PENGUIN BOOKS

THE PENGUIN GUIDE TO JAZZ ON COMPACT DISC

Praise for the First Edition

'It must be one of the most elegantly written and useful books ever to have appeared about jazz' – Adam Lively in the *Mail on Sunday*

'Suitably monumental . . . admirably thorough . . . an impressive achievement – any serious collector of jazz recordings ought to have it on his or her shelf' – James Maxfield in *Cadence*

'A considerable achievement and entirely recommendable' – *Sunday Telegraph*

'Highly recommended . . . the book is a valuable reference tool, a thorough catalogue, and a credible guide through the ocean of discs that flood the stores' – *Fanfare*

'One of the most comprehensive jazz reference books around – a must' – Nick Gibson in the *Daily Mirror*

'Comprehensive, endlessly fascinating and informative . . . I was lost in admiration' – *Literary Review*

'This masterpiece of compilation . . . provides the newcomer with an easy to use and accessible introduction . . . for the regular jazz collector it is the first truly comprehensive and critical reference source (of its kind)' – Sinan Carter Savaskan in *The Times Educational Supplement*

ABOUT THE AUTHORS

RICHARD COOK was born in Kew in 1957. He began accumulating records when he still had milk teeth and has since continued in the bizarre quest to hear virtually every jazz record ever made. He started writing about music in the '70s and has exasperated more than one generation of listeners with his views on a wide range of sonics. He still contributes to various magazines and newspapers and is sometimes to be heard on the airwaves too. He has made his home in west London for a number of years, and so far is still there.

BRIAN MORTON is slightly older than Mr Cook but is not unduly self-conscious about it. In his teens he was struck to discover a Morton among the founders of jazz and resolved to stay in the family business. After nearly 25 years collecting records, the joists and foundations of his house are no sounder than his bank balance. He has been an academic and journalist and, more recently, a freelance writer and broadcaster. He presents BBC Radio 3's jazz magazine, *Impressions*, as well as the posher *In Tune*. Since May 1996 he has been senior producer of Radio Scotland's arts strand, *The Usual Suspects*. He fulfils one cynic's definition of a gentleman: owning several saxophones, but now seldom playing them. The soccer and boxing metaphors are his; all references to 'googlies', 'Chinamen' and 'cover drives' are attributable to his co-author. Their private Esperanto is compounded of jazz, horse-racing and malt whisky.

The Penguin Guide to Jazz on Compact Disc

Richard Cook and Brian Morton

PENGUIN BOOKS

PENGUIN BOOKS

Published by the Penguin Group
Penguin Books Ltd, 27 Wrights Lane, London W 8 5 T Z, England
Penguin Books USA Inc., 375 Hudson Street, New York, New York 10014, USA
Penguin Books Australia Ltd, Ringwood, Victoria, Australia
Penguin Books Canada Ltd, 10 Alcorn Avenue, Toronto, Ontario, Canada M 4 V 3 B 2
Penguin Books (NZ) Ltd, 182–190 Wairau Road, Auckland 10, New Zealand
Penguin Books Ltd, Registered Offices: Harmondsworth, Middlesex, England

First edition 1992
Second edition 1994
Third edition 1996
10 9 8 7 6 5 4 3 2 1

Copyright © Richard Cook and Brian Morton, 1996
All rights reserved

The moral right of the authors has been asserted

Set in 8/9pt Monotype Times New Roman
Typeset, from data supplied, by RefineCatch Limited, Bungay, Suffolk
Made and printed in Great Britain by Clays Ltd, St Ives plc

Except in the United States of America, this book is sold subject
to the condition that it shall not, by way of trade or otherwise, be lent,
re-sold, hired out, or otherwise circulated without the publisher's
prior consent in any form of binding or cover other than that in
which it is published and without a similar condition including this
condition being imposed on the subsequent purchaser

Contents

Introduction

The origins of jazz are as cloudy and unspecific as those of any other kind of music, but scholars usually agree that the recordings made by the Original Dixieland Jazz Band in 1917 mark the starting point for jazz on record. We shall never know what Buddy Bolden, the first 'king' of New Orleans cornet playing, sounded like, since he never recorded; and many other opportunities were also missed by the American industry. King Oliver and Jelly Roll Morton, both prominent figures before 1917, didn't arrive in the studios until the 1920s; Freddie Keppard, whose band was a sensation in the 1910s, allegedly refused to make records lest anyone steal his sound. In fact, very little significant recording was done in New Orleans, the supposed birthplace of jazz, until the 1940s. So a white band in New York made 'Darktown Strutters' Ball' in January 1917: at that time, they were described on the record labels as 'Original Dixieland Jass Band'.

Now 80 years have passed since then, and jazz (or jass) has become as widely documented on record as any music. It has rushed through its history – from traditional jazz to swing to bebop to free jazz and back again – in less than a century, and the gramophone has enjoyed the unique position of being able to document it at almost every step along the way. Although jazz itself continues to be regarded by many as some kind of specialist music, difficult to comprehend without a wide-ranging knowledge of the form, its impact on twentieth-century music as a whole is incalculable. It has nurtured some of the finest composers and performers of our times, in any musical genre; its influence on other musics, through the principles of jazz improvisation and composition, is immense; and it paved the way for rock and soul and all their various sub-genres that have emerged in the last 40 years.

Although many will always hold that jazz is primarily a live music, at its best created in the immediacy of a concert setting of some kind, it has long been disseminated, listened to and argued about via the medium of records. Jazz was, indeed, the first music to be dramatically affected *by* records. As the 78-r.p.m. medium gave way to the LP format, the confining bonds of the three-minute disc were abandoned and jazz performance became longer, less contained, more multifarious. Jazz recordings are relatively economical to make when compared with the studio time which rock and classical records seem to demand and, while the major companies have an almost traditional antipathy towards putting significant resources behind a music they tend to see as marginal, countless independent operators have sprung up who have recorded and released the music with an almost obsessive fervour. The advent of the compact disc brought new life to many a neglected jazz archive, too. Most of the major catalogues of the past – RCA's Bluebird, Warner Bros' Atlantic, the great modern archives of Blue Note, Verve and Prestige – have been restored to circulation via CD. As many of the earlier recordings have fallen out of copyright, independent enterprises such as JSP and Classics have embarked on extensive CD reissues of the jazz of the 1920s and '30s. The current outlook suggests that the steady flow of reissues will be maintained, if not accelerated, in the foreseeable future, and the value of such extensive catalogues is at last being recognized by the big players of the record industry. Meanwhile the thirst for recording new music seems unquenchable.

As in our first two editions, our aim here has been to try to provide as comprehensive an overview as possible of this vast and bewilderingly diverse area of recorded music. Newcomers to jazz – and there have been many in recent years, with the music acquiring a much wider casual listenership than it has had since, perhaps, the trad boom of the 1950s – are always hard-pressed to know both where to start and where to proceed from there. Most will have heard of Miles Davis's *Kind Of Blue* or John Coltrane's *Giant Steps*, two of the most famous jazz albums ever released. But both those musicians have enormous discographies, and this presents a formidable problem to collectors on a limited budget or to those who wish to acquire just a few examples of Davis or Coltrane on record. At the same time, more experienced fans and collectors deserve a detailed summary and evaluation of what exactly is available by both major and minor figures in the jazz field. That is what we've tried to do here.

The richness and diversity of music covered by the term 'jazz' is extraordinary, and that point has once again been brought home to us more forcefully than ever in compiling our third edition. We have attempted to list and discuss as many records currently available in the field as possible – but, since jazz itself is a difficult area to define, this has inevitably led to problems over what to include and what to leave out. Although jazz and blues are inextricably bound up in each other, we have omitted such musicians as Bessie Smith and Joe Turner, even though their records are listened to and enjoyed by countless 'jazz fans': the blues demands a volume to itself, which should be documented by safer hands than ours. Singers, too, are difficult to make clear judgement-calls on: the old argument as to what is a jazz singer has never been resolved, and it could be contended that, if we have included Mel Torme (as we have), then why not Peggy Lee, or even Bing Crosby? Often we have been guided by the nature of the accompaniments, and in some cases we have chosen to include only the jazz-directed output of a particular artist. In the case of Nat Cole, for instance, we've omitted the bulk of his vocal recordings, while his instrumental ones have remained; much the same applies to George Benson. We don't wish to discriminate against an artist seeking pop status, but we try to stick to discussing jazz records.

The advent of 'free music' has placed a further strain on jazz classification: the work of such musicians as Derek Bailey and Billy Jenkins may, often at their own insistence, have little to do with any jazz tradition. But the connections between jazz and improvised music are indisputable, and there is no feasible reason to discriminate against free music by excluding it from this book.

It hardly needs saying that it's impossible to include every jazz record from every part of the globe. We've tried to cover every significant record we could find that was available at the time of our cut-off point (spring 1996), but there are sure to be many records missing, for a variety of reasons.

Budget-priced collections of dubious provenance have largely been omitted: readers who think they've found a bargain in some nefarious-looking release of unidentified origin might like to remember that the musicians involved probably aren't benefiting from the issue in any way. In situations where there is a big overlap in the reissues of early material, as is now the case with some major artists, we've simply tried to choose the best records to list. We have again chosen to dismiss many records which amount to little more than easy-listening, instrumental or vocal music with only the vaguest of jazz connotations. While there's an awkward line to draw here, we've attempted to inscribe it. There's a substantial grey area between jazz and contemporary composition: some musicians, such as Fred Rzewski or John Lewis, move freely between these genres, and there are many records – particularly from such companies as Bvhaast and hat ART – which count jazz as an element (though not perhaps the defining one) in their make-up. Again, we've used our discretion here as best we can. Other discs may have arrived too late for inclusion, or may be so difficult to locate that listing them will prove to be more frustrating than helpful to most readers. Others we may have deemed too poor to be even worth listing. Some we may have been unable to get hold of ourselves, or have simply missed altogether. A few of our correspondents take obvious delight in pointing out discs which we've left out, to which we can only say, well, nothing's perfect.

Our intention continues to be to make this as practical a book as possible. None of the judgements herein is cast in stone: further listening and pondering on the music may yield different opinions in the fullness of time, and here and there assiduous readers may again spot a slight change of opinion from our previous edition. In that respect, we share a characteristic that is surely common to all jazz listeners: that of living and developing with this music as it continues to evolve and grow. We have tried not to be sentimental about our evaluations: it is all too tempting to overrate some records on the basis that the jazz musician's lot is trying enough without having to endure negative criticism. But the first responsibility of a *Guide* such as this is to the listeners and record-buyers. Building a comprehensive library of jazz CDs is an expensive business, and most enthusiasts will be able to invest in only a fraction of what is available to them in the current record marketplace. Our primary aim has been to assist in deciding how best to make that choice and to suggest areas of the music which may yield hitherto unrealized pleasures.

Evaluation

While some may consider it iniquitous to define the merits of a record using a star-system, we feel that it's simply the most useful shorthand as a starting point for discussing the disc in question. But we cannot stress too strongly that the reader should consult the text in addition to the star rating for our overall evaluation of the record. We have chosen to make use of between one and four stars: parentheses round a single star indicate that some small reservation prevents our placing it in the higher category. Parentheses round all the stars indicate that some more fundamental reservation exists which prevents us giving a wholehearted recommendation: usually this will relate to some aspect of the recording or presentation of the disc in question, but again we advise the reader to consult the text.

**** Very fine: an outstanding record that yields consistent pleasure and demands a place in any comprehensive collection

***(*) A fine record, with some exceptional music, although it's one which we have some slight reservations about

*** A good if middleweight set; one that lacks the stature or consistency of the finest records, but which is certainly rewarding on its own terms

**(*) There are worthwhile things here, and admirers of the artist in question will enjoy it, but a number of drawbacks tell against it

** Some good points, but this should detain only the curious or the completist

*(*) Seriously flawed; hardly worth bothering with

* An absolute disgrace, whoever's fault it is

In a *very* few cases we have, like our colleagues on *The Penguin Guide To Compact Discs*, chosen to award a special token of merit; in our *Guide*, it takes the form of a crown. This is to denote records we feel a special admiration or affection for: a purely personal choice, which we hope our readers will indulge.

Recording Quality

Our first concern is with the music itself, and most contemporary jazz records are engineered to the customary high standards which are the norm for the industry; they therefore require little further comment – although, whenever there is some particular felicity or problem with the production, we have noted it as such. Far more important, however, is the question of the remastering of older material for CD reissue. We have been disturbed to discover how erratic and unreliable standards of remastering for CD are, among major and independent companies alike. Time and again we have encountered examples of shoddy and ill-informed work, particularly with regard to remastering from 78s. Set against this is the magnificent work which has been done by, in particular, the British engineer, John R. T. Davies – for Hep, Collector's Classics and JSP – and Robert Parker, some of whose stereo re-creations for CDS records have been outstanding. We have attempted to be as scrupulous as possible in our evaluation of this issue. We might also mention that we have frequently discovered many instances when the CD version of even a relatively modern record offers no noticeable improvement over the LP issue. Overall, however, we are glad to note that, as the CD era has matured, standards of remastering have become much more consistent and more often than not there is evidence of real craftsmanship in a typical CD reissue.

Running Time: Never Mind the Width . . .

Our decision to ignore the question of CD running-time may vex some readers, since it continues to bother a number of pundits. The compact disc can comfortably accommodate some 80 minutes of music, yet most jazz CDs fail to use the full capacity of the disc and, in the case of many reissues, no attempt is made to beef up the running-time of the original LP by adding extra material. That said, a considerable number of issues *do* include extra tracks by way of alternative takes or previously rejected pieces. But such material is often of dubious value, and an ordinary LP is unlikely to become an extraordinary CD by the addition of three or four more-of-the-same tunes. Our criterion continues to be that the quality of the music determines the desirability of the disc, not its running-time. An outstanding 40-minute record remains outstanding, even if it does run to only half of what could be put on the CD. The mysterious means-test of 'value for money' is not worth addressing here. In our experience, most CDs are too long, not too short.

Pricing

While it is tempting to denote records which are available at less than full price, in practice this is a difficult area to be accurate about. Many reissues are made available in some kind of mid-price range, but the bargain bracket which is a commonplace in the field of classical discs holds very few jazz records, and most of those are frequently of dubious worth. In addition, a mid-price issue in one country may list at full price when it is imported into another. It's clearly a matter of checking with individual retailers.

Layout of Text

Here is a typical record-entry:

*** Red Garland Trio With Eddie 'Lockjaw' Davis Vol. 1 Original Jazz Classics OJC 360
   Garland; Eddie 'Lockjaw' Davis (*ts*); Sam Jones (*b*); Art Taylor (*d*). 12/59.

The star-rating is followed by the title of the record, its label and catalogue number. (If the recording is available in a format other than compact disc, that fact is also noted here.) Next we list the musicians who are playing on the disc, together with their instrumental credits, and – where available – the date of the recording (month/year). All personnel are listed collectively – that is, it shouldn't be implied that every musician listed for a record is featured on every track. A full list of instrument abbreviations follows this introduction. Where there are multiple records in an entry, each change in personnel is duly noted – although, rather than listing the same musicians over again, subsequent details may begin with 'As above, except . . .'. Sometimes, where there may be some minor changes between complex lists of personnel, we have chosen to say 'similar to above' or suchlike. Where the recording dates span a number of different sessions, as is the case for many compilations, they are listed as, for example, 5/74–10/80. While we've tried to present the clearest possible picture of who recorded what and when, this is a guide, not a discography, and we've attempted to be sensible over the listing of minutiae. We hope our readers will indulge any slight discrepancies of style which may result.

   We have tried to be as accurate as possible over listing catalogue numbers, but neither we nor our publishers can be held responsible for mistakes which may have eluded our checking. By and large, we have attempted to simplify the situation as far as possible by concentrating on the 'core' number which most records are assigned. Many CDs now show a seemingly baffling array of digits, but often these refer to bar-code configurations as well as the core number. It has become an industry standard to use the suffix -2 to denote a CD issue. Independent companies often use very simple systems of cataloguing – which we wish the major companies availed themselves of!

The situation is complicated further by the inclusion of many America-only or Europe-only releases in the book. The reader is warned that such releases, from smaller companies in particular, may be much more difficult to obtain; but most collectors will know all too well that securing a particular jazz record from a non-specialist retailer can often be a frustrating business anyway. Most record companies are seeking to standardize their catalogue-number system to ensure that a worldwide release uses the same central number.

We always advise that, when ordering records, readers state in full the title and artist and desired format, as well as the catalogue numbers. Most experienced dealers will be able to spot any possible confusion over the number when furnished with these extra details.

Formats: Goodbye Vinyl, Sayonara Cassette . . .

It's not only vinyl which has disappeared from this edition: we have chosen to eliminate discussion of what little remains on cassette as well. Cassettes are still acquired in large quantities, but usually as blanks these days: pre-recorded jazz cassettes, particularly at full price, are rapidly dwindling in number. After some soul-searching, we have decided to concentrate exclusively on CD for this edition. Since both DCC and Mini-Disc have also made no real impact on the marketplace, we have also left these formats out of consideration for now. The development of high-density CD looks likely to be the next priority in sound-carrier evolution. Time must decide.

Deletions

A book like this can never be as up to date as we would wish. Many records will have appeared since our manuscript went to press, and a number of those listed here may have fallen victim to the deletions axe. Records often stay in circulation even after they have been officially deleted: dealers and independent distributors may hold stocks, and a diligent search can often locate a supposedly extinct item. All this will be familiar to experienced collectors, who know how difficult it can be to locate a particular record; but we counsel that a patient reader should try more than one source if confronted with an initial response that a record is deleted and therefore impossible to obtain. For that purpose we have included a list of distributors at the end of this introduction.

Mosaic Records

The programme of high-quality reissues run by Mosaic Records of Stamford, Connecticut, has continued since our last edition. Once again, we have omitted most of these editions from our listing since they are specialist items available only from the company itself or from the small number of retailers who stock them. However, we once again applaud Mosaic's work and would suggest that interested parties get in touch with the company direct for information regarding current releases. Their address is 35 Melrose Place, Stamford, CT 06902, USA (Tel.: 06902-7533)

Acknowledgements

Once again, our burden in compiling this third obese volume has been greatly lightened by the kindness and affable co-operation of many friends involved in the jazz business, both in the UK and abroad. Our special thanks in this connection go to Trevor Manwaring, Steve Sanderson, Wendy Furness, Mark Gillinson, Leonard Newman, Graham Griffith, Eddie Wilkinson, Kirsten Mackness, John Jack, Adam Sieff and Terri Hinte. The extraordinary diligence of our peerless copy editor, Roger Wells, has once again been invaluable. Ravi Mirchandani and his successor, Alistair Rolfe, have been souls of benevolence as our editors at Penguin Books. But, as usual, we reserve our warmest affection for Lee Ellen, Pam and Fiona, whose patience and sweetness in the face of a third onslaught of thousands of CDs were a source of inspiration to us both.

Richard Cook
Brian Morton

Distributors

The following UK distributors may be able to help in obtaining records. We have appended the names of some of the labels they deal with, where appropriate.

New Note Distribution, Electron House, Cray Avenue, Orpington, Kent BR5 3RJ (Tel.: 01689 877884; Fax: 01689 877891): Chesky, Concord, ECM, Enja, Gramavision, GRP/Decca, Hep, Impulse!, Jazz City, Landmark, Muse, Paddlewheel, Strata East, Theresa, Timeless, Triloka, Tutu

Harmonia Mundi Ltd, 19–21 Nile Street, London N1 7LR (Tel.: 0171 253 0863; Fax: 0171 253 3237): Black Saint, Criss Cross, DIW, Flapper, hat ART, Philology, Red, Soul Note

Cadillac Distribution, 61–71 Collier Street, London N1 9DF (Tel.: 0171 278 7391; Fax: 0171 278 7394): Bvhaast, Capri, Collector's Classics, Dragon, FMP, Ear-Rational, Frog, Geestgronden, Gemini, ICP, Incus, JSP, Jazz Hour, Moers, Ogun, Olufsen, Phono Suecia, Phontastic, Reservoir, Storyville

Koch International, 23 Warple Way, London W3 0RX (Tel.: 0181 749 7177): Black & Blue, Black Lion, IDA, ITM, Yazoo

Spotlite, 103 London Road, Sawbridgeworth, Herts CM21 9JJ (Tel.: 01279 724572): Sackville, Spotlite

Discovery Records, Old Church Mission Room, Kings Corner, Pewsey, Wilts SN9 5BS (Tel.: 01672 63931; Fax: 01672 563934): Classics, Cool N Blue, Fresh Sound, Sunnyside

Conifer Records, Horton Road, West Drayton, Middx UB7 8JL (Tel.: 01895 440450): Denon, Savoy, Telarc

Impetus Distribution, 587 Wandsworth Road, London SW8 3JD (Tel.: 0171 720 4460): Jazz, Nine Winds, Open Minds, Splasc(h), Steeplechase

Direct Distribution, 50 Stroud Green Road, London N4 3EF (Tel.: 0171 281 3465; Fax: 0171 281 5671): Challenge, Delmark, Lake, Retrieval

Support your local record shop! However, since mail order is often the only available option for many, we recommend: Crazy Jazz, 5 Prospect Road, Cheshunt, Herts EN8 9QX (Tel.: 01992 625436; Fax: 01992 640644).

Abbreviations

acc	accordion	g	guitar
acl	alto clarinet	gfs	goofus
af	alto flute	g-syn	guitar synthesizer
ahn	alto horn	hca	harmonica
arr	arranger	hn	horn
as	alto saxophone	hp	harp
b	bass	hpd	harpsichord
ban	bandoneon	ky	keyboards
bar hn	baritone horn	kz	kazoo
bb	brass bass	mand	mandolin
bcl	bass clarinet	mar	marimba
bf	bass flute	mel	mellophone
bhn	baritone horn	ob	oboe
bj	banjo	org	organ
bs	baritone saxophone	p	piano
bsn	bassoon	perc	percussion
bsx	bass saxophone	picc	piccolo
b-t	bass trumpet	picc t	piccolo trumpet
btb	bass trombone	pkt-t	pocket-trumpet
c	cornet	sno	sopranino saxophone
cbcl	contrabass clarinet	sou	sousaphone
cbsx	contrabass saxophone	srspn	sarrusophone
cbsrspn	contrabass sarrusophone	ss	soprano saxophone
cel	celeste	syn	synthesizer
cl	clarinet	t	trumpet
clo	cello	tb	trombone
Cmel	C-melody saxophone	tba	tuba
comp	composer	thn	tenor horn
cond	conductor	ts	tenor saxophone
cor	cor anglais	uke	ukulele
d	drums	v	vocal
elec	electronics	vib	vibraphone
eng hn	english horn	vla	viola
euph	euphonium	vn	violin
f	flute	vtb	valve trombone
flhn	flugelhorn	wbd	washboard
frhn	french horn	xy	xylophone

Abash GROUP

***(*) **Abash** Dragon DRCD 249
> Anders Ekholm (*ts*); Tommy Skotte (*b*); Nils Danell (*d*). 6/93.

As usual, Sweden finds its own way. This trio approaches an open canvas with a fine blend of fresh ideas and hard-won acumen. Skotte and Danell are the more experienced pair, and the drummer's noisily swinging style merges handsomely with Skotte's fundamentally lyrical free playing. Ekholm, though sometimes a bit diffident, usually plays with a brimming energy that his attractively scratchy tone tempers and scales down to the intimacy of the setting. He is responsible for six of the 11 themes and there's plenty of ingenuity here, as in the endless melody of 'P1', to take a single example. Humour, too – 'Caravan' is a surprising, funny rendition of the Ellington chestnut, which contrasts nicely with the hard-bitten, rather bleak handling of 'Out Of Nowhere'.

Greg Abate ALTO, SOPRANO AND TENOR SAXOPHONES, FLUTE

*** **Bop City – Live At Birdland** Candid CCD 79513
> Abate; James Williams (*p*); Rufus Reid (*b*); Kenny Washington (*d*). 7/91.
*** **Straight Ahead** Candid CCD 79530
> Abate; Claudio Roditi (*t, flhn*); Hilton Ruiz (*p*); George Mraz (*b*); Kenny Washington (*d*). 9/92.
(*) **Dr Jekyll And Mr Hyde Candid CCD 79715
> Abate; Richie Cole (*as*); Chris Neville (*p*); Paul Del Nero (*b*); Artie Cabral (*d*). 11/94.

Abate worked as a section player in big bands for nearly 20 years before making these small-group albums for Candid. *Bop City* is a breezy session which affirms a basic interest in bebop saxophone, since the leader is apparently at home on any of the models. Alto is his main preoccupation, but his tenor features on 'Peaks Beaks' and 'Gemini Mood' are convincing, and the soprano on 'Opportunity' reveals a lesson absorbed from Coltrane. It's a pick-up rhythm section, but they know exactly what they're doing. *Straight Ahead* re-runs the formula with Roditi as sparring partner, but his sometimes anonymous facility is more of a distraction than a counterweight: the best music is created between Abate and another heavyweight rhythm section. *Dr Jekyll And Mr Hyde* offers a second repeat of the formula, with Cole on board, but this time it's starting to wear thin and the impression at the end is of nothing much at all except facility. More like *Dr Jekyll And Dr Jekyll*.

Ahmed Abdullah (born 1947) TRUMPET

(*) **Liquid Magic Silkheart SHCD-104
> Abdullah; Charles Brackeen (*ts*); Malachi Favors (*b*); Alvin Fielder (*d*). 2/87.
*** **Ahmed Abdullah And The Solomonic Quintet** Silkheart SHCD-109
> Abdullah; David S. Ware (*ts*); Masuhjaa (*g*); Fred Hopkins (*b*); Charles Moffett (*d*).

Abdullah's original inspiration was Louis Armstrong, but his main areas of activity have more to do with the free playing of the 1970s and '80s. The two Silkheart albums are interesting if inconclusive. Tersely organized, the six tunes on *Liquid Magic* reflect a Colemanesque feel which suits the folk-like melodies. But the trumpeter is, frankly, the least impressive player here: Brackeen's fierce yet lightly shaded solos make a more powerful impression, and Favors and Fielder generate a loose yet convincingly swinging pulse. The second disc has a similar problem: the leader is outclassed by his own band. The rhythm section is wonderfully alert and inventive, with Masuhjaa's guitar an especially individual presence, and Ware is a gritty improviser. Abdullah's writing is at its best in the Latin lope of 'El Canto II', and altogether this must be his strongest record.

Kaoru Abe (1948–78) ALTO AND SOPRANINO SAXOPHONES, HARMONICA, GUITAR, PIANO

*** **Duo** 1971 PSFD-67
> Abe; Huiroshi Yamazaki (*d*). 1/71.
***(*) **Solo** PSFD-66
> Abe (*as* solo). 7/72.
*** **Live At Gaya Vol. 1** DIW 371
> Abe (*sno, as* solo). 9–12/77.
*** **Live At Gaya Vol. 2** DIW 372
> Abe (*sno, as, p* solo). 1/78.

*** **Live At Gaya Vol. 3** DIW 373
>Abe (*as* solo). 3/78.

*** **Live At Gaya Vol. 4** DIW 374
>Abe (*sno, as* solo). 4/78.

** **Live At Gaya Vol. 5** DIW 375
>Abe (*sno, hca, p* solo). 5/78.

(*) **Live At Gaya Vol. 6 DIW 376
>Abe (*sno, as, hca* solo). 5–6/78.

*** **Live At Gaya Vol. 7** DIW 377
>Abe (*sno, as* solo). 6/78.

*** **Live At Gaya Vol. 8** DIW 378
>Abe (*as* solo). 7/78.

*** **Live At Gaya Vol. 9** DIW 379
>Abe (*as* solo). 7/78.

(*) **Live At Gaya Vol. 10 DIW 380
>Abe (*sno, g* solo). 8/78.

(*) **Last Date DIW 335
>Abe (*as, g, hca* solo). 8/78.

Abe is scarcely known outside Japan, in part due to his early death, and until recently there was nothing accessible on CD. This remarkable burst of releases from DIW and PSFD has suddenly placed him in a far wider currency: 12 solo albums of mostly saxophone improvisation, plus one duo recording with drummer Yamazaki. Abe's style is one of near-total extremes, and he may well earn an honoured place in the affections of today's generation of Japanese noise-makers, such as The Boredoms. The first *Solo* disc consists of three mouth-splitting exercises on alto, phrases that sound scalded on his own lips, and though he actually resorts to overblowing only infrequently his phrasing is gnarled, squalling, of indeterminate shape. Sometimes he starts with an actual melody: though uncredited, the second piece on *Solo* is based on 'Fly Me To The Moon', and the Gaya series includes a cruel sopranino disquisition on 'Chim Chim Cheree' (Vol. 4), while Vol. 9 consists of a single alto improvisation on 'Lover Come Back To Me'. Abe is quite unafraid to use space: some solos contain huge chunks of silence, others seem to crawl along at a tempo that suggests a music of no momentum at all and, though he seems unaware of imperatives such as beginning, middle and end, one finds oneself adjusting to his peculiar timelessness when sitting through long sections of this music. Of less interest are the pieces on guitar (scratchy and home-made-sounding), piano (bass-chord thunder, of no discernible consequence) and harmonica (which seems like nothing more than mere sucking and blowing). But his alto and sopranino pieces have their own strange vocabulary, and it is surely not fanciful to place them in a Japanese tradition of spare, intensely refined music-making. Even as they exist in a parallel universe to Albert Ayler.

Of these 13 discs, we would cautiously recommend *Solo*, Volumes 1, 4, 7 and 9 of the *Gaya* sequence, and (for a little variety) the duos with Yamazaki, a conventional but energetic free drummer. *Last Date* has its own poignancy in view of the circumstances, but the guitar and harmonica pieces which take up 40 minutes or so are of modest interest.

John Abercrombie (born 1944) GUITAR, GUITAR SYNTHESIZERS, ELECTRIC MANDOLIN, GUITAR MANDOLIN

***(*) **Timeless** ECM 1047
>Abercrombie; Jan Hammer (*p, ky*); Jack DeJohnette (*d*). 6/74.

(*) **Night ECM 1272
>Abercrombie; Mike Brecker (*ts*); Jan Hammer (*ky*); Jack DeJohnette (*d*). 4/84.

***(*) **Current Event** ECM 1311
>Abercrombie; Marc Johnson (*b*); Peter Erskine (*d*). 9/85.

ECM had been around for nigh on five years when the first of these top-drawer sets was cut, and all the qualities that distinguish Manfred Eicher's label are firmly in place. It seems unlikely that Abercrombie would have been so sensitively and sympathetically treated elsewhere, and he's become a major constituent in what people still think of as the ECM sound. Most of his catalogue is now on CD. The only major exceptions – *Abercrombie Quartet* and *M*, from 1980 – are easily the weakest things he ever did, and they're scarcely missed.

Timeless is a superb album, brimming with interesting ideas and textures. DeJohnette is probably the finest drummer of his generation – or why not say one of the finest musicians of his generation? Hammer is a vastly underrated keyboard player, with a strong all-round conception (face it, everyone gets a buzz off the *Miami Vice* theme). At this point he still seems to be adjusting to normal altitude, having just descended from Mount Mahavishnu, and there is a tendency to overplay; but DeJohnette and Abercrombie seem to be in complete agreement, and the guitarist's fingering is typically exact and his lyricism more than usually forceful.

DeJohnette and Abercrombie sealed their very fruitful association in a trio (completed by Dave Holland) that came to be known as Gateway after the first record. At this point, Gateway (q.v.) merits a separate entry. The drummer is, however, again the key on the surprisingly funky *Night*, a good trio session into which a slightly surprised Brecker seems to have walked out of the darkness. Blinking a little in the sudden glare, he peers at the charts. Edit him out and this fine album would be none the worse.

Current Event introduces one of Abercrombie's most sympathetic and effective partnerships, better even than the slightly fitful combination of Holland and DeJohnette. They do a beautiful version of 'Ralph's Piano Waltz', a guitar piece by Ralph Towner, Abercrombie's duo partner on the item below. Nothing else quite comes up to that, but the standard is very high nonetheless.

*** Sargasso Sea ECM 1080
Abercrombie; Ralph Towner (*classical g, 12-string g, p*). 5/76.
Though the abstractions of the title-track are intriguing, this is a slightly disappointing set. In contrast to Towner's duos with Larry Coryell on *The Restful Mind* (Vanguard), which is a magnificent stylistic compromise on both parts, Towner and Abercrombie are perhaps too similar to do more than cancel each other out. Towner's piano, increasingly important to his conception at that point in his career, adds an attractive element, but 'attractive' is the strongest this set merits. Five years later, they met up again and cut *Five Years Later* (ECM 1207); Towner's name came first that time . . .

***(*) Characters ECM 1117
Abercrombie (*g* solo). 11/77.
Before the advent of Bill Frisell, this was as good as contemporary solo guitar playing got. The mood is generally elegiac and there are sufficient internal indications to suggest that Abercrombie is working through at least some of his influences. There are strong echoes of Tal Farlow and Jim Hall in the beautiful opening 'Parable', in the writing and conception rather than the articulation, and there are signs elsewhere that Abercrombie has absorbed Django Reinhardt's overlapping rhythm.

***(*) Getting There ECM 1321
Abercrombie; Michael Brecker (*ts*); Marc Johnson (*b*); Peter Erskine (*d*). 4/87.
At first glance this might almost be a Michael Brecker album. The two front men are so different temperamentally one wonders whether the music will gel or whether Abercrombie will be swamped, though this wasn't the case on the earlier *Night*. In fact, he calls most of the shots, playing with controlled power and making some of the most effective use of guitar synthesizer you'll ever hear. The remainder of the group is, of course, well attuned to Abercrombie's approach and the ensembles are beautifully etched.

*** John Abercrombie ECM 1390
Abercrombie; Marc Johnson (*b*); Peter Erskine (*d*). 4/88.
***(*) Animato ECM 1411
Abercrombie; Vince Mendoza (*syns*); Jon Christensen (*d*). 10/89.
Not known as a big standards player (but then, that's what they used to say about Keith Jarrett), Abercrombie turns in a beautiful 'Stella By Starlight' here, perfectly weighted this side of sentimentality, and an unforgettable version of the less well-known Dietz/Schwartz 'Haunted Heart'. Johnson and Erskine make a convincing team (and were properly given equal billing on the sleeve), though the former shouldn't have been indulged an airing of his 'Samurai Hee-Haw', nor the latter an over-extended drum solo.

With *Animato*, the exact opposite applies. Christensen can be listened to all night, the lightest, nimblest drummer Europe has produced, rivalling DeJohnette for sheer swing and intelligence. Mendoza's six (out of eight) compositions are spot-on and he seems to have steered Abercrombie towards a more confident use of electronics. Both albums feature the leader's guitar synthesizer, a machine that too often stands in the way of creative thought. Abercrombie deploys it intelligently, using it to vary the textures, supplying unexpected glissandi and dramatic upward shifts or to add a more forceful chordal pulse. Strongly recommended.

**** While We're Young ECM 1489
Abercrombie; Dan Wall (*org*); Adam Nussbaum (*d*). 6/92.
***(*) Speak Of The Devil ECM 1511
As above. 7/93.
Nobody expected this. It's difficult to tell whether Abercrombie is thinking about Wes Montgomery's classic trios or the steaming jazz-rock of Tony Williams's Lifetime. Whichever, it sounds *great*. Wall's churning but somehow delicate Hammond provides shading for the guitar lines and the big rolling bass

which is evident in his generous share of the writing credits. Nussbaum is almost irrelevant, but he takes the opportunity to play some gorgeously free accents and some typically intricate stick-work close in to the cymbal clamps, producing tight, ringing sounds that blend well from opposite directions with organ and guitar.

One suspects that the second disc contains more writing done specifically for this trio. However, it lacks some of the thump of its predecessor, and parts of it are actually quite dull and plodding. Abercrombie sounds to be enjoying himself, though, and is a lot looser-limbed than he had become in previous years.

*** **Now It Can Be Played** Steeplechase SCCD 31314
    Abercrombie; Andy LaVerne (*p*); Steve LaSpina (*b*); Jeff Hirshfield (*d*). 4/92.
*** **Farewell** Musidisc 500462
    Abercrombie; Andy LaVerne (*p*); George Mraz (*b*); Adam Nussbaum (*d*). 4/93.
The first of these is jointly credited to Abercombie and LaVerne and includes a good deal of the pianist's quirky and angular writing. The long 'Cat Nap' and 'Waltz King' stand out as unusual items in the guitarist's output, and there's something about the recording that makes him sound more acid and compressed than usual, enough to make one wonder whether he's best served by Jan Erik Kongshaug's limpid engineering any more. (*While We're Young* was recorded in New York, and there, too, the guitarist has or is given a much sharper tone than usual; one entirely appropriate to that particular session.)

The Musidisc is more immediately recognizable, but the result is that it sounds like a low-budget effort to produce an ECM session. Mraz had featured in the disappointing 1980 band and sounds no more in tune with the music here; or, rather, he sounds as though he's trying to do Abercrombie's job for him. They do a rather drab 'Ralph's Piano Waltz' (see *Current Event*) which is sentimental rather than romantic. Much better is Abercrombie's own similarly conceived 'John's Waltz' on *Now It Can Be Played*; it's repeated in a very different reading on *November*, and the comparison gives a pretty good impression of the direction Abercrombie's been travelling since the late '80s.

**** **November** ECM 1502
    Abercombie; John Surman (*ss, bs, bcl*); Marc Johnson (*b*); Peter Erskine (*d*). 11/92.
A lovely, lovely record, with just the hint of impending chill the title suggests. In what has become standard practice at ECM, the group is used in various configurations, giving the music lots of space and maximizing the range of voices.

Surman brings in a range of bleakly lyrical accents. He's superb on the freely improvised opening piece, 'The Cat's Back'. Johnson's 'Right Brain Patrol' is marched a little harder than on his own record. The title-piece is one of the freest things the long-standing trio have attempted, and they sound completely comfortable with it.

Rabih Abou-Khalil OUD, FLUTE

**** **Between Dusk And Dawn** MMP 170886
    Abou-Khalil; Charlie Mariano (*as, ss*); Christian Burchard (*mar*); Michael Armann (*p*); Glen Moore (*b*); Glen Velez (*frame d, bodhran, darabukka, perc*); Ramesh Shotham (*tavil, ghatam, mouth hp, dholak, kanjira, perc*). 86.
***(*) **Nafas** ECM 1359
    Abou-Khalil; Selim Kusur (*nay, v*); Glen Velez (*frame d*); Setrak Sarkissian (*darabukka*). 2/88.
**** **Bukra** MMP 170889
    Abou-Khalil; Sonny Fortune (*as*); Glen Moore (*b*); Glen Velez (*frame d, perc, v*); Ramesh Shotham (*South Indian d, perc*). 3/88.
***(*) **Al-Jadida** Enja 6090
    Abou-Khalil; Sonny Fortune (*as*); Glen Moore (*b*); Ramesh Shotham (*South Indian d, perc*); Nabil Khaiat (*frame d, perc*). 10/90.
*** **Roots And Sprouts** MMP 170890
    Abou-Khalil; Selim Kusur (*nay*); Yassin El-Achek (*v*); Glen Moore (*b*); Glen Velez (*frame d*); Mohammad Al-Sous (*darabukka*). 11/90.
**** **Blue Camel** Enja 7053
    Abou-Khalil; Charlie Mariano (*as*); Kenny Wheeler (*t, flhn*); Steve Swallow (*b*); Milton Cardona (*perc*); Nabil Khaiat (*frame d*); Ramesh Shotham (*Indian d, perc*). 5/92.
***(*) **Tarab** Enja 7083
    Abou-Khalil; Selim Kusur (*nay*); Glen Moore (*b*); Nabil Khaiat (*frame d, perc*); Ramesh Shotham (*Indian d, perc*). 2–3/92.

*** **The Sultan's Picnic** Enja 8078
> Abou-Khalil; Kenny Wheeler (*t, flhn*); Charlie Mariano (*as*); Howard Levy (*hca*); Michel
> Godard (*tba, serpent*); Steve Swallow (*b*); Mark Nauseef (*d*); Milton Cardona, Nabil Khaiat
> (*perc*). 3/94.

Jazz is only one of the world's great improvising traditions. Within Arab music, there has always been a substantial area of freedom for the virtuoso performer, and the 11-string oud has occupied a role in classical and more popular forms roughly analogous to that of the piano and guitar in the West. Abou-Khalil is a young Lebanese master forced into exile in 1978 by the increasingly chaotic civil war. A follower of the great Wadih Al-Safi, he has maintained a passionate commitment to the 'new music' (*al-jadida*; 'new' not just in the sense of modern, but also in the sense that Western homophony was once dubbed 'new') while taking account of the singing and playing traditions of Western jazz.

From the point of view of a jazz-literate listener, it is clear that the first and last items above are likely to be the least familiarly accessible and their ratings reflect that rather than their perceived quality. One of the main points of contact on the middle three items is the presence of jazz improvisers Charlie Mariano, Sonny Fortune and Oregon (*q.v.*) bassist, Glen Moore, all of whom have made the same cultural journey as Abou-Khalil, but in reverse, west to east. There is an impressive absence of pastiche or self-conscious eclecticism. A composition like 'Ornette Never Sleeps' (*Al-Jadida*) gives off no obvious irony; like much of Abou-Khalil's work, it is intended as sincere *hommage*. Those well disposed towards Oregon's proto-'world music' will feel most comfortable with the magnificent *Between Dusk And Dawn*, but *Bukra* is in some regards more challenging.

Like early jazz, much of the emphasis is on ensemble improvisation rather than more obviously virtuosic soloing. Apart from the leader's cleanly picked multi-directional lines, it's also worth mentioning Moore's marvellously sonorous bass and Mariano's familiarly 'Eastern' mode. Fortune is more of a revelation; staying mainly with the alto saxophone, which is perhaps a more promising choice in this harmonic context, he sounds absolutely familiar with the idiom, and it's the saxophonist who gives *Bukra* much of its compelling power; his unaccompanied introduction to 'Kibbe' is breathtaking, matched for sheer surprise only by Glen Velez's perfectly controlled overtone singing on 'Remember . . . The Desert'.

Restored to the catalogue just as the early *Bitter Harvest* on MMP was disappearing, *Nafas* is most notable for a brilliant performance by Selim Kusur, a leading performer on the bamboo *nay* flute. Recent sets have also leant heavily on guest players, as Abou-Khalil's own playing increasingly takes a backseat to a more ensemble approach with occasional vivid highlighting. *Blue Camel*, with Wheeler, Swallow and Mariano again all guesting, might on the surface appear to be his 'jazz' album, but the mix is very much as usual. *Tarab* returns unequivocally to a highly traditional style, as if to refute any suspicion of commercial sell-out, but again the slightly disappointing *Sultan's Picnic* looks to be aimed at a cross-over audience. Even so, because it is so uncompromised, it is hard to see this music ever reaching a mass audience, but it is highly attractive none the less, and the laminated card-covers Enja have now seemingly reserved for Abou-Khalil are among the most attractive around.

Muhal Richard Abrams (born 1930) PIANO, KEYBOARDS, CLARINET, COMPOSER, EDUCATOR

*** **Levels And Degrees Of Light** Delmark DD 413
> Abrams; Anthony Braxton (*as*); Maurice McIntyre (*ts*); Leroy Jenkins (*vn*); Gordon Emmanuel
> (*vib*); Charles Clark, Leonard Jones (*b*); Thurman Barker (*d*); David Moore, Penelope Taylor
> (*v*). 1 & 7/67.
*(*) **Duet** Black Saint 120051
> Abrams; Amina Claudine Myers (*p*). 5/81.
*** **Duets And Solos** Black Saint 120133
> Abrams; Roscoe Mitchell (*f, reeds*). 3/90.

Hugely influential, Abrams is one of the most important catalytic forces in contemporary jazz and improvisation and, like any physical catalyst, seems curiously unchanged and unmoved by the forces he has set in motion. His own performing and compositional style remains fixed in his original and very personal synthesis of black music styles. He ranges from stride to freely improvised structures, bebop to a kind of proto-funk, echoes of field hollers to dim annunciations of the European classical avant-garde.

Levels And Degrees Of Light has an oddly prayerful quality, encapsulated on the opening track by Penelope Taylor's wavering *vocalise* (which gives way to Abrams's unvirtuosic but effective clarinet). The lyrical content of the very long 'Bird Song' is much less effective; Jenkins and Jones join the others (Cranshaw sits it out), giving an almost orchestral depth of focus that contrasts with the percussive quality of the other two tracks. Braxton and McIntyre play modestly but with feeling throughout, and Barker is absolutely excellent.

Abrams's understanding with Roscoe Mitchell goes back a long way. In duet, they are inclined to elide much that would have been more effective if stated explicitly, and there is a sense that the whole thing becomes private and uncommunicative. It is, all the same, a fascinating eavesdrop, recommendable to fans of either gentleman.

In sharp contrast to his rapport with Mitchell (and elsewhere with another Art Ensemble member, Malachi Favors), Abrams simply lets Amina Claudine Myers get in his way. Piano duos are rarely successful, and this one seems more laden and leaden than most. CD transfer sharpens and separates the sound usefully – as it does on several more of the Black Saint sessions, below – but in this case not enough to lift the rating.

(*) 1-OQA+19 Black Saint 120017
  Abrams; Anthony Braxton (*as, sno, f, cl, v*); Henry Threadgill (*as, ts, f, v*); Leonard Jones (*b, v*); Steve McCall (*d, perc, v*). 11–12/77.
*** Spihumonesty Black Saint 120032
  Abrams; George Lewis (*tb, sou, syn*); Roscoe Mitchell (*as, f*); Amina Claudine Myers (*p, electric p, org*); Leonard Jones (*b*); Jay Clayton (*v*); Youssef Yancey (*theremin*). 7/79.

Myers's contribution to *Spihumonesty* (a typically punning title that recalls the gnomic and esoteric titles of bebop, like 'Klactoveesedstene') is a good deal more acute. The drummerless band moves through the charts like information through a printed circuit, and there is an intriguing simultaneity to some of the cues that suggests – rightly or wrongly – something like Braxton's wholly-composed conception. In truth, Abrams isn't a great soloist in the conventional sense. But that doesn't mean that he attempts to submerge more assertive musical personalities in a bland collective logic. Here the balance of ensemble and solo is well maintained and the timbral range impressively extended by Lewis's computer/synth and the peculiar sound of the theremin (the woo-woo bit in the Beach Boys' 'Good Vibrations'). Abrams did finer things in the '80s, but this is well worth tracking back.

The earlier set has, on the face of it, a more impressive starting line-up. Though Threadgill is a much less demanding player than Mitchell, Anthony Braxton is one of the certain masters of modern jazz and perhaps Abrams's most gifted pupil. The music they make is complex, scurryingly allusive and seldom directly appealing. Braxton's title composition is compellingly handled, and so is 'Charlie In The Parker' (compare George Lewis's similarly conceived homage on Black Saint BSR 0029), but there are question marks over some of the rest. May take longer to absorb than is strictly worthwhile.

** Mama And Daddy Black Saint 120041
  Abrams; Baikida Carroll (*t, flhn*); Vincent Chauncey (*hn*); Wallace McMillan (*as, bs, ts, f, perc*); Andrew Cyrille (*perc*); George Lewis (*tb*); Bob Stewart (*tba*); Leroy Jenkins (*vn*); Brian Smith (*b*). 12/79.
**(*) Rejoicing With The Light Black Saint 120071
  Abrams; Baikida Carroll (*t, flhn*); Vincent Chauncey (*hn*); Wallace McMillan (*as, bs, ts, f, perc*); Andrew Cyrille (*perc*); Marty Ehrlich (*as, f, cl*); Patience Higgins (*cl, acl, bs*); Jean-Paul Bourelly (*g*); Abdul Wadud (*clo*); Rick Rosie (*b*); Warren Smith (*vib, timp, perc*). 1/83.

These are slightly uneasy records, by no means his most impressive work, but perhaps suggestive of the effort Abrams was putting into the application of his basic language to much larger structures and ensembles. The presence of Baikida Carroll, George Lewis and, on *Rejoicing With the Light*, a soon-to-be Abrams regular, Patience Higgins, guarantees interesting moments, albeit widely spaced.

**(*) View From Within Black Saint 120081
  Abrams; Stanton Davis (*t, flhn*); John Purcell (*as, ss, f, ts, bcl*); Marty Ehrlich (*picc, f, as, ts, cl, bcl*); Warren Smith (*vib, mar, perc*); Rick Rosie (*b*); Thurman Barker (*d, perc*); Ray Mantilla (*perc*). 9/84.

Like the slightly later *Colors In Thirty-Third*, *View From Within* sounded like a much more personal statement than previous records. The multi-instrumental approach lends it a fluid, unsettled quality that is rectified only by Thurman Barker's typically inspirational percussion and by Abrams's own patient articulation.

***(*) The Hearinga Suite Black Saint 120103
  Abrams; Ron Tooley, Jack Walrath, Cecil Bridgewater, Frank Gordon (*t*); Clifton Anderson, Dick Griffin (*tb*); Jack Jeffers, Bill Lowe (*btb*); John Purcell (*ts, f, cl*); Marty Ehrlich (*as, picc, f, cl*); Patience Higgins (*ts, bcl*); Courtnay Wynter (*bsn, bcl, ts*); Charles Davis (*bs, ss*); Dierdre Murray (*clo*); Fred Hopkins (*b*); Andrew Cyrille (*d*). 1/89.

One can now almost hear Abrams pushing towards something much larger and more cohesive. Pieces like 'Hearinga' itself, 'Seesall' and 'Bermix' are as perfectly self-contained and full of meat as fresh eggs. The only qualification is that one might almost prefer to hear this music in a looser, more open-ended form, with the saxophonists in particular given their head. Hard to fault, though, and an important way-station on the way to the mature compositions of the '90s.

**** **Blu Blu Blu** Black Saint 120117
> Abrams; Joel Brandon (*whistle*); Jack Walrath (*t*); Alfred Patterson (*tb*); Mark Taylor (*frhn*); Joe Daley (*tba*); John Purcell (*as, f, bcl*); Robert De Bellis (*as, cl, bcl*); Eugene Ghee (*ts, cl, bcl*); David Fiuczynski (*g*); Lindsey Horner, Brad Jones (*b*); Warren Smith (*vib, tim*); Thurman Barker (*d*). 11/90.

Abrams's best album for some considerable time is a showcase for the extraordinary – and initially unsettling – talents of whistler Joel Brandon (also featured on David Murray's recent big-band album, DIW 851). At first hearing, Brandon's high swooping lines sound remarkably like the MiniMoog features Jan Hammer used to contribute to the Mahavishnu Orchestra, only much more quickly delivered. 'One For The Whistler' is a *tour de force*, but elsewhere on the album Brandon demonstrates his own and his instrument's viability in an improvising context.

Abrams really gets going as a pianist only on the final 'Stretch Time', leaving most of the foreground to a tonally varied and adventurous band. The title-track is a dedication to McKinley Morganfield (better known as the late, great Muddy Waters). Fiuczynski's howling guitar initially sounds out of place, but it settles back into a typically sophisticated and historically aware chart which underlines Abrams's commitment to the wider spectrum of black music. Walrath is forceful among the brasses and Barker moves fluently between abstraction and big-band swing. Set alongside Sun Ra's later work and Butch Morris's 'conduction' experiments, this is among the most important contemporary big-band records, a far more accomplished set than the currently deleted *Hearinga Suite*. Highly recommended.

***(*) **Family Talk** Black Saint 120132
> Abrams; Jack Walrath (*t*); Patience Higgins (*ts, bcl, eng hn*); Warren Smith (*vib, timp, mar, gongs*); Brad Jones (*b*); Reggie Nicholson (*d, mar, bells*). 3/93.

A fine record, despite some reservations about individual contributions. As a player, Higgins is nothing much, but he provides some agreeable sound-colours on his bass clarinet and cor anglais. His tenor solo on 'Illuso' is laughable. By contrast, Walrath is too effusive and powerful. On the long 'DizBirdMonkBudMax' he sounds poised and at ease, but he's the wrong man for the moodier and more complex tracks like 'Drumbutu', where he simply re-works the cod-Gothick effects he has patented on his own recordings.

Family Talk really belongs to the rhythm section. Abrams sounds more anchored than ever, and the addition of an extra percussionist allows him to play quite abstractly whenever the opportunity presents itself; he reserves the synthesizer in the main for introductory sketches and background washes, but it adds an important element to the overall sound. Smith is excellent on vibes and marimba. The woodier tones mix well with Jones's bass.

**** **One Line, Two Views** New World 80469
> Abrams; Eddie Allen (*t, perc, v*); Marty Ehrlich (*as, bcl, perc, v*); Patience Higgins (*ts, bcl, perc, v*); Mark Feldman (*vn, perc, v*); Tony Cedras (*acc, perc, v*); Anne LeBaron (*hp, perc, v*); Bryan Carrott (*vib, perc, v*); Lindsey Horner (*b, perc, v*); Reggie Nicholson (*d, perc, v*). 6/95.

A new label and a marvellous start. For us, this is the record Abrams has been promising for years, marked by tight, highly intelligent charts, an imaginative approach to timbre and registration, and a headlong freedom that remains intact from the early days. As before, Higgins is the key individual, but the recruitment of Marty Ehrlich brings in a new range of sounds, and Abrams finds interesting things for harpist LeBaron and accordionist Cedras to do. At the heart of the set, a brief, heartfelt threnody to Julius Hemphill and Don Pullen, fellow-composers who left in a hurry. The longer pieces never drag, though there are moments on the closing 'Ensemble Song' which border on self-indulgence. A triumph, though, and essential purchase for Abrams enthusiasts.

*** **UMO Plays The Music Of Muhal Richard Abrams** UMO CD 101
> Chuck Findley, Simo Salminen, Esko Heikkinen, Heikki Haimila (*t*); Markku Veijonsuo, Mircea Stan, Juhani Aalto, Mikael Lángbacka (*tb*); Pentti Lahti, Teemu Salminen, Eero Koivistoinen, Kari Heinilä, Pertti Päivinen (*sax*); Seppo Kantonen (*p*); Kirmo Lintinen (*syn*); Lars Danielsson (*b*); Klaus Suonsaari (*d*); Mongo Aaltonen (*perc*). 5/88.

Arguably, this should be discussed under a separate entry for the Finnish big band but, since Abrams charts are absolutely of the essence, it makes sense to include this very interesting and beautifully recorded disc here. UMO are a long-standing, government-sponsored outfit whose work ranges from fairly light standards repertoire right through to the avant-garde. There is a slight sense that both are tackled with more professionalism and exactitude than fire and passion, but almost everything the orchestra does is worth listening to, and this is certainly one of their more enterprising recorded outings. Compositions include 'Ritob', 'Fortex', 'Melancholia' and 'Symtre', and there is an Abrams arrangement of Duke's 'Melancholy' for contrast. It appears that the composer supervised the sessions, but technical credits really have to go to the engineers in Helsinki and re-mix wizard Dave Baker in New York, who gave the record its undeniable presence. Worth searching for.

Bob Ackerman SOPRANO, ALTO AND TENOR SAXOPHONES, FLUTES, CLARINET AND PIANO

*** **Old & New Magic** Silkheart SHCD 138
    Ackerman; Wilber Morris (b); Dennis Charles (d). 1/93.
(*) **If I Think Of Something, You'll Let Me Know Progressive Winds PW1001
    As above, except add Pam Purvis (v). 5/93.

Ackerman is a reed specialist, expert in old saxes and flutes, who wears his scholarship lightly on these enjoyable if unexceptional records. The trio date, cut almost off-the-cuff in one four-hour session, finds Morris and Charles creating a fluid backdrop to the leader's energetic free playing, scratching around tone centres and toying with overtones but never quite going for any avant-garde jugular. A concentrated tenor feature such as 'Tranein' In' is rather more impressive than one of the long pieces in which he jumps from horn to horn (the sleeve-notes suggest that two titles have been transposed in the running order). The subsequent disc, where the trio is joined by vocalist Purvis, is let down by some feeble choices of material, including a dolorous 'Angel Eyes' and Don McLean's miserable 'Vincent'. Despite the gushing sleeve-notes, neither record sounds particularly outstanding in sonic terms, with both bass and drums lacking in body and presence.

Bruce Adams (born 1951) TRUMPET, FLUGELHORN

** **One Foot In The Gutter** Big Bear CD36
    Adams; John Clarke (p); Len Skeat (b); Bobby Orr (d). 11/91–1/92.
(*) **Side-Steppin' Big Bear CD38
    Adams; Alan Barnes (as, bs); Brian Dee (p); Len Skeat (b); Bobby Orr (d). 8/93.
*** **Let's Face The Music** . . . Big Bear ESSCD 269
    As above. 12/94.

A harum-scarum stylist on trumpet, Adams came up through British variety, and it seems to show on the first album – he sounds as much like Eddie Calvert as he does any jazz trumpet hero. A big, brassy but rather ineffectual sound leaves no more than a surface bruise on a lot of decent standards, and the annoyingly resonant echo on the horn doesn't help. The next two albums are by the regular band he's formed with Alan Barnes, who stabilizes the front line. They still sound faintly comic on the very fast numbers intended as showstoppers, Barnes turning to his glib rather than his thoughtful side; but on the slow-to-mid tunes – on some of which Barnes picks up the baritone – they cruise nicely enough through a blend of small-group swing with some bebop touches. The third album matures the band further; Barnes writes some slight but appealing material, Adams scales down his playing a little further (though he still overdoes it when he feels like it), and something like Strayhorn's 'Raincheck' comes off on a pleasing lilt. Still rather dislikeable studio sound.

George Adams (1940–92) TENOR SAXOPHONE, FLUTE, BASS CLARINET

(*) **Don't Loose Control Soul Note 1211004
    Adams; Don Pullen (p); Cameron Brown (b); Dannie Richmond (d). 11/79.
*** **Live At The Village Vanguard** Soul Note 1211094
    As above. 8/83.
*** **Live At The Village Vanguard 2** Soul Note 1211144
    As above. 8/83.
*** **Earth Beams** Timeless SJP 147
    As above. 81.
*** **Life Line** Timeless SJP 154
    As above. 8/80.
*** **City Gates** Timeless SJP 181
    As above. 3/83.
*** **Decisions** Timeless SJP 205
    As above. 2/84.
(*) **Live At Montmartre Timeless SJP 219
    As above, except add John Scofield (g). 4/85.

This was one of the most successful long-standing units working in contemporary jazz. Co-led with

Don Pullen – the Blue Note sessions list the pianist's name first – the quartet combines a convincing unity of purpose with tremendous individuality of response. Adams was a powerful player with a huge, fruity tone that occasionally overwhelmed lesser sidemen. Pullen's forceful right-hand chords are a perfect complement and foil. Richmond, with the weight of many years with Charles Mingus behind him, has no problems with powerful personalities and always plays superbly in these settings, as on the co-led *Hand To Hand* (see below). He is particularly fine on the rumbustious *Village Vanguard* sessions which see the band stretch out the tight, Monk-inspired structures of the studio sets in order to explore some of the freer areas Adams and Pullen enter in their duo work (see below).

Adams's technique often suggested a hybrid of Albert Ayler and Sonny Rollins. He had Ayler's power but, more tellingly, much of Rollins's superb instinct for the structural logic of a song or of a chord progression. He was at home with material ranging from Stephen Foster and traditional hymns to the wilder shores of atonality (and Pullen's Taylorish free play describes a similar arc).

Completists will, of course, want the lot. Newcomers might well start with *City Gates*, which includes a version of 'Thank You Very Much, Mr Monk' (the kick-off piece on the slightly later *Village Vanguard* double-set), a Mingus tribute, a samba, and a reading of 'Nobody Knows The Trouble I've Seen'. Taken together, that's a fair cross-section of what they do. The subsequent Timeless albums are qualitatively pretty much of a piece, though John Scofield's contribution to *Live At Montmartre* seems a little supernumerary.

(*) Melodic Excursions Timeless SJP 166
> Adams; Don Pullen (*p*). 6/82.

This is perhaps more influenced by Pullen's conception than was usually the case in the quartets. It is a curious album, demanding without being particularly involving. There is a hot, gospelly 'God Has Smiled On Me' (the shortest track) and six originals, almost all of which play on the inbuilt dichotomies of the duo format. It's probably unfortunate that the dichotomies insist more strongly than the unities in this case; unusually, and however responsive they seem to be, the two players give every sense of working on parallel tracks rather than in tandem.

(*) Hand To Hand Soul Note 1211007
> Adams; Jimmy Knepper (*tb*); Hugh Lawson (*p*); Mike Richmond (*b*); Dannie Richmond (*d*). 2/ 80.

(*) Gentlemen's Agreement Soul Note 1211057
> As above. 2/83.

Co-led by the drummer, these sets are marked by fine writing and some ambitious structures, redolent of Mingus bands where five could be made to sound like a dozen and every solo suggested an entire section at play. The 'Symphony For Five' on *Gentlemen's Agreement* moves into Dolphy territory, as does 'Prayer For A Jitterbug'. The tonality is broader than on the quartet sessions; Knepper's playing is reminiscent of Vic Dickenson, an almost regressive style that ignores much of the Bebop 'Bone Book and keeps the trombone closer to the saxophone's timbral range and attack. Lawson is an intelligent and lyrical pianist, but he isn't in Pullen's class, and these sets are nowhere like as compelling as the Adams/ Pullen quartets.

Pepper Adams (1930–86) BARITONE SAXOPHONE

*** **The Cool Sound Of Pepper Adams** Savoy SV-0198
> Adams; Bernard McKinney (*euph*); Hank Jones (*p*); George Duvivier (*b*); Elvin Jones (*d*). 11/ 57.

*** **10 To 4 At The 5-Spot** Original Jazz Classics OJC 031
> Adams; Donald Byrd (*t*); Bobby Timmons (*p*); Doug Watkins (*b*); Elvin Jones (*d*). 4/58.

The baritone sax was as unpopular with the hard-bop musicians as it was with original boppers and, come to that, with the swing-era saxophonists. Pepper Adams, more than anyone, came close to making it a congenial instrument in the hothouse environment of hard bop. He had a dry, unsentimental tone – very different from either Serge Chaloff or Gerry Mulligan – and a penchant for full-tilt solos that gave no shred of concession to the horn's 'cumbersome' reputation. The live session, made with a frequent partner at the time, Donald Byrd, is typical of Adams's kind of date, with muscular blow-outs of the order of 'Hastings Street Bounce' sitting next to a clear-headed ballad reading of 'You're My Thrill'. That said, it's sometimes only the novelty value of hearing a baritone in the ensembles that lifts the music out of a professional hard-bop routine. *The Cool Sound Of Pepper Adams* is hardly an appropriate title for a session by this leader, although the plodding tempos of three of the four pieces here certainly don't generate much heat. Only 'Like What Is This?' brings out the best in Adams, with a typically trenchant improvisation; the rest rolls genially along, with McKinney's low brass and Jones's urbane fills barely escaping the background.

*** **Stardust** Bethlehem 6018-2
 Adams; Donald Byrd (*t*); Tommy Flanagan (*p*); Kenny Burrell (*g*); Paul Chambers (*b*); Louis Hayes (*d*). 60.
*** **Out Of This World** Fresh Sound FSR-CD 137
 Adams; Donald Byrd (*t*); Herbie Hancock (*p*); Teddy Charles (*vib*); Laymon Jackson (*b*); Jimmy Cobb (*d*). 61.

Though sometimes listed under either Byrd's name or Adams's, we have elected to include these albums under the saxophonist's entry. Though one might expect a bluff, no-nonsense kind of hard bop, these sessions tend to spotlight the gentler side of the two leaders. The Fresh Sound date, tracks originally released on Warwick and produced by Teddy Charles, is the better bet since it has more music and some genuinely lyrical touches: Adams's solo turn on 'Day Dream', for instance, with a pleasing early solo by Hancock. But the Bethelehem set isn't far behind, in the same mould.

*** **Pepper Adams Plays Charlie Mingus** Fresh Sound FSR-CD 177
 Adams; Thad Jones (*t*); Bennie Powell (*tb*); Charles McPherson (*as*); Zoot Sims (*ts*); Hank Jones (*p*); Paul Chambers, Bob Cranshaw (*b*); Dannie Richmond (*d*). 9/63.

Adams led this date with his usual unfussy authority. There are nine Mingus tunes and a mixture of Mingusians and – in the case of Zoot Sims – at least one musician about as far removed from being a Mingus sideman as one could imagine, though Zoot deals with the situation as imperturbably as always. The results, split between a quintet and an octet, are akin to a pocket-size edition of a typical Mingus band: 'Haitian Fight Song' and 'Fables Of Faubus' are as swinging as any Mingus version (Chambers is at the top of his game), but 'Better Git In Your Soul' (*sic.*) is comparatively watery and Jones is a lot more dapper than a Mingus pianist might have been. A solid jazz record.

***(*) **Conjuration: Fat Tuesday's Session** Reservoir RSR 113
 Adams; Kenny Wheeler (*t, flhn*); Hank Jones (*p*); Clint Houston (*b*); Louis Hayes (*d*). 8/83.

A heartening farewell to Adams's career on record, this live set emphasizes his virtues – the muscularity of sound, oversized tone and plangent phrasing – so decisively that one overlooks any scent of routine in the playing. Kenny Wheeler, an unlikely partner, adds sparkle and some good material, and Hank Jones is sublimely buoyant, as are Houston and Hayes. Three extra tracks have been added to the original LP issue, bringing the running time to 66 minutes.

Terry Adams PIANO, ORGAN

(*) **Terrible New World 80464
 Adams; Dave Gordon (*t*); Donn Adams, Tyrone Hill, Roswell Rudd (*tb*); Marshall Allen, Noel Scott (*as, f*); Jim Hoke (*as, ss, f*); Jim Gordon (*hca*); John Sebastian, Johnny Spampinato (*g*); Greg Cohen, Joey Spampinato, Pete Toigo (*b*); Tom Ardolino, Bobby Previte (*d*). 1/95.

Adams comes from a rock background, having led the innovative and often jazz-orientated NRBQ for many years. He has also worked with Carla Bley and David Sanborn. During the band's history it performed and recorded some Sun Ra material, and a relationship developed between Adams and Arkestra members, who feature on some tracks here. (The connection is celebrated on an Adams composition, 'Le Sony'r'.) From a jazz fan's point of view, it is their contributions and that of trombonist Roswell Rudd on a couple of tracks which make this album worth considering. For the most part it comes across as offbeat boogie, using augmented rhythms and awkward semi-dissonances which restore raw edges to what is essentially a very slick product. Hard as it is to dislike, it's not easy to get too excited about *Terrible*.

Julian 'Cannonball' Adderley (1928–75) ALTO SAXOPHONE

*** **Presenting Cannonball** Savoy SV-0108
 Adderley; Nat Adderley (*c*); Hank Jones (*p*); Paul Chambers (*b*); Kenny Clarke (*d*). 7/55.
***(*) **Sophisticated Swing** Verve 528408-2 2CD
 Adderley; Nat Adderley (*c*); Junior Mance (*p*); Sam Jones, Al McKibbon (*b*); Specs Wright, Jimmy Cobb (*d*). 7/56–3/58.
*** **Jump For Joy** Verve 528699-2
 Adderley; Emmett Berry (*t*); Bill Evans (*p*); Barry Galbraith (*g*); Milt Hinton (*b*); Jimmy Cobb (*d*). 10/55–8/58.
**** **Somethin' Else** Blue Note CDP 746338-2
 Adderley; Miles Davis (*t*); Hank Jones (*p*); Sam Jones (*b*); Art Blakey (*d*). 3/58.

*** **Portrait Of Cannonball** Original Jazz Classics OJC 361
   Adderley; Blue Mitchell (*t*); Bill Evans (*p*); Sam Jones (*b*); Philly Joe Jones (*d*). 7/58.
***(*) **Things Are Getting Better** Original Jazz Classics OJC 032
   Adderley; Wynton Kelly (*p*); Milt Jackson (*vib*); Percy Heath (*b*); Art Blakey (*d*). 10/58.
*** **Cannonball And Coltrane** Emarcy 834588-2
   Adderley; John Coltrane (*ts*); Wynton Kelly (*p*); Paul Chambers (*b*); Jimmy Cobb (*d*). 2/59.
(*) **Cannonball Takes Charge Landmark 1306
   Adderley; Wynton Kelly (*p*); Paul Chambers, Percy Heath (*b*); Jimmy Cobb, Albert 'Tootie'
   Heath (*d*). 4–5/59.

Long a critically undervalued figure, Cannonball Adderley's status as a great popularizer and patron
spirit of the music has, if anything, increased since his sadly early death. The blues-soaked tone and
hard, swinging delivery of his alto lines are as recognizable and communicative a sound as anything in
the aftermath of bebop and, while many have been quick to criticize his essentially derivative manner –
Cannonball always fell back on clichés, because he just liked the sound of them – there's a lean, hard-
won quality about his best playing which says a lot about one man's dedication to his craft. Everything
was already in place at the time of his 1955 debut, with brother Nat playing the eternal second fiddle: in
sprucely remastered sound, the music sounds like an excerpt from almost any stage of the leader's career
(there are some alternative takes to be found on the compilation *Discoveries*, SV 0251). When he joined
Miles Davis, Adderley's cameo appearances on *Milestones* and *Kind Of Blue* were somewhat outclassed
by the leader's returning-the-favour guest spot on *Somethin' Else*, which features some of Davis's most
pithy improvising. But something else distinguishes the Adderley sessions of this period: the superb line-
up of supporting players. There is marvellous sparring with Milt Jackson on *Things Are Getting Better*,
with Kelly, Heath and Blakey in great form too; and 'The Sidewalks Of New York' is an inspired
revision which only Ellington's incomparable 1940 version can surpass. *Cannonball Takes Charge* is
perhaps only ordinary, but *Portrait Of Cannonball* (which includes three alternative takes on the CD
issue) finds Blue Mitchell taking some welcome limelight – though he sounds no more facile than the
oft-maligned Nat – and an early glimpse of Bill Evans feeling his way through 'Nardis'. The session with
Coltrane is really the Miles Davis band without Miles, and it's a bit of good fun, both hornmen flexing
their muscles on the blues and a ballad feature apiece. There isn't really a dud record in this batch.
   Verve have filled in the picture of this period by putting together Cannonball's Emarcy sessions.
Sophisticated Swing pulls together all of the LPs *Sophisticated Swing*, *Cannonball En Route* and
Cannonball's Sharpshooters, plus Nat's date, *To The Ivy League From Nat*, in a double-disc reissue. The
clipped, punchy format of most of the tracks suits the playing, and there is some of the altoist's freshest
music hidden in some otherwise unpromising songs. *Jump For Joy* puts Cannonball with Richard
Hayman's strings for the first half, and it's not the happiest of combinations, though the sheer alacrity
of Adderley's sound energizes some otherwise tepid writing. The second half, arranged by Bill Russo to
accommodate a string quartet beside a familiar rhythm section, works better, and there is some felicitous work by all hands. Excellent remastering of both discs.

*** **In San Francisco** Original Jazz Classics OJC 035
   Adderley; Nat Adderley (*c*); Bobby Timmons (*p*); Sam Jones (*b*); Louis Hayes (*d*). 10/59.
*** **Them Dirty Blues** Landmark 1301
   As above, except add Barry Harris (*p*). 2–3/60.
*** **Cannonball And The Poll Winners** Landmark 1304
   Adderley; Victor Feldman (*p, vib*); Wes Montgomery (*g*); Ray Brown (*b*); Louis Hayes (*d*). 5–6/
   60.
***(*) **At The Lighthouse** Landmark 1305
   Adderley; Nat Adderley (*c*); Victor Feldman (*p*); Sam Jones (*b*); Louis Hayes (*d*). 10/60.
*** **What Is This Thing Called Soul** Original Jazz Classics OJC 801
   As above. 11/60.

Adderley's regular quintet has often been damned with such faint praise as 'unpretentious' and 'soulful'. This was a hard-hitting, rocking band which invested blues and blowing formulae with an intensity
which helped to keep one part of jazz's communication channels open at the time of Ornette Coleman,
Eric Dolphy and other seekers after new forms. The two earlier live albums, cut in San Francisco and at
the Hermosa Beach Lighthouse, are memorably rowdy and exciting sessions. *In San Francisco* is a little
overstretched, with four tracks nudging the 12-minute mark and some of the solos running out of steam
too soon, but *At The Lighthouse* is crisper and wittier: Feldman, who contributes the engaging 'Azule
Serape' to the band book, is a lot more interesting than Timmons, and the Adderleys are in rousing
form: Cannonball's six choruses on 'Sack O' Woe' distil some of the best of himself. *Them Dirty Blues*
introduces two classic set-pieces in 'Dat Dere' and 'Work Song' – and the originals are still the best –
while Barry Harris sits in for half of the set. The *Poll Winners* date is a brief vacation for Cannonball,
and he trades licks with Wes Montgomery to piquant effect. *What Is This Thing Called Soul* is taken

from European concerts: the band is on cracking form on Jimmy Heath's 'Big P', and the rest of the set is up to scratch.

*** **African Waltz** Original Jazz Classics OJC 258
> Adderley; Clark Terry, Ernie Royal, Joe Newman, Nick Travis (*t*); Nat Adderley (*c*); Bob Brookmeyer (*vtb*); Melba Liston, Arnet Sparrow, George Matthews, Jimmy Cleveland, Paul Faulise (*tb*); George Dorsey (*as, f*); Jerome Richardson, Oliver Jackson (*ts, f*); Arthur Clarke (*bs*); Wynton Kelly (*p*); Sam Jones (*b*); Don Butterfield (*tba*); Louis Hayes, Charli Persip (*d*); Ray Barretto, Olatunji (*perc*). 2–5/61.

A departure from and an extension of what the Adderleys were doing in their small groups. Ernie Wilkins arranges a set of fulsome, top-heavy charts which Adderley has to jostle with to create their own space, and the music's worth hearing for its sheer brashness and impact. But the simple clarity of the Adderley small groups is a casualty of the setting, and the altoman isn't as convincingly at home here as he is in the *Great Jazz Standards* album with Gil Evans, one of his finest hours.

*** **Know What I Mean?** Original Jazz Classics OJC 105
> Adderley; Bill Evans (*p*); Percy Heath (*b*); Connie Kay (*d*). 1–3/61.

*** **Cannonball Adderley Quintet Plus** Original Jazz Classics OJC 306
> Adderley; Nat Adderley (*c*); Victor Feldman (*p, vib*); Wynton Kelly (*p*); Sam Jones (*b*); Louis Hayes (*d*). 5/61.

(*) **In New York Original Jazz Classics OJC 142
> Adderley; Nat Adderley (*c*); Yusef Lateef (*ts, ob*); Joe Zawinul (*p*); Sam Jones (*b*); Louis Hayes (*d*). 1/62.

*** **Cannonball In Europe!** Landmark 1307
> As above. 8/62.

(*) **Jazz Workshop Revisited Landmark 1303
> As above. 9/62.

(*) **Cannonball's Bossa Nova Landmark 1302
> Adderley; Pedro Paulo (*t*); Paulo Moura (*as*); Sergie Mondez (*p*); Durval Ferreira (*g*); Octavio Bielly (*b*); Dom Um Romao (*d*). 12/62.

*** **Nippon Soul** Original Jazz Classics OJC 435
> Adderley; Nat Adderley (*c*); Yusef Lateef (*ts, ob, f*); Joe Zawinul (*p*); Sam Jones (*b*); Louis Hayes (*d*). 7/63.

*** **Dizzy's Business** Milestone MCD-47069-2
> As above. 9/62–7/63.

*** **Lugano 1963** TCB TDE 02032
> As above. 3/63.

Cannonball continued to turn out records for Riverside at a cracking pace and, while there are no classics here, his own big-hearted playing seldom falters. At this point, though, the regimen of tours and records begins to fossilize some aspects of his own playing. Having stratified bop licks and set the pace for so-called 'soul jazz', Adderley found there wasn't much left to do but play them over again. If he plays with undiminished verve, the power of his improvising declines. The quartet date with Bill Evans was one of the last chances to hear him as sole horn, and he sounds fine; *Plus* brings in Wynton Kelly on a few tracks, enabling Feldman to play some more vibes, but it's otherwise a routine Adderley band date. Bringing in Joe Zawinul and Yusef Lateef energized the band anew, but the records are all vaguely disappointing. Zawinul is still no more than a good bandsman, and Lateef's touches of exotica – such as the oboe solo on 'Brother John' (*Nippon Soul*) or his furry, Roland Kirk-like flute improvisations – are an awkward match for the sunnier disposition of the customary material. Nevertheless *Nippon Soul* and *In Europe* are perhaps the best of this bunch; the bossa nova set is a perfunctory nod to prevailing breezes. *Dizzy's Business* patches together some out-takes from the sessions for *Jazz Workshop Revisited* and *Nippon Soul*: not bad, with the title-track a solidly turned cooker. The Lugano date is another characteristic concert from one of the hardest-working bands of their era: familiar songs, though done as well as anywhere, and one nice note with 'Jessica's Birthday'. Recorded by Swiss Radio and in good fidelity. The men who earn exemption from criticism on all these records are Sam Jones and Louis Hayes: seldom remembered as a major rhythm section, their unflagging tempos and generosity of spirit centre the music at all times.

** **Cannonball In Japan** Capitol B21Y-93560
> Adderley; Nat Adderley (*c*); Joe Zawinul (*p*); Victor Gaskin (*b*); Roy McCurdy (*d*). 8/66.

*** **Mercy, Mercy, Mercy** Capitol 829915-2
> As above. 10/66.

*** **The Best Of Cannonball Adderley: The Capitol Years** Capitol CDP 7954822
> As above, except add Yusef Lateef, Charles Lloyd (*ts*); Sam Jones, Walter Booker (*b*); Louis Hayes (*d*). 8/62–10/69.

*** **Deep Groove!** Blue Note 830725-2
    As above discs. 62–69.
*** **Inside Straight** Original Jazz Classics OJC 750
    Adderley; Nat Adderley (*c*); Hal Galper (*p*); Walter Booker (*b*); Roy McCurdy (*d*); King
    Errisson (*perc*). 6/73.

Adderley kept on recording regularly until his death, but his later albums are currently in limbo so far as the catalogues are concerned. Close to 20 Capitol albums have been boiled down to one live set from Tokyo and the best-of, which actually starts with two tracks from Riverside sessions. Given that many of the later records were misfire attempts at fusion of one sort or another, maybe it's not such a bad thing. *Cannonball In Japan* is another live show in a favourite location: the group play well enough, but it won't enrich any who already have other Adderley records. The Capitol best-of is short on surprise and concentrates mostly on Zawinul's additions to the band's book, including their hit 'Mercy Mercy Mercy' and 'Country Preacher', which has a rare glimpse of the leader on soprano. But the most interesting thing is the lengthy '74 Miles Away', which suggests the distant influence of late Coltrane, with Cannonball's solo straying into what are for him very remote regions. That the group finally don't know what to do with the situation says something about the limits of their ambitions. *Deep Groove!* is another clutch of Capitol sides (despite the Blue Note logo) and features a couple of rarities to keep collectors happy, though overall it's a shade behind the other best-of. *Mercy, Mercy, Mercy* is a hard-swinging live album with one of Cannon's hottest outings in 'Sticks'; you can find this and 'Games' on *Deep Groove!*, though.

    Inside Straight is a welcome addition to latter-day Cannon on CD. This was one of his live-in-the-studio sessions with a late edition of the band: Galper plays smart, probing electric piano, and Booker and McCurdy generate considerable heat. The tunes are a little more severe than before: only the title-track can be called a typical Adderley slice of soul-jazz. 'Inner Journey', 'Snakin' The Grass' and 'Second Son' are more sidelong looks at the band's playing methods, and more interesting for it. No masterpiece, but a hint of other paths the group might have explored.

Nat Adderley (born 1931) CORNET, TRUMPET

*** **That's Nat** Savoy SV 0146
    Adderley; Jerome Richardson (*ts, f*); Hank Jones (*p*); Wendell Marshall (*b*); Kenny Clarke (*d*).
    7/55.
**** **Work Song** Original Jazz Classics OJC 363
    Adderley; Bobby Timmons (*p*); Wes Montgomery (*g*); Keter Betts, Sam Jones (*b*); Louis Hayes,
    Percy Heath (*d*).
***(*) **That's Right** Original Jazz Classics OJC 791
    Adderley; Julian 'Cannonball' Adderley (*as*); Yusef Lateef (*ts, f, ob*); Jimmy Heath, Charlie
    Rouse (*ts*); Tate Houston (*bs*); Wynton Kelly (*p*); Jim Hall, Les Spann (*g*); Sam Jones (*b*);
    Jimmy Cobb (*d*). 9/60.
***(*) **In The Bag** Original Jazz Classics OJC 648
    Adderley; Julian 'Cannonball' Adderley (*as*); Nat Perrilliat (*ts*); Ellis Marsalis (*p*); Sam Jones
    (*b*); James Black (*d*). 62.

The Adderley brothers helped keep a light burning for jazz when rock'n'roll was dominating the industry 'demographics'. Neither was ever particularly revolutionary or adventurous in style, but saxophonist Cannonball's enormous personality and untimely death, together with his participation in such legendary dates as Miles's *Kind Of Blue*, have sanctified his memory with young fans who would have found his live performances rather predictable.

    Nat was always the more incisive soloist, with a bright, ringing tone that most obviously drew on the example of Dizzy Gillespie but in which could be heard a whole raft of influences from Clark Terry to Henry 'Red' Allen to the pre-post-modern Miles of the 1950s.

    'I Married An Angel', on *That's Nat*, suggests that Bobby Hackett be added to that roster. A gorgeously toned ballad performance which keeps referring to the original tune, it's perhaps the best single track on a beautifully remastered recording. Jones's comping is inch-perfect throughout and Clarke is right on the case, often following Adderley outside the basic count for a phrase or two.

    In the late 1950s the cornetist was playing at his peak, and these sessions do genuinely merit the 'classic' tag, though 'original' is probably stretching things a bit. *Work Song* is the real classic, of course, laced with a funky blues feel but marked by some unexpectedly lyrical playing (on 'Violets For Your Furs' and 'My Heart Stood Still') from the leader. Montgomery manages to produce something more enterprising than his trademark octave-runs and hits a tense, almost threatening groove. Timmons is more predictable, but just right for this sort of set; compare *In San Francisco* (OJC 035), which was made under Cannonball's name. *In The Bag* is welcome for a further glimpse of the brothers playing together but isn't specially exciting. Watch out for the little-known Perrilliat, who plays a firm-toned and steady tenor, with some interesting quirks. The CD added a couple of rather inconsequential bonus tracks.

That's Right is a bit of an oddity, with Nat's cornet placed in front of what was billed, quite accurately, as the Big Sax Section. Lateef's multi-instrumentalism is kept to a minimum. He leads the ensemble on flute for 'My Old Country' but switches back to tenor for a rich, folksy solo. His oboe doesn't quite work out on 'Night After Night'; back in 1960 there weren't that many soprano specialists around to take a part made for one of them. Heath and Rouse are well featured, taking fine solos either side of Nat and the pianist on Heath's own 'Chordnation'. One of the high points of a thoroughly enjoyable record.

**(*) Don't Look Back Steeplechase SCCD 31059
    Adderley; Ken McIntyre (*as, bcl, ob, f*); John Stubblefield (*ts, ss*); Onaje Allan Gumbs (*p, ky*); Fernando Gumbs (*b*); Ira Buddy Williams (*d*); Victor See Yuen (*perc*). 8/76.

Adderley's reputation as a mainstream traditionalist takes a knock with sets like these. Unfortunately the results aren't by any means commensurate with the daring of the line-up. McIntyre is an important catalyst in the re-voicing of jazz horns, but like a true catalyst he remains largely untouched by what goes on round him and solos as if alone. Stubblefield is fierier and provokes some of the leader's best returns of fire. Whatever Onaje Allen Gumbs's qualities, he's patently wrong for this gig, and the rest of the group circle round him somewhat uneasily. A bold effort, but not quite there. (There is still an audiophile pressing of the LP, for collectors of such arcana.)

*** On The Move Evidence ECD 22064
    Adderley; Sonny Fortune (*as*); Larry Willis (*p*); Walter Booker (*b*); Jimmy Cobb (*d*). 83.
***(*) Blue Autumn Evidence ECD 22035
    As above. 83.

A fair proportion of listeners who played either of these cold would plump for Cannonball as the altoist, which suggests it may have been an attempt to re-create that cheerfully bouncing sound. In many respects Fortune is a more interesting player, inserting oddly angular ideas and figures into relatively innocuous contexts, stretching out with ideas that Cannonball would have dismissed with the back of his hand. The group as a whole is very strong and, while there might be quibbles about the sound-quality on the first of the pair, which was formerly listed as a Theresa release, there are none whatsoever about the music.

At just 40 minutes, *Blue Autumn* gives slightly short measure, but there's plenty packed in. Sonny Fortune's 'For Duke And Cannon' is a great opener and Adderley responds warmly to it. Larry Willis claims the lion's share of writing credits with both 'Blue Autumn' and 'Tallahassee Kid', but these are not much more than blowing ideas and they're treated accordingly, with Fortune in particular offering his own perspective on them.

*** We Remember Cannon In + Out 7012
    Adderley; Vincent Herring (*as*); Art Resnick (*p*); Walter Booker (*b*); Jimmy Cobb (*d*). 11/89.
**** Work Song Sweet Basil 660.55.007
    As above, except add Sonny Fortune (*as*); replace Resnick with Rob Bargad (*p*). 5/90.
***(*) Autumn Leaves Sweet Basil 660.55.013
    As for *Work Song*. 7/90.
**(*) Talkin' About You Landmark LCD 1528 2
    As for *Work Song*, except omit Fortune. 11/90.
***(*) The Old Country Enja 7027
    As for *Talkin' About You*, except omit Booker and Cobb; add James Genus (*b*); Billy Drummond (*d*). 12/90.

Recorded in Switzerland, *We Remember Cannon* is pretty much state of the art for the late-'80s band. There's a high quota of slower themes, including 'Soul Eyes' and 'Autumn Leaves', and the near obligatory tribute to Cannonball. However, there's a slightly tired air to the rhythm section, who get far less from Resnick than from the more dynamic Bargad, who signs up for the remainder of the trip.

Work Song and *Autumn Leaves* are the product of a long residency at Sweet Basil in New York. The latter set has a leftovers feel, but *Work Song* has some of the energy of its illustrious namesake, though the title-track has its rough spots. Randy Weston's 'Hi-Fly' is rousingly good-humoured. 'In A Sentimental Mood' gives Adderley a chance to emote, and 'Jive Samba' rounds it off. A thoroughly satisfying disc.

Astonishingly slow to get going (almost as if it were an unedited take of a live set) and marred by intonation problems with both horns, *Talkin' About You* develops into a storming session with Eddie Vinson's 'Arriving Soon'. Adderley's tone is better on medium-tempo themes like Victor Feldman's swinging 'Azule Serape' but he doesn't have a sure enough lip for the moody 'Ill Wind', a theme tailored to Herring's melting delivery. The rhythm section is faultless and the digital recording is of the highest quality.

Genus and Drummond do a marvellous job on the last of the three, and the two horns are well synchronized and brightly registered. Adderley's solo on 'Stella By Starlight' has a candied edge, but (set at the opposite end of the session from the optimistic title-track) it's the version of 'Nippon Soul' which will appeal most to Adderley fanatics, with Herring doing brisk Cannonball runs and bluesy punctuations.

Ron Affif (born 1965) GUITAR

*** **Ron Affif** Pablo PACD 2310-949-2
  Affif; Brian O'Rourke (*p*); Andy Simpkins (*b*); Colin Bailey (*d*). 10/92.
***(*) **Vierd Blues** Pablo PACD 2310-954-2
  As above, except add Ron Anthony (*g*), Brian Kilgore (*d*). 12/93–2/94.
It's a little surprising to read that Affif was never a rock player, since his hard tone is at odds with the sweeter, warmer jazz feel of Montgomery, Pass or Hall, three clear role-models to judge from the interesting debut set, *Ron Affif*. There's something of a pull between the guitarist's obvious chopsmanship and his reluctance to take all the limelight: O'Rourke is just as readily featured, and nothing Affif does takes up too much space. Nevertheless this is still a fundamentally traditional-modern guitar programme, with standards the main bill of fare. *Vierd Blues* is an advance which is even more surprising. The programme is all Miles Davis tunes or dedications, and Affif goes at it with a startling blend of irreverence and homage. 'Solar' is turned into a helter-skelter samba tune; 'So What' is genuinely hardbitten, a striking antidote to the many softer versions of the past 30 years. Affif puts some fresh light on most of the tunes, and his gutsy playing is capable enough to silence any talk of mere disrespect. In any case this is fundamentally straight-ahead jazz. O'Rourke's keen support is a further bonus, and Simpkins and Bailey are no slackers.

Affinity GROUP

**** **Plays Nine Modern Jazz Classics** Music & Arts CD 834
  Joe Rosenberg (*ss*); Rob Sudduth (*ts*); Richard Saunders (*b*); Bobby Lurie (*d*). 93.
Originally a limited-edition release, this excellent set always deserved wider exposure. The quality of playing starts high with a fierce burn through Lee Morgan's 'Afrique' (losing nothing through the absence of brasses) and quickly resolves into a sustained dialogue between Rosenberg's plain-speaking but harmonically subtle soprano work and Joe Sudduth's nervier tenor solos.

The interplay is both dense and exact on Ornette Coleman's rarely attempted 'Little Symphony', catching some of the quality of Ornette and Cherry, but it takes on an unexpected, old-style swing for Ellis Marsalis's 'After'. The choice of material is impeccable: Konitz's drily affable 'Subconsciouslee', Monk's 'Evidence', two numerical compositions by Braxton including a rousing reduction of the big-band march, 'Composition No. 58', and one of Dolphy's loveliest conceptions, 'Miss Ann'. Some doubt on the sleeve as to who (re)wrote 'Three Blind Mice', Curtis Fuller or Cedar Walton; no doubts whatever about the playing, which is impeccable, particularly in this case from drummer Lurie.

Rosenberg served a patient apprenticeship in this repertoire and has earned the right to tackle it in his own distinctive accent. All the same, Affinity isn't merely his working quartet; like all creative jazz groups, it's a genuinely collaborative venture.

Afro-Asian Music Ensemble GROUP

*** **Tomorrow Is Now** Soul Note 121117
  Fred Houn (*bs, leader*); Sam Furnace (*as, ts*); Sayyd Abdul Al-Khabyr, Al Givens (*ss, ts, f*); Richard Clements, Jon Jang (*p*); Kyoto Fujiwara (*b*); Taru Alexander (*d*); Carleen Robinson (*v*). 85.
(*) **We Refuse To Be Used And Abused Soul Note 1211167
  Fred Houn (*bs, ss, f*); Sam Furnace (*as, ss, f*); Hafez Modir (*ts, f*); Jon Jang (*p*); Kyoto Fujiwara (*b*); Royal Hartigan (*perc*). 11/87.
This is powerfully advocated activist music from a 'rainbow coalition' of fine young players, led by the young baritone saxophonist Fred Houn. Houn, an Asian-American like pianist Jang, has a big, powerful sound reminiscent of Harry Carney, and this sets the tone for the ensemble, which has a strongly Ellingtonian cast.

The title of the first album sets up all sorts of expectations – from Ornette Coleman's *Tomorrow Is The Question* to Max Roach's *Freedom Now* suite – which are not so much confounded as skirted. There would seem to be little place for prettiness in music as aggressively programmatic as this, but the band plays with surprising delicacy and unfailing taste. CD transfer flatters Houn's skills as an orchestrator.

The later album is more bitty and has a much less coherent sound. There is also a degree of stridency completely missing from the earlier set. Together, though, they represent an interesting development beyond the politicized jazz of Charlie Haden's Liberation Music Ensemble. An object lesson for America's new New Frontier in the dismal '80s.

Afro Blue Band GROUP

(*) **Impressions Milestone MCD-9237-2
> Melton Mustafa (*t*); Mario Rivera (*c, f*); Papo Vasquez (*tb*); Dave Liebman (*ss*); Mel Martin (*as, ts, bcl, f, picc*); Arthur Barron (*as, ts*); Hilton Ruiz, Mark Levine (*p*); Nicole Yarling (*vn, v*); Steve Neil (*b*); Phoenix Rivera (*d*); Jerry Gonzalez, Glen Cronkhite, Steve Berrios (*perc*). 12/94–5/95.

This three-way one-off, put together in New York, San Francisco and Fort Lauderdale, features players from three distinct musical scenes and blends a particular kind of metropolitan jazz with an Afro-Cuban base. Problematically, though, a good idea is often squandered through poor preparation and plain lack of finesse. The title-track is an impassioned but unconvincing mess, Yarling's inadequate vocals spoil 'Lonnie's Lament' and it's only when the more demanding contributions of Liebman and Ruiz – easily the most authoritative voices here – are thrown into relief that the undoubted energy and exuberance assume any genuine stature. This comes out best in 'Latin Jazz Dance', though Horace Silver's 'Senor Blues' isn't a bad effort.

After The End Of The World Coretet GROUP

** **Quaternity** Crystal Egg CE 06670
> Annelise Zamula (*ss, as, f*); Tracy McMullen (*ts, v*); Bill Noertker (*b*); Dave Mihaly (*d*); 5–12/91.
*** **13** AEWC Records AE0013
> As above, except Jon Birdsong (*t*) replaces McMullen. 3–9/94.

Barely known outside their native San Francisco, this unassuming free-bop group take very cautious steps on their first disc. Zamula and McMullen are a hesitant front line, and they tiptoe through their solos rather than making any mark. Pleasant to find a cover of James Blood Ulmer's 'Big Tree', and the playing is open enough to suggest a fresh, humane approach to free playing but they sound like amateurs too often for comfort.

There is some real advance with *13*. Zamula's tenor playing is still sometimes awkward but Birdsong's spare, lyrical manner is nicely complementary, and bassist and drummer work with much more confidence. The timbre is still rather introverted, but that works the oracle on a charming miniature such as 'Forsythia'.

Air / New Air GROUP

(*) **Live Air Black Saint 120034
> Henry Threadgill (*as, ts, f, bf, hubkaphone*); Fred Hopkins (*b*); Steve McCall (*d, perc*). 10/77.
*** **Air Mail** Black Saint 120049
> As above. 12/80.
(*) **New Air: Live At Montreal International Jazz Festival Black Saint 120084
> As above, except add Pheeroan akLaff (*d, perc*). 7/83.

One of the less shambolic units to come out of the AACM and, on its day, a far more interesting band than the Art Ensemble of Chicago. There are signs, though, that their day has passed. With each passing year, this music seems consigned more and more firmly to a finished chapter in American jazz. That, however, is not to denigrate the group's achievements. Though Threadgill, the *de facto* leader, is a far less complex musician than either Roscoe Mitchell or Joseph Jarman, he shows a far clearer and more sophisticated understanding of form, and an awareness (even more noticeable on the earlier, deleted *Air Song*, *Air Raid* and *Air Time*) of the need to conceive music for the band *democratically* but also *dramatically* (Air was formed to provide incidental music for a play about Scott Joplin, and the now deleted *Lore* was a fascinating free meditation on compositions by Joplin and Jelly Roll Morton) in such a way that the drums are conceived as another voiced and pitched instrument. Perhaps only with McCall would this have been practicable. Unlike almost any of his contemporaries, he is able to play ametrically, with almost no quantifiable pulse, at the same time as Hopkins is shadowing the saxophonist's marvellous lines.

McCall's successor, akLaff, is a rather different proposition, motoric, closer to Sunny Murray than to Andrew Cyrille, less concerned with finessing Threadgill's melodic textures than with finding the correct gear ratio that gives the band its undoubted impetus. New Air, almost inevitably, came across rather more immediately and compellingly, but the Montreal sessions do not capture the band at their best. The tributes – to Charles Clarke and Leo Smith on *Live Air*, to the late Ronnie Boykins, Cecil Taylor and Jimmy Lyons on *Air Mail* – are heartfelt and very powerful; Hopkins's 'R. B.' is a low, sonorous eulogy to a fellow-bassist. It's one of the finest things in the Air catalogue. Time, perhaps, to make available again the wonderful 'No. 2' and 'Dance Of The Beast' from the missing early albums.

Toshiko Akiyoshi (born 1929) PIANO, COMPOSER

*** **Live At Birdland** Fresh Sound FSRCD 1021
    Akiyoshi; Charlie Mariano (*as*); Gene Cherico (*b*); Eddie Marshall (*d*). 4/60, 10/61.
*** **Toshiko–Mariano Quartet** Candid 79012
    As above. 12/60.
When she moved to the United States in 1956, under Oscar Peterson's patronage, Toshiko Akiyoshi was already the most highly regarded arranger-composer to emerge in the post-war commercial music revival in her native Japan.

Akiyoshi met Charlie Mariano while at Berklee and the couple married in 1959, just over a year before the Candid session. Her playing, based closely but not slavishly on Bud Powell's, is forceful and intelligent, and the only sign of 'orientalism' in the small-group playing (there are engaging oddities of scoring in the big-band arrangements) is a willingness to mix modes, as on the Mariano-composed 'Little T', dedicated to her, and on the closing 'Long Yellow Road'.

Recorded with an established band (the excellent Eddie Marshall had signed up a few months before), the set has a coherence of tone and enthusiasm which provides Mariano with the impetus for some of his best recorded playing. Supervised by Nat Hentoff, the balances and registrations are ahead of their time.

The Birdland sets, one before and one after the studio recording, are worthwhile in themselves, but they also offer a useful way of judging how much the band developed in its short life. A later version of 'Blues For Father' (introduced by stand-in compère Maynard Ferguson on the April 1960 date as a new composition) is taken rather slower and Mariano's solo opens on a sequence of held notes that feed directly off Akiyoshi's accompaniment, rather than varying the melody. Unfortunately, the sound is much poorer on the later session, roughening his tone and significantly muting the piano and bass.

*** **Finesse** Concord CCD 4069
    Akiyoshi; Monty Budwig (*b*); Jake Hanna (*d*). n. d.
*** **Interlude** Concord CCD 4324
    Akiyoshi; Dennis Irwin (*b*); Eddie Marshall (*d*). 2/87.
It's a pity that Akiyoshi should have cluttered herself with a rhythm section for at least the second of these sets. She is such an interesting player that she barely needs an external context – even one as sympathetic as that provided by Irwin and Marshall.

The earlier set is marginally the more impressive and there is a slightly perfunctory quality to the 1987 cuts. Working an unpromising theme like 'Solveig's Song', which can turn to mush without undue trouble, her harmonic rigour is impressive. Nor is she troubled by the demands of such very different standards as 'Mr Jelly Lord' and 'You Go To My Head'. 'American Ballad' is one of her best performances, beautifully judged.

The later trio seems tighter, but much less conscious, as if the whole business had become second nature. The closing 'You Stepped Out Of A Dream' is the high spot. Some doubts about the recording levels on both sets (is this endemic to Concord?) but no loss of clarity.

***(*) **Sumi-e** Insights 32 CJ-1
    Akiyoshi; Lew Tabackin (*ts, f*); Steve Huffsteter, Bobby Shew, Larry Ford, Mike Price (*t*); Randy Aldcroft, Bill Reichenbach, Rick Culver, Phil Teele (*tb*); Gary Foster, Dick Spencer (*as*); Tom Peterson (*ts*); Bill Byrne (*bs*); John Heard (*b*); Peter Donald (*d*); Kisaku Katada (*perc*). 2/79.
Dating from just after the material documented on the deleted Novus compilation by the Akiyoshi–Tabackin big band, this one suggests that Akiyoshi and Tabackin were prepared to consolidate and retrench somewhat. Even so, the ethos of this band is still experimental, and it is fascinating to compare alternative takes of both 'Quadrille, Anyone?' (an Akiyoshi favourite) and the more radical 'A-10-205932', one of her more adventurous compositions of the period. The recording is particularly good, with a bright brass sound and a full but not exaggerated role for the rhythm section.

***(*) **Wishing Peace** Ken/Bellaphon 660 56 001
    Akiyoshi; John Eckert, Brian Lynch, Joe Mosello, Chris Pasin (*t*); Conrad Herwig, Kenny Rupp, Hart Smith (*tb*); Matt Finders (*btb*); Frank Wess (*as, ss, f*); Lew Tabackin (*ts, f, picc*); Jim Snidero (*as, cl, f*); Walt Weiskopf (*ts, cl*); Mark Lopeman (*bs, bcl*); Jay Anderson (*b*); Jeff Hirschfield (*d*); Daniel Ponce (*perc*). 7/86.

'Liberty Suite', which takes up a substantial proportion of this fine record, was written as part of the centenary celebrations for the Statue of Liberty. It opens with a piano-and-flute duet between Akiyoshi and Tabackin, whose touch on his 'second' horn is now near-perfect. Akiyoshi's preference for high voicings is also reflected in a later segment, entitled 'Wishing Peace', where the flute part is taken by Frank Wess, a bluesier player with a stronger but less sophisticated tone. The preceding 'Lady Liberty' develops the opening duet into a powerful orchestration, marked by fine solos from Brian Lynch (in much better form here than on his disappointing Criss Cross albums) and Jim Snidero (ditto). The East Coast band, recruited when Akiyoshi and Tabackin moved their base to New York, are spot-on throughout, and the two non-suite tracks, Akiyoshi's 'Feast In Milano' and Tabackin's beautiful 'Unrequited Love', are both magnificent performances. For anyone interested in the development of big-band playing in the 1980s, this is an essential purchase.

***(*) **Remembering Bud / Cleopatra's Dream** Evidence ECD 22034
    Akiyoshi; George Mraz, Ray Drummond (*b*); Lewis Nash, Al Harewood (*d*). 7 & 8/91.

Bud Powell played a significant role in Akiyoshi's development as a jazz pianist. They met in New York in 1964, in the last phase of the great pianist's life, and there are echoes of Powell's classic trios all through her work. In 1990 she recorded this tribute album, a mixture of Powell tunes – 'Tempus Fugit', 'Parisian Thoroughfare', 'Budo' and 'Dance Of The Infidels' – along with her own composition, 'Remembering Bud', which had already been recorded by Akiyoshi's orchestra.

    Throughout the session, she maintains strong rhythmic patterns which sometimes seem to rule out the need for a bassist and drummer altogether. The most successful permutation of personnel (all the tracks are for trio) would seem to be those involving Mraz, who adds intriguing middle-register fills to Akiyoshi's forceful solos, and a magnificent solo on 'I'll Keep Loving You'.

    The only negative points relate to a certain predictability around the beginnings and ends of Akiyoshi's solos, almost as if she needs a nudge and then a safety net. But these are minor quibbles. A lovely set that Budophiles can also listen to with profit.

***(*) **Carnegie Hall Concert** Columbia 472925
    Akiyoshi; Mike Ponella, John Eckert, Greg Gisbert, Joe Magnarelli (*t*); Herb Besson, Conrad Herwig, Larry Farrell (*tb*); Matt Finders (*btb*); Frank Wess (*as, f*); Jim Snidero (*ss, f, picc, cl*); Lew Tabackin (*ts, f*); Walt Weiskopf (*ts, ss, f, cl*); Scott Robinson (*bs, bcl*); Peter Washington (*b*); Terry Clarke (*d*). 9/91.

*** **Desert Lady** Columbia 477880
    As above, except omit Clarke, Farrell, Finders, Washington, Wess; add Luis Bonilla (*tb*); Jerry Dodgion (*as, ss, f*); Doug Weiss (*b*); Terry Clarke (*d*); Daniel Ponce (*perc*). 12/93.

How to sum up the differences between the Akiyoshi–Tabackin bands of the 1970s and their more recent incarnation? Purely technical considerations don't really explain much. It is more a matter of maturity of vision; the recent records are wonderfully centred and poised, and yet constantly open to outside influence. Listen to how Freddie Hubbard alters his own well-established idiom on 'Chasing After Love', a guest spot on the Carnegie Hall disc. This was recorded in September 1991, a mixture of recent band-book material and two commissioned pieces originally for the cities of Yokohama and Kukuoka. The opener features Japanese instruments – tsuzumi and ohkawa – in the context of a Western orchestra, a little like straight composer the late Toru Takemitsu's *November Steps*. Tabackin's flute and tenor solos by this point are poised almost exactly between East and West.

    He, Hubbard and Wess are the most prominent soloists. Toshiko barely features herself at all, with only relatively limited excursions on 'I Know Who Loves You' and 'Kourakan'. She's more to the fore on *Desert Lady*, an elegant studio confection that lacks the sheer drive and immediacy of the concert date but offers an impressive insight nevertheless into her recent thinking for large ensemble. The arrangements are undeniably powerful, with a strong emphasis on flute and high woodwinds as usual; Tabackin, again the principal soloist, is in very good voice indeed. The title-piece is one of her loveliest exotica.

***(*) **At Maybeck** Concord CCD 4635
    Akiyoshi (*p* solo). 7/94.

For piano players, the Maybeck recital has become a sort of professional milestone. Akiyoshi comes 36th in the series that began with another female musician, JoAnne Brackeen, and tackles the challenge with similar *savoir faire* and a slightly muted self-confidence. Hearing her without a rhythm section and outside her more familiar role as a bandleader, Akiyoshi still sounds startlingly original. Almost as a signal of intent, she opens with an original, 'The Village', that establishes her voice and stylistic mannerisms. The trajectory from there to the staple 'Quadrille, Anyone?', and a closing interpretation of Bud Powell's 'Tempus Fugit', is more conventional and standards-based than expected. She finds room for Diz's 'Con Alma', on which she manages to avoid the usual horn-derived clichés, and two Duke tunes – 'Come Sunday' and 'Sophisticated Lady' – are particularly suited to her delivery. For the most part, though, this is a very straightforward, perhaps even slightly diffident, set; there are intimations that, even at this point in her career, Akiyoshi isn't entirely happy with this degree of exposure.

Joe Albany (1924–88) PIANO, VOCAL

***(*) **The Right Combination** Original Jazz Classics OJC 1749
  Albany; Warne Marsh (ts); Bob Whitlock (b). 57.

Albany was a frustrating enigma. Legendary in his time, as the sleeve to this album proclaims, he was allegedly one of Parker's favourite accompanists but never made a studio recording with him. In fact he didn't make any kind of studio sessions until the 1970s. This reissue was spliced together from an impromptu session at engineer Ralph Garretson's home, which caught Albany and Marsh jamming together on seven standards (the last of which, 'The Nearness Of You', is only a fragment). While the sound is very plain and the piano in particular is recessed, the music is intermittently remarkable. Albany's style is a peculiar amalgam of Parker and Art Tatum: the complexity of his lines suggests something of the older pianist, while the horn-like figures in the right hand might suggest a bop soloist. Yet Albany's jumbled, idiosyncratic sense of time is almost all his own, and his solos are cliff-hanger explorations. Marsh is at his most fragmentary, his tone a foggy squeal at some points, yet between them they create some compelling improvisations: 'Body And Soul', done at fast and slow tempos, is as personal as any version, and a dreamy, troubled 'Angel Eyes' shows off Albany's best work. No wonder, with the next 25 years spoiled by narcotic and personal problems, that Albany seemed like a wasted talent.

** **Birdtown Birds** Steeplechase SCCD 1003
  Albany; Hugo Rasmussen (b); Hans Nymand (d). 4/73.
(*) **Two's Company Steeplechase SCCD 1019
  Albany; Niels-Henning Orsted-Pedersen (b). 2/74.

Once rediscovered, first through a home-made tape which forms the basis of *Joe Albany At Home*, a now-deleted comeback album on Spotlite, and then on subsequent European sojourns and New York appearances, Albany made a dozen or so albums during the 1970s. While much talked-up at the time, none of them is very satisfying now. The best music comes on *Two's Company*, where the duets with bassist NHOP are elaborately conceived and confidently dispatched. But many of his ideas are beset by misfingerings, and the famously off-kilter conception of time can sometimes sound more like clumsiness than anything else. It seems churlish to criticize one of the few bop-orientated pianists to take Parker's ideas in a different direction, but Albany's records sound like an unfulfilled ideal.

(*) **Live In Paris Fresh Sound FSCD-1010
  Albany; Alby Cullaz (b); Aldo Romano (d). 77.

This recent discovery sheds no special new light on Albany, but there are some rather more impressive things here: the long Jerome Kern medley which opens the solo section (six titles; there are five more with the trio) shows the pianist's dense, heavily allusive style at its best, and it's a severe disappointment when he follows this with a terribly maudlin vocal treatment of 'Lush Life' (he also sings 'The Christmas Song'). Cullaz and Romano accompany as best they can, but this was clearly a trio that needed more work. The sound is a bit flat, but not too bad, for what seems to be a private club recording.

*** **Bird Lives** Storyville STCD 4164
  Albany; Art Davis (b); Roy Haynes (d). 1/79.

Davis and Haynes play particularly well and ensure that there's no loss of focus on what is one of the best sets that Albany laid down. The strong emphasis on blues lines – most of the songs are Parker originals, but most are based on the blues – might have led to a lack of variety, but they're more useful in keeping Albany's mind on the job, perhaps. A decent piano and respectable sound.

Albion Jazz Band GROUP

** **One For The Guv'nor** Stomp Off 12O6
  Tony Pringle (c, v); Jim Klippert (tb, v); Gerry Green (cl); Bob Pelland (p); Mike Cox (bj, v); Mike Fay (b); Mike McCombe (d). 3/90.

(*) They're All Nice Tunes Stomp Off 1249
> As above. 3/92.

A couple of waggish trad sessions by a troupe of cheerful British luddites, transported to Vancouver for the occasion (both times). The first album is a tribute to Ken Colyer and is pretty effortful stuff, with Colyer's dogged primitivism overshadowing their more sprightly moments. The subsequent *They're All Nice Tunes* is a smidgeon more lively and gets an extra notch for the sheer cheek of turning the Beatles' 'I'll Follow The Sun' into a George Lewis-like dirge. Some of the horn playing is stunningly ham-fisted, but the band have a knack of sticking an extra chorus on to the end of most of the tunes, which always seem to pick up a ragged second wind as a result.

Alvin Alcorn (born 1912) TRUMPET

*** **Sounds Of New Orleans Vol. 6** Storyville STCD 6012
> Alcorn; Jack Delaney, Bill Matthews (*tb*); Raymond Burke (*cl*); Stanley Mendelson (*p*); Lawrence Marrero (*bj*); Chink Martin, Sherwood Mangiapane, Alcide 'Slow Drag' Pavageau (*b*); Abbie Brunies (*d*). 12/52–11/53.

*** **Live At Earthquake McGoon's Vol. 1** GHB BCD-238
> Alcorn; Big Bill Bissonnette (*tb*); Paul 'Polo' Barnes (*cl, as*); James 'Sing' Miller (*p*); Jim Tutunjian (*b*); Alec Bigard (*d*). 7/69.

(*) **Live At Earthquake McGoon's Vol. 2 GHB BCD-239
> As above. 7/69.

Alcorn has been lightly recorded as a leader, and he might almost be termed a cool hornman in comparison with some of his New Orleans peers. His contributions to Storyville's archive series of sessions consists of two live dates from Joe Mares's Place and an informal studio session by the Alcorn Jazz Babies, all using largely the same personnel, in listenable sound. As so often, the group plays with more spirit than finesse, but Alcorn's controlled lead (he is never much of a soloist) settles a certain steady-rolling fluency on much of the playing.

In 1969, at Turk Murphy's club, four New Orleanians sat down with Bissonnette and played through a stack of old numbers. The music has its ragged edges, but what compensates is a gentlemanly cama-raderie that is rather different from the fierceness of much authentic New Orleans playing. Alcorn still sounds better as ensemble man than as improviser, and Bissonnette's barking trombone can sound overly heated; it's Barnes's charmingly old-fashioned alto playing which is the most distinctive thing. History may be glad that there are two volumes, but most will settle for the first. Bissonnette has cleaned up the original tapes quite respectably.

Howard Alden (born 1958) GUITAR

*** **Swing Street** Concord CCD 4349
> Alden; Dan Barrett (*tb*); Chuck Wilson (*as, cl*); Frank Tate (*b*); Jackie Williams (*d*). 9/86.

*** **The A.B.Q. Salutes Buck Clayton** Concord CCD 4395
> As above. 6/89.

Alden's polished manner places him in the swing-to-modern lineage of Herb Ellis, and he has mastered the style as well as anybody. In this band of young fogeys, the musicians don't so much re-create swing styles as reinvigorate them, adding a modern lick or two to classic material and classy arrangements, and throwing the occasional curve, such as a lucid treatment of Monk's 'Pannonica', into the gameplan. Barrett, a superbly accomplished player, is the star of these sessions, but the group is uniformly com-manding and relaxed. The session devoted to material associated with Buck Clayton is marginally superior, if only because of the interesting concept.

(*) **The Howard Alden Trio Plus Special Guests Concord CCD 4378
> Alden; Warren Vaché (*c*); Ken Peplowski (*ts, cl*); Lynn Seaton (*b*); Mel Lewis (*d*). 1/89.

Vaché sits in with Alden's trio for five tracks, Peplowski for three, and the music has less cohesion than the ABQ record, although no less freshness. Vaché rewards Ellington's 'Purple Gazelle' with special radiance.

*** **Snowy Morning Blues** Concord CCD 4424
> Alden; Monty Alexander (*p*); Lynn Seaton (*b*); Dennis Mackrel (*d*). 4/90.

Alexander's customary enthusiasm puts a little more pep into Alden's music, though not enough to coarsen the guitarist's fundamentally lightweight variations on swing material. The programme is well chosen to include some lesser-known Ellington and Monk tunes, but the Concord recording tends to smooth away the most interesting edges.

*** **Misterioso** Concord CCD 4487
    Alden; Frank Tate (*b*); Keith Copeland (*d*). 4/91.
***(*) **A Good Likeness** Concord CCD 4544
    Alden; Michael Moore (*b*); Alan Dawson (*d*). 8/92.

Like such older Concord hands as Scott Hamilton and Warren Vaché, Alden is starting to assume his methods so convincingly that the prettiness and formal grace of his playing are taking on an ironclad quality. *Misterioso* was certainly his most effective record to date: 'We See' and 'Misterioso' don't so much simplify Monk as put the crusty elegance of his tunes in the forefront, and everything else – including such bedfellows as 'Flying Down To Rio' and Jelly Roll Morton's 'The Pearls' – is delivered with the same fine touch. But it's outdone by *A Good Likeness*, which finds Alden brimming with ideas and drive. The tunes are another surprising bunch – Bud Freeman's 'The Eel's Nephew', Monk's 'Crepuscule With Nellie', Willie Smith's 'Echoes Of Spring' – and this time Alden lets rip at fast tempos as he never has before on record, with the rippling grace of a solo 'Single Petal Of A Rose' as the other side of the coin.

*** **13 Strings** Concord CCD 4464
    Alden; George Van Eps (*g*); Dave Stone (*b*); Jake Hanna (*d*). 2/91.
(*) **Hand-Crafted Swing Concord CCD 4513
    As above. 6/91.
** **Seven & Seven** Concord CCD 4584
    As above, except omit Stone and Hanna. 12/92.

It's interesting to hear Alden playing alongside a man who himself played alongside Eddie Lang more than 60 years ago. Van Eps prefers stately chord-based playing and, while it might not inhibit the younger man, Alden certainly scales down his approach to accommodate his senior (he also had a seven-string guitar made in the fashion of van Eps's instrument). The first record is nice and the second pleasant, but the third is dull: without any rhythm players to egg them on, they're too slow and quiet, and the sluggish tempos tend to push the music into the background.

**** **Your Story – The Music Of Bill Evans** Concord CCD 4621
    Alden; Frank Wess (*ts, f*); Michael Moore (*b*); Al Harewood (*d*). 5/94.
*** **Encore!** Concord CCD 4654
    Alden; Ken Peplowski (*cl, ts*); Jeff Chambers (*b*); Colin Bailey (*d*). 8/94.

Alden continues to expand his range and ambition. The Evans album is quite beautifully done, a considerably more involving record than John McLaughlin's tribute album. The bluesier side of Evans's playing isn't neglected, with the surprise choice of Frank Wess sitting in on three tracks; but, for touch, line and texture, it's hard to top the exquisite way the trio has with 'Time Remembered' and 'Your Story', with a bass/guitar duet on 'Two Lonely People' as a charming coda.

    Encore! is slighter stuff, a concert in which Peplowski and Alden josh around on a catholic set of material – 'It All Depends On You', Konitz's 'Palo Alto', 'The Dolphin'. When bass and drums come in, as on the closing romp through 'You', it's close to burning.

Eric Alexander (born 1968) TENOR SAXOPHONE

*** **Straight Up** Delmark 461
    Alexander; Jim Rotondi (*t*); Harold Mabern (*p*); John Webber (*b*); George Fludas (*d*). 8/92.
*** **New York Calling** Criss Cross 1077
    Alexander; John Swana (*t, flhn*); Richard Wyands (*p*); Peter Washington (*b*); Kenny Washington (*d*). 12/92.
*** **Up, Over And Out** Delmark 476
    Alexander; Harold Mabern (*p*); John Ore (*b*); Joe Farnsworth (*d*). 8/93.
*** **Full Range** Criss Cross 1098
    Alexander; John Swana (*t*); Kenny Barron (*p*); Peter Bernstein (*g*); Peter Washington (*b*); Carl Allen (*d*). 1/94.
*** **Stablemates** Delmark DE-488
    Alexander; Lin Halliday (*ts*); Jodie Christian (*p*); Dan Shapera (*b*); Wilbur Campbell (*d*). 95.

Alexander stands four-square in the tradition of big Chicago tenors: the first disc was made on local turf, the second in the city of the title, and in either milieu he sounds completely assured. This is old-fashioned tenor playing: fat, bruising, wide-bodied, but limber enough to handle bebop tempos and inner complexities, even if Alexander prefers a more seasoned tradition. His laggardly way with the beat makes one think of Dexter Gordon. Still, neither of these records is a world-beater, and the next two – again, one from Chicago, one from New York – show no specific advance. Each of the Delmark albums includes some professorial work from Mabern, even while the other players are unexceptional: *Up, Over*

And Out is arguably the best of the four for its tough, uncompromising take on Monk's 'Eronel' and – the other side of Alexander's persona – the tender trap of 'The Nearness Of You'. Both the Criss Cross dates are good value yet neither really lifts itself out of the blowing-session convention that is wearing after a few tracks. Alexander's writing shows only modest promise and he sounds more like an executant than a leader; but it will be interesting to hear him marshal a properly prepared record. *Stablemates* is more an off-the-cuff interlude than anything. Alexander shares front-and-centre with veteran tenorman Halliday in a specific attempt to revitalize the two-tenor fisticuffs of yore. They certainly strike sparks on the up-tempo pieces and there is a fetching ballad medley of 'Polka Dots And Moonbeams' and 'Old Folks', but otherwise this goes down as little more than a good potboiler.

Monty Alexander (born 1944) PIANO

**** Three Originals MPS 523 526 2CD
    Alexander; Ernest Ranglin (*g*); Andy Simpkins, Eberhard Weber (*b*); Kenny Clare, Frank Gant (*d*); Vincent Taylor (*steel d*); Charles Campbell (*perc*). 10/74, 9/77.
***(*) Live At The Montreux Festival MPS 817 487
    Alexander; John Clayton (*b*); Jeff Hamilton (*d*). 6/76.
**(*) Live In Holland Verve 835627
    Alexander; John Clayton (*b*); Jeff Hamilton (*d*). 3/77.
*** Facets Concord CCD 4108
    Alexander; Ray Brown (*b*); Jeff Hamilton (*d*). 8/79.
** Full Steam Ahead Concord CCD 4287
    Alexander; Ray Brown (*b*); Frank Gant (*d*). n. d.
*** Trio Concord CCD 4136
    Alexander; Herb Ellis (*g*); Ray Brown (*b*). 8/80.
**(*) Triple Treat Concord CCD 4193
    As above. 3/82.
**(*) Triple Treat II Concord CCD 4338
    As above, except add John Frigo (*vn*). 6/87.
*** Triple Treat III Concord CCD 4394
    As for *II*. 6/87.

Long associated with Milt Jackson and Ray Brown, Alexander now has an impressive back-catalogue of (mostly trio) recordings which reveal an exuberant sensibility schooled – sometimes a little too doctrinairely – in the School of Oscar Peterson. Typical of that tendency, he has a tone which is both percussive and lyrical, heavy on the triplets and arpeggiated chords, melodically inspired in the main (i.e. no long, chordal ramblings), maximal but controlled.

The connection with Peterson is cemented by the recordings on *Three Originals* which, like Oscar's *Exclusively For My Friends*, began life at Hans Georg Brunner-Schwer's home in Villingen, Germany; the latter pair were made in the MPS studios. These albums were originally released as *Love And Sunshine* (which is the approximate emotional temperature of all three), *Estate* (which is very definitely the season) and *Cobilimbo* (which sounds exotic enough to capture the mood). Alexander is paired with the legendary Ranglin, one of the great unsung guitarists in jazz and Caribbean music, and together they swing in an entirely individual way, splitting four-to-the-bar sequences in unexpected ways, syncopating and compressing. A good deal of the material on the first pair is based on standards and pop tunes. There is a slightly darker timbre to the originals on *Cobilimbo*, and it here that one gets the first taste of another Alexander staple, the steel pans. How much of what makes him distinctive is cosmetic and extrinsic remains difficult to say, but nobody will have any difficulty identifying him from any of these tracks, and they remain some of his best on record. A very good buy.

Though the trio is the ideal context for Alexander's playing, it's a little difficult to assess the permutations in these groups, beyond the observation that Gant seems better suited to the faster tempos, whereas Hamilton plays with a greater feel for the melody. The best of the bunch is the earliest, recorded at a vintage Montreux Festival. Alexander opens with Ahmad Jamal's 'Nite Mist Blues' and closes with the 'Battle Hymn Of The Republic', and he doesn't put a foot wrong in between. Clayton is the only weak link – but only relative to the astonishingly high standard of bass playing the pianist has usually been able to call on. Brown, where he appears, is so beyond reproach as to be *sui generis*.

Alexander obviously encourages his bassists to play *arco*, favouring big-toned pedals against which he can punch out sometimes surprisingly complex augmented chords. In the drummerless *Triple Treat*, he used the violinst, John Frigo, alongside Brown and Herb Ellis, to similar effect. Though they were recorded at the same time, *III* is a more interesting record, and the quartet interpretation of 'My One And Only Love' stands out. The rather lowly rating largely stems from a very poor sound, with everything jumbled together towards the middle.

There are wonderful things on *Trio* (the opening 'I'm Afraid The Masquerade Is Over') and *Triple Treat* ('Body And Soul' and, ahem, the 'Flintstones' theme). The sequel is a shade disappointing, given the weight of campaign medals, but there is a gorgeous quartet reading of 'Smile' and a fine trio 'It Might As Well Be Spring'.

*** **Ivory And Steel** Concord CCD 4124
    Alexander; Othello Molineaux (*steel d*); Gerald Wiggins (*b*); Frank Gant (*d*); Robert Thomas Jr (*perc*). 3/80.
*** **Jamboree** Concord CCD 4359
    Alexander; Othello Molineaux, Len 'Boogsie' Sharpe (*steel d*); Marshall Wood, Bernard Montgomery (*b*); Robert Thomas Jr (*perc*); Marvin 'Smitty' Smith (*d*). 2–3/88.
One of the most interesting aspects of Alexander's career has been his attempt to assimilate the steel-drum sound of his native Jamaica to the conventional jazz rhythm section. In the earlier pair, the new sound is still a little tacked-on and Gant in particular seems slightly uneasy, but the balance of instrumentation is good and Alexander finds sufficient space on *Ivory And Steel* to rattle off some of his most joyous solos.

Jamboree is a marvellous record, partly because the playing is so good, but also because of the imaginative selection of covers. Bob Marley's 'No Woman, No Cry' and Joni Mitchell's 'Big Yellow Taxi' have not previously figured too prominently in the average fake book; indeed, with the very considerable exception of avant-garde trumpeter Leo Smith, reggae has made remarkably little impact on contemporary jazz. 'Smitty' Smith was an inspired addition on the later date, and he lifts the energy level a further notch. Both are highly recommended, but go for *Jamboree*. One–love.

***(*) **The River** Concord CCD 4422
    Alexander; John Clayton (*b*); Ed Thigpen (*d*). 10/85.
No confusing this with the Bruce Springsteen product of the same name. This is the unsentimental one, played largely in key. Alexander's reading of hymn tunes (all except the title-track and Ellington's 'David Danced') is as bold as anything he has tried since the 'Ivory and Steel' sets. Mostly played with a rolling, gospelly fervour, there is space for a little schmaltz on 'Ave Maria' (aching bowed bass from Clayton) and some surprisingly abstract drum and piano effects on the closing traditional 'How Great Thou Art'. Thigpen is magnificent throughout. A really beautiful record.

*** **Threesome** Soul Note 121152
    Alexander; Niels-Henning Orsted-Pedersen (*b*); Grady Tate (*d, v*). 11–12/85.
Well used to top-drawer rhythm sections, Alexander makes the most of this one, turning in a sparkling set with sufficient variety to suggest his responsiveness to others. The version of 'All Blues' is interesting, but the material is otherwise a little lacklustre.

*** **Caribbean Circle** Chesky JD 80
    Alexander; Jon Faddis, E. Dankworth (*t*); Slide Hampton (*tb*); Frank Foster (*ts*); Dave Glasser (*as*); Ira Coleman, Anthony Jackson (*b*); Othello Molineaux (*steel d*); Herlin Riley, Steve Perrone (*d*); Robert Thompson Jr, Marjorie Whylie (*perc*). 6/92.
An extension of his work with Ivory & Steel and the nearest thing to a big band Alexander has mustered so far, this is a jolly, romping session that slightly overplays the Jamaican accent Alexander jokingly phoneticizes in his sleeve-notes. Credit for the arrangements goes to Hampton. They're characteristically bright and uncluttered, and features like Dankworth's solo on a bluebeat version of 'When The Saints' or Marjorie Whylie's one-woman-band percussion-breaks fit neatly into them. What don't are Alexander's own solos, which tend to go off in odd directions, a bit like his jivey monologues, which you'll find either charming or plain irritating, like the 'Cowboy Ska Melody'. A tribute to Miles called 'Oh Why?' shows the pianist still capable of writing and playing feelingly, but it's exceptional.

***(*) **Maybeck Recital Hall Series: Volume 40** Concord CCD 4689
    Alexander (*p* solo). 94.
The series may have been tiring by this point, but Alexander was determined to make it clear that he wasn't. Perhaps he responds to the surroundings with a little more reserve and solemnity than one might usually expect of him, but that is not to detract one jot from a fine, forceful performance that will delight his fans and satisfy anyone putting together a piano library on the strength of this series.

Jan Allan (born 1934) TRUMPET

***(*) **Sweet And Lovely** Dragon DRCD 254
    Allan; Rune Gustafsson (*g*); Georg Riedel (*b*). 3/92.

Allan's small number of records as a leader is an inadequate showing for one of the most eminent Swedish modernists: poised between a cool lyricism and a bashful affection for the long melodic line, the trumpeter's unfussy and effortless playing refuses to draw attention to itself. It can make his improvising a little too quiescent at times, but here, with two very old friends, he sketches a sequence of wonderful miniatures. Since Lars Gullin, Reinhold Svensson and Jan Johansson – three major contemporaries of Allan's – are all represented as composers, the record also stands as a meditation on the achievements (still sorely undervalued) of one of the great schools of modern jazz in Europe. Some may be reminded of many of Chet Baker's later sessions; but Allan, Gustafsson and Riedel, all in prime, easy-going form, sustain the flow of these 14 tunes with few difficulties.

Byron Allen ALTO SAXOPHONE

*** **Byron Allen Trio** ESP Disk ESP 1005
Allen; Maceo Gilchrist (b); Ted Robinson (d). 9/64.
ESP Disk recorded Allen's debut on Ornette Coleman's say-so. The compliment is returned in 'Decision For The Cole-Man' and in just about every note the saxophonist plays. Though Coltrane's influence was less widespread at the time than it was to become posthumously, it was still relatively unusual to find a saxophonist prepared to confront Ornette's enigmatic challenge (even Eric Dolphy, who died in the summer of '64, had approached the Texan's work with some trepidation).

Allen plays the part to the hilt. Unsupported by a harmony instrument (though Gilchrist doles out big fat chords), Allen has to rely on strong melodic invention, and this sometimes fails him. At this point in his career he seems a little fixated on futuristic clichés, so, in place of Ornette's *Tomorrow Is The Question* and *The Shape Of Jazz To Come*, we get 'Time Is Past', 'Three Steps In The Right Direction' and 'Today's Blues Tomorrow'. Interesting enough as an act of homage, the album failed to transcend its main influence, and Allen conspicuously failed to make that next step.

Carl Allen DRUMS

*** **The Pursuer** Atlantic 82572-2
Allen; Marcus Printup (t); Steve Turre (tb, shells); Vincent Herring (ss, as); Teodross Avery (ss, ts); George Coleman (ts); Ed Simon (p); Ben Wolfe (b). 9/93.
*** **Testimonial** Atlantic 82755-2
Allen; Nicholas Payton (t); Vincent Herring (ss, as); Cyrus Chestnut (p, org); Anthony Wonsey (p); Mark Whitfield (g); Christian McBride, Reuben Rogers (b); Daniel Sadownick (perc); Kevin Mahogany (v). 12/94.
Polished, inventive music from drummer Allen and a stellar personnel mustered across the two discs. *The Pursuer* is modern bop delivered with a steely, notably aggressive stance: the title-piece, 'Hidden Agenda' and 'A Difference Of Opinion' are bruisers, though Herring's soprano feature, 'Alternative Thoughts', settles things down and the horn arrangements are thoughtfully prepared. Avery is good, but everyone is smoked by the tremendous Coleman on his one appearance. *Testimonial* is much more good-humoured and to that degree a little less exciting. 'Foot Pattin'' and 'Storefront Revival' are sanctified interludes in which Allen duets with Chestnut on organ, and 'Tuesday Night Prayer Meeting' and 'A City Called Heaven' continue the theme with mixed results. Nothing tops the opener, a leisurely but handsomely realized version of 'Come Sunday' where everyone shines. Allen himself throttles back a little at the drums. Enjoyable stuff.

Eddie Allen TRUMPET

*** **R&B** Enja 9033
Allen; Donald Harrison (as); Anthony Wonsey (p); Christian McBride (b); Marvin 'Smitty' Smith (d). 1/95.
Don't be misled by the title. Though Allen's roots are squarely in the rhythm-and-blues field (his first recordings were with local Milwaukee bands), the range of material on this debut as leader is very much wider. He's worked with, among others, trombonist Craig Harris, Muhal Richard Abrams, Louis Hayes and Charli Persip, and he's been a charter member of Lester Bowie's Brass Fantasy. No tyro, then, and no slouch.

The spectrum of rhythms alone takes in hard bop, Latin and Afro-jazz, while the *B* is by no means restricted to the blues. Allen is a superb ballad-player, for instance, with a delicate, almost free-form approach to the material. He takes constant liberties with the basic count of a piece, often appearing at entirely unexpected moments and slithering in beguiling little phrases when it seems a solo is over, as on the opening 'Frick And Frack'.

He is, of course, abetted by an absolutely excellent band. Smitty is in cracking form and seems to have had quite an influence on the layout of the session. His opening on 'As Quiet As It's Kept' is one for the book. The only name likely to be unfamiliar is the 24-year-old Wonsey, a bright youngster from New York who studied with Mulgrew Miller and cut his teeth with the likes of Christopher Hollyday and Kenny Garrett. The ever-dependable Harrison does his usual confident job and Chris McBride is full-voiced and robust in his passage-work and has seldom soloed better.

There are, inevitably, hints of immaturity. It isn't the best-balanced set ever recorded, but compositions like 'Schism', 'Seduction' and 'The Quest' all suggest that Allen is going places. Keep the name in mind.

Geri Allen PIANO

***(*) **The Printmakers** Minor Music 8001
    Allen; Anthony Cox (b); Andrew Cyrille (d). 2/84.
**** **Home Grown** Minor Music 8004
    Allen (p solo). 1/85.
Geri Allen is one of the most individual pianists of the younger generation. Though initially involved with M-Base (from which she has recently attempted to distance herself), she has a broad stylistic range that takes cues from Ellington, Bud Powell, Mary Lou Williams, lesser-known figures like Herbie Nichols, non-piano players like Eric Dolphy, and (on her own instrument again, albeit in a very different bag) elements of Cecil Taylor.

The more avant-garde elements of her style were on show in *The Printmakers*, and Cyrille's presence certainly accounts for some of that. There's no standard material and, though Allen plays lyrically and with restrained fire throughout, it's an oddly spiky set that may dismay some listeners who have heard only her later work with Haden and Motian. The solo set is much more accommodating and gains as much from the familiarity of the repertoire – 'Bemsha Swing', 'Round About Midnight', 'Alone Together' – as from the freshness of Allen's address.

***(*) **Etudes** Soul Note SN 1162
    Allen; Charlie Haden (b); Paul Motian (d). 9/87.
*** **Segments** DIW-833
    As above. 4/89.
*** **In The Year Of The Dragon** JMT 834428
    As above; add Juan Lazaro Mendolas (quena). 3/89.
**** **Live At The Village Vanguard** DIW 847
    As above, except omit Mendolas.
Strictly speaking, *Etudes* was credited to the Haden/Motian trio, with Geri Allen as featured artist. A single hearing establishes it unequivocally as her album, not because her two senior colleagues merely fulfil backing duties, but because she is so obviously calling the shots. The obvious parallel is Bill Evans, who 'led' by unassertive example, and there are similarities of manner (not least the presence of Paul Motian) with the vintage Evans Trio.

Allen is without equal in her ability to play quietly, sometimes as softly as *ppp*, without becoming indistinct and losing the cool, almost intellectual intensity which is her signature. Only Paul Bley – with whom she shares certain tonal characteristics – manages to invest diminuendo passages with such dramatic freight. Motian almost notoriously inclines to the subliminal, but Haden's ability to play in these registers is seldom acknowledged.

The set isn't without humour. Ornette's 'Lonely Woman' is offset by the much less obvious 'Shuffle Montgomery', a little-played Herbie Nichols tune, and there is an unexpected warmth and gentleness to 'Dolphy's Dance', which belies the sardonic, Monkish delivery.

Segments is by no means an anticlimax, though it lacks the immediate impact of the earlier set. It is certainly a more polished and professional performance from a trio rapidly acquiring 'in demand' status from promoters and record producers. There are hints, in the closing original 'Rain', of a slightly soft centre to Allen's playing that bodes ill. On the other hand, 'Segment', a not-quite-canonical Charlie Parker tune from 1949, is given a superb reading, as is 'Marmaduke', two untypical examples of Allen's bebop approach. Haden's 'La Pasionaria', like most of his work, is too vital a tune to suffer fatal damage from a lacklustre performance.

The Village Vanguard session is vintage and one of the best piano-trio records of the last ten years. *Live* is both accessible and inexhaustible, making its appeal at all sorts of unexpected levels, with a saving tinge of humour. Allen relaxes and speeds away in the club setting and, though the piano doesn't sound out of the best catalogue, it is responsive and eloquent enough for her needs. *In The Year Of The Dragon* is a disappointment. For the first time, Allen sounds mannered and deliberate; compare the version of 'No More Mr Nice Guy' on *Home Grown*. Motian and Haden (particularly) sound a little jaded; as if to compensate, the sound is very forward and peaky.

***(*) **Twenty One** Somethin' Else 830028-2
    Allen; Ron Carter (*b*); Tony Williams (*d*). 3/94.
It didn't seem likely that the Haden/Motian trio would ever be topped, but this dream line-up just about manages it. Allen is forceful and very direct but doesn't allow herself to be trapped into mere display. Every solo is invested with feeling and meaning, and her re-interpretation of 'Lullaby Of The Leaves' is masterful, unsentimental, boiled down and assertive. She brings a certain intellectual rigour to 'Old Folks' and the trio tackles 'Tea For Two' as if Tatum were sitting in front – a glorious performance. The originals are less individual, more workmanlike, than previously, and there are signs that Allen is already beginning to make changes to her approach, relying more on melody, less on sheer technique.

Harry Allen (born 1966) TENOR SAXOPHONE

(*) **How Long Has This Been Going On? Progressive 7082
    Allen; Keith Ingham (*p*); Major Holley (*b*); Oliver Jackson (*d*). 6/88.
*** **Someone To Light Up My Life** Mastermix CHECD 00100
    Allen; John Horler (*p*); Peter Morgan (*b*); Oliver Jackson (*d*).
*** **I Know That You Know** Mastermix CHECD 00104
    Allen; John Colianni (*p*); Michael Moore (*d*). 1/92.
*** **I'll Never Be The Same** Mastermix CHECD 00106
    Allen; Howard Alden (*g*); Simon Woolf (*b*). 11/92.
***(*) **Jazz Im Amerika Haus Vol. 1** Nagel-Heyer 011
    Allen; John Bunch (*p*); Dennis Irwin (*b*); Duffy Jackson (*d*). 5/94.
Allen has been acclaimed by an audience waiting for the Four Brothers to come back, if not the big bands. His full-blooded tenor-sound offers countless tugs of the forelock to Zoot, Ben, Lester, Hawkins and whichever other standard-issue swing tenor one can think of, and it's hardly surprising that these enjoyable records have been given the kind of approbation heaped on the early Scott Hamilton albums. Allen plays nothing but standards, delivers them with a confidence and luxuriance that belie his twenty-something age, and generally acts as if Coltrane and Coleman had never appeared at all. On their own terms, there is much to enjoy in all of these records: the two earlier discs are a little too stratified by tenor-and-rhythm clichés but, by cannily removing any sign of a drummer on the later records, Allen frees himself up just enough to suggest that he might eventually do more than act the young fogey. Certainly the interplay with Alden, who has also found a way of investing more of himself into mainstream vocabulary, offers some piquant moments.

    Allen has been doing some solid sideman duty of late, but his entry in the *Jazz Im Amerika Haus* series suggests he's getting more authoritative all the time. His improvisation on 'Deed I Do' has a steamrollering sense of swing, and he's sewing phrases and licks together with the kind of assurance once associated with Zoot Sims. Since the rhythm section goes along with the same ineluctable purpose, this has to go down as Allen's best to date.

Henry 'Red' Allen (1908–1967) TRUMPET, VOCAL

**** **Henry 'Red' Allen And His New York Orchestra 1929–1930** JSP CD 332
    Allen; Otis Johnson (*t*); J. C. Higginbotham (*tb*); Albert Nicholas, William Blue (*cl, as*); Charlie Holmes (*cl, ss, as*); Teddy Hill (*cl, ts*); Luis Russell (*p, cel*); Will Johnson (*bj, g, v*); Pops Foster (*b*); Paul Barbarin (*d*); Victoria Spivey, The Four Wanderers (*v*). 7/29–2/30.
**** **Henry 'Red' Allen And His New York Orchestra Vol. 2** JSP CD 333
    As above. 29–30.
**** **Henry 'Red' Allen & His Orchestra 1929–1933** Classics 540
    As above, except add James Archey, Dicky Wells, Benny Morton (*tb*); Russell Procope, Edward Inge (*cl, as*); Hilton Jefferson (*as*); Coleman Hawkins, Greely Walton (*ts*); Don Kirkpatrick, Horace Henderson (*p*); Bernard Addison (*g*); Bob Ysaguirre (*bb, b*); Ernest Hill (*bb*); Walter Johnson, Manzie Johnson (*d*). 7/29–11/33.
***(*) **Henry Allen Collection Vol. 1** Collector's Classics COCD 1
    Allen; Jimmy Lord (*cl*); Pee Wee Russell (*cl, ts*); Joe Sullivan, Fats Waller (*p*); Eddie Condon (*bj*); Jack Bland (*g*); Al Morgan, Pops Foster (*b*); Zutty Singleton (*d*); Billy Banks (*v*). 4–10/32.

*** Henry 'Red' Allen–Coleman Hawkins 1933 Hep 1028
> As above, except add Russell Smith, Bobby Stark (*t*); Claude Jones (*tb*), John Kirby (*b*), omit
> Blue, Johnson, Higginbotham, Archey, Russell, Holmes, Walton, Johnson, Foster, Barbarin,
> Spivey. 3–10/33.

**** Henry 'Red' Allen 1929–1936 Jazz Classics in Digital Stereo RPCD 610
> Allen; plus groups led by Fats Waller, Luis Russell, Billy Banks, Walter Pichon, Spike Hughes,
> Horace Henderson, Benny Morton, Mills Blue Rhythm Band. 29–36.

Henry Allen was once described as 'the last great trumpet soloist to come out of New Orleans', but that
was before Wynton Marsalis and his followers. He was, though, the last to make a mark on the 1920s,
recording his astonishing debut sessions as a leader for Victor in the summer of 1929 and immediately
causing a stir. The four tracks are 'It Should Be You', 'Biff'ly Blues', 'Feeling Drowsy' and 'Swing Out',
and there is a total of ten takes of them on the first JSP disc, while the Classics CD, which commences a
chronological survey of Allen in the 1930s, is content with the master takes in each case. Either way,
these four titles are magnificently conceived and executed jazz, with the whole band – actually the
nucleus of the Luis Russell Orchestra, where Allen had already set down some superb solos – playing
with outstanding power and finesse, while Allen's own improvisations outplay any trumpeter of the day
aside from Louis Armstrong. While his playing is sometimes a little unfocused, Allen's ideas usually run
together with few seams showing, and the controlled strength of his solo on 'Feeling Drowsy' is as
impressive as the more daring flights of 'Swing Out'. The beautifully sustained solo on 'Make A
Country Bird Fly Wild' sees him through a tricky stop-time passage, and shows how he was both like
and unlike Armstrong: there's the same rhythmic chance-taking and nobility of tone, but Allen is often
less predictable than Armstrong and can shy away from the signalled high notes which Louis always
aimed at. He can even suggest a faintly wistful quality in an otherwise heated passage. The tracks for
Victor, though, are abetted by his choice of companions: Higginbotham is wonderfully characterful on
trombone, agile but snarlingly expressive, and the vastly underrated Charlie Holmes matches the young
Johnny Hodges for a hard-hitting yet fundamentally lyrical alto style. Foster and Barbarin, too, are
exceptionally swinging. This was an outstanding band which should have made many more records than
it did.

The JSP discs, superbly remastered by John R. T. Davies, are indispensable. Some may prefer the
Classics approach, which carries on through the first sessions by the Allen–Coleman Hawkins
Orchestra. Both men were then working with Fletcher Henderson, and this could have been an explosive
combination, but their records are comparatively tame, with pop-tune material and Allen's admittedly
engaging vocals taking up a lot of space. The Hep CD includes all the Allen–Hawkins tracks (the final
three are on the next Classics disc), and adds the 1933 session under Horace Henderson's leadership,
which includes what might be the most swinging 'Ol' Man River' on record and a splendid feature for
Hawkins in 'I've Got To Sing A Torch Song'. More excellent remastering here: the Classics CD is
patchy in comparison but most will find it very listenable. The first volume of the Collector's Classics
edition brings together all the tracks released under the nominal leadership of Billy Banks and Jack
Bland; if you can stomach Banks's singing, there's some very hot playing from what is basically an
Eddie Condon group. Superb transfers.

Robert Parker's Jazz Classics compilation fills in some useful gaps – the very obscure session with the
vaudeville singer Walter Pichon, for instance, and a date under Benny Morton's leadership – and picks
some favourites by the Luis Russell band and Allen's own groups. A useful supplement to the Classics
series, although concentrating on all the otherwise-unavailable titles would have made it even more
collectable. Parker's resonant transfers may not appeal to all, but they're very wide-ranging in their
sonic detail.

*** Henry 'Red' Allen 1933–1935 Classics 551
> Allen; Pee Wee Irwin (*t*); J. C. Higginbotham, Dicky Wells, Benny Morton, Keg Johnson,
> George Washington (*tb*); Buster Bailey, Cecil Scott, Albert Nicholas (*cl*); Edward Inge (*cl, as*);
> Hilton Jefferson (*as*); Coleman Hawkins, Chu Berry (*ts*); Horace Henderson (*p*); Bernard
> Addison (*bj, g*); Lawrence Lucie (*g*); Bob Ysaguirre (*bb*); John Kirby (*b, bb*); Elmer James, Pops
> Foster (*b*); Manzie Johnson, Kaiser Marshall, Walter Johnson, Paul Barbarin, George Stafford
> (*d*). 11/33–7/35.

*** Henry Allen Collection Vol. 2 Collector's Classics COCD 2
> Similar to above. 10/32–7/35.

*** Henry 'Red' Allen 1935–1936 Classics 575
> Allen; J. C. Higginbotham (*tb*); Albert Nicholas (*cl*); Rudy Powell, Hildred Humphries (*cl, as*);
> Cecil Scott (*cl, ts*); Pete Clark, Tab Smith (*as*); Happy Caldwell, Joe Garland, Ted McRae (*ts*);
> Edgar Hayes, Norman Lester, Jimmy Reynolds, Clyde Hart (*p*); Lawrence Lucie (*g*); Elmer
> James, John Kirby (*b*); O'Neil Spencer, Cozy Cole, Walter Johnson (*d*). 11/35–8/36.

*** **Henry Allen Collection Vol. 3** Collector's Classics COCD 10
  Similar to above. 35–36.
*** **Henry 'Red' Allen 1936–1937** Classics 590
  Allen; Gene Mikell, Buster Bailey, Glyn Paque (*cl*); Tab Smith (*as*); Ted McRae, Sonny
  Fredericks, Harold Arnold (*ts*); Clyde Hart, Billy Kyle, Luis Russell (*p*); Danny Barker (*g*);
  John Kirby, John Williams (*b*); Cozy Cole, Alphonse Steele, Paul Barbarin (*d*). 10/36–4/37.
*** **Henry Allen Collection Vol. 4** Collector's Classics COCD 15
  Similar to above. 10/36–6/37.
***(*) **Henry 'Red' Allen 1937–1941** Classics 628
  Allen; Benny Morton, J. C. Higginbotham (*tb*); Glyn Paque, Edmond Hall (*cl*); Tab Smith (*as*);
  Harold Arnold, Sammy Davis (*ts*); Luis Russell, Billy Kyle, Lil Armstrong, Kenny Kersey (*p*);
  Danny Barker, Bernard Addison (*g*); John Williams, Pops Foster, Billy Taylor (*b*); Paul
  Barbarin, Alphonse Steele, Zutty Singleton, Jimmy Hoskins (*d*). 6/37–7/41.
*** **Original 1933–1941 Recordings** Tax S-3-2
  As above Classics discs. 33–41.
**** **Swing Out** Topaz TPZ 1037
  As above discs, plus tracks with Luis Russell, Spike Hughes, King Oliver and Fletcher
  Henderson. 29–35.

Maybe Allen was a man out of time: he arrived just too late to make a significant impact on the first jazz decade, and he had to work through the Depression – and the early part of the swing era – recording what were really novelty small-group sessions, most of which are little-known today. Like Armstrong and Waller, he had to record at least as many bad songs as good ones and, though he was an entertaining singer, he couldn't match either Fats or Louis as master of whatever material came his way. Still, the chronological Classics and Collector's Classics sequences are a valuable and pretty consistent documentation. The groups tend to be rough-and-ready but, whenever he's partnered by the superb Higginbotham, Allen comes up with marvellously exuberant jazz. And sometimes unpromising material releases a classic performance: hear, for instance, the completely wild version of 'Roll Along, Prairie Moon' on Classics 551/COCD 2, in which the trombonist blows such a fine solo that Allen insists on handing over his own solo space. The CDs in the middle of the sequence have too many duff tunes on them, but the 1937–41 set is stronger, since Allen switched labels (to Decca) in 1940 and started recording uncompromised jazz again. Sessions with Ed Hall, Zutty Singleton and Benny Morton are a little too brash, perhaps, but Allen's own playing is stirring throughout.

  The Tax CD offers a somewhat mystifying selection of tracks from the period. The sound on all five Classics CDs is mostly very good, with just a few transfers suffering from noticeable blemishes, but they are outdone by the excellent new Collector's Classics edition, which gets our first choice.

  The Topaz compilation is a very sensible selection of tracks from Allen's Victors, the Luis Russell band, Oliver, Henderson and Spike Hughes's 'Firebird'. A rounded and exciting portrait of the great stylist, and the transfers are fastidiously done.

Rex Allen (born 1952) TROMBONE, VIBES

*** **Keep Swingin'** Nagel-Heyer CD 016
  Allen; Dan Barrett (*t*); Jim Rothermel (*cl, ss, as*); Harry Allen (*ts*); Mark Shane (*p*); Bucky
  Pizzarelli (*g*); Frank Tate (*b*); Gregor Beck (*d*); Terrie Richards (*v*). 10/94.
Volume Five in Hans Nagel-Heyer's sequence of CDs recorded at Hamburg's Musikhalle features a man who must be one of the few musicians to double on trombone and vibes. Allen leads a group called the Swing Express, and with material like 'Back Bay Shuffle' and 'Opus 1' it's not hard to figure out where his tastes lie. The amazingly versatile Barrett forsakes his usual trombone for trumpet, Allen is urbanity personified, and Rothermel does equally well on his three horns. There are one or two nice ideas for a tune – Quincy Jones's 'Pleasingly Plump', unheard since Basie days, is one – and if the audience is sometimes a little intrusive, well, everybody was swinging, after all.

Tex Allen TRUMPET, VOCAL

*** **Late Night** Muse MCD 5492
  Allen; Jesse Davis (*as*); Jacky Terrasson (*p*); Ugonna Okagu (*b*); Eddie Gladden (*d*); Lawrence
  Killian (*perc*). 7/91.
Allen plays and sings like Chet Baker on a different prescription. Remembered for some interesting moments with Gil Evans, he fares – let's say, interestingly – in two slightly different quintet settings. When the gifted Davis is on hand, the mix is richer and more coherent. Terrasson still over-elaborates,

and he probably always will; he just seems a touch more reserved with two horns in front of him. 'You Don't Know What Love Is' brings out the best in all three, while Bruno Martno's 'Estate' is the outstanding track from the other line-up, with Killian making up the fifth rather inconsequentially. The bassist with the name that sounds like a Glasgow threat is a new one to us, but he plays very creditably. Nice beefy recording, even if the drums are a touch loud.

Mose Allison (born 1927) PIANO, VOCAL, TRUMPET

***(*) **Back Country Suite** Original Jazz Classics OJC 075
    Allison; Taylor LaFargue (*b*); Frank Isola (*d*). 3/57.
*** **Local Color** Original Jazz Classics OJC 457
    Allison; Addison Farmer (*b*); Nick Stabulas (*d*); 11/57.
***(*) **Creek Bank** Prestige PRCD-24055-2
    Allison; Addison Farmer (*b*); Nick Stabulas, Ronnie Free (*d*). 1–8/58.
*** **Greatest Hits** Original Jazz Classics OJC 6004
    As above three records. 3/57–2/59.
**** **Sings And Plays** Prestige CDJZD 007
    As above. 3/57–2/59.

Mose Allison grew up in Mississippi, played trumpet in high school and listened to a lot of blues and swing; by the time he came to listen to bebop, a little of which creeps into his playing, he was already hooked on the light and steady kind of swing playing which Nat Cole's trio exemplified. Mose has always been a modernist: his hip world-weariness and mastery of the wry put-down ('When you're walking your last mile/Baby, don't forget to smile') have always been paired with a vocal style that is reluctantly knowing, as though he tells truths which he has to force out. Coupled with a rhythmically juddering, blues-directed piano manner, he's made sure that there's been no one else quite like him – aside from such second-generation stylists as Georgie Fame.

Back Country Suite, his debut, remains arguably his best record as an instrumentalist and composer: the deft little miniatures which make up the 'suite' are winsome and rocking by turns, and LaFargue and Isola read the leader's moves beautifully. *Local Color* is nearly as good, with a rare glimpse of Allison's muted trumpet on 'Trouble In Mind', an unusual Ellington revival in 'Don't Ever Say Goodbye' and his first and best treatment of Percy Mayfield's 'Lost Mind'. *Creek Bank* couples the album of that name with the slightly earlier *Young Man Mose* and is an excellent package: more standards, blues and Allison vignettes in generous playing time. *Greatest Hits* concentrates on Allison the singer/recitalist rather than the pianist/composer: a well-planned selection, but it bows to John Crosby's excellent compilation, *Sings And Plays*, which brings together all his vocal cuts for Prestige as well as ten instrumentals on an excellent-value 23-track CD.

***(*) **High Jinks** Columbia/Epic/Legacy J3K 64275 3CD
    Allison; Addison Farmer, Henry Grimes, Aaron Bell, Bill Crow (*b*); Paul Motian, Jerry Segal,
    Osie Johnson, Gus Johnson (*d*). 12/59–9/60.

Recorded across four different sessions, this three-disc set collects three original LPs – *I Love The Life I Live*, *V-8 Ford Blues* and *The Transfiguration Of Hiram Brown* – and adds a smattering of unreleased extras to each disc. The 'Hiram Brown' suite which takes up half of one of the discs is Allison's best intrumental work outside of the 'Back Country Suite', another tough, charming evocation of country-meets-the-city, while each of the other discs has its share of gems: 'A Pretty Girl Is Like A Melody', 'Life Is Suicide', 'Make Yourself Comfortable'. Nice remastering, a reminiscent note by Mose on each one, and some neat packaging.

**** **I Don't Worry About A Thing** Rhino/Atlantic R2 71417
    Allison; Addison Farmer (*b*); Osie Johnson (*d*). 3/62.

No real change or advance, but this is perhaps the classic Allison album. Here are the first versions of two of his sharpest pieces, 'Your Mind Is On Vacation' and the title-song; one of his best Nat Cole treatments, 'Meet Me At No Special Place'; and three of his own oblique pieces of Americana for piano, bass and drums. Short shrift on playing time, but extra tracks would have spoiled the balance of a marvellous record.

*** **Middle Class White Boy** Discovery 71011
    Allison; Joe Farrell (*ts, f*); Phil Upchurch (*g*); Putter Smith (*b*); John Dentz (*d*); Ron Powell
    (*perc*). 82.

From the first of several 'comebacks', if one can be so impertinent to a timeless warrior. Spoilt by the clanky sound of the Yamaha piano he plays on most of the tracks, perhaps, but this is still buoyed up by some terrific Allisonisms – 'How Does It Feel (To Be Good Looking)?' and 'Hello There, Universe' are but two – and the music is consistently chipper.

*** **Ever Since The World Ended** Blue Note B21Y-48015
> Allison; Bob Malach (*as, ts*); Arthur Blythe (*as*); Bennie Wallace (*ts*); Kenny Burrell (*g*); Dennis Irwin (*b*); Tom Whaley (*d*). 5–6/87.

*** **My Backyard** Blue Note B21S-93840
> Allison; Tony Dagradi (*ts*); Steve Masakowski (*g*); Bill Huntington (*b*); John Vidacovich (*d*). 12/89.

*** **The Earth Wants You** Blue Note 827640-2
> Allison; Randy Brecker (*t*); Joe Lovano (*as*); Bob Malach (*ts*); Hugh McCracken (*hca*); John Scofield (*g*); Ratzo Harris (*b*); Paul Motian (*d*); Ray Mantilla (*perc*). 94.

After 30-plus years in the studios, some of Mose's world-view has become institutionalized, and his slip-on brand of fatalism might seem old hat to some. These are good, solid Allison albums, nevertheless. Blue Note's efforts to update him a little aren't especially successful: the guest-star turns on *Ever Since The World Ended* add weight but no special substance to the music, and the New Orleans team that supports him on *My Backyard* has its own agenda as well as following the leader. Allison's distinctive touch still comes through on 'The Gettin' Paid Waltz' and 'I Looked In The Mirror'.

After a further break came *The Earth Wants You*. Another cast of Blue Note heavies make themselves useful, none more so than the unerringly versatile Scofield, whose blues fills on 'You Can't Push People Around' and 'Natural Born Malcontent' make solid sense. Motian's return to the Allison fold after 30-odd years is another pleasure, and 'Certified Senior Citizen' is as canny a lyric as Mose has ever come up with. Excellent fun.

Karin Allyson VOCAL, PIANO

***(*) **I Didn't Know About You** Concord CCD 4543
> Allyson; Gary Sivils (*c*); Mike Metheny (*flhn*); Joe Cartwright, Russ Long, Paul Smith (*p*); Rod Fleeman, Danny Embrey (*g*); Bob Bowman, Gerald Sparts (*b*); Todd Strait (*d*); Doug Auwarter (*perc*); Bryan Hicks (*v*). 92.

*** **Sweet Home Cookin'** Concord CCD 4593
> Allyson; Randy Sandke (*t*); Bob Cooper (*ts*); Alan Broadbent, Paul Smith (*p*); Rod Fleeman (*g*); Putter Smith, Bob Bowman (*b*); Sherman Ferguson, Todd Strait (*d*). 6–9/93.

*** **Azure-Te** Concord CCD 4641
> Allyson; Stan Kessler (*t, flhn*); Mike Metheny (*flhn*); Kim Park (*as, ts*); Randy Weinstein (*hca*); Paul Smith, Laura Caviani (*p*); Claude Williams (*vn*); Rod Fleeman, Danny Embrey (*g*); Bob Bowman, Gerald Sprats (*b*); Todd Strait (*d*). 11/94.

The debut album established Allyson's sexy, fresh-faced delivery as something different in the small group of new jazz singers. With a background rather vaguely rooted in rock, she doesn't feel uptight about including material from writers like Randy Newman or Janis Ian, but her zestful rhythmic sense and solid scat capabilities let her walk in the tradition when she wants. A small-hours blues such as Newman's 'Guilty' sounds terrific here, but all the standards she tackles come off well, and her large cast of supporting players create a wide variation of settings. If *Sweet Home Cookin'* was a slight disappointment as a follow-up, it's because it's that much more homogeneous, with Alan Broadbent's arrangements and horn charts fashioning a more familiar West Coast feel to the situations. Allyson herself still sounds fine. The same with *Azure-Te*, though again the material seems less catholic and more classic, with standards and bop tunes making up the programme. Heartbreaker: the slowly sighing 'Some Other Time'.

Mikhail Alperin PIANO, MELODICA, VOICE

(*) **Wave Over Sorrow ECM 1396
> Alperin; Arkady Shilkloper (*flhn, frhn, v*). 7/89.

The Lester Young retort – 'Yes, very impressive, kid, but what's your story?' – applies here in spades. This is an elegantly performed and (of course) exquisitely recorded set, but it reeks of inconsequence. Occasional outbreaks of irony do not a meaningful story make and, after just a couple of tracks, it becomes possible to second-guess just about every move and counter-move. Lovely all the same, but far from satisfying.

Maarten Altena (born 1943) BASS, CELLO

** Quotl hat Art 6029
> Altena; Marc Charig (*t, ahn*); Wolter Wierbos (*tb*); Michael Moore (*as, cl, bcl*); Peter Van Bergen (*ts, bcl*); Maartje Ten Hoorn (*vn*); Michel Scheen (*p*); Michael Vatcher (*perc*). 8/87.

**(*) Rif hat Art 6056
> As above, except Guus Janssen (*p, syn*) replaces Scheen. 12/88.

*** Cities And Streets hat Art 6082
> As for *Quotl*, except Christel Postma (*vn*) replaces ten Hoorn. 10/89.

Tremendously interesting things have been done in the Netherlands over the past two or three decades by composers deeply influenced by jazz and improvisational traditions. One thinks mainly of Louis Andriessen and Misha Mengelberg. That Altena's writing is much less certain than either of these is evident in *Quotl*'s heavyweight seriousness. Nine densely packed compositions – of which five are credited to the bassist – are played by a flexible ensemble that seems to be attempting big-band gestures with insufficient resources. There are rather too many send-for-reinforcements occasions, and too many moments when the already sparse solos come across like desperate vamping while the rest of the band reshuffle their sheet music. Only the most self-effacing curate would fail to balk at such an egg.

Cities And Streets, by the sharpest of contrasts, is like a walk through the ethnic hotch-potch of the cultural market district. Though again devised as a series of systems for improvisation, it has a steady, ambulatory progress that makes the album resemble a large-scale suite: there are quiet squares, threatening alleys and sudden, barking thoroughfares. The effect resembles Charles Ives and Mingus, filtered back through much of the technical innovation of the last 75 years. The album also features a much-transformed re-run of 'Rif' from the fine 1987 set; put side by side, they provide a useful object-lesson in Altena's conception of the borders of composition and improvisation. Unlike the Willem Breuker Kollektief, there is little obvious satirical intent, but there are moments of calculated banality, which must be heard in context. Despite the imbroglio of *Quotl*, Altena's is a music of the highest contemporary significance.

**(*) Code hat Art CD 6094
> Altena; Wolter Wierbos (*tb*); Peter Van Bergen (*ts, bcl, cbcl*); Jacques Palinckx (*g*); Christel Postma (*vn*); Michel Scheen (*p*); Michael Vatcher (*perc*); Jannie Pranger (*v*). 12/90.

With *Code*, Altena's insistent self-examination moves to a new level. The Ensemble line-up has changed again, paring down the sectional feel of the earlier band, adding Palinckx's quite aggressive guitar sound and Pranger's post-Berberian vocabularies, giving the sound a tougher but also more conservatively modernist feel. In keeping with Altena's growing interest in 'coding', three tracks – 'Slange', 'Prikkel' and 'Rij' – are reprised from the excellent *Cities And Streets*. There are also compositions from British 'punk' composer, Steve Martland – the opening 'Principia' – and from Gilius van Bergerjik, a companion-piece to the earlier 'Scène Rurale' called 'Scène De Mort'.

Like many current leader/composers, Altena is concerned with the interface between notated and improvised musical language and the title-track (part of a series again) is based on structural cues calling for either imitation of basic materials or else free improvisation. The result there is very much more interesting than the 'squeaky door' effects of earlier tracks. By this point in his career, Altena's music may require more effort and cross-reference than most casual listeners will be prepared to give it. This isn't necessarily a vice, but it is an obstacle – and one has to wonder if the means of communication (successive CDs that overlap, thematically and methodologically) is the right one. For most people, the code will remain not just unbreakable but unappealingly enigmatic.

Barry Altschul (born 1943) DRUMS, PERCUSSION

*** Virtuosi Improvising Artists Inc 123 844 2
> Altschul; Paul Bley (*p*); Gary Peacock (*b*). 6/67.

**(*) That's Nice Soul Note 1211115
> Altschul; Glenn Ferris (*tb*); Sean Bergin (*as, ts*); Mike Melillo (*p*); Andy McKee (*b*). 11/85.

Altschul is one of the finest percussionists in contemporary jazz, an intelligent, analytical man who has moved from an early free-form and avant-garde idiom to embrace virtually all the major world traditions (except, interestingly, the unaccented musics of East Asia). He has written persuasively about drumming, but if there is anything that mars his recorded output, it is a slightly didactic insistence which can make his playing a little stiff. The early *Virtuosi* sounds – and is – very much like Bley's own trio work of the period. There are two compositions by Annette Peacock, each of which forms the basis for a long, freely associating improvisation. Bley still tends to dominate proceedings, though Altschul's continuous flow of ideas would be impressive were it registered more distinctly; not even CD gives a faithful rendition of some of his softer figures and effects.

Altschul's Soul Note albums have taken a bit of a pasting in the last few years. *For Stu*, *Somewhere Else* and *Irina* have disappeared, to be replaced by the less-than-compelling *That's Nice*, a record that labours under the weight of too many 'drummer's album' peccadilloes. A longish tribute 'For "Papa" Jo, "Klook" And "Philly", Too' gets to grips with the ancestors but turns into a succession of licks and pastiches. The addition of Melillo for the title-track and one other softens the rather barking sound that Ferris and Bergin go in for, but the damage is already done. Wait in hope that *For Stu* will be back in circulation before too long.

Franco Ambrosetti (born 1941) TRUMPET, FLUGELHORN

***(*) **Gin And Pentatonic** Enja 4096-2
    Ambrosetti; Lew Soloff, Mike Mossman (*t*); Steve Coleman (*as*); Michael Brecker (*ts*); Howard Johnson (*bs, tba*); Alex Brofsky, John Clark (*frhn*); Tommy Flanagan, Kenny Kirkland (*p*); Dave Holland, Buster Williams (*b*); Daniel Humair (*d*). 12/83–3/85.
*** **Movies** Enja 5035-2
    Ambrosetti; Geri Allen (*p*); John Scofield (*g*); Michael Formanek (*b*); Daniel Humair (*d*); Jerry Gonzalez (*perc*). 11/86.
(*) **Music For Symphony And Jazz Band Enja 6070-2
    Ambrosetti; Daniel Schnyder (*ss*); Greg Osby (*as*); Simon Nabatov, Vladislaw Sendecki (*p*); Ed Schuller (*b*); Alfredo Glino (*d*); NDR Radio-Orchestra, Hannover. 10/90.
***(*) **Live At The Blue Note** Enja 7065-2
    Ambrosetti; Seamus Blake (*ts*); Kenny Barron (*p*); Ira Coleman (*b*); Victor Lewis (*d*). 7/92.
Ambrosetti divides his time between industrial management and jazz – 'after a couple of days of intense industrial management I look for a jazz gig'. He seems to prefer flugelhorn to trumpet and holds his ground impressively with some distinguished musicians on all these dates. *Gin And Pentatonic* conflates the best of two albums, *Wings* and *Tentets*, into a fat-free single disc, all concerned playing with real enthusiasm. *Movies* is film music, treated with amused and just slightly irreverent hospitality by Ambrosetti and some American friends. It's hardly as dramatic a disintegration as a John Zorn session, but the players have fun, and Ambrosetti again impresses as an inventive soloist. The meeting with the NDR Orchestra is about as successful as most such things, which is to say not very. The most striking record is perhaps the live session at New York's Blue Note. This kind of venture – visitor pals up with American hirelings, makes solid and forgettable live date – is old hat, but Ambrosetti plays with real authority, and there are other virtues: Blake, making one of his first appearances on record, is far from the usual hard-bop fledgeling, taking some baroque, surprising solos; Coleman and Lewis are unbeatable; and Barron, who contributes two tunes, is a notch above his normal professional self. His unforgettable theme, 'Phantoms', receives an outstandingly fine reading, even at nearly 20 minutes in length.

American Jazz Quintet GROUP

***(*) **From Bad To Badder** Black Saint 1201142
    Alvin Batiste (*cl*); Harold Battiste (*ts*); Earl Turbinton (*as*); Ellis Marsalis (*p*); Richard Payne (*b*); Ed Blackwell (*d*). 11/87.
The American Jazz Quintet first got together in New Orleans in 1956. They teamed up again for a one-off gig at the 1987 Edward Blackwell Festival in Atlanta. Some of the material from that occasion is already available as Old and New Dreams's *A Tribute To Blackwell* (Black Saint 120113), but this is even better, a total surprise from start to finish.

The night belonged to Alvin Batiste by acclaim, and that's certainly borne out here. His twisting, lifting choruses and sudden, single-note shuffles leave everyone else standing. Turbinton, standing in for the late Nat Perilliatt, has an effusive manner that complements Harold Battiste's more subdued mien. For once Ellis Marsalis, normally a very dominant player, was reduced to the role of mere accompanist as the rhythm section gravitated (quite properly) to Blackwell, who added a wonderfully clanky cowbell to his kit.

Batiste is sensational on his own 'Imp'n Perty Too', chopping out bop-tinged choruses in a register that stays the right side of shrill. Once Payne recognized that Marsalis was content to keep house, he set about having himself a good time; his finger-work is impressive enough, but his *arco* playing is wonderful. The star of the event doesn't sound as though the pressure was getting to him. He's rarely been so relaxed, and his fills on 'Mozarten' are quietly appreciative thank-yous to a bunch of old friends.

AMM IMPROVISING ENSEMBLE

***(*) **AMMMUSIC 1966** Matchless/rer no number
    Cornelius Cardew (*p, transistor radio*); Lou Gare (*ts, vn*); Eddie Prévost (*d*); Keith Rowe (*g, transistor radio*); Lawrence Sheaff (*cl, acc, cl, transistor radio*). 6/66.

**** **The Crypt – 12th June 1968** Matchless MRCD 05 2CD
    Cornelius Cardew (*p, clo*); Lou Gare (*ts, vn*); Christopher Hobbs, Eddie Prévost (*perc*); Keith Rowe (*g, elec*). 6/68.

***(*) **To Hear And Back Again** Matchless MRCD 03
    Lou Gare (*ts*); Eddie Prévost (*d*). 6/73, 11/74, 4/75.

*** **It Had Been An Ordinary Enough Day In Pueblo, Colorado** ECM Japo 60031
    Eddie Prévost (*d*); Keith Rowe (*g, elec*). 79.

***(*) **Generative Themes** Matchless MRCD 06
    Eddie Prévost (*d*); Keith Rowe (*g, elec*); John Tilbury (*p*). 12/82, 4/83.

*** **Combine + Laminates + Treatise '84** Matchless MRCD 26
    Keith Rowe (*g, elec*); Eddie Prévost (*d*); John Tilbury (*p*). 84.

***(*) **The Inexhaustible Document** Matchless MRCD 13
    Eddie Prévost (*d*); Keith Rowe (*g, elec*); Rohan De Saram (*clo*); John Tilbury (*p*). 87.

**** **The Nameless Uncarved Block** Matchless MRCD 20
    Lou Gare (*ts*); Eddie Prévost (*d*); Keith Rowe (*g, elec*); John Tilbury (*p*). 4/90.

**** **Newfoundland** Matchless MRCD 23
    Keith Rowe (*g, elec*); John Tilbury (*p*); Eddie Prévost (*d*). 7/92.

Commercial recording is in almost every practical and ethical respect inimical to this extraordinary music, which has helped shape the instincts of two generations of British improvisers and their supporters. Organized on a collective basis, AMM self-transformed within two years from a free-jazz outfit into a process-dominated improvising group, influenced by a very British combination of materialist and spiritualist philosophies (and, somewhat implicitly, by left-wing politics). Performances attained such a level of intensity and rapport, with the 'audience' as well as among the players, that recordings can offer only a very partial and compromised impression of the group's music.

One of the practical problems to be confronted was that, before the advent of the CD era, extended improvisations could be accommodated to LP only by heavy editing. In recent years, Prévost has been reissuing the material on CD, adding material from other sources in order to bring original LPs up to length. *Ammmusic 1966* usefully restores material excluded from the original (Elektra EUK 265) release. Both *To Hear And Back Again* and *Generative Themes* incorporate performances from other dates.

The music itself, though unremittingly abstract, still calls upon musical and semantic (i.e. radio-sampled) reference points, which give the music an element of irony it entirely lacks later. This may well be down to Cardew's presence; it's also noticeable on the very important Crypt performances recorded in June 1968. Though the two-LP boxed set (Matchless MR5) is now very collectable, these have recently been digitally restored and reissued with additional material on a double-CD set. Prévost points out in a superb liner-note to *Ammmusic* (which also reproduces the 13 aphorisms that accompanied the original LP) that *Jazz Journal* attributed the record to the 'Cornelius Cardew Quartet' – patent nonsense anyway, given the non-hierarchical nature of the music – but still more so, given Cardew's formal preoccupations and ideological unease. As a more orthodox composer from the serialist tradition, Cardew found the selflessness and abnegation of AMM performances (which occasionally took place in pitch dark) difficult to comprehend. Cellist Rohan de Saram, a member of the pivotal, new-music Arditti String Quartet, seems to have had no such difficulties in AMM (he appears only on *The Inexhaustible Document*, in an instrumental role similar to Cardew's) but it's perhaps fair to suggest that de Saram comes from a very different philosophical tradition, in which suspension of the self, of ego and intention, is more readily accepted.

Identifying the participants on record (not, after all, so very different from one of the early live performances) is a little like watching for meteor showers on a moonless night. Sources are identifiable but their incidence is not, and there is constant activity elsewhere on the aural plane; digital sound exposes more and more layers of activity. Over time, though, it becomes clear that the central dialogue is between the stupendously gifted Prévost and Keith Rowe (or with Gare on the recently reissued *To Hear And Back Again*, the first but not the last time AMM functioned as a duo). Prévost and Rowe's duetting on the wonderfully titled *Pueblo, Colorado*, a rare instance of studio recording under the auspices of a large(ish) label, is quite exceptional.

The arrival of pianist John Tilbury reintroduced some of the contradictions experienced with past changes of personnel, but Tilbury is so polymorphous in technique as to overcome any danger of separatism, and his role on *Generative Themes*, *Combine and Laminates/Treatise* (the latter piece a radical re-composition of a Cardew composition and not included on the original Pogus LP) and on the marvellous recent *Nameless Uncarved Block* is reassuringly seamless.

By 1990, the music has become absolute, physical rather than abstract, calling on nothing outside itself, but not falling into the Cagean formlessness (with its silences and 'found' devices) of earlier years. Uncarved or not, the music is the product of identifiable forces, just as the 'sedimentary', 'igneous' and 'metamorphic' strata of the album's three tracks (two massive, one brief) are the product of enormous proto-historical pressures. Prévost's percussion constantly and logically alters the physical dynamics of performance; to identify him as leader is now more than justified, an empirical response to the music as played.

Critics, who have always found it difficult to describe that music and who often resort to comment on titles, were quick to dub *Nameless Uncarved Block* as AMM's 'rock album'. The approach has actually (and with the important qualifications mentioned above) changed remarkably little over 25 years; it certainly hasn't been susceptible to stylistic fashion. AMM music is *sui generis* and needs to be encountered not so much with an open mind as with a mind from which certain critical blind-alleys have been carefully closed off. The 1990 album and the newly restored 1966 debut and Crypt performances are among the essential documents of contemporary free music, and should be heard.

AMM's visit to North America in 1992 was a high point for the ensemble, attracting considerable sympathetic attention. The standard of performance was also very high. *Newfoundland* was recorded at the School of Music in St John's. At more than 75 minutes, it's a particularly intense and focused example of AMM in action. In a sleeve-note the composer Howard Skempton points out the futility of verbalizing the music, the danger of using a little information about the provenance to extrapolate largely meaningless descriptions and categorizations. More than ever it's necessary to surrender oneself to these remarkable sounds and not to speculate on their origins or function. If improvisation still is the *terra incognita* of modern culture, this is some sort of landfall.

Albert Ammons (1907–49) PIANO

***(*) **Albert Ammons 1936–1939** Classics 715
>   Ammons; Guy Kelly (*t*); Dalbert Bright (*cl, as*); Ike Perkins (*g*); Israel Crosby (*b*); Jimmy Hoskins (*d*). 2/36–10/39.

One-third of the great boogie-woogie triumvirate (with Pete Johnson and Meade Lux Lewis), Albert Ammons was arguably the least individual of the three, though he lacked nothing in power and swinging. The Classics CD usefully rounds up all his tracks from the 1930s: there are two Decca sessions by his Rhythm Kings, but the meat is in the 18 piano solos, cut for Vocalion, Solo Art and Blue Note, with a session of airshots from Chicago making up the balance. 'Shout For Joy' and 'Boogie Woogie Stomp' are classics of boogie-woogie exuberance, but his 1939 Solo Art session proved he was a considerable blues piano man, too: 'Chicago In Mind' contemplates the form with genuine insight. The CD offers mixed reproduction, mostly not bad.

Gene Ammons (1925–74) TENOR SAXOPHONE

*** **Red Top – The Savoy Sessions** Savoy SV 0242
>   Ammons; Howard McGhee, Johnny Coles (*t*); Lino Murray (*tb*); Mack Easton (*ts, bs*); Leo Parker (*bs*); Junior Mance, John Houston (*p*); Gene Wright, Ben Stuberville (*b*); Chuck Williams, George Brown (*d*). 10/47–6/53.

(*) **The Gene Ammons Story: The 78 Era Prestige PRCD-24058-2
>   Ammons; Bill Massey, Nate Woodyard (*t*); Matthew Gee, Eli Dabney, Benny Green, Henderson Chambers (*tb*); Sonny Stitt, Rudy Williams, McKinley Easton (*bs*); Duke Jordan, Charlie Bateman, Junior Mance, Clarence Anderson, John Houston (*p*); Gene Wright, Earl May, Ernie Shepard, Ben Stuberville, Tommy Potter (*b*); Art Blakey, Wes Landers, Teddy Stewart, George Brown (*d*); Earl Coleman (*v*). 4/50–2/55.

(*) **All Star Sessions Original Jazz Classics OJC 014
>   Ammons; Art Farmer, Bill Massey (*t*); Al Outcalt (*tb*); Lou Donaldson (*as*); Sonny Stitt (*ts, bs*); Duke Jordan, Junior Mance, Charles Bateman, Freddie Redd (*p*); Tommy Potter, Gene Wright, Addison Farmer (*b*); Jo Jones, Wes Landers, Teddy Stewart, Kenny Clarke (*d*). 3/50–6/55.

*** **The Happy Blues** Original Jazz Classics OJC 013
>   Ammons; Art Farmer, Jackie McLean (*as*); Duke Jordan (*p*); Addison Farmer (*b*); Art Taylor (*d*); Candido Camero (*perc*). 4/56.

(*) **Jammin' With Gene Original Jazz Classics OJC 211
>   Ammons; Donald Byrd (*t*); Jackie McLean (*as*); Mal Waldron (*b*); Doug Watkins (*b*); Art Taylor (*d*). 7/56.

*** **Funky** Original Jazz Classics OJC 244
 As above, except Art Farmer (*t*) replaces Byrd, add Kenny Burrell (*g*). 1/57.
** **Jammin' In Hi Fi** Original Jazz Classics OJC 129
 Ammons; Idrees Sulieman (*t*); Jackie McLean (*as*); Mal Waldron (*p*); Kenny Burrell (*g*); Paul
 Chambers (*b*); Art Taylor (*d*). 4/57.
*** **The Big Sound** Original Jazz Classics OJC 651
 Ammons; John Coltrane (*as*); Paul Quinichette (*ts*); Pepper Adams (*bs*); Jerome Richardson (*f*);
 Mal Waldron (*p*); George Joyner (*b*); Arthur Taylor (*d*). 1/58.
*** **Groove Blues** Original Jazz Classics OJC 723
 As above. 1/58.
(*) **Blue Gene Original Jazz Classics OJC 192
 Ammons; Idrees Sulieman (*t*); Pepper Adams (*bs*), Mal Waldron (*p*); Doug Watkins (*b*); Art
 Taylor (*d*); Ray Barretto (*perc*). 5/58.

The son of Albert Ammons made a lot of records, and a surprising number are now in print on CD,
thanks mainly to the extensive OJC/Prestige reissue programme. The Savoy set collects the results of
four dates over a six-year period. Some of it is ancient bebop history, particularly the 1947 session with
McGhee and Leo Parker, but the later tracks offer an interesting glimpse of the young Johnny Coles and
the already maturing Ammons well into his stride. OJC's series of reissues has so far dealt mainly with
his jamming sessions of the mid- and late-1950s; they are entertaining but often flabby blowing dates
which number as many clichés as worthwhile ideas in the playing. The leader's own style had been
forged as a first-generation bopper, first with Billy Eckstine, then under his own name, but his early
records find him walking a line between bop and R&B honking: the second disc listed above, *The 78 Era*,
is rough-and-ready music, and listening to it is like thumbing coins into a jukebox of the day. Jug liked
to enjoy his music, and perhaps the darker passions of a Parker were beyond him. The earliest tracks on
All Star Sessions are also typical of the kind of stuff he recorded prior to the LP era, roistering through
two-tenor battles with Sonny Stitt, a close kindred spirit. A later date with Farmer and Donaldson is
more restrained until the collective whoop of 'Madhouse'.

 The next six records all follow similar patterns: long, expansive tracks – at most four to a record – and
variations on the blues and some standards for the material. Ammons himself takes the leading solos,
but he so often resorts to quotes and familiar phrases that one is left wishing for a less open-ended
environment; of the other players involved, McLean and Waldron are the most reliably inventive.
Jammin' In Hi Fi is the weakest of the six, the whole session sounding like a warm-up, while *Jammin'
With Gene* has a very long and overcooked 'Not Really The Blues' balancing two superior slow pieces.
Funky and *Blue Gene* are decent if unremarkable, but the session that makes up both *The Big Sound* and
Groove Blues has a couple of interesting points in featuring one of John Coltrane's few appearances on
alto (undistinguished though it is) and some unexpectedly piquant flute solos by Richardson to vary the
palette a little. These all count as playable but unexceptional discs.

*** **The Gene Ammons Story: Organ Combos** Prestige PRCD-24071-2
 Ammons; Joe Newman (*t*); Frank Wess (*ts, f*); Jack McDuff, Johnny 'Hammond' Smith (*org*);
 Wendell Marshall, Doug Watkins (*b*); Art Taylor, Walter Perkins (*d*); Ray Barretto (*perc*). 6/60–
 11/61.
*** **Boss Tenor** Original Jazz Classics OJC 297
 Ammons; Tommy Flanagan (*p*); Doug Watkins (*b*); Art Taylor (*d*); Ray Barretto (*perc*). 6/60.
*** **Jug** Original Jazz Classics OJC 701
 Ammons; Richard Wyands (*p*); Clarence 'Sleepy' Anderson (*org*); Doug Watkins (*b*); J. C.
 Heard (*d*). 1/61.
***(*) **The Gene Ammons Story: Gentle Jug** Prestige PRCD-24079-2
 Ammons; Richard Wyands, Patti Bown (*p*); George Duvivier, Doug Watkins (*b*); J. C. Heard,
 Ed Shaughnessy (*d*). 1/61–4/62.
(*) **Live! In Chicago Original Jazz Classics OJC 395
 Ammons; Eddie Buster (*org*); Gerald Donovan (*d*). 8/61.
*** **Up Tight!** Prestige PRCD-24140-2
 Ammons; Walter Bishop Jr, Patti Bown (*p*); Arthur Davis, George Duvivier (*b*); Arthur Taylor
 (*d*); Ray Barretto (*perc*). 10/61.
** **Preachin'** Original Jazz Classics OJC-792
 Ammons; Clarence 'Sleepy' Anderson (*org*); Sylvester Hickman (*b*); Dorral Anderson (*d*). 5/62.
*** **Jug And Dodo** Prestige PRCD-24021-2
 Ammons; Dodo Marmarosa (*p*); Sam Jones (*b*); Marshall Thompson (*d*). 5/62.
(*) **Bad! Bossa Nova Original Jazz Classics OJC 351
 Ammons; Hank Jones (*p*); Bucky Pizzarelli, Kenny Burrell (*g*); Norman Edge (*b*); Oliver
 Jackson (*d*); Al Hayes (*perc*). 9/62.

**(*) We'll Be Together Again Original Jazz Classics OJC 708
    Ammons; Sonny Stitt (*as, ts*); John Houston (*p*); Buster Williams (*b*); George Brown (*d*). 68.
**(*) The Boss Is Back! Prestige PRCD-24129-2
    Ammons; Prince James, Houston Person (*ts*); Junior Mance (*p*); Sonny Phillips (*org*); Billy
    Butler (*g*); Buster Williams, Bob Bushnell (*b*); Frankie Jones, Bernard Purdie (*d*); Candido
    Camero (*perc*). 11/69.

There is a lot of Gene Ammons available again. It's sad that the albums are so spotty and inconsistent,
but that seemed to be his way: great performances can follow weary ones, even on the same record, and
there doesn't seem to be a particular setting that turns him on to his best form. The clinkers here are
Preachin', a set of gospel tunes that he can barely be bothered to blow through, and *The Boss Is Back!*,
which combines the original *Boss Is Back* (not bad) and *Brother Jug* (rotten). *We'll Be Together Again*
should have been an incendiary meeting with Sonny Stitt, but it leaves a trail of smoke rather than any
fire – the tracks are cut off short before they can really work up steam. *Bad! Bossa Nova* sounds like a
duff corporate idea, setting him to work on bossa nova rhythms, but he blows hard enough to make it
worthwhile. *Boss Tenor*, *Jug* and especially *Organ Combos* (which combines the original albums,
Twisting The Jug and the fine *Angel Eyes*) are solid and worth the shelf-space. The best records, though,
are probably *Jug And Dodo*, an unlikely, sometimes compelling meeting with Dodo Marmarosa in one
of the pianist's rare recordings, and the splendid *Gentle Jug*. This at last puts on CD one of his very best
Prestige dates, *The Soulful Moods Of Gene Ammons*, where he plays with Hawkins-like authority, and
adds the similarly inclined *Nice An' Cool* session from a year earlier. *Up Tight!* is the most recent
addition to the sequence, collecting the contents of two 1961 LPs, *Up Tight* and *Boss Soul*. A couple of
good ones, too, though if anyone feels confused by the similarity of all these titles, much the same can be
said about a lot of the music.

**(*) Greatest Hits, Vol. 1: The Sixties Original Jazz Classics OJC 6005
    Ammons; Joe Newman (*t*); Frank Wess (*ts*); Jack McDuff, Johnny Hammond Smith (*org*);
    Richard Wyands, Hank Jones, Tommy Flanagan (*p*); Kenny Burrell, Bucky Pizzarelli (*g*); Doug
    Watkins, Norman Edge, Wendell Marshall (*b*); Art Taylor, Oliver Jackson, Walter Perkins (*d*);
    Ray Barretto, Al Hayes (*perc*). 61–69.
*** Soul Summit Prestige PRCD-24118-2
    Ammons; various others. 6/61–4/62.

Two useful if sometimes frustrating compilations. The *Hits* collection isn't a bad trawl through some of
his 1960s sessions, though any of the better albums listed above would do just as well as a sampling of
Ammons in this decade. *Soul Summit* is shared with Sonny Stitt and Jack McDuff, and Jug turns up on a
couple of tracks with a big band as well as sparring with Stitt.

Curtis Amy (born 1927) TENOR AND SOPRANO SAXOPHONES

*** Peace For Love Fresh Sound FSR 5004
    Amy; Steve Huffsteter (*t, flhn*); Bob McChesney (*b*); Frank Strazzeri (*p*); Donn Wyatt (*ky*);
    John B. Williams (*b*); Leon Ndugu Chancler (*d*); Merry Clayton, Jessie Williams (*v*). 6/94.
Nice to have this likeable old pro back in the racks with a record under his own name. Amy is a Texas
tenor who missed out on many of the plaudits – his half-dozen Pacific Jazz albums are currently in
limbo, though *Meetin' Here* has been on CD in the past – and this easy-going date, while never striking
more than a few sparks, is the jazz equivalent of comfort food. Amy's thick, soft tenor lines and
insinuating tone are fine, but the best features are the astute writing for the three-horn front line and the
slowly unfolding groove which the splendid rhythm section put together for most of the tunes. Mrs Amy,
Merry Clayton, adds wordless vocals to track one.

Arild Andersen (born 1945) DOUBLE BASS, ELECTRIC BASS, OTHER INSTRUMENTS

***(*) Sagn ECM 1435
    Andersen; Bendik Hofseth (*ts, ss*); Frode Alnaes (*g*); Bugge Wesseltoft (*ky*); Nana Vasconcelos
    (*perc, v*); Kirsten Braten Berg (*v*). 8/90.
*** If You Look Far Enough ECM 1493
    Andersen; Ralph Towner (*g*); Nana Vasconcelos (*perc*); Audun Klieve (*d*). Spring 88, 7/91, 2/92.
One of Europe's finest musicians, and certainly one of a handful of international-class bass players,
Andersen is sadly under-recorded as a leader. These two albums, though, and the 1985 *Bande A Part*
(ECM 1319) by his band, Masqualero, are sufficient to establish his credentials. Two other records on
ECM – *Green Shading Into Blue* and *A Molde Concert* – are currently in limbo.

Like so many Scandinavians, Andersen is powerfully influenced by Miles Davis (the first of those deleted titles contains an unmistakable reference), writing and adapting oblique melodies which are separated from kitsch only by the most exact intonation and absence of undue elaboration. The spread-out dates on the later release suggest its bittiness. The title-pieces – 'If You Look' and 'Far Enough' – were written for the soundtrack of a Norwegian film, *Blücher*, and have that vaguely expressionistic quality one expects of film music. Andersen uses real-time delay and reverb devices to give his bass a rounded, 'orchestral' sound. Later pieces, with Towner prominently featured, draw on Norwegian folk music, in similar vein to *Sagn*.

Immediately reminiscent of Jan Garbarek's recent explorations in the boundaries of jazz and Nordic folk-music, *Sagn* – 'Saga' – stands up to the comparison remarkably well. Andersen structures his commissioned piece with great care, incorporating Kirsten Braten Berg's reconstructed Telemark folk-songs alongside elements of mainstream and modern jazz and rock (the latter largely communicated by Alnaes, not always with perfect taste). Berg hasn't the purity and simplicity of tone of Agnes Buen Garnas, Garbarek's collaborator, but she has considerable presence in the overall shape of the piece, which is deeply moving and satisfying.

Cat Anderson (1916–81) TRUMPET, FLUGELHORN

*** **Plays W. C. Handy** Black & Blue 59163 2
> Anderson; Booty Wood (*tb*); Norris Turney (*as*); Harold Ashby (*ts*); Gerard Badini (*ts, cl*); Philippe Baudouin, Raymond Fol, André Persiany (*p*); Aaron Bell, Michel Gaudry (*b*); Sam Woodyard (*d*). 6/77, 5/78.

There has long been a tendency to dismiss Anderson as just another high-wire act, an exhibitionist who traded on his extraordinary five-octave reach to the detriment of more thoughtful play in the vital middle trumpet register. Anderson's coloratura solos were features of Ellington shows, and carefully pitched numbers like 'El Gato' were contrived to afford him as much sky as he wanted; at such moments, Anderson was like a cat who had traded souls with a bird.

Underneath, though, he was a tense perfectionist who studied music with an intensity that belied his occasionally histrionic playing. In his solo ventures before and after Ellington's death, he demonstrates an intelligence and sense of structure that utterly confound the usual complaint that his solo-development was immature or banal. On the 1958 'Concerto For Cootie' – originally written for his arch-rival on the Ellington trumpet benches, Cootie Williams – he demonstrates considerable taste and tact, and the 'Black And Tan Fantasy' from the same 1958 sessions is one of the finest small-group performances on record. Never well served by furiously compensating sound-engineers, Anderson's recorded performances can sound rather brittle.

Recorded in France with a mixture of locals and Ellingtonians, the Black & Blue CD is decently representative. The resolute traditionalism of the material allows Anderson to explore harmonic and timbral devices which in the late 1970s were identified with the avant-garde (Anderson had a brief and, by all accounts, productive flirtation with experimental techniques) but which relate back directly to the growls, slurs and squeezed notes of the classic cornetists. The opening cadences of 'Yellow Dog Blues' betray absolutely no stint in his ability to do high-note intros. His wah-wah solo on 'Careless Love' is a rarer, middle-register effort, but none the less impressive for being relatively contained. (The CD reissue brings in two non-Handy numbers from an earlier session.)

There has never been any doubt about Anderson's technique, but there is a nudging sense that, even by the early 1960s, he had become slightly typecast as a high-note man and that his attempts to shake off a tired script and take account of some of the more interesting recent developments in trumpet-playing – Miles and Clifford Brown most obviously – were a little too late. As with Armstrong, people came along to hear him clearing top C and would have been queueing at the refund desk if he hadn't.

Ernestine Anderson (born 1928) VOCAL

*** **Ernestine Anderson** Mercury 514076-2
> Anderson; orchestra directed by Pete Rugolo. 58.

(*) **Hello Like Before Concord CCD 4031
> Anderson; Hank Jones (*p*); Ray Brown (*b*); Jimmie Smith (*d*). 76.

(*) **Live From Concord To London Concord CCD 4054
> As above, except add John Horler (*p*), James Richardson (*b*); Jake Hanna, Roger Sellers (*d*); Bill Berry Big Band; omit Smith. 8/76–10/77.

*** **Sunshine** Concord CCD 4109
    Anderson; Monty Alexander (*p*); Ray Brown (*b*); Jeff Hamilton (*d*). 8/79.
*** **Never Make Your Move Too Soon** Concord CCD 4147
    Anderson; Monty Alexander (*p*); Ray Brown (*b*); Frank Gant (*d*). 8/80.
*** **Big City** Concord CCD 4214
    Anderson; Hank Jones (*p*); Monty Budwig (*b*); Jeff Hamilton (*d*). 2/83.
(*) **When The Sun Goes Down Concord CCD 4263
    Anderson; Red Holloway (*ts*); Gene Harris (*p*); Ray Brown (*b*); Gerryck King (*d*). 8/84.
*** **Be Mine Tonight** Concord CCD 4319
    Anderson; Benny Carter (*as*); Marshall Otwell (*p*); Ron Eschete (*g*); Ray Brown (*b*); Jimmie
    Smith (*d*). 12/86.
*** **Boogie Down** Concord CCD 4407
    Anderson; Clayton–Hamilton Jazz Orchestra. 9/89.
*** **Live At The 1990 Concord Jazz Festival – Third Set** Concord CCD 4454
    Anderson; Marshall Royal (*as*); Frank Wess (*ts*); Gene Harris (*p*); Ed Bickert (*g*); Lynn Seaton
    (*b*); Harold Jones (*d*). 8/90.

Ernestine Anderson isn't the kind of singer one expects to find on Concord: she's more of a rhythm-and-blues shouter (she sang with Johnny Otis's band in the late 1940s), and her 1958 debut for Mercury was a typical girl-singer date in which she sounded fine on the belters and less sure with the ballads, though Rugolo's smart arrangements wear well. The suave situations she's been placed in at Concord, the suavest of jazz recording operations, on the face of it may seem to be inappropriate. Yet the least satisfying session here is the most 'bluesy', *When The Sun Goes Down*, which wastes the subtleties in Anderson's voice on lesser material, with Holloway and Harris also sounding stuck in routine. None of these records counts as a classic but each has its own particular interest. The two with Hank Jones benefit from the pianist's ingenious accompaniments, although *Hello Like Before* suffers from a couple of weak song choices. *Never Make Your Move Too Soon* also has too many familiar tunes on it, but Alexander's knowing vivacity is a tonic. Benny Carter's stately appearance on *Be Mine Tonight* adds some extra interest, and here the songs are chosen perfectly, including 'Christopher Columbus', 'London By Night' and 'Sack Full Of Dreams'. Anderson's voice isn't the strong, smoky instrument it was on her Mercury album, but she often takes hold of a song with a kind of infectious intensity that is exciting; her ballads, by contrast, are either compelling or heavy-going. *Boogie Down*, with a full big band behind her, is suitably rollicking music, and she can show Diane Schuur, for one, how to make such a situation work best for a singer. The Concord Festival set from 1990 is par for this particular course – Royal and Wess make statesman-like guest appearances, and there is a lot of applause.

Fred Anderson TENOR SAXOPHONE

*** **Vintage Duets: Chicago 1.11.1980** Okkadisk OD 12001
    Anderson; Steve McCall (*d*). 1/80.

Blimey, but this takes a while to get going. Anderson's opening statements sound disconcertingly like a scales-and-shapes warm-up before the mics go on. Typically, though, of his unpretentious talent, he doesn't just dive in with big, flagrant gestures, all sound and fury signifying damn-all, but works his way patiently into his thing, which is thoughtful, lyrical and involving.

    McCall, meanwhile, has set off on his own parallel course, lots of tight rolls and splashy cymbals, with next to nothing (audible at any rate) on the bass drum. He's immediately distinguishable from all the other players in this field – Moye, Cyrille, Graves, Thurman Barker, Hamid Drake – for sticking much closer to a basic swing conception, using the elasticity of his count to change the shape of his partner's phrasing. It's not been wonderfully well recorded or transferred, and it's McCall who suffers.

    Anderson worked with Joseph Jarman on *Song For* and has been part of the AACM orbit since the 1960s, working away quietly and without much critical brouhaha. 'Within' and 'Wandering', the two long tracks that make up these 1980 duets, suggest he's perhaps too self-effacing a player ever to have made it big time, but he repays attention all the same. Worth a try.

Ray Anderson (born 1952) TROMBONE, ALTO TROMBONE, OTHER BRASS AND PERCUSSION

*** **Old Bottles – New Wine** Enja 4098
    Anderson; Kenny Barron (*p*); Cecil McBee (*b*); Dannie Richmond (*d*). 6/85.
*** **Right Down Your Alley** Soul Note 1211087
    Anderson; Mark Helias (*b*); Gerry Hemingway (*d*). 2/84.

(*) It Just So Happens Enja 5037
>   Anderson; Stanton Davis (*t*); Bob Stewart (*tba*); Perry Robinson (*cl*); Mark Dresser (*b*); Ronnie Burrage (*d*). 86.

*** **Blues Bred In The Bone** Enja 5081
>   Anderson; John Scofield (*g*); Anthony Davis (*p*); Mark Dresser (*b*); Johnny Vidacovich (*d*). 3/88.

***(*) **Every One Of Us** Gramavision R2 79471
>   Anderson; Simon Nabatov (*p*); Charlie Haden (*b*); Ed Blackwell (*d*). 6/92.

***(*) **Big Band Record** Gramavision R2 79497
>   Anderson; Lew Soloff, Ryan Kisor, John D'Earth, Herb Robertson (*t*); Art Baron, Dave Bargeron (*tb*); Dave Taylor (*btb*); Howard Johnson (*tba, bs*); Tim Berne, Sal Giorgianni (*as*); Marty Ehrlich (*as, ss, cl, bcl*); Larry Schneider (*ts*); George Gruntz (*p*); Mark Feldman (*vn*); Drew Grass (*b*); Tom Rainey (*d*). 1/94.

*** **Don't Mow Your Lawn** Enja 8070
>   Anderson; Lew Soloff (*t*); Jerome Harris (*g*); Gregory Jones (*b*); Tommy Campbell (*d*); Frank Colón (*perc*). 3/94.

***(*) **Heads and Tails** Enja 9055
>   As above. 5/95.

***(*) **Azurety** hat ART CD 6155
>   Anderson; Christy Doran (*g*); Han Bennink (*d*). 4/94.

**** **Cheer Up** Hat ART CD 6175
>   As above. 3/95.

Just over a decade ago, Ray Anderson headed the usually under-contested trombone category in the *downbeat* critics' poll and won a 'Talent Deserving Wider Recognition' citation into the bargain. Since then he has rapidly established himself as the most exciting slide brass player of his generation, effortlessly switching between free improvisation and funk, humorous and intense by turns, always challenging and always identifiably himself.

Though his biggest commercial success has been the Latinized funk of his band, Slickaphonics (*q.v.*), he has an impressive back-catalogue both as sideman and leader, working with the (un)likes of Barry Altschul, Anthony Braxton, Barbara Dennerlein and others. His preferred sidemen – Dresser, Hemingway, Helias, Burrage – all play in what could be described as an advanced rock idiom and Cecil McBee on the outstanding *Old Bottles – New Wine* demonstrates the untroubled eclecticism that made the Charles Lloyd quartets of the late '60s and early '70s so important to the jazz–rock crossover. Anderson plays very cleanly, almost like a valve player, but has a massive repertoire of smears, multiphonics, huge portamento effects, which fit equally comfortably into his funk and abstract idioms. Anderson's blues understanding, sharpened by a fruitful stint with saxophonist Bennie Wallace's revivalist project, is strongly featured on the very fine *Blues Bred In The Bone*. Anderson's partnership with Scofield on the haunting, self-written '53rd And Greenwood' is hard to fault, as is the fully-blown 'A Flower Is A Lovesome Thing'. Jazz was bred in the cornet, the clarinet, and the 'bone; Anderson is putting flesh on the tradition.

Right Down Your Alley is taut and to the point, and a slap in the face to those who regard solo trombone as a hubristic embarrassment in flight from its 'proper' section role in one of the back rows of the band. Here, as in the similarly constituted *Bass Drum Bone*, he plays with great discipline and control. *It Just So Happens* is perhaps his least well-defined recording to date, but it is adventurous and provocative in its remarkably traditionalist deployment of instrumental voices.

Anderson has had a happy time with Gramavision, though his non-exclusive deal there also seems to have accelerated his desire to diversify. Jim Anderson gives him a big-hearted sound, and the label seems more than broadly sympathetic to the trombonist's developing concern for environmental issues. The *Big Band Record* with George Gruntz's well-drilled outfit is excellent, and it's good to hear a player of Anderson's sensibilities working in this sort of context. From one perspective at least, it suits him better than the more skittish and free-form small groups. Certainly, the arrangement of 'Don't Mow Your Lawn', by now an Anderson staple, is superior to the version on the eponymous Enja, below. The high points on *Every One Of Us* are the original 'Muddy And Willie', one of Anderson's most sustained inventions, and a beautiful reading of Coltrane's 'Dear Lord'. The group is one of the best he's put together for years. Balancing Nabatov's super-committed approach, Haden and Blackwell tackle the session like veterans, unwilling to break sweat until they absolutely have to.

Perhaps typically, they sometimes – Haden especially – make it sound more like a job of work rather than a fun gig. On *Azurety* (less with the puns, already!), Doran and Bennink are more obviously matched to the leader's personality. The satirical side is catered for, most notably in titles like 'March of the Hipsters', but there is also some great, if hardly straightforward, playing. Bennink is a master drummer and hard to beat for sheer inventiveness of sound. Doran, as always, can conjure up a whole orchestra with his pedals and delays, but he can also pick delicate counterpoints. The follow-up *Cheer*

Up is better still, with some gloriously off-the-wall playing from all concerned on the long, presumably improvised 'Tabasco Cart' and the shorter 'Buckethead' (a tribute to one of the most enigmatic figures on the American scene). Some wonderfully tight writing, too, on things like 'My Children Are The Reason Why I Need To Own My Publishing' and 'Like Silver', confirming Anderson's uncomplicated musical intelligence. Doran plays a greater part this time around and gets an appopriate nod with the title-track, one of his own most confident creations. They even manage to squeeze in a version of Horace Silver's 'Melancholy Moods'.

The Alligatory Band, on *Don't Mow Your Lawn* and *Heads And Tails*, is generically closer to Slickaphonics than to the rest of the material here, but it fatally lacks the earlier group's what-the-hell insouciance and charm. Episodically, *Lawn* is a fine record, albeit with most of the interesting episodes credited to Soloff, but the singing is a turn-off and one's left with the feeling that Anderson can do better than this in his sleep . . .

. . . as proves to be the case with the follow-up, which is tightly constructed and sharp as a tack. The lyric on 'Tough Guy' is still a yawn (bow your head, Jackie Raven) but it's more than made up for by the recent of the set, which begins with a suite of four excellent compositions, grouped together as 'The Four Reasons' and including the quite superb 'Hunting And Gathering'.

Wessell Anderson ALTO AND SOPRANINO SAXOPHONES

*** **Warmdaddy In The Garden Of Swing** Atlantic 82657-2
    Anderson; Eric Reed (*p*); Ben Wolfe (*b*); Donald Edwards (*d*). 5/94.
*** **The Ways Of Warmdaddy** Atlantic 82860-2
    Anderson; Antoine Drye (*t*); Ellis Marsalis (*p*); Taurus Mateen (*b*); Donald Edwards (*d*). 6–7/ 95.

'Warmdaddy' Anderson's big, oleaginous sound spreads like molasses over the rhythms on the first record. It's a surprise that he starts the disc with a sopranino outing, 'The Black Cat', but the title blues tells more of what he's about. For the most part, the record is a dialogue between himself and Reed (a fellow bandmate in the Wynton Marsalis group), since Wolfe and Edwards play a very subsidiary role; and the problem here is the pianist's sometimes irritating manner of taking the trickiest path he can possibly find on an otherwise simple sequence. When they set down an actual duet, 'Go Slow For Mo'', they sound deadly serious.

The Ways Of Warmdaddy is a step forward. The material seems more focused, less wound-up: 'Change Of Heart' is a boppish blues executed with a fine bounce, 'Rockin' In Rhythm' is done with some panache, and the trio tracks in which Ellis Marsalis sits out are shouldered to good effect by the leader – 'Desimonae' sounds particularly fine. But so far Anderson hasn't solved a problem which seems to beset a number of Marsalis associates: he wants to play with the kind of unfettered, rocking swing that was second nature to pre-boppers, but he can't throw off the self-consciousness which that approach has built into it today. He could also use a second horn to strike sparks with: Drye's sole appearance on the second disc seems desultory.

Krister Andersson TENOR SAXOPHONE, CLARINET

***(*) **About Time** Flash Music FLCD 1
    Andersson; Ion Baciu (*p*); Torbjorn Hultcrantz, Markus Wikstrom (*b*); Leif Wennerstrom, Jan Robertson (*d*); Malando Gassama (*perc*). 93.

A rare outing as leader for this very accomplished Swedish tenorman. One of his models is Joe Henderson: the long, looping phrases and faintly querulous tone are familiar from the American's music. But Andersson is his own man. He thinks a long way ahead, mapping out improvisations with shrewd foresight so that they feel all of a piece, as spontaneous as they sound. 'How High The Moon' is coolly dismantled, an old bop blowing vehicle with all the clichés cleared away. The rhythm sections add anonymous support, somewhat in the manner of Tristano-school players, and it would be interesting to hear Andersson in the company of more assertive musicians. Gassama's guest presence on one track is also a mistake, since he sounds entirely wrong. Otherwise a fine record.

Leny Andrade VOCALS

(*) **Embraceable You Timeless CD SJP 365
    Andrade; Angelo Verploegen (*flh*); João Carlos Coutinho (*ky*); Lucio Nascimento (*b*); Adriano De Oliveira (*d*). 7/91.

*** **Maiden Voyage** Chesky J D 113
> Andrade; Fred Hersch (*p*); Dave Dunaway (*b*); Helio Schjiavo (*d*). 12/93.

Andrade has a pleasant if unexceptional voice and she tends to approach standard material by the numbers, rarely deviating from the most straightforward line of attack. She doesn't swing much herself and leaves a lot for her accompanists to do. The two quartet tracks with Verploegen added on flugelhorn are consistently more interesting than the trios, and it's a shame there aren't more of them. Oddly, the sound-balance is better, too, with Andrade placed a foot or two further from the mike. *Maiden Voyage* benefits from Fred Hersch's typically impeccable playing, nudging and cajoling the singer, and Andrade responds with some of her best work on a programme of standards and wistful Latin tunes.

Ernie Andrews (born 1927) VOCAL

*** **No Regrets** Muse MCD 5484
> Andrews; Houston Person (*ts*); Junior Mance (*p*); Jimmy Ponder (*g*); Ray Drummond (*b*); Michael Carvin (*d*). 8/92.

Nice to have a record in the catalogue by this journeyman vocalist. He's lost little of his blustering delivery, which sounded so effective in his cameo role on Kenny Burrell's *Ellington Is Forever*, and the blues comes naturally to a voice like this. Houston Person produced the session without much subtlety but with everyone encouraged to overplay; however, on 'When They Ask About You' and 'I'll Never Be Free' it musters the kind of saloon-singer feel everyone was after.

Peter Appleyard (born 1928) VIBES

** **Barbados Heat** Concord CCD 4436
> Appleyard; Rick Wilkins (*ts*); Bucky Pizzarelli (*g*); Major Holley (*b*); Butch Miles (*d*). 2/90.
(*) **Barbados Cool Concord CCD 4475
> As above. 2/90.

Appleyard is a veteran who has spent most of his playing life away from any jazz limelight, working in Canada and Bermuda. He played with Benny Goodman in the 1970s, and his Hampton-derived style obviously stood him in good stead there. These are the only records under his own name in print, both cut at a Barbados concert, and the uncomplicated swing makes for a typical Concord date. The sound-mix favours Miles, which is an advantage, since his rather noisy style gives the music some extra kick. Hackneyed material dominates the first record, although Wilkins gives a good account of 'Body And Soul'. Pizzarelli's feature on 'Passion Flower' ups the ante on *Cool*, but both records are potboilers.

Arcado GROUP

(*) **Arcado JMT 8344239
> Mark Dresser (*b*); Hank Roberts (*clo*); Mark Feldman (*vn*). 2/89.
***(*) **Behind The Myth** JMT 834441 As above. 3/90.

Arcado follow in the path of Billy Bang's String Trio of New York (and, by no means incidentally, new music prodigies, the Kronos Quartet) in exploring a range of instrumentation still considered problematic in small-group jazz. The debut album oozed promise, but it was with *Behind The Myth* that Arcado established themselves as something quite exceptional. The long title-track has moments of breathtaking beauty, with Feldman stretching above the lower strings. Though all the tracks are self-written, along the way they touch on influences as various as Django Reinhardt, Charles Mingus and, on the closing 'Somewhere', hints of Jimi Hendrix (for which they may well be indebted to the Kronos). Jazz with no horns? . . . no piano? . . . no drums? Purists will whisper anathemas, and will be the losers. Highly recommended.

*** **For Three Strings And Orchestra** JMT 849 152
> Mark Dresser (*b*); Mark Feldman (*vn*); Hank Roberts (*clo*); Kölner Rundfunkorchester. 6/91.

Not strictly a jazz album at all, but a fascinating experiment in large-scale writing by this adventurous group. There's no sense in which it's even an *un*orthodox triple concerto. The three principals seem to develop material unrelated to the background of each composition (one apiece and one, 'In Cold Moonlight', credited to Manfred Niehaus), with the exception of Feldman's long 'Naked Singularities' which has a persuasively cumulative logic that makes more effective use of (presumably) free elements than the other pieces. Perhaps a little too close to squeaky-door music for some tastes, but undeniably challenging.

Jimmy Archey (1902–67) TROMBONE

*** **Dr Jazz Vol. 4** Storyville STCD 6044
> Archey; Henry Goodwin (*t*); Benny Waters (*cl, ss, as*); Dick Wellstood (*p*); Pops Foster (*b*);
> Tommy Benford (*d*). 1–4/52.

** **Reunion** GHB BCD-310
> Archey; Punch Miller (*t*); Albert Burbank (*cl*); Dick Griffith (*bj*); Dick McCarthy (*b*); Sammy
> Penn (*d*). 2/67.

Rare examples of this redoubtable 'bone man as leader. The Storyville disc is from the *Dr Jazz* series of
radio broadcasts, and though as usual the band was encouraged to play overheated Dixieland, some
excellent moments survive. Waters, not often in the limelight at this stage of his career, is in top form,
and the rarely heard Goodwin stands comfortably beside the leader.

Archey was from Virginia, but the *Reunion* with a group of New Orleans players actually took place in
Connecticut. The material is bedraggled – and so, alas, is much of the playing: Burbank's agile phrasing
is flawed by his terribly squeaky tone, and Punch Miller was having an indifferent day. Archey's spirited,
melodic solos are much more encouraging, though, and the rhythm players make sure that the music
clatters along.

Julian Arguëlles (born 1966) TENOR SAXOPHONE

*** **Phaedrus** Ah Um 010
> Arguëlles; John Taylor (*p*); Mick Hutton (*b*); Martin France (*d*). 91.

***(*) **Phaedrus** Babel BDV 9503
> Arguëlles; Mike Walker (*g*); Steve Swallow (*b*); Martin France (*d*). 5/95.

The Arguëlles brothers – Julian and Steve – are, along with the Mondesirs, the Traceys and the
Bancrofts in Scotland, the closest thing to a significant family dynasty in British jazz. Both are richly
talented; both have created music of considerable individuality. *Phaedrus* is an encouragingly personal
sax-and-rhythm date for the young British saxophonist. Abjuring obvious role-models has apparently
led him in the direction of such players as Warne Marsh and some of the modern European masters, but
he tempers any danger of humourless expertise with some typically off-kilter melodies which Taylor, in
particular, underlines with harmonic and textural strength. While there are hints of deliberate foolish-
ness in some of the writing – a trait that continues to be a besetting sin among many British players – it
livens up the sometimes portentous Taylor no end, and Hutton and France play with plenty of enjoyment too.

If Arguëlles is a Good Thing, then so, too, is Oliver Weindling's Babel label, which has dedicated itself
to some of the most creative music around. It is a measure of the reputation of young Brits like
Arguëlles and guitarist Mike Walker that Steve Swallow should find time in a busy schedule to come and
record a session like this. To be frank, he makes it. Weaving in and around both Walker and Arguëlles, he
creates a skein of sound that is almost too beguiling, and the listener may end up pulled away from the
main action.

Steve Arguëlles (born 1963) DRUMS

*** **Blue Moon In A Function Room** Babel BDV 9402
> Arguëlles; Stuart Hall (*g, v*); Billy Jenkins (*g*); Steve Watts (*b*). 90.

*** **Busy Listening** Babel BDV 9406
> Arguëlles; Julian Arguëlles (*as*); Stuart Hall (*g, v*); Huw Warren (*acc*); Mick Hutton (*b*). 9/93.

***(*) **Recyclers / Rhymes** ZZ 84111
> Arguëlles; Noel Akchote (*g*); Benoit Delbecq (*p*). 93.

So richly and sympathetically has Britain nourished and nurtured talent like Arguëlles's that he has had
to move to France to find an acceptable amount of paid work. A familiar story, and a very galling one.
Fortunately, though he is less often to be heard at home, Arguëlles can now be found on CD. The
earliest of these goes back some way and is still a little self-conscious, bearing the stamp of Jenkins's
maverick genius. Items like 'Vision On', theme music to a British television programme for deaf children, seem unlikely in a jazz context, alongside 'Tiger Rag', 'Lady Be Good' (which is segued with
'Johnny B. Goode') and 'Ruby (Don't Take Your Love To Town)'. Hugely entertaining, but not by any
means as interesting as the material with Recyclers and on *Busy Listening*, both of which are splendidly
mature but not solemn, and packed with ideas without becoming po-faced. Arguëlles lays down a
crackling groove for his colleagues on both sets. Some of the laddishness has worn off, and the music is
all the better for it.

Lil Armstrong (1898–1971) PIANO, VOCAL

*** Lil Hardin Armstrong And Her Swing Orchestra 1936–1940 Classics 564
> Armstrong; Joe Thomas, Shirley Clay, Ralph Muzillo, Johnny McGee, Reunald Jones, Jonah
> Jones (*t*); Al Philburn, J. C. Higginbotham (*tb*); Buster Bailey, Tony Zimmers (*cl*); Don Stovall
> (*as*); Russell Johns, Prince Robinson, Robert Carroll, Chu Berry (*ts*); Frank Froeba, James
> Sherman, Teddy Cole (*p*); Arnold Adams, Huey Long, Dave Barbour (*g*); John Frazier,
> Wellman Braud, Haig Stephens (*b*); O'Neil Spencer, Sam Weiss, George Foster, Manzie Johnson
> (*d*); Midge Williams, Hilda Rogers (*v*). 10/36–3/40.

The former Mrs Armstrong was never much of a piano player, which may be why keyboard duties were
entrusted to others on most of these sessions. But her vocal talents were more likeable, and on these now
largely forgotten sides she comes on like a precursor of Nellie Lutcher and other, vaguely racy, post-war
singers. The accompaniments offer a rough distillation of small-band swing and rather older styles,
suggested by the presence of such veterans of the 1920s as Robinson and Clay, alongside the more
modernistic Thomas and Berry. Titles such as '(I'm On A) Sit-down Strike For Rhythm' have a self-
explanatory charm, and there's a more distinctive jazz content in the typically hot and fluent playing of
Bailey. On the final, 1940 date, Mrs Armstrong returns to the piano and leaves the singing to others. A
mixed bag as far as reproduction goes but mostly dubbed from decent originals.

*** Lil Hardin Armstrong – Chicago: The Living Legends Original Jazz Classics OJC 1823
> Armstrong; Bill Martin, Roi Nabors, Eddie Smith (*t*); Preston Jackson, Al Wynn (*tb*); Darnell
> Howard, Franz Jackson (*cl*); Pops Foster (*b*); Booker Washington (*d*). 9/61.

This collection of old-timers plays with astonishing vitality, even mania, on some of these tracks. 'Royal
Garden Blues' has seldom had such a shaking-down as it gets here: Howard's clarinet goes from a
woody moan to a near-shriek, and the trumpeters all take their turn to rattle the roof. There is also some
solid blues, an enjoyable feature for Lil's singing on 'Clip Joint', and 'Boogie Me', where she duets with
Washington and makes one wonder why she didn't play piano like that with the Hot Five. Hardly subtle,
but much merriment.

Louis Armstrong (1901–71) TRUMPET, CORNET, VOCAL

**** Louis Armstrong 1923–1931 Jazz Classics In Digital Stereo RPCD 618
> Armstrong; Zilmer Randolph, Otis Johnson, Henry Allen (*t*); King Oliver (*c*); John Thomas,
> Honore Dutrey, Preston Jackson, Jack Teagarden, J. C. Higginbotham, Fred Robinson (*tb*);
> Johnny Dodds (*cl*); Albert Nicholas, Charlie Holmes, Don Redman (*cl, as*); Jimmy Strong (*cl,
> ts*); Bert Curry, Crawford Wethington (*as*); Teddy Hill, Happy Caldwell (*ts*); George James,
> Albert Washington, Lester Boone (*reeds*); Lil Armstrong, Earl Hines, Joe Sullivan, Luis Russell,
> Charlie Alexander (*p*); Lonnie Johnson, Eddie Lang, Will Johnson (*g*); Bud Scott, Johnny St
> Cyr, Mancy Cara, Mike McKendrick (*bj*); Pete Briggs (*bb*); Joe Lindsay, Pops Foster (*b*); Baby
> Dodds, Zutty Singleton, Kaiser Marshall, Paul Barbarin, Tubby Hall (*d*). 6/23–11/31.

Knowing where to start with Armstrong's music on record is something of a problem for newcomers to
jazz, since his vast output has now been comprehensively reissued – but, alas, in a far from coherent
manner. This is the only compilation which starts with Armstrong in the King Oliver band and goes
through to his big-band work of the early 1930s. The 16 tracks are almost uniformly magnificent: three
of the finest Hot Seven sides, six Hot Fives including 'West End Blues' and 'Muggles', 'Symphonic
Raps' with the Carroll Dickerson band and 'Knockin' A Jug' from a 1929 all-star small-group date. But
the arbitrary nature of the record overall emphasizes that Armstrong's 1920s records are consistently
too valuable to be scattered across compilations. Even so, a fine introduction and, since Robert Parker
has remastered the disc for a second time, using the nearest-to-mint originals he could find, the sound is
now as fine as that of any reissue.

**** Louis Armstrong And The Blues Singers 1924–1930 Affinity AFS 1018-6 6CD
> Armstrong; Charlie Green, Aaron Thompson, Charlie Irvis, Kid Ory, Tommy Dorsey (*tb*);
> Sidney Bechet (*cl, ss*); Don Redman (*cl, as*); Jimmy Strong (*cl, ts*); Buster Bailey, Jimmie Noone,
> Artie Starks, Jimmy Dorsey (*cl*); Coleman Hawkins (*ts*); Fred Longshaw (*harm, p*); Justin Ring
> (*p, cel*); Fletcher Henderson, Lil Armstrong, James P Johnson, Richard M. Jones, Earl Hines,
> Hersal Thomas, Clarence Williams, Gene Anderson (*p*); Harry Hoffman, Joe Venuti (*vn*); Eddie
> Lang (*g*); Charlie Dixon, Buddy Christian, Johnny St Cyr, Mancy Cara (*bj*); Kaiser Marshall,
> Zutty Singleton (*d*); Ma Rainey, Virginia Liston, Eva Taylor, Alberta Hunter, Margaret
> Johnson, Sippie Wallace, Maggie Jones, Clara Smith, Bessie Smith, Trixie Smith, Billy Jones,
> Coot Grant, Wesley Wilson, Perry Bradford, Bertha 'Chippie' Hill, Blanche Calloway, Hociel
> Thomas, Baby Mack, Nolan Welsh, Butterbeans and Susie, Lillie Delk Christian, Seger Ellis,
> Victoria Spivey, Clarence Todd, Jimmie Rodgers (*v*). 10/24–7/30.

An astonishing collection. Armstrong worked as an accompanist to a number of singers in the 1920s, and although his records with Bessie Smith are well known, most of the others are familiar only to experienced Armstrong collectors. Yet there is enough material to fill six CDs, and this handsomely mounted set includes all of it. There are sessions with some of the greatest of the 'classic' blues singers, including Clara Smith, Trixie Smith, Chippie Hill, Alberta Hunter and Ma Rainey, as well as with more vaudeville-orientated singers such as Butterbeans and Susie, Eva Taylor and Lillie Delk Christian (who is backed by what was basically the Hot Five). Affinity have also rounded up oddities such as the beautiful 'Blue Yodel No. 9', where Armstrong plays a gorgeous accompaniment to country singer Jimmie Rodgers, and the amazing 'I Miss My Swiss', in which the Fletcher Henderson orchestra backs Billy Jones on a novelty tune which Armstrong utterly transforms with a glittering solo. The trumpeter often provides the only interest on many of the recordings and it's his ability to create parts of almost offhand radiance that sustains a listener even through six entire CDs. The remastering has been done using the CEDAR process and, while this sometimes has mixed results on recordings of varying original quality, there must be few complaints about the overall ambience of the sound. For specialists rather than general listeners, perhaps, but we give this the highest recommendation to anyone interested in Armstrong's work away from his most renowned sessions.

**** **The Hot Fives Vol. 1** Columbia 460821-2
    Armstrong; Kid Ory (*tb*); Johnny Dodds (*cl*); Lil Armstrong (*p*); Johnny St Cyr (*bj*). 11/25–6/26.
**** **The Hot Fives And Hot Sevens Vol. II** Columbia 463052-2
    As above, except add John Thomas (*tb*), Pete Briggs (*bb*); Baby Dodds (*d*), May Alix (*v*). 6/26–5/27.
  **** **Hot Fives And Sevens Vol. 1** JSP 312
    As above. 11/25–11/26.
**** **The Complete Hot Fives And Sevens Vol. 1** EMI Jazztime 781083-2
    As above. 11/25–11/26.
**** **Louis Armstrong 1925–1926** Classics 6
    As above. 11/25–11/26.
**** **The Hot Fives And Hot Sevens Vol. III** Columbia 465189-2
    As above, except add Lonnie Johnson (*g*). 5–12/27.
  **** **Hot Fives And Sevens Vol. 2** JSP 313
    As above. 5–12/27.
**** **The Complete Hot Fives And Hot Sevens Vol. 2** EMI Jazztime 781084-2
    As above. 11/25–12/27.
**** **Louis Armstrong & His Hot Five & Hot Seven** Classics 585
    As above. 5–12/27.
**** **Louis Armstrong And Earl Hines Vol. IV** Columbia 466308-2
    Armstrong; Fred Robinson (*tb*); Jimmy Strong (*cl, ts*); Don Redman (*cl, as, v*); Earl Hines (*p, cel, v*); Mancy Cara (*bj, v*); Zutty Singleton (*d*). 6–12/28.
  **** **Hot Fives And Sevens Vol. 3** JSP 314
    Armstrong; Homer Hobson (*t*); Fred Robinson, Jack Teagarden (*tb*); Bert Curry, Crawford Wethington (*as*); Jimmy Strong (*cl, ts*); Happy Caldwell (*ts*); Earl Hines (*p, cel, v*); Joe Sullivan (*p*); Carroll Dickerson (*vn*); Eddie Lang (*g*); Dave Wilborn (*bj, g*); Mancy Cara (*bj, v*); Pete Briggs (*bb*); Zutty Singleton, Kaiser Marshall (*d*). 6/28–2/29.
**** **The 25 Greatest Hot Fives And Hot Sevens** ASV AJA 5171
    As above. 25–29.

These are some of the most famous of all jazz recordings, and their power to astonish and invigorate listeners is undiminished, even after more than six decades. One is envious of those who hear master-pieces such as 'Potato Head Blues' or 'Hotter Than That' for the first time, for their beauty and intensity provide the most thrilling experiences to anyone who comes fresh to jazz. Countless listeners must have been converted into jazz fans by these tracks. The Hot Five and the subsequent larger group, the Hot Seven, were units which existed only in the recording studios, and their sessions were hurriedly arranged, but they showcase Armstrong's blossoming genius with brilliant clarity. His improvisations, ensemble parts and vocals are all imbued with an iconoclastic majesty which is sustained through almost all of their individual records. While the early sides feature a rough exuberance, Armstrong still finding his way but superbly creative on the likes of 'Cornet Chop Suey' and 'Jazz Lips', the Hot Seven tracks move with an almost furious power, exemplified in the overwhelming solo on 'Wild Man Blues', which in turn leads to the poetic, perhaps mollified grandeur of 'West End Blues', 'Muggles' and 'Tight Like This'. A detailed summary is beyond the scope of this book, but we must insist that any who are still unaware of these records make their acquaintance as soon as possible.

They have been reissued many times over the years, and OKeh's excellent studio sound has been faithfully transferred to a number of LP editions from the 1960s onwards. In the main we are disappointed with Columbia's transfers, which render some parts of the ensembles with poor clarity and generally lose much of the original life of the music (the disclaimer that 'it has been impossible to find clean copies of the 78-r.p.m. discs' is preposterous: as jazz 78s go, these are not rare records). They're not unlistenable, just short on what the records can deliver. John R. T. Davies's remastering of the material for JSP is, however, a superior effort which shames the Columbia engineering, and it's to these we award our 'crown'. The third volume includes the two tracks by Carroll Dickerson's Savoyagers, a sort of augmented Hot Five, and ends with the meeting of Armstrong with Teagarden, Eddie Lang and Joe Sullivan in the beautiful 'Knockin' A Jug'. Again, the transfers – though wholly unafraid of surface hiss – are marvellously clear and lifelike. The latest entries are the two discs in the French EMI Jazztime series, which follow the usual order and (so far) go up to 'Savoy Blues' from 1927. The sound here is quite truthful and lively. The Classics CDs commence a comprehensive overview of all of Armstrong's pre-war work under his own leadership, but again the sound is inferior to the JSP discs.

The ASV disc isn't far behind the best in terms of sound and, as a single-disc representation of some of the best in the series, this works pretty well.

**** **Louis In New York Vol. V** Columbia 466965-2
    Armstrong; Homer Hobson (*t*); Fred Robinson, Jack Teagarden, J. C. Higginbotham (*tb*); Jimmy Strong (*cl, ts*); Albert Nicholas, Charlie Holmes, Bert Curry, William Blue, Crawford Wethington (*as*); Happy Caldwell (*ts*); Joe Sullivan, Luis Russell, Buck Washington (*p*); Eddie Lang, Lonnie Johnson (*g*); Eddie Condon (*bj*); Pops Foster (*b*); Paul Barbarin, Kaiser Marshall (*d*); Hoagy Carmichael (*v*). 3/29–4/30.

**** **Big Bands Vol. 1** JSP 305
    Armstrong; Ed Anderson, Leon Elkins, George Orendorff, Harold Scott (*t*); Henry Hicks, Lawrence Brown, Luther Graven (*tb*); Bobby Holmes (*cl, as*); Castor McCord, Charlie Jones (*cl, ts*); Les Hite (*as, bs*); Theodore McCord, Leon Herriford, Willie Stark, Marvin Johnson (*as*); William Franz (*ts*); Joe Turner, Buck Washington, L. Z. Turner, Henry Prince (*p*); Bernard Addison, Bernard Prince (*g*); Ceele Burke (*bj*); Lavert Hutchinson, Reggie Jones (*bb*); Joe Bailey (*b*); Lionel Hampton (*d, vib*); Willie Lynch (*d*). 4/30–4/31.

**** **St Louis Blues Armstrong Vol. VI** Columbia 467919-2
    As above. 12/29–8/30.

**** **Big Bands Vol. 2** JSP 306
    Armstrong; Zilmer Randolph (*t*); Preston Jackson (*tb*); George James (*cl, ss, as*); Lester Boone (*cl, as*); Albert Washington (*cl, ts*); Charlie Alexander (*p*); Mike McKendrick (*g, bj*); John Lindsay (*b*); Tubby Hall (*d*). 4/31–3/32.

**** **You're Driving Me Crazy Vol. 7** Columbia 472992-2
    Similar to above. 10/30–4/31.

**** **Louis Armstrong & His Orchestra 1928–1929** Classics 570
    Personnel as listed under appropriate dates above. 6/28–3/29.

**** **Louis Armstrong & His Orchestra 1929–1930** Classics 557
    Personnel as listed under appropriate dates above. 3/29–5/30.

**** **Louis Armstrong & His Orchestra 1930–31** Classics 547
    Personnel as listed under appropriate dates above. 5/30–4/31.

**** **Louis Armstrong & His Orchestra 1931–32** Classics 536
    Personnel as listed under appropriate dates above. 11/31–3/32.

Following the final Hot Five records, Armstrong recorded almost exclusively as a soloist in front of big bands, at least until the formation of the All Stars in the 1940s. Although the records became much more formal in shape – most of them are recordings of contemporary pop tunes, opened by an Armstrong vocal and climaxing in a stratospheric solo – the finest of them showcase Louis as grandly as anything he'd already recorded. The Columbia *Louis In New York* is a close duplicate of Classics 557, though with fewer titles, and mainly covers the period when Armstrong was fronting the Luis Russell band. 'Black And Blue', 'Dallas Blues' and 'After You've Gone' offer superb improvisations against bland but functional backdrops, and while some of the sheer daring has gone out of Armstrong's playing, he's become more poised, more serenely powerful than before. Finer still, though, are the records made in Los Angeles in 1930 with, among others, the young Lionel Hampton. There are few Armstrong performances superior to 'Body And Soul', 'I'm A Ding Dong Daddy From Dumas' and 'Memories Of You', where his singing is as integral and inventive as his trumpet-playing, and the sequence culminates in the moving and transcendent playing of 'Sweethearts On Parade'. The 1931–2 sessions find him in front of another anonymous orchestra and, although arrangements and performances are again merely competent, they serve to throw the leader's own contributions into sharper relief, with 'Star Dust', 'Lawd, You Made The Night Too Long' and 'Chinatown, My Chinatown' among the outstanding tracks. These were his final recordings for OKeh before a move to Victor in 1933.

While the Columbia engineers have generally been a little more successful with these later records, we must again primarily recommend the excellent JSP transfers, although their packaging is less substantial. The Classics sequence, though, has the merit of uninterrupted chronological presentation at an attractive price and, while their transfers aren't always of the finest, there are no serious problems with the overall sound.

***(*) **Laughin' Louis 1932–1933** Bluebird ND 90404
    Armstrong; Louis Bacon, Louis Hunt, Billy Hicks, Charlie Gaines, Elmer Whitlock, Zilmer Randolph (*t*); Charlie Green, Keg Johnson (*tb*); Pete Clark, Scoville Brown, George Oldham (*cl, as*); Edgar Sampson (*as, vn*); Louis Jordan, Arthur Davey (*as*); Budd Johnson (*cl, ts*); Elmer Williams, Ellsworth Blake (*ts*); Don Kirkpatrick, Wesley Robinson, Teddy Wilson (*p*); Mike McKendrick (*bj, g*); John Trueheart (*g*); Ed Hayes, Bill Oldham (*bb, b*); Elmer James (*b*); Chick Webb, Benny Hill, Yank Porter (*d*). 12/32–4/33.

**** **Louis Armstrong & His Orchestra 1932–33** Classics 529
    As above. 12/32–4/33.

**** **Young Louis Armstrong (1930–1933)** RCA Tribune 15517-2 2CD
    As above. 30–33.

Armstrong's Victor records of 1932–3 are among his most majestic statements. If he had simplified his style, the breadth of his tone and seeming inevitability of timing and attack have been fashioned into an invincible creation: the way he handles 'I Gotta Right To Sing The Blues' or 'Basin Street Blues' makes them seem like conclusive offerings from jazz's greatest virtuoso. Even so, weaker material was already starting to creep into his repertoire, and even the title-track of *Laughin' Louis* gives some indication of what was happening to his music. The Bluebird collection is incomplete in terms of dealing with this period, but it's the best possible cross-section and the sound, although the NoNoise process won't be to all tastes, is dry but substantial. The Classics series continues apace and gathers in most of the Victor material on to one CD. RCA's two-disc set in their Tribune series covers 32 tracks and, though the remastering hasn't been improved from the variable LP edition, it still makes a tempting package.

**** **Louis Armstrong & His Orchestra 1934–36** Classics 509
    Armstrong; Jack Hamilton, Leslie Thompson, Leonard Davis, Gus Aiken, Louis Bacon, Bunny Berigan, Bob Mayhew (*t*); Lionel Guimaraes, Harry White, Jimmy Archey, Al Philburn (*tb*); Pete Duconge (*cl, as*); Sid Trucker (*cl, bs*); Henry Tyre, Henry Jones, Charlie Holmes, Phil Waltzer (*as*); Alfred Pratt, Bingie Madison, Greely Walton, Paul Ricci (*ts*); Herman Chittison, Luis Russell, Fulton McGrath (*p*); Maceo Jefferson, Lee Blair, Dave Barbour (*g*); German Artango, Pops Foster, Pete Peterson (*b*); Oliver Tynes, Paul Barbarin, Stan King (*d*). 10/34–2/36.

***(*) **Rhythm Saved The World** MCA GRP 16022
    Largely as above. 10/35–2/36.

***(*) **Louis Armstrong & His Orchestra 1936–37** Classics 512
    As above, except add Snub Mosley, Bobby Byrne, Joe Yukl, Don Mattison (*tb*); Jimmy Dorsey, Jack Stacey (*cl, as*); Fud Livingston, Skeets Herfurt (*cl, ts*); Bobby Van Eps (*p*); George Archer, Harry Baty (*g, v*); Roscoe Hillman (*g*); Sam Koki (*stg*); Andy Iona (*uke, v*); Jim Taft, Joe Nawahi (*b*); Ray McKinley, Lionel Hampton (*d*); Bing Crosby, Frances Langford, The Mills Brothers (*v*). 2/36–4/37.

**** **Louis Armstrong & His Orchestra 1937–38** Classics 515
    Armstrong; Shelton Hemphill, Louis Bacon, Henry Allen (*t*); George Matthews, George Washington, J. C. Higginbotham, Wilbur De Paris (*tb*); Pete Clark, Charlie Holmes, Rupert Cole (*as*); Albert Nicholas, Bingie Madison (*cl, ts*); Luis Russell (*p*); Lee Blair (*g*); Pops Foster, Red Callender (*b*); Paul Barbarin (*d*); The Mills Brothers (*v*). 6/37–5/38.

***(*) **Louis Armstrong & His Orchestra 1938–39** Classics 523
    As above, except add Bob Cusamano, Johnny McGee, Otis Johnson, Frank Zullo, Grady Watts, Sonny Dunham (*t*); Al Philburn, Murray McEachern, Russell Rauch, Pee Wee Hunt (*tb*); Sid Stoneburn (*cl*); Art Ralston, Clarence Hutchinrider (*as*); Pat Davis, Dan D'Andrea, Joe Garland (*ts*); Kenny Sargent (*bs*); Nat Jaffe, Howard Hall (*p*); Jack Blanchette, Dave Barbour (*g*); Haig Stephens, Stan Dennis (*b*); Sam Weiss, Big Sid Catlett, Tony Briglia (*d*). 5/38–4/39.

*** **Vol. 2 – Heart Full Of Rhythm** Decca/MCA GRD-620
    As above discs. 4/36–12/38.

***(*) **Vol. 3 – Pocketful Of Dreams** Decca/MCA GRD-649
    As above. 10/35–6/38.

*** **Louis Armstrong 1939–1940** Classics 615
    Armstrong; Shelton Hemphill, Otis Johnson, Henry Allen, Bernard Flood (*t*); Wilbur De Paris, George Washington, J. C. Higginbotham (*tb*); Charlie Holmes, Rupert Cole (*cl, as*); Joe Garland, Bingie Madison (*ts*); Luis Russell (*p*); Lee Blair (*g*); Pops Foster (*b*); Big Sid Catlett (*d*); The Mills Brothers (*v*). 4/39–4/40.

***(*) Louis Armstrong 1940–1942 Classics 685

As above, except add Gene Prince, Frank Galbreath (*t*); Claude Jones, Norman Greene, Henderson Chambers, James Whitney (*tb*); Sidney Bechet (*cl, ss*); Carl Frye (*as*); Prince Robinson (*cl, ts*); Bernard Addison, Lawrence Lucie (*g*); John Simmons, Hayes Alvis, Wellman Braud (*b*); Zutty Singleton (*d*). 5/40–4/42.

Armstrong's Decca recordings in the 1930s have been a maligned and undervalued group, seldom reissued and often written off as a disastrous pop period. While there are many throwaway songs and plain bad ideas – even Louis couldn't do much with 'She's The Daughter Of A Planter From Havana' and its sorry ilk – he does rise above the circumstances much as Fats Waller and Billie Holiday do in the same period: the sheer *sound* of Armstrong, whether singing or playing trumpet, is exhilarating. The sequential Classics issues are therefore very welcome. The 1934–5 disc includes a memorable session made in Paris with a local band including the very fine pianist, Herman Chittison, with a terrific 'St Louis Blues'; from there, Armstrong is backed mostly by a Luis Russell band, and it performs very creditably, with some members stepping forward for occasional solos. 1936–7 includes two tremendous pieces in 'Swing That Music' and 'Mahogany Hall Stomp' as well as a peculiar meeting with a Hawaiian group and two dates with the Mills Brothers. The fine session from January 1938 is on the next disc, with Albert Nicholas almost stealing the occasion on 'Struttin' With Some Barbecue' until Louis's own solo. The 1938–9 record has a session with the Casa Loma Orchestra, another with a rather white-toned gospel group, the lovely 'My Walking Stick' with the Mills Brothers and a concluding date which remakes 'West End Blues' and Don Redman's 'Save It, Pretty Mama'. Classics 615 has some miserable stuff of the order of 'Me And Brother Bill' but peaks on a new 'Confessin'', a fine 'Wolverine Blues' and a stunning new 'Sweethearts On Parade'. The final disc in the sequence, Classics 685, is again rather dated, although it includes the complete reunion date with Bechet from May 1940 and has a majestic 'When It's Sleepy Time Down South' – not the last track, but a suitable climax. We must award all these high marks, if only for the occasions when the material, music and Armstrong himself are all strong. The transfers are mainly very good. The first MCA compilation takes a look at one of the most enjoyable of this run of sessions, from 1935–6, with 'I've Got My Fingers Crossed', 'Solitude' and 'I'm Putting All My Eggs In One Basket' among the standouts. Having creamed off the best of those, the second disc, *Rhythm Saved The World*, is a little less consistent, though there are still half a dozen tracks that any Armstrong collector should have; together, these two make a good sampler of the period. Some may prefer the highly cleaned-up sound of these transfers using the NoNoise system. It sounds even better on *Vol. 3: Pocketful Of Dreams*, which suggests that the engineers are getting the measure of this process. This concentrates on 1938 dates and presents them in exceptionally clean sound, and what should tempt most Armstrong collectors is the presence of four alternative takes, including one of 'Got A Bran' New Suit' from one of the 1935 dates.

*** On The Sunny Side Of The Street Jazz J-CD-19

Armstrong; Shelton Hemphill, Frank Galbreath, Bernard Flood, Robert Butler, Louis Gray, Fats Ford (*t*); George Washington, Henderson Chambers, James Whitney, Russell Moore, Waddet Williams, Nat Allen, James Whitney (*tb*); Don Hill, Amos Gordon, Rupert Coile (*as*); Dexter Gordon, Budd Johnson, John Sparrow (*ts*); Ernest Thompson (*bs*); Prince Robinson, Joe Garland, Carl Frye (*saxes*); Luis Russell, Earl Mason, Gerald Wiggins (*p*); Elmer Warner, Lawrence Lucie (*g*); Art Simmons, Arvell Shaw (*b*); Chick Morrison, Edmond McConney, Jesse Price (*d*); The Mills Brothers, Velma Middleton, Jimmy Anderson, Ann Baker, Bea Booze (*v*). 6/38–8/46.

A very entertaining compilation of broadcast and soundtrack material. Three shows for forces radio feature plenty of mugging and a degree of great trumpet, though a soundtrack reading of 'Jeepers Creepers' also has a strong solo, and a closing and very frantic 'Hot Chestnuts' is surprisingly wild. Sound-quality is very clean for all except two tracks, which suffer from some distortion.

**** From The Big Band To The All Stars (1946–1956) RCA Tribune ND 89279 2CD

Armstrong; Bobby Hackett, Manny Klein, Zeke Zarchey, Louis Bacon, Louis Hunt, Williams Hicks (*t*); Jack Teagarden (*tb, v*); Kid Ory, Charlie Green, Si Zentner, Ed Kusby, George Roberts (*tb*); Barney Bigard (*cl*); Peanuts Hucko (*cl, ts*); Ernie Caceres (*cl, bs*); Jack Dumont, Edgar Sampson (*as*); Ronnie Lang, Babe Russin, Elmer Williams (*ts*); Chuck Gentry (*bs*); Johnny Guarnieri, Gerald Wiggins, Don Kirkpatrick (*p, cel*); Dick Cary, Charlie Beal (*p*); Bud Scott, Al Casey, John Trueheart, Al Hendrickson (*g*); Bob Haggart, Red Callender, Elmer James, Joe Comfort, Al Hall (*b*); George Wettling, Minor Hall, Cozy Cole, Chick Webb, Irving Cottler (*d*). 12/32–8/56.

***(*) Town Hall Concert Plus RCA 13036-2

As above, except add Charlie Shavers, Neal Hefti (*t*); Jimmy Hamilton (*cl*); Johnny Hodges (*as*); Don Byas (*ts*); Duke Ellington, Billy Strayhorn (*p*); Remo Palmieri, Allan Reuss (*g*); Red Callender (*b*); Zutty Singleton (*d*). 1/46–6/47.

**** **The Complete Town Hall Concert** RCA Tribune ND 89746 2CD
      Armstrong; Bobby Hackett (*t*); Jack Teagarden (*tb, v*); Peanuts Hucko (*cl*); Dick Cary (*p*); Bob
      Haggart (*b*); George Wettling, Big Sid Catlett (*d*). 5/47.

After some years of comparative neglect, Armstrong bounced back via the film *New Orleans*, which was
made during the period covered by the earliest tracks here, and the formation of the All Stars, a move
initiated by the 1947 New York Town Hall concert. With vintage jazz undergoing something of a
revival, Armstrong sounded like a pillar: his playing here on 'Back O'Town Blues', 'Jack-Armstrong
Blues' and another 'Mahogany Hall Stomp' has riveting intensity. Teagarden matches him with his own
playing, and the full recording of the concert is a prime document of the period. Contemporaneous
small-band recordings make up most of the other RCA Tribune set, with two stray 1956 tracks and
(inexplicably) an odd one from 1932 at the end. Great music from a master still at the top of his game.
Town Hall Concert Plus takes nine tracks from these sessions, plus three from various other dates,
including an Esquire Award Winners date, where Pops met Duke on record for the first time. A somewhat oddball issue that follows an original LP edition.

***(*) **Plays W. C. Handy** Columbia 450981-2
      Armstrong; Trummy Young (*tb*); Barney Bigard (*cl*); Billy Kyle (*p*); Arvell Shaw (*b*); Barrett
      Deems (*d*); Velma Middleton (*v*). 6/54.
*** **Satch Plays Fats** Columbia 450980-2
      As above. 4–5/55.

Two of Louis's best studio records of the 1950s. When granted an intelligent choice of programme,
Armstrong still sounded in imperious command, and the Handy collection in particular sounds like a
master delivering a definitive interpretation of a sequence of standards. While he sounds more comfortable on the slower numbers – such as a stately 'Hesitating Blues' – his singing is eloquent throughout,
and just as fine on the Waller collection, although here the showbiz characteristics which stick to many
of the tunes renege on their jazz content. The All Stars were playing well enough, but Young is scarcely a
strong replacement for Teagarden, no matter how lax the latter might become, and the ratings for almost
all the All Stars records from this point refer only to Louis himself: without him, the band would
amount to nothing at all. Remastering of both discs is good.

**** **The California Concerts** MCA GRP 4 6132 4CD
      Armstrong; Jack Teagarden, Trummy Young (*tb, v*); Barney Bigard (*cl, v*); Earl Hines, Billy Kyle
      (*p*); Arvell Shaw (*b*); Barrett Deems, Cozy Cole (*d*); Velma Middleton (*v*). 1/51–1/55.
***(*) **Chicago Concert** Columbia 471870-2 2CD
      As above, except add Ed Hall (*cl*), Dale Jones (*b*); omit Teagarden, Bigard, Hines, Shaw, Cole
      and Middleton. 6/56.

Armstrong's period with the All Stars has also been treated unfairly over the years. While there have
been many indifferent and low-fi concert recordings floating around on dubious labels, these well-
packaged and handsomely remastered collections call for a new appraisal of the group. The superb
MCA set, spread across four CDs, covers two dates four years apart: the original All Stars with
Teagarden and Hines, and the more familiar later group with Young and Kyle. Pops is in good form
throughout and, though the vaudevillian aspects of the group often take precedence, there is always
some piece of magic from the leader that transforms routine; his singing, as nearly always, is beyond
reproof. There are many previously unreleased tracks and a good deal of straight-ahead jazz. The
Chicago Concert date is slighter stuff, but there are still memorable takes of 'Black And Blue', 'Tenderly'
and 'Struttin' With Some Barbecue'.

*** **Satchmo A Musical Autobiography Vol. 1** Jazz Unlimited JUCD 2003
      Armstrong; Yank Lawson (*t*); Jack Teagarden, Trummy Young (*tb*); Ed Hall, Barney Bigard
      (*cl*); Dick Cary, Earl Hines, Billy Kyle (*p*); Everett Barksdale, George Barnes (*g*); Squire Gersh,
      Arvell Shaw (*b*); Cozy Cole, Big Sid Catlett, Barrett Deems (*d*); Velma Middleton (*v*). 11/47–1/
      57.
*** **Satchmo A Musical Autobiography Vol. 2** Jazz Unlimited JUCD 2004
      As above, except add Lucky Thompson (*ts*), George Dorsey (*as, f*), Dave McRae (*bs, basx*),
      Kenny John (*d*), omit Teagarden, Cary, Hines, Catlett, Bigard. 1/51–1/57.
*** **Satchmo A Musical Autobiography Vol. 3** Jazz Unlimited JUCD 2005
      As above, except omit Lawson and John. 1/55–1/57.

Armstrong tells something of his life and career in the spoken intros to most of the tracks on these three
CDs. This should have been some of the most worthwhile Armstrong of the period, with the material
including plenty of tunes he hadn't returned to for many years, but the arrangements by Bob Haggart or
Sy Oliver are a bit tight and Dixielandish, with the tempos a shade too taut to suit him. That said, it's
still a pleasure to hear him go back to the likes of 'Knockin' A Jug'. The remastered sound is a little thin
compared with that of the Columbia discs of the period.

*** **Satchmo The Great** Columbia 476896-2
> Armstrong; Trummy Young (*tb*); Edmond Hall (*cl*); Billy Kyle (*p*); Arvell Shaw, Dale Jones (*b*); Barrett Deems (*d*); Lewisohn Stadium Symphony Orchestra with Leonard Bernstein. 10/55–11/57.

A fascinating documentary piece, based around a film with Ed Murrow commentating. A few All Stars tracks mingle with a beguiling chat with Louis, his triumphant arrival in Accra for an African visit, and the celebrated orchestral concert version of 'St Louis Blues' with Bernstein conducting and W. C. Handy watching from the audience. Not a record to get off the shelf very often, but indispensable Armstrong trivia.

*** **Porgy And Bess** Verve 827475-2
> Armstrong; Ella Fitzgerald (*v*); Russell Garcia Orchestra. 8/57.

(*) **Louis Armstrong: The Silver Collection Verve 823446-2
> Armstrong; Russell Garcia Orchestra. 8/57.

*** **Louis Armstrong Meets Oscar Peterson** Verve 825713-2
> Armstrong; Oscar Peterson (*p*); Herb Ellis (*g*); Ray Brown (*b*); Louie Bellson (*d*). 7–10/57.

*** **Verve Jazz Masters: Louis Armstrong** Verve 519818-2
> Armstrong; Trummy Young (*tb*); Ed Hall (*cl*); Billy Kyle, Oscar Peterson (*p*); Herb Ellis (*g*); Ray Brown, Dale Jones (*b*); Louie Bellson, Barrett Deems (*d*); Ella Fitzgerald (*v*); Russell Garcia Orchestra. 8/56–10/57.

*** **Verve Jazz Masters: Ella Fitzgerald & Louis Armstrong** Verve 521851-2
> As above discs.

*** **Jazz Around Midnight: Louis Armstrong** Verve 843422-2
> As above, except add Tyree Glenn (*tb*), Buster Bailey (*cl*), Marty Napoleon (*p*), Alfred Di Lernia (*bj*), Buddy Catlett (*b*), Danny Barcelona (*d*). 7/57–5/66.

***(*) **Let's Do It** Verve 529017-2 2CD
> As above discs, except add Big Chief Russell Moore (*tb*), Joe Darensbourg (*cl*), Everett Barksdale (*g*), Arvell Shaw (*b*). 8/57–9/64.

Verve recorded Armstrong with a little more initiative as regards concepts, but it didn't always work out. The two-handed version of *Porgy And Bess* didn't suit either Ella or Louis very well: it's too stiff and formalized for either one to loosen up either vocally or instrumentally, some nice moments notwithstanding. *The Silver Collection* finds Armstrong fronting Russell Garcia's hearty though not graceless orchestra with his usual aplomb, and comparing, say, 'I Gotta Right To Sing The Blues' with his version of some 25 years earlier isolates the maturity of Armstrong's later art: he hasn't the chops for grandstand improvisations any more, but his sense of timing and his treatment of pure melody are almost as gratifying. Yet some of the songs end up as merely dull. The meeting with Oscar Peterson's trio is another very mixed success: not because Peterson is too modern for Armstrong, but because he can't avoid his besetting pushiness. On the slower tunes, though, especially 'Sweet Lorraine' and 'Let's Fall In Love', the chemistry works, and Louis is certainly never intimidated. Both of the two compilations are quite thoughtfully chosen and, with the spotlight primarily on Louis's singing, the VJM disc is a good sampler of the period.

Dan Morgenstern's selection and notes for *Let's Do It*, a comprehensive overview of Louis with Verve, make a good case for reconsidering this period. If one wants a single selection here, this is certainly the one to go for, with some of his very best moments with Ella, Russ Garcia and Peterson carefully sequenced.

*** **Mack The Knife** Pablo 2310941
> Armstrong; Trummy Young (*tb*, *v*); Edmond Hall (*cl*); Billy Kyle (*p*); Squire Gersh (*b*); Barrett Deems (*d*). 7/57.

(*) **Basin Street Blues Black Lion BLCD 760128
> As above, except add Dale Jones (*b*). 8/56–10/57.

There seem to be many, many All Stars concerts which have survived on tape, and these two are no better or worse than any for the period. They're also all pretty much the same, songwise and treatmentwise. But the Pablo set, which includes a slightly more concentrated amount of jazz material, is marginally the better, with certainly the better sound.

*** **Ella And Louis Again Vol. 1** Verve 825373-2
> Armstrong; Oscar Peterson (*p*); Herb Ellis (*g*); Ray Brown (*b*); Louie Bellson (*d*); Ella Fitzgerald (*v*). 57.

*** **Ella And Louis Again Vol. 2** Verve 825374-2
> As above. 57.

*** **Verve Jazz Masters 24: Ella Fitzgerald & Louis Armstrong** Verve 521851-2
> As above discs. 56–57.

There's something too respectful about the various meetings of these great singers on record: Fitzgerald never gets ripe the way Velma Middleton does and, while that may be asking too much of such a stately singer, there's only the slightest sense of interaction during this lengthy session. But hearing the two great voices on the same record is still rather fine, even if it doesn't live up to potential. The *Jazz Masters* disc chooses some of the best from their various meetings.

**(*) Americans In Sweden Tax CD 3712-2
> Armstrong; Trummy Young (*tb, v*); Peanuts Hucko (*cl*); Billy Kyle (*p*); Mort Herbert (*b*); Danny Barcelona (*d*); Velma Middleton (*v*). 1/59.

The Stockholm concert is an unusually crisp and forthright example of a latter-day All Stars performance: the sound is clear and well balanced, and Louis's singing is impeccable, although most of the instrumental spots are given over to the band.

**** Louis Armstrong & Duke Ellington: The Complete Sessions Roulette CDP 793844-2
> Armstrong; Trummy Young (*tb*); Barney Bigard (*cl*); Duke Ellington (*p*); Mort Herbert (*b*); Danny Barcelona (*d*). 4/61.

These sessions have never been highly regarded: Ellington is more or less slumming it with the All Stars, and some of his piano parts do sound eccentrically isolated. Yet this is Armstrong's date, not his, even with all the material composed by Duke: Louis stamps his imprimatur on it from the first vocal on 'Duke's Place'. His occasional frailties and the sometimes tired tempos only personalize further his single opportunity to interpret his greatest contemporary at length. On the extraordinarily affecting 'I Got It Bad And That Ain't Good' or the superbly paced 'It Don't Mean A Thing', Louis reflects on a parallel heritage of tunes which his traditional proclivities perhaps denied him; and the results are both moving and quietly eloquent. The sound is excellent on CD, although the music is also spread across two LPs, *Together For The First Time* (Roulette ROU 1007) and *The Great Reunion* (Roulette ROU 1008).

**(*) The Real Ambassadors Columbia 476897-2
> Armstrong; Trummy Young (*tb, v*); Joe Darensbourg (*cl*); Billy Kyle, Dave Brubeck (*p*); Gene Wright, Irving Manning (*b*); Joe Morello, Danny Barcelona (*d*); Carmen McRae, Annie Ross, Dave Lambert, Jon Hendricks (*v*). 9–12/61.

A sort of oratorio, nearly an opera, a bit of this and that, cobbled together by Brubeck to feature his band, the All Stars, McRae, Lambert, Hendricks and Ross, and especially Armstrong himself. With lyrics by Iola Brubeck, the whole is like a dated fantasy on a Bill of Rights, but somehow Louis overcomes the fluff and adds dignity, which McRae, in her imperious way, also grafts something on to. Some bits of awesome kitsch mingle with some genuinely judicious and impressive music.

** Masters Of Jazz: Louis Armstrong Storyville SLP 4101
> Armstrong; Trummy Young (*tb*); Joe Darensbourg (*cl*); Billy Kyle (*p*); Billy Cronk (*b*); Danny Barcelona (*d*). 8/62.

* Louis Armstrong & The All Stars 1965 EPM Musique FDC 5100
> As above, except Eddie Shu (*cl*) and Arvell Shaw (*b*) replace Darensbourg and Cronk; add Jewel Brown (*v*). 3/65.

By the mid-1960s, Armstrong's powers as a trumpeter were finally in serious decline, and there are sad moments among the glimmers of greatness which remain. The Storyville date isn't bad, but the band sound overcome by ennui, while the other disc, recorded at concerts in Prague and East Berlin, is poorly recorded and, aside from a moving version of Fats Waller's 'Black And Blue', scarcely worth hearing.

** What A Wonderful World Bluebird ND 88310
> Armstrong; studio orchestra. 70.

The final studio recordings have little to do with jazz but much to do with Armstrong, since his voice is by now so inimitable that it transcends any material which could be put before it. Nevertheless, it is in other respects a record of few pleasures.

Dag Arnesen PIANO

*** Renascent Odin NJ 4030-2
> Arnesen; Bjorn Kjellemyr (*b*); Sven Christiansen (*d*). 5/84.

** The Day After Taurus TRCD 829
> As above, except add Odd Riisnaes (*ss, ts*), Wenche Gausdal (*v*). 2/90.

** Photographs Taurus TRCD 830
> As above, except Terje Gewelt (*b*) replaces Kjellemyr and Riisnaes.

*** Movin' Taurus TRCD 832

As above, except omit Gausdal. 1–2/94.

Arnesen's romantic kind of post-bop falls easily on the ear. The trio session (an earlier sextet LP, *N Y Bris*, Odin LP02, is worth seeking out) has some boldly lyrical writing where the lush voicings and ear-catching melodies are reinforced by the assurance of the playing, with Kjellemyr and Christiansen absolutely behind him. Only a fey treatment of Monk's 'Played Twice' lets him down. But the Taurus albums take a different route with the arrival of vocalist Gausdal, who co-writes much of the material. Despite some fine work by the players on both records, Gausdal's studied pronunciation, flimsy lyrics and plain lack of authority are deeply unfortunate. *Movin'* gets the pianist back on the track: this is a strong trio and, though Arnesen's composing is no more than functional, the calibre of the playing engages the ear. Gewelt also contributes the most interesting tune, 'Maybe'.

Kenneth Arnstrom (born 1946) TENOR SAXOPHONE, CLARINET

*** Saxcess Phontastic NCD 8836

Arnstrom; Jan Stolpe (*t*); Pelle Larsson (*p*); Dan Berglund (*b*); Hasse Linskog (*d*); Sabina Have (*v*). 1–7/95.

The enigmatic Arnstrom disappeared from Swedish jazz for 15 years, having established a name for himself as a big-toned tenorman in the classic manner (he founded the Kenneth label). This seems to be a first album under his own name, tempted back to playing after working as a carpenter, and only the cursory support and off-the-cuff tune choices withhold a higher commendation: his own playing is in the top class. He musters a fluent delivery, but it's edged by a black tone that intensifies when his phrases turn vehement – scarcely a solo goes by without some seemingly angry turn of expression. Partnered by Stolpe, who comes on like Louis Armstrong was still everybody's main influence on the horn, this gives the front line a rare virility. The rhythm section are much more polite and Have's three vocals sound almost demure. This one will surprise anyone expecting a sunny mainstream date.

Art Ensemble Of Chicago GROUP

**** Art Ensemble 1967–68 Nessa NCD-2500 5CD

Lester Bowie (*t, flhn, perc*); Roscoe Mitchell (*saxes, perc*); Joseph Jarman (*saxes, bsn, cl*); Malachi Favors (*b, zith*); Charles Clark (*b*); Phillip Wilson, Thurman Barker, Robert Crowder (*d*). 67–68.

*** Tutankhamun Black Lion BLCD760199

As above, except omit Clarke, Wilson, Barker and Crowder. 6/69.

Those who know the Art Ensemble of Chicago only by their considerable reputation may be disappointed by their work as it's been documented on record. Bowie, Jarman, Favors and Mitchell, later joined by percussionist Famoudou Don Moye, have been celebrated as among the most radical and innovative musicians in the intensely creative environment which was centred on Chicago's AACM movement in the 1960s. Unsurprisingly, they had to uproot and head for Europe in order to find work and recording opportunities at the time, and most of their music remains on European labels. As a mix of personalities, the Ensemble has always been in a crisis of temperament, with Bowie's arsenal of sardonic inflexions pitched against Mitchell's schematic constructions, Jarman's fierce and elegant improvising and Favors's other-worldly commentaries from the bass. Satire, both musical and literal, has sustained much of their music; long- and short-form pieces have broken jazz structure down into areas of sound and silence. At their best, they are as uncompromisingly abstract as the most severe European players, yet their materials are cut from the heart of the traditions of black music in Chicago and St Louis.

The Nessa five-disc set (which is a limited though very expensive edition) compiles three previously issued LPs – Mitchell's *Congliptious* and *Old/Quartet*, and Bowie's *Numbers 1 & 2* – along with some 2½ hours of previously unreleased workshop tapes, alternative takes and some demos. Historically, with relatively little of the Chicago free masters having been documented at the time, this is of great importance and, while the best music is probably that heard on those original albums, there are some fascinating things in the sometimes messy alternative tracks and rehearsals, with the legendary Clark and drummers Crowder and Barker making rare appearances. For specialists, arguably, but there is much here that deserves wider circulation – especially as a spate of recording in France in 1969 is currently out of print, aside from the recently reissued *Tutankhamun*. Typical of the Ensemble's hit-and-miss strategies, this collects three noisy, reflective, ambitious pieces and can almost act as a sampler of the period.

*** Live Delmark DE-432
   As above, plus Famoudou Don Moye (*d*). 1/72.
*** Nice Guys ECM 1126
   As above. 5/78.
*** Full Force ECM 1167
   As above. 1/80.
**** Urban Bushmen ECM 1211/1212 2CD
   As above. 5/80.

The Ensemble made only a handful of discs in the 1970s, all now hard to find. But the live session recorded at Chicago's Mandel Hall in 1972 has recently been remastered for CD. This was something of a homecoming affair and there is much jubilation in the playing, but the recording remains imperfect, the detail skimped, and in a continuous 76-minute performance there are inevitable dead spots which the Ensemble have never truly found a way of avoiding. It wasn't until they secured a deal with ECM that they were finally given the opportunity to record in the sonic detail which their work has always demanded. Even so, the two studio albums were good yet unexceptional instances of the group at work. *Nice Guys* has two absorbing Jarman pieces in '597-59' and 'Dreaming Of The Master' but the attempt at a ska beat in 'JA' is unconvincing and much of the music seems almost formulaic, the improvisation limited. *Full Force* is a little more outgoing without cutting loose, and the lengthy 'Magg Zelma' seems long-winded rather than epic in its movement. The Ensemble's concert appearances could still generate music of blistering power, which made their apparently desultory records all the more frustrating. So the live *Urban Bushmen*, while still somewhat muted and inevitably deprived of the theatrical impact of the Ensemble's in-person charisma, proved to be their most worthwhile record for many years. Spread over 90 minutes, the group displayed their virtuosity on a vast panoply of devices (Jarman alone is credited with playing 14 different wind instruments, along with sundry items of percussion) and the patchwork of musics adds up to a tying together of their many endeavours in form and content. Certainly the best introduction to their work.

**(*) The Third Decade ECM 1273
   As above. 6/84.

A dispiriting continuation after another longish absence from the studios. Embarking on their third decade together suggested nothing so much as the atrophy of a once-radical band. The horn players are as spikily creative as ever in the moments where the Ensemble parts to reveal them, but the crucial decline is in the quality of interaction: several of these pieces dispel the collective identity of the group rather than binding it together.

*** Live In Japan DIW 8005
   As above. 4/84.
*** The Complete Live In Japan DIW 8021/2 2CD
   As above. 4/84.

The AEOC commenced a new contract with the Japanese DIW company with this worthwhile though hardly enthralling live set (the first record is a distillation of the concert, which appears in its completeness on the subsequent double-album and CD). Some of the earlier ECM material appears in concert form: the differences in emphasis are interesting, if little more. Acceptable rather than outstanding sound.

*** Naked DIW 8011
   As above. 11/85–7/86.
**(*) Vol. I: Ancient To The Future DIW 8014
   As above, plus Bahnamous Lee Bowie (*ky*). 3/87.

The group's recording for DIW continued with records which, because of their limited distribution, caused little excitement. But the music continued to be a revisiting of old haunts rather than anything strikingly new. Mitchell and Bowie were, in any case, more active elsewhere. A taste for fanciful, zig-zagging hard bop lightens some of *Naked*, and the impeccable recording affords some pleasure in just listening to the sound of Jarman, Mitchell and Favors in particular. But the attempts at rounding up 'the tradition' on DIW 8014 include poorly conceived stabs at 'Purple Haze' and 'No Woman No Cry' which mock their mastery.

**** The Alternate Express DIW 8033
   As above. 1/89.

When it seemed the AEOC was all but spent, they pulled out this tremendously powerful session. The huge, blustering 'Kush' rekindles the wildness of their best improvising; 'Imaginary Situations' is a ghostly collective sketch; 'Whatever Happens' catches Bowie at his melancholy best, while Mitchell's title-piece is a fine tribute to the group's in-bred spirit. A valuable and welcome document that might be called a comeback.

**(*) Art Ensemble Of Soweto DIW 837
    As above, plus Elliot Ngubane (*v, ky, perc*); Joe Leguabe (*v, perc*); Zacheuus Nyoni, Welcome
    Max Bhe Bhe, Kay Ngwazene (*v*). 12/89–1/90.
This might have seemed like a logical collaboration, between the Ensemble and the African male chorus
Amabutho, but the results tend to declare the differences betwen the two groups rather than their
allegiances. The harmonic dignity of Amabutho stands alone on the three tracks which they're featured
on, while the best instrumental music comes on Mitchell's 'Fresh Start', an invigorating blast of free
bop. Worth hearing, but not the grand encounter which must have been intended.

*** Live At The Eighth Tokyo Music Joy 1990 DIW 842
    Lester Bowie, Stanton Davis, E. J. Allen, Gerald Brazel (*t*); Vincent Chauncey (*frhn*); Steve Turre,
    Clifton Anderson (*tb*); Roscoe Mitchell, Joseph Jarman (*reeds*); Bob Stewart (*tba*); Malachi
    Favors (*b*); Famoudou Don Moye, Vinnie Johnson (*d*). 2/90.
A meeting between two great ensembles, the AEOC and Bowie's Brass Fantasy. Each has three tracks
of its own and there are four collective pieces, of which Steve Turre's arrangement of 'The Emperor'
seems to prove the idea that he is the real leader of Brass Fantasy – or, at least, the one who knows how
to make it work for the best. A celebratory meeting but not an altogether successful one.

*** Dreaming Of The Masters Vol. 2: Thelonious Sphere Monk DIW 846
    Lester Bowie (*t*); Roscoe Mitchell, Joseph Jarman (*reeds*); Cecil Taylor (*p*); Malachi Favors (*b*);
    Famoudou Don Moye (*d*). 1–3/90.
*** Dreaming Of The Masters Suite DIW 854
    As above, except omit Taylor. 1–3/90.
It seems a curiously neo-classic device for the Ensemble to be so specifically paying tribute to senior
spirits, which is on the face of it the kind of laborious dues-paying which Bowie in particular has been
critical of in many of today's younger players. Their approach is, of course, different: the colouristic
interchanges between Mitchell and Jarman, Bowie's now inimitable irreverence and the patient, other-
worldly bass of Favors all ensure that. But neither of these records is anything much more than a
reminder that the AEOC are still here and still playing; certainly no specific new ground is broken, and
in that sense the encounter with Cecil Taylor is a disappointment, although Taylor's singing is actually a
fascinating embellishment of the Ensemble's own tradition. When he plays piano, the two sides –
perhaps inevitably – don't really meet. Oddly, neither record is much about its respective dedicatees:
there are only two Monk tunes and three by Coltrane here, though 'Impressions' is a fine repertory
performance. Both are excellently recorded.

Dorothy Ashby (1932–86) HARP

*** The Jazz Harpist Savoy SV 0194
    Ashby; Frank Wess (*f*); Eddie Jones (*b*); Ed Thigpen (*d*). 8/56.
***(*) In A Minor Groove Prestige PCD 24120
    Ashby; Frank Wess (*f*); Eugene Wright, Herman Wright (*b*); Roy Haynes, Art Taylor (*d*). 3 &
    12/58.
The New Grove Dictionary of Jazz describes Ashby as 'the only important bop harpist', which might
seem a rather empty accolade, given a rather scant subscription to the instrument in this music. On
balance, though, it's fair comment. Ashby came to notice in her early twenties, playing with no less a
man than Louis Armstrong. Remarkably, she saw a place for herself in the new idiom and managed to
fit her seemingly unwieldy instrument to the contours of an essentially horn-dominated style. There are
affinities between her harp playing and some contemporary guitar stylings, notably Wes Montgomery's,
but she also learned something from bebop pianists like Bud Powell, bringing an unusually dark tonality
and timbre to a notoriously soft-voiced instrument.
    Ashby's determination to lead her own groups allowed her to develop a personal language and style.
Although she recruited such fine players as Roy Haynes and Jimmy Cobb, her most fruitful association
was with Frank Wess, whose flute playing (still much undervalued) was perfect for her. Their interaction
on 'Dancing On The Ceiling' and 'Stella By Starlight', both on the excellent Savoy, deserves careful
notice, but the best of their partnership can be sampled on the slightly later Prestige. This found her
working with two equally good rhythm sections, Haynes and Gene Wright, Art Taylor and Herman
Wright, against which Jones and Thigpen didn't quite match up. The absence of a more familiar piano
or guitar left some of the harmonies quite open, and there are unexpected chromatic sweeps in some of
these tracks – 'It's A Minor Thing' and 'Alone Together' – which seem ahead of their time.
    'Important' may be stretching it a bit, even allowing for the size of the constituency, but there is no
doubt that Ashby did some intriguing work, for which she deserves wider recognition. Either of these
would suffice.

Harold Ashby (born 1925) TENOR SAXOPHONE

*** **The Viking** Gemini GM 60
> Ashby; Norman Simmons (*p*); Paul West (*b*); Gerryck King (*d*). 8/88.

*** **What Am I Here For?** Criss Cross 1054
> Ashby; Mulgrew Miller (*p*); Rufus Reid (*b*); Ben Riley (*d*). 11/90.

*** **I'm Old Fashioned** Stash ST-CD-545
> Ashby; Richard Wyands (*p*); Aaron Bell (*b*); Connie Kay (*d*). 7/91.

*** **On The Sunny Side Of The Street** Timeless SJP 385
> Ashby; Horace Parlan (*p*); Wayne Dockery (*b*); Steve McCraven (*d*). 1/92.

A late arrival in the Duke Ellington orchestra, Harold Ashby was really Ben Webster's replacement: he still has the Webster huff on ballads and the grouchy, just-woke-up timbre on up-tempo tunes. Quicker tempos don't bother him as much as they did Ben, but he likes to take his own time, and he fashions storytelling solos which can freshen up the material. It's all done consistently enough to ensure that there's little to choose between these four records for four labels. *What Am I Here For?* is an ideal programme of Ellingtonia and, though the disc is a little too long to sustain interest, the playing is jauntily assured from track to track. The Gemini set sounds perkier, perhaps because the rhythm section is less of a signed-up star group and because Ashby sounds expansive and happy with the four original lines he came up with for the date ('Hash' sounds unsurprisingly like 'Dash', which is on the Stash record). The Timeless album revisits some more Ellington and a handful of failsafe standards: 'It's The Talk Of The Town' is a favourite tenorman's set-piece. Horace Parlan, imperturbable as ever, beds everything down with a hint of the blues.

Asian America Jazz Trio GROUP

*** **Sound Circle** Paddle Wheel KCJ 105
> Kei Akagi (*p*); Rufus Reid (*b*); Akira Tana (*d*). 2/91.

Akagi spent some time with the late-'80s Miles Davis band and, on the present showing, was rather wasted as a mere scene-painter on synths. Like a lot of Japanese, he has a secure technique and a slightly chill delivery. This lends itself well to material like 'Nefertiti', 'ESP' and 'Nem Um Talvez', on which a paler tonality sits comfortably, but it sounds decidedly off on more straight-ahead material like 'Dear Old Stockholm'. Reid and Tana are as instinctively in tune as the guard and centre in a basketball team and they pop ideas back and forth with an almost insolent calm.

Svend Asmussen (born 1916) VIOLIN, VIBES, VOCAL

*** **Musical Miracle 1935–1940** Phontastic PHONTCD 9306
> Asmussen; Svend Hauberg (*t, cl, g*); Olaf Carlson (*t*); Kai Ewans (*cl*); Aage Voss, Kai Moller, Johnny Campbell (*as*); Henry Hagemann, Banner Jansen, Valdemar Nielsen (*ts*); Kjeld Bonfils (*p, vib*); Kjeld Norregaard (*p*); Hans Ulrik Neumann, Helge Jacobsen, Jimmy Campbell, Borge Ring (*g*); Niels Foss, Christian Jensene, Alfred Rasmussen (*b*); Bibi Miranda, Erik Frederiksen, Rik Kragh (*d*). 11/35–12/40.

Asmussen should be celebrated as one of the major jazz violinists, yet he remains relatively little-known outside his native Denmark. Like, say, Bengt Hallberg, his musical tastes stretch to areas of music remote from jazz and have led him into light-music byways that have perhaps not done his reputation much good. Nevertheless he remains preposterously neglected by CD reissues, and a listen to some of the tracks on this early collection will make one wonder why: he is at least as fluent as Grappelli or South, and with little of the sweetness or strictness that sometimes mars their work. Try, for example, the rigorous variation on the theme of 'Limehouse Blues' (1938), or the flawless impetus of 'After You've Gone' (1940). The earliest tracks feature him as sideman, but the majority are by small groups designed to feature him as violinist, occasional vibesman and an agreeable if Armstrong-derived vocalist. Aside from Aleman, present on only two tracks, none of the guitarists really challenges him the way Reinhardt did Grappelli, and there's a hint of café society kitsch here and there. Otherwise this is an excellent programme. Remastering is a little tubby in the bass and 'Jazz Potpourri 2' is from a swishy original 78, but the sound is fine in most respects.

*** **Fiddling Around** Imogena IGCD 039
> Asmussen; Jacob Fischer (*g*); Jesper Lundgaard (*b*); Aage Tanggaard (*d*). 3/93.

Interesting, but Asmussen's originals here are insubstantial and the arrangements of the more familiar material are inconsistent: a slow, thoughtful 'Cherokee' is set beside a merely silly 'Alabama Barbecue'. Still, the rest of the group are in good fettle and the violinist has lost none of his panache.

Astreja GROUP

(***) **Music From Davos** Leo CD LR 181

> Sofia Gubaidulina, Viktor Suslin, Mark Pekarsky (*various inst.*); Valentina Ponomareva (*v*). 8/
> 91.

Gubaidulina and Suslin are both composers; Pekarsky leads one of Russia's most distinguished percussion ensembles; Ponomareva is a dramatic singer of gypsy extraction. The latter pair are here guesting with a group which began in the underground improvisation scene of the mid-1970s. Founding member Vyacheslav Artemov is no longer involved.

Originally the group functioned as a composition workshop, allowing the composers to free themselves from the tyranny of notation. Since they have also been freed from the tyranny of state control the music has begun to sound a little self-indulgent. However, their intense interest in the nature of sound and its spiritual implications gives these performances an impact that fully compensates for the appalling recording-quality. An unfortunate return, this, to the good old days of smuggled tapes and *samizdat* imprints; odd, though, because Davos in 1991 was scarcely inaccessible.

Lovie Austin (1887–1972) PIANO

*** **Lovie Austin 1924–1926** Classics 756

> Austin; Tommy Ladnier, Bob Shoffner, Natty Dominique (*c*); Kid Ory (*tb*); Jimmy O'Bryant,
> Johnny Dodds (*cl*); Eustern Woodfork (*bj*); W. E. Burton (*d*); Ford & Ford, Edmonia
> Henderson, Viola Bartlette, Henry Williams (*v*). 9/24–8/26.

A remarkable woman, and one of the first female musicians to make a significant contribution to jazz, the Tennessee-born Austin became house-pianist at Paramount in the early 1920s. She settled in Chicago, but after the end of the decade she scarcely recorded again until the early '60s. There are 17 surviving sides by her Blues Serenaders, plus various accompaniments to blues and vaudeville singers, and they're all on this valuable CD. Austin's music was a tight, sophisticated variation on the barrelhouse style that was prevalent in Chicago at the time. The two sides by the trio of Austin, Ladnier and O'Bryant create a densely plaited counterpoint which seems amazingly advanced for its time. The quartet and quintet sides are harsher, with Burton's clumping drumming on what sounds like a military side-drum taking unfortunate precedence, but the simple breaks and stop-time passages have a rough poetry about them that transcends the very grimy recording. This CD adds to the old Fountain LP by including nine tracks in which Austin and some of her colleagues accompany various blues singers. The transfers are a very mixed bag, as usual with Classics: two tracks by Edmonia Henderson are terribly noisy, and none of the original Paramount recordings are better than average; but practised ears will listen through the noise to some classic Chicago jazz of its day.

In 1961, when in her seventies, Austin was persuaded to record again, as accompanist to Alberta Hunter. The results are available on Original Blues Classics OBC-510.

Available Jelly GROUP

*** **In Full Flail** Ear-rational ECD 1013

> Eric Boeren (*t, c*); Michael Moore (*cl, bcl, as, p, mar, mca, bells*); Gregg Moore (*tb, tba, b, mand*);
> Michael Vatcher (*d, dulc, mar*). 6/88.

*** **Al(l)Ways** NOM CD00110

> As above, except add Tobias Delius (*ts, mca*), Eric Calmes (*b, perc*). 11/89.

*** **Monuments** Ramboy 07

> As above, except add Jimmy Sernesky (*t*), Alexei Levin (*p, org, acc*). 8–10/93.

Michael Moore and Eric Boeren mastermind most of the material for this band, which grew out of a band that worked as accompanists to a mime troupe in the 1970s. Judging from the expanding personnel, it's still growing. *In Full Flail* has a theatrical feel to it, with 11 of the 21 pieces done and dusted in less than three minutes, some of them tossed out like a spontaneous idea. Yet most of it is impeccably organized, especially the pair of sad, funny, faintly satirical tunes at the heart of the disc, Boeran's 'Waggery' and Moore's 'Beauty'. Boeren plays with a fat, brassy intensity that can crack into a chuckling aside, while Moore can play any style, anywhere. Gregg Moore and Vatcher follow them with wit and guile. But it remains a tad arch. *Al(l)ways* is their best record, though it's on the hard-to-find NOM label. The expanded personnel has a number of consequences: it takes the arrangements a step away from jazz and towards the kind of art-rock espoused by Frank Zappa and Henry Cow, it frees up Gregg Moore to play more trombone, and it allows brother Michael to include perfectly logical tributes to Steve Lacy and Thelonious Monk (in the shape of three seldom-played Monk tunes). Some of the short tracks seem like space-wasters, and three melodica players is two too many; but there are many lovely, tart moments. Special highlight: a drowsy treatment of Neal Hefti's 'Girl Talk'.

Monuments overdoes it. The new members add extra weight, but they sometimes seem like excess baggage. The firecracker playing that Boeren contributed to the first disc seems to have been swamped by the arrangements, some of which are merely lugubrious, and the concert-hall ambience of the sound-mix doesn't suit them. But there are still some moments to savour, such as Moore's doleful 'Shotgun Wedding', a classic sad-sack dirge, and a couple of Boeren's neatest miniatures.

Teodross Avery TENOR AND SOPRANO SAXOPHONES

*** In Other Words GRP 97982

    Avery; Roy Hargrove (*t, flhn*); Charles Craig (*p*); Reuben Rogers (*b*); Mark Simmons (*d*). 94.

***(*) My Generation Impulse! IMP 11812

    Avery; John Scofield, Peter Bernstein, Mark Whitfield (*g*); Charles Craig (*p*); Rodney Whitaker (*b*); Greg Hutchinson (*d*); Andrew Daniels (*perc*); Black Thought (Tariq Trotter) (*v*). 10/95.

Image and externals first. Look at the cover of Teodross Avery's second album: the familiar thick orange spine of Impulse!, the fold-out monochrome shot of the young saxophonist *in excelsis*, offering thanks to the Creator, and then the track-titles, 'Addis Ababa', 'Mode For My Father', 'Theme For Malcolm', and so on. It's pretty clear that we're being asked to think of this talented young man as a latter-day Coltrane or Pharoah. What, though, of the more important matter: the music inside? Heard blindfold, without those visual clues, and most people will still put the date around 1966 or 1967; not Coltrane himself, too untroubled, slightly too round in tone, but definitely from within that orbit.

This is a lot to be saddled with in your early twenties. Avery's debut was greeted with rapturous enthusiasm; along with Joshua Redman, he was unmistakably a Next Big Thing, and the raw edges of *In Other Words* almost perversely proved the point. Unlike Trane, who really had little use for McCoy Tyner after *A Love Supreme* and built his later explorations on Elvin and Rashied, Avery has a relatively undeveloped rhythmic awareness and often sounds as if he's playing on a different track. His understanding with the very fine Craig, the only survivor from the first record, is well attuned, but Avery is already looking at different possibilities, and the guitar players who share out the seven non-piano tracks between them give him a much more open and ambiguous accompaniment. In response, his playing this time is more abstract, less melodic than on the opening record. Perhaps ironically, perhaps because of Impulse!, the Coltrane mannerisms are even more pronounced, to the point of regression on 'Mode', which is an interesting enough conception, played with less than adequate imagination and spoiled by a drab drum solo.

Hargrove brought some interesting sounds to the first record, playing flugelhorn in the main and using a rounder, less cutting tone than usual. What impresses about Avery is that he makes the guest players do what *he* needs, rather than having them just as starry walk-ons. It's to be earnestly hoped that he is allowed to develop at his own pace and not be pushed into formula projects; the single rap track is quite enough of a nod to 'my generation'. Five years ago, the Coltrane tribute album would have seemed inevitable; given that the big anniversaries are past, he may be spared that particular showdown.

Axon GROUP

**(*) Perceptions Random Acoustics RA 008

    Phil Minton (*v, t*); Marcio Mattos (*clo, elec*); Martin Blume (*d*). 12/93.

Minton's brand of abstract scat either excites or gets on the nerves in exact ratio to how much of it you've actually heard. It's a shame that it has so thoroughly downgraded his unidiomatic but always exciting trumpet work, which nowadays takes a lazy second place. Equine snorts, lip-farts and Donald Duck tantrums are all very well, but one constantly waits for him to match the delicate subtlety of what the undermixed Mattos is doing (far) behind him, or the controlled urgency of Blume's drumming.

To this extent, *Perceptions* is a frustrating record. It does, though, succeed despite its limitations. The long 'Passages' is apt to sound like just that, a slice of improv piecework that on occasion veers close to clock-watching. The two following pieces, 'Doors Of Perception' and 'Soma', occupy only half the space each, but they're packed with meat and muscle. Minton abandons his more tiresome mannerisms and actually gets involved in the drama of the thing, listening and responding rather than just getting off on his own. There are good things on the shortish opening track, too, but if these are delivered in the order in which they were performed at Hans-Martin Müller's LOFT in Cologne, that would explain the slightly tentative warm-up feel.

Albert Ayler (1936–70) TENOR SAXOPHONE, ALTO SAXOPHONE, SOPRANO SAXOPHONE

*** My Name Is Albert Ayler Black Lion BLCD 760211
> Ayler; Niels Bronsted (*p*); Niels-Henning Orsted-Pedersen (*b*); Ronnie Gardiner (*d*). 1/63.

*** Goin' Home Black Lion BLCD 760197
> Ayler; Call Cobbs (*p*); Henry Grimes (*b*); Sunny Murray (*d*). 2/64.

***(*) Witches And Devils Freedom 741018
> Ayler; Norman Howard (*t*); Henry Grimes, Earl Henderson (*b*); Sunny Murray (*d*). 4/64.

There is an almost Aeschylean inevitability to Albert Ayler's life and death. The final tragedy has been dressed up as almost everything from murder to recall by the planet Zog, but is now known to have been plain, exhausted suicide. Ayler's style has been subjected to just as many conspiracy theories but is now generally considered to be a highly personal amalgam of New Orleans brass, rhythm and blues (to which Ayler unapologetically returned in his last two years) and some of the more extreme timbral innovations of the '60s New Thing.

The first recordings (made in Denmark and not currently available) are astonishingly sparse. With no harmony instrument and a concentration on stark melodic variations in and out of tempo, they sound influenced by early Ornette Coleman; but what is immediately distinctive about Ayler is the almost hypnotic depth of his concentration on a single motif, which he repeats, worries, splinters into constituent harmonics, until even familiar standards are virtually unrecognizable.

Back in the USA, Ayler cut a session for Debut Records' Ole Vestergaard Jensen; it was released as *My Name Is Albert Ayler* and, like much of the saxophonist's output, has enjoyed only rather uncertain circulation. *Goin' Home* contains the rest of the session. It finds Ayler at his most 'primitive', digging deep into traditional Americana for themes like 'Down By The Riverside' and 'Swing Low, Sweet Chariot' and 'When The Saints Go Marchin' In', with 'Old Man River' thrown in; all but 'Saints' are offered in two versions, forgivable padding for such an important document. Working with a pianist constrained Ayler a touch, though later Cobbs was to contribute a distinctive harpsichord part to *Love Cry*. The saxophone lines are gloriously unadorned and *Goin' Home* is doubly valuable for a rare glimpse of Ayler's soprano sound.

On his return from Europe, where he had moved to find work and cut a tentative debut, Ayler bunked for a time with the trumpeter Norman Howard, who had been a friend since schooldays. There he met Earl (or Errol) Henderson, a sax player who had turned, it seems wisely, to playing bass. Jensen arranged a recording in New York City. This might be seen as Albert's real debut, but Howard was more of a sympathetic friend than a genuinely challenging musician, and he seems no more certain of Ayler's direction than the Scandinavian sidemen on the deleted *First Recordings*. However, he had the basic chops and a sufficient measure of respect for his friend to throw himself into the project, and he plays more than competently on 'Saints', 'Witches And Devils', 'Holy Holy' and, the track that gave the original release its title, 'Spirits'.

A bare three months before the mammoth achievement of *Spiritual Unity*, Ayler sounds poised and confident, the Sonny Rollins mannerisms of the first record still evident. Henderson and Grimes combine for 'Witches And Devils', giving the saxophonist the weight of sound he was looking for and was to get from Gary Peacock. The recording quality was surprisingly good, with the two horns well balanced and the rhythm section spread across the background.

**** Spiritual Unity ESP Disk 1002
> Ayler; Gary Peacock (*b*); Sunny Murray (*d*). 7/64.

The poet Ted Joans likened the impact of this trio to hearing someone scream the word 'fuck' in St Patrick's Cathedral. Subjectively, there may be some validity in this, but it makes a nonsense of what was actually going on in this group. The intensity of interaction among the three individuals, their attentiveness to what the others were doing, ruled out any such gesture. Even amid the noise, the 1964 Ayler trio was quintessentially a listening band, locked in a personal struggle which it is possible only to observe, awe-struck, from side-lines.

If one single item justifies the return of the admittedly patchy ESP catalogue, this is it. The first 'variation' of 'Ghosts' lifts that bare, unadorned theme into realms that no previous jazz musician had ever dared, and superlatives simply run out in trying to find a terminology for its bleak power and – never let it be forgotten – control. Though the horn inevitably dominates a mono recording (the engineer had assumed they were still warming up), CD transfer reveals how much this was an ensemble performance. Peacock's huge bass shapes are more evident than they were on the original release and are clearly essential to what Ayler is doing. Murray's role is more ambiguous, but he is entirely absorbed in the music, achieving a level of rapport on 'Transfiguration' and the second variation of 'Ghosts' that equals – and in places exceeds – the almost telepathic sympathy between John Coltrane and his drummers, Elvin Jones and Rashied Ali. *Spiritual Unity* is one of the essential recordings of the new jazz and should be in every serious collection.

*** **Vibrations** Freedom 741000
>   Ayler; Don Cherry (*t*); Gary Peacock (*b*); Sunny Murray (*d*). 9/64.
*** **The Hilversum Session** Coppens CCD 6001
>   As above. 11/64.

The chief problem with the Ayler discography – quite apart from the record companies' unwillingness until recently to keep it up to date – is his remarkably slender basic repertoire; there was not much of it and what there was tended to be melodically skeletal, almost folkish. Versions of 'Ghosts' turn up on this pair, played pretty much straight and in line with his growing sense that the exact notes mattered considerably less than the amount of emotional charge that could be put across the poles of a melody.

Cherry was, as with Ornette, his most sympathetic interpreter, a more responsive and clear-sighted musician than the saxophonist's brother, trumpeter Donald Ayler, with whom he was to form his next band, this time in the USA. Both 1964 sessions are well recorded and transfer well to CD (the shift of medium is particularly advantageous to Peacock, whose critical contribution tends to get lost on vinyl).

***(*) **Bells / Prophecy** ESP Disk 1010
>   Ayler; Donald Ayler (*t*); Charles Tyler (*as*); Lewis Worrell, Gary Peacock (*b*); Sunny Murray (*d*).
>   5/65, 6/64.
**** **Spirits Rejoice** ESP Disk 1020
>   Ayler; Donald Ayler (*t*); Call Cobbs (*hpd*); Henry Grimes, Gary Peacock (*b*); Sunny Murray (*d*).
>   9/65.
***(*) **New York Eye And Ear Control** ESP 1016
>   Ayler; Don Cherry (*t*); Roswell Rudd (*tb*); John Tchicai (*as*); Gary Peacock (*b*); Sunny Murray
>   (*d*). 9/65.

On May Day 1965, Ayler and his brother Donald led a band on stage at Town Hall. The 20-minute 'Bells' was subsequently released as a one-sided LP, pressed on translucent plastic. More people remember that than the music, which was ragged and shapeless where *Spiritual Unity* had been so entire and coherent. Donald's trumpet playing is edgy and uneven, and he frequently resorts to bugle calls and fanfares. Murray plays like a man isolated from the others, wailing along with whatever is going on in his head. Ayler himself sounds as damaged and self-absorbed as Quasimodo. *Bells* is one of his rare ugly moments.

In reissuing it, ESP have included material recorded at a New York club date with the Peacock/Murray trio and subsequently issued by Bernard Stollman's label as a posthumus LP. This is particularly important material, coming from the end of his most productive period. There is a further version of 'Ghosts (First Variation)' and of 'Spirits', which are worth comparing in some detail with the performances on *Spiritual Unity*, which they predate by almost a month. It is clear that the empathy of the studio album was worked at over time; it did not simply occur by chance.

Spirits Rejoice was recorded in Judson Hall, scene of so much New Thing activity. The most important new component in the sound is Call Cobbs's harpsichord (later to make an appearance on the underrated *Love Cry*). The original intention had been to use vibes, but the softly jangling keyboard effect Cobbs gets now seems just right, conjuring up the spirit world in Ayler's most directly Christian statement. 'The Holy Family' and 'Prophet' are subtly different from what had gone before, pointing a new direction which was to occupy the saxophonist for most of the rest of his life.

It isn't immediately evident on *New York Eye And Ear Control*, also recorded in September 1965. It isn't strictly an Ayler album but a collaborative soundtrack project for Michael Snow's now-forgotten film of the same name. It would have been interesting to hear Ayler work with another trumpeter, particularly the one who contributed so much to Ornette Coleman's music, but Cherry is having an off-day. It's Rudd who surprises, and the slightly diffident Tchicai who steals most of the honours.

*** **Lörrach / Paris 1966** hat Art 6039
>   Ayler; Donald Ayler (*t*); Michel Sampson (*vn*); William Folwell (*b*); Beaver Harris (*d*). 11/66.

The 1966 band was probably Ayler's most dramatic move in the direction of complete abstraction, and it was an uneasy affair. Ayler was visibly battling to reconcile the demands of arhythmic and atonal free jazz with traditional black music, and he was succeeding only partially.

The nature of the material left from this time makes a full assessment rather difficult, and some of the releases are of questionable provenance. Even on the valuable hat Art issue, the registration is muzzy, with little clear sense of what the rhythm section is being asked to do. Most of the queries, though, relate to Ayler's treatment of his themes. The live version of 'Bells', which had just appeared on ESP-Disk, is mostly unproblematic, but the addition of a second stringed instrument only contributes to an often-remarked sense of incompleteness in Ayler's work. 'Spirits' and two versions of 'Ghosts' – or 'Ghost', as it is listed – are unquestionably performances of great power by Ayler, but again the recording quality makes it difficult to assess the pieces as a whole.

**** In Greenwich Village Impulse AS 9155/254635

> Ayler; Donald Ayler (*t*); Michel Sampson (*vn*); Joel Friedman (*clo*); Alan Silva, William Folwell, Henry Grimes, (*b*); Beaver Harris (*d*). 2/67, 12/67.

Whatever technical and aesthetic shortcomings the Lörrach and Paris sessions may have had (there is a nihilistic, fragmentary quality to the latter), the Village Theater and Village Vanguard sessions are hugely affirmative and satisfyingly complete without losing a jot of Ayler's angry and premonitory force. *In Greenwich Village* is one of the essential post-war jazz albums, and features some of Ayler's best playing on both alto ('For John Coltrane', ironically or self-protectively), and tenor (the apocalyptic 'Truth Is Marching In'). For comparison, try the closing version of 'Our Prayer' here, with the version recorded in Germany, above. The addition of a second bass, in addition to either violin or cello, actually sharpens the sound considerably, producing a rock-solid foundation for Ayler's raw witness. If his reputation hangs on any single recording, it is this one.

*** Love Cry Impulse GRP 11082

> Ayler; Donald Ayler (*t*); Call Cobbs (*hpd*); Alan Silva (*b*); Milford Graves (*d*). 8/67, 2/68.

Love Cry began six weeks after John Coltrane's painful death from liver cancer. Ayler had been quick to identify himself with the Holy Ghost in Coltrane's Trinity. In the time left to him, he moved with unnerving swiftness from the torrential outpourings of *Bells* and *Spirits Rejoice* towards the irredeemably banal R&B of *New Grass*. What was wrong with the last studio album was the pinched, inelastic beat. No such problems with *Love Cry*, which isn't entirely satisfactory but which, given recent depredations in the Ayler catalogue, demands a hearing and emerges as a work of qualified brilliance. Reissue on CD considerably enhanced its standing. Not only is 'Universal Indians', with its odd whooping vocal, restored to its full nine and three-quarter minutes, the set contains alternative takes of it and the gospelly 'Zion Hill', the clearest indication on the set as to where Ayler was headed next. It also includes a confusingly titled 'Love Cry II', which is a different composition from the original piece. 'Love Cry' features another vocal, in a disturbing Spanish-Moorish wail. Only on it and the issued take of 'Zion Hill' does Ayler play his alto saxophone. Listening to the fierce tenor line on 'Ghosts', played unusually fast, and the tender protestations on 'Dancing Flowers' and 'Love Flower', it's easier to see what Ayler's most distinguished disciple, David Murray, took and what he chose to leave behind.

It may not be Ayler's finest moment, but it's elevated by the extraordinary polystylistic work of Milford Graves, one of the heroes of the New Thing, a percussionist of inexhaustible resource who could call up anything from huge tribal calls-to-arms to quiet, filigreed patterns. He sounds restless, but also completely contained. A word, too, for Silva, who plays magnificently.

Azimuth GROUP

**** Azimuth / The Touchstone / Départ ECM 1546/7/8 3CD

> John Taylor (*p, ky, org*); Norma Winstone (*v*); Kenny Wheeler (*t, flhn*); Ralph Towner (*g* on *Départ* only). 3/77, 6/78, 12/79.

** Azimuth '85 ECM 1298

> As above, except omit Towner. 3/85.

***(*) 'How it was then . . . never again' ECM 1538

> As above. 4/94.

The repackaging of Azimuth's first three records, and the appearance of a new disc after a break of some years, offers a chance to re-assess the work of a notably understated trio whose live appearances (at least one gig every year since 1977; no mean achievement in this branch of music) are often far more rugged and sharply inflected than the recorded product would suggest.

Initially, the group was a duo format for the then-married Taylor and Winstone. On the debut album, her voice floats with a characteristic balance between freedom and control over Taylor's minimalistic piano figures. Any doubts that these are jazz-trained and jazz-centred performers are immediately dispelled, and the second track, called simply 'O', is not much more than a blowing shape, over which Winstone and Wheeler (whose inclusion was suggested by ECM producer and demiurge, Manfred Eicher, with a characteristic instinct for the appropriate touch) improvise freely. The very next track, significantly the title-cut, is the first to use the studio as a compositional device, building up layers of keyboard, voice and trumpets into a grand acoustic edifice that constantly reveals new areas of interest.

The most obvious difference between the first and third albums and the middle one of the original group is that on *Touchstone* there is no lyric component as such. Here Winstone vocalizes, turning her voice into a third and equal part in the mix. Taylor abandons the synthesizer swirls of *Azimuth* in favour of the organ's richly *breathing* sound. The result is perhaps the group's masterpiece, combining jazz, classical and contemporary composition, and sheer sound in a mix that is as invigorating as it is thought-provoking. Outstanding track? Without a doubt the glorious 'See'.

Azimuth and Ralph Towner met at ECM's Oslo studios, where the guitarist was finishing an album of his own. The end of the 1970s probably marked the high-water mark of the label's more experimental ethos, with Eicher encouraging previously untried permutations. Much as he does on Weather Report's *I Sing The Body Electric*, Towner sounds as if he comes from outside the basic conception of the group, but with a genuine understanding and appreciation of what it's all about. His contribution is perhaps most emphatic on 'Arrivée', which is a companion-piece to the title-track, linking the whole disc into a continuous suite. As such, it's perhaps slightly too mannered and deliberate, but none the less effective for that.

Succeeding years presented fewer opportunities to record as a unit, presumably to some extent because Wheeler in particular was busy on projects of his own. Azimuth's return to the studio was the pretty disappointing *'85*. With *'85*, Azimuth fell into the trap Towner's Oregon has always avoided: that of making style an end in itself. There is no fixed requirement that musicians or bands 'develop' stylistically, but, for all the quality of writing and performance, *Azimuth '85* did seem to be an unconfident step back.

It was then nearly a decade before the group recorded again, an awkward gap of time in critical and commercial terms. The signs are, though, that the energies of the first record have been significantly re-channelled and re-directed. '*How It Was Then . . . Never Again*' suggests a backward-looking and even nostalgic sub-text; the music within is as progressive and empirical as anything the group has done in 20 years. Taylor restricts himself to piano and to a compositional style that has acquired a new, though entirely non-linear, logic. Titles like 'Whirlpool' and 'Full Circle' very accurately convey his ability to infuse harmonic and melodic stasis with hints of tremendous energy. Winstone's voice is as pure and reed-like as ever, and the only question marks relate to Wheeler, who increasingly seems to be speaking in a different musical language. For the time being, that makes for an exciting pluralism, as on the opening and closing numbers, 'How It Was Then' and 'Wintersweet', but one wonders where Azimuth can go with it next.

Ab Baars CLARINET, SOPRANO, TENOR AND BARITONE SAXOPHONES

** **Krang** Geestgronden 2
        Baars (solo). 12/87–6/89.
(*) **3900 Carol Court Geestgronden 12
        Baars; Wilbert De Joode (*b*); Martin Van Duynhoven (*d*). 3–6/92.
*** **Sprok** Geestgronden 14
        As above. 2–5/94.

Baars, a Dutchman who's worked in Maarten Altena's groups, makes very heavy weather of the solo album. Rather than improvising in any specific direction, his solos tend to circle in on themselves or reach a spurious climax of increasingly harsh repetitions. This makes the soprano solo, 'Geel en Rood', barely listenable, a different application of Steve Lacy's methods to sometimes grisly ends. But the blustering weight of the baritone on 'Spaat' or the false pathos of the tenor on the title-track are interesting.

There's another version of 'Krang' on the trio album, which is a little more worthwhile. After the abstractions of the solo record, it comes as a mild shock to hear him with an almost conventionally swinging rhythm section on John Lewis's 'Plastic Dreams'. But the other pieces, revolving round remote kinds of interplay among the three players, are more typical of what Baars is after. The leader's solos still tend to grind through curtly defined areas of timbre and phrasing, but at least they're leavened by the inquiring bass and drum parts.

Sprok seems like a loosening-up and a further clarifying at the same time. Baars makes his clarinet and tenor sound more dry and stone-faced than ever, but bass and drums shift smoothly between free playing and courtly, strict time. Not bad at all; by the next one, Baars may almost raise a smile.

Babkas GROUP

*** **Babkas** Songlines 1502-2
        Briggan Krauss (*as*); Brad Schoeppach (*g*); Aaron Alexander (*d*). 1/93.
*** **Ants To The Moon** Songlines 1505-2
        As above. 2/94.

Entertaining variations on the power trio by the not-quite-splenetic Babkas. Schoeppach is the principal writing force and the major musical personality: he tends to set the tone for each of their pieces, with decoration by Krauss and pulse and splashing rhythm from Alexander. The earlier disc is less unified, more diverse. 'Czugy Stodel' sounds like a Hungarian dance, and they then proceed to cover a genuine one, No. 20 by Brahms. Punky outbursts like 'Piglet' are measured against long, dense explorations. Schoeppach favours lots of thick-toned fuzz on this disc; he prefers a more open tone on the next disc, which is more composed and poised, though not necessarily superior – some of the pieces go on a bit, and Krauss's squalling delivery has its limitations exposed. Decades from now, scholars will look back on this kind of record as everyday post-mod jazz life, *circa* the early '90s.

Alice Babs (born 1924) VOCAL, PIANO

*** **Swing It!** Phontastic PHONTCD 9302

Babs; Thore Ehrling, Gosta Redlig, Gosta Torner, Rolf Ericson, Rune Ander, Olle Jacobson, Nisse Skoog, Anders Sward (*t*); Georg Vernon, Bertil Jacobson, Sven Bohman, Karl-Erik Lennholm, Sverre Oredson (*tb*); Sven Gustafsson, Ove Lind, Putte Wickman, Charlie Redland (*cl*); Casper Hjukstrom (*cl, as*); John Bjorling, Ove Ronn, Arne Domnérus, O. Thalen (*as*); Carl-Henrik Norin, Gunnar Lunden-Welden, Gosta Theselius, Curt Blomqvist (*ts*); Lars Schonning (*bs*); Stig Holm, Allan Johansson, Rolf Larsson, Charles Norman, Rolf Svensson (*p*); Bosse Callstrom (*vib*); Erik Frank, Nisse Lind (*acc*); Rolf Berg, B. Larsson, Folke Eriksberg, Sven Stiberg, Jonny Bossman, Nils-Erik Sandell, Sten Carlberg, Kalle Lohr (*g*); Thore Jederby, Henry Lundin, Gunnar Almstedt, Romeo Sjoberg, Simon Brehm, Rolf Bengtsson (*b*); Ake Brandes, Andrew Burman, Henry Wallin, Gosta Heden, Thord Waerner, Gosta Oddner (*d*). 5/39–4/53.

(*) **Metronome-Aren 1951–1958 Metronome 4509-93189-2 2CD

Babs; orchestras of Charlie Norman, Harry Arnold, Gunnar Lunden-Welden, Anders Burman, Ernie Englund. 51–58.

*** **Far Away Star** Bluebell ABCD 005

Babs; Money Johnson, Johnny Coles, Barry Lee Hall, Willie Cook, Mercer Ellington, Americo Belotto, Bertil Lovgren, Jan Allan, Hakan Nyqvist (*t*); Vince Prudente, Chuck Connors, Art Baron, Torgny Nilsson, Lars Olofsson, Bertil Strandberg, Sven Larsson (*tb*); Harry Carney, Russell Procope, Harold Minerve, Harold Ashby, Parcy Marion, Arne Domnérus, Claes Rosendahl, Lennart Aberg, Ulf Andersson, Erik Nilsson (*reeds*); Duke Ellington, Nils Lindberg (*p*); Rune Gustafsson (*g*); Joe Benjamin, Red Mitchell (*b*); Quentin White Jr, Nils-Erik Slorner (*d*). 6/73–5/76.

*** **There's Something About Me** . . . Bluebell ABCD 052

As above, except omit Ellington personnel; add Jan Allan (*t*), Anders Lindskog (*ts*), Erik Nilsson (*bs*), Davor Kajfes (*ky*), Red Mitchell (*b*), Rune Carlsson (*d*). 5/73–9/78.

Along with the very different stylist, Monica Zetterlund, Alice 'Babs' Nilson is Sweden's most renowned vocalist in the jazz world – although, like Zetterlund, she has often touched only peripherally on jazz surroundings. Her early tracks feature on the useful compilation, *Swing It!*, which is in many ways the most jazz-orientated of all four discs. She tackles everything from 'Some Of These Days' and 'Darktown Strutters Ball' to 'Yodel In Swing' and 'Opus In Scat', in settings that range from accordion trios to impressive big bands. Three airchecks with a small group including Rolf Ericson (terrific on 'Truckin'') offer some of the best music, but the entire disc has much to enjoy, not least Babs's light but amazingly confident handling of the English lyrics. The earliest track dates from before her sixteenth birthday, yet she seems fearless in all this music. The Metronome two-disc set is of much more limited appeal. Sung mainly in Swedish, this includes a lot of pop material which has marginal jazz content and, though Babs is unfailingly charming, in parts it can be a struggle.

She first worked with Ellington in 1963, and she remained a favourite with Duke: the four 1973 tracks with the band on *Far Away Star* are a souvenir of one of their final collaborations, though the tracks from an Ellington memorial concert the following year with a Swedish group are actually rather better. So is *There's Something About Me* . . ., which has some more Ellington material – 'Checkered Hat', 'Me And You' and the title-piece – but which is most interesting for five songs co-written by John Lewis. Babs, whose cool, slightly impassive but fundamentally emotional delivery seems well suited to this material, produces some of her best work here. There is much more still awaiting reissue.

Back Bay Ramblers GROUP

*** **'Leven Thirty Saturday Night** Stomp Off CD 1262

Peter Ecklund (*c*); Bob Connors (*tb*); Steve Wright (*cl, as, ts, bs, bsx*); Bill Novick (*cl, as*); Butch Thompson (*p*); Peter Bullis (*g, bj*); Stu Gunn (*tba, b*); Bill Reynolds (*d*); Karen Cameron (*v*). 1/93

*** **My Mamma's In Town!** Stomp Off CD 1279
    As above, except Mark Shane, Bob Pilsbury (*p*) and Vince Giordano (*tba, bsx, b*) replace
    Thompson and Gunn, add Andy Stein (*vn*), Jimmy Mazzy (*v*). 1/94.
Of the many repertory bands recording for Stomp Off, the Ramblers pay the most dutiful homage to
their inspirations – usually the hot dance music of the 1920s, rather than the out-and-out jazz of the
period. So the first CD includes arrangements drawn from the books of Bob Haring, Jack Pettis and
Spike Hughes, while the second relies heavily on the work of Jean Goldkette, Annette Hanshaw and Ted
Lewis. None of the players makes a special impression by himself – they're playing for the band, and the
lilt and deferential swing of this music is its reason to exist. Ecklund has some agreeable 16-bar interludes, Connors is splendidly versatile, and Novick and Wright are skilled interpreters of the old-time
reedsman's role. That said, the music can seem almost airlessly polite at times. Cameron sings sweetly,
Mazzy with a bit more gusto on the second disc. Little to choose between the two discs, and it's a churl
who would deny that it's pleasant to find a group ready to perform something like Phil Napoleon's 'You
Can't Cheat A Cheater' in the Godless '90s.

Benny Bailey (born 1925) TRUMPET, FLUGELHORN

*** **Big Brass** Candid CCD 79011
    Bailey; Julius Watkins (*hn*); Phil Woods (*as, b cl*); Les Spann (*f, g*); Tommy Flanagan (*p*); Buddy
    Catlett (*b*); Art Taylor (*d*). 11/60.
** **Islands** Enja 2082
    Bailey; Sigi Schwab (*g, sitar*); Eberhard Weber (*b*); Lala Kovacev (*d*). 5/76.
*** **For Heaven's Sake** Hot House HHCD 1006
    Bailey; Tony Coe (*ts, cl*); Horace Parlan (*p*); Jimmy Woode (*b*); Idris Muhammad (*d*). 88.
*** **Live At Grabenhalle, St Gallen** TCB 8940
    Bailey; Carlo Schoeb (*as*); Peter Eigenmann (*g*); Reggie Johnson (*b*); Peter Schmidlin (*d*). 4/89.
***(*) **While My Lady Sleeps** Gemini GMCD 69
    Bailey; Harald Gundhus (*ts*); Emil Viklickáy (*p*); František Uhlír (*b*); Ole-Jacob Hansen (*d*). 4/
    90.
Bailey is probably best known as first trumpet in the Kenny Clarke/Francy Boland big bands of the
1960s, but he is also an impressive and entertaining soloist, with a number of distinguishing marks on
his musical passport, noticeably his much-commented-upon octave plummets and his attraction to
enigmatic lines that seem from moment to moment to have neither melodic nor harmonic significance,
just a strangely specific logic all their own.
    His bebop background is still evident on *Big Brass*, certainly his finest available record (though the
deleted *Serenade To The Planet* is considered essential documentation). The themes have begun to
stretch out, though, into long, quasi-modal strings that contain any number of potential resolutions.
Flanagan is a sympathetic accompanist. Woods and Rouse could hardly be more different, but Bailey
responds magnanimously to the challenge posed by each. Only *Islands* seems a little vacuous. Weber's
bass is not quite right, and Schwab's guitar and sitar seem almost surplus to the more straightforward
themes.
    The quartet on *While My Lady Sleeps* are completely attuned to Bailey's music, combining an attractive
obliqueness with some wonderfully concentrated ballad playing on 'While My Lady Sleeps'; Gundhus
solos impressively and the rhythm section sustain a long, throbbing accompaniment. Two originals by
Viklickáy (the disappointing opening 'Vino, Oh Vino!') and Uhlír ('Expectation') are redeemed by
Bailey's thoughtful commentaries; but the meat of the album is kept for last with the long version of the
title-track and a tight reading of Benny Golson's 'Along Came Betty'. Recording was done at the
Rainbow Studio in Oslo by Jan Erik Kongshaug, both associated with ECM; the quality is exactly what
you'd expect. Recommended.
    The record with Tony Coe is as lovely as one would expect it to be, and very decently recorded, though
some of Bailey's solos seem excessively closely miked. Those same solos are without exception intelligent, elegant and finely crafted, so no complaints there.

Derek Bailey (born 1930) GUITAR

*** **Solo Guitar: Volume 1** Incus CD10
    Bailey (*g solo, syn*). 2/71.
*** **Cyro** Incus CD01
    Bailey; Cyro Baptista (*perc*).

***(*) **Han** Incus CD02
    Bailey; Han Bennink (*perc*).
**** **Figuring** Incus CD05
    Bailey; Barre Phillips (*b*). 5/87, 9/88.
***(*) **Solo Guitar: Volume 2** Incus CD11
    Bailey (*g* solo). 6/91.
***(*) **Village Life** Incus CD09
    Bailey; Thebe Lipere (*perc, v*); Louis Moholo (*d, perc, v*). 9/91.
***(*) **Playing** Incus CD14
    Bailey; John Stevens (*d, mini-t*). 8/92.

Though scarcely a household name (or likely to become one) Derek Bailey has won almost universal acclaim from fellow improvising musicians on both sides of the Atlantic. His sometimes forbidding but always challenging music, premised on the avoidance of any groove (whether rhythmic, harmonic or melodic), illuminates certain important differences between European and American improvisers. Whereas American free jazz and improvisation have tended to remain individualistic – the most convenient image is the soloist stepping forward from the ensemble – European improvisers have tended to follow a broadly collectivist philosophy which downplays personal expression in favour of a highly objectified or process-dominated music.

Perhaps the best concrete illustration of the difference can be found in Bailey's duo performances with the multi-instrumentalist Anthony Braxton (*q.v.*). Despite considerable mutual admiration, these confirm the old saw about Europeans and Americans being divided by a common language; Braxton's formulations are still conditioned by the deep structures of jazz, Bailey's according to a mysterious metalanguage by which a performance offers few guidelines as to its presumed origins and underlying processes. (The guitarist did once record a splendidly ironic version of 'The Lost Chord'.)

Like a good many European improvisers, Bailey underwent an accelerated and virtually seamless transition from jazz to free jazz to free music. He has performed with such innovative groups as Josef Holbrooke and Iskra 1903, but since 1976 his activities have centred on solo and duo work (where he is most influential as a performer) and on his loosely affiliated collective, Company (*q.v.*), locus of some of the most challenging musical and para-musical performance of recent years. Company has been sufficiently unlimited to draw in musicians from a 'straight' jazz background (most strikingly Lee Konitz), avant-garde composer-performers such as trombonist Vinko Globokar, and even dancer Katie Duck, as well as long-standing associates Evan Parker, Jamie Muir, Barre Phillips, Han Bennink and Tristan Honsinger, with all of whom Bailey has made significant duo recordings.

It has always been a matter of some controversy whether music conceived as Bailey's is belongs in the repeatable, reified grooves of a record (and now CD, *mutatis mutandis*). Against the argument that improvisation belongs to the moment of creation only is Bailey's own conviction that it should be documented. Incus Records was co-founded with saxophonist Evan Parker to do just that. Its output is non-commercial and uncompromising, but the surviving releases above are far from ephemeral; remaining vinyl stocks are, however, dwindling fast. Bailey's music resists exact description and evaluation. Eschewing special effects (apart from a swell pedal on his amplified performances and a one-off use of VCS3 synthesizer on *Solo Guitar: Volume One*), he plays intensely and abstractly, a musical discourse that is far removed from the chatty 'conversational' style of much duo jazz. Given certain reservations about his collaborations with Braxton, and allowing that his relationship with Parker (now no longer directly involved with Incus) is exceptional, he has generally preferred to work in the company of percussionists, and a quick comparison of his recordings with the elegant Baptista, the forceful and witty Bennink, and on *Village Life* with African modernists Thebe Lipere and Louis Moholo, and on the recent set with John Stevens demonstrates how thoughtfully contextualized all his work is. Dialogue in the conventional musical sense rarely occurs (with Braxton it sounds like a dialogue of the deaf), but with Phillips on the excellent *Figuring* there is evidence of a to-and-fro of ideas which makes it perhaps the most accessible of the duos.

Despite a long association with Stevens, there was almost no duo material until *Playing* was recorded. Concentrated and flowing, it offers an ideal opportunity, as Steve Beresford points out in his liner-note, to examine at close quarters how this music works. Beresford's analogy to the 'buttterfly effect', in which tiny events have disproportionately significant outcomes at considerable physical or temporal distances, is completely apt.

However, it's still Bailey's solo performances that afford the clearest impression of his pitchless, metreless playing, but these are extremely forbidding and are perhaps best approached only when *Figuring* and *Han* have been absorbed and Bailey's initially unfriendly tongue assimilated. As a crib and consolation, his 1980 book, *Improvisation*, is indispensable.

**** **Drop Me Off At 96th** Scatter 02
    Bailey (*g* solo). 5/86.

*** **Wireforks** Shanachie 5011
    Bailey; Henry Kaiser (*g*). 95.
***(*) **Banter** OO Discs 20
    Bailey; Gregg Bendian (*perc*). 95
***(*) **Harras** Avant AVAN 056
    Bailey; John Zorn (*as*); William Parker (*b*). 95.
**** **The Last Wave** DIW 903
    Bailey; Bill Laswell (*b*); Tony Williams (*d*). 95

The last few years have been extremely productive ones in Bailey's life, though recent indifferent health has curtailed his playing (we wish him a continued recovery) and thrown more emphasis than usual on the CD output. Fortunately, this has remained at a high level, and all of the above are worth having. The duets with Kaiser and Bendian are interesting in the context of our earlier comments about the difficulties he has sometimes had squaring his very radical conception with the more groove-based work of American players. With neither of these players does he have any problem, nor with the self-aware but cartoonish post-bop of Zorn on the apparently big-selling *Harras* CD, which is a recommended place for newcomers to approach the later work. Of the others, Bendian is a fantastically open-minded musician whose interests embrace straight composition, folk forms, free jazz and more straight-ahead, pulse-driven things, while Kaiser is an eccentric (in the strict sense) who is always able to put his instincts out on the line and take chances.

On all three of these discs it is the absolute *concentration* of Bailey's playing that compels attention. The solo session is one of the most intense he has ever recorded, and sceptics who are convinced that this manner of playing is just a matter of rationalized haphazardry are well advised to have a careful listen.

The real shocker is *The Last Wave*, which can be described as a post-modern revenant of Williams's notorious Lifetime by a group officially known as Arcana. One simply isn't used to hearing Derek Bailey in a context like this. It is both exhilarating and rather unsettling, like seeing a favourite uncle give up chitting seed potatoes and debudding chrysanthemums in order to take up ju-jitsu.

Mildred Bailey (1904–51) VOCAL

***(*) **That Rockin' Chair Lady** Topaz TPZ 1007
    Bailey; Bunny Berigan, Jimmy Jake, Zeke Zarchey, Barney Zudecoff, Manny Klein, Charlie Margulis, Gordon Griffin, Bill Hyland, Stew Pletcher, Eddie Meyers, Eddie Sauter, Jimmy Blake (*t*); Tommy Dorsey, Sonny Lee, Leo Moran, Al Mastren, Wes Hein (*tb*); Jimmy Dorsey, Hank D'Amico, Benny Goodman (*cl*); Slats Long (*cl, as*); Frank Simeone, Len Goldstein, Johnny Hodges (*as*); Charles Lamphere (*as, ts*); Larry Binyon, Coleman Hawkins, Herbie Heymer, Jerry Jerome, Chu Berry (*ts*); Fulton McGrath, Arthur Schutt, Teddy Wilson, Joe Liss, Bill Miller, Mary Lou Williams (*p*); Red Norvo (*xy*); Dick McDonough, Alan Hanson, Allan Reuss, Floyd Smith (*g*); Artie Bernstein, Grachan Moncur, Pete Peterson, John Williams (*b*); Stan King, Eddie Dougherty, Maurice Purtill, George Wettling, Dave Tough (*d*). 11/31–3/39.
***(*) **The Rockin' Chair Lady** MCA GRP 16442
    Bailey; Bunny Berigan, Joe Hostetter, Bo Ashford, Bobby Jones, Billy Butterfield, John Best (*t*); Pee Wee Hunt, Billy Ruach, Jack Jenney, Murray McEachern, Hoyt Bohannon, Ed Kusby, Si Zentner (*tb*); Glen Gray, Clarence Hutchenrider, Kenny Sargent, Pat Davis, Johnny Hodges, Ted Nash, Jimmy Lytell, Sal Franzella, Rudy Herman, John Rotella, Wilbur Schwartz (*reeds*); Mel Jenssen (*vn*); Joe Hall, Teddy Wilson, Herman Chittison, Billy Kyle, Willy Usher (*p*); Gene Gifford, Dave Barbour, Carmen Mastren, Al Hendrickson (*g*); Stanley Dennis, Grachan Moncur, Charlie Barbour, Frenchy Covetti, Joe Mondragon (*b*); Tony Briglia, Jimmy Hoskins, Irv Cottler, O'Neil Spencer (*d*); Deep River Boys (*v*). 9/31–4/50.
**** **Rockin' Chair: The Legendary V-Disc Sessions** Vintage Jazz Classics VJC-1006-2
    Bailey; Roy Eldridge, Yank Lawson, Mickey McMickle (*t*); Vernon Brown, Ward Silloway (*tb*); Aaron Sachs, Benny Goodman (*cl*); Reggie Merrill, Hymie Schertzer (*as*); Art Rollini, Wolf Tayne (*ts*); Ernie Caceres (*bs*); Teddy Wilson, Ellis Larkins, Danny Negri (*p*); Red Norvo (*xy*); Tommy Kay, Remo Palmieri, Carmen Mastren, Gene Fields (*g*); Clyde Lombardi, Gene Traxler, Beverley Peer (*b*); Eddie Dell, Specs Powell (*d*); plus various unidentified personnel. 43–51.
*** **Me And The Blues** Savoy SV-0200
    Bailey; Irving Randolph (*t*); Henderson Chambers (*tb*); Hank D'Amico (*cl*); Ellis Larkins (*p*); Barry Galbraith (*g*); Al Hall, Beverley Peer (*b*); Specs Powell, Jimmy Crawford (*d*); strings. 3/46–47.

Mildred Bailey has at last secured some decent representation on CD, though, since her own discography is somewhat scattered, perhaps it's no surprise that it's taken a while for this fine singer to be properly anthologized in the format. She had claims to be fêted on a par with Holiday and Fitzgerald –

and she started recording well before either of them, with her first version of her signature, 'Rockin' Chair', dating back to 1931 – yet she was more of a transitional figure than either of those giants. Her early records suggest a singer struggling, gently, with the old style of Broadway belting (difficult enough for someone with a small voice), while some of the later ones are almost too placid and formal; yet she never lost the vaudevillian tang of the classic blues singers of the 1920s, which helped her put over risqué numbers like 'Jenny' or the wartime novelty 'Scarp Your Fat'. Lacking either Holiday's modern pathos or Fitzgerald's monumental swing, her art is modest, stylized and innately graceful, and over these four discs it is often quietly intoxicating.

Luckily, there is little duplication among these discs and they make up a useful portrait of Bailey. The Topaz compilation concentrates on the 1930s and covers some fine sessions with the Dorsey brothers (including Berigan in fine form), the superb 'Junk Man' with Benny Goodman, several tracks with then-husband Red Norvo and two rather muffled and low-fi tracks with a Mary Lou Williams group. Transfers are patchy – the Brunswicks sound excellent, the Columbias and Vocalions are boomy in the bass – but mostly acceptable. The MCA compilation offers surprisingly bright and clear sound (aside from the rather scratchy 1931 session) but concentrates on later tracks from 1941 to 1950. Both discs include the very fine 1935 date with Hodges, Berigan and Wilson. MCA's tracks which feature Mildred with the Delta River Boys are something of an acquired taste, but the disc is almost worth having just for the lovely 'Lover Come Back To Me' with Herman Chittison on piano.

Ironically, it's the VJC scrapbook of V-Disc titles which features some of the very best of Bailey. Four tracks from 1943, with Wilson as sole accompanist (and how much finer he sounds here than he usually did with Holiday!) are so sublime that they earn four stars on their own, especially the absolutely definitive version of 'Rockin' Chair'. But there is also a track with a Benny Goodman all-star band, a gorgeous 'Someday Sweetheart' with a Red Norvo quintet, a charming 'I'll Close My Eyes' with Ellis Larkins, and two songs cut in the year of Bailey's death which still find her in fine form. Sound is inconsistent, though never distracting.

The Savoy CD is a brief but still impressive set of ten songs dating from the mid-'40s, half with orchestra, half with another Ellis Larkins group. This is short measure, like most of the Savoy CDs. Yet several of these interpretations, such as a heart-sore 'Can't We Be Friends', can stand with the best of Bailey's music. There is no one quite like her in jazz singing.

Chet Baker (1929–88) TRUMPET, FLUGELHORN, VOCAL

** Live At The Trade Winds 1952 Fresh Sound FSCD-1001
Baker; Ted Ottison (t); Sonny Criss (as); Wardell Gray, Jack Montrose, Dave Pell (ts); Les Thompson (hca); Jerry Mandell, Al Haig (p); Harry Babasin (clo); Bob Whitlock, Dave Bryant (b); Lawrence Marable, Larry Bunker (d). 3–8/52.

*** LA Get Together Fresh Sound FSRCD 1022
Baker; Stan Getz (ts); Russ Freeman (p); Joe Mondragon, Carson Smith (b); Larry Bunker, Shelly Manne (d). 6 & 12/53.

*** Witch Doctor Original Jazz Classics OJC 609
Baker; Rolf Ericson (t); Bud Shank (as, bs); Jimmy Giuffre, Bob Cooper (ts); Russ Freeman, Claude Williamson (p); Howard Rumsey (b); Max Roach, Shelly Manne (d). 9/53.

*** Ensemble And Sextet Fresh Sound FSRCD 175
Baker; Bob Brookmeyer (tb); Jack Montrose, Phil Urso (ts); Herb Geller (as, ts); Bob Gordon, Bud Shank (bs); Russ Freeman, Bobby Timmons (p); Jimmy Bond, Joe Mondragon, Carson Smith (b); Peter Littman, Shelly Manne (d). 12/53, 9/54, 7/56.

*** Big Band Pacific Jazz 781202
Baker; Norman Raye, Conte Candoli (t); Bob Burgess, Frank Rosolino (tb); Bob Brookmeyer (vtb); Art Pepper, Fred Waters (as); Bud Shank (as, bs); Phil Urso (ts, bs, as); Bob Graf, Bill Perkins (ts); Bill Hood (bs); Russ Freeman, Bobby Timmons (p); Jimmy Bond, Carson Smith (b); Peter Littman, James McLean, Shelly Manne, Lawrence Marable (d). 9/54, 10/56.

*** My Funny Valentine Pacific Jazz 828262
Baker; Bob Brookmeyer (vtb); Bud Shank (f); Herb Geller (as, ts); Jack Montrose (ts); Bob Gordon (bs); Russ Freeman, Pete Jolly (p); Corky Hale (hp); Jimmy Bond, Red Mitchell, Joe Mondragon, Carson Smith, Leroy Vinnegar, Bob Whitlock (b); Larry Bunker, Stan Levey, Peter Littman, Shelly Manne, Lawrence Marable, Bob Neel, Bobby White (d). 7/53–7/56.

There was considerable surprise first time around at the sheer size of Chet Baker's discography. It has altered very little since then. Some later items have disappeared (the material on Philology, for instance, has rather intermittent currency); some more live material has turned up, and will continue to do so. The most important initiative has been Pacific's rationalization of some of the mid-'50s material. Compilations will doubtless continue to proliferate. Newcomers may want to start with the better of them, or else to work their way through some of the more positively reviewed discs listed below.

Chet's crucial years came right at the beginning of his career, 1952–3, when he played with Charlie Parker (undocumented in the studios) and in Gerry Mulligan's pianoless quartet; Stan Getz joined Chet in a similar group at The Haig in LA in June 1953 (recorded on *LA Get Together*), returning that Christmas for a more conventional, piano-driven quintet. Some of the Monday-night jam sessions at the Trade Winds Club in Inglewood, California, produced the music collected on the Fresh Sound CD: scrappily recorded, it doesn't make much of an album, but Baker already sounds like himself – cool, restrained, diffidently lyrical – and Criss is very much himself, a fire-engine next to Baker's roadster. Gray, Montrose and the mysterious Les Thompson garner other features, but it's nothing special. *Witch Doctor* was recorded at the Lighthouse and sounds superior, though again the diffuseness of the jam-session atmosphere tends to militate against it standing up as a record in its own right.

Ensemble And Sextet cobbles a bunch of Jack Montrose and Bill Holman arrangements, recorded in Hollywood in 1953 and 1954 (and originally released on a 10-inch LP), with a single track from a later Forum Theatre engagement which is reviewed below. The September 1954 material also appears on the Pacific *Big Band* CD, which pairs it with the ensemble tracks from an October 1956 band recording. It's unfortunate that the material falls the way it does, because collectors will certainly want to have all these sessions, irrespective of the overlap. Both are mono sets, but the Pacific probably has a shade more oomph.

MFV is one of a proliferating sub-genre of (mainly) vocal compilations. Individual sessions can probably be identified by reference to dates, but this is unlikely to be of interest to serious collectors. Insomniac romantics may well find it pleasing.

***(*) **The Best Of Chet Baker Plays** Pacific Jazz CDP 7971612
    Baker; Conte Candoli, Norman Faye (*t*); Frank Rosolino (*tb*); Bob Brookmeyer (*vtb*); Bud Shank (*as, bs*); Herb Geller, Art Pepper (*as*); Richie Kamuca, Jack Montrose, Phil Urso, Bill Perkins (*ts*); Russ Freeman, Bobby Timmons, Pete Jolly, Carl Perkins (*p*); Carson Smith, Joe Mondragon, Curtis Counce, Leroy Vinnegar, Jimmy Bond (*b*); Larry Bunker, Lawrence Marable, Shelly Manne, Stan Levey, Peter Littman (*d*); Bill Loughborough (*perc*). 7/53–10/56.

**** **Let's Get Lost: The Best Of Chet Baker Sings** Pacific Jazz CDP 79299322
    Baker; Russ Freeman (*p*); Carson Smith, Jimmy Bond, Joe Mondragon (*b*); Shelly Manne, Bob Neel, Lawrence Marable, Peter Littman (*d*). 2/53–10/56.

*** **The Route** Pacific Jazz CDP 7929312
    Baker; Art Pepper (*as*); Richie Kamuca (*ts*); Pete Jolly (*p*); Leroy Vinnegar (*b*); Stan Levey (*d*). 7/56.

*** **Playboys** Pacific Jazz CDP 7944742
    Baker; Art Pepper (*as*); Phil Urso (*ts*); Carl Perkins (*p*); Curtis Counce (*b*); Lawrence Marable (*d*). 10/56.

*** **At The Forum Theater** Fresh Sound FSRCD-168
    Baker; Phil Urso (*ts*); Bobby Timmons (*p*); Jimmy Bond (*b*); Peter Littman (*d*). 7/56.

***(*) **Chet Baker And Crew** Pacific Jazz 781205
    As above. 7/56.

*** **Chet Baker Cools Out** Boplicity CDBOP 013
    As above, except add Art Pepper (*as*), Richie Kamuca (*ts*), Pete Jolly (*p*), Leroy Vinnegar (*b*), Stan Levey (*d*). 7/56.

Richard Bock began recording Baker as a leader when the quartet with Mulligan began attracting rave notices and even a popular audience, and the records the trumpeter made for Pacific Jazz remain among his freshest and most appealing work. The material is currently a little scattered across the seven releases listed above, two of which are best-ofs, and one – *The Route* – which was subsequently put together from tracks strewn across various compilations over the years. *Playboys*, co-credited to Pepper and Baker, is good if under-powered: somehow the results never quite match up to what were the ingredients for a superb band, with Jimmy Heath's tunes offering apparently no more than workmanlike inspiration for the soloists. *The Route* is stronger: Kamuca is strong enough to match the other horns, and the rhythm section does a surprisingly better job on what are mostly standards. On *Forum Theater* and *Cools Out*, Urso's almost mentholated tenor is an apposite foil, but the music is rather under-achieved and all too similar to many of the sessions being cut in the city in this period. A couple of tracks duplicate each other on these two CDs (not all the tracks were made for Pacific), and the Boplicity disc includes a single item from the *Route* band. The appearance in 1993 of *And Crew*, with two previously unissued tracks and material formerly issued on Jazz West Coast and Crown, offers pretty definitive coverage of this material, and there's no earthly reason to plump for the Fresh Sound instead.

To hear the best of Baker himself, one must turn to the other records. Controversy has simmered over the extent of Baker's powers: a poor reader, a restrained technician, he sticks to the horn's middle range and picks at bebop lines as if they were something that might do him harm; yet he can play with sometimes amazing accomplishment. The blues 'Bea's Flat' (on *The Best Of Chet Baker Plays*), a scintillating line by Russ Freeman, provokes a solo of agility enough to dismiss charges of Baker's incompetence as ludicrous. It was on the various quartet sessions with Freeman that Baker did most of his best work for Pacific, and it's a pity that they are currently available only in the excellent Mosaic boxed-set (see Introduction). The five tracks on *Plays* will have to suffice. The rest of the compilation makes an intelligent choice from the trumpeter's other sessions, and – as the title suggests – it's all trumpet and no vocals.

The other disc contains what are still Baker's most popular recordings, his first vocal sessions for Pacific. The 20 tracks include all of the original *Chet Baker Sings* LP, which is a modest classic in its way. Baker's soft, pallidly intimate voice retained its blond timbre to the end of his life, but here – with his phrasing and tone uncreased by any trace of hard living – it sounds as charming as it ever would, and a song such as 'There Will Never Be Another You' is so deftly organized for voice, trumpet and rhythm section (Freeman's role here is as crucial as it is on the instrumental sessions) that it is very hard not to enjoy the music, even if it has become as buttressed by glamorous legend as much of Billie Holiday's later output.

***(*) **Chet Baker In Paris Volume 1** Emarcy 837474-2
  Baker; Richard Twardzik, Gerard Gustin (*p*); Jimmy Bond (*b*); Peter Littman, Bert Dale (*d*). 10/55.

***(*) **Chet Baker In Paris Volume 2** Emarcy 837475-2
  As above, except add Benny Vasseur (*tb*), Jean Aldegon (*as*), Armand Migiani (*ts*), William Boucaya (*bs*), René Urtreger (*p*). 10/55.

***(*) **Chet Baker In Paris Volume 3** Emarcy 837476-2
  Baker; Benny Vasseur (*tb*); Reddy Ameline (*as*); Bobby Jaspar, Jean-Louis Chautemps, Armand Migiani (*ts*); William Boucaya (*bs*); René Urtreger, Francy Boland (*p*); Eddie De Haas, Benoit Quersin (*b*); Jean-Louis Viale, Charles Saudrais, Pierre Lemarchand (*d*). 12/55–3/56.

*** **Chet Baker In Paris Volume 4** Emarcy 837477-2
  As above three discs. 10/55–3/56.

*** **Live In Europe, 1956** Accord 556622
  Baker; Jean-Louis Chautemps (*ts*); Francy Boland (*p*); Eddie De Haas (*b*); Charles Saudrais (*d*). 1/56.

***(*) **Verve Jazz Masters 32** Verve 840632
  Baker; Benny Vasseur (*tb*); Jean Aldegon (*as*); Frank Strozier (*as, f*); Stan Getz, Armand Migiani, Jean-Louis Chautemps, Phil Urso (*ts*); William Boucaya (*bs*); Leon Cohen, Wilford Holcombe, Henry Freeman, Seldon Powell, Alan Ross (*reeds*); Francy Boland, Jodie Christian, Dick Twardzik, Hank Jones, Hal Galper, Gerard Goustin, Bob James, René Urtreger (*p*); Everett Barksdale (*g*); Caterina Valente (*g, v*); Jimmy Bond, Eddie De Haas, Richard Davis, Michael Fleming, Victor Sproles (*b*); Nils-Bertil Dahlander, Connie Kay, Charlie Rice, Charles Saudrais, Marshall Thompson (*d*) 10/55–6/65.

Baker's Parisian sessions are among his finest and most considered work. The celebrated association with Richard Twardzik – abruptly terminated by the latter's ugly narcotics death – is followed on Volume 1, with tantalizing Twardzik originals such as 'The Girl From Greenland' and almost equally interesting writing from Bob Zieff to engage Baker's interest. The drift of the sessions varies from spare and introspective quartet music to more swinging larger groups, and it's by no means all pale and melancholic: what's striking is the firmness of Baker's lines and his almost Tristano-like logic on occasion. There is some very downcast music in the session immediately following Twardzik's death, but otherwise lyricism and energy usually combine to high effect. Of the four Emarcys, only the last, which is a supplemental set of alternative takes, is comparatively inessential. For non-specialists, though, the *Jazz Masters* compilation is good value for money. It includes a track from the October '55 sessions, with later European material and a group of tracks recorded back in America in 1964 and 1965; the best of these are probably the four songs recorded with Urso and Strozier in New York, November 1964, a highlight for that period. The Accord is unexpectedly bright and precise for its time and place and contains excellent (if not classic Chet) solos on 'Stella By Starlight' and 'You Don't Know What Love Is'.

*** **It Could Happen To You** Original Jazz Classics OJC 303
  Baker; Kenny Drew (*p*); George Morrow, Sam Jones (*b*); Dannie Richmond, Philly Joe Jones (*d*). 8/58.

*** **Chet Baker In New York** Original Jazz Classics OJC 207
  Baker; Johnny Griffin (*ts*); Al Haig (*p*); Paul Chambers (*b*); Philly Joe Jones (*d*). 9/58.

*** **Chet** Original Jazz Classics OJC 087
  Baker; Herbie Mann (*ts, f*); Pepper Adams (*bs*); Bill Evans (*p*); Kenny Burrell (*g*); Paul Chambers (*b*); Connie Kay, Philly Joe Jones (*d*). 3/59.

*** **Plays The Best Of Lerner & Loewe** Original Jazz Classics OJC 137
> Baker; Herbie Mann (*ts, f*); Zoot Sims (*ts, as*); Pepper Adams (*bs*); Bill Evans, Bob Corwin (*p*); Earl May (*b*); Clifford Jarvis (*d*). 7/59.

Perhaps Baker wanted nothing more than to be a part of the modern-jazz mainstream; certainly, after his earlier adventures, his records were taking on the appearance of another bebop trumpeter wandering from session to session. These are all worthwhile records, but without any regular cast of players Chet sounds like a man trying to be one of the boys. He has no problem with the assertiveness of the group on *In New York*, which shows how far he'd come from the supposed early fumblings (never very apparent from the actual records). But this set, and the Lerner & Loewe collection and the similarly directed *Chet*, aren't very different from the standard bop outings of the time: good, but working off a solid routine. *It Could Happen To You* is more of a singing record, and it includes a couple of his most charming efforts on 'Do It The Hard Way' and 'I'm Old Fashioned'.

*** **Italian Movies** Liuto LRS 0063
> Baker; Piero Umiliani Band. 58–62.

No revelations or stylistic jumps of the sort effected by Miles Davis in his score for *L'Ascenseur pour l'échafaud* but excellent and idiomatic music nevertheless. All the pieces are written by pianist Umiliani for a variety of settings from small group to orchestra. The recordings are soaked in atmosphere, sometimes at the expense of hearing Chet correctly, but this does not significantly diminish the impact of these attractive sessions.

*** **With Fifty Italian Strings** Original Jazz Classics OJC 492
> Baker; Mario Pezzotta (*tb*); Glauco Masetti (*as*); Gianni Basso (*ts*); Fausto Papetti (*bs*); Giulio Libano (*p, cel*); Franco Cerri (*b*); Gene Victory (*d*). 9/59.
(*) **In Milan Original Jazz Classics OJC 370
> Baker; Glauco Masetti (*as*); Gianni Basso (*ts*); Renato Sellani (*p*); Franco Cerri (*b*); Gene Victory (*d*). 9–10/59.

Back in Europe, Baker lived in Italy, where he eventually ended up in jail. The strings album is a rather good one of its kind: it was inevitable that Baker would go with this treatment eventually, and by now he was assured enough not to let the horn solos blow away on the orchestral breeze. 'Violets For Your Furs', for instance, makes the most of both the melody and the changes. *In Milan* features a good band – Basso was one of the leading Italians of the day – but it's an uneventful session.

*** **The Italian Sessions** RCA Bluebird 82001
> Baker; Bobby Jaspar (*ts, f*); Amadeo Tommasi (*p*); René Thomas (*g*); Benoit Quersin (*b*); Daniel Humair (*d*). 62.
*** **Somewhere Over The Rainbow** RCA Bluebird 90640
> As above. 62.

A fine group – it was mostly Bobby Jaspar's, with local man Tommasi sitting in – and Baker has to work hard to get some room. Quersin and Humair are a grooving rhythm section, Thomas gets in some voluble solos, and Jaspar is his usual mix of detachment and intensity; Baker, though, seems undecided whether to play hot or cool. *Somewhere Over The Rainbow* offers a budget-price version of the same music, minus two tracks.

*** **Baker's Holiday** EmArCy 838 204
> Baker; Alan Ross, Henry Freeman, Seldon Powell, Leon Cohen, Wilford Holcombe (*reeds*); Everett Barksdale (*g*); Hank Jones (*p*); Richard Davis (*b*); Connie Kay (*d*). 65.

Chet on flugelhorn and as a vocalist obeying what he thought was the most impressive aspect of Billie Holiday's singing, that she never raised her voice. It's a warm, swinging session that is kept quite deliberately low-key. On the bigger horn, Chet actually doesn't sound so very different, a little broader, a little less clipped in faster passages, but essentially the same. Richard Davis emerges much more clearly than on the LP, and he and Jones provide the springboard for graceful solos on 'Travelin' Light' and 'That Ole Devil Called Love', our personal favourites from an album with a box of chocolates flavour.

*** **You Can't Go Home Again** A&M 396997
> Baker; Paul Desmond (*as*); Michael Brecker (*ts*); Hubert Laws (*f, bf, picc*); John Scofield (*g*); Richie Beirach (*p, ky*); Kenny Barron, Don Sebesky (*ky*); Ron Carter (*b*); Alphonso Johnson, Tony Williams (*d*); Ralph McDonald (*perc*); strings. 5/72.
(****) **My Funny Valentine** Philology W 30 2
> Baker; Stan Getz (*ts*); Nicola Stilo (*f*); Philip Catherine (*g*); Nino Bisceglie, Kenny Drew, Gil Goldstein, Michael Graillier, Mike Melillo, Enrico Pieranunzi (*p*); Furio Di Castri, George Mraz, Edy Olivieri, Jean-Louis Rassinfosse, Larry Ridley (*b*); David Lee, Victor Lewis, Ilario De Marinis (*d*). 80–87.

In 1968, having moved to San Francisco, Chet was attacked and severely beaten, suffering the kind of injuries to his mouth that horn players dread. The incident has been explained as a random mugging, and as a 'reminder' of defaulted drug payments by a local supplier. Whatever the explanation, the loss of several teeth and a nearly unbreakable narcotics habit gave his face that caved-in, despairing look that it wears on a score of album covers from the 1980s. If Chet began as a golden youth, he ended his days as a death's-head.

F. Scott Fitzgerald wrote that there were no second acts in American lives. To an extent, Chet bore that out. The years between 1970 and his rather mysterious death in 1988 were a prolonged curtain. What they did confirm was the truth of another literary tag, Thomas Wolfe's 'You can't go home again', which was used for a wonderful quartet piece, recorded by the slowly rehabilitating trumpeter in 1972 with Paul Desmond, by far the best thing on the A&M album, though by no means representative of its rather slick, fusion-tinged product. America really didn't know what to do with him, other than wrap him up in no-substance parcels like this, and he left for Europe again in 1975.

For the remainder of his life, Chet lived out of a suitcase. He enjoyed cult status in Europe and followed an exhausting and seemingly futile itinerary, 'going single' with local musicians. Having moved over to flugelhorn after his beating, he gradually restored his lip. The late sound is frail, airy, almost ethereal. Usually assumed to be a development of Miles Davis's style (and Chet followed a similar repertoire of standards), it was actually more reminiscent of Fats Navarro at his most delicate and attenuated. Unlike Miles, Chet did not favour mutes but developed a quiet, breathy delivery that made such accessories irrelevant.

His singing voice, which took on an increasingly significant role in his work, was a perfect match for his playing, a slight, hurt tenor, with a wistful vibrato. Though his singing was valued out of all proportion to its real worth, it served as a reminder of how important an understanding of the lyrics was to Chet, who often sounds as if he is softly enunciating the words through his horn. No song characterized his last years more fully than 'My Funny Valentine', another Miles-associated tune that he played and sang at almost every concert he gave. It appears with absolute predictability on the majority of the live albums and was the encore to the last full-scale concert he gave.

The Philology compilation brings together seven different performances of the song and illustrates a significant point about 'late Chet'. Though the material was increasingly repetitive, Chet's treatment of it was rarely formulaic, but adapted itself to the demands of particular contexts and moods. There is, then, a dramatic difference between the all-star confrontation with Stan Getz at the Jazzhus Montmartre in 1983 and the very long version recorded with a drummerless quartet in Senigallia the year before he died. In contrast to its nearly 16 minutes, a July 1975 performance with Kenny Drew and a bebop-based rhythm section at Pescara is untypically boiled down. Performances range from the straightforward and melodic to the near-abstract, and this is characteristic of the late years. There is a huge mass of material, but it is more various than initially appears. There is almost always something of interest, and only patient sampling will separate the corn from the chaff, the tough-minded music from the sentimental corn.

*** **In Concert** India Navigation IN 1052
   Baker; Lee Konitz (*as*); Michael Moore (*b*); Beaver Harris (*d*). 74.
Not a label on which one would expect to find either of the two frontmen, concentrating as it did largely on avant-garde music. This set, apparently Chet's first in America for some time, was recorded at Ornette Coleman's New York City loft. It's standard bop fare, freeze-dried and then set to the quite demanding rhythm set up by Moore and Harris. Sonny Rollins's 'Airegin' gets things moving and a long 'Au Privave' completes the first side. Later tracks are more representative of Chet's style, and he shapes some lovely solos on 'Body And Soul' (demonstrating that it's not just a tenor saxophonist's number), 'Willow Weep For Me' and 'Walkin''. The sound is rather poor, and there's quite a lot of surface noise on the LPs, but the music is interesting enough and fills in an awkward gap in the current discography.

*** **She Was Good To Me** Epic 450954
   Baker; Paul Desmond (*as*); Hubert Laws (*f*); Romeo Penque (*f, ob*); George Marge (*af, ob*); David Friedman (*vib*); Bob James (*p*); Lewis Eley, Max Ellen, Barry Finclair, Paul Gershman, Harry Glickman, Emmanuel Green, Harold Kohon, David Nadien, Herbert Sorkin (*vn*); Warren Lash, Jesse Levy, George Ricci (*clo*); Ron Carter (*b*); Jack DeJohnette, Steve Gadd (*d*). 7, 10 & 11/74.

*** **Carnegie Hall Concert, Volume 1 & 2** CTI EPC 450554
   Baker; Gerry Mulligan (*bs*); Ed Byrne (*tb*); Dave Samuels (*vib*); Bob James (*p*); John Scofield (*g*); Ron Carter (*b*); Harvey Mason (*d*). 11/74.
In the main, Sebesky's arrangements are flattering, but the violins are a bit sticky and Chet's solos tend to sit on top like decorations on a cake. Desmond's presence should, perhaps, have led to something special, but he sounds restrained and even hesitant. What wouldn't we give to hear just Baker with Desmond, Carter and DeJohnette, with a sympathetic piano player or guitarist.

That almost happens at the twentieth-anniversary reunion of the Mulligan/Baker group, except that, hey, far from pianoless, this one's got piano, vibes *and* guitar. Though listed here, it's probably more appropriately reviewed under Mulligan's name, and it can also be found there.

***(*) Once Upon A Summertime Original Jazz Classics O J C 405
Baker; Greg Herbert (*ts*); Harold Danko (*p*); Ron Carter (*b*); Mel Lewis (*d*). 2/77.

Originally released on Galaxy, this is a fine, straightforward jazz session. Herbert isn't particularly well known, but he acquits himself with honour in a no-frills ballad style, with occasional glimpses of a tougher, hard-bop diction peeking through. Chet plays very cleanly and sounds in better lip than at any time for the previous ten years. The rhythm section can't be faulted. Good versions of 'E.S.P.' and 'The Song Is You', with Danko well to the fore on the latter.

**** Live At Nick's Criss Cross Jazz Criss 1027
Baker; Phil Markowitz (*p*); Scott Lee (*b*); Jeff Brillinger (*d*). 11/78.

**(*) Two A Day Dreyfus Jazz Line F D M 365092
Baker; Phil Markovitz; Jean-Louis Rassinfosse (*b*); Jeff Brillinger (*d*). 12/78.

Distinguished by a notably fresh choice of material, this is another fine jazz set. Richie Beirach's 'Broken Wing' was written specially for Chet, but the long version of Wayne Shorter's 'Beautiful Black Eyes' (it can also be heard on the later France's Concert session) is the product of an unexpected enthusiasm that fed the trumpeter with new and relatively untried material. Markowitz is an admirably responsive accompanist and fully merits 'featured' billing on the sleeve. The Shorter track is by far the longest thing on the session, though two CD bonuses, the relatively predictable standards 'I Remember You' and 'Love For Sale', are both over ten minutes. Gerry Teekens is too sophisticated and demanding a producer to have settled for just another ballad album and, with the exception of the two last tracks, this is extremely well modulated, one of a mere handful of records from the last two decades of Chet's career that have to be considered essential.

By contrast, the live session from Hérouville, France, is pretty nondescript, though recorded only a month later and with essentially the same band. Those who saw Chet on this trip will confirm that 'two a day' wasn't the reality of the situation at all, and it shows in the playing. Where *Live At Nick's* finds him crisp and pointed (albeit according to his own laid-back standard), the later session is merely messy and not helped by a cack-handed recording.

***(*) The Touch Of Your Lips Steeplechase 1122
Baker; Doug Raney (*g*); Niels-Henning Orsted-Pedersen (*b*). 6/79.

*** Daybreak Steeplechase 1142
As above. 10/79.

*** This Is Always Steeplechase 1168
As above. 10/79.

*** Someday My Prince Will Come Steeplechase 1180
As above. 10/79.

Chet greatly relished this format (and returned to it to even greater effect with Philip Catherine and Jean-Louis Rassinfosse in the mid-1980s). The absence of a drummer allowed him to develop long, out-of-tempo lines that were reminiscent of Miles Davis's ballad experiments in the 1950s in which bar-lines were largely ignored and phrases were overlapped or elided. This broke down the conventional development of a solo, replacing it with a relatively unstructured sequence of musical incidents, all of them directly or more obliquely related to the main theme. This was easier to do on ballads, and Chet's dynamics became increasingly restrictive in the last few years. *Chet's Choice*, below, is more varied in pace, but in 1979 Chet was still suffering some intonation problems, presumably as a result of losing teeth, and he fluffs some of the faster transitions. On slower material he sounds masterful and is ably accompanied by Raney's soft-bop guitar and NHOP's towering bass (a studio duo album with the big Dane would have been something to hear). Steeplechase are often guilty of issuing poorly recorded *audio vérité* sessions with little adjustment of balance or volume. This, though, is admirably done, though there's more than an element of overkill in the other three sessions, apparently from later that same year, where there really isn't enough good material for more than one carefully edited CD, a double at most.

*** All Blues Arco 3 ARC 102
Baker; Jean-Paul Florence (*g*); Henri Florence (*p*); James Richardson (*b*); Tony Mann (*d*); Rachel Gould (*v*). 9/79.

Chet recorded surprisingly rarely with other singers. The tracks with Rachel Gould would be more interesting if she had a more appealing voice. There are two versions of 'Valentine' and two takes of 'Round About Midnight', a tune he tackled only rather rarely despite a considerable affection for the more lyrical side of Monk. The Florences play effectively, but they are not kindly served by a very dry acoustic. Generally good.

*** **No Problem** Steeplechase SCCD 31131
    Baker; Duke Jordan (*p*); Niels-Henning Orsted-Pedersen (*b*); Norman Fearrington (*d*). 10/79.
A more than usually boppish set for this vintage. Though none of the material is orthodox bebop, there
is something about Chet's phrasing, and Jordan's tight, unelaborate comping, that looks back to a much
earlier period. That may recommend the session to those who find the later material too far removed
from the blues. Others may feel that Chet had moved too far beyond this kind of approach to be able to
return to it comfortably.

***(*) **Burnin' At Backstreet** Fresh Sound FSR CD 128
    Baker; Drew Salperto (*p*); Mike Formanek (*b*); Art Frank (*d*). 2/80.
Unconsciously or no, this turns into a tribute by the white Miles Davis to the original and only Miles
Davis. Three Davis compositions – 'Tune Up', 'Milestones' and 'Four' – and a version of 'Stella By
Starlight' that twice quotes from the classic version. Baker often did these tunes, but seldom with this
concentration. He had behind him a very good young band, including the excellent Formanek, and he
had at the time (so it is said) a belief that every date could be his last. There was to be nearly a decade
more of last dates and missed deadlines, but there were few better nights than this. The sound is our only
problem with it. Recorded in the Backstreet Club in New Haven, it is no better than it might be, and
there are a few off-mike moments that disturb the flow of solos. Strongly recommended, all the same.

** **And The Boto Brasilian Quartet** Dreyfus Jazz Line 849228
    Baker; Richard Galliano (*acc*); Riqué Pentoja (*p*); Michel Peyratoux (*b*); José Boto (*d, perc*). 7/
    80.
The combination of electric piano and bass guitar gives this a very dated sound, and Chet sounds rather
diffident on a programme of unfamiliar Brazilian themes. Nevertheless the session does emphasize once
again the number of very different settings in which either inclination or circumstance found him in
these years.

***(*) **Live At Fat Tuesday's** Fresh Sound FSR CD 131
    Baker; Bud Shank (*as*); Hal Galper, Phil Markovitz (*p*); Ron Carter (*b*); Ben Riley (*d*). 4/81.
A great shame that Shank wasn't able to sit in on 'You Can't Go Home Again', thus wakening memories
of the superb Baker–Desmond version; but there's no doubt that the altoist gives Chet a shot in the arm
on their two tracks together. 'In Your Own Sweet Way' is handled with more fire than normal. Shank's
tone (well captured on CD) is clear and bright, and Chet sounds more pungent and full-bodied than
usual. Warmly recommended.

**** **Peace** Enja CD 4016
    Baker; David Friedman (*vib, mar*); Buster Williams (*b*); Joe Chambers (*d*). 82.
By far the most interesting of the later studio sessions, *Peace* consists largely of David Friedman
originals. The exceptions are 'The Song Is You' and a feeling interpretation of the title-piece, a Horace
Silver composition. 'Lament For Thelonious' has an elaborate-sounding melody, built up out of very
simple elements. As on 'Peace', it's Williams rather than Friedman who takes responsibility for sustaining the chord progression, leaving the vibraharpist to elaborate the theme. His response to Chet's first
couple of choruses is softly ambiguous. Chambers also takes a simple but effective solo. The CD has an
alternative take of the opening '3 + 1 = 5', a confident post-bop structure that deserves to be covered
more frequently. Remixed in 1987, the album sounds sharp and uncluttered.

*** **Everything Happens To Me** Timeless SJP 176
    Baker; Kirk Lightsey (*p*); David Eubanks (*b*); Eddie Gladden (*b*). 3/83.
Stars for Lightsey, who has a good proportion of the album to himself, and his characteristically
respectful readings of Wayne Shorter themes. Chet comes in for 'Ray's Idea' and the title-piece, making
more of an impact than he does on many a longer set. Worth buying for Lightsey alone, but collectors
will welcome Chet's trumpet and vocal contributions.

*** **Mister B** Timeless SJP 192
    Baker; Michel Graillier (*p*); Philip Catherine (*g*); Riccardo Del Frà (*b*).
*** **Sings Again** Timeless SJP 238
    As above, except omit Catherine; add John Engels (*d*). 5/83.
Catherine unfortunately shows up on only a single track, the far from typical 'Father Christmas'.
However, the trio sessions on *Mister B* are good enough. Graillier was a sympathetic pianist in the lush,
romantic manner (Danko, Beirach, Galper, Lightsey) which Chet preferred and which one associates
with pianists who accompany singers. The absence of a drummer on the first album is more than made
up for by Del Frà, who is brought through very strongly on this remixed issue, which also includes the
bonus 'White Blues' and the Catherine track. All the same points apply to the *Sings Again* session,
except that Del Frà has been relegated to the background in favour of Engels's notably soft touch,
largely on brushes.

***(*) **Chet Baker At Capolinea** Red CD 123206
>   Baker; Diane Varvra (*ss*); Nicola Stilo (*f*); Michel Graillier (*p*); Riccardo Del Frà (*b*); Leo
>   Mitchell (*d*). 10/83.

*** **A Night At The Shalimar** Philology W 59 2
>   Baker; Nicola Stilo (*f*); Mike Melillo (*p*); Furio Di Castri (*b*). 5/87.

Flute was an integral feature of many of the 1980s groups, and Stilo had a particular facility for the long, slightly shapeless lines that the trumpeter was looking for. These are all attractive sets in a rather lightweight way, but only the Red offers much challenge. Varvra's soprano is used, like the flute, to filigree the backgrounds, allowing Graillier to play slightly more percussively than usual, much as the guitarist plays on the rather good West Winds. The first of these includes material by Richie Beirach, Jimmy Heath, Enrico Pieranunzi, Bud Powell and Miles Davis, which gives a measure of how far afield Chet was searching at the time.

Of the group, the Red is the one to go for. The opening 'Estate' is one of the most imaginative available readings of the Bruno Martino tune and (typical of Chet's unflagging ability to pull out unexpected themes) there is an excellent version of J. J. Johnson's little-heard 'Lament'.

*** **Let's Get Lost** Novus PD 83054
>   Baker; Nicola Stilo (*f, g*); Frank Strazzeri (*p*); John Leftwich (*b*); Ralph Penland (*d, perc*).

Stilo unfortunately appears on only one track here, the evocative 'Zingaro'. Most of the titles are for drummerless trio and are slightly uncertain in register. Things are a little sharper when Penland is playing and 'Every Time We Say Goodbye' and 'I Don't Stand A Ghost Of A Chance With You' are done without undue sentimentality.

**** **Blues For A Reason** Criss Cross Jazz Criss 1010
>   Baker; Warne Marsh (*ts*); Hod O'Brien (*p*); Cecil McBee (*b*); Eddie Gladden (*d*). 9/84.

It has always been a matter of considerable debate whether or not Chet belongs in the 'Cool School', is a Tristano disciple, or has the authentic 'West Coast sound'. Just as it's now recognized in most quarters that Tristano was a much more forceful and swinging player than the conventional image allows, so it's clear that the near-abstraction and extreme chromaticism of Chet's last years were a perfectly logical outgrowth of bebop. Warne Marsh's style has been seen as equally problematic, 'cold', 'dry', 'academic', the apparent antithesis of Chet's romantic expressionism. When the two are put together, as on this remarkable session, it's clear that unsubstantiated generalizations and categorizations quickly fall flat.

While Chet is quite clearly no longer an orthodox changes player, having followed Miles's course out of bop, he's still able to live with Marsh's complex harmonic developments. *Blues For A Reason* stands out from much of the work of the period in including relatively unfamiliar original charts, including three by Chet himself. The best of these, 'Looking Good Tonight', is heard in two versions on the CD option, demonstrating how the trumpeter doesn't so much rethink his whole strategy on a solo as allow very small textural changes to dictate a different development. Marsh, by contrast, sounds much more of a *thinking* player and, to that extent, just a little less spontaneous. The saxophonist's 'Well Spoken', with which the set begins, is perhaps the most challenging single item Chet tackled in his final decade, and he sounds as confident with it as with the well-worn 'If You Could See Me Now' and 'Imagination'. This is an important and quietly salutary album that confounds the more casual dismissals of the trumpeter's latter-day work.

** **My Foolish Heart** I R D T D M 002
>   Baker; Fred Raulston (*vib*); Floyd Darling (*p*); Kirby Stewart (*b*); Paul Guerrero (*d*); Martha
>   Burks (*v*).

** **Misty** I R D T D M 003
>   As above.

** **Time After Time** I R D T D M 004
>   As above. 1/85.

Exhaustive and mostly futile documentation of two nights in Dallas. The performances are well below par and the group sounds self-conscious and slightly contrived. Almost all of the material is familiar, and Martha Burks is merely dull. I R D don't currently list any other titles.

***(*) **Diane** Steeplechase 1207
>   Baker; Paul Bley (*p*). 2/85.

Considerably undervalued as a standards player, Bley is exactly the right duo partner for Chet. His accompaniments frequently dispense with the chords altogether, holding on to the theme with the lightest of touches and allowing the basic rhythm to stretch out and dismantle itself. Typically of this period, the material is quite straightforward, but the treatments are far from orthodox and *Diane* would certainly merit an unqualified fourth star were it not for rather murky sound.

**** **Chet's Choice** Criss Cross Jazz Criss 1016
>Baker; Philip Catherine (*g*); Jean-Louis Rassinfosse (*b*); Hein Van De Geyn (*b*). 6/85.
***(*) **Strollin'** Enja 5005
>As above, except omit Van De Geyn.
(*) **Chet Baker In Bologna Dreyfus Jazz Line 191 133
>As above.

This was the most productive year of Chet's last decade, and in the association with Catherine he hit a purple patch. It was a format he liked and had used to great effect in the 1979 sessions with Doug Raney and NHOP. The Criss Cross session is the most completely satisfying studio record of the period. Playing a basic standards set, he sounds refocused and clear-voiced, with a strength and fullness of tone that is undoubtedly helped by Gerry Teeken's typically professional production job. All three players are recorded in tight close-up, but with excellent separation. Three long tracks – 'My Foolish Heart', Pettiford's 'Blues In The Closet' and 'Stella By Starlight' – are not on the LP.

The Enja performances are equally good, but the live sound isn't quite so distinct and it's a very much shorter set. One interesting link reflects Baker's outwardly unlikely enthusiasm for Horace Silver compositions, 'Doodlin'' on *Choice*, the title-piece on *Strollin'*. Their built-in rhythmic quality is ideal for players like Baker and Catherine who tend to drift out of metre very quickly, developing long, carefully textured improvisations with only a very basic pulse. Both of these sessions are strongly recommended.

The Bologna session is the weakest of the three. The trio doesn't sound comfortably played in, Chet seems to be having intonation problems, even on familiar stuff like 'Valentine' and 'My Foolish Heart', and the sound-balance is frequently awry. Completists only.

** **Symphonically** Soul Note SN 121134
>Baker; Mike Melillo (*p*); Massimo Moriconi (*b*); Giampaola Ascolese (*d*); Orchestra
>Filarmonica Marchigiana. 7/85.

Baker often performed well in front of big orchestras, but this was an over-produced and rather heavy-handed session and contains little of interest. The sound is very slushy and Chet is made to sound rather cavernous.

***(*) **Live From The Moonlight** Philology W 10/11 2 2CD
>Baker; Michel Graillier (*p*); Massimo Moriconi (*b*). 11/85.

More than two and a half hours (on CD) from a single night at the Moonlight Club, Macerata. The extra material comprises three tracks from a third, presumably later, set, and a long rehearsal perform-ance of 'Polka Dots And Moonbeams'. Chet is in good lip and reasonable voice. There isn't a track under ten minutes and most are longer than a quarter of an hour. This, depending on the trumpeter's state of mind, was either his most serious vice or, as here, his most underrated virtue, for he was capable of remarkable concentration and, ironically, compression of ideas, and his up-close examination of themes like 'Estate' and Richie Beirach's 'Night Bird' (CD only) is extremely impressive. As an insight into how Chet worked over an entire evening, this is hard to beat. Without a drummer, the music can start to sound a little rarefied, and Moriconi often isn't clearly audible. A fine document, nevertheless. For a change the liner document includes something more useful than the usual over-emotional '*ciao*, Chet, *mille grazie*', a discography from 1952 to 1988 that lists a sobering 198 items; specialists will doubtless be able to add more to that.

*** **Silent Nights** Dinemec CD CD 04
>Baker; Christopher Mason (*as*); Mike Pellera (*p*); Jim Singleton (*b*); Johnny Vidacovich (*d*).
>1/86.

Given the sheer profusion and range of this discography, it would be more surprising if Chet *hadn't* made a Christmas album. This session was put together as a favour to the young Mason (and one of the authors once had similar reason to be grateful to Chet's generosity in this respect). The trumpeter's only proviso was that the music should be reverent . . . and, lo and behold, another side to Chet revealed. After the Roland Kirk version of 'We Three' – or 'Free' – 'Kings', it might seem difficult to treat it with any sort of reverence in a jazz context but Chet and the young group manage without a blush, and the two versions of 'Silent Night' are quite breathtaking. A backwater project, of course, but one to be enjoyed

***(*) **When Sunny Gets Blue** Steeplechase SCCD 31121
>Baker; Butch Lacy (*p*); Jesper Lundgaard (*b*); Jukkis Uotila (*d*). 2/86.

A rather melancholic session, but one of the better ones from the period. Lacy is a much-underrated piano player. He gives Chet a great deal of room, leaving chords suspended in unexpected places and rarely resorting to predetermined structures even on very familiar tunes. Indeed, he sets up conventional expectations on 'Here's That Rainy Day' and 'You'd Be So Nice To Come Home To' and then con-founds them utterly with altered tonalities and out-of-tempo figures. Lundgaard and Uotila are both thoroughly professional and contribute to a fine, unpredictable set.

(*) **As Time Goes By Timeless SJP 251/2
> Baker; Harold Danko (*p*); Jon Burr (*b*); Ben Riley (*d*). 12/86.
(*) **Cool Cat Timeless SJP 262
> As above.
** **Heartbreak** Timeless SJP 366
> As above, except add Michael Graillier (*p*); Richardo Del Frà (*b*); John Engels (*d*); strings. 86–
> 88, 91.

The first two were recorded at a single session, with considerable emphasis on Chet's singing. Given that his chops sound in very poor shape, this may not have been a matter of choice. Posthumously adding strings to a selection of tunes from the Timeless catalogue clearly was. The editing on *Heartbreak* hasn't been well done and there are joins all over the place, particularly obvious to anyone who knows the original sessions. These are slight enough, though Danko is a fine, lyrical player. Further sweetening doesn't redeem or enliven some very weary material.

***(*) **Memories: Chet Baker In Tokyo** Paddle Wheel K32Y 6270
> Baker; Harold Danko (*p*); Hein Van Der Geyn (*b*); John Engels (*d*). 6/87.
*** **Four: Live In Tokyo – Volume 2** Paddle Wheel K32Y 6281
> as above. 6/87.

Despite crowd-pleasing versions of 'Stella By Starlight' and 'Valentine', the material and arrangements are by no means as predictable as on similar live sets. On Volume 1 there is a brisk reading of Jimmy Heath's staple, 'For Minors Only', a long, long version of Jobim's 'Portrait In Black And White' with Danko eating up the soft bossa rhythm, and then there's a surprise. Like Miles, Chet kept his eyes open for new pop standards and had enjoyed a brief association with Elvis Costello, playing an unforgettable, delay-laden solo on Costello's own version of his anti-Falklands War anthem, 'Shipbuilding'. Chet returns the compliment with a sharp, well-thought-out version of Costello's 'Almost Blue', a song that offers a combination of romantic sentiment and hard-edged melody. This is an excellent set, slightly remote but very true, and the inclusion of a drummer, as so often, gives Chet a much-needed impetus. Volume 2 strongly suggests that the best of the material has already been heard, but anyone who feels enthusiastic about the first set will also want the second, which includes Richie Beirach's lovely 'Broken Wing' and a slightly unusual arrangement of 'Seven Steps To Heaven'. Recommended.

*** **Naima** Philology W 52 2
> Baker; Mario Concetto Andriulli, Pino Caldarola, Martino Chiarulli, Tom Harrell, Mino
> Lacirignola (*t*); Nino Besceglie, Nucci Guerra, Giovanni Pellegrini, Muzio Petrella (*tb*);
> Giovanni Congedo, Franco Lorusso, Silvano Martina, Nicola Nitti, Pino Pichierri (*reeds*); Hal
> Galper, Hank Jones, Kirk Lightsey, Edy Olivieri, Enrico Pieranunzi (*p*); Steve Gilmore, Rocky
> Knower, Ilario De Marinis, Red Mitchell, Massimo Moriconi (*b*); John Arnold, Bill Goodwin,
> Shelly Manne, Vincenzo Mazzone (*d*). 6/83, 9/85, 7, 8 & 11/87.

Billed as Volume 1 of a sequence called 'Unusual Chet', this certainly has some unusual discographical quirks. Two tracks, valuable big-band readings of Benny Golson's 'Killer Joe', 'Lover Man' and Thad Jones's 'A Child Is Born' from 1985 are identified as 'never on record'. Two others, though, including a long version of the Coltrane title-piece with Lightsey, are described as 'never recorded', which presents a philosophical problem or suggests that they're coming from the Other Side.

Essentially, this grab-bag set brings together live tapes of compositions that Chet rarely played or hadn't put on official releases. The big-band tracks are surprisingly strong, though the tone suggests he might be playing a flugelhorn. Much of the rest, like the opening blues scat with Jones, Mitchell and Manne, is rather scrappy. Despite its length, 'Naima' seems rather attenuated. A collector's set, but an interesting sidelight on Chet for non-specialists as well.

*** **The Heart Of The Ballad** Philology W 20 2
> Baker; Enrico Pieranunzi (*p*). 2/88.
***(*) **Little Girl Blue** Philology W 21 2
> Baker; Enrico Pieranunzi (*p*); Enzo Pietropaoli (*b*); Fabrizio Sferra (*d*). 3/88.

Billed as Chet's last studio recordings, these encounters with Pieranunzi and his thoroughly professional Space Jazz Trio were recorded less than a week apart. Predictably, there are no late reversals or epiphanies, just a straightforward reading of some uncontroversial charts. On the group session, Chet counts each tune in but slows up progress after the theme in almost every case, not so much out of hesitancy as an apparent desire to linger over the melody. There are exceptions: 'Old Devil Moon' is quite upbeat and Wayne Shorter's 'House Of Jade', which had been a regular item in Chet's book for a long time, is given a smoothly swinging reading. Pieranunzi brings a crisp formality to his solos. The CD bonus is a long (presumably rehearsal) meditation on 'I Thought About You', which is placed first. It's slightly shapeless but includes some fine passages from Chet that one wouldn't have liked to have missed. The duos aren't particularly compelling, but Pieranunzi is a careful, quietly challenging accompanist and leaves a sufficient number of chords hanging or incompletely resolved to generate a measure of tension that's largely missing on the group set. It's unfortunate there are no tunes in common with the Paul Bley duets, above. Pieranunzi certainly lacks the Canadian's brittle sensitivity and rarely risks anything like Bley's departures from conventional tonality. Generally, though, he shapes up pretty well.

(*) **Live In Rosenheim Timeless SJP 233
> Baker; Nicola Stilo (*g, f*); Marc Abrams (*b*); Luca Flores (*d*). 4/88.

There's a slightly distasteful but commercially understandable desire among record labels to be able to release the last word from a great artist. This, following the final studio session, was billed as the last *quartet* recording. It's pretty thin stuff. Chet takes a turn at the piano, quite inconsequentially, and though the material is reasonably enterprising ('Funk In Deep Freeze', 'Arborway', 'Portait In Black And White') it's played with an almost total lack of conviction. The sound is respectable, though Stilo's flute, long a feature of Chet's groups, is sometimes overpoweringly vibrant.

*** **My Favourite Songs** Enja 5097
> Baker; L. Axelsson, H. Habermann, B. Lanese, M. Moch (*t*); W. Ahlers, E. Christmann, M. Grossman, P. Plato (*tb*); Herb Geller (*as*); A. Boether, H. Ende, K. Nagurski, E. Wurster, John Schröder (*g*); Walter Norris (*p*); W. Schlüter (*vib*); Lucas Lindholm (*b*); Aage Tanggaard (*d*); Radio Orchestra Hannover. 4/88.

*** **Straight From The Heart** Enja 6020
> As above. 4/88.

*** **The Last Concert: Volume I & II** Enja 6074 2CD
> As above. 4/88.

Billed as 'The last great concert' (Volume 1) and 'The great last concert' and only quibbles about one word. This was certainly something more than just another small-group recording, but by no stretch of the imagination does it merit any imputation of greatness. The photograph on the sleeve, repeated in reverse on Volume 2, is quite ghastly, a shrunken, pucker-mouthed shell of a man who looks ten years older than his actual 59 everywhere but the eyes, which still have the soft, faraway look they had back in the 1950s when Chet seemed like the freshest thing out. The horn with the big mouthpiece (pictured dewed with water on the cover of *Naima*, above) still looks burnished and pristine, but it only takes a track or two to realize that by the last year of his life Chet was trading on nothing more than pure sound and reputation. There are no new ideas any more, and the old ones lack the morning freshness that was their greatest lasting stock-in-trade.

There are small-group, big-band and orchestra tracks. There isn't much to choose among them, but for the fact that on the few quintet sessions one listens more attentively to Geller and Walter Norris than to Chet. The run of material is pretty standard, with Miles's 'All Blues', John Lewis's 'Django', 'Summertime', Brubeck's 'In Your Own Sweet Way', Monk's 'Well, You Needn't' and the inevitable 'Valentine' all on Volume 1; the sequel covers slightly less familiar ground, but, yes, the encore is 'My Funny Valentine' again. There's no obvious reason why the two single discs are still listed when a double-CD of the whole event (with no bonus tracks) is now in catalogue – but, as will be obvious from the pages above, unnecessary profusion seems to be the order of the day with this artist and, one way and another, it was the impossibility of maintaining the precarious balance between profusion and empty lack that killed him. Two weeks after the Hannover concert, Chet Baker fell from an Amsterdam hotel window. The exact circumstances of his death have never been satisfactorily explained.

Ginger Baker (born 1939) DRUMS, PERCUSSION

(*) **African Force ITM 1417
> Baker; Ludwig Götz (*tb*); Wolfgang Schmidtke (*ss, ts, bs*); Jan Kazda (*b, g, ky*); J. C. Commodore (*perc, v*); Ampofo Acquah (*perc, g, v*); Ansoumana Bangoura (*perc*); Francis Kwaku A. Mensah (*perc, v*).

*** **Palanquin's Pole** ITM 1433
> Baker; Ampofo Acquah (*perc, g, v*); Ansoumana Bangoura (*perc*); Thomas Akuru Dyani (*perc*); Francis Kwaku A. Mensah (*perc, v*). 5/87.

*** **No Material** ITM 1435
> Baker; Peter Brötzmann (*reeds*); Sonny Sharrock, Nicky Skopelitis (*g*); Jan Kazda (*b*). 3/87.

*** **The Album** ITM 1469
> Baker; Ludwig Götz (*tb*); Courtney Pine (*ts*); Wolfgang Schmidtke (*ts, ss, bs*); Eric Clapton, Dr X. Labaré, Bireli Lagrene, John Mizzarolli (*g*); Jan Kazda (*g, ky*); Jack Bruce, Marco Rikeri (*b*); Art Blakey (*d*); Ampofo Acquah, Ansoumana Bangoura, J. C. Commodore (*perc, v*); Francis Kwaku A. Mensah (*perc*). 11/68, 72, 12/82, 7/85, 87.

**** **Goin' Back Home** Atlantic 7567 82652
     Baker; Bill Frisell (*g*); Charlie Haden (*b*). 3/94.
When the 'supergroup' Cream split up in 1969, there were dark mutterings from the two members who were still talking that it had always 'really' been a jazz group, and not really their thing at all. Eric Clapton and Ginger Baker went on to form Blind Faith and, after its brief (one album, one massive gig) career, Baker found himself tired of supergrouping, formed a percussion-laden outfit called Airforce, which included the still-viable Phil Seamen, and then found he was tired of the whole bloody business and went off to open a studio in Nigeria. *The Album* tells the story in fast forward, with the original 'Sunshine Of Your Love' from Cream, and the deutero-Cream thrash of 'Energy' (also to be found, should you feel strong enough, on the Traditional Line CD), tacked on to a 1972 drum battle with Art Blakey and various African projects from later years.

    Whatever the internal stresses and stated objectives of Cream, Baker has always seemed a jazzer *manqué*, a Charlie Watts figure under whose relentless 4/4s beat a heart tuned to something else entirely. Baker's African Force is a percussion band of formidable energy, occasional sophistication and considerable charm. Whether what they play is 'really' jazz or not is a metaphysical question.

    In addition to the African drummers, the original *African Force* featured all but the drummer (naturally) of the German band, Das Pferd. The polyrhythms bog down a little in the Europeans' more linear approach and the potential for a genuinely creative synthesis is largely missed. *Palanquin's Pole* repeats two of the tracks – 'Brain Damage' and 'Ansoumania' (a punning eponym for one of the drummers) – but the treatment is altogether brighter and more inventive. 'Ginger's Solo' is overlong but, God knows, a lot shorter than the notorious 'Toad' of Cream days, which allowed punters to go for a pint, a three-course dinner and a haircut before Clapton and Bruce picked up their guitars again.

    Second track in, Baker gravely informs the audience that, at this juncture, he and his colleagues would like to administer brain damage. Those interested should skip briskly on to *No Material*, so named as a nod to Bill Laswell's band, Material, and because there was no set list for the concert documented. Baker's project, which lasted for exactly one week in 1987, was the rump of an ambitious three-way collaboration between African Force, Last Exit and Material. Laswell's absence on more lucrative chores meant the recruitment of Skopelitis and, from Das Pferd again, bassist Jan Kazda.

    Fans of Last Exit shouldn't bother listening for anything like Shannon Jackson's polydirectional drumming. Baker plays it unwaveringly straight. Sharrock and Skopelitis crunch and clang away, and Brötzmann squeals furiously. It probably sounded absolutely great at the time. It wears a little thin on subsequent hearings, though nothing like as wearingly as *Unseen Rain*, which hangs in like a convention of Jehovah's Witnesses; but it does confirm Baker's often unrecognized sense of artistic challenge.

    Going Back Home is a refreshing surprise. Teamed up with two top-drawer eclectics, Ginger sounds as if he's having a whale of a time. Nearly 40 years after his debut in Dixieland bands, he's back in a more or less straight jazz context. The interplay among the three on 'Straight, No Chaser' is a revelation; how many people would identify the percussionist blindfold? The set opens with Frisell's Latin-tinged 'Rambler' (not to be confused with 'Ramblin'' later on), but darkens rapidly through the North African tonalities of 'I Lu Kron', and the astonishing epiphanies of Haden's composition, 'In The Moment', on which Frisell finally unleashes his full battery of effects. It's followed by another of the bassist's compositions, the delicate waltz-time 'Spiritual', before going out on Ginger's fierce condemnation of colonialist exploitation in 'East Timor', a disconcertingly antagonistic conclusion to such an unexpectedly expressive record. An improbable partnership, maybe, but well worth checking out.

Jon Balke PIANO, KEYBOARDS

***(*) **Further** ECM 1517
     Balke; Jens Petter Antonsen (*t*); Per Jorgensen (*t, v*); Morten Halle (*as*); Tore Brunborg (*ts, ss*); Anders Jormin (*b*); Audun Klieve (*d*); Marilyn Mazur (*perc*); Gertrud Okland (*vn*); Trond Villa (*vla*); Jonas Franke-Blom (*clo*). 6/93.
This locates itself somewhere on the continuum that links Jan Garbarek and Edward Vesala. Balke favours slow developments, dense textures and a very open-ended harmonic approach. There are New Age longueurs but, given that most of the tracks are brief and to the point, these rarely get in the way. Apart from the leader, soloing is relatively sparse. Brunborg, Halle and Jorgensen are featured in the central section of what is effectively a continuous suite; otherwise the emphasis is on ensemble playing.

    The entrance of the strings – played pizzicato – on 'Horizontal Song' shows how crafty Balke can be. Many of these pieces function as wry musical puzzles, deceptively straightforward at first hearing, but constantly opening up layers of interest. Well worth a try.

Kenny Ball (born 1930) TRUMPET, VOCAL

** **Greensleeves** Timeless TTD 505
Ball; Joe Bennett (*tb, v*); Andy Cooper (*cl, v*); Duncan Swift (*p*); John Fenner (*bj, g*); John
Benson (*b*); Ron Bowden (*d*). 11/82.
** **The Very Best Of Kenny Ball** Timeless TTD 598
As above, except Hugh Ledigo (*p*) replaces Swift. 91–95.

British jazz has never been short of vaudevillians, and Ball is among the most eminent. In between stints
on TV variety shows (well, that was some time ago) he has played trumpet in clubs and cabaret in every
conceivable locale in the UK. It has never got much beyond that, though the peculiarly European
affection for British trad has held him in some esteem, too. His greatest three minutes came with the
unforgettable 'Midnight In Moscow' (no wonder they loved him on his first visit there in 1985), but the
hits have been fewer since then. Actually, he plays a decent, brassy horn, and this edition of the Ball
Jazzmen do all right on the earlier CD. The new compilation of Ball's 1990s recordings is a bit less
appealing since the front line sounds increasingly prone to either fluffs or fatigue, even as the rhythms
sound bouncier than ever. A new recording of 'Midnight In Moscow' sounds more like next morning's
hangover.

Iain Ballamy TENOR SAXOPHONE, SOPRANO SAXOPHONE

***(*) **All Men Amen** B&W BW065
Ballamy; Django Bates (*p, ky, E flat hn*); Steve Watts (*b*); Martin France (*d, perc*). 3 & 4/93.

Ballamy's disappearance from the second edition of this *Guide* may have prompted some to think that
early bets may have been misplaced. After *Balloon Man* on Editions EG in 1989, there was an ominous
silence on the record front, apart from credits under other leaders, notably Bill Bruford's Earthworks.
Needless to say, judging a young jazz musician's progress simply by his recorded output is a fool's
errand. It would have been nice to see Ballamy picked up by a major label, but he scarcely wasted the
intervening time, working at his craft and developing a voice second only to Bates (who joins him here)
for sheer individuality.

The unpredictable grooves of 'Serendipity' and 'Haunted Swing' are the product not of mere caprice but
of many, many nights on the stand. The group sounds played-in, intimate *and* communicative, and
Bates's piano playing is some of the best he has ever committed to record, full-voiced and unfussy. He
comes close on occasion to hijacking the whole session, except that Ballamy himself is playing so well,
and completely in charge of things. His theme and development on the jovially pastoral 'Meadow' is
gorgeous (Bates contributes a horn part which is just right) and there is an intellectual sophistication to
'Blennie' which has not been heard from him before. Production is pin-sharp but also very warm; credit
to Peter Schulze at Radio Bremen (and, yes, why did it have to be Bremen and not Birmingham or
Brent?).

Jon Ballantyne (born 1964) PIANO

*** **Sky Dance** Justin Time JUST-30
Ballantyne; Joe Henderson (*ts*); Neil Swainson (*b*); Jerry Fuller (*d*). 12/88.
*** **A Musing** Justin Time JUST 39-2
Ballantyne; Paul Bley (*p*); Dave Laing (*d*). 2/91.

Ballantyne is an accomplished Canadian pianist, but he's also rather chameleonic: the major stylistic
trait of these two rather good records is his ability to sound like whoever else he fancies, though luckily
there's enough good humour about it to make him stand aside from many of the post-Tyner pianists.
The meeting with Henderson is distinguished by the saxophonist's now almost predictable inventiveness
and lustrous solos, with a good blues in 'BYO Blues' and a nicely sonorous ballad performance of the
title-track. With Bley, who sits in on five tunes – there are two solos and two duets with Laing –
Ballantyne finds that his mischievous streak is rather akin to Bley's own, and there is some suitably
elliptical playing by both men, though Ballantyne's solo, 'Question', seems almost slavishly Bley-like.
The best things happen on the two duos with Laing, whose rather circumspect and deftly stroked
playing adds subtle rhythmic colour rather than impetus to Ballantyne's own playing.

Billy Bang (born 1947) VIOLIN

**** Rainbow Gladiator Soul Note 121016
    Bang, Charles Tyler (*as, bs*); Michele Rosewoman (*p*); Wilber Morris (*b*); Dennis Charles (*d*). 6/
    81.
** Invitation Soul Note 121036
    As above, except Curtis Clark (*p*) replaces Rosewoman. 4/82.
*** The Fire From Within Soul Note 121086
    Bang; Ahmed Abdullah (*t*); Oscar Sanders (*g*); William Parker (*b*); Thurman Barker (*mar,
    perc*); John Betsch (*d*); Charles Bobo Shaw (*perc*).
*** Live At Carlos 1 Soul Note 121136
    As above, except omit Abdullah, Betsch and Shaw; add Roy Campbell (*t*); Zen Matsuura (*d*);
    Eddie Conde (*congas*). 11/86.
***(*) Valve No. 10 Soul Note 121186
    Bang; Frank Lowe (*ts*); Sirone (*b*); Dennis Charles (*d*). 2/88.
***(*) A Tribute To Stuff Smith Soul Note 121216
    Bang; Sun Ra (*p*); John Ore (*b*); Andrew Cyrille (*d*). 9/92.

Titular head of the unfortunately named Bang Gang, the most significant jazz violinist of his day
reverses the old cliché about Chicago gangsters going around with Thomson machine-guns in their
fiddle cases. Bang's rapid-fire approach stems partly from the work Ramsey Ameen did with Cecil
Taylor, approaching strings much as Taylor approaches piano: as a percussion instrument.

Rainbow Gladiator is one of the finest records of the 1980s, and is certainly Bang's most convincing
recording. Rhythmic and polycultural, it has a highly distinctive instrumental coloration (echoed somewhat more artificially on his later albums) and an urgency that is somewhat tamed on the subsequent
Invitation, a more immediately appealing set that palls with repeated hearings. Rosewoman plays
superbly and is better recorded than on some of her own sessions; as always, Soul Note's Giovanni
Bonandrini gets an evenly democratic final mix which sounds even better, now that these have been
transferred to CD.

The horn/guitar/marimba combination on *The Fire From Within* is highly unusual and very effective as a
setting for Bang's skittering lines. An even more noticeable swing here towards African – or, more
strictly, Middle Eastern and North African – rhythms and cells. Abdullah's keying is faintly reminiscent
of Leo Smith's but much more limber and somewhat less sure of tone. Betsch, who played with Bang on
Marilyn Crispell's fine *Spirit Music*, is a tighter and more traditional player than Matsuura, but there's
little to choose between them, or between the albums. (No point looking for 'Live At Carlos Volume 2'.
Carlos 1 was a club in Greenwich Village.)

Without question Bang's best work of recent years, *Valve No. 10* has a balance and precision equal to its
intensity. It is certainly one of the violinist's most deeply felt recordings. 'Bien-Hoa Blues' is named after
the army post where Bang served in Vietnam; the music suggests Southern fields and rice paddies,
Spanish moss and monkey jungle by dizzying turns. Even more intense are the two tributes to Coltrane,
recorded to commemorate the twentieth anniversary of the saxophonist's death. 'September 23rd'
(Coltrane's birth-date) is less successful, a combination of music and spoken verse that drifts towards
banality and does little more than name-check Trane and rerun the 'Love Supreme' chant. The long,
concluding 'Lonnie's Lament' is more heart-felt. The tune adapts well to Bang's violin, and Sirone – too
rarely in a recording studio these days – plays beautifully underneath him. Lowe's breathy delivery stems
from a generation or two before Coltrane, but sounds quite in keeping.

The other tracks are rather more abstract. 'Improvisation For Four' has awkward moments when
Charles comes unstuck trying not to play the obvious cadence, but he is absolutely on the case on the
opening 'P.M.', where solos are deployed irregularly and asymmetrically, starting in the middle of one
chorus and leaking over into the middle of a later one, overlapping or leaving oddly syncopated gaps.
It's an impressive start to a thoroughly intriguing album.

The Stuff Smith tribute is unique in having Sun Ra as a sideman. It's a one-off, and a rather remarkable
one. Sun Ra had played with Smith in the early 1950s and was familiar with tunes like 'Only Time Will
Tell' and 'Bugle Blues'. Bang played briefly in the Arkestra in 1981, an experience that was marked by
his first exposure to large amounts of standard material. That's reflected in this set. The remaining
material includes 'Deep Purple', Duke's 'Satin Doll', 'Yesterdays', 'April In Paris', 'Lover Man' and 'A
Foggy Day'. It isn't the repertoire one normally associates with Smith, and the album will be foxing
blindfold testees for years.

Cyrille's brightly patterned drumming and Sun Ra's slightly stolid piano, together with Ore's flat-
bottomed bass sound, are ideal for Bang's purposes; and he gets off on the old tunes every bit as much
as he has on more aggressive contemporary material. Recommended.

Paul Barbarin (1899–1969) DRUMS

*** Streets Of The City 504 CD 9
Barbarin; Ernest Cagnalotti, John Brunious (*t*); Eddie Pierson, Worthia Thomas (*tb*); Albert Burbank, Willie Humphrey (*cl*); Lester Santiago (*p*); Edmond Souchon (*bj, v*); Richard McLean, Ricard Alexis (*b*). 9/50–4/56.
*** Paul Barbarin And His Band Storyville STCD 6008
As above, except omit Brunious, Thomas, Burbank, Souchon, Alexis, add Johnny St Cyr (*bj*). 51.
*** Paul Barbarin And His New Orleans Band Atlantic 90977-2
Barbarin; John Brunious (*t*); Bob Thomas (*tb*); Willie Humphrey (*cl*); Lester Santiago (*p*); Danny Barker (*bj*); Milt Hinton (*b*). 55.
*** Oxford Series Vol. 15 American Music AMCD-35
As above except Ricard Alexis (*b*) replaces Hinton. 3/56.

One of the major New Orleans drummers, Paul Barbarin was most visibly active in the 1930s, when he played and toured with such leaders as Louis Armstrong and Luis Russell; but it was the revival of interest in New Orleans jazz which let him record as a leader. He had a hard yet restless manner of playing the beat, and his bands swing with a kind of relentlessness that can be very exciting. The Storyville disc catches his group at a peak: the horns are all excellent soloists as well as vivid ensemble players, with Pierson a shouting trombonist, Burbank terrifically agile and Cagnolatti making light work of sounding tough and imaginative at the same time. There's an uproarious version of 'Clarinet Marmalade' and, though all the material is staple Dixieland repertoire, they play it all with seasoned rather than hackneyed dedication. The sound is a little flat but perfectly acceptable. *Streets Of The City* collects three sessions by two bands: with Cagnolatti and Burbank the music is more deeply traditional, with Brunious and the versatile Humphrey, a blend of looking back and glancing forward. Barbarin himself, a four-square traditionalist even though he worked on some very modern sessions two decades earlier, adds gravitas to every passage.

The 1955 edition of the group – which includes some major New Orleanians – is perhaps less exciting than the one which made the 1951 sessions. The music is otherwise much as before, though Hinton's flexible bass gives the underlying rhythms a more varied sense of swing, and this is certainly the clearest sound of Barbarin's available music. The Oxford sesson, by basically the same band, suffers from a wobbly balance, but the dominant musician here is certainly Humphrey, whose graceful lines are para-digmatic of New Orleans clarinet. All four discs are worth hearing and keeping.

Chris Barber (born 1930) TROMBONE, BASS TRUMPET, VOCALS

***(*) Live In 1954/5 Limelight 820878
Barber; Pat Halcox (*c*); Monty Sunshine (*cl*); Lonnie Donegan (*bj*); Jim Bray (*b, bb*); Ron Bowden (*d*); Ottilie Patterson (*v*). 10/54, 1/55.
*** The Original Copenhagen Concert Storyville STCD 5527
As above. 10/54.
***(*) Ottilie Patterson With Chris Barber's Jazzband, 1955–1958 Lake LACD 30
As above, except add Eddie Smith (*bj*); Dickie Bishop (*b*). 3 & 9/55, 7 & 12/56, 8 & 9/57, 1/58.
**** The Chris Barber Concerts Lake LACD 55/56 2CD
As above, except omit Bray, Donegan; add Eddie Smith (*bj*); Graham Burbidge (*d*); Dick Smith (*b*). 12/56, 1 & 3/58.
**** 30 Years Chris Barber: Can't We Get Together Timeless TTD 517/8 2CD
Barber; Pat Halcox (*t, v*); Monty Sunshine, Ian Wheeler (*cl*); John Crocker (*ts*); Dr John (Mac Rebennack) (*p, v*); Eddie Smith (*bj*); Roger Hill (*g*); Dick Smith (*b*); Vic Pitt (*tba*); Ron Bowden, Norman Emberson, Johnny McCallum (*d*). 12/56–11/84.
*** The Traditional Jazz Scene: Volume 2 Teldec 43997
Barber; Pat Halcox (*t*); Monty Sunshine (*cl*); Eddie Smith (*bj*); Dick Smith (*d*); Graham Burbidge (*d*); Ottilie Patterson (*v*). 1 & 9/59, 1/60.
***(*) The Classic Concerts: 1959/1961 Chris Barber Collection CBJBCD 4002
Barber; Pat Halcox (*t*); Monty Sunshine (*cl*); Joe Harriott (*as*); Eddie Smith (*bj*); Dick Smith (*b*); Graham Burbidge (*d*); Ottilie Patterson (*v*). 5/59, 3/61.
*** Hot Gospel Lake LACD 39
Barber; Pat Halcox (*t*); Ian Wheeler (*cl, as*); Alex Bradford (*p, v*); Stu Morrison, Eddie Smith (*bj*); John Slaughter (*g*); Micky Ashman, Dick Smith (*b*); Graham Burbidge (*d*); Alex Bradford Singers, Kenneth Washington (*v*). 1/63, 66, 67.

*** **Collaboration** Jazzology BCD 40
    Barber; Pat Halcox (*t*); Ian Wheeler (*cl, as*); Graham Paterson (*p*); Stu Morrison (*bj*); Brian
    Turnock (*b*); Barry Martyn (*d*). 9/66.
***(*) **Live In East Berlin** Black Lion BLCD 760502
    Barber; Pat Halcox (*t*); John Crocker (*as, cl*); John Slaughter (*g*); Stu Morrison (*bj*); Jackie
    Flavelle (*b, v*); Graham Burbidge (*d*). 11/68.
*** **The Grand Reunion Concert** Timeless TTD 553
    Barber; Pat Halcox (*t, flhn, v*); Monty Sunshine (*cl*); John Crocker (*cl, as, v*); Lonnie Donegan
    (*bj, g, v*); Johnny McCallum (*bj, g*); John Slaughter (*g*); Jim Bray (*b*); Ron Bowden, Graham
    Burbidge (*d*). 6/75.
*** **Echoes Of Ellington: Volume 1** Timeless TTD 555
    Barber; Pat Halcox (*t, flhn*); John Crocker (*cl, as, ts*); Russell Procope (*cl, as*); Wild Bill Davis (*p*);
    John Slaughter (*g*); Johnny McCallum (*g, bj*); Jackie Flavelle (*b*); Pete York (*d*). 6/76.
*** **Echoes Of Ellington: Volume 2** Timeless TTD 556
    As above. 6/76.
*** **Jazz Zounds: Chris Barber** Zounds 2720008 2CD
    Barber; Pat Halcox (*t, v*); John Crocker (*cl, as, ts*); Ian Wheeler (*cl, as*); John Slaughter (*g*);
    Johnny McCallum (*bj, g*); Vic Pitt (*b*); Norman Emberson (*d*); Rundfunkorchester Berlin.
*** **Concert For The BBC** Timeless TTD 509/10
    Barber; Pat Halcox (*t*); Ian Wheeler (*cl, as*); John Crocker (*cl, as, ts, hca*); Johnny McCallum (*g,
    bj*); Roger Hill (*g*); Vic Pitt (*b*); Norman Emberson (*d*). 6/82.
*** **Live In '85** Timeless TTD 527
    As above. 11/85.
***(*) **Chris Barber Meets Rod Mason's Hot Five** Timeless TTD 524
    Barber; Rod Mason (*c, v*); Klaus Dau (*tb*); Helm Renz (*cl, as*); Ansgar Bergmann (*p*); Udo
    Jagers (*bj*). 8/85.
*** **Stardust** Timeless TTD 537
    As for *Come Friday*. 5/88.

In his memoir, *Owning Up*, George Melly describes how Chris Barber 'prettified' the fundamentalist jazz
of the 'holy fool', Ken Colyer. Colyer had been jailed in New Orleans, actually for overstaying his
permit, but in the eyes of his acolytes for having dared to play with black musicians. In Melly's view,
Colyer alone could never have brought about the British trad boom that lasted from the mid-1950s until
rock and pop took a solid hold of the music industry a decade later. Melly presented the trad revolution
as if it were the Reformation, purging jazz of solos and arrangements, bringing it back to the primitive
collectivism of the Delta. 'It was [Ken] who established the totems and taboos, the piano-less rhythm
section, the relentless four-to-the-bar banjo, the loud but soggy thump of the bass drum. Ken invented
British traditional jazz. It wasn't exactly ugly' – as Picasso's primitivist canvases were thought to be ugly
– 'on the contrary, it was quite often touchingly beautiful, but it was clumsy. It needed prettifying before
it could catch on. Chris Barber was there to perform the function.'

Barber had been leading bands while still in his teens, but his first serious attempt was a co-operative
group pulled together in 1953 during Colyer's extended 'vacation' in New Orleans. Colyer, who had
some reason to feel that a *coup d'état* had taken place behind his back, was invited to join, and he did for
a time, until he found himself out of tune with Lonnie Donegan's grandstanding (Donegan was soon to
become a star in his own right) and what he thought of as the (gasp!) bebop mannerisms that were
creeping in. Pat Halcox, who had declined the offer first time around, joined up and has grown in
Barber's company from the slightly raw voice heard on *Live In 1954/5* into a first-rate performer with a
ringing and occasionally vocalized tone of some power.

The early live material on London includes two skiffle features for Donegan, whose 'Rock Island Line'
was to become a million-seller. The jazz material (which on *Echoes* takes in a little-known Ellington
tune, 'Doin' The Crazy Walk') is not so much prettified as a 'middle way' between modern jazz (with
accoutrements like solos and formal arrangements) and the grim nonconformist Protestantism of
Colyer's approach. It's hard to over-estimate the significance of Barber's contribution at this period, or
that of Donegan's skiffle, which became the musical foundation for the Beatles and Herman's Hermits.
Melly's description of the music holds good for *Live In 1954/5*. It's awkwardly recorded, the banjo chugs
relentlessly and there's a plodding predictability to the bass drum beat.

Things are much better on the *Concerts* discs. The Lake documents what was, just 40 years ago, the
biggest musical draw in Britain, filling the Royal Festival Hall ten days before Christmas 1956 and
packing venues elsewhere round the country with that full-hearted sound. Ottilie Patterson's occasional
spots are uneven but tend to confirm her blues credentials. The Philips is actually shared with material
under Pat Halcox's and Ottilie Patterson's leadership, but Barber is the dominant presence; 'Revival'
and 'We Shall Walk Through The Streets Of The City' are essential performances, marked by his
generously toned tailgating style. A 1962 trio version of 'Body And Soul', not usually thought to be a

trad anthem, offers a measure of one of Barber's greatest qualities: his shrewd adaptability. Not to question the sincerity of product like *Hot Gospel*, which is actually culled from often poorly documented or undated sessions, it provides an ideal example. When rock and the British blues scene took off, he added electric basses and guitars to his band, rechristened it the Chris Barber Jazz & Blues Band and secured a haven between what already seemed to be irreconcilable musical tendencies. In the 1980s he has recorded very successfully with the New Orleans legend, Dr John, who (as 'The Night Tripper') was an icon of psychedelic blues in the later '60s; *Take Me Back To New Orleans* (Black Lion BLCD 760163 CD), with Dr John and bass drummer Freddie Kohlman, is not currently in the catalogue, but Dr John can be heard on 'Good Queen Bess' on *30 Years Chris Barber*, a slightly misleading compilation that brings together material from 1956 (a film soundtrack for *Holiday*) and from 1984, but not from the intervening period; so it isn't a handy sampler.

Barber's groups were at their peak in the late 1950s, a period usefully and authentically caught on the Teldec compilation. At the end of the decade they became the first British group to play the blue-riband Ed Sullivan Show. There's no mistaking the raw authenticity of the May 1959 sell-out concert at the Deutschhalle in Berlin. There were allegedly 3,000 East Germans in the audience, and it's important to recognize with what respect and seriousness Barber's brand of jazz was regarded in the Eastern bloc; a measure of that respect is the collaboration with the Rundfunkorchester Berlin on the rather overcooked *Jazz Zounds*. In the communist countries, traditional jazz was the spontaneous music of an oppressed proletariat, uncomplicated by formalism or individualism, created collectively. Barber's later *Live In East Berlin* rarely reaches the heights of Ottilie Pátterson's unaccompanied intro to 'Easy, Easy, Baby' or the rocking optimism of 'Gotta Travel On', but 'Royal Garden Blues' and 'Sweet As Bear Meat' have an authentic energy that highlights the leader's unironic populism. The East Berlin set also features a superb version of 'Revival' by Joe Harriott, the West Indian-born saxophonist who seemed able to play in any context from trad to free. Harriott guests on 'Revival' at the 1961 London Palladium concert (*Classic Concerts*), which was a celebration of *Jazz News* poll winners. By 1968, Harriott was a forgotten figure, 'going single' round Britain, a reminder of the kind of suffering and neglect out of which jazz came.

Just because he was successful, Barber never forgot the origins of the music he loved. He has become an important practical historian of early 'hot' music in Britain and has constantly purified his own style, though not to the extent of shunning contact with other styles (witness the 1976 Ducal sessions, recorded in St Ives, with Ellingtonian Russell Procope) and he keeps a weather eye on shifts in public taste. In important essentials, though, Barber's approach has not changed in nearly four decades; adaptability has never meant compromise. The later material, notably *Reunion* and *Live In '85*, albeit recorded a decade apart, betrays some signs of rote playing from some of the band, but Sunshine (who went off to make a career of his own on the back of 'Petite Fleur', a 1959 clarinet feature on which Barber did not solo but which became a major band hit) is an elegant and often moving performer, and Halcox has grown in stature with the years. The *Collaboration* with drummer Martyn is an interesting by-blow (taped by the late Doug Dobell, who was something of a legend on the British jazz scene), and the later record with Rod Mason's drummerless but piano'd Hot Five is also well worth checking out.

Barber is one of the major figures in British popular music. His longevity is not that of a survivor but of a man whose roots go too deep to be disturbed by mere fashion. He has, of course, had to keep up. *Concert '80* is a first digital live recording. It brings the familiar sound into unexpected close-up, more so than on succeeding discs, interestingly, though the BBC gig, recorded in Derby, has the same sharp focus. Some will like the sharpness and clarity; some may feel that the charm has been smoothed away in some part.

(***) **Under The Influence Of Jazz** Timeless TTD 569
    Barber; Bill Houghton, Mark Bennett (*t*); Chris Larkin (*frhn*); Jim Casey (*tb*); Steve Wick (*tba*). 5 & 6/89.
**** **Panama!** Timeless CD TTD 568
    Barber; Wendell Brunious (*t, v*); Pat Halcox (*t*); Ian Wheeler (*cl, as*); John Crocker (*cl, ts*); Johnny McCallum (*bj, g*); Vic Pitt (*b*); John Slaughter (*g*); Russell Gilbrook (*d*). 1/91.
*** **Chris Barber And His New Orleans Friends** Timeless TTD 573
    Barber; Percy Humphrey (*t*); Willie Humphrey (*cl*); Jeanette Kimball (*p*); Frank Fields (*b*); Barry Martyn (*d*). 8/91.
(*) **Chris Barber With Zenith Hot Stompers Timeless TTD 582
    Barber; Tony Davis (*c*); Alan Bradley (*tb*); Roy Hubbard (*cl*); Ken Freeman (*p*); Brian Mellor (*bj*); Phil Matthews (*b, tba*); Derek Bennett (*d*). 7/92.

Barber faced up to his fifth decade in the business with renewed energy and enterprise. Again, he was ever watchful for new wrinkles on the old routine. *Under The Influence*, with the Gabrieli Brass Ensemble, was an interesting one-off. Basically what happened was that Barber joined them for a jazz-tinged 'classical' piece and then they played some trad arrangements. The results are predictably uneven, but Wick for one knows what jazz is all about and there's a convincing bounce to the whole thing.

The August 1991 meeting with members of the legendary Preservation Hall Band is as much of a disappointment as most of their activities. These may be the senior practitioners of the New Orleans style, but they make it sound a lot more pedestrian in the charmed air of New Orleans (albeit in a campus auditorium at Tulane University) than Barber's regular band can do in a small-town arts centre in the Home Counties, or in a school in Derby, in the case of the Zenith Hot Stompers. It's relatively unusual to hear him backed by a piano, but Jeanette Kimball isn't a particularly unusual player; indeed, she seems content to stay within reach of half a dozen trademark chords and runs at all times.

There's certainly nothing more 'authentic' about the way the Preservation Hall laureates play the music than the Zenith Hot Stompers do it. Less accomplished than Barber's regular group and a bit heavy-handed when it comes to varying dynamics, they play with the enthusiasm that's almost essential for this game. The sound's average for a Barber production.

Panama! is really a showcase for the young New Orleanian trumpeter, who supplants the long-serving Halcox on most of the solo slots. Brunious builds a lovely solo on the extended 'Georgia On My Mind' and sings in a mournful, wavery mid-tenor. 'Careless Love' features clarinet before the vocal and then continues with a soft, cry-baby wah-wah chorus on trumpet (presumably from Brunious) that drops behind a delicate banjo and bass accompaniment; McCallum doubles the time on his own intriguingly jittery solo line. Typically well crafted and intelligent, Barber's arrangements of 'Oh! Lady Be Good' and William Tyers's title-tune reflect traditional jazz at its best. Barber fans shouldn't miss it and trad enthusiasts should jump at the opportunity to hear Brunious in sympathetic company.

*** **Forty Years Jubilee At The Opera House, Nürnberg** Timeless TTD 590
> Barber; Pat Halcox (*t*); Monty Sunshine (*cl*); Ian Wheeler, John Crocker (*cl, as*); John Slaughter (*g*); Lonnie Donegan, Johnny McCallum (*bj*); Jim Bray, Vic Pitt (*b*); Ron Bowden, Russell Gilbrook (*d*). 5/94.

The old gang's back in town. Two resurrected bands revisit one of their old stamping-grounds (and this corner of Europe is very much a hotbed of Barber loyalism), sounding in pretty good form. The chops, inevitably, aren't quite what they were but the inclusion of Sunshine and a fit-sounding Donegan (who'd had cardiac problems) pushes the energy level well up. Delightful stuff from start to finish, though a better bet for collectors and nostalgists than for newcomers who might find it all a bit old-pals-ish.

Leandro 'Gato' Barbieri (born 1934) TENOR SAXOPHONE, FLUTE, PERCUSSION, VOICE

***(*) **In Search Of The Mystery** ESP Disk ESP 1049
> Barbieri; Calo Scott (*clo*); Sirone (*b*); Robert Kapp (*d*). 3/67.

Barbieri is a classic victim of what is known as Rodin's Syndrome: being best known for your least representative work. Bernardo Bertolucci's *Last Tango In Paris*, as well as working some pretty far-fetched variations on 'The Kiss', was graced by one of the most remarkable soundtrack scores of recent times, performed by Barbieri with orchestra. A staple ever since, despite long deletion, *Last Tango* has tended to cloud Barbieri's significance and doubtless helped push him towards the tiresome disco vein of the later '70s.

Two decades before, he had been one of the most innovative young horn players working in Europe, where he cut a classic set with Don Cherry, *Complete Communion*, and the intermittently available *In Search Of The Mystery* (also known as *Obsession*, after one of the tracks) under his own name, before establishing himself in the Jazz Composers' Orchestra.

The restored ESP suggests a surprising kinship between Barbieri and Ayler. Clearly *Mystery* is no *Spiritual Unity* but it is in very similar vein, and it's unfair to let Barbieri's subsequent lapse from grace cloud his achievement. The Argentinian spends a considerable portion of his time in the 'false' upper register and, with Scott's cello acting as second horn and harmony instrument, the emphasis is on long, dissonant drones. 'Michelle' is less frantic, but also much less interesting, and there's a noticeable loss of conviction on the final 'Cinématheque'. A pity there's no unreleased material to fill out a short-weight session from an under-represented artist, but there it is. The ESP at least restores Barbieri the avant-gardist to a measure of credibility.

***(*) **Chapter Three: Viva Emiliano Zapata** Impulse GRP 11112
> Barbieri; Randy Brecker, Bob McCoy, Victor Paz, Alan Rubin (*t, flhn*); Ray Alonge, Jimmy Buffington (*frhn*); Buddy Morrow (*tb*); Alan Ralph (*btb*); Howard Johnson (*tba, flhn, bcl*); Seldon Powell (*f, picc, af, as, bs*); Eddie Martinez (*p, ky*); George Davis, Paul Metzke (*g*); Ron Carter (*b*); Grady Tate (*d*); Ray Armando, Luis Mangual, Ray Mantilla, Portinho (*perc*). 6/74.

In the early 1970s Barbieri steadily turned his back on abstraction in an effort to reacquaint himself with his own cultural roots. The breakthrough albums were *The Third World* and *El Pampero*, but then – with *Last Tango In Paris* briefly and lucratively intervening – the saxophonist recorded a sequence of four

'Chapters', the albums that are collectively his most significant. The first, *Latin America*, had an almost wholly 'ethnic' feel, with Barbieri roaring and wailing over a swarming carpet of unusual percussion effects. *Chapters Two* and *Four* are, in their way, much more mainstream; the latter, *Alive In New York*, is one of the great jazz albums of the mid-1970s, alas deleted. Its best moments were a reworking of 'La China Leoncia' from *Chapter One* and 'Milonga Triste' from *Viva Emiliano Zapata*. The latter is a Cuban-derived *habañera*, thematically very simple. Barbieri builds up the emotion steadily, shifting key and rhythm in relentlessly logical stages, climaxing with one of his false upper-register flag-wavers. The softer cha-cha rhythm of 'Lluvia Azul' allows the subtle orchestration to show through. 'El Sublime' is in Barbieri's favourite double waltz time, a metre that permits the most flexible phrasing and occasional syncopation of notes. It's unusual to find Barbieri playing a standard, but the arrangement of 'What A Difference A Day Makes' goes under the unfamiliar title 'Cuando Vuelva A Tu Lado' and does so without a trace of an accent. The closing title-track has no explicit programme, but it's clear from Barbieri's burning solo that he isn't just spraying slogans on walls for the hell of it.

(*) Caliente! A & M 394 597
>Barbieri; Marvin Stamm, Bernie Glow, Randy Brecker, Irvin Marvovitz (*t*); Wayne Andre, David Taylor, Paul Faulise (*tb*); Don Grolnick, Eddie Martinez (*ky*); Joe Beck, Eric Gale, David Spinozza (*g*); Gary King (*b*); Lenny White (*d*); Ralph MacDonald, Cachete Maldonado, Mtume (*perc*); strings. 76.

Caliente! catches Barbieri half-way into his disco-god mode. There is some excellent playing, as usual, though oddly the upper-register stuff sounds far more overheated in this context than it ever did in the more way-out sessions, and the orchestrations (by Jay Chattaway) are as tight and crisp as anything that came out of the fusion movement. Whatever else, Herb Alpert knows how to produce this sort of thing, and there can be few quibbles on technical grounds. However, apart from the opening 'Fireflies' and the evocative 'Behind The Rain', which contains a tiny, almost subliminal reference to a similarly titled Coltrane piece, there is not much of any great substance here.

Bardo State Orchestra GROUP

**** **The Ultimate Gift** Impetus IMP CD 19425
>Jim Dvorak (*t, perc, v*); Marcio Mattos (*b, clo, perc*); Ken Hyder (*d, perc, khoomei, v*). 10 & 11/ 94.

A rather grand name for such a small group, but what a range! All three men have studied Eastern musics in addition to jazz. This is what Jim Dvorak would call 'spirit music', dense, joyous sounds that seem to belong to no tradition exclusively. Hyder, who has led Talisker for many years, has worked extensively with shamans in Siberia as well as studying Tuvan throat-singing. Dvorak has studied chanting under the Tibetan masters, and the Brazilian-born Mattos is a confirmed Buddhist.

Lest this sound too other-worldly, there is a visceral physicality to the group's interaction, a toughness and humour which give long improvisations like 'On The Mend', 'Inside Out' and the opening 'No Harm Done' an almost matey, conversational quality. How much of the music is predetermined remains difficult to judge. And hardly matters.

A. Spencer Barefield GUITAR, 12-STRING GUITAR, SYNTHESIZER

(*) Live At Nickelsdorf Konfrontation sound aspects 007
>Barefield; Anthony Holland (*as, ss*); Tani Tabbal (*d, perc*). 6/84.
*** **Live At Leverkusener Jazztage** sound aspects 0039
>Barefield; Oliver Lake (*as*); Andrew Cyrille (*d*). 10/89.

These are slightly tentative sets, full of good ideas and fine playing, but ultimately a little diffuse. Barefield, perhaps best known for his work with Roscoe Mitchell's Sound/Space Ensembles, is a fine guitarist who works at the opposite pole from the Sonny Sharrock/James 'Blood' Ulmer *Sturm und Drang* school. His acoustic figures are almost classical in execution. He combines well with both Lake and Holland, saxophonists of like persuasion, while Tabbal and Cyrille knock out the kind of metre he appears to prefer. The trio on the 1989 festival disc gets right down to basics from the off, and the guitarist sounds much more focused and enthusiastic. Barefield is well worth catching live; these are for converts only.

Rob Bargad PIANO

*** Better Times Criss Cross CRISS 1086

Bargad; Eddie Henderson (*t, flhn*); Tom Williams (*t*); Steve Wilson (*as, ss*); Donald Harrison (*as*); Peter Washington (*b*); Billy Drummond (*d*); Daniel G. Sadownick (*perc*). 12/92, 12/93.

Bargad cut his professional teeth in Nat Adderley's quintet. Behind him he has rock and blues and, in the family background, cantorial singing, none of which is immediately discernible but all of which somehow contribute to the overall sound and conception. There's something refreshingly simple but studied in Bargad's approach, and it's testimony to his powers as a writer of themes that the seven originals on *Better Times* all sound like things other bandleaders should pick up on. A duo performance of one of them, 'Is It Love?', on which he is partnered by Eddie Henderson, has the *déjà-écouté* quality of something that sounds as though it must have been around for years.

Bargad has been singularly fortunate in his fellow-musicians on this debut recording. Henderson is a fierce and swinging trumpeter who manages to maintain beauty of tone even at full stretch. Wilson is an excellent partner. The two tracks from a December 1992 session – both standards, interestingly enough – feature Williams and Harrison instead and, while the former is in cracking form on 'When I Fall In Love', the partnership wouldn't be quite right for Bargad's own material. Of it, 'The Snake', 'Little J. J.' and 'Tears' are the most memorable themes, the last of them perfectly illustrating what the composer has learnt from rock. Some listeners may question Sadownick's role, which often does seem like one flavour too many. However, he does add a few angles to a rhythm section which – taking its cue from the composer/arranger, we tend to think – sounds uncharacteristically chunky and foursquare, even when the count is more complex.

Guy Barker (born 1957) TRUMPET

***(*) Isn't It? Spotlite SPJ-CD 545

Barker; Jamie Talbot (*ss*); Nigel Hitchcock (*as, ts*); Peter King (*as*); Julian Joseph, Stan Tracey (*p*); Jim Mullen (*g*); Alec Dankworth (*b*); Clark Tracey (*d*). 7–8/91.

Barker's standing as the doyen of Britain's younger trumpeters has scarcely resulted in a flood of recordings under his own name, but this belated effort as leader bristles with fine music. His own three originals suggest a witty composer as well as a polished musical mind, with the title-track a particularly lucid and clever line, while the trumpet-and-rhythm setting of 'Amandanita' strikes a measured balance between poise and tenderness. Some of his solos err on the side of self-consciousness, such as that on 'Sheldon The Cat', where both he and the garrulous saxman Hitchcock are outdone by Jim Mullen's flowing improvisation; but there is trumpet playing of sometimes awesome finesse scattered through the session. No complaints about anyone else's contribution, either. The sound is beautifully clear, if a little acidulous.

**** Into The Blue Verve 527 656

Barker; Sigurdur Flosason (*as*); Bernardo Sassetti (*p*); Alec Dankworth (*b*); Ralph Salmins (*d*). 12/94, 2/95.

Barker's debut for Verve is no rushed, back-of-an-envelope affair, put together with a band of safely bankable names. Instead, it's a carefully thought-out and patiently executed set, intended to introduce an artist whose personal style is deeply embedded in jazz history. Barker's thoughtful involvement with the tradition is reflected in cuts like 'Oh Mr Rex!', which takes as its starting point phrases of Rex Stewart's, and 'Weather Bird Rag', an Oliver/Armstrong classic done here as a duo with bassist Dankworth. A more recent inspiration (and employer) is acknowledged in 'This Is The Life', a vigorous dedication to Stan Tracey.

Barker's ballad playing has long been his trump suit, and on 'Low Down Lullaby' and the more familiar 'Ill Wind' he plays with poise and intelligence. These qualities are reflected in an intriguingly inter-national band – Flosason is Icelandic, Sassetti Portuguese – which already sounds confidently seasoned and sure-footed. The saxophonist is perhaps inclined to dwell on pure tone for much of his impact, and Sassetti is occasionally tempted into puzzlement and riddling (as his composition 'Enigma' might suggest), but together they give Barker just the blend he needs, and this is a band one can look forward to seeing develop and strengthen.

(It's even more of a pleasure than a relief to one of the authors to be able to register so positive a response, since his colleague is credited as joint producer of *Into The Blue*. Interest, as they say, duly declared.)

Dale Barlow TENOR SAXOPHONE

***(*) **Hipnotation** Spiral Scratch 0009
> Barlow; Eddie Henderson (*t*); Kevin Hays (*p*); Essiet Okun Essiet (*b*); Billy Drummond (*d*). 7/
> 90.

*** **Jazz Juice** Hipnotation 001
> Barlow; Kenny Barron (*p*); Ray Drummond (*b*); Ben Riley (*d*). 9/92.

An Australian who divides his time between Sydney and New York, Barlow's flexible style gets contrasting airings across these two discs. The earlier date, cut while he was still with the Jazz Messengers, is a grand and attacking session where the players are all full-on from the first. Drummond and Essiet don't rush the tempos, but there's an abiding sense of bulldozing power about the playing that Barlow's appealing tunes mediate just sufficiently for the music not to overwhelm. 'Thick As Thieves', 'Hipnotation' and 'Bunyip' are all strong themes which both horns appropriate to their own ends: Barlow here sounds much in his adopted Blakey tradition, while Henderson's mix of grace and fire is especially effective. *Jazz Juice* seems almost laid-back in the comparison. It's oddly appropriate that Barlow should choose to cover Hank Mobley's 'This I Dig Of You', since this time his sound has some of the foggy lightness of Mobley's own. A charming 'Never Let Me Go' is also very fine, but at times the rest of the date sounds a trifle under-characterized, though that may be a consequence of the restrained studio mix.

Charlie Barnet (1913–91) TENOR, ALTO AND SOPRANO SAXOPHONES

***(*) **Cherokee** RCA Bluebird ND 61059
> Barnet; Charles Huffine, Bobby Burnet, Marshall Mendel, Johnny Owens, Billy May, Lyman Vunk, George Esposito (*t*); Ben Hall, Don Ruppersberg, Bill Roberston, Spud Murphy, Ford Leary (*tb*); Don McCook (*cl, as*); Gene Kinsey, Skippy Martin, Leo White, Conn Humphries (*as*); Kurt Bloom (*ts*); Jimmy Lamare (*bs*); Bill Miller, Nat Jaffe (*p*); Bus Etri (*g*); Phil Stephens (*b*); Wesley Dean, Ray Michaels, Cliff Leeman (*d*). 39–41.

**** **Drop Me Off In Harlem** MCA GRP 16122
> Barnet; Peanuts Holland, Irving Berger, Joe Ferante, Chuck Zimmerman, Al Killian, Jimmy Pupa, Lyman Vunk, Roy Eldridge, Art House, Johnny Martel, Jack Mootz, Everett McDonald, George Seaberg, Ed Stress, Paul Webster, Art Robey (*t*); Russ Brown, Kahn Keene, Wally Baron, Bill Robertson, Eddie Bert, Ed Fromm, Spud Murphy, Bob Swift, Porky Cohen, Tommy Pederson, Ben Pickering, Charles Coolidge, Gerald Foster, Dave Hallett, Burt Johnson, Frank Bradley, Lawrence Brown (*tb*); George Bone, Conn Humphries, Murray Williams, Buddy DeFranco, Ray DeGeer, Harold Herzon, Joe Meisner, Gene Kinsey, Les Robinson (*as*); Kurt Bloom, Mike Goldberg, Ed Pripps, Kenny Dehlin, Dave Mathews (*ts*); James Lamare, Danny Bank, Bob Poland, Bob Dawes (*bs*); Bill Miller, Dodo Marmarosa, Al Haig, Sheldon Smith (*p*); Tommy Moore, Turk Van Lake, Barney Kessel, Dennis Sandole (*g*); Jack Jarvis, Russ Wagner, Andy Riccardi, Howard Rumsey, John Chance, Morris Rayman, Irv Lang (*b*); Cliff Leeman, Harold Hahn, Mickey Scrima (*d*); Frances Wayne, Kay Starr (*v*). 4/42–6/46.

Although a handful of Barnet's records – especially his big hits, 'Cherokee' and 'Skyliner' – stand as staples of the big-band era, he's generally been less than well served critically and by jazz collectors: only these two albums remain easily available, and all his later work for Capitol is out of print. His own playing – which always points to Johnny Hodges as a first influence, and splendidly so – is usually restricted to a few telling bars, but he was an enthusiastic advocate of other, greater players, and remains one of the few bandleaders to have virtually ignored racial distinctions. It may have cost him dear in career terms, too, though Barnet (from a very wealthy background) never seems to have cared very much.

The Bluebird set (an earlier, more comprehensive disc of his Bluebird period has recently been deleted, though copies may still be in circulation) is a fine introduction: the 11 tracks are more like skilful patchworks of other orchestras, especially those of Basie and Ellington, than original frameworks; but the sparkle of 'Redskin Rumba', 'The Count's Idea' and the original hit reading of 'Cherokee' have weathered the years very well. Maybe his 'Rockin' In Rhythm' sounds mechanized next to the natural swing of any Ellington version, but Barnet's admiration for his contemporary was genuine, and it makes the band sound at a level a long way ahead of such commercial rivals as Glenn Miller.

The tracks collected on the MCA compilation are, though, better still. Arranger Andy Gibson (ex-Basie) turned in charts, such as that for 'Shady Lady', which find new tone-colours for the sections; key soloists included Roy Eldridge and Dodo Marmarosa, and lead-trumpeter Al Killian gave the brass a stratospheric punch which would be equalled in the next decade only by the young Maynard Ferguson. Of the 20 tracks collected here, the pick include the still-glorious hit 'Skyliner', Eldridge's murderous romp through 'Drop Me Off In Harlem', Barnet's own not undistinguished playing on 'West End Blues', the tongue-in-cheek menace of 'Pow-Wow' and, above all, Ralph Burns's astonishing arrangement to feature Marmarosa on 'The Moose', a chart that anticipates so much of bebop (both men were still only teenagers at the time, which gives the lie to the 'modern' movement of jazz masters barely involved in manhood). Many of Barnet's records still lacked the last shred of individuality which would have allotted him a place right next to Ellington or Basie, but he was already starting to sound more riskily modern than either of those leaders. The remastering of both records has been capably done: there is no scratch on the MCA tracks, though some of the reproduction is a little muffled; and the Bluebird music, while cheerfully radiating a little crackle, is perhaps a shade more lively.

*** **1941** Circle CCD-65
> Barnet; Bernie Privin, Bob Burnet, George Esposito, Lyman Vunk (*t*); Spud Murphy, Don Ruppersberg, Bill Robertson, Ford Leary (*tb*); Leo White, James Lamare, Conn Humphries (*as*); Kurt Bloom (*ts*); Bill Miller (*p*); Bus Etri (*g*); Phil Stevens (*b*); Cliff Leeman (*d*); Lena Horne, Bob Carroll (*v*). 1/41.

A Lang–Worth transcription date featuring a strong edition of Barnet's band, even if it lacks a little in star soloists. It's the gutsy ensemble playing that endured, even when the programme is biased towards the sweeter end of Barnet's repertoire, as it often is here. Carroll is a lugubrious crooner on his features but the young Lena Horne makes an impact in her two songs, and there are some useful Billy May arrangements, as well as several originals by 'Dale Bennett' (a Barnet *nom de plume* that he used to help him out with his alimony problems). Excellent remastering.

*** **Cherokee** Evidence ECD 22065
> Barnet; Charlie Shavers, Marky Markowitz, Clark Terry, Al Stewart, Jimmy Nottingham (*t*); Bill Byers, Frank Sarroco, Bobby Byrne, Ed Price (*tb*); Vinnie Dean (*as*); Pete Mondello (*as, ts, bs*); Dick Hafer, Kurt Bloom (*ts*); Danny Bank (*bs*); Nat Pierce (*p*); Chubby Jackson (*b*); Terry Snyder (*d*); Bunny Briggs (*v*). 8/58.

Full of pep and fizz. The arrangements, by Bill Holman, Jimmy Nottingham, Billy May and Bille Moore, emphasize swing energy over tonal sophistication and leave lots of room for soloing; with Shavers and Terry on hand, there's plenty to listen to. Barnet's own contributions reassert the Hodges influence, but there's a boppish edge too, on 'Cherokee' and 'Skyliner'. Barnet didn't stand still.

Joey Baron (born 1955) DRUMS, ELECTRONICS

*** **Miniature** JMT 834423
> Baron; Tim Berne (*as*); Hank Roberts (*clo, elec, v*). 3/88.

***(*) **Tongue In Groove** JMT 849158
> Baron; Steve Swell (*tb*); Ellery Eskelin (*ts*). 5/91.

*** **R A Isedpleasuredot** New World 80449
> As above. 2/93.

Baron has an interesting list of credits, taking in sessions for Jim Hall and Toots Thielemans, as well as most of the leading lights of the downtown, post-Ornette school of noise-orientated sophisticates who record for JMT. *Miniature* is strongly influenced by Coleman's harmolodic revolution, but it's also a melodists' album that takes in elements of Bill Frisell's fractured country sound ('Circular Prairie Song' is dedicated to the guitarist) as well as black, hip-hop and free elements. Co-credited to Berne and Roberts, both excellent writers, it's accessible and well recorded.

Tongue In Groove – or, more plausibly, in cheek – is characterized as an 'all-acoustic, all-live, no mix, no edit, gutbucket digital recording', which is pretty much how it sounds, all sharp, splintery edges and untrimmed takes with a lot of fuzz and dirt in all the places where one might like to hear the detail unimpeded. Baron sounds thrashier than usual and the unusual instrumentation makes very few compromises. Sixteen tracks and only two topping five minutes, so the pace is quite ferocious. Fascinating music, but a cleaned-up mix wouldn't have hurt.

R A Isedpleasuredot comes under New World's 'Counter Currents' rubric, and one can see why. It's a most unusual instrumentation (the band is known as Barondown) and the music is virtually uncategorizable, alternating thrashy punk-jazz outbreaks with longer and more thoughtful excursions. As the closing 'Girl From Ipanema Blues' perhaps suggests, the music is inclined to be arch, pointing to its own cleverness; but the point is that it is very clever indeed, and one somehow doesn't mind being reminded of it. Swell is a great ensemble player, but he also functions well in this outside-edge enterprise, staying out in front of Eskelin, who almost does accompanist's duties at some points.

Dan Barrett TROMBONE, CORNET

*** **Strictly Instrumental** Concord CCD 4331
> Barrett; Warren Vaché (*c*); Chuck Wilson (*as*); Ken Peplowski (*cl, ts*); Howard Alden (*g*); Dick
> Wellstood (*p*); Jack Lesberg (*b*); Jackie Williams (*d*). 6/87.

Dan Barrett is a formidably talented technician on the most problematic of jazz instruments, but he has
a shrewd musical mind too. This session is perhaps a little too smoothly mainstream in the accredited
Concord manner but, by mixing standards with surprise choices ('Quasimodo' and 'Minor Infraction'),
Barrett tips one off that he doesn't think everything stops with swing. The band is a blend of youth and
experience, too, with the leader, Vaché and Peplowski a strong front line and the dependable Wellstood
underscoring the variations in texture. Barrett will surely have more adventurous records ahead of him.

*** **Jubilesta!** Arbors 19107
> Barrett; Ray Sherman (*p*); David Stone (*b*); Jake Hanna (*d*). 12/91–2/92.
*** **Reunion With Al** Arbors ARCD 19124
> As above, except add Al Jenkins (*tb, v*), Rick Fay (*cl, ss, ts*). 3/93.

Barrett doesn't sound much like Teagarden, but his manner makes one think of the great man: he plays
a melody with a singer's grace and vibrancy. This session is beautifully done, horn and rhythm section in
simple, effective empathy; but the drowsy material takes the edge off, and even when he picks up the
plunger mute Barrett doesn't really push himself. Or so one thinks. Barrett has done a ton of sideman
work of late, but he turns up again as nominal leader on *Reunion With Al*, which seems meant primarily
as a comeback showcase for octogenarian trombonist Jenkins. Despite the lavish praise in the sleeve-
notes, Jenkins sounds unsurprisingly slow and careful in his playing, but the music still goes off at an
agreeable lilt, and with Barrett sticking to cornet this time the front line has a pleasing balance.

Arthur Barron TENOR SAXOPHONE

(*) **Arthur Barron / Hilton Ruiz Dragon Rose DR R0756
> Barron; Pete Minger (*flhn*); Hilton Ruiz (*p*); Pepe Aparico, David Wertman (*b*); Oscar Salas,
> John Yalring (*d*); Osieku Danell (*perc*). 94.

Those who enjoy meat-and-two-veg sax blowing may warm to Barron's splenetic approach to the horn.
Only four tracks in almost 70 minutes of music, so nothing stinted on the solos in this set, cut live at
Rose's Bar in Florida, but Barron's methodology will tire all but the most ardent supporters of the
Pharoah Sanders style. The main point is to hear the now less frequently encountered Ruiz, who is as
mercurial as usual, if less pointed. Minger adds some useful seasoning with his cameo appearance on
'All Blues'.

Bill Barron (1932–90) TENOR AND SOPRANO SAXOPHONE

*** **The Tenor Stylings Of Bill Barron** Savoy SV-0212
> Barron; Ted Curson (*t*); Kenny Barron (*p*); Jimmy Garrison (*b*); Frankie Dunlop (*d*). 2/61.
*** **The Next Plateau** Muse M 5368
> Barron; Kenny Barron (*p*); Ray Drummond (*b*); Ben Riley (*d*). 3/87.

Less renowned than his pianist brother Kenny, Bill Barron was a hard-bop tenorman with a grouchy
tone and a broad vocabulary of short, legato phrases that made him resemble a less amiable Dexter
Gordon. He appeared on Cecil Taylor's 1959 *Love For Sale* session but seldom recorded in the years
prior to his death. The Savoy reissue brings back a raw, exploratory session that suggests some of the
outward-looking jazz of the day fusing awkwardly with more orthodox hard bop. Dunlop's noisy
drumming is a mixed blessing – sometimes exciting, often annoyingly directionless. But the buzzing
tenor solos of the leader, streaked with odd intervals and unexpected hollow notes, are intriguing, and
Curson's similarly energetic trumpet is a strong partner.

The Next Plateau, Barron's final record, is a fine, mature statement of modern hard bop, with six
interesting original tunes and the fluent support of a rhythm section that knew the leader well. Barron
invests his material with considerable intellectual fire without sacrificing the excitement or swing.

Kenny Barron (born 1943) PIANO

***(*) **Sunset To Dawn** Muse MCD 6014
> Barron; Warren Smith (*vib, perc*); Bob Cranshaw (*b*); Freddie Waits (*d*); Richard Landrum
> (*perc*). 73.

**** Green Chimneys Criss Cross Jazz Criss 1008
  Barron; Buster Williams (*b*); Ben Riley (*d*). 7/83.
***(*) Scratch Enja 4092
  Barron; Dave Holland (*b*); Daniel Humair (*d*). 3/85.
*** What If Enja 5013
  Barron; Wallace Roney (*t*); John Stubblefield (*ts*); Cecil McBee (*b*); Victor Lewis (*d*). 2/86.
*** Live At Fat Tuesday's Enja 5071
  Barron; Eddie Henderson (*t*); John Stubblefield (*ts*); Cecil McBee (*b*); Victor Lewis (*d*). 1/88.
**(*) Rhythm-A-Ning Candid CCD 79044
  Barron; John Hicks (*p*); Walter Booker (*b*); Jimmy Cobb (*d*). 9/89.
*** The Only One Reservoir RSR CD 115
  Barron; Ray Drummond (*b*); Ben Riley (*d*). 90.
*** Invitation Criss Cross Criss 1044
  Barron; Ralph Moore (*ts*); David Williams (*b*); Lewis Nash (*d*). 12/90.
*** Live At Maybeck Recital Hall, Volume 10 Concord CCD 4466
  Barron (*p* solo). 12/90.
*** Quickstep Enja 6084
  Baron; Eddie Henderson (*t*); John Stubblefield (*ts*); David Williams (*b*); Victor Lewis (*d*). 2/91.
*** Sambao Emarcy 512 736
  Barron; Toninha Horta (*g*); Nico Assumpcao (*b*); Victor Lewis (*d*); Mino Cinelu (*perc*). 5, 5 & 7/92.

Barron came to notice during a short stint with multi-instrumentalist Yusef Lateef in 1961, having previously played in R&B bands with his elder brother, Bill Barron. At nineteen, he replaced Lalo Schifrin in Dizzy Gillespie's group and worked with the trumpeter for nearly five years, subsequently rejoining Lateef and playing with Freddie Hubbard.

Barron has a funky, angular style that owes something to Monk, but is highly adept at lighter samba lines, romantic ballads and orthodox minor blues. His versatility is well attested in scores of recordings, mostly as sideman but with a substantial number under his own name. The Muses are consistently good, with fine, inventive programmes and excellent sound. Barron fans may feel that *Sunset To Dawn*, the only one of the generally good Muses to have been transferred to CD, still sounds rather better on vinyl, minus the rather brittle edge that digitalization sometimes brings. It's a fine album, if a little less adventurous than later trio sessions with Dave Holland and Daniel Humair, Cecil McBee and Al Foster, Buster Williams and Ben Riley.

The later 1980s work is somewhat disappointing but, like many musicians of his generation, Barron had a sudden boost at the start of the new decade. *Invitation* and the Maybeck solo recital were recorded within three weeks of one another and both are well worth having. The only common track is Barron's own 'And Then Again' (that's the way he plays, setting out an idea, stating its converse, trying it out on the band if he has one, and then, as often as not, replacing it with the second subject or counter-melody rather than merely recapitulating). It's a brisk blues with the strong bebop overtones Barron brings to most of his work. The Maybeck recital has him playing three originals, but also looking back to influences earlier than Bud Powell, Tatum especially.

The trio on *Lemuria-Seascape* also features some good original material. The two title-tunes, at top and bottom of the programme, are more impressionistic than usual, though the rhythm section keeps the music driving forward. Riley's brushwork is prominently featured on 'Have You Met Miss Jones?'. The same 'and then again . . .' effect transforms Monk's 'Ask Me Now' into an altogether less spiky number. *Lemuria-Seascape* is one of Barron's most attractively romantic sessions, a lighter and less rooted conception. Though none of them scales the heights, there are of course good things on almost all of these records, and Barron, who has suffered the kind of critical invisibility that comes with ubiquity, shouldn't be overlooked.

Jean-Philippe Allard gives Barron a beautiful sound on *Sambao*, but it's marred by the rather fuzzy group playing (Lewis excepted) around it. All the tunes are Barron originals, many of them in the same quasi-Latin mould of 'Lemuria', and it would have been good to have heard them a little more plainly. A trio with just Horta and Lewis would have been intriguing.

**** Other Places Verve 519699-2
  Barron; Ralph Moore (*ss, ts*); Bobby Hutcherson (*vib*); Rufus Reid (*b*); Victor Lewis (*d*); Mino Cinelu (*perc*). 2/93.

This wipes out at a single stroke any problems the previous session might have had. Moore is in firm, probing voice, the rhythm section are wonderfully sharp and swinging, but it's the magnificent interplay between Hutcherson – still in absolutely prime shape – and Barron that marks this one down as a classic. The pianist saved some excellent writing for the date: 'Anywhere', 'Other Places' and 'Ambrosia' are deft, lyrical, unfussy themes that blossom into fine vehicles for improvising, and the chiming chord-structures set up by both piano and vibes ring long and loud in the memory. The duet between Hutcherson and Barron on 'For Heaven's Sake' is simply one of the most gorgeous ballad performances of recent times. Unmissable.

***(*) **Wanton Spirit** Verve 528634-2
> Barron; Charlie Haden (b); Roy Haynes (d). 2/94.

Scarcely any less outstanding, and an affirmation of Barron's increasing stature as leader after countless sessions as loyal sideman. Ellington's sly blues, 'Take The Coltrane', gets a perfectly layered treatment, swung off its feet by Barron's attack, and from there the music opens out into alternately passionate and reflective settings. Haden and Haynes are a practised team by now, and they follow every line: they don't push Barron as a younger pair might, but it suits the wisdom inherent in the music.

Gary Bartz (born 1940) ALTO SAXOPHONE; ALSO SOPRANO SAXOPHONE, CLARINET, FLUTE, WOOD FLUTE

(*) **Monsoon Steeplechase SCCD 31234
> Bartz; Butch Lacy (p); Clint Houston (b); Billy Hart (d). 4/88.

** **Reflections Of Monk** Steeplechase SCCD 1248
> Bartz; Eddie Henderson (t); Bob Butta (p); Geoff Harper (b); Billy Hart (d); Jenelle Fisher, Mekea Keith (v). 11/88.

In 1972, Bartz was collecting poll wins like beer mats. By the end of the decade he was playing, er, disco, a shift of idiom perhaps blessed by his one-time boss, Miles Davis, and one by no means out of keeping with the tenor – or, in this case, alto – of the times.

What was galling was that Bartz had quickly been identified, by Max Roach and Art Blakey before Miles, as one of the finest young saxophone voices of the time, perhaps the best since Jackie McLean. These recent sets mark a partial return to form. Whether at near-fifty he still cuts it like he used to remains more or less non-proven. Both albums seem slightly tentative, a little uncertain in register and far from instantly compelling. There is a fine 'Soul Eyes' on *Monsoon*, but the Monk covers are slightly robotic despite Eddie Henderson's fine contribution. The superadded vocals on 'Monk's Mood' and 'Reflections' were a mistake (Jenelle Fisher's no Abbey Lincoln). Enough of the *Wunderkind* survives in Bartz to guarantee listenability, but not much more than that.

***(*) **West 42nd Street** Candid CCD 79049
> Bartz; Claudio Roditi (t, flhn); John Hicks (p); Ray Drummond (b); Al Foster (d). 3/90.

Sometimes, just sometimes, when a saxophone player climbs the stand at Birdland and lays a reed on his tongue, a tubby ghost wobbles unsteadily out of the shadows and whispers in his ear. Bartz plays like a man inspired, turning 'It's Easy To Remember' into a huge romantic edifice, from which he soars into 'Cousins' and a surprisingly Coltraneish 'The Night Has A Thousand Eyes'. Hicks is the best piano player Bartz has come across in years, and Al Foster sends little whiplash flicks down the line of the metre, coaxing the three main soloists on to even better things. Slightly exhausting, in the way a hot club set teeters between euphoria and growing weariness, but a more than welcome confirmation of Bartz's long-latent qualities. Strongly recommended.

**** **There Goes The Neighbourhood!** Candid CCD 79506
> Bartz; Kenny Barron (p); Ray Drummond (b); Ben Riley (d). 11/90.

Bartz's finest hour. The opening 'Racism' is a boiling blues in double B flat minor, an original played with an increasingly noticeable Coltrane inflexion. The first of two Tadd Dameron compositions, 'On A Misty Night', was originally recorded in the mid-1950s by a band that included Coltrane; the mid-point of the set is a severe interpretation of 'Impressions'. Bartz's homage isn't limited to a growing repertoire of anguished cries and dissonant transpositions. He has also paid attention to how the younger Coltrane framed a solo; working against the trajectory of Dameron's theme, he constructs an ascending line that culminates each time in a beautifully placed false note.

Johnny Mercer's 'Laura' receives a serene and stately reading, with Drummond featured. Bartz's coda restatement is masterful. He tackles 'Impressions' in the most boiled-down way, with only minimal rhythmic support, concentrating on the basic musical information. Barron returns to the foreground for 'I've Never Been In Love' and the closing 'Flight Path', his own composition. Throughout, his touch is light but definite, freeing his accompaniments of any excess baggage.

Though previously Charles McPherson and Bobby Watson have laid claim to Parker's alto crown, Bartz appears to have come into his kingdom at last. A superb album that will grace any collection; recorded live at Birdland, it's beautifully balanced and free from extraneous noise.

***(*) **Shadows** Timeless CD SJP 379
>Bartz; Willie Williams (*ts*); Benny Green (*p*); Christian McBride (*b*); Victor Lewis (*d*). 6/91.

The purple patch continues. No real complaints about this one, except that on occasion Bartz and the bustling Williams get in each other's way. The choice of material is also a bit questionable, with 'Holiday For Strings' not quite coming off as a curtain-piece. There is, to balance that, a riveting performance of Coltrane's 'Song Of The Underground Railroad'. McBride and Lewis are superlative, and Green makes his mark without fuss or histrionics. There are better moments, but this is well up to scratch.

**** **Alto Memories** Verve 523 268
>Bartz; Sonny Fortune (*as*); Kenny Barron (*p*); Buster Williams (*b*); Jack DeJohnette (*d*). 6/93.

*** **Children Of Harlem** Challenge JAZZ CHR 70001
>Bartz; Larry Willis (*p*); Buster Williams (*b*); Ben Riley (*d*). 1/94.

There's nothing on *Children Of Harlem* in terms of emotional urgency or social polemic that Bartz hadn't already done on *There Goes The Neighbourhood!*. The session is dedicated to Paul Laurence Dunbar, tagged with lines by Countee Cullen, another poet of the Harlem Renaissance, and kicked off with a version of the Amos-'n'-Andy theme. An unlikely parallel maybe, but where Charlie Haden's Quartet West project works precisely because it is so determinedly unapologetic in its sentimentality, Bartz seems inclined to throw in ironic nods and winks, quotes and antagonistic outbursts that don't really fit the mood of the thing. That said, the playing is generally very good (if recorded a bit crudely, by Rudy van Gelder's usual high standard), and the long 'If This Isn't Love' stands upsides with anything Bartz has done in recent years. This must be a glorious band in a club setting, but it rather sits in the shadow of *Alto Memories*.

Bartz has very happily shared the front spot with other alto men before. One thinks of Jackie McLean, Charlie Mariano and even Lee Konitz. In Sonny Fortune he has a near-perfect foil, someone who can combine the qualities of all three: the boppish fire, the non-Western idioms, the unexpectedly cool. The rhythm section could hardly be improved upon. Williams is *huge* (and mixed well forward, unlike the van Gelder session) while DeJohnette could almost have taken the place of a piano player less focused and well-characterized than Barron. They stick to standard material pretty much, but it is 'Lonely Woman', Ornette Coleman's most durable composition, that stands out a mile. Getting on for indispensable.

***(*) **The Red and Orange Poems** Atlantic 7567 82720
>Bartz; Eddie Henderson (*t, flhn*); John Clark (*frhn*); Mulgrew Miller (*p*); Dave Holland (*b*);
>Greg Bandy (*d*); Steve Kroon (*perc*).

Ambitious and rich, but Bartz sounds slightly fettered by the format, and it is Henderson (whose critical reputation has been on a parallel branch-line for many years) who steals the honours. Miller is a little busy and hyperactive, compared to previous incumbents, and some of the bass lines, with Clark shadowing, are overdone, even given Bartz's obvious preference for a very resonant sound. He's on a roll, for sure, but this one doesn't quite succeed.

Count Basie (1904–84) PIANO, ORGAN

**** **The Original American Decca Recordings** MCA GRP 36112 3CD
>Basie; Buck Clayton, Joe Keyes, Carl Smith, Ed Lewis, Bobby Moore, Karl George, Harry 'Sweets' Edison, Shad Collins (*t*); Eddie Durham (*tb, g*); George Hunt, Dan Minor, Benny Morton, Dicky Wells (*tb*); Jack Washington (*as, bs*); Caughey Roberts, Earl Warren (*as*); Lester Young, Herschel Evans (*cl, ts*); Chu Berry (*ts*); Claude Williams, Freddie Green (*g*); Walter Page (*b*); Jo Jones (*d*); Jimmy Rushing, Helen Humes (*v*). 1/37–2/39.

**** **Listen . . . You Shall Hear** Hep CD 1025
>As above. 1–10/37.

**** **Do You Wanna Jump . . . ?** Hep CD 1027
>As above. 1–11/38.

**** **Basie Rhythm** Hep CD 1032
>As above, except add Harry James (*t*), Jess Stacy (*p*). 10/36–2/39.

**** **Count Basie Volume One 1932–1938** Jazz Classics In Digital Stereo RPCD 602
>As above, except add Hot Lips Page, Dee Stewart (*t*), Ben Webster (*ts*), Leroy Berry (*g*), Willie McWashington (*d*). 12/32–6/38.

*** **Jive At Five** ASV AJA 5089
>As above. 12/32–2/39.

**** **Count Basie 1936–1938** Classics 503
>As MCA disc, except omit Collins, Edison, Wells, Berry and Humes. 10/36–1/38.

**** Count Basie 1938–39 Classics 504
    As above, except omit Keyes, Smith, Hunt, Roberts and Williams, add Harry 'Sweets' Edison,
    Shad Collins (*t*), Dicky Wells (*tb*), Helen Humes (*v*). 1/38–1/39.
(***) Lester–Amadeus Phontastic CD 7639
    As above discs. 10/36–9/38.
(***) Rock-A-Bye-Basie Vintage Jazz Classics VJC-1033
    As above discs. 38–39.

The arrival of the Count Basie band – on an East Coast scene dominated by Ellington, Lunceford and Henderson – set up a new force in the swing era, and hearing their records from the late 1930s is still a marvellous, enthralling experience. Basie's Kansas City band was a rough-and-ready outfit compared with the immaculate drive of Lunceford or Ellington's urbane mastery, but rhythmically it might have been the most swinging band of its time, based around the perfectly interlocking team of Basie, Green, Page and Jones, but also in the freedom of soloists such as Lester Young, Buck Clayton and Herschel Evans, in the intuitive momentum created within the sections (famously, Basie had relatively few written-out arrangements and would instead evolve head arrangements on the stand) and in the best singing team of any working with the big bands, Helen Humes and the incomparable Jimmy Rushing. There are paradoxical elements – the minimalism of the leader's piano solos that is nevertheless as invigorating as any chunk of fast stride piano, Green's invisible yet indispensable chording, the power of the band which still seems to drift rather than punch its way off the record. Yet they all go to make up an orchestra unique in jazz.

There are too many great individual records to cite here, and instead we shall note only that there are two significant early periods covered by reissues, the Decca tracks (1937–9) and the subsequent recordings for Vocalion, OKeh and Columbia (1939–42). A contractual oddity is that Basie's first session – credited to Jones-Smith Inc., and marking the astonishing debut of Lester Young on record – was made for Columbia rather than Decca, yet the Columbia reissues haven't even put the four tracks together. Two of them are on the hotchpotch *Jive At Five*, but the first Classics CD has them all together. For a definitive study of the Decca sides, one must look to either the Hep or the MCA CDs. The Hep discs have now been added to with *Basie Rhythm* and, besides having the four Jones-Smith Inc. tracks, the valuable thing here is the addition of eight tracks under the nominal leadership of Harry James but with Basie personnel dominating the line-up. James himself sounds better than he does on most of his own records, but otherwise the outstanding figure is saxophonist Herschel Evans, always at least as interesting as Lester Young. The MCA is complete to 1939 on three CDs. There is actually very little to choose between the transfers: the Hep remastering is sometimes a little more full-bodied, but the MCA is mostly smoother and often a little brighter. But given the completeness and the handsome packaging on the MCA discs, we have awarded them top marks for what is desert-island music.

The Classics CDs, as usual, ignore any 'label' boundaries and simply go through all the music chronologically, although no alternative takes are included. The transfers here are unpredictable. Some seem to have a lot of reverberation, which suggests second-hand tape transfers, and, while all the discs sound good enough, they can't compete with the Hep or MCA sets. A fourth CD issue has also been commenced by the French EPM label, and is now up to four discs (*The Golden Years Vols 1–4*), but the remastering isn't notably different from those discs listed above.

The Phontastic CD, though named for Lester Young, is nearly all Basie airshots and concert material. There are some rarities, such as two allegedly unreleased tracks from a 1938 Carnegie Hall concert, but sound-quality is often very poor; for fanatics only.

Rock-A-Bye-Basie, which is all airshots, also comes in very rough fidelity, but the standard of performances is high enough to warrant giving it an audition: if you can stand sound that sounds like it's crackling out of a pre-war receiver, this will be an exciting, surprising disc. There are some very fine treatments and individual spots by the usual stars, as well as undervalued performers such as Jack Washington. Edison especially gets a better shot in than on many of the studio sides: hear his chrous of trumpet on 'Moten Swing'.

*** The Essential Count Basie Vol. 1 Columbia 460061-2
    As above. 10/36–6/39.
*** The Essential Count Basie Vol. 2 Columbia 460828-2
    As appropriate discs below. 8/39–5/40.
*** The Essential Count Basie Vol. 3 Columbia 461098-2
    As appropriate discs below. 8/40–4/41.
***(*) Count Basie 1939 Classics 513
    Basie; Buck Clayton, Ed Lewis, Harry 'Sweets' Edison, Shad Collins (*t*); Dicky Wells, Benny
    Morton, Dan Minor (*tb*); Earl Warren (*as*); Jack Washington (*as, bs*); Chu Berry, Buddy Tate,
    Lester Young (*cl, ts*); Freddie Green (*g*); Walter Page (*b*); Jo Jones (*d*); Jimmy Rushing, Helen
    Humes (*v*). 1–4/39.

***(*) **Count Basie 1939 Vol. 2** Classics 533
    As above, except omit Berry. 5–11/39.
*** **Count Basie 1939–1940** Classics 563
    As above, except add Al Killian (*t*), Tab Smith (*ss, as*), omit Collins. 11/39–10/40.
*** **Count Basie 1940–1941** Classics 623
    As above, except add Ed Cuffee (*tb*), Paul Bascomb, Coleman Hawkins (*ts*). 11/40–4/41.
*** **Count Basie 1941** Classics 652
    As above, except add Robert Scott, Eli Robinson (*tb*), Kenny Clarke (*d*), Paul Robeson, Lynne
    Sherman (*v*); omit Hawkins. 5–11/41.
*** **Count Basie 1942** Classics 684
    As above, except add Jerry Blake (*cl, as*), Caughey Roberts (*as*), Henry Nemo (*v*); omit Minor,
    Cuffee, Robeson. 5/41–7/42.
***(*) **Count Basie Volume 2** Jazz Classics In Digital Stereo RPCD603
    As above discs. 38–40.

It's a pity that Basie's second wave hasn't been as well served by Columbia as his first has been by other companies. The three volumes of 'Essential' Basie haven't been treated with the kind of care which the 'essential' should merit: muddy transfers do a disservice to the music, which is almost but, irritatingly, not quite chronological or complete. Docked a star each. The Classics CDs are again uneven but are basically a better bet.

The great change which commenced this Basie era was the sad death of Herschel Evans, 'the greatest jazz musician I ever played with in my life', as Jo Jones remembered him. In many ways the band was never the same again. Evans's partnership with Lester Young had given the reed section its idiosyncratic fluency, and perhaps his death marked the end of the original Basie era, when the band relied on its individual players to combine and create the instinctive Basie sound. That said, Chu Berry was a more than capable replacement for Evans, and the orchestra was still approaching a technical peak. Other arrivals – Shad Collins, Tab Smith (who also did some strong arrangements) and, later, Buddy Tate (when Berry also departed) – also had an impact on the band, and emerging arrangers (Andy Gibson, Buck Clayton) had a beneficial effect. But Basie was already steeped in a routine of riffs, conventional harmonies and familiar patterns, which even the soloists (including the finally disenfranchised Young) couldn't really transcend, let alone transform. Taken a few at a time, these tracks are fine, but all together they can sometimes be as dull as full-length records.

Highlights to listen for are 'Evil Blues', a memorable band performance, Lester Young's solo on 'Taxi War Dance' (both Classics 513), 'Clap Hands, Here Comes Charlie' and the Kansas City Seven date of September 1939 (all Classics 533), 'Blow Top' (Classics 563), Clayton's 'Love Jumped Out' and Helen Humes's delightful vocal on 'My Wanderin' Man' (both Classics 623). There are plenty of other interludes and solos to savour: this was too good a band to lack interest. Coleman Hawkins also makes a guest appearance on two tracks on Classics 623. But the paucity of genuinely memorable compositions and Basie's own leaning towards ensemble punch and exactness over personal flair sows the seeds of the band's decline.

There are also Basie's own piano 'solos' (actually with the rhythm section), ten of which were recorded in 1938–9 (they are split among Classics 503, 504 and 513). Basie had long since started to pare away the more florid and excitable elements of his early stride style and by now was cutting down to the bone. It works best on the elegance of 'How Long' and the almost playful feel accorded to 'Fare Thee Well, Honey, Fare Thee Well'. They also let the great rhythm section display itself away from the confines of the band, and one can hear how perfectly the team interlocks. But they also expose something of the repetitiousness and sometimes false economies of Basie's playing, even at the curtailed 78-r.p.m. length.

The two latest Classics compilations take the story up to 1942. Classics 652 shows the band playing with unimpaired vitality, but the material is often grim: saving graces include 'Diggin' For Dex' and 'Platterbrains', and there is Paul Robeson's one jazz appearance on 'King Joe'. Classics 684 is considerably better: some excellent Rushing blues performances, eight titles by the Basie All-American Rhythm Section (all traditional blues), with Clayton and Byas featured on four of them, and a final date that produced a minor classic in Clayton's arrangement of 'It's Sand, Man!'.

Robert Parker's second volume of Basie (RPCD 603) is a strong selection in his customary superb sound. A fine companion piece to his first.

***(*) **The Jubilee Alternatives** Hep CD 38
    Basie; Harry 'Sweets' Edison, Al Killian, Ed Lewis, Snooky Young (*t*); Eli Robinson, Robert
    Scott, Louis Taylor, Dicky Wells (*tb*); Jimmy Powell, Earl Warren (*as*); Buddy Tate, Lester
    Young, Illinois Jacquet (*ts*); Rudy Rutherford (*bs, cl*); Freddie Green (*g*); Rodney Richardson
    (*b*); Jo Jones, Buddy Rich (*d*); Thelma Carpenter, Jimmy Rushing (*v*). 12/43–10/44.
*** **Old Manuscripts: Broadcast Transcriptions 1944–45** Music & Arts CD-844
    Similar to above. 43–45.

*** Count Basie 1943–1945 Classics 801
Similar to above discs, except add Buck Clayton, Al Stearns, Joe Newman (*t*), Lucky Thompson (*ts*), Jack Washington (*bs*), Shadow Wilson (*d*). 7/43–1/45.

Splendidly remastered in very crisp sound, these studio 'alternatives' to AFRS Jubilee show broadcasts give a useful impression of a transitional Basie band. Buddy Rich and Illinois Jacquet replace Jones and Young on some tracks, and the brass section is largely different from the previous commercial studio tracks. There are some good charts here – Andy Gibson's freshly paced 'Andy's Blues', Clayton's excellent 'Avenue C' and Tab Smith's 'Harvard Blues', one of the best of the later Columbias, with a repeat performance of the *tour de force* vocal by Jimmy Rushing – and many of the soloists sound in unusually lively form.

The Music & Arts disc collects another set of transcriptions. There are a handful of rarities, including 'Dance Of The Gremlins', but plenty of familiar things to please Basie's core audience. Reproduction varies rather wildly, but the best tracks sound clear and strong.

Classics pick up their story again with a group of V-Discs and one Columbia session. This covers some of the VJC material (below) and, as usual, no sources are listed for the transfers.

***(*) Beaver Junction Vintage Jazz Classics VJC-CD-1018
As above, except add Karl George (*t*), J. J. Johnson (*tb*), Joe Marshall (*d*). 44–46.

More Jubilee and V-Disc material, in excellent shape and featuring all the strengths of the mid-1940s band. Similar material to the above, but there are one or two previously unavailable tracks and, with all the remastering done from clean glass acetates, the sound is uncommonly bright and clear.

*** Count Basie And His Orchestra – 1944 Circle CCD-60
Similar to above. 1/44.

Cut in a single three-hour session, these are 16 transcriptions from the Lang-Worth service. Another solid Basie session with staples from his then-current book, three rather gooey ballads sung by Earl Warren and only two features for Rushing. Hardly essential, but the sound of the transcriptions is exceptionally clear and fresh.

**(*) Count Basie And His Orchestra 1944 & 1945 Circle CCD-130
Similar to above. 1/44–2/45.

Another 17 transcriptions, remastered in very good sound. Too many vocals, perhaps, even though two of them are by Rushing, and jazz survives only in a couple of unremarkable Dickie Wells tunes, Earl Warren's predictable 'Rockin' The Blues' and Al Killian's boisterous 'Let's Jump'.

*** Brand New Wagon RCA Bluebird ND 82292
Basie; Harry 'Sweets' Edison, Ed Lewis, Emmett Berry, Snooky Young (*t*); Bill Johnson, Ted Donnelly, George Matthews, Dicky Wells, George Simon, George Washington, Eli Robinson (*tb*); Preston Love, Rudy Rutherford, C. Q. Price (*as*); Paul Gonsalves, Buddy Tate (*ts*); Jack Washington (*bs*); Freddie Green (*g*); Walter Page (*b*); Jo Jones (*d*); Jimmy Rushing (*v*). 1–12/47.

*** Basie's Basement RCA Bluebird ND 90630
As above, except add Clark Terry, Gerald Wilson, Jimmy Nottingham (*t*), Earl Warren, W. Parker (*as*), S. Palmer (*b*), Butch Ballard (*d*). 1/47–7/49.

Basie signed a three-year contract with Victor in 1947, and the results have usually been regarded as something of a low point in his discography. But this set of 21 tracks from that initial year presents some good Basie performances, even if they show little sign of any marked change from the formula which had been enveloping the orchestra over the previous seven years. Gonsalves, seldom remembered as a Basie-ite, turns in some strong solos, 'Swingin' The Blues' and 'Basie's Basement' trim the band down to a small group without losing any impact, and there is the usual ration of features for Jimmy Rushing, always worth hearing. The sound hasn't been best served by the NoNoise process of remastering but will suffice. The subsequent *Basie's Basement* takes ten tracks from the earlier CD and adds a single 1949 recording. The sound is bigger but also seems over-resonant and booms in the bass.

*** Shoutin' Blues RCA Bluebird 07863 66158 2
Basie; Harry 'Sweets' Edison, Emmett Berry, Clark Terry, Gerald Wilson, Jimmy Nottingham (*t*); Ted Donnelly, Dicky Wells, George Matthews, Melba Liston (*tb*); C. Q. Price, Earl Warren (*as*); Paul Gonsalves, Weasel Parker, George Auld (*ts*); Gene Ammons (*ts, bs*); Jack Washington (*bs*); Freddie Green (*g*); Singleton Palmer, Al McKibbon (*b*); Butch Ballard, Gus Johnson (*d*); Jimmy Rushing, Billy Valentine, Taps Miller, Google Eyes (*v*). 4/49–2/50.

*** The Indispensable Count Basie RCA ND 89758 2CD
As above discs. 1/47–2/50.

The final sessions before Basie disbanded the orchestra in 1950. Bop sidles into some of the arrangements here, notably 'Slider' and 'Normania', and it gives Basie's men no trouble – after all, this was one of the most accomplished of bands. There is some dreadful stuff as far as material is concerned, and it's only on the various permutations of the blues that the music settles down and grooves. Good moments for Wells, Edison and Rushing, as ever, and mostly fine remastering. The RCA Tribune two-disc set collects the two Bluebirds in one package, but the remastering (copies straight from the original LP edition) isn't on a par, convenient though this format is.

*** **The Essential** Columbia 467143-2
> As appropriate discs above, plus Clark Terry (*t*), Buddy DeFranco (*cl*), Charlie Rouse, Wardell Gray (*ts*), Jimmy Lewis (*b*), Buddy Rich (*d*). 8/39–11/50.

A solid compilation of Basie's Columbia years, although the later selections are a peculiar lot – 'For The Good Of Your Country' is a strange one, and the four final tracks by the 1950 small group with Terry, DeFranco, Rouse and Chaloff don't really belong, interesting though they are.

*** **Americans In Sweden Vol. 1** Tax CD 3701-2
> Basie; Reunald Jones, Joe Wilder, Wendell Culley, Joe Newman (*t*); Bill Hughes, Henry Coker, Benny Powell (*tb*); Marshall Royal (*as, cl*); Ernie Wilkins (*as, ts*); Frank Wess (*ts, f*); Frank Foster (*ts*); Charlie Fowlkes (*bs*); Freddie Green (*g*); Eddie Jones (*b*); Gus Johnson (*d*). 3/54.

*** **Americans In Sweden Vol. 2** Tax CD 3702-2
> As above. 3/54.

** **Class Of '54** Black Lion BLCD 760924
> As above, except Thad Jones (*t*) replaces Wilder. 9/54.

Basie had been obliged to work with an octet rather than a full band in 1950–51, but he put a new orchestra together the following year, and from then on he always remained in charge of a big band. It was the start of the 'modern' Basie era. By taking arrangements from a new team, of whom the most important was Neal Hefti, Basie made the most of a formidable new reed section, trumpets that streamlined the old Basie fire with absolute precision, and the first of a line of effusive drummers, Gus Johnson. The new soloists were showstoppers, but in a rather hard, sometimes brittle way, and Basie's belief in the primacy of the riff now led inexorably to arrangements which had screaming brass piled on top of crooning reeds on top of thunderous drums: it was a fearsome and in its way very exciting effect.

The two Tax CDs come from what was Basie's first European tour, and the sound is very good for the period, with only a few balance problems for the rhythm section: the brass and reeds come through very strikingly. In set-pieces like Foster's flag-waving solo on 'Jumpin' At The Woodside', Hefti's glittering charts for 'Fancy Meeting You' and 'Two Franks', and similarly punchy efforts by John Mandel and Buster Harding, all the gusto of the new Basie band comes powering through. The Black Lion CD mixed tracks by a nonet drawn from the band and others from a 1954 radio concert, though the sound is much less attractive on this disc, and the Tax CDs give a much better impression of the band as it then was.

*** **April In Paris** Verve 825575-2
> Basie; Reunald Jones, Thad Jones, Joe Newman, Wendell Culley (*t*); Benny Powell, Henry Coker, Matthew Gee (*tb*); Marshall Royal (*cl, as*); Bill Graham (*as*); Frank Wess (*ts, f*); Frank Foster (*ts*); Charlie Fowlkes (*bs*); Freddie Green (*b*); Eddie Jones (*b*); Sonny Payne (*d*); Joe Williams (*v*). 1/56.

*** **Basie In London** Verve 833805-2
> As above. 9/56.

**** **Count Basie Swings, Joe Williams Sings** Verve 519852-2
> As above, except Bill Hughes (*tb*) replaces Gee. 7/55–6/56.

***(*) **The Greatest!!** Verve 833774-2
> As above. 57.

(*) **Count Basie At Newport Verve 833776-2
> As above, except add Roy Eldridge (*t*), Illinois Jacquet, Lester Young (*ts*), Jo Jones (*d*), Jimmy Rushing (*v*). 7/57.

Facsimile editions of some of the most significant of Basie's Verve albums from the 1950s – *Dance Session No. 1* and *No. 2*, and *The Band Of Distinction* – have yet to appear. Of the three originals now on CD, *April In Paris* and *Basie In London* are typical Basie fare of the period, bustling charts, leathery solos and pinpoint timing. *At Newport* is a fun reunion with some of Basie's old sidemen (though Young sounds as wayward as he usually then was) and features Eldridge going several miles over the top on 'One O'Clock Jump'. The outstanding albums are probably the two featuring Joe Williams. The debut appearance on 519852-2 is a classic of big-band singing: the original versions of 'Alright, OK, You Win', 'Every Day I Have The Blues' and 'In The Evening', material on which Williams made his name, still have terrific zip and élan, and the remastered sound has real clout. *The Greatest!!* concentrates on standards but is another faultless performance. Rich-toned, as oleaginous as Billy Eckstine could be, yet with a feeling for the blues which at least came some way near the irreplaceable Rushing, Williams's smoothness and debonair manner fitted the new Basie band almost perfectly.

**** **The Complete Atomic Mr Basie** Roulette CDP 7932732
>   Basie; Joe Newman, Thad Jones, Wendell Culley, Snooky Young (*t*); Benny Powell, Henry
>   Coker, Al Grey (*tb*); Marshall Royal, Frank Wess (*as*); Eddie 'Lockjaw' Davis, Frank Foster
>   (*ts*); Charlie Fowlkes (*bs*); Freddie Green (*g*); Eddie Jones (*b*); Sonny Payne (*d*). 10/57.

*** **Sing Along With Basie** Roulette B21Y-95332-2
>   As above, except add Dave Lambert, Jon Hendricks, Annie Ross, Joe Williams (*v*). 5–9/58.

*** **Basie / Eckstine Inc** Roulette 828636-2
>   As above, except George Duvivier (*b*) replaces Jones, add Billy Eckstine (*v*). 5–7/59.

*** **Basie Swings, Bennett Sings** Roulette B21Y-93899-2
>   As above, except add Ralph Sharon (*p*), Tony Bennett (*v*). 1/59.

(*) **Kansas City Suite Roulette B21Y-94797-2
>   As above. 9/60.

Basie opened his contract for Roulette with the great showstopping album that this band had in it, *The Atomic Mr Basie* (complete with mushroom cloud on the cover, a cold war classic). It might be the last great Basie album. He had Neal Hefti (who already had scored most of the hottest numbers in the band's recent book) do the whole record, and Hefti's zesty, machine-tooled scoring reached its apogee in 'The Kid From Red Bank', 'Flight Of The Foo Birds', 'Splanky' and the rest. But it also had a guest soloist in the great Lockjaw Davis, whose splenetic outbursts gave just the right fillip to what might otherwise have been a too cut-and-dried effort. The record has at last been reissued in its full form, properly remastered (early pressings were flawed), with all the available extra tracks.

Thereafter, the Roulette albums become as prosaic and sensible as the rest of Basie's latter-day output. The meeting with Tony Bennett will please Bennett fans more than Basie admirers, but it's a very enjoyable record, as is the meeting with Eckstine – mostly the singer's old favourites, plushly orchestrated in Basie's luxury class, which is the sort of thing Eckstine thrived on. *Sing Along With Basie* is perhaps the one occasion where the band has sounded good with singers other than their regulars: Lambert, Hendricks and Ross swing infectiously through ten Basie staples, with Ross's work on 'Lil' Darlin'' particularly delightful.

***(*) **Count On The Coast Vol. 1** Phontastic PHONT CD 7574
>   Basie; Snooky Young, Thad Jones, Wendell Culley, Joe Newman (*t*); Benny Powell, Henry
>   Coker, Al Grey (*tb*); Frank Wess (*as, f*); Billy Mitchell, Frank Foster (*ts*); Charlie Fowlkes (*bs*);
>   Freddie Green (*g*); Eddie Jones (*b*); Sonny Payne (*d*); Joe Williams (*v*). 6–7/58.

***(*) **Count On The Coast Vol. 2** Phontastic PHONT CD 7575
>   As above. 6–7/58.

*** **Fresno, California** Jazz Unlimited JUCD 2039
>   As above. 4/59.

***(*) **Live 1958–59** Status STCD 110
>   As above, except add John Anderson (*t*), Marshall Royal (*as, cl*). 6/58–11/59.

These are exceptionally strong live recordings. The two Phontastic CDs and the Status disc are all in such clear and powerful sound that the recordings belie their age; and Basie's men sound in particularly muscular and good-humoured form, especially on the Status set, which includes a few uncommon parts of the Basie repertoire and some dry runs for the Roulette sessions that were coming up. Foster is a titan among the soloists, but Powell, Wess and Newman also have their moments, and Williams is very good on the Phontastic discs. The date in Fresno caught another good one by the band, though the way the applause has been trimmed out you'd hardly know there was any encouragement for them. Sound is a little harsh, as if brightened from a dull master-tape, but listenable.

*** **Basie In Sweden** Roulette B21Y-95974-2
>   Basie; Thad Jones, Sonny Cohn, Fip Ricard, Al Aarons, Benny Bailey (*t*); Benny Powell, Ake
>   Persson, Henry Coker, Quentin Jackson (*tb*); Marshall Royal, Frank Wess, Frank Foster, Eric
>   Dixon, Charlie Fowlkes (*reeds*); Freddie Green (*g*); Ike Isaacs (*b*); Louie Bellson (*d*); Irene Reid
>   (*v*). 8/62.

*** **Lil' Ol' Groovemaker . . . Basie!** Verve 821799-2
>   As above, except add Don Rader (*t*), Grover Mitchell, Urbie Green (*tb*), Buddy Catlett (*b*),
>   Sonny Payne (*d*); omit Jones, Bailey, Persson, Jackson, Isaacs, Bellson, Reid. 4/63.

** **This Time By Basie** Reprise 45162
>   As above, except add Edward Preston, Wallace Davenport, Sam Noto (*t*), Henderson Chambers,
>   Al Grey, Bill Hughes, Gordon Thomas (*tb*), Eddie 'Lockjaw' Davis, Bobby Plater (*reeds*), Wyatt
>   Ruther (*b*), Louie Bellson (*d*), Leon Thomas (*v*). 1/63–12/64.

*** **More Hits Of The Fifties And Sixties** Verve 519849-2
>   Similar to above discs. 4/63–1/65.

*** **Our Shining Hour** Verve 837446-2
> Probably similar to above, except add Sammy Davis Jr (*v*). 65.

Basie was at a low ebb in the mid-1960s, and many of his studio albums were dedicated to Beatles tunes, among others. *This Time By Basie* is one of the misguided attempts to make the Count go pop. Competent, but any decent radio orchestra could have done just as good a job. *Our Shining Hour* is more showbiz in a collaboration with Sammy Davis, but the singer plays up to the occasion so much – and elevates the band in doing so – that it's hard not to enjoy. *Basie In Sweden* is a late Roulette disc and quite a good one, although most of the best live Basie recordings for the label are in the Mosaic de-luxe edition (see Introduction). *Lil' Ol' Groovemaker* is another – and this time a rather better – set of Quincy Jones charts, with 'Pleasingly Plump' turning out to be a rather gracious ballad and the swingers taking off effectively. *More Hits* proves to be a series of covers of Frank Sinatra successes and, though the band is contained within precise arrangements and largely inflexible parts, the delivery is sometimes stunningly achieved. One of the better dates from a largely undistinguished period.

*** **Verve Jazz Masters: Count Basie** Verve 519819-2
> As appropriate discs above. 8/54–10/65.

Old favourites and the obvious choices from Basie's Verve tenure – 'April In Paris', 'Shiny Stockins', Sent For You Yesterday' and 13 more.

*** **Basie Jam** Pablo 2310-718
> Basie; Harry 'Sweets' Edison (*t*); J. J. Johnson (*tb*); Eddie 'Lockjaw' Davis (*ts*); Zoot Sims (*ts*); Irving Ashby (*g*); Ray Brown (*b*); Louie Bellson (*d*). 12/73.

*** **The Bosses** Original Jazz Classics OJC 821
> Basie; Harry 'Sweets' Edison (*t*); J. J. Johnson (*tb*); Eddie 'Lockjaw' Davis, Zoot Sims (*ts*); Irving Ashby (*g*); Ray Brown (*b*); Louie Bellson (*d*); Joe Turner (*v*). 12/73.

*** **For The First Time** Pablo 2310-712
> Basie; Ray Brown (*b*); Louie Bellson (*d*). 5/74.

*** **For The Second Time** Original Jazz Classics OJC 600
> Basie; Ray Brown (*b*); Louie Bellson (*d*). 8/75.

(*) **Satch And Josh Pablo 2310-722
> Basie; Oscar Peterson (*p*); Freddie Green (*g*); Ray Brown (*b*); Louie Bellson (*d*). 12/74.

***(*) **Basie & Zoot** Original Jazz Classics OJC 822
> Basie; Zoot Sims (*ts*); John Heard (*b*); Louie Bellson (*d*). 4/75.

** **Jam Session At Montreux 1975** Pablo 2310-750
> Basie; Roy Eldridge (*t*); Johnny Griffin (*ts*); Milt Jackson (*vib*); Niels-Henning Orsted-Pedersen (*b*); Louie Bellson (*d*). 7/75.

*** **Basie Big Band** Pablo 2310-756
> Basie; Pete Minger, Frank Szabo, Dave Stahl, Bob Mitchell, Sonny Cohn (*t*); Al Grey, Curtis Fuller, Bill Hughes, Mel Wanzo (*tb*); Bobby Plater (*as, f*); Danny Turner (*as*); Eric Dixon, Jimmy Forrest (*ts*); Charlie Fowlkes (*bs*); Freddie Green (*g*); John Duke (*b*); Butch Miles (*d*). 8/75.

(*) **Basie And Friends Pablo 2310-925
> Basie; Oscar Peterson (*p*); Freddie Green (*g*); Ray Brown, John Heard, Niels-Henning Orsted-Pedersen (*b*); Louie Bellson (*d*). 12/74–11/81.

It hardly seemed likely that, at 70, Basie would embark on a new career; but that was more or less what happened when Norman Granz signed him to his new Pablo label and began taking down Basie albums more prolifically than ever before, some three dozen in the last ten years of the bandleader's life. Eight of them were set down in the first 18 months. *The Bosses* was a fine beginning, setting Basie alongside Joe Turner, who is in mellow but not reticent mood: there are too many remakes of his old hits here, but Turner and Basie make a magisterial combination, and the horns aren't too intrusive. *Basie Jam* was the first and perhaps the best of a series of studio jam sessions. The formula is, let it be said, predictable: fast blues, slow blues, fast blues, slow blues . . . sort-of-fast blues. Basie plays as minimally as he ever has, but he presides grandly from the rear, and there are entertaining cameos from Johnson, Sims and Davis. The *Montreux Jam* is a bore, with Eldridge past his best and the others simply going on too long, while *Basie Big Band* was his first set for Pablo with the regular orchestra. This was a more than encouraging start. Sam Nestico, who wrote all nine charts, offered no radical departures from the Basie method, but at least he looked for more interesting harmonies and section colours, and there were some fine players in the band again: Jimmy Forrest, Bobby Mitchell, Curtis Fuller. Butch Miles, the least self-effacing of Basie's drummers, had also arrived, but was so far behaving, and Granz's dry studio sound suited the clean and direct lines rather well.

As far as Basie the pianist went, he made his first trio album in *For The First Time* (a formula repeated on *For The Second Time*) and traded licks with Oscar Peterson, his stylistic opposite, in the amusing *Satch And Josh*. Neither record was exactly a revelation, since Basie basically carried on in the style he'd played in for the last 40 years, but as fresh areas of work after 25 years of making the same kind of record, it must have been invigorating; and he plays as if it was. *Basie And Friends* is a collection of out-takes from various sessions, mainly made in this period, though a couple date from later on.

One of the best of all of Basie's Pablos is the meeting with Zoot Sims on *Basie & Zoot*. It's almost worth having just for the snorting blues choruses they put down on 'Hardav'. Basie gets a bit too ripe when he turns to the organ for a wallow through 'I Surrender Dear' but Sims always has a swinging line to put down, and this was a well-made match.

*** **I Told You So** Original Jazz Classics OJC 824
    As above, except John Thomas, Jack Feierman (*t*) replace Szabo and Stahl. 1/76.
*** **Basie Jam No. 2** Original Jazz Classics OJC 631
    Basie; Clark Terry (*t*); Al Grey (*tb*); Benny Carter (*as*); Eddie 'Lockjaw' Davis (*ts*); Joe Pass (*g*); John Heard (*b*); Louie Bellson (*d*). 5/76.
(*) **Basie Jam No. 3 Original Jazz Classics OJC 687
    As above. 5/76.
(*) **Prime Time Pablo 2310-797
    Basie; Pete Minger, Lyn Biviano, Bob Mitchell, Sonny Cohn (*t*); Al Grey, Curtis Fuller, Bill Hughes, Mel Wanzo (*tb*); Danny Turner, Bobby Plater (*as*); Jimmy Forrest, Eric Dixon (*ts*); Charlie Fowlkes (*bs*); Nat Pierce (*p*); Freddie Green (*g*); John Duke (*b*); Butch Miles (*d*). 1/77.
** **Montreux '77** Original Jazz Classics OJC 377
    As above, except Waymon Reed (*t*), Dennis Wilson (*tb*) replace Minger and Fuller. 7/77.
*** **Jam Montreux '77** Original Jazz Classics OJC 379
    Basie; Roy Eldridge (*t*); Vic Dickenson, Al Grey (*tb*); Benny Carter (*as*); Zoot Sims (*ts*); Ray Brown (*b*); Jimmie Smith (*d*). 7/77.
*** **Kansas City Five** Original Jazz Classics OJC 888
    Basie; Milt Jackson (*vib*); Joe Pass (*g*); John Heard (*b*); Louie Bellson (*d*). 1/77.
*** **Satch And Josh . . . Again** Pablo 2310-802
    Basie; Oscar Peterson (*p*); John Heard (*b*); Louie Bellson (*d*). 9/77.

If Basie hadn't made too many records in the early 1970s, he was certainly making up for lost time now. The two further *Basie Jam* albums are lesser editions of the previous set, though, like all such records, they have a moment or two when things start happening. Carter and Davis are the most reliable soloists on hand. *I Told You So* and *Prime Time* were the second and third full-orchestra albums for Pablo and, while the first one is solid, the second misfires a few times: 'Bundle O'Funk' was exactly the kind of modishness which Basie's return to traditionalism should have eschewed, and some of the soloists sound tired. But it's better than the desperately routine live set from Montreux which wanders joylessly through a stale Basie set. The small-band jam from the same year is much better: Carter's gorgeous solo on 'These Foolish Things', Sims wherever he plays, and even the by-now-unreliable Eldridge all make something good out of it. The second *Satch And Josh* album follows the same sort of pattern as the first and takes much of its energy from the grooving beat laid down by Heard and Bellson: 'Home Run', for instance, is deliciously spry and merry. *Kansas City Five* sets the unpretentious pairing of Basie and Jackson on their inevitable programme of blues and jazz chestnuts so old they ought to be roasted to a crisp by now. The old campaigners still find a wrinkle or two. Especially warm: 'Frog's Blues'.

*** **Live In Japan '78** Pablo 2308-246
    Basie; Pete Minger, Sonny Cohn, Noland Smith, Waymon Reed (*t*); Mel Wanzo, Bill Hughes, Dennis Wilson, Alonzo Wesley (*tb*); Bobby Plater, Danny Turner (*as*); Eric Dixon (*ts, f*); Kenny Hing (*ts*); Charlie Fowlkes (*bs*); Freddie Green (*g*); John Clayton (*b*); Butch Miles (*d*). 5/78.
*** **Night Rider** Original Jazz Classics OJC 688
    Basie; Oscar Peterson (*p*); John Heard (*bb*); Louie Bellson (*d*). 2/78.
*** **The Timekeepers** Original Jazz Classics OJC 790
    Basie; Oscar Peterson (*p*); John Heard (*b*); Louie Bellson (*d*). 2/78.
(*) **Yessir, That's My Baby Pablo 2310-923
    As above. 2/78.
*** **On the Road** Original Jazz Classics OJC 854
    Basie; Pete Minger, Sonny Cohen, Paul Cohen, Raymond Brown (*t*); Booty Wood, Bill Hughes, Mel Wanzo, Dennis Wilson (*tb*); Charlie Fowlkes, Eric Dixon, Bobby Plater, Danny Turner, Kenny Hing (*reeds*); Freddie Green (*g*); Keter Betts (*b*); Mickey Roker (*d*). 7/79.
*** **Get Together** Pablo 2310-924
    Basie; Clark Terry (*t, flhn*); Harry 'Sweets' Edison (*t*); Budd Johnson (*ts, bs*); Eddie 'Lockjaw' Davis (*ts*); Freddie Green (*g*); John Clayton (*b*); Gus Johnson (*d*). 9/79.

The Japanese concert must have been a happy experience for the band since they sound in excellent spirits, and familiar charts take on a springier life. The sound is unfortunately slightly constricted and certainly isn't as wide-bodied as the punchy crescendos secured on *On The Road*, which is another of the better live albums from this stage of Basie's career. The sheer wallop of 'Wind Machine' and 'Splanky' sums up the kind of unhindered and creaseless power which Basie's orchestra worked to secure and, while it says little of any personal nature, taken a few tracks at a time it certainly knocks the listener over. The three albums with Peterson are good enough on their own terms but anyone who has either of the earlier discs won't find anything different here. Peterson carries most of the weight, and Basie answers with his patented right-hand fills and occasional brow-furrowing left-hand chords. If anything makes the music happen, though, it's again the exemplary swing of Heard and Bellson. *Get Together* is yet another small-group jam on a few old favourites, but the presence of the great Budd Johnson adds a few more felicitous moments than usual.

*** **Kansas City Seven** Original Jazz Classics OJC 690
>   Basie; Freddie Hubbard (*t*); J. J. Johnson (*tb*); Eddie 'Lockjaw' Davis (*ts*); Joe Pass (*g*); John Heard (*b*); Jake Hanna (*d*). 4/80.

(*) **Kansas City Shout Pablo 2310-859
>   Basie; Pete Minger, Sonny Cohn, Dale Carley, Dave Stahl (*t*); Booty Wood, Bill Hughes, Dennis Wilson, Grover Mitchell, Dennis Rowland (*tb*); Eddie Vinson (*as, v*); Eric Dixon, Bobby Plater (*as*); Danny Turner, Kenny Hing (*ts*); John Williams (*bs*); Freddie Green (*g*); Cleveland Eaton (*b*); Duffy Jackson (*d*); Joe Turner (*v*). 4/80.

*** **Warm Breeze** Pablo 2312-131
>   As above, except add Bob Summers, Willie Cook, Harry 'Sweets' Edison, Frank Szabo (*t*), Harold Jones, Gregg Field (*d*); omit Rowland, Stahl, Minger. 9/81.

*** **Farmers Market Barbecue** Original Jazz Classics OJC 732
>   As above, except Chris Albert (*t*), James Leary (*b*), replace Eaton, Jackson, Vinson, Jones and Turner. 5/82.

*** **Me And You** Pablo 2310-891
>   As above, except Steve Furtado, Frank Szabo (*t*), Eric Schneider (*ts*), Chris Woods (*as*), Dennis Mackrel (*d*) replace Albert, Rowland, Hing, Dixon, Plater, Field. 2/83.

(*) **88 Basie Street Pablo 2310-901
>   As above. 5/83.

(*) **Fancy Pants Pablo 2310-920
>   As above, except Jim Crawford (*t*) replaces Furtado. 12/83.

*** **Kansas City Six** Original Jazz Classics OJC 449
>   Basie; Willie Cook (*t*); Eddie Vinson (*as, v*); Joe Pass (*g*); Niels-Henning Orsted-Pedersen (*b*); Louie Bellson (*d*). 11/81.

*** **Mostly Blues . . . And Some Others** Pablo 2310-919
>   Basie; Snooky Young (*t*); Eddie 'Lockjaw' Davis (*ts*); Joe Pass (*g*); Freddie Green (*g*); John Heard (*b*); Roy McCurdy (*d*). 6/83.

Basie carried on, regardless of encroaching arthritis, eventually working the stage from a wheelchair. The big-band records from this patch are some of his best Pablos, for the simple reason that Granz was recording the band to more telling effect: studio mixes had improved, the weight and balance of the orchestra came through more smoothly and arrived with a bigger punch and, since those virtues counted for more with Basie than did individual solos or any other idiosyncrasy, the band just sounded bigger and better. The arrangements on the final albums are shared among a number of hands. Sam Nestico was again responsible for most of *Warm Breeze* and *Fancy Pants*, while other band-members contributed to the other three discs, which also featured numbers by Ernie Wilkins and Basie himself. *Warm Breeze* is a particularly shapely album, with Willie Cook featured on a couple of tunes, Harry 'Sweets' Edison guesting on 'How Sweet It Is' and the themes standing among Nestico's more melodic efforts. *Me And You* and *Farmers Market Barbecue* are both split between full-band and some tracks by a smaller edition of the orchestra: the latter has a splendid 'Blues For The Barbecue' and fine tenor by Kenny Hing on 'St Louis Blues', while the former includes an overripe Booty Wood solo on a dead slow 'She's Funny That Way' as well as a look all the way back to 'Moten Swing'. *88 Basie Street* and *Fancy Pants* are a little more routine, but the slickness and precision are unfaltering. *Kansas City Shout* and *Six* are fun albums with Vinson and Turner vying for attention and Basie refereeing with stately calm at the piano. But the two best records from this closing period are probably *Kansas City Seven* and *Mostly Blues . . . And Some Others*. The former features a cracking line-up and, though Hubbard sometimes goes too far and Hanna's cymbals are annoyingly over-busy, it makes for some steaming music. The latter is as slow, full-flavoured and hefty as Basie seemed to want his blues to be: Pass and the imperturbable Green make a memorable combination, and Young and Davis blow things that turn out just fine. The pianist, of course, does his usual.

*** **Fun Time** Pablo 2310-945
>   Basie; Sonny Cohn, Frank Szabo, Pete Minger, Dave Stahl, Bob Mitchell (*t*); Al Grey, Curtis Fuller, Mel Wanzo, Bill Hughes (*tb*); Eric Dixon, Danny Turner, Bobby Plater, Jimmy Forrest,

Charlie Fowlkes (*reeds*); Freddie Green (*g*); John Duke (*b*); Butch Miles (*d*); Bill Caffey (*v*). 7/75.

The first of what could be many more Basie records yet, depending on what Pablo has in its unreleased stockpile. This is the orchestra at Montreux in 1975, a very grand edition of the band, and delivering on all cylinders. Big and clear concert sound.

*** **The Best Of Count Basie** Pablo 2405-408
*** **The Best Of The Count Basie Big Band** Pablo 2405-422
Two solid compilations from a vast trove of recordings. The first concentrates on the small groups, the second on the orchestra, and either will serve as a sampler of the later Basie.

*** **Long Live The Chief** Denon 33CY-1018
Byron Stripling, Bob Ojeda, Sonny Con, Melton Mustafa (*t*); Dennis Wilson, Clarence Banks, Mel Wanzo (*tb*); Bill Hughes (*btb*); Danny Turner, Danny House (*as*); Eric Dixon, Kenny Hing, Frank Foster (*ts*); John Williams (*bs*); Tee Carson (*p*); Freddie Green (*g*); Lynn Seaton (*b*); Dennis Mackrel (*d*); Carmen Bradford (*v*). 7/86.

*** **Live At El Morocco** Telarc CD-83312
Mike Williams, Melton Mustafa, Derrick Gardner, Bob Ojeda (*t*); Mel Wanzo, Clarence Banks, Robert Trowers, Bill Hughes (*tb*); Danny Turner (*as, picc*); Manny Boyd (*as, f*); Kenny Hing, Doug Miller (*ts, f*); Frank Foster (*ts*); John Williams (*bs, bcl*); George Caldwell (*p*); Charlie Johnson (*g*); Cleveland Eaton (*b*); David Gibson (*d*). 2/92.

*** **Basie's Bag** Telarc CD-83358
As above. 11/92.

Given that the big band as it stood under Basie in the final years was as sleek and hard as polished steel, the idea of a ghost band seems more plausible than an Ellington, Goodman or Herman survival group. Frank Foster has worked hard to maintain the standards of the group and these records are convincing reminders of Basie's legacy, even if they don't shake the earth. The studio set is too dispassionate to stir the blood, but the live disc warms up a bit. *Basie's Bag* has a grand set-piece in the 'Count Basie Remembrance Suite' and a few solid reshuffles from the band book: Foster, by now an eminence of Basie-esque stature himself, presides with fine authority.

Piero Bassini (born 1952) PIANO, KEYBOARDS

(*) **Into The Blue Red 123218-2
Bassini; Flavio Boltro (*t*); Michele Bozza (*ts*); Riccardo Fioravanti (*b*); Giampiero Prina (*b*). 11/87.

(*) **Lush Life Splasc(h) H 341-2
Bassini (*p* solo); with Erminio Cella (*ky*). 6/90.

Bassini's earlier records for Red are out of print, but he plays a useful role in the quintet session, which is otherwise under no single leader. All six tunes are based round the blues and, given the plain speaking of the group, the results are inevitably sound but unexceptional, with Boltro and Bozza sounding facile, rather than involving. *Lush Life* is an energetic solo album that's let down somewhat by the hard piano-sound which accentuates Bassini's already percussive, almost belligerent manner – not much of his underlying romanticism comes through, though 'Night Moon' is a composition worth saving.

Django Bates (born 1960) PIANO, KEYBOARDS, TENOR HORN

*** **Summer Fruits (And Unrest)** JMT 514 008
Bates; Sid Gauld, Chris Batchelor (*t*); Roland Bates (*tb*); Richard Henry (*btb*); Dave Laurence (*frhn*); Eddie Parker (*f, bf*); Sarah Homer (*cl, bcl*); Iain Ballamy (*ss, as*); Steve Buckley (*ss, as, bcl*); Mark Lockheart (*ts*); Barak Schmool (*ts, picc, bsx*); Julian Arguëlles (*bs*); Stuart Hall (*g, vn, bjo*); Steve Watts, Michael Mondesir (*b*); Martin France (*d*); Thebe Lipere (*perc*).

*** **Autumn Fires (And Green Shoots)** JMT 514 014
Bates (*p* solo). 2/94.

***(*) **Winter Truce** JMT 514 021
Similar to *Summer Fruits*. 95.

For a number of years Bates laboured under the slightly ambiguous designation of 'best unsigned jazz artist of his generation'. On the face of it, it was odd that a musician of such formidable talent should have issued only one record – and that the rather unsatisfactory *Music For The Third Policeman* – since the demise of Loose Tubes. There was a compounding irony in the fact that when he did release a disc, under contract to JMT, the similarities with Loose Tubes were so great.

Summer Fruits alternates big-band arrangements with pieces by Bates's small group, Human Chain. It's not an entirely successful combination and, for once, one feels a need for two discs on which to reflect on what sound like very different aspects of his musical personality. The vices of Loose Tubes are still in evidence: over-writing, a rather bloke-ish exuberance, and a suspicion of straightforward expressiveness. Bates freely admits that he likes dense scores, and the pieces for Delightful Precipice (as he calls his big band) are thickly – sometimes redundantly – notated. They're undeniably lively, but the circus pieces, inspired by an earlier collaboration with a troupe, are too glibly ironic, and some of the most virtuosic scoring is lost in off-the-cuff gestures. The Human Chain pieces, notably 'Food For Plankton (In Detail)' and 'Little Petherick' (the latter sparking off the leader's best solo of the disc), are much more coherent and expressive, and one might hope that in future Bates could combine the virtues of the two groups.

He does so to a degree on the solo piano record, which represents a significant extension of what he has been willing to do as a player. The textures are still rich, but capriciously varied, and there are signs that he is achieving a better balance between full scoring and improvisational freedom, something that isn't at all well calibrated on *Summer Fruits* but which comes together triumphantly on *Winter Truce*, which contains some of the most nakedly emotional music Bates has yet allowed us to see. There is still the rather irritating collegiate joshing and some truth in the often-quoted argument that Bates hasn't advanced significantly since Loose Tubes days, but this at least is a mature and poised record, divided as before between a big band and Human Chain, who between them represent the two poles of Bates's musical thought.

Alvin Batiste (born 1937) CLARINET

***(*) **Bayou Magic** India Navigation IN1069
Batiste; Emile Vinette, Maynard Batiste (*p*); Chris Severen (*b*); Herman Jackson (*d*). 88.
*** **Late** Columbia CK 53314
Batiste; Wessell Anderson (*as*); Kenny Barron, Fred Sanders (*p*); Rufus Reid, Elton Heron (*b*); Herman Jackson (*d*); Donald Edwards (*perc*). 93.

Whatever attention Don Byron and others may have garnered, Batiste – along with John Carter – was the real architect of the clarinet in any avant-garde jazz environment. His mere handful of recordings have told against any wider currency in the music, but these two discs go some way to establishing his reputation beyond the circles he teaches in. *Bayou Magic* is a rather extraordinary record which seems to come from nowhere as a manifesto. Batiste tackles a programme that covers bop, folk and even systems music: the uncredited synthesizer on 'Venus Flow' partners a clarinet line that sounds amazingly close to minimalist composition. The title-piece is a bebop fantasy of brilliant colour, but the exceptional piece is 'Picou', presumably a tribute to that clarinet master and an example of old roots flowering into an extremist improvisation. Batiste's sound is rather unlovely – he gets little of the woodiness of some players, bypasses the chalumeau timbres and prefers a pinched, exhortative approach – and that makes the standards 'I Want To Talk About You' and 'A Child Is Born' less impressive. But his playing has a baronial authority that invests his solos with compelling weight and intensity. Problematically, the studio sound is unacceptably flat, reducing Jackson's drums to mere boxes, and piano and bass are no more than competent. Otherwise, a remarkable record.

The Columbia album is more mediated, less spontaneous: there's a second version of 'Imp And Perry', an unconvincing 'When The Saints', and the star rhythm section don't seem right for the date (Sanders and Heron play on one track only). But Batiste's own playing remains uniquely involving, nagging at jazz's stylistic barriers with the least fashionable of instruments. Hear him out.

Milton Batiste (born 1934) TRUMPET, FLUGELHORN, VOCAL

*** **Milton Batiste With The Rue Conti Jazz Band** Lake LACD31
Batiste; Mike Peters (*t*); Mick Burns (*tb, v*); George Berry (*cl, as, ts*); Andy Young (*bj, d*); Terry Knight (*b*); Jim Young (*tba*); Ron Darby (*d*); Paul Adams (*perc*). 3/93.

Batiste is a New Orleans maverick. His repertoire is right in the New Orleans trad pocket, but, with Clifford Brown as a major influence and an upbringing in R&B, he is scarcely a conventional Louisiana brassman. Unpredictable rips and squashed notes mark his style, but he can also play controlled, severe trumpet, as on 'In The State Of Blues'. He was captured in the middle of a British tour with the local Rue Conti group and, while the band sometimes stumble more than is warranted, the playing is spirited and raffishly hot. There are one or two overworked pieces, as fresh as Batiste sounds on them, but surprises like Dudu Pukwana's 'Tula Sana' take up the slack. At least British trad is far better served now by modern recording than it ever was in the past: the mix is tough and vibrant without losing that certain griminess which this music lives by.

Stefano Battaglia (born 1966) PIANO

*** **Auryn** Splasc(h) H 161-2
Battaglia; Paolino Dalla Porta (*b*); Manhu Roche (*d*). 5/88.
***(*) **Explore** Splasc(h) H 304-2
Battaglia; Tony Oxley (*d*). 2/90.
***(*) **Confession** Splasc(h) H 344-2
Battaglia; Paolino Dalla Porta (*b*); Roberto Gatto (*d*). 3/91.

Battaglia is a formidable young player from Italy's impressive contemporary movement. His first album for Splasc(h), *Things Ain't What They Used To Be*, has yet to appear on CD, but the programme of original material on *Auryn* is a reasonable place to start: the rubato structure of 'The Real Meaning (Of The Blues)' and the Jarrett-like melodies elsewhere are vehicles for full-blooded and essentially romantic improvisations, though sometimes one feels they aren't really going anywhere. The two later discs suggest a wider range of interests, starting with the unexpected meeting with Oxley. Most of the duo pieces on *Explore* are quite brief and contained, and structurally there's little sense of anything but careful preparation; yet spontaneity runs all through the music, whether in full-tilt, crashing interplay with the drummer or in small-voiced dialogue which shows great sensitivity. *Confession* is a much more closely developed trio music than that of his earlier releases, all three men taking virtually equal roles in a triologue that they sustain with few problems over the course of several very long tracks. These are distinctive and worth seeking out.

*** **Bill Evans Compositions Vol. One** Splasc(h) H 400-2
Battaglia; Paolino Dalla Porta (*b*); Aldo Romano (*d*). 12/92.
*** **Bill Evans Compositions Vol. Two** Splasc(h) 410-2
As above. 12/92.

The relatively small number of direct homages to Evans – as compared with the countless ones to Monk or Ellington – hints at the difficulty of getting inside the skin of his music, as opposed to decorating its surface. Battaglia looks to celebrate rather than scrutinize, and he sounds fully at ease on the likes of 'Five', 'Loose Bloose' and 'Nardis'. But when it comes to 'Time Remembered' or 'My Bells', the luminosity of the originals is what one thinks of, as charmingly as Battaglia plays. The second volume follows a similar pattern.

***(*) **Life Of A Petal** Splasc(h) 422
Battaglia (*p* solo). 5/93.

Despite the occasional air of New Age wandering, Battaglia's solo work continues to impress. The dozen pieces here offer further evidence of his wide-ranging tastes (one piece is called 'Tatum') and if they sometimes seem like exercises in technique, that proficiency is so superb that Battaglia can't help but dazzle. Besides, he has a gift for melodic shaping which is the bequest of a generation of Italian piano masters.

Bobby Battle (born 1944) DRUMS

*** **The Offering** Mapleshade 01332
Battle; David Murray (*ts*); Larry Willis (*p*); Santi Debriano (*b*). 11/90.

David Murray's caressing treatment of 'One For Frederick', in dedication to Freddie Waits, is one of his most accomplished ballad performances, and after that everything else on this date is a bit of an anti-climax. Willis executes his parts with customary grace – his own 'To Wisdom, The Prize' gets a perfectly measured treatment – and Debriano and Battle blend easily. The results, though, are merely very good; if it had all been on the level of the opener, this would have turned out a classic. Good sound, though Battle's cymbals are made to seem splashy.

Conrad Bauer (born 1943) TROMBONE, ELECTRONICS

*** **Toronto Tone** Victo CD017
Bauer (*tb, elec* solo). 10/91.
*** **Three Wheels – Four Directions** Victo CD023
Bauer; Peter Kowald (*b*); Gunter Sommer (*d* etc.). 10/92.

***(*) **Bauer Bauer** Intakt CD 040

 Bauer; Johannes Bauer (*tb*).

**** **Plie** Intakt CD 037

 Bauer; Ernst-Ludwig Petrowsky (*as, cl, f*); Ulrich Gumpert (*p*); Gunter Sommer (*d*). 2/94.

Working out of the DDR for many years, Bauer is perhaps the least-known of the great European trombone impressionists. Heard in successive years at Canada's Victoriaville Festival, he makes a good if less than outstanding account on these souvenirs of the occasions. The solo engagement finds him colouring his improvisations with a variety of electronics: chorus effects, loops, echo. Sometimes one feels that the FX are used for impressionistic rather than musical effect though – as with similar projects by Bill Frisell or Eberhard Weber – the results can be entertaining enough to overcome doubts. As a plain soloist, Bauer can't match Paul Rutherford or Gunter Christmann for sheer inventiveness, but his folksy blares and long, sung tones have their own impact.

With Kowald and Sommer he uses the unadorned slide trombone. There are four group improvs and a solo apiece: Sommer's soliloquy is merely silly, and his lumpy kind of momentum can hold the group back, but there is some excellent stuff on 'Trio Goes East' and 'Trio Goes North'. Kowald, as usual, is beyond reproach, and his *arco* solo is intense enough to blister paint.

Bauer Bauer is a duo concert with his brother Johannes, recorded in the room inside Leipzig's Monument to the Battle of Nations, where there's a natural twenty-second echo. The results are almost predictably beautiful, given the sonorities involved, and it must have been a temptation to remain with the long-held notes and counterpoint of 'Dialog 1' and 'Dialog 4' for the whole set; but there is some taut, snickering interplay elsewhere, and the senior Bauer uses some electronics to spare and judicious effect on his solo (there are six duets and a solo apiece).

Plie should properly be credited to the Zentralquartett, since this band of old cronies go under that name when working together. In the aftermath of free jazz (not to mention the DDR), the four players work through a bad-tempered kind of free bop that seems to blossom reluctantly into lyricism at the most unexpected moments. Fragments of blues piano, hard bop, hot solos and harsh ensemble-work permeate what turns out to be an absolutely engrossing record. Cantankerous and highly entertaining sleeve-notes by Christian Broecking fit the record perfectly.

Johannes Bauer TROMBONE

***(*) **Organo Pleno** FMP CD 56

 Bauer; Fred Van Hove (*p, acc*); Annick Nozati (*v*). 7/92.

Not to be confused with Conrad 'Connie' Bauer (who plays the same instrument). Johannes is a blunter and less discursive player, these days wholly dedicated to free-improvised music. The present trio is relatively long-standing by the usual measure of such things, and *Organo Pleno* bespeaks considerable understanding among the members. Van Hove is an enormously underrated player whose continued involvement in other areas of musical enterprise may be reflected in his patiently normative role, roping in the group's wilder excesses.

As is the way of such things, the trio swing between spiky, open-form blasts that ruthlessly avoid anything resembling a groove and gentler, almost song-like patterns, such as 'Pars IV', on which piano gives way to organ, starbursts and broken-glass runs to soft, wheezy washes. In general the mood is fairly laid-back. There are plenty of sub-two-minute miniatures, and one mammoth work-out which approaches half an hour in length. Nozati tires and runs low on ideas here, and it is left to Bauer's post-Mangelsdorff phrase-making to give the thing a sense of direction. He is a wonderfully clean articulator, with a very distinctive attack and a real dramatic presence.

Jim Beard PIANO, SYNTHESIZER, PERCUSSION

*** **Lost At The Carnival** Lipstick LIP 89027

 Beard; Bill Evans (*ts, ss*); Stan Harrison (*cl, bcl, f, af*); Jon Herington (*g, hca, perc*); Ron Jenkins, Steve Rodby (*b*); Scooter Warner, Mike Mecham, Billy Ward (*d*). 94.

Beard has worked extensively with the Breckers, Sco and John McLaughlin, and a prejudiced eye wonders why he didn't try to get one or more of them in on this solo project. The results are actually more interesting than they promise to be. The album has a rough concept, held together by fairground organ; the device allows Beard to wander, slightly distractedly, through the 'carnivalized' world of contemporary jazz, rock and funk, touching on styles and approaches, committing to none, discarding none. It's quite exhilarating in a headachey sort of way; but the voicings on 'Chunks And Chairknobs' are interesting enough to hear again, and 'Poke' has an insistent harmonic oddity that quickly overcomes its initial cheesy impression.

Sidney Bechet (1897–1959) SOPRANO SAXOPHONE, CLARINET; ALSO TENOR SAXOPHONE, BASS SAXOPHONE, PIANO, BASS, DRUMS

*** Sidney Bechet: Complete Edition – Volume 1, 1923 Media 7 MJCD 5
Bechet; Thomas Morris (*c*); Charlie Irvis, John Mayfield (*tb*); Clarence Williams (*p*); Narcisse Buddy Christian (*d, bjo*); Rosetta Crawford, Margaret Johnson, Sara Martin, Mamie Smith, Eva Taylor (*v*). 7, 8, 9 & 10/23.

*** The Complete 1923–6 Clarence Williams Sessions: 1 EPM Musique FDC 5197
As above.

*** Sidney Bechet, 1923–1936 Classics 583
Bechet; Clarence Brereton, Wendell Culley, Demas Dean, Tommy Ladnier (*t*); Billy Burns, Chester Burrill, Teddy Nixon (*tb*); Chauncey Haughton (*cl, as*); Ralph Duquesne, Rudy Jackson (*cl, as, ss*); Ramon Usera (*cl, ts*); Jerome Pasquall, Gil White (*ts*); Harry Brooks, Henry Duncan, Lloyd Pinckney, Clarence Williams (*p*); Oscar Madera (*vn*); Buddy Christian, Frank Ethridge (*bj*); Jimmy Miller (*g*); Wilson Myers (*b, v*); Edward Coles (*bb*); Jimmy Jones (*b*); Jack Carter, Wilbert Kirk, Morris Morland (*d*); Billy Banks, Lena Horne, Billy Maxey, Noble Sissle (*v*). 10/23–3/36.

***(*) Sidney Bechet, 1937–1938 Classics 593
Bechet; Clarence Brereton, Wendell Culley, Demas Dean, Charlie Shavers (*t*); Chester Burrill (*tb*); Chauncey Haughton (*cl, as*); Jerome Pasquall, Gil White (*ts*); Ernie Caceres (*bs*); Oscar Madera (*vn*); Dave Bowman, Harry Brooks, Erskine Butterfield, Sam Price (*p*); Teddy Bunn, Jimmy Miller, Leonard Ware (*g*); Richard Fullbright, Jimmy Jones, Henry Turner (*b*); Wilbert Kirk, Zutty Singleton (*d*); O'Neil Spencer (*d, v*); Billy Banks, The Two Fishmongers, Trixie Smith (*v*). 4/37, 2, 5 & 11/38.

'When one has tried so hard and so often in the past to discover one of the figures to whom we owe the advent of an art . . . what a moving thing it is to meet this very black, fat boy with white teeth and that narrow forehead who is very glad one likes what he does, but who can say nothing of his art save that it follows his "own way" and then one thinks his "own way" is perhaps the highway the world will swing along tomorrow.' Thus the Swiss conductor Ernest Ansermet recorded his first impressions of the Southern Syncopated Orchestra and their clarinet player in an essay entitled 'On a Negro Orchestra' in the October 1919 issue of *Revue Romande*. Ansermet's article has become one of the central reference-points of Bechet's early career, and it helped establish his increasingly extravagant European reputation. Even so, it's fraught with oddities: was Bechet 'very black'? (he was actually a light-skinned Creole); why insist on the narrowness of his forehead (over in Munich a frustrated house-painter was putting together a theory based on such 'observations'); and was Bechet really as naïve and untutored in his approach to music as Ansermet implies?

On the last point, Bechet himself contributed to the heav'n-taught image. His autobiography, *Treat It Gentle*, is a masterpiece of contrived ingenuousness – the opposite, one might say, of Charles Mingus's ruthlessly disingenuous rants in *Beneath the Underdog*. The fact is that Bechet was an exceptionally gifted and formally aware musician whose compositional skills greatly outshine those of Louis Armstrong, his rival for canonization as the first great jazz improviser. Armstrong's enormous popularity – abetted by his sky-writing top Cs and vocal performance – tended to eclipse Bechet everywhere except in France. Yet the musical evidence is that Bechet was an artist of equal and parallel standing. His melodic sense and ability to structure a solo round the harmonic sequence of the original theme (or with no theme whatsoever) have been of immense significance in the development of modern jazz. Bechet made a pioneering switch to the soprano saxophone (a stronger-voiced and more projective instrument than the clarinet) in the same year as Ansermet's essay, having found a second-hand horn in a London shop. Within a few years his biting tone and dramatic tremolo were among the most distinctive sounds in jazz.

Bechet made a relatively slow start to his recording career. His first cuts as 'leader' are as accompanist on two tracks made in New York in October and credited to Rosetta Crawford & the King Bechet Trio. The early sessions with Clarence Williams and a variety of modestly talented singers (also available under Williams's name) include carefully annotated breaks and solos from Bechet, largely on soprano saxophone; but these sessions are of specialist interest in the main. His clarinet style (on tracks with Eva Taylor) is still strongly coloured by that of Alphonse Picou and Lorenzo Tio, who gave the precocious Bechet lessons, and is markedly less individual than his saxophone playing.

The *Chronological* compilation is less detailed but it includes material with Noble Sissle's orchestra not included on either of the other available options. In fact, only the two Rosetta Crawford tracks are in common. The sound is rather abrasive and these early sessions are essential only for a brief, brilliant soprano solo on 'Loveless Love'. According to John Chilton, Bechet is also responsible on this and two other tracks (he solos only on the initially rejected 'In A Café On The Road To Calais') for the bass saxophone parts, which are not credited in the Classics notes. The session of 15 September 1932 is one of Bechet's best yet, with superb solos on 'I Want You Tonight' and 'Maple Leaf Rag'. The later disc is generally more professional and every bit as compelling musically. Bechet reached a new high with two quintet tracks credited to Noble Sissle's Swingsters, an offshoot of the main band. His solos on 'Okey-Doke' and 'Characteristic Blues' are classic performances, full of extravagantly bent notes, trills and time changes. Using both clarinet and soprano saxophone, Bechet creates an atmosphere of considerable tension that is discharged only during a phenomenal solo on 'Characteristic Blues'. Later, in 1938, there was controversy over the exact authorship of 'Hold Me Tight', which Bechet claimed was based on his earlier 'I Want Some Seafood, Mama', but which was declared obscene and withdrawn from radio stations. The real controversy, however, was directed towards what seemed to be a new way of playing jazz, and in that context the session of April 1937 is absolutely critical, not just to Bechet's development but to that of jazz itself.

**** **The Complete Sidney Bechet: Volumes 1 & 2 – 1932–1941** RCA ND 89760 2CD
    Bechet; Gus Aiken, Henry 'Red' Allen, Henry Goodwin, Tommy Ladnier, Henry Levine, Sidney De Paris, Charlie Shavers (*t*); Rex Stewart (*c*); Vic Dickenson (*tb, v*); Jack Epstein, J. C. Higginbotham, Teddy Nixon, Sandy Williams (*tb*); Claude Jones (*tb, v*); Alfred Evans, Albert Nicholas (*cl*); Mezz Mezzrow (*cl, ts*); Rudolph Adler, Happy Caldwell, Lem Johnson (*ts*); Don Donaldson, Hank Duncan, Earl Hines, Cliff Jackson, Mario Janarro, Willie 'The Lion' Smith, James Toliver, Sonny White (*p*); Jelly Roll Morton (*p, v*); Teddy Bunn, Tommy Collucci, Lawrence Lucie, Everett Barksdale, Charlie Howard (*g*); Wellman Braud, Elmer James, John Lindsay, Wilson Myers, Harry Patent, Ernest Williamson (*b*); Wilson Myers (*b, v*); Big Sid Catlett, Kenny Clarke, Baby Dodds, J. C. Heard, Arthur Herbert, Manzie Johnson, Wilbert Kirk, Nat Levine, Morris Morland, Zutty Singleton (*d*); Herb Jeffries, William Maxey (*v*). 32–41.

**** **The Complete Sidney Bechet: Volumes 3 & 4 – 1941** RCA ND 89759 2CD
    Selectively as above. 41.
***(*) **The Complete Sidney Bechet: Volume 5 – 1941–1943** RCA ND 155192 2CD
    Selectively as above. 38–39, 41–43.

Nothing more clearly establishes Bechet's credentials as a harmonic improviser in the modern sense than his remarkable excursion on 'Shag', an athematic exploration from 1932 of the 'I Got Rhythm' chords. Bechet's tearing, urgent solo has to be seen as one of the earliest foretastes of what was to be standard bebop practice (and many of the bop standards were also based on the Gershwin tune). Even when dealing with a relatively conventional structure like 'Maple Leaf Rag', also with Tommy Ladnier and the 1932 Feetwarmers, he busts the harmonic code wide open, and it's useful-to-valuable to compare his treatment of the Joplin tune with avant-gardist Anthony Braxton's approach on *Duets 1976*.

The 1939 sessions really belong in the Jelly Roll Morton discography, but they feature some fine Bechet accompaniments and two intriguing comparative studies in alternative takes of 'O Didn't He Ramble' and 'Winin' Boy Blues'. A 1940 trio, 'Blues In Thirds', with Earl Hines (the composer) and Baby Dodds is by far the best track from a curiously up-and-down session that features cornetist Rex Stewart, bassist John Lindsay and vocalist Herb Jeffries (who makes William Maxey's abstract scatting on 'Shag' and 'Maple Leaf Rag' sound even better).

In April 1941 Bechet fulfilled the logic of his increasingly self-reliant musical conception (Hines suggested that his quietly 'evil' mood on the day of the 1940 sessions was characteristic of New Orleans players at the time when dealing with Northerners) by recording two unprecedented 'one-man-band' tracks, overdubbing up to six instruments. 'Sheik Of Araby' is for the full 'band' of soprano and tenor saxophones, clarinet, piano, bass and drums; so time-consuming was the process that a second item, 'Blues For Bechet', had to be completed without bass or drums, leaving a fascinating fragment for RCA to release.

In September of the same year, Bechet made another classic trio recording, this time with Willie 'The Lion' Smith and the relative unknown, Everett Barksdale, on electric guitar. Though the two sidemen provide no more than incidental distractions, the trio sessions were more compelling than the full band assembled on that day (Charlie Shavers plays monster lines on 'I'm Coming Virginia' as on the October 'Mood Indigo', but is otherwise ill-suited); 'Strange Fruit' is one of Bechet's most calmly magisterial performances, and the two takes of 'You're The Limit' seem too good to have been dumped in the 'unreleased' bin, though perhaps the absence on either of a commanding solo from Bechet (who may not have liked Smith's uncomplicated tune) put the label off.

But what did they know? A month later, in the same session that realized 'Mood Indigo', Bechet cut the utterly awful 'Laughin' In Rhythm', a New Orleans version of 'The Laughing Policeman' that, despite a taut soprano solo, hardly merits revival. Dickenson, whose humour was usually reliable, also plays beautifully on 'Blue In The Air', one of the finest of Bechet's recorded solos and one that merits the closest attention.

CD transfer has in some cases improved the sound-balance (Tommy Ladnier had been disappointed by his position in the early mixes but he is largely restored here) and in some cases has wiped out elements of the background. Understandably, the major emphasis always falls on the main subject. Though there is, inevitably, some dross, these invaluable mid-period documents contain nearly 100 tracks from a score of sessions. Essential Bechet material that no serious fan should be without. Repackaging this material into three double-CD sets has allowed RCA to round out the picture in some interesting directions. Volume five only requires a little padding; disc two is devoted to earlier material recorded under the leadership of Mezz Mezzrow and Tommy Ladnier (jointly) in December 1938 and Frankie Newton the following January. The black and white Jazz Tribune imprint – with its newspaper motif – isn't all that pleasing to the eye, but these records could hardly be improved upon discographically.

*** Sidney Bechet In New York, 1937–40 JSP CD 338

Bechet; Louis Armstrong, Clarence Brereton, Charlie Shavers (t); Claude Jones (tb); Gil White (cl, ts); Harry Brooks, Sammy Price, Luis Russell (p); Bernard Addison, Teddy Bunn, Jimmy Miller (g); Wellman Braud, Richard Fullbright, Jimmy Jones (b); Wilbert Kirk, Zutty Singleton, O'Neil Spencer (d); Coot Grant, Kid Wesley Wilson (v). 4/37, 2 & 5/38, 5/40.

The Bechet discography is now a puzzling network of overlapping CDs. This one contains some of the Noble Sissle material from the 1937–8 and 1938–40 *Chronologicals*, together with examples of his accompanist's role with Coot Grant and Kid Wesley Wilson (May 1938), and a session under Louis Armstrong's leadership which is also, quite properly, passed over by Classics; both issues, for some mysterious reason, find room for Bechet's work with singer Trixie Smith. What's good about these sides is the quality of the remastering. John R. T. Davies has made a considerable name for himself as an audio restorer, and the results here are well up to scratch. Unfortunately, the nature of the material is such that it isn't going to make a huge difference to perceptions of Bechet's playing.

***(*) Sidney Bechet, 1938–1940 Classics 608

Bechet; Tommy Ladnier, Frankie Newton, Kenneth Roane (t); J. C. Higginbotham (tb); Mezz Mezzrow (cl, ts); Meade Lux Lewis, Willie 'The Lion' Smith, Sonny White (p); Teddy Bunn, Charlie Howard (g); Elmer James, Olin Aderhold, Wilson Myers, John Williams (b); Big Sid Catlett, Kenny Clarke, Manzie Johnson, Leo Warney (d). 11/38.

*** Sidney Bechet, 1940 Classics 619

Bechet; Sidney De Paris (t); Muggsy Spanier (c); Sandy Williams (tb); Cliff Jackson (p); Bernard Addison, Teddy Bunn, Carmen Mastren (g); Josh White (g, v); Wellman Braud, Pops Foster, Wilson Myers (b); Big Sid Catlett (d). 3, 4 & 6/40.

***(*) Sidney Bechet, 1940–1941 Classics 638

Bechet; Gus Aiken, Henry 'Red' Allen, Henry Goodwin, Henry Levine, Charlie Shavers (t); Rex Stewart (c); Jack Epstein, Vic Dickenson, J. C. Higginbotham, Sandy Williams (tb); Alfie Evans (cl); Rudolph Adler, Lem Johnson (ts); Don Donaldson, Earl Hines, Cliff Jackson, Mario Janarro, Willie 'The Lion' Smith, James Toliver (p); Everett Barksdale, Tony Colucci (g); Wellman Braud, John Lindsay, Wilson Myers, Harry Patent, Ernest Williamson (b); Baby Dodds, J. C. Heard, Arthur Herbert, Manzie Johnson, Nat Levine (d); Herb Jefferies (v). 9 & 11/ 40, 1, 4, 9 & 10/41.

A lot of this material is available elsewhere: the Bluebirds from 1938, the Blue Notes, much of the Victor stuff. However, it's always good to have the simply and exactly documented Classics discs, and there are some useful inclusions and corrections, like the correct attribution of 'Ti Ralph' and 'Meringue D'Amour' from the Willie 'The Lion' Smith date of November 1939; these have been inverted on most reissues in recent times. The 'Original Haitian Music' with Smith is an oddity from a decidedly odd band, and one has a strong sense that Bechet was finding it harder over this period following his brief sabbatical in 1938 to set up completely sympathetic sessions. More and more often one finds him in bands where piano, not guitar, dominates the rhythm section, and he is paired with other saxophone players. It was always characteristic of Bechet's VSOP sound that it didn't marry well with sharper vintages, however potent they were in isolation. One would still want to recommend these discs, but with the proviso that they have their downs as well as ups.

***(*) Jazz Classics: Volume 1 Blue Note 789384

Bechet; Bunk Johnson, Max Kaminsky, Frankie Newton, Sidney De Paris (t); Jimmy Archey, Vic Dickenson, J. C. Higginbotham, George Lugg, Sandy Williams (tb); Albert Nicholas (cl); Art Hodes, Cliff Jackson, Meade Lux Lewis (p); Teddy Bunn (g); Pops Foster, John Williams (b); Big Sid Catlett, Manzie Johnson (d); Fred Moore (d, v). 6/39, 3/40, 12/44, 3/45, 2/46, 11/51.

*** Jazz Classics: Volume 2 Blue Note 789385

As above.

Bechet and Blue Note make an irresistible combination, but not an immediately obvious one. Though the label had its roots in earlier R&B and jazz, having recorded both Albert Ammons and Meade Lux

Lewis, its stock-in-trade was to be hard bop and the more accommodating aspects of the avant-garde. Bechet had approached Alfred Lion, wanting to record a long version of 'Summertime' (*Volume 1*, also available on Classics, above), something he had not been able to do for another label. The session of June 1939, the earliest of the dates represented on these compilations, isn't vintage Bechet by any stretch of the imagination, but there are some striking moments. With Lewis all over the place, Bunn lays down a wonderfully simple accompaniment and, with no other horn to hand, Bechet plays a vivid solo that was to boost the original 78 into hit sales. The 1939 session came shortly after the death of Tommy Ladnier and the full band recorded a less than morose 'Blues For Tommy' (*Volume 2*) on which only Bechet sounds as if he might honestly miss his old partner.

The association with Blue Note continued intermittently over the next few years. In March 1940, with the excellent Bunn again on hand, Bechet recorded 'Dear Old Southland' (*Volume 1*). The 1944 cuts with Sidney de Paris, Vic Dickenson and Art Hodes are less than wholly compelling; but the saxophon- ist's encounter with the enigmatic Bunk Johnson in March 1945 is a different matter. Bechet sounds cautiously respectful; Bunk sounds like a man whose mind is elsewhere. Nevertheless 'Milenberg Blues' and 'Days Beyond Recall' have a historic significance that goes well beyond their intrinsic value as performances.

The final Blue Note session was recorded a dozen years after the first, and it's a mellowing Bechet who plays the appropriately titled 'Changes Made' with de Paris again, and trombonist Jimmy Archey. Looked at objectively, these sides have taken on a certain sheen purely because of the label that recorded them. Technically, they're first class; historically, they're full of interest; but musically, they're second- order Bechet.

*** New Orleans Jazz Columbia 462954

Bechet; Bob Wilber (*cl*); John Glasel (*c*); Bob Mielke (*tb*); Dick Wellstood (*p*); Charles Traeger (*b*); Dennis Strong (*d*). 7/47.

Just four tracks on a record otherwise devoted to Kid Ory. Recorded with Bob Wilber's Wildcats, they were originally released on a CBS LP called *The Sidney Bechet Story*. It was his first session for Columbia and a coup for Wilber's young band. It would be possible to drive one of the London buses Bechet so much admired through the gap between the maestro and the band, and Wilber himself sounds as though he's parroting his mentor. It all falls apart a bit on 'Polka Dot', but Bechet sails on oblivious. By this time in his life, often paid by the number, he was disinclined to stop for retakes, and it's unlikely that he troubled to listen to a playback.

***(*) Spirits Of New Orleans Vogue 113408

Bechet; Bill Coleman (*t*); Jimmy Archey (*tb*); Mezz Mezzrow (*cl*); Frank Goodie (*ts*); Charlie Lewis (*p*); Pierre Michelot (*b*); Kenny Clarke (*d*). 10/49.

This is a compilation album consisting of six Bechet tracks, eight by clarinettist Albert Nicholas and five by Mezz Mezzrow, the latter seeming only a grace-and-favour representative of the New Orleans spirit. The axis of the Bechet sessions is the partnership with Clarke, a founding exponent of bebop but patently also at his ease in this company. 'Klook's Blues' is an outstanding track; not well known in the Bechet canon, it demonstrates how he continued to develop throughout his long career. 'American Rhythm' is another fine duet, with (despite the title) strong African elements. Bechet's interpretation of 'Out Of Nowhere', a favourite ballad of the bebop generation, is exquisite.

*** We Dig . . . Dixieland Jazz Savoy SV 0197

Bechet; Humphrey Lyttelton (*t*); Keith Christie (*tb*); Wally Fawkes (*cl*); George Webb (*p*); Buddy Vallis (*bj*); John Wright (*b*); Bernard Seward (*d*). 11/49.

While visiting Europe in 1949, Bechet visited London, where the promoter Bert Wilcox arranged a concert and a recording session for Melodisc (enterprise which made him liable to prosecution under a Ministry of Labour ruling about American musicians in Britain). The band assigned to work with Bechet was Humphrey Lyttelton's. They sound a bit edgy and mechanical behind the great man, but Fawkes and Lyttelton himself respond with great solos, both of them performing with style on 'Who's Sorry Now'; the trumpeter also shone on 'Georgia On My Mind'. Bechet himself kept his best for 'Black And Blue'.

What spoils an otherwise enjoyable session is the unrelenting chug of Buddy Vallis's (not Wallis, as sometimes listed) banjo, and the rest of the rhythm section's unwillingness to keep the beat moving forward. The remainder of the disc is made up of material by Joe Marsala's group. Unspectacular, but certainly of more than mere historical interest.

*** In The Groove Jazz Society (Vogue) 670506

Bechet; Claude Luter (*cl*); Pierre Dervaux (*t*); Claude Philippe (*cl, bj*); Mowgli Jospin, Guy Longnon, Bernard Zacharias (*tb*); Christian Azzi (*p*); Roland Bianchini (*b*); François Moustache Galepides (*d*). 10 & 11/49, 10/50, 5/51, 1/52.

***(*) **Salle Pleyel: 31 January 52** Vogue 655001

Bechet; Claude Luter (*cl*); Claude Rabanit (*t*); Guy Longnon, Bernard Zacharias (*tb*); Christian Azzi (*p*); Claude Philippe (*bj*); Roland Bianchini (*b*); François Moustache Galepides (*d*). 1/52.

*** **In Concert** Vogue 655625

Bechet; Claude Luter (*cl*); Pierre Dervaux, Giles Thibaut (*t*); Benny Vasseur (*tb*); Yannick Singery (*p*); Claude Philippe (*bj*); Roland Bianchini (*b*); Marcel Blanche (*d*). 12/54.

Luter was a surprisingly confident and self-assured partner for the newly emigrated Bechet, who regarded his move to France as the fulfilment of racial destiny rather than as escape from an unfeeling and unappreciative environment. Even so, Bechet's reputation in America never matched the adulation he received in France. With the exception of the leader, the French band give him an easy ride, offering *carte blanche* for either relatively pat solos or more developed excursions, as the mood took him. 'Ghost Of The Blues' and 'Patte De Mouche' (with Bechet taking over at the piano) are rare gems and 'Les Oignons' is a delight. Generally, though, quite low-key.

The Salle Pleyel concert was a noisy, vociferous affair but also surprisingly inward-looking and musicianly. Introduced by Charles Delaunay, it features favourites like 'Les Oignons' again, 'Petite Fleur', 'St Louis Blues', 'Frankie And Johnny', 'Maryland My Maryland' and alternative versions of both 'Sweet Georgia Brown' and 'Royal Garden Blues' that are of more than incidental documentary interest. Recommended.

The later concert record has some interesting elements (Bechet's solos on 'Buddy Bolden Stomp' and 'On The Sunny Side Of The Street' are contrastingly good) but with a slightly bland air which isn't helped by a very skew-whiff recording that makes everyone sound as if they're moving around onstage.

***(*) **Sidney Bechet At Storyville** Black Lion BLCD 760902

Bechet; Vic Dickenson (*tb*); George Wein (*p*); Jimmy Woode (*b*); Buzzy Drootin (*d*). 10/53.

A tight and professional set from mid-way through a residency at George Wein's Boston club. There is a slight sense of motions being gone through on some of Bechet's briefer breaks, but every now and then, as on 'Crazy Rhythm', he will make subtle changes of direction that Wein, for one, doesn't seem to have noticed. Sound-balances are erratic in places, but everyone can be heard and Woode in particular gains over his showing on the original Storyville LP release. Recommended.

*** **La Nuit Est Une Sorcière** Vogue 113414

Bechet; Jacques Bazire, Gerard Calvi (*cond*). 5/53, 64.

La Nuit Est Une Sorcière was a dreamy and impressionistic ballet score, based on a book by André Coffret who had had the inspiration of presenting it to Bechet. The work achieved only modest success on its first production in 1953, but it was successfully revived at the Théâtre des Champs Elysées two years later, winning the soloist, Bechet, considerable acclaim. After his weaving preface, Bechet's part is only notionally woven into James Toliver's arrangements. The young pianist (the liner-note identifies him as a saxophonist, with two 'll's) understood Bechet's music well, but there is an element of pastiche about the whole suite which resembles one of those 'jazz-influenced' orchestral pieces that had been fashionable in the 1930s and enjoyed a renewed vogue in Europe after the war.

The disc is rounded out by another ballet-rhapsody called *La Colline Du Delta*, orchestrated by Gerard Calvi and featuring Claude Luter as soloist; Bechet had been dead some years when it was recorded. Bechet had derived the piece from his 'Negro Rhapsody No. 1', written in Paris in 1928 in memory of his native state. Pianist Charlie Lewis helped to transcribe the piece. Its place in the saxophonist's discography is slightly ambiguous, but it is an attractive enough piece in its way and Luter gives the part an unashamedly Bechet coloration.

Gordon Beck (born 1938) PIANO, ELECTRIC PIANO, SYNTHESIZERS

** **Dreams** JMS 049

Beck; Rowanne Mark (*v*). 5–6/89.

**** **For Evans' Sake** JMS 059

Beck; Didier Lockwood (*vn*); Dave Holland (*b*); Jack DeJohnette (*d*). 9/91.

**** **One For The Road** JMS 077

Beck (*kys* solo). 5/95.

For all his extravagant talent – his acuity as a composer has been acknowledged on record by the finicky Gary Burton – Gordon Beck has never broken through to the wider audience he deserves. In recent years, after shifting his centre of operations to the French jazz scene, he has undergone a revival of fortunes, producing excellent records on JMS and Owl with guitarist Allan Holdsworth and singer Helen Merrill (for whom, see the relevant entries), which perfectly highlighted his remarkable technique and facility for complex melodic invention, coupled with an inner metronome programmed by Horace Silver and the ghost of Art Tatum.

Dreams, though, is a rather disappointing set, far too involuted and personal to communicate fully its unashamedly sentimental vision. Keyboard-generated bass and drum effects are never entirely satisfactory and there is a stiffness in the pulse which mars some fascinating and adventurous writing which is occasionally reminiscent of Chick Corea in style-switching mood. Rowanne Mark's vocal contributions are attractive but could, for the most part, just as easily have been created by a sampling keyboard. Holdsworth's production is impeccable.

The excellent *One For The Road* notwithstanding (and more on it in a moment), it may be that Beck simply needs more challenging musical company, not more challenging than Ms Mark, but more than a bank of keyboards can possibly offer. *For Evans' Sake* immediately shows why he has such a high standing in the profession. At last, a band and a session commensurate with his remarkable talents. If the excitement of the opening 'You Are All The Things', with Lockwood's violin squealing away like a row of saxophones, isn't maintained, it primes the listener for a thoughtful and often very moving tribute to Bill Evans. Interestingly, Beck uses nothing by Evans himself. Miles Davis's 'Blue In Green' is the only familiar piece, and that is an unaccompanied bass solo from Holland, in good form. Beck has been accumulating this material for many years. 'Trio Type Tune Two?' was written as long ago as 1966. As Evans's example has sunk in and been assimilated, Beck has become ever more sophisticated as a composer. 'Re: Mister E', far from pastiche, is a virtuosic performance with a complex harmonic and rhythmic profile to which all three performers contribute in full measure, and there's no mistaking the certainty of the closing 'He Is With Us Still'.

Lockwood doesn't play on every track, sensibly; when he does, he often surprises with the grace and precision of his ravelling, intricate lines. DeJohnette is now so completely in command of his drums that he can appear to be playing strict time when the basic metre is changing bar to bar. Players get used to this kind of service, and one sees why in the past decade Beck has felt obliged to continue with his solo multi-tracked recordings.

One For The Road mixes Steinway, Fender Rhodes, Hammond and Korg into subtle and elegant shades. Nine Beck compositions of absolute poise, executed with skill and flair. Titles like 'Beautiful, But' suggest the extent to which he remains aware of standard repertoire while working his own drily romantic furrow. There probably isn't quite enough straight piano for the purists, but the blend, overseen by JMS boss Jean-Marie Salhani, is so professional and seamless that even sceptics will be won over.

Marcus Becker PIANO

*** Lacuna L + R CDLR 45043
Becker; Peter Bolte (*as, ss*); Paul Imm (*b*); John Schroeder (*d*). 6/91.
With players of proven quality like Imm and Schroeder, Lacuna are well up to the leader's challenging ideas. The closest parallel, in terms of structure and sound-world, is Klaus Ignatzek, except that Becker is less straight-ahead, more oblique and allusive. The main, self-titled piece and the mysterious 'Brothers Of Redemption' are worth sampling, but speculative purchasers won't be disappointed.

Harry Beckett (born 1935) TRUMPET, FLUGELHORN

***(*) All Four One Spotlite SPJ CD 547
Beckett; Chris Batchelor, Jon Corbett, Claude Deppa (*flhn*); Alistair Gavin (*p*); Fred T. Baker (*b*); Tony Marsh (*d*); Jan Ponsford (*v*). 91.
**** Images Of Clarity Evidence EVCD 315
Beckett; Didier Levallet (*b*); Tony Marsh (*d*). 12/92.
Too vital a presence to be merely a father-figure, Beckett lent a rugged, avuncular blessing to the reintegration of young black musicians into post-free British jazz. Like many of the African- and Caribbean-born musicians who fell within the circle of Chris McGregor's Brotherhood of Breath, Beckett moves without strain between free and mainstream improvisation. His essential qualities are an untroubled romanticism and a brightly lyrical tone (to which he adds gruff asides and occasionally startling rhythmic punctuations).

Though some of the best of Beckett's work is on sessions for other leaders, his re-emergence as a recording artist (no more than his deserts, albeit on small labels) finds him consolidating his strengths as an improviser. A pity he hasn't recorded more frequently in this sparse but richly contoured setting. Levallet has a gorgeous touch (and chips in with two lovely themes it would be nice to hear again). Marsh is among the most musical of European drummers, embellishing softly without ever losing track of an already delicate pulse. Beckett sounds pensive and slightly wry, and he keeps a thread of humour running through the set, as he has throughout his career.

Beckett's All Four One project is based on a four-flugelhorn front line, an instrumentation capable of great richness but also, one fears and quickly hears confirmed, too little variety. There are some excellent moments. Mingus's 'Better Git It In Your Soul' is just right for this group and 'The Outstanding Light', a very Beckettian original, sits perfectly for the group, but it might have been better to have made an album on which this personnel appeared once or twice. They don't, alas, sustain the full distance. A partially successful idea, then, that nevertheless confirms this much-loved musician's continuing desire to experiment.

Bix Beiderbecke (1903–31) CORNET

*** **Bix Beiderbecke And The Wolverines** Timeless CBC 1-013
    Beiderbecke; Jimmy McPartland (*c*); Miff Mole, Tommy Dorsey, George Brunies, Al Gandee (*tb*); Don Murray (*cl*); Jimmy Hartwell (*cl, as*); Frankie Trumbauer (*Cmel*); George Johnson (*ts*); Dick Voynow, Rube Bloom, Paul Mertz (*p*); Bob Gillette, Howdy Quicksell (*bj*); Min Leibrook (*tba*); Vic Moore, Tom Gargano (*d*). 2–12/24.
*** **Bix Beiderbecke And The Chicago Cornets** Milestone MCD-47019-2
    As above, except add Muggsy Spanier (*c*), Guy Carey (*tb*), Volly DeFaut (*cl*), Mel Stitzel (*p*), Marvin Saxbe (*bj, g*), Vic Berton (*d*). 2–12/24.

Bix Beiderbecke, the cornetist from Davenport, Iowa, remains among the most lionized and romanticized of jazz figures, more than 60 years after his death. Beiderbecke's understated mastery, his cool eloquence and precise improvising, were long cherished as the major alternative to Louis Armstrong's clarion leadership in the original jazz age, and his records have endured remarkably well – even though comparatively few of them were in the uncompromised jazz vein of Armstrong's studio work. These CDs collect virtually everything he made in his first year in the studios, with the Wolverine Orchestra, the Sioux City Six and Bix's Rhythm Jugglers. With no vocalists to hinder them, these young white bands were following in the steps of the Original Dixieland Jazz Band and, although they sometimes seem rather stiff and unswinging, the ensembles are as daring as almost anything that was being recorded at the time. Yet despite the presence of such players as Mole, Dorsey and Murray, only Beiderbecke's solos have retained much independent life: the beautiful little contribution to 'Royal Garden Blues', for instance, shines through the dull recording and staid surroundings. The record also includes two tracks made after McPartland had replaced Bix in the Wolverines. Some of the original Gennett masters will never sound better than dusty and muffled, but for Timeless, John R. T. Davies has done his usual peerless job on the remastering and there is a fine essay by Beiderbecke scholar Richard Sudhalter. Milestone's *Chicago Cornets* disc includes all this material but also adds five tracks by Chicago's Bucktown Five, fronted by the teenaged Muggsy Spanier – a not inconsiderable bonus, though overall the remastering isn't quite as good as that on the Timeless CD.

***(*) **Bix Beiderbecke 1924–1930** Jazz Classics in Digital Stereo RPCD 620
    Beiderbecke; Ray Lodwig, Eddie Pinder, Charles Margulis, Bubber Miley (*t*); Andy Secrest (*c*); Jack Teagarden, Bill Rank, Tommy Dorsey (*tb*); Don Murray (*cl*); Benny Goodman, Jimmy Dorsey, Jimmy Hartwell, Irving Friedman, Frankie Trumbauer (*cl, saxes*); Arnold Brilhart (*as*); Bud Freeman, George Johnson, Charles Strickfadden (*ts*); Adrian Rollini (*bsx*); Irving Brodsky, Frank Signorelli, Lennie Hayton, Hoagy Carmichael, Roy Bargy, Tommy Satterfield (*p*); Joe Venuti, Matty Malneck (*vn*); Eddie Lang (*g*); Min Leibrook (*tba, bsx*); Harry Goodman (*tba*); Mike Trafficante (*b*); Chauncey Morehouse, Hal McDonald, Stan King, Gene Krupa, Harry Gale, Vic Moore (*d*); Irene Taylor, Hoagy Carmichael, The Rhythm Boys (*v*). 24–30.
*** **Bix Lives!** Bluebird ND 86845
    Personnel largely as above; others present include Fred Farrar, Henry Busse (*t*); Boyce Cullen (*tb*); Pee Wee Russell (*cl, as*); Wes Vaughan, Jack Fulton (*v*). 27–30.
*** **The Beiderbecke File** Saville CDSVL 201
    Personnel largely as above discs. 10/24–9/30.
*** **The Indispensable Bix Beiderbecke 1924–1930** RCA ND 89572 2CD
    Personnel largely as above. 24–30.

With Beiderbecke's recordings now out of copyright, reissues have recently emerged from several sources. Robert Parker's Jazz Classics compilation, taken from very fine originals, secures an admirable clarity of sound. The 16 tracks offer a somewhat hotch-potch collection of Beiderbecke, from the Wolverines up to his very last session with Hoagy Carmichael; it's a strong single-disc compilation, but it lacks such important sides as 'Singing The Blues' and 'I'm Coming Virginia'. The Bluebird collection, numbering 23 tracks, covers only his Victor sides with the Jean Goldkette and Paul Whiteman orchestras, along with the final date under his own name. Bix was rather buried amidst dance-band arrangements of pop tunes of the day and has to be enjoyed in eight- and sixteen-bar solos, but the record does collect virtually everything important that he did with Whiteman, bar the *Show Boat* medley which has yet to appear on CD. The sound is very clean, using BMG's NoNoise technique, although some may find the timbres a little too dry. RCA have issued what amounts to a rival version to their own disc with the reappearance of the Black & White double-CD, which covers much of the same ground as *Bix Lives!*, though with a few more tracks. The sound here is harsher, though the bass is quite lively and makes it sound more like the original 78s.

The Beiderbecke File mixes 1924–5 tracks with seven with Trumbauer, two with Whiteman and six of the Bix And His Gang titles. A sensible survey, and the sound is quite clean, though John Wadley's transfers seem a bit recessed and lacking in much spark.

**** Bix Beiderbecke Vol. I Singin' The Blues Columbia 466309-2
> Beiderbecke; Hymie Farberman (*t*); Bill Rank (*tb*); Don Murray (*cl, bs*); Jimmy Dorsey (*cl, as*); Frankie Trumbauer (*Cmel*); Red Ingle, Bobby Davis (*as*); Adrian Rollini (*bsx*); Paul Mertz, Itzy Riskin, Frank Signorelli (*p*); Eddie Lang (*g*); Joe Venuti (*vn*); John Cali (*bj*); Joe Tarto (*tba*); Chauncey Morehouse, Vic Berton (*d*); Sam Lanin (*perc*); Irving Kaufman, Seger Ellis (*v*). 2–9/27.

**** Bix & Tram Vol. 1 JSP CD 316
> As above. 2–9/27.

Both these compilations follow Beiderbecke chronologically through 1927, arguably his greatest year in the studios, and both include precisely the same tracks, although the Columbia disc includes an extra in the form of his curious piano solo, 'In A Mist'. Most of them are under Frankie Trumbauer's leadership, and his own slippery, imaginative solos are often as inventive as Bix's, demonstrating why Lester Young named him as a primary influence. But most listeners will be waiting for the shining, affecting cornet improvisations on 'Singin' The Blues', 'Clarinet Marmalade', 'For No Reason At All In C' and the rest. The contributions of Lang and Dorsey are a further bonus. The Columbia sound is lighter and clearer than the JSP, which some listeners may prefer, but John R. T. Davies's remastering on the latter certainly has a fuller presence.

**** Bix Beiderbecke Vol. II At The Jazz Band Ball Columbia 460825-2
> Beiderbecke; Charlie Margulis (*t*); Bill Rank (*tb*); Pee Wee Russell (*cl*); Jimmy Dorsey, Izzy Friedman, Charles Strickfadden (*cl, as*); Don Murray (*cl, bs*); Frankie Trumbauer (*Cmel*); Adrian Rollini, Min Leibrook (*bsx*); Frank Signorelli, Arthur Schutt (*p*); Tom Satterfield (*p, cel*); Joe Venuti, Matty Malneck (*vn*); Carl Kress, Eddie Lang (*g*); Chauncey Morehouse, Harold MacDonald (*d*); Bing Crosby; Jimmy Miller, Charlie Farrell (*v*). 10/27–4/28.

**** Bix And Tram Vol. 2 JSP CD 317
> As above. 10/27–4/28.

The survey of Beiderbecke's OKeh recordings has the advantage of eliminating the Whiteman material and concentrating on his most jazz-directed music; these discs (again basically the same in content) include some of the best of the Bix And His Gang sides, including the title-piece, 'Jazz Me Blues' and 'Sorry', plus further dates with Trumbauer. As a leader, Beiderbecke wasn't exactly a progressive – some of the material harks back to the arrangements used by the Original Dixieland Jazz Band – but his own playing is consistently gripping. Both sets of remastering sound good.

*** Bix Beiderbecke 1924–1927 Classics 778
> As appropriate discs above. 2/24–10/27.

*** Bix Beiderbecke 1927–1930 Classics 788
> As appropriate discs above. 10/27–9/30.

The world waits for a fully comprehensive Beiderbecke collection, properly remastered and from a reputable source. Classics enter the fray with two discs that start with the Wolverines' titles, go on through all of the Bix And His Gang tracks, and finish with the 1930 sessions for Hoagy Carmichael and Irving Mills, together with the final three Victors under his own name. As so often with this series, reproduction is rather up-and-down. While these are sound enough for those collecting the Classics titles in sequence, one should go to Timeless and then either Columbia or JSP for the best edition of this music so far, while Parker's collection remains the best-sounding of the compilations.

Richie Beirach (born 1947) PIANO, KEYBOARDS

*** Richie Beirach–Masahiko Togashi–Terumasa Hino Konnex KCD 5043
> Beirach; Terumasa Hino (*t, flhn*); Masahiko Togashi (*d, perc*). 9/76, 6/78.

** Emerald City Core COCD 9.00522 0
> Beirach; John Abercrombie (*g-syn*). 2/87.

(*) **Common Heart Owl 048
    Beirach (*p* solo). 9/87.
Entirely successful in the context of bands like Lookout Farm and Quest, Beirach's liquescent keyboard style (partially derived from his experiments with electric piano) cloys dreadfully in solo performance. The logic is all there, but the lines are cluttered with grace-notes and over-ripe sustains. Generally an impressive duo player – as he has proved with Dave Liebman, Frank Tusa and others – he fails utterly to gel with Abercrombie, leaving a sense of discontinuous textures and undeveloped ideas. There are far better things in the second-hand racks.

    The duos with Hino and Togashi are a little strange but repay patient attention. Hino is better versed in jazz and gives a firm, Chet Baker-tinged account of 'What Is This Thing Called Love?'. The tracks with the drummer are more evanescent and non-Western; 'Tsunami' isn't quite as overwhelming as the title suggests it ought to be, and there's even something slightly ridiculous about it.

    The solo session is recorded rather distantly and in an uncomfortably dry acoustic. Better to skip straight on to the Maybeck Hall disc, below.

*** **Some Other Time** Triloka 180 2
    Beirach; Randy Brecker (*t, flhn*); Michael Brecker (*ts*); John Scofield (*g*); George Mraz (*b*); Adam Nussbaum (*d*). 4/89.
*** **Self-Portrait** CMP CD 51
    Beirach (*p* solo). 5/90.
***(*) **Convergence** Triloka 185 2
    Beirach; George Coleman (*ts, ss*). 11/90.
***(*) **Maybeck Recital Hall Series, Volume 19** Concord CCD 4518
    Beirach (*p* solo). 1/92.
Some Other Time is a tribute to Chet Baker, who hired Beirach in the early 1970s and recorded two of his compositions, 'Broken Wing' and 'Leaving', both recorded here. The group is as good as the affection for Chet's music is patently sincere, but the real star is Mraz (who also contributed 'For B.C.' – impresario Bradley Cunningham – to *Convergence*). He anchors the music brilliantly with a technique that is ageless and individual. Apart from the Beirach originals, the material is fairly predictable, with a final flourish on 'My Funny Valentine'. No mush; just a thoroughly professional performance all round.

    Convergence documents an outwardly improbable partnership which actually works wonderfully well. It opens with a first glimpse of Coleman on soprano, a complex, polyrhythmic arrangement of Gordon Parish's 'The Lamp Is Low' that feeds both players' considerable harmonic daring. They alternate four-bar sequences on an unusual and highly effective reading of Miles Davis's 'Flamenco Sketches', from *Kind Of Blue*. There are three fine Beirach originals, of which the best is the blues 'Rectilinear', on which Coleman again plays his soprano. He completes the set on the higher horn, appropriately on a version of Wayne Shorter's 'Infant Eyes'.

    Beirach uses typically dense textures but seems to have lost some of the heavy lushness that he brought to duos with Dave Liebman. Coleman is a revelation on the straight horn, and nine out of ten people won't guess who it is. The recording itself is immaculate, a tribute to Paul Sloman's loving attention to detail at Triloka/Living Proof.

    Concord boss Carl Jefferson publicly compared the CMP and Maybeck Hall records as representative of Beirach's 'way out' and 'straight' tendencies respectively. Listening to them, the suspicion is that his style is a bit of a two-headed coin. There's not really that much to compare. He probably uses more out-and-out dissonance on the CMP, but 'Elm', the closing number and only original on the Concord, is as floaty and abstract as anything he's done on record. His standards playing is always just a touch elaborate and he adopts a rather grandmasterish gambit on some of the tunes, a bit like a schoolmaster who'll talk about 'pedal appendages' rather than feet. Coincidentally, Beirach's a brilliant user of the piano pedals, damping off notes sharply and then letting the harmonics run under the next delicately etched phrase. It's too arch a device to use too often, but it's lovely when it comes off.

***(*) **Trust** Evidence ECD 22143
    Beirach; Dave Holland (*b*); Jack DeJohnette (*d*). 2/93.
Beirach has never had a trio this good and, if we were to recommend a way of introducing yourself to his work, this would be it. Apart from Shorter's 'Nefertiti' and a track apiece by Dave Holland and fellow-bassist Gary Peacock, all the material is new. This significantly adds to the attraction of the record, because Beirach has on occasion become bogged down in a set repertoire and seems to need a fresh challenge. This is very definitely it. But for a sound-mix that squashes a lot of DeJohnette's top accents, top marks.

Bob Belden (born 1958) TENOR SAXOPHONE, KEYBOARDS

(*) Treasure Island Sunnyside SSC 1041D

Belden; Jim Powell, Tim Hagans (*t, flhn*); John Fedchock (*tb*); George Moran (*btb*); Peter Reit (*frhn*); Tim Ries, Craig Handy (*ss, ts*); Chuck Wilson (*cl, f*); Mike Migliore (*as, f, picc*); Ron Kozak (*bcl, f*); Glenn Wilson (*bs*); Marc Cohen (*ky*); Carl Kleinsteuber (*tba*); Jay Anderson (*b*); Jeff Hirshfield (*d*). 8/89.

A young arranger from Illinois, Belden has gone the accustomed route from college schooling to big-band experience (with Woody Herman) to being an active sideman in New York. His first record as a leader may be belated, but it's not terribly exciting. His own 'Treasure Island Suite' is a cumbersome piece of scoring without anything thematically interesting, and the rest of this well-recorded CD (which runs for nearly 80 minutes) offers an eclectic bunch of modern big-band workouts. Migliore and Wilson, at least, add purposeful improvising.

*** Straight To My Heart Blue Note B41Z-95137

Belden; Jim Powell (*t, flhn*); Tony Kadleck, Tim Hagans (*t*); John Fedchock (*tb*); George Moran (*btb*); Peter Reit (*frhn*); Tim Ries (*ss, ts, bf*); Mike Migliore (*as, f, bf, picc*); Chuck Wilson (*cl, f, af*); Bobby Watson (*as*); Rick Margitza, Kirk Whalum (*ts*); Glenn Wilson (*bs*); Joey Calderazzo, Marc Copland, Benny Green, Kevin Hays (*p*); Doug Hall, Adam Holzman (*ky*); Pat Rebillot (*org*); Jim Tunnell (*g, v*); John Hart, John Scofield, Fareed Haque (*g*); Darryl Jones, Jay Anderson (*b*); Dennis Chambers, Jeff Hirshfield (*d*); Abraham Adzeneya, Ladji Camara, Jerry Gonzales, David Earle Johnson (*perc*); Dianne Reeves, Phil Perry, Mark Ledford (*v*). 12/89–5/91.

Eleven compositions by Sting arranged by Belden and performed by an all-star cast drawn from the current Blue Note roster. The material is steeped in what might be called pop sophistication: simple tunes and constructions with underlying harmonic detail to make it interesting for superior players, and Belden utilizes the original structures in interesting ways. 'Roxanne', for instance, has its melody deconstructed and turned into a haunting concerto for Hagans, repetition used with mesmerizing effectiveness. But airplay-orientated touches let down parts of the project: the vocal tracks are tedious and, of the soloists, only Hagans and the superb Margitza – on 'They Dance Alone', easily the best track – make an individual impression.

While Belden's subsequent project, *When Doves Cry: The Music Of Prince* (Metro Blue 829515-2), has much interesting music, it probably stands *just* outside the borders of this book. He is now tremendously in demand as an arranger and his work will be found on several other records herein.

Louie Bellson (born 1924) DRUMS

*** Live At Flamingo Hotel 1959 Jazz Hour JH-1026

Bellson; Guido Basso, Johnny Frock, Ralph Clark, Wally Buttogello, Fred Thompson (*t*); Juan Tizol, Earl Swope, Nick Di Maio (*tb*); Joe Di Angelis (*frhn*); Frank Albright, Herb Geller (*as*); Aaron Sachs, Nick Nicholas (*ts*); George Perry (*bs*); Ed Diamond (*p*); Lawrence Lucy (*g*); Truck Parham (*b*); Jack Arnold (*vib, perc*). 6/59.

(*) Jam With Blue Mitchell Original Jazz Classics OJC 802

Bellson; Blue Mitchell (*t, flhn*); Pete Christlieb (*ts*); Ross Tompkins (*p*); Bob Bain (*g*); Gary Pratt (*b*); Emil Richards (*vib, perc*). 9/78.

** Cool, Cool Blue Original Jazz Classics OJC 825

Bellson; Ted Nash (*ss, ts*); Matt Catingub (*ss, as*); Frank Strazzeri (*p*); George Duvivier (*b*). 11/82.

(*) The Best Of Louie Bellson Pablo 2405-407

Bellson; Blue Mitchell, Snooky Young, Bobby Shew, Dick Mitchell, Dick Cooper, Cat Anderson, Conte Candoli, Walter Johnson, Ron King (*t*); Nick Di Maio, Gil Falco, Ernie Tack, Mayo Tiana, Bob Payne, Alan Kaplan, Dana Hughes (*tb*); Don Menza, Pete Christlieb, Dick Spencer, Larry Covelli, Bill Byrne, Ted Nash, Andy Mackintosh (*reeds*); Nat Pierce, Ross Tompkins (*p*); Emil Richards (*vib, perc*); Mitch Holder, Grant Geissman, Bob Bain (*g*); John Williams, Joel Dibartolo, Gary Pratt (*b*); Paulo Magalhaes, Dave Levine, John Arnold, Gene Estes (*perc*). 5/75–9/78.

** The Louis Bellson Explosion Original Jazz Classics OJC 728

Similar to above. 5/75.

Louie Bellson is among the most meritorious of swing drummers, one of the last survivors of a breed of tough and tirelessly energetic men who powered big bands and small groups with the same mix of showmanship and sheer muscle. His comprehensive work with the big-band elite – including Goodman,

Basie, James and especially Ellington – gave him a nearly unrivalled experience, and his own groups are marked out by an authority which is often masked by Bellson's comparatively restrained style: virtuoso player that he is, he always plays for the band and seldom overwhelms in the manner of Buddy Rich.

The Jazz Hour CD resurrects a typical hotel engagement by his band as it stood at the end of the 1950s. Location sound is excellent and the authentic whomp of the Bellson kit fires up the band, though soloists are left precious little space to shine: Basso and Geller get some time to themselves in 'Blast Off', but there isn't much more than that.

Many of Bellson's records from the 1970s and '80s are blemished by a shallow attempt at crossover and unhappy eclecticism. Several have now returned on CD. The pick is probably the *Jam* date with Mitchell, even though Blue isn't his old self, and Christlieb supplies the most reliable solos. *Cool, Cool Blue* has very little going on. The *Best Of* is no great shakes, but it distils some of the superior moments from what were otherwise dispensable records. The 1975 *Explosion* has its moments but the best of them are on the compilation.

*** **Dynamite!** Concord CCD 4105
> Bellson; Nelson Hatt, Bobby Shew, John Thomas, Walt Johnson, Ron King (*t, flhn*); Nick Di Maio, Alan Kaplan, Dana Hughes, Bob Payne (*tb*); Dick Spencer, Matt Catingub, Andrew Mackintosh, Gordon Goodwin, Don Menza (*saxes*); Frank Collett (*p*); John Chiodini (*g*); John Williams Jr (*b*); Jack Arnold (*vib, perc*). 8/79.

(*) **Live At Joe Segal's Jazz Showcase Concord CCD 4350
> Bellson; Don Menza (*f, ts*); Larry Novak (*p*); John Heard (*b*). 10/87.

Of Bellson's eight albums for Concord, a much more consistent sequence than his Pablo records, these two are currently the only ones in the catalogue. The big-band date is solidly satisfying without living up to its title, and the main interest probably lies in the gripping section-work by the brass and reeds. The quartet date finds Louie with his trusted sideman and arranger, Don Menza, a hard-swinging and gruff tenor soloist whose amiable drive finds decent if unspectacular assignment here. Both are very cleanly recorded, as is usual with the company.

** **The Originals** Stash STB-CD-2509
> Bellson; Jon Faddis (*t, flhn*); Bob Malach (*ts*); Hank Jones (*p*); Bucky Pizzarelli (g); Milt Hinton (*b*); New York Saxophone Quartet. n.d.

An oddly clinical session by a useful team which never gets very far. Two extra tracks with the New York Sax foursome are similarly uneventful. Missable.

**** **Hot** Musicmasters 5008-2
> Bellson; Robert Millikan, Larry Lunetta, Danny Cahn, Glenn Drewes (*t*); Clark Terry (*flhn*); Don Mikkelsen, Hale Rood, Clinton Sharman, Keith O'Quinn (*tb*); Joe Roccisano (*as, f*); George Young (*ss, as, f*); Don Menza (*ts*); Jack Stuckey (*bs, bcl*); Kenny Hitchcock (*ts, cl, f*); John Bunch (*p*); Jay Leonhart (*b*). 12/87.

***(*) **East Side Suite** Musicmasters 5009-2
> As above. 12/87.

A delightful pair of records which revitalize Bellson in the studios. Superbly engineered and produced, the sound gives the band both warmth and a sheen of top-class professionalism, and the arrangements – by Menza, Rood, Roccisano and Tommy Newsom – return the favour. There are storming features for the leader – 'Blues For Uncommon Kids', the opener on *East Side Suite*, is an absolute knockout – but just as memorable are the smooth changes of gear, the lovely section-work on 'Peaceful Poet' (*Hot*), the spots allotted to guest horn Clark Terry, the sense that the band always has something extra in its pocket. A must for big-band admirers.

***(*) **Jazz Giants** Musicmasters 5035-2
> Bellson; Conte Candoli (*t*); Buddy DeFranco (*cl*); Don Menza (*ts*); Hank Jones (*p*); Keter Betts (*b*). 4/89.

Bellson's records have taken such a turn for the better that it's annoying to think of wasted opportunities in the last two decades. Here he's leading a top-flight sextet on a European tour at their Swiss stopover, and as a festival blowing date this is about as good as it gets. The soloists make a nicely contrasting front-line – DeFranco's punctiliousness, Candoli's light fire, Menza's muscularity – and Louie fires them up with superb and never overbearing drumming.

*** **Airmail Special** Musicmasters 5038-2
> Bellson; Bob Milligan, Danny Cahn, Glenn Drewes, Joe Wilder, Joe Mosello, Marvin Stamm (*t, flhn*); Keith O'Quinn, James Pugh, Hale Rood, Dave Taylor (*tb*); George Young, Joe Roccisano, Don Menza, Ken Hitchcock, Scott Robinson (*reeds*); Derek Smith (*p*); Charlie Descarfino (*vib, perc*); Remo Palmieri (*g*); Jay Leonhart (*b*). 2/90.

Just a shade disappointing after the last few. Bellson is still in commanding form and the band alternately steam and glide through these scores, but another tribute to other bandleaders' hits isn't the most striking notion in jazz at this point and only the handful of originals really get much above professional smarts.

*** **Black, Brown & Beige** Musicmasters 65096-2
    Bellson; Clark Terry, Marvin Stamm, Robert Millikan, Barry L. Hall, Anthony Kadleck (*t*); Britt Woodman, Arthur Baron, Dave Bargeron (*tb*); Alan Ralph (*btb*); Frank Wess, Phil Bodner, Bill Easley, Scott Robinson, Ted Nash, Joe Temperley (*reeds*); Lesa Terry (*vn*); Harold Danko (*p*); Gene Bertoncini (*g*); John Beal (*b*).92.
*** **Live From New York** Telarc 83334
    Bellson; Clark Terry (*flhn*); Marvin Stamm, Robert Millikan, Danny Cahn, Glenn Drewes, Darryl Shaw (*t*); Larry Farrell, Mike Savis, Keith O'Quinn (*tb*); Herb Besson (*btb*); Joe Roccisano, Steve Wilson (*as*); Ted Nash, Scott Robinson (*ts*); Jack Stuckey (*bs*); Derek Smith (*p*); Harvie Swartz (*b*). 12/93.

Recorded 50 years after the premiere, this *BB&B* is a tad disappointing. Despite the presence of several Ellingtonians in the cast, the orchestra – perhaps consciously – makes no attempt at Ducal impersonation. Problematically, though, it finds no real character as a substitute. The band plays a polished treatment of the score and, while Duke might have admired it, he would surely have been bothered that no maverick touches bring it properly to life. Bellson's original piece, 'Ellington–Strayhorn Suite', which acts as a makeweight, is similarly precise and unadventurous.

Live From New York features another set of Bellson originals played by a proficient team, with Terry guesting on two tracks. This is archetypal, big, bruising stuff, though never quite as overbearing as a typical Buddy Rich date.

Gregg Bendian PERCUSSION

*** **Definite Pitch** Aggregate CD 001
    Bendian (*perc* solo). 94.
***(*) **Counterparts** CIMP 105
    Bendian; Paul Smoker (*t, flhn*); Vinny Golia (*sno, cl, bcl*); Mark Dresser (*b*). 1/96.

Like Gerry Hemingway, whom he in many ways resembles, Bendian was originally excited by rock music, before discovering the richness of percussion-aware composers like Edgard Varèse. Bendian has pointed out that the main influences on his development of a solo improvisational approach were not other percussionists but free players like Cecil Taylor (who has recorded some Bendian compositions) and Derek Bailey (with whom he has since recorded, see above). With one exception the pieces on *Definite Pitch* are all written for tuned instruments, hence the title; Bendian uses chimes, timps, chromatic boobams, electronic keyboard percussion, vibes, but only on one track does he attempt to create an ensemble effect by moving among different instruments. This is a work-in-progress recording with an emphasis on repaying debts. There are tributes to Bailey associate Jamie Muir, one of the most extravagant contemporary percussion improvisers, to Captain Beefheart/Don Van Vliet, to film-maker Stan Brakhage, physicist Richard Feynmann and others.

Brakhage and Beefheart are interesting figures to acknowledge because much of Bendian's work is surreal and associative, and this is very much the mood of his first group-recording, in which he takes a more conventional drummer's part but reinterprets it in that same, rather maverick way. Smoker, Golia and Dresser are very much kindred spirits in this. The pieces (rather dimly recorded, it should be said, on Caden magazine's own label) are for the most part long, open-formed and integrate arranged themes with what sound like totally free passages. Precisely where one begins and the other ends remains unclear and there is a constant sense, as in Braxton's works, of multiple subjects being engaged, sometimes sequentially, sometimes overlapping slightly, sometimes simultaneous as in a palimpsest. CIMP's dedication to this music is admirable, but their as-it-happens approach to the sound is a little troubling and might be addressed in future issues. These are, after all, expensive items and not everyone wants the warts and all.

Don Bennett (born 1941) PIANO

***(*) **Chicago Calling!** Candid CACD 79713
    Bennett; Arthur Hoyle, Steve Smyth (*t*); Art Porter (*as, ss*); Eddie Peterson (*ts*); Erich Hochberg (*b*); Paul Wertico, Darryl Ervin (*d*). 5/90.
*** **Solar** Candid CACD 79723
    Bennett; James Long (*b*); Douglas Sides (*d*). 8/94.

A fascinating story. Bennett gave up music for a decade and spent part of his off-time working as a private investigator. On his return, *Chicago Calling!* was released on the small Illinois label, Southport; it garnered positive notices and was picked up by Candid boss Alan Bates. One wonders what a larger label would have done with Bennett, perhaps throwing him into a studio with a couple of celebrity horns and the house rhythm section. The pianist has preferred to work with players who are known to him but little known outside the Windy City. Peterson heads the music department at the University of Illinois, and turns out to be a persuasive soloist and tight ensemble player. Likewise, Arthur Hoyle, who didn't last out the session, having to retire with busted chops and cede his place to young Smyth. Before he went, though, he recorded the lovely bridge solo on Bennett's 'Sleeping Child'. The composer's own contribution is very striking, terse but not unexpressive, and leaning heavily on the melody. This is his great strength. On 'Love Found Me' he conjures the sort of song that sounds as though it must have been around for generations. Porter's avowed Lucky Thompson influence is very evident in his soprano solo.

Though Parker's 'Au Privave' and the long bonus 'All The Things You Are' (added for the CD) are intensely exciting, it is the highly personalized originals that attract attention on the comeback record. For the trio recording that followed, Bennett put considerably more emphasis on other people's writing. He takes a typically unpredictable route through Miles's title-piece and 'Tune Up', and he closes with vividly renewed versions of 'Blue Moon' and 'A Night In Tunisia'. Gorgeous as both are, they're still in danger of being eclipsed by 'In Search Of . . .' and 'Blues For Nikki'. Like 'Prayer For Sean' and 'Steven's Song' on *Chicago Calling!*, these are not politely bland dedications but profoundly felt pieces in which the personality and perhaps even the voice of the dedicatees can be heard. Our only reservation about *Solar* is the way the trio is recorded: very big and unsubtle, with a boxy bass sound and uncertain miking on the kit.

George Benson (born 1943) GUITAR, VOCAL

*** **The New Boss Guitar** Original Jazz Classics OJC 460
 Benson; Red Holloway (*ts*); Jack McDuff (*org*); Ronnie Boykins (*b*); Montego Joe (*d*). 5/64.
The huge success he earned in the 1970s and '80s as a light soul vocalist has obscured some of the impact of Benson's guitar playing. He is a brilliant musician. His first records were made when Wes Montgomery was alive and the acknowledged master of the style which Benson developed for his own ends: a rich, liquid tone, chunky chording which evolved from Montgomery's octave technique, and a careful sense of construction which makes each chorus tell its own story. At his best he can fire off beautiful lines and ride on a 4/4 rhythm with almost insolent ease; strain is never a part of his playing. Almost any record that he plays guitar on has its share of great moments, although this early date with his then-boss McDuff is comparatively routine, its short tracks and meagre playing-time very much in the organ-combo genre which churned out scores of records in the early and middle '60s. But it's still very good.

*** **The Silver Collection** Verve 823450-2
 Benson; Jimmy Owens (*t, flhn*); Clark Terry, Ernie Royal, Snooky Young (*t*); Garnett Brown (*tb*); Alan Ralph (*btb*); Arthur Clarke, George Marge (*ts, f*); Pepper Adams (*bs*); Buddy Lucas (*hca*); Herbie Hancock, Paul Griffin (*p*); Jimmy Smith (*org*); Eric Gale (*g*); Jack Jennings (*vib, perc*); Bob Cranshaw, Ron Carter, Chuck Rainey (*b*); Billy Cobham, Jimmy Johnson Jr, Idris Muhammed, Donald Bailey (*d*); Johnny Pacheco (*perc*); strings. 1/67–11/68.
After leaving McDuff, Benson cast around for success without really breaking through. His clean, funky but restrained style was hardly the thing in Hendrix's era, and the easy-listening option which Montgomery fell prey to had yet to envelop him while at Columbia and Verve. This set is an intelligent cross-section of Benson's small number of recordings in the period: a hot quintet with Hancock, Carter and Cobham glide through 'Billie's Bounce' and 'Thunder Walk', while 'I Remember Wes' is a sensitive tribute to the lately deceased Montgomery. The tracks with a larger band are ordinary; but it hints at Benson's growing versatility, and suggests that he was already seen as Montgomery's natural successor.

*(*) **Shape Of Things To Come** A&M CD-0803
 Benson; Joe Shepley, Marvin Stamm (*t, flhn*); Burt Collins (*t*); Wayne Andre (*tb, bhn*); Alan Ralph (*tb, vtb, tba*); Buddy Lucas (*ts, hca*); George Marge, Romeo Penque, Stan Webb (*f*); Herbie Hancock, Hank Jones (*p*); Charles Covington (*org*); Jack Jennings (*vib*); Bernard Eichen, Charles Libove (*vn*); David Markowitz (*vla*); George Ricci (*clo*); Richard Davis, Ron Carter (*b*); Leo Morris (*d*); Johnny Pacheco (*perc*). 8/67–10/68.
*** **Beyond The Blue Horizon** CTI ZK-40810
 Benson; Clarence Palmer (*org*); Ron Carter (*b*); Jack DeJohnette (*d*); Michael Cameron, Albert Nicholson (*perc*). 2/71.

** **White Rabbit** Columbia 450555-2
   Benson; John Frosk, Alan Rubin (*t, flhn*); Wayne Andre (*tb, bhn*); Jim Buffington (*frhn*); Hubert
   Laws (*f, picc*); Phil Bodner (*f, ob, cor*); George Marge (*f, cl, ob, cor*); Romeo Penque (*cl, bcl, ob,
   cor, f*); Jane Taylor (*bsn*); Herbie Hancock (*p*); Gloria Agostini (*hp*); Phil Kraus (*vib, perc*); Jay
   Berliner, Earl Klugh (*g*); Ron Carter (*b*); Billy Cobham (*d*); Airto Moreira (*perc, v*). 11/71.
** **Body Talk** CTI ZK-45222
   Benson; Jon Faddis, John Gatchell, Waymon Reed (*t, flhn*); Gerald Chamberlain, Dick Griffin
   (*tb*); Frank Foster (*ts*); Harold Mabern (*p*); Earl Klugh (*g*); Ron Carter, Gary King (*b*); Jack
   DeJohnette (*d*); Mobutu (*perc*). 7/73.
** **Bad Benson** Columbia 450892-2
   Benson; John Frosk, Alan Rubin, Joe Shepley (*t*); Wayne Andre, Garnett Brown, Warren
   Covington (*tb*); Paul Faulise (*btb*); Jim Buffington, Brooks Tillotson (*frhn*); Phil Bodner (*cl, f,
   cor*); George Marge (*f, picc, cor*); Al Regni (*cl, f*); Kenny Barron (*p*); Margaret Ross (*hp*); Phil
   Upchurch (*g, b*); Ron Carter (*b*); Steve Gadd (*d*); strings. 5/74.
(*) **In Concert At Carnegie Hall Columbia 460835-2
   Benson; Hubert Laws (*f*); Ronnie Foster (*ky*); Wayne Dockery, Will Lee (*b*); Marvin Chappell,
   Steve Gadd, Andy Newmark (*d*); Ray Armando, Johnny Griggs (*v*). 1/75.
(*) **Benson & Farrell CTI ZK-44169
   Benson; Joe Farrell (*ss, f*); Eddie Daniels, David Tofani (*f*); Don Grolnick, Sonny Bravo (*p*);
   Eric Gale, Steve Khan (*g*); Will Lee, Gary King (*b*); Andy Newmark (*d*); Nicky Marrero (*perc*).
   3–9/76.
*** **George Benson: Verve Jazz Masters 21** Verve 521861-2
   Similar to above discs, except add Jimmy Smith (*org*). 2/68–11/69.
Creed Taylor, who ran things at CTI, certainly thought Benson should carry on where Montgomery
had left off. The A&M album, which quickly bogs down in Don Sebesky's typically ponderous
arrangements, is a wet run for what came next, a sequence of strong-selling albums which found Benson
gamely making the best of a near-hopeless situation. Given Taylor's proclivities for stupefying charts
and tick-tock rhythms, it's surprising that there's as much decent music as there is here. *Beyond The Blue
Horizon* is an attractive, smoochy session with Carter and DeJohnette surrounding the guitarist with
shrewdly paced rhythms; 'So What' and a very pretty 'The Gentle Rain' are among the high points of
Benson's CTI work. *White Rabbit*, *Body Talk* and *Bad Benson* find him ambling through the likes of
'California Dreaming' and 'Top Of The World' while reeds pipe soothingly behind him. Benson still
finds interesting fills, but it's a terribly weak assignment for a man who was playing on *Miles In The Sky*
a few years earlier. The live album is inevitably livelier, and the date with Joe Farrell, although the latter
is confined mostly to the flute, has some spunky playing; yet it scarcely adds up to a strong manifesto for
the man who might have been the premier straight-ahead jazz guitarist of the moment. *Beyond The Blue
Horizon* will do for anyone who wants to hear the pick of Benson's CTI work.
    The *Jazz Masters* disc isn't a bad selection from both the Verve and early CTI years. 'Tuxedo Junction'
with Jimmy Smith reminds one of Benson's skill in the guitar/organ combo set-up, and three of Creed
Taylor's productions are at least palatable. But the best is still 'Thunder Walk', from *Giblet Gravy*, which
could stand a reissue in its own right.

*** **Breezin'** Warner Bros 256199
   Benson; Ronnie Foster, Jorge Dalto (*ky*); Phil Upchurch (*g*); Stanley Banks (*b*); Harvey Mason
   (*d*); Ralph McDonald (*perc*); strings. 1/76.
** **In Flight** Warner Bros 256327
   As above. 8–11/76.
*** **Weekend In L.A.** Warner Bros 3139-2 2CD
   As above, except omit strings. 2/77.
Breezin' was the first jazz album to go platinum and sell a million copies, but more important for the
listener was its reconciliation of Taylor's pop-jazz approach with a small-group backing which Benson
could feel genuinely at home in: Claus Ogerman's arrangements are still fluffy, and the tunes are thin if
not quite anodyne, but Benson and his tightly effective band get the most out of them. It's a very
pleasurable listen. *In Flight* reintroduces Benson as vocalist (he actually began as a singer in the 1950s),
and 'Nature Boy' blueprints the direction he would take next, but the record is too patently a retread of
the previous one. *Weekend In L.A.* is a live set that shows how the band can hit a groove outside the
studio. Benson's treatment of 'On Broadway' is an infectious classic because he lives out the song; the
session as a whole is a bit deodorized, but smoothness is the guitarist's trademark, and his solos are full
of singing melodies, tied to their own imperturbable groove.

** **Tenderly** Warner Bros 25907
   Benson; McCoy Tyner (*p*); Ron Carter (*b*); Louis Hayes, Al Foster (*d*). 89.

** **Big Boss Band** Warner Bros 26295

        Benson; Bob Ojeda, Byron Stripling, Randy Brecker, Jon Faddis, Lew Soloff, Larry Farrell (*t*);
Paul Faulise, Earl Gardner, Keith O'Quinn, James Pugh (*tb*); David Glasser (*as*); Frank Foster
(*ts*); Barry Eastmond, Richard Tee, Terry Burrus, David Witham (*ky*); Ron Carter (*b*); Carmen
Bradford (*v*); Count Basie Orchestra; Robert Farnon Orchestra. 90.

Most of Benson's records after *Weekend In L.A.* fall outside the scope of this book, although many rate
as high-calibre light-soul. But of late he's been investigating a return to more jazz-orientated material,
possibly as a result of a somewhat waning general popularity. Guest appearances as a sideman with such
friends as Earl Klugh and Jimmy Smith haven't yielded much, though, and these two sets must be
counted great disappointments. *Tenderly* is far too relaxed: Benson's singing sounds tired, and his
playing is as uneventful as that of the others involved, although such seasoned pros always deliver a few
worthwhile touches. Weaker still is *Big Boss Band*, a collaboration with Frank Foster's Count Basie
band that runs aground on fussy arrangements, material Basie himself wouldn't have touched (the
soporific 'How Do You Keep The Music Playing'), and one track with Robert Farnon's band ('Portrait
Of Jennie') which suggests a shot at Nat Cole's repertoire may be the next thing on George's agenda. His
guitar playing takes an entirely minor role.

Alison Bentley VOCALS

*** **Alison Bentley Quartet** Slam SLAMCD 211

        Bentley; Mornington Lockett (*ts*); Jonathan Gee (*p*); Dave Jones (*b*); Paul Cavaciutti (*d*). 12/94.
Alison Bentley is an elegant lyricist with an unspectacular but warm and subtle vocal delivery. Her songs
are perhaps better than these particular performances of them. It's an oddity of the record that after it
finishes one wants to hear it played again, but differently.

   It's no coincidence that the strongest tracks are those on which Lockett plays. At the mid-point of the
set, 'Angels On A Pin' is a high point, reminiscent of Norma Winstone's 1970s' work, albeit with a
folksier strain. Lockett's statement appears to chaff the song's ambiguities, before dissolving into its
own. Gee, as always, is a sensitive and responsive accompanist, one of the best partners a singer could
hope for.

   Don't be put off. This is good stuff, but it just lacks that little extra spark.

Bob Berg (born 1951) TENOR SAXOPHONE, SOPRANO SAXOPHONE

*** **Short Stories** Denon CY 71768

        Berg; David Sanborn (*as*); Mike Stern (*g*); Don Grolnick (*p, org, syn*); Jeff Andrews, Will Lee
(*b*); Bobby Kilgore (*syn*); Peter Erskine (*d*).

*** **In The Shadows** Denon CY 76210

        Berg; Randy Brecker (*t*); Mike Stern (*g*); Jim Beard (*ky*); Lincoln Goines, Will Lee (*b*); Dennis
Chambers (*d*).

(*) **Back Roads Denon CY 79042

        Berg; Jim Beard (*p, ky*); Mike Stern (*g*); Lincoln Goines (*b*); Dennis Chambers, Ben Perowsky
(*d*); Manolo Badrena (*perc*). 91.

***(*) **Enter The Spirit** Stretch GRS 00052

        Berg; Chick Corea, Jim Beard, David Kikoski (*p*); James Genus (*b*); Dennis Chambers (*d*).

*** **Virtual Reality** Denon CY 75369

        Berg; Jim Beard (*p, org, syn*); Joe Herington (*g, mand*); James Genus, Will Lee (*b*); Dennis
Chambers (*d*); Arto Tuncboyaci (*perc*). 8/92.

***(*) **Riddles** Stretch GRS 00112

        Berg; Gil Goldstein (*acc*); Jim Beard (*p, org, ky*); Joe Herington (*g, mand*); Victor Bailey, John
Patitucci (*b*); Steve Gadd (*d*); Arto Tuncboyaci (*perc, v*). 94.

A stint with Miles Davis, far from pushing Berg into the limelight, set his always-promising solo career
back a good album or two. Miles, for reasons obvious from his earlier CV, has been less than generous
to his latter-day reedmen, obviously looking on the sax as a regressive instrument *vis-à-vis* happening
things like 'lead' bass guitars, synths and drum machines.

   Berg is a hugely talented mainstream player with a well-assimilated Coltrane influence who could never
realistically have been expected to fit into Miles's avant-disco conception. What he was expected to put
in is now history, but what did he take away with him? On the strength of the currently unavailable *Short
Stories*, not a great deal. However, Berg has worked steadily and patiently, and even his less successful
ventures have an undercurrent of enterprise and enquiry that is satisfying over time, even when it isn't
initially impressive.

That's certainly true of *In The Shadows*. Berg's enunciation seems just a notch tauter, and Stern plays with authority. The band is well balanced, and 'Autumn Leaves' is well worth the wait. The nagging sense that Berg is playing entirely within himself rather than taking chances, an impression ironically reinforced by his avoidance of standards, may in retrospect be an incidental function of his patience. Even when he 'let go', as he did from time to time on *Short Stories*, there was still a measure of reserve.

If the late-'80s records suggested it was time to come out of the shadows, *Back Roads* was discouraging indeed. The title-track, which opens the set, is no more than variations up and down the scale of a sweet, brief theme reminiscent of Sadao Watanabe's 'My Dear Life', the kind of smoothed-out fusion that has been keeping Denon in business. Most of the rest is played with a bland, jeans-advert feel that lifts only briefly on 'When I Fall In Love' (which is convincingly romantic) and the closing 'Nighthawks', by which time the harm has been done. Very disappointing.

Enter The Spirit is a more-than-welcome return to form, though it isn't clear from the record *when* this actually took place. Recorded on Chick Corea's label, it's far more musicianly and far less packaged than the earlier records. Berg lets his imagination take him along on the more extended themes – notably Chick Corea's enticing 'Snapshot' and 'Promise' – and dispatches more familiar repertoire like 'I Loves You Porgy' and Rollins's 'No Moe' with great élan. Berg still doesn't write very appetizingly, and 'Blues For Béla' is hardly worthy of a jazz studies undergraduate. But his playing is getting there and, with this guy, that's what matters.

Riddles marks a step forward. There is turbulence that one doesn't detect on the more recent records and a power in the soloing that seems to come from deep within. Unlike, say, Michael Brecker, who always manages to sound completely in command of his material, Berg is best when he is on the brink of letting everything fall drastically apart and there is considerable excitement and not a little of the enigmatic on this most recent record.

Thilo Berg DRUMS

** Footing Mons 1878
> Berg; Thomas Vogel, Ingolf Burkhardt, Stefan Zimmermann, Thomas Bendzko, Sepp Meier (*t*); Ludwig Nuss, Jochen Scheerer, Patrick Mattes, Georg Maus (*tb*); Stefan Pfeiffer, Jens Neufang, Jorg Kaufmann, Matthias Erlewein, Rainer Heute (*reeds*); Hubert Nuss, Thilo Wagner (*p*); Uwe Gehring (*g*); Ingmar Heller, Kai Eckhardt-Karpeh (*b*); Freddy Santiago (*perc*). 90.

*** Carnival Of Life Mons 1887
> As above, except add Till Bronner (*t*), Slide Hampton, Dan Gottshall, Mark Nightingale, Ingo Luis (*tb*), Paul Heller (*reeds*); omit Bendzko, Meier, Scheerer, Mattes, Maus, Erlewein, Hubert Nuss, Gehring, Eckhardt-Karpeh and Santiago. 3/91.

**(*) Blues For Ella Mons 1902
> Berg; Thomas Vogel, Gerard Presencer, Martin Shaw, Thorsten Benkenstein (*t*); Ludwig Nuss, Mark Nightingale, Jochen Scheerer, Georg Maus (*tb*); Stefan Pfeiffer, Peter Bolte, Paul Heller, Jorg Kaufmann, Reiner Haute (*reeds*); Thilo Wagner (*p*); Martin Wind (*b*); Barbara Morrison (*v*). 92.

Berg's big band (mostly German, but with a few international guests across the three albums) runs to very precise timetables – too much so on *Footing*, which is so careful and clean-cut that the music has a character deficiency; for most of the time it sounds like any good radio orchestra. But the follow-up, *Carnival Of Life*, is much stronger. Slide Hampton comes in as *éminence grise* and main arranger, with six interesting charts, although the highlight is probably Bobby Shew's memorial to Blue Mitchell, 'Blue', with a gorgeous flugelhorn essay by Ingolf Burkhardt. Still, the orchestra continues to err on the side of caution. *Blues For Ella* was recorded live, though there's not much that could be described as a rough edge and Berg's meticulous leadership again lacks any persuasive identity, for all his expertise. Barbara Morrison guests as featured vocalist, and her blues-to-jazz swagger adds a little grit.

Anders Bergcrantz (born 1961) TRUMPET

*** Live At Sweet Basil Dragon DRCD 225
> Bergcrantz; Rick Margitza (*ts*); Richie Beirach (*p*); Ron McClure (*b*); Adam Nussbaum (*d*). 2/92.

**(*) In This Together Dragon DRCD 261
> As above, except omit Margitza. 8/94.

Bergcrantz is a gifted hard-bop trumpeter with a popping attack and a penchant for short, pecked-off phrases. Some earlier records for Dragon have yet to make it to CD, and this enjoyable CD is unfortunately something of a pot-boiler. Bergcrantz is among peers for this New York visit, and he takes a firm lead with two interesting originals of his own and a striking recasting of 'Body And Soul' among other themes, but the sound of the group lacks the clear weave of his Swedish bands and the music isn't as tautly sustained as his earlier records. Margitza makes a useful partner – there's a nice touch of European bleakness about his tone – and Beirach, McClure and Nussbaum are dependable and classy rather than inspired. The sound is a little fuzzy when it ought to bite.

In This Together is very, very good. In the studio, the quartet comes together perfectly: Beirach plays in his most concentrated style, and McClure and Nussbaum swing mightily. Bergcrantz takes a more measured course than usual, pacing himself through his solos and finding a mellow, woodsmoked sound on flugelhorn. He comes up with tones and phrasings which no American trumpeter would play and, set against the strong yet thoughtful pulse of the others, the result is a rare kind of post-bop. Even so, it's difficult to sustain a trumpet quartet date for an hour, and just here and there one wishes for another horn for some piquancy, or to propel Bergcrantz in a fresh direction. Exemplary recording, done in New York.

Karl Berger (born 1935) VIBRAPHONE, PIANO

*** **We Are You** Enja 6060
   Berger; Peter Kowald (*b*); Allen Blairman (*d, perc*); Ingrid Sertso (*v*). 11/71.
***(*) **Transit** Black Saint BSR 0092
   Berger; Dave Holland (*b*); Ed Blackwell (*d*). 8/86.
*** **Crystal Fire** Enja 7029
   As above. 4/91.
*** **Conversations** In + Out IOR 77027
   Berger; Ray Anderson (*tb*); Carlos Ward (*as, f*); Mark Feldman (*vn*); James Blood Ulmer (*g*); Dave Holland (*b*); Ingrid Sertso (*v*). 94.

Berger made an unforgettable contribution to John McLaughlin's *Where Fortune Smiles* but has recorded surprisingly little on his own account. The group with Kowald and Blairman finds him in free-ish mode, a vibes style that has as much in common with Gunter Hampel as with Bags or Hutcherson. Sertso is an attractive enough singer but is apt to sound like a poor man's Linda Sharrock and rarely does anything truly surprising.

The best of Berger's recorded output lies in the trio with Holland and Blackwell. 'Dakar Dance' and 'Ornette' on *Transit* are both open-hearted and expressive. The second record is much more inward-looking. Parts of the 'Crystal Fire Suite' are frankly boring and there's too much of Berger's alternately plonky and histrionically flowing piano (he sounds as though he spent his piano lessons skipping from 'Chopsticks' to 'Rustle Of Spring'). Holland is a completely sympathetic collaborator; this is very much his territory. One wonders about the choice of Blackwell, rather than a European drummer adapted to these abstractions. There's a sense that he's having to work harder than the others, giving the quieter tracks a rather tense quality that presumably isn't intentional.

Because of its relative lightness, the vibraphone makes an excellent duo instrument and the partnerships on *Conversations*, some long-standing, some new, show Berger off at his best. Inevitably, he only seems as good as his opposite number allows him to be, and Ulmer's contribution is (to say the least) unilluminating; but on balance this is a very fine album, up with his best.

Totti Bergh (born 1935) TENOR SAXOPHONE

***(*) **I Hear A Rhapsody** Gemini GMCD 48
   Bergh; Per Husby, Egil Kapstad (*p*); Terje Venaas (*b*); Egil Johansen, Ole Jacob Hansen (*d*). 8/85.
*** **Tenor Gladness** Gemini GMCD 53
   As above, except add Al Cohn (*ts*); omit Husby and Johansen. 8/86.

Bergh plays with all the authority, weight and tenderness of the great tenor romantics but, coming from Norway as he does, he's hardly known beyond a local coterie of admirers. These amiable discs will please mainstream followers of whatever nationality. *I Hear A Rhapsody* is a luscious set of ballads, the tenor curling round the melodies and huffing through solos that barely bother to move; lovely stuff, though, and the rhythm sections are good enough never to let the music bog down in treacle. Bergh's meeting with Al Cohn calls to mind the many Zoot-and-Al partnerships, perhaps slightly to Bergh's disadvantage, though Cohn (near the end of his life) was also taking things steady that day: both men sound a little harsher than usual, but there is still much to savour.

Borah Bergman PIANO

**** **A New Frontier** Soul Note 121030
    Bergman (*p* solo). 1/83.
*** **The Fire Tale** Soul Note 121252
    Bergman; Evan Parker (*ss*).
***(*) **The Human Factor** Soul Note 121212
    Bergman; Andrew Cyrille (*d*). 6/92.
**** **First Meeting** Knitting Factory Works KFW 175
    Bergman; Roscoe Mitchell (*as, ss*); Thomas Buckner (*v*). 12/94.

Record companies insist that no overdubs, multi-tracking or tape-speeding have been used on their records only when something rather special is going on inside. That is certainly the case with Borah Bergman, whose initial impact as a player can be likened – however lame a cliché this has become – only to that of Cecil Taylor. Bergman is both a composer and an improviser, and it is often difficult to draw lines between the two. What he has done is to break down any residual distinction between left- and right-hand functions in piano playing. His astonishing solo performances on the Chiaroscuro label instantly reawaken the 'two pianists' illusion associated with Art Tatum, though in a fragmentary and disorderly sound-world far removed from Tatum's or that of the stride and ragtime pianists who are also part of Bergman's background.

Earlier in his career, Bergman concentrated for a time exclusively on pieces for the left hand only, thus building up a strength, suppleness and right-brain co-ordination which now underpin his formidable technique. On the two large-scale pieces which make up *A New Frontier* he sets up huge whirling shapes with each hand, which then engage in dialogue – often confrontational dialogue, at that. There is something slightly mechanistic about the playing on 'Night Circus' that makes one think of the player-piano pieces of Conlon Nancarrow, but this is eliminated on the remarkable 'Time For Intensity', a more richly coloured pair of contrasting pieces, the second of which, 'Webs And Whirlpools', must be one of the most purely astonishing piano performances of all time.

In contrast to these, the duos with Evan Parker are almost conventional, conforming to the basic idiomatic conventions of improvised music. Nevertheless there is a scope to 'The Fire Tale', a piece about the survival and extinction of creativity, and to 'Red Desert', which Bergman has recorded before, for which only classical parallels effectively apply. If some of the solo pieces are symphonic, the duos have to be heard as bizarre concertos in which the element of contention has once again taken over from simple concord.

The disc with Cyrille is both exhilarating and exhausting. Framed by two approaches to the title-theme and, more surprisingly, two takes of 'Chasin' The Trane' (why didn't he record that with Parker?), it is both visceral and intellectually challenging. 'Red Shadows' reappears from the earlier record, and Bergman enthusiasts must already be aware how doggedly and self-critically he pursues certain ideas. Even with Cyrille in harness, Ayler might perhaps be a more accurate analogy than Taylor, though for sheer thump there's not much in it.

Even given the variety of the foregoing, what a complete surprise *First Meeting* is. Coming to it with expectations based on the earlier records, on some knowledge of Mitchell's fierce saxophone poetry, or simply on reputation, one is astonished by the delicacy and precision, the sheer *quietness* of these pieces. 'Clear Blue' particularly has a limpid quality, as if every note had been gently diluted in water before being exposed to the air. Mitchell's breath-sounds are often louder than the actual reed-notes. Thomas Buckner was there as producer only, but it was decided that he should take part, and he did so unrehearsed on the suite, 'One Mind', bringing a further dimension to a riveting, gentle and perfectly centred hour of creative music.

Jerry Bergonzi (born 1947) TENOR AND SOPRANO SAXOPHONE

(*) **Jerry On Red Red 123224
    Bergonzi; Salvatore Bonafede (*p*); Dodo Goya (*b*); Salvatore Tranchini (*d*). 5/88.
*** **Inside Out** Red 123230-2
    Bergonzi; Salvatore Bonafede (*p*); Bruce Gertz (*b*); Salvatore Tranchini (*d*).
(*) **Lineage Red 123237
    Bergonzi; Mulgrew Miller (*p*); Dave Santoro (*b*); Adam Nussbaum (*d*). 10/89.
*** **Tilt** Red 123245-2
    Bergonzi; Andy Laverne, Salvatore Bonafede (*p*); Bruce Gertz (*b*); Salvatore Tranchini (*d*). 5/90.

Bergonzi is cast in the familar mould of modern tenorman, consistently in hock to Rollins and Coltrane and doing his best to struggle free of them. From moment to moment his records impress, but over the full stretch they usually lack the singularity that marks the stand-out recital. None of these is truly outstanding (with the possible exception of *Tilt*) and Bergonzi's harshness and false-register cries are often more ugly than powerful. *Lineage* keeps up a high level of energy and inventiveness on its own terms. The best records, though, are *Inside Out* and *Tilt*. Gertz and Tranchini create a solid foundation with few distractions, and Bergonzi's rather spare writing works best in this context: 'Jones', from *Tilt*, makes the most of its simple bass motif, and the other tunes provide just enough material to keep the long, dissonant tenor solos on a particular track.

*** **Etc Plus One** Red 123249-2
>   Bergonzi; Fred Hersch (*p*); Steve LaSpina (*b*); Jeff Hirshfield (*d*). 3/91.
***(*) **Signed By** Deux Z 84104
>   Bergonzi; Joachim Kühn (*p*). 10/91.
*** **Peek A Boo** Evidence 22119
>   Bergonzi; Tiger Okoshi (*t, flhn*); Joachim Kühn (*p*); Dave Santoro (*b*); Daniel Humair (*d*). 10/92.

Bergonzi's records have been growing in stature. *Etc Plus One* documents his meeting with Fred Hersch's trio, the pianist's elegance of line a shrewd counter to the saxophonist's spilling energy and hard sound. The result is a record that tends to drift between sensibilities, interesting if never quite compelling; and there are probably a few tracks where an extra take could have secured a higher result.

The duet with Kühn grips from the first, with 'Manipulations' asking Bergonzi to go as far out as he ever has over Kühn's vamping bass figure. One is reminded of both the Shepp/Parlan and Barbieri/Ibrahim duets, except that Bergonzi is a more accurate, specific executant than either of those saxophonists. His big tone has never been caught better than it is here and, though some of the pieces seem diffuse, the best of them act as both meditation and fierce interaction between the two men.

Peek A Boo, though Kühn is on board again, is more conventional. Bergonzi's command of the horn is one of the striking qualities here, and the expertise of this quintet can be enjoyed by itself, though again nothing in the set really stands out as unmissable.

Bunny Berigan (1908–42) TRUMPET

** **I Can't Get Started** Pro Arte CDD 554
>   Berigan; Bud Freeman (*ts*); Frank Trumbauer (*as, Cmel*); Mildred Bailey, Red McKenzie, Herb Weil (*v*); other personnel unknown. 34–38.
*** **Swingin' High** Topaz TPZ 1013
>   Berigan; Nick Kazebier, Joe Aguanno, John Fallstitch, Irving Goodman, George Johnston, Steve Lipkins, Ralph Muzillo, Jerry Neary, Charlie Spivak, Jimmy Welch, Karl Warwick, Joe Bauer, Bob Cusumano, Johnny Napton (*t*); Glenn Miller, Morey Samuel, Red Ballard, Jack Lacy, Marc Pasco, Al Jennings, Ray Conniff, Bob Jenny, Tommy Dorsey, Red Bone, Al George, Sonny Lee, Les Jenkins (*tb*); Johnny Mintz, Matty Matlock, Benny Goodman (*cl*); Fred Stulce, Clyde Rounds, Henry Saltman, Toots Mondello, Hymie Schertzer, Charlie DiMaggio, Jack Goldie (*as*); Gus Bivona, Murray Williams, Sid Pearlmutter, Joe Dixon, Joe Dixon (*cl, as*); Eddie Miller (*cl, ts*); Bud Freeman, Georgie Auld, Dick Jones, Don Lodice, Harry Walsh, Arthur Rollini, Dick Clark, Stewart Anderson (*ts*); Frank Froeba, Joe Lippman, Claude Thornhill, Fats Waller, Edwin Ross, Joe Bushkin (*p*); Eddie Condon, Larry Hall, Dick McDonough, Carmen Mastren, Tommy Moore, Tom Morgan, George Van Eps, Dick Wharton, Allan Reuss (*g*); Harry Goodman, Arnold Fishkind, Delmar Kaplan, Grachan Moncur, Pete Peterson, Mort Stulhmaker, Gene Traxler, Hank Wayland (*b*); Ray Bauduc, Cozy Cole, Paul Collins, Eddie Jenkins, Gene Krupa, Dave Tough, George Wettling (*d*); Wingy Manone, Jack Leonard (*v*). 4/35–11/39.
*** **Portrait Of Bunny Berigan** ASV Living Era AJACD 5060 CD
>   As above, except add Paul Hamilton and His Orchestra; Frankie Trumbauer and His Orchestra. 32–37.
***(*) **The Chronological Bunny Berigan, 1935–1936** Classics 734
>   Berigan; Jack Lacey (*tb*); Joe Marsala, Slats Long, Artie Shaw, Paul Ricci (*cl*); Edgar Sampson (*cl, as*); Eddie Miller (*cl, ts*); Forrest Crawford, Art Drelinger, Bud Freeman, Herbie Haymer (*ts*); Joe Bushkin, Frank Froeba, Cliff Jackson (*p*); Dave Barbour, Bobbie Bennett, Eddie Condon, Clayton Duerr (*g*); Artie Bernstein, Artie Shapiro, Mort Stuhlmaker, Grachan Moncur (*b*); Ray Bauduc, Maurice Purtill, Cozy Cole, Dave Tough (*d*); Chick Bullock, Tempo King, Midge Williams. (*v*). 12/35–8/36.
***(*) **Bunny Berigan And The Rhythm Makers: Volume 1 – Sing! Sing! Sing!** Jass J-CD 627
>   Berigan; Irv Goodman, Steve Lipkins, Ralph Muzillo, Harry Preble (*t*); Ray Conniff, Nat Lobovsky, George Mazza, Artie Foster (*tb*); Artie Shaw (*cl*); Joe Dixon, Mike Doty, Carl Swift (*cl, as*); Georgie Auld, Artie Drelinger, Clyde Rounds (*ts*); Joe Bushkin, Joe Lippman (*p*); Dick

Wharton (*g*); Morty Stuhlmaker, Hank Wayland (*b*); Johnny Blowers, Bill Flanagan (*d*); Ruth
Gaylor, Peggy Lawson, Bernie Mackey (*v*); other personnel unidentified. 7/36, 6/38.

***(*) **Bunny Berigan, 1936–1937** Classics 749

Berigan; Irving Goodman, Harry Greenwald, L. Brown, Cliff Natalie, Steve Lipkins (*t*); Morey
Samuel, Sonny Lee, Frank D'Annolfo, Ford Leary, Red Jessup (*tb*); Matty Matlock (*cl*); Sid
Pearlmutter, Joe Dixon, Slats Long, Henry Freling (*cl, as*); Toots Mondello, Hymie Schwertzer
(*as*); Art Drelinger, Babe Russin, Clyde Rounds, Georgie Auld (*ts*); Joe Bushkin, Les Burness,
Joe Lippman (*p*); Eddie Condon, Tom Morgan (*g*); Arnold Fishkind, Mort Stuhlmaker (*b*);
Manny Berger, George Wettling (*d*); Art Gentry, Ruth Bradley, Johnny Hauser, Carol McKay,
Sue Mitchell (*v*). 11/36–6/37.

**** **Bunny Berigan, 1937** Classics 766

Berigan; Irving Goodman, Steve Lipkins (*t*); Morey Samuel, Sonny Lee, Al George (*tb*); Mike
Doty, Sid Pearlmutter, Joe Dixon (*cl, as*); Clyde Rounds, George Auld (*ts*); Joe Lippman (*p*);
Tom Morgan (*g*); Arnold Fishkind, Hank Wayland (*b*); George Wettling (*d*); Ruth Bradley,
Gail Reese (*v*). 6–12/37.

**** **Bunny Berigan, 1937–1938** Classics 785

As above, except add Ray Conniff, Nat Lobovsky (*tb*); Graham Forbes, Fulton McGrath (*p*);
Dick Wharton (*g*); Dave Tough (*d*); Ruth Gaylor (*v*). 12/37–5/38.

***(*) **Bunny Berigan, 1938** Classics 815

As above, except add John Napton (*t*); George Bohn, Gus Bivona, Milton Schatz, Murray
Williams (*cl, as*); Buddy Rich (*d*); Jayne Dover, Kathleen Lane, Bernie Mackey (*v*). 6–11/38.

*** **Gangbusters** Hep CD 1036

Berigan; Steve Lipkins, Irving Goodman, George Johnston, Jake Koven, Johnny Napton (*t*);
Nat Lobovsky, Ray Conniff, Bob Jenney, Andy Russo (*tb*); Gigi Bohn, Milton Schatz, Hank
Saltman, Murray Williams (*as*); Gus Bivona (*cl, as*); Georgie Auld, Don Lodice (*ts*); Clyde
Rounds, Larry Walsh (*ts, bs*); Joe Bushkin (*p*); Dick Wharton, Allan Reuss (*g*); Hank
Wayland (*b*); Eddie Jenkins, Buddy Rich (*d*); Jayne Dover, Kitty Lane, Bernie Mackey (*v*). 9/
38–3/39.

(*) **1938 Broadcasts from the Paradise Restaurant Jazz Hour J H 1022

Berigan; Georgie Auld (*ts*); Dave Tough (*d*); personnel unknown but probably from above. 38.

*** **The Complete Bunny Berigan Volume III** Bluebird NL 90439 2CD

Berigan; Irving Goodman, Steve Lipkins (*t*); Ray Conniff, Al George, Sonny Lee, Nat Lovobsky
(*tb*); Georgie Auld, Mike Doty, Joe Dixon, Clyde Rounds (*reeds*); Joe Lippman (*p*); Tom
Morgan, Dick Wharton (*g*); Hank Wayland (*b*); Johnny Blowers, George Wettling (*d*); Ruth
Gaylor, Gail Reese (*v*). 10/37–6/38.

*** **Bunny Berigan And The Rhythm Makers: Volume 2 – Devil's Holiday!** Jass JCD 638

Berigan; Steve Lipkins, Irving Goodman (*t*); Ray Conniff, Nat Lobovsky (*tb*); Mike Doty, Joe
Dixon (*cl, as*); George Auld, Clyde Rounds (*ts*); Joe Bushkin (*p*); Dick Wharton (*g*); Hank
Wayland (*b*); Johnny Blowers (*d*); Ruth Gaylor (*v*). 6/38.

*** **Bunny Berigan, 1938–1942** Classics 844

Berigan; Joe Aguanno, John Fallstitch, Irving Goodman, Bobby Mansell, Arthur Mellor, Johnny
Napton, Freddy Norton, Jack Koven, George Johnston, Karl Warwick (*t*); Ray Conniff, Max
Smith, Charlie Stewart, Mark Pasco, Al Jennings, Bob Jenny (*tb*); Gus Bivona, Charlie
DiMaggio, Jack Goldie, Henry Saltman, Walt Mellor, George Quinty, Murray Williams (*cl, as*);
Georgie Auld, Stewart Anderson, Larry Walsh, Don Lodice, Neil Smith, Red Lang, Larry Walsh
(*ts*); Joe Bushkin, Eugene Kutch, Edwin Ross (*p*); Tommy Moore, Allan Reuss (*g*); Mort
Stuhlmaker, Tony Estren, Hank Wayland (*b*); Paul Collins, Eddie Jenkins, Buddy Rich, Jack
Sperling (*d*); Kathleen Long, Danny Richards, Nita Sharon (*v*). 1/38–1/42.

Bunny Berigan's only flaw, in Louis Armstrong's opinion, was that he didn't live long enough. At the
height of his career as an independent bandleader, he was making impossible demands on an uncertain
constitution. As a leader, he was wildly exciting, cutting solos like 'I Can't Get Started' (there are two
versions, but the 1937 one is the classic), one of the lads, but utterly inept as an organizer. Stints with
disciplinarians like Goodman and Tommy Dorsey (who valued his genius too much to pitch him out)
didn't change his ways.

Though he died prematurely burnt out, Berigan left a legacy of wonderful music. The Topaz compilation is a pretty good introduction, basically chronological and nicely paced, better on the early years
but not going quite as far back as the ASV Living Era package, which isn't so precisely documented;
hard to pick between them. Converts, though, will certainly want the Classics documentation in full.
Berigan's tone was huge and 'fat', a far cry from the tinny squawk with which he started out. The 1936
material on Jass was recorded for NBC's Thesaurus series of 16-inch electrical transcriptions. The
arrangements are mostly very bland and the only thing that holds the attention is Berigan's horn, either
open or muted, cutting through the pap with almost indecent ease. Typical devices are his use of 'ghost'

notes and rapid chromatic runs that inject a degree of tension into music that often sounds ready to fall asleep.

By contrast, the small groups anthologized on the first Classics volume are sparky, tight and wholly inventive. Chick Bullock's vocals are no great asset, except on those occasions when they give Berigan the chance to mimic his singer's phrasing. The disc also includes six tracks under Frank Froeba's leadership and featuring Midge Williams, who later went on to make her own records. Pretty obscure stuff, this, but worth having for Berigan's buoyant fills.

That Berigan's time-sense and ability to play instant countermelodies were God-given there is no doubt, but it's also clear that he studied Armstrong closely and learned a great deal from him. That's evident from the solos on 'Sing! Sing! Sing!' and 'On Your Toes'. The second volume continues with the June 1938 sessions and kicks off with the best track yet, a rousing 'Shanghai Shuffle' with Auld and Dixon bracketing Berigan himself; Dixon returns for another couple of choruses on alto at the end. Ray Conniff is featured on 'I Never Knew (I Could Love Anybody)' but it's not so much the solos that stand out as the section playing, which often sounds like a much bigger band, yet is also marvellously detailed. That's testimony to the sound restoration, which is fine on both discs. An excellent buy.

As is the Hep set. It covers the period between the two Jass dates with a detailed documentation of autumn 1938, which must be considered a final peak before Berigan's financial and alcoholic slide of the following year. The Pro Arte compilation is a lot patchier. There's some overlap with the Jasses but, more critically, none of the earlier material is up to scratch.

There's a conventional wisdom that Berigan's best work bloomed unseen in the desert air of Hal Kemp's and Paul Whiteman's orchestras and that he was already a spent force by the time he recorded on his own account. This is pure mythology of the Bolden/Bix type; a certain type of fan always likes to think that the *really* good stuff is just over some discographical event-horizon. There is also a substantial mythology attached to Berigan's drinking. Looking at the 1938 recording schedule suggests he may have been as much a workaholic as an alcoholic. The falling away, perfectly evident on the final Classics volume, was doubtless tragic, but it came after a period of sustained excellence, a body of work attained by few who lived twice as long.

The high point, undoubtedly, came in 1937 and 1938, and serious enthusiasts should make the relevant Classics volumes their priority. Long for its time at four minutes and forty seconds, 'I Can't Get Started' is exemplary jazz playing, with that mix of sheer bravura and pathos that was Berigan's signature. His solo on 'The Wearin' Of The Green' on the 1937–38 volume is a nod to Irish ancestry, blustering and demonstrative, but also touchingly guileless.

Three stars, let it be said, for Berigan only on the Bluebird set. Wading through these tracks is a little like the heron-patient waiting that Bix buffs willingly undergo for occasional glimmers of the man himself. The arrangements are generally better than those Bix had to suffer, but the material is pretty lame (Berigan eased himself out of the Paul Whiteman orchestra, where he had replaced Beiderbecke, in disgust at the band-book and distribution of solos) and much of the supporting play is nothing to write home about. Berigan, though, is remarkably fresh and a lot closer to Miles's minimal approach than anyone else dared attempt in those furiously competitive days. Berigan's ability to sustain power throughout his impressive range was one of his most durable characteristics, and he retains the ability to say more in fewer notes than any of his rivals. His development is logical, and impressively simple; he tackles 'Russian Lullaby' without the onion-y emotion most players of the time brought to Irving Berlin's tune, and his deep-toned solo on 'A Serenade To The Stars' is as moving as trumpet gets before Miles Davis came along.

These days, certainly among younger listeners and recent jazz converts, Berigan is little known. It's a pity that Bluebird, having set up a 'complete' and taken the trouble to commission a long and intelligent essay from Richard Sudhalter, should have let the first two volumes lapse.

Dick Berk (born 1939) DRUMS

***(*) **Bouncin' With Berk** Nine Winds NWCD 0142
      Berk; Andy Martin (*tb*); Mike Fahn (*vtb*); Tad Weed (*p*); Ken Filiano (*b*). 6/90.
***(*) **Let's Cool One** Reservoir RSR 122
      Berk; Andy Martin (*tb*); Jay Collins (*ts*); Tad Weed (*p*); Jeff Littlejohn (*b*). 9/91.
*** **East Coast Stroll** Reservoir RSR 128
      Berk; Jay Collins (*ts*); John Hicks (*p*); Dan Faehnle (*g*); Ray Drummond (*b*). 2/93.
Berk, a capable drummer in the hard-bop manner, calls his bands The Jazz Adoption Agency, although the fluctuating personnel militates against the sequence of records creating their own dynasty. *Bouncin' With Berk* is in some ways the most interesting: the two trombones are a telling match, both quiet virtuosos with a needling edge to their playing, and on thoughtfully revised bop set-pieces such as 'Lament' and 'Jive Samba' the quintet secure a real identity. Much of the credit goes to Weed, who acts

as MD for the first two records and arranges the material in surprising ways. On *Let's Cool One*, he fashions a stop-go treatment of 'My Favourite Things', cools off the customary heat of 'A Night In Tunisia' and puts in a couple of smart originals in 'Judy, Judy' and 'Food Club'. Collins is a youthful saxophonist but he plays with grouchy maturity, and Martin repeats his fine turn from the previous disc. Sound on the Nine Winds album is regrettably thin and lacking in impact; on *Let's Cool One* it's congested but more full-bodied.

East Coast Stroll suffers a little from Weed's absence: Hicks and Drummond play with their usual skill, but they're doing session-man chores rather than being part of the band. Worthwhile, but something of a pressure drop.

Bernard Berkhout CLARINET

*** Airmail Special Timeless SJP 360
Berkhout; Frits Landesbergen (*vib*); Jeroen Koning (*g*); Frans Bouwmeester (*b*); Bob Dekker (*d*). 7/90.

A group of young fogeys from Holland, centred round the swinging and stimulating partnership of Berkhout and Landesbergen, both of whom have a knack for taking not quite the expected route through their solos. The programme is Goodmanesque and the timbres of the group not very different from a classic B. G. line-up, yet Berkhout's variety of shadings – from a Getzian breathiness to dirty notes and sudden boppish flares – and Landesbergen's clear-headed virtuosity aim for something else. They don't always make it happen, since clarinet, vibes and soft-spoken rhythms will never move too far from the cocktail lounge, but it's interesting to hear them try. Beautiful studio sound.

**** Royal Flush Timeless SJP 425
Berkhout; Ian Cooper (*vn*); Ian Date, Horst Weber (*g*); Frans Van Geest (*b*). 5/94.

Berkhout's gift is to take a jazz setting of foregone conclusion and resolve it in a wholly unexpected way. The opening track, 'Who ?', is almost lubricious in its delivery, and throughout the disc the five players make deep, sensuous work out of what looks like a palm court programme and a hotel-lounge instrumentation. Berkhout's inspired playing – agile, yearning, without a hint of routine – is matched by Cooper's violin, which takes the Grappelli approach without overdoing the sweetness. Guitars and bass create a rich textural interplay below, as well as pushing the music forward when they have to. A memorable surprise for anyone who hears it.

Berlin Contemporary Jazz Orchestra GROUP

**** Berlin Contemporary Jazz Orchestra ECM 1409
Benny Bailey, Thomas Heberer, Henry Lowther (*t*); Kenny Wheeler (*t, flhn*); Henning Berg, Hermann Breuer, Hubert Katzenbeier (*tb*); Ute Zimmermann (*btb*); Paul Van Kemenade, Felix Wahnschaffe (*as*); Gerd Dudek (*ts, ss, cl, f*); Walter Gauchel (*ts*); Ernst Ludwig Petrowsky (*bs*); Willem Breuker (*bs, bcl*); Misha Mengelberg, Aki Takase (*p*); Günter Lenz (*b*); Ed Thigpen (*d*); Alex von Schlippenbach (*cond*). 5/89.

Much as Barry Guy's London Jazz Composers Orchestra (*q.v.*) has turned in recent years to large-scale composition, the Berlin Contemporary Jazz Orchestra presents its conductor/organizer with a more formal and structured resource for presentation of large-scale scored pieces with marked tempi for improvising orchestra. One outwardly surprising inclusion in the line-up is drummer Ed Thigpen, normally associated with conventional mainstream jazz. This superb set, as yet the only recorded output of the BCJO, features one long piece by Canadian trumpeter Kenny Wheeler and two rather less melancholy pieces by Misha Mengelberg.

Wheeler's 'Ana' is a long, almost hymnic piece whose mournful aspect nevertheless doesn't soften some powerful soloing; Thomas Heberer, Aki Takase and Gerd Dudek are just the most notable contributors, and the piece is held together as much by Thigpen's robust swing as by Wheeler's detailed score.

Mengelberg's 'Reef Und Kneebus' and 'Salz' are very much in the line of a post-war Dutch style in which jazz is almost as dominant an element as serial procedures. Mengelberg's music is frequently satirical, then unexpectedly melancholy. Benny Bailey's bursting solo on 'Salz' prepares the way for some determined over-blowing on the second piece, which fits jazz themes into a 'Minuet', 'Rigaudon', 'Bourrée' matrix. (If the middle element is less familiar, it relates to another seventeenth-century dance-form with a sharp rhythmic hop at the opening and a central bridge passage which sharply changes the direction of both music and dancers. Of such turns are both of Mengelberg's compositions made.) Outstanding solos from Dudek again and Van Kemenade, while, on 'Salz', Breuker almost matches Bailey for sheer brass – or, in this case, woodwind. Thoroughly enjoyable and thought-provoking music.

Tim Berne (born 1954) ALTO SAXOPHONE, VOICE

*** **The Ancestors** Soul Note 121061
   Berne; Clarence Herb Robertson (*t, pocket t, c, flhn*); Ray Anderson (*tb, tba*); Mack Goldsbury
   (*ts, ss*); Ed Schuller (*b*); Paul Motian (*d, perc*). 2/83.

*** **Mutant Variations** Soul Note 121091
   As above, except omit Anderson, Goldsbury. 3/83.

*** **Fractured Fairy Tales** JMT 834 431
   Berne; Herb Robertson (*t, c, laryngeal crowbar*); Mark Feldman (*vn, baritone vn*); Hank Roberts
   (*clo, electric clo, v*); Mark Dresser (*b, giffus, bungy*); Joey Baron (*d, CZ-101, shacktronics*). 6/89.

*** **Peace Yourself** JMT 834 442
   Berne; Herb Robertson (*t, flhn, c, f, v*); Steve Swell (*tb*); Marc Ducret (*g*); Mark Dresser (*b*);
   Bobby Previte (*d*). 11/90.

**** **Diminutive Mysteries** JMT 514 003
   Berne; David Sanborn (*as, sno*); Marc Ducret (*g*); Hank Roberts (*clo*); Joey Baron (*d*). 9/92.

***(*) **Nice View** JMT 514 013
   As for *Peace Yourself*, except add Django Bates (*p, ky, E flat horn*). 12/93.

**** **Lowlife: The Paris Concert** JMT 514 019
   Berne; Chris Speed (*ts, cl*); Marc Ducret (*g*); Michael Formanek (*b*); Jim Black (*d*). 9/95.

*** **Poisoned Minds: The Paris Concert** JMT 514 020
   As above.

*** **Memory Select: The Paris Concert** JMT 514 029
   As above.

Tim Berne called his first album *The Five Year Plan*. He released it himself, apparently unwilling to wait around for the bigger labels to get their heads together and totally unwilling to spend five or ten years hacking it as a sideman. *The Ancestors* is his fifth album, and a first sign that he was willing to slow down, look about him and take stock. Recorded live, it's a measured, authoritative set, rhythmically more coherent than previous and later sessions, with passages of almost Asiatic beauty from Berne and some classic trombone from the still-developing Anderson. Berne's charts are increasingly adventurous, and ensemble passages are well played and registered in a typically professional Soul Note production.

   The set's coherence might be credited to the veteran Motian (he takes a fine solo on one piece and holds together the excellent *Mutant Variations*, with its leaner, punchier line-up), who makes a very effective rhythmic anchor with Schuller, a veteran of Berne albums. Dresser, by contrast, is a less rhythmic, stringier player and is called on to play a very different role on *Fractured Fairy Tales*, collaging textures with Roberts and Feldman (the three fiddlers have recorded recently as Arcado). Unfortunately, though, the sound is muddied and the interplay imprecise. The electronic input is uneasy and largely superfluous, clogging Berne's logic to the point of thrombosis at a couple of points.

   On *Peace Yourself*, he has a working band – now called Caos Totale – capable of sustaining highly developed ideas without time out for hot solos. 'Bass Voodoo' and 'The Noose' are typical Berne performances, with Robertson clowning up-front, Previte knocking out steady but constantly changing figures, and Ducret filling in with strong crescendi. The band are still there for *Nice View*, a disc that contains material written for a British tour in 1993 and recorded in the studio shortly afterwards. Bates's role is more substantial and focused than it was on the tour, when his keyboard playing at least seemed completely directionless. As then, so now; his peckhorn is his most effective voice and it blends in nicely with Swell's old-fashioned sound.

   Perhaps the best of the bunch is *Diminutive Mysteries*. Conceived as a homage to Berne's first and most influential teacher, Julius Hemphill, it includes a long composition called 'The Maze' which impersonates Hemphill rather effectively. Berne's still not a virtuosic saxophonist and often sounds like a beginner who knows what he wants to say but hasn't quite the technical wherewithal to get it out. It's testimony to his basic musicianship that he is able to do what he does without sounding gauche. All the other tracks on the record are by Hemphill himself, still one of the most unregarded composers in contemporary jazz.

   The big selling-point was, of course, Sanborn. To avoid a bland and predictable two-alto front line, Berne doubles on baritone and Sanborn makes a recording debut on the tiny sopranino, on which he sounds entirely like himself, pushed up an octave and a bit. Exchanging Dresser for Roberts means that the sound is still, but also more staccato, and this suits Hemphill's writing admirably. This is the one to go for first.

   The Paris 'concert' was actually a short residency at Montreuil as part of *Instants chavires*. All the better since the selection of material is that bit more varied and generous. Not quite enough to sustain three discs, we feel. The best is certainly contained on the first disc, the long 'Bloodcount' (not the Strayhorn classic) which gives the excellent new band its name and the exceptionally long 'Prelude: The Brown Dog Meets The Spaceman'. 'Eye Contact' on *Memory Select* is longer still at not much under the hour and, though it is episodically interesting, it hardly sustains this amount of attention. Speed is an oddly diffident player; the real heat in this outfit, or perhaps we should say the real source of red blood-cells, is the Berne–Ducret–Formanek trio. The leader has never been a particularly virtuosic soloist, but he deals in interesting ideas and has a very definite sense of what he is looking for as a totality.

Peter Bernstein (born 1967) GUITAR

(*) Somethin's Burnin' Criss Cross CRISS 1079
    Bernstein; Brad Mehldau (*p*); John Webber (*b*); Jimmy Cobb (*d*). 12/92.
*** Signs Of Life Criss Cross CRISS 1095
    Bernstein; Brad Mehldau (*p*); Christian McBride (*b*); Gregory Hutchinson (*d*). 12/94.
Bernstein's anonymous tone and easy fluency send this blameless session on the way to mediocrity. Precious little here really burns – Mehldau's jabbing solos are a good deal more interesting than the leader's, who tends to come off the Grant Green axis without much to call his own. The follow-up is an improvement, though Bernstein has to lean very heavily on Mehldau and McBride to keep up the level of interest. Some promising signs of life, though.

Bill Berry (born 1930) TRUMPET, CORNET

(*) Hello Rev Concord CCD 4027
    Berry; Cat Anderson, Gene Goe, Blue Mitchell, Jack Sheldon (*t*); Britt Woodman, Jimmy Cleveland, Benny Powell, Tricky Lofton (*tb*); Marshall Royal, Lanny Morgan, Richie Kamuca, Don Menza, Jack Nimitz (*saxes*); Dave Frishberg (*p*); Monty Budwig (*b*); Frank Capp (*d*). 8/76.
*** Shortcake Concord CCD 4057
    Berry; Bill Watrous (*tb*); Marshall Royal (*as, f*); Lew Tabackin (*ts, f*); Mundell Lowe (*g*); Alan Broadbent, Dave Frishberg (*p*); Chuck Berghofer, Monty Budwig (*b*); Frank Capp, Nick Ceroli (*d*). 78.
Berry, a journeyman mainstream trumpeter who once worked with Ellington, presides over a big-band record that searches for an Ellingtonian feel and gets some of the way there. The group performs with cheerful swing on an effectively chosen programme, including such lesser-known Ducal pieces as 'Tulip Or Turnip', and the live recording is quite kind, but it's finally too much like many another midstream big-band date to demand much attention. Berry himself did much better with the engaging small-group record *Shortcake*, recently restored to the catalogue and certainly the best place to sample this engaging musician.

Chu Berry (1910–41) TENOR SAXOPHONE

**** Blowing Up A Breeze Topaz TPZ 124
    Berry; Henry 'Red' Allen, Mario Bauza, Emmett Berry, Buck Clayton, Leonard Davis, Harry Edison, Roy Eldridge, Dizzy Gillespie, Jonah Jones, Ed Lewis, Howard Scott, Russell Smith, Joe Thomas, Shad Collins, Dick Vance, Lamar Wright (*t*); Fernando Arbello, Ed Cuffee, Tyree Glenn, J. C. Higginbotham, Quentin Jackson, Claude Jones, Keg Johnson, Dicky Wells, Benny Morton, Dan Minor, Wilbur De Paris, George Washington, De Priest Wheeler (*tbn*); Buster Bailey (*cl*); Benny Carter (*cl, as, ss*); Jerry Blake, Chauncey Haughton, Andrew Brown, Howard Johnson (*cl, as*); Scoops Carey, Hilton Jefferson, Earl Warren (*as*); Jack Washington (*as, bs*); Wayman Carver (*cl, as, f*); Coleman Hawkins, Walter Thomas, Ben Webster, Elmer Williams, Lester Young (*ts*); Count Basie, Clyde Hart, Fletcher Henderson, Benny Paine, Red Rodriguez, Teddy Wilson (*p*); Lionel Hampton (*vib*); Danny Barker, Albert Casey, Charlie Christian, Bob Lessey, Lawrence Lucie (*g*); Danny Barker, Israel Crosby, Freddie Green, Ernest Hill, Milt Hinton, John Kirby, Walter Page, Artie Shapiro (*b*); Big Sid Catlett, Cozy Cole, Walter Johnson, Jo Jones, Harry Jaeger (*d*). 5/33–9/41.
***(*) Chu Berry, 1937–1941 Classics 784
    Berry; Roy Eldridge, Hot Lips Page, Irving Randolph (*t*); Keg Johnson, George Mathews (*tbn*); Buster Bailey (*cl*); Charlie Ventura (*ts*); Horace Henderson, Clyde Hart, Benny Payne (*p*); Danny Barker, Al Casey (*g*); Israel Crosby, Milt Hinton, Al Morgan, Artie Shapiro (*b*); Big Sid Catlett, Cozy Cole, Leroy Maxey, Harry Yeager (*d*). 3/37–9/41.
Half a century after his premature death, Berry's reputation is still in eclipse. He died just a little too soon for the extraordinary revolution in saxophone playing that followed the end of the war. He had a big sound, not unlike that of Coleman Hawkins – who considered him an equal – with a curiously fey

inflexion that was entirely his own and which appealed strongly to Young Turks like Frank Lowe, who began to listen to Berry again in the 1970s.

For someone who recorded a good deal, the catalogue has always been sparse. Classics have made some restitution but it is the Topaz compilation which is more useful, going right back to Berry's apprenticeship with Spike Hughes as a 23-year-old. A self-effacing sort of character, Berry often found himself in the shadow of more celebrated figures such as Herschel Evans, Basie's right-hand man until his premature death. Berry was only ever a dep in the Basie orchestra, but he turned in one classic, 'Lady Be Good'. He had more prominence in the Calloway outfit, with whom he was employed at the time of his death; Berry came very much to the fore on ballad material like 'Ghost Of A Chance', another of the excellent things on *Blowing Up A Breeze*. Too often under other leaders he was restricted to brief excursions from the woodwind bench, and Berry was a player who needed time and space to have his say.

The partnership with Roy Eldridge was a matey, happy affair, and the 'Little Jazz' Ensembles of November 1938 (just three out of the four documented tracks on the Topaz, but rather better mastered) are among Chu's best small-group performances. The missing item is 'Body And Soul', a version which sits very well alongside the great ones. The opening number, 'Sittin' In', is introduced conversationally by the two principals. Talking or playing, they're both in rumbustious form, and the warmth of the partnership was equalled only by the late sessions with Hot Lips Page, made within weeks of the road accident which ended his short life. 'On The Sunny Side Of The Street' had Page laying out, and it's an interesting place to study Berry as an improviser. Neither of the existing releases includes an alternative take, but these do exist, and here and elsewhere they expose a rather thin sense of structure; solos always seemed to follow much the same trajectory. Chu was a wonderfully complete player in every other regard, and with a strong band behind him he was up with the very best. When he died, they left his chair in the Cab Calloway band sitting empty.

Eddie Bert (born 1922) TROMBONE

*** **Musician Of The Year** Savoy SV 0183
        Bert; Hank Jones (*p*); Wendell Marshall (*b*); Kenny Clarke (*d*). 5/55.
***(*) **Encore** Savoy SV 0229
        Bert; J. R. Monterose (*ts*); Hank Jones (*p*); Joe Puma (*g*); Clyde Lombardi (*b*); Kenny Clarke
        (*d*). 6–9/55.

Bert is one of the undervalued masters of the trombone. His career has been divided between big bands, small groups and studio work quite democratically, and the only pity is that there've been few albums under his own leadership. The two Savoys are impeccably delivered slices of cool bop. Bert's articulation isn't quite as clean as J. J. Johnson's but, for agility and coherence, he isn't far behind, and it's only when he hits lower notes – where he gets the fatter, more vocal sound of the swing era players – that his wider allegiances come through. The quartet session with Hank Jones is let down only by a certain prosaic feel here and there, but there's little to complain about on *Encore*. Four brief tracks with Joe Puma attain a beautiful balance between bebop attack and a more filigree sensitivity. Three longer pieces offer a valuable glimpse of Monterose in his most creative period, contrapuntally jousting with the leader. Excellent remastering throughout. The contemporary *Let's Dig Bert!* session was reissued on vinyl in recent years but seems to have slipped into limbo again.

*** **Live At Birdland** Fresh Sound FSR-CD 19
        Bert; J. R. Monterose (*ts*); Ben Aronov (*p*); Bill Crow (*b*); Eddie Locke (*d*). 9/91.

Together again, the years slip away for Bert and Monterose. In the end, though, this is sometimes disappointing. The genteel pace set for Dizzy Gillespie's 'Ow!' suggests that the horns are obliged to take it relatively easy, and the rhythm section shade in a perfunctory swing. But if Monterose has lost the best of his fluency, his solos have the grouchy, quizzical bent of better late-period Lester Young, and Bert himself is watchful, dapper and exuberant by turns, both men at their best on material such as Shorty Rogers's 'What Known?' (alias 'Cool Sunshine').

Ben Besiakov (born 1956) PIANO

** **You Stepped Out Of A Dream** Steeplechase SCCD-31265
        Besiakov; Ron McClure (*b*); Keith Copeland (*d*). 3/90.

Besiakov is a Dane who has recorded as a sideman with Doug Raney. His style is a familiar mixture of post-bop pianists, unemphatic for the most part and agreeable without suggesting much depth. At 72 minutes, the CD is perhaps over-generous. McClure, in fact, has almost as much space as the leader to improvise, and actually sounds more in command.

Tony Bevan TENOR SAXOPHONE, SOPRANO SAXOPHONE

*** **Original Gravity** Incus CD 03
> Bevan; Greg Kingston (*g, rec, tapes, toys*); Matt Lewis (*perc, bird calls*). 9/88.

**** **Bigshots** Incus CD 08
> Bevan; Paul Rogers (*b*); Steve Noble (*perc*). 7/91.

Bevan is a gritty British improviser, who's managed to spell out an idiom sufficiently different from the dominant but hard-to-emulate Evan Parker style. The earlier of these two sessions is engagingly spiny and good-humoured, with a few nods (Lewis's duck-calls most obviously) in the direction of John Zorn's freestyle. The beery track titles – '1044°–1050°', 'Original Gravity', 'Best Before End' – are a bit of a giveaway, for there's a boys'-night-out feel to the proceedings which makes you wonder if it wasn't a lot more fun for the participants than it could ever be for CD listeners.

That certainly isn't true of *Bigshots*, which is wonderfully controlled and dramatic, three absolutely compatible players working at full stretch, listening carefully to one another without surrendering a shred of autonomy. Rogers, as so often in these settings, is the dominant voice, and it's sometimes difficult not to home in exclusively on his rumbling lines. Bevan himself has started to play more smoothly, even lyrically in passages, and it suits him. Only on the long closing 'The Last Shot' does he appear to run out of ideas, though, listening to the track again, one almost wonders if it wasn't actually an initial try-out rather than a curtain-call, so tentative are some of its components. The title-track is much more compelling. Noble comes into his own with a vengeance and Bevan truffles up ideas of real originality. Recommended.

Ed Bickert (born 1932) GUITAR

(*) **I Wished On The Moon Concord CCD 4284
> Bickert; Rick Wilkins (*ts*); Steve Wallace (*b*); Terry Clarke (*d*). 6/85.

Bickert's self-effacing style masks a keen intelligence. His deceptively soft tone is the front for a shrewd, unexpectedly attacking style that treats bebop tempos with the same equanimity as a swing-styled ballad. This was one of the best of several Concord albums (other earlier dates have drifted out of print). Although the music is rather too evenly modulated to sustain attention throughout, Bickert adds interest by choosing unhackneyed material, and this disc in particular has a fine programme of rare standards. Wallace and Clarke make useful foils.

*** **Third Floor Richard** Concord CCD 4380
> Bickert; Dave McKenna (*p*); Neil Swainson (*b*); Terry Clarke (*d*). 1/89.

*** **This Is New** Concord CCD 4414
> Bickert; Lorne Lofsky (*g*); Neil Swainson (*b*); Jerry Fuller (*d*). 12/89.

Bickert's most recent records for the label continue the formula but, like so many other Concord artists, he's inhabiting the style so completely that the records are taking on a special elegance and grace. *Third Floor Richard* returns McKenna to a Bickert date, though he is in – for him – a quiescent mood, and the playing is sumptuously refined. The quartet with Lofksy, though, is a little sharper, with 'Ah-Leu-Cha' pacifying the contrapuntalism of the playing without surrendering all of the bebop fizz which underlines it. Very agreeable.

*** **Mutual Street** Jazz Alliance TJA-10003
> Bickert; Rob McConnell (*tb*). 3/82–5/84.

A rare combination indeed, at least in this kind of jazz circle, but Bickert and McConnell make it sound easy. Since neither man is exactly a grandstander, the lack of aggression pushes the music into the background, which discourages hard listening – and yet there are interesting discoveries which repay close attention. As a pleasant, noodling dialogue between two modest personalities, it sounds fine as well – or at least better than much of today's easy-listening radio jazz. The unfussy studio sound is just what's needed.

The Big 18 GROUP

***(*) **Live Echoes Of The Swinging Bands** RCA 13032-2
> Billy Butterfield, Buck Clayton, Charlie Shavers, Yank Lawson (*t*); Rex Stewart (*c*); Lawrence Brown, Vic Dickenson, Lou McGarity, Dicky Wells, Bob Ascher, Sy Berger (*tb*); Peanuts Hucko (*cl*); Walt Levinsky (*cl, as*); Hymie Schertzer (*as*); Sam Donahue, Boomie Richman (*ts*); Ernie Caceres (*bs*); Johnny Guarnieri (*p*); Barry Galbraith (*g*); Milt Hinton, Russ Saunders (*b*); Jimmy Crawford, Don Lamond (*d*). 6–7/58.

*** **More Live Echoes Of The Swinging Bands** RCA 13033-2
    As above. 6–7/58.
The idea was to re-create some of the big-band scores of the 1940s in 1958, using crack sidemen, most of them veterans of one or other original recordings. Although Charlie Shirley's arrangements were perfunctory, the sound and swing of the orchestra are exhilarating and, with such formidable brass sections, there is a string of good solos – although the stars are sometimes outdone by less familiar stagers like Richman on 'Easy Does It' or Schertzer on 'Blues On Parade'. The two records were cut together at five different sessions, but the first has a slight edge for some of the most appealing scores ('Liza' outswings anything else on the date) and two great set-pieces in 'Tuxedo Junction' and 'Easy Does It'. The remastering is some of the best RCA has done on music from this period, handsomely cast.

Barney Bigard (1906–80) CLARINET

** **Barney Bigard And The Pelican Trio** Jazzology JCD-228
    Bigard; Duke Burrell (p); Barry Martyn (d). 76.
The place to hear Bigard is with Ellington, Morton, Armstrong . . . not really here, though. The great clarinettist was basically in retirement and well past his best when these tracks were made. He might have been a New Orleans man, but Martyn's full-blooded Crescent City drumming doesn't suit, and Burrell's cheerful piano is also on the overwhelming side. Bigard gargles some notes and his phrasing falters at times, though here and there some of the old magic returns.

Big World GROUP

** **Angels** Nine Winds NWCD 0145
    Bill Plake (ss, ts, f, af); Rick Helzer (p); Jeanette Wrate (d). 8–9/91.
Despite some longueurs and a structural approach that encourages the long rambling line, this trio have an impassioned kind of free bop almost within their grasp. The very pretty flute feature, 'Mingus In Watercolor', is a surprising beginning, and the terseness of 'Connecting' or parts of 'The Concept Of Possession' is well conceived. Elsewhere, though, Wrate's singing on 'I'd Like To Go Alone', heartfelt though it may be, or the African-orientated 'Spirit Offering', which could use a bass, are discordant efforts at a wider vision.

Mr Acker Bilk (born 1929) CLARINET

**** **Mr Acker Bilk And His Paramount Jazzband** Lake LACD 48
    Bilk; Ken Sims (t); John Mortimer (tb); Jay Hawkins, Roy James (bj); Ernest Price (b); Ron McKay (d). 3, 5 & 7/58, 1/59.
***(*) **The Traditional Jazz Scene: Volume 1** Teldec 43996
    Bilk; Ken Sims, Colin Smith (t); John Mortimer (tb); Stan Greig (p); Roy James (bj); Ernest Price (b); Ron McKay (d). 1/59–1/63.
***(*) **Blaze Away** Timeless TTD 543/4 2CD
    Bilk; Mike Cotton (t); Campbell Burnap (tb); Colin Wood (p); Tucker Finlayson (b); Richie Bryant (d). 1/87.
*** **Chalumeau – That's My Home** Apricot Music CD 001
    Bilk; Colin Smith (t); Mickey Cooke (tb, v); Colin Wood (p); Tucker Finlayson (b); Richie Bryant (d, perc). 93.
Barber, Ball and Bilk – the 'Three Bs' – were the heirs of Ken Colyer's trad revolution. If Barber 'prettified' Colyer's rough-edged approach, Bilk brought an element of showmanship and humour, speaking in a disconcerting Zummerzet accent, dressing his Paramount Jazz Band in Edwardian waistcoats and bowlers, notching two enormous hits with 'Summer Set' (a further punning reference to the county of his birth) and 'Stranger On The Shore', a tune still much requested at autumnal wedding receptions.
    The idea had come from producer Dennis Preston, who wanted Bilk to record with strings. The clarinettist reworked a theme that was originally dedicated to his daughter, recorded it with the Leon Young String Chorale, saw it picked up as the signature tune to a similarly titled television serial, and counted the royalties. Bilk's success – 'Stranger' sold more than two million copies – and photogenic presentation attracted an inevitable mixture of envy and disdain and it's often forgotten how accomplished and 'authentic' a musician he actually is. Working with Colyer in the mid-1950s, he played in a raw-edged

George Lewis style very different from the silky, evocative vibrato he cultivated in later years.

The choice of a single Bilk album for a sample collection of British trad is made easier by the appearance on Lake of sessions from the Nixa 'Jazz Today' collection. These dates from 1958 and 1959 capture the Paramount Jazz Band at its best, doing blues and rags with a raw, unembellished quality. 'Willie The Weeper' is pretty authentic and things like 'Blaze Away' and 'Higher Ground' give the band plenty of scope for raucous to-and-froing.

A hint of the rawer sound can be heard on the Teldec. It's more of a purist's sound, with many of the clichés of doctrinaire trad (like the banjo going *chung, chung, chung* exactly on the beat, as George Melly describes in *Owning Up*), and those not weaned on this kind of thing may well prefer the more varied instrumental spectrum of later years that found room for a piano and even (horrors!) a saxophone. The late Bruce Turner, the 'dirty bopper' who attracted such hostility from the trad lobby in the 1950s, played with Bilk towards the end of the '60s, and it's a pity that none of this stuff is currently available. Turner's departure was welcomed like the passing of a plague by Bilk's occasionally too vociferous fans, but he added a certain mainstream punch to a band that was in some risk of dead-ending itself.

The excellent Colin Smith was replaced first by Rod Mason (whose Hot Five was a fine revivalist outfit) and later by Mike Cotton, a more intense and subtle player who wasn't content to do Bunk Johnson impressions all night. The Timeless set highlights his talents and those of Campbell Burnap, who replaced John Mortimer. Bilk likens 'Stranger' to a pension plan and willingly keeps up payments on it. It appears on *Blaze Away*, as does the numbing 'Aria', another big hit; but that shouldn't detract from some rather less predictable fare, like 'Black And Tan Fantasy' which is played with impressive freshness and enough jazz 'feel' for anyone.

Bilk is an impressive middle-register player who seldom uses the coloratura range for spurious effect, preferring to work melodic variations on a given theme. Though he repeats certain formulae, he tends to do so with variations that stop them going stale. A major figure in British jazz, Bilk has to be separated from a carefully nurtured image. On record, he's consistently impressive and, as the last of the items on this list suggests, has continued to produce the goods right into the 1990s.

Walter Bishop Jr (born 1927) PIANO

(*) Milestones Black Lion BLCD 760109
  Bishop; Jimmy Garrison (*b*); G. T. Hogan (*d*). 3/61.
***** Summertime** Fresh Sound FSCD 11
  Bishop; Butch Warren (*b*); Jimmy Cobb (*d*). 64.

Bishop's dad composed 'Swing, Brother, Swing', but it was W. B. Junior who gave many of the classic bebop sessions their vigorous chordal propulsion and a duly radicalized version of Erroll Garner's distinctive right-hand effects. Oddly for a man so well thought of in the counsels of bop, it was not until 1961 that Bishop made a record as leader. The results are finely crafted rather than startling, though alternative takes of 'Sometimes I'm Happy', Pettiford's 'Blues In The Closet' and 'Speak Low' suggest a subtle imagination at work. There is a long take of 'On Green Dolphin Street' that is as good as anything in the piano literature on that overworked subject, and a fine title-track, in which Garrison and the underrated Hogan display a sophisticated understanding of Miles's theme. Recording quality is approximately par for the course, with a slight dulling in the bass, but otherwise bright and clear.

Bishop's always been attracted to romantic themes. *Summertime* almost sounds like one of big Dave McKenna's thematic programmes, except that the love songs are delicately and sensitively handled. It's interesting to compare this trio with one recorded more than a quarter of a century later (see below), which is much less flowing but also more adventurous in its tonality.

***(*) What's New** DIW 605
  Bishop; Peter Washington (*b*); Kenny Washington (*d*). 10/90.
*** Midnight Blue** Red RR 123251
  Bishop; Reggie Johnson (*b*); Doug Sides (*d*). 12/91.

The older Bishop takes more chances, leaves more unstated or merely implicit, but is equally resistant to cliché. The originals on the Red – 'Lady Barbara', 'Farmer's Delight', 'Midnight Blue' – are a bit identikit, but they're put together without awkward joins and bear all the marks of Bishop's ability to take what he needs from other material but to mould it entirely to his personal needs. He recasts elements of 'Sweet And Lovely' and 'Autumn In New York', seemingly in order to give both a bit more poke. Back in '64, he was less willing to do that; 'Love For Sale' and 'Falling In Love With Love' are left pretty much intact until the solo kicks in.

What's New is great, a poised and seemingly effortless evening's work by a master technician who's able to throw in enough surprises to lift a set of basically familiar material – 'I'll Remember April', 'Things Ain't What They Used To Be', Shorter's 'Speak No Evil', Dorham's 'Una Mas' – up out of the ordinary.

The Washington brothers fulfil their parts more than competently and the sound is as bright and present as if they were in your front room.

Ketil Bjørnstad (born 1952) PIANO

*** **Water Stories** ECM 1503
> Bjørnstad; Terje Rypdal (g); Bjorn Kjellemyr (b); Jon Christensen, Per Hillestad (d). 1/93.
***(*) **The Sea** ECM 1545
> Bjørnstad; David Darling (clo); Terje Rypdal (g); Jon Christensen (d). 9/94.

Bjørnstad is a classically trained pianist who was turned on to jazz by Miles's *In A Silent Way* and hasn't looked back since. *Water Stories* is by no means a straight jazz session but a linked sequence of pieces inspired by the natural landscape (and seascapes) round Rosendal in the west of Norway. The first few pieces evoke the glacier cutting its path through the mountains. This section is tense, held back, and Rypdal's guitar is deliberately held in check. The second part is much more open and propulsive, and that's partially explained by the changeover of drummers. Per Hillestad, an ECM debutant, has a rock background, including a stint with underrated heart-throbs, A-Ha. He brings a cruder (arguably) but more unfettered quality, which gives the second half its freewheeling impact, as if musical gravity has taken over. Rypdal is magnificent, as he always is on such dates, but Christensen (who normally scores highly in these pages) is frankly a disappointment, palpably not in tune with the music.

The Sea (still harping on water) sounds very much like a retread, but it is a much more coherent record all round and we suggest those tempted to try Bjørnstad's gentle and evocative sound-world should start here.

Black Eagle Jazz Band GROUP

*** **Don't Monkey With It** Stomp Off CD1147
> Tony Pringle (c); Stan Vincent (tb); Billy Novick (cl, ss, as); Bob Pilsbury (p); Peter Bullis (bj); Eli Newberger (tba); Pam Pameijer (d). 6/87.
***(*) **Jersey Lightning** Stomp Off CD1224
> As above. 6/90.
(*) **On Tour In England Stomp OffCD1257
> As above, except Ray Foxley (p) replaces Pilsbury. 8/92.

The Black Eagles celebrate their 25th anniversary in 1996, and their status as trad eminences is well-supported by their records for Stomp Off (there is a lengthy back-catalogue on LP, plus three CDs on their own BE label which, unfortunately, we haven't heard). The discs to hand are all live recordings and portray a band that knows exactly how it wants to deal with the vast legacy of old jazz: programmes that mix staples with rarities, a very occasional original, an emphasis on ensemble-work over solos but space enough for gentle improvisation, and a particularly fine judgement of tempo. They can play incredibly slowly at times and never make it sound like a crawl: try the stately version of 'Wild Man Blues' on the first disc in which Pilsbury's piano solo is some kind of miracle of trad minimalism. There's little enough to choose among the three records, but we have made a token differentiation. *Jersey Lightning* has the smartest choice of material and some of the best playing, but it's only a notch ahead of the first disc. The British date is a whit less appealing since the recording isn't quite so good and here and there the redoubtable Pringle seems shakier than usual.

Cindy Blackman (born 1959) DRUMS

** **Arcane** Muse MCD 5341
> Blackman; Wallace Roney (t); Kenny Garrett (as); Joe Henderson (ts); Larry Willis (p); Buster Williams (b). 8–12/87.
*** **Trio + Two** Free Lance FRL CD 015
> Blackman; Greg Osby (as); Dave Fiuczynski (g); Santi Debriano (b); Jerry Gonzalez (perc). 8/90.
** **Code Red** Muse MCD 5365
> Blackman; Wallace Roney (t); Steve Coleman (as); Kenny Barron (p); Lonnie Plaxico (b). 10/90.
*** **Telepathy** Muse MCD 5437
> Blackman; Antoine Roney (ss, ts); Jacky Terrasson (p); Clarence Seay (b). 9/92.

Blackman plays with as much force, noise and bravado as any drummer today, even if she keeps to within a fairly conservative hard-bop framework. As tempestuously as she fills the spaces in her rhythms with massive rolls, cymbal explosions and the like, the underlying pulse always seems to want to be in 4/4, and her admiration for Art Blakey is never obscured by any strangeness of metre or pulse. Her records as a leader are a mixed bunch. *Arcane* wasn't a great start: too many faceless themes and not much for the horns to pin their committed statements on. Much more interesting is the Free Lance album, a free-flowing jam between Blackman, Debriano and Fiuczynski – the latter two much more interesting than on Debriano's thin *Soldiers Of Fortune* date – and, though the guitarist sometimes turns up his amplifier and heads for freak-out, the drummer's ruthless precision and round after round of press rolls keep time and order in equal measure. Osby blows a few spools of melody on three tracks.

Code Red was an overheated continuation. The ugly studio sound and neurotically overdriven playing suggested that Blackman was pushing even this stellar personnel too hard. There is some excitement in the session, but of the kind that bludgeons the ears into submission. *Telepathy* is much the superior record. The sound-mix is still rather odd, but here the quartet sound like a real, interactive group: Roney's playing is flexible but strong enough to let him stand his ground, and Terrasson's rich voicings and nimble fingering are fine enough to make one itch to hear his forthcoming Blue Note album. Blackman herself still tends to overdo it on the punchiest numbers, but on the ballad 'Missing You' (where she instructed everyone to play as quietly as possible) and the astutely structured 'Club House' she varies the blend to much greater success. 'Well You Needn't' is also a good, tough Monk interpretation. Certainly her best to date.

Black Market Jazz Orchestra GROUP

*** Art Attack Sea Breeze CDSB-2057

Marvin McFadden, Louis Fasman, Brian Boothe, Steve Campos, Brad Catania (*t*); Kevin Porter, John Gove, Dave Martell, Mark Anderson, Chip Tingle (*tb*); Colin Wenhardt, Nik Phelps, Tod Dickow, Dave Rikenberg, Jim Dukey (*saxes*); John Rosenberg (*p*); Brian Pardo (*g*); John Shifflett (*b*); Jeff Nuss (*d*); Lee Durley (*v*). 1/94.

A retro project in that, according to Nuss's sleeve-note, the aim was to capture the feel and timbre of the big-band ensemble style of the 1940s and '50s while still playing a set of contemporary charts. Unlike some of the Sea Breeze big bands, this one is assuredly in the jazz tradition, and all 13 scores resound with top-notch section-work and pithy solos. The sharpest piece is probably Sammy Nestico's 'The Blues Machine', but the quirkier 'Clyde In The Basement' makes its mark; otherwise workmanlike rather than inspired, which might be the fate of every outfit following this lead.

Ed Blackwell (1929–92) DRUMS

*** What It Is? Enja ENJ 7089

Blackwell; Graham Haynes (*c*); Carlos Ward (*as, f*); Mark Helias (*b*). 8/92.

Like a lot of drummers, Blackwell appeared on a huge number of records, but very rarely indeed as leader. He features prominently in duos with Dewey Redman and Don Cherry, but this is the only current release bearing his name. It was recorded at a festival in Oakland, California, celebrating the life of another great drummer, Eddie Moore, who's played with Redman and many others. Blackwell was barely functioning at the date, suffering appallingly from the long-standing kidney ailment which had curtailed his activities for many years and which was to end his life only two months later. His contribution is inevitably a little muted.

The most straightforward feature for the drummer is Carlos Ward's 'Mallet Song', a ritualized sequence of drum-calls punctuated by horns and bowed bass. Helias's tunes, 'Beau Regard' and 'Thumbs Up', are more energetic but marked by free-ish singing lines from the bass, across which Blackwell plays his own melodies. 'Nette' is a tribute to the man whose work the drummer had explored in *Old And New Dreams*. Ward's theme has a typically African cast, his alto as fiery as his flute is softly lyrical on 'Beau Regard'. Haynes, the youngest of the group by a decade, has an almost quaintly old-fashioned sound on his cornet.

Realistically, the record belongs to the group as much as to the nominal leader. One wishes there were more from Blackwell on his own account.

Ran Blake (born 1935) PIANO, KEYBOARDS, COMPOSER

*** Solo Improvising Artists Incorporated IAI 123848

Blake (*p* solo). 76.

*** **Duke Dreams** Soul Note 121027
    Blake (*p* solo). 5/81.
(*) **Suffield Gothic Soul Note 121077
    Blake (*p* solo); Houston Person (*ts*). 6/81.
***(*) **Epistrophy** Soul Note 121177
    Blake (*p* solo). 4/91.
Since 1973 Blake has headed the Third Stream music department at the New England Conservatory.
Cynics will say that only in the quieter backwaters of New England is Third Stream still considered a
viable synthesis. Arguably only Blake and NEC president Gunther Schuller remain strict-
constructionists.

Blake is a scholar, and something of a gentleman, with an approach to the music very far removed from
the seat-of-the-pants gigging mentality of most jazz musicians. His solo performances – and he has
generally preferred to work without sidemen – are thoughtful, precisely articulated, but always
intriguingly varied, combining jazz standards, original compositions of great interest, ethnic musics
from all over the world (though Blake has a special interest in Spanish/Castilian Sephardic themes, as on
the unfortunately deleted *Painted Rhythms*). If he has a single influence from within jazz, it is Monk
(though they seem temperamentally quite different), even if the Soul Note *Duke's Dreams* has some
wonderful treatments of Ellington and Strayhorn. *Epistrophy* is probably the most representative of
Blake's records currently available (though the tribute to Monk's daughter Barbara, see below, must not
be missed). He touches bass with the title-tune no fewer than three times on the record and adopts
characteristically acute angles on the others. Something of Monk's method of improvising on surprisingly limited motives can be heard even when Blake is working with standards, as on *Suffield Gothic*. His
collaboration there with saxophonist Houston Person is intriguing but a little detached. Since his days
with Arthur Blythe, though no one's suggesting any conection, Blake has tended to steer clear of
saxophonists, and only his ex-NEC student Ricky Ford has worked out a viable *modus operandi*.

*** **Improvisations** Soul Note 121022
    Blake; Jaki Byard (*p*). 6/81.
Piano duos can be messily unsatisfactory affairs; one thinks of the Cecil Taylor/Mary Lou Williams
imbroglio in particular. This, though, is exceptional. Blake and Byard don't so much share a common
conception as an ecumenical willingness to meet one another half-way, a characteristic noted on Byard's
remarkable Festival Hall, London, encounter with the British improviser, Howard Riley. The formalism
of 'Sonata For Two Pianos' is mostly in the title; it's a limber, well-spaced piece with considerable
harmonic interest. Almost inevitably, there is a taut, academic undercurrent to 'Tea For Two' and 'On
Green Dolphin Street'. The pianos don't register quite as well as they might in some of the more
exuberant passages but the sound is generally good, given the difficulties of recording this kind of
music; a little more crispness in the bass might have helped; but the music is good enough to merit a
sprinkle of stars.

**** **Painted Rhythms: Volume 1** GM 3007
    Blake (*p* solo). 12/85.
**** **Painted Rhythms, Volume 2** GM 3008
    As above. 12/85.
Like trumpeter Franz Koglmann, Blake takes a highly personal stance on the jazz tradition, reinterpret-
ing classic material with a curious mixture of respectful precision and free-floating innovation. The most
striking instances of that are the *four* versions of 'Maple Leaf Rag' that straddle these two remarkable
discs. The third of them, bringing Volume One to a close, is dislocated, rediscovering Joplin's tune from
a whirlpool of atonality and fractured rhythms. The second, by contrast, is played with a kind of sweet
abandon that's the other side to Blake's sometimes rather severe approach.

Volume One is largely concerned with jazz repertoire, originals like Duke's 'Azure' and 'Skrontch',
Mary Lou Williams's 'What's Your Story, Morning Glory?', more recent things like George Russell's
'Ezzthetic' and the Stan Kenton tune that gives the set its name. Part Two casts the net a lot wider,
searching for that 'Spanish tinge' that Jelly Roll Morton thought was a constant in jazz. As noted above,
Blake has long been interested in Sephardic music, and its distinctive harmonies (parallel to those
familiar from the blues and jazz) provide this volume with new colours. Volume Two also features Blake
the composer. 'Shoah!' and 'Storm Warning' both seem to hint at historical urgency, an impression
heightened by the quotes from Shostakovich in the second, and by Blake's adaptation of Olshanetsky
and Wolfson's *klezmer*-based 'Vilna', a mourning tune memorializing the victims of a Nazi massacre.
'Babbitt', presumably dedicated to the composer, is a more abstract exploration of sound and silence,
each pushed to the limit in its power to communicate with the immediacy of images.

**** **Short Life Of Barbara Monk** Soul Note 1211127
    Blake; Ricky Ford (*ts*); Ed Felson (*b*), Jon Hazilla (*d*). 8/86.

This is a truly marvellous album, which makes Blake's apparent unwillingness to work in ensemble settings all the more galling. The first side ends with the title-piece, dedicated to Thelonious Monk's daughter, Barbara, who died of cancer in 1984. It's a complex and moving composition that shifts effortlessly between a bright lyricism and an edgy premonition; Blake plays quite beautifully, and his interplay with the young but supremely confident rhythm section is a revelation.

A death also lies behind the closing track on side two. 'Pourquoi Laurent?' expresses both a hurt need to understand and a calm desire to heal, written in the face of French jazz critic Laurent Goddet's suicide. 'Impresario Of Death' is equally disturbing but so intelligently constructed as to resolve its inner contradiction perfectly. 'Vradiazi' by the Greek composer Theodorakis is a favourite of Blake's, as is the Sephardic melody, 'Una Matica De Ruda' (two eye-blink takes), which also features on *Painted Rhythms II* (above).

To lighten the mix a little, there are astonishing versions of Stan Kenton's theme, 'Artistry In Rhythm', and, as an entirely unexpected opener, 'I've Got You Under My Skin'. Blake's Falcone Concert Grand sounds in perfect shape and the session – a single day of concentrated music-making – is superbly recorded and pressed.

***(*) **That Certain Feeling** hat Art 6077
    Blake; Steve Lacy (*ss*); Ricky Ford (*ts*). 90.
The *real* distorters of Gershwin are those who reduce him to a sticky harmonic paste. Blake keeps the *shape* of the songs, if not intact, then at least plastically viable. The 'Overture', played twice, bears no obvious relationship to the rest of the material, except in that it underlines the pianist's highly original and unquantifiable use of non-standard, almost Moroccan intervals. 'Strike Up The Band' brings in both saxophonists, who also duet with Blake elsewhere. It's a noisy and initially off-putting performance, but it yields great prizes, as does the *faux-naïf* 'I Got Rhythm' (Ford may not be faking, but Blake certainly is, and he gets away with it majestically). The music is full of oblique, inverted and sometimes probably imaginary references to Gershwin's corpus. It's a record to be swallowed whole, then nibbled at and digested over time.

*** **Round About** Music & Arts CD 807
    Blake; Christine Correa (*v*). 12/92, 8/93.
Some of the records on which Mal Waldron accompanies singers have made us think that Mal himself may prove to be a more expressive interpreter of a song than the lady (though not, of course, the Lady) herself. This project similarly. Correa has a strong and evocative voice, but she does rather diverge from the expected path of the lyric, and Blake seems too much involved in his own interpretations to steer her back. The top things are exactly those you'd expect: a re-working of 'Short Life Of Barbara Monk' and 'Blue Monk' ahead of it. Good as these are, they don't supersede Blake's earlier readings.

Seamus Blake (born 1969) TENOR SAXOPHONE, SOPRANO SAXOPHONE

*** **The Call** Criss Cross CRISS 1088
    Blake; Kurt Rosenwinkel (*g*); Kevin Hays (*p*); Larry Grenadier (*b*); Bill Stewart (*d*). 12/93.
As with Ralph Moore before him, the United Kingdom can claim a small stake in Seamus Blake. Born in England, he grew up in Canada and studied in the US at Berklee College, before falling in with drummer Victor Lewis, who's been his backer and spur.

Blake has recorded before, also on Criss Cross with Billy Drummond's group, and it's characteristic of label boss Gerry Teekens that he should have given the youngster such an early opportunity to record under his own steam. Interestingly, on this occasion neither Teekens nor Blake seems to have felt a need to lay on a big-name rhythm section (apologies to Stewart, perhaps) as both insurance and a commercial draw. Blake stands tall on his own account. The title-track confirms his vocation in the music; Blake's own contribution is outweighed by the guitarist's, but the shape and logic of the thing are entirely his own. Another original, the long 'On Cue' rambles uncomfortably, but 'Zydeco' and 'Mercy Days' are both thoughtfully written and executed, the latter a winding, ambiguous soprano exercise with almost an excess of emotional freight.

The disc opens and closes with alternative versions of 'Vanguard Blues', apparently written as a tribute to Joe Lovano and to the Village Vanguard in New York. It very effectively captures the young man's excitement and sheer buzz at coming face to face with musical heroes (fellow-Canadian Kenny Wheeler is also name-checked) but without succumbing to undue influence. Blake is someone to watch.

Art Blakey (1919–90) DRUMS

**** A Night At Birdland Vol. 1 Blue Note B21Y-46519-2
   Blakey; Clifford Brown (*t*); Lou Donaldson (*as*); Horace Silver (*p*); Curley Russell (*b*). 2/54.
**** A Night At Birdland Vol. 2 Blue Note B21Y-46520-2
   As above. 2/54.

It was still called the 'Art Blakey Quintet', but this was the nexus of the band that became The Jazz Messengers, one of the most durable bywords in jazz, even if the name was first used on a Horace Silver album-cover. Blakey wasn't as widely acknowledged as Max Roach or Kenny Clarke as one of the leaders in establishing bop drumming, and in the end he was credited with working out the rhythms for what came after original bebop, first heard to significant effect on these records. Much of it is based on sheer muscle: Blakey played very loud and very hard, accenting the off-beat with a hi-hat snap that had a thunderous abruptness, and developing a snare roll that possessed a high drama all its own. As much as he dominates the music, though, he always plays for the band, and inspirational leadership is as apparent on these early records as it is on his final ones. Both horn players benefit: Donaldson makes his Parkerisms sound pointed and vivacious, while Brown is marvellously mercurial, as well as sensitive on his ballad feature 'Once In A While' from Volume 1 (Donaldson's comes on 'If I Had You' on the second record). Silver, too, lays down some of the tenets of hard bop, with his poundingly funky solos and hints of gospel melody. The sound has been capably transferred to CD, although owners of original vinyl needn't fear that they're missing anything extra.

***(*) At The Café Bohemia Vol. 1 Blue Note B21Y-46521-2
   Blakey; Kenny Dorham (*t*); Hank Mobley (*ts*); Horace Silver (*p*); Doug Watkins (*b*). 11/55.
***(*) At The Café Bohemia Vol. 2 Blue Note B21Y-46522-2
   As above. 11/55.

A very different band but results of equal interest to the Birdland session (the second volume of the Bohemia date was made 12 days after Volume 1). Hank Mobley is a somewhat unfocused stylist, and nothing quite matches the intensity which the Quintet secured at Birdland, yet the playing is finally just as absorbing. Dorham's elusive brilliance was seldom so extensively captured, his 'Yesterdays' ballad feature displaying a rare tenderness which faces off against the contentious dynamism of his fast solos, which seem to forge a link between Dizzy Gillespie and Miles Davis. Long, mid-tempo pieces such as 'Soft Winds' and 'Like Someone In Love' find Silver and Blakey in reflective competition, but the drummer never slackens his grip: listen to what he does behind Dorham on 'Minor's Holiday'. The recording captures the atmosphere very truthfully, and there's some added charm in the announcements by Mobley and Dorham before their features.

*** The Jazz Messenger Columbia 467920-2
   Blakey; Donald Byrd, Bill Hardman (*t*); Jackie McLean (*as*); Ira Sullivan, Hank Mobley (*ts*);
   Horace Silver, Sam Dockery, Kenny Drew (*p*); Spanky DeBrest, Doug Watkins, Wilbur Ware
   (*b*). 5–12/56.

Compiled from three Columbia albums, this finds Blakey's band in transition. The impact McLean had on the group is clearly illustrated by the first two tracks: after the elegant, rather dapper 'Ecaroh', with Byrd and Mobley in the front line, McLean and Hardman tear things up on 'Cranky Spanky'. That sort of yin and yang is maintained through the first seven tracks, with a measured debut for McLean's standard 'Little Melonae', before a third edition of the band appears at the end, with Byrd and Sullivan in the front line on 'The New Message'. Shrewdly compiled, this makes the best of three sometimes routine original records. The remastering is very clean.

*** Hard Drive Bethlehem BET 6001-2
   Blakey; Bill Hardman (*t*); Johnny Griffin (*ts*); Junior Mance, Sam Dockery (*p*); Spanky DeBrest
   (*b*).
*** Big Band Bethlehem BET 6002-2
   Blakey; Donald Byrd, Idrees Sulieman, Bill Hardman, Ray Copeland (*t*); Melba Liston, Frank
   Rehak, Jimmy Cleveland (*tb*); Sahib Shihab, Bill Graham (*as*); Al Cohn, John Coltrane (*ts*); Bill
   Slapin (*bs*); Walter Bishop (*p*); Wendell Marshall (*b*). 12/57.

Blakey's two Bethelehem albums are welcome if inessential reissues. *Hard Drive* finds the Messengers in transition, with Hardman's peppery trumpet not quite the ideal foil for the ever-hungry Griffin, and some of the tracks sound a little cut-off. The big-band date is a rarity in Blakey's discography, but it's blemished by what sounds like very little rehearsal: the sloppiness in some of the section playing sounds like a giveaway. That said, Blakey directs with customary enthusiasm and some of the tracks work up something interesting, with Liston's 'Late Date' and Cohn's 'The Outer World' sounding best. Most interesting of all, though, is the chance to hear Coltrane as a surrogate Jazz Messenger: he lines up alongside Byrd for two quintet tracks, and they both make an impression on 'Tippin''. Excellent remastering on both discs.

*** **Midnight Session** Savoy SV-0145
    Blakey; Bill Hardman (*t*); Jackie McLean (*as*); Sam Dockery (*p*); Spanky DeBrest (*b*). 3/57.
Savoy's solitary Blakey entry delivers half a dozen workouts by the group, playing with an energy that
seems prosaic next to that shown by some of the other great Blakey line-ups, perhaps underlining that
this was one of Blakey's lesser outfits, even with McLean in the front line.

**** **Art Blakey's Jazz Messengers With Thelonious Monk** Atlantic 781332-2
    Blakey; Bill Hardman (*t*); Johnny Griffin (*ts*); Thelonious Monk (*p*); Spanky DeBrest (*b*). 3/57.
Blakey appeared on several of Monk's seminal Blue Note sessions, and he had a seemingly intuitive
knowledge of what the pianist wanted from a drummer. Griffin, volatile yet almost serene in his mastery
of the horn, was another almost ideal yet very different interpreter of Monk's music. This set of five
Monk tunes and one by Griffin is a masterpiece. If Hardman wasn't on the same exalted level as the
other three, he does nothing to disgrace himself, and DeBrest keeps calm, unobtrusive time. The continuous dialogue between Blakey and Monk comes out most clearly in passages such as Monk's solo on
'In Walked Bud', but almost any moment on the session illustrates their unique empathy. Both use
simple materials, which makes the music unusually clear in its layout, yet the inner complexities are
astonishing, and as a result the music retains an uncanny freshness 35 years later; no passage is like
another, and some of the tempos, such as those chosen for 'Evidence' and 'I Mean You', are almost
unique in the annals of Monk interpretations. The CD remastering is mostly fine, although DeBrest
seems very remote in the mix. Absolutely indispensable jazz.

***(*) **Moanin'** Blue Note B21Y-46516-2
    Blakey; Lee Morgan (*t*); Benny Golson (*ts*); Bobby Timmons (*p*); Jymie Merritt (*b*). 10/58.
*** **1958 Paris Olympia** Fontana 832659-2
    As above. 11–12/58.
*** **Des Femmes Disparaissent / Les Tricheurs** Fontana 834752-2
    As above. 12/58.
*** **Les Liaisons Dangereuses 1960** Fontana 812017-2
    Blakey; Lee Morgan (*t*); Barney Wilen (*ss, ts*); Duke Jordan, Bobby Timmons (*p*); Jymie Merritt
(*b*); John Rodriguez, Williams Rodriguez, Tommy Lopez (*perc*). 7/59.
Benny Golson wasn't a Jazz Messenger for very long – this was his only American album with the band
– but he still contributed three of the most enduring themes to their book, all of them on *Moanin'*: the
title-track, 'Blues March' and 'Along Came Betty'. These versions might seem almost prosaic next to
some of the grandstand readings which other Blakey bands would later create, but Golson's own
playing shows great toughness, and the ebullient Morgan, also making his Messengers debut, is a
splendid foil. The set played at the Paris Olympia follows a similar pattern: Golson plays with riveting
urgency (if imperfect control), and only the more distant sound keeps this one on the B list of
Messengers albums. The soundtrack for Eduardo Molinaro's *Des femmes disparaissent* is one of the
least-known of Blakey's albums, directed mainly by Golson: the album is made up of fragments of
Messengers tunes, motifs, drum-rolls and blues. It scarcely hangs together as a Messengers session, but
the components are impeccably conceived and finished, and the superb studio sound allows a close-up
hearing of how this band worked.
    Another soundtrack, *Les Liaisons Dangereuses*, offers a brief look at Barney Wilen in the band. The
music is less than abundant in terms of material (most of it gets played twice for the purposes of the
film) but Wilen acquits himself courageously, his tenor on 'Valmontana' and soprano on 'Prelude In
Blue' both impressive.

***(*) **At the Jazz Corner Of The World** Blue Note 828888-2 2CD
    Blakey; Lee Morgan (*t*); Hank Mobley (*ts*); Bobby Timmons (*p*); Jymie Merritt (*b*). 4/59.
A brief interlude with Hank Mobley in the tenor chair. He sounds comfortable enough – and gets to
contribute three tunes of his own, even if they're hardly in the class set by the next tenorman to step in.
Any live event with The Messengers in this period was worth saving, and this one sounds terrifically
loud, up-front and spirited, with the master of the traps in imperious form. Originally on two separate
LPs, now on a double-CD set.

*** **The Big Beat** Blue Note B21Y-46400
    Blakey; Lee Morgan (*t*); Wayne Shorter (*ts*); Bobby Timmons (*p*); Jymie Merritt (*b*). 3/60.
***(*) **A Night In Tunisia** Blue Note B21Y-784949-2
    As above. 8/60.
After Golson came Shorter, the most individual of composers and an invaluable source for The
Messengers. Of the seven Blue Note albums with Morgan and Shorter in the front line, only the above
are available and only *A Night In Tunisia* is still in the UK catalogue. Luckily, it's perhaps the best of the

three: besides the wildly over-the-top version of the title-tune, there's Shorter's lovely 'Sincerely Diana' and two charming Lee Morgan themes. Shorter's playing had a dark, corrosive edge to it that turned softly beseeching when he played ballads, but some of his solos don't come off: that on 'The Chess Players' from the patchy *The Big Beat* never gets started. *Like Someone In Love*, made at the same sessions as *Tunisia*, includes two takes of the haunting 'Sleeping Dancer Sleep On', and the other themes are attractive but more conventional. The CD remastering is very good.

*** **Live In Stockholm 1959** DIW 313
    Blakey; Lee Morgan (*t*); Wayne Shorter (*ts*); Walter Bishop Jr (*p*); Jymie Merritt (*b*). 11/59.
*** **Live In Stockholm 1959** Dragon DRCD 182
    As above. 11/59.
*** **Live In Stockholm 1960** DIW 344
    As above, except Bobby Timmons (*p*) replaces Bishop. 12/60.
*** **Unforgettable Lee!** Fresh Sound FSCD-1020
    As above. 4–6/60.
*** **More Birdland Sessions** Fresh Sound FSCD-1029
    As above, except add Walter Davis Jr (*p*). 6–11/60.

Though one might imagine live Messengers recordings to be hotter than their studio counterparts, the band was able to generate the same intensity in both locations. Still, these live sessions from a couple of European visits are useful supplements to the Blue Note albums. There is little variation between the three Stockholm sets – although the 1959 Dragon issue includes some more interesting themes, recorded on the same day as the DIW disc but apparently using some different material – but the Royal session includes a couple of rarer items in Shorter's 'Nelly Bly' and 'The Midgets'. With the recordings probably emanating from radio tapes, the sound is consistently clear, if not as full-bodied as the studio sessions; and Morgan and Shorter are in any event always worth hearing as a youthful partnership, creating the kind of idiosyncratic front line which seems lost among today's more faceless technicians. The Fresh Sound disc sorts together nine tracks from various Birdland sessions in the spring of 1960 (it is nominally credited to Morgan and has his picture on the CD sleeve) and although anyone who has the other discs listed here will have the material in other versions, this catches the Messengers in very hot form. A brief 'Justice' finds Morgan in explosive form on his solo, and he sounds particularly exciting on most of the tracks on a generously packed CD. The sound, though, is rather grainy and suffers from some drop-outs. *More Birdland Sessions* sweeps together some more offcuts from the same year: Shorter is at his most eccentric in the 'Lester Left Town' solo, but there is interesting stuff from both him and Morgan throughout. Indifferent sound, though.

** **Jazz Messengers** MCA/Impulse! 33103
    Blakey; Freddie Hubbard (*t*); Curtis Fuller (*tb*); Wayne Shorter (*ts*); Cedar Walton (*p*); Jymie Merritt (*b*). 6/61.
**** **Mosaic** Blue Note B21Y-46523-2
    As above. 10/61.
**** **Buhaina's Delight** Blue Note 784104-2
    As above. 11–12/61.
*** **Caravan** Original Jazz Classics OJC 038
    As above, except Reggie Workman (*b*) replaces Merritt. 10/62.
***(*) **Ugetsu** Original Jazz Classics OJC 090
    As above. 6/63.
**** **Free For All** Blue Note B21Y-84170
    As above. 2/64.
*** **Kyoto** Original Jazz Classics OJC 145
    As above. 2/64.

Exit Morgan, enter Hubbard and Fuller. By now it was clear that Blakey's Jazz Messengers were becoming a dynasty unto themselves, with the drummer driving from the rear. As musical director, Shorter was still providing some startling material, which Hubbard and Fuller, outstanding players but undercharacterized personalities, could use to fashion directions of their own. Cedar Walton was another significant new man: after the lightweight work of Bobby Timmons, Walton's deeper but no less buoyant themes added extra weight to the band's impact.

    In some ways, this was the most adventurous of all Messengers line-ups. The three masterpieces are the amazingly intense *Free For All*, which reasserts Blakey's polyrhythmic firepower as never before and finds Shorter at his most ferocious on the title-tune and 'Hammer Head'; *Mosaic*, where the complex title-piece (by Walton) shows how the expanded voicings of the band added orchestral sonority to rhythmic power; and *Buhaina's Delight*, opening on the swaggering 'Backstage Sally' and leading to Shorter's stone-faced 'Contremplation' and vivid arrangement of 'Moon River'. Hubbard's feisty brightness and Fuller's sober, quickfire solos are a memorable counterweight to Shorter's private, dark improvisations. The tenorman is less evident on *Kyoto*, a breezier session dominated by Fuller and Hubbard, and although the live-at-Birdland *Ugetsu* is fine, it doesn't catch fire in quite the way the band might have been expected to in concert, though Shorter's feature on 'I Didn't Know What Time It Was' is ponderously impressive. *Caravan* is another solid though slightly less imposing set. The earliest date, for Impulse!, seems to have been organized more by the producer than the musicians, since it consists almost entirely of standards, and though capably done it's not what this edition of the band was about. All of these dates have been well remastered.

*** **A Jazz Message** MCA/Impulse! MCAD-5648
    Blakey; Sonny Stitt (*as, ts*); McCoy Tyner (*p*); Art Davis (*b*). 6/63.
A rare instance of Blakey as a leader away from the Messengers, but it's basically a Stitt-plus-rhythm date, as characteristically as the drummer plays. A couple of blues and some standards, with Tyner strolling through the date and Stitt playing hard and well.

**** **The Best Of Art Blakey And The Jazz Messengers** Blue Note CDP 793205-2
*** **The Best Of Art Blakey** Emarcy 848245-2
    Blakey; Lee Morgan, Chuck Mangione, Valery Ponomarev (*t*); Bobby Watson (*as*); Benny
    Golson, Barney Wilen, Wayne Shorter, Frank Mitchell, David Schnitter (*ts*); Bobby Timmons,
    Walter Davis Jr, Keith Jarrett, James Williams (*p*); Jymie Merritt, Reggie Johnson, Dennis Irwin
    (*b*). 12/58–2/79.
The Blue Note compilation is well chosen, with 'Moanin'', 'Blues March' and 'Dat Dere' covering the most popular Messengers tunes and 'Mosaic', 'Free For All' and 'Lester Left Town' their most challenging. 'A Night In Tunisia' is also here. Emarcy's collection includes four tracks with Barney Wilen opposite Morgan in the 1958–9 band, a 1966 reading of 'My Romance' which is included mainly for the presence of Keith Jarrett, and a somewhat desultory 1979 version of 'Blues March' by a less than distinguished line-up; a patchwork but worthwhile disc.

(*) **Child's Dance Prestige PCD 24130-2
    Blakey; Woody Shaw (*t*); Buddy Terry (*ss*); Ramon Morris (*ts, f*); Carter Jefferson (*ts*); Manny
    Boyd (*f*); George Cables, Cedar Walton, John Hicks, Walter Davis (*p*); Essien Nkrumah (*g*);
    Stanley Clarke, Mickey Bass (*b*); Nathaniel Bettis, Sonny Morgan, Pablo Landrum, Emmanuel
    Rahim, Ray Mantilla, Tony Waters (*perc*). 3/73.
This Messengers period is scarcely represented in the catalogues at all at present. They cut three albums for Prestige at this time; the balance of two of them is presented here, with a long-unreleased track as a bonus. Musically it's pretty poor stuff. The ramshackle percussion tracks, modish electric pianos, preponderance of flutes and generally rambling solos give little focus to a band that was stuck between past and future. The one figure of substance (aside from Blakey himself) is Shaw, who cuts out a few hard-edged solos and gives a slightly overcooked but mainly convincing reading of 'I Can't Get Started' as the anachronistic but solid centre of the disc.

** **In My Prime Vol. 1** Timeless SJP 114
    Blakey; Valery Ponomarev (*t*); Curtis Fuller (*tb*); Bobby Watson (*as*); David Schnitter (*ts*);
    James Williams (*p*); Dennis Irwin (*b*); Ray Mantilla (*perc*). 12/77.
(*) **In This Korner Concord CCD 4068
    As above, except omit Fuller and Mantilla. 5/78.
The long gap in Blakey's discography is symptomatic of the commercial decline of jazz in the 1960s and '70s. Some good Messengers line-ups, featuring Chuck Mangione, Woody Shaw, Bill Hardman and others, made only a few records in the period, and no studio dates are currently in print. This 1977 band was workmanlike rather than outstanding, although the redoubtable Fuller lends class and Watson lends firepower. The music, though, seems to have fallen into routine. There wasn't much improvement in the first of several live sessions Blakey was to cut at San Francisco's Keystone Korner: Watson's 'Pamela', later a staple in his repertoire, is engaging, but the rest is so-so.

*** **Live At Montreux And Northsea** Timeless SJP 150
    Blakey; Valery Ponomarev, Wynton Marsalis (*t*); Robin Eubanks (*tb*); Branford Marsalis (*as,*
    bs); Bobby Watson (*as*); Bill Pierce (*ts*); James Williams (*p*); Kevin Eubanks (*g*); Charles
    Fambrough (*b*); John Ramsey (*d*). 7/80.
***(*) **Album Of The Year** Timeless SJP 155
    Blakey; Wynton Marsalis (*t*); Bobby Watson (*as*); Bill Pierce (*ts*); James Williams (*p*); Charles
    Fambrough (*b*). 4/81.
*** **In Sweden** Evidence ECD 22044
    As above. 3/81.
***(*) **Straight Ahead** Concord CCD 4168
    As above. 6/81.

***(*) **Keystone 3** Concord CCD 4196
>   As above, except Branford Marsalis (*as*) replaces Watson, Donald Brown (*p*) replaces Williams.
>   1/82.

Wynton Marsalis's arrival was a turning point for both Blakey and jazz in the 1980s. His peculiar assurance and whipcrack precision, at the age of nineteen, heralded a new school of Messengers graduates of rare confidence and ability. He plays only a minor role in the big-band album, which is devoted mainly to Watson's themes and is an exuberant round-robin of solos and blustering theme statements, with Eubanks appearing as the first guitarist in a Messengers line-up. Once Marsalis took over as MD, the ensembles took on a fresh bite and the soloists sound leaner, more pointed. The live set from Stockholm is solid stuff, if a notch behind *Album Of The Year*: Watson's feature on 'Skylark' is the best thing here, and a reminder that his time in the band has been unfairly eclipsed by Wynton's arrival. Both *Straight Ahead* and *Keystone 3* were recorded live at San Francisco's Keystone Korner (though on separate occasions), and both find a renewed involvement from Blakey himself, who's well served by the crisp recording. Watson's departure was a shade disappointing, given the tickle of creative confrontation between himself and Marsalis, but brother Branford's arrival, though he sounds as yet unformed, lends another edge of anxiety-to-please to the ensembles.

*** **Oh – By The Way** Timeless SJP 165
>   - Blakey; Terence Blanchard (*t*); Donald Harrison (*as*); Bill Pierce (*ts*); Johnny O'Neal (*p*);
>   Charles Fambrough (*b*). 5/82.
***(*) **New York Scene** Concord CCD 4256
>   Blakey; Terence Blanchard (*t*); Donald Harrison (*as*); Jean Toussaint (*ts*); Mulgrew Miller (*p*);
>   Lonnie Plaxico (*b*). 4/84.
(*) **Blue Night Timeless SJP 217
>   As above. 3/85.
*** **Live At Sweet Basil** Paddle Wheel K28P 6357
>   As above. 3/85.
*** **Live At Kimball's** Concord CCD 4307
>   As above. 4/85.
***(*) **New Year's Eve At Sweet Basil** Paddle Wheel K28P 6426
>   As above, except add Tim Williams (*tb*). 12/85.
*** **Dr Jeckyl** Paddle Wheel K28P 6462
>   As above. 12/85.
*** **Farewell** Paddle Wheel KICJ 41/41 2CD
>   As above. 3–12/85.
***(*) **Art Collection** Concord CCD 4495
>   As Concord albums above. 78–85.

Even after Marsalis departed the band, The Messengers continued their winning streak. Blanchard, whom one might call the first post-Marsalis trumpeter, proved another inspiring MD, and his partnership with Harrison made the front line sizzle. Two trumpet solos on the *New York Scene* set, on 'Oh By The Way' and 'Tenderly', show off intelligence, fire and perfectly calculated risk in some abundance. Miller and Plaxico renewed the rhythm section with superlative technique, and the old man sounds as aggressive as ever. Only *Blue Night* is routine. Although all the live sessions are good, *New York Scene* and the first *New Year's Eve* set are particularly hot, with the band sounding very rich and full on the last Paddle Wheel albums. Toussaint's brawny solos are closely in the Messengers tradition, and only Williams sounds a little out of his depth. *Farewell* was released after Blakey's death and, although these are clearly leftovers from the previously released live sets, there is at least one performance to match with the best of those records: a tempestuous reading of Bill Pierce's attractive 'Sudan Blue'. The playing time, at about 85 minutes, is rather short for a double-CD, though. *Art Collection* is a best-of culled from five of the Concord albums, and the shrewd programming and sensible choice of tracks make this a useful one-disc introduction to what Blakey was doing in the early 1980s.

*** **Hard Champion** Paddle Wheel K28P 6472
>   As above, except add Philip Harper (*t*); Kenny Garrett (*as*); Javon Jackson (*ts*); Benny Green
>   (*p*); Peter Washington (*b*); omit Williams. 3/85–5/87.
(*) **Not Yet Soul Note SN 1105
>   Blakey; Philip Harper (*t*); Robin Eubanks (*tb*); Javon Jackson (*ts*); Benny Green (*p*); Peter
>   Washington (*b*). 3/88.
(*) **Standards Paddle Wheel 292 E 6026
>   As above. 9/88.
** **I Get A Kick Out Of Bu** Soul Note SN 12155
>   As above, except Leon Dorsey (*b*) replaces Washington. 11/88.

The Blanchard/Harrison edition of The Messengers is responsible for most of *Hard Champion*, which includes a scrupulously intense reading of Shorter's 'Witch Hunt', but the new team arrive in time for one track, and they are responsible for the next four albums. Blakey's status as a bandmaster for all seasons was now as widely celebrated as anything in jazz, and taking a place in The Messengers was one of the most widespread ambitions among young players. Of those in this edition, only Jackson seems less than outstanding, with Eubanks splendidly peppery, Harper another Marsalis type with a silvery tone, and Green one of the funkiest pianists since the band's earlier days. Yet they never made a truly outstanding Messengers record together. By this time much of the excitement about neo-classic jazz had subsided and the players had a hard time escaping the scent of technique-over-feeling which was beginning to invade a lot of precision-orientated young bands. Blakey's own playing remains thunderously powerful, and he makes a lot of things happen which might otherwise have slipped away, yet the Soul Note records seem made by rote, the *Standards* set is focused only by the familiar material, and there's an overall feeling of transition which Blakey himself was too late in his career to move forward.

** **One For All** A&M 395329-2
>   Blakey; Brian Lynch (*t*); Steve Davis (*tb*); Dale Barlow, Javon Jackson (*ts*); Geoff Keezer (*p*); Essiet Okon Essiet (*b*). 4/90.
(*) **Chippin' In Timeless SJP 340
>   As above, except Frank Lacy (*tb*) replaces Davis.

Keezer aside, the final Messengers line-up is a bit disappointing: Lynch, Barlow and Jackson are all in the front of the second division, but they can't strike sparks the way the best Messenger bands could. It's hard to avoid the feeling that Blakey, too, is slowing down, though he's trying his damnedest not to let anyone know it. Nevertheless, the Timeless session includes some strong new themes, and Lacy and Keezer have energy enough to stake places in the Messengers lineage. These are decent rather than exceptional farewell records from a master.

Pierre Blanchard (born 1956) VIOLIN

*** **Music For String Quartet, Jazz Trio, Violin And Lee Konitz** Sunnyside SSC 1023
>   Blanchard; Lee Konitz (*ss, as*); Alain Hatot (*ss*); Alain Jean-Marie (*p*); Vincent Pagliarin, Hervé Cavalier (*vn*); Michel Michalakakos (*vla*); Hervé Derrien (*clo*); Césarius Alvim (*b*); André Ceccarelli (*d*). 11–12/86.

Blanchard's writing for the string players results in ripe and sometimes indulgently rhapsodic textures, for which the more sour notes and tones of Konitz are a welcome antidote. The two long pieces, 'Mani-Pulsations' and 'XVIII Brumaire', come on as too much of an inventive thing, but a reworking of Coltrane's 'Moment's Notice' finds a sharp balance between severity and lushness, and the more conventional shapes of Konitz's 'Chick Came Around' are easier to grasp. Blanchard's own playing is full of cavalier virtuosity and gallantry, and he infuses plenty of life into the other players. A word, too, for Hatot, who is barely credited yet takes a neat little solo on 'Mani-Pulsations'.

*** **Gulf String** OMD CD 1538
>   Blanchard; Vincent Pagliarin (*vn*); Claude Terranova (*ky*); Hervé Derrien (*clo*); Claude Mouton (*b*); Laurent Robin (*d*); Minino Garay (*perc*). 11/92.

If the violin weren't still such an unfashionable jazz instrument, Blanchard might find himself much better known than he is. This is an ingenious programme of themes that conflate different ideas about fusion, hard bop and world music into a single energetic package. 'Koid'9' sets up a kind of acoustic jazz-funk on a sequence of very fine improvisations by the group, and it contrasts nicely with folkish romps such as 'Folklores' and 'Isidora' or the lightly menacing 'Lithops'. Pagliarin is as tempestuous a soloist as the leader and, though Terranova's electric keyboards sometimes induce hints of elevator music, Blanchard usually introduces a new twist at the right moment. There are a couple of duds, but it's well worth investigating.

Terence Blanchard (born 1962) TRUMPET, PIANO

*** **Terence Blanchard** Columbia CK 47354
>   Blanchard; Branford Marsalis, Sam Newsome (*ts*); Bruce Barth (*p*); Rodney Whitaker (*b*); Troy Davis, Jeff Waits (*d*). 91.
*** **Simply Stated** Columbia 471364-2
>   Blanchard; Antonio Hart (*as*); Sam Newsome (*ts*); Bruce Barth (*p*); Rodney Whitaker (*b*); Troy Davis, Billy Kilson (*d*). 92.

*** **The Billie Holiday Songbook** Columbia CK 57793
    Blanchard; Bruce Barth (*p*); Chris Thomas (*b*); Troy Davis (*d*); Jeanie Bryson (*v*); orchestra. 10/
93.
**** **Romantic Defiance** Columbia 480489
    Blanchard; Kenny Garrett (*ts*); Edward Simon (*p*); Chris Thomas (b); Troy Davis (*d*). 12/94.
The titles say it all. Blanchard plays with a minimum of fuss and with admirable directness, simple and
declarative: name, rank and number – though, if you're looking for a fancier way to describe what he
does and how he sounds, 'romantic defiance' serves very well. If he looks more and more like Dizzy as
the years go by, his sound seems to come from an earlier generation, Sweets Edison and Buck Clayton
foremost. An intriguing segue from the original 'Glass J' to 'Mo' Better Blues' and thence to Ornette's
'Lonely Woman' on *Simply Stated* serves as a brief but effective history lesson.

    Blanchard took over Wynton Marsalis's chair in the Jazz Messengers (that was where he met sidekick,
Donald Harrison, who'd stepped into Branford Marsalis's shoes), but though there are superficial
similarities of approach, he's a more open-hearted player, less hung up on self-defeating standards of
authenticity. He also swings more convincingly, even on a gentle dedication to his baby daughter, 'Little
Miss Olivia Ray' (*Simply Stated* again), where he switches briefly to piano. Perhaps because Newsome is
such an uninspiring player, and because Hart's contribution is so brief (restricted to 'Dear Old
Stockholm' only), these cuts lack the punch of the Blanchard–Harrison sessions. There's some good
music nevertheless.

    One wonders how exactly the Billie Holiday project was A&R'd. 'Songbook' albums are very popular
again and, though Lady was no composer, she gave the material she sang such a highly personal cast
that a whole raft of songs – not just 'Strange Fruit' – seem eternally associated with her. At what point,
though, was Jeanie Bryson brought in as soloist? Was it to rescue a dismally bland record? Or simply
because she was available? Or was it part of the gameplan from the off? Whatever, it's the key to this
extremely patchy session. Blanchard finds interesting things to do with 'Good Morning Heartache', a
tune that sits comfortably for a brass player, and solos with some emotion on 'I Cover The Waterfront'.
But the band trudges through the rest, and it's only on Bryson's five songs that things get seriously
interesting.

    'Strange Fruit' is always a bit of a gamble for other singers. Only Nina Simone has ever got a hold of its
sheer weirdness, but Bryson takes it very simply and unaffectedly, unlike her dizzy reading of 'What A
Little Moonlight Can Do'. Encouragingly, it's an album that gets better as it goes along. The closing
'Lady Sings The Blues' instrumental gets at the elements of Herbie Nichols's tune that are often
overlooked, and Blanchard provides a nice coda.

    Romantic Defiance is the best of the bunch. It sounds as though it was recorded by a seasoned working
band. Garrett, who has been growing on his own account in recent years, plays with tremendous poise
and conviction and the rhythm section is subtly different in emphasis from the Marsalis-orbit players
who have been round Blanchard up till now. A smashing record by any standard.

(****) **X** Columbia 472806
    Blanchard; James Hynes, John Longo, Joseph Wilder (*t*); Britt Wodman, Mike Davis, Keith
O'Quinn, Timothy Williams (*tb*); Katie Dennis, Linda Blacken (*frhn*); Howard Johnson (*tba*);
Jerry Dodgion, Jerome Richardson (*as*); Branford Marsalis (*ts, ss*); Virgil Blackwell (*cl*); Blair
Tindall (*ob*); Paula Bing (*f*); Shelley Woodworth (*eng hn*); Sir Roland Hanna (*p*); Simon Shaeen
(*oud*); Tarus Mateen, Nedra Wheeler (*b*); Troy Davis, Brian Grice, James Saporito, Warren
Smith, Eugene Jackson Jr (*d*); Sue Evans, Gordon Gottlieb, Eli Fountain, Michael Baklook
(*perc*); Sanford Allen, Sandra Billingslea, Larissa Blitz, Gayle Dison, Barry Finclair, Cecilia
Hobbs Gardner, Winterton Garvey, Joyce Hammam, Rebekah Johnson, Ann Labin, Charles
Lobove, Louann Montesi, Sandra Park, Marion Pinheiro, John Pintavalle, Elliot Rosoff, Laura
Seaton, Myra Segal, Dale Stuckenbruck, Yuri Vodovoz, Belinda Whitney-Barratt (*vn*); Richard
Brice, Alfred Brown, Juliet Haffner, Lois Martin, Maxine Roach, Richard Spencer, Rebecca
Young, Harry Zaratzian (*vla*); Diane Barere, Buck Carol, David Calhoun, Anne Callahan,
Eileen Folson, Erik Friedlander, Batia Lieberman, Alvin McCall, Bruce Wang (*clo*); Joe
Bongiorno, Jacquie Danilow, Melanie Punter, Deb Spohnheimer (*b*); Boys Choir of Harlem (*v*).
92.
Almost hidden in the huge string section is the name, Maxine Roach, whose father, Max, 30 years before
recorded the fiercely activist *We Insist! Freedom Now Suite*. Blanchard's music inevitably lacks the tense
urgency of that time, but it hasn't been Hollywoodized to mere pulp. The soundtrack is an integral part
of director Spike Lee's conception and *X*, a project that had huge symbolic potency for an Afro-
American artist, was clearly going to require a sympathetic hand.

    Much of the music is, of course, in dramatic fragments, the most effective of which are perfect mini-
atures; one thinks of Branford Marsalis's soprano spots on 'Earl's Death' and 'Firebomb', the chilling,
snaky spit of the oboe on 'Assassination', the clattering drums on 'Chickens Come Home', symbolizing

the escalating cycle of violence that whirled America into a maelstrom of assassinations and backlashes. There are purely colouristic passages, like the Arabic effects backing Malcolm's pilgrimage to Mecca, and more or less conventional string interludes.

Interspersed with these, though, are powerful moments of jazz from a group that detaches from the orchestra. Only on 'The Old Days' do they get anything like enough room to stretch out, and they sound like a band one would want to hear more from. Hanna's engine-room piano contains unmistakable echos of Duke, just as Blanchard often appears to be thinking that he's stepped into Miles's shoes. Which, in a way, he has. As a wordless spokesman for black America, he has made a strong statement with the music for *X*. Unlike Anthony Davis's opera of the same name, he has avoided collageing familiar themes and reference points, concentrating instead on small, evocative themes and elements of *leitmotif* such as the quiet, contained phrases that signal Malcolm's presence. Hard to assess as a jazz album, but a major piece of work nevertheless.

Carla Bley (born 1938) PIANO, ORGAN, SYNTHESIZERS, COMPOSER

*** Escalator Over The Hill JCOA/ECM 839 310 2 2CD

Bley; Michael Mantler (*t, vtb, p*); Enrico Rava, Michael Snow (*t*); Don Cherry (*t, f, perc, v*); Sam Burtis, Jimmy Knepper, Roswell Rudd (*tb*); Jack Jeffers (*btb*); Bob Carlisle, Sharon Freeman (*frhn*); John Buckingham, Howard Johnson (*tba*); Peggy Imig, Perry Robinson (*cl*); Souren Baronian (*cl, dumbec*); Jimmy Lyons, Dewey Redman (*as*); Gato Barbieri (*ts*); Chris Woods (*bs*); Sam Brown, John McLaughlin (*g*); Karl Berger (*vib*); Don Preston (*syn, v*); Jack Bruce (*b, solo v*); Charlie Haden, Ron McClure, Richard Youngstein (*b*); Leroy Jenkins (*vn*); Nancy Newton (*vla*); Calo Scott (*clo*); Bill Morimando (*bells*); Paul Motian (*d*); Roger Dawson (*perc*); Jane Blackstone, Paul Jones, Sheila Jordan, Jeanne Lee, Timothy Marquand, Tod Papageorge, Linda Ronstadt, Bob Stewart, Viva (*solo v*); Jonathan Cott, Steve Gebhardt, Tyrus Gerlach, Eileen Hale, Rosalind Hupp (*v*). 11/68, 11/70, 3 & 6/71.

Though she was initially influenced by the likes of Monk and Miles, with all that implies, Carla Bley's imagination seems to have been heavily conditioned by European models. She quickly became disenchanted with free-form improvisation and, from the late 1960s onwards, began experimenting with large-scale composition. No jazz composition – except perhaps Mingus's 'Epitaph' – is as large and ungainly as her massive 'chronotransduction' *Escalator Over The Hill*, which is more wonderful to have heard than to listen to. A surreal, shambolic work, to an impenetrable libretto by Paul Haines, it is more closely related to the non-linear, associative cinema of avant-garde film-makers Kenneth Anger, Stan Brakhage, Maya Deren and Jonas Mekas (at whose Cinematheque some of the sessions were recorded) than to any musical parallel. The repetitious dialogue – 'again' is repeated *ad infinitum* – is largely derived from Gertrude Stein and it's perhaps best to take Stein's Alice-in-Wonderland advice and treat everything as meaning precisely what one chooses it to mean. Musically, it's a patchwork of raucous big-band themes like the opening 'Hotel Overture' (many of the events take place in Cecil Clark's Hotel with its pastiche Palm Court band), which has fine solos from Barbieri, Robinson, Haden and Rudd, heavy rock numbers like the apocalyptic 'Rawalpindi Blues' (McLaughlin, Bruce, Motian), ethnic themes from Don Cherry's Desert Band, and mysterious, ring-modulated 'dream sequences'. There is an element of recitative that, as with most opera recordings, most listeners will prefer to skip, since it doesn't advance understanding of the 'plot' one millimetre, and it's probably best to treat *Escalator* as a compilation of individual pieces with dispensable continuity. The slightly earlier *A Genuine Tong Funeral* is a genuine masterpiece on a slightly less ambitious scale and it, rather than *Escalator* (which was as much Paul Haines's work as Bley's), established her musical idiom of the 1970s.

*** Dinner Music Watt 6

Bley; Michael Mantler (*t*); Roswell Rudd (*tb*); Bob Stewart (*tba*); Carlos Ward (*as, ts*); Richard Tee (*p*); Eric Gale, Cornell Dupree (*g*); Gordon Edwards (*b*); Steve Gadd (*d*). 7, 8 & 9/76.

*** European Tour 1977 Watt 8

Bley; Michael Mantler (*t*); Roswell Rudd (*tb*); John Clark (*frhn*); Elton Dean (*as*); Gary Windo (*bs*); Terry Adams (*p*); Hugh Hopper (*b*); Andrew Cyrille (*d, perc*).

*** Musique Mecanique Watt 9

Bley; Michael Mantler (*t*); Roswell Rudd (*tb*); John Clark (*frhn*); Bob Stewart (*tba*); Alan Braufman (*f, cl, as*); Gary Windo (*bcl, ts*); Terry Adams (*p, org*); Eugene Chadbourne (*g, radio*); Steve Swallow (*b*); D. Sharpe (*d*); Karen Mantler (*glock*). 8 & 11/78.

The disappearance of *Tropic Appetites* – not yet on CD – slightly skews this early trawl through the Watt catalogue. To some degree these are much of a muchness, harmonically quirky, sometimes plain eccentric song shapes, delivered with a maximum of spin. The Brits on the European tour seemed to get the point straight away, paving a course for Carla's European bands of the 1980s and after. Earlier editions give a more detailed breakdown of these records; time makes it harder to choose between them.

(*) **Social Studies Watt/11
    Bley; Michael Mantler (*t*); Gary Valente (*tb*); Joe Daley (*euph*); Earl McIntyre (*tba*); Carlos Ward (*as, ss*); Tony Dagradi (*cl, ts*); Steve Swallow (*b*); D. Sharpe (*d*). 12/80.

***(*) **Live!** Watt/12
    Bley; Michael Mantler (*t*); Gary Valente (*tb*); Vincent Chauncey (*frhn*); Earl McIntyre (*tba, btb*); Steve Slagle (*as*); Tony Dagradi (*ts*); Arturo O'Farrill (*p, org*); Steve Swallow (*b*); D. Sharpe (*d*). 8/81.

It's at this point that Bley's imagination makes a sharp left, away from the European art-music models which haunted her throughout the 1970s, and towards a more recognizable jazz idiom which may be less authentically individual but which gains immeasurably in sheer energy. *Live!* is a treat, representing one of the finest performances by her and Mantler on record. *Social Studies* shouldn't be missed; a bookish cover masks some wonderfully wry music.

** **I Hate To Sing** Watt/12$^1_2$ LP
    Bley; Michael Mantler (*t*); Gary Valente (*tb*); Vincent Chauncey (*frhn*); Earl McIntyre (*tba, btb, v*); Steve Slagle (*as*); Tony Dagradi (*ts*); Arturo O'Farrill (*p, org, v*); Steve Swallow (*b, d*); D. Sharpe (*d, v*). 8/81–1/83.

** **Heavy Heart** Watt/14
    Bley; Michael Mantler (*t*); Gary Valente (*tb*); Earl McIntyre (*tba*); Steve Slagle (*f, as, bs*); Hiram Bullock (*g*); Kenny Kirkland (*p*); Steve Swallow (*b*); Victor Lewis (*d*); Manolo Badrena (*perc*). 9–10/83.

(*) **Night-Glo Watt/16
    Bley; Randy Brecker (*t, flhn*); Tom Malone (*tb*); Dave Taylor (*btb*); John Clark (*frhn*); Paul McCandless (*ob, eng hn, ss, ts, bcl*); Hiram Bullock (*g*); Larry Willis (*p*); Steve Swallow (*b*); Victor Lewis (*d*); Manolo Badrena (*perc*). 6–8/85.

This is a disappointing vintage in Bley's music. Despite the undoubted popularity of *I Hate To Sing*, it is one of her least imaginative small-group albums, heavily reliant on a limited range of ideas that are far more heavily embellished than usual, with camouflaging percussion and timbral effects. *Heavy Heart* is similarly disappointing, though the arrangements and voicings are beautiful and transfer well to CD. *Night-Glo* is by far the best of the trio; Oregon's Paul McCandless produces some striking woodwind effects and Hiram Bullock's guitar, not yet promoted beyond NCO status, is used more sensibly than on the first item below. Completists – and there must be lots – will be happy enough. New listeners would do better elsewhere.

(*) **Sextet Watt/17
    Bley; Hiram Bullock (*g*); Larry Willis (*p*); Steve Swallow (*b*); Victor Lewis (*d*); Don Alias (*perc*). 12/86–1/87.

*** **Duets** Watt/20
    Bley; Steve Swallow (*b*). 7–8/88.

Towards the end of the 1980s, Bley's emphasis shifted towards smaller and more intimate units. Though never a virtuosic soloist, she grew in stature as a performer. *Sextet* was unusual in having no horns, but Bley's chords are so voiced as to suggest whole areas of harmonic interest that here and in the *Duets* with Swallow remain implicit rather than fully worked out. Bullock is perhaps too insistent a spokesman, though he takes his more promising cues from the veteran bassman. By this time there is an almost telepathic understanding between Bley and Swallow (the compliment is returned in *Carla* (Xtra Watt/2), recorded under his name); the duets make an ironic but uncynical commentary on the cocktail-lounge conventions of piano-and-bass duos. It's an entertaining album and an ideal primer on Bley's compositional and improvising techniques.

***(*) **Fleur Carnivore** Watt/21 839 662
    Bley; Lew Soloff, Jens Winther (*t*); Frank Lacy (*frhn, flhn*); Gary Valente (*tb*); Bob Stewart (*tba*); Daniel Beaussier (*ob, f*); Wolfgang Puschnig (*as, f*); Andy Sheppard (*ts, cl*); Christof Lauer (*ts, ss*); Roberto Ottini (*bs, ss*); Karen Mantler (*hca, org, vib, chimes*); Steve Swallow (*b*); Buddy Williams (*d*); Don Alias (*perc*). 11/88.

This is something like a masterpiece. Having concentrated pretty much on small bands during the 1980s, Bley returned wholeheartedly to large-scale scoring and arranging, touring with a Big Band and a Very Big Band, working in an idiom that was not only unmistakably jazz but also plain unmistakable. The relation of parts to whole is far more confident than in times gone by and the solos are uniformly imaginative, with Lauer, Soloff and Mantler, K., deserving special commendation. The writing is acute and the concert recording manages to balance 'live' energy with studio precision and fullness of sound.

*** **The Very Big Carla Bley Band** Watt/23
    Bley; Guy Barker, Steven Bernstein, Claude Deppa, Lew Soloff (*t*); Richard Edwards, Gary
    Valente, Fayyaz Virji (*tb*); Ashley Slater (*btb*); Roger Janotta (*ob, f, cl, ss*); Wolfgang Puschnig
    (*as, f*); Andy Sheppard (*ts, ss*); Pete Hurt (*ts, cl*); Pablo Calogero (*bs*); Karen Mantler (*org*);
    Steve Swallow (*b*); Victor Lewis (*d*); Don Alias (*perc*). 10/90.

A stirring live outfit, the Very Big Band translate well to record, with plenty of emphasis on straightforward blowing from featured soloists Soloff, Valente, Puschnig and Sheppard. 'United States' opens
with splashy percussion, low, threatening brass figures, with the theme only really hinted at in Lew
Soloff's sensuous growl solo. The riff and horn voicings that follow are unmistakably Bley's, as is the
sudden, swinging interpolation of an entirely new theme. 'Strange Arrangement' opens with an almost
childish piano figure, which gives way to huge, shimmering harmonics that instantly explain its logic.
'Who Will Rescue You?' grows out of an almost gospelly vamp, but by this time the album has lost at
least some of its initial impetus, and 'Lo Ultimo' is a rather limping curtain-piece.

*** **Go Together** Watt 24
    Bley; Steve Swallow (*b*). Summer 92.

An intriguingly relaxed and unhurried survey of (mostly) older material, this includes beautifully judged
performances of 'Sing Me Softly Of The Blues', 'Mother Of The Dead Man' and 'Fleur Carnivore'.
Students of Bley – and there are growing numbers, even in academia – will find much of interest in these
slender, relatively unadorned arrangements. Everyone else can simply enjoy them.

*** **Big Band Theory** Watt 25
    Bley; Lew Soloff, Guy Barker, Claude Deppa, Steve Waterman (*t*); Gary Valente, Richard
    Edwards, Annie Whitehead (*tb*); Ashley Slater (*btb*); Roger Janotta (*ss, f*); Wolfgang Puschnig
    (*as, f*); Andy Sheppard (*ts, ss*); Pete Hurt (*ts*); Julian Arguëlles (*bs*); Karen Mantler (*org*); Steve
    Swallow (*b*); Dennis Mackrel (*d*). 7/93.

This never quite fulfils the promise of some exciting arrangements (notably of Mingus's 'Goodbye Pork
Pie Hat') and a rash of hot soloists, including regulars Sheppard, Soloff, Puschnig and Swallow, and
guest Alex Balanescu, who gets down to it with a will. 'Birds Of Paradise' was a commission for the
Glasgow Jazz Festival and was a serious disappointment there. Typically, though, it has been reworked
and sharpened up considerably, and it comes across much more forcefully on record.

    The main reservation about *Big Band Theory* stems from the overall balance of the recording. Though
in a warm, expansive analogue, it muffles and blurs some of the horn passages and exaggerates the
rhythm tracks, often to the detriment of subtle voicings.

*** **Songs With Legs** Watt 26
    Bley; Andy Sheppard (*ts, ss*); Steve Swallow (*b*). 5/94.

A matey trawl round Europe by three chums with a bag of songs. It isn't much more complicated than
that and just sometimes it conveys precisely that had-to-be-there feel which can be off-putting if you
weren't. Carla's compositions have become modern classics and it is fascinating to hear 'Real Life Hits'
and 'Wrong Key Donkey' given this stripped-down treatment. She doesn't put a foot wrong throughout,
but then these performances were hand-picked from six different locations, so the selection process
obviously played a part.

Paul Bley (born 1932) PIANO

***(*) **Introducing Paul Bley** Original Jazz Classics OJC 201
    Bley; Charles Mingus (*b*); Art Blakey (*p*). 11/53.
***(*) **The Fabulous Paul Bley Quintet** Musidisc MU 500542
    Bley; Don Cherry (*t*); Ornette Coleman (*as*); Charlie Haden (*b*); Billy Higgins (*d*). 7/58.
**** **Touching** Black Lion BLCD 760195
    Bley; Kent Carter, Mark Levinson (*b*); Barry Altschul (*d*). 11/65, 11/66.
**** **Open, To Love** ECM 1023
    Bley (*p* solo). 9/72.
(*) **Alone Again DIW 319/Improvising Artists Inc IAI 123840
    As above. 8/74.
***(*) **Axis** Improvising Artists Inc 123853
    Bley (*p* solo). 7/77.
*** **Tango Palace** Soul Note 1211090
    As above. 5/83.
***(*) **Solo** Justin Time Just 28
    As above. 87.

*** **Solo Piano** Steeplechase SCCD 31236
    As above. 4/88.
*** **Blues For Red** Red Records RR 123238
    As above. 5/89.
***(*) **Changing Hands** Justin Time Just 40
    As above. 2/91.
***(*) **Caravan Suite** Steeplechase SCCD 31316
    As above. 4/92.
*** **Paul Bley At Copenhagen Jazz House** Steeplechase SCCD 31348
    As above. 11/92.

There is probably no other pianist currently active with a stylistic signature as distinctively inscribed as Paul Bley's – which is ironic, for he is a restless experimenter with an inbuilt resistance to stopping long in any one place. It is difficult to formulate exactly what unifies his remarkable body of work, beyond a vague sense that Bley's enunciation and accent are different from other people's, almost as if he strikes the keyboard differently. He favours curiously ambiguous diminuendo effects, tightly pedalled chords and sparse right-hand figures, often in challengingly different metre; working solo, he creates variety and dramatic interest by gradually changing note-lengths within a steady pulse (a device introduced to keyboard literature by a minor German improviser called Ludwig van Something), and generates considerable dramatic tension by unexpectedly augmenting chords, shifting the harmonic centre constantly.

Though he has played in a number of classic groups – notably with Jimmy Giuffre and Steve Swallow, that astonishing debut with Mingus and Blakey, on which he sounds edgy and a little cautious on the standards but absolutely secure in his technique, and, more recently, with John Surman and Bill Frisell – Bley is still perhaps best heard as a solo performer. The 1958 Hillcrest Club session has an almost legendary status, by no means hindered by the shaky recording. Though it is often discussed as if it were an Ornette Coleman record (and indeed the saxophonist dominates it), it was Bley's date. Having sacked vibraphonist Dave Pike to recruit Ornette and Cherry, Bley then had to absorb their radical new music at high speed; *Something Else* had been released a short time before and, though he was winning a critical following, Ornette was still considered a radical outsider.

The first track was a version of 'Klactoveesedstene', which proceeds in a predictable bebop manner until the saxophonist takes off into his solo, at which point it is immediately obvious something revolutionary is taking place. Bley audibly does his best to stick with it but, of course, even at this stage Ornette had very little use for an orthodox accompanist. The piano solo is a little spindly, but CD transfer has put a certain amount of meat on it. Bley's contributions to the two Ornette compositions, 'The Blessing' and 'Free', are much less assured. This is clearly an important record and, technical deficiencies aside, it should be in all modern collections. However, it isn't central to Bley's recorded output.

A decade apart, the two earlier solo sets neatly overstep the most uncomfortably eclectic phase of Bley's career, when he turned to electronics in a largely unsuccessful bid to increase his tonal vocabulary.

Bley claims that he only listens to his own records nowadays. Tongue in cheek or not, there are certainly enough of them on the backlist to occupy the bulk of his non-playing time (if bulk is the right word for a musician so promiscuously active). There are also signs that Bley listens to his past records in a quite constructive sense, constantly revising and modifying his thematic development (as in these intense reveries), constantly alluding to other melodies and performances. There is, perhaps, inevitably a hint of *déjà vu* here and there, but the terrain is always much too interesting for that to become a problem.

The 1965 sessions on Black Lion were once available on an Arista Freedom double-LP which featured one of the most unpleasant covers in the history of recorded music. The playing was superb, though, and it's a great shame that the whole disc hasn't been reproduced. Long tracks like 'Mister Joy' are missing, though other Annette Peacock and Carla Bley tracks are strongly in evidence, and Paul Bley's own 'Mazatalan' suggests that he's no slouch as a writer when he so chooses. Carter and Altschul offer solid support, but the focus is all on the piano.

Solo and *Changing Hands* are uniquely thoughtful piano solos recorded back home in Montreal on a beautifully tempered instrument (and producer Jim West has to be congratulated for the immediacy and precision of the sound). Any suspicion that Bley may have become one-dimensionally meditative is allayed by the vigorous 'Boogie' on *Solo* and *Changing Hands'* remarkable interpretation of 'Summertime'. If it came down to a hard choice, the earlier album is marginally to be preferred; don't be seduced by the prettier cover.

Improvising Artists Inc was Bley's own label, releasing a wide range of innovative music (piano and otherwise) in the later 1970s. *Alone, Again* was originally released on that imprint and may still be found bearing its number. Bley's own *Axis*, named after the studio in New York's SoHo, is one of his most 'outside' performances. The title-track is not unremittingly abstract, however, and there are beautifully lyrical touches on 'Porgy', 'Music Matador' and 'El Cordobes', the tunes which made up side two of the original LP. Here's the problem: 30 minutes of music has to be considered a bit thin for a present-day CD – full price, too.

Much of his recorded output has been on similarly scaled European labels, many of them in Italy, like the *Blues* set on Red. (See also *Lyrics*, below, on Splasc(h), which mixes vocal tracks by Tizia Ghiglioni with solo pieces.) *Blues For Red* is typical in all but content. Bley doesn't normally play as much in a blues mode as this, and it's pretty effective, though by no means orthodox.

There are fine things on the Soul Note session (also recorded in Italy), but it is a mellow, after-dinner affair compared to the iced-vodka shocks of *Open, To Love*, one of Bley's finest-ever performances and the beginning of a productive relationship with ECM that only really flowered much later. Stand-out track is a fresh reading of ex-wife Carla Bley's uneasy 'Ida Lupino'. The 1988 Steeplechase has excellent sound and features the pianist in meditative mood; his reading of 'You Go To My Head' is so oblique as to suggest another tune entirely. Nevertheless there is little of the vapid meandering that afflicts so much piano improvisation; Bley is a tremendously disciplined improviser and this is one of his most intellectually rigorous albums.

The recent *Caravan Suite* is an extended examination on Ellington. There's a long version of 'In My Solitude', notably sombre accounts of 'I Got It Bad And That Ain't Good' and 'I'm Beginning To See The Light', and an extended, four-part meditation on 'Caravan'. The Steeplechase piano (a new one, we believe) is very crisp and exact, suiting the material admirably. It's certainly a better instrument than the one at the Jazz House, which has a couple of unpleasant idiosyncrasies, not helped by the close-up recording of the top end. Good playing, though.

*** Paul Bley With Gary Peacock ECM 1003
Bley; Gary Peacock (*b*); Paul Motian, Billy Elgart (*d*). 4/63.
*** Japan Suite Improvising Artists Inc 123849
As above. 7/76.

In November 1953, Bley had recorded a disc for Charles Mingus's Debut label, now available on a 12-CD compilation of all the Debut performances. A trio consisting of Charles Mingus and Art Blakey was a pretty decent coming-of-age present for a 21-year-old from Montreal, and it gave Bley a taste he was never to lose for strongly individual, not just blandly supportive sidemen. There are good things, too, from what was to be Bley's established trio. It really matured with the 1976 *Japan Suite*, a live recording that saw Bley stretching out in a more relaxed and gently textured variation of the kind of music he had made for ESP Disk. Bley's avoidance of cadences and clear tonal centres gives the piece a flowing, abstract feel quite appropriate to the oriental setting. Though a festival recording, the sound is pretty decent and has been very capably mixed. Up until that point, most of the trio's best work seems to have gone unrecorded. The ECM label's third release – following a superb Mal Waldron session and a thoroughly forgettable band led by the enigmatic Alfred Harth – highlighted 'When Will The Blues Leave', a version that bears careful comparison with the petrol-injected, steroid-laden reading on . . .

*** Footloose Savoy SV 0140
Bley; Steve Swallow (*b*); Pete LaRoca (*d*). 8/62 & 9/63.

A valuable reissue of an important session, and it's hard, listening to it after nearly 20 years, to understand why there was so very much excitement about Bill Evans when Bley was producing far more interesting and challenging piano-trio music, sometimes only a couple of blocks away. Swallow is every bit as interesting as Scott LaFaro, and LaRoca was simply one of the best drummers around.

***(*) Barrage ESP Disk ESP 1008
Bley; Dewey Johnson (*t*); Marshall Allen (*as*); Eddie Gomez (*b*); Milford Graves (*d, perc*). 10/64.
**** Closer ESP Disk ESP 1021
Bley; Steve Swallow (*b*); Barry Altschul (*d*). 12/65.

By 1964, Bley was unambiguously an avant-gardist, and it's fascinating to hear him in this company. *Barrage* is successful in a way that comes when players of wildly disparate philosophies manage to pool enough common ground to make things work. Graves in particular sounds quite restrained and formal, often seeming to take his leads from Gomez. Allen, who was to be one of the most loyal of Sun Ra's interpreters, is disconcertingly weak, and it's Johnson, a spangly, circus voice, who makes the session buzz. The best reference-point here is the verson of 'Ictus', a tune that always brings out the best and most individual in Bley.

The 1965 record should be in every collection. It's comparable in its democratic intensity and high melodic content to Chick Corea's *Song Of Singing*. Bley had, of course, worked with Swallow before, but in Altschul he was doubly blessed: a drummer who could move without strain between free playing and almost melodic straightness of line. The material here is more familiar: Carla Bley's 'Ida Lupino', Annette Peacock's 'Cartoon', 'Batterie' again from the earlier ESP.

**(*) The Paul Bley Group Soul Note 1211140
Bley; John Scofield (*g*); Steve Swallow (*b*); Barry Altschul (*d*). 3/85.

*** **Fragments** ECM 1320
     Bley; John Surman (*ss, b cl, bs*); Bill Frisell (*g*); Paul Motian (*d*). 1/86.
*** **The Paul Bley Quartet** ECM 1365
     As above.

Fragments is denied a further star only by the width of the band-book. As on the Soul Note session, recorded a year before, the writing and arranging are surprisingly below par and the recording isn't quite as clean as it might be. The Soul Note features a fine reading of Bley's staple 'Mazatalan', but little else of really compelling interest; Scofield and Swallow blend almost seamlessly, and Altschul has always been the perfect conduit for Bley's more advanced rhythmic cues. By contrast, the ECM band seems all texture, and much less structure; Frisell's almost apologetically discordant lines and reverberations blend unexpectedly well with Surman's almost equally introspective lines, and Motian – with whom Bley has duo'd to great effect – varies his emphases almost by the bar to accommodate whoever is to the forefront. The long 'Interplay' on the later, eponymous set, is disappointing enough to ease that album back a stellar notch. All three, though, are fine examples of a remarkable musician at work without preconceptions, doctrinaire stylistic theories or ego.

*** **Questions** Steeplechase SCCD 1205
     Bley; Jesper Lundgaard (*b*); Aage Tanggaard (*d*). 2/85.
*** **My Standard** Steeplechase SCCD 1214
     As above; but replace Tanggaard with Billy Hart (*d*). 12/85.
(*) **Live Steeplechase SCCD 1223
     As above, except omit Hart. 3/86.
*** **Live Again** Steeplechase SCCD 1230
     As for *Live*.
**** **Indian Summer** Steeplechase SCCD 31286
     Bley; Ron McClure (*b*); Barry Altschul (*d*). 5/87.

The mid-'80s trios for Steeplechase mark a consistent high point in Bley's now capacious output. The Danish rhythm section isn't all that special on *Questions* but it functions more than adequately. The duos with Lundgaard are pretty dry; oddly, the best performances have been held over for the follow-up *Live Again*. Bley needs a bassist with a little more poke (step forward Swallow, Peacock and the better-known Dane, NHOP – see below) or a drummer who doesn't get swamped by the sheer profusion of Bley's notes. Hart tends to drive things along quite hard, and it's only really on *Indian Summer* that one feels the chemistry is just right. This is one of the pianist's periodic blues-based programmes. Engineered by Kazunori Sigiyama, who's responsible for DIW's output, it registers brightly, essential for music which is as softly pitched as much of this is. The high points are Bley's own 'Blue Waltz' and an ironic 'The More I See You', in which he works through variations in much the same way as he had on *Caravan Suite* for the same label, reconstructing the melodies rather than simply going through the changes. It's a fine record by any standards, but it stands out prominently among the later trios.

*** **Paul Bley / NHOP** Steeplechase SCCD 31005
     Bley; Niels-Henning Orsted-Pedersen (*b*).
*** **Notes** Soul Note SN 1190
     Bley; Paul Motian (*d*). 7/87.

Years of standing behind Oscar Peterson did nothing to blunt NHOP's appetite for the job. He complements Bley's haunting chords perfectly, and on the inaugural 'Meeting' constructs an *arco* solo of great beauty over huge, ringing piano pedals (played on the electric instrument which reappears to good effect on the closing 'Gesture Without Plot' by Annette Peacock). 'Later' is perhaps the best-balanced duo performance; followed by the lively and intriguingly oblique 'Summer', it underlines once again Bley's sensitivity to his fellow-players and the emotional range of his playing.

     He is, nevertheless, absolutely distinctive. The opening notes of 'Meeting' could not be by anyone else, and a random sampling of any track uncovers his signature within half a dozen bars. The piano is appropriately well recorded and the bass is well forward with no flattening of the bottom notes (which is where NHOP works best) and no teeth-jangling distortion of his bridgework.

     Motian is always wonderful, seeming to work in a time-scale all his own, conjuring tissues of sound from the kit that seem to have nothing to do with metal or skin. Their interplay in the most demanding of all improvisational settings is intuitive and perfectly weighted.

***(*) **Rejoicing** Steeplechase SCCD 31274
     Bley; Michal Urbaniak (*vn*); Ron McClure (*b*); Barry Altschul (*d*). 5/89.

The vibrant amplified sound of the Polish-born violinist works very effectively in the context of Bley's music. Add a rhythm section as sympathetic as McClure and Altschul, and you have a formula for something rather different and unpredictable. The Monk opening is certainly unexpected and leaves Urbaniak standing, but he recovers well enough to steal a couple of well-trodden standards – 'I Can't

Get Started' and 'All The Things You Are' – and to make a dramatic contribution to 'Ictus', a tune that Bley had recorded with Jimmy Giuffre and Steve Swallow back in 1961 and again on the ESP Disk.

A slightly unusual item in Bley's list, this is nevertheless well worth sampling. Recorded live at Sweet Basil, it has a convincing live feel without too much dirt in the sound.

**** **BeBopBeBopBeBopBeBopBeBop** Steeplechase SCCD 31259
Bley; Bob Cranshaw (*b*); Keith Copeland (*d*). 12/89.

The two most distinctive performances in recent times of Charlie Parker's classic 'Now's The Time' have been by Prince (a diminutive, purple-obsessed rock person) and Paul Bley. There's a certain irony in the fact that the man who headed the palace coup that overthrew bebop at the Hillcrest Club in 1958 (the date is often credited to Ornette Coleman, but Bley was the nominal leader) should be the one to produce the most exacting and forward-looking variations on bop language in the last decade.

Far from a nostalgia album, or an easy ride for soloist and sidemen, *BeBop* is a taxingly inventive and constantly surprising run through a dozen kenspeckle bop tunes, including (a circular tribute to the label) 'Steeplechase'. Bley's chording and lower-keyboard runs on 'My Little Suede Shoes' pull that rather banal theme apart; Cranshaw's solo is superb. 'Ornithology' and 'The Theme' receive equally extended attention; the closing '52nd Street Theme' is a suitably elliptical commentary on the whole era.

This is one of the finest piano-trio records of the last ten years – or the next, depending on how you view its revisionism.

*** **The Nearness Of You** Steeplechase SCCD 1246
Bley; Ron McClure (*b*); Billy Hart (*d*). 11/88.

For those who find Bley a shade too dry, 'Take The "A" Train' rousts along like it was trying to make up time between stops. By sharp contrast, the title-track is a long reverie punctuated by angry inter-polations, almost as if a whole relationship is replaying on some inner screen. Compelling music as always, with an uncharacteristically laid-back rhythm section that on a couple of cuts might just as well have sat out and left the pianist to do his own remarkable thing. Good, well-rounded sound.

***(*) **12 (+6) In A Row** hat Art 6081
Bley; Hans Koch (*reeds*); Franz Koglmann (*flhn*). 5/90.

Arnold Schoenberg was once told that composers everywhere were adopting his twelve-tone method: 'Ah, but do they make music with it?' Most jazz musicians are highly resistant to systems and have found Schoenberg's lack of rhythmic nous distinctly off-putting; as a consequence, orthodox serialism has remained only a rather peripheral experimental temptation for eclectics like Gunther Schuller and Don Ellis. Only among jazz pianists – perhaps inevitably, given the conformation of the instrument – have serial procedures taken hold.

It's clear that even Cecil Taylor's celebrated 'atonality' is only episodic, part of a determined expansion of traditional jazz harmony. Roland Hanna, Jaki Byard and Ran Blake have nodded towards Schoenberg in much the same spirit. Paul Bley's remarkable album has to be seen in the context of a current rehabilitation of the so-called Third Stream, and of such marginalized jazz experimenters as Jimmy Giuffre. Drawing on tone-rows (non-repeating sequences of the entire chromatic scale) by Schoenberg and Anton Webern, Bley has created structures for trio improvisation that are as chal-lenging as Anthony Braxton's, and as clearly hooked into jazz tradition.

The 18 tracks – none of which is over five minutes – are divided into Bley solos, together with duos and trios in all the available permutations. The music combines highly abstract improvisation in minimalist (but, again, non-repeating) patterns with sudden blues figures, stride and boogie left-hand lines and snatches of melody, somewhat in the manner of the latter-day Giuffre/Bley/Swallow trio. The two horns have more immediate access to microtones and high harmonics, but Bley has devised a number of techniques (not all of them discernible from listening, but including currently *de rigueur* activity inside his instrument) to overcome the well-tempered resistance of the piano. It's challenging and important music. It's also highly listenable and strongly recommended.

**** **Memoirs** Soul Note 121240
Bley; Charlie Haden (*b*); Paul Motian (*d*). 7/90.

A dream line-up that promises much and delivers royally. If anything pricks the bubble of the concur-rent trio featuring Geri Allen, it is this fine set. Bley's finely spun chromatic developments are now so well judged as to give an impression of being quite conventionally resolved. Given the title and the strategically placed 'Monk's Dream' and Ornette's 'Latin Genetics', it's tempting to read the set as an attempt to summarize Bley's career over the past three decades. Haden's 'Dark Victory' and 'New Flame' and Bley's own 'Insanity' suggest how far Bley, Haden and Motian have pushed the con-ventional piano trio. Tremendous stuff.

*** **Lyrics** Splasc(h) CD H 348-2
Bley; Tiziana Ghiglioni (*v*). 3/91.

Ghiglioni's rather strained delivery does little more than point out the melody on the vocal tracks. These are interspersed by instrumental originals, which are a commentary (though recorded prior to the vocal track) on five otherwise uneventful standards. It's these re-readings which lift this rather low-key set. They're further testimony to Bley's remarkable harmonic imagination and it may that Ghiglioni felt constrained rather than inspired by them. The idea is an intriguing one, but one would like to hear him try it with a more sophisticated vocal artist, like Sheila Jordan.

***(*) In The Evenings Out There ECM 1488

Bley; John Surman (*bs, bcl*); Gary Peacock (*b*); Tony Oxley (*d*). 9/91.

It's not clear quite how to attribute this one, since material from the same session has been released under Surman's name as *Adventure Playground*. The music is entirely collaborative and there are solo tracks, duos and trios, with only one substantial group track, so the emphasis is on intimate communications across small but significant musical distances. Oxley might not at first seem to be the ideal drummer for Bley, having played regularly with Cecil Taylor and in an almost antagonistic branch of the music. They play face to face only briefly, but it is enough to suggest that Bley's style is at least capable of re-incoporating some aspects of the free jazz he appeared to have left behind.

***(*) Paul Plays Carla Steeplechase SCCD 31303

Bley; Marc Johnson (*b*); Jeff Williams (*d*). 12/91.

This contains a number of tunes by ex-wife Carla Bley that have criss-crossed Bley's playing career from the beginning. They still fall comfortably under his fingers. It's possible to trace through some of the tunes, 'Vashkar' and 'Ictus' particularly, how and where Bley's playing has changed over the years. His left-hand accents are now stronger and more insistently rhythmic than would once have been the case, and he has largely stripped away the grace notes and embellishments that once would have surrounded the solo line. It's all much cleaner and more exact, without in any way losing its romantic lilt.

**** Annette hat ART CD 6118

Bley; Franz Koglmann (*t, flhn*); Gary Peacock (*b*). 4/92.

Bley's tribute to the composer who, arguably more than any other, has shaped his output, begins and ends with takes of a theme which is almost his signature tune. Little is known (or nowadays heard) about Annette Peacock; her own career has been erratic in the extreme. However, there is no doubting the fecundity of her musical imagination, second only to Carla Bley's. *Annette* includes two versions of 'Touching' and also of 'Blood', performances of old favourites like 'El Cordobes', 'Cartoon', and 'Mister Joy'.

Koglmann's slightly frosty trumpet and flugelhorn drift across the surface of each theme, detached and utterly disenchanted, leaving the drama to be played out between Bley and Gary Peacock. The bassist's terse figures are often little more than displaced fragments of the original material, and it is these that Bley seizes upon, elaborating them into fresh themes. The trumpeter is more obviously jazz-inspired here than on *12 (+6) In A Row* and on several of his own records, but he often sounds as if he's trying to push Miles Davis's abstract modalities one final stage further. The problem for him, perhaps, is just how commanding Annette Peacock's compositions actually are.

***(*) If We May Steeplechase SCCD 31344

Bley; Jay Anderson (*b*); Adam Nussbaum (*d*). 4/93.

Not perhaps as successful as the slightly earlier Steeplechase trios (for which, see above) but a sterling performance all the same, and further testimony to Bley's willingness to reinvent himself and his repertoire. Nussbaum gives him a spacious rhythm, allowing him to stretch out on 'All The Things You Are' and 'Confirmation', two of his best-crafted solos of recent years. Once again the Steeplechase studio delivers the goods triumphantly, digital recording of marked sensitivity and warmth.

*** Know Time Justin Time JUST 57

Bley; Herbie Spanier (*t, flhn*); Geordie McDonald (*d, perc*). 8/93.

A free session by three Canadians whose paths have crossed in different permutations over the years but who have never been able to preserve this type of gig on tape. McDonald is the wild card, a composer–improviser with a huge range of sounds at his disposal. Though the stated aim is the old one of finding a basis for improvisation that goes far beyond conventional song form, there is a persistent sense that this is exactly what lies behind these 13 shortish pieces. However, items like 'Seascape', 'Cave Painting' and 'Matrix' do suggest that the prevailing analogy is not musical at all but the visual arts, and that these are not so much songs as images. They are less static than this suggests, and it is possible to hear Bley in particular hesitate between linear logic (never something he has been wedded to) and a more impressionistic, flat-plane sound that generates very different patterns of sound.

Though in some respects it sounds unresolved and even uncertain, in years to come this may be seen as one of Bley's most important later recordings, signalling yet another change of direction.

**** Time Will Tell ECM 1537
  Bley; Evan Parker (*ts, ss*); Barre Phillips (*b*). 1/94.
Superb. This is the kind of group that makes you wish you ran a festival or owned a club. The material is
divided into seven trios, two duets pairing Bley with Phillips or Parker, and two excellent Parker/Phillips
encounters. These are not apprentice players in a hurry, but mature artists who can afford the time to let
their music unfold organically. Every piece gives off a sense of having evolved spontaneously.

  The original intention was to create a setting very similar to the then recently reconvened Giuffre/Bley/
Swallow trio (whose first two records had been reissued on ECM), but the strong personalities of three
players who had not worked as a trio before very quickly asserted themselves. What is striking is how
much recent musical history, association direct or respectful with some of the giants of modern jazz.
'Poetic Justice' has a more restless quality than the rest, but the title-track is a near-perfect illustration of
the way three senior players with yard-long CVs and utterly distinctive voices are still able to touch base
with their own musical upbringing. Parker's Coltrane inflexions are only the most obvious example;
Bley and Phillips dig deep into their own memories as well. A superb album, recommendable to anyone.

*** Outside In Justin Time JUST 69
  Bley; Sonny Greenwich (*g*). 7/94.
A very spontaneous and – apparently – unrehearsed studio session following one of the guitarist's
relatively rare concert appearances at the Festival International de Jazz de Montréal in 1994. The aim
was to explore a batch of songs from without and within, working in both directions simultaneously.
The process is easier to follow on the standard and repertoire material, a very oblique interpretation of
'These Foolish Things' and versions of Eldridge's 'I Remember Harlem', Rollins's 'Pent Up House' and
Charlie Parker's 'Steeplechase', a nod in the direction of Bley's other sponsoring label. Some of the
material is clearly improvised on the spot or is based on material run down at the concert earlier.

  The playing is calm, detailed and resolutely un-intense. If improvising players now try to resist the
'conversational' analogy for what they do, this record seems to restore it. It's full of the elisions,
repetitions, non-sequiturs and sheer playfulness found in any dialogue between friends, old or new.

***(*) Synth Thesis Postcards POST 1001
  Bley (*syn*). 8/94.
A year after *Know Time* and just six months after the triumph of *Time Will Tell*, Bley recorded this
fascinating set of synth pieces. In the 1970s he had been one of the most accomplished and idiomatic
electric piano players, but his association with what is after all an amplified clavichord and thus severely
limiting did not last very long and he quickly re-established his commitment to the acoustic piano.

  The technology caught up with Bley in a sense. These tracks are subtle, imaginative and endlessly
various, with not a cliché in sight. 'Poetic License' reappears from the *Time Will Tell* session, but
transformed into a softly spoken electronic manifesto that, following 'Gentle Man' and preceding
'Augmented Ego', confirms the sense that Bley is searching for new ways of making the technology
function – as another great Canadian put it – as 'extensions of the self'. Unless you're already committed to sounds of this persuasion, it's perhaps best to sample *Synth Thesis* a track or two at a time. No
shortage of ideas, but the sound-world is still much less complex than that of a decent Steinway, or the
spanking new piano at Steeplechase, and it would be easy and wrong to be put off by that.

Urs Blochlinger (died 1995) SAXOPHONES, REEDS, PIANO, ORGAN, GUITAR, ETC.

*** Kuttel Daddel Du Plainisphare PL 1267-61
  Blochlinger; Jacques Demierre (*p*); Olivier Magnenat (*b*). 10/82.
*** Rona Unit UTR 4053
  Blochlinger; Peter Landis (*ss, ts*); Jan Schlegel (*b*). 8/92.
*** Just The One Plainisphare 1267-97
  Blochlinger; Martin Gantenbein (*d*). n.d.
Although Swiss musicians have scarcely made an international mark on jazz to date, Blochlinger man-
aged to secure a modest international platform, and his suicide closed the chapter on a very interesting
voice in the saddest way. His interests lay in the noise-making of the American avant-garde, while his
roots in European composition led to a tug-of-war between the two areas. With Magnenat and
Demierre he plays only alto, but he still favours an energetic melange of free licks and tortuous,
Braxtonian logic. His partners seem unperturbed and make the bridge between form and freedom with
calm, almost placid logic, even though the playing gets quite excitable at some points. The trio Legfek,
which is responsible for *Rona*, is harder to predict, less amiable, and Schlegel's guitar-like lines make a
nutty counterpoint between the huffing and wheezing of the two saxophonists (Blochlinger brings out
his beloved bass sax here). Neither disc is a masterpiece, but both showed an inquiring mind and an able
musician seeking unclaimed ground. The final Plainisphare disc is basically a solo recording and fea-

tures Blochlinger's reed voices refracted through the recording process into a dense mosaic. Textures are altered, darkened or lightened with restless speed, and Blochlinger uses keyboards and other instruments for colour, bass line, anything he needs. Overlapping riffs supply the heart of many of the pieces, but there is still room for particular improvisation, with the bass sax work on 'Huber' outstanding.

Jane Ira Bloom (born 1953) SOPRANO SAXOPHONE

*** **Mighty Lights** Enja 4044 807519
> Bloom; Fred Hersch (*p*); Charlie Haden (*b*); Ed Blackwell (*d*). 11/82.

***(*) **Art And Aviation** Arabesque AJ0107
> Bloom; Kenny Wheeler (*t, flhn*); Ron Horton (*t*); Kenny Werner (*p*); Rufus Reid, Michael Formanek (*b*); Jerry Granelli (*d*). 7/92.

Ms Bloom is one of the handful of musicians who play exclusively on the soprano sax, more frequently used as a secondary instrument by tenor or baritone sax players. Recent recordings – two quickly deleted albums for Columbia, which found her dabbling with electronics – suggested she was becoming disenchanted with the possibilities of the instrument in a straight-ahead jazz format; but the earlier disc is a distinctive acoustic setting. She has a sparse, considered delivery, eschewing vibrato and sentimentality: Leroy Anderson's 'Lost In The Stars' is awarded an attractively tart reading. Particularly impressive are two tracks in which Hersch sits out and Bloom, Haden and Blackwell hit a propulsive groove.

After a quiet period, Bloom returned with the fine *Art And Aviation*. The seven originals are titled to suggest a concept of flying through dark, outer-space skies and, with the peripatetic Wheeler in wonderful form and spare, sharply attuned playing by the rhythm players, the music does indeed soar and glide when it wants to. The plangency of Wheeler's brass and Bloom's acerbic delivery grant a pleasingly frosty feel to much of the playing, as if they really were performing in a still, cold atmosphere. 'Hawkins' Parallel Universe' dovetails the two horns so acutely that they might be figure-skating the melodies. In context, the cover of Monk's 'Straight No Chaser' and the farewell of 'Lost In The Stars' work perfectly; and the occasional flicker of live electronics is much better adapted than on Bloom's earlier records.

Blue Notes GROUP

*** **Live In South Africa, 1964** Ogun OGCD 007
> Chris McGregor (*p*); Mongezi Feza (*t*); Dudu Pukwana (*as*); Nick Moyake (*ts*); Johnny Dyani (*b*); Louis Moholo (*d*). 64.

The dateline tells you much of what you need to know. Two years after Sharpeville, a mixed-race group (Chris McGregor was white) playing jazz in Durban. Not long after this recording was made, the Blue Notes went to Europe to perform at the St Juan-les-Pins Jazz Festival and never returned to a country which had enacted such gloriously euphemistic legislation as the Reservation of Separate Amenities Act and other laws intended to prevent miscegenation and preserve 'morality'.

The early Blue Notes were more mixed stylistically than hindsight might have suggested. This is essentially a swing band, playing mostly in common time and with very few bebop accents. Moholo, later to be a fantastically lateral drummer, mainly keeps it straight, and the solos are delivered straight with none of the boiling dissonance that was to be a feature of later groups like Pukwana's Spear and Zila. They, of course, were founded amidst the agonies of exile and it would be idle to speculate how these six musicians (of whom only Moholo is still playing) might have developed – or not – had they lived untroubled in a liberal climate.

As the set progresses, a mixture of McGregor and Pukwana tunes, with 'I Cover The Waterfront' featuring a Gonsalves-like Moyake, it becomes possible to hear some intimations of the later style. Pukwana's 'B My Dear' has a tender plangency that was to be reasserted when the piece was re-arranged for the Dedication Orchestra in 1993 (see below). Feza is less assertive than one expects and the bulk of the solo space is devoted to alto and piano. Acoustically, the quality is no worse than one might expect, given the circumstances. Dyani is quite audible relative to McGregor, and the Kid's trumpet seems to be pointing away in another direction, which might offer some insight into the position of the mike. These are secondary issues, though. This is an important historical release for anyone interested in the development of the South African strain in British and European jazz. It conveys, particularly on the closing 'Dorkay House', something of the raw excitement of those extraordinary years.

Hamiet Bluiett (born 1940) BARITONE SAXOPHONE, ALTO CLARINET

***(*) **Resolution** Black Saint 120014
    Bluiett; Don Pullen (*p*); Fred Hopkins (*b*); Famoudou Don Moye (*perc*). 11/77.
*** **EBU** Soul Note 121088
    Bluiett; John Hicks (*p*); Fred Hopkins (*b*); Marvin Smith (*d*). 2/84.

The baritone saxophone enjoyed a brief but historically unspecific boom in the 1950s. Why then? Harry Carney had turned it into a viable solo instrument; there were probably more good ensemble players around, conscious equally of the run-down on paying gigs with big bands and of the attractions of a little solo spotlight; lastly, the prevailing role-models on alto and tenor were, perhaps, a little too dominant. By contrast, no established baritone style developed; Gerry Mulligan was as different from Serge Chaloff as Chaloff was from Pepper Adams; and round the fringes there were players like Sahib Shihab and Nick Brignola doing very different things indeed.

Currently, the situation is much the same. The three most interesting baritonists all play in markedly different styles. The young Amerasian Fred Houn is very much a Carney disciple; Britain's John Surman blows baritone as if it were a scaled-up alto (which by and large it is); Hamiet Bluiett, on the other hand, gives the big horn and his 'double', alto clarinet, a dark, Mephistophelian inflexion, concentrating on their lower registers. A fine section-player – and his work with the World Saxophone Quartet is an extension of that – he is a highly distinctive soloist.

Compared to the clutter (or exuberance – tastes vary) of the later, Africanized albums, the earlier recordings are stripped down (or downright sparse – ditto), muscular and sometimes chillingly abrasive. The *Resolution* quartet are perhaps heard to better effect on the deleted *SOS* (India Navigation IN 1039), a live New York set of near-identical vintage, but the studio cuts are still absolutely compelling. Bluiett, on baritone only, is in sterling form, relaxed in perhaps the most conducive company he has assembled on record. Pullen and Hopkins are masters of this idiom, and Moye curbs his occasionally foolish excesses. Production values aren't as hot as on the Soul Note sessions, but the music is way out in front.

A generous mix and better-than-average registration of the lead horn (the CD is first class) redeems *EBU*'s rather slack execution and raises it to front rank. Hicks is a much lighter player than Pullen and is perhaps too much of an instinctive lyricist to combine well with Bluiett's increasingly declamatory responses. The rhythm section sometimes lacks incisiveness, fatally so on a rather odd 'Night In Tunisia'.

*** **Dangerously Suite** Soul Note 121018
    Bluiett; Bob Neloms (*p*); Buster Williams (*b*); Billy Hart (*d*); Chief Bey (*African perc*); Irene Datcher (*v*). 4/81.
*** **Nali Kola** Soul Note 121188
    Bluiett; Hugh Masekela (*t, flhn*); James Plunky Branch (*ss*); Billy Spaceman Patterson (*g*); Donald Smith (*b*); Okeryema Asante, Chief Bey, Titos Sompa, Seku Tonge (*perc*); Quincy Troupe (*poet*). 7/87.

Bluiett's pan-Africanism of the early 1980s opened up for him a whole book of new rhythmic codes that helped ease him out of the still impressive but palpably finite resources of his original post-bop orientation. *Dangerously* is a transitional exercise in that it merely grafts African percussion and voice on to the basic horn/piano/rhythm quartet. It is a fine album none the less, neither tentative nor blandly 'experimental'. *Nali Kola* is certainly not tentative, but it lacks the clearly methodological premises someone like Marion Brown brings to projects of this type. The awkward instrumentation is intriguingly handled and well recorded – though the channel separation is a little crude – and Bluiett seems comfortable in his interplay with the still-adventurous Masekela and the little-known Branch and Smith, who are casual additions to the long title-track. It also features the 'verse' of Quincy Troupe, now better known for his ghosting of Miles's autobiography. As a whole, it is somewhat reminiscent of Archie Shepp's remarkable 1969 collaboration with Philly Joe Jones (America 30 AM 6102). And none the worse for that!

**** **The Clarinet Family** Black Saint 120097
    Bluiett; Dwight Andrews (*sno cl, s cl*); Don Byron, Gene Ghee, John Purcell (*s cl, bcl*); Buddy Collette (*s cl, acl*); J. D. Parran (*sno cl, s cl, acl, contralto cl*); Sir Kidd Jordan (*cbcl*); Fred Hopkins (*b*); Ronnie Burrage (*d*). 11/84.

Utterly remarkable. The ten-minute egg of hard-boiled clarinet revivalism. Bluiett's inspired project may initially sound like a discursive guide to the woodwinds; in practice, it's a deeply celebratory, almost pentecostal rediscovery of the clarinet – once the jazz voice *par excellence* – and its preterite cousins and second cousins. Kidd Jordan's hefty contrabass instrument, hitherto associated only with Anthony Braxton, must count as a second cousin, twice removed; pitched at double B flat, it has an extraordinary tonality, as on 'River Niger', a Jordan composition that conjures up oddly disconnected echoes of Paul Robeson in *Sanders of the River*.

There's a strong sense of tradition through this fine live set, recorded in Berlin: two long tributes to Machito – a very different 'Macho' from the one credited to Steve Turre on the Brass Fantasy's ECM *Avant Pop* – and Duke Ellington, well-shared-out compositional credits, a startling bass solo from Hopkins, and, following it, a beautifully judged climax. After *Resolution* and the better of the WSQ albums, this is the essential Bluiett album, albeit one in which he plays a collective and slightly understated role.

*** **You Don't Need To Know . . . If You Have To Ask** Tutu CD 888 128
 Bluiett; Thomas Ebow Ansah (*g, v*); Fred Hopkins (*b*); Michael Carvin (*d*); Okeryema Asante (*perc, v*). 2/91.
***(*) **Sankofa / Rear Garde** Soul Note 121238
 Bluiett; Ted Dunbar (*g*); Clint Houston (*b*); Ben Riley (*d*). 10/92.
The title refers to a celebrated riposte of Louis Armstrong's when asked what jazz really was. In the context of that his quotation of the celebrated waltz theme at the beginning of 'Black Danube', a tune described by drummer Carvin as 'James Brown in 3/4 time', has to be seen as slightly ironic in the context of Bluiett's now thoroughly Africanized approach to jazz performance. The rhythmic base, whether by Carvin or Asante, is in most cases the essence of the piece, over which Bluiett improvises with considerable freedom. His alto flute makes an effective opening to 'If Only We Knew' and Asante's percussion line bridges the piece with 'T. S. Monk, Sir' on which the baritone and bass punch out a respectful pastiche of the great pianist. Guitarist Thomas Ebow Ansah's vocal 'Ei Owora Befame-Ko' is built on a syncopated chord-sequence of the sort Bluiett instinctively heads for in his own compositions, and the two voices harmonize superbly, with Bluiett punctuating the melody with great bull-roar effects.

 The last-but-one track of the session is perhaps the most straightforward and the most conventionally jazz-orientated. 'The Gift: One Shot From The Hip' has the kind of headlong, thunderous urgency that Bluiett can generate as a soloist, with Hopkins and Carvin tucked in behind like a three-man bob team. The bassist gets his big feature on 'Goodbye Pork Pie Hat', but it's on 'The Gift' that his long-standing commitment to Bluiett's music pays its most generous dividends.

Arthur Blythe (born 1940) ALTO SAXOPHONE

***(*) **In Concert** India Navigation IN 1029
 Blythe; Ahmed Abdullah (*t*); Bob Stewart (*tba*); Abdul Wadud (*clo*); Steve Reid (*d*);
 Muhammad Abdullah (*perc*). 2/77.
Arthur Blythe has attracted almost as much 'what went wrong' copy as Desert Orchid and Barry McGuigan. His India Navigation sets of the late 1970s were breathtakingly original and his form-sheet included demanding and chops-quickening stints with Gil Evans and Horace Tapscott. In 1979, he signed with Columbia. *Lenox Avenue Breakdown* was a masterpiece of imaginative instrumentation; there were two more fine albums, and then Blythe's wind went.

 It's good to have *In Concert*, with its two major pieces, 'Metamorphosis' and 'The Grip', back in the catalogue. The band has the sort of dark, experimental feel of Tapscott's West Coast collectives. The use of Stewart is brilliant and the absence of a string bassist irrelevant in face of his robust *legato* playing. Ahmed Abdullah is sharp and forceful, combining elements of Pops with Roy Eldridge and Charlie Shavers (and, frankly, nothing more contemporary than that). Blythe's solo formation isn't always entirely secure, but he is brimming over with ideas and attempts to string them together at least logically.

*** **Hipmotism** Enja ENJ 6088
 Blythe; Hamiet Bluiett (*bs*); Kelvyn Bell (*g*); Gust William Tsilis (*vib, mar*); Bob Stewart (*tba*);
 Arto Tuncboyaci (*perc, v*); Famoudou Don Moye (*d*). 3/91.
*** **Retroflection** Enja ENJ 8046
 Blythe; John Hicks (*p*); Cecil McBee (*b*); Bobby Battle (*d*). 6/93.
For all the personal references and dedications, Blythe still betrays a lack of essential spirit on *Hipmotism*. There are also signs, most seriously on the opening trio and the concluding, unaccompanied 'My Son Ra', that his articulation problems are becoming more evident. The Village Vanguard session that makes up *Retroflection* finds him in better voice, technically speaking, but decidedly short of ideas. A more or less routine re-run of 'Lenox Avenue Breakdown' is relieved by crisp, sensitive playing from the group. Hicks is a total professional and McBee is absolutely on the spot, both harmonically and rhythmically. No complaints whatever there, but still an unsatisfyingly hollow centre.

 The blend of instrumental voices on *Hipmotism* is intriguing enough to carry the day. There are only three all-in tracks, 'Matter Of Fact' and 'Bush Baby', both of them notably abstract, and the title-piece, which is simple and roistering. Blythe sounds good on them all, feeding off the deeper, darker sounds of Stewart's tuba and guest Bluiett's brassy baritone. The sparser settings expose him mercilessly and 'Miss

Eugie', for alto saxophone, tuba and Tuncboyaci's percussion and voice, requires a more forceful performance.

A partial return to form, well conceived and produced. And there's a bonus for CD purchasers who loathe those brittle plastic boxes and yearn for old-style album sleeves: the new Enjas come in attractive fold-out laminated card with a plastic insert for the disc. Almost like the real thing again.

Peter Bocage (1887–1967) TRUMPET, VIOLIN

** Peter Bocage With His Creole Serenaders And The Love–Jiles Ragtime Orchestra Original Jazz Classics OJC 1835-2

> Bocage; Charlie Love (*t*); Homer Eugene, Albert Warner (*tb*); Louis Cottrell, Paul Barnes (*cl*); Benjamin Turner (*p*); Sidney Pflueger (*g*); Emanuel Sayles (*bj*); McNeal Breaux, Auguste Lanoix (*b*); Alfred Williams, Albert Jiles (*d*). 6/60–1/61.

One of the weakest entries in Riverside's *New Orleans: The Living Legends* series, and it does no justice to a brassman who first recorded with A. J. Piron in the early 1920s. Bocage sounds faltering and shaky on the tracks where he leads his Creole Serenaders and, though Cottrell provides some bright moments, this is pretty lame stuff. Bocage plays violin as a sideman in the Love–Jiles group, which handles five rags without a great deal of panache – Warner in particular plays some atrocious trombone. Definitely one for hardcore specialists only.

Claudio Bolli TRUMPET, FLUGELHORN

*** Empty Jazz Quintet & Octet Splasc(h) H 371-2

> Bolli; Luca Begonia, Alessio Nava (*tb*); Claudio Chiara (*as*); Fulvio Albano (*ts*); Marco Visconti Prasea (*bs*); Paolo Brioschi (*p*); Roberto Piccolo (*b*); Ferdinando Farao (*d*). 7–9/91.

The group name is asking for trouble, but this is light, bright post-bop from a mixed confederacy of old and young hands. Bolli himself plays an Art Farmer-like horn, reticent rather than pushy, and the other players all seem reluctant to take a firm lead. As far as co-operative spirit goes, though, it's amiably up to the mark.

Sharkey Bonano (1904–72) TRUMPET, CORNET, VOCAL

*** Sharkey Bonano 1928–1937 Timeless CBC 1-001

> Bonano; Santo Pecora, Moe Zudecoff, Julian Lane, George Brunies (*tb*); Meyer Weinberg (*cl, as*); Sidney Arodin (*cl, tin whistle*); Joe Marsala, Irving Fazola (*cl*); Hal Jordy (*as, bs*); Dave Winstein (*ts*); Johnny Miller, Clyde Hart, Joe Bushkin, Stan Wrightsman, Freddy Newman, Armand Hug (*p*); Joe Cupero, Frank Federico, Eddie Condon (*g*); Bill Bourjois (*bj, g*); Steve Brou (*bj*); Luther Lamar (*tba, b*); Chink Martin, Ray Bonitas, Thurman Teague, Artie Shapiro, Hank Wayland (*b*); Monk Hazel (*d, mel, v*); Leo Adde, Augie Schellange, Ben Pollack, George Wettling, Al Sidell, Riley Scott (*d*). 4/28–4/37.

Bonano is conventionally placed as a New Orleans man, but though he was a native of the town his early career points elsewhere – he tried out as replacement for Beiderbecke with both The Wolverines and Jean Goldkette, for instance. The first two (little-known) sessions here, though, are among the very few home-grown New Orleans sessions of the 1920s – both showing an ironic New York influence, but with fine clarinet by Sidney Arodin and Bonano proving that he had a light but curiously engaging lead as a cornetist. A jump forward to 1936 brings a more Dixieland-orientated sound, and three further sessions from 1936–7 find him in New York with a band largely made up of Condonites. Four tracks by a Santo Pecora group with Shorty Sherock on trumpet round off the disc. Bonano's vaudevillian vocals dominate several tracks, but when his trumpet emerges he sounds in good fettle, and there are useful glimpses of the New Orleans clarinet of Fazola. A mixed but entertaining bag, and the remastering is fine.

*** Sharkey Bonano At Lenfant's Lounge Storyville STCD 6015

> Bonano; Jack Delaney (*tb*); Bujie Centobie (*cl*); Stanley Mendelson (*p*); Arnold 'Deacon' Loyacano (*b*); Abbie Brunies, Monk Hazel (*d*); Lizzie Miles (*v*). 8–9/52.

*** Sharkey Bonano And His Band Storyville STCD 6011

> As above, except omit Hazel and Miles. 12/52.

Bonano almost inevitably returned to New Orleans and spent most of the rest of his life there, working and recording frequently in the aftermath of the New Orleans revival of the 1940s and '50s. Location recordings catch his able band in lively form. The leader's own playing suggests that he was more convincing as a front man than as a soloist: if he tries to push too hard, his tone thins out and his phrases buckle. But Delaney and Centobie are both perfectly assured soloists, and Bonano sensibly gives them the lion's share of the attention. Lizzie Miles sings a couple of vocals on the first record and shouts encouragement too. The recordings are clear enough, though they don't have much sparkle, but the swing of the band stands up well: another valuable document of a genuine New Orleans outfit, playing to orders – the material is very familiar – but making the most of it.

Bone Structure GROUP

(*) **Bone Structure Calligraph CLG 020

> Mark Nightingale, Richard Edwards, Colin Hill, Andy Hutchinson (*tb*); Nigel Barr (*btb*); Pete Murray (*p*); Mike Eaves (*g*); Don Richardson (*b*); Chris Barron (*d*); Lorraine Craig (*v*). 4–5/88.

There have been all-trombone front lines before, courtesy of J. J. Johnson, Slide Hampton and others, but this British group approach the task with a flair and nicely deadpan wit which alleviate the built-in blandness of their sound. It's hard to make trombones sound interesting across the length of a record if they set out to avoid the expressionist approach, and Nightingale's team tend to impress through dexterity and timing. Nor do they truly sidestep the novelty aspects of the group, a trait which has plagued British trad and mainstream: Horace Silver's 'Doodlin'' is taken at a silly, ambling pace, and the sonorous treatment of 'Lush Life' seems designed more to elicit gee-whiz reactions than anything else. But their up-tempo pieces are delivered with a punch that overcomes doubts about musical integrity: if, at times, one longs to hear them loosen up, that may have more to do with the metronomic feel of the rhythm section.

Ntshukumo Bonga ALTO SAXOPHONE, CLARINET, VOCALS

***(*) **Tshisa! Urban Ritual** Slam CD 213

> Bonga; Marcio Mattos (*clo, b*); Ken Hyder (*d, perc, v*). 9 & 12/94.

The key track here is 'Mzangwa, Mzangwa', a thirteen-minute tribute to Ntshuks Bonga's most obvious stylistic influence, the late Dudu Pukwana. Like an earlier generation of South African exiles in Britain, Bonga shows a remarkable facility in both patterned and free music; though he also works in more established African contexts (albeit dismissive of the notion that South African music is reducible to kwela), it is as a spontaneous improviser that he is most effective.

In Xhosa, 'Tshisa' means 'to burn' or 'to set alight', and there is an incendiary quality in Bonga's playing which, like Pukwana's on occasion, yields more heat than light. The presence of Mattos and Hyder, though, tempers the more flagrant aspects considerably and in the process gives the music a much darker and more penetrating quality. Bassist and drummer are both deeply interested in oriental forms, and Hyder's now long-standing involvement in trans-Siberian, shamanistic music comes across in hauntingly vocalized passages and in his remarkably open-minded and uncluttered sense of musical space. Mattos's cello provides drones from a similar source.

Pieces like 'Ancient Whispers' and 'Before The Snow' point in the direction this music always promises to go, without ever quite delivering the sheer impact of a trio who, in a live context, roar along like the most unfettered free-jazz group.

Raymond Boni GUITAR

***(*) **Le Goût Du Jour** CELP C18

> Boni; Jean Luc Cappuzzo (*t, bugle*); Jacques Veille (*tb*); Michèle Fernandez (*ss, v*); Pascal Lloret (*p, syn*); Geneviève Sorin (*acc*); Bernard Abeile (*b*); Michel Boiton (*d, perc*). 8/91.

Like Louis Sclavis and Henri Texier, Boni works in an area that cannot narrowly be defined as jazz but certainly can't be pigeonholed as world music. He makes use of folk themes, waltzes and tangos, but places them in improvisational settings that maximize performers' freedom. As in Joe McPhee's Po Music ensemble, of which Boni is an important member, the balance between structure and freedom is very delicately maintained.

Le Goût Du Jour begins boldly with 'S'bo', a vestigial theme grafted on to Michel Boiton's long, surprisingly basic drum solo. The next track, 'Bateau De Mes Rêveries', is a feature for trombonist Veille, but Boni is always there or thereabouts, laying down clangorous guitar riffs and patterns. The opening of 'La Promesse' is a good example of the heavily amplified but reined-in style that he favours. Geneviève Sorin is the featured artist on 'Zé', which is influenced by North African music. 'Le Repos Du

Danseur' is a dark, throbbing finale, with Patrick Williams's poem 'Le Studio Ensoleillé' inserted as a coda, spoken by Michèle Fernandez over a simple bass pattern.

The disc makes an impressive start to Boni's solo career. Like Marc Ducret, he will always be in demand as a sideman, offering an alternative to the prevailing Bill Frisell approach. But he also shows a considerable musical intelligence and a gift for marshalling disparate musics and performance styles into a satisfying whole.

Luis Bonilla TROMBONE, BASS TROMBONE

*** **Pasos Gigantes** Candid CCD 79507
    Bonilla; Tony Lujan (*t, flhn*); Kenny Goldberg (*as, bs, f*); Justo Almario (*ts, ss, f*); Otmaro Ruiz (*p, syn*); Abe Laboriel (*b*); Alejandro Neciosup Acuna (*d, perc*); Michito Sanchez (*perc*). 2/91.
A member of Lester Bowie's saxless Brass Fantasy, Bonilla is a trombone revivalist who's nodded to J. J. Johnson and Ray Anderson as influences. His own debut is a lively Latin-jazz session without much in the way of surprise. The arrangement of 'Giant Steps', which provides the album's title, is nice, if a bit obvious; and it's clear that the trombonist knows his way round those graduation-class changes.

Unfortunately the rest of the group doesn't quite match up. Except perhaps Laboriel, they sound a little as if they're trying to keep up with unfamiliar charts, and there's too much pointless time-filling on the straight Latin numbers. Anyone who's seen Bonilla with Brass Fantasy knows that he's capable of far, far more than he's been able to deliver on record until now.

Joe Bonner (born 1948) PIANO

**** **Parade** Steeplechase SCCD 31116
    Bonner; Johnny Dyani (*b*); Billy Higgins (*d*). 2/79.
***(*) **Suite For Chocolate** Steeplechase SCCD 31215
    Bonner; Khan Jamal (*vib*); Jesper Lundgaard (*b*); Leroy Lowe (*d*). 11/85.
*** **New Life** Steeplechase SCCD 31239
    Bonner; Hugo Rasmussen (*b*); Aage Tanggaard (*d*). 8/86.
**** **The Lost Melody** Steeplechase SCCD 31227
    Bonner; Bob Rockwell (*ts*); Jesper Lundgaard (*b*); Jukkis Uotila (*d*). 3/87.
*** **Impressions Of Copenhagen** Evidence ECD 22024
    Bonner; Eddie Shu (*t*); Gary Olson (*tb*); Holly Hoffman (*f*); Paul Warburton (*b*); J. Thomas Tilton (*d*); Carol Michalowski (*vn*); Carol Garrett (*vla*); Beverley Woolery (*clo*).
Bonner is an impressive modernist whose occasional resemblance to Thelonious Monk probably stems from the fact that he has listened and paid attention to the same swing-era players that Monk did. He has a surprisingly light touch (too light on some of the Steeplechases, where the miking sounds a bit remote) and he can seem a little diffident. He is, though, a fine solo performer, with a rolling, gospelly delivery, and an adventurous group leader. Much of his most distinctive work has been with the late Johnny Dyani, not all of it currently available; over several albums they developed a rapport that seems to cement ever more strongly as they move outwards from settled bop progressions and into freer territory. The African elements also emerge in the lovely *Suite For Chocolate*, which shouldn't be overlooked or dismissed as a soundtrack album.

The Lost Melody is a good group session, marked by strong charts and just the right element of freedom for Rockwell, a fine soloist within his own square of turf, but apt to flounder beyond it. *Impressions Of Copenhagen* is now on Evidence, with a bonus version of 'Lush Life'. There are some effectively impressionistic moments and the use of strings is quite original and uncluttered, but it's a bit of a by-blow and not really consistent in either tone or quality with Bonner's impressive jazz output.

René Bottlang PIANO

*** **The Lausanne Concert** Plainisphare PL 1267-39
    Bottlang; Mal Waldron (*p*). 12/87.
(*) **Voyages Divers Plainisphare PL1267-70
    Bottlang; Jean Querlier (*ss, as*). 4/91.
***(*) **Round About Boby** Plainisphare PL 1267-91
    Bottland; Jean Querlier (*as*); Claude Tchamitchian (*b*); Youval Micemacher (*d*); Phil Minton (*v*). 10/92.
As might be expected from Waldron's part in it, *The Lausanne Concert* is essentially minimalist in

approach, but grandly, almost classically, expressive nevertheless. The Swiss is a fine technician who solos with confidence and, though he doesn't have Waldron's mastery of Monk tunes – 'Evidence' and 'Epistrophy' – he gets stuck in anyway and pulls out a few plums all on his own. *Voyages Divers* is an introverted and rather odd sequence of duets with the similarly reserved Querlier and, since the sound is so remote – the saxophonist often sounds like he's miles away – what little impact there could have been is dissipated. That said, there is some keen intelligence at work in the structure and unfolding of these pieces.

Better still is the concert recording dedicated to Boby Lapointe. This is a memorable group, Bottlang's precise pianistics and Querlier's rather prim freedom banked alongside the looser, swinging rhythms of Tchamitchian and Micemacher. Minton's particular brand of vocal madness enters this world with surprising ease and there are all sorts of felicitous passages: try the way the group builds towards the very fine bass solo in 'Marcelle', for a single example. This time the sound-mix is very vivid and effective.

Ralph Bowen TENOR SAXOPHONE

***(*) **Movin' On** Criss Cross Criss 1066
      Bowen; Jim Beard (*p*); Jon Herington (*g*); Anthony Jackson (*b*); Ben Perowsky (*d*). 12/92.
An able and in-demand sideman, Bowen took his time before recording a debut solo album. It was worth the wait. Bowen has been writing and putting by original themes since he was in his teens, and it's a symptom of his remarkable self-possession that he should have picked seven of them for *Movin' On* rather than opting for more familiar repertoire material.

The title-piece is entirely characteristic, a lean but lyrical tune that propels him into the first of what is to be a batch of fine solos. Apprenticeship with Horace Silver has left an unmistakable mark on Bowen's writing, but it is Silver the melodist who predominates. Bowen rarely forces the pace, allowing each theme to dictate its own momentum. 'A Little Silver In My Pocket' is the most direct homage, and Jim Beard draws a completely idiomatic solo with a brisk, bouncy left-hand part.

Only on the longish 'Just Reconnoitering' does Bowen start to repeat himself. To some extent the piece draws on Coltrane's 'sheets of sound' approach, but this isn't a comfortable route, and the piece resolves itself much more conventionally. Mixed well up, the two guitars bring a soulful groove to 'Thru Traffic'; Herington draws heavily on Pat LaBarbera licks, but it's Jackson who impresses with a fluid legato.

It's rare to come across a debut record so comfortably in possession of its own language. If in the past there's been a suspicion that producer Gerry Teekens has given undue prominence to journeyman horn-players with no more to say for themselves than you might hope to hear on an average club date, Bowen's debut stands up resolutely on its own merits.

Lester Bowie (born 1940) TRUMPET, FLUGELHORN

*** **The Fifth Power** Black Saint 120020-2
      Bowie; Arthur Blythe (*as*); Amina Claudine Myers (*p, v*); Malachi Favors (*b*); Phillip Wilson (*d*). 4/78.
Bowie's 1970s band provides a more straightforward kind of post-Chicago jazz, but this quintet is loaded with expressive talent. Blythe and Myers are the outsiders here, yet their different kinds of playing – Blythe is swaggeringly verbose, Myers a gospellish spirit – add new flavours to Bowie's sardonic music. The 18 minutes of 'God Has Smiled On Me' are several too many, although the ferocious free-for-all in the middle is very excitingly done, while '3 In 1' finds a beautiful balance between freedom and form.

*** **The Great Pretender** ECM 1209
      Bowie; Hamiet Bluiett (*bs*); Donald Smith (*ky*); Fred Wilson (*b*); Phillip Wilson (*d*); Fontella Bass, David Peaston (*v*). 6/81.
(*) **All The Magic! ECM 1246/7 2CD
      As above, except Ari Brown (*ss, ts*), Art Matthews (*p*) replace Bluiett and Smith. 6/82.
This was a disappointing band, at least on record: in concert, David Peaston's rendition of 'Everything Must Change' was astonishingly uplifting, but the version on *All The Magic!* is disarmingly tame. *The Great Pretender* began Bowie's exploration of pop standards as vehicles for extended free-jazz satire, but it tends to go on for too long. Perhaps the typically resplendent ECM recording didn't suit the group, although 'Rios Negroes' is a fine feature for the leader. The second half of *All The Magic!*, though, multitracks Bowie's trumpet into a gallery of grotesques: his style has matured into a lexicon of smears, growls, chirrups and other effects, and here he uses it as an expressionist cartoon.

**(*) I Only Have Eyes For You ECM 1296
> Bowie; Stanton Davis, Malachi Thompson, Bruce Purse (*t*); Steve Turre, Craig Harris (*tb*); Vincent Chauncey (*frhn*); Bob Stewart (*tba*); Phillip Wilson (*d*). 2/85.

**(*) Avant Pop ECM 1326
> As above, except Rasul Siddik (*t*) and Frank Lacy (*tb*) replace Purse and Harris. 3/86.

*** Serious Fun DIW 834/8035
> Bowie; Stanton Davis, E. J. Allen, Gerald Brezel (*t*); Steve Turre, Frank Lacy (*tb*); Vincent Chauncey (*frhn*); Bob Stewart (*tba*); Vinnie Johnson, Ken Cruchfield (*d*); Famoudou Don Moye (*perc*). 4/89.

These records are by Bowie's group, Brass Fantasy, a band with an unprecedented instrumentation – at least, in modern jazz. The brass-heavy line-up has obvious echoes of marching bands and the oldest kinds of jazz, however, and one expects a provocative kind of neo-traditionalism with Bowie at the helm. But Brass Fantasy seldom delivers much more than a lightweight irreverence on record. The first two albums have some surprising choices of covers, including Whitney Houston's 'Saving All My Love For You' and Lloyd Price's 'Personality', but the studio seems to stifle some of the freewheeling bravado of the ensemble, and Bowie himself resorts to a disappointing self-parody. Just as one thinks it can go no further, though, the DIW disc displays a fresh maturity: the brass voicing acquires a broader resonance, the section-work sounds funkier and, although the improvising is still too predictable, it suggests altogether that the group still has plenty left to play.

*** Works ECM 837 274
> Bowie; various groups. 81–86.

A respectable compilation from Bowie's four ECM records, plus one track ('Charlie M') from the AEOC's *Full Force*.

*** The Organizer DIW 821
> Bowie; Steve Turre (*tb*); James Carter (*ts*); Amina Claudine Myers (*org*); Famoudou Don Moye, Phillip Wilson (*d*). 1/91.

Bowie strips out the horns and adds Amina Myers on organ: it's really an update of his Fifth Power band of the 1970s, and it works out fine, though the music trades the visceral punch of organ-soul jazz for a more rambling and discursive impact. Turre, as usual, gets in some of the best shots on trombone.

***(*) My Way DIW 835
> Bowie; Stanton Davis, E. J. Allen, Gerald Brazel, Earl Garner (*t*); Steve Turre (*tb, conch*); Frank Lacy (*tb, v*); Gregory Williams (*frhn*); Bob Stewart (*tba*); Vinnie Johnson, Ken Crutchfield (*d*); Famoudou Don Moye (*perc*). 1/90.

**** The Fire This Time In + Out IOR 7019-2
> As above, except add Tony Barrero (*t*), Louis Bonilla (*tb*), Vincent Chauncey (*frhn*); omit Davis, Turre, Williams, Garner and Crutchfield. 5/92.

In the past this project seemed like an amusing – if not especially productive – vehicle for Bowie to mess around with. These two releases snap the whole thing into focus. The three originals which lead off *My Way* explore the sonorities of the band as never before; the playing glitters with a new finesse, and the improvising has real gravitas. 'My Way' itself should have been too cornball and obvious, but the superb central solo by Turre denies all that. 'I Got You' really is too obvious, but the closing 'Honky Tonk' is a good one.

The live album, performed the day after the Los Angeles riots, is properly uproarious – some more fine charts, covers that stretch from Jimmie Lunceford's 'Siesta For The Fiesta' to Michael Jackson's 'Black Or White', and the climactic 'The Great Pretender' is the version to top them all. About time.

Ronnie Boykins BASS, SOUSAPHONE

** Ronnie Boykins ESP Disk 3026
> Boykins: Daoud Haroon (*tb*); Joe Ferguson (*f, ss, ts*); Jimmy Vass (*f, as, ss*); Monty Waters (*as, ss*); Art Lewis (*d, perc*); George Avaloz (*perc*). 2/75.

Boykins's most significant recording credit came with Sun Ra's *Heliocentric Worlds* sessions for ESP Disk. There are signs that he has attempted to capture the Arkestra's strange compromise between discipline and anarchy on his own first solo record, but it doesn't quite work. The playing is fine, with good things from the dark-voiced Haroon in particular, but the material is uniformly duff and the recording (even tidied up for CD release) reduces an already over-egged saxophone section to mush. ESP was a pretty tired operation by 1975 and this must be one of the drabbest items in the revived catalogue.

Charles Brackeen (born 1940) TENOR SAXOPHONE, SOPRANO SAXOPHONE

*** Rhythm X Strata East 660.51.019
    Brackeen; Don Cherry (*t*); Charlie Haden (*b*); Ed Blackwell (*d*). 1/68.
*** Bannar Silkheart SH 105
    Brackeen; Dennis Gonzalez (*t*); Malachi Favors (*b*); Alvin Fielder (*d*). 2/87.
*** Attainment Silkheart SH 110
    Brackeen; Olu Dara (*c*); Fred Hopkins (*b*); Andrew Cyrille (*d, perc*); Dennis Gonzalez (*perc*).
    11/87.
**** Worshippers Come Nigh Silkheart SH 111 As above; 11/87.
In 1986 the managing director of the recently founded Silkheart Records tracked down the reclusive Brackeen and persuaded him to record again. Over the following year, the saxophonist cut three astonishing albums for the label that are as fine as anything released in the late 1980s.

If Coltrane was the overdetermining presence for most saxophonists of the period, Brackeen seems virtually untouched, working instead in a vein reminiscent alternately of Ornette Coleman (as in the stop-start melodic stutter of 'Three Monks Suite' on *Bannar*) and Albert Ayler ('Allah' on the same album). He favours a high, slightly pinched tone; his soprano frequently resembles clarinet, and his tenor work is punctuated by Aylerish sallies into the 'false' upper register. The 'Three Monks Suite' is wholly composed and Brackeen really lets go as a soloist on *Bannar* only with 'Story', a limping melody with enough tightly packed musical information to fuel two superb solos from the horns.

The two November 1987 sessions are even more remarkable. Gonzalez is a fine, emotive trumpeter but he lacks the blowtorch urgency of Dara's more hotly pitched cornet. 'Worshippers Come Nigh' is as exciting a jazz piece as any in the catalogue, underpinned by Hopkins's fine touch (less spacious than Favors but generously responsive) and Cyrille's percussion. 'Bannar' confusingly finds its way on to this album rather than the one named after it, but all three have to be seen as a unit. *Attainment* is the least satisfying, but only because there are no solos on a par with 'Worshippers' and 'Story'. However, it does include the fascinating sax/bass/drums trio 'House Of Gold'.

Recently restored to the catalogue, *Rhythm X* is a valuable glimpse of the earlier, pre-sabbatical Brackeen. The risk of confusion with Ornette's *Song X* is likely to be compounded by the presence of Cherry, Haden and Blackwell, three-quarters of one of the great jazz groups of all time, and by Brackeen's still largely unreconstructed Texan sound. Though nowhere near as individual as the later Silkhearts, the 1968 record is packed with gritty detail.

JoAnne Brackeen (born 1938) PIANO

*** New True Illusion Timeless SJP 103
    Brackeen; Clint Houston (*b*). 7/76.
*** AFT Timeless SJP 115
    As above, but add Ryo Kawasaki (*g*). 12/77.
**** Havin' Fun Concord CCD 4280
    Brackeen; Cecil McBee (*b*); Al Foster (*d*). 6/85.
*** Fi-Fi Goes To Heaven Concord CCD 4316
    As above, but add Terence Blanchard (*t*); Branford Marsalis (*ss, as*). 10/86.
***(*) Live At Maybeck Recital Hall, Volume 1 Concord CCD 4409
    Brackeen solo. 6/89.
**** Where Legends Dwell Ken 660 56 021
    Brackeen; Eddie Gomez (*b*); Jack DeJohnette (*d*). 3 & 4/91.
*** Breath Of Brazil Concord CCD 4479
    Brackeen; Eddie Gomez (*b*); Duduka Fonseca (*d*); Waltinho Anastacio (*perc*). 4/91.
***(*) Take A Chance Concord CCD 4602
    As above. 6/93.
**** Power Talk Turnipseed Music TMCD 08
    Brackeen; Ira Coleman (*b*); Tony Reedus (*d*). 4/94.
Always useful as a jazz trivia stumper: what white woman played piano for the Jazz Messengers? JoAnne Brackeen hung on to the piano chair with Blakey between 1969 and 1971; a poorly recorded spell, so, just to prove she could do it, she recorded *Fi-Fi Goes To Heaven*. Despite her formidable gifts, Brackeen has been shamefully overlooked by the critics. She even disappeared – mysteriously but symbolically – from the first edition of this book. Since then, there's been some movement in her list, not least the appearance of *Where Legends Dwell*, which is perhaps the most impressive of the bunch.

Raised in California, she moved to New York, following her divorce from saxophonist Charles Brackeen, and found there a music scene much in keeping with her own unsettled, exploratory talent.

With a restless, unrooted delivery, Brackeen has always gravitated towards strong, very melodic bass players. The two early discs with Houston expose some of his crudities – compare his playing on 'Solar' with the standard set by Eddie Gomez – but confirm impressive strength and presence, qualities which are rather muffled on the trio set with guitarist Kawasaki.

The trio with McBee and Foster immediately gains from a sympathetic hand at the controls. The sound is lovely, with lots of definition on both bass and percussion. Foster is perhaps a little straight-ahead for this type of thing, but McBee (who gets a thank-you later with 'Can This McBee?') is absolutely solid and sings along under the piano vamp on 'Manha De Carnaval'. The larger group misfires, replacing subtlety with sheer strength. Instead of keeping in line, Marsalis and Blanchard jostle and barrack out front, and the ensembles are disappointingly uncoordinated.

So it's refreshing at last to turn to Brackeen as a solo performer. Her Maybeck recital turns out to be a significant moment, kicking off a series that has become almost definitive in its coverage of contempor-ary jazz piano. Brackeen seems to have been responsible for getting Concord boss Carl Jefferson to record in the little Berkeley hall in the first place, a telephone conversation memorialized in 'Calling Carl'. She certainly didn't let him down. From the opening bars of 'Thou Swell' to a jovial and ironic 'Strike Up The Band' at the finish, she sounds completely in command. 'Dr Chu Chow', 'African Aztec' and 'Curved Space' demonstrate her capacity for unfamiliar tonalities and rhythmic patterns, while 'Yesterdays' sheds almost all its romantic ballast to re-emerge as a big, bold statement of intent.

Brackeen's fine balance of abstraction and straightforward melody is amply demonstrated on *Where Legends Dwell*. The title-track is complex and intense, with an enormous part for Gomez. 'Picasso', 'Helen Song' and the rapid-fire 'Cosmic Ties And Mud Pies' push out the envelope further still, fractur-ing chords and building new lines on top. Gomez's bow-work is as good as ever and DeJohnette sounds as if he's been playing these charts for ever. Brackeen moves briefly inside the piano to set up the mood for 'Asian Spell', then has fun with cod-Chinese effects in a modified pentatonic scale. She's in similar territory on the Latin album, which is essentially a duo with added percussion but sets some of the agenda for *Take A Chance*. Her own playing is a touch below par and there are some muddy passages that perhaps ought to have been ironed out. *Breath Of Brazil* is a rather reserved and thoughtful set underneath all the noise and bustle, sign perhaps of a change of direction (already partly signalled by the Maybeck set) towards a more lyrical approach.

The concert documented on *Power Talk* takes the wheel on an extra turn. Opening with a magnificent stop-action reading of 'There Is No Greater Love', she powers through a mostly standards trio, repeat-ing 'Picasso' and 'Cosmic Ties And Mud Pies' from *Where Legends Dwell* and giving both the big treatment. Her young colleagues don't show her undue deference, forging ahead a couple of times as she pauses to elaborate points and then defiantly accelerating again as she changes pace to catch up. It must have been an exhilarating night. Incidentally, Turnipseed Music operates out of Metairie, Louisiana. So now you know.

Don Braden (born 1964) TENOR SAXOPHONE

*** **The Time Is Now** Criss Cross Criss 1051
  Braden; Tom Harrell (*t, flhn*); Benny Green (*p*); Christian McBride (*b*); Carl Allen (*d*). 1/91.
***(*) **Wish List** Criss Cross Criss 1069
  As above, except add Steve Turre (*tb*). 12/91.

Braden is a swinging mainstream player with a sophisticated harmonic sense and a good deal of taste. He proved his worth as an accompanist on Betty Carter's Grammy winner, *Look What I Got*, and more recently has worked effectively with another, much mellower singer, Jeanie Bryson.

His own debut album, *The Time Is Now*, was widely praised, but it wasn't a patch on *Wish List*, an elegant set of standards and refreshingly straightforward originals. Instead of overloading themes with harmonic changes, Braden builds in bridge sections which shift the tempo from fours to threes. He's an intelligent arranger, too. Turre and Harrell wouldn't on the face of it be everyone's notion of a *simpatico* brass-line, but Braden has them working in easy tandem without diluting what each does best. Harrell is unwontedly fiery on 'Just The Facts', a schematic minor blues with a gentle twist in its tail. It's the title-track, appropriately closing the record, that confirms Braden's enormous potential, a dreamy, almost wistful song that steadily uncovers its hidden riches.

Braden has already played with the best – Carter, Tony Williams, Wynton Marsalis – so this record isn't a 'wish list' date in that sense. Braden palpably doesn't need the support of star names, just the company of like-minded and equally dedicated players.

**** **After Dark** Criss Cross Criss 1081
  Braden; Scott Wendholt (*t, flhn*); Noah Bless (*tb*); Steve Wilson (*as*); Darrell Grant (*p*);
  Christian McBride (*b*); Carl Allen (*d*). 5/93.

Braden's third Criss Cross record marks a sudden and dramatic maturing of his style. Not only is he playing as well as before; suddenly his writing and arranging skills seem to have made a quantum step forward. There is a nocturnal programme to the record which gives it a darker and more sombre emphasis. Originals like the uneasy 'R.E.M.' and the gently upbeat 'Dawn' are interspersed with 'You And The Night And The Music', 'Monk's Dream' and Stevie Wonder's 'Creepin''. The group plays well, and trombonist Bless must have staked a claim with producer Gerry Teekens for a solo outing of his own.

*** **Organic** Columbia 481258
> Braden; Tom Harrell (*t, flhn*); David Newman (*ts*); Jack McDuff, Larry Goldings (*org*); Russell Malone (*g*); Cecil Brooks III, Winard Harper (*d*); Leon Parker (*perc*). 9–12/94.

Braden's bow for a major label is entertainingly delivered, but it scarcely measures up to the innate promise of the Criss Cross discs. The opening duet with Malone on 'Moonglow' is lovely, and some of the other pieces hit a productive groove in the organ/soul-jazz mode. Otherwise this feels disappointingly close to a man in mid-career casting around for a fresh idea. If Braden still gets off some strong solos, the real star here is Malone, whose guitar adds grit as well as polish when he takes a solo.

Bobby Bradford (born 1934) TRUMPET, CORNET

** **Lost In LA** Soul Note 121068
> Bradford; James Kousakis (*as*); Roberto Miguel Miranda (*b*); Mark Dresser (*b*); Sherman Ferguson (*d*). 6/83.
** **One Night Stand** Soul Note 121168
> Bradford; Frank Sullivan (*p*); Scott Walton (*b*) Billy Bowker (*d*). 11/86.
** **Comin' On** hat Art 6016
> Bradford; John Carter (*cl*); Don Preston (*p, synth*); Richard Davis (*b*); Andrew Cyrille (*d*). 5/88.

Twenty years ago, Bradford was recording with Ornette Coleman (he appears on *Broken Shadows* and the underrated *Science Fiction*), having replaced Don Cherry in the regular quartet ten years earlier. Ironically, he is now probably most often cited as a 'guest' improviser with the British-based Spontaneous Music Ensemble, where he fitted in not quite seamlessly.

His best work with Ornette is supposed to have gone the way of desert flowers, and the recordings made under his own name are curiously unsatisfactory, full of good things (like his superbly constructed solos) but ultimately underachieved. Don Preston seems a wildly improbable choice for the 1988 hat Art session and combines only poorly with Davis and Cyrille, both of whom are uncharacteristically bland. Bradford's interplay with clarinettist Carter falls a long way short of their long-deleted mid-1960s collaborations, and his tone seems muffled and indistinct.

Lost In LA has some striking moments and the single-horn format of *One Night Stand* prompts some more of his bravura and his most thoughtful solos. An important and adventurous player, Bradford has yet to recapture the brilliance of the 1973 *Secrets* with Carter; even the live sets seem to lose something of their burnish at the mixing desk.

Carmen Bradford VOCALS

*** **With Respect** Evidence ECD 22115
> Bradford; Charles Owens (*ts, f*); Donald Brown, Cedar Walton (*p*); Wali Ali, Dori Caymmi, Michael O'Neill (*g*); Steve Nelson (*vib*); Robert Hurst, James Leary (*b*); Ralph Penland (*d*); Bill Summers (*perc*). 7/93.

'With respect' is what you say when you're just about to disagree with someone and make your own point, politely but firmly. You feel that's very much the way Ms Bradford approaches the tradition. With the better part of a decade as vocalist for the Basie Orchestra, she hardly lacks a grounding in the basics, but it's worth noting that she brought herself to the Count's attention and suggested it would be in *his* best interests to give her a job.

No shrinking violet, then, but not a hard-bitten roadster either. She sings with a very natural, upbeat intonation, allowing the song to swing without pushing the lyric out of view. The arrangements, by Walton, Donald Brown, Dori Caymmi and John Clayton, are judged just right to give her a push without exposing some obvious frailties too cruelly. Her R&B approach is somewhat questionable on the strength of 'Ain't No Use'; she hasn't really the power for this kind of thing. On the other hand, her pared-down reading of 'Nature Boy', with just guitarist O'Neill for accompaniment, bespeaks a depth of experience, not just of the musical sort. In purely musicianly terms, her scat on 'Mr Paganini' is masterful, a brisk reminder that this is trumpeter Bobby Bradford's daughter. Not to be messed with.

Tim Brady GUITAR, SYNTHESIZER

*** **Visions** Justin Time JTR 8413-2
>   Brady; Kenny Wheeler (*t, c, flhn*); Montreal Chamber Orchestra. 11/85–6/88.

** **Double Variations** Justin Time JTR-8415-2
>   Brady; John Abercrombie (*g, g-syn*). 11/87–12/89.

(*) **Bradyworks Justin Time JTR 8433-2
>   Brady; John Surman (*ss, bs*); Simon Stone (*saxes, f*); Christopher Best (*clo*); Barre Phillips (*b*);
>   Marie Josée Simard, Pierre Tanguay (*perc*). 11/88–4/91.

Brady is a Montreal-based guitarist and composer whose jazz affiliations are only a part of a wide-ranging schema. *Visions* consists of a five-movement work for orchestra, with Wheeler as soloist, plus two duets by Wheeler and Brady and four solos by the guitarist. The orchestral piece doesn't instil much impression beyond the familiar one when faced by such an effort – that here is an orchestral piece by an occasional 'serious' composer – but Wheeler gives it his full attention and creates some passages of striking empathy with the material. Certainly anyone who likes a Keith Jarrett record such as *Luminescence* will want to explore this. The solos and duos suggest a more stop-motion approach to improvising, with Brady exploring textures and sound-barriers a step at a time. *Double Variations* is a sort of combination of both approaches, with Abercrombie pressed into the 'traditional' soloist's role while Brady sets up banks of electronic sound. Comparisons with Abercrombie's records with Ralph Towner are misleading, for this is much less of a yin–yang situation, and the continuously blurred articulation and use of multi-tracking create an overlapping of sound which is finally rather wearisome. *Bradyworks* continues what is a four-part sequence (based on ideas in Jacques Attali's *Bruit*) in much the same style, with a grander cast but a similar dependence on synthesizer samples. It's a thoughtful and scrupulously prepared piece of work, but there seems little here which – since they're both present – Surman and Phillips haven't done better on their own forays into this area.

Ruby Braff (born 1927) CORNET, TRUMPET

(*) **Hustlin' And Bustlin' Black Lion BLCD 760908
>   Braff; Vic Dickenson (*tb, v*); Dick LeFave (*tb*); Al Drootin (*cl, ts*); Edmond Hall (*cl*); Kenneth
>   Kersey, Sam Margolis (*ts*); George Wein (*p*); John Field, Milt Hinton (*b*); Bobby Donaldson, Jo
>   Jones (*d*). Summer 51, 5/54, 6/54.

*** **Hi-Fi Salute To Bunny** RCA 2118250
>   Braff; Benny Morton (*tb*); Pee Wee Russell (*cl*); Dick Hafer (*ts*); Nat Pierce (*p*); Steve Jordan
>   (*g*); Walter Page (*b*); Buzzy Drootin (*d*). 3 & 4/57.

***(*) **Easy Now** RCA 2118522
>   Braff; Emmett Berry, Roy Eldridge (*t*); Bob Wilber (*cl, ts*); Hank Jones (*p*); Mundell Lowe (*g*);
>   Leonard Gaskin (*b*); Don Lamond (*d*). 8/58.

Braff was born a generation too late and spent much of what should have been his most productive years in the 1950s with a great deal less to do than his talent deserved. His cornet playing has an almost vocal agility that balances delicacy of detail with a strong underlying pulse and harmonic richness. Like Eldridge, who joins him on some of the *Easy Now* tracks, he is a player who bridges the gap between early jazz and swing, and then between swing and (hard as it may be to credit, given his status as a rearguard traditionalist) bebop; listen to the phrasing on *Hi-Fi Salute To Bunny*, ostensibly a tribute to the ill-fated Berigan, and it is possible to hear strong intimations of Fats Navarro and even that other style-switcher, Charlie Shavers.

The early material on Black Lion is more conservatively angled. The opening 'Hustlin' And Bustlin'' is associated with Louis Armstrong and binds Braff to the mainstream that went underground with Dizzy Gillespie and Clifford Brown. 'Shoe Shine Boy' has a bright polish and the self-written 'Flaky' an intriguingly ironic edge. And it's perhaps in that irony, that nod to the audience that he knows he is dealing in relative archaisms, that Braff's great creativity lies.

The two RCAs see him develop into a somewhat different player and certainly in embryo the protean stylist he was to remain into the 1990s. Comparing these (over)lushly remastered sessions with a recent Concord does the RCA technical department no great favours, but it also confirms that Braff's mature style was in place almost from the beginning rather than coming along later in a bid to keep pace with the youngsters. One further indication of his bridge-building capacity is that old-school players like Morton and Russell manage to sound comfortable alongside the bustly Hafer.

***(*) **Hear Me Talkin'** Black Lion BLCD 760161
>   Braff; Alex Welsh (*t*); Roy Williams (*tb*); Al Gay (*ts*); Johnny Barnes (*bs*); Jim Douglas (*g*); Fred
>   Hunt (*p*); Ron Rae (*b*); Lennie Hastings (*d*). 11/67.

Recorded in London at the tail-end of a mouth-watering 'Jazz Expo' package which introduced British players to some of their American idols. The Welsh band had been playing with Wild Bill Davison at the 100 Club before these sessions were recorded, and something of Davison's brisk attack creeps into the brass chase that ends 'No One Else But You'. Though Welsh mostly defers to Braff as far as solo space is concerned, the real star of the set is trombonist Roy Williams, who plays a marvellous solo on 'Ruby Got Rhythm' and even more outstandingly on 'Smart Alex Blues', both originals put together by Braff for the set. His own finest moment is on the long 'Between The Devil And The Deep Blue Sea', where he plays in his equally distinctive lower register.

The Welsh band was probably the finest mainstream unit of its time and had recently had an opportunity to prove its quality in international company at Antibes (Newport beckoned for 1968). It offers Braff spirited company, with sparks of real class from both Williams and Welsh; the music is faithfully reproduced on this valuable reissue.

(*) Ruby Braff – Buddy Tate With The Newport All Stars Black Lion BLCD 760138
    Braff; Buddy Tate (*ts*); George Wein (*p*); Jack Lesberg (*b*); Don Lamond (*d*). 10/67.
Braff slips into Pops mode for this Newport All Stars compilation, made in a London studio. There are alternative takes of quite a bit of the music – 'Mean To Me', 'Take The "A" Train' and 'The Sheik Of Araby' – but they don't reveal much more than the slightly programmed quality of Braff's music at this time. Tate plays very well indeed, except that it seems to be his fluffing that lies behind the call for further takes of tunes that to all intents and purposes have been solidly run down.

***(*) Live At The New School** Chiaroscuro CRD 126
    Braff; George Barnes, Wayne Wright (*g*); Michael Moore (*b*). 4/74.
*** **Plays Gershwin** Concord CCD 6005
    As above. 7/74.
(*) **Plays Rodgers & Hart Concord CCD 6007
    As above.
In the end, despite the amiably waspish chat on the first of these, they couldn't get along together, but while they were playing (rather than squabbling) Braff and Barnes produced some of the best small-group jazz of the day. Needless to say, the critics were looking in the other direction at the time.

The Chiaroscuro documents an entire concert at the prestigious New School for Social Research, a recording made by the audio engineering class. It was actually the last gig in an influential series known as Jazz Ramble and it seems appropriate that it should have been a group touching so many stylistic bases that rang down the curtain. Braff's sponsorship of the young wasn't limited to having students in the booth. The inclusion of young Michael Moore in the quartet was a master-stroke, bringing forward one of the best mainstream-modern bassists of his generation and taxing him to the limit. You can almost *hear* Moore learning on some of the less familiar material, things like 'With Time For Love' and Don Redman's 'Nobody Else But You', just two of ten tracks which were not included on the original release. A doubly valuable document, then, of a short-lived group which continued for only another few months, basically long enough to make the Concords and to work with Tony Bennett.

The first of the pair for Carl Jefferson's recently established label isn't just another 'Goishwin' route-march but a genuine attempt to get inside the tunes and unpick their still far too little understood progressions. Unfortunately, if Braff is on his usual plateau of excellence, there is something slightly unresolved about Wayne Wright's rhythm guitar and Moore's bass.

The mix is perhaps better on the Rodgers/Hart set. 'Spring Is Here' is completely masterly and Barnes seems happier with this material than with the Gershwin. On a toss-up, though, Gershwin's writing breaks the deadlock.

*** **Mr Braff To You** Phontastic CD 7568
    Braff; Scott Hamilton (*ts*); John Bunch (*p*); Chris Flory (*b*); Phil Flanigan (*d*). 12/83.
The title offers an insight into Braff's – shall we say robust? – personality, but it also shows him capable of sending himself up. This early encounter with Hamilton is one of their best. There's an almost folksy quality to Braff's theme statements, and it's this that Hamilton picks up on, leaning back into relaxed, saloon-bar solos on 'Ida, Sweet As Apple Cider', 'Poor Butterfly' and 'Miss Brown To You' with complete relaxation. Bunch is a tower of strength throughout, to the extent that Flory and Flanigan are almost superfluous.

*** **A First** Concord CCD 4274
    Braff; Scott Hamilton (*ts*); John Bunch (*p*); Chris Flory (*g*); Phil Flanigan (*b*); Chuck Riggs (*d*). 2/85.
*** **A Sailboat In The Moonlight** Concord CCD 4296
    As above. 2/85.
Two fine albums from the same 1985 sessions. Hamilton, a generation younger, is a co-religionist in his refusal to accept the orthodoxy of bop or its aftermath. He and Braff blend as effectively as any one

reed player he has partnered over the years, and the two albums move with an unstinted eloquence, punctuated by moments of real fire.

*** **Me, Myself And I** Concord CCD 4381
    Braff; Howard Alden (*g*); Jack Lesberg (*b*). 6/88.
*** **Bravura Eloquence** Concord CCD 4423
    As above.

Braff's tone is still ringingly strong, the allusions and melodic palimpsests as thought-provoking as ever; particularly effective are the segues from 'Smile' to 'Who'll Buy My Violets?' and in the long, superb 'Judy [Garland] Medley', which contains not just the inevitable 'Rainbow' but 'If I Only Had A Brain'. On *Me, Myself And I* he even takes a shot at the big toon from *Swan Lake*. Lesberg and Alden provide sterling support. Two of those 'nice warm feeling' records that don't starve the grey cells.

*** **Music From My Fair Lady** Concord CCD 4393
    Braff; Dick Hyman (*p*). 7/89.
*** **Younger Than Swingtime** Concord CCD 4445
    As above. 6/90.

America The Beautiful, a duo Braff made with Hyman on organ, has now disappeared, but these show-tune records are an acceptable alternative for the moment. The music is familiar to the point of banality and the only substantial variations on it seem to involve taking the tempos unusually fast or slow (as on 'With A Little Bit Of Luck', which gets both treatments). It all seems worth it when you get to the final track and hear Braff's curmudgeonly romantic huff and grizzle 'I've Grown Accustomed To Her Face'.

The *South Pacific* material is more accessibly lyrical and is confronted in a much more conventional way, with few of the little quirks and asides that Braff uses to propel the other session. Here it's Hyman who takes a lot of the responsibility and, in acknowledgement, he plays 'There Is Nothing Like A Dame' solo, making an effective job of it too. 'Bali Ha'i' frames the session nicely. For choice, the first record is more interesting, but the second may well be more immediately appealing. The choice, as they say on TV, is yours.

***(*) **And His New England Songhounds: Volume 1** Concord CCD 4478
    Braff; Scott Hamilton (*ts*); Dave McKenna (*p*); Frank Tate (*b*); Alan Dawson (*d*). 4/91.
***(*) **And His New England Songhounds: Volume 2** Concord CCD 4504
    As above. 4/91.

Braff and McKenna last did a studio session together in 1956, when the cornetist cut the fine *Braff!* for Epic. The chemistry still works. The hand-picked band offers Braff a warmly swinging background for one of his best performances of recent years. The original 'Shō-Time' is dedicated to Scott Hamilton's son, a relatively rare writing credit for Braff but further evidence of his skill as a melodist. Stand-out tracks have to be 'My Shining Hour', Billie's 'Tell Me More', and the brief closing 'Every Time We Say Goodbye'. Mainstream jazz at its best.

Volume 2 was always going to be worth the wait, and it delivers royally. Braff's clipped, brusque delivery on 'Indian Summer' tempers the sugariness that always threatens to come through, and that's what's happening throughout the record. Oddly, Hamilton sounded better on the first volume, but the Songhounds have really clicked into gear and one hopes there'll be more soon.

***(*) **Cornet Chop Suey** Concord CCD 4606
    Braff; Ken Peplowski (*cl*); Howard Alden (*g*); Frank Tate (*b*); Ronald Zito (*d*). 3/91.

This is essentially a trio record, with Peplowski and Zito guesting on just five of the dozen tracks. Given the obvious *simpatico* of the well-established Braff–Alden–Tate Trio, it might have been as well to hold them in reserve for another session altogether. These are remarkable performances. Lead lines are swapped about and played back re-harmonized on the spot; Tate and Alden seem to enjoy a rapport that provides Braff with exactly the sort of ambiguous context he thrives on. To give one clear example: Louis Armstrong's 'Cornet Chop Suey' is played at a furious pace, far faster than by Pops, and with a variant in the melody that, as Braff himself suggests, aligns it to Charlie Parker and bebop.

It wouldn't do to overstate this line of argument, but it makes better sense of this highly inventive and thoughtful player than does the received view of him as a curmudgeonly reactionary who stopped listening to anything recorded after the Hot Fives.

***(*) **Live At The Regattabar** Arbors ARCD 19131
    Braff; Gray Sargent, Jon Wheatley (*g*); Marshall Wood (*b*). 11/93.
*** **Controlled Nonchalance At The Regattabar** Arbors ARCD 19134
    As above, except omit Wheatley; add Scott Hamilton (*ts*); Dave McKenna (*p*); Chuck Riggs (*d*). 11/93.

The earlier of these – by just a few days – was recorded on the thirtieth anniversary of John Kennedy's assassination and in the heart of Kennedy country; the Regattabar is in the Charles Hotel, Cambridge, Massachusetts. Though there is no mention of the date's significance on the record, can it be that it contributed something to the quiet centredness of the session, which conveys a mood closer to melancholy than to nonchalance? Control, though, definitely. Braff's activities had been curtailed somewhat in the previous couple of years by attacks of the wind player's curse, emphysema; but he is fit enough to take charge of both these groups, leading them through two superbly crafted programmes of standard material.

'No One Else But You' is revived and gives Jon Wheatley his most effective feature, and here Braff's increasingly obvious interest in playing saxophone lines on cornet (Ben Webster is his avowed model) is given full rein. Gray Sargent has a more plangent, blues-influenced style, which is effectively deployed on 'Give My Regards To Broadway' and on the brand-new 'Orange', a departure in the Braff canon in that the composer introduces it on piano. That nicely warms up the instrument for big Dave McKenna four nights later with the augmented group. Qualitatively there really isn't much to choose between these groups, but one misses the stillness and precision of the drummerless quartet and the slight sense that, except for 'Struttin' With Some Barbecue' (played with a Latin spin) and 'Sunday', both of which are triumphant, Braff is partially eclipsed by the others.

**** Inside & Out Concord CCD 4691
  Braff; Roger Kellaway (*p*). 9/95.
Songful, bright and shady, above all *detailed* and full of invention, this is a beautiful set that makes a virtue of simplicity. Kellaway has a solid left hand and an unfailing feel for the essential drama of a song. His accompaniment on 'Between The Devil And The Deep Blue Sea' is masterful, following Braff's radical reinvention every step of the way. 'I Got Rhythm' receives the attention and respect it deserves; but it is on 'Yesterdays' – far and away the most striking single item on the set – that the chemistry begins to fizzle. It doesn't come a lot better than this.

Anthony Braxton (born 1945) ALTO SAXOPHONE, ALL OTHER SAXOPHONES AND CLARINETS, FLUTE, ELECTRONICS, PERCUSSION

*** Three Compositions Of New Jazz Delmark DS 423
  Braxton; Leo Smith (*t, perc*); Leroy Jenkins (*vn, vla, perc*); Muhal Richard Abrams (*p, clo, cl*). 68.
Anthony Braxton records are a little like No. 12 buses: there'll always be another one along in a moment. He is, perhaps, the most extensively documented contemporary improviser – remarkably so, given the dauntingly cerebral character of at least some of his output. There is a further problem: is Braxton's music jazz at all, since a large proportion of his work, solos and all, is – gasp! – scored?

Whatever the prevailing definition of jazz (and, as the man said, if you have to ask . . .), Braxton's music conforms majestically: rhythmic, virtuosic, powerfully emotive, constantly reinventing itself. He has been able to translate his solo concept (in the late 1960s, he pioneered unaccompanied saxophone performance) to the largest orchestral scale.

The dateline on this one is significant. Braxton's first major statement – indeed his recording debut as leader – came in the year of revolutions (or at least of revolutionary thinking throughout America and Europe) and openly declares itself as standing at the end of a played-out cultural tradition. Though he can expect to rake over the ashes of that tradition for some time, this is the critical historical moment which Braxton's music addresses.

The disc contains three compositions of decreasing length, two by Braxton, one by Smith. As John Litweiler suggests in a useful biographical liner-note, the middle piece is the one in which the new language that Braxton, Smith and Abrams are articulating can most readily be accessed. The saxophonist still sounds hot and fierce, the disciple of Parker and Dolphy rather than of the cooler, whiter voices (Desmond, Marsh) he turned to in the '80s. All the same, these graduation exercises by the 1968 AACM show class. The loose, drummerless concept works well for all three, and the music, though still slightly raw, stands up well after 25 years.

*** Composition 113 sound aspects 003
  Braxton solo. 12/83.
** 19 (Solo) Compositions 1988 New Albion Records NA023
  As above. 4/88.
***(*) Wesleyan (12 Altosolos) 1992 hat ART CD 6128
  As above. 11/92.
In 1968 Braxton set the jazz world back on its heels with an album of solo saxophone improvisations entitled *For Alto*. There was nothing fundamentally new about unaccompanied saxophone – Coleman

Hawkins had done it years before with the intriguingly abstract 'Picasso' – but *For Alto* was stingingly powerful, abstract and daring. It was, perhaps, Braxton's finest hour.

Composition 113, which is scored for soprano saxophone and a couple of props, is one of Braxton's most effective conceptual pieces. Surprisingly moving in a live setting – the soloist stands beside a photograph of a deserted railway station with a train lantern suspended above him – it transfers well to record and has a meditative calm which is rare with Braxton.

The New Albion set, product of yet another new recording deal, is thin stuff indeed, almost as if that remarkable technique has become a polished manner which can be taken on and off at will. 'Compositions' they may be; pointlessly enigmatic they certainly are. Things are infinitely better on the material from Wesleyan University (where Braxton has found a niche). For comparison with the New Albion set, there is a further version of 'Composition No. 106d', this time overlaid with one of the Opus 170 pieces of which the set is largely made up. Where the standards on *19 (Solo) Compositions* had seemed ironic, collaged as they were with dry generic or technical labels ('ballade', 'long', 'intervallic', 'triplet diatonic'), those on *Altosolos* are pointedly idiomatic. 'Charlie's Wig' is one of Braxton's most detailed examinations of bebop harmony.

**(*) In The Tradition Steeplechase 31015
    Braxton; Tete Montoliu (*p*); Niels-Henning Orsted-Pedersen (*b*); Albert 'Tootie' Heath (*d*). 5/74.
**(*) In The Tradition Steeplechase 31045
    As above.
***(*) Eight (+3) Tristano Compositions 1989 hat Art 6052
    Braxton; Jon Raskin (*bs*); Dred Scott (*p*); Cecil McBee (*b*); Andrew Cyrille (*d*). 12/89.
**** Six Monk's Compositions (1987) Black Saint 120 116
    Braxton; Mal Waldron (*p*); Buell Neidlinger (*b*); Bill Osborne (*d*). 7/87.

Braxton more than most had eventually to prove himself as a performer of standards. The Monk sessions are a triumph. Far from the usual pastiche, these are reinvented versions of a half-dozen obscurer items from the monastic *œuvre*. Pianist Mal Waldron is there to confirm the apostolic succession, but Braxton's readings are thoroughly apostate, furiously paced and unapologetically maximal.

In The Tradition, his first sustained essay in revisionism, was less successful, partly because the piano player, the blind Catalan Tete Montoliu, so patently misunderstood his intentions. Braxton's lyrical lines – on shibboleths like 'Ornithology' and 'Goodbye Pork Pie Hat' – are so clearly drawn as to render the chords and Montoliu's embellishments almost redundant. The bass and drums are by contrast almost ideally adapted to Braxton's needs, a particular tribute to NHOP's resilience and catholicity of taste.

If *In The Tradition* remains a collectable curiosity with occasional flashes of brilliance, as in Braxton's statements on 'Marshmallow', *Eight (+3) Tristano Compositions* is another small masterpiece in the same mould as the Monk set. Intended as a tribute to the late Warne Marsh, a less than immediately obvious influence on Braxton, it adds Marsh's 'Sax Of A Kind', Irving Berlin's 'How Deep Is The Ocean' and Vincent Youmans's 'Time On My Hands' – all Cool School standbys – to a roster of Tristano originals. Though Braxton (restricted to alto and sopranino saxophones and flute) manages to get inside the tunes, it's not clear that the second saxophonist, John Raskin, fully understands the idiom. No hesitancy, though, from Dred Scott (whose historical namesake enjoys a significant libertarian niche in American history) or from a marvellously adaptive veteran rhythm section. If Braxton's own compositions have started to re-centre our definitions of jazz scoring and structure, his treatment of standards is no less radical. Recommended.

***(*) Town Hall (Trio & Quintet), 1972 hat ART CD 6119
    Braxton; John Stubblefield (*ts, f, bcl, perc*); Dave Holland (*b*); Barry Altschul, Phillip Wilson (*d*). 5/72.
***(*) Dortmund (Quartet) 1976 hat Art 6075
    Braxton; George Lewis (*tb*); Dave Holland (*b*); Barry Altschul (*d*). 76.
***(*) Donaueschingen (Duo) 1976 hat ART CD 6150
    As above, except omit Holland and Altschul. 10/76.
*** Performance (Quartet) 1979 hat Art 6044
    Braxton; Ray Anderson (*tb*); John Lindberg (*b*); Thurman Barker (*b*). 9/79.

The 1970s were a difficult decade for Braxton in many respects. Though his music was developing rapidly, it still met with considerable critical resistance, objections to its supposed lack of swing, its cerebralism and Braxton's controversial (though hardly unique) use of wholly scored solos.

The earliest of these discs was originally released on LP and then on CD in Japan. It's an important record of one of Braxton's first major concerts and a rare instance of his playing with just bass and drums (see *Seven Compositions*, above). Apart from 'All The Things You Are', the set consisted of compositions drawn from the 'coordinate music structures' written between the mid-1960s and 1972. Identified as 'Composition 6' (parts N, O and P are performed), these were mostly abstract cells and lines but with hints of the more codified approach of later years. The trio sessions are taut but not unromantic, and the gentle, almost ballad-like 'Composition 6(O)', dedicated to Frederic Rzewski, features beautiful playing by Wilson, who died horrifically in 1990, murdered by a burglar. The quintet tracks (with Altschul in for Wilson) are dominated by Jeanne Lee, for whom Braxton wrote '6(P)'. The first section is vocalise, but in the second part she sings Braxton's characteristically intense lyrics. Stubblefield's multi-instrumentalism adds nothing substantial to the music but it varies Braxton's typically pale saxophone colours rather attractively. (The set includes a facsimile poster from the original gig, which is a nice touch.)

The Dortmund set finds Braxton at the top of his form, and it prompts a nagging doubt as to whether his playing – as opposed to his still-remarkable compositional and conceptual strides – has ever been better. Braxton's 'other' trombonist, Lewis, is a notoriously capricious player in a free context (though it's often forgotten how much he owes to the likes of Vic Dickenson and Dicky Wells) but capable of quite extraordinarily beautiful lines, especially on the thumping 'Composition 40B', which also highlights the superb rhythm section. Lest anyone doubt the existence of such a creature as the contrabass saxophone, heard at the beginning of the set introducing 'Composition 40F', there is a yes-it's-true picture in the liner booklet.

The Donaueschingen duos with Lewis were released in 1994 and listening to them with a measure of hindsight suggests again how much of Braxton's mature or 'later' language was actually in place very early on. There is nothing here that could not have been reconciled to the language of the 1968 record on Delmark (above) or that couldn't have been integrated with one of the more recent large-ensemble projects. There are just two tracks, a detailed collage of Lewis's 'Fred's Garden' and one of Braxton's 'Kelvin' pieces, with 'Composition 6F' and '64'; as a tailpiece, a brief run-through of 'Donna Lee'. There is an intricate closeness in the performances that one doesn't encounter again until Braxton's 1993 collaboration with the other Parker, for which, see below.

In one significant sense, Braxton is the archetypal CD artist. This is less a matter of sound-quality *per se* than of durations, for it is increasingly important to hear how an entire concert set develops. Ironically, despite the huge range of material available, there is very little yet in catalogue from the classic quartet with Kenny Wheeler. Much of this material is on Arista and Moers CDs and has not (yet) appeared on CD.

Performance (Quartet) 1979 represents, as Graham Lock discusses in his highly informed liner-note, a transitional stage in Braxton's career, linking the more oppositional work of the 1970s to the composer's increasing interest in collage forms and 'pulse track structures' (which alternate notated sequences with freely improvised 'spaces', radically shifting the axes of bebop and post-bop improvisation). The 1979 group is one of the funkiest Braxton ever assembled, but it is also, paradoxically, one of the most cerebral. 'Composition 40F' is generically part of the sequence consolidated on *Three Compositions (Trio) 1989* and should be heard in conjunction with that remarkable record.

Alongside work like this, Braxton's 'standards' and 'in the tradition' work begin to sound like redundant special pleading. By the end of the 1970s Braxton *is* the tradition, albeit a new tradition, and those unforgivingly numbered compositions, perhaps destined never to be repertoire pieces, are the contemporary standards.

**** **Creative Orchestra (Koln) 1978** hat ART CD 61711/2 2CD

Braxton; Rob Howard, Michael Mossman, Leo Smith, Kenny Wheeler (*t*); Ray Anderson, George Lewis, James King Roosa (*tb, tba*); Dwight Andrews, Marty Ehrlich, Vinny Golia, J. D. Parran, Ned Rothenberg (*sax, cl, f, picc*); Marilyn Crispell (*p*); Birgit Taubhorn (*acc*); James Emery (*g*); Robert Ostertag (*syn*); John Lindberg, Brian Smith (*b*); Thurman Barker (*perc, mar*). 5/78.

A vintage performance by a wonderful band. It isn't always possible to pick out soloists and it isn't always desirable, so intense and seamless are these performances. It is hard to think that the opening 'Language Improvisations' are not close to an ideal rendering of Braxton's basic compositional devices. The march, 'Composition No. 45' had only been heard on the *Eugene* disc before these tapes were issued in 1995. It comes across here, in its earlier version, as one of Braxton's most subversively intelligent palimpsests, a subtle historical gloss on a style of music often dismissed as 'martial' or strictly utilitarian and, in most regards, inimical to the freedoms of jazz, but of course deeply bound up with its early history.

'Composition No. 55' was originally included on Braxton's *Creative Music Orchestra 1976*, which can probably still be found as a budget Novus CD. It's a piece that concentrates a great many of his ideas about the scaling-up of bebop lines for large ensembles, and its debt to both Ellington and, more particularly, Mingus is pretty inescapable. All these appear on the first of the two CDs. The second, which includes compositions 59, 51 and 58 (in that order) is much less compelling and, though they clearly belong to the same project, might have been retained for later release. As it stands, most listeners will find themselves returning to disc one much more often.

(***(*)) **8KN-(B-12)IR10 For String Quartet** sound aspects SAS 009
    Braxton; Robert Schumann String Quartet. 11/79.
A tricky one, this, for much of the music emphatically isn't in the jazz idiom or anything close to it. It is, however, quite remarkable musically and does include some very fine solo Braxton, as well as alternative versions – with and without saxophone – of his densely conceived string quartet. Recommended (with caution).

***(*) **Composition No. 96** Leo CD LR 169
    Braxton (*cond*); Dave Scott, James Knapp (*t*); Julian Priester, Scott Reeves (*tb*); Richard Reed (*frhn*); Rick Byrnes (*tba*); Nancy Hargerud, Rebecca Morgan, Denise Pool (*f*); Aileen Munger, Laurri Uhlig (*ob*); Bob Davis (*eng hn*); Marlene Weaver (*bsn*); Paul Pearse, Bill Smith (*cl*); Ray Downey (*bcl*); Denny Goodhew (*as*); Julian Smedley, Mathew Pederson, Jeannine Davis, Libby Poole, Jeroen Van Tyn, Sandra Guy, Becky Liverzey, Mary Jacobson (*vn*); Betty Agent, Jean Word, Sam Williams, Beatrice Dolf (*vla*); Page Smith-Weaver, Scott Threlkold, Marjorie Parbington (*clo*); Scott Weaver, Deborah De Loria (*b*); Motter Dean (*hp*); Ed Hartman, Matt Kocmieroski (*perc*). 5/81.
Dating from the end of the 1970s, *Composition No. 96* is a large-scale composition dedicated to Karlheinz Stockhausen and reflecting Braxton's interest in the relationship between 'dynamic symbolism' (the Jungian archetypes, close enough) and planetary change. The symbols are realized as photographic slides of actual physical phenomena, which are then projected as part of a strict parallelism between perceptual systems.

    Braxton's earlier experiments with large-scale orchestral 'composition' – difficult to hear any of it as uniformly scored – were not particularly happy. It's ironic that while one of the routine criticisms levelled at his small-group work is that it is too rigidly formalized, his orchestral works can sound unproductively chaotic. *Composition No. 96*, which comes from a particularly fruitful phase in Braxton's career, is a huge, apocalyptic thing that might serve as a soundtrack for some post-creationist epic of the Next Frontier.

    Graham Lock's immensely detailed liner-note explains the genesis and structure of the music, but essentially *Composition No. 96* consists of 16 separate elements and their numerological product, seven distinct parts, which move from the vibrant collisions of the opening through slower and faster sections, punctuated by *fermata* or pauses like those which signal the beginning of cadenzas in classical concertos.

    Braxton's large-scale works were a logical extension of what he had been doing throughout the 1970s, but they were also part of his effort to raise Afro-American music out of the 'jazz' ghetto. Even at the level of pure sound, with no reference to its complex structural synchronization, *Composition No. 96* is an impressive achievement. The Composers and Improvisers Orchestra has a rather *ad hoc* feel, and some of the transitions sound fudged and incomplete. The only recognizable jazz name in the ensemble is trombonist Julian Priester, and one wonders how sympathetic some of the players actually were to Braxton's conception. There are places when the playing is more exact and 'legitimate' than the context seems to demand; but such perceptions may be the result of residual expectations of what jazz musicians are 'supposed' to sound like, and for that reason alone should be resisted.

*** **Composition No. 98** hat Art 6062
    Braxton; Hugh Ragin (*t, flhn, picc t*); Ray Anderson (*tb, atb*); Marilyn Crispell (*p*). 1/81.
The key element here, interestingly, is not Braxton at all, but the interplay between Ragin's high scribbly trumpet and the fruitier sounds produced by Anderson. There are hints of Sousa marches, of Varèse's writing for winds, of bebop (as usual), and a superadded, almost narrative quality, a line that can't quite be abstracted analytically but which holds this extraordinary piece together. We have rated it a little lower than some only because Braxton's own playing is under-powered. The others are exceptional.

*** **Four Compositions (Quartet) 1984** Black Saint 120086
    Braxton; Marilyn Crispell (*p*); John Lindberg (*b*); Gerry Hemingway (*d*). 9/84.
***(*) **Quartet (London) 1985** Leo CD LR 200/201 2CD
    As above, except Mark Dresser (*b*) replaces Lindberg. 11/85.
***(*) **Quartet (Birmingham) 1985** Leo CD LR 202/3 2CD
    Braxton; Marilyn Crispell (*p*); Mark Dresser (*b*); Gerry Hemingway (*d*). 11/85.
**** **Quartet (Coventry) 1985** Leo CD LR 204/205 2CD
    As above. 11/85.
(*) **Five Compositions (Quartet) 1986 Black Saint 120106
    As above, except David Rosenboom (*p*) replaces Crispell. 7/86.
For all his compositions for amplified shovels, 100 tubas and galactically dispersed orchestras, the core of Braxton's conception remains the recognizably four-square jazz quartet. This is where he was heard

to best advantage in the 1980s. The minimally varied album-titles are increasingly confusing; for instance, *Four Compositions (Quartet) 1983* with George Lewis has now disappeared, leaving the near-identical-sounding set above). Fortunately, there is a straightforward rule of thumb. If Marilyn Crispell is on it, buy it. The Braxton Quartet of 1984–5 was of remarkable vintage and Crispell's Cecil Taylor-inspired but increasingly individual piano playing was one of its outstanding features. There are unauthorized recordings of this band in circulation, but the Leo sets are absolutely legitimate, and pretty nearly exhaustive; the CDs offer good-quality transfers of the original boxed set, six sides of quite remarkable music that, in conjunction with the other quartet sessions, confirm Braxton's often stated but outwardly improbable interest in the Lennie Tristano school, and in particular the superb harmonic improvisation of Warne Marsh. Those who followed the 1985 British tour may argue about the respective merits of different nights and locations, but there really isn't much to separate the London, Coventry and Birmingham sets for the non-specialist. For reference, the material performed on each pair of discs is as follows: London – Compositions 122 (+ 108A), 40(O), 52, 86 (+ 32 + 96), 115, 105A, piano solo from 96, 40F, 121, 116; Birmingham – 110A (+ 96 + 108B), 69M (+ 10 + 33 + 96), 60 (+ 96 + 108C), 85 (+ 30 + 108D), 105B (+ 5 + 32 + 96), 87 (+ 108C), 23J, 69H (+ 31 + 96), 40(O); Coventry – 124 (+ 30 + 96), 88 (+ 108C + 30 + 96), piano solo from 30, 23G (+ 30 + 96), 40N, 69C (+ 32 + 96), percussion solo from 96, 69F, 69B, bass solo from 96, 6A. It will be noted how often compositions in the above list are 'collaged' with 'Composition No. 96', the 'multiple-line' orchestral piece listed above. It serves as a reference point, most obviously in the Coventry concert. This also includes an intriguing conversation interview with Braxton, conducted by Graham Lock and covering such subjects as Frankie Lymon, John Coltrane, Warne Marsh, chess, the blues, and the nature of music itself.

Though the Birmingham set reaches a hectic climax with an encore performance of 'Kelvin 40(O)' that does further damage to Braxton's undeserved reputation as a po-faced number-cruncher, the extra half-star has to go to Coventry, first for the interview material, but also for the most sheerly beautiful performance in Braxton's entire recorded output, the peaceful clarinet music on 'Composition No. 40(N)' that ends the first set. Nothing else on the remaining five discs quite reaches that peak of perfection.

Rosenboom is a poor substitute for Crispell on the 1986 set, but the rhythm section of Dresser or Lindberg and Hemingway was beginning to sound custom-made by this stage, perfectly attuned to the music.

*** **Composition 99, 101, 107 and 138** hat Art 6019
    Braxton; Garrett List (*tb*); Marianne Schroeder (*p*).
Not by any means a classic Braxton album, but distinguished by some fine solo and duo performances from the classically leaning Schroeder, who has a lighter and more diffuse touch than Crispell but is nevertheless an effective performer in this idiom. The trio music doesn't entirely convince, but there is some fine solo Braxton on 'Composition 99B' which, Cage-like, incorporates simultaneous elements of four other compositions.

*** **Open Aspects (Duo) 1982** hat ART CD 6106
    Braxton; Richard Teitelbaum (*syn, elec*). 3/82.
** **Kol Nidre** sound aspects SAS 031
    Braxton; Andrew Voigt (*saxophones, f*). 12/88.
*** **Duets Vancouver 1989** Music & Arts 611
    Braxton; Marilyn Crispell (*p*). 6/89.
Duetting with Braxton must be a daunting gig. His London appearances in the 1970s with Derek Bailey (*mutatis mutandis*) were frankly disappointing, largely again because Braxton's idiom is still jazz and Bailey's is something else; the saxophonist's 1976 partnership with Muhal Richard Abrams, a living conduit of the black musical tradition, makes for telling comparison. In that regard Crispell more than holds her own, with a sympathetic awareness that contrasts sharply with the arrogant insouciance one heard from the likes of George Lewis. The Vancouver duets are as warmly approachable as anything Braxton has done. There is no soft-pedalling from Crispell, and she may even be the more compelling voice. There are some signs, minor here, fatal to *Kol Nidre* with ROVA man Voigt, that Braxton is settling into an uneasy alternation between a relatively fixed style and sudden, nihilistic eruptions. The two-saxophone format doesn't work on this ocasion, though it succeeds triumphantly on the 1990s duo album with Evan Parker; for which, see below.

Recently issued on CD, *Open Aspects* recalls the period of Braxton's involvement with the radical improvisation group, Musica Elettronica Viva, and with a non-acoustic sound source. Restricted to just alto and sopranino, the saxophonist often sounds rather shrill, and the set itself is rather unrelieved and one-dimensional, even when both players strive for variation in the overall colouration.

*(*) **The Aggregate** sound aspects SAS 023
    Braxton; ROVA Saxophone Quartet. 88.

A well-intentioned but rather desiccated collaboration with the ground-breaking saxophone quartet. As on *Kol Nidre*, there is too much horning in on each other's space, though Braxton seems surprisingly comfortable in the setting. One for completists only.

**** Seven Compositions (Trio) 1989 hat Art CD 6025
    Braxton; Adelhard Roidinger (*b*); Tony Oxley (*d*). 89.
In our judgement, this is still the finest small-group performance. Recorded in London, it has a spare majesty seldom equalled and seldom possible in the more luxuriant context of the quartets. Tony Oxley, a veteran of the British free-jazz movement of the 1960s, plays superbly and is beautifully recorded, a typically metallic, urgent sound that complements the slightly brooding quality of Roidinger's bass.

Braxton runs through his usual gamut of horns, including the antiquated C-melody saxophone, and sounds assured and confident. There's even a standard, a powerful 'All The Things You Are', which is something of a *locus classicus* for examining the relationship between Braxton's 'own' music and the changes-based harmonic language he inherits from jazz. If you've room for only one Braxton, or are about to do 'Desert Island Discs', look no further; no question at all as to the validity of this particular release.

***(*) 2 Compositions (Jarvenpaa) 1988 Leo CD LR 233
    Braxton; Mircea Stan (*tb*); Seppo Baron Paakkunainen (*ts, bs, f*); Pentti Lahti (*as, ss, f*); Pepa Paivinen (*ts, ss, bcl, f*); Mikko-Ville Luolajan-Mikkola (*vn*); Teppo Hauta-Aho (*b, clo*); Jukka Wasama (*d*). 11/88.

**** Eugene (1989) Black Saint 120137
    Braxton; Rob Blakeslee, Ernie Carbajal, John Jensen (*t*); Mike Heffley, Tom Hill, Ed Kammerer (*tb*); Thom Bergeron, Jeff Homan, Carl Woideck (*reeds*); Mike Vannice (*reeds, p*); Toddy Barton (*syn*); Joe Robinson (*g*); Forrest Moyer (*b*); Charles Dowd (*vib, perc*); Tom Kelly (*perc*). 1/89.

***(*) Two Compositions (Ensemble) 1989/1991 hat ART CD 6086
    Ensemble Modern: Tony Cross, Julian Brewer (*t*); Uwe Dierksen, Norbert Hardegren (*tb*); ·
    Dietmar Wiesner, Anne La Berge (*f*); Catherine Milliken (*ob*); Vanessa King, Achim Reus (*eng hn*); Roland Diry, John Corbett, Joachim Klemm (*cl*); Wolfgang Stryi (*sax, bcl*); Veit Scholz (*bsn*); Karin Schmeer (*hp*); Ueli Wiget, Hermann Kretzschmar (*p*); Klaus Obermaier (*g*); Sebastian Gottschick, Thomas Hofer, Peter Rundel, Hilary Sturt (*vn*); Werner Dickel, Almut Steinhausen (*vla*); Michael Stirling, Friedemann Dähn (*clo*); Thomas Fichter (*b*); Diego Masson (*cond*); & Creative Music Ensemble: Torsten Maas, Hermann Ss, Tobias Netta (*t*); Ferdinand Von Seebach, Heinz-Erich Gödecke (*tb*); Dizi Fischer (*tba*); Adam Zablocki (*f*); Wolfgang Schubert (*eng hn*); Vlatko Kucan (*ss*); Klaus Roemer (*as*); Bernd Reinecke (*bs*); Georgia Charlotte Hoppe (*bcl*); Buggy Braune (*p*); Bernd Von Ostrowski (*vib*); Dirk Dhonau (*mar*); Andreas Nock (*g*); Hans Schüttler (*syn*); Nicola Kruse, Mauretta Heinzelmann, Dorothea Geiger (*vn*); Mike Rutledge (*vla*); Cornelia Gottberg, Ralf Werner (*clo*); Peter Skriptschinsky, Johannes Huth, Peter Niklas Wilson (*b*); Dieter Gostischa, Heinz Lichius, Björn Lücker, Martin Engelbach (*perc*); conducted by Braxton. 10/89, 2/91.

In the autumn of 1988, Braxton toured Finland with an *ad hoc* group called Ensemble Braxtonia. It is to their credit – considerable collective experience notwithstanding – that they coped so well with numbers 144 and 145, and the ease with which these were communicated to a highly enthusiastic audience at the Tampere Jazz Happening (Jarvenpaa is Sibelius's home and a point of pilgrimage for Finnish musicians) gives some sense of the movement of Braxton's work from the far periphery to something near the hub of contemporary creative music. There is nothing here that would frighten the horses, just intense, very focused music of a high order. Only the recording lets it down.

Eugene is one of Braxton's finest discs, and certainly the most accessible of the larger-group recordings; this features eight compositions dating from 1975 to the present day, and was recorded in Eugene, Oregon, during a 'creative orchestra' tour of the Pacific North-West. Much of the credit for the project has to go to trombonist Mike Heffley, who originally proposed and subsequently organized the tour.

The earliest of the pieces, 'Composition No. 45', was written for a free-jazz festival in Baden-Baden and is defined by Braxton in his *Composition Notes C* as 'an extended platform for the challenge of post-Coltrane/Ayler functionalism'. A march, it anticipates the more complex 'Composition No. 58' (not included here) but demonstrates how creatively Braxton has been able to use the large-scale 'outdoor' structures he draws from Henry Brant, Sun Ra and traditional marching music, to open up unsuspected areas of improvisatory freedom; the link with Ayler's apocalyptic 'Truth Is Marching In' is immediately obvious. 'Composition No. 91' is a delicately pointillistic piece with a much more abstract configuration. Less propulsive than 'No. 45' or the more conventional ensemble-and-soloists outline of 'No. 71', it underlines the composer's brilliant grasp of instrumental colour; synthesizer and electric guitar provide some unfamiliar tonalities in the context of Braxton's work and, perhaps in reaction, he limits his own playing to alto saxophone.

Braxton's work has taken on an increasingly ritualistic quality, as in the processional opening and steady two-beat pulse of the most recent piece, 'Composition No. 134'. As such, it stands beside the work of Stockhausen and the composers mentioned above. If its underlying philosophy is millennial, its significance is commensurate with that. That's confirmed by *Two Compositions (Ensemble)*, a recording which straddles the start of a new decade and marks Braxton's emergence as a composer of major significance. It also takes him somewhat outside the range of this book, except that the programmatic content of both pieces ('Composition No. 147' with the Ensemble Modern most obviously) takes him back into the cultural environment of bebop and the explosive musical language spawned by it. 'Composition No. 151' is prefaced by a curious narrative involving a character called Harvey, a cop called Zuphthon and a city of shining glass and chrome. The work attempts to disassemble identity and then reconstitute it on ever higher levels of temporal organization. The playing is certainly not as crisp as the Ensemble Modern's, and the piece lacks the focus of the earlier work's three solo clarinets. Even so, along with *Eugene*, the set marks a formidable step forward in Braxton's ability to marshal large orchestral forces.

*** **Eight Duets – Hamburg 1991** Music & Arts CD 710
    Braxton; Peter Niklas Wilson (*b*). 2/91.
**** **Duo (London) 1993** Leo CD LR 193
    Braxton; Evan Parker (*ts, ss*). 7/93.
The duets with Wilson are a bit of a throwback, recalling a set recorded with John Lindberg in the 1980s and released on Cecma. Braxton, who was working in Hamburg on 'Composition No. 151' (see above), often sounds as if he is simply filling in time, though when he does fire, as in 'Composition No. 153' when his alto burns fiercely, the music is very impressive indeed. Braxton uses four instruments twice in all; in addition to alto, he plays flute (brilliantly on the well-established '40(A)'), contrabass clarinet (on which he often recalls Dolphy's duets with Richard Davis) and soprano saxophone, which pairs only rather uneasily with Wilson's refreshingly fleet bass playing.

**** **Willisau (Quartet) 1991** hat ART 4 61001/2/3/4 4CD
    Braxton; Marilyn Crispell (*p*); Mark Dresser (*b*); Gerry Hemingway (*d*). 6/91.
A whopper. Two double-CDs, one recorded in the studio, one in concert. Half a decade after the now-classic 1985 quartets, Braxton's music seems to be moving in a more sequential, almost narratological, direction. That is obvious in the new material, but it also influences his approach to such familiar reference-points as the opus 40 pieces, and numbers 23 and 69.

There is considerably more than four hours of music on the set, much of it reaching as high as anything Braxton has done, but there is also a fair degree of mere journeywork and signs of rather pat collageism in the multiple pieces. Crispell is by now so strong and individual a performer that she fits into the music only by suppressing (sometimes audibly) her most characteristic qualities. Hemingway, too, doesn't always sound completely attuned to the new approach, though it probably allows him a freer hand than before. Fascinating stuff, and beautifully played, but it certainly doesn't supersede the 1985 sessions.

**** **Four (Ensemble) Compositions** Black Saint 120124
    Braxton; Robert Rumboltz (*t*); Roland Dahinden, John Rapson (*tb*); Don Byron (*cl, bcl*); Marty Ehrlich (*f, picc, cl, as, ts*); J. D. Parran (*f, cl, bcl, acl, bamboo f*); Randy McKean (*cl, as, bcl*); Ted Reichmann, Guy Klucevesek (*acc*); Amina Claudine Myers (*org, v*); Jay Hoggard (*vib, mar*); Lynden Achee, Warren Smith (*perc*). 92.
***(*) **Composition No. 165** New Albion NA 050
    Braxton; University of Illinois Creative Music Orchestra: Thomas Tait, Jeff Helgesen, Judd G. Danby (*t*); Erik Lund, Douglas Farwell, Keith Moore (*tb*); Jesse Seifert-Gram (*tba*); Paul Martin Zonn (*as, cl, slide sax*); Graham Kessler (*as, cl*); Andrew Mitroff (*ts, f*); Kevin Engel (*ts, bsn, cl*); Mark Barone (*bs, bcl*); Tom Paynter (*p*); Mark Zanter (*g*); Drew Krause (*syn*); Adam Davis (*b*); Justin Kramer, Tom Sherwood (*perc*). 2/92.
The material on *Four (Ensemble) Compositions* is a combination of brand-new compositions – numbers 163 and 164 – with a fascinating performance of the pivotal 'Composition No. 96'. This time, the orchestra includes time-served jazz players and improvisers, and the piece takes on a limber, relaxed charm that it can't altogether claim on the Leo recording. 'Composition No. 165', on the New Albion, is surprisingly direct and unfussy, but it lacks the element of sheer shock that Braxton used to bring, and there are moments when it is drifts perilously close to cosy classicism. Once again, one wonders to what extent these players understand where Braxton is coming from. The wonderful thing about the ensemble on the Black Saint is that they've all been there, too.

These sessions, like some of their predecessors, pose one intriguing question about Braxton's future work. Will he come to see himself more and more as a composer/conductor, less and less as an improvising instrumentalist; or does he believe that he can sustain both strands? For the sake of improvised music, one hopes so.

*** Duets (1993) Music & Arts CD 786

    Braxton; Mario Pavone (*b*). 1/93.

Pavone has still not made the impact one would have expected, either as a leader (see below under his name) or as a sideman. His response to 'Composition No 6(O)', which has become standard Braxton fare, is highly individual and even idiosyncratic, preserving the unmistakable contours of one of the saxophonist's most expressive conceptions but also steering it in a new and unexpected direction, where pure melody becomes an issue again. Braxton has played better, and now and again he lapses into a pointless *sotto voce* which tends to lose the thread. A more than acceptable session, though, and dedicated collectors will certainly not be disappointed.

**** Duo (London) 1993 Leo CD LR 193

    Braxton; Evan Parker (*ts*). 5/93.

**** Trio (London) 1993 Leo CD LR 197

    As above, except add Paul Rutherford (*tb*). 5/93.

Braxton has been quoted as saying that these recordings gave him more solace in times of doubt and uncertainty than anything he had played for many years. Contrary to expectation, both men sound cool and thoughtful. The understanding with Parker is almost telepathic as intricate, bleached lines spiral upwards at ever higher levels of organization. Parker in particular sounds as though he has awakened ancestral ghosts, at a couple of points sounding disconcertingly like one of Braxton's masters, Warne Marsh, and hovering on the verge of harmonic improvisation throughout the set. In strict harmonic terms, he may even be ahead of his partner in this sort of project. He seems to be able to hear harmonics two places above the ostensible playing position and to bring them into play quite seamlessly and unforcedly.

    He is doing the same thing on the trio set, recorded at the same London festival. Rutherford's contribution is to make the music more abstract. Any intention on Braxton's part to restore elements of jazz language is confounded and, as so often in a European environment, he is pushed out into unfamiliar and very challenging territory, where he is obliged to examine his procedures note by note. These are exhilarating performances, among his most radical small-group works.

***(*) Charlie Parker Project 1993 hat ART CD 2-6160 2CD

    Braxton; Paul Smoker (*t, flhn*); Ari Brown (*ts, ss*); Misha Mengelberg (*p*); Joe Fonda (*b*); Han Bennink, Pheeroan akLaff (*d*). 10/93.

This would seem to take Braxton back direct to one of his most fundamental sources. As is probably already obvious, Parker has been supplanted, or at least sidelined, as an influence for much of the last decade and a half, but yet has remained the shadowy Ur-text from which nearly everything derives. On this double CD (what else?) Braxton plays Parker material, first in concert with Bennink at the drums, and then, on the very next day, in studio with akLaff. Whether the Dutchman was on a promise elsewhere or fell out with the boss isn't clear, but his presence is decidedly disturbing, and the difference between the common tracks – 'Klactoveesedstene', 'Night In Tunisia' – suggests that he wasn't the ideal choice for the gig.

    It's fascinating to hear Braxton work his way inside less well-known themes like 'An Oscar For Treadwell' and 'Sippin' At Bell's', and the presence of the enigmatic Smoker and Mengelberg adds to a shifting, almost evanescent atmosphere that is both close and alien to what we know about Parker. Consistently fascinating from start to finish.

(***) Composition No 174 Leo CD LR 217

    Arizona State University Percussion Ensemble. 2/94.

Though we stand by our assertion that Braxton's music is readily accommodatable on CD, one wonders about this piece, which is written for percussion ensemble and constructed environment and which seems to concern a party of mountaineers and an expedition that is a cross between *The Ascent of F6* and a virtual reality primer to Braxton's compositional method. There are oddities in the registration of the instruments – a broad-ranging percussion ensemble – which beg the question as to whether the music is played accurately or whether hitches and uncertainties have persisted in this premiere performance. Unless you are Anthony Braxton, impossible to judge.

*** Knitting Factory (Piano / Quartet): Volume 1 Leo CD LR 222/223 2CD

    Braxton; Marty Ehrlich (*as, ss, cl*); Joe Fonda (*b*); Pheeroan akLaff (*d*). 94.

*** Piano Quartet, Yoshi's, 1994 Music & Arts CD 849 4CD

    As above, except omit akLaff; add Arthur Fuller (*d, perc*). 6/94.

It was no surprise to anyone who has heard him play keyboard that Braxton should want to release something of this sort; he is also an accomplished drummer, and we can't rule out a future percussion project. What is astonishing is that he should have permitted the release of *six* CDs, with the explicit promise of more – volumes two, three? more? – on Leo.

    These are exclusively jazz repertoire sessions, a detailed and highly respectful examination of composers who have affected Braxton and his music. The range of material is astonishing: Mingus, Brubeck, Monk, Golson, Noble, Miles, Dolphy, Gryce, and (on the Leo) Shorter, Mingus and Monk again, Ellington, Tristano. It is difficult to gauge how we might assess these performances if the pianist were anyone but Braxton. In a sense, he does not sound 'like himself'. The switch of register, the harmonic resource, the relative unfamiliarity, all make a profound difference, and yet it is clear that he is directing operations in a quite interventionist way. Ehrlich is a strong player but not a particularly passionate structuralist, and he seems to follow where Braxton leads, allowing his pitching and coloration to be determined quite explicitly

(***) Composition No. 173 Black Saint 120166
> Braxton; Melinda Newman (*ob*); Brandon Evans (*sno, bcl*); Jennifer Hill (*cl*); Bo Bell (*bsn*); Nickie Braxton, Danielle Langston (*vn*); Brett W. Larner (*koto*); Kevin O'Neil (*g*); Sandra Miller, Jacob Rosen (*clo*); Dirck Westervelt (*b*); Joe Fonda (*b*); Josh Rosenblatt (*perc*); actors. 12/94.

'"I hear an influence coming in from the CKA areas," cried Miss Tishingham' is about the most illuminating commentary on this one. Another of Braxton's multi-media pieces, it transfers to disc no more incompletely and insecurely than its successor (which was recorded first). Like 'No. 174', it has moments of real musical beauty, especially here when the woodwinds are soloing; but to what extent the 'score' can be separated from the *mise en scène* and the stage apparatus is beyond our competence. It may still be jazz music, but not as we know it, Jim.

Joshua Breakstone (born 1955) GUITAR

*** Evening Star Contemporary CCD-14040-2
> Breakstone; Jimmy Knepper (*tb*); Tommy Flanagan (*p*); Dave Shapiro (*b*); Keith Copeland (*d*).

*** Self-Portrait In Swing Contemporary CCD-14050-2
> Breakstone; Kenny Barron (*p*); Dennis Irwin (*b*); Kenny Washington (*d*).

*** 9 By 3 Contemporary CCD-14062-2
> As above, except omit Barron.

**(*) I Want To Hold Your Hand (The Compositions Of The Beatles Vol. 1) Paddle Wheel KICJ 122
> As above, except add Kenny Barron (*p*). 6/92.

**(*) Oh! Darling (The Compositions Of The Beatles Vol. 2) Paddle Wheel KICJ 123
> As above. 6/92.

*** Remembering Grant Green Paddle Wheel KICJ 169
> Breakstone; Kenny Barron (*p*); Jack McDuff (*org*); Ray Drummond (*b*); Al Harewood, Keith Copeland (*d*). 1–3/93.

*** Sittin' On the Thing With Ming Capri 74042-2
> As above, except omit Mcduff and Harewood. 1/93.

Breakstone loves the sound of traditional jazz guitar, as in cool, clear, single-note lines delivered with a soft articulation and a tone that insinuates rather than jumps out of his amplifier. He can peel melodies off the frets with little effort, but sometimes his manner is so relaxed that his improvisations go to sleep; with impeccable but deferential rhythm sections on most of these records, that's a small but significant problem. *Evening Star* has Jimmy Knepper to add some spice to the line-up, but more typical are the several sessions with Barron at the piano. *Self-Portrait In Swing* is perhaps the best of them, since the tempos have an extra ounce of bounce, while the two discs of Beatles tunes, though sweet-toned and balmy in feel, suffer from the pop familiarity of the melodies: one ends up waiting to see how Breakstone will jazz a melody that western civilization has locked in its collective memory. But at least these are much better than Basie's *Beatle Bag*. Barron sits out on *9 By 3*, which was cut straight after a tour in which Breakstone had no pianist on hand, and the session is slightly looser as a result – though not necessarily better.

Remembering Grant Green is a rare homage – when guitarists remember anyone these days, it's usually Wes Montgomery. Breakstone had already paid a modest tribute by recapitulating Green's original solo on 'I Want To Hold Your Hand' on the first of his Beatles albums, and here he tackles half a dozen pieces of Greenery with calm assurance. McDuff adds apposite organ licks, Rudy Van Gelder produces, and Paddle Wheel even copy the Blue Note cover-art style; but the record still sounds like a pleasant diversion rather than required listening. Unfortunately, one could say much the same about *Sittin' On The Thing With Ming*, which goes off at a busy pace with the title-tune and shifts through the expected cadences of such a session without much surprise. All but one of the tunes are originals, which is something of a departure for the guitarist, but his writing is scholarly rather than exciting. Barron, Drummond and Copeland add the extra notch with their unimpeachable class.

Michael Brecker (born 1949) TENOR SAXOPHONE, EWI

*** **Michael Brecker** Impulse! MCA 5980
>   Brecker; Kenny Kirkland (*ky*); Pat Metheny (*g*); Charlie Haden (*b*); Jack DeJohnette (*d*). 87.

(*) **Don't Try This At Home Impulse! MCA 42229-2
>   Brecker; Don Grolnick, Herbie Hancock, Joey Calderazzo (*p*); Mark O'Connor (*vn*); Mike Stern (*g*); Charlie Haden, Jeff Andrews (*b*); Jack DeJohnette, Adam Nussbaum, Peter Erskine (*d*). 88.

The sax-playing one of the Brecker brothers has appeared on some 500 record dates but has made only a handful of discs as sole leader. He is, nevertheless, one of the most admired and emulated saxophonists of the day. He began playing in rock and soul bands in the late 1960s, worked with Horace Silver and Billy Cobham in the '70s and put together the very successful Steps Ahead group in 1979. His tenure as a session man has polished his style into something superbly confident and muscular, a Coltrane without the questing inner turmoil. His steely, brilliant sense of structure ensures that almost every solo he plays is impressive; whether he is emotionally involving may depend on the listener's willingness to believe.

Michael Brecker, his 1987 debut, suggested that he had been unreasonably shy about recording as a leader: his own compositions, 'Sea Glass' and 'Syzygy', are attractive if not exactly haunting, while producer Don Grolnick's tunes elicit some suitably herculean solos. The interplay with DeJohnette inevitably recalls something of the Coltrane–Elvin Jones partnership, while Kirkland, Haden and the unusually restrained Metheny combine to create a super-session of genuine commitment. But *Don't Try This At Home* seemed like a too casual follow-up, with several of the pieces sounding like left-overs from the first session and Brecker cruising through the record in his session-man identity rather than imposing a leader's presence.

*** **Now You See It . . . (Now You Don't)** GRP GR-9622
>   Brecker; Jim Beard, Joey Calderazzo (*ky*); Jon Herington (*g*); Victor Bailey, Jay Anderson (*b*); Adam Nussbaum, Omar Hakim (*d*); Don Alias, Steve Berrios, Milton Cardona (*perc*). 90.

Brecker's third record as a leader is a mixed success. Too few of the eight themes are truly memorable or demanding on anything other than a technical level, and some of the synthesizer orchestration is a distraction rather than a benefit. The best jazz comes in the tracks where the saxophonist gets a clear run at the listener: on 'Peep', which turns into a kind of abstract funk, and 'The Meaning Of The Blues', which is unadorned tenor-plus-rhythm. The slow intensification of the saxophonist's improvisation on 'Minsk' is the one moment where Brecker best displays his mastery: it's staggeringly well played. Don Grolnick's production is snappy and clean without being as glaring as many fusion records.

Randy Brecker (born 1945) TRUMPET

*** **In The Idiom** Denon 33CY 1483
>   Brecker; Joe Henderson (*ts*); David Kikoski (*p*); Ron Carter (*b*); Al Foster (*d*). 10/86.

** **Mr Max!** Nabel CD 4637
>   Brecker; Wolfgang Engstfeld (*ts*); Gunnar Plümer (*b*); Peter Weiss (*d*). 5/89.

Brecker is less generously talented than his saxophone-playing younger sibling, but he is still an impressive soloist whose style has mellowed and matured since the barnstorming fusion days of the Brecker Brothers. *In The Idiom*'s top-drawer line-up suggested a strong desire to move back into the jazz mainstream, and the chops to pull it off. Henderson and the pedigree rhythm section give him lots of time and room, and Brecker plays two or three strongly authentic solos, marked by an unhurried exploration of basic (but by no means banal) harmonic ideas.

The Nabel session is pretty forgettable. Engstfeld shares top billing and gets more than his fair share of solo space. If a diluted version of Michael Brecker can be imagined (and it ought to be; it's pretty ubiquitous) then that's about right for this. 'On Green Dolphin Street' could be by an average pub band.

Dave Brennan BANJO, GUITAR

(*) **Take Me To The Mardi Gras Lake LACD 20
>   Brennan; Pat O'Brien (*t, v*); Dave Vickers (*tb*); Frank Brooker (*cl, as, ts*); Mick Kennedy (*b*); Terry Kennedy (*d*). 4/90–2/91.

Dave Brennan has been leading his Jubilee Jazz Band for 30 years, though records have been very few. This anniversary set is scarcely a milestone in British trad, but it sums up both the pros and cons of the genre. The material is determinedly unhackneyed and includes Henry Allen's 'Ride Red Ride', 'Rip 'Em Up Joe', 'Eccentric Rag' and 'Dauphine Street Blues'; the playing ranges from rumbustious energy to a surprisingly delicate touch on the filigree treatment of 'Mood Indigo'; the echoes of George Lewis and

Bunk Johnson are integrated into a home-grown spirit which is by now just as 'authentic'; and the best of the individual contributions, particularly Dave Vickers's trombone solos, are impressive. On the other side of the coin are the vocals (still the least appealing aspect of British trad); the frequently flat dynamics; and a sense of ennui which the restrictive practices of the genre encourage rather than exonerate. But it would be churlish to deny the best of this music. The recording is truthful and lifelike.

John Wolf Brennan PIANO, KEYBOARDS, ELECTRONICS, COMPOSER

(*) **Mountain Hymn L + R 45002
  Brennan; Urs Leimgruber (*ts, ss, bs s, bamboo f, etc.*). 9/85.
** **Entupadas** Creative Works CW 1013
  Brennan; Corina Curschellas (*v, dulcimer, kalimba, acc, f, police siren, perc*). 11/85.
*** **An Chara** L + R 45007
  As above. 1/86.
*** **Henceforward** Core COCD 900871 0
  Brennan; Christy Doran (*g*). 5/88.
*(*) **Polyphyllum** L + R 45013
  As above. 5/89.
(*) **MAP (Music For Another Planet) L + R 45021
  As above, except add Norma Winstone (*v*). 8/88 & 5/89.
(*) **The Beauty Of Fractals Creative Works CW 1017 1
  Brennan (*ky* solo). 12/88.
(*) **Iritations Creative Works CW 1021
  Brennan (*ky* solo). 4/90.
*** **Ten Zentences** L + R CDLR 45066
  Brennan; Daniele Patumi (*b*). 5/91.
*** **Text, Context, Co-Text, Co-Co-Text** Creative Works CW 1025
  Brennan (*p* solo). 94.
***(*) **Shooting Stars And Traffic Lights** Bellaphon CDLR 45090
  Brennan; John Voirol (*ts, ss*); Tscho Theissing (*vn*); Daniele Patumi (*b*); Alex Cline (*d, perc*). 95.
John Wolf Brennan was born and raised in Ireland, lives and works in Switzerland, and bears a startling resemblance from certain angles to Gene Pitney. This is, as they say, a complex fate.

His music combines the romanticism of the one place with the watchmaker exactness of the other. It is approachable but somehow also irreducible and manages to avoid a fatal descent into New Age blandness only by the thickness of Brennan's remarkable aptitude for the unexpected. The solo *Beauty Of Fractals*, which combines studio and live recordings, and the 'nonsolopiano' *Iritations* (which combines standard and prepared piano with Martin Spuhler's environmental sound objects) are perhaps the best introduction to his style, but the duos with Leimgruber and with Doran particularly are powerful and affecting; Leimgruber's extreme tonal range fits in perfectly both with the folkish material of the earlier sets and with the increasing abstraction of *Polyphyllum* and *MAP*. The addition of Norma Winstone's remarkable voice adds a dimension to a handful of cuts on *MAP*; by contrast, Corina Curschellas tends to overpower. The more recent *Ten Zentences* involves a less absorbing partnership, but Patumi has the ability to string together arresting miniatures and to use space and silence in an attractively abstract way. (Brennan has also recently composed a cycle of art songs called *Bestiarium* to be performed by other players. These are certainly neither jazz nor improvised pieces, but they merit a listen.)

Shooting Stars And Traffic Lights has a settled group feel, reinforcing the impression that Brennan works best *as a player* in collective settings, whether or not these constrain his more extravagant outpourings. Compare his playing on the two new listings. *Shooting Stars* is as open and fresh as *Text* (what a title! we should co-co) is broodingly internalized. That isn't to say that it fails to communicate, merely that it communicates in a much less direct fashion than the group record, or his more recent work with Pago Libre.

Brennan is a thoughtful composer, not merely a slick executor. Where some of the solo pieces are over-intellectualized, his collaborations tend to steer him in the welcome direction of a simpler lyricism, which is convincing, entire and very beautiful. We've thought on about the question of this music's exact angle on the jazz mainstream. It still doesn't matter.

Willem Breuker (born 1944) SAXOPHONES, CLARINETS, RECORDER

***(*) **Baal Brecht Breuker Handke** BVHAAST CD 9006
  Breuker; Cees Klaver (*t*); Bernard Hunnekink (*tb*); Jan Wolff (*hn*); Donald Blakeslee (*tba*); Bob

Driessen (*as*); Herman De Wit (*ts*); Louis Andriessen (*p, org, hpd*); Maarten van Regteren Altena (*b*); Han Bennink (*d, tap dance*). 10/73, 10/74.

*** **Bertolt Brecht / Herman Heijermans** BVHAAST CD 9003

Breuker; Ad Klink, Jos Kieft (*t*); Bernard Hunnekink (*tb*); Leonore Pameijer (*f, picc*); Rob Bouwmeester (*ob*); Leon Bosch (*cl*); Wim Jonas (*bsn, cbsn*); Henk De Jonge (*p, acc*); Jan Erik van Regteren Altena, Lorre Trytten (*vn*); Eduard van Regteren Altena (*clo*); Ernst Glerum (*b*); Rob Verdurmen (*perc*). 9/73.

**** **De Onderste Steen** Entr'acte CD 2

Breuker; Andy Altenfelder, Cees Klaver, Boy Raaymakers (*t*); Iman Soetemann, Jan Wolff (*frhn*); Bernard Hunnekink (*tb, tba*); Gregg Moore (*tb*); Willem Van Manen (*tb, v*); Dil Engelhardt (*f*); André Goudbeek (*as*); Peter Barkema (*ts, bs*); Emil Keijzer, Reinbert De Leeuw, Bert Van Dijk (*p*); Leo Cuypers (*p, mca*); Henk De Jonge (*p, acc, ky*); Louis Andriessen (*p, org, hpd*); Johnny Meyer (*acc*); Michael Waisvisz (*syn*); Sytze Smit (*vn*); Maarten van Regteren Altena, Arjen Gorter (*b*); Han Bennink, Martin Van Duynhoven, Rob Verdurmen (*perc*); Frits Lambrechts, Olga Zuiderhoek (*gamelan*); Mondriaan Strings; Ernö Ola String Quartet; Daniël Otten String Group. 74–91.

*** **De Illusionist, Kkkomediant** BVHAAST CD 9205

Breuker; Jos Kieft, Ad Klink, Jelle Schouten, Carlo De Wild (*t*); Bernard Hunnekink, Chris Abelen, Hans Van Balen (*tb*); Roel Koster (*frhn*); Loes Kerstens, Leonore Pameijer (*f, picc*); Fred Man (*Pan f*); Rob Bouwmeester, Evert Weidner (*ob*); Rob Bouwmeester (*eng hn*); André Kerver (*cl*); Guus Dral, Jos De Lange, Wim Jonas (*bsn*); Hens Otter (*tarogato*); Henk De Jonge (*p, ky, acc*); Julian B. Coco, Jan De Hont (*g*); Ernestine Stoop (*hp*); Jan Vermeulen, Thom De Ligt (*b*); Rob Verdurmen, Martin Van Duynhoven (*perc*); Rami Koch, Stanislaw Lukowski (*vn*); Michel Samson (*vla*); Henk Lambooij (*clo*); B. Borden, Ananda Goud, Hans Pootjes, Richard Zook, Hans Vermeulen, Jody Pijper (*v*). 3 & 4/83, 2/85.

***(*) **To Remain** BVHAAST CD 8904

Breuker; Andreas Altenfelder, Boy Raaymakers (*t*); Chris Abelen, Bernard Hunnekink, Garrett List, Gregg Moore (*tb*); André Goudbeek (*as*); Peter Barkema, Maarten Van Norden (*ts*); Henk De Jonge (*p, ky*); Arjen Gorter (*b*); Rob Verdurmen (*d, perc*). 9/83, 12/84, 1–4/89.

**** **Bob's Gallery** BVHAAST CD 8801

Breuker; Boy Raaymakers (*t*); Chris Abelen (*tb*); Bernard Hunnekink (*tb, tba*); André Goudbeek (*as*); Peter Barkema (*ts*); Henk De Jonge (*p, syn*); Arjen Gorter (*b*); Rob Verdurmen (*perc, xyl*); Peter Kuit Jr (*tapdance*). 12/87.

*** **Metropolis** BVHAAST CD 8903

Breuker; Andreas Altenfelder, Boy Raaymakers (*t, v*); Gregg Moore (*tb, v*); Bernard Hunnekink (*tb, tba, v*); André Goudbeek (*as, v*); Peter Barkema (*as, ts, bs*); Henk De Jonge (*p, cel, syn*); Arjen Gorter (*b*); Rob Verdurmen (*perc*); Toby Rix (*Toeterix, hca*); Mondriaan Strings: Jan Erik van Regteren Altena, Erik Kromhout, Alison Wallace (*vn*); Aimée Versloot, Jan Schoonenberg (*vla*); Wieke Meyer, Eduard van Regteren Altena (*clo*). 11/87, 12/88, 1–4/89.

***(*) **Parade** BVHAAST CD 9101

As for *Metropolis*, except omit Rix; add Alex Coke (*ts, f*). 12/90.

**** **Heibel** BVHAAST CD 9102

As for *Parade*, except omit Coke; add Greetje Bijma (*v*); Lorre Trytten (*vn*). 12/90, 5/91.

*** **Meets Djazzex** BVHAAST 9513

As above, except omit Bijma, Trytten. 5/92.

**** **Deze Kant Op, Dames / This Way, Ladies** BVHAAST CD 9301

As for *Parade*, except omit Mondriaan Strings; replace Verdurmen with Arend Niks (*perc*); Loes Luca (*v*). 12/92.

*** **Sensemaya** BVHAAST CD 9509

Breuker; Andy Altenfelder, Boy Raaymakers (*t*); Nico Nijholt (*tb*); Bernard Hunnekink (*tb, tba*); Alex Coke (*ts, f*); Peter Barkema (*as, ts*); Han De Vries (*ob*); Henk De Jonge (*p, syn*); Arjen Gorter (*b*); Rob Verdurmen (*d*); Greetje Kauffeld (*v*); strings. 6/95.

**** **The Parrot** BVHAAST CD 9601

Drawn from listing above. 80–95.

If the Dutch soccer side of the 1970s played 'total football', then this is 'total jazz'. Joachim Berendt likens Breuker's use of Dutch and Low German folk music to Roland Kirk's unironic and loving use of the less elevated music of the black tradition. Eclecticism of this sort has been a feature of post-war Dutch music. Composers like Louis Andriessen (who appears on *De Onderste Steen*) and Misha Mengelberg have made extensive use of jazz and rock forms as a way of breaking down the tyranny of serialism and of rigid formal structures. Like the late Frank Zappa, whom Breuker in some respects resembles and whose strange critical marginality he shares, the Dutchman was turned on to classical music by hearing Varèse, whose enthusiastic embrace of chaos is very much a part of what Breuker and

Mengelberg are about; but Breuker has made a point of guying the more pompous aspects of all the musics he has a hand in. In structural terms, he does so by simple juxtaposition, placing popular melodies alongside quasi-classical themes. In terms of instrumental colour, he relies on the populist associations of saxophones, tubas; on *Baal*, ukuleles and mandolins, elsewhere invented (non)instruments like Toby Rix's. Clearly, a good deal of this music fits only rather uncomfortably into a 'jazz' category. Breuker's Kollektief is a performance band in the fullest sense. Whether the music transfers successfully to record will depend largely on personal taste and on a level of sympathy with what Breuker is about. However, it is necessary to point out that most of the performances listed, even the concert recordings by the Kollektief, depend to some extent on visual components which the listener at home has no access to.

Breuker has also frequently been likened to Kurt Weill (he includes 'Pirate Jenny's Song' from *Die Dreigroschenoper* on *Driesburgen-Zeist*) and is as likely to use harmonic devices, structural principles, and occasionally straight quotes, from concert music ('Prokof' on *In Holland* is a good example) as from popular sources; he is also a fundamentally theatrical composer, and several of these records are of music written for dramatic performance or for films, as in the case of *De Illusionist, Kkkomediant*, which represents the sountracks to two movies by Freek de Jonge, whose work is never going to trouble Orson Welles, even on a good day.

Another obvious parallel is with Brecht and Weill, whose experiments in total theatre have been absorbed into the mainstream only rather slowly. A melody from Weill's *Lady In The Dark* opens *Metropolis*, but the most extended examinations are the music for Brecht's *Baal*, and for his parable of fascism, *The Resistible Rise Of Arturo Ui*, which is paired with music for a television documentary on the novelist and playwright, Herman Heijermans. The *Baal* disc also contains a score for the Austrian novelist Peter Handke's hallucinatory drama, known in English as *The Ride Over Lake Constance*. In all of these, the music is ironic, referential, collaging a bizarre variety of materials, such as 'White Cliffs Of Dover' on *Baal*, tags from hymns and national anthems on *Parade*. This is the most formal of the records in some respects, developing material by Satie and Weill ('Aggie's Sewing Machine Song' from *Johnny Johnson*) alongside music written more specifically for the Kollektief. The title-piece on *Metropolis* is a realization of a piece by Ferde Grofé, whose *Grand Canyon Suite* is a concert favourite. The remainder of the programme consists of a typically diverse (not to say perverse) array of materials, including Haydn's 1796 'Trumpet Concerto', in which the soloist's part is taken by former singing cowboy, Toby Rix, with his patented Toeterix, an instrument constructed out of chromatically tuned car-horns. It reappears on the closing 'I Want To Be Happy'; Rix also plays harmonica on two traditional songs arranged by Breuker.

It's unfortunate that a number of the saxophonist's more improvisational records are not currently on release. Of the Kollektief albums, by far the best known (and probably the best initial bet) is the FMP/ BVHAAST co-release, *Live In Berlin*, which is still worth looking out for and which will doubtless reappear soon. The obvious model is Ellington; Breuker uses his soloists in the same individualistic but still disciplined way (one wonders how 'anarchic' these bands *really* are). Recorded versions of 'Creole Love Call', and other straight repertoire like the Gershwin arrangements on a currently unavailable 1987–8 tribute, are played remarkably straight – though such is the imaginative tension the Kollektief generates that one finds oneself listening more intently than usual, in constant expectation of a sudden chorus of raspberries or a dramatic swerve of tone. It's possible that critics and even Breuker have overplayed the comic hand; *To Remain*'s 11 movements suggest that his reputation as a *farceur* is (like Roland Kirk's) emphasized at the expense of understanding his remarkable technical and structural abilities.

Though it's now being overtaken by a vigorous new CD programme, *De Onderste Steen* is still an indispensable sampling of Breuker's improvised and compositional work over a decade and a half. The opening piece is a traditional Indian melody; the next is the magnificent threnody for Duke Ellington, marked by an emotional growl solo by Raaymakers (who has obviously absorbed Rex Stewart and Cootie Williams) over a throbbing, dead-march ostinato. There are two tangos, a gamelan, some cod Vivaldi, and a bizarre swing blues called 'My Baby Has Gone To The Schouwburg', which eventually collapses in harmonic(a) chaos, a Satie-influenced composition for Reinbert de Leeuw (a distinguished interpreter of Satie piano pieces) and two theatre pieces. Musically, it's the best available profile of Breuker's work over nearly 20 years, but availability may very well be a moot point.

It should be easier to find Breuker's own sampling of his work on *The Parrot*. This really covers the early 1980s, with just a single track, 'Potsdamer Stomp', from 1995, offering a perspective that would be slightly skewed were the Kollektief not so absolutely consistent in their unpredictability. It does seem that just about any point of entry makes no less sense than any other, so it is often a good idea just to jump in.

Even so, the next best choices for the newcomer are undoubtedly *To Remain* and *Bob's Gallery*. On the latter, the wonderfully skew-whiff title-track, which is inspired by a Gary Larson cartoon, features magnificent solos by Goudbeek, Raaymakers and Breuker. 'Morribreuk', with Altenfelder and

Raaymakers processing from the back of the hall to the stage, is a dedication to Ennio Morricone. There is also a dedication to the offbeat jazz pianist and composer (has Breuker ever done 'Yellow Waltz'?) Richard Twardzik, and a selection of pieces from the theatre work, *Thanks, Your Majesty*, making this one of the jazzier Kollektief records. That's a factor that may appeal to those who find his media-mixing a turn-off. However, the two '90s recordings are also extremely attractive. *This Way, Ladies* is a musical, co-written with Ischa Meijer. It concerns the silver anniversary celebrations of Louise (played by Loes Luca) and the Count Guillaume de Breuckelaere (a figure who presents a disconcerting resemblance to our hero, the saxophonist and composer). Much of the action takes place in his concussed brain as a notably democratic celebration carries on around him. The dreamlike action and several of the themes, notably 'Dirge For An Insignificant Musician', suggest that Breuker may have been drinking at the same well as Carla Bley: shades of her *Genuine Tong Funeral* and *Escalator Over The Hill*. However, the pace and the wry dynamics of the thing are Breuker's own and, for once, the absence of the theatrical element doesn't seem to matter unduly.

The curiously packaged *Heibel* (it comes in a cheese box) combines a concert recording by the Kollektief with superb solo contributions from Raaymakers on the Ellington threnody, 'Duke Edward/Misère', and from the redoubtable Verdurmen. The second half of the set consists of another mini-opera, this time for the astonishing voice of Greetje Bijma, a solo singer of great presence and range. It's a slighter – if rather more sober – piece than *This Way, Ladies* and depends more on the soloists (Lorre Trytten has a prominent part) than on the usual Breuker mayhem.

Nick Brignola (born 1936) BARITONE, SOPRANO, TENOR AND ALTO SAXOPHONES, CLARINET, ALTO CLARINET, BASS CLARINET, FLUTE, PICCOLO

*** L. A. Bound Night Life SB 2003/CD NLR 3007
Brignola; Bill Watrous (*tb*); Dwight Dickerson (*p*); John Heard (*b*); Dick Berk (*d*). 10/79.
Opening on Horace Silver's 'Quicksilver', delivered at a hurricane tempo, this is a good way to get to know the playing of a journeyman who's never had a clear shot at the major league, recording almost exclusively for small labels. Though he doubles on all the reeds – and plays some soprano here – Brignola's key horn is the baritone, and he gets an unusually lambent tone from it which allows him to create fast-moving solos with no loss of coherence. The programme here could be straight off a Blue Note session and it's played with admirable panache by the quintet, Watrous as agile as Brignola is.

*** A Tribute To Gerry Mulligan Stash STCD 574
Brignola; Randy Brecker (*t*); Paul Johnson (*vib*); Don Friedman (*p*); Sal Salvador (*g*); Gary Mazzaroppi (*b*); Butch Miles (*d*). 11/82–11/84.
A reissue of two albums originally put out under Sal Salvador's name, now with Brignola co-credited – appropriate, since he is easily the outstanding player. Salvador's own playing tends towards glibness, padding solos out with irritating quotes, and Brecker's turns show little interest. In contrast, Brignola plays with a dependable aggression that doesn't disavow the good humour of Mulligan's tunes, and he also makes the most of 'Blue Monk'. Five tracks without him elicit a quick, trim sound from the group, and here Salvador seems more at ease.

*** Raincheck Reservoir RSR CD 108
Brignola; Kenny Barron (*p*); George Mraz (*b*); Billy Hart (*d*). 9/88.
**** On A Different Level Reservoir RSR CD 112
Brignola; Kenny Barron (*p*); Dave Holland (*b*); Jack DeJohnette (*d*). 9/89.
*** What It Takes Reservoir RSR CD 117
Brignola; Randy Brecker (*t*); Kenny Barron (*p*); Rufus Reid (*b*); Dick Berk (*d*). 10/90.
Three good records. Brignola's facility goes hand in hand with a consistently imposing sound – as fluently as he plays, he always makes the baritone sound like the big horn that it is – and the flat-out burners are as tonally effective as the big-bodied ballads which are dotted through these sessions. *Raincheck* is a trifle diffuse, since Brignola turns to clarinet and soprano every so often, and *What It Takes* brings on Randy Brecker for a little variation in the front line, which is bought at the expense of the music's more personal feel (and the leader again doubles on the other reeds). *On A Different Level*, though, is suitably head-and-shoulders above the others. Brignola sticks to baritone as his sole horn here, and the solos on 'Tears Inside', 'Hot House' and 'Duke Ellington's Sound Of Love' are sustained with fantastic strength, mirrored in the playing of the rhythm section, which is the kind of team that makes any horn player sound good. Brignola's shrewd choice of tunes here encapsulates a pocket history of jazz baritone – from Carney on 'Sophisticated Lady' to Adams on the Mingus tune – but he puts it all under his own flag, with DeJohnette and Holland marking superb time behind him. A great modern baritone set.

*** **It's Time** Reservoir RSR CD 123
> Brignola; Kenny Barron (*p*); Dave Holland (*b*). 2/91.

A singular feat of overdubbing – Brignola brings out not only the baritone but also all of his clarinets,
flutes, other saxes and a piccolo. Mike Holober's arrangements create intelligent variations on the
standard reed section and introduce all sorts of counterpoint and texture. But producer Mark Feldman
doesn't secure a convincing enough mix: there's too much artifice here, as naturally and enthusiastically
as Brignola approaches the project. 'Dusk' and 'Renewal' are pleasing scores, and there are a couple of
straighter blows on 'Speak Low' and a clarinet treatment of 'I Thought About You'. Holland, as usual,
is marvellous, especially on 'Dusk'.

*** **Live At Sweet Basil, First Set** Reservoir RSR CD 125
> Brignola; Mike Holober (*p*); Rich Syracuse (*b*); Dick Berk (*d*). 8/92.

Given that he deliberately avoided having a drummer on the previous date, there's some irony about this
date: all the real dialogue goes on between Brignola and drummer Dick Berk, whose hefty, momentous
style is a fine foil for the burliness of the leader's baritone. The soprano comes out on 'Mahjong' and the
alto for part of 'Sister Sadie', but otherwise it's all baritone, on a clear-eyed 'Everything Happens To
Me', a nicely paced 'I Hear A Rhapsody' and a grandly articulated 'East Of The Sun'. Occasional club-
date longueurs, but otherwise this is a fine continuation of possibly the best sequence of baritone
records of recent times.

***(*) **Like Old Times** Reservoir RSR CD 133
> Brignola; Claudio Roditi (*t, flhn*); John Hicks (*p*); George Mraz (*b*); Dick Berk (*d*). 5/94.

Another great one. This time the tenets of the blowing date are followed without any suspicion of
routine. The two long blow-outs on 'When Lights Are Low' and 'The Night Has A Thousand Eyes' are
marked by perfectly controlled dynamics, with no loss of excitement as one solo passes into another.
Roditi is in rare form – Brignola is also a welcome guest on the trumpeter's own Reservoir date,
Freewheelin' – and Hicks supplies all the right leads, but the saxophonist surrenders nothing to either of
them, with a pointed clarinet meditation on 'More Than You Know' and his terrific solo on 'Thousand
Eyes' as particular highlights. Rudy Van Gelder still doesn't put enough air round the horns, and this
cuts back on the music's impact to a degree.

Alan Broadbent (born 1947) PIANO

**** **Live At Maybeck Recital Hall Vol. 14** Concord CCD 4488
> Broadbent (*p* solo). 5/91.

**** **Alan Broadbent / Gary Foster Duo Series Vol. 4** Concord CCD 4562
> Broadbent; Gary Foster (*as, ts*). 3/93.

There's a great clarity of thought about Alan Broadbent's playing: his interpretations of jazz and show
standards seem thought through and entire and, while that may suggest a lack of spontaneity, he also
manages to make the music sound fresh. These are very satisfying records. Broadbent, who is a native of
New Zealand, studied at Berkeley in the 1960s and then joined Woody Herman's band, before leading
groups of his own; he hasn't recorded much under his own leadership. The pianist takes his first cues
from Parker and Powell, yet one seldom thinks of bop while listening to him: there is much interplay
between the hands, a sly but considerate cunning and a striking concern to develop melodies which are
entirely faithful to the material. Good as his earlier trio albums are, it's the Maybeck Hall setting which
has brought out the best in the pianist to date: Broadbent's internal rhythms are springy enough to keep
even his ballads on a simmering heat, and the neatly tucked readings of such as 'Oleo' (most of the
pieces run out to only three or four minutes each) or the cleverly shaded 'Sweet And Lovely' are
genuinely fascinating. The sound is as fine as is customary for this series. In conversation with the
similarly undervalued Foster, Broadbent shines just as convincingly. Foster's languorous sound and
silky phrasing disguise an acute musical mind, and when the two start spinning out contrapuntal lines
on bebop themes it's at least as telepathic as a Konitz–Tristano encounter. Hoagy Carmichael's lovely
'One Morning In May' is one end of the seam, Parker's 'Relaxin' At Camarillo' the other, and there's
not a wasted moment in any of the improvising. Excellent location sound.

***(*) **Pacific Standard Time** Concord CCD 4664
> Broadbent; Putter Smith (*b*); Frank Gibson Jr (*d*). 1/95.

The only drawback here is in the choice of material: some of the themes are just a shade too familiar
and, since Broadbent's way is to personalize by small, well-chosen gestures, the trio don't quite characterize each piece as strongly as they might. That said, this is still a very fine record. Broadbent's touch is
so lucid and refined that he makes one hear every note as a specific choice, and his sense of swing is good
enough to lift slow tempos and mediate fast ones. Smith and Gibson are unadventurous but completely

in sympathy with him. 'Summer Night', 'Django' and 'Easy To Love' are about as close to perfect as they can be.

Bosse Broberg TRUMPET

*** West Of The Moon Dragon DRCD 235

Broberg; Joakim Milder (*ts*); Gosta Rundqvist (*p*); Red Mitchell (*b*); Martin Löfgren (*d*). 2/92. Broberg has been around Swedish jazz for decades, so this is another in the sequence that Dragon enjoys, the belated leadership debut. He plays well, if a little thunderously and without the control he must once have had: brassy and short-breathed, but full of enjoyable punch, his solos sound like he's always looked up to Clark Terry and some of the late-swing masters. Mitchell was an old chum, and their duet on 'I Cover The Waterfront' is delicious. But Milder (present on three of the six tracks) and the nicely unpredictable Rundqvist are scene-stealers too. They close out on a rollicking 'Blues For O' that everyone will enjoy.

Bob Brookmeyer (born 1929) VALVE TROMBONE, PIANO

***(*) The Dual Role Of Bob Brookmeyer Original Jazz Classics OJC 1729

Brookmeyer; Jimmy Raney (*g*); Teddy Charles (*vib*); Teddy Kotick (*b*); Mel Lewis, Ed Shaughnessy (*d*); Nancy Overton (*v*). 1/54, 6/55.

*** Quintets Vogue 2111503

Brookmeyer; Henri Renaud (*p*); Jimmy Gourley (*g*); Red Mitchell (*b*); Frank Isola (*d*). 6/54.

*** The Ivory Hunters Blue Note CDP 827324

Brookmeyer; Bill Evans (*p*); Percy Heath (*b*); Connie Kay (*d*). 3/59.

*** Oslo Concord CCD 4312

Brookmeyer; Alan Broadbent (*p, ky*); Eric Von Essen (*b*); Michael Stephans (*d*).

**(*) Dreams Dragon DRCD 169

Brookmeyer; Gustavo Bargalli, Jan Kohlin, Lars Lindgren, Fredrik Norén, Stig Persson (*t, flhn*); Mats Hermansson, Mikael Raberg, Bertil Strandberg (*tb*); Sven Larsson (*btb*); Dave Castle (*as, ss, cl*); Hakan Broström (*as, ss, f*); Johan Alenius, Ulf Andersson (*ts, ss, cl*); Hans Arktoft (*bs, bcl*); Anders Widmark (*p, ky*); Jan Adefeldt (*b*); Johan Diedelmans (*d*). 8/88.

*** Electricity Act 892 192

Brookmeyer; John Abercrmbie (*g*); Rainer Bruninghaus, Frank Chastenier (*ky*); Dieter Ilg (*b*); Danny Gottlieb (*d*); WDR Big Band. 3/91.

Almost the first sounds to be heard on the classic *Jazz On A Summer's Day* soundtrack are the mellow tones of Bob Brookmeyer's valve trombone interweaving with Jimmy Giuffre's clarinet on 'The Train And The River'. It's a curiously formal sound, almost academic, and initially difficult to place. Valve trombone has a more clipped, drier sound than the slide variety, and Brookmeyer is probably its leading exponent, though Maynard Ferguson, Stu Williamson and Bob Enevoldsen have all made effective use of it.

Late-1950s recordings, like his own *Traditionalism Revisited*, saw Brookmeyer exploring classic material with an augmented version of Giuffre's Newport trio and in an idiom the clarinettist was to christen 'folk jazz'. On 'Honeysuckle Rose' there are some choruses in which he accompanies himself on piano without double tracking, a rather extreme example of the 'dual role' he has adopted throughout his performing career. The record with Evans is a useful way of gauging his keyboard playing up against one of the real masters. Rather artificially panned left and right, it's easy to hear what each is doing. Brookmeyer inevitably is rather more limited than his partner, but he takes his fair share of leads and isn't found wanting in any department.

Brookmeyer was a founding member and arranger for the influential Thad Jones–Mel Lewis band and played with both Clark Terry and Gerry Mulligan. He shared piano duties with the latter and is a very considerable keyboard player, as he proves on the OJC. 'Rocky Scotch' and 'Under The Lilacs' are both readily categorized as 'cool' jazz, but there is a surprising degree of variation in Brookmeyer's tone. In legato passages (inevitably harder to execute on a valve instrument) he can sound almost like an alto saxophonist – Lee Konitz, say – at the lower end of his range, but he mingles this with sly growls and purrs (as on 'With The Wind And The Rain In Your Hair' on *Oslo*) and austere, almost toneless equations that sound more like a formula for music than a realized performance. He is also capable of quite broad humour and isn't above adding the odd Dicky Wells effect to an otherwise straightforward solo. Perhaps the biggest criticism and irony of Brookmeyer's *later* work is that it has become humourless as his tone has relaxed and broadened.

Beyond these, there really isn't very much. *Quintets* is shared with Lee Konitz, but the trombonist's four tracks are extremely vivid, and one wonders if there are alternative takes in the vaults; there are *seven* Konitz rejects on the disc, three of 'I'll Remember April' alone. *Dreams* is best seen as an example, and not a particularly inspiring one, of his work as an arranger. It's a dull piece, lifted by one or two passages on 'Cats' and 'Missing Monk'.

Based in Europe, Brookmeyer found more opportunities for large-scale sessions than he ever had back home. *Electricity* isn't, to be frank, a particularly wonderful set, but it is immaculately arranged and recorded and, of the soloists, Brookmeyer and Abercrombie are capable of something special, even when the material doesn't appear to be promising. Bob's tone has lightened a touch over the years (unless it is simply modern microphones) and he often now puts more notes into a phrase than he did before.

Cecil Brooks III DRUMS

*** **The Collective** Muse MCD 5377
    Brooks; Greg Osby (*as*); Gary Thomas (*ts*); Geri Allen (*p*); Lonnie Plaxico (b). 3/89
*** **Hangin' With Smooth** Muse MCD 5428
    Brooks; Philip Harper (*t*); Justin Robinson (*as*); Craig Handy (*ts*); Benny Green (*p*); Peter
    Washington, Kenneth Davis (*b*). 12/90.
*** **Neck Peckin' Jammie** Muse MCD 5504
    Brooks; Terell Stafford (*t*); Justin Robinson (*as*); Craig Handy (*ss, ts*); Geoff Keezer (*p*);
    Christian McBride (*b*). 1/93.

On all these sessions, Brooks has assembled top-flight bands of blossoming talent and, although one sometimes feels that the music is dedicated more to working out than anything else, it's clever, energetic, sometimes involving. The tunes on the first record are more self-consciously 'modern' than those on the second: jolting melodic parts, abstruse counterpart, polyrhythmic aggression from Brooks underneath. Harper, Robinson and Handy are more conservative players, and Green is certainly less challenging than Allen, which makes *Hangin' With Smooth* lighter, less fraught. There's even a ballad medley for each of the horns, as on an old Jazz Messengers date, as well as a feeble pop tune called 'Adreena'. That unsureness as to which material works and which doesn't seeps into *Neck Peckin' Jammie* as well. Stevie Wonder's 'Creepin'' isn't very good, and the reggae beat chosen for Wayne Shorter's 'One By One' is hopeless. After the adventurousness of the first date, Brooks seems to be retrenching in the Blakey tradition, and it takes most of the sting out of the music. But there is a good blues march in 'Blues Citizens', the harmonization of 'Without A Song' is pretty, and Handy's solos are always worth waiting for.

Roy Brooks (born 1938) DRUMS, PERCUSSION, SAW

***(*) **Duet In Detroit** Enja 7067 2
    Brooks; Woody Shaw (*t*); Geri Allen, Don Pullen, Randy Weston (*p*). 8/83, 5/84.

Brooks cut his musical teeth in the 1959 Horace Silver band, subsequently taken over by trumpeter Blue Mitchell. His first major recording session was Mitchell's *Blue's Moods*, a gritty, uncomplicated session that still stands up well. Since then, he's worked as a jobbing drummer, mostly in New York, but attracting modest fame during Charles Mingus's stormy 1972 European tour, when Brooks charmed the pants off French audiences with his musical saw.

He brings it out here to add some colours to a spirited duet with Don Pullen, the most immediately effective of these head-to-head encounters, two tracks each. The others take a little more work, but Brooks quickly establishes a strong empathy, particularly with Shaw on the long 'Elegy For Eddie Jefferson'. Though a generation younger and not obviously in sympathy with all of Brooks's New Thing mannerisms, Allen has no difficulty keeping up, and their opening 'Samba Del Sol' is a delight.

A long-time member of Max Roach's percussion circus, M'Boom, Brooks runs his own 17-piece drum ensemble, called the Aboriginal Percussion Choir, and a group called the Artistic Truth. Reports are that both are steamingly good. Time perhaps for a more generous representation on record.

Brotherhood Of Breath GROUP

***(*) **Live At Willisau** Ogun OGCD 001
    Chris McGregor (*p, leader*); Harry Beckett, Marc Charig, Mongezi Feza (*t*); Nick Evans, Radu
    Malfatti (*tb*); Dudu Pukwana (*as*); Evan Parker, Gary Windo (*ts*); Harry Miller (*b*); Louis
    Moholo (*d*). 1/73.

The trick was to keep breathing, because Death was always near by. One of the truly legendary modern jazz big bands, the Brotherhood was formed in 1970 by South African pianist and composer, Chris McGregor, who had come to Europe in mid-decade with the equally legendary Blue Notes and stayed on till apartheid itself seemed ready to give up the ghost. McGregor's passing and Dudu Pukwana's, and before them Johnny Mbizo Dyani's, Harry Miller's and Mongezi Feza's, confirmed that there was a shadow across this music, as if the life that was breathed into it had to be paid for in some way.

For anyone who grew up with this music, as we did, it is hard to be objective. The Brotherhood was an initiation, a freemasonry of the spirit that had nothing to do with technical exactness or acoustic precision. From the opening moments of 'Do It', with its searing Evan Parker solo, to the relative ease of the closing 'Funky Boots', this is affirmative music of a rare sort, bringing together African *kwela*, post-Ellington swing, free jazz, and even touches of classicism in a boiling mix that grips the heart throughout. Pukwana, Charig and Feza are perhaps the dominant soloists, but the two trombone players have their moment in the sun on 'Kongi's Theme' (a McGregor original for Malfatti) and 'Andromeda'. The only player under-represented on this particular occasion is the survivor, Moholo, who carries on the Blue Notes/Brotherhood tradition into the new, post-apartheid age.

Peter Brötzmann (born 1941) ALL SAXOPHONES AND CLARINETS, TAROGATO

**** Machine Gun FMP CD 24
    Brötzmann; Willem Breuker, Evan Parker (*ts*); Fred Van Hove (*p*); Buschi Niebergall, Peter Kowald (*b*); Han Bennink, Sven Ake Johansson (*d*). 5/68.
Brötzmann's influence over the European free-music scene is enormous, and many of his pioneering achievements have only recently been acknowledged in the wider domain. He was playing free jazz in the early 1960s and by the time of this astounding album – originally pressed and distributed by the saxophonist himself – was a stylist whose intensity and sureness of focus were already established. The huge, screaming sound he makes is among the most exhilarating things in the music, and while he has often been typecast as a kind of sonic terrorist, that does insufficient justice to his mastery of the entire reed family. The only precedents for his early work are to be found in the contemporary records of Albert Ayler, but Brötzmann arrived at his methods independently of the American. His first trio record (currently out of print) is of a similar cast to, say, Ayler's *Spiritual Unity*, a raw, ferocious three-way assault, yet it is surpassed by *Machine Gun*, one of the most significant documents of the European free-jazz underground. The three saxophonists fire off a ceaseless round of blasting, overblown noise, built on the continuous crescendo managed by Bennink and Johansson, and, as chaotic as it sounds, the music is informed by an iron purpose and control. Although the recording is crude, the grainy timbre is a fitting medium for the music. In 1990, *Machine Gun* was reissued on CD with two alternative takes which match the original versions in their fearsome power.

*** The Berlin Concert FMP CD 34/35 2CD
    Brötzmann; Albert Mangelsdorff (*tb*); Fred Van Hove (*p*); Han Bennink (*cl, d, perc*). 8/71.
The Berlin Concert, originally released as three separate albums, was culled from two days of performance at the Berlin Free Music Market, where the (long-standing) trio was augmented by trombonist Albert Mangelsdorff, whose experience in many other areas of jazz left him unintimidated by the demands of this group. Sound is again only average, but the vigour and earthy bravado of the quartet sustain the listener through the unglamorous circumstances of the music-making. There's little to choose among the various improvisations, but there is a long, compelling feature for Mangelsdorff in 'Alberts', and 'Couscouss De La Mauresque' includes some finely detailed playing by van Hove, even though his piano is often obscured.

*** Reserve FMP CD 17
    Brötzmann; Barre Phillips (*b*); Gunter Sommer (*d*). 11/88.
A big jump forward from 1971, since the deletion of FMP's catalogue on vinyl has decimated the Brötzmann discography, at least for the time being. Here, on relatively conventional turf, with the more gently inclined Phillips at the bass, Brötzmann digs through three long improvisations. Even on CD, sound is still only reasonable in fidelity, but the music has some attractive empathy, particularly between the leader and Phillips.

*** Last Home Pathological n/n
    Brötzmann; Caspar Brötzmann (*g*). 90.
This is a remorseless meeting between father and son, the younger Brötzmann emulating his elder's ferocity on a distortion-drenched electric guitar. There's no real 'interplay', more a collision between two elemental forces; even with amplification at his disposal, the younger man can't overpower his partner, though. Whether one hears it as energizing or tedious, it's quite devastating. There are several extra tracks on the CD.

*** **Wie Das Leben So Spielt** FMP CD 22
    Brötzmann; Werner Lüdi (*as*). 9/89.
Lüdi has drifted in and out of free playing for many years, but he sounds enthusiastic enough about
being added to Brötzmann's pack of sparring partners on record. Playing only alto, while Brötz runs
through his whole arsenal of reeds, Lüdi concocts a stuttery romanticism (of sorts) to set against his
companion's fields of fire. Highly invigorating, as usual.

***(*) **No Nothing** FMP CD 34
    Brötzmann. 8/90.
The saxophonist still has plenty of new things to say on his third solo album, perhaps the most quiescent
of the three yet often exploding into a logical catharsis. He changes between various saxes and clarinets
during the 14-track programme and manages to sustain close to 75 minutes of music, all of it faithfully
recorded by Jost Gebers.

***(*) **Dare Devil** DIW 857
    Brötzmann; Haruhiko Gotsu (*g*); Tetsu Yahauchi (*b*); Shoji Hano (*d*). 10/91.
Yet another sensational – and sensationally effective – blow-out. Recorded live in Tokyo with what
sounds like some kind of Japanese hardcore band, Brötzmann sounds completely at home and enjoying
every second of the challenge. Hano, who produced the record, beats out minimal but brazenly effective
tattoos and Gotsu is a modest master at making riffs into feasible compositions. Brötzmann just goes at
it head first.

*** **The Marz Combo** FMP CD 47
    Brötzmann; Toshinori Kondo (*t*); Paul Rutherford, Hannes Bauer (*tb*); Werner Lüdi, Larry
    Stabins (*saxes*); Nicky Skopelitis, Caspar Brötzmann (*g*); William Parker (*b*); Anton Fier (*d*). 2/
    92.
Not, perhaps, one of the great Brötzmann sessions: the saxophonists are scarcely a match for the leader,
or a useful contrast; and while Rutherford is as magnificent as ever, few of the others really rise to the
challenge of sharing time with Peter himself. Yet there are still moments of incandescence during the 74
minutes of music, and the energy level rarely drops below invigorating.

*** **Songlines** FMP CD 53
    Brötzmann; Fred Hopkins (*b*); Rashied Ali (*d*). 10/91.
***(*) **Die Like A Dog** FMP CD 64
    Brötzmann; Toshinori Kondo (*t, elec*); William Parker (*b*); Hamid Drake (*d*). 8/93.
*** **Sacred Scrape** Rastascan BRD-015
    Brötzmann; William Parker (*b*); Gregg Bendian (*d*). 92.
As an elder statesman of free playing, Brötzmann is working steadily but not carelessly: his records are
still soaked in the intensity which he's been pursuing for 30 years and, like Bailey or Parker, he alights on
new situations and turns them to fit some part of an entrenched but flexible aesthetic. *Die Like A Dog* is
the starkest, most Gothic of these three discs, a harrowing meditation on the life and work of Albert
Ayler, whose earliest work mirrored Brötzmann's own. This is fuming and at times almost intractable
stuff, but its spiritual measure is palpable, and the quartet play with stunning commitment. *Songlines* is
more a 'traditional' free trio, the American team of Ali and Hopkins playing with a flair and (indeed!)
swing which Brötzmann uses for shape and context with his own severe kind of lyricism. *Sacred Shape*
sets him alongside another generation of American improvisers, and this is a more scattershot battle of
wits, Bendian's broken mass of rhythm and noise cracking around the reedman's grand oratory. Parker,
a veteran of many a Cecil Taylor scrap, calmly finds his own space in the music. Three good ones.

Clifford Brown (1930–56) TRUMPET

***(*) **The Beginning And The End** Columbia 477737
    Brown; Vance Wilson (*as, ts*); Ziggy Vines, Billy Root (*ts*); Sam Dockery, Duke Wells (*p*); Eddie
    Lambert (*g*); James Johnson, Ace Tisone (*b*); Osie Johnson, Ellis Tolin (*d*); Chris Powell (*v,
    perc*).
*** **Clifford Brown Memorial** Original Jazz Classics OJC 017
    Brown; Art Farmer, Idrees Sulieman (*t*); Herb Mullins, Ake Persson (*tb*); Arne Domnérus, Gigi
    Gryce (*as*); Benny Golson (*ts*); Oscar Estell, Lars Gullin (*bs*); Tadd Dameron, Bengt Hallberg
    (*p*); Percy Heath, Gunnar Johnson (*b*); Philly Joe Jones, Jack Noren (*d*); collective personnel. 6
    & 9/53.
**** **Clifford Brown Memorial Album** Blue Note CDP 781526 2CD
    Brown; Lou Donaldson (*as*); Gigi Gryce (*as, f*); Charlie Rouse (*ts*); Elmo Hope, John Lewis (*p*);
    Percy Heath (*b*); Art Blakey, Philly Joe Jones (*d*). 6 & 8/53.

***(*) **Clifford Brown Quartet In Paris** Original Jazz Classics OJC 357
    Brown; Henri Renaud (*p*); Pierre Michelot (*b*); Benny Bennett (*d*). 10/53.
***(*) **Clifford Brown Sextet In Paris** Original Jazz Classics OJC 358
    Brown; Gigi Gryce (*as*); Henri Renaud (*p*); Jimmy Gourley (*g*); Pierre Michelot (*b*); Jean-Louis
    Viale (*d*). 10/53.
***(*) **The Complete Paris Sessions: Volume 1** Vogue 114561
    Brown; Gigi Gryce (*as*); Henri Renaud (*p*); Jimmy Gourley (*g*); Pierre Michelot (*b*); Jean-Louis
    Viale (*d*). 10/53.
***(*) **The Complete Paris Sessions: Volume 2** Vogue 114562
    As above, except add Art Farmer, Walter Williams, Quincy Jones (*t*); Jimmy Cleveland (*tb*);
    Anthony Ortega (*as*); André Dabonneville, Clifford Solomon (*ts*); William Boucaya (*bs*). 10/53.
*** **The Complete Paris Sessions: Volume 3** Vogue 114872
    As above. 10/53.

In the days after Clifford Brown died – Richie Powell with him – and as the news filtered through to clubs and studios up and down the country, hardened jazz musicians put away their horns and quietly went home to grieve. Only 26, Brown was almost universally liked and admired. Free of the self-destructive 'personal problems' that haunted jazz at the time, he had seemed destined for ever greater things when his car skidded off the turnpike.

To this day, his influence on trumpeters is immense, less audibly than Miles Davis's, perhaps, because more pervasive. Though most of his technical devices – long, burnished phrases, enormous melodic and harmonic compression within a chorus, internal divisions of the metre – were introduced by Dizzy Gillespie and Fats Navarro, his two most significant models, it was Brownie who melded them into a distinctive and coherent personal style of great expressive power. Almost every trumpeter who followed, including present-day figures like Wynton Marsalis, has drawn heavily on his example; few though have managed to reproduce the powerful singing grace he took from the ill-starred Navarro.

After a first, near-fatal car accident, Brown gigged in R&B bands (the tail-end of that period is documented on the Columbia) and then worked briefly with Tadd Dameron, before touring Europe with Lionel Hampton towards the end of 1953, on which he enjoyed a good-natured and stage-managed rivalry with Art Farmer, and recorded the excellent quartet, sextet and big-band sides now reissued on OJC and sampled on *Blue And Brown*. By this time, he had already recorded the session on the confusingly titled *Memorial* (OJC) and *Memorial Album* (Blue Note). The former combined European and American sessions and isn't the most compelling of his recordings, though Dameron's arrangements are as challenging as always, and there are some fine moments from the Scandinavians on the September date.

The Complete Paris Sessions volumes are full of interesting material, but nowhere does the trumpeter really knock sparks off any of the themes, and he seems hampered by busy or hesitant arrangements. Perhaps the best of the tracks are the two sextet takes of 'All The Things You Are' and the three quartet versions, each subtly different, of 'I Can Dream, Can't I?'. *Blue And Brown* doesn't offer either, but it might seem an attractive alternative, if only for the fact that its selection of tracks from the 1953 Paris sessions is so determinedly perverse. There have to be some doubts about the French rhythm section, experienced as it was, but it shapes up pretty well in comparison to the Scandinavian players on *Memorial*.

The Blue Note is essential. Brown still sounds slightly blurred on 'Cherokee', but his solo on Gryce's 'Hymn Of The Orient' and his medium-paced delivery on 'Minor Mood' are exceptional. The original second side featured a session with Lou Donaldson and then-rising star, Elmo Hope. The opening 'Brownie Speaks' is (along with 'Hymn') perhaps the most accessible introduction to the trumpeter's style and method. Quarter and eighth notes are played square to the very vigorous rhythm without any loss of lyrical force and without any hesitation. 'You Go To My Head' underlines his sensitivity as a ballad player. Much of this material was supplemented by a valuable collection of *Alternate Takes* which so far hasn't made the transition from vinyl. Good as most of these masters are (and they also include a single track, 'Get Happy', from a J. J. Johnson date), they do also indicate how inexperienced and occasionally callow 1954's *downbeat* 'New Star' could still be. Fortunately, Brown's best work was still to come.

**** **Jazz Immortal** Pacific Jazz CDP 7468502
    Brown; Stu Williamson (*vtb*); Zoot Sims (*ts*); Bob Gordon (*bs*); Russ Freeman (*p*); Joe
    Mondragon, Carson Smith (*b*); Shelly Manne (*d*). 7 & 8/54.

While playing on the West Coast with Max Roach, Brown was asked to record a session for Dick Bock's Pacific Jazz. The arrangements are all by Jack Montrose and, though they're slighter, less demanding harmonically, more 'West Coast' than what Brownie was used to with Roach, they brought out some of his most relaxed and mellow playing. His solo on Montrose's 'Finders Keepers' is a model of uncomplicated and mellifluous invention. Zoot Sims slides in next with some lovely choruses in a drier than usual tone. 'Joy Spring', like the opening 'Daahoud', underlines how resilient and adaptable Brown's themes could be; a third, 'Bones For Jones', is a rarity, perhaps a dedication to Quincy Jones, but not recorded elsewhere, and there are two takes of the ironically formal 'Tiny Capers', another little-known Brown composition. Perhaps his best solo is reserved for 'Blueberry Hill', from the August session.

**** **Brownie** Emarcy 838 306-16 10CD
     Brown; Maynard Ferguson, Clark Terry (*t*); Herbie Mann (*f*); Danny Bank (*f, bs*); Herb Geller, Joe Maini (*as*); Walter Benton, Harold Land, Paul Quinichette, Sonny Rollins (*ts*); Kenny Drew, Jimmy Jones, Junior Mance, Richie Powell (*p*); Barry Galbraith (*g*); Joe Benjamin, Keter Betts, Curtis Counce, Milt Hinton, George Morrow (*b*); Oscar Pettiford (*b, clo*); Bobby Donaldson, Roy Haynes, Osie Johnson, Max Roach (*d*); Helen Merrill, Dinah Washington, Sarah Vaughan (*v*); strings arranged and conducted by Neal Hefti; collective personnels. 8/54–2/56.
**** **Jazz Masters: Clifford Brown** Emarcy 842933
     Brown; as above. 2/54–2/56.
**** **Alone Together** Verve 526 373-2
     Brown; Harold Land, Hank Mobley, Paul Quinichette, Sonny Rollins (*ts*); Danny Bank (*bs*); Herbie Mann (*f*); Ray Bryant, Jimmy Jones, Richie Powell (*p*); Barry Galbraith (*g*); Joe Benjamin, Milt Hinton, George Morrow (*b*); Roy Haynes, Osie Johnson, Max Roach (*d*); Helen Merrill, Sarah Vaughan (*v*); strings. 8/54–1/56.

Brownie gathers together all the material Brown recorded for Emarcy between 2 August 1954 and 16 February 1956. It includes no fewer than nine previously unreleased takes, together with a number of alternative takes that have appeared in other contexts. The research was done by the indefatigable Kiyoshi Koyama and the recordings remastered digitally from the originals held at the Polygram Tape Facility at Edison, New Jersey. The liner-notes are by Dan Morgenstern and are impeccably detailed.

Inevitably, the best of the music is in the Roach–Brown sessions. The drummer's generosity in making the younger man co-leader is instantly and awesomely repaid. On the earliest of the sessions (Discs 1 and 2, originally released as *Brown And Roach Incorporated*), there is a brilliantly impressionistic arrangement of Bud Powell's 'Parisian Thoroughfare' (whose onomatopoeic effects are echoed on a 'Take The "A" Train' from February 1955, Disc 9), a superb 'Jordu', and an offcut of Brown soloing on 'Sweet Clifford', a reworking of the 'Sweet Georgia Brown' changes. Whether cup-muted or open, he sounds relaxed and completely confident. Land plays a more than supportive role and is generously featured on 'Darn That Dream'.

The next session (Discs 3 and 4) was a studio jam recorded a week or so later, with Herb Geller, the un-chancey Joe Maini and Walter Benton all on saxophones, and Kenny Drew, Curtis Counce and Roach filling out the band. There are three takes (the first incomplete) of a blues called 'Coronado' (Disc 3), then extended versions of 'You Go To My Head', 'Caravan' – and a fragmentary variant, 'Boss Man' – and 'Autumn In New York'. Posthumously released as *Best Coast Jazz* and *Clifford Brown All Stars*, they contain some of the trumpeter's weakest and most diffuse playing. Always eminently disciplined, his solos lost much of their shape in this context. However, it's worth it for Maini's contribution.

The 14 August jam with Dinah Washington (Discs 5 and 6) includes over-long versions of 'What Is This Thing Called Love', 'Move' and 'I'll Remember April', but there are two fine medleys and Brown is superb on 'It Might As Well Be Spring', which extends his accompanist's role. He has less space round Sarah Vaughan (Disc 7), but he compresses his responses to the vocal line into beautifully polished choruses and half-choruses; Paul Quinichette is magnificent. Brown also accompanies Helen Merrill (Disc 8) on her debut recording; this is slighter, even prettified, and Quincy Jones's arrangements are definitely overcooked, but the trumpeter's contributions are gently effective.

The *Clifford Brown With Strings* sessions (Disc 8, originally released as Emarcy MG 36005) are very much in the Bird mould. Brown sounds almost philosophically calm on a range of ballads, tightened up by Hefti's firmly organized string backings and the Brown–Roach Quintet rhythm section, somewhat unnecessarily beefed up by guitarist Barry Galbraith. This session is also available as a West Wind CD, but the remastering doesn't sound as clean or true.

The first quintet sessions for six months (Disc 9) find the group in rattling form. *Study In Brown* marks the trumpeter's emergence as an individual star of formidable magnitude. He takes 'Cherokee' at a dangerous pace and doesn't fudge a single note (there are bootleg recordings of him doggedly alternating and inverting practice phrases). Throughout the album, his entries have real *presence* and his delivery floats over the rhythm section without ever losing contact with Roach's compelling metres. 'Jacqui' is relatively unusual fare, and it may be significant that Land, with his West Coast roots, handles it most comfortably. This was the saxophonist's last studio date with the band. His replacement, Sonny Rollins, has at this point in his career a slightly crude approach. He is nevertheless bursting with ideas that push the group's capabilities to the utmost and his first statement on 'Gertrude's Bounce' may suggest recourse to the review button, so daring is it in conception and execution. Brown himself sounds as though he must be reading off prearranged sequences, firing out eight-, four- and two-bar statements that seem to contain more and more musical information the shorter they get. This is the material released as *At Basin Street*.

Koyama has dug out previously unsuspected masters of 'Love Is A Many Splendored Thing' (taken at a distinctly unslushy pace) and of 'Flossie Lou' (which reworks 'Jeepers Creepers'). A rehearsal fragment of the latter is included on a 3-inch bonus CD single, like the cherry on top of the cake. *Brownie* is a bulky and, inevitably, expensive work of documentation. The trumpeter has scarcely a bad moment, but there is a lot of material to digest, and newcomers might prefer to begin with the excellent *Jazz Masters* compilation, which draws from all but the unfeasibly long jam sessions and consists of 'The Blues Walk', 'I Get A Kick Out Of You', 'Jordu', 'Parisian Thoroughfare', 'Daahoud', 'It's Crazy', 'Stardust', 'I'll Remember April', 'I've Got You Under My Skin', 'Yesterdays' and the original release of 'Flossie Lou'. For accessibility and sheer value it could hardly be bettered. At least some of those who invest will want to move on to the Complete Works. Brown's qualities ring out on every bar.

Alone Together, it should be made clear, consists of one CD of Brownie material (much of it with Roach) and one CD of somewhat later Roach recordings; these latter are discussed in the appropriate place. As a package it makes a very attractive introduction to both artists. Of Brownie, there is the magnificent 'Joy Spring' from August 1954, the February 1955 'Cherokee' from *A Study In Brown*, 'Gertrude's Bounce' from January 1956 with 11 other tracks from the Emarcy sessions. No surprises, but elegantly packaged and very desirable.

*** **Brownie's Eyes: Volume 1 – Nice Work If You Can Get It** Philology W 1000
> Personnel unknown or unconfirmed; includes Sonny Rollins (*ts*); Richie Powell (*p*); George Morrow (*b*); Max Roach (*d*).

*** **Brownie's Eyes: Volume 2 – Blues** Philology W 1001
> Personnel unknown or unconfirmed as above; add Harold Land (*ts*); Eric Dolphy (*as*).

Bird's Eyes, Philology's long-standing sweeping-up of Charlie Parker ephemera, has at time of writing reached Volume 22, which may well strike up a mixture of anticipation and fiscal panic in Clifford Brown fans. Like its predecessor, this series will consist of lo-fi airshots, practice tapes and other oddments likely to be of value to the student and the specialist listener, but probably not to anyone who simply wants to listen to finished performances. Volume 2 has the attraction of a jam session, teaming Brown with another short-lived legend, Eric Dolphy; and both volumes have examples of Brownie running down ideas and scales on 'Cherokee' and 'Dizzy Atmosphere' (trumpet) and 'Au Privave' (piano). It seems on the face of it unlikely that Brown's short and generally well-documented career will yield as much in the way of *obiter dicta* as Bird's. Enthusiasts will, though, still need to do a little cost-benefit analysis.

Donald Brown PIANO

*** **Early Bird** Sunnyside SSC 1025D
> Brown; Bill Mobley (*t, flhn*); Donald Harrison (*f*); Steve Nelson (*vib*); Bob Hurst (*b*); Jeff Tain Watts (*d*). 87.

*** **The Sweetest Sounds** Jazz City 660.53.008
> Brown; Steve Nelson (*vib*); Charnett Moffett (*b*); Alan Dawson (*d*). 6/88.

(*) **Sources Of Inspiration Muse MCD 5385
> Brown; Eddie Henderson (*t, flhn*); Gary Bartz (*as*); Buster Williams (*b*); Carl Allen (*d*). 89.

Donald Brown followed James Williams into the piano chair for the Jazz Messengers in 1981 but he has made comparatively few recordings since, owing to problems with arthritis. Each of these sessions, though, is rewarding, and they seldom get stuck in the sometimes over-zealous groove which many later Messengers graduates fall prey to. *Early Bird* is a little careful and civilized, but it's interesting to hear Harrison dealing primarily with the flute, and Brown reveals a very mature grasp of Tadd Dameron's 'If You Could See Me Now', which he takes as a piano solo. *Sources Of Inspiration* sounds more hastily prepared, and Henderson and Bartz are only intermittently persuasive as improvisers. But Brown's best to date is the excellent quartet date for Jazz City. The piano sound is very bright and clear, and Nelson's vibes are complementary rather than contradictory on the four tracks he appears on. Moffett curbs his occasional tendency to overplay – he hits a perfect groove on 'I Used To Think She Was Quiet' – and the rarely sighted Dawson makes a convincing return to the studios. But it's two solo ballads – 'Betcha By Golly Wow' and a dramatic reshaping of 'Killing Me Softly With His Song' – which prove Brown's personal evaluations of rhythm and harmony to best effect.

*** **People Music** Muse MCD 5406
> Brown; Tom Harrell (*t, flhn*); Vincent Herring (*as, f*); Steve Nelson (*vib*); Bob Hurst (*b*); Samarai Celestial (*d, v*); Daniel Sadownick (*perc*); Lenora Helm (*v*). 3/90.

*** **Cause And Effect** Muse MCD 5447
     Brown; Joe Henderson (*ts*); James Spaulding (*f*); Steve Nelson (*vib, mar*); Ron Carter (*b*); Carl
     Allen (*d*); Rudy Byrd, Donald Eaton (*perc*); Marlon Saunders, Lenora Helm (*v*). 4/91.
***(*) **Send One Your Love** Muse MCD 5479
     Brown; Tom Williams (*flhn*); Steve Wilson (*ss, as, f*); Charnett Moffett (*b*); Louis Hayes, Eric
     Walker (*d*); Rudy Byrd (*perc*). 6/92.

Brown's music continues to diversify: his intention on *People Music*, according to the sleeve-notes, was
to reflect the many rhythmic styles of black music, and the clipped, funky 'The Biscuit Man' and Latin-
flavoured pop of 'I Love It When You Dance That Way' display range at least. Harrell and Herring are a
cleverly chosen front line, the former coolly vigorous, the latter blues-drenched and irresistibly colourful.
Nelson, too, adds some deft remarks. But the impression remains that Brown's own playing isn't well
served by a group that features so many others who are eager to play: his one feature, 'Booker T', is a
marvellous, sanctified piano solo that makes one ache to hear a Brown solo record. The stellar cast on
Cause And Effect also get in the way on occasion, and Brown's concern for singers is less interesting than
his straight-ahead settings. But Henderson's refresher course on his own 'Black Narcissus' and the
excellent work by the rhythm section still make the record strong.

    Send One Your Love sounds like Brown's best to date, though. He introduces fresh rhythmic slants with
every session, and here there are passages that seem to combine hard bop, soul and even Afro-Latin
metres with few apparent stitches showing. 'Whisper Not' is a typically mature revision of a bedrock
jazz tune, but Brown's latest thoughts on the blues ('Blues For Harold') are just as absorbing, and the
joyful grooves of 'Theme For Malcolm' and 'Girl Watching' are rootsy and urbane. Wilson and
Williams are used sparingly, and effectively.

Jeri Brown VOCAL

*** **Mirage** Justin Time JUST 38
     Brown; Fred Hersch (*p*); Daniel Lessard (*b*). 2 & 3/91.
**** **'Unfolding' The Peacocks** Justin Time JUST 45
     Brown; Michel Dubeau (*ss, shakuhachi*); Peter Leitch (*g*); Kirk Lightsey (*p*); Rufus Reid (*b*);
     Wali Muhammad (*d*); Shawn Smith, Suzanne Doucet (*v*). 2/92.
**** **A Timeless Place** Justin Time JUST 70
     Brown; Jimmy Rowles (*p, v*); Eric Von Essen (*b*). 5/94.

The gorgeous Ms Brown makes light of a few technical shortcomings. She's a classy, sophisticated
singer, unafraid to try unusual material. Her scatting is subtle, unhistrionic and as true as an oboe; the
only singer who sounds much like her is Britain's Norma Winstone, and on the 1994 record she covers
Norma's words to Rowles's 'A Timeless Place'.

    He is a big inspiration. The centrepiece of *'Unfolding'* is a long vocalized improvisation on Jimmy
Rowles's 'The Peacocks', with Michel Dubeau's shakuhachi mimicking the melancholy call of the male
bird. Even the more conventional vocal material is fresh and original, and the arrangements (by Brown
and fellow-Canadian Leitch, who plays superbly throughout) are designed to bring out the shape of the
song, not to swamp it in extraneous detail. 'Orange Coloured Sky' has a breezy bounce, and Bob
Dorough's 'Wouldn't You' almost exceeds the original. Lightsey leads the rhythm section with his usual
dark-toned concentration on essentials. Dubeau figures on only two tracks but makes his presence felt
on 'Jean' with his soprano. The two backing singers turn up on the closing number, a haunting, wordless
version of Abdullah Ibrahim's chorale 'Tuang Guru'.

    Mirage is more conventional. This is a jazz record first and foremost – 'Good Bait', 'Ebb Tide', 'The
Sunny Side Of The Street' – with just the closing 'Ten Twenty', a collaboration with the excellent
Hersch, showing signs of mould-breaking progress. Other observers, not least Hersch, don't share our
sense of a slightly fragile technique. Melodically, she's sure-fire, but there is a slight uncertainty about
the rhythmic count here and there which, paradoxically, gives lyrics a very immediate, almost conversational quality. That's most evident on the session with Rowles, which is as distinguished for his
wonderful playing as for her voice. Stuff like 'Morning Star', co-written with Johnny Mercer, 'My
Mother's Love' and the vocal duet on 'Don't Quite Now' simply melts the heart. Catch up with Jeri
Brown without delay.

Marion Brown (born 1935) ALTO SAXOPHONE

***(*) **Marion Brown Quartet** ESP Disk ESP 1022
     Brown; Alan Shorter (*t*); Reggie Johnson, Ronnie Boykins (*b*); Rashied Ali (*d*). 11/65.

**** **Porto Novo** Black Lion BLCD 760200
    Brown; Leo Smith (*t*); Maarten Altena (*b*); Han Bennink (*d*). 12/67, 12/70.
**** **Why Not?** ESP Disk ESP 1040
    Brown; Stanley Cowell (*p*); Sirone (*b*); Rashied Ali (*d*). 10/66.
**** **Recollections – Ballads And Blues For Saxophone** Creative Works CW 1001
    Brown (*as* solo). 87.

Possessed of a sweet, slightly fragile tone and a seemingly limitless melodic resource, Brown is neverthe-less one of the most undervalued of contemporary saxophonists. There is a certain poignant irony in the fact that his finest recorded work should be solo saxophone, for he is a dedicated educator with a long-standing commitment to collective – and often untrained or amateur – music-making. Brown's one and only recording for ECM, *Afternoon Of A Georgia Faun*, came out of that ethos. The LP has now been deleted and one of Brown's most adventurous records has yet to appear on CD.

In its place, though, two sessions cut for ESP Disk, which became the only CD items currently available from before the 1980s. Recorded in the same month as Sun Ra's *Heliocentric Worlds*, Brown's debut has the same slightly unearthly quality, grafted over a basically very simple harmonic and melodic concep-tion. The charm of his work has almost always lain in the sound of his saxophone playing, rather than in very advanced ideas; even his concept of 'interchangeable discourse' (which reached its high point on *Georgia Faun*) was revealed to be a quite conventional round of ensembles and solos. '27 Cooper Square' commemorates one of the many buzz addresses of the New Thing, and it's the most substantial achievement on the record, with strong statements from Alan Shorter and Ali. On 'Capricorn Moon', which remained a favourite of Brown's, he uses two bassists, a cliché of the time which he at least seems to know how to deploy effectively. (One oddity: saxophonist Bennie Maupin was listed as having played on 'Exhibition', but seems not to have done.)

The later ESP is much stronger and more coherent. Cowell brings in a much more upbeat sense of time, and the themes – 'La Sorella', 'Fortunato', 'Why Not' and 'Homecoming' – are much more direct and personal, with long lyrical lines cast in repetitive, subtly changing contexts. Ali is probably a mismatch for this kind of music. Either Roger Blank or Tom Price, neither of them well known but both on the ESP roster, might have been a better choice.

Porto Novo offers the irresistible attraction of hearing Brown and Smith together, a meeting between two musical eccentrics, neither of whom hears pitch quite the same way as anyone else. 'Sound Structure' is immensely powerful, fuelled by Bennink's offbeat swing and Altena's fruity bass chords. A surprise and a delight. Good to have it back in circulation.

Recollections shouldn't be overlooked at any price. A near-perfect set of standards – ranging from 'Angel Eyes' and 'Black And Tan Fantasy' to 'Blue Monk' and 'After The Rain' – it poignantly exposes Brown in reverie. His blues are technically watertight and, though the tempo is varied only minimally, the whole set communicates a wide range of emotions. Very warmly recommended indeed.

Ray Brown (born 1926) DOUBLE BASS

*** **Brown's Bag** Concord CCD 6019
    Brown; Blue Mitchell (*t*); Richie Kamuca (*ts*); Dave Grusin, Art Hillery (*p*); John Collins (*g*); John Guerin, Jimmie Smith (*d*). 12/75.
*** **Something For Lester** Original Jazz Classics OJC 412
    Brown; Cedar Walton (*p*); Elvin Jones (*d*). 6/77.
*** **As Good As It Gets** Concord CCD 4066
    Brown; Jimmy Rowles (*p*). 12/77.

Bassists seem to job quite promiscuously, and bassists of Brown's calibre are hard to find. As with Paul Chambers and Ron Carter, the Brown discography is enormous; he was the most cited musician in the first edition of the *Guide*. Unlike the other two, however, his output as a leader is proportionally and qualitatively substantial.

He is almost certainly best heard in any of the trios featuring pianist Gene Harris, his most sympathetic collaborator, but this relaxed session features some fine moments from the still-undervalued Kamuca and the lamented Blue Mitchell. The sound is a shade flat, but the music is well up to Brown's impressive standard.

The OJC is an old Contemporary release, with that label's openness of sound. Jones isn't perhaps the ideal drummer and he gets in the way on 'Georgia On My Mind', but all in all this is a very enjoyable session and Brown's introductory statements on 'Love Walked In' are pure class.

As Good As It Gets is an accompanists' master class. Rowles used to work for Billie Holiday and others; Brown was Ella Fitzgerald's husband. Together, they play quietly and lyrically, tracing out a programme of favourite tunes – 'Alone Together', 'Sophisticated Lady', 'Like Someone In Love' – with consummate professionalism.

** **Live At The Concord Jazz Festival** Concord CCD 4102
    Brown; Monty Alexander (*p*); Jeff Hamilton (*d*); Ernestine Anderson (*v*). 79.
With his foot off the gas, Brown can be as ordinary as the next guy. Most of the running here seems to come from the interplay between Alexander and the impressive Hamilton, but that impression may be unfairly compounded by an uneasy sound-mix. Ernestine Anderson is an acquired taste which not everyone may have the patience to acquire. She shares something of the great Al Hibbler's surrealist diction but little of his latterly wacky charm. The stars are mostly for Hamilton.

*** **Soular Energy** Concord CCD 4268
    Brown; Gene Harris (*p*); Gerryck King (*d*); Red Holloway (*ts*); Emily Remler (*g*). 8/84.
A really fine album which only needs Jeff Hamilton in his usual slot behind the drums to lift it into minor classic status. King is a fine drummer but lacks sparkle and is inclined to hurry the pulse unnecessarily.

    Perhaps in retaliation, Brown takes the '"A" Train' at a pace which suggests privatization may be around the corner. Slowed down to an almost terminal grind, it uncovers all manner of harmonic quirks which Brown and the attentive Harris exploit with great imagination. Red Holloway and – rather more anonymously – the late Emily Remler sign up for a shortish and slightly inconsequential 'Mistreated But Undefeated Blues'. Brown's counter-melody figures on 'Cry Me A River' and, especially, the closing 'Sweet Georgia Brown' could almost be taped as his calling card. Exemplary.

** **Bye Bye Blackbird** Paddle Wheel K28P 6303
    Brown; Ichiro Masuda (*vib*); Cedar Walton (*p*); Mickey Roker (*d*); Emi Nakajima (*v*). 4/85.
** **Don't Forget The Blues** Concord CCD 4293
    Brown; Al Grey (*tb*); Ron Eschete (*g*); Gene Harris (*p*); Grady Tate (*d*). 5/85.
*** **The Red Hot** Concord CCD 4315
    Brown; Gene Harris (*p*); Mickey Roker (*d*). 11 & 12/85.
The second is a cheery 'all-star' – so why Eschete? – session that never really amounts to much. Tate is another in a line of first-class drummers to have recorded under Brown's leadership. In some regards he is the most conventional, though Tate is no revolutionary either, and there is a slightly stilted quality to some of the medium-tempo tracks. *Blackbird* never gets off its stilts and totters badly as a result. This is probably Brown's least impressive work as leader.

    Just when things were looking bleak for 1985, Brown turns in *Red Hot*, a strong, gamey trio with one of his most effective partners, the highly adaptable Harris. 'Love Me Tender' is a bit of fluff, but 'Have You Met Miss Jones?' and 'Street Of Dreams' are both substantial performances.

***(*) **Bam Bam Bam** Concord CCD 4375
    Brown; Gene Harris (*p*); Jeff Hamilton (*d*). 7/88.
*** **Summer Wind** Concord CCD 4426
    As above. 12/88.
Two superb live sets from an excellent working trio who interweave seamlessly and earn their solo spaces many times over. Brown's writing and arranging have been much more confident of late. The version of 'A Night In Tunisia' on *Bam Bam Bam* is quite remarkable, featuring hand percussion from Hamilton, and the tributes on both albums to Sonny Rollins ('T. S. R.'), Victor Feldman ('Rio'), and Art Blakey ('Buhaina Buhaina') are intelligent reinventions of some unexpected stylistic associations. Brown's blues stylings get more assured with each passing year. Originals like 'The Real Blues', the eponymous 'Bam Bam Bam' and Milt Jackson's oblique, bebop-flavoured 'Bluesology' all repay careful attention. 'If I Loved You', 'Summertime' and 'Days Of Wine And Roses' all comfortably fit the former Mr Ella Fitzgerald, while 'It Don't Mean A Thing', 'Mona Lisa' and 'Put Your Little Foot Right Out' uncover quite different aspects of Brown's increasingly complex musical persona.

**** **Black Orpheus** Paddle Wheel KICJ 109
    Brown; Gene Harris (*p*); Jeff Hamilton (*d*). 5/89, 2/91.
***(*) **3 Dimensional** Concord CCD 4520
    As above. 8/91.
***(*) **Moore Makes 4** Concord CCD 4477
    As above, except add Ralph Moore (*ts*). 91.
Vintage stuff from the very best of Brown's groups. This line-up has the easy cohesion of Oscar Peterson's trios, and Brown's busy lines often suggest Peterson's approach to a melody. Following on from an Ellington medley, Coltrane's 'Equinox' on *3 Dimensional* is a rare stab at the post-bop repertoire, and the group handle it comfortably. There are signs, though, that Brown is over-eager to diversify, and the album's a bit shapeless.

    Black Orpheus represents the trio's club programme of the time and hangs together very much better. Brown is under-mixed in places, despite the fact that the music has been recorded through the PA (or so it seems); there are a couple of places where it might have been better to overdub a studio line. Other than that, it's an excellent romantic disc.

Does Moore make more? On balance, yes. The cover depicts a saxophone standing in as fourth leg of a tea-table. The Brown trio has stood up on its own for years now and scarcely needs the help. On the other hand, Moore's forceful tenor adds such an effective element to 'My Romance' and the superb 'Stars Fell On Alabama' that one wonders what filled those spaces before. Brown's bass-lines are still among the best in the business, and the desk-slide was pushed well up to catch them. A return fixture seems inevitable.

Rob Brown (born 1962) ALTO SAXOPHONE

*** **Breath Rhyme** Silkheart SHCD-122
    Brown (*as*); William Parker (*b*); Dennis Charles (*d*). 4/89.
*** **Youniverse** Riti CD3
    Brown; Joe Morris (*g*); Whit Dickey (*d*). 6/92.

Brown's allegiances are to the free jazz of the 1960s, of Ayler and Jimmy Lyons, although he demurs at the mention of both names as influences. *Breath Rhyme* does, nevertheless, offer a powerful reminder of the kind of skirling declamations which those musicians would deploy against a rhythm section which works in rhythmic waves: Charles, especially, rolls out a beat that derives from Sunny Murray. Brown's own playing is a litany of overblown wails and long, anguished cries, although he is more temperate on the slower pieces. The sense of disorder is deceptive, for closer listening reveals subtle differentiations between pieces and a shrewd sense of detail – but that doesn't prevent some of the longer pieces from becoming monotonous. Slower, briefer episodes such as 'Stillness' may be more convincing for some. Parker is immensely interesting, but unfortunately the sound-balance does him few favours.

The most telling difference with *Youniverse* is the presence of Joe Morris, whose playing abjures obvious influences and displaces jazz, rock and other guitar traditions. Dickey, a pupil of Milford Graves, is right in the free tradition. The result is a clearer, more songful music that retains its intensity.

Ted Brown (born 1927) TENOR SAX

** **Free Spirit** Criss Cross Jazz Criss 1021
    Brown; Hod O'Brien (*p*); Jacques Schols (*b*). 10/87.

Criss Cross Jazz have made a speciality of rekindling the careers of some forgotten players, but in the case of Ted Brown the new records don't do much justice to a semi-legendary figure. He recorded with Warne Marsh and Art Pepper in the 1950s but has seldom been heard from since; this date reveals a musician whose loyalty to Lester Young has been unswerving for an entire career. Some of his solos come together in just the way that Young's successful later ones do: rhythmically suspended on the brink of disaster, the melodic ideas sew the improvisation together. His tone is also much like Young's hesitant, half-formed timbre. But without Lester's tragic mystique, the music doesn't add up to very much. His temperamental reserve means that the trio date of *Free Spirit* is sorely under-characterized.

Dave Brubeck (born 1920) PIANO

***(*) **The Dave Brubeck Octet** Original Jazz Classics OJC 101
    Brubeck; Dick Collins (*t*); Bob Collins (*tb*); Paul Desmond (*as*); Dave Van Kriedt (*ts*); Bill Smith (*cl, bs*); Ron Crotty (*b*); Cal Tjader (*d*). 48–49.
*** **The Dave Brubeck Trio** Fantasy F 24726
    Brubeck; Ron Crotty (*b*); Cal Tjader (*d, perc*).
***(*) **Dave Brubeck – Paul Desmond** Fantasy F 24727
    Brubeck; Paul Desmond (*as*); Ron Crotty, Wyatt Ruther (*b*); Herb Barman, Lloyd Davis, Joe Dodge (*d*). 52, 53, 54.
*** **Stardust** Fantasy F 24728
    As above, except add Norman Bates, Fred Dutton (*b*).
**** **Jazz At Oberlin** Original Jazz Classics OJC 046
    Brubeck; Paul Desmond (*as*); Ron Crotty (*b*); Lloyd Davis (*d*). 3/53.
*** **Jazz At The College Of The Pacific** Original Jazz Classics OJC 047
    Brubeck; Paul Desmond (*as*); Ron Crotty (*b*); Joe Dodge (*d*).
*** **In Concert** Fantasy 60-013
    As above. 6/53.

Often derided as a white, middle-class formalist with a rather buttoned-down image and an unhealthy obsession with classical parallels and clever-clever time signatures, Brubeck is actually one of the most significant composer-leaders in modern jazz. Tunes like 'Blue Rondo A La Turk', 'Kathy's Waltz' and Paul Desmond's 'Take Five' (which Brubeck made an enormous hit) insinuated their way into the unconscious of a whole generation of American college students. Though he has contributed very little to the 'standards' gene-pool ('In Your Own Sweet Way' is probably the only Brubeck original that is regularly covered), he has created a remarkable body of jazz and formal music, including orchestral pieces, oratorios and ballet scores. The Brubecks constitute something of a musical dynasty. His elder brother, Howard, is a 'straight' composer in a rather old-fashioned Francophile vein, while his sons, bassist and trombonist Chris, drummer Danny, and keyboard player Darius, have all played with him.

It used to be conventional wisdom that the only Brubeck records which mattered were those that featured the liquid alto of Paul Desmond. Such was the closeness – and, one might say, jealousy – of the relationship that it was stated in Desmond's contract that his own recordings had to be pianoless. What no one seemed to notice was that Desmond's best playing was almost always with the Brubeck group. Brubeck himself was not a particularly accomplished soloist, with a rather heavy touch and an unfailing attachment to block chords, but his sense of what could be accomplished within the bounds of a conventional jazz quartet allowed him to create an impressive and often startling body of music that demands urgent reassessment.

The early Octet catches Brubeck at the height of his interest in an advanced harmonic language (which he would have learnt from Darius Milhaud, his teacher at Mills College); there are also rhythmic transpositions of a sort that popped up in classic jazz and were subsequently taken as read by the 1960s avant-garde, but which in the 1950s had been explored thoroughly only by Max Roach. Relative to Gerry Mulligan, Brubeck has been not been widely regarded as a writer-arranger for larger groups, but the better material on this rather indifferently recorded set underline how confidently he approached the synthesis of jazz with other forms. Tracks like 'Serenades Suite' and 'Schizophrenic Scherzo' are a great deal more swinging than most products of the Third Stream, a movement one doesn't automatically associate with Brubeck's name.

The trios are bubbly and smoothly competent but lack the luminous quality that Desmond brought. The saxophonist joined in 1951 and immediately transformed the group. His duos with Brubeck on the later Fantasy are a measure of their immediate mutual understanding; 'Over The Rainbow' is one of the loveliest improvisations of the period, caught in a whispery close-up. Tjader is still an interestingly varied player at this period, far from the bland stylist he was to become later.

The quartets with Crotty (he succeeded Norman Bates; no, not that one) and Davis aren't considered to be the classic Brubeck groups; that was the later line-up with Wright and Morello, but they were excellent on their own less ambitious terms. There's an intriguing rehearsal version of the 'Trolley Song' on Fantasy 24727 that suggests something of what went into this music. *Stardust* is more of a grab-bag and is perhaps the dullest compilation from this early period; there are, though, fine Desmond perform-ances throughout, and Brubeck fans will want to have some less familiar material collected there.

Jazz At Oberlin was an enormous success on its first release and is still durable 40 years later, with some of Brubeck's and Desmond's finest interaction; one of the pianist's innovations was in getting two musicians to improvise at the same time, and there are good examples of that on the Oberlin College set. It's all standard material, and there are excellent performances of 'Perdido', 'Stardust' and 'How High The Moon' which adumbrate Brubeck's later interest in unconventional time-signatures. The other 1953 set (and the location underlines what Brubeck's constituency was) and the CD-only *In Concert* are less compelling at first glance. Desmond is having a slightly quieter night on the first, but Brubeck is in exceptional form, playing well within himself but showing all his class and sophistication. Repeats of 'Stardust' and 'All The Things You Are' on *In Concert* confound the notion that this was a 'reading' band, too stiff to improvise. The sound on all three is a bit remote and Crotty isn't always clearly audible.

***(*) Interchanges '54 CBS 467917

Brubeck; Paul Desmond (*as*); Bob Bates (*b*); Joe Dodge (*d*).

Originally released as *Brubeck Time*, this was recorded round a film shoot by the celebrated Gjon Mili and George Avakian's brother Aram (who went on to film *Jazz on a Summer's Day*). A purist to his suede shoes, Mili had taken a good deal of convincing that Brubeck was a worthy subject but had relented. There is a story that Mili's dismissiveness spurred Brubeck to angry heights not normally associated with him. Certainly, 'Stompin' For Mili' sounds as if he might have meant the preposition to read 'On'.

There is some fabulous music on the disc. Desmond's solo on 'Why Do I Love You' is brilliantly subtle and 'Audrey' (a soft minor blues intended to counterbalance the thudding Mili piece) is delicate to the point of fragility. This really was Brubeck time. He appeared on the cover of *Time* magazine, and was pushing jazz's demographics into territory no one had anticipated. The music stands up pretty well, too.

(*) Dave Brubeck Plays And Plays And Plays . . . Original Jazz Classics OJC 716
    Brubeck (*p* solo). 2/57.
. . . and is pretty uninspiring over this distance. The CD bonus of 'Two Sleepy People' will tip all but the
most ardent fan over into slumber.

*** **Dave Digs Disney** Columbia 471250
    Brubeck; Paul Desmond (*as*); Norman Bates (*b*); Joe Morello (*d*). 6 & 8/57.
Sun Ra did a Disney set, so don't be too quick to dismiss this one. 'When You Wish Upon A Star' is, of
course, a gift for players of Brubeck's and Desmond's delicacy and 'Some Day My Prince Will Come'
was brought into the jazz mainstream by Miles Davis. Among the remaining material, oddities like
'Heigh Ho', which gives Desmond one or two problems, and 'Give A Little Whistle', whose stop-start
melody is simply irritating. However, it is the little-known 'Very Good Advice' from *Alice in Wonderland*
and 'So This Is Love' from *Cinderella* which really top off this easily overlooked, non-novelty set by a
group at the top of its powers.

*** **Reunion** Original Jazz Classics OJC 150
    Brubeck; Paul Desmond (*as*); Dave Van Kriedt (*ts*); Norman Bates (*b*); Joe Morello (*d*). 2/57.
*** **Brubeck A La Mode** Original Jazz Classics OJC 200
    Brubeck; Bill Smith (*cl*); Eugene Wright (*b*); Joe Morello (*d*). 5 & 6/60.
From the end of his association with Fantasy (he'd signed for Columbia in 1954) *Reunion* brings back
the full-voiced Van Kriedt and Bates from the early bands. There's a greater preponderance of 'classical'
tags – 'Pieta', 'Prelude', 'Divertimento', 'Chorale' – most of them interpreted rather loosely. *A La Mode*
introduced another regular associate, fellow-Californian Smith, who has a lumpier touch than Desmond
and a far less sophisticated improvisational sense. Interesting writing on the vinyl-only *Near-Myth*, but
both the playing and the reproduction are a shade muted. None of these should be considered essential,
though Van Kriedt is worth checking out.

*** **Jazz Impressions Of Eurasia** Columbia 471249
    As for *Newport '58*. 7 & 8/58.
Very much in the same vein as Ellington's overseas suites (possibly even influencing them). There's no
'Isfahan', and nothing that really sets the pieces apart programmatically. It's not clear what distinguishes
'Brandenburg Gate' from 'Marble Arch', 'Calcutta Blues' from 'The Golden Horn'; and Brubeck
himself never sounds like anything but an American abroad, lacking Ellington's ability to relax, if not
exactly get inside, other milieux. Not as good as *Jazz Impressions Of Japan* or *New York*, which are now
available only in excerpt on the encyclopaedic *Time Signatures*, below, but it's atmospheric enough,
though in a Cook's tour sort of way.

***(*) **The Great Concerts** Columbia 462403
    Brubeck; Paul Desmond (*as*); Eugene Wright (*b*); Joe Morello (*d*). 3/58, 2/63.
This pulls together the double-LP, *At Carnegie Hall*, with *Brubeck In Amsterdam*. 'Great' is pushing it a
bit for the earlier of the two, but the Dutch gig is quite special, and the recordings are miles better than
the amateurish Moons. Morello's easy swing on 'Wonderful Copenhagen' (from 1958) sets the pace and
the standard for most of the disc, which is more than usually even in tempo and might have benefited
from a more judicious trawl through the material. Good value for money, though.

**** **Time Out** Columbia 460611-2
    Brubeck; Paul Desmond (*as*); Eugene Wright (*b*); Joe Morello (*d*). 6, 7 & 8/59.
Catalogued as a 'Historic Reissue' (industry-speak for a golden egg), this is the music everyone associates with Brubeck. So familiar is it that no one actually hears what's going on any more. As the title
suggests, Brubeck wanted to explore ways of playing jazz that went a step beyond the basic 4/4 that had
remained the norm long after jazz threw off the relentless predictability of B flat. The opening 'Blue
Rondo A La Turk' (with its Mozart echoes) opens in an oddly distributed 9/8, with the count rearranged
as 2-2-2-3. It's a relatively conventional classical *rondo* but with an almost raucous blues interior. 'Take
Five' is in the most awkward of all key signatures, but what is remarkable about this almost iconic slice
of modern jazz is the extent to which it constantly escapes the 5/4 count and swings. Morello's drum
solo is perhaps his best work on record (though his brief 'Everybody's Jumpin'' solo is also excellent)
and Brubeck's heavy vamp has tremendous force. Though it's almost always identified as a Brubeck
tune, 'Take Five' was actually written by Desmond.
    Most of the other material is in waltz and double-waltz time. Max Roach had explored the idea
thoroughly on *Jazz In 3/4 Time*, but not even Roach had attempted anything as daring and sophisticated
as the alternations of beat on 'Three To Get Ready' and 'Kathy's Waltz', which is perhaps the finest
single thing on the album. Desmond tends to normalize the count in his solo line, and it's easy to miss
what is going on in the rhythm section if one concentrates too exclusively on the saxophone. The
Desmond cult may be fading slightly and as it does it may be possible to re-establish the Brubeck

Quartet's claim *as a unit* to be considered among the most innovative and adventurous of modern-jazz groups.

*** Gone With The Wind Columbia 450984
As for *Time Out*. 4/59.

We're into concept-album territory here, the first of many thematic sets like the *Jazz Impressions* dates on which the quartet dined out for some years. This is 'Brubeck Goes South', a chipper but slightly flat-footed tribute to Dixie. Desmond doesn't sound enamoured of 'Camptown Races' or 'Short'nin' Bread', but he delivers a perfectly weighted solo on 'Georgia On My Mind' with Brubeck in close attendance.

*** Take Five Vipers Nest VN 160
Brubeck; Paul Desmond (*as*); Joe Dodge, Eugene Wright (*b*); Joe Morello, Norman Bates (*d*).

No firm date or location for these live sets from the later 1950s. A nice blend of familiar and less familiar material, with 'Take Five' taking its rightful place towards the end in the midst of 'New Material In New Tempi'. The biggest single statement is Brubeck's 'Two Part Contention', as clever a piece of part-writing as he ever conceived. There are two takes of ' "A" Train' and a lovely performance of 'Gone With The Wind', the first track on the album to feature Morello rather than Bates, and what a difference it makes!

*** Brubeck Plays Music From West Side Story And . . . Columbia 450410
Brubeck; Paul Desmond (*as*); Eugene Wright (*b*); Joe Morello (*d*). 2/60, 6 & 7/62, 12/65.

The 'and' is more than useful padding, since the Bernstein tunes sound a little rinky-dink, played like this. The other material, mainly by Cole Porter, is more finely judged, and played with a degree more commitment. In January 1960 Brubeck had worked with Bernstein and the New York Phil. on a set that was originally released as *Bernstein Plays Brubeck Plays Bernstein*; see *Time Signatures*, below.

**(*) Greatest Hits Columbia 32046
Brubeck; Paul Desmond (*as*); Eugene Wright (*b*); Joe Morello (*d*).

Fairly predictable packaging of standard fare. For the record: the single-album set includes 'Take Five', 'It's A Raggy Waltz', 'Camptown Races', 'Unsquare Dance', 'Mister Broadway', 'I'm In A Dancing Mood', 'The Trolley Song', 'In Your Own Sweet Way' and 'Blue Rondo A La Turk'.

*** The Last Set At Newport Atlantic 81382
Brubeck; Gerry Mulligan (*bs*); Jack Six (*b*); Alan Dawson (*d*). 7/71.

*** We're All Together Again For The First Time Atlantic 81390
As above, except add Paul Desmond (*as*). 10/72, 11/72.

Brubeck and Desmond teamed up again for one-shot tours all through the early 1970s, and they played to huge crowds. Something of the magic had gone, though. Desmond's playing still provokes a thrill, especially when he weaves round Mulligan on 'Rotterdam Blues' on the *All Together Again* European tour compilation. Mulligan fitted perfectly into Brubeck's conception, swinging hard in uneven measures when there was a call for it, caressing a ballad the next moment. The Newport session is mostly upbeat, a show-stopping bravura performance that lacks subtlety but confirms Brubeck's remarkable ability to work a crowd. Desmond, one suspects, was happier in more intimate settings. He often sounds slightly frail on the European dates.

*** All The Things We Are Atlantic 81399
Brubeck; Lee Konitz, Anthony Braxton (*as*); Jack Six (*b*); Alan Dawson, Roy Haynes (*d*). 7/73, 10/74.

The eye-popping presence of avant-gardist Anthony Braxton in the line-up is not a misprint. This perhaps helps put into context his much-discussed affection for the cool, 'white' saxophone sound of Paul Desmond and Warne Marsh. On 'In Your Own Sweet Way' he sounds very much like a younger, more accommodating version of himself. Paired with Konitz on 'All The Things You Are', he's more conventionally boppish, and the combination is pleasantly awkward. Haynes adds a bit of beef to the engine room, sounding very much like old swingers like Krupa and Dave Tough. There's actually only one track from the July '73 session, a trio medley of Jimmy Van Heusen songs; pleasant, but hardly startling.

*** Paper Moon Concord CCD 4178
Brubeck; Jerry Bergonzi (*ts, b*); Chris Brubeck (*b, btb*); Randy Jones (d). 9/81.

**(*) Concord On A Summer Night Concord CCD 4198
Brubeck; Bill Smith (*cl*); Chris Brubeck (*b, tb*); Randy Jones (*d*). 8/82.

**(*) For Iola Concord CCD 4259
As above. 8/84.

*** **Reflections** Concord CCD 4299
    As above. 12/85.
(*) **Blue Rondo Concord CCD 4317
    As above. 11/86.
*** **Moscow Night** Concord CCD 4353
    As above. 3/87.
*** **New Wine** Musicmasters 5051-2
    As above. 7/87.

The Concord years suggest that whatever Brubeck once had has now been thoroughly run to ground. Only the most dedicated fans will find much to get excited about on these albums, though there are lovely things on *Paper Moon* which hark back to the old days. 'We Will All Remember Paul' on *Reflections* is a heartfelt tribute to Desmond (who died in 1977) and the surrounding material seems to be lifted by it. *Moscow Night* also seems to be up a gear and the versions there of 'Three To Get Ready', 'Unsquare Dance' and 'St Louis Blues' are the best for years. Otherwise non-essential. Brubeck *fils* and Jones are curiously stiff and unswinging, and Smith's initial promise seems (temporarily at least) to have evaporated; he is probably a less sophisticated player now than he was in 1960. Jerry Bergonzi was one of a number of young radicals introduced to Dave by Chris and Danny. It's still clear whose record it is, but there are signs that Brubeck was able to take on board new ideas, often far removed from his primary concerns.

(*) **Trio Brubeck Musicmasters 844 337
    Brubeck; Chris Brubeck (*b, btb*); Danny Brubeck (*d*). 88.

Musically, the third brother was hardly missed (Darius lives in South Africa), but this still needs something to give it a bit of substance. The two Brubeck sons are competent players, with odd sparks of fire here and there; but the only thing that keeps the music from being entirely static is Dave's remarkable energy. He carries the whole thing.

*** **Quiet As The Moon** Musicmasters 65057-2
    Brubeck; Bob Militello (*as, ts, f*); Jack Six (*b*); Chris Brubeck (*b, btb*); Matthew Brubeck (*clo*); Danny Brubeck, Randy Jones (*d*). 9/88, 12/89, 5/91.
**** **Once When I Was Very Young** Musicmasters 65083-2
    Brubeck; Bill Smith (*cl*); Jack Six (*b*); Randy Jones (*d*). 5/91.

Despite some health problems, Brubeck entered the 1990s like so many musicians of his generation, artistically rejuvenated and enjoying renewed attention and critical respect. *Quiet* cobbles together material from a thirty-month period and is inevitably patchy. The reunion with Six prompts some of the happiest music, though Militello is never much more than Desmond-and-water. Smith, despite the reservations above, emerges as very much his own man. *Very Young* is one of Brubeck's most centred and coherent performances since the 1950s, one of those records that seem to exist as an entity, almost irrespective of the distribution of tracks and personnel. Smith's rich *chalumeau* can sound very like Desmond, but he lacks the saxophonist's other side, the 'dry martini' chill that could be a little forbidding. A very welcome return to form.

**** **Time Signatures: A Career Retrospective** Columbia/Legacy 52945 4CD
    Brubeck; Dick Collins (*t*); Bob Collins (*tb*); Paul Desmond (*as*); Bobby Militello (*as, f*); Dave Van Kriedt, Jerry Bergonzi (*ts*); Gerry Mulligan (*bs*); Bill Smith, Perry Robinson (*cl*); Darius Brubeck, Billy Kyle (*p*); Bob Bates, Norman Bates, Joe Benjamin, Chris Brubeck, Ron Crotty, Charles Mingus, Jack Weeks, Dave Powell, Wyatt Ruther, Jack Six, Eugene Wright (*b*); Herb Barman, Danny Brubeck, Lloyd Davis, Alan Dawson, Joe Dodge, Randy Jones, Joe Morello (*d*); Cal Tjader (*vib, d, perc*); Salvatore Agueros, Howard Brubeck, Teo Macero, John Lee (*perc*); Louis Armstrong, Carmen McRae, Jimmy Rushing, Lambert, Hendricks and Ross (*v*); New York Philharmonic Orchestra conducted by Leonard Bernstein. 46–91.

This is *the* stocking-filler for a Brubeck fan, a magnficently packaged four-CD box with immaculately reproduced liner photographs and a detailed booklet breaking down each and every track. There is also a long biographical essay by Juul Anthonissen.

    The recordings (items marked with a † not currently available) are drawn from the 1946 *Old Sounds From San Francisco*†, *Trio Featuring Cal Tjader*, *Octet*, *Brubeck–Desmond*, *Jazz At Storyville*†, *Jazz At Oberlin*, *Jazz Goes To College*†, *Brubeck Time*, *Jazz: Red, Hot And Cool*†, *Brubeck Plays Brubeck*†, *And Jay And Kai At Newport*†, *Jazz Impressions Of The USA*†, the underrated *Dave Digs Disney*, *In Europe*, *Newport 58*, *Jazz Impressions Of Eurasia*, *Gone With The Wind*, *Time Out* (of course!), *Southern Scene*† (a companion to *Gone*), *The Riddle*†, *Brubeck And Rushing*†, *Bernstein Plays Brubeck Plays Bernstein*, *Tonight Only!*†, the inevitable follow-ups *Time Further Out*†, *Time Changes*† and *Time In*†, *Countdown Time In Outer Space*†, *Brandenburg Gate: Revisited*†, *The Real Ambassadors*† (with Louis Armstrong), *Summit Sessions*†, *Bossa Nova USA*†, *At Carnegie Hall*, *Jazz Impressions Of Japan*†, and of *New York*†, *Angel Eyes*†, *Anything Goes!*†, *Bravo! Brubeck!*†, *The Last Time We Saw Paris*†, *Compadres*† and *In Berlin*† (with Mulligan), *Brother, The Great Spirit Made Us All*† (with the sons and unexpected Brubeckians, Perry Robinson and Jerry Bergonzi), and the recent *Quiet As The Moon* and *Once When I Was Very Young*. There is also a previously unreleased live session from Moscow, recorded in the spring of 1987. From the collector's point of view, it's a shame that there isn't far more unreleased material; but the point is, as this astonishing list shows, that Brubeck has been unusually well documented over the years. There has undoubtedly been stuff left on the editing-room floor and in the vaults, but there has also been an unusually severe quality-control process.

There are wonderful oddities in the playlist: the duo with Mingus on 'Sectarian Blues', the 12-tone rumba from *Jazz Impressions Of New York*, the vocal items with Pops, Carmen and Jimmy Rushing, the odd 'Lost Waltz' from 1965's *Time In*. What they reveal is not so much an 'experimental' or an unexpected Brubeck as a man propelled by what John Aldridge called 'the energy of new success' into the centre of the musical culture and allowed to pick and choose, and to initiate, the projects which interested him.

Time Signatures has been selected with the music, not the matrix numbers, in mind, and it offers an ideal introduction to one of the music's most popular and enduring figures.

Thierry Bruneau ALTO SAXOPHONE, BASS CLARINET, BASSOON

*** **Live At De Kave** Serene SER 01
      Bruneau; Mal Waldron (*p*); Carlos Barretto (*b*); John Betsch (*d*). 9/89.
(*) **Tribute Serene SER 02
      Bruneau; Ken McIntyre (*f, as, ob, bsn*); Severi Pyysalo (*vib*); Richard Davis (*b*); Jean-Yves
      Colson (*d*). 11/90.
Both the multi-instrumentalist and his home label are dedicated to the spirit of Eric Dolphy; 'Serene' was a Dolphy blues. For these sessions, Bruneau commands the experience of two of his mentor's former cohorts, Waldron and Davis, notoriously brooding players who contribute to the rather murky overall sound. *Live At De Kave* is, however, a surprisingly brisk set that includes such Dolphy touchstones as 'Bee Vamp' and '245'. They're played impressively well. Captured at the 1990 Tourcoing Festival in France, *Tribute* includes 'GW' and 'The Cry'. Less impressive; one feels the lack of something with the bite of Booker Little's trumpet. Bruneau and McIntyre get in each other's way and Pyysalo isn't a convincing substitute for Bobby Hutcherson.

Bruneau's bass clarinet playing won't really do, but he is a fine, idiomatic saxophonist, and his bassoon captures most of the darker tones he's after. It's essentially heart-on-sleeve stuff, but it certainly makes a refreshing change from all the wannabe Coltrane stuff that's still around.

Alain Brunet TRUMPET

(*) **Rominus Label Bleu LBLC 6541
      Brunet; Denis Badault (*p*); Didier Lockwood (*vn*); Patrick Rollin (*g*); Yves Torchinsky (*b*);
      Francis Lassus (*d*). 91.
This is basically a quartet album, with Lockwood making only two appearances and Rollin confined to accompanying the trumpeter on a minute-and-a-half reading of 'Caravan'. The most striking thing is a version of 'Ode To Billie Joe', which recasts Bobbie Gentry's song as a medium-tempo shuffle and makes the most of the tune. If anything, it shows up the rest of the material as merely clever exercises in sort-of-bebop writing, and Brunet, who has a tone much akin to Chet Baker's and a deadpan line in humour which he slips into his playing – there is a tick-tock version of 'St Thomas' which some will find intensely irritating – sounds like a character player in search of a good leader. 'Rominus' itself, though, initiates a striking partnership with the mercurial Lockwood and makes one wish he'd been more involved in the rest of the record.

Jimmy Bruno GUITAR

(*) **Sleight Of Hand Concord CCD-4532
      Bruno; Pete Colangelo (*b*); Bruce Klauber (*d*); Edgardo Cintron Orchestra. 4–5/91.
*** **Burnin'** Concord CCD 4612
      Bruno; Craig Thomas (*b*); Craig Holloway (*d*). 2/94.
Bruno is a Philadelphia homebody whose playing sits squarely in the big-toned electric tradition. He's more fond of chords, octave playing and parallel lines than of single-string solos, and it gives his

improvisations a meaty texture that fleshes out his simple tunes. That said, the record is impressively skilful but not very exciting. The 'orchestra' is a Latin rhythm section that sits in on two tracks for a useful change of pace; but otherwise Bruno has to carry everything himself, since Colangelo and Klauber offer anonymous support. *Burnin'* goes up a notch since Thomas and Holloway bring some muscle of their own to the date. Two deft solos by Bruno include a thoughtful revsion of Coltrane's 'Central Park West' that's quietly effective.

Ray Bryant (born 1931) PIANO

*** **Golden Earrings** Original Jazz Classics OJC 793
    Bryant; Ike Isaacs (*b*); Specs Wright (*d*).
*** **Hot Turkey** Black and Blue BLE 233089
    Bryant; Major Holley (*b*); Panama Francis (*d*). 10/75.
***(*) **Montreux 77** Original Jazz Classics OJC 371
    Bryant (*p* solo). 12/76, 7/77.
***(*) **Plays Basie And Ellington** Emarcy 832235
    Bryant; Rufus Reid (*b*); Freddie Waits (*d*). 2/87.
***(*) **Blue Moods** Emarcy 842438
    As above. 2/87, 1 & 6/88.
***(*) **All Mine All Yours** Emarcy 510423
    Bryant; Rufus Reid (*b*); Winard Harper (*d*). 10/89.
**** **Through The Years: Volume 1** Emarcy 512764
    Bryant; Rufus Reid (*b*); Grady Tate (*d*). 3/92.
**** **Through The Years: Volume 2** Emarcy 512933
    As above. 3/92.
**** **No Problem** Emarcy 522 387
    Bryant; Kenny Burrell (*g*); Peter Washington (*b*); Kenny Washington (*d*). 2/94.

Bryant is not an orthodox bopper in the way Hampton Hawes once was, and his solo performances are even further away from the predominant Bud Powell model of bop piano. Noted for an imaginative and influential alteration of the basic 12-bar-blues sequence on his 'Blues Changes', Bryant is a distinctive pianist who resembles Hawes superficially but who, unlike the older man, has been content to record solo. Unfortunately, the fine OJC *Alone With The Blues* is now available only in very depleted vinyl stock. Fortunately, the rather good *Golden Earrings* has come back into circulation, with fine versions of 'Daahoud' and 'Django'.

The solo and trio material on the slightly later *Hot Turkey* is also worthy of attention, though there's still a slight feeling of uncertainty about, as if Bryant wasn't yet sure what direction his revived career was going to take. That was to become much clearer over the next few years, with a signing to Pablo (unfortunately all this material is now vinyl only) and then to Emarcy.

Bryant got off to a cracking start with the Basie and Ellington set. *Blue Moods*, which looks back to the earlier blues sessions, cemented a partnership with Reid and Waits which was sundered only by the drummer's untimely death. Tate is a more solidly rhythmic replacement, sometimes to the detriment of Bryant's relaxed delivery, but the two *Through The Years* volumes, recorded to celebrate Bryant's sixtieth birthday, are absolutely top drawer, and there's nothing to pick between them. Favourites like 'Cold Turkey', 'Round Midnight', 'Oleo' and 'Satin Doll' (all *Volume 1*) and 'St Thomas', 'Cry Me A River' and 'Django' make this the set of choice. Bryant's breakthrough at this time can only be compared to Joe Henderson's, almost equally belated but the product of patient application rather than over-deliberate 'relocation' and hype. Unfairly, Bryant hasn't enjoyed a quarter of the attention and praise heaped on the saxophonist, and he is still regarded in some quarters as a poor cousin of the man he replaced at Montreux all those years ago.

No Problem is a reflection of his can-do approach to life and music. With Burrell playing those lean boppish lines all around him, Ray is able to stretch out and groove in perfect relaxation. You can feel him enjoying himself, and when he turns Benny Goodman's 'Soft Winds' into a secular hymn you're on your feet in sheer respect for this uncomplicated genius.

Rusty Bryant ALTO AND TENOR SAXOPHONES

(*) **Rusty Bryant Returns Original Jazz Classics OJC 331
    Bryant; Sonny Phillips (*org*); Grant Green (*g*); Bob Bushnell (*b*); Herbie Lovelle (*d*). 8/69.

*** **Fire Eater** Prestige 10014-2
> Bryant; Bill Mason, Leon Spencer Jr (*org*); Wilbert Longmire (*g*); Idris Muhammed (*d*). 72.
*** **Friday Night Funk For Saturday Night Brothers** Prestige 10054-2
> Bryant; Kennth Moss (*p, org*); Harold Young (*g*); Eddie Brookshire (*b*); Fred Masey (*d*);
> Norman Jones (*perc*). 73.

Bryant's records have long been out of print, but a clutch of reissues has recently brought him back to the racks. He plays in a hard-hitting, soul-sax style, not very productive on *Returns* but a little more exciting on the two subsequent dates for Prestige. The four tracks on *Fire Eater* follow the same pattern of bluesy licks over toasted organ grooves, but there's a little more variety on *Friday Night Funk*, with a greasy 'Mercy Mercy Mercy' and a splendid set-piece in 'Blues For A Brother', which climaxes on a storming organ solo from Moss.

Jeanie Bryson VOCALS

***(*) **I Love Being Here With You** Telarc CD 83336
> Bryson; Wallace Roney (*t*); Don Braden (*ts*); Kenny Barron, Ted Brancato (*p*); Steve Nelson
> (*vib*); Vic Juris (*g*); Bob Crane, Ray Drummond (*b*); Ron Davis (*d*); Rudy Bird (*perc*). 1/93.
*** **Tonight I Need You So** Telarc CD 83348
> As above, except omit Roney, Barron, Drummond; add Claudio Roditi (*t*); Jay Ashby (*tb*);
> Paquito D'Rivera (*as*); Danilo Perez (*p*); Christian McBride (*b*); Ignacao Berroa (*d*). 94.

Not all publicity is good publicity. Bryson's excellent debut record was somewhat overshadowed by her unfortunately timed claim that she was the child of Dizzy Gillespie. DNA testing hasn't generally played much part in jazz criticism, and speculation about Bryson's parentage (and the notably uxorious Gillespie's extra-marital activities) tended to cloud any recognition that she was the most impressive new vocal talent for years.

Like its successor, the first album benefited hugely from the presence of top-flight players. Barron is exemplary, and Braden and Roney provide tough *yang* counterbalances to her unexpected fragility. 'Bittersweet' and 'A Sleeping Bee' – ironically the two tracks on which Brancato replaces Barron – are exceptional performances, but there is scarcely a false note throughout the session; a word also has to go to Ray Drummond for his lush, full-bodied accompaniment, filling in a part of the vocal spectrum where Bryson is apt to sound uncertain.

On *Tonight* he is replaced by the now equally ubiquitous McBride, who also brought along his electric bass for a couple of soul numbers: Stevie Wonder's 'Too Shy To Say' and Luther Vandross's 'What Can A Miracle Do?' It would have been fascinating to have heard a simple voice–bass duet – perhaps 'Alone Together'? – to highlight what sounds like a very fruitful relationship. Roditi is a very different kind of player from Roney, but his warm, reservedly passionate sound is perfect for a session of this sort, and he holds in check the busier and more assertive D'Rivera and Braden.

A glorious debut, with the promise of a long career to come. It would be a pity if Bryson were only remembered for non-musical reasons.

Milton Buckner (1915–77) PIANO, ORGAN, VIBRAPHONE, VOCALS

*** **Them There Eyes** Black and Blue BLE 233023
> Buckner; Buddy Tate (*ts*); Wallace Bishop (*d*). 12/67.
*** **Green Onions** Black and Blue BLE 59.087
> Buckner; Roy Gaines (*g*); André Persiany (*p*); Roland Lobligeois (*b*); Panama Francis (*d*). 2/75,
> 7/76.

Milt Buckner's musical roots lay in the broad-brush band arrangements of the 1920s and '30s, rather than in small-group jazz. His father Ted had played alto saxophone with Jimmie Lunceford, and Buckner Junior held two campaign medals from gruelling stints with Lionel Hampton in the 1940s (most of them) and early '50s.

His pioneering use of electric organ was in part an attempt to bring some of the energy and power of a full horn section to small-group playing, and his old skills as an arranger are more in evidence on the quartet/quintet tracks than any technical virtuosity.

It would have been good to hear Buckner with Tate and Bishop in a well-engineered studio. In these settings they sound full of energy but the performances have the subtlety of the proverbial blunt instrument; 'Mack The Knife' and 'Stompin' At The Savoy' on *Them There Eyes* are the best of them. Panama Francis was a great swing drummer and he gives the sessions a relaxed beat that encourages a more refined and lyrical expression. The two-tenor tracks are disastrous.

It's a curiously skewed legacy for such an able and likeable musician, and difficult to assess objectively.

Uncommitted samplers could start almost anywhere, though *Them There Eyes* would seem to be the best bet.

John Bunch (born 1921) PIANO

***(*) **John Bunch Plays Kurt Weill** Chiaroscuro CD(D) 144
> Bunch (*p* solo). 5/75–1/91.

*** **The Best Thing For You** Concord CCD 4328
> Bunch; Phil Flanigan (*b*); Chuck Riggs (*d*). 6/87.

Despite his seniority, John Bunch was a little-known sideman, accompanist and orchestra pianist until he was in his fifties. In the 1970s and '80s he secured wider attention as a member of the mainstream clan championed by Concord, though to date he has only the trio album listed above on that label. There's nothing demonstrative about his style, which is in the aristocratic swing tradition of Teddy Wilson, but he can play with bruising power when he wants, as well as with fingertip delicacy.

The *Kurt Weill* album is a rare and highly imaginative project: only a handful of Weill's tunes have entered the jazz repertoire, and Bunch's thoughtful settings – some at ballad tempo, others with a flavour of stride, some delivered with Monk-like rhythms – make all of them sound like plausible vehicles. The original (1975) sessions have been extended with six tracks cut in 1991, and there's amazingly little to choose between them in terms of both sound and interpretation. The Concord album is good if rather so-so, in the unemphatic manner of the company.

Jane Bunnett SOPRANO SAXOPHONE, FLUTE

*** **New York Duets** Music & Arts CD 629
> Bunnett; Don Pullen (*p*). 89.

*** **Live At Sweet Basil** Denon CAN 9009
> Bunnett; Larry Cramer (*t*); Don Pullen (*p*); Kieran Overs (*b*); Billy Hart (*d*).

*** **Spirits Of Havana** Denon CAN 9011
> Bunnett; Larry Cramer (*t, flhn*); Frank Emilio, Flynn Rodríques, Gonzalo Rubalcaba, Hilario Durán Torres (*p*); Ahmed Barroso (*g*); Kieran Overs (*b*); Oqduardo Díaz Anaya, Justo M. Garcia Arango, Orlando Lage Bozva, Guillermo Barreto Brown, Ignacio Ubicio Castillo, Jacinto Soull Castillo, Ernesto Rodríquez Guzman, Francisco Hernández Mora, Roberto García Valdes (*perc*); Merceditas Valdés, Grupo Yoruba Andabo (*v*). 9 & 10/91.

(*) **Rendez-Vous Brazil / Cuba Justin Time JUST 74
> Bunnett; Larry Cramer (*t, flhn*); Sabine Boyer (*af*); Hilario Durán Torres (*p*); Filo Machado (*g, v, perc*); Carlitos Del Puerto (*b*); Celso Machado (*perc*). 6/95.

Like Steve Lacy, her acknowledged model on soprano saxophone, Canadian Jane Bunnett has led a band almost wholly dedicated to Monk themes. Don Pullen, who clearly recognizes talent when he hears it, gives her the quirky harmonies and off-centre count that she hears in them. On the duets, he coaxes and provokes, encouraging Bunnett's unstuffy progressions; together, they make an interesting job of 'Bye Ya' and 'Little Rootie Tootie'. Pullen takes a less prominent role on the live session, content to comp away in his inimitable blocky style with its organ player clusters, leaving the main action to Bunnett and her companion, Cramer. There are some signs here that Bunnett still doesn't quite hack it as an improvising player. The opening is stunning (if a little contrived), but the long set tends to break down into its constituents and the writing isn't quite strong enough to carry some very un-together playing.

Bunnett's chill soprano is better suited to the more abstract duet settings than to a relatively straightforward blowing session. She concentrates largely on textures, leaving the piece to plod its own way home. Pullen's deliciously unexpected outbursts keep the ingredients stirring and the pace unpredictable, but there's nothing more than the odd off-centre voicing coming from the trumpeter, and the rhythm section sounds oddly mechanized.

Bunnett's 'In Dew Time' (title-track of an earlier LP, now deleted) gets an airing and she does some lovely flute work on 'You Don't Know What Love Is', but she's trying to make silk purses when she needs to concentrate on the basic fabric which simply isn't robust enough. Perhaps the most teasingly original new saxophone voice on the scene, but no one's written her a good script yet.

She's adamant that *Spirits Of Havana* isn't just another Latin jazz date but a genuine attempt to bring Cuban music within her own constantly widening purview. She was already listening to and playing salsa before making her all-important first trip to Havana, and she seems immediately at ease in an idiom which puts conventional (that is, jazz- and bop-derived) soloing at a premium, shifting emphasis towards the overall sound of the group. The opening 'Hymn' is a flute tribute to the spirit of Miles

Davis, who had just died. There is a searing version of 'Epistrophy', with Cuban percussion not so much added as incorporated into the fabric of the composition. For the rest, the material is nearly all traditional Afro-Caribbean or written in collaboration with the late Guillermo Barreto Brown, who masterminded the project.

Bunnett's soprano and flute figures are haunting on 'La Luna Arriba', by her close associate, Larry Cramer, who is superb on the Monk tune. Frank Emilio's 'G. M. S.' opens with pan-American flute but gets lost in a thicket of percussion. Merceditas Valdés's vocals will not be to everyone's taste, but they're integral to a fascinating project. It would be interesting to hear Bunnett extend the 'Epistrophy' experiment, taking in compositions by Andrew Hill and her sometime associate, Don Pullen, who has also recently worked in a parallel idiom.

The *Brazill/Cuba* project is dominated by Filo Machado compositions, and he is clearly the effective co-leader of a session that almost puts Bunnett's solo skills at a discount in favour of a highly rhythmic and dance-orientated group sound. It's all doubtless very authentic, and Cramer could find work in wedding bands any day of the week, growing a lot more comfortable with this type of material every time he goes out, but one wonders whether it's the most effective direction for the young Canadians.

Albert Burbank (1902–76) CLARINET

*** **Albert Burbank With Kid Ory And His Creole Jazzband** Storyville STCD 6010
      Burbank; Alvin Alcorn (*t*); Kid Ory (*tb*); Don Ewell (*p*); Ed Garland (*b*); Minor Hall (*d*). 5–7/
54.

Burbank scarcely ever left New Orleans, and it's an irony that the only disc currently under his own name should have been recorded elsewhere (he toured briefly with Ory's band and returned home the same year). These tracks, culled from six different 1954 concerts at San Francisco's Club Hangover, were made under Ory's leadership and it's rather a matter of paying respects that they appear under Burbank's name: Ory and Alcorn have just as major a role in the music. But the clarinettist has much to say, too. He was a dramatic player, switching between long and short phrases and possessing an odd, shrimpy vibrato which gives his high notes a peculiarly affecting quality. There are fine solos on 'Fidgety Feet' and the rest of a frankly ordinary set of material, but the epic 'Blues For Jimmie Noone', which runs for 11 minutes, has a funereal grandeur that is only finally undercut by Garland's disastrous *arco* passage. Alcorn is, as ever, in rousing form, too. Fair recording, given the source material.

Raymond Burke (1904–86) CLARINET

(***) **Raymond Burke's Speakeasy Boys 1937–1949** American Music AMCD-47
      Burke; Wooden Joe Nicholas, Vincent Cass (*t*); Joe Avery (*tb*); Louis Gallaud, Woodrow Rousell
(*p*); Johnny St Cyr (*g*); Austin Young (*b*); Bob Matthews (*d*). 37–5/49.

Burke's clarinet playing stands in the line of the New Orleans masters: he had the sweet-toned delivery of Percy Humphrey, but could be as elaborate and blues-inflected as Johnny Dodds when he wished. Some of this can be gleaned from a very rough CD in the American Music series. Most of the tracks come from 1949 acetates by a band from which Burke stands out: Nicholas sounds terribly weak and shaky when he struggles to the front, and Avery's trombone is inept enough to make one wince (even the sleeve-notes describe him as 'ratty'). The loudest person in the band is St Cyr. Despite all that, Burke still weaves some lovely solos out of the situation. The other tracks are even more obscure: a 1937 'Solitude' with George Hartman's (unknown) band, a couple of duets with Woodrow Rousell, and four dusty tracks with Vincent Cass's (unknown) band. Sound-quality ranges from dire to moderately decent (two final acetates were turned up in a New Orleans flea market in 1993). For New Orleans scholars only.

***(*) **Raymond Burke And Cie Frazier With Butch Thompson In New Orleans** 504 CDS27
      Burke; Butch Thompson (*p*); Cie Frazier (*d*). 8/79.

This is more like the way Raymond Burke should be remembered. Though already late in life, he was still playing very well in 1979, his understated delivery the mark of a man whose unassuming approach to his art has helped it endure. In itself, the music is nothing much: a battery of tunes, played at more or less the same tempo, with Frazier marking out a steady pulse and Thompson comping and taking easy-going solos. But scarcely any of the 15 tunes are too familiar – there are New Orleans rarities like A. J. Piron's 'I Want Somebody To Love', 'Gypsy Love Song' and 'Oh Daddy' – and each is played with genuine pleasure by the three men. Thompson never pushes too hard, and Burke's musing solos have an eloquence all their own. On a hot day, with a jug of iced tea to hand, this can sound like the very heart of jazz.

Ronnie Burrage (born 1959) DRUMS, PERCUSSION, KEYBOARDS, VOICE

*** **Shuttle** Sound Hills SSCD 8052
> Burrage; Frank Lacy (*tb, flhn*); Hamiet Bluiett (*bs*); Cyrus Chestnut (*p, perc*); Joe Ford (*as, ss, f*); Charnett Moffett (*b*); Doc Gibbs (*perc*). 4/93.

A very decent debut indeed from the likeable Burrage, who's put together a challengingly blunt and unobvious group. Bluiett, Ford and Lacy belong up at the sharp end of things; Chestnut is much more mainstream and there are times when he doesn't quite seem to follow what's going on – or to care for it. Moffett is an irritating, scribbly player, but he actually fits into these busy themes (which are presumably Burrage's; no composer credit is visible and the liner-notes are in Japanese) remarkably well. Worth a listen.

Dave Burrell (born 1940) PIANO, KEYBOARDS

**** **High Won – High Two** Black Lion BLCD 760206
> Burrell; Sirone (*b*); Bobby Kapp, Sonny Murray (*d*); Pharoah Sanders (*perc*). 2 & 9/68.

*** **Plays Ellington and Monk** Denon DC 8550
> Burrell; Takahashi Mizuhashi (*b*). 4/78.

**** **Windward Passages** hat ART CD 6138
> Burrell (*p* solo). 9/79.

*** **Daybreak** Gazell GJCD 4002
> Burrell; David Murray (*ts*). 3/89.

*** **Brother To Brother** Gazell GJCD 4010
> As above.

**** **In Concert** Victo CD016
> As above. 10/91.

*** **Jelly Roll Joys** Gazell GJCD 4012
> Burrell (*p* solo).

Burrell has never fallen easily into any stylistic categories. In the late 1960s, he was much involved with the avant-garde while retaining an affection for standards jazz and for non-jazz styles such as ragtime, calypso and, at more of a sceptical distance, elements of the so-called 'Third Stream'. It is only really possible to say that Burrell himself represents a fourth or umpteenth stream. On *High Won – High Two*, his medley, 'Theme Stream', touches on many of these components, reworking five of the other tracks on the record into a single, consecutive piece. Among those it absorbs are 'Dave Blue', 'Bittersweet Reminiscence' and 'Margie Pargie', a cross between a rag and a morning *raga*. The long 'East Side Colors' replaces Kapp (this whole group was part of Noah Howard's rhythm section) with the more fluent but no less fierce Murray. Sanders, for those who are confused by the instrumentation, only plays tambourine.

Windward Passages is the solo version of a large-scale jazz opera co-written with Burrell's wife, Monika Larsson; it was the largely autobiographical account of a young musician growing up in Hawaii and suffering the various tokens of dispossession that haunt non-white Americans. An intensely private work, it communicates well as a solo piano performance, showing off Burrell's remarkable syncretism of black musics. He combines bop, rag, stride, blues and free elements with complete ease. 'Punaluu Peter', with its calypso syncopations, has become a favourite of David Murray's and is a figure of unacknowledged importance in recent attempts to recolonize the earlier history of jazz after the scorched-earth policy of the 1960s' radicals. He has worked with Marion Brown, Giuseppi Logan, Archie Shepp and Sonny Sharrock, among many others.

Though his take on Morton is surprisingly linear and straightforward, Burrell's approach to standards playing is by no means conventional. In his own work he follows a course that takes him pretty close to Monk and Ellington anyway, and he adapts well to them. ''Round Midnight' acquires an exotic cast and 'A Flower Is A Lovesome Thing' develops oriental appendages. It's essentially another solo performance. The Japanese bassist signs on for 'Blue Monk', 'Straight, No Chaser', 'In A Sentimental Mood', and 'Come Sunday', but Burrell scarcely seems to need the extra impetus.

The 1991 Victoriaville duo and its rather stilted predecessor on Gazell were widely and perhaps inevitably received as two more David Murray albums. While both are collective performances, there's some justification in claiming them for Burrell, whose discography as leader is thinner than ever with the disappearance of his large-scale *In:Sanity*, not yet transferred to Black Saint's CD list.

The pianist contributes all but one of the compositions on *Daybreak* and three out of five on *In Concert* (which includes 'Punaluu Peter' and 'Teardrops For Jimmy', a threnody to Coltrane's bassist, Jimmy Garrison, both from *Windward Passages*).

It's clear that Murray's revisionist approach to the black music tradition has been much influenced by the man who plays on many of his best records. The stride accompaniments on 'Punaluu Peter' suddenly erupt into volcanic outbursts of sound that suggest something of the pressure that always comes up from below in Burrell's work. Murray's well-worked 'Hope Scope' almost becomes a feature for the pianist, but on 'Ballad For The Black Man' that is reversed, with Burrell patiently comping for Murray's calm statement of his own theme and then sustaining a harmonic base for some incredibly sustained upper-register whistles. 'Intuitively' and 'Teardrops For Jimmy' bring the performance to a moving and effective close. The sound is excellent for a live recording, with no distortion or drop-out at either end of the dynamic scale. Strongly recommended as an introduction to either man.

There's nothing with quite that level of intensity on *Daybreak*, but the long 'Blue Hour' has a hypnotic quality, and the bass clarinet duo on Murray's own vestigial 'Sketch No. 1' is one of his best things on the big horn.

Kenny Burrell (born 1931) GUITAR

*** **All Night Long** Original Jazz Classics OJC 427
    Burrell; Donald Byrd (*t*); Hank Mobley (*ts*); Jerome Richardson (*ts, f*); Mal Waldron (*p*); Doug Watkins (*b*); Art Taylor (*d*). 12/56.
*** **All Day Long** Original Jazz Classics OJC 456
    Burrell; Donald Byrd (*t*); Frank Foster (*ts*); Tommy Flanagan (*p*); Doug Watkins (*b*); Art Taylor (*d*). 1/57.
*** **Blue Moods** Original Jazz Classics OJC 019
    Burrell; Cecil Payne (*bs*); Tommy Flanagan (*p*); Doug Watkins (*b*); Elvin Jones (*d*). 2/57.
*** **The Cats** Original Jazz Classics OJC 079
    Burrell; Idrees Sulieman (*t*); John Coltrane (*ts*); Tommy Flanagan (*p*); Doug Watkins (*b*); Louis Hayes (*d*). 4/57.
*** **Kenny Burrell & John Coltrane** Original Jazz Classics OJC 300
    Burrell; John Coltrane (*ts*); Tommy Flanagan (*p*); Paul Chambers (*b*); Jimmy Cobb (*d*). 3/58.
Burrell's playing is tied to bebop and rhythm-and-blues, yet he's the most gentlemanly of musicians, never losing his grip on a playing situation and in command of a seemingly inexhaustible supply of interesting licks. He has a tone as lulling as that of Joe Pass, but shies away from that player's rococo extravagances. It's difficult to pick out the best of Burrell, for his earliest sessions are as maturely formed as his later ones, and while he's played with a vast number of musicians, he manages to fit seamlessly into whatever the context happens to be. In the 1950s he was a popular man to have on blowing dates, and his early work for Prestige is mostly in that mould. The sessions that were designated as all-day and all-night don't actually go on that long, but some of the solos seem to, and there's little to recommend them beyond a few livelier moments. *Blue Moods* is a reflective canter through a typical programme of blues and standards, with a feature for Jones on 'Drum Boogie'. OJC 300 finds Coltrane in his restless early period, but Burrell seems to be a calming influence, and they have a beautifully shaded duet on 'Why Was I Born?'. *The Cats* benefits from Flanagan's leadership, and the pianist's shapely contributions add further lustre to the music, all of it very well engineered.

***(*) **On View At The Five Spot Café Vol. I** Blue Note B21Y-46538
    Burrell; Tina Brooks (*ts*); Bobby Timmons, Sir Roland Hanna (*p*); Ben Tucker (*b*); Art Blakey (*d*). 8/59.
*** **Blue Lights Vol. 1** Blue Note B21Y-81596
    Burrell; Louis Smith (*t*); Tina Brooks (*ts*); Duke Jordan, Bobby Timmons (*p*); Sam Jones (*b*); Art Blakey (*d*). 5/58.
Burrell's live recordings, unusually, don't fan the flames any more brightly than his studio sessions. But the Five Spot date is a particularly strong one for the presence of the seldom-recorded Brooks, whose solos strike a truce between urgency and relaxation, and the exhortative Blakey. *Blue Lights* is at a slightly lower temperature, although the soloists still create feelingful music.

*** **Midnight Blue** Blue Note 746399-2
    Burrell; Stanley Turrentine (*ts*); Major Holley (*b*); Bill English (*d*); Ray Barretto (*perc*). 1/63.
Just what the title says, and a sketch for a quiet classic in its way. Turrentine breezes over the changes as if he's trying to huff out a flame flickering somewhere across the room, and Burrell simply pads around him. Kenny's solo 'Soul Lament' makes a nice party-piece.

*** **Soul Call** Original Jazz Classics OJC 846-2
    Burrell; Will Davis (*p*); Martin Rivera (*b*); Bill English (*d*); Ray Barretto (*perc*). 4/64.
Burrell's reluctance to assert any special kind of leadership tells against him on a date like this, where the

supporting players have little to say by themselves. The title-piece and 'Mark One' are solid slow blues, and all the licks are smoothly executed. Otherwise, little to remember.

***(*) Guitar Forms Verve 825576-2

> Burrell; Johnny Coles, Louis Mucci (*t*); Jimmy Cleveland, Jimmy Knepper (*tb*); Andy Fitzgerald, George Marge (*cor, f*); Ray Alonge, Julius Watkins (*frhn*); Steve Lacy (*ss*); Ray Beckenstein (*as, f*); Lee Konitz (*as*); Richie Kamuca (*ts, ob*); Bob Tricarico (*bsn, f*); Roger Kellaway (*p*); Bill Barber (*tba*); Ron Carter, Joe Benjamin (*b*); Elvin Jones, Charli Persip, Grady Tate (*d*); Willie Rodriguez (*perc*). 12/64–4/65.

This is arguably the closest Burrell has come to a singular achievement, even if it is more by association with Gil Evans, who arranged it. Burrell's tonal pallor and sanguine approach might make him a less characterful soloist than those who've handled other of Evans's concerto set-pieces, but in some ways that works to the music's advantage: without misleading emotional resonances of the kind associated with, say, Miles Davis cracking notes, the purity of Evans's veils of sound emerges the more clearly in the likes of 'Lotus Land'.

*** Kenny Burrell: Jazz Masters 45 Verve 527652-2

> As above, except add Jimmy Nottingham, Thad Jones, Ernie Royal, Marvin Stamm, Joe Shepley (*t*), Wayne Andre, Urbie Green, Tony Studd (*tb*), Jerome Richardson (*woodwinds*), Harvey Philips (*tba*), Phil Woods (*as*), Richard Wyands, Herbie Hancock (*p*), Jimmy Smith (*org*), Vince Gambella (*g*), Ron Carter (*b*), Mel Lewis, Donald McDonald (*d*), Johnny Pacheco (*perc*). 64–69.

This creams off some of *Guitar Forms* along with tracks from *A Generation Ago Today*, *Blues: The Common Ground*, *For Charlie Christian And Benny Goodman*, *Asphalt Canyon Suite* and *Night Song*, so there's a fair amount of otherwise-unavailable Burrell here. That said, several of those discs weren't among his finest hours, and he sounds as happy here on a single track with Jimmy Smith as he does on his own-name projects. *Guitar Forms* is a better bet as a single disc, but collectors will certainly want this one too.

*** Soulero Chess GRP 18082

> Burrell; Richard Wyands (*p*); Marty Rivera (*b*); Oliver Jackson (*d*); orchestra and strings arranged by Richard Evans. 4/66–9/67.

A reissue of a couple of Cadet albums, *The Tender Gender* and *Ode To 52nd Street*. The earlier date with the quartet includes some terrific playing on 'Mother-In-Law' and 'Hot Bossa', with the sweeter tunes slipping neatly alongside; Wyands gets in some nice touches of his own. The arranged pieces are more like snooze music, although Burrell's class brings a mild edge to the situation. A worthwhile rescue.

**** Ellington Is Forever Vol. 1 Fantasy FCD-79005-2

> Burrell; Jon Faddis, Snooky Young (*t*); Thad Jones (*c, flhn*); Jerome Richardson (*ss, ts*); Joe Henderson (*ts*); Jimmy Jones (*p*); Jimmy Smith (*org*); Jimmie Smith (*d*); Mel Lewis, Richie Goldberg (*perc*); Ernie Andrews (*v*). 2/75.

Burrell's greatest album looks unpromising from a distance, after countless tribute records have become such a catch-all theme in the past 20 years. But this salute to Ellington remains one of the great examples of the genre. Cut at a couple of loose-knit sessions over two days, the cast is a shifting one, from 12 men on a hard-hitting 'Caravan' to a Burrell solo on 'Jump For Joy' and Jimmy Jones's moving soliloquy on 'Take The "A" Train'. 'C Jam Blues' sets Faddis and Thad Jones against the rhythm section, a blues medley allows a rare sighting of Snooky Young as a soloist, and Henderson is splendid on 'I Didn't Know About You'. Most affecting of all is the absolutely definitive treatment of 'My Little Brown Book' by Ernie Andrews and Jimmy Jones. Burrell may be just a bystander at times, but he presided over a magnificent session.

*** Ellington is Forever Vol. 2 Fantasy 79008-2

> As above, except add Nat Adderley (*c*), Quentin Jackson (*tb*), Gary Bartz (*cl, as*), Sir Roland Hanna (*p*), Stanley Gilbert, George Mraz, Monk Montgomery (*b*), Philly Joe Jones (*d*); omit Jimmie Smith, Lewis, Goldberg. 11–12/75.

The return match was a disappointment, even though there are delightful moments: Smith's lovely glide through 'Solitude', and Jones and Young together on 'Come Sunday'. Too many of the other pieces sound routine or merely very good.

***(*) Ellington A La Carte Muse MCD 5435

> Burrell; Rufus Reid (*b*). 8/83. ˙

A better set of Ellington, this time at New York's Village West. The crowd is a little intrusive, but Burrell and Reid are miked so close that it isn't bothersome. The playing on nine Ellington chestnuts and a blues is about as *simpatico* as one can get, and all the tempos seem perfectly judged.

(*) Guiding Spirit Contemporary 14065
    Burrell; Jay Hoggard (*vib*); Marcus McLaurine (*b*); Yoron Israel (*d*). 8/89.
Burrell continued to work through the 1970s and '80s in his patient, unhurried way, and there is a string of albums on Muse yet to appear on CD. So here he is in 1989: still pretty, still bebop, still no trouble, still fine; not that great, unless one needs a late-night painkiller.

***(*) Sunup To Sundown** Contemporary CCD-14065-2
    Burrell; Cedar Walton (*p*); Rufus Reid (*b*); Lewis Nash (*d*); Ray Mantilla (*perc*). 6/91.
A good one. 'Out There' hits a fine groove from the outset, and it's quickly apparent that Walton, Reid and Nash are bringing the best out of the nominal leader, whose solos find an extra pinch of energy and grit without surrendering any of his smoothest moves.

*** **Midnight At The Village Vanguard** Paddle Wheel KICJ 178
    Burrell; James Williams (*p*); Peter Washington (*b*); Sherman Ferguson (*d*). 9/93.
Not quite on a par with the previous Contemporary, but this is another top-line rhythm section and the music, though never in as swinging a groove as it might be, is solidly enjoyable.

*** **The Best Of Kenny Burrell** Blue Note 830493-2
    As Blue Note albums above, except add Grover Washington (*ss*), Frank Foster, Hank Mobley (*ts*), Seldon Powell (*f*), Tommy Flanagan, Horace Silver, Herbie Hancock, Hank Jones (*p*), Bobby Broom, Rodney Jones (*g*), Ben Tucker, Dave Jackson, Reggie Workman, Doug Watkins, Milt Hinton, Oscar Pettiford (*b*), Shadow Wilson, Louis Hayes, Osie Johnson, Jack DeJohnette, Kenny Washington (*d*), Ray Barretto (*perc*). 3/56–10/86.
Thirty years (on and off) of Burrell on Blue Note. A couple of rarities – a single release of 'Loie' and a quartet track with Hancock – plus some familiar fodder from the early days, along with tracks from the so-so *Togethering* and *Generation* albums.

Abraham Burton (born 1972) ALTO SAXOPHONE

***(*) Closest To The Sun** Enja ENJ 8047
    Burton; Marc Cary (*p*); Billy Johnson (*b*); Eric McPherson (*d*). 94.
With so many young saxophone players attempting to fly at the altitude of John Coltrane, it's no surprise that many have repeated Icarus's fall. Burton has taken a more modest course, but a no less expressive one, drawing his inspiration very largely from Jackie McLean. The young man's sound is fierce and passionate, as young men are meant to sound, but tempered with an admirable reserve and intelligence. It's evident from the opening number, McLean's 'Minor March', onwards that here is a very special talent, capable of working in a straight changes context, but also interested in the development of melody and a more linear style of improvisation. Apparently Burton had scarcely worked with this band before recording. That makes his debut all the more impressive.

Gary Burton (born 1943) VIBRAPHONE

*** **The New Quartet** ECM 1030
    Burton; Mick Goodrick (*g*); Abraham Laboriel (*b*); Harry Blazer (*d*). 3/73.
*** **Real Life Hits** ECM 1293
    Burton; Makoto Ozone (*p*); Steve Swallow (*b*); Mike Hyman (*d*). 1/82, 11/84.
Ever since the late 1960s, and the band that established his name and mature style, Burton has shown a marked preference for the quartet format, and for working with guitarists. The 1967 band included Larry Coryell, Steve Swallow and Bob Moses, and it remains perhaps his most consistently inventive unit. Swallow has been a steady presence and provides a consistent but imaginative bottom line for Burton's occasionally flyaway approach. The New Quartet was a more or less self-conscious attempt to synthesize the earlier band; the newcomers are by no means faceless epigoni, and the resulting album is robustly conceived and performed, and is marked by some of the best writing Burton had to work with. There are pieces by Carla Bley, Gordon Beck and Michael Gibbs; 'Olhos De Gato' and Beck's 'Mallet Man' are masterly.
    Real Life Hits is understated almost to the point of blandness, but it is also one of Burton's most interesting sets of compositions, and merits close attention.

*** **Ring** ECM 1051
    Burton; Mick Goodrick, Pat Metheny (*g*); Steve Swallow (*b*); Bob Moses (*d*). 74.

(*) Dreams So Real ECM 1072
  As above, except add Eberhard Weber (*b*). 75.
*** **Passengers** ECM 1092
  Burton; Pat Metheny (*g*); Steve Swallow, Eberhard Weber (*b*); Dan Gottlieb (*d*). 11/76.
*** **Reunion** GRP 95982
  Burton; Pat Metheny (*g*); Mitch Forman (*p, ky*); Will Lee (*b*); Peter Erskine (*d*). 5/89.

Burton's mid-1970s albums with rising star Metheny and the distinctive Weber now sound a little tarnished but their blend of country softness and Weber's slightly eldritch melody lines still make for interesting listening, even if the group never sounds quite as enterprising as it did live. The three ECMs are pretty much of a piece, but *Passengers*, actually co-credited to Weber, is probably the one to go for initially.

Burton makes a considerable virtue out of what might have become an awful clutter of strings and percussion. The themes are open and clearly stated, even when they are relatively complex, as on 'The Whopper', and Weber's forceful, wailing sound is strongly contrasted to those of the two guitarists; Swallow as usual plays bass guitar with a pick, getting a clean, exact sound whose coloration is totally different from Metheny's rock-influenced sustains. Weber's own composition, 'Yellow Fields' (see ECM 1066), undergoes an attractive variation.

The Burton–Metheny *Reunion* is rather good, too, but is marred by a very ripe mix and the rather compromising introduction of Forman.

(*) Whiz Kids ECM 1329
  Burton; Tommy Smith (*ts*); Makoto Ozone (*p*); Steve Swallow (*b*); Martin Richards (*d*). 6/86.

Though Ozone (who has a fine CBS album to his credit) resurfaced to great effect on *Whiz Kids*, all the buzz was about the Scottish *Wunderkind* Smith, another pupil of Burton's at Berklee, and just at this time beginning to receive serious critical attention on the other side of the Atlantic. The results (perhaps inevitably, given all the hype) are a shade disappointing. Burton has never been easy with saxophone players (see his two tracks with Michael Brecker on *Times Like These*), and the lead voices clutter and compete furiously, without any logic or drama. Ozone keeps things more or less tidy, but it is an uncomfortable set and definitely missable.

*** **Matchbook** ECM 1056
  Burton; Ralph Towner (*g*). 7/74.
**** **Hotel Hello** ECM 1055
  Burton; Steve Swallow (*b*). 5/74.
(*) Duet ECM 1140
  Burton; Chick Corea (*p*). 10/78.

At first blush, the Burton/Corea partnership looked like a marriage made in heaven, and they toured extensively. In practice, and at least on record, the collaboration fell foul of the inevitable similarity between piano and vibraphone and of the performers' out-of-synch musical personalities. The earlier *Crystal Silence* is more properly credited to Corea, since he is the chief writer. On *Duet*, the pianist never seems far from whimsicality, and it is interesting to see how much more positively and forcefully Burton responds to Towner's light but well-anchored style. *Matchbook* is surprisingly disciplined and coherent for all its lacy textures and delicate, almost directionless transitions; *Slide Show* (ECM 1306) reversed the performers' names on the cover and so – by our ruthlessly alphabetical rubric – stops for T. Disappointing, though.

Hotel Hello is by far the most impressive of Burton's two-handers and an ideal opportunity to examine the vibist in close-up. The overture and vamp to 'Hotel Hello' are worthy of Carla Bley. This is one of the high points of ECM's distinguished catalogue. Why it was ever out of circulation is a mystery.

*** **Works** ECM 823267
  Burton; Chick Corea (*p*); Mick Goodrick, Pat Metheny, Ralph Towner (*g*); Abe Laboriel, Steve
  Swallow, Eberhard Weber (*b*); Harry Blazer (*d*); Bob Moses (*perc*); orchestra. 72–80.

Works is one of the better balanced of ECM's 15th-anniversary artist samplers, with a good range of material from what some would consider his vintage years. Virtually all the material is readily available elsewhere, though.

(*) Times Like These GRP 95069
  Burton; Michael Brecker (*ts*); John Scofield (*g*); Marc Johnson (*b*); Peter Erskine (*d*).
(*) Cool Nights GRP 9643
  Burton; Bob Berg (*ts*); Bob James (*ky*); Wolfgang Muthspiel (*g*); Will Lee (*b, perc*); Peter
  Erskine (*d, perc*). 91.

For all the sophistication of Burton's writing, these are drab, middle-of-the-road sets. *Cool Nights* is too laid-back by half and is further blurred by a muzzy, rock-album mix, out of which Brecker, Berg, Scofield and, less often, the Austrian-born Muthspiel occasionally emerge to do rather self-conscious solo spots and twiddles. *Times Like These* is marginally better, as the line-up would suggest, but it's still very disappointing.

(*) Six Pack GRP 96852
    Burton; Bob Berg (*ts*); Jim Hall, Mulgrew Miller (*p*); Kevin Eubanks, B. B. King, Kurt
    Rosenwinkel, John Scofield, Ralph Towner (*g*); Paul Shaffer (*p, org*); Larry Goldings (*ky, org*);
    Steve Swallow (*b*); Jack DeJohnette (*d*). 10/91–4/92.

Burton's continuing love affair with the guitar goes public with this rather odd line-'em-up. The title-track and 'Double Guatemala' with B. B. King are a joke, Rosenwinkel is pretty anonymous, and only Sco and Hall really seem to know what they're about. Burton's own playing has gone to pot, in the sense that he seems content to string together bits and pieces from old solos. There are, of course, moments of interest, but for the most part this is a rummage sale.

John Butcher TENOR, SOPRANO AND BARITONE SAXOPHONES

**** Thirteen Friendly Numbers** Acta 6
    Butcher (*ss, ts, bs* solo). 3–12/91.

A British improviser whose playing is highly accomplished and strikingly individual, Butcher's recital is unlike any other solo-saxophone record. Nine of the 13 tracks are real-time solos on either tenor or soprano, while the other four create some unprecedented sounds and textures through overdubbing: 'Bells And Clappers', for instance, piles up four tenors into a brittle choir of humming overtones that has a chilling, sheet-metal sound, while the amplification introduced into the very brief 'Mackle Music' is peculiarly disturbing. On the more conventional solo tracks, Butcher's mastery of the instrument creates a vocabulary which can accommodate pieces as disparate as 'Notelet', which is like a single flow of melody, and the explorations of single aspects of performing technique, as on 'Humours And Vapours' and 'Buccinator's Outing'. Assisted by a very clear and suitably neutral recording, this is a masterful record which should be investigated by anyone interested in free playing.

***(*) Concet Moves** Random Acoustics RA 011
    Butcher; Phil Durrant (*vn*); John Russell (*g*). 11/91–9/92.

Butcher's sparse discography is to be regretted since he is obviously in his prime; a typical Braxton documentation would have had this as at least a three-disc set, and the group is great enough to stand it. Lyrical when you expect frenzy, light and airy when darkness seems about to fall, the trio don't confound expectations so much as create freshness from moment to moment. Russell almost always plays quietly; Durrant prefers a vocabulary of small, scratchy gestures; so it's left to Butcher to use the largest range of device, songful high motifs, circular riffs, blatted notes, slap-tongue devices, all sorts of everything. It is as fine a set of free playing as one could encounter in recent times, with a piece such as 'Playfair's Axiom' almost a model of what-can-be-done, though it probably won't convert anyone to this aesthetic. Docked a fraction for the soundmix: Russell is further away than even he would surely prefer.

Henry Butler PIANO

***(*) For All Seasons** Atlantic 82856-2
    Butler; Steve Turre (*tb*); Dave Holland (*b*); Herman Jackson (*d*). 6/95.

Butler has made an earlier record for MCA, but this is his first on a new contract for Atlantic. Compared with other New Orleans homeboys such as Marcus Roberts, Butler is all extravagance and energy at the keyboard. His take on the tradition is to hammer it open: the solo version of 'St Louis Blues' becomes an opulent fantasy in which the blues is a mere component. That much he gets from McCoy Tyner – the interplay between both hands, the grand, trilling delivery. But he tackles his material with a nice irreverence, too: 'How Insensitive' becomes a New Orleans bounce. Holland is as outstanding as always, Jackson is as keen as a terrier, and Turre plays a nicely hammy cameo on one track. Only 'A Winter's Blues' outstays its welcome at nearly 15 minutes.

Jaki Byard (born 1922) PIANO

***(*) Blues For Smoke** Candid CCD 79018
    Byard (*p* solo). 12/60.
*** Live! At Lennie's On The Turnpike** Prestige PCD 24121
    Byard; Joe Farrell (*ts, ss, f*); George Tucker (*b*); Alan Dawson (*d, vib*). 4/65.

*** **Empirical** Muse MCD 6010
    As above. 12/72.
(*) **To Them, To Us Soul Note 121025
    Byard (*p* solo). 5/81.
*** **Phantasies** Soul Note 121075
    Byard; The Apollo Stompers: Roger Parrett, Al Bryant, John Eckhert, Jim White (*t*); Steve
    Wienberg, Steve Swell, Carl Reinlib, Bob Norden (*tb*); Stephen Calia (*btb*); Bob Torrence,
    Manny Boyd (*as*); Jed Levy, Alan Givens (*ts*); Preston Trombly (*bs*); Dan Licht (*g*); Ralph
    Hamperian (*b*); Richard Allen (*d*); Denyce Byard, Diane Byard (*perc, v*). 9/84.
*** **Foolin' Myself** Soul Note 121125
    Byard; Ralph Hamperian (*b*); Richard Allen (*d*). 8/88.
***(*) **Phantasies II** Soul Note 121175
    Byard; The Apollo Stompers: as above, but omit Eckhert, Wienberg, Norden, Boyd, Givens,
    Trombly, Licht, Denyce Byard; replace with Graham Haynes (*t*), Rick Davies (*tb*), Susan Terry
    (*as*), Bud Revels (*ts*), Don Slatoff (*bs*); Peter Leitch (*g*), Vincent Lewis (*v*). 8/88.
***(*) **At Maybeck: Maybeck Recital Hall Series, Volume 17** Concord CCD 4511
    Byard (*p* solo). 9/91.

Byard's enormous power and versatility are grounded on a thorough knowledge of brass, reeds, drums and guitar, as well as piano, and there are passages in solos which suggest some attempt to replicate the phrasing of a horn rather than a keyboard instrument. On a straight comparison between two solo sets two decades apart, it seems that Byard does now play more pianistically, though the distinctive left- and right-hand articulation of themes – based on a highly personal synthesis of ragtime and stride, bop and free jazz – is still strongly evident in 1981. *Blues For Smoke* is a minor classic, with the wonderful 'Aluminium Baby', originally written for trumpeter/bandleader Herb Pomeroy, and 'Diane's Melody'. There is a more generous register (perhaps down to a more responsive piano) on the Soul Note set, but it lacks some of the percussive energy of the Candid. Both are recommended, as is the live quartet from 1965, which highlights the seriously underrated Farrell in one of his most attractive and sympathetic settings. The charts are rather sketchy and a couple of them sound like run-throughs; it's the musicianship rather than anything in the writing that makes them work.

    Byard's solo performances are perhaps his best and most characteristic. The Concord set is one of the 'out'-est of a high-quality but generally mainstream series. Byard's 'Tribute To The Ticklers', 'European Episode' and 'Family Suite' are characteristically expansive, and the Monk collage is judged to perfection. More romantic material like 'My One And Only Love' is gruffly unsentimental. The Muse from 1972 is more uncompromising and marked by some of Byard's most unchecked blues playing. Of the solo sets, it's probably the closest to the sound he cultivated around Mingus, and that may appeal to some listeners.

    Byard is inclined to swamp sidemen with weather-changes of idiom or mood. No such problems with *Foolin' Myself*. Hamperian and Allen have grown into Byard's music and become confident interpreters. The set's full of oblique harmonies and wonderfully off-centre themes; the CD offers a big sound with a lot of warmth, typical of Giovanni Bonandrini's in-house production at Soul Note.

    Working with Maynard Ferguson and then Mingus gave Byard some insight into how to steer at high speed. Without any doubt, his excellence as a section player fed into his solo and small-group playing as well. *Phantasies* is an uncomfortable big-band excursion with vocals from Byard's Denyce and Diane (she of the melody – see above); though well produced and more than adequately executed, the album runs pastiche a little too close for comfort and lands somewhere among at least three stylistic stools. That said, it contains some great ensemble work on the Ellington material, and some of the modernist things – 'Lonely Woman', 'Impressions' – are excitingly done. A change of heart since the first edition, prompted by the emergence of *Phantasies II*, an altogether better-structured and more together exercise in nostalgia. Byard's skills as a comping pianist and bandleader are seen nowhere better than on 'Concerto Grosso', a playful look at a Baroque form within the context of a jazz band. Vincent Lewis does a convincing job as an Apollo crooner, with a rich baritone that owes something to Eckstine. Musically, though, the most interesting thing is 'II IV I', a title which refers to the cadence minor/dominant/major which dominates the piece. It takes Byard back to the great days of the Harlem stride pianists.

Don Byas (1912–72) TENOR SAXOPHONE

**** **Lover Man** Vogue 2115470
    Byas; Martial Solal, Maurice Vander (*p*); Fats Sadi (*vib*); Pierre Michelot (*b*); Benny Bennett,
    Pierre Lemarchand (*d*). 11 & 12/53, 5/55.

*** **Americans In Europe** Impulse! GRP 11502
> Byas; Idrees Sulieman (t); Bud Powell (p); Jimmy Woode (b); Joe Harris (d). 1/63.

(*) **A Night In Tunisia Black Lion BLCD 760136
> Byas; Bent Axen (p); Niels-Henning Orsted-Pedersen (b); William Schiopffe (d). 1/63.

(*) **Walkin' Black Lion BLCD 760167
> As above. 1/63.

Somewhat in eclipse these days, Byas was regarded as the foremost tenor player of the late war years and immediate post-war period. He had a broad, chocolatey tone that collapsed when the tempo exceeded a canter, so he preferred, as in most of the above, to stick to a late-night stroll, never stepping on the cracks (his on-the-beat articulation made some impact later on John Coltrane), less aimless and more purposeful than at first appears. It's said that Byas transposed some of Tatum's harmonic language to the saxophone; he is undoubtedly a wonderfully intelligent player.

In 1946, having toured Europe with Don Redman, the first American jazz musicians to visit after the war, he emigrated, first to France, then to Holland. He died in Amsterdam in 1972. The best of the records is the early Vogue, without question. Solal is a hugely intelligent accompanist with taste to spare, and his work on the title-track is absolutely exemplary. The upbeat 'I Can't Give You Anything But Love' illustrates our point about Byas at speed, but generally on these sides he sounds comfortable and well in command.

Since good material is in dearth, it is worth mentioning the compilation, *Americans In Europe*, which brings together the work of several distinguished expats at a concert in Koblenz. The Byas material – 'All The Things You Are' and 'I Remember Clifford' – stands out on the disc, which is very collectable. *Walkin'* includes a version of 'A Night In Tunisia' which easily outstrips earlier, more assertive recordings of a favourite bebop theme. There is also a smoothly vibrant 'Billie's Bounce' and 'All The Things You Are', on which he appears to quote Paul Gonsalves.

For Byas, beauty of sound was everything. Once that had faded, there wasn't a great deal left.

Charlie Byrd (born 1925) GUITAR

*** **Jazz Recital** Savoy SV 0192
> Byrd; Tom Newson (f, ts); Al Lucas (b); Bobby Donaldson (d). 2/57.

***(*) **Midnight Guitar** Savoy SV 0247
> Byrd; Keter Betts (b); Gus Johnson (d). 8/57.

*** **Byrd At The Village Vanguard** Original Jazz Classics OJC 669
> Byrd; Keter Betts (b); Buddy Deppenschmidt (d). 61.

*** **Bossa Nova Pelos Pássaros** Original Jazz Classics OJC 107
> Byrd; Keter Betts (b); Bill Reichenbach (d). 62.

** **Byrd At The Gate** Original Jazz Classics OJC 262
> As above, except add Clark Terry (t); Seldon Powell (ts). 5/63.

The release in 1962 of the evergreen *Jazz Samba* with Stan Getz, and the legal kerfuffle that followed, put Charlie Byrd firmly on the map. Like all hugely successful products, there was an element of *ersatz* about it, and Byrd's Latin stylings have never sounded entirely authentic and are often quite rheumaticky in articulation. Here, though, is a historically valuable selection of albums, the last one full of that characteristically American syndrome that John Aldridge called 'the energy of new success' and which comes just before what the French call the *crise de quarante*. Byrd sounds full-toned and quick-fingered, and the themes still have a bloom they were to lose all too quickly in the years that followed.

Midnight Guitar is probably the best of the whole bunch, a fleet, disarming trio session, a little too elegantly segued, but packed with sheer musicianship. A pity there was not to be too much more in this vein. 'Recital' in the title of the earlier Savoy might ring one or two warning bells. The problem with Byrd was that, even at the Village Vanguard, he always sounded as if he was preparing for Carnegie Hall.

*** **Tambu** Fantasy FCD 9453
> Byrd; Cal Tjader (vib); Mike Wolff (p); John Heard (b); Joe Byrd (b); Michael Stephans, Dick
> Berk (d, perc); Mayoto Correa (perc). 9/73.

Like a lot of jazz records from around this time, *Tambu* is constrained not by indifferent playing but by certain giveaway tics in the sound. Wolff's electric piano and Joe Byrd's duh-duh-duh bass guitar conspire with an overlit and glaringly contrastive mix to bleach all the character out of Byrd's playing. Tjader was the co-leader on this date, and the vibes, too, are all over the place, jingling like a bead-curtain and then improbably tolling down at the bass end. It all mars some very good playing, from virtually all concerned.

*** **Three Guitars** Concord 6004
>   Byrd; Barney Kessel, Herb Ellis (*g*); Joe Byrd (*b*); Johnny Rae (*d*). 7/74.

Promoters and A&R men have always recognized that there's an audience for guitar specials like this. Put together any three saxophonists of similar stature, and the take on the door or through the record-shop tills will be significantly smaller. Musically, it's polished and shiny and ever so polite. Kessel and Ellis play a duo, Byrd plays with his own trio, rents it out to the other pair for 'Slow Burn', and then they all get together for 'Undecided', 'Topsy' and 'Benny's Bugle'. Honours just about even.

** **Blue Byrd** Concord CCD 4082
>   Byrd; Joe Byrd (*b, v*); Wayne Phillips (*d*). 8/78.

** **Sugarloaf Suite** Concord CCD 4114
>   As above. 8/78.

** **Isn't It Romantic** Concord CCD 4252
>   As above, except replace Phillips with Chuck Riggs (*d*). 8/79.

Byrd had a dull time for much of the 1970s. These discs find him less becalmed than usual and, on *Blue Byrd*, occasionally inspired. He handles mainstream standards well, surprising now and again with a figure completely out of left field; but the trio format leaves him much too exposed for comfort, and the up-close recording almost parades his stiffness.

(*) **Brazilville Concord CCD 4173
>   Byrd; Bud Shank (*as*); Joe Byrd (*b*); Charles Redd (*d*). 5/81.

(*) **It's A Wonderful World Concord CCD 4374
>   Byrd; Scott Hamilton (*ts*); John Goldsby (*b*); Chuck Redd (*d*). 8/88.

Byrd's quality in a horn-led band suggests that he was done only economic favours by having greatness thrust upon him so suddenly, 30 years ago. With both Shank and Hamilton he plays elegantly and with considerable taste. Both albums show a marked centring of Byrd's stylistic range; by no means everything is automatically Latinized and on *Wonderful World* in particular he displays an improvisational confidence that seemed to have deserted him in the 1970s. Nobody looks to Byrd for fire and brimstone, but there's an edgy, slightly restless quality to both of these that belies their bland packaging and suggests a genuinely improvisatory spirit at work. The Ellington and Arlen pieces are particularly fine.

(*) **Byrd & Brass Concord CCD 4304
>   Byrd; Joe Byrd (*b*); Chuck Redd (*d*); Annapolis Brass Quintet. 4/86.

A surprisingly sharp and swinging set from an offbeat and unpromising line-up. Byrd pushes things along with unwonted enthusiasm; the brass is generously voiced and the rhythm work tighter than Byrd normally favours. Well recorded, too.

* **The Charlie Byrd Christmas Album** Concord CCD 42004
>   Byrd (*g* solo). 6/82.

This is fine for those who like this sort of thing, as Jean Brodie might say. Almost everyone else will hate it with a passion.

*** **The Bossa Nova Years** Concord CCD 4468
>   Byrd; Ken Peplowski (*ts, cl*); Dennis Irwin (*b*); Chuck Redd (*d*); Michael Spiro (*perc*). 4/91.

One of the astonishing things about Byrd's career is his relentless conservatism in the choice of material. One would hardly expect an artist of his inclinations or stature to desert an established audience by adopting Jimi Hendrix songs, but one might reasonably expect him to challenge that audience a little more often than he does. *The Bossa Nova Years* contains precisely the roster of soft-centred Jobim/Gilberto themes you probably began whistling as you read the title. What makes it more galling is that they're all played superbly, in the sense that there isn't a hair out of place on any of them. Peplowski can usually be relied on for a bit more than he offers here. As a performance, this is brushed and pomaded to the point of anonymity. A shame, really.

*** **Charlie Byrd / The Washington Guitar Quintet** Concord CCD 42014
>   Byrd; Carlos Barbosa-Lima, Howard Alden, Washington Guitar Quintet: John Marlow, Jeffrey Meyerriecks, Myrna Sislen, Larry Snitzler (*g*); Joe Byrd (*b*); Chuck Redd (*d*). 4/92.

What's disappointing about this brilliantly arranged and very beautiful record is how numbingly obvious the programme turns out to be: 'Nuages', 'Django', *Concierto De Aranjuez* segued with Chick Corea's 'Spain', Stanley Myers's 'Cavatina' from *The Deerhunter*, another Reinhardt tune, Jobim, Almeida. With a little more imagination this could have been a masterpiece. Instead, it all too swiftly runs aground. Only when Alden's electric guitar is introduced for three numbers before the end – Cole Porter's 'Easy To Love' and Kurt Weill's 'I'm A Stranger Here Myself' and 'Speak Low' – is there much in the way of dramatic variation. The other members of the Washington Guitar Quintet (Byrd himself makes up the five) try to invest the earlier tunes with a bit of percussive spice, but again the material draws them down.

** **Aquarelle** Concord CCD 42016
> Byrd; Ken Peplowski (*cl*); Carlos Barbosa-Lima, Jeffrey Meyerriecks, Myrna Sislen, Larry Snitzler (*g*). 8/93.

This collaboration with the Washington Guitar Quintet is pastelly and insipid, soft-focus washes of colour overlaid on some notably bland and sentimental melodies. The analogy with wallpaper won't stay in its basket.

*** **Moments Like This** Concord CCD 4627
> Byrd; Ken Peplowski (*cl*); Bill Douglass (*b*); Chuck Redd (*d, vib*). 94.

Immediately and wholly better. The blend of guitar, bass, clarinet and (mostly) vibraphone is very appealing and Byrd exploits the possibilites to the maximum. His chording on 'Rose Of The Rio Grande' is highly distinctive, often moving outside the natural sequence, and Douglass is a willing assistant in keeping many of the pieces from becoming predictable. A fine record by a musician whose career has taken some odd turns over the years.

Donald Byrd (born 1932) TRUMPET, FLUGELHORN

** **First Flight** Delmark 407
> Byrd; Yusef Lateef (*ts*); Barry Harris (*p*); Bernard McKinney (*euph*); Alvin Jackson (*b*); Frank Gant (*d*). 8/55.

(*) **Byrd's Word Savoy SV-0132
> Byrd; Frank Foster (*ts*); Hank Jones (*p*); Paul Chambers (*b*); Kenny Clarke (*d*). 9/55.

First Flight is the first album under Byrd's own name, recorded at a concert in Detroit, and, while it gave a smart indication of his own promise, it's Lateef's more commanding solos that take the attention. Harris, perhaps the quintessential Detroit pianist, is also imposing, although he has to contend with a poor piano, and the location sound is disappointingly muddy. *Byrd's Word* comes in fine remastered sound, but it adds up to another routine Savoy blowing date: Foster plays with intermittent enthusiasm and the rhythm section show some sparkle, but one feels that some of them were watching the clock.

(*) **Fuego Blue Note B21Y-46534
> Byrd; Jackie McLean (*as*); Duke Pearson (*p*); Sam Jones (*b*); Lex Humphries (*d*). 10/59.

*** **At The Half Note Vol. 1** Blue Note B21Y-46539
> Byrd; Pepper Adams (*bs*); Duke Pearson (*p*); Laymon Jackson (*b*); Lex Humphries (*d*). 11/60.

*** **Free Form** Blue Note B21Y-84118
> Byrd; Wayne Shorter (*ts*); Herbie Hancock (*p*); Butch Warren (*b*); Billy Higgins (*d*). 12/61.

By the time he signed a deal with Blue Note in 1958, Byrd had already made more records than any of the other up-and-coming trumpeters of the day. It was his easy-going proficiency which made him sought-after: like Freddie Hubbard, who was to the early 1960s what Byrd had been to the previous five years, he could sound good under any contemporary leader without entirely dominating the situation. His solos were valuable but not disconcertingly personal, dependably elegant but not strikingly memorable. His records as a leader emerged in much the same way: refined and crisp hard bop which seems to look neither forward nor backwards. Choosing from the above selection – all of them available only as US releases at present – is more a matter of which of the accompanying musicians is most appealing, since Byrd's own performances are regularly polished – almost to the point of tedium, some might say. *Byrd In Hand* and *Fuego* are typical Blue Note blowing sessions, the latter slightly more rewarding thanks to the reliable Adams, a frequent partner of the trumpeter; *Fuego* has some good McLean, but the tunes are dull. The live sessions at New York's Half Note are impeccably played and atmospherically recorded, but they tend to show the best and worst of Byrd: on the first number on Volume 1, 'My Girl Shirl', he peels off chorus after chorus of manicured licks, and this process gets repeated throughout. One is impressed but dissatisfied, and Humphries's less than outstanding drumming is another problem, although Adams is again splendid. *Free Form* puts Byrd among altogether more difficult company, and there's an unflattering contrast between his prim solo on the gospel cadences of 'Pentecostal Feeling' and Shorter's bluff intensity. But he plays very prettily on Herbie Hancock's 'Night Flower' (which sounds like 'I Left My Heart In San Francisco') and the more severe leanings of the title-track suit Byrd's punctilious manner well.

***(*) **Groovin' For Nat** Black Lion BL 760132
> Byrd; Johnny Coles (*t*); Duke Pearson (*p*); Bob Cranshaw (*b*); Walter Perkins (*d*). 1/62.

** **A New Perspective** Blue Note 7841242
> Byrd; Hank Mobley (*ts*); Herbie Hancock (*p*); Donald Best (*vib*); Kenny Burrell (*g*); Butch Warren (*b*); Lex Humphries (*d*); choir. 12/63.

*** **Kofi** Blue Note CDP 831875-2
    Byrd; William Campbell (*tb*); Lew Tabackin (*ts, f*); Frank Foster (*ts*); Duke Pearson (*p*); Ron
    Carter, Bob Cranshaw (*b*); Mickey Roker (*d*); Airto Moreira, Dom Um Romao (*perc*). 12/69–
    12/70.
(*) **Blackbyrd Blue Note B21Y-84466
    Byrd; Alan Barnes (*ts, ob, f*); Kevin Toney (*p*); Barney Perry (*g*); Joe Hill (*b*); Keith Kilgo (*d*);
    Perk Jacobs (*perc*). 74.
***(*) **Early Byrd** Blue Note 789606-2
    Byrd; various line-ups. 60–72.
*** **The Best Of Donald Byrd** Blue Note CDP 798638-2
    Byrd; various line-ups. 69–76.
After dozens of straightforward hard-bop dates, Byrd branched out with mixed success. *Groovin' For
Nat* is measure for measure one of his most enjoyable records: Coles, a splashier but characterful player,
spars with him through a dozen duets, and the unusual combination of two trumpets and rhythm proves
to be a joyous rather than a one-dimensional setting. Nevertheless it's Coles who steals the record with a
very expressive turn through 'Friday's Child'. The Black Lion CD includes three previously unavailable
alternative takes, and the sound is very persuasive.

   A New Perspective has remained popular and contains the seeds of Byrd's wider success in the 1970s: his
own playing is set against large-scale scoring and the use of a choir and, while there was talk at the time
of gospel-inspired fusions, it seems clear that the music aimed for an easy-listening crevice somewhere
between soul-jazz and mood music. Set against the stricter tenets of the records which came before it,
it's dispensable. The previously unreleased *Kofi* fares better, cut at two sessions a year apart but with
basically the same band on each occasion. Byrd's four pieces are vague stabs at a modal/African
impressionism, but it's the pragmatic Tabackin and Foster who come off best: sounds as if Byrd had
been listening to Miles more than the musicologists he mentions in the self-serving comments on the
sleeve, though to no terrific effect. *Blackbyrd* is modishly arranged round a concept of soul-jazz that
struck a resonantly harmonious note at the time: it sold past the million mark and outdid all of Blue
Note's previous releases. Twenty years on, it sounds much the same: simple, lightweight crossover, with
Byrd masking his declining powers as an improviser with a busy group. To paraphrase Swamp Dogg, he
wasn't selling out, he was buying in. More of all that on *The Best Of Donald Byrd*. But *Early Byrd* is, by
contrast, a cracking set of tracks from some Byrd albums that shouldn't be in limbo: here are the title-
pieces from *Mustang*, *Slow Drag* and *Blackjack*, although the album peters out with the rambling 'The
Weasel' and 'The Emperor'.

*(*) **Donald Byrd And 125th Street, N.Y.C.** Discovery 1046-71019-2
    Byrd; Ernie Watts (*f*); Pete Christlieb (*ts*); Clare Fischer (*ky*); William Duckett (*g*); Marcus
    Carlisle (*st-g*); Ronnie Garrett (*b*); Victor Azevedo (*d*); Michael Campbell, Jim Gilstrap, Mitch
    Gordon, John Lehman, Joyce Michael, Zedric Turnbough (*v*); strings.
Flatulent funk and cooing singers dominate an album that should have stayed in vinyl limbo. One of
Byrd's worst.

(*) **Harlem Blues Landmark LCD-1516
    Byrd; Kenny Garrett (*as*); Mulgrew Miller (*p*); Mike Daugherty (*ky*); Rufus Reid (*b*); Marvin
    'Smitty' Smith (*d*). 9/87.
(*) **Gettin' Down To Business Landmark LCD-1523
    Byrd; Kenny Garrett (*as*); Joe Henderson (*ts*); Donald Brown (*p*); Peter Washington (*b*); Al
    Foster (*d*). 10/89.
(*) **A City Called Heaven Landmark LCD-1530
    Byrd; Joe Henderson (*ts*); Bobby Hutcherson (*vib*); Donald Brown (*p*); Rufus Reid (*b*); Carl
    Allen (*d*); Lorice Stevens (*v*). 1/91.
Most of Byrd's 1970s albums have disappeared from the catalogue, and his return to the studios for
Orrin Keepnews's Landmark operation has been inauspicious. A cloudier tone, unsure vibrato and
intonation problems mar all of these records and, on the evidence of the latest, *A City Called Heaven*,
matters seem to be getting worse rather than better. Frustratingly, everyone else on these sessions plays
particularly well as if to compensate. The new-generation outfit on *Harlem Blues* play with typical
button-down drive; Garrett and Henderson mesh with purpose and take some fine solos on *Gettin'
Down To Business* and, despite a couple of intrusive vocals by Stevens, the sextet on the latest record
seems to have power to spare: Hutcherson continues his Indian summer in the studios with swarming,
harmonically dense lines, and Henderson's profoundly cast solos evince all the grand maturity which
seems to have eluded Byrd.

Don Byron CLARINET, BASS CLARINET

**** Tuskegee Experiments Elektra Nonesuch 79280

Byron; Bill Frisell (*g*); Joe Berkovitz, Edsel Gomez (*p*); Kenny Davis, Lonnie Plaxico, Reggie Workman (*b*); Richie Schwarz (*mar*); Pheeroan AkLaff, Ralph Peterson Jr (*d*); Sadiq (*v*). 11/90, 7/91.

***(*) Plays The Music Of Mickey Katz Elektra Nonesuch 79313

Byron; Dave Douglas (*t, v*); Josh Roseman (*tb, v*); J. D. Parran (*cl, bcl, ss, f*); Mark Feldman (*vn, v*); Uri Caine (*p, v*); Brandon Ross (*g*); Jay Berliner (*mand*); Steve Alcott (*b*); Richie Schwarz (*d, perc, xyl*); Jerry Gonzalez (*perc*); Lorin Sklamberg, Avi Hofman, Loretta Malta, Rosalie Gerut (*v*). 9/92.

***(*) Music For Six Musicians Nonesuch 7559 79354

Byron; Graham Haynes (*c*); Edsel Gomez (*p*); Bill Frisell (*g*); Lonnie Plaxico, Kenny Davis (*b*); Ben Wittman, Ralph Peterson Jr (*d*); Jerry Gonzalez (*perc*); Sadiq (*v*). 94.

One of the first young players to emerge with a bang in the 1990s, Byron's rapidly growing reputation reflected a widespread revival of interest in jazz clarinet. Relative to the amount of press attention, the discography is still not large, though Byron has become one of the most in-demand guest players around. Second thoughts are a luxury but, relative to the hype the young clarinettist has received, perhaps essential. *Tuskegee Experiments* is a remarkable record; in our last edition, we described it as 'masterful, one of the most exciting debuts in more than a decade'. While it would be curmudgeonly to rob the album of, or even qualify, its fourth star, the passage of time has rubbed off some of the initial burnish.

As a debut record it was always intended to be more than just a showcase for Byron's wide-ranging talents, but it suffers (then as now) from its own ambition. Ending with a straight reading of Robert Schumann's '*Auf einer Burg*' is a rather self-conscious gesture. Nor do many jazz records name-check Diego Rivera, the Mexican muralist who so influenced American artists in the 1930s and '40s; this is the period that seems to interest Byron. The one standard he covers is Duke Ellington's 'Mainstem'. The title-piece relates to a bizarre and shocking 'medical' programme conducted in Alabama from 1932, by which black syphilitics were neither treated for nor even informed of their condition, in order to document their prognosis. The second experiment involved subjecting intelligent black men of military age to systematic humiliation in order to prove that they were not suitable to fly military aircraft. Byron's anger is impressively contained, though a vocal by the Detroit poet, Sadiq, comes close to violating the dignity of his response. 'Tuskegee Experiment' is scored for a quintet, with piano, marimba, electric bass and drums generating a threatening, percussive sound. On the opening 'Tuskegee Strutter's Ball', 'Next Love' and the beautiful 'Tears', Byron establishes his theme in unison with Frisell, favouring a bright coloratura and spiky, stop–start phrasing. Elsewhere, on 'Diego Rivera' and 'In Memoriam: Uncle Dan' (the latter a duet with Workman), he doubles on bass clarinet and switches to the longer line and romantic phrasing first heard on the unaccompanied 'Waltz For Ellen' that starts the record.

However eclectic *Tuskegee Experiments* was, nothing quite prepared Byron's growing body of fans for what followed. It had been known that one of his earliest stamping grounds had been a *klezmer* group in New York; Byron's was the only black face. This was widely thought to be the jazz equivalent of a Woody Allen joke. However, Byron's participation raised significant questions about the cultural identity of American popular music. In the odd twilight between the swing and rock'n'roll eras, the American public cast about for new and exotic musical styles. 'Tzena, Tzena, Tzena', 'Vaya Con Dios', 'Oh Mein Papa' were big hits, the 'Incan princess' Yma Sumac was a star, and *klezmer* composer Mickey Katz saw satirical potential in the Yiddishization of Americana. With a humour not unlike that of Peter Schickele (aka P. D. Q. Bach) or Kinky Friedman later, he turned familiar tunes around: 'Home On The Range' became 'Heim Afen Range', Khachaturian's 'Sabre Dance' became 'Seder Dance', and so on with 'Mechaye War Chant', 'Paisach In Portugal' and 'Kiss Of Meyer'. Byron's covers of these are played pretty straight, with only the opening and closing 'Tears' recalling the earlier record.

Plays Mickey Katz was received as a jokey aberration, a one-joke record with the joke pushed a little too hard. However, there is far more continuity with the earlier record than at first appears, and it does make a serious point about American popular culture (Byron's liner-note is, again, extremely intelligent) and its tendency to consume and digest 'sub-cultures' without regard for their essential historical nature.

Somehow, the *klezmer* record was going to make sense only when it was known what Byron intended to do next. The no-nonsense, composerly title of *Music For Six Musicians* was probably intended to defuse criticism, if indeed it was Byron's own choice, for the individual cuts are as pungent and *engagé* as anything on the first record, name-checking the likes of 'third party' presidential candidate Ross Perot, the man who helped redefine 'reasonable force', Rodney King, the Reverend Al Sharpton, and the late Bob Marley. Along with Byron, the most forceful instrumental voice is that of cornettist Graham Haynes, the son of drummer Roy. He has a bright, staccato sound that sits well with Byron's own and which has an ironclad inner logic that makes up for some deficiencies in the rhythm section.

A single track, 'I'll Chill On The Marley Tapes', appears to be left over from the *Tuskegee* session and features Frisell, Plaxico and Peterson again. It's not markedly stronger than the rest of the session, but it somehow confirms the irony of Byron's choice of the lower-case name *nottuskegeelike* for his publishing company, since at this point in his career he seems perfectly content to reprocess ideas from his debut disc. There is even another quasi-classical performance, this time of Manuel Ponce's 'La Estrellita'. A liner-note points out that – Ponce apart – the music was commissioned by the American Museum of the Moving Image, which might partly explain the feeling that a lot of this music seems to be functioning as accompaniment to other agenda rather than in its own right.

Reservations and hindsight/backlash apart, Byron is still a formidable musician who has already made a sizeable impact both as exponent of an unfashionable horn and as a provocative composer/bandleader. It would be a shame if he were pressured into growing up *too* fast.

George Cables (born 1944) PIANO

*** **Circles** Contemporary C 14015
    Cables; Joe Farrell (*f*); Ernie Watts (*ts*); Tony Dumas, Rufus Reid (*b*); Peter Erskine, Eddie Gladden (*d*). 3/79.
*** **Cables Vision** Original Jazz Classics OJC 725
    Cables; Freddie Hubbard (*t, flhn*); Ernie Watts (*ts, ss*); Bobby Hutcherson (*vib*); Tony Dumas (*b*); Peter Erskine (*d*); Vince Charles (*perc*). 12/79.
**** **Phantom Of The City** Contemporary C 14014
    Cables; John Heard (*b*); Tony Williams (*d*). 5/85.
***(*) **By George** Contemporary C 14030
    Cables; John Heard (*b*); Ralph Penland (*d*). 2/87.
***(*) **Cables Fables** Steeplechase SCCD 31287
    Cables; Peter Washington (*b*); Kenny Washington (*d*). 3/91.
***(*) **Night And Day** DIW 606
    Cables; Cecil McBee (*b*); Billy Hart (*d*). 5/91.
***(*) **Beyond Forever** Steeplechase SCCD 31305
    Cables; Joe Locke (*vib*); Santi Debriano (*b*); Victor Lewis (*d*). 12/91.
*** **I Mean You** Steeplechase SCCD 31334
    Cables; Jay Anderson (*b*); Adam Nussbaum (*d*). 4/93.
***(*) **Maybeck Recital Hall Series: Volume 35** Concord CCD 4630
    Cables (*p* solo). 1/94.
*** **Quiet Fire** Steeplechase SCCD 31357
    Cables; Ron McClure (*b*); Billy Hart (*d*). 4/94.

Still probably best known for his duo performances with the late Art Pepper on the marvellous Galaxy *Goin' Home*, Cables is a fine accompanist who has been consistently underrated as a soloist. His touch can be rather sharp and there is sometimes an awkward bounce to his chording at fast tempi, but he is a fine solo and trio performer.

He plays an electric instrument with great taste and economy throughout *Cables Vision* with the exception of a single acoustic duo with Bobby Hutcherson called 'The Stroll', which deserves to be more widely known. The 1987 Gershwin set is richly sophisticated and the solo performances of 'Embraceable You' and 'Someone To Watch Over Me' are excellent examples of his innate rhythmic sense. It's this, even more than the choice of material and his sure-footed progress round the keys, that makes the Maybeck recital such an interesting listen. He plays 'Someone' again, holding back on the beat and then nudging forward urgently (compare the version on *By George*), and turning 'Bess, You Is My Woman Now' into a tense little drama.

Switching labels in later years has served Cables only rather ambiguously. DIW's production flatters him no more than his due and some might find *Night And Day* a little hard and unresonant. The selection of material is much more imaginative than usual, mixing well-worn standards like 'Night And Day' (given a little twist in the middle chorus), 'I Love You' and 'I Thought About You', with more enterprising numbers like Rollins's 'Doxy', Bill Evans's 'Very Early' (another possible source for Cables's keyboard approach), and Jaco Pastorius's misterioso funk 'Three Views Of A Secret'. An able composer, Cables has tended to keep this side of his work under wraps, writing for others but sticking to standards on his own records; 'Ebony Moonbeams' on *Night And Day* suggests that this is a pity.

Steeplechase certainly don't give their product the gloss one expects from the Japanese DIW, but it may be that their roomier sound is more sympathetic to Cables. *Beyond Forever* is a delight, centred on a moving version of 'I Fall In Love Too Easily'. Hutcherson's 'Little B's Poem' is a feature for Joe Locke, predictably. The trios are more uneven in quality, and the reason has to be the rhythm pairings. The namesake Washingtons are as much in synch as if they *were* brothers, or even twins, but Nussbaum and the less experienced Anderson don't hit it off on the Monk tune and the three originals, apparently unfamiliar with the latter. Only when the pace drops for 'Lush Life' do they sound as if they're on the same team.

The recent *Quiet Fire* is lovely: a cracking group and a riveting choice of material, including John Hicks's 'Naima's Love Song', and Freddie Hubbard's seldom-covered 'The Decrepit Fox'. They close a session that hasn't lost pace or momentum, or lacked for expressive variety from the very start. McClure seems to grow in stature every time he turns out.

Perhaps the best news for Cables enthusiasts, though, is the reappearance of *Phantom Of The City* and *Circles*. In our first edition we could give the LP version of the former only a qualified accolade because of its messy sound. On CD it comes across much more positively, with Williams's drums where they ought to be in the mix and tweaked down enough to leave everything else audible. Heard (no cheap association of ideas intended) has always been a sympathetic colleague, and this is one of his very best recorded performances. 'Dark Side, Light Side' is the outstanding track. In contrast to the intense concentration of *Phantom*, the other reissue is scrappy and shapeless; all surviving moments of Joe Farrell are to be treasured, but this is not one of the shining ones.

All in all, though, a good haul of stuff now from Cables. He'll continue to win fans and convert critics. Anyone with lingering doubts could perhaps start – as with so many piano players – at the Maybeck Recital Hall.

Mike Cain (born 1966) PIANO

** **Strange Omen** Candid CCD 79505
    Cain; Bruce Saunders (*g*); Glen Velez (*perc*). 11/90.
Cain's interest in world music and composition makes Velez's appearance less of a surprise than it might be with most of today's younger pianists; and Saunders, while rather subliminally placed, contributes the two most focused compositions in 'Follow Through' and 'The Way Things Work'. Cain himself has a precise and fine touch, but too many of the pieces here – particularly the four solo 'Piano Sketch' themes, which offer a slight recall of Chick Corea's ECM records – sound like home exercises rather than real compositions. Only on 'Bestido Al Cielo De Noche', where the trio work up a real interplay, are expectations fulfilled.

*** **What Means This?** Candid CCD 79529
    Cain; Anthony Cox (*b*); Marvin 'Smitty' Smith (*d*); Paul Hannah (*perc*). 3/91.
A tighter rhythm section assist Cain no end. Cox and Smith (Hannah appears on only one track) play with boundless energy and crisp, almost crystalline detail: the rhythm work on 'Figure Of Speech' is so sharp and clear that one almost forgets about the piano. Cain's writing is a lot more precise this time, though, and the catchiness of 'As I Gazed' is symptomatic of a mild advance. But his own playing continues either to meander, as on 'Meander', or to seem inexplicable, as on 'How So?'. See also the, er, title-track.

Uri Caine PIANO

***(*) **Sphere Music** JMT 514 007
    Caine; Graham Haynes (*c*); Don Byron (*cl*); Gary Thomas (*ts*); Kenny Davis (*b*); Ralph
    Peterson (*d*). 4 & 5/92.
**** **Toys** JMT 514 022
    Caine; Dave Douglas (*t*); Joshua Roseman (*tb*); Don Byron (*bcl*); Gary Thomas (*ts*); Dave
    Holland (*b*); Ralph Peterson (*d*); Don Alias (*perc*). 2 & 3/95.
As a soloist, he has more in common with Herbie Hancock than with anyone else, underlined by the inclusion of 'Cantaloupe Island' on *Toys*. As a writer and bandleader, he is already and formidably his own man. It would be hard to look for two more confidently inscribed visiting cards than these discs.

Caine had recorded previously with vibist Gust William Tsilis, workmanlike performances that gave only a limited sense of his potential. It's slightly surprising that he should have left his synthesizer at home for both *Sphere Music* and *Toys*. He uses electronics tastefully and with acute perceptiveness. For his debut, though, he obviously favoured a bluntly resonant acoustic sound, picking his players accordingly. Byron provides the coloratura, whistling away above Caine's forceful vamps on 'Mr BC' and on the beautifully conceived 'Jelly', a pair of titles that may well help point the listener to the pianist's strong sense of jazz history.

Thomas is a less *simpatico* partner, always sounding as if he wants to wrest the tune – 'When The Word Is Given' and 'Jan Fan' are his two credits here – in his own hip-hop-tinged direction. Graham Haynes's brittle cornet sound provides a welcome diversion on the latter track, a much more idiomatic range for Caine. It's Byron again, though, who sneaks in a little mid-set showstopper, duetting with Caine on 'Round Midnight'; just when you thought that old warhorse should be put out to grass . . .

There are a couple of trio tracks, one a tribute to Philly Joe Jones, the other a thing called 'We See' which is the best starting place for anyone who wants to study Caine's technique in close-up. The rhythm section is spot on; Peterson's deceptive cymbal work and off-beat accents are an ideal foil to Cox's round, Carter-influenced bass lines.

Of the second album there is little to say, except even better all round. The replacement of Cox with Holland has some interesting implications, and again it is in the trios that the interaction is most effective; 'Herbal Blue' and 'Or Truth?' are sensibly placed back-to-back early in the set, and there's another outing, with Alias added, towards the end. There's a re-run of the Byron–Caine duo, this time on the Hancock composition, and the leader also duets with trumpeter Dave Douglas (one of the best contemporary horn players) on 'I'm Meshugah For My Sugah (And My Sugah's Meshugah For Me)', which might almost bespeak a John Zorn influence. The extra horn provides a bit of width on 'The Prisoner' and 'Toys' itself, but Roseman doesn't get much opportunity to show off his stuff. Two excellent albums; the next one should be considered a must-hear.

Joey Calderazzo (born 1966) PIANO, KEYBOARDS

*** **Secrets** Audioquest AQ 1036

>   Calderazzo; Tim Hagans (*t, flhn*); John Clark (*frhn*); Earl McIntyre (*btb, tba*); Tim Ries (*ss, f*); Charlie Pillow (*ts, bcl, cor*); Fareed Haque (*g*); Tomas Ulrich (*clo*); James Genus (*b*); Clarence Penn (*d*). 1/95.

Calderazzo came to prominence as a Michael Brecker sideman, but his three albums as a leader for Blue Note didn't create much excitement. While pivoted around himself, Genus and Penn, this session for Audioquest has the extra colour of arrangements for a multifarious ensemble by Bob Belden on most of the tracks. Belden chooses an eastern tinge for Miles Davis's 'Filles De Kilimanjaro' and Vince Mendoza's 'Scriabin', and sets his other charts to various points of the compass; but none of them seem to do much more than cloud around Calderazzo's piano. Ironically, the leader's own playing, while sometimes still too effusive, is mostly more thoughtful and insidious than it ever was on the Blue Note records.

Cab Calloway (1907–94) VOCAL

***(*) **Cab Calloway & The Missourians 1929–1930** JSP CD 328

>   Calloway; R. Q. Dickerson, Lamar Wright, Reuben Reeves (*t*); De Priest Wheeler (*tb*); George Scott, Thornton Blue (*cl, as*); Andrew Brown (*cl, ts*); Walter Thomas (*cl, ts, bs*); Earres Prince (*p*); Morris White (*bj*); Jimmy Smith (*bb, b*); Leroy Maxey (*d*); Lockwood Lewis (*v*). 6/29–12/30.

The rough, almost violent playing of The Missourians, a black dance band recording in New York but drawing most of its talent from the Mid-West, is as impassioned as any band of the day, and their thinly disguised blues constructions, freakishly wild ensembles and occasional snarling solos (by Wheeler and Dickerson especially) are still exciting to listen to. Their dozen records are splendidly remastered here, along with two alternative takes, as well as the first ten tracks featuring the man who took the band over, Cab Calloway. At his very first session – in July 1930, with an astonishingly virtuoso vocal on 'St Louis Blues' – he served notice that a major jazz singer was ready to challenge Armstrong with an entirely different style.

*** **Cab Calloway 1930–1931** Classics 516

>   Calloway; R. Q. Dickerson, Lamar Wright, Reuben Reeves, Wendell Culley (*t*); De Priest Wheeler (*tb*); Thornton Blue, Arville Harris (*cl, as*); Andrew Brown (*bcl, ts*); Walter Thomas (*as, ts, bs, f*); Earres Prince, Bennie Payne (*p*); Morris White (*bj*); Jimmy Smith (*bb, b*); Leroy Maxey (*d*). 7/30–6/31.

***(*) **Cab Calloway 1931–1932** Classics 526

>   As above, except add Edwin Swayzee, Doc Cheatham (*t*), Harry White (*tb*), Eddie Barefield (*cl, as, bs*), Al Morgan (*b*), omit Dickerson, Culley, Prince and Blue. 7/31–6/32.

***(*) **Cab Calloway 1932** Classics 537

>   As above, except add Roy Smeck (*g*), Chuck Bullock (*v*), omit Reeves and Smith. 6/32–12/32.

*** **Cab Calloway 1932–1934** Classics 544

>   As above, except omit Smeck and Bullock. 12/32–9/34.

It didn't take long for Calloway to sharpen up the band, even though he did it with comparatively few personnel changes. Unlike the already-tested format of a vocal feature within an instrumental record, Calloway's arrangers varied detail from record to record, Cab appearing throughout some discs, briefly on others, and usually finding space for a fine team of soloists. Some of the discs are eventful to an extraordinary extent: listen, for instance, to the 1935 'I Ain't Got Nobody' or the dazzling 1930 'Some Of These Days' to hear how enthusiastically the band tackled its charts. The lexicon of reefers, Minnie the Moocher and Smokey Joe, kicking gongs around and – of course – the fabulous language of hi-de-ho would have soon become tiresome if it hadn't been for the leader's boundless energy and ingenious invention: his vast range, from a convincing bass to a shrieking falsetto, has remained unsurpassed by any male jazz singer, and he transforms material that isn't so much trite as empty without the investment of his personality. This was a very popular band, long resident at the Cotton Club, and the stability of the personnel says much about the good pay and working conditions. The prodigious number of records they made both during and after the Depression was scarcely matched by any other bandleader, and it has taken the Classics operation no fewer than ten well-filled CDs to cover them all. Unfortunately, reproduction is rather a mixed bag. The earlier sides were made for Banner and other budget labels and suffer from some booming recording; but there is a fair amount of surface noise, too. The first volume duplicates the last ten tracks on the JSP CD, and reproduction is clearly inferior on the Classics issue. However, there's nothing unlistenable here and, since Calloway's music is at its freshest, casual listeners may choose one of these earlier discs as representative.

(***) **Cab Calloway 1934–1937** Classics 554

As above, except add Shad Collins, Irving Randolph (*t*), Claude Jones, Keg Johnson (*tb*), Garvin Bushell, Thornton Blue (*cl, as*), Ben Webster (*ts*), Milt Hinton (*b*). 9/34–3/37.

***(*) **Cab Calloway 1937–1938** Classics 568

As above, except add Chu Berry (*ts*), Chauncey Haughton (*cl, as*), Danny Barker (*g*), omit Swayzee, Culley, Cheatham and Morgan. 3/37–3/38.

*** **Cab Calloway 1938–1939** Classics 576

As above, except add June Richmond (*v*), Cozy Cole (*d*), omit Webster and White. 3/38–2/39.

***(*) **Cab Calloway 1939–1940** Classics 595

As above, except add Dizzy Gillespie, Mario Bauza (*t*), Tyree Glenn (*tb, vib*), Quentin Jackson (*tb*), Jerry Blake (*cl, as*), omit Maxey, Bushell and Richmond. 3/39–3/40.

*** **Cab Calloway 1940** Classics 614

As above, except omit Collins, Randolph, Jones and Blue. 3–8/40.

*** **Cab Calloway 1940–1941** Classics 625

As above, except add Jonah Jones (*t*). 3/40–7/41.

Calloway progressed through the 1930s with unquenchable enthusiasm. He took fewer risks on his vocals and chose to set down some more straightforward ballad interpretations on several of the later sides, but the singing is still exceptional, and there are new points of interest among the soloists: Ben Webster appears on several tracks on the 1934–7 disc, and Chu Berry follows him in as a regular soloist, while Gillespie, Jackson and Jefferson also emerge. The 1940 disc features some arrangements by Benny Carter and the bizarre 'Cupid's Nightmare' score by Don Redman, a mystifying mood-piece. Jonah Jones, the last great soloist to arrive in this era, sparks several of the 1941 tracks. Reproduction is mostly clean if sometimes lacking in sparkle on the later discs, but the 1934–7 disc is marred by preposterously heavy surface-noise on the opening tracks and we must issue a caveat in this regard.

*** **Cab Calloway & Co** RCA ND 89560 2CD

As appropriate discs above, except add Jonah Jones (*t*), Tyree Glenn, John Ewing (*tb*), S. A. Stewart, Leon Washington, Hilton Jefferson, Sam Taylor (*saxes*), Dave Rivera (*p*); Milt Hinton (*b*), Panama Francis (*d*). 9/33–11/49.

(*) **Hi-De-Hi-De-Ho RCA 74321 18524 2

Calloway; Bernie Glow, Jimmy Maxwell, Joe Wilder, James Nottingham, Doc Severinsen (*t*); Urbie Green, Chauncey Welsh, Richard Hixson, Thomas Mitchell, Joe Bennett, James Dahl (*tb*); Sam Marowitz, Charles O'Kane, Abraham Richman, Sam Donahue, Stanley Webb, Sol Schlinger (*saxes*), Hank Jones (*p*); Everett Barksdale (*g*); Milt Hinton, Joe Reisman (*b*); J. C. Heard (*d*). 12/58.

***(*) **Cruisin' With Cab** Topaz TPZ 1010

As above discs. 12/30–43.

The two-disc compilation in the RCA Tribune series is good value and a sensible cross-section of Cab's Victor tracks, with most of the famous hits and an interesting makeweight of three sessions by sister Blanche Calloway and two tracks by Billy Banks. There is also a 1949 date with four tracks in which Calloway is trying out in the post-bop era. The sound is, as usual for this series, listenable if less than ideal.

Hi-De-Hi-De-Ho found Calloway remaking some of his old hits with a then-modern entourage. He is still in good voice, and the players do their best to approximate the old style, but this was a showman who needed an audience and it feels like his time had already gone – even though he would still be performing into the 1990s. The glory days are neatly captured on the single Topaz disc, which is a smartly chosen retrospective of 20 tracks from the period 1930–41, with a single Broadcast of 'Cruisin' With Cab' to cap the collection. In good sound, this makes a case as the best single introduction to Cab's work.

Michel Camilo PIANO

*** **Why Not?** Electric Bird K28P 6371
> Camilo; Lew Soloff (*t*); Chris Hunter (*as, ts*); Anthony Jackson (*b*); Dave Weckl (*d*); Sammy Figueroa, Guarionex Aquino (*perc*). 2/85.
*** **In Trio** Electric Bird K28P 6445
> Camilo; Anthony Jackson (*b*); Joel Rosenblatt, Dave Weckl (*d*). 6/86.
***(*) **Michel Camilo** Portrait PRT 463330
> Camilo; Marc Johnson, Lincoln Jones (*b*); Joel Rosenblatt, Dave Weckl (*d*); Mongo Santamaria (*perc*). 1–2/88.

Camilo grins broadly as he plays, almost palpably enjoying the music he makes. Born in the Dominican Republic and formally schooled, he had been a fixture on the New York club scene and a word-of-mouth star long before he won a major record deal. He is possessed of a formidable technique with very few traces of the conservatory left in it, beyond his fondness for occasional Bartók-isms in his folkier themes. Hurricane-fast, he sings along with himself, not in Bud Powell's anguished cry or with Jarrett's exaggerated passion, but in sheer exuberance.

The Portrait is perhaps his best showing to date on record, a headlong set mainly of originals, but with an intriguing piano/conga version of Kenny Dorham's 'Blue Bossa' which confirms Camilo's jazz credentials and his impressive individuality at a stroke. 'Caribe' is also particularly strong, and evidence of Camilo's ability to mix vintages as well as genres.

The earlier trio recording is a little less sure of itself and is certainly not so well produced, with a slight hazing of the top notes and percussion accents. The Latin component is also more prominent, which will please some and repel others.

An accomplished big-band and orchestral arranger, Camilo sounds quite easy round horns. He has worked with Soloff and his regular Jackson/Weckl rhythm section before, under the name *French Toast* (Electric Bird K28P 6314). It's a fine album.

***(*) **On The Other Hand** Columbia 477753-2
> Camilo; Michael Phillip Mossman (*t*); Ralph Bowen, Chris Hunter (*as*); Michael Bowie (*b*); Cliff Almond (*d*); Sammy Figueroa (*perc*); D. K. Dyson (*v*).

Camilo attempts something more ambitious on the long 'Suite Sandrine: Part 3', which occupies nearly nine minutes of the second side, but the really impressive tracks are a version of Jaco Pastorius's 'City Of Angels' and Camilo's own thundering 'Impressions', which would have made an excellent climax but is buried in the middle of the CD. There are, perhaps inevitably, some dullish fusion elements to negotiate, and D. K. Dyson's late-nite vocal on 'Forbidden Fruit' seems a touch *ersatz*. Otherwise, though, beyond reproach musically, and marred only by a rather loud, cranky sound-mix, which might sound good through a club system, but isn't easy to adjust on home stereo.

Gary Campbell TENOR AND SOPRANO SAXOPHONES

*** **Intersection** Milestone MCD-9236-2
> Campbell; Mike Orta (*p*); Nicky Orta (*b*); Ignacio Berroa (*d*); Rafael Solano (*perc*). 12/93.

A journeyman reed specialist, renowned as teacher and theorist, Campbell bases himself in south Florida and has taken a special interest in finding a fresh slant on Latin/jazz fusion. It's idiosyncratic enough that this small-group date sounds quite unlike the accustomed crossover: instead of vamps and overheated solos, Campbell looks for subtle pulses that can trigger different kinds of improvisation. 'Lago Turvo' and 'Hair Of The Dog' open and close the disc in lively fashion, but more typical are the pensive 'Almost Lost', the odd mix of pep and sobriety in 'J. A.' (dedicated to John Abercrombie) and the stern tranquillity of 'Tango'. If anything, the music seems a little too studied in its attempts to get away from cliché, and it doesn't help that Campbell has a stone-faced quality to his playing which disengages the power of some otherwise interesting solos.

John Campbell PIANO

**** After Hours Contemporary 14053
    Campbell; Todd Coolman (*b*); Gerry Gibbs (*d*). 89.
*** Turning Point Contemporary 14061
    Campbell; Clark Terry (*t*); Jay Anderson (*p*); Joel Spencer (*d*). 90.
***(*) John Campbell At Maybeck: Maybeck Recital Hall Series, Volume 29 Concord CCD 4581
    Campbell (*p* solo). 5/93.

Campbell is a fresh-faced mid-Westerner whose farmboy demeanour may arouse musical expectations closer to his namesake Glen than to the reality of his tough but sophisticated bop playing. The Maybeck disc, as so often, is the best place to sample him. Like many of his predecessors in the series, he uses the occasion as an opportunity to show off a couple of test-pieces (like the opening interpretation of 'Just Friends' with its odd turn-arounds and harmonic nervousness) or simply to enjoy old favourites (like 'You And The Night And The Music', to which again he gives an unusual twist). 'Emily' is more straightforwardly romantic, though not without its reserves of guile.

    The trios with Coolman and Gibbs are uniformly good, especially the partially deconstructed 'Donna Lee'. Its successor, unfortunately, is pretty feeble. Terry probably thinks it's all a bit high-falutin' and, in a strange way, it is.

Roy Campbell (born 1952) TRUMPET, FLUGELHORN, CORNET, POCKET-TRUMPET

**(*) Other Dimensions In Music Silkheart SHCD 120
    Campbell; Daniel Carter (*as, ts, f, t*); William Parker (*b*); Rashid Bakr (*d*). 4/89.
***(*) New Kingdom Delmark DE-456
    Campbell; Zane Massey (*ts*); Riccardo Strobert (*as, f*); Bryan Carrott (*vib*); William Parker (*b*); Zen Matsuura (*d*). 10/91.
*** La Tierra Del Fuego Delmark DE-469
    Campbell; Alex Lodico (*tb*); Riccardo Strobert (*as, f*); Zane Massey (*ts*); Klaas Hekman (*bs*); Rahn Burton (*p*); Hideji Taninaka (*b*); Reggie Nicholson (*d*); Talik Abdullah (*perc*). 12/93.
*** Communion Silkheart SHCD 139
    Campbell; William Parker (*b*); Reggie Nicholson (*d*). 9/94.

Campbell plays like the offspring of Lee Morgan, who was actually his teacher, but imbued with a hankering to go much further outside than Morgan ever would have. He loves lyrical playing and, on Parker's piece dedicated to Cecil Taylor, 'For C.T.', he counters the inspiration by playing some of his sweetest horn. But the idea of *New Kingdom* is to create music that salutes the tradition and still pays heed to the avant garde. The three trio pieces for Campbell, Parker and Matsuura are an expertly constructed bridge, and beautifully played by all three men. Massey and Strobert are sound, if relatively unremarkable saxophonists, but Carrott is a fine participant, moving smoothly between roles as colourist, ensemble man and fleet improviser.

    La Tierra Del Fuego is an intermittently exciting stew of traditions and new ideas, with nods to Booker Little and various threads of Afro-Cuban jazz and the hottest modal bands of the 1960s. Campbell assembles a rather ragtag cast for this one, with the surprising Hekman a wild card, and as a result it comes off hit and miss. He empties out the studio for *Communion*, which spotlights his freest playing, and this time evokes – perhaps all too obviously – some of Don Cherry's small-group recordings. Probably ten or fifteen minutes' too much here, since the record palls a little over the full stretch; inventively as Parker and Nicholson play, one hears graft and perspiration rather than flair. But Campbell remains a gratifying and lyrical performer, even at his furthest out.

    Other Dimensions is a democratic record which we've listed under Campbell's name for convenience. It's a loosely organized free-bop date of no special character but one speckled with the expected flashes of excellence.

Tony Campise TENOR, ALTO AND SOPRANO SAXOPHONES, FLUTE, BASS FLUTE

**(*) First Takes Heart 021
    Campise; Rick Jackson (*p*); Erich Avinger (*g*); Bill Miller (*b*); Steve Allison (*d*). 90.
**(*) Once In A Blue Moon Heart 04
    As above, except Joe Locascio (*p*) replaces Jackson and Avinger. 12/90.
*** Ballads Blues Bebop And Beyond Heart 006
    Campise; Dennis Dotson (*t*); John Milles (*ts, bs*); Joe Locascio, Sandy Allen, Doug Hall (*p*); Mitch Watkins, Erich Avinger (*g*); Evan Arredondo, Chris Marsh, Dave Morgan (*b*); Steve

Summer, A. D. Mannion (*d*). 94.
Campise's bluff, open-hearted approach to the sax – his primary horn seems to be the tenor, but there is alto and soprano as well as flute on these discs – is cheering in small doses but a little unconvincing over the long haul. He piles into his solos as if worried that he won't have the time to say all he wants, and the results can be predictably exhausting, something between Trane-like intensity and the swaggering line of the great Texas tenors (Campise is from Houston). The first two albums are rough-and-ready mixtures of standards, blues and the occasional original line, and on both of them the weight falls on Campise, with mixed results. *Ballads Blues Bebop And Beyond* is the best by a narrow margin: Watkins, excellent as usual, adds tonal contrast to the five tracks he appears on, Dotson is useful on 'Teo' and (a brave stab at this one) Mingus's 'Haitian Fight Song', and there is a hell-for-leather blow-out on 'Impressions' which is genuinely exciting.

Canal Street Ragtimers GROUP

**(*) Canal Street Ragtimers GHB BCD-4
Roy Bower, Tony Smith (*t*); Chris Brown (*tb*); Martin Rodger (*cl*); John G. Featherstone (*p*); Derek Gracie (*bj*); Colin Knight (*b*); Derek Hamer, Mo Green (*d*). 10/61–1/62.
Some irony in that it took a Louisiana-based label to record this pick-up band of Manchester trad stalwarts back in the early 1960s. For those with memories of the scene, it's a nice souvenir, but on its own terms the record doesn't deliver that much. The nine tunes ('Old Rugged Cross' appears twice) were well-worn even then, and if the Ragtimers give them an enthusiastic ragging it's not much more than an echo now. Dusty sound affects the drums in particular.

Conte Candoli (born 1927) TRUMPET

**(*) Double Or Nothin' Fresh Sounds FSR-CD197
Candoli; Lee Morgan (*t*); Frank Rosolino (*tb*); Benny Golson, Bob Cooper (*ts*); Dick Shreve, Wynton Kelly (*p*); Red Mitchell, Wilfred Middlebrooks (*b*); Stan Levey, Charli Persip (*d*). 2/57.
*** Sweet Simon Best Recordings BR 92101-2
Candoli; Pete Christlieb (*ts*); Frank Strazzeri (*p*); Monty Budwig (*b*); Ralph Penland, Roy McCurdy (*d*). 92.
Conte Candoli is one of the great West Coast brassmen. Often as content to be a foot-soldier as a leader, he's seldom helmed his own dates, and these discs (a generation apart) suggest an unassumingly likeable style. The first is a Howard Rumsey date co-credited to Conte and Lee Morgan, but neither man really has much space to shine: Morgan's youthful swashbuckling is penned in by the charts and, though Golson contributes three good tunes, the material is flatly delivered. Golson and Morgan take some good choruses on 'Blues After Dark', but the two-trumpet tracks are disappointingly tame, and this is hardly Candoli's show. Still awaited on CD from this period are his 1954 quartet date for Bethlehem and Atlantic's cracking *West Coast Wailers* with Lou Levy and Bill Holman.
Sweet Simon is a veteran bopper's notebook. He graciously covers two tunes by his old friend, Frank Rosolino, adds a couple of Frank Strazzeri originals and two of his own, picks out a neat Al Cohn piece called 'Travisimo' and turns it all into an hour of good-humoured blowing. 'Lush Life' doesn't really suit the trumpeter, and he probably cedes too much space to the others, especially bluff tenorman Christlieb; but the pleasure he takes in his own playing shows how much Conte enjoys his work. Impeccable studio sound.

Frank Capp (born 1931) DRUMS

**(*) Juggernaut Concord CCD 4040
Capp; Blue Mitchell, Gary Grant, Bobby Shew (*t*); Buster Cooper, Britt Woodman, Alan Kaplan (*tb*); Bill Green, Marshall Royal (*as*); Richie Kamuca, Plas Johnson (*ts*); Quin Davis (*bs*); Nat Pierce (*p*); Al Hendrickson (*g*); Chuck Berghofer (*b*); Ernie Andrews (*v*). 79.
**(*) Live At Century Plaza Concord CCD 4072
Capp; Al Aarons, Bobby Shew, Frank Szabo, Bill Berry (*t*); Garnett Brown, Buster Cooper, Alan Kaplan, Britt Woodman (*tb*); Bob Cooper, Bill Green, Lanny Morgan, Herman Riley, Marshall Royal (*reeds*); Nat Pierce (*p*); Ray Pohlman (*g*); Chuck Berghofer (*b*); Joe Williams (*v*).
** Juggernaut Strikes Again! Concord CCD 4183
Capp; Bill Berry, Snooky Young, Johnny Audino, Frank Szabo, Al Aarons, Warren Luening (*t*); Alan Kaplan, Buster Cooper, George Bohannon, Mel Wanzo (*tb*); Marshall Royal, Joe

Roccisano, Jackie Kelso (*as*); Pete Christlieb, Bob Cooper, Bob Efford (*ts*); Bill Green (*ss, bs*); Nat Pierce (*p*); Bob Maize (*b*); Ernie Andrews (*v*). 10–11/81.

**(*) Live At The Alley Cat Concord CCD 4336
Capp; Bill Berry, Snooky Young, Frank Szabo, Conte Candoli (*t*); Charles Loper, Garnett Brown, Buster Cooper (*tb*); Dave Edwards, Joe Romano (*as*); Red Holloway, Bob Cooper (*ts*); Bill Green (*bs*); Nat Pierce (*p*); Ken Pohlman (*g*); Chuck Berghofer (*b*); Ernestine Anderson (*v*). 6/87.

*** In A Hefti Bag Concord CCD 4655
As above, except add Bob Summers (*t*), Andy Martin, Thurman Green, Alan Kaplan (*tb*), Marshall Royal, Lanny Morgan, Danny House, Rickey Woodard, Pete Christlieb, Jack Nimitz (*reeds*), Gerry Wiggins (*p*), Dennis Budimir, John Pisano (*g*); omit Loper, Brown, Cooper, Edwards, Romano, Holloway, Cooper, Pierce, Pohlman, Anderson. 11/94–3/95.

Co-led by Capp, a drummer loaded with big-band experience, and Pierce, *Juggernaut* is essentially a troupe of sessionmen out for a good time on the stand. Because they're such proficient players, there's nothing casual about the music; but that also means that it never becomes quite as freewheeling as the musicians might imagine. Too many of the arrangements rely on stock devices pulled from the Basie and Herman books, while the section playing is sometimes overwound, especially on *Strikes Again!*. Nevertheless, so many good players are on hand that the results are seldom less than enjoyable, and when somebody cuts loose – as, say, Buster Cooper does on 'Things Ain't What They Used To Be', on Concord CCD 4183 – it's as thrilling as they intend. The first live record features the majestic Williams, the second Anderson, and she is in fair voice, and never as fulsome as Andrews is on the other two discs. *In A Hefti Bag* finds Capp's men piling through 'authentic' Basie charts; as a polished piece of repertory – with the sax section now stronger than the band has ever shown, too – it's an impressive show, with choice moments for Young, Woodard and Candoli, and a farewell blow from Marshal Royal.

*** Frank Capp Presents Rickey Woodard Concord CCD 4469
Capp; Rickey Woodard (*as, ts*); Tom Ranier (*p*); Chuck Berghofer (*b, v*). 91.

Capp lends his name to a date that's really a showcase for the splendid Woodard, a stylist whose dedication to swing is as strong as his allegiance to bebop. The material is straightforward stuff, but Woodard characterizes it all with full-blooded enthusiasm.

Arrigo Cappelletti PIANO

**** Samadhi Splasc(h) H 111
Cappelletti; Roberto Ottaviano (*ss, as*); Piero Leveratto (*b*); Massimo Pintori (*d*). 4/86.
*** Pianure Splasc(h) H 308-2
Cappelletti; Giulio Visibelli (*ss*); Maurizio Deho (*vn*); Gianni Coscia (*acc*); Hami Hammerli, Luca Garlaschelli (*b*). 3–5/90.
***(*) Singolari Equilibri Splasc(h) H 390-2
Cappelletti; Hami Hammerli (*b*); Billy Elgart (*d*). 4/92.

Cappelletti is a not perhaps a very original voice – his underlying romanticism is tempered by a linear approach to improvised melody which, especially on *Singolari Equilibri*, can make him closely akin to Paul Bley – but he's a skilful and unusually clear thinker at the keyboard. There's little waste in his compositions, which are unfailingly lyrical, and his harmonies are sparsely voiced, as if he's anxious not to obscure the sonority of individual notes. He asks for highly developed interplay from companions, and the quartet and trio sessions are both memorably characterful. Ottaviano has seldom sounded better than he does on *Samadhi*, which includes two good tunes of his own as well as a thoughtful treatment of John Taylor's 'Windfall' and Cappelletti at his composing best in 'Neve' and 'Incipit'. The trio record is over-full at 77 minutes but there is much ingenuity from all three men, with Elgart's improvisations as interesting as those of the others. *Pianure* is a modest departure, with Cappelletti looking to try his hand at the tango music of Astor Piazzolla: there are many fine moments, but it feels relatively polite and tame next to the passions which Piazzolla himself could generate, and the other players can't match the leader in the quality of their solos.

Thomas 'Mutt' Carey (1891–1948) TRUMPET

*** Mutt Carey And Lee Collins American Music AMCD-72
Carey; Lee Collins (*t*); Hociel Thomas (*p, v*); Lovie Austin, J. H. Shayne (*p*); Johnny Lindsay (*b*); Baby Dodds (*d*); Bertha 'Chippie' Hill (*v*). 2–8/46.
Carey was an early giant of New Orleans trumpet, but his representation on record is relatively slight,

certainly in terms of being in the limelight. His contribution to the one CD under his name consists of six accompaniments to the piano and vocals of classic blues singer Thomas, still in good voice even though she'd been living in obscurity for many years at that point. This isn't some of Carey's best work, though. He sounds surprisingly uncomfortable at several points and much of the playing seems hesitant, but there's some superb interplay on 'Go Down Sunshine', and Thomas herself does very well. Collins, another frequently unsung trumpeter, sounds rather better on his eight tracks, where he plays behind another veteran, Chippie Hill. This is all rough music and it gets close to the core. Good restoration from the original Circle masters.

Judy Carmichael PIANO

*** **Pearls** Jazzology JCD-204
    Carmichael; Warren Vaché Jr (*c*); Howard Alden (*g*); Red Callender (*b*). 9/85.
Carmichael is something of a rarity, a woman playing stride and old-time piano, and she performs the classic repertoire here with much affection and dedication. She tends to do better by old standards such as 'Lulu's Back In Town' than with piano set-pieces such as Morton's 'The Pearls', where the composition gets a beating rather than an interpretation – she doesn't go for the light touch. Of the four solos, Johnson's 'Mule Walk' is perhaps the best. But all the quartet tracks have the blessing of Vaché's suave cornet, with Alden (then not much out of his teens) strumming alongside. The stretch to CD length adds eight extra tracks to the original album, but unfortunately all but one of them are alternative takes of earlier tracks.

Mike Carr ORGAN

*** **Good Times And The Blues** Cargogold CGCD 191
    Carr; Dick Morrissey (*ts*); Jim Mullen (*g*); Mark Taylor (*d*). 3/93.
Three British venerables (Mark Taylor isn't quite as senior) having fun on blues and bop lines and getting a good record out of it. While the writing is merely functional, the solos work up a rare head of steam, with Morrissey and Mullen eschewing the politely funky licks of their jazz-funk past and digging in. Carr likes to put the Hammond on a rasping, trebly setting and it gives some of his lightning runs an agreeably spine-tingling quality. An outside producer might have served them better, though, and given Taylor a superior drum sound.

Baikida Carroll (born 1947) TRUMPET

**** **Shadows And Reflections** Soul Note 121023
    Carroll; Julius Hemphill (*as, ts*); Anthony Davis (*p*); Dave Holland (*b*); Pheeroan akLaff (*d*). 1/82.
***(*) **Door Of The Cage** Soul Note 121123
    Carroll; Erica Lindsay (*ts*); Steve Adegoke Colson (*p*); Santi Debriano (*b*); Pheeroan akLaff (*d*). 3/94.
These are high ratings for a musician who is not generally very well known. He grew up in St Louis and became a leading force in the Black Artists Group (BAG), sacrificing a good deal in professional terms to commit himself to radical community music-making when his bright chops and fertile ideas would surely have won him considerable prominence as a leader. As it was, Carroll didn't record on his own account until the late 1970s before he cut *Shadows And Reflections*, like so many of his advanced contemporaries, for the Italian IREC group, the umbrella organization for Soul Note and Black Saint.

    'This project was born out of sheer dedication.' It has repaid handsomely: Carroll has assembled a superb group of musicians. Hemphill is returning the favour of an important solo part on his *Dogon A.D.*, but it is Holland who emerges as the key player, rooting the music in something dark and tremulously substantial, great shadowy bass-lines that seem to push the two horns ever higher on 'Jahi Sundance Lake' and the long Pharoah Sanders-like 'Pyramids'.

    It's more than a decade before Carroll emerges as a leader again. *Door Of The Cage* is almost inevitably a slight disappointment after the sheer excellence of its predecessor, but it is still an enormously impressive record. Lindsay appears only once elsewhere in this book, with her own Candid record. Astonishingly, she hasn't recorded more; it's a rich, warm-toned sound with a hard edge when called for. It's called for less on this second record. In keeping with the times, Carroll favours a more line-driven, melodic approach and a softer, more plangent tone. There is still a brassy bite on numbers like 'King' and 'At Roi', which was originally written for Hemphill (whose chosen name was Roi Boye) in friendly revenge for some of the charts he gave the young trumpeter to play.

Paolo Carrus PIANO

*** **Sardegna Oltre Il Mare** Splasc(h) CDH 373-2

> Carrus; Paolo Fresu (*t, flhn*); Giorgio Baggiani (*flhn*); Pietro Tonolo (*ss*); Massimo Carboni (*ts*); Andrea Pinna (*launeddas*); Salvatore Majore (*b*); Billy Secchi (*d*). 7/90–1/92.

Carrus is a Sardinian whose principal aim here is to blend his local culture into a broader jazz perspective. The results are mixed, and perhaps it's unfair to say that the record works best when it's at its least obviously Sardinian. The main intrusion is the sound of the launeddas, the triple clarinet that makes a skirling, bagpipe-like addition to five of the ten tracks. It's a memorable noise, but since the talented Pinna is never actually allowed to fit in as part of the ensemble – he mostly plays march-like statements at some point in the tune when the other horns drop out – it can seem a little peculiar. The solo piece, 'Ballo In Minore', is certainly his most vivid appearance. Elsewhere, though, there is some beautifully sensitive post-bop, with Fresu in characteristically Milesian mode on the ballad 'No' and Tonolo appearing on one tune, 'Apri'. Carrus has taken care to let native melodies colour his writing, and if that hardly makes the record stand out, the players still have plenty to say.

Benny Carter (born 1907) ALTO SAXOPHONE, TRUMPET, CLARINET, VOCALS

***(*) **Benny Carter, 1929–1933** Classics 522

> Carter; Louis Bacon, Shad Collins, Leonard Davis, Bill Dillard, Frank Newton, Howard Scott, Bobby Stark, Rex Stewart (*t*); J. C. Higginbotham, Wilbur De Paris, George Washington, Dicky Wells (*tb*); Jimmy Harrison (*tb, v*); Howard Johnson (*as*); Don Redman (*as, v*); Wayman Carver (*as, f*); Chu Berry, Coleman Hawkins (*ts*); Horace Henderson, Red Rodriguez, Luis Russell, Fats Waller, Teddy Wilson (*p*); Benny Jackson, Lawrence Lucie (*g*); Richard Fullbright, Ernest Hill (*b*); John Kirby (*b, bb*); Cyrus St Clair (*bb*); Big Sid Catlett (*d, vib*); Kaiser Marshall, George Stafford (*d*); other personnel unidentified. 9/29–5/33.

***(*) **Benny Carter, 1933–1936** Classics 530

> Carter; Henry Allen (*t, v*); Dick Clark, Leonard Davis, Bill Dillard, Max Goldberg, Otis Johnson, Max Kaminsky, Eddie Mallory, Tommy McQuater, Irving Randolph, Howard Scott, Russell Smith, Duncan Whyte (*t*); Ted Heath, Keg Johnson, Benny Morton, Bill Mulraney, Floyd O'Brien, Wilbur De Paris, Fred Robinson, George Washington, Dicky Wells (*tb*); Howard Johnson, Andy McDevitt (*cl, as*); Wayman Carver (*cl, as, f*); Glyn Pacque, E. O. Pogson, Russell Procope, Ben Smith (*as*); Coleman Hawkins (*cl, ts*); Chu Berry, Buddy Featherstonehaugh, Johnny Russell, Ben Webster (*ts*); Pat Dodd, Red Rodriguez, Teddy Wilson (*p*); George Elliott, Clarence Holiday, Lawrence Lucie (*g*); Al Burke, Ernest Hill, Elmer James (*b*); Big Sid Catlett, Ronnie Gubertini, Walter Johnson (*d*); Charles Holland (*v*). 5/33–4/36.

***(*) **Benny Carter, 1936** Classics 541

> Carter; Max Goldberg, Tommy McQuater, Duncan Whyte (*t*); Leslie Thompson (*t, tb*); Lew Davis, Ted Heath, Bill Mulraney (*tb*); Freddie Gardner, Andy McDevitt (*cl, as*); E. O. Pogson (*as*); Buddy Featherstonehaugh (*ts*); Pat Dodd, Billy Munn, Gene Rodgers (*p*); George Elliott, Albert Harris, Ivor Mairants (*g*); Al Burke, Wally Morris (*b*); George Elrick, Ronnie Gubertini (*d*). 4, 6 & 10/36.

***(*) **Benny Carter, 1937–1939** Classics 552

> Carter; Jack Bulterman, Sam Dasberg, Rolf Goldstein, Tommy McQuater, Lincoln Mills, Joe Thomas, Leslie Thompson, George Van Helvoirt, George Woodlen, Cliff Woodridge (*t*); Jimmy Archey, Lew Davis, George Chisholm, Vic Dickenson, Bill Mulraney, Harry Van Oven, Marcel Thielemans (*tb*); Tyree Glenn (*tb, vib*); Freddy Gardner, Andy McDevitt, Andre Van der Ouderaa, Wim Poppink, Jimmy Williams (*cl, as*); Fletcher Allen, Carl Frye, James Powell, Louis Stephenson (*as*); Alix Combelle, Sal Doof, George Evans, Buddy Featherstonehaugh, Coleman Hawkins, Bertie King, Castor McCord, Ernie Powell, Jimmy Williams (*ts*); Eddie Heywood Jr, Freddy Johnson, Eddie Macauley, Nich De Roy, York De Souza (*p*); Albert Harris, Ulysses Livingston, Django Reinhardt, Ray Webb (*g*); Len Harrison, Alvis Hayes, Wally Morris, Jack Pet (*b*); Al Craig, Kees Kranenburg, Robert Montmarche, Henry Morrison (*d*). 1/37–6/39.

***(*) **The Various Facets Of A Genius** Black & Blue BLE 59.230

> Carter; Henry 'Red' Allen, Bill Coleman, Shad Collins, Sam Dasberg, Bill Dillard, Harry James, Max Kaminsky, Joe Smith, Russell Smith, Otis Johnson, Lincoln Mills, Irving Randolph, Sidney De Paris, Leonard Davis, Bobby Stark, Joe Thomas, Cliff Woodridge, Rolf Goldstein, George

Woodlen (*t*); Jimmy Archey, George Chisholm, Vic Dickenson, Harry Van Oven, Jimmy
Harrison, Benny Morton, Keg Johnson, Floyd O'Brien, Claude Jones, Gene Simon, Dicky
Wells, Wilbur De Paris, George Washington, Sandy Williams, Milton Robinson (*tb*); Tyree
Glenn (*tb, vib*); Wayman Carver, Howard Johnson, Don Redman (*cl, as*); André Ekyan, George
Dorsey, Jimmy Powell, Carl Frye, Dave Matthews, Ben Smith, Russell Procope, Louis
Stephenson (*as*); Chu Berry, Alix Combelle, Herschel Evans, Coleman Hawkins, Bertie King,
Ernie Powell, Jimmie Williams, Ted McCord, Babe Russin, Stafford Simon, Sammy Davis, Ben
Webster (*ts*); Stéphane Grappelli, Horace Henderson, Eddie Heywood, Freddy Johnson, Billy
Kyle, Luis Russell, Sonny White, Teddy Wilson (*p*); Fats Waller (*p, cel*); Lionel Hampton (*vib*);
Clarence Holiday, Ray Webb, Ulysses Livingston, Lawrence Lucie, Django Reinhardt (*g*);
Benny Jackson, Dave Wilborn (*bjo*); John Kirby (*tba, b*); Hayes Alvis, Len Harrison, Eugene
D'Hellemes, Ernest Hill, Elmer James, Billy Taylor (*b*); Tommy Benford, Big Sid Catlett, Cozy
Cole, Walter Johnson, Kaiser Marshall, Mezz Mezzrow, Robert Montmarche, Keg Purnell (*d*);
Nan Wynn (*v*). 11/29–5/40.

**** Benny Carter, 1940–1941 Classics 631

Carter; Emmett Berry, Doc Cheatham, Bill Coleman, Roy Eldridge, Jonah Jones, Lincoln Mills,
Sidney De Paris, Rostelle Reese, Russell Smith, Nathaniel Williams (*t*); Jimmy Archey, Joe
Britton, Vic Dickenson, John McConnell, Benny Morton, Milton Robinson, Madison Vaughan
(*tb*); Eddie Barefield, George Dorsey, Chauncey Haughton, Ernie Purce, Bill White (*as*); George
James (*as, bs*); George Auld, Alfred Gibson, Coleman Hawkins, George Irish, Fred Mitchell,
Ernie Powell, Stafford Simon, Fred Williams (*ts*); Sonny White (*p*); Bernard Addison, Everett
Barksdale, William Lewis, Ulysses Livingston, Herb Thomas (*g*); Hayes Alvis, Charles Drayton,
John Kirby, Wilson Myers, Ted Sturgis (*b*); Big Sid Catlett, J. C. Heard, Yank Porter, Keg
Purnell, Berisford Shepherd, Al Taylor (*d*); Roy Felton, Maxine Sullivan, Joe Turner, The Mills
Brothers (*v*). 5/40–10/41.

By 1930, Carter was being widely recognized as a gifted young arranger and multi-instrumentalist.
Carter's charts, like his playing, are characteristically open-textured and softly bouncing, but seldom
lightweight; though he had a particular feel for the saxophone section, as is often noted, and he
pioneered a more modern approach to big-band reeds, his gifts extend throughout the orchestra. As a
soloist, he developed in a direction rather different from that of Johnny Hodges, who explored a darker
register and a less buoyant sensibility.

Carter's earliest recordings with the Chocolate Dandies (the band included Coleman Hawkins) and with
McKinney's Cotton Pickers put considerable emphasis on his multi-instrumentalism. Set against trom-
bonist Quentin Jackson's surprisingly effective vocals, he sounds poised and elegant – the essential
Carter qualities – whatever his horn; and two takes each of 'Do You Believe In Love At First Sight' and
'Wrap Your Troubles In Dreams' demonstrate how beautifully crafted and custom-made his choruses
habitually were.

None of these performances is included on the Classics format which is, on the face of it, rather
surprising, since Volumes 1 and 2 include sides Carter recorded with Spike Hughes's Negro Orchestra.
In the early 1930s Carter's band had been increasingly identified as a proving ground for young talent,
and the number of subsequently eminent names appearing in Carter sections increases as the decade
advances. In 1936 the urbane young American took up a post as staff arranger for the BBC Dance
Orchestra, then under Henry Hall. The London period saw some excellent recording with the local
talent, including 'Swingin' At Maida Vale', and there are two separate Vocalion sessions with Elisabeth
Welch, the first yielding the classic 'When Lights Are Low', the later and better superb arrangements of
'Poor Butterfly' and 'The Man I Love'.

Later sets with Kai Ewans' orchestra and a variety of European bands are less striking, perhaps because
after five well-filled discs, Carter's particular mastery does, unjustifiably, begin to pall. There is little
tension in a Carter solo, which is presented bright and fresh like a polished apple, and his seemingly
effortless approach is rather hard to square with a new construction of jazz improvisation which came in
with bebop. However, these sides and those following on in the early 1940s are significant because, for
much of the next two and a half decades, Carter concentrated on lucrative film music and small groups.

The personnels to the Black and Blue compilation may have a rather redundant, usual-suspects air, but
this is actually a very valuable anthology of material that would sit very well with *All Of Me* (below) for
anyone who didn't want a completist shelf-load of Carter. Nothing, oddly, from 1936, but there is a
Coleman Hawkins Jam Band session from Paris in the following year, with the Hot Club stars present,
and dates under Hamp's and Teddy Wilson's leadership, recorded the following year. A track each from
the Cotton Pickers and Carter's Chocolate Dandies, one from Spike Hughes's Negro Orchestra, and so
on, right through to the Gentlemen of Jazz package in 1940. Good value for money.

*** When Lights Are Low Conifer/Happy Days CDHD 131

Carter; Max Goldberg, Tommy McQuater, Duncan Whyte (*t*); Leslie Thompson (*t, tb*); Lew

Davis, Ted Heath, Bill Mulraney (*tb*); Freddie Gardner, Andy McDevitt (*cl, as*); E. O. Pogson
(*as*); Buddy Featherstonehaugh (*ts*); Pat Dodd, Billy Munn, Gene Rodgers (*p*); George Elliott,
Albert Harris, Ivor Mairants (*g*); Al Burke, Wally Morris (*b*); George Elrick, Ronnie Gubertini
(*d*). 4, 6 & 10/36.

A useful abstract of the London sessions Carter made for Vocalion. Conifer have even managed to
unearth one track – a rejected take of 'Gin And Jive' – not covered by Classics' completism. Oddly,
though, they skip two better tracks, 'Scandal In A Flat' and 'Accent On Swing', from the same session.
Carter returned to 'Gin And Jive' in January 1937 and cut a vastly superior version with essentially the
same band. Swings and roundabouts again, but the Conifer reissue will appeal to anyone who has a
particular interest in the development of hot music in Britain in the 1930s.

*** Devil's Holiday JSP JSPCD 331

Carter; Dick Clark, Shad Collins, Leonard Davis, Bill Dillard, Freddie Goodman, Ben Gusick,
Otis Johnson, Reunald Jones, Max Kaminsky, Eddie Mallory, Chelsea Quealey, Irving
Randolph, Russell Smith (*t*); J. C. Higginbotham, Floyd O'Brien, Wilbur De Paris, Keg
Johnson, Benny Morton, Fred Robinson, George Washington (*tb*); Mezz Mezzrow (*cl, as*);
Howard Johnson, Glyn Paque, Russell Procope, Ben Smith (*as*); Wayman Carver (*as, f*); Chu
Berry, Bud Freeman, Johnny Russell, Ben Webster (*ts*); Nicholas Rodriguez, Willie 'The Lion'
Smith, Teddy Wilson (*p*); Clayton Duerr, Clarence Holiday, Lawrence Lucie (*g*); Pops Foster,
Ernest Hill, Elmer James, John Kirby (*b*); Walter Johnson, Jack Maisel, Chick Webb (*d*); Big Sid
Catlett (*d, vib*); Charles Holland (*v*). 3–12/34.

The excellent 1933 sessions with the Chocolate Dandies and Carter's own orchestra are already available
on Classics and Charly, as are the December 1934 sessions. A useful addition to these well-transferred
sides are the tracks recorded in May 1934 with Mezz Mezzrow (who is alleged to have played drums on
the earlier 'Krazy Kapers'). These represent a third of the album and will be useful for collectors, with
fine performances on 'Dissonance' and 'Old Fashioned Love'. Otherwise, nothing to recommend this
over the items discussed above.

**** **All Of Me** Bluebird ND 83000

Carter; Henry 'Red' Allen, Emmett Berry, Pete Candoli, Don Fagerquist, Maury Harris, Doc
Cheatham, Robert Cheek, Richard Clark, Neal Hefti, Max Kaminsky, Reunald Jones, Chelsea
Quealey, Eddie Mallory, Lincoln Mills, Russell Smith, Sidney De Paris, Rostelle Reese, Jonah
Jones, Bobby Williams (*t*); Edgar Battle (*t, vtb*); John Haughton, Robert Horton, Eddie
Durham, Vic Dickenson, Jimmy Archey, Joe Britton, Pete Carpenter, John McConnell, J. C.
Higginbotham, Joe Howard, Benny Morton, Floyd O'Brien, George Roberts, Milt Robinson,
Frank Rosolino, Madison Vaughan (*tb*); Tyree Glenn (*tb, vib*); Castor McCord, Artie Shaw
(*cl*); George Dorsey, Ernie Purce, Eddie Barefield, Chauncey Haughton, Glyn Paque, Stanley
Payne, Bill White (*as*); George James (*as, bs*); George Irish, Fred Mitchell, Bud Freeman,
Alfred Gibson, Stafford Simon, Ben Webster, Johnny Russell, Fred Williams, Ernie Powell,
Lucky Thompson (*ts*); Robert Lawson (*bs*); Reginald Beane, Dodo Marmarosa, Willie 'The
Lion' Smith, Sonny White, John Williams, Teddy Wilson (*p*); Arnold Adams, Danny Barker,
Everett Barksdale, William Lewis, Barney Kessel, Jimmy Shirley, Herb Thomas (*g*); Charles
Drayton, Hayes Alvis, John Kirby, Louis Thompson, Milt Hinton, Red Callender, Red
Mitchell, Joe Mondragon, Billy Taylor (*b*); J. C. Heard, Jack Mills, Keg Purnell, Shep
Shepherd, Alvin Stoller, Al Taylor, Chick Webb (*d*); Maxine Sullivan, Ethel Waters (*v*); strings.
5/34–3/59.

Not quite 'all' of him, of course, but a tremendously valuable synopsis of perhaps the most creative
phase of Carter's long and multi-faceted career. With the exception of an early and not terribly interesting '35th And Calumet' with Mezz Mezzrow's group, and a 'Sheik Of Araby' with Willie Bryant, all the
material comes from the period after Carter's return Stateside. The greater bulk of the disc is taken up
with the material he made in 1940 and 1941 for RCA Bluebird.

'All Of Me' was the first tune cut at the session of 19 November 1940, and it's one of his finest
performances, a supremely elegant statement by a master craftsman. 'Cuddle Up, Huddle Up' and
'Babalu', recorded a couple of months later, are more prosaic, but the band is engagingly eccentric, and
a step ahead of the April 1941 line-up which recorded two vocal tracks with Maxine Sullivan.

Serious collectors of Carter marginalia will be interested in two tracks which have not, to our knowledge, ever been issued elsewhere: 'Ev'ry Goodbye Ain't' from January 1941 and a first take of 'Ill Wind'
from October of that year. There are a couple of other things which have appeared only on French
RCA releases. One-off tracks from sessions with Ethel Waters (in good voice), Artie Shaw and Lucky
Thompson add a bit of variety, and there are four selections from a 1959 soundtrack session for the
television series, *M Squad*, worth including for what is apparently Carter's only recorded solo on
soprano saxophone, conductor Stanley Wilson's composition, 'Lonely Beat'. Atmospheric, but not
earth-shaking.

All in all, though, this is a most worthwhile compilation, judiciously selected, effectively but not intrusively remastered, and packaged with Bluebird's usual decent attention to detail.

*** **Groovin' High In LA, 1946** Hep CD 15
Carter; Miles Davis, Fred Trainer (?), Calvin Strickland (?); Walter Williams (?), Ira Pettiford (?) (*t*); Al Grey, Charley Johnson, Johnny Morris, Candy Ross (*tb*); Willard Brown, Joe Epps (*as*); Harold Clark, Bumps Myers (*ts*); Bob Graettinger (*bs*); Sonny White (*g*); James Cannady (*b*); Thomas Moultrie (*b*); Percy Brice (*d*). 7/46.

Carter returned to the United States in 1938, by which time the big-band era was well under way. His sterling talents seem to have appealed more to other musicians than to the public at large and, as the war progressed, he switched coasts.

Metronome concluded around this time that Carter's bands died so slowly that *rigor mortis* had no chance to set in. From the point of view of the dance floor, he offered little enough, but his arrangements have more than survived transfer to unforgiving CD, and there is some astonishing musicianship.

Miles Davis appears on the Hep compilation of Armed Forces Radio Service Jubilee transcriptions, a disc shared with the West Coast bands of Wilbert Branco, Gerald Wilson and Jimmy Mundy. Perhaps of greater historical than musical interest, these capture a very specific moment in jazz, the final flowering of the big swing bands before economic constraints began to bite and before bop took over the running.

**** **Benny Carter, 1928–1952** RCA ND 89761
Similar to sessions listed above. 28–52.

This is probably the best single-option item available for the non-specialist collector. A generous selection of 32 tracks covers material for Ethel Waters and Una Mae Carlisle, as well as for Charlie Johnson's Paradise Orchestra and Mezz Mezzrow's group of the early 1930s. Despite these, there are obviously very substantial overlaps with the Classics material above, but the transfers are very much cleaner and more faithful to Carter's limpid sound. Quite properly, there's an emphasis on Benny's own orchestra of 1940 and 1941, an outfit with the likes of Doc Cheatham, Sidney de Paris and Vic Dickenson in its ranks. 'When Lights Are Low' and 'All Of Me' are classic performances by any standard. Strangely, perhaps, only one previously unissued item, an oddly drab and below-par 'Georgia On My Mind' from the insecurely identified orchestra of 1952.

**** **3, 4, 5: The Verve Small Group Sessions** Verve 849395
Carter; Don Abney, Oscar Peterson, Teddy Wilson (*p*); Herb Ellis (*g*); Ray Brown, George Duvivier (*b*); Louie Bellson, Jo Jones, Bobby White (*d*).

***(*) **Cosmopolite: The Oscar Peterson Sessions** Verve 521 673
Carter; Bill Harris (*tb*); Oscar Peterson (*p*); Herb Ellis, Barney Kessel (*g*); Ray Brown (*b*); J. C. Heard, Buddy Rich, Bobby White (*d*). 9 & 12/52, 9 & 11/54.

Irritatingly, no exact dates are provided for the sterling *3, 4, 5* sessions for Norman Granz's label. The trio sides with Teddy Wilson and Jo Jones are seeing the light of day only after 40 years in the vaults; mysteriously, because a similar session with Art Tatum and Louie Bellson *was* released. Far from wondering at the absence of a bass player (and Wilson wasn't one of the big left-hand men), one might almost wish that the under-recorded Jones had been left out altogether, so bright is the interplay between alto and piano. Wilson is supreme on 'June In January' and the Parker/Sanicola/Sinatra 'This Love Of Mine', a perfect vehicle for Carter's sinuous para-bop phrasing.

An 'audio disclaimer' pointing out 22 seconds of 'slight wow and warbling' on 'Moonglow' has to be considered somewhat diversionary, for the music on the middle quartet section really isn't up to the rest of the album. Originally released as *Moonglow: Love Songs By Benny Carter And His Orchestra* (sic.), the material is a bit lame, however beautifully played.

The final three tracks, also unreleased, come from a super-session with rising star, Oscar Peterson. Again, the drummer – added for the date – makes very little mark on the music, which includes the intriguing 'Don't You Think', written by Stuff Smith. Despite some reservations about the middle tracks, this makes a superb introduction to Carter the player (there's not a single writing credit) at a fine stage in his distinguished career.

Cosmopolite brings together material from the LPs *Benny Carter Plays Pretty*, *Alto Saxes* and *New Jazz Sounds*, as well as the one whose title has been recycled. They are by no means as compelling as the earlier reissue, but there are, inevitably, some precious moments, as on 'The Song Is You' with trombonist Harris, Ellis, Brown and Rich, a lovely, centred performance with not a hint of strain.

Together these records cover an important period and association in Carter's career. Only the first is obviously essential, but Carter fans will be satisfied only with both.

**** **Jazz Giant** Original Jazz Classics OJC 167
Carter; Frank Rosolino (*tb*); Ben Webster (*ts*); André Previn, Jimmy Rowles (*p*); Barney Kessel (*g*); Leroy Vinnegar (*b*); Shelly Manne (*d*). 6, 7 & 10/57, 4/58.

*** **Swingin' The Twenties** Original Jazz Classics OJC 339
    Carter; Earl Hines (*p*); Leroy Vinnegar (*b*); Shelly Manne (*d*). 11/58.
Carter's trumpet playing was still sounding remarkably adept at this stage; it tailed off a bit in later years, though he was still able to maintain what is always thought of as the most difficult instrumental 'double' right into the 1990s. The material on *Swingin'* is generally pretty bland, though 'A Monday Date' and 'Laugh, Clown, Laugh' uncover some interesting harmonic wrinkles. The rhythm section was one of the best money could buy at the time, nicely balancing old and new. *Jazz Giant* is one of Carter's best small-group records, full of imagination and invention, and the interchanges with Webster are classic. Originally released on Contemporary, it's very much in line with that label's philosophy of easy swing. The CD of *Swingin'* includes some interesting alternative takes.

**** **The King** Pablo 2310768
    Carter; Milt Jackson (*vib*); Joe Pass (*g*); Tommy Flanagan (*p*); John B. Williams (*b*); Jake Hanna (*d*). 2/76.
Jackson is another brilliant improviser whose mellifluous approach has led detractors to suspect him of giving short weight. Here again, he underlines his genius with a dozen blues choruses of immense sophistication. The closing D flat blues opens up the kind of harmonic territory on which Carter and Flanagan both thrive, and the set ends with a ringing affirmation. Williams is rather anonymous and Pass seems to miscue slightly on a couple of faster ensembles. Otherwise hard to fault.

*** **Carter Gillespie Inc** Original Jazz Classics OJC 682
    Carter; Dizzy Gillespie (*t*); Joe Pass (*g*); Tommy Flanagan (*p*); Al McKibbon (*b*); Mickey Roker (*d*). 4/76.
***(*) **Wonderland** Pablo 2310922
    Carter; Harry 'Sweets' Edison (*t*); Eddie 'Lockjaw' Davis (*ts*); Ray Bryant (*p*); Milt Hinton (*b*); Grady Tate (*d*). 11/76.
Remarkable to think that as long ago as 1976 Carter was approaching his seventieth birthday. There's a slightly ponderous, aldermanic quality to the AGM with Diz, much polite deference, some cheerful banter but not a great deal of classic music. He sounds in better form on the relaxed *Wonderland*, ably accompanied by Edison (Carter let others handle the brass duties by this stage) and an uncharacteristically cool Lockjaw Davis. 'Misty' was to remain a favourite, played with curious emphases and a wry unsentimentality.

***(*) **Montreux '77** Original Jazz Classics OJC 374
    Carter; Ray Bryant (*p*); Niels-Henning Orsted-Pedersen (*b*); Jimmie Smith (*d*). 7/77.
***(*) **Live And Well In Japan** Original Jazz Classics OJC 736
    Carter; Cat Anderson, Joe Newman (*t*); Britt Woodman (*tb*); Budd Johnson (*ts*); Cecil Payne (*bs*); Nat Pierce (*p*); Mundell Lowe (*g*); George Duvivier (*b*); Harold Jones (*d*). 77.
1977 was a monster year at Montreux, and a good deal of the music performed over the main weekend has been preserved on live Pablo releases (and subsequently on OJC). The Carter set is one of the best of them. Though his soloing here doesn't quite match up to some choruses on a Count Basie jam from the following day, 'Three Little Words', 'Body And Soul' and 'On Green Dolphin Street' are absolutely sterling. The band swings comfortably and NHOP plays delightful countermelodies on 'In A Mellow Tone'.

    Turning seventy, Carter seemed eager to dismiss biblical estimates of an average lifespan by playing like a man half his age. In an all-star line-up in Japan (a country he has come to love and where he is treated like a minor deity), he trades superbly crafted licks with all and sundry. The sound is rather cavernous but there's great atmosphere, and the playing makes up for all other deficiencies.

*** **Summer Serenade** Storyville STCD 4047
    Carter; Kenny Drew (*p*); Jesper Lundgaard (*b*); Ed Thigpen (*d*); Richard Boone (*d*). 8/80.
Carter's small-group encounters, like this Scandinavian session, were a well-polished act; but it takes a certain genius to make the umpteenth version of quite banal tunes like 'Back Home In Indiana' and 'When Lights Are Low' sound quite as freshly minted as Carter does here. The rhythm section is admirably professional and Boone holds his wheesht for all but one track, which is all to the good.

(*) **The Best Of Benny Carter Pablo PACD 2405
    Carter; Cat Anderson, Harry 'Sweets' Edison, Joe Newman (*t*); Britt Woodman (*tb*); Eddie 'Lockjaw' Davis, Budd Johnson (*ts*); Cecil Payne (*bs*); Ray Bryant (*p*); Mundell Lowe (*g*); George Duvivier, Milt Hinton, Niels-Henning Orsted-Pedersen (*b*); Harold Jones, Jimmie Smith, Grady Tate (*d*).
Odd and uninspired choice of material. Better to stick to the original Pablos.

*** **Skyline Drive And Towards** Phontastic PHONTCD 9305
    Carter; Jan Allan (*t*); Arne Domnérus (*as*); Plas Johnson (*ts*); Jerome Richardson (*ts, ss*); Putte

Wickman (*cl*); Bengt Hallberg (*p*); Rune Gustafsson (*g*); Georg Riedel (*b*); Magnus Persson (*d*); other personnel. 1929–39, 1982.

This is essentially a Swedamerican All Stars record with eight early tracks pasted on to make up a reasonably proportioned CD. The 1982 material is smoothly professional and as good as Carter is solo to solo. The archive stuff, which includes 'I'd Love It' by McKinney's Cotton Pickers and 'I'm In The Mood For Swing' under Hamp's leadership, may prove useful for anyone who hasn't already got some early Carter. Others may feel that this isn't distributed quite right and decide to pass.

***(*) A Gentleman And His Music Concord CCD 4285
Carter; Joe Wilder (*t, flhn*); Scott Hamilton (*ts*); Ed Bickert (*g*); Gene Harris (*p*); John Clayton Jr (*b*); Jimmie Smith (*d*). 8/85.

A wonderfully urbane set which puts Carter in the company of the young traditionalist, Scott Hamilton, whose tone and relaxed inventiveness are perfectly in keeping with Carter's own. No real surprises; just a generously proportioned album of first-rate jazz music, professionally performed and recorded.

***(*) Meets Oscar Peterson Pablo 2310926
Carter; Oscar Peterson (*p*); Joe Pass (*g*); Dave Young (*b*); Martin Drew (*d*). 86

How much more interesting this might have been as a duo. Even allowing for some melodic breaks from Pass, the rhythm backings are bland and undynamic enough to seem superfluous. 'Baubles, Bangles And Beads' moves at the gentle lope both men seem to prefer nowadays, and Peterson's statement of the theme is about as straightforward as he's ever been.

***(*) In The Mood For Swing Musicmasters 65001-2
Carter; Dizzy Gillespie (*t*); Sir Roland Hanna (*p*); Howard Alden (*g*); George Mraz (*b*); Louie Bellson (*d*). 11/87.

A pally but still communicative set of gently paced tunes, designed to let the four main soloists – Carter, Gillespie, Alden and Hanna – stretch out at their leisure. There's nothing self-indulgent about it. Carter's as crisp as ever, though Diz goes a bit OTT on 'South Side Samba'. Good, warm sound.

**(*) Central City Sketches Musicmasters 65030-2
Carter; All-American Jazz Orchestra. 87.

The least attractive of the Limelights. With the exception of the ballad, 'People', which became 'People Time' on *My Man Benny*, below, the writing is pretty drab, and the playing sounds too well-oiled to be engaging.

*** My Kind Of Trouble Pablo 2310935
Carter; Art Hillery (*p*); Joe Pass (*g*); Andy Simpkins (*b*); Ronnie Bedford (*d*). 88.

Disappointing only because the band is. The rhythms never quite cohere and on 'Berkeley Bounce' and 'Gee, Baby, Ain't I Good To You', Carter appears to be leading the count rather than playing on top of it. Nevertheless, he is in finer voice than seems decent for a man entering his eighties and well past his fiftieth year of climbing on and off bandstands.

*** Cooking At Carlos I Musicmasters 65033-2
Carter; Richard Wyands (*p*); Lisle Atkinson (*b*); Al Harewood (*d*). 10/88.

Record-shop staff are well used to punters coming in with queries along the lines of: 'I really liked *Live / Blues / Round Midnight / Whatever At Carlos I*. Can you tell me if volume two is out yet?' Carlos 1 was actually a much-loved New York City jazz club, one of the few beacons of the music during the '80s. Lest *Cookin'* suggests something like boiling intensity, it might be more accurate to characterize Carter's visit as a slow simmer. His playing on 'All The Things You Are' and 'Key Largo' is almost statesmanly, and the excellent rhythm section pay him considerable respect throughout, relaxing the tempo, almost always easing back on the throttle after Wyands, bursting with ideas as always, has taken a solo spot. Carter gets out his trumpet for the final 'Time For The Blues'.

*** My Man Benny, My Man Phil Musicmasters 65036-2
Carter; Phil Woods (*as, cl*); Chris Neville (*p*); George Mraz (*b*); Kenny Washington (*d*). 11/89.

Not quite the mutual admiration society that the two title-pieces might suggest. Carter's lyric tribute has to be heard to be believed, though: 'Adolphe Sax / Before he made that horn / Knew some day, somewhere, / A Phil Woods would be born', and so on. Musically, there's some great stuff. Carter dusts off his trumpet again, Woods his woefully underexposed clarinet, for 'We Were In Love', and Carter sticks with brass for his own 'People Time'. Two takes of 'Just A Mood' give a sense of how *happy* a session this obviously was.

***(*) All That Jazz – Live At Princeton Musicmasters 65059-2
Carter; Clark Terry (*t, flhn, v*); Kenny Barron (*p*); Rufus Reid (*b*); Kenny Washington (*d*); Billy Hill (*v*). 11/90.

Carter first played at Princeton University in 1928, as a member of the Fletcher Henderson Orchestra. In the late 1970s, he became a visiting professor and was awarded an honorary doctorate. This 1990 concert was treated as a triumphant homecoming. Thelonious Monk's 'Hackensack' was played cold, after Clark Terry hummed the melody to Carter as they walked onstage. The band get in behind and off they all go. 'I'm Beginning To See The Light' and 'Misty' were more familiar themes to the saxophonist, but he gives the Garner/Burke tune a curious off-balance feel that is unexpectedly witty. 'Now's The Time' is renowned as a Parker tune, though the theme is known to be much older. Carter delves down into its roots and comes up with something that seems to unite swing and bop approaches. Terry growls round him like a friendly dog pretending to be tough. Most Carter enthusiasts would have willingly dispensed with the services of Billy Hill, who comes on for the last four tunes. The title-track has some vocals from the two horn men but the charm is strictly limited.

***(*) **Harlem Renaissance** Musicmasters 65080-2 2CD
    Carter; John Eckert, Richard Grant, Virgil Jones, Michael Mossman (*t*); Eddie Bert, Curtis Hasselbring, Benny Powell, Dennis Wilson (*tb*); Frank Wess, Ralph Bowen (*as, f*); Loren Schoenberg, Jeff Rupert (*ts*); Danny Bank (*bs, f*); Chris Neville (*p*); Remo Palmieri (*g*); Lisle Atkinson (*b*); Kenny Washington (*d*); Rutgers University Orchestra. 2/92.

Picture-in-the-attic time now, surely? Carter's level of energy is, for a man in his ninth decade, quite astonishing. This double-CD is a recording of a major concert he gave at the invitation of the Rutgers Institute of Jazz Studies. To celebrate the 85th birthday, Carter was commissioned to write a new piece. Suggesting a combination of jazz big band and chamber orchestra, he actually set about *two* pieces with the twin themes of Japan and Harlem.

The 'Tales Of The Rising Sun Suite' is conventionally pictorial and slightly wan in colour, with a few interesting shapes breaking through on 'Samurai Song' and 'Chow Chow', the last two pieces. The 'Harlem Renaissance Suite' is more interesting. Harking back to the burgeoning black culture of the 1920s, it takes up the challenge of Paul Whiteman's long-discredited 'symphonic jazz' (James P. Johnson worked in a similar vein) and the Carnegie Hall concerts of James Reece Europe's celebrated band. To his credit, Carter has done something more than simply drape a few solos over coathanger themes. The suite has a good deal of inner consistency. What it probably lacks is the bustle and frenetic activity one associates with the period he is celebrating. Here, undoubtedly, the orchestra hold him back a bit, defeating even his peerless arranging skills. Though the strings and woodwinds are integrated into the main fabric of the piece (rather than serving merely as a backdrop, as in most 'with strings' projects), the execution is rather lifeless.

Carter himself solos with a good deal of pep, and most fans will prefer the first disc which has him in front of the big band, grazing down a menu of attractive originals (his own 'Vine Street Rumble', Sao Paolo' and the beautiful 'Evening Star', which prompts the most coherent solo of the disc), with a couple of standards thrown in for good measure. A set of two halves, as the football commentators say.

**** **Elegy In Blue** MusicMasters 65115
    Carter; Harry 'Sweets' Edison (*t*); Cedar Walton (*p*); Mundell Lowe (*g*); Ray Brown (*b*); Jeff Hamilton (*d*). 5/94.

Check out the date. This is a man who has been making fine music for a biblical lifespan, still playing gloriously lyrical jazz. On this record, he's keeping the sort of company that almost guarantees quality. There's still a fiery dynamism to Sweets' trumpeting, and the rhythm section is not inclined to defer to age and let things slip. Hamilton has a deceptively easy but insistent swing, and Lowe is a very under-rated musician, who has spent large periods of time away from jazz proper but who always comes back fired up with ideas. BC remains the focus, though, quoting Hodges on 'Good Queen Bess' and 'Prelude To A Kiss', sounding dogged and unflustered on 'Blue Monk' and touchingly unsentimental on the closing title-piece. A beautiful record that would grace any jazz collection.

Betty Carter (born 1930) VOCALS

***(*) **I Can't Help It** Impulse! GRP 11142
    Carter; Ray Copeland, Kenny Dorham (*t*); Melba Liston (*tb*); Gigi Gryce, Jimmy Powell (*as*); Benny Golson (*ts*); Jerome Richardson (*ts, f, bcl*); Sahib Shihab (*bs*); Wynton Kelly (*p*); Sam Jones, Peck Morrison (*b*); Specs Wright (*d*). 2/58, 8/60.
**** **At The Village Vanguard** Verve 519 851
    As above. 5/70.
  **** **The Audience With Betty Carter** Verve 835684 2CD
    Carter; John Hicks (*p*); Curtis Lundy (*b*); Kenny Washington (*d*). 79.

**** **Look What I Got** Verve 835661
    Carter; Don Braden (*ts*); Stephen Scott (*p*); Michael Bowie, Ira Coleman (*b*); Winard Harper, Lewis Nash (*d*). 88.
**** **Droppin' Things** Verve 843991
    Carter; Freddie Hubbard (*t*); Craig Handy (*ts*); Geri Allen, Marc Cary (*p*); Tarus Mateen (*b*); Gregory Hutchinson (*d*). 5 & 6/90.
**** **It's Not About The Melody** Verve 513870
    Carter; Craig Handy (*ts*); Cyrus Chestnut, John Hicks, Mulgrew Miller (*p*); Christian McBride, Ariel J. Roland (*b*); Lewis Nash, Clarence Penn, Jeff Tain Watts (*d*). 92.
**** **Feed The Fire** Verve 523 600
    Carter; Geri Allen (*p*); Dave Holland (*b*); Jack DeJohnette (*d*). 10/93.
Billie Holiday once said that she didn't feel like she was singin', she felt like she was playin' a horn. So, too, with Betty Carter, who transcended the 'bop vocalist' tag and created a style which combined the fluent, improvisational grace of an alto saxophone with an uncanny accuracy of diction. Even when her weighting of a lyric is almost surreal, its significance is utterly explicit and often sarcastically subversive. The latter quality has allowed her to skate on the thin ice of quite banal standard material, much of which has acquired a veneer of 'seriousness' from nowadays being heard only as instrumentals; 'Body And Soul' is the obvious example. Carter can sound remarkably dead in a studio, as on the ballad duet with Geri Allen on the recent *Droppin' Things*; compare their version of 'If I Should Lose You' on the live *Feed the Fire*.

Because she needs a crowd to bounce off just as much as she needs rhythmically and harmonically subtle accompanists (and she recruits only the best), the title of *The Audience With Betty Carter* is a multiple pun. She works the room with consummate skill, sliding from the slightly squeaky *faux-naïf* mannerisms that prompted Lionel Hampton to call her 'Betty Bebop' (a less condescending and more accurate nickname than she liked to acknowledge) to soaring climbs up off the bottom that wouldn't disgrace Sarah Vaughan. Her feminism is explicit not so much in the choice or creation of material ('30 Years' on *Droppin' Things* is a relatively untypical original) as in the way she subverts all expectations about female singers, and about women in the bebop business, where they occupied a notoriously marginal and subservient role.

One important index of Carter's independence was her desire to make and issue records on her own terms. *At The Village Vanguard* originally appeared on her own Bet-Car label, released at a time when jazz was profoundly embattled. It did no better than the beautifully arranged sessions on *I Can't Help It*, most of which appeared on the small Texan gospel label, Peacock. Only in recent times, with the leverage to insist on full creative responsibility, has she been able to find a secure major-label niche. The recent Verves are certainly smoother and more sophisticated than the earlier discs but, just as *I Can't Help It* doesn't lack subtlety (*By The Bend Of The River*' is, at just over two minutes, glorious), so too the later stuff maintains a high energy level. Again, though, the better things tend to be the live cuts rather than the more thought-out and prefabricated studio performances.

Carter's trios are always vital to her conception. The wild opening to 'Girl Talk' on *Finally* and virtually the whole of *Feed The Fire* offer perfect examples of how she breaks up the accepted conventions of singer-and-accompaniment. The arrival of Hubbard and Handy on *Droppin' Things* whistles in a whole new ball game, and her diction changes yet again, probably subconsciously. Handy also makes two brief appearances on *It's Not About The Melody*, just edged by the October 1993 set from London's Royal Festival Hall as the most attractive of the post-*Audience* crop. Interestingly, he's featured on two tunes associated with another saxophonist, Bobby Watson. Watson's wife Pamela wrote 'The Love We Had Yesterday' and he's been featured on the Hicks theme, 'Naima's Love Song', to which Carter adds her own lyric. She has two other songs on the set: 'Make Him Believe' and 'Dip Bag' are funny, sly, knowing, funky, unpretentiously feminist, all the things she is.

Above are some of the finest vocal jazz albums ever made, and everyone should give at least a couple of them a sympathetic airing.

James Carter (born 1969) ALTO SAXOPHONE, TENOR SAXOPHONE, BARITONE SAXOPHONE

***(*) **JC On The Set** DIW 875
    Carter; Craig Taborn (*p*); Jaribu Shahid (*b*); Tani Tabbal (*d*). 4/93.
*** **Jurassic Classics** DIW/Columbia 478612
    As above. 94.
**** **The Real Quietstorm** Atlantic 782742
    As above, except add Dave Holland (*b*); Leon Parker (*d*). 10 & 11/94.
No messing. Jackets are doffed. Music is played. Street clothes are re-assumed. Immense promise in three shifts. If much less was written and heard about Carter than about contemporaries like the much-

touted Josh Redman, that has already begun to change. Carter is the kind of player who seems to emerge fully formed, like his solos. These have a breathtaking onrush, whether they are fierce altissimo raves or tender ballads. The young Detroiter's appearances with the Tough Young Tenors gave only a one-dimensional impression of his skills. These three records reveal him to be a mature, thoughtful artist who will surely be one of the most signficant saxophone players of his talented generation.

The vivid, almost explosive sound is strongly reminiscent of Frank Lowe (with whom he has recorded) and similarly draws sustenance from the work of earlier giants like Chu Berry and Don Byas. The choice of a Byas tune, 'Worried And Blue', on the debut recording is a sign that he's making his own choices. No less intriguing, he chooses to cover Sun Ra's 'Hour Of Parting' (how often have other musicians tackled it?), the little-known Texan John Hardee's 'Lunatic', and Duke's 'Caravan' and 'Sophisticated Lady', which highlight his Carney-influenced baritone work. The opening bars of his own 'Blues For A Nomadic Princess' suggest some long-forgotten by-blow of Ellington's; the climax salutes Coltrane and Ayler.

Nothing cumbersome about *Jurassic Classics*, but it does sound like a record too soon and, though the laddish reworking of Ellington, Monk, Rollins and Coltrane material is highly professional and often very stirring, it doesn't sound like anything more than leavings from the first record, despite being made some months later. Carter has kept that band together and given them the most constructive brief. None are quite as seasoned as he, and so none receives quite the coverage, as seems appropriate at this stage. Though they are replaced on a couple of tracks by Holland and Parker, their appearance on the most recent record gives every earnest of rapid development, certainly in the context of this unit.

Carter is already an accomplished multi-instrumentalist: his rehearsal room is allegedly full of bass saxes, clarinets and other horns. What's striking, on the strength of the three deployed here, is how much like himself he sounds on all of them, even when he's explicitly paying homage to saxophonists of the past. David Murray has made it easier for young guys to work in this vein and on *The Real Quietstorm* Carter chalks up a set that has the dimensions and the calm intensity of a Murray album. Over nine tracks, he uses soprano (twice), alto, tenor, baritone (twice), bass clarinet and bass flute, the last of these in a wonderful setting, 'Ballad For A Doll', with Holland creaking atmospherically behind and Parker just playing cymbal. Significantly or not, the two most substantial performances are 'The Stevedore's Serenade', an unexpectedly beautiful tenor monologue, and the cringingly titled 'Intimacy Of My Woman's Beautiful Eyes' on alto. However, there is no sign that he uses alternative horns just to show them off. The opening and closing baritone duets with Taborn on 'Round Midnight' and with Shahid on 'Eventide' are gloriously evocative, though it was a mistake to kick the album off with the old Monk groaner. A splendid record on a new label; it will be interesting to see what the new post-Ertegun Atlantic makes of him.

John Carter (1929–91) CLARINET, ALTO SAXOPHONE

**** Seeking hat ART 6085
    Carter; Bobby Bradford (*t*); Tom Williamson (*b*); Buzz Freeman (*d*). 1/69.
John Carter emerged from the Fort Worth community, which also spawned Ornette Coleman and Ed Blackwell, and his playing was certainly as free and inquiring as Coleman's own. But Carter preferred to concentrate on the clarinet rather than the alto, and his music offers a refraction of that instrument's jazz history while remaining essentially modern: few contemporary players can match Carter's combination of old, woodsy timbre with sharply modern conceptions. The records under his own name, though, achieve a somewhat mixed success. Nothing currently available surpasses the two excellent discs made for Revelation in the late 1960s, in which Carter and Bradford created some of the most inventive variations on the 'classic' free-jazz setting. Their appearance together on *West Coast Hot* (listed in our last edition, but currently in limbo) and *Seeking* (which was recorded a fortnight later) serves to underline yet again how utterly wrong-headed is the view of 1950s and '60s California as given to crew-cut and buttoned-down 'cool'. The work of Bradford and Carter suggests that the reality was different, blacker and more radical.

*** A Suite Of Early American Folk Pieces Moers Music 02086
    Carter (*cl* solo). 8/79.
*** Dauwhe Black Saint BSR 0057
    Carter; Bobby Bradford (*c*); Charles Owens (*ss, cl, ob*); James Newton (*f*); Red Callender (*tba*); Roberto Miguel Miranda (*b*); William Jeffrey (*d*); Luis Peralta (*perc*). 2–3/82.
*** Castles Of Ghana Gramavision 8603
    Carter; Bobby Bradford (*c*); Baikida Carroll (*t, v*); Benny Powell (*tb*); Marty Ehrlich (*bcl, perc*); Terry Jenoure (*vn, v*); Richard Davis (*b*); Andrew Cyrille (*d*). 11/85.
The latter two records are part of a set of five by Carter, entitled 'Roots And Folklore', which purports

to create an episodic history of native American music as the composer sees and hears it. Unfortunately, the third instalment, *Dance Of The Love Ghosts*, and the concluding parts, *Fields* and *Shadows On A Wall*, are currently out of print. But each disc stands in its own right as a history-lesson-cum-celebration of black Americana, as Carter has it, creating a sense of repertory, with their evocations of folk tunes, blues and gospel strains and their contemporary parallel in the expert free improvising of the differing groups.

In these settings, Carter was able to avoid the slightly professorial voice that turned his *Suite Of Early American Folk Pieces* into something of an ethnomusicology lecture in which the elements of popular culture – cakewalk, blues, funk – sound contrived and illustrative rather than integral. In a group setting, as he was to prove with Horace Tapscott again in the late 1980s, Carter was a master.

Ron Carter (born 1937) DOUBLE BASS, BASS GUITAR, CELLO; OTHER INSTRUMENTS

*** **Where?** Original Jazz Classics OJC 432
    Carter; Eric Dolphy (*as, bcl, f*); Mal Waldron (*p*); George Duvivier (*b*); Charli Persip (*d*). 6/61.
*** **Peg Leg** Original Jazz Classics OJC 621
    Carter; Jerry Dodgion, Walter Kane, George Marge (*reeds*); Jay Berliner (*g*); Kenny Barron (*p*); Buster Williams (*b*); Ben Riley (*d*). 11/77.
** **Pastels** Original Jazz Classics OJC 665
    Carter; Kenny Barron (*p*); Hugh McCracken (*g, hca*); Harvey Mason (*d*); strings. 10/76.
***(*) **Uptown Conversation** Embryo/Rhino 7567 81955
    Carter; Hubert Laws (*f*); Herbie Hancock (*p*); Sam Brown (*g*); Grady Tate, Billy Cobham (*d*).
**** **Third Plane** Original Jazz Classics OJC 754
    Carter; Herbie Hancock (*p*); Tony Williams (*d*). 78.
*** **Patrao** Original Jazz Classics OJC 778
    Carter; Chet Baker (*t*); Amaury Tristao (*g*); Kenny Barron, Aloisio Aguiar (*p*); Jack DeJohnette, Edison Machado (*d*); Nana Vasconcelos (*perc*). 5/80.

If 'piccolo bass' isn't a contradiction in terms, then it probably ought to be. As befits perhaps the most technically adept bassist of recent times, the Carter discography is colossal, well in excess of 500 albums, and still counting. Though in the greater bulk of these, of course, as sideman, Carter has also made a respectable number of albums as leader. It's a pity that these should be of such mixed quality, marred by Carter's flirtation with electric bass guitar (on which he is a surprisingly indifferent player) and the aforementioned octave-divided instrument which allows a bassist to mimic a lead guitarist. The irony is that Carter, such a fleet and resonant player on the acoustic instrument, becomes very anonymous when electricity is involved.

Peg Leg is excellent, with a first-rate version of Monk's 'Epistrophy' (piccolo bass and all), though the overall sound is a little floaty and indistinct in register. The quality set is *Where?*, which must also count as a significant item in the Dolphy discography. It's dominated by a brilliant bass/clarinet duet of the sort Dolphy worked many times with Charles Mingus, and by a fine, unsentimental reading of 'Softly As In A Morning Sunrise'. Carter plays cello on 'Really' and 'Saucer Eyes' as he had on Dolphy's second album, *Out There*, also originally released on New Jazz. Waldron and (on the two cello tracks) Duvivier give firm support, and Persip once again displays the skills that should have guaranteed him a higher rating than he currently receives in histories of the music.

Of the later records, *Third Plane* stands out like a beacon. Commercial pressures being what they were, it wasn't easy for players of Hancock's and Williams's generation to make an acoustic piano record in 1978. The drummer hasn't quite got the hang of the setting and he thrashes about a bit at inopportune moments, but Carter's big gloopy fills on 'Stella By Starlight' and Hancock's 'Dolphin Dance' are absolutely perfect for the job. The most interesting tracks on *Uptown Conversation* vary the trio slightly, with Billy Cobham in for Williams, but doing essentially the same job. It's a slightly odd record, with brooding, abstract trios and solo bass (indexed but unlisted and untitled) interspersed with cheesy jazz funk. The reisue has been filled out with alternative takes which don't add anything of substance; even without, it would have been a worthwhile purchase.

No quibbles either about most of the stuff on *Patrao*. It's a slightly wet Latin date, but in the middle there are three tracks by just Baker, Barron, Carter and DeJohnette which stand out as strongly as anything in this list. A pity about the rest, but no matter.

History will doubtless draw a discreet veil over *Pastels* and, while there is nothing inherently suspect about a 'with strings' album (Charlie Parker made some, after all), a strings album entitled *Pastels* should ring a warning bell somewhere.

*** **Heart And Soul** Timeless SJP 158
    Carter; Cedar Walton (*p*). 12/81.

*** **Live At Village West** Concord CCD 4245
    Carter; Jim Hall (*g*). 11/82.
*** **Telephone** Concord CCD 4270
    As above; 8/84.

Carter's bass is unmistakably a *string* instrument. That is made clear on his unexpected and thoroughly impressive collaboration with the Kronos Quartet and by the fine duos. The Hall sets are absolutely top-drawer, with superb standard performances of 'All The Things You Are', 'Embraceable You', 'Bags' Groove', 'Baubles, Bangles And Beads' and Sonny Rollins's 'St Thomas', while *Telephone* includes a lovely 'Stardust' and the obligatory duo, 'Alone Together'.

Walton doesn't quite achieve Hall's rapport, but *Heart And Soul* is none the less exemplary, with the pianist's long melodic lines sparking some of Carter's most interestingly lateral playing.

***(*) **Etudes** Discovery 71012
    Carter; Art Farmer (*flhn*); Bill Evans (*sax*); Tony Williams (*d*). 9/82.

Rather a special record: understated and elegant on the one hand, fiery and impatient on the other. If one wanted to psychologize or personalize it, the Carter/Farmer axis appears to be the philosophical half, not so much brooding as thoughtful, while young Evans and Williams try to pick up the pace and roar away. It's all done with consummate taste, however, and not a note wasted in a full, uprettified mix.

Michael Carvin (born 1944) DRUMS

(*) **Between Me And You Muse MCD 5370
    Carvin; Cecil Bridgewater, Claudio Roditi (*t, flhn*); Ron Bridgewater, John Stubblefield (*ts*); Cyrus Chestnut (*p*); Calvin Hill (*b*). 9/89.
*** **Revelation** Muse MCD 5399
    As above, except add Sonny Fortune (*as*); John Hicks (*p*). 12/89.
** **Each One Teach One** Muse MCD 5485
    Carvin; Antoine Roney, Claudio Roditi (*t*); Houston Person (*ts*); Carlton Holmes (*p*); David Williams (*b*). 10/92.

Carvin's pinpoint technique and easeful approach to a wide variety of settings have granted him a valued if somewhat anonymous position among contemporary drummers. He played plenty of jazz-rock in the 1970s, but his one date as a leader from that era, an album for Steeplechase, is out of print. In the 1980s he involved himself heavily in teaching, but his occasional albums for Muse have resulted in some enjoyable if rather carelessly focused music. Rudy van Gelder's engineering rarely serves the band's drummer as well as it might, and the sound sometimes reduces Carvin to a splashy noisemaker. But he enthuses his sidemen, and there are some fine improvisations scattered through the three records. *Between Me And You* is a bit diffuse and suffers from a lack of either strong originals or interesting standards; the Bridgewaters too are a less than challenging front line. But *Revelation* is a good deal stronger. Fortune immediately raises the general game, blazing through the title-track (and inspiring Roditi to his best work) and smouldering on a very fetching 'Body And Soul', while the contrasts between Bridgewater's nervy horn and Roditi's confident brilliance result in useful creative tension. *Each One Teach One* comes as an anticlimax. The silly staccato beat for 'Surrey With The Fringe On Top' sounds like the notion of a band lost for good ideas, and most of the tracks have the half-finished feel typical of a Muse project.

Marc Cary (born 1967) PIANO

*** **Cary One** Enja ENJ 9023
    Cary; Roy Hargrove (*t*); Ron Blake (*ts*); Yarborough Charles Laws (*f*); Dwayne Burno (*b*); Dion Parson (*d*); Charlene Fitzpatrick (*v*). 1/94.

If musicians were to be issued with diplomas, Cary could claim to have graduated from two of the toughest and most stretching bands around: Arthur Taylor's Wailers and Betty Carter's supporting group, a well-respected academy for young players. In more recent times Cary has been part of trumpeter Hargrove's set-up, which explains his presence on three tracks here and the choice of Hargrove's 'The Trial' as a test piece. Cary's only subtlety as a writer can be gauged from 'The Vibe' (which he has also recorded with Hargrove), a bright, optimistic theme with an ominous shadow at its tail. He looks to Sonny Clark for inspiration and digs out 'Melody In C', a seldom-covered piece which elicits the same light/dark balance. 'He Who Hops Around' is Cary's most explicit examination here of his Native-American ancestry. Y. C. Laws and Charlene Fitzpatrick make only a rather incidental contribution. The real action – when Hargrove isn't around – is piano, bass and drums and, though Cary probably isn't quite ready to take that step yet, one day he will and it will surely prove a fascinating development for him.

Al Casey (born 1915) GUITAR

(*) **Jumpin' With Al Black & Blue 233056
    Casey; Arnett Cobb, Candy Johnson (*ts*); Jay McShann (*p*); Milt Buckner (*org*); Roland Lobligeois (*b*); Paul Gunther, Michael Silva (*d*). 7–8/73.

The former Fats Waller sideman worked busily in the 1980s, but these sides were recorded at a rather quiet point in his career. The quartet sides with McShann, an old *compadre*, are the most successful, with Casey humming along à la Slam Stewart to his crustily picked solos; he plays acoustic for most of the record, but there are three bouncing work-outs on electric with Buckner and Johnson in simmering fettle. Cobb sits in for two tracks and sounds even more cantankerous than usual. Dry, closely miked recording which suits the music quite well.

Bruno Castellucci DRUMS

(*) **Bim Bim Koala/Quetzal IRS 970.339/QZ 101
    Castellucci; Johannes Faber (*t, flhn*); Toots Thielemans (*hca*); Michel Herr, Jorg Reiter (*p, ky*); Jasper Van't Hof (*p*); Peter Tiehuis (*g*); Riccardo Del Frà, Michel Hatzigeorgiou (*b*); Bart Fermie, Chris Joris (*perc*). 7/89.

An album of bits rather than a coherent conception, but nevertheless an attractive package of themes by the drummer, Herr and van't Hof, with a couple of standards thrown in. Thielemans is wonderful on an upbeat rearrangement of Coltrane's 'Naima', contributing a solo that confirms what a wonderful improviser he is, not just a colour-and-effects man. Unfortunately for *Bim Bim*, the album is almost entirely defined by moments like this. The dominant voice throughout is Tiehuis's, who to his credit varies his guitar sound very considerably from full-on amplification to gentler finger-style accompaniments; van't Hof plays beautifully on his own 'Instant' and Faber pops up for a couple of tracks, including 'Fold Your Hands', for which he is credited as co-composer. Not much continuity. No real sense of what Castellucci himself is about. Pleasant, but hardly a priority purchase.

Castle Jazz Band GROUP

** **The Famous Castle Jazz Band** Good Time Jazz GTCD 10030-2
    Don Kinch (*t*); George Bruns (*tb*); Bob Gilbert (*cl*); Freddie Crews (*p*); Monte Ballou (*bj, v*); Bob Short (*tba*); Homer Welch (*d*). 8/57.

Stragglers from the Lu Watters-inspired revival of the 1940s, these traditionalists re-formed for the purposes of this 1957 record date. It might have appeased their original fans, but the music sounds like second-hand revivalism today, and the players perform with a rather gauche humour in their delivery. There is one rarity in 'I've Been Floating Down The Old Green River'; but everything else has been done better elsewhere, both before and since. The remastering is fine, though it emphasizes how lightweight the band was.

Philip Catherine (born 1942) GUITAR, ELECTRIC GUITAR, GUITAR SYNTHESIZER

***(*) **Sleep, My Love** CMP CD 5
    Catherine; Charlie Mariano (*ss, as, f, nagaswaram*); Jasper Van't Hof (*ky, kalimba*). 12/78 & 2/79.

Catherine is of mixed English/Belgian parentage. His first guitar influence, apart from the unavoidable Django Reinhardt, was the brilliant Belgian René Thomas (who died prematurely in 1975), but he was quick to respond to the jazz-rock techniques of both John McLaughlin and Larry Coryell.

Sleep, My Love is absolutely gorgeous, a near-perfect blend of instrumental voices. Catherine had still not emerged as a fully mature composer at this point; his 'Janet' (repeated on the Elektra below) is very personal and slightly guarded, and his most significant compositional input is a remarkable arrangement of Schoenberg's expressionistic *Verklärte Nacht*. Mariano, as always, is superb.

*** **Babel** Elektra ELK K 5244
    Catherine; Jean-Claude Petit (*ky, syn*); Yannick Top (*b*); André Ceccarelli (*d, perc*); Isabelle Catherine, Janet Catherine (*v*); string quartet. 80.

Catherine's larger-ensemble work has never had quite the same impact as his duos and trios (surprisingly, he is a not altogether confident solo performer), but *Babel* manages largely to belie the suggestion of chaotic cross-talk in the title. Well arranged by keyboard player Petit, it has some of the impetus that Catherine is often tempted – not for want of rhythmic sense – to abandon in favour of sheer texture.

*** Transparence Inak 8701
> Catherine; Hein Van de Geyn (*b*); Aldo Romano (*d*); Michel Herr (*ky*); Diederik Wissels (*p*). 11/86.

*** September Sky September 5106
> As above, except omit Herr and Wissels. 9/88.

'René Thomas' repays an early debt, and *Transparence* (originally released as Timeless SJP 242) is an album of often moving *hommages*. 'Father Christmas' is dedicated to Charles Mingus and 'Galeries St Hubert' to the ghost of Django Reinhardt; there is also an unexpected tribute to the British multi-instrumentalist, Victor Feldman, which opens up another putative line of descent for the guitarist.

September Sky is an album of (mainly) standards, but what is immediately obvious in both these backward-looking sets is how confidently in possession of his own voice and interpretative skill Catherine now is. On the earlier album, 'L'Eternel Désir' may bear a more than striking thematic resemblance to Ralph Towner's 'Silence Of A Candle', but it is far more deeply suffused with the blues than Towner has ever been, and far more dramatically modulated. Of the standards, 'Body And Soul', 'Stella By Starlight' and 'All Blues' stand out.

***(*) I Remember You Criss Cross Criss 1048
> Catherine; Tom Harrell (*flhn*); Hein Van de Geyn (*b*). 10/90.

***(*) Moods: Volume 1 Criss Cross Criss 1060
> As above, except add Michael Herr (*ky*). 5/92.

*** Moods: Volume 2 Criss Cross Criss 1061
> As for *Volume 1*. 5/92.

Recorded as a tribute to the late Chet Baker, *I Remember You* reunites the line-up that made *Chet's Choice* for Criss Cross in 1985, with Tom Harrell's floating melancholic flugelhorn steering dangerously close to Baker's weary, self-denying diction. Harrell contributes two fine originals – the softly swinging 'From This Time, From That Time' and 'Songflower' – Van de Geyn one and Catherine two. The opening 'Nardis' serves as an unintended farewell to Miles. Hank Mobley's 'Funk In Deep Freeze' and the closing 'Blues For G. T.' are slightly unexpected in this context but, drummerless, take on the same slightly enervated quality that is raised only by Catherine's astonishingly accurate rhythm guitar. 'My Funny Valentine'? Well, yes, of course; they could hardly have got away without it. Harrell's statement and subsequent solo are pretty much in the Baker vein, and again it's the guitarist who lifts the performance a notch, using his pedals imaginatively. A beautiful album.

Attractive as they are in many regards, one wonders if the *Moods* sessions really yielded enough for two full-length discs. As the title doubtless unconsciously hints, there is a just a crickle of suspicion that Catherine is drifting towards an elegantly jazzy mood-music. The three interesting tracks on Volume 2, significantly, are the Tom Harrell compositions whose rather deprecating titles, 'The Waltz' and 'Twenty Bar Tune', disguise a considerable expenditure of imaginative effort.

*** Art Of The Duo Enja ENJ 8016
> Catherine; Niels-Henning Orsted-Pedersen (*b*). 2/91.

Class meets class. Two players of quietly understated brilliance, recorded in a Swiss jazz club. Therein lies the problem. The whole session is so gracefully undemonstrative and unassertive that it is difficult to sustain the appropriate level of attention throughout a substantial set. Appropriate, because these are both improvisers who get right inside a tune, not just the chord structure but also the melody, and courteously reinvent it. 'All The Things You Are', 'My Foolish Heart' and 'Stella By Starlight' are each subjected to subtly complex variations, none of which sound predetermined but utterly spontaneous and, if not vivid, never less than intelligent. For refined tastes only.

André Ceccarelli DRUMS

*** From The Heart Verve 529 851
> Ceccarelli; Denis Leloup (*tb*); Sylvain Beuf (*ts, ss*); Bernard Arcadio, Jean-Michel Pilc (*p*); Thomas Bramerie, Remy Vignolo (*b*); Louis-César Ewande (*djembe*); Dee Dee Bridgewater, Oumou Kouyate, Margan Diabate (*v*). 9/95.

Remarkable how many French sidemen who, after years spent making themselves unobtrusively useful, pop up and turn in work of genuine originality. *From The Heart* is quietly but insistently idiosyncratic, fuelled by Ceccarelli's relaxed but insistent pulse and Jean-Michel Pilc's engagingly dissonant single-note outbursts and raw comping, which sounds as though Bud Powell had come alive again and taken up citizenship papers.

   Ceccarelli carries the beat mostly on the cymbals, with tom-toms and bass drum used almost exclusively for embellishment and accent; Kenny Clarke might be the obvious ancestor, and the Frenchman uses the same extra-long sticks with exactly the same precision and delicacy. Beuf is not widely known. He has a slightly rasping, plangent tone that some may not take to immediately, but it is spot on for this music. The two add-on tracks are an Afro-tinged thing with djembe and vocals, and a song feature for Dee Dee Bridgewater, that underlines how good an accompanist Ceccarelli has been; they've worked together before and it's fascinating to hear how the relationship shifts when he's calling the shots.

Oscar 'Papa' Celestin (1884–1953) CORNET, VOCAL

**** Papa Celestin & Sam Morgan Azure AZ-CD-12
   Celestin; Kid Shots Madison, Ricard Alexis, George McCullum, Guy Kelly (*c*); Williams Ridgley, August Rousseau, William Matthews, Ernest Kelly (*tb*); Willard Thoumy, Paul Barnes, Earl Pierson, Sid Carriere, Clarence Hall, Oliver Alcorn (*reeds*); Manual Manetta, Jeanette Salvant (*p*); John Marrero, Narvin Kimball (*bj*); Simon Marrero (*b, bb*); Abby Foster, Josiah Frazier (*d*); Charles Gills, Ferdinand Joseph (*v*). 1/25–12/28.

Little enough music was actually recorded in New Orleans in the 1920s to make any surviving tracks valuable. But the sessions led by Celestin and Morgan (the latter dealt with under his own entry) would be remarkable anyway. Despite the importing of devices from dance-band trends elsewhere, particularly in the later tracks, they really sound like no other jazz of the period. The first three tracks are by the Original Tuxedo Jazz Orchestra, with Madison and Celestin as the front line, and the deliriously exciting 'Original Tuxedo Rag' is a blazing fusion of ragtime, jazz and dance music that makes one ache to hear the band as it might have sounded live. The 13 subsequent titles from 1926–8 are less frantic and are occasionally troubled by the mannerisms of the day, weak vocals in particular. But the reed sections manage their curious blend of sentimentality and shrewd, hot playing – a New Orleans characteristic – with surprising finesse; the ensembles are consistently driving, and the two-cornet leads are frequently as subtle and well-ordered as those of King Oliver's band. Celestin himself, a great veteran of the city's music even then, has been undervalued as a soloist: he plays very well on 'My Josephine' and the superb slow piece 'It's Jam Up'. Taken together with the equally fine Sam Morgan tracks, we rate this as a five-star record, especially given the outstandingly clear and powerful remastering.

Henri Chaix (born 1925) PIANO

*** Jumpin' Punkins Sackville SKCD2-2020
   Chaix; Alain Du Bois (*b*); Romano Cavicchiolo (*d*). 10/90.
*** Jive At Five Sackville SKCD2-2035
   As above. 8/93.

'A listener could close his eyes and never believe that this is a Swiss playing in Geneva' – thus did Rex Stewart commend Henri Chaix's playing in 1967. Chaix became Switzerland's mainstream leader in the 1940s, and he backed many American visitors. But his own circumstances have seldom taken him to international audiences. *Jumpin' Punkins* finds him in vigorous form, touching few intensities but taking a satisfyingly personal route through jazz-piano tradition. His favourite manner is a medium-tempo stride, a variation which is faithful to James P. Johnson's methods, and he makes 'Yesterdays' and 'All God's Chillun Got Rhythm' into believable stride vehicles. Yet his unassumingly romantic treatment of 'Ruby My Dear' suggests that more demanding jazz material holds few terrors for him. Du Bois and Cavicchiolo stay out of his way, and the recording pays handsome regard to the Bösendorfer piano.

   Jive At Five is nothing more or less than a second helping, three years on. The material is more mainstreamed than ever, and one could wish that Chaix would look around for one or two more interesting tunes. But this is his style and he's right at home in it.

Serge Chaloff (1923–57) BARITONE SAXOPHONE

***(*) We The People Bop: Serge Chaloff Memorial Cool & Blue C&B CD 102
   Chaloff; Sonny Berman, Miles Davis, Gait Preddy, Red Rodney (*t*); Ernie Royal (*t, v*); Mert Goodspeed, Bennie Green, Bill Harris, Earl Swope (*tb*); Woody Herman (*cl, v*); Charlie Mariano (*as*); Al Cohn, Allen Eager, Flip Phillips, Sonny Stitt (*ts*); Al Haig, Ralph Burns, Barbara Carroll, Lou Levy, Bud Powell, George Wallington (*p*); Terry Gibbs (*vib*); Artie

Bernstein, Chubby Jackson, Oscar Pettiford, Curley Russell, Frank Vaccaro, Chuck Wayne (*b*); Denzil Best, Tiny Khan, Don Lamond, Max Roach, Pete DeRosa (*d*). 9/46, 1 & 3/47, 11/48, 3, 4 & 12/49.

***(*) **The Fable Of Mabel** Black Lion BLCD 760923
    Chaloff; Capazutto, Herb Pomeroy (*t*); Gene DiStachio (*tb*); Charlie Mariano, Boots Mussulli (*as*); Varty Haritounian (*ts*); Russ Freeman, Dick Twardzik (*p*); Ray Oliver, Jimmy Woode (*b*); Buzzy Drootin, Jimmy Zitano (*d*). 6 & 9/54.

Hugely talented, but the career was riven by 'personal problems' and the end was dreadful. Chaloff's approach to the unwieldy baritone was restrained rather than virtuosic (the result of an extended apprenticeship with Jimmy Dorsey, Georgie Auld and Woody Herman), and concentrated on the distinctive timbre of the instrument rather than on outpacing all opposition. Nevertheless, he was an agile improviser who could suddenly transform a sleepy-sounding phrase with a single overblown note.

Astonishingly, very little of Chaloff's work is currently available. *Boston Blow Up!* and the later, classic *Blue Serge* have not yet been reissued on CD by Affinity. Two takes of 'Blue Serge' itself are included on the memorial record, which contains a good selection of Chaloff in the studio and on stage, over some of his most productive years. Some effort has been made to fillet out tracks that feature him strongly, such as 'Serge's Urge' with Red Rodney, and one comes away with a surprisingly clear sense of his stormy musical personality.

Recorded before the onset of a final decline which was interrupted only by the brilliance of *Blue Serge*, *The Fable Of Mabel* reflects the blocked intensity of his playing. A Chaloff solo, as on the three takes of 'The Fable Of Mabel', two of 'Eenie Meenie Minor Mode', always seems about to tear its own smooth fabric and erupt into something quite violent; 'Blue Serge' was, oddly, an exception. Harmonically and rhythmically subtle, they also seem to represent a triumph of self-control. The later All Stars sessions, from which these tracks come, are in every way superior to the quintet tracks recorded in June, which are rather bland. Though his phrasing is quite conventional, Mariano's alto sound is wild and penetrating and Dick Twardzik's crabby piano is perfect for the setting. With the exception of Pomeroy, the rest of the band are virtually unknown.

Gerry Mulligan once walked into a studio while Chaloff was recording. Seeing the younger baritonist in the listening booth, Chaloff executed a perfect imitation of his fledgling style and then savagely reduced it to a heap of down and feathers. Relative to the enormous Mulligan discography, the older man, who gave the baritone saxophone its greatest impetus since Harry Carney, is seriously neglected.

Joe Chambers (born 1942) DRUMS

***(*) **Phantom Of the City** Candid CCD 79517
    Chambers; Philip Harper (*t*); Bob Berg (*ts*); George Cables (*p*); Santi Debriano (*b*). 3/91.

Joe Chambers has featured in post-bop jazz mostly as a drummer, but he is a gifted composer as well, and several of his earlier themes – particularly the four he wrote for Bobby Hutcherson's *Components* (Blue Note) – deserve to be better known than they are. He numbers Jimmy Giuffre as a crucial influence, and there's certainly a parallel between the thinking of both men regarding free and formal structures. That said, only two of the themes on this recent date are Chambers compositions: 'For Miles Davis', a serene yet vaguely ominous *in memoriam*, and the brighter 'Nuevo Mundo'. Chambers the drummer has become a thoughtful, interactive performer, seldom taking a driving-seat initiative and preferring a careful balancing of tonal weights and measures. He has a near-perfect band for his needs here: Berg's tenor is habitually analytical, Cables is a romantic with a terse streak of intelligence, and Harper's Berigan-like low notes and dryly spun lyricism – featured on an extended reading of 'You've Changed' – add further spice. The live recording, from New York's Birdland, is clear and full-bodied.

Thomas Chapin ALTO SAXOPHONE, FLUTE, SOPRANO SAXOPHONE

***(*) **Radius** Mu MUCD 1005
    Chapin; Ronnie Mathews (*p*); Ara Dinkjian (*oud*); Ray Drummond (*b*); John Betsch (*d*); Sam Turner (*perc*). 90.

*** **Third Force** Knitting Factory KFWCD 103
    Chapin; Mario Pavone (*b*); Steve Johns (*d*). 11/90, 1/91.

*** **Anima** Knitting Factory KFWCD 121
    As above, except add Michael Sarin (*d*, etc.). 12/91.

***(*) **Insomnia** Knitting Factory KFWCD 132
    As above, except add Al Bryant, Frank London (*t*); Curtis Fowlkes, Peter McEachern (*tb*); Marcus Roja, Ray Stewart (*tba*). 12/92.

*** **I've Got Your Number** Arabesque AJ 0110
    Chapin; Ronnie Mathews (*p*); Ray Drummond (*b*); Steve Johns (*d*); Louis Bauzo (*perc*). 1/93.
***(*) **You Don't Know Me** Arabesque AJ 0115
    Chapin; Tom Harrell (*t, flhn*); Peter Madsen (*p*); Kiyoto Fujiwara (*b*); Reggie Nicholson (*d*). 8/
    94.

Lively, inventive post-bop from a well-respected figure on the 'downtown' New York scene who has now confirmed our initial enthusiasm and hit very credible stride as a recording artist. In addition to the *Radius* quartet, Chapin has also worked with Lionel Hampton and Chico Hamilton. His flute playing on 'Forgotten Game' recalls another Hamilton graduate, Eric Dolphy, and the following 'Jitterbug Waltz' (played on the unusually pitched mezzo-soprano sax) sounds like a cross between Dolphy and Cannonball Adderley. The addition of an oud to 'Forgotten Game' recalls the world music interests that have quietly matured over the past few years.

    The Enemy set is gruffer and in some respects less adventurous, adhering to a narrower groove, often trading on rather limited ideas. 'Ahab's Leg' is the strongest individual item, but the set as a whole works well cumulatively, and the combination of Pavone and Johns boded well for future projects.

    Anima provides further live performances and offers three unwontedly stretched-out tracks on which the saxophonist solos at length, though with a minimum of actual development, ceding the foreground to the rhythm section for much of the time. Chapin's sound is ever more refined, and certainly by no means as blunt as formerly; but the Dolphy influence is still in place on both versions of 'Lift Off' and has allowed him to explore the limits of harmonic organization, while staying inside essentially jazz structures.

    Chapin isn't usually as smoothly accommodating as on *I've Got Your Number*, and it makes one wonder whether he wouldn't have received wider recognition if he had stuck to mainstream agenda. He sounds superficially like Richie Cole, but on Bud Powell's 'Time Waits' he reverts to a version of his Jackie McLean delivery. It's a most effective record, with a generally able band (though Ray Drummond must have had round shoulders by the end of the afternoon, having carried them throughout). It comes a bare month after the live project documented on *Insomnia*, where Chapin experiments with a larger group for the first time on disc. It's a jolly good record by any standard but, relative to the saxophonist's output, a rather important one, suggesting that he may yet develop into a significant mainstream/modern composer and arranger, full as it is of arresting ideas.

    In a very real sense, *You Don't Know Me* is its logical sequel, a beautifully crafted set which finds Chapin at his most expressive and open-hearted. Interesting to hear him working outside the comfort zone of the Pavone/Johns/Sarin axis, and with a piano player. Far from impeding him, it seems to have broadened his harmonic range considerably. Harrell is masterful, of course, and adapts surprisingly quickly to the opening sequence of numbers identified as 'Safari Notebook', on which Chapin moves into Sonny Fortune territory. This is perhaps the most sympathetically recorded of the discs to date, a good representation of this very original and impressive talent.

Teddy Charles (born 1928) VIBES, PIANO

***(*) **Collaboration: West** Original Jazz Classics OJC 122
    Charles; Shorty Rogers (*t*); Jimmy Giuffre (*ts, bs*); Curtis Counce (*b*); Shelly Manne (*d*). 8/53.
*** **Evolution** Original Jazz Classics OJC 1731
    As above, plus J. R. Monterose (*ts*); Charles Mingus (*b*); Gerry Segal (*d*). 8/53–1/55.
*** **Coolin'** Original Jazz Classics OJC 1866
    Charles; Idrees Sulieman (*t*); John Jenkins (*as*); Mal Waldron (*p*); Addison Farmer (*b*); Jerry
    Segal (*d*). 4/57.

When remembered at all – he has scarcely been a ubiquitous figure in post-war jazz – Charles is usually respected as a harbinger of Coleman's free music: the first two records aim for an independence of bebop structure which still sounds remarkably fresh. The two 1953 sessions, spread across the two discs, explore contrapuntal textures in a way which only Lennie Tristano had already tried, and there is a wonderful sense of interplay with Rogers and Manne especially. 'Variations On A Theme By Bud' from *Collaboration: West*, is a small classic of anticipatory freedom, the music played around key centres rather than a framework of chords. But Charles's interest in harmony and arrangement required larger groups than these, and the quartet session with Mingus, Monterose and Segal is less impressive. *Coolin'* features a surprising line-up of rarely encountered horns in a programme of evenly divided originals. Charles takes a relatively back-seat role, contributing only one tune and taking his turn in the round-robin of solos. This is a more conventional hard-bop session, but the tunes have some piquant interest: Waldron's off-centre 'Staggers' and 'Reiteration', a typical piece of minor-key brooding, are worth reviving. Jenkins plays with splendid intensity, but Sulieman's solos are mere bop convention, quotes and all.

**** **The Teddy Charles Tentet** Atlantic 790983-2
      Charles; Art Farmer (*t*); Eddie Bert (*tb*); Gigi Gryce, Hal Stein (*as*); Robert Newman, J. R.
      Monterose (*ts*); George Barrow, Sol Schlesinger (*bs*); Jimmy Buffington (*frhn*); Hall Overton,
      Mal Waldron (*p*); Jimmy Raney (*g*); Don Butterfield (*tba*); Addison Farmer, Teddy Kotick,
      Charles Mingus (*b*); Joe Harris, Ed Shaughnessy (*d*). 1–11/56.

Charles's masterpiece has been truthfully transferred to CD with the bonus of three tracks from the
comparably fine *Word From Bird* album, made the same year – although that one should be made
available in its entirety. Besides Charles's own scores, including the stunning 'The Emperor' and a
bizarre transformation of 'Nature Boy', there are arrangements by Jimmy Giuffre, Brookmeyer,
Waldron, Gil Evans and George Russell, whose heated 'Lydian M-1' is one of his sharpest pieces of the
era. With its density of incident, acute solos and arresting textures, this music relates closely to Russell's
Jazz Workshop recordings of the same period. Yet Charles is more than a Svengali, taking an important
instrumental part in several of the themes.

** **Live At The Verona Jazz Festival 1988** Soul Note SN 121183
      Charles; Harold Danko (*p*); Ray Drummond (*b*); Tony Reedus (*d*). 6/88.

An indifferent comeback by Charles, who had effectively retired from music for many years. He plays
well with an imposing rhythm section, but, as noted above, this kind of casual blowing session is hardly
his forte, and the live recording isn't distinguished.

Doc Cheatham (born 1905) TRUMPET, VOCALS

*** **Hey Doc!** Black & Blue BLE 59.090
      Cheatham; Gene Conners (*tb*); Ted Buckner (*as*); Sam Price (*p*); Carl Pruitt (*b*); J. C. Heard (*d*).
      5/75.

***(*) **Duets And Solos** Sackville SKCD-5002 2CD
      Cheatham; Sam Price (*p*). 11/76–11/79.

***(*) **The Fabulous Doc Cheatham** Parkwood PW 104
      Cheatham; Dick Wellstood (*p*); Bill Pemberton (*b*); Jackie Williams (*d*). 10/83.

Adolphus 'Doc' Cheatham is one of the most enduring of all living jazz musicians. He was effectively
rediscovered in the 1970s after many years of society band work, having been among the most esteemed
of lead trumpeters in the big-band era. He was recording in the late 1920s and his studio work of some
60 years later shows amazingly little deterioration in the quality of his technique, while the ideas and
appetite for playing remain wholly unaffected by the passage of time. It's not so much that one feels a
sentimental attachment to such a veteran, but that Cheatham's sound represents an art which has
literally died out of modern jazz: the sweet, lyrically hot style of a swing-era man. Prior to his records in
the 1980s, Cheatham's main work was with Cab Calloway in the 1930s, Eddie Heywood in the '40s
(often backing Billie Holiday), and in various settings in the 1950s and '60s; but it wasn't until these
albums that he was heard at length as a leader.

    Hey Doc! was recorded in Paris with a troupe of fellow veterans, though none of them were quite of
Doc's vintage, and while the group sounds a bit rough and ready Cheatham's elegance sets much of the
tone. *Duets And Solos* is arguably Cheatham's most valuable recording, since it both recalls the earlier
age which he seems so much a part of – the trumpet/piano format recalls Armstrong and Hines, and the
material mixes rags, stomps, blues and whiskey pop – and sits comfortably in modern sound and with a
knowing air of sagacity. Price (whose session of 12 solos fills up spare space on the two-disc set) is fine,
and often better than he is on his own featured recordings, although his solo showpieces are less
impressive as rather mechanical blues and light boogie. The Parkwood album is good, too. Here
Cheatham's solos have a classical economy and a courageous spring to them, and the tiny shakes and
inflexions in his sound only help to make it uniquely his own, with a songful high register and choruses
which, after 60 years of playing, he knows exactly how to pace. The session benefits a little from
Wellstood's attacking piano, and Cheatham's dapper, delicate vocals on several tracks only add to the
fun.

*** **At The Bern Festival** Sackville 2-3045
      Cheatham; Roy Williams (*tb*); Jim Galloway (*ss*); Ian Bargh (*p*); Neil Swainson (*b*); Terry
      Clarke (*d*). 4/83–1/85.

This live session finds Cheatham unfazed by a hard-swinging and quite modern-sounding band, with
Roy Williams sitting in on the first six tracks – he has a delightful feature on 'Polka Dots And
Moonbeams' – and Galloway's soprano measuring the distance between Sidney Bechet and Steve Lacy.
Three later tracks were taped on more local ground in Toronto. If the rhythm section sometimes crashes
rather more than it might for Cheatham's taste, he still sounds invigorated by the setting, and his hand-
muted playing on 'Creole Love Call' or the firm, silvery solos on 'Cherry' and 'Love Is Just Around The

Corner' are commanding examples of his best work.

*** **The Eighty-Seven Years Of Doc Cheatham** Columbia 474047-2
> Cheatham; Chuck Folds (*p*); Bucky Calabrese (*b*); Jackie Williams (*d*). 9/92.

With his regular band, the group he plays with every week in New York, Doc continues to defy Father Time. He is fading a little on some of the tracks, although one notices it more in his singing than in his trumpet playing, which retains so much of his cultivated delivery that he still turns back the clock to an earlier age. The detailed, dynamic treatment of Benny Carter's 'Blues In My Heart' proves that he is more than just a history act. The regular team provide faithful support, and Phil Schaap's clean production is perfectly apposite.

*** **Swinging Down In New Orleans** Jazzology JCD-233
> Cheatham; Brian O'Connell (*cl*); Butch Thompson (*p*); Les Muscutt (*g, bj*); Bill Huntington (*g, b*); Peter Badie (*b*); Ernest Elly (*d*). 92.

(*) **You're A Sweetheart Sackville SKCD2-2038
> Cheatham; Sarah McElcheran (*t*); Jim Galloway (*ss, vbs*); Jane Fair (*cl, ts*); Norman Amadio (*p*); Rosemary Galloway (*b, v*); Don Vickery (*d*). 3–11/92.

Doc seems no more or less than his usual self on both of these, so it comes down to the settings as to which is preferable: no real contest. Jazzology's seasoned team of veteran modern traditionalists (if that doesn't sound too absurd) provide a springy, amiable and perfectly appropriate background for the trumpeter's lean, sometimes puffy solos and singing, with Thompson a model of deftness. They play plenty of tunes from the old town and make them all sound as if they're worth the attention. The Canadian sessions captured on the Sackville disc are more routine and, though there's a very sweet ballad in 'Under The Moonlight Starlight Blue', most of this is rather too ordinary.

Jeannie Cheatham PIANO, VOCAL and
Jimmy Cheatham BASS TROMBONE, VOCAL

*** **Sweet Baby Blues** Concord CCD 4258
> Jimmy Cheatham; Jeannie Cheatham; Snooky Young (*t, v*); Jimmie Noone (*ss, cl*); Charles McPherson (*as*); Curtis Peagler (*as, ts*); Red Callender (*b, tba*); John 'Ironman' Harris (*d*); Danice Tracey, Chris Long (*v*). 9/84.

*** **Homeward Bound** Concord CCD 4321
> As above, except Eddie Vinson (*as, v*) and Dinky Morris (*ss, ts, bs*) replace McPherson, Tracey and Long. 1/87.

*** **Back To The Neighbourhood** Concord CCD 4373
> Cheatham; Cheatham; Clora Bryant (*t, flhn*); Curtis Peagler (*as, ts*); Jimmie Noone (*ss, ts, cl*); Herman Riley (*ss, ts*); Dinky Morris (*bs*); Papa John Creach (*vn*); Red Callender (*b*); John 'Ironman' Harris (*d*). 11/88.

*** **Luv In The Afternoon** Concord CCD 4429
> As above, except add Nolan Smith (*t, flhn*); omit Bryant, Riley and Creach. 5/90.

*** **Basket Full Of Blues** Concord CCD 4501
> As above, except add Rickey Woodard (*as, ts, cl*) and Frank Wess (*ts, f*); omit Noone. 11/91.

*** **Blues And Boogie Masters** Concord CCD 4579
> As above, except add Snooky Young (*t*), Charles Owens, Hank Crawford (*as*), Richard Reid (*b*); omit Wess, Peagler, Callender. 7/93.

Like many of their somewhat younger counterparts on Concord, the Cheathams have now been doing this kind of record for the label long enough to create their own little genre. Some may find Concord's spotless recording not much in keeping with the rougher spirits of what is a variation on jump-band blues, but the horns are perfectly cast and the material is smartly chosen to get the most out of the formula. Jeannie Cheatham's singing is a nice blend of girlishness and acting tough, and husband Jimmy plays Butterbeans to her Susie. Very little to choose among the records, but the first is probably the freshest, and *Basket Full Of Blues* benefits from the presence of Woodard, an inspired addition to the group, and who now seems to be a fixture.

Don Cherry (1936–95) POCKET TRUMPET, WOODEN FLUTES, DOUSSN'GOUNI,
MISCELLANEOUS INSTRUMENTS AND PERCUSSION, VOICE

*** **El Corazon** ECM 1230
> Cherry; Ed Blackwell (*d*). 2/82.

A musical gypsy, Cherry has defined his art as that of people 'listening and travelling'. Like many travellers, he has been treated with suspicion, and record companies have been notably reluctant to cross his palm with silver. His unconventional choice of instruments makes him an easy mark as a temporary recruit for 'colour' – Cherry favours a tiny pocket trumpet, bamboo flutes, and the Malian *doussn'gouni*, a calabash guitar with rattles attached – but the errant lifestyle seems to suit his world-view and there is something about his staccato, declamatory style that lends itself to brief interjection rather than to developed 'performance'. Cherry conspicuously lacks the self-consciousness of most improvisers.

After Coleman and the ill-fated Collin Walcott in later years, Cherry's closest and longer-lasting artistic association has been with Ed Blackwell. Their most significant collaboration was on *Mu*, recorded in 1969 but now unavailable. It was a remarkable exploration of relatively untried territory; the New Thing had freed percussionists from mere time-keeping and reminded Afro-Americans of their heritage in percussion-based music.

The later session is much more obviously lyrical, as one might expect from the label, and includes what by that time had become a rare Cherry performance of a jazz staple, 'Bemsha Swing', a Thelonious Monk/Denzil Best tune which Cherry returned to on his jazz and big-label comeback, *Art Deco*, below. Though the material is somewhat different from the later Old and New Dreams group (which special-ized very largely in Ornette Coleman material), the approach is broadly similar and *El Corazon* may be read as a germ or distillation of what the quartet were to do later in the 1980s.

**** **Art Deco** A & M 395258
Cherry; James Clay (*ts*); Charlie Haden (*b*); Billy Higgins (*d*). 8/88.
Cherry was a pioneer of world music before the term acquired capital letters, market-niche status, and a weight of opprobrium that even Cherry has found it hard to shake off. Later years saw him working with 'ethnic' and pop musicians, including Ian Dury and the Blockheads, Lou Reed and his own step-daughter Neneh, and thus by critical inference further and further removed from jazz (Old and New Dreams can be conveniently dismissed as a 'nostalgic' reconstruction of the original Ornette Coleman Quartet).

It was, though, surprising to find Cherry recording a relatively conventional jazz album that sees him concentrate on trumpet playing opposite a remarkably straightforward 'Texas tenor'. Alongside Coleman tunes like 'The Blessing' and 'Compute' which invite a freer approach, there are standards like 'When Will The Blues Leave', 'Body And Soul' and a further, rather indifferent, version of 'Bemsha Swing'. Clay has had a quiet career since the 1950s and has only recently garnered much critical notice; he plays beautifully, sounding like an ancestor of Ornette-on-tenor. Cherry, mostly playing muted, seemed to have reverted to a cross between his old, rather tentative self and mid-period Miles Davis.

***(*) **Multi Kulti** A & M 395323
Cherry; Bill Ortiz (*t, v*); James Harvey (*tb*); Jeff Cressman (*tb, v*); Bob Stewart (*tba*); Carlos Ward (*as*); Jessica Jones, Tony Jones (*ts*); Peter Apfelbaum (*ts, ky, perc*); Peck Allmond (*bs*); Will Bernard, Stan Franks (*g*); David Cherry, Frank Serafine (*syn*); Karl Berger (*mar*); Bo Freeman, Mark Loudon Sims (*b*); Ed Blackwell, Deszon X. Claiborne (*d*); Joshua Jones V (*d, perc, v*); John L. Price (*d programming*); Frank Ekeh, Robert Buddha Huffman, Nana Vasconcelos (*perc*); Anthony Hamilton, Ingrid Sertso (*v*); collective personnel. 12/88–2/90.
Very much closer to what one has come to expect of a Don Cherry album, perhaps too self-consciously so. Yet Cherry's eclecticism is confident enough to rid this poly-stylistic collection of any suspicion of mere artistic tourism. In Carlos Ward he finds a particularly sympathetic partner, and he clearly drew considerable sustenance from his stepdaughter's street-wise and commercially successful hip-hop and rap styles. User-friendly and thoroughly enjoyable.

*** **Dona Nostra** ECM 1448
Cherry; Lennart Aberg (*sax, f*); Bobo Stenson (*p*); Anders Jormin (*b*); Anders Kjellberg (*d*); Okay Temiz (*perc*). 3/93.
Three years on, the old fires are momentarily rekindled on a set that sees brief flashes of brilliance embedded in a solid but slightly prosaic ECM setting. The wind that stirs the coals, significantly, is Ornette Coleman, two of whose pieces are included. In the autumn of 1993, Cherry toured with Ornette and an acoustic group on a historic reunion tour. Experiences were mixed, and the trumpeter's own performances ranged from the quirky to the minimal. Here, though, he sounds in full, strong voice. Restricting himself to trumpet, he eases through 'Race Face' with less fury than the composer brings to it, produces a singing tone on 'Fort Cherry' and 'Prayer' (the outstanding cut) and leads the pack on the closing 'Ahayu-Da' which, like much of the material, is collectively composed. The record is quite properly also credited to Aberg and Stenson, both of whom play very well indeed. The technical quality, it goes without saying, is superb; one wishes that Jan Erik Kongshaug had been around in 1958.

Ed Cherry (born 1954) GUITAR

***(*) **First Take** Groovin' High 519 942
    Cherry; Jon Faddis (*t*); Paquito D'Rivera (*cl*); David Jensen (*ts*); Kenny Barron (*p*); Peter
    Washington (*b*); Marvin 'Smitty' Smith (*d*). 1/93.
A long-time associate of Dizzy Gillespie, Cherry was recording *First Take* when the trumpeter succumbed to cancer in January 1993. Dizzy's spirit shines through from the very first two tracks. Freddie
Hubbard's 'Little Sunflower' gives Jon Faddis scope for one of his dizzily high solos, while 'Lorenzo's
Wings', celebrating a defector who returned to Cuba to rescue his wife and kids, slips into the dancing
samba rhythm Gillespie loved. 'Third Stone From The Sun' puts Cherry squarely in the generation that
grew up with Hendrix. The following track, Pheeroan akLaff's 'Serious', is wackily contemporary. At
that point, the guitarist turns right around and heads back to source, with a lovingly re-created version
of 'In A Sentimental Mood'. Barron (who sat out the last two), Washington and Smith are absolutely on
the case. D'Rivera's guest slot is elegantly phrased. The only drawback is the lack of a truly memorable
solo from Cherry himself. A fine group player, he stiffens up a bit in the spotlight.

Cyrus Chestnut PIANO

*** **Revelations** Atlantic 82518-2
    Chestnut; Christopher J. Thomas (*b*); Clarence Penn (*d*). 6/93.
A fine debut. Chestnut, Thomas and Penn were the members of one of Betty Carter's recent rhythm
sections, and the deftness of this trio certainly bespeaks mutual familiarity. The opening 'Blues For
Nita' is a beautifully controlled workout in which Chestnut controls the dynamics as sagaciously as any
keyboard veteran. Instead of coming from the post-bop piano masters, he looks back to those who
bridged swing and bop, in particular Oscar Peterson: 'Little Ditty' features a trademark show of
virtuosity, while the gospel inflexions of 'Lord, Lord, Lord' might have come from Ray Bryant. The
down-side of this direction is a certain sameness and predictability about some of his solos, as if he'd
already fallen into patterns of playing. But the quiet gravity of his solo ballad, 'Sweet Hour Of Prayer',
suggests that he has other sides to develop, too. Impeccable studio sound throughout.

***(*) **Dark Before The Dawn** Atlantic 82719-2
    As above, except Steve Kirby (*b*) replaces Thomas. 8/94.
One of the interesting things about Chestnut is his take on gospel roots. So few modern jazz pianists
have tackled the issue of gospel melody and harmony within a post-bop context – beyond the customary
'soulful' clichés – that Chestnut's meditative approach is something of a rarity. Here, on 'It Is Well
(Within My Soul)', he plays a beautifully modulated treatment of a traditional hymn, but more important is the way he integrates gospel materials into his overall approach. It lends a distinctive touch to
most of the pianism on show here, and plays a notable part of his choice of dynamics: he can play
remarkably delicately, but – and he's physically a very big man – he can really thump the keyboard when
he wants to. That range is splendidly exploited by the variety of the themes on display, and Kirby and
Penn offer exemplary support. Still, there are contrivances here and there which suggest that Chestnut
has yet to deliver a consistent masterpiece, even if this strong record will do for now.

Herman Chittison (1909–67) PIANO, VOCALS

(*) **Herman Chittison, 1933–1941 Classics 690
    Chittison; Ikey Robinson (*g, v*); Arita Day (*v*). 33–41.
Chittison's great mistake was to take on Tatum and Waller at their own game, trying to accelerate his
ragtime and stride approach to such an extent that he was able to play very fast but only rather vapidly.
These are valuable sides, the bulk of them recorded in France. The solo 'Honeysuckle Rose' is
unashamedly Walleresque and very nearly works. The solo stuff is almost always better, and the album
might receive a slightly higher rating if it weren't for the dreary material with Robinson and the two
tracks with Day, who shouldn't be confused with Anita O'Day (and wouldn't be if you could hear her
sing).

Ellen Christi VOCAL

** **Dreamers** Splasc(h) H 311
    Christi; Claudio Lodati (*g*). 4/90.

*** **A Piece Of The Rock** Splasc(h) H 393-3
    Christi; Masahiko Kono (*tb*); Carlo Actis Dato (*ts, bs, bcl*); Enrico Fazio (*f*); Fiorenzo Sordini (*d*). 1/91.

Born in Chicago, Christi made these records in Italy, where she seems to be a more popular figure. She's an improvising vocalist in the manner of Jeanne Lee and Urszula Dudziak, and she hovers between words and sounds in a confident but sometimes unappealing manner: neither a committed improviser like Maggie Nicols nor a convincing bop-scat singer, she doesn't always characterize her material with enough certainty to persuade a listener that she really knows what she's doing. The duet session with Lodati sounds dated, relying on overdubs and cooing textures which suggest a throwback to some of the improvising experiments of the 1970s. But *A Piece Of The Rock* is far superior. Christi has worked with Dato before, on the vinyl-only *Senza Parole*, and both of them are part of a convincing bop-to-free group that gets extra weight from Kono's sombre trombone and the crisp rhythms of Fazio and Sordini (who is credited as co-leader). Christi's vocabulary of groans may still turn some listeners off, but the music holds some power.

Charlie Christian (1916–42) GUITAR

**** **The Genius Of The Electric Guitar** Columbia 460612-2
    Christian; Alec Fila, Irving Goodman, Cootie Williams (*t*); Cutty Cutshall, Lou McGarity (*tb*); Gus Bivona, Skippy Martin (*as*); Georgie Auld, Pete Mandello (*ts*); Bob Snyder (*bs*); Lionel Hampton (*vib*); Count Basie, Dudley Brooks, Johnny Guarnieri, Fletcher Henderson (*p*); Artie Bernstein (*b*); Nick Fatool, Harry Jaeger, Jo Jones, Dave Tough (*d*). 39–41.
**** **Solo Flight** Topaz TPZ 1017
    As above, except add Henry 'Red' Allen, Ziggy Elman, Dizzy Gillespie, Johnny Martell, Jimmy Maxwell (*t*); Red Ballard, Vernon Brown, J. C. Higginbotham, Ted Vesley (*tb*); Edmond Hall (*cl*); Earl Bostic, Benny Carter, Buff Estes, Skippy Martin, Boots Mondello, Hymie Schertzer (*as*); Bus Basey, Coleman Hawkins, Jerry Jerome, Ben Webster (*ts*); Clyde Hart, Ken Kersey (*p*); Meade Lux Lewis (*clo*); Israel Crosby, Milt Hinton (*b*); Sid Catlett, Cozy Cole (*d*). 39–41.

Who actually invented bebop? Parker and Gillespie seemed to arrive at near-identical solutions to the blind alley of jazz harmony. Thelonious Monk was never an orthodox bopper, but he had his two cents' worth. And then there was Charlie Christian, who in some accounts was the first to develop the long lines and ambitious harmonic progressions of bop. Christian's appetite for booze and girls was only ever overtaken by his thirst for music. He once improvised 'Rose Room' for nearly an hour and a half, a feat which prompted Benny Goodman to hire him.

    Though Christian's greatest contributions, in terms of musical history, were the historic jams at Minton's in New York out of which bebop emerged, his role in the Goodman and Lionel Hampton bands, documented rather well on *Solo Flight*, represent the bulk of what is left to us. There are versions around of the Minton's material, but they enjoy a slightly uncertain existence. Christian's first commercial outings were the September 1939 sides with Hampton. A single track from it ('One Sweet Letter From You') and one from a month later ('Haven't Named It Yet') give a sense of the excitement the bandleader obviously felt at this freshly discovered young voice.

    Christian was the first guitarist to make completely convincing use of an electric instrument and, though his style blended Texas blues riffing with Lester Young's long-limbed strolls, he was able to steer a path away from the usual saxophone-dominated idiom and towards something that established guitar as an improvising instrument in its own right. Goodman clearly recognized that and gave him considerable solo space on the sextet, also in October 1939. Amplification meant that the guitar could be heard clearly, and Christian's solos on 'Rose Room' and 'Star Dust' remain models for the instrument. There is considerable overlap between the two records, but the absence of 'Air Mail Special' on the Topaz might just swing things in favour of the Columbia . . . except that it includes another excellent Goodman big-band number, 'Honeysuckle Rose', and – a fascinating sidelight on a short career – Christian's contribution to a February 1941 session by clarinettist Edmond Hall, on which no less than Meade Lux Lewis plays celeste; 'Profoundly Blue' is a one-off, but it is a very lovely singleton.

    As one might expect, there is some pretty routine passage-work on both records – 'I Surrender Dear' from April 1940 is the first time Christian sounds prepared to recycle his own ideas – but the best of it (and we might add the tersely swinging 'Seven Come Eleven' from November 1939 to that list) requires a place in any properly representative collection of modern jazz.

Jodie Christian (born 1932) PIANO

***(*) **Experience** Delmark DD-454
 Christian; Larry Gray (b); Vincent Davis (d). 5/91–2/92.
*** **Rain Or Shine** Delmark DE-467
 As above, except add Paul McKee (tb); Roscoe Mitchell (ss, as, ob), Art Porter (as), Ernie
 Adams (d), George Hughes (d), Francine Griffin (v). 5/91–12/93.

Christian opens the first record with a Byzantine exploration of the blues on 'Bluesing Around', and it
gives the impression that he couldn't wait to get stuck into his first date as a leader, on the cusp of his
sixtieth birthday. A local Chicagoan through and through, he can play for anybody, yet, unlike all too
many such sidemen, he has a distinction of his own. More than half of the CD is solo piano, with a very
slow 'Mood Indigo' and a lovely original called 'Faith' as particular standouts; and Christian's decisive
touch and complex but clear voicings bespeak a talent that has absorbed everything it needs from the
jazz tradition. Gray and Davis help out assiduously on the four trio tracks.

 The follow-up is by comparison a bit disappointing. 'Let's Try' is a fine opener with sterling work by
McKee and Porter – who sounds quite different from his Verve Forecast self – and the ballad medley
works well, with an especially impressive turn by the trombonist on 'Polka Dots And Moonbeams'. But
the tracks with Roscoe Mitchell, who sounds notably sour and argumentative, just don't fit in, no matter
how nobly Christian tries to bring them round. Griffin sings on two tracks and Jodie himself croons one
number.

Denny Christianson TRUMPET

*** **Suite Mingus** Justin Time JUST 15
 Christianson; Pepper Adams (bs); Roger Walls, Danile Doyon, Ron Di Lauro, Jocelyn Laponte
 (t); Patrice Dufour, Muhammad Abdul Al-Khabyyr, André Verreault (tb); Bob Ellis (btb); Joe
 Christie Jr (as, f, cl, ss, picc); Pat Vetter (as, cl, f); Richard Beaudet (ts, f, cl); Jean Lebrun (ts, f, ss,
 picc); Jean Frechette (bs, bcl); Kenny Alexander (p); Richard Ring (g); Vic Angelillo (b); Pierre
 Pilon (d). 8/86.
***(*) **Shark Bait** Justin Time JUST 60
 Christianson; Roger Walls, Jocelyn Couture, Richard Gagnon, Robert Piette (t, flhn); André
 Verreault, Muhammad Abdul Al-Khabyyr, Kelsley Grant (tb); Colin Murray (btb); Jean-Pierre
 Zanella (as, ss, f, cl); François D'Amour (as, ss, f); Richard Beaudet (ts, f); Jacques Lelievre (ts, f,
 cl); Colin Biggin (bs, bcl); Jan Jarczyk (p); Richard Ring (g); Vic Angelillo, Sylvain Gagnon (b);
 Jim Hillman (d). 11 & 12/93.

Christianson is an accomplished Canadian trumpeter with a tone startlingly close to that of compatriot,
Kenny Wheeler, but with a more straight-ahead approach to improvisation. In the earlier of the pair, he
expertly fronts his well-schooled big band in a showcase for baritonist Pepper Adams, a former Mingus
sideman. The main event is a suite by Curt Berg called 'Three Hats', which largely consists of three
original Mingus compositions – 'Slop', 'Fables Of Faubus' and '1 × Love' – with a linking theme.
Adams's bronchial tone stands out rather too starkly from Christianson's smooth arrangements. It
works beautifully on an arrangement of 'My Funny Valentine' – in the non-Mingus part of the programme – but palls a little over the long haul. Christianson himself solos with authority on 'Faubus' and
two of the Alf Clausen themes that open the set, but he is relatively modest in his claim on solo space.

 His main contributions to the later record are a moving flugelhorn solo on his own composition, 'Monking', and a crisper duet with Walls on 'Back To The Office'. For the most part, he is happy to leave the
spotlight to others, and there are excellent band contributions: Al-Khabyyr's on 'Blenda Lee' and
'Geezers On Parade' (another Berg composition), Zanella's Sonny Fortune-like alto on 'C'est Quoi?'.
The band is nicely balanced and very professionally recorded with a natural, 'acoustic' sound that gives
the music a lot of presence.

Keith Christie (1931–80) TROMBONE and
Ian Christie (born 1927) CLARINET

***(*) **Christie Brothers Stompers** Cadillac SGC/MEL CD 201
 Christie; Christie; Ken Colyer (c); Dickie Hawdon (t); Pat Hawes, Charlie Smith (p); Nevil
 Skrimshire (g); Ben Marshall (bj); Micky Ashman, Denny Coffee (b); George Hopkinson,
 Bernard Saward, Pete Appleby (d); Bill Colyer (wbd); Neva Raphaello (v). 6/51–8/52.

This captures the sometimes crazed intensity of original British trad better than any of the recent
Colyer, Lyttelton or Barber reissues. The Christies originally put together the group with players from

the Lyttelton and Crane River bands, and the CD collects tracks from various sessions for Melodisc, along with four live tracks from a previously unknown acetate. Though the first few numbers suffer from poor sound, they belt along with bewildering power. Colyer's lead is less self-consciously 'authentic' than he would later become, and Keith Christie delivers some hair-raising solos. The later sessions with Dickie Hawdon in for Colyer are comparatively steady, but the fierce rhythm sections, Ian Christie's gargling but supple solos and the queer blend of high spirits and grim determination which seems to typify this music keep everything fresh. Remastering has been very capably done from some less-than-ideal sources. The CD is also beautifully packaged and annotated.

Pete Christlieb (born 1945) TENOR SAXOPHONE

*** **Conversations With Warne Vol. 1** Criss Cross 1043
    Christlieb; Warne Marsh (*ts*); Jim Hughart (*b*); Nick Ceroli (*d*). 9/78.
*** **Live** Capri 74026-2
    Christlieb; Bob Cooper (*ts*); Mike Wofford (*p*); Chuck Berghofer (*b*); Donald Bailey (*d*). 2/90.
Christlieb's proficiency as sessionman and section-player with numerous West Coast big bands has let his status as soloist drift over the years. These two dates, each with another tenorman, present him as the energy source on both occasions, even though Cooper and Marsh come over as far more individual. Next to Marsh's serpentine, querulous solos, Christlieb's improvisations sound almost simple, but the senior man plays with much more attack and a rather less pinched tone than usual. Whether this dissipates any of the characteristic Marsh qualities is a moot point, but the playing – on a series of sequences devised by Christlieb and Hughart – has a prodigious intensity.
    Next to that, the club recording with Cooper is easy-going music. They both burn through 'Shaw 'Nuff', but Cooper's solo turns on 'Come Sunday' and the mid-tempo 'Touch Of Your Lips' are more typical. The location recording is rather muted.

June Christy (1926–90) VOCAL

**** **Something Cool** Capitol B21Y-96329
    Christy; Pete Rugolo Orchestra. 53–55.
**** **The Misty Miss Christy** Capitol 798452-2
    Christy; Pete Rugolo Orchestra. 55.
June Christy's solo recordings, following her stint with the Stan Kenton orchestra, have been reissued in various forms over the years, but *Something Cool*, a compilation from two albums, several uncollected singles and two previously unreleased tracks, and the original *The Misty Miss Christy* are a beautiful celebration of one of the most undervalued singers of the post-swing era. Christy's wholesome but peculiarly sensuous voice is less an improviser's vehicle than an instrument for long, controlled lines and the shading of a fine vibrato. Her greatest moments – the heartbreaking 'Something Cool' itself, 'Midnight Sun', 'I Should Care' – are as close to creating definitive interpretations as any singer can come. Rugolo's arrangements are nicely inventive without getting in her way and, although some of the compilation tracks are more like collectable items (the cooing male vocals on 'Why Do You Have To Go Home', for instance) than essential ones, there are very few less-than-exceptional moments on the record, which includes all of the original *Something Cool* LP among its 24 tracks. The remastering is bright and well defined. *The Misty Miss Christy* is perfectly programmed, from lighter material such as 'Sing Something Simple' to a glorious, immaculately controlled ''Round Midnight', and Rugolo is again a master of the situation. These are essential vocal records.

(*) **A Lovely Way To Spend An Evening Jasmine JASMCD 2528
    Christy; Stu Williamson (*t*); Herb Geller (*as*); Russ Freeman (*p*); Monty Budwig (*b*); Shelly
    Manne (*d*); Jerry Gray Orchestra. 57–59.
Poor documentation and thin packaging make this collection of Christy's late-1950s performances look cheaply presented. The sound is thin and weakly spread, too; but the performances find the singer in inventive and bright form, and both the tracks with Manne's group and with the Jerry Gray band are hip and swinging affairs.

Clarinet Summit GROUP

*** **In Concert At The Public Theater** India Navigation IN 1062
    Alvin Batiste, John Carter, Jimmy Hamilton (*cl*); David Murray (*bcl*). 82 or 83.

***(*) **Southern Bells** Black Saint 120107
    As above. 3/87.
This is one of those one-off projects – the concert documented on the India Navigation disc – that proved so durable that the group re-convened as often as individual commitments permitted. What made the line-up fascinating was the appearance side by side of two mainstream-traditionalists (Batiste, Hamilton) alongside two modernists of markedly individual temperament. Murray's voice is, inevitably, the easiest to pick out of the throng, but the three B-flat clarinets are woven so closely together that it is only when a trademark device emerges, like Hamilton's softly decelerating phrases towards the end of a chorus, that it is possible to identify who is playing.
    'Jeep's Blues' acknowledges Hamilton's swing loyalties, but the most enticing single performance is 'Groovin' High', in which Carter takes a prominent lead. 'Sweet Lovely' gives Murray a chance to show off his more lyrical side and features some great ensemble playing as well. There is more emphasis on individual expression on the follow-up, but with the same mix of styles: 'Mbizo' alongside 'Perdido', 'I Want To Talk About You' before 'Beat Box'. These are beguiling juxtapositions and this is a much better-recorded disc, which means that the very different textures of the four horns are much more evident. Either one will delight.

Clarion Fracture Zone GROUP

*** **Blue Shift** VeraBra 2075-2
    Sandy Evans (*ts, ss*); Tony Gorman (*as, ts, cl, perc*); Alister Spence (*p, syn*); Steve Elphick (*b*); Andrew Dickeson (*d*). 3/90.
*** **Zones On Parade** Rufus Records R F 001
    As above, except for Elphick add (*tba*); replace Dickeson with Louis Burdett (*d*); add Tony Buck, Lucien Boiteaux (*d*). 3 & 4/92.
***(*) **What Love Can Do** Rufus R F 010
    As above, except replace Elphick with Lloyd Swanton (*b*), Burdett with Toby Hall (*d*); add Greg Sheehan (*perc*); omit Buck and Boiteaux. 11/93.
Strong, slightly moody contemporary sounds from a Scottish/Australian group who have become a solid live act. The husband-and-wife front line exchange featured roles with seemly even-handedness, though Sandy Evans, composer of the suite, *What This Love Can Do*, has emerged as the stronger voice. Initially a good deal of responsibility was devolved to Spence; on the debut album he shows a relaxed touch that tempers the slight fussiness of some of the arrangements. The sound on *Zones On Parade* is immediately better, with a businesslike, road-tested feel, abetted by a more professional mix. Further changes to the rhythm section for record number three, and it's here that things are quite clearly not 100 per cent. CFZ have yet to present a convincing drum-sound, and there isn't enough propulsion from the back. Ironically, the *What Love* suite might have worked better with a drummerless concept and with a couple of guest spots for brass. Gorman wisely sticks to alto and gives his clarinets more prominence; a better texture up front. Spence, as always, is unflustered and competently expressive. Plaudits to Evans, though, for an impressive composition.

John Clark (born 1944) FRENCH HORN

(*) **Il Suono CMP 59
    Clark; Lew Soloff (*t*); Dave Taylor (*btb*); Alex Foster (*ts*); Jerome Harris (*g*); Anthony Jackson (*b*); Kenwood Dennard (*d*). 92.
A much-requested sideman, Clark produces the sort of sound which, if it were a wine, would be described as round and flowery. A touch more tannin would make him a more interesting soloist. In contrast to Tom Varner, the other leading contemporary exponent of this rather neglected horn, he is a shade one-dimensional and, though the instrumental range of this group is unusual to say the least, the impact fades very rapidly indeed. Soloff, Foster and Taylor could all have been used to greater effect, though the saxophonist has some good moments on 'Groove From The Louvre', while Jackson (on contrabass guitar) and Dennard provide a solid enough foundation for a more fluent and upbeat session.

Mike Clark DRUMS

*** **Give The Drummer Some** Stash ST-CD-22
    Clark; Jack Walrath (*t*); Ricky Ford (*ts*); Neal Kirkwood (*p*); Jack Wilkins (*g*); Chip Jackson (*b*). 89.

*** **The Funk Stops Here** Tiptoe 888811-2
  Clark; Kenny Garrett (ss, as); Jeff Pittson (ky); Paul Jackson (b). 4/91.
Clark's versatile drumming bridges funk and jazz time with rare aplomb. The first album starts from a
tough hard-bop base and leans towards groove playing; the second beds down in the straight funk
rhythms of Clark and Jackson and uses Garrett's arsenal of licks to turn back towards jazz. Walrath
and Ford are failsafe soloists in this kind of situation and they eat up the changes on *Give The Drummer
Some*. Garrett and Pittson probably have less to say, but they have energy and chops to spare, too. On
both records, the rhythm section makes cheerful, engaging music by itself.

Sonny Clark (1931–63) PIANO

**** **Cool Struttin'** Blue Note 746513
  Clark; Art Farmer (t); Jackie McLean (as); Paul Chambers (b); Philly Joe Jones (d). 1/58.
***(*) **Leapin' And Lopin'** Blue Note 784091
  Clark; Tommy Turrentine (t); Ike Quebec, Charlie Rouse (ts); Butch Warren (b); Billy Higgins
  (d). 11/61.
It's slightly difficult now to remember that Clark was once the piano player of choice in the Blue Note
studios. He debuted on record with Wardell Gray, for Prestige this time, played with Dexter Gordon,
Sonny Rollins and Charles Mingus, and worked on Serge Chaloff's classic *Blue Serge* date for Capitol.
His short career was punctuated by lapses all too familiar from the period, and his last few years were
spent on an awful pendulum back and forth between heroin addiction and alcoholism (the latter contracted in a failed bid to cure himself of the former).
  Perhaps surprisingly, Clark's music betrays very little sign of the darkness of his life. In sharp contrast
to Bud Powell, who was still the dominant model for post-bop piano players, Clark gave off a sense of
effortless ease. Original melodies and variations on standards seemed to flow from his fingers and the
only player one might possibly confuse him with is Hampton Hawes, who also very seldom performed
solo.
  The Blue Notes are both excellent, albeit the rump of a larger documentation. In the light of a new issue
of *Cool Struttin'*, we have slightly tempered our enthusiasm for *Leapin' And Lopin'*, which has him in the
sympathetic company of Turrentine and Rouse, and, for one track only, Ike Quebec; a sample track can
be found on the *Art Of Ike Quebec* compilation. Though 'Voodoo' stands out as a brilliant original
composition, 'Deep In A Dream' is Clark's classic performance, choruses of beautifully inventive piano
following one another without the slightest hint of strain. Nothing else quite comes up that standard. As
a whole, though, *Cool Struttin'* is more coherent. Farmer and McLean play with the same passionate
insouciance and there are moments on 'Blue Minor' and 'Deep Night' when the music virtually levitates.
  For all his exuberant self-confidence, he never quite seemed a convincing professional, but rather an
inspired amateur, happy when there was a piano in the corner, a bottle open on top, and some business
to be attended to in a back room.

Kenny Clarke (1914–85) DRUMS, XYLOPHONE

***(*) **Special Kenny Clarke, 1938–1959** Jazz Time 799 702
  Clarke; Benny Bailey, Bernard Hullin, Ack Van Rooyen, Clark Terry (t); Nat Peck, Billy Byers,
  Benny Vasseur (tb); Hubert Fol, John Brown, Jean Aldegon, Mickey Nicholas (as); Rudy Powell
  (cl, as); Lucky Thompson, Georges Grenu, Pierre Gossez (ts); Eric Dixon (ts, f); Tony Scott (ts,
  cl); Cecil Payne, Armand Migiani (bs); Ralph Schecroun, Raymond Fol, Edgar Hayes, Bernard
  Pfeiffer, Art Simmons, Maurice Vandair (p); Elek Bacsik, Eddie Gibbs (g); Jean Bouchety,
  Michel Gaudry, Coco Darling, Al McKibbon, Pierre Michelot (b); James Anderson, Billie Poole
  (v). 3/38, 3/48, 10/49, 6, 9 & 10/57, 3/58, 11/59.
*** **Telefunken Blues** Savoy SV 0106
  Clarke; Henry Coker (tb); Frank Morgan (as); Walter Benton (ts); Frank Wess (ts, f); Charlie
  Fowlkes (bs); Milt Jackson (vib, v); Gerry Wiggins (p); Percy Heath, Eddie Jones (b). 11/54, 2/
  55.
***(*) **Kenny Clarke And Ernie Wilkins** Savoy SV 0222
  Clarke; Eddie Bert (tb); Ernie Wilkins (as, ts); George Ballow (ts, bs); Cecil Payne (bs); Hank
  Jones (p); Wendell Marshall (b). 3/55.
***(*) **Bohemia After Dark** Savoy SV 0107
  Clarke; Nat Adderley (c); Donald Byrd (t); Cannonball Adderley (as); Jerome Richardson (ts,
  f); Hank Jones, Horace Silver (p); Paul Chambers (b). 6 & 7/55.

*** **Discoveries** Savoy SV 0251
    Clarke; Nat Adderley (*c*); Donald Byrd (*t*); Cannonball Adderley (*as*); Jerome Richardson (*f,
    ts*); Horace Silver (*p*); Paul Chambers (*b*). 6/55.
*** **Jazz Men Detroit** Savoy SV 0176
    Clarke; Pepper Adams (*bs*); Kenny Burrell (*g*); Tommy Flanagan (*p*); Paul Chambers (*b*). 4 & 5/
    56.
*** **Meets The Detroit Jazz Men** Savoy SV 0243
    As above.
*** **Transatlantic Meetings** Vogue 211512
    Clarke; Jimmy Deuchar (*t*); Bill Byers (*tb*); Allen Eager (*ts*); Martial Solal (*p*); Benoit Quersin
    (*b*). 10/54.
**** **Plays André Hodeir** Philips 834 542
    Clarke; Roger Guérin (*t*); Billy Byers, Nat Peck (*tb*); Hubert Rostaing (*as*); Armand Migiani
    (*bs*); Martial Solal, René Urtreger (*p*); Pierre Michelot, Jean Warland (*b*). 10 & 11/56.

'Klook', so called because of the distinctive 'klook-mop' sound of his favourite cadence, is one of the most influential drummers of all time. There are those who allow him a hand in the invention of bebop, and certainly in recent times the focus of the bebop revolution has shifted away from the horn-men and towards the rhythm section that gave bop its ferocious energy and drive. While working with Dizzy Gillespie in the early 1940s, having made his recording debut at 24 in Sweden (see *Special*) with the dire James Anderson on vocals, Clarke began to depart from normal practice by marking the count on his top cymbal and using his bass drum only for accents. With his left hand he rattled out the counter-rhythms that weave their way through all these records. It became the distinctive sound of bebop, imitated and adapted by Blakey and Roach, who came to the music with rather different presuppositions about it, and it remains essential background work for drummers even today. Clarke had a strong but also quite delicate sound. The cover of *Plays André Hodeir* shows him wielding extra-long sticks, as he did from time to time throughout his career; they enabled him to get around his kit and to pick out a highly nuanced sound that lesser drummers could never duplicate.

The Savoys are generally good, but the Jazz Time compilation is a valuable starting point, covering Clarke's works from those early Swedish sessions right through to 1959, by which time he was established in Paris. *Special* includes sessions made under the leadership of Hubert Fol and Art Simmons, and one 1957 session devoted to Pierre Michelot compositions – and remarkably good they are, too. Clarke's solo on 'Iambic Pentameter' with Fol is a good example of where he was at in the late '40s. Historically, though, the four tracks recorded with Lucky Thompson, Solal and Michelot in September 1957 (they include Parker's 'Now's The Time', Miles's 'Four' and Tadd Dameron's 'Squirrel') are of great interest, showing how logically the whole 'cool' school evolved out of bebop, and was even inscribed in it.

CD transfer means that Clarke comes through a bit better than of yore, but no great effort has been made on any of these records to lift him up with horns. Fortunately, Clarke always raised his game when he was playing with loud and forceful players, and the Detroit encounter (actually recorded in Hackensack) has him working round Pepper Adams and Burrell like a dancing master. This material has been repackaged with an additional 'Tricotism' as *Meets*; potential customers would be well advised to check that they're not duplicating (and should note that the session is sometimes credited to Kenny Burrell). They should also be aware that *Discoveries* is shared with material under Adderley's leadership and that the Clark/Solal tracks share space with a 1954 transatlantic encounter between fellow-drummer Roy Haynes and pianist Henri Renaud.

Clarke and Milt Jackson trade fascinating ideas on *Telefunken Blues* (the Swedish debut had featured Klook as a xylophonist), but the essential record is *Bohemia After Dark*, featuring the Adderleys at their antagonistic best and Byrd still sounding like a man who'd drunk at Dizzy's cup. These are perhaps Clarke's finest hour, certainly as a leader, and 'Late Entry', which Byrd sits out, should be in everybody's collection. The Hodeir arrangements, of 'Round Midnight', 'When Lights Are Low' and other tunes, are fascinating. What the collective personnel above doesn't reveal is that the October 1956 session was with a brass-only sextet, no saxophones. It's a rare and exciting sound. The later dates are much less original, and the deficiencies of Rostaing and Migiani don't help; but, with Solal and Michelot on hand, the engine-room is in perfect running order. The final session, scored for just trumpet, trombone and baritone saxophone, is more successful, and Migiani excels himself on 'Bemsha Swing' and the tailor-made 'Blue Serge'.

The more recently reissued Clarke/Wilkins session from 1955 rounds out this splendidly well-documented period. A powerful, dark-toned group, they give dark, full-voiced readings of tunes by Wilkins and session supervisor Ozzie Cadena (who proves to be no mean composer). One of the most remarkable things in the entire catalogue is Clarke's solo gloss on Parker's 'Now's The Time' (the great man having passed away a little over two weeks previously); Clarke makes no attempt to play the melody, but his statement of the rhythm is clean-lined and uncomplicated, a remarkably disciplined performance.

***(*) **Pieces Of Time** Soul Note 121078
    Clarke; Andrew Cyrille, Milford Graves, Famoudou Don Moye (*d, perc*). 9/83.
Though the record was hailed on release as a much-needed reminder that Milford Graves was still alive and functioning, Klook was the elder statesman at this astonishing confrontation, and he more or less steals the show with a seemingly effortless display that has the younger guys diving into their bags for ever more exotic wrinkles on the same basic sound. Not to all tastes, perhaps, but an intriguing and historic record nevertheless.

Clarke-Boland Big Band GROUP

*** **Three Adventures** MPS 529 095
    Kenny Clarke (*d*); Francy Boland (*p*); Benny Bailey, Idrees Sulieman, Milo Pavlovich, Jimmy Deuchar, Dusko Goykovich (*t*); Ake Persson, Nat Peck, Erik Van Lier (*tb*); Derek Humble, Phil Woods, Johnny Griffin, Ronnie Scott, Tony Coe, Sahib Shihab (*reeds*); Jimmy Woode, Jean Warland (*b*); Kenny Clarke, Shake Keane, Albert 'Tootie' Heath, Tony Inzalaco, Sabu Martinez (*perc*). 8 & 12/68.
Three large-scale pieces – 'Latin Kaleidoscope', 'Cuban Fever' and 'Fellini 712' – by one of the most exciting big bands of the post-war years. Joint leadership did them nothing but good. Boland steered the harmonies, Clarke piled on the coal and steamed. It was a near-perfect combination of strengths and it lasted them for many years. These are welcome reissues, missing for many years. Studio sound is roomy and generous, with plenty of space round bass and drums, though an odd spatial separation here and there among the horns on the Fellini suite which may be deliberate but has no obvious rationale.

The Classic Jazz Quartet GROUP

**** **The Complete Recordings** Jazzology JCD-138/139 2CD
    Dick Sudhalter (*c*); Joe Muranyi (*cl, ss*); Dick Wellstood (*p*); Marty Grosz (*g, v*). 11/84–3/86.
The Classic Jazz Quartet – they preferred their original name, The Bourgeois Scum – were one of the pioneer outfits who helped create the renewed taste for old(er) jazz repertory in the 1980s and '90s. This package is a comprehensive set of their work – two studio LPs, plus about an LP's worth of previously unreleased, live-without-an-audience music – set down before Wellstood's untimely death ended the group. They resuscitate much neglected material from the 1920s and '30s, fill in with the odd chestnut and sneak by a few originals. The range of arrangement and dynamic which a quartet can touch on is surprising at this length, and the band always surprises, though the Germanic treatment of 'Mississippi Mud' will be tiresome to some. Grosz's wit has become relatively familiar in the last ten years, but the feel of this music has a freshness about it that some subsequent revivalism has missed; Sudhalter does a fine line in neo-Bix, the undervalued Muranyi is consistently strong; and 'the engine, the generator, driving the whole contraption', Wellstood shows why the band went down when he did. The notes in the booklet are rather exhaustingly clever, and the remastered sound is very fine.

James Clay (born 1935) TENOR SAXOPHONE

*** **The Sound Of The Wide Open Spaces** Original Jazz Classics OJC 257
    Clay; David Newman (*ts*); Wynton Kelly (*p*); Sam Jones (*b*); Art Taylor (*d*). 4/60.
*** **A Double Dose Of Soul** Original Jazz Classics OJC 1790
    Clay; Nat Adderley (*c*); Vic Feldman (*vib*); Gene Harris (*p*); Sam Jones (*b*); Louis Hayes (*d*). 10/60.
Clay is a semi-legendary figure whose reported influence on Ornette Coleman is interesting but scarcely borne out by these early records. *The Sound* gets into the brawling spirit typical of such two-tenor encounters but offers only a glimpse of Clay as a distinctive force. *A Double Dose* is only marginally more interesting, given that the date is organized as little more than a rote hard-bop affair, but Feldman's vibes are an unusual foil on three tunes and 'Linda Serene' and 'Lost Tears' are mildly interesting originals.

Buck Clayton (1911–91) TRUMPET

***(*) **The Classic Swing Of Buck Clayton** Original Jazz Classics OJC 1709
    Clayton; Dicky Wells, Trummy Young (*tb*); Buster Bailey, Scoville Brown (*cl*); George Johnson

(*as*); Jimmy Jones, Billy Taylor (*p*); Brick Fleagle, Tiny Grimes (*g*); John Levy, Al McKibbon, Sid Weiss (*b*); Cozy Cole, Jimmy Crawford (*d*). 46.

***(*) **Buck Special** Vogue 2111513
Clayton; Bill Coleman, Aimé Haruche, Alex Renard, Pierre Selin, André Simon, Merrill Steppter (*t*); René Godard, George Kennedy, Jean-Jacques Léger (*as, bs*); Don Byas, Alix Combelle, Armand Conrad (*ts*); Henri Mast (*bs*); Charlie Lewis, Jean-Claude Pelletier, André Persianny (*p*); Roger Chaput (*g*); George Hadjo, Yvon Leguen (*b*); Wallace Bishop, Christian Garros (*d*). 10 & 11/49, 10/53.

*** **Jam Sessions From The Vaults** Columbia 463336
Clayton; Billy Butterfield, Ruby Braff, Joe Newman (*t*); Henderson Chambers, Bennie Green, Urbie Green, Dicky Harris, J. C. Higginbotham (*tb*); Tyree Glenn (*tb, vtb*); Lem Davis (*as*); Julian Dash, Coleman Hawkins, Buddy Tate (*ts*); Charlie Fowlkes (*bs*); Kenny Kersey, Sir Charles Thompson, Al Waslohn (*p*); Freddie Green, Steve Jordan (*g*); Milt Hinton, Walter Page (*b*); Bobby Donaldson, Jo Jones (*d*); Jimmy Rushing (*v*). 53-56.

*** **Copenhagen Concert** Steeplechase SCCD 36006/7 2CD
Clayton; Emmett Berry (*t*); Dicky Wells (*tb*); Earl Warren (*as, cl*); Buddy Tate (*ts*); Al Williams (*p*); Gene Ramey (*b*); Herbie Lovelle (*d*); Jimmy Rushing (*v*). 9/59.

***(*) **Buck & Buddy** Original Jazz Classics OJC 757
Clayton; Buddy Tate (*ts*); Sir Charles Thompson (*p*); Gene Ramey (*b*); Mousie Alexander (*d*). 12/60.

***(*) **A Buck Clayton Jam Session** Chiaroscuro CRD 132
Clayton; Doc Cheatham, Joe Newman (*t*); Urbie Green (*tb*); Earl Warren (*as*); Budd Johnson, Zoot Sims (*ts*); Joe Temperley (*bs*); Earl Hines (*p*); Milt Hinton (*b*); Gus Johnson (*d*).

*** **Buck Clayton Meets Big Joe Turner** Black BLCD 760170
Clayton; Bosko Petrovic (*vib*); Davor Kajfes (*p*); Kresimir Remeta (*b*); Silvije Glojnaric (*d*); Big Joe Turner (*v*). 6/65.

*** **Ben And Buck** Sackville SKCD 22037
Clayton; Ben Webster (*ts*); Henri Chaix (*p*); Alain Du Bois (*g*); Isla Eckinger (*b*); Romano Cavicchiolo (*d*). 67.

*** **A Swingin' Dream** Stash STCD 16
Clayton; Spanky Davis, Paul Cohen, Johnny Letman (*t*); Dan Barrett, Bobby Pring (*tb*); Chuck Wilson (*as, cl*); Kenny Hing, Doug Lawrence (*ts*); Joe Temperley (*bs*); Mark Shane (*p*); Chris Flory (*g*); Ed Jones (*b*); Mel Lewis (*d*). 10/88.

Clayton is one of the great players of mainstream jazz. Responsible for no particular stylistic innovation, he managed to synthesize much of the history of jazz trumpet up to his time with a bright, brassy tone and an apparently limitless facility for melodic improvisation, which made him ideal for open-ended jams like the Columbia reissue of *All The Cats Join In* (which is approximately how it sounds) and the rather good one on Chiaroscuro. He played with Basie until 1946, the year of the fine *Classic Swing* sessions, and after a stint in the army struck off on his own again, forming a productive association with shouter Jimmy Rushing which survived long enough for the European tour featured on the Steeplechase set. Clayton was a superb vocal accompanist and his fills and subtle responses are always tasteful, but he's heard to better effect on the instrumental All Stars tracks from the same occasion, tackling 'Moonglow' with consummate artistry and taste.

Buck Special finds him at the peak of his powers. While touring in France in 1949, he recorded two sessions for Vogue, one with a smaller group, one with a trombone-less, mid-size band (the liner-notes get a little tied up over this point) which lends 'Uncle Buck', 'B.C. & B.C.', 'Perdido' and the title-tune a ringing sonority that sets off the solos beautifully. The recording has great presence. The big-band recordings, made in 1953 while Clayton was in France with Mezz Mezzrow, were actually under Alix Combelle's leadership and feature Buck's arrangements of eight Combelle tunes. The Frenchman was a Coleman Hawkins disciple with an enviable technique and an interesting grasp of blues harmony; 'Blues En Cuivres' is the best example. *Pace* Claude Carrière's note, this band did have trombones, but they're kept subordinate to the same rippling front line.

The association with Buddy Tate, a saxophonist of similar lineage, was a happy one for Buck. Much of the music on *Buck & Buddy* was formerly on the Prestige double LP, *Kansas City Nights*. Originally recorded for Swingville, it gives a near-perfect sense of where Buck was at the end of his last really productive decade before the trumpeter's curse, persistent lip problems, began to curtail his activity. There's certainly no sign of difficulty here. He traded figures with Tate on 'Birdland Betty' and more romantic shapes on 'When A Woman Loves A Man'.

The partial reappearance of the Columbia material helps balance up the picture but these are still not complete, and in default of the rest it would be worth considering the OJC. 'Harlem Cradle Song', with Young and Wells, has a lovely, easy swing, and there is a fine instrumental version of 'I Want A Little Girl' that avoids the slightly crass quality of the Rushing version.

Another singer in that same bellowing mould appears on the Black Lion, though rather more briefly than the title would suggest, and it seems a little cynical to have billed the set this way. Essentially, it's Buck with vibist Petrovic's well-drilled group, recorded in Zagreb. The Yugoslavs play with the faintly hysterical concentration of men who know they're not going to believe this in the morning; but they don't let the guest down, even if they crowd him a little here and there. On 'I Can't Get Started', he simply ignores the beat and lets his solo find its own route and pace.

Buck wasn't playing at all towards the end. He suffered a serious collapse immediately after the *Ben and Buck* concert and after that was never up to soloing with any sort of attack or pressure. On *A Swingin' Dream*, just a couple of years away from the end, he conducts a small big band (same size as Chick Webb's at its peak) in a selection of mostly new or recent compositions. Only 'Avenue C' is an oldie, though almost any of the numbers – the ballad 'Smoothie', for instance – might have come from the old days with Basie. For non-specialist collectors, the limiting factor here is Buck's position as leader and conductor rather than soloist, but big-band fans will be well satisfied and will echo Earl Warren's enraptured shout of 'All right! All right!' at the close of the blues, 'Margaux'.

Jay Clayton VOCALS

*** The Jazz Alley Tapes Hep CD 2046
        Clayton; Jay Thomas (*t, as*); Jeff Hay (*tb*); Don Lanphere (*ts*); Marc Seales (*p, ky*); Chuck Deardorf (*b*); Dean Hodges (*d*). 9/88.

Clayton is a vividly gifted vocal improviser whose feel for a lyric is perhaps less convincing than her ability to mimic horn lines. Though rooted in bebop, she's also capable of tackling more demanding harmony, like the version of 'Equinox' on the same record, and the variations of Coltrane's 'Mr P.C.' on *Tapes*. Oddly, she sounds too close to Don Lanphere's saxophone for that now well-established relationship to work as well as they seem to feel it does. They obviously play comfortably together (Clayton is also featured on his *Go . . . Again*), but there's something rather too bland and pat about it. Another of the singer's associations worth following up is her partnership with the String Trio of New York, for whom see below.

Clayton–Hamilton Jazz Orchestra GROUP

*** Groove Shop Capri 74021
        Bobby Bryant, Snooky Young, Oscar Brashear, Clay Jenkins (*t, flhn*); George Bohannon, Ira Nepus, Thurman Green (*tb*); Maurice Spears (*btb*); Jeff Clayton (*ss, as, ts, ob, f*); Bill Green (*as, cl, f*); Rickey Woodard (*ts, cl*); Charles Owens (*ts, cl*); Lee Callet (*bs, bcl*); Bill Cunliffe (*p*); Doug MacDonald (*g*); John Clayton (*b*); Jeff Hamilton (*d*). 4/89.
*** Heart And Soul Capri 74028
        As above, except Jim Hershman (*g*) replaces MacDonald. 2/91.
*** Absolutely! Lake Street LSR 52002
        As above, except add Chuck Findley (*t*) and Dave Bjur (*b*). 94.

It's the arranging, by ex-Basieite John Clayton, which gives this blithe orchestra its character: there are some good soloists here, especially Snooky Young and Rickey Woodard, but the integration and polish of the sections are what makes the music come alive. Clayton seeks little more than grooving rhythms and call-and-response measures, and they all figure dutifully enough in the arrangements, though occasionally – as on the very slow and piecemeal variation on 'Take The "A" Train' on *Heart And Soul* – the band have something more out-of-the-ordinary to play. Detailed and full-blooded recording lets one hear how all the wheels go round. The most recent album, *Absolutely!*, continues this serene sequence. The opening Basie-like 'Blues For Stephanie' is a grand manifesto which some of the later tracks don't quite carry off – 'Prelude To A Kiss' and 'A Beautiful Friendship' are rather ordinary – but the enthusiasm of the band seems undiminished, and the straightforward arrangements are a modest tonic at a time when big-band charts seem to be growing more like obstacle courses.

Gilles Clement GUITAR

**(*) Wes Side Stories Musidisc 500492
        Clement; Alain Jean-Marie (*p*); Yves Torchinsky (*b*); Eric Dervieu (*d*). 5/93.

Attractively unpretentious guitar jazz, broadly in the style of the master, with a few unexpected wrinkles thrown in by Jean-Marie, who has seen service with Abbey Lincoln, Teddy Edwards and, out in left field, Charles Tolliver. The mix of originals and Montgomery compositions is varied by a Thelonious Monk composition ('Hackensack'), and by 'Close Your Eyes', which the pianist may have brought in from Abbey's book. Unfortunately, it isn't quite varied enough, and it's a slightly worrying situation when you sit up and take notice of bass solos rather than the front man.

Alex Cline (born 1956) DRUMS, PERCUSSION

*** **The Lamp And The Star** ECM 1372
> Cline; Aina Kemanis, Nels Cline (*v*); Jeff Gauthier (*vn, vla, v*); Hank Roberts (*clo, v*); Wayne Peet (*p, org*); Eric Von Essen (*b*); Susan Rawcliffe (*didjeridu*). 9/87.

The Clines – Alex and guitarist Nels – used to trade under the name Quartet Music, partnered by Gauthier and von Essen. The music they make with an augmented line-up is even further from academia, full of lush textures and strange transitions that don't conform to any recognizable logic. *The Lamp And The Star* has an unspecifically devotional programme, characterized by Cline's imagistic titles – 'A Blue Robe In The Distance', 'Emerald Light', 'Accepting The Chalice' – but there is nothing mushy or New Age-ish about the music, which has a strong and very individual resonance. Well worth checking out.

Nels Cline (born 1956) GUITAR, ELECTRIC GUITAR

*** **Angelica** Enja 5063
> Cline; Stacy Rowles (*t, flhn*); Tim Berne (*as*); Eric Von Essen (*b*); Alex Cline (*d*). 8/87.

*** **Silencer** Enja 6098
> Cline; Mark Loudon Sims (*b*); Michael Preussner (*d*). 12/90.

These could almost be by a Charlie Haden band of the early 1970s, with Cline picking as gently and fluently as Sam Brown and Berne summoning up something close to Carlos Ward's muezzin quaver. To continue the parallel, twin brother Alex Cline, who has gigged and recorded with Haden, works in a seam originally opened up by Paul Motian, but with a far heavier accent.

Worth searching out, *Angelica* is a series of dedications – to Maria Farandouri, to the Chilean martyr Victor Jara, to bandoneon virtuoso Dino Saluzzi, to Vinny Golia (who does a superb production job) and, on the superb long 'Fives And Sixes', to trumpeter Booker Little.

Two years after *Angelica* and with a regularly working band, Cline seems to have found the balance he wants between rock'n'roll pyrotechnics and a much more atmospheric and minimalist guitar-trio sound. Set alongside some of Terje Rypdal's recent trios, *Silencer* seems much more thoughtful and considered, examining textures and slow transitions rather than heading straight for Rypdal's all-out ferocity. The opening 'Las Vegas Tango' (a Gil Evans composition) and the two-part 'Lapsing' are the most evocative, the latter suggesting something of Cline's growing stature as a composer. The sound is slightly muzzy, like a picture taken through a Vaselined lens, but that suits the progress of the music rather well.

Rosemary Clooney (born 1928) VOCAL

*** **Blue Rose** Mobile Fidelity MFCD-850
> Clooney; Willie Cook, Ray Nance, Clark Terry, Cat Anderson (*t*); Gordon Jackson, Britt Woodman, John Sanders (*tb*); Johnny Hodges (*as*); Russell Procope (*as, cl*); Jimmy Hamilton (*cl, ts*); Paul Gonsalves (*ts*); Harry Carney (*bs*); Duke Ellington (*p*); Jimmy Woode (*b*); Sam Woodyard (*d*). 56.

Ellington's collaborations with singers were few, and the pairing with Rosemary Clooney was, on the face of it, surprising. In fact, she overdubbed her parts on to already-recorded Ellington tracks. Yet it works very well: as a pop stylist who recognized rather than courted jazz-singing principles, she handles Ellington's often difficult (for a singer) songs with attentive finesse, and it culminates in one of the most gracious and thought-through versions of 'Sophisticated Lady' on record.

*** **Everything's Coming Up Rosie** Concord CCD 4047
> Clooney; Bill Berry (*t*); Scott Hamilton (*ts*); Nat Pierce (*p*); Monty Budwig (*b*); Jake Hanna (*d*). 77.

*** **Here's To My Lady** Concord CCD 4081
> As above, except add Warren Vaché (*c*). 79.

***(*) **Sings The Lyrics Of Ira Gershwin** Concord CCD 4112
> Clooney; Warren Vaché (*c, flhn*); Scott Hamilton (*ts*); Roger Glenn (*f*); Nat Pierce (*p*); Cal Collins (*g*); Chris Amberger (*b*); Jeff Hamilton (*d*). 10/79.

*** **With Love** Concord CCD 4144
    Clooney; Warren Vaché (*c, flhn*); Scott Hamilton (*ts*); Nat Pierce (*p*); Cal Tjader (*vib*); Cal
    Collins (*g*); Bob Maize (*b*); Jake Hanna (*d*). 11/80.
*** **Sings The Music Of Cole Porter** Concord CCD 4185
    As above, except add David Ladd (*f*). 1/82.
***(*) **Sings The Music Of Harold Arlen** Concord CCD 4210
    Clooney; Warren Vaché (*c*); Scott Hamilton (*ts*); Dave McKenna (*p*); Ed Bickert (*g*); Steve
    Wallace (*b*); Jake Hanna (*d*). 1/83.

Clooney virtually quit music in the 1960s and went through some difficult personal times, but her re-emergence with Concord in the 1970s and '80s has been one of the most gratifying returns of recent years. Not all of her 16 albums for the label have yet made it to CD, but the best of them – and they're a very consistent run – set a very high standard. If she is not, at her own insistence, a jazz singer, she responds to the in-house team with warm informality and the breadth of her voice smooths over any difficulties with some of the more intractable songs. Her voice has a more matronly and less flexible timbre than before, but pacing things suits her style, and good choices of tempo are one of the hall-marks of this series. The 'Songbook' sequence is one of the best of its kind: the Arlen and Gershwin records are particularly fine. *With Love* has some indifferent 'contemporary' tunes from the likes of Billy Joel, but the rest of it more than matches up. Countless cameos from Hamilton, Vaché and the others lend further class.

*** **My Buddy** Concord CCD 4226
    Clooney; Scott Wagstaff, Mark Lewis, Paul Mazzio, Bill Byrne, Dan Fornero (*t, flhn*); Gene
    Smith, John Fedchock (*tb*); Randy Hawes (*btb*); Woody Herman (*cl, as*); Frank Tiberi (*ts*);
    Mark Vinci, Jim Carroll (*ts, f*); Nick Brignola (*bs*); John Oddo (*p*); John Chiodini (*g*); John
    Adams (*b*); Jeff Hamilton (*d*). 8/83.
*** **Sings The Music Of Irving Berlin** Concord CCD 4255
    Clooney; Warren Vaché (*c, flhn*); Scott Hamilton (*ts*); John Oddo (*p*); Ed Bickert, Chris Flory
    (*g*); Phil Flanigan (*b*); Gus Johnson (*d*). 6/84.
***(*) **Rosemary Clooney Sings Ballads** Concord CCD 4282
    As above, except Chuck Israels (*b*) and Jake Hanna (*d*) replace Flory, Flanigan and Johnson. 4/
    85.
*** **Sings The Music Of Jimmy Van Heusen** Concord CCD 4308
    As above, except Michael Moore (*b*) and Joe Cocuzzo (*d*) replace Israels and Hanna; add Emily
    Remler (*g*). 8/86.
**** **Sings The Lyrics Of Johnny Mercer** Concord CCD 4333
    As above, except Dan Barrett (*tb*) replaces Remler. 8/87.
***(*) **Show Tunes** Concord CCD 4364
    Clooney; Warren Vaché (*c*); Scott Hamilton (*ts*); John Oddo (*p*); John Clayton (*b*); Jeff
    Hamilton (*d*). 8–11/88.
*** **Sings Rodgers, Hart And Hammerstein** Concord CCD 4405
    Clooney; Jack Sheldon (*t, v*); Chauncey Welsh (*tb*); Scott Hamilton (*ts*); John Oddo (*p*); John
    Clayton (*b*); Joe LaBarbera (*d*); The L.A. Jazz Choir (*v*). 10/89.

John Oddo began working regularly with Clooney with the Woody Herman album, and has been MD of most of the records since. But the steady, articulate feel of the records is a continuation of what came before. The Johnny Mercer is perhaps the single best record Clooney has ever done: the choice of songs is peerless, and she has the measure of every one. *Show Tunes*, though something of a mixture, is another very good one, and the *Ballads* and Jimmy Van Heusen discs are full of top-rank songs. Very little to choose among any of these sets, though the Mercer would be our first choice for anyone who wants just a taste of what Rosie can do.

(*) **For The Duration Concord CCD 4444
    Clooney; Warren Vaché (*c*); Scott Hamilton (*ts*); John Oddo (*p*); Chuck Berghofer, Jim
    Hughart (*b*); Jake Hanna (*d*); strings. 10/90.
*** **Girl Singer** Concord CCD 4496
    Clooney; Warren Luening, George Graham, Larry Hall, Bob Summers (*t, flhn*); Chauncey
    Welsh, Bill Booth, Bill Elton, George Roberts (*tb*); Brad Warnaar (*frhn*); Dan Higgins (*c, as, ts,
    f*); Joe Soldo (*cl, as, f*); Gary Foster (*as, af, f*); Pete Christlieb (*cl, ts, f*); Bob Cooper (*ts, f*); Bob
    Tricarico (*bs, bcl, f*); John Oddo (*ky*); Tim May (*g*); Tom Warrington (*b*); Joe LaBarbera (*d*); Joe
    Porcaro (*perc*); Monica Mancini, Ann White, Mitchel Moore, Earl Brown, Mitch Gordon (*v*).
    11–12/91.

If anything, these are slightly disappointing. *For The Duration* is a set of wartime songs similar to one attempted by Mel Torme and George Shearing, and Clooney belabours what is occasionally trite (or at least over-exposed) material. *Girl Singer* features an orchestra which has one thinking about the small group of the earlier records: if that formula had perhaps been used to the point of diminishing returns, this one is a top-heavy alternative which suits Clooney's voice less well. Still, Oddo's arrangements leave room for some solos from the horns, and the singer moves from Dave Frishberg to Duke Ellington to Cy Coleman songs with her customary resilience.

***(*) **Do You Miss New York?** Concord CCD4537
    Clooney; Warren Vaché (*c*); Scott Hamilton (*ts*); John Oddo (*p*); John Pizzarelli (*g, v*); Bucky
    Pizzarelli (*g*); David Finck (*b*); Joe Cocuzzo (*d*). 9/92.
*** **Still On The Road** Concord CCD-4590
    Clooney; Warren Luening, Rick Baptist, George Graham, Larry Hall, Larry McGuire (*t, flhn*);
    Chauncey Welsh, Bill Elton, Charley Loper, Phil Teele, Lew McCreary (*tb*); Gary Foster, Nino
    Tempo, Joe Soldo, Tommy Newsom, Bob Tricarico, Dan Higgins, Don Ashworth (*reeds*); John
    Oddo (*ky*); Tim May, Steve Lukather (*g*); Chuck Berghofer (*b*); Jeff Hamilton (*d*); Joe Porcaro,
    Dan Greco (*perc*); Earl Brown, Jack Sheldon (*v*). 11/93.
Turning 65, Rosie still sounds in very good form, although some of Concord's production decisions seem designed to push her towards kitsch rather than great singing situations. *Do You Miss New York?* is an album of Big Apple memories and her best since *Show Tunes* – excellent material, the Concord house-team in strong form and the singer notably relaxed and amiable. 'As Long As I Live' and a duet with John Pizzarelli on 'It's Only A Paper Moon' work out very well. *Still On The Road* is one of those travelogue albums (Rosie did a similar one years ago with Bing Crosby) and benefits from some high-stepping, big-band charts, but Willie Nelson and Paul Simon are composers she shouldn't bother with, and guest spots by Earl Brown and Jack Sheldon were misguided ideas.

*** **Demi-Centennial** Concord CCD 4633
    As above, except add Wayne Bergeron (*t*), Fred Simmons (*tb*), Ron Jannelli, Vince Trombetta
    (*reeds*), Thomas Warrington (*b*), Steve Houghton (*d*); omit Hall, McRearey, Tempo, Newsom,
    Tricarico, Lukather, Hamilton, Greco, Brown, Sheldon. 10–11/94.
*** **Dedicated To Nelson** Concord CCD 4685
    As above, except add George Roberts (*tb*), Gene Cipriano (*reeds*), Dennis Budimir (*g*), Gregg
    Field (*d*); omit Simmons, Jannelli, Warrington, Houghton, Teele, Higgins, Ashworth, May,
    Porcaro. 9/95.
Demi-Centennial celebrates Clooney's fiftieth anniversary as a performer, and all the songs have personal ties. Some of the record comes close to drowning in American schmaltz, but it's hard not to find some of the songs affecting, and the sincerity of the singing is a given. Both this and the subsequent *Dedicated To Nelson* are so sumptuously recorded that it's possible just to enjoy the production values by themselves. For her latest, Clooney goes back to some transcriptions of arrangements which Nelson Riddle did for an old TV series: stretched to recordable length, they're brought to life by Oddo's crack team of studio pros. Very well done, and the singer enjoys herself, though her voice has lost some of the bloom of her earlier Concords.

Clusone 3 GROUP

*** **Clusone 3** Ramboy 02
    Michael Moore (*cl, bcl, as, mca, cel*); Ernst Reijseger (*clo*); Han Bennink (*d, perc*). 90.
***(*) **I Am An Indian** Ramboy/Gramavision GCD 79505
    As above. 6 & 12/93.
**** **Soft Lights And Sweet Music** hat ART CD 6153
    As above. 11/93.
This astonishing trio has been around for some time – since 1980, in fact – but it was only in 1988 when cellist Ernst Reijseger put together a quartet for the Clusone Festival in Italy that it took on its settled present form; pianist and composer Guus Janssen withdrew from the group shortly afterwards and it continued as a trio, though the more neutral '3' is still the preferred term.

    It makes sense of the music, too, since this is an improbable coalition. For all his showmanship – which famously includes a janitor routine, the wackiest use of 'brushes' you'll see or hear – Bennink is a great jazz drummer, with an impeccably elastic sense of time. Reijseger comes from a straighter tradition, but in a sense he is the real wild card here, playing his cello like a big guitar or squawking out raw *arco* outlines that don't seem to belong anywhere outside one of Rembrandt's slaughterhouse pictures. The expat. Moore is a calmer presence, but his playing is scarcely conventional, spinning nervy or ironically self-important little monologues as if into a mirror.

    The 1990 tour was still part of a getting-together process. It's only with the marvellous *I Am An Indian* – the back-cover adds the word *Too*, as in the Irving Berlin song – that the group really starts to sound like itself rather than an occasional get-together. There are originals (mostly improvised), standards (mostly

Berlin), and a range of off-beat jazz repertory pieces like Duke's 'Angelica (Purple Gazelle)', Bud Powell's 'Celia', Herbie Nichols's 'The Gig' and Dewey Redman's fierce 'Qow'. One suspects that these are chosen partly for their sheer unfamiliarity, but the group works its chemistry on them all.

The hat ART disc is devoted entirely to Berlin, except for 'Cuckoo In The Clock' and a piece by South African saxophonist (and erstwhile associate), Sean Bergin. Much in the way that label-mate Franz Koglmann rethinks and recolours classic jazz material, so the approach here is poised somewhere between respect and irreverence. 'I Am An Indian, Too' is the longest track, a weird, revisionary reprise. For the most part, the songs are performed straight, but refracted by a sort of naïve anti-technique that is genuinely unsettling and often both funny and moving. It's very hard to hear 'Let's Face The Music And Dance' in any other way again.

Johnny Coates Jr (born 1938) PIANO

*** **Portrait** Savoy SV 0234
Coates; Wendell Marshall (b); Kenny Clarke (d). 11/55, 5/56.
Something of a prodigy, Coates had his union card by age twelve and was gigging regularly through his teens, before recording this album with a top-flight bassist and drummer. The material is extraordinarily mixed: two originals – 'Coates Oats' and 'Sha-Ga-Da-Ga-Da' – and a mixture of standard songs in a mostly melancholy and sombre vein. 'Let's Get Lost' has something of the spare fragility Chet brought to it, while 'Skylark' and 'Little Girl Blue' have a sweetness that makes 'Ding Dong, The Witch Is Dead' (from *The Wizard Of Oz*) all the more startling.

Arnett Cobb (1918–89) TENOR SAXOPHONE

*** **Blow, Arnett, Blow** Original Jazz Classics OJC 794
Cobb; Strethen Davis (p); George Duvivier (b); Arthur Edgehill (d). 59.
*** **Party Time** Original Jazz Classics OJC 219
Cobb; Ray Bryant (p); Wendell Marshall (b); Arthur Taylor (d). 5/59.
*** **Blue And Sentimental** Prestige PRCD 24122
Cobb; Red Garland (p, cel); George Duvivier, George Tucker (b); J. C. Heard (d). 11/60.
*** **Again With Milt Buckner** Black and Blue BLE 59.052
Cobb; Milt Buckner (org); Candy Johnson (ts); Clarence Gatemouth Brown (g); Michael Silva (d). 7 & 8/73.
*** **The Wild Man from Texas** Black and Blue BLE 233099
Cobb; Wallace Davenport (t); Frank Buster Cooper (tb); Eddie Chamblee (ts); Earl Warren (as); Milt Buckner (org, vib); Lloyd Glenn, André Persianny (p); Tiny Grimes, Roland Lobligeois (b); Panama Francis (d). 5/74, 5/76.
*** **Arnett Cobb is Back** Progressive PCD 7037
Cobb; Derek Smith (p); George Mraz (b); Billy Hart (d). 6/78.
(*) **Live Timeless SJP 174
Cobb; Rein De Graaff (p); Jacques Schols (b); John Engels (d). 11/82.
*** **Show Time** Fantasy F 9659
Cobb; Dizzy Gillespie (t); Clayton Dyess (g); Paul English (p, org); Kenny Andrews, Sammy Price (p); Derrick Lewis (b); Malcolm Pinson, Mike Lefebvre (d). 8/87.
Cobb overcame serious illness and a crippling motor accident (several covers picture him propped on his crutches as he plays) to keep his career afloat in the 1960s and after. A powerful saxophonist in the so-called 'Texas tenor' tradition, he was an ideal big-band player – with Lionel Hampton mostly – who never scaled down quite enough for small-group work. On *Blow, Arnett, Blow* and the following *Party Time*, he is clearly still suffering the after-effects of the accident, playing awkwardly and doing not much more than going through the motions, however much sheer energy and drive he managed to muster.

The Paris date, co-led with Tiny Grimes, is pleasantly shambolic and the French crowd clearly had a ball. Grimes, though, had never entirely recovered from the great days with Tatum and is inclined to go his own way regardless. There is a good deal more French material on the Black and Blues, most of it fairly routine, but the stuff with Buckner is pretty exciting, and there are lovely moments on the *Midnight Show* session; '(I Don't Stand) A Ghost Of A Chance' also appears on the Progressive and, with a more sophisticated rhythm section, sounds remarkably close to some of Coltrane's early ballad performances.

Going Dutch suits Cobb pretty well. De Graaff is a fine, responsive accompanist who will go to his grave with a bent back from having carried so many visiting 'singles' over the years. Cobb plays well, if a little fruitily, and the sound is mostly adequate. The material on Fantasy is pretty late and frail. Cobb shares the Houston stage and the disc with Dizzy Gillespie and the singer, Jewel Brown. Two years before his death the tone is still intact, but there really isn't much to say any more and there's a queasy sense of going through the motions once too often. Newcomers might like to start with either of the 1973 discs.

***(*) **Tenor Tribute** Soul Note 121184
   Cobb; Jimmy Heath (*ts, ss, f*); Joe Henderson (*ts*); Benny Green (*p*); Walter Schmocker (*b*); Doug Hammond (*d*). 4/88.
(*) **Tenor Tribute, Volume 2 Soul Note 121194
   As above. 4/88.

Though this was always conceived as a collective project with a three-saxophone front line, Cobb gets the nod on grounds of alphabetical priority, seniority, and not least because this Nuremberg concert came in the last full year of the Texan's life. Like most similar things, this is full of exciting and entertaining episodes but won't hang together as a whole. Cobb sounds pretty good, considering. His choruses on 'Smooth Sailing' and during a lengthy ballad medley (all on Volume One) are nicely weighted and well – perhaps too well – thought out. However, he's comprehensively blown away by the two youngsters, who both sound full of vim and ideas. He does better on 'Cottontail', which opens Volume Two, but there isn't enough top-flight stuff to support a second disc, and it palls very quickly; even 'Flying Home' at curtain time lacks sparkle.

   Heath's lighter tone and occasional forays into soprano and flute broaden the range a bit, for this is otherwise pretty heavy fare. Green does his best to push it along, but there's not much manoeuvrability in a band like this and he has to rein in quite sharply more than once. Avid collectors only.

Junie Cobb (1896–1970) CLARINET, SOPRANO AND TENOR SAXOPHONES, VIOLIN, PIANO, VOCAL

***(*) **The Junie Cobb Collection, 1926–29** Collector's Classics COCD-14
   Cobb; Jimmy Cobb (*c, t*); Cicero Thomas (*t*); Arnett Nelson (*cl, ts*); Angelo Fernandez, Johnny Dodds, Darnell Howard (*cl*); Ernie Smith (*bs, bsx*); George James (*as, bs*); Tiny Parham, Jimmy Blythe, Frank Melrose, Alex Hill, Earl Frazier (*p*); Tampa Red (*g*); Eustern Woodfork (*bj*); Walter Wright (*tba*); Bill Johnson (*b*); Jimmy Bertrand (*d, xy, slide-whistle*); Clifford Jones (*d, kz*); Tommy Taylor, Harry Dial (*d*); W. E. Burton, Georgia Tom Dorsey (*v*). 6/26–10/29.

This is classic Chicago jazz of its period. Cobb was a jobbing musician on the local scene and, although he led groups as a reed specialist, he also played banjo and ended his career as a club pianist and accompanist. His groups – The Hometown Band, The Grains Of Corn and the Kansas City Tin Roof Stompers are three of those here – bounce along in a rough-and-ready barrelhouse manner, never touching the sophistications of Armstrong or Dodds (who turns up as sparring partner for Cobb on two early tracks) but creating their own peculiar exhilaration. Cobb's saxophone style, an idiosyncratic mix of slap-tongueing and the more progressive manner of Hawkins, gets a wild momentum going on some tracks; and reliable stompers such as Blythe, Melrose and Hill keep the music hot in the rhythm section, as does Woodfork's banjo. Jimmy Cobb plays most of the trumpet parts, often surprisingly effectively. There are also (among a generous 24 tracks) three cuts from a hitherto lost 1929 session for Vocalion. The transfers show variable levels of surface noise, but the remastering is lively and vivid throughout.

(*) **Chicago The Living Legends: Junie C. Cobb And His New Hometown Band Original Jazz Classics OJC 1825-2
   Cobb; Fip Ricard (*t*); Harlan Floyd (*tb*); Leon Washington (*cl, ts*); Ikey Robinson (*bj*); Walter Hill (*b*); Red Saunders (*d*); Annabelle Calhoun (*v*). 9/61.

Rediscovered in 1961, Cobb had given up clarinet in favour of piano. The pick-up band assembled for this session is mostly younger hands rather than old-timers (Robinson and Saunders are the exceptions), and some of the music sounds like tourist trad. But Cobb's enthusiasm carries much of the music, even if Washington is a comparatively ordinary substitute as reedsman.

Billy Cobham (born 1944) DRUMS, PERCUSSION, ELECTRONICS

***(*) **Spectrum** Atlantic 781428
   Cobham; Jimmy Owens (*t, flhn*); Joe Farrell (*as, ss, f*); Jan Hammer (*p, ky*); Tommy Bolin, John Tropea (*g*); Ron Carter, Lee Sklar (*b*); Ray Barretto (*perc*). 5/73.
** **Warning** GRP GRD 9528
   Cobham; Dean Brown (*g, g syn*); Gerry Etkins (*ky*); Baron Browne (*b*); Sa Davis (*perc*). 85.

(*) **Power Play GRP D 9536
    As above, except add Onaje Allan Gumbs (*ky*). 86.
*** **Picture This** GRP GRD 9551
    Cobham; Randy Brecker (*flhn*); Grover Washington (*saxes*); Michael Abene (*p*); Gerry Etkins
    (*ky*); Tom Scott (*lyricon*); Ron Carter (*b*); Victor Bailey, Abraham Laboriel (*b*); Sa Davis
    (*congas*). 87.

To some extent, the jury is still out on Billy Cobham. A superb technician and clearly a man of great
musical intelligence and resource, he has nevertheless committed some awful clunkers to record.
Whereas *Spectrum*, his debut as leader, was one of the finest records of the jazz-rock era, a record to set
alongside *Birds Of Fire*, *Head Hunters* and the earlier Return To Forever discs, much of what has
followed has been remarkably hazy. The cliché about Cobham – that he is all fire and fury and 20-minute
drum solos – has never stood up to scrutiny. In actuality, he is a somewhat introspective drummer whose
compositions are often blurry and unmemorable.

    Of the available albums, the best by far are the three late-1980s sets dominated by Gerry Etkins's fine,
robust keyboards and, in the case of *Picture This* (perhaps the best of the bunch), Grover Washington's
very underrated saxophone playing. Washington contributes a plangent but anger-edged solo line to the
beautiful 'Same Ole Love' and Prince's 'Sign O' The Times', and the old 'Taurian Matador' seems to
remember most of his most extravagant passes.

    The sad truth remains, though, that Cobham is much too good a drummer for most of the material he is
working with. The self-written things are full of interesting ideas (and the solo percussion 'Danse For
Noh Masque', again on *Picture This*, is highly inventive). The cross-over gestures of *Funky Thide*, *Flight
Time* and *Stratus* now seem wildly dated and Cobham unable to develop the dialect that had seemed so
fresh and strong with Miles Davis and the Mahavishnu Orchestra. *Observations* is particularly limp, and
Life And Times a small masterpiece of miscasting.

*** **The Best Of Billy Cobham** Atlantic 781588
    Cobham; Glenn Ferris (*tb, btb*); Randy Brecker (*t*); Michael Brecker (*sax*); John Abercrombie,
    Tommy Bolin, Cornell Dupree, John Scofield (*g*); Jan Hammer (*p, ky*); Milcho Leviev (*ky*);
    George Duke (*ky, v*); Alex Blake, Alphonso Johnson, Lee Sklar (*b*).
** **Billy's Best Hits** GRP 9575
    Cobham; Randy Brecker (*flhn*); Grover Washington (*saxes*); Michael Abene (*p*); Gerry Etkins
    (*ky*); Dean Brown (*g, g syn*); Tom Scott (*lyricon*); Baron Browne, Ron Carter (*b*); Victor Bailey,
    Abraham Laboriel (*b*); Sa Davis (*congas*). 85, 87.

There can't be many 'best of . . .' albums that really are. The Atlantic brings together materials from the
1970s, including such favourite tracks as 'Snoopy's Search', 'Red Baron' and 'Quadrant', all of which,
coincidentally, highlight the band that featured Jan Hammer and the late, lamented Tommy Bolin.
Culled from just two previous releases – *Warning* and *Picture This* – *Best Hits* puts together a very
acceptable package of latter-day Cobham funk-jazz that should do very well for all but dedicated
completists.

Michael Cochrane PIANO

***(*) **Elements** Soul Note SN 1151
    Cochrane; Tom Harrell (*t*); Bob Malach (*ts*); Dennis Irwin (*b*); James Madison (*d*). 9/85.

The ensembles are keenly pointed, the solos have great contextual power, and Cochrane's tunes are all
just slightly out of the ordinary: this is in sum a very interesting post-bop record by a leader looking
hard for new ground. 'Tone Row Piece No. 2' is the most surprising theme, the melody organized with
strict adherence to 12-tone technique, and, although it's a little less fluid than the other pieces, one can't
fault Cochrane's ambitions. Or his own playing – he has a terse, improvisational flair tempered by a
romantic streak. Harrell and the fine and underrated Malach sound in very good shape, and the contrast
between the boisterous 'Reunion' and the steadily darkening 'Waltz No. 1' shows the extent of the range
on offer here. Recommended.

*** **Song Of Change** Soul Note 121251-2
    Cochrane; Marcus McLaurine (*b*); Alan Nelson (*d*). 11/92.

Not exactly a retreat, but Cochrane's latest session pulls back on his ambitions to some degree, as the
sleeve-notes seem to aver ('no agenda, no ideology, no big ideas'). He still sounds convincing without the
cover of horns, and the trio work up some impressive interplay within the ensembles, even in such
lightweight material as 'Once I Loved'. But the five standards receive comparatively straightforward
piano-trio treatment, and Cochrane's four originals are a shade less compelling than some of his
previous writing. It goes out on a very swinging 'Bemsha Swing' indeed – but, all in all, a very slight
disappointment after the previous Soul Note.

Codona GROUP

***(*) **Codona** ECM 1132
>Don Cherry (*t, f, doussn'gouni, v*); Collin Walcott (*sitar, tabla, hammered dulcimer, sanza, v*);
>Nana Vasconcelos (*berimbau, perc, v*). 9/78.

*** **Codona 2** ECM 1177
>As above. 5/80.

*** **Codona 3** ECM 1243
>As above. 9/82.

In 1978, at Collin Walcott's behest, three musicians gathered in Tonstudio Bauer, Ludwigsburg, and recorded one of the iconic episodes in so-called (but never better called) 'world music'. Any tendency to regard Codona's music, or Walcott's compositions, as floating impressionism is sheer prejudice, for all these performances are deeply rooted in modern jazz (Coltrane's harmonies and rhythms, Ornette Coleman's melodic and rhythmic primitivism) and in another great and related improvisational tradition from Brazil.

Nothing done subsequently quite matches the impact of the original *Codona*. It featured three long Walcott pieces (most notably the closing 'New Light'), the collectively composed title-track, and a brief, witty medley of Ornette Coleman tunes and Stevie Wonder's 'Sir Duke'. The permutations of instrumental sound are astonishing, but rooted in a basic jazz-trio format of horn, harmony and percussion. All three men contribute string accompaniment: Walcott on his sitar, Vasconcelos on the 'bow-and-arrow' berimbau, Cherry on the Malian *doussn'gouni*. The interplay is precise and often intense.

The members' developing interests and careers created a centrifugal spin on the later albums, which are by no means as coherent or satisfying. At their best, though, which is usually when Walcott's writing is at its best, they are still compelling. 'Walking On Eggs' on *Codona 3* is one of his and their best performances.

Tony Coe (born 1934) TENOR SAXOPHONE, CLARINET, SOPRANO SAXOPHONE, BASS CLARINET

*** **Coe, Oxley & Co: Nutty On Willisau** hat Art 6046
>Coe; Chris Laurence (*b*); Tony Oxley (*d*). 8/83.

***(*) **Canterbury Song** Hot House HHCD 1005
>Coe; Benny Bailey (*t*); Horace Parlan (*p*); Jimmy Woode (*b*); Idris Muhammad (*d*). 88.

These discs confirm what fellow-players have been saying about Tony Coe for years. One of the finest saxophonists/clarinettists ever to grace these shores, he must also be one of the most ubiquitous (he played the lead saxophone part on Henry Mancini's 'Pink Panther' theme) and stylistically the most adaptable. *Canterbury Song* is a relaxed – sometimes deceptively relaxed – session, combining a near-perfect choice of material with a well-pedigree'd band of Americans, with some of whom Coe had previously worked in Europe (where his standing is even higher than at home) and in the Clarke–Boland Band. There are two fine originals, 'Canterbury Song' and 'Lagos'. The closing 'Morning Vehicle' is an intriguing theme highlighting Coe's superb clarinet. Parlan's taut chording (a childhood bout of polio allegedly, but only allegedly, restricts his right-hand play) opens out on a duo 'Blue 'N' Green' that re-invents some of the harmonic terrain and on 'Re: Person I Knew' (another theme with Bill Evans's hand on it; compare the trio version on *Nutty On Willisau*) where Coe's distinctive soprano tones are perfectly deployed.

Like all the hyphenate reed players – Sidney Bechet, Barney Bigard, Jimmy Giuffre – Coe assimilates the qualities of one horn to another; his clarinet punchy and full-throated, his soprano and tenor making complex legato runs with no loss of breath. He is equally adept at switching idioms, always in a recognizably personal accent. The 1983 double album links him with perhaps the finest improvising percussionist in Europe. Oxley's contribution to the standards is breathtaking, introducing an element of abstraction to 'Re: Person I Knew' and to a majestically simple 'Body And Soul'. Chris Laurence is undoubtedly the junior partner but plays as if he's looking for a seat on the board.

Both albums, different as they are, come warmly recommended.

Al Cohn (1925–88) TENOR SAXOPHONE

*** **Cohn's Tones** Savoy SV 0187
>Cohn; Nick Travis (*t*); George Wallington, Horace Silver (*g*); Tommy Potter, Curley Russell (*b*);
>Tiny Kahn, Max Roach (*d*). 7/50, 6/53.

*** **The Progressive Al Cohn** Savoy SV 0249
    As above. 7/50, 6/53.
*** **Broadway** Original Jazz Classics OJC 1812
    Cohn; Hal Stein (*as*); Harvey Leonard (*p*); Red Mitchell (*b*); Christy Febbo (*d*). 7/54.
*** **Either Way** Evidence ECD 22007
    Cohn; Zoot Sims (*ts*); Mose Allison (*p*); Bill Crow (*b*); Gus Johnson (*d*); Cecil Collier (*v*). 2/61.
Virtually all one needs to know about Al and Zoot's long-standing association can be found on the
sober-sounding 'Improvisation For Two Unaccompanied Saxophones' on the less than sober-sounding
Hot Tracks For Cool Cats, which is not currently in circulation. All the virtues – elegant interplay, silk-
smooth textures – and all the vices – inconsequentiality and Sims's tendency to blandness – are firmly in
place. A and Z were apt to cover the whole expressive gamut from A to B, as Dorothy Parker once
memorably said about Miss Hepburn. There's a little more muscle in the early Savoys and, as gardeners
will tell you, savoys always taste better for a little frost. It's difficult to locate Cohn's stylistic direction at
this point. Websterisms nudge up against Don Byas phrases; there's something of Lester Young's
languid phrasing in the middle chorus of 'How Long Has This Been Going On'; there's even a tiny
quote from the classic Hawkins 'Body And Soul' on the original 'Ah Moore'. It isn't so derivative as to
be disagreeable, though, and there is a hard edge and an ironclad logic which seldom surface in the
relationship with Sims. No one will doubt, even at this stage, that it is Cohn who is playing.
    The Evidence set is sparky enough, if only because Allison is such an enlivening presence. Still wholly
underrated as a pianist and misplaced in the history of the music – filed under 'vocal', or 'easy listening'
in one major store of our acquaintance – Allison brings a touch of acidity to the slightly sweet harmonies Sims for one seems to prefer. Cohn was always a more adventurous player, and he responds well
to the pianist's sly, stealthy cues. With the whole Xanadu catalogue currently *hors de combat* and
awaiting CD transfer, this session and the quartet/quintet material packaged half and half on *Tones* and
Progressive become all the more valuable and all the harder to distinguish qualitatively
    The *Broadway* disc is exceedingly well behaved, even dull, until Cohn launches into a ballad medley that
simply takes one's breath away. Stein is virtually unknown; he's recorded with Teddy Charles and fellow-
altoist Phil Woods, and on the basis of this performance might have expected to make more of a splash
on his own account. The rest of the band do their jobs like men on an hourly rate.

*** **Body And Soul** Muse MCD 5356
    Cohn; Zoot Sims (*ts, ss*); Jaki Byard (*p*); George Duvivier (*b*); Mel Lewis (*d*). 3/73.
The later *Body And Soul* is much more striking, largely because the supporting cast is so good. Byard
has all his big-band instincts on show and plays superbly. Duvivier and Lewis hold the tempo up well
and the main soloists are occasionally goaded into something slightly more acid than usual. Certainly
the best thing that partnership ever put on record.

*** **Nonpareil** Concord CCD 4155
    Cohn; Lou Levy (*p*); Monty Budwig (*b*); Jake Hanna (*d*). 4/81.
(*) **Tour De Force Concord CCD 4172
    Cohn; Scott Hamilton, Buddy Tate (*ts*); Cal Collins (*g*); Dave McKenna (*p*); Bob Maize (*b*);
    Jake Hanna (*d*). 8/81.
*** **Standards Of Excellence** Concord CCD 4241
    Cohn; Herb Ellis (*g*); Monty Budwig (*b*); Jimmie Smith (*d*). 11/83.
A brilliant arranger, Cohn hasn't always been the most convincing soloist, leaving his own most compelling ideas rather hanging in the air. This latter-day set has him in fine voice, with a tougher, more
segmented delivery than previously. The bossa nova stylings bear comparison with the rather muffled
versions recorded with Zoot Sims.
    Ellis is a less satisfactory foil than Levy, and he overcooks some of the simpler transitions. Generally,
though, standards of excellence are well up to form and Cohn sounds deliciously relaxed on
'Embraceable You', a wonderful tune with a consistency somewhere between marshmallow and quick-
sand that has lured and lost many a soloist.
    Tour De Force is something of a throwback to the multi-tenor sessions Cohn made with Zoot, Brew
Moore, Allen Eager and Stan Getz back in 1949; it's engaging enough stuff, but surely not sufficiently
compelling to merit the critical raves it received on its appearance in 1981. Fifteen years on, it definitely
sounds a bit thin.

*** **Al Cohn Meets Al Porcino** Red Baron JK 57334
    Cohn; Frank Beyerer, Al Porcino, Claus Reichstaller, Peter Tuscher (*t*); Gerd Fink, Erwin
    Gregg, Jon Welch (*tb*); Auwi Geyer (*btb*); Thomas Faist, Otto Staniloy (*as*); Petri Kral, Herman
    Martlreiter (*ts*); Thomas Zoller (*bs*); Roberto Di Gioia (*p*); Paulo Cardoso (*b*); Wolfgang
    Haffner (*d*). 3/87.

*** **Keeper Of The Flame** Jazz House JHCD 022
  Cohn; Dick Pearce (*t, flhn*); Pete Beachill (*tb, vtb*); Andy Mackintosh (*as*); Dave Hartley (*p*); Chris Laurence (*b*); Quinny Laurence (*d*). 5/87.
***(*) **Rifftide** Timeless SJP 259
  Cohn; Rein De Graaff (*p*); Koos Serierse (*b*); Eric Ineke (*d*). 6/87.

It wasn't the final final performance, of course, though that was how some labels tried to market the concert of 30 March 1987 in Karlsruhe. Cohn carried on into the winter of 1988 before finally succumbing. Over the last few years, most of the recordings were made in Europe. The mostly German big band does him proud on the Red Baron, which has also been listed on RAZmTAZ, though it's Al Porcino's inspired leadership that gives the set its taut energy. The quartet 'Body And Soul' is one of the best Cohn has recorded; the Lester Young influences seem ever more recessive and irrelevant. He sounds like a man who has recovered his own diction. Docked a star for very disappointing sound, even on the CD, which is very harsh and flat.

Rifftide is an absolutely marvellous set, with Cohn's brooding tone working an unhurried magic over 'Speak Low', 'Blue Monk' and 'Hot House', as surprising and moving a group of tunes as he's ever recorded. Three other tracks are less familiar but, if anything, better played, with 'We'll Be Together Again' and the title-tune underlining how subtle an accompanist de Graaff can be. Further proof, if any were needed, of Cohn's creative stamina.

The London recording was made in a studio rather than in concert, but it has the easy flow of a sympathetic gig. The Jazz Seven play 'Keeper Of The Flame' in tribute and Cohn takes a couple of tracks with rhythm only. These are the most effective of all – which is no surprise. He sounds calm, untroubled and completely on top of things. Less than a year later, he was gone.

George 'Kid Sheik' Cola (born 1908) TRUMPET, VOCAL

** **Kid Sheik With Charlie Love And His Cado Jazz Band – 1960** 504 CDS 21
  Cola; Charlie Love (*t*); Albert Warner (*tb*); Emile Barnes (*cl*); Louis Gallaud (*p*); Emanuel Sayles (*bj*); Albert Jiles (*d*). 8/60.
** **In Boston And Cleveland** American Music AMCD-69
  Cola; Louis Nelson, Albert Warner (*tb*); John Handy (*cl, as*); James Sing Miller, Louis Gallaud (*p*); Fred Minor (*bj*); Chester Zardis, John Joseph (*b*); Alex Bigard, Cie Frazier (*d*). 61–69.
*** **First European Tour** GHB BCD-187
  Cola; Jack Weddell (*tb*); Sammy Rimington (*cl*); Paul Sealey (*bj*); Barry Richardson (*b*); Barry Martyn (*d*). 6/63.
*(*) **Kid Sheik & Brother Cornbread In Copenhagen** Jazz Crusade JCCD-3002
  Cola; Peter Goetz (*tb*); Joe 'Brother Cornbread' Thomas (*cl*); Peter Nissen (*bj*); Niels Henrik Ross-Petersen (b); Keith Minter (*d*). 11/74.

Kid Sheik Cola was much loved in the ranks of New Orleans brassmen, and the notes to several of these discs detail the affection he inspired on his travels. CD listeners will find his music hard going, though. He plays in the mould of the short-breathed frontman and packs a punch only occasionally: solos tend to be self-effacing, and he usually lets someone else drive things along. This mixed bag of records doesn't fare too well. The 504 date offers a band which sounds almost enfeebled at times, even as weathered New Orleans music goes. Charlie Love is the bandleader, and Kid Sheik sits out on six tracks – but even when he's there the music flickers into real life only occasionally, as on a rickety but spirited 'Down In Honky Tonk Town'. The American Music set includes two knockabout sessions which are largely dominated by Handy: sound-quality is indifferent and there's some awful singing, but it's listenable. The pick is surely *First European Tour*, in which Kid Sheik was chaperoned by Martyn and Rimington through a spirited session that still sounds good. Recorded at Egham Cricket Club.

The notes to the Jazz Crusade set remember the occasion of the recording with much nostalgia, which makes the fairly awful music a terrible disappointment. The main culprit is Brother Cornbread's clarinet, which flies out of tune at every opportunity, though nobody seems to care much. Obviously a happy night, but you definitely had to be there.

Freddy Cole PIANO, VOCAL

(*) **I'm Not My Brother, I'm Me Sunnyside SSC 1054
  Cole; Ed Zad (*g*); Eddie Edwards (*b*). 4/90.
*** **Always** Fantasy FCD-9670-2
  Cole; Byron Stripling (*flhn*); Robin Eubanks (*tb*); Jeff Scott (*frhn*); Frank Perowsky (*ss, ts, f*); Grover Washington (*ss*); William Kerr (*as, f*); Antonio Hart (*as, ts*); Javon Jackson (*ts*); Roger

Rosenberg (*bs*); Mel Martin (*af*); Cyrus Chestnut (*p*); Lionel Cole (*ky*); Joe Locke (*vib*); Tom Hubbard, George Mraz (*b*); Yoron Israel, Russ Kunkel (*d*); Steve Berrios (*perc*); strings. 12/94.

*** **I Want A Smile For Christmas** Fantasy FCD-9672-2
> Cole; Joe Ford (*ss*); Larry Willis (*p*); Joe Locke (*vib*); Jerry Byrd (*g*); Tom Hubbard (*b*); Steve Berrios (*d*). 7/94.

The brother is Nat, and the voice is close, though the piano is lightweight. Freddy seems to be falling over to invite comparisons on the first album, what with 'He Was The King' and a Nat medley among the titles, and the trio format is a not disagreeable update on his brother's pioneering work. But there seems little enough to make one want to return. The Fantasy records, though, are superior, prepared with great care and thoughtfulness by producer, Todd Barkan. There's a glittering line-up of names on the first disc, set to work on meticulously arranged standards: nobody really has any space to cut loose, but the splendid Chestnut is magisterial at the piano, Washington (especially fine on 'You Must Believe In Spring') and Hart take apposite cameos, and the result is a laid-back but not soporific entry. Cole stays away from the piano and sticks to husking through the lyrics, somewhat without Nat's guile but not without style. There are a couple of clinkers – 'The Rose' seems to have strayed in from another project altogether. The Christmas collection is, surprisingly, almost as good, centred round the small group listed in the personnel. Willis plays with quiet dignity and Ford, a surprise choice for sole horn, traces filigree lines over the sometimes unpromising Yuletide material. It's to Cole's credit that when they get to 'The Christmas Song' he sings it in a way that's nothing like Nat.

Nat Cole (1917–65) PIANO, VOCAL

*** **Nat King Cole 1936–1940** Classics 757
> Cole; Kenneth Roane (*t*); Tommy Thompson (*as*); Bill Wright (*ts*); Oscar Moore (*g*); Wesley Prince, Eddie Cole (*b*); Jimmy Adams, Lee Young (*d*); Bonnie Lake, Juanelda Carter (*v*). 7/36–2/40.

*** **Nat King Cole 1941–1943** Classics 786
> Cole; Lester Young (*ts*); Oscar Moore (*g*); Wesley Prince, Red Callender, Johnny Miller (*b*). 7/41–11/43.

*** **Nat King Cole 1943–1944** Classics 804
> Cole; Shad Collins (*t*); Illinois Jacquet (*ts*); Oscar Moore (*g*); Johnny Miller, Gene Englund (*b*); J. C. Heard (*d*). 11/43–3/44.

***(*) **Sweet Lorraine** Vintage Jazz Classics VJC 1026-29 4CD
> Cole; Oscar Moore (*g*); Wesley Prince (*b*). 10/38–2/41.

The discographer Brian Rust has pointed out that while Nat 'King' Cole made many records between 1943 and 1966, 'there is virtually no jazz music on any of them'. This kind of slight has been conferred on Cole's output for literally decades. While we have omitted most of his later, vocal records from this book, there should be no doubt that this great pianist never really left jazz behind. He began with deceptively lightweight, jiving music (sample titles: 'Scotchin' With The Soda', 'Ode To A Wild Clam') which masked the intensity of his piano style to a large extent. Smooth, glittering, skating over melodies, Cole's right-hand lines were breaking free of his original Earl Hines influence and looking towards a dashing improvisational freedom which other players – Powell, Haig, Marmarosa – would turn into the language of bebop. Cole was less inclined towards that jagged-edge approach and preferred the hip constrictions of songs and good-natured jive. With pulsing interjections from Moore and Prince (subsequently replaced by Miller), this was a surprisingly compelling music. Classics start their usual chronological survey with four obscure 1936 titles by a group led by Eddie Cole. The trio proper begins in 1939 with 12 titles cut in a single day and moves on through a session with Lester Young and Red Callender (Classics 786) and a single quintet date with horns (Classics 804). The latter disc is probably the best single representation of Cole's early music, with hits such as 'Straighten Up And Fly Right' and some deft interpretations of standards. Transfers, from unlisted sources, seem good.

The superb collection of transcriptions offers nearly 4½ hours of music on four CDs. The surprising thing is that, taken even at a long stretch, listener-fatigue doesn't set in. The hipness of the sound, the playing and the singing makes even the most trifling songs endure. A fine package, and the skilful remastering brings it all to life.

*** **World War II Broadcast Transcriptions** Music & Arts CD-808
> Cole; Oscar Moore (*g*); Johnny Miller (*b*); Anita O'Day, Ida James, Anita Boyer (*v*). 41–44.

*** **The Jazzman** Topaz TPZ 1012
> As above, except add Wesley Prince (*b*), omit vocalists. 40–44.

**** The Best Of The Nat King Cole Trio Capitol 7982882
    Cole; Oscar Moore, Irving Ashby (*g*); Johnny Miller, Joe Comfort (*b*); Jack Costanza (*perc*). 11/
    43–3/49.

*** Straighten Up And Fly Right! Vintage Jazz Classics VJC-1044
    Cole; Oscar Moore (*g, v*); Johnny Miller (*b, v*); Frank Sinatra (*v*). 12/42–1/48.

***(*) Jazz Encounters Capitol 796693-2
    Cole; Dizzy Gillespie, Bill Coleman, Ernie Royal, Ray Linn (*t*); Bill Harris (*tb*); Buddy
    DeFranco, Buster Bailey (*cl*); Coleman Hawkins, Charlie Barnet, Flip Phillips, Herbie Haymer
    (*ts*); Benny Carter (*as*); Heinie Beau, Fred Stulce, Harry Schuman (*reeds*); Billy Bauer, Irving
    Ashby, Oscar Moore, Dave Barbour (*g*); Eddie Safranski, Johnny Miller, Joe Comfort, Art
    Shapiro, John Kirby (*b*); Buddy Rich, Max Roach, Nick Fatool, Earl Hyde (*d*); Woody
    Herman, Jo Stafford, Nellie Lutcher, Johnny Mercer, Kay Starr (*v*); Stan Kenton Orchestra. 12/
    47–1/50.

*** Lush Life Capitol 780595 2
    Cole; orchestra arranged by Pete Rugolo. 3/49–1/52.

Cole made a tremendous number of recordings with his trio; the definitive collection is the awe-inspiring collection of 18 CDs or 27 LPs issued by Mosaic, which covers his entire output for Capitol with the group. Capitol's *Best Of*, though, is a fine introduction which covers instrumental-only tracks and highlights Cole's swing and dextrous touch and his intelligently varied arrangements for the Trio and their wonderfully responsive following of his leads. Moore is, indeed, almost Cole's equal on an executive level, and their best playing often runs in dazzling, parallel lines. The VJC collection pulls together a collection of airchecks which act as a counterweight to the studio material. The 'Route 66' here predates the Capitol studio version by a matter of days, and Sinatra turns up to sing on 'I've Found A New Baby' (not really him) and 'Exactly Like You' (a shade more appropriate). Music & Arts have compiled a set of broadcast transcriptions which settles mostly for Cole's variations on standards, with the occasional guest spot by a vocalist, notably Anita O'Day. Meticulously remastered, this is a good choice for those who prefer less of Cole's jiving persona. The Topaz disc covers tracks from Capitol, Decca and seven airchecks and is a capable selection, though the field is starting to get crowded for this material.

   Capitol's Jazz Encounters disc is a remarkable demonstration of Cole's versatility, bringing together seven dates in which he acted in the main as a sideman yet still usually dominated the tracks. Two pieces with the Metronome All Stars – including Gillespie and Harris – are followed by one with Kenton and a session with the swing-styled Capitol International Jazzmen, where Hawkins is outstanding but Cole takes the honours. A beautiful set of Jo Stafford songs, a couple of jive routines with Woody Herman and a date with Capitol boss Johnny Mercer make the record essential for Cole's admirers. *Lush Life* shows him moving inexorably towards his singing success: the trio is still here, but Rugolo's arrangements – though often very swinging, as in 'You Stepped Out Of A Dream' – are straightening out the jive element.

*** Anatomy Of A Jam Session Black Lion BLCD 760137
    Cole; Charlie Shavers (*t*); Herbie Haymer (*ts*); John Simmons (*b*); Buddy Rich (*d*). 6/45.

Not a great deal of music here – 38 minutes, and that includes six alternative takes – but it's a swinging interlude in the normal run of Cole's records of the time, with Haymer and Shavers in knockabout form and Rich at his most brusque. Cole himself is unperturbed by the surrounding racket and makes cool, elegant space for himself. The sound is mostly good, with only some surface noise present.

**(*) The King Cole Trios Live: 1947–48 Vintage Jazz Classics VJC-1011-2
    Cole; Duke Ellington (*p*); Oscar Moore, Irving Ashby (*g*); Johnny Miller (*b*); Clark Dennis, The
    Dinning Sisters, Pearl Bailey, Woody Herman (*v*). 3/47–3/48.

Taken from *King Cole Time* broadcasts, the routine here is that each guest on the show chats with Nat, 'chooses' songs, and does one number with the Trio. Main interest, inevitably, is on Ellington, who sounds under-rehearsed but does a neat solo on 'Mood Indigo', while the other singers offer slighter stuff. The rest is no more or less than Cole and the Trio on their regular form, though several of the tunes are despatched very quickly. Sound quality varies from fairly terrible on the Pearl Bailey and Dinning Sisters shows to quite good with Herman and Ellington. For dedicated Cole fans only.

***(*) Big Band Cole Capitol 7962592
    Cole; Count Basie, Stan Kenton Orchestras. 50–58.

A compilation of sessions with Basie's band (minus Basie) and two tracks with the Kenton orchestra, plus two other songs with a top-flight studio band. Cole should have made more big-band jazz records than he did – for all the beauty and warmth of his 'straight' records – and this compilation shows the missed opportunity. Cole doesn't swing noticeably harder here than he does normally, but set-pieces such as 'The Blues Don't Care' and 'Wee Baby Blues' establish a very different mood from his normal regimen, and he sounds as comfortable and good-humoured as he ever did elsewhere. Beautifully remastered, this is highly recommended.

Nat's later Capitol albums are without exception dedicated to his singing and, although we have opted not to list them here, they are uniformly recommended as examples of great vocal records.

Richie Cole (born 1948) ALTO AND TENOR SAXOPHONES

** New York Afternoon Muse MCD 5119
    Cole; Mickey Tucker (*p*); Vic Juris (*g*); Rick Laird (*b*); Eddie Gladden (*d*); Ray Mantilla (*perc*); Eddie Jefferson (*v*). 10/76.
**(*) Alto Madness Muse MCD 5155
    As above, except Harold Mabern (*p*) replaces Tucker, add Steve Gilmore (*b*). 12/77.
** Hollywood Madness Muse MCD 5207
    Cole; Dick Hindman (*p*); Marshall Hawkins, Bob Magnusson (*b*); Les Demerle (*d*); Michael Spiro (*perc*); Eddie Jefferson, Manhattan Transfer (*v*). 4/79.
**(*) Side By Side Muse MCD 6016
    Cole; Phil Woods (*as*); Eddie 'Lockjaw' Davis (*ts*); John Hicks (*p*); Walter Booker (*b*); Jimmy Cobb (*d*). 7/80.
*** Pure Imagination Concord CCD 4314
    Cole; Vic Juris (*g*); Ed Howard (*b*); Victor Jones (*d*); Ray Mantilla (*perc*). 11/86.
*(*) Popbop Milestone 9152
    Cole; Dick Hindman (*p*); Vic Juris (*g*); Marshall Hawkins, Eddie Howard (*b*); Victor Jones (*d*); Kenneth Nash, Tim Hauser (*perc*). 87.
** Signature Milestone 9162
    Cole; Ben Sidran (*ky*); Tee Carson (*p*); Vic Juris (*g*); Keith Jones, Marshall Hawkins (*b*); Mel Brown (*d*); Andy Narell, Babatunde Olatunji (*perc*). 88.
**(*) Bossa Nova International Milestone 9180
    Cole; Hank Crawford (*as*); Emily Remler (*g*); Marshall Hawkins (*b*); Victor Jones (*d*). 6/87.
**(*) Profile Heads Up HUCD 3022
    Cole; Dick Hindman (*p*); Rich Kuhns (*ky*); Henry Johnson (*g*); Seward McCain, Frank Passantino (*b*); Scott Morris (*d*). 4/93.
There was a time when Richie Cole seemed on the verge of some kind of international jazz stardom, but his impact has waned dramatically since the late 1970s and early '80s, when most of these records were made. A former student of Phil Woods, at his best he sounds like a good version of Woods, which – when the original has so many records available – tends to raise the question as to whether it's worth listening to a good copy. A little unfair, perhaps, but none of these records has the kind of sustained interest that makes one want to return to them very often. *Side By Side*, where he actually plays with Woods, is a barnstorming encounter, but it's wearisome over the full stretch, and it's the studio sessions which usually work out for the best, particularly *Alto Madness*, although Eddie Jefferson's singing is another acquired taste. A move to Milestone hasn't reaped any greater artistic rewards – *Popbop* is as disastrous as its title suggests, and *Signature* forsakes bebop heat for damp soul-jazz – but *Bossa Nova International* benefits from the felicitous presence of Emily Remler, whose comping binds the music together. Some personal problems have kept Cole out of the limelight in recent years, but the Heads Up album is his cautious return to active duty. His alto playing has much of the old bounce, though tempered with time, and on a tune like 'One For Monterey' he seems to have reconciled pace with elegance more effectively than before. Even 'Volare' sounds rather nice, and Tom Waits's 'A Foreign Affair' was a good choice for a ballad. But there is some gloop, too – 'Sarah' is a feeble tribute to Sarah Vaughan, and the sidemen make no impression.

Bill Coleman (1904–81) TRUMPET

***(*) Hangin' Around Topaz TPZ 1040
    Coleman; Henry 'Red' Allen, John Butler, Shad Collins, Bill Dillard (*t*); Billy Burns, J. C. Higginbotham, Dicky Wells (*tb*); George Johnson, Albert Nicholas (*cl, as*); Andy Fitzgerald, Joe Marsala (*cl*); Edgar Courance, Frank Goudie (*cl, ts*); Pete Brown, Willie Lewis, Joe Hayman (*as*); Charlie Holmes (*as, ss*); Coleman Hawkins, Teddy Hill (*ts*); Herman Chittison, Garnet Clark, John Ferrier, Ellis Larkins, Luis Russell (*p*); Stéphane Grappelli (*vn, p*); Oscar Aleman (*g*); Will Johnson (*bj, g*); Al Casey, Carmen Mastern, John Mitchell, Django Reinhardt, Joseph Reinhardt (*g*); June Cole, Eugene D'Hellemes, Pops Foster, Richard Fullbright, Wilson Myers, Oscar Pettiford, Gene Traxler (*b*); Paul Barbarin, Bill Beason, Tommy Benford, William Diemer, Ted Fields, Shelly Manne (*d*). 9/29, 11/35, 1/36, 7, 10 & 11/37, 9/38, 4/40, 12/43.

*** **Bill Coleman, 1936–1938** Classics 764

Coleman; Christian Wagner (*cl, as*); Eddie Brunner, Edgar Courance, Frank Goudie (*cl, ts*); Alix Combelle, Noel Chiboust (*ts*); Herman Chittison, John Ferrier, Emile Stern (*p*); Stéphane Grappelli (*vn, p*); Oscar Aleman, John Mitchell, Django Reinhardt, Joseph Reinhardt (*g*); Roger Graset, Eugene D'Hellemes, Wilson Myers, Lucien Simoens (*b*); Tommy Benford, William Diemer, Ted Fields, Jerry Mengo (*d*). 1/36, 11/37, 6 & 9/38.

*** **Bill Coleman Meets Guy Lafitte** Black Lion BLCD 760182

Coleman; Guy Lafitte (*ts*); Marc Hemmeler (*p*); Jack Sewing (*b*); Daniel Humair (*d*). 7/73.

Many people encounter this fine trumpeter only in the context of sessions with the great Django Reinhardt. Having worked with Don Redman and Luis Russell, he first went to Paris in 1933 and finally settled there three years after the war. The Topaz includes one early track recorded under Russell's leadership in 1929. Though his contribution is brief and outclassed by Allen's, it is enough to mark him down as a player to be followed. The next tracks jump on to the Paris sojourns, activity with Garnet Clark's Hot Clubs Four and a duo with Herman Chittison on 'I'm In The Mood For Love', one of the things that overlap with the Classics volume. There is obviously a good deal of overlap between these, though the Classics set kicks off with only a slightly earlier (a week, to be exact) encounter between the pair, with bassist Eugene d'Hellemes in support on 'What's The Reason' and 'After You've Gone'.

Classics omit the material recorded under the leadership of Dickie Wells and Willie Lewis but, for some reason (the quality of the solos presumably), do include five tracks made with clarinettist and tenorman Eddie Brunner, and of course the Topaz extends forward in time to the war years. Of the years in common, the only big loss is a storming version of 'I Got Rhythm' for Dickie Wells, with Django powering the band along. If his is the dominant voice on the instrument in this time period, the Argentinian, Oscar Aleman, suggests a range of alternatives and an arresting solo style on the same January 1936 session as the Chittison/d'Hellemes cuts.

Coleman has a bright, uncomplicated tone and delivery, and a nice singing voice. He probably reached his peak in the mid- to late 1930s, but he had the sort of chops that can go on pretty much for ever, unpressured, distinct and slightly discursive. The later material with Guy Lafitte, recorded when this American-in-Paris was rising seventy, is pretty lightweight festival stuff, but there is no mistaking who is playing, even in the opening choruses of 'Blue Lou', which he reharmonizes slightly. Using the same Montreux rhythm section as Stéphane Grappelli, he swings lightly and rather politely, but there is no mistaking that he is still swinging.

George Coleman (born 1935) TENOR SAXOPHONE, ALTO SAXOPHONE

*** **Amsterdam After Dark** Timeless SJP 129

Coleman; Hilton Ruiz (*p*); Sam Jones (*b*); Billy Higgins (*d*). 12/78.

(*) **Manhattan Panorama Evidence ECD 22019

Coleman; Harold Mabern (*p*); Jamil Nasser (*b*); Idris Muhammad (*d*). 82 or 83.

***(*) **At Yoshi's** Evidence ECD 22021

Coleman; Harold Mabern (*p*); Ray Drummond (*b*); Alvin Queen (*d*). 8/87.

Like his near-namesake of the boxing ring, George Coleman plays a little weight-bound but gets in the odd spectacular punch. The records are few and far between only because Coleman looks on record producers the way some prize-fighters look on Don King: with the justified suspicion that they don't have his interests entirely at heart. Consequently, the few records that have appeared have tended to be self-produced, and always reliably packed with the muscular soloing that has influenced some of the younger generation of British tenor players who heard him at Ronnie Scott's in 1978 on the same European stint as Timeless SJP 129.

Given the long and sometimes rough ride the city's given him, it's hard to tell how sincere Coleman's love affair with the Big Apple really is. Woody Allen turned the same skyline into a wry, Gershwin-drenched poem. Coleman, with an eye on 'El Barrio' and the 'New York Housing Blues', is by no means so dewy-eyed; the inevitable 'Manhattan' and 'I Love New York' are both in place, but there's also a vocal tribute to 'Mayor Koch' that suggests a much tougher perspective, and there's a chill wind blowing through 'Autumn In New York' on the Timeless album. The Mabern/Muhammad rhythm axis fuels some fine solos from Coleman, who also plays his alto on this date with a fleet diction that belies any charges of ponderousness.

The Dutch cityscape is even finer, with an absolutely superb rhythm section and a beautiful registration that picks up all the tiny, grainy resonances Coleman gets across his reed. Ruiz and Higgins play with perfect understanding and Sam Jones must be one of the best slow-tempo players on the scene.

Yoshi's is a small club in Oakland, California, which puts the emphasis on music rather than mark-up at the bar. Coleman feels comfortable playing there, and it shows on the Evidence set. Again, the band has the hand-picked feel and telepathic understanding of good cornermen, and Coleman's playing is full of instinctive invention, as when he knocks off the oddly metred 'Laig Gobblin' Blues' standing up. There are three long tracks that feature most of the group: 'They Say It's Wonderful', Freddie Hubbard's 'Up Jumped Spring' and Mal Waldron's 'Soul Eyes' which brings the set to an entirely satisfactory end. It isn't the sort of album that makes reputations, but it confirms that big George is still very much a contender.

** **Meditation** Timeless SJP 110
    Coleman; Tete Montoliu (*p*). 4/77.
A not entirely successful collaboration. Coleman's meditative mode is still a little tense and, without the backing of a section, he seems uncertain about metres. Montoliu is a much less linear player, and there are moments when the two seem to be occupying different musical spaces. Coleman fans will find it intriguing, though.

*** **Playing Changes** Ronnie Scott's Jazz House JHCD 002
    Coleman; Hilton Ruiz (*p*); Ray Drummond (*b*); Billy Higgins (*d*). 4/79.
For anyone who has worn smooth their copy of the old Pye LP, *Ronnie Scott Presents George Coleman 'Live'*, mentioned above, this could be a fair substitute. Recorded during the same 1979 residency at Frith Street, *Playing Changes* consists of just three – two *long*, one shorter – takes. Coleman's attack is typically robust and veined with unexpected harmonic ore. However, anyone whose copy of the original LP survives may feel that they already have the best of the deal. The long 'Laura' is, at 23 minutes plus, a tad *too* long, and slightly overgenerous to both Ruiz and the still-inexperienced Drummond; by contrast, 'Stella By Starlight', which occupies a whole side of the Pye, is a much more coherent performance. The second track, 'Siorra', is an unconvincing Coleman original, and the best of the saxophonist's work occurs when he moves sideways of the given changes and into his inventive high harmonic mode. There are either misfingerings or symptoms of a weary reed in the closing ensembles of the end-of-set 'Moment's Notice' which detract a little from an intriguing variation on the Coltrane original. On balance, it might have been better to put together a stronger 65-minute CD integrating the best of the two sessions. Scratches aside, most listeners will be returning to the Pye a lot more often than to this.

**** **My Horns Of Plenty** Birdology 837278
    Coleman; Harold Mabern (*p*); Ray Drummond (*b*); Billy Higgins (*d*). 3/91.
Far and away the best Coleman record currently available, it finds him with a top-class rhythm section who really couldn't be improved upon for sheer responsiveness. 'The Sheik Of Araby' is an exquisite performance, checking licks from Bechet and Ben Webster along the way, the solo moving in a steady, almost relentless progression from chorus to chorus, in a way that revives the prize-fighter analogy. 'Lush Life', which Mabern always does beautifully, is an even grander conception, done perhaps a bit faster than usual but with no less emotion and presence. The closing 'Old Folks' is a convincing demonstration of how, for all his highly sophisticated harmonics (his own device, not at all a Coltrane borrowing, as some have suggested), big George is a melodist at heart. A lovely record.

Ornette Coleman (born 1930) ALTO SAXOPHONE, TRUMPET, VIOLIN, TENOR SAXOPHONE

*** **Something Else!!** Original Jazz Classics OJC 163
    Coleman; Don Cherry (*t*); Walter Norris (*p*); Don Payne (*b*); Billy Higgins (*d*). 2/58.
*** **Tomorrow Is The Question** Original Jazz Classics OJC 342
    Coleman; Don Cherry (*t*); Percy Heath, Red Mitchell (*b*); Shelly Manne (*d*). 1, 2, 3/59.
Though the 1958 Hillcrest Club sessions under Paul Bley's nominal leadership represent something of a crux in Coleman's development, it is still startling to hear him work with a pianist. He got the first of these sessions at Red Mitchell's behest and it suffers from all the vices of a hasty pick-up; problems that were largely ironed out on the more thoughtful *Tomorrow Is The Question*, a set which includes 'Tears Inside', perhaps the most beautiful single item in the whole Coleman canon – and sucks to all the critics who considered him a raucous circus act. *Tomorrow* is also notable for Shelly Manne's impeccably hip contribution; an unlikely recruitment on the face of it, even given his tenure at Contemporary, but absolutely bang up to the moment.

**** **The Shape Of Jazz To Come** Atlantic 781339-2
    Coleman; Don Cherry (*pkt-t*); Charlie Haden (*b*); Billy Higgins (*d*). 10/59, 10/59, 7/60.
**** **Change Of The Century** Atlantic 781341
    As above. 10/59.
***(*) **Art Of the Improvisers** Atlantic 90978-2
    As above, except add Jimmy Garrison, Scott LaFaro (*b*). 59–60.

**** Free Jazz Atlantic 781347
> Coleman; Don Cherry (*pkt-t*); Freddie Hubbard (*t*); Eric Dolphy (*bcl*); Charlie Haden, Scott
> LaFaro (*b*); Ed Blackwell, Billy Higgins (*d*). 12/60.

**** Beauty Is A Rare Thing Rhino/Atlantic R2 71410 6CD
> As above discs, except add Eric Dolphy (*as, f, bcl*); Robert DiDomenica (*f*); Bill Evans (*p*);
> Eddie Costa (*vib*); Jim Hall (*g*); George Duvivier (*b*); Sticks Evans (d); The Contemporary
> String Quartet. 5/59–3/61.

These are the classic Coleman quartet sessions. It is slightly hard to quantify their 'influence'. There
were a score and more of dime-store Coltranes for every one alto player with Coleman's sharp harmonic
astigmatism. The slightly hectoring and apocalyptic tone of the album-titles isn't entirely borne out by
the music inside, which is far more introspective and thoughtful than is often suggested. The first two
were released slightly out of chronological sequence; if 'progress' and 'development' can show inside a
month, then *The Shape Of Jazz To Come* really is a major step forward.

CD transfer is slowly changing perceptions of these and later sets, uncovering the extent to which the
bands worked collectively and from the bottom up, never entirely dominated by the two horns. On vinyl,
Haden in particular has to be listened for very carefully indeed.

Most of the essential Coleman pieces are to be found here: 'Lonely Woman' and 'Congeniality' on
Shape, 'Una Muy Bonita' on *Change*, 'Blues Connotation' on (currently deleted) *This Is Our Music*,
with a wonderful revisionist 'Embraceable You' on the last of the three – which underlines its consolidating place in Coleman's output. Hard to think that any of these is less than essential.

The original Jackson Pollock cover to *Free Jazz* was a fairly accurate summation of a common *Zeitgeist*.
It's gestural music, splashing instrumental colour about with a total indifference to accurate figuration.
Coleman's huge double quartet, with its blandly generic title, set a course for large-scale 'comprovisa-
tion' over the next decade, and notably Coltrane's grandly metaphysical *Ascension* (Impulse! GRD
21132). Free it may have been harmonically, but it was still locked into an oddly mechanical theme-and-
solos format which, with eight sturdy egos to massage, takes a bit of time. What redeems *Free Jazz* and
elevates it to senior status in the modern canon is the extraordinary variety of sound-colour that comes
from the twinned soloists. Dolphy's fruity-bass clarinet is a perfect specific to Coleman's thin, slightly
flat tone. Hubbard and Cherry could hardly be less alike. LaFaro's out-of-tempo playing contrasts well
with Haden's Ware-influenced, long-legged gait. Separating Blackwell and Higgins requires an almost
ornithological attention to detail and is, in any case, largely for the birds. Both are superb.

The individual issues are cornerstones of the modern jazz collection but, with *Ornette On Tenor* and
Ornette! both missing, most will be more than tempted by the astonishing *Beauty Is A Rare Thing*, one
of the most handsome of all jazz reissue projects. The six CDs cover every scrap of surviving music
from Ornette's Atlantic period: all the original sessions appear in chronological order; there are 45
minutes of never-before-heard music – of which 'Proof Readers', with LaFaro, and 'Rise And Shine' are
quite magnificent – and the packaging is sumptuous. CD sound clears up a lot of the clouds round the
musicians (unless you have pristine original vinyl and a $30,000 turntable to play it on) and lets one hear
the bassists and the drummers (especially) as never before. The contrasting timbres of trumpet and
saxophone are also made radically clear. All the music sounds fresh-minted, timeless, invincibly melodic.
An essential collection.

***(*) Town Hall 1962 ESP Disk ESP 1006
> Coleman; David Izenzon (*b*); Charles Moffett (*d*); Selwart Clarke, Nathan Goldstein (*vn*); Julian
> Barber (*vla*); Kermit Moore (*clo*). 12/62.

This is an important document, recorded at a point of change in Coleman's work. It would be difficult
to exaggerate the influence that Izenzon had on his work at this time. He is quite unlike his predecessors,
and quite unlike any other jazz bassist of the period. Bowing much more than most, he has an entirely
original rhythmic concept which frequently works in flat contradiction to whatever else is going on in the
group. This, and his ability to improvise in quarter-tones, may be an early indication of what Coleman
came to describe as 'harmolodics'. On 'Sadness', Izenzon does something quite extraordinary to the
tune's relatively conventional blues changes, while on 'The Ark' the three performers work in parallel,
each creating a discourse that has no obvious connection with the others. Only 'Doughnut' sounds like a
regular jazz tune; when the trio include it in their programme at the Fairfield Halls in Croydon, England,
three years later (a concert that has also been issued on disc), it has an almost satirical simplicity, as if
Ornette is saying: you want straight jazz? here's straight jazz. (On that same occasion in Croydon, he
had reacted to barracking from an uncomprehending crowd by suddenly breaking into 'Cherokee'.)

It's unfortunate that more of the Town Hall concert hasn't been issued. One would love to hear
Izenzon's solo bass piece, which might well confirm his importance to Coleman's music, and it would
help fill out a thin period in this notoriously patchy discography. What the album does include is a
'classical' piece for string quartet, which itself has a satirical edge, plucking a conventional ending out of
a whirlwind of dissonance. With the best will in the world, it's hard to find much in it beyond that, and

the recording isn't sufficiently full-bodied to appreciate what sounds like robust playing by four modernists.

*** **Chappaqua Suite** Columbia COL 480584
 Coleman; Pharoah Sanders (*ts*); David Izenzon (*b*); Charles Moffett (*d*); other personnel
 unidentified. 6/65.
It should be made clear at the outset that Ornette Coleman never wanted this music to be released. It was made to accompany a project by avant-garde film-maker Conrad Rooks, who apparently offered the saxophonist/composer enough cash to overcome his resistance. The finished product was, Rooks claimed, so striking that it would have detracted from the images – he may well have been right – and, in a piece of exquisite rationalization, deserved to be heard separately and in its own right. Perversely, having delayed and prevaricated over other Coleman recordings, Columbia (France/Japan) issued the soundtrack in an edited form, with the emphasis on Coleman.

It's an odd piece of work, ambiguous orchestral textures from an ensemble conducted by Joseph Tekula suddenly breaking out into boppish sequences from Ornette and the group. Though Sanders is credited, he actually gets very little of the limelight. The unusual circumstances of its creation, its slightly shadowy existence since, and, one suspects, wonderfully striking cover photography have given *Chappaqua Suite* a cachet out of all proportion to its real merits. It remains a curiosity, part of the story, but unmistakably a minor part.

**** **At The Golden Circle, Stockholm: Volume 1** Blue Note B21Y 84224
 Coleman; David Izenzon (*b*); Charles Moffett (*d*). 65.
**** **At The Golden Circle, Stockholm: Volume 2** Blue Note B21Y 84225
 As above.
Marvellous live sessions from Coleman's most stripped-down touring band. Moffett is a thrasher, but Izenzon's cantorial cries, already heavily laced with the tragedy that was to dog his life, provide a perfect grounding for some of Coleman's best solo work on record. Guess-the-next-note pieces like 'European Echoes' work less well than 'Morning Song' and 'The Riddle', and the obligatory fiddle-and-trumpet feature, 'Snowflakes And Sunshine', is unusually bland. Otherwise, the material is excellent.

The sound is surprisingly good for a club recording and for Coleman's spare, almost minimalist music, certainly better balanced than some of the classic Atlantics. CD underscores Izenzon's merits and Moffett's defaults in roughly equal measure, and long-standing fans may prefer to hang on to pristine vinyl, which softens the shriller overtones of the leader's alto.

One of the slight myths of Coleman's career is that he 'hears' changes and progressions according to some inner logic and doesn't require the conventional supports of piano accompaniment or pedal notes on the bass. In fact, as with Dewey Redman in years to come, Coleman here relies heavily on Izenzon, working along pathways laid out by the bassist's deep-rooted chords, often quite conventionally.

***(*) **Dancing in Your Head** A & M 396 999
 Coleman; Bern Nix, Charles Ellerbee (*g*); Jamaaladeen Tacuma (*b*); Ronald Shannon Jackson
 (*d*); Robert Palmer (*cl*); Master Musicians of Joujouka. 1/73, 12/75.
This controversial record effectively set the agenda – both artistic and critical – for the second half of Coleman's career. Purists were appalled by the relentlessly thudding rhythm of the two long 'variations' on 'Theme From A Symphony', but there is no doubt that a whole generation, innocent of the great Atlantics, and even of the Izenzon/Moffett trio, were turned on to what Ornette was doing. The harmolodic method, in which an absolute democracy applies among all the voices and all the constituent parameters of the music – rhythm, melody, harmony – perhaps receives its most definitive statement in these two tracks, but they need to be heard as an extension of what was going on at Town Hall (see above) and in some ways a tentative draft of what was to happen over the next decade and a half with the electrified Prime Time band. They also need to be heard in the context of a much longer session, recorded in Paris, that yielded the first release on Coleman's own Artist's House label, *Body Meta*.

It's misleading to describe this music as rock-influenced, since the whole approach to rhythm is actually antagonistic to rock's accenting of strong beats. In practice, almost everything is attempted at some point: swing, march cadences, stop-time, long unbroken sequences in the bass with virtually no audible sub-divisions, hints of reggae and ragtime. Though *Dancing* can initially sound unrelieved and one-dimensional, it repays careful listening.

There is a brief extra track in which Coleman plays with clarinettist Robert Palmer and the Master Musicians of Joujouka, who had been an enthusiasm of Rolling Stone Brian Jones and who fulfilled many of Coleman's own aesthetic ideals.

*** **Virgin Beauty** Columbia RK 44301
 Coleman; Bern Nix, Charles Ellerbee, Jerry Garcia (*g*); Al McDowell, Chris Walker (*b*);
 Denardo Coleman (*ky, d, perc*); Calvin Weston (*d*). 87–88.
Thought by some to be a commercial sell-out even more heinous than *Dancing In Your Head* (a

complaint very largely stirred by the presence of Grateful Dead guitarist Jerry Garcia on some tracks), *Virgin Beauty* is the least troublous and ironic Coleman recording in the lists. But it is by no means a peripheral or unsatisfactory project, and the mild rock/funk sound camouflages a further round of experiment, as so often with Coleman. His own willingness to play is evident from the unaccompanied introduction to 'Unknown Artist', but it is in such tracks as 'Bourgeois Boogie', with its quasi-Motown groove, and the medium-up 'Happy Hour' (a latter-day cousin of 'Doughnut') that one hears him experimenting with contemporary grooves; if there is less irony in evidence than usual, the experiment is no less valid.

It is worth mentioning the circumstances in which Garcia came to work with the group. Coleman and Cecil Taylor had visited a Grateful Dead concert and were astonished at the unswerving devotion of Deadheads. For Coleman, it was an object lesson in the social construction of music, and he has always been an artist as concerned with the reception and commercial definition of his music as with its pure aesthetics.

***(*) **Tone Dialing** Verve/Harmolodic 527 483
    Coleman; Dave Bryant (*ky*); Chris Rosenberg, Ken Wessell (*g*); Al McDowell, Bradley Jones
    (*b*); Denardo Coleman (*d*); Badal Roy (*perc*). 95.

A major initiative for the 65-year-old: his own imprint within the Polygram empire and a relatively free hand to issue and A&R his own choice of material. The first record is very much of a piece with Prime Time's output over the previous decade. Much was made of the fact that Coleman was working with a keyboard player for the first time in decades. Significantly or not, Bryant receives pretty scant attention in the finished product. A piano introduction to 'Search For Life' gets the ears pricked, but it's almost immediately swept away in the now familiar guitar and bass funk, this time with a rap/recitation. He's back at the front of the old favourite, 'Kathelin Gray', a long, lyrical intro that occupies a good half of the track before Ornette comes in with the keening, offset phrases. Elsewhere, it's single-note runs and soft arpeggiations on the guitars that set up the themes.

As before, he seems keen to reinvent, ironize and subvert, but again in a more accessible and un-antagonistic framework. The players (with the exception of Denardo) are about as anonymous and poorly individualized as guitarists in a Glenn Branca orchestra, but collectively they produce a sound that is absolutely unique and full of character, testimony to the vision behind these outwardly formulaic musics. In historical terms, this can only be seen – as *Dancing In Your Head* was – as a new phase in Ornette's recorded output. It will be fascinating to hear it unfold and evolve.

Steve Coleman ALTO SAXOPHONE, SOPRANO SAXOPHONE, VOCALS

***(*) **Motherland Pulse** JMT 834401
    Coleman; Graham Haynes (*t*); Geri Allen (*p*); Lonnie Plaxico (*b*); Marvin Smitty Smith (*d*). 3/
    85.

*** **Five Elements** JMT 834405
    Coleman; Graham Haynes (*t*); Kelvyn Bell (*g, v*); Kevin Bruce Harris (*b, v*); Geri Allen (*ky*);
    Mark Johnson, Marvin Smitty Smith (*d, perc*); Cassandra Wilson (*v*). 1 & 2/86.

*** **World Expansion** JMT 834410
    Coleman; Graham Haynes (*t*); Robin Eubanks (*tb, v*); Geri Allen (*p, ky*); Kelvyn Bell (*g*); Kevin
    Bruce Harris (*b*); Mark Johnson (*d*); D. K. Dyson, Cassandra Wilson (*v*). 11/86.

(*) **Rhythm People Novus PD 83092
    Coleman; Robin Eubanks (*tb*); James Weidman (*p, ky*); Dave Holland, Reggie Washington (*b*);
    Marvin Smitty Smith (*d, perc*); Cassandra Wilson (*v*). 2/90.

*** **Black Science** Novus PD 83119
    Coleman; David Gilmore (*g, g syn*); James Weidman (*p*); Dave Holland, Reggie Washington
    (*b*); Marvin Smitty Smith (*d*); Cassandra Wilson (*v*). 12/90.

***(*) **Phase Space** DIW 865
    Coleman; Dave Holland (*b*). 1/91.

***(*) **Rhythm In Mind** Novus PD 90654
    Coleman; Kenny Wheeler (*t, flhn*); Von Freeman (*ts*); Kevin Eubanks (*g*); Tommy Flanagan
    (*p*); Dave Holland (*b*); Ed Blackwell (*d*); Ed Blackwell, Marvin Smitty Smith (*d, perc*). 4/91.

*** **Drop Kick** Novus PD 63144
    Coleman; Greg Osby (*as*); Lance Bryant (*ts*); Don Byron (*cl, bcl*); Andy Milne, Andy Weidman
    (*p, ky*); David Gilmore (*g, g syn*); Reggie Washington, Meshell Johnson (*b*); Marvin Smitty
    Smith, Camille Gainer (*d*); Michael Wimberley (*perc*); Cassandra Wilson (*v*). 1/92.

**** **The Tao Of Mad Phat / Fringe Zones** Novus 63160
    Coleman; Roy Hargrove (*t*); Josh Roseman (*tb*); Andy Milne (*p, ky*); David Gilmore (*g, g syn*);

Kenny Davis, Matthew Garrison, Reggie Washington (*b*); Oliver Gene Lake Jr (*d, perc*); Junior Gabu Wedderburn (*perc*). 93.

Coleman's most interesting work to date has been with bassist Dave Holland's band on a group of interesting ECMs, recorded after these rather erratic and tentative sessions. Coleman has a crisp diction with an attractive sourness of tone, and he is a surer technician than his label-mate, tenorist Gary Thomas.

Thomas shares a broad commitment to M-Base's syncretism of jazz, funk, hip-hop, beatbox and other black urban musics, but he makes his approach from the opposite angle, as it were. Coleman is unmistakably a jazz player whose unique melodic developments suggest a sophisticated musical intelligence. *Motherland Pulse* is the best of the earlier discs, but there is a quantum jump after *Black Science* and *Drop Kick*, both of which now seem to be transitional records, marking a significant advance in his compositional interests.

Typically, Coleman uses a range of black rhythms as a basis for complex melodies that ride, sometimes precariously, atop often unvayring patterns. This has become slightly mannered on *World Expansion*, which is credited to Five Elements, a name derived from the earlier disc. Smith is an able accompanist in all branches of black music, but Allen's keyboard figures are maddeningly inconsistent, brightly inventive one moment, bland enough for an MOR pop album the next. Cassandra Wilson's vocals have a joyous, soaring quality and the band always sounds best when it falls in behind her.

Guitarist David Gilmore becomes an important component after 1990, replacing Kelvyn Bell's rather hackneyed funk approach with sharp, staccato figures and broader-brush stuff on the guitar synthesizer. By *The Tao of Mad Phat*, he's become Coleman's right-hand man. The duo album with Dave Holland, recorded right on the back of *Black Science*, confirms the enduring value of an earlier relationship. The saxophonist plays with great assurance, and also more freely, in the sense that he appears confident enough with his partner not to stick to one settled groove. There's a suspicion, though, that the disc should more properly be credited to the bassist, so dominant is he.

Rhythm In Mind is a more traditionally minded, less bluntly 'contemporary' set. The presence of Wheeler, Freeman, Holland and (particularly) Flanagan sigificantly alters the overall sound (Blackwell and Smith turn out to be pretty much interchangeable), but Coleman still cuts the mustard very confidently in this august company. Eubanks and Holland contribute material, but the saxophonist also tests himself on two Thad Jones tunes, 'Zec' and 'Slipped Again', both of which call for a significant measure of restraint.

Holland's guest appearances on *Black Science* don't make a great deal of difference, but (perhaps by association only) it's possible to hear the continuity between what Steve Coleman is doing now and Miles Davis's electric bands of the late 60s. 'Black Phonemics' (*sans* Holland) is a strong track and there are isolated episodes here and there throughout the remainder that command attention. It's certainly a more coherent statement than the (literally) anonymous *Rhythm People*.

Coleman brings the confident freedom principle he seems to have imbibed from the bassist to the next Five Elements disc, the excellent if oddly named *Mad Phat*. Here the group documents the process of 'collective meditation that had played a part in their live appearances for some time. Sequenced into a loose suite, the shifting interplay of individual and ensemble elements is constantly interesting and there are signs that Coleman has carried the process over into more formally written material, like the title piece and 'Polymad Nomads'. 'Alt-Shift-Return' sees him switch to piano, to no particular purpose, but 'Incantation', which dispenses with Gilmore, is an interesting examination of musical space.

Johnny Coles (born 1926) TRUMPET

**** New Morning Criss Cross Criss 1005

Coles; Horace Parlan (*p*); Reggie Johnson (*b*); Billy Hart (*d*). 12/82.

A marvellous record from the one-time Mingus and Gil Evans sideman who rarely found time or inclination to make discs of his own. When he did, as on the long-deleted Blue Note *Little Johnny C*, sparks flew. *New Morning* catches him well played-in, visiting Europe with the posthumous Mingus Dynasty. Coles has a round, slithery tone which sounds great on the blues but which drops down well for ballads.

Opening with Charles Davis's 'Super 80', an unusual but effective curtain-raiser, they tackle the rarely played Wayne Shorter theme, 'United', Mingus's 'Sound Of Love' (a brisk, unsentimental interpretation) and three Coles originals, of which the title-track is the most substantial in thematic terms. The closing 'I Don't Know Yet' is improvised from scratch, a performance possible only with a rhythm section of this pedigree. Parlan seems to be behind the leader every step of the session, coaxing, teasing with incomplete chords and out-of-tempo passages, fuelling Coles's more fiery passages (if that isn't too many puns in one phrase).

John Colianni (born 1963) PIANO

*** **John Colianni** Concord CCD-4309
    Colianni; Joe Wilder (*t*); Emily Remler (*g*); Bob Field (*b*); Connie Kay (*d*). 8/86.
(*) **Blues-O-Matic Concord CCD-4367
    Colianni; Lew Tabackin (*ts, f*); Lynn Seaton (*b*); Mel Lewis (*d*). 8/88.
*** **Maybeck Recital Hall Vol. 37** Concord CCD 4643
    Colianni (*p* solo). 94.

Younger than he plays, Colianni learned his trade in Washington piano bars and with Lionel Hampton's big band. The most impressive thing about this youthful mainstreamer is his rock-steady rhythm: that confidence means he can take a slow-to-mid-tempo tune such as Ray Brown's engaging 'Soft Shoe', on *John Colianni*, and make it swing. The first record is divided into solo, trio and quartet tracks, with Wilder sitting in for one tune, and it's all bright and affectionate music. The second session is a fraction less appealing, since Tabackin seems a vaguely distracted participant, and the pianist is a tad less decisive. His Maybeck session is about par for the course and, though Colianni plays as well as he ever has on record, there's not a great deal of special distinction about it.

Buddy Collette (born 1921) REEDS AND WOODWINDS

(*) **Man Of Many Parts Original Jazz Classics OJC 239
    Collette; Gerald Wilson (*t*); Dave Wells (*bt*); Bill Green (*as*); Jewell Grant (*bs*); Gerald Wiggins, Ernie Freeman (*p*); Barney Kessel (*g*); Gene Wright, Red Callender, Joe Comfort (*b*); Max Alright, Bill Richmond, Larry Bunker (*d*). 2–4/56.
*** **Nice Day With Buddy Collette** Original Jazz Classics OJC 747
    Collette; Don Friedman, Dick Shreve, Calvin Jackson (*p*); John Goodman, Leroy Vinnegar (*b*); Bill Dolney, Shelly Manne (*d*). 11/56–2/57.
(*) **Jazz Loves Paris Original Jazz Classics OJC 1764
    Collette; Frank Rosolino (*tb*); Howard Roberts (*g*); Red Mitchell (*b*); Red Callender (*tba*); Bill Douglass (*d*). 1/58.

Buddy Collette had the misfortune to be a pioneer on an instrument whose jazz credentials remain in doubt: though he was a capable performer on alto, tenor and clarinet, he became renowned as a flautist and consequently got stuck in the role of novelty sessionman in the West Coast scene of the mid-1950s. On his own dates, at least, he got to handle the rest of the instruments from his music room. *Man Of Many Parts*, originally issued on Contemporary, is gimcracked around his multi-instrumentalism and is mildly enjoyable without catching much fire. A shade better is the entertaining *Nice Day*: his prime instrument here is clarinet, his woodsy sound isn't so far from Jimmy Giuffre's, and it makes an interesting gambit on the minor blues, 'Minor Deviation' (on which the little-known Shreve plays an outstanding solo), and the queer arrangement of 'Moten Swing'. The record is let down a little by switching among three different rhythm sections, but it ends usefully on the tenor feature, 'Buddy Boo'. Excellent remastering. The players can't do very much with *Jazz Loves Paris*, a pretty thin concept, based round songs about, er, Paris. Callender's tuba introduces a novelty element and all the tracks are too short to let the players breathe, but there are still a few nice moments: Roberts on 'La Vie En Rose', the hopped-up reading of 'The Last Time I Saw Paris' and any of Rosolino's brief turns out front. Four alternative takes beef up the CD reissue.

*** **Flute Talk** Soul Note SN 1165
    Collette; James Newton (*f*); Geri Allen (*p*); Jaribu Shahid (*b*); Giampiero Prina (*d*). 7/88.

Collette's return to the studios, recorded on an Italian tour, is hurried but agreeable enough, and this is probably the best group he's ever led on record. The meeting with Newton is more respectful than combative, and Allen is her usual unpredictable self, alert in places, asleep in others. The recording could be sharper.

Max Collie (born 1931) TROMBONE, VOCALS

*** **Frontline / Backline** Timeless TTD 504/508
    Collie; Phil Mason (*t*); Jack Gilbert (*cl*); Jim McIntosh (*bj*); Trefor Williams (*b*); Ron McKay (*d*). 12/82.
** **Sensation** Timeless TTD 530
    As above, except replace Gilbert with Paul Harrison (u), McKay with Peter Cotterill (*d*); add J. Johnson (*p, v*). 7/86.

(*) **Latest And Greatest Reality RCD 113
>As above, except replace Harrison with Steve Mellor (*cl*), McIntosh with Chris Marney (*bj*),
>Johnson with Lord Arsenal (*p*); add Pauline Pearce, Marilyn Middleton Pollock (*v*). 9/93.

This sort of music doesn't really sound right on a CD and, if there is such an entity as the 'CD generation', they probably don't buy it anyway. Collie works at the blue-collar, Transit van end of the Bilk–Ball–Barber spectrum, a rough-diamond revivalist with a big strong tone, notably tight and well-schooled bands and an entertainment potential that goes off the scale. These albums do little more than provide tasters of the live act.

Far from awarding himself a sabbatical on reaching his fifties, Collie has been working harder than ever. Perversely, he was better documented on record ten years ago. The 1982 recording is one of his best, cheerfully unfashionable and utterly untroubled by any recent rethink of traditionalism in jazz. There are no fiery solos, no fancy arrangements. Songs are simply counted off and played. Full stop.

The '86 band has a rather more 'authentic' feel (whatever that means) than its immediate predecessor, whose output is now only to be found on second-hand vinyl; replacing Denny Ilett's sharp, brassy cornet with Mason's more polished sound did the group no particular favours. Fine performances, though, better material and a clearer pick-up on the rhythm section.

Interestingly, the rationale behind *Latest And Greatest* was to provide a representative CD sampling of Collie material for fans who had just bought a player. Simple enough formula: just turn up and play lots of the old stuff. The inclusion of Pearce and Middleton Pollock was doubtless intended as a plus but, unlike Ottilie Paterson's contribution to Chris Barber records, it doesn't work out quite like that. 'Dippermouth Blues', 'Fidgety Feet', 'When You And I Were Young, Maggie', 'Shimmee Sha Wabble', and so on, and so forth. Wholly undisturbing fun.

Cal Collins (born 1933) GUITAR

(*) **Ohio Style Concord CCD 4447
>Collins; Jerry Van Blair (*flhn*); Lou Lausche (*b*); Tony Sweet (*d*). 11/90.

None of the previous six albums for Concord by Cal Collins remains in the catalogue. Of the many swing-styled guitarists which the company has recorded, Collins is rather more exciting than most: a former bluegrass player and a rather late developer, his manner owes much to Django Reinhardt, although he follows Tal Farlow's lead more closely. What comes out is a kind of down-home swing-to-bop, a manner that lets him create some crackling improvisations at fast tempos, although he tends towards sleepy gentility on a ballad. This recent session pairs him with cornetist Van Blair in a setting which sounds much like a Ruby Braff–George Barnes date or something involving Bobby Hackett. There isn't that level of class here, but it's well done in its way.

Jay Collins (born 1968) TENOR SAXOPHONE

*** **Uncommon Threads** Reservoir RSR CD 135
>Collin; Kenny Barron (*p*); Joe Locke (*vib*); Rufus Reid (*b*); Ben Riley (*d*). 6/92.

The saxophonist holds his own in distinguished company on his leadership debut. A native of the Portland, Oregon, scene, he plays with the acid-jazz combo, TUBA, and was a sometime break-dancer – none of which squares with the big, almost classical sound of his tenor playing, steeped in the tradition. Three nice originals, a version of 'Dearly Beloved' that spins off a funky bass vamp and a rare Monk tune, 'Played Twice', are the prime elements in an interesting programme. Collins shines in some of his solos but sounds a little rote in others: he never characterizes 'You've Changed', done as a duet with Barron, with enough guts, and some of the tempos encourage a noodling rather than a purposeful feel. The others sound fine, and Locke is his usual challenging self. Nobody is that well served by the listless studio mix, though.

Lou Colombo TRUMPET

** **I Remember Bobby** Concord CCD 4435
>Colombo; Dave McKenna (*p*); Gray Sargent (*g*); Phil Flanigan (*b*); Keith Copeland (*d*). 6/90.

The 'Bobby' is Bobby Hackett, but Colombo isn't much like that master, nor is he especially interesting as a leader-soloist. A proficient player, but there's nothing in this pleasant mainstream session which couldn't have been done as well by many other section trumpeters. McKenna and the others offer their customary capable support.

John Coltrane (1926–67) TENOR, ALTO AND SOPRANO SAXOPHONES, FLUTE

*** **Dakar** Original Jazz Classics OJC 393
    Coltrane; Cecil Payne, Pepper Adams (bs); Mal Waldron (p); Doug Watkins (b); Art Taylor (d). 4/57.

*** **Coltrane** Original Jazz Classics OJC 020
    Coltrane; Johnny Splawn (t); Sahib Shihab (bs); Mal Waldron (p); Paul Chambers (b); Albert 'Tootie' Heath (d). 5/57.

*** **Lush Life** Original Jazz Classics OJC 131
    Coltrane; Donald Byrd (t); Red Garland (p); Earl May (b); Art Taylor, Louis Hayes, Albert 'Tootie' Heath (d). 5/57–1/58.

*** **Traneing In** Original Jazz Classics OJC 189
    Coltrane; Red Garland (p); Paul Chambers (b); Art Taylor (d). 8/57.

***(*) **Blue Train** Blue Note CDP 7460952
    Coltrane; Lee Morgan (t); Curtis Fuller (tb); Kenny Drew (p); Paul Chambers (b); Philly Joe Jones (d). 9/57.

*** **Coltranetime** Blue Note CDP 7 84461
    Coltrane; Kenny Dorham (t); Cecil Taylor (p); Chuck Israels (b); Louis Hayes (d). 10/58.

*** **The Art Of John Coltrane** Blue Note CDP 799175
    As above, except add Donald Byrd (t). 9/56–10/58.

Coltrane had moved from obscurity to front-ranking stardom in a matter of two years. When he joined the Miles Davis quintet, he rapidly asserted a primal voice on the tenor saxophone: a hard, iron tone, a ceaseless, tumbling flow of phrases, a sense of some great architecture in the making. He had already played big-band section-work for years, and his work with Davis now sounds transitional – although, in a sense, so does all of his music. His early sessions as a leader for Prestige are mere stopovers on the journey, expansive, prolific, but never finally achieved in the way that his great later works would be. In 1957, the year he also worked with Thelonious Monk, whose influence on him is important but hard to pin down, he made these five sessions under his own name. (The Blue Note compilation overlaps *Blue Train* with some related material from the time.) All of the OJC reissues (from Prestige originals) are enjoyable without leaving a lasting impression. *Dakar* is timbrally unusual, with its rumbling two-baritone front line (in the excellent remastering the music emerges as quite a feast of low-register grumbling and growling), but Coltrane sounds out of place, even on the three interesting originals by session supervisor Teddy Charles. *Coltrane* and *Lush Life* are full of powerful tenor: the latter is interesting for three tracks with just bass and drums support, but Trane never uses this as the challenge which Sonny Rollins took up at the Village Vanguard in the same year (it only came about, in any case, because the pianist never showed up). *Traneing In*, with the Davis rhythm section, features a tumultuous solo on the title-track and the lovely, deep-set ballad playing on 'You Leave Me Breathless' which is the untarnished virtue of the Prestige sessions and one of the things which attract many to Coltrane in the first place. More significant, though, is his sole date for Blue Note; *Coltranetime* was originally released on United Artists. *Blue Train* has one of his most coherent early solos on the title-track. The rest of the band are inappropriate players for the occasion, though Fuller tears off a great outburst on 'Locomotion': the underlying strength of 'Moment's Notice', which has since become a standard, is reduced to hard-bop cliché here. But there is always a sense of Coltrane having something tremendous almost within sight. *Coltrane* and *Lush Life* have also been combined on a single, UK-issue CD.

    Coltranetime is valued mostly for the chance to hear two giants of the new music in session together. As with Monk, it isn't clear what Coltrane heard or got from Taylor, and much of this session is played on a polite middle ground that neither of them found especially engaging. One listens with most interest, ironically, to Israels, who might well have become a more significant part of this story in different circumstances. He's a remarkable player and seems highly responsive to the saxophonist's needs.

(*) **Tenor Conclave Original Jazz Classics OJC 127
    Coltrane; Paul Quinichette, Hank Mobley, Al Cohn, Zoot Sims (ts); Red Garland (p); Paul Chambers (b); Art Taylor (d). 9/56.

*** **Cattin' With Coltrane And Quinichette** Original Jazz Classics OJC 460
    Coltrane; Paul Quinichette (ts); Mal Waldron (p); Julian Euell (b); Ed Thigpen (d). 5/57.

*** **Wheelin' And Dealin'** Original Jazz Classics OJC 672
    Coltrane; Frank Wess, Paul Quinichette (ts); Mal Waldron (p); Doug Watkins (b); Art Taylor (d). 57.

One of Coltrane's chores for Prestige was to blow his way through sundry encounters with other tenors. The *Tenor Conclave* album is moderately good fun, but the essential pointlessness of the exercise is shown up by the looseness of the material and arrangements, even if professionalism does win out. The meeting with Quinichette is rather better, Trane's intensity making a good match for Quinichette's lighter and more carefree (but still bluesy) mannerisms. 'Cattin'' itself is a great up-tempo swinger. *Wheelin' And Dealin'* returns to the tenors-all-out formula, and is respectable enough.

***(*) **Soultrane** Original Jazz Classics OJC 021
> Coltrane; Red Garland (*p*); Paul Chambers (*b*); Art Taylor (*d*). 2/58.

***(*) **Settin' The Pace** Original Jazz Classics OJC 078
> As above. 3/58.

(*) **Black Pearls Original Jazz Classics OJC 352
> As above, except add Donald Byrd (*t*). 5/58.

*** **The Standard Coltrane** Original Jazz Classics OJC 246
> As above, except Wilbur Harden (*t, flhn*), Jimmy Cobb (*d*) replace Byrd and Taylor. 7/58.

*** **The Stardust Session** Prestige 24056
> As above. 7/58.

*** **Bahia** Original Jazz Clasics OJC 415
> As above, except add Art Taylor (*d*). 12/58.

*** **The Last Trane** Original Jazz Classics OJC 394
> Coltrane; Donald Byrd (*t*); Red Garland (*p*); Paul Chambers, Earl May (*b*); Art Taylor, Louis Hayes (*d*). 8/57–3/58.

***(*) **John Coltrane And The Jazz Giants** Prestige 60104
> Coltrane; Donald Byrd, Miles Davis, Wilbur Harden (*t*); Tadd Dameron, Red Garland, Thelonious Monk (*p*); Paul Chambers, Jamil Nasser, Wilbur Ware, John Simmons (*b*); Shadow Wilson, Jimmy Cobb, Philly Joe Jones, Louis Hayes, Art Taylor (*d*). 56–58.

Even as Coltrane grew in stature, with the celebrated 'sheets of sound' – covering every possible permutation of one chord before the next arrived – as the dominant part of his sound and delivery, the circumstances of his recording tenure at Prestige stubbornly refused to open up to him, with the casual nature of the sessions reinforced by sole use of standards and blues as the blowing material. *Soultrane*, with its first version of a later favourite, 'I Want To Talk About You', and *Settin' The Pace*, featuring a spearing assault on Jackie McLean's 'Little Melonae' and a glowing 'If There Is Someone Lovelier Than You', are both outstanding tenor-and-rhythm dates where Coltrane gives himself as much rope as he feels he can find. *Black Pearls* is let down by the overlong and tedious 'Sweet Sapphire Blues', and *Bahia* – though it has a couple more excellent Coltrane ballad treatments – is also routine. *The Standard Coltrane* dwells on ballads and will please any who prefer the more tractable side of Coltrane's music, while *The Last Trane* pulls together four out-takes from earlier sessions, 'Come Rain Or Come Shine' standing up particularly well. *The Stardust Session* includes all of *Standard Coltrane*, two tracks from *Bahia* and 'Stardust' and 'Love Thy Neighbour'. There is little in these records of genuinely outstanding calibre, and the compilation *John Coltrane And The Jazz Giants* – which includes tracks with Davis and Monk – is as good a way as any of geting to know this period without toiling through what are mostly verbose and disorganized records. But Coltrane's sound, of course, endures.

**** **Giant Steps** Atlantic 781337-2
> Coltrane; Tommy Flanagan (*p*); Paul Chambers (*b*); Art Taylor (*d*). 5/59.

A fresh start – almost a debut album – and perhaps Coltrane's most playable, memorable and best-sustained record. The tunes are uniformly marvellous, riffs or steps or even melodies which have all – except for 'Spiral' – become integral parts of the modern jazz book. Coltrane's tone has lost some of its remorselessness, and it gives the ballad 'Naima' a movingly simple lyrical intent. It's almost like an interlude on Coltrane's journey, this record, a summing up of past achievements in sparer, easier forms, before the great steps forward of the next few years. 'Giant Steps' itself has a sunny quality which its rising theme embodies; 'Mr P.C.' is a blowing blues which is idiomatic enough to have become the most frequently blown blues in the repertory. 'Syeeda's Song Flute' explores the possibilities of a single long line. There is very able support from Flanagan, Chambers and Taylor, and the CD edition includes four alternative takes.

**** **Coltrane Jazz** Atlantic 781344
> Coltrane; Wynton Kelly, McCoy Tyner (*p*); Paul Chambers, Steve Davis (*b*); Jimmy Cobb, Elvin Jones (*d*). 11–12/59.

*** **The Avant-Garde** Atlantic 90041-2
> Coltrane; Don Cherry (*t*); Charlie Haden, Percy Heath (*b*); Ed Blackwell (*d*). 6–7/60.

Coltrane had had some important dental work done and had to redevelop his embouchure: 'Harmonique' on *Coltrane Jazz* features split tones that suggest the saxophonist testing out what he could do. On the same record he began doubling on soprano. *Coltrane Jazz* is largely a continuation of the spirit of *Giant Steps* without quite securing the same consistency of result, and there is a stray track, 'Village Blues', from a session by the later quartet. Nevertheless there is some magnificent tenor playing. *The Avant-Garde* found him meeting Don Cherry in an approximation of the freedoms of the Coleman quartet, but Coltrane's responses are tentative, and he sounds too bulky and grandiose to fly around as easily as Cherry does in this situation. He sounds happiest on Monk's 'Bemsha Swing'.

**** **My Favorite Things** Atlantic 782346-2
      Coltrane; McCoy Tyner (*p*); Steve Davis (*b*); Elvin Jones (*d*). 10/60.
**** **Coltrane's Sound** Atlantic 1419-2
      As above. 10/60.
**** **Coltrane Plays The Blues** Atlantic 1382-2
      As above. 10/60.
**** **Olé Coltrane** Atlantic 1373-2
      Coltrane; Freddie Hubbard (*t*); Eric Dolphy (*as, f*); McCoy Tyner (*p*); Art Davis, Reggie
      Workman (*b*); Elvin Jones (*d*). 5/61.

The new quartet – Steve Davis didn't last long, and would soon be replaced by Jimmy Garrison – pitched Coltrane into his next phase, but the last four albums for Atlantic are in some ways transitional, with Elvin Jones not yet embarking on the great polyrhythmic dialogues he would later conduct with the leader. *My Favorite Things* is dominated by the leader's soprano sax improvisation on the title-track, a theme he would return to over and over again: the important thing here is that both Coltrane and McCoy Tyner reduce the material to a couple of scales and ignore the changes, without forgetting to return to the theme. This gives the music a suitably endless feel, helps Coltrane push far beyond the normal performance durations, and sustains him into what would eventually be marathon performances (this one is a mere 13 minutes or so). The music also echoes the joyfulness of the lyric and points towards the searching for ecstasy that would also come to characterize some parts of later Coltrane.

Plays The Blues is six versions of the blues, split between tenor and soprano; *Coltrane's Sound* includes a crushingly intense tenor solo on 'Liberia' and a very dark 'The Night Has A Thousand Eyes'. These are forbiddingly powerful records (both records were cut on two very long days in the studio). Jones has begun to develop his singular role at the drums, and Tyner his thumpingly overdriven block chords and flurries of right-hand figures.

Olé Coltrane includes just three pieces, and was cut two days after one of the sessions for *Africa/Brass*. By comparison with that date, this is a lesser affair, but the title-theme and 'Dahomey Dance' evoke some of the orchestral swirl which Coltrane (and Dolphy) were aiming to secure in these bigger works. The CD issues of all these records sound faithful to the mastertapes, though they present no noticeable improvement over original vinyl.

**** **The Best Of John Coltrane** Atlantic 781366
      As above. 5 & 12/59, 10/60.

An ideal, single-volume selection for the newcomer, or as a greatest hits second copy for the car or Discman. It contains 'Giant Steps', 'Naima', 'Cousin Mary', 'My Favorite Things', 'Central Park West', 'Equinox', so no surprises there. Valuable as it is, it should on no account be used to fob off anyone who asked for the item below as a Christmas present.

**** **The Heavyweight Champion** Atlantic/Rhino 8122 71984 7CD
      Personnel as for Atlantic recordings above. 1/59–5/61.

It would be tempting to dock this massive documentation of the ultimate apotheosis just on the grounds of its ugly title. Its price is neither more nor less than one can expect to pay for seven CDs packaged as exquisitely as these are. The only problem arises for the collector who already has the material on CD (all the above are still available) and who only really wants the additional material to be found on the last disc, which is in a mock-up of an old tape-box. Some variants have, of course, already been available on *Alternate Takes* (including such cruces as 'Giant Steps', 'Naima' and 'Body And Soul') and *The Coltrane Legacy* brought forward a couple of untitled pieces from the *Coltrane's Sound* session of 24 October 1960 and the *Olé* recordings nine months later. The difference here, packaging apart, is the sheer density of additional studio material.

For 'Giant Steps', there are now no fewer than ten alternative takes; the previously heard one (issued on the compilation noted above) is with the released performance on disc one, but it should be noted that it is being played by a different, unfamiliar group, with Cedar Walton at the piano and Lex Humphries drumming. The remaining takes are grouped on the out-take disc, and fascinating listening they make, as two groups (one redated 26 March 1959, the other, with Tommy Flanagan, a couple of months later) work through this most demanding of modern jazz themes. As often as not, it is the composer who seems ill at ease with the changes, and it is he who brings a couple of takes to an abrupt close.

Alternative versions of 'Naima' and 'Like Sonny' were also on the LP compilation, but these are filled out substantially, though with less obvious historical significance than with 'Giant Steps'. The studio talk is relaxed and funny but offers no profound further insight into the way these extraordinary recordings were made. (One final note: two tracks – 'Lady Bird' and 'In Your Own Sweet Way' – are omitted from the *Coltrane's Sound* material on the unimpeachable logic that Coltrane does not play on them. So, depending on how one views the ground-rules of completism, to be completely complete one needs that CD as well.)

***(*) **The Complete Africa / Brass Sessions** Impulse! 21682 2CD
      Coltrane; Freddie Hubbard, Booker Little (*t*); Charles Greenlea, Julian Priester, Britt Woodman (*tb*); Donald Corrado, Bob Northern, Robert Swissel, Julius Watkins (*frhn*); Bill Barber (*tba*); Carl Bowman (*euph*); Eric Dolphy (*as, bcl*); Pat Patrick (*reeds*); McCoy Tyner (*p*); Paul Chambers, Art Davis (*b*); Reggie Workman (*b*); Elvin Jones (*d*). 5 & 6/61.
This was Coltrane's first recording for Impulse!. Eric Dolphy has long been credited with the brass arrangements (which are of an unprecedented scale in Coltrane's work), but it's clear that most of the structures were fully worked by Coltrane and Tyner, leaving the other saxophonist little to do but straightforward orchestration for the baritone horns and conducting the take. Coltrane's desire to experiment with rhythm (most of his work had been in basic 4/4, with occasional waltz-time pieces like 'My Favorite Things') was fostered by an interest in African music, and the 16-minute 'Africa' is an experiment with altered signatures and an implied chord-structure. This remains very much in the background, freeing the saxophonist for some of his most powerful and unfettered solo work to date. The second tune could hardly be more different. 'Greensleeves' is played pretty straight as a 3/4 arrangement for soprano saxophone, much like 'My Favorite Things' and the later 'Chim Chim Cheree' (*Plays*, below). 'Blues Minor' is an uncomplicated blowing theme, with an easy swing and some attractively altered chords.

    A second volume, *Africa/Brass*, consisting mainly of alternative takes, was released in the mid-1970s. The traditional 'Song Of The Underground Railroad', recorded in a single take, hadn't been issued before, but there were significant variant performances of 'Greensleeves' (a slightly longer second take) and 'Africa' (a preliminary take with a rather tentative solo from Coltrane). The reissue – and subsequent CD compilation – have refocused attention on what is increasingly seen as one of Coltrane's most adventurous experiments. This latest completist repackaging actually adds only two tracks, but it spreads the material over two discs. There is an alternative version of 'Africa' from the 7 June session, where it is slowed up further and given a more orthodox jazz swing, perhaps to iron out whatever seemed to be blocking the flow of ideas. It makes for a fascinating study piece and a valuable insight into the way Coltrane was thinking on this unique orchestral project. The only other new item is the only non-Coltrane/Dolphy/Tyner arrangement. It's a piece called 'The Damned Don't Cry' by Coltrane's friend, Cal Massey, arranged (not altogether successfully) by Romulus Franceschini, easily the weakest thing on the disc; it previously appeared on the compilation, *Trane's Modes*, and might very usefully have been left there. Having got the thing to this stage, one can't imagine that GRP will find any more ways of repackaging it.

**** **Live At The Village Vanguard** MCA MCAD 39136
      Coltrane; Eric Dolphy (*bcl*); McCoy Tyner (*p*); Reggie Workman (*b*); Elvin Jones (*d*). 11/61.
***(*) **Impressions** MCA MCAD 5887
      As above, except add Jimmy Garrison (*b*). 11/61, 9/62, 4/63.
Coltrane told Impulse! producer Bob Thiele that he liked the intimacy and human contact of a club setting, where direct communication with an audience was possible. The opening 'Spiritual' has a preaching immediacy that Dolphy picks up in his extraordinary, vocalized bass clarinet solo. He follows Coltrane on soprano, who returns to finish off a number he based on an actual spiritual heard many years before and stored away. There were only three tracks on the original album. After the relatively conventional 'Softly As In A Morning Sunrise' (Dolphy drops out, but Coltrane remains on soprano), the scorching blues of 'Chasin' The Trane' comes as an almost physical shock. There had been nothing quite like this in jazz; no one had dared to create a solo as freely stressed, polytonal, downright ugly, as this since the days of the early blues men. The difference was that Coltrane was able to sustain inventiveness in that genre for nearly 16 minutes, an achievement that became the immediate target of hostile criticism. There is a hint of Philip Larkin's celebrated feeling (directed at the *Live In Birdland* record, which he confessed to liking) that Coltrane spends too much time 'rocking backwards and forwards as if in pain between two chords', but there is little doubt that the pain is genuine.

    Further material from Coltrane's Village Vanguard residency is included on *Impressions*, which, like the first album, features Dolphy on bass clarinet for just one fine track ('Indiana') and, like the later *Live At Birdland*, also includes studio material. 'After The Rain', recorded with Garrison on bass in April 1963, is a hymnic ballad with a repetitive structure that builds up emotion to an almost unbearable extent and then dies away into nothing. (Purchasers should be aware that *Live At The Village Vanguard Again*, currently available on a European CD reissue, relates to a 1966 session by the later group which included Alice Coltrane, Pharoah Sanders and Rashied Ali. Other material from the classic 1961 Vanguard sessions is scattered around; no sign yet of any attempt to bring it all together on a single-CD set.)

***(*) **Coltrane** MCA MCAD 5883
    Coltrane; McCoy Tyner (*p*); Jimmy Garrison (*b*); Elvin Jones (*d*). 4 & 6/62.
Less well known than its immediate predecessors, this was the first full-scale studio record by the classic Coltrane quartet. It's a curious album, led off by the magnificent 'Out Of This World', one of Coltrane's greatest achievements. This was followed by Mal Waldron's lovely 'Soul Eyes', and then the album slips. How many even enthusiastic Coltrane listeners would list 'Tunji' and 'Miles' Mode' in the front rank of the saxophonist's work? 'The Inch Worm', an irritating Frank Loesser theme from *Hans Christian Andersen*, is the regulation show-tune arrangement for soprano. The album stands and falls, though, on that magnificent reading of the old Harold Arlen/Johnny Mercer tune and is well worth having on the strength of that alone.

***(*) **From The Original Master Tapes** MCA MCAD 5541
    As for *Coltrane* and *Africa/Brass*; with Garvin Bushell (*ob*); Ahmed Abdul-Malik (*oud*); Reggie Workman (*b*); Roy Haynes (*d*). 61–62.
Digitally remastered from first-generation stereo masters, this is as much a tribute to Bob Thiele as to Coltrane himself. 'Song Of The Underground Railroad', from the *Africa/Brass* sessions, is included, along with 'Soul Eyes', 'Dear Lord', 'Big Nick' and 'Vilia', one of Coltrane's less well-known subversions of pop material. There are also previously unreleased performances of 'Spiritual' and of 'India' with Dolphy, Bushell and Abdul-Malik lending the latter theme an exotic sound-palette. The reproduction is predictably good (which means mainly that Garrison and Workman can be heard properly) and it stands as a fine reminder of Thiele's very considerable contribution to Coltrane's most dramatic years.

***(*) **The European Tour** Pablo Live 2308222
    Coltrane; McCoy Tyner (*p*); Jimmy Garrison (*b*); Elvin Jones (*d*). 62.
*** **Bye Bye Blackbird** Original Jazz Classics OJC 681
    As above. 62.
*** **The Paris Concert** Original Jazz Classics OJC 781
    As above. 62.
*** **Ev'ry Time We Say Goodbye** Natasha NI-4003
    As above. 11/62.
A comprehensive documentation of live material from a rather troubled year, which nevertheless saw unprecedented public exposure. The Pablo Live *European Tour* is a good choice from this vintage, with 'The Promise' unrepresented elsewhere. OJC 681 consists of just two mammoth performances, 'Bye Bye Blackbird' and 'Traneing In'. *The Paris Concert* opens up on a long, boiling 'Mr P.C.', but the subsequent 'Inch Worm' and 'Ev'ry Time We Say Goodbye' are more mortal and less lapel-grabbing. The Natasha album is drawn from one of the Graz concerts which have appeared on several issues previously: the expected set, in the usual indifferent sound. Anyone building a CD collection from scratch would be well advised to concentrate on Impulse! releases only for the time being.

*** **Live At Birdland And The Half Note** Cool & Blue C&B CD 101
    Coltrane; McCoy Tyner (*p*); Jimmy Garrison (*b*); Elvin Jones (*d*). 5/62, 2/63, 5/65.
***(*) **Coltrane Live At Birdland** Impulse! MCAD 33109
    As above. 10, 11/63.
To gain a sense of how rapidly Coltrane developed in the early 1960s, the main focus of comparison here should be 'I Want To Talk About You', originally recorded on *Soul Trane*, above. There are versions on both the Birdland sets, recorded eight months apart in 1963. Though Coltrane's sound on the 1963 recordings is harsher, restless, unsettlingly sombre, far from the Getz-like ballad phrasing of the Prestige sessions, the real, structural differences relate every bit as much to the rest of the band. Compare Jones's shredded rhythms, Garrison's drones and Tyner's every-which-way polytonality with the relatively conventional accompaniments of Garland, Chambers and Taylor, and it's again clear that the Coltrane *Quartet* should be studied as a whole, not as a secondary aspect of the saxophonist's lonely struggle.

    He sounds isolated enough on the unaccompanied coda, and it's clear that there's no end to the turbulence. The album is actually slightly mis-titled, for two of the tracks – one of them of considerable stylistic importance – were recorded in the studio just over a month after the club sessions. 'Alabama' was inspired by the murder of four black children in a church bombing. Fuelled by an almost militaristic pulse from Jones, it's a sad, stately ballad theme that rides at an angle to the basic tempo. Where a player like Archie Shepp might have turned such inspiration into a scream of pain, Coltrane attempts to find a route to transcendence, a way up out of the vicious mire of the modern South. Set opposite the long 'Afro-Blue', a soprano feature built up out of eerily unfamiliar intervals and a repetitive, almost *raga*-like theme, and 'The Promise', it makes this one of the most emotionally satisfying records of the period. Only the final track, 'Your Lady', seems rather slight, though it features some very telling unaccompanied exchanges between Coltrane and Jones that in some respects set a precedent for the later *Interstellar Space* with Rashied Ali.

The Cool & Blue set is a mixed bag, with New York performances ranging over nearly three years. The long 'Song Of Praise' (May 1965) is perhaps the most valuable single track, unmistakably in the 'late' style, but 'My Favorite Things' and 'Body And Soul' (June 1962) are very welcome as well, and the sound is quite respectable for a club recording.

***(*) **Ballads** Impulse! MCAD 5885
    Coltrane; McCoy Tyner (*p*); Jimmy Garrison (*b*); Elvin Jones (*d*). 9–11/62.
*** **John Coltrane And Johnny Hartman** Impulse! MCAD 5661
    As above, except add Johnny Hartman (*v*). 3/63.
***(*) **The Gentle Side Of John Coltrane** Impulse! GRD 107
    As above, except add Duke Ellington (*p*); Aaron Bell (*b*); Roy Haynes, Sam Woodyard (*d*).
It was apparently producer Bob Thiele who suggested the *Ballads* and Hartman projects to Coltrane, who had been experiencing articulation problems and was unable to play as accurately at speed as he wished. It was certainly Thiele who set up the historic encounter with Duke which is recorded on Impulse! MCAD 39103 (reviewed elsewhere), which is marked by a superb reading of 'In A Sentimental Mood'. Coltrane had always been an affecting ballad player and there was a sound market logic in an album of this type. He was less experienced working with a singer, but the sessions with Hartman have a satisfaction all their own and it's a shame that (with the exception of 'Lush Life', which Coltrane had recorded with Donald Byrd and Red Garland in 1958) the set doesn't include a vocal version of one of the standard songs in Trane's regular repertoire.

Most of the songs on *Ballads* are relatively little used as jazz standards, though 'Nancy (With The Laughing Face)', 'You Don't Know What Love Is' and 'Too Young To Go Steady' have all been favoured at one time or another. To some extent this is Tyner's session. He floods the tunes with chords and lush flurries of single notes, with Garrison placing long, cello-like tones underneath him. Jones is inevitably at something of a premium, but plays very tunefully, with a hint of Max Roach in his stick-work on the cymbals.

The Gentle Side is a reasonable option for anyone who really can't take Coltrane's flat-out style. Apart from the Ellington and Hartman tracks, it includes 'Soul Eyes', 'Wise One' from *Crescent*, 'After The Rain' from *Impressions* and 'Dear Lord' from *Transition*. Thirteen tracks in all, and good value if you don't mind duplications.

**** **Afro Blue Impressions** Pablo Live 2620101 2CD
    Coltrane; McCoy Tyner (*p*); Jimmy Garrison (*b*); Elvin Jones (*d*).
The 1963 tour was slightly anti-climactic compared to those of the previous two years. This one comes close to being essential. Coltrane and (somewhat less audibly) Garrison play powerfully on 'Lonnie's Lament' (a foretaste of the *Crescent* sessions the following spring), there's a good version of 'Cousin Mary', and staple fare like 'My Favorite Things', 'Naima' and 'Impressions'. Strongly recommended.

***(*) **Crescent** Impulse! MCAD 5889
    Coltrane; McCoy Tyner (*p*); Jimmy Garrison (*b*); Elvin Jones (*d*). 4, 6/64.
In the spiritual odyssey of Coltrane's last years, *Crescent* has always been cast as the dark night of the soul, coming before the triumphant affirmation of *A Love Supreme*, below. It is certainly Coltrane's most melancholy record, dominated by the mournful 'Wise One' and the haunting blues ballad, 'Lonnie's Lament'. If 'Crescent' was meant to suggest growth, it's a hesitant, almost blindfolded progress, with little of the soaring joy that Coltrane usually brought to such themes. 'Bessie's Blues' is a brightly bubbling three and a half minutes that seems almost out of place on an album so sombre, but it served as a brief feature for the unsettled Tyner. 'Lonnie's Lament' contains one of Garrison's best solos on record, and the closing 'Drum Thing' is largely devoted to Elvin Jones, who plays a less than usually prominent part elsewhere.

    **** **A Love Supreme** MCA DMCL 1648
    Coltrane; McCoy Tyner (*p*); Jimmy Garrison (*b*); Elvin Jones (*d*). 12/64.
Great albums are usually made by groups who have attained a certain measure of mutual understanding. Very great albums are almost always made by groups on the brink of splitting asunder. By the autumn of 1964, the quartet had reached a point where further development along the free-modal path they had been exploring since the November 1961 Village Vanguard dates seemed impossible.

A Love Supreme was Coltrane's most profoundly spiritual statement and cannot (despite at least one generation of text-free sleeves) be separated from a passionate statement of belief on the gatefold and the free-verse text that accompanies it. The fourth movement, 'Psalm', was intended as a 'musical narration' of this text and is the point towards which the whole sequence gravitates.

Coltrane's spirituality was more than usually hard-won. A mere seven years before, he had been seriously addicted to heroin and alcohol, and in a very real sense *A Love Supreme*, coming at the end of a cycle of years, is a document of his struggle to extricate himself from that slough. Coltrane suffered agonizing dental problems and had considerable difficulty with his mouthpiece in 1961 and 1962. The pure, vibrato-less tone of earlier years has gone, to be replaced with a tearing, rather brutal delivery replete with false notes, splintery harmonics and harsh, almost toneless breath-noises. The vocal parallels to parts of *A Love Supreme* are in keeping with his desire (already evident on *Live At The Village Vanguard*) to recapture something of the highly vocalized sound of the blues, field shouts, and the unaccompanied psalms of the primitive Black Church.

The sequence begins with a calmly untroubled fanfare of 'Acknowledgement'. This gives way to a stately 8-bar theme which serves as background for one of the short motifs out of which Coltrane constructed much of his music at this period. The four notes stated and restated by Jimmy Garrison and then echoed by Coltrane in a questioning variation of keys are probably the best known in the whole of modern jazz. They create much of the material for Coltrane's shifting, gradually ascending solo and then the famous, husky iteration of 'a love supreme' by the four players. Jones's drumming is absolutely extraordinary, using double-time figures of considerable complexity, while Garrison and Tyner sustain a background ostinato that prevents the whole piece from falling apart.

'Resolution' increases the emotional temperature very considerably, with Jones simplifying the rhythm somewhat and stoking up the dynamics mercilessly. Coltrane, again led by Garrison, cuts loose with a scalding solo that brought the first half of the original LP to a seemingly unsurpassable climax. 'Pursuance' is a dark blues, with a nervously fragmented rhythm, which becomes increasingly untenable as the piece develops. This paves the way for the extraordinary final movement.

The final movement has always been seen as continuing a line established by 'Alabama' on the Birdland album. 'Psalm' is an out-of-tempo ballad with the most beautiful saxophone playing on the album. Coltrane's sound is still rather acerbic, but his non-verbal narration of a deeply felt credo is expressed in tones of great majesty. At the very end, in an episode much discussed by Coltrane fans, a second saxophone (perhaps Archie Shepp's) joins with a two-note figure corresponding to the final 'amen' of Coltrane's text. Coltrane responds with a fragment of the opening fanfare, bringing the music full circle.

The greatest jazz album of the modern period? Or the most overrated? *A Love Supreme* is certainly one of the best known and among the most personal, factors that make objective assessment rather problematic. On that account, it may be forgivable that the album was credited to Coltrane alone rather than to the quartet (whose full names and instruments are not even given on the original sleeve). However, it's vital to appreciate the contribution that they made to the music. Though he was much more prominently featured elsewhere, *A Love Supreme* was arguably Garrison's finest hour with Coltrane, and it was certainly one of Jones's. If anyone showed slight signs of dissatisfaction with the way the music was progressing, it was Tyner, a feeling reinforced on the European tour of summer 1965, which has to be seen as a kind of denouement for perhaps the most influential single jazz group of the post-war period.

***(*) **Dear Old Stockholm** Impulse! GRD-123
   Coltrane; McCoy Tyner (*p*); Jimmy Garrison (*b*); Roy Haynes (*d*). 4/63–5/65.
Haynes was the drummer of choice whenever Jones was 'indisposed', and a handful of live and studio recordings survive to show how he fared at the kit. These were all studio takes. 'Dear Lord' is simply, graciously beautiful in a way that Coltrane didn't often let himself be, and 'One Down, One Up' is a piledriver that showed how Haynes could compel the others into the spikiest form as well as Jones: 'I'd have to think of more things and get ideas from what he was playing. When I'm with Trane, I don't want to let him down. I want to keep him inspired.'

**** **The John Coltrane Quartet Plays** Impulse! MCAD 3310
   As for *Coltrane*, except add Art Davis (*b*). 5/65.
The title should strictly read . . . *Plays 'Chim Chim Cheree', 'Song Of Praise', 'Nature Boy', 'Brazilia'*, all of which was printed on the original sleeve in inch-high letters; but the album has always been known as *Plays* and there is something appropriate in that, for after the sky-scraping affirmations of *A Love Supreme* it sounds as if the group have got down to some basic jazz playing again, themes, choruses, standard tunes. There are, of course, clear signs of Coltrane's growing concerns. 'Song Of Praise', actually played last, is a towering hymn in the line of 'Psalm', and the addition of a second bassist for the well-worn 'Nature Boy' is an often overlooked indication of Coltrane's desire to break down the conventional time-keeping role of the rhythm section.

The most interesting track, though, is the *Mary Poppins* tune, another of Coltrane's soprano features. The poet and critic LeRoi Jones (now known as Amiri Baraka) has persuasively shown how Coltrane's subversive aesthetic is based on the deceptive co-option of mass-cultural materials, followed by their complete subversion. It's possible to argue, along Jones's lines, that 'My Favorite Things', which begins this particular line of inquiry, 'The Inch Worm' and 'Chim Chim Cheree' are Coltrane's *most* radical improvisations. The last of the three is certainly the most ferociously deconstructed. The weird, slightly off-pitch sound of the soprano turns the familiar tune into something more closely resembling an Indian *raga* or a Korean court theme, and the rhythm section piles up an enormous flurry of sound behind him. Despite the apparently conventional division of themes and solos, the quartet is playing as a whole in a way that points unambiguously forward to the collective experiments of the last years. This is an often overlooked item in the Coltrane discography, but it's a very important one.

**** The Major Works Of John Coltrane Impulse! GRD 21132 2CD
    As for *Coltrane*, except add Freddie Hubbard, Dewey Johnson (*t*); Marion Brown, John Tchicai (*as*); Pharoah Sanders, Archie Shepp (*ts*); Donald Garrett (*bcl, b*); Joe Brazil (*f, perc*); Frank Butler (*d*); Juno Lewis (*perc, v*). 6/65, 10/65.

The short pattern of notes played by Coltrane at the beginning of 'Ascension' was a clear reference to the fanfare that opened 'Acknowledgement' on *A Love Supreme*. To those who had asked where Coltrane might go after the December 1964 album, the two versions of *Ascension* were the answer. The circumstances of their release are now hopelessly muddied and at one point MCA actually got the liner-notes reversed. Coltrane had originally OK'd release of the first, 40-minute take, and this was issued as *Ascension* Impulse A-95 in late 1965. Then the saxophonist decided that the 'wrong' master had been issued, and the second take was substituted, leaving *Ascension – Edition I* as a piece of discographical apocrypha until MCA put the two together on this important but still oddly named compilation.

The oddity stems only from the fact that, however significant *Ascension* is, the other items included, 'Om', 'Kulu Se Mama' (both of which once fronted albums of those names) and 'Selflessness', would not initially seem to belong in the same league and are unlikely to spring first to mind when asked to set out Coltrane's 'major works'. However, 'Om', with its initial chant again recalling *A Love Supreme*, is clearly derived from the complex sound-world of *Ascension*, with two bassists weaving complementary and sometimes overlapping lines and Joe Brazil's flute adding a mysterious quality to structures of great 'plasticity' (the term was Coltrane's).

'Kulu Se Mama' was recorded on the West Coast as a musical objectification of Juno Lewis's Afro-Creole poem. The chanting is slightly off-putting and Coltrane is rather muted; it's something of a relief to turn to the relatively familiar outline of 'Selflessness'.

What they all share, with the partial and instructive exception of the last track, is a developing commitment to collective improvisation. In a very real sense, *Ascension* was alien to the American spirit of individualistic performance in improvised music; even Ornette Coleman's *Free Jazz* resolved very rapidly into a sequence of separate solo features. *Ascension*, though, was much closer to a European aesthetic of collective improvisation (which drew sustenance, of course, from early jazz). Coltrane organized his augmented group (similarly constituted to Coleman's) in such a way that he was able to give signals for switches of mode that implied new scalar and harmonic patterns. These were sketched out by Hubbard and Tyner respectively, but left individual players to develop their own material in an apparently chaotic field of sound that sometimes sounds like a dense canvas of pointillist gestures, sometimes like a huge wall of rhythmic sound, pushing ever forwards, sometimes like enormous blocks of static noise with no obvious structural rationale. The success of the piece lay quite explicitly in Coltrane's ability to steer the individual freedoms of his players in accordance with the code established in the first few bars.

There are, of course, solos, but these serve a very different purpose from those on *Free Jazz*. There, soloists emerge out of the ensemble and impose a rather normative structure on the collective improvisations. Here, the soloists create internal commentaries on the progress of the music, which is genuinely transcendent. The main obvious difference between the two versions of *Ascension* lies in the sequence of solos: the revised release (Edition II) runs Coltrane, Johnson, Sanders, Hubbard, Brown, Shepp, Tchicai, Tyner, and a bass duet; Edition I relocates Shepp and Tchicai in front of Brown and adds an Elvin Jones solo at the end. On purely aesthetic grounds there is remarkably little to separate them and over time they come to resemble the same piece of landscape from a subtly adjusted viewing point.

If Coltrane had never recorded another note of music, he would be guaranteed greatness on the strength of *Ascension* alone. Compiling the two versions with the slightly later material from 1965 makes considerable sense, certainly more so than the original location of the later pieces. Though *Ascension*, an admittedly demanding, even 'difficult', work, has tended to be eclipsed in popularity by *A Love Supreme*, its importance has long been recognized; and this version comes without the ludicrous fade-edits on the first European CD that marked the end of the original LP sides. The sound is surprisingly good, though it must have been a nightmare to record. What is needed now is a full-scale reassessment of 'Om', 'Kulu Se Mama' and 'Selflessness' in the light of an entirely new construction of what a jazz group was capable of.

***(*) Transition Impulse! GRP 11242
    Coltrane; McCoy Tyner (*p*); Jimmy Garrison (*b*); Elvin Jones (*d*). 6/65.

The title says it all, with the great quartet about to consume itself – and the headlong charge into the maelstrom which the title-track sets up certainly has a seed of self-destruction in it – but going down blazing. The studio sound is one of the best Impulse! secured for Coltrane, with the iron tone and regal delivery beautifully caught. The peaceable coda, 'Welcome', settles everyone down, but the ominous

'Vigil' ('I mean watchfulness against elements that might be destructive – from within or without') sets the album's final keynote. In simple terms, another great one.

*** New Thing At Newport Impulse! GRD 105
Coltrane; McCoy Tyner (*p*); Jimmy Garrison (*b*); Elvin Jones (*d*). 7/65.

July 1965 saw the quartet performing at two major festivals. The Newport session was shared with Archie Shepp and originally contained only 12 minutes of Coltrane ('One Down, One Up' is the same theme as 'One Up And One Down' on the Cool & Blue compilation). CD reissue adds a brutal reading of 'My Favorite Things' which was formerly available only in the grab-bag *Mastery Of John Coltrane* series. The MC identifies Elvin Jones as 'a newcomer to jazz', which seems a quite incredible piece of condescension, and may explain some of the rhythmic fury that follows.

***(*) Sun Ship Impulse! IMP 11672
As above. 8/65.

Arguably one of the least well-known Coltrane albums, tucked away in the high summer of a packed year but marking, as ever, another stage in this extraordinary group's progress. There is a short nugget of conversation before 'Dearly Beloved', a minor-key ballad which sees Coltrane (as he partially explains) working over the top of a softly unfolding continuous rhythm. The title-track is more angular and splintery, based on just four notes and powered along by Jones and Tyner, who set the mood for Coltrane's high-altitude full-throttle entry. It isn't a solo that many people will identify and guess first time, but it's as fascinating an exploration of altissimo playing as any in the studio (there are plenty of concert moments around in this listing: *In Japan, In Seattle,* elsewhere). 'Attaining' is by contrast a heavily modified minor blues, rhythmically unfettered and, as David Wild points out, generically related to several of Trane's other folk-tradition pieces. Its climax is extraordinary. *Sun Ship* represents an absolutely authentic quartet performance, claiming its place with better-known recordings.

***(*) Live In Seattle Impulse! WMC 5 116
Coltrane; Pharoah Sanders (*ts*); Donald Garrett (*bcl*); McCoy Tyner (*p*); Jimmy Garrison (*b*); Elvin Jones (*d*). 9/65.

**(*) Om Impulse! MCAD 39118
As above, except add Joe Brazil (*f*). 10/65.

Apocalyptic, and just verging on the preposterous. 'Evolution' clocks in at 36 minutes and takes in some of the worst and some of the most innovative Coltrane on record. For much of its length the piece is marking time in the curiously uninvolving flat-out register that became the norm after *A Love Supreme*. Then, before the chanting begins, there's a marvellous passage for all three horns and Garrison (who can just about be heard clearly) improvising the interweaving lines that had been the essence of *Ascension*. 'Cosmos' gets things going at an extraordinary altitude; Tyner sounds lost from the word go and, for a change, Jones doesn't dominate proceedings. Though he's far back in the mix, he's also quieter than on many a session, and Coltrane's main dialogues are with Sanders.

The subsequent studio recording, *Om*, now available separately, is discussed under *The Major Works* entry, above.

***(*) Meditations Impulse! MCAD 39139
As for *Coltrane*, except add Pharoah Sanders (*ts*); Rashied Ali (*d*). 11/65.

**** First Meditations Impulse! GRP 11182
As for *Coltrane*. 2/65.

These two sessions, covering essentially the same material, bridge the end of the classic quartet and the opening phase of the new, augmented group with Sanders and Ali. In February 1965 Coltrane and the quartet recorded a preliminary version of a new five-part suite consisting of 'Love', 'Compassion', 'Joy', 'Consequences', 'Serenity'. When he returned to the studio in November, the saxophonist substituted the unbelievably turbulent 'The Father And The Son And The Holy Ghost' for the original opening movement, and moved 'Love' to what was the start of the continuous second side on the released LP. The most immediate difference between the two versions, apart from the extraordinary change in the rhythm section wrought by the introduction of Ali's pure-sound percussion, is that the movements are run together almost seamlessly, with quite long transitional sections, whereas on *First Meditations* the breaks are distinct though played through without a pause. On grounds of simple beauty, the first version is still to be preferred, though it clearly no longer represented what Coltrane wanted to do with his group and would experiment with on the critical *Ascension*.

Set alongside *A Love Supreme*, it becomes more obvious how formulaic and predetermined some of Coltrane's large-scale composition was becoming. Much as *Ascension* develops out of a a simple fanfare figure like that on the December 1964 album, so, too, does the original *Meditations* seem to develop out of coded harmonic and rhythmic patterns set out by Garrison and Jones, which have become far more deeply embedded in the ensembles of the release version.

The CD of the February session includes an alternative version of 'Joy', the piece that sets in motion the final, multi-art movement. It's obvious that Coltrane is already trying to escape the sticky webs that Jones weaves for him. Had the old and new drummers been able to play together (there is evidence of considerable tension), 'Father/Son/Holy Ghost' suggests that something quite out of the ordinary might have developed. As it is, Ali was closer to Coltrane's new conception of pure sound and a haunted, runaway rhythm sustained by the horns, not by the bass and drums, and the shift between the two versions is a first dramatization of his final break with the bop idiom and its descendants.

**** **Live At The Village Vanguard Again!** Impulse! 254647
    Coltrane; Pharoah Sanders (*ts*); Alice Coltrane (*p*); Jimmy Garrison (*b*); Rashied Ali (*d*);
    Emmanual Rahid (*perc*). 5/66.
Back at the Vanguard with a new band and the only weak link is the one survivor from the 1961 sessions. Garrison's long unaccompanied intro to 'My Favorite Things' is prosaic in the extreme, but what follows is the most comprehensively dissected version Coltrane ever put on record (and that includes the marathon version below). The real high spot of the set is a wonderful, roiling 'Naima', originally dedicated to Trane's first wife, not the lady comping spacily behind him, but gradually transformed into a billowing expression of love *per se*. The addition of a percussionist greatly increases the rhythmic shimmer, but it also ironically pushes Ali back towards something like the old duelling style associated with Jones. This is sometimes thought to be from the same sessions as the 1961 album. The briefest of samples underlines how far Coltrane had come in the five years in between. That sense of intimacy and communication with the audience had certainly not been lost, but was continuing at an ever higher and more invasive level. If the first album was subject to hostile misprision, the reception accorded this one frequently went off the scale: arch-conservative Philip Larkin thought it the quintessence of the 'blended insolence and ugliness' of the New Wave, and it does for the first time seem to have taken a full step off the classic jazz tradition which was Larkin's absolute standard and into an unexplored void.

*** **Live In Japan** Impulse! GRP 4-102 4CD
    Coltrane; Pharoah Sanders (*ts*); Alice Coltrane (*p*); Jimmy Garrison (*b*); Rashied Ali (*d*). 7/66.
Three and a half hours of music. It was quickly clear that the recruitment of Ali allowed Coltrane to break his last ties to bebop phrasing and chorus structure (however elongated both had become). His performances here, with or without Sanders in close proximity, are essentially duets with the drummer of the sort he developed in the studio for *Interstellar Space*, and it's easy to see why cosmic titles and analogies sprang to mind, so little tied to earth does it all seem. There is an *hour-long* version of 'My Favorite Things', which takes it as far from the original song as seems conceivable. An interesting development is Coltrane's first documented use of alto saxophone (apparently a plastic model like Ornette Coleman's or the one Bird used at Massey Hall) since the late 1950s. Garrison contributes very little, even when he *is* completely audible, and Alice arpeggiates furiously, but adds nothing essential to the music. There must be some niggles of doubt about the viability of music as unflaggingly humourless and god-bothering as this. *Live In Japan* could hardly have been much more tiring to play than it is to listen to.

**** **Interstellar Space** Impulse! GRP 11102
    Coltrane; Rashied Ali (*d*). 2/67.
The final masterpiece. It's now conventional wisdom that Coltrane took the harmonic development of post-bop jazz as far as it could be taken, and then some. What is often forgotten is the attention the saxophonist paid to *rhythm*, and the Impulse! years – from *Africa/Brass* to *Interstellar Space* – are very largely devoted to a search for the time beyond time, an uncountable pulse which would represent a pure musical experience not chopped up into bars and choruses. Though Ali is more than just a sound-effects man on this extraordinary set, it's clear that Coltrane is leading from the front. With no bass and piano in competition (as it increasingly seemed), he's recorded in dramatic close-up and with none of the off-mike wavers that afflicted the Seattle and Tokyo concerts.

    'Mars', first of the planetary sequence, is characterized as the 'battlefield of the cosmic giants' and that is exactly how it sounds, with huge, clashing brass tones and a thunderous clangour from the drum kit. 'Venus', by contrast, is delicate, amorous and almost fragile, with Ali barely skiffing his cymbals with wire brushes. 'Jupiter (Variation)' was known to Coltrane fans even when *Interstellar Space* was out of catalogue, from being included on one of the *Mastery Of John Coltrane* compilations of out-takes and ephemera. The release version is the shortest item on the set, a stately expression of 'supreme wisdom', coming immediately before the climactic evocation of joy on 'Saturn'. 'Leo' is known in a live version from the Tokyo concerts, but wasn't on the original album.

    Interestingly, Coltrane sticks with his tenor saxophone throughout, eschewing soprano for the first time in very many years and not following up the alto experiments of *Live In Japan*.

*** **Expression** Impulse! MCA 254646
    As for *Live In Japan*. 2 & 3/67.

(*) Stellar Regions Impulse! IMP 11692
    As above.
It would be wonderfully neat if the final studio session really had represented the final wisdom of the greatest saxophonist since Parker, but *Expression* and the additional material recently issued for the first time as *Stellar Regions* (like the track titles, named long after the event by Alice Coltrane) is a murky, often undistinguished work. There's some interest in hearing Coltrane on flute ('To Be') and there are a couple more instrumental quiddities, but what little of the music really convinces occurs on 'Offering' and 'Expression' itself, both of which represent elements of Trane's calm-after-storm lyricism.

    The suspicious thing about *Stellar Regions* is that its best track is 'Offering' again, not an alternative, but the version already available on *Expression*. This might torpedo it irreparably, but for the quality of some of the playing. The most compelling point of debate is 'Tranesonic' (two takes). Though Coltrane is credited with playing tenor throughout (no further flute excursions), the sound on this track is somehow smaller and more sharply focused, and the pitching suggests a different horn. The only candidates are the rarely heard C melody saxophone or Coltrane's first instrument, the alto, which he is documented playing again in the last years. That is our best guess, and it is confirmed by fellow-saxophonist and Coltrane expert, Evan Parker.

    Oddly, and quite unlike the much-improved *Interstellar Space*, *Expression* sounds if anything worse on the CD, with long passages quite indistinct. *Stellar Regions* is an improvement, though back-to-back playings of 'Offering', will suggest that it isn't by much. The recording sessions bracket the session with Ali and the contrast between the two strongly suggests that Coltrane had finally exhausted the horn–piano–rhythm format that had totally dominated jazz since the advent of bebop. Where he might have gone next is anyone's guess.

**** **A John Coltrane Retrospective – The Impulse! Years** Impulse! GRP 31192 3CD
    Coltrane; various groups as above. 5/61–2/67.
'Greensleeves', 'Naima', 'Impressions', 'Spiritual', 'Chasin' The Trane', 'Soul Eyes', 'Miles' Mode', 'What's New', 'In A Sentimental Mood', 'Take The Coltrane', 'My One And Only Love', 'After The Rain', 'Afro-Blue', 'I Want To Talk About You', 'Alabama', 'Crescent', 'Bessie's Blues', 'A Love Supreme Part One', 'Nature Boy', 'Chim Chim Cheree', 'Dear Lord', 'Living Space', 'Welcome', 'Offering'. The music is unanswerable. But remember that all the original albums are also available.

Ken Colyer (1928–88) CORNET, TRUMPET, GUITAR, VOCAL

*** **In The Beginning** Lake LACD 014
    Colyer; Chris Barber, Ed O'Donnell (*tb*); Acker Bilk, Monty Sunshine (*cl*); Lonnie Donegan, Diz Disley (*bj*); Jim Bray, Dick Smith (*b*); Stan Greig, Ron Bowden (*d*). 9/53–9/54.
*** **The Unknown New Orleans Sessions** 504 CD 23
    Colyer; Albert Artigues (*t*); Jack Delaney (*tb*); Raymond Burke (*cl*); Stanley Mendelson (*p*); Edmond Souchon (*g, v*); Bill Huntington, Lawrence Marrero (*bj*); Dick Allen (*tba*); Alcide Pavageau (*b*); Harold 'Katz' Maestri, Charles Merriweather, Abbie Brunies (*d*). 12/52–2/53.
** **The Decca Skiffle Sessions** Lake LACD 07
    Colyer; Bob Kelly (*p*); Alexis Korner (*g, mand*); Johnny Bastable (*g, bj*); Mickey Ashman, Ron Ward (*b*); Bill Colyer, Colin Bowden (*wbd*). 6/54–11/57.
*** **Sensation!** Lake LACD1
    Colyer; Mac Duncan (*tb*); Ian Wheeler (*cl*); Ray Foxley (*p*); Johnny Bastable (*bj*); Dick Smith, Ron Ward (*b*); Stan Greig, Colin Bowden (*d*). 4/55–5/59.
*** **Marching Back To New Orleans** Lake LACD 21
    As above, except add Bob Wallis, Sonny Murray (*t*); Mick Clift (*tb*); Dave Keir (*as*); Derek Easton (*ts*); Maurice Benn (*tba*); Neil Millet; Stan Greig (*d*). 4/55–9/57.
*** **Up Jumped The Devil** Upbeat URCD114
    Colyer; Mac Duncan (*tb*); Ian Wheeler (*cl*); Ray Foxley (*p*); Johnny Bastable (*bj*); Ron Ward (*b*); Colin Bowden (*d*). 57–58.
*** **The Famous Manchester Free Trade Hall Concert 1957** 504 CD51/2
    As above, except add George Lewis (*cl*). 4/57.
Colyer was one of the most interesting figures British jazz ever produced. At a time when the trad boom of the 1950s was just getting under way, he abjured such 'modern' role models as Armstrong and Morton and insisted on the earlier New Orleans methods of George Lewis and Bunk Johnson. Colyer's records from the period emerge as an intriguing muddle of stiff British orthodoxy and something that finds a genuine if limited accord with the music that obsessed him. These discs give some idea of the impact Colyer had. The 504 sessions were made on Colyer's fabled visit to New Orleans and find the

young cornetist sitting in with various local players. The tracks were lost for years and this is the first appearance for most of them: there's a real vitality and a bluff panache about the playing, with Colyer's deliberately primitive lead firmed up by the sheer force of his obsessions. Listeners should be warned, though, that the sound is inevitably pretty dingy. *In The Beginning* stands as an important document for British jazz if only for the musicians involved – Barber, whose subsequent disagreements with the trumpeter led him to assume command of a different edition of the band; Bilk, whose erratic clarinet had yet to acquire the distinctive glow of his later records; Sunshine, who stayed with Barber and has since enjoyed an immortal reputation with European trad audiences; and Donegan, who became the major name in skiffle. If the music is comparatively stilted, its formal strictness pays off in the music's terseness.

Having established the blueprint, Colyer worked hard at refining it during the 1950s. The most useful reissues, though, are *Lonesome Road, Marching Back To New Orleans* and *Sensation!*, effectively an alternative live version of the unavailable *Colyer Plays Standards*, although much of the material – 'Underneath The Bamboo Tree' and 'Bluebells Goodbye', to name two – would hardly be classed as standards in most band books. *Marching Back To New Orleans* opens with seven tracks from the session which produced *Sensation!* – including an uproarious 'Red Wing' – and then includes the entire date by the Omega Brass Band, where Colyer tried his hand at an 'authentic' New Orleans parade band: shambling, stentorian, it's a bizarre sound, and actually surprisingly close to the genuine article. Typically, Colyer refused to pick obvious tunes, and chose instead 'Isle Of Capri', 'Tiger Rag' and 'Gettysburg March', which occasionally rise in an almost hysterical crescendo. *Sensation!* collects various single and EP tracks, including all four from the sought-after *They All Played Ragtime* EP, which is in some ways Colyer's most distinctive achievement: it includes such rarities as 'Kinklets' (recorded by Bunk Johnson at his final session), 'Fig Leaf Rag' and what might be the first jazz version of 'The Entertainer', many years before Joshua Rifkin and *The Sting*. This is an ensemble music: Colyer wasn't a great soloist, and although Wheeler and Duncan are lively they struggle a bit when left on their own. Foxley is actually the most impressive improviser on the basis of *Lonesome Road*, reissued on LP some years ago but still to reach CD. Colyer's steady, unflashy lead, and the four-square but oddly hypnotic beat of the rhythm section (using a banjo to the end), still manage to add their own character. The one avoidable disc is *Skiffle Sessions*, which enshrines Colyer's heartfelt if bizarre interest in that movement. His own guitar playing goes on like a machine, and though Korner, who at least knew how to play feasible blues, is also on hand, this is for the curious only.

Up Jumped The Devil documents various live sessions at Studio 51. This was one of the best Colyer bands and, though the sound is rather muffled, their hard-won vitality breaks through to surprising effect. They manage to sustain 'Milneburg Joys' for chorus after chorus and, as sometimes happens in this kind of jazz, the sheer determination of the music becomes almost hypnotic. The concert tour with George Lewis was another legendary moment, and 504's documentation of their Manchester show, spread across two CDs, reeks of authenticity. The enthusiasm of the audience is infectious, and Lewis himself responds with his best form, even on chestnuts he'd played countless times. The sound is sometimes distant but mostly quite clear and clean.

(*) **When I Leave The World Behind Lake LACD 19
    Colyer; Geoff Cole (*tb*); Sammy Rimington (*cl*); Johnny Bastable (*bj*); Ron Ward (*b*); Pete Ridge (*d*). 3/63.
***(*) **Colyer's Pleasure** Lake LACD 34
    As above. 62–63.
If everything on *When I Leave The World Behind* was as good as a terrifically swinging account of J. C. Higginbotham's 'Give Me Your Telephone Number', this would be a classic record. As it is, it's an interesting memento of Colyer's 1960s band, playing a broad range of rags, King Oliver tunes, and other odds and ends. Rimington weaves interesting lines all through the music, Cole is a strong, hardbitten trombonist; only the rhythm section, bothered by the pedestrian Ridge, is weaker. The recording, salvaged by Paul Adams from some private tapes, is variable and rather boomy, but it's listenable enough.

Much better is *Colyer's Pleasure* – indeed, this has claims to be Colyer's best available CD. The band never sounded better in a studio (actually a pub back room), with Colyer and Rimington loud and clear, and the excellent set-list gets a varied and inventive treatment: 'Dardanella' is a classic performance. The original LP (once issued on the old budget label, Society) is augmented by five previously unissued acetates by the same band.

** **One For My Baby** Joy JOY-CD-1
    Colyer; Geoff Cole (*tb*); Tony Pyke (*cl*); John Bastable (*bj*); Bill Cole (*b*); Malcolm Murphy (*d*). 1–2/69.

** **Spirituals Vol. 1** Joy JOY-CD-5
    As above, except Ken Ames (*b*) replaces Cole. 69.
** **Spirituals Vol. 2** Joy JOY-CD-6
    As above. 69.
** **Watch That Dirty Tone Of Yours – There Are Ladies Present** Joy JOY-CD-3
    As above. 5/70.
** **At The Thames Hotel** Joy JOY-CD-4
    As above. 5/70.
(*) **Ragtime Revisited Joy JOY-CD-2
    As above, except add Ray Smith (*p*). 70.

These are solid examples of Colyer at work and there's little here to detain any but the fanatic: the 1950s music is fresher, and the band with Rimington had a superior front line. Even Colyer himself lacks the stamina to sustain an album's worth of material. Still, there are better moments on most of the records. The first *Spirituals* has a firmer grip, the *Thames Hotel* live set has a neat set-list, and the *Ragtime Revisited* disc continues Colyer's grappling with the rag form to create a viable bridge between styles. The sound is much as it was on the original LPs and, for those who were there, the two live sets (*Thames Hotel* and *One For My Baby*) will rekindle the atmosphere.

(*) **More Of Ken Colyer And His Handpicked Jazzmen Ken Colyer Trust KCT3CD
    Colyer; Mike Sherbourne (*tb*); Jack Gilbert (*cl*); Jim McIntosh (*bj*); Ray Holland (*b*); Tony
    Scriven (*d*). 1/72.
*** **Won't You Come Along With Me** Ken Colyer Trust KCT5CD
    Colyer; Dave Vickers (*tb*); Chris Blount (*cl*); Pete Trevor (*p*); John Bly, Dave Brennan (*bj*);
    Harry Slater (*b*); Mike Ellis (*d*). 10/73–12/77.
*** **Ken Colyer In Holland** Music Mecca 1032-2
    Colyer; Cor Fabrie (*tb*); Butch Thompson (*cl*); Jos Koster (*bj*); Ad Van Beerendonk (*b*); Emiel
    Leybaert (*d*). 11/76.
*(*) **Painting The Clouds With Sunshine** Black Lion 760501
    Colyer; Mike Sherbourne (*tb*); Bruce Bakewell (*cl*); Ray Smith (*p*); Bill Stotesbury (*bj*); Alyn
    Shipton (*b*); Colin Bowden (*d*). 10/79.

Colyer disbanded his regular group in 1971, partly due to illness, and these are mementoes of the motley situations he found himself in after that. The earlier KCT disc comes in good, clean sound and the band sound very enthusiastic, but this is a ragbag affair which could use a little finesse. Colyer played with Chris Blount's pro-am group many times in the early to mid-'70s and *Won't You Come Along With Me* is a collection of scraps from various surviving live tapes. Much of the playing is pretty shambolic but there are some queerly affecting moments, such as the wistful singing by Colyer on 'Basin Street Blues' and the atmosphere of the East Midlands in the 1970s which seems to permeate tracks that were cut in pubs in Derby, Ilkeston and Fadler Gate. *In Holland* finds Ken joining the long-established Storyville Jazzband, who sound rather better than he does: much of his trumpet work from this period seems to get by on irascibility alone. A solid programme, in listenable sound. The 1979 date is nothing like as good. The rhythm section provides Colyer's favoured chugging momentum, but the horns are frankly unmemorable.

*** **Blame It On The Blues** Azure AZ-CD-33
    Colyer; Jean-François Bonnel (*cl*); Paul Sealey (*bj, g*); Ken Ames (*b*). 1/85.
** **Too Busy** CMJ 008
    Colyer; Les Hanscombe (*tb*); Dave Bailey (*cl*); Tim Phillips (*bj*); Keith Donald (*b*); John Petters
    (*d*). 2/85.
(*) **Together Again Lake LACD 53
    Colyer; Les Hanscombe (*tb*); Acker Bilk (*cl*); Pat Hawes (*p*); Brian Mitchell (*bj*); Julian Davies
    (*b*); Pete Lay (*d*). 7/85.

Colyer's illness cut him down in the end, and his later recordings are a mix of sad decline and a reflective, almost introspective approach as he adapted his circumstances to his music. There's no better example than *Blame It On The Blues*, which features a gentle, airy quartet working patiently through ten favourites at London's Pizza Express. Bonnel is a deferential partner and the sound is lovely. *Too Busy* is missable: Colyer guests with the John Petters group, and he is clearly taking things very gingerly. The band plays decent, fat-free trad, but the trumpeter's own contribution is unexceptional. He is, alas, also the weak link on *Together Again*, a surprise reunion with Bilk, again at the Pizza Express. Hawes has a bad time with the awful 'old' PE piano and Colyer's lead sounds very shaky; the stars are for Acker, returning to some heartland repertoire and proving himself again one of our best jazzmen.

Company FLEXIBLE IMPROVISING ENSEMBLE

*** **Music Improvisation Company, 1968/70** Incus CD 17
    Derek Bailey (*g*); Evan Parker (*ss*); Hugh Davies (*elec, org*); Jamie Muir (*perc*).
**** **Company 6 & 7** Incus CD07
    Derek Bailey (*g*); Leo Smith (*t, f*); Anthony Braxton (*as, ss, f, cl*); Evan Parker (*ts, ss*); Lol
    Coxhill, Steve Lacy (*ss*); Steve Beresford (*p, g*); Tristan Honsinger (*clo*); Maarten van Regteren
    Altena (b). 5/77.
**** **Once** Incus CD04
    Derek Bailey (*g*); Lee Konitz (*as, ss*); Richard Teitelbaum (*ky*); Carlos Zingaro (*vn*); Tristan
    Honsinger (*clo*); Barre Phillips (*b*); Steve Noble (*perc, bugle*). 5/87.
**** **Company 91** Incus CD16
    Yves Robert (*tb*); John Zorn (*as*); Derek Bailey, Buckethead (*g*); Alexander Balanescu (*vn*);
    Paul Rogers (*b*); Paul Lovens (*perc*); Pat Thomas (*elec, ky*); Vanessa Mackness (*v*). 91.
**** **Company 91** Incus CD17
    As above. 91.
***(*) **Company 91** Incus CD18
    As above. 91.

At the end of his very important book, *Improvisation: Its Nature and Practice in Music*, Derek Bailey collages a number of quotations that might be said to hold the key to what his improvising collective, Company, is about: for Leo Smith, improvisation is an individual's 'ability to instantaneously organize sound, silence and rhythm with the whole of his or her creative intelligence'; Peter Riley defines the process much more crisply as 'the exploration of occasion'.

Incus, the label Bailey co-founded in 1970 with saxophonist Evan Parker and drummer Tony Oxley, has dedicated much of its catalogue to the documentation of those explorations and those occasions (once annual, otherwise as occasion demanded) when Bailey brought together groups of British and international improvisers, some with a free-jazz background, some coming more from a classical environment, for a weekend or week of unstructured improvisation. Company was founded in 1976 (the first item, above, explores its pre-history) and has been the most important locus of free improvisation in Britain since then. It is, of course, moot whether existential performances which admit of no gap between conception and execution and which are completely conditioned by intuition really belong on record. What is remarkable about the above records (and the vanished LPs recorded at other events) is the extent to which they remain compellingly listenable long after the occasion of their performance is past; newcomers are directed particularly to *Once* and *6 & 7* which seem to encapsulate the challenges and beauties of Company in equal measure.

The music is extremely difficult to quantify or categorize. It was clear from the earlier encounters that it was necessary to negotiate a divide between free music which owned to no generic ties and a deep structure drawn from jazz. The first Company Week proper was in 1977, and is fondly remembered for the then rare chance to see important overseas players like Braxton, Smith and Lacy playing with the Europeans. However, the visiting Americans (notably Braxton) appeared to find the radical and collective freedom on which Bailey quietly insisted rather unsettling; against that, both Steve Lacy and, much more surprisingly, former Tristano disciple Lee Konitz (who took part in the 1987 Company documented on *Once*) have managed to assimilate their notably dry approach to Bailey's. It's very instructive to compare what Parker does with Braxton here and on their 1993 London duo released on Leo (for which, see under Braxton's entry). As so often, it's the smaller combinations that stick in the mind. Tristan Honsinger's duo with Leo Smith on the same record is a tiny masterpiece.

Perhaps because Company Weeks are no longer annual events, the 1991 gathering is remembered with especial clarity and affection and amply merits such full documentation. As always, the line-up included players not usually associated with the free-music scene, and the set begins, appropriately, with a duo by the classically trained Vanessa Mackness and classical violinist Alex Balanescu who, having got the remaining starch out of his instrument, simply goes for it. His duo with Bailey on Volume 2 is almost equally good.

One of the oddities of 91 was the inclusion of the heavy metal guitarist, Buckethead, who performs in mask and costume. The trio on Volume 2 which features him with Zorn and the young British improviser, Pat Thomas, was one of the highpoints of the week, though the chemistry didn't work quite so well when the guitarist joined Rogers and Balanescu (a duo would have been good) at the end of that same disc.

The final part documents the Friday and Saturday. Historically, musical relationships are expected to develop as the week advances. There were signs in 91, though, that some were unravelling. The performances on Volume 3 are by no means so well calibrated, and there are signs of weariness in the American ranks. That said, this disc is dominated by Zorn, first in duo with Robert (a quirky and unpredictable performer) and then with various larger combinations. The set ends with a noisy exchange between Bailey and Buckethead to which the audience makes an equally noisy contribution.

Concord All Stars GROUP

*** **Tour De Force** Concord CCD 4172
> Al Cohn, Scott Hamilton, Buddy Tate (*ts*); Dave McKenna (*p*); Cal Collins (*g*); Bob Mate (*b*); Jake Hanna (*d*). 8/81.

*** **Take 8** Concord CCD 4347
> Warren Vaché (*c*); Dan Barrett (*tb*); Red Holloway (*as*); Scott Hamilton (*ts*); Dave McKenna (*p*); Steve Wallace (*b*); Jimmie Smith (*d*). 11/87.

*** **Ow!** Concord CCD 4348
> As above, except add Ed Bickert (*g*); Ernestine Anderson (*v*). 11/87.

(*) **On Cape Cod Concord CCD 4530
> Scott Hamilton (*ts*); Dave McKenna (*p*); Gray Sargent (*g*); Marshall Wood (*b*); Chuck Riggs (*d*); Carol Sloane (*v*). 5/92.

Casually organized but informed by the innate discipline of some of the best-focused players in the mainstream, these civilized jam sessions may lack the brawling excitement of Jazz at the Philharmonic, but they also expunge the excessive solos and ragged ensembles in that kind of jazz. *Tour De Force* concentrates on the three tenors, and Hamilton holds his own with Cohn and Tate without problems: 'Tickle Toe', 'Broadway' and 'Rifftide' are classic tenors-all-out features, but the slower moments let them wear hearts on sleeves too. The other session is basically the Vaché–Hamilton band with Holloway as an extra front-line guest, and this unit's suave manner with standards and swing staples is effortlessly maintained. Anderson joins in for three tracks of *Ow!*, finishing on 'Down Home Blues'. After a five-year vacation, the name was revived for a hotel engagement by the latest edition of the All Stars. Everyone plays comfortably on a familiar-looking programme, Carol Sloane strolls in for the last three songs, it's all nicely done, and one is tempted to ask, so what?

Eddie Condon (1905–73) GUITAR

**** **Eddie Condon 1927–1938** Classics 742
> Condon; Jimmy McPartland, Bobby Hackett (*c*); Max Kaminsky, Leonard Davis (*t*); George Brunies, Floyd O'Brien, Jack Teagarden (*tb*); Mezz Mezzrow, Frank Teschemacher, Pee Wee Russell (*cl*); Bud Freeman, Happy Caldwell (*ts*); Joe Sullivan, Alex Hill, Jess Stacy, Joe Sullivan (*p*); Art Miller, Jim Lannigan, Artie Bernstein, Artie Shapiro, Art Miller (*b*); George Wettling, Gene Krupa, Johnny Powell, George Stafford, Big Sid Catlett (*d*). 12/27–4/38.

**** **Eddie Condon 1938–1940** Classics 759
> As above, except add Muggsy Spanier (*c*), Marty Marsala (*t*), Miff Mole, Vernon Brown (*tb*); Brad Gowans (*vtb*); Joe Bushkin, Fats Waller (*p*), Clyde Newcombe (*b*), Lionel Hampton, Dave Tough (*d*); omit McPartland, Davis, O'Brien, Mezzrow, Teschemacher, Caldwell, Hill, Lannigan, Bernstein, Miller, Krupa, Powell, Stafford, Catlett. 4/38–11/40.

***(*) **Eddie Condon 1942–1943** Classics 772
> As above, except add Yank Lawson (*t*), Benny Morton (*tb*), Gene Schroeder (*p*), Al Morgan, Bob Casey (*b*), Tony Sbarbaro (*d*); omit Spanier, Marsala, Mole, Brown, Waller, Newcombe, Hackett, Hampton, Tough, Teagarden. 1/42–12/43.

**** **Dixieland All Stars** MCA GRP 16372
> Condon; Max Kaminsky, Billy Butterfield, Bobby Hackett, Yank Lawson (*t*); Wild Bill Davison (*c*); Brad Gowans (*vtb*); Jack Teagarden, Lou McGarity (*tb*); Pee Wee Russell, Edmond Hall, Tony Parenti (*cl*); Ernie Caceres, Joe Dixon (*cl, bs*); Bud Freeman (*ts*); Joe Sullivan, Joe Bushkin, Gene Schroeder (*p*); Clyde Newcombe, Jack Lesberg, Bob Haggart, Sid Weiss (*b*); Johnny Blowers, Dave Tough, George Wettling (*d*). 8/39–3/46.

*** **Chicago Style** ASV AJA 5192
> As above discs. 27–40.

*** **Windy City Jazz** Topaz TPZ 1026
> As above. 27–42.

*** **The Definitive Eddie Condon And His Jazz Concert All Stars: Volume 1** Stash ST-CD-530
> Condon; Bobby Hackett, Muggsy Spanier (*c*); Billy Butterfield, Max Kaminsky (*t*); Hot Lips Page (*t, v*); Lou McGarity, Benny Morton (*tb*); Ernie Caceres (*cl, bs*); Edmond Hall, Pee Wee Russell (*cl*); Gene Schroeder, Jess Stacy (*p*); Bob Haggart (*b*); Joe Grauso, George Wettling (*d*); Liza Morrow, Lee Wiley (*v*). 6 & 10/44.

*** **We Dig Dixieland Jazz** Savoy SV-0197
   Condon; Bobby Hackett (*c*); Frank Orchard (*tb*); Joe Marsala (*cl*); Gene Schroeder (*p*); Bob
   Casey (*b*); Rollo Laylan (*d*). 3/44.
(*) **Ringside At Condon's Savoy SV-0231
   Condon; Wild Bill Davison (*c*); Cutty Cutshall (*tb*); Edmond Hall (*cl*); Gene Schroeder (*p*); Bob
   Casey (*b*); Buzzy Drootin (*d*). 1–12/52.
*** **Dixieland Jam** Columbia 465680-2
   Condon; Wild Bill Davison (*c*); Billy Butterfield (*t*); Cutty Cutshall, Vic Dickenson (*tb*); Bob
   Wilber (*cl*); Gene Schroeder (*p*); Leonard Gaskin (*b*); George Wettling (*d*). 8 & 9/57.
***(*) **Eddie Condon In Japan** Chiaroscuro GRD 154
   Condon; Buck Clayton (*t*); Vic Dickenson (*tb*); Bud Freeman (*ts*); Pee Wee Russell (*cl*); Dick
   Cary (*p, ahn*); Jack Lesberg (*b*); Cliff Leeman (*d*); Jimmy Rushing (*v*).

A brilliant entrepreneur and colourful raconteur with a good head for whisky, Condon was the focus of
Chicago jazz from the 1920s to the 1940s, garnering a personal reputation that far exceeds his actual
musical significance. Condon is now best seen as a catalyst, a man who made things happen and in the
process significantly heightened the profile of Dixieland jazz in America. Condon was rarely anything
more than a straightforward rhythm guitarist, generally avoiding solos, but he had a very clear sense of
what his role ought to be and frequently 'laid out' to give the piano player more room. His chords have a
rather melancholy ring, but are always played dead centre.

   The Classics discs offer a chronological overview of a career that didn't really get seriously under way on
record until the 1940s. The five sessions from the '20s are key staging-posts in the evolution of Chicago
jazz, starting with the four classic titles cut by the McKenzie–Condon Chicagoans in 1927, in which
McPartland and the ill-fated Teschemacher made up a superbly vibrant front line. Two 1929 sessions
feature some top-notch early Teagarden, and the 1933 band date includes the original versions of
Freeman's famous turn on 'The Eel'. But it then goes quiet up until the first sessions for Commodore in
1938. These take up most of the remaining two discs: relaxed but smart, graceful and hot at the same
moment, Condon's various bands made eloquent jazz out of what were already becoming Dixieland
warhorses. The four-part version of 'A Good Man Is Hard To Find' from 1940 is a little masterpiece,
but almost anything from these sessions has its memorable moments, and players like Kaminsky,
Brunies and Bushkin never found a better context to work in. All these discs are recommended, but
transfers (from unlisted sources) are, as usual, a mixed bunch – though Commodore's own recording
could vary from session to session. The Topaz and ASV compilations are each a good bet for anyone
wanting a single disc from the period: ASV cover most of the early dates and add some titles by Billy
Banks, Joe Marsala and Bud Freeman, while Topaz offer the earliest sessions and some of the
Commodore tracks.

   Then go to the excellent MCA compilation of studio sessions from the early 1940s. Here are most of the
Condon stalwarts playing to three-minute, 78-r.p.m. length, tucking small, gem-like solos into otherwise
powerhouse ensembles – the rhythm sections were always good – and making all the choruses count.
They may have had dubious reputations off the bandstand, but Condon's men were disciplined about
their kind of jazz. The first of the two Savoy discs is another good if brief and muzzy-sounding date,
featuring beautiful work from Hackett and the underrated Marsala and Schroeder. The second is
marred by shabby recording and dubbed-in applause, though Davison and Hall still play hard.

   The 1944 transcriptions on Stash are straightforward Condon fare, played with considerable professionalism, and marked by some fine solos from Russell, Page, Morton (with his vintage-style trills on
'Royal Garden Blues') and the lyrical Hackett, but with a slight chill about them, too. There are some
first takes and breakdowns, but three of the latter amount to less than five seconds apiece and really
don't merit inclusion in a compilation of this type.

   Condon enjoyed a long and very successful association with Columbia, who released a substantial body
of work in the 1950s. *Dixieland Jam*, featuring two different bands a month apart, is a relaxed, joyous
affair, on which Condon can be heard encouraging the players, ordering drinks, wisecracking, doing
everything in fact except playing very much guitar. He's rather lost in the digital remix, which greatly
favours the horns, putting a polish on Billy Butterfield's solos on 'When A Woman Loves A Man' and
'Why Was I Born?'. The live set from Japan is poorly balanced and some of the playing sounds a little
makeshift. However, it's generally up to scratch and a good buy for anyone who doesn't have the multi-
disc Jazzology sessions below.

***(*) **The Town Hall Concerts Vol. 1** Jazzology JCD 1001/2 2CD
   Collective personnel for this and following eight discs: Condon; Muggsy Spanier, Dick Cary (*c*);
   Billy Butterfield, Sterling Bose, Bobby Hackett, Jonah Jones, Hot Lips Page, Max Kaminsky,
   Wingy Manone (*t*); Jack Teagarden, Bill Harris, Benny Morton, Miff Mole, Lou McGarity (*tb*);
   Pee Wee Russell, Joe Marsala, Edmond Hall (*cl*); Ernie Caceres (*bs, cl*); Gene Schroeder, James
   P. Johnson, Willie 'The Lion' Smith, Norma Teagarden, Jess Stacy, Cliff Jackson (*p*); Carl Kress

(*g*); Bob Haggart, Bob Casey, Jack Lesberg, Johnny Williams, Sid Weiss (*b*); George Wettling, Joe Grauso, Cozy Cole, Gene Krupa (*d*); Lee Wiley, Red McKenzie, Harry The Hipster Gibson (*v*). 6/44.

***(*) **The Town Hall Concerts Vol. 2** Jazzology JCD 1003/4 2CD
As above. 6/44.

**** **The Town Hall Concerts Vol. 3** Jazzology JCD 1005/6 2CD
As above. 7/44.

***(*) **The Town Hall Concerts Vol. 4** Jazzology JCD 1007/8 2CD
As above. 8/44.

***(*) **The Town Hall Concerts Vol. 5** Jazzology JCD 1009/1010 2CD
As above. 9/44.

*** **The Town Hall Concerts Vol. 6** Jazzology JCD 1011/2 2CD
As above. 10/44.

**** **The Town Hall Concerts Vol. 7** Jazzology JCD 1013/4 2CD
As above. 11/44.

*** **The Town Hall Concerts Vol. 8** Jazzology JCD 1015/6 2CD
As above. 12/44.

***(*) **The Town Hall Concerts Vol. 9** Jazzology JCD 1017/8 2CD
As above. 1/45.

***(*) **Live At Town Hall** Jass J-CD-634
Condon; Billy Butterfield, Hot Lips Page, Max Kaminsky (*t*); Miff Mole (*tb*); Pee Wee Russell, Edmond Hall (*cl*); Joe Bushkin, Cliff Jackson (*p*); Bob Casey, Pops Foster (*b*); George Wettling, Kansas Fields (*d*). 3/44.

Condon's Town Hall concerts became an institution on radio during 1944–5, and many of them have survived as airshots. The earliest is actually the Jass disc, which is one of the best-sounding of these sessions and makes a curtain-raiser to the long series of double-CD sets which Jazzology have issued. Each of these packages contains four half-hour shows, compered with a mixture of genial bonhomie and irascibility by Condon himself. He credits every player, sets the beat up for every number, kids around at the expense of most of the others (but especially the benighted Pee Wee Russell) and makes sure that standards of Dixieland are maintained at all times. Choosing among the discs is a little invidious since all of them are patchy, all are occasionally troubled by the sound (which is, though, usually quite listenable) and each falls back on routine instead of inspiration at some point. But the general standard of music is surprisingly high, given the showbiz feel of some of the situations. The second volume has a tribute to Fats Waller, the third a tribute to Bix Beiderbecke. If Russell is consistently the star player, there are often precious glimpses of men who would seldom make much more music in the studios: Spanier, Mole, Marsala, Manone. *Volume 7*, which features Jack and Norma Teagarden as guest stars, is a very good one, and perhaps the best to sample; but all of them have period feel and excellent music in great measure, a lasting tribute to Condon's bluff expertise.

*** **Dr Jazz Vol. 1: Eddie Condon With Johnny Windhurst, No. 1** Storyville STCD 6041
Johnny Windhurst (*t*); Cutty Cutshall (*tb*); Edmond Hall (*cl*); Gene Schroeder (*p*); Bob Casey, Bill Goodall (*b*); Cliff Leeman, Buzzy Drootin, Monk Herbert (*d*). 1–6/52.

*** **Dr Jazz Vol. 8: Eddie Condon With Johnny Windhurst No. 2** Storyville STCD 6048
As above, except add Condon; omit Goodall, Herbert. 1–5/52.

*** **Dr Jazz Vol. 5: Eddie Condon With Wild Bill Davison** Storyville STCD 6045
As above, except add Wild Bill Davison (*c*), Ralph Sutton (*p*), Don Lamond (*d*), Bill Goodall (*b*), George Wettling (*d*); omit Windhurst. 12/51–3/52.

Radio broadcasts from Eddie's club, dating from the early '50s. Sound is occasionally scruffy but decent enough. The main point of the first two discs is to hear the seldom-recorded Windhurst whose blend of Armstrong and Hackett gave his playing a lovely dancing quality that still manages to power a front line. Obvious material, but worth a listen; as is the disc with Davison – though, given his ubiquitous discography, this scarcely goes down as essential. Condon doesn't play on the first disc, but he turns up here and there on the other two.

Harry Connick Jr (born 1968) VOCAL, PIANO

** **Harry Connick** Columbia CK 40702
Connick. 87.

(*) **20 Columbia 462996-2
Connick; Dr John (*org, v*); Robert Hurst (*b*); Carmen McRae (*v*). 5–6/88.

*** **We Are In Love** Columbia 466736-2
    Connick; Branford Marsalis (*ss, ts*); Russell Malone (*g*); Ben Wolfe (*b*); Shannon Powell (*d*); strings. 3–5/90.
** **Lofty's Roach Soufflé** Columbia CK 46223
    Connick; Ben Wolfe (*b*); Shannon Powell (*d*).
(*) **Blue Light, Red Light Columbia 469087-2
    Connick; Jeremy Davenport, Leroy Jones, Dan Miller, Roger Ingram (*t*); Mark Mullins, Craig Klein (*tb*); Lucien Barbarin (*tb, sou*); Joe Barati (*btb*); Louis Ford (*cl*); Brad Leali, Will Campbell (*as*); Jerry Welden, Ned Goold (*ts*); David Schumacher (*bs, bcl, f*); Russell Malone (*g*); Ben Wolfe (*b*); Shannon Powell (*d*). 6–7/91.
** **25** Columbia CK 53172
    Connick; Ned Goold (*ts*); Ellis Marsalis (*p*); Ray Brown (*b*); Johnny Adams (*v*). 10/92.

Barely out of his teens, this New Orleans singer and pianist became the most commercially successful jazz musician of his generation in a whirlwind romance with the public. Cannily promoted around a hit soundtrack (*When Harry Met Sally*), matinee idol looks and a vicarious appeal to an audience too young to remember demob suits and pre-rock crooning, Connick has cleaned up with a flair and showmanship which are actually – given his marketing-man's-dream aura – surprisingly hard to dislike. He is a rather pointlessly eclectic pianist, his solos an amiable but formless amalgam of Monk, Garner and Hines influences; and his real talent (reversing the jazz norm) is surely his singing, which is rather affected and overloaded with mannerisms on *20*, the first record he sang on, but is still good enough to deliver an unexpectedly poignant treatment of 'Imagination'. *Lofty's Roach Soufflé* wasn't so much premature – it was released, more or less simultaneously with *We Are In Love*, as a 'jazz' instrumental album paired with the songs collection – as half-baked. Any good piano-trio record will outdo this one. But *We Are In Love* is much better, a neat blend of copycat originals and carefully pitched standards, with Marsalis taking a couple of guest solos. Connick's voice is maturing all the time, as *Blue Light, Red Light* shows, and, although this set of all-original songs is pretty thin fare, the arrangements for a young big band are encouragingly untypical of middle-of-the-road big-band scoring, even if some of the charts sound a little wilfully odd. Connick sings even the tritest of the lyrics with care. But it's hard to see him 'developing' in the showbiz spotlight, on the basis of the latest progress report, *25*. This is *20* re-run in a less charmed atmosphere, and Connick's gathering-up of piano cliché (at least he gets Ellis Marsalis to play for him on one track) is increasingly tiresome. He has since released his basement tapes on *Eleven* (Columbia CK 53171), but this is getting ridiculous. His latest direction is towards a Meters-style New Orleans funk on the often rather enjoyable *She* (Columbia 476816-2), but this weather bird is now pointing the way out of this book.

Chris Connor (born 1929) VOCAL

**** **Sings The George Gershwin Almanac Of Song** Atlantic 2-601 2CD
    Connor; Joe Newman, Doc Severinsen (*t*); Eddie Bert, Jimmy Cleveland, Jim Thompson, Warren Covington (*tb*); Sam Most, Peanuts Hucko (*cl*); Herbie Mann (*f*); Eddie Wasserman, Al Cohn (*ts*); Danny Bank (*bs*); Ralph Sharon, Stan Free, Hank Jones (*p*); Barry Galbraith, Joe Puma, Mundell Lowe (*g*); Milt Jackson (*vib*); Wendell Marshall, Milt Hinton, Oscar Pettiford, Vinnie Burke (*b*); Osie Johnson, Ed Shaughnessy, Ronnie Free (*d*); Johnny Rodriguez (*perc*).

The cool vocalist par excellence. Her records for Bethlehem and Atlantic showcased the ex-Kenton singer in a way that led to some definitive interpretations: her versions of 'Ev'ry Time', 'It's All Right With Me', 'I Wonder What Became Of Me' and several more are unlikely to be bettered. Her phrasing, the limpid quality of her tone and the dramatic effect of her vibrato remain uniquely hers. Most of Connor's marvellous series of Atlantic albums are out of print, but at least this superb collection has been reissued on a double-CD, with previously unreleased sides as a bonus. The vocalist works comprehensively through the Gershwin songbook in the company of seven different instrumental groups, and the results are probably superior even to Ella Fitzgerald's similar recordings of the period. Trifles such as 'Bla Bla Bla' or 'I Can't Be Bothered Now' are graced with thoughtful readings, the swingers despatched unhurriedly, the ballads lingered over; despite the size of the project, there's no sense of routine. The remastering has been admirably done.

***(*) **Lover Come Back To Me** Evidence 22110
    Connor; Fred Hersch (*p*); Steve LaSpina (*b*); Tony Tedesco (*d*). 9/81.

A New York club show. Chris still sounds in her prime. Hersch's team accompany with a completely *simpatico* outlook and a choice set of standards comes up just fine. It closes on her concert set-piece of 'My Heart Stood Still', but all the songs are well chosen.

***(*) **Classic** Contemporary C-14023

> Connor; Claudio Roditi (*t, flhn*); Paquito D'Rivera (*as*); Michael Abene, Richard Rodney Bennett (*ky*); Rufus Reid (*b*); Akira Tana (*d*). 8/86.

A fine return to the studios for Connor. Although some of the accompaniments are a shade too bright, the material is a refined choice of standards, and the vocalist shows few signs of advancing years. She revisits 'Blame It On My Youth' with poignant sincerity and elsewhere handles the pulse of Bennett's arrangements with undiminished skill.

(*) **New Again Contemporary C-14038

> Connor; Claudio Roditi (*t, flhn*); Bill Kirschner (*ss, as, ts, f, cl*); Dave Valentin (*f*); Michael Abene, Richard Rodney Bennett (*ky*); Michael Moore (*b*); Buddy Williams (*d*); Sammy Figueroa (*perc*). 8/87.

Something of a let-down after the sublime *Classic*. The band is a little too pushy and loud for the singer to come through clearly, and some of the songs are inappropriate choices for a vocalist whose strengths lie in more traditional interpretation. But a handful of tunes, especially 'I Wish I'd Met You', approach Connor's best form.

***(*) **As Time Goes By** Enja 7061-2

> Connor; Hank Jones (*p*); George Mraz (*b*); Keith Copeland (*d*). 4/91.

Connor has never before made such a straight-ahead jazz album and, with blue-chip accompaniment from the incomparable Jones, this session swings even at slow tempos. Yet the singer's concentrated readings of 'As Time Goes By', 'Gone With The Wind' and 'Goodbye' are on the level of her classic recordings.

Bill Connors (born 1949) GUITAR

*** **Theme To The Guardian** ECM 1057

> Connors (*g* solo). 11/74.

*** **Of Mist And Melting** ECM 1120

> Connors; Jan Garbarek (*ts, ss*); Gary Peacock (*b*); Jack DeJohnette (*d*). 77.

*** **Swimming With A Hole In My Body** ECM 1158

> As above. 8/79.

(*) **Step It Core COCD 9.00818

> Connors; Steve Khan (*g*); Tom Kennedy (*b*); Dave Weckl (*d*). 6 & 10/84.

(*) **Step It Evidence ECD 22080

> As above.

(*) **Double Up Core COCD 9.00826

> Connors; Tom Kennedy (*b*); Kim Plainfield (*d*). 85.

(*) **Double Up Evidence ECD 22081

> As above.

*(*) **Assembler** Core COCD 9.00519

> As above. 6/87.

Once Chick Corea's guitarist in Return To Forever, Connors shares his old boss's galling tendency to short-change exceptional technical ability with rather bland and self-indulgent ideas. The later trios have a certain energy and immediacy, but they're crude in comparison to the Corea-influenced solo projects. Connors's acoustic work is finely detailed and there are some interesting things on *Swimming*, albeit worked out in a shut-off, self-absorbed away that, like a lot of Alan Holdsworth's work, may appeal to guitar technicians but which can be curiously off-putting for everyone else. *Theme*, long in the tooth now, was probably the most satisfactory of the bunch until *Of Mist And Melting* reappeared on CD; the presence of Garbarek and of a rhythm section that cooks along in a dark strain adds quantifiably to the range, yielding more of his typically tense atmospheric pieces. Even allowing for the success of this record, it may be that Connors has yet to find a sympathetic group setting that will allow him to play more simply without descending to the awful banalities of *Assembler*.

Contemporary Piano Ensemble GROUP

***(*) **The Key Players** DIW/Columbia 475646

> James Williams, Geoff Keezer, Harold Mabern, Mulgrew Miller, Donald Brown (*p*); Christian McBride (*b*); Tony Reedus (*d*). 8/93.

How does this work? *Four* pianos, with bass and drums? Not all at the same time, surely? That was certainly the assumption when James Williams first put together this keyboard summit. Early versions featured a kind of relay or Consequences set-up, with one player handing over to another, with perhaps a few four-handed sections thrown in. In 1990 there was an album called *For Pianos, For Phineas*, a dedication to the late Phineas Newborn Jr, but this seems to have been released only in Japan, and it was essentially a collection of four quite distinct piano trios.

What we have with *The Key Players* is a genuine ensemble project, and it is a credit to Williams, co-producer Kazunori Sugiyama and, above all, engineer Jim Anderson that it is listenable at all. There are solos, of course, and listeners may find the liner-notes indispensable in identifying who's doing what, and when. However, it is clear that these are musicians with very distinct musical characters; any notion that the piano is not a 'personality' instrument, like the saxophone, is dispelled very quickly. Mabern's blues loyalism, Williams's own fire and passion, Keezer's brisk investment of the McCoy Tyner legacy he shares with Miller, the lesser-known Brown's very individual slant when he steps in: all these come through strongly.

All of them bring original compositions. Miller's 'P.N.J.' is the most obvious throwback to the Newborn tribute and features a hectic trading session. Keezer's 'Hibiscus' is the most sheerly attractive, but for rhythmic muscle and ensemble co-ordination it would be hard to pass a roistering interpretation of Ray Brown's 'Up There'. It is. Mabern sits out one tune that would seem to have been ideal for him, Bobby Timmons's 'Moanin'', played, intriguingly, without drums. One has to feel a little for the rhythm section, but they're fairly and audibly represented in a stereo field that individualizes all the participants. More than just technically adroit, this succeeds artistically as well.

Contraband GROUP

***(*) **Live At The Bimhuis** Bvhaast CD 8906

> Toon De Gouw, Louis Lanzing, Ad Gruter (*t*); Willem Van Manen, Hans Sparla, Hans Visser (*tb*); Theo Jorgensmann, Paul Van Kemenade, Rutger Van Otterloo, Maarten Van Norden, Eckard Koltermann (*reeds*); Ron Van Rossum (*p*); Hein Offermans (*b*); Martin Van Duynhoven (*d*). 11/88.

***(*) **De Ruyter Suite** Bvhaast CD 9104

> As above, except Chris Abelen (*tb*), Jeroen Van Vliet (*p*) and Eric Van der Westen (*b*) replace Sparla, Van Rossum and Offermans. 4/91.

Contraband is Willem van Manen's 'occasional' big band. The trombonist and veteran of Holland's post-bop and free-music scene is a skilled and dynamic composer-arranger, and these records – one live, one studio, and both written almost entirely by van Manen – are packed with incident. The group swings and shouts with all the power and finesse of the great big bands, and it glories in soloists who crackle their way out of complex charts. But sometimes there are hints of strain or of over-familiar effects – clustering muted trumpets or high reeds, for instance, or fast cutting from passages of rigid orthodoxy to all-out freedom – which suggest that it's a best of both worlds which the band can't quite grasp. It would be churlish, though, to deny the vividness, sweep and panache of a band which ought to be far better known than it is. 'Contra-Suit' from the live record, and the three-part title-piece of *De Ruyter Suite*, dedicated to Dutch critic Michiel de Ruyter, are grand yet wholly coherent big-scale structures, and the soloists – especially Jorgensmann on clarinet and van Kemenade on alto – refuse to dilute the intensity of the whole band. Both discs are sumptuously recorded.

Junior Cook (1934–92) TENOR SAXOPHONE

***(*) **Somethin's Cookin'** Muse MCD 5470

> Cook; Cedar Walton (*p*); Buster Williams (*b*); Billy Higgins (*d*). 6/81.

*** **The Place To Be** Steeplechase CCD 31240

> Cook; Mickey Tucker (*p*); Wayne Dockery (*b*); Leroy Williams (*d*). 11/88.

*** **On A Misty Night** Steeplechase SCCD 31266

> As above, except Walter Booker (*b*) replaces Dockery. 6/89.

*** **You Leave Me Breathless** Steeplechase SCCD 31304

> Cook; Valery Ponomarev (*t*); Mickey Tucker (*p*); John Webber (*b*); Joe Farnsworth (*d*). 12/91.

Junior Cook's work with Horace Silver and a few other leaders revealed a tenorman of staunch loyalty to the hard-bop language and, though he never quite broke through to the front rank, he left many inventive solos on record. As a leader, he was rather less than successful, and a few earlier records were easily forgotten. He came into his own again during the final decade of his oddly underachieving career. The Muse session is not just recommended because of the rhythm section (which is splendid) but because Cook himself makes such an excellent set of it. Alternative takes of 'Detour Ahead',

'Hindsight' and 'Fiesta Espanol' give some pointers to his thinking at this time, but it is Cook's solo on 'Heavy Blue' that really establishes a continuity with his Silver Age.

Sadly, there was never to be a golden one. Steeplechase has been a profitable home for many a journey-man hard-bopper, with the label's comfortable house sound and familiar menus making plenty of otherwise disenfranchised musicians feel at home. Cook's records for the company worked out rather well, but none of them can be claimed to be a classic. If the saxophonist's dependability was his strongest suit, he nevertheless manages to find enough in the way of ear-catching ideas to give his up-tempo workouts an edge of involvement which grants even something as simple as 'Cedar's Blues' on *The Place To Be* a tough credibility. His powers were also in decline to some extent, but that tends to lend such a professional player a further challenge: how does he deal with it? Cook's answer seems to be to shy away from over-familiar material and to turn to more timbral variation than he would have bothered with as a younger man. *On A Misty Night* is marked by a considered choice of material – 'By Myself', 'Make The Girl Love Me', 'My Sweet Pumpkin' – and the leader's thoughts on the title-tune, once associated with Coltrane, stake his place in the grand tenor lineage. *You Leave Me Breathless* was his last date, made a few months before his death, and although there is some rambling – a few solos have one chorus too many, for instance – Cook's playing has a candid, clear-eyed quality which is quite affecting. Ponomarev is rather ordinary; but all three records are greatly assisted by the presence of Tucker, sympathetic, and driving when he has to be.

Marty Cook TROMBONE

***(*) **Nightwork** Enja ENJ 5031
   Cook; Jim Pepper (*ts*); Essiet Okon Essiet (*b*); John Betsch (*d*). 10/86, 1/87.
*** **Red White Black And Blue** Enja 5067
   Cook; Jim Pepper (*ts*); Mal Waldron (*p*); Ed Schuller (*b*); John Betsch (*d*). 11/87.
***(*) **Borderlines** Tutu 888 122
   Cook; Monty Waters (*as*); Paul Grabowsky (*p*); Ed Schuller (*b*); Art Lewis (*d*). 12/90.
*** **Phases Of The Moon** Tutu 888 160
   Cook; Rudi Mahall (*bcl, turntables*); Bill Bickford (*g*); Ed Schuller (*b*); Jim Black (*d, perc*). 11/93.

If Ray Anderson is way out on his own, Cook could be leading the contemporary trombone pack. Whatever their respective merits, there is certainly no quantitative comparison between their respective outputs. Anderson is everywhere, while Cook's most noted recorded work before the mid-1980s was a too-brief appearance on *Out From Under*, a typically enigmatic Gunther Hampel release from the fissiparous Birth label.

Cook's Enja sets showed that he has considerable qualities as both soloist and leader: bright articula-tion, inexhaustible ideas, sharp arrangements and an impressive structural awareness. In Jim Pepper, the Amerindian composer of 'Witchi Tai To', he has the perfect instrumental complement. *Nightwork* has been restored to the catalogue, thankfully. Betsch is the key element on 'Apocatastasis' and 'Idiosyncratic', drumming with great control and rigour. Essiet brings a darkness of tone that his successor never quite achieves. Waldron, on *Red White . . .*, is a virtual guarantee of quality; no mistak-ing which part of the musical spectrum he represents.

In Monty Waters, Cook has brought forward a player who really ought to be much better known. He has an astonishing alto tone, peeled raw, alternately harsh and tender, surprisingly close to Pepper's vocalized sound, but closer to the blues in spirit. Cook's 'O.C.' was written for Waters but conjures up another influence on the saxophonist. The two title-pieces, 'Borderlines' (plus alternative take) and 'Bordercross', colonize the edgy territory the trombonist negotiates between African and European influences, 'black' and 'white' constructions of jazz, order and freedom, the same agenda as *Red White Black And Blue*.

Phases Of The Moon is an odd set (as titles like the opening 'Kicking Monster And The Vagina Girls' might suggest), a seeming attempt to get to grips with street sounds and the whole HipHop idiom. It certainly isn't Cook's forte, and the album is never more than the sum of, on the whole, rather interest-ing parts.

Al Cooper (1911–81) CLARINET, ALTO AND BARITONE SAXOPHONES and
The Savoy Sultans GROUP

*** **Al Cooper's Savoy Sultans 1938–1941** Classics 728

Cooper; Pat Jenkins (*t, v*); Sam Massenberg (*t*); Rudy Williams (*as*); Ed McNeil, Sam Simmons, Irving 'Skinny' Brown, George Kelley (*ts*); Oliver Richardson, Cyril Haynes (*p*); Paul Chapman (*g, v*); Grachan Moncur (*b*); Alex 'Razz' Mitchell (*d*); Helen Procter, Evelyn White (*v*). 7/38–2/41.

The Sultans usually played opposite the Chick Webb band at Harlem's Savoy Ballroom, and visiting bands were wary of competing with them, since they were so popular with the dancers. The records are another matter: simple head arrangements, average solos and merely capable playing makes one wonder why they were held in such high regard. But playing through these 24 tracks, one can hear some of the simple appeal of what wasn't really a big band but a small, mobile, flexible unit which covered whatever base the customers wanted. Pat Jenkins is the best soloist. Transfers start out very clean, but some of the tracks have plenty of original surface noise.

Bob Cooper (1925–93) TENOR SAXOPHONE, OBOE

*** **Coop! The Music Of Bob Cooper** Original Jazz Classics OJC-161

Cooper; Conte Candoli, Pete Candoli, Don Fagerquist (*t*); Frank Rosolino, John Halliburton (*tb*); Lou Levy (*p*); Victor Feldman (*vib*); Max Bennett (*b*); Mel Lewis (*d*). 8/57.

Because he chose to spend much of his career away from any leadership role, Cooper's light has been a little dim next to many of the West Coast players of the 1950s, especially as he often worked as an accompanist to his wife, vocalist June Christy. His flute-and-oboe sessions with Bud Shank are out of print, but this sole feature album, recorded for Contemporary, displays a light, appealing tenor style and arrangements which match rather than surpass the West Coast conventions of the day. The drily effective recording is typical of the studios of the period.

*** **Milano Blues** Fresh Sound FSR-CD 179

Cooper; Hans Hammerschmid, Pim Jacobs (*p*); Rudolf Hansen, Ruud Jacobs (*b*); Victor Plasil, Wessel Ilcken (*d*). 3–4/57.

Two sessions from a European visit, both with local rhythm sections, a studio date in Milan and a live show in Holland. Cooper sounds a little over-relaxed on the Italian date, but the livelier 'Cappuccino Time' is sinuously done and the live tracks feature a fine tenor blow on 'Indiana'. A couple of oboe features don't assert a great jazz role for the instrument. Goodish sound throughout, though the drums are a bit thin on the studio date.

*** **For All We Know** Fresh Sound FSR-CD 167

Cooper; Lou Levy (*p*); Monty Budwig (*b*); Ralph Penland (*d*). 8/90.

Cooper made rather sporadic returns to the studios in the 1980s and '90s, but he remained a guileful player, his tone deceptively languid: when the tempo picks up, the mastery of the horn asserts itself, and he gets the same kind of even-handed swing which the more demonstrative Zoot Sims or Al Cohn could muster. He was working right up until his sudden death in 1993. The wistful *For All We Know* stands as an honest farewell: typically thoughtful preparation by Cooper and Levy, on good and unhackneyed standards and with quartet arrangements that make the most of the various combinations of players.

Jim Cooper (born 1950) VIBES

(*) **Tough Town Delmark DD-446

Cooper; Ira Sullivan (*ts*); Bob Dogan (*p*); Dan DeLorenzo (*b*); Charlie Braugham (*d*); Alejo Poveda (*perc*). 91.

*** **Nutville** Delmark DD-457

As above, except Sullivan also plays *t* and *ss*. 11/91.

Cooper's fluency and drive on the vibes lend piquancy to his music, but these records are too diffuse to make any significant impact. The original compositions are musicianly rather than melodically compelling, while bebop updates such as 'Cheryl' and 'Bemsha Swing' aren't strong enough to transcend mere repertory playing. The best moments come in Dogan's contributions to the second record, notably the complex but hard-swinging 'Sui Fumi' and 'Cabbie Patch'. Sullivan is his usual chameleonic self, although he sticks to tenor for the first record; and occasionally one feels that a more decisive horn would be a better partner for Cooper, who sometimes drifts into clouds of notes. The music isn't well served by a flat production on both discs, but *Nutville* is worth trying for vibes lovers – it's still a seldom-featured instrument in jazz terms, and Cooper is a dedicated exponent.

Marc Copland PIANO, KEYBOARDS

***(*) **All Blues At Night** Jazz City 660.53.026
    Copland; Tim Hagans (*t, flhn*); Gary Peacock (*b*); Bill Stewart (*d*). 9/90.
*** **Tracks** L + R CDLR 45050
    Copland; Dieter Ilg (*b*); Ralph Penland (*d*). 11/91.
*** **Never At All** Future Music FMR CD05 28193
    Copland; Stan Sulzmann (*as, ss, f*). 2/92.
As a composer, Copland is drily attractive. It's a quality which transfers to his work on standards –
much of *All Blues At Night* and 'Rhythm-A-Ning' on *Tracks* – which is reined-in, disciplined, almost
analytical, yet capable of great shouting surges of emotion. A complex performer.
    The group on *All Blues* has the kind of response speed Copland needs. By no means an orthodox jazz
player, he calls for a level of detail Ilg for instance isn't qualified to offer him but which a player of
Peacock's experience and values regards as second nature. Hagans has the right trumpet-tone for these
settings, enunciating almost like a Baroque player. The session with Sulzmann was an 'old pals'
encounter and the pieces were put down more or less spontaneously. Predictably, Copland's use of
synthesizers is both individual and tasteful. The highlight perhaps is the flute chase on 'Phobos And
Demos', though Copland's 'Guinevere', which closes the album, is lovely, too.

Chick Corea (born 1941) PIANO, KEYBOARDS, COMPOSER

*** **Piano Improvisations Vols 1 & 2** ECM 1014/1020
    Corea (*p* solo); Ida Kavafian (*vn*); Fred Sherry (*clo*). 4/71.
(*) **Children's Songs ECM 1267
    As above. 7/83.
Corea is a pianist and composer of remarkable range and energy, combining a free-ish jazz idiom with a
heavy Latin component and an interest in more formal structures. The obvious parallel is with his ECM
stable-mate, Keith Jarrett, an even more prolific keyboard improviser with a similar facility for melodic
invention within relatively conventional popular forms or in more loosely conceived improvisatory
settings; they also share a certain ambivalence about audiences. Corea's stated ambition is to assimilate
the 'dancing' qualities of jazz and folk musics to the more disciplined structures of classical music. He
has written a half-dozen classic melodies, notably the much-covered 'La Fiesta', 'Return To Forever'
and 'Tones For Joan's Bones'.
    There is certainly a world of difference between the miniatures on *Piano Improvisations* and Jarrett's
hugely rambling excursions. Corea is superficially less demanding, but he still repays detailed attention. If his taste was to lapse in the following years, he was surely never more decorously apt than in
these 1971 sessions, which after 20 years are still wearing well. *Children's Songs* is a much less
compelling set.

*** **A.R.C.** ECM 1009
    Corea; Dave Holland (*b*); Barry Altschul (*d*). 1/71.
*** **Trio Music** ECM 1232/33
    Corea; Miroslav Vitous (*b*); Roy Haynes (*d*). 11/81.
(*) **Trio Music, Live In Europe ECM 1310
    As above. 9/84.
The trios offer the best internal evidence of Corea's musical and philosophical trajectory. The early
Sings/Sobs is a fine, solid jazz set with some intelligently handled standard material. A bare three years
later, Corea, falling under the influence of the Scientology movement, was playing altogether more
experimentally, with a searching, restless quality that he lost in later years. *The Song Of Singing* (arguably Corea's best record and, like *Tones For Joan's Bones*, awaiting restoration to the catalogue) is
marked by fine melodic invention and some remarkably sophisticated group interplay which demands
that the record be seen as a trio performance, not just as Corea plus rhythm. The two 'Ballads',
numbered I and III, are credited to the three musicians and are presumably improvised over predetermined structures; one wonders how many were left on the editing-room floor. Corea's two compositions,
'Rhymes' and 'Flesh', are slightly vapid but sharpen up on familiarity. *A.R.C.* isn't entirely successful,
but the quality of Holland and Altschul renders it a credible essay that Corea was never fully to develop.
He left the demanding Circle (whose single record contained versions of Holland's 'Toy Room' and
Wayne Shorter's 'Nefertiti', both covered on *The Song Of Singing*) later in 1971, convinced that the
music was losing touch with its audience. This is the beginning of the pianist's awkward populism,
which was to lead him to a commercially successful but artistically null flirtation with fusion music of
various sorts. (It's worth noting that 'Tones For Joan's Bones', title-track of the LP mentioned above, is

available on an Atlantic CD devoted to Corea, Herbie Hancock, Keith Jarrett and McCoy Tyner: 7567 81402.)

The later trio perfectly illustrates Corea's change in attitude. Vitous and Haynes are both superbly gifted players, but they take no discernible chances, sticking close to a conception laden with Corea's increasingly vapid philosophizing. By 1984, there isn't much left on Old Mother Hubbard's shelves.

**** Return To Forever ECM 1022
    Corea; Joe Farrell (*ss, f*); Stanley Clarke (*b*); Airto Moreira (*d, perc*); Flora Purim (*v, perc*). 2/72.
**** Light As A Feather Polydor 2310247
    As above. 10/72.
*** Hymn Of The Seventh Galaxy Polydor 825 336
    Corea; Bill Connors (*g*); Stanley Clarke (*b*); Lenny White (*d, perc*). 8/73.
**(*) Where Have I Known You Before Polydor 2310354
    Corea; Al DiMeola (*g*); Stanley Clarke (*b*); Lenny White (*d, perc*). 7–8/74.
** My Spanish Heart Polydor 2669034 2CD
    Corea; 17-piece band, including strings; Jean-Luc Ponty (*vn*); one track of Corea; Stanley Clarke (*b*); Narada Michael Walden (*perc*). 10/76.
**(*) The Mad Hatter Verve 519 799
    Corea; John Thomas, Stuart Blumberg, John Rosenberg (*t*); Ron Moss (*tb*); Charles Veal, Kenneth Yerke (*vn*); Denyse Buffum, Michael Nowack (*vla*); Dennis Karmazyn (*clo*); Herbie Hancock (*ky*); Joe Farrell (*ts, f, picc*); Eddie Gomez, Jamie Faunt (*b*); Steve Gadd, Harvey Mason (*d*); Gayle Moran (*v*).
*** Friends Polydor 849 071
    Corea; Joe Farrell (*ts, ss, f*); Eddie Gomez (*b*); Steve Gadd (*d*). 78.

Lightweight it may be in some regards, but *Light As A Feather* is a perennial favourite, with Corea bouncing joyously and unselfconsciously over themes like '500 Miles High', 'Captain Marvel' and the ubiquitous 'Children's Song'. The earlier record is better still, more improvisational in cast but still constructed around song forms. Purim's voice was never better, and Clarke keeps his lead guitarist ambitions to himself for the present. Moreira is rarely heard on a regular drum kit, and he offers an unconventional pulse that gives both sets a distinctive tilt. He plays a particularly strong role on 'Return To Forever' and on the long, buoyant 'Sometime Ago/La Fiesta'.

The following year, Corea formed an electric group called Return to Forever. Not to be confused with the group that made the EDM record; only Clarke remains. There's something very '70s about *Hymn Of The Seventh Galaxy* and *Where Have I Known You Before*. Compared to the Mahavishnu Orchestra, which was very cheeseclothy and intense, Return to Forever was rather closer to a dance group, and the very buoyancy of the music often glossed over its occasional subtleties. Though both records are painfully dated, certainly in technical terms and even despite careful remastering, they do retain some of the freshness and energy of the earlier, acoustic band, and it's perfectly possible to shut one's eyes to Corea's quasi-mystical titles.

Things went a little awry thereafter. *The Leprechaun* was so intent on being charming that it ended up deeply charmless. It marked some sort of a return to acoustic jazz, though Corea himself lined up a bank of then state-of-the-art keyboards, most of which now sound no more contemporary than a clavichord might. He added horns and a few strings and tied himself up in a drab fantasy realm that muffled even the sub-Bartókian melodies that had emerged from time to time in Corea's work and had their apotheosis in the *Children's Songs* (above, and – numbers five and fifteen – on *Friends*). *The Mad Hatter* was in the same dismal vein, with horns and strings clogging up some of the most promising material. The one bright spot is Joe Farrell's part on 'Humpty Dumpty', a typically elegant and feeling tenor break.

Friends was the one with the embarrassing Smurfs cover which must have put off hundreds of potential buyers. Perversely, it's better than the two previous items. The long 'Smaba Song' and the title-track are close to his best for this vintage, and Farrell and Gomez give the session a considerable boost. Corea was still publicly thanking L. Ron Hubbard for his 'continual inspiration', but it was never clear how exactly the fantasy realm into which these works dipped was the product of a clear – or Clear – vision that went beyond verbalized or abstract concepts and to what extent they were a sign of creative exhaustion.

My Spanish Heart was a rare instance of Corea working with a large band. It gives every impression of having been got up for the tourists. It's a rather ersatz Latin concoction that never seems to earn its climaxes or justify the band's rather strained enthusiasm.

** Corea Hancock Polydor 835360
    Corea; Herbie Hancock (*p*). 2/78.
*** Crystal Silence ECM 1024
    Corea; Burton (*vib*). 10/79.

** In Concert, Zurich, October 28, 1978 ECM 1182/3
> As above.
* Lyric Suite For Sextet ECM 1260
> As above, except add string quartet. 9/82.

Interesting duo performances of 'La Fiesta' and 'Maiden Voyage' on *Corea Hancock* (a compositional credit apiece), but by no means a compelling album, with some of Hancock's notions baffling in the extreme. *Crystal Silence* is a lot more substantial than it initially sounds and the music holds up well on the subsequent concert performance, which for a time was a worthwhile substitute, though CD has given the sound a cleaner and more distinctive edge. 'Senor Mouse' and 'Crystal Silence' reappear from the studio disc and there is a fine eponymous Bud Powell tribute that is well worth the admission price.

The *Lyric Suite* recalls Ravel more readily than Alban Berg, which is no bad thing. It's delicate, attractive music, sensibly limited in scope, firmly executed and, as always, beautifully executed. Less baroquely ambitious than Jarrett's classical compositions, it comes across as something of a by-blow.

*** Tap Step Stretch GRS 00092
> Corea; Alan Vizutti (*t, flhn*); Joe Henderson (*ts*); Joe Farrell (*ts, ss*); Hubert Laws (*f, picc*); Bunny Brunel, Stanley Clarke, Jamie Faunt (*b*); Tommy Brechtlein (*d*); Don Alias, Airto Moreira, Laudir Oliveira (*perc*); Nani Vila Brunel, Shelby Flint, Flora Purim, Gayle Moran (*v*). 12/79, 1/80.

The Stretch Collector series was planned as a way of releasing previously unheard or unavailable Corea material, partly (as in the case of the item below) to offset bootleg issues, partly, one suspects, as a reaction to the pianist's rather difficult relationship with the recording industry.

The stuff on *Tap Step* is pretty much of a muchness; a heavy emphasis on electric piano, synth and clavinet, a fondness for rock settings, Latin percussion and, here and there, voices. Only on 'Grandpa Blues' with Brunel on fretless bass and Stanley Clarke on his piccolo bass is there anything that really grabs the attention. The few glimpses of Joe Farrell are welcome as always, and Joe Henderson, who in these years was quite close to Corea (see below), contributes a typically unstuffy and intelligent part to 'Flamenco', which belongs in the *Light As A Feather* league. Other than these two tracks, little of distinction to report.

***(*) Live In Montreux Stretch GRS 00122
> Corea; Joe Henderson (*ts*); Gary Peacock (*b*); Roy Haynes (*d*). 81.

Chick wore a T-shirt emblazoned with the legend 'EAT CARROTS'. Haynes played throughout as if on a diet of raw steak. Henderson and Peacock just snacked away happily. This is a further dip into the Corea archive for Stretch, a supergroup encounter introduced with due sense of occasion by Montreux organizer, Claude Nobs, who just about gets off-stage quick enough before the fireworks begin. Though things like 'Folk Song' and 'Psalm' are not in themselves demanding, the standard of musicianship required to last in this company is awesome. On 'Hairy Canary' (which may be an oblique reference to Charlie Parker's music), the four jostle a bit and generally check one another out. The main weight of the session falls to the two tracks already mentioned and an extended improvisation on 'Trinkle Tinkle', a version of Chick's 'Quintet No. 2' and Peacock's 'Up, Up, And . . .'.

Even though the horn sound is often rather uncertain and indistinct, Henderson remains the key to the whole proceedings, an improviser of undimmed resource and patience, required to work in a notably floaty and uncertain harmonic landscape. Not a great recording, but a splendid record all the same.

*** Works ECM 825426-2
> Corea (*p* solo and with various bands). 71–83.

A well-selected sample of the pianist's decade-plus with ECM. Not many surprises, though it's interesting how thin the short piano improvisations from ECM 1014 and 1020 sound when heard out of context.

** Voyage ECM 1282
> Corea; Steve Kujala (*f*). 7/84.
** Septet ECM 1297
> As above, except add strings and french horn. 7/84, 10/84.

Voyage is a flimsy confection that is very difficult to take entirely seriously. Part of the problem is that the two players take it very seriously indeed, when what it cries out for is a little lightness of touch. *Septet* is no more pulse-quickening, but it has the benefit of a certain variation of register and timbre that is episodically quite interesting.

** Elektrik Band GRP 95352
> Corea; Scott Henderson, Carlos Rios (*g*); John Patitucci (*b*); Dave Weckl (*d, perc*).
* Light Years GRP 95462
> Corea; Eric Marienthal (*sax*); Frank Gambale (*g*); John Patitucci (*b*); Dave Weckl (*d*).

* Eye Of The Beholder GRP 95642
   As above.
* Inside Out GRP 96012
   As above.
** Beneath The Mask GRP 96492
   Corea; John Patitucci (*b*); Dave Weckl (*d*).
Products of a rush of blood to the head known as the Elektrik Band (yes, the Akoustik Band was not far behind), these do Corea no kredit whatever. Though many of the compositional ideas remain intriguing, particularly on *Beneath The Mask*, the arrangments and solos are numbingly bland. It will, of course, be argued that it was the very popularity of this group that induced Corea to persist with it. So be it.

*** Akoustic Band GRP 95822
   Corea; John Patitucci (*b*); Dave Weckl (*d*).
**(*) Alive GRP 96272
   As above.
From the very first notes of 'My One And Only Love' and 'Bessie's Blues' on the first of these, Corea is unmistakable. For better or worse, he still has perhaps the most distinctive stylistic signature in contemporary jazz piano, a rippling fullness of sound that cloys very quickly. Here, then, the promised Akoustic Band and a mainly standards set. Compared to what Keith Jarrett has done with similar repertoire, the thinness of Corea's conception becomes clearer. *Akoustic Band* has its moments, mostly on original material, and *Alive* is an uncomplicated, entertaining set; the pianos both sound first rate and the production is spot-on.

*** Three Quartets Stretch GRS 00032
   Corea; Michael Brecker (*ts*); Eddie Gomez (*b*); Steve Gadd (*d*). 1 & 2/81.
Stretch is Corea's own imprint, licensed through GRP, and devoted not just to archive material like the Montreux concert (above) but to new recording as well. The *Three Quartets* were structured jazz compositions with a wide range of classical influences, and they see Corea exploring some of the territory Bill Evans (who had died prematurely the year before) left uncolonized. 'Quartet No. 2' is the only one broken down into parts – dedications, respectively, to Duke Ellington and John Coltrane – and it is harmonically the most varied. The other two are unmistakable Corea, mixing funky lines with a floating, very classical sound which the Bösendorfer Grand richly accentuates.
   After the main session ended, the band filled in studio time with a few untried originals and an off-the-cuff run-through of Charlie Parker's 'Confirmation'. Though they don't quite fit in with the three main items for the original LP, they contain (perversely enough) some of the leader's best playing on the record. Michael Brecker was still developing what has since become the most ubiquitous contemporary tenor sound after John Coltrane and Jan Garbarek, and he still sounds adventurous and forceful.

**(*) Touchstone Stretch 00042
   Corea; Al Vizzutti (*t*); Lee Konitz (*as*); Steve Kujala (*ts, f*); Al DiMeola, Paco De Lucia (*g*);
   Carlos Benavent, Stanley Clarke, Bob Magnusson (*b*); Lenny White (*d*); Carol Shrive (*vn*); Greg
   Gottlieb (*vla*); Alex Acuña, Don Alias, Laudir De Oliveira (*perc*); Gayle Moran (*v*).
Prefaced by a nutty fable about the Singing Woman and Rivera, 'Touchstone' itself has the same soapy unreality as Hollywood fantasies like *Legend*. Scored for keys, guitar, voice, bass and percussion, it is no more than a couple of slight themes, lent a papier-mâché superstructure and then vaguely jazzed up. There are more interesting things on the record. Lee Konitz's contribution to 'Duende' is a reminder of Getz's *Sweet Rain*, and 'Compadres' reunites Return to Forever for an overlong but attractive blow. The main problem with *Touchstone* is its bittiness. There is more musical substance than on *The Mad Hatter*, but as a disc it's all over the place and can really be seen only as a haphazard sampler.

***(*) Expressions GRP 900732
   Corea (*p* solo). 93.
Significant on two counts, the first solo record for some time and a very welcome return to standards. Corea includes only two of his own compositions (a wonderful reading of 'Armando's Rhumba'), but he scans the history of modern piano jazz with a typically eclectic range of vision. The second original is a 'Blues For Art' and the whole session is dedicated to Tatum. There are tunes by Strayhorn, Monk and Bud Powell, but in each case it's the Tatum strand that is most evident.
   It's beautifully recorded (Corea is listed as both producer and 'recordist') with a full, old-fashioned sound, pleasantly different from GRP's usual glitter.

***(*) Time Warp Stretch GRS 00152
   Corea; Bob Berg (*ts, ss*); John Patitucci (*b*); Gary Novak (*d*). 4/95.
A quasi-narrative suite with a sci-fi story-line, bog-standard stuff: purplish glows, names with too few

vowels, unbidden transitions from place to place, a little philosophy and dogma . . . and yet, one of the best and straightest Corea albums for some time. There is little obvious musical connection between the numbers, nor needs there to be, but Corea has woven the whole package into a suite with interpolated cadenzas from saxophone – bridging 'The Wish' and 'Terrain', his own intro to 'New Life', by far the most important track on the disc – and Patitucci's switch to Garrison mode to set 'Discovery' in motion.

'New Life' is as boldly optimistic and as quietly chastened as anything since the scandalously deleted *Song Of Singing* on Blue Note. It was a trio, and in some ways this record has the feel of a trio performance with Berg superadded, mostly effectively as here, but sometimes more jarringly where it seems clear that he is working his own agenda. The mystery – other than what exactly is going on in the story of Arndok – is why Corea should have felt drawn to a drummer as leaden and hostile as Novak. But for him, and a few raw edges elsewhere, this would be up with Corea's very best, rather than teetering problematically on the fringes.

Larry Coryell (born 1943) GUITAR

*** **Twin House** Act 9202
  Coryell: Philip Catherine (*g*); Joachim Kühn (*p*). 76, 77.
'Schizophrenic' is a wildly misused critical adjective, but if there was ever a split musical personality, it is Coryell. The guitarist never seemed able to make up his mind whether he wanted to be Chet Atkins, Jimi Hendrix or Segovia; and there were always doubts about his chops as an improviser.

Indifferently recorded in London and Hamburg, these are mainly guitar duets, with just one opening for Kühn. Coryell leads off a great version of 'The Train And The River', and there's a companionable 'Nuages'; but for the most part the material is original and very fresh. The two guitars are rather crudely separated and could do with narrowing a bit, but there are passages where it's impossible to judge who's playing what, though generally Catherine plays with a fuller, less rhythmic intonation.

(*) **Comin' Home Muse MCD 5303
  Coryell; Albert Dailey (*p*); George Mraz (*b*); Billy Hart (*d*); Julie Coryell (*v*). 2/84.
***(*) **Equipoise** Muse MCD 5319
  Coryell; Pamela Sklar (*f*); Stanley Cowell (*p*); Buster Williams (*b*); Billy Hart (*d*). 1/85.
*** **Toku Du** Muse MCD 5350
  Coryell; Stanley Cowell (*p*); Buster Williams (*b*); Beaver Harris (*d*). 9/87.
**** **Shining Hour** Muse MCD 5360
  Coryell; Kenny Barron (*p*); Buster Williams (*b*); Marvin 'Smitty' Smith (*d*). 10/90.
Coryell's sessions for Muse during the 1980s marked a return to jazz playing at the highest level and an – at least temporary – abandonment of his apparent desire to be all things to all men. The balance of originals to standards has shifted in the direction of tradition and there's more emphasis on blues sequences than before but, with Cowell and Barron in the line-up, it's unlikely that things will get too programmed and predictable.

The session with Dailey is a bit disappointing, and Julie Coryell's voice seems to belong to a different age. All the rest, though, can be recommended without reservation. *Toku Du*, named after a fine Buster Williams piece, offers convincing proof of Coryell's credentials as a traditionalist, while 'Nefertiti' and 'The Sorcerer' on *Shining Hour* see him tackle more contemporary repertoire (Shorter and Hancock respectively) with equal aplomb. Rudy van Gelder's hand at the controls is as sure as always.

(*) **A Quiet Day In Spring Steeplechase SCCD 31187
  Coryell; Michal Urbaniak (*vn*); Jesper Lundgaard (*b*). 11/83.
This was an interesting pairing. The Polish-born fusion violinist has had a fairly up-and-down career and can sound rather sentimental in a more intimate setting like this. However, Coryell gets him going on tunes like his own 'Polish Reggae' and two lovely waltzes, on which he combines delicate open-string passages with rich, triple-stopped chords that conjure up the Polish Romantic composers. Coryell takes a back seat where necessary, as on the violinist's feature, 'Stuff's Stuff', but is at his expressive best on 'Rue Gregoire Du Tour', picking out soft, sustained variations on the melody.

*** **Together** Concord CJ 4289
  Coryell; Emily Remler (*g*). 8/85.
Emily Remler's death from a heart attack, aged only 32, robbed America of one of its foremost instrumental voices and a jazz musician of considerable stature. *Together* delivers handsomely, a warm, approachable album which does not lack for subtleties. Recommended.

***(*) **Live From Bahia** CTI 1005
  Coryell; Marcio Montarroyos (*t*); Donald Harrison (*as, ss*); Luiz Avellar (*ky*); Dori Caymmi

(*g, v*); Romero Kubambo (*g*); Nico Assumpção, Francisco Centeno (*b*); Billy Cobham (*d*); Bashiri Johnson, Monica Millet, Tiao Oliveira (*perc*). 92.

A warm, relaxed session from Creed Taylor's Latin-leaning imprint, this brings Coryell back into contact with Billy Cobham (who plays superbly) and with New Orleans saxophonist Donald Harrison who, as always, reacts positively to contact with yet another aspect of the Afro-American tradition. Guitar duties are shared with composer Dori Caymmi, who also handles the vocals, and an extended rhythm section sets up a shifting backdrop against which melody lines move in an intriguingly cross-grained way. The long 'Bahian Night Walk' degenerates into a bit of a jam, and the more compelling tunes tend to be from the *norteamericanos*: Harrison's 'Oshum, Goddess Of Love' has a brooding quality that suggests the Old Religion. It would be good to hear more of Coryell in this company, though one suspects this was something of a one-off.

**(*) Fallen Angel CTI 1014
>   Coryell; Chris Hunter (*as*); Richard Elliot (*ts*); Mulgrew Miller, Ted Rosenthal (*p*); Jeanie Bryson, Klyde Jones (*v*).

Despite the presence of Miller, and a couple of the notoriously patchy Hunter's best recorded moments, this is a fairly drab and inconsequential session on which Coryell devolves a lot of solo responsibility to his colleagues. Only on 'Bumpin' On Sunset', 'Monk's Corner' and 'The Moors' (where he mimics Ralph Towner) does he kick back and play at full stretch. The rest of the time it's strictly pipe-and-slippers stuff, professionally done but unlikely to excite.

Giuseppe Costa BASS

**(*) Picture Number Two Splasc(h) H 325-2
>   Costa; Flavio Boltro (*t, flhn*); Danilo Terenzi, Stefano Scalzi (*tb*); Sandro Satta (*as*); Andrea Beneventano (*p*); Pippo Cataldo (*d*). 5/90.

One of two records (*Picture Number One* is vinyl only) co-led by the bass and drums partnership of Giuseppe Costa and Pippo Cataldo. While both used the odd instrumentation of trumpet, two trombones, alto and rhythm section, they're quite different from each other. *Picture Number Two*, which has the more familiar cast of new Italian jazzmen, is much smoother than the earlier disc and, while it's better played all through, some of the impetuousness has been disadvantageously lost. Boltro's lovely playing on 'To Gil' makes up for what's gone missing, though.

Louis Cottrell (1911–78) CLARINET

*** The Louis Cottrell Trio Original Jazz Classics OJC 1836-2
>   Cottrell; Emanuel Sayles (*g*); McNeal Breaux, Alcide Slow Drag Pavageau (*b*). 1/61.

One of the least-known albums in Riverside's *New Orleans: The Living Legends* series featured this charming trio music by a clarinettist far less remembered than most of the city's favourite sons on this horn. Cottrell's style has none of the harshness of the George Lewis manner: he preferred the soft tone and modest vibrato that typified the old-fashioned elegance of the Lorenzo Tio style. He never had a better showcase than this one, with the spirited strum of Sayles and the no-frills line of Breaux (Pavageau appears on only one brief track) alongside. On some songs he seems careless about his phrasing and falters here and there, but on others – 'Rose Room' is a good instance – the purling variations on the tune secure a surprising intensity. Two tracks, previously available only on an anthology LP, have been added to the original programme for the CD reissue.

Curtis Counce (born 1926) BASS

*** You Get More Bounce Original Jazz Classics OJC 159
>   Counce; Jack Sheldon or Gerald Wilson (*t*); Harold Land (*ts*); Carl Perkins (*p*); Frank Butler (*d*). 10/56.

***(*) Landslide Original Jazz Classics OJC 606
>   As above. 4/57.

*** Carl's Blues Original Jazz Classics OJC 423
>   As above. 8/57.

** Sonority Contemporary C 7655
>   As above. 1/58.

'More bounce' promised, more bounce delivered. Elasticity aplenty in Counce's late-1950s quintet, one of the better and more resilient bands working the West Coast scene at the time. Perhaps the best of the albums, *Exploring The Future*, appeared on Dooto/Boplicity and is currently unavailable, but *Landslide* is a fine substitute, showcasing Land's beefy tenor and Sheldon's very underrated soloing. Perkins, remembered best for his weird, crab-wise technique, was probably on better form with this band than anywhere else on record, but the real star – a point recognized by the drum solo 'The Butler Did It' on *Carl's Blues* and 'A Drum Conversation' on the bin-end *Sonority* – was Frank Butler, a powerful technician who shared Counce's own instinctive swing. Most of the material stems from the same half-dozen sessions, but is none the worse for that.

Stanley Cowell (born 1941) PIANO, ELECTRIC PIANO

***(*) Travellin' Man Black Lion BLCD 760178

Cowell; Steve Novosel (*b*); Jimmy Hopps (*d*). 6/69.

A supremely gifted player who bridges Bud Powell with the free movement of the 1960s, Cowell has received far less than his due of critical attention. His recorded output was for a long time restricted to work as a jobbing sideman for the Galaxy label – his own 1978 Galaxy LP, *Equipoise*, is now out of print – backing Art Pepper, John Klemmer, and Johnny Griffin, among others.

Recorded in London by Alan Bates, *Travellin' Man* was itself out of circulation for some time, but it offers a good synopsis of what he was doing during his first full decade as a professional musician, a period when he gigged with Marion Brown and Max Roach. 'You Took Advantage Of Me' is a tribute to Art Tatum, who apparently visited the Cowell home in Toledo, Ohio, and hammered the family piano into submission; see also 'Jitterbug Waltz' on the Maybeck session, below. Cowell's gentler side comes out in the title-track which, like 'Blues For The Viet Cong', is taken on electric piano, an instrument he played with great sensitivity.

The two long tracks, 'The Shuttle' and the oddly titled 'Photon in a Paper World', are both quite densely structured, with internal reverses and subtly varied repeats. Novosel and Hopps battle gamely but give no real sense of understanding what's expected of them. The sound is about scratch for the period, but comes across rather brusquely on CD.

***(*) We Three DIW 807

Cowell; Buster Williams (*b*); Frederick Waits (*d*). 12/87.

As the title suggests, this was issued as a collaborative trio rather than a straightforward Cowell session. Waits and the fecund Williams contribute half of the charts between them, and the high points tend to come on Williams pieces; 'Air Dancing' and 'Deceptacon' are good enough to be in anyone's book. Cowell's own main statement comes on 'Sienna', which is an on-going compositional essay. This is a particularly fine rendition of it, though the composer's solo on the version below just edges it into second place.

Waits died less than a year after the session and remains an unsung hero, a drummer with the lyrical touch Cowell always seemed to search out after his days with Roach. Waits's 'My Little Sharif' has a touching charm that recalls Cowell's own 'Wedding March' on *Travellin' Man*.

**** Sienna Steeplechase SCCD 31253

Cowell; Ron McClure (*b*); Keith Copeland (*d*). 7/89.

The two opening tracks – a passionate tribute to trumpeter/composer 'Cal Massey' (which also appears on the solo Maybeck Hall recital, below), and the gentle ballad, 'I Think It's Time To Say Goodbye' – take the measure of Cowell's extraordinary range. Copeland seems a little out of place on slower tracks, which might well have been done as duos, but his abrupt unison accents on 'Evidence' are startlingly effective. This is quite the best version of Monk's tune since the master's own and it represents a peak from which the album can only decline, in relative terms at least. A long 'I Concentrate On You' adds nothing in particular to the hundreds that have gone before, and it's only with the title-piece (one of a cycle of differently subtitled 'Sienna' compositions) and the last-but-one track, 'Dis Place', that Cowell lets loose his remarkable harmonic and rhythmic intelligence. An excellent album, recorded in slightly uncomfortable close-up.

*** Back to the Beautiful Concord CCD 4398

Cowell; Steve Coleman (*as, ss*); Santi Debriano (*b*); Joe Chambers (*d*). 7/89.

For some reason, this wasn't available at the time of our last edition. That reason may just be a recognition on someone's part that this is a below-par performance (we're talking about a vintage period from here to the mid-1990s) from a band that seems ill-adapted to Cowell's needs. Coleman is the main culprit, roaring through some of the subtler lyrical passages of 'But Beautiful', 'Prayer For Peace' and 'A Nightingale Sang In Berkeley Square', and rarely sounding accurately in tune with the piano. The trio functions pretty well, with one or two reservations about Debriano's sense of time, but there are too many distractions for the thing to stand up as a whole. A galling near-miss.

***(*) **Live At Maybeck Recital Hall** Concord CCD 4431
    Cowell solo. 6/90.
This is the fifth, and one of the best, of Concord's series of piano recitals in the beautiful acoustic of a small hall in Berkeley, California. Cowell features himself as a composer only sparingly – 'I Am Waiting', 'Little Sunny' and the concluding 'Cal Massey', a dedication to the neglected trumpeter/ composer (*q.v.*) – concentrating instead on demanding reinterpretations of standards and bebop staples. 'Softly, As In a Morning Sunrise' opens the set in a uncontroversially pianistic C minor, but then undergoes an astonishing *twelve* changes of key; the effect is not just blandly virtuosic but offers considerable insight into Cowell's harmonic imagination and way of approaching the subsequent pro- gramme. 'Stella By Starlight' and 'I'll Remember April', 'Out Of This World', 'Autumn Leaves' and 'Django' receive subtly off-centre readings. Wayne Shorter's 'Nefertiti' is a *tour de force*, rarely attempted by an unaccompanied pianist, and Charlie Parker's 'Big Foot' (or 'Air Conditioning') is a finger-breaker. An excellent set by a master at the height of his considerable powers.

**** **Close To You Alone** DIW 603E
    Cowell; Cecil McBee (*b*); Ronnie Burrage (*d*). 8/90.
No sense of anti-climax with this one, which catches the pianist in the middle of a purple streak. It begins with dramatic bass chords from McBee on his own '"D" Bass-ic Blues'. Cowell's entry is reminiscent of 1950s Cecil Taylor but ripples off in his characteristic Bud Powell vein. McBee and Burrage account for four of the seven tracks between them and, with 'Stella By Starlight' finishing the set, it's another example of Cowell's apparent unwillingness to foreground his own material. 'Equipoise' makes a welcome reappearance, its curiously balanced, rather static initial theme sounding almost as if it is built out of some five-note Chinese scale (and Cowell's stiff-fingered, chopsticks attack increases the effect) but then breaking out into a good-natured funk roll. Few current pianists are more interesting to listen to; Cowell seems quite genuinely to be expanding the improvising vocabulary of his instrument while remaining within relatively conventional jazz structures. High marks for McBee and Burrage, too, though the drummer's compositional skills are not yet fine-tuned.

***(*) **Departure No. 2** Steeplechase SCCD 31275
    Cowell; Walter Booker (*b*); Billy Higgins (*d*). 10/90.
*** **Games** Steeplechase SCCD 31293
    Cowell; Cheyney Thomas (*b*); Wardell Thomas (*d*). 8/91.
Cowell finished 1990 on a bit of a roll. Turning fifty, he seemed to have discovered new sources of energy. Recorded in Denmark, *Departure* is his most jagged and pugnacious recording for some time. 'Photon In The Paper World' and 'Splintered Ice' are both as technically impressive in their way as 'Softly' on the Maybeck record, and they manage to sustain a similar expressiveness. 'Four Harmonizations Of The Blues', however, on the later set, is almost as mechanical as it sounds. There's always been a strain of sheer cleverness in Cowell's playing, games with false symmetries and weird harmonic regresses; when it breaks through as obviously as this, it's decidedly tiresome.

    There's no doubt he's let down by the rhythm section on the later date. Thomas has a nice tone, but he never quite clicks with the drummer. There are some majestic episodes on 'From The Rivers Of Our Father', but they fail to add up to anything larger. 'Sienna: Welcome To This New World' is perfunctory and bland, and the new material fails to get things moving.

**** **Angel Eyes** Steeplechase SCCD 31339
    Cowell (*p* solo). 4/93.
*** **Bright Passion** Steeplechase SCCD 31328
    Cowell; Cheyney Thomas (*b*); Wardell Thomas (*d*). 4/93.
Angel Eyes offers a solid hour of near flawless piano jazz. From the opening, Coltrane-tinged 'Night Has A Thousand Eyes' to the small group of more demanding originals at the close – 'Akua', 'The Ladder', 'Abscretion' – Cowell grips the attention. The house piano at Steeplechase sounds rather light to us; it certainly isn't one of those great woofing concert things, but it's responsive enough for Cowell to weave a subtly inflected spell. Even John Lennon's 'Imagine', a pretty unpromising theme at the best of times, is turned into something rather special, without the original song's irritatingly winsome programme.

    The trio session is more than acceptable by any decent standard but, relative to the rest of the stuff Cowell was producing at this time, it's less than top-notch. We had some reservations about Thomas and Thomas; nothing fatal, but a definite air of un-finish and incomplete focus, which leaves the attention wandering long before the end.

***(*) **Setup** Steeplechase SCCD 31349
    Cowell; Eddie Henderson (*t*); Dick Griffin (*tb*); Rick Margitza (*ts*); Peter Washington (*b*); Billy Hart (*d*). 10/93.
Cowell has never seemed an excessively brooding player, but this is joyously upbeat by any standard. The

key track is 'Sendai Sendoff', featured in solo form on *Angel Eyes* but here arranged for an excellent and thoroughly sympathetic band. Henderson is in sterling form, always at his best when relieved of the responsibilities of leadership. A word, too, for the unsung Griffin, who gives the ensemble passages a rich, caramelly texture. The saxophonist is less well adapted to Cowell's idiom, and there are moments when he sounds uncertain and less than fully rehearsed. The Steeplechase sound, though, is flawless these days, and Nils Winther has clearly managed to create a *simpatico* environment in which musicians are encouraged to play as they feel, rather than keeping their eye on the clock and an ominously clicking meter. Cowell has seldom sounded so relaxed.

Lol Coxhill (born 1932) SOPRANO SAXOPHONE

***(*) **The Dunois Solos** Nato 95
    Coxhill (*ss* solo). 81.
***(*) **Three Blokes** FMP CD 63
    Coxhill; Steve Lacy, Evan Parker (*ss*). 94.
*** **Halim** Nato DK 018.53031
    Coxhill; Pat Thomas (*p, elec*). 92, 93.
*** **One Night In Glasgow** Scatter 03
    As above. 7/94.

It has been said that Coxhill is not so much an improviser as an instant composer, with a busker's (and that's what he used to be) instinct for the next thing to play. Having earned a crust with rock singer Kevin Ayers's Whole World group, he flirted with the avant-garde, formed a retro swing/chanson group called the Melody Four, and an overstrength combo known as the Johnny Rondo Duo, and in recent years has been a regular fixture emceeing (and, more infrequently, playing) at festivals in Britain and elsewhere. Perhaps as a result, he is a considerably underrated performer. His very distinctive style on soprano cannot be traced back to any of the obvious specialists on that instrument. Hearing him alongside Evan Parker and Steve Lacy, the two main title-contenders, makes it obvious that Lol has found his own way of playing the treacherous straight horn. His improvisations are direct, almost songlike, and constantly refer back to jazz. 'I Can't Get Started', included on the Nato duets with recent chum Thomas, is a Coxhill staple and the *locus classicus* for his wonderfully terse and unaffected changes playing. He kicks off the same album with 'That Old Black Magic', the kind of song that brings out his most skittish side. The Glasgow Jazz Festival gig is more subdued, but the musicianship is, if anything, more provocative and contained.

   The relationship with Thomas has been very fruitful in recent times, but Coxhill is most effective as a solo performer and the Dunois album, full of *in situ* responses, is still arguably his best, two long, slightly rambling improvisations that have the intimacy of conversation and the self-absorption of monologue in equal measure. It is interesting to go from these to the Thomas duos, with their generous sound-palette, and to the FMP session with its brittly uncompromising approach. The original concert was a mixture of solos, duos and trios, and it is possible to hear Coxhill functioning a little as Dewey Redman did in the Ornette groups of the 1970s, rationalizing and normalizing, finding the melody in the midst of fierce dissonance. It is a vivid, rather beautiful performance, and there is no sense in which he is overshadowed by his two technically more advanced partners. Proper recognition has come only slowly and has often had to combat patronizing lip-service; he is a complete original and a musician of real substance.

Crane River Jazz Band GROUP

(*) **The Legendary Crane River Jazz Band Lake LACD 57
    Ken Colyer (*t, v*); Sonny Morris (*t*); John R. T. Davies (*tb, bass c, cornopean*); Monty Sunshine
    (*cl*); Pat Hawes (*p*); Ben Marshall (*bj*); Julian Davies (*b*); Colin Bowden (*d*). 4–6/72.

Legendary indeed, but this isn't the record by which they'd want to be remembered. It's a 1972 reunion of the stalwarts who helped kick off the British trad scene some 20 years earlier. John R. T. Davies recorded it for fun and the results are as one would expect – sloppy, disjointed, inconsistent – but quite engaging if British trad is your meat. Colyer is as erratic as usual in his later days, the material is obvious and the only surprise concerns the peculiar bass-brass instruments that Davies brought along to play. Certainly there's only a trace of the sometimes manic intensity of original trad. Remastering from the home-brewed tapes is sound enough.

Hank Crawford (born 1934) ALTO AND BARITONE SAXOPHONES

*** **Midnight Ramble** Milestone MCD-9112-2
Crawford; Waymon Reed, Charlie Miller (*t*); Dick Griffin (*tb*); David Newman (*ts*); Howard Johnson (*bs*); Dr John (*ky*); Calvin Newborne (*g*); Charles Greene (*b*); Bernard Purdie (*d*). 11/82.

(*) **Indigo Blue Milestone MCD-9119-2
Crawford; Martin Banks, Danny Moore (*t*); David Newman (*ts*); Howard Johnson (*bs*); Melvin Sparks (*g*); Wilbur Bascomb (*b*); Bernard Purdie (*d*). 8/83.

** **Mr Chips** Milestone MCD-9149-2
Crawford; Randy Brecker, Alan Rubin (*t*); David Newman (*ts*); Howard Johnson (*bs*); Richard Tee (*ky*); Cornell Dupree (*g*); Wilbur Bascomb (*b*); Bernard Purdie (*d*). 11/86.

*** **Night Beat** Milestone MCD-9168-2
Crawford; Lew Soloff, Alan Rubin (*t*); David Newman (*ts, f*); Howard Johnson (*bs*); Dr John (*ky*); Melvin Sparks (*g*); Wilbur Bascomb (*b*); Bernard Purdie (*d*). 9–10/88.

*** **Groove Master** Milestone MCD-9182-2
Lou Marini (*ts*) replaces Newman, add Gloria Coleman (*org*), others as above. 2–3/90.

Hank Crawford says that he tries 'to keep the melody so far in front that you can almost sing along', and that irresistibly vocal style lends his simple approach to the alto a deep-rooted conviction. His records are swinging parties built on the blues, southern R&B – Crawford apprenticed in the bands of Ike and Tina Turner and Ray Charles – and enough bebop to keep a more hardened jazz listener involved. He recorded 12 albums for Atlantic in the 1960s, but none of them is currently in the catalogue, and his renewed career has been thanks to the initiative of Milestone, who have provided him with consistently sympathetic settings. There's little to choose between the albums listed above, all of them smartly organized around Crawford's libidinous wail: *Mr Chips* gets lower marks for a mundane choice of material, while *Midnight Ramble*, *Night Beat* and *Groove Master* are enlivened by the inspiring presence of Dr John on piano and organ. Typical of Crawford's mature command is the way he empowers Whitney Houston's 'Saving All My Love For You' on *Groove Master* with a real authority.

*** **Soul Survivors** Milestone MCD-9142-2
Crawford; Jimmy McGriff (*ky*); George Benson, Jim Pittsburg (*g*); Mel Lewis, Bernard Purdie (*d*). 1/86.

(*) **Steppin' Up Milestone MCD-9153-2
Crawford; Jimmy McGriff (*ky*); Billy Preston (*p*); Jimmy Ponder (*g*); Vance James (*d*). 6/87.

(*) **On The Blue Side Milestone MCD-9177-2
As above. 7/89.

Crawford shares leadership duties with McGriff on these small-group albums, and between them they update the sound of the 1960s organ combo without surrendering the juice and fire of the original music. *Soul Survivors* is the best of the three because the renewed partnership is at its freshest, and Benson is for once employed in a worthwhile jazz context; but, taken a few tracks at a time, all three discs are exhilarating.

(*) **Portrait Milestone MCD-9192-2
Crawford; David 'Fathead' Newman (*ts*); Johnny Hammond (*org*); Jimmy Ponder (*g*); Vance James (*d*). 90.

*** **South-Central** Milestone MCD-9201-2
Crawford; Stan Hope, Dr John (*p*); Gloria Coleman (*org*); Melvin Sparks (*g*); Peter Martin Weiss, Wilbur Bascomb (*b*); Grady Tate, Bernard Purdie (*d*). 2/90–8/92.

Crawford soldiers on with more out of the same locker. While there's little danger of his delivering a duff record in this style, there's nothing in either of these sets that will be required listening for any who've heard one or two out of the previous half-dozen. Still, *South-Central* racks up some good results; a couple of especially fulsome ballads (winding up with a Christmas tune that strayed in from another date) and a rollicking 'Splanky' give it an extra nudge.

***(*) **Heart And Soul** Rhino/Atlantic R2 71673 2CD
As above Milestone albums, plus: Marcus Belgrave, Lee Harper, Phil Guilbeau, John Hunt, Fielder Floyd, Joe Newman, Ernie Royal, Bernie Glow, Snooky Young (*t*); Jimmy Cleveland, Benny Powell, Tom Malone (*tb*); Frank Wess (*as*); Seldon Powell, James Clay, Harvey Thompson, Abdul Baari, Wendell Harrison (*ts*); Leroy Cooper, Howard Johnson, Pepper Adams, Alonzo Shaw, Ronnie Cuber, Jim Horn (*bs*); Ray Charles, Richard Tee, Clayton Ivey (*p*); Lucky Peterson (*org*); Frankie Crawford (*ky*); B. B. King (*g, v*); Steve Cropper, Will McFarlane, Sonny Forrest, Eric Gale, Hugh McCracken (g); Edgar Willis, Charlie Green, Ron Carter, Gary King, Willie Weeks (*b*); Richie Goldberg, Milt Turner, Bruno Carr, Bernard Purdie, Roger Hawkins (*d*); Etta James (*v*). 7/58–5/92.

Another handsome package in the Rhino/Atlantic series gives us something close to the definitive Hank Crawford retrospective. It starts, fittingly, with the Ray Charles band at Newport, but the key early tracks on disc one are those from the *More Soul*, *Soul Clinic* and *From The Heart* albums (otherwise unavailable on CD). Here is the fulsome, slow, blues-drenched Crawford sound on 'Angel Eyes' and 'Misty', plus the peppery grooves of 'The Peeper' and 'Read 'Em And Weep'. Crucially, the arrangments are horn-based and use no keyboards, so the charts take on a declamatory, gospelized strain that underlines the soul only in the alto solos. It's a grand formula, but a formula none the less, and it palls a little over two long CDs. So the second disc, after a few Creed Taylor rhapsodies from the 1970s, turns to the Milestone albums for the rest of the compilation. Tracks with B. B. King and Etta James restore to Crawford his righteous role as a signifying sideman and pretty much close the circle on this middle-weight's gratifying career. Remastering is exemplary throughout, with the Atlantic tracks sounding as good as new.

Ray Crawford (born 1924) GUITAR

(*) **Smooth Groove Candid 79028
    Crawford; Johnny Coles (*t*); Cecil Payne (*bs*); Junior Mance (*p*); Ben Tucker (*b*); Frankie Dunlop (*d*). 2/61.
Easily overlooked, Crawford followed a course midway between Grant Green's clean, single-note lines and Kenny Burrell's meatier and more ringing sound. It was a modest but unpretentious talent. This single disc under his own name (Crawford also saw service with Gil Evans and Sonny Stitt) has little of the tense propulsion he brought to the rhythm section on Evans's *Out Of The Cool*. Pushed to the forefront, he marks time as often as not, leaving the more dramatic solo statements to Payne, Mance and the vastly underrated Coles.

    The recording is a little too middle-ish to pick out much detail in the ensembles. The title-track is rather fuzzy, and there really isn't enough momentary detail in 'The Compendium Suite' to merit the promin-ence it's given. However, Crawford isn't at all well known, and *Smooth Groove* is still worth checking out, especialy by jazz guitar enthusiasts.

Marilyn Crispell (born 1947) PIANO

*** **Live In Berlin** Black Saint BSR 120069
    Crispell; Billy Bang (*vn*); Peter Kowald (*b*); John Betsch (*d*). 11/82.
Crispell seems destined to become a major presence in the '90s. In retrospect, the Coltrane and Cecil Taylor influences weighed much less heavily on her earliest recordings than was routinely thought and, though she has regularly returned to Coltrane in particular as a kind of guiding spirit (see below), she is certainly not a slavish imitator.

    She holds up strongly in some pretty rugged company in this early set from the Total Music Meeting. The shift to CD has lifted the piano considerably and effects a bit of separation and space in the background. The set is dominated by a huge piece, 'ABC', dedicated to her next most important influence, Anthony Braxton, with whom she has worked very profitably for many years. Her background in classical, and particularly Baroque, music is still clearly audible as she negotiates oblique contra-puntal passages and wild, seamless fugues. The two string-players seem worlds apart and don't interact very effectively. Kowald replaced guitarist Wes Brown, who had appeared on an earlier Cadence LP called *Spirit Music* and seemed much more in tune with Crispell's conception.

**** **For Coltrane** Leo CDLR 195
    Crispell (*p* solo). 7/87.
***(*) **Live In San Francisco** Music & Arts 633
    As above. 10/89.
Solo performances by Crispell are dramatic, harmonically tense and wholly absorbing. Though the excellent *Rhythms Hung In Undrawn Sky* has disappeared from the Leo catalogue, along with *And Your Ivory Voice Sings*, a duo with percussionist Doug James, they have been replaced by a recording of a remarkable concert given in London in the summer of 1987, when Crispell supported Alice Coltrane and the two Coltrane boys, Ravi and Omar, with a solo set dedicated to Alice's late husband. Opening with a torrid 'Dear Lord' and closing with the billowing 'After The Rain', she improvised a series of 'collages' in memory of the great saxophonist. She also performed a piece called 'Coltrane Time', a title of convenience for a sequence of rhythmic cells on which the saxophonist had been experimenting in the period immediately before his death.

A beautiful record, *For Coltrane* is a companion-piece to the deleted *Labyrinths* on Victo and is more immediately appealing than the San Francisco session. Recorded shortly after the Californian earthquake of 1989, it alternates the subdued aftershocks and beatific restorations of her own 'Tromos' and Coltrane's 'Dear Lord' with some unexpectedly light and romantic touches. 'When I Fall In Love' has a hesitant shyness that makes the theme statement all the more moving; the same applies to the humour of Monk's 'Ruby, My Dear', which underlines Crispell's impressive rhythmic awareness. (Interestingly, the CD also contains two 'sampler' tracks from other Music & Arts titles featuring Crispell: the long 'Composition 136' with Anthony Braxton from the Vancouver duets record mentioned above (CD 611) and a shorter group track with another senior collaborator, Reggie Workman, and his highly inventive ensemble (CD 634).)

*** **The Kitchen Concert** Leo LR 178
    Crispell; Mark Dresser (*b*); Gerry Hemingway (*d*). 2/89.
This marks a slight but significant change of direction for Crispell. In place of free or structured improvisation, *The Kitchen Concert* documents a first, rather tentative, confrontation with written forms of her own. Her own recorded misgivings are reflected to some degree in the music itself, which exposes areas of hesitancy rarely encountered in her improvised performances. The tonalities are a little forced, in sharp contrast to her normal instinctive 'centring' of a piece. By her own remarkable standards a less than wholly successful album, it still merits close attention, not least for the contributions of Dresser and of Hemingway, whose insistent (if rather similar) solos on 'Ahmadu/Sierra Leone' and the Tristano-dedicated 'For L. T.' lend the music a much-needed impulse.

**** **Gaia** Leo Records LR 152
    Crispell; Reggie Workman (*b*); Doug James (*d, perc*). 3/87.
*** **Live In Zurich** Leo Records LR CDLR 122
    As above, except omit James; add Paul Motian (*d, perc*). 4/89.
Gaia is one of the finest composition/improvisation records of the 1980s, a hymn to the planet that is neither mawkish nor sentimental, but tough-minded, coherent and entire. Spared conventional rhythm-section duties, Workman and James combine extremely well, producing both a dense ripieno for Crispell's dramatic concertante effects and a powerful drama of their own. *Live In Zurich* finds her working against a much more conventional rhythm (though Motian shares James's delicacy of touch). Though it consists of individual pieces (including the obligatory Coltrane, 'Dear Lord'), the Zurich set comes to resemble a single suite, opening with some haunting North African *vocalise* (an equally obligatory nod in Taylor's direction) and developing strongly into one of her finest recorded piano performances.

**** **Overlapping Hands: Eight Segments** FMP CD30
    Crispell; Irene Schweizer (*p*). 90.
***(*) **Piano Duets** Leo CD LR 206/207 2CD
    Crispell; Georg Gräwe (*p*). 10 & 12/91.
Like much of Crispell's best work, *Overlapping Hands* is a concert performance, and a duo at that. There are moments when it might almost be one person playing, so close is the understanding between the two women, but for the fact that they do sound very different. Schweizer's sound is sharper and more Europeanized; Crispell's draws deeper on an American tradition and constantly refers to tonal centres that her collaborator wants to push away to the very boundaries of the music. The recording is near perfect, and a tremendous advance on some of FMP's more Heath Robinsonish concert efforts; the music is a joy.

The duos with Gräwe are fascinating, largely for the second disc, on which they play detuned pianos. Pitched a quarter-tone apart in the middle register, with upper and lower strings sharped and flatted respectively in accordance with Thomas Henke's 'diagonal tuning' system, they sound alien and unfamiliar. The improvisations are understandably more textural than usual, obviating the minor culture clash of the performances with Schweizer. Unfortunately, the recording levels are too fierce to register all the finer detail and, though there are substantial individual contributions from both players (who are not difficult to distinguish), it's a pity that Crispell hasn't had an opportunity to explore this line of inquiry more fully and in a purely solo context. The duets provide an information overload.

*** **Duo** Knitting Factory KFWCD 117
    Crispell; Gerry Hemingway (*perc*). 92.
***(*) **Marilyn Crispell Trio: Highlights From The 1992 American Tour** Music & Arts CD758
    Crispell; Reggie Workman (*b*); Gerry Hemingway (*d*). Summer 92.
**** **Santuerio** Leo CD LR 191
    Crispell; Mark Feldman (*vn*); Hank Roberts (*clo*); Gerry Hemingway (*d*). 5/93.
The 1990s saw a change in Crispell's work and a gradual movement towards more structured com-

position. The main substance of the music is, however, still generated by improvisation, and that is particularly noticeable on the first two items.

The trio with Reggie Workman is marked by slow harmonic transformations that largely develop in the bass register, accented by piano right hand and percussion. Though several of the pieces remain 'open', there is a developing emphasis on determinant form, as in the 'Suite For Trio' and the quite brief 'Mouvements Changeables' which appears (perhaps accidentally) to quote from the Dutch composer Ton de Leeuw's *Mouvements rétrogrades*.

Hemingway is the common factor in the group. A strong but by no means aggressive player, he concentrates in the spaces in the music, stippling them with detail. On the duo, it becomes almost too self-conscious a mannerism. It works wonderfully well in the combination with Workman, for which Hemingway (true to his surname) strips down to essentials.

The most recent of the discs marks Crispell's full emergence as a composer. Again, much of the music is improvised, but it is linked by elemental structures – pieces include 'Air / Fire', 'Water', 'Burning Air / Wood', 'Red Shift', 'Repercussions Of Air And Light' – and a visionary spirit. The opening 'Entrances Of Light', inspired by a Nathaniel Mackey poem, would fit comfortably into a programme of contemporary composition. Introduced by a rapturous Mark Feldman solo, it develops slowly and quietly, anticipating the underlying drama of the 13-minute title-track which lies at the centre of the disc. Here the central action is between Crispell and Hemingway. The drummer's solo is stunning, but what follows is even more impressive: a long, restless tussle between percussion and piano. Cello and violin break in with heavy ostinato shapes, and Feldman briefly rises out of the mêlée with an echo of his opening phrases. Like *Gaia*, *Santuerio* tackles huge themes, but there is nothing grandiose or overblown about it. The music is beautifully controlled and specific. Crispell's finest hour.

(****) **Stellar Pulsations / Three Composers** Leo CD LR 194
 Crispell; Don Byron (*cl*); Ellen Polansky (*p*); Gerry Hemingway (*d*); WDR Radio Orchestra, David de Villiers (*cond*). 7/92.
Equally marvellous, but a further step away from the immediate concerns of this *Guide*, *Stellar Pulsations* represents the work of three composers who are exploring the borderlines of improvisation and formally scored music. Manfred Niehaus's *Concerto For Marilyn* has a wholly scored and fixed orchestral part, with partial notation for the piano player in the first movement. This part is called 'Concerto For Chico'; movements three and four also refer to the Marx Brothers. The second movement is a swaying 'unhoused tango' in which piano and orchestra conjoin in open-ended tempo. 'Concerto For Harpo' is a piano/harp duet. A timpanist joins in for 'Concerto To Provoke Groucho', leading to a final cadenza for Crispell.

Pozzi Eschot's *Mirabilis II* draws on music by Mother Hildegard (a figure much admired by both Crispell and Anthony Braxton) to create a framework for trio improvisation. As before, Crispell and Hemingway seem to be in complete communication, but Don Byron's part is a little less sure-footed and often sounds as if he's merely reading off. The balance of composition and improvisation is clearer in Robert Cogan's *Costellar Pulsations*, which starts the disc. Here Crispell improvises over Ellen Polansky's notated (but not immutable) score, from which the performer can select and re-order elements. Echoing the language and ideas of *Overlapping Hands* (above), Crispell allows the piece to divide naturally into expressive segments, some of which strongly suggest tonality, others the orderly but indefinable progress of natural (or cosmic) events.

Though less likely to appeal to straight jazz fans, this is another beautiful record and, in its way, another important stage in Crispell's development as an artist.

***(*) **Hyperion** Music & Arts CD 852
 Crispell; Peter Brötzmann (*sax, cl, tarogato*); Hamid Drake (*d, hand d*). 6/92.
*** **Cascades** Music & Arts CD 853
 Crispell; Barry Guy (*b*); Gerry Hemingway (*d, vib, gamelan*). 6/93.
Two contrasting trios documenting Crispell's growing stature as darling of the festival circuit. Both were recorded in Canada but at different locations. *Cascades* reunites her with Hemingway, who increasingly sees himself not just as a drummer but also as a tuned percussionist, contributing vibes and gamelan to the mix; Guy is also a highly structured and often tuneful player, and the combination is sometimes too cluttered, though the bassist also understands better than the two Americans how to leave light and shade, space and air, in this music. The trio with Peter Brötzmann and Hamid Drake is, predictably, more intense and frenetic, though the saxophonist does also have his delicately lyrical side, and he defers at moments during 'Hyperion I' to Crispell's desire to take the music down a more expressive path. Which is not to say he has to defer to her 'feminine' side. She sets off like an express train as usual and, as often in the past, it's difficult to gauge how responsive, how much of a listening player she now is. Solo performance (see below) may still be her forte.

**** **Spring Tour 1994** Alice ALCD 13
    Crispell; Anders Jormin (*b*); Raymond Strid (*d*). 94.
Well, the season seems completely apposite for music as fresh and affirmative as this. There used to be – probably still is – an awful test-piece for pianists by Christian Sinding called 'Rustle Of Spring'. No one need ever perform or listen to it again . . . Where often Crispell can sound slightly dense and introspective, here she dares to play somewhat more simply and directly. She is undoubtedly encouraged by her two colleagues. Strid has a brisk, beery exuberance (and does a famous line in homebrew, incidentally) which doesn't invite tortured, existential dramatics, while the bassist is quite simply one of the most beautiful stylists currently working on the instrument. Heady, uplifting stuff, perhaps more immediately winning than the excellent things below.

**** **Band On The Wall** Matchless MRCD 25
    Crispell; Eddie Prévost (*d, perc*). 5/94.
***(*) **Destiny** Okka OD 12003
    Crispell: Fred Anderson (*ts*); Hamid Drake (*d, perc*). 8/94.
Recorded live during the 'Women of New Music' festival in Chicago, the Okka set is marred – Crispell-wise – only by having the piano mixed down too low and occasionally swamped by saxophone and percussion. Otherwise it finds her in thoroughly sympathetic company. Anderson's diction is Coltrane-influenced but generously varied and thoroughly personalized. As with Braxton and Prévost (below), this seems like a relationship written in the stars, and it allows them to build up whole areas of interaction in which the exchange of ideas is almost too fast to follow. Drake provides sterling accompaniment and, like Prévost, often takes the initiative in breaking up Crispell's long, suspended lines into shorter, more discursive sections.

    The Matchless disc was also recorded live, at the Manchester venue called Band on the Wall. It's a fiery, sometimes almost violent performance, in which ideas are run together with a challenging insouciance. Extravagant as she often is, Crispell has rarely sounded so thoroughly unfettered; oddly, perhaps, because Prévost is a highly disciplined drummer and certainly one of the most swinging in a free idiom. One slight oddity of the set is the inclusion of the Denny Zeitlin composition, 'Quiet Now', towards the end. How many repertory pieces has this pairing explored?

***(*) **Live at Mills College, 1995** Music & Arts CD 899
    Crispell (*p* solo). 1/95.
Very much a showcase performance, back on a campus which in many respects helped define the type of music Crispell plays. 'As Our Tongues Lap Up The Burning Air' reappears from the session with Prévost, in an even more incendiary version, despite the appearance of restraint. There is a further nod to the Coltrane heritage with a wonderful medleyed version of 'The Night Has 1,000 Eyes', and a slightly congested Monk cover, 'Reflections'. 'Song For Abdullah' is a relatively long-standing original, having been written for the Leo set, *Rhythms Hung In Undrawn Sky*, more than a decade ago.

    Neither the hall acoustic nor the piano sounds quite right for a recital hall at a major music college, but it's possible that the poor thing is going out of tune as she plays. It has been known.

Sonny Criss (1927–77) ALTO SAXOPHONE, SOPRANO SAXOPHONE

*** **California Boppin'** Fresh Sound FSR CD 156
    Criss; Al Killian, Howard McGhee (*t*); Teddy Edwards, Wardell Gray (*ts*); Charlie Fox, Russ Freeman, Hampton Hawes, Dodo Marmarosa (*p*); Barney Kessel (*g*); Harry Babasin, Red Callender, Addison Farmer (*b*); Tim Kennedy, Jackie Mills, Roy Porter (*d*). 4, 6, 7 & 10/47.
***(*) **Memorial Album** DIW 302
    Criss; Al Killian, Clark Terry (*t*); Dexter Gordon, Wardell Gray (*ts*); Gil Barrios, Jimmy Bunn, Charles Fox, Hampton Hawes (*p*); Dave Bryant, Billy Hadnott, Shifty Henry, Clarence Johnson (*b*); Frank Butler, Tim Kennedy, Billy Snyder, Chuck Thompson (*d*); Damita Jo (*v*). 10/47, 8/50, 9/52, 6/65.
***(*) **Sonny Criss Quartet, 1949–1957** Fresh Sound FSRCD 64
    Criss; Hampton Hawes (*p*); Iggy Shevack, Buddy Woodson (*b*); Chuck Thompson (*d*). 9/49, 11/57.
Criss was perhaps a little too tightly wrapped for the destiny that seemed to await him. Though it was the altogether more robust Sonny Stitt – with whom Criss is occasionally confused – to whom Charlie Parker promised 'the keys of the Kingdom', it was Criss out on the West Coast who inherited most of the ambiguities of Parker's legacy.

    California wasn't a happy place for Bird, by and large, and there's something hectic, almost desperate, in Criss's super-fast runs and soaring, high-register figures. The earliest of material is rather derivative but provides several excellent opportunities to hear Criss's pure, urgent tone and delivery; he comes in behind Wardell Gray on 'Groovin' High' almost impatiently, with a little flurry of notes, before stretching out and shaping those distinctive wailing passages and held notes. The June 1947 material, with the rhythm section that backed Parker at the Hi-De-Ho in Los Angeles earlier that year (Hawes, Farmer, Porter) is probably the best on the disc, with a particularly fine version of 'The Man I Love' that also features Teddy Edwards and Howard McGhee. Two long jam-sessions have lots of episodic interest but are marred by Al Killian's dreary high-note work.

The DIW memorial is an excellent buy, offering a bitty but reasonably comprehensive survey of the whole career with the exception of Criss's brief Indian summer of the mid-'70s. Unfortunately, there's an overlap with *California Boppin'*, and quite a substantial one; doubly unfortunately, it's the October 1947 Portland jam with Killian and Wardell Gray. However, the record's worth having for the 1965 material with Hampton Hawes (see below), and a one-off track from 1950 ('I Can't Give You Anything But Love') with Clark Terry and Dexter Gordon, on which Criss more than holds his own. Hawes spurs him.

He's on hand for both the sessions on the other Fresh Sound, playing a little neatly on the 1949 tracks, which have a brittle politeness suggestive of buried tensions in the studio, but opening out majestically on the two standards which start the November 1957 session. On 'Willow Weep For Me', Criss delivers a gently sorrowful solo, spoken with manly regret and without a wasted gesture. Hawes matches him, and bassist Woodson – an unremarked player – comes in with a fluent statement of his own. In this still small discography, this has to be considered a significant release.

***(*) **This Is Criss!** Original Jazz Classics OJC 430
  Criss; Walter Davis (*p*); Paul Chambers (*b*); Alan Dawson (*d*). 66.
**** **Portrait Of Sonny Criss** Original Jazz Classics OJC 655
  As above. 67.
These are probably the two best Criss albums currently available. His ability to invest banal tunes with real feeling (see *I'll Catch The Sun!*, below, for real alchemy) is evident on 'Sunrise, Sunset', a tune from *Fiddler On The Roof* given a brief but intense reading on *This Is Criss!*. Criss does something similar, though at greater length, to 'Days Of Wine And Roses', adjusting his timbre subtly throughout the opening choruses.

'Wee' on *Portrait* takes him back to bop days, an astonishing performance that manages to skate over a lack of solid ideas with sheer virtuosity. 'Smile' bears comparison with Jackie McLean's readings, but the real stand-out tracks are 'On A Clear Day', which is hugely emotional, and 'God Bless The Child'. The CD also offers a bonus 'Love For Sale', which probably deserved to be left out first time round. The band is good and Davis (who wrote 'Greasy' on *This Is Criss!* and 'A Million Or More Times' on *Portrait*) is the mainstay.

**** **Sonny's Dream** Original Jazz Classics OJC 707
  Criss; Conte Candoli (*t*); Dick Nash (*tb*); Ray Draper (*tba*); David Sherr (*as*); Teddy Edwards
  (*ts*); Peter Christlieb (*bs*); Tommy Flanagan (*p*); Al McKibbon (*b*); Everett Brown Jr (*d*). 68.
This is a most welcome CD reissue of a project subtitled 'Birth Of The New Cool' and featuring six Horace Tapscott compositions and arrangements. Though he has only recently begun to receive wider recognition, Tapscott's influence on the West Coast has been enormous, and this was a rare chance for Criss to play in front of a carefully orchestrated mid-size band.

'Sonny's Dream' is an astonishing opener, with luminous solos from both Criss and Tommy Flanagan. Criss switches to soprano for the brief 'Ballad For Samuel', dedicated to a respected teacher, but profoundly marked by Coltrane (who had recently died). Tapscott's inventiveness and political sensibilities are equally engaged on 'Daughter Of Cochise' (a unusually relaxed solo from Criss) and 'Black Apostles', originally dedicated to Arthur Blythe (another Angelean saxophonist who made a personal accommodation with Bird's idiom) but transformed into a brooding and ferocious lament for the three martyrs of the black liberationist movement.

A remarkable album that lapses only to the extent that the band is sometimes reduced to providing highly coloured backdrops for Tapscott's American history lessons and Criss's soloing (which bears comparison with Parker's on the 'With Strings' sessions).

***(*) **I'll Catch The Sun!** Prestige PR 7628
  Criss; Hampton Hawes (*p*); Monty Budwig (*b*); Shelly Manne (*d*). 1/69.
Something of a comeback for Criss and perhaps the most amenable and sympathetic band he ever had, reuniting him with Hawes. The material is vile but players like these made a living out of turning sows' ears into silken purses, and both 'California Dreaming' and 'Cry Me A River' have a genuine depth of focus. Criss sounds composed and confident in this company, and solos with impressive logic and considerable emotion.

*** **Crisscraft** Muse MCD 6015
  Criss; Ray Crawford (*g*); Dolo Coker (*p*); Larry Gales (*b*); Jimmie Smith (*d*). 2 & 10/75.

***(*) **Out Of Nowhere** Muse MCD 5089
      As above, except omit Crawford. 10/75.
During the early 1970s, Criss tried to bury his own troubles, working with juvenile alcoholics in the Watts ghetto. His return to playing finds his tone unimpaired and more and more marked by Coltrane devices. Long, harmonically dense lines pile up on top of one another, almost as if he is trying to fit in too much musical information in the time available.

    Crisscraft cobbles together a rather forced and effusive session featuring guitarist Crawford with a single out-take from the October session on *Out Of Nowhere*: an alternative take of 'All The Things You Are' which doesn't add anything to the original release. The standards are all excellent and the saxophonist's solos on 'My Ideal' and the title-tune are beautifully crafted, with a gentle, slightly winsome quality. The shadows were gathering, though; in 1977, brought to the brink yet again, Sonny Criss shot himself dead.

John Crocker CLARINET, ALTO AND TENOR SAXOPHONES, VOCAL

(*) **Easy Living Timeless TTD 561
      Crocker; Roger Munns (*p*); Vic Pitt (*b*); Jimmy Tagford (*d*). 6/89.
(*) **All Of Me Timeless TTD 585
      As above. 4/93.
A stalwart of Chris Barber's groups, Crocker's style hews closely to a dated rather than a neo-classic idea of what swing-style clarinet should sound like – exaggerated phrasing, plush tone but a glibness standing in for fluency. On tenor, when he tries to do a Websterish treatment of 'I Can't Get Started', it sounds all wrong, and the alto treatment of 'I Hadn't Anyone Till You' isn't much more appealing. But Goodman staples like 'Avalon' and 'Rose Room' turn out better: Crocker knows this stuff well, and he plays it well. The rhythm section play cheerfully behind him. *All Of Me* follows a similar line, and does it that bit better. Docked a notch for the vocals, though.

Hal Crook TROMBONE

*** **Only Human** RAM RMCD 4506
      Crook; John Lockwood (*b*); Bob Gullotti (*d*). 6/93.
Crook has been a member of Phil Woods' group for some time and seemingly hasn't felt moved to record under his own name until now. This is a tough discipline; brass and rhythm without a harmony instrument requires a very confident approach, and Crook seems to take it in his stride. Most of the material is his own, and it sounds relaxed and thoughtful. The only exceptions are Ary Barroso's 'Brazil' (a mistake) and 'Suddenly It's Spring' (which is gorgeous). The opening 'Show' is something of a warm-up, but the title-piece, at almost identical length, is packed with meaty music and very expressive playing. Lockwood and Gullotti are first class and, with so much weight thrown on them, are admirably willing to shoulder a lot of the playing.

Bob Crosby (1913–93) VOCAL, LEADER

*** **You Can Call It Swing** Halcyon DHDL121
      Crosby; Yank Lawson, Phil Hart, Zeke Zarchey, Andy Ferretti (*t*); Ward Silloway, Art Foster, Warren Smith, Mark Bennett (*tb*); Gil Rodin, Matty Matlock (*cl, as*); Noni Bernardi (*as*); Eddie Miller (*cl, ts*); Dean Kincaide (*ts*); Bob Zurke, Gil Bowers, Joe Sullivan (*p*); Nappy Lamare (*g*); Bob Haggart (*b*); Ray Bauduc (*d*); Judy Garland, Connie Boswell (*v*). 4/36–2/37.
*** **A Strange New Rhythm In My Heart** Halcyon DHDL122
      As above, except add Billy Butterfield (*t*), Bill DePew, Joe Kearns (*as*), Kay Weber (*v*); omit Hart, Foster, Bowers, Sullivan, Garland and Boswell. 2–11/37.
*** **You're Driving Me Crazy** Halcyon DHDL123
      As above, except add Charlie Spivak (*t*), Connie Boswell (*v*); omit Ferretti, Bennett, Bernardi, Kincaide. 11/37–2/38.
*** **How Can You Forget?** Halcyon DHDL125
      As above, except add Irving Fazola (*cl*); omit Boswell. 2–3/38.
**** **Bob Crosby 1937 To 1938** Jazz Classics In Digital Stereo RPCD 631
      Yank Lawson, Charlie Spivak, Billy Butterfield, Zeke Zarchey, Sterling Bose, Andy Ferretti (*t*); Ward Silloway, Mark Bennett, Warren Smith (*tb*); Irving Fazola (*cl*); Matty Matlock (*cl, as*); Noni Bernardi, Joe Kearns (*as*); Eddie Miller (*cl, ts*); Gil Rodin, Dean Kincaide (*ts*); Bob Zurke (*p*); Nappy Lamare (*g*); Bob Haggart, Haig Stephens (*b*); Ray Bauduc (*d*). 37–38.

***(*) **Bob Crosby** Zeta/Jazz Archives ZET 766
    As above. 36–38.
***(*) **Bob Crosby's Bob Cats Vol. One 1937–1938** Swaggie CD 501
    Yank Lawson, Billy Butterfield, Sterling Bose (*t*); Warren Smith (*tb*); Matty Matlock, Irving
    Fazola (*cl*); Eddie Miller (*cl, ts*); Bob Zurke (*p*); Nappy Lamare (*g, v*); Bob Haggart (*b*); Ray
    Bauduc (*d*); Connie Boswell, Marion Mann (*v*). 11/37–10/38.
*** **Bob Crosby's Bob Cats Vol. Two 1939** Swaggie CD 502
    As appropriate records above. 11/37–9/39.
*** **Bob Crosby's Bob Cats Vol. Three 1940** Swaggie CD 503
    Crosby; Billy Butterfield, Max Herman (*t*); Muggsy Spanier (*c*); Warren Smith, Floyd O'Brien
    (*tb*); Irving Fazola, Hank D'Amico (*cl*); Eddie Miller (*ts*); Jess Stacy (*p*); Nappy Lamare (*g, v*);
    Bob Haggart (*b*); Ray Bauduc (*d*); Marion Mann, Bing Crosby, The Merry Macks (*v*). 2–12/40.
*** **I Remember You** Vintage Jazz Classics VJC-1046
    Crosby; Yank Lawson, Max Herman, Lyman Vunk (*t*); Floyd O'Brien, Elmer Smithers, Buddy
    Morrow, Bruce Squires, Pete Carpenter (*tb*); Matty Matlock (*cl*); Art Mendelsohn, Arthur
    Rando, Ted Klein (*as*); Eddie Miller (*ts, cl*); Gil Rodin (*ts*); Jess Stacy (*p*); Nappy Lamare (*g*);
    Bob Haggart (*b*); Ray Bauduc (*d*); Liz Tilton, Gloria DeHaven, Muriel Lane, Lee & Lyn Wilde,
    David Street (*v*). 41–42.

Crosby's band – fronted by the handsome crooner himself, brother of Bing and a charming vocalist, if
hardly a jazz singer – worked an unusual furrow among the swing-era bands. Their small-group sides,
under the name The Bob Cats, were cast in a tempestuous Dixieland style, the music a throwback to the
best hot music of a decade before, and many of the full band's best sides – 'South Rampart Street
Parade', 'Royal Garden Blues', 'Wolverine Blues' – were made from the same mould. The fuming
trumpet of Yank Lawson, Eddie Miller's fluently hot tenor, the New Orleans-styled clarinets of Irving
Fazola and Matty Matlock – all created an authenticity which, say, Tommy Dorsey's Clambake Seven
could only hint at. Yet, as usual, so many of the orchestra's records were tainted by schmaltz and
novelty that the integrity of the best music is always compromised in any chronological survey. Crosby
was game enough to give his men their share of solo space, on the lesser tracks as well as the jazz-
directed ones, which means that all is seldom lost. But in the end even The Bob Cats were playing the
miserable likes of 'Adios Americano', 'Oh Mistres Mine' and 'You Oughta Hang Your Heart In Shame'.
    The compilations listed above should satisfy all but the most dedicated Crosby followers. Robert
Parker's Jazz Classics set is one of the best examples of his remastering and offers many of the very best
tracks. The Halcyon discs are a complete ongoing survey in chronological order, but that means that the
best sides are mixed with the mediocre, and the shoddy packaging and sometimes dull remastering make
this one for specialists only. Swaggie have collected all the Bob Cats tracks on their three discs (some
tracks by the full 1937 band are included on the second volume as a makeweight) and the remastering is
very fine. *Volume One* includes the tremendous debut session by the small group, and the first six tracks
almost garner four stars on their own, but the rest is let down by the likes of 'Big Bass Viol'. The Zeta
collection is another solid cross-section of tracks from the band's best period. *I Remember You* features
rare material by the wartime band – some material of the 'We're Riding For Uncle Sammy Now' ilk, but
the band can still boil water when it wants.

Connie Crothers PIANO

(*) **Perception Steeplechase SCCD 31022
    Crothers; Joe Solomon (*b*); Roger Mancuso (*d*). 74.
*** **Swish** New Artists NA1001
    Crothers; Max Roach (*d*).
*** **Concert At Cooper Union** New Artists NA1002
    Crothers (*p* solo). 1/84.
*** **Duo Dimension** New Artists NA1003
    Crothers; Richard Tabnik (*as*). 85.

Crothers is a former student of Lennie Tristano, and her immersion in the language and lore of that
giant is total enough to generate a feeling that she is merely following in his footsteps (intimidating
though that might be). But just as the best of the young hard-boppers have found new wrinkles in that
currency, Crothers has much of her own to say and, given the still-unexplored expanse of Tristano's
methods, it still sounds fresh, even as repertory music. The Steeplechase album, recently reissued on
CD, finds her taking tentative steps towards her own style, with a preponderance of literal translations
of themes such as 'Perception'. Solomon and Mancuso are a functional assist. But the start of a
sequence of records for the New Artists label marks a much more interesting documentation. The
meeting with Roach finds the pianist far from overwhelmed by her illustrious partner on six improvised

duts; the solo record is an open-handed display of thoughtful virtuosity; and the duets with the (inevitably) Konitz-like Tabnik run along probing paths. Crothers plays with the familiar evenness and uses the long, steady, deliberate lines of the style, but her dynamics offer unexpected contrasts of touch and her chordings can build to massive weight and intensity.

***(*) **Love Energy** New Artists NA1005
    Crothers; Lenny Popkin (*ts*); Cameron Brown (*b*); Carol Tristano (*d*). 4/88.
***(*) **New York Night** New Artists NA1008
    As above. 12/89.
*** **In Motion** New Artists NA1013
    As above. 11/89.
***(*) **Jazz Spring** New Artists NA1017
    As above. 3/93.

The formation of this excellent quartet, little-known though it is, has been a valuable means of exploring Tristano's music as repertory. Lenny Popkin builds on Warne Marsh's grey, scratchy tone with fretful cadences of his own, Carol Tristano secures a quietly propulsive swing, and Brown's unobtrusively forceful lines eliminate any sense that the music could grow static, either rhythmically or harmonically. Crothers plays for the band yet manages to make her best improvisations distinctive and freely developed, while still minding the essential logic of the form. This is tough, serious jazz, a little self-regarding in its selflessness, but none the worse for that. If Popkin is – so far – never quite the individual voice that he might be, he's still a determined improviser. *In Motion* gets a fractionally lower score for the foreshortened delivery of most of the pieces; but any of the discs offers a fine portrait of the group.

Cruel Frederick GROUP

*** **We.Are.The.Music.We.Play.** SST CD-290
    Walter Zooi (*t*); Hermann Buhler (*as*); Lynn Johnston (*reeds*); Guy Bennett (*b*); Mike Ezzo (*d*).
    10/90.

Although their home is the alternative-rock label SST, this trio (guests Zooi and Buhler sit in on two tracks) play noisy, broken free jazz that comes as a tonic in small doses. They open with a foul-tempered, blundering version of Monk's 'Little Rootie Tootie' and, once past the controlled hysteria of the second, title, track, one wonders what else they can do. The answer is that Johnston picks up his clarinet and they go quiet for a bit. Good dynamics sustain the record, with Ezzo's snare rolls and Bennett's booming electric bass always meeting in different ways, and they overcome a relatively monochrome competence with bursts of the relatively unexpected. Ornette Coleman's 'Dee Dee' is another nice choice for a cover version, too.

The Crusaders GROUP

    Wayne Henderson (*tb*); Wilton Felder (*sax*); Joe Sample (*ky*); Stix Hooper (*d*).
**** **The Golden Years** GRP 50072 3CD
    As above, except add Oscar Brashear, Robert O. Bryant Sr (*t*); Garnett Brown (*tb*); Maurice
    Spears (*btb*); Robert Bryant Jr (*ts*); Bill Green (*bs*); Arthur Adams, Roland Bautista, Larry
    Carlton, Paul M. Jackson Jr, B. B. King, Dean Parks, Billy Rogers, David T. Walker (*g*); Max
    Bennett, Jimmy Bond, Robert Popwell, Leroy Vinnegar, Buster Williams (*b*); Paulinho Da
    Costa, Efraim Logreira, Ralph MacDonald (*perc*); Randy Crawford (*v*); strings. 62–73.
*** **Old Socks, New Shoes / New Socks, Old Shoes** MoJazz 530 307
    As above, except add Arthur Adams, Freddie Robinson (*g*). 9/70.
*** **Pass The Plate** MoJazz 530 308
    As above. 5/71.
(*) **Hollywood MoJazz 530 306
    As above, except add Arthur Adams, David T. Walker (*g*); Reggie Johnson, Chuck Rainey (*b*). 7/
    72.
*** **Chain Reaction / Those Southern Knights** MCA MCAD 5841
    As above, except add Larry Carlton (*g*); Robert Popwell (*b*). 75–76.

Dropping the word 'jazz' from the name was, of course, a form of critical suicide; it happened in 1971, and since then the Crusaders have been a sour byword for sell-out and commercial compromise. Despite which, the group has maintained a consistency and occasionally perverse integrity of purpose since first emerging in 1961 out of a Houston high-school band. The basic line-up – Felder, Hooper, Sample,

Henderson – has been in place from the start, despite individual projects and excursions, fallings-out and Star Chamber reshuffles. The Crusaders offer a solidly funky quasi-jazz which might almost have been programmed by a computer; it hinges on Sample's bar-room piano, Felder's and Henderson's uncomplicated horn lines, and Hooper's accurate but curiously undynamic drumming. No less, and seldom any more.

The addition of outside players – guitarists and bassists most obviously – seldom disrupted the basic formula; Larry Carlton was *de facto* 'fifth Crusader' for many years. The subsequent years, covering such classic recordings as *Young Rabbits* and *Those Southern Knights* are covered on the excellennt GRP compilation, which is all most people will need. There is, however, a doubled-up CD version of *Knights* and *Chain Reaction*, which may be more acceptable to purists. The model was supposedly Art Blakey's Jazz Messengers but Hooper was much too robotic for that to hold and the Crusaders' instincts were always for the dance floor.

The three single-album reissues will be priority purchases for committed fans, but these records pall very quickly, suffering from too much makeweight material and a fizzy rock-and-roll mix. Almost everything of lasting value – 'Young Rabbits', 'Thank You' (from *Old Socks, New Shoes*), 'Chain Reaction', 'Street Life' – is available on the GRP and this is the one we recommend.

Ronnie Cuber (born 1941) BARITONE, ALTO AND TENOR SAXOPHONES, FLUTE

*** **Cubism** Fresh Sound FSRCD 188
    Cuber; Joe Locke (*vib, ky*); Bobby Broom (*g*); Michael Formanek (*b*); Ben Perowsky (*d*); Potato Valdez (*perc*). 12/91.
*** **Airplay** Steeplechase SCCD 31309
    Cuber; Geoff Keezer (*p*); Chip Jackson (*b*); Ben Perowsky (*d*). 4/92.
***(*) **The Scene Is Clean** Milestone 9218
    Cuber; Lawrence Feldman (*f*); Geoff Keezer (*ky*); Joey DeFrancesco (*org*); George Wadenius (*g*); Tom Barney, Reggie Washington (*b*); Victor Jones (*d*); Manolo Badrena, Milton Cardona (*perc*). 12/93.

Cuber has played on scores of sessions as a section-man, but his records as leader are down to a handful. He gets a light, limber feel out of the baritone when he wants to, though he will make it sound gruff and monstrous if he has to, and his odd adaptability to Latin rhythms means that his own discs usually have more than a few traces of Brazilian bop about them. The feel on *Cubism* is directed towards a lite kind of jazz-funk, but Locke's typically shrewd playing and a few worthwhile licks from the valuable Broom lift it out of the rut that Cuber was in on some of his earlier releases. *Airplay*, despite the somewhat ironic title, puts Cuber back into hard bop with Keezer's fine work as his line to earth. Most of the tunes work a rather old-fashioned groove, as if this were a tribute to the great days of Blue Note and Prestige, but the baritone work is as forthright and full-bodied as Cuber has ever sounded. *The Scene Is Clean* is another blend of styles: the Dameron title-tune, the modal jazz theme, 'Song For Pharoah', and the winsome 'Flamingo' are more traditionally sewn, but the bristling Latin tunes again carry an infectious spirit. Cuber picks up tenor and alto here and there, but the big horn is what holds his soul and he sounds appreciative on this date.

Laurent Cugny ARRANGER, CONDUCTOR, KEYBOARDS

***(*) **Yesternow** Verve 522 511
    Cugny; Claude Egea, Claus Stotter (*t*); Stéphane Belmondo (*t, flhn*); Denis Leloup (*tb*); Bernard François (*frhn*); Philippe Legris (*tba*); Denis Barbier (*f, af*); Pierre-Olivier Govin (*bs, as, ss*); Philippe Sellam (*as, ss*); Julien Lourau (*ts, as*); Lionel Benhamou (*g*); Benoit De Mesmay (*ky*); Lucky Peterson (*org*); Hilaire Penda, Frédéric Monino (b); Stéphane Huchard (*d*). 5/94.

A suite of Miles Davis compositions, compiled by the author of *Electrique Miles Davis, 1968–1975*, and there's a clue in the title, because all but fairly dedicated Milesians will be thrown by tracks headed 'Red China Blues', 'Right Off', 'Fun' and 'Lonely Fire'. Not perhaps first-run compositions, and yet they come from one of the most creative and still largely misunderstood – or at least controversial – periods of Miles's career.

'It's About That Time' from *In A Silent Way* is effectively the climax, before a reprise of 'Yesternow' itself, and here Cugny and soloist Benhamou bring together many of the elements that have gone to make up this fascinating project. The Orchestre National de Jazz is a skilled unit, and the arranger has them playing some challenging material. It begins with a theme from *Jack Johnson*, a transcription of an ensemble passage that casual listeners may not even have registered under Miles's foregrounded trumpet. Here, it becomes a keynote theme to a set of variations that call on unexpected elements of the originals (like the horns on 'Red China Blues' from *Get Up/With It*, or the bass theme from 'Right Off' (*Jack Johnson* and *Agharta*). It's fascinating stuff, crisply played, and some of the best evidence yet for a reappraisal of Miles *as a composer*. Not the least important thing about it is that it will send listeners straight back to a pile of Miles records – 1968 to 1975 – with fresh ears.

Ted Curson (born 1935) TRUMPET, POCKET TRUMPET

***(*) **Plays Fire Down Below** Original Jazz Classics OJC 1744
> Curson; Gildo Mahones (*p*); George Tucker (*b*); Roy Haynes (*d*); Montego Joe (*perc*). 12/62.

***(*) **Tears For Dolphy** Black Lion BLCD 760190
> Curson; Bill Barron (*ts, cl*); Herb Bushler (*b*); Dick Berk (*d*). 8/64.

Thin representation for a highly significant innovator who came to prominence with Mingus, wrote the beautiful 'Tears For Dolphy' and then spent much of his time in Europe. A radical with a strong interest in classic jazz, Curson's work on piccolo trumpet often resembles Rex Stewart, though he's closer to Fats Navarro on the concert horn. *Fire Down Below* is a reasonable representation of his pungent, unsentimental style. Mahones laces a basically conventional approach with figures reminiscent of Carl Perkins. Tucker and Haynes might explain a resemblance to Eric Dolphy's debut album on New Jazz, on which they played, and they're equally impressive here. The drummer is quietly forceful on the two quartet tracks, 'The Very Young' and 'Only Forever', but he sounds slightly cramped by the addition of congas on the remainder.

Tears For Dolphy was recorded a month or so after the death of its dedicatee, and there is a raw sorrow in the title-tune that was less evident in later versions. Barron provides solid support and chips in with four strong charts, including the Dolphyish '7/4 Funny Time' and 'Desolation'. The rhythm section is also very solid, but it is Curson's high, slightly old-fashioned sound on the small trumpet that commands attention. 'Searchin' For The Blues' is the other highlight. Enthusiasts for Curson need to get hold of *Blue Piccolo And Fireball* from 1976 and *The Ted Curson Trio* from 1979 (both currently deleted); there is also a fine tribute to Mingus and a rare 1962 live set from La Tête de l'Art in Toronto, originally released on Trans World and briefly reissued on Can-Am.

Leo Cuypers (born 1947) PIANO

*** **Zeeland Suite & Johnny Rep Suite** Bvhaast 9307
> Cuypers; Willem Van Manen (*tb*); Bob Driessen (*ss, as, bs*); Willem Breuker (*ss, as, ts, bcl*); Piet Noordijk (*as*); Hans Dulfer (*ts*); Harry Miller, Arjen Gorter (*b*); Martin Van Duynhoven, Rob Verdurmen (*d*). 9/74–9/77.

Cuypers is known internationally only as one of Willem Breuker's cronies, but these two vintage sessions from the Bvhaast catalogue, usefully reissued on a single CD, give him some modest limelight as a leader. That said, the 'Zeeland Suite' in particular is much like a Breuker cross-section of riffs and ideas and is more impressive as a framework for the players – Gorten and Miller on 'Two Bass Shit', Breuker and Driessen on 'Bach II And Bach ' – than as any thematic sequence. The 'Johnny Rep Suite' is again dominated by Breuker himself, delivering 'Kirk' as a roaring tribute to the eponymous Kirk; but at least Cuypers gets a couple of pieces more or less to himself at the end. The original recording is rather rough and a little unkind to the piano.

*** **'Songbook'** Bvhaast 9502
> Cuypers (*p* solo). 8/95.

A comeback after a number of years of retreat. Cuypers prepared a studio album, but on hearing the tape of this informal recital preferred this off-the-cuff session. There are 17 original tunes, some little more than embellished vamps but others showing the most acute and inventive harmonic thinking. A handful seem like flawless gems, such as the haunting 'Joplin' or 'Bouquet Mélancholique'; others have a nearly throwaway air about them. Cuypers seems rusty at some moments, virtuosic at others; one follows the record through, wondering what will emerge next. A welcome return.

Andrew Cyrille (born 1939) DRUMS

***(*) **Metamusicians' Stomp** Black Saint 120025
> Cyrille; Ted Daniel (*t, flhn, wood f*); David S. Ware (*ts, f*); Nick DiGeronimo (*b*). 9/78.

**** **Nuba** Black Saint 120030
> Cyrille; Jimmy Lyons (*as*); Jeanne Lee (*v*). 6/79.

**** **The Navigator** Soul Note 121062
 Cyrille; Ted Daniel (*t, flhn*); Sonelius Smith (*p*); Nick Di Geronimo (*b*). 9/82.
***(*) **Galaxies** Music & Arts CD 672
 Cyrille; Vladimir Tarasov (*d, perc, elec*). 6/90.
***(*) **My Friend Louis** DIW 858
 Cyrille; Hannibal (*t*); Oliver Lake (*as, ss*); Adegoke Steve Colson (*p*); Reggie Workman (*b*). 11/91.
***(*) **The X-Man** Soul Note 121262
 Cyrille; James Newton (*f*); Alex Tit Pascal (*g*); Anthony Cox (*b*). 5/93.

Cyrille was a mainstay of what was probably Cecil Taylor's most influential group. Together they explored a significant redefinition of jazz as a non-Western music, one largely based on percussive techniques and sonorities. 'Whence I Came' on *What About?* (an Affinity set that marked his debut as leader but which is now, sadly, deleted) had him using vocal techniques, mostly sighs evocative of loss and enslavement, to convey his sense of place in the wider spectrum of Afro-American history and culture; 'mouth percussion' has become a staple of his solo work since then. The moving *Nuba* is now perhaps the most purely musical of the works under his own name. Jeanne Lee's setting of a poem from her own *The Valley of Astonishment and Bewilderment* is as powerful a statement as she has made on record, and the late Jimmy Lyons marches through the set with the same stoical calm he brought to everything he did.

Cyrille has steadily moved back from the free/abstract idiom he originally espoused, towards an outwardly more conventional music that draws on orthodox jazz structures. All the same, *Nuba* cannot be defined uncomplicatedly as a jazz album. It is richer and more various than that, delving far more deeply into the ore of African and Afro-American experience. It resembles a miniature opera in which the 'mad scene' is the whole dark pre-history of one continent's servitude to another.

Its return to the catalogue helps to restore a rather battered discography. *The Navigator* was also *hors de combat* for some time. Of all Cyrille's records, it is the one that most deliberately synthesizes his vision of a new/ancient form based on the drum and the voice with the jazz tradition. The title-piece is a suite in which each of the players introduces a section in his own instrumental voice; it grows out of a shapeless whirlpool of sound and gradually resolves into currents and counter-currents, tide-races and sudden unexpected calms. By contrast, 'So That Life Can Endure . . . PS With Love' is a delicate ballad with more than a hint of Ellington in it. But perhaps the most accurate index of where Cyrille was at *vis--à-vis* Duke is the off-centre blues, 'The Music in Us', an intriguing performance. Daniel plays beautifully on his own 'Module', but the set belongs to the leader.

Metamusicians' Stomp keeps him in the frame and *My Friend Louis* offers encouraging evidence that Cyrille is still active and creative, and producing eventful music. The earlier record offers pretty short measure, but what there is of it reaches a high standard. Cyrille called this band Maono. Ware and Daniel are sympathetic partners, deriving their approach from Albert Ayler and Don Cherry respectively, though Daniel also sounds like his namesake, Ted Curson. All four musicians are credited with having a 'foot' in the proceedings, a reference to the reverberant stomping on the title-track. Cyrille introduces one unusual standard, Kurt Weill's 'My Ship', a tune which Earl Hines used to play. The final track is a long, discursive suite called 'Spielegasse 14', and it's here that Cyrille's great sense of drama takes over.

My Friend Louis is dominated by Lake, who plays absolutely wonderfully throughout and gets tremendous support from Cyrille, Workman and the too rarely seen Colson, who gets a feature on his own 'South Of The Border Serenade'. Everyone else chips in with a tune, Lake's 'Tap Dancer' the most memorable, and there's a rugged cover of Dolphy's 'The Prophet'. The dedication is to South African drummer Louis Moholo, and the disc ends with a long exploration of the drummers' shared language, a many-sided but never impenetrable dialect of Afro-free that remains as potent today as it ever was.

The California-based Music & Arts label is acquiring a growing reputation, not least for programming challenging duos of this sort, mainly recorded at the Vancouver Jazz Festival. Tarasov, formerly the drummer with the Ganelin Trio and an often overlooked influence on that important group's sound, offers three significant compositions. 'Galaxies' and 'Action V' are performed together, with unobtrusive electronic washes and ostinati filling in the background. Cyrille's own 'No. 11' seems to represent an autobiographical statement, tracing his own re-accommodation to the jazz tradition, a stance that is undoubtedly also problematic for Tarasov. Perhaps the place to start, though, is the final track, disproportionately shorter than the two main performances and still only half the length of Tarasov's short 'Summit'; it's a version of John Coltrane's 'One Up, One Down', reflecting Cyrille's detailed study of Coltrane's late experiments in metre, an aspect of the saxophonist's work that has begun to be fully recognized only recently. *Galaxies* is a dense, detailed album that may well tax the attention of listeners not entirely persuaded as to the merits of solo percussion. It should, perhaps, be listened to track-by-track rather than as an uninterrupted whole.

The recent *X-Man* takes up the main story-line again. These days, though, Cyrille is more than ever inclined to dispense with the waffle and cut to the chase. The improvised title-track is a remarkable performance by any standard. Newton's imagination runs on a parallel course to the drummer's and here they seem to be in telepathic contact. There are more conventional moments, of course: relatively tuneful things like Newton's 'E-Squat', with its bebop stylings, and Cyrille's own plainly stated 'Simple Melody'. There's no sense that these are either fillers or sops to radio playlists. In fact the very same rhythmic and harmonic procedures are in evidence on the purportedly 'simpler' cuts. A great drummer; a fine writer; and a wonderful bandleader; you pass him by at your peril.

Tony Dagradi TENOR AND SOPRANO SAXOPHONE

*** **Dreams Of Love** Core COCD 9.00798 O
  Dagradi; David Torkanowsky (*ky*); Steve Masakowski (*g*); Jim Singleton (*b*); John Vidacovich (*d*). 9/87–1/88.
***(*) **Images From The Floating World** Core COCD 9.00727
  As above, except omit Torkanowsky and Masakowski. 90.
***(*) **Live At The Columns** Turnipseed TMCD 07
  As above, except Masakowski returns. 93.

A New Orleans tenorman of swaggering, bullish temperament, Dagradi communicates a mixture of local tradition and outward-bound thinking in these records. He seems content to let himself get a little penned in on *Dreams Of Love*: now and again one hears him straining at the barriers of the tunes. But slimming the group down to a trio affords Dagradi the space and freedom to turn *Images From The Floating World*, despite the ominous title, into a terrific blowing session. 'Parading', which was also on the last record, becomes a boastful New Orleans march, 'O.F.O.' is a convincing tribute to Ornette Coleman, and there's nothing wasted in the long and impassioned exchanges between the leader and his partners on the other pieces. *Live At The Columns* finds the trio on home turf in New Orleans and enjoying themselves. Dagradi continues to retain an air of freedom while contenting himself with familiar structures, and his confidence in his own powers as an improviser radiates through an hour of music. Masakowski guests on a fine 'Body And Soul'.

Roland Dahinden TROMBONE, VOICE

*** **Trombone Performance** Amadeo 841330-2
  Dahinden; Christian Muthspiel (*tb, v*). 7/89.

A brimming display of trombone virtuosity, this two-man show is funny, thoughtful, slyly creative. Dahinden and Muthspiel use all of the techniques pioneered by Mangelsdorff, Rutherford and Christmann many years earlier, but their terse organization (none of the pieces runs for more than six minutes, unthinkably short in free-music terms) and precise dialogue bespeak a different aim: this is as fine-tuned as a Basie arrangement. Not all of it works, and the monumental drone of 'First Etude' will try the patience of some; but madcap episodes like the human-beat-box nonsense of 'Last Etude' break up the flow, and the music on 'Canard Rose' is championship playing by any standard.

Del Dako (born 1955) BARITONE AND ALTO SAXOPHONES

(*) **Balancing Act Sackville SKCD2-2021
  Dako; Richard Whiteman (*p*); Dick Felix (*b*); Mike McClelland (*d*). 3–11/90.

A Canadian known only to local audiences, Dako waited until he was 35 before making his debut album. Although he plays alto in places, notably on the thoughtful original 'Steve The Weave' which opens the record, Dako's primary horn is the baritone, which he employs with a gruff, bull-headed swing: he loves the grouchiness of baritone timbre, and his solo on 'Just Don't Slip With That Axe' is a memorable string of complaints. But the music is rhythmically less assured, Dako not quite authoritative enough to command the best from a so-so rhythm section, and it results in a bit of a potboiler.

Meredith D'Ambrosio VOCAL, PIANO

*** **Lost In His Arms** Sunnyside SSC 1081D
  D'Ambrosio; Ray Santisi (*p*); Norman Coles (*g*); Chris Rathbun (*b*). 7–10/78.

*** **Another Time** Sunnyside SSC 1017D
    D'Ambrosio. 2/81.
***(*) **Little Jazz Bird** Sunnyside SSC 1040D
    D'Ambrosio; Phil Woods (*cl, as*); Hank Jones (*p*); Gene Orloff, Fred Buldrini (*vn*); Julian
    Barber (*vla*); Fred Slatkin (*clo*); Steve Gilmore (*b*); Bill Goodwin (*d*). 3/82.
**** **It's Your Dance** Sunnyside SSC 1011
    D'Ambrosio; Harold Danko (*p*); Kevin Eubanks (*g*). 3/85.
(*) **The Cove Sunnyside SSC 1028D
    D'Ambrosio; Lee Konitz (*as*); Fred Hersch (*p*); Michael Formanek (*b*); Keith Copeland (*d*).
***(*) **South To A Warmer Place** Sunnyside SSC 1039D
    D'Ambrosio; Lou Colombo (*t*); Eddie Higgins (*p*); Don Coffman (*b*); Danny Berger (*d*). 2/89.
***(*) **Love Is Not A Game** Sunnyside SSC 1051D
    D'Ambrosio; Eddie Higgins (*p*); Rufus Reid (*b*); Keith Copeland (*d*). 12/90.
*** **Shadowland** Sunnyside SSC 1060D
    D'Ambrosio; Ron Kozak (*f, bcl*); Blair Tindall (*cor, ob*); Eddie Higgins (*p*); Johnny Frigo (*vn*);
    Erik Friedlander (*clo*); Jay Leonhart (*b*); Ben Riley (*d*). 7/92.
(*) **Sleep Warm Sunnyside SSC 1063
    D'Ambrosio (*p, v*). 2/91.

Literate, polished singing from a vocalist whose approach is so soft and unemphatic that sometimes she barely seems to be present at all. But her choice of songs is so creative and the treatments so consistently refined that the records are unexpectedly absorbing. *Another Time* is a reissue of a privately produced session, and its bare-bones approach is perhaps a little too austere, but it's still an impressive recital of 18 songs. Another recent reappearance is the 1978 session, *Lost In His Arms*, which unfolds at the steady, thoughtful pace of all of her music. *Little Jazz Bird*, despite an eccentric studio production by Rudy van Gelder, is ingeniously programmed to accommodate Woods and the string quartet, and the songs encompass Dave Frishberg, Gene Lees, Loonis McGloohan and two exceptional pieces by Deborah Henson-Conant, 'How Is Your Wife' and 'When The End Comes'. *It's Your Dance* is arguably D'Ambrosio's most fully realized record: with only Danko and Eubanks (who's never played better) in support, D'Ambrosio maintains a supernal glow throughout the record. Almost all the songs are unusual, from her own lyrics to 'Giant Steps' and Dave Brubeck's 'Strange Meadowlark' to Al Cohn's 'The Underdog', the title-track's reworking of John Carisi's 'Israel' and the lovely Burke–Van Heusen rarity, 'Humpty Dumpty Heart'. The vocalist's choice of material and the hip understatement of her singing create the core of her work. Her voice is too small and unambitious to make any play for jazz virtuosity, but she achieves a different authenticity through economies of scale.

   That said, it goes a little wrong on *The Cove*, which is too composed and sleepy, the playing sounding fatigued rather than laid-back. But *South To A Warmer Place* restores her run: Colombo plays a Bobby Hackett-like role and, since many of the songs are relatively familiar, this may be the best place to start hearing D'Ambrosio's enchanting work. *Love Is Not A Game* has some more memorable treatments: 'Autumn Serenade', J. J. Johnson's 'Lament', Denny Zeitlin's 'Quiet Now'. On 'Oh Look At Me Now', she extends the song into a coda which has her composing new lyrics for a variation on the tune, and that approach is carried over into five of the twelve tunes on *Shadowland*, perhaps with mixed success. She still sounds at her best on the introspective, soliloquy-like material, such as Burton Lane's 'A Rainy Afternoon', and Noël Coward's 'Zigeuner' is another surprising and successful choice. Eddie Higgins, her husband, provides sympathetic piano throughout, although her own playing isn't negligible. *Sleep Warm* is for more specialized tastes, perhaps, since it is mainly a set of modern and old-fashioned lullabies for a child.

Tadd Dameron (1917–65) COMPOSER, BANDLEADER, PIANO

***(*) **Fats Navarro Featured** Milestone M 47041
    Dameron; Fats Navarro (*t*); Kai Winding (*tb*); Rudy Williams (*as*); Allen Eager (*ts*); Milt
    Jackson (*vib*); Curley Russell (*b*); Kenny Clarke (*d*). 48.
*** **Cool Boppin'** Fresh Sound FSCD 1008
    Dameron; Miles Davis (*t*); Kai Winding (*tb*); Sahib Shihab (*as*); Benjamin Lundy (*ts*); Cecil
    Payne (*bs*); John Collins (*g*); Curley Russell (*b*); Kenny Clarke (*d*); Carlos Vidal (*perc*). 2/49.
*** **Clifford Brown Memorial** Original Jazz Classics OJC 017
    Dameron; Clifford Brown, Idrees Sulieman (*t*); Herb Mullins (*tb*); Gigi Gryce (*as*); Benny
    Golson (*ts*); Oscar Estell (*bs*); Percy Heath (*b*); Philly Joe Jones (*d*). 6/53.
*** **Fontainebleau** Original Jazz Classics OJC 055
    Dameron; Kenny Dorham (*t*); Henry Coker (*tb*); Sahib Shihab (*as*); Joe Alexander (*ts*); Cecil
    Payne (*bs*); John Simmons (*b*); Shadow Wilson (*d*). 3/56.

*** **Mating Call** Original Jazz Classics OJC 212
>   Dameron; John Coltrane (ts); John Simmons (b); Philly Joe Jones (d).

(*) **The Magic Touch Original Jazz Classics OJC 212
>   Dameron; Ernie Royal, Charlie Shavers, Clark Terry, Joe Wilder (t); Jimmy Cleveland, Britt
>   Woodman (tb); Julius Watkins (frhn); Jerry Dodgion, Leo Wright (as, f); Jerome Richardson (ts,
>   f); Johnny Griffin (ts); Tate Houston (bs); Bill Evans (p); Ron Carter (b); Philly Joe Jones (d);
>   Barbara Winfield (v). 2–4/62.

It's Dameron's fate to be remembered now largely for a handful of compositions – 'Hot House' and
'Lady Bird' pre-eminently – which became standards. As such, Dameron is a much-underrated performer who stands at the fulcrum of modern jazz, midway between swing and bebop. Combining the
broad-brush arrangements of the big band and the advanced harmonic language of bop, his own
recordings are difficult to date blind. Encouragingly, and despite the fact that the discography hasn't
grown spectacularly, the work has become more visible over the past few years, a process of re-
familiarization for which the late Philly Joe Jones's Dameronia project (see below) must claim some of
the credit.

Fats Navarro played as well with Dameron as he did with anyone; the Blue Note sets issued as *The
Fabulous Fats Navarro* (781531/2) should strictly be credited to the Tadd Dameron Sextet/Septet and to
Bud Powell's Modernists, but became known as a posthumous tribute to the brilliant young trumpeter
who died in 1950. Navarro's big, ringing brass-tone is superb on a second take of 'Anthropology'
(Dameron features on the first), two takes of 'Good Bait' and a witty 'Oh! Lady Be Good'. The overall
sound is a little too muzzy to catch some of Dameron's more sophisticated voicings – but then 1948 was
a rather uncertain year for everyone in the music, and Navarro peals out of the fog quite beautifully.

Another young genius took a significant stride forward under Dameron's wing. John Coltrane's solo on
'Soultrane' and the ballad construction on 'On A Misty Night' are among the best things in his early
career. Though *Mating Call* is often discussed as if it were a Coltrane album, it's the pianist who's firmly
in the driving seat, directing an ensemble sound subtly different from anything else that was coming out
of bebop. Though dedicated to the memory of another ill-fated trumpet genius, the Brown memorial set
(shared with a Brown/Farmer session from Stockholm, recorded later the same summer) is also valuable
for insights into Dameron's methods. 'Theme Of No Repeat', 'Dial "B" For Beauty' and 'Philly J. J.' are
relatively little known compared to 'Lady Bird' and 'Good Bait', but they evidence a consummate grasp
of instrumental voicing; the last of the three also stands up well on the Dameronia recording reviewed
below. Also shared is *Cool Boppin'*, which fuels debate about the real parentage of Cool School jazz by
pairing Dameron's Royal Roost session of February 1949 with Miles Davis's residency there the previous autumn and winter; Miles also plays with Dameron's group. 'Good Bait' isn't a vintage performance, but the treatments of 'April In Paris' and 'Webb's Delight' point in interesting directions that help
refocus appreciation of Dameron's art.

Fontainebleau originates from Dameron's last full year of freedom before the term of imprisonment that
more or less ended his career. It's a fine set, with no clutter in the horns. The title-piece is wholly written
out, with no scope for improvising, but there is plenty of fine individual work elsewhere, notably from
Dorham. Never a virtuoso soloist, Dameron prefers to work within the very distinct chord-progressions
of his tunes, big, lush confections that are too sharp-edged ever to cloy.

Dameronia GROUP

***(*) **Live At The Théâtre Boulogne-Billancourt, Paris** Soul Note 121202
>   Don Sickler, Virgil Jones (t); Benny Powell (tb); Frank Wess (as, f); Clifford Jordan (ts); Cecil
>   Payne (bs); Walter Davis Jr (p); Larry Ridley (b); Kenny Washington (d). 5/89.

The original idea for Dameronia came from drummer Philly Joe Jones, who wanted to see Tadd
Dameron's achievement properly recognized. The work of transcription and re-orchestration from
records (the original MSS had gone missing years before) was done by Don Sickler, who conducts on
this concert performance, and by pianist John Oddo. They did a strikingly good job. The group's first
LP was issued on the small Uptown label, but it was live appearances in New York that attracted all the
critical attention.

By the time the group got together again in 1989, Philly Joe was dead, so these sessions serve a further
memorial function. Like Mingus Dynasty and Big Band Charlie Mingus, the intention is to represent
the composer's music accurately, but with the same level of freedom for soloists to express themselves.
Clearly neither Sickler nor Virgil Jones has the passionate ring of a Fats Navarro, who interpreted the
blues 'Good Bait' and 'The Squirrel' in the late 1940s, but their performances are more than routine on
both. The star turn on 'The Squirrel' is Cecil Payne, who represents the last remaining line of succession.
His barrel-chested tone had been heard on *Fontainebleau* in 1956. The 1989 version of Dameron's little
suite is beautifully orchestrated and balanced, with a delicate touch from everybody concerned.

Faultless performances all round, and a special word for Washington, who stepped into the founder's shoes without a moment's hesitation.

Paolo Damiani BASS, CELLO, VOCAL

*** **Poor Memory** Splasc(h) HP 07
> Damiani; Paolo Fresu (*t, flhn*); Gianluigi Trovesi (*ss, as, bcl*); Claude Barthelemy (*g*); Aldo Romano (*d*). 7/87.

*** **Eso** Splasc(h) H 404
> As above, except Danilo Rea (*p*), Antonio Iasevoli (*g*), Roberto Gatto (*d*), Raffaela Siniscalchi, Sabina Macculi (*v*) replace Bathelemy and Romano. 93.

Poor Memory is a fine concert recording, featuring several of the brightest contemporary talents in Italian jazz. Fresu continues to impress as a lyrical voice, but Trovesi's hard-hitting reed solos and Barthelemy's harsh, rock-directed guitar provide piquant contrast. Damiani's compositions find a suitable middle ground between hard bop and freer modes, and the live recording is agreeably rough-edged and human-sounding.

Eso has a few unexpected vocal contributions, including those by the leader, although Siniscalchi is the one with the outstanding voice. In the main, this is the mix as before, with Fresu and Trovesi both in excellent voice.

Franco D'Andrea (born 1941) PIANO, KEYBOARDS

*** **Kick Off** Red 123225-2
> D'Andrea; Giovanni Tommaso (*b*); Roberto Gatto (*d*). 4/88.

*** **Earthcake** Label Bleu L BLC 6539
> D'Andrea; Enrico Rava (*t, bugle*); Miroslav Vitous (*b*); Daniel Humair (*d*). 1/91.

*(*) **Enrosadira** Red 123243-2
> D'Andrea; Luis Agudo (*perc*). 91.

**** **Airegin** Red 123252-2
> D'Andrea; Giovanni Tommaso (*b*); Roberto Gatto (*d*). 4/91.

*** **Flavours** Penta Flowers CDPIA 024
> D'Andrea; Glenn Ferris (*tb*); Tino Tracanna (*ts*); Saverio Tasca (*vib*); Attilo Zanchi (*b*); Gianni Cazzola (*d*); Naco (*perc*). 5/92.

*** **Current Changes** Penta Flowers CDPIA 035
> D'Andrea; David Boato (*t*); Naco (*perc*). 12/93.

*** **Live In Perugia** Penta Flowers CDPIA 41
> D'Andrea (*p* solo). 7/94.

D'Andrea's several solo records and earlier trio sessions for Red have yet to be reissued on CD. He's a senior figure among Italy's post-bop musicians; his playing has a scholar's penchant for irony and dramatic construction and, while there's plenty of Mediterranean fire in his music, he is just as partial to a meditative frame of expression. Either of the two trio sessions for Red, with two of his favourite partners, will make a good place to start hearing D'Andrea's jazz. *Kick Off* offers comparatively short measure with only five tunes, and the sound-balance isn't too kind to the piano, but the trio demonstrate a very refined empathy, the balance of initiative shifting almost from measure to measure. *Airegin*, though, is even better. There are some superb reworkings of the jazz repertoire on 'Epistrophy', 'Doxy', 'Airegin' and 'Blue In Green', as well as some fine originals, with Tommaso's 'My Dear One' and D'Andrea's own 'Things Called'. The pianist takes a lot of trouble to reharmonize or otherwise vary the delivery of the familiar pieces without making it seem effortful.

The Label Bleu disc is something of an all-star session and, while nothing extraordinary happens, it's a significantly democratic affair, with compositions from each man and the title-piece standing as a highly articulate and detailed improvisation. *Enrosadira*, though, is eminently avoidable, a muddle of electronic keyboards pitched against Agudo's splashy percussion: good therapy for D'Andrea, perhaps, but tedious to listen to. *Flavours* is a new recording by the quintet that D'Andrea has led for several years, with Tracanna, Zanchi and Cazzola, embellished by contributions from Ferris and Naco. The music is pitched somewhere between D'Andrea's personalized hard bop and a touch of Afro-jazz on five long tunes and one coda. Some of the pieces trail rather aimlessly on, but the pianist plays an authoritative role in pulling them round with an incisive solo or fragment of arrangement. Well worth hearing.

The previous brush with electronics on *Enrosadira* was so discouraging that one views *Current Changes* with alarm – D'Andrea returns to the Clavinova keyboard synthesizer for this trio outing. But Boato's refreshingly bright playing and Naco's gently propulsive percussion set up an amiable atmosphere, and

D'Andrea uses the keyboard with restraint. Not without appeal. His first solo set for some time, *Live In Perugia*, is better, though: two themes common to both discs sound firmer and more characterful on the acoustic piano. Rhythmically, D'Andrea isn't always the most ingenious of players, and some of these pieces have to rely on harmonic substance to sustain what can be rather stolid performances. But his reduction of a Mahler *adagietto* is charming.

Putney Dandridge (1902–46) PIANO, VOCALS

(*) Putney Dandridge, 1935–1936 Classics 846
> Dandridge; Henry 'Red' Allen, Richard Clarke, Shirley Clay (*t*); Buster Bailey (*cl, as*); Tom Mace, Gene Sedric (*cl, ts*); Chu Berry, Kenneth Hollon, Johnny Russell (*ts*); Harry Grey, Teddy Wilson (*p*); Arnold Adams, Dave Barbour, Clarence Holiday, Nappy Lamare (*g*); John Kirby, Artie Bernstein, Ernest Hill, Grachan Moncur (*b*); Bill Beason, Cozy Cole, Walter Johnson, Manzie Johnson (*d*). 3/35–3/36.

Fame is a fickle thing, but only rarely does she withdraw her favours quite as totally as she did from Dandridge. In the mid-1930s he was quite a considerable entertainer, having once accompanied Bill Bojangles Robinson and been able to call on musicians as accomplished as Allen, Berry, Eldridge and Wilson, and on an appealingly tongue-in-cheek vocal style that was about two-thirds vaudeville. His piano playing would never have set the room on fire, and for all but the first two tracks here he was able to rely on Wilson's calm professionalism. The earliest cut is 'You're A Heavenly Thing', enlivened by a chorus or two on celeste; nothing is known about the other musicians involved, though everyone who has listened carefully has a theory. Three months later, an impeccably pedigreed group backed him on a totally hokey 'Nagasaki' (dig those crazy Japanese voices), 'Chasing Shadows' (a lovely break from Berry) and 'When I Grow Too Old To Dream'. After that, or maybe after 'I'm In The Mood For Love' with Red Allen (a.k.a. 'Gabriel') and Buster Bailey, all but dedicated fans will start wondering what to play next.

Peter Danemo DRUMS

*** **Baraban** Dragon DRCD 206
> Danemo; Inge Petersson (*ts*); Esbjorn Svensson (*ky*); Klaus Hovman (*b*). 5/91.

A session very much in the house style of the company – drifting, modal jazz with a hard centre, expertly recorded. Danemo wrote most of the 11 themes here and, while they start with simple materials, the quartet transmute them into frequently intense explorations of a motif or a mood. The opening 'Below The Surface', for instance, is built into an impressively intense ensemble piece. Solos tend to emerge as part of the overall fabric: Petersson, another in the line of fine Swedish tenors, plays a co-operative rather than a front-line role, and Svensson, who contributes two charming compositions, is a thoughtful source of support. There are almost 67 minutes of music on the CD.

Dee Daniels VOCALS

(*) **All Of Me September CD 5101
> Daniels; Jack Van Poll (*p*); John Clayton (*b*); Bruno Castellucci (*d*). 5/91.
*** **Close Encounters Of The Swingin' Kind** Timeless CD SJP 312
> Daniels; Johan Clement (*p*); Koos Wiltenburg (*b*); Fred Kress (*d*). 9/91.

Attractively uncomplicated jazz singing. Both trios are highly professional and the choice of material – 'Nigerian Marketplace' on the Timeless, 'Midnight Strangers' on the more conventional *All Of Me* – is sufficiently varied to keep things interesting. Both recordings are good.

Eddie Daniels (born 1941) CLARINET, TENOR SAXOPHONE

(*) **First Prize! Original Jazz Classics OJC 771
> Daniels; Roland Hanna (*p*); Richard Davis (*b*); Mel Lewis (*d*). 9/66.

Daniels was allegedly once told by Tony Scott to stick to the tenor saxophone, advice he subsequently ignored, as the clarinet records listed below bear witness to. Even on tenor, though, he wasn't terribly exciting. Five tracks on sax, three on clarinet, and the scarcity of the original album suggests that Daniels wouldn't have been all that missed on either instrument in the long run. Competent but uninvolving playing.

** **Breakthrough** GRP 95332

    Daniels; London Philharmonia Orchestra, Ettore Strata (*cond*). 86.

(*) **To Bird With Love GRP 95442

    Daniels; Fred Hirsch, Roger Kellaway (*ky*); John Patitucci (*b*); Al Foster (*d*); Steve Thornton (*perc*). 87.

** **Memos From Paradise** GRP 95612

    Daniels; Roger Kellaway (*ky*); David Nadien, Elena Barbere (*vn*); Lamar Alsop (*vla*); Beverly Lauridsen (*clo*); Eddie Gomez (*b*); Al Foster, Terry Clarke (*d*); Glen Velez (*perc*). 12/87–1/88.

Flawless technician that he is, Daniels seems happiest when creating the most trivial kind of light chamber-jazz. He might be a master of the instrument, but his earlier GRP discs failed to direct those skills to any purposeful ends. On these intermittently playable records, Daniels creates various acceptable faces on ideas that might have called for more stringent resources. *To Bird With Love* is bebop without any teeth, and the two albums with strings pander to saccharine values while pretending to a sterner virtuosity. A dreary sequence, made more so by the plush recording.

** **Nepenthe** GRP 96072

    Daniels; Chuck Loeb (*g*); John Patitucci (*b*); Dave Weckl, Adam Nussbaum (*d*); Sammy Figueroa (*perc*). 12/89.

Daniels becomes an innovator: the first clarinettist fully to embrace fusion, though it's no more significant than any of Herbie Mann's similarly perky records. The session-men in support play with their usual exhausting aplomb, but Daniels's original material is forgettable.

** **This Is Now** GRP 96352

    Daniels; Billy Childs (*p*); Tony Dumas, Jimmy Johnson (*b*); Ralph Penland, Vinnie Colaiuta (*d*). 90.

Daniels in a traditional, acoustic setting, but there's nothing to trouble anyone's slumbers here. There is a mildly galling comparison between his version of 'Body And Soul' and the Coleman Hawkins classic, but otherwise there's nothing offensive in this clean and spotlessly delivered set. Nothing very interesting, either.

*** **Benny Rides Again** GRP 96652

    Daniels; Gary Burton (*vib, xy*); Mulgrew Miller (*p*); Marc Johnson (*b*); Peter Erskine (*d*). 1/92.

** **Under The Influence** GRP 97172

    Daniels; Alan Pasqua (*ky*); Michael Formanek (*b*); Peter Erskine (*d*). 92.

Benny Rides Again is easily Daniels' best record although, since he comes on more as a sideman than a leader, it may not confer that much honour on him. Burton and the superb rhythm section hijack what's meant to be a tribute to Goodman, and the sheer muscle of the back line – as well as Burton in rather funky form – blows past the lithe but perfunctory clarinet parts. *Under The Influence* is a pointless return to the tenor saxophone for much of the record, supposedly at the urging of admirers. It's well enough done, but when jazz is filled with so many fine tenor players there's little reason to listen to this.

Lars Danielsson BASS, KEYBOARDS

***(*) **New Hands** Dragon DRCD 125

    Danielsson; David Liebman (*ss*); Bobo Stenson (*p*); Goran Klinghagen (*g, ky*); Jon Christensen (*d*). 12/85.

**** **Poems** Dragon DRCD 209

    As above, except omit Klinghagen. 4/91.

This is a very fine group, and *New Hands* is certainly the equal of any of Liebman's records with Quest. The bassist's six compositions range from a mysterious electronic lament on 'Chrass' to the memorable ballads of 'It's Your Choice' and 'Johan', the former featuring a bass solo of astonishing virtuosity. Stenson and Christensen live up to their reputation as two of the most outstanding Europeans on their respective instruments, and Liebman's work is typically broad in its sympathies, from gnarled volleys of notes to long-breathed lines of high lyrical beauty.

    Poems, recorded after a brief 'reunion' tour by the band, is a degree finer even than *New Hands*. Liebman contributes the funky, brittle 'Little Peanut' and two other tunes, while the bassist turns in some of his best writing for the haunting 'Crystalline' and 'Suite'; but it's the interaction of four mastermusicians which engenders the magic here: there really are no joins to be seen and, with Christensen at his most robustly inventive, the rhythmic layers are as songful as those created by Liebman and Stenson. Richly recorded and highly recommended.

***(*) **Fresh Enough** L + R CDLR 45051

    Danielson; Dave Liebman (*ss*); Bill Evans (*ts*); Niels Lan Doky (*p*); John Scofield, Ulf Wakenius (*g*); Jack DeJohnette (*d*). 1/91.

The first two tracks on album three suggest that Danielsson has traded his elusiveness for Big Apple muscle, a power trio with Scofield and DeJohnette and another slugfest with Evans and Doky joining in too. But after those knockabouts comes a typically serene ballad called 'Far North', and Liebman and Wakenius displace the uptown brawn of the other music. Liebman turns 'Autumn Leaves' into one of the challenging revisions that he has become a master of when it comes to standards, and there are two other thoughtful originals apiece by Danielsson and Doky. More top-flight playing that wears its virtuosity lightly.

*** **European Voices** Dragon DRCD 268 2CD
> Danielsson; Niels-Petter Molvaer (*t*); Nils Lindgren (*tb*); Sven Fridolfsson (*as*); Joakim Milder (*saxes*); Michael Riessler (*cl, bcl, sno*); Lars Jansson (*p*); Tobias Sjogren, Elvind Aarset (*g*); Marilyn Mazur (*d*). 12/93.

*** **... Continuation** L + R CDLR 45085
> Danielsson; John Abercrombie (*g*); Adam Nussbaum (*d*). 1/94.

European Voices is two discs of various groupings, improvisations and compositions, boiled down from seven hours of material. Perhaps surprisingly, the range of moods is actually more limited than on some of Danielsson's other discs – the tone stretches from pastel calm to craggy, restless discord, but rhythmically it's rather flat and unmoving. There are some beautiful passages, such as the carefully wrought 'Eden' or the vigorous 'Falling Down'; but overall this feels like a project that's of more importance to its maker than to his audience. A couple of the same tunes turn up on ... *Continuation*, but this is a lighter, brisker date, centred round the interplay among the three men and inevitably rather dominated by Abercrombie and his vocabulary of guitar sounds. Danielsson's own playing here is as good as he's ever given, though one misses some of the freshness of the first records.

Palle Danielsson (born 1946) DOUBLE BASS

*** **Contra Post** Caprice CAP 21440
> Danielsson; Joakim Milder (*ts, ss*); Rita Marcotulli (*p*); Goran Klinghagen (*g*); Anders Kjellberg (*d*). 94.

One loses count of the number of top-flight jazz bassists coming out of Scandinavia. Danielsson has an enormous CV and a huge range of session credits, including some of the finest Jan Garbarek recordings of earlier years. This, though, is his first record as leader. Some of the material – including an unaccompanied solo – is recorded at home near Stockholm, but the rest was taped at the renowned Rainbow Studio in Oslo, where Jan-Erik Kongshaug has established an unbeatable technical standard. Not all the material lives up to that standard. Rita Marcotulli's minimalist '7 Notes, 7 Days, 7 Planets' has an attractively mysterious quality, and Milder is similar enough in basic tonality to Garbarek to reinforce the 'ECM feel' on some tracks. The best of the material, though, recording quality notwithstanding, is home-produced, notably a fine duo, 'Monk's Mood', with Klinghagen.

Harold Danko (born 1947) PIANO

*** **Mirth Song** Sunnyside SSC 1001
> Danko; Rufus Reid (*b*). 4/82.

*** **Alone But Not Forgotten** Sunnyside SSC 1033
> Danko; Marc Johnson, Michael Moore (*b*); Joe LaBarbera (*d*); Bob Dorough (*v*); strings arranged by John LaBarbera. 11/85, 2 & 5/86.

(*) **The First Love Song Jazz City 660 53 011
> Danko; Tom Harrell (*t, flhn*); Rufus Reid (*b*); Mel Lewis (*d*).

*** **Next Age** Steeplechase SCCD 31350
> Danko; Rich Perry (*ts*); Scott Colley (*b*); Jeff Hirshfield (*d*). 10/93.

Danko is a quiet, lyrical player, much too understated to make a vulgar splash, but underrated none the less. Don't expect fireworks, just beautifully crafted jazz tinged with Danko's slightly academic approach to composition.

His debut for the Jazz City label never quite peaks. The opening version of Bob Brookmeyer's gently oblique 'The First Love Song', with Harrell floating muted whole-note progressions above a bare statement of the chords, underlines Danko's ability to build solos of genuine significance and considerable beauty out of relatively limited resources; there is also a lovely bowed solo by Reid, who's a highly sympathetic partner. Originals like 'Swift Shifting' and the contrasting slow 'To Start Again' allow him to work against the basic pulse to good effect. 'Eleanor Rigby', like most jazz transcriptions of Lennon–

McCartney tunes, is a schmaltzy lost cause. Danko was pianist with the Thad Jones–Mel Lewis big band and returns the compliment with a gig for the underused Lewis, who plays tidily but without much fire.

The association with Reid delivered perhaps Danko's best recorded performances on *Mirth Song*, which kicked off the Sunnyside imprint. Opening with 'In Walked Bud' has to be seen as a statement of intent. The rate of delivery hardly falters thereafter, with sterling versions of Jackie McLean's 'Omega', Charlie Parker's 'Red Cross' and Wayne Shorter's 'Penelope', which points to one significant, though hardly obvious, source for Danko's unique phrasing and harmonic sense.

Alone But Not Forgotten is a softly romantic session with a good deal more musical substance than initially appears. Danko's interest in Brazilian music – Jobim, the percussionist Edison Machado, and singer Elis Regina – is reflected in the title-piece and Edu Lobo's 'O Circo Mistico', his European roots in the lovely ballad 'Martina'. His admiration for Bill Evans is reflected in almost every note, but more specifically in a vocal version of 'Laurie', while the opening 'Wayne Shorter' confirms the connection. The string arrangements – by the drummer's brother – are a model of their kind and should be studied by all producers who want to orchestrate ballad albums.

Can it be that Danko's main problem as a recording artist has been the lack of a genuinely sympathetic producer? Nils Winther at Steeplechase seems to have found a way to get the best out of him. A pity *Next Age* (the tune optimistically dedicated to Bill Clinton) wasn't a trio set, but the circumstances are that this was a return fixture for the group which recorded under saxophonist Rich Perry's leadership six months earlier. Perry is very much a Danko-hued reed player, soft and thoughtful. He contributes enormously to 'For Bud', but he seems (to our ears) less appropriate on the more adventurous contra-facts like 'Gregarious Solitude' and 'Silk Lady'. There is another tribute to Edison Machado in 'Subindo' – rising, ascending – which is paired with another, originally 'straight', concert piece called 'Luz Caverna'. Characteristically intelligent, both, and strangely beguiling.

Jacqui Dankworth VOCALS

*** **First Cry** EFZ 1010
Dankworth; Anthony Kerr (*vib*); Stan Sulzmann (*f*); Paul Clarvis (*d*); Bosco De Oliveira (*perc*). 93, 94.

No disrespect to Ms Dankworth, but this is notable mainly for some elegantly lyrical vibes from Kerr, who in a few short years has turned into an able, sympathetic accompanist for singers, and a soloist of some substance. Dankworth herself has a full but somehow not very resonant voice, which may have something to do with the studio and desk on this record, because her live performances sound very different. Kerr contributes most of the musical material, Dankworth the words, a successful chemistry which yields nicely balanced and unforced songs that might have been around for years, always a promising sign. Sulzmann's flute is always a welcome guest, but what the record actually needs is a touch of one of his saxophones; it's a little too light and delicate.

Stefano D'Anna (born 1959) TENOR SAXOPHONE

**** **Leapin' In** Splasc(h) H 374-2
D'Anna; Enzo Pietropaoli (*b*); Fabrizio Sferra (*d*). 12/91.

D'Anna says that he admires the 'sculpture-like clarity' of Sonny Rollins's improvising, and his own playing strives to secure the same lucidity. If he is in Rollins's debt, though, he also goes to exceptional lengths to evade modern saxophone cliché. Rhythmically, he eschews easy double-time passages or tonal distortions: there's an evenness to his line which gives his solos an irresistible flow, and a steely clarity to his tone that doesn't detract from his lyricism. His seven compositions here all differ from one another, and three standards are scrupulously remodelled: 'I've Grown Accustomed To Her Face' is strikingly different from the classic Rollins reading, 'Be-Bop' is fantastically fast and biting, and 'Body And Soul', done as a duo for tenor and uncredited soprano, refers to the melody hardly at all and reminds us of a Konitz–Marsh collaboration. A stunning recital all round.

James Dapogny PIANO

*** **Laughing At Life** Discovery 74006
Dapogny; Jon-Erik Kellso (*t*); Bob Smith (*tb*); Kim Cusak (*cl, as, v*); Russ Whitman (*ts, bs, v*); Rod McDonald (*bj, g*); Maike Karoub (*b*); Wayne Jones (*d*). 92.
**** **Original Jelly Roll Blues** Discovery 74008
As above, except add Paul Klinger (*c*), Peter Ferran (*ss, as, cl*), Mike Walbridge (*tba*). 7/93.

Dapogny's Chicago Jazz Band make light work of these exemplary adventures in jazz repertory. Dapogny himself is a scholar of the music whose understanding spreads to the feel of playing it, as well as the nuts and bolts of how it's done. The result is an unusually loose-limbed kind of traditionalism that respects the fragility of some of this music as well as its robustness. *Laughing At Life* is a blend of styles – Chicago, New Orleans, New York – from both the 1920s and '30s, and as a result is something of a mixed bag; but the second disc is a masterful look at Jelly Roll Morton's music. Dapogny is a Morton specialist and comes as close as anyone has to reconvening the feel and texture of Jelly's sound. He orchestrated seven titles which the Red Hot Peppers never recorded, including 'Mamanita', 'Seattle Hunch' and 'Frog-I-More Rag', and even among the other tunes there are seldom-encountered pieces: 'Midnight Mama', 'Little Lawrence', 'Boogaboo'. The rocking pulse of the rhythm section – with Dapogny himself an indispensable element – is well-nigh perfect for the task, and tempos never become hectic, while the horns honour their forebears without settling for anonymity. Critically, they get a superb, rich, full sound in the studio, the kind of thing that's usually been denied to this kind of band. Which leaves no excuse for modern ears to leave this music alone.

Giovanni D'Argenzio SOPRANO AND TENOR SAXOPHONES

**(*) Domestic Standards Splasc(h) H 358-2
D'Argenzio; Aldo Farias (*g*); Angelo Farias (*b*); Umberto Guarino (*d*). 2–4/91.
A pleasing set of Italian pop tunes (with Lehár's 'You Are My Heart's Delight' apparently also qualifying), prettily played by this quartet of jazzmen from Campania. On a few occasions the rhythm section settle for a rock beat, which doesn't turn out so well, but D'Argenzio's tenor strikes a few impassioned sparks out of the unlikely material, and his soprano has a wiry elegance. Lightweight, but not without charm.

David Darling (born 1941) CELLO, ELECTRIC CELLO, PERCUSSION

**(*) Journal October ECM 1161
Darling (*clo* solo). 10/79.
** Cycles ECM 1219
Darling; Jan Garbarek (*ts, ss*); Steve Kuhn (*p*); Oscar Castro-Neves (*g*); Arild Andersen (*b*); Collin Walcott (*perc, sitar, tabla*). 11/81.
***(*) Cello ECM 1464
Darling (*clo* solo). 11/91, 1/92.
Sir Thomas Beecham once snapped in fury at a woman cellist: 'You have between your legs the most sensitive instrument known to man and all you can do is sit there and scratch it.' At first blush, there isn't much more to David Darling's music than rather haphazard scratchings that border on self-absorption if not self-abuse. Repeated hearings confirm that, far from abusing his enormous technical talent, Darling is striving for a music commensurate with it.

There is, of course, already a substantial body of jazz cello: Oscar Pettiford, Ron Carter, Dollar Brand, Dave Holland, Tristan Honsinger. Perhaps inevitably, Darling's basic conception, particularly when he uses his 8-string, solid-bodied, amplified instrument, is closest to that of ECM stablemate Eberhard Weber, who has considerably extended the timbral and tonal range of amplified bass playing. Darling's music is less dynamic and more textural; it is certainly more 'classical' in structure and may prove a little too evanescent for tastes conditioned by jazz rhythms and structures.

Though *Cycles* is probably the closest thing one could find to an identikit ECM record – shapelessly impressionistic themes and poster-print ethnic soundscapes, redeemed only by Jan Garbarek's unmistakable voice – *Cello* really is very good indeed. This is the record one would like to have heard first, suggesting a learning curve that wasn't in evidence on the earlier records. Where *Journal October* sounded like eavesdropped musical jottings, the new record has an almost cinematic precision of focus. Interestingly, ECM producer and film-maker Manfred Eicher is listed as co-composer on a couple of tracks, one of them a dedication to movie director, Jean-Luc Godard.

Carlo Actis Dato REEDS

***(*) Ankara Twist Splasc(h) H 302
Dato; Piero Ponzo (*cl, bcl, as, bs, f*); Enrico Fazio (*b*); Fiorenzo Sordini (*d*). 10/89.
Though Dato plays some tenor, he is most at home on baritone and bass clarinet, and he's a volatile and unpredictable player with a compensating brilliance of timing: just when one thinks he's gone too far in

a solo, he pulls it around and returns to the structure. As a composer, he writes themes that suggest some bridging-point between jazz and Balkan folk music, and the bucolic air of, say, 'Moonlight In Budapest' on *Oltremare* (currently on LP only and in need of CD transfer) is counterpointed by the very next tune on the record, 'Portorico Smog'. The tracks on this quartet album are rather brief and have a programmatic feel to them, but they're played with great verve and enthusiasm by the group: Ponzo is a useful foil to the leader, Fazio is authoritative, Sordini full of bustle.

***(*) **Dune** Splasc(h) H 354-2
     Dato; Laura Culver (*ss, clo, berim*); Alex Rolle (*xy, perc*), Massimo Barbiero (*d, mar*). 2/91.
Rolle and Barbiero join in the fun and the quartet take some aspects of 'world music' to the cleaners: march and tango rhythms are mischievously undercut by Carlo's tendency to jump into bawling improvisations – he lets off another almost brutal baritone assault on 'Ketchup' – and by Laura's deadpan drones and vamps on the cello. The two percussionists are pressed into subsidiary roles, leavening the sometimes sparse arrangements, and sometimes the action seems a little too contrived on a very long (74 minutes) CD: 'Mar Del Plata' is rather stiffly delivered. But the crackerjack liveliness of the best playing is a delight.

*** **Tree** Penta Flowers CDPEL 0139
     Dato; Laura Culver (*ss, clo*); Alex Rolle (*d*). 6/93.
Another hour of tangos, blues, jazz and so forth from Dato and his gang. This time, though, it's delivered not quite so irrepressibly. The solo spots tend to expose Culver's limitations as an improviser, Rolle offers minimalist percusssion, and even Dato himself sounds contained. The best music still has flair and invention, but fans of the earlier discs may be a little disappointed.

*** **Urartu** Leo 220
     Dato (*bs, bcl, ts* solo). 3/94.
Dato's first solo set is a typically mercurial and imaginative effort. He caricatures his reeds and loves to make excessive, elaborate noise with them, using circular breathing, slap-tonguing and whatever else he can think of and, though he plays a couple of standards, they come out rather cold. Most of the pieces seem like lightning sketches and once he's finished with the idea, it's done. Maybe not an important Dato record but another very enjoyable one.

Wolfgang Dauner (born 1935) PIANO, KEYBOARDS

** **Changes** Mood 33.613
     Dauner (*ky* solo). 3–9/78.
(*) **Solo Piano Mood 33.600
     Dauner (*p* solo). 82.
*** **Two Is Company** Mood 33.614
     Dauner; Albert Mangelsdorff (*tb*). 12/82.
(*) **Meditation On A Landscape – Tagore Mood 33.622
     Dauner; Charlie Mariano (*as, f*); Ernst Stroer (*perc*). n.d.
***(*) **One Night In '88** Mood 33.623
     As above, except Dino Saluzzi (*acc*) replaces Stroer. 4/88.
**** **Pas De Trois** Mood 33.630
     As above. n.d.
Dauner's back-catalogue on Mood has been making its way on to CD and affords a closer look at a somewhat neglected figure. His importance to European free music in the 1960s was scarcely accounted for on record, and the 1978 solo album is not the happiest of places to start, the music sounding akin to the meanderings of the decade's art rock with synthesizer sounds that now seem antiquated. The multi-tracked pianos of *Solo Piano* are more interesting, although this too sounds academically inclined: much exercise, little development. His stentorian manner makes a nice foil for Mangelsdorff, though, on the live *Two Is Company*. Dauner ladles out bluff, staccato passages while the trombonist writhes on top, sometimes noodling to himself but always making an intriguing noise. Less-than-perfect live sound doesn't matter too much.

The three albums with Charlie Mariano suggest that Dauner has found a soulmate of a kind. *Meditation On A Landscape* is a bit solemn and slow, the music done for a film on the life of Rabindranath Tagore, and only when Stroer adds some livelier percussion does the sound get much beyond a drone. But the two albums with Saluzzi are superb stuff. *One Night In '88* has a loose, largely improvisatory feel, the music structured round four longish and free-flowing triologues, but the more firmly centred *Pas De Trois* is beautifully modulated and balanced among the three voices: Mariano's achingly lovely 'Randy' is the clearest highlight, but all this music is almost ecstatically rich and songful.

Dauner is often no more than anchor, but his playing honours the situation, and Mariano returns to the alto for most of both discs, his most searching horn by far.

Kenny Davern (born 1935) CLARINET

***(*) **Stretchin' Out** Jazzology JCD-187
    Davern; Dick Wellstood (*p*); Chuck Riggs (*d*). 12/83.
***(*) **Never In A Million Years** Challenge CHR 70019
    As above except omit Riggs. 1/84.
***(*) **Playing For Kicks** Jazzology JCD-197
    Davern; Martin Litton (*p*); John Petters (*d*). 11/85.
*** **One Hour Tonight** Musicmasters 5003-2
    Davern; Howard Alden (*g*); Phil Flanigan (*b*); Giampaolo Biagi (*d*). 1/88.
*** **I'll See You In My Dreams** Musicmasters 5020-2
    Davern; Howard Alden (*g*); Phil Flanigan (*b*); Giampaolo Biagi (*d*). 1/88.
*** **My Inspiration** Musicmasters 65077-2
    Davern; Howard Alden (*g*); Bob Haggart (*b*); Bobby Rosengarden (*d*); strings. 9/91.
*** **East Side, West Side** Arbors ARCD 19137
    Davern; Dan Barrett (*c, tb*); Joel Helleny (*tb*); Bucky Pizzarelli (*g*); Bob Haggart (*b*); Tony DeNicola (*d*). 6/94.
*** **Kenny Davern & The Rhythm Men** Arbors ARCD 19147
    As above, except omit Barrett and Helleny; add John Bunch (*p*). 6/95.

Kenny Davern has recorded infrequently as a leader, and his records are the more valuable and surprising because of it: there's no waste in his execution, as garrulous as his playing often is, and he succeeds in playing in what is essentially a swing-based clarinet style while suggesting that he's also perfectly aware of every jazz development that has taken place since (he once recorded with Steve Lacy, Steve Swallow and Paul Motian on the now-deleted *Unexpected*, Kharma PK-7). He plays soprano with Bob Wilber in the Soprano Summit group, but on these records he sticks to the clarinet. *Stretchin' Out* is perhaps the single best showcase for his own playing, starting with a mellifluous and perfectly paced 'The Man I Love' and proceeding through five more standards with unflagging inventiveness. Wellstood is a superb partner, harrying and supporting him in equal measure, but the drawback is the presence of Riggs, who's not only too loud in the mix but superfluous to what should have been a duo session. The recently issued *Never In A Million Years* finds Davern and Wellstood alone together at New York's Vineyard Theatre and, though the bare format is a little dry across CD length, there is some marvellous sparring between the two men. *Playing For Kicks* goes back to the trio and, while Litton isn't remotely up to Wellstood's standard, it's another great clarinet set, with the ancient ('Willie The Weeper') and the comparatively modern ('Lullaby Of The Leaves') on the agenda. Much the same happens on both *One Hour Tonight* and *I'll See You In My Dreams*, though with Alden on hand rather than a pianist the music has a lighter, more fluid feel to it, and the treatment of some of the older pieces – especially 'Riverboat Shuffle' – strikes up something of the chamber-jazz feel of a Venuti–Lang group. Again, Davern himself is irreproachable. *My Inspiration* features string arrangements by Bob Haggart, dreamily played, with Davern relishing his opportunity and submitting his most graceful and romantic horn; yet the production isn't quite right, Rosengarden's drums oddly miked, and the balance tips into schmaltz just fractionally enough to waylay some of the tunes. *East Side, West Side* and *Rhythm Men* are two recent Davern sessions for Arbors. Barrett is a valuable front-line partner, playing cornet for the most part, though he picks up his slide for a very ripe duet with Helleny on 'Sidewalks Of New York'. Davern seems in good spirits on both sessions, and the rhythm section fits like a comfortable shoe. In the end, though, both dates sound a little hindered by their lack of preparation – expert playing, fine solos, but nothing to lift them a notch above what is now a bulging bracket of mainstream records.

Anthony Davis (born 1951) PIANO, KEYBOARDS, COMPOSER

*** **Lady Of The Mirrors** India Navigation IN 1047
    Davis (*p* solo). 80.
(*) **I've Known Rivers Gramavision 8201
    Davis; James Newton (*f*); Abdul Wadud (*clo*). 4/82.
*** **Hemispheres** Gramavision 8303
    Davis; Leo Smith (*t, steelophone, perc*); George Lewis (*tb*); Dwight Andrews (*f, picc, ss, cl*); J. D. Parran (*cl, cbcl*); Dave Samuels (*vib, mar*); Shem Guibbory (*v*); Eugene Friesen (*clo*); Rick Rozie (*b*); Pheeroan akLaff (*d, perc*). 7/83.

(*) **Middle Passage Gramavision 8401
    Davis (*p* solo). 84.
Inclined to be slightly abstract and structure-bound in his solo performances (a legacy of his work with the new-music outfit, Episteme), Davis loosens up considerably in freer company. Newton's Dolphyish flute contrasts very sharply with Davis's mannerly runs and long, discursive progressions in and out of harmony. Wadud combines bass and left-hand piano functions on his cello, using heavy bow pressure, and a percussive, resonant attack in more rhythmic passages.

Hemispheres brings together the two sides (!) of Davis's approach more successfully than anything else he has done to date. In overall impact it resembles a user-friendly version of Anthony Braxton's explorations of post-bop and post-serial language. AkLaff's drumming is powerfully idiomatic, and the horns are dominated by Smith's extraordinary diction; Parran's contrabass clarinet boldly goes where only Braxton had gone before, and Davis himself plays with great intelligence and control, as he does on *Middle Passage*.

In the late 1980s, Davis's attention was largely taken up with *X*, an opera on the life of the Black Muslim radical, Malcolm X. The later of the two solo albums represents his not-too-programmatic account of the Africans' coming to America and their uneasy confrontation with a new and alien culture. Resonantly recorded and beautifully played, it suffers only from an occasional lapse back into discursiveness (which may well be the fault of composers Ursula Oppens and Earle Howard). *Lady Of The Mirrors* may be a more successful – because more metaphorical and oblique – expression of broadly the same ideas. Not for all tastes by any means, but Davis is a powerfully individual voice at the more formal end of contemporary jazz.

Art Davis (born 1934) BASS

*** **Life** Soul Note 121143
    Davis; Pharoah Sanders (*ts*); John Hicks (*b*); Idris Muhammed (*d*). 10/85.
The sole album under the leadership of this hugely experienced bassist belongs primarily to Sanders, whose gruffly magisterial sound tends to conquer any surroundings it finds itself in. The spare, modal structures open the music out, and there is an extract from Davis's large-scale 'Concertpiece For Bass', but it's Sanders (and the powerful Hicks) that one remembers.

Charles Davis TENOR SAXOPHONE

*** **Reflections** Red 123247-2
    Davis; Barry Harris (*p*); Peter Washington (*b*); Ben Riley (*d*). 2/90.
Not usually a tenor specialist, Davis trades on his expertise in other horns to push his range up into a rather dry alto, or down into a huffing baritone, as on 'Monking'. He solos fluently, staying fairly close to the melody line. It's Harris, playing clattery little accelerandos or longer and more lyrical excursions (as on his own 'To Duke With Love', the only composition not by Davis), who ranges beyond. Question marks about the recording, which has Riley way up front and Washington, an ideal bassman for this kind of session, largely buried, even when he takes a couple of choruses on his own.

Davis has an impressive track record that takes in Cecil Taylor and Shirley Scott, Abdullah Ibrahim and Steve Lacy (for whose *Straight Horn* session he provided contrasting baritone lines). He's probably at his best working against different-sounding players, as Harris is here, and it's hard to imagine listening to him for long with a more conventional rhythm section.

Eddie 'Lockjaw' Davis (1922–86) TENOR SAXOPHONE

***(*) **The Cookbook Vol. 1** Original Jazz Classics OJC 652
    Davis; Jerome Richardson (*ts, f*); Shirley Scott (*org*); George Duvivier (*b*); Arthur Edgehill (*d*). 6/58.
*** **Smokin'** Original Jazz Classics OJC 705
    As above. 9–12/58.
*** **The Cookbook Vol. 2** Original Jazz Classics OJC 653
    As above. 12/58.
*** **The Cookbook Vol. 3** Original Jazz Classics OJC 756
    As above. 12/58.
*** **Gentle Jaws** Prestige PRCD-24160-2
    As above, except add Red Garland (*p*), Sam Jones (*b*), Arthur Taylor (*d*). 60.

One of the great saxophone pugilists, Eddie Davis made more or less the same record as a leader for 30 years. His apprenticeship in New York big bands in the 1940s led him towards rhythm-and-blues rather than bebop, but it was as either a section soloist (notably with Count Basie, where he starred on several 1950s sessions) or a jazz combo leader that Jaws functioned best. He spent the late 1950s leading the group which made the OJC reissues listed above. The records are formulaic – blustering solos over bluesy organ riffs – but endowed with a no-nonsense spirit that makes the discs highly enjoyable, taken one at a time. All three *Cookbook* albums are entertaining displays of good-natured fisticuffs, with the food theme followed through in all the titles ('The Chef', 'Skillet', 'In The Kitchen' and so on) and Jaws taking the lid off on 'Have Horn, Will Blow', which garners an extra notch for the first disc. Richardson's flute is a needless cooling-off device on most of the tracks, but these are fun records. *Gentle Jaws*, if that title doesn't sound like a contradiction, puts together a couple of small-hours sessions where the man huffs and hustles his way through a selection of top-notch ballads, sentiment without slop.

**** **Very Saxy** Original Jazz Classics OJC 458
>   Davis; Coleman Hawkins, Arnett Cobb, Buddy Tate (*ts*); Shirley Scott (*org*); George Duvivier (*b*); Arthur Edgehill (*d*). 4/59.

Prestige called in three other tenormen on their books to sit in with the Davis–Scott combo, and the results were barnstorming. The programme is all simple blues, but the flat-out exuberance of the playing is so exhilarating that it would be churlish to give it anything less than top marks, particularly in the excellent remastered sound. As competitive as it might appear, nobody is bested, and the clout of Davis and Cobb is matched by the suaver Tate and the grandiloquent Hawkins. Their 'Lester Leaps In' is a peerless display of saxophone sound.

(*) **Afro-Jaws Original Jazz Classics OJC 403
>   Davis; Clark Terry, Ernie Royal, Phil Sunkel, John Bello (*t*); Lloyd Mayers (*p*); Larry Gales (*b*); Ben Riley (*d*); Ray Barretto (*perc*).

*** **Trane Whistle** Original Jazz Classics OJC 429
>   Davis; Clark Terry, Richard Williams, Bob Bryant (*t*); Melba Liston, Jimmy Cleveland (*tb*); Jerome Richardson, Oliver Nelson, Eric Dolphy, George Barrow, Bob Ashton (*reeds*); Richard Wyands (*p*); Wendell Marshall (*b*); Roy Haynes (*d*). 9/60.

*** **Streetlights** Prestige PRCD 24150-2
>   Davis; Don Patterson (*org*); George Duvivier (*b*); Paul Weedon, Billy James (*d*). 11/62.

Afro-Jaws puts the saxophonist in front of brass and percussion to no very telling effect. But *Trane Whistle*, a set of Oliver Nelson arrangements for a cracking big band, puts him in his element and, though the charts are perhaps too functional to make the record a classic, the knock-out power of Davis's blowing is thrilling. An Ernie Wilkins arrangement of 'You Are Too Beautiful' shows off his skills with a ballad, too. *Streetlights* puts him back in the organ–combo setting with the slightly more 'modern' style of Patterson. Nobody puts themselves out particularly, and the tunes are mostly obvious, but the playing is hard to fault.

***(*) **Eddie 'Lockjaw' Davis With Michel Attenoux** Storyville STCD 5009
>   Davis; Patrick Artero (*t*); Claude Gousset (*tb*); Michel Attenoux (*as*); Gabriel Garvanoff (*p*); Jean-Pierre Mulot (*b*); Teddy Martin (*d*). 7/75.

*** **Jaws Strikes Again** Black & Blue 59.004 2
>   Davis; Wild Bill Davis (*org*); Billy Butler (*g*); Oliver Jackson (*d*). 1/76.

(*) **Swingin' Till The Girls Come Home Steeplechase SCS 1058
>   Davis; Thomas Clausen (*p*); Bo Stief (*b*); Alex Riel (*d*). 3/76.

*** **Straight Ahead** Original Jazz Classics OJC 629-2
>   Davis; Tommy Flanagan (*p*); Keter Betts (*b*); Bobby Durham (*d*). 5/76.

*** **Montreux '77** Original Jazz Classics OJC-384
>   Davis; Oscar Peterson (*p*); Ray Brown (*b*); Jimmie Smith (*d*). 7/77.

Davis went the journeyman route of wandering freelance through the 1970s and '80s. Of the European records, the Black & Blue session is superior through the reunion with Davis, whose energy is as infectious as the leader's. The Steeplechase session is a little routine. The real stars of the Montreux concert recording are Peterson and Brown, whose hard clarity creates a formidable platform for the nominal leader; but Davis himself sounds somewhat below par, his solos overwrought, and the music is only inconsistently exciting.

The pick of the bunch is certainly the Storyville session with a team of French mainstreamers. Impromptu as the session was – Davis simply harmonized his parts with Attenoux on the scores – it's played with enormous gusto by all seven men, the horns matching Jaws in their surly attack, and rollicking events like Neal Hefti's 'Midnite Blue' get a good thrashing. Yet there are three terrrific ballad solos by the tenorman on 'Moonlight In Vermont', 'What's New?' and 'Lush Life'. Excellent sound.

*** **Eddie Lockjaw Davis** Enja 3097

> Davis; Horace Parlan (*p*); Reggie Johnson (*b*); Oliver Queen (*d*). 2/81.

Davis was still a commanding player up until his unexpected death in 1986. His recording regimen was a casual one, and his later discs have a pot-luck quality, but the leader himself secures an unusual level of commitment: all his records manage to be recommendable for his own tenor playing. The Enja date matches him with a fine trio and is excellently recorded. But there is much more good Jaws out of print at present.

Jesse Davis ALTO SAXOPHONE

(*) **Horn Of Passion Concord CCD 4465

> Davis; Antoine Roney (*ts*); Mulgrew Miller (*p*); Rufus Reid, Tyler Mitchell (*b*); Jimmy Cobb, Eric McPherson (*d*). 1/91.

(*) **As We Speak Concord CCD 4512

> Davis; Robert Trowers (*tb*); Peter Bernstein (*g*); Jacky Terrasson (*p*); Dwayne Burno (*b*); Leon Parker (*d*). 2/92.

*** **Young At Art** Concord CCD 4565

> Davis; Ted Klum (*as*); Brad Mehldau (*p*); Peter Bernstein (*g*); Dwayne Burno (*b*); Leon Parker (*d*). 3/93.

***(*) **High Standards** Concord CCD 4624

> Davis; Nicholas Payton (*t*); Robert Trowers (*tb*); Dado Moroni (*p*); Peter Washington (*b*); Lewis Nash (*d*). 6/94.

Admirable as Davis's wish to avoid fashionable extremes of register in favour of a 'clean', middle-register delivery may be, his purchase on basic harmonic principles isn't always secure, and there is a repetitive, almost formulaic quality to his soloing on the first two albums. *Horn Of Passion* is split between quartet and quintet (with Roney) tracks and, though the playing has a nice bite and precision, a certain tiresomeness invades the frame from track to track.

In photographs, he bears a striking resemblance to Charlie Parker and he's Bird's man through and through, though his straight blues playing, as on the self-penned 'Recession Blues', suggests he's been listening to Cannonball Adderley as well. Bernstein's single-note lines on both *As We Speak* and *Young At Art* are a bit off the peg – Grant Green, Blue Note, *circa* 1965 – but he isn't helped by a rather erratic mix which tends to bury him under the horns. Trowers, like Davis a graduate of the Illinois Jacquet big band, is a sympathetic partner who swings well but never sounds like much more than a section man (except on 'Lush Life'). Davis's finest moment comes on Bird's 'Quasimodo', where he tackles the altered changes with a hint of more kept in reserve, springing one or two surprises in the final chorus.

The two more recent albums turn out for the best, without quite suggesting that Davis is really ready for anyone's front rank. The excellent Mehldau adds many finesses to the earlier album, and the duet with fellow altoman Klum on a swinging 'One For Cannon' hits the mark. *High Standards* brings back Trowers and enlists the big, brassy sound of Payton for the front line, and the compositions are an eclectic lot: Shorter's 'The Big Push', Dameron's 'On A Misty Night', the smart Trowers original 'Rush Hour', Junior Mance's 'Jubilation'. The result is a really rather impressive blueprint for a modern Messengers session – cracking solos, super-smart ensembles. Davis hardly stamps his individuality on the date, but maybe that's the point.

Miles Davis (1926–91) TRUMPET, FLUGELHORN

*** **Bopping The Blues** Black Lion BLCD 760102

> Davis; Gene Ammons (*ts*); Connie Wainwright (*g*); Linton Garner (*p*); Tommy Potter (*b*); Art Blakey (*d*); Earl Coleman, Ann Hathaway (*v*). 10/46.

**** **Birth Of The Cool** Capitol CDP 792862

> Davis; Kai Winding, J. J. Johnson (*tb*); Junior Collins, Sandy Siegelstein, Gunther Schuller (*frhn*); Lee Konitz (*as*); Gerry Mulligan (*bs*); John Barber (*tba*); John Lewis, Al Haig (*p*); Joe Shulman, Al McKibbon, Nelson Boyd (*b*); Max Roach, Kenny Clarke (*d*); Kenny Hagood (*v*). 1/49–3/50.

***(*) **The Real Birth Of The Cool** Bandstand BDCD 1512

> As above, except Mike Zwerin (*tb*) replaces Winding and Johnson, Curley Russell (*b*) replaces Shulman and Boyd; Siegelstein, Schuller, Haig and Clarke absent. 9/48.

***(*) **Cool Boppin'** Fresh Sound FSCD-1008

> As above, except add Kai Winding (*tb*), Sahib Shihab (*as*), Benjamin Lundy (*ts*), Cecil Payne (*bs*), Tadd Dameron (*p*), John Collins (*g*), Kenny Clarke (*d*), Carlos Vidal (*perc*). 9/48–2/49.

Davis's first records under his own name, in 1947, can be located in Charlie Parker's entry. The Black Lion sessions, which are not even specified in Ian Carr's meticulous discography, are easily ignorable. The groundbreaking *Birth Of The Cool* band – the record actually consists of three sessions recorded over the span of a year – was strikingly new to bebop listeners at the time, and it still sounds particularly fresh. Davis at the time presided over a group of young explorers based in New York, and the music by this nine-piece band (though a commercial failure) included some of the pioneering efforts by arrangers Mulligan and Gil Evans and composer John Carisi: the results were allusive, magical scores that channelled the irresistible energy of bop into surprising textures and piquant settings for improvisation. Davis and Konitz played as if a new world were almost within their grasp. The availability of the original LP has fluctuated over the years, but the capable if no more than adequate remastering for CD should ensure its current catalogue life. The Bandstand record brings to CD airshot recordings from the Royal Roost club, where Davis's band made a brief engagement: the sound is comparatively poor, but it's a valuable look at how these arrangements came alive in person, and the soloists are spontaneously exciting, especially the leader. Nine of the same tracks open *Cool Boppin'*, but the remaining six are by a ten-piece Tadd Dameron group which makes an interesting addendum to the Davis sessions: 'Focus', 'Webb's Delight' and 'Casbah' display Dameron's askew lyricism to sometimes ponderous effect, but Davis's own improvisations hit some daringly high notes for him, and it makes for an interesting contrast to the Nonet tracks. Sound is about the same as on the Bandstand disc.

*** **Quintet With Lee Konitz; Sextet With Jackie McLean** Fresh Sound FSCD 1000
    Davis; Don Elliott (*mel, vib*); Lee Konitz, Jackie McLean (*as*); John Lewis, Gil Coggins (*p*);
    Curley Russell, Connie Henry (*b*); Max Roach, Connie Kay (*d*); Kenny Hagood (*v*). 9/48–5/52.
Useful glimpses of Davis in action away from the studios, at a period when he wasn't getting much done on legitimate recordings. The 1948 session features him with Konitz on four titles, and aside from a lugubrious 'You Go To My Head' all are fast and exciting. Davis hits some improbable high notes and is in ebullient mood, while Konitz's serpentine elegance is already individual, if attuned to a more straight-ahead bop vision than he would later apply. The sextet date is a bit cluttered but still offers some strong bop-styled playing: the best performance is a Davis original, 'Out Of The Blue', with an impassioned and agile trumpet solo and the young McLean in eager form. Sound for both sessions is typically muddy but listenable enough.

(*) **Miles Davis With Horns Original Jazz Classics OJC 053
    Davis; Bennie Green, Sonny Truitt (*tb*); Sonny Rollins, Al Cohn, Zoot Sims (*ts*); John Lewis (*p*);
    Leonard Gaskin, Percy Heath (*b*); Roy Haynes, Kenny Clarke (*d*). 1/51–2/53.
*** **Dig** Original Jazz Classics OJC 005
    Davis; Jackie McLean (*as*); Sonny Rollins (*ts*); Walter Bishop Jr (*p*); Tommy Potter (*b*); Art
    Blakey (*d*). 10/51.
Davis's first sessions for Prestige are scarcely harbingers of what was to come: the earliest is doleful and undistinguished, and while there are a couple of challenging trumpet solos on 'My Old Flame' and 'Blueing', the second isn't a great deal better; sound-balance favours the horns at the expense of the rhythm section. The 1953 date, arranged by Cohn, finds Davis in atypical but obviously enjoyable surroundings, since he plays brightly alongside the two-tenor partnership; on their own terms, these four tracks offer slight but exuberant entertainment.

*** **Collectors' Items** Original Jazz Classics OJC 071
    Davis; Sonny Rollins, Charlie Parker (*ts*); Walter Bishop Jr, Tommy Flanagan (*p*); Percy Heath,
    Paul Chambers (*b*); Philly Joe Jones, Art Taylor (*d*). 1/53–3/56.
*(*) **At Last! Miles Davis And The Lighthouse All Stars** Original Jazz Classics OJC 480
    Davis; Rolf Ericson, Chet Baker (*t*); Bud Shank (*as*); Bob Cooper (*ts*); Lorraine Geller, Russ
    Freeman (*p*); Howard Rumsey (*b*); Max Roach (*d*). 9/53.
The 1953 session with Parker on tenor is a curio, and it makes an odd makeweight for the accompanying, later quintet date with Rollins, which includes a skilful solo by the saxophonist on 'Vierd Blues' and a fine investigation of Brubeck's 'In Your Own Sweet Way' by Davis. This session, along with *Blue Moods* (OJC 043, see below), may also still be available as the double-LP *Collectors' Items* (Prestige P 24022). The live jam session recorded at the Lighthouse is best forgotten by admirers of the trumpeter, whose desultory playing was hardly worth preserving on ponderous versions of 'Infinity Promenade' and 'Round Midnight'; the others do better, but not much. Surprisingly well-recorded under the circumstances.

***(*) **Miles Davis: Volume 1** Blue Note CDP 7815012
    Davis; J. J. Johnson (*tb*); Jackie McLean (*as*); Jimmy Heath (*ts*); Gil Coggins, Horace Silver (*p*);
    Oscar Pettiford, Percy Heath (*b*); Kenny Clarke, Art Blakey (*d*). 5/52–3/54.

***(*) **Miles Davis: Volume 2** Blue Note CDP 7815022
    As above.
*** **The Best Of Miles Davis** Blue Note CDP 7982872
    As above Blue Note and Capitol sessions, except add Cannonball Adderley (*as*), Hank Jones
    (*p*), Sam Jones (*b*). 1/49–3/58.
While these are inconsistent records, they're also Davis's most personal and clear-sighted statements up
to this point, both as a soloist and as an emerging small-group leader. Although still suffering heroin
addiction when the first two sessions were made, and with his professional life in considerable disarray,
Davis was beginning to move beyond the confines of small-group bop. The tracks on the earlier dates
are still brief in duration with pithy and well-turned solos, but the emotional timbre is different from
bop – intense yet restrained, cool yet plangent. The first date seems comparatively hurried, but the
second, with fine compositions from Johnson, Heath and Bud Powell included, is indispensable. The
third, featuring Davis as sole horn, includes some of his best playing to date, with fast, eventful solos on
'Take Off' and 'The Leap' and a potent reading of Monk's 'Well You Needn't'.
    The jumbled sequencing of the original LPs has been corrected for CD release: the first and third
sessions are complete on the first volume and the second is on Volume 2. The sound is a little fresher if
not noticeably superior in the remastering.
    The *Best Of* collection covers the Blue Note albums, *Birth Of The Cool* and 20 minutes of material from
Cannonball Adderley's *Somethin' Else* session from 1958. A fine selection, but the original discs are all
but indispensable.

*** **Blue Haze** Original Jazz Classics OJC 093
    Davis; Dave Schildkraut (*as*); John Lewis, Charles Mingus, Horace Silver (*p*); Percy Heath (*b*);
    Kenny Clarke, Art Blakey, Max Roach (*d*). 5/53–4/54.
**** **Walkin'** Original Jazz Classics OJC 213
    Davis; J. J. Johnson (*tb*); Dave Schildkraut (*as*); Lucky Thompson (*ts*); Horace Silver (*p*); Percy
    Heath (*b*); Kenny Clarke (*d*). 4/54.
***(*) **Bags' Groove** Original Jazz Classics OJC 245
    Davis; Sonny Rollins (*ts*); Milt Jackson (*vib*); Thelonious Monk, Horace Silver (*p*); Percy Heath
    (*b*); Kenny Clarke (*d*). 6/54.
**** **Miles Davis And The Modern Jazz Giants** Original Jazz Classics OJC 347
    Davis; John Coltrane (*ts*); Milt Jackson (*vib*); Thelonious Monk, Red Garland (*p*); Percy Heath,
    Paul Chambers (*b*); Kenny Clarke, Philly Joe Jones (*d*). 12/54–10/56.
The *Blue Haze* set is split between a merely good quartet date from 1953 and three altogether excellent
tracks from the following March, by the same quartet that cut the final date for Blue Note. Plus a single
track from the April 1954 session with the undervalued Schildkraut on alto. *Walkin'* and *Bags' Groove*
find the great leader of post-bop jazz hitting his stride. The former session includes two clear-cut
masterpieces in the title-track and 'Blue 'N' Boogie': the solos here are brilliantly sharp, dazzlingly
inventive. Most of the *Bags' Groove* set is by a quintet with Rollins, which produced fine if slightly less
enthralling music, though the trumpeter uses the Harmon mute sound which was to become a trademark for the first time on 'Oleo'. Two compelling takes of the title-track round off the record, but these
come from the Christmas Eve date which is otherwise contained on OJC 347, the only official meeting
between Davis, Monk and Jackson. The clash between Jackson's typically fleet lines and the different
kinds of astringency represented by Monk and Davis made for a tense and compelling situation. This
disc is, in turn, completed by a very fine 'Round Midnight' by the quintet with John Coltrane.

(*) **The Musings Of Miles Original Jazz Classics OJC 004
    Davis; Red Garland (*p*); Oscar Pettiford (*b*); Philly Joe Jones (*d*). 6/55.
*** **Blue Moods** Original Jazz Classics OJC 043
    Davis; Britt Woodman (*tb*); Teddy Charles (*vib*); Charles Mingus (*b*); Elvin Jones (*d*). 7/55.
***(*) **Quintet / Sextet** Original Jazz Classics OJC 012
    Davis; Jackie McLean (*as*); Milt Jackson (*vib*); Ray Bryant (*p*); Percy Heath (*b*); Art Taylor (*d*).
    8/55.
Davis's final quartet session prior to the formation of his famous quintet is a surprisingly lacklustre
affair (Jones and Pettiford were allegedly exhausted or, in Pettiford's case, drunk). Davis holds the music
together but sounds rather sour. The brief *Blue Moods* session, though poor value on a single disc, offers
an instrumentation which Davis never tried again, and has a desolate version of 'Nature Boy' that
prepares one for the melancholy poetry of his later ballads. The August 1955 session is something of a
farewell to Davis's most carefree music, with four pacy and involving workouts on mostly blues
material, though at little more than 30 minutes this is also poor value for a single CD.

(*) **Hi-Hat All Stars Fresh Sound FSRCD 13
    Davis; Jay Migliori (*ts*); Bob Freeman, Al Walcott (*p*); Jimmy Woode (*b*); Johnny Zitano (*d*). 55.

Eavesdroppings from Boston, the bootleg capital of America. Miles's insufficiency as a bebopper is still in evidence here, and the band are giving him no help whatever. Though there is much of historical interest on it, this is a pretty dreary airshot with not much to recommend it to non-specialists.

***(*) **Miles** Original Jazz Classics OJC 006
    Davis; John Coltrane (*ts*); Red Garland (*p*); Paul Chambers (*b*); Philly Joe Jones (*d*). 11/55.
**** **Cookin'** Original Jazz Classics OJC 128
    As above. 10/56.
**** **Relaxin'** Original Jazz Classics OJC 190
    As above. 5/56–10/56.
**** **Workin'** Original Jazz Classics OJC 296
    As above. 5/56–10/56.
**** **Steamin'** Original Jazz Classics OJC 391
    As above. 5/56–10/56.
**** **Miles Davis Chronicle: The Complete Prestige Recordings, 1951–1956** Prestige PRCD 102 8CD
    As above.
Despite an initially unfavourable reaction from musicians and listeners, Davis's 1956 quintet quickly established a major following, and their five albums for Prestige (actually recorded to fulfil a contract before Davis could move to Columbia) have endured as some of the most famous documents of the music as it stood in the mid-1950s. They are uneven in inspiration and there is no single standout record, but the sense of spontaneity and of a combative group in brilliant creative flux is surpassed by no other jazz records. The greatest contrast is between Davis – spare, introspective, guileful – and the leonine, blustering Coltrane, who was still at a somewhat chaotic stage of his development. But equally telling are the members of the rhythm section, who contrive to create a different climate behind each soloist and sustain the logical flow of the tunes. Recorded at a handful of marathon sessions, each record has its own special rewards: a slow, pierced 'My Funny Valentine' on *Cookin'*, the supple swing of 'I Could Write A Book' and revitalized bebop in 'Woody'n You' from *Relaxin'*, a haunted trumpet reading of 'It Never Entered My Mind' on *Workin'*. All five, however, should be a part of any significant jazz collection.
    Rudy van Gelder's splendid engineering and Bob Weinstock's production have ensured that the music has survived in excellent condition, and the CD reissues – although the individual OJC editions are all rather short measure – sound well enough, if a little compressed. The English company Ace has, however, coupled *Cookin'* and *Relaxin'* on a single CD (Ace/Prestige CDJZD 003), a considerable bargain.

***(*) **Round About Midnight** Columbia 460605
    As above. 10/55–9/56.
A Columbia footnote to the Prestige sessions, with six tracks culled from three sessions, cut in the middle of the Prestige tenure. The playing is probably as fine, but somehow the music doesn't cast quite the consistent spell which the Prestige records do.

**** **Miles Ahead** Columbia 460606
    Davis; Bernie Glow, Ernie Royal, Louis Mucci, Taft Jordan, John Carisi (*t*); Frank Rehak,
    Jimmy Cleveland, Joe Bennett (*tb*); Tom Mitchell (*btb*); Willie Ruff, Tony Miranda (*frhn*); Lee
    Konitz (*as*); Romeo Penque, Sid Cooper (*woodwinds*); Danny Bank (*bcl*); Bill Barber (*tba*); Paul
    Chambers (*b*); Art Taylor (*d*); Gil Evans (*cond*). 5/57.
Davis's first full-length collaboration with arranger Gil Evans remains the best, if not the best known of their recordings. While the ensemble as directed by Evans isn't always note-perfect – a failing even more obvious on the later *Porgy And Bess* – the interlinking of the tracks with written bridge passages and subsequent splicing is impeccably done, and Davis the soloist provides continuity and spontaneous illumination of the scores, which make manifest the neo-classical leanings of such previous ensembles as the 'Birth Of The Cool' nonet. The excitement which the record created – as a long-playing record, a 'concerto', and a vehicle for Davis's lyric side, spotlit by his use of flugelhorn throughout the album – survives the passage of time. Now available again in its original format.

**** **L'Ascenseur Pour L'Echafaud** Fontana 836305
    Davis; Barney Wilen (*ts*); René Urtreger (*p*); Pierre Michelot (*b*); Kenny Clarke (*d*). 12/57.
Miles responded instinctively when asked to contribute music to Louis Malle's bleak thriller, ostensibly a murder story but actually about the claustrophobic impact of social technology. The film would certainly not now be widely remembered, were it not for Miles's music, his first significant exercise in composition and hailed as a pointer towards the abstract, themeless experiments of the following decade. Most of the fragments are slow and moody, though there are also a couple of fast tracks (one of them the inevitable motorway number) in which he plays with barely controlled intensity. Interesting as it is on record, this music really makes complete sense only when combined with Malle's images. So

successful was Miles's scoring that he effectively redraws the movie's inner landscape, accentuating its psychological elements and the philosophical calm of its somewhat fugitive subtext.

**** **Milestones** Columbia 460827
> Davis; Cannonball Adderley (*as*); John Coltrane (*ts*); Red Garland (*p*); Paul Chambers (*b*); Philly Joe Jones (*d*). 4/58.

Milestones is as essential as any Miles Davis of the period. While usually considered a transitional album, between the quintet period and the modal jazz initiated fully in *Kind Of Blue*, it stands as a superb record by itself. Davis's contrasting solos on 'Sid's Ahead' – a brooding, coolly mournful improvisation – and 'Milestones' itself – a sharply ambiguous and dancing treatment – are enough to make the record important, but the standard of writing and playing by everyone involved makes this an outstanding group record as well as one of Davis's strongest sessions.

***(*) **Miles And Coltrane** Columbia 460824
> Davis; John Coltrane (*ts*); Cannonball Adderley (*as*); Bill Evans, Red Garland (*p*); Paul Chambers (*b*); Jimmy Cobb, Philly Joe Jones (*d*). 10/55–7/58.

***(*) **'58 Miles** Columbia 467918
> Davis; Cannonball Adderley (*as*); John Coltrane (*ts*); Bill Evans (*p*); Paul Chambers (*b*); Jimmy Cobb (*d*). 58.

***(*) **Mostly Miles** Phontastic NCD 8813
> As above. 7/58.

The two 1955 tracks, 'Little Melonae' and 'Budo', are leftovers from an earlier session. Most of the other material on the CBS record is from a live set at the 1958 Newport Festival. There is much effervescence in the live setting and Coltrane, especially, is in tremendous form on 'Ah-Leu-Cha' and 'Bye Bye Blackbird'; the contrasts with Davis's spareness were seldom as striking as here. Evans and Adderley also play well, the former taking a fine solo on 'Straight No Chaser', but it's the two principal protagonists who make the record.

The 1958 compilation brings together material that was formerly on *Black Giants* and *Jazz At The Plaza*, the latter a brilliant live date that has been out of catalogue for some time. Miles's performances on 'My Funny Valentine' and a melting 'Oleo' are good to have back in catalogue, as is the Newport Festival set on *Mostly Miles*.

**** **Porgy And Bess** Columbia 450985
> Davis; Louis Mucci, Ernie Royal, John Coles, Bernie Glow (*t*); Jimmy Cleveland, Joseph Bennett, Richard Hixon, Frank Rehak (*tb*); Daniel Banks, Cannonball Adderley (*as*); Willie Ruff, Julius Watkins, Gunther Schuller (*frhn*); Philip Bodner, Romeo Penque, Jerome Richardson (*f*); Bill Barber (*tba*); Paul Chambers (*b*); Philly Joe Jones, Jimmy Cobb (*d*). 7–8/58.

Gil Evans scored Gershwin's masterpiece in glowing terms, using flutes and horns in place of saxes to create a palette of delicacy as well as toughness. Davis rose to the occasion, sounding at his most majestic in the contemplative improvisations on 'Summertime' and even making the brief passages such as 'Gone, Gone, Gone' into something singular and memorable. If the record falls a trifle short, it's in the imperfections of the ensemble, which mar some of the more difficult passages. The remastering is well enough done but adds little to the clarity of the original LP.

*** **Jazz At The Plaza** Columbia 471510
> Davis; Cannonball Adderley (*as*); John Coltrane (*ts*); Bill Evans (*p*); Paul Chambers (*b*); Philly Joe Jones (*d*). 9/58.

Probably the stand-out track on this glitzy session from the New York City Hotel is 'My Funny Valentine', which features just Miles and rhythm. Unlike some of the official live sessions, this lacks a sense of history and comes across now merely (merely!) as an excellent gig by one of the premier working bands of the day. For an artist of Miles's world-historical dimensions that somehow doesn't seem enough. Fascinating as the interplay with Coltrane and Adderley is, and within the year it was to yield *Kind Of Blue*, it isn't an album to put high on a shopping list.

**** **Kind Of Blue** Columbia 460603
> Davis; Cannonball Adderley (*as*); John Coltrane (*ts*); Bill Evans, Wynton Kelly (*p*); Paul Chambers (*b*); Jimmy Cobb (*d*). 3–4/59.

One of the two or three most celebrated albums in jazz history still lives up to its reputation, especially in this fine remastering for CD. The key presence may be that of Bill Evans (Kelly plays only on the blues, 'Freddie Freeloader') whose allusive, almost impressionist accompaniments are the ideal platform for the spacious solos created by the horns, in what was the first widely acknowledged 'modal jazz' date. Tension is consistently established within the ensembles, only for Davis and Coltrane especially to resolve it in songful, declamatory solos. The steady mid-tempos and plaintive voicings on 'So What' and 'All Blues' establish further the weightless, haunting qualities of the music, which no collection, serious or casual, should be without. Columbia have now also released a fine 'Mastersound' edition of the session (CK 64403).

***(*) **Sketches Of Spain** Columbia 460604
    Davis; Bernie Glow, Ernie Royal, John Coles, Louis Mucci, Taft Jordan (*t*); Frank Rehak, Dick Hixon (*tb*); John Barrows, Jimmy Buffington, Earl Chapin, Joe Singer, Tony Miranda (*frhn*); Albert Block, Eddie Caine, Harold Feldman, Romeo Penque (*woodwinds*); Jack Knitzer (*bsn*); Danny Bank (*bcl*); Bill Barber (*tba*); Janet Putnam (*hp*); Paul Chambers (*b*); Jimmy Cobb, Elvin Jones (*d*). 11/59–3/60.

Though it has many moments of luminous beauty, it's hard to evade the feeling that this is an overrated record. Despite – or perhaps because of – far more time in the studios than was used on the earlier collaborations with Gil Evans, the feel of the record seems ill-focused, with the ambitious 'Concierto De Aranjuez' sounding sometimes like inflated light music, with only Davis's occasional intensities driving energy into the whole. The dialogue between trumpet and ensemble in 'Solea' is the best sequence on the session. Although the trumpeter is giving of his best throughout, the sometimes haphazard percussion tracks and muzzy ensembles suggest a harbinger of some of the electric trance music which Davis would later delve into in the 1970s. The original sound – never very good, as far as the orchestra was concerned – receives a rather dry remastering for CD.

***(*) **Miles Davis In Stockholm Complete** Dragon DRCD 228 4CD
    As above, except add Sonny Stitt (*as, ts*). 3 & 10/60.

A number of live recordings exist from this period, away from Davis's officially sanctioned releases, and the material on Dragon – excellently recorded by Swedish Radio – affords valuable glimpses of two European sojourns in 1960. The concert with Coltrane (which includes a six-minute interview with the saxophonist) suggests a battle of giants: Trane piles in with all his most abandoned lines, while Davis remains – especially in a nearly anguished 'All Blues' – aloof. The rhythm section play with impervious jauntiness and it adds up to a tremendous concert recording. The session with Stitt is only slightly less effective. Stitt, admittedly, wrestles with no dark demons, but his plangency and itch to play are scarcely less powerful than Coltrane's, and his switching between alto and tenor offers more light and shade. Davis is again bitingly inventive, even on material which he must already have played many times over.

*** **Some Day My Prince Will Come** Columbia CK 466312
    Davis; Hank Mobley, John Coltrane (*ts*); Wynton Kelly (*p*); Paul Chambers (*b*); Philly Joe Jones, Jimmy Cobb (*d*). 3/61.

***(*) **Friday Night At The Blackhawk: Volume 1** Columbia 463334
    As above, except omit Coltrane and Jones. 4/61.

***(*) **Saturday Night At The Blackhawk: Volume 2** Columbia 465191
    As above. 4/61.

Although a fine, individual tenor player, Hank Mobley never sounded right in the Davis band – at least, not after Coltrane, whose 'guest' appearance on the somewhat lethargic *Some Day My Prince Will Come* is astonishing: he plays two solos, on the title-track and on 'Teo', which put everything else in the shade. The live sessions from The Blackhawk were Davis's first attempts at an official live album, and although Mobley plays well – he negotiates the tempo of a rocketing 'Walkin'' without any bother – he sounds at some remove from the rest of the group, which was sparking with Miles. The leader's solos, both muted and open, mix a spitting intensity with thoughtful, circling phrases, at both fast and medium tempos. The outstanding recording of the original albums has been capably transferred to CD.

***(*) **Miles Davis At Carnegie Hall 1961** Columbia 472357 2CD
    Davis; Bernie Glow, Ernie Royal, Louis Mucci, Johnny Coles (*t*); Frank Rehak, Dick Hixon, Jimmy Knepper (*tb*); Julius Watkins, Paul Ingraham, Bob Swisshelm (*frhn*); Bill Barber (*tba*); Hank Mobley (*ts*); Jerome Richardson, Romeo Penque, Eddie Caine, Bob Tricarico, Danny Bank (*reeds, woodwinds*); Wynton Kelly (*p*); Paul Chambers (*b*); Janet Putnam (*hp*); Bobby Rosengarden (*perc*). 5/61.

Davis's Carnegie Hall concert of 1961 set the seal on his emergence as a jazz superstar during the previous five years. Split between music by the quintet and Evans's arrangements of some of the material from their albums together, the night was distinguished by the leader's own playing – he plays with more incisiveness on the Evans material than he does on the studio versions, and 'Teo' and 'No Blues' feature compelling solos – but Mobley is again no match for what Coltrane might have done, and 'Concierto De Aranjuez' sounds no more convincing in this setting.

After some time when the material was available only on two separate discs, the original release and a 'more of' sequel called *Live Miles*, the whole concert is now available on a double CD. Coming to it again after a break and entire, one is startled by the sheer grandeur of the conception. Even in 1961, at what must be considered the peak of his career, no jazz musician could have expected a setting as sumptuous as Gil gives him and it whets the appetite for the one major item still awaiting release, the promised multi-volume compilation of all their work together. When it appears, it will represent one of the pillars of jazz history and a key moment in the discography. Until then, this rather special occasion will suffice.

*** Seven Steps To Heaven Columbia 466970

> Davis; George Coleman (*ts*); Victor Feldman, Herbie Hancock (*p*); Ron Carter (*b*); Tony Williams, Frank Butler (*d*). 4 & 5/63.

Two oddities on this: Miles playing with a West Coast band, and including such classic jazz pieces as 'Basin Street Blues' and 'Baby, Won't You Please Come Home'. The later session unveiled his new group, with Tony Williams and Herbie Hancock. They sound relatively sure-footed on *Seven Steps*, and Hancock certainly understands the need for subtler harmonic – or rather chromatic – shading in the music. It's possible to hear in these sessions the seeds of change, but it's an abum that is much more illuminating retrospectively, once Miles's later and more revolutionary work has been absorbed.

**(*) Quiet Nights Columbia COLCD 85556

> Davis; Ernie Royal, Johnny Coles, Bernie Glow, Louis Mucci (*t*); Jimmy Knepper, Dick Hixon, Frank Rehak (*tb*); John Barrows, Julius Watkins, Paul Ingraham, Robert Swisshelm (*frhn*); Bill Barber (*tba*); Steve Lacy (*ss*); Romeo Penque, Jerome Richardson, Eddie Caine, Bob Banks, Bob Tricarico (*reeds*); George Coleman (*ts*); Janet Putnam (*hp*); Victor Feldman (*p*); Ron Carter, Paul Chambers (*b*); Frank Butler, Jimmy Cobb, Elvin Jones (*d*); Bobby Rosengarden (*perc*); Gil Evans (*cond*). 7, 8 & 11/62.

Miles was furious when this record was released, accusing Teo Macero of working behind his back. It is pretty thin stuff, rather anonymous big-band arrangements with just one small-group track, 'Summer Night', recorded in Los Angeles with the *Seven Steps To Heaven* sextet. Some of the tunes, 'Corcovado' and 'Slow Samba', are very beautiful, but this is the nearest Miles ever got to easy listening.

**** Miles In Antibes Columbia 462940

> Davis; George Coleman (*ts*); Herbie Hancock (*p*); Ron Carter, Richard Davis (*b*); Tony Williams (*d*). 6/63, 5/66.

***(*) My Funny Valentine Columbia 471276

> As above. 2/64.

**** The Complete Concert, 1964 Columbia 471246 2CD

> As above. 2/64.

In Antibes is a very fine concert set from a generally undervalued period in Davis's discography. Some of the excellent albums with Coleman on tenor have yet to appear on CD, but this one, recorded only a few weeks after the band had been formed, is unpredictable and exciting.

At Antibes, Coleman's muscular, scouring style proves surprisingly effective and the new, young rhythm section, powered by the thunderous rhythm of Williams, draws Davis into taking fresh risks. Even though the material is much the same as it had been for the last five years, the treatments are newly abstract or expressionist by turns.

Recorded at the Philharmonic Hall in New York, *My Funny Valentine* has a moody and elegiac quality which Miles attributed to President Kennedy's death, the previous November. Certainly the group plays with almost ritual stateliness and there is a plangent, wounded quality to the trumpet-sound that was to emerge only rarely thereafter. The double-CD set brings together *My Funny Valentine* with *Four & More*. Excellent value.

***(*) Miles In Berlin Columbia CD62976

> As above, except Wayne Shorter (*ts*) replaces Coleman. 9/64.

Wayne Shorter's arrival stabilized the new group, since Shorter was a major composer as well as soloist. Although the set in Berlin is the standard one of 'So What' and so on, the pungency of Davis's solos is matched by a new depth of interplay with the rhythm section, as well as by Shorter's phenomenally harsh-sounding parts. The highlight is a superbly intense reading of 'Autumn Leaves'. There is a huge amount of bootleg material from this period; not as much as of the 1980s band, but still in distracting quantities. We have in the past noted some questionable issues, simply because of their historical importance, but readers should be aware that few of the live albums (and certainly almost none with unfamiliar label names) have been authorized, and many are acoustically sub-standard. *Caveat emptor*.

**** E.S.P. Columbia 467899

> As above. 1/65.

**** Miles Smiles Columbia 471004

> As above. 10/66.

***(*) Sorcerer Columbia 474369

> As above. 5/67.

***(*) **Nefertiti** Columbia 467089
    As above. 6–7/67.
*** **Miles In The Sky** Columbia 472209
    As above, except add George Benson (*g*). 1 & 5/68.
*** **Filles De Kilimanjaro** Columbia 467088
    As above, except add Chick Corea (*ky*), Dave Holland (*b*). 6–9/68.
*** **Circle In The Round** Columbia 467898 2CD
    Davis; Cannonball Adderley (*as*); John Coltrane, Hank Mobley, Wayne Shorter (*ts*); Herbie
    Hancock, Chick Corea, Red Garland, Wynton Kelly, Joe Zawinul, Bill Evans (*p*); George
    Benson, Joe Beck (*g*); Paul Chambers, Ron Carter, Dave Holland (*b*); Philly Joe Jones, Jimmy
    Cobb, Tony Williams (*d*). 10/55–1/70.

Miles Smiles and *Sorcerer* were long out of print, leaving a hiatus in an already hard-to-read period.
Restored, this group charts the extraordinary progress of the most mysterious of all of Davis's bands.
The trumpeter returns to his tactic with Coltrane, of paring away: sometimes he doesn't even take a
solo, as on the slowly simmering 'Nefertiti', which the horns pace out over Williams's boiling rhythms.
On *Sorcerer*, he contributes nothing to the writing, leaving most of it to Shorter. Only with *Miles In The
Sky*, another of the trumpeter's transitional works, does he start writing again.

    Miles Smiles had opened up areas that were to be Miles's main performing territory for the next few
years, arguably for the rest of his career. The synthesis of complete abstraction with more or less
straightforward blues-playing (Shorter's 'Footprints' is constructed with brilliant simplicity) was to
sustain him right through the darkness of the 1970s bands to the later period when 'New Blues' became
a staple of his programmes. After *Smiles*, *E.S.P.* is probably the best album, with seven excellent original
themes and the players building a huge creative tension between Shorter's oblique, churning solos and
the leader's private musings, and within a rhythm section that is bursting to fly free while still playing
time. *Nefertiti* is nearly as strong, if a little too cool, but *Filles De Kilimanjaro* is a little stiffer, with the
quintet at the point of break-up (Corea and Holland arrive for two tracks).

    The live albums are different – the programmes continue to look back to standard Davis sets, and the
long, exhaustive treatments of the likes of 'Stella By Starlight' and 'All Blues' sometimes ramble yet
seem to have a different subtext for every player. There is always something happening. The real *sine qua
non* for this period is the material recorded at the Plugged Nickel in Chicago, which we formerly
included in this group. Those sessions have now been issued entire and are noted below.

    Circle In The Round is an interesting if seldom compelling set of out-takes from Davis's Columbia
albums over a 25-year period. The long title-track is an attempt at a mesmerizing mood piece which
works for some of the time but tends to fade in and out of the listener's attention. Earlier pieces with the
great quintet, plus a marvellous 'Love For Sale' from 1958, are more vital. The CD omits some of the
music from the original double-LP.

    **** **The Complete Live At The Plugged Nickel** Columbia CXK 66955 7CD
    Davis; Wayne Shorter (*ts*); Herbie Hancock (*p*); Ron Carter (*b*); Tony Williams (*d*). 12/65.

When future histories of jazz are written (and it would be possible to write a history of jazz between
1945 and 1990 from the point of view of Miles's part in it), these sessions will be adduced as a turning
point, and a closely documented one. Arguably Miles's best ever group, working its way out of one
phase and into another in which time and harmony, melody and dynamics were radically rethought. The
improvisations here would have been inconceivable a mere couple of years earlier; three years later, they
fed directly into Miles's electric revolution and the beginning of what was to be his long final phase.

    To set the time and place, these were recorded (officially, by Columbia engineers) at the Plugged Nickel
club in Chicago. Unlike the Blackhawk sessions, the registration was almost as good as in a studio. At
first glance, and with an eye to the predictably high price, one might wonder whether so repetitive a
documentation would be worth either the cash or the patience (or the time and strength, just to complete Herman Melville's trinity-plus-one). The short answer is: yes, and unambiguously so, because here
it is possible to observe at the closest quarters Miles and his musicians working through their ideas set by
set in ways that make the named material, the songs, more or less irrelevant. Even when it is clear he is
working from 'Stella By Starlight' or 'My Funny Valentine', Miles is moving out into areas of
harmonic/melodic invention and performance dynamics which were unprecedented in the music, and
doing so within the concentrated span of two nights at the club.

    Unlike the two original LPs, on which Columbia had forgivably presumed to deliver up the 'best' of the
sessions, it is possible to hear Carter clearly. His role is absolutely crucial and there are times when one
can almost visualize Miles flicking from one solid outcrop of sound to another like a caddis fly.
Hancock occasionally sounds diffident and detached, and he is the only one of the group who resorts to
repeated licks as the sets progress; he may have been tired, but he may also, as McCoy Tyner was to do at
almost exactly the same time, have realized that he was to some extent external to the real drama of this
music.

These are genuinely historic recordings. It would be better to go without a dozen – make that two dozen – run-of-the-mill jazz records in order to be able to afford this elegant box.

**** **In A Silent Way** Columbia 450982
> Davis; Wayne Shorter (*ts*); Chick Corea (*p*); Joe Zawinul (*p, org*); John McLaughlin (*g*); Dave Holland (*b*); Tony Williams (*d*). 2/69.

As an artefact, *In A Silent Way* is already a very long way even from the increasingly abstract sessions of the preceding couple of years. It was in every sense a collage, using 'found objects', put together with a view to the minimum detail and coloration required to make an impact. Two of the 'objects' were John McLaughlin, recruited on the nod and apparently unheard by the trumpeter, and Joe Zawinul, whose 'In A Silent Way' became a centre-piece of the album.

Three electric instruments give the band a sound completely unlike the previous incarnation, though it is clear that there are very significant continuities between this record and *Miles Smiles* or *E.S.P.*, and these should not be overlooked. In order to bring the performances up to LP length, Teo Macero stitched repeats of certain passages back into the fabric of the music, giving it continuity and a certain hypnotic circularity. Once again, a practical contingency (Miles was apparently happy with the short chunks that had been recorded) resulted in a new creative development, no less significant than Charles Mingus's overdubbing on *The Black Saint And The Sinner Lady*. The path was cleared for something even more extraordinary.

**** **Bitches Brew** Columbia 460602 2CD
> Davis; Wayne Shorter (*ss*); Bennie Maupin (*bcl*); Chick Corea, Joe Zawinul, Larry Young (*p*); John McLaughlin (*g*); Harvey Brooks, Dave Holland (*b*); Charles Alias, Jack DeJohnette, Lenny White (*d*); Jim Riley (*perc*). 8/69.

Less beautiful than *In A Silent Way* and far more unremittingly abstract, this is one of the most remarkable creative statements of the last 50 years, in any form. It is also profoundly flawed, a gigantic torso of burstingly noisy music that absolutely refuses to resolve itself formally. There are stories (authenticated by Macero) that the recordings were made under the cloud of an enormous dust-up between producer and star. Certainly Miles plays with a dour aggression, but also, on 'Sanctuary' (apparently the first to be recorded), with an odd vulnerability which surfaced only occasionally during his later career.

The most significant change in personnel from previous bands was the replacement of Williams (a very linear drummer) with DeJohnette. The rhythms are immediately more shifting and uncertain, matching the complete polytonality of much of the music. It is rarely possible to decide what key the pieces are in, once they are under way; and there is never much consistency between the key of a 'solo', if such they are, and what the rest of the band is about. The electric keyboards (with Young drafted in to play his distinctive clusters) create a shimmer out of which Miles stabs out some of his most maximal trumpet playing on record, hordes of ideas packed together into a relatively small space on 'Miles Runs The Voodoo Down' and 'Bitches Brew'.

Zawinul and McLaughlin don't play on every track, but the naming of a piece after the guitarist suggests how important he had become to this sound. Again, the whole package is less of a performance in the old-fashioned sense than an artefact, the details of which are secondary to the overall effect. And that – for all the sheer awkwardness of some passages and internal inconsistency of much of the music – is shattering.

**** **Jack Johnson** Columbia 471003
> Davis; Steve Grossman (*ss*); Herbie Hancock (*ky*); John McLaughlin (*g*); Michael Henderson (*b*); Billy Cobham (*d*). 4 & 11/70.

A hugely underrated item in the canon, to a large extent it resolves some of the unfinished business of *Bitches Brew*. Made for a movie soundtrack, like *L'Ascenseur Pour L'Echafaud* before it, *Jack Johnson* offers a perfect example of Miles's imagination being channelled and focused by a project. The opening track, 'Yesternow' (one side of the original LP), has a boiling intensity that perfectly matches the clubbing power and cat-like grace Johnson showed in the ring. Miles was, of course, greatly interested in the fight game and he appreciated the social and cultural dimension of Johnson's life story as well. The later session, recorded in the autumn, is more spacious and delicate, an almost perfect balance to the first half. It may well be that, in time to come, this will be regarded as one of the trumpeter's finest statements (he is playing fantastically well, with a huge, confident tone) and *Bitches Brew* will be relegated to the ambiguous ranks of failed masterpieces.

***(*) **Get Up With It** Core/Line CLCD 9.009827/8 2CD
> Davis; Sonny Fortune (*as, f*); Carlos Garnett, John Stubblefield (*as*); Steve Grossman (*ss*); David Liebman (*f*); Wally Chambers (*hca*); Cedric Lawson (*p, org*); Herbie Hancock, Keith Jarrett (*ky*); Pete Cosey, Cornell Dupree, Dominique Gaumont, Reggie Lucas, John McLaughlin (*g*); Khalil Balakrishna (*sitar*); Michael Henderson (*b*); Billy Cobham, Al Foster, Bernard Purdie

(*d*); Airto Moreira, Mtume, Badal Roy (*perc*); additional brass and rhythm arrangements by Wade Jarcus and Billy Jackson. 70–74.

Miles's first attempt to make Ellington dance with Stockhausen. Dedicated to the recently deceased Duke and dominated by a huge, mournful tribute, *Get Up With It* is more coherent than its immediate predecessors and very much more challenging. Recorded over a period of four years, it traces Miles's growing interest in a whole range of apparently irreconcilable musics. In his ghosted autobiography, he explains his growing attachment to Sly Stone's technologized Afro-funk on the one hand and Stockhausen's brooding music-as-process on the other. What united the two, beyond an obvious conclusion that pieces no longer needed to end or be resolved, was the idea that instrumental sound could be transformed and mutated almost infinitely and that the interest of a performance could be relocated from harmonic 'changes' and settled on the manipulation of sound textures over a moving carpet of rhythm. Since *Bitches Brew*, and very noticeably on an album like *Jack Johnson*, Miles had been willing to consider the studio and the editing room a further instrumental resource. With *Get Up With It* and the two live albums that follow, Miles went a step further, putting together bands that create similar phases and process-dominated 'improvisations' in real time.

There is a conventional wisdom that Miles's trumpet playing was at a low ebb during this period; health problems are adduced to shore up the myth of a tortured genius robbed of his truest talent, clutching at even the most minimal musical opportunities. Even those who *had* heard the mid-1970s albums, which acquired an added mystique by being the last before Miles's five-year 'retirement', were apt to say that he 'no longer played any trumpet'. Though distorted by wah-wah pedals and constantly treading water in its own echo, Miles's horn was still doing precisely what the music required of it; the same applied to his resort to organ ('Rated X') and piano ('Calypso Frelimo'). The poorer tracks ('Maishya' and 'Red China Blues' start off very late-nite) give only a misleading representation of how finely balanced Miles's radical populism actually was; a live version of 'Maishya' from the infamous Osaka gig is altogether tougher.

The essence of the 'new' Miles is to be found on the Duke tribute, 'He Loved Him Madly', a swarthy theme that sounds spontaneously developed, only gradually establishing a common pulse and tone-centre, but replete with semi-conscious, almost dreamed references to Ellington's work. 'Honky Tonk', by contrast, is an actual throwback to the style and personnel of *Jack Johnson* (which, like *Lift For The Scaffold* before it, greatly exceeded its occasion in musical significance, even if that was recognized only retrospectively). Though put together piecemeal and with Miles apparently willing to let Teo Macero edit greater or lesser chunks out of extended performances, *Get Up With It* is of considerable historical importance, looking forward not just to the apocalyptic live performances of 1975 but to the more polished and ironic pop-jazz of the comeback years.

** On The Corner Columbia 474371

> Davis; Teo Macero (*as*); Dave Liebman, Carlos Garnett (*ts*); Chick Corea, Herbie Hancock, Harold I. Williams (*ky*); David Creamer, John McLaughlin (*g*); Collin Walcott (*sitar*); Michael Henderson (*b*); Badal Roy (*tabla*); Jack DeJohnette (*d*); William W. Hart (*d, perc*); Don Alias, James Mtume (*perc*). 72.

The notorious Corky McCoy cover, featuring Miles's constituency of latter-day zoot-suiters, Afros, gays, steatopygous chicks in hot-pants, and Willie The Pimp look-alikes. The trumpet has a flex and plug. The wah-wah pedal remains firmly depressed throughout. The critics hated it.

Mostly they were right. *On The Corner* is pretty unrelieved, chugging funk, and one has to dig a little bit for the experimental subtleties that lie in even his most unpromising records. Where electronics gave Miles a sinister, underground sound on *Agharta* and *Pangaea*, here the sound is tinny and unattractive. The supporting cast is one of the least effective Miles ever put together, and unfortunately it steered Garnett (a promising player) into similar projects of his own.

***(*) Agharta Columbia 467897

> Davis; Sonny Fortune (*as, ss, f*); Pete Cosey (*g, syn, perc*); Reggie Lucas (*g*); Michael Henderson (*b*); Al Foster (*d*); Mtume (*perc*). 2/75.

**** Pangaea Columbia 467087 2CD

> As above.

It bears repeating: Miles's trumpet playing on these astonishing records is of the highest and most adventurous order, not the desperate posturing of a sick and cynical man. The use of a wah-wah pedal – routinely interpreted as part of the same turn towards a pop market signalled by Corky McCoy's much-sneered-at cover-art for *On The Corner* – is often fantastically subtle, creating surges and ebbs in a harmonically static line, allowing Miles to build huge, melismatic variations on a single note. The truth is that the band, Fortune apart, aren't fully understanding of the leader's conception; Henderson in particular tends to plod, and the two guitarists are inclined to get off on long spotlit solos that are almost laughably tame and blustery when set alongside Miles's knifefighter's reserve and reticence.

A re-run 'Maishya' and a long edit from the *Jack Johnson* theme (miscredited on the original release of

Agharta) underlines the importance of two underestimated earlier albums. The music scarcely touches any longer on European norms, adding Stockhausen's conception of a 'world music' that moves like creeping tectonic plates ('Pangaea' and 'Gondwana' are the names palaeo-geographers give to the primeval super-continents) to Afro-American popular forms. 'Gondwana' is the most consistent performance on either album. It opens on Fortune's surprisingly delicate flute and proceeds trance-like, with Miles's central trumpet episode bracketed by shimmering organ outlines and sullen, percussive stabs. It is difficult music to divide. Key centres are only notional and deceptive; most of the rhythmic activity – unlike Ornette Coleman's Prime Time bands – takes place along a single axis, but with considerable variation in the intensity and coloration of the pulse; the solos – like Weather Report's – are constant but also inseparable from the main thrust of the music. There is a growing appreciation of these admittedly problematic recordings (which were originally released only in Japan) but time will tell how significant they are in the overall trajectory of Miles's music.

** **The Man With The Horn** Columbia 468701
> Davis; Bill Evans (*ss*); Barry Finnerty (*g*); Rod Hill (*g, v, ky*); Robert Irving III (*p, ky*); Felton Crews, Marcus Miller (*b*); Al Foster, Vince Wilburn (*d*); Sammy Figueroa (*perc*). 81.

(*) **We Want Miles Columbia 469402
> Davis; Bill Evans (*ss*); Mike Stern (*g*); Marcus Miller (*b*); Al Foster (*d*); Mino Cinelu (*perc*). 6 & 7/81.

*** **Star People** Columbia 25395
> As above, except add John Scofield (*g*), Tom Barney (*b*). 83.

Glittery, mechano-funk, from a painful comeback trail, on which the trumpeter was playing little of real note. *The Man With The Horn* was a desperately tired performance. 'Back Seat Betty' was a concert favourite and is played again on the live *We Want Miles*, where it sits alongside the cheeky 'Jean-Pierre', one of his most engaging signature pieces. There's also a bravura pastiche on a theme from *Aida* and, on the live disc, a rare standard for this time: a huge and strangely evocative performance of 'My Man's Gone Now'.

   Star People at first glance is dispiriting but gradually yields up music of great sophistication and subtlety, which picks up on Miles's apparently reviving interest in the jazz tradition. Punctuated by pre-recorded organ interludes, it sets swing-era choruses over Motown riffs, dark blues shapes and passages that seem to hark all the way back to Buddy Bolden. An astonishing performance, marred by cluttered arrangements and a very unspecific mix.

   These are difficult records to assess, largely because of the circumstances in which they were made, but they can safely be left at the bottom of any shopping list, with the possible exception of *Star People*, which grows in stature every time it is heard.

** **Decoy** Columbia 468702
> Davis; Branford Marsalis (*ss*); John Scofield (*g*); Darryl Jones (*b*); Robert Irving III (*syn*); Al Foster (*d*); Mino Cinelu (*perc*). 84.

Decoy shouldn't be much more of a priority. Recorded up in Canada, where Davis sensationally snubbed the trumpet star of the new decade, Wynton Marsalis, brother of his insultingly under-used saxophonist on this record (Miles had a deep-seated problem with saxophone players). The music is hard, brittle and unlovely, and there are passages when almost anyone might be playing, or even no one, so programmed and pre-set is the sound.

***(*) **You're Under Arrest** Columbia 468703
> Davis; Bob Berg (*ss*); Robert Irving III (*ky*); John McLaughlin, John Scofield (*g*); Darryl Jones (*b*); Al Foster (*d*); Steve Thornton (*perc*); Marek Olko, Sting (*v*). 85.

The final studio release with Columbia (issued with a preposterous cover-picture of a sick-looking Miles posing grouchily with what looks like a toy long-stock pistol) has acquired classic status on the strength of two of his best latter-day transformations of pop material. His version of Cyndi Lauper's 'Time After Time', a medium-tempo waltz, is straightforwardly lovely, etched in melting top notes and passionate soars; but the finest performance on the record is the version of Michael Jackson's 'Human Nature'. The title-track is set up with some engaging 'read him his rights' / 'you got one phone-call' nonsense from the guest 'vocalists' and there's some steaming funk on 'Katia'. McLaughlin and Scofield vie for attention, but the dominant sound is the solid whoomph of Darryl 'The Munch' Jones's thumb-slap bass. Entertainment-wise, perhaps the best of the late albums.

*** **Tutu** Warner Brothers 925 490
> Davis; George Duke (*ky, etc.*); Adam Holzman, Bernard Wright (*ky*); Michal Urbaniak (*vn*); Marcus Miller (*b, ky*); Omar Hakim (*d, perc*); Paulinho Da Costa, Steve Reid (*perc*). 86.

***(*) **Amandla** Warner Brothers 925 873
> Davis; Kenny Garrett (*as*); Rick Margitza (*ts*); Jean-Paul Bourelly, Michael Landau, Foley McCreary, Billy Spaceman Watson (*g*); Joe Sample (*p*); Joey DeFrancesco, George Duke (*ky*);

Marcus Miller (*ky, b, etc.*); Al Foster, Omar Hakim, Ricky Wellman (*d*); Don Alias, John Bigham, Mino Cinelu, Paulinho Da Costa, Bashiri Johnson (*perc*). 89.

Miles's first post-CBS albums were an uneasy blend of exquisite trumpet miniaturism and drab cop-show funk, put together with a high production gloss that camouflaged a lack of real musical substance. Though he was acutely sensitive to any perceived put-down by middle-class whites, little was known about Miles's specific political beliefs at this or any previous time. Talking to a French interviewer, he said that naming albums for Bishop Tutu and after the ANC battle-cry was the only contribution he could make to the liberation struggle in South Africa; Miles also namechecks Mandela on 'Full Nelson', though this both relates back to an earlier 'Half Nelson' and simultaneously signals a reawakening interest in blues and bop harmonies, which was to be interrupted only by his death.

The horn sounds as deceptively fragile as ever, but it's made to dance in front of shifting sonic backdrops put together in a cut-and-paste way that succeeds very much better on *Amandla* than on the earlier set. 'Big Time' and 'Jilli' have a hectic, thudding energy, while at the other end of the spectrum Miles's dedication to the late 'Mr Pastorius' catches him in convincingly lyrical form. There's no mistaking the ultimate provenance of Marcus Miller's vivid techno-arranging. In particular, his use of synthesized percussion on 'Hannibal' recalls 'La Nevada' on Gil Evans's *Out Of The Cool*, an influence that became explicit to the point of pastiche on the item below.

(*) Music From Siesta Warner Brothers 925 655

Davis; Marcus Miller (*ky, b, etc.*).

By this time, Marcus Miller had taken over writing and arranging duties and Miles was beginning to take on an unaccustomed Grand Old Man demeanour and a series of guest appearances. *Siesta*, based on a Patrice Chaplin novel, was a flop as a movie, and Miles's free-hand Spanish sketches have subsequently taken on a life of their own. However they related to the film's imagery, they are now appealingly abstract, if a little undemanding. By no means an essential item in the discography, but pleasant enough.

**** **Aura** Columbia 463351

Davis; Palle Bolvig, Perry Knudsen, Palle Mikkelborg, Benny Rosenfeld, Idrees Sulieman, Jens Winther (*t, flhn*); Jens Engel, Ture Larsen, Vincent Nilsson (*tb*); Ole Kurt Jensen (*btb*); Axel Windfeld (*tba, btb*); Niels Eje (*ob, eng hn*); Per Carsten, Bent Jaedig, Uffe Karskov, Flemming Madsen, Jesper Thilo (*reeds*); Thomas Clausen, Ole Koch-Hansen, Kenneth Knudsen (*ky*); John McLaughlin, Bjarne Rouypé (*g*); Lillian Tbernqvist (*hp*); Niels-Henning Orsted-Pedersen, Bo Stief (*b*); Lennart Gruvstedt, Vince Wilburn (*d*); Marilyn Mazur, Ethan Weisgaard (*perc*); Eva Thaysen (*v*). 85.

Miles's first big-band record since the Gil Evans albums in the late 1950s. In 1984, he was awarded the prestigious Sonning Prize by the Danish government, an accolade normally accorded only to 'straight' composers. In recognition, and as a personal tribute to the influence of Miles's music, Palle Mikkelborg composed 'Aura' and persuaded the trumpeter to appear as soloist. CBS promptly sat on it for three years.

The piece, a suite of eight 'colour poems' with an introduction and a wonderful variation on 'Red', is built up out of a slightly bizarre 10-tone scale – stated by John McLaughlin in a brief 'Intro' – derived from the letters of Miles's name. This in turn yields a chord and a basic theme, which is then transformed by all the usual processes of serial composition, and by Miles's familiar alchemy.

Miles's inclusion clearly lent the music a considerable fillip and cachet, and Mikkelborg (a gifted trumpeter with a particular expertise in electronic shadings and transformations) might just as readily have taken the lead role himself. It is, though, marvellous to have Miles ranged against a large group again, and Mikkelborg's arrangements (particularly on 'Green', which is an explicit tribute) are clearly influenced by Gil Evans's grouping of instruments and interest in non-standard sonorities.

Miles's duet with NHOP on 'Green' is one of the finest moments on the record, spacious and delicately executed. He's almost as good on 'Orange', which makes explicit references to the *Bitches Brew* period, and on the two versions of 'Red'/'Electric Red', where he tries out the theme a second time, muted, and moves outside the structure entirely to lay bright watercolour washes over the insistent riff. Mikkelborg's intention seems to have been to inscribe Davis and his music yet more firmly into the history of American music. The solitary musings of 'White' are repeated with Mikkelborg's carefully stacked horns on 'Yellow' (which also restates the M.I.L.E.S. D.A.V.I.S. row), drawing the trumpeter into the musical community that he helped to create. There are more-or-less-explicit references to such touchstones as *Kind Of Blue* and *Sketches Of Spain*. There are also plenty of generic references: hints of bebop harmony, subtle modes and, on 'Blue', reggae. The closing 'Violet' is a blues, an idiom to which Miles returned more and more frequently in his last years. It's also, though, a tribute to two former Sonning winners, Igor Stravinsky and Olivier Messiaen (whose colour mysticism Mikkelborg adapts). In referring to them, and to Charles Ives on the pivotal 'Green', Mikkelborg also allows Miles to take his place in a broader musical continuum, not just in the condescending by-way that came to be known (though not by Miles) as 'jazz'.

Unique among his later records, *Aura* has an unexpected power to move.

***(*) The Miles Davis Selection Columbia 465699 5CD
Davis; personnels as for Columbia records above. 55–60.

*** The Miles Davis Selection Columbia 471623 3CD
Davis; personnels as for Columbia records above. 59–69.

Confusingly titled but apparently non-overlapping packages from the Columbia years. We have not had an opportunity to review these compilations (ratings are based on the material listed) and purchasers are recommended to compare what is on offer with what they may already have in their collections. For complete tyros, both look quite attractive.

**(*) Ballads CBS 461099
Davis; personnels as for *Quiet Nights, Seven Steps To Heaven, In Person Friday Night At The Blackhawk*. 61–63.

A very weak cull of material from a spotty period. There's nothing much to recommend this record.

***(*) Mellow Miles Columbia 469440 2
Davis; various personnels as above.

When Norman Mailer was asked if he thought he was getting mellower with age, he replied, 'Well, I guess I'm about as mellow as old camembert.' There's still a sharp whiff of risk and enterprise coming up off this outwardly bland, life-style packaging of late-night Davis hits, but it's unlikely in itself to send anyone hitherto unfamiliar with the trumpeter's work scuttling out for a copy of *Milestones* or *Agharta*. There is, needless to say, nothing from the latter included here, but it does kick off with 'Miles' (aka 'Milestones') and runs a reasonably predictable course from there: 'So What' and 'Freddie Freeloader' from *Kind Of Blue*, 'Summertime' and 'It Ain't Necessarily So' from *Porgy And Bess*, the title-tune of *Miles Ahead*, ''Round Midnight' and 'Bye Bye Blackbird' from *Round About Midnight*, 'Pfrancing' from *Someday My Prince Will Come* and, jumping a whole generation, 'Human Nature' and 'Time After Time' from *You're Under Arrest*. Reasonable value, but most true believers will still prefer their own mental compilation of 'Hostile Miles'.

*** Dingo Warner Brothers 7599 264382
Davis; Chuck Findley, Oscar Brashear, Ray Brown, George Graham (*t*); George Bohannon, Thurman Green, Jimmy Cleveland, Lew McGreary, Dick Nash (*tb*); David Duke, Marnie Johnson, Vince De Rosa, Richard Todd (*frhn*); Buddy Collette, Kenny Garrett, Bill Green, Jackie Kelso, Marty Krystall, Charles Owens, John Stephens (*reeds*); Kei Akagi, Michel Legrand, Alan Oldfield (*ky*); Mark Rivett (*g*); Foley, Abraham Laboriel, Benny Rietveld (*b*); John Bigham, Harvey Mason, Alphonse Mouzon, Ricky Wellman (*d, perc*). 91.

Though Rolf de Heer's movie will undoubtedly draw a little extra resonance from the casting of Miles as trumpeter/shaman 'Billy Cross', the music may again be a little more vital than the images it was written to accompany, as with *Siesta*. Michel Legrand's scores and orchestrations are predictably slick and rather empty, but there are some nice touches and a couple of sly echoes (presumably intentional) to Miles's work for Louis Malle's *L'ascenseur pour l'échafaud*. Lest anyone be alarmed at what has happened to Miles's lip on the opening 'Kimberley Trumpet', solo duties are shared with Chuck Findley, in the role of 'Dingo Anderson'. Attractive, but a slightly sad memorial of a dying man.

*** Doo-Bop Warner Brothers 7599 26938 2
Davis; Easy Mo Bee, J. R., A. B. Money (*v*); other personnel not specified. 91.

Almost the end. Perhaps inevitably, it isn't of earth-shaking significance but, equally predictably, it finds Miles taking another ostensibly rejuvenating stylistic turn. Unfortunately, Easy Mo Bee's doo-wop/rap stylings are so soft-centred and lyrically banal – 'Let's kick a verse for my man called Miles / Seems to me his music's gonna be around for a long while / 'Cuz he's a multi-talented and gifted musician / Who can play any position' – as to deny 'The Doo-Bop Song', 'Blow' and the 'posthumous' 'Fantasy' any credibility. Miles brought in material recorded in the late 1980s and known as the RubberBand session, and this final set might be likened to the grab-bag approach of *Get Up With It*, though without its retrospective promise of fresh fields to explore.

Miles plays well, sometimes with surprising aggression, but the backgrounds are uniformly trite and the samples (from Kool & The Gang, James Brown, Donald Byrd's 'Street Lady', Gene Ammons's 'Jungle Strut', among others) are used unimaginatively. As a studio curtain-call, it's a severe disappointment.

*** Miles Davis & Quincy Jones Live At Montreux Warner Bros 45221
Davis; Lew Soloff, Miles Evans (*t*); Benny Bailey, Marvin Stamm, John D'Earth, Jack Walrath, Wallace Roney, Manfred Schoof, Ack Van Rooyen (*t, flhn*); Tom Malone, Roland Dahinden, Conrad Herwig (*tb*); David Barageron, Earl McIntyre (*tb, euph*); Dave Taylor (*btb*); Alex

Brofsky, John Clark, Tom Varner, Claudio Pontiggia (*frhn*); Howard Johnson (*tba, bs*); Sal Giorgianni (*as*); Bob Malach (*ts, f, cl*); Larry Schneider (*ts, ob, f, cl*); Jerry Bergonzi (*ts*); Alex Foster (*as, ss, f*); George Adams (*ts, f*); Anne O'Brien (*f*); Julian Cawdry (*f, af, picc*); Michael Weber (*cl*); Christian Gavillet, Roger Rosenberg (*bcl, bs*); Tilman Zahn, Dave Seghezzo, Xavier Duss, Judith Wenziker (*ob*); Christian Rabe, Reiner Erb (*bsn*); Xenia Schindler (*hp*); George Gruntz (*p*); Gil Goldstein, Delmar Brown (*ky*); Carlos Benavent, Mike Richmond (*b*); Kenwood Dennard, Grady Tate (*d*). 7/91.

His last bow. Miles and Quincy had never worked together. For years the trumpeter had refused to retread his great material. Presto! The ultimate wish-list booking for a 25th anniversary event. It was clear that Miles was ailing at the time, and his solos often find him short of breath (though not of ideas) and lacking in stamina. The arrangements are grandly overdone, but there's no mistaking the rapturous nature of the reception the concert received from the crowd at Montreux.

It was a career retrospective up to *Sketches Of Spain*. After 'Boplicity' from *Birth Of The Cool*, the band launches into medleys from *Miles Ahead* and *Porgy And Bess*. It doesn't take long to recognize that Quincy Jones is no Gil Evans, and it's a pity that the smaller Evans group (a ghost band now, alas) couldn't have been entrusted with the music, instead of being augmented with the huge George Gruntz Concert Jazz Band (*and* guests) who play with typical precision and the sort of dead-centredness one expects of studio house-bands.

Jones hailed him as a great 'painter', and there is a sense in which that is exactly what Miles Davis was. He left some masterpieces, some puzzling abstracts, and a pile of fascinating sketches. The Leonardo of our time.

Nathan Davis (born 1937) TENOR SAXOPHONE, SOPRANO SAXOPHONE

** London By Night DIW 813
> Davis; Dusko Goykovich (*t, flhn*); Jean Toussaint, Stan Robinson (*ts*); Kenny Drew (*p*); Jimmy Woode (*b*); Al Levitt (*d*). 8/87.

The same session yielded Dusko Goykovich's own *Celebration* and, again, it's the quality of the largely Europe-based rhythm section that really makes the difference. The two quartet performances – 'I Thought About You' and 'But Beautiful' – are relaxed and free-swinging, with Drew's extended and almost unbarred right-hand lines rightly forward in the mix. 'Shades', arranged for three saxophones and rhythm, is far less successful, but the quintet tracks could almost be from an undiscovered Jazz Messengers tape. Goykovich's flugelhorn has a fat, luxuriant quality that blends well with Davis, and there are fine, controlled solos all round, notably on 'Dr Bu', where the Blakey/Messengers debt is most openly acknowledged.

Richard Davis (born 1930) DOUBLE BASS

***(*) Persia My Dear DIW 805
> Davis; Sir Roland Hanna (*p*); Frederick Waits (*d*). 8/87.
***(*) One For Frederick Hep CD 2047
> Davis; Cecil Bridgewater (*t*); Ricky Ford (*ts*); Sir Roland Hanna (*p*); Frederick Waits (*d*). 7/89.
*** Dealin' Sweet Basil 660.55.011
> Davis; Cecil Bridgewater (*t*); Ricky Ford (*ts*); Sir Roland Hanna (*p*); Ronnie Burrage (*d*). 8/90.

Stravinsky's favourite bass player, Davis draws heavily on the example of fellow-Chicagoan Wilbur Ware, bringing considerable rhythmic virtuosity and a tremendous range of pitches and timbres to solo performances. Whatever the merits of his pizzicato work (and there are those who find him much too mannered, relative to Ray Brown and Ron Carter), there is no one to touch him as a soloist with the bow. His *arco* statements on 'Manhattan Safari', the opening track of the excellent studio *Persia My Dear*, rather take the sting out of Hanna's funky lines, but Hanna too shares an ability to mix dark-toned swing with a sort of classical propriety, as he shows on three compositions.

On the later set, recorded live at Sweet Basil, bass and piano combine particularly well for 'Misako', a Monk-influenced Davis original which also appears on the excellent *Four Play*, with Clifford Jordan, James Williams, Ronnie Burrage and Davis. The same influence is even more explicit on 'De Javu Monk', which offers probably the best representation on record of Davis's unaccompanied style, all weird intervals and changes of metre. As on the closing 'Strange Vibes' (a Horace Silver tune), Hanna comes in to balance the bassist's tendency to abstraction. The Hep album is dedicated to drummer Waits, who died four months after the recording. His introduction to 'City Bound' (and to the album) is very strong, and he turns in a fine, accelerated solo on 'Brownie Speaks', one of the stronger tracks on *Persia My Dear*.

The Sweet Basil session is a strong club date. Burrage is a fine replacement for Waits, but he lacks the older man's gift for silence, and there are moments during 'On The Trail' when his intrusiveness can't be put down to poorly balanced recording – which, generally speaking, it isn't.

Wild Bill Davis (born 1918) ORGAN, PIANO

(*) Impulsions Black & Blue 590372
> Davis; Floyd Smith (g); Chris Columbo (d). 5/72.

Most of Davis's work on record has been with other leaders. He had 20 years of arranging behind him when he began to attract serious attention as an organist, his most celebrated association being the partnership with Johnny Hodges in the early 1960s. Though he made several records as a sideman in Europe in the early '70s, this is the only one under his own name. The 14 tracks take a solid, unadventurous course through swing and blues and are a conservative variation on the more hard-hitting manner of organists of the Jimmy Smith school. Floyd Smith is generously featured, along with the leader. The recording is clear, if a little lacking in crispness.

Wild Bill Davison (1906–90) CORNET

*** **This Is Jazz** Jazzology JCD-42
> Davison; Jimmy Archey (tb); Albert Nicholas, Edmond Hall (cl); Ralph Sutton, James P. Johnson (p); Danny Barker (g); Pops Foster (b); Baby Dodds (d). 47.

*** **Showcase** Jazzology JCD 83
> Davison; Jiri Pechar (t); Jimmy Archey, Miloslav Havranek (tb); Garvin Bushell (cl, bsn); Josef Reiman (as, cl); Karel Mezera (ts); Ivor Kratky (bs); Ralph Sutton, Pavel Klikar (p); Miroslav Klimes (g, bj); Zdenek Fibrish (tba); Sid Weiss (b); Morey Feld, Ales Sladek (d). 12/47–10/76.

***(*) **Wild Bill Davison & His Jazzologists** Jazzology JCD-2
> Davison; Lou McGarity (tb); Tony Parenti (cl); Hank Duncan (p); Pops Foster (b); Zutty Singleton (d).

*** **Surfside Jazz** Jazzology JCD-25
> Davison; Tom Saunders (c); Guy Roth (tb); Jim Wyse (cl); George Melczek (p); Frank Harrison (b); Gene Flood (d). 8/65.

*** **After Hours** Jazzology JCD-22
> Davison; Kenny Davern (cl); Charlie Queener (p); George Wettling (d). 66.

(*) **Jazz On A Saturday Afternoon Vol. 1 Jazzology JCD-37
> Davison; Wray Thomas (tb); Herman Foretich (cl); Ernie Carson, Eustis Tompkins (p); Jerry Rousseau (b); Mike Hein (d). 6/70.

(*) **Jazz On A Saturday Afternoon Vol. 2 Jazzology JCD-38
> As above. 6/70.

** **Just A Gig** Jazzology JCD-191
> Davison; Slide Harris (tb, v); Tom Gwaltney (cl); John Eaton (p); Van Perry (b); Tom Martin (d); Johnson McRee (kz, v). 11/73.

***(*) **'S Wonderful** Jazzology JCD-181
> As above, except add Vic Dickenson (tb), Buster Bailey (cl), Dick Wellstood (p), Willie Wayman (b), Cliff Leeman (d).

(*) **Lady Of The Evening Jazzology JCD143
> Davison; various groups as above, 65–81.

*** **Solo Flight** Jazzology JCD-114
> Davison; Paul Sealey, Denny Wright (g); Harvey Weston (b). 10/81.

Born in Defiance, Ohio, Wild Bill Davison looks to have slung the town sign round his neck as a badge of identity. His work has appeared in all sorts of situations, but the Jazzology issues offer a long look at this famous brass pugilist, a hornman equally unfazed by either Sidney Bechet or a team of local trad ear-bashers.

The early stuff on JCD-42 and JCD-83 is typical This Is Jazz fare, with a good if workmanlike band (Sutton is the outstanding player) and a frowsy Davison vocal on 'Ghost Of A Chance'. Clean sound on both releases; the second is shared with a curious 1976 session, made in a Czech castle with a local team who aren't up to the challenge, even if Davison sounds in good spirits. McGarity and Parenti are admirable and underrated players, and they make up a very good front line with Bill on the Jazzologists date: as righteous Dixieland goes, this is arguably the best record of the bunch. The Surf Side Six were a local band working in Detroit when Davison muscled in on their gig (a habitual occurrence) and shook the rafters on a few tunes. Nothing fancy, but some nice music. Much the same scenario with the *After*

Hours date, where Bill drove by a gig where George Wettling was in charge, sat in, taped it, and counted his royalties. The footwork with Davern is rather good.

The two *Saturday Afternoon* gigs are rather less exciting, an Atlanta group providing the backdrop for the Davison horn, and the following *Just A Gig* is just as it says, this time hailing from downtown Manasas, Virginia. Some very shaky sidemen on this one (and we don't just mean their vibrato). A couple of leftovers turn up on *'S Wonderful*, which is by a much superior group: Davison and Dickenson are a dream front line, the snarling bite of the one with the droll, loping gait of the other, and, if neither is quite at his best, it's a tonic after some of the other playing on these CDs. *Lady Of The Evening* is a hotchpotch collection of one session with rhythm section from 1971 and several out-takes from some of the prior dates: some strong, bruising horn on the main date, though.

Solo Flight finds him in London in 1981. Wright, Sealey and Weston make so much reverberant noise that at times even Davison has to struggle to make himself heard. It's worth the effort, though, since, despite some fluffs, he battles on with the kind of fierce licks that, rasp by rasp, made up an unrepeatable jazz persona.

*** **Sweet And Lovely** Storyville STCD 4060
    Davison; strings. 8/76.
(*) **Together Again! Storyville STCD 8216
    Davison; Ole Fessor Lindgreen (*tb*); Jesper Thilo (*cl, ss, ts*); Ralph Sutton (*p*); Lars Blach (*g*); Hugo Rasmussen (*b*); Svend-Erik Norregaard (*d*). 5/77.
(*) **All-Stars Timeless TTD 545
    Davison; Tom Saunders (*t, v*); Bill Allred (*tb*); Chuck Hedges (*cl*); Danny Moss (*ts*); Johnny Varro (*p*); Isla Eckinger (*b*); Butch Miles (*d*); Banu Gibson (*v*). 10/86.

With the *All Stars* album, Davison marked his arrival in the CD era. Like Armstrong, he had suffered serious lip problems, allegedly caused by a blow from a Schlitz bottle (this is the only known instance of an empty bottle touching Davison's lips). At eighty, and with an unforgiving playback, his articulation isn't all it used to be (!), and the line-up and repertoire not entirely in his usual line. His energy and raw humour are nevertheless undiminished. The singing is very so-so indeed.

The inimitable snarl is present and sounds intermittently correct on the album with strings, a blissful carpet of violins that Davison, well, spits on. This, indeed, is jazz.

New to CD is the Storyville reunion with Ralph Sutton – pity, though, that this wasn't a great moment for either man. Bill sounds a bit out of sorts, the material is a little too sloppy for his tastes, and Sutton is poorly recorded. Still a few good blasts in the locker, and four alternative takes as a bonus.

Elton Dean (born 1945) ALTO SAXOPHONE, SAXELLO

*** **Unlimited Saxophone Company** Ogun OGCD 002
    Dean; Trevor Watts (*as*); Paul Dunmall, Simon Picard (*ts*); Paul Rogers (*b*); Tony Levin (*d*). 89.
***(*) **The Vortex Tapes** Slam CD 203
    Dean; Nick Evans (*tb*); Trevor Watts, Simon Picard, Jerry Underwood (*sax*); Keith Tippett, Howard Riley (*p*); Marcio Mattos, Paul Rogers (*b*); Louis Moholo, Tony Levin, Nigel Morris, Mark Sanders (*d*). 9/90.
*** **If Dubois Only Knew** Voiceprint VP 194
    Dean; Paul Dunmall (*ts, ss, Cmel*). 2/95.
***(*) **Silent Knowledge** Cuneiform RUNE 83
    As above, except add Sophia Domancich (*p*); Paul Rogers (*b*); Tony Levin (d). 9/95.

The man – believe it or not – from whom Elton John borrowed his stage moniker, Dean is a powerful free-jazz player who gets a Roland Kirk-like tone out of the curved saxello and maintains an individual dialogue with tenor heavyweights like Coltrane, Pharoah Sanders and Joe Henderson. Dean's Ninesense big band was one of the most exciting units of the desiccated late '70s in Britain. In recent years, despite an enthusiastic following for his smaller groups, he has been heard less often.

For much of the period covered above, Dean has been closely involved with the members of Mujician, an improvising group consisting of Keith Tippett, Paul Dunmall, Paul Rogers (who subsequently moved to France) and Tony Levin. It is an ideal partnership, though Dean's own ideas tend to be more structured and songlike. There are even hints of Ellington's small-group organization on the tape-only *EDQ Live* (which Dean distributes from home) and the augmented *Unlimited Saxophone Company*. Watts and Dean run no risk of cancelling one another out; they are very different players, and Dean's tight-sounding saxello broadens the timbral spectrum considerably. Picard is largely supernumerary, but Rogers and Levin are at their best on 'Small Strides' and 'One Three Nine'. Just because you won't find them on the High Street doesn't mean you shouldn't try them.

In September 1990, Dean could have been found just off Stoke Newington High Street in north

London, leading a short season of improvisations at the Vortex club. In documenting the best of the series, Slam has provided a valuable opportunity to hear younger and unrecorded players like Underwood, Sanders and Morris (all of whom played very well indeed) as well as established masters like Tippett, Moholo, Rogers and Riley. Though the language in currency is by no means new, *The Vortex Tapes* feel like a rejuvenating breeze in British improvisation.

Dean's new Quintet is almost a version of Mujician, with Sophia Domancich in for Keith Tippett and with Dean's high, almost anguished lines scribbling in the air above Dunmall, who sticks to tenor throughout. Four long pieces, of which the second and last seem to be wholly improvised. The opening track is by far the longest, almost a half-hour of intense ensemble music called 'Gualchos'. The only (mild) reservation is that Dean and Dunmall dominate proceedings almost as thoroughly as on the fascinating home-recorded duos. On this occasion Dunmall swaps round his soprano and C-melody saxophones, bringing a mix of sounds to this very demanding setting. The fact that both men seem so untroubled by it is a testimony to their capability, but also a faint warning sign regarding the Quintet, which still sounds like a duo superimposed on a trio rather than a fully communicative group.

John D'Earth TRUMPET

(*) One Bright Glance Enja 6040
    D'Earth; John Abercrombie (*g*); Marc Johnson (*b*); Howard Curtis (*d*). 7/89.
D'Earth is a thoughtful trumpeter whose list of credits suggests a wide range of interests – Gunter Hampel, Emily Remler and Bob Moses are some of the leaders he's recorded with. This session has some pleasing moments, and the leader's lucid tone and agile phrasing mesh well with Abercrombie's more soft-edged lines. But the music lacks a deeper character: it slips unassumingly by.

December Jazz Trio GROUP

*** **The Street One Year After** Splasc(h) H 329-2
    Giorgio Occhipinti (*p*); Guiseppe Guarella (*b*); Francesco Branciamore (*d*). 8/90.
*** **Concert For Ibla** Splasc(h) H 359-2
    As above, except add Pino Minafra (*t, flhn*). 1/91.
It's appropriate that the trio is democratically named, for this is genuine group music, a highly accomplished and detailed mixture of form and improvisation, touching on jazz and avant-garde elements alike. The key player is, in many ways, Branciamore whose propulsive and momentous playing suggests an orchestral concept and who never lets the music settle into random doodling. Occhipinti varies his contributions from locked-hands passages to long, meandering lines, but seldom seems at a loss for an idea, even over some very long tracks on both records; and Guarella plays with unassuming virtuosity. Minafra's guest role on the live recording is sometimes recorded a little remotely, and the overall sound on the studio disc is significantly superior, but both feature a great deal of interesting music.

The Dedication Orchestra GROUP

***(*) **Spirits Rejoice** Ogun OGCD 101
    Guy Barker, Harry Beckett, Kenny Wheeler (*t*); Claude Deppa (*t, v*); Dave Amis, Malcolm Griffiths, Radu Malfatti, Paul Rutherford (*tb*); Dave Powell (*tba*); Django Bates (*E– horn*); Neil Metcalfe (*f*); Lol Coxhill (*ss, ts*); Ray Warleigh (*as, f*); Elton Dean (*as*); Evan Parker, Alan Skidmore (*ts*); Chris Biscoe (*bs*); Keith Tippett (*p*); Paul Rogers (*b*); Louis Moholo (*d, v*). 1/92.
***(*) **Ixesha (Time)** Ogun OGCCD 102/103 2CD
    Harry Beckett, Claude Deppa, Ian Hamer, Pat Higgs, Henry Lowther, Kenny Wheeler (*t*); Jim Dvorak (*t, v*); Marc Charig (*c, thn*); Dave Amis, Roland Bates, Malcolm Griffiths, Paul Rutherford (*tb*); Andy Grappy, Dave Powell (*tba*); Neil Metcalfe (*f*); Lol Coxhill (*ss, ts*); Elton Dean, Mike Williams (*as*); Evan Parker (*ts*); Sean Bergin (*ts, as*); Chris Biscoe (*bs*); Keith Tippett (*p*); Paul Rogers (*b*); Louis Moholo (*d, v*). 1/94.
On New Year's Day, 1992, the less hung-over of London's jazz fans piled into the 100 Club in Oxford Street to hear a gig by a stellar band that encompassed two generations of British improvisers. The intention was to commemorate lost comrades: saxophonist Dudu Pukwana, trumpeter Mongezi Feza, composer Chris McGregor and bassists Johnny Mbizo Dyani and Harry Miller; and also to launch the Spirits Rejoice Trust, a fund to help support and develop young talent in their native South Africa.

Others were being remembered, too, but it was the music of these men (with a final piece by drummer Louis Moholo, now the last surviving member of the legendary Blue Notes) that went to the making of

Spirits Rejoice. Two days after the 100 Club gig, the orchestra reconvened in a London studio and recorded a set every bit as scorching and beautiful as the concert versions. Arrangements were by Keith Tippett (who makes a beautiful job of Miller's 'Dancing Demon'), Kenny Wheeler (ditto for the gentle 'B My Dear', one of Pukwana's most affecting themes), Eddie Parker, John Warren, Jim Dvorak, Django Bates, Radu Malfatti and John Warren.

Outstanding among the soloists are Harry Beckett on Pukwana's 'Hug Pine', Jim Dvorak on his own arrangement of Feza's 'Sonia' and Evan Parker and Keith Tippett on McGregor's 'Andromeda'. A throwback to days when conglomerations like this were still economically viable, *Spirits Rejoice* has a pleasingly old-fashioned sound (albeit crisply produced by Steve Beresford with Evan Parker) and will awaken nostalgic memories of great days in British jazz. However, the whole purpose of the project is to look to the future and carry on the work of the composers being celebrated. Buying it also represents an investment in a new generation of South Africans, some of whom Moholo was able to work with in the months that followed.

Ixesha was recorded two years on, with a slightly different orchestra but in the same format. If anything, the compositions and arrangements are even better, nothing on a par with 'B My Dear', but Johnny Dyani's 'Wish You Sunshine' and McGregor's 'The Serpent's Kindly Eye' (arranged by Alex Maguire and John Warren respectively) are excellent. The only slight quibble this time relates to the playing. There's more of a Buggins's turn feel, and some tracks are overcrowded with solo spots. The best are still very fine, inevitably, but this is a long record and it might have been tackled in a more relaxed way. Both sets, though, should be considered priority purchases for anyone interested in the legacy of the five great South Africans.

Joey DeFrancesco (born 1971) ORGAN, PIANO, SYNTHESIZER, TRUMPET, VOCAL

*** **Live At The 5 Spot** Columbia 474045-2
>   DeFrancesco; Jim Henry (*t, flhn*); Robert Landham (*as*); Illinois Jacquet, Kirk Whalum, Grover Washington, Houston Person (*ts*); Jack McDuff (*org*); Paul Bollenback (*g*); Byron 'Wookie' Landham (*d*). 93.

(*) **All About My Girl Muse MCD 5528
>   DeFrancesco; Houston Person (*ts*); Paul Bollenback (*g*); Byron 'Wookie' Landham (*d*). 3/94.

(*) **The Street Of Dreams Big Mo 20252
>   As above, except add Bruce Gates, Rick Sigler (*t*), Rick Lillard, Doug Elliott (*tb*), Dudley Hinote (*btb*), Pete Berrenbregge (*ts*), Keter Betts (*b*), omit Person. n.d.

Organ players are a rarer breed than before, although the Hammond B-3 has made a surprise comeback in the age of synthesizers and samplers, and DeFrancesco might be the youngest of the new tribe. He plays respectable trumpet, too, and handles piano with equal facility, but it's his organ playing (he actually uses a modified C-3) which is his calling-card. Not far into his twenties, he already has five major-label albums under his belt, but the earlier discs for Columbia have already gone and he has departed for independent companies. The surviving *Live At The 5 Spot*, though, is probably the best thing DeFrancesco has done, if only because it snatches up much of the excitement that this kind of jazz exists to create. Whistle-stop appearances by Jacquet (grandfatherly), Turrentine (imperious), Whalum (surprisingly tough) and Person (sly old dog) add to the fun, and when Jack McDuff clambers up to trade punches on a rollicking 'Spectator' it's pretty splendid. Perhaps not one to stand up to too many plays, though. *All About My Girl* takes DeFrancesco to a label which has done a lot of these sort of records, and this is deep in that pocket: fat, buttery licks from the organ, blooming, many-noted runs on guitar, and blues-soaked asides from the tenor. Person can play this in his sleep, and maybe DeFrancesco can by now, too. *The Street Of Dreams* adds a horn section to some tracks and there's a notably tough and focused version of Wayne Shorter's 'Black Nile'. What will make or break the disc, though, are the four vocals by the leader. A departure to be sure: Messrs Smith, McGriff, Patton, McDuff, etc. never felt this particular need.

Buddy DeFranco (born 1923) CLARINET

*** **The Buenos Aires Concerts** Hep CD 2014
>   DeFranco; Jorge Navarro (*p*); Richard Lew (*g*); Jorge López-Ruiz (*b*); Osvaldo López (*d*). 11/80.

*** **Hark** Pablo 2310915
>   DeFranco; Oscar Peterson (*p*); Joe Pass (*g*); Niels-Henning Orsted-Pedersen (*b*); Martin Drew (*d*). 4/85.

*** Holiday For Swing Contemporary 14047
     DeFranco; Terry Gibbs (*vib*); John Campbell (*p*); Todd Coolman (*b*); Gerry Gibbs (*d*). 8/88.
***(*) Like Someone In Love Progressive PCD-7014
     DeFranco; Derek Smith (*p*); Tal Farlow (*g*); George Duvivier (*b*); Ronnie Bedford (*d*). 3/89.
*** Five Notes Of Blues Musidisc 500302
     DeFranco; Alain Jean-Marie (*p*); Michel Gaudry (*b*); Philippe Cobelle (*d*). 12/91.
*** Chip Off The Old Bop Concord CCD 4527
     DeFranco; Joe Cohn (*g*); Larry Novak (*p*); Keter Betts (*b*); Jimmy Cobb (*d*). 7/92.
Nobody has seriously challenged DeFranco's status as the greatest post-swing clarinettist, although the instrument's desertion by reed players has tended to disenfranchise its few exponents. Only Benny Goodman and Artie Shaw matched DeFranco in terms of technical virtuosity: his incredibly smooth phrasing and seemingly effortless command are unfailingly impressive on all his records. But the challenge of translating this virtuosity into a relevant, post-bop environment has left his career on record somewhat unfulfilled.

The sessions with Sonny Clark remain DeFranco's finest works and can be found in a well-presented Mosaic box set (see introduction). For the rest, his output on record has been rather sporadic. DeFranco issued little in the 1960s and '70s while teaching and bandleading, but he has made something of a comeback in recent years. The Pablo album shows that all his facility is still present, but in the company of Oscar Peterson, with whom he had recorded in 1955, it sounds merely like empty facility, capable though the playing is. DeFranco's association with the exuberant Terry Gibbs, though, has given him a better focus and, although there are better things listed under Gibbs's own name, *Holiday For Swing* bounces through a well-chosen programme in which the clarinettist creates some febrile improvisations.

Like Someone In Love is, by a squeak, perhaps the best of the more recent studio dates. The rhythm section is guided in the main by the effortless Duvivier and, with Farlow at his most beguiling in a guest role, DeFranco sounds perfectly relaxed and on top of the programme. The fast pieces show the expected flair, but it's the almost honeyed interpretations of the title-tune and 'How Long Has This Been Going On?' which impress the most.

The live concerts caught on the Hep and Musidisc releases offer good, lively music, and DeFranco tends to take more chances in this situation: he really takes apart 'Billie's Bounce' in Buenos Aires and responds vigorously to a pushy rhythm section. In Paris, with the local rhythm section he plays a more quiescent set, which includes a finely caressed 'Early Autumn'. Neither disc is ideally recorded, though, and the Argentinian players probably get more space than is comfortable.

Concord threw a line to players of DeFranco's sensibilities. He jumps at the chance and lays down one of his most carefree offerings, partnered by Al Cohn's boy and a workmanlike piano trio who sound astonishingly like the 1953 band with Drew and Hinton. In sum, not an ideal picture of DeFranco's work to date, but these have to do until the superb sessions for Verve are back in full circulation.

Rein De Graaff PIANO, KEYBOARDS

*** Be-Bop, Ballads & Blues Timeless CD SJP 354
     De Graaff; Charlie Rouse (*ts*); Henk Haverhoek, Koos Serierse (*b*); John Engels, Eric Ineke,
     Leroy Williams (*d*). 10/76, 4/80, 9/81, 7/84, 5/85.
*** New York Jazz Timeless CD SJP 130
     De Graaff; Tom Harrell (*t, flh*); Ronnie Cuber (*bs*); Sam Jones (*b*); Louis Hayes (*d*). 2/79.
**(*) Jubilee Timeless CD SJP 294
     De Graaff; Jarmo Hoogedijk (*t*); Bart Van Lier (*tb*); Dick Vennik (*ts*); Koos Serierse (*b*); Eric
     Ineke (*d*). 2/89.
A superb accompanist, with a real flair for the contours of a vocal line or a saxophone solo, De Graaff has rarely sounded as convincing on his own account. His chops are beyond scrutiny, but often he seems to lack a convincing plot. *Be-Bop, Ballads & Blues* is an attractive compilation of different personnels over a near-decade span, and the quintet with Harrell is gorgeous whether at an accelerated tempo ('Au Privave') or on one of the slower tracks, coaxing De Graaff into one of his spun-out, lyrical notions. The last of the group is a bit overpowered by co-leader Vennik's unremarkable saxophone, but even here there are good things to be found.

Jack DeJohnette (born 1942) DRUMS, PIANO, KEYBOARDS, MELODICA

**(*) The DeJohnette Complex Original Jazz Classics OJC 617
     DeJohnette; Bennie Maupin (*ts, f*); Stanley Cowell (*electric p*); Eddie Gomez, Miroslav Vitous
     (*b*); Roy Haynes (*d*). 12/68.

Playing with Charles Lloyd threw DeJohnette very suddenly into the spotlight. Recording under his own name a month after his first studio shift with Miles Davis, he still sounds a bit up in the air. His melodica is rather too heavily featured and has an uneasy, ersatz tone. The second day's music-making – minus Haynes – put DeJohnette back on the drum stool, where he sounds considerably more together and offers intriguing hints of the work that was to come. Otherwise rather forgettable.

*** **Pictures** ECM 1079
    DeJohnette; John Abercrombie (*g*). 2/76.
The duos with Abercrombie are more satisfying than the solo performances with piano, organ and drums. The guitarist has a light, fleet approach, very lyrical and tightly woven even when moving at slow tempos. DeJohnette was clearly at this time still wrestling with the tension between his own sterling musicianship and the requirement to be first and foremost a good sideman, with its unremovable implication of secondary status. Whether he has ever quite reconciled the two is unclear; it seems acute on this, albeit attractive, record.

*** **New Directions** ECM 1128
    DeJohnette; Lester Bowie (*t*); John Abercrombie (*g, mand g*); Eddie Gomez (*b*). 6/78.
***(*) **New Directions In Europe** ECM 1157
    As above. 6/79.
In Europe is one of DeJohnette's finest albums, and there may be a message in the live provenance. DeJohnette never seems to play his own material with this amount of conviction in the studio and there's a noticeable contrast in the basic dynamic of the two albums. The thinnish air of Willisau hasn't cut his wind or Bowie's, though Abercrombie sounds a little cyanosed and plays a relatively modest background role, reserving his energy for the final, group-devised 'Multo Spiliagio', where he stutters out a nervous cross-beat to DeJohnette's hissing cymbals and free-ish tom-tom accents; his solos are caught a lot more cleanly in the studio. DeJohnette opens the long and very beautiful 'Bayou Fever' on piano, building up the temperature much more effectively than on the original version.

*** **Special Edition** ECM 1152
    DeJohnette; David Murray (*ts, bcl*); Arthur Blythe (*as*); Peter Warren (*b, clo*). 3/79.
(*) **Inflation Blues ECM 1244
    DeJohnette; Baikida Carroll (*t*); John Purcell (*picc, af, acl, cl, bcl, as, bs*); Chico Freeman (*ss, ts, bcl*); Rufus Reid (*b*). 9/82.
*** **Tin Can Alley** ECM 1189
    DeJohnette; Chico Freeman (*ts, f, bcl*); John Purcell (*as, bs, f*); Peter Warren (*b, clo*).
*** **Album Album** ECM 1280
    DeJohnette; David Murray (*ts*); John Purcell (*as, ss*); Howard Johnson (*tba*); Rufus Reid (*b*). 6/84.
(*) **Audio Visualscapes Impulse! MCA 8029
    DeJohnette; Gary Thomas (*ts, f, bcl*); Greg Osby (*as, ss*); Mick Goodrick (*g*); Lonnie Plaxico (*b*). 2/88.
**** **Earth Walk** Blue Note CDP 7 96690
    As above, except add Michael Cain (*p, electric p, syn*), Joan Henry (*animal noises*). 6/91.
After 1979 and ECM 1152, Special Edition became DeJohnette's name for a series of markedly different working bands, united by his growing interest in quite extreme instrumental sonorities – tuba, bass clarinet, baritone saxophone – and by quite complex charts. The original *Special Edition* featured some of Arthur Blythe's last decent playing before his mysterious decline; the opening tribute, 'One For Eric' (which can also be found on a *Works* compilation, not listed in this edition but still presumably available) foregrounds Murray's surprisingly Dolphyish bass clarinet.

John Purcell's multi-instrumentalism, kept in check on the two later recordings, works well in the context of the more experimental and less achieved *Inflation Blues*, softening Carroll's rather acidulous attack and complementing Chico Freeman's linear approach. One of the least known of DeJohnette's albums, *Tin Can Alley* is certainly one of the very best, with Freeman's increasingly rock- and funk-coloured approach balancing Purcell's rather more abstract styling and Warren's imaginative, off-line patterns and rich timbre. DeJohnette's solo spot – a peril of drummer-led albums – is the vivid 'Gri Gri Man'.

The band featured on *Audio Visualscapes* is probably the most road-hardened DeJohnette has been able to take into the studio (with *New Directions* it worked the other way round). If anything, it's the material that is at fault. Greg Osby's M-Base approach to composition doesn't suit DeJohnette's more complex, multi-dimensional style. There is a long, perhaps over-long, reading of Ornette's 'The Sphinx' and a re-run of 'One For Eric' that adds nothing to the original recording. The closing title-track is a mish-mash.

It's difficult to judge whether *Earth Walk* has benefited most from the move to Blue Note or simply from the additional couple of years that this version of Special Edition has had together. The band sounds tighter and the soloing more confidently grounded; the production, by DeJohnette himself, is impeccable. Having handed over keyboard duties to the solidly imaginative Michael Cain, DeJohnette concentrates on some of the best drumming of his recording career, and certainly the best on any album under his own name. His figuring on 'Where Or Wayne' and the long title-track has an almost algebraic precision; throughout the album he alternates a powerful, straightforward count with hiddens and unknowns. DeJohnette is credited with all nine full-length compositions (there is a brief coda) and seems to have better assimilated the funk and rap influences that pervaded *Audio Visualscapes*. 'Earth Walk', with its slightly stale *Zebra*-droppings (the drummer recorded a soundtrack album of that name with Lester Bowie), is over-long and a shade repetitive at 13 minutes but, with four of the tracks nearing or topping 10 minutes, there are remarkably few compositional longueurs. DeJohnette has emerged as a rounded and successful performer/composer/leader.

***(*) **Dancing With Nature Spirits** ECM 1558
    DeJohnette; Steve Gorn (*ss, cl, f*); Michael Cain (*p, ky*). 5/95.

So much potential for mimsy mysticism here, elegantly avoided by DeJohnette's beautifully modulated new trio. Judicious use of keyboards and Gorn's horns (including a richly toned Bansuri flute) gives the group a generous range of sounds, and all contribute compositional materials. Gorn's main input is 'Anatolia', the most self-consciously 'ethnic' piece in the set; Cain's 'Emanations' is, as it sounds, more abstract, but the main bulk of the record is taken up with two long, largely improvised pieces. The title-track is richly textured and surprisingly logical in its development, not at all impressionistic; 'Healing Song For Mother Earth' is a little longer, and feels more so, tailing off at around 16 or 17 minutes into a slightly repetitive roster of ideas. Otherwise, though, a splendid return to form by DeJohnette, who stays behind his drumkit and percussion set throughout, significantly or not.

Peter Delano (born 1976) PIANO

*** **Peter Delano** Verve 519602-2
    Delano; Tim Hagans (*t*); Gary Bartz (*as, ss*); Michael Brecker (*ts*); Ira Coleman (*p*); Jay
    Anderson (*b*); Lewis Nash (*d*). 4/93.
***(*) **Bite Of The Apple** Verve 521869-2
    Delano; Tim Hagans (*t*); Gary Bartz (*as*); Chris Potter, Craig Handy (*ts*); Dick Oatts, Chuck
    Wilson (*f*); Joe Locke (*vib*); Eddie Gomez, Marc Johnson, Gary Peacock, Peter Washington (*b*);
    Joe Chambers, Jeff Hirshfield, Victor Lewis, Adam Nussbaum, Bill Stewart (*d*); Ray Mantilla
    (*perc*). 94.

Delano is still at an age when it is OK simply to show off a technique that will have some older players eyeing the chainsaw or the lathe as alternative ways of using their fingers, or dispensing with them altogether. There will be plenty of time to worry about all the other things that are currently lacking, like a plot or an emotional gamut that goes past C. Verve has the chequebook to put the youngster in with top talent, and both albums are interesting, first of all for the procession of names and only then, alas, for the quality of the music actually played.

   However, however, however, when Delano is engaged and focused and in *simpatico* company, as with Brecker on 'Reminiscence' (on the eponymous debut) or the ever-wonderful Locke on 'Sunrise Remembered' (*Bite*), he exhibits an unaffected maturity and grace that will surely develop and come to something in future years. 'Promise' is a weaselly concept, but Delano has it by the bagful and he could prove to be one of Verve's most exciting recent signings.

Barbara Dennerlein (born 1964) ORGAN, KEYBOARDS

*** **Orgelspiele** Bebab 003
    Dennerlein; Jorg Widmoser (*vn*); Peter Wolpl (*g*); Harald Ruschenbaum (*d*). 5/84.
*** **Bebab** Bebab 250964
    Dennerlein; Hermann Breuer (*tb*); Allan Praskin (*as*); Jurgen Seefelder (*ts*); Joe Nay (*d*). 7/85.
** **'Live' On Tour!** Bebab 250965
    Dennerlein; Oscar Klein (*t, cl, g*); Charly Antolini (*d*). 1/89.

Her first four releases marked Dennerlein out as a compelling, surprising performer. It's rare enough to find anyone taking up the organ as their main keyboard – and she doesn't even sound like any of the acknowledged masters of the Hammond – but her interest in different settings is just as unusual. *Orgelspiele* has its novelty elements, including rather kitschy versions of Chopin's Prelude No. 4 and Bach's 'Jesu, Joy Of Man's Desiring', but the unusually thoughtful reading of Chick Corea's 'Spain' is intriguing, and Wolpl and Widmoser have plenty of their own to say. *Bebab* offers more conventional organ-band hard bop, chirpily performed with infectious enthusiasm. The live session with Klein and Antolini, two veterans of the German scene, is a rather odd meeting, since Dennerlein's bristling energy on the likes of 'Au Privave' sounds in a different world from that of her companions' more mainstream thinking.

***(*) **Straight Ahead!** Enja 5077
 Dennerlein; Ray Anderson (*tb*); Mitch Watkins (*g*); Ronnie Burrage (*d*). 7/88.
***(*) **Hot Stuff** Enja 6050
 Dennerlein; Andy Sheppard (*ts*); Mitch Watkins (*g*); Mark Mondesir (*d*). 6/90.
Straight Ahead! belies its title with some unexpectedly adventurous music: the blues accounts for three of the compositions, but they're blues blown open by Anderson's yawning trombone expressionism, Watkins's post-modernist funk and Burrage's wide range of rhythms. Dennerlein sounds happiest on the up-tempo numbers, such as the heroically delivered title-piece, but her use of organ colour maximizes the potential of a cumbrous instrument.
 Hot Stuff is in some ways more conventional, with Sheppard a less wayward spirit than Anderson, but the band cooks harder than before and the compositions – especially 'Wow!', 'Birthday Blues' and 'Polar Lights' – take organ-band clichés and turn them on their head. Mondesir's excitable drumming adds to the intensity.

*** **That's Me** Enja 7043-2
 Dennerlein; Ray Anderson (*tb*); Bob Berg (*ts*); Mitch Watkins (*g*); Dennis Chambers (*d*). 3/92.
With some of the cast of *Straight Ahead!* coming back into the frame, this is a good but non-committal album from Dennerlein. The presence of Berg and Chambers tends to up the testosterone count at the expense of some of the freewheeling exuberance which marks the organist's best music: they beef up the tempos and the sonic weight without adding anything else of much moment. Anderson grows ever more outlandish – his 'One For Miss D' is over the top, even for him – and a finale like 'Downtown N. Y.' hints that Dennerlein might be looking towards cop-show themes as her next forte. But there is still much gutsy, entertaining playing here.

*** **Take Off!** Verve 527664-2
 Dennerlein; Roy Hargrove (*t, flhn*); Ray Anderson (*tb*); Mike Sim (*ss, as, ts, bs*); Mitch Watkins (*g*); Joe Locke (*vib*); Lonnie Plaxico (*b*); Dennis Chambers (*d*); Don Alias (*perc*). 3/95.
With another illustrious band, Dennerlein makes her major-label move. It's to her credit that she remains the centre of the music and the main force behind it: as prodigious as her colleagues here are, nobody outplays her. On the other hand, there are times, on some of the longer, up-tempo themes, where one wishes that someone would step forward and dominate what are otherwise cheerful workouts. The most vivid piece is 'Purple', in which Dennerlein's sense of line and texture elevates an otherwise conventional ballad.

Karl Denson SOPRANO, ALTO AND TENOR SAXOPHONES, FLUTE

(*) **Blackened Red Snapper Minor Music MM801024
 Denson; Ron Stout (*t*); Deron Johnson, Reginald Webb (*p*); Jeff Littleton, John Patitucci, Jesse Murphy (*b*); Don Littleton (*d*); Munyungo, Milton Commeaux (*perc*). 92.
*** **Herbal Turkey Breast** Minor Music MM801032
 As above, except Nedra Wheeler (*b*), Tom White (*d*) and Bruce Cox (*d*) replace Webb, Littleton, Patitucci, Murphy, Littleton and Munyungo. 5/93.
***(*) **Chunky Pecan Pie** Minor Music MM801041
 Denson; Pee Wee Ellis (*ts*); Gust William Tsilis (*mar*); Dave Holland (*b*); Jack DeJohnette (*d*). 1/94.
Denson has played with Fred Wesley's band and stands somewhere between funk and hard bop on the balance of these discs. The first two offer a boppish mix that shades from competent to good across the two albums: none of his companions is especially outstanding and, with Denson himself lacking the last ounce of inventiveness, the music never takes on a convincing enough cast. Stout copes well enough and the second record closes on a brief, piercing 'Goodbye Porkpie Hat'. This hardly prepares one for the sudden upswing of *Chunky Pecan Pie*, though. Most of the session is tenor–bass–drums in the tradition of the Rollins Vanguard sessions and, while Denson is hardly up to that model, he's plenty more inspired than before: 'Waltz For Leslie' has real assertion in every part of its 3/4 make-up, 'Heart Of The Wanderer' is a wrenching slow tune (even if it does sound like 'A Whiter Shade Of Pale') and the duel with guest star Ellis on 'Blue-Eyed Peas' is a likeable dose of tenor madness. What lifts things is the

superlative playing of Holland and DeJohnette who each play out of their skins, even if this is a sessionman ticket for both of them. DeJohnette in particular takes the roof off on 'Is It A Bell?'. Presumably coffee and *petits fours* will come next on the menu.

Paul Desmond (1924–77) ALTO SAXOPHONE

*** Quintet / Quartet Featuring Don Elliott Original Jazz Classics OJC 712
> Desmond; Don Elliott (*t, mellophone*); Dave Van Kriedt (*ts*); Jack Weeks, Barney Kessel (*g*); Norman Bates, Bob Bates (*b*); Joe Chevrolet, Joe Dodge (*d*); Bill Bates Singers. 2/56, 57.

*** East Of The Sun Discovery DSCD 840
> Desmond; Jim Hall (*g*); Percy Heath (*b*); Connie Kay (*d*). 59.

**** Two Of A Mind Bluebird ND 90364
> Desmond; Gerry Mulligan (*bs*); John Beal, John Benjamin, Wendell Marshall (*b*); Connie Kay, Mel Lewis (*d*). 62.

**** Easy Living Bluebird ND 82306
> Desmond; Jim Hall (*g*); Eugene Cherico, Percy Heath, Eugene Wright (*b*); Connie Kay (*d*). 63–64.

***(*) Polka Dots And Moonbeams Bluebird ND 90637
> As above. 63–64.

*** Paul Desmond And The Modern Jazz Quartet Columbia JK 57337
> Desmond; Milt Jackson (*vib*); John Lewis (*p*); Percy Heath (*b*); Connie Kay (*d*). 2/71.

*** Like Someone In Love Telarc 83319
> Desmond; Ed Bickert (*g*); Don Thompson (*b*); Jerry Fuller (*d*). 3/75.

It's still fashionable among the more categorical sort of jazz enthusiast to anathematize anything committed to record by Dave Brubeck *unless* it also features Paul Desmond. In addition to downplaying Brubeck's considerable significance, this rather overplays Desmond's occasionally self-conscious style and rather begs the question why most of his better performances tended to be with Brubeck in any case. Desmond did, however, strike up a fruitful association with the members of the MJQ and made some excellent recordings with them, of which some good samples remain.

Desmond's own-name outings were, by verbal agreement with Brubeck, always made without piano. There are hints on both *East Of The Sun* and the earlier sessions with Don Elliott of Gerry Mulligan's piano-less quartets. There was also the added plus of Jim Hall, who perfectly fitted Desmond's legato approach and interest in top harmonics (an approach that improbably influenced Anthony Braxton). Bickert is, almost needless to say, no match for Hall, but the later album has a warmth and regained confidence that recalls Desmond's finest performances. The Bluebird compilations are essentially the same, except that *Polka Dots* has been shorn of four tracks and digitally remastered as a 35-minute budget 'Masters Of Jazz'. It makes a fine introduction to Desmond's limpid work – but, for most people, *Easy Living* will be the preferred option.

Ted Des Plantes PIANO, VOCAL

**** Midnight Stomp Stomp Off CD1231
> Des Plantes; Leon Oakley (*c*); Jim Snyder (*tb, v*); Larry Wright (*cl, as, ts, ocarina, v*); John Otto (*cl, as, v*); Frank Powers (*cl, as*); Mike Bezin (*tba, v*); Jack Meilahn (*bj*); Hal Smith (*wbd, d*). 3–4/91.

Never a dull moment with this superb studio trad outfit, barrelling through a connoisseur's choice of classic material in Ohio. They have the measure of all 18 tracks, and even at over 70 minutes the record never runs out of puff. Individually, each man has the right blend of chops and enthusiasm: nobody pretends to outright virtuosity, but there are no painful mistakes either. Oakley is a properly salty cornet lead, Snyder is a ripe 'bone man, but it's Wright and Otto, their styles harking back to the oldest Chicago masters as if bebop had never happened, who lend a rare authenticity. Smith's washboard (the group is actually called The Washboard Wizards, though Des Plantes is the genial leader) lends a rare crispness to the rhythms, and even the singing is more than passable. Des Plantes chooses real obscurities from the oldest days of the music, including tunes from the books of Bennie Moten, Perry Bradford, Doc Cook, Alex Hill and The Pods of Pepper, and everything sounds fresh-minted in outstanding studio sound. Essential modern trad.

*** Ain't Cha Got Music? Jazzology JCD-225
> Des Plantes; Chris Tyle (*t, v*); David Sager (*tb*); Tom Fischer (*cl, as, ts*); Barry Wratten (*cl*); John Gill (*bj*); Tom Saunders (*b, tba*); Hal Smith (*d, wbd, v*). 5/92.

The time-frame moves forward about eight years to the early swing-era styles here, with Des Plantes' Louisiana Swingers re-creating the manner of that day on another 17 songs. If this one seems more ordinary, it's because the material is sometimes more familiar and the approach already mined: Marty Grosz does this kind of thing with perhaps an ounce more character and, while the New Orleans-based group have the measure of Henry Allen's 'Algiers Stomp' and James P. Johnson's title-track, they don't do so well by 'The Touch Of Your Lips'. That aside, the playing is still pleasantly hot and swinging.

***(*) **Ohio River Blues** Stomp Off CD 1290
> Des Plantes; Leon Oakley (c); John Otto (cl, as); Larry Wright (cl, as, ts); Ken Keeler (g, bj); Ray Cadd (tba); Hal Smith (d, wbd). 10/94.

Des Plantes strikes again with a fresh team and another set of archaeological discoveries: King Oliver's repertoire gets a shakedown (though none of the obvious titles), and there's even a nod to our own Fred Elizalde in 'Stomp Your Feet'. Back at home in the 1920s, Ted's team sound in great nick, and the only disappointment is that there isn't more of his ridiculous singing.

Giorgio Diaferia DRUMS

(*) **Doctor In Jazz Splasc(h) H 388-2
> Diaferia; Felice Reggio (t); Hal Stein, Bob Bonisolo (ts); Paolo Birro (p); Brad Buethe, Luigi Tessarollo (g); Marco Vaggi, Piero Leveratto (b); Jennie Stein (v). 11/91–5/92.

A hotchpotch of instrumentations – trio, quartet, voice and rhythm – which Diaferia presides over with unassuming authority. While it doesn't make any special sense as an album, there are some fine moments from several strong Italian voices: Birro contributes two interesting themes, Leveratto's lovely 'Deserti' is a charming pastorale, and the contrasting, rugged tenors of Stein and Bonisolo have their moments. Reggio's treatment of 'My Foolish Heart' is also good, though the three vocal tracks suggest that Jennie Stein is no more than a competent singer.

Furio Di Castri (born 1955) BASS, PIANO

*** **What Colour For A Tale** Splasc(h) H 351-2
> Di Castri; Stefano Cantini (ss, perc); Ramberto Ciammarughi (ky); Manhu Roche (d). 4/91.
*** **Urlo** YVP 3035
> Di Castri; Paolo Fresu (t, flhn, elec). 1–2/93.
***(*) **Mythscapes** Soul Note 121257-2
> As above, except add Jon Balke (p), Pierre Favre (d). 1/95.

The bassist is an inquisitive stalwart of the contemporary Italian scene. Across the very long *What Colour For A Tale*, Di Castri displays a fine ear for nuance and interplay in a quartet that features the most delicate electronic additions from the mainly acoustic Ciammarughi and pert, fiery soprano from Cantini. One standard, Jimmy Van Heusen's 'Nancy', turns up in the middle, but otherwise the tunes are mostly penned by the leader.

He has frequently worked with Paolo Fresu, and the duo record *Urlo* is an absorbing account of their partnership, sketched across 27 miniatures (some no more than a few seconds long), embellished by occasional electronics and the merest touch of overdubbing. Perhaps inevitably, this comes out as piecemeal: they develop an immaculate interplay on longer pieces such as 'Blind Streets', but at other times the tunes seem like props for the two players to show off the exquisite sound they get. Not that that's unpleasant.

The quartet record, *Mythscapes*, is democratically credited, though the two Italians take the lion's share of the composing credits. Di Castri's strong ear for melody breaks through on his tunes, especially the very fetching 'Suenos', which sounds like a sketch straight from Spain. Fresu, naturally, does his Miles impersonation here and there, though Balke's incisive piano parts and Favre's ingenious drums avert any idea of pastiche. Formless here and there, but all beautifully done.

Robert Dick FLUTES

*** **Venturi Shadows** O.O Records 7
> Dick; Mary K. Fink (f); Ned Rothenberg (shakuhachi); Steve Gorn (bansuri); Neil B. Rolnick (elec). 91.
**** **Tambastics** Music & Arts CD 704
> Dick; Denman Maroney (p); Mark Dresser (b); Gerry Hemingway (d). 1/92.

*** **Steel And Bamboo** O.O Records 12
    Dick; Steve Gorn (*bamboo f*). 92.
**** **Third Stone From The Sun** New World 80435
    Dick; Marty Ehrlich (*bcl*); Jerome Harris (*b, g*); Jim Black (*d*); Shelley Hirsch (*v*); Soldier String
    Quartet: Laura Seaton, Dave Soldier (*vn*); Ron Lawrence (*vla*); Mary Wooten (*clo*). 1/93.
**** **Worlds Of If** Leo CDLR 224
    Dick; Ned Rothenberg (*as*). 2/94.

Dick is an avant-garde concert flautist who has also found a niche in improvisation and the outer reaches of jazz. A superb performer on all the flutes (he can even make the F contrabass instrument sound feasible), he has a huge tonal and timbral range which he uses to maximum effect on these records.

His jazz-based activities are best sampled on the Music & Arts disc featuring Tambastics (those who already know the work of Dresser and Hemingway will be able to gauge the approximate territory) and he is also a member of an as yet undocumented group called ADD Trio with drummer Steve Arguëlles and guitarist Christy Doran. He is also a member of New Winds.

The material on *Venturi Shadows* is closer to his 'straight' repertoire. Rolnick's sampling locates 'A Black Lake With A Blue Coat In It' in the midst of a huge sonic landscape. By contrast, 'Further Down' and 'Heart Of Light' are unaccompanied solo pieces on flute and piccolo respectively. Dick duets with Steve Gorn on 'Bassbamboo', with Mary K. Fink on 'Recombinant Landscapes', and with Rothenberg on 'Daytime'. The final track is a mish-mash of overdubbed sounds, disconcertingly undisciplined from a player of Dick's taste and precision.

The duets with *bansuri* master Gorn on *Steel And Bamboo* are interesting rather than involving. The contrast in timbre palls rather quickly and there are passages when the two participants seem be thinking and working in entirely opposite directions. Students of flute will undoubtedly be fascinated and should be aware that all of Dick's scores and transcriptions are available from his publishing house, Multiple Breath.

There have been many jazz-centred Hendrix tributes over the last few years, but *Third Stone From The Sun* is one of the most unexpected and imaginative. Dick and arranger Dave Soldier give 'Pali Gap', 'Purple Haze' and 'Voodoo Chile' workouts that are obviously influenced by the Kronos Quartet's tongue-in-cheek approach but which are far more inventive musically. Producer Marty Ehrlich and Shelley Hirsch play on the title-track only, giving it an extra dimension the whole album could do with. Not to be missed, though.

For sheer, astonishing impact, *Worlds Of If* is the Dick record to start with. It begins with percussive, hollow sounds on the F bass flute (it might almost be some sort of marimba), stalking a range a full octave beyond a conventional bass instrument. 'Sea Of Stories', dedicated to novelist Salman Rushdie, shows how far Dick has come with the concept of overdubbing. Here, he weaves a mysterious carpet of sound in which threads of melody pop up in unexpected places, like characters returning from some distant enchantment. 'Eleven In Use' is a duo with Ned Rothenberg, the man Dick describes as the 'Jules Verne of the saxophone'; whatever it means, great music comes of it. There are other literary inspirations, as well, ideas from science-fiction writers Philip K. Dick and Ron Goulart (*Worlds of If* was the name of an influential SF magazine), but there is no mistaking the absolute musicality of Dick's approach. He makes a palimpsest of Edgard Varèse's 'Density 21.5', playing it straight, but multi-tracking additional interpretations, written as if Varèse himself had lived long enough to hear (and doubtless appreciate) Hendrix. That influence, with substantial input from Ornette Coleman, comes out on 'Lapis Blues', scored for 'harmolodic flute ensemble'. To borrow a tag from some other SF comics, *Astounding*, *Amazing* and *Fantastic*!

Vic Dickenson (1906–84) TROMBONE

**** **Gentleman Of The Trombone** Storyville STCD 5008
    Dickenson; Johnny Guarnieri (*p*); Bill Pemberton (*b*); Oliver Jackson (*d*). 7/75.

Much of the contemporary trombone vocabulary comes from the playing of Vic Dickenson. His bravura range of sounds on the horn laid the groundwork for everything that players such as Ray Anderson and Craig Harris do. At present, only the wonderful Storyville is in the catalogue, with the bonus of three previously unissued tracks. The tunes are nearly all standards or blues, but Dickenson liked a wide repertoire and, even when one of the tunes might seem a dull choice, he makes it new: there are few versions of 'Bye Bye Blackbird' that can stand next to this one. The peppery delivery, unpredictable accents, huffing low notes and barking high ones, even his charmingly doleful singing: all are essential parts of a great jazzman who always gave his best. For all the humour in his work, there's an underlying feeling for blues that deepens all his solos, and his own composing is represented by the typically wistful

'Just Too Late'. The trio play very well, though some of Guarnieri's more elaborate flourishes may irritate some, and the studio balance is a little eccentric; but four stars for Vic, without question.

Walt Dickerson (born 1931) VIBRAPHONE

*** **This Is Walt Dickerson** Original Jazz Classics OJC 1817
 Dickerson; Austin Crowe (*p*); Bob Lewis (*b*); Andrew Cyrille (*d*). 3/61.
(*) **A Sense Of Direction Original Jazz Classics OJC 1794
 Dickerson; Austin Crowe (*p*); Edgar Bateman (*b*); Ernest Guillemet (*d*). 5/61.
*** **Serendipity** Steeplechase SCCD 31070
 Dickerson; Rudy McDaniels (*b*); Edgar Bateman (*d*). 8/76.
***(*) **Peace** Steeplechase SCCD 31042
 Dickerson; Lisle Atkinson (*b*); Andrew Cyrille (*d*). 11/76.
** **To My Queen Revisited** Steeplechase SCCD 31112
 Dickerson; Albert Dailey (*p*); Andy McKee (*b*); Jimmy Johnson (*d*). 7/78.
Despite a recent revival of enthusiasm for his vividly original vibes approach, Walt Dickerson has never enjoyed the kind of critical praise heaped on Bobby Hutcherson's head. While Hutcherson is unquestionably the more innovative player, with a direction that diverges sharply from the orthodoxy laid down in the late 1940s and early '50s by Milt Jackson, Dickerson is arguably the more interesting player, with a style that combines something of Jackson's piano-based approach with Lionel Hampton's exuberantly percussive sound and an ear for tunes that head off in unexpected directions like the wonderful 'Time' and 'Death And Taxes' on *This Is*. Cyrille was an early interpreter; on the best of the Steeplechases, *Peace*, he drives things along with great generosity of spirit. The addition of Albert Dailey, a pianist of comparatively limited conceptual range, to an already successful trio was a tactical error. Vibes and piano are apt to cancel each other out; when they don't on *To My Queen Revisited*, they merely sound mismatched.

*** **Divine Gemini** Steeplechase SCCD 31089
 Dickerson; Richard Davis (*b*). 2/77.
*** **Tenderness** Steeplechase SCCD 31213
 As above. 2/77.
(*) **Visions Steeplechase SCCD 31126
 Dickerson; Sun Ra (*p*). 7/78.
The duo was probably Dickerson's ideal performing context. A busy player, he nevertheless revelled in space (and not always the kind of space that a collaboration with Sun Ra implies). For all its cosmic subtexts, *Visions* is remarkably restrained, with Ra playing some of his most intimate and earthbound piano. Once considered a minor classic (and certainly Dickerson's most playlisted recording), it has lost a lot of its original sheen.

 Richard Davis is a well-practised duo improviser – most notably with Eric Dolphy – and he falls in at once with Dickerson's conception, giving the whole session a rich, almost symphonic depth of tone and breadth of development. Along with *Peace*, these are the Dickerson albums that should prevail. For the moment, though, he remains a rather 'outside' presence.

Neville Dickie PIANO

*** **The Piano Has It** Stomp Off CD1269
 Dickie; Micky Ashman (*b*); John Petters (*d*). 4–9/93.
Britain's answer to Don Ewell and Ralph Sutton gets one of his most sympathetic outings here, though the concept is a mite dusty: 21 treatments of piano-roll solos, all played in faithful approximation to the originals, often solo but sometimes with the support of Ashman and Petters. This is a scholar's record and stands up well on that count, with Dickie obviously enjoying himself and the best of the pieces – James P. Johnson's 'Modernistic', for instance – securing a strong virtuosity. It *is* all rather samey, though, and, capable though he is, Dickie doesn't quite have the bullish impact of his heroes. This kind of piano needs a soupçon of bluster to make it come fully alive.

Guido Di Leone (born 1964) GUITAR

*** **All For Hall** Splasc(h) H 323-2
 Di Leone; Paolo Fresu (*t*); Attilo Zanchi (*b*); Ettore Fioravanti (*d*). 7/90.
Lovingly crafted guitar music, with the bonus of Fresu's muted horn on five tracks. The title is a giveaway that Di Leone is a Jim Hall disciple and, while he prefers Hall's gentility over his incisiveness,

the music has substance as well as tranquillity. Zanchi and Fioravanti are always looking to play more than a simple bottom line: hear, for instance, the drummer's dramatic work on 'Auschwitz'. A grower.

Gene Dinovi (born 1928) PIANO

***(*) **Renaissance Of A Jazz Master** Candid CACD 79708
    DiNovi; Dave Young (b); Terry Clarke (d). 3/93.

It might be easier to list the great players Gene DiNovi *hasn't* worked with. He made his debut with Joe Marsala while still in his teens, trading on a precocious, cocksure talent that quickly brought him to the attention of Boyd Raeburn, Buddy DeFranco, Artie Shaw and Lester Young. His only other reference in this volume is as pianist on the Benny Goodman recording of 'Stealin' Apples', with the ill-starred Fats Navarro and Wardell Gray.

Though drawn into Charlie Parker's sometimes fatal orbit, DiNovi survived both personally and professionally, becoming a successful composer/arranger in Hollywood and New York. In the 1970s he emigrated to Canada and gradually began to reconstruct his stalled career as an improvising player. *Renaissance* is a beautifully balanced set, with the emphasis on upbeat, forward-looking themes. Opening with 'A Cockeyed Optimist', the late John Carisi's 'Springsville', 'Till The Clouds Roll By' and 'Right As The Rain' suggests a pretty sanguine stance and somehow belies the Bud Powell inflexions that hover round the perimeter of solos. 'Elegy' shouldn't be confused with the Powell tune; it's one of three DiNovi originals ('Have A Heart' is co-credited to Johnny Mercer, no less) and the difference in emotional temper is instructive.

DiNovi is above all an elegant player who loves songs and never lets the melody disappear behind mere harmonic artifice. His colleagues have a wealth of experience, not least Young's stints with Oscar Peterson, and the rhythm lines are both accurate and relaxed.

Joe Diorio (born 1936) GUITAR

*** **Double Take** RAM RMCD 4502
    Diorio; Riccardo Del Frà (b). 4/92.
***(*) **We Will Meet Again** RAM RMCD 4501
    Diorio (g solo). 5/92.
*** **The Breeze And I** RAM RMCD 4508
    Diorio; Ira Sullivan (f, af, ss, as, perc). 6/93.
***(*) **More Than Friends** RAM RMCD 514
    Diorio; Steve LaSpina (b); Steve Bagby (d). 6/93.

He knows all the tunes, obviously loves them immoderately, but still manages always to impart a little personal spin and variation to even the most hackneyed warhorse standard. These are all supremely elegant, affectionate and mainly thoughtful, and it is immensely difficult to draw qualitative distinctions between subtly different sessions. In our judgement, the duos with Mick Goodrick (listed under Goodrick's name) are less appetizing than the trio discs or the pairing with Sullivan, a player who trades up a limited stock of ideas by the sheer variety of sounds he can command on his horns. The other duo session, with del Frà, is alternately exquisite and drab (two takes of 'Summertime' isn't quite gilding the lily). Like it, most of the sessions consist of standards, but graced with so much intelligence that almost all sound as if they have just been written. And then there are the unexpected coups, like 'The Summer Knows' on *The Breeze And I*, which jolt the whole thing into a new dimension.

Diorio keeps going in and out of focus as a solo artist. This recent batch is a pretty good sample of the vintage, an artist who has a very personal take on harmonic improvisation (see his book *Intervallic Designs*) and who has managed to reconcile it comfortably with straight chordal accompaniment, polyphonic ideas and some carefully selected aspects of free improvisation.

Dirty Dozen Brass Band GROUP

*** **My Feet Can't Fail Me Now** Concord CCD 3005
    Gregory Davis, Efrem Towns (t); Charles Joseph (tb); Roger Lewis (ss, bs); Kevin Harris (ts); Kirk Joseph (tba); Jenell Marshall, Benny Jones (d). 84.
*** **Live: Mardi Gras In Montreux** Rounder RR 2052
    As above, except Lionel Batiste (d) replaces Jones. 7/85.

Positioned between novelty group, authentic revivalists and neoconservative brass masters, this New Orleans ensemble make exciting and funny and clever records without finally convincing the listener that they're delivering as much as they seem to promise. The playing is too slick to approximate the unaffected character of the great New Orleans bands of the past, but the individual players don't suggest that they have anything important to say away from the voicings and the spirited beats and bass lines of the arrangements. Their first two albums, both recorded live, are surely the best ones to get, because this isn't a music – or at least a band – that was meant to 'develop' itself very far. Each disc captures much of the fun which their concerts provide.

*** **Open Up (Whatcha Gonna Do For The Rest Of Your Life?)** Columbia 468365-2
    As above, except add Raymond Webber (*d*). 1–4/91.
Open Up opens them up to procedural music: Raymond Webber's 'conventional' drum parts anchor the rolling rhythms of the band to a steadier beat, and there's some tension between the parping eccentricities of the solo horns and the straighter beats below. It's not especially better or worse than any earlier DDBB session, though.

(*) **Jelly Columbia 473059-2
    Gregory Davis (*t, perc*); Efrem Towns (*t*); Revert Andrews (*tb, perc*); Roger Lewis (*ss, bs, perc*); Kevin Harris (*ts*); Keith Anderson (*sou, tb*); Eddie Bo (*p*); Jenell Marshall, Lionel Batiste Jr (*d*); Kenyatta Simon, Big Chief Smiley Ricks (*perc*); Danny Barker, George French (*v*). 8/92–1/93.
A tribute to Jelly Roll Morton that at least gives them context, if not real purpose. They reinterpret Morton's tunes as thumping, mostly one-dimensional marches and stomps and, while it's one side of his legacy, one misses the decorative beauty his piano always inserted. Aside from a brief, blustering 'Shoe Shiner's Drag', most of these tunes are no more or less than another stack of DDBB jollities. Danny Barker's spoken comments add a dash of documentary that palls over repeated listening.

Bruce Ditmas DRUMS

**** **What If** Postcards POST 1007
    Ditmas; Sam Rivers (*ss, ts*); Paul Bley (*p*); John Abercrombie (*g*); Dominic Richards (*b*). 12/94.
An unobtrusive sideman in all sorts of previous playing situations, Ditmas's sole entry as leader is enormously impressive. As usual with releases on the Postcards imprint, the band assembled is a dream ticket that manages to live up to the billing. On the astounding title-track Ditmas pilots a course that suggests a spontaneous improvisation among the quintet which still musters the structure and refinement of a finished composition. Compare this with the closing track, a mystery song with speckles of rhythm and droplets of melody, an ECM-like watercolour. Yet elsewhere Ditmas has inveigled the recently reserved Abercrombie into his most dynamic and explosive form since the original *Gateway* albums of 20 years before; has Bley playing in an atypically outgoing and attacking frame of mind; and bridges old and new in the oddball tribute to New Orleans capsuled in the three-part '3348 Big Easy'. Rivers plays an almost deferential role on most of his appearances, but check the harsh timbres of 'Power Surge'. Swinging, yet uncompromisingly contemporary, this is a very fine disc.

Bill Dixon (born 1925) TRUMPET, FLUGELHORN, PIANO

***(*) **Bill Dixon In Italy: Volume 1** Soul Note 121008
    Dixon; Arthur Brooks, Stephen Haynes (*t*); Stephen Horenstein (*ts, bs*); Alan Silva (*b*); Freddie Waits (*d*). 6/80.
**** **November 1981** Soul Note 121038
    Dixon; Mario Pavone, Alan Silva (*b*); Lawrence Cook (*d*). 11/81.
** **Thoughts** Soul Note 121111
    Dixon; Marco Eneidl (*as*); John Buckingham (*tba*); Peter Kowald, William Parker, Mario Pavone (*b*); Laurence Cook (*d*). 5/85.
*** **Son Of Sisyphus** Soul Note 121138
    As above, except omit Eneidl, Kowald and Parker. 6/88.
***(*) **Vade Mecum** Soul Note 121208
    Dixon; Barry Guy, William Parker (*b*); Tony Oxley (*d*). 8/93.
Having made a substantial mark with Cecil Taylor – notably on *Conquistador* – Dixon's own work seemed to languish somewhat during the 1970s and it was only the enthusiasm of Giovanni Bonandrini (blessings rain on him for many mercies) that gave the trumpeter an outlet commensurate with his gifts. Even so, the discography is still rather patchy and incomplete.
    The 1980 disc – a studio recording, despite what the title may imply – is very much in the Taylor line, and the closing suite ('Anacrusis' / 'Conversation' / 'New Slow Dance') is dedicated to the pianist. Dixon typically doesn't feature himself all that prominently, spreading much of the higher voicing across the

three-trumpet front line. Horenstein has an unenviable job keeping up and is much more effective on his baritone. Silva and Waits generate a maelstrom underneath.

November 1981 may well be Dixon's masterpiece, patiently conceived and executed, and generously proportioned. Dixon likes to build his statuesque ideas on rich drones and has often worked with two bass players. Silva is a very considerable artist in his own right, adhering to a style of bass playing (Richard Davis is the best example) that is clearly premissed on orchestral requirements. As ever, the trumpet is used quite sparingly, often doing little more than sustaining quasi-pedal points against which the bassists move restlessly. Music as concentrated as 'Penthesilea' or the 'Llaattiinnoo Suite' require certain adjustments of musical expectation, but they are consistently satisfying and Bonandrini provides a generous, albeit intimate, sound which suits Dixon very well indeed.

Pavone and Cook survive from the earlier grouping, but *Thoughts* lacks the impact of the earlier disc and drifts off into inconsequential and even slightly pretentious ramblings (for which, see 'For Nelson And Winnie: A Suite In Four Parts'). Here again, Dixon's own playing is at a discount and is often lost in a disconcertingly scrunched-up mix that for once blurs a lot of detail. No obvious reason for this: hurry? budgetary squeeze?

Son Of Sisyphus (the title refers to an earlier large-scale composition) is superior in almost every regard. It opens with a brooding duo for bass and Dixon on piano. 'Silences For Jack Moore' is a threnody for a dancer friend, cast in the familiar bass range Dixon favours. The sonorities are even darker on the long title-track, where Buckingham's tuba fills the role accorded a trio of string bassists on *Thoughts*, but the overriding impression is of tremendous space and movement, and there's a sense in which Dixon's melancholically graceful soloing conforms to Cecil Taylor's much-quoted assertion that his own improvisations imitate the leaps that a dancer makes in space. It also has much in common with the trumpeter's other great passion; Dixon's paintings are featured on the covers of more than one of his records, richly gestural abstracts based on an intelligently restricted palette.

Behind almost all of Dixon's small-group performances there is a sort of dark, inner pressure, like the imprint of a much larger conception that has been denied expression. That is profoundly evident again on *Vade Mecum*, in which he is joined by Britons Guy and Oxley. It might be argued that both men are too 'strong' in conception (however sympatic) to conform easily to Dixon's exceptionally disciplined approach. This is a highly effective record, but it does on occasion seem to be moving in too many directions at once.

Baby Dodds (1898–1959) DRUMS, VOCAL

(****) **Baby Dodds** American Music A M C D-17
    Dodds; Bunk Johnson, Kid Shots Madison, Wooden Joe Nicholas (*t*); Jim Robinson, Joe Petit (*tb*); George Lewis, Albert Burbank (*cl*); Adolphe Alexander Jr (*bhn*); Isidore Barbarin (*ahn*); Lawrence Marrero (*bj*); Red Clark, Sidney Brown (*tba*); Alcide Pavageau (*b*). 44–45.
One of the best examples of living history in the catalogue, *Baby Dodds* features the leading drummer of New Orleans jazz talking at some length about his traps, his cymbals, his style and how it all comes together – for jazz bands, marching bands, funeral parades and whatever else a drummer had to play for. Most of the music is actually lifted from other records, notably Bunk Johnson's American Music CDs, but this is the place to hear Baby's history lesson. Some of it is horse sense that still holds good – 'Tiger Rag is played too fast,' he grumbles, and then we hear the tempo he liked to play for it – and when he talks us through a lesson in technique, the good-natured generosity of the man comes alive again, four decades after his death. Remastering of all the speech/drum tracks is excellent and, though the music comes in mainly for illustration, the compilers have chosen some fine slices of New Orleans to go with the talk.

Johnny Dodds (1892–1940) CLARINET, ALTO SAXOPHONE

**** **Johnny Dodds, 1926** Classics 589
    Dodds; Freddie Keppard, George Mitchell (*c*); Kid Ory, Eddie Vincent (*tb*); Junie Cobb (*cl*); Joe Clark (*as*); Lockwood Lewis (*as, v*); Lil Hardin Armstrong, Jimmy Blythe, Arthur Campbell, Tiny Parham (*p*); Curtis Hayes, Cal Smith, Freddy Smith (*bj*); Eustern Woodfork, Johnny St Cyr (*bj, v*); Clifford Hayes (*vn*); W. E. Burton (*wbd, v*); Earl McDonald (*jug, v*); Jimmy Bertrand, Jasper Taylor (*d, perc*); Papa Charlie Jackson, Trixie Smith (*v*). 5–12/26.
**** **Johnny Dodds, 1927** Classics 603
    Dodds; Freddie Keppard (*c*); Eddie Ellis (*tb*); Lil Hardin Armstrong, Jimmy Blythe, Tiny Parham (*p*); Jasper Taylor (*d*); Baby Dodds (*wbd*). 1–10/27.

**** Johnny Dodds, 1927–8 Classics 617
> Dodds; Natty Dominique, George Mitchell (*c*); R. Q. Dickerson (*t*); Honoré Dutrey, Kid Ory,
> John Thomas (*tb*); Charlie Alexander, Jimmy Blythe (*p*); Bud Scott (*bj*); Bill Johnson (*b*); Baby
> Dodds (*d*); W. E. Burton (*wbd, v*); Julia Davis (*v*). 10/27–7/28.

*** Johnny Dodds, 1928–40 Classics 635
> Dodds; Natty Dominique, Herb Morand (*c*); Charlie Shavers (*t*); Honoré Dutrey, Preston
> Jackson (*tb*); Charlie Alexander, Lil Hardin Armstrong, Jimmy Blythe, Richard M. Jones,
> Frank Melrose (*p*); Teddy Bunn, Lonnie Johnson (*g*); Junie Cobb (*g, v*); Bill Johnson, John
> Kirby, John Lindsay (*b*); O'Neil Spencer (*d, wbd, v*); Baby Dodds (*d, wbd*). 7/28–5/40.

**** Johnny Dodds & Jimmy Blythe, 1926–1928 Timeless CBC 015
> Dodds; Louis Armstrong, Natty Dominique, Freddie Keppard (?), Punch Miller (*c*); Roy Palmer
> (*tb*); Jimmy Blythe (*p*); Bud Scott (*bjo*); Jimmy Bertrand (*wbd*); W. E. Burton (*wbd, v*); Jasper
> Taylor (*d, wbd*); Trixie Smith (*v*). 5/26–3/28.

***(*) King Of The New Orleans Clarinet, 1926–1938 Black & Blue 59.235
> Dodds; Natty Dominique, George Mitchell, Herb Morand, Charlie Shavers (*t*); John Thomas,
> Honoré Dutrey, Kid Ory (*tb*); Joe Clark (*as*); Charlie Alexander, Lil Hardin Armstrong, Frank
> Melrose (*p*); Teddy Bunn, Johnny St Cyr (*bjo*); Bud Scott (*g*); Bill Johnson, John Kirby (*b*);
> Baby Dodds (*d, wbd*); O'Neil Spencer (*d, wbd, v*). 7/26–1/38.

Johnny Dodds was the model professional musician. He rehearsed his men, frowned on alcohol and drugs, and watched the cents. In 1922 he was a member of King Oliver's Creole Jazz Band at Lincoln's Garden in Chicago, a band that included Louis Armstrong, Lil Hardin Armstrong, trombonist Honoré Dutrey, and Dodd's wayward younger brother, Warren 'Baby' Dodds. The clarinettist left in 1924, after a quarrel about money, and set out on a highly successful recording career of his own that faltered only with the beginnings of the swing boom. Dodds died in 1940 and was promptly canonized by the revivalists.

His tone was intense and sometimes fierce, rather removed from the soft introspections of Jimmie Noone or George Lewis's folksy wobble. Like Jimmy Giuffre two generations later, Dodds favoured the lower – *chalumeau* – register of the instrument in preference to the piercing *coloratura*. He doubles briefly on alto saxophone on July 1926 cuts (CD2 above) with Jimmy Blythe. The switch may have been an attempt to get some change out of Paramount's insensitive microphones for, unlike Sidney Bechet, Dodds never seriously considered a full turn to the saxophones.

Though much of his best work was with Louis Armstrong's Hot Five and Seven, the Classics compilations are (or will be when the former is complete) the essential Dodds documents. They contain work for Brunswick, Columbia, Gennet, the ropey Paramount, Victor and Vocalion. The real classics are the cuts made for Columbia with the New Orleans Wanderers/Bootblacks, a line-up that included George Mitchell, Kid Ory, Joe Clark, Johnny St Cyr and Lil Hardin Armstrong. There are fine clarinet duets with Junie Cobb (and without brass) from 26 August which have been rather overlooked in the rush of enthusiasm for the Wanderers/Bootblacks performances of the previous month.

Inevitably, very little matches up to these classics, but Dodds's reconciliation with King Oliver in September for a single track ('Someday Sweetheart') underlines the great might-have-been of their interrupted association. Dodds by this time was making too much regular money in Burt Kelly's Stables, a South Side club much frequented by Italian businessmen (if you follow), to pursue or accept a longer recruitment. A pity, because there's a definite falling-off after 1926. The duets with Tiny Parham are interesting, and there are excellent things on the Vocalion trios of April 1927; too many pick-up bands, though, and on a lot of the material Dodds is overpowered by other voices, notably Louis Armstrong (in for a Black Bottom Stompers session that also included Barney Bigard and Earl Hines) and Jelly Roll Morton. The Classics format omits the two Morton tracks but does reinstate a number, 'Cootie Stomp', from the State Street Ramblers session of August 1927, and includes a rare June 1928 session with the vocalist Julia Davis (allegedly half her entire recorded output) and trumpeter R. Q. Dickerson.

The 1927–8 disc does, though, include some of the material excerpted on the Bluebird *Blue Clarinet Stomp*, below, omitting an alternative take of the title-track. This is a no-nonsense feature of the Classics series as a whole and one that may recommend it to more casual listeners. The final Classics volume ends with a bit of a rush and there really isn't much in it that even those who love Dodds's music will greatly treasure, beyond a trio 'Indigo Stomp' with Lil Hardin Armstrong and Bill Johnson from February 1929.

The Black & Blue and Timeless compilations cover the same ground in different permutations. Both are quite decently done and neither will disappoint anyone who isn't interested in following the *Chronological* sequence right through to its heartbreaking banal end. The personnel and dates attached to each disc are the best guide to possible overlaps, but the Timeless is particularly good on alternative takes.

There is considerable controversy over the remastering of early jazz. On this occasion, the Classics is very much to be preferred, with a warm sound. However, the NoNoise system used by Bluebird (see below) certainly carries the day. John R. T. Davies's surgery on the Timeless disc typically leaves not so much as a tuck or stitch in sight. Non-specialists may – for the time being, at any rate – opt for the perfectly acceptable Bluebird compilation, which overlaps on only a few tracks and which has a slightly sweeter delivery.

***(*) **South Side Chicago Jazz** MCA 42326
   Dodds; Louis Armstrong, Natty Dominique, Herb Morand (*c*); Roy Palmer, John Thomas (*tb*); Barney Bigard (*ts*); Charlie Alexander, Lil Hardin Armstrong, Jimmy Blythe, Earl Hines, Frank Melrose (*p*); Bud Scott (*g, bj*); Jimmy Bertrand, W. E. Burton (*wbd*); Baby Dodds (*d, wbd*). 4 & 10/27, 3/28. 7/29.
**** **Blue Clarinet Stomp** Bluebird ND 82293
   Dodds; Natty Dominique (*c*); Honoré Dutrey (*tb*); Lockwood Lewis (*as*); Charlie Alexander, Lil Hardin Armstrong, Jelly Roll Morton (*p*); Clifford Hayes (*vn*); Curtis Hayes, Emmitt Perkins, Cal Smith (*bjo*); Bill Johnson (*b*); Baby Dodds (*d, wbd*); H. Clifford, Earl McDonald (*jugs*). 12/26, 6/27, 7/28, 1 & 2/29.
***(*) **Blue Clarinet Stomp** Frog DGF 3
   Dodds; Natty Dominique (*c*); Honoré Dutrey (*tb*); Charlie Alexander, Lil Hardin Armstrong (*p*); Bill Johnson (*b*); Baby Dodds (*d, wbd*). 7/28, 1 & 2/29.

Though nominally a thematic compilation, *South Side Chicago Jazz* is in effect a useful Dodds anthology, since he plays on every track. It reduplicates a good deal of the material from the more detailed compilations above, notably 1927 material by Dodds's Trio and Black Bottom Stompers, Jimmy Blythe's Owls and Blythe's and Jimmy Bertrand's Washboard Wizards; but it is attractive as an across-the-board sample of early Dodds work with a variety of bands, though there's only one item, a 1929 'Forty And Tight' with Herb Morand, not (yet) covered by either of the fuller documents. The Bluebird *Blue Clarinet Stomp* may be the better buy (though its namesake isn't bad either). Processed by the computerized NoNoise system, ND 82293 lets the musical information come through almost without interference and, if there's a suspiciously 'modern' extra dimension to the bass, it's neither intrusive nor excessively overdone. The vintage trio tracks with Jelly Roll Morton from 1927 are another plus. MCA have a good holding of Dodds material right through to his death in 1940, and they have scoured the archive quite intelligently, with a good mix of styles, from the appealingly raucous Beale Street Washboard Band to the slightly earlier sets with Louis Armstrong and Lil Hardin Armstrong.

There are several things which make the Frog desirable: having the Victor sessions together, having them relatively untinkered with, having the (seemingly) correct discographical story of 'Pencil Papa' for which dates and sessions seem to have been transposed. All to the good. Collectors will be satisfied; newcomers can feel they have a reasonable sampling of the classic material.

Christian Minh Doky DOUBLE BASS

*** **Appreciation** Storyville STCD 4169
   Doky; Thomas Schneider (*ts*); Thomas Clausen (*ky*); Larry Petrowsky (*d*). 1/89.
*** **The Sequel** Storyville STCD 4175
   Doky; Ulf Wakenius (*t*); Bill Evans (*sax*); Niels Lan Doky (*p, ky*); Adam Nussbaum (*d*). 90.
***(*) **Letters** Storyville STCD 4177
   Doky; Randy Brecker (*t, ky*); Niels Lan Doky (*p, ky*); Hans Oxmond (*g*); Adam Nussbaum (*d*). 2 & 4/91.

Brother of and frequent collaborator with the brilliant young piano player, Niels Lan Doky, Minh Doky has a firm, controlled tone on the bass and the kind of popping smoothness in faster runs that is derived from the better bass guitarists. Like his fellow-Dane, the great NHOP, Minh Doky favours the lower register of his instrument and moves down the bridge only for occasional dramatic accents. The opening album is polished but not particularly inspired and the later, Shorter-tinged writing hasn't yet made much impact. In fact the best things on *Appreciation* are a lilting but unsentimental version of 'When You Wish Upon A Star' and an original version of the bassist's warhorse, 'Alone Together'. The second album is a disappointment but is also clearly transitional, placing greater emphasis on collective skills. In mood and structure it is fleetingly reminiscent of similar projects by Ron McClure.

With *Letters*, Minh Doky really comes into his own. Brecker's spare lines are effectively used on the opening title-track and thereafter, and the bassist's brother plays crisply and with his now familiar ability to work quite abstractly within the confines of a melody. Oxmond provides Scofield-derived guitar touches on two tracks, and the closing traditional 'Lullaby' is a bass solo with just washes of synthesizer for accompaniment. The finest track, however, is the gentle ballad 'Please, Don't Leave Me', on which Minh Doky develops a minimal idea at length over a shifting, steadily changing background.

As producer, he has given himself a resonant acoustic, with a strong touch of echo, which suits his tone very well indeed.

Niels Lan Doky (born 1963) PIANO

***(*) **Here Or There** Storyville STCD 4117
  Doky; Niels-Henning Orsted-Pedersen (b); Alvin Queen (d). 1/86.
*** **The Target** Storyville STCD 4140
  Doky; Niels-Henning Orsted-Pedersen (b); Jack DeJohnette (d). 11/86.
(*) **The Truth Storyville STCD 4144
  Doky; Bob Berg (ts); Bo Stief (b); Terri Lyne Carrington (d). 6/87.
*** **Daybreak** Storyville STCD 4160
  Doky; John Scofield (g); Niels-Henning Orsted-Pedersen (b); Terri Lyne Carrington (d). 9/88.
***(*) **Close Encounter** Storyville STCD 4173
  Doky; Gary Peacock (b); Alex Riel (d). 7/89.

Doky seems set to be the next Danishman to carve an international jazz reputation after NHOP. He plays with dazzling fluency, has a biting, percussive touch, relishes fast tempos and has a decisive, linear manner. He writes terrific riff tunes, too. Storyville's five albums are all strong examples of what he can do, brusquely recorded to show off his sound. While there's little to choose among the three trio dates, all of which are made up of originals plus a favourite standard or two, we've given the edge to the debut record for the sheer excitement that seems to energize every minute of the music. *The Truth*, a live session, loses some immediacy over the course of four long pieces, but it's an accomplished quartet, even if Berg's occasionally faceless tenor isn't an ideal match. *Daybreak* adds Scofield's dependably handsome guitar to the proceedings and 'Jet Lag' and 'Natural' find Doky's writing at its wittiest.

*** **Dreams** Milestone MCD-9178-2 C
  Doky; Randy Brecker (t); Bob Berg (ts); John Scofield (g); Christian Minh Doky (b); Adam Nussbaum (d). 8/89.
***(*) **Friendship** Milestone MCD-9183-2
  Doky; Randy Brecker (t); Bill Evans (ss); Rick Margitza (ts); John Abercrombie, Ulf Wakenius (g); Christian Minh Doky, Niels-Henning Orsted-Pedersen (b); Adam Nussbaum, Alex Riel (d). 8–9/90.

Doky had already graduated from Berklee in 1984 and moved to New York in the mid-1980s. So his 'American' albums are scarcely a departure from his earlier work. *Dreams* has two of his catchiest themes in 'That's It' and 'Faxed', and the writing is generally good enough to overcome any hint of ennui which the star sidemen might have introduced. But *Friendship* is even better, split between sessions in Copenhagen and New York, with Doky's native crew outdoing the New Yorkers for bravura and unity and the album produced (by Doky himself) in stunningly upfront sound.

*** **Paris By Night** Soul Note 121206-2
  Doky; Randy Brecker (t); Christian Minh Doky (b); Daniel Humair (d). 2/92.

Something of a holding operation until the next studio project (though Doky seems to be busy producing other artists at present), this on-the-hoof live date from Paris is nothing more or less than an accomplished blow on some jazz standards, with Brecker in firm voice and the brothers displaying their usual seamless drive.

Eric Dolphy (1928–64) ALTO SAXOPHONE, FLUTE, BASS CLARINET, CLARINET

*** **Outward Bound** Original Jazz Classics OJC 022
  Dolphy; Freddie Hubbard (t); Jaki Byard (p); George Tucker (b); Roy Haynes (d). 4/60.

Eric Dolphy's recording debut was with the Roy Porter band in California in early 1949. The session afforded him an almost apostolic contact with the roots of bebop. Thereafter, though, the desert. It was to be nearly a decade before he was asked to record again, when he joined the Chico Hamilton band. After leaving Hamilton at the end of 1959, he did some sessions with Sammy Davis Jr ('no solos', as the discographies laconically put it) where he met the bassist, George Tucker. It's thought that Tucker used his contacts to sign Dolphy up for his first session as leader.

  Outward Bound was recorded on April Fool's Day, 1960. Issued with a murkily surreal sleeve, it is immediately and unsettlingly different from anything Dolphy had attempted before. If it lacks the sudden, alienating wallop of an equivalent dose of Ornette Coleman or Cecil Taylor, it's no less challenging. Though his alto playing was still marked by occasional Parkerisms, his work on bass clarinet pointed in an entirely new direction, as on an introspective ramble down 'Green Dolphin Street'.

***(*) **Out There** Original Jazz Classics OJC 023
> Dolphy; Ron Carter (*clo*); George Duvivier (*b*); Roy Haynes (*d*). 8/60.

The rest of 1960 was almost absurdly overbooked: Dolphy was to play on a staggering 18 albums before the year's end. His own second album as leader was recorded in August. Still far more conventionally tonal than most New Wave jazz, Dolphy was already hearing dimensions to chords few other musicians and very few critics were attuned to hear. *Out There* marked a significant stage in his exploration of timbre and sonority; this time he dispensed with piano, replacing it with Ron Carter's eerily effective cello. If the disturbing example of Ornette Coleman – a nemesis Dolphy had yet to confront – lay behind the jagged rhythms of the first album, *Out There* was very much a tribute to Charles Mingus, with whom Dolphy enjoyed probably his closest, if least probable, artistic partnership.

Disguised, like its predecessor, behind an ersatz, Dali-and-water sleeve-design, *Out There* really did sound different. The blues-based 'Serene' is one of his finest compositions and the Mingus-inspired 'Eclipse' affords a rare and intriguing glimpse of his work on a normal, concert-pitched clarinet.

(*) **Other Aspects Blue Note B21Y 48041
> Dolphy; Ron Carter (*b*); Gina Lalli (*tabla*); Roger Mason (*tamboura*); other musicians unidentified. 7 & 11/60, 62.

Dolphy's only other Blue Note album, *Out To Lunch*, is a masterpiece, but this is a collection of oddments, not released until the 1980s, fascinating for the light it casts on Dolphy's restless experimentalism but not entirely satisfying in itself. The long 'Jim Crow', whose personnel is not known, is a powerful piece that has Dolphy on all three of his horns, carving something positive out of protest. The two 'Inner Flight's are highly personal flute meditations that don't communicate quite convincingly; there is also some distortion of sound on the original tapes. 'Dolphy-N' is a fine alto/double-bass duet with Ron Carter. The Indian-influenced 'Improvisation And Tukras' contains some fascinating music, as Dolphy anticipates some of Joe Harriott's work on *Indo-Jazz Fusions*. Despite the title, much of the music sounds as if it has been worked out in advance. Essential for serious Dolphy collectors, this will otherwise be of limited interest.

**** **Far Cry** Original Jazz Classics OJC 400
> Dolphy; Booker Little (*t*); Jaki Byard (*p*); Ron Carter (*b*); Roy Haynes (*d*). 12/60.
**** **At The Five Spot: Volume 1** Original Jazz Classics OJC 133
> Dolphy; Booker Little (*t*); Mal Waldron (*p*); Richard Davis (*b*); Ed Blackwell (*d*).
***(*) **At The Five Spot: Volume 2** Original Jazz Classics OJC 247
> As above.
**** **Memorial Album** Original Jazz Classics OJC 353
> As above. 7/61.

When trumpeter Booker Little died in October 1961, Dolphy was robbed of one of his most promising and sympathetic artistic partnerships. All the same, it's somehow rather telling that the most striking track on *Far Cry*, his only studio album as leader with Little (there was a return bout the following March, released as *Out Front*), should be for unaccompanied alto saxophone. 'Tenderly' is one of the truly remarkable performances in modern jazz; it draws a firm line from Coleman Hawkins's 'Picasso' to Anthony Braxton's innovative 'For Alto'.

Side one sees Dolphy paying respectful but now more distant homage to Charlie Parker, a suite of three loosely connected tracks culminating in the title-piece. By the end of 1960, Dolphy had long left the nest and was attempting altitudes that Parker wouldn't have dreamt of, as on a re-run of the blues, 'Serene', which wasn't included on the original release but only on the interesting but now unavailable label compilation, *25 Years Of Prestige*.

Nor would Parker have felt easy with the sustained harmonic invention of Dolphy's live sets with Little. The skittering 'Fire Waltz' and 'Bee Vamp' show what Dolphy was capable of with a top-of-the-range rhythm section; Waldron's chords are just ambiguous enough, and Davis's orchestral-sounding bass opens up the harmonic texture even more. For once a 'memorial album' really does merit the title, though it serves as a more immediate epitaph to Little. By no means a pound-of-flesh release, the two long tracks are of consistently high quality (as, more surprisingly, is the sound-quality), with Dolphy exploring some of his most intriguing harmonic ideas and Little playing exquisitely. Volume 1 of *At The Five Spot* has a valuable alternative of 'Bee Vamp'. This material was formerly also available on a three-LP Prestige set called *The Great Concert Of Eric Dolphy*.

(*) **Berlin Concerts Enja 3007 2CD
> Dolphy; Benny Bailey (*t*); Pepsi Auer (*p*); Jamil Nasser (*b*); Buster Smith (*d*). 8/61.

Dolphy in the city where he died, dying only occasionally in the arms of a willing but short-winded rhythm section. Benny Bailey's contributions to the long opening 'Hot House' and the closing 'I'll Remember April' are characteristically impressive, but once again the highlights come only when Dolphy's magnificent bass clarinet is picked out solo, as in the by then *de rigueur* 'God Bless The Child' and a long trio version of Benny Carter's 'When Lights Are Low', with just bass and drums in support.

(*) **In Europe: Volume 1 Original Jazz Classics OJC 413
　　Dolphy; Erik Moseholm, Chuck Israels (*b*); Bent Axen (*p*); Jorn Elniff (*d*). 9/61.
(*) **In Europe: Volume 2 Original Jazz Classics OJC 414
　　As above.
(*) **In Europe: Volume 3 Original Jazz Classics OJC 416
　　As above.
(*) **Stockholm Sessions Enja 3055
　　Dolphy; Idrees Sulieman (*t*); Knud Jorgensen, Rune Ofwerman (*p*); Jimmy Woode (*b*); Sture
　　Kalin (*d*). 9/61.

Recorded less than a month after the *Berlin Concerts* and an object lesson in the perils of 'going single'. The first and second are overlapping releases. The OJC sets (which sound tinnier on CD) include versions of 'Miss Ann' and 'Don't Blame Me' and 'Glad To Be Unhappy'. They also include a rather inconsequential three-parter called 'In The Blues'.

The Danish rhythm section, nominally led by Moseholm but bearing all the symptoms of advanced rhythmic and harmonic disorientation, flounder in Dolphy's increasingly insouciant wake. By this time, he had – like Charlie Parker before him – learned to ignore inadequate settings and go his own way. There is another wonderful 'God Bless The Child', less terse and stripped down, but gamier in articulation, and a fine duo with bassist Chuck Israels – where did he spring from? – on 'Hi-Fly', another intriguing point of comparison with the Berlin set, where it gets a trio reading. Collectable, and for completists self-evidently essential, but by no manner of means classic performances. In value-for-money terms, the OJC CDs are a better bet, though they lack the warmth of the old Prestige *Copenhagen Concert* on vinyl.

The Swedes are a little more adventurous and Jorgensen's chording in particular suggests greater familiarity with the idiom, but Dolphy appears to be having some articulation problems and there is a tiredness even in familiar themes like 'Miss Ann', 'G.W.' and, yes, 'God Bless The Child'. On balance, though, not least with the advantage of nicely fronted CD sound, the Swedish sessions are the ones to plump for.

*** **Softly As In A Morning Sunrise** Natasha NI 4001
　　Dolphy; McCoy Tyner (*p*); Reggie Workman (*b*); Mel Lewis (*d*). 12/61.

Much bootlegged, and sounding decidedly *sub rosa* even in this reasonably respectable issue, this justifies its inclusion on historical grounds. Recorded at Studio 15 in Munich, three months after the Swedish sessions, Dolphy is playing supremely well on a standards programme – 'On Green Dolphin Street', 'Softly As In A Morning Sunrise', 'The Way You Look Tonight' and Rollins's 'Oleo'. He sticks to bass clarinet throughout, for reasons not specified. Some doubts, too, about the exact circumstances of the gig. Mel Lewis was in for Elvin Jones, who had been having what are euphemistically described as 'passport problems', but there is a persistent story that the piano player on 'The Way You Look Tonight' is not McCoy Tyner but the other Lewis, John. Even repeated listens offer no absolute stylistic confirmation, but we accept it's a possibility and, as such, an intriguing sidebar to the Dolphy discography.

**** **Out To Lunch!** Blue Note CDP 746522
　　Dolphy; Freddie Hubbard (*t*); Bobby Hutcherson (*vib*); Richard Davis (*b*); Tony Williams (*d*). 2/
　　64.

Out to Lunch! is one of the handful of absolutely essential post-war jazz records. Perhaps predictably, the conjunction of Dolphy and Blue Note (and the only one, apart from the indifferent *Other Aspects*) resulted in something extraordinary.

Though Dolphy had played better, he had never had a more cohesive or responsive band. His control on the opening 'Hat And Beard', dedicated to Thelonious Monk, is extraordinary, but the real power of the track comes from the wonderfully fragmented rhythm section: Tony Williams's broken-field drumming, Richard Davis's big, freely pulsed bass and, where once there would have been a piano, Bobby Hutcherson's furiously percussive vibes. 'Something Sweet, Something Tender' is marked by a wonderful unison between Dolphy (on bass clarinet) and Richard Davis. On 'Out To Lunch' all semblance of a fixed metre breaks down; Williams plays almost entirely 'free' (though the basic count appears to be a taxing 5/4) and Davis ignores the bar-lines altogether, allowing the group to improvise unrestrictedly around a brief, staccato theme. 'Straight Up And Down' has a lop-sided, knockabout feel that isn't entirely successful. If Dolphy's flute-playing was the last of his three instrumental disciplines to mature, then 'Gazelloni' is its apotheosis, a wonderful performance after which jazz flute could never be the same again.

The album is a near-perfect example of 'pure' invention on a remarkably slight foundation of melodic ideas that have only implicit harmonic support and which are not governed by strict time-signatures. *Out To Lunch!* seems to reorganize modern jazz around itself: Charlie Parker's vertical take-offs from the top of the chord; Ornette Coleman's morse-code melody; John Coltrane's hugely expansive harmonic reach; even a touch of Cecil Taylor's all-out atonality. Yet it resists anything as drearily repetitive as a personal 'style'. Rudy van Gelder's engineering is inch-perfect and, of all Dolphy's recordings, *Out To Lunch!* is the most coherently conceived and packaged (right down to Reid Miles's distinctive artwork). It almost doesn't look or sound like Dolphy's record at all. It was always hard to locate Dolphy in his music, almost as if it really wasn't his but an item of unclaimed property which reverts to us each time it goes on the turntable. As it should at very regular intervals.

**(*) Candid Dolphy Candid 9033

> Dolphy; Benny Bailey, Ted Curson, Roy Eldridge, Lonnie Hillyer, Booker Little (*t*); Jimmy Knepper, Julian Priester (*tb*); Charles McPherson (*as*); Walter Benton, Coleman Hawkins (*ts*); Nico Bunink, Kenny Dorham, Tommy Flanagan, Don Friedman, Mal Waldron (*p*); Ron Carter, Art Davis, Charles Mingus, Peck Morrison (*b*); Jo Jones, Dannie Richmond, Max Roach (*d*); Roger Sanders, Robert Whitley (*perc*); Abbey Lincoln (*v*). 10 & 11/60, 2, 3 & 4/61.

This is how curates like their eggs done. Parts of it – like the first take of 'Stormy Weather' with Mingus – are excellent; the Abbey Lincoln parts are horrid. The long solo opening to 'Stormy Weather' is one of the best things Dolphy ever did, and the sessions with Little helpfully represent his next most fruitful artistic partnership. As an index of the extremes to which Dolphy's playing career was subjected, it's a useful compilation.

** Vintage Dolphy Enja 5045

> Dolphy; Edward Amour, Don Ellis, Nick Travis (*t*); Jimmy Knepper (*tb*); Phil Woods (*as*); Benny Golson (*ts*); Lalo Schifrin (*p*); Barry Galbraith, Jim Hall (*g*); Warren Chiasson (*vib*); Art Davis, Richard Davis, Chuck Israels, Barre Phillips (*b*); Gloria Agostini (*hp*); Sticks Evans, J. C. Moses, Charli Persip (*d*); string quartet. 3/62, 3/63, 4/63.

By no possible stretch of the imagination 'vintage' anything. The first – jazz – side has some fine solo material from Dolphy, notably on 'Iron Man', but nothing that re-centres the original, 'official' discography. Side two, but for a so-so 'Donna Lee' (notable only for Dolphy's confrontation with the radical Don Ellis), documents his involvement with Gunther Schuller's Third Stream movement, a jazz-meets-serialism *rapprochement* that was always slightly more interesting as an idea than in actuality. The recording quality has an *audio vérité* shakiness and, though some of the pieces have a clever, palindromic logic, Dolphy never sounds entirely easy with Schuller's atonal scores. Though now thought to be a relatively important way-station in Dolphy's progress, this shouldn't be considered an urgent acquisition.

**(*) Here & There Original Jazz Classics OJC 673

> Dolphy; as for OJC 022; Prestige 34002; OJC 413.

A useful if slightly raggedy collection of out-takes. 'Status Seeking' and (yet) another 'God Bless The Child', slightly below par, round out the *Great Concert* sessions without adding significantly to their stature. There is a second bash at 'Don't Blame Me' from the Copenhagen sessions, with another fine effort from Dolphy on flute, and the same manful struggle from the local rhythm section.

Most intriguing is a quartet track (i.e. no Freddie Hubbard) from Dolphy's debut as leader, *Outward Bound*. Under the title-of-convenience 'April Fool', a reference to the day in 1960 when the album was recorded, it's the equal of anything on the original release and, but for Hubbard's absence, might well have been included. Worth having.

*** The Essential Eric Dolphy Prestige 60022

> Dolphy; Freddie Hubbard, Booker Little, Richard Williams (*t*); Oliver Nelson (*as, ts, cl*); Booker Ervin (*ts*); Jaki Byard, Mal Waldron, Richard Wyands (*p*); Ron Carter (*clo*); Joe Benjamin, George Duvivier, George Tucker (*b*); Roy Haynes, Charli Persip (*d*). 4, 5, 8 & 12/60, 1 & 6/61.

'Les' from *Outward Bound*, 'Feathers' from *Out There*, 'Ode To Charlie Parker' and 'Bird's Mother' from *Far Cry*, 'Status Seeking' from Mal Waldron's *The Quest*, and 'The Meetin'' and 'Ralph's New Blues' from Oliver Nelson's *Screamin' The Blues* and *Straight Ahead* respectively. A worthwhile collation of material that might appeal to a newcomer.

*** Last Date Emarcy 5101242

> Dolphy; Misha Mengelberg (*p*); Jacques Schols (*b*); Han Bennink (*d*). 6/64.

A welcome reappearance. Though the items above were actually recorded later, this long-deleted disc has entered the mythology as Dolphy's last word to the world, a feeling sustained by the words he speaks as the final notes of 'Miss Ann' die away: 'When you hear music, after it's over, it's gone in the air. You can never recapture it again.' Dolphy's reading of 'Epistrophy' is typically angular and devastatingly precise, and for once on his European travels he has a rhythm section who are with him almost all the way. Bennink in particular is highly responsive and puts in some lovely fills and accents on 'South Street Exit' and 'Miss Ann'. Not his greatest performance ever, but one to cherish nevertheless.

Arne Domnérus (born 1924) ALTO SAXOPHONE, CLARINET, BARITONE SAXOPHONE

***(*) **Portrait** Phontastic PHONT CD 9313
> Domnérus; other personnel includes Clifford Brown, Rolf Ericson, Art Farmer, Clark Terry (*t*);
> Putte Wickman (*cl*); Benny Carter (*as*); Rolf Blomquist, Jerome Richardson (*ts, f*); Lars Gullin
> (*bs*); Bengt Hallberg (*p, org*); Lars Erstrand (*vib*); Sture Akerberg, George Mraz, Georg Reidel
> (*b*); Rune Carlsson, Oliver Jackson, Johan Lofcrantz (*d*). 46–93.

*** **In Concert** Phontastic PHONT CD 9303
> Domnérus; Rolf Ericson (*t*); Claes Rosendahl (*f, ts*); Bengt Hallberg (*p*); Rune Gustafsson (*g*);
> Georg Riedel (*b*); Egil Johansen (*d*). 8/78.

(***) **Blåtoner Fra Troldhaugen** FXCD 65
> Domnérus; Rune Gustafsson (*g*); Bengt Hallberg (*p*); Georg Riedel (*b*). 9/86.

*** **Dompan At The Savoy** Phontastic PHONT CD 8806
> Domnérus; Ulf Johansson (*p, tb, v*); Sture Akerberg (*b*); Aage Tanggaard (*d*). 9/90.

(*) **Sugar Fingers Phontastic PHONT CD 8831
> Domnérus; Jan Lundgren (*p*); Lars Estrand (*vib*); Sture Akerberg (*b*); Johan Lofcrantz (*d*). 7/93.

One of the finest Scandinavian jazz musicians of his generation, Domnérus oversaw a shift away from the heavily bop-influenced Scandinavian idiom of the early 1950s and towards something more straight-forwardly romantic and impressionistic. The early sessions are not presently available, but they reveal Domnérus sounding closer to Benny Carter than to Parker in his phrasing, with a wan, meditative quality that frequently refers to diatonic folk themes and hymn tunes. (It may be Domnérus whom the ageing bopper is thinking about in the great jazz movie, *Sven Klangs Kvintett*, when he says that the only places you could hear jazz in Scandinavia in the 1970s were churches. For a time at least, Domnérus performed in 'sacred concerts' that combined jazz and liturgical materials.)

His typical sound, even on the alto and clarinet, is low, soft and somewhat undynamic. In later life, this has become even more pronounced though, like Lee Konitz, Domnérus is occasionally able to surprise with brief episodes of dissonance. *Sugar Fingers*, recorded at the Swedish Academy of Music rather than in church, has a politely respectful, elder-statesman feel, and the band hover round him like courtiers. Pianist Lundgren's title-track sounds almost tailor-made for the leader but, ironically, it's the one number he sits out.

With *Blåtoner*, Domnérus has tackled a figure almost as sacrosanct in Scandinavia as the liturgical themes he was examining at the end of the 1970s. This beautiful chamber session, recorded without a drummer, is based entirely on compositions by Edvard Grieg, mostly the *Lyric Pieces*, the *Nordic Dances*, the inevitable *Peer Gynt Suite* (which yields the lovely 'Solveig's Song') and *Norwegian Folk Tunes*. It's light, delicate, with only a rather attenuated jazz content, and most of Domnérus's impro-visations are along the lines of conventional Romantic variations, with little vertical-harmonic inven-tiveness. Worth trying, though it gives only a rather poor account of the Swede's skills as a jazzman.

These are very much better attested on the other three Phontastics. *In Concert* Domnérus presents much more convincingly. His solo on 'Isfahan' isn't quite out of the book, but it's close enough and sits well in a section of the concert played 'with Duke in mind'. The folklore side is accounted for in Bengt Hallberg's 'Visa fran Utanmyra', a piano solo. There are also three guest spots for trumpeter Ericson, back visiting his ancestral homeland; he sat in on Monk's 'Well You Needn't', followed by 'You've Changed' and the closing 'Stony Lonesome', lifting the proceedings a notch.

Dompan At The Savoy is unusual in that Hallberg is absent. In his place is Ulf Johansson, who came in to jam and show off his multi-instrumentalism by contributing trombone solos to 'Honeysuckle Rose' and 'Solitude'. It's a relaxed, affectionate session ('Dompan' is the saxophonist's nickname in Sweden) that doesn't purport to offer much more than easy, mid-paced swing. No sign at all of Domnérus's more acerbic, Konitz-influenced side, and as such not a particularly representative or flattering point of contact.

Portrait, as it suggests, is a career profile, 18 tracks covering the period from the end of the war (a single cut from a Sonora disc called *Ben's Music*, 1946) right up to *Sugar Fingers*. There's a quite extraordinary performance of Strayhorn's 'Blood Count', played as a duet with long-term associate Hallberg at the organ of the Stockholm Konserthus, and there is a single track from their New York trip, *Downtown Meeting*, where they recorded with Clark Terry, George Mraz and Oliver Jackson. There's return traffic on the Quincy Jones-conducted Swedish All-Stars session of 1953, an Art Farmer vehicle also featuring Clifford Brown and the great Swede, Lars Gullin. There's also a Swedamerican summit from 1982 with the veteran Benny Carter, originally released as *Skyline Drive And Towards*.

Useful as *Portrait* is for a career summary, it makes for unsatisfactory listening as a continuous whole. It's a slightly ramshackle sampling, put together more with an eye to coverage than to the creation of a well-balanced CD; an aircheck from the Salle Pleyel in Paris, May 1949, makes it in only as a historical oddity and, second track in, it's a touch off-putting. These misgivings apart, it's still the best Domnérus album, or we should say *surviving* album. The best of all is the 1977 duo with Hallberg, *Hypertoni*. Enthusiasts can have fun looking for that.

Miles Donahue TRUMPET, TENOR SAXOPHONE

**(*) Double Dribble Timeless SJP 392
　　Donahue; Kenny Werner (*p*); Bruce Gertz (*b*); George Schuller (*d*). 4/92.
*** The Good Listener RAM RMCD4510
　　As above, except Adam Nussbaum (*d*) replaces Schuller; add Jerry Bergonzi (*ts*). 6/93.

Donahue may be a new name to the leadership ranks, but he's been around and is now in his fifties. Both discs were recorded at New Hampshire college gigs a year apart, and each has a lot of enjoyable contemporary blowing, without touching any special highs or lows. Like most who double on brass and reeds, Donahue sounds stronger on the saxophone, and he plays that horn for most of the earlier session: a tough 'Inner Urge' and the surprisingly cantankerous treatment of 'When I Fall In Love' which closes the show are the picks, but some of the tracks bog down in rhetoric and Werner plays so many notes that it seems he's trying to take over. The quintet date is stronger, though Bergonzi tends to outplay the leader: 'Tab' is a nicely bruising mêlée for the two horns. Yet Donahue's solo tenor turn on 'I'm Old Fashioned' has a furry beauty to it, and his more generous allocation of trumpet sits well with Bergonzi's tendency to collar the situation. Better recording on the second disc, too.

John Donaldson PIANO

*** Meeting In Brooklyn Babel BDV 9405
　　Donaldson; Iain Ballamy (*ts, ss*); Ray Drummond (*b*); Victor Lewis (*d*). 9/93.

En route to California, Britons Donaldson and Ballamy stopped off to cut this refreshingly spontaneous, unfussy and often deeply interesting session with two excellent American players who've rubbed shoulders with the best. The sheerest mark of their quality is the total simplicity and unaffectedness of approach, Drummond patiently chording behind Ballamy's delightful arrangement of 'Scarborough Fair', before handing over to Lewis to whip through the double-time second section. Donaldson's solo doesn't depart very far from the melody, but then he is primarily a melodist, as his two compositions on *Meeting In Brooklyn* demonstrate.

Quite where he is coming from as a melodist isn't absolutely clear. There are hints of Django Bates's approach in 'Big Loss In Lewisham' and 'Medjugorje' (a pilgrim destination in the former Yugoslavia), but Donaldson likes to play it pretty straight and shows little of Bates's appetite for pure sound. He plays elegantly and with feeling on Cole Porter's 'All Of You', but even here one has to conclude that he has been thoroughly upstaged by his colleagues.

Lou Donaldson (born 1926) ALTO SAXOPHONE

**(*) Blues Walk Blue Note B21Y-46525
　　Donaldson; Herman Foster (*p*); Peck Morrison (*b*); Dave Bailey (*d*); Ray Barretto (*perc*). 7/58.
** Alligator Boogaloo Blue Note B21Y-84263
　　Donaldson; Melvin Lastie Sr (*c*); Lonnie Liston Smith (*org*); George Benson (*g*); Leo Morris (*d*).
**(*) Everything I Play Is Funky Blue Note 831248-2
　　Donaldson; Eddie Williams (*t*); Charles Earland (*org*); Melvin Sparks (*g*); Jimmy Lewis (*b*); Idris Muhammad (*d*).
** The Scorpion: Live At The Cadillac Club Blue Note 831876-2
　　Donaldson; Fred Ballard (*t*); Leon Spencer Jr (*org*); Melvin Sparks (*g*); Idris Muhammad (*d*). 11/70.
*** The Righteous Reed! The Best Of Poppa Lou Blue Note 830721-2
　　As above discs. 60–70.

Lou Donaldson was and has remained among the most diligent of Charlie Parker's disciples. His playing has hardly altered course in 40 years of work: the fierce tone, quickfire phrasing and blues colourings remain constant through the 1950s and '60s and, if he's as unadventurous as he is assured, at least his records guarantee a solid level of well-executed improvising. He replaces Parker's acidity with a certain sweetness which can make his work pall over extended listening, but it's an engaging sound.

Donaldson's stack of Blue Note albums have drifted in and out of circulation. *Blues Walk*, true to its title, is Donaldson at his bluesiest, and Bailey and Barretto make a propulsive combination; the material, though, is rather dull. *Alligator Boogaloo* comes from the period when the saxophonist was trying to make the best of the soul-jazz trend, without much success on this occasion – routine playing on lightweight back-beat music, though the album was a hit in its day and has remained popular. *Everything I Play* is marginally better, since the rhythm section dig in a little more and stop trying to pretend to be stuck on 4/4 jazz rhythms; but this whole thing was already a disintegrating formula, and the live set captured on *The Scorpion* is about as fiery as last week's chili dogs. The curious are directed to the best-of collection, which is still basically a clumsy and repetitive record but manages to sort out some of the best licks the originals had to offer.

** **Forgotten Man** Timeless SJP 153
>   Donaldson; Herman Foster (*p*); Geoff Fuller (*b*); Victor Jones (*d*). 7/81.
** **Live In Bologna** Timeless SJP 202
>   As above. 1/84.
The title of the earlier Timeless record is a little indulgent, since Donaldson is more widely represented in the catalogue than many of his peers. Both of these sessions, with the faithful Herman Foster still on the piano bench, have nothing surprising in them, from the material to Lou's favourite licks, but they probably say as much for the survival of original bebop mannerism in the 1980s as anything else recorded at the time.

(*) **Play The Right Thing Milestone MCD 9190
>   Donaldson; Lonnie Smith (*org*); Peter Bernstein (*g*); Bernard Purdie (*d*); Ralph Dorsey (*perc*). 90.
** **Birdseed** Milestone MCD-9198-2
>   Donaldson; David Braham (*org*); Peter Bernstein (*g*); Fukushi Tainaka (*d*); Ralph Dorsey (*perc*). 4/92.
(*) **Caracas Milestone MCD 9217-2
>   Donaldson; Lonnie Smith (*org*); Peter Bernstein (*g*); Kenny Washington (*d*); Ralph Dorsey (*perc*).
Lou's flame burns a little more brightly here, but he's still sounding a bit worn out after 40 years of bebop: most of his old attack has gone, the articulation furred over. Smith is a feeble prop and Bernstein plays many of the best licks on *Play The Right Thing*, although the organist sounds in better form on *Caracas*. Everyone sounds all-in on *Birdseed*, which is something Parker wouldn't have tolerated; but matters perk up a degree on *Caracas*. There's no shape to the albums, though, just casual blowing; maybe Lou needs a new producer.

(*) **Sentimental Journey Columbia 278177-2
>   Donaldson; Lonnie Smith (*org*); Peter Bernstein (*g*); Fukushi Tainaka (*d*); Ray Mantilla (*perc*). 8/94.
Yet another chance for Lou to shine. The sleeve-notes talk about a back-to-basics approach, but Donaldson's art has never been anything but. Producer Todd Barkan gets the prettiest sound Lou's had in the studio for a while, comfortingly wide, but the musicians do little of any great interest with it, and when the leader quotes 'English Country Garden' on 'What Will I Tell My Heart' one feels like giving up.

Michel Doneda SOPRANO SAXOPHONE

*** **Open Paper Tree** FMP CD 68
>   Doneda; Paul Rogers (*b*); Le Quan Ninh (*perc*). 5/94.
This must have been a remarkable set – performed at Berlin's Free Music Workshop in 1994 – but, as so often with great improvisations, something's been lost in the translation. For once, Jost Gebers doesn't seem to have secured a very faithful sound, and the grand range of Le Quan's percussion parts has been withheld. Rogers also suffers. The surviving document still has a raw, wound-up quality, which makes for unsettling listening over a long disc. Doneda's soprano begs no great virtuosity and he makes an awkward voice with the others, yet this makes the music the more intense and hard-won. There's little obvious textural interest, more a drawn-out struggle among three rather disparate voices, or entities. Tough work, and absorbing stuff for those who like a challenge.

Dorothy Donegan (born 1922) PIANO, VOCAL

*** **Makin' Whoopee** Black & Blue 59146-2
>   Donegan (*p* solo). 3/79.

** **Sophisticated Lady** Ornament CM-8011
    Donegan; Georg Linges (*b*); Tony Mann (*d*). 1/80.
** **The Explosive Dorothy Donegan** Audiophile ACD-209
    Donegan; Jerome Hunter (*b*); Ray Mosca (*d*). 3/80.
** **I Just Want To Sing** Audiophile ACD-281
    As above. 3/80.
(*) **Live At The 1990 Floating Jazz Festival Chiaroscuro CD(D) 312
    Donegan; Jon Burr (*b*); Ray Mosca (*d*). 10–11/90.
(*) **Live At The 1991 Floating Jazz Festival Chiaroscuro CR(D) 318
    As above, except add Dizzy Gillespie (*t*). 10/91.
*** **Live At the Floating Jazz Festival 1992** Chiaroscuro CR(D) 323
    As above, except Clark Terry (*t*) replaces Gillespie. 10/92.

A veteran whose greatest fame has come very late in her career, Donegan is a pianist whose exuberance and sometimes hysterical virtuosity make her difficult to assess. *Makin' Whoopee* is the most temperate of these recordings and, while it explores the range of her talent – taking in Tatum, Garner, stride, cocktail-lounge playing and an extravagant sense of humour – the scaled-down approach makes it the most approachable of these discs. Her version of 'Yesterday', for instance, manages a unique take on the song without destroying its lyricism. The two Audiophiles, both taken from the same session, are much less successful, gathering together a muddle of standards and medleys in unattractive sound, on a day when Donegan's least sensitive instincts were in charge. *Sophisticated Lady*, recorded live, also suffers from a clattery mix and rambles around to no useful purpose.

Her show-stopping appearances on Hank O'Neal's Floating Jazz cruises have brought her some useful notoriety in the 1990s. The 1990 session includes her celebrated impersonations of Lena Horne, Pearl Bailey, Eartha Kitt and (dead on) Billie Holiday, which are worth hearing once. But there's also some strong piano, and this rhythm section knows her well enough to make the music swing and stay together. Gillespie makes only the most desultory appearance on the 1991 date, which also has a very engaging 'Tea For Two'. Terry is more generously featured on his guest role the following year, and this is probably the one to get out of the three, although her spoken reminiscences at the end of the previous two discs make an interesting postscript. She is a phenomenon, whatever one thinks about the music, and a sensible best-of culled from all these recordings would be something to hear.

Armen Donelian (born 1949) KEYBOARDS

(*) **Trio '87 Odin 4024-2
    Donelian; Carl Morten Iversen (*b*); Audun Klieve (*d*). 7/87.
(*) **Secrets Sunnyside SSC 1031
    Donelian; Barry Danielian (*t, flhn*); Dick Oatts (*ss, ts*); Anthony Cox (*b*); Bill Stewart (*d*); Arto Tuncboyaci (*perc*). 2/88.

Donelian makes elaborate work of some of his chosen themes on the trio record, and while it sometimes pays off – as in the bright, finely judged treatment of Dave Brubeck's 'In Your Own Sweet Way' – his admittedly considerable technique masks the feeling that it's hard to discern the point of some of his ideas. Iversen and Klieve, though, add a muscular third dimension to the music.

While *Secrets* is a difficult record to warm to – Donelian's themes can sound pointlessly tricky, and he sacrifices melodic warmth for textural density – the musicians perform the music with a lot of heart. Danielian and Oatts move from in to out with believable fluency, Oatts in particular using the material to forge some wiry improvisations, and Cox and Stewart (along with the excitable Tuncboyaci on two tracks) deliver their parts with fine crispness. Danielian's long-phrased solo on 'New Blues' is nearly worth the admission price. Bright and full-bodied recording.

Brigeen Doran ALTO, TENOR AND SOPRANO SAXOPHONES

** **Bright Moments** B & W BW020
    Doran; Christy Doran (*g*); Fernando Saunders (*b, v*); Dave Doran (*d, ky, perc, v*). 11/90.

There used to be a British television programme called *Family Band*, on which smiling kinsfolk cranked out performances distinguished only by the fact that the bass player was the trumpeter's grandmother. *Bright Moments* features three Doran siblings, but what (apart from affection and loyalty to sis) Christy is doing on this plodding slab remains a mystery. One might have expected him to rumple things up a bit, or to have brought something a touch more imaginative to the seven (out of nine) tunes credited to him.

    Brigeen has an unpleasing, kazoo-ish tone, but that never stopped Candy Dulfer making a career of it.

Compared even to someone like Gretchen Langheld, who has a similar starting-point, this is pretty unimaginative fare. Not *too* many bright moments, then.

Christy Doran (born 1949) GUITARS, EFFECTS

*** **Red Twist & Tuned Arrow** ECM 1342
    Doran; Stephan Wittwer (*g, syn, elec*); Freddy Studer (*d*). 11/86.
*** **Henceforward** Leo Lab CD 015
    Doran; John Wolf Brennan (*p, prepared strings*). 5/88.
***(*) **Phoenix** hat Art 6074
    Doran; Ray Anderson (*tb*); Marty Ehrlich (*cl, ts, as*); Urs Leimgruber (*ss*); Hank Roberts (*clo*).
    12/89–4/90.

A superb technician with considerable imaginative range, Doran has, like his Irish compatriot and fellow exile, John Wolf Brennan, come uncomfortably close on occasion to an awkward New Ageism. There are moments on *Henceforward*, notably the opening bars of 'Waltz For Erik Satie', when he appears to be bent on nothing more than ersatz 'Gymnopédies' for the 1990s. But Doran is too uncompromising an improviser for lassitude and complacency. He has a fierce and occasionally biting tone which complements Brennan's complex arpeggiations (the opening track is nothing but) and is unembarrassed about placing plain, folksy strums in open tunings among all the effects.

    Grouped with Wittwer and Studer, he sounds a little less adventurous. ECM production is invariably faultless, though, and the album survives some rather indifferent material. Doran seems to work best in dialogue rather than in more obviously hierarchical conformations. The *Phoenix* duets are intelligently conceived and beautifully played. It's rather a pity there can't be an all-in jam at the end, in the spirit of Derek Bailey's improvising collective Company, for individual contributions seem to be itching towards some higher principle of organization. Ray Anderson is superb, worth the price of admission alone.

***(*) **Corporate Art** JMT 849155 2
    Doran; Gary Thomas (*ts, f*); Mark Helias (*b*); Bobby Previte (*d*). 4, 5 & 6/91.

Doran seems more than usually effectual as a member of a hard-hitting modern-jazz outfit. He's still the dominant voice, though Thomas makes some powerful statements on saxophone and (particularly) flute, and his dark, school-of-Hendrix feedback storm on 'Chiaroscuro' is the single most impressive thing on the record. Helias and Previte are a top-drawer rhythm section, lifted well to the front of Stefan Winter's hard-edged mix. Strong stuff, *Corporate Art* makes some of Doran's solo work seem rather inconsequential.

*** **Musik Für Zwei Kontrabasse, Elektrische Gitarre Und Schlagzeug** ECM 1436
    Doran; Bobby Burri, Olivier Magnenat (*b*); Freddy Studer (*d*). 5/90.

Doran's second ECM album is an uncomfortable and ultimately unsatisfactory affair which veers between hard, almost industrial sound and a nervous, algebraic discourse. The formal 'new music' title isn't really reflected in the eight tracks (one of which is by Burri and only two of which, 'Chemistries I/ II', are related – by name only). Doran's sound is as pumped up as usual, and it's tempting to speculate whether the music would have had greater impact had the *zwei Kontrabasse* been stood down for the afternoon. Recording twin basses is an engineer's nightmare; but for a rather crude channel separation, they are virtually indistinguishable. Production is credited to the band; one wonders how ECM chief Manfred Eicher might have handled it.

***(*) **What A Band** hat Art CD 6105
    Doran (*g* solo). 6/91.

Using delay devices in real time, Doran is able to improvise over ostinati or simple chords, thereby creating an impression of many simultaneous voices. The opening 'Solomutations' whirls off into the kind of flamenco-coloured territory John McLaughlin has been exploring in recent years, but the real highlight of the set is the second track, a cranked-up electric version of 'She Moved Through The Fair', which is more explicitly drawn from Hendrix's feedback anthems.

    Technical virtuosity at this level is inclined to pall rather quickly, and *What A Band* is perhaps best sampled a track at a time rather than listened to continuously. It certainly shouldn't be missed.

Pierre Dørge (born 1946) GUITAR

** **Ballad Round The Left Corner** Steeplechase 1132
    Dørge; John Tchicai (*ss, as*); Niels-Henning Orsted-Pedersen (*b*); Billy Hart (*d*). 10/79.

The Dane is an experienced performer in jazz-rock and free settings, although his guitar tone is bright and clear, almost in a mainstream jazz tradition. But these small-group settings don't suit him very well.

The duo session with Dickerson blends counterpoint almost too cleanly and tends to pall rather quickly; while the quartet date, despite the promising line-up – Tchicai has been a frequent collaborator with the guitarist – is depressingly low in vitality, the compositions given only a perfunctory treatment.

*** **Brikama** Steeplechase SCCD 31188
> Dørge; Michael Marre (*t, euph*); Kenneth Agerholm, Niels Neergaard (*tb*); John Tchicai (*ts, bcl*); Jesper Zeuthen (*as*); Morten Carlsen (*ts, bcl, bsx, ney, tarogato*); Doudou Gouirand (*as, ss*); Bent Clausen (*vib, perc*); Irene Becker (*ky*); Johnny Dyani (*perc, v*); Hugo Rasmussen (*b*); Thomas Akuru Dyani (*perc*); Marilyn Mazur (*d, perc*). 3/84.

***(*) **Very Hot – Even The Moon Is Dancing** Steeplechase SCCD 31208
> Dørge; Harry Beckett (*t, flhn*); Kenneth Agerholm, Niels Neergaard (*tb*); Soren Eriksen, Doudou Gouirand (*ss, as*); Jesper Zeuthen (*as*); John Tchicai (*ts, v*); Morten Carlsen (*ts, bsx, f, tara, cl, zurna*); Irene Becker (*ky, perc, v*); Bent Clausen (*vib, perc*); Johnny Dyani (*b, p, v*); Hugo Rasmussen (*b*); Marilyn Mazur (*d*); Ahmadu Jarr (*perc*). 7/85.

***(*) **Johnny Lives** Steeplechase SCCD 31228
> As above, except omit Neergaard, Eriksen, Gouirand, Dyani and Jarr; add Hamid Drake (*d*), Thomas Dyani (*perc*). 4/87.

These albums are by New Jungle Orchestra, the nearly-big band under Dørge's leadership, which is among the most enterprising and unpredictable outfits of its kind. Dørge explores the idea of a global jazz village by pushing what is basically a post-bop orchestra into African, European and any other climes he can assimilate: roistering horn parts might emerge from a lush percussive undergrowth, or heartbreaking ballads may be brightened by Dørge's own sparkling high-life guitar solos. Inevitably there are moments on the records that sound misconceived, or cluttered, but these are surprisingly few: what one remembers is the joyful swing of the ensembles, the swirling tone-colours and rhythmic pep. There are fine soloists too in Tchicai, Carlsen and Beckett. *Brikama* is absolutely stunning, with vivid voicings and a bewildering range of instrumental characters. *Very Hot* is slightly fresher, with a winning reworking of Ellington's 'The Mooche' and two very long yet convincing pan-global jams; but it would be unwise to pass up *Johnny Lives*, dedicated to the late Johnny Dyani, which has some beautiful writing and playing in such as 'Lilli Goes To Town' and 'Mbizo Mbizo'. The CD issues of both records include extra material, and each is expansively recorded, while retaining a lively feel.

(*) **Live In Denmark Olufsen DOC 5077
> Dørge; Jan Kaspersen (*p, picc*). 9/87.

A surprisingly sober and careful meeting between two of the more madcap spirits in Danish jazz. They work as a kind of chamber duo on a selection of self-composed and standard material, with three variations on Satie's 'Gnossiennes' typical of the sort of feel of the programme. The best things are a reflective piece by Kaspersen called 'Snail Trail' and a bittersweet reading of 'Blue Monk', though the oddball duets on altohorn and piccolo at the end of the record bring the most applause! The sound is a little chilly and recessed.

***(*) **Different Places, Different Bananas** Olufsen DOC 5079
> As previous Steeplechase session, except Aage Tanggaard (*d*), Gert Mortensen and Ivan Hansen (*perc*) replace Mazur and Drake. 11/88.

Further rollicking adventures from the New Jungle Orchestra. The compositions are the accustomed rag-bag of riffs, African rhythms and jazz in-jokes, which some of the titles suggest: 'Fats Waller In The Busch Of Leipzig', for instance, or 'Sun Ra Over La Luna'. The latter includes some deliciously grumpy bass sax from Clausen, but singling out soloists is unfair – everybody plays well. Tchicai's 'Largo Lapidarius' may be the most memorable theme they've been given to play, too. The Olufsen recording is quite as good as that for Steeplechase.

*** **Live In Chicago** Olufsen DOC 5122
> Dørge; Harry Beckett (*t*); John Tchicai (*ss, ts*); Jesper Zeuthen (*as, bcl, f*); Irene Becker (*ky*); Harrison Bankhead (*b*); Hamid Drake (*d*). 7/90.

As boisterous as ever, but this is a mildly disappointing session: the live versions of 'The Mooche' and 'Mbizo Mbizo' add little to the studio treatments, and the sound-quality is bottom-heavy and missing in essential detail. A nice souvenir for any who saw this edition of the band, but not important in its own right.

Kenny Dorham (1924–72) TRUMPET

***(*) **Kenny Dorham Quintet** Original Jazz Classics OJC 113
> Dorham; Jimmy Heath (*as, bs*); Walter Bishop Jr (*p*); Percy Heath (*b*); Kenny Clarke (*d*). 12/53.

*** **Afro-Cuban** Blue Note 7468152

> Dorham; J. J. Johnson (*tb*); Hank Mobley (*ts*); Cecil Payne (*bs*); Horace Silver (*p*); Oscar Pettiford (*b*); Art Blakey (*d*); Carlos Patato Valdez (*congas*). 1/55, 3/55.

Dorham never sounded more like Dizzy Gillespie than on *Afro-Cuban*, punching out single-note statements across the rhythm. The marvellous 1953 quintet features gulping blues passages that manage to thrive on the thinnest harmonic oxygen; never a mere showman, it is Dorham's mental stamina that impresses, a concentration and attention to detail that make him one of the most coherent and structurally aware of the bebop players. He is also one of the better composers, a fact – 'Blue Bossa' apart – which is generally overlooked.

***(*) **'Round About Midnight at the Café Bohemia** Blue Note 781524 2CD

> Dorham; J. R. Monterose (*ts*); Kenny Burrell (*g*); Bobby Timmons (*p*); Sam Jones (*b*); Arthur Edgehill (*d*). 5/56.

. . . and at around midnight a sequence of minor keys would seem to be in order. Whatever else, Dorham always had a predilection for a unified mood, and this session, combining the Monk tune, 'Autumn In New York', and 'A Night In Tunisia' with three originals (more fuel to our conviction that he is a neglected writer) manages to sustain a slightly brooding, intensely thoughtful atmosphere. As a foil, Monterose was an excellent recruitment, most notably on the opening 'Monaco', but also on ''Round About Midnight' itself. Burrell swings with the usual horn-like attack and Timmons vamps righteously, though without ever really showing his mettle.

Dorham's own solos are models of grace and tact, always giving an impression of careful construction and development, and an unfailing sense of texture. Francis Wolff's subtly doctored cover shot offers an intriguing impression of the man, showing Dorham in a bright check jacket, but with a faraway look in his eyes as he clutches the microphone; above him, a ghostly image of an American townscape, vivid but also fleeting.

*** **Jazz Contrast** Original Jazz Classics OJC 028

> Dorham; Sonny Rollins (*ts*); Hank Jones (*p*); Oscar Pettiford (*b*); Max Roach (*d*); Betty Glamann (*hp*). 5/57.

*** **Two Horns / Two Rhythm** Original Jazz Classics OJC 463

> Dorham; Ernie Henry (*as*); Wilbur Ware (*b*); Granville T. Hogan (*d*). 11/57, 12/57.

The piano-less horn-and-rhythm experiment posed interesting problems for Dorham. Ware's big bass almost fills in the gap; but what is interesting about the set as a whole is how Dorham adjusts his delivery, counting rests much more carefully, filling in with a broader intonation on ensemble passages. Henry and Hogan are by no means passengers, but the real drama of the recording is played out across the three octaves that divide trumpet and bass on some of the bridging passages.

Rollins wasn't at first glance the ideal partner for Dorham, but he began to steer him in the direction of an altogether different approach to thematic variation which really became evident only towards the end of the decade. *Horns/Rhythm* gains a star for boldness; *Jazz Contrast* drops back one for the wishy-washy sound.

*** **This Is The Moment** Original Jazz Classics OJCCS 812

> Dorham; Curtis Fuller (*tb*); Cedar Walton (*p*); Sam Jones (*b*); G. T. Hogan, Charli Persip (*d*). 7 & 8/58.

Like Chet Baker, Dorham always considered his singing to be an integral part of what he was and did as a musician. He had sung with Dizzy's band in the 1940s but had made the decision to concentrate on his horn. Even here, it's his trumpet playing that counts and, while it's tempting to reverse the emphasis and say that it's as lyrical as his singing is improvisatory and horn-like, almost the reverse is the case. Dorham doesn't sing like a horn man, but gives the lyric almost deliberate weight and emphasis, closer to speech rhythms than to top-line jazz. Unlike many hyphenate players, he makes a hard and fast distinction between the two 'voices'. 'From This Moment On' is done as an instrumental but 'I Remember Clifford' is adorned with the Jon Hendricks lyric, when it might have been more interesting the other way round. Both horns are muted throughout, lending the whole a soft, staccato bounce that is no less attractive for being determinedly understated.

Historically, the album is significant for being Cedar Walton's first recording. He's not yet the presence he was to be in future years, a sapling rather than the solidly rooted sideman-for-all-seasons that he was to become. Nevertheless his soloing is adroit and uncliché'd and his accompaniment firm without being domineering. A telling debut.

*** **Blue Spring** Original Jazz Classics OJC 134

> Dorham; David Amram (*frhn*); Julian Cannonball Adderley (*as*); Cecil Payne (*bs*); Cedar Walton (*p*); Paul Chambers (*b*); Jimmy Cobb or Philly Joe Jones (*d*). 1/59, 2/59.

*** **Quiet Kenny** Original Jazz Classics OJC 250
    Dorham; Tommy Flanagan (*p*); Paul Chambers (*b*); Art Taylor (*d*). 11/59.
*** **The Arrival Of Kenny Dorham** Fresh Sound FSRCD 200
    Dorham; Charles Davis (*bs*); Tommy Flanagan (*p*); Butch Warren (*b*); Buddy Enlow (*d*). 1/60.
(*) **West 42nd Street Black Lion BLCD 760119
    Dorham; Rocky Boyd (*ts*); Walter Bishop Jr (*p*); Ron Carter (*b*); Pete LaRoca (*d*). 3/61.
*** **Osmosis** Black Lion BLCD 760146
    Dorham; Curtis Fuller (*tb*); Frank Haynes (*ts*); Tommy Flanagan (*p*); Ben Tucker (*b*); Dave
    Bailey (*d*). 10/61.

Dorham enjoyed a brief resurgence towards the end of the 1950s, and any of the above would serve as a reasonable introduction to his more deliberate, Miles-influenced approach of that period. *Quiet Kenny* is a minor masterpiece. The blues-playing is still as emotional as ever, but there is a more relaxed approach to the basic metres, and Tommy Flanagan in particular invites a quieter and more sustained articulation of themes. *Arrival* sees him in good voice, tooting through a light but demanding programme that includes Rollins's favourite 'I'm An Old Cowhand' and 'Stella By Starlight' with the most open tone he'd produced. *West 42nd Street*, good as it is, isn't a Dorham album. It was recorded and originally released on Jazztime under the leadership of tenor player, Rocky Boyd, which rather explains the order and emphasis of the solos. The two takes each of 'Stella By Starlight' and 'Why Not?' soon dispel a faint aroma of marketing cynicism.

    Osmosis is rather better, if a little more padded out. Partnered this time by the callow but developing Curtis Fuller and the all-but-unknown Frank Haynes (whose obscurity seems, on this showing, entirely understandable), Dorham plays with a good deal of fire, often more or less stealing the limelight from his colleagues and at least twice copping an extra couple of choruses, to Flanagan's evident surprise. No one could blame him; the group aren't exactly stiff, but they aren't wildly exciting either; as for Dorham, he was having a good night.

***(*) **Matador / Inta Somethin'** Blue Note CDP 7844602
    Dorham; Jackie McLean (*as*); Walter Bishop, Bobby Timmons (*p*); Teddy Smith, Leroy
    Vinnegar (*b*); J. C. Moses, Art Taylor (*d*). 1/61, 4/62.
*** **Trompeta Toccata** Blue Note B21Y 84181
    Dorham; Joe Henderson (*ts*); Tommy Flanagan (*p*); Richard Davis (*b*); Albert 'Tootie' Heath
    (*d*). 9/64.
** **Short Story** Steeplechase SCCD 36010
    Dorham; Allan Botschinsky (*flhn*); Tete Montoliu (*p*); Niels-Henning Orsted-Pedersen (*b*);
    Alex Riel (*d*). 12/63.
** **Scandia Skies** Steeplechase SCCD 6011
    As above, except replace Botschinsky with Rolf Ericson (*t, flhn*). 12/63.

Despite the sustained energy of *Una Mas* (recently available only as a limited edition) and of *Trompeta Toccata* (both of which paired the trumpeter's brightly burnished tone with the muscular tenor of Joe Henderson), Dorham seemed to be running out of steam in 1963; 'one more time' was beginning to sound like once too often. The Steeplechases are essentially footnote albums to a remarkable career which still had nearly a decade to run, in purely chronological terms at least. Artistically, Dorham was already recycling desperately. Both albums are perfectly respectable and eminently listenable but lack the profound emotional urgency that was Dorham's trademark, whether he was playing fast, high-register runs or sustained blues cadences. The writing is good but increasingly precise and Dorham's occasional 'classical' experiments, the beautifully cadenced 'Trompeta Toccata' and, on the Latin-influenced *Matador*, a Villa-Lobos prelude for Dorham and the unsuitable Timmons, don't quite effect the kind of syntheses he managed in Henderson's company. Produced in the wake of a South American tour, *Matador* (originally released on United Artists) is touched by Brazilian rather than Afro-Cuban rhythms. McLean plays beautifully, especially an anguished introduction to 'Lover Man' that recalls Parker's disastrous Dial recording of the tune.

*** **Zodiac: The Music Of Cecil Payne** Strata East 660.51.021
    Dorham; Cecil Payne (*as, bs*); Wynton Kelly (*p*); Wilbur Ware (*b*); Albert 'Tootie' Heath (*d*). 12/
    68.

There is some justification – obvious from title and line-up – for considering this a Payne album. Whoever claims the main credit, it's really very good, with Dorham playing well and Payne sounding more in command of his own idiom than he was on *Afro-Cuban*, almost a decade-and-a-half earlier. This was a sort of dream band for the trumpeter, and he responds fully to the challenge. There's a certain twilight quality to his tone, which lacks the bright, brassy ring of earlier days, but it's by no means unattractive; and the familiar dark keys which are a component of Payne's thinking as well suit the occasion very well indeed. There were later things, but this will do for now as a curtain piece.

Jimmy Dorsey (1904–56) ALTO AND BARITONE SAXOPHONES, CLARINET, TRUMPET

**(*) Pennies From Heaven ASV AJA 5052

Dorsey; George Thow, Toots Camarata, Joe Meyer (*t*); Don Mattison (*tb, v*); Bobby Byrne, Joe Yukl, Bruce Squires (*tb*); Fud Livingston (*as, ts*); Jack Stacey, Len Whitney (*as*); Skeets Herfurt, Charles Frazier (*ts*); Bobby Van Eps, Freddy Slack (*p*); Roc Hillman (*g, v*); Slim Taft, Jack Ryan (*b*); Ray McKinley (*d, v*); Bob Eberle, Frances Langford (*v*). 3/36–6/37.

**(*) At The 400 Restaurant 1946 Hep CD 41

Dorsey; Bob Alexy, Claude Bowen, Ray Linn, Tonny Picciotto, Nathan Solomon, Seymour Baker, Irving Goodman, Louis Mucci (*t*); Simon Zentner, Thomas Lee, Nick Di Maio, Anthony Russo, Fred Mancusi, Don Mattison, Bob Alexander (*tb*); Jack Aiken, Frank Langone, Bill Covey, Cliff Jackson (*as*); Bobby Dukoff, Charles Frazier, Charles Travis, Gill Koerner (*ts*); Bob Lawson, Johnny Dee (*bs*); Marvin Wright, Lou Carter (*p*); Herb Ellis, Teddy Walters (*g*); Jimmy Middleton, Norman Bates (*b*); Adolf Shutz, Karl Kiffe (*d*); Dee Parker, Paul Chapman (*v*). 1/46.

The elder Dorsey brother was a saxophonist of the highest technical accomplishment, though it tended to lead him to merely show off on many of the records he made as a sessionman in the 1920s, such as 'Beebe' and 'I'm Prayin' Humble', which have yet to make it to CD. The band he formed in 1935 after splitting up with his brother was a commercial dance band rather than any kind of jazz orchestra, but the group could swing when Dorsey wanted it to, and there was some impeccable section-playing, particularly from the trombones. The ASV disc pulls together 18 tracks from this period, a mixture of vocal features for Eberle, Langford and McKinley and more jazz-orientated titles. 'Dorsey Dervish' harks back to the leader's technical exercises of the decade before, but 'Stompin' At The Savoy' is creditable enough, and Bobby Byrne's beautiful lead trombone on 'In A Sentimental Mood' (contrary to the sleeve-notes, Byrne doesn't sing on this tune) outdoes even Tommy Dorsey for mellifluousness. It's a pity, though, that titles such as 'Swamp Fire', 'Major And Minor Stomp' and 'Cherokee' are omitted. The remastering is rather lifeless.

The Hep CD is a lot more modernistic: among the opening four tracks, which date from 1944, is a Dizzy Gillespie arrangement of 'Grand Central Getaway'. The remainder are airshots taken from a New York engagement two years later, and while the band has nothing very outstanding about it there are one or two worthwhile solos from Bob Avery and the leader, whose attractive score 'Contrasts' hints at directions which he never really followed. Generally, though, there is rather more jazz-inflected material here than on the earlier CD, and remastering makes the best of the broadcast recording.

***(*) Contrasts MCA GRP 16262

Dorsey; George Thow, Toots Camarata, Joe Meyer, Shorty Sherock, W. C. Clark, Ralph Muzillo, Nate Kazebier, Johnny Napton, Shorty Solomon, Jimmy Campbell, Paul McCoy, Bill Oblak, Ray Linn, Bob Alemsky, Phil Napoleon, Marky Markowitz (*t*); Bobby Byrne, Don Mattison, Joe Yukl, Bruce Squires, Sonny Lee, Jerry Rosa, Nat Lobovsky, Phil Washburn, Andy Russo, Billy Pritchard, Nick Di Maio (*tb*); Dave Matthew, Fud Livingston, Skeets Herfurt, Jack Stacy, Leonard Whitney, Noni Bernardi, Milt Yaner, Herbie Haymer, Sam Rubinowich, Frank Langone, Don Hammond, Babe Russin, Chuck Gentry, Bill Covey, Bob Lawson, Charles Frazier (*reeds*); Bobby Van Eps, Freddy Slack, Joe Lippman, Johnny Guarnieri, Dave Mann (*p*); Roc Hillman, Guy Smith, Allan Reuss, Tommy Kay (*g*); Slim Taft, Jack Ryan, Bill Miller (*b*); Ray McKinley, Buddy Schutz (*d*); June Richmond, Helen O'Connell, Bob Eberly (*v*). 7/36–10/43.

At last, a well-chosen compilation of some of the best from one of the most undersung of the big swing bands. Dorsey's own demanding musicianship made his bands into formidably schooled orchestras, and his sax sectons in particular were a match for any of his rivals. He was a little short on star soloists but the shrewd arrangements emphasized the steely power of the band and they had the vocal class of Bob Eberly and Helen O'Connell to take care of commercial appeal. It's surprising to note that in fact Dorsey's sales were strong enough to rival Glenn Miller's in the early 1940s. Of the 20 tracks here, the highlights must include the knockout arrangement of 'I Cried For You', a steaming update of 'The Darktown Strutters Ball', O'Connell's gorgeous vocal on 'All Of Me', the harder, more expressive sound of the 1940 'Dolemite' and the final, perfectly controlled revision of Morton's 'King Porter Stomp', whicb takes the story up to 1943. Dorsey's own playing still emerges as impressively forthright in his featured solos. There is surely another disc or two of fine tracks to be compiled from this prolific band, but this is a fine start.

Leon Lee Dorsey BASS

*** **The Watcher** Landmark LCD-1540-2
> Dorsey; Vincent Herring (*ss, as*); Don Braden (*ts*); Lafayette Harris Jr (*p*); Cecil Brooks III, Jimmy Madison (*d*). 2/94.

Dorsey's compositions – the first seven tracks here – are so fierce and unsmiling that it's rather a relief when the band relaxes into 'Cheek To Cheek'. They're played with undeniable chops and commitment: Braden and Herring are nobody's slouches, and the solos they trade on the title-track would rouse a cataleptic. But the music could use some melodic substance to centre it all. 'River Of The Fire' works off a nice bass vamp, and Dorsey himself is content to stand at the back most of the time, which is where the rather unpromising production put him. Solid modern blowing.

Tommy Dorsey (1905–56) TROMBONE, TRUMPET

*** **Tommy Dorsey 1928–1935** Classics 833
> Dorsey; Manny Klein, Andy Ferretti, Sterling Bose, Bill Graham (*t*); Joe Ortolano, Ben Pickering, Dave Jacobs (*tb*); Jimmy Dorsey, Sid Stoneburn (*cl, as*); Noni Bernardi (*as*); Clyde Rounds (*as, ts*); Johnny Van Eps (*ts*); Paul Mitchell, Fulton McGrath, Frank Signorelli (*p*); Arthur Schutt (*harm*); Eddie Lang, Mac Cheikes (*g*); Gene Traxler, Jimmy Williams (*b*); Sam Rosen, Sam Weiss, Stan King (*d*); Edythe Wright, Eleanor Powell (*v*). 11/28–11/35.

Classics' opening disc takes in Dorsey's great 1928–9 dates where he plays trumpet – a bit shaky, but tremendously fierce, with terrific Eddie Lang support. These sound very clean and bright, which is why the rotten quality of the 1935 orchestra dates is so disappointing. These can't have been direct transfers. Either way, Dorsey got off to a modest start with five fairly nondescript sessions – though the fourth released his hit theme, 'I'm Getting Sentimental Over You'.

*** **Yes, Indeed!** Bluebird ND 904499
> Dorsey; Yank Lawson, Pee Wee Irwin, Andy Ferretti, Mickey Bloom, Jimmy Blake, Ray Linn, Clyde Hurley, Ziggy Elman, Chuck Peterson, Al Stearns, Manny Klein, Jimmy Zito, Roger Ellick, Mickey Mangano, Dale Pierce, George Seaberg, Charlie Shavers, Gerald Goff (*t*); Dave Jacobs, Elmer Smithers, Ward Silloway, Lowell Martin, George Arus, Les Jenkins, Walter Mercurio, James Skiles, Walt Benson, Nelson Riddle, Tex Satterwhite, Karle De Karske, William Haller, Richard Noel (*tb*); Johnny Mince, Fred Stulce, Skeets Herfurt, Dean Kincaide, Babe Russin, Hymie Schertzer, Paul Mason, Don Lodice, Heinie Beau, Manny Gershman, Bruce Snyder, Harry Schuchman, Buddy DeFranco, Sid Cooper, Gale Curtis, Al Klink, Bruce Branson, Babe Fresk, Dave Harris, Gus Bivona, Vido Musso (*saxes*); Howard Smith, Joe Bushkin, Milt Raskin, Milt Golden, John Potoker, Duke Ellington (*p*); Carmen Mastren, Clark Yocum, Bob Bain, Sam Herman (*g*); Joe Park (*tba*); Gene Traxler, Sid Weiss, Phil Stevens, Sid Block (*b*); Dave Tough, Cliff Leeman, Buddy Rich (*d*); Edythe Wright, Sy Oliver, Jo Stafford (*v*). 6/39–5/45.

*** **The Song Is You** Bluebird 66353-2 5CD
> Basically as above. 40–41.

*** **Tommy Dorsey & His Orchestra With Frank Sinatra** RCA Tribune 15518-2 2CD
> Similar to above. 40–42.

This compilation of Tommy Dorsey's big-band recordings for Victor only hints at the surprisingly consistent excellence of the trombonist's groups. Orrin Keepnews's compilation chooses a sequence of mostly instrumental, mostly jazz-orientated tracks, with a cross-section of work by arrangers Paul Weston, Sy Oliver and Bill Finegan, and there are such hits as 'Opus No. 1', 'Swing High' and Oliver's remarkable transformation of 'Swanee River', alongside adventurous charts like 'Stomp It Off' and 'Loose Lid Special'. There are but few glimpses of the 'sentimental' style which buttered Dorsey's bread for most of the swing era, and his somewhat underrated skills as a soloist emerge best on 'Mandy, Make Up Your Mind'. The sound is as clean as the NoNoise process allows, though some may prefer the occasionally more sprightly sound of earlier LP reissues, as patchy as they often were.

The Song Is You is of relatively peripheral interest, since it puts together a complete edition of all Frank Sinatra's vocals with Dorsey. Inevitably, jazz takes a back seat to the band's smoochier style but, if it's Sinatra you want to hear, this is as good a set as one could hope for, and the painstaking remastering should please all but those who have access to a set of mint originals. The Tribune set boils it down to a couple of discs' worth.

(*) **The Music Goes Round And Round Bluebird ND 83140
> Dorsey; Sterling Bose, Max Kaminsky, Pee Wee Irwin, Yank Lawson, Jimmy Blake, Charlie Shavers, Ziggy Elman (*t*); Joe Dixon, Johnny Mince, Buddy DeFranco (*cl*); Bud Freeman, Sid

Block, Babe Russin, Boomie Richman (*ts*); Dick Jones, Howard Smith, John Potoker, Teddy Wilson (*p*); Bill Schaeffer, Carmen Mastren, Sam Herman, Billy Bauer (*g*); Gene Traxler, Sid Block (*b*); Dave Tough, Maurice Purtill, Graham Stevenson, Cliff Leeman, Alvin Stoller (*d*); Edythe Wright, Hughie Prince, Sy Oliver, Hanna Williams (*v*). 12/35–2/47.

*** **The Panic is On!** Vipers Nest VN-154

Dorsey; Max Kaminsky (*t*); Joe Dixon (*cl*); Sid Block (*ts*); Dick Jones (*p*); William Schaffer (*g*); Gene Traxler (*b*); Dave Tough (*d*); Edythe Wright (*v*). 3–4/36.

While there are a few marvellous sides here – including the instrumentals 'The Sheik Of Araby' and 'Chinatown, My Chinatown' – too many numbers in this collection by Dorsey's small group, The Clambake Seven, fall victim to corny material and time-wasting vocals, although Edythe Wright's singing has a lot of charm. Some of the kitsch numbers, especially 'Rhythm Saved The World', with its irresistible sign-off, and the heated 'At The Codfish Ball', are elevated by what were even then old-fashioned hot treatments of the kind Dorsey graduated on in the 1920s. If it's a period piece, it still includes plenty of compelling moments from soloists such as Freeman, Kaminsky and Dorsey himself. The CD remastering will sound muffled to those who've heard the original 78s but will probably satisfy everybody else.

The Panic is On! offers airshots from the same period. Some of these have some fine spots for Dorsey and Kaminsky, and 'I'll Bet You Tell That To All The Girls' is untypically hot and swinging. Some of the material is pretty awful, but overall this is probably the best glimpse of the Clambake Seven in serious action. Sound is faded but not too dusty.

(*) **Palladium 1940 & Raleigh Show 1943 Jazz Hour JH-1035

Personnel unlisted. 40–43.

(*) **1942 War Bond Broadcast Jazz Hour JH-1013

Personnel unlisted. 7–10/42.

Both these discs of airshots are for hardcore followers only. The earlier set has some good if rusty 1940 material with Sinatra and, though the 1943 show is in surprisingly bright and clear hi-fi, the band sounds jolted and there's a lot of irrelevant speech-making. The 1942 disc starts off in poor sound, which gets increasingly worse until half-way through, when the October programme cleans up and works off a couple of nice if familar Sy Oliver arrangements.

*** **The Carnegie Hall V-Disc Session April 1944** Hep CD 40

Dorsey; Pete Candoli, George Seaberg, Sal La Perche, Dale Pearce, Bob Price, Ralph Santangelo, Mickey Mangano (*t*); Walter Benson, Tommy Pedersen, Tex Satterwhite, Nelson Riddle (*tb*); Buddy DeFranco, Hank D'Amico (*cl, as*); Sid Cooper, Leonard Kaye (*as*); Gale Curtis, Al Klink, Don Lodice, Mickey Sabol (*ts*); Bruce Branson, Manny Gershman (*bs*); Dodo Marmarosa, Milt Raskin (*p*); Dennis Sandole, Bob Bain (*g*); Joe Park (*tba*); Sid Block (*b*); Gene Krupa, Maurice Purtill, Buddy Rich (*d*); Bing Crosby, Frances Langford, Georgia Gibbs, Bob Allen, The Sentimentalists, Bonnie Lou Williams (*v*); plus string section. 10/43–9/44.

(*) **The All Time Hit Parade Rehearsals Hep CD 39

As above, except omit Candoli, Price, Santangelo, D'Amico, Kaye, Klink, Gershman, Raskin, Sandole, Krupa and Purtill, Crosby and Gibbs; add Judy Garland, Frank Sinatra (*v*). 6–9/44.

Although there isn't a great deal of jazz on these records, they give a clearer idea of the sound of Dorsey's band, since John R. T. Davies's superb remastering puts the Bluebird records to shame. *All Time Hit Parade* is drawn from acetate transcriptions of rehearsals for a radio show of that name and, while they tend to display the sweeter side of Dorsey's band, the smooth power of the sections is smartly put across by the sound. Sinatra has a couple of fine features in 'I'll Walk Alone' and 'If You Are But A Dream', and there's a showcase for Marmarosa on 'Boogie Woogie'. The V-Disc material, again in splendid restoration, is rather more exciting, with a number of spots for La Perche, DeFranco and Klink. Crosby and Langford deliver a couple of messages to the troops as a bonus.

** **Tommy Dorsey Plays Sweet And Hot** Tax CD 3705-2

Dorsey; Zeke Zarchey, Lee Castaldo, Jimmy Blake (*t*); Ward Silloway, Lowell Martin (*tb*); Johnny Mince (*cl, as*); Fred Stulce, Les Robinson (*as*); Babe Russin, Paul Mason (*ts*); Bob Kitsis (*p*); Bob Heller (*g*); Gene Traxler (*b*); Buddy Rich (*d*); Frank Sinatra, Jo Stafford, The Pied Pipers (*v*). 2/40.

***(*) **Well, Git It!** Jass J-CD-14

Dorsey; Pete Candoli, Bob Price, George Seaberg, Sal La Perche, Vito Mangano, Dale Pierce, Gerald Goff, Charlie Shavers, Paul McCoy, Mickey Mangano, Cy Baker, Chuck Genduso (*t*); Walter Benson, Tommy Pedersen, Tex Satterwhite, Nelson Riddle, Richard Noel, Karl DeKarske, Al Esposito, Bill Siegel, Bill Schallen, Sam Levine (*tb*); Hank D'Amico, Buddy DeFranco, Gus Bivona (*cl, as*); Sid Cooper, Leonard Kaye (*as*); Bruce Branson (*ts, as, bs*); Hank Lodice, Gale Curtis, Mickey Sabol, Al Klink, Babe Fresk, Boomie Richman (*ts*); Manny

Gershman (*bs*); Milt Raskin, Jess Stacy, Dodo Marmarosa, Johnny Potoker (*p*); Sam Herman, Danny Sandoli (*g*); Sid Block, Joe Park (*b*); Alvin Stoller, Buddy Rich, Gene Krupa (*d*); Skip Nelson, Stuart Foster, Bonnie Lou Williams, The Sentimentalists (*v*). 43–46.

There could hardly be a more striking contrast than there is between these two discs of airshots. The Tax CD offers a complete show from the Meadowbrook Ballroom in New Jersey from February 1940, and it's all sweet and not very hot: there are corny arrangements of college songs, novelty tunes and a few worthwhile ballads – with Sinatra and Jo Stafford perhaps the main points of interest in the broadcast. There isn't much jazz, but the sound of the band is caught very clearly by Jack Towers's fine remastering of the material. The Jass collection is a little rougher, but it's infinitely more exciting, opening on a wildly over-the-top 'Well, Git It!' featuring guest Gene Krupa (Buddy Rich has his own turn on another version at the end of the disc). In between are new versions of many of Dorsey's better hits, a few of the superior sweet items, and solo spots for DeFranco, Shavers, Candoli and more. A first-class compilation of its kind.

*** Live In Hi-Fi At Casino Gardens Jazz Hour JH-1018
Personnel unlisted. 6–8/46.

The first show here is OK but nothing special, with Charlie Shavers's feature on 'At The Fat Man' the only standout; but the second, with extended workouts on six good charts by Bill Finegan and others, is much more like it. There's a lot of badinage between Tom and the announcer, which will either charm or repel, but the music's strong and the sound, if not exactly 'hi-fi', is quite listenable.

**(*) At The Fat Man's 1946–1948 Hep CD 43
Dorsey; Jack Dougherty, Mickey Mangano, George Seaberg, Ziggy Elman, Charlie Shavers, Claude Bowen, Vern Arslan, Chuck Peterson (*t*); Larry Hall, Tex Satterwhite, Greg Philips, John Youngman, Charles La Rue, Red Benson, Nick Di Maio, Dick Noel (*tb*); Buddy DeFranco, Billy Ainsworth, Marshall Hawk, Louis Prisby (*cl, as*); Sid Cooper, Bruce Branson (*as*); Boomie Richman, Don Lodice, Babe Fresk, Corky Corcoran, Marty Berman (*ts*); Joe Koch (*bs*); John Potoker, Rocky Coluccio, Paul Smith (*p*); Sam Herman, Tony Rizzi (*g*); Sid Block, Sam Cheifetz, Norman Seelig (*b*); Alvin Stoller, Louie Bellson (*d*); Stuart Foster, Denny Dennis, Lucy Ann Polk, Gordon Polk, The Sentimentalists (*v*). 5/46–12/48.

***(*) The Post-War Era Bluebird 07863 66156 2
Similar to above, except add Charlie Shavers, Paul McCoy, Cy Baker, Irving Goodman, Johnny Martel, Bernie Glow, Hal Ableser, Chris Griffin, Stan Stout, Doc Severinsen, Ray Wetzel, Billy Butterfield, Art Depew, Johnny Amoroso (*t*); Bill Siegel, Sam Levine, Bill Schallen, Larry Hall, Sol Train, Al Mastren, Buddy Morrow, Dean Kincaide, Will Bradley, Bill Pritchard, Ange Callea (*tb*); Abe Most, John Rotella, Billy Ainsworth, George Kennon, Walt Levinsky, Hugo Lowenstein, Sol Schlinger, Danny Bank, Jerry Winner (*reeds*); Gene Kutch, Lou Levy (*p*); Ward Erwin, Bob Baldwin (*b*); Buddy Rich (*d*). 1/46–6/50.

Dorsey's later records deserve a wider hearing than they've been given by posterity. He had no more hits on the scale of 'Marie' or 'Song Of India', but he remained – as then-new arranger Bill Finegan, responsible for the best arrangements on the Bluebird CD, asserts in the sleeve-note – a keen-eared musician and less conservative than many of his contemporaries. *The Post-War Era* is a splendid cross-section of the pick of Dorsey in the 1940s, with smart scores such as 'Hollywood Hat', with its amazing brass figures, or 'Tom Foolery' sounding as good as anything in his earlier work. There are some previously unissued tracks among the 22 on offer, and the sound, though dry, is much better than on the earlier Bluebird discs. The Hep compilation suffers from some very variable sound-sources and, though these airchecks feature some fine alternative versions of some of the scores on the Bluebird disc (as well as a couple of delicious vocals by Lucy Ann Polk), it stands very much in the shadow of the studio disc.

(***) The Best Of Tommy Dorsey Bluebird ND90587
Fifteen favourites from Dorsey's golden era, with all the obvious hits to hand. A pity that the remastering is erratic, indifferent and sometimes resembling a brutal restoration: there is much better sound to be had from grade-A original 78s, which shouldn't have been too hard for the compilers to locate.

Dorsey Brothers Orchestra GROUP

*** Harlem Lullaby Hep CD 1006
Manny Klein, Sterling Bose, Bunny Berigan (*t*); Tommy Dorsey (*tb*); Larry Binyon (*cl, as, ts*); Jimmy Dorsey (*cl, as*); Joe Venuti, Harry Hoffman, Walter Edelstein, Lou Kosloff (*vn*); Joe Meresco, Fulton McGrath (*p*); Dick McDonough (*g*); Artie Bernstein (*b*); Stan King, Chauncey Morehouse, Larry Gomar (*d*); Bing Crosby, Mae West, Ethel Waters, Mildred Bailey, Lee Wiley (*v*). 2–7/33.

The Dorsey brothers co-led a band before making separate careers as swing-era bandleaders, and while many of their 78s are still awaited on CD, this compilation offers the chance to hear them backing four vocalists of the day. Mae West's pair of titles are little more than a not especially tuneful extension of her man-eating persona, and Wiley's session shows the singer still in raw shape, but the four tracks with Crosby show how much the singer had learnt from jazz players and the eight featuring Mildred Bailey are delightful, her light and limber voice gliding over the music with little effort. There are brief solos for the Dorseys and Berigan here and there, but the record belongs mostly to the singers. First-class remastering throughout.

(*) **The Dorsey Brothers Orchestra – 1935 Circle CCD-20
 Dorsey; Dorsey; George Thow, Jerry Neary, Charlie Spivak (*t*); Joe Yukl, Don Matteson (*tb*);
 Jack Stacey (*as*); Skeets Herfurt (*ts*); Bobby Van Eps (*p*); Roc Hillman (*g*); Delmar Kaplan (*b*);
 Ray McKinley (*d*); Bob Crosby (*v*). 1/35.
Thirteen transcriptions for WBC, with the orchestra in fine fettle. Crosby is restricted to four vocals and the emphasis is on the band, but the charts tend towards the sweet rather than the hot, and when they do tackle a fast one – as with 'Sugar Foot Stomp' or 'Eccentric' – the ensemble sound and a certain rhythmic squareness suggest the Dorseys hadn't yet got their feet out of the 1920s. The sound is clean if a little muffled. The rest of the CD is given over to 12 tracks by Arnold Johnson's orchestra.

** **'Live' In The Big Apple 1954/5** Magic DAWE44
 Charlie Shavers (*t*); Tommy Dorsey, Jimmy Henderson (*tb*); Jimmy Dorsey (*cl, as*); Buddy Rich
 (*d*); Johnny Amoroso, Billy Raymond, Dick Haymes, Kitty Kallen, Lynn Roberts (*v*); rest
 unknown. 1/54–10/55.
While the brothers were famous for quarrelling, they patched up their differences and joined forces again in the 1950s, although the orchestra here was principally Tommy's. Neither man was long for this world, and the jazz content here is low: a swinging 'Puddlewump' and 'Skirts And Sweaters' have to fight for space with some feeble vocals (aside from Dick Haymes's beautiful 'Our Love Is Here To Stay') and dining and dancing music. Most of the band is appropriately anonymous. Culled from various radio broadcasts, the sound is lo-fi but listenable.

Double Trio GROUP

***(*) **Green Dolphy Suite** Enja 9011
 Armand Angster (*cl, bcl, cbcl*); Louis Sclavis, Jacques Di Donato (*cl, bcl*); Mark Feldman (*vn*);
 Ernst Reijseger (*clo*); Mark Dresser (*b*). 9/94.
It would be tempting and, on the face of it, quite reasonable to attribute this project album to either Sclavis or the long-established Arcado, who provide the string component. However, by dint of time, cash and patience, and the unmistakable strength of individual contributions, *Green Dolphy Suite* adds up to considerably more than the sum of its parts.

 The group(s) first came together in 1993, at the Banlieues Bleues festival in Paris. This was clearly a meeting of minds. Sclavis has long been interested in synthesizing a new 'tradition' in European jazz, while Arcado and new man Reijseger (who replaces Hank Roberts) had severally been exploring new ways of integrating 'classical' voices with an improvised idiom. The first and longest test of the collaboration is the title-piece, an elegantly shaped quarter-hour of music that picks up on Dolphy's dramatic emancipation of the bass clarinet, and intelligent use of the cello as both ancillary horn and rhythm instrument.

 Nothing else on the set *quite* matches up, but even if the remaining five tracks were to be heard independently, they would still be worthy of notice. Reijseger's 'Buhu' steers closest to the free improvisational contexts the Dutchman has favoured, but it is also, ironically, the most formally shaped. Dresser's 'Bosnia' has a richly pictorial strain and does most to draw out the instruments' ethnic characters. The only disappointment is Angster's closing 'Suite Domestique', whose parts never quite manage to tot up.

Dave Douglas (born 1964) TRUMPET

***(*) **The Tiny Bell Trio** Songlines SGL 1504
 Douglas; Brad Schoeppach (*g*); Jim Black (*d*). 12/93.
**** **Constellations** hat Art CD 6173
 As above. 2/95.

**** **In Our Lifetime** New World NW 80471
>   Douglas; Josh Roseman (*tb*); Chris Speed (*cl, ts*); Marty Ehrlich (*bcl*); Uri Caine (*p*); James
>   Genus (*b*); Joey Baron (*d*).

**** **Five** Soul Note 121276
>   Douglas; Mark Feldman (*vn*); Erik Friedlander (*clo*); Drew Gress (*b*); Michael Sarin (*d*). 8/95.

Like Bill Frisell, Douglas went from being an interesting outsider to a ubiquitous sideman-of-choice in
what seemed like no time at all. Perhaps most prominently, he has been a key member of John Zorn's
Masada group, but the credits pile up elsewhere as well. Half a minute spent with either of these or with
any of his records with others will reveal how deep and thoughtful is the young trumpeter's musical
engagement. He is, above all, a contemplative player and a very emotional one. *The Tiny Bell Trio*
(which is the working name of this group) is seemingly motivated by the death of children in Sarajevo
(as is 'Taking Sides' on the other record) and is full of dark references, like Kosma's 'Girl Of Steel' –
'*Fille d'acier*' – and Kurt Weill's 'The Drowned Girl'. He is also able to mix in classical references, not
just his own composition 'Scriabin', but also actual arrangements – an 'Arabesque' by Germaine
Tailleferre of Les Six and Schumann's 'Vanitatus Vanitatum' (on *Constellations*), alongside songs by
Brassens and jazz archaeology like Herbie Nichols's 'The Gig' (also on the hat Art).

A trio of this configuration is pretty exacting for a brass player, but Douglas floats over the guitarist's
raw metallic chords and peppery runs with immense grace and clarity, a very beautiful sound. There is
certainly no indication that he needs the usual scaffolding and support. The larger group on *In Our
Lifetime* (Ehrlich, it should be said, is restricted to just one track) slightly muffles his approach and puts
a limit on his appetite for broad atonal jumps (somehow harder to pull off against a piano player). The
musicianship also seems a little less engaged, lacking the intense concentration on senses on
Constellations. Some of hat Art's output – the ostensibly similar work of Franz Koglmann, for instance
– strikes jazz purists as too ethereal, abstract, cool, ironic. They should be reassured that Douglas is an
altogether more pungently traditional performer, even on *Five*, where he's accompanied by yet another
harmonic variant, a string trio this time, led by experienced improviser Feldman. At least some of the
music recalls the dark, Hebraic sound of the Masada group (and 'Mogador' is dedicated to Zorn), but
there are dedications as well to Woody Shaw ('Actualities'), Wayne Shorter ('Going, Going') and Steve
Lacy ('Seven'), which suggest some of the other directions from which Douglas is taking cues..

Down Home Jazz Band GROUP

*** **Dawn Club Joys** Stomp Off CD1241
>   Bob Schulz (*c, v*); Chris Tyle (*c*); Tom Bartlett (*tb, v*); Bob Helm (*cl, v*); Ray Skjelbred (*p*); Jack
>   Meilahn (*bj*); Mike Bezin (*tba*); Hal Smith (*d*). 7/91.

*** **Back To Bodega** Stomp Off CD1273
>   Chris Tyle (*t, v*); Bob Mielke (*tb*); Bob Helm (*cl, ss, bcl, v*); Wally Rose (*p*); Carl Lunsford (*bj, v*);
>   Mike Walbridge (*tba*); Hal Smith (*d*); Barbara Dane (*v*). 8/93.

Chris Tyle's group has been a fixture in West Coast traditional circles for many years, though there was a
ten-year disbandment in the 1970s. Both of these discs pay tribute to the Lu Watters Yerba Buena sound
which had a huge impact on revivalists in the US. There are a few oddities – such as 'When Ragtime
Rufus Rags The Humoresque' on *Back To Bodega*! – but much of the material is from a relatively
familiar pocket. The distinction comes in the tight syncopation of the ensembles, the particular jig-jog
rhythm and the blend of knowingness and genuine enthusiasm which American trad relies on. It helps
that original Yerba Buena man Helm is on hand for an extra drop of authenticity. Excellent, crisp studio
sound.

Mark Dresser (born 1952) DOUBLE BASS

*** **The Cabinet Of Dr Caligari** Knitting Factory Works KFWCD 155
>   Dresser; Dave Douglas (*t*); Denman Moroney (*prepared p*).

**** **Force Green** Soul Note 121273
>   As above, except add Phil Haynes (*d*); Theo Bleckmann (*v*). 9/94.

Like his colleagues in the Anthony Braxton Quartet – Marilyn Crispell and Gerry Hemingway – Dresser
has musical ideas of his own. He studied bass with the great classical virtuoso, Bertram Turetzky, and
has always incorporated ideas from that realm into his thinking about jazz. Though he does not overdo
arco playing, there is something very proper and legitimate about his plucked lines: he uses them to
create a mood on the first of these, written as live accompaniment to the cult silent film. Prepared piano
gives a dry, alienating sound that is ideally suited to the bleak expressionism of *Caligari*, and the
ubiquitous Douglas conveys an urgency and sense of menace, allied perhaps to his own passionate
response to recent war and violence.

On 'Bosnia', one of the tracks on *Force Green*, he utters despairing, pain-racked cries over Dresser's harmonic squeaks and rumbles, an intense evocation of both men's (Dresser is the composer) humanitarian reaction; Bleckmann, who is used as a second horn rather than a lyric vocalist, comes in with muezzin cries and wails that reinforce the Balkan/Middle Eastern tonality. The previous track, 'Ediface', is a more obviously jazz-based structure and allows Douglas to stretch out, counterpointed by Bleckmann's slightly nasal scats.

The long 'Castles For Carter' is an elaborate fantasy for the late clarinettist, John Carter, and a passing reference to his *Castles Of Ghana* album. Tightly organized round a series of pan-tonal themes, it never sounds like a blowing piece, nor as if it is wholly written out; and it's here for the first time on the set that the young Moroney and Haynes come into their own. Up to that point it could almost have been another trio. Douglas blows a thoughtful remembrance of his great predecessor on 'For Miles', with a sly quote from a famous solo, before Bleckmann reverts to falsetto for a gorgeous dialogue that consigns Dresser to the background for a few minutes. Moroney experiments with preparation again, creating a strange, sitar-like tone. This is otherwise very much the bassist's record, but only in the proper sense that he steers the music. Co-producer Tim Berne keeps him properly located in the mix – even the unaccompanied intro to 'Castles' is naturally balanced – and the total effect is of an ensemble rather than a loose coalition of individuals, which is what this music requires.

Kenny Drew (1928–93) PIANO

**(*) The Kenny Drew Trio Original Jazz Classics OJC 065
    Drew; Paul Chambers (*b*); Philly Joe Jones (*d*). 9/56.
Drew's earliest-available album as a leader is no better or worse than many another piano-trio date of the day: light, bluesy variations on a flock of standards. Chambers and Jones are typically strong in support, but the material is under-characterized.

**(*) This Is New Original Jazz Classics OJC 483
    Drew; Donald Byrd (*t*); Hank Mobley (*ts*); Wilbur Ware (*b*); G. T. Hogan (*d*). 3–4/57.
*** Pal Joey Original Jazz Classics OJC 1809
    Drew; Wilbur Ware (*b*); Philly Joe Jones (*d*). 10/57.
Nothing very new here, despite both the title and the period; this sort of hard-bop fare was already becoming a standard repast in 1957. It may say something for the principals involved that the most interesting presence appears to be Ware, who is constantly inventive. The recording is somewhat reticent in dealing with the horns. *Pal Joey* is a typical jazz-goes-to-Broadway album of the day: it earns an extra notch, though, for Ware's hungry, probing lines and the crisper lines that this trio secures. There is also a compilation LP, *Trio/Quartet/Quintet* (OJC 6007 CD), which selects tracks from all the above discs.

*** Duo Steeplechase SCCD 31002
    Drew; Niels-Henning Orsted-Pedersen (*b*); Ole Molin (*g*). 4/73.
*** Duo 2 Steeplechase SCCD 31010
    As above, except omit Molin. 2/74.
*** Duo Live In Concert Steeplechase SCCD 31031
    As above. 6/74.
**(*) Everything I Love Steeplechase SCCD 31007
    Drew (*p* solo). 10–12/73.
Drew left America for Europe in 1961 and worked and recorded there until his death. His numerous records for Steeplechase are modest successes, but the pianist's very consistency is perhaps his undoing: it's frequently hard to tell one disc – or even one performance – from another. The three duo sessions with NHOP are the best, if only because there is a fine clarity of interplay and the bassist doesn't settle for Drew's plainer modes of expression. The solo date is rather too quiescent.

** Morning Steeplechase SCCD 31048
    Drew; Niels-Henning Orsted-Pedersen (*b*); Philip Catherine (*g*). 9/75.
**(*) Lite Flite Steeplechase SCCD 31077
    Drew; Thad Jones (*c*); Bob Berg (*ts*); George Mraz (*b*); Jimmy Cobb (*d*). 2/77.
*** In Concert Steeplechase SCCD 31106
    Drew; Niels-Henning Orsted-Pedersen (*b*); Philip Catherine (*g*). 2/77.
**(*) Ruby My Dear Steeplechase SCCD 31129
    Drew; David Friesen (*b*); Clifford Jarvis (*d*). 8/77.
Although Drew recorded in a variety of settings for Steeplechase, a certain blandness continued to detract from his sessions as a leader. The quintet date with Jones and Berg is amiable but no more

exciting than the trio records, of which *In Concert* is the best, benefiting from the in-person atmosphere. Drew's powers as an accompanist are best demonstrated elsewhere, in his sessions with Dexter Gordon.

**(*) And Far Away Soul Note 121081
Drew; Philip Catherine (*g*); Niels-Henning Orsted-Pedersen (*b*); Barry Altschul (*d*). 2/83.
Drew made several records for the Japanese Baystate company in the early 1980s, as well as this session for Soul Note: his compositions continue to work a slight, pretty seam to rather soporific ends, but the record benefits from the presence of Altschul, whose ear for texture helps to create a more integrated and purposeful sound to such Drew originals as 'Rianne'.

*** Recollections Timeless SJP 333
Drew; Niels-Henning Orsted-Pedersen (*b*); Alvin Queen (*d*). 5/89.
It might be thanks to digital sound of tremendous impact, but this set sounds like a revitalization of Drew's music. Whether tackling standards or originals, he digs in with a verve and a decisive attack which will surprise anyone familiar with the earlier trio dates. NHOP and Queen respond with appropriate vigour of their own.

Kenny Drew Jr PIANO

*** A Look Inside Antilles 314 514 211
Drew; Joshua Redman, David Sanchez (*ts*); Charnett Moffett, George Mraz (*b*); Codaryl Moffett, Lewis Nash (*d*). 6/92.
***(*) At Maybeck: Volume 39 Concord CCD 4653
Drew (*p* solo). 8/94.
***(*) Portraits of Mingus and Thelonious Monk Claves 50 1194
Drew; Lynn Seaton (*b*); Marvin 'Smitty' Smith (*d*). 94.
'Junior' no longer, of course; since 1993 he has been the senior Drew, and they've been years of accelerated progress. The three Jazz City albums (for which, see the previous edition of the *Guide*) are out of catalogue, leaving the slate wiped pretty much clean as far as recordings are concerned. Both of the above suggest that important steps have already been taken.

Kenny Jr never really sounded like his dad, who would never have owned up to allowing 'a little Schoenberg or Messiaen' sneak into his playing. Classically trained, young Kenny uses non-blues intervals to a far greater extent and has a less percussive attack. His approach to the Maybeck recital is, though, refreshingly unacademic; not a classical *étude* in sight (though there is a meditation on the name 'HAYDN' included in the Antilles set) and half-way through he pairs up a composition each from son and father – 'Coral Sea' and 'Images' respectively – a gesture which seems intended to cement his ongoing debt.

Players seem to approach Maybeck programmes in one of two ways: they either take leave to experiment or else remain very squarely in the tradition. Kenny takes the latter tack, and very convincingly too; his closing 'Autumn Leaves' is absolutely conventional and almost flawless, and the two Monk tunes, 'Ugly Beauty' and 'Straight, No Chaser', could be improved upon only if the great man were to reach down and muss the youngster's hair up a bit; they're both a little too studied and earnest, and it's time that Drew had the self-possession to let go a bit.

No particular sign that he's ready for that on *A Look Inside*. He goes back to 'Ugly Beauty' in a duo with Josh Redman, and another Monk, 'San Francisco Holiday (Worry Later)', both spin-offs from the sons-of-famous-fathers quartet responsible for 'Mr P.C.'. Quite predictably, the other quartet – Sanchez, Mraz, Lewis – and its subdivisions sound more coherent, even if the saxophonist is inclined to reinvent the wheel every time he solos. Nevertheless, the outstanding single item is the closing 'Giant Steps', cast as a trio with the two Moffetts.

With a first solo record under his belt, Drew need no longer feel apprehensive about venturing out without the cover of a trio. 'Light Blue' and 'Weird Nightmare' on the *Mingus/Monk* disc are both unaccompanied solos, and very impressive too, subtly modulated and multi-dimensional. The trio is slightly too busy for comfort, with Smith doing his characteristic hurry-up act, but the recording is so good and true that one scarcely notices. Drew comes of age (perhaps again) with this one.

Paquito D'Rivera (born 1948) ALTO, SOPRANO AND TENOR SAXOPHONES, CLARINET

*** Tico! Tico! Chesky 034
D'Rivera; Danilo Perez (*p*); Fareed Haque, Romero Lobambo, Tibero Nascimiento (*g*); David Finck, Nilson Matta (*b*); Portinho, Mark Walker (*d*). 7–8/89.
D'Rivera was the first of the recent wave of Cuban musicians to defect to the US (in 1980), and his

intensely hot, infectiously runaway style on alto has enlivened quite a number of sessions. He has the same difficulty which besets his compadre, Arturo Sandoval: finding a consistently productive context for a talent which is liable to blow away on the winds of its own virtuosity. D'Rivera is never short of a string of firecracker phrases, but they can often be as enervating to a listener as the most laid-back of jazz easy-listening dates. His Columbia albums tended to end up as Latinized hard bop, no better or worse than a typical neo-classical session if a little more sparky than most. But this Chesky album suggests ways that D'Rivera can make a more convincing kind of fusion. The bolero, waltz and bossa nova rhythms are integrated into a setting which sifts bebop into an authentic South American stew, and the leader turns to the clarinet as well as the alto (and a little tenor) to decorate the pulse. Chesky's brilliant sound only heightens the sunny qualities of Paquito's music.

*** **Havana Café** Chesky JD 80
       D'Rivera; Danilo Perez (*p*); Fareed Haque, Ed Cherry (*g*); David Finck (*b*); Jorge Rossy (*d*);
       Sammy Figueroa (*perc*).
More of the same, really. But the very quick tempos tend to underline D'Rivera's difficulty in finding a context: he can handle these rapid-fire speeds, but other members of the band – Perez and Haque in particular – find it difficult both to sustain the pace and to have anything interesting to say. Two classical pieces, 'Improvisation' and 'Contradanza', offer a little more variety, and this time D'Rivera brings out his soprano rather than his tenor.

*** **Who's Smoking?** Candid CCD79523
       D'Rivera; Claudio Roditi (*t, flhn*); Mark Morganelli (*flhn*); James Moody (*ts*); Danilo Perez,
       Pedriot Lopez (*p*); Harvie Swartz (*b*); Al Foster (*d*). 5/91.
Lots more gilt-edged hard bop, heavy on smoke, glittter and flash but short on anything beyond the showmanship. D'Rivera and Roditi strike sparks off each other until they're practically smouldering, and there is a rather good 'Giant Steps' which emerges out of it all. Taken moment by moment, fair game.

Billy Drummond DRUMS

*** **Native Colours** Criss Cross Jazz Criss 1057
       Drummond; Steve Wilson (*ss, as*); Steve Nelson (*vib*); Renée Rosnes (*p*); Ray Drummond (*b*). 3/
       91.
***(*) **The Gift** Criss Cross Jazz Criss 1083
       Drummond; Seamus Blake (*ts, ss*); Renée Rosnes (*p*); Peter Washington (*b*). 12/93.
Drummond is the partner of Canadian-born pianist Renée Rosnes. That would probably assist his employment prospects were he not already recognized as a crisp, accurate player who can make fascinating things happen without moving away from his cymbals. When he seems in danger of overdoing one range of sound to the exclusion of the rest, he suddenly drops in a sharp tom-tom accent, or else – even more effectively – switches to a harder, more emphatic attack on the edge of the metal. That he should draw attention away from players of the quality of Rosnes, Nelson and Wilson on the debut disc is a sign of his pedigree, but it is only on *The Gift*, a far better-intergrated session, that he begins to shine as a leader.

    Drummond leaves the writing to Rosnes, by and large, but his own imaginative approach can be gauged from the unusual material he picks up, preferring strong, medium-pace bop tunes by the likes of Harold Land and Clifford Jordan to Broadway standards. Blake is certainly not a player of Wilson's character and range, but he takes to Land's 'Ode To Angela' as if it was written for him, and he does interesting things, too, with Charles Lloyd's open-form 'Apex' (a wonder more leaders haven't programmed this lovely thing). Rosnes occasionally sounded uneasy picking her way round the vibes and the other Drummond's heavy bass sound on *Native Colours*. She likes a bit more space than that, and Peter Washington is a sympathetic partner.

Ray Drummond BASS

*** **Camera In A Bag** Criss Cross Jazz 1040
       Drummond; David Newman (*ts, f*); Kenny Barron (*p*); Steve Nelson (*vib*); Marvin 'Smitty'
       Smith (*d*). 12/89.
*** **Excursion** Arabesque AJ0106
       Drummond; Craig Handy (*ss, as, ts, f*); Joe Lovano (*ss, ts, f*); Danilô Perez (*p*); Marvin 'Smitty'
       Smith, Mor Thiam (*d*). 6/92.
Drummond has appeared on numerous sessions as sideman, but his outings as a leader are rarer. The

Criss Cross session works out very well, although nothing exactly arrives with a bang. Newman plays as much flute as tenor and sounds full and funky on both instruments, while Nelson functions peripherally; the strongest music, though, comes from the rhythm section, which develops a tremendously assured momentum across the nine compositions, four of them by Drummond. *Excursion* is a complete contrast. The polished post-bop of the earlier date is traded for a looser, noisier ensemble sound in which Mor Thiam's percussion sets the tone. Handy's wild solos are a polar opposite to Lovano's considered improvising, and Perez contributes his carefully heated piano manner to what is a thick, percussive ensemble sound. But Drummond's writing doesn't quite have a handle on the situation: it's enjoyable from moment to moment, yet the music sounds confused as often as it is exhilarating.

***(*) **Continuum** Arabesque A J O11
> Drummond; Randy Brecker (*t*); Thomas Chapin (*f*); John Scofield (*g*); Kenny Barron (*p*); Steve Nelson (*vib*); Marvin 'Smitty' Smith (*d*); Mor Thiam (*perc*). 1/94.

Drummond's best record works on grounds of both simplicity and detail. The continuum is the blues, which provides the source for most of these pieces, be they a simple melodic line such as the leader's own 'Blues From The Sketchpad' or the Japanese chords of 'Sakura'. There is great blowing by a band stuffed with masters, but Drummond was smart enough to vary the textures by keeping Chapin on flutes rather than alto and bringing the chime of Nelson's vibes into the picture. Here and there, as in the fine turbulence of Strayhorn's 'Intimacy Of The Blues', the music moves far beyond boppish origins into a thickly textured stew. The only reservation might be the sometimes unspecific sound-mix which the leader favours as producer.

The Dry Throat Fellows GROUP

*** **Do Something** Stomp Off CD 1226
> René Hagmann (*c, tb, cl, as, bsx*); Jacques Ducrot (*cl, ss, as, v*); Bertrand Neyroud (*cl, ts, gfs, v*); Pierre-Alain Maret (*g, bj*); Michel Rudaz (*tba*); Raymond Graisier (*wbd, perc, v*). 11–12/90.

Since trad has long since colonized Europe, it should come as no surprise that this wry troupe of Swiss players should be as adept as they are. If this is the humorous side of traditional playing, though, how come their version of Clarence Williams's 'Red River Blues' cuts anyone else's? Secret weapon René Hagmann, who does most of the arranging, is equally at home with brass or reeds; Bertrand Neyroud plays the most vibrant clarinet this side of Don Byron; and new recruit Jacques Ducrot (there are two earlier LPs on Stomp Off) sounds right at home with an alto style that seems to have heard of nothing after 1932. He also puts a ridiculous vocal on 'Sweet Sue (Just You)'. Sounds daft on a CD player, but sounds pretty good anywhere.

Marc Ducret GUITAR, GUITAR-SYNTHESIZER

*** **La Théorie Du Pilier** Label Bleu L BL 6508
> Ducret; Michel Benita (*b*); Aaron Scott (*d*). 87.
***(*) **Le Kodo** Label Bleu L BL 6519
> Ducret; Larry Schneider (*ss, ts*); Michel Benita (*b*); Adam Nussbaum (*d*). 12/88.
*** **Gris** Label Bleu L BLC 6531
> Ducret; Enrico Rava (*t*); Yves Robert (*tb*); François Jeanneau (*ss*); Andy Emler (*p*); Michel Benita, Renaud Garcia Fons (*b*); Joel Allouche (*d*). 5/90.

Ducret should be in the forefront of those guitarists who've fused rock, jazz and blues accents into an accessible new genre, but, hidden away on small European labels, his work lags far behind that of Scofield or Frisell in terms of reputation. *La Théorie Du Pilier* is a temperate trio record, concentrating on the interplay of the group, with Ducret sticking mostly to a clean, traditional guitar tone; but *Le Kodo* is a far tougher and more exciting session, the underrated Schneider piling through his solos and Ducret upping the ante on his own playing by several notches. Nussbaum plays with all the requisite energy, but sometimes one wishes for a drummer with a little more finesse. *Gris* varies the pace again: 'Elephanta' is a guitar–drums duet, Rava, Emler, Jeanneau and Robert drift in and out of the other tracks, and both bassists appear on 'Danser'. All three records have their share of good tunes as well as intelligent solos: Ducret pens a pleasing melody.

*** **News From The Front** J M T 849148-2
> Ducret; Herb Robertson (*t, flhn*); Yves Robert (*tb*); François Verly (*d*). 6–7/91.

A surprising step forward, although the record is finally let down by some questionable judgements. After the straight 'jazz guitar' of the previous discs, this first for a new company finds Ducret choosing a range of different guitar sounds and a dispersal of the jazz/rock time which had governed his previous discs. Verly is employed for percussive colour (via a drum machine) as much as for timekeeping, and the most serious relationship here is between Ducret's guitars and Robertson's mocking, splintery trumpet and flugelhorn. Their opening duet on 'Pour Agnes', with Ducret on acoustic 12-string, sounds eerily like an echo of some old Ralph Towner meditation, but the bigger pieces such as the title-track and the long – perhaps too long – 'Fanfare' splay electric solos against a background of brass noise in still space. Robert doesn't have much to do, but his trombone chords on 'Wren Is Such A Strange Name' (the titles suggest an, er, concept) add another note of mystery. It isn't fully sustained, and passages such as the closing 'Golden Wren' sound more like an elevated kind of art-rock than anything, but Ducret is taking a courageous shot at the outside. Find him also on Tim Berne's JMT albums.

Gerd Dudek (born 1938) SOPRANO SAXOPHONE, TENOR SAXOPHONE, FLUTE

***(*) **After All** Konnex KCD 5022
    Dudek; Ali Haurand (*b*); Rob Van Den Broeck (*p*).
Dudek's tenor sound has become one of the most distinctive of the 1980s (with an individualized Coltrane influence evident on the superb 'Alabama') and it's rather shocking that he remains so little known and so poorly represented as a leader. The remaining material is more ambitious for a drummer-less trio, but all three players contribute to the maintenance of a solid but elastic pulse.

Ted Dunbar (born 1937) GUITAR

(*) **Gentle Time Along Steeplechase SCCD 31298
    Dunbar; Mickey Tucker (*p*); Ray Drummond (*b*); David Jones (*d*). 12/91.
Dunbar's restrained and even dynamic, coupled with his soft-toned picking style, makes him a jazz guitarist somewhat at odds with the current school. He and Tucker work well together, perhaps a little too well – it's the sort of empathy that sends the music to sleep rather than making fresh points. Superior sound opens out the subtlety of the guitarist's ideas, though, and the rhythm section keep a watchful eye on the back line.

Paul Dunmall SAXOPHONES, CLARINET

***(*) **Soliloquy** Matchless MR 15
    Dunmall (solo *reeds*). 10 & 12/86.
*** **Folks** Slam CD 212
    Dunmall; Paul Rogers (*b*); Polly Bolton (*v*). 12/89, 9/93.
***(*) **Quartet and Sextet / Babu (Trio)** Slam CD 207 2CD
    Dunmall; John Corbett (*c*); Simon Picard (*ts*); John Adams (*g*); Paul Rogers (*b*); Tony Levin (*d*). 9/93.
A powerful soloist, Dunmall soliloquizes on the earliest of these with nary a hint of introspection. Multi-tracking allows him to build contrapuntal lines and stark harmonic intervals, but perhaps the most striking effects are created when, as on 'Human Atmospheres', he plays a long, unaccompanied bridge using squally extremes of pitch. On the much shorter 'Elementals' he swaps his long, developed lines for a dense, pointillistic effect; 'Holocaust' opens with anguished 'unison' blares, before opening out into an intense tenor soliloquy that is admirably controlled. 'Clarinet And Ocarina' is not as slight as its resources might suggest; but the real star piece is 'Voyage', which nine out of ten blindfold-tested listeners would guess was Surman until the long *a cappella* soprano solo pushes the music in a very different direction. Intelligently conceived and performed, *Soliloquy* is well worth having.

    The duos with Rogers, who also used to be a member of Mujician with Keith Tippett and Tony Levin, are as matily instinctive as one would expect them to be. It's interesting to consider what changes time has wrought in the two Pauls' relationship; perhaps Dunmall is a little more confidently assertive in the later pieces? Rogers uses both 4- and 5-string basses, and Dunmall his full range of clarinets, saxes and whistles, though there is clearly something wrong with the track listings given, which do not match up to the instruments heard. Polly Bolton's contribution is limited to a single track, but there is obviously scope for a vocal component in music of this kind, and Slam's interest in song/jazz crossovers is already well attested.

    The two-CD Slam set offers a fuller range of playing contexts and Dunmall again reveals himself to be a responsive group-player, constantly listening to what is going on around him. The trio Babu is essentially Mujician without Keith Tippett. It's a sparer sound, with much less harmonic detail, and Dunmall uses it as a showcase for his C-melody, tenor, baritone and soprano saxophones. His interest in more developed or composed forms is served by the two larger groups, though only the sextet (a single track called 'Apocalypse Now And Then') includes a harmony instrument. The two-saxophone quartet with Picard includes some hairy moments; unison passages on 'In The Haddock' and 'The Devil's Chair' are as good as anything he's done, and the concentration on tenor is all to the good. At pushing on for two hours of fairly intense music, this is a good buy.

Johnny Mbizo Dyani (1945–86) DOUBLE BASS

*** **Witchdoctor's Son** Steeplechase SCCD 31098
        Dyani; John Tchicai (*as, ss*); Dudu Pukwana (*as, ts*); Alfredo Do Nascimento (*g*); Luiz Carlos
        De Sequeira (*d*); Mohamed Al-Jabry (*perc*). 3/78.
*** **Song For Biko** Steeplechase SCCD 31109
        Dyani; Dudu Pukwana (*as*); Don Cherry (*c*); Makaya Ntoshko (*d*). 7/78.
(*) **Afrika Steeplechase SCCD 31186
        Dyani; Ed Epstein (*as, bs*); Charles Davis (*as*); Thomas Ostergren (*b*); Gilbert Matthews (*d*);
        Rudy Smith (*steel d*); Thomas Akuru Dyani (*congas*). 10/83.
*** **Angolian Cry** Steeplechase SCCD 31209
        Dyani; Harry Beckett (*t, flhn*); John Tchicai (*ts, bcl*); Billy Hart (*d*). 7/85.
The late Johnny Dyani was calmly visionary, with a deep swelling of anger and irony underneath; technically robust; stylistically various. More than any of the South African exiles, Dyani absorbed and assimilated a wide variety of styles and procedures. He spent much of his active life in Scandinavia where he forged close artistic relationships with John Tchicai, Don Cherry and with Dollar Brand (Abdullah Ibrahim), with whom he shared a particular vision of Africa.

   The music is strongly politicized but never programmatic. *Witchdoctor's Son* and *Song For Biko* come from Dyani's most consistently inventive period. Some of the early 1980s material is a little more diffuse and, though Pukwana – another who has since re-entered Azania beyond life – is a powerfully compelling solo voice, he always seemed to mute Dyani's more inventive progressions.

   Afrika is probably the weakest of Dyani's records, marred by an ill-matched rhythm section and out-of-character horns. Dyani never found another drummer with Ntoshko's instincts and empathy, but he came briefly close with Churchill Jolobe and then again towards the end of his life with Billy Hart. *Angolian Cry* is a marvellous record, brimming with the pathos and joy that marked *Song For Biko*. Beckett is an uncut national treasure and it's interesting to hear Tchicai on the less familiar tenor.

Jon Eardley (born 1928) TRUMPET, FLUGELHORN

(*) **From Hollywood To New York Original Jazz Classics OJC 1746
        Eardley; J. R. Monterose (*ts*); George Syran (*p*); Teddy Kotick (*b*); Nick Stabulas (*d*). 12/54.
Uncontroversial swing from the sometime Chet Baker doppelgänger, who shares a frail intensity with his one-time partner. *From Hollywood To New York* was fronted by Eardley and the ever-about-to-be-rediscovered Monterose, who is one of the more adventurous of the middle-generation tenor players; the rhythm section is robust, and turned out to be durable, producing a near-identical groove on the later recording.

   It's hard to be categorical about Eardley because he doesn't make categorical music. On its own unambitious terms, unexceptionable.

Charles Earland (born 1941) ORGAN

***(*) **Black Talk!** Original Jazz Classics OJC 335
        Earland; Virgil Jones (*t*); Houston Person (*ts*); Melvin Sparks (*g*); Idris Muhammad (*d*); Buddy
        Caldwell (*perc*).
*** **Leaving This Planet** Prestige PRCD-66002-2
        Earland; Freddie Hubbard (*t, flhn*); Eddie Henderson (*t*); Joe Henderson (*ts*); Dave Hubbard (*ss,
        ts, af*); Patrick Gleeson (*ky*); Eddie Arkin, Greg Crockett (*g*); Brian Brake, Harvey Mason (*d*);
        Larry Killian (*perc*); Rudy Copeland (*v*). 12/73–1/74.
*** **Front Burner** Milestone M 9165
        Earland; Virgil Jones (*t*); Bill Easley (*ts*); Bobby Broom (*g*); Rudy Williams (*d*); Frank Colon
        (*perc*). 6/88.
(*) **Third Degree Burn Milestone MCD-9174-2
        Earland; Lew Soloff (*t*); David Newman, Grover Washington (*ss, ts*); Bobby Broom (*g*); Buddy

Williams (*d*); Ralph Dorsey (*perc*). 5/89.
(*) **Whip Appeal Muse MCD 5375
Earland; Johhny Coles (*flhn*); Jeffrey Newell (*ss, as*); Houston Person (*ts*); Robert Block (*g*);
Marvin Jones (*d*); Lawrence Killian (*perc*). 5/90.
*(*) **Unforgettable** Muse MCD 5455
Earland; Kenny Rampton (*t*); Clifford Adams (*tb*); Eric Alexander (*ss, ts*); Houston Person (*ts*);
Oliver Nevels (*g*); Gregory Williams, Buddy Williams (*d*); Lawrence Killian (*perc*). 12/91.
The recent revival of interest in 'traditional' jazz organ has rekindled Earland's career. He made a key
album at the very end of the 1960s, *Black Talk!*, which has finally made it to CD. Earland updated the
heavier style of players such as Jack McDuff and Jimmy Smith, chose more pop-orientated material and
delivered it with a percussive attack. Jones and Person are useful props, but Earland drives the music –
even an unpromising piece like 'Aquarius' becomes a convincing, bluesy groove piece. *Leaving This
Planet*, though it comes with some of the excess baggage of the era – dopey space effects, wah-wah
guitars and the like – isn't far behind, and summons a first-rate cast to hammer through what's really a
blowing session with some space-age debris. Hubbard's own set-piece, 'Red Clay', also features.
    The later crop of amiable records doesn't really show him at his best, and diminishing returns seem to
have set in. There's some fluff on the first date – the theme to *Moonlighting*, for example – and matters
get worse rather than better as he switches from Milestone to Muse, where producer Houston Person
doesn't have any fresh course to put him on. *Whip Appeal* is a bit tougher, but *Unforgettable* is dreary,
and only the startlingly big and juicy sound of the youthful Alexander on tenor makes much impression.

Earthbound GROUP

** **Unity** Leo CD LR 189
Alexandros (*p*); Alex Foster (*ss*); Andy McKee (*b*); Victor Jones (*d*); Cosa Ross (*perc*). 4/92.
Possibly the most disappointing record ever to be issued by this normally enterprising label. It has a
rehearsal/workshop feel and a dismal low-fi sound that will prove off-putting to many. Foster is an
interesting player moment to moment, and Jones has some very worthwhile ideas. One suspects that
leader Alexandros – no forename – might be more unfettered playing on his own, without the need to
create dialogues.

Bill Easley REEDS

(*) **Wind Inventions Sunnyside SSC 1022
Easley; Mulgrew Miller (*p*); Victor Gaskin (*b*); Tony Reedus (*d*). 9/86.
This talented multi-instrumentalist is a proven asset as a sideman, but his debut as a leader is a trifle
colourless. He performs most of this programme on clarinet and, while it's a welcome change from
hearing yet another prodigious saxophonist, his improvisations are facile rather than compelling. The
sleeve-note compares the date to Buddy DeFranco's '50s records, but Easley doesn't approach
DeFranco's piercing insight, and his swing-into-bop manner sounds bland across the length of an
album. The soft-edged sound doesn't assist him.

*** **First Call** Milestone MCD-9186-2
Easley; Bill Mobley (*t*); George Caldwell (*ky*); Roland Hanna, James Williams (*p*); J. J. Wiggins,
Dave Jackson (*b*); Grady Tate (*d*). 10/90.
The lavish tenor treatment of 'It's All In The Game' gets the record off to a fine start, and Easley is
enjoying himself here in the company of two different quintets, Hanna and Williams changing places at
the piano. Standard material and the easy-going fluency of both pianists give the date a lighter, more
knowing air than the debut and, while there's still nothing remarkable here, it's persuasive music.

Eastern Rebellion GROUP

**** **Eastern Rebellion** Timeless SJP 101
Walton; George Coleman (*ts*); Sam Jones (*b*); Billy Higgins (*d*). 12/75.
***(*) **Eastern Rebellion 2** Timeless CD SJP 106
As above, except Bob Berg (*ts*) replaces Coleman.
***(*) **Mosaic** Musicmasters 65073-2
Walton; Ralph Moore (*ts*); David Williams (*b*); Billy Higgins (*d*). 12/90.
***(*) **Simple Pleasure** Musicmasters 518 014
As above. 6/92.

**** Just One Of Those . . . Nights At The Village Vanguard MusicMasters 65116-2
        As above. 95.
Led by pianist Walton, Eastern Rebellion is a more collective enterprise than his solo records, though he is still the main composer. The group's essentially a piano trio but, in line with the earlier Walton band of which Clifford Jordan became an integral part, there has always been a place for a hornman. Higgins has been a stalwart from the start and is probably the main point of continuity with Walton's other records. The original *Eastern Rebellion* is still arguably the finest record Walton has put his hand to; the version of 'Naima', with Coleman sounding magisterial as he cuts through the harmonies, compares more than favourably with that on the excellent *Bluesville Time* (see under Walton), where Dale Barlow takes the lead.

    The addition of British-born Ralph Moore brings a fresh, vocalized tone, first heard to effect on 'John's Blues' on *Mosaic*, a track that also shows off Higgins's formidable talents. There are fewer highs and lows on *Simple Pleasures*, a more straightforward blowing date, but the musicianship is consistently high and the empathy among the three senior members is as close as ever. By the time of the Village Vanguard sessions, it sounds unquestionably like a well-established group. Moore is wholly integrated and often very impressive indeed, and there are signs that he is stamping his personality on the music as well as following his elders. Again, much of the material is Walton's, but there are expansive versions of Thad Jones's 'A Child Is Born' and John Lewis's 'Django' and the long, long 'Seven Minds', a Sam Jones piece, is as full of drama, light and shade as one could wish.

Jon Eberson GUITAR

** Stash Odin 19
        Eberson; Bjorn Kjellemyr (*b*); Audun Klieve (*d*). 8/86.
Jon Eberson has the problem of being Norway's 'other' guitarist after Terje Rypdal, and it's likely to be compounded by his decision to use Rypdal's Chasers rhythm section for this brawny but not especially distinctive set. The 13 compositions often boil down to decorated riffs and, while their brevity at least prevents stasis setting in, it means that nothing gets developed very far either.

Rinde Eckert VOCALS, PIANO, ORGAN, ACCORDION, KEYBOARDS

*** Finding My Way Home DIW 859
        Eckert; Will Bernard, Bill Frisell (*g*); Rob Vlack (*ky*); Suzy Thompson (*vn*); Clark Suprynowicz (*b*); Jerry Granelli, Jim Kassis (*d*). 92.
Extraordinary, but also extraordinarily difficult to categorize. Eckert's big, raw-boned voice will remind listeners of nothing more strongly than Marianne Faithfull or Diamanda Galas in blues-singing mood. He draws something from the old-style blues shouters, and one of the best tracks on the record is a reworking – almost atonal in quality – of Howlin' Wolf's 'Sittin' On Top Of The World'. Besides that, there is a strange solo version of 'Amazing Grace'. It comes in the middle of a suite, 'Crossing The Country', which appears to have a profound autobiographical impetus, coming from as deep inside as the closing 'Heaven In His Eyes'. Superb as some of this is, and accomplished as the nerdy-looking Compleat Strangers (Frisell has the right spectacles to claim membership) can be, it's not entirely clear whether it belongs in the jazz racks. Worth searching out nevertheless.

Peter Ecklund TRUMPET, CORNET

***(*) Ecklund At Elkhart Jazzology JCD-246
        Ecklund; Dan Barrett (*tb*); Bobby Gordon (*cl*); Mark Shane (*p*); Marty Grosz (*g, v*); Greg Cohen (*b*); Hal Smith (*d*). 7/94.
Though under Peter Ecklund's nominal leadership, this is really nothing more or less than another of the ineffably hot and good-humoured jazz parties which always seem to take place when Marty Grosz and his pals are on hand. Another 15 chestnuts from 1918 to 1939, some of which only the Grosz gang would dare go near these days, especially the once-frightful 'Trees', here given a peppery rendition. Barrett and Gordon have plenty of good solos and Shane is a model of light-fingered swing, but Ecklund does take marginal honours with cornet playing of finesse and pukka good cheer. Recorded at various points during the Elkhart Jazz Festival of 1994, once when only three people were present. That's no comment on the music.

Billy Eckstine (1914–93) VOCAL

***(*) **Billy's Best!** Verve 526440-2
  Eckstine; orchestras of Hal Mooney, Bobby Tucker. 8/57–9/58.
*** **Imagination** Emarcy 848162-2
  Eckstine; Pete Rugolo Orchestra. 58.
*** **At Basin Street East** Emarcy 832592
  Eckstine; Benny Bailey, Clark Terry, Ernie Royal (*t*); Curtis Fuller (*tb*); Julius Watkins (*frhn*);
  Phil Woods (*as*); Jerome Richardson, Eric Dixon (*ts, f*); Sahib Shihab (*bs*); Patti Bown (*p*); Don
  Elliott (*vib*); Don Arnone (*g*); Stu Martin (*d*). 61.
**** **Everything I Have Is Yours** Verve 819442-2 2CD
  Eckstine; various groups, 47–57.
***(*) **Verve Jazz Masters: Billy Eckstine** Verve 519693-2
  Eckstine; various groups, 49–58.

Eckstine had the ripest, most luxuriant voice in black music and, though his later records suggest a man who was fundamentally a conservative, one shouldn't forget how radical a role it was for a black singer to adopt such a romantic persona in the 1940s. His peerless bebop big band made few records and they are still awaited on CD; so one must start with these discs. Eckstine's many records for Mercury from the 1950s and '60s have until recently been neglected. Of the surviving 'original' albums, *At Basin Street East* is a rousing encounter with Quincy Jones's big band. The contrast here is between Eckstine's opulent, take-my-time delivery and the scintillating punch of what was a fierce, slick, note-perfect organization. *Imagination* is more in the slicked-down ballad mode, and some of these tunes have never oozed quite so much; Rugolo provides limousine-class charts. *Billy's Best* is a beauty which we have petitioned for reissue in the past, so it is a special pleasure to welcome it in such splendid remastering. 'When The Sun Comes Out' shows how Eckstine could handle a high-stepping arrangement without seeming to require any exertion of his own, and the following 'I Got Lost In Her Arms' presents ardour as the most gentlemanly of emotions. The arrangements walk a line between vigour and schmooze, and there are six bonus tracks added to the original LP programme.

First choice here, though, must go to the two-disc set, *Everything I Have Is Yours*, which charts Eckstine's course with all his hits and a few plum rarities of the order of 'Mister You've Gone And Got The Blues'. The *Jazz Masters* disc boils it down to 16 tracks and throws in a previously unissued obscurity to tempt diehard collectors, 'I Lost My Sugar In Salt Lake City'.

**** **No Cover No Minimum** Roulette B21S-98583-2
  Eckstine; Charlie Walp (*t*); Bucky Manieri (*tb*); Charlie McLean, Buddy Balboa (*saxes*); Bobby
  Tucker (*p*); Buddy Grievey (*d*). 8/60.

A superlative example of Eckstine's art, and arguably his best record in print. Recorded at a Las Vegas lounge, the 21 tracks (12 of them previously unissued) luxuriate in Bobby Tucker's simple arrangements and bask in the grandeur of Eckstine's voice and phrasing. 'Moonlight In Vermont' has never sounded more richly expansive, 'Lush Life' is a proper ode to barfly poetry, and the swingers are delivered with an insouciance and a perfect mastery of metre which creates shivers of delight. A few trumpet solos are the least we can forgive him for, although actually they're not bad. The remastering is very full and vivid on what is an indispensable issue.

Harry 'Sweets' Edison (born 1915) TRUMPET

*** **Jawbreakers** Original Jazz Classics OJC 487
  Edison; Eddie 'Lockjaw' Davis (*ts*); Hugh Lawson (*p*); Ike Isaacs (*b*); Clarence Johnston (*d*). 4/
  62.
*** **Edison's Light** Original Jazz Classics OJC 804
  Edison; Eddie 'Lockjaw' Davis (*ts*); Count Basie, Dolo Coker (*p*); John Heard (*b*); Jimmie
  Smith (*d*). 5/76.
(*) **Sweets And Jaws Black & Blue 233106
  Edison; Eddie 'Lockjaw' Davis (*ts*); Gerald Wiggins (*p*); Major Holley (*b*); Oliver Jackson (*d*).
  2/77.
(*) **Simply Sweets Pablo 2310806
  Edison; Eddie 'Lockjaw' Davis (*ts*); Dolo Coker (*p*); Harvey Newmark (*b*); Jimmie Smith (*d*). 9/
  77.

Ubiquitous as an accompanist/soloist, Edison has made surprisingly few records of his own, given the length of his career. Like many players of his type, he often sounds better on other people's sessions than on his own, though the presence of Basie on *Edison's Light* audibly inspires him (compare the rather lacklustre tracks made on the same day with Coker). The 1970s association with Lockjaw Davis produced some of the best of his work, a bright, bursting sound which can also be quite reserved and contemplative; *Jawbreakers* comes highly recommended, a big, raw session that springs a romantic version of 'A Gal In Calico' which contrasts well with the tough funk of 'Oo-ee!'. The Pablos have a good, full sound and there's no great bonus in the Black & Blue CD transfer, though it does have the best of several available readings of 'There Is No Greater Love', an Edison staple.

***(*) **For My Pals** Pablo 2310934
    Edison; Buster Cooper (*tb*); Curtis Peagler (*as, ts*); Art Hillery (*p, org*); Andrew Simpkins (*b*); Albert 'Tootie' Heath (*d*). 12/88.
*** **Swing Summit** Candid CCD 79050
    Edison; Buddy Tate (*cl, ts*); Frank Wess (*ts, f*); Hugh Lawson (*p*); Ray Drummond (*b*); Bobby Durham (*d*). 4/90.
*** **Swingin' Sweets** L + R CDLR 45076
    Edison; Frank Wess (*ts, f*); Hugh Lawson (*p*); Lindy Huppertsberg (*b*); Alvin Queen (*d*). 3/92.
*** **Live At Ambassador Auditorium** Concord CCD 4610
    Edison; Ken Peplowski (*cl, ts*); Howard Alden (*g*); Ben Aronov (*p*); Murray Wall (*b*); Tom Melito (*d*). 2/94.
Edison's artistic longevity has been remarkable; his ability and willingness continually to develop is nothing short of miraculous. *For My Pals*, with a larger than usual group, marks a welcome return to form; 'Lover Man' and 'There Is No Greater Love' are both top-notch performances and the sound is immaculate. *Swing Summit* contains less interesting material, but is brightly and faithfully recorded, and excellent value.

    The L + R has a candid, eavesdropping quality, a lack of deliberation and polish that may well be the best way to catch Sweets nowadays. His drop-in with the Ken Peplowski group at the Ambassador Auditorium in Pasadena is masterfully timed and judged. Like all great statesmen, he says nothing of substance but gives even vacancy a kind of grandeur.

Teddy Edwards (born 1924) TENOR SAXOPHONE, CLARINET

***(*) **Steady With Teddy** Cool N' Blue C & B CD 115
    Edwards; Benny Bailey, Howard McGhee (*t*); Iggy Shevack (*tb*); Dexter Gordon (*ts*); Duke Brooks, Hampton Hawes, Dodo Marmarosa, Jimmy Rowles (*p*); Arvin Garrison (*g*); Red Callender, Addison Farmer, Bob Kesterson (*b*); Roy Porter (*d*). 10/46, 7 & 12/47, 8/48.
***(*) **Teddy's Ready** Original Jazz Classics OJC 1785
    Edwards; Joe Castro (*p*); Leroy Vinnegar (*b*); Billy Higgins (*d*). 8/60.
*** **Back To Avalon** Contemporary CCD 14074
    Edwards; Nathaniel Meeks (*t*); Lester Robertson (*tb*); Jimmy Woods (*as*); Modesto Brisenio (*bs*); Danny Horton (*p*); Roger Alderson (*b*); Lawrence Marable (*d*). 12/60.
**** **Together Again!** Original Jazz Classics OJC 424
    Edwards; Howard McGhee (*t*); Phineas Newborn Jr (*p*); Ray Brown (*b*); Ed Thigpen (*d*). 5/61.
***(*) **Good Gravy** Original Jazz Classics OJC 661
    Edwards; Danny Horton, Phineas Newborn Jr (*p*); Leroy Vinnegar (*b*); Milton Turner (*d*). 8/61.
*** **Heart And Soul** Original Jazz Classics OJC 177
    Edwards; Gerry Wiggins (*org*); Leroy Vinnegar (*b*); Milton Turner (*d*). 62.
*** **Nothin' But The Truth** Original Jazz Classics OJC 813
    Edwards; Walter Davis Jr (*p*); Phil Orlando (*g*); Paul Chambers (*b*); Billy Higgins (*d*), Montego Joe (*perc*). 12/66.
*** **Out Of This World** Steeplechase SCS 1147
    Edwards; Kenny Drew (*p*); Jesper Lundgaard (*b*); Billy Hart (*d*). 12/80.
** **Good Gravy** Timeless SJP 139
    Edwards; Rein De Graaff (*p*); Henk Haverhoek (*b*); John Engels (*d*). 12/81.
Unrated as a soloist, Edwards is still one of the most influential voices around. He came through in his early twenties on the West Coast, playing with Howard McGhee, Benny Bailey , and in front of the likes of Dodo Marmarosa and Hampton Hawes, boppers who put a lyrical spin on the familiar changes. Tracks like 'Dilated Pupils' from the 1946 session (a McGhee composition, significantly) suggest the sort of background he was working against. Though he has had his ups and downs, Edwards's relaxed, imperturbable manner has sustained him well; 'steady with Teddy' has been the watchword. His reunion with a cleaned-up Howard McGhee in 1962 led to one of the best mainstream albums of the post-war years. *Together Again!* is beautifully and almost effortlessly crafted. The ultra-straight 'Misty' showcases Edwards's moody ballad approach and there is a fine 'You Stepped Out Of A Dream'. Three months

later, and without a second horn, Edwards waffles and digresses engagingly but doesn't quite get into the frame. Horton depped for Newborn for much of the three-day session; he's a bright enough lad, but lacks horsepower and swing. Vinnegar is as surefire as ever.

Recorded in 1960, *Back To Avalon* was an interesting attempt at arrangement for a mid-size band. The problem is that the Octet doesn't generate quite the head of steam the blandness of these charts requires in compensation, and there isn't enough going on on the solo front, including a rather subdued and preoccupied Edwards. Even the workhorse 'Good Gravy' fails to raise a cheer. Lester Koenig's recording can't shoulder any significant blame, and the remix for CD restores a lot of detail.

Nothing quite compares, then, to the session with McGhee, though *Teddy's Ready* (originally on Contemporary) has a timeless vigour that makes it endlessly repeatable. It followed a period of ill-health – unrelated, it should be said, to the usual perils of a jazzman's life in those days – and one can hear the relief and delight in the slightly too hasty attack on 'Scrapple From The Apple' and 'Take The "A" Train'. In later years, Edwards was reliably to be found *behind* the beat. Not a great deal is known nowadays about Arizonan Castro and he tends to be thought of as an accomplished accompanist (Anita O'Day and June Christy) who never quite made it as a straight jazz player. On this showing he's more than worthy, and the support of his two colleagues here goes without saying.

The rather later *Nothin' But The Truth* is similarly well manned but, with the exception of 'But Beautiful' and the title-track (to but no more buts than that), it's a rather routine set. Even with a rhythm section of this quality, Edwards doesn't sound inclined to hurry or be infused with anything more dynamic than his usual step-up-and-play approach. The 1980s material is pretty much of a piece, but Edwards isn't on form for the confusingly titled *Good Gravy*. He also lacks a convincing bass player. Spoilt by Leroy Vinnegar, Edwards never again found someone who could put so much relaxed spring into his solo gait. Haverhoek copes manfully but hasn't the lyricism to match the firmly accented pulse.

There's no point by-passing *Together Again!*. Subsequent ports of call should be *Teddy's Ready* and *Out Of This World*, in that order.

** Mississippi Lad Verve 511 411
Edwards; Nolan Smith (*t*); Jimmy Cleveland (*tb*); Art Hillery (*p*); Leroy Vinnegar (*b*); Billy Higgins (*d*); Ray Armando (*d*); Tom Waits (*v*). 3/91.

** Blue Saxophone Verve 517 298
Edwards; Frank Szabo, Oscar Brashear, James B. Smith (*t*); Thurman Green, Maurice Spears (*tb*); Art Hillery (*p*); Andrew Simpkins (*b*); Mel Brown (*d*); Brenton Banks, Michael White, Mark Cargill (*vn*); Dan Weinstein (*vla*); Melissa Hasin (*clo*); Carol Robbins (*hp*); Lisa Nobumoto (*v*). 6/92.

Tom Waits is much like olives. People either love him or *really* dislike him. He actually appears on only two songs, the disconcerting opener, 'Little Man', and the later 'I'm Not Your Fool Anymore', both with music and lyrics by Edwards. It's also clear, by way of a further consolation to the olive-haters, that Edwards, denied his share of recording opportunities in recent years, probably couldn't have made *Mississippi Lad* without Waits's enthusiastic imprimatur and crossover marketability.

In practice, the album is a sorry mish-mash of up-tempo Latino dance-numbers, oozing ballads and a couple of good, straightforward jazz pieces. 'Symphony On Central' opens promisingly with Vinnegar's instantly recognizable walking bass and Higgins's incisive cymbal pattern; both later solo, and Higgins fans will be reassured to think he had nothing to do with the idiotic percussion solo on 'Safari Walk'. By and large, though, 'Symphony' and the following 'Ballad For A Bronze Beauty' are features for the leader and rhythm, with the other horns and Señor Armando out. A disappointing album but, as the man said, parts of it are excellent.

Blue Saxophone goes downhill steadily from Edwards's unaccompanied 'Prelude'. There are flashes: his solo on 'Lennox Lady' and the clarinet feature on 'Serenade In Blue'. However, his self-touted lyrics border on the mawkish. His monologue on 'Blue Saxophone' itself is just rather banal, and Nobumoto doesn't have the character or presence to establish herself in the session. A disappointment, but one with a few moments to treasure.

*** La Villa: Live In Paris Verve 523 495
Edwards; Christian Escoude (*g*); Alain Jean-Marie (*p*); Thomas Bramerie (*b*); Alvester Garnett (*d*); Spanky Wilson (*v*); strings. 11/93.

What's the old chap's ideal of bliss these days? A box of reeds where more than one in four makes a musical sound, a spot of dinner, and a friendly crowd. At almost seventy, Edwards approaches a gig with complete relaxation, on the basis that if he's enjoying himself, we probably will too. This was recorded over two nights – not quite a week apart – at the eponymous club in Paris. Escoude is a bonus, but we're not entirely sure that the strings or vocalist Spanky Wilson add much of any substance. On familiar stuff like 'Lover Man' and 'Good Gravy', Edwards just goes his own blissful way, elegantly melodic, reliably inventive, completely laid back. It's hard not to like a record like this, but it would be possible to underestimate or simply to miss the mature artistry hidden away on it.

Marty Ehrlich (born 1955) REEDS, FLUTES

*** The Welcome sound aspects sas 002

Ehrlich; Anthony Cox (*b*); Pheeroan akLaff (*d*). 3/84.

Ehrlich maintains a consistent level of excellence on all his instruments – he's a pungent improviser with a colourful imagination – but it's his work on B-flat and bass-clarinets which is most striking, since he uses them as often as he does the more familiarly contemporary alto sax and flute. An interest in collective improvisation and a taste for folkish melodies give this trio a feel comparable to Ornette Coleman's mid-1960s group, and Ehrlich, Cox and akLaff respond keenly to each other's playing. The recording is a little dry.

**** Pliant Plaint Enja 5065

Ehrlich; Stan Strickland (*ss, ts, f*); Anthony Cox (*b*); Bobby Previte (*d*). 4/87.

***(*) The Traveller's Tale Enja 6024

As above, except Lindsey Horner (*b*) replaces Cox. 5–6/89.

Ehrlich's Enja albums provide entertaining samplers for the breadth of contemporary jazz. His compositions are eclectic in the best way, drawing on different rhythmic and formal backgrounds but impressed with his own spirited playing. Strickland, a gutsy and agile tenor player, is an excellent foil for the leader and both rhythm sections are fine, though Cox is marginally more responsive than Horner. We prefer *Pliant Plaint* for its sense of variety: there's an impeccable composed piece, 'After After All', played by Ehrlich alone in a series of overdubs, and an enchanting flute duet on 'What I Know Now', along with more familiar thematic improvising on the other pieces. *The Traveller's Tale* is nearly as good, though, with Ehrlich sounding strong on four different reeds.

***(*) Side By Side Enja 5065-2

Ehrlich; Frank Lacy (*tb*); Wayne Horvitz (*p*); Anthony Cox (*b*); Andrew Cyrille (*d*). 1/91.

*** Falling Man Muse MCD 5398

Ehrlich; Anthony Cox (*b*). 90.

Side By Side continues an exceptionally rewarding sequence of records. Ehrlich's instinct for good tunes accompanies ensemble playing and direction which go about as far out from hard-bop orthodoxy as they can: it's highly melodic and rhythmically liberated free playing, with enough arranged detail to keep a composer's sensibility happy. Lacy and Ehrlich are all over their horns, and the rhythm section play just as strongly. *Falling Man* reduces the cast to two, with a certain loss of individuality as a result: by himself, Ehrlich isn't so interesting a soloist, and there's only so much that he can find to say in tandem with Cox, though 'You Don't Know What Love Is' – a retrospective nod at Mingus and Dolphy, two very kindred influences – is very good.

*** Emergency Peace New World NW 80409

Ehrlich; Muhal Richard Abrams (*p*); Abdul Wadud (*clo*); Lindsey Horner (*b*). 12/90.

Ehrlich sets himself another difficult programme here, with the contrasting resonances of Wadud and Horner making an intriguing bottom-line (Abrams plays piano on only two of the nine tracks). Ehrlich can't help but recall Julius Hemphill in duo with Wadud, and when they actually do a Hemphill tune ('The Painter') the comparison doesn't really favour him. Ehrlich calls this group the 'Dark Woods Ensemble', a useful image, and when the three of them (Ehrlich on bass clarinet) execute the grave dance of 'Unison', they make a real identity out of it. But some of it either merely meanders or runs on too long.

***(*) Can You Hear A Motion? Enja 8052-2

Ehrlich; Stan Strickland (*ts, f*); Michael Formanek (*b*); Bobby Previte (*d*). 9/93.

*** Just Before The Dawn New World/CounterCurrents 80474

Erhrlich; Vincent Chauncey (*frhn*); Erik Friedlander (*clo*); Mark Helias (*b*); Don Alias (*perc*). 94.

Ehrlich invites many comparisons in his playing, but the spirit which is starting to seem closest to his is Anthony Braxton's. While the opening clarinet tune on *Can You Hear A Motion?* is a dedication to John Carter, it's Braxtonian tone and logic one hears. Ehrlich humanizes the approach: he gets bite and swing out of this woodsy-sounding quartet and inculcates a rural feel into a team which includes such urbanites as Formanek and Previte. 'The Welcome' pivots on a township-like melody, while 'Ode To Charlie Parker' is a chamber-piece for clarinet, flute and bass, and a lovely one too. This probably counts as Ehrlich's best disc since *Pliant Plaint*. The latest Dark Woods Ensemble record, *Just Before The Dawn*, is as highly coloured but a shade less vivacious in the playing: sometimes the group gets a little hung up on its own sounds and shadings, perhaps.

Thore Ehrling (born 1912) TRUMPET, VOCAL

*** Jazz Highlights Dragon DRCD 236

Ehrling; Gosta Redlig, Gosta Pettersson, Gosta Torner, Rune Ander, Yngve Nilsson, Olle Jacobson, Arnold Johansson, Putte Bjorn, John Linder, Nisse Skoog (*t*); Georg Vernon, Sverre Oredson, Sven Hedberg, Andreas Skjold (*tb*); Ove Rann, Curt Blomquist, Erik Andersson, John Bjorling, Carl-Henrik Noren, Casper Hjukstrom, Stig Gabrielsson, Gunnar Lunden-Welden, Arne Domnérus, Harry Arnold, Fritz Fust, Rolf Londell, Georg Bjorklund, Mats Borgstrom (*reeds*); Stig Holm, Mats Olsson (*p*); Folke Eriksberg, Sven Stiberg (*g*); Thore Jederby, Hasse Tellemar (*b*); Anders Solden, Gosta Heden, Uffe Baadh, Henry Wallin, Bertil Frylmark (*d*). 1/39–12/55.

**(*) Swedish Swing 1945–1947 Ancha ANC 9503-2

Similar to above. 3/45–7/47.

A sizeable slice of Swedish jazz history is packed on to this 26-track CD, decently remastered from some rare originals. Ehrling had already worked in dance bands for many years before forming his first orchestra in 1938 – he had been a Benny Carter sideman two years earlier – and, although his band made as many concessions to popular taste as did Basie and Ellington, they made enough good jazz-directed records to grant this retrospective more than a passing interest. Among the early tracks, a very swinging 'Roses Of Picardy' and a Dorsey-like 'Meditation' are impressive. Carl-Henrik Norin's arrival brought his interesting tunes to the book, including the Ellingtonian 'Mississippi Mood', but the later tracks suggest that Ehrling never got much further than the solidly competitive swing style that was established by the early 1940s. Soloists are more functional than inspiring, although Ove Ronn's Hodges-like alto is always worth catching, as is Norin, and Domnérus appears on one track. A pleasing tribute to a great name in Swedish jazz.

The Ancha disc is for more dedicated tastes, since it covers a couple of broadcasts from the mid-'40s. The first is all Ellington, done with a surprising amount of panache, though the arrangements seem like slavish copies. The second is by a nonet, with Bjorling's clarinet taking a significant role and a couple of kitsch items betraying the music's dance-hall origins. The second set is a bit crackly, but sound is otherwise clear enough.

8 Bold Souls GROUP

** 8 Bold Souls Open Minds SOM 2409-2

Robert Griffin (*t, flhn*); Isaiah Jackson (*tb*); Edward Wilkerson (*as, ts, bs, cl*); Mwata Bowden (*ts, bs, cl*); Aaron Dodd (*tba*); Naomi Millender (*clo*); Richard Brown (*b*); Dushun Mosley (*d*). 86.

***(*) Sideshow Arabesque AJO103

As above, except Harrison Bankhead (*b*) replaces Brown. 11/91.

***(*) Antfarm Arabesque AJO114

As above.

This big, surprising group made real progress with its second record. We were unimpressed by the first record in our first edition, although prolonged acquaintance and cleaner CD sound have revealed a more interesting core: by emphasizing the unusual timbres of the instrumentation, Chicagoan Edward Wilkerson's group creates a singular ensemble sound that is finally more interesting than the often impassioned solos. The use of low brass (Dodd is a key player) and the ponderous tempos are more interesting than the sometimes incoherent faster pieces on the debut. But *Sideshow* is more impressive in every way. Wilkerson takes his time – there are only five pieces on a record running well over an hour – and the opening 'Black Herman' is an ominous masterpiece, grown from a simple riff into a fascinating series of contrasting groupings, with the leader's severe tenor solo as the icing on a rich cake. It's slightly disappointing that he grants himself only one further improvisation on the record, and the very long rendition of Coleman's 'Lonely Woman' is a shade unconvincing in its explosive central section; but the contributions from Griffin, Bowden, Dodd and Millender are vivid compensation, and the stealthy, deliberate pace of the record is finally hypnotic.

Antfarm is a fine continuation. Again, Wilkerson refuses to hurry himself, with the title-piece running at 16 minutes and the shortest of the others reaching 8 minutes 27 seconds. His debt to Henry Threadgill's early work is perhaps even more clear, with his own tenor solo on 'Half Life' re-creating the atmosphere of a classic Air performance, and the rumbustious ensembles and bizarre contrasts walk in Henry's footsteps. But the group has its own democratic character: Jackson, Bowden and Griffin impress as individual voices, growing in stature, and the leader's writing always seems to have a surprise up its sleeve. Another valuable report from Chicago in the 1990s.

Either/Orchestra GROUP

*** Dial E Accurate AC-2222
Tom Halter, Dave Ballou, Bob Sealy, Dan Drexter (*t*); Russell Jewell, Josh Roseman (*tb*); Rob Rawlings, Bob Sinfonia (*as*); Russ Gershon (*ts*); Steve Norton (*bs*); Kenny Freundlich (*ky*); John Dirac (*g*); Mike Rivard (*b*); Jerome Deupree (*d*). 7/86.

***(*) Radium Accurate AC-3232
Tom Halter, John Carlson (*t, flhn*); Russell Jewell, Curtis Hasselbring (*tb*); Rob Rawlings (*as*); Russ Gershon (*ss, ts*); Charlie Kohlhase (*bs*); Kenny Freundlich (*ky*); John Dirac (*g*); Mike Rivard (*b*); Jerome Deupree (*d*). 8/87–1/88

***(*) The Half-Life Of Desire Accurate AC-3242
As above, except add Douglas Yates (*ss, as*), Dave Finucane (*bcl*), John Medeski (*ky*), Mark Sandman (*g, v*). 89.

**** The Calculus Of Pleasure Accurate AC-3252
As above, except add Bob Nieske (*b*) and Matt Wilson (*d*), omit Freundlich, Dirac, Rivard, Deupree, Finucane, Sandman. 4–6/90.

**** The Brunt Accurate AC-3262
As above, except add Dan Fox (*tb*), Andrew D'Angelo (*as, bcl, cl*), Chris Taylor (*ky*), John Turner (*b*), omit Hasselbring, Yates, Medeski, Nieske. 5/93.

A modest-sized big band full of outsize talents, Either/Orchestra have made scarcely any international impact. Leader Russ Gershon has squeezed these CDs out of the impossible restrictions which modern budgets have set for this kind of band if it wants to work and make records: it's a heroic accomplishment that the group is as swinging, exciting and cheerfully cutting-edge as it is. All three records are a rag-bag of favourite cover versions, bristling originals and complexities which only the most skilful and hungry players could go for broke with. *Dial E*, their debut, has made it to CD only recently: comparatively rough-and-ready compared with the finesse of the later discs, it's still an exciting and unpredictable record. Rollins's 'Doxy' is turned into an outlandish shuffle, they have the chutzpah to take apart 'Brilliant Corners', and the extravagantly extended '17 December' is an early manifesto of what the band could do. *Radium* is all live and runs the gamut from a tragedian's version of 'Willow Weep For Me' to a madcap distillation of 'Nutty' and 'Ode To Billie Joe', with Roscoe Mitchell's 'Odwalla' as a bonus. *The Half-Life Of Desire* expands the palette a little by dint of Medeski's arrival: this brilliant keyboardist has a sure grasp of which electronics will and which won't work in a neo-trad context, and on Gershon's 'Strange Meridian' he blends acoustic and electric parts with perfect aplomb. Rock and 'world' musics get only a modest look-in on this group's work: their materials come largely from within jazz language itself, which sets them a little apart from such groups as Peter Apfelbaum's ensemble. Yet they still manage to cover the King Crimson metal blow-out, 'Red', and tamper with Miles Davis's 'Circle In The Round' on the same record.

The Calculus Of Pleasure, part live and part studio in origin, is arguably their best to date. There is an astonishing arrangement of Horace Silver's 'Ecaroh', previously a piano-trio tune, and a sour, lavish update of Benny Golson's 'Whisper Not' which is an object lesson in renewing stale jazz repertory. Julius Hemphill's 'The Hard Blues' also comes in for a grandly decadent interpretation, brass and reeds fattening up the harmonies as never before – which leaves five originals from within the band's own ranks. Mention should also be made of soloists such as Medeski, Hasselbring, Yates and Kohlhase, foot-soldiers and front-liners alike.

There is no falling-off in quality with *The Brunt*. Though both Hasselbring and Medeski have departed, the team remains terrifically strong as a playing unit: the complexities of 'Notes On A Cliff' and the swaggering 'Permit Blues' are shrugged off, and the title-piece, a bequest by Hasselbring, is a feast of overlapping ideas. One of their most dramatic repertory adventures takes place in Mal Waldron's 'Hard Talk', and only the Ellington piece, 'Blues For New Orleans', disappoints – but that is classic Ellington. The charming retread of Bob Dylan's 'Lay Lady Lay' is a fitting finale and reminds that the band's secret may lie in acting good-humoured rather than merely being humorous. This is also their best-recorded CD.

Roy Eldridge (1911–88) TRUMPET, VOCAL, PIANO

***(*) The Big Sound Of Little Jazz Topaz TPZ 1021
Eldridge; Al Beck, Bill Coleman, Torg Halten, Mickey Mangano, Norman Murphy, Joe Thomas, Dick Vance, Graham Young (*t*); Fernando Arbello, Joe Conigliaro, Ed Cuffee, John Grassi, Jay Kelliher, Babe Wagner, Dicky Wells (*tb*); Buster Bailey, Benny Goodman, Cecil Scott (*cl*); Omer Simeon (*cl, as, bs*); Russell Procope (*cl, as*); Sam Musiker (*cl, ts*); Scoops Carey, Benny Carter, Joe Eldridge, Ben Feman, Andrew Gardner, Hilton Jefferson, Howard Johnson,

Rex Kittig, Jimmy Migliore, Clint Neagley, Mascagni Ruffo (*as*); Tom Archia, Walter Bates, Chu Berry, Don Brassfield, Coleman Hawkins, Teddy Hill, Ike Quebec, Ben Webster, Elmer Williams, Dave Young (*ts*); Sam Allen, Teddy Cole, Rozelle Gayle, Clyde Hart, Horace Henderson, Bob Kitsis, Joe Springer, Jess Stacy, Teddy Wilson (*p*); Bernard Addison, Danny Barker, Ray Biondi, John Collins, Bob Lessey, Lawrence Lucie, Allan Reuss, John Smith (*g*); Biddy Bastien, Israel Crosby, Richard Fullbright, John Kirby, Ed Mihelich, Truck Parham, Artie Shapiro, Ted Sturgis (*b*); Bill Beason, Big Sid Catlett, Cozy Cole, Gene Krupa, Zutty Singleton, Harold 'Doc' West (*d*). 2/35–11/43.

*** **Roy Eldridge, 1935–1940** Classics 766
Similar to above.

***(*) **After You've Gone** G R P Decca 16052
Eldridge; Gus Aiken, Henry Clay, Paul Cohen, Sidney De Paris, Andy Ferretti, Bill Graham, Tom Grider, John Bugs Hamilton, Marion Hazel, Elton Hill, Yank Lawson, Sylvester Lewis, Robert Mason, Jimmy Maxwell, Dave Page, Pinky Savitt, Jim Thomas, Clarence Wheeler, Elmon Wright (*t*); Nat Atkins, Will Bradley, Wilbur De Paris, Vic Dickenson, Richard Dunlap, Charles Greenlea, Ted Kelly, John McConnell, Hal Matthews, Fred Ohms, Albert Riding, Fred Robinson, George Robinson, Ward Silloway, George Stevenson, Sandy Watson, Sandy Williams, Gerald Wilson (*tb*); Buster Bailey (*c*); Curby Alexander, Mike Doty, Ray Eckstrand, Joe Eldridge, Andrew Gardner, Edmond Gregory (Sahib Shihab), Chris Johnson, Porter Kilbert, Sam Lee (*as*); Tom Archia, Chu Berry, Charles Bowen, Al Green, Franz Jackson, George Lawson, Walt Lockhart, Don Purvance, Ike Quebec, Mike Ross, Hal Singer, Harold Webster (*ts*); Ernie Caceres, Dave McRae, Cecil Payne, Al Townsend (*bs*); Dave Bowman, Ted Brannon, Tony D'Amore, Teddy Cole, Rozelle Gayle, Buster Harding, Duke Jordan (*p*); Sam Allen, Mike Bryan, John Collins, Luke Fowler (*g*); Louis Carrington, John Kirby, Carl Pruitt, Rodney Richardson, Ted Sturgin, Billy Taylor, Carl Wilson (*b*); Lee Abrams, Big Sid Catlett, Cozy Cole, Les Erskine, Earl Phillips, Mel Saunders, Harold West (*d*). 2/36–9/46.

**** **Heckler's Hop** Hep CD 1030
Similar to above, except add Prince Robinson, Franz Jackson (*ts*); Panama Francis (*d*); Helen Ward, Gladys Palmer, Laurel Watson (*v*). 36–39.

Roy Eldridge has been widely acknowledged as the bridge between swing and bebop trumpet. Listening to Dizzy Gillespie at the (in)famous Massey Hall concert with Charlie Parker, Charles Mingus, Bud Powell and Max Roach, there is very little doubt about the ancestry of the trumpeter's high-register accents. However, Eldridge can't just be seen as Moses who led his people out of the desert of late swing and up to the borders of bop's promised land. Eldridge did his thing longer and more consistently than the modernists' version of the story would have you believe.

Eldridge moved to New York in 1934 and was quickly recognized as a new star. The introductory bars of '(Lookie, Lookie, Lookie) Here Comes Cookie', first item on the valuable Topaz compilation, offers a glimpse of the excitement the youngster must have caused. His ability to displace accents and play questionable intervals with perfect confidence and logic is immediately evident. More than just a high-note man, Eldridge combined remarkable rhythmic intuition with an ability to play intensely exciting music in the middle and lower register, often the acid test that separates the musicians from the instrumentalists. His solo on 'Blue Lou', recorded with the Fletcher Henderson band in March 1936 (see *After You've Gone*) is a perfect case in point. He does the same kind of thing with the Teddy Wilson band on 'Blues In C Sharp Minor', fitting his improvisation perfectly to the moody key; Chu Berry's follow-up and Israel Crosby's tensely throbbing bass complete a masterful performance. At the other end of the emotional spectrum, there are the starburst top Cs (and beyond) of 'Heckler's Hop', high point of an excellent set as leader with a band anchored on Zutty Singleton's tight drumming. The vocal tracks with Mildred Bailey are often quite appealing and show how responsive an accompanist Eldridge was, again able to play quietly and in contralto range when called upon. A solitary Billie Holiday track – 'Falling In Love Again' – gives a flavour only of that association, which is more fully documented under her name.

After You've Gone is a valuable compilation of 'Little Jazz' 's American Decca recordings of the late war years, with one brief glimpse back at the sessions with clarinettist Buster Bailey and tenor saxophonist Chu Berry two years before the more familiar Little Jazz Ensemble dates on Commodore Classics' valuable Chu Berry compilation, *A Giant Of The Tenor Sax*. The set includes some material never before released commercially, like a 'St Louis Blues' used on a 1965 Decca promotional for *Life* magazine (doubtless pitched in *Life*'s inimitably condescending way). The transfers are done on the Sonic Solutions' NoNoise system, which leaves the masters clean but a little bleached-out in some areas. Eldridge occupies most of the foreground, whacking out top notes like Satchmo had never been heard of; the opening of (an unissued) 'I Surrender, Dear' is almost absurdly skyscraping. Unfortunately, Eldridge has been saddled with the reputation of being a high-note man. His muted 'stroll' opening to his own composition, 'The Gasser', is equally typical, giving way to a fine soulful solo from Ike Quebec, and then Eldridge again in more familiar mode on open horn.

The sound is less crystalline on the Topaz (and decidedly muddy in places on the weirdly inconsistent Classics), but both of these cover pretty much the same material. As the massed personnels will again suggest, it selects from the broadest range of bands and sessions, starting with Teddy Hill, taking in Krupa, Henderson, the Little Jazz Ensemble with Chu, the Chocolate Dandies with Carter, and the other Teddy, the urbane Wilson. In just over an hour it offers a pretty straightforward and representative account of the first decade of activity.

Long before he became known as a JATP stalwart and itinerant sitter-in, Eldridge had sounded comfortable in front of big bands, where his reaching tone and simple phrasing sounded less forced than they can in smaller groups. There is a lovely 'Body And Soul' (compare the version with Berry, above) and a fine 'I Can't Get Started' with the October 1944 line-up that yields the teasing, stop-start 'After You've Gone' (it's the only piece with an alternative take, though there are a couple of incompletes). 'Embraceable You' from the following year is equally fine; but the quality thins badly around this point in the compilation. None of the later tracks matches up to the astonishing ripping intensity of his tone on 'Star Dust' with the 1943 group, which counts as one of his finest performances ever, studded in the middle chorus with a single high note.

There is much to recommend the Hep selection, not least a high-quality transfer that renders such notes with absolute clarity and minimum distortion. Though it covers a shorter chronological span and puts undue emphasis on less than startling singers, its immediacy and presence (check out the end of 'After You've Gone', a classic Eldridge moment) make it the item of choice for us.

Given the dominance of Dizzy and the alternative direction opened up by Miles, Eldridge's work has been at something of a premium in recent years. These, though, are essential – and usefully complementary – documents of modern jazz and offer a salutary lesson for anyone who still tends to think of the music as a sequence of upper-case historical styles.

***(*) **Nuts** Vogue 115468
> Eldridge; Zoot Sims (*ts*); Dick Hyman, Gerald Wiggins (*p*); Pierre Michelot (*b*); Kenny Clarke, Eddie Shaughnessy (*d*); Anita Love (*v*). 6/50.

*** **French Cooking** Vogue 115469
> Eldridge; Benny Vasseur (*tb*); Don Byas, Albert Ferreri (*ts*); William Boucaya (*bs*); Claude Bolling, Raymond Fol, Gerald Wiggins (*p*); Guy De Fatto, Pierre Michelot, Barney Spieler (*b*); Robert Barney, Kenny Clarke, Armand Molinetti (*d*). 50–51.

The two Vogues catch the trumpeter in his first year-and-a-bit of exile, insulated from the virtual gang-warfare of big-band jazz Stateside in which Eldridge – as brittle as he was aggressive – got badly cut. The earlier disc uses a group made up of Goodman bandsmen, with Michelot recruited from the local register. It's a session with quality written all over it, replete with alternative takes, a couple of false starts on the tricksy 'Undecided' and every sign that the wee guy was enjoying himself greatly. His lip sounds sure and in shape from the opening number onwards, but 'The Man I Love', played once with authentic anguish, then again with a bit more finish, and 'Wrap Your Troubles In Dreams' are the high points. He's muted for 'Undecided' but otherwise seems to prefer to play open. The later session, recorded five days later, is much less polished. Though all four are playing well, nothing seems to click.

The October 1950 band didn't have the pedigree of its predecessors. Vasseur, Ferreri and Boucaya were decent enough section players but they didn't have two original ideas to rub together, and Eldridge is left to do all the hard work. The sessions with Don Byas and Claude Bolling are excellent, and there are two fascinating duos – 'Fireworks' and 'Wild Man Blues' – with the pianist. These were made just as Roy was preparing to go back to the United States and were done as a kind of tribute to the legendary Armstrong–Hines recordings. At the end of the disc are three tracks made by Eldridge at the piano. He sounds a bit like Dizzy at the keyboard, unfussy and direct, with a nice left hand.

**** **Little Jazz: The Best Of The Verve Years** Verve 523 338
> Eldridge; Joe Ferrante, Bernie Glow, Ernie Royal, Nick Travis (*t*); Jimmy Cleveland, J. J. Johnson, Fred Ohms, Kai Winding, Benny Morton, Vic Dickenson (*tb*); Eddie Barefield (*cl*); Sam Marowitz, Hal McKusick, Benny Carter, Johnny Hodges, Sonny Stitt (*as*); Aaron Sachs, Eddie Shu, Coleman Hawkins, Ben Webster (*ts*); Danny Bank (*bs*); Oscar Peterson (*p, org*); Dave McKenna, Dick Wellstood, Billy Strayhorn, Bruce Macdonald, Hank Jones, Ronnie Ball (*p*); Barney Kessel, Barry Galbraith, Herb Ellis (*g*); Ray Brown, John Drew, Walter Page, John Simmons, Jimmy Woode, Bennie Moten, George Duvivier (*b*); Jo Jones, J. C. Heard, Gene Krupa, Alvin Stoller, Buddy Rich, Sam Woodyard, Eddie Locke, Mickey Sheen (*d*); Anita O'Day (*v*); Russell Garcia Orchestra, George Williams Orchestra. 12/51–6/60.

Say what you like about Norman Granz, he gets the best people to his parties. The Verve years were happy and productive for Little Jazz. There is hardly a dull track on this excellent compilation. Only the opening number, Roy's classic 'I Remember Harlem', is disappointing, not because the trumpeter is less than superb but because the George Williams Orchestra is less than ideally registered. The live cut with Stitt, Peterson and Ellis at the 1957 Newport Festival is good enough to have merited more than a single representative from that triumphant day, and the same goes for the March 1955 stuff with Benny Carter, who induces Eldridge to play more quietly and thoughtfully.

Peterson proves to have been the most sympathetic accompanist, whether on piano or organ (the latter, memorably, on 'Blue Moon') but the late group with Ronnie Ball does some wonderful things with 'Dreamy' and 'When I Grow Too Old To Dream'. He never did.

***(*) **Roy And Diz** Verve 521 647
> Eldridge; Dizzy Gillespie (*t, v*); Oscar Peterson (*p*); Herb Ellis (*g*); Ray Brown (*b*); Louie Bellson (*d*). 10/54.

They enjoyed this. A little friendly sparring, with just enough edge to get the juices on the move. Alongside the man who influenced his style more than any other, Dizzy sounds comfortable and in good humour. On 'Pretty Eyed Baby' they take turns at accompanying the other's scat chorus, but the gloves are off for 'Limehouse Blues', where they try to cut one another like a pair of teenagers. Though thoroughly bested, Gillespie gets off a sarky quote from Eldridge's 'Heckler's Hop', only to find it taken up, turned around and thrown back with interest.

Despite the obvious kinship, it's interesting to compare their styles. Gillespie gets cornered on the long blues only because he's taken some chances with the sequence. Eldridge, by contrast, stays as close as possible to the original melody, embroidering it and turning it around, but not veering off into quite distant keys as the bop-nurtured Diz does almost as a matter of course. Peterson gives both hornmen a solid leg-up from time to time, but it's clear that his sympathies are mainly with Little Jazz. An old-fashioned, unpretentious session, and a good one.

*** **Just You, Just Me – Live In '59** Stash 531
> Eldridge; Coleman Hawkins (*ts*); Don Wilson (*p*); Bob Decker (*b*); Buddy Dean (*d*). 59.
**** **The Nifty Cat** New World 80349
> Eldridge; Benny Morton (*tb*); Budd Johnson (*ts, ss*); Nat Pierce (*p*); Tommy Bryant (*b*); Oliver Jackson (*d*). 11/70.
***(*) **Montreux '77** Original Jazz Classics OJC 373
> Eldridge; Oscar Peterson (*p*); Niels-Henning Orsted-Pedersen (*b*); Bobby Durham (*d*). 7/77.
*** **Roy Eldridge & Vic Dickenson** Storyville STCD 8239
> Eldridge; Vic Dickenson (*tb*); Budd Johnson (*ts*); Tommy Flanagan (*p*); Major Holley (*b*); Eddie Locke (*d*). 5/78.
*** **Happy Time** Original Jazz Classics OJC 628
> Eldridge; Oscar Peterson (p); Joe Pass (*g*); Ray Brown (*g*); Eddie Locke (*d*).
*** **Jazz Maturity . . . Where It's Coming From** Pablo 2310928
> Eldridge; Dizzy Gillespie (*t*); Oscar Peterson (*p*); Ray Brown (*b*); Mickey Roker (*d*).

Much of Eldridge's recorded output was for a time tucked away on trumpet compilations and festival albums. The major compilations above have done much to improve the situation; perhaps only the Benny Carter discography has been so comprehensively turned round in the same period. Even so, there is quite a lot of valuable Eldridge to be found on one-off sessions from later years. The Pablo with Diz and Peterson is pretty much a reworking of studio associations, but there were occasions in later years when the trumpeter found himself not so much reliving his old amities as reinventing them. The connection with Budd Johnson was a good case in point. The 1978 concert in St Peter's Church on Storyville is very relaxed and mild, but there are moments on the New World disc (an unexpected place to find Eldridge material) which are quite startling in their harmonic language, a further sign that Roy was always prepared to try new angles. Johnson doesn't hustle and bluster as Hawkins tended to do at this period, so there is every encouragement for the wee guy to proceed with some interestingly wayward stuff.

Along with the New World, perhaps the best of the later stuff is the Montreux set, part of a good series documenting what was considered to be a vintage year. The trumpeter appears to have regained some of his fire and sparkle and doesn't seem to require much notice for the upper-register stabs.

Eliane Elias (born 1960) PIANO

(*) **Plays Jobim Blue Note 793089-2
> Elias; Eddie Gomez (*b*); Jack DeJohnette (*d*); Nana Vasconcelos (*perc*). 12/89.
*** **Fantasia** Blue Note 796146-2
> Elias; Eddie Gomez, Marc Johnson (*b*); Jack DeJohnette, Peter Erskine (*d*); Nana Vasconcelos (*perc*); Ivan Lins, Amanda Elias Brecker (*v*). 91.
*** **Paulistana** Blue Note 789544-2
> As above, except add Jim Beard (*syn*), Cafe, Portinho (*perc*), Malcolm Pollack (*v*). 92

***(*) **Solos And Duets** Blue Note 832073-2
    Elias; Herbie Hancock (*p*). 11–12/94.
Elias's sequence of Blue Note albums make up an unashamedly enjoyable and increasingly personal synthesis of Latin and American jazz. If the *Plays Jobim* album seemed a mere confection, the subsequent records suggested that Elias was creating a good-natured but well-crafted interpretation of the best of her native Brazilian music which is more subtle and impressive than at first hearing. On each record she uses top-notch support in the bass and drums department, with the Gomez/DeJohnette and Johnson/Erskine teams grooving through multiple variations of bossa nova, samba and 4/4 jazz rhythms, while she chooses the most princely compositions by Jobim, Nascimento, Bonfa, Barroso and others alongside an occasional original of her own. The surprising revisions of 'The Girl From Ipanema' and 'No More Blues' on *Fantasia* and 'Black Orpheus' on *Paulistana* show a pleasing attempt to sidestep the clichés those tunes have built round themselves, and her discreet use of synthesizer and her own voice add further variety.
    Solos And Duets is perhaps even stronger. Although Hancock sits in for six entertaining duets, her own solo pieces are at least as impressive, with the spirited 'Autumn Leaves' and lush harmonies of 'Asa Branca' particularly appealing. The most 'American' of her records, but still attractively tinged with a Brazilian lilt.

The Elite Syncopators GROUP

*** **Ragtime Special** Stomp Off CD1286
    Terry Parrish (*p*); James Marshall (*bj*); Steve Ley (*tba*); Mike Schwimmer (*wbd, v*). 4–5/94.
Ragtime piano as a singleton enterprise is specialized enough, but placing it in the context of a repertory group is quite something in the 1990s. Of the 26 tracks here, all but three are original rags, two-steps or cakewalks of differing vintages, and it's some tribute to the expertise of the quartet – and that of the composers – that the music doesn't go stale across the duration of a long CD. The sometimes unvarying jollity of ragtime is tempered by intelligent programming – an occasional vocal, or the juxtaposition of reflectively melodic as opposed to pop-tune rags – and the graceful syncopation of the playing. Parrish's liner-notes offer useful background on all the tunes for hardcore scholars and, though this is a lot to take in at one sitting, determined cakewalkers will find it an indispensable primer.

Art Ellefson (born 1932) TENOR AND SOPRANO SAXOPHONES

*** **As If To Say** Sackville SKCD2-2030
    Ellefson; Lee Ellefson (*g*); Russell Botten (*b*); Buff Allen (*d*). 2/92.
Hidden away in British Columbia, Ellefson, who lived and played in the UK through most of the 1950s and '60s, is an accomplished hybrid of swing player and bopper. He has a way of phrasing a line that is almost nerveless in its placid inevitability, but there's a darker side to his tone that can make an improvisation turn sour at the edges. In this piano-less quartet, with his son Lee on guitar, the music has an air of abstraction which undercuts the songful melodies without defeating them. It's a little too unambitious and workmanlike, and Botten and Allen are content to play within themselves but the music is absorbing enough, and the 11 original themes are shot through with interesting touches.

Duke Ellington (1899–1974) PIANO

*** **Duke Ellington 1924–1927** Classics 542
    Ellington; Bubber Miley, Pike Davis, Harry Cooper, Leroy Rutledge, Louis Metcalf, June Clark (*t*); Jimmy Harrison (*tb, v*); Charlie Irvis, Joe 'Tricky Sam' Nanton (*tb*); Don Redman (*cl, as*); Otto Hardwick (*Cmel, as, ss, bs*); George Thomas (*as, v*); Edgar Sampson (*as*); Prince Robinson, Rudy Jackson (*ts, cl*); Harry Carney (*cl, ts, bs*); George Francis, Fred Guy (*bj*); Mack Shaw, Henry 'Bass' Edwards (*bb*); Sonny Greer (*d, v*); Alberta Jones, Irving Mills, Adelaide Hall (*v*). 11/24–11/26.
Ellington's story on record remains the most commanding legacy in the music, impossible to surpass. After the enormous and comprehensive LP reissues of the 1970s – specifically the multiple-disc sets issued by French RCA and CBS, as well as numerous and lengthy sequences of broadcast material from private labels – the industry has finally made headway with reissuing all this material on CD. With the copyright lapsed on all the pre-1940 records, smaller labels are now taking up the challenge of chronological reissues. The Classics sequence, meanwhile, currently stands at 27 discs, covering the period up to 1942; more will doubtless be available by the time we are in print. The Hot 'N Sweet

operation is also starting from scratch; for reasons of space (and more limited availability) we are not listing them separately here; but so far they have released 12 volumes leading up to 1932.

Classics are content to stick to the band sides leading up to the Victor version of 'Black And Tan Fantasy' in 1927; they have omitted a handful of obscure early accompaniments to singers. However, the very early material will be of interest only to scholars and the merely curious. Poor recording – the mastering of several tracks is rough and, in the absence of hearing high-quality originals ourselves, we're unsure as to how good a job has been done on some of the items – and a primitive, clumsy ensemble will be almost shocking to any who've never been acquainted with the earliest Ellington. Certainly the stiff rhythms and feeble attempts at solos on all the pre-1926 records are sometimes painful to hear, and if it weren't for Bubber Miley, the man who made Ellington 'forget all about the sweet music', there'd be nothing to detain anyone here. Yet Miley is already distinctive and powerful on his solo on The Washingtonians' 'Choo Choo' from November 1924. With 'East St Louis Toodle-oo', from the first important Ellington session, the music demands the attention. Any comprehensive edition will include much duplication, since Ellington spread himself around many different record labels: he recorded for Broadway, Vocalion, Gennett, Columbia, Harmony, Pathé, Brunswick, OKeh and Victor in the space of a little over three years. It also includes the first two versions of 'Black And Tan Fantasy', Ellington's first masterpiece, and Adelaide Hall's vocal on 'Creole Love Call'. Remastering is occasionally indifferent.

***(*) **Duke Ellington 1927–1928** Classics 542
    Ellington; Bubber Miley, Jabbo Smith, Louis Metcalf, Arthur Whetsol (*t*); Joe 'Tricky Sam' Nanton (*tb*); Otto Hardwick (*ss, as, bs, bsx*); Rudy Jackson, Barney Bigard (*cl, ts*); Harry Carney (*bs, as, ss, cl*); Fred Guy (*bj*); Wellman Braud (*b*); Sonny Greer (*d*); Adelaide Hall (*v*). 10/27–3/28.

***(*) **Duke Ellington 1928** Classics 550
    As above, except add Lonnie Johnson (*g*), Baby Cox, The Palmer Brothers (*v*); omit Jackson, Smith. 3–10/28.

*** **Duke Ellington 1928–29** Classics 559
    As above, except add Freddy Jenkins (*t*), Johnny Hodges (*cl, ss, as*), Ozie Ware, Irving Mills (*v*); omit Metcalf, Cox and Palmers. 10/28–3/29.

***(*) **The Complete Brunswick Recordings Vol. 1** MCA MCAD 42325
    As above three discs. 3/27–1/29.

Ellington progressed quickly from routine hot-dance records to sophisticated and complex three-minute works which showed a rare grasp of the possibilities of the 78-r.p.m. disc, a trait which he developed and exemplified better than anyone else in jazz from then until the 1950s. Yet during these years both Ellington and his band were still seeking a style that would turn them into a genuinely distinctive group. Having set down one or two individual pieces such as 'Black And Tan Fantasy' didn't mean that Duke was fully on his way. The 1926–8 records are still dominated to a high degree by the playing of Bubber Miley, and on a track such as 'Flaming Youth' (Classics 559), which was made as late as 1929, it is only Miley's superb work that makes the record of much interest. Arthur Whetsol made an intriguing contrast to Miley, his style being far more wistful and fragile: the way he plays 'The Mooche' on the 1928 Victor version is in striking contrast to Miley's delivery (all versions are on Classics 550), and his treatment of the theme to 'Black Beauty' (also on Classics 550) is similarly poignant. Joe Nanton was a shouting trombonist with a limited stock of phrases, but he was already starting to work on the muted technique which would make him into one of Duke's most indispensable players. It was already a great brass team. But the reeds were weaker, with Carney taking a low-key role (not always literally: he played as much alto and clarinet as baritone in this era), and until Bigard's arrival in 1928 it lacked a distinctive soloist. Hodges also didn't arrive until October 1928. When the Ellington band went into the Cotton Club at the end of 1927, the theatricality which had begun asserting itself with 'Black And Tan Fantasy' became a more important asset, and though most of the 'Jungle' scores were to emerge on record around 1929–30, 'The Mooche' and 'East St Louis Toodle-oo' show how set-piece effects were becoming important to Ellington. The best and most 'Ellingtonian' records of the period would include 'Blue Bubbles' (Classics 542), 'Take It Easy' and 'Jubilee Stomp' (1928 versions, on Classics 550), and 'Misty Mornin'' and 'Doin' The Voom Voom' (both Classics 559), but even on the lesser tunes or those tracks where Ellington seems to be doing little more than copying Fletcher Henderson, there are usually fine moments from Miley or one of the others. The Classics CDs offer admirable coverage, with a fairly consistent standard of remastering, and, though they ignore alternative takes, Ellington's promiscuous attitude towards the various record companies means that there are often several versions of a single theme on one disc (Classics 542, for instance, has three versions of 'Take It Easy'). MCA's Brunswick disc has the merit of conscientious if not always very lively remastering, while it covers only the tracks made for that label in the period.

***(*) **Duke Ellington 1929** Classics 569
    Ellington; Cootie Williams (*t, v*); Arthur Whetsol, Freddy Jenkins (*t*); Joe 'Tricky Sam' Nanton
    (*tb*); Barney Bigard (*cl, ts*); Johnny Hodges (*ss, as, cl*); Harry Carney (*bs, cl, as*); Fred Guy (*bj*);
    Wellman Braud (*b*); Sonny Greer (*d, v*); Ozie Ware (*v*). 3–7/29.
*** **Duke Ellington 1929–1930** Classics 577
    As above, except add Juan Tizol (*vtb*), Teddy Bunn (*g*), Bruce Johnson (*wbd*), Harold Randolph,
    Irving Mills (*v*); omit Ware. 8/29–1/30.
*** **Duke Ellington 1930** Classics 586
    As above, except add Cornell Smelser (*acc*), Dick Robertson (*v*); omit Bunn, Johnson and
    Randolph. 1–6/30.
*** **Duke Ellington 1930 Vol. 2** Classics 596
    As above, except add Charlie Barnet (*chimes*), Sid Garry, Jimmy Miller, Emmanuel Paul (*v*);
    omit Smelser. 6–11/30.
*** **Duke Ellington 1930–1931** Classics 605
    As above, except add Benny Paine (*v, p*), Chuck Bullock, Frank Marvin, Smith Ballew (*v*); omit
    Barnet, Robertson, Miller and Paul. 11/30–1/31.
*** **The Brunswick Recordings Vol. 2** MCA MCAD 42348
    Similar to above Classics discs. 1/29–1/31.
***(*) **The OKeh Ellington** Columbia 466964-2 2CD
    As appropriate discs above. 3/27–11/30.
***(*) **Jubilee Stomp** Bluebird 74321 101532
    As appropriate discs above. 3/28–1/34.

The replacement of Bubber Miley by Cootie Williams was the key personnel change in this period: Williams was a leaner, less outwardly expressive version of Miley, but equally fiery; his scat singing was a fast development of Armstrong's vocal style, and he gave the brass section a new bite and brightness, even if he lacked Miley's ability to growl quite so intently. Hodges and Carney, too, were coming into their own and, along with the increasing mastery of Ellington's handling of his players, the band was now growing in assurance almost from session to session. The Victor date of 7 March 1929 (Classics 569) exemplifies many of the new powers of the orchestra. 'Hot Feet' includes a superb Hodges solo, Williams singing and playing with great authority, and the band moving out of the older hot style without sacrificing any drive. It was the now extraordinarily powerful swing of the rhythm section that was responsible for much of this advance: the same session is a fine instance of what they could do, from Braud's subtly propulsive drive on the excellently scored 'The Dicty Glide' to his outright stomping line on 'Hot Feet', with Greer taking a showman's role on his cymbals and traps and the remarkable Guy strumming a quick-witted counterpoint that made the banjo seem far from outdated (he would, though, soon switch to guitar). The two important Victor sessions on this disc (a third, two parts of a Cotton Club medley, is less substantial) make this a valuable issue, and there are two fascinatingly different versions of the small-group blues, 'Saratoga Swing', as well as little-known Ellington attempts at 'I Must Have That Man' and an accompaniment to singer Ozie Ware.

    Ellington was recording at a prodigious pace, surprisingly so given the state of the industry at that time, and there are some three CDs' worth of material from 1930. Classics 586 includes some tunes that reek of Cotton Club set-pieces – 'Jungle Nights In Harlem', 'Jungle Blues' – and some thin novelty tunes, but new versions of 'The Mooche' and 'East St Louis Toodle-oo' and new originals like 'Shout 'Em Aunt Tillie', 'Hot And Bothered' and 'Cotton Club Stomp' are more substantial. Classics 596 has three different versions of 'Ring Dem Bells', each with outstanding solos by Williams, three of 'Old Man Blues', and a first try at 'Mood Indigo'. Classics 605 has three versions of 'Rockin' In Rhythm', each showing a slight advance on the one before, the tempo brightening and the reeds becoming smarter, and a slightly ironic reading of 'Twelfth Street Rag' which hints at Duke's later treatment of other people's jazz standards. But the record closes with his first lengthy work, the two-part 'Creole Rhapsody', where for perhaps the first time the soloists have to take a firm second place to the arrangement (this is the ten-inch 78 version; the subsequent 12-inch version is on the next disc in the Classics sequence). Remastering is mainly good and full-bodied: some of the records from more obscure companies sound a little rougher, there are some tracks in which bass boom overcomes mid-range brightness, and frequent hints that these are not first-hand dubbings. Still, only more demanding ears may be particularly troubled by the mixed transfer quality. The second volume of MCA's Brunswick series is generally cleaner, taking the story up to 'Creole Rhapsody', the same place where Classics 605 stops. Columbia's OKeh set includes 49 titles ranging from 'East St Louis Toodle-oo' up to 'Rockin' In Rhythm' in a comprehensive account of the OKeh series. It's capably remastered. Whether one wants to isolate the recordings by company in this way must be a matter for the individual collector. Bluebird, too, are confined to Victor masters for *Jubilee Stomp*, but this is a strong set: 'Saratoga Swing', 'Stevedore Stomp', 'The Dicty Glide', 'Ebony Rhapsody' and 18 others, in clear, firm sound.

*** **Duke Ellington 1931–1932** Classics 616
    Ellington; Arthur Whetsol, Freddy Jenkins, Cootie Williams (*t*); Joe 'Tricky Sam' Nanton,
    Lawrence Brown (*tb*); Juan Tizol (*vtb*); Johnny Hodges (*as, ss, cl*); Barney Bigard (*cl, ts*); Harry
    Carney (*bs, cl*); Fred Guy (*bj, g*); Wellman Braud (*b*); Sonny Greer (*d*); Frank Marvin, Ivie
    Anderson, Bing Crosby (*v*). 1/31–2/32.
*** **The Brunswick Sessions 1932–1935 Vol. 1** Jazz Information CAH 3001
    As above, except add Otto Hardwick (*as, bsx*); omit Marvin. 2–5/32.
*** **Duke Ellington 1932–1933** Classics 626
    As above, except add Ray Mitchell, Adelaide Hall, The Mills Brothers, Ethel Waters (*v*); omit
    Crosby. 5/32–1/33.
*** **The Brunswick Sessions 1932–1935 Vol. 2** Jazz Information CAH 3002
    As above, except add Joe Garland (*ts*); omit Mitchell, Hall, Mills Bros, Waters. 5/32–5/33.
**** **The Brunswick Sessions 1932–1935 Vol. 3** Jazz Information CAH 3003
    As above, except add Rex Stewart, Charles Allen (*t*), Billy Taylor Sr (*b, bb*), Hayes Alvis (*b*). 5/
    33–3/35.
***(*) **Duke Ellington 1933** Classics 637
    Similar to above. 2–8/33.
***(*) **Duke Ellington 1933–1935** Classics 646
    Similar to above. 9/33–3/35.

The second 'Creole Rhapsody' opens Classics 616, a longer and better-played though still imperfect
version, but the rest of the disc is more conventional Ellington, with 'It Don't Mean A Thing' and 'Lazy
Rhapsody' the highlights in a programme which is mostly made up of other writers' songs. The arrival
of both Lawrence Brown and Ivie Anderson is more important: Brown gave the brass section a new
mellifluousness, and Anderson was probably the best regular singer Duke ever employed. Classics 626
has ten Ellington themes out of 23 tracks, and loses impetus at the end with sundry accompaniments to
singers, but there are four substantial pieces in 'Slippery Horn', 'Blue Harlem', 'Ducky Wucky' and
especially 'Lightnin'', though the orchestra often sounds sloppy here.

    The three Jazz Information albums, with fine remastering from original 78s and excellent sleeve-notes,
cover all of Duke's work for Brunswick (he was still also recording for Columbia and Victor in the same
period, though to a lesser extent) up to 1935. Most of the first two discs are also on the final two Classics
discs, but remastering here is rather better. The third volume, though, is essential. Two Ellington standards make their debut here – 'Sophisticated Lady' and 'Solitude' – and there are at least four more major
pieces in 'Bundle Of Blues', 'Harlem Speaks', 'Saddest Tale' and 'Sump'n 'Bout Rhythm'. Stewart and
Allen arrive in time for four tracks and Stewart already makes a mark on the brass sound of the
orchestra on 'Margie'. Classics 637 and 646 divide this material between them, and 646 covers a number
of important Victor sessions as well: 'Stompy Jones', the locomotive classic, 'Daybreak Express', 'Blue
Feeling'.

***(*) **Early Ellington 1927–1934** RCA Bluebird 86852
    As appropriate discs above. 27–34.
***(*) **Jungle Nights In Harlem** RCA Bluebird 82499
    As appropriate discs above. 12/27–2/32.
*** **Jazz Cocktail** ASV AJA 5024
    As appropriate discs above. 10/28–9/32.
(*) **Rockin' In Rhythm ASV AJA 5057
    As appropriate discs above. 3/27–7/36.
*** **The Duke Plays Ellington Vol. 1** Topaz TPZ 1020
    As above. 3/27–6/38.
**** **Great Original Performances 1927–1934** Jazz Classics In Digital Stereo RPCD 624
    As appropriate discs above. 27–34.
**** **Swing 1930 To 1938** Jazz Classics In Digital Stereo RPCD 625
    As appropriate discs above, except add Wallace Jones, Harold Baker (*t*), Ben Webster (*ts*). 11/30–
    1/38.

Of the various compilations of early Ellington, we have examined the above discs. The two ASV discs
aren't really competitive since the remastering is rather grey and undefined, especially on ASV AJA
5057. Both the Bluebird compilations, though, are shrewdly chosen from Duke's Victor output: the first
is a mixed bag of mostly better-known material, while the second concentrates more on the 'theatrical'
Ellington and includes several Cotton Club set-pieces such as the title-track, 'Haunted Nights' and two
medleys. Both are among the better examples of the NoNoise system of remastering. Topaz do a decent
job with their 19-track set, with the obvious favourites and a couple of idiosyncratic choices. Robert
Parker's two Jazz Classics compilations use the finest original 78s for remastering and, while we must
include the usual reminder that Parker's use of a very slight reverberation to simulate concert-hall

conditions may be unpleasing to some ears, these are exceptionally fine, clear and full-bodied transfers, among his finest efforts to date. The tracks are a well-chosen selection from a dozen years of Ellingtonia.

***(*) **Duke Ellington 1935–1936** Classics 659
> Ellington; Charlie Allen, Cootie Williams, Arthur Whetsol (*t*); Rex Stewart (*c*); Joe 'Tricky Sam' Nanton, Lawrence Brown (*tb*); Juan Tizol (*vtb*); Johnny Hodges (*cl, ss, as*); Harry Carney (*cl, as, bs*); Otto Hardwick (*as*); Barney Bigard (*cl, ts*); Ben Webster (*ts*); Fred Guy (*g*); Hayes Alvis, Billy Taylor (*b*); Fred Avendorf, Sonny Greer (*d*); Ivie Anderson (*v*). 4/35–2/36.

***(*) **Duke Ellington 1936–1937** Classics 666
> As above, except add Pete Clark (*as*), Brick Fleagle (*g*); omit Allen, Avendorf. 2/36–3/37.

***(*) **Duke Ellington 1937** Classics 675
> As above, except add Wallace Jones (*t*), Sandy Williams (*tb*), Bernard Addison (*g*), Chick Webb (*d*); omit Whetsol, Clark and Fleagle. 3–5/37.

**** **Duke Ellington 1937 Vol. 2** Classics 687
> As above, except add Freddy Jenkins (*t*), Jack Maisel (*d*); omit Sandy Williams, Webb. 5–10/37.

**** **Duke Ellington 1938** Classics 700
> As above, except add Harold Baker (*t*), Mary McHugh, Jerry Kruger (*v*); omit Jenkins and Maisel. 1–4/38.

**** **Duke Ellington 1938 Vol. 2** Classics 717
> As above, except add Scat Powell (*v*). 4–8/38.

***(*) **Duke Ellington 1938 Vol. 3** Classics 726
> As above, except omit Anderson, Kruger, McHugh and Powell. 8–12/38.

Ellington's mid- and late-'30s output is a blend of commerce and art, as in most of his work; but it's astonishing how seldom he lets a duff track slip through. Even the most trifling pieces usually have something to commend them. Classics 635 is important for the four-part original recording of 'Reminiscing In Tempo' a dedication to Ellington's mother that was one of the first of his extended works; but it also has the joyful 'Truckin'', and two early 'concerto' pieces in 'Clarinet Lament' for Bigard and 'Echoes Of Harlem' for Cootie Williams. Classics 666 starts with some unpromising material magically illuminated: Rex Stewart's filigree touches on 'Kissin' My Baby Goodnight', the lovely scoring on 'Maybe Someday'. Several tracks here are small-group crossovers with the Columbia discs (see below), but there are top-drawer records by the full group, including 'In A Jam', 'Uptown Downbeat', the rollicking 'Scattin' At The Kit Cat' and an example of Ellington's revisionism in 'The New East St Louis Toodle-oo'. One of the best in this sequence.

In contrast, Classics 675 is a bit thin so far as the full-band tracks are concerned, though two versions of 'Azure' shouldn't be missed. Much stronger is Classics 687, which peaks on the still remarkable first recording of 'Diminuendo And Crescendo In Blue' but which also has the tremendous 'Harmony In Harlem', 'Chatterbox' and 'Jubilesta', as well as several of the small-group sessions. Classics 700 includes a lot of distinctive Ellingtonia that has been obscured by some of his obvious hits: 'Braggin' In Brass', 'The Gal From Joe's', the new version of 'Black And Tan Fantasy', superbly played by the band which transforms itself from dance orchestra to complex jazz ensemble – and back again. Though seldom commented on, the rhythm section of Guy, Taylor or Alvis and Greer is unobtrusively fine. There are more neglected winners on Classics 717, including 'I'm Slappin' Seventh Avenue' (which Cecil Taylor always admired), 'Dinah's In A Jam', the lovely treatment of 'Rose Of The Rio Grande' and the very fine 'The Stevedore's Serenade'. The next disc might be a little behind in class, but there are more fine small-group sides led by Hodges (see below) and further lesser-known Ellington originals. The remastering in this series is inconsistent but, for the most part, very listenable; as a sequence of records, it's of a very high calibre.

**** **The Duke's Men: Small Groups Vol. I** Columbia 468618 2CD
> Ellington; Cootie Williams, Freddy Jenkins (*t*); Rex Stewart (*c, v*); Lawrence Brown, Joe 'Tricky Sam' Nanton, Sandy Williams, George Stevenson (*tb*); Juan Tizol (*vtb*); Johnny Hodges (*ss, as*); Rudy Powell (*cl, as*); Otto Hardwick (*as*); Barney Bigard, Bingie Madison (*cl, ts*); Harry Carney (*bs*); Roger 'Ram' Ramirez, Tommy Fulford (*p*); Fred Guy, Bernard Addison, Brick Fleagle, Ceele Burke (*g*); Billy Taylor Sr, Hayes Alvis, Wellman Braud (*b*); Sonny Greer, Chick Webb, Jack Maisel (*d*); Charlie Barnet (*perc*); Sue Mitchell (*v*). 12/34–1/38.

**** **The Duke's Men: Small Groups Vol. II** Columbia 472994-2 2CD
> Basically as above. 3/38–3/39.

Ellington's sidemen recorded a number of small-group dates under the nominal leadership of one or other of them during the late 1930s, and these superb compilations bring many of these dates together. Some of the thunder of these sets has been stolen by the Classics compilations listed above, but the presentation here is impressive. There are a few undistinguished arrangements of pop tunes, but for the most part this is inventive and skilful small-group jazz of the period. Duke is at the piano as often as not and there are a number of scarce Ellington tunes here; but many of the sides are features for Stewart,

Bigard or Williams, who are the three main leaders (Hodges is credited with only two tracks, but most of his great work comes later, for Victor). 'Caravan', 'Stompy Jones', 'Back Room Romp', 'Tea And Trumpets', 'Love In My Heart' and 'Echoes Of Harlem' are all essential slices of Ellingtonia, but all 45 tracks have at least something of interest. Columbia have made one of their better efforts at remastering, and there is an excellent accompanying essay by Helen Oakley Dance, who was involved in producing many of the records.

The second volume maintains the high standard of the first. The Hodges session of March 1938 has 'Jeep's Blues' and 'I Let A Song Go Out Of My Heart', but that for August of the same year is even better: six little classics. Most of the other tracks are under the stewardship of Cootie Williams, but the second disc wraps up with a pleasing date under Rex Stewart as leader. A shade behind the earlier set in track-for-track quality, but still excellent stuff, in good sound.

***(*) **Braggin' In Brass – The Immortal 1938 Year** Columbia 465464 2CD
    Ellington; Harold 'Shorty' Baker, Wallace Jones, Cootie Williams (*t*); Rex Stewart (*c*); Lawrence Brown, Joe 'Tricky Sam' Nanton (*tb*); Juan Tizol (*vtb*); Barney Bigard (*cl, ts*); Johnny Hodges (*ss, as, cl*); Otto Hardwick (*as*); Harry Carney (*bs, as, cl*); Fred Guy (*g*); Hayes Alvis, Billy Taylor Sr (*b*); Sonny Greer (*d*). 1–12/38.

A valuable set from a very fine if not quite immortal year. One could argue that the really outstanding Ellington themes here number only a few – 'Boy Meets Horn', a scintillating feature for Rex Stewart, 'Dinah's In A Jam', 'T. T. On Toast', 'I Let A Song Go Out Of My Heart' – and many of the others get by on orchestral twists or quality solos. But there are a good number of those and, as suggested above, it's amazing how sharp Ellington was in skirting dud material. The remastering is good if not quite as lively as it might have been.

***(*) **Duke Ellington 1939** Classics 765
    As above, except add Billy Strayhorn (*p*); omit Baker and Alvis. 3–6/39.
***(*) **Duke Ellington 1939 Vol. 2** Classics 780
    As above. 6–10/39.
**** **Duke Ellington 1939–1940** Classics 790
    As above, except add Ben Webster (*ts*), Jimmy Blanton (*b*); Ivie Anderson (*v*). 10/39–2/40.
**** **Duke Ellington 1940** Classics 805
    As above. 2–8/40.
**** **Duke Ellington 1940 Vol. 2** Classics 820
    As above, except add Herb Jeffries (*v*). 9–11/40.
**** **Duke Ellington 1940–1941** Classics 837
    As above, except Ray Nance (*t*) replaces Williams. 11/40–7/41.
**** **Duke Ellington 1941** Classics 851
    As above, except add Junior Raglin (*b*).7–12/41.
    **** **The Blanton–Webster Band** RCA Bluebird 74321 13181 2 3CD
    Ellington; Wallace Jones, Cootie Williams, Ray Nance (*t*); Rex Stewart (*c*); Joe 'Tricky Sam' Nanton, Lawrence Brown (*tb*); Juan Tizol (*vtb*); Barney Bigard, Chauncey Haughton (*cl*); Johnny Hodges (*ss, as, cl*); Harry Carney (*bs, cl, as*); Otto Hardwick (*as, bsx*); Ben Webster (*ts*); Billy Strayhorn (*p*); Fred Guy (*g*); Jimmy Blanton, Junior Raglin (*b*); Sonny Greer (*d*); Ivie Anderson, Herb Jeffries (*v*). 3/40–7/42.
(****) **In A Mellotone** RCA 13029-2
    As above. 5/40–6/42.

With much late-'30s Ellington now back in print, it's easier to see that he was working towards this exceptional period for the band for a long time. Ellington had been building a matchless team of soloists, his own composing was taking on a finer degree of personal creativity and sophistication and, with the arrival of bassist Jimmy Blanton, who gave the rhythm section an unparalleled eloquence in the way it swung, the final piece fell into place. The 6 May 1940 session, which opens this three-disc set, is one of the great occasions in jazz history, when Ellington recorded both 'Jack The Bear' (a feature for Blanton) and the unqualified masterpiece, 'Ko Ko'. From there, literally dozens of masterpieces tumbled out of the band, from originals such as 'Harlem Air Shaft' and 'Main Stem' and 'Take The "A" Train' to brilliant Ellingtonizations of standard material such as 'The Sidewalks Of New York' and 'Clementine'. The arrival of Billy Strayhorn, Ellington's closest collaborator until Strayhorn's death in 1967, is another important element in the music's success.

With the Classics sequence of discs now stretching through this period as well, the RCA collections have some competition. The three discs covering 1939 include many of the small-group dates led by Bigard, Hodges and Williams, and those who have the Columbia sets may not want to duplicate this material. But Classics 790 includes some important stuff: the Ducal solo 'Blues' and the duets with Blanton, 'Blues' and 'Plucked Again'. Thereafter, the 1940–41 discs cover much the same ground as the three-disc Bluebird set. All this is four-star material and, for those who would prefer to have it a disc at a time, this isn't a bad way forward. Transfers are all right, though no improvement on Bluebird's, and sources are as usual unlisted.

Bluebird's set collects 66 tracks over a two-year period, which many hold as Ellington's greatest on record, and it's certainly the summation of his work within the three-minute confines of the 78-r.p.m. record. There are one or two minor errors in the set, and the remastering is showing its age a bit: surely it's time for someone to take another look at the original masters of these discs and do them again. But we cannot feasibly withhold a 'crown' recommendation for some of the finest twentieth-century music on record.

In A Mellotone creams off 16 tracks from the period and is a straight reissue of a 1950s LP. Somewhat redundant in the face of the other issues.

**** **Fargo, ND 11/7/40** Vintage Jazz Classics VJC-1019/20 2CD
       As above, except omit Haughton, Strayhorn and Raglin. 11/40.
**** **Fargo 1940 Vol. 1** Tax CD 3720-2
       As above. 11/40.
**** **Fargo 1940 Vol. 2** Tax CD 3721-2
       As above. 11/40.
Of the many surviving location recordings of the Ellington band, this is one of the best, catching over two hours of material from a single dance date in North Dakota, part of it broadcast but most of it simply taken down by some amateur enthusiasts. The sound has been extensively cleaned up by both VJC and Tax and there is little to choose between the two editions, though the VJC version is available only as a double set. Here is the great Ellington orchestra on a typical night, with many of the best numbers in the band's book and the most rousing version of 'St Louis Blues' to climax the evening. The sound is inevitably well below the quality of the studio sessions, but it's a very fine supplement to them.

***(*) **Take The 'A' Train** Vintage Jazz Classics VJC-1003-2
       As above, except omit Williams, add Junior Raglin (*b*). 1–12/41.
A fascinating set of studio transcriptions. There are eight tunes which Duke never recorded in the studio again, including 'Madame Will Drop Her Shawl' and Strayhorn's 'Love Like This Can't Last', a pretty feature for Webster on 'Until Tonight' and unexpected things like a boisterous 'Frenesi', a Rex Stewart feature called 'Easy Street' and debut recordings of 'West Indian Stomp', 'Moon Mist' and 'Stomp Caprice'. The sound is mostly clear and fine, if a fraction below first-class.

**** **The Great Ellington Units** RCA Bluebird ND86751
       Ellington; Cootie Williams, Ray Nance (*t*); Rex Stewart (*c*); Lawrence Brown (*tb*); Juan Tizol
       (*vtb*); Johnny Hodges (*ss, as*); Ben Webster (*ts*); Harry Carney (*as, bs*); Billy Strayhorn (*p*);
       Jimmy Blanton (*b*); Sonny Greer (*d*). 11/40–9/41.
These small-group dates aren't far behind the full-orchestra sides of the same period. The sessions led by Rex Stewart and Barney Bigard are slighter stuff, but the eight tracks led by Johnny Hodges are superlative features for his own playing, immensely swinging on 'Squatty Roo', suitably passionate on 'Passion Flower'. Ellington and Strayhorn add little touches of their own, and the remastering is firm and clear.

**** **Black, Brown And Beige** RCA Bluebird 86641 3CD
       Ellington; Taft Jordan, Cat Anderson, Shelton Hemphill, Ray Nance, Rex Stewart, Francis
       Williams, Harold 'Shorty' Baker (*t*); Claude Jones, Lawrence Brown, Joe 'Tricky Sam' Nanton,
       Tommy Dorsey, Wilbur De Paris (*tb*); Jimmy Hamilton (*cl, ts*); Otto Hardwick (*as*); Johnny
       Hodges (*as*); Al Sears (*ts*); Russell Procope (*cl, ts*); Harry Carney (*bs*); Fred Guy (*g*); Junior
       Raglin, Sid Weiss, Oscar Pettiford, Al Lucas, Bob Haggart (*b*); Sonny Greer, Big Sid Catlett (*d*);
       Al Hibbler, Joya Sherrill, Kay Davis, Marie Ellington, Marian Cox (*v*). 12/44–9/46.
While this ultimately stands a notch below the music on *The Blanton–Webster Band*, it is still an essential Ellington collection. Besides numerous further examples of the composer's mastery of the three-minute form, there are the first of his suites to make it to the studios, including most of 'Black, Brown And Beige' – which was never finally recorded in its entirety in the studio – and 'The Perfume Suite'. New Ellingtonians include Cat Anderson and Taft Jordan – two brilliantly individual members of the brass section – as well as the lyrical Shorty Baker, Al Sears and Russell Procope. Ellington's confidence may have been sagging a little from the loss of major soloists – Webster, Williams – and the indifference to some of his higher ambitions as a composer, but the orchestra itself is still inimitable. Remastering is kind enough, even if not always wholly respectful of the music, but most will find it acceptable.

*** **Sophisticated Lady** RCA Bluebird ND 90625
       As above Bluebird discs. 2/41–9/46.
Eleven tracks filched from the two big sets for a snapshot hits collection. Unanswerably great music, but

docked a star for a few mundane choices: it wouldn't have hurt to have had 'Harlem Air Shaft' or 'Ko Ko' in here instead of 'Just Squeeze Me' or 'Caravan'.

RCA have also released four two-disc sets in their Tribune series, covering Ellington from 1940 to 1946. This is exactly the ground covered above and will probably tempt only those collecting discs in that particular series. Sound is no different from the original LP editions.

***(*) **Duke Ellington & His Orchestra Vols 1–5** Circle CCD-101/2/3/4/5 (5CD, only available separately)
      Basically as above discs in this period, 43–45.
Since the American recording ban was in full swing, Ellington's studio work was limited to material like this, transcriptions in the World Broadcast Series. Circle have included what seems to be every available fragment from these sessions, which means multiple takes and many false starts. If this detracts from a general recommendation, it ought to be remembered that this was the greatest Ellington orchestra in top form, and there are countless things to marvel at in the likes of (to pick a few of our personal favourites) 'Air Conditioned Jungle', 'Let The Zoomers Drool', 'Blues On The Double', 'In A Jam', 'Blue Cellophane', 'Three Cent Stomp' and many more. Besides, the many breaks allow an intriguing insight into Duke's way of working. Excellent notes and impressive remastering.

***(*) **The Duke Ellington Carnegie Hall Concerts January 1943** Prestige 34004 2CD
      Ellington; Rex Stewart, Harold 'Shorty' Baker, Wallace Jones (*t*); Ray Nance (*t, vn*); Joe 'Tricky Sam' Nanton, Lawrence Brown (*tb*); Juan Tizol (*vtb*); Johnny Hodges, Ben Webster, Harry Carney, Otto Hardwick, Chauncey Haughton (*reeds*); Fred Guy (*g*); Junior Raglin (*b*); Sonny Greer (*d*); Betty Roche (*v*). 1/43.
***(*) **The Duke Ellington Carnegie Hall Concerts December 1944** Prestige 24073 2CD
      As above, except add Shelton Hemphill, Taft Jordan, Cat Anderson (*t*), Claude Jones (*tb*), Al Sears, Jimmy Hamilton (*reeds*), Hillard Brown (*d*), Kay Davis, Marie Ellington, Al Hibbler (*v*); omit Baker, Wallace Jones, Webster, Haughton, Greer, Roche. 12/44.
***(*) **The Duke Ellington Carnegie Hall Concerts January 1946** Prestige 24074 2CD
      As above, except add Francis Williams (*t*), Wilbur De Paris (*tb*), Al Lucas (*g*), Oscar Pettiford (*b*), Sonny Greer (*d*), Joya Sherrill (*v*); omit Stewart, Nanton, Guy, Raglin, Brown, Marie Ellington. 1/46.
***(*) **The Duke Ellington Carnegie Hall Concerts December 1947** Prestige 24075 2CD
      As above, except add Harold 'Shorty' Baker, Al Killian (*t*), Tyree Glenn (*tb, vib*), Russell Procope (*reeds*), Fred Guy (*g*), Junior Raglin (*b*); omit Jordan, Anderson, De Paris, Hamilton, Lucas, Sherrill. 12/47.
***(*) **Carnegie Hall November 1948** Vintage Jazz Classics VJC-1024/25 2CD
      As above, except add Quentin Jackson (*tb*), Ben Webster (*ts*); omit Jones. 11/48.
Ellington's Carnegie Hall appearances began in 1943 and continued on an annual basis. The only surviving recordings are mainly in indifferent condition and none of the Prestige CDs can really be called hi-fi, despite extensive remastering work. Nevertheless, Ellington scholars will find them essential, and even casual listeners should find much to enjoy. The 1943 concert premiered 'Black, Brown And Beige' and its lukewarm reception became a notorious snub that decimated Ellington's confidence in the work. These surviving extracts are fascinating but inconclusive. The rest of the programme includes many greatest hits and one or two scarcer pieces. The 1944 concert includes many less-familiar tunes – 'Blutopia', 'Suddenly It Jumped', 'Blue Cellophane' – plus more 'Black, Brown And Beige' and the debut of 'The Perfume Suite', as well as a glorious finale showcase for Nanton on 'Frankie And Johnny'. Notable in the next concert were a reworking of 'Diminuendo And Crescendo In Blue' and some fine miniatures including 'Magenta Haze', Joya Sherrill's fine interpretation of 'The Blues' and a euphoric treatment of 'Solid Old Man'. The 'Liberian Suite' is one of the principal items of the 1947 set, but the Ray Nance feature in 'Bakiff', Duke's own spot on 'The Clothed Woman' and Carney on 'Mella Brava' are of equal interest. While all the concerts have their weak spots, each has enough fine Ellington to make it more than worthwhile. The recently released 1948 concert features a guest return by Ben Webster and a rare recording of 'Lush Life'; sound-quality is again imperfect but listenable.

*** **The Great Chicago Concerts** Limelight 844401-2 2CD
      Ellington; Shelton Hemphill, Taft Jordan, Cat Anderson, Harold Baker, Ray Nance, Francis Williams, Bernard Flood (*t*); Lawrence Brown, Claude Jones, Wilbur De Paris (*tb*); Otto Hardwick, Johnny Hodges, Jimmy Hamilton, Harry Carney, Al Sears (*reeds*); Django Reinhardt, Fred Guy (*g*); Oscar Pettiford (*b*); Sonny Greer (*d*). 1–11/46.
A couple of Chicago dates in unusually good sound for the period, though there are the usual anomalies in balancing the sections. The January date is a shade ordinary, but the November concert has a strongly played version of 'The Deep South Suite' and features guest Django Reinhardt sitting in on four tunes. Worthwhile.

***(*) **Happy-Go-Lucky Local** Musicraft 70052-2
> As above, except omit Flood, Reinhardt. 10–12/46.

Ellington's Musicraft records have been in and out of the catalogue over the years, but this CD edition is a sound one and, though the remastering still seems to have introduced some top-end distortion here and there, it's probably about as clear as these tracks will sound. Some very witty writing in the likes of 'Jam A Ditty', one of the loveliest Hodges features of the period in 'Magenta Haze', and the two-part 'Beautiful Indians' making its debut.

**** **The Complete Duke Ellington & His World Famous Orchestra** Hindsight HBCD501 3CD
> Ellington; Shelton Hemphill, Francis Williams, Harold 'Shorty' Baker, Ray Nance, Dud Bascomb, Bernard Flood, Cat Anderson (*t*); Lawrence Brown, Claude Jones, Tyree Glenn, Joe 'Tricky Sam' Nanton (*tb*); Russell Procope, Johnny Hodges, Jimmy Hamilton, Al Sears, Harry Carney, Otto Hardwick (*reeds*); Billy Strayhorn (*p*); Fred Guy (*g*); Oscar Pettiford, Wilson Myers (*b*); Sonny Greer (*d*); 3/46–6/47.

These transcriptions have drifted in and out of circulation over many years, but this fine three-disc set brings them all together in mostly clean and quite lively sound. There are a host of rarities – 'Violet Blue', 'Park At 106th', Ray Nance doing 'St Louis Blues', Al Sears tearing up 'The Suburbanite', Harry Carney's 'Jennie' . . . and so on. Quite a feast, and a fine addendum to the studio tracks of the period.

*** **Liberian Suite** Columbia 469409-2
> As above, except add Al Killian, Herman Grimes (*t*), Wilbur De Paris (*tb*), Edgar Brown, Junior Raglin (*b*); omit Flood, Bascombe, Nanton, Hardwick, Myers. 12/47.

*** **Masterpieces By Ellington** Columbia 469407-2
> Ellington; Nelson Williams, Andrew Ford, Ray Nance, Harold Baker, Cat Anderson (*t*); Quentin Jackson, Lawrence Brown, Tyree Glenn (*tb*); Russell Procope, Harry Carney, Johnny Hodges, Jimmy Hamilton, Paul Gonsalves (*ts*); Billy Strayhorn (*p*); Wendell Marshall (*b*); Sonny Greer (*d*); Yvonne (*v*). 12/50.

Now available separately from the above issues, *Liberian Suite* suffers from inadequate recording and a conception that Ellington would come to grips with far more successfully in his various long works from the 1960s, but the opening 'I Like The Sunrise' still has great nobility as Al Hibbler sings it. The most successful piece on *Masterpieces* is probably 'The Tattooed Bride', a whirl of tone-colours and melodic lines that are handled with some skill by the band, even if it could use a shade more finesse. The long versions of 'Mood Indigo', 'Solitude' and 'Sophisticated Lady' gain less from the big treatment.

(*) **Great Times! Original Jazz Classics OJC 108
> Ellington; Billy Strayhorn (*p, celeste*); Wendell Marshall, Lloyd Trottman (*b*); Oscar Pettiford (*clo*); Jo Jones (*d*). 9, 11/50.

A curiosity, but a valuable one. Ellington duets on the overworked '"A" Train' with its creator, Strayhorn, who plays celeste; Pettiford saws away in the near background over bass and drums. There are eight two-piano tracks of mixed success, and an odd pair – 'Perdido' and 'Blues For Blanton' – minus Strayhorn. A chance recording, maybe, it conveys something quite profound about the chemistry at work between the two pianist/composers. Aspects of a single self?

*** **The Seattle Concert 1952** RCA 66531-2
> Ellington; Clark Terry, Cat Anderson, Willie Cook (*t*); Ray Nance (*t, vn*); Quentin Jackson, Britt Woodman (*tb*); Juan Tizol (*vtb*); Jimmy Hamilton (*cl, ts*); Willie Smith, Russell Procope (*as*); Paul Gonsalves (*ts*); Harry Carney (*bs*); Wendell Marshall (*b*); Louie Bellson (*d*). 3/52.

The first-ever legitimate release of an Ellington concert when it originally appeared, this hasn't worn quite as well as others of the period (or later). The main point is 'Harlem Suite', which still stands up as one of the best of Duke's longer pieces, but filler material like 'Skin Deep', 'The Hawk Talks' and the medley of hits lets the rest down. Sound is rather cloudy for the period.

(*) **Live At Birdland 1952 Jazz Unlimited JUCD 2036
> Ellington; Clark Terry, Willie Cook, Ray Nance, Cat Anderson (*t*); Quentin Jackson, Britt Woodman (*tb*); Juan Tizol (*vtb*); Hilton Jefferson, Jimmy Hamilton, Russell Procope, Harry Carney (*reeds*); Wendell Marshall (*b*); Louie Bellson (*d*); Betty Roche, Billy Grissom (*v*). 11/52.

A complete Birdland broadcast, marred by very intrusive announcements (it was a programme in honour of Duke's 25th anniversary, and they never let us forget it) and repetitive material. But 'Monologue' and 'The Tattooed Bride' seldom turn up in live recordings. Clear sound for the period.

***(*) **Piano Reflections** Capitol B21Y-92863-2
> Ellington; Wendell Marshall (*b*); Butch Ballard, Dave Black (*d*); Ralph Colier (*perc*). 4–12/53.

Ellington's apparent reluctance to document himself extensively as a pianist must be a source of regret, but these 1953 sessions find him pondering on 14 of his own tunes (and Mercer's 'Things Ain't What They Used To Be'). Most of them are too short to show any great development from the original themes, and Duke's habitual cat-and-mouse with the listener takes some of the pith out of the session; but it shows how distinctive his touch had become, how mannerism could become even more inimitable than Basie's minimalism, and how Ellington could fashion moving little episodes out of mere fragments.

*** **Duke Ellington Presents . . .** Bethlehem BET 6004-2
    Ellington; Cat Anderson, Willie Cook, Clark Terry (*t*); Ray Nance (*t, vn*); Quentin Jackson, Britt Woodman (*tb*); John Sanders (*vtb*); Johnny Hodges (*as*); Russell Procope (*as, cl*); Paul Gonsalves (*ts*); Jimmy Hamilton (*cl, ts*); Harry Carney (*bs, bcl*); Jimmy Woode (*b*); Sam Woodyard (*d*). 2/56.
Six standards and five Ellington staples, from a brief association with Bethlehem. The expected features for Hodges and Carney turn out well and the studio sound is very appealing, with the band jousting through a 'Blues' to cap the session.

**** **Ellington At Newport** Columbia 450986-2
    Ellington; Cat Anderson, Willie Cook, Ray Nance, Clark Terry (*t*); Quentin Jackson, John Sanders, Britt Woodman (*tb*); Johnny Hodges, Russell Procope (*as*); Paul Gonsalves, Jimmy Hamilton (*ts*); Harry Carney (*bs*); Jimmy Woode (*b*); Sam Woodyard (*d*). 7/56.
*** **Duke Ellington & The Buck Clayton All Stars At Newport** Columbia 477320-2
    As above. 7/56.
*** **Duke And Friends, Connecticut Jazz Festival 1956** IAJRC 1005
    As above, except add Buck Clayton (*t*), Willie 'The Lion' Smith, Hank Jones (*p*), Jimmy Grissom (*v*). 7/56.
The 1956 Newport Festival marked a significant upswing in Duke's critical and commercial fortunes. In large part, the triumph can be laid to Paul Gonsalves's extraordinary 27 blues choruses on 'Diminuendo And Crescendo In Blue', which CBS producer George Avakian placed out of sequence at the end of what was to be Ellington's best-selling record. Gonsalves's unprecedented improvisation (which opened up possibilities and set standards for later tenor saxophonists from John Coltrane to David Murray) was clearly spontaneous. There were two theories at the time as to how he had managed to play so long and so well. One was that the veteran drummer Jo Jones, sitting sidestage, had egged him on by slapping out the rhythm with a rolled-up magazine, further fuelling the crowd's enthusiastic shouts. Another was that Gonsalves was serenading a beautiful blonde in a black dress who had got up to dance uninhibitedly to his solo. Since the saxophonist's eyes were clamped shut in the near-ecstasy, that has become the image of the improvising genius.

    Gonsalves himself has suggested that a particularly competitive edge to the band that night was the real reason. Johnny Hodges had just returned to the fold after a brief stint as an independent bandleader. His beautiful, almost stately solo on 'Jeep's Blues' was intended as the climax to the concert, but Hodges found himself upstaged in the subsequent notices (and by Avakian's reprogramming) and the concert firmly established Gonsalves as one of the leading soloists in jazz.

    Unfortunately, much of the solo was played badly off-mike and it's slightly difficult to get a complete sense of its extraordinary impact. It does, nevertheless, dominate the album, overshadowing Hodges and, more significantly, the three-part 'Festival Suite' which Ellington and Strayhorn had put together for the occasion. The first part, 'Festival Junction', is more or less a blowing theme for a parade of soloists, including an incisive first excursion by Gonsalves, who gives notice of what's to come with some blistering choruses (though not 27) on the third part, 'Newport Up'. An essential Ellington album, *At Newport* documents a rejuvenating experience for the band and the impetus for the experiments of the 1960s.

    The second volume covers four other numbers played at the show and is something of an anticlimax; the rest of the disc is filled with a Buck Clayton jam-session sequence with Coleman Hawkins and J. J. Johnson.

    The Connecticut set was played 22 days later. Ellington's 'Newport Jazz Festival Suite' gets another airing, but the rest is a bit of a mess, with throwaway versions of some of the hits and some blues, plus a fairly uproarious Nance feature of 'Her Cherie'. Of some interest are extra tracks with Clayton fronting a small Ellington group and three numbers by The Lion. Good concert sound.

**** **Such Sweet Thunder** Columbia 469140-2
    As above disc. 8/56–5/57.
The wit and sagacity of his nod to Will Shakespeare makes for one of the most delightful of all Ellington records. Hard to choose between the pleasures of hearing Clark Terry cough out the words (or so it seems) 'Lord, what fools these mortals be' through his horn at the end of 'Up And Down'; or Britt Woodman's remarkable solo on 'Sonnet To Hank Cinq'; or Hodges's heartbreaking delineation of 'Star-Crossed Lovers'. Sweet, swinging, perfect Ellingtonia.

(*) **Ellington Indigos Columbia 463342-2
    As above, except add Rick Henderson (*as*), Ozzie Bailey (*v*). 10/57.

This sounds like a chore for the company. Ten smoochy ballads, only three of them by Duke, with the band set on snooze. The players play themselves rather than playing, so to speak. But Shorty Baker is still a marvel on 'Willow Weep For Me'.

*** A Drum Is A Woman Columbia 471320-2

As above, except add Betty Glamann (*hp*), Candido Camero, Terry Snyder (*perc*), Margaret Tynes, Joya Sherrill (*v*). 57.

Ellington's 'history of jazz' is a sly oratorio with virtuoso singing by Tynes and Sherrill, as well as an amusing commentary on jazz history by Duke as narrator and composer. Somewhat dated, perhaps, though not a bad antidote to the earnest history-mongering of the '90s from one of the music's sharpest intellects.

***(*) Live At The 1957 Stratford Festival Music & Arts 616

Ellington; Cat Anderson, Willie Cook, Clark Terry (*t*); Ray Nance, (*t, vn*); Quentin Jackson, Britt Woodman (*tb*); John Sanders (*tb, vtb*); Russell Procope (*as, cl*); Johnny Hodges (*as*); Jimmy Hamilton (*ts, cl*); Paul Gonsalves (*ts*); Harry Carney (*bs, bcl*); Jimmy Woode (*b*); Sam Woodyard (*d*). 57.

Unusual and highly inventive material, beautifully remastered for CD with a bright, clear mono sound that puts space round individual voices in the ensembles and gives the rhythm section a better-than-average profile. A slightly larger band than its immediate predecessor, it produces a denser sound, with a lot more resolution in the bass and a shade more colour in the horns. Tracks include 'Harlem Air Shaft' and 'La Virgin De La Macarena'.

***(*) The Girl's Suite / The Perfume Suite Columbia 469139-2

As above, except add Ed Mullens (*t*), Lou Blackburn, Chuck Connors (*tb*), Aaron Bell (*b*). 12/57–1/61.

Ellington often played 'The Perfume Suite' in public, but only bits and pieces of 'The Girl's Suite', which mixed 'Clementine', 'Dinah', Sweet Adeline', 'Diane' and 'Peg O' My Heart' with five ladies of his own. Though apparently throwaway, the music has hidden resource and all sorts of ingenious folds and tucks to tie the melodies together. 'The Perfume Suite' dates back to the Carnegie Hall shows of the 1940s but gets a near-definitive reading here, with highly charged treatments of 'Strange Feeling' and 'Dancers In Love'. A good one.

***(*) Newport 58 Columbia 468436-2

Ellington; Cat Anderson, Harold Baker, Ray Nance, Clark Terry (*t*); Quentin Jackson, John Sanders, Britt Woodman (*tb*); Harry Carney, Paul Gonsalves, Jimmy Hamilton, Johnny Hodges, Gerry Mulligan, Russell Procope (*reeds*); Jimmy Woode (*b*); Sam Woodyard (*d*); Ozzie Bailey (*v*). 58.

Not quite the triumph of two years before, but a fine set nevertheless. 'Jazz Festival Jazz' may have its tongue in its cheek, but for the most part the set is as straightforward as one ever hears an Ellington band. The crowd-pleasers, 'El Gato' and 'Hi Fi Fo Fum', traditionally a Woodyard feature, are given big licks, but the real highlight is a guest appearance by Mulligan and a marvellous duet with fellow-baritonist Carney on 'Prima Bara Dubla'. A good-value set, carefully transferred and with a more reliable sound-mix than its illustrious 1956 predecessor.

*** Jazz At The Plaza Vol II Columbia 471319-2

Ellington; Harold Baker, Clark Terry, Cat Anderson (*t*); Ray Nance (*t, v*); Quentin Jackson, John Sanders, Britt Woodman (*tb*); Harry Carney, Paul Gonsalves, Jimmy Hamilton, Johnny Hodges, Russell Procope (*reeds*); Jimmy Woode (*b*); Sam Woodyard (*d*); Jimmy Rushing, Billie Holiday (v). 58.

Taken down at a record company show at New York's Plaza Hotel, the band are in good fettle here. The major piece is the 'Jazz Festival Suite', written for the 1958 Newport Festival, with crackling contributions from Hamilton, Baker and Gonsalves; but intriguing are a medley featuring Jimmy Rushing, in great heart, though not favoured by the microphones, and another with Billie Holiday, who clearly wasn't in any kind of heart, yet somehow pulled out an impressive performance. Scrappy, but an interesting set.

***(*) Live At Newport 1958 Columbia C2K53584 2CD

As above, except omit Rushing and Holiday; add Gerry Mulligan (*bs*), Mildred Falls (*p*), Mahalia Jackson, Ozzie Bailey, Lil Greenwood (*v*). 7/58.

The original *Newport 1958* LP was actually a studio re-creation cut a few weeks later. This set restores the original performances and covers plenty of extra ground. Some useful rarities such as 'Princess Blue', the Clark Terry feature, 'Juniflip', and a track where the guesting Mulligan spars with Harry Carney, 'Prima Bara Dubla'. Mahalia Jackson is another unlikely drop-in and she belts out an impressive 'Come Sunday'. There are plenty of loose ends, as with most Festival shows, but this is a good one to have restored.

**** **Back To Back** Verve 823637-2

> Ellington; Johnny Hodges (*as*); Harry 'Sweets' Edison (*t*); Les Spann (*g*); Al Hall, Sam Jones (*b*); Jo Jones (*d*). 2/59.

**** **Side By Side** Verve 821578-2

> As above, except add Roy Eldridge (*t*), Lawrence Brown (*tb*), Ben Webster (*ts*), Billy Strayhorn (*p*); Wendell Marshall (*b*). 58–59.

Welcome reissue of a marvellous 'play the blues' session jointly credited to Ellington and Hodges. The opening 'Wabash Blues' sets an attractive 32-bar theme over an initially disconcerting Latin rhythm that goes all the way back to W. C. Handy's experiments with tango measures in a blues context. Hodges and Edison take contrasting approaches on their solos, with the trumpeter working the changes in fairly orthodox fashion, Hodges sticking very much closer to the melody. 'Basin Street Blues' features Spann in a slightly wavering but completely authentic solo, after which Hodges comes in with two delightfully varied choruses. Ellington's own solo is a curious affair, with a slightly wistful quality but also marked by repeated references to his own youthful style, in particular the descending arpeggios that became something of a tic.

The varied 12-bar form of 'St Louis Blues' is further developed in Ellington's fast, accurate introduction. The two horns do a call-and-response routine that further underlines their different approaches. Duke is the featured soloist again on 'Loveless Love' ('Careless Love'), a traditional tune with some kinship to the blues, but not a strict blues at all. Fittingly, though, the set ends with 'Royal Garden Blues', an orthodox 12-bar structure given a deliberately basic (Basie-like?) treatment.

The companion piece, *Side By Side*, brings Strayhorn in for Ellington at the piano and enlists Webster, Eldridge and Brown. Hodges dominates again, though his friends all have some pertinent remarks, and though the material is jam-session stuff as usual, it falls open to the expertise on show here. Three tracks from the session with Duke, including a classic 'Stompy Jones', are carried over to this one.

** **The Duke D.J. Special** Fresh Sound 141

> Ellington; Cat Anderson, Shorty Baker, Clark Terry (*t*); Ray Nance (*t, vn*); Quentin Jackson, John Sanders, Britt Woodman (*tb*); Jimmy Hamilton (*cl,ts*); Russell Procope (*cl, as*); Johnny Hodges (*as*); Paul Gonsalves (*ts*); Harry Carney (*bs*); Jimmy Woode (*b*); Jimmy Johnson (*d*). 3/59.

*** **Live At The Newport Jazz Festival '59** Emarcy 842071-2

> Ellington; Cat Anderson, Shorty Baker, Fats Ford, Clark Terry (*t*); Ray Nance (*t, vn*); Quentin Jackson, John Sanders, Britt Woodman (*tb*); Jimmy Hamilton (*cl, ts*); Russell Procope (*cl, as*); Johnny Hodges (*as*); Paul Gonsalves (*ts*); Harry Carney (*bs*); Jimmy Woode (*b*); Sam Woodyard (*d*). 7/59.

***(*) **Live At The Blue Note** Roulette 828637-2 2CD

> As above, except add Billy Strayhorn (*p*), Johnny Pate (*b*), Jimmy Johnson (*d*). 8/59.

The Emarcy is a lively concert performance with the trumpets in particularly good throat. Juan Tizol's 'Perdido' makes a welcome return to the band-book. The CD transfers are good, with very little dirt. The slightly earlier *Special* has a near-identical band in lower gear and with an occasionally slipping clutch. While it's comforting to know that Homer nods, there's no compelling need to have him doing it on your stereo.

The session at Chicago's Blue Note is drawn from three sets on a single night. Overhead mikes caught the performances, which consequently have a live but slightly askew feel, as if we're listening from the gods. Four tunes from the *Anatomy Of A Murder* score get a welcome outing, Strayhorn comes on to do a duet, Stan Kenton and June Christy drop by to say hello . . . a typical night's work for the master. Best moment: the perennially underrated Shorty Baker blowing as sweet as he could on 'Almost Cried'.

**** **Blues In Orbit** Columbia 460823-2

> Ellington; Cat Anderson, Shorty Baker, Clark Terry (*t*); Ray Nance (*t, vn*); Quentin Jackson, John Sanders, Britt Woodman, Booty Wood (*tb*); Matthew Gee (*bhn*); Harry Carney, Paul Gonsalves, Bill Graham, Jimmy Hamilton, Johnny Hodges, Russell Procope (*reeds*); Billy Strayhorn (*p*); Jimmy Woode (*b*); Jimmy Johnson, Sam Woodyard (*d*). 2/58, 2/59.

Teo Macero took control of the sound booth for the first time on an Ellington session for the bulk of these stratospheric studio sessions. It would be convenient to argue that the huge separation between Ellington's chips-of-ice piano and the chesty, distant horns on the title-track was a typical Macero touch but for the fact that the first two items were produced by the Duke's old friend and collaborator, Irving Townshend. If 'Blues In Orbit' was some sort of Ducal welcome to the age of Sputnik, the previously unreleased 'Track 360' is an elegant train-ride, Pullman-class and with a nod in the direction of Honegger's popular concert-opener 'Pacific 231', swaying over a track laid down by Sam Woodyard; the drummer fell ill shortly afterwards and isn't heard on the rest of the album.

There are two more tracks which weren't on the original release. 'Brown Penny' is a state-of-the-art Hodges solo, played in imitation of Kay Davis's earlier vocal version and sounding as if it is being poured out of a bottle. The other also features Hodges, on a slightly too syrupy reading of 'Sentimental Lady' (aka 'I Didn't Know About You'). Hodges rather dominates the album, even being featured on 'Smada', which was usually a Hamilton spot. Hamilton himself has mixed fortunes, sounding anonymous on tenor on his own 'Three J's Blues' and 'Pie Eye's Blues', a rackety 12-bar that compares badly with the subsequent 'C Jam Blues', where he goes back to clarinet, rounding off a sequence of solos that includes excellent work by Gonsalves, the little-known Matthew Gee and Booty Wood. A very fine album, with just enough new compositional input – 'Blues In Blueprint' and 'The Swinger's Jump' – to vary a slightly predictable profile.

*** **Anatomy Of A Murder** Columbia 469137-2
　　　As above, except add Gerald Wilson (*t*); omit Gee and Woodyard. 5–6/59.
*** **At the Bal Masqué** Columbia 469136-2
　　　As above. 59.
Ellington's score for Otto Preminger's film strikes a moderate number of sparks. The main-title theme shows he could write thriller material as strong as anything Pete Rugolo and Shorty Rogers were turning out for Hollywood, but the more impressionistic stuff tends to sound like middleweight Ellington. The *Bal Masqué* music (with an audience nonsensically dubbed in) stacks up some more Ducal transformations of everything from 'Laugh Clown Laugh' to 'Spooky Takes A Holiday'. Nobody is taking this too seriously, but the soloists have fun on the tunes.

***(*) **Piano In The Background** Columbia 468404-2
　　　Ellington; Cat Anderson, Andres Meringuito, Eddie Mullins, Gerald Wilson (*t*); Ray Nance (*t, v*); Quentin Jackson, Booty Wood, Britt Woodman (*tb*); Juan Tizol (*vtb*); Jimmy Hamilton, Russell Procope (*cl, as*); Johnny Hodges (*as*); Paul Gonsalves (*ts*); Harry Carney (*bs, cl*); Aaron Bell (*b*); Sam Woodyard (*d*); Lil Greenwood (*v*). 5–6/60.
Piano In The Background was designed to beat the drum for Duke's piano: he takes a chorus at the start of each tune and closes the numbers himself. No new material, but the input is all fresh and he comes up with many a twist from the keyboard (with, oddly, 91 keys on it). 'Rockin' In Rhythm' and 'I'm Beginning To See The Light' are too fast, but never mind.

*** **Peer Gynt Suites** Columbia 472354-2
　　　As above, except add Paul Horn (*reeds*). 6–10/60.
A strange one: Grieg meets Duke, and nobody seems much the wiser at the end of it. At least the fill-up is the Ellington–Strayhorn 'Suite Thursday', four bright new pieces. This is also the point at which to mention *The Nutcracker Suite* (Columbia 472356-2), another unlikely jazz-meets-the-classics project.

***(*) **Live At Monterey 1960** Status DSTS 1008
　　　As above, except add Willie Cook (*t*); omit Anderson, Wilson, Horn. 9/60.
*** **Live At Monterey 1960 Part Two** Status DSTS 1009
　　　As above, except add Jimmy Rushing (*v*). 9/60.
In fine concert sound, here's some previously unheard Ellington from 1960. Volume One has several seldom-encountered tunes; the second disc is slighter stuff, with Rushing doing three amiable turns and a run across 'Red Carpet' (the rest of the disc features the Cannonball Adderley group). Wally Heider did the original recording and, though some of the soloists drift off, the clout of the band comes over very well.

*** **The Ellington Suites** Original Jazz Classics OJC 446
　　　Ellington; Cat Anderson, Harold Baker, Mercer Ellington, Money Johnson, Eddie Preston, Clark Terry (*t*); Ray Nance (*t, vn*); Quentin Jackson, Vince Prudente, John Sanders, Malcolm Taylor, Booty Wood, Britt Woodman (*tb*); Johnny Hodges, Harold Minerve, Norris Turney (*as*); Russell Procope (*as, cl*); Jimmy Hamilton (*ts, cl*); Russ Andrews, Harold Ashby, Paul Gonsalves (*ts*); Harry Carney (*bs, bcl*); Joe Benjamin, Wulf Freedman, Jimmy Woode (*b*); Jimmy Johnson, Rufus Jones (*d*). 2/59–10/72.
An interesting collection of extended and medley pieces from the 1959 'Queen's Suite' to the late and indifferent 'Uwis Suite'. Significantly or not, the most arresting track on the whole album, which has good sound-quality throughout, is 'The Single Petal Of A Rose', a duo for Ellington and bassist Jimmy Woode.

*** **Hot Summer Dance** Red Baron AK 498631
　　　Ellington; Willie Cook, Fats Ford, Eddie Mullens (*t*); Ray Nance (*c, v*); Lawrence Brown, Booty Wood, Britt Woodman (*tb*); Russell Procope (*as, cl*); Johnny Hodges (*as*); Jimmy Hamilton (*ts, cl*); Paul Gonsalves (*ts*); Harry Carney (*bs, bcl*); Aaron Bell (*b*); Sam Woodyard (*d*). 7/60.
Recorded at the Mather Air Force Base in California, this is very immediate stuff, with an entirely convincing live feel. After the obligatory ' "A" Train', Ellington tries out a new 'Paris Blues', a couple of arrangements from *The Nutcracker Suite*, 'Such Sweet Thunder' and, for a climax, Paul Gonsalves's

party piece, which on this occasion gets a slightly strained reading. Being a dance gig, most of the tracks are taken at a brisk clip and the band squeeze in 16 tunes (or 15 and a medley) in just over an hour. The tapes have been decently handled and the soloists all come across strongly, with Jimmy Hamilton in particularly strong form on 'Tenderly'.

(*) **The Feeling Of Jazz Black Lion BLCD 760123
> Ellington; Cat Anderson, Harold Baker, Bill Berry, Roy Burrowes, Ray Nance (*t*); Lawrence Brown, Chuck Connors, Leon Cox (*tb*); Jimmy Hamilton (*cl, ts*); Johnny Hodges, Russell Procope (*as*); Paul Gonsalves (*ts*); Harry Carney (*bs*); Aaron Bell (*b*); Sam Woodyard (*d*). 2, 5 & 7/62.

A very unexceptional mixed programme of old and newer material. Even at third or fourth hearing, it seems indistinguishable from half a dozen early-1960s concert recordings, and even the solos come straight off the peg. Serious collectors only.

*** **All American In Jazz** Columbia 469138-2
> As above, except add Eddie Mullens (*t*); omit Burrowes. 1/62.

This kind of thing must have been a contractual chore for Ellington, but one would hardly know that from the sparkle and finesse of the performances. None of the tunes from what was once a hit musical have really survived in the popular memory, and the melodies aren't exactly riveting, but Ellington shapes it as a charming set of miniatures.

**** **Afro Bossa** Discovery 71002
> Ellington; Cat Anderson, Roy Burrowes, Cootie Williams (*t, perc*); Ray Nance (*c, vn*); Lawrence Brown, Buster Cooper (*tb*); Chuck Connors (*b tb*); Russell Procope (*as, cl*); Johnny Hodges (*as*); Jimmy Hamilton (*cl, ts*); Paul Gonsalves (*ts*); Harry Carney (*bs, bcl, cl*); Billy Strayhorn (*p, perc*); Ernie Shepard (*b*); Sam Woodyard (*d*). 11 & 12/63, 1/63.

Afro Bossa is not the best-known of the 1960s Ellingtons but one of the more interesting. The band don't always seem entirely easy with the more roistering tempos and the extra percussion is sometimes all over the place, but the material is brilliantly coloured and highly imaginative: working in miniature, Duke constructed a dozen brief scores that look towards some of the Afro-American ponderings of the Marsalis clan in the 1990s (and Marsalis has declared his admiration for this set in particular). There are fine solo passages from Hodges, Carney and Nance especially.

*** **Featuring Paul Gonsalves** Original Jazz Classics OJC 623
> Ellington; Cat Anderson, Bill Berry, Roy Burrowes, Ray Nance (*t*); Lawrence Brown, Chuck Connors, Leon Cox (*tb*); Russell Procope (*cl, as*); Johnny Hodges (*as*); Paul Gonsalves (*ts*); Jimmy Hamilton (*cl, ts*); Harry Carney (*bs*); Aaron Bell (*b*); Sam Woodyard (*d*). 5/62.

A deserved album feature for a saxophonist who contributed enormously to the Ellington sound and who has made a considerable impact on contemporary players like David Murray, but whose reputation has been somewhat eclipsed by that of Johnny Hodges. The tenorist's solo material is typically extended and supremely logical, and his tone, sometimes a little muffled and lacking in individuality, is razor-sharp here. Whether the 'name' ranking was planned beforehand or awarded in recognition of particularly inspired playing isn't clear, but this this is a significant set by one of the unsung geniuses of the saxophone, who joins Warne Marsh and Richie Kamuca in the ranks of those who have been passed over by noisier talents.

*** **Midnight In Paris** Columbia 468403-2
> As above, except omit Burrowes. 1–6/62.

Only two Ellington tunes on this tribute to the city (the title-song is by Strayhorn), and the material is often pure slush; but Duke makes light of another A&R idea by turning the orchestra into the big, romantic instrument he sometimes liked it to be. Sumptuous sound, and some great bits of Gonsalves in particular.

*** **Duke Ellington Meets Coleman Hawkins** Impulse 11622
> Ellington; Ray Nance (*c, vn*); Lawrence Brown (*tb*); Johnny Hodges (*as*); Coleman Hawkins (*ts*); Harry Carney (*bs, bcl*); Aaron Bell (*b*); Sam Woodyard (*d*). 8/62.

The sketchy nature of this meeting of giants finally tells against it. The good-natured fun of 'Limbo Jazz' is the tonic note of the date and, while there is much entertaining playing by the small band on hand, one wishes for some of the gravitas which at least got into the date with Coltrane (see below). 'Solitude' is added to the original LP programme.

***(*) **Duke Ellington And John Coltrane** Impulse! MCAD 39103
> Ellington; John Coltrane (*ts, ss*); Aaron Bell, Jimmy Garrison (*b*); Elvin Jones, Sam Woodyard (*d*). 9/62.

It's known that Coltrane was going through a difficult transitional phase when this remarkable opportunity was presented to him. Six months before, he had recorded the simply titled *Coltrane* with what was to be the classic quartet. He was, though, stretching for something beyond its surprisingly relaxed lyricism and had managed to wreck his mouthpiece (no minor loss for a saxophonist) trying to improve its lay. His work around this time is, in retrospect, quite conventional, certainly in relation to what was to follow, and it's often Ellington, as so often in the past, who sounds the 'younger' and more adventurous player. It is, for all that, a slightly disappointing record, which peaks early with a brilliant reading of 'In A Sentimental Mood', but never reaches such heights again.

***(*) **Money Jungle** Blue Note B21Y-46398
　　Ellington; Charles Mingus (*b*); Max Roach (*d*). 9/62.
Set up by United Artists, this was intended to put Duke in the company of two modernists of the next generation, both of whom (Mingus especially) had drawn particular sustenance from his example. It was the first trio recording the bassist had done since the 1957 Jubilee sessions with Hampton Hawes and Dannie Richmond and, despite his apparent misgivings before and during the session, he completely steals the show, playing complicated countermelodies and dizzying, out-of-tempo runs in every register. Much of the material seems to have been put together at speed and inevitably relies quite heavily on the blues. 'Money Jungle' itself and 'Very Special' are both reasonably orthodox 12-bars and both sound improvised. 'La Fleurette Africaine' is clearly developed from a very simple melodic conception, stated at the beginning by the piano. Long-standing Ellington staples, 'Warm Valley' and 'Caravan', are rather less successful and it isn't clear on the former whether a rather agitated Mingus is unfamiliar with the changes or whether he is suffering one of the minor huffs Ellington recounted later. Throughout, Roach plays with the kind of ordered freedom that is characteristic of him. Unfortunately, he is poorly served by the recording and even on CD sounds rather tinny. A fascinating set, though, which will be of particular interest to Mingus fans and collectors.

*** **Recollections Of The Big Band Era** Atlantic 7 90043 2
　　Ellington; Cat Anderson, Bill Berry, Roy Burrowes, Eddie Preston, Cootie Williams (*t*); Ray
　　Nance (*t, vn*); Lawrence Brown, Chuck Connors, Buster Cooper (*tb*); Russell Procope (*cl, as*);
　　Jimmy Hamilton (*cl, ts*); Johnny Hodges (*as*); Paul Gonsalves (*ts*); Harry Carney (*bs, cl, bcl*);
　　Ernie Shepard (*b*); Sam Woodyard (*d*). 11/62.
Something of a novelty set, bringing together some of the most famous theme and signature tunes of the pre- and immediately post-war bands. Billy Strayhorn's arrangement of Don Redman's 'The Chant Of The Weed' and piano part on the Harry James-associated 'Ciribiribin' are noteworthy, but there are also name-checks for Woody Herman ('The Woodchopper's Ball'), Erskine Hawkins ('Tuxedo Junction'), Louis Armstrong ('When It's Sleepy Time Down South'), Paul Whiteman (Gershwin's 'Rhapsody In Blue') and, inevitably, Basie's 'One O'Clock Jump' and Cab Calloway's 'Minnie The Moocher'. Thoroughly enjoyable, and something more than just a nostalgic wallow. Some of Ellington's own arrangements are strikingly original, virtually re-conceiving the material.

***(*) **The Great Paris Concert** Atlantic SD 2-304
　　Ellington; Cat Anderson, Roy Burrowes, Cootie Williams (*t*); Ray Nance (*c, v*); Lawrence
　　Brown, Chuck Connors, Buster Cooper (*tb*); Johnny Hodges (*as*); Russell Procope (*cl, as*);
　　Jimmy Hamilton (*cl, ts*); Paul Gonsalves (*ts*); Harry Carney (*bs, cl*); Ernie Shepard (*b*); Sam
　　Woodyard (*d*). 2/63.
Great? Very nearly. Oddly, perhaps, the quality of this set doesn't lie so much in the solos as in the ensembles, which are rousing to an almost unprecedented degree. 'Suite Thursday' is an unexpected gem for anyone who hasn't encountered it before, and there are lovely settings of 'Rose Of The Rio Grande' and the *Asphalt Jungle* theme. The sound is big and resonant, as it presumably was in the hall, and, more than almost any of the live recordings of the time, it conveys something of the excitement of a concert performance.

*** **The Great London Concerts** Limelight 518446-2
　　As above, except add Rolf Ericson, Herbie Jones (*t*), Milt Grayson (*v*). 1/63–2/64.
A re-run at the same temperature, but with somewhat less interesting material: the only tunes outside the Ellington hits canon are 'Harlem' and 'Single Petal Of A Rose'. But the playing has rare enthusiasm (Duke liked London) and the sound is very lively.

*** **Piano In The Foreground** Columbia 474930-2
　　Ellington; Aaron Bell (*b*); Sam Woodyard (*d*). 63.
Another attempt to focus on Duke the pianist, though this time with his regular rhythm section. Far less combative than his meeting with Mingus and Roach, there's a perhaps inevitable doodling feel to most of these pieces, as if this were a sketch for a project he could hardly be bothered to finish. What survive are the harmonic and rhythmic throwaways that he is trying out for later, grander ideas.

*** **My People** Columbia/Red Baron A K 52759
>   Billy Berry, Ray Nance, Ziggy Harrell, Nat Woodward (*t*); Britt Woodman, John Sanders, Booty
>   Wood (*tb*); Russell Procope, Rudy Powell, Bob Freedman, Harold Ashby, Pete Clark (*reeds*);
>   Billy Strayhorn (*cel*); Jimmy Jones (*p*); Joe Benjamin (*b*); Louie Bellson (*d*); Juan Amalbert
>   (*perc*); Jimmy Grissom, Lil Greenwood, Jimmy McPhail, Bunny Briggs, Joya Sherrill, Irving
>   Burton Singers (*v*). 63.

One of Ellington's extended vocal/orchestral works, with the composer participating only as narrator.
Some more background on the piece would have been helpful (there is a rambling note by Stanley
Crouch instead) and Ellington's sometimes doubtful choice of vocalists militates against some of the
pieces having the impact they might; as do parts of the libretto. The reworkings of 'Come Sunday' and
'The Blues Ain't' have grandeur and fire, though; even as sketches for a longer and more ambitious
work, it should be heard by serious Ellington followers.

*** **Harlem** Pablo 2308-245
>   Ellington; Cat Anderson, Rolf Ericson, Herbie Jones, Cootie Williams (*t*); Lawrence Brown,
>   Buster Cooper, Chuck Connors (*tb*); Russell Procope (*as, cl*); Johnny Hodges (*as*); Jimmy
>   Hamilton (*cl, ts*); Paul Gonsalves (*ts*); Harry Carney (*bs, bcl, cl*); Major Holley, Jimmy Woode
>   (*b*); Sam Woodyard (*d*). 64.

In 1964 Ellington made a triumphal return to Carnegie Hall, scene of the famous (and slightly overblown) wartime concerts. The two latter-day sets, respectably transferred, include the marvellous
'Harlem', a concert selection from *The Far East Suite* (see below), including 'Depk', 'Amad', 'Agra',
'Bluebird Of Delhi' and, on Volume 2, a lovely 'Isfahan', a tune made in heaven for Johnny Hodges. The
similarly vintaged Pablo material is better ordered and more sharply transferred and, but for archival
purposes, is the one to go for.

***(*) **In The Uncommon Market** Pablo 2308-247
>   Ellington; Cat Anderson, Roy Burrowes, Cootie Williams (*t*); Ray Nance (*t, vn*); Lawrence
>   Brown, Chuck Connors, Buster Cooper (*tb*); Johnny Hodges (*as*); Russell Procope (*as, cl*);
>   Jimmy Hamilton (*ts, cl*); Paul Gonsalves (*ts*); Harry Carney (*bs*); Ernie Shepard (*b*); Sam
>   Woodyard (*d*).

Undated, but this probably comes from the same period as the above. Challengingly unfamiliar scores –
'Bula', 'E.S.P.', 'Silk Lace' – and trio performances of two concepts of 'The Shepherd' make this a
valuable session. The soloing is not so much below par as clearly subordinated to collective values, and
the ensembles repay the closest attention.

*** **New York Concert** Musicmasters 65122-2
>   Ellington; Willie 'The Lion' Smith, Billy Strayhorn (*p*); Peck Morrison (*b*); Sam Woodyard (*d*).
>   5/64.

A rare example of Ellington the pianist in the spotlight. Much of this is infected by the way he chose to
distract attention from his individual instrumental skills – he just doesn't take anything very seriously.
The Lion and Strayhorn turn up to do a couple of party pieces, but it's not until the final few numbers –
'Melancholia/Reflections In D', 'Bird Of Paradise' and 'The Single Petal Of A Rose' – that the piano
player sets himself any genuine interpretative challenges. Inessential and perhaps revealing of how little
Ellington was prepared to reveal.

**** **The Afro-Eurasian Eclipse** Original Jazz Classics O J C 645
>   Ellington; Mercer Ellington, Money Johnson, Eddie Preston, Cootie Williams (*t*); Chuck
>   Connors, Malcolm Taylor, Booty Wood (*tb*); Russell Procope (*cl, as*); Norris Turney (*as*);
>   Harold Ashby, Paul Gonsalves (*ts*); Harry Carney (*bs*); Joe Benjamin (*b*); Rufus Jones (*d*).

'World music' of a very high order. Ellington's understanding of non-Western forms was often limited
to a grasp of unusual tone-colours, but here, on 'Chinoiserie', 'Didjeridoo' and 'Afrique', he produces
something that sounds genuinely alien. The original Fantasy release sounded veiled and mysterious, but
the CD reissue is quite bright, perhaps too much so for music of this sort. However, sharper resolution
does confirm a strong impression that, far from being a by-blow, these pieces are essential items in the
Ellington canon.

(*) **Yale Concert Original Jazz Classics O J C 664
>   Ellington; Cat Anderson, Herbie Jones, Cootie Williams, Mercer Ellington (*t*); Lawrence Brown,
>   Chuck Connors, Buster Cooper (*tb*); Russell Procope (*as, cl*); Johnny Hodges (*as*); Jimmy
>   Hamilton (*ts, cl*); Paul Gonsalves (*ts*); Harry Carney (*bs*); Jeff Castleman (*b*); Sam Woodyard
>   (*d*). 4/65.

The *Yale Concert* has its moments but suffers from the surfeit of available Duke-in-concert: apart from
'A Chromatic Love Affair' and a beautiful Hodges medley, there's nothing worth cutting classes for.

(*) Live At The Greek Theatre Status DSTS 10143
    As above, except omit Castleman; add Jimmy Jones (*p*), Jim Hughart, John Lamb (*b*), Ed
    Thigpen (*d*), Ella Fitzgerald (*v*). 9/66.
Duke's spoken intros sound like he's broadcasting from Mars, but the band sound all right, and they do
a typical tour of service for the period. Ella sings a short set with her trio and does 'Cotton Tail' with the
band. Hardly a deathless discovery.

(*) Masters Of Jazz – Volume 6 Storyville STCD 4106
    Ellington; Cat Anderson, Shorty Baker, Bill Berry, Eddie Mullen, Ray Nance (*t*); Lawrence
    Brown, Chuck Connors, Leon Cox (*tb*); Jimmy Hamilton (*cl, ts*); Russell Procope (*as, cl*);
    Johnny Hodges (*as*); Paul Gonsalves (*ts*); Harry Carney (*bs, cl, bcl*); Aaron Bell (*b*); Sam
    Woodyard (*d*). 62, 66.
The performances here are pretty much *comme il faut*, but again it's Ellington's solo medley, recorded
somewhat later than the rest, which really catches the ear. The complexity of his delivery is quite
astonishing, even when it is clearly calculated to beguile. Not a great album, but enthusiasts will want
the solo spot.

**** The Far East Suite** Bluebird ND 87640
    Ellington; Cat Anderson, Mercer Ellington, Herbie Jones, Cootie Williams (*t*); Lawrence Brown,
    Chuck Connors, Buster Cooper (*tb*); Harry Carney, Paul Gonsalves, Jimmy Hamilton, Johnny
    Hodges, Russell Procope (*reeds*); John Lamb (*b*); Rufus Jones (*d*). 12/66.
It should really have been *The Near East Suite*. In 1963, the State Department sent the Ellington band
on a tour that took in Ceylon, India and Pakistan, most of the Middle East, and Persia. The tour was
eventually interrupted by the assassination of JFK, but Duke and co-writer Strayhorn slowly absorbed
the sights and tone-colours of those weeks, and nearly three years later went into the studio to record
the suite. Typical of Ellington's interpretation of the genre, it is really little more than a well-balanced
programme of individual songs but with a greater-than-usual degree of overall coherence, summed up
at the end by 'Amad'. 'The Tourist Point Of View' serves as overture and reminder of the Duke's
characteristic sound, and introduces two of the most important solo voices, Anderson and Gonsalves.
'Bluebird Of Delhi' relates to a mynah that mocked Billy Strayhorn with a beautiful song (played by
Jimmy Hamilton) and then brought him down with the resounding raspberry one hears at the end of the
piece.
    What follows is perhaps the most beautiful single item in Ellington's and Strayhorn's entire output.
Hodges's solo on 'Isfahan' is like attar of roses, almost (but not quite) *too* sweet and, once smelt,
impossible to forget. Critical attention has almost always focused on Hodges, but it's important to be
aware of the role of the backing arrangements, a line for the saxophones that seems as monumental as
the place it celebrates. The other unquestionable masterpiece of the set is 'Mount Harissa', a soft,
almost spiritual opening from Ellington, building up into a sinuous Gonsalves solo over a compulsive
drum-and-cymbal pattern and huge orchestral interjections. An evocation of Agra, location of the Taj
Mahal, is quite properly assigned to Harry Carney, in superb voice.
    Ellington's ability to communicate points of contact and conflict between cultures, assimilating the
blues to Eastern modes in tracks like 'Blue Pepper (Far East Of The Blues)' never sounds editorialized
or excessively self-conscious. This remains one of the peaks of post-war Ellington. There is now also a
'special mix' available, which presents the music with several alternative takes (Bluebird 66551-2).

***(*) The Intimacy Of The Blues** Original Jazz Classics OJC 624
    Ellington; Cat Anderson, Willie Cook (*t*); Lawrence Brown (*tb*); Norris Turney (*f*); Johnny
    Hodges (*as*); Harold Ashby, Paul Gonsalves (*ts*); Harry Carney (*bs*); Wild Bill Davis (*org*); Joe
    Benjamin, Victor Gaskin, Paul Kondziela, John Lamb (*b*); Rufus Jones (*d*). 3/67–6/70.
Delightful small-group settings of which the 1967 'Combo Suite', incorporating the title-piece, 'Out
South', 'Near North' and 'Soul Country', is far and away the best. Even in restricted settings like this,
Ellington still manages to get a tremendous depth of sound, and the disposition of horns is such that
Carney's line often suggests that a whole section is at work. The tenor is contrastingly quieter and less
forceful, which has the same effect.

**** . . . And His Mother Called Him Bill** Bluebird ND 86287
    Ellington; Cat Anderson, Mercer Ellington, Herbie Jones, Cootie Williams (*t*); Clark Terry
    (*flhn*); Lawrence Brown, Chuck Connors, Buster Cooper, John Sanders (*tb*); Harry Carney,
    Johnny Hodges, Paul Gonsalves, Jimmy Hamilton, Russell Procope (*reeds*); Aaron Bell, Jeff
    Castleman (*b*); Steve Little, Sam Woodyard (*d*). 8, 9 & 11/67.
This is Ellington's tribute to Billy Strayhorn, who died in May 1967. The mood is primarily one of loss
and yearning, and Strayhorn titles like 'U.M.M.G.', standing for 'Upper Manhattan Medical Group',
and 'Blood Count' bear poignant witness to his prolonged final illness. Hodges's solo on the latter is
almost unbearable, and is surpassed in creative terms only by the later 'Day-Dream'. 'U.M.M.G.' has an

urgent, ambulance-ride quality, largely conveyed by Ellington's clattering piano that sets it in sharp opposition to the easy swing of the opening 'Boo-Dah'.

The CD has four previously unreleased tracks, including 'Smada', 'My Little Brown Book' and (another Hodges feature) 'Lotus Blossom'; but the main interest focuses on the tracks mentioned above and on the astonishing 'All Day Long', which counts as one of Duke's most devastating orchestral conceptions, as daring as anything in the modern movement.

In a brief written tribute, dated on the day of Strayhorn's death, Ellington states that his collaborator's 'listening-hearing self was totally intolerant of his writing-playing self when, or if, any compromise was expected or considered expedient'. Fortunately, Ellington's notion of expedience was arrogance itself where music was concerned. Strayhorn couldn't have hoped for a finer memorial.

(*) **The Intimate Ellington Original Jazz Classics OJC 730
    Ellington; various line-ups, 1969–71.
Definitions of intimacy must vary. This isn't an obvious choice for last thing at night with a glass of malt and the dimmer turned down. Apart from the feeble 'Moon Maiden', on which Ellington plays celeste, it's an averagely appealing album with some assured big-band playing and a useful sample of Ellington's still-underrated trio performances (which may yet come to seem more significant than essays on the scale of 'Symphonette'). The sound wobbles a bit from track to track, an almost inevitable problem on compilations for quite various forces, and there is a problem with the bass register. Otherwise good.

*** **Second Sacred Concert** Prestige P 24045
    Ellington; Cat Anderson, Mercer Ellington, Cootie Williams (*t*); Lawrence Brown, Buster
    Cooper (*tb*); Harry Carney, Paul Gonsalves, Johnny Hodges, Russell Procope (*reeds*); Jeff
    Castleman (*b*); Sam Woodyard (*d*); voices. 68.
Ellington's last few years were often spent writing liturgical music. The first of the sacred concerts, based on the piece *In The Beginning, God*, was performed in Grace Cathedral, San Francisco. The second is equally moving, its blend of jazz, classical and black gospel materials profoundly influenced by the large-scale Masses and praises of Mary Lou Williams, Ellington's only serious rival in jazz composition on the large scale. Despite the dimensions of the piece and the joyous, ringing concords, it is a surprisingly dark work, with a tragic sub-theme that constantly threatens to break through. Non-believers will still appreciate the extraordinary part-writing; for Christians of whatever persuasion, it remains an overwhelming musical experience.

(*) **Up In Duke's Workshop Original Jazz Classics OJC 633
    Ellington; Johnny Coles, Willie Cook, Mercer Ellington, Money Johnson, Jimmy Owens, Eddie
    Preston, Alan Rubin, Fred Stone, Cootie Williams (*t*); Tyree Glenn, Bennie Green, Benny
    Powell, Julian Priester, Vince Prudente, Malcolm Taylor, Booty Wood (*tb*); Russell Procope (*as,
    cl*); Johnny Hodges, Harold Minerve, Buddy Pearson, Norris Turney (*as*); Harold Ashby, Paul
    Gonsalves (*ts*); Harry Carney (*bs*); Joe Benjamin, Victor Gaskin, Paul Kondziela (*b*); Rufus
    Jones (*d*). 4/69–12/72.
The line-ups don't actually vary very much, but there are a number of relatively unfamiliar names, notably those trying to fill Johnny Hodges's shoes, for which they should have been assigned rabbit's feet. As the title implies, these are working sessions – and slightly tentative ones at that. The early 'Black Butterfly' and the interesting 'Neo-Creole' are significant pieces, but in only eight cuts there's a fair bit of slack.

Duke Ellington: The Private Collection 10CD as follows:
**** **Volume 1: Studio Sessions, Chicago 1956** Saja 791041 2
    Ellington; Cat Anderson, Willie Cook, Ray Nance, Clark Terry (*t*); Quentin Jackson, John
    Sanders, Britt Woodman (*tb*); Johnny Hodges (*as*); Russell Procope (*cl, as*); Jimmy Hamilton
    (*cl, ts*); Paul Gonsalves (*ts*); Harry Carney (*bs, cl*); Jimmy Woode (*b*); Sam Woodyard (*d*). 3 &
    12/56.
*** **Volume 2: Dance Concerts, California, 1958** Saja 791042 2
*** **Volume 6: Dance Dates, California, 1958** Saja 791230 2
    Ellington; Harold Baker, Clark Terry (*t*); Ray Nance (*t, v, vn*); Quentin Jackson, John Sanders,
    Britt Woodman (*tb*); Russell Procope (*as, cl*); Bill Graham (*as*); Paul Gonsalves (*ts*); Jimmy
    Hamilton (*ts, cl*); Harry Carney (*bs, cl, bcl*); Jimmy Woode (*b*); Sam Woodyard (*d*); Ozzie Bailey
    (*v*). 3/58.
*** **Volume 3: Studio Sessions, New York, 1962** Saja 791043 2
    Ellington; Cat Anderson, Bill Berry, Roy Burrowes, Ray Nance, Cootie Williams (*t*); Lawrence
    Brown, Chuck Connors, Buster Cooper, Britt Woodman (*tb*); Johnny Hodges, Russell Procope
    (*as*); Paul Gonsalves (*ts*); Jimmy Hamilton (*ts, cl*); Harry Carney (*bs*); Aaron Bell (*b*); Sam
    Woodyard (*d*); Milt Grayson (*v*). 7 & 9/62.

*** **Volume 4: Studio Sessions, New York, 1963** Saja 791044 2
    Ellington; Ray Nance (*c*); Cat Anderson, Rolf Ericson, Eddie Preston, Cootie Williams (*t*); Lawrence Brown, Chuck Connors, Buster Cooper (*tb*); Johnny Hodges, Russell Procope (*as*); Jimmy Hamilton (*cl, ts*); Paul Gonsalves (*ts*); Harry Carney (*bs*); Ernie Shepard (*b*); Sam Woodyard (*d*). 4, 5 & 7/63.

***(*) **Volume 5: The Suites, New York, 1968 & 1970** Saja 791045 2
    Ellington; Cat Anderson, Dave Burns, Willie Cook, Mercer Ellington, Al Rubin, Fred Stone, Cootie Williams (*t*); Chuck Connors, Cliff Heathers, Julian Priester, Booty Wood (*tb*); Johnny Hodges (*as*); Russell Procope (*as, cl*); Norris Turney (*as, f*); Harold Ashby, Paul Gonsalves (*ts*); Harry Carney (*bs*); Joe Benjamin, Jeff Castleman (*b*); Rufus Jones (*d*); Dave Fitz, Elayne Jones, Walter Rosenberg (*perc*). 11 & 12/68, 5 & 6/70.

*** **Volume 7: Studio Sessions, 1957 & 1962** Saja 791231 2
    Ellington; Cat Anderson, Bill Berry, Roy Burrowes, Willie Cook, Ray Nance, Clark Terry (*t*); Lawrence Brown, Chuck Connors, Leon Cox, Quentin Jackson, John Sanders, Britt Woodman (*tb*); Harold Ashby, Harry Carney, Paul Gonsalves, Jimmy Hamilton, Johnny Hodges, Russell Procope (*reeds*); Billy Strayhorn (*p*); Aaron Bell, Jimmy Woode (*b*); Sonny Greer, Sam Woodyard (*d*); Milt Grayson (*v*). 1/57, 3, 5 & 6/62.

*** **Volume 8: Studio Sessions, 1957, 1965–7, San Francisco, Chicago, New York** Saja 791232 2
    Ellington; Nat Adderley, Cat Anderson, Willie Cook, Mercer Ellington, Herbie Jones, Howard McGhee, Ray Nance, Clark Terry, Cootie Williams (*t*); Lawrence Brown, Chuck Connors, Buster Cooper, Quentin Jackson, John Sanders, Britt Woodman (*tb*); Harry Carney, Paul Gonsalves, Jimmy Hamilton, Johnny Hodges, Russell Procope (*reeds*); John Lamb, Jimmy Woode (*b*); Louie Bellson, Chris Columbus, Rufus Jones, Steve Little, Sam Woodyard (*d*). 1/57–7/67.

***(*) **Volume 9: Studio Sessions, New York, 1968** Saja 791233 2
    Ellington; Cat Anderson, Willie Cook, Money Johnson, Cootie Williams (*t*); Lawrence Brown, Chuck Connors, Buster Cooper (*tb*); Harold Ashby, Harry Carney, Paul Gonsalves, Johnny Hodges, Russell Procope (*reeds*); Jeff Castleman (*b*); Rufus Jones (*d*); Trish Turner (*v*). 11–12/68.

*** **Volume 10: Studio Sessions, New York & Chicago, 1965, 1966 & 1971** Saja 791234 2
    Ellington; Cat Anderson, Mercer Ellington, Money Johnson, Herbie Jones, Eddie Preston, Paul Serrano, Cootie Williams, Richard Williams (*t*); Ray Nance (*c, v*); Lawrence Brown, Chuck Connors, Buster Cooper, Malcolm Taylor, Booty Wood (*tb*); Harold Ashby, Harry Carney, Jimmy Hamilton, Johnny Hodges, Buddy Pearson, Russell Procope, Norris Turney (*reeds*); Joe Benjamin, John Lamb (*b*); Rufus Jones, Sam Woodyard (*d*); Tony Watkins (*v*). 3/65–5/71.

Duke Ellington was one of the first composers – in any field – to recognize the aesthetic implications of recording. His own forays into the industry were not marked with unqualified success; his investment in both Musicraft and Sunrise (a gamble prompted by the post-war recording ban) was largely lost, and the later Mercer label, administered by his son, was a flop. It did, though, become Ellington's practice to document his work on tape and this remarkable ten-CD set represents the Duke's personal archive of compositions and arrangements. Given its bulk and the availability elsewhere of most of the compositions covered, it's chiefly for serious Ellington scholars. However, discs can be purchased individually, and the best of them have sufficient intrinsic merit to be attractive to more casual listeners.

Best of all, perhaps, is Volume 1, devoted to a vintage year for the Ellington band. Johnny Hodges had just returned to the band after his solo foray, and Newport in the summer was to be the scene of Ellington's greatest triumph. At the festival, Paul Gonsalves played one of the historic solos of modern jazz, a staggering 27 choruses on 'Diminuendo And Crescendo In Blue'. Appropriately, it's Gonsalves, rather than the returned prodigal, Hodges, who dominates the Chicago *Studio Sessions*. He is brilliant on 'Satin Doll' and 'In A Sentimental Mood' and takes over from Ray Nance on Mercer's 'Moon Mist', a theme originally composed for Ben Webster but which became inextricably associated with the fiddle-playing trumpeter. Hodges stakes his claim with a beautiful chorus on 'Prelude To A Kiss'.

Hodges and Cat Anderson don't appear on the 1958 dance concerts, which are spread across Volumes 2 and 6, the latter disc covering a second night at the Travis Air Force base in California. Both are jolly, rather shambolic affairs, beautifully recorded by Wally Heider but somewhat lacking in substance. On the first of the pair, Nance sings a second version of 'Take The "A" Train' and there's a wild, impromptu arrangement of 'Oh! Lady Be Good'. Perhaps the best track, ironically, is an arrangement of Basie's 'One O'Clock Jump' theme, with Ellington taking off his friendly rival in the opening statement and the ensembles rocking along in good Kansas City fashion. Baker's solo on 'Willow Weep For Me' looks like being the highpoint of Volume 6, until Ray Nance steps in with a perfectly crafted solo on 'Caravan'. The version of 'Blues In Orbit' is longer and more open-textured than the issued version, above, and Ellington's piano work is supreme.

'E.S.P.' was written as a feature for Gonsalves, who tries it out on Volume 3 with characteristic self-confidence and speed of thought. In the same way, Johnny Hodges's reading of the classic 'Isfahan' on the 1963 New York sessions (Volume 4) is a try-out for the magnificent *Far East Suite*. The great satisfaction of these recordings is in being able to hear Duke work out new and challenging arrangements. 'Take It Slow', again from New York in 1962, is scored for three trombones, three saxophones and rhythm, and it steers a wistful course under Gonsalves's fine solo. 'Cordon Bleu' is interesting in that Ellington and Strayhorn alternate at the piano and duet briefly when Duke arrives back from a spot of conducting. Cootie Williams had just returned to the fold and was welcomed back with a 'New Concerto' and with a ranking solo on 'September 12th Blues'.

'The Degas Suite' on Volume 5 was written for the soundtrack of a film about the French Impressionist painter. When the project ran out of money, Ellington was given back the score in recompense. It's a brightly lit work, scored for a much smaller band than usual, with a lot of humour and dabbed with detail that close up or on a score would make no sense, but which contributes perfectly to the overall impact. Volume 5 is completed with a run-down of an original danced score, *The River*, commissioned for the American Ballet Theater. It's a meditative, rather inward work, bubbling up from the 'The Spring', a solo piece by the piano player, and then flowing down towards Carney's deep, dark solo on 'Her Majesty The Sea', taking in obvious geographical features on the way, but also touching human settlements like 'The Neo-Hip-Hot Kiddies Communities' and the contrasting 'Village Of The Virgins' along the way. It's hard to judge which community Duke would have felt most at home in.

Like Volume 6, the last four discs jump back in time somewhat, taking in a decade's worth of studio material, leading up to the death of Billy Strayhorn in 1967. Some of the tapes have deteriorated rather badly and the sound is somewhat unreliable, but they give a fascinating glimpse of Ellington in a workshop setting and represent a valuable checklist of his compositional output throughout his career. Highlights? Hodges's 'Sophisticated Lady' with just rhythm on Volume 9 and his rather inward 'Something Sexual' on 7; Anderson's blood'n'sand 'El Viti' on 8; and the sections from *Black, Brown And Beige* on the final volume.

No one had ever or has since done more with the jazz orchestra, and these recordings (some of them merely torsos, some of commercially unacceptable sound-quality) are a fitting monument to Ellington's genius. They are also something more important: a living laboratory for musicians, composers and arrangers, which was Ellington's other purpose. The 'stockpile', as he called it, was expected to pay dividends of one sort or another.

**** New Orleans Suite Atlantic 1580-2
    Ellington; Cootie Williams, Money Johnson, Al Rubin, Fred Stone (*t*); Booty Wood, Julian
    Priester, Chuck Connors (*tb*); Dave Taylor (*btb*); Russell Procope, Norris Turney, Harry
    Carney, Paul Gonsalves (*reeds*); Wild Bill Davis (*org*); Joe Benjamin (*b*); Rufus Jones (*d*). 4–5/
    70.

Arguably the final masterpiece, though the disc immediately below is an important one. Ellington looked to create another of his quasi-historical overviews here, but there was no commentary, just a sequence of intensely beautiful vignettes. The rollicking 'Blues For New Orleans' which opens the set features Davis in a very effective cameo, but the wellspring of this album is the sound of the orchestra rather than individual soloists: the reed section is truly on song for the last time (Hodges died during the making of the album and is absent from the final tracks). Gonsalves and Carney abide, though, and the scoring for 'Second Line', 'Bourbon Street Jingling Jollies' and 'Portrait Of Mahalia Jackson' is sadly beautiful, exceptionally expressive. 'Portrait Of Wellman Braud' is also a fascinating rhythmic exercise.

***(*) Latin American Suite Original Jazz Classics OJC 469
    Ellington; Lawrence Brown, Buster Cooper (*tb*); Johnny Hodges (*as*); Paul Gonsalves (*ts*);
    Harry Carney (*bs*); only soloists identified. 72.

Typically, this late suite is not an attempt to reduplicate the sounds and rhythms Ellington and his band heard on their first trans-equatorial trip in 1968 (surprisingly late in his career, on the face of it). Rather, it records the very personal impressions the southern half of the Americas made on a mind so fine that it was never violated by anything as vulgar as a new influence, and never so closed-off as to reject any new stimulus. Where most composer/bandleaders would have packed the rhythm section with congas, shakers and timbales, as Stanley Dance points out, Ellington conveys a strong Latin feel with his regular rhythm section. On the short 'Tina', an impression of Argentina, he uses a small rhythm group with two bassists and works a bluesy variation on the tango. (Elsewhere on the album, the bass is so heavily recorded that it sounds very much like an electric instrument; unfortunately, the personnel are not identified.) The bass is again important on the jovial 'Latin American Sunshine', paired with Ellington on a rather untypical theme statement. The opening 'Oclupaca', a title that follows the jazz cliché of reversing names, is a bright, danceable theme that recalls the Latin-influenced big bands of the 1930s and '40s. And that is the overall impression of the set. Perhaps fittingly, there is a nostalgic feel underneath its typically adventurous arrangements and voicings. There's a wistful quality to 'The Sleeping Lady And The Giant Who Watches Over Her', ostensibly the two mountains overlooking Mexico City; but one wonders if Ellington wasn't thinking about Latin America and the neo-colonial United States, with its cultural dominance and magpie eclecticism, and expressing a tinge of regret that he hadn't plunged into the music of the southern continent earlier in his career.

*** Never-Before-Released Recordings, 1965–1972 Musicmasters 65041-2
> As discs listed above, 65–72.

A very enjoyable *pot-pourri* of oddments from the workshop. There are two preliminary tries at three of the 'New Orleans Suite' pieces, as well as surprisingly effective features for Wild Bill Davis.

**(*) Live At The Witney Impulse 11732
> Ellington; Joe Benjamin (*b*); Rufus Jones (*d*). 4/72.

Another rare concert featuring the piano player – entirely by himself on many of the tunes. Nine rambling minutes of 'New World A-Coming' and a tune called 'A Mural From Two Perspectives', which is so clumsily played that it seems even Duke doesn't know it, are rather discouraging. There is much kidding aroud with the audience on the up-tempo pieces and the hits, and he even chucks in a minute or so of 'Soda Fountain Rag', his first composition. The piano-sound is bass-heavy and there is an audible hum during quiet passages.

** Duke's Big 4 Pablo 2310703
> Ellington; Joe Pass (*g*); Ray Brown (*b*); Louie Bellson (*d*). 73.

A jolly, matey sort of set that put little demand on the improvisational instincts of any of the participants. This was the sort of stuff they could all do blindfold at festivals and, apart from some of Duke's chording, which is typically unpredictable, there's not much to listen to.

***(*) Digital Duke GRP GRD 9548
> Mercer Ellington (*cond*); Kamau Adilefu, Barry Lee Hall, Lew Soloff, Clark Terry, Ron Tooley (*t, flhn*); Al Grey, Britt Woodman (*tb*); Chuck Connors (*btb*); Norris Turney (*as*); Jerry Dodgion (*as, cl*); Branford Marsalis (*ts*); Eddie Daniels, Herman Riley (*ts, cl*); Charles Owens (*bs, cl, bcl*); Roland Hanna, Gerald Wiggins (*p*); Bucky Pizzarelli (*g*); J. J. Wiggins (*b*); Louie Bellson, Rocky White (*d*). 87.

*** Music Is My Mistress Musicmasters 65013-2
> Barrie Lee Hall, John Longo, Tony Barrero, Tony Garruso, Kamau Adilefu (*t*); Ed Neumeister, Muhammed Abdul Al-Khabyyr, Britt Woodman, Raymond Harris (*tb*); Chuck Connors (*btb*); Sayyd Abdul Al-Khabyyr, Kenny Garrett, Victor Powell, Harold Minerve, Patience Higgins, Herman Riley, Bill Easley, Danny Bank, Joe Temperley (*reeds*); Sir Roland Hanna, Mulgrew Miller (*p*); Thomas James (*ky*); Kenny Burrell (*g*); Gerald Wiggins (*b*); Quentin White (*d*); Rudolph Bird, Ken Philmore (*perc*). 89.

Like most of the big bands that are great, the Ellington orchestra continued to perform after the leader's death. Frank Foster carried on the Basie band with great success, but Ellington had a literal heir among his musicians. Mercer Ellington took up the most daunting mantle in jazz with great professionalism. *Digital Duke* is perhaps the finest tribute to his work and, though some potential (or even actual) purchasers may feel let down when they realize the eponymous Duke is no longer present in the flesh, these latter-day performances of absolutely standard Ellington fare are not to be sneezed at.

Roland Hanna clearly isn't Ellington, but he mimics enough of the master's approach to the opening bars of 'Satin Doll' to more than pass muster. Elsewhere, he shares the solo space with Gerald Wiggins. Soloff makes a convincing high-note man ('Cottontail') but Clark Terry is the real thing on '22 Cent Stomp' (the US postage stamp of that denomination, celebrating Ellington, is on the cover) and 'Perdido'. Turney is another who had worked with the Duke in life, and he sounds poised and reflective in the Hodges role. Herman Riley and Branford Marsalis stand in for Gonsalves. Michael Abene's 32-track production is cracklingly precise, sometimes a little too up-front, ironically exposing just a hint of one-dimensionality in the arrangements, which completely lack Duke's mysterious ambiguities and daringly voiced chords. But it's a perfectly valid set.

As an encore, *Music Is My Mistress* is more ambitious but a shade less persuasive. Mercer finally tiptoes into the spotlight with three charts, including the extended title-piece, but one of these is a revision of his father's 'Azure', and the big work is a somewhat mixed success. But the band play with great gusto, the recording does well by the textures – a fine 'Jack The Bear' is a convincing interpretation of a classic Ellington sound – and this is certainly more impressive than the work Frank Foster has done with the ghost Basie band.

**(*) Only God Can Make A Tree Musicmasters 65117-2
> Barry Lee Hall Jr, Tony Barrero, John Longo, Anthony Garruso, Ron Tooley, James Zollar (*t*); Muhammed Abdul Al-Khabyyr, Raymond Harris, Art Barron, Brad Shigeta, Gregory Paul (*tb*); Charlie Young, Mark Gross, Sayyd Abdul Al-Khabyyr (*as*); Shelly Paul, Zane Zachoroff (*ts*); Jay Brandford (*bs*); Thomas James, Shuzuko Yokoyama (*p*); Steve Fox (*g*); Hassan Abdul Ash-Shakur, Peter Wiggins (*b*); Quentin White, Max Roach (*d*). 95.

Though titled as if it were another sacred concert, this mix of the spiritual and the profane is Mercer's farewell, since he died in January 1996. It doesn't much sound like any Ellington band one remembers and, though there are some intriguing choices of Ducal material – 'Ballet Of The Flying Saucers', 'Calyph', 'Matumbe' – this sequence of pieces associated with specific places is a colourful and enthusiastically played set. Not a very distinctive one, though. 'Caravan' and 'Trees' add the extra weight of the Brooklyn Philharmonic; Steve Fox's pieces are quite anonymous. The weakness lies in the rhythmic element: drawing beats out of rock, Latin and other pulses may be a modern necessity, but it's scarcely a progressive one, and it tends to make the band sound like any capable college outfit.

Don Ellis (1934–78) TRUMPET

*** . . . **How Time Passes** . . . Candid 9004
    Ellis; Jaki Byard (*p, as*); Ron Carter (*b*); Charli Persip (*d*). 10/60.
*** **Out Of Nowhere** Candid 9032
    Ellis; Paul Bley (*p*); Steve Swallow (*b*). 4/61.
*** **New Ideas** Original Jazz Classics OJC 431
    Ellis; Al Francis (*vib*); Jaki Byard (*p*); Ron Carter (*b*); Charli Persip (*d*). 6/61.
**** **Electric Bath** Columbia 472620
    Ellis; Glenn Stuart, Alan Weight, Ed Warren, Bob Harmon (*t*); Ron Myers, Dave Sanchez, Terry Woodson (*tb*); Ruben Leon, Joe Roccisano (*as, ss, f*); Ira Schulman (*ts, f, picc, cl*); Ron Starr (*ts, f, cl*); John Magruder (*bs, f, bcl*); Mike Lang (*p, ky*); Ray Neapolitan (*b, sitar*); Frank De la Rosa, Dave Parlato (*b*); Steve Bohannon (*d*); Chino Valdes, Mark Stevens, Alan Estes (*perc*). 9/67.
(*) **Autumn Columbia 472622
    Ellis; Glenn Stuart, Stu Blumberg, John Rosenberg, Bob Harmon (*t*); Ernie Carlson, Glenn Ferris, Don Switzer, Terry Woodson (*tb*); Doug Bixby, Roger Bobo (*tba*); Ira Schulman, Frank Strozier (*as*); Ron Starr (*as, f*); Sam Falzone, John Klemmer (*ts*); John Magruder (*bs*); Mike Lang, Pete Robinson (*ky*); Ray Neapolitan, Dave Parlato (*b*); Ralph Humphrey (*d*); Gene Strimling, Lee Pastora (*perc*). 68.

'I believe in making use of as wide a range of expressive techniques as possible.' Ellis never lost sight of his own artistic credo, making some of the most challenging music of recent times. Draw a line from Jimmy Giuffre to Maynard Ferguson and somewhere around its imaginary mid-point you might find Don Ellis; he has been alternately praised and decried as a latter-day Kenton, but he actually belongs to a much older and more jazz-centred tradition. *How Time Passes* was made before the Third Stream finally ran dry. Half the album is devoted to 'Improvisational Suite No. 1', in which the soloists are asked to extemporize, not on chord progressions or standard melodies, but on a relatively orthodox 12-tone row, distributed among the instruments and out of which chords can be built. The material is less reminiscent of Arnold Schoenberg, who'd spent his last years in Ellis's native California, than of Ernst Krenek, another European exile to the West Coast. Miraculously, it still swings.

The title-track is loosely inspired by Stockhausen's views on musical duration. The extraordinary accelerations and decelerations of tempo are initially almost laughable; but it's a highly significant piece, and Ellis's own solo (with Byard following less convincingly on his alto saxophone 'double') is superbly structured. The ballad 'Sallie' has a more straightforward modal theme.

Out Of Nowhere is much more conventional and standards-based, but Ellis plays lines and melodic inversions of considerable inventiveness, always striking out for the microtonal terrain he was to colonize later in the 1960s when he began to work on a four-valve quarter-tone trumpet. 'All The Things You Are' – a fifth take, incidentally – is quite extraordinary, running from free abstract patterns round the subdominant to fast, almost Delta-ish runs in quadruple time. The two versions of 'I Love You' show how he miscues occasionally here – but always in pursuit of metrical accents no one else was attempting at the time. Bley plays superbly, though unfortunately Swallow is a bit recessed in the mix.

On *New Ideas* Ellis moves effortlessly between the D flat blues of 'Uh Huh', the atonal 'Tragedy', the strict canon of 'Imitation' and the stark, improvisational approach of 'Despair To Hope' and a piece for unaccompanied trumpet. Even with a more conventional jazz context, the opening 'Natural H' and 'Cock And Bull' are strikingly original, with Ellis demonstrating an ability to assimilate advanced harmonic ideas to jazz. Challenging, provocative music, sympathetically recorded by Rudy van Gelder. The band are on the case from start to finish, with a particular word of praise for Francis, who has a demanding role. Ellis's own liner-notes are very informative about his methods.

The two Candids and the OJC are recommended to anyone interested in the technical development of modern jazz, but it's *Electric Bath* that will make the greatest impact. Ellis's commitment to extending the technical resources available to jazz players is perhaps most clearly traced in his use of the quarter-tone trumpet and in the extraordinary loop-delayed solo passage on 'Open Beauty', in which he creates huge swirls of sound out of the simplest harmonic elements. Even Palle Mikkelborg's experiments in the same vein have not been as startling.

Rhythmically, *Electric Bath* is pretty much of its time, except that rock drummers (Jethro Tull's apart) were rarely expected to play in 5 or 7. The band are all excellent readers and imaculately rehearsed. Even where the structural permutations are very complex, as on 'New Horizons' where a 17-bar theme is divided 5–5–7 and internally varied as well at each recapitulation so that the microtonality is also matched by fractional rhythms, there is no sign of stickiness or uncertainty in the ensembles. One intriguing aspect of the record is how often Ellis alludes to classic jazz: call-and-response choruses, a New Orleans coda to the 'Indian Lady', and jaunty boogie vamps amidst the alien landscape of 'New Horizons'.

Rarely can there have been such an effective use of electric piano in a big-band context: a soft tolling between G# and A in the same piece, each note placed exactly in the space; long abstract trills; chiming chords. Glorious stuff.

Though recorded the same year, *Autumn* is a disappointment. Too much Maynard, not enough Giuffre, one might say. It's a loud, directionless set in which the special effects and the off-kilter rhythms merely sound eccentric and wilful. Why there should be such a turn-around in such a short space of time, nobody can say. Where Ellis himself is delicate and rather precise, Glenn Stuart, the other featured soloist, blares at full throttle from the off and milks even the most elegant themes of their subtleties. In this version, even 'Indian Lady' sounds rather crass. Ellis lived only another decade. Given a new receptiveness to the kind of thing he was attempting in the 1960s, had he survived he might nowadays be considered an innovator on a par with George Russell and Gil Evans, rather than a somewhat peripheral experimenter.

Herb Ellis (born 1921) GUITAR

****** Nothin' But The Blues** Verve 521674-2
    Ellis; Roy Eldridge, Dizzy Gillespie (*t*); Stan Getz, Coleman Hawkins (*ts*); Oscar Peterson (*p*); Ray Brown (*b*); Stan Levey, Gus Johnson (*d*). 10/57–5/58.

The classic Ellis album is this one, cut in 1957 with a small group of Eldridge, Getz, Brown and Levey in tow. Despite the magisterial presence of the horns – Eldridge is absolutely commanding, peeling off some scalding open-horn choruses and a lovely, stealthy one with the mute on 'Tin Roof Blues', and Getz does his stomping-tenorman bit as well as the lyrical one – it's the guitarist who sets the tone: soft-spoken but swinging, artfully pushing the music forward, colouring the harmonies and opening up the piano-less group's sound, Ellis leads from behind and takes some of his best solos too. There are eight terrific tracks like this, with four makeweights from a session for some film music, where Gillespie and Hawkins also have brief cameos. In beautiful remastered sound.

***** Jazz / Concord** Concord CCD 6001
    Ellis; Joe Pass (*g*); Ray Brown (*b*); Jake Hanna (*d*). 72.
****(*) Seven Come Eleven** Concord CCD 6002
    As above. 7/73.
***** Soft Shoe** Concord CCD 6003
    Ellis; Harry 'Sweets' Edison (*t*); George Duke (*p*); Ray Brown (*b*); Jake Hanna (*d*). 74.
**** Rhythm Willie** Concord CCD 60
    Ellis; Ross Tompkins (*p*); Freddie Green (*g*); Ray Brown (*b*); Jake Hanna (*d*). 75.
***** Hot Tracks** Concord CCD 6012
    Ellis; Harry 'Sweets' Edison (*t*); Plas Johnson (*ts*); Mike Melvoin (*ky*); Ray Brown (*b*); Jake Hanna (*d*). 76.
****(*) Soft And Mellow** Concord CCD 4077
    Ellis; Ross Tompkins (*p*); Monty Budwig (*b*); Jake Hanna (*d*). 8/78.
***** Doggin' Around** Concord CCD 4372
    Ellis; Red Mitchell (*b, v*). 3/88.
***** Roll Call** Justice JR 1001-2
    Ellis; Jay Thomas (*flhn, ts*); John Frigo (*vn*); Mel Rhyne (*org*); Jake Hanna (*d*). 91.

Ellis was one of the early members of the Concord stable, and his first discs for the label set something of the house style: tempos at an easy jog, standard programmes with one or two eccentric choices ('Inka Dinka Doo' on *Soft Shoe*, 'Squatty Roo' on *Hot Tracks*), and bands that are like an assembly of old rogues joshing one another about old glories. The two albums with Edison and Brown are probably the best, with Ellis digging in a little harder than usual, the trumpeter turning in some of his wryest solos, and Brown insuperably masterful as always. The discs with Pass and Green tend to go the way of all such encounters, the pleasantness of the sound cancelling out most of the musical challenges, and the disc with Green is almost somnambulistic in parts. *Soft And Mellow* is another one that tends to live up to its title. But *Doggin' Around*, made after Ellis had been away from the label for some time, is probably the most engaging album of the lot. Red Mitchell thrives in this kind of open and relaxed situation, which gives him the chance to unearth some of his ripest licks, and Ellis sounds keen-witted in a way that he perhaps disguises on the earlier records. His playing at its best is as swinging and hard-hitting as that of more modern guitarists such as Farlow and Raney, but he can send himself to sleep at times. Still, any of these sessions will go down well as a late-night palliative after a hard day. The Justice record pulls together an unlikely personnel for a good-natured set that bounces between blues, hoedown (courtesy of Frigo) and small-hours swing. There's even a touch of gospel at the end with 'Amazing Grace', though that might not have been such a good idea.

Ziggy Elman (1914–68) TRUMPET

*** **Ziggy Elman And His Orchestra 1947** Circle CCD-70
   Elman; Harry DeVito (*tb*); Clint Garvin (*cl*); Johnny Hayes (*ts*); Virginia Maxey, Bob Manning (*v*); rest unlisted. 3–4/47.

Benny Goodman's other great trumpet mainstay in the 1930s (the first was Harry James, if you discount the errant Bunny Berigan), Ziggy Elman led bands of his own without a great deal of luck. There are some good pick-up sides from the late '30s collected on an Affinity CD, *Zaggin' With Zig* (AFS 1006), but this has already slipped out of circulation. This set of 1947 Lang–Worth transcriptions marks a brief period during which Ziggy was signed to MGM. The music is solid, functional swing, enlivened by spots from Hayes and DeVito and some respectable singing, especially from the Dick Haymes-like tenor of Bob Manning. Elman's brashly exuberant trumpet poses questions of taste, but the big sound of the band is persuasive enough. The remastering has been capably done.

Kahil El'Zabar DRUMS, PERCUSSION, FLUTE

(*) **The Ritual sound aspects sas 011
   El'Zabar; Lester Bowie (*t*); Malachi Favors (*b*). 11/85.
*** **Sacred Love** sound aspects sas 021
   As above, except add Raphael Garrett (*cl, perc*). 11/85.
*** **Another Kind Of Groove** sound aspects sas 016
   El'Zabar; Billy Bang (*vn, bells*); Malachi Favors (*b, perc*). 5/86.
*** **Ancestral Song** Silkheart SH 108
   El'Zabar; Joseph Bowie (*tb, mar, perc*); Edward Wilkerson (*ts, cl, perc*). 5/87.
***(*) **Hang Tuff** Open Minds 2405
   As above. 11/90.
**** **Dance With The Ancestors** Chameleon 8808
   As above. 91.
*** **Big Cliff** Delmark DE-477
   El'Zabar; Ari Brown (*ts, p*); Billy Bang (*vn*); Malachi Favors (*b*). 9/94.

El'Zabar is a percussionist with a knack for creating exciting musical situations out of elemental materials. He often refers to his groups as the Ethnic Heritage Ensemble, and the Silkheart and Chameleon releases listed above go under that name (unfortunately, the debut album by the group, the splendid *Three Gentlemen From Chicago* on Moers 01076, is not yet available on CD). *The Ritual* rambles on rather too much, consisting of a single, 42-minute improvisation, with the usual quota of dead spots as well as some more telling interplay. When he is joined by Garrett, in a session recorded on the same occasion, the music becomes more expressive, more sonorously powerful, with the coda of 'There Is No Greater Love' sounding oddly poetic. *Another Kind Of Groove* adds another maverick voice, that of Billy Bang, to El'Zabar's mix: his tersely swinging violin parts sit well with the rhythm team, though an extra horn might have have alleviated the occasional dryness in the trio's sound.

   The three releases by the trio of El'Zabar, Bowie and Wilkerson suggest a group that has grown in stature with each release. *Ancestral Song* was a somewhat modest start, with Bowie's lines offering only cautious counterpoint to Wilkerson's intensities, and the following *Hang Tuff* has a quiet, chamberish quality which suggests that the horn players felt slightly constrained by El'Zabar's concentration on texture. *Dance With The Ancestors*, though, makes clear the relationships within the group: Bowie acts more as a bassman than as second horn, with most of the themes pivoting round him, while El'Zabar's percussion parts lend colour and melodic variations as well as rhythm. Wilkerson, in mighty form on tenor, commands the real attention in improvising terms. Whether marching through 'Take The "A" Train' or one of their own, somewhat enigmatic, free pieces, the group suggests fresh avenues for Chicago jazz to turn down next.

Big Cliff gets its biggest kicks out of the title-piece, in which Bang and Brown take boiling solos, and the funky fun of 'Another Kind Of Groove', where the sawing violin over the hypnotic bomp rhythms starts to get a hypnotic happening under way. Though the music is dedicated to El'Zabar's late father, this is celebratory music and, if scarcely a new take either on what he's done before or on Chicago jazz itself, it's a very satisfying record.

Jorgen Emborg (born 1953) PIANO

***(*) **Over The Rainbow** Storyville STCD 4183

Emborg; Fredrik Lundin (*ss, ts*); Steve Swallow (*b*); Alex Riel (*d*); Lisbeth Diers (*perc*). 3/92.

This disc was commissioned as part of the annual JAZZPAR awards, made by Skandinavisk Tobakskompagni and the Danish Jazz Centre, Emborg inviting Swallow to work with him. The result is an airy, graceful, modern set of wonderful lyricism. Emborg's cultivated touch and flowing line pay their dues to the Evans school and, with a translucent version of 'Peace Piece' in the programme, that debt is almost too obvious. But rhythmically he's his own man, and the balance of the group is beautifully poised, the ensembles spacious but with plenty of inner life. Swallow and Riel are something of a dream team at the back, with the bassist doubling guitar-like runs with solid formations and Riel scampering around the time. Lundin is a shade less interesting, though the five closing tracks, each a duet for sax and piano, are a purposeful meditation. Strongly recommended.

Andy Emler PIANO, KEYBOARDS, VOICE

*** **Headgames** Label Bleu LBLC 6553

Emler; Michel Massot (*tba, v*); Philippe Sellam (*as, ss, v*); Simon Spang-Hanssen (*ts, ss, v*); Nguyen Le (*g, syn, v*); François Moutin (*b, v*); Tony Rabeson (*d, v*); François Verly (*perc, mar, tabla, v*). 6 & 9/92.

Emler's Megaoctet develops from fairly unpromising beginnings, irritating synth-processed voices and noodling keyboards, going nowhere. The opening sequence is overlong by a good couple of minutes but, astonishingly, turns into something almost majestic. Emler is a subtle, clever craftsman who distrusts mere show and display, favouring intelligent ensemble work. Guitarist Le is given due prominence, but *Headgames* is otherwise refreshingly free of cult-of-personality flourishes. Good, but needs work.

Giuseppe Emmanuele PIANO

*** **A Waltz For Debby** Splasc(h) H 200

Emmanuele; Paolo Fresu (*t, flhn*); Pietro Tonolo (*ss, ts*); Nello Toscano (*b*); Pucci Nicosia (*d*). 1/90.

*** **Reflections In Jazz** Splasc(h) H 389-2

As above, except Orazio Maugeri (*as*), Paolo Mappa (*d*) replace Fresu and Nicosia. 12/91.

A Waltz For Debby is a lovely record. Emmanuele is a Bill Evans admirer, and the quintet's version of the title-song pays suitable homage to its composer; but the four originals by the pianist show a light but clear watermark of his own, and he plays with strength as well as delicacy: the solo on an unusually sunny reading of Lennie Tristano's 'Wow' even suggests some of the energy of the young Tristano himself. Fresu and Tonolo, though, are probably the most accomplished players here and both have plenty of chances to shine. *Reflections In Jazz* is perhaps a degree less involving: Maugeri is a bustling player, but Fresu's elegance is missed and, though there is a limpid version of Ellington's 'On A Turquoise Cloud' to commence with, Emmanuele's music seems a fraction less beguiling this time. Tonolo, though, continues to impress.

Sidsel Endresen VOCALS

***(*) **So I Write** ECM 1048

Endresen; Nils Petter Molvaer (*t, flhn, perc*); Django Bates (*p*); Jon Christensen (*d*). 6/90.

***(*) **Here The Moon** ECM 1524

As above, except add Jens Bugge Wesseltoft (*ky*); David Darling (*clo*). 8/93.

Working rather obliquely outwards from a jazz/folk/improvised idiom, Endresen sings with a deceptive range that pushes her up into the lyric-soprano register and down into contralto accents on the more sombre songs. Jon Balke's settings on the first record, to 'So I Write', 'This Is The Movie' and

'Dreamland', perfectly suit her slightly prosaic lyrics. There are no up-tempo tracks but, whether singing exactly on the beat or drawing out the words without any pretext of verse-metre, Endresen seems completely confident, and the accompanying group is superb though often minimal in gesture. Bates – who's credited with the two weakest compositions – plays beautifully: no electronics, no horn, no additional percussion, just beautifully modulated stylings which accord with the accompanist's duty to point up the words without swamping them.

Bates takes his tenor horn along for the later date, which has a much richer instrumental palette. Endresen's singing is stronger and more pointedly articulated, so there is no risk of her being over-powered. The songs are interspersed with variations in which Darling plays a big part. A very solid consolidation of a most impressive debut.

The Enja Band GROUP

*** **Live At Sweet Basil** Enja ENJ 8034
> Willie Williams (*ts, ss*); Gust William Tsilis (*vib, mar*); Uri Caine (*p*); Michael Formanek (*b*);
> Cecil Brooks III (*d*). 12/92.

Rather a good label band as label bands go; as the CD title indicates, this isn't just a prowl around the studio but a serious showcase gig in a top-drawer club. Each of the participants is a composer and bandleader in his own right and the evening was undoubtedly intended to draw attention to their issued work and to generate anticipation of forthcoming contractual fulfilments. However, as reviewers noted at the time, it was clear that this band enjoyed a sensitive – and occasionally roistering – empathy usually heard only in more settled outfits.

Tsilis and Williams claim the bulk of the writing credits. The opening pair – 'The Unnameable' and 'Purse' – offer contrasting insights into the vibes player's rather brooding creative personality. It's clear that he himself probably wouldn't have recruited a saxophonist like Williams; since he's there, though, both themes take unexpected and unexpectedly bluesy turns that must have intrigued the composer. Their free-form introduction to Formanek's 'Snalking' suggests future collaborations shouldn't be ruled out.

'Snalking' is a fierce, winding theme that is sure to have attracted the notice of more ambitious leaders sitting in the crowd. The bassist is perhaps the key element in the group. The less experienced Caine here and there sounds tentative, even on his own generously proportioned 'Form An X', and Brooks's clattering solo on 'Snalking' contains nothing rhythmically that wasn't already hinted at in the intro. For sheer beauty, Tsilis captures the honours with 'The Duke And Mr Strayhorn', an open-ended, con-temporary ballad with lots of room for all the participants.

Still most useful as an introduction to five disparate talents, but don't overlook this one.

Enten Eller GROUP

*** **Antigone** Splasc(h) H 352-2
> Mario Simeoni (*ts, f*); Carlo Actis Dato (*ts, bs, bcl*); Ugo Boscain (*p*); Giovanni Maier (*b*);
> Massimo Barbiero (*d*); Alex Rolle, Andrea Stracuzzi (*perc*). 1/91.

This band is from Piedmont, which has spawned several of the best new Italian groups (Enrico Fazio, Claudio Lodati, Carlo Actis Dato). *Antigone* is their second album and is, if anything, even more brawling than their rough-and-ready earlier set, with the opening tracks, 'Il Mago' and 'Pragma', blown open by Actis Dato and Simeoni, but a lengthy set includes ballads too, and the basic quintet know each other's moves to make this blend of modal, bop and fusion leanings into an entertaining whole.

Ed Epstein (born 1946) BARITONE, TENOR AND SOPRANO SAXOPHONES

*** **The Art Of Survival** Olufsen DOCD 5131
> Epstein; Erling Kroner (*tb*); Peter Epstein (*ss, as*); Jan Lundgren, (*p*); Thomas Oveson (*b*);
> Jonas Johansen (*d*); Lisbeth Diers (*perc*). 6–7/90.

Epstein is a Texan saxophonist who decamped for Sweden at the end of the 1960s. This recent session reveals a conservative but energetic stylist who harks back to swing and mainstream tenor as well as to the familiar post-bop models. His son, Peter, is a happy choice as front-line partner (Kroner plays on only three tracks) and Epstein Senior's most distinctive horn proves to be the baritone, which he solos on with as much gusto as he does tenor. The all-original material is no great shakes but there's plenty of good-humoured blowing here.

Rolf Ericson (born 1922) TRUMPET

*** **Rolf Ericson & The American Stars 1956** Dragon DRCD 255
Ericson; Lars Gullin, Cecil Payne (*bs*); Duke Jordan, Freddie Redd (*p*); John Simmons, Tommy Potter (*b*); Art Taylor, Joe Harris (*d*); Ernestine Anderson (*v*). 6–7/56.
*** **Stockholm Sweetnin'** Dragon DRCD 256
Ericson; Nils Sandstrom (*ts, p*); Claes Crona (*p*); Goran Lindberg (*b*); Mel Lewis (*d*). 8/84–7/85.
*** **Ellington & Strayhorn** Sittel SITCD 9223
Ericson; Lennart Aberg (*ss, ts, f*); Bobo Stenson (*p*); Goran Klinghagen, Max Schultz (*g*); Dan Berglund (*b*); Egil Johansen (*d*); Rose-Marie Aberg (*v*). 1/95.

Sweden's elder statesman of jazz trumpet, whose fairly astonishing career has taken in playing with everyone from Parker to Ellington. The 1956 recordings date from a tour when Rolf was asked to front a band of Americans for a Swedish visit. The first tour was wrecked by the narcotic problems of two of the visitors, and only four tracks by this sextet survive. The bulk of the disc has Ericson and Gullin in the front line, with Redd, Potter and Harris in the rhythm section. Despite the problems, the tour was instrumental in bringing a wave of hard bop into Sweden, previously drawn more to American cool. Ericson and Gullin are in brimming form, though the live recording isn't ideal. Anderson sings on six tracks.

Ericson was still in fine fettle on the 1984 date for Dragon: a good, juicy selection of jazz tunes and standards by a useful little band, with Sandstrom's Lestorian tenor a fine foil; there are four previously unreleased trumpet–piano duets with Crona as a bonus. He takes things a little more gingerly on the set of Ellington and Strayhorn tunes for Sittel, but it's an even better band – Aberg's solemn tenor, Stenson's unfailingly intelligent piano, the light, deep rhythm section. One or two too-obvious choices, but a couple of nice rarities – and the studio sound is gorgeous: try Rolf's muted work on 'Star-Crossed Lovers'.

Peter Erskine (born 1954) DRUMS

*** **Peter Erskine** Original Jazz Classics OJC 610
Erskine; Randy Brecker (*t, flhn*); Michael Brecker (*ts*); Bob Mintzer (*ts, bcl*); Don Grolnick, Kenny Kirkland (*p*); Mike Mainieri (*vib*); Eddie Gomez (*b*); Don Alias (*perc*). 6/82.
Erskine is (justifiably) among the most sought-after drummers of the contemporary American circuit: besides his formidable technique, he's gregarious enough to handle virtually any musical situation and is a thoughtful composer to boot. His first record as a leader found him in charge of a relatively straight-forward post-bop session; but, with such a heavyweight gathering of studio craftsmen all on their toes, the results are impressive if a little too brawny here and there.

**** **Transition** Denon 33CY-1484
Erskine; Joe Lovano (*ss, ts*); Bob Mintzer (*ts*); Peter Gordon (*frhn*); Kenny Werner, Don Grolnick (*ky*); John Abercrombie (*g, g-syn*); Marc Johnson (*b*). 10/86.
*** **Motion Poet** Denon CY 72582
Erskine; Randy Brecker, Lew Soloff, Joe Mosello (*t, flhn*); Dave Bargeron (*tb, tba*); Matt Finders (*btb*); Peter Gordon, Jerry Peel, John Clark (*frhn*); Lawrence Feldman (*ss, as, f*); Bob Mintzer (*ts, f*); Michael Brecker (*ts*); Roger Rosenberg (*bs*); Jim Beard, Eliane Elias (*ky*); John Abercrombie (*g, gsyn*); Jeff Mironov (*g*); Will Lee, Marc Johnson (*b*). 4–5/88.
Erskine outdid his leadership potential with these very fine records. He achieves the seemingly impos-sible task of diversifying the music without making it seem eclectic, giving himself considerable space without turning the sessions into mere 'drummer's records'. *Transition* is outstanding: richly melodic and detailed compositions by Erskine and Vince Mendoza, intensely committed playing by all hands, a lovely reading of 'My Foolish Heart' by the Erskine/Abercrombie/Johnson trio, and quite stunning digital sound. By comparison, *Motion Poet* is slightly less interesting, with a brass section used to no very telling effect, but there's an impeccable revision of Joe Zawinul's 'Dream Clock' and a fine Erskine ballad in 'Not A Word'. Both records prove what New York's finest studio players can do when they have a challenging assignment before them.

(*) **Big Theatre Ah Um 004
Erskine; Vince Mendoza (*t, flhn*); Peter Gordon, Jerry Peel (*frhn*); Don Grolnick (*ky*); Will Lee (*b, v*); Paulinho Da Costa (*perc*). 86–89.
Erskine has been commissioned to do a number of theatre scores, and this is the music from three different Shakespeare plays. Harmless, pretty putterings from the workshop, with sweet synthesizer dances and other fragments, most of them no more than a moment or two long; only Will Lee's vocal on

'O Mistress Mine' (no Elizabethan, he!) is unpalatable. But it's hardly much more than a distraction, or light background music.

***(*) Sweet Soul RCA Novus PD 90616
> Erskine; Randy Brecker (*t*); Joe Lovano (*ss, ts*); Bob Mintzer (*ts*); Kenny Werner (*p*); John Scofield (*g*); Marc Johnson (*b*). 3/91.

*** You Never Know ECM 1497
> Erskine; John Taylor (*p*); Palle Danielsson (*b*). 7/92.

***(*) Time Being ECM 1532
> As above. 11/93.

On his regular sessions Erskine continues to set a formidable standard. The lovely rearrangement of William Walton's 'Touch Her Soft Lips And Part' on Novus is another Shakespearean borrowing, and a more practical one: Lovano's bewitching drift is as haunting as anything he's done. Other credits are split between Erskine, Werner and Vince Mendoza, and there's not a weak tune in the pack. Improvisations grow naturally from their surroundings and even such over-exposed players as Brecker and Scofield function at their best. *You Never Know* is disappointing, perhaps, in that Erskine himself defers so much to Taylor: there is but a single composition by the leader, with four by Taylor and three (very good) by Vince Mendoza; this is really a piano album in which Erskine does conscientious time and duty. Taylor's lean pastoralisms are always interesting, seldom compelling. *Time Being* follows the same path but is more interesting. One reason is a greater sense of group identity, with the three men finding a teetering balance between their parts; another is the wider variation in material, with Staffan Linton's 'Liten Visa Till Karin' a particularly delightful choice; another is Danielsson's increasing involvement, his bass parts securing an eminent voice inside the trio. Impeccable.

Lars Erstrand VIBES

*** Two Sides Of Lars Erstrand Opus 3 8302
> Erstrand; Roland Jivelid (*ts*); Knud Jorgensen (*p*); Bertil Fernqvist (*g*); Arne Wilhelmsson (*b*); Pelle Hulten (*d*). 5–6/83.

*** Lars Erstrand And Four Brothers Opus 3 8402
> As above. 6/84.

*** Tribute To Benny Goodman Quartet Opus 3 8603
> Erstrand; Ove Lind (*cl*); Rolf Larsson (*p*); Pelle Hulten (*b*). 12/86.

**(*) Dream Dancing Opus 3 9101
> Erstrand; Kjell Ohman (*org*); Tommy Johnson (*b*); Gus Dhalberg (*d*). 2/91.

*** Beautiful Friendship – The First Set Sittel SITCD 9204
> As above, except add Ken Peplowski (*cl, ts*), Frank Vignola (*g*). 6/92.

*** Beautiful Friendship – The Second Set Sittel SITCD 9205
> As above. 6/92.

Erstrand's enduring admiration for the Lionel Hampton style – as best evidenced in their meeting on *Two Generations*, Phontastic 8807 – disguises a rather broader range of interests. *Two Sides* also touches on bebop in 'Sweet And Hot Mop' and even traces of European echoes of the MJQ in such as the Bach 'Invention In C Major'. This and the *Four Brothers* disc feature an entertaining band – Jivelid's nicely Lestorian tenor floats agreeably over the rhythm players, and Jorgensen unobtrusively steals the show on several tracks with some quick-witted improvisations. The Goodman tribute is an accurate-sounding evocation, with Lind's wonderfully supple lines twining round the vibes apparently effortlessly. The organ band with Ohman puts the pots on, at least compared with the other discs, and it encourages the vibesman to dig in more wholeheartedly than he does on some of the other records. *Dream Dancing* suffers from a few more laid-back and almost sleepwalking ballads, but the two live albums on Sittel have some genuine fire in the belly on the up-tempo tunes: 'Jim Dawgs' is almost over the top in its energies and 'Lady Be Good' personifies the swinging small combo. Peplowski is an unlikely man for a grooving organ/tenor band, but he puts his romantic hat on for the ballads and 'I Thought About You' on the first disc is a charmer. Second guest Vignola prefers strumming over single notes. But both discs have a sound-problem: the organ sounds either tinny or buzzy at different moments, and the overall mix seems rougher than it should have been. Erstrand enjoys it all, though.

Booker Ervin (1930–70) TENOR SAXOPHONE

*** Cookin' Savoy SV 0150
> Ervin; Richard Williams (*t*); Horace Parlan (*p*); George Tucker (*b*); Dannie Richmond (*d*). 11/60.

*** **Down In The Dumps** Savoy S V 0245

    As above, except add Billy Howell (*t*); Nat Phipps (*p*); Al Harewood (*d*); Barbara Long (*v*). 10/ 60, 1/61.

***(*) **That's It** Candid CCD 79014

    Ervin; Horace Parlan (*p*); George Tucker (*b*); Al Harewood (*d*). 1/61.

***(*) **The Song Book** Original Jazz Classics OJC 779

    Ervin; Tommy Flanagan (*p*); Richard Davis (*b*); Alan Dawson (*d*). 64.

***(*) **The Blues Book** Original Jazz Classics OJC 780

    Ervin; Carmell Jones (*t*); Gildo Mahones (*p*); Richard Davis (*b*); Alan Dawson (*d*). 64.

**** **The Freedom Book** Original Jazz Classics OJC 891

    Ervin; Jaki Byard (*p*); Richard Davis (*b*); Alan Dawson (*d*). 64.

***(*) **Setting The Pace** Prestige PRCD 24123

    Ervin; Dexter Gordon (*ts*); Jaki Byard (*p*); Reggie Workman (*b*); Alan Dawson (*d*). 65.

***(*) **Lament For Booker Ervin** Enja ENJ 2054

    Ervin; Kenny Drew, Horace Parlan (*p*); Niels-Henning Orsted-Pedersen (*b*); Alan Dawson (*d*). 10/65, 5/75.

It's slightly hard to credit that 'When You're Smiling' and 'The Trolley Song' on the recently restored *Down In The Dumps* and the sessions for the magnificent *That's It* were recorded on successive days. On the Candid album, Ervin is in full, fierce voice, blending elements of Don Byas and John Coltrane into a typical Texan shout. 'Uranus' is his finest ballad performance. George Tucker's deliberate introduction to 'Booker's Blues' takes the music down into some South-western storm cellar, where it spins out its unhurried message. To avoid contractual problems, Parlan was originally credited (with rather arcane literary humour) as 'Felix Krull', but there is nothing fraudulent about his playing on the album. He was always Ervin's most sympathetic sideman, and it was Parlan who spun out the 'Lament' for Ervin on the Enja, adding a sad, posthumous afterthought to a 1965 European session that rounds out the story with teasing intimations of what might have been.

    The reissued Savoy is just about as 'straight-ahead' as it comes. There's not much subtlety to the arrangements, which are played with a jumpy regularity, but Ervin and Williams both solo strongly, and the saxophonist's long meditation with rhythm only on 'You Don't Know What Love Is' is perhaps the most affecting extended performance on the record.

    The Prestiges, now available again on OJC (though *The Space Book* hasn't returned from orbit) are consistently excellent and mark the core of Ervin's output. Davis and Dawson are strong rhythm players of the kind the saxophonist needed, and their ability to play gently on the ballad album is as impressive as their driving beat on 'No Booze Blooze'. *The Freedom Book*, with its wider remit, is probably the best of the lot, with Byard a more robustly percussive and blues-aware pianist. Ervin commanded great loyalty and respect. With his catalogue brought up to date, it is easy to see why.

Christian Escoude GUITAR

*** **Gypsy Waltz** EmArCy 838772

    Escoude; Paul Challain, Jimmy Gourley, Frederic Sylvestre (*g*); Marcel Azzola (*acc*); Vincent Courtois (*clo*); Alby Cullaz (*b*); Philippe Combelle (*d*). 5/89.

**** **Cookin' In Hell's Kitchen** Verve 526 743

    Escoude; Tom Harrell (*t, flhn*); Rodney Kendrick (*p*); Michael Bowie (*b*); Alvester Garnett (*d*); Chi Sharpe (*d*). 11/94.

There are other Escoude records available on Emarcy (including the inevitable 'plays Django' date), but these may be the most widely available, and they offer a reasonable sampling of his range. The earlier record is squarely in the Reinhardt tradition, though Escoude sounds nothing like the master, favouring a more smoothly picked line. The 1994 album is much more obviously jazz-centred and the bigger band coaxes him into higher gear and a more fulsomely expressive style that cuts through even Kendrick's tastier accompaniments. Harrell, as always, is a master, working his own variations on relatively stand-ard changes and doing so in a voice of compelling grace and maturity. There are moments on all his records when Escoude drifts close to the shoals of easy listening; this one alone would be enough to guarantee serious attention.

Dave Eshelman TROMBONE

***(*) **Deep Voices** Sea Breeze SB 2039

    Eshelman; Rich Theurer, Bill Resch, Dave Bendigkeit, Steve Campos (*t, flhn*); John Russell, Mike Humphrey, Chris Braymen, Phil Zahorsky (*tb*); Mary Park (*as, f*); Rory Snyder (*as, f, cl*);

Daniel Zinn (*ts, f*); Glenn Richardson (*ts, f, cl, picc*); Joe Henderson (ts); Bob Farrington (*bs, f, cl, bcl*); Smith Dobson (*p*); Bruce Forman (*g*); Seward McCain (*b*); Russ Tincher (*d*). 10/88.

*** **When Dreams Come True** Sea Breeze S B 2045

Eshelman; Marvin McFadden, Bill Resch, Steve Campos, Dan Buegelsen (*t, flhn*); John Russell, Dave Martell, Chip Tingle, Dave Gregoric (*tb*); Phil Zahorsky (*btb*); Larry Osborne (*frhn*); Mary Fettig, Rory Snyder, Paul Contos, Dan Zinn, Bob Farrington, Bennett Friedman, Dominic Teresi, Steve Parker (*reeds*); Susan Muscarella, Smith Dobson (*p*); Tom Volpicella (*g*); Dennis Cooper (*vib*); Seward McCain (*b*); Russ Tincher (*d*); Michael Spiro (*perc*). 12/91–1/92.

Southern California has been a spawning ground for a number of interesting bands in the past 20 years, with such West Coast hold-outs as Gerald Wilson maintaining a West Coast tradition, which groups like Eshelman's Jazz Garden Big Band – a San Francisco fixture through the late 1970s and '80s – have amplified further. These are unflashy, thoughtful sessions which are beautifully performed without resorting to slickness or facile racing. A trombonist himself, Eshelman gets a fine, singing timbre out of his 'bone section, and he pitches it to scintillating effect against the trumpets and woodwinds: sample the fascinating arrangement of 'Softly As In A Morning Sunrise' on *Deep Voices*. This album takes the lead for a couple of guest spots by Joe Henderson and Bruce Forman, whose guitar solo on 'To Catch A Rainbow' is a thrilling beat-the-clock feat. Even the title-work on *Deep Voices*, which tackles the favourite Californian topic of whale-song, sidesteps bathos. If the more recent *When Dreams Come True* is a shade behind, it's only because the soloists in it make a more functional mark than their illustrious predecessors on the earlier disc. Eshelman's own writing continues to put his personal stamp on what is often a glib, overslick genre: the beautiful reshaping of 'Invitation' and 'Old Folks' is as accomplished as his amusing Latin pastiche, 'Tumbao Nuevo'.

Ellery Eskelin (born 1959) TENOR SAX

*** **Forms** Open Mind 2403

Eskelin; Drew Gress (*b*); Phil Haynes (*d*). 3/90.

**** **Figure Of Speech** Soul Note 121232-2

Eskelin; Joe Daley (*tba*); Arto Tuncboyaci (*perc*). 7/91.

***(*) **Premonition** Prime Source 2010

Eskelin (*ts* solo). 7/92.

*** **Jazz Trash** Songlines SG L 1506-2

Eskelin; Andrea Parkins (*acc, sampler*); Jim Black (*d*). 10/94.

While there are countless young tenor players making records, Eskelin is one who deserves more than a single glance. Gress and Haynes are regular working partners with Eskelin; as a unit, the trio plays with unusual empathy. The saxophonist has a querulous tone and likes to stretch phrases into elongated shapes that push against what are otherwise fairly conventional parameters: he chooses standards or simple thematic constructions to play on, and sounds to be good at moving in and out of familiar tonalities. Gress and Haynes don't so much follow as run along parallel paths, commenting and abstracting ideas of their own: Haynes can be rather carefree with his cymbals, but it's a trio in which everybody talks.

Forms is superior to their debut LP for Cadence (not yet on CD) – better played, better recorded, with five originals plus Ellington's 'African Flower' and Gillespie's 'Bebop'. The trio's collective intensity is best caught on 'Blues' and 'In Three', while 'Ballad' has Eskelin exploring the horn with plangent authority. It's still redolent of sketchwork in parts, and a couple of the tracks are simply too long, but these are clearly musicians with something to say.

Figure Of Speech is a real breakthrough, though. Eskelin's purposeful avoidance of the obvious routes of improvisation – specifically, theme-and-variation structures – brings a rare sense of something new to this project in particular. Daley's tuba and Tuncboyaci's quiet, pattering percussion are important voices, but their essentially simple figures throw the detail and complexity of Eskelin's own playing into very sharp relief. The tunes revolve round carefully coded motifs or structural ideas without depending on them: the improvisations usually form separate entities of their own, contrasting with (rather than commenting on) the written material. This is a rare kind of freedom, negotiated with superb assurance by all three men.

The solo album, *Premonition*, might be for more rarefied tastes, but there's no doubting Eskelin's mastery of the horn or his ingenuity in dealing with the chosen material here. While there are three improvisations that deal with timbral extremes, wide intervals and rhythmic variations, the three further solos based on standard tunes are even more remarkable, culminating in a bizarre demolition of 'Besame Mucho'. Much is reminiscent here of an early David Murray solo album, particularly Eskelin's big tone and busker's vibrato, but this is less obviously experimental, more achieved.

Jazz Trash has 'interesting' writ large, but goes little further. Eskelin skirmishes with Parkins and Black rather than creating any tangible interplay and, while there are numerous intriguing moments – 'Rain' is a nicely abstruse essay on ballad form, for instance – there's a certain paucity to the textures which makes it hard to sustain over the 70-odd minutes.

John Etheridge GUITAR

** Ash The Jazz Label TJL 103
Etheridge; Steve Franklin (*p, ky*); Dudley Phillips, Henry Thomas (*b*); Mark Fletcher (*d*). 93.
Founder Danny Thompson's list of professional credits on the inside sleeve may suggest to some that The Jazz Label (an admirable undertaking on its own terms) isn't at all what it claims to be. Five minutes of John Etheridge's smoothly intelligent fusion will have boppers reaching for the STOP button. This is a working band, with a lot of miles under its feet; unfortunately most of the artistic itinerary is contained within a time and idiom that most people thought had ended with the 1970s. Etheridge tries to vary the diet with Brubeck's 'In Your Own Sweet Way', compositions by Cedar Walton ('Ugetsu'), Wayne Shorter ('Infant Eyes'), and Ron Carter ('81'), roughens up the usual latter-day approach to Hendrix's 'Little Wing', and tries to give the set a semblance of conceptual coherence with an intro and outro that do no more than confirm its basic blandness and uniformity.

Kevin Eubanks (born 1957) GUITAR, ELECTRIC GUITAR

*** Guitarist Discovery 1046 71006
Eubanks; Robin Eubanks (*tb*); Ralph Moore (*ts*); Charles Eubanks (*p*); David Eubanks (*b*); Ronnie Burrage, Tommy Campbell, Roy Haynes (*d*). 83.
**(*) Face To Face GRP D 9539
Eubanks; Dave Grusin (*DX7 computer*); Ron Carter, Marcus Miller (*b*); Buddy Williams (*d*); Crusher Bennett, Paulinho Braga, Ralph McDonald (*perc*). 86.
** The Heat Of Heat GRP 9552
Eubanks; Onaje Allan Gumbs, Patrice Rushen (*ky*); Ron Carter, Rael Wesley Grant (*b*); Gene Jackson (*d*); Don Alias (*perc*). 87.
* Shadow Prophets GRP 9565
Eubanks; Victor Bailey, Rael Wesley Grant (*b*); Tommy Campbell, Gene Jackson (*d*); Mark Ledford (*v*); Onaje Allan Gumbs (*syn strings*). 1/88.
*(*) The Searcher GRP 9580
Eubanks; Edward Simon (*p*); Victor Bailey, Kenny Davis (*b*); Dennis Chambers, Gene Jackson (*d*); Mark Ledford (*v, v perc*); Duane Cook Broadnax (*beatbox drum v*). 11/88.
**(*) Promise Of Tomorrow GRP 9604
Eubanks; Edward Simon (*p, ky*); Kenny Davis (*b*); Gene Jackson, Marvin 'Smitty' Smith (*d*). 11/89.
*** Turning Point Blue Note CDP 798170
Eubanks; Kent Jordan (*af*); Dave Holland, Charnett Moffett (*b*); Mark Mondesir, Marvin 'Smitty' Smith (*d*). 12/91.
**** Spirit Talk Blue Note CDP 7 89286
Eubanks; Robin Eubanks (*tb*); Kent Jordan (*af*); Dave Holland (*b*); Mark Mondesir (*d*); Marvin 'Smitty' Smith (*d, perc, v*). 4/93.
Dripping with talent and technique, Kevin Eubanks has yet to produce anything on record genuinely commensurate with either. All too often the albums drift off into soft elevator funk, laced with mawkish dedications (notably to Krishnamurti) and superadded 'effects'. Long-term residency on the *Tonight* show probably hasn't helped his progress. All the more irritating when, as an unaccompanied 'Blue In Green' on *Guitarist* shows, he is capable of some delicacy and invention when the mood takes him.

There is a very definite shift and change in Eubanks's output, a long, slow dip into drear fusion that makes the excellence of the first album here (in parts) and the later Blue Note sets all the more puzzling. There are adventurous duos with Ron Carter on 'Relaxin' at Camarillo' and the Krishnamurti-inspired 'Silent Waltz', but for the most part he shuts down this aspect of his playing for the remainder of the decade; 'Poem For A Sleeping Child', which closes *The Searcher*, is a piece of New Age thistledown. The glycerined-bicep guitar hero cover-shot to *The Heat Of Heat* (Eubanks is a big sports and iron-pumping enthusiast) is coupled with dire warnings of a 'rock guitar solo' among the credits. In reality, and in body-building parlance, the solo has very poor def indeed: a lot of posing and fake-sweat, no stamina or lasting muscle.

Eubanks is a more than competent composer: he understands advanced harmony and has pushed through and beyond his initial dedication to George Benson. Even so, he suffers recurrent lapses of judgement. *Shadow Prophets* is certainly the nadir, opening with sampled voices and the unrelieved keyboard surf that constantly swamps Eubanks's fleet lines. 'Cookin'', on *The Searcher*, treads basically the same path with sub-McFerrin vocal percussion and ultra-bland octave guitar effects.

Promise Of Tomorrow brings some relief. The guitar gets back on top of the wave again, and there is A Standard (!), 'In A Sentimental Mood', played with gentle conviction, acoustic piano well up. Some of these qualities are carried over to the first Blue Note, where (as per label policy, he finds himself surrounded by quality British and American players. The in-demand Mondesir is a revelation on 'Freedom Child' and 'One Way To Paradise' and there are exceptionally mellow noises from Jordan's big flute. A turning point? . . .

. . . Seems so in retrospect. *Spirit Talk* is arguably his first straight jazz record, and very good it is too. As so often in the past, the relationship that really counts is with brother Robin, who makes a powerful intervention on 'Union', while Jordan sustains the dialogue elsewhere. Dave Holland is utterly solid and inventive, as ever, and fellow-Brit Mondesir continues his march into legend with another sterling performance, good enough to knock the ubiquitous Smitty into the proverbial cocked hat. A happy disc, packed to the brim with music, easy on the special FX. Watch this space.

Robin Eubanks (born 1959) TROMBONE, BASS TROMBONE, KEYBOARDS

*** Different Perspectives JMT 834424
Eubanks; Michael Phillip Mossman (*flhn*); Clifton Anderson, Slide Hampton (*tb*); Douglas Purviance (*btb*); Steve Coleman (*as*); Kevin Eubanks (*g*); James Weidman (*p, syn*); Peter Washington, Rael Wesley Grant (*b*); Terri Lyne Carrington, Jeff Tain Watts (*d*).

*** Dedication JMT 834433
Eubanks; Steve Turre (*tb*); Mulgrew Miller (*p, syn*); Francesca Tanksley (*syn*); Charnett Moffett (*b*); Tommy Campbell, Tony Reedus (*d*); Jimmy Delgado (*congas, perc*). 4/89.

**(*) Karma JMT 834446
Eubanks; Earl Gardner (*t*); Greg Osby (*as*); Branford Marsalis (*ts*); Kevin Eubanks (*g*); Renée Rosnes, Ken Werner (*ky*); Dave Holland (*b, v*); Lonnie Plaxico (*b*); Marvin 'Smitty' Smith (*d*); Mino Cinelu (*perc, v*); Kimson Kism Albert, Cassandra Wilson, Stefan Winter (*v*). 5/90.

*** Mental Images JMT 514017
Eubanks; Antonio Hart (*as, ts*); Kevin Eubanks (*g*); Michael Cain (*p*); Kenny Davis, Dave Holland (*b*); Gene Jackson, Marvin 'Smitty' Smith (*d*); Kimati Dinizulu (*perc*). 4/94.

Harder-edged and much more clearly conceived than any of his brother Kevin's albums to date, *Different Perspectives* is an impressive effort, well worth checking. The title-track is the straightest performance of the set, with a good mix of horns and no electronics. 'Walkin'' brings in Hampton and Anderson for a big trombone revivalist meeting. The veteran's clean delivery is immediately distinguishable from the leader's more legato and slurred approach. Very much a studio session, with instrumentations tailored exactly for each track, it continually poses the question of what any one grouping might have sounded like live. Which is probably a good sign.

Co-led with fellow-trombonist Steve Turre, *Dedication* looks almost like an attempt at Jay and Kai for the early 1990s. The two horns lock firmly on 'Trance Dance' and 'Perpetual Groove', not always easy to separate. The synthesizer backgrounds are somewhat elided and spare, and Campbell's distinctive drumming sounds very sure and straightforward.

If the name implies a certain superficial trendiness, the reality is not so far removed from that. *Karma* is a little heavier on the vocals, with raps all round on the title-track and a somewhat raggedy chorus behind Eubanks's trombone on 'Minoat'. The trios with Holland and Smith are excellent, and the Art Blakey tribute, 'Remember When', strikes just the right chord, an M-Base response to the Jazz Messengers' great example. A fine album, with a few rough corners.

Mental Images is stronger still, a mixture of large-scale M-Base grooves and Afro-influenced improvisations that feature the leader most prominently on both his regular and electric trombone. Brecker, Smitty and brother Kev all contribute hugely. An excellent statement from a constantly developing musician.

Eureka Brass Band GROUP

(****) New Orleans Funeral And Parade American Music AMCD-70
Percy Humphrey, Willie Pajeaud, Edie Richardson (*t*); Albert Warner, Sunny Henry (*tb*); George Lewis (*cl*); Ruben Roddy (*as*); Emanuel Paul (*ts*); Joseph 'Red' Clark (*sou*); Arthur Ogle, Robert 'Son' Lewis (*d*). 8/51.

Probably the most authentic example of old New Orleans music in its original environment, even if this recording of traditional funeral and parade music was recorded in a French Quarter alleyway rather than actually on the job. The regulars of the Brass Band, as they then were, were augmented by Lewis for the day, although he plays flat, and the brass are similarly wayward in their intonation. The recording is musty, the tempos ragged, the extra takes of four of the numbers come as an anticlimax and some of the dirges threaten to dissolve altogether. But many will find this a moving, rather magnificent recording – seldom has the old music sounded so affecting, the workmanlike attitude of the players lending something like nobility to it all. The remastering has actually been done very well, considering the source material, and the superb documentation – by Alden Ashforth, the then-teenage enthusiast who recorded the session – adds to the undeniable mystique.

European Jazz Ensemble GROUP

**(*) Live Ear-Rational 1011
> Manfred Schoof, Allan Botschinsky (*t, flhn*); Steve Galloway (*tb*); Ernst Ludwig Petrowsky (*as, cl*); Gerd Dudek (*ss, ts, f*); Rob Van den Broeck (*p*); Ali Haurand (*b*); Tony Oxley (*d*); Uschi Bruning (*v*). 8/87.

*** At The Philharmonic Cologne M A Music A-800
> As above, except Enrico Rava (*t, flhn*), Stan Sulzmann (*ss, ts*), Philip Catherine (*g*) and Tony Levin (*d*) replace Galloway and Oxley. 4/89.

While this isn't a genuinely pan-European band, it's an unusual cross-section of players, and any idea that they would aim for an MOR modernism is quickly dispelled by the first track on *Live*, Petrowsky's bizarre exercise in extremities of register, 'Skizzen', which features Bruning's only vocal on the disc. Petrowsky and Dudek are certainly given free rein: even on a relatively conventional theme such as Botschinsky's 'Folkmusic Nr', Petrowsky's howling clarinet solo ruptures the seams. Oxley's diffuse rhythms never let matters settle down, and the Ensemble tend to split up into smaller groupings rather than playing as an entirety: it's an altogether very free set, although the concert recording is rather remote and unfocused. The second session offers more of the same, though the new players temper some of the freedoms, and the larger group has a bigger sound.

European Music Orchestra GROUP

*** Featuring Kenny Wheeler Soul Note 121299
> Kenny Wheeler, Andrea Bellotti, Gianluca Carallo, Yllich Fenzi, Maurizio Scamparin (*t, flhn*); Alessandro Azzolini, Toni Constantini, Stefano Giuliani (*tb*); Moreno Milanetto (*btb*); Guido Bombardieri (*as, ss*); Rosarita Crisafi (*as*); Claudio Fasoli (*ts, ss*); Marco Strano, Nicholas Camardi (*ts*); Gianluca Carollo (*vib*); Paolo Birro, Sergio Pietruschi (*p*); Ermanno M. Signorelli (*g*); Stefano Liudello (*b*); Enzo Carpentieri, Aldo Romano (*d*); Luca Palmarin (*perc*). 1/94.

Though the soloist is kept in fairly constant focus throughout this absorbing set, the section work by some of Italy's finest contemporary players is equally satisfying and provides Wheeler with the perfect setting for his floating, ethereal lines. There isn't as much straightforward drive and energy as one might look for in an American band, but on its own terms the EMO (note no reference to jazz, which may be telling) is spot-on, and the version of Wheeler's favourite 'W. W.' could hardly be bettered.

Bill Evans (1929–80) PIANO

*** New Jazz Conceptions Original Jazz Classics OJC 035
> Evans; Teddy Kotick (*b*); Paul Motian (*d*). 9/56.

The most influential pianist of modern times began with a fine, comfortable set of boppish trio performances which created little stir at the time (the record sold some 800 copies over the course of one year). Orrin Keepnews, the producer, was convinced to record Evans by hearing a demo tape played over the telephone, and the pianist's distinctive touch and lovely tone are already apparent: he makes bop material such as Tadd Dameron's 'Our Delight' into comprehensive structures, and the three tiny solos – including the very first 'Waltz For Debby', his most renowned original – hint at what was to come. But it's clearly a talent in its early stages.

**** Everybody Digs Bill Evans Original Jazz Classics OJC 068
> Evans; Sam Jones (*b*); Philly Joe Jones (*d*). 12/58.

Perennially reluctant, busy with the Miles Davis group, Evans didn't record as a leader for another two years. This superb record was worth the wait, though. Jones and Jones back him with enough spirit to bring out his most energetic delivery, and the assertiveness he'd found with Davis lent Evans an assur-

ance which makes 'Night And Day' and 'Oleo' into driving performances. But 'Peace Piece', a translucent reshaping of the opening phrases of 'Some Other Time', which Evans came up with in the studio,
is one of his most affecting soliloquies, and the ballad reading of 'Young And Foolish' is an almost
astonishing contrast to the up-tempo pieces. 'Some Other Time', which was omitted from the original
LP, is present on the CD version of the reissue.

**** **Portrait In Jazz** Original Jazz Classics OJC 088
       Evans; Scott LaFaro (*b*); Paul Motian (*d*). 12/59.
**** **Explorations** Original Jazz Classics OJC 037
       As above. 2/61.
  **** **Sunday At The Village Vanguard** Original Jazz Classics OJC 140
       As above. 6/61.
  **** **Waltz For Debby** Original Jazz Classics OJC 210
       As above. 6/61.
**** **At The Village Vanguard** Riverside 60-017
       As above. 6/61.

Evans was having trouble finding good bassists, but LaFaro's arrival precipitated the advent of one of
the finest piano trios jazz has ever documented. The bassist's melodic sensitivity and insinuating sound
flowed between Evans and Motian like water and, while notions of group empathy have sometimes been
exaggerated in discussion of this music – it was still very much directed by Evans himself – the playing
of the three men is so sympathetic that it set a universal standard for the piano–bass–drums set-up
which has persisted to this day. Both *Portrait In Jazz* and *Explorations* have their small imperfections:
there's an occasional brittleness in the latter, possibly a result of the quarrel which LaFaro and Evans
had had just before the session, and the recording of both does less justice to LaFaro's tone and delivery
than it might. But 'Autumn Leaves', 'Blue In Green', 'Beautiful Love' and the transformation of John
Carisi's 'Israel' to the trio format are as sublimely integrated and inspiring as this kind of jazz can be.
Yet the two records culled from a day's work at the Village Vanguard are even finer. Evans's own playing
is elevated by the immediacy of the occasion: his contributions seem all of a piece, lines spreading
through and across the melodies and harmonies of the tune, pointing the way towards modality yet
retaining the singing, rapturous qualities which the pianist heard in his material (Evans retained a
relatively small repertoire of favourite pieces throughout his career). All the Vanguard music is informed
by an extra sense of discovery, as if the musicians were suddenly aware of what they were on to and were
celebrating the achievement. They didn't have much time: LaFaro was killed in a car accident ten days
later. There are extra tracks and alternative takes on the CD editions of all the above and, because the
trio finally left very little music behind them, they are indispensable. *At The Village Vanguard* offers
nothing new, simply ten tracks culled from the other two records – a nice single-disc representation, but
the others must be heard in their entirety.

***(*) **Moon Beams** Original Jazz Classics OJC 434
       Evans; Chuck Israels (*b*); Paul Motian (*d*). 5–6/62.
**** **How My Heart Sings!** Original Jazz Classics OJC 369
       As above. 5–6/62.

Chuck Israels replaced LaFaro, although Evans was at first so upset by the bassist's death that he
stopped playing for a while. After some months of work, the pianist felt they were ready to record, and
Keepnews, who'd wanted to get an all-ballad album out of Evans, cut both the above discs at the same
sessions, alternating slow and up-tempo pieces and saving the ballads for *Moon Beams*. There are five
Evans originals – 'Very Early' and 'Re: Person I Knew' on *Moon Beams*, 'Walking Up', 'Show-Type
Tune' and '34 Skidoo' on *How My Heart Sings!* – and the slightly unfocused readings by the trio can be
accounted for by the fact that the pianist revealed them to the others only at the dates. But this was
otherwise a superb continuation of Evans's work. Israels plays pushy, hard-bitten lines and meshes very
capably with Motian, and it spurs Evans into a sometimes pugnacious mood: 'Summertime' numbers
among the more dramatic revisions of this standard, and 'In Your Own Sweet Way', present on the CD
of *How My Heart Sings!* in two different takes, negotiates Brubeck's theme with a hint of asperity. Not
that the ballads are wispy: 'Stairway To The Stars', for instance, is a model of firm melodic variation.

**** **Undercurrent** Blue Note 790538-2
       Evans; Jim Hall (*g*). 4–5/62.
*** **Interplay** Original Jazz Classics OJC 308
       Evans; Freddie Hubbard (*t*); Jim Hall (*g*); Percy Heath (*b*); Philly Joe Jones (*d*). 7/62.

Temperamentally, Evans and Hall hit it off perfectly in the studios. Their duet album is a masterpiece of
quiet shadings, drifting melancholy and – perhaps surprisingly – hard swinging, the latter quality
emerging on a particularly full-blooded 'I'm Getting Sentimental Over You'. But it's the nearly hallucinatory ballads, 'Dream Gypsy' and 'Romain', which stick in the mind, where harp-like tones and

gently fingered refrains establish a rare climate of introspection. The *Interplay* session, organized by Keepnews to keep Evans in funds, is comparatively desultory, but Hubbard plays rather well, and 'When You Wish Upon A Star' retains its powdery charm.

***(*) **At Shelly's Manne Hole** Original Jazz Classics OJC 263
    Evans; Chuck Israels (*b*); Larry Bunker (*d*). 5/63.
An understated yet tremendously intense 'Round Midnight' is among the highlights of this considerable club recording. Bunker and Israels were again given sight of some of the material only on the night of the recording, and their concentration adds to the tense lyricism which Evans was spinning out at the piano. A couple of rare excursions into the major blues, 'Swedish Pastry' and 'Blues in F/Five', complete a very strong programme, and the recording is particularly fine and well balanced.

**** **The Solo Sessions Vol. 1** Milestone M 9170
    Evans. 1/63.
***(*) **The Solo Sessions Vol. 2** Milestone M 9195
    Evans. 1/63.
Both of these solo records were made on the same evening, as part of a contract-fulfilling exercise, and they lay unreleased for over 20 years. The music finds Evans at his most exposed (the tunes include 'Why Was I Born?' and 'What Kind Of Fool Am I?'), and there's an underlying tone of aggressive disquiet – which has to be set against some deliriously lyrical passages. Two medleys, of 'My Favourite Things / Easy To Love / Baubles, Bangles And Beads' and 'Love Theme From Spartacus / Nardis', are particularly revealing (both are on *Volume 1*) and there's a reading of 'Ornithology' on the second disc which sounds as vital and energized as anything which Evans recorded for Riverside.

**** **The Complete Riverside Recordings** Riverside 018 12CD
    Personnel collected from all above-listed OJC records. 56–63.
This huge collection is certainly a breathtaking monument to Evans's art, and it would earn a fifth star if the individual albums weren't so easily available. It includes all the music listed on the OJC albums above, as well as the two solo discs on Milestone, which originally made their first appearance in this boxed set.

***(*) **Empathy / A Simple Matter Of Conviction** Verve 837757-2
    Evans; Monty Budwig, Eddie Gomez (*b*); Shelly Manne (*d*). 8/62–10/66.
Although Budwig is excellent, and Gomez, making his debut with Evans, is superb, it's the partnership with Manne which is the most interesting thing about these records. Evans seldom responded to a hard-driving drummer – a meeting with Tony Oxley in the 1970s was fairly disastrous – but Manne's canny momentum creates sparks of interplay without disturbing the pianist's equilibrium. That said, the high spontaneity of these sessions sometimes misses the clarity of thought which is at the core of Evans's music, and although there's a flashing ingenuity on their playing on, say, 'With A Song In My Heart' with its mischievous coda, the more considered strengths of the pianist's regular trios are finally more satisfying. But Evans fans mustn't miss it.

***(*) **Conversations With Myself** Verve 8219884-2
    Evans (*p* solo). 1–2/63.
***(*) **Trio '64** Verve 815057-2
    Evans; Gary Peacock (*b*); Paul Motian (*d*). 12/63.
These discs show how much music Evans was coming up with in this period: an entire album of overdubbed three-way piano, something only Tristano had tried before, and another new trio taking on a striking set of fresh material. *Conversations* has aroused sometimes fierce views both for and against its approach, but in an age where overdubbing is more or less the norm in record-making, its musicality is more important. Carefully graded, each line sifted against the others, this is occasionally too studied a record, and the follow-up *Further Conversations With Myself* (currently missing from print) is arguably more graciously realized; but 'Theme From Spartacus' and a fine-grained 'Round Midnight' are pieces where Evans seems to gaze at his own work and find it compelling. The trio record features Peacock's only official appearance with Evans, and the empathy is stunningly adventurous: on 'Little Lulu', for instance, the reach of the bassist's lines and his almost flamenco-like rhythms score brilliant points against the pianist's own energetic choruses. Motian, for once, seems subdued.

*** **Trio '65** Verve 519808-2
    Evans; Chuck Israels (*b*); Larry Bunker (*d*). 2/65.
*** **Bill Evans Trio With Symphony Orchestra** Verve 821983-2
    Evans; Chuck Israels (*b*); Larry Bunker, Grady Tate (*d*); strings, directed by Claus Ogerman. 9–12/65.
Trio '65 documents a good rather than great edition of the trio on a middling day in the studios, although it still sounds better than most piano-trio dates. The tempos sound rather brusque – this is a

good one to play to people who still think Evans was pure marshmallow – and some of the tracks seem to be curtly dismissed, but there is still a good ''Round Midnight' and a fine 'If You Could See Me Now'. The album with arrangements by Claus Ogerman is very pretty, if hardly a milestone in jazz meets the symphony. Ogerman's charts are sweetly romantic rather than overbearing, and this gives the trio some space to work in; if the confections which the arranger makes out of Bach, Chopin, Fauré and Granados are scarcely challenging, he manages to make it sound a plausible backdrop to the pianist's musings, and 'Time Remembered' and 'My Bells' sound fine, too.

***(*) **At Town Hall** Verve 831271-2
    Evans; Chuck Israels (*b*); Arnold Wise (*d*). 2/66.
***(*) **At The Montreux Jazz Festival** Verve 827844-2
    Evans; Eddie Gomez (*b*); Jack DeJohnette (*d*). 6/68.
*** **Alone** Verve 833801-2
    Evans (*p* solo). 9–10/68.
*** **The Best Of Bill Evans On Verve** Verve 527906-2
    As above Verve discs. 5/63–12/69.

Evans's period with Verve went on to produce two further in-concert albums and his first officially released solo record, aside from the multi-tracked albums. *At Town Hall* includes some exquisite playing on his favourite standards, together with the long 'Solo – In Memory Of His Father', a requiem that includes 'Turn Out The Stars'. Wise makes his only appearance in the Evans canon and keeps out of the way. The Montreux disc was a Grammy winner in its day and is another one-time-only appearance for DeJohnette – hardly the ideal man for the position – but, along with fellow recruit Gomez, he pushes Evans into his most tigerish form. 'Nardis' and 'A Sleepin' Bee' sound particularly strong. Much of the solo album's music sounds low-voltage, even for Evans, but the very long (over 14 minutes) exploration of 'Never Let Me Go' investigates what would become Keith Jarrett territory, with both prowess and resource to spare. The CD includes alternative takes of three of the pieces.

    The Best Of Bill Evans On Verve is a taster for the complete edition of 18 CDs which Verve have scheduled for release at the end of 1996. This picks a dozen tracks from 12 albums to make a very playable sampler. If one returns to his Riverside albums as the best of Evans, the Verve sequence has plenty of treasure, usefully dipped into here.

*** **You're Gonna Hear From Me** Milestone 9164
    Evans; Eddie Gomez (*b*); Marty Morell (*d*). 11/69.
*** **Montreux II** Columbia 481264-2
    As above. 6/70.
(*) **The Bill Evans Album Columbia CK 30855/480989-2
    As above. 5/71.
*** **The Tokyo Concert** Original Jazz Classics OJC 345
    As above. 1/73.
*** **Live In Tokyo** Columbia 481265-2
    As above. 1/73.
(*) **Live In Europe Vol. I EPM FDC 5712
    As above. 74.
(*) **Live In Europe Vol. II EPM FDC 5713
    As above. 74.

Some of the steam had gone out of Evans's career on record at this point, after the astonishing consistency of his first ten years in the studio. Gomez, a great technician, has an immediately identifiable, 'soulful' sound which tends to colour his lines a mite too highly: his interplay with the leader assumes a routine excellence which Morell, a fine if self-effacing drummer, tends to play alongside rather than inside, and bass and piano take more conspicuously solo turns rather than seeking out the three-way interplay of the earlier trios. On their own terms, the individual albums are still usually very good and highly enjoyable. *You're Gonna Hear From Me*, cut live at Copenhagen's Montmartre, is a lively date, with 'Waltz For Debby' taken at possibly its fastest-ever tempo, a surprisingly light-hearted 'Round Midnight' and an excellent 'Nardis' in a generally bountiful session. Evans dabbles with a little electric piano on *Album*, but both Japanese concerts are straight-ahead and flow with ideas: 'Up With The Lark' on the OJC is a marvellous piece, and the Columbia version is almost as good. The problem with the two EPM discs seems to be an erratic speed level: many of the tracks sound as if they're playing back too fast. *Bill Evans Album* was always a weak note in the Evans discography and the latest edition sounds no better. *Montreux II* is fine on its own terms, but this is a very familiar programme and nothing especially stands out.

*** **Symbiosis** MPS 523381-2
    Evans; orchestra directed by Claus Ogerman. 2/74.

Another jazz-meets-the-classics project, even if the parties involved would demur at the tag. Ogerman's two-movement orchestration creates a backdrop that is shakily kaleidoscopic: it's not as if this is a display of range, more a ragbag of many elements. Evans seems interested enough, though he plays a particularly reverberant electric piano for much of the piece, which tends to date the whole enterprise. An interesting diversion, but a footnote in the Evans discography.

*** **Since We Met** Original Jazz Classics OJC 622
    Evans; Eddie Gomez (*b*); Marty Morell (*d*). 1/74.
*** **Re: Person I Knew** Original Jazz Classics OJC 749
    As above. 1/74.
*** **Jazzhouse** Milestone M 9151
    As above. 74.
*** **Blue In Green** Milestone M 9185
    As above. 74.
*** **Intuition** Original Jazz Classics OJC 470
    As above, except omit Morell. 11/74.
*** **Montreux III** Original Jazz Classics OJC 644
    As above. 7/75.

Evans signed to Fantasy (the source of the OJC material listed above) and with his assiduous producer, Helen Keane, created a big body of work that lasted through the 1970s. *Since We Met* and *Re: Person I Knew* both come from a single Village Vanguard engagement, and though Gomez and Morell don't erode memories of LaFaro and Motian, the music speaks with as much eloquence as this trio could muster. *Jazzhouse* and *Blue In Green* are more recent 'discoveries' of Evans concerts, which tell us nothing new about him and must be considered for collectors only, even if the playing is mostly impeccable. Consistency had become Evans's long suit, and he seemed content to tinker endlessly with his favourite pieces, disclosing little beyond the beauty of his touch, which by now was one of the most admired and imitated methods in piano jazz. The three albums with Gomez as sole partner explore a wider range of material – *Montreux III* is a particularly well-turned concert set – but one still misses the extra impetus of a drummer.

***(*) **Alone (Again)** Original Jazz Classics OJC 795
    Evans (*p* solo). 12/75.
*** **Crosscurrents** Original Jazz Classics OJC 718
    Evans; Lee Konitz (*as*); Warne Marsh (*ts*); Eddie Gomez (*b*); Eliot Zigmund (*d*). 2–3/77.
(*) **Quintessence Original Jazz Classics OJC 698
    Evans; Harold Land (*ts*); Kenny Burrell (*g*); Ray Brown (*b*); Philly Joe Jones (*d*). 5/76.
*** **I Will Say Goodbye** Original Jazz Classics OJC 761
    Evans; Eddie Gomez (*b*); Eliot Zigmund (*d*). 5/79.
*** **Eloquence** Original Jazz Classics OJC 814
    Evans; Eddie Gomez (*b*). 11/73–12/75.
*** **The Complete Fantasy Recordings** Fantasy 1012 9CD
    As all Fantasy/OJC sessions listed above. 73–79.

The Fantasy material isn't on a par with the magnificent complete Riverside set, but it has many rewards and includes two bonuses: an interview with Marian McPartland from her *Piano Jazz* radio series, and a 1976 date in Paris. A few recent reissues have brought some other Fantasy sessions back into general circulation. *Crosscurrents* is another interesting if ultimately unremarkable meeting with two great horn players; *I Will Say Goodbye* finds the trio tackling some relatively unfamiliar material in 'A House Is Not A Home', 'Quiet Light' and 'Seascape'. But it's good to have the neglected *Alone (Again)* as a separate release. This features some very fine Evans on five favourite standards, with a long and wide-ranging exploration of 'People' as the highlight. *Quintessence* provided some answer as to what Evans would have done if he'd recorded more frequently with a bigger group in his later years: he would have made an amiable and not especially interesting Evans-plus-horns date. *Eloquence* is a mixture of solos and duets with Eddie Gomez, some studio, some live. Losing the drummer doesn't do anything special for the situation but two ballads, 'In A Sentimental Mood' and 'But Beautiful', are notably effective.

**** **The Tony Bennett / Bill Evans Album** Original Jazz Classics OJC 439
    Evans; Tony Bennett (*v*). 6/75.

Pairing Evans with Tony Bennett was an inspired idea which pays off in a session which has an illustrious kind of after-hours feel to it. Bennett, as big-hearted as always, lives out the helpless-Romeo lyrics of such as 'When In Rome', and sounds filled with wonder when working through a gorgeous 'The Touch Of Your Lips'. He also sings what's surely the definitive vocal version of 'Waltz For Debby', where the corn of Gene Lees's lyric suddenly sounds entirely right. Evans plays deferentially but creates some lovely accompaniments and seems to read every mood with complete accuracy.

*** **Letter To Evan** Dreyfus 191064-2
    Evans; Marc Johnson (*b*); Joe LaBarbera (*d*). 7/80.
**** **The Brilliant** Timeless CDSJP 329
    As above. 8–9/80.
***(*) **Consecration 1** Timeless SJP 331
    As above. 8–9/80.
***(*) **Consecration 2** Timeless SJP 332
    As above. 8–9/80.

Evans's final years were full of personal problems, yet his music seemed set on fresh paths of discovery. Several months with Philly Joe Jones at the drums seem to have gone undocumented, but Johnson and LaBarbera eventually proved to be a challenging team which propelled the pianist through a remarkable burst of creativity. He compared this group to his original band with LaFaro and Motian, and there's certainly a sense of an evolving music, with the three men playing as a close-knit ensemble and Evans stretching out in improvisations which were roaming much more freely than before. Even long solos had hitherto kept a relatively tight hold of the thematic material underpinning them but, in all the concerts which these discs cover, Evans sounds unencumbered by frameworks, and such pieces as 'Letter To Evan' (*The Brilliant*) are as close to clear freedom as he ever came. The Timeless records all come from an engagement at San Francisco's Keystone Korner and chart a very high level of playing, with Johnson especially challenging memories of the many great bassmen who had worked with Evans. Fine recording. *Letter To Evan* is marred by confused sound, but there's still some very committed and powerful music here.

Bill Evans (born 1958) TENOR AND SOPRANO SAXOPHONES

**** **Moods Unlimited** Paddle Wheel KICJ 65
    Evans; Hank Jones (*p*); Red Mitchell (*b*). 10/82.

Evans – the third Bill Evans to make a name for himself in jazz, after Bill Evans (piano) and Bill Evans (alias Yusef Lateef, saxes) – was the saxophonist in the Miles Davis 'comeback' band around the time of this session. With Miles, he always seemed frozen-off in a corner, mysteriously ignored by the leader, yet he was surely among the best sidemen the trumpeter had in the 1980s: in possession of a hard, piercing tone and a compelling rhythmic assurance, Evans cut through fusion backbeats with little trouble. Here, he sounds superb in an entirely different situation, an immaculately recorded after-hours session with two masters of an earlier generation. The three of them mull over five standards at their leisure, but there's nothing undercooked here: the long, ruminative trawl through 'In A Sentimental Mood' must be accounted one of the greatest on record, with Jones creating a peerless improvisation and Evans's soprano underscoring every heartfelt step of the melody. Mitchell's wonderfully idiosyncratic bass marks out all the other lines. Highly recommended.

*** **Summertime** Jazz City 66053018
    Evans; Gil Goldstein (*ky*); Chuck Loeb (*g*); Marc Johnson (*b*); Danny Gottlieb (*d*). 2–4/89.
(*) **Let The Juice Loose Jazz City 66053001
    Evans; Jim Beard (*ky*); Chuck Loeb (*g*); Darryl Jones (*b*); Dennis Chambers (*d*). 9/89.
(*) **The Gambler Jazz City 66053025
    Evans; Mitchell Forman (*ky*); Victor Bailey (*b*); Richie Morales (*d*). 9/90.
(*) **Petite Blonde Lipstick 89012-2
    Evans; Mitch Forman (*ky*); Chuck Loeb (*g*); Victor Bailey (*b*); Dennis Chambers (*d*). 7/92.
(*) **Push Lipstick 89022-2
    Evans; Chris Botti, Dave Stahl (*t*); Mike Davis, Keith O'Quinn, Conrad Herwig (*tb*); Gary Smulyan (*bs*); Clifford Carter, Philippe Saisse (*ky*); Bruce Hornsby (*p*); Chuck Loeb, Jeff Glub, Nick Moroch (*g*); Christian Minh Doky, Marcus Miller (*b*); Billy Ward, Max Risenhoover (*d*); voices. 93.
(*) **Live In Europe Lipstick 89029-2
    Evans; Charles Blenzig, Jon Werking (*ky*); Gary Poulson, Adam Rogers (*g*); Ron Jenkins (*b*); Scooter Warner (*d*); K. C. Flight, Marc Allison (*v*). 94.
*** **Escape** Escapade ESC 03650-2
    Evans; Wallace Roney (*t*); Jim Beard (*ky*); Lee Ritenour, Jon Herington, Gary Poulson, Nick Moroch (*g*); Victor Bailey, Marcus Miller, Mark Egan, Ron Jenkins (*b*); Billy Kilson, Steve Ferone (*d*); Manolo Badrena (*perc*); MC 900 Ft Jesus, Mark Ledford, Ahmed Best (*v*). 12/95–1/96.

After leaving Miles Davis, Evans worked with John McLaughlin and Herbie Hancock and cut a couple of (now-deleted) records of his own. The Jazz City albums are entertaining examples of Evans in action

– the later two were both recorded live in Tokyo – but none of them suggests a particularly commanding leadership, and without the saxophonist these would be very bland records indeed. *Summertime* suggests a variation on Pat Metheny's lyrical-pastoral fusion bent, and 'Chatterton Falls' might be a ringer for anything off a mid-period Metheny record. But the leader keeps his own playing at a high level of invention, concentrating mainly on soprano on a generally acoustic record. The two Tokyo sessions feature much flexing of muscles: Jones and Chambers have some jaw-dropping moments on the first disc and Evans takes some long, calculatedly impassioned solos, but the record is too long and the live sound, while clear, is somewhat recessed. *The Gambler* has a bigger soundstage and the music sounds more pointed, perhaps as a result. Forman, though, is too much of a doodler to make Evans work very hard, and it's Bailey's showstopping 'Kid Logic' that will appease fusion fans the most.

Petite Blonde is another hard-hitting concert set. For sheer beef the opening 'Two Price Hit' takes some beating and, with the redoubtable Chambers on board, it's obvious that the session is going to turn into a slugging match. Nothing else on the record packs quite such a wallop, but even at cruising speed the band sound hard. Effective, but only for those who like a lot of testosterone. Evans's touring band, Push, are responsible for the next two, though *Push*, the studio set, is more a collection of studio exercises – shots of impressionism such as 'Nightwing' and 'Road To Run' come off well, but the more self-consciously funky music is less impressive. Much the same applies to the tour record, which comes unstuck when K. C. Flight starts rapping and Evans is reduced to the role of accompanist. This backs off from the sheer wallop of *Petite Blonde* but there isn't that much in its place.

Jim Beard's artful production enhances *Escape*, which is typical of the new breed of art-jazz that's starting to come out of what used to be straight-ahead fusion dates. Beard adds lots of touches to the mix, cocooning Evans and the other soloists in glittering keyboard and percussion surrounds. A piece such as 'Coravilas' is pure studio dreamtime, and Evans decorates the environment very prettily. That said, it's difficult to hear this as either deep or enduring.

Gil Evans (1912–88) PIANO, ARRANGER, COMPOSER

(*) **Gil Evans And Ten Original Jazz Classics OJC 346
Evans; John Carisi, Jack Loven, Louis Mucci (*t*); Jimmy Cleveland, Bart Varsalona (*tb*); Willie Ruff (*hn*); Lee Konitz (*as*); Steve Lacy (*ss*); Dave Kurtzer (*bn*); Paul Chambers (*b*); Jo Jones, Nick Stabulas (*d*).

**** **Out Of The Cool** MCA MCACD 9653
Evans; Johnny Coles, Phil Sunkel (*t*); Keg Johnson, Jimmy Knepper (*tb*); Tony Studd (*btb*); Bill Barber (*tba*); Ray Beckenstein, Eddie Cane (*as, f, picc*); Budd Johnson (*ts, ss*); Bob Tricarico (*f, picc, bsn*); Ray Crawford (*g*); Ron Carter (*b*); Elvin Jones, Charli Persip (*d*). 12/60.

*** **Into The Hot** Impulse! MCAD 39104
Evans; John Carisi, John Glasel, Clark Terry, Joe Wilder (*t*); Bob Brookmeyer, Urbie Green (*tb*); Jimmy Buffington (*hn*); Gene Quill, Phil Woods (*as*); Eddie Costa (*p, vib*); Barry Galbraith (*g*); Art Davis, Milt Hinton (*b*); Osie Johnson (*d*); and Cecil Taylor (*p*); Ted Curson, Roswell Rudd (*tb*); Jimmy Lyons (*as*); Archie Shepp (*ts*); Henry Grimes (*b*); Sunny Murray (*d*); collective personnel. 9–10/61.

***(*) **The Individualism Of Gil Evans** Verve 833804
Evans; Ernie Royal, Johnny Coles, Bernie Glow, Louis Mucci (*t*); Jimmy Cleveland, Tony Studd (*tb*); Ray Alonge, Jimmy Buffington, Gil Cohen, Don Corado, Robert Northern, Julius Watkins (*frhn*); Bill Barber (*tba*); Al Block, Garvin Bushell, Eric Dolphy, Andy Fitzgerald, Steve Lacy, George Marge, Jerome Richardson, Wayne Shorter, Bob Tricarico (*reeds*); Kenny Burrell, Barry Galbraith (*g*); Bob Maxwell, Margaret Ross (*hp*); Paul Chambers, Richard Davis, Milt Hinton, Gary Peacock, Ben Tucker (*b*); Osie Johnson, Elvin Jones (*d*). 9/63, 4 & 7/64.

*** **Verve Jazz Masters 23: Gil Evans** Verve 516728
Similar to above.

They used to say it was an anagram of Svengali. Certainly Evans's influence on other musicians (the notoriously solipsistic Miles only most obviously) was quite remarkable. The sessions on *Gil Evans And Ten*, recorded four months after his epochal arrangements for *Miles Ahead*, are oblique, intelligent modern jazz, with Carisi's trumpet prominent, Lee Konitz and Steve Lacy lending the reed parts the floating feel typical of an Evans chart. *Into The Hot* is a slightly odd album, credited to the Gil Evans Orchestra and then to its individual constituents, a large and a smaller band led by John Carisi and Cecil Taylor respectively. The compositions are also by Carisi and Taylor. What Evans brings is a kind of tutelary genius with the harmonic structure of a theme (and Carisi's 12-note materials become tonal only by a kind of undogmatic sleight) and a brilliant grasp of instrumentation.

As was to be typical of his own later bands, Evans welds disparate materials into a single, absolutely solid structure which maintains an *appearance* of freedom. Taylor's atonal commentaries on bebop are demanding even after 30 years of more extreme revisions, but they're so absolutely self-consistent and achieved that they become totally absorbing rather than alienating.

Out Of The Cool is Evans's masterpiece under his own name (some might want to claim the accolade for some of his work with Miles) and one of the best examples of jazz orchestration since the early Ellington bands. It's the soloists – Coles on the eerie 'Sunken Treasure', a lonely-sounding Knepper on 'Where Flamingoes Fly' – that most immediately catch the ear, but repeated hearings reveal the relaxed sophistication of Evans's settings, which give a hefty band the immediacy and elasticity of a quintet. Evans's time-sense allows Coles to double the metre on George Russell's 'Stratusphunk', which ends palindromically, with a clever inversion of the opening measures. 'La Nevada' is one of his best and most neglected (but see *Rhythm-A-Ning*, below) scores, typically built up out of quite simple materials. The sound, already good, has been enhanced by digital transfer, revealing yet more timbral detail.

Individualism is a looser album, made with a pool of overlapping ensembles, perfectly tailored to the compositions, and all securely grounded in the bass. The solos are now mainly improvised rather than written, and stray more freely from the original composition, in anticipation of the 1980s bands. 'Hotel Me' is an extraordinary performance, basically very simple but marked by throaty shouts from the brass that set up Evans's own churchy solo. 'El Toreador' again features Coles, less certain-sounding than on *Out Of The Cool*, but still a soloist of considerable imagination. Remarkable as the music is, there's an oddly unfinished feel to the record, as if it has been put together out of previously rejected bits and pieces. It isn't just a CD round-up, though. The Jazz Masters doesn't pretend to be anything else, but it's actually a well-paced and wholly convincing survey, ideal for anyone coming at Gil's music with no previous acquaintance or no stock of old vinyl.

** Blues In Orbit Enja 3069

Evans; Johnny Coles, Mike Lawrence, Ernie Royal, Snooky Young (*t*); Garnett Brown, Jimmy Cleveland, Jimmy Knepper (*tb*); Ray Alonge, Julius Watkins (*hn*); Howard Johnson (*bs, tba*); Hubert Laws (*f*); George Marge (*f, ss*); Billy Harper (*f, ts*); Joe Beck (*g*); Gene Bianco (*hrp*); Herb Bushler (*b*); Elvin Jones, Alphonse Mouzon (*d*); Sue Evans, Donald McDonald (*perc*); collective personnel. 69, 71.

Highly regarded, but now wearing rather badly. Evans's instincts seem for once to have deserted him. The arrangements are a touch ragged and the solos have a centrifugal energy that leaves the ensembles firmly earthbound. A rather bright register kills a lot of interesting activity down in the bass.

*** Where Flamingos Fly A & M 390 831

Evans; John Coles, Hannibal Marvin Peterson, Stan Shafran (*t*); Jimmy Knepper (*tb*); Billy Harper (*ts*); Trevor Koehler (*bs, ss*); Howard Johnson (*bs, flhn, tba*); Phil Davis, Don Preston (*syn*); Joe Beck (*g, mand*); Bruce Johnson (*g*); Harry Lookofsky (*tenor vn*); Herb Bushler, Richard Davis, Bill Quinze (*b*); Bruce Ditmas, Lenny White (*d*); Sue Evans (*perc, mar*); Airto Moreira, Flora Purim (*v, perc*). 71.

Originally released on Ornette Coleman's Artists House label, at which time one of the tracks, 'Jelly Rolls', was mis-labelled 'Hotel Me'. A minor point, but not untypical of the rather sloppy treatment accorded to Gil's output down the years. This was a version of the band he took into the Village Vanguard, starting life as a gigging bandleader only rather late. Transferred to the studio, and with some capacity for overdubs and sweetening, it sounds close to how the composer presumably conceived this material. The long tracks, 'Zee Zee', which is a spiky 5/4 blues, and Kenny Dorham's 'El Matador', prominently feature Harper and the seemingly omnicompetent Johnson, and both are notable as fore-runners of the more loosely constructed and individualistic performances of the next decade. A fine record left to rust in obscurity too long, but all the more welcome for that.

***(*) Svengali ACT 9207

Evans; Tex Allan, Hannibal Marvin Peterson, Richard Williams (*t*); Joseph Daley (*tb, tba*); Sharon Freeman, Peter Levin (*frhn*); David Sanborn (*as*); Billy Harper (*ts, f*); Trevor Koehler (*ss, bs, f*); Howard Johnson (*bs, tba, flhn*); David Horovitz (*syn*); Ted Dunbar (*g*); Herb Bushler (*b*); Bruce Ditmas (*d*); Sue Evans (*perc*). 73.

'Zee Zee' reappears on *Svengali* as a feature for the incendiary Peterson, who turns it into a prolonged cry of anger, exhilaration and commanding abstraction, surprisingly different from his usual run of things. The other big number is Harper's own 'Cry Of Hunger', a companion piece on this concert recording, prominently featuring the composer and apparently reassembled at the production stage by Evans, who thus becomes an *ex post facto* composer in the way that he and Teo Macero often were on Miles projects. The sound is very good, given the live provenance, and the horns all come through with striking clarity. Not so some aspects of the extended rhythm section, which often sounds distant and out of focus.

***(*) Play The Music Of Jimi Hendrix Bluebird ND 88409

Evans; Hannibal Marvin Peterson, Lew Soloff (*t, flhn*); Tom Malone (*tb, btb, f, syn*); Peter

Gordon (*frhn*); Pete Levin (*frhn, syn*); Howard Johnson (*tba, bcl, b*); David Sanborn (*ss, as, f*); Billy Harper (*ts, f*); Trevor Koehler (*as, ts, f*); David Horovitz (*p, syn*); Paul Metzke (*syn, b*); Joe Gallivan (*syn, perc*); John Abercrombie, Ryo Kawasaki, Keith Loving (*g*); Warren Smith (*vib, mar*); Don Pate, Michael Moore (*b*); Bruce Ditmas (*d*); Sue Evans (*perc*). 6/74, 4/75.

A title like that probably did raise eyebrows in 1974. Evans's championing of Hendrix's compositions – 'Little Wing' most immortally – was a controversial but ultimately career-stoking decision. It's a little difficult to tell, while listening to these powerful tracks, whether the quality of the music is testimony to Hendrix's genius as a composer or Evans's as an arranger, or to some strange posthumous communication between the two. Some of the tunes are inevitably moved a long way from source; '1983 A Merman I Should Turn To Be' takes on a new character, as does 'Up From The Skies', two takes of which are included. 'Little Wing' remains the touchstone, though, and the recording, from the following spring, is superb.

**(*) Little Wing DIW 329

Evans; Lew Soloff (*t, picc t*); Terumasa Hino (*t*); Gerry Niewood (*as, ss, f*); George Adams (*ts, f, perc*); Bob Stewart (*tba*); Pete Levin (*syn*); Don Pate (*b*); Bob Crowder (*d*). 10/78.

Evans's wish to record with Hendrix was thwarted by the guitarist's death. His interest in the music continued, and by the late 1970s 'Stone Free' and 'Little Wing' became staple items in his concert performances. None of these sets should be considered essential, but they do underline Evans's growing commitment to a more open, improvisational approach.

There have been a good many bootleg or, at best, questionable issues of material from the 1976 tour, but we are no longer listing these, even at the price of a rather smaller entry for Evans. The rather later DIW is recommendably kosher in provenance and the performances are both highly professional and modestly adventurous; Adams is in full, not to say vociferous, voice throughout.

**(*) Live At The Public Theater Volume 1 Storyville STCD 5003

Evans; Jon Faddis, Hannibal Marvin Peterson, Lew Soloff (*t*); George Lewis (*tb*); Dave Bargeron (*tb, tba*); Arthur Blythe (*as, ss*); Hamiet Bluiett (*bs, a f*); John Clark (*hn*); Masabumi Kikuchi, Pete Levin (*syn*); Tim Landers (*b*); Billy Cobham (*d*). 2/80.

**(*) Live At The Public Theater Volume 2 Storyville STCD 5005

As above. 2/80.

A transitional band in most regards, with all the lags and hesitancies that implies. Individual performances are generally good, but there's a lack of excitement about the music and a greater abstraction than in preceding and later line-ups. Hendrix sits very comfortably alongside Evans's favourite Mingus, 'Orange Was The Color Of Her Dress . . .'

Everyman Band GROUP

*** Everyman Band ECM 1234

Marty Fogel (*ss, ts*); David Torn (*g*); Bruce Yaw (*b*); Michael Suchovsky (*d*). 3/82.

*** Without Warning ECM 1290

As above. 12/84.

A couple of strong records in the thinly populated field of impressionist jazz-rock: the spare textures of the quartet, blessedly free of keyboards, are thickened by Torn's occasional recourse to an orchestral palette; but there is an interesting emphasis on group form and improvisation, and Fogel is a determined force, even when restrained by the engineering. The compositions prefer tunefulness to bombast, although nothing is quite as strong as some of the pieces Fogel composed for his CMP recording.

Don Ewell (1916–83) PIANO

*** Music To Listen To Don Ewell By Good Time Jazz 12021-2

Ewell; Darnell Howard (*cl*); Minor Hall (*d*). 3/56.

*** Man Here Plays Fine Piano! Good Time Jazz 10043-2

Ewell; Pops Foster (*b*); Minor Hall (*d*). 2/57.

*** Live At The 100 Club Solo Art SACD-89

Ewell (*p* solo). 2/71.

The much-recorded Ewell hasn't been well served by CD so far, but the recent GTJ reissues restore some of his eminence. A structured, disciplined practitioner of stride piano, Ewell took his cues from New Orleans musicians – his early sessions in the 1940s were with Bunk Johnson and George Lewis – without succumbing to any raggedly 'authentic' mannerisms. One hears an almost prim sense of detail in his playing, the tempos unerringly consistent, the left hand a meticulous counterpoint to the right, the variations as refined and logical as in ragtime. The pair of GTJ reissues find him with the great New Orleans drummer, Minor Hall, and between them they offer a seasoned kind of classic jazz piano, without the music ever losing its balance.

Ewell's manner can make him a little dull to listen to at length, and perhaps a solo recital isn't an ideal memorial, but, taken a few tracks at a time, the Solo Art session, cut on a visit to London in 1971 and crisply recorded, is quite involving. His treatment of Fats Waller, not his natural métier, was somewhere between fanciful and respectful: 'Keepin' Out Of Mischief Now' is almost rococo in some of its designs, while the following 'Handful Of Keys' is very fast, and seems to pirouette on tiptoe.

Excelsior Brass Band GROUP

***(*) **Jolly Reeds And Steamin' Horns** GHB BCD-290
  Teddy Riley, James May (*t*); Gregory Stafford (*c*); Fred Lonzo, Clement Tervalon (*tb*); Michael White (*cl*); Oscar Rouzan (*as*); David Grillier (*ts*); Walter Payton (*bb*); Freddie Kohlman, Calvin Spears, Stanley Stephens (*d*). 10/83.
The rich yet highly restricted tradition of New Orleans brass bands is slowly getting through to CD, and this disc by perhaps the oldest institution in the genre – the EBB was originally formed in 1880 – is a very fine example of the tradition as it stands today (or, at least, in 1983). The digital sound allows one to hear all the detail which scrappy old recordings eliminated, and the ineffable bounce of the drummers (two on snare, one on bass), the old-fashioned tremble of the reeds and the sheer brassiness of the brass create some sense of a living tradition, on material which is profoundly historical ('Just A Closer Walk With Thee', 'Amazing Grace', 'Down In Honky Tonk Town', 'Just A Little While To Stay Here' and so on). At the same time, the primitivism of the band can only be affected: players such as White, Lonzo and Riley can probably go bebop if they wanted to, which one could never say about original brass-band stalwarts. Whether that matters may be up to the ear of the behearer. It still makes for a very spirited and enjoyable session, adding four tracks to the earlier LP issue.

Jon Faddis (born 1953) TRUMPET, FLUGELHORN

(*) **Legacy Concord CCD 4291
  Faddis; Harold Land (*ts*); Kenny Barron (*p*); Ray Brown (*b*); Mel Lewis (*d*). 8/85.
Three out of four blind-tested subjects will tell you that Jon Faddis is Dizzy Gillespie. The influence is still transparent, but in the near-decade that separates the precocious but now unavailable *Youngblood* from the more measured *Legacy* the technique has become far more individual and, though the 'A Night In Tunisia' solo on the later session makes explicit (though possibly unconscious) allusions to Gillespie at the legendary Massey Hall concert, Faddis seems to have steered a new course somewhere between Miles and Clark Terry.

Chris Fagan ALTO SAXOPHONE

*** **Lost Bohemia** Open Minds 2411
  Fagan; Bobby Bradford (*c*); Reggie Workman (*b*); Andrew Cyrille (*d*). 1/91.
A solid free-bop date. Fagan has enlisted a blue-chip team and everybody plays well, though in the end the session turns out to be something of a potboiler: nobody takes a firm lead, yet the group has little to say as a unit. Bradford's spiky cornet improvisations are the main reason to listen, since he remains neglected as a recording artist, while Fagan's own alto parts are a capable foil.

Peter Fairclough DRUMS

*** **Shepherd Wheel** ASC CD 1
  Fairclough; Peter Whyman (*as, ss, cl*); Paul Dunmall (*ts, ss, Cmel*); Pete Saberton (*p*); Rick Bolton (*g*); Tim Holmes (*b*); Tim Harries (*b*); Richard Newby (*d, perc*); Christine Tobin (*v*). 1/95.
Credited to The Fairclough Group rather than to the drummer himself, *Shepherd Wheel* is an engaging group effort which mixes some fine jazz with folksong and elements of straight composition (doubtless absorbed during the leader's long stint with Mike Westbrook). The two horn players are strong personalities, fiery but also lyrical, and Tobin has a haunting voice that adapts well to what are on paper unpromising lyrics. A word too for Saberton, a much-respected figure on the London scene who has

never received his due of praise. The recording is very direct and unfussy, enhancing these excellent performances.

Digby Fairweather (born 1946) TRUMPET, CORNET, MELLOPHONE, VOCALS

*** **A Portrait Of Digby Fairweather** Black Lion BLCD 760505
  Fairweather; Stan Barker, Brian Lemon (*p*); Ike Isaacs, Denny Wright (*g*); Ted Taylor (*ky, syn*); Len Skeat (*b*); Stan Bourke (*d*); Chris Ellis (*voc*). 7 & 12/79, 84.
*** **With Nat In Mind** Jazzology JCD 247
  Fairweather; Pete Strange (*tb*); John Barnes (*cl, as, bs*); Pat Smuts (*ts*); Dave Lee (*p*); Paul Sealey (*g*); Jack Fallon (*b*); John Armatage (*d*); Wild Bill Davison, Lisa Lincoln (*v*). 94.
***(*) **Squeezin' The Blues Away** Spirit Of Jazz SOJ CD 10
  Fairweather; Tony Compton (*acc, d machine*); Lisa Lincoln (*v*).
Digby Fairweather's embouchure has been baffling fans and trumpet students for years. Like Ziggy Elman's, it appears to project from just under his right ear. However odd the angle, though, it hasn't adversely affected Fairweather's sound, which is richly toned and curiously delicate, especially at slower tempos.

It's unfortunate that this most articulate communicator isn't better represented on disc, but the situation has improved since our last edition. The Black Lion *Portrait* brings together two sessions from what must be considered the beginning and end of Fairweather's golden period. He became a full-time musician only in the late '70s, but by 1984 he was already losing his initial momentum. The partnership with Barker was a regular gig, resulting in the fine *Let's Duet* LP, and it's perhaps these tracks that should be sampled first, if for no other reason than to get the full flavour of the leader's cornet playing. The sextets and quartets contain few surprises, though there are phrases on 'Cherokee' which suggest that, given a different set of circumstances, Fairweather might have gravitated towards a more contemporary idiom.

His tribute to the veteran Nat Gonella is eloquent, nicely paced and includes some of his most characteristic playing. The guest stars span the generations, establishing a link back to Nat's Georgians and their origins in the Lew Stone orchestra. Nat's theme, 'Georgia On My Mind', is given a fulsome airing, with Wild Bill taking the vocal. 'I Must See Annie Tonight' carries associations of the old master's association with American greats like Benny Carter, and it's treated with due respect. There are less expected things as well: 'I'm Feelin' Like A Million' is arranged from Nat's original solo, and 'September Song', which he never actually recorded but which here offers him an opportunity to express his satisfaction with the proceedings.

The duos with Compton take a moment or two to get used to, but they are consistently fascinating thereafter. Fairweather plays with a breezy, unfussy clarity, and the accordion wheezes and chugs after its manner, an undersubscribed sound in jazz but one with plenty of untapped potential. Lisa Lincoln, also featured on the Nat tribute, contributes two lovely vocals. (We could, frankly, have done without the drum machine.)

Dalia Faitelson GUITAR, VOICE

*** **Common Ground** Storyville STCD 4196
  Faitelson; Susi Hyldgaard (*ky, acc*); Johannes Lundberg (*b*); Niels Werner Larsen (*d*); Marilyn Mazur (*perc*). 4–5/94.
It would be a pity to pass by this thoughtful, measured record on account of its unfamiliar names. Faitelson's pitch is a kind of impressionist fusion and, while there are a couple of misplaced attempts at rocking out, most of the music is quiet and intelligent. The leader is shy about putting herself out front, and there is at least as much improvising space for the effective Hyldgaard and the agile Lundberg, who closes the record with a fine solo over Faitelson's calm strumming. The production is somewhat flat, though that may be in keeping with the players' intentions.

Charles Fambrough (born 1950) DOUBLE BASS

***(*) **The Proper Angle** CTI R2 79476
  Fambrough; Roy Hargrove, Wynton Marsalis (*t*); Roy Ford, Branford Marsalis (*ts, ss*); Kenny Kirkland (*p*); Jeff Watts (*d*); Jerry Gonzalez, Steve Berrios (*perc*). 5/91.
(*) **The Charmer CTI 1010
  Fambrough; Roy Hargrove (*t*); Kenny Garrett (*as*); Grover Washington Jr (*ss*); Abdullah

Ibrahim, Stephen Scott (*p*); Bill O'Connell (*p, ky*); Billy Drummond, Yoron Israel, Jeff Watts (*d*); Doc Gibbs, Bashiri Johnson (*perc*). 9/92.

*** **Blues At Bradley's** CTI 10113
Fambrough; Steve Turre (*tb, shells*); Donald Harrison (*as*); Joe Ford (*ss*); Bill O'Connell (*p*); Bobby Broom (*g*); Ricky Sebastian (*d*); Steve Berrios (*perc*). 2/93.

*** **Keeper Of The Spirit** Audioquest AQ 1033
Fambrough; John Swana (*t, EWI*); Grover Washington (*ss*); Ralph Bowen (*ts, ss, f*); Art Webb (*f*); Joel Levine (*recs*); Edward Simon (*p*); Adam Holzman, Jason Shatill (*ky*); Lenny White (*d*); Marlon Simon (*d, perc*); Joe Gonzalez (*perc*). 12/94.

When the Philadelphia-born bassist first recorded under his own name, he was already 41. By then, though, he had a substantial CV, including stints with the Messengers and with McCoy Tyner's band. Experience showed. *The Proper Angle* is a smooth and sophisticated session, and Fambrough's ability to call on a stellar array of guest players gives the disc plenty of local interest. Wynton Marsalis's solo on 'The Dreamer' is a high spot; he features on another six tracks, including the respectful 'Our Father Who Art Blakey', an old boys' reunion. The quartet tracks with just Ford, Kirkland and Watts offer the best opportunity to hear Fambrough working in space. He favours a solid, lower-register sound that sometimes recalls Paul Chambers, sometimes Mingus; and there's certainly a hint of Mingus in the Latin-tinged themes. Arranging credits are shared, and there are one or two queston marks here, with some tracks faded down rather than ending satisfactorily.

This becomes more of an issue on *The Charmer*, which lives up to its title rather too assiduously. Despite another impressive line-up, the music has become disconcertingly bland. Washington solos with his usual facility, and you'd be forgiven for thinking you'd stumbled across one of the saxophonist's own records. Even Abdullah Ibrahim, guesting on his own 'Beautiful Love', can't inject any sense of urgency. Garrett roughens things up a little with his latter-day Sonny Stitt phrasing and tone, but he gets going properly only on the long closing 'Sparks', by which time *The Charmer* has probably been consigned to the late-nite pile.

If one thing was significantly lacking, it was the chance to hear Fambrough and his music stretched out in a live setting. On the evidence of *Blues at Bradley's*, he's more than capable of sustaining interest over the long haul. The opening items weigh in at 15 and 13 minutes respectively and are as full of meat as double-yolked eggs. Bradley's in New York City is the present-day home of Paul Desmond's much-loved piano (and O'Connell twice appears to quote from 'Polka Dots And Moon Beams', unless the old chap still haunts the room and dictates that his signature be heard), and its wooden walls afford a warm, resonant acoustic for Fambrough's rebuilt but three-centuries-old bass. Steve Turre contributes the concluding blues and is as evocative as ever in his solo.

Keeper Of The Spirit embraces some unlikely sounds, including tenor recorder on 'Save That Time' and the ever-irritating wheeze-and-squeak of EWI throughout. In some respects this is a more ambitious album than its predecessors, but it lacks the straightforwardness and precision that make the others such compelling listening. Washington, a much underrated soloist, provides the leaven, but there is a drabness and lack of vitality which is depressing after earlier highs. The beautiful cover photo will pull you in, willy-nilly.

Massimo Farao PIANO

*** **For Me** Splasc(h) H 337-2
Farao; Flavio Boltro (*t, flhn*); Aldo Zunino, Dado Moroni (*b*); Gianni Cazzola (*d*). 12/90.

A boisterous and pleasing display of piano which starts out like a grooving Junior Mance or Bobby Timmons session on 'That's How We Like It!' then softens up with a long, languorous treatment of 'It's Easy To Remember'. Boltro sits in on a blues and an original called 'The Flea', but it's Farao's record, elegant in an Italian way (he even does a version of Lehár's 'Yours Is My Heart Alone') but keenly characterized throughout.

Tal Farlow (born 1921) GUITAR

**** **Tal Farlow: Jazz Masters 41** Verve 527365-2
Farlow; Bob Enevoldsen (*vtb*); Bill Perkins (*ts*); Bob Gordon (*bs*); Claude Williamson, Eddie Costa (*p*); Red Mitchell, Ray Brown, Monty Budwig, Oscar Pettiford, Vinnie Burke, Bill Tackus, Knobby Totah (*b*); Stan Levey, Chico Hamilton, Joe Morello, Jimmy Campbell (*d*). 1/55–3/58.

***(*) **The Return Of Tal Farlow** Original Jazz Classics OJC 356
Farlow; John Scully (*p*); Jack Six (*b*); Alan Dawson (*d*). 9/69.

One could hardly tell from the catalogue that Farlow is one of the major jazz guitarists, since most of his records – as both leader and sideman – are currently out of print. His reticence as a performer (he has been semi-retired for many years) belies his breathtaking speed, melodic inventiveness and pleasingly gentle touch as a bop-orientated improviser. His tenure at Verve included some marvellous sessions and, though all the individual dates are still in limbo, the Jazz Masters disc creams off the pick of seven original albums. Trios with Eddie Costa and Vinnie Burke are especially fine, but so is the date with Gerry Wiggins, Ray Brown and Chico Hamilton, which features one of the fastest treatments of 'Cherokee' ever recorded. Unassumingly though he plays, one never feels intimidated by Farlow's virtuosity, even when he takes the trouble to reharmonize a sequence entirely or to blitz a melody with single-note flourishes. An indispensable compilation. *The Return* is hardly less fine, and Farlow plays just as quickly, with comparable insight: try the lovely variations on 'My Romance'.

*** **Trinity** Columbia 476580-2
    Farlow; Mike Nock (*p*); Lynn Christie (*b*); Bob Jaspe (*d*). 9/76.
*** **A Sign Of The Times** Concord CCD 4026
    Farlow; Hank Jones (*p*); Ray Brown (*b*). 77.
***(*) **Chromatic Palette** Concord CCD 4154
    Farlow; Tommy Flanagan (*p*); Gary Mazzaroppi (*b*). 1/81.
*** **Standards Recital** FD Music 151932
    Farlow; Philippe Petit (*g*). 11/91.

These are the only two of several Concord albums to make it to CD so far. On *A Sign Of The Times* the music's delivered with pristine accuracy and brightness by these infallible pros, but somehow there's a spark missing. Even though they've gone to the trouble of arranging a dark, contrapuntal framework for 'You Don't Know What Love Is', for instance, or treating 'Stompin' At The Savoy' in a unique way, one misses the sizzle of Farlow's older work. Sumptuously recorded and balanced among the three players, though, and hard not to enjoy. *Chromatic Palette* is just a shade better. Flanagan digs in a little harder than he often does, and Farlow's own playing has a majestic breadth to it on some of the tunes, all of which are dispatched quickly and with few frills. Mazzaroppi sounds somewhat like a more youthful Red Mitchell on the bass. Try the hard-bitten 'Nuages' as a sample.

The Columbia album sets Farlow alongside the surprise choice of Mike Nock, who does a more than creditable job: though this is mainly a trio date, with Jaspe present on only one tune, it might have been even better as a meditation between Farlow and Nock, judged on the utterly beautiful duo take on 'If I Should Lose You'.

Farlow has seldom encountered other guitarists (on record, at least) and his gentlemanly encounter with Petit is graceful and suffused with bonhomie. Like most such records, it's a little too polite to sustain a long programme unless one is hung up on harmonic subtleties, but there's no denying the empathy of the players. Farlow gets a three-tune medley to himself at the end and sounds, amusingly, like two players.

Art Farmer (born 1928) FLUGELHORN, TRUMPET

*** **Art Farmer Septet** Original Jazz Classics OJC 054
    Farmer; Jimmy Cleveland (*tb*); Clifford Solomon, Charlie Rouse (*ts*); Oscar Estell, Danny Bank (*bs*); Quincy Jones, Horace Silver (*p*); Monk Montgomery, Percy Heath (*b*); Art Taylor, Sonny Johnson (*d*). 7/53–6/54.
***(*) **When Farmer Met Gryce** Original Jazz Classics OJC 072
    Farmer; Gigi Gryce (*as*); Freddie Redd, Horace Silver (*p*); Addison Farmer, Percy Heath (*b*); Kenny Clarke, Art Taylor (*d*). 5/54–5/55.
**** **The Art Farmer Quintet** Original Jazz Classics OJC 241
    Farmer; Gigi Gryce (*as*); Duke Jordan (*p*); Addison Farmer (*b*); Philly Joe Jones (*d*). 10/55.
(*) **Two Trumpets Original Jazz Classics OJC 018
    Farmer; Donald Byrd (*t*); Jackie McLean (*as*); Barry Harris (*p*); Doug Watkins (*b*); Art Taylor (*d*). 8/56.
*** **Farmer's Market** Original Jazz Classics OJC 398
    Farmer; Hank Mobley (*ts*); Kenny Drew (*p*); Addison Farmer (*b*); Elvin Jones (*d*). 11/56.

Art Farmer began his recording career with the ten-inch album *Work Of Art*, the contents of which are on OJC 018. Although pitched around Farmer's trumpet solos, the music is as much in debt to the composing and arranging of Jones and Gryce, and witty originals such as 'Elephant Walk', 'The Little Band Master' and 'Wildwood' make up the programme. Yet Farmer's skilful contributions elevate the scores and it's clear that his style was already firmly in place: a pensive restraint on ballads, a fleet yet soberly controlled attack on up-tempo tunes, and a concern for tonal manipulation within a small range of inflexions. If he was comparatively unadventurous, then as later, it didn't stop him from developing an individual style.

This begins to come clear in the small-group work of the mid-1950s. The group he led with Gigi Gryce has been somewhat forgotten in recent years, but the two OJC reissues are both impeccable examples of a more considered approach to hard-bop forms. While *When Farmer Met Gryce* is the better known, it's slightly the lesser of the two: *Art Farmer Quintet* has some of Gryce's best writing in the unusual structures of 'Evening In Casablanca' and 'Satellite', while 'Nica's Tempo', constructed more from key centres than from chords, might be his masterpiece; in the sequence of long solos, Farmer turns in an improvisation good enough to stand with the best of Miles Davis from the same period. The rhythm section, too, is the most sympathetic of the three involved.

The two-trumpet meeting with Byrd is capable but routine, a typical Prestige blowing session of the period, while *Farmer's Market* suffers slightly from unexpectedly heavy tempos and an erratic performance from Mobley, although Kenny Drew takes some crisp solos. The remastering of all these reissues is cleanly done.

**** Portrait Of Art Original Jazz Classics OJC 166
    Farmer; Hank Jones (p); Addison Farmer (b); Roy Haynes (d). 4–5/58.
Though as unassumingly handled as everything in Farmer's discography, this one has long been signposted as a classic. The rhythm section is beautifully balanced and offers exemplary support to the leader, whose playing summons elegance, fire and craftsmansip in almost perfect accord, with his ballad-playing particularly refined. Never as fêted as any comparable session by Miles Davis, this is still jazz trumpet playing on an exalted level and should be acknowledged as such.

**** Modern Art Blue Note 784459-2
    Farmer; Benny Golson (ts); Bill Evans (p); Addison Farmer (b); Dave Bailey (d). 9/58.
***(*) Live At The Half Note Atlantic 90666
    Farmer; Jim Hall (g); Steve Swallow (b); Walter Perkins (d). 12/63.
The Blue Note album, originally on United Artists and finely remastered, is one of Farmer's most successful records of the period. Golson contributes one excellent theme, 'Fair Weather', but most of the others involve subtle reworkings of familiar standards: a surprisingly jaunty 'The Touch Of Your Lips', a beguilingly smooth reading of Junior Mance's 'Jubilation', a stately 'Like Someone In Love'. The presence of Evans makes a telling difference: his solos are so finely thought out that it makes one wish he'd become the regular man in the Jazztet.

Not much of Farmer's work as a leader in the 1960s remains easy to find. The empathy between Farmer and Jim Hall makes the live Half Note session a compelling occasion: long and unflagging renditions of 'I Want To Be Happy' and 'Stompin' At The Savoy' feature both men in vibrant improvisations, and each has an engaging ballad feature.

*** On The Road Original Jazz Classics OJC 478
    Farmer; Art Pepper (as); Hampton Hawes (p); Ray Brown (b); Shelly Manne, Steve Ellington (d). 7–8/76.
An exceptional band, although the music is not quite as good as one might have hoped. The sole outstanding group performance is 'Namely You', where Farmer and Pepper both turn in superb solos, while 'Will You Still Be Mine?' and 'What Am I Here For?' are merely very good. Pepper, entering his Indian summer in the studios, was still a little unfocused, and Hawes is not quite at his best. But Farmer is as consistently fine as ever, by now using the flugelhorn almost exclusively, and the recording captures much of the quality of his tone.

**(*) Foolish Memories L + R 45008
    Farmer; Harry Sokal (ts); Fritz Pauer (p); Heiri Keinzig (b); Joris Dudli (d). 8/81.
***(*) Manhattan Soul Note SN 1026
    Farmer; Sahib Shihab (ss, bs); Kenny Drew (p); Mads Vinding (b); Ed Thigpen (d). 11/81.
***(*) Mirage Soul Note SN 1046
    Farmer; Clifford Jordan (ts); Fred Hersch (p); Ray Drummond (b); Akira Tana (d). 9/82.
*** Warm Valley Concord CCD 4212
    As above, except omit Jordan. 9/82.
Farmer spent the early part of the 1980s recording, like so many of his colleagues, for European rather than American companies. The L + R date would be very routine if it weren't for his presence, but the leader turns in his usual conscientious performance. The two Soul Note dates are much more interesting. *Manhattan* blends excellent original material from Drew, Horace Parlan and Bennie Wallace with a jaunty reading of Parker's 'Passport', and Shihab is an unexpected but rumbustious partner in the front line; *Mirage* is perhaps a shade better, with Jordan at his most fluent, Hersch numbering among Farmer's most sympathetic accompanists and another Parker tune, 'Barbados', taken at an ideal tempo. Drummond and Tana are also splendid. The Concord date misses only the stimulation of another front-

line horn to set off against Farmer's most introspective playing, although Hersch's finely wrought ballad, 'And Now There's You', is the kind of track which makes any record worth keeping for that alone. All three discs are recorded with great presence and very sharp clarity.

*** **Maiden Voyage** Denon 38C38-7071
>   Farmer; Sato Masahiko (*p*); Ron Carter (*b*); Jack DeJohnette (*d*); strings conducted by David Nadien. 4/83.

(*) **In Concert Enja 4088-2
>   Farmer; Slide Hampton (*tb*); Jim McNeely (*p*); Ron McClure (*b*); Adam Nussbaum (*d*). 8/84.

*** **You Make Me Smile** Soul Note SN 1076
>   Farmer; Clifford Jordan (*ts*); Fred Hersch (*p*); Rufus Reid (*b*); Akira Tana (*d*). 12/84.

It was inevitable that Farmer's beautiful tone would again bedeck a record with strings, and the Denon session (a CD reissue) is as well done as this sort of thing can be, favouring strong jazz material – 'Ruby My Dear', 'Goodbye Pork Pie Hat' – over standards. The Enja concert recording from the following year is inauspicious, a less than scintillating day in the players' lifetimes, although Farmer turns on his ballad mode for 'Darn That Dream' to agreeable effect. The music on *You Make Me Smile* is a mite disappointing after the exemplary earlier Soul Notes – but only by those standards, since Farmer and Jordan are basically their usual pedigree selves.

*** **The Jazztet: Moment To Moment** Soul Note SN 1066
>   Farmer; Curtis Fuller (*tb*); Benny Golson (*ts*); Mickey Tucker (*p*); Ray Drummond (*b*); Albert 'Tootie' Heath (*d*). 5/83.

***(*) **Real Time** Contemporary CCD-14034-2
>   As above, except Marvin 'Smitty' Smith (d) replaces Heath. 2/86.

***(*) **Back To the City** Original Jazz Classics OJC 842
>   As above. 2/86.

The occasionally re-formed Jazztet is rather more of a showcase for Golson – as both composer and performer – than it is for Farmer. Their Soul Note session is a somewhat perfunctory return, with the six themes passing in prescribed fashion, but the Contemporary album, recorded live at a single residency at New York's Sweet Basil, gives a vivid idea of the group's continued spirit. *Real Time* offers lengthy readings of Golson staples such as 'Whisper Not' and 'Are You Real'. There's also an expansive treatment of 'Autumn Leaves' which finds all the soloists at their best. Coltrane's influence on Golson is arguably never more clear than in this music; Farmer is keenly incisive with the muted horn, romantically ebullient with it open; and Tucker emerges as a considerable soloist and accompanist: his solo on 'Autumn Leaves' is sweepingly inventive. Smith, the most audacious drummer of his generation, is the ideal occupant of the drum stool. *Back To The City* is now back on CD and features some lesser-known items from the band's book – including a rare outing for Farmer as composer, 'Write Soon'.

(*) **Azure Soul Note SN 1126
>   Farmer; Fritz Pauer (*p*). 9/87.

Although Farmer clearly enjoys the company of Pauer, these nine duets are not very compelling listening. One can't avoid the feeling that Farmer relaxes more in the company of a full rhythm section and, adept as Pauer is at filling the rhythmic and harmonic backdrops, the results seem a little stiff here and there, despite showcasing Farmer's flugelhorn tone at its most beguiling.

**** **Something To Live For** Contemporary CCD-14029-2
>   Farmer; Clifford Jordan (*ts*); James Williams (*p*); Rufus Reid (*b*); Marvin 'Smitty' Smith (*d*). 1/87.

**** **Blame It On My Youth** Contemporary CCD-14042-2
>   As above, except Victor Lewis (*d*) replaces Smith. 2/88.

**** **Ph. D** Contemporary CCD-14055-2
>   As above, except Marvin 'Smitty' Smith (*d*) replaces Lewis; add Kenny Burrell (*g*). 4/89.

As he entered his sixties, Art Farmer was playing better than ever. The three albums by this wonderful group speak as eloquently as any record can on behalf of the generation of players who followed the first boppers (Farmer, Jordan) yet can still make modern music with a contemporary rhythm section (Williams, Reid, Lewis, Smith). The first record, dedicated to Billy Strayhorn's music, is a little doleful on the ballads but is otherwise perfectly pitched. *Blame It On My Youth*, though, is a discreet masterpiece. Art's reading of the title-track is one of his very finest ballad interpretations, even by his standards; Jordan plays with outstanding subtlety and guarded power throughout and has a memorable feature of his own on 'I'll Be Around'; Williams leads the rhythm section with consummate craft and decisiveness. But it's Lewis who, like Smith, shows amazing versatility and who really makes the music fall together, finding an extra ounce of power and crispness in every rhythm he has to mark out. *Ph. D* doesn't quite maintain this exalted level but, with Burrell guesting in jovial mood, it's as good-humoured and fluent as the others. Outstanding production work from Helen Keane.

*** **Central Avenue Reunion** Contemporary CCD-14057-2
> Farmer; Frank Morgan (*as*); Lou Levy (*p*); Eric Von Essen (*b*); Albert 'Tootie' Heath (*d*). 5/89.
The reunion is between Farmer and Morgan, friends from the Los Angeles scene of the early 1950s, yet never together on record before. The music, from a live engagement at Kimball's East in California, is finally disappointing: Morgan's keening and late-flowering interest in what extremes he can reach on his horn isn't a very apposite partner for Farmer's unflappable flugelhorn, and the rhythm section have few ambitions beyond comping. Some fine moments amidst a generally routine record.

*** **Soul Eyes** Enja 7047-2
> Farmer; Geoff Keezer (*p*); Kenneth Davis (*b*); Lewis Nash (*d*). 5/91.
Beguiling, graceful, this is Farmer cruising amiably through the autumn of his career. The tempos are on the stately side, and the man with the horn feels no need to rush a tune like 'Soul Eyes' or 'Isfahan', one of several interesting choices – but the closing 'Straight No Chaser' is rather warmer. Keezer continues to impress, Nash is one of today's great drummers. Recorded live at one of Japan's Blue Note clubs.

*** **The Company I Keep** Arabesque AJ0112
> Farmer; Tom Harrell (*t, flhn*); Ron Blake (*ss, ts*); Geoff Keezer (*p*); Kenny Davis (*b*); Carl Allen (*d*). 1/94.
The title is appropriate in a slightly discomfiting way. Farmer sounds like the senior citizen of this party, and virtually all the best strokes are pulled by his much younger companions. Harrell takes most of the brass honours, Blake is fleet and incisive, Keezer is masterful: his harmonically intriguing 'Song Of The Canopy' is certainly the best original here. Art takes measured, dark solos, but he sounds more like a patron than a leader.

Allen Farnham (born 1961) PIANO

(*) **5th House Concord CCD 4413
> Farnham; Tom Harrell (*t, flhn*); Joe Lovano (*ss, ts*); Drew Gress (*b*); Jamey Haddad (*d*). 10/89.
*** **Play-cation** Concord CCD 4521
> As above, except add Dick Oatts (*ss, as, ts*); Rufus Reid (*b*); omit Lovano and Harrell. 5/92.
*** **The Common Thread** Concord CCD 4632
> Farnham; Joe Lovano (*ts*); Jamey Hadad (*b*); Drew Gress (*d*). 1/86–7/94.
*** **At Maybeck Recital Hall Vol. 41** Concord CCD 4686
> Farnham (*p* solo). 6/94.
Farnham's dexterity masks a certain indecisiveness about what he wants to do, at least on the first record. An eclectic muddle of tunes stretches from Shorter and Coltrane to a Farnham original called 'Despair', with Lovano and Harrell putting in desultory appearances. For Concord, though, this is really left-field stuff, and the subsequent *Play-cation* is much more confident and unified. Gress and Haddad make a lively rhythm section (though bass chores are partly entrusted to Reid on the second set) and the talented, slippery playing of Oatts sits very compatibly on the music, distinguished this time by some sharper writing: the title-piece especially is an inventive one. *The Common Thread* is a set of leftovers of varying vintages: six tracks come from a 1986 session with Lovano, two more date from *Play-cation* and two makeweight solos were cut in 1994. This is a darker, at times almost lugubrious session: lots of minor keys, ginger tempos and nocturnal sonorities, the one exception coming in an almost explosive solo treatment of Jobim's 'No More Blues'. Lovano has a terrific outing on the title-piece and there are interesting trio versions of tunes by Ralph Towner and Steve Swallow, but the record's doleful bent is a bit oppressive. Farnham's turn in the Maybeck spotlight displays a chameleonic bent: on Evans, Brubeck and McPartland tunes he sounds like he's following the composers without imposing too much of himself. A blues and two original sketches show an adept if fundamentally derivative tack. A solid entry in the series but hardly one of the essential ones.

Joe Farrell (1937–86) TENOR SAXOPHONE, SOPRANO SAXOPHONE, FLUTE

***(*) **Sonic Text** Original Jazz Classics OJC 777
> Farrell; Freddie Hubbard (*t, flhn*); George Cables (*p*); Tony Dumas (*b*); Peter Erskine (*d*). 11/79.
(*) **Vim 'n' Vigor Timeless SJP 197
> Farrell; Louis Hayes (*d*); Rob Van Den Broeck (*p*); Harry Emmery (*b*). 11/83.
Farrell's painful death in 1986 silenced a voice probably best known for the life-raft it threw Chick Corea's original 'Return To Forever', and consistently undervalued ever since. Farrell's best album, *Sonic Text*, originally on Contemporary, has appeared only belatedly on CD. It captures perfectly his

adventurous modal approach and his interest in pure sound. His flute part on Cables's 'Sweet Rita Suite' is both effective and unusual. He was perhaps a better flautist than saxophonist, but his soprano work always had what one-time colleague Flora Purim describes as a 'singing' quality that eliminates the horn's often rather shrill character. Hubbard may be too assertive a player for Farrell's music – the trumpeter's own 'Jazz Crunch' is slightly out of character for the set as a whole – but when he switches to flugelhorn for 'When You're Awake' and the slightly melancholy 'If I Knew Where You're At', which might almost be by Chick Corea, he sounds spot on. The closing 'Malibu', reminiscent of some of the things with Corea, is Farrell's best testament.

Vim 'n' Vigor is co-led by Louis Hayes, who toured with Farrell for two years before moving on to the McCoy Tyner Trio. Farrell's Rollins debts are still audible in the phrasing on 'Miles Mode', but the intonation is very much his own, and his flute style (occasionally reminiscent of Prince Lasha) is quite individual. This is a fine album that might have been improved by the addition of a more sympathetic drummer.

Claudio Fasoli TENOR AND SOPRANO SAX

*** **Cities** Ram RMCD4503
    Fasoli; Mick Goodrick (*g*); Paolino Dalla Porta (*b*); Billy Elgart (*d*). 93.
*** **Ten Tributes** Ram RMCD4517
    As above, except add Kenny Wheeler (*t, flhn*), Henri Texier (*b*), omit Dalla Porta. 4/94.
Fasoli's earlier records suggested a musician who enjoyed differing jazz styles but didn't seem especially at ease in all of them. When he tries to go outside familiar parameters, as on the edgy 'Surfaces' on *Cities*, his broken phrasing can sound contrived. But this is an interesting session, made up of ten dedications to different metropolises. Goodrick's versatile range is a more authoritative force than the leader's playing, binding the parts together and taking liquid, affably lyrical solos in his own time. Dalla Porta and Elgart play restlessly, unwilling to settle into any simple groove; yet when the four of them find the same pulse – '20121' is a good example – the results are very pleasing. *Ten Tributes* is slow and thoughtful and just a bit heavy-going: Fasoli blends five standards and five originals and takes the trouble to alter slightly the fabric of each of the familiar tunes. It's interesting – 'Yesterdays' adds a bar of silence to each eight measures, like a regular pause for thought – but some may find it a degree too painstaking to enjoy. Wheeler is his usual diligent self and Raimondo Lupi gets a lovely sound in the studio.

Riccardo Fassi (born 1955) KEYBOARDS

(*) **Notte Splasc(h) H 345-2
    Fassi; Claudio Corvini, Aldo Bassi, Flavio Boltro (*t*); Roberto Rossi (*tb, shells*); Mario Corvini (*tb*); Michel Audrisso (*ss*); Sandro Satta (*as*); Torquato Sdrucia (*bs*); Antonello Salis (*acc*); Fabio Zeppetella (*g*); Luca Pirozzi, Francesco Puglisi (*b*); Massimo D'Agostino, Alberto D'Anna, John Arnold (*d*); Alfredo Minotti (*perc, v*). 2/91.
(*) **Toast Man Splasc(h) H 307
    Fassi; Flavio Boltro (*t, flhn*); Dario La Penna (*g*); Massimo Morriconi (*b*); Alberto D'Anna (*d*); Massimo Rocci, Alfredo Minotti (*perc*). 2–4/90.
*** **One For Leonardo** Splasc(h) H 379-2
    Fassi; Flavio Boltro (*t, flhn*); Riccardo Luppi (*ss, ts, f, af*); Sandro Cerino (*bcl, cbcl*); Massimo Moriconi, Paolino Dalla Porta (*b*); Alberto D'Anna (*d*); Alfredo Minotti (*perc*). 4/92.
Fassi works both in small-group settings and with his big Tankio Band, which is responsible for *Notte*. His orchestral scores are colourful and fluent but not especially individual and, as so often, it's the soloists who make *Notte* catch fire, even if only here and there. British readers will be reminded of Kenny Wheeler with John Taylor when they hear 'Octopus' and 'La Foresta' on *Toast Man*. Some of the other tracks here, though, aim for a studious kind of fusion, Fassi turning to synthesizer over piano, and his lyrical bent is obscured by those settings, although Boltro is attractively elegant throughout. The trumpeter gets even more space on *One For Leonardo*, which is probably Fassi's best work to date. There is only a dash of electronics this time and the soundscape is widened by the bass reeds of Cerino: not all the sonic effects are convincingly integrated into Fassi's arrangements, and he seems short on real melodic invention, but Boltro and the useful Luppi play with great purpose on the date.

*** **New York Trio** YVP 3036
    Fassi; Rufus Reid (*b*); Marvin 'Smitty' Smith (*d*). 12/92.

*** **Plays The Music Of Frank Zappa** Splasc(h) 428
> Fassi; Claudio Corvini, Mike Applebaum, Giancarlo Ciminelli, Flavio Boltro (*t*); Massimo Pirone (*tb, tba*); Mario Corvini (*tb*); Sandro Satta, Michel Audrisso, Torquato Sdrucia, Francesco Marini, Riccardo Luppi (*reeds*); Fabio Zeppetella (*g*); Francesco Lo Cascio (*vib, mar*); Antonello Salis (*acc*); Luca Pirozzi (*b*); Alberto D'Anna (*d*). 5/94.

The New York album is unexpectedly straight-ahead, lean, immediate: Fassi brought a portfolio of strong themes to the stduio, and Reid and Smith play up to their best form in support. The Zappa tribute album returns Fassi to the Tankio Band format. He chooses a group of Zappa favourites – all from the 1960s output, though – and sets them up as something between blowing vehicles and smartly arranged pastiches. As homage, it's probably too respectful, but it does get a lot of good jazz out of the likes of 'Twenty Small Cigars'.

Zusaan Kali Fasteau SOPRANO SAXOPHONE, FLUTES, PIANO, PERCUSSION, VOICE

*** **Worlds Beyond Words** Flying Note FNCD 9001
> Fasteau; James C. Jamison II (*g*); Elizabeth Panzer (*hp*); Bob Cunningham (*b*); Rashied Ali (*d*); Paul Leake (*tabla*); David Cornick (*perc*). 89.

A New Yorker, Fasteau spent much of her early career abroad, absorbing a huge range of musics and refining her quite remarkable multi-instrumentalism. On *Worlds Beyond Words* she alternates tough, Coltrane-influenced trio performances with Ali and Cunningham (of which the long 'From Above' is the most coherent) and 'world music' pieces that use multitracking to suggest ensemble performance. She's a fine flautist, with an authentic-sounding tone on the difficult shakuhachi ('Dolphin Meditation'), and has a strong, grainy voice ('Appreciating People', 'Spiritual Kinship'). Flying Note has also released other material of Fasteau's; it may be difficult to track down, but it is certainly worth the effort.

Dan Faulk (born 1969) TENOR SAXOPHONE, SOPRANO SAXOPHONE

***(*) **Focusing In** Criss Cross Criss 1076
> Faulk; Barry Harris (*p*); Rufus Reid (*b*); Carl Allen (*d*). 21/92.

Benny Golson contributes an appreciative liner-note, and at first hearing Faulk might well be a player of Golson's generation and experience. The young Philadelphian has a big, slightly old-fashioned tone to go with his racy delivery of new and standard material. His own 'Quintagon' quickly demonstrates his ability to push bebop chords a step further. Faulk frequently departs from the basic harmonic structure but in ways that give even 'wrong' notes an aura of relatedness. Harris is, of course, an ideal collaborator in this, and the partnership comes into its own on two Monk tunes, 'Nutty' and 'Epistrophy'; 'Barry's Tune' is offered by way of thanks.

Though the liner details list only tenor, Faulk shifts to the straight horn for one of the oddest takes on 'I Love Paris' ever committed to disc. Allen is at his best here and on 'Lover', laying off threes against fours, speeding up, then softening the count. If, as Golson suggests, ballads offer the most accurate index of a young player's chops, then Faulk is definitely on the up, with a long and flawless version of Horace Silver's 'Peace' that constantly finds new things to do with the tune. This is an excellent album. The only quibble with it is that the sound is a little too condensed and central, an arrangement that masks Reid's contribution and frequently finds Harris and the leader right on top of each other. A minor drawback; otherwise warmly recommended.

Pierre Favre (born 1937) DRUMS, PERCUSSION

** **Singing Drums** ECM 1274
> Favre; Paul Motian (*d, gongs, crotales, calabashes, rodbrushes*); Freddy Studer (*d, gongs, log d, cym*); Nana Vasconcelos (*berimbau, tim, congas, water pot, shakers, bells, voice*). 5/84.

*** **Window Steps** ECM 1584
> Favre; Kenny Wheeler (*t, flhn*); Roberto Ottaviano (*ss*); David Darling (*clo*); Steve Swallow (*b*). 6/95.

One of the most innovative percussionists in Europe, Favre hasn't always been heard to best advantage on his own recordings. All-percussion albums are always a problem and *Singing Drums* rapidly degenerates into an acoustically pristine sampling of effects and devices with no sense of centre and very little coherent development. Ironically, on such a crowded canvas, the music seems to call out for horns or strings to draw the various strands together.

If the first of the pair appeals only to rather specialist tastes, the second is accessible to all. The presence of Wheeler and the much-admired Ottaviano guarantees music of interest, and this session has to be considered one of Darling's most focused and aware. Favre is himself seldom out of focus, but he is never intrusive and he holds the long 'Lea' together with great intelligence.

Wally Fawkes (born 1924) CLARINET, SOPRANO SAXOPHONE

*** **Fidgety Feet** Stomp Off CD1248
> Fawkes; Tony Davis (*t, v*); Alan Bradley (*tb*); Roy Hubbard (*cl, v*); Ken Freeman (*p*); Brian Mellor (*bj*); Phil Matthews (*tba*); Brian Lawrence (*b*); Derek Bennett (*d*). 1–2/92.

Trog has seldom taken leadership duties in the recording studios, but he gets top billing here as guest with the Zenith Hot Stompers. The band don't exactly break into a muck sweat, but there's plenty of vim on the upbeat numbers and Fawkes forms a neat partnership with Hubbard on several of the tunes. Trog gargles the odd note, but for the most part he is still in great nick and this 'Trog's Blues' is probably as good as any he's given of late. Recorded in dry but lively sound at the Bull's Head by redoubtable Dave Bennett.

Rick Fay TENOR, ALTO AND SOPRANO SAXOPHONES, CLARINET, VOCAL

(*) **Live At Lone Pine Arbors 19101
> Fay; David Jones (*c*); George Palmer (*tb*); Bob Leary (*g, bj, v*); Lee Richardson (*sou*); Pat Doyle (*d*). 9/89.

*** **Hello Horn** Arbors 19102
> Fay; Ernie Carson (*c, v*); Charlie Bornemann (*tb, v*); Tom Baldwin (*p*); Paul Scarvarda (*bj, g*); Lee Richardson (*sou*); Pat Doyle (*d*). 4/90.

*** **Memories Of You** Arbors 19103
> Fay; Ernie Carson (*c*); Dan Barrett (*tb*); Johnny Mince (*cl*); Tom Baldwin (*p*); Bob Leary (*g, bj, v*); Lee Richardson (*sou*); Pat Doyle (*d*). 1/91.

(*) **Glendena Forever Arbors 19104
> Fay; Jackie Coon (*flhn, v*); Charlie Bornemann (*tb*); Bob Phillips (*p*); Eddie Erickson (*g, bj, v*); Lee Richardson (*sou, b*); Eddie Graham (*d*). 5/91.

*** **This Is Where I Came In** Arbors 19106
> Fay; Jon-Erik Kellso, Peter Ecklund (*c*); Dan Barrett (*tb*); Bobby Gordon (*cl*); Keith Ingham (*p*); Marty Grosz (*g, v*); Greg Cohen (*b*); Hal Smith (*d*). 6/91.

*** **Rollin' On** Arbors 19108
> Fay; Jon-Erik Kellso (*t*); Dan Barrett (*tb*); Chuck Hodges (*cl*); Dick Cary (*p, ahn*); Paul Scarvarda, Howard Alden (*g, bj*); Lou Mauro (*b*); Joe Ascione (*d*). 12/91.

*** **Live At The State** Arbors 19112
> As above, except Chuck Folds (*p*), Bob Haggart (*b*) and Eddie Graham (*d*) replace Cary, Scarvarda, Alden, Mauro and Ascione. 4/92.

(***) **Sax-O-Poem Poetry With Jazz** Arbors 19113
> Fay; Johnny Varro (*p*); Doug Mattocks (*g*); David Stone (*b*); Gene Estes (*d*). 9/92.

Rick Fay's unassuming brand of Dixie-into-swing has now been extensively documented by the Arbors label, and there's some amusing and good-hearted music on all of these discs. The first three lean more towards revivalism, with Fay's Hot Five handling the Lone Pine date in good spirits, though without a deal of finesse. Carson's energetic and rasping manner is a useful fillip on *Hello Horn* and *Memories Of You*, and the latter benefits further from the arrival of the catalytic Barrett to bring the group up to an octet (Fay's Big Eight). *Glendena Forever* is marred by too many vocals, shared between Fay, Coon and Erickson, and some of the material here is a bit shopworn, but the next three albums are more particular. *This Is Where I Came In* features the strongest band Fay has organized (credited this time as his Summa Orchestra) and the subsequent *Rollin' On* follows up with somewhat rarer material and a singularly smart arrangement of Beiderbecke's 'In The Dark'. The live date returns to more familiar Dixieland terrain, but Kellso and Hedges sound in notably good fettle.

Fay himself stands in the swing tenor tradition of the likes of Eddie Miller and Boomie Richman, a big sound but a light and fluent way with it. When he picks up soprano, he worships Sidney Bechet. The final disc shows off his poetry: he starts each track with a reading, with the music fading up from underneath, and though his declamations are a bit flat, the end result is not without charm. An acquired taste, and much the same can be said about his singing, which some of the tracks on several of these discs can probably do without.

Enrico Fazio BASS

***(*) **Mirabilia!** Splasc(h) H 327-2
  Fazio; Alberto Mandarini (*t*); Lauro Rossi (*tb*); Francesco Aroni Vigone (*ss, as*); Carlo Actis
  Dato (*ts, bs, bcl*); Fiorenzo Sordini (*d, vib, mar*); Franca Silveri (*v*). 7/89.
*** **Favola** CMC 9921-2
  Fazio; Alberto Mandarini (*t*); Floriano Rosini (*tb*); Sergei Letov (*ss*); Francesco Vigone (*ss, as*);
  Piero Ponzo (*as, bs, cl, bcl*); Andrea Chenna (*ob*); Eleonora Nervi (*tba*); Giuliano Palmieri (*elec*);
  Fiorenzo Sordini (*d*); Vittorio Bestoso (*v*). 11/90.

Fazio loves an exciting, kinetic band, full of carnival colours and offbeat energies. Fazio, Actis Dato and
Sordini all work together in the reed players' group, but here the bassist's themes are equally full of
surprise and prime improvisational flair. While the longest section of *Euphoria* is a·tribute to Charles
Mingus which incorporates four Mingus themes, it doesn't sound much like a Mingus band: trombone,
bassoon and oboe make only fleeting appearances, but the central unit of three horns, bass and drums
swarms all over Fazio's pleasing melodies enough to convince that there's a bigger band at work here
than the numbers suggest. Mandarini is very different from the cool trumpeters who set today's brass
norm: notes seem to topple out of his horn, and long, barely controlled lines spiral crazily over the
ensemble. Actis Dato's typically zesty ripostes and Vigone's brusque, pinchy alto lines fill in the rest.
Favola is a festival commission, a 12-part suite with vocal commentary by Bestoso and some more
strong writing by the leader. Ponzo and Letov are worthy substitutes for Actis Dato, but the music is a
little more constrained and less freewheeling this time.

John Fedchock TROMBONE

**** **New York Big Band** Reservoir RSRCD 138
  Fedchock; Tony Kadleck, Greg Gisbert, Barry Ries, Tim Hagans (*t, flhn*); Keith O'Quinn, Clark
  Gayton, George Flynn (*tb*); Jon Gordon (*ss, as*); Mark Vinci (*as*); Rich Perry, Rick Margitza
  (*ts*); Scott Robinson (*bs*); Joel Weiskopf (*p*); Lynn Seaton (*b*); Dave Ratajczak (*d*); Jerry
  Gonzalez (*perc*). 9/92.

A glance through the personnel shows immediately that this is far from being another anonymous
studio big band: Fedchock has creamed off some of the sharpest of New York's contemporary players
and created a meticulous, skilful yet passionate orchestra. The leader spent seven years with Woody
Herman and knows his trade: he has a sonorous if not especially distinctive style as a soloist, which
gives the featured treatment of 'Ruby, My Dear' a glistening quality, but he leaves the showstopping
moments to players such as Perry, Robinson, Hagans, Margitza and Gisbert. 'Limehouse Blues' is a
brilliant flag-waver, tempestuous but perfectly controlled; 'La Parguera' is melodically lovely, far more
than the typical Latin potboiler; and when they end on the dreaded *Flintstones* theme, Fedchock takes
the trouble to reharmonize it and actually takes the parodic element out. Glittering digital recording
lends extra attack. A prime statement from a certain strand of contemporary New York jazz.

Victor Feldman (1934–87) PIANO, VIBRAPHONE, DRUMS

***(*) **Suite Sixteen** Original Jazz Classics OJC 1768
  Feldman; Jimmy Deuchar, Dizzy Reece, Jimmy Watson (*t*); Ken Wray (*t, bt*); John Burden
  (*frhn*); Jim Powell (*tba*); Derek Humble (*as*); Tubby Hayes, Ronnie Scott (*ts*); Harry Klein (*bs*);
  Tommy Pollard, Norman Stenfalt (*p*); Lennie Bush, Eric Peter (*b*); Tony Crombie (*d, p*); Phil
  Seamen (*d*). 8 & 9/55.

It was probably inevitable that Feldman would move to America, but there's enough fine musicianship
on *Suite Sixteen* to suggest he might just as easily have stayed and played at home had London just
offered enough adventurous paying gigs. Divided into big-band, septet and quartet tracks, *Suite Sixteen*
was cut just prior to his first American trip. It isn't a classic like *Arrival*, which is also remembered as a
precious addition to the brief Scott LaFaro discography and will soon be available on CD; but it's a fine
record all the same. As a cross-section of the local talent – Deuchar, Scott, Hayes, Crombie, Seamen,
Reece – it's a remarkable document. Musically, it doesn't come up to some of the later, American
sessions, but it features four excellent Feldman originals (the ambitious title-piece was actually written
by Tony Crombie), Allan Ganley's 'Duffle Coat', Dizzy Reece's exuberant 'Maenya', which makes a fine
closer, and Kenny Clarke's and Gerald Wiggins's 'Sonar'.

  Feldman plays all three of his instruments, but concentrates on vibes, with excellent solos on his own
brief 'Elegy', where he follows the fiercely melancholic Deuchar, and on 'Maenya'. It's an interesting
aspect of his solo work that its quality always seems to be in inverse proportion to its length. Feldman

was a master of compression who often lost his way beyond a couple of choruses. The septet and quartet tracks are less buoyant, though 'Brawl For All', which features the leader's only piano contribution, is excellent. The sound is good but needs to be adjusted according to personnel.

*** Merry Olde Soul Original Jazz Classics OJC 402
     Feldman; Hank Jones (*p*); Sam Jones, Andy Simpkins (*b*); Louis Hayes (*d*). 60, 61.
Scandalously, Feldman's best record, *The Arrival Of*, is still not available on CD. This is only a rather second-rate and, one hopes, temporary substitute. Altogether more predictable and perhaps an indication of the toll exacted by Feldman's time as an in-demand session player. 'Bloke's Blues' contains flashes of originality (though Hank Jones didn't seem to know what it was all about) and there's a wonderful shimmering quality to the vibes on 'Serenity'. Otherwise, it's rather bland standards fare.

**(*) The Artful Dodger Concord CCD 4038
     Feldman; Jack Sheldon (*t, v*); Monty Budwig, Chuck Domanico (*b*); Colin Bailey (*d*).
As with Hampton Hawes, the switch to electric piano at the end of the 1960s did Feldman no favours, robbing him of that characteristically percussive touch and blurring the edges of his lines. This is an agreeable and sometimes surprising set but, apart from a very direct 'Limehouse Blues' and the title-piece, it errs on the fussy side and isn't helped by a soft-focus mix which is very much of its time.

Simon H. Fell (born 1958) BASS

**** Foom! Foom! Bruce's Fingers BF5
     Fell; Alan Wilkinson (*ss, as, bs*); Paul Hession (*d*). 2/92.
**** The Horrors Of Darmstadt Shock SX025
     As above. 6/93.
*** Music For 10(0) Leo Lab 013
     Fell; Guy Llewellyn (*frhn*); Charles Wharf, Pete Minns, Mick Beck, Alan Wilkinson (*reeds*); Mary Schwarz (*vla*); Paul Buckton (*g*); John McMillan (*b*); Paul Hession (*d*); Ben Watson (*v*). 11/93.
The best precedent for this music is the old Brötzmann trio with Van Hove and Bennink: exploding, tumultuous, improvised sound by one of the most exciting groups in the music today. There is little point in trying to describe the sound of Wilkinson's saxophones (primarily baritone, for which he is creating a valuable new outlook) as they roar over the top of Fell's bass and Hession's drums, or the amazing internal dialogues which the trio manages to create even as they break the sound barrier. It's a welcome, cold-shower experience at a time when acoustic free-jazz has dropped many of its confrontational aspects: these men revivify the intensities of Ayler, Brötzmann and others in the small but noble tradition of great noise. A CD is a poor substitute for a live performance, but *Foom! Foom!* (six pieces, from the lengthy 'Ballad Of Otis Twelvepersons' to the almost snapshot-like 'The Alphabet Poised Like Twenty-Six Frozen Ducklings') is a fine place to start, and the live *The Horrors Of Darmstadt* (recorded at the legendary Leeds Termite Club) is the essential in-concert aftermath, opening on the 32-minute mayhem of the title-track. Recording on the live CD is indifferent, but both are splendid records.
    Music For 10(0) celebrates a decade of achievement at the Termite Club with a symphony for ten improvisers and one poet. Though close listening reveals much scrupulous organization by Fell, the music writhes in ways that sound utterly spontaneous, and many of the textures and juxtapositions are as dramatic and undiscovered as anything free music can throw out. Though the full-scale version of the work runs for about 90 minutes, this one works perfectly well at some 75 minutes. The libretto is provided (and shouted) by Ben Watson, a sequence of love letters to or tirades about the various record shops which exist in the city. Watson's bellowing may discourage repeat plays, but it's all pretty hilarious and great and ludicrous in roughly equal measure.

Eric Felten TROMBONE

***(*) T-Bop Soul Note 121196
     Felten; Jimmy Knepper, Tom Everett, Evan Dobbins (*tb*); Joshua Redman (*ts*); Jonny King (*p*); Paul La Duca, Paul Henry (*b*); Jorge Rossy (*d*). 4/91.
Felten has the music in his genes. His grandfather, dedicatee of 'Blues For Lester DuBree', played in territory bands back in the 1920s, and apparently still blows a trombone. Felten has the stinging, brassy tone that went out of fashion for a while after J. J. Johnson devised a new, rapid-action delivery that was chiefly inspired by the saxophone. Felten's solos are notably spare and unfussy and, if he lacks his senior partner's glorious facility, he has other virtues on which to trade: strength, evenness and very exact pitching.

It might be thought that *T-Bop* was merely an attempt to cash in on the trombone's recent rejuvenation by cobbling together a latter-day Jay and Kai session. Misleading, though; it's clear from the opening track (on which Knepper quite properly leads off) that they're working in a very different vein, weaving together subtly voiced lines rather than alternating harmonized unisons and cutting session chases. Like a good deal of new jazz, it looks back to early jazz and bop-era styles. The title-track is audibly based on the changes to 'Stompin' At The Savoy', and there are quotes throughout the record to lots of other music. As Art Lange points out in his liner-note (which is disappointingly thin on biographical info about Felten), 'Delphi' is an attempt to create something in Wayne Shorter's pre-Weather Report idiom; allowing Redman to lead off the solos underscores the lineage.

Knepper doesn't so much keep to the background as avoid crowding the youngster. When they solo on the same track, as on 'T-Bop' and 'Ontology', there's not much between them technically, but it's perfectly clear who has the greater poise and experience. Perhaps their most effective partnership comes on an absolutely lovely 'Stella By Starlight' on which the two other brasses briefly feature. Felten has a couple of tracks all to himself with just bass for company, the original 'Love Muffin' and 'I Guess I'll Hang My Tears Out To Dry'.

Maynard Ferguson (born 1928) TRUMPET, FLUGELHORN, VALVE TROMBONE, BARITONE HORN, BANDLEADER

***(*) **Jazz Masters 52: Maynard Ferguson** Verve 529 905
> Ferguson; Buddy Childers, Don Palladino, Ray Linn, Pete Candoli, Tom Slaney, John Bello, Joe Burnett (*t*); Milt Bernhart, Bobby Burgess, Jimmy Cleveland, Herbie Harper (*tb*); Jimmy Ford, Anthony Ortega (*as, ts*); Bud Shank (*as, f*); Bob Cooper (*ts, ob*); Georgie Auld, Bill Holman, Ben Webster, Al Cohn, Ernie Wilkins, Willie Maiden, Nino Tempo, Willie Maiden (*ts*); Benny Carter, Herb Geller (*as*); Bob Gordon (*bs, bcl*); Tate Houston (*bs*); Russ Freeman, Lorraine Geller, Bobby Timmons, Gerry Wiggins (*p*); Howard Roberts (*g*); Ray Brown, Curtis Counce, Richard Evans, John Kirby, Red Mitchell, Joe Mondragon (*b*); Gary Frommer, George Jenkins, Shelly Manne, Alvin Stoller (*d*); Larry Bunker (*d, vib*); Irene Kral (*v*). 12/51–8/57.

*** **Live At Peacock Lane, Hollywood** Jazz Hour JH 1030
> Ferguson; personnel includes Herb Geller (*as*); Richie Kamuca (*ts*); Mel Lewis (*d*); others not indicated. 1/57.

*** **Two's Company** Roulette 852068
> Ferguson; Bill Berry, Rolf Ericson, Chet Feretti (*t*); Kenny Rupp, Ray Winslow (*tb*); Lanny Morgan (*as, f*); Willie Maiden (*ts, cl*); Joe Farrell (*ts, ss, f*); Frank Hittner (*bs, bcl*); Jaki Byard (*p*); John Neves (*b*); Rufus Reid (*d*); Chris Connor (*v*). 6/61.

There are few sights more impressive in animal physiology than the muscles in Maynard Ferguson's upper thorax straining for a top C. Unfortunately, on record there are no such distractions; putting a Ferguson disc on the turntable evokes sensations ranging from walking into a high wind to being run down by a truck.

The Verve compilation fills in what had been until recently a missing part of the story, the early stuff for Emarcy on *Dimensions*, *Round The Horn* and *Boy With Lots Of Brass*. The earliest item of all is actually from a Ben Webster session arranged by Benny Carter, in whose august company Ferguson sounds a touch too brassy and brash. There is also a track, 'Can't We Talk It Over?', from a Mercury album by arranger Pete Rugolo. The rest, though, is pure double-smelted Ferguson.

The material on Jazz Hour gives a fairly reliable account of what the MF Orchestra sounded like (to change the metaphor yet again) at its hormonal peak: brash, brazen, curiously likeable even when it is slapping the listener jovially round the mouth. There is as little point commenting analytically on these tracks – say, for example, 'Stand Up And Preach' – than it is to analyse a rainstorm or the tide: it's just there, and you have to deal with it or not. What may be slower to register is the sheer grace and elegance of some of the leader's gentler features, like 'My Funny Valentine'.

It's always been known that Ferguson can also play pretty. His middle-register work is often remarkably subtle, with unexpected inflexions reminiscent of his apparent opposite, Don Ellis (whose big-band experiments nevertheless betray a reciprocal Ferguson influence). Chris Connor is the finest band singer of her generation, and the band are duly respectful, leading her through a typically unhackneyed programme with some finesse.

*** **The New Sounds Of Maynard Ferguson And His Orchestra** Fresh Sound FSRCD 2010
> Ferguson; Rick Kiefer, Dusko Goykovich, Harry Hall, Nat Pavone (*t*); Don Roane, Kenny Rupp (*tb*); Lanny Morgan (*f, as*); Willie Maiden, Frank Vicari (*ts*); Ronnie Cuber (*bs*); Mike Abene, Roger Kellaway (*p*); Linc Milliman (*b*); Tony Inzalaco, Rufus Jones (*d*); Willie Rodriguez (*perc*); other percussionists unidentified. 64.

This was a smaller, rather subtler and more coherently inflected Ferguson outfit than many before or since. Benefiting from arrangements by Don Sebesky, Oliver Nelson, Bill Holman and others, and sticking to short, pungent durations (rather than the blowsier format of the live act, it packs 20 tracks into a generous 75 minutes that will delight converts and leave the uninitiated still a little winded. It's the usual blend of contemporary material (Hancock's 'Watermelon Man' and Alex North's 'Anthony and Cleopatra Theme') with jazz staples like Golson's 'Whisper Not' and Basie's 'One O'Clock Jump', together with non-mainstream items like 'The Londonderry Air'.

*** **Live At The Great American Music Hall** Status DSTS 1004
>   Ferguson; Lyn Biviano, Wayne Naus, John DeFlon, Bob Summers (*t*); Billy Graham (*tb, vtb*); Eddie Byrne (*vtb, btb*); Andy Mackintosh (*as*); Tony Buchanan (*ts*); Bruce Johnstone (*bs*); Pete Jackson (*ky*); Joel Di Bartolo (*b*); Randy Jones (*d*). 3/73.

*** **Live At The Great American Music Hall: Volume 2** Status DSTS 1007
>   As above. 3/73.

This was the period when it was virtually *de rigueur* to cover pop hits, so 'MacArthur Park' (a big hit for Ferguson) and 'Hey Jude' take their place alongside 'Take The "A" Train'. The energy level is as high as always on this closely but accurately recorded live record, which is high on atmosphere, if occasionally wanting in respect of subtle improvisational activity. Interestingly, even at this point a good deal of the solo space is devolved to other players, notably the ecclesiastically named but decidedly unpriestly Billy Graham and Brubeck's one-time standby, drummer Randy Jones.

   This is probably the closest thing on offer to the experience of a live MF gig. You have been warned.

(*) **Storm TBA TBCD 8052
>   Ferguson; no personnel or recording details.

(*) **Live From San Francisco TBA TBCD 8077
>   Ferguson; Hoby Freeman, Hugh Ragin, Alan Wise (*t*); Chris Braymen, Steve Wiest (*tb*); Tim Ries (*as*); Daniel Jordan (*ts, f*); Denis Di Blasio (*bs, f*); Rod Pedley (*ky*); Matt Bissonette (*b*); Greg Bissonette (*d*). 5/83.

Ferguson's revival in the 1980s has been interesting to watch. There's no less reliance on bruising volume, but Ferguson has slowly been revising the basic textures. The charts are more solidly grounded in large-scale bass patterns and the textures are no longer merely passive launching pads for strato-spheric solos. Difficult to pick between the two.

*** **Maynard Ferguson '93 – Footpath Café** Hot Shot HSR 8312
>   Ferguson; Roger Ingram, Jon Owens, Brian Thompson (*t*); Dante Luciani (*tb*); John Kricker (*btb*); Scaglione (*as*); Chip McNeil (*ts, ss*); Matt Wallace (*as, ts*); Glen Kostur (*bs*); Doug Bickel (*p, ky*); Dennis Marks (*b*); Jim White (*d*). 7/92.

Attention all shipping in sea areas Dogger, Wight and Portland: Hurricane Maynard blowing in from Heist-op-den-Berg in Belgium. The Big Bop Nouveau Band contains the changes and improvements of recent years. Ferguson switches to flugelhorn more than of yore and gets a rich, squeezed sound out of it, like hot taffy being spun out of a sugar boiler. The pace is still ferocious, but there are a few signs of elder statesmanly reserve creeping in.

(*) **Live From London Avenue Jazz R2 71631
>   Ferguson; Roger Ingram, Craig Johnson, Brian Thompson, Walter White (*t*); Keith Oshiro (*tb*); Joe Barati (*btb*); Dave Pietro (*as*); Matt Wallace (*as, ts*); Chip McNeill (*ts, ss*); Glenn Kostur (*bs*); Christian Jacob (*p, ky*); Nathan Berg (*b*); Chris Brown (*d*). 93.

One of the editors contrived to be present when some of this was recorded, at Ronnie Scott's club in Soho, and a pretty robust evening's music it turned out to be. Ferguson still likes to revert to the full frontal approach of earlier years, but the difference between hearing this band in a small(ish) venue, where the wind from the horns threatened hairpieces at the bar, and hearing it again on record is quite instructive. Though cleanly recorded and remixed with what sound like a few can't-hear-the-join edits, these tracks plod a little bit. The opening 'A Night In Tunisia' has the feel of a work-out, as does 'St Thomas' a little later. It's only with 'My One And Only Love' that Ferguson begins to knuckle down and play expressively rather than combatively. His own flugelhorn and trumpet solo is as good a recorded moment as there has been for years . . . for about two and a half choruses.

Rachelle Ferrell VOCALS

*** **First Instrument** Blue Note CDP 8 27820
>   Ferrell; Terence Blanchard (*t*); Wayne Shorter (*ts*); Alex Foster (*ss*); Eddie Green, Michel Petrucciani (*p*); Gil Goldstein, Pete Levin (*syn*); Stanley Clarke (*b*); Lenny White (*d*). 12/89, 1 & 2/90.

A well-judged debut from a singer who is already considerably more than the sum of her influences. There's a little Billie, no small amount of Shirley Horn and Betty Carter, and just a touch of the cooler white swingers like June Christy or Chris Connor. For this debut recording, which seems to have made an odd progress through the Capitol machine, she has mixed standards with original material which is musically sharp if lyrically a bit wanting. Her own trio of Green, Brown and Nally is (ironically) a bit colourless, though no one can complain that it doesn't swing hard. The guests make a significant difference. Alex Foster's soprano part on 'Inchworm' makes the track, and Blanchard is smoothly expressive on 'With Every Breath I Take'. The big convention of celebs on 'Autumn Leaves' (arranged for Shorter, Petrucciani, Clarke, producer White, with Levin and Goldstein providing extra tones) is slightly thrown away, but it points forward to other possibilities, a richer, more ornamented sound. Perhaps the most interesting performance of the lot is a duet with drummer Nally on 'What Is This Thing Called Love'. Her one attempt to ape Ms Horn and combine piano and vocal falls a bit flat, though 'Extensions' is by far her most interesting song. Lots of promise there.

Firehouse Five Plus Two GROUP

** **The Firehouse Five Plus Two Story** Good Time Jazz 2GTJCD-22055-2 2CD
>   Johnny Lucas, Danny Alguire (*t*); Ward Kimball (*tb*); Clark Mallory, Tom Sharpsteen, George Probert (*cl*); Ed Penner (*bs, tba*); Frank Thomas (*p*); Dick Roberts (*g, bj*); Harper Goff (*bj*); Jim McDonald, Monte Mountjoy, Jerry Hamm (*d*). 5/49–2/50, 10/50–7/51, 3/51–3/54.
(*) **Goes South! Good Time Jazz GTJCD-12018-2
>   As above, except omit Mallory, Sharpsteen and Hamm. 1/54–10/56.
(*) **Dixieland Favourites Good Time Jazz GTJCD-10040-2
>   As above, except Ralph Ball, George Bruns, Don Kinch (*tba, b*) replace Penner; Eddie Forrest (*d*) replaces McDonald. 9/59–3/60.
** **Goes To Sea** Good Time Jazz GTJCD-100282
>   As above. 2–11/57.
** **At Disneyland** Good Time Jazz GTJCD-10049-2
>   As above. 7/62.
** **Twenty Years Later** Good Time Jazz GTJCD-10054-2
>   As above, except K. O. Ecklund (*p*) replaces Thomas, Bill Newman (*uke*) replaces Roberts; add George Bruns (*tba*). 10/69.

It's difficult to offer a serious criticism of this group, which was always a semi-professional band: it was formed by Ward Kimball and its personnel was originally drawn from the staff at Walt Disney's animation studios. The music seldom varies from record to record, even from track to track – it's Dixieland done with vigorous enthusiasm rather than panache, and it's as formulaic as anything done by British trad groups. Yet there's a certain degree of authenticity which the group conferred on itself, largely through sheer persistence. The earlier versions of the band play with clockwork momentum, and there is an almost Spike Jones-like feel to their music, occasionally underlined by Kimball's use of sirens and washboards to point up what was already a kitsch act. The personnel which settled down in the later 1950s, though, made some rather more personal and quite successful records, notably the *Dixieland Favourites* set and *Goes South!*. The brass players were often rather reticent about taking solos, and it was mainly left to Probert to be the chief improviser: his playing is often sour and he can't sustain solos for very long, but there's an interestingly quirky edge to his best moments . . . which tends to go for the band as a whole, too. Whatever their shortcomings, the popularity of this pro-am group is attested by the fact that they still have several records in the catalogue.

First House GROUP

** **Erendira** ECM 1307
>   Ken Stubbs (*as, ss*); Django Bates (*p, thn*); Mick Hutton (*b*); Martin France (*d*). 7/85.
(*) **Cantilena ECM 1393
>   As above. 3/89.

First House were always a very different proposition from Human Chain, Bates's other extracurricular sortie from the surprisingly demanding keyboard and writing/arranging desk at Loose Tubes. It's a more thoughtful band, relying less on sheer energy and more on Bates's intelligent structures. Stubbs is by no means a charismatic player, but the results are adequate to the occasion. Hutton and France combine well.

The later *Cantilena* is more thoroughly achieved and lacks some of the pretentiousness and rough edges of *Erendira* and of Bates's subsequent recording and concert band, Powder Room Collapse.

Clare Fischer (born 1928) PIANO, KEYBOARDS

** **Lembrancas** Concord CCD 4404
    Fischer; Dick Mitchell (*reeds*); Brent Fischer (*b*); Tris Imboden (*d*); Michito Sanchez, Luis
    Conte (*perc*). 6/89.

In great demand as an arranger, Fischer's own playing has had little exposure on record of late. There
are some fine and important records for Revelation and MPS, all of them languishing in the vinyl
wasteland. Fischer's interest in Latin rhythms has been important in his career, but it's also encouraged
a populist streak which has resulted in some more recent records being as fluffy and inconsequential as
his earlier ones were lean and intense. The Concord session is unfortunately typical: Fischer plays only
synthesizer, and the music is a pretty concoction of light Latin fusion styles, pleasant and forgettable.
We still await much of Fischer's back-catalogue on CD.

Ella Fitzgerald (1917–96) VOCAL

(***) **Ella Fitzgerald** ASV AJD 055 2CD
    Fitzgerald; Taft Jordan, Mario Bauza, Bobby Stark, Gordon Griffin, Zeke Zarchey, Ziggy
    Elman (*t*); Sandy Williams, Nat Story, Claude Jones, Murray McEachern, Red Ballard (*tb*);
    Benny Goodman (*cl*); Teddy McRae, Louis Jordan, Pete Clark, Edgar Sampson, Elmer
    Williams, Wayman Carver, Garvin Bushell, Chauncey Haughton, Hymie Schertzer, Bill DePew,
    Arthur Rollini, Vido Musso (*reeds*); Tommy Fulford, Joe Steele, Jess Stacy (*p*); John Trueheart,
    Allan Reuss, Bobby Johnson (*g*); Beverley Peer, Bill Thomas, Harry Goodman (*b*); Chick Webb,
    Gene Krupa (*d*). 10/35–12/37.
*** **The Early Years Vol. 1** Decca GRD 2-618 2CD
    As above. 35–37.
(*) **Ella Fitzgerald 1935–1937 Classics 500
    As above, plus Frankie Newton (*t*), Benny Morton (*tb*), Chu Berry (*ts*), Teddy Wilson (*p*),
    Leemie Stanfield (*b*), Cozy Cole (*d*). 6/35–1/37.
(*) **Ella Fitzgerald 1937–1938 Classics 506
    As above, except omit Griffin, Zarchey, Elman, McEachern, Ballard, Goodman, Schertzer, De
    Pew, Rollini, Musso, Stacy, Reuss, Goodman, Newton, Morton, Berry, Wilson, Stanfield and
    Cole; add George Matthews (*tb*), The Mills Brothers (*v*). 1/37–5/38.
*** **Ella Fitzgerald 1938–1939** Classics 518
    As above, except add Dick Vance (*t*) and Hilton Jefferson (*as*); omit The Mills Brothers. 5/38–2/
    39.
** **Ella Fitzgerald 1939** Classics 525
    As above, except add Bill Beason (*d*). 2–6/39.
*** **Ella Fitzgerald 1939–1940** Classics 566
    As above, except add Irving Randolph (*t*), John Haughton, Jimmy Archey, Floyd Brady, John
    McConnell (*tb*), Sam Simmons (*ts*), Roger Ramirez (*p*); omit Webb. 8/39–5/40.
*** **Ella Fitzgerald 1940–1941** Classics 644
    Similar to above, except add John McConnell, Earl Hardy (*tb*), George Dorsey (*as*), Elmer
    Williams (*ts*), Ulysses Livingston (*g*), Jesse Price (*d*); omit Sandy Williams and Ramirez. 5/40–7/
    41.
** **Live From The Roseland Ballroom New York 1940** Jazz Anthology 550032
    Fitzgerald; Dick Vance, Taft Jordan, Bobby Stark (*t*); George Matthews, Nat Story, Sandy
    Williams (*tb*); Garvin Bushell (*cl, ss*); Hilton Jefferson (*as*); Wayman Carver (*as, ts, f*); Teddy
    McRae (*ts, bs*); Tommy Fulford (*p*); John Trueheart (*g*); Beverley Peer (*b*); Bill Beason (*d*). 40.

Fitzgerald's fabled break came when she won an Apollo Theatre talent contest in 1934, still aged only
seventeen, and by the following year she was singing for Chick Webb's band. When Webb died in 1939,
the singer inherited leadership of his band, for by this time she was its undoubted star. But her recordings of the period are often hard to take because the material is sometimes insufferably trite: after Ella
had a major hit with the nursery-rhyme tune, 'A Tisket A Tasket', she was doomed – at least, until the
break-up of the band – to seek out similar songs. The Classics CDs offer a chronological survey of her
work up to 1941 and, while the calibre of her singing is consistent enough – the voice at its freshest, her
phrasing straightforward but sincerely dedicated to making the most of the melody – the tracks seem to
spell the decline of what was, in the mid-1930s, one of the most swinging of big bands. The arrangements are often blandly supportive of the singer rather than creating any kind of partnership, and when
the material is of the standard of 'Swinging On The Reservation' it's difficult to summon up much
enthusiasm. But there are perhaps many minor successes. The 1937–8 CD includes the session which
produced Webb's only 12-inch 78, 'I Want To Be Happy' and 'Halleleujah', arranged by Turk Van Lake,

and 'Rock It For Me' and 'Bei Mir Bist Du Schön' look forward to the authority which Fitzgerald would bestow on her later records. The 1939–40 disc, although it sports 'My Wubba Dolly', has a number of swinging features such as 'After I Say I'm Sorry', 'I'm Not Complainin'' and a fine 'Baby, Won't You Please Come Home?'. Fitzgerald tends to treat all the songs the same – there's little of Billie Holiday's creative approach to the beat – but the lightness of her voice lets her float a lyric without losing her grip on it.

The remastering of all these discs is very mixed. The earlier discs vary almost from track to track, some laden with hiss, some foggy, others crisp. 'A Tisket A Tasket', on the 1937–8 volume, is dreadfully brassy. Only the 1939–40 set has consistently clear transfers. The ASV two-disc set offers a cross-section from Ella's earliest sessions, but the remastering is bass-heavy and listening isn't much fun. Far better is the new MCA/Decca anthology, which may be the benchmark set, once it's completed: good documentation, solid sound. With all this material out of copyright, there are other sets on the market, too: a three-disc Affinity compilation, *The Complete Recordings 1935–39*, and a double-set on Memoria, Savoy Ambassadors. Collectors can choose at their leisure, but we commend the Decca set for completists. The Jazz Anthology set captures a 1940 airshot which mixes superior material – 'Royal Garden Blues', 'Sugar Blues' – with tunes of the order of 'Chewin' Gum', but it's not without period charm, though the sound is indifferent.

*** **Ella Fitzgerald 1941–1944** Classics 840
  Fitzgerald; John McGhee (*t*); Eddie Barefield (*as*); Teddy McRae (*ts*); Tommy Fulford, Bill
  Furness, Bill Doggett (*p*); Ulysses Livingston, Slim Furness, Bernie Mackey (*g*); Peck Furness,
  Beverley Peer, Bob Haggart (*b*); Bill Beason, Kenny Clarke, Ernie Hatfield, Johnny Blowers (*d*);
  The Ink Spots (*v*). 10/41–11/44.
The start of Ella's 'solo' career, away from the Chick Webb band. It starts with a lovely version of 'Jim', and the first three sessions have some excellent material, but the 1942 dates with The Four Keys are more novelty-orientated, and two sessions with The Ink Spots are missable. The 1944 tracks see her with an orchestra again. Transfers are from unlisted sources and are good enough.

*** **75th Birthday Celebration** MCA GRP 26192 2CD
  Fitzgerald; small groups feature Louis Armstrong (*t, v*); Taft Jordan, Aaron Izenhall, Leonard
  Graham (*t*); Sandy Williams (*tb*); Louis Jordan (*as, v*); Josh Jackson, Hilton Jefferson, Teddy
  McRae (*reeds*); Bill Doggett (*p, org*); Billy Kyle, Bill Davis, Ellis Larkins, Don Abney, René
  Knight, Hank Jones, John Lewis (*p*); Carl Hogan, John Trueheart, Bill Jennings, Hy White,
  Bernie Mackay, Jimmy Shirley (*g*); Arnold Fishkind, Jesse Simpkins, Ray Brown, Haig
  Stephens, Bob Bushnell, Joe Mondragon, Beverley Peer, Bob Haggart, Junior Raglin (*b*); Larry
  Bunker, Sylvester Payne, George Wettling, Chick Webb, Johnny Blowers, Eddie Byrd, Joe
  Harris, Rudy Taylor (*d*); Dick Jacobs, Harry Dial, Vic Lourie (*perc*); The Ink Spots (*v*); plus
  orchestras of Bob Haggart, Chick Webb, Vic Schoen, Sy Oliver, Gordon Jenkins, Benny Carter
  and Toots Camarata. 5/38–8/55.
*** **The War Years 1941–1947** Decca GRP 26282 2CD
  Similar to above. 41–47.
***(*) **The Legendary Decca Years** Decca GRP 46482 4CD
  Similar to above. 38–55.
***(*) **Ella – The Best Of Ella Fitzgerald** GRP 16592
  Similar to above. 5/38–5/55.
**** **Pure Ella** MCA GRP 16362
  Fitzgerald; Ellis Larkins (*p*). 9/50–3/54.
Now that MCA have finally opened the vaults to their Ella recordings, the balance of her career comes into clearer perspective. The birthday collection (although packaged more like a wedding album) is an intermittently convincing cross-section of her best for Decca over some 17 years. The early tracks are given short shrift since there are only two tracks with Webb and, accurate though it may be as a portrait of her Decca period, there's too much pap chosen from the 1940s – rubbish with The Song Spinners and The Ink Spots, and thinly spread jive with Louis Jordan. Premium scat on 'Lady Be Good' and a gorgeous duet with Pops on 'Dream A Little Dream Of Me' salvage the day, and the '50s stuff is better, with a full session of Benny Carter charts and one track from the collaboration with Larkins. Two further sets have slightly complicated the picture. *The War Years* covers her uncertain early period at Decca more comprehensively, while *Legendary Decca Years* (a somewhat dubious title) goes for the whole period. This last is probably the one to get, so far as dedicated Fitzgerald collectors are concerned, but most may simply want to settle for *Pure Ella* as her best work of the time. *Ella – The Best Of* is yet another single-disc compilation, a pleasing choice, though often arbitrarily done.

Pure Ella is a masterpiece, her first great album (*Ella Sings Gershwin*) coupled with *Songs In A Mellow Mood*, all of it with Larkins's gentle, perfect accompaniments. Her voice bridges the girlish timbre of her early days with the grander delivery she moved on to for her Verve albums; and on this almost ideal programme of standards there is nothing out of place. Fine remastering and an essential Fitzgerald item.

**** Ella Sings Arlen Vol. 1 Verve 817527-2
    Fitzgerald; Billy May Orchestra. 8/60–1/61.
**** Ella Sings Arlen Vol. 2 Verve 817528-2
    Fitzgerald; Billy May Orchestra. 8/60–1/61.
**** The George & Ira Gershwin Songbook Verve 821024-2 3CD
    Fitzgerald; Nelson Riddle Orchestra. 1–3/59.
*** The Johnny Mercer Songbook Verve 821247-2
    Fitzgerald; Nelson Riddle Orchestra. 10/64.
**** The Rodgers And Hart Songbook Vol. 1 Verve 821579-2
    Fitzgerald; Buddy Bregman Orchestra. 8/56.
*** The Rodgers And Hart Songbook Vol. 2 Verve 821580-2
    Fitzgerald; Buddy Bregman Orchestra. 8/56.
*** The Jerome Kern Songbook Verve 821669-2
    Fitzgerald; Nelson Riddle Orchestra. 63.
**** The Cole Porter Songbook Vol. 1 Verve 821989-2
    Fitzgerald; Buddy Bregman Orchestra. 2/56.
**** The Cole Porter Songbook Vol. 2 Verve 821990-2
    Fitzgerald; Buddy Bregman Orchestra. 2–3/56.
***(*) The Irving Berlin Songbook Vol. 1 Verve 829534-2
    Fitzgerald; Paul Weston Orchestra. 3/58.
***(*) The Irving Berlin Songbook Vol. 2 Verve 829535-2
    Fitzgerald; Paul Weston Orchestra. 3/58.
**** Sings The Duke Ellington Songbook Verve 837035-2 3CD
    Fitzgerald; Cat Anderson, Willie Cook, Clark Terry, Harold Baker (*t*); Quentin Jackson, Britt
    Woodman, John Sanders (*tb*); Jimmy Hamilton (*cl, ts*); Johnny Hodges (*as*); Russell Procope (*cl,*
    as); Ben Webster, Paul Gonsalves, Frank Foster (*ts*); Harry Carney (*bs, bcl, cl*); Duke Ellington,
    Paul Smith, Oscar Peterson (*p*); Stuff Smith (*vn*); Barney Kessel, Herb Ellis (*g*); Jimmy Woode,
    Joe Mondragon, Ray Brown (*b*); Alvin Stoller, Sam Woodyard (*d*). 9/56–10/57.
*** The Songbooks Verve 823445-2
    As above discs. 56–64.
**** Best Of The Songbooks Verve 519804-2
    As above discs. 56–64.
***(*) Best Of The Songbooks – The Ballads Verve 521867-2
    As above discs. 56–64.
*** Day Dream: Best Of The Duke Ellington Songbook Verve 527223-2
    As Ellington set, above. 9/56–10/57.
*** Oh, Lady Be Good! Best Of The Gershwin Songbook Verve 529581-2
    As Gershwin set, above. 3/59.
**** The Complete Songbooks Verve 519832-2 16CD
    As above discs. 56–64.

In January 1956, Fitzgerald began recording for Norman Granz's Verve label, and the first release, *The Cole Porter Songbook*, became the commercial rock on which Verve was built. It was so successful that Granz set Ella to work on all the great American songwriters, and her series of 'songbook' albums are an unrivalled sequence of their kind. The records work consistently well for a number of reasons: Fitzgerald herself was at a vocal peak, strong yet flexible, and her position as a lyric interpreter was perfectly in tune with records dense with lyrical detail; each disc carefully programmes familiar with lesser-known material; the arrangers all work to their strengths, Bregman and May delivering hard-hitting big-band sounds, Riddle the suavest of grown-up orchestrations; and the quality of the studio recordings was and remains outstandingly lifelike and wide-ranging on most of the discs, although some of the earlier sessions are more constricted in scope.

The single most awe-inspiring piece is the Gershwin set, once a five-LP box, now a resplendent three-CD set, which works patiently through 53 songs without any suspicion of going through the motions. The delight in listening to these discs one after another lies in hearing some almost forgotten tunes – 'The Half Of It, Dearie, Blues', 'You've Got What Gets Me', even 'Just Another Rhumba' – alongside the premier Gershwin melodies, and Fitzgerald's concentration is such that a formidable standard is maintained. The Harold Arlen and Cole Porter sets are, though, barely a step behind, even if the much-loved Porter discs now sound less profound through the sometimes perfunctory arrangements. Arlen's songs are among a jazz singer's most challenging material, though, and Fitzgerald is ebulliently part-nered by Billy May, who sounds more pertinent here than he did on some of the sessions he did with

Sinatra. The Mercer record is slightly disappointing after the previous Gershwin triumph with Riddle, and the Kern collection, though fine enough, is also a secondary choice. The two discs dedicated to Berlin are a bit patchy, but the first volume starts off with a quite unsurpassable reading of 'Let's Face The Music And Dance', in which Ella negotiates all the changes in backdrop without the slightest hint of discomfort, and goes on to wonderfully tender versions of 'Russian Lullaby' and 'How Deep Is The Ocean'. The second disc works further wonders with 'Isn't This A Lovely Day' and 'Heat Wave'. The discs dedicated to Rodgers and Hart are also slightly less than perfect: Fitzgerald's plain speaking doesn't always fully realize the ingenuity of Hart's lyrics. But the first disc is virtually unmissable for the famous readings of 'Manhattan' and 'With A Song In My Heart'.

The collection made with Duke Ellington is a somewhat different matter, with the composer himself working with the singer. It's been an undervalued record in the past, with charges of under-rehearsal flying about, and there's certainly a major difference between these sessions and the others: Riddle would surely never have tolerated the looseness of some of the playing, or Sam Woodyard in any circumstances. Yet the best of the disc finds Ellington inspired, with such as 'Caravan' evoking entirely new treatments and swingers like 'Drop Me Off In Harlem' fusing Ella's imperturbable time with the rough-and-ready movement of the band in full cry. Some of the tracks feature her with a small group, and there is an 'I Got It Bad And That Ain't Good' which finds Ben Webster almost oozing out of the speakers. Highly recommended.

The best-of pick on *The Songbooks* isn't bad, with 19 tracks and a little over an hour of music, but it emphasizes how little fat there is in the original albums. The more recent *Best Of The Songbooks* is a neat pocket-edition, with some lesser-known tracks alongside the obvious winners. There are also the subsequent *The Ballads* and single-disc editions filleted from the Ellington and Gershwin sets. But the addictive qualities of these albums often leave one hankering for more, and the solution to that problem is the 16-CD set which collects the whole lot.

**** **Like Someone In Love** Verve 511524-2
    Fitzgerald; Ted Nash (*as*); Stan Getz (*ts*); Frank DeVol Orchestra. 10/57.
*** **At The Opera House** Verve 831269-2
    Fitzgerald; Roy Eldridge (*t*); J. J. Johnson (*tb*); Sonny Stitt (*as*); Coleman Hawkins, Stan Getz,
    Flip Phillips (*ts*); Oscar Peterson (*p*); Herb Ellis (*g*); Ray Brown (*b*); Connie Kay (*d*). 9–10/57.
**** **Ella Swings Lightly** Verve 517535-2
    Fitzgerald; Don Fagerquist, Al Porcino (*t*); Bob Enevoldsen (*vtb*); Bud Shank (*as*); Bill Holman
    (*ts*); Lou Levy (*p*); Mel Lewis (*d*). 58.
*** **Clap Hands, Here Comes Charlie!** Verve 835646-2
    Fitzgerald; Lou Levy (*p*); Herb Ellis (*g*); Joe Mondragon, Wilfred Middlebrooks (*b*); Stan
    Levey, Gus Johnson (*d*). 1-6/61.
*** **Mack The Knife (Ella In Berlin)** Verve 519564-2
    Fitzgerald; Paul Smith (*p*); Jim Hall (*g*); Wilfred Middlebrooks (*b*); Gus Johnson (*d*). 2/60.
*** **Ella Returns To Berlin** Verve 837758-2
    Fitzgerald; Lou Levy, Oscar Peterson (*p*); Herb Ellis (*g*); Wilfred Middlebrooks, Ray Brown
    (*b*); Gus Johnson, Ed Thigpen (*d*). 2/61.
***(*) **Ella Wishes You A Swinging Christmas** Verve 827150-2
    Fitzgerald; Frank DeVol Orchestra. 60.
*** **These Are The Blues** Verve 829536-2
    Fitzgerald; Roy Eldridge (*t*); Wild Bill Davis (*org*); Herb Ellis (*g*); Ray Brown (*b*); Gus Johnson
    (*d*). 10/63.
***(*) **The Intimate Ella** Verve 829838-2
    Fitzgerald; Paul Smith (*p*). 60.
*** **Ella In Rome (The Birthday Concert)** Verve 835454-2
    Fitzgerald; Oscar Peterson, Lou Levy (*p*); Herb Ellis (*g*); Ray Brown, Max Bennett (*b*); Gus
    Johnson (*d*). 4/58.
***(*) **Ella Swings Brightly With Nelson** Verve 519347-2
    Fitzgerald; Nelson Riddle Orchestra. 59–61.
*** **Ella Swings Gently With Nelson** Verve 519348-2
    Fitzgerald; Nelson Riddle Orchestra. 61–62.
***(*) **Ella And Basie** Verve 821576-2
    Fitzgerald; Joe Newman, Al Aarons, Sonny Cohn, Don Rader, Fip Ricard (*t*); Henry Coker,
    Grover Mitchell, Benny Powell, Urbie Green (*tb*); Marshall Royal (*as, cl*); Eric Dixon (*ts, f*);
    Frank Wess (*ts, as, f*); Frank Foster (*ts*); Charlie Fowlkes (*bs*); Freddie Green (*g*); Buddy Catlett
    (*b*); Sonny Payne (*d*). 7/63.
***(*) **Verve Jazz Masters: Ella Fitzgerald** Verve 519822-2
    Fitzgerald; various groups, 55–62.

The 'songbook' albums may be Fitzgerald's best-remembered at Verve, but there were many more good ones, and a fair number of them are still in print. Essential: *Like Someone In Love*, a very fine programme of major standards and rarities, with Getz taking solos on four tracks; *Ella Swings Lightly*, arranged by Marty Paich with his West Coast band handling the backings; the meeting with Basie, which is a little more fun than her encounters with Ellington, brash and exciting but tempered by the invulnerable machine that was Basie's band; *The Intimate Ella*, a one-on-one meeting with underrated pianist Paul Smith, and a good instance of the big voice being shaded down; and the Christmas album, the least affected and most swinging seasonal jazz album ever made. Good ones: *At The Opera House*, which is a bit of a typical JATP rave-up but has its moments; *Clap Hands, Here Comes Charlie!*, a swinging small-group encounter, and something of a rarity in her record dates from this period; and the recently issued *Returns To Berlin*, which comes in excellent sound. The original *Berlin* set has been beefed up with some extra tracks in its latest incarnation and it includes the famous version of 'Mack The Knife'. Disappointing, but still worth hearing, are *These Are The Blues*, which tends to prove that Ella is no great queen of the blues, despite the nicely simmering back-ups from Davis and Eldridge, and the Rome concert. The *Swings Brightly* / *Swings Gently* albums with Riddle are welcome recent appearances on CD: the *Brightly* set is the superior one, if only for the irresistible treatment of 'Don't Be That Way'; but the ballads disc is fine, too. The Verve Jazz Masters disc picks its way past some of the other Ella compilations and delivers an interesting summary for those who don't want to trawl through the whole Verve catalogue. Her albums with Louis Armstrong are listed under his name.

*** **Ella At Duke's Place** Verve 529700-2
> Fitzgerald; Cat Anderson, Herbie Jones, Cootie Williams (*t*); Lawrence Brown, Buster Cooper, Chuck Connors (*tb*); Jimmy Hamilton (*cl, ts*); Russell Procope (*cl, as*); Johnny Hodges (*as*); Paul Gonsalves (*ts*); Harry Carney (*bs*); Duke Ellington (*p*); John Lamb (*b*); Sam Woodyard (*d*). 10/65.

If only the whole album had been as good as the opening, a wonderful reading of 'Something To Live For'. The other ballads in the first half are nearly as good. But the up-tempo pieces show both singer and band at something less than their best, Ellington's notorious weakness for inappropriate speeds getting the better of him and Ella not quite on top of the situation. But the good things were worth salvaging.

*** **Take Love Easy** Pablo 2310-702
> Fitzgerald; Joe Pass (*g*). 73.
(*) **Fine And Mellow Pablo 2310-829
> Fitzgerald; Clark Terry (*t, flhn*); Harry 'Sweets' Edison (*t*); Eddie 'Lockjaw' Davis, Zoot Sims (*ts*); Tommy Flanagan (*p*); Joe Pass (*g*); Ray Brown (*b*); Louie Bellson (*d*). 1/74.
***(*) **Ella In London** Pablo 2310-711
> Fitzgerald; Tommy Flanagan (*p*); Joe Pass (*g*); Keter Betts (*b*); Bobby Durham (*d*). 4/74.
*** **Montreux 1975** Pablo 2310-751
> As above, except omit Pass. 7/75.
***(*) **Ella And Oscar** Pablo 2310-759
> Fitzgerald; Oscar Peterson (*p*); Ray Brown (*b*). 5/75.
*** **Fitzgerald And Pass . . . Again** Pablo 2310-772
> Fitzgerald; Joe Pass (*g*). 1–2/76.
** **Dream Dancing** Pablo 2310-814
> Fitzgerald; Nelson Riddle Orchestra. 6/72–2/78.
(*) **Lady Time Pablo 2310-825 D
> Fitzgerald; Jackie Davis (*org*); Louie Bellson (*d*). 6/78.
*** **A Perfect Match** Pablo 231-2110
> Fitzgerald; Pete Minger, Sonny Cohn, Paul Cohen, Raymond Brown (*t*); Booty Wood, Bill Hughes, Mel Wanzo, Dennis Wilson (*tb*); Kenny Hing, Danny Turner (*ts*); Eric Dixon, Bobby Plater (*as*); Charlie Fowlkes (*bs*); Count Basie (*p*); Freddie Green (*g*); Keter Betts (*b*); Mickey Roker (*d*). 7/79.
*** **A Classy Pair** Pablo 2310 132
> As above, except add Nolan Smith (*t*), John Clayton (*b*); Butch Miles (*d*); omit Cohen, Betts and Roker. 2/79.

Back with Norman Granz again, Ella recorded steadily through the 1970s; but there was little to suggest that she would either repeat or surpass the best of her earlier music. If encroaching age is supposed to impart a greater wisdom to a singer of songs, and hence into the interpretation of those songs, it's a more complex matter with Fitzgerald, who has never been much of a purveyor of lyrics, more a musician who happens to sing. Her scatting has grown less fluent and more exaggerated, but no less creative in its construction; her manipulation of time and melody has become more obvious because she has to push herself harder to make it happen. There are still many good records here, but no really great ones, and all of them miss a little of the grace and instinctive improvisation which float off all her older records.

Granz recorded her in several settings. With Joe Pass, the bare-strings accompaniment is initially intimate but finally dull: Pass can't devise enough variation to make the music stay awake, and Fitzgerald isn't always sure how strongly she's able to come on. Their duet albums are nice enough, but one is enough. *Fine And Mellow* is a rather noisy and brash session, but the title-track is a very good version of the Holiday favourite, which sounds just as good in Ella's hands. The Montreux and Nice live sets are merely OK, and much better is the London date from 1974: probably the final chance to hear Ella in a club setting, and it's a racy and sometimes virtuosic display by the singer, a fine souvenir of what was a memorable visit. Of the big-band dates, *Dream Dancing* features Nelson Riddle at his sententious worst, and is missable, while the two sets with Basie are boisterous if comparatively uneventful. *Lady Time* is an unusual setting which tries Ella out as a kind of club-class blueswoman; she makes a game go of it. The other must-hear record, though, is the duet (almost – Ray Brown offers discreet support) with Oscar Peterson, *Ella And Oscar*. The pianist plays as hard as usual, but instrumentalist and vocalist bring out the best in each other, and there are at least three near-classics in 'Mean To Me', 'How Long Has This Been Going On?' and 'Midnight Sun'.

(*) **Ella Abraça Jobim Pablo 2630-201
    Fitzgerald; Clark Terry (*t*); Zoot Sims (*ts*); Toots Thielemans (*hca*); Mike Lang, Clarence McDonald, Terry Trotter (*ky*); Joe Pass, Oscar Castro-Neves, Paul Jackson, Mitch Holder, Roland Bautista (*g*); Abe Laboriel (*b*); Alex Acuna (*d*); Paulinho Da Costa (*perc*). 9/80.

(*) **The Best Is Yet To Come Pablo 2312-138
    Fitzgerald; Al Aarons (*t*); Bill Watrous (*tb*); Marshall Royal (*as*); Bob Cooper (*ts*); Jimmy Rowles (*p*); Art Hillery (*org*); Joe Pass, Tommy Tedesco (*g*); Jim Hughart (*b*); Shelly Manne (*d*); strings and woodwinds. 2/82.

(*) **Nice Work If You Can Get It Pablo 2312-140
    Fitzgerald; André Previn (*p*). 5/83.

*** **Speak Love** Pablo 2310-888
    Fitzgerald; Joe Pass (*g*). 3/83.

*** **Easy Living** Pablo 2310-921
    As above.

** **All That Jazz** Pablo 2310-938
    Fitzgerald; Clark Terry, Harry 'Sweets' Edison (*t*); Al Grey (*tb*); Benny Carter (*as*); Mike Wofford, Kenny Barron (*p*); Ray Brown (*b*); Bobby Durham (*d*). 3/89.

*** **The Best Of Ella Fitzgerald** Pablo 2405-421
The 1980s saw Fitzgerald slackening off her workload as illness and perhaps sheer tiredness intervened. The Jobim collection came too late, since every other singer had already had their shot at this kind of thing; *The Best* was another tiresome set of Nelson Riddle arrangements; and the duo album with Previn was a pointless bit of star-matching. Which left two more albums with Pass and what will surely prove to be a farewell set in the strained and unconvincing *All That Jazz*. At least the best-of is a good selection from the pick of the above.

***(*) **The Concert Years** Pablo 4414-2 4CD
    Basically as Pablo albums above. 53–83.
Distilled from Fizgerald's live appearances as a headliner and with JATP, this is a very strong four-disc set which should be the first stopping-point for those who want to hear Ella the improviser and jazz musician. Starting with JATP material from the 1950s, it takes in three different shows with Ellington, the 1974 set at Ronnie Scott's club, three Montreux appearances from the 1970s, and a final (1983) show in Tokyo. If there are occasional lapses in judgement, where her scatting or phrasing can become almost parodic, the quality of her musicianship wins through. Cameos from many famous names add to the interest.

Five A Slide GROUP

*** **Strike Up The Band!** Black Lion BLCD 760509
    John Beecham, Campbell Burnap, Roy Crimmins, Jim Shepherd, Roy Williams (*tb*); Stan Greig (*p*); Peter Skivington (*b*); Johnny Richardson (*d*). 1/81.
With up to six slide brass on some numbers (regular dep. Roy Crimmins was brought in for the recording session), this rivals Kai Winding's six-trombone front lines of the '50s. The effect is actually a lot less muddled. The arrangements are quite crisp and the reading of 'Lush Life', unexpectedly in among the traddier stuff, is quite powerful and much too brief. That also goes for a beautifully rendered 'Jubilee', which must have sounded great as part of the live act. Burnap takes the vocal and a chipper

solo on 'I Gotta Right To Sing The Blues', a tune associated with his idol, Jack Teagarden. The 'Pink Panther' theme is the only bit of pure hokum, but even that has a fine solo from Roy Williams. Fine, but certainly not enough to justify Alun Morgan's liner-note claim that Williams is 'probably the greatest jazz trombonist in the world today'. Not even probably.

Paul Flaherty ALTO AND TENOR SAXOPHONES

***(*) **Fat Onions** Cadence CJR 1054

> Flaherty; James 'Chumly' Hunt (*t, pkt-t*); Stephen Scholz (*vn*); Mike Murray (*g*); Richard Downs (*b*); Randall Colbourne (*d*). 11/93.

*** **Visitants** Zaabway 2001

> As above, except omit Hunt and Scholz. 3/94.

Flaherty (who appeared in our first edition but missed out last time) is an irascible-sounding saxophonist who takes his cues from the unadorned energy playing of the 1960s and early '70s. He co-leads these groups with drummer Colbourne, and together they marshal a music which forms around dense, braying collectives, sometimes recalling the heterophony of the Ayler ensemble, sometimes a golden-age FMP session, and sometimes creating something peculiarly their own. It's an exhilarating experience and an exhausting one, handled over CD length; but endemic to this kind of listening is a sense of shared work-experience with the players. Hence the slightly superior rating for *Fat Onions*, with its bigger ensemble and heavier, cloudier music, because it's harder work. There are moments of lyricism and quiet, though these are soon enough dispersed, and the group breaks into a kind of hymnal mode when it wants to sound celebratory. For the committed only, perhaps, but it's pleasing to know that this kind of jazz is still being explored and created. Recording is good, if on the dry side on both sessions.

Tommy Flanagan (born 1930) PIANO

*** **The Cats** Original Jazz Classics OJC 079

> Flanagan; Idrees Sulieman (*t*); John Coltrane (*ts*); Kenny Burrell (*g*); Doug Watkins (*b*); Louis Hayes (*d*). 4/57.

*** **The Complete 'Overseas'** DIW 305

> Flanagan; Wilbur Little (*b*); Elvin Jones (*d*). 8/57.

*** **Jazz . . . It's Magic** Savoy SV 0153

> Flanagan; Curtis Fuller (*tb*); Sonny Red (*as*); George Tucker (*b*); Louis Hayes (*d*). 9/57.

If it's difficult to make fine qualitative distinctions within Tommy Flanagan's discography, it isn't difficult to distinguish his output from the average piano trio of the last 30 years. The earlier albums date from a period before he became known as one of the finest accompanists in the business, backing Tony Bennett and, more memorably, Ella Fitzgerald in her great late-1960s resurgence. *The Cats* is officially a Prestige All Stars session, but it is Flanagan's stewardship of the house rhythm section that makes the gig his own, and there is a wonderful 'How Long Has This Been Going On' for trio which clinches the deal. He is always at the heart of the action, helping out the hornmen when they lose their way, once or twice cutting through the verbiage to get back to the song. There is also material from this period and from similar lineups on other discs.

   Flanagan's touch at this point lacks the fabled delicacy it acquired later, but he has a fine, boppish attack that is complemented by Jones on the excellent European sessions, and by the adaptable Hayes. Fuller adds an interesting dimension to the Savoy session, riding the rails with Flanagan on 'Club Car' with the kind of precarious ease both seem to specialize in. Unfortunately the saxophonist is pretty dreary (though he seems to have been drinking from the same spring as the young Coltrane) and the trio tracks on the same disc are well below par for Flanagan.

*** **The Tommy Flanagan Trio** Original Jazz Classics OJC 182

> Flanagan; Tommy Potter (*b*); Roy Haynes (*d*). 5/60.

This plain-label session is as blunt and straightforward as the title suggests and helps plug a longish gap in the available documentation. Flanagan rolls his sleeves up and wades straight into a nicely judged programme of standards with an emphasis on medium-paced ballads. He's at his best on 'In The Blue Of The Evening' and 'In A Sentimental Mood', the opening and closing numbers, while 'You Go To My Head' underlines his determination to stay in sight of the lyric at all times.

(*) **The Tommy Flanagan Tokyo Recital Original Jazz Classics OJC 737

> Flanagan; Keter Betts (*b*); Bobby Durham (*d*). 2/75.

*** **The Best Of Tommy Flanagan** Pablo PACD 2405 410
    As above. 2/75 & 7/77.
** **Something Borrowed, Something Blue** Original Jazz Classics OJC 473
    As above, except Jimmie Smith (*d*) replaces Durham. 1/78.
*** **Eclipso** Enja 2088
    Flanagan; George Mraz (*b*); Elvin Jones (*d*). 2/77.
(*) **Confirmation Enja 4014
    Flanagan; George Mraz (*b*); Elvin Jones (*d*). 2/77 & 11/78.
*** **Alone Too Long** Denon DC 8572
    Flanagan (*p* solo). 12/77.
***(*) **Our Delights** Original Jazz Classics OJC 752
    Flanagan; Hank Jones (*p*). 1/78.
*** **Ballads And Blues** Enja 3031
    Flanagan; George Mraz (*b*, duo). 11/78.
(*) **Together Denon DC 8573
    Flanagan; Kenny Barron (*p*). 12/78.
(*) **Plays The Music Of Harold Arlen DIW 328
    Flanagan; George Mraz (*b*); Connie Kay (*d*); Helen Merrill (*v*). n.d.
*** **Communication: Live At Fat Tuesday's, New York** Paddle Wheel KICJ 73
    Flanagan; Jerry Dodgion (*as, ss*); Red Mitchell (*b*). 11/79.
***(*) **Super Session** Enja 3059
    Flanagan; Red Mitchell (*b*); Elvin Jones (*d*). 2/80.
*** **You're Me** Phontastic CD 7528
    As above, except omit Jones. 2/80.
**** **Giant Steps: In Memory Of John Coltrane** Enja 4022
    Flanagan; George Mraz (*b*); Al Foster (*d*). 2/82.
(*) **Thelonica Enja 4052
    Flanagan; George Mraz (*b*); Art Taylor (*d*). 12/82.
Throughout the 1970s and early '80s, Flanagan explored aspects of harmony most closely associated with the late John Coltrane, often stretching his solos very far from the tonal centre but without lapsing into the tuneless abstractions that were such a depressing aspect of Coltrane's legacy.

Elvin Jones's presence and multidirectional approach are always a plus on Flanagan dates. *Eclipso* (and *Confirmation*, which uses up some unreleased masters from the February 1977 session) develops the relationship further; *Super Session* brings it to a peak; recorded three weeks later, *You're Me* manages to hang on to some of the same energy. Increasingly, though, it is the partnership of Flanagan and bassist Mraz which dominates and Jones who tends to follow. *Ballads And Blues* is a piano–bass duo, and again the residual material is on *Confirmation*; only Red Mitchell has managed to equal Mraz's superb harmonic response to Flanagan's long, almost unsupported lines (Betts, by contrast, is very much a rhythm player). Mitchell is to the fore on the rather unusual *Communication*, to which Dodgion, a fine ensemble player, contributes only fitfully. The duos with Barron might just as easily have been two separate solo sessions, and there's a slight dialogue-of-the-deaf edge to a couple of the tracks where each man seems to be going in an opposite direction. Not so the excellent – and brightly recorded – *Our Delights*, which has all the signs of a real meeting of minds. As usual, not a particularly adventurous roster of tunes: 'Our Delight', 'Jordu', 'Lady Bird', two takes of 'Robbins Nest', 'Autumn Leaves' – but beautifully crafted all the same.

The Best Of . . ., which brings together much of the preceding Pablo with another, deleted, live session from Montreux '77, might more usefully have been labelled a Strayhorn tribute, since he is the main composer represented. Flanagan sounds bright and airy but also a little empty of ideas, and some of his colleagues' work is decidedly pedestrian and uninspired.

It's often forgotten that it was Flanagan who accompanied John Coltrane on (most of) the original *Giant Steps*. The quartet sessions with Harden occasionally recall those days, but not particularly memorably; the homage to Coltrane, though, is one of the finest piano-trio albums of the last 20 years. Flanagan repeats several of the tracks from *Giant Steps*, adds 'Central Park West', and tackles 'Naima', which Coltrane had entrusted to Wynton Kelly on a later session. Flanagan's reinterpretations are emotive, often harmonically clearer, and very beautiful. As is the most recent of these records: featuring Mraz again and the brightly swinging Kenny Washington. Flanagan's a wonderfully lyrical performer, with the widest imaginable range of diction and association. There is not a dull or fudged set in the bunch, but it's hard to go past *Giant Steps* or *Jazz Poet*, below.

**** **Jazz Poet** Timeless SJP 301
    Flanagan; George Mraz (*b*); Kenny Washington (*d*). 1/89.
'Jazz poet' would be a fair passport entry for what Flanagan does. A beautifully judged and perfectly

performed record you'll find yourself playing often. Though a studio session, it has the relaxed but subtly challenging feel of one of Flanagan's club dates. Outstanding tracks include the opening 'Raincheck', 'Caravan', and an unexpected performance of 'St Louis Blues'. Mraz is at the top of his powers and Washington doesn't attempt to muscle in but keeps to his business patiently and accurately. Lovely.

***(*) **Beyond The Bluebird** Timeless SJP 350
    Flanagan; Kenny Burrell (*g*); George Mraz (*b*); Lewis Nash (*d*). 4/90.

After concert and recorded tributes to Ellington and Coltrane, Flanagan turns back to bebop and the spirit of Charlie Parker. The pianist, though, has always been conscious that music is very precisely mediated by time and place, specific contexts. The Bluebird Inn in Detroit was a significant bop locus; Flanagan and Elvin Jones both played in the house band there, as did Barry Harris, whose 'Nascimento' anchors the second half of the disc. The first half of the set is dedicated to it and the music played there: two (relatively unfamiliar) Parker compositions, 'Bluebird' and 'Barbados', a long 'Yesterdays' featuring Burrell at his most contemplative, Benny Carter's 'Blues In My Heart' and '50-21' (the Bluebird's address) by trumpeter/bandleader Thad Jones, like his brother a stalwart of the club.

The second half of the set is, in the words of Flanagan's title-piece, 'Beyond The Bluebird', dispelling any imputation of mere nostalgia, and further bracketed by Burrell's closing 'Bluebird After Dark'. 'Something Borrowed, Something Blue' reappears from the old Galaxy session reissued on OJC 473, above, a fine reinvention. Typical of Flanagan's eclectic approach is the inclusion of Dizzy Reece's rarely played 'The Con Man', whose unusual blues tonality provides a vivid setting for remarkable solos by Flanagan and George Mraz.

**** **Let's** Enja ENJ 8040
    Flanagan; Jesper Lundgaard (*b*); Lewis Nash (*d*). 4/93.
***(*) **Lady Be Good** Groovin' High 521 617
    Flanagan; Peter Washington (*b*); Lewis Nash (*d*). 7/93.

Let's is interesting. Thad Jones's music, most famously 'A Child Is Born', has been well covered by big bands and by horn groups, but never before by a piano trio. (Mal Waldron has covered Jones tunes on club dates, but never with this degree of concentration.) Flanagan knew Thad years ago when they were both starting out. One suspects that they were temperamentally similar, and these treatments bespeak a warm sympathy. It's a generous programme; as well as the title-piece and 'Child', there are performances of 'Mean What You Say', 'To You', 'Bird Song' and 'Scratch' (Nash standing out prominently on these), 'Thadrack', 'Three In One', 'Quietude', 'Zec' and, finally, 'Elusive', which closes the record on a high. The disc was made as part of the 1993 Jazzpar project in Denmark.

    Lady Be Good is a tribute to the now retired Ella; this is an affectionate run through a set of songs not so much associated with her as calling for her voice to round them out. Their partnership was, as Flanagan confirms, a learning experience. He gives 'Rough Ridin'', in which Ella had a hand, a gently ironic twist and clatters out the 'Cherokee' theme with the tongue-twisting poise that she had as a younger singer. Washington and Nash sound well versed in this music and both take modest but well-judged features.

Bob Florence (born 1932) PIANO, ARRANGER

*** **Name Band – 1959** Fresh Sound FSCD 2008
    Florence; Johnny Audino, Tony Terran, Jules Chaikin, Irv Bush (*t*); Bob Edmondson, Bobby Pring, Don Nelligan, Herbie Harper (*tb*); Bob Enevoldsen (*vtb*); Herb Geller, Bernie Fleischer (*as*); Bob Hardaway (*ts*); Don Shelton (*ts, cl*); Dennis Budimir (*g*); Mel Pollan (*b*); Jack Davenport (*d*). 11/58.
*** **Westlake** Discovery DSCD-832
    Florence; George Graham, Rick Baptist, Warren Luening, Steve Huffsteter, Nelson Hatt (*t, flhn*); Chauncey Welsh, Charlie Loper, Herbie Harper (*tb*); Kim Richmond, Ray Pizzi, Pete Christlieb, Bob Cooper, Bob Hardaway, Lee Callet (*woodwinds*); Joel DiBartolo (*b*); Nick Ceroli (*d*). 3/81.
**** **Jewels** Discovery 74005
    As above, except add Buddy Childers, Gene Goe (*t, flhn*), Rick Culver, Don Waldrop (*tb*), Bob Efford, John Lowe, Dick Mitchell, Lanny Morgan, Bill Perkins (*woodwinds*), Peter Donald (*d*), Mike Stephans (*perc*), Julie Andrews (*v*). 6/79–11/86.
*** **Treasure Chest** USA 680
    As above, except add Larry Ford (*t, flhn*), Rob McConnell (*vtb*), Bob Militello (*woodwinds*), Tom Warrington (*b*), Luis Conte (*perc*), omit Childers, Goe, Baptist, Hatt, Welsh, Loper, Harper, Perkins, Cooper, Pizzi, Christlieb, Hardaway, DiBartolo, Ceroli, Stephans and Andrews. 90.

***(*) **Funupmanship** Mama MMF 1006

As above, except add Wayne Bergeron, Charlie Davis (*t, flhn*), Alex Iles (*tb*), Steve Houghton (*d*), omit McConnell, Militello, Donald, Conte. 92.

*** **With All The Bells And Whistles** Mama MMF 1011

As above, except add Carl Saunders (*t, flhn*), Bob McChesney (*tb*), Terry Harrington, Bob Carr (*woodwinds*), Brian Kilgore (*perc*), omit Ford, Culver. 2/95.

Florence has done sterling work as a big-band arranger, leader and performer over nearly 40 years. His bread has been buttered in Los Angeles studio work, but none of these records sounds compromised by that background: he likes big, swinging, powerful bands, and his charts are stuffed with activity. Soloists seldom get by without counterpoint or some other sort of support, and – unusually for the Californian orchestral tradition – he's as interested in long-form writing as he is in punchy three- and four-minute numbers. 'One Two, Three', on *Westlake* extends for nearly 15 minutes and is sustained almost effort-lessly. His bands are usually staffed by the best executants, with two or three knockout soloists as a bonus, and the Fresh Sound reissue shows that that's been the case from the start. There are marvellous turns by Herb Geller and Bob Enevoldsen here, but the section-work, though filled with unfamiliar names, lacks nothing in polish and attack. The disc is stuffed with alternative takes, but there's plenty of interest throughout.

Florence resumed his recording in the late 1970s with seven albums for Discovery: *Westlake* is a lone survivor, but *Jewels* is a splendid compilation, including the pile-driving 'Carmelo's By The Freeway', one of the standout big-band performances of the era. 'The Bebop Treasure Chest' is a witty compil-ation of original bop licks, Julie Andrews turns up on 'Jewels' itself, and 'Bebop Charlie' is another extended arrangement of cumulative power. *Westlake* is good, but the compilation is the one to get from this period.

Treasure Chest offers more good fun in the title-piece, a history lesson on the big bands of yore, and if such hints of kitsch don't appeal there's always the straight-ahead shakedown of Ellington's 'Main Stem'. *Funupmanship* gains an extra ounce of energy from the live recording, and here Florence really puts the band on its mettle: 'Slimehouse' comes out of the stalls ferociously, and 'Come Rain Or Come Shine' is smart enough to have would-be arrangers scratching their heads. Among the soloists, Kim Richmond plays a key role: a modernist with sufficient tradition in him to uphold and transcend his surroundings. After that, *With All The Bells And Whistles* seems like a pressure drop, and 'Teach Me Tonight' is too arch to convince. Compensations include the rough-housing by the two saxes of Mitchell and Harrington on 'Tenors, Anyone?', which just about makes up for its title.

This is a splendid sequence of records, not very fashionable but cooked through with an expertise and intensity that are often as thrilling as big-band music should be.

Chris Flory GUITAR

*** **For All We Know** Concord CCD 4403

Flory; Mike LeDonne (*p, org*); Phil Flanigan (*b*); Chuck Riggs (*d*). 1/88.

*** **City Life** Concord CCD 4589

Flory; John Bunch (*p*); John Webber (*b*); Chuck Riggs (*d*). 3/93.

A member of the Concord repertory of young mainstreamers, Flory's cool phrasing and ambiguous tone (soft when you expect a hardness, and vice versa) lends an attractive piquancy to his improvisa-tions. He sounds easily in command of both these records: the first has a touch of variety lent by LeDonne playing both piano and organ, the second has a more interesting programme of originals and standards (his swinging treatment of 'Besame Mucho' is particularly engaging). But there's little in either record that makes one take notice of anything beyond the merely very good playing.

Marty Fogel TENOR SAXOPHONE, SOPRANO SAXOPHONE, CLARINET

(*) **Many Heads Bobbing, At Last . . . CMP CD 37

Fogel; David Torn (*g*); Dean Johnson (*b*); Michael Shrieve (*d, perc*). 3/89.

Fogel has a suprisingly blunt tone which goes well in this rock-tinged setting. Torn's guitar is a little more restrained than usual, and some of his chord work on 'Unlikely Beast Slayer' is reminiscent of the great riffmeister himself, Frank Zappa. 'Luminous Energy' and the closing 'Cool It' are more obviously vehicles for the leader, who, like Torn, sounds much more to the point here than in their Everyman Band discs for ECM. Production values are no less to the fore at CMP, but the results are crisper, underlining the strength of Fogel's writing.

Ricky Ford (born 1954) TENOR SAXOPHONE

(*) Saxotic Stomp Muse MCD 5349
  Ford; James Spaulding (*as, f*); Charles Davis (*bs*); Kirk Lightsey (*p*); Ray Drummond (*b*); Jimmy Cobb (*d*). 9/87.
*** **Manhattan Blues** Candid CCD 79036
  Ford; Jaki Byard (*p*); Milt Hinton (*b*); Ben Riley (*d*). 3/89.
***(*) **Ebony Rhapsody** Candid CCD 79053
  As above. 6/90.

An erratic but occasionally brilliant player, Ford is best known for his work with Ran Blake and Abdullah Ibrahim. His own records are ambitious in extent, covering a range of idioms from bop, modal-to-free harmony, and back to a broad swing style. On the 1989 *Manhattan Blues* his breadth of reference is instantaneously answered by the eclectic Byard and by the bassist and drummer; Ford's soloing is thoughtful but still curiously uninvolving. *Ebony Rhapsody*, with the same line-up, irons out the occasional awkwardnesses and finds Ford with a band that seems increasingly responsive to his changes of direction; 'Mirror Man', a duet with Milt 'The Judge' Hinton, has an authority worthy of Coleman Hawkins, and the other originals bespeak a growing compositional talent.

Saxotic Stomp has little of its successors' bite and polish. The three horns lock rather inconsequentially, and Spaulding in particular sounds slightly off, a far cry from his own *Brilliant Corners*. Cobb is wonderfully at ease, but Lightsey sounds constrained at times, noticeably on 'For Mary Lou' (which may be no surprise, given the dedication).

*** **Hard Groovin'** Muse MCD 5373
  Ford; Roy Hargrove (*t*); Geoff Keezer (*p*); Bob Hurst (*b*); Jeff Watts (*d*). 89.

Arnold Schoenberg freely conceded that, despite the advent of serialism, there was still a lot of good music to be written in C major. One might say much the same sort of thing about hard bop. If there's an element of young-fogeyism to the generation of musicians who've abandoned the avant-garde to rally under a banner inscribed 'Forward to the 1950s', Ford gives his revivalism a curiously magisterial gravitas, almost as if he were giving a lecture on the evolution of jazz saxophone.

There are some symptoms of reinvention of the wheel on *Hard Groovin'*, a title clearly intended to leave potential purchasers with no misgivings that they're going to be fobbed off with any experimental nonsense. This is so straight-ahead that it has creases in its jeans. Keezer keeps the stew simmering and contributes the most intriguing composition in 'Masaman' (one would like to hear it covered by older-generation players), and Hargrove belts out impressive Hubbard-influenced lines that just occasionally work themselves under an overhang and have to inch shamefacedly back the way they came. Can't say it's an 'advance' on past performances, since advance doesn't seem to be the point.

***(*) **Hot Brass** Candid CCD 79518
  Ford; Lew Soloff, Claudio Roditi (*t*); Steve Turre (*tb*); Danilo Perez (*p*); Christian McBride (*b*); Carl Allen (*d*). 4/91.
**** **American-African Blues** Candid CCD 79528
  Ford; Jaki Byard (*p*); Milt Hinton (*b*); Ben Riley (*d*). 9/91.

Or at least it didn't until these two sets popped up. Ford has never lacked for prestigious sidemen, but the September 1991 quartet, recorded live at Birdland again, puts him in the frame with three sympathetic seniors who quite clearly enjoyed the experience. Hinton gets his own feature on 'Mostly Arco', originally written for Stafford James, but the emphasis otherwise falls on Ford himself, playing with a growing maturity with each passing year and interestingly showing no inclination to double his horns with soprano or flute. The two versions of 'American-African Blues' which bracket the session are the most passionate and intelligent things he has done. There are Coltrane and Rollins references, but for the most part the voice is Ford's own.

The studio album is not quite so impressive, but only because it features less of the leader out front. The arrangements are sharp and pungent. 'Banging, Bashing, Bowing and Blowing' is a superb band work-out, and '11/15/91' is a chromatic lament for Martin Luther King Jr, written at the time of the Gulf War, while 'Carbon 14' draws its inspiration from Ford's interest in Afro-Americana and the theory that black Africans may have discovered America long before Columbus. These days he's digging ever deeper into those roots. The results are hugely impressive.

Bruce Forman (born 1956) GUITAR

*** **There Are Times** Concord CCD 4332
  Forman; Bobby Hutcherson (*vib*); George Cables (*p*); Jeff Carney (*b*); Eddie Marshall (*d*). 8/86.

**(*) Pardon Me Concord CCD 4368
> Forman; Billy Childs (*p*); Jeff Carney (*b*); Eddie Marshall (*d*). 10/88.

All the guitarists who record for Concord seem to come from the same brotherhood: a clean, modulated tone, quick attack and a detailed fluency in their solos; a swing-based style with a streak of bebop complexity running through it. It's appropriate that the company released the later records of Tal Farlow, who is the exemplar of the style. Bruce Forman, a much younger guitarist, is nevertheless entirely of the same persuasion and, as capable as he is, it's hard to glean much excitement or consistent interest from these records. The date with Hutcherson is the best, simply because the vibesman is such a great-hearted musician; but most of the music is well turned out and not much more.

Mitchell Forman KEYBOARDS

** Childhood Dreams Soul Note SN 1050
> Forman (*p* solo). 2/82.

** Only A Memory Soul Note SN 1070
> Forman (*p* solo). 8/82.

**(*) What Else? Novus PD90664
> Forman; Bill Evans (*ss*); John Patitucci (*b*); Terri Lyne Carrington (*d*). 9/91.

Forman's credentials as a sessionman and fusion-band keyboardist don't seem to have prepared him adequately for these unfocused and doodling solo albums. The first is all done on acoustic piano, the second adds some organ washes, and neither makes any impression on an already overcrowded area of endeavour, the solo-piano record. The more recent *What Else?* is an advance, given that Forman's melodies have a hook to many of them (he has spent years in jazz-funk groups of various stripes), and Patitucci and Carrington make a reliable team; Evans also has four cameo appearances. But it's still lightweight from first to last.

***(*) Now And Then Novus 163165
> Forman; Eddie Gomez (*b*); Jack DeJohnette (*d*). 92.

This is much more like it, a tribute to Bill Evans played very much in the idiom but with enough personal input from Forman (and, needless to say, his two fine sidemen) to make it an interesting session. Gomez is wonderful in situations like this and he puts a lot of thought and care into covering some of Forman's less happy excursions. DeJohnette is as supremely musical as always, but it would be unfair to let credit for bass and drums overshadow the leader's own excellent contribution.

**(*) Metro LIP 890232
> Forman; Chuck Loeb (*g*); Anthony Jackson (*b*); Wolfgang Haffner (*d*); Roland Peil (*perc*). 3/94.

A bit of a disappointment after the last record, to put it only mildly. In his defence this isn't strictly Forman's record, but a collaborative group with Loeb, the overheated Jackson, and Haffner. On keyboards again, Forman sounds indistinguishable from any half-dozen other players. Though nicely recorded, musically it's pretty thinly spread.

Michael Formanek (born 1958) BASS

***(*) Wide Open Space Enja ENJ 6032
> Formanek; Greg Osby (*ss, as*); Wayne Krantz (*g*); Mark Feldman (*vn*); Jeff Hirshfield (*d*). 1/90.

*** Extended Animation Enja ENJ 7041
> As above, except Tim Berne (*as, bs*) replaces Osby. 11/91.

***(*) Loose Cannon Soul Note 121261
> As above, except omit Krantz and Feldman. 10/92.

**** Low Profile Enja ENJ 8050
> Formanek; Dave Douglas (*t*); Kuumba Frank Lacy (*tb*); Tim Berne (*as, bs*); Marty Ehrlich (*cl, bcl, as, ss*); Salvatore Bonafede (*p*); Marvin 'Smitty' Smith (*d*). 10/93.

Formanek's unassuming leadership is the lynchpin of these provocative, entertaining records from New York's left field; 'low profile' just about sums him up. He plays funky, grooving acoustic bass for much of the time, even when the signature is something peculiar, and his partnership with Hirshfield is strong enough to carry all the music: there are points on *Loose Cannon*, when Berne sits out, that are fine enough to make one wish for a whole set of bass and drums alone. But he's an interesting writer, too, with a range of moods and thematic styles to keep impatient listeners (and players) absorbed. The band on *Wide Open Space* is a cracker: Osby always sounds better on other people's records, and his playing here is unaffected and lively. But both of the Enja albums are elevated by the excellent team of Krantz and Feldman, string players for a new era. *Extended Animation* is sometimes let down by the front-and-centre role taken by Berne, whose sour, rattled alto takes the edge off Formanek's natural lyricism. But the saxophonist sounds much better on *Loose Cannon*, where he also writes five of the eight themes: 'Almost Normal' is one of his best tunes.

Formanek really hits his groove on *Low Profile*. It's a marvellous band, marked out by Douglas and Lacy's ringing brass, especially on 'Paradise Revisited', and the undervalued simplicity of Berne's baritone playing; his alto is also prominently featured on the long 'Great Plains', the track which affords Formanek himself most leeway for improvisation in his characteristic open-formed style. The only member of the group not likely to be familiar is Bonafede, but he quickly establishes a presence and acquits himself every bit as well as his more celebrated colleagues. In some respects an old-fashioned record, looking back to the free jazz of the early 1960s, it manages never to sound merely retro or nostalgic, and every one of the musicians has definite things to say.

Jimmy Forrest (1920–80) TENOR SAXOPHONE

(*) Forrest Fire Original Jazz Classics OJC 199
> Forrest; Larry Young (*org*); Thornel Schwartz (*g*); Jimmie Smith (*d*). 8/60.

*** Most Much! Original Jazz Classics OJC 350
> Forrest; Hugh Lawson (*p*); Tommy Potter (*b*); Clarendon Johnson (*d*); Ray Barretto (*perc*). 10/61.

Understandably, much of the interest of these centres on a pre-Weather Report Joe Zawinul and the late, great Larry Young, but Forrest is an intriguing performer. For reasons never satisfactorily explained, there weren't that many tenor saxophonists in the bebop revolutions. Like Big Nick Nicholas and Lucky Thompson, Forrest was something of a players' player, with only a rather marginal following now. That's a pity for, as these two sets amply demonstrate, his playing was full of character, a little rough-hewn in places but capable of greater subtlety than his big hit, 'Night Train', might suggest. Forrest is the mid-point, stylistically if not quite geographically, between Charlie Parker and Ornette Coleman.

Forrest Fire pits him against the brimstone stomp of Young's Hammond; between them, they roll up the floor. It's the biggest possible contrast to the lighter and more detailed sound of *Out Of The Forrest*, which has slipped out of sight, but in most respects this is the right context for the saxophonist, who had no desire to play delicately detailed changes.

Most Much! is a fine set, restoring two tracks from the same session previously released only as part of *Soul Street* on New Jazz. More than anything, it demonstrates what a developed time-feel Forrest had. The first three tracks could hardly be more different in emphasis. 'Matilda' is a traditional calypso, given a forceful reading, with the saxophonist closely backed by the unsung Hugh Lawson. 'Annie Laurie' is similarly upbeat but seldom departs from the melody. 'Autumn Leaves' is full of glassy harmonies and a first taste of the curious rhythmic displacements and imaginative harmonic inflexions that make him such a significant way-station between bop and the New Thing. The closing 'Most Much' is a tough rocker, with strong upper-register effects. The recording isn't really up to standard but, as usual, it's 'only' Tommy Potter who suffers unduly.

Sonny Fortune (born 1939) ALTO SAXOPHONE, FLUTE

***(*) Laying It Down Konnex KCD 5030
> Fortune; Kenny Barron (*p*); Cecil McBee (*b*); Billy Hart (*d*). 89.

*** It Ain't What It Was Konnex KCD 5033
> Fortune; Mulgrew Miller (*p*); Santi Debriano (*b*); Billy Hart (*d*). 91.

*** Monk's Mood Konnex KCD 5048
> Fortune; Kirk Lightsey (*p*); David Williams (*b*); Joe Chambers (*d*). 1/93.

Fortune was in the 1975 Miles Davis group that made the darkly exotic *Agharta*. Miles's illness curtailed its activities, but that same year Fortune recorded a fine solo album, *Awakening*, for A&M which suggested that, like Gary Bartz before him, he was destined for great things. In the event, things have proceeded more quietly. An in-demand sideman who specializes in a sharp, keening tone that recalls Asian or African music – he'd previously recorded with McCoy Tyner, notably on *Sahara* – Fortune seemed to have fallen through the net until he popped up with these two suprisingly straight-ahead sessions. It may well be that they were intended to demonstrate his competence as a jazz player rather than merely as an exotic colourist.

The earlier rhythm section suits him rather better. McBee favours drone-like effects that work well underneath Fortune's quarter-tones and indefinite slides, and Barron has always (recent appearances aside) favoured Afro-Asian contexts. Fortune has guested with Santi Debriano's group; the bassist is a limber, fast-moving player but he lacks McBee's subtlety, and Miller (if you'll forgive the pun) is too light. The two familiar repertoire pieces on *It Ain't*, 'Lush Life' and Coltrane's 'Straight Street', are both competently played without suggesting that Fortune's rating as a improviser needs to be altered significantly.

Monk's Mood benefits immeasurably from Lightsey's presence; he's springily rhythmic on the title-track, softly romantic elsewhere, and his solo statements are always spot-on. Fortune himself allows the pace to lag a bit and once or twice gets sidetracked into rather unpromising digressions. Generally, though, well up to scratch.

***(*) Four In One Blue Note 828243
>   Fortune; Kirk Lightsey (*p*); Buster Williams, Santi Debriano (*b*); Billy Hart, Ronnie Burrage (*d*). 1/94.

Fortune's second consecutive album of Monk tunes suggests he is making up for lost time: his sleeve-note comments reveal that he didn't even look at Monk's music until 1990. The results have an appealing freshness, as if some of the tunes were new discoveries, and Fortune earns further marks for choosing the more obscure items: the title-piece, 'Hornin' In', 'Criss Cross' and others. Some of the music doesn't quite happen – the flute-and-bass duet on 'Pannonica' doesn't go anywhere – and Fortune seems deceived by a few Monkian twists; but Lightsey is as strong here as he was on the Konnex date, and the studio sound is better here too.

Frank Foster (born 1928) TENOR AND SOPRANO SAXOPHONE

*** No Count Savoy SV 0114
>   Foster; Henry Coker (*t*); Benny Powell (*tb*); Frank Wess (*ts, f*); Kenny Burrell (*g*); Eddie Jones (*b*); Kenny Clarke (*d*). 3/56.

***(*) Shiny Stockings Denon DC 8545
>   Foster; Sinclair Acey, Virgil Jones, Joe Gardner, Don McIntosh, Chris Albert (*t*); Kiane Zawadi, Charles Stephens, Janice Robinson (*tb*); William Lowe (*btb*); Willie J. Davis (*tba*); Leroy Barton (*as*); Bill Saxton, Bill Cody, Douglas Harris, Charles J. Williams (*ts*); Kenny Rogers (*bs*); Mickey Tucker (*p*); Ted Dunbar (*g*); Earl May (*b*); Charli Persip (*d*); Roger Blank, Babafunyi Akunyon (*perc*). 11/77, 11/78.

*** The House That Love Built Steeplechase SCS 1170
>   Foster; Horace Parlan (*p*); Jesper Lundgaard (*b*); Aage Tanggaard (*d*). 9/82.

**(*) Frankly Speaking Concord CCD 4276
>   Foster; Frank Wess (*as, ts, f*); Kenny Barron (*p*); Rufus Reid (*b*); Marvin 'Smitty' Smith (*d*). 12/84.

Although Frank Foster made his name with Count Basie's orchestra in the 1950s – and a less bop-orientated band one couldn't wish to find – he had assimilated enough of the music of Charlie Parker into his playing to make him stand out as a particularly vivid soloist in that tightly integrated unit. The pun in *No Count* points to the heightened boppishness of the Savoy material, though there's nothing no--'ccount about the music within. Since he has assumed leadership of the Basie band following the Count's death, small-group recording under his own name has recently taken a back seat, and it isn't clear what has happened to his own big band, The Loud Minority, who made two excellent discs and were firm festival favourites.

   The early-1980s sessions are entertaining examples of Foster's mighty swing and full-blooded improvising, yet the settings somehow don't demand enough of him to make him give of his absolute best. Despite comprising mostly original material, the Steeplechase quartet date emerges as much like any other modern tenor-plus-rhythm session, although 'I Remember Sonny Stitt' is an imposing tribute to the then recently departed saxophonist. The meeting with Frank Wess, another Basie colleague to whom Foster seems wedded through all eternity, is rather carefully conceived, as if the players were trying too hard to avoid the blowing clichés which sometimes dominate such records. Wess is a subtler and more varied player, but Foster is a crafty character and often has the last word.

Gary Foster ALTO SAXOPHONE, FLUTE

*** Make Your Own Fun Concord CCD 4459
>   Foster; Jimmy Rowles (*p, v*); John Heard (*b*); Joe LaBarbera (*d*). 1/91.

It's become a standard requirement that if you want to play Jimmy Rowles's 'The Peacocks', you get the great man along to see the job is done right. Rowles is the main attraction throughout this attractive set by a saxophonist and flautist who occasionally sounds like the other reed-playing Foster, but with more overt West Coast touches and flourishes. His versions of 'Nica's Dream', the smooth 'Warne-ing' and

'Alone Together' suggest a player of some character who could do with loosening up and varying the pace a touch.

The Four Brothers GROUP

*** Together Again! RCA 743121 13040

Al Cohn, Zoot Sims, Herbie Steward (*ts*); Serge Chaloff (*bs*); Elliot Lawrence (*p*); Buddy Jones (*b*); Don Lamond (*d*). 2/57.

The original 'Four Brothers' – Herbie Steward, Zoot Sims, Jimmy Giuffre and Stan Getz – represented two-thirds of Woody Herman's saxophone section. Herman himself played alto and clarinet, and one Sam Marowitz, now remembered only by serious collectors, made up the numbers, but the fraternal association of four tenors with Tommy de Carlo on trumpet and a rhythm section behind enjoyed an existence independent of the Herman band.

The name 'Four Brothers' was enshrined in a Giuffre composition that capitalized on the players' precise co-ordination and limpid tone. It was inevitable that this should be one of the first tunes out of the hat when the grouping was revived for this record almost a decade on; 'Ten Years Later' and 'A Quick One' were specially written for the session. Giuffre and Getz had moved on to other things, so Al Cohn and Serge Chaloff were brought in to take their place. Chaloff was ill and in a wheelchair following surgery, which lends some credence to the suggestion that fellow baritonist Charlie O'Kane filled in for half of the tracks, though the featured solo on 'Aged In Wood' sounds very much like Chaloff, albeit in unsparkling form.

The standard criticism of the original Four Brothers was that they traded in individuality for a rather bland uniformity. There's no real difficulty (*pace* the Chaloff/O'Kane question) in distinguishing between the players here. Cohn emerges as the dominant voice; he and arranger Manny Albam bring in most of the new material. Even so, Herbie Steward, the least well-known of this latter-day bunch, makes his presence felt on 'So Blue', swinging confidently through the minor-key turns. The rhythm section is spot on, if a little antiseptic, and the sound, overseen by Bob Rolontz of the Vik label (who released the original), is better than par for 1957: full-voiced, well separated and accurately registered.

Panama Francis (born 1918) DRUMS

***(*) Gettin' In The Groove Black & Blue 233320

Francis; Francis Williams, Irving Stokes (*t*); Norris Turney (*as, cl*); Howard Johnson (*as*); George Kelly (*ts*); Red Richards (*p*); John Smith (*g*); Bill Pemberton (*b*). 1 & 2/79.

Like Tony Williams a generation later, Francis was a teenage prodigy at the drumkit, making his debut as early as 1932. He served a long apprenticeship with Lucky Millinder's band and then graduated to Cab Calloway's, where he stayed for five years. Like a lot of players of his generation, he dropped out of the scene for a long time during the 1960s and early '70s, returning to active service later in the decade only when he had got together the Savoy Sultans, the band featured on this disc.

From his first entrance on 'Song Of The Islands', it is evident how utterly polished a drummer Francis is. He has the loose-wristed delivery of the great swing players and an ability to give even a quite uncomplicated beat a huge range of expression simply by altering the dynamics and by hitting the skins near the rim or dead centre. Much of the material on the record – tracks like 'Rhythm Dr Man', 'Boats', 'Frenzy' and 'Looney' – are by Al Cooper, after whose band the Sultans were named. There are a couple of things by Millinder, and Norris Turney (better known as an Ellingtonian) contributes 'Checkered Hat'. The other saxophonist, George Kelly, is responsible for the arrangements. Drum solos are kept to a decent minimum, but they're full of interest and not a second over-long.

Tomas Franck (born 1958) TENOR SAXOPHONE

*** Tomas Franck In New York Criss Cross Jazz Criss 1052

Franck; Mulgrew Miller (*p*); Kenny Washington (*b*); Billy Drummond (*d*). 12/90.

A stalwart of the Danish Radio Big Band, Franck sounds much like many another hard-bop tenorman, heavily in hock to Coltrane, Gordon and so forth. But it must be admitted that he has the style down as well as most, and the prospect of recording this quartet date on a first trip to New York seems to have held no terrors for him at all. Miller is his usual courteous and thoughtful self, and Washington and Drummond keep good time. Four Franck originals suggest nothing special in the way of composing, but he knows how to get the best out of himself as an improviser: the long solo on the opening 'Triton' shows no lack of ideas. The playing time is a little long, though, at 68 minutes.

Rebecca Coupe Franks (born 1963) TRUMPET, FLUGELHORN

*** **Suit Of Armor** Justice JR 0901-2
>   Franks; Joe Henderson (*ts*); Kenny Barron (*p*); Leni Stern (*g*); Buster Williams (*b*); Ben Riley
>   (*d*); Carolyn Brandy (*perc*). 2/91.
(*) **All Of A Sudden Justice JR 0902-2
>   Franks; Javon Jackson, Donny McCaslin (*ts*); Kevin Hays (*p*); Scott Colley (*b*); Yoron Israel
>   (*d*); Rita Lackey, Tish Sainz, Gwen Warran (*v*). 2/92.

Female trumpet players are rare birds indeed, and a larger than was strictly fair proportion of the press surrounding release of *Suit Of Armor* was of the pretty-girl-with-a-horn sort. An equally unjustified proportion of the remainder was directed at the big-name band newcomers Justice had put together for her debut. Interestingly, though, where perhaps most young players showcased in this way tend to freeze, Franks plays very much more confidently with Henderson, Baron, Williams and Riley than she does a year later with her own band.

Her trumpet playing is unashamedly in thrall to Miles Davis, to whom *All Of A Sudden* is dedicated. She has something of the same ability to infuse an isolated note or phrase with considerable dramatic force, and in solos she lingers over ideas rather than hurrying on to something new. Her partnership with Henderson (a card-carrying feminist) on the earlier record is particularly fruitful. The long 'Elephant Dreams' is perhaps her major statement to date, an outwardly ponderous but in practice quite graceful theme that somehow reconciles the rather vulnerable and anxious persona projected in 'Suit Of Armor'.

Franks's rock and soul slip shows only once or twice on the first record. 'U-bitch' and Leni Stern's 'Back Out' aren't as tough as they pretend and demand a thicker mix than Justice's rather spartan live-to-2-track format. Unfortunately, *All Of A Sudden* is largely in this style. The vocal tracks are pretty feeble, and Franks's own playing misses the smack of the earlier record. Once again she slots in an Ellington tune, 'I Let A Song Go Out Of My Heart'; but, compared to 'Beginning To See The Light' on *Suit*, the arrangement is merely capricious, and the rhythm section turn it into a schmaltzy plod.

Franks is obviously going places, but she's certainly outgrown her label and now deserves a more professional set-up.

Hugh Fraser PIANO, TROMBONE

***(*) **Looking Up** Jazzimage JZCD 115
>   Fraser; Campbell Ryga (*ss, as*); Phil Dwyer (*ss, ts, p*); Chris Nelson (*b*); Buff Allen (*d*). 88.
**** **Pas De Problèmes** CBC 2-0119
>   As above, except Blaine Wikjord (*d*) replaces Allen. 89.

Fraser plays some trombone on these records, but it's as pianist and arranger that this Canadian makes his mark, and he gets a formidable sound out of a superbly accomplished quintet. Sample 'Sanctus Agnus Dei' on the first record to hear how grand Fraser can make five instruments sound, or hear how the riff of 'Who'd Of Thunk' is worked into a coherent theme. Ryga and Dwyer are talented saxophonists, the latter getting a big, tempestuous sound out of the tenor and doubling on piano when needs be; but Fraser stamps his personality on the group to the degree that individual contributions form a logical part of an impressive whole. The second album is slightly ahead for the bigger studio sound-stage and Wikjord's imposing drumming, and in the memorable 'Mode To McCoy' the leader displays amazing chops at the piano: he really does have Tynerish authority. Recommended.

Free Jazz Quartet GROUP

**** **Premonitions** Matchless MR18
>   Paul Rutherford (*tb*); Harrison Smith (*ts, ss, bcl*); Tony Moore (*clo*); Eddie Prévost (*d*). 7/89.

If the group's title is a wry reference to the Modern Jazz Quartet (see also Prévost's punning Supersession), it takes in Ornette Coleman's seminal *Free Jazz* as well. The terminology is used advisedly, for this superb recording is more obviously rooted in one of the dialects of post-bop than, say, the process-dominated free improvisation of AMM. The underlying motif of *Premonitions* is warning: 'Red Flags', 'Roman Geese', 'Gathering Clouds', 'Cry Wolf', 'Tocsin' and even 'Old Moore's' (an oblique reference to the trombonist's *Old Moore's Almanack* album). The music is tense and often powerfully dramatic, strung along highly attenuated motivic threads. Prévost's drumming is as good as he has ever been on record and Rutherford is, as always, good enough to listen to on his own. Just as politically Prévost and his circle have tended to reject the bland triumphalism of the doctrinaire left, so musically he clearly rejects the anything-goes attitude that gives free improvisation a bad name. This is intense and concentrated music. A warning: please do not 'understand' it too quickly.

Bud Freeman (1906–91) TENOR SAXOPHONE, CLARINET

**** Great Original Performances, 1927–1940 Jazz Classics in Digital Stereo RPCD 604
Freeman; Jimmy McPartland (*c*); Joe Bauer, Andy Ferretti, Bunny Berigan, Pee Wee Erwin, Charlie Spivak, Max Kaminsky, Johnny Mendel (*t*); Glenn Miller, Will Bradley, Tommy Dorsey, Red Bone, Les Jenkins, Floyd O'Brien (*tb*); Jack Teagarden (*tb, v*); Brad Gowans (*vtb*); Benny Goodman, Bud Jacobson, Pee Wee Russell, Frank Teschemacher (*cl*); Johnny Mince, Jim Cannon, Fred Stulce, Mike Doty, Milt Yaner (*cl, as*); Dave Matthews (*as*); Adrian Rollini (*bsx*); Dave North, Dave Bowman, Jose Sullivan, Howard Smith, Jess Stacy, Claude Thornhill (*p*); George Van Eps, Dick McDonough, Carmen Mastren (*g*); Eddie Condon (*g, bj*); Norman Foster (*bj*); Joe Venuti (*vn*); Jim Lannigan, Artie Bernstein, John Mueller, Grachan Moncur, Clyde Newcombe, Delmer Caplan, Artie Shapiro, Mort Stuhlmaker, Gene Traxler (*b*); Danny Alvin, Cozy Cole, Big Sid Catlett, Gene Krupa, Neil Marshall, Morey Feld, Dave Tough (*d*). 12/27–7/40.

***(*) Bud Freeman, 1928–1938 Classics 781
Freeman; Bobby Hackett (*c*); Bunny Berigan, Johnny Mendel (*t*); Joe Bushkin (*t, p*); Floyd O'Brien (*tb*); Bud Jacobson, Pee Wee Russell (*cl*); Dave Matthews (*as*); Dave North, Jess Stacy, Claude Thornhill (*p*); Eddie Condon (*g*); Norman Foster (*bj*); Grachan Moncur, John Mueller, Artie Shapiro (*b*); Cozy Cole, Gene Krupa, Marty Marsala, Dave Tough, George Wettling (*d*); Red McKenzie, Minerva Pious (*v*). 12/28–11/38.

***(*) Bud Freeman, 1939–1940 Classics 811
Freeman; Max Kaminsky (*t*); Jack Teagarden (*tb, v*); Brad Gowans (*vtb*); Pee Wee Russell (*cl*); Dave Bowman (*p*); Eddie Condon (*g*); Clyde Newcombe, Pete Peterson, Mort Stuhlmaker (*b*); Danny Alvin, Morey Feld, Al Sidell, Dave Tough (*d*). 7/39–7/40.

***(*) Chicago / Austin High School Jazz In Hi-Fi RCA 13031
Freeman; Jimmy McPartland (*c*); Billy Butterfield (*t*); Tyree Glenn (*tb*); Jack Teagarden (*tb, v*); Peanuts Hucko, Pee Wee Russell (*cl*); Dick Cary, Gene Schroeder (*p*); Al Casamenti (*g*); Leonard Gaskin, Al Hall, Milt Hinton (*b*); George Wettling (*d*). 3, 4 & 7/57.

*** Something To Remember You By Black Lion BLCD 760153
Freeman; Dave Frishberg (*p*); Bob Haggart (*b*); Don Lamond (*d*). 1/62.

Freeman was perhaps the first truly significant white tenor player. If he looked, and chose to behave, like the secretary of some golf club in the Home Counties – episode one of his autobiography was called *You Don't Look Like A Musician* – his saxophone walked all over the carpets in spikes, a rawer sound than Lester Young's (to which it is often likened) and with a tougher articulation.

Freeman developed late, worked in some unpromising contexts, and ended up one of the most distinctive tenorists of all time (and any colour). Until recently the available discography was pretty thin. The situation improved with the appearance of Robert Parker's superbly remastered Jazz Classics in Digital Stereo compilation. This is the essential Freeman record for the CD collector. It contains all his best work of the period, including the November 1933 'The Eel' and a marvellous tune called 'The Buzzard', recorded with Bunny Berigan. There is inevitably a large overlap of material on the Classics imprint, though these will be preferred (sound quality notwithstanding) by collectors who want a more complete and idiosyncratic selection, or who are dismayed by Parker's bonging reverb. Where Parker goes for excellent performances, even under other leaders like Joe Venuti and Eddie Condon, Classics tend to stick to just those sessions where Freeman was leading his Windy City Five, his Gang, or his later Summa Cum Laude orchestra (who reprised 'The Eel' in 1939).

Classics (*1928–1938*) include one astonishing oddity, a piece of ham acting by Freeman and the bizarrely named Minerva Pious; no description will quite suffice . . . The 1938 trio with Stacy and Wettling is excellent evidence for Freeman's gifts as a highly focused improviser. His harmonic shifts and deceptively easy chromatic transitions on 'I Got Rhythm' (January of that year and an astonishing performance) and 'Three Little Words' (a later session, in November) have a cut-out-and-keep quality that will endear them to all saxophone players.

Almost as welcome is the reappearance of the 1957 'Austin High School Gang' dates, featuring Freeman's Summa Cum Laude orchestra. These sides included some of his most unrestrained and relaxed solos. Pieces like LaRoca's 'At The Jazz Band Ball', something of an anthem for the Chicago players, is absolutely on the money, with Teagarden playing at his best and Peanuts Hucko diving around the two slower-moving men at the front. The cuts with Russell are almost equally good, but there's no version of 'The Eel', a Freeman favourite which became a bit of a millstone round his neck. The Black Lion is fine as far as it goes, but a rash of alternative takes includes nothing of any devastating novelty and the set is rather pinched by Frishberg, an entertaining player at the best of times, playing at top form here. Until OJC see fit to bring back the 1960 *All Stars* with Shorty Baker, this is all that remains of one of the longest and most prolific careers in the business.

Chico Freeman (born 1949) TENOR SAXOPHONE, SOPRANO SAXOPHONE, BASS CLARINET, CLARINET, FLUTE

*** **Beyond The Rain** Original Jazz Classics OJC 479
> Freeman; Hilton Ruiz (*p*); Juni Booth (*b*); Elvin Jones (*d*). 6/77.

***(*) **Chico** India Navigation IN 1031
> Freeman; Muhal Richard Abrams (*p*); Cecil McBee (*b*); Steve McCall (*d*); Tito Sampa (*perc*). 77.

**** **Chico Freeman Quartet** India Navigation IN 1042
> Freeman; John Hicks (*p*); Cecil McBee (*b*); Jack DeJohnette (*d*). 78.

***(*) **Spirit Sensitive** India Navigation IN 1070
> Freeman; John Hicks (*p*); Jay Hoggard (*vib*); Cecil McBee (*b*); Billy Hart, Famoudou Don Moye (*d*). 78.

***(*) **No Time Left** Black Saint 120036
> Freeman; Jay Hoggard (*vib*); Rick Rozie (*b*); Famoudou Don Moye (*d*). 6/79.

**** **Destiny's Dance** Original Jazz Classics OJC 799
> Freeman; Wynton Marsalis (*t*); Bobby Hutcherson (*vib*); Dennis Moorman (*p*); Cecil McBee (*b*); Ronnie Burrage (*d*); Paulinho Da Costa (*perc*). 81.

** **You'll Know When You Get There** Black Saint 120128
> Freeman; Eddie E. J. Allen (*t, flhn*); Von Freeman (*ts, p*); Geri Allen (*p, ky*); Don Pate (*b*); Victor Jones (*d*); Norman Hedman (*perc*); Joel Brandon (*whistling*). 8/88.

***(*) **Luminous** JazzHouse JHCD 010
> Freeman; Arthur Blythe (*as*); John Hicks (*p, ky*); Donald Pate (*b*); Victor Jones (*d*); Norman Hedman (*perc*). 2/89.

*** **Up And Down** Black Saint 120136
> Freeman; Mal Waldron (*p*); Rocky Knauer (*b*); Tiziana Ghiglioni (*v*). 7/89.

***(*) **The Unspoken Word** Jazz House JH 9 & 10/93.
> Freeman; Arthur Blythe (*as*); Julian Joseph (*p*); Curtis Lundy (*b*); Idris Muhammad (*d*). 9 & 10/93.

**** **Focus** Contemporary CCD 14073
> Freeman; Arthur Blythe (*as*); George Cables (*p*); Santi Debriano (*b*); Yoron Israel (*d*). 5/94.

For a radical, Chico Freeman has a highly developed sense of tradition. In the late 1970s, when most of his contemporaries were highly resistant to the notion, he recorded a set of standards (*Spirit Sensitive*) at the same time as he was pushing away at his own angular conception, and he has continually resorted to the tradition since then, often with a strange, Doppler-shift effect, as if heard across great distances. Perhaps because availability has been intermittent, Freeman's India Navigation records of the late '70s have been sorely undervalued; they are exciting, full of character and impeccably well played. With partners like Hicks, who reappears on the 1989 live recording from Ronnie Scott's, with Arthur Blythe co-starring, he can hardly go wrong. Like his artistic cousin, David Murray, Freeman seemed to draw inspiration from unfashionable sources, like Ellington's 'other' great saxophonist, Paul Gonsalves. The Ellington album is a fine and sensitive effort, with a reading of 'Sophisticated Lady' on unaccompanied tenor saxophone to put alongside more conventional ensemble pieces.

Despite an impressive line-up that includes his father, Von Freeman, and Geri Allen, *You'll Know . . .* is curiously muted. *Destiny's Dance*, on the other hand, is among the essential jazz albums of the 1980s, building on the foundation of the earlier sets. The 1981 record is Freeman's masterpiece, with an all-star supporting cast and a devastating programme of originals.

The Black Saint from 1989 has also been rather overlooked since its appearance. Though betraying signs of having been put together at short notice (who, for instance, is Rocky Knauer, and why is he allowed out with a contrabass?), it contains some fascinating exchanges between the saxophonist and a characteristically dark-toned Waldron, one of the great contemporary pianists. It repays the search.

The recent association with Arthur Blythe has been very fruitful. Blythe has gone through similar doldrums and becalmings over the years, and the two men seem to have reached a strong creative understanding that yields some very powerful music. Monk's 'Rhythm-A-Ning' is common to both records, as is Cecil McBee's 'Peacemaker' and an original, 'Playpen'. The later studio recordings see Blythe in particular stretch out and warm to his task, while Freeman palpably feeds off the live atmosphere at Ronnie Scott's club and the rich, fruity accompaniment he is getting from young British pianist Joseph, no mean soloist himself.

These are very encouraging records, suggesting that Freeman has recalibrated some of his harmonic thinking, working straighter and more linearly, using his impressive circular breathing as on Don Pullen's eulogy to the late George Adams, 'Ah, George, We Hardly Knew Ya', with taste and discretion, and allowing the music to flow through him rather than forcing it out.

*** **Freeman & Freeman** India Navigation I N 1070
> Freeman; Von Freeman (*ts*); Muhal Richard Abrams, Kenny Barron (*p*); Cecil McBee (*b*); Jack DeJohnette (*d*). 4/81.

The family firm. The Freemans play well together, with Von's sliding tonalities closing the gap between his more mainstream blues approach and Chico's pure-toned modernism. Their gruff partnership on 'The Shadow Of Your Smile' invests a hokey tune with considerable dignity, and 'I Can't Get Started' is an excellent performance from both. A fascinating band, held together by DeJohnette's endlessly interesting figures and powerful surges; the two keyboard men undertake a concise exercise in comparative pianistics, Chicago *v.* Philly, with Barron coming out fractionally ahead on points.

** **The Mystical Dreamer** In + Out 7006
> Freeman; Brainstorm: Delmar Brown (*ky, v*); Chris Walker (*b, ky, v*); Archie Walker (*d, ky*); Norman Hedman (*perc*). 5/89.

** **Sweet Explosion** In + Out 7010
> Freeman; Brainstorm: Delmar Brown (*ky, p, v*); Norman Hedman (*perc*); Alex Blake (*b*); Tommy Campbell (*d*). 4/90.

*** **Threshold** In + Out 7022
> Freeman; Jack Lee (*g*); Vincent Leroy Evans (*p, ky*); Dave Dyson (*b*); Gene Jackson (*d*); Norman Hedman (*perc*); Ada Dyer, Urszula Dudziak, Rodney Harris, Thulise Khumalo, Andrea Re (*v*). 10/92.

For all his professed hostility to 'compromise' music, Freeman has long wiggled his toes in a rather dismal funk idiom that gives his extraordinary talent precious little room for manoeuvre. *The Mystical Dreamer* by his Brainstorm group has a refreshing crispness – and eye-catching cover-art. If Freeman is rather wasted, the synthesizer stabs and racketing percussion maintain interest. The live performances that make up *Sweet Explosion* were recorded at Ronnie Scott's club in London. There is a long version of 'On The Nile' from the first album, which gives Freeman a chance to stretch out, but there is also a vocal track so banal as to defy description or categorization and which makes 'I'll Be There' from *Mystical Dreamer* sound like *Winterreise*.

There's a lot more to chew on with the third record. Dudziak's agile voice is a very definite plus, and Freeman seems inclined to play across the rhythm line more often and with a much more pronounced jazz feel. 'Blues For Miles' and 'Oleo' are both in a fairly standard jazz idiom and the band play all the better for it, with Lee in particular concentrating on getting his chords right and spending less time bending notes and racketing away like a rock-and-roller.

Von Freeman (born 1922) TENOR SAXOPHONE

*** **Serenade And Blues** Chief CD 3
> Freeman; John Young (*p*); David Shipp (*b*); Wilbur Campbell (*d*). 6/75.

*** **Walkin' Tuff** Southport S-SSD 0010
> Freeman; Jon Logan, Kenny Prince (*p*); Carroll Crouch, Dennis Carroll (*b*); Wilbur Campbell, Mike Raynor (*d*). 89.

***(*) **Never Let Me Go** Steeplechase SCCD 31310
> Freeman; Jodie Christian (*p*); Eddie De Haas (*b*); Wilbur Campbell (*d*). 5/92.

***(*) **Lester Leaps In** Steeplechase SCCD 31320
> As above. 5/92.

Opening with Glenn Miller quotes may be, as the fashion advisers say, 'very ageing', but Von Freeman has never been impressed by trends. While his son and fellow-tenorist, Chico, has explored sometimes baffling extremes of free jazz and neo-funk, Von Freeman has stuck with a curious down-home style that occasionally makes his saxophone sound as if it is held together with rubber bands and sealing wax. Stylistically it is closer to Ornette Coleman than to Lester Young (and it fitted quite seamlessly into Chico's band in the 1980s), but in the sense that Ornette is himself a maverick traditionalist.

Serenade And Blues is a relaxed and wholly untroubled set of standards, cut with a friendly rhythm section; the session was originally released, shorn of a track, on the parent Nessa as *Have No Fear*. It's also 15 years old; the decision to stay back in Chicago did nothing for Freeman's recording schedule. 'Von Freeman's Blues' and the strong closing 'I'll Close My Eyes' were, for long enough, the closest thing on record to a Freeman set at the Enterprise Lounge. Since then, though, two additions to the list. The studio selections on *Walkin' Tuff* are obviously meant to sound as in-yer-face and immediate as a club date. Logan/Crouch/Campbell are the first-string linebackers: punchy, up-front and slightly cavalier about the rule book. When the pace slows a bit, and the *dee*-fence are called on, Messrs Prince, Carroll and Raynor take the field. They claim an assist on both 'Nature Boy' and 'But Beautiful', but get a bit waylaid on 'Blues For Sunnyland'. Half-way through, the saxophonist goes on a long solo run, playing 'How Deep Is The Ocean' completely unaccompanied. Very effective, too.

Any fears that Freeman was going to be John Lee Hookered, turned into an overnite sensation just in time for his bus-pass, failed to materialize. His more recent career has been a self-confident demonstration that a recording contract is a spoonful of jam, but not necessarily bread and butter to a jazz musician. However, for his seventieth birthday, the old boy treated himself to a Paris trip, on which *Never Let Me Go* and *Lester Leaps In* were recorded. Both discs have a resolutely old-fashioned air and might easily have been recorded in 1975. This has something to do with the sound of Christian's electric piano, but also the very foursquare beat that Campbell favours. The Rollins accents that Freeman brings to 'The End Of A Love Affair' and 'I'll Remember April' on *Never*, and still more noticeably to 'A Nightingale Sang In Berkeley Square' on *Lester Leaps In*, haven't been so much in evidence before. The delicacy that used to be only sparsely dusted over ballads is now a major component of the sound, and there are touches of near-genius on the chestnut, 'Alone Together', and the heart-on-sleeve Cole Porter 'I Love You' which alone make this a vintage performance.

Paolo Fresu TRUMPET, FLUGELHORN, CORNET

*** **Ostinato** Splasc(h) H 106-2
    Fresu; Tino Tracanna (*ss, ts*); Roberto Cipelli (*p*); Attilo Zanchi (*b*); Ettore Fioravanti (*d*). 1/85.
*** **Inner Voices** Splasc(h) H 110-2
    As above, plus David Liebman (*ss, f*). 4/86.
***(*) **Mamut: Music For A Mime** Splasc(h) H 127-2
    As above, except omit Liebman; add Mimmo Cafiero (*perc*). 11/85–5/86.
*** **Quatro** Splasc(h) H 160-2
    As above, except omit Cafiero. 4–6/88.
*** **Live In Montpellier** Splasc(h) H 301-2
    As above. 7/88.

An outstanding exponent of the new Italian jazz, Fresu is in much demand as a sideman, but his records as a leader offer some of the best views of his music, even if there is no masterpiece yet. Fresu's quintet includes the agile Tracanna and the expert bassist Zanchi, and together they follow an energetic yet introspective kind of jazz that suggests a remote modern echo of an early Miles Davis group – the trumpeter does, indeed, sound like the Davis of the mid-1950s often enough to bother some ears. Most of the time the resulting music is engaging rather than compelling: the soloists have more to say than the compositions and, although the group works together very sympathetically, the records never quite take off. Liebman is soon at home on the session he guests on; the live record from Montpellier is scrappy yet often more exciting than the others; and *Quatro* has some bright originals. *Mamut*, though, is the best of these records: although the programme is a collection of fragments for the theatre, the miniatures include some of Fresu's most vivid writing, and the title-piece and 'Pa' are themes which hang in the memory. Fresu even finds something new to say on a solo reading of 'Round Midnight'.

***(*) **Ensalada Mistica** Splasc(h) 415
    Fresu; Gianluigi Trovesi (*as, cl, bcl*); Tino Tracanna (*ss, ts*); Roberto Cipelli (*p*); Attilo Zanchi
    (*b*); Ettore Fioravanti (*d*). 5/94.

A decade of work has made this into a very confident, imposing group. Fresu is generous about sharing space, but his is still the most impressive single voice: luxurious brass sound, firm delivery, staunchly flow of ideas. Still, Trovesi and Tracanna make a formidable front line, and the rhythm section continue to grow. This is elegant and eloquent post-bop which speaks in any language and this is a group that can stand on any world stage.

Dave Friedman (born 1944) VIBES, MARIMBA

*** **Of The Wind's Eye** Enja 3089
    Friedman; Jane Ira Bloom (*ss*); Harvie Swartz (*b*); Daniel Humair (*d*). 7/81.
(*) **Shades Of Change Enja 5017
    Friedman; Geri Allen (*p*); Anthony Cox (*b*); Ronnie Burrage (*d*). 4/86.

Friedman's methods are unusual among vibes players in that he seems as interested in the percussive and rhythmic qualities of the instrument as he is in harmony and melody. He also uses the marimba as often as he does the vibraphone. It adds up to a purposeful style that deglamorizes the often shallow prettiness which the vibes can settle into, although Friedman's own romantic streak can allow his playing to meander to nowhere in particular.

His work as a leader in the 1970s and '80s – he also co-led the group Double Image with Dave Samuels –

is interesting rather than especially memorable. The best album, *Of The Wind's Eye*, is now on CD: the quartet respond well to the programme, with Humair outstandingly vivid on 'A Swiss Celebration' and Bloom in piquant form. Allen, Cox and Burrage are a close-knit trio, and Friedman sounds as if he's decorating their lines rather than integrating with them: tonally this is a rather bland group, although the Enja recording is as resonant as usual.

Don Friedman (born 1935) PIANO

*** **A Day In The City** Original Jazz Classics OJC 1775
    Friedman; Chuck Israels (*b*); Joe Hunt (*d*). 6/61.
*** **Hot Pepper And Knepper** Progressive PCD 7036
    Friedman; Jimmy Knepper (*tb*); Pepper Adams (*bs*); George Mraz (*b*); Billy Hart (*d*). 6/78.
**** **I Hear A Rhapsody** Stash ST CD 577
    Friedman (*p* solo). 9/84.
***(*) **At Maybeck: Volume 33** Concord CCD 4608
    As above. 93.

Friedman's experimentalism is of a relaxed, Californian sort. He started out as a relatively orthodox West Coaster, bringing aspects of the Bill Evans style to work with Shorty Rogers, Jimmy Giuffre and others, but increasingly he has incorporated elements of classical composition and twelve-tone technique, as well as abstraction, to his playing. As with many contemporary pianists, it was a Maybeck recital that gave him renewed prominence.

It's clear that he enjoys the sweet-tempered piano and the quiet, respectful atmosphere of the hall. His own 'Memory For Scotty' is a classically conceived piece replete with echos and allusions to the great Evans/LaFaro exchanges on the Riverside sessions. His choice of standards is predictably romantic – 'I Concentrate On You', 'How Deep Is The Ocean', and a Friedman favourite, 'I Hear A Rhapsody' – and there is a surpassingly elegant interpretation of Duke's 'Prelude To A Kiss', which has an almost operatic emotional range.

The *leitmotif* that governs *A Day In The City* is actually kept well disguised. Subtitled 'Six Variations On A Theme' and devoted to the hours from dawn through rush hour to the mildly threatening hush of the night, it isn't so much a theme-with-variations as a piece that never quite declares its central subject but toys with several possibilities. Elegantly and atmospherically played, it could almost be an Evans session; certainly the nocturne has that feel.

Hot Knepper And Pepper is not entirely characteristic and has to be co-credited to the horn men name-checked. Adams brings the original 'Hellure', there is a cover of Rollins's 'Audubon' (plus a very good alternative take) and a long medley that strings together 'Alfie', 'Laura', 'Prelude To A Kiss' (another Friedman enthusiasm) and 'I Got It Bad (And that Ain't Good)'. In addition, two takes of 'I'm Getting Sentimental Over You' and 'Beautiful Love', both of which show how restless an improviser Friedman can be, and how fettered he patently is by the conventional round of themes and solos. Half-way through the longer first take of 'Beautiful Love', he sounds as if he is going to take the whole thing off in an entirely new direction but the inertia of the band holds him back, and the B minor tonality reasserts itself.

It would be difficult to pick between the Maybeck session and *I Hear A Rhapsody*. Both have their merits, but there is a swinging intelligence to the Stash which prompts us to give it the nod. Friedman unveils his touch as a composer with 'Olivia' (worthy of Kern) and 'Half and Half', a Rollins-tinged theme, and throws in an intriguing free improvisation which the majority of blindfolded listeners would guess was Paul Bley of a slightly earlier vintage, but for the distinctive parallel chords and rich chromaticism. The closing 'Gentle Rain' is magnificent, perhaps Friedman's finest hour on record.

The Fringe GROUP

***(*) **It's Time For The Fringe** Soul Note 121205
    George Garzone (*sax*); John Lockwood (*b*); Bob Gullotti (*d*); Nick Racheotes (*v*). 4/92.
*** **Live** A.V. Arts ADJ CD 004
    As above, except omit Racheotes. 3/93.

The Fringe play a pleasantly old-fashioned variety of free bop that is rather reminiscent of 1960s British bands like Trevor Watts's Amalgam trio. Garzone is probably a more diverse player in the sense that he gravitates much less to fixed tonalities. The caveman poses on the cover of *It's Time For* are doubly ironic, since this is such civilized improvisation, polite even when Garzone is screeching up in the false register. (The cover shot is, incidentally, a reference to 'Neanderthal Man', on which guest performer Racheotes delivers an, ahem, recitation.)

It isn't clear why the live record is attributed to the George Garzone Trio, since the personnels are identical and The Fringe still seems to be functioning as a unit. Taped at Catania, it offers the group's sunnier side; it also offers a standard, 'My One And Only Love', interpreted with just enough eccentricity to save it from tedium.

Bill Frisell (born 1951) GUITAR, ELECTRIC GUITAR, BANJO, GUITAR SYNTHESIZER, EFFECTS

*** **In Line** ECM 1241
    Frisell; Arild Andersen (*b*). 8/82.
*** **Smash And Scatteration** Minor Music 005
    Frisell; Vernon Reid (*g, syn*); duos, solos. 12/84.
There are always murmurs of 'Hendrix, Hendrix' whenever a new electric guitarist of more than modest inventiveness hits the scene, and they're usually inaccurate. However warmly he may have responded to Jimi Hendrix as an example, Bill Frisell's playing is much closer to Frank Zappa's licks-based and treatment-heavy style. However concerned he appears to be with textures, Frisell concentrates on the exact figuration of brief but often quite complex melodic shapes, out of which a whole piece grows. With repeated hearings, it is these shapes that insist.

The process is more evident on *In Line*, which is essentially a solo album and the best place to start. The basic ideas could be jotted down on a couple of sides of stave paper, but the developments open up whole ranges of musical language; the best track, 'Throughout', so appealed to the British composer, Gavin Bryars, that he turned it into an atmospheric concert-piece called 'Sub Rosa'. For the most part, though, Frisell's free modal themes are geared to open improvisation. Paired with Vernon Reid (with whom the 'Hendrix' labels make a deal of sense) he sounds brawnier, and the ideas, presumably cooked up quickly for the session, are left just on the raw side of underdone. Good crossover appeal, though; Living Color fans might take note.

*** **Rambler** ECM 1287
    Frisell; Kenny Wheeler (*t, c, flhn*); Bob Stewart (*tba*); Jerome Harris (*b*); Paul Motian (*d*). 8/84.
***(*) **Lookout For Hope** ECM 1351
    Frisell; Hank Roberts (*clo, v*); Kermit Driscoll (*b*); Joey Baron (*d*). 3/87.
*** **Before We Were Born** Elektra Musician 960843
    Frisell; Billy Drewers, Julius Hemphill (*as*); Doug Wieselman (*bs*); Arto Lindsay (*g, v*); Peter Scherer (*ky*); Hank Roberts (*clo, v*); Kermit Driscoll (*b*); Joey Baron (*d, perc*); Cyro Baptista (*perc*).
*** **Is That You?** Elektra Musician 960956
    Frisell; Dave Hofstra (*t, tba*); Wayne Horvitz (*ky, b*); Joey Baron (*d*). 8/89.
(*) **Where In The World? Elektra Nonesuch 7559 61181
    As above. 91.
Rambler doesn't succeed at every level – it has a disconcertingly soft centre – but it is a beautifully structured album with a fascinating instrumental blend. Frisell's experiments in that direction continue with *Lookout For Hope*, his best album to date. Rough samples of a wide variety of styles (including a previously unexploited enthusiasm for Country 'n' Western) recall the emergence of Larry Coryell, but where Coryell was a quick-change artiste rather than a genuine synthesizer, Frisell boils every resource down to usable basics. His is a completely individual voice, without a hint of pastiche.

Until, that is, *Where In The World?* which, despite an identical line-up, sounds curiously self-absorbed and anything but interactive. All the usual infusion of country and folk themes (though these are turned head over heels on 'Rob Roy'), bludgeoning blues and abstractionist devices, but there's a polymorphous New Age quality to much of the music that from a player of Frisell's gifts seems downright perverse.

It worked better on *Is That You?*, which was a rather self-conscious dive down into the guitarist's roots, taking in country trashings, big generous sweeps of abstract sound, jazz and free structures. The programming is almost as random as that on Frisell's Elektra debut, *Before We Were Born*, which gives his gentle eclecticism and occasional bad-boy tantrums an almost postmodern sheen. The second album might just as well have been a solo set, so incidental does the 'band' appear; the musicians are better used on *Born*, if only because Lindsay's contributions are so utterly no-shit and apposite. The switch of labels doesn't seem to have done the guitarist any non-fiscal favours. ECM's occasionally absolutist purity constrained him very little; Elektra's market trufflings are, on this showing, doing him no good at all.

*(*) **Works** ECM 8372732
    Frisell; various line-ups.
Premature, and by no means adequately representative.

***(*) **This Land** Elektra Nonesuch 7559 79316
    Frisell; Curtis Fowlkes (*tb*); Don Byron (*cl, bcl*); Billy Drewes (*as*); Kermit Driscoll (*b*); Joey
    Baron (*d*). 10/92.
**** **Have A Little Faith** Elektra Nonesuch 79301
    As above, except omit Fowlkes, Drewes; add Guy Klucevesek (*acc*). 3/93.
On *This Land* Frisell experiments further with stylistic hybrids, putting together elements of jazz and
country music, abstract shapes and tuneful miniatures that have the resonant familiarity of the melodies
in Aaron Copland's *Appalachian Spring* and *Billy the Kid*. Sonically, it's a fascinating combination, with
Fowlkes and Byron often combining to produce elegant dissonances (as on 'Jimmy Carter, Part 1') that
are taken over by accordion master Klucevesek on *Have A Little Faith*.

    Frisell's marvellous examination of Americana takes in Stephen Foster, Sousa, Ives, Copland, Sonny
Rollins, Bob Dylan, and, most controversially, Madonna. There's no attempt to debunk or satirize, and
even Madonna's 'Live To Tell', despite a heavily distorted cadenza with all Frisell's switches and pedals
on, sticks pretty close to the original. As was noted on their tour of Britain, Byron's role was rather
marginal, and it's Klucevesek and Baron whom one particularly remembers, both enjoying themselves
mightily.

    Perhaps the only reservation about its predecessor is a slight sententiousness that seems at odds with
most of Frisell's compositions. The repertoire and pop pieces on *Faith* encourage a more playful
approach and make for a less coherent but far more varied record.

*** **Live** Gramavision GCD 79504
    Frisell; Kermit Driscoll (*b*); Joey Baron (*d*). 10/ 91.
***(*) **Go West: Music From The Films Of Buster Keaton** Elektra Nonesuch 979350
    As above. 95.
One would have thought that a live album by an artist of Frisell's current eminence, and from a label
with reasonable resources at its disposal, might have done something handsomer than this rather weedy
effort, which seems to come straight off the mixing desk. This was a group reaching not so much the end
of its natural span as that moment when the constituent personalities began to move outwards in their
own personal quests, the responsiveness paradoxically increased song on song. The end result is a poor
documentation of what was clearly a wonderful concert in Seville. It may be that a recording was not
originally intended, in which case this is a very welcome souvenir of a great band – sample 'Have A
Little Faith In Me' – which in more amenable settings could sound very special indeed.

    The Keaton project – one of a slew inspired by silent movies – is immaculately recorded and as a result is
convincing enough to overcome the tattiness of much of the material. One of the problems of this sort
of thing is that there really isn't enough for the players to get their teeth into. Frisell battles and wins.
Baron, as so often, is a revelation, clattery but with an unfailing swing and sense of the shape of a
melody. Driscoll, who suffered most from the ungenerous balance on *Live*, comes through full-chested
and resonant, and where much of Frisell's effects-based work was not properly registered on the Seville
tapes, he is absolutely on the case here.

*** **American Blood / Safety In Numbers** veraBra vBr 2064
    Frisell; Brian Ales (*elec*); Victor Bruce Godsey (*v*). 94.
'All sounds on this recording are made by the guitar or the human voice.' *Safety In Numbers* is the result
of Ales's sampling and manipulation of a 27-minute guitar solo by Frisell, who seems then to have
played a live guitar part over the resultant tape. *American Blood* features lyrics by Godsey with somewhat less totalizing manipulation from Ales. The results are two dense collage pieces, very much in
keeping with Frisell's other work as far back as *Smash And Scatteration*, but also subtly differentiated by
the input of his two collaborators. Interesting, rather than compellingly involving.

David Frishberg (born 1933) PIANO, VOCAL

**** **Classics** Concord CCD 4462
    Frishberg; Steve Gilmore (*b*); Bill Goodwin (*d*). 12/82–3/83.
***(*) **Live At Vine Street** Original Jazz Classics OJC 832
    Frishberg (*p, v* solo). 10/84.
*** **Can't Take You Nowhere** Fantasy FCD 9651
    Frishberg (*p* solo). 87.
*** **Let's Eat Home** Concord CCD 4402
    Frishberg; Snooky Young (*t*); Rob McConnell (*vtb*); Jim Hughart (*b*); Jeff Hamilton (*d*). 1/89.
*** **Where You At?** Bloomdido BL 010
    Frishberg; Glenn Ferris (*tb*); Turk Mauro (*bs*); Michel Gaudry (*b*). 3/91.

*** **Double Play** Arbors ARCD 19118
     Frishberg; Jim Goodwin (*c*). 10/92.

Although Frishberg himself notes that a supply sergeant once told him that 'Jazz is OK, but it ain't got no words', he has done his best to deliver hip songwriting in a form that fits with his individual brand of mainstream piano. If he's become best known as a cabaret recitalist, Frishberg nevertheless has a strong, swinging keyboard style that borrows from the swing masters without making him seem like a slavish copyist. He has worked extensively as a sideman and seems most suited to swing-styled groups with enough space for him to let loose his favourite, rolling, two-fisted solos. Of those recordings under his own name currently in print, *Classics* is the best, since it gathers all his best-known songs together on a single CD (which is a reissue of two LPs made for Omnisound). Sparsely but crisply presented by the trio, here are the prototype versions of such Frishberg favourites as 'My Attorney Bernie', 'Dodger Blue' and 'Do You Miss New York?', bittersweet odes which he is very good at investing with both warmth and wryness. The sound has been dried out by CD remastering but isn't disagreeable.

    A fine live set for Fantasy has now made it to CD in the OJC series. It's a useful souvenir of an evening with Frishberg: some of his smartest songs, a Johnny Hodges medley where he gets to show off his pianism, and the corncrake voice put to work on his wryest lyrics. A special favourite of ours is the opener, 'You Would Rather Have The Blues', but any of his nine songs here sound good. *Can't Take You Nowhere* is a few more pages from Frishberg's notebooks of Americana, as is the recent Concord set, although the horns are more of a distraction than a bonus. Actually, the three other participants on the Bloomdido session add some useful seasoning. This time there are medleys dedicated to Ellington and (a nice touch) Ivie Anderson.

    Double Play is one where he keeps his voice down, and plays alongside the salty cornet of Jim Goodwin. They make a good fist of a fine clutch of old songs ('One, Two, Button My Shoe' was an inspired choice) and Goodwin's thick, rasping tone is unfailingly entertaining, but sometimes the sameyness of Frishberg's piano deflates the occasion.

Frisque Concordance GROUP

***(*) **Spellings** Random Acoustics RA 001
     John Butcher (*ts, ss*); Georg Gräwe (*p*); Hans Schneider (*b*); Martin Blume (*d*). 10/92.

Founded by the classically-inclined Gräwe, this free-music group hinges on the relationship between the pianist and the young British saxophonist who has become one of the most roundedly accomplished European players in this idiom. The fact that Gräwe runs the label (this item is issued in a plain, grey card cover) in no way compromises quality control. All five lettered 'Spellings', of steadily increasing length, seem to combine the title's promise of linguistic straightforwardness and magic combined. There is a certain amount of Morse and background traffic on 'A' and 'B' but, once the pace has picked up – and we are assuming that the music is tracked in the order recorded – there is a whirling intensity and mystery which owners of Butcher's *Thirteen Friendly Numbers* will recognize. Our only slight reservations relate to the bassist and drummer, who sometimes seem to drift away from the main action.

Tony Fruscella (1927–69) TRUMPET

*** **Tony's Blues** Cool N' Blue CD107
     Fruscella; Chick Maures, Phil Woods (*as*); Bill Triglia, Hank Jones (*p*); Red Mitchell, Wendell Marshall, Paul Chambers (*b*); Dave Troy, Shadow Wilson, Roy Hall (*d*). 12/48–11/55.

Despite a formidable reputation among some collectors, Fruscella has remained an obscure figure. This CD patches together much of his small legacy of recording and makes a modest case for his standing. The studio session with Chick Maures (previously on Spotlite SPJ 126) forms the central body of work: pale, interesting bebop with a glance towards Tristano, and the two horns play carefully spun improvisations that at least take a different tack from bop convention. The rest is live material from 1955: a blues with Hank Jones, pleasingly done, and three somewhat desultory jams with a quintet including Phil Woods, whose usual ebullience is the opposite of Fruscella's deferential playing. The sound on these is scruffy but listenable. We still await the reissue of Fruscella's sole album for Atlantic, which is surely his best work. The trumpeter died a melancholy death in 1969, many years wasted through addiction.

Wolfgang Fuchs SOPRANINO SAX, CLARINET, BASS CLARINET, CONTRABASS CLARINET

(*) **FinkFarker FMP CD 26
     Fuchs; Georg Katzer (*elec*). 6/89.

***(*) **Binaurality** FMP CD 49
>   Fuchs; Gunter Christmann, Radu Malfatti (*tb*); Peter Van Bergen (*ts, bcl, cbcl*); Luc Houtkamp
>   (*as, ts, cl*); Phil Wachsmann (*vn, elec*); Melvyn Poore (*tba*); Torsten Muller (*b*); Paul Lytton (*d,
>   elec*); Georg Katzer (*elec, computer*). 6/92.

Fuchs is an improviser who's especially interested – as his choice of instruments suggests – in timbral
extremes. He gets squalling, hysterical sounds out of the sopranino and the bass-clarinet, phrases diced
into the smallest fragments, and, while one can construe lines out of the sonic splinters, deconstruction
is Fuchs's speciality. *FinkFarker* operates across wide soundscapes, the reed player combating Katzer's
electronics in pieces entitled 'Vicious', 'Confrontation' and so on. Interesting but rarefied.

Binaurality is by Fuchs's larger group, King Ubu Orchestra. As big as the ensemble is, Fuchs has clearly
thought very carefully about the balance of instruments and the differing nature of the players, and the
result is a free group of unusually specific empathies. The cloudy nature of the brass instruments
contrasts with the filigree, pecking lines of the reed players, with Wachsmann's elegance and the
unpredictable elements of Lytton and Katzer adding to the flavour without distorting any lines of
communication. As always with this kind of music, there are dead ends and disappointments as well as
achievements: 'Translation No. 4', for instance, loses its way at the half-way mark after an utterly
riveting development – it peters out into typical free-jazz crescendo and diminuendo. Yet there are so
many fascinating passages here that the record demands a full hearing.

Curtis Fuller (born 1934) TROMBONE

*** **New Trombone** Original Jazz Classics OJC 077
>   Fuller; Sonny Red (*as*); Hank Jones (*p*); Doug Watkins (*b*); Louis Hayes (*d*). 5/57.
*** **Blues-ette** Savoy SV 0127
>   Fuller; Benny Golson (*ts*); Tommy Flanagan (*p*); Jimmy Garrison (*b*); Al Harewood (*d*). 5/59.

Curtis Fuller made his mark on one of the most memorable intros in modern jazz, the opening bars of
Coltrane's 'Blue Train', and, for many, the story stops there; ironically, since it was hardly a representative moment in his career. Fuller's contribution to that rather overrated album was well below par and
he was probably not an ideal choice for the gig in the first place. Possessed of an excellent technique, if
slightly derivative of J. J. Johnson, he occasionally found it difficult to develop ideas at speed and tended
to lapse back (as on 'Blue Train') into either repetition or sequences of bitten-off phrases that sounded
either diffident or aggressive, depending on the context. Generally he has a soft-focus, almost
saxophone-like delivery, mixed in with rich bell notes and a trademark enharmonic slide that often
creates an ambiguity not accessible to keyed and valved horn players.

Blues-ette is far and away his finest available album (three good Blue Notes are currently missing in
action). Fuller sounds much more confident than on the early – and honestly titled – *New Trombone*,
which has promise rather than finish. Golson is a strong and supportive player and Flanagan's quick
fills more than make up for any residual shortcomings in the longer solos.

*** **The Curtis Fuller Jazztet** Savoy SV 0134
>   Fuller; Lee Morgan (*tb*); Benny Golson (*ts*); Wynton Kelly (*p*); Paul Chambers (*b*); Charli
>   Persip (*d*). 8/59.
*** **Imagination** Savoy SL 0128
>   Fuller; Thad Jones (*t*); Benny Golson (*ts*); McCoy Tyner (*p*); Jimmy Garrison (*b*); Dave Bailey
>   (*d*). 12/59.
*** **Images of Curtis Fuller** Savoy SL 0129
>   Fuller; Wilbur Harden, Lee Morgan (*t*); Yusef Lateef (*ts, f*); McCoy Tyner (*p*); Jimmy Garrison,
>   Milt Hinton (*b*); Bobby Donaldson, Clifford Jarvis (*d*). 6/60.

For those familiar with Fuller's work on *Blue Train*, his introductory solo on 'Accident', first track on
Images, will strike an immediate chord. Its big, vocalized blues tonalities are typical of his work of the
period, and these reissues (along with *Blues-ette*) represent the trombonist's most coherent and successful playing. Golson is a particularly sympathetic partner, as are the trumpeters, and Lateef produces a
beautiful intro and solo on flute (not credited on the re-packaging) to 'Darryl's Minor'.

What emerges most strongly from these albums is the strength and individuality of the trombonist's
writing. Numbers such as the mysterious 'Lido Road' (*Imagination*) and the impressionistic 'Arabia'
(*Jazztet*) bespeak a remarkable talent. The remasterings are rather 'dead' and unresonant, but in that
regard do little more than reproduce the shortcomings of the original releases, which completely lacked
the vibrancy one associates with Blue Note. The liner-notes – with original art-work included – are
unreliable and occasionally inconsistent.

** **Four On The Outside** Timeless SJP 124
>   Fuller; Pepper Adams (*bs*); James Williams (*p*); Dennis Irwin (*b*); John Yarling (*d*). 9/78.

(*) **Meets Roma Jazz Trio Timeless SJP 204
 Fuller; Danilo Rea (*p*); Enzo Pietropaoli (*b*); Roberto Gatto (*d*). 12/82.
Fuller's career drifted into the doldrums after the mid-1960s and took some time to recover. Though the band is unexceptionable, *Four On The Outside* is curiously uncommunicative and Fuller's normally reliable medium blues phrasing sounds slightly off. The later Italian job is really much more interesting; Fuller has a lot of time to play with and judges his solo passages with greater ease.

***(*) **Blues-ette: Part II** Savoy SV 75624
 Fuller; Benny Golson (*ts*); Tommy Flanagan (*p*); Ray Drummond (*b*); Al Harewood (*d*). 1/93.
Thirty-five years on – half a lifetime – and the old gang reconvenes, minus Garrison, for a run-through of some familiar charts. There isn't quite the pep and bounce of the original session, but Fuller still has that lovely wuffly tone, as if the horn is wrapped in velvet, and Flanagan has become so urbane in the intervening years that the session has almost an ambassadorial gravity and solidity. Golson's contribution is sterling as always, though he is a little too forthright on 'Bluesette '93' for the balance of the piece.

Full Monte GROUP

*** **Spark In The Dark** Slam CD 209
 Chris Biscoe (*as, ss, acl*); Brian Godding (*g, g syn*); Marcio Mattos (*b*); Tony Marsh (*d, perc*). 11/90, 12/93.
Biscoe and Godding were regular playing partners in the Mike Westbrook Orchestra; Mattos and Marsh are mainstays of British free jazz. As a unit, they cover a lot of bases. The great beauty of the sound is its textural variety. Godding and Mattos take a great deal of credit for that, but not all of it, for Marsh is an atmospheric drummer and Biscoe makes full use of his horns (including the increasingly popular alto clarinet) to give each track a distinctive character.

 Formed in 1988, the group has the old shoe feel you get only from settled combinations. All but two of the tracks have been in the can for some time (dating from the time of Slam's *Saxophone Phenomenon* compilation), but the longer of the two recent cuts (the other, 'Wind Dance', is only two minutes long) suggests that they've continued to get to know one another over the intervening time. 'Spiritual Cleavage II' is testimony to the members' spiritual empathy.

Fun Horns GROUP

*** **Surprise** Jazzpoint JP 1029
 Joachim Hesse (*t, flhn*); Jorg Huke (*tb*); Volker Schlott (*ss, as, f, af*); Thomas Klemm (*ts, f, v*). 7/90.
**** **Live In South America** Klangraume 30060
 As above, except Rainer Brennecke (*t, flhn*) replaces Hesse. 3–5/92.
(***) **Weihnachtsoratorium** Klangraume 30090
 As above, except add Karl Scharnweber (*org*), Wolfgang Schmiedt (*g*). 8/93.
Whoever did the christening got it right. These bare-faced Germans (they bare rather more on the cover of *Live In South America*) have the cheek to establish a four-man quartet that's neither all-sax nor all-brass and then proceed to demonstrate an encyclopedic knowledge of improv, classical and even some jazz techniques. *Surprise* is an occasionally cautious start – some of the tracks are charmingly inconsequential, like the sweetly voiced 'Berceuse', and others fly past too quickly; but there is some marvellous stuff in the longer tracks – counterpoint, bizarre harmony, top-class soloing. They are most fun (and most Fun) in concert, which makes the *South America* album essential: the enormous 'Suite For F-Horns' is a masterpiece, the winsome 'Fei Gett'n-Tanz' is gorgeous, and their blues pastiche had them rolling in the aisles. Imperfect sound, but no matter. The recent collaboration with organist Scharnweber on an extended and surprisingly straight transcription of Bach is a bit of a shock, and scarcely belongs here, but the curious may find it rewarding. Meanwhile, the world waits for their collision with Billy Jenkins (already consummated in concert).

Stéphane Furic DOUBLE BASS

*** **Kishinev** Soul Note 121215
 Furic; Chris Cheek (*ts, ss*); Patrick Goraguer (*p*); Jim Black (*d*). 7/90.
***(*) **The Twitter-Machine** Soul Note 121225
 As above. 5/92.

French born bassist Furic's debut includes material by Lil Hardin Armstrong ('Two Deuces'), Ornette Coleman ('The Sphinx'), as well as original themes, which include an eponymous tribute to Wayne Shorter. It's a bold and remarkably self-possessed beginning which very definitely registers his concern with a wider jazz tradition and with aspects of the idiom – collective improvisation, melodic development – that sometimes seem to be marginalized in contemporary playing.

With an identical line-up, *The Twitter-Machine* delivers on the earlier record's promise and, on reflection, probably does the job more convincingly. The title comes from a Paul Klee graphic of a mechanical singing bird, four voices conjoined to a single mechanism. That's broadly the impact of the music. Chris Cheek, soloing impressively throughout, contributes the opening 'Could You Be There?'. Furic's own writing is muted and often quite complex, suggesting nothing more than Austrian trumpeter Franz Koglmann's wry palimpsests on the jazz tradition. The most remarkable of his pieces is the brief 'Harvest Song', a tense and dramatic theme inspired by Coltrane's duets with Rashied Ali, and also by the drones in Pakistani music. Jim Black's 'The Moon Breathed Twice' could almost be a Koglmann title, but for its essential simplicity of statement. There is a gloriously sober version of Prince's 'Diamonds And Pearls', with Furic mimicking a thumb-struck electric bass. It's a further reminder, as Kevin Whitehead points out in his liner-note, that the bassist's first inspiration was Miles Davis, not just the classic '50s quintet but the latter-day eclectic as well.

Slim Gaillard (1916–90) PIANO, GUITAR, VOCAL

(*) **Original 1938 Recordings – Volume 1 Tax S 1
> Gaillard; Slam Stewart (*b, v*); Kenneth Hollon (*ts*); Sam Allen (*p*); Pompey Dobson (*d*). 2–11/38.

(*) **Original 1938–9 Recordings – Volume 2 Tax S 2
> As above, except add Al Killian, Cyril Neman (*t*); Herman Flintall (*as*); Loumell Morgan (*p*); William Smith (*b*); Herbert Pettaway (*d*). 11/38–4/40.

(*) **Original 1940–2 Recordings – Volume 3 Tax S 3
> Similar to above. 40–42.

*** **Slim Gaillard, 1937–1938** Classics 705
> As the above. 37–38.

***(*) **Slim Gaillard, 1939–1940** Classics 724
> Gaillard; Henry Goodwin, Cyril Newman, Al Killian (*t*); Garvin Bushell (*cl*); Herman Flintall (*as*); Kenneth Hollon (*ts*); Loumell Morgan (*p*); William Smith (*b*); Herbert Pettaway (*d*). 9/39–8/40.

*** **Slim Gaillard, 1940–1942** Classics 787
> Similar to the above. 40–42.

*** **Trio – Quartet – Orchestra** Jazz Anthology 550282
> Gaillard; Karl George, Howard McGhee (*t*); Teddy Edwards, Wild Bill Moore, Lucky Thompson (*ts*); Dodo Marmarosa, Fletcher Smith (*p*); Tiny Bam Brown (*b*); Zutty Singleton (*d*); Leo Watson (*d, v*). 45.

***(*) **Laughing In Rhythm: The Best Of The Verve Years** Verve 521 651
> Gaillard; Taft Jordan (*t*); Bennie Green (*tb*); Buddy Tate, Ben Webster (*ts*); Tiny Bam Brown, Cyril Haynes, Maceo Williams (*p*); Ray Brown, Clyde Lombardi (*b*); Milt Jackson, Charlie Smith (*d*); Jim Hawthorne (*v*). 4/46–1/54.

*** **The Legendary McVouty** Hep CD 6
> Gaillard; Jay Thomas (*t*); Digby Fairweather (*c*); Buddy Tate, Jay Thomas (*ts*); Jay McShann (*p*); Peter Ind (*b*); Allan Ganley (*d*). 10/82.

Gaillard must be the only jazz musician ever quoted in public by Ronald Reagan. Which gives Democrats an easy out. Gaillard's presence on the Savoy Parkers makes it harder for the purists, much as they may prefer, to ignore him. An element of sheer capriciousness – verbal, musical, personal – was always at the heart of the bebop movement and the hipster lifestyle it purported to distil and reflect. Gaillard was probably the last and most unreconstructed survivor of that era, a reminder of its lighter side. His brand of humour, centred largely on a hip dialect known as 'vout', either tickles you or it doesn't, but it's hard to maintain reserve in the face of 'Laughin' In Rhythm', 'Sploghm' and 'Hit That Mess', and it's clear that Gaillard's more purely musical output, and particularly the highly popular sessions with Slam Stewart, deserve and have recently received a posthumous rethink.

The Verves are a little more contrived, but there is still some astonishing musicianship buried in these hectic sessions. The long 'Opera In Vout (Groove Juice Symphony)' is a *tour de force*, and 'Genius' has Gaillard out-sidneying Bechet with a one-man-band overdub of manic proportions. The 1951 tracks (including 'Chicken Rhythm') incorporate various Ellingtonians, and the Shintoists group conjured some slight but mellowly beautiful solos out of Ben Webster.

The 1982 Hep sessions reintroduced Gaillard to a younger audience. His energy is extraordinary and his mind constantly, laterally inventive. His mainly British sidemen (Gaillard eventually settled in London) are not too po-faced about the whole thing, and it chugs along splendidly. The 1945 thing isn't as spontaneously wacky as the earlier material. You get the feeling that 'vout' had become a marketable and packageable act. It still swings, but do it swing like it useta?

There's not much overlap between the Taxes and the *Chronological* compilation, so they're all worth having unless you're allergic to vout. The Tax CDs are identical with the earlier *Slim And Slam* LPs, give or take an alternative take-oroonie. You picks your licks.

Larry Gales (born 1936) BASS, VOCAL

(*) A Message From Monk Candid CCD 79503
> Gales; Claudio Roditi (*t*); Steve Turre (*tb*); Junior Cook (*ts*); Benny Green (*p*); Ben Riley (*d*). 6/90.

There could hardly be a more appropriate rhythm section for a tribute to Monk than this one, since both Gales and Riley were veterans from the master's own quartet. It's a pity, then, that this otherwise quite spirited set, recorded live at New York's Birdland, has a few crucial failings. Cook in particular sounds tired and ill-prepared, and yet he is the most featured of the horns: as a result 'Off Minor' and 'Ruby My Dear' sound ragged. Turre is easily the most characterful soloist, with pungent improvisations on 'Straight No Chaser' and the one Gales original, 'A Message From The High Priest'; and Roditi also takes some pleasing risks on the latter tune. Green tries to work his way out of seeming like the Monk substitute and does well enough, and Gales and Riley play dependably; but Larry's vocal on ''Round Midnight' wasn't the best idea in the world. The location recording is well managed.

Richard Galliano ACCORDION, PIANO, KEYBOARDS, TROMBONE

***(*) Spleen** Dreyfus Jazz Line FDM 36513
> Galliano; Dennis Leloup (*tb*); Eric Giausserand (*flhn*); Franck Stibon (*p, syn, v*); Jean-Marc Jafet (*b*); Luiz Augusto (*d, perc*). 6/85.
*** **Coloriage** Quadrivium SCA 031
> Galliano; Gabriele Mirabassi (*cl*). 7/92.
*** **Viaggio** Dreyfus Jazz Line FDM 36562
> Galliano; Bireli Lagrene (*g*); Pierre Michelot (*b*); Charles Bellonzi (*d*). 6/93.
**** **Laurita** Dreyfus Jazz Line FDM 36572
> Galliano; Michel Portal (*bcl*); Didier Lockwood (*vn*); Toots Thielemans (*hca*); Palle Danielsson (*b*); Joe Baron (*d*). 11/94.

It is, on the face of it, surprising that there have not been more top-flight jazz accordionists. Galliano is a master of the instrument, a compelling improviser with a wonderfully expressive sound and a subtle swing, mostly in three-quarter time and tango rhythms. He is by no means in thrall to Astor Piazzolla but, like any accordion player, draws heavily on the master for compositions (notably 'Libertango' on the very wonderful *Laurita*).

Original material like 'Spleen' and 'Il Viaggio' is well trodden, and the very pared-down instrumentation on the Quadrivium disc is a good place to sample both these pieces and to get a measure on Galliano's style. The earliest album is something of a collage, pieced together in a slightly ramshackle way that has distinct charm but lacks an element of finish. The group with Lagrene, on the contrary, is a blowing gig, with plenty of solo space for all concerned. We like *Laurita* for the way it puts the two together. Galliano uses his guests tastefully and intelligently. Portal's brooding sound lifts the opening number, a Hermeto Pascoal; Thielemans is mistily beautiful on the title-piece and then Lockwood lifts 'Decisione' and whirls it away like a cross between Grapelli and a New Orleans clarinet player. Exhilarating stuff, beautifully recorded.

Joe Gallivan DRUMS, PERCUSSION

***(*) Innocence** Cadence CJT 1051
> Gallivan; Guy Barker, Claude Deppa, Gerard Presencer (*t*); Paul Rutherford (*tb*); Ashley Slater (*btb*); Neil Metcalfe (*f*); Elton Dean (*as, saxello*); Evan Parker (*ts, ss*); Marcio Mattos (*b*). 8/91.

Cast in cycles of form, freedom and surrender, Gallivan's suite of pieces concerns the innocence of creative music-making in an essentially pragmatic culture. Though the basic structures are scored, they are left open for both the ensemble and the soloists to explore their own natures and thereby renounce control to the flow of ideas and inspirations.

Grandiose, perhaps, but it works. Gallivan has assembled a band of old friends from his years in London (he is now based in Hawaii), with the addition of younger players like Presencer and Deppa and, a last-minute recruit, flautist Neil Metcalfe, who brings an air of thoughtful simplicity to the opening 'Materialism'. On 'Voices Of Ancient Children', Evan Parker combines darkly with Elton Dean, establishing a sonority that will run through the rest of the session. Much of the action centres on bass and drums, with horns freely voiced on top. Gallivan states openly that he regards his rhythm-section partner, Marcio Mattos, as the most important person in the band. The bassist's cadenza on 'Marcio's Maze' is magnificent, as poised and centred as if it had been written out, but searching too.

Gallivan has two or more instruments introduce each piece, setting up dialogues which then determine the flow of ideas in the main action. The method's strongly reminiscent of Gil Evans, the drummer's friend and great inspiration. The ultimate compliment for *Innocence* would be to say that Evans would have appreciated it.

Jim Galloway (born 1936) SOPRANO SAXOPHONE

*** **Kansas City Nights** Sackville SKCD 2 3057
      Galloway; Sandy Barter, Arnie Chycoski, Dave Johnson, Brigham Phillips (*t*); Lawrie Bower, Doug Gibson, Scott Suttie (*tb*); Gordon Evans, Ingrid Stitt (*as*); Bob Brough, Fraser MacPherson (*ts*); Del Dako (*bs*); Jay McShann (*p*); Martin Loomer (*g*); Rosemary Galloway (*b*); Jake Hanna (*d*). 4/93.

Galloway was born in Scotland (in the former mining region of Ayrshire) and moved to Canada aged 28. He has a slightly rough-hewn, Bechet-influenced style on the soprano but is a capable soloist who seldom wastes a point; Ayrshire men seldom do. Some of his best work can be found in the company of Art Hodes, and this live session by Galloway's Wee Big Band is mainly interesting for the inclusion of McShann, Hann and MacPherson, who are listed as guests. The veteran KC pianist certainly lifts the rhythm section with his easy swing, and Hanna would be more of a joy to listen to if the recording – straight to two-track DAT at the Montreal Bistro – were a little better modulated. A pretty routine trawl of Galloway's favourite repertoire: the title-song, 'Blue And Sentimental', a very good 'Moten Swing' and a rousing finish on 'One O'Clock Jump'. Thoroughly enjoyable.

Hal Galper (born 1938) PIANO, KEYBOARDS

***(*) **Reach Out** Steeplechase CCD 31067
      Galper; Randy Brecker (*t*); Mike Brecker (*ts, f*); Wayne Dockery (*b*); Billy Hart (*d*). 11/76.
*** **Now Hear This** Enja 2090
      Galper; Terumasa Hino (*t, flhn*); Cecil McBee (*b*); Tony Williams (*d*). 2/77.
(*) **Ivory Forest Enja 3053
      Galper; John Scofield (*g*); Wayne Dockery (*b*); Adam Nussbaum (*d*). 10–11/79.
(*) **Dreamsville Enja 5029
      Galper; Steve Gilmore (*b*); Bill Goodwin (*d*). 3/86.
**** **Portrait** Concord CCD 4383
      Galper; Ray Drummond (*b*); Billy Hart (*d*). 2/89.
(*) **Live At Maybeck Recital Hall Concord CCD 4438
      Galper (*p* solo). 7/90.
***(*) **Invitation To A Concert** Concord CCD 4455
      Galper; Todd Coolman (*b*); Steve Ellington (*d*). 11/90.
*** **Tippin'** Concord CCD 4540
      As above, except Wayne Dockery (*b*) replaces Coolman. 11/92.

Galper's wide, sweeping keyboard style needs bass and drums to salt a touch of sugariness that creeps in from time to time. The solo Maybeck Hall set is unusually self-sufficient in this regard. Galper's touch is exact; the ideas come unimpeded but rarely glibly. There is, though, a lack of any real drama, and the set doesn't repay repeated hearings.

Reach Out is a vivid, hard-hitting set. The Brecker brothers have seldom combined so effectively under anyone else's leadership, and the arrangements are razor-fine. The later *Speak With A Single Voice* lacks tension and sounds slightly slack on vinyl. Though Hino is a limited soloist with a narrow improvisational range, McBee and Williams lift *Now Hear This* all on their own.

Of the trios, *Portrait* stands out, for a wonderfully profound 'Giant Steps' that rivals Tommy

Flanagan's. The Randy Weston tune is also worked over on *Dreamsville*, but the drummer sounds slightly off and the vinyl-only format is a bit lacking in resonance and bounce.

The star of the fine *Ivory Forest* is Scofield, who plays a brilliant, unaccompanied 'Monk's Mood' that cuts through the thicket with almost brutal efficiency. Galper plays a duo with the guitarist ('Continuity') and with Dockery ('Yellow Days'), and there are three strong quartet tracks.

The post-Maybeck Concords (A M and P M have become important historical benchmarks for piano players) are both very smooth, but without the florid chromatic embellishment that Galper might once have resorted to. He's still an immensely elegant player, but a growing understanding of ancestors like Monk has straightened out his conception very considerably, and much to his benefit.

***(*) **Just Us** Enja E NJ 8058
      Galper; Jerry Bergonzi (*ts*); Pat O'Leary (*b*); Steve Ellington (*d*). 9/93.
This is a pretty straightforward session, but not without subtleties and elegance. At first blush, Bergonzi doesn't sound quite the right kind of horn player for Galper's conception, but he fits in from the off and contributes very considerably to a relaxed and very swinging set. The high point is unquestionably the leader's solo on 'Lover Man', a tissue of pianistic references that confirms his familiarity with the literature. As always, it is Galper's intelligence and taste that we applaud. Fireworks can be exhilarating, but these are more lasting satisfactions.

Ganelin Trio GROUP

    **** **Catalogue: Live In East Germany** Leo CD LR 102
        Vyacheslav Ganelin (*p, basset, g, perc*); Vladimir Chekasin (*as, ts, basset cl, cl, ob, v, perc*);
        Vladimir Tarasov (*d, perc*). 77–82.
    **** **Poco A Poco** Leo CD LR 101
        As above.
    ***(*) **Encores** Leo CD LR 106
        As above. 6/78, 10/80, 11/81.
    **** **. . . Old Bottles** Leo CD LR 112
        As above. 6/82, 3/83.
    ***(*) **Non Troppo** hat Art CD 6059
        As above.
One of the genuinely significant moments in recent jazz history occurred in March 1984 at the Bloomsbury Theatre in London, when the Ganelin Trio, an improvising group from the Soviet Union, played a concert organized under the auspices of the Arts Council Contemporary Music Network and attended by an unprecedented claque of musicians (whose expectations were, in the event, confounded and disappointed), arts administrators, journalists and mysterious raincoats from the Soviet Embassy. The Ganelin Trio's work was already known in Britain through the good offices of Leo Feigin, who had released smuggled tapes of the group on his Leo Records, and it had acquired a certain *samizdat* mystique which almost outweighed the impact of what was certainly the most dramatic development in jazz performance since the New Thing of the 1960s.

The Trio had been performing together for nearly 13 years when the London performance took place but had received Soviet release only in 1976, following a successful appearance at the Jazz Jamboree in Warsaw. The Trio's output was a series of improvised suites, most of them bearing deceptively neutral titles, drawn from classical music performance but developed in a way which diverges sharply both from 'classical' orthodoxies and from the surprisingly restrictive conventions of jazz. In the first place, it is clear that underlying the work of the Ganelin Trio – as of Sergey Kuryokhin and other Russian musicians released by Leo Feigin – is a strong element of theatricality, a tradition of licensed foolery that (carried to pretty severe lengths, it has to be admitted) alienated much of the audience at the Bloomsbury Theatre in 1984. Chekasin's outbursts of lunacy and Tarasov's deliberately undynamic drumming opened the Trio to charges of wilful perversity and aesthetic nihilism that are wholly contradicted by the body of music now available on record, which is densely structured (though not according to orthodox Western principles) and expressive.

For all its evident dependence on bebop as a basic musical language, the Ganelin Trio is probably closer in spirit to the multi-instrumentalism and competitively tinged collectivism of the earliest jazz groups. There are, though, obvious parallels with figures such as Rahsaan Roland Kirk (Chekasin has adopted the simultaneous performance of two horns as a stage device), the Art Ensemble of Chicago, and even the Dave Brubeck Quartet (whose 'classical' approach made a big impact on Soviet jazz fans). What one sees in a Trio performance is an insanely accelerated history of jazz compressed into brief spans, each of which relates to the other in an ongoing process. Its apparent freedoms are relatively circumscribed and the group always clearly regarded performances as expositions of a composed work rather than spontaneous creations; there are now alternative performance recordings of several important pieces, affording a better understanding of the group's working methods.

Leo Feigin's label has been important not just in making the music available, but also in clearing up persistent misunderstandings about specific pieces and performances. For instance, the admirable Werner Uehlinger confused a long performance in Prague of the first part of *Ancora da Capo* with performances of parts one and two and of another work, *Non Troppo*, and inadvertently released them as such; they are grouped together on CD and listeners can simply ignore the incorrect track-titling. The appearance on Leo of a long Berlin performance of *Non Troppo*, paired with the previously issued *New Wine* . . . is a major step in sorting out the Trio's canon; *Non Troppo* is perhaps the group's darkest and grandest moment, and the Berlin performance has a physicality as well as intellectual sophistication that makes the music seem almost overwhelming, even on record. Enthusiasts should on no account miss this disc.

Newcomers should certainly begin with the first of Feigin's Ganelin Trio releases. *Catalogue* was created in 1981 as a summation of their first decade. This is one of the very important jazz records of recent times, despite the inadequacies of the recording; even on compact disc; the sound-quality is exceptionally poor, and it should clearly be understood that the high rating indicated above is based solely on its importance as a historical document. The tapes of *Catalogue* were brought to the West clandestinely and released with a disclaimer intended to protect the Trio from any association with a Western recording. The CD reissue includes a perceptive review by the critic, Efim Barban, originally published in the underground magazine *CHORUS*.

The piece is performed in a continuous cycle and alternates quiet, remarkably formal sections using what sounds like a formal, serial construction and only occasional eruptions of improvisational frenzy, with intense outbursts of sound in which Chekasin's saxophone is the main component. Like almost all the Trio's work, and most notably *Non Troppo*, the music is predominantly dark and tragic, and makes only a very specialized use of the traditional theme-and-variation format of jazz performance.

This technique *does*, however, play an important part in the second parts of both *Non Troppo* and *Ancora da Capo*, both of them profoundly healing pieces in which the presentation of a melodic theme (in the case of *Non Troppo* a standard, 'Too Close For Comfort') is seen as the culmination rather than the starting point of performance and may even have been done as a slap in the face to critics who criticized the group for their 'inability' to play standards-derived jazz. *Non Troppo* was also the basis of the 1984 Bloomsbury performace (a second piece from the concert, entitled *Old Bottles* and related to the *New Wine* suite, is available on Leo's encyclopaedic *Document: New Music From Russia – The '80s*).

One of the definitive characteristics of the Trio's sound is a dry, unpropulsive rhythm, an aspect that can make their work difficult for jazz fans to appreciate. Tarasov deliberately avoids any settled groove. There is no conventional bass either, though Ganelin makes very individual use of the basset. This is not to be confused with the basset-horn, or with the basset-clarinet played by Chekasin; it is in fact a small keyboard instrument which mimics the sound of a double bass but which lacks the rhythmic bounce that a string bass has, giving the Trio's 'bass line' a curiously lifeless initial impact that requires to be unpacked and rethought for listeners weaned on jazz bass.

In purely instrumental terms, the group probably never again reached the heights of *Catalogue: Live In East Germany*, where Chekasin's saxophone and bass clarinet playing is stunning. One doesn't want to draw attention and recognition away from Leo Feigin's achievement in bringing this music to the West, or to gloss over the inaccuracies of presentation, but hat Art's *Non Troppo* CD was a major technical step forward and set the acceptable standard for later releases. A number of LP releases *may* still be available direct from Leo Feigin, but supplies are now very scarce and second-hand racks may well be your best bet. The appearance of the *Encores* set plugs a few more gaps, with an important Moscow performance of *Con Fuoco*, the rather unlikely sound of the Ganelin Trio playing standards (*sic*!).

*** **San Francisco Holidays** Leo CD LR 208/209 2CD
    As above, but add ROVA Saxophone Quartet: Andrew Voigt (*as*); Larry Ochs (*ts*); Bruce
    Ackley (*ss*); Jon Raskin (*bs*). 6/86.
This catches the Trio in somewhat unguarded and relaxed form, much as the title suggests, on their first visit to the United States. A prevailing critical cliché compared what Ganelin, Tarasov and Chekasin were doing to the work of the Art Ensemble of Chicago, with much apologetic shuffling about its 'Russianness'. This had clearly less to do with the actual music played than with the whole ethos of performance. For musicians, to whom music does not in the first instance 'communicate', to perform in an environment where communication is of the essence requires a complete mental revolution, and there is little sign that the Trio was able or disposed to make it. Much of the tension has gone out of the music and there is an anxiously discursive quality to Ganelin's playing. The man sounding most at home is Tarasov, anticipating some of the work he was to do later with free-jazz luminaries like Andrew Cyrille. Chekasin, as always, remains an enigma.

There is a long, rather lifeless version of 'New Wine' and a very long piece called 'Ritardando', which is too persistently evasive and reticent to sustain interest over its 45-minute span. The Trio performs a rare standard, 'Moritat' or 'Mack The Knife', done with less irony than might be expected. Assessments of the two collaborative pieces with the ROVA Quartet (who had been in turn the first American avant-gardists to visit the Soviet Union) are likely to depend on how one feels about their usual fare. This was a symbolic moment rather than an effective musical combination and should be heard as such.

***(*) Opuses Leo CD LR 171
As above, except add Uri Abramovitch (*v*). 12/89.
In the mid-1980s, 'Slava' Ganelin defected to the West and took up residence in Israel. The music from this period is markedly different from the predominantly tragic and highly theatrical music of the original Trio. It is austere, sometimes to the point of frostiness, a development that is perhaps reflected in Ganelin's acquisition of a synthesizer, which he utilizes with notable restraint and to largely abstract effect, though more recent work has seen him develop in a more composerly direction (see below). The singing tones of 'Cantabile' and 'Cantus', Opus 3 of the excellent CD, are immediately less alien than any of the Russian-period pieces and a certain tension seems to have gone out of the music (in keeping, perhaps, with Sergey Kuryokhin's view that the lifting of cultural repression in the Soviet Union was a mixed blessing from a purely artistic point of view). On its own terms, though, this is a beautiful record, with moments that equal anything in the earlier catalogue. If *Catalogue*, *New Wine* or *Non Troppo* remain impenetrable, *Opuses* has a user-friendliness one doesn't find on the earlier material. It lacks some of the humour, unfortunately, but that is one of the prices one pays for freedom.

**** On Stage . . . Backstage Leo CD LR 216
Ganelin solo. 4/92, 7/93.
Throughout his career Slava Ganelin has always seemed to be pushing against the limitations of the instruments available to him. There was a faintly Heath Robinson, Rube Goldberg quality to the early work of the Trio but, if anything, it tended to camouflage just how ambitious a musician Ganelin himself was. The first fruits of his belated encounter with electronics were surprisingly tentative but, with the advance of the 1990s, he began to push off into areas of experiment that recalled nothing more strongly than his compatriot Aleksander Skryabin's desire to write for a giant super-instrument.

Skryabin never lived to see and hear his 'Mysterium' performed, but Ganelin has recently been able to work with a remarkable 'backstage' set-up, comprising digital sound-modules, synthesizers and multi-track recorders, that affords him similar dramatic potential. The dense, complex sound he makes 'onstage' with piano, synth and drums (one long, one short piece from Munich in spring 1992) is as nothing compared to the 'orchestrated improvisations' he creates with his integrated electronic system.

His ability to synthesize instrumental combinations – string quartet and percussion, viola and wind quartet, flugelhorn, tuba and drums, orchestra and chorus – and to have each permutation 'perform' at a level far beyond human capacity creates a musical language of immense potential . . . and some risk. At moments, the 'backstage' portions resemble nothing more than Frank Zappa's Synclavier epics on *Jazz From Hell* and are no less coldly brittle and forbidding. It's not clear from this vantage where Ganelin can go with this technology; the fear must be that the technology will run away with him.

Jan Garbarek (born 1947) TENOR SAXOPHONE, SOPRANO SAXOPHONE, BASS SAXOPHONE, FLUTES, KEYBOARDS, PERCUSSION

***(*) Afric Pepperbird ECM 1007
Garbarek; Terje Rypdal (*g, bugle*); Arild Andersen (*b*); Jon Christensen (*d*). 9/70.
*** Sart ECM 1015
As above, except add Bobo Stenson (*p*). 4/71.
Jan Garbarek's high, keening saxophone is perhaps the most readily universalized instrumental sound in contemporary music, regularly pressed into service on documentary soundtracks to evoke almost anything from the Chernobyl-blighted Lappish tundra to the African desert. He is also almost unique in being a one-label jazz artist. Their destinies have been so closely intertwined that it is difficult to tell whether ECM shaped Garbarek or he gave definitive voice to that chimera of contemporary music, the 'ECM sound'.

Afric Pepperbird was an astonishing label debut. By far his most 'out' recording, it exposes Garbarek's early Coltrane obsession at its most extreme, but also as it collides with other influences, notably Ayler's multiphonic intensity and Dexter Gordon's phrasing; his flute has a thin, folky timbre that is particularly effective when overblown. The rhythm partnership of Andersen and Christensen was hard to beat at the time (though Eberhard Weber and Palle Danielsson became the bassists of choice in future), and Rypdal's abstract, unmetrical chime-chords are more or less perfect. Production, as with virtually all that follows, can't be faulted.

Sart suffers considerably by comparison. On its own terms, it's a strong set. Garbarek again uses flute and bass saxophone in addition to his more familiar tenor (but at this stage, not the Wayne Shorter-inspired soprano that was to make such an impact on *Dansere* and *Dis*).

**** Triptykon ECM 1029
> Garbarek; Arild Andersen (*b*); Edward Vesala (*d, perc*). 11/72.

This is Garbarek's most 'outside' recording, and he isn't immediately recognizable to listeners who came up after *Dis*. There are signs already that both the saxophonist and Vesala are dissatisfied with free music, and Andersen is unmistakably hesitant about it, breaking up his rhythm shapes with the deliberateness of a man speaking a foreign language in which he is word-perfect but not quite idiomatic. The record also offers a very rare opportunity to hear Garbarek the multi-instrumentalist, doubling on soprano, baritone saxophone (a hint of Gullin, perhaps?) and flute. Ultimately, though, attention is diverted to the Finn, who plays brilliantly from start to finish; from the point of view of future projects, *Triptykon* says more about him.

** Red Lanta ECM 1038
> Garbarek; Art Lande (*p*). 11/73.

Garbarek's least-known ECM recording is an odd, dimly speculative affair that seems to go in no particular direction. Lande's keyboard style is quite abstract and only intermittently effective.

***(*) Witchi-Tai-To ECM 1041
> Garbarek; Bobo Stenson (*p*); Palle Danielsson (*b*); Jon Christensen (*d*). 11/73.
*** Dansere ECM 1075 / 8291932
> As above. 11/75.

Recorded at the same time as *Red Lanta*, *Witchi-Tai-To* is a more satisfactory album in almost every respect. Garbarek's intonation is much more relaxed, with a less pressurized embouchure and more sense of playing in distinct breath-groups or verses. Jim Pepper's surprise hit makes an appealing centre-piece to the album.

Dansere is as much Stenson's album as Garbarek's, and it would be good to hear more of the trio, which moves restlessly and often out of metre under some of Garbarek's most plaintive lines.

**** Dis ECM 1093
> Garbarek; Ralph Towner (*g, 12-string g*); wind harp; brass sextet. 12/76.
**** Places ECM 1118
> Garbarek; Bill Connors (*g*); John Taylor (*org*); Jack DeJohnette (*d*). 12/77.
*** Photo With Blue Sky ECM 1135
> Garbarek; Bill Connors (*g*); Eberhard Weber (*b*); Jon Christensen (*d*). 12/78.
*** Eventyr ECM 1200
> Garbarek; John Abercrombie (*g, 12-string g, mand*); Nana Vasconcelos (*talking d, perc, v*). 12/80.
*** Paths, Prints ECM 1223
> Garbarek; Bill Frisell (*g*); Eberhard Weber (*b*); Jon Christensen (*d*). 12/81.
*** Wayfarer ECM 1259
> As above, except omit Christensen; add Michael DiPasqua (*d, perc*). 3/83.

The end of the 1970s saw a pattern established whereby Garbarek went into the studio at each year's end to consolidate and capture what had been learnt in performance and to send out new feelers for the year ahead. One constant aspect of these albums (which are otherwise quite unalike) is Garbarek's use of a guitarist; see the beautiful *Folk Songs* (ECM 1170) with Charlie Haden and guitarist Egberto Gismonti. The early sessions with Rypdal were unrepeatable, and perhaps only Bill Frisell comes close; Towner and Abercrombie are strongly atmospheric players, but Connors is a trifle prosaic for this music.

Places is a small masterpiece, again dominated by one long track (a pattern that recurs throughout Garbarek's output). 'Passing' begins with misterioso organ from Taylor, tense drum rips from DeJohnette, and an unresolved, questioning figure on the guitar. Garbarek's entry picks it up without variation. There was by this point almost no linear argument in a Garbarek solo, just a static and very occasionally ponderous meditation on a figure of runic simplicity and mystery. Much of the power of *Dis*, Garbarek's most plundered album, works in a similar way, with a windharp and a brass group offering unstructured Aeolian backgrounds for plangent spells and riddles on soprano saxophone and wood flute.

** Aftenland ECM 1169
> Garbarek; Kjell Johnsen (*org*). 12/79.

On a checklist of ECM and Garbarek clichés, this scores quite highly. Nordic? Unmistakably. Moody? Certainly. Atmospheric? Definitely. But funky and swinging it surely isn't. Reminiscent of similar experiments by Keith Jarrett, it conspicuously lacks Jarrett's arrogant and insouciant self-confidence.

*** **It's OK To Listen To The Gray Voice** ECM 1294
> Garbarek. 84.

By this point in his career, Garbarek is possessed of an unmistakably individual voice. The weirdly titled *It's OK* (the reference is to a poem by Tomas Tranströmer) represents a consolidation rather than a new initiative. There are decided longueurs, but in sum it's classic Garbarek.

** **All Those Born With Wings** ECM 1324
> Garbarek (*saxes* solo). 8/86.

As with the wholly orchestral *Luminessence*, no longer listed, it was perhaps inevitable that Garbarek would attempt something like this. It is probably his weakest album since *Red Lanta*, with a dull aftertaste of introversion that is conspicuously missing from even his most meditative work elsewhere.

*** **Legend Of The Seven Dreams** ECM 1381
> Garbarek; Rainer Bruninghaus (*ky*); Eberhard Weber (*b*); Nana Vasconcelos (*perc, v*). 7/88.

*** **Rosensfole** ECM 1402
> Garbarek; Agnes Buen Garnas (*v*). 88.

*** **I Took Up The Runes** ECM 1419
> Garbarek; Rainer Bruninghaus (*p*); Eberhard Weber (*b*); Manu Katche (*d*); Nana Vasconcelos (*perc*); Bugge Wesseltoft (*syn*); Annte Ailu Gaup (*v*). 8/90.

Towards the end of the 1980s, Garbarek began to explore Nordic folk musics and myth in a more structured way, thus turning the casually unsubstantiated generalizations about his 'Nordic' style into a conveniently self-fulfilling critical prophecy. *Rosensfole* is really Garnas's album and is none the worse for that, Garbarek limited in the main to providing a shifting, minimal stage set for her rather dramatic singing. The opening 'He Comes From The North' on *Legend* is based on a Lappish *joik*, converted into state-of-the-art 'world music' by Vasconcelos's unplaceable percussion and vocal. There are also three brief, unaccompanied tracks, two on soprano saxophone, one on flute, to demonstrate how Garbarek has pared down his harmonic conception.

   Runes is in very much the same vein, but the experiment of adding a rock drummer and synthesizer player to the basic core trio of saxophone, piano and drums was an inspired one, and the long central track is one of Garbarek's most ambitious works to date. The energy of the live performances doesn't quite come across on the record, but there is more than enough of interest to bridge occasional repetitive lapses. The cassette format is above average throughout the ECM catalogue.

***(*) **Star** ECM 1444
> Garbarek; Miroslav Vitous (*b*); Peter Erskine (*d*). 1/91.

Initial expectations of a welcome return to serious jazz playing are slightly confounded by the disappointingly woolly opening track, the sole Garbarek composition, which does little more than lay out a palette of tone-colours. These, though, are imaginatively employed in a democratic trio session whose stripped-down configuration suits the saxophonist perfectly. The tone is still pristine, and Garbarek manages to infuse his tenor playing with the sort of brittle-edged fragility one normally associates with soprano. There is still a slight tendency to place long notes like monograms, but the signature is in a new, bolder sans-serif which reads as freshly as *Triptykon* did 20 years ago (20 years!). Vitous's playing has become much more purposive and surely grounded; it's interesting to note that the clouds are in the mountains now, not vice versa. Erskine doesn't at first seem the obvious choice for this session, but the obvious alternative – Jon Christensen – hasn't the simplicity and directness the session seems to call for. The (presumably) improvised 'Snowman' is indicative of how far Garbarek has progressed during his folksy sabbatical from blowing jazz, and it may even be a satirical response to all the editorial blah about his 'Nordic' cool and stiffness. It hardly seems necessary to say that the sound is superb; bass and drums well to the front.

***(*) **Ragas And Sagas** ECM 1442
> Garbarek; Manu Katché (*d*); Ustad Shaukat Hussain (*tabla*); Ustad Nazim Ali Khan (*sarangi*); Ustad Fateh Ali Khan, Deepika Thathaal (*v*). 5/90.

***(*) **Madar** ECM 1515
> Garbarek; Anouar Brahem (*oud*); Ustad Shaukat Hussain (*tabla*). 8/92.

By the turn of the 1990s, Garbarek's voice was the most completely internationalized in contemporary music. It sounded 'Nordic' only if one knew he was Norwegian. But as it began to slip its moorings to that rather reductive characterization, critics began to adduce other possibilities. Garbarek's father was Polish, so was he also 'Slavic'? Did his interest in Sami culture allow us to suggest an 'Asiatic' bent? And so forth.

   These two records are 'world music' in the most positive sense. They demonstrate the essential irreducibility of what Garbarek is about. Various Karnatic ideas had cropped up in his work before, and there are certain *raga*-like sequences even in the early albums. *Ragas And Sagas* was a perfectly logical step. It succeeds for the most part a good deal better than the collaboration with *oud* player Brahem (for whose records Garbarek has also recorded), but only because Garbarek himself is in better voice. Though the combination of Norwegian and non-European styles is every bit as seamless on both, Garbarek simply plays better with Hussain and his colleagues and dries up a little with Brahem.

**** Twelve Moons ECM 1500
> Garbarek; Rainer Bruninghaus (*ky*); Eberhard Weber (*b*); Manu Katché (*d*); Marilyn Mazur (*perc*); Agnes Buen Garnas, Mari Boine (*v*). 9/93.

Appropriately, it was Garbarek who was chosen to mark ECM's 500th release with this magnificently packaged offering. Musically it finds Garbarek at an interesting point of development, still exploring the folklore materials of *Rosensfole*, but also easing his way back into a more jazz-orientated programme. There's a very heavy emphasis on soprano saxophone, perhaps to blend better with the voices.

Katché is essentially a rock drummer with a crude but immensely vibrant delivery. It's closer to Vesala's heavy sound than to Christensen, and it seems to serve the saxophonist very well. This time around, in addition to the Sami *joik*s, he includes an arrangement of national composer Edvard Grieg's gentle 'Arietta', and a new version of the late Jim Pepper's 'Witchi-Tai-To', which has been a staple piece for much of his career. A beautiful record, and a credit to all concerned.

(****) Officium ECM New Series 1525
> Garbarek; Hilliard Ensemble (*v*). 9/93.

There is a certain irony in the detail that Garbarek's most successful recording to date is not a jazz date at all but an album of fourteenth- and fifteenth-century church music, arranged for vocal ensemble and saxophonist. *Officium* has huge appeal in keeping with the recent vogue for 'faith minimalism' and the New Age revival of ecumenicized liturgical music. Immaculately recorded as always, the record is so sheerly beautiful that few will not be moved by it, while not a few will wonder what place it has in Garbarek's artistic progress and in the development of late-twentieth-century music.

*** Visible World ECM 1585
> Garbarek; Rainer Bruninghaus (*p, ky*); Eberhard Weber (*b*); Marilyn Mazur (*d, perc*); Manu Katché (*d*); Trilok Gurtu (*tabla*); Mari Boine (*v*). 6/95.

As if to keep his way clearly marked out, Garbarek followed *Officium* with a record that quite consciously cemented long-standing relationships. The majority of the tracks are trios, with either Bruninghaus or Weber and Katché or Mazur. There are also some searching duos, including 'The Creek' with Katché, in which Garbarek appears to be experimenting in a quiet way with new rhythmic ideas. The longest track, 'Aftenlandet', was originally written as a music-video collaboration; featuring Boine and Mazur, it has a delicately mysterious quality. Garbarek briefly plays clarinet on this disc, suggesting that he may also be interested in hearing new colours and sounds. No overt sign of those emerging in the foreground, but lots of possibilities sketched into this essentially consolidating record.

Red Garland (1923–84) PIANO

*** A Garland Of Red Original Jazz Classics OJC 126
> Garland; Paul Chambers (*b*); Art Taylor (*d*). 8/56.
*** Groovy Original Jazz Classics OJC 061
> As above. 12/56–8/57.
*** Red Garland's Piano Original Jazz Classics OJC 073
> As above. 3/57.
*** Manteca Original Jazz Classics OJC 428
> As above, plus Ray Barretto (*perc*). 4/58.
*** Rediscovered Masters Vol. 1 Original Jazz Classics OJC 768
> As above. 6/58.
*** All Kinds Of Weather Original Jazz Classics OJC 193
> As above. 11/58.
*** Red In Bluesville Original Jazz Classics OJC 295
> As above, except Sam Jones (*b*) replaces Chambers. 4/59.
*** Rojo Original Jazz Classics OJC 772
> Garland; George Joyner (*b*); Charli Persip (*d*); Ray Barretto (*perc*). 8/58.
*** At The Prelude Vol. 1 Prestige 24132
> Garland; Jimmy Rowser (*b*); Specs Wright (*d*). 10/59.

Unassuming, graceful, yet authentically bluesy, Red Garland's manner was flexible enough to accommodate the contrasting styles of both Miles Davis and John Coltrane in the Davis quintet of the mid-1950s. His many records as a leader, beginning at about the same period, display exactly the same qualities. His confessed influences of Tatum, Powell and Nat Cole seem less obvious than his debts to

Erroll Garner and Ahmad Jamal, whose hit recording of 'Billy Boy' from the early 1950s seems to sum up everything that Garland would later go on to explore. All of the above trio sessions feature the same virtues: deftly fingered left-hand runs over bouncy rhythms coupled with block-chord phrasing which coloured melodies in such a way that Garland saw no need to depart from them. Medium-uptempo treatments alternate with stately ballads, and Chambers and Taylor are unfailingly swinging, if often constrained, partners. The later sessions feature a slightly greater empathy, but there is really very little to choose among these nine records, and favourite choices may depend on the tunes on each record, some of which are presented thematically (*All Kinds Of Weather*, for instance, is made up of 'Rain', 'Summertime', and so on). The guest role for Barretto on *Manteca* is a mostly peripheral one – he plays a quiet second line of percussion – although he's given a couple of lively features with Taylor on the title-tune and 'Lady Be Good'. The remastering is clean, although Chambers, while conspicuously present, is seldom awarded anything better than a dull bass sound. *At The Prelude* is a snapshot of Garland at work in a New York club, though he doesn't sound appreciably different away from the studios.

*** **All Mornin' Long** Original Jazz Classics OJC 293
    Garland; Donald Byrd (*t*); John Coltrane (*ts*); George Joyner (*b*); Art Taylor (*d*). 11/57.
***(*) **Soul Junction** Original Jazz Classics OJC 481
    As above. 11/57.
***(*) **High Pressure** Original Jazz Classics OJC 349
    As above. 11–12/57.
(*) **Dig It! Original Jazz Classics OJC 392
    As above, plus Paul Chambers (*b*). 3/57–2/58.

Garland's recordings with Coltrane are typical of the long, relaxed blowing sessions which Prestige were recording at the time, and some of the tracks are very long indeed: 'All Mornin' Long' runs for 20 minutes, 'Soul Junction' and 'Lazy Mae' from *Dig It!* for 16 apiece. There are inevitable longueurs in this approach, and Byrd, though accomplished, lacks the greater authority which he would bring to his later Blue Note albums. But there are some solos of immense power from the tenor saxophonist, and the playing on *Soul Junction* and *High Pressure* especially is as purposeful as the format allows (all the recordings from November 1957 were made on the same day). *Dig It!*, patched together from three sessions and including a fairly routine trio version of 'Crazy Rhythm', is slightly inferior. All four records have been remastered well.

***(*) **Rediscovered Masters Vol. 2** Original Jazz Classics OJC 769
    Garland; Richard Williams (*t*); Oliver Nelson (*as, ts*); Doug Watkins, Peck Morrison (*b*); Specs Wright, Charli Persip (*d*). 8/59–3/61.
(*) **Red Garland Trio With Eddie 'Lockjaw' Davis Vol. 1 Original Jazz Classics OJC 360
    Garland; Eddie 'Lockjaw' Davis (*ts*); Sam Jones (*b*); Art Taylor (*d*). 12/59.
(*) **Solar Original Jazz Classics OJC 755
    Garland; Les Spann (*g, f*); Sam Jones (*b*); Frank Grant (*d*). 1/62.
*** **When There Are Grey Skies** Original Jazz Classics OJC 704
    Garland; Wendell Marshall (*b*); Charli Persip (*d*). 9/62.

Davis appears on only three tracks of OJC 360, but it's enough to enliven an otherwise somnolent LP of ballads, originally issued in Prestige's Moodsville series; a stentorian reading of 'When Your Lover Has Gone' works especially well. The second volume of *Rediscovered Masters* couples a very good session by Red's favourite trio, with Watkins and Wright, strolling through a quickfire 'Blues In The Closet' and a long, languorous 'Mr Wonderful', with a scarce quintet date featuring Williams and Nelson in the front line: nothing extraordinary, but Nelson's sombre tenor makes a pleasing foil to Williams's more exuberant horn. *Solar* returns him to a rhythm format, although Les Spann's presence isn't very useful; and *When There Are Grey Skies* was to be Red's last album for nearly ten years. He delivers one of his most considered interpretations here in the almost painstaking exploration of 'Nobody Knows The Trouble I've Seen', beautifully sustained over some 12 minutes.

*** **Crossings** Original Jazz Classics OJC 472
    Garland; Ron Carter (*b*); Philly Joe Jones (*d*). 12/77.
(*) **Red Alert Original Jazz Classics OJC 647
    Garland; Nat Adderley (*c*); Harold Land, Ira Sullivan (*ts*); Ron Carter (*b*); Frank Butler (*d*). 12/77.
** **Misty Red** Timeless SJP 179
    Garland; Jamil Nasser (*b*); Frank Gant (*d*). 4/82.

Most of the few records Garland made in the 1970s and '80s have been deleted, and those that remain show his style unchanged, although some of the litheness went out of his touch. *Red Alert* is a decent if impersonal attempt at recapturing one of Red's old Prestige blowing dates: nice enough cameos by the horns, but the prettiest music is when they sit out and let the pianist play 'It's Impossible'. *Crossings* features such fine support from the rhythm section that the music gathers its own momentum, but the Timeless album is eventually rather dull.

Erroll Garner (1926–77) PIANO, HARPSICHORD

** Erroll Garner 1944 Classics 802
 Garner (*p* solo). 11–12/44.
**(*) Erroll Garner 1944 Vol. 2 Classics 818
 Garner (*p*); John Simmons (*b*); Doc West (*d*). 12/44.
** Erroll Garner 1944 Vol. 3 Classics 850
 Garner; Inez Cavanaugh (*v*). 12/44.
**(*) Serenade To Laura Savoy SV-0221
 Garner; John Levy, John Simmons (*b*); George De Hart, Alvin Stoller (*d*). 9/45–3/49.
*** Penthouse Serenade Savoy SV-0162
 As above. 9/45–3/49.
** Separate Keyboards Savoy SV-0223
 Garner; John Simmons, Leonard Gaskin (*b*); Alvin Stoller, Charlie Smith (*d*). 3–8/49.
**(*) Yesterdays Savoy SV-0244
 Garner; Mike Bryan (*g*); John Simmons, Leonard Gaskin, Slam Stewart (*b*); Doc West, Alvin
 Stoller, Charlie Smith (*d*). 1/45–6/49.
*** Long Ago And Far Away Columbia 460614-2
 Garner; John Simmons (*b*); Shadow Wilson (*d*). 6–10/50.
*** Body And Soul Columbia 467916-2
 As above. 1/51–1/52.

Erroll Garner was one of a kind. He was as outré as the great beboppers, yet bop was alien to him, even though he recorded with Charlie Parker. He swung mightily, yet stood outside the swing tradition; he played orchestrally, and his style was swooningly romantic, yet he could be as merciless on a tune as Fats Waller. He never read music, but he could play a piece in any key, and delighted in deceiving his rhythm sections from night to night. His tumbling, percussive, humorous style was entirely his own.

Garner's earliest recordings were done semi-privately and, though issued on Blue Note in the 1950s, they're in often atrocious sound, and one has to be either scholar or devoted fan to get much out of them. Most of his style is in place, even though these are often rambling and discursive pieces compared with what came later, and one can hear his debt to Tatum already. The three Classics discs include what there is of these survivals, and it's a difficult listen.

His first serious bout of studio recording was for Savoy, and he already sounds like himself. The tracks are all over rather quickly, running to the typical 78-r.p.m. playing-time, and Garner is deprived of the chance to stretch out as he later liked to; but as miniatures these have a certain charm. The transfers are less happy: there are one or two speed problems with some of the masters ('Rosalie' on *Separate Keyboards* sounds completely off) and variable levels of surface- or tape-hiss. Of the three original albums, *Penthouse Serenade* is probably the best; *Separate Keyboards* is only half Garner, with six tracks devoted to Billy Taylor. *Yesterdays* has an annoying session with Slam Stewart but a couple of swinging ones from 1949. The two Columbia albums round up his earliest sessions for the company, with the compatible team of Simmons and Wilson: still pinned to three-minute lengths, but the improved studio sound grants a better look at his early style.

*** Erroll Garner Collection Vol. 3: Too Marvellous For Words Emarcy 824419-2
 Garner; Wyatt Ruther (*b*); Eugene 'Fats' Heard (*d*). 5/54.
***(*) The Original Misty Mercury 834910-2
 As above. 7/54.
*** Mambo Moves Mercury 834909-2
 As above, plus Candido Camero (*perc*). 7/54.

By this period Garner had settled into his format as well as his style – swashbuckling trios which plundered standards with cavalier abandon. Bass and drums have only to keep up with Garner, but they provide a deceptively important anchor, for otherwise his treatments might simply wander off. The drummer's role is particularly important: as percussive as the pianist is, he leaves many accents to the man with the traps, and Heard has to concentrate hard to keep up. Garner's heartiness, his fondness for extravagantly arpeggiated ballads and knockabout transformations of standards can grow wearisome over the length of an album, and his favourite mannerisms become irritating. But there are undervalued aspects to these records, too. He is a quirky but resonant blues player; he keeps the melody sacrosanct, even at his most mischievous; he always swings. *Mambo Moves* has the extra heat of Candido's congas, which generate a terrific momentum on 'Mambo Garner', the opening piece, while *The Original Misty* has the first and finest version of his deathless composition. The *Collection* albums are all of previously unreleased material.

**** The Erroll Garner Collection Volumes 4 & 5: Solo Time! Emarcy 511821-2 2CD
> Garner (*p* solo). 7/54.

***(*) Solitaire Mercury 518279-2
> Garner (*p* solo). 3/55.

*** Soliloquy / At The Piano Columbia 465631-2
> Garner (*p* solo). 2/52–2/57.

Garner made few solo records, but these sessions are among his finest. The *Solo Time!* collection was set down in a single afternoon of one-take performances at a Detroit radio station. Garner indulges himself in long, immoderate performances that show his imagination at its most free-spirited and abundant. The treatment of 'It Might As Well Be Spring' is archetypal: over 8½ minutes he changes keys, builds huge orchestral crescendos, throws in a waltz-time passage, mocks and cherishes the melody, and finishes with an edifice that stands alone. Most of the tracks are variations on that manner, to a greater or lesser degree, and even when he falls back on Garnerisms the energy and spontaneity are something to marvel at. Only a shade behind is the 'proper' studio session which produced *Solitaire*: here are 10 minutes of 'Over The Rainbow', and perhaps the only jazz treatment of 'When A Gypsy Makes His Violin Cry'. Excellent remastering in both cases, the piano sounding a shade harder on *Solitaire*. The Columbia album doubles up a couple of solo dates five years apart, both characteristically mercurial, if slightly less lavish.

***(*) Concert By The Sea Columbia 451042-2
> Garner; Eddie Calhoun (*b*); Denzil Best (*d*). 9/55.

Garner's most famous album, and one of the biggest-selling jazz records ever made, *Concert By The Sea* is essentially no more or less than a characteristic set by the trio in an amenable setting. Moments such as the teasing introduction to 'I'll Remember April', the flippant blues of 'Red Top' and the pell-mell 'Where Or When' find Garner at his most buoyant; but rather more interesting is his well-shaped treatment of 'How Could You Do A Thing Like That To Me'. The recording was never outstanding but the reissue serves it well enough.

*** Paris Impressions Columbia 475624-2
> Garner; Eddie Calhoun (*b*); Kelly Martin (d). 3–5/58.

A souvenir of Garner's visit to Paris a few months earlier, even if it was recorded in New York. The tunes have suitable connections – 'The French Touch', 'La Vie En Rose', 'Left Bank Swing' and so on – and Garner must have enjoyed his trip, since it sounds particularly affectionate.

*** Dreamstreet / One World Concert Telarc CD-83350
> Garner; Eddie Calhoun (*b*); Kelly Martin (*d*). 59–8/63.

*** That's My Kick / Gemini Telarc CD-83332
> Garner; Arthur Ryerson, Wally Richardson (*g*); Ernest McCarty, Milt Hinton (*b*); George
> Jenkins, Herbie Lovelle, Jimmie Smith (*d*); Johnny Pacheco, Jose Mangual (*perc*). 66–72.

Telarc have pulled these out of the lengthy list of Garner albums lying in the back-catalogue; as two-for-one deals on CD, they're decent value. That said, none of these four sessions is likely to stir much excitement except among hardcore devotees. *Dreamstreet* is nice, the *One World* show notably lively, *That's My Kick* has a slightly augmented band with guitar and percussion, and *Gemini* found Erroll taking a turn at the harpsichord. Garner remains interesting from moment to moment, but over CD length his style's limitations tend to show up on ordinary albums, which is basically what these are.

***(*) Erroll Garner Collection Vol. 1: Easy To Love Emarcy 832994-2
> Garner; Eddie Calhoun (*b*); Kelly Martin (*d*).

*** Erroll Garner Collection Vol. 2: Dancing On The Ceiling Emarcy 834935-2
> As above. 6/61–8/65.

With much of Erroll's work out of print, the appearance of previously unreleased material may seem like a luxury; but this is quality Garner. Both discs round up nuggets from various early-'60s sessions, and there are some fine things on both, such as the dizzying opening to 'It Had To Be You' or the prime after-hours Garner of 'Like Home'.

*** Plays Gershwin & Kern Mercury 826224-2
> Garner; Eddie Calhoun, Ike Isaacs (*b*); Kelly Martin, Jimmie Smith (*d*). 8/64–2/68.

*** Jazz Around Midnight – Erroll Garner Verve 846191-2
> Garner; Red Callender, John Simmons, Leonard Gaskin, Wyatt Ruther (*b*); Lou Singer, Harold
> West, Charlie Smith, Eugene 'Fats' Heard (*d*). 12/45–3/55.

*** **Erroll Garner: Jazz Masters 7** Verve 518197-2
 Garner (*p*); Wyatt Ruther (*b*); Eugene Heard (*d*); Candido Camero (*perc*). 54–55.
Many of Garner's albums from the late 1950s and '60s have been lost from the catalogue, and the
Gershwin and Kern set is no more than typical of the period. But Garner is well served by the *Around
Midnight* compilation, which closes with the very long and unpredictable 'Over The Rainbow' from
Solitaire; and the *Jazz Masters* disc is sound value, a smart choice of solo and trio pieces from the
Mercury sessions.

Kenny Garrett ALTO SAXOPHONE, FLUTE

*** **Introducing Kenny Garrett** Criss Cross 1014
 Garrett; Woody Shaw (*t, flhn*); Mulgrew Miller (*p*); Nat Reeves (*b*); Tony Reedus (*d*). 12/84.
(*) **Garrett 5 Paddle Wheel K32Y 6280
 Garrett; Wallace Roney (*t*); Mulgrew Miller (*p*); Charnett Moffett (*b*); Tony Reedus (*d*); Rudy
 Bird (*perc*). 9/88.
*** **Prisoner Of Love** Atlantic 82046
 Garrett; Miles Davis, Barry Lee Hall Jr (*t*); Muhammad Abdul Al-Khabyyr (*tb*); Sayydah
 Garrett (*cl*); Foley, Darryl Jones, Marcus Miller (*b*); Ricky Wellman (*d*); Rudy Bird, Mino
 Cinelu (*perc*); vocal choir. 89.
*** **African Exchange Student** Atlantic 82156
 Garrett; Mulgrew Miller (*p*); Ron Carter, Charnett Moffett (*b*); Elvin Jones, Tony Reedus (*d*);
 Rudy Bird, Tito Ocasio, Steve Thornton (*perc*). 90.
**** **Black Hope** Warner Bros 9362 45017
 Garrett; Joe Henderson (*ts*); Kenny Kirkland (*p, syn*); Donald Brown (*syn*); Charnett Moffett
 (*b*); Brian Blade, Ricky Wellman (*d*); Don Alias (*perc*). 92.
**** **Triology** Warner Bros 9 45731
 Garrett; Kiyoshi Kitagawa, Charnett Moffett (*b*); Brian Blade (*d*). 95.
It was in Garrett's company that Miles Davis felt most inclined of late to return to the blues. The young
saxophonist has a warm, vibrant delivery that works best in short, fairly discontinuous passages; Davis
once accused him of wearing 'Sonny Stitt's dirty drawers'. Had he lived long enough to hear some of the
more recent of these records, he might have had cause to alter his view. Garrett has acquired considerable stature and a voice that is unmistakably his own.

 Woody Shaw plays wonderfully on the debut album, a far more amenable partner than the younger and
gruffer Roney, whose Miles-influenced sound for once sounds rather acid and obstreperous. Garrett's
bluesy phrasing fits the bill perfectly and his habit of lingering on low tones just a fraction longer than
you expect gives his solos a very solid, anchored presence, which has allowed him to work on occasion
without a harmony instrument. There is an excellent piano-less trio with Ron Carter and Elvin Jones on
African Exchange Student, good enough to make one wish for a whole album of it, not that the rest of
the album is lacking in any way.

 Its predecessor, *Prisoner Of Love*, is an ambitious, well-crafted record, and of course it gains special
cachet from a guest appearance by Miles himself, who rents out his band – Foley, Ricky Wellman,
Marcus Miller – for the gig. Even so, taking his cue from Marcus, Garrett plays all instruments on three
tracks, including an affecting 'Lift Ev'ry Voice And Sing'. That apart, it's all predictably in the late-
Miles mode and, but for the prominence of the saxophone, many will guess that they are listening to
out-takes. This isn't to decry Garrett's contribution, but there is a slight sense here that he is swamped
by more dominant partners.

 He certainly isn't put off by the presence of Henderson for 'Transit Dance' and 'Bye Bye Blackbird' on
the excellent *Black Hope*, though perhaps having worked with Miles Davis makes all future encounters
pretty straightforward. Henderson's solo construction is so magisterial that any partner runs the risk of
sounding banal, but Garrett more than holds his own, and the lessons inculcated pay huge dividends on
Triology. This is a very special record, made with his working trio (and with a couple of tracks featuring
old pal Moffett). Garrett is still content to play standards and repertoire pieces and brings fresh angles
to Brubeck's 'In Your Own Sweet Way' and the old lip-buster, 'Giant Steps', which he plays with a
respectful insouciance, as if it really doesn't matter should he stumble. There's refreshingly little ego on
these discs, just the work of a young master musician who clearly recognizes the way he has to go and
the towering example of those who've passed before him. The dedication to Henderson and Rollins on
Triology is perhaps a sign of where his thinking now lies. Certainly, *pace* 'Giant Steps', he is not one of
the Coltrane school but prefers to keep close contact to the basic melody rather than spool off endless
harmonic variations. An exciting career to keep track of as it continues to develop.

Michael Garrick (born 1933) PIANO

**** A Lady In Waiting Jazz Academy JAZA 1
  Garrick; Dave Green (*b*); Alan Jackson (*d*). 93.
When the Big Audit is done, Britain may well find itself in trouble for not having disclosed a national
asset on the scale of Michael Garrick, or for not having found an appropriate response to his multifarious talents. To be fair, Garrick's own activities as a teacher, writer and administrator have often prevented him from showing off his elegant compositions and fleet, uncomplacent keyboard style. Garrick
is above all a melodist and a colourist and, if his preferred palette and medium tend to be the softer
watercolours, there is nothing at all watery about his playing, or about this trio.

  It has the feel of a seasoned, highly instinctive group (Green and Jackson are also national treasures), at
home with Garrick's demanding charts as well as standards and jazz repertory. 'The Royal Box' is a
large-scale suite written for big band; though Garrick has sometimes been able to work with full-size
ensembles, more often he has been obliged to rearrange compositions for smaller groups. It works well
here, but the better things are staples like Herbie Hancock's 'Dolphin Dance' and John Lewis's wonderfully pianistic 'Two Degrees East, Three Degrees West'. The group is clearly and uncomplicatedly
recorded, with lots of presence in the bass and no distortion from the kit. When they're all three working
at full speed, it's an exhilarating experience.

Giorgio Gaslini (born 1929) PIANO, KEYBOARDS

**** Gaslini Plays Monk Soul Note 1020
  Gaslini (*p* solo). 5/81.
*** Schumann Reflections Soul Note 1120
  Gaslini; Piero Leveratto (*b*); Paolo Pellegatti (*d*).
*** Multiple Soul Note 1220
  Gaslini; Roberto Ottaviano (*as, ss, sno s, bcl*); Claudio Fasoli (*ts, ss*); Bruno Tommaso (*b*);
  Giampiero Prina (*d*). 10/87.
***(*) Ayler's Wings Soul Note 1270
  Gaslini (*p* solo). 7/90.
***(*) Masks Soul Note/Musica Jazz SNMJ 002
  Gaslini; Alberto Mandarini, Guido Mazzon (*t*); Pino Minafra (*t, didjeridu*); Lauro Rossi (*tb*);
  Giancarlo Schiaffini (*tb, tba*); Sebi Tramontana (*tb, euph*); Martin Mayes, Claudio Pontiggia
  (*frhn*); Rudy Migliardi (*tba*); Eugenio Colombo (*ss, f*); Roberto Ottaviano, Mario Schiano (*as*);
  Claudi Lugo (*as, ss*); Gianluigi Trovesi (*as, cl*); Claudio Allifranchini (*as, f*); Daniel Cavallanti
  (*ts*); Claudio Fasoli, Giancarlo Porro (*ts, ss*); Gianluigi Trovesi (*cl, as*); Oretta Orengo (*ob, eng
  hn*); Roger Rota (*bsn*); Luca Gusella (*vib*); Massimo Coen, Renato Geremia (*vn*); Bruno Nidasio
  (*vla*); Paolo Damiani, David Zaccaria (*clo*); Attilo Zanchi, Bruno Tommaso (*b*); Fulvio Marras,
  Vincenzo Mazzone, Giampiero Prina (*d*). 3 & 9/90, 3 & 6/91.
**** Lampi Soul Note 121290
  Gaslini; Daniele Di Gregorio (*vib, mar, perc*); Roberto Bonati (*b*); Giampiero Prina (*d*). 1/94.
Monk has received no more sensitive and intelligent reading than Gaslini's remarkable 1981 homage.
He makes no attempt to mimic the style, just to get inside those mysterious and deceptive tunes.
Schumann would seem to be a more intractable subject, but Gaslini exploits considerable harmonic and
contrapuntal ingenuity to bring it off. The quintet session has a better rhythm section and progress is a
little brisker. Transcribing Albert Ayler, the most anti-pianistic of improvisers, would seem to be an
almost absurdly quixotic task. Gaslini converts Ayler's fierce microtonality into ripples and arpeggios
that are as provocative as they are unexpectedly appealing. Superimposing 'Omega Is The Alpha' over
'Bells' is the only slight oddity (but it works), and the versions of 'Ghosts' and 'Truth Is Marching In'
acquire a Bachian simplicity and exactness.

  A joint production, *Masks* includes four long suites of Gaslini's. Imagine an Italianate cross between
Duke Ellington and Willem Breuker, and you're close. 'Scena Dalla Commedia Dell'Arte' is smoothly
elegant, with carefully distributed dissonances. Scored for a small saxophone-led group, it has an intimate, low-key sound that contrasts sharply with the large-group effects on 'Pierrot Solaire', a piece which
the Italian Instabile Orchestra have released on their own record from the same performance. The
textures on 'African Masks' are very vivid, and each piece is tailored to a small internal group of
soloists, as on Ellington's overseas suites. The final piece is a 'Masquerade' for Jean Genet, as polymorphous and perverse as its dedicatee.

  One of Gaslini's most characteristic devices is a sudden dead halt over a heavy drum beat. On *Lampi* it
resembles the shocked pause after a bolt of lightning (that's what the title means) before the rumble of
thunder, with only the heart racing. Gaslini plays strange tricks with the pulse rate, whipping it along

with brawling ensembles and then collapsing into tiny, breathless interludes, before getting its second wind and rushing off in another direction. The range of textures on all these records is extraordinary. Though he only rarely uses exotic instruments like Moe-Moe Yee's Burmese harp (Breuker, by contrast, is addicted to Kagel-ish exotica), he voices passages in such a way that they sound quite outside their normal range or register. Gaslini's is a quite astonishing output that urgently deserves wider coverage. Recent releases only confirm that.

Jeff Gauthier VIOLIN

*** **Internal Memo** Nine Winds NWCD 0164

Gauthier; David Witham (*ky*); Eric Von Essen (*b, hca*); Alex Cline (*d*). 9/93.

Gauthier's favoured ground is at the sweet end of jazz violin: his tone and delivery are amiable enough to sit soundly in a QHCF situation. But this is a Nine Winds date and, though it doesn't always suit him, he seems more interested in a long, tough, abstract piece like the closing 'Olivier's Nightmare'. The dedication to Richard Grossman, 'Seriously Twisted Blues', is a successful narrowing of range: when Witham drops out and the trio dig in, the music finds a real intensity. Elsewhere, on the charming pastorale of 'Astor' and the gracious 'Refuge', the group concoct a brainy sort of mood music. An appealing if inconsistent mixed bag.

Charles Gayle (born 1939) TENOR SAXOPHONE

(*) **Always Born Silkheart 115

Gayle; John Tchicai (*as, ts*); Sirone (*b*); Reggie Nicholson (*d*). 4/88.

*** **Homeless** Silkheart 116

Gayle; Sirone (*b*); Dave Pleasant (*d*). 4/88.

***(*) **Spirits Before** Silkheart 117

As above. 4/88.

Gayle has lived the life of a street musician in Manhattan for some years, and these three records were all recorded in the same week on what was effectively a field trip by Silkheart. Gayle is like a folk musician in other ways, too: he harks back to unreconstructed energy music of the 1960s, blowing wild, themeless lines with an abandon that sometimes sounds neurotic, sometimes pleading, occasionally euphoric. He seems oblivious to all 'fashions' in jazz, keeps faith with only a few players – drummer Pleasant, whose fractured and weirdly illogical time is a prime feature of the two records he appears on, and bassist Sirone appear to be two of them – and questions the status quo with unblinking certainty. *Always Born* is a well-meaning failure through Tchicai's efforts: Gayle wasn't really meant to play with another saxophonist, even a venerable veteran of the wave which he harks back to. *Homeless* and, especially, *Spirits Before* are the real, hard stuff, with 'Give' a particularly knotty and troubling performance.

**** **Touchin' On Trane** FMP CD 48

Gayle; William Parker (*b*); Rashied Ali (*d*). 10–11/91.

**** **Repent** Knitting Factory Works KFWCD 122

Gayle; Vattel Cherry, Hilliard Greene (*b*); David Pleasant (*d*). 1–3/92.

**** **More Live** Knitting Factory Works KFWCD 137 2CD

As above, except add William Parker (*b, cel, vn*), Michael Wimberley, Marc Edwards (*d*); omit Greene and Pleasant. 1–2/93.

**** **Consecration** Black Saint 120138-2

As above, except omit Edwards. 4/93.

***(*) **Translations** Silkheart SHCD 134

As above. 1/93.

***(*) **Raining Fire** Silkheart SHCD 137

As above. 1/93.

*** **Kingdom Come** Knitting Factory Works KFW157

Gayle; William Parker (*b*); Sunny Murray (*d*). n.d.

***(*) **Unto I Am** Victo CD032

Gayle (*ts, p, bcl, d* solo). 9/94.

These astounding records catapult Gayle into the vanguard of the music today. He is still working as a street musician in New York, and he has clearly developed the iron chops that go with playing in the open for hours on end, but the conception and realization of these records is monumental. His holy, holy delivery inevitably makes one think of both Coltrane and Ayler in their most conously spiritual guise, and a performance like 'Jesus Christ And Scripture' (*Repent*) has all the biblical intensity that one might imagine; but there is also Gayle's own superbly harsh lyricism to go with that. He is unusually adept at both the highest register of the tenor and control of the most outlandish overblowing: even David Murray must bow to extremism of this calibre. Solos are not so much fashioned as drawn straight from the moment: all that seems to be created in advance is an instantaneous planning of a performance that might run on seemingly without end. The rhythm players on the Knitting Factory and Black Saint records are all little known, apart from the admirable Parker, who is as central to events as he is becoming with Cecil Taylor; but they are wonderfully behind Gayle all the way. The opening of 'Deliverance' (*More Live*) suggests that they would be quite an ensemble even without him.

The outright masterpiece is the FMP album, which seems likely to be a central document in the free music of the decade: the three men touch on Coltrane from moment to moment (and Ali renews his old relationship in triumph) but this is new, brilliant, eloquent free playing. The two records cut live at New York's Knitting Factory are exhausting manifestos (particularly the double-disc set), which struggle towards ecstasy or chaos, depending on one's own tolerance. A piece such as 'Sanctification' (*More Live*) certainly goes further in building on Ayler's legacy than even Brötzmann ever has. *Consecration* catches them in the studio and shows only the slightest scaling-down, with 'Justified' another *tour de force*.

It might seem as if Gayle is suddenly being too widely documented, and it's true that his records tend to follow similar patterns. But they are all unlike one another. The two new Silkheart releases document more by his working quartet and, though two discs without much relief is probably too much even for Gayle addicts, it can't be denied that there's some awesomely powerful interaction here. The only weak spot is Gayle's taste for instruments which don't really suit him: he fiddles away on a viola for some of the time, and it's no more enlightening than Ornette Coleman's violin playing.

Kingdom Come gets its power from three serene, muscular encounters with Murray and Parker. The drummer doesn't seem to be quite the force of old, but he does well enough, and Gayle marches almost obliviously on. Two piano solos and a trio are less inspiring. The all-solo Victo release has a dispensable drum solo and a middling workout on piano again; but the two tenor solos and the bass-clarinet item are astoundingly heavyweight pieces. Gayle has never sounded as close-up and direct as he does here, the saxophone terrorizing the microphone. And the quality of his thinking is remarkable, even as he appears to lose himself in the music.

Gianni Gebbia SOPRANO SAXOPHONE, ALTO SAXOPHONE, BARITONE SAXOPHONE

***(*) **Cappuccini Klang** Splasc(h) CDH 383
    Gebbia; Peter Kowald (*b*); Günther Baby Sommer (*d*). 3/92.
Gebbia is an enterprising musician who had already recorded an all-solo programme for his own Sound Event label before being taken up by Splasc(h). The leader's soprano playing is agile rather than especially distinctive or expressive, and much of his work still seems to be concerned with working out abstract ideas. Kowald and Sommer are a blessing to him. He benefits immeasurably from the discipline of group playing and in these two seniors he has found the ideal teachers. The 'Cappuccini Suite' is exemplary, with some wry pseudo-classical gestures that may recall his fellow-countryman, Giorgio Gaslini.

Herb Geller (born 1928) ALTO SAXOPHONE, SOPRANO SAXOPHONE, FLUTE, VOCALS

**** **That Geller Feller** Fresh Sound FSR CD 91 ╱
    Geller; Kenny Dorham (*t*); Harold Land (*ts*); Lou Levy (*p*); Ray Brown (*b*); Lawrence Marable (*d*). 3/57.
** **A Jazz Songbook Meeting** Enja 6006
    Geller; Walter Norris (*p*); John Schroeder (*g*); Mike Richmond (*b*); Adam Nussbaum (*d*). 7/88.
***(*) **Birdland Stomp** Fresh Sound FSRCD 174
    Geller; Kenny Drew (*p*); Niels-Henning Orsted- Pedersen (*b*); Mark Taylor (*d*). 5/90.
**** **The Herb Geller Quartet** VSOP 89
    Geller; Tom Ranier, Jimmy Rowles (*p*); John Leitham (*b*); Louie Bellson (*d*). 8/93.
Relatively untroubled by fashion, Geller set out as an orthodox, Parker-influenced bopper – *rara avis* on the West Coast in those days – before turning towards a more broadly based and decidedly cooler style which incorporated elements of Paul Desmond, Johnny Hodges and even Benny Goodman, with whom he worked in the later 1950s. Until recent years, he's been hard to spot, buried in a German radio big band and other groups.

That Geller Feller is the best of the available sets. The originals – 'S'Pacific View', 'Marable Eyes', 'An Air For The Heir' and 'Melrose And Sam' – are tightly organized and demand considerable inventiveness from a group that frequently sounds much bigger than a sextet. Dorham plays a lovely, crackling solo on the opening track but is otherwise rather anonymous when out on his own. Geller's own introduction to 'Jitterbug Waltz' is wonderfully delicate, with more than a hint of Benny Carter in the tone and phrasing. He also does a fine version of the Arlen–Gershwin rarity 'Here's What I'm Here For', which John Williams picked up on later in 1957 on the excellent *Plays The Music Of Harold Arlen*. The quintet sessions on *Songbook* are slightly disappointing, largely because Geller's soloing is just off-line.

Confusingly titled, given the existence of an Enja record of the same name, *Birdland Stomp* is way ahead on quality. At 62, Geller has a beautiful tone and the Ellington–Strayhorn medley with which the Spanish-recorded session ends suggests he has renewed his debt to Hodges. His articulation on Parker's 'Cheryl' isn't all it might be, and even the capable Drew sounds a bit sticky, but both are magnificent on the title-tune and 'Autumn Nocturne'. Recorded with a heavy emphasis on NHOP's bass, this is nevertheless one of Geller's best latter-day recordings, topped only by the VSOP.

Ruby Braff calls one recent CD *Controlled Nonchalance*. It's a title that would double very happily for the most recent Geller release. At 65 he sounds utterly relaxed and in command of his craft. Of the originals, 'Chromatic Cry' and 'Stand-Up Comic' stand out. The first, an exquisite ballad, sounds like something that may have popped into his head during a solo or else in the rehearsal room; the second is a wry look at another group of improvising entertainers – 'Comedy is not the same / social critic is the game' – a vocal tribute topped by a piquant soprano solo. Geller's forte these days is the evocative ballad. 'Isfahan' is totally restructured in the middle section, otherwise played *à la* Hodges. Jimmy Rowles guests on his own evergreen, 'The Peacocks', with its softly eldritch cries and brooding mystery. A wonderful record by a seldom acknowledged master who charted his own course out of orthodox bebop.

German Jazz Orchestra GROUP

*** **First Take** Mons 6458

> Thomas Vogel, Thorsten Benkenstein, Claus Reichstaller, Torsten Maas, Stefan Zimmermann, Herman Marstatt (*t*); Ludwig Nuss, Peter Feil, Bjoern Strangmann, Georg Maus (*tb*); Klaus Graf, Jens Neufang, Andreas Maile, Mathias Erlewein, Steffen Schorn, Wolfgang Bleibel, Peter Weniger (*reeds*); Hubert Nuss (*p*); Henning Sieverts (*b*); Holger Nell (*d*); Roland Peil (*perc*); Jiggs Whigham (*cond*). 6/94.

The impersonal name masks a big band fashioned to showcase a new generation of German players and composers. There are nine pieces here by eight hands and, while there's nothing spectacularly attention-grabbing, the music yields plenty of felicities on the way. Thorsten Wollmann's 'Concerto For Soprano Saxophone', with Weniger the very skilful soloist, is the obvious standout, although Frank Reinshagen's 'In The Best Tradition' runs it close, thanks to Steffen Schorn's fine feature role on, of all things, bass saxophone. Avuncular presence: Jiggs Whigham, who conducts.

Bruce Gertz DOUBLE BASS, ELECTRIC BASS

(*) **Blueprint Freelance FRL CD 017

> Gertz; Jerry Bergonzi (*ts*); John Abercrombie (*g*); Adam Nussbaum (*d*). 2 & 3/91.

*** **Third Eye** RAM RMCD 4509

> As above, except add Joey Calderazzo (*p*). 10/92.

Unlike, say, Ed Schuller, another young bassist-leader, Gertz lacks a roundness of musical personality. The writing is actually quite interesting, but almost every track on the earlier record leaves the listener with an uncomfortable yearning to hear exactly the same tune played by a totally different group. Abercrombie carries the whole thing along on his shoulders, with occasional effective interjections by Bergonzi. The two live dates on the RAM disc are more effective. Abercrombie is not quite so dominant; the group sounds seasoned and collaborative, and the two standards, 'Alone Together' and 'In Your Own Sweet Way', are sufficiently different from the usual run to suggest that there may yet be more of interest from this source.

Stan Getz (1927–91) TENOR, SOPRANO AND BARITONE SAXOPHONES

*** **Early Stan** Original Jazz Classics OJC 654
> Getz; Shorty Rogers (*t*); Earl Swope (*tb*); George Wallington, Hall Overton (*p*); Jimmy Raney (*g*); Curley Russell, Red Mitchell (*b*); Shadow Wilson, Frank Isola (*d*). 3/49–4/53.

(*) **The Brothers Original Jazz Classics OJC 008
> Getz; Zoot Sims, Al Cohn, Allen Eager, Brew Moore (*ts*); Walter Bishop Jr (*p*); Gene Ramey (*b*); Charlie Perry (*d*). 4/49.

*** **Prezervation** Original Jazz Classics OJC 706
> Getz; Kai Winding (*tb*); Al Haig (*p*); Gene Ramey, Tommy Potter (*b*); Roy Haynes, Stan Levey (*d*); Junior Parker, Blossom Dearie (*v*). 6/49–2/50.

*** **Stan Getz Quartets** Original Jazz Classics OJC 121
> Getz; Al Haig, Tony Aless (*p*); Gene Ramey, Tommy Potter, Percy Heath (*b*); Stan Levey, Roy Haynes, Don Lamond (*d*). 6/49–4/50.

After starring as one of Woody Herman's 'Four Brothers' sax section, and delivering a luminous ballad solo on the 1948 'Early Autumn', Getz went out on his own and at first seemed much like the rest of the Lester Young-influenced tenormen: a fast, cool stylist with a sleek tone and a delivery that soothed nerves jangled by bebop. The 'Brothers' idea was pursued in the session on OJC 008 (the rest of the disc is devoted to a Zoot Sims–Al Cohn date): the five tenors trade punches with panache and it's a fun session, if hardly an important one (the CD includes three alternative takes not on the LP issue). *Early Stan* finds Getz as a sideman with a septet led by Terry Gibbs and a quartet under Jimmy Raney's direction. Bright, appealing cool-bop on the Gibbs date, but the Raney session, from 1953, is more substantial, the quartet whisking through four stretching exercises including 'Round Midnight'.

Prezervation rounds up some odds and ends, including an improbable alliance with Junior Parker on two tracks and a Haig sextet date with Winding and two vocal duets by Jimmy Raney and Blossom Dearie! Not very important. But the *Quartets* set is an attractive dry run for the upcoming four-piece sessions for Roost, and it features the tenorman in very lithe form. The sound on most of these issues was fairly indifferent to start with, and these latest editions emerge well enough.

**** **The Best Of The Roost Years** Roulette 7981142
> As above, except add Sanford Gold, Duke Jordan (*p*); Johnny Smith (*g*); Eddie Safranski, Teddy Kotick, Bill Crow, Leonard Gaskin, Bob Carter (*b*); Frank Isola, Tiny Kahn, Roy Haynes, Don Lamond, Morey Feld (*d*). 5/50–12/52.

**** **At Storyville** Blue Note B21Y-94507
> Getz; Al Haig (*p*); Jimmy Raney (*g*); Teddy Kotick (*b*); Tiny Kahn (*d*). 10/51.

It's a moot point as to when Getz did his finest work on record, but it's possible to argue that these are his best records. The side-length of 78-r.p.m. discs lent a terseness and conviction to his improvisations which perhaps drifted away in the LP era, and even on club dates – as those at Boston's Storyville show, four tracks of which are on the best-of disc – Getz kept himself on a tighter rein. The lovely, mottled tone which he displays blinks through even the sometimes indifferent Roost recording, although the engineers have done an excellent job in making the music come up bright and clear; and bebop energy and surprise inform all the up-tempo pieces, some of which go off at a fearful pace. Haig and Silver both play splendidly. The *Storyville* disc is a classic club session cut in Boston. The best-of samples from this and adds tracks from a quartet session with Jimmy Raney. It also includes the gorgeous 'Moonlight In Vermont' from a session with guitarist Johnny Smith. All command the highest recommendation.

(***) **At Carnegie Hall** Fresh Sound FSCD 1003
> Getz; Kai Winding (*tb*); Al Haig, Duke Jordan (*p*); Jimmy Raney (*g*); Bill Crow, Tommy Potter (*b*); Frank Isola, Roy Haynes (*d*). 12/49–11/52.

(***) **Birdland Sessions** Fresh Sound FSR-CD 149
> Getz; Horace Silver, Duke Jordan (*p*); Jimmy Raney (*g*); Nelson Boyd, Charles Mingus, Gene Ramey (*b*); Phil Brown, Connie Kay (*d*). 4–8/52.

There's some excellent Getz on both these discs – but we have to withhold a firm recommendation because of the sound-quality. He sounds in prime form at both of the two Carnegie Hall concerts on FSCD 1003, but the sound deteriorates (frustratingly, after a good start) to complete muddiness by the end of the 1952 show. Jordan tends to toss out clichés, but the interplay with Raney is as subtle as usual. The Birdland recordings have been available on various pirate LPs over the years, and this edition is about as listenable as the others. For Getz addicts only.

*** **Together For The First Time** Fresh Sound FSCD-1022
> Getz; Chet Baker (*t*); Russ Freeman, Donn Trenner (*p*); Carson Smith, Joe Mondragon, Gene Englund (*b*); Larry Bunker, Shelly Manne, Jimmy Pratt (*d*). 9/52–12/53.

An interesting discovery: the Mulligan quartet at the Haig with Getz subbing for the leader. He sounds perfectly at home with Baker, Smith and Bunker, and there are some forthright variations on six tunes, including 'Half Nelson' and 'Yardbird Suite'. A subsequent quintet version of 'All The Things You Are' is a lot more dispirited, and there are four quartet airshots from 1952 to fill up the disc, which is in surprisingly good sound for the most part, the Haig titles having been apparently recorded by Richard Bock.

***(*) **Stan Getz Plays** Verve 833535-2

Getz; Jimmy Rowles, Duke Jordan (*p*); Jimmy Raney (*g*); Bob Whitlock, Bill Crow (*b*); Frank Isola, Max Roach (*d*). 12/52–1/54.

**** **At The Shrine** Verve 513753-2

Getz; Bob Brookmeyer (*vtb*); John Williams (*p*); Bill Anthony (*b*); Art Madigan, Frank Isola (*d*). 11/54.

Getz's long association with Norman Granz and Verve starts here. *Plays* features some of the best recording he was given in the period, and much of the playing is as fine as it is on the Roost dates, with the 1954 quartet session with Rowles particularly pretty. But it's the live sessions from The Shrine in Los Angeles, long a collector's-item album, which stand out. Getz plays with unstinting invention throughout, Brookmeyer is a witty and unfailingly apposite partner, and the remastered sound is fine.

*** **Stan Getz And The Oscar Peterson Trio** Verve 827826-2

Getz; Oscar Peterson (*p*); Herb Ellis (*g*); Ray Brown (*b*). 10/57.

*** **At The Opera House** Verve 831272-2

Getz; J. J. Johnson (*tb*); Oscar Peterson (*p*); Herb Ellis (*g*); Ray Brown (*b*); Connie Kay (*d*). 10/57.

*** **Getz Meets Mulligan In Hi-Fi** Verve 849392-2

Getz; Gerry Mulligan (*bs, ts*); Lou Levy (*p*); Ray Brown (*b*); Stan Levey (*d*). 10/57.

*** **Stan Getz & Dizzy Gillespie: Jazz Masters 25** Verve 521852-2

Getz; Dizzy Gillespie (*t*); J. J. Johnson (*tb*); Paul Gonsalves, Coleman Hawkins (*ts*); John Lewis, Lalo Schifrin, Wynton Kelly (*p*); Herb Ellis (*g*); Ray Brown, Art Davis, Wendell Marshall (*b*); Max Roach, Stan Levey, Chuck Lampkin, J. C. Heard (*d*); Candido Camero (*perc*). 12/53–11/60.

Getz's 1950s tracks for Verve aren't yet on CD as comprehensively as they might be, but the classic *West Coast Jazz* and *More West Coast Jazz* should be released by the time this edition is in print. The session with Peterson is as ebullient as expected, and the Opera House concert with J. J. Johnson includes some extrovert playing from everyone, especially on a snorting romp through Bud Powell's 'Blues In The Closet'. Listening to this kind of playing makes one wonder at Getz's reputation for being a featherlight stylist (he preferred 'stomping tenor-man'). The session with Mulligan is beautifully dovetailed: although, somewhat notoriously, they chose to swap instruments for part of the session, the sound of the two horns speaks of a tonal fraternity which sounds rare and entrancing. The *Jazz Masters* disc picks four tracks from two studio dates with Gillespie, plus a JATP piece and a jovial meeting with Gonsalves and Hawkins in 1957.

***(*) **In Sweden 1958–60** Dragon DRCD 263 2CD

Getz; Benny Bailey (*t*); Ake Persson (*tb*); Erik Norström, Bjarne Nerem (*ts*); Lars Gullin (*bs*); Jan Johansson, Bengt Hallberg (*p*); Gunnar Johnson, Ray Brown, Torbjorn Hultcrantz, Georg Riedel (*b*); William Schiopffe, Sune Spangberg, Joe Harris (*d*). 8–9/58.

A spell in Stockholm led to some recording with Swedish musicians, and these admirable sessions were the result, a Swedish variation on the cool manner with Getz sounding perfectly comfortable in Hallberg's and Johansson's charts. Gullin and Hallberg himself shine too – and so does the remarkable Johansson, whose status as the lost master of Swedish jazz is further enhanced by his playing here. The previous edition of this music has now been beefed up with some concert and radio material from 1960 and it's a close to indispensable package.

*** **Stan Getz With Cal Tjader** Original Jazz Classics OJC 275

Getz; Cal Tjader (*vib*); Vince Guaraldi (*p*); Eddie Duran (*g*); Scott LaFaro (*b*); Billy Higgins (*d*). 2/58.

A one-off session with Cal Tjader which looks forward with some prescience to the bossa nova records that were to come: certainly the coolly pleasant backings of Tjader's rhythm section make up a cordial meeting-ground for tenor and vibes to play lightly appealing solos, and the charming version of 'I've Grown Accustomed To Her Face' is a winner.

***(*) **Stan Getz At Large Plus! Vol. 1** Jazz Unlimited JUCD 2001

Getz; Jan Johanssen (*p*); Daniel Jordan (*b*); William Schiopffe (*d*). 1/60.

***(*) **Stan Getz At Large Plus! Vol. 2** Jazz Unlimited JUCD 2002

As above. 1/60.

Two very rare Getz albums, recorded in Copenhagen with a local team, and he sounds in wonderful form throughout. The opening 'Night And Day' on the first disc is delivered with heavenly grace and is sustained over chorus after chorus at a perfect tempo. There are some interesting choices of material – by Johnny Mandel, Al Cohn, Harold Land – and though both albums are weighted towards slow to mid-tempos, Getz stays concentrated and inspired throughout. The rhythm section are capable rather than challenging, and the sound is slightly less than ideal, but the music is terrific.

*** **Cool Velvet / Voices** Verve 527773-2
> Getz; Herbie Hancock, Hank Jones (*p*); Dave Hildinger (*vib*); Jim Hall (*g*); Blanchie Birdsong (*hp*); Freddy Dutton, Ron Carter (*b*); Sperie Karas, Grady Tate (*d*); Artie Butler, Bobby Rosengarden, Bill Horwath (*perc*); strings, voices. 3/60–12/66.

It was inevitable that Getz would do a full-blown encounter with strings, and Russ Garcia's arrangements for the *Cool Velvet* album are workmanlike settings for the lovely sound. *Voices* was arranged by Claus Ogerman, and in the brief frameworks he devises Getz sounds professionally involved though not much more. Pleasant music, but hardly a competitor to the indispensable *Focus*.

***(*) **Jazz Samba** Verve 810061-2
> Getz; Charlie Byrd (*g*); Keter Betts (*b*); Gene Byrd (*g, b*); Buddy Deppenschmidt, Bill Reichenbach (*d*). 2/62.

*** **Big Band Bossa Nova** Verve 825771-2
> Getz; Doc Severinsen, Bernie Glow, Joe Ferrante, Clark Terry (*t*); Tony Studd, Bob Brookmeyer, Willie Dennis (*tb*); Ray Alonge (*frhn*); Gerald Sanfino, Ray Beckenstein (*f*); Eddie Caine (*af*); Babe Clark, Walt Levinsky (*cl*); Romeo Penque (*bcl*); Hank Jones (*p*); Jim Hall (*g*); Tommy Williams (*b*); Johnny Rae (*d*); Jose Paulo, Carmen Cossa (*perc*). 8/62.

***(*) **Jazz Samba Encore** Verve 823613-2
> Getz; Antonio Carlos Jobim (*g, p*); Luiz Bonfa (*g*); George Duvivier, Tommy Williams, Don Payne (*b*); Paulo Ferreira, Jose Carlos, Dave Bailey (*d*); Maria Toledo (*v*). 2/63.

**** **Getz / Gilberto** Verve 810048-2
> Getz; Antonio Carlos Jobim (*p*); Joao Gilberto (*g, v*); Tommy Williams (*b*); Milton Banana (*d*); Astrud Gilberto (*v*). 3/63.

*** **Getz Au Go Go** Verve 821725-2
> Getz; Gary Burton (*vib*); Kenny Burrell (*g*); Gene Cherico (*b*); Joe Hunt, Helcio Milito (*d*); Astrud Gilberto (*v*). 64.

***(*) **The Girl From Ipanema** Verve 823611-2 4CD
> As above discs, except add Steve Kuhn (*p*); Laurindo Almeida (*g*); Edison Machado, Jose Soorez, Luiz Parga (*perc*). 62–64.

***(*) **Round Midnight: Stan Getz** Verve 841445
> As above. 62–64.

Getz's big commercial break. However much he protested that he played other stuff besides the bossa nova in later years, his most lucrative records – and some of his best playing – were triggered by the hit versions of first 'Desafinado' from the first album and then 'The Girl From Ipanema' with Gilberto, the tune which a thousand wine-bar bands have had to play nightly ever since. The original albums still hold up very well. Getz actually plays with as much pungency and alertness as anywhere else, and even though the backings sometimes threaten to slip into a sleepwalk, there's always an interesting tickle from the guitar or the bass to keep the music alive; and the melodies, by Bonfa, Gilberto and Jobim, have proved their quality by how well they've endured. *Jazz Samba* and *Jazz Samba Encore* are excellent, but the famous Getz/Gilberto, which has hummed seductively round cafés, wine-bars and bedrooms for 30 years, remains peerless. The big-band set has some clever arrangements by Gary McFarland, but sundering the intimacy of these whispery settings seems a fairly pointless exercise. And *Getz Au Go Go*, which had the vocals by Gilberto dubbed in subsequently, sounds just a mite too forceful, as though Getz were hurrying to push on to something else. Astrud Gilberto's singing isn't so much an acquired taste as a languid, ghostly sound on the breeze; many will prefer Maria Toledo on the third record listed. *The Girl From Ipanema* collects all the music plus the session for *Stan Getz/Laurindo Almeida*. The *Round Midnight* disc is a functional one-volume sampler with all the hits.

**** **Nobody Else But Me** Verve 521660-2
> Getz; Gary Burton (*vib*); Gene Cherico (*b*); Joe Hunt (*d*). 3/64.

Unreleased for 30 years, this one's a marvel. Supposedly put on the shelf so as not to cause any distraction from Getz's bossa nova hit-making, the music here – amazingly, the only studio recording by a group that was a popular concert attraction – is lush and romantic with the backbone of a master improviser's intelligence. Burton contributes '6-Nix-Pix-Flix' and opens up the harmonic base just enough to give Stan clear, lucid space for his solos. 'Summertime' is a classic, 'Waltz For A Lovely Wife' is rapture, but there's nothing less than great here.

*** Stan Getz & Bill Evans Verve 833802-2
    Getz; Bill Evans (*p*); Richard Davis (*b*); Elvin Jones (*d*). 5/64.
A curiously unsatisfying match. If one expected feathery ballads and lavishly romantic music, the results were the complete opposite: the only real ballad is 'But Beautiful'; the rest go from mid-tempo to stomp, and Davis and Jones break up the beat and harry the two nominal leaders. Both can handle it, but it's disappointing that something on the level of the almost telepathic Evans–Jim Hall records wasn't secured. The CD has several alternative and unissued takes.

**** Focus Verve 821982-2
    Getz; Eddie Sauter Orchestra. 4–6/65.
Nobody ever arranged for Getz as well as this, and Sauter's luminous and shimmering scores continue to bewitch. This isn't art-jazz scoring: Sauter had little of Gil Evans's misterioso power, and he was shameless about tugging at heartstrings. But within those parameters – and Getz, the most pragmatic of soloists, was only too happy to work within them – he made up the most emotive of frameworks. It doesn't make much sense as a suite, or a concerto; just as a series of episodes with the tenor gliding over and across them. In 'Her', the tune dedicated to Getz's mother, the soloist describes a pattern which is resolved in the most heartstopping of codas. This was surely Getz's finest hour. The CD remastering hasn't eliminated much of the tape hiss, but it sounds good enough.

***(*) Sweet Rain Verve 815054-2
    Getz; Chick Corea (*p*); Ron Carter (*b*); Grady Tate (*d*). 3/67.
We were too hard on this in our first edition – it's a beauty. Corea is still arguably too sweet and noodling at times, but 'O Grande Amor' and 'Windows' blend the brightness of Getz's bossa nova years with a spare, precise lyricism, and Carter and Tate have the measure of the situation.

***(*) Dynasty Verve 839117-2 2CD
    Getz; Eddie Louiss (*org*); René Thomas (*g*); Bernard Lubat (*d*). 1–3/71.
Recorded at a live engagement in London, Getz was in happy and swinging form here, and the quartet stretch out as far as they want on the material. Louiss is far more flexible and discreet than most jazz organists and Getz is untroubled by anything the instrument produces, while the reliable Thomas takes some excellent solos.

***(*) The Best Of The Verve Years Vol. 2 Verve 517330-2 2CD
    Getz; various groups as above. 52–71.
***(*) Verve Jazz Masters: Stan Getz Verve 519823-2
    Getz; various groups, as above.
The double-CD compilation goes for a wide-ranging, packed retrospective, from the earliest Verve material up to Dynasty; the VJM disc is more modest but includes 'Her', 'Desafinado', 'Shine' and 'Ipanema'. Each would be a fine introduction to this big period of Getz's music.

**(*) Captain Marvel Columbia 468412-2
    Getz; Chick Corea (*p*); Stanley Clarke (*b*); Tony Williams (*d*); Airto Moreira (*perc*). 3/72.
** Best Of Two Worlds Columbia CK 33703
    Getz; Albert Dailey (*p*); Joao Gilberto (*g. perc, v*); Oscar Neves (*g*); Clint Houston, Steve Swallow (*b*); Billy Hart, Grady Tate (*d*); Airto Moreira, Ruben Bassini, Ray Armando, Sonny Carr (*perc*); Heloisa Buarque de Hollanda (*v*). 5/75.
*** The Master Columbia 467138-2
    Getz; Albert Dailey (*p*); Clint Houston (*b*); Billy Hart (*d*). 10/75.
*** Live At Montmartre Steeplechase SCS 1073 2CD
    Getz; Joanne Brackeen (*p*); Niels-Henning Orsted-Pedersen (*b*); Billy Hart (*d*). 1/77.
**(*) Another World Columbia 471513-2
    Getz; Andy Laverne (*p*); Mike Richmond (*b*); Billy Hart (*d*); Efrain Toro (*perc*). 9/77.
*(*) Children Of The World Columbia 468811-2
    Getz; strings etc. 12/78–3/79.
*** The Essential Stan Getz Columbia 460819-2
    As above discs.
*** The Lyrical Stan Getz Columbia 471512-2
    As above discs.
*** New Collection Columbia 471513-2
    As above discs.
This wasn't a vintage period for Getz. The Columbia albums range from perfunctory to mildly engaging: nothing very wrong with the settings (aside from *Best Of Two Worlds*, which is a very pallid re-run of the bossa nova years), but Getz's own playing has taken on a wayward, purposeless quality, and the licks he sometimes fell back on when bored recur frequently enough to be troublesome. *Captain*

Marvel was meant to be an energetic new beginning, but the noise created by Moreira drowns out even Williams at times, and Getz never sounds at ease, despite some of his old gumption breaking through. The Montmartre set suffers from a rhythm section that don't really work with him, and *Another World* found him drifting towards easy listening: Laverne's bland pianistics dissemble the firmer rhythms of Richmond and Hart, and the situation seems to be tranquillizing everyone. Matters turn towards outright disaster on *Children Of The World*, a grim confection of lite-fusion, world musics, anything. *The Master*, though, is a better record; it doesn't shake the earth but finds the leader very comfortable on the bed of rich chords which Albert Dailey lays down.

Columbia have three separate anthologies available and, though *The Essential* duplicates tracks with the other two, each is a quite attractive selection from this somewhat spotty period. *The Lyrical* would just get the nod since it concentrates on what the title suggests.

***(*) **Billy Highstreet Samba** Emarcy 838771
  Getz; Mitch Forman (*ky*); Chuck Loeb (*g*); Mark Egan (*b*); Victor Lewis (*d*); Bobby Thomas (*perc*).
***(*) **The Dolphin** Concord CCD 4158
  Getz; Lou Levy (*p*); Monty Budwig (*b*); Victor Lewis (*d*). 5/81.
***(*) **Spring Is Here** Concord CCD 4500
  As above. 5/81.
**** **Pure Getz** Concord CCD 4188
  Getz; Jim McNeely (*bp*); Marc Johnson (*b*); Victor Lewis (*d*). 1/82.
**** **Blue Skies** Concord CCD 4676
  As above. 1/82.
***(*) **Live In Paris** Dreyfus FDM 36577-2
  As above. 82.

Not so much a miraculous return to form as an artist reasserting his artistry. Getz passed fusion leanings by and moved back to his greatest strength, tenor and rhythm section, of which the Concord albums are triumphant illustrations. *The Dolphin* and its recently issued companion, *Spring Is Here*, offer live sessions with a first-class band: Getz is at his most expansive here, reeling off very long but consistently expressive and well-argued solos, his tone a shade harder but still with a misty elegance that softens phrases at key moments. *Pure Getz*, recorded in the studio, is perhaps even better: there is a celebrated version of Billy Strayhorn's 'Blood Count', which alternates between harsh cries and soft murmurings, and which became a staple part of Getz's live set at the time; but the variations on 'Come Rain Or Come Shine' and a terse 'Sippin' At Bells' are probably even more masterful. But *Billy Highstreet Samba* is by no means a second-rate Getz album: here, for once, he adapted well to what could have been a fusion-led project. The material (by Loeb and Forman) is unusually perspicacious, and Getz responds with bright and committed playing against a group more concerned with playing music than licks. There is also a strong 'Body And Soul' and a couple of rare outings for Getz on soprano.

Blue Skies is a new discovery, dating from the same sessions as *Pure Getz*, and though we might have given it a fractionally lower rating there is still some transcendant playing, especially on the slower pieces: Getz's gravitas on a ballad was never more perfectly revealed than in the likes of 'How Long Has This Been Going On?'. The live date is a valuable pendant to the studio sessions, and this was clearly a band in top gear: the only slight drawback is some extra reverb added to the remix, with McNeely's piano also sounding imperfect.

**** **Anniversary** Emarcy 838769-2
  Getz; Kenny Barron (*p*); Rufus Reid (*b*); Victor Lewis (*d*). 7/87.
**** **Serenity** Emarcy 838770-2
  As above. 7/87.

Getz's last great records are pristine examples of his art. Sometimes it seems as if there is nothing there but his sound, the 'incredibly lovely sound', as he once murmured to himself, and it's possible to find an emptiness at the heart of this music. Certainly he had no pretence to playing anything but long, self-regarding lines that had little to do with anything going on around him: as impeccably as both of these rhythm sections play, their function is purely to sketch in as painless a backdrop as possible for the unfurling of Getz's sound. But it is such a breathtaking beauty that he creates that these might be the most sheerly pretty jazz albums of their day. The two Emarcy sets are the definitive ones, splendidly recorded and letting the listener bathe in the rapturous sound of the tenor.

*** **Apasionado** A&M 395297-2
  Getz; orchestra. 89.

Though already troubled by his terminal illness, Getz still plays handsomely on this superior example of mood music. His earlier records with strings wait to be reissued, so this one – with keyboards substituting for the string parts and a mélange of soft rhythms and whispering brass in support – will serve to illustrate this most soothing side of his art.

***(*) **People Time** Emarcy 510134-2 2CD
Getz; Kenny Barron (*p*). 3/91.

Cut not long before his death, Getz has his moments of struggle on this imposing, double-length series of duets with Kenny Barron, his last keyboard partner. Some of the butter has run out of his tone, and unlike many valedictory recordings there isn't a compensating ardour of delivery to go with it: he sounds as if he's just trying to be the same old Getz. But knowledge of his impending death still, inevitably, lends a poignancy to this music which even those previously unmoved by the saxophonist's work may find themselves responding to. Nor should Barron be relegated to the role of mere accompanist: he is a full-fledged partner in these pieces, and turns in some of the best improvising.

*** **A Life In Jazz: A Musical Biography** Verve 535119-2
Getz; various Verve sessions as listed above. 1/52–3/91.

Released to tie in with a Getz biography, this is an interesting hotchpotch rather than a definitive sampler. It rescues a few rarities – 'Hymn To The Orient' from *Plays*, a solo with Ella Fitzgerald from her *Like Someone In Love* album, and the sultry backing to Abbey Lincoln on 'I'm In Love' from her *You Gotta Pay The Band*. For someone who doesn't have too much Stan, this is a nice variation on the normal hits selection.

Tiziana Ghiglioni VOCAL

(*) **Streams Splasc(h) H 104
Ghiglioni; Luca Bonvini (*tb*); Maurizio Caldura Nunez (*ss, ts*); Luca Flores (*p*); Franco Nesti (*b*); Alessandro Fabbri (*d*). 12/84.
*** **Onde** Splasc(h) H 133
Ghiglioni; Carlo Actis Dato (*ts, bs, bcl*); Claudio Lodati (*g*); Enrico Fazio (*b*); Fiorenzo Sordini (*d, perc, mar*). 6/87.
*** **Yet Time** Splasc(h) H 150
Ghiglioni; Roberto Ottaviano (*ss*); Stefano Battaglia (*p*); Paolino Dalla Porta (*b*); Tiziano Tononi (*d*). 3/88.
*** **Lyrics** Splasc(h) H 348
Ghiglioni; Paul Bley (*p*). 3/91.
*** **Something Old, Something New, Something Borrowed, Something Blue** Splasc(h) H 370
Ghiglioni; Enrico Rava (*t*); Giancarlo Schiaffini (*tb*); Steve Lacy (*ss*); Umberto Petrin (*p*); Attilo Zanchi (*b*); Tiziano Tononi (*d, perc*). 4 & 5/92.

Since she seems to appear in a quite different setting almost from record to record, it's a little difficult to focus on the merits of Tiziana Ghiglioni's singing. Her albums for Splasc(h) find her both fronting groups and working as an integral element within them: she is almost peripheral to *Onde*, where she guests with Actis Dato's Art Studio band, yet her singing on 'Rosso Di Sera' and 'Voci' is a striking wordless invention. *Streams* and *Yet Time* find her taking a Norma Winstone-like role of alternating pastoral scat with cool readings of lyrics. She has a big, rangy voice which she's reluctant to use in a big way, so many of her vocal improvisations sound restrained; fluency doesn't come easy to her, either. Yet the improvisation on Ornette Coleman's 'Round Trip' on *Yet Time* is sustained with great skill, and her meeting with Schiaffini, which includes bare-bones readings of 'When I Fall In Love' and 'All Blues' as well as more *outré* material, shows her unfazed by working alone with an improvising trombonist. Her enunciation always makes one aware that she's not singing in her native language, and her self-written lyrics are awkward, but she's a charismatic performer.

*** **Somebody Special** Soul Note SN 1156
Ghiglioni; Steve Lacy (*ss*); Franco D'Andrea (*p*); Jean-Jacques Avenel (*b*); Oliver Johnson (*d*). 4/86.
*** **I'll Be Around** Soul Note 121256
Ghiglioni; Enrico Rava (*t*); Mal Waldron (*p*). 7–8/89.

Ghiglioni's albums for Soul Note seek out a more conservative context, with mixed results. Steve Lacy's iron presence is the dominant feature of *Somebody Special* and, while Ghiglioni is a better singer than Irene Aebi, and the quartet are in excellent form, the vocalist doesn't make a strong case for besting Lacy's sometimes intractable forms. *I'll Be Around* is dedicated to Billie Holiday, an inspiration rather than an influence, and in this collection of deathly slow ballads the singer does surprisingly well with Waldron and Rava, the latter especially at his most hauntingly poignant.

(*) **Goodbye, Chet Philology W 22-2
    Ghiglioni; Chet Baker (*t*); Mike Melillo, E. Olivieri (*p*); M. Moriconi, I. De Marinis (*b*);
    Giovanni Ascolese, V. Mazzone (*d*). 7/85–3/88.
A pretty strange record, even by the often oddball standards of Philology. Ghiglioni was to make a
record with Baker but never did, and here instead is a set of eight standards by the singer with Melillo,
followed by a rehearsal tape of Baker with Melillo's trio and an orchestra, which then leads into two
versions of J. J. Johnson's 'Lament' by Baker with Ghiglioni's quartet at Bari harbour, taped in offhand
circumstances by Paolo Piangiarelli. The songs with Melillo are well done by the singer, but whether one
wants to go through the rest of it – Baker sounds as weary as usual in his final years – is another matter.

*** **Sings Gaslini** Soul Note 121297-2
    Ghiglioni; Renato Geremia (*vn*); Roberto Bonati (*b*); Giampiero Prina (*d*); string ensemble. 1–2/
    95.
The songs, lyrics and arrangements are all by Giorgio Gaslini, and they provoke Ghiglioni's most
measured, thoughtful work. Sometimes one wishes that she'd let go a little, in the manner of some of her
less formal records: the singing is beautifully done, and the arrangements are impeccable, but this is a
very temperate climate and across a CD's length it's a little becalmed. The most *outré* moments are
actually provided by the eccentric violin of Geremia.

Maurizio Giammarco (born 1952) TENOR SAXOPHONE

***(*) **Inside** Soul Note 121254
    Giammarco; Mauro Grossi (*p, ky*); Piero Leveratto (*b*); Andrea Melani (*d*). 7/93.
Like his late, much-lamented countryman, Massimo Urbani, Giammarco brings something quite fresh
and unexpected to the saxophone, a quality of intonation or *accent* one would simply not hear from an
American player. Ten years ago Giammarco attracted attention with a symphonic arrangement of
pieces by Enrico Rava. He has also led a notably vibrant electric group called Lingomania. His free-
tonal compositions and improvisations alternate unfamiliar-sounding progressions with chromatic
blues that often recall Joe Lovano's more way-out pieces.
    Inside features the group he calls his Heart Quartet, a band centred on Leveratto's rattly, plucked bass
and Melani's Motian-influenced cymbals. The opening 'Urgency' establishes the pace and idiom without wasting a gesture, setting up for a more relaxed and swinging mood in the remaining nine tracks.
Grossi sounds like a dozen European keyboard players, but he never puts a foot wrong in the context of
this particular music and his solo on 'Inside News' is a model of spareness and logic.
    Giammarco himself favours a nasal, vocalized tone on both tenor and soprano. It sounds perfect on
things like Carlo Alberto Rossi's 'E Se Domani', which closes the set, but it isn't quite limber enough for
the faster items. The recording is well up to Soul Note's unfussy standard, and all four players are well
registered.

Shannon Gibbons VOCAL

*** **Shannon Gibbons** Soul Note 121163
    Gibbons; Cecil Bridgewater (*t, flhn*); Kenny Barron (*p*); Rufus Reid (*b*); Ben Riley (*d*). 5/87.
Gibbons has a big, rich voice and sufficient improvisational capacity to make these sides worthwhile.
The material is not especially inspired, but the band is absolutely top notch and Bridgewater's arrange-
ments couldn't be faulted on any count. Barron in particular is a constant revelation.

Michael Gibbs (born 1937) BANDLEADER

**** **The Only Chrome Waterfall Orchestra** Ah Um 009
    Gibbs; Derek Watkins, Ian Hamer, Kenny Wheeler, Henry Lowther (*t*); Chris Pyne (*tb*); Ray
    Warleigh, Stan Sulzmann (*as*); Charlie Mariano (*as, nagaswaram*); Tony Coe (*ts, bcl*); Alan
    Skidmore (*ts*); Philip Catherine (*g*); Steve Swallow (*b*); Bob Moses (*d*). 75.
***(*) **By The Way . . .** Ah Um 016
    John Barclay, Kenny Wheeler, Richard Iles, Steve Sidwell (*t*); Pete Beachill (*tb*); Dave Stewart
    (*btb*); John Rooke, Cormac OhAhodain, Andrew Clark (*frhn*); Julian Arguëlles, Iain Dixon, Iain
    Ballamy, Evan Parker, Charlie Mariano (*reeds*); John Taylor, Nikki Iles (*p*); Mike Walker, John
    Parricelli (*g*); Oren Marshall (*tba*); Steve Swallow (*b*); Bob Moses, John Marshall (*d*). 4–5/93.
Thanks to such patrons as Stan Getz and Gary Burton, some of this Rhodesian-born composer's
themes have achieved a wider currency, but almost all of his (infrequent) records are out of the

catalogue. Gibbs was early interested in the possibilities of jazz with rock, and there's no discomfort in his use of funk rhythms and the guitarists: Gibbs was and remains a pioneer of a 'pure' kind of fusion: rock instruments and rhythms used to extend rather than diminish the scope of the improvisations. He always makes one feel the breadth and power of a big band, though, insisting on its weight and sonic force rather than breaking it down or using simple solo/accompaniment strategies.

Only Chrome Waterfall Orchestra is his most Gil Evans-like work. As with Gil, the secret is a combination of quality soloists and finely constructed compositions. Tony Coe's solo on 'Antique' is a perfect case in point, and elsewhere Mariano's Indian horn and Catherine's tasteful chromatic shapes are played over backgrounds that demand careful attention. There is a version of one of Gibbs's 'Lady Mac' pieces and the superb 'Unfinished Sympathy', which is one of his most ambitious creations.

The other Ah Um is a new recording rather than a reissue. There are fine moments for Mariano again, for Wheeler and Parker and, although the predominantly British orchestra sometimes plays with characteristic reserve, this is mostly vivid and exciting music, and a hint that Gibbs's earlier music deserves a CD comeback.

Terry Gibbs (born 1924) VIBRAPHONE, DRUMS

*** **Dream Band** Contemporary CCD 7647
> Gibbs; Conte Candoli, Al Porcino, Ray Triscari, Stu Williamson (*t*); Bob Enevoldsen (*vtb*); Vernon Friley (*tb*); Joe Cadena, Med Flory, Bill Holman (*ts*); Joe Maini, Charlie Kennedy (*as*); Jack Schwartz (*bs*); Pete Jolly (*p*);); Max Bennett (*b*); Mel Lewis (*d*). 3/59, 11/59, 3 & 11/59.

(*) **The Sundown Sessions Contemporary CCD 7562
> As above, except add Johnny Audino (*t*), Bob Burgess (*tb*). 11/59.

*** **Flying Home** Contemporary CCD 7654
> As above, except add Frank Higgins (*t*), Lou Levy (*p*), Buddy Clark (*b*). 3 & 11/59.

***(*) **Main Stem** Contemporary CCD 7656
> Gibbs; Conte Candoli, Frank Huggins, Al Porcino, Ray Triscari, Stu Williamson (*t*); Bob Edmondson, Vern Friley, Frank Rosolino (*tb*); Charlie Kennedy, Joe Maini (*as*); Richie Kamuca, Bill Perkins (*ts*); Jack Nimitz (*bs*); Pat Moran (*p*); Buddy Clark (*b*); Mel Lewis (*d*). 1/61.

*** **The Big Cat** Contemporary CCD 7657
> As above.

The Gibbs bands combined the high-energy swing of Lionel Hampton with the sophistication of the Thad Jones/Mel Lewis outfits (Mel Lewis straddled the drum stool during Gibbs's most productive period). Apart from some material on a Savoy compilation, these are the earliest things currently available. The arrangements, by Marty Paich, Lennie Niehaus and others, are all good, but with an uneasy emphasis on the higher horns. Gibbs's playing is closer to Hampton's percussive bounce than to any of the competing influences, and he solos with considerable verve; the two later sets are perhaps to be preferred and Gibbs's choruses on 'Ja-Da' (with Candoli) and 'Sweet Georgia Brown' (with Triscari) are the highlights of *Main Stem*. Even so, it's a style that draws a great deal from bop and it's no less well adapted to the small-group performances on . . .

*** **Chicago Fire** Contemporary 14036
> Gibbs; Buddy DeFranco (*cl*); John Campbell II (*p*); Todd Coolman (*b*); Gerry Gibbs (*d*). 7/87.

*** **Holiday For Swing** Contemporary 14047
> As above. 8/88.

*** **Air Mail Special** Contemporary 14056
> Gibbs; Buddy DeFranco (*cl*); Frank Collett (*p*); Andy Simpkins (*b*); Jimmie Smith (*d*). 10/81.

***(*) **Memories Of You** Contemporary 14066
> Gibbs; Buddy DeFranco (*cl*); Herb Ellis (*g*); Larry Novak (*p*); Milt Hinton (*b*); Butch Miles (*d*). 4/91.

*** **Kings Of Swing** Contemporary CCD 14067
> As above. 4/91.

Lively latter-day sets from a player who must be taking multi-vitamins. All of these feature him in the company of fellow New Jerseyan DeFranco in a series of friendly but competitive sets, which were also repeated with the clarinettist as (strictly nominal) leader, but what's a credit among friends? *Memories Of You* is perhaps the best all-round set, with an excellent reading of 'Flying Home' and a romantic but un-schmaltzy 'Poor Butterfly'. *Kings Of Swing* is the poorer half of the same sessions. Of the remainder, *Air Mail Special* ('Love For Sale', 'Blues For Brody', 'Body And Soul') is particularly recommended, with *Chicago Fire* (unexpected versions of 'Giant Steps' and the '52nd Street Theme'). The big-band stuff is the most wholly authentic, but Gibbs's small groups are perhaps more in tune with prevailing tastes.

John Gill BANJO, VOCAL

**(*) Smile, Darn Ya, Smile Stomp Off CD 1227
    Gill; Charles Fardella (*t*); David Sager (*tb, v*); Lynn Zimmer (*ss, ts, cl*); Tom Fischer (*as, cl*);
    Steve Pistorius (*p, v*); Debbie Markow, Elliot Markow (*vn*); Tom Saunders (*tba*); Hal Smith (*d*).
    12/90.
*** Headin' For Better Times Stomp Off CD 1270
    As above, except add Dan Levinson (*ts, cl*). 7/91–12/92.

Shading between revivalism and a straight and strict re-creation of hot dance music, Gill's outfit errs on the side of the latter, which will tend to switch off all but the more dedicated archivists. There are two or three tunes on both discs that build up a bigger head of steam, and both ride out on a hot one: 'Here Comes The Hot Tamale Man', which Freddie Keppard once blew on, was a good idea for the second record. For the rest, though, it's often re-created schmaltz. Which still sounds like schmaltz, however much ironic salt and pepper gets milled over the melodies.

Dizzy Gillespie (1917-1993) TRUMPET, PERCUSSION, PIANO, VOCAL

**** Groovin' High Savoy SV-0152
    Gillespie; Dave Burns, Ray Orr, Talib Daawud, John Lynch, Kenny Dorham, Elmon Wright,
    Matthew McKay (*t*); Al Moore, Leon Comeghys, Charles Greenlea, Gordon Thomas, Taswell
    Baird (*tb*); Charlie Parker, Sonny Stitt (*as*); Dexter Gordon (*ts*); Howard Johnson, John Brown,
    Ray Abrams, Warren Luckey, Pee Wee Moore, Scoops Carey, James Moody, Billy Frazier, Leo
    Parker (*saxes*); Frank Paparelli, Clyde Hart, Al Haig, John Lewis (*p*); Milt Jackson (*vib*); Chuck
    Wayne, Remo Palmieri (*g*); Murray Shipinsky, Ray Brown, Curley Russell, Slam Stewart (*b*);
    Shelly Manne, Cozy Cole, Big Sid Catlett, Kenny Clarke, Joe Harris (*d*); Gil Fuller (*v*). 2/45–11/
    46.
**** Shaw Nuff Musicraft 1046-70053-2
    As above. 11/45–2/46.
*****   The Complete RCA Victor Recordings Bluebird 66528-2 2CD
    As above, except add Bill Dillard, Shad Collins, Lamar Wright, Willie Cook, Benny Harris,
    Miles Davis, Fats Navarro (*t*); Dicky Wells, Ted Kelly, J. J. Johnson, Kai Winding (*tb*); Buddy
    DeFranco (*cl*); Benny Carter, Russell Procope, Ernie Henry (*as*); Yusef Lateef, Coleman
    Hawkins, Ben Webster, Charlie Ventura, Don Byas, Robert Carroll, Teddy Hill (*ts*); Al Gibson,
    Ernie Caceres (*bs*); Lionel Hampton (*vib*); Lennie Tristano, Sam Allen, James Foreman (*p*);
    Charlie Christian, Billy Bauer (*g*); Milt Hinton, Richard Fullbright, Al McKibbon, Eddie
    Safranski (*b*); Bill Beason, Teddy Stewart (*d*); Vince Guerra, Sabu Martinez, Chano Pozo (*perc*);
    Johnny Hartman (*v*). 5/37–1/49.
***(*) Dizzy Gillespie Vols 1 & 2 RCA Tribune ND89763 2CD
    Similar to above. 46–49.

John Birks Gillespie had already been recording for almost a decade when he made the earliest of these tracks, and in the Cab Calloway and Teddy Hill bands he cut the outline of a promising Roy Eldridge disciple. His associations with Thelonious Monk and Charlie Parker, though, took him into hitherto uncharted realms. While he continued to credit Parker as the real inspirational force behind bebop, Gillespie was the movement's scholar, straw boss, sartorial figurehead and organizer: his love of big-band sound led him into attempts to orchestrate the new music which resulted in some of the most towering jazz records, particularly (among those here) 'Things To Come' and 'Cubano Be-Cubano Bop'. But his own playing is at least as powerful a reason to listen to these tracks. Gillespie brought a new virtuosity to jazz trumpet just as Parker created a matchless vocabulary for the alto sax. It scarcely seems possible that the music could have moved on from Louis Armstrong's 'Cornet Chop Suey' to Gillespie's astonishing flight on 'Dizzy Atmosphere' in only 20 years. A dazzling tone, solo construction that was as logical as it was unremittingly daring, and a harmonic grasp which was built out of countless nights of study and experimentation: Gillespie showed the way for every trumpeter in post-war jazz. His Musicraft recordings include a single sextet track with Dexter Gordon ('Blue 'N' Boogie'), seven with Parker, four with Sonny Stitt and Milt Jackson, and the balance with his big band; some of these are unfortunately missing from these editions. The Musicraft has the edge on better packaging.

    The RCA set sweeps the board as the cream of Gillespie's studio work in the period. The big-band tracks are complete and in good sound, all the small-group sessions are here, there are pre-history tracks with Teddy Hill and Lionel Hampton as a taster for things to come, and four tracks with the Metronome All-Star bebop group, where Dizzy lines up with Miles, Bird, Fats and J. J. Absolutely indispensable and some of the most exciting jazz of the era. The RCA Tribune set seems like a spoiler next to this, but it may tempt those on a budget, since it includes most of the same tracks.

***(*) **Pleyel 48** Vogue 74321 134152
>   Gillespie; Dave Burns, Benny Bailey, Lamar Wright, Elmon Wright (*t*); Ted Kelly, Bill Shepherd
>   (*tb*); Howard Johnson, John Brown (*as*); George Gales, Big Nick Nicholas (*ts*); Cecil Payne (*bs*);
>   John Lewis (*p*); Al McKibbon (*b*); Kenny Clarke (*d*); Chano Pozo (perc); Kenny Hagood (v). 2/
>   48

***(*) **Dizzy Gillespie & His Big Band In Concert** GNP Crescendo GNPD 23
>   As above, except add Willie Cook (*t*), Cindy Duryea, Jesse Tarrant (*tb*), Ernie Henry, James
>   Moody (*reeds*), James Foreman (*p*); Nelson Boyd (*b*), Teddy Stewart (*d*); omit Bailey, Lamar
>   Wright, Kelly, Johnson, Nicholas, Lewis, McKibbon, Clarke, Hagood. 48.

Although the big band made only a small number of studio records, it was caught on the wing at a
number of concerts, even if seldom in hi-fi conditions. These are two splendid gigs though, and only the
exasperatingly imperfect sound holds them back from top ratings. Although much of the material is
duplicated across the two concerts, some of it is strikingly different: the Pasadena (GNP) concert has a
three-minute 'Round Midnight' while the one from Paris runs to almost nine minutes. Gillespie's interest in Latin rhythms brought semi-legendary percussionist Pozo (killed not long after these concerts)
into the fold, and there is typically exciting stuff on 'Manteca'. If the orchestra never moves with the
neurotic immediacy of small-group bebop, it's still a remarkable sound.

(*) **School Days Savoy SV 0157
>   Gillespie; J. J. Johnson (*tb*); John Coltrane (*as, ts*); Bill Graham (*as, bs*); Budd Johnson (*ts*);
>   Wynton Kelly (*p*); Milt Jackson (*vib, p*); Kenny Burrell (*g*); Percy Heath, Bernie Griggs (*b*); Al
>   Jones, Kansas Fields, Art Blakey (*d*); Joe Carroll, Freddy Strong, Melvin Moore (*v*). 1/51–7/52.

*** **The Champ** Savoy SV 0170
>   As above, except add Stuff Smith (*vn*). 1/51–7/52.

First issued on his own Dee Gee label, this was small-group music featuring Gillespie as bebop showman rather than trumpet innovator, looking for success in the slack aftermath of bebop's decline.
Hardcore bop pickings are relatively slim: 'The Champ', 'Tin Tin Deo', 'Birk's Works', all of them on
The Champ. There's a lot of suspect material of the 'Umbrella Man' ilk. Gillespie's good humour and
sly spirits usually save the day, but it can be discouraging.

*** **Pleyel Concert 1953** Vogue 74321 154662
>   Gillespie; Bill Graham (*bs*); Wade Legge (*p*); Lou Hackney (*b*); Al Jones (*d*); Joe Carroll (*v*). 2/
>   53.

*** **Ooh-Shoo-Be-Doo!** Natasha NI-4018
>   As above. 3–4/53.

When economics required Gillespie to dissolve the big band, he carried on with small groups. Operating
at something of a tangent to bop – he still performed with Parker on a few occasions, and there is a
superb session for Verve with Monk and Bird, as well as the famous Massey Hall concert of 1953 – his
playing began to take on a grandeur which sounded even more ravishing than Parker's alto did when
confronted with strings. At the same time he continued to delight in on-stage horseplay, and this record
of a French concert includes plenty of interplay with Joe Carroll on the likes of 'Ooh-Shoo-Be-Doo-
Be'. What's missing is anyone to challenge him in the way Parker or Powell could. The Natasha album
collects tracks from Birdland broadcasts of the same period: there are four versions of 'Ooh-Shoo-Be-
Doo-Be', which is probably three too many, and flashes of great trumpet amid a lot of enjoyable
nonsense. How well one responds is a matter of how Gillespified one wants to be.

*** **Diz And Getz** Verve 833559-2
>   Gillespie; Stan Getz (*ts*); Oscar Peterson (*p*); Herb Ellis (*g*); Ray Brown (*b*); Max Roach (*d*). 12/
>   53.

(*) **For Musicians Only Verve 837435-2
>   As above, except add Sonny Stitt (*as*), John Lewis (*p*), Stan Levey (*d*); omit Peterson and Roach.
>   10/56.

*** **Sonny Side Up** Verve 825674-2
>   Gillespie; Sonny Stitt, Sonny Rollins (*ts*); Ray Bryant (*p*); Tommy Potter (*b*); Charli Persip (*d*).
>   12/57.

These all-star encounters have perhaps been overrated. It's interesting to hear Gillespie on what was
effectively mainstream material on *Diz And Getz* – two Ellington tunes, three standards and a single
Latin theme – but the group strike a surprisingly shambolic note in places, seldom managing to play
together, and the superfast blues 'Impromptu' is a virtual disaster. Worth salvaging are a lovely trumpet
treatment of 'It's The Talk Of The Town', some moments from the otherwise audibly ruffled Getz, and
a version of 'It Don't Mean A Thing' in which the tempo is actually matched by the intensity of the
playing. The music has never sounded like a great feat of engineering, and the latest CD transfer
improves little on previous editions. *For Musicians Only* is even more of a blow-out, with 'Be-Bop' and

'Dark Eyes' running over 12 minutes each and Stitt treating it as a carving session: the tempos are almost uniformly hell-for-leather. Exhilarating in small doses, but it's hardly as significant a date as it might have been with a little preparation. *Sonny Side Up* is pretty desultory stuff, too, but with Rollins in his greatest period and Stitt as combative as usual, the two long blues tracks strike some sparks, and Rollins's solo on the brief 'I Know That You Know' is prime cut. Dizzy referees with aplomb.

**** Birks Works Verve 527900-2 2CD
> Gillespie; Joe Gordon, Quincy Jones, E. V. Perry, Carl Warwick, Talib Daawud, Lee Morgan (*t*); Melba Liston, Frank Rehak (*tb*); Rod Levitt, Ray Connor (*btb*); Jimmy Powell, Phil Woods, Ernie Henry (*as*); Billy Mitchell, Benny Golson, Ernie Wilkins (*ts*); Mart Flax, Billy Root, Pee Wee Moore (*bs*); Walter Davis Jr, Wynton Kelly (*p*); Paul West, Nelson Boyd (*b*); Charli Persip (*d*); Austin Comer (*v*). 6/56–7/57.

Long-awaited in a comprehensive edition, these tracks cover the work of a band that Gillespie toured with as a cultural ambassador, though this is all studio work. Studded with great players, the orchestra also benefits from some of the most perceptive scoring of the day – by Liston, Wilkins, Jones, Golson and other hands – and with Gillespie in stratospheric form as soloist, the band could hardly have failed. Yet the three original albums remain comparatively forgotten, or at least neglected, which makes the reissue even more welcome.

*** At Newport Verve 513754-2
> Gillespie; Lee Morgan, Ermit Perry, Carl Warwick, Talib Daawud (*t*); Melba Liston, Al Grey, Chuck Connors (*tb*); Ernie Henry, Jimmy Powell (*as*); Billy Mitchell, Benny Golson (*ts*); Pee Wee Moore (*bs*); Wynton Kelly, Mary Lou Williams (*p*); Paul West (*b*); Charli Persip (*d*). 7/57.

**** Gillespiana / Carnegie Hall Concert Verve 519809-2
> Gillespie; John Frosk, Clark Terry, Nick Travis, Carl Warwick, Ernie Royal, Joe Wilder (*t*); Urbie Green, Frank Rehak, Britt Woodman, George Matthews, Arnet Sparrow, Paul Faulise (*tb*); Jimmy Buffington, Al Richman, Gunther Schuller, Julius Watkins, John Barrows, Richard Berg (*frhn*); Leo Wright (*f, as*); Lalo Schifrin (*p*); Don Butterfield (*tba*); Art Davis (*b*); Chuck Lampkin (*d*); Candido Camero, Willie Rodriguez, Ray Barretto, Julio Collazo, Jose Mangual (*perc*); Joe Carroll (*v*). 11/60–3/61.

*** Round Midnight: Dizzy Gillespie Verve 510088-2
> Gillespie; various groups. 6/54–11/64.

***(*) Dizzy's Diamonds The Best Of The Verve Years Verve 513875-2 2CD
> Gillespie; various groups. 54–64.

***(*) Verve Jazz Masters: Dizzy Gillespie Verve 516319-2
> Gillespie; various groups. 52–64.

Gillespie's Verve contract was arguably a little disappointing in that it produced no single indispensable record. The big- and small-band dates were pot-pourris of dazzling breaks and solos which never quite gelled into the long-playing masterpiece Gillespie surely had in him at this time. Having already outlived many of his key contemporaries in bebop, he was beginning to be a player in search of a context. The best single disc is certainly the one that couples *Gillespiana* – a marvellous assemblage of orchestral charts by Lalo Schifrin, some of his finest work on record, to which Gillespie rises superbly – and the subsequent *Carnegie Hall Concert* of a few months later, not quite so memorable, though this 'Manteca' and the extravagant 'Tunisian Fantasy' are exhilarating. The Newport set from 1957 has some great moments – a fine 'I Remember Clifford', the chunks from Mary Lou Williams's 'Zodiac Suite' with the composer sitting in – and some concert schtick. But at least the *Dizzy's Diamonds* set offers a comprehensive overview, with one disc of big bands, one of small groups and one of Afro-Cuban, bossa nova and calypso fusions. The latter disc is occasionally stretched a bit thin, but the first two are loaded with great things. There are plenty of other Gillespie Verve albums that still await their turn for reissue. Meanwhile the *Round Midnight* and VJM sets make useful individual primers, with the latter taking in Parker as well as big-band and other small-group work.

***(*) Dizzy Gillespie And The Double Six Of Paris Philips 830224-2
> Gillespie; James Moody (*as*); Kenny Barron, Bud Powell (*p*); Chris White, Pierre Michelot (*b*); Kenny Clarke, Rudy Collins (*d*); The Double Six Of Paris (*v*). 7–9/63.

This almost-forgotten record doesn't deserve its obscurity. The tracks are small-group bop, with the Double Six group dubbing in supremely athletic vocals later – normally a recipe for aesthetic disaster, but it's done with such stunning virtuosity that it blends credibly with the music, and the interweaving is done with some restraint. Gillespie himself takes some superb solos – the tracks are compressed into a very short duration, harking back to original bop constraints, and it seems to focus all the energies – and even Powell, in his twilight, sounds respectable on the ten tracks he plays on.

***(*) The Monterey Festival Jazz Orchestra Blue Note CDP 780370-2
> Gillespie; Harry 'Sweets' Edison, Melvin Moore, Fred Hill, Johnny Audino (*t*); Lester Robinson,

Francis Fitzpatrick, Jim Amlotte (*tb*); Herman Lebow, Sam Cassano, David Burke, Alan Robinson (*frhn*); Buddy Collette, Gabe Baltazar, Bill Green, Carrington Visor Jr, Jack Nimitz (*reeds*); Phil Moore (*p*); Bobby Hutcherson (*vib*); Dennis Budimir (*g*); Jimmy Bond (*b*); Earl Palmer (*d*). 65.

Gil Fuller's charts for this band miss some of the freewheeling excitement he gave to the first Gillespie big band in the 1940s, but there's real glitter and polish in the playing that the trumpeter responds to with some acrid, pinpoint improvising. It's over too soon.

*** **Live At The Village Vanguard** Blue Note CDP 780507-2 2CD
Gillespie; Garnett Brown (*tb*); Pepper Adams (*bs*); Chick Corea (*p*); Ray Nance (*vn*); Richard Davis (*b*); Mel Lewis, Elvin Jones (*d*). 10/67.

One of the oddest line-ups Gillespie ever figured in – Nance and Brown swap places, Jones sits in on two tunes, but otherwise the band is as listed. These are club jams rather than thought-out situations, and there are the usual dead spots; but Gillespie takes some magisterial solos – his thoughts on the blues in 'Blues For Max' are worth a close listen – and Adams in particular is in tough, no-nonsense form.

***(*) **Dizzy Gillespie's Big 4** Original Jazz Classics OJC 443
Gillespie; Joe Pass (*g*); Ray Brown (*b*); Mickey Roker (*d*). 9/74.

(*) **The Trumpet Kings Meet Joe Turner Original Jazz Classics OJC 497
Gillespie; Roy Eldridge, Clark Terry, Harry 'Sweets' Edison (*t*); Connie Crayton (*g*); Jimmy Robbins (*b*); Washington Rucker (*d*); Joe Turner (*v*). 9/74.

** **The Trumpet Kings At Montreux '75** Original Jazz Classics OJC 445
Gillespie; Roy Eldridge, Clark Terry (*t*); Oscar Peterson (*p*); Niels-Henning Orsted-Pedersen (*b*); Louie Bellson (*d*). 7/75.

*** **At The Montreux Jazz Festival 1975** Original Jazz Classics OJC 739
Gillespie; Eddie 'Lockjaw' Davis, Johnny Griffin (*ts*); Milt Jackson (*vib*); Tommy Flanagan (*p*); Niels-Henning Orsted-Pedersen (*b*); Mickey Roker (*d*). 7/75.

** **Dizzy's Party** Original Jazz Classics OJC 823
Gillespie; Rodney Jones (*g*); Benjamin Franklin Brown (*b*); Mickey Roker (*d*); Paulinho Da Costa (*perc*). 9/76.

(*) **Montreux '77 Original Jazz Classics OJC 381
Gillespie; Jon Faddis (*t*); Milt Jackson (*vib*); Monty Alexander (*p*); Ray Brown (*b*); Jimmie Smith (*d*). 7/77.

*(*) **Free Ride** Original Jazz Classics OJC 740
Gillespie; band arranged by Lalo Schifrin. 2/77.

(*) **The Trumpet Summit Meets The Oscar Peterson Big 4 Original Jazz Classics OJC 603
Gillespie; Freddie Hubbard, Clark Terry (*t*); Oscar Peterson (*p*); Joe Pass (*g*); Ray Brown (*b*); Bobby Durham (*d*). 3/80.

*** **The Alternate Blues** Original Jazz Classics OJC 744
As above. 3/80.

** **The Best Of Dizzy Gillespie** Pablo 2405-411

Gillespie's Pablo period marked a return to regular recording after some years of neglect in the studios. The *Big 4* album was the first session he did, and it remains perhaps the best. There is a superb display of trumpet chops in 'Be Bop', a very good ballad in 'Hurry Home' and an intriguing revision of 'Jitterbug Waltz' in which Pass and Gillespie push each other into their best form. The other records seem to betray Norman Granz's indecision as to how best to employ Dizzy's talents. The four Trumpet Kings/Summit encounters are typical of their kind: brilliant flashes of virtuosity interspersed with rhetoric and mere showing-off. The best is probably the Joe Turner meeting, where the great R&B singer puts everyone through their paces. *Montreux '77* is Gillespie featuring his young protégé, Jon Faddis, who xeroxes the young Gillespie style but comes up with a remark or two of his own. The earlier set, from 1975, includes some righteous jousting with Davis and Griffin, though it tends to go the way of all such festival showdowns. The best-of set is weak, picking some tracks off records that have thankfully disappeared. *Free Ride* is a hopeless collaboration with Lalo Schifrin that comes as a nasty shock after the great *Gillespiana* from 25 years earlier. *Dizzy's Party* is another one where there's no need to weep over a lost invite.

*** **Dizzy Gillespie Meets Phil Woods Quintet** Timeless SJP 250
Gillespie; Tom Harrell (*t*); Phil Woods (*as*); Hal Galper (*p*); Steve Gilmore (*b*); Bill Goodwin (*d*). 12/86.

(*) **Live At the Royal Festival Hall Enja 6044
Gillespie; Arturo Sandoval, Claudio Roditi (*t*); Slide Hampton (*tb*); Steve Turre (*tb, conch*); Paquito D'Rivera (*as, cl*); James Moody (*ts, f, as*); Mario Rivera (*ss, ts, perc*); Danilo Perez (*p*);

Ed Cherry (*g*); John Lee (*b*); Ignacio Berroa (*d*); Airto Moreira, Giovanni Hidalgo (*perc*); Flora Purim (*v*). 6/89.

The haphazard nature of Gillespie's recording regimen in the 1980s brings home how much the industry wasted the opportunity to provide a meaningful context for such a creative musician. Perpetually on the road, perhaps Dizzy simply wasn't so interested in making records; but the point remains that his legacy of genuinely great records is disappointingly small and is mainly concentrated at the other end of his career. His guest appearance with the Phil Woods band is respectable fare as such things go: there is yet another ''Round Midnight' of little interest, and Tom Harrell (uncredited) takes all the really strong trumpet parts, but it's a goodish Woods album with Dizzy making a few remarks. The Festival Hall concert catches something of the exuberance which continues to attend this kind of global-summit band and, though it's best approached as a souvenir for anyone who heard the group in concert, there are felicitous moments from a band very eager to please their boss.

***(*) **Max + Dizzy, Paris 1989** A&M 6404 2CD
Gillespie; Max Roach (*d*). 3/89.

A unique, moving, exciting experience. Bop's most eminent surviving champions reflect on close to 50 years of their music in an encounter which is as free as either man will ever play. Across some 90 minutes of music (the final section features the two of them talking it over), Roach sometimes pushes Dizzy a shade uncaringly, for the trumpeter's powers aren't what they were; but most of the horn playing is astonishingly clean and unmarked for a man in his seventies. As a kind of living history lesson, or a record of two of jazz's great personalities having a final exchange of ideas, it's a singular and generously entertaining occasion. Excellent sound.

(*) **To Bird With Love Telarc CD-83316
Gillespie; Paquito D'Rivera (*as, cl*); Jackie McLean, Antonio Hart (*as*); Clifford Jordan, David Sanchez, Benny Golson (*ts*); Danilo Perez (*p*); George Mraz (*b*); Lewis Nash (*d*); Bobby McFerrin (*v*). 1/92.

*** **To Diz With Love** Telarc CD-83307
Gillespie; Wynton Marsalis, Charlie Sepulveda, Claudio Roditi, Red Rodney, Wallace Roney, Jon Faddis, Doc Cheatham, Lew Soloff (*t*); Junior Mance (*p*); Peter Washington (*b*); Kenny Washington (*d*). 1–2/92.

From the concerts which were meant to inaugurate a year of celebration for Dizzy's 75th birthday and which instead turned out to be his final appearances. The trumpet feast on the second disc has the edge, with a hint of cutting contest in the air, whereas some of the sax players burn each other out on the first record. Diz sounds frail but unprepared to admit it.

Ginger Pig New Orleans Band GROUP

*** **The Ginger Pig New Orleans Band Featuring Sammy Remington** [sic.] GHB BCD-232
Jim Holmes (*t*); Dale Vickers (*tb*); Sammy Rimington (*cl, as*); John Hale (*cl*); John Richardson (*p*); John Coles (*bj*); Annie Hawkins (*b*); Colin Richardson (*d*). 12/87.

Another group of Brits masquerading as New Orleans players, the Ginger Pig combo play an august sort of trad, with guest Rimington lending some authentic flavour. On a more 'modern' piece such as 'Mahogany Hall Stomp' they lack the necessary finesse, but a slow piece such as 'Till Then' is quite convincingly done, and the sound of the record – it was made at Northampton's Black Bottom Club – is reverberantly evocative of a proper Louisiana setting.

Vince Giordano TUBA, BASS SAXOPHONE, BASS

*** **Bill Challis' The Goldkette Project** Circle CCD-118
Giordano; Peter Ecklund (*t, c*); Spanky Davis, Dave Gale, Randy Rinehart (*t*); Stew Pletcher (*c*); Dan Barrett, Herb Gardner, Spiegel Wilcox (*tb*); Mark Lopeman, Ted Nash, Jack Stuckey (*cl, as, bs*); Bob Wilber (*ts, cl*); Dick Wellstood (*p*); Stan Kurtis (*vn*); James Chirillo, Frank Vignola (*bj, g*); Arnie Kinsella (*d*). 88.

***(*) **Quality Shout!** Stomp Off CD1260
Giordano; Peter Ecklund, Jon-Erik Kellso (*c*); Herb Gardner (*tb*); Jack Stuckey, Scott Robinson, Dan Block (*reeds*); Jeremy Kahn (*p*); John Gill, Matt Trimboli (*bj, g*); Arnie Kinsella (*d*). 9/92–3/93.

A band that names their record, made in the '90s, after a track by Paul Howard's Quality Serenaders should be of interest to all inquiring jazz listeners. As the first-call man on bass instruments for any revivalist project in the New York area, Giordano has cornered the market in bass sax and tuba specialities. His band, The Nighthawks (name borrowed from the Coon–Sanders outfit), take a line in revivalism that would be fanatical but for their good humour and magically light touch. All 22 tracks on *Quality Shout!* are based on original records, all cited in the sleeve-notes, and archivists will be astonished at finding transcriptions of the likes of Cliff Jackson's 'The Terror', Sam Wooding's 'Bull Foot Stomp' and Alex Hill's 'Southbound'. In some cases they even follow the transcribed solos, as with the California Ramblers' Edison version of 'Zulu Wail'. As a repertory record, it's beautifully done – Ecklund and Kellso are a sparkily brilliant front line, the reeds have their original vibratos down pat, and the rhythm feels poised between something clockwork and something a little looser, which feels just right for the period. Recommended to ears of any vintage.

The Goldkette album is a more specific homage, recorded under the eye of Goldkette's arranger, Bill Challis, and with the coup of having original Goldkette sideman Wilcox in the band. They get a beautiful sound in the studio, old-fashioned and immediate at the same time; but anyone who knows the original Goldkette records might find some of these re-creations tame: they miss the terrific rush of 'My Pretty Girl', probably Goldkette's best record, and some of the individual parts falter – Stan Kurtis, for instance, sounds no match for Joe Venuti on 'I'd Rather Be The Girl In Your Arms'. But it's a charming and enjoyable tribute.

George Girard (1930–57) TRUMPET, VOCAL

*** **George Girard** Storyville STCD 6013
Girard; Santo Pecora, Bob Havens (*tb*); Raymond Burke, Harry Shields (*cl*); Lester Bouchon (*ts*); Jeff Riddick (*p, v*); Bob Discon (*p*); Emile Christian, Chink Martin (*b*); Monk Hazel, Paul Edwards (*d*). 9/54–7/56.

Girard, who died young after contracting cancer, was a very fine trumpeter. He made his name in the Basin Street Six with Pete Fountain, but these recordings – one session made at the Municipal Auditorium in 1954, the other at the Parisian Room in 1956, only a few months before his death – offer formidable evidence of a great, idiosyncratic New Orleans hornman, somewhat in the manner (if not the style) of Henry Allen. Girard's firm lead is countered by his unpredictable solos, which may suddenly flare up into wild high notes or stay in a sober middle range: he's hard to second-guess, even on warhorse material such as the tunes played at the 1956 session, which also has excellent work from Havens and Shields. The earlier date is marred by the recording, which is poorly balanced and muffled, and by the feeble tenor work of Bouchon; but Girard and Pecora are both very good: the trumpeter's brilliant solo on 'A Good Man Is Hard To Find' is a small masterpiece of controlled tension. The 1956 recordings are more than adequate, and it's hard to believe that Girard's playing is the work of a man who was already very ill.

Greg Gisbert (born 1966) TRUMPET

*** **Harcology** Criss Cross Criss 1084
Gisbert; Chris Potter (*ts, ss*); John Campbell (*p*); Dwayne Burno (*b*); Gregory Hutchinson (*d*). 12/92.

This bright, unfussy date is strongly marked by the example of Clark Terry, Thad Jones and Tom Harrell, the most obvious influences on the thirty-year-old Gisbert's trumpet style. He plays clean, uncomplicated lines in a frankly old-fashioned style. Over almost exactly an hour there is nothing that will frighten the horses, and nothing that is not resolutely tasteful and coherent. His big solos are on the title-piece (a solitary Gisbert original), Campbell's 'Turning Point' and the standard 'Autumn In New York'. For much of the remainder he is happy to sit back and let colleagues take front stage. An engaging set by yet another of Criss Cross's seemingly endless supply of new hornmen.

Jimmy Giuffre (born 1921) CLARINET, TENOR SAXOPHONE, SOPRANO SAXOPHONE, FLUTE, BASS FLUTE

***(*) **The Jimmy Giuffre 3** Atlantic 90981
Giuffre; Jim Hall (*g*); Jim Atlas, Ralph Pena (*b*). 12/56.
***(*) **Hollywood & Newport, 1957–1958** Fresh Sound FSCD 1026
Giuffre; Bob Brookmeyer (*vtb*); Jim Hall (*g*); Ralph Pena (*b*). 1/57, 7 & 10/58.

Cultivating a brown *chalumeau* register on his clarinet and defending the aesthetic benefits of simple quietness, Giuffre created what he liked to call 'folk jazz'. *The Jimmy Giuffre Clarinet* and *Music Man*, recorded for Atlantic in the 1950s, evoked a middle-America which had hitherto played little part in jazz. Giuffre's soft meditations and homely foot-tapping on the earlier album suggested a man playing out on his front porch, sufficiently solitary and unselfconscious to forget the rules and try out unfamiliar tonalities.

The Jimmy Giuffre 3 contains some of the essential early material, notably a fine version of 'The Train And The River', on which Giuffre moves between baritone and tenor saxophones and clarinet, and the long 'Crawdad Suite', which intelligently combines blues and folk materials. Giuffre's out-of-tempo playing recalls the great jazz singers. Jim Hall was his longest-standing and most sympathetic cohort; they were partnered either by trombonist Bob Brookmeyer or a bassist, most successfully Ralph Pena or Buddy Clark (Jim Atlas plays on only two bonus tracks on the Atlantic CD).

The Giuffre–Brookmeyer–Hall trio appears behind the credits on the great movie, *Jazz on a Summer's Day* (the top of Hall's head is just about visible), playing 'The Train And The River'. The Fresh Sound captures that whole set, together with earlier and later material from the West Coast, where this kind of jazz seemed to have a more natural home. Brookmeyer's slightly lazy, wall-eyed delivery was an ideal foil for Giuffre. He kept to the same end of the tonal spectrum and shared a love of easy tempos.

**** 1961 ECM 1438/9 2CD
    Giuffre; Paul Bley (*p*); Steve Swallow (*b*). 3 & 8/61.
**** Emphasis, Stuttgart 1961 hat Art CD 6072
    As above. 11/61.
***(*) Flight, Bremen 1961 hat Art CD 6071
    As above. 11/61.
  **** Free Fall Columbia 480708
    As above. 62.

Giuffre's subsequent drummerless trios and cool, almost abstract tonality created nearly as much stir as Gerry Mulligan's pianoless quintets and encountered considerable critical resistance at the end of the 1950s. Nothing that had come along before quite prepares us for the astonishing work that Giuffre created with Paul Bley and Steve Swallow in two 1961 albums called *Fusion* (a term which hadn't yet taken on its 1970s associations) and *Thesis* (which seemed equally unpromising as the title of a jazz album). Paired and remastered as *1961*, they constitute ECM's first ever reissue; it's interesting, first, how modern the music sounds after 30 years (compare it with the Owl sets, below), and then how closely it seems to conform to ECM's familiar aesthetics of great formal precision and limpid sound. Herb Snitzer's session photographs have often been commented on. In deeply shadowed and evocatively focused black and white, they say something about the music. It's arguable that Giuffre's playing is equally monochrome and its basic orientation uncomfortably abstract; but again one notices its sometimes urgent but always compelling swing. The slightly earlier *Fusion* is perhaps the more daring of the two sets, balancing starkly simple ideas, as on 'Jesus Maria' and 'Scootin' About' with some complex harmonic conceptions (to which all three contribute). *Thesis*, though, is tighter and more fully realized, and tunes like 'Ictus' and 'Carla' (the former written by the dedicatee of the latter, Bley's then wife, Carla Bley) have been an inexhaustible element of the pianist's concert improvisations ever since. By contrast, the music on *Fusion* seems fixed in and of its moment.

Free Fall, by contrast, is a trickier and more insidious sound altogether. A mixture of Giuffre solos (including some of his most piercing and antagonistic recorded statements) with duos and trios, it catches the group late on in its brief initial history. After the European tour documented on the hat ART CDs, some hard thinking and talking was obviously done and the internal dynamics of the group change. Remarkable to think of Columbia taking on a project like this in 1962 but, whatever the exact intention of the title, it was clear that the studiousness and philosophical calm which overlaid the previous discs was no longer to be expected. What you're hearing is something that has almost run its course in practical terms but which creatively is far from exhausted. Swallow's fiery scrabbles and sharply plucked single-note runs lend the music a new momentum and the sort of energy to be found in free jazz. Bley may be the most least comfortable of the three by this stage, but he has always been a restless experimenter and by 1962 his eye was probably on the next step. Giuffre often sounds as if he is in a world of his own, intensely focused, totally aware, but communicating ideas for which there was no ready-made language or critical rhetoric.

These – and *Free Fall* especially – are essential documents in the development of a broader jazz idiom that refused to see bop as the only recourse. Giuffre's pioneering has only slowly been recognized and it's valuable to jump straight from these sessions to *Diary Of A Trio*, below. Almost nothing has changed, except that Giuffre's tone has lost its slightly discursive quality, an effect underlined by his use of soprano saxophone, and Steve Swallow has renounced upright bass, on which he creates throbbing lines and interjections (these are, perhaps, the most dramatic sounds on *1961*), in favour of bass guitar.

The group ran into a critical brick wall in the United States but were briefly taken up in Europe where they toured that same year, arousing strong (though admittedly sometimes hostile) notice wherever they went. The Stuttgart concert is the better of the two on hat Art. It may be that the strains of what was obviously a very charged tour have started to take their toll by the time the trio played in Bremen, a fortnight later. 'Cry, Want', 'Stretching Out' (a specially devised 'Suite For Germany'), 'Venture', 'Sonic' and 'Whirrr' are common to both sets, but Bley's determination not to repeat prefabricated licks means that they sound very different on both records. Giuffre is more of a licks player (as wind instrumentalists often are) and he seems to have dropped into certain repetitive structures. What's impressive, though, is his ability to shade a phrase microscopically (or perhaps microtonally) so that it sits on the piano and bass chords differently each time. These are remarkable documents.

***(*) Giuffre / Konitz / Connors / Bley Improvising Artists Inc IAI 37.38.59

Giuffre; Lee Konitz (as); Bill Connors (g); Paul Bley (p). 5/78.

The 1970s were Giuffre's wilderness years but, contrary to what is sometimes suggested, he had not given up playing altogether. These pieces were recorded for Paul Bley's IAI label at the IAI Festival in 1978, a nodal point for creative musicians at that time and the seed that grew into some of the more positive innovations of the next decade.

Giuffre and Konitz, on tenor and alto respectively, duet on Pettiford's 'Blues In The Closet', then Giuffre switches to the throbbing bass flute for the improvise, 'Sad Time'. The remaining tracks are also duos. He improvises 'Spanish Flames' on clarinet with Connors, moves on to soprano for 'Enter, Ivory' with Bley, and returns to tenor for the last piece with Konitz again. It's a virtuoso performance, and it served to remind many people that, 20 years after the Newport triumph, Giuffre was not only still alive but was playing at the very highest level. A very valuable record.

*** Quasar Soul Note 1108

Giuffre; Pete Levin (ky); Bob Nieske (b); Randy Kaye (d). 5/85.

*** Liquid Dancers Soul Note 1158

As above. 4/89.

For much of the later 1960s and 1970s, the most intuitive improviser of his generation was obliged to teach improvisation to college students, gigging only in relative obscurity. Randy Kaye was a loyal and dependable supporter in those days, and he adds just the right kind of softly enunciated percussion to Giuffre's 1980s quartet albums (a third Soul Note, *Dragonfly*, is currently unavailable).

Bob Nieske's 'The Teacher', on *Liquid Dancers*, pays no less a tribute. Scored for Giuffre's bass flute, it has a crepuscular, meditative quality that isn't altogether typical of a lively and almost self-consciously ('Move With The Times') contemporary set. Levin's keyboard stylings are perhaps a little too blandly atmospheric, but they open up the texture for Giuffre's familiar chalumeau clarinet and a surprisingly agile soprano saxophone.

The earlier *Quasar* is equally fine and the writing may even be a little better.

***(*) Eiffel CELP C6

Giuffre; André Jaume (bcl, sax). 11/87.

The best of these thoughtful, often delicate duos recall the best of Giuffre's work with Brookmeyer. Jaume has the same intensity and dry wit, and the register of his bass clarinet is not so far from that of the trombone. Recorded in concert, *Eiffel* consists of scored and improvised duets, none longer than five and a half minutes, most around three. Jaume's saxophone on 'Stand Point' tends to break the mood a little, but the studied, contemplative tone otherwise remains intact and Giuffre's articulation and tone have seldom been more compelling.

**** Diary Of A Trio: Saturday Owl 059

Giuffre; Paul Bley (p); Steve Swallow (b). 12/89.

**** Diary Of A Trio: Sunday Owl 060

As above. 12/89.

***(*) Fly Away, Little Bird Owl 068

As above. 4/92.

When Jimmy Giuffre went back into the studio with Paul Bley and Steve Swallow in December 1989, the first notes he improvised were identical to a figure he had played on their last meeting, nearly 30 years before. Whether conscious or not, the gesture helps underline not just the intervening period of (for Giuffre) relative neglect but also the tremendous understanding that developed in the trio that produced *Free Fall, Fusion* and *Thesis*.

Diary Of A Trio is an astonishing achievement, whatever the chronology. A series of solos, duos and trio pieces, it has considerable spontaneity and freedom. There are, of course, significant changes from the early records. Swallow is now wholly converted to electric bass, and is perhaps the leading bass guitarist in improvised music; Bley, though, has passed through his romance with electronics and now concentrates almost exclusively on acoustic piano. Giuffre, who was always a formidable tenor player as well as clarinettist, has added soprano saxophone, relishing both its directness and its untameable 'wildness' of pitch. Not least of the differences is a willingness to play standards, which they do with a characteristically oblique touch. Most highly recommended.

Owl's attempt to repeat the experiment in 1992 comes off only partially. Giuffre sounded tired, as he did throughout the European tour of that year, and much of the emphasis falls on exchanges between Bley and Swallow, with mere elaborations from saxophone and clarinet. They included some standards to keep the purists quiet. 'All The Things You Are', 'Sweet And Lovely', 'Lover Man' and 'I Can't Get Started': if only they'd thought to do that in 1961, Giuffre's CV and discography might well have read very differently!

***(*) **River Station** CELP C 26
> Giuffre; Joe McPhee (*tb*); André Jaume (*ts, bcl*). 9/91.

Repeating the triumphs of 30 years before, Giuffre found himself an honoured elder in Europe. With the exception of Bley and Swallow, it was nearly always Frenchmen who wanted to perform with him. This session has an air of relaxed preparedness. Some of the duos recall the Giuffre/Konitz encounter of 1978 (see above) and the walk-on contribution of Joe McPhee with his trombone on 'Three Way Split' sounds like a long after-echo of the classic Brookmeyer trio. Giuffre's wife had been writing a good deal of music before this time, and she contributes the outstanding 'When Things Go Wrong'. The only thing that has gone wrong with the recording is that both players seem to be placed at opposite ends of the studio. A little 'false mono' might actually have helped.

It's worth cross-referencing here to another CELP release led by Joe McPhee and called *Impressions Of Jimmy Giuffre*. It's reviewed under McPhee's entry.

Ole Amund Gjersvik BASS

*** **A Voice From The Past** Acoustic ACR 9001
> Gjersvik; Jan Kare Hystad (*ss*); Ole Jacob Hystad (*ts*); Helge Lilletvedt (*p*); Ole Thomsen (*g, g-syn*); Geir Svinnset (*d*). 2/90.
***(*) **Appasionata Criminelle** Acoustic ACR 9201
> As above. 6/91.
*** **Around The Fountain** Acoustic ACR 9504
> As above. 8/93–1/94.

Gjersvik's group is based in Bergen and they play a thoughtful and not too laid-back variation on the pastoral jazz that seems to get classed as a Norwegian speciality. In truth, there is more of Pat Metheny than of Jan Garbarek in these records, with the gently shuttling rhythms and carefully voiced unison horns plaiting closely with Thomsen's familiar-sounding guitar and guitar-synth licks. But it's done with plenty of style. The saxophonists turn in some of the best improvising: Jan Kare Hystad's forlorn soprano on 'Yaqui' on the second record, his namesake's tenor on the charming 'Follow Swallow' on the earlier date. *Appasionata Criminelle* edges ahead for the greater variety in composition and a sense that these men are crafting this currency in their own authentic way: 'Joik', for instance, sounds worldly and localized at the same moment. *Around The Fountain* shows no special advance but is again very satisfying: melodic, absorbing music, somewhere between a boppish sensibility and a fusion outlook. The final track, a live cut by the tenor–bass–drums trio alone, is more free-flowing and suggests a fresh path for the future.

Globe Unity Orchestra GROUP

***(*) **Rumbling** FMP CD 40
> Manfred Schoof, Kenny Wheeler (*t*); Paul Rutherford, Albert Mangelsdorff (*tb*); Evan Parker (*ss, ts*); Steve Lacy (*ss*); Peter Brötzmann (*as, ts, bsx*); Gerd Dudek (*bs, bcl, f*); Alex Von Schlippenbach (*p*); Peter Kowald (*b*); Paul Lovens (*d*). 3/75.
**** **20th Anniversary** FMP CD 45
> Manfred Schoof, Kenny Wheeler (*t*); Gunter Christmann, Paul Rutherford (*tb*); Peter Brötzmann, Rudiger Carl, Gerd Dudek, Evan Parker, Michael Pilz (*reeds*); Alex Von Schlippenbach (*p*); Derek Bailey (*g*); Peter Kowald (*b, tba*); Han Bennink (*d, perc, cl*); Paul Lovens (*d*). 11/86.

Only two discs to show for 20 years of work by an incomparable free-music institution. Formed in 1966, the Globe Unity Orchestra has had to sustain itself with rare concerts and even rarer records, an unworthy fate for arguably the finest group to attempt to reconcile big-band forms with free improvisation. Although there has been a revolving cast of players throughout the group's existence, a few hardy spirits (notably Alex Schlippenbach, the original organizer) act as a point of reference. The *Rumbling* CD is by what is more like a contingent from the orchestra. There is Monk's title-tune, a march by Misha Mengelberg and a tune by Lacy, while 'Into The Valley' is a nearly continuous 38-minute piece.

The latter is the best demonstration of the group's powers, moving through solo and duet passages between the horns to thunderous all-in tussles. Problematically, the original LP editions of this music sounded grey and boxy, but the sound is much bigger and more convincing here.

To celebrate their twentieth anniversary, the Orchestra held a Berlin concert at which the 66-minute work on FMP CD 45 was played. While a shade below their 1977 masterpiece, *Pearls*, this is still a vivid, bristling assemblage of ideas and individual spontaneities: Schlippenbach's hand is on the tiller, but each man asserts his individual mastery in his personal way. A very good way of making acquaintance with many of the great modernists of the past 30 years.

Larry Goldings ORGAN

*** **Intimacy Of The Blues** Minor Music 801017
> Goldings; David 'Fathead' Newman (*ts*); Peter Bernstein (*g*); Bill Stewart (*d*). 91.

*** **Light Blue** Minor Music 801026
> As above, except omit Newman. 92.

The virtue of Goldings's approach to the Hammond B–3 is its easeful simplicity. Both albums are thoughtfully titled, given the plain, small-hours moods which Goldings prefers to evoke instead of all-stops-out virtuosity. The subtly shaded solo treatment of 'Here, There And Everywhere' on *Light Blue* is typical. Bernstein plays the Grant Green role with loose-limbed skill, and Stewart is guileful at the drums, while Newman makes three cameo appearances on the first record. All that said, there's very little here that hasn't been done on a McGriff or Smith record: only the big-screen digital sound is a novelty, when most of the classic organ-jazz records date from the 1960s.

*** **Caminhos Cruzados** Novus 01241 63184-2
> Goldings; Joshua Redman (*ts*); Peter Bernstein (*g*); Bill Stewart (*d*); Guilherme Franco (*perc*). 12/93.

***(*) **Whatever It Takes** Warner Bros 945996-2
> As above, except add Fred Wesley (*tb*), David Sanborn, Maceo Parker (*as*); Richard Patterson (*b*); omit Franco. 95.

The Novus album is more of the same as the Minor Music records, though more healthily energetic: 'So Danco Samba', normally taken at a tempo that would slow most dancers to a crawl, skips along. Redman appears on three tracks and blows some hearty solos. *Whatever It Takes*, though, is more cannily presented. The material is biased towards funky pop – Stevie Wonder, Sly Stone, Ray Charles – and the spots by Sanborn, Parker, Wesley and Redman (again) add a touch of class without sounding too much like here-comes-the-guest-star. But it's not done at the expense of Goldings' cool blue side, since 'Slo-Boat' and 'Willow Weep For Me' handle that very effectively. Excellent, full-blooded studio sound seals the deal.

Per Goldschmidt BARITONE SAXOPHONE

*** **Cage Rage** Olufsen DOCD 5095
> Goldschmidt; Erling Kroner (*tb*); Nikolaj Bentzon (*p*); Klaus Hovman (*b*); Preben Petersen (*d*). 11/88.

*** **Another Night, Another Day** Olufsen DOCD 5129
> As above. 11/88.

*** **The Frame** Timeless SJP 290
> Goldschmidt; Niels Lan Doky (*p*); Lonnie Plaxico (*b*); Jack DeJohnette (*d*). 2/87.

*** **Frankly** Milestone MCD-9224-2
> As above, except Alvin Queen (*d*) replaces DeJohnette, Niels-Henning Orsted-Pedersen (*b*) replaces Plaxico; add Tom Harrell (*t, flhn*). 12/93.

Goldschmidt is no romantic fool on the baritone. He loves its weight and impact and powers along with few concessions to its size: even on ballads he prefers to take a terser line than Mulligan or Chaloff ever would have done. Structurally, he's a hard bopper who can't abide the clichés of the genre. Some of the tunes on the Olufsen albums are mere sketches to blow on, but he never takes the easy line, chopping his phrasing, bouncing off the drive of the rhythm section, wrestling with himself to make it turn out new.

Not that any of these is a masterpiece. The Olufsens were recorded back-to-back in one marathon session – the second ends with an alternative take of track one on the first – and their sheer rough-and-tumble merits applause. Bentzon is wildly excitable at the piano, playing with Pullen-like intensity, and Petersen hammers and rolls through the rhythms. Kroner is sober, almost deadpan, and that sits usefully with Goldschmidt's sometimes blustering improvising. The horns are weakened by the indifferent mix and the records never peak, but they're an exhilarating pair.

The Timeless album assembles a classier band. Goldschmidt plays with fine energy and purpose and the band are behind him, but the music misses a decisiveness that sometimes results in rambling: the ironic bossa nova of 'Loneliness', for instance, merely turns hollow. Nor is Doky's production very agreeable. He also produces the Milestone session, which sounds terrific, and there are some marvellous moments here: 'Theme For Eve', for baritone, bass and drums only, is exquisitely modulated, and Goldschmidt plays with extra swagger and resilience on the up-tempo tracks. But the concept, playing songs associated with Frank Sinatra, seems intended to tame the leader's most adventurous side, and Harrell, if dependable, seems a notch below his best.

Vinny Golia CLARINETS, FLUTES, SAXOPHONES, SHAKUHACHI, ETC.

***(*) **Pilgrimage To Obscurity** Nine Winds NWCD 0130
    Golia; John Fumo, Ralf Rickert, Sal Cracchiolo (*t, flhn*); Mike Vlatkovich, Doug Wintz, John Rapson (*tb*); David Stout (*tb*); Mike Acosta, Steve Fowler, Wynell Montgomery, David Ocker (*reeds*); David Johnson (*vib, mar*); Eric Messerschmidt (*tba*); Ken Filiano, Roberto Miranda (*b*); Billy Mintz (*d*); Alex Cline (*perc*). 12/85.

*** **Worldwide And Portable** Nine Winds NWCD 0143
    Golia; Wayne Peet (*p*); Ken Filiano (*b*). 2/86.

**** **Regards From Norma Desmond** Fresh Sound FSNT 008
    Golia; John Fumo (*t*); Wayne Peet (*p*); Ken Filiano (*b*); Alex Cline (*d*). 10/86.

***(*) **Decennium Dans Axlan** Nine Winds NWCD 0140
    Golia; Mark Underwood, John Fumo, Rob Blakeslee (*t, flhn*); Bruce Fowler, George McMullen (*tb*); Phil Teele (*btb*); Emily Hay, Steve Fowler, Bill Plake, David Ocker (*reeds*); Wayne Peet (*ky*); Jeff Gauthier (*vn*); Jonathan Golove, Dion Sorell (*clo*); Ken Filiano, Joel Hamilton (*b*); Alex Cline (*d*); Brad Dutz (*perc*). 4/92.

***(*) **Commemoration** Nine Winds NWCD 0150/0160 2CD
    As above, except add Marissa Benedict (*t*), Mike Vlatkovich (*tb*), Kim Richmond (*reeds*), Harry Scorzo (*vn*), Greg Adamson, Matt Cooker (*clo*), William Roper (*tba*), David Johnson (*perc*). 91–92.

*** **Haunting The Spirits Inside Them** . . . Music & Arts CD-893
    Golia; Joelle Leandre, Ken Filiano (*b*). 4/92.

***(*) **Against The Grain** Nine Winds NWCD 0159
    Golia; Rob Blakeslee (*t*); Nels Cline (*g*); Ken Filiano (*b*); Billy Mintz (*d*). 10/93.

Vinny Golia has been a central figure in the West Coast avant-garde for many years, and with his Nine Winds label he's been undertaking virtually a one-man documentation of the improvising underground of California – far less 'fashionable' than anything out of New York, but no less significant in the grain of American free jazz. There are a number of earlier Nine Winds LPs featuring Golia as both leader and sideman, but so far these are the only CDs under his own name on the label. The two discs by the Large Ensemble are fragments from ten years of work with this vast orchestra which Golia apparently keeps going out of his own pocket. Out of more than 100 pieces the Ensemble has managed to record a scant few, but both of these discs are very worthwhile. The group moves like some sea-going leviathan: ponderous, sluggish at times, but suddenly raising itself and achieving grace and beauty. Golia always insists on the weight and thick sonority of the orchestra: sections call and respond to one another somewhat in the big-band tradition, but there is little that one can call swinging, more the contrast of great blocks of sound, the emergence of a soloist to say his piece, the chattering of brass or lowering of a bass reed section. *Pilgrimage To Obscurity* – self-effacing to be sure – alternates between rousing all-hands-on pieces and thinned-out, dirge-like textures. The recent *Decennium Dans Axlan* starts even more slowly, with the gradually accumulating power of 'Tapestry Of Things Before', and ends on the similarly inclined 'Man In A Bottle'; in between, there are some beautiful solos by Rob Blakeslee, Bruce Fowler and Steve Fowler from the round-robin of improvisers. *Commemoration*, though a more recent release, was in part recorded prior to *Decennium Dans Axlan*. Again, Golia marshals his forces around key points, waving in some instruments, keeping others under wraps, and only rarely going for the big climax – though when he does, as on the towering 'Tumulus Or Griffin', it's mightily impressive. None of the three sets really stands out from the others, and the problem with all three is the second-rate recording, that perennial obstacle for the independent label.

By himself, in the small-group context, Golia reveals an obsession with doubling on numerous instruments: he plays 11 different woodwinds on *Worldwide And Portable*, changing the weave with each different reed. He calls this group The Chamber Trio, and the mood is assuredly sober, the ambitions of the group seemingly based around texture rather than individual lines. The most swinging piece, peculiarly enough, is a dedication to Kafka! But Golia, Peet and Filiano know each other's work very well, and there is much subtlety of interaction. *Against The Grain* is another admirable outing for his quintet: Golia's fascination with long form comes out in the 24-minute 'Presents To Savages/Alternation', and there is some superb contrapuntalism in 'SBB-CFF'. He sticks to sopranino and soprano saxes and two clarinets here; on the meeting with Filiano and Leandre, a chance session following a concert, he plays only flutes, clarinets, piccolo, ocarina, shakuhachi and sheng. This is a whispery, introverted music, the two basses somewhat distant in the soundmix and Golia laying out as often as pitching in, with sometimes mixed results.

It might seem perverse to pick out a rare record for another label as one of Golia's best. But the recently issued 1986 session for Fresh Sound is a corker. Golia sticks to baritone sax throughout *Regards From Norma Desmond*, and with one of his favourite line-ups they blaze through 50 minutes of free bop that's gripping from first to last, with the outstanding threnody for Booker Little, 'The Cry', particularly fine.

Benny Golson (born 1929) TENOR SAXOPHONE

*** **Benny Golson's New York Scene** Original Jazz Classics OJC 164
    Golson; Art Farmer (*t*); Jimmy Cleveland (*tb*); Julius Watkins (*frhn*); Gigi Gryce (*as*); Sahib Shihab (*bs*); Wynton Kelly (*p*); Paul Chambers (*b*); Charli Persip (*d*). 10/57.

*** **The Modern Touch** Original Jazz Classics OJC 1797
    Golson; Kenny Dorham (*t*); J. J. Johnson (*tb*); Wynton Kelly (*p*); Paul Chambers (*b*); Max Roach (*d*). 12/57.

***(*) **Gone With Golson** Orignal Jazz Classics OJC 1850
    Golson; Curtis Fuller (*tb*); Ray Bryant (*p*); Tom Bryant (*b*); Al Harewood (*d*). 6/59.

**** **Groovin' With Golson** Original Jazz Classics OJC 226
    Golson; Curtis Fuller (*tb*); Ray Bryant (*p*); Paul Chambers (*b*); Art Blakey (*d*). 8/59.

*** **Gettin' With It** Original Jazz Classics OJC 1873
    Golson; Curtis Fuller (*tb*); Tommy Flanagan (*p*); Doug Watkins (*b*); Art Taylor (*d*). 12/59.

*** **The Other Side Of Benny Golson** Original Jazz Classics OJC 1750
    Golson; Curtis Fuller (*tb*); Barry Harris (*p*); Jymie Merritt (*b*); Philly Joe Jones (*d*). 11/58.

He is still best known as an arranger and composer – of such standards as 'I Remember Clifford', 'Whisper Not' and 'Stablemates' – so Benny Golson's powers as a saxophonist have been somewhat undervalued as a result. Although he has contributed several of the staple pieces in the hard-bop repertoire, his own playing style originally owed rather more to such swing masters as Hawkins and Lucky Thompson: a big, crusty tone and a fierce momentum sustain his solos, and they can take surprising and exciting turns, even if the unpredictability sometimes leads to a loss of focus. The earlier of the two 1957 sessions concentrates on the more reflective side of his work, with three tracks by a nonet, three by a quintet with Farmer, and a ballad interpretation of 'You're Mine You' with the rhythm section alone: all well played but comparatively reserved. *The Modern Touch* is impeccably tailored hard bop, bedecked with good writing by the leader and suave playing by the sextet, but it's uneventful rather than exciting. The later discs contain the seeds of the group which would, when joined full-time by Farmer, become the Jazztet. The best is *Groovin'*, titled appropriately since the band hit a splendid pace from the start, and Golson and Fuller turn in inspired solos. *Gone With Golson* is only a notch behind: Golson fashions a catchy arrangement of Bryant's 'Staccato Swing', takes an impassioned course through 'Autumn Leaves' and turns in a fine 'Blues After Dark'. *Gettin' With It* is rather too casual here and there, starting with a 'Baubles, Bangles And Beads' which is so relaxed it scarcely comes off the starting blocks. There's consolation in 'Tippin' On Thru' and a very slow and consummately controlled 'April In Paris'. *The Other Side* is also at a lower temperature but is still very worthwhile.

*** **California Message** Timeless SJP 177
    Golson; Oscar Brashear (*t*); Curtis Fuller, Thurman Green (*tb*); Bill Mays (*p*); Bob Magnusson (*b*); Roy McCurdy (*d*). 10/80.

*** **Time Speaks** Timeless SJP 187
    Golson; Freddie Hubbard, Woody Shaw (*t*); Kenny Barron (*p*); Cecil McBee (*b*); Ben Riley (*d*). 12/84.

(*) **This Is For You, John Timeless SJP 235
    Golson; Pharoah Sanders (*ts*); Cedar Walton (*p*); Ron Carter (*b*); Jack DeJohnette (*d*). 12/83.

Golson aged in an interesting way. Though his tone has weakened and taken on a querulous edge, his playing hasn't so much declined in stature as changed its impact. He had traded his swing influences for Coltrane 20 years earlier and, by the 1980s – after a sabbatical in film and TV scoring – it had resulted in the kind of introspective passion which marks out some of Coltrane's music, even if Golson chose a more conservative set of aims. These three Timeless albums include some top-drawer sidemen, but

Golson is invariably the most interesting presence on each session. *California Message* is a good if rather routine date; *Time Speaks* is better, with the stellar line-up clearly enjoying itself. Golson's solo on the opening 'I'll Remember April' is a textbook example of how he adapted Coltrane's methods to his own ends. Unfortunately the interplay between Hubbard and Shaw is rather splashy, and the piano is too remote in the mix (a characteristic Rudy van Gelder trait). *This Is For You, John* should have been a classic meeting with Sanders, with Golson confronting Coltrane's influence to the full, yet the session too often degenerates into rambling solos to maintain real interest.

*** **Stardust** Denon 33CY-1838
    Golson; Freddie Hubbard (*t, flhn*); Mulgrew Miller (*p*); Ron Carter (*b*); Marvin 'Smitty' Smith (*d*). 6/87.
Golson in confident if sometimes discursive form. *Stardust* has him co-leading a blue-chip group with Hubbard, and originals such as 'Gypsy Jingle-Jangle' are strong enough to put the band on its mettle; the session is finally a little ordinary, though, if only because Hubbard lacks front-line substance on this occasion.

***(*) **Live** Dreyfus 191057-2
    Golson; Mulgrew Miller (*p*); Peter Washington (*b*); Tony Reedus (*d*). 2/89.
***(*) **Domingo** Dreyfus 191132-2
    Golson; Jean-Loup Longnon (*t*); Curtis Fuller (*tb*); Kevin Hays (*p*); James Genus (*b*); Tony Reedus (*d*). 11/91.
Golson sounds in wonderful voice on the live session, captured on a European stopover in Porto Maggiore. There's a feathery, rippling treatment of 'I Remember Clifford' which makes it clear that, although there've been countless versions of this ballad, the composer himself still has fresh things to say about it. 'Jam The Avenue' is the kind of blow-out that has to have everyone's chops in good order, and Golson has no trouble there. 'Sweet And Lovely' shows that he is still learning from Coltrane, too. The studio date features an impressive quintet (Longnom turns up only for 'Blues March') and continues the long and intriguing partnership between Golson and Fuller, a dialogue seldom remarked on but as productive as any in the post-bop era. The title-track was originally arranged for Lee Morgan in the 1950s and has hardly been heard from since, but Golson comes up with a fine new arrangement, and it's a pity that he otherwise contributes only one new piece, 'Thinking Mode'; the rest are staples from his book, as well as Fuller's spirited 'A La Mode' and Brubeck's 'In Your Own Sweet Way'. Some thin patches, but Golson remains a fascinating source and a great tenor player.

Eddie Gomez (born 1944) BASS

*** **Gomez** Denon DC 8562
    Gomez; Chick Corea (*p, syn*); Steve Gadd (*d*); Yasuaki Shimizu (*ts*); Kazumi Watanabe (*g*). 1–2/84.
***(*) **Live In Moscow** B&W Music BW 038
    Gomez; Michael Okun (*p*); Steve Amirault (*p, syn*); Ronnie Burrage (*d*). 10/92.
(*) **Next Future Stretch GRS 00062
    Gomez: Rick Margitza (*ts, ss*); Jeremy Steig (*f*); James Williams (*p*); Chick Corea (*p, syn*); Lenny White (*d*). 93.
A veteran of the Bill Evans Trio and a staggering roster of free(ish)-modern to fusion line-ups since then, Gomez hasn't been extensively recorded as leader. *Gomez* moves close to the company (and production values) he deserves. Corea is immediately responsive, notably on the two duo tracks, and Gomez also duets effectively with Gadd. The Japanese saxophonist and guitarist are responsible for some mildly interesting aesthetic mismatches, but neither is sufficiently individual to carry it off regardless. An unqualified three stars for the best of it; mild reservations about the remainder.

    Recorded during a Moscow–Rio–New York festival, the second disc, like its predecessor, brings a range of cultures together under the umbrella of a tribute to Bill Evans. Gomez is playing magnificently, opening in duo with Okun on 'Alice In Wonderland', 'Stella By Starlight' and 'Someday My Prince Will Come', before introducing Amirault for the remainder of the set. The bassist introduces the love-theme from *Spartacus* with the bow, over soft synthesizer patterns, and then follows up with sweeping interpretation of the melody. The set ends with two Miles Davis tunes closely associated with Evans: 'Nardis' and 'Solar'. An unexpected record in every way, but a finely crafted session nonetheless.

    Next Future is pretty drab, a bland studio set redeemed only by the two Chick Corea tunes, 'Lost Tango', a lament for Astor Piazzolla, and 'Basic Trane-ing'. Margitza is an uninspiring choice for this set-up, but Williams plays rhythmically and well in a modified version of Corea's own piano idiom.

Nat Gonella (born 1908) TRUMPET, VOCALS

*** **Nat Gonella And His Georgians** Flapper PAST CD 9750

Gonella; Bruts Gonella, Johnny Morrison, Chas Oughton, Jack Wallace (*t*); Miff King (*tb*); Jack Bonser, Jock Middleton, Joe Moore, Ernest Morris, Mickey Seidman, Albert Torrance (*cl, as, bs*); Pat Smuts, Don Barigo (*ts*); Harold Hood, Monia Liter, Norman Stenfalt (*p*); Roy Dexter, Jimmy Mesene (*g*); Will Hemmings (*b*); Bob Dryden, Johnny Roland (*d*). 1/35–10/40.

Nat's Georgians – in which brother Bruts played Joe Oliver to his Pops – was one of the most successful British hot bands of the pre-war years. There have been various 'Georgian' revivals (the title was taken from his big hit, 'Georgia On My Mind') since that time and in the 1980s Nat was still singing, though no longer playing his horn. The Armstrong influence is so overt as to be unarguable, and yet Gonella brought something of his own as well, a wry, philosophical shrug as he threw off neat aphoristic solos with the biting tone and earthy humour his fans loved.

The Flapper disc is a very good selection of early material. Nat spent a little time in America at the end of the decade and its influence can be heard in the bluesier and more relaxedly rhythmic swing of the later cuts. The New Georgians stuff from 1940 is – heretical though it may be – superior to the original band's output. There's a novelty edge to many of the tracks, but Nat's vocal on 'The Flat Foot Floogie' and even 'Ol' Man River' is never less than musical and in the latter case quite moving. A bit of an institution, who will be fondly remembered by anyone over the age of 60 and who may prove mystifying to anyone under.

Paul Gonsalves (1920–74) TENOR SAXOPHONE

**** **Gettin' Together** Original Jazz Classics OJC 203

Gonsalves; Nat Adderley (*t*); Wynton Kelly (*p*); Sam Jones (*p*); Jimmy Cobb (*d*). 12/60.

*** **Jazz Till Midnight** Storyville STCD 4123

Gonsalves; Jan Johansson (*p, org*); Bob Cranshaw (*b*); Albert 'Tootie' Heath (*d*). 1/67.

*** **Just A-Sittin' And A-Rockin'** Black Lion BLCD 760148

Gonsalves; Ray Nance (*t, vn, v*); Norris Turney (*as, cl*); Raymond Fol, Hank Jones (*p*); Al Hall (*b*); Oliver Jackson (*d*). 8/70.

*** **Meets Earl Hines** Black Lion BLCD 760177

Gonsalves; Earl Hines (*p*); Al Hall (*b*); Jo Jones (*d*). 12/70, 11/72.

*** **Mexican Bandit Meets Pittsburg Pirate** Original Jazz Classics OJC 751

Gonsalves; Roy Eldridge (*t, v*); Cliff Smalls (*p*); Sam Jones (*b*); Eddie Locke (*d*). 8/73.

A staggeringly underrated player who stands in a direct line with earlier masters like Chu Berry and Don Byas, and with young Turks like Frank Lowe and David Murray. It would be absurd to compare his influence with Coltrane's, but it's now clear that he was experimenting with tonalities remarkably similar to Coltrane's famous 'sheets of sound' long before Coltrane; it's also unarguably true that more people heard Gonsalves (albeit in his more straight-ahead role as an Ellington stalwart). His fabled 27 choruses on 'Diminuendo And Crescendo In Blue' at the Newport Jazz Festival in 1956 can be considered the first important extended saxophone solo in modern jazz. Whatever the impulse, its impact was very considerable.

Gettin' Together is a remarkable album, beautifully played and recorded. Wynton Kelly's piano playing on 'Walkin'' and 'I Cover The Waterfront' (a Gonsalves favourite) is of the highest quality, and Adderley's slightly fragile, over-confident tone fits in perfectly. Most strongly recommended.

Hines delivers more reliably than the saxophonist at their 1970 encounter (there's actually just one brief track from '72). Gonsalves saves his best shot for 'Moten Swing', where he plays three choruses of pure invention, before Hines tugs the whole tune away in a new direction. 'Over The Rainbow' is whispery and delicate, just one run through the tune with a minimum of embellishment, but at a pace in which every note is made to count.

'I Cover The Waterfront' is again the stand-out track on Black Lion's relaxed, old-pals reunion. Nance is a less dramatic soloist than Gonsalves's more familiar foil, Cat Anderson, and his singing and fiddle-playing are less than compelling, but he blends beautifully in the ensembles and is imaginative enough to essay out-of-tempo sequences and slurred sounds around the saxophonists. Turney, a not quite time-served Ellington employee, plays exceedingly well.

The last of the group makes sad listening after the earlier sessions or any of the great Ellington occasions. Gonsalves at this point had less than a year to live and, while a meting with the incendiary trumpeter might have been marvellous 15 years earlier, the tenor playing sounds fractious and tired. Eldridge has a few characteristic squalls to deliver, but seam out the other discs first.

Dennis Gonzalez TRUMPET, POCKET TRUMPET, FLUGELHORN, OTHER INSTRUMENTS

**** Stefan Silkheart SHCD 101

> Gonzalez; John Purcell (*bcl, bf, eng hn, syn, v*); Henry Franklin (*b, v*); W. A. Richardson (*d*). 4/86.

***(*) Namesake Silkheart SHCD 106

> Gonzalez; Ahmed Abdullah (*t, flhn, balafon*); Charles Brackeen (*ts, perc*); Douglas Ewart (*bcl, as, f*); Malachi Favors (*b*); Alvin Fielder (*d*). 2/87.

***(*) Catechism Music & Arts CD 913

> Gonzalez; Rob Blakeslee (*t*); Kim Corbet (*tb*); Elton Dean (*as, saxello*); Keith Tippett (*p*); Marcio Mattos (*b*); Louis Moholo (*d*). 7/87.

**** Debenge, Debenge Silkheart SHCD 112

> Gonzalez; Marlon Jordan (*t*); Charles Brackeen (*ts*); Kidd Jordan (*sno, as, bcl*); Malachi Favors, Henry Franklin (*b*); Alvin Fielder, W. A. Richardson (*d*). 2/88.

***(*) The Desert Wind Silkheart SHCD 124

> Gonzalez; Kim Corbet (*tb*); Charles Brackeen (*ts, ss*); Michael Session (*ss, ts, as*); Michael Kruge (*clo*); Henry Franklin (*b*); Alvin Fielder (*d*). 4/89.

Gonzalez's recordings for the Silkheart label are part of a determined effort to wrest initiative back from New York and the West Coast and to restore the South's, and particularly the Delta's, slightly marginal standing in the new jazz. The band assembled for *Debenge, Debenge* goes under the uncomfortably agglutinative name New Dallasorleanssippi, that for *Desert Wind* New Dallasangeles, formulae which give no sense at all of their coherence and directness of statement. Gonzalez's other great achievement is to have tempted the great tenor player, Charles Brackeen, out of a self-imposed semi-retirement.

Stefan is probably the trumpeter's masterpiece. The opening 'Enrico', dedicated to the Italian trumpeter, Enrico Rava, opens a path for magnificent flugelhorn figurations over a bass/bass-clarinet accompaniment. 'Fortuity' is calm and enigmatic, like the title-track (a dedication to Gonzalez's son) a simple theme on open chords, but with a strange, dramatic interlude for voices. 'Hymn For Don Cherry' is based on 'At The Cross' and reflects two more of Gonzalez's influences. 'Boi Fuba', the briefest and least successful track, explores Brazilian materials, while John Purcell's closing 'Deacon John Ray' features his Dolphyish alto, and the trumpeter is superbly instinctive on the borders of total harmonic abstraction. A masterful record.

Namesake only suffers by comparison, but it shouldn't be missed. The long title-piece is a complex 7/4 figure that manages to sound completely coherent and also as if it were being played by a very much larger band, as if Gonzalez had been listening to Mingus's appropriations of Ellington on *The Black Saint And The Sinner Lady*. 'Separation Of Stones' is tranced and dreamy, and the solos are softly enunciated, with Gonzalez muted and the Armstrong-influenced Abdullah on flugelhorn. A percussion overture sets up a mood of combined grief and triumph in anticipation of 'Hymn For Mbizo', a threnody for South African bassist Johnny Dyani, but is interrupted by the lightweight 'Four Pigs And A Bird's Nest', on which Gonzalez plays his Cherry-patented pocket trumpet, muted on this occasion.

Debenge, Debenge, along with Brackeen's own *Banaar* and *Worshippers Come Nigh* (Silkheart 105 & 111), quickly consolidated the label's quality and confirmed Gonzalez's considerable musical intelligence. The multi-talented Kidd Jordan builds a bridge between Gonzalez's ringing, sometimes slightly sharp-toned trumpet and Brackeen's powerful tenor; his son, Marlon Jordan, is a fresh new voice and the Art Ensemble of Chicago veteran, Favors, shows more of his formidable technique than for some time. A superb record, beautifully engineered and produced.

The most recent of the Silkhearts, *Desert Wind*, opens with a mournful 'Hymn For Julius Hemphill'. Kruge's cello establishes the mood, before Brackeen, then Gonzalez, come in with turbulent solos. They're joined by Session, the other main soloist, again on 'Aamriq'aa' and 'The Desert Wind'. For the latter, Brackeen shifts to soprano and a keening, Middle Eastern tonality. The record tails off a bit after that, and Fielder's drum solo on 'Max-Well' is a bit of a bore.

The earlier *Catechism*, recorded in London, is rawer and the British free-scene players dictate a greater emphasis on collective improvisation. Dean and Tippett are the most prominent as soloists. The writing (two *kwelas* dedicated to the trumpeter's wife, Gerard Bendiks's delightfully titled 'The Sunny Murray–Cecil Taylor Dancing Lesson', and 'Catechism', written for the Creative Opportunity Orchestra in Austin, Texas) is of consistently high quality, and only a rather flat sound and the likelihood of limited availability keeps this one down to 3½ stars.

***(*) Hymn For The Perfect Heart Of A Pearl Konnex KCD 5026

> Gonzalez; Carlos Ward (*as, f*); Tim Green (*ts*); Paul Plimley (*p*); Paul Rogers (*b*); Louis Moholo (*d*). 4/90.

A shift both of label and of emphasis for Gonzalez, this sees him re-enter the free-jazz idiom hinted at on *Catechism*, but mostly kept at arm's length there. 'Angels Of The Bop Apocalypse' is a group improvisation, with the European-based Rogers and Moholo prominent (as they are throughout the set) and Plimley guesting in Cecil Taylor mode.

The long suite of the title has an Ellingtonian surge and diversity of detail, with sections apparently tailor-made for individual soloists. Curiously, perhaps, Ward and Green seem to have greater prominence than the leader, who tends to restrict himself to taut, almost antagonistic perorations. Rogers follows him on both the title-piece and the second movement, 'Astonishing Emptiness', a piece which evokes the same parched beauty of the Silkheart bands, but with a much more abstract edge. There is a 'Hymn For Louis Moholo', on which the horns ride precariously over the drummer's wonderfully splintery and unpredictable lines.

Plimley reappears for his own 'Parachute', sounding disconcertingly like another Brit, Keith Tippett (also on *Catechism*), and then the final movement is an all-in New Orleans stomp with emphatic gestures from the whole group, which Gonzalez has called his Band of Sorcerers. (A minor quibble: Konnex's idea of a readable sleeve-note needs looking at.)

**** The Earth And The Heart Konnex KCD 5028
> Gonzalez; Nels Cline, Mark Hewins (*g*); Ken Filiano (*b*); Alex Cline (*d, syn*); Andrew Cyrille (*d*). 7 & 12/89.

***(*) Welcome To Us GOWI CDG 10
> Gonzalez; Nils Petter Molvaer (*t*); Bugge Wesseltoft (*p, syn*); Terje Gewelt (*b, tabla*); Pal Thowsen (*d, perc*); Sidsel Endresen (*v*). 3/93.

The mystical strain in Gonzalez's imagination becomes ever more evident. *The Earth And The Heart* consists largely of a suite written to celebrate the tenth birthday of the Creative Opportunity Orchestra. The pervasive theme of tension between earth and heaven – or between material and spiritual natures – is one that seems to haunt the trumpeter, and which is ideally suited to his intense, bugling tone.

More than ever before, he seems the heir of Don Cherry on these records. His gift for putting together unexpected bands in whatever locale circumstance finds him echoes Cherry's gypsy temperament. The spontaneity and freshness of the solos on *The Earth And The Heart* is breathtaking. Cyrille performs magnificently, as do the Cline brothers, and the lesser-known Hewins plays with taste and quiet sophistication on the opening movement and on Cyrille's 'Simple Melody'. The LA sessions with the Clines are rather more polished and lack something of the immediacy of the New York date. Even so, this is a beautifully balanced album, and Gonzalez finds the right sound for each of the participants.

The Nordic Wizards band is issued on a Polish label and includes elements of another suite, 'Warszawa'. Another stylistic parallel immediately springs to mind, that of Tomasz Stańko. Gonzalez is more oblique and softer-toned than usual, and the overall accent of the record is one of muted gentleness. Molvaer does much of the straight trumpet playing, but they might almost be creative twins. There are perhaps too many texts, but Endresen's voice is consistently interesting, as in her own recordings, and the additional material – Asian percussion, a choir of refugee Afghani children – is not intrusive. A lovely, if slightly untypical, record.

Jerry Gonzalez (born 1949) TRUMPET, FLUGELHORN, PERCUSSION

*** The River Is Deep Enja 4040
> Gonzalez; Steve Turre (*tb, btb*); Papo Vasquez (*tb*); Wilfredo Velez (*as*); Jorge Dalto (*p*); Edgardo Miranda (*g*); Andy Gonzalez (*b,v*); Steve Berrios (*d, v*); Gene Golden, Hector 'Flaco' Hernandez, Nicky Marrero, Frankie Rodriguez (*perc*). 11/82.

*** Obalata Enja 5095
> Gonzalez; John Stubblefield (*ts*); Larry Willis (*p*); Edgardo Miranda (*g*); Andy Gonzalez (*b*); Steve Berrios (*d*); Nicky Marrero, Milton Cardona, Angel 'Papa' Vacquez (*perc*). 11/88.

Jerry Gonzalez has been surpassed in popularity by Arturo Sandoval but he is a trumpeter of comparable gifts, whose efforts at blending jazz and Latin genres have all the necessary ingredients: zesty, explosive rhythm sections, pellucid brass breaks, sunny melodies and an element of kitsch: one of his records included a version of the *I Love Lucy* theme. But Gonzalez likes to interpret Thelonious Monk and Wayne Shorter and, though he sometimes turns their compositions into unsuitably happy-go-lucky vehicles, there's a sensitive streak in his treatment of 'Footsteps' (*Obalata*). The earlier record is the more energetic, while *Obalata* benefits from the considerable presence of Stubblefield and the thoughtful Willis in a slightly smaller band.

*** Rumba Para Monk Sunnyside SSC 1036
> Gonzalez; Carter Jefferson (*ts*); Larry Willis (*p*); Andy Gonzalez (*b*); Steve Berrios (*d*). 88.

***(*) Earthdance Sunnyside SSC 1050
> As above, except add Joe Ford (*ss, as*). 10/90.

***(*) **Moliendo Café: To Wisdom The Prize** Sunnyside SSC 1061
    As above. 9/91.
**** **Crossroads** Milestone MCD 9225
    As above, except replace Jefferson with John Stubblefield (*ts*). 4 & 5/94.
Gonzalez has stabilized the personnel of this band and it's shown real growth on record, though it hardly matches the excitement it can generate live. The earliest of the bunch is an attempt to filter back out some of the Latin influences on Monk's rhythmic conception. 'Monk's Mood', 'Bye-Ya', 'Ugly Beauty' and 'Little Rootie Tootie' are transformed into south-of-the-border flag-wavers without sustaining any damage or bowing to compromise. There is a slight feeling that, having established his premise, Gonzalez doesn't quite know how to go any further with it, and some of his own soloing is very limited in scope. However, the sheer *joie de vivre* of the session gets it through a lot.

On the later records Jefferson and Ford make a canny front line, reminiscent of the horn sections McCoy Tyner worked with in his 1970s bands, and while neither man seems especially individual it suits the democratic blend of the group. Willis is the cooling ingredient in a rhythm section that's always ready to stoke the polyrhythmic fires, and Gonzalez himself plays eloquent or fiery horn as the occasion demands. There are more glances towards Monk and Shorter (a very fine 'El Toro' on *Moliendo Café*), and the later album also includes 'Summertime' and 'Corcovado' – kitsch choices that the band very nearly pull off. The earlier disc is slightly stronger, but either one has a lot of joyful music.

If *Crossroads* is the best of the bunch, that's largely because Stubblefield adds a whole new dimension. On the two parts of 'Rumba Columbia', he is a revelation, roaring away happily in the sourest and most piquant tonality imaginable, a sound that is absolutely complementary to Gonzalez's own. Jefferson seemed an essential part of the Fort Apache mix, but he turns out to be replaceable after all, whether temporarily or as a regular thing we are not sure.

Brad Goode (born 1964) TRUMPET

*** **Shock Of The New** Delmark DD 440
    Goode; Lin Halliday, Ed Petersen (*ts*); Jodie Christian (*p*); Fareed Haque (*g*); Rob Amster,
    Dennis Carroll, Angus Thomas (*b*); Bob Rummage, Jeff Stitely, Paul Wertico (*d*); strings. 88.
Neither particularly new nor in any sense shocking, the young Chicagoan's debut nevertheless reflects a talent that is going places fast. He has listened with more care than most Browniephiles to the source material; the influence is not so much in the phrasing – which is already distinctive – as in the way solos are built up by steadily augmenting core statements and relatively simple ideas. Halliday and Christian are both well-respected players, but one has the sense that they weren't given much leeway on these dates, and neither lives up to reputation.

Benny Goodman (1909–86) CLARINET

***(*) **B.G. And Big Tea In NYC** MCA GRP 16092
    Goodman; Red Nichols, Leo McConville, Ruby Weinstein, Charlie Teagarden, Manny Klein,
    Dave Klein, Ray Lodwig (*t*); Bix Beiderbecke (*c*); Jack Teagarden, Glenn Miller, Bill Trone (*tb*);
    Benny Goodman (*cl, as*); Arthur Rollini, Larry Binyon, Babe Russin (*ts*); Sid Stoneburn (*as*);
    Adrian Rollini (*bsx*); Ed Bergman, Wladimir Solinsky, Matty Malneck, Joe Venuti (*vn*); Arthur
    Schutt, Joe Sullivan, Jack Russin, Frank Signorelli, Howard Smith (*p*); Eddie Lang, George Van
    Eps, Carl Kress (*g*); Treg Brown (*bj*); Ward Lay, Art Miller, Artie Bernstein (*b*); Stan King, Neil
    Marshall, Gene Krupa (*d*). 4/29–10/34.
None of these sides was recorded under either Goodman's or Teagarden's leadership, but they dominate much of the record, in bands led by Nichols, Rollini and Irving Mills. The great exception is the superb Lang–Venuti All Star Orchestra date of 1931, in which the nominal leaders play their tails off, though Goodman has a fine solo on 'Farewell Blues'. This is all polished New York Dixieland of its day, and well worth reviving.

*** **Benny Goodman 1928–1931** Classics 693
    Goodman; Wingy Manone (*t*); Jimmy McPartland (*c*); Tommy Dorsey, Glenn Miller (*tb*); Fud
    Livingston, Larry Binyon (*cl, ts*); Sid Stoneburn (*cl, as*); Bud Freeman (*ts*); Vic Breidis, Joe
    Sullivan, Mel Stitzel (*p*); Eddie Lang, Dick Morgan (*g*); Herman Foster (*bj*); Harry Goodman
    (*b*); Bob Conselman, Gene Krupa (*d*); Harold Arlen, Grace Johnston, Scrappy Lambert, Paul
    Small (*v*). 1/28–2/31.
*** **Benny Goodman 1931–1933** Classics 719
    Goodman; Charlie Teagarden, Manny Klein, Shirley Clay, Bunny Berigan (*t*); Jack Teagarden,

Tommy Dorsey, Glenn Miller (*tb*); Sid Stoneburn (*cl, as*); Larry Binyon (*cl, ts, f*); Art Karle (*ts*); Irving Brodsky, Joe Sullivan (*p*); Eddie Lang, Dick McDonough (*g*); Artie Bernstein (*b*); Gene Krupa, Ray Bauduc, Johnny Williams (*d*); Billie Holiday, Smith Ballew, Paul Small, Dick Robertson (*v*). 3/31–12/33.

Goodman's earliest dates as a leader are rough-and-ready New York jazz, with McPartland's gruff lead adding to the grit, and with Benny doubling on alto and baritone. The notorious 'Shirt Tail Stomp', in which the group lampooned the jazz clichés of the time, became a minor hit. His two solos, 'That's A Plenty' and 'Clarinetitis', are virtuoso stuff, and a subsequent date in Chicago yielded two more gutsy small-group titles with Manone and Freeman. After that, though, his New York sessions, which take up the rest of Classics 693 and all of 719, are polite, inconsequential dance music. Elements of swing start to creep in as time goes on, but the often stellar personnel have trouble getting any jazz into the records, and the most notable thing is the arrival of young Billie Holiday on two of the final tracks. Sound is mixed – very rough and scratchy on some of the transfers, particularly on the latter sessions on Classics 693.

(*) **Benny Goodman 1934–1935** Classics 744
> Goodman; Manny Klein, Charles Margulis, Charlie Teagarden, George Thow, Russ Case, Jerry Neary, Sam Shapiro, Pee Wee Irwin, Art Sylvester, Ralph Muzillo (*t*); Sonny Lee, Jack Teagarden, Red Ballard, Jack Lacey (*tb*); Hymie Schertzer, Ben Kantor, Toots Mondello (*as*); Coleman Hawkins, Hank Ross, Arthur Rollini, Dick Clark (*ts*); Claude Thornhill, Arthur Schutt, Frank Froeba, Teddy Wilson (*p*); Dick McDonough, George Van Eps, Benny Martel (*g*); Artie Bernstein, Harry Goodman, Hank Wayland (*b*); Ray McKinley, Sammy Weiss, Gene Krupa (*d*); Mildred Bailey, Ann Graham, Helen Ward, Buddy Clark (*v*). 2/34–1/35.

*** **Benny Goodman 1935** Classics 769
> Goodman; Jerry Neary, Pee Wee Irwin, Bunny Berigan, Nate Kazebier, Ralph Muzillo (*t*); Red Ballard, Jack Lacey, Jack Teagarden, Joe Harris (*tb*); Toots Mondello, Hymie Schertzer (*as*); Arthur Rollini, Dick Clark (*ts*); Frank Froeba (*p*); Allan Reuss, George Van Eps (*g*); Harry Goodman (*b*); Gene Krupa (*d*); Helen Ward, Ray Hendricks, Buddy Clark (*v*). 1–7/35.

*** **Benny Goodman 1935–1936** Classics 789
> As above, except add Harry Geller (*t*), Bill De Pew (*as*), Teddy Wilson, Jess Stacy (*p*); omit Neary, Lacey, Teagarden, Van Eps, Hendricks, Clark. 7/35–4/36.

*** **Benny Goodman 1936** Classics 817
> As above, except add Chris Griffin, Manny Klein (*t*), Murray McEachern (*tb*); omit Mondello, Froeba. 4–8/36.

***(*) **Benny Goodman 1936 Vol. 2** Classics 836
> As above, except add Sterling Bose, Zeke Zarchey, Ziggy Elman (*t*), Vido Musso (*ts*), Lionel Hampton (*vib*); omit Klein, Geller. 8–11/36.

***(*) **Benny Goodman 1936–1937** Classics 858
> As above, except add Irv Goodman, Harry James (*t*), George Koenig (*as*), Margaret McCrae, Jimmy Rushing, Frances Hunt (*v*); omit Bose, Zarchey. 12/36–7/37.

*** **Benny Goodman 1935 Vol. 1** Tax CD 3708-2
> Goodman; George Erwin, Nathan Kazebier, Jerry Neary (*t*); Red Ballard, Jack Lacey (*tb*); Toots Mondello, Hymie Schertzer (*as*); Arthur Rollini, Dick Clark (*ts*); Frank Froeba (*p*); Allan Reuss (*g*); Harry Goodman (*b*); Gene Krupa (*d*). 6/35.

*** **Benny Goodman 1935 Vol. 2** Tax CD 3709-2
> As above. 6/35.

*** **The Birth Of Swing (1935–1936)** RCA Bluebird ND90601 3CD
> Goodman; Bunny Berigan, Pee Wee Erwin, Ralph Muzillo, Jerry Neary, Nathan Kazebier, Harry Geller, Chris Griffin, Manny Klein, Sterling Bose, Ziggy Elman, Zeke Zarchey (*t*); Red Ballard, Jack Lacey, Jack Teagarden, Murray McEachern (*tb*); Toots Mondello, Bill De Pew, Hymie Schertzer (*as*); Arthur Rollini, Dick Clark, Vido Musso (*ts*); Frank Froeba, Jess Stacy (*p*); George Van Eps, Allan Reuss (*g*); Harry Goodman (*b*); Gene Krupa (*d*); Helen Ward, Ella Fitzgerald, Joe Harris, Buddy Clark (*v*). 4/35–11/36.

Goodman was struggling as a bandleader until the mystical night of 21 August 1935 when the swing era apparently began, following his broadcast from Los Angeles. He already had a good band: the reed section was skilful, the trumpets – boosted by the arrival of Bunny Berigan, who had a terrific impact on Goodman himself – strong, and the book was bulging with material. The two Tax CDs, of transcriptions for radio, contain 50 numbers yet were recorded in a single day's work. There were Fletcher Henderson arrangements which would help to make Goodman's fortune – 'Blue Skies', 'King Porter Stomp', 'Basin Street Blues' – and Jimmy Mundy and Edgar Sampson charts of a similar calibre. There was Gene Krupa at the drums and Goodman, perhaps the first great virtuoso of the swing era, himself.

It may surprise some, at this distance, to hear how Goodman actually played more of an ensemble role than that of a star leader – at least in terms of the sound of his clarinet and its place on the records. Solos are usually quite short and pithy and, though he takes the lion's share, that was only right and proper – he was far and away the best improviser (Berigan aside, who didn't last very long) in his own band. What one notes about the records is their smooth, almost ineluctable power and fleetness: Krupa's drumming energized the orchestra, but its brass and reed sections were such fine executants (only Lunceford's band could have matched them) that they generated their own kind of inner swing. Henderson, Mundy and Sampson all supplied arrangements which, in a gesture that has dominated big-band writing to this day, pointed up those strengths without looking for fancy textures or subtleties.

The Classics series, moving chronologically through the Columbia and Victor sessions, offers a comprehensive overview. Classics 744 finds the band still in an awkward, transitory phase, which is more or less resolved by the end of Classics 769 – here are the first Henderson arrangements, the classic reading of 'King Porter Stomp' and the big hit, 'Blue Skies'. The sound of the band, comparatively muffled on the Columbia sessions (though the erratic Classics' remastering doesn't help) is smoother, bigger and more sophisticated by the time the Victor dates were properly under way. Classics 789 also includes the first tracks by the BG trio, and though this disc also marks Berigan's departure – leaving Goodman short of a major trumpeter until the arrival of Harry James – one can hear the orchestra growing in stature. Classics 817 and 836 see Jimmy Mundy coming on board as arranger; Ziggy Elman's arrival in the trumpet section in October 1936 adds some extra firepower to the brass. Classics 858 sees Harry James coming into the band, and the record ends on the studio version of 'Sing, Sing, Sing', one of the most familiar set-pieces of the whole swing era. There is the occasional clinker in terms of material, but for the most part Goodman was able to record songs and charts of a consistently high quality and, even where Helen Ward's vocals dominate a record, the band's eminence is obvious. Transfers of the Victor material are usually strong and without much surface noise.

The Tax CDs (broadcast transcriptions) are in excellent sound, and though there are plenty of second-rate tunes and occasional dead passages the standard stays surprisingly high, with Goodman in good to inspirational form. The Bluebird three-CD set should be the definitive document of the start of the swing era, but it's badly let down by inconsistent remastering: a handful of tracks (including 'Blue Skies') sound as if they were recorded under water, and the general standard, though listenable enough, is varied almost from track to track. That said, it's of consistent musical interest and Loren Schoenberg's excellent notes add to the impact of the set.

***(*) **The Harry James Years Vol. 1** Bluebird 07863 66155 2
    Goodman; Harry James, Ziggy Elman, Gordon Griffin (*t*); Red Ballard, Murray McEachern, Vernon Brown (*tb*); Hymie Schertzer, Bill De Pew, George Koenig (*as*); Babe Russin, Arthur Rollini, Vido Musso (*ts*); Jess Stacy (*p*); Allan Reuss (*g*); Harry Goodman (*b*); Gene Krupa (*d*). 1/37–2/38.

**** **The Harry James Years Vol. 2** Bluebird 07863 66549 2
    As above, except add Irv Goodman, Corky Cornelius (*t*), Bruce Squires (*tb*), Noni Bernardi, Dave Matthews, Milt Yaner (*as*), Lester Young, Jerry Jerome, Bud Freeman (*ts*), Freddie Green, Ben Heller (*g*), Walter Page (*b*), Dave Tough, Buddy Shutz (*d*); Martha Tilton (*v*); omit McEachern, Koenig. 3/38–5/39.

Two good slices of the band in its prime. The arrangements are by Henderson, Mundy, James, Sampson, Basie and even Mary Lou Williams – Goodman took them from many hands. Much better sound than on many earlier Bluebird discs. Volume 2 starts with a session where various Basieites sat in, takes in the arrival of Bud Freeman and Dave Tough, and includes two rare takes of otherwise familiar items. As samplers of Goodman's output in the 1930s, these two are hard to beat, though the Hep discs, below, also have a strong claim.

**** **Plays Fletcher Henderson** Hep 1038
    As appropriate discs above. 4/35–4/39.
**** **Plays Jimmy Mundy** Hep 1039
    As appropriate discs above. 9/35–11/37.

These two excellently remastered discs offer a good way of exploring the key points of Benny's music in the 1930s. It was Henderson's arrangements, still rooted in his favourite call-and-response patterns, that gave Goodman's band their first real identity, and the best of them are collected here. Mundy's charts follow on from Henderson's and are scarcely more subtle: his favourite riff devices occur again and again, and only in some of his saxophone writing is there any genuine freshness; but the band's superb craftsmanship makes the arrangements fit snugly into what Goodman wanted. None of this music challenges the best of Ellington, Basie or Lunceford, but the particular crispness of Goodman's band is undeniable. Recommended.

*** The Complete Madhattan Room Broadcasts Vols 1–6 Viper's Nest VN 171/2/3/4/5/6
  Goodman; Harry James, Ziggy Elman, Chris Griffin (*t*); Red Ballard, Vernon Brown (*tb*);
  Hymie Schertzer, George Koenig (*as*); Arthur Rollini, Vido Musso (*ts*); Jess Stacy, Teddy
  Wilson (*p*); Lionel Hampton (*vib*); Allan Reuss (*g*); Harry Goodman (*b*); Gene Krupa (*d*);
  Martha Tilton (*v*). 10–11/37.
*** More Camel Caravans Phontastic PHONTCD 8841/2 2CD
  As above, except add Murray McEachern (*tb*); omit Brown. 8/37.
*** More Camel Caravans Phontastic PHONTCD 8843/4 2CD
  As above, except Brown returns, add Will Bradley (*tb*), Dave Matthews, Noni Bernardi (*as*), Ben
  Heller (*g*), Dave Tough (*d*); omit Schertzer, Koenig, McEachern. 11/37–9/38.
*** More Camel Caravans Phontastic PHONTCD 8845/6 2CD
  As above, except add Corky Cornelius (*t*), Bruce Squires (*tb*), Toots Mondello, Buff Estes (*as*),
  Bus Bassey, Jerry Jerome, Bud Freeman (*ts*), Fletcher Henderson (*p*), Arnold Coivey (*g*), Art
  Bernstein (*b*), Nick Fatool (*d*), Louise Tobin (*v*); omit Bradley, Musso, Reuss, Tilton. 9/38–9/39.
*** Air Checks 1937–1938 Columbia 472990-2 2CD
  Goodman; Ziggy Elman, Harry James, Irving Goodman, Chris Griffin (*t*); Red Ballard, Murray
  McEachern, Vernon Brown (*tb*); Bill De Pew, Hymie Schertzer, Noni Bernardi, George Koenig,
  Dave Matthews (*as*); Vido Musso, Arthur Rollini, Bud Freeman (*ts*); Jess Stacy, Teddy Wilson
  (*p*); Lionel Hampton (*vib*); Allan Reuss, Ben Heller (*g*); Harry Goodman (*b*); Dave Tough,
  Gene Krupa (*d*); Martha Tilton (v). 36–38.
*** Camel Caravan Broadcasts Vol. 1 Phontastic 8817
  As above, except add Cy Baker (*t*), Jack Teagarden (*tb, v*), Joseph Szigeti (*vn*), Johnny Mercer,
  Billie Holiday, Leo Watson (*v*). 1/39.
*** Camel Caravan Broadcasts Vol. 2 Phontastic 8818
  As above, except omit Baker, Teagarden, Szigeti, Mercer, Holiday and Watson. 2–3/39.
*** Camel Caravan Broadcasts Vol. 3 Phontastic 8819
  Similar to above. 3–4/39.

Airshots have survived in copious quantities as far as the Goodman band is concerned, and these hefty
reissues ought to satisfy the most diligent devotee. They are taken from various sources on the Columbia
set, and from broadcasts sponsored by Camel on the three Phontastic CDs. The sound is sometimes
rather clunky on the Columbia set but it's superior to many an airshot from the period; on the
Phontastic 'Camel' discs it's clean, if rather fusty. The latter CDs call for a lot of patience since there are
frequent interruptions from the sponsor, dialogue and other distractions; that aside, the group play
handsomely, though there's the usual quota of feeble titles. Since our last edition, Phontastic have dug
up three more two-disc sets which cover the earlier years of this Camel-sponsored show and, though
there are numerous exhortations to smoke, the music more or less wins through. Better, though, are the
looser and usually more swinging 'Madhattan Room' broadcasts, available on six separate discs from
Viper's Nest. Each disc has a share of charts and songs which Goodman otherwise never recorded, and
the sound is marginally better than the Phontastic discs can offer. The Columbia set weeds out distractions, although chaff of the order of 'That Naughty Waltz' has got in somehow. The VJC discs listed
below are still the best airshots around, but those listed above will interest the dedicated.

**** After You've Gone RCA Bluebird ND 85631
  Goodman; Lionel Hampton (*vib*); Teddy Wilson (*p*); Gene Krupa (*d*). 7/35–2/37.
***(*) Avalon RCA Bluebird ND 82273
  As above, except add Jess Stacy (*p*); John Kirby (*b*); Buddy Schutz, Dave Tough (*d*). 7/37–4/39.
Goodman's small groups set a new standard for 'chamber jazz', the kind of thing Red Nichols had tried
in the 1920s, but informed with a more disciplined – and blacker – sensibility. That said, Goodman's
own playing, for all its fineness of line and tonal elegance, could be blisteringly hot, and he is by far the
strongest personality on all their records, the presence of domineering figures like Hampton and Krupa
notwithstanding. The earliest sides are among the best, but both these Bluebird compilations come
highly recommended. Perhaps the Trio sessions, made before Hampton's arrival, are the most satisfying,
since the brilliant empathy between Goodman and Wilson – one of the great unspoken jazz partnerships
– is allowed its clearest expression. Certainly the likes of 'After You've Gone' and 'Body And Soul'
express a smooth yet spontaneously refined kind of improvisation. Hampton made the music 'swing' a
little more obtrusively, yet he often plays a rather quiet and contained ensemble role, the vibes shimmering alongside Wilson's playing, and it created a fascinating platform for Goodman's lithest playing.
While this quickly became formulaic jazz, it was a very good formula. The NoNoise remastering isn't
ideal, but it lets all the players stand clearly in the mix. RCA also have *The Complete Small
Combinations Volumes 1/2* and *3/4* in their two-CD Jazz Tribune series, which covers exactly the same
ground.

***(*) **Live At Carnegie Hall** Columbia 450983-2 2CD
    Goodman; Ziggy Elman, Buck Clayton, Harry James, Gordon Griffin (*t*); Bobby Hackett (*c*);
    Red Ballard, Vernon Brown (*tb*); Hymie Schertzer, George Koenig, Johnny Hodges (*as*); Arthur
    Rollini, Lester Young, Babe Russin (*ts*); Harry Carney (*bs*); Jess Stacy, Teddy Wilson, Count
    Basie (*p*); Lionel Hampton (*vib*); Allan Reuss, Freddie Green (*g*); Harry Goodman, Walter
    Page (*b*); Gene Krupa (*d*). 1/38.

A very famous occasion indeed, and the music still stands up extraordinarily well. This was one of those
events – like Ellington at Newport nearly two decades later – where jazz history is spontaneously
changed, even if Goodman had clearly planned the whole thing as a crowning manoeuvre. Unmissable
points: Krupa's fantastically energetic drumming throughout, leading to the roof coming off on 'Sing,
Sing, Sing', an Ellington tribute and a jam on 'Honeysuckle Rose' with various guests from other bands
(George Simon called it 'ineffectual', but it's very exciting), Ziggy Elman powering through 'Swingtime
In The Rockies' and the original quartet going through their best paces. But the whole affair is atmos-
pheric with the sense of a man and a band taking hold of their moment.

**** **Solo Flight** Vintage Jazz Classics VJC-1021-2
    Goodman; Cootie Williams (*t*); George Auld (*ts*); Lionel Hampton (*vib*); Fletcher Henderson,
    Johnny Guarnieri, Count Basie (*p*); Charlie Christian, Freddie Green (*g*); Artie Bernstein,
    Walter Page (*b*); Jo Jones, Gene Krupa, Nick Fatool (*d*). 8/39–6/41.

**** **Roll 'Em!** Vintage Jazz Classics VJC 1032-2
    Goodman; Jimmy Maxwell, Billy Butterfield, Cootie Williams, Slim Davis (*t*); Lou McGarity,
    Cutty Cutshall (*tb*); Gene Kinsey, Clint Neagley (*as*); George Berg, Vido Musso, Pete Mondello
    (*ts*); Skip Martin, Chuck Gentry (*bs*); Mel Powell (*p*); Tommy Morganelli (*g*); Walter Iooss,
    Johnny Simmons, Marty Blitz (*b*); Big Sid Catlett (*d*). 7–10/41.

Two fabulous collections of airshots and V-Discs. Various breakdowns and alternative takes sunder the
flow on *Roll 'Em!* to some extent, but the band sound absolutely mercurial, careering through a sensational 'Henderson Stomp' and coming through loud and clear in excellent remastering. The collection
with Christian features the guitarist in wonderful extended solos, but Goodman himself matches him
blow for blow and, though the sound is dustier, it's perfectly listenable. Essential supplements to a
Goodman collection.

**** **Sextet Featuring Charlie Christian** Columbia 465679-2
    Goodman; Cootie Williams (*t*); George Auld (*ts*); Fletcher Henderson, Johnny Guarnieri,
    Count Basie (*p*); Lionel Hampton (*vib*); Artie Bernstein (*b*); Nick Fatool, Jo Jones, Dave Tough
    (*d*). 39–41.

*** **The Rehearsal Sessions 1940–1941** Jazz Unlimited JUCD 2013
    As above, except add Ken Kersey (*p*), Harry Jaeger (*d*); omit Henderson, Guarnieri, Hampton,
    Fatool, Tough. 11/40–1/41.

*** **Small Groups 1941–1945** Columbia 463341-2
    Goodman; Lou McGarity, Cutty Cutshall (*tb*); Red Norvo (*vib*); Teddy Wilson, Mel Powell (*p*);
    Tom Morgan, Mike Bryan (*g*); Slam Stewart, Sid Weiss (*b*); Morey Feld, Ralph Collier (*d*);
    Peggy Lee (*v*). 10/41–2/45.

Christian was a once-in-a-lifetime collaborator with Goodman, who had bad luck with some of his best
sidemen (Christian, Berigan, Hasselgård – all of whom came to untimely ends). The first *Sextet* compilation is full of finely pointed small-group jazz, hinting every now and then at bop, but not so much as to
give anyone any trouble. Equally interesting is the mixture of personalities – Williams, Goodman,
Christian, Auld, Basie – which gives the sextet performances a blend of coolness and resilience which
seems to be a direct extension of the leader's own ambitions. Goodman had led a nearly perfect double-
life with the small groups and the big band, balancing dance material and 'listening' jazz and making
both commercially and artistically successful; and part of that freshness which the small groups created
may be due to the fact that several participants – Wilson, Hampton, Christian – weren't regular members of the big band. But after a reorganization in 1941 he started using regular band-members, who
turn up on the *Small Groups 1941–45* compilation. While this is a less impressive set than the earlier
small-band discs, with Cutshall and McGarity standing as curious choices and the timbre of most of the
tracks sounding like a slightly paler echo of what had gone before, Goodman still plays very well.
Respectable remastering on both discs. The *Rehearsal Sessions* brings together multiple takes on four
tunes plus a remarkable 27-minute track that details the sextet working towards a finished version of
'Benny's Bugle' (where Cootie Williams eventually has to play the intro 23 times). For Goodman
scholars rather than the general collector, but intriguing stuff.

***(*) **Featuring Peggy Lee** Columbia 473661-2
    Goodman; Jimmy Maxwell, Billy Butterfield, Al Davis, Cootie Williams, Joe Ferrante, Bernie
    Privin (*t*); Lou McGarity, Cutty Cutshall (*tb*); Skip Martin, Clint Neagley, Julie Schwartz, Sol

Kane (*as*); Vido Musso, George Berg (*ts*); Chuck Gentry (*bs*); Mel Powell (*p*); Tommy Morgan
(*g*); Johnny Simmons, Marty Blitz, Sid Weiss (*b*); Big Sid Catlett, Ralph Collier (*d*); Peggy Lee,
Art Lund (*v*). 8–12/41.

It was a good idea to collect Lee's best vocals with Goodman, and this one brings together 16 of them,
from the nervous-sounding 'Elmer's Tune' to the lush treatment of 'Ev'rything I Love' and 'Not Mine'.
Eddie Sauter's arrangements come almost as a bonus, but they highlight the dexterity and serene
confidence of Goodman's players at this point.

***(*) **Goodman – The Different Version Vol. 1** Phontastic NCD 8821 2CD
As discs above. 39–40.

***(*) **Goodman – The Different Version Vol. 2** Phontastic NCD 8822 2CD
As above. 41.

***(*) **Goodman – The Different Version Vol. 3** Phontastic NCD 8823 2CD
As above. 41–42.

***(*) **Goodman – The Different Version Vol. 4** Phontastic NCD 8824 2CD
As above. 42–45.

***(*) **Goodman – The Different Version Vol. 5** Phontastic NCD 8825 2CD
As above. 45–47.

*** **The Permanent Goodman Vol. 1** Phontastic CD 7659
As above. 26–38.

***(*) **The Permanent Goodman Vol. 2** Phontastic 7660
As above. 39–45.

There is some irony in that, while no comprehensive edition of Goodman's proper studio releases exists
(though Classics will be there soon), enterprises like this have appeared instead. The five-volume
Phontastic set covers ten CDs of alternative takes to the more familiar studio sides – virtually all of it
from legitimate, V-Disc or transcription sessions, so the sound-quality is consistently good, if not quite
as lively as some reissue projects. The documentation is detailed and superbly organized and, although
the alternative takes themselves seldom tell anything strikingly new about Goodman's work – changes
amount to matters of precise detail, rather than glaring contrasts – it makes a very impressive series of
programmes. So, too, are the alternatives offered up on the other two *Permanent Goodman* discs, which
follow a similar course but go back to 1926 (some of the early Ben Pollack sessions) and somehow avoid
any duplication with these other sets. A remarkable undertaking, previously released as a long series of
LPs but welcome in the new format.

***(*) **'Way Down Yonder** Vintage Jazz Classics VJC-1001-2
Goodman; Lee Castle, Frank Muzzillo, Charlie Frankhauser, Johnny Dee, Frank Berardi,
Mickey Mangano (*t*); Bill Harris, H. Collins, Al Mastren (*tb*); Heinie Beau, Eddie Rosa, Hymie
Schertzer, Leonard Kaye (*as*); Al Klink, Zoot Sims (*ts*); Ernie Caceres, Eddie Beau (*bs*); Jess
Stacy, Mel Powell, Teddy Wilson (*p*); Red Norvo (*vib*); Sid Weiss (*b*); Morey Feld, Gene Krupa,
Johnny DeSoto (*d*); Lorraine Elliott (*v*). 12/43–1/46.

More broadcast material. Goodman hadn't lost the keys to the kingdom, but his popularity was past its
peak and the big bands were starting to enter their steep decline. Nevertheless this collection of V-Discs
includes some very impressive and hard-hitting performances, and some new faces – Zoot Sims, for one
– add further interest. Very good transfers, considering the source of the material.

*** **Sextet** Columbia 450411-2
Goodman; Teddy Wilson (*p*); Terry Gibbs (*vib*); Johnny Smith (*g*); Bob Carter (*b*); Charles
Smith (*d*). 50–52.

More latterday sextet sessions. Goodman was at a rather low ebb, like every other fallen giant of the
decade before, and Wilson and Gibbs play with professional calm rather than passion, but there's the
usual quota of neatly swinging music.

*** **The Essential** Columbia 467151-2
Goodman; various groups as above. 10/39–1/51.

Aside from some rather unusual 1951 tracks in which the band played some (already) ancient
Henderson arrangements, this is a hotchpotch of Goodman's Columbia material: several obvious
choices and a few idiosyncratic ones ('Mission To Moscow', 'Scarecrow').

*** **Benny's Bop** Hep CD 36
Goodman; Howard Reich, Doug Mettome, Al Stewart, Nick Travis (*t*); Milt Bernhart, Eddie
Bert, George Monte (*tb*); Stan Hasselgård (*cl*); Mitch Goldberg, Angelo Cicalese (as); Wardell
Gray, Eddie Wasserman (*ts*); Larry Molinelli (*bs*); Mary Lou Williams, Buddy Greco, Barbara
Carroll (*p*); Billy Bauer, Francis Beecher (*g*); Clyde Lombardi (*b*); Mel Zelnick, Sonny Igoe (*d*);
Louis Martinez (*perc*); Jackie Searle, Terry Swope (*v*). 7/48–3/49.

Goodman was interested by the new music but he never felt very comfortable with it, and Hasselgård, present on three tracks here, was much more at home in bop's surroundings. There isn't anything here that would have troubled Parker and Gillespie. More involving is some superb playing from Wardell Gray. This is V-Disc and broadcast material, conscientiously remastered, and the leader (aside from one clinker) plays imperturbably well.

**** **Undercurrent Blues** Capitol 832086-2

As above, except add Nate Kazebier, Manny Klein, Zeke Zarchey, Joe Triscari, Irv Goodman, Ziggy Schatz, John Wilson, Fats Navarro (*t*), Tommy Pederson, Lou McGarity, Ed Kusby, Bill Byers, Mario Daone (*tb*), Gus Bivona, Heinie Beau (*as*), Babe Russin, Jack Chaney (*ts*); Chuck Gentry, Bob Dawes, Joe Casalaro (*bs*); Jess Stacy (*p*); Allan Reuss, Mundell Lowe (*g*), Larry Breen, Bob Carter (*b*), Sammy Weiss (*d*). 1/47–10/49.

Loren Schoenberg's notes make an eloquent case for reconsidering Goodman's allegedly miserable relationship with bebop, and the music on the disc makes an even better one. Two arrangements by Mary Lou Williams offer him a superb showcase in 'Lonely Moments', the sextet swinger 'Shirley Steps Out' is a near-classic, but the version of 'Stealing Apples', where he jousts with Navarro and Gray, is a real ear-opener for those who haven't heard it before. The remaining material includes some more fine small-group stuff and some fine Chico O'Farrill arrangements. If Goodman left bop alone again at this point, it wasn't exactly because he couldn't play it. The remastering has been done superbly, with the music sounding vibrant and clear.

**** **B.G. In Hi-Fi** Capitol B21Y-92684-2

Goodman; Ruby Braff, Charlie Shavers, Chris Griffin, Carl Poole, Bernie Privin (*t*); Will Bradley, Vernon Brown, Cutty Cutshall (*tb*); Al Klink, Paul Ricci, Boomie Richman, Hymie Schertzer, Sol Schlinger (*saxes*); Mel Powell (*p*); Steve Jordan (*g*); George Duvivier (*b*); Bobby Donaldson, Jo Jones (*d*). 11/54.

Goodman left the big-band era with his finances and his technique intact and, although this was a more or less anachronistic programme of trio, quintet and big-band sides in 1954, the playing is so good that it's a resounding success. A few Goodman staples are mixed with Basie material such as 'Jumpin' At The Woodside', and Benny's readings are by no means outdone by the originals. Shavers, Braff, Richman and Powell all have fine moments, but Goodman himself is peerless. The sound is a trifle dry but otherwise excellent, and the CD reissue adds four tracks – including a beautiful trio version of 'Rose Room' – to the original LP.

*** **Yale Archives Vol. 2: Live At Basin Street** Musicmasters 5006-2

Goodman; Ruby Braff (*t*); Urbie Green (*tb*); Paul Quinichette (*ts*); Teddy Wilson (*p*); Perry Lopez (*g*); Milt Hinton (*b*); Bobby Donaldson (*d*). 3/55.

This recording, from Goodman's personal collection now in Yale University, catches a characteristic club engagement by a typical Goodman band, only eight in number but big enough to suggest the swing of the leader's orchestras. The material is old-hat, even for Goodman, but the unusual gathering of names lends a fresh twist, and Braff and Green sound in particularly good shape. Well recorded and remastered.

***(*) **The Benny Goodman Story** Capitol 833569-2

Goodman; Chris Griffin, Billy Butterfield, Doc Severinsen, Jimmy Maxwell, Carl Poole, Harry James, Bernie Glow, Jon Durante, Bernie Privin, Ruby Braff (*t*); Urbie Green, Will Bradley, Lou McGarity (*tb*); Hymie Schertzer, Phil Bodner, Milt Yaner (*as*); Al Klink, Peanuts Hucko, Boomie Richman (*ts*); Dick Hyman, Morris Wechsler, Mel Powell (*p*); Lionel Hampton (*vib*); Tony Mottola, Al Caiola (*g*); George Duvivier, Milt Hinton (*b*); Bobby Donaldson, Don Lamond (*d*); Martha Tilton (*v*). 12/55.

Occasioned by his film life-story, this remodelling of some old favourites was well done. 'Sing Sing Sing' was a necessary chore, 'And The Angels Sing' didn't improve with time, and there is some other so-so music; but the sound of the orchestra was handsomely caught by the Capitol engineers, and the small-group tracks at the end are handled with stinging aplomb. Excellent remastering.

*** **Happy Session** Columbia 476523-2

Goodman; John Frosk, Allen Smith, Ermit Perry, Benny Ventura (*t*); Rex Peer, Hale Rood, Buster Cooper (*tb*); Herb Geller, James Sands, Bob Wilber, Babe Clark, Pepper Adams (*reeds*); André Previn, Russ Freeman (*p*); Barney Kessel, Turk Van Lake (*g*); George Duvivier, Milt Hinton, Leroy Vinnegar (*b*); Shelly Manne (*d*).

Happy but not ecstatic. This sounds like Goodman meets the West Coast: Californian brass and reed sounds styled around the King's somewhat isolated clarinet. Plenty to hear, but hardly a great Goodman record.

*** Yale Archives Vol. 3 Musicmasters 65007-2

Goodman; Billy Hodges, Taft Jordan, John Frosk, Ermit Perry (*t*); Vernon Brown, Willie Dennis, Rex Peer (*tb*); Al Block, Ernie Mauro (*as*); Zoot Sims, Seldon Powell (*ts*); Gene Allen (*bs*); Roland Hanna (*p*); Billy Bauer (*g*); Arvell Shaw (*b*); Ray Burns (*d*); Ethel Ennis, Jimmy Rushing (*v*). 5/58.

The band is a bit of a ragtag troupe, lacking the kind of punctilious precision one expects of a Goodman ensemble, and they can't finesse their way through some of the more risky moments in the scores. But it's still an interesting orchestra and, on what are familiar Goodman programmes, the leader summons enough spirit of his own to see them through.

**(*) Yale Archives Vol. 4: Big Band Recordings Musicmasters 65017-2

Goodman; John Frosk, Allen Smith, E. V. Perry, Benny Ventura, Jimmy Maxwell, Mel Davis, Al Mairoca, Fern Caron, Joe Wilder, Joe Newman, Tony Terrar, Ray Triscari, Jimmy Zito, Taft Jordan, Billy Butterfield, Buck Clayton (*t*); Rex Peer, Harry DeViuto, Vern Friley, Bob Edmondson, Jimmy Knepper, Willie Dennis, Wayne Andrew, Hale Rood, Buster Cooper, Vernon Brown, Eddie Bert (*tb*); Herb Geller, Jimmy Santucci, Bob Wilber, Babe Clark, Pepper Adams, Gene Allen, Walt Levinsky, Al Block, Budd Johnson, Bill Slapin, Phil Woods, Jerry Dodgion, Zoot Sims, Tommy Newsom, Skeets Furfurt, Herbie Steward, Teddy Edwards, Bob Hardaway (*reeds*); Pete Jolly, Russ Freeman, Roland Hanna, Hank Jones, John Bunch (*p*); Kenny Burrell, Turk Van Lake, Benny Garcia, Steve Jordan (*g*); Milt Hinton, Henry Grimes, Irv Manning, Bill Crow, Monty Budwig (*b*); Mousie Alexander, Shelly Manne, Roy Burns, Mel Lewis, Colin Bailey (*d*); Martha Tilton, Mitzi Cottle (*v*). 11/58–6/64.

There's some dreary stuff – including a terrible version of 'People' – on this hotchpotch of leftovers from bands that Goodman led in the late 1950s and early '60s. Many major players involved here, and some of them take the odd solo, but Goodman is at centre stage and the main interest remains on his own solos. For Goodman collectors only, who'll have to salvage bits and pieces.

*** In Stockholm 1959 Phontastic NCD 8801

Goodman; Jack Sheldon (*t*); Bill Harris (*tb*); Jerry Dodgion (*as, f*); Flip Phillips (*ts*); Red Norvo (*vib*); Russ Freeman (*p*); Jimmy Wyble (*g*); Red Wootten (*b*); John Markham, John Poole (*d*); Anita O'Day (*v*). 10/59.

Although the leader plays very well on this souvenir of a European tour which Goodman scholars credit as a peak period in his later work, the rather desultory presentation of the music – too many offhand introductions by Benny, and the inclusion of crowd-pleasing pieces like 'Sing Sing Sing' and the hits medley – take some of the fizz out of the record. The band aren't granted too much individual space – which is frustrating, since Sheldon, Norvo and Freeman all sound excellent – and Goodman's habit of whistling through other people's solos is caught by the mostly very clear recording, which suffers from only occasional drop-outs.

***(*) Yale University Archives Vol. 5 Musicmasters 65040-2 2CD

Goodman; Jack Sheldon, Bobby Hackett (*t*); Bill Harris, Urbie Green (*tb*); Jerry Dodgion (*as, f*); Flip Phillips (*ts*); Modesto Bresano (*ts, f*); Red Norvo (*vib*); Gene DiNovi, John Bunch (*p*); Jimmy Wyble (*g*); Steve Swallow, Red Wootten, Jimmy Rowser (*b*); John Markham, Ray Mosca (*d*). 11/59–6/63.

*** Yale University Archives Vol. 7 Musicmasters 65058-2

Goodman; Bill Harris (*tb*); Flip Phillips (*ts*); Marty Harris (*p*); Leo Robinson (*g*); Al Simi (*b*); Bob Binnix (*d*). 8/59.

***(*) Yale University Archives Vol. 8 Musicmasters 65093-2

Goodman; Bernie Privin, Manny Klein, Conrad Gozzo, Irv Goodman, Don Fagerquist (*t*); Joe Howard, Murray McEachern, Milt Bernhart, Lou McGarity (*tb*); Toots Mondello, Herb Geller, Bud Shank (*as*); Zoot Sims, Buddy Collette, Dave Pell (*ts*); Chuck Gentry (*bs*); André Previn, Hank Rowland, Mel Powell, Russ Freeman (*p*); Eddie Costa (*vib*); Tony Mottola, Al Hendrickson, Barney Kessel (*g*); Leroy Vinnegar, George Duvivier (*b*); Frank Capp, Roy Burnes, Morey Feld (*d*); Martha Tilton (*v*). 9/58–2/61.

More from Goodman's own archive. There is some happy and spirited playing by these sometimes improbably constituted small groups. The first band on *Volume 5* features Phillips, Norvo and Sheldon, and generates some agreeable swing re-creations, but the second is graced by the lovely trumpet-playing of Bobby Hackett and merits an extra notch on the ratings. The line-up on *Volume 7* is a little more routine, but the group play very capably. *Volume 8* includes a session of Hawaiian tunes from 1961 (improbable but rather good), a small group with Previn (flat), and two exquisitely shaped medleys with Mel Powell. Plus one big-band shot, a blossoming 'Bei Mir Bist Du Schön', with Martha Tilton back as vocalist. A good one.

*** Yale University Archives Vol. 6 Musicmasters 65047-2
>   Goodman; Joe Newman, Doc Cheatham (*t*); Zoot Sims (*ts*); Bernie Leighton, Herbie Hancock
>   (*p*); Les Spann, Attila Zoller (*g*); George Duvivier, Al Hall (*b*); Morey Feld, Joe Marshall (*d*);
>   Annette Saunders (*v*). 6/66–6/67.

Two very strange line-ups for these live dates from the Rainbow Grill: one has Herbie Hancock and Doc
Cheatham together on the stand. That both of them are plausible Goodman bands says something,
perhaps, about the leader's inflexible will. He allows no stretching out – only three tracks run over the
five-minute mark – and little adventure. But the playing conforms to the usual stern standard.

*** Jazz Masters 33 Verve 844410-2
>   Goodman; Warren Vaché (*t*); George Young (*as*); Scott Hamilton, Zoot Sims, Buddy Tate,
>   Frank Wess (*ts*); Mary Lou Williams (*p*); Lionel Hampton (*vib*); Percy Heath (*b*); Connie Kay
>   (*d*). 70–78.

*** 40th Anniversary Concert – Live At Carnegie Hall London 820349-2 2CD
>   Goodman; Victor Paz, Warren Vaché, Jack Sheldon (*t*); Wayne André, George Masso, John
>   Messner (*tb*); George Young, Mel Rodnon (*as*); Buddy Tate, Frank Wess (*ts*); Sol Schlinger (*bs*);
>   Mary Lou Williams, Jimmy Rowles, John Bunch (*p*); Lionel Hampton (*vib*); Cal Collins, Wayne
>   Wright (*g*); Michael Moore (*b*); Connie Kay (*d*); Martha Tilton, Debi Craig (*v*). 1/78.

Goodman's enduring facility as a clarinettist is the most absorbing thing about these sessions, on both
sets. The Jazz Masters disc collates material from various appearances during the 1970s including a
number of different generations involved, and makes a worthwhile sampler of Goodman's final period.
At Carnegie Hall the band played a functional rather than challenging role, the job being to replicate
standard scores as flawlessly as the leader wished and, although there are many fine players involved,
Goodman's iron hand stifles anything freewheeling which might have emerged. But he drives himself as
hard as the others: the clarinet still sounds august, refined, imperious.

***(*) Yale Archives Vol. 1 Musicmasters 65000-2
>   Goodman; Ermit Perry, Taft Jordan, Buzz King, John Frosk, Joe Newman, Ruby Braff, Allen
>   Smith, Benny Ventura, Jack Sheldon, Joe Mosello, Randy Sandke, John Eckert (*t*); Vernon
>   Brown, Eddie Bert, Harry DeVito, Urbie Green, Bill Harris, Buster Cooper, Rex Peer, Hale
>   Rood, Matt Finders, Dan Barrett (*tb*); Ernie Mauro, Skippy Colluchio, Jerry Dodgion, Herb
>   Geller, Jimmy Sands, Jack Stuckey, Chuck Wilson (*as*); Zoot Sims, Buddy Tate, Dick Hafer,
>   Flip Phillips, Bob Wilber, Babe Clark, Paul Quinichette, Ken Peplowski, Ted Nash (*ts*); Gene
>   Allen, Pepper Adams (*bs*); Bernie Leighton, Roland Hanna, Dave McKenna, Martin Harris,
>   Gene DiNovi, Russ Freeman, Teddy Wilson, Ben Aronov (*p*); Red Norvo (*vib*); Attila Zoller,
>   Chuck Wayne, Steve Jordan, Leo Robinson, Jimmy Wyble, Turk Van Lake, Perry Lopez, Billy
>   Bauer, James Chirillo (*g*); George Duvivier, Henry Grimes, Tommy Potter, Al Simi, Red
>   Wootten, Milt Hinton, Arvell Shaw, Murray Wall (*b*); Joe Marshall, Roy Burns, Bobby
>   Donaldson, Bob Binnix, John Markham, Shelly Manne, Don Lamond, Louie Bellson (*d*). 9/55–
>   1/86.

What was the first collection from Goodman's personal archive is a fascinating cross-section of work,
most of it from the 1950s, but with two tracks by a 1967 septet featuring Joe Newman and Zoot Sims
and one by the 1986 big band that must be among his final testaments. That his playing on that final
session is as impeccable as ever says much for Goodman's tireless devotion both to the clarinet and to
the rigorous, swinging music which he believed was his métier. Small groups of five, seven and eight
predominate in this selection and, although there's little which can be called surprising, the themes
chosen – including 'Macedonia Lullaby', 'Marching And Swinging' and 'Diga Diga Doo' – are at least
unfamiliar Goodman fare. A delightful 'Broadway' with Bill Harris and Flip Phillips is one highlight,
and shrewd programming makes the CD consistently interesting, with all the recordings, despite their
differing vintage, sounding well.

Mick Goodrick (born 1945) GUITAR

*** In Passing ECM 1139
>   Goodrick; John Surman (*ss, bs, bcl*); Eddie Gomez (*b*); Jack DeJohnette (*d*). 11/78.
***(*) Biorhythms CMP CD 46
>   Goodrick; Harvie Swartz (*b*); Gary Chaffee (*d*). 10/90.
*** Rare Birds RAM RMCD 4505
>   Goodrick; Joe Diorio (*g*). 4/93.

Goodrick's brand of electric-guitar impressionism has been slow to make an impact, at least in comparison to that of such peers as Frisell and Metheny (Goodrick worked with Metheny in Gary Burton's
mid-1970s band). He seems to have fewer ambitions as a leader, but both these records reveal an

intelligent grasp of form and a shrewd management of resources. The 1978 session is a little more diffuse: Surman is a more dominant voice than Goodrick, and the music aspires to the pastel tones of a typical ECM session. *Biorhythms* is a follow-up that took a long time to emerge, but it's a feast of guitar playing, with excellent support from Swartz and Chaffee, who can play jazz or funk time with equal aplomb. Goodrick's themes range from the peppy groove of the title-tune and 'Groove Test' through to a reflective sequence for Emily Remler, 'Bl'ize Medley', and the lavish farewell of '(I'll) Never Forget'. Restrained use of overdubs and crystal-clear sound by engineer Walter Quintus ensure that the music holds the interest even across generous CD length. The pairing with Joe Diorio on *Rare Birds* is a meeting of minds which are seemingly a little too alike: with each man using long, liquid sustain and a rippling melodic flow, the six standards and half-dozen improvisations have a seamless but soporific beauty about them. Here and there, as on a particularly lovely 'Blue In Green', the music intensifies just a fraction.

Dexter Gordon (1923–89) TENOR SAXOPHONE, SOPRANO SAXOPHONE

*** Jazz West Coast Live – Hollywood Jazz, Volume 1 Savoy 0164
Gordon; Howard McGhee (*t*); Trummy Young (*tb*); Sonny Criss (*as*); Wardell Gray (*ts*); Hampton Hawes (*p*); Barney Kessel (*g*); Leroy Gray (*b*); Connie Kay, Ken Kennedy (*d*). 7/47.
*** Dexter Rides Again Savoy SV 0120
Gordon; Leonard Hawkins (*t*); Leo Parker (*bs*); Tadd Dameron, Sadik Hakim, Bud Powell (*p*); Gene Ramey, Curley Russell (*b*); Art Blakey, Eddie Nicholson, Max Roach (*d*). 10/45, 1/46, 12/47.
**** Dexter Gordon On Dial: The Complete Sessions Spotlite SPJ CD 130
Gordon; Melba Liston (*tb*); Teddy Edwards, Wardell Gray (*ts*); Jimmy Bunn, Charles Fox, Jimmy Rowles (*p*); Red Callender (*b*); Roy Porter, Chuck Thompson (*d*). 6/47.

One of the giants (literally) of modern jazz, Gordon made an impact on players as dissimilar as Sonny Rollins and John Coltrane, but himself remained comparatively unrecognized until a comeback in the 1960s (Gordon had lived and worked in Scandinavia in the early half of the decade), by which time many of the post-Lester Young stylistic devices he had introduced were firmly in place under others' patents.

Gordon's on-off partnership with fellow-tenorist Wardell Gray was consistently productive, pairing him for much of the late 1940s with another Lester Young disciple who had taken on board most of the modernist idiom without abandoning Young's mellifluously extended solo style. The Dial sessions – with Gray and, at Christmas 1947, Teddy Edwards – are pretty definitive of what was going on on the West Coast at the time. The Spotlite brings together all the material, including a track with just Edwards up front. 'The Chase' was a studio version of the saxophone contests that Dexter and Gray had been conducting night after night in LA's Little Harlem.

The earliest of the sessions features Melba Liston, who was presumably recruited for her skill as an arranger. The charts to 'Mischievous Lady' and 'Lullaby In Rhythm' sound tight and well organized, more coherent than the ultimately rather tiresome 'Chase'. On the same day as it, Gordon also laid down three tracks with just rhythm, of which 'Chromatic Aberration' is perhaps the most interesting vis-à-vis the development of bebop, but 'It's The Talk Of The Town' is the occasion for one of his most expressive ballad solos of these years. The final Dial session, with Rowles at the piano, was made just before the AFM recording ban began the brief eclipse which skews our perception of what was going on stylistically at this point.

The second of the Savoys also includes the saxophonist's signature-theme, 'Long Tall Dexter', and the equally well-known '. . . Rides Again' and '. . . Digs In' are from a fine session with Bud Powell and Max Roach, which also featured the little-known Leonard Hawkins. Best of all, though, is a rousing 'Settin' The Pace', where Gordon repeats the 'chase' sequences of the sets with Gray, but this time in the company of Leo Parker, whose jaunty baritone-sound is a good foil. The still-underrated Tadd Dameron comps impressively and Blakey stokes up the engines. The last of the three sessions is slightly muted. Argonne Thornton, later known as Sadik Hakim, was supposedly present at Charlie Parker's classic Savoy recordings. On the strength of these four sides with Gordon, one can see why Dizzy Gillespie (*sic*!) was called in as a pianist. Denon have redistributed their Savoy holdings somewhat, but there are more interesting things in the vaults than have turned up so far. Some masking of the sound has been eliminated, though, and the price is attractive enough to make up for any other deficiencies.

*** The Bethlehem Years Fresh Sound FSR 154
Gordon; Conte Candoli (*t*); Frank Rosolino (*tb*); Kenny Drew (*p*); Leroy Vinnegar (*b*); Lawrence Marable (*d*). 9/55.

*** **Daddy Plays The Horn** Bethlehem BET 6005
     As above. 9/55.
*** **Dexter Blows Hot And Cool** Boplicity CDBOP 006
     Gordon; Jimmy Robinson (*t*); Carl Perkins (*p*); Leroy Vinnegar (*b*); Chuck Thompson (*d*). 55.
Not normally thought of as a West Coast man in the stylistic sense, Gordon enjoyed his sojourn back in
California during 1955. Charlie Parker's death in March created a vacuum at the head of the saxophone
rankings and Gordon looked like an ideal contender. *The Bethlehem Years* compilation is good value for
money. Neither Candoli nor Rosolino is a charismatic soloist, but they spur Gordon on and lend 'Ruby
My Dear' a beefy resonance. Drew and Vinnegar play exceptionally well, and the CD transfer is
generally good. In 1955 Gordon had already cemented the style he was to utilize virtually to the end of
his career. Its easy, but never shallow, expressiveness and light, springy time-feel were directly related to
Lester Young, and the presence of the short-lived Perkins gives the Boplicity disc (originally made for
Dootone) an intriguing angularity, on 'Cry Me A River' especially, which lifts it out of the ordinary and
underlines how original was Dexter's take on bebop idiom. He was, though, playing in the interim
between two drug-related prison sentences that more or less wound up the 1950s, which should have
been his decade.

**** **Doin' Alright** Blue Note CDP 784077
     Gordon; Freddie Hubbard (*t*); Horace Parlan (*p*); George Tucker (*b*); Al Harewood (*d*). 5/61.
Back in the world and doing all right. Gordon's first recording after a long and painful break is one of
his best. Critics divide on whether Gordon was influenced by Coltrane at this period or whether it was
simply a case of the original being obscured by his followers. Gordon's phrasing on *Doin' Alright*
certainly suggests a connection of some sort, but the opening statement of 'I Was Doin' Alright' is
completely individual and quite distinct, and Gordon's solo development is nothing like the younger
man's. This is one of Gordon's best records and should on no account be missed.

*** **Dexter Calling** Blue Note B21Y 46544
     Gordon; Kenny Drew (*p*); Paul Chambers (*b*); Philly Joe Jones (*d*). 5/61.
Recorded three days later and reflecting the same virtues. With a better-drilled but slightly more conventional band, Gordon is pushed a little wider on the solos, ranging much further away from the stated
key (as on a memorable mid-chorus break on 'Ernie's Tune') and varying his timbre much more than he
used to. As indicators of how his harmonic language and distinctive accent were to develop, the two
1961 Blue Notes are particularly valuable. The sound is a little better on the later record.

*** **Go!** Blue Note CDP 746094
     Gordon; Sonny Clark (*p*); Butch Warren (*b*); Billy Higgins (*d*). 8/62.
*** **A Swingin' Affair** Blue Note CDP 784133
     As above.
Typically good husbandry on the part of Blue Note to get two albums from this not altogether riveting
date, one of the first since his return to normal circulation. *Swingin' Affair* stands and falls on a lovely
version of 'You Stepped Out Of A Dream'. *Go!* includes Gordon's simplest and finest reading of 'Where
Are You', a relatively little-used standard with interesting changes and a strong turn in the middle. The
hipsters' motto (pinched from novelist John Clellon Holmes) was meant to suggest relentless improvisatory progress. Gordon was to play better, but rarely with such directness, and it's not entirely idle to ask
whether he felt himself hampered by a rhythm section that was not always responsive.

** **Cry Me A River** Steeplechase SCCD 36004
     Gordon; Atli Bjorn (*p*); Benny Nielsen, Marcel Rigot (*b*); Finn Frederiksen, William Schiopffe
     (*d*). 11/62, 6/64.
A pretty dismal album by any standard, much of it is given over to Bjorn's own trio. The title-track
receives a predictably fulsome and emotive reading, but Bjorn seems to be all over his keyboard in
contrast to Gordon's discipline and reserve. Not an album for the A-list.

**** **Our Man In Paris** Blue Note CDP 746394
     Gordon; Bud Powell (*p*); Pierre Michelot (*b*); Kenny Clarke (*d*). 5/63.
Gordon's 'purest' bebop album since the early 1950s, *Our Man* also shows how much he had continued
to absorb of the pre-bop sound of Lester Young and Johnny Hodges. There are hints of both in his
ballad playing, and in the winding, almost incantatory solo on 'Night In Tunisia', which is one of his
finest performances on record. A classic.

***(*) **One Flight Up** Blue Note B21Y 84176
     Gordon; Donald Byrd (*t*); Kenny Drew (*p*); Niels-Henning Orsted-Pedersen (*b*); Art Taylor (*d*).
     6/64.
Three extended performances, dominated by 'Darn That Dream' (see also *Ballads*, below) and the
turned-sideways 'Coppin' The Haven' theme. Byrd was still an impressive player at this period, though

he's rarely as adventurous as Hubbard, and Drew is a brilliant accompanist. It's easy to see, particularly on 'Darn', how Gordon continued to influence John Coltrane's harmonic development.

***(*) Gettin' Around Blue Note B21Y 46681

Gordon; Bobby Hutcherson (*vib*); Barry Harris (*p*); Bob Cranshaw (*b*); Billy Higgins (*d*). 5/65. *Gettin' Around* benefits enormously from the inclusion of Hutcherson. He makes Gordon play more simply, in the sense of going for fewer notes, but he provides a far more challenging harmonic background than Harris, and the big man has to negotiate some intriguingly non-standard changes on 'Who Can I Turn To' and 'Everybody's Somebody's Fool'.

***(*) The Panther! Original Jazz Classics OJC 770

Gordon; Tommy Flanagan (*p*); Larry Ridley (*b*); Alan Dawson (*d*). 7/70.
Dexter's visit to the USA in 1970 confirmed his growing stature (so to speak). He played at Newport and, following the success of *The Tower Of Power!*, recorded *The Panther!*. It is generally thought that one of the panther's most effective characteristics is its silence, which makes the exclamation mark slightly redundant. In point of fact, the 1970 record marks a stage in Gordon's development in which he was able and willing to play more quietly, using fewer notes, a greater dynamic range and a willingness to dwell on effective phrases rather than rush them past like trolleybuses.

'Body And Soul' is, almost inevitably, the touchstone here again, a delicate, almost kaleidoscopic reading, with Flanagan's immaculate accompaniment using altered chords. 'Mrs Miniver' is an original and is one of the saxophonist's most interesting and little-known tunes; medium tempo and song-like, it has a brilliantly simple bridge and coda that confirms the strength of Gordon's conception at this point in his career.

**(*) Cheese Cake Steeplechase SCCD 36008

Gordon; Tete Montoliu (*p*); Benny Nielsen, Niels-Henning Orsted-Pedersen (*b*); Alex Riel (*d*). 6/64.
*** King Neptune Steeplechase SCCD 36012
As above. 6/64.
*** I Want More Steeplechase SCCD 36015
As above. 7/64.
*** Love For Sale Steeplechase SCCD 36018
As above. 7/64.
**(*) It's You Or No One Steeplechase SCCD 36022
As above. 8/64.
**(*) Billie's Bounce Steeplechase SCCD 36028
As above. 8/64.
*** Stable Mable Steeplechase SCCD 31040
Gordon; Tete Montoliu, Horace Parlan (*p*); Benny Nielsen, Niels-Henning Orsted-Pedersen (*b*); Alex Riel, Tony Inzalaco (*d*). 11/74.
**(*) Bouncing With Dex Steeplechase SCCD 31060
Gordon; Tete Montoliu (*p*); Benny Nielsen, Niels-Henning Orsted-Pedersen (*b*); Alex Riel, Billy Higgins (*d*). 3/75, 9/75.
**(*) Something Different Steeplechase SCCD 31136
Gordon; Philip Catherine (*g*); Niels-Henning Orsted-Pedersen (*b*); Billy Higgins (*d*). 9/75.
Newly settled in Scandinavia, Gordon turns the tap on full. There's still the emotional equivalent of an airlock, slightly spluttering hesitations alternating with sudden, scalding flows, but it all starts to fit together as this fascinating sequence of albums progresses. A more comprehensive pianist, Parlan or Flanagan, might have varied the structures a little, but Montoliu is sympathetic and very lyrical.

The touchstone 'Body And Soul' is beautifully enunciated on *King Neptune* and the band gels in the ensemble passages, with little of the slightly mechanistic pulse that afflicted the earlier *Cheese Cake* session. *I Want More* and *Love For Sale* are the best of this group. Gordon's understanding with the players seems increasingly telepathic and his approach to themes correspondingly inventive. Considered as a set, this is some of Gordon's best work, documented at close quarters on good pressings and CD transfers.

Bouncin' With Dex takes essentially the same band forward a decade. By the time of *Swiss Nights* (below), the act is consummately polished. Montoliu sounds relaxed and confident and plays with considerable authority. The addition of guitarist Catherine adds a new band of the spectrum to *Something Different*. From the opening 'Freddie Freeloader' till it closes with 'Polka Dots And Moonbeams' and 'Yesterday's Mood', it exudes bonhomie and relaxed invention.

*** Both Sides Of Midnight Black Lion BLCD 760103

Gordon; Kenny Drew (*p*); Niels-Henning Orsted- Pedersen (*b*); Albert 'Tootie' Heath (*d*). 7/67.

***(*) **Body And Soul** Black Lion BLCD 760118
    As above. 7/67.
(*) **Take The 'A' Train Black Lion BLCD 760133
    As above. 11/74.
** **The Apartment** Steeplechase SCCD 31025
    As above, except Alex Riel (*d*) replaces Heath. 8/75.
*** **Swiss Nights – Volume 1** Steeplechase SCCD 31050
    As above. 8/75.
*** **Swiss Nights – Volume 2** Steeplechase SCCD 31090
    As above. 8/75.
(*) **Swiss Nights – Volume 3 Steeplechase SCCD 31110
    As above. 8/75.
(*) **Lullaby For A Monster Steeplechase SCCD 31156
    As above, except omit Drew. 6/76.

Both Sides and *Body And Soul* are vintage albums from a two-shift session in July 1967. ' "A" Train' uses up some of the alternative takes ('For All We Know' from the former, and 'Blues Walk' from the second) and is a little dilute as a consequence. Drew is a more rhythmic pianist than Montoliu, and the metre of Gordon's solos tends to stretch, fragment, re-integrate at great speed when in his company. *Lullaby*, a piano-less trio and thus unusual for Gordon, sees him trying rather unsuccessfully to bridge the gaps that Drew's absence leaves. It contains some of his freest solos, notably 'On Green Dolphin Street', but there's an element of constancy lacking.

There's a slight break in the continuity between 1967 and 1974. *The Apartment* isn't one of Gordon's best records; it sounds curiously timebound now, far more than anything else he did, and there's a flatness to some of the solo work. Whatever the reason, the three volumes of *Swiss Nights* sound vigorous, pumped-up and highly coherent. There probably wasn't enough material for three albums, though the last is justified by 'Sophisticated Lady'. Together, they make a fine set and a good summation of what this quartet was about.

(*) **Tower Of Power Original Jazz Classics OJC 299
    Gordon; James Moody (*ts*); Barry Harris (*p*); Buster Williams (*b*); Albert 'Tootie' Heath (*d*). 4/
    69.

The 'battle of the tenors' format never suited Gordon's extended delivery. Though this is subtler than an old-fashioned cutting contest, Moody tends to impede rather than spur Gordon; fortunately his contribution is restricted to a single track, 'Mon Maestre'. The quartet numbers are better, but Gordon isn't firing on all cylinders.

** **The Shadow Of Your Smile** Steeplechase SCCD 31206
    Gordon; Lars Sjøsten (*p*); Sture Nordin (*b*); Fredrik Norén (*d*). 4/71.
(*) **After Hours Steeplechase SCCD 31226
    As above, except add Rolf Ericson (*t*).

These are weak performances by Gordon's high and consistent standard. 'Polka Dots And Moonbeams' on *Shadow* suffers some difficulties in the first dozen measures, mostly down to the Danish rhythm section. Not usually lacking in proportion, Gordon sounds merely grandstanding on 'Secret Love' and never quite gets hold of 'Shadow Of Your Smile'; there's a much better (1961) version of the latter with Dizzy Reece, Slide Hampton and Kenny Drew on the Verve sampler, *Jazz Club – Tenor Sax*. Ericson has a bold, swinging tone, but it cuts across Gordon's development on 'All The Things You Are' quite disconcertingly. Two to miss with a clear conscience.

***(*) **Round Midnight** Steeplechase SCCD 31290
    Gordon; Benny Bailey (*t*); Lars Sjösten (*p*); Torbjörn Hultcrantz (*b*); Jual Curtis (*d*). 74.

Bailey was a terrific partner: tight, energetic and unfailingly lyrical. To a large extent they ignore the well-intentioned accompaniment of the Swedish trio (Sjösten is an able player, the others not) and head off on a companionable jaunt round a set of themes that fall easily under their respective approaches. Gordon is completely at home on 'Round About Midnight' and 'Stella By Starlight'; Bailey takes the initiative on 'Blue 'N' Boogie' and 'What's New', and fans of the little trumpeter (one wonders what they must have looked like side by side on the stand) will find this one of the most profitable of his live recordings.

***(*) **Biting The Apple** Steeplechase SCCD 31080
    Gordon; Barry Harris (*p*); Sam Jones (*b*); Al Foster (*d*). 11/76.

Prodigal comes home. Hugs and forgiveness on all sides, and then the party. In 1976, Gordon made a rare return visit to the States. The response was so overwhelmingly positive that he decided to end his exile permanently. 'Apple Jump' is a joyous homecoming and 'I'll Remember April' one of his loveliest performances. Harris, Jones and Foster fit in comfortably, and the sound is good.

**** More Than You Know Steeplechase SCCD 31030
> Gordon; Palle Mikkelborg, Allan Botschinsky, Benny Rosenfeld, Idrees Sulieman (*t, flhn*);
> Richard Boone, Vincent Nilsson (*tb*); Axel Windfeld (*btb*); Ole Molin (*g*); Thomas Clausen (*p,
> electric p*); Kenneth Knudsen (*syn*); Niels-Henning Orsted-Pedersen (*b*); Alex Riel, Ed Thigpen
> (*d*); Klaus Nordsoe (*perc*); chamber winds and strings. 2–3/75.

** Strings And Things Steeplechase SCCD 31145
> Gordon; Allan Botschinsky, Markku Johansson (*t*); Eero Koivistoinen, Pekka Poyry (*reeds*);
> George Wadenius, Ole Molin (*g*); Niels-Henning Orsted-Pedersen (*b*); unknown ensemble. 2/65,
> 5/76.

*** Something Different Steeplechase SCCD 31136
> Gordon; Philip Catherine (*g*); Niels-Henning Orsted-Pedersen (*b*); Billy Hart (*d*). 9/75.

**(*) Sophisticated Giant Columbia 450316
> Gordon; Benny Bailey, Woody Shaw (*t, flhn*); Wayne Andre, Slide Hampton (*tb*); Frank Wess (*f,
> as, picc*); Howard Johnson (*tba, bs*); Bobby Hutcherson (*vib*); George Cables (*p*); Rufus Reid
> (*b*); Victor Lewis (*d*). 6/77.

Beautifully arranged and orchestrated (by Mikkelborg), *More Than You Know* sets Gordon in the middle – as it sounds – of a rich ensemble of textures which are every bit as creatively unresolved and undogmatic as his solo approach. 'Naima' rarely works with a large band, but this is near perfect and Gordon responds with considerable emotion and inventiveness. The cassette sound is a little flat, but the CD shouldn't be missed.

Gordon rarely played with a guitarist, but Catherine was an inspired choice for the September 1975 session, alternating warm, flowing lines with more staccato, accented figures towards the top of his range. NHOP responds with firmly plucked and strummed figures and Gordon rides on top in a relatively unfamiliar programme for him – Miles's 'Freddie Freeloader', 'When Sunny Gets Blue', 'Polka Dots And Moonbeams'.

Sophisticated Giant is an energetic but occasionally oblique album that shows off more of Gordon's Coltrane mannerisms. The arrangements – by Slide Hampton – and the typically overmixed CBS sound mask some of the subtlety of Gordon's soloing and the true sound of his soprano. The trumpets are a trifle brittle and this might be considered a later gap-filler rather than an essential buy.

Strings And Things is a diffident, rather shapeless compilation of material with none of the bite of Mikkelborg's usually intelligent orchestration.

**(*) American Classic Discovery 71009
> Gordon; Grover Washington Jr (*ss*); Kirk Lightsey (*p*); Shirley Scott (*org*); David Eubanks (*b*);
> Eddie Gladden (*d*). 3/82.

As always, Dexter rises above a rather indifferent setting, and the brief interview at the end of 'Skylark' makes this an attractive acquisition. Though Lightsey is with him every inch of the way, Shirley Scott is overpowering; and Washington, attractively toned as always, seems to be playing on another session altogether, almost as if his contribution were overdubbed. This set was originally released on Elektra Musician in 1982; good as Discovery's intentions undoubtedly are, it doesn't really merit reissue.

**(*) The Other Side Of Round Midnight Blue Note 746397
> Gordon; various line-ups. 86.

Soundtrack material from French movie director Bertrand Tavernier's sentimentalized treatment of a composite black musician (played with Methodical conviction by Gordon) slowly unwinding his life. The music, curiously, is far more atmospheric on its own. Good contributions from Bobby Hutcherson, John McLaughlin and Herbie Hancock; very up-close, how you say? intimate sound. *The Other Side* is pretty much the same as this one.

Frank Gordon TRUMPET

***(*) Clarion Echoes Soul Note 121096
> Gordon; Bobby Watson (*as*); Ari Brown (*ts*); James Williams (*p*); Rufus Reid (*b*); Carl Allen
> (*d*). 6/85.

A hint of cleverness just takes the edge off Gordon's debut. The opening 'Take Off' touches on aspects of atonality in a manner reminiscent of Don Ellis's 1960s experiments and seems a little too pleased with itself. Gordon's on firmer ground with 'Libra', which jumps into polytonality. If there's a slight sense that every track illustrates an -ism, the playing is usually bright enough to deflect attention.

A latter-day Clifford Brown disciple, Gordon has terrific control at the top and bottom of the range. The improvised title-track is not much more than a showcase for the trumpeter's skills but, like Brownie's practice tapes, there's lots going on. Significantly, 'I Remember Clifford' inspires the most confident and searching solo of the night; a few more repertoire pieces might have been advisable for a first record.

Bobby Watson makes an effective partner and the rhythm section are thoroughly competent, though Ari Brown's role is slightly more questionable. Little has been seen or heard of Gordon on the recording front since 1985. This and an appearance with Charli Persip's Superband remain the only items currently available.

Joe Gordon (1928-63) TRUMPET

*** **West Coast Days** Fresh Sound FSCD 1030
    Gordon; Richie Kamuca (*ts*); Russ Freeman (*p*); Monty Budwig (*b*); Shelly Manne (*d*). 7/58.
***(*) **Lookin' Good** Original Jazz Classics OJC 174
    Gordon; Jimmy Woods (*as*); Dick Whittington (*p*); Jimmy Bond (*b*); Milton Turner (*d*). 7/61.
With impeccable credentials from the New England Conservatory and an extended apprenticeship with Georgie Auld, Lionel Hampton and Charlie Parker, Gordon was considered one of the finest trumpeters of his day. A slightly brittle tone, always pitched a little sharp, but affectingly vocalized and never less than expressive. He was a Jazz Messenger for a short time and appeared in the film *The Proper Time* with Shelly Manne. Like Woody Shaw, he mismanaged – or failed to manage – his solo career and his life; at the age of 35 he burned to death in a rooming-house fire that was apparently started by a cigarette on his mattress.

The recorded legacy is thin but impressive. *Lookin' Good* isn't quite the unpretentious blowing session it pretends to be. There are subtle, thoughtful things on it as well, including the 'Non-Viennese Waltz Blues', which flirts with all sorts of new-fangled things, and 'Terra Firma Irma', a blustery opener which could end up almost anywhere. Here at least, Gordon is prominently featured. On the Fresh Sound (which is in any case shared with Scott LaFaro material), he takes a second place to Kamuca and Freeman and never quite settles to the task. The recordings are average for the time (1958) and place (the legendary Lighthouse), though 'Poinciana' finds him several hundred yards off-mike. There is better sound and music, if a little smoothed out, on the OJC.

Jon Gordon ALTO SAXOPHONE

*** **The Jon Gordon Quartet** Chiaroscuro CR(*D*) 316
    Gordon; Phil Woods (*as*); Kevin Hays (*p*); Scott Holley (*b*); Bill Stewart (*d*). 3/92.
*** **Spark** Chiaroscuro CR(*D*) 330
    Gordon; Benny Carter, Phil Woods (*as*); Bill Charlap (*p*); Sean Smith (*b*); Tim Horner (*d*). 4/94.
***(*) **Ask Me Now** Criss Cross CRISS 1099
    Gordon; Tim Hagans (*t*); Bill Charlap (*p*); Larry Grenadier (*b*); Billy Drummond (*d*). 12/94.
Much admired by Joe Lovano (who contributes a fulsome liner-note on *Ask Me Now*), Gordon is a young player gifted with an irrepressibly joyous sound and a wise head. Nothing seems beyond his range and none of it sounds effortful or pretentious. His cover of Lovano's far from straightforward 'Land Of Ephysus' on the first record is a good case in point. The two Chiaroscuros (and the label name may point to one minor misgiving) were sold largely on the strength of the guest artists, but it is Gordon's fleet, eloquent voice which captures the attention from the very first number. 'Spark' is an original composition, breezily unpredictable and combustible, the first of several pieces that relate to fire ('Prometheus Syndrome' and 'Phoenix' are the others on this disc).

So, the obvious canard? More heat than light? Well, to some extent, yes. There isn't (yet) enough light and shade in Gordon's playing, which always seems to come from the same approximate band of the emotional spectrum. Even after a brief moment of the two old-timers on *Spark* (which was recorded on a cruise ship in the Caribbean – tough at the top, guys, tough at the top) it's clear that he has a way to go in terms of emotional depth and resonance. However, the basics are unshakeably in place, and it seems unlikely that Gordon will not fulfil the rich promise of *Ask Me Now*, where he follows his own 'Joe Said So' with a hair-raising ride through 'Giant Steps', bowing out on the Monk title tune. It's all in front of him . . .

Liz Gorrill PIANO, VOCAL

*** **Phantasmagoria** New Artists NA1004
    Gorrill; Andy Fite (*g*, *v*). 3/88.
*** **A Jazz Duet** New Artists NA1007
    Gorrill; Charley Krachy (*ts*). 10/89.

*** **Cosmic Comedy** New Artists NA1012
     Gorrill; Andy Fite (*g*). 3/90.
*** **Dreamflight** New Artists NA1010
     Gorrill (*p* solo). 5/90.

Gorrill is a part of the small but dedicated enclave of new Tristano-ites, although – unlike Connie Crothers, who seems to follow directly in the master's footsteps – she casts her range more widely. Her left-hand parts can be thunderously heavy and dark, and such favourite standards of this circle as 'You'd Be So Nice To Come Home To' – which appears in two utterly different versions in this sequence, one on *A Jazz Duet* and another on *Dreamflight* – aren't so much restructured as demolished by the weight of their new identity. Her approach to rhythm can be pedantic in its dogged avoidance of traditional swing: 'It Could Happen To You', also on *Dreamflight*, is a shipwreck rather than any floating of a new idea. But at least her methods eschew simple clichés, without surrendering an often graceful pianism.

The solo album is perhaps her best single record, but both the duet sessions with Fite are well worth hearing: *Phantasmagoria* is a blend of standards and brief, almost staccato originals, while the concert recording of *Cosmic Comedy* lets them stretch out on nine seemingly improvised pieces. Some of the interplay sounds static, even repetitive, but they can also lock into a glowering kind of groove that is exhilarating, too. The slightly eerie vocals on two tracks of the earlier album may be a bonus for some listeners. With Krachy, who resembles a gruff and somewhat shopworn edition of Warne Marsh, Gorrill is the dominant partner, though the best of their duets are again fiercely original. Three of the discs were recorded at New York's Greenwich House, in sometimes less-than-perfect sound: the session with Krachy in particular suffers from top-end distortion.

Simon Goubert DRUMS

**** **Haïti** Seventh SRA 7
     Goubert; Jean-Michel Couchet (*as*); Steve Grossman (*ts, ss*); Laurent Fickelson (*p*); Stéphane Persiani (*b*). 2/91.
(*) **Encierro Seventh SRA 18
     Goubert; David Sauzay (*ts, ss*); Jean-Michel Couchet (*as, ss*); Arrigo Lorenzi (*ss*); Michel Graillier (*p*); Stéphane Persiani (*b*). 8/95.

Goubert is a regular member of Steve Grossman's trio and has played a significant role in re-energizing the saxophonist's career. On *Haïti* the favours are reversed. Grossman isn't over-used and spends much of his time lazily doodling round Couchet's relaxed but forceful alto. They combine well on the long title-track (a Goubert composition), but the real star-turns are covers of Coltrane's ballad, 'Naima', and a breathtaking version of Paul Desmond's 'Take Five', which gives a rather unfashionable MOR favourite more than a degree of cred.

It may be that *Haiti* was something of a one-off. The follow-up is a flat disappointment, competent hard bop with over-mixed drums, predictable, guess-the-next-note solos and – except on the long 'Sunrise' by guest Lorenzi – little of the breezy grace of the earlier record.

Frank Goudie (1899–1964) CLARINET, VOCAL

(*) **Frank 'Big Boy' Goudie With Amos White American Music AMCD-50
     Goudie; Amos White (*t*); J. D. Banton (*ts*); Jimmy Simpson, Burt Bales (*p, v*); Al Levy (*g*); Al Conger (*b*); James Carter (*d*). 9/60–3/61.

Goudie is an obscure figure, even among New Orleans musicians, but he was much admired by Albert Nicholas, and these somewhat grimy recordings reveal an idiosyncratic, vigorous clarinettist (his previous spell in the limelight came with a date in Paris in 1937, with Bill Coleman and Django Reinhardt, which produced 'Big Boy Blues'). Five tracks with White, Banton, Simpson, Levy and Carter are unexceptional New Orleans dance-hall music – though recorded, like all the tracks, in San Francisco – but the four duets and three trios with Bales and Conger are more substantial. Goudie chews over the melody lines rather than elaborating on them, and there's a folkish lilt to some of his ideas. Recommended, though to New Orleans specialists only.

Dusko Goykovich (born 1931) TRUMPET, FLUGELHORN

***(*) **Swinging Macedonia** Enja 4048
     Goykovich; Eddie Busnello (*as*); Nathan Davis (*ts, ss, f*); Mal Waldron (*p*); Peter Trunk (*b*); Cees See (*d*). 8/66.

One of the most convincing attempts to synthesize jazz and the curious scalar progressions of Balkan folk music. Born in Yugoslavia, Goykovich studied at Berklee and saw action with Maynard Ferguson, Woody Herman and with the Clarke–Boland big band. His most characteristic work, though, has been with smaller groups. He is a bright, rhythmic player, with a full, rather folksy sound that draws some-what selectively on the bop trumpet tradition.

Swinging Macedonia was a bold stroke, with an impact akin to that of Ivo Papasov's much-hyped Bulgarian Wedding Band. Goykovich, though, is more purely a jazz player, and a more adventurous improviser. He's ably supported by an international line-up that hinges on the two American exiles. Waldron deals splendidly with some unfamiliar chord changes, Davis sounds authentically Slavonic (indeed, much like Papasov) and the little-known Busnello makes three or four very effective interven-tions. More than just an oddity, this deserves to be known more widely.

***(*) **Celebration** DIW 806
> Goykovich; Kenny Drew (*p*); Jimmy Woode (*b*); Al Levitt (*d*). 8/87.
**** **Soul Street** Enja ENJ 8044
> Goykovich; Jimmy Heath (*ts*); Tommy Flanagan (*p*); Eddie Gomez (*b*); Mickey Roker (*d*). 93.
**** **Bebop City** Enja ENJ 9015
> Goykovich; Abraham Burton (*as*); Ralph Moore (*ts*); Kenny Barron (*p*); Ray Drummond (*b*); Alvin Queen (*d*). 95.

There weren't many better mainstream-to-modern rhythm sections doing the rounds in the late 1980s than Drew, Woode and Levitt. Behind Goykovich, they are seamless and sympathetically responsive to his still occasionally surprising harmonic shifts. This, though, is his most Western album (one can't strictly say 'American'), with hints of everything from the Ellington small groups to the Jazz Messengers. Goykovich negotiates 'Blues In The Closet' and 'The Touch Of Your Lips' with admirable self-confidence. The originals have a clean bop edge, with just a hint of that indefinable Adriatic tinge that isn't quite Middle Eastern, but certainly isn't 'European' either. That is even more in evidence on the excellent *Soul Street*, which is probably Goykovich's best record. It has the sterling advantage of an absolutely top-class rhythm section and a guest appearance by Jimmy Heath, who sounds relaxed and assured. The record is intended as a tribute to Miles Davis, who had died not long before. Unlike many who laid flowers at the great trumpeter's grave, Goykovich doesn't attempt to emulate him. His approach still seems to stem from an earlier age, but the 'Ballad For Miles' includes one or two of the very slyest quotes and a tiny moment where Goykovich slips a semitone exactly in the great man's accent.

The most recent record is equally elegant and unfussy. This is the best band Goykovich has been able to put together, a rhythm section of surpassing quality and hungry young hornmen who divide up duties. The darkness is more evident this time around, a throb at the centre of the music that bespeaks something more than just blues and bebop changes. These must have been difficult years for Goykovich as his old country tore itself apart. He has maintained a dignified application to his art. *Nazdravie*.

Paul Grabowsky PIANO, SYNTHESIZER

*** **Tee Vee** VeraBra vBr 2050
> Grabowsky; Simon Kent (*tb*); Ian Chaplin (*as, ss*); Dale Barlow (*ts*); Ed Schuller (*b*); Niko Schauble (*d*). 92.
(*) **Viva Viva East West 994167
> Grabowsky; Scott Tinkler, Bobby Venier (*t*); Stephen Grant (*c*); Simon Kent (*tb*); Ian Chaplin (*as, ss*); Timothy Hopkins (*ts*); Ren Walters (*g*); Doug DeVries (*dobro*); Gary Costello, Ed Schuller (*b*); Andrew Gander, Niko Schauble (*d*). 93.

Grabowsky is an able young Australian who writes good tunes but hasn't quite got the technique or the band to deliver them with sufficient panache. Our hope that Grabowsky might be 'mainstreamed' by a major jazz label hasn't quite happened. The East West record is immaculately produced, with a sharp edge, but it takes him a further step away from jazz. As the portraits of Elvis on the front cover suggest, *Viva Viva* draws on other sources of inspiration, equally valid, but taking him further and further away from what we judge to be his forte.

Schuller is still a major asset, and the horns are cleverly varied; Grabowsky seems to have a particular affection for the way a trombone lies relative to piano, and it would be good to hear him develop this further in a straight blowing context, except that we suspect this isn't the way his ambitions lie. A pity.

Teddy Grace (1905–92) VOCAL

***(*) **Teddy Grace** Timeless CBC 1-016
> Grace; Charlie Shavers, Max Kaminsky (*t*); Bobby Hackett (*c*); Jack Teagarden, Sonny Lee,
> Moe Zudecoff (*tb*); Brad Gowans (*vtb*); Milt Yaner, Sal Franzella, Don Watt (*cl, as*); Buster
> Bailey, Pee Wee Russell (*cl*); John Sadola, Bud Freeman (*ts*); Frankie Froeba, Billy Kyle, Dave
> Bowman (*p*); Dave Barbour, Eddie Condon (*g*); Haig Stephens, Delmar Kaplan, Pete Peterson
> (*b*); Al Sidell, O'Neil Spencer, Morey Feld (*d*). 10/37–9/40.

An overdue reissue of 22 tracks by a nearly forgotten singer of the 1930s. Teddy Grace worked for Mal
Hallett and Bob Crosby as a band singer, but the sides under her own name show a commanding,
surprisingly tough vocalist whose smooth delivery and striking improvisation are enough to make one
wonder how she's been neglected. The six sessions include some outstanding accompaniments: Jack
Teagarden (who had passed out drunk by the end of the date) is on one, which includes a stunning 'Love
Me Or Leave Me', and Bud Freeman leads his Summa Cum Laude group through the last. But the
centrepiece is made up of three 1939 sessions of blues material with Shavers, Bailey and Kyle. Grace
tackles it with no trace of the affectation that some white singers of the period founder on. The
remastering is mostly very good, although loud passages still cause some blasting here and there. A very
fine reissue, with a splendid accompanying essay by David McCain, who located Teddy Grace almost at
the end of her life.

Bob Graf (1927–81) TENOR SAXOPHONE

(*) **At Westminster Delmark DD-401
> Graf; Ron Ruff (*ts, f*); Jimmy Williams (*p*); Bob Maisel (*b*); Al St James (*d*). 1/58.

A faded but entertaining memento of the modern scene in St Louis in the late 1950s. Both Graf and
Ruff were Lester Young disciples, though the nominal leader had a slightly more boppish feel to his
delivery, and their light-toned, slithery lines decorate the plain-speaking work of the rhythm section
with plenty of inventive intensity. There are too many slips and wrong turnings in the solos, but it's
sometimes a relief after listening to a lot of the rote hard bop of the day. The recording, though, is only
about as good as that on an average bootleg. It comes from a concert that should have featured
trumpeter Bill Buxton and the group's original themes, but Buxton was ill and they played standards.
We'll never know what the group might have sounded like, because they never recorded again.

Grand Dominion Jazz Band GROUP

*** **San Jacinto Stomp** Stomp Off CD1268
> Bob Jackson (*t*); Jim Armstrong (*tb, v*); Gerry Green (*cl, as*); Bob Pelland (*p*); Mike Cox (*bj, v*);
> Mike Duffy (*b*); Mike McCombe (*d*). 1/93.

Somewhat in the style of Ken Colyer's revivalism, this is a sturdy and impressive group of (mainly) trad
veterans. With most of the tracks rolling expansively past the six- and seven-minute mark, they generate
a steadily building momentum that's very effective on the likes of 'Bugle Boy March' and Adrian
Rollini's 'Old Fashined Swing'. Jackson is a rather wiry, short-breathed soloist, but Green's wide-bodied
alto is nice and the rhythm section play with great heart. Excellent sound.

Jerry Granelli DRUMS

*** **Koputai** ITM Pacific 970058
> Granelli; Julian Priester (*tb*); Denny Goodhew (*as*); Robben Ford (*g*); Ralph Towner (*syn*);
> Charlie Haden (*b*); Jay Clayton (*v*). 11/88.
(*) **Forces Of Flight ITM Pacific 970061
> Granelli; Glenn Moore (*b*); Annabel Wilson (*v*). 90.
*** **A Song I Thought I Heard Buddy Sing** ITM Pacific 970066
> Granelli; Julian Priester (*tb*); Denny Goodhew (*ss*); Kenny Garrett (*as*); Bill Frisell (*g, bj*);
> Robben Ford (*g*); Anthony Cox, J. Granelli (*b*). 1 & 2/92.
***(*) **Another Place** VeraBra vBr 2130
> Granelli; Julian Priester (*tb*); Jane Ira Bloom (*ss*); David Friedman (*vib, mar*); Anthony Cox (*b*).
> 92.

Granelli's most obvious influence would seem to be Paul Motian, a delicate but never lightweight
approach that caught the attention of guitarist/pianist Ralph Towner who recruited him and at one

point (or so it is rumoured) considered him to replace Collin Walcott in Oregon. Towner appears on the first of these records, playing synth unfortunately, and bassist Glenn Moore turns up on the second of the ITMs, a disappointing piece of nonsense that wouldn't get any of them a gig anywhere. One of the big pluses of these records is the appearance of Priester, an under-recorded trombonist with a markedly modernist style who was briefly sponsored by ECM but has recorded only rather sporadically in recent years.

He makes a substantial difference to *A Song . . .*, tucking into a slightly busy front line with great economy and a wonderfully full, uncomplicated tone. The VeraBra finds him in a sparser setting, and it suits him admirably. Bloom solos with greater conviction than on her own recent records, and Friedman's tuneful percussion is a perfect complement to the leader's. Worth sampling.

Stéphane Grappelli (born 1908) VIOLIN

**** Grappelli Story Verve 515 807 2CD
Grappelli; Django Reinhardt, Philip Catherine, Larry Coryell, Pierre Cavalli, Diz Disley, Leo Petit, Roger Chaput, René Duchaussoir, Joe Deniz, Dave Wilkins, Alan Hodgkiss, Ike Isaacs, Eugène Vees, Jack Llewellyn, Sid Jacobson, Chappie D'Amato (*g*); Stan Andrews (*t, vn*); Bill Shakespeare (*t*); Frank Weir (*cl*); Dennis Moonan (*cl, ts, vla*); Stanley Andrews (*vn*); Harry Chapman (*hp*); Reg Conroy, Roy Marsh, Michel Hausser (*vib*); Frank Baron, Raymond Fol, Charlie Pude, George Shearing, Yorke De Sousa, Marc Hemmeler, Maurice Vander (*p*); George Gibbs, Hank Hobson, Joe Nussbaum, George Senior, Louis Vola, Benoît Quersin, Guy Pedersen, Lennie Bush, Coleridge Goode, Pierre Michelot, Isla Eckinger, Niels-Henning Orsted-Pedersen, Eberhard Weber (*b*); Arthur Young (*novachord*); Tony Spurgin, Dave Fullerton, Kenny Clare, Rusty Jones, Alan Levitt, Jack Jacobson, Daniel Humair, Jean-Baptiste Reilles, Jean-Louis Viale, John Spooner (*d*); Beryl Davis (*v*); orchestra conducted by Michel Legrand. 1/ 38–5/92.
*** Stéphane Grappelly, 1935–1940 Classics 708
Similar to above.
***(*) Stéphane Grappelly, 1941–1943 Classics 779
Similar to above.
***(*) Special Stéphane Grappelli, 1947–1961 Jazz Time CDP 794481
Grappelli; Joseph Reinhardt, Roger Chaput, Henri Crolla, Jimmy Gourley, Georges Megalos (*g*); Jack Dieval (*p*); Pierre Spiers (*hp*); Pierre Michelot, Benoît Quersin, Emmanuel Soudieux (*b*); Armand Molinetti, Baptiste Reilles (*d*). 10/47–3/61.
***(*) Jazz Masters 11: Stéphane Grappelli Verve 516 758
As above, except add Alex Riel (*d*). 9/66–5/92.
***(*) Anniversaire Musidisc 500412
Grappelli; Baden Powell, Philip Catherine, Roger Chaput, Eugène Vees, Ernie Cranenburgh, Gérard Niobey, Lennie Bush, Pierre Ferret, Jimmy Gourley, Georges Megalos, Joseph Reinhardt (*g*); Bill Coleman (*t*); Marc Hemmeler, Alan Clare, Oscar Peterson (*p*); Eddie Louiss, Maurice Vander (*org*); François Jeanneau (*syn*); Pierre Spiers (*hp*); Jean-Luc Ponty (*vn*); Tony Bonfils, Niels-Henning Orsted-Pedersen, Louis Vola, Pierre Michelot, Guy Pedersen (*b*); Armand Molinetti, André Ceccarelli, Kenny Clarke, Pierre-Alain Dahan, Michel Delaporte, Daniel Humair, Louis Vola, Jorge G. Rezende, Clément De Waleyne (*d*). 5/36–10/77.
*** Special Jazztime 251286
Grappelli; Roger Chaput, Henri Crolla, Jimmy Gourley, Georges Megalos, Joseph Reinhardt (*g*); Jack Dieval (*p*); Pierre Spiers; (*hrp*); Pierre Michelot, Benoît Quersin, Emmanuel Soudieux (*b*); Armand Molinetti, Baptiste Reilles (*d*). 47–61.

Grappelli's association with Django Reinhardt and the Quintet du Hot Club de France is one of the legendary stories of jazz. It has been Grappelli's pleasure and burden equally to carry that legend forward into one decade after another, a player of enormous range and facility linked by a mystical band to another artist who, by all accounts, made his life extremely difficult.

Grappelli's limber, graceful style is so familiar that it hardly needs to be described. Because jazz fiddlers are relatively thin on the ground, he may be the most instantly recognizable jazz musician in the world – an astonishing situation if true. The Classics volumes do their usual good job of dotting *i*s and crossing *t*s without worrying too much about the quality of recording or transfer, and there can be no better way of familiarizing oneself with that legacy than the Verve double-CD set which covers everything from the pre-war years to a high-budget recording session with Michel Legrand in 1992, Grappelli's 85th year. It's almost pointless to rehearse the treasures within: 'Nuages', 'Body And Soul','Fascinating Rhythm', the 'Nocturne' with Django. There is nothing that will disappoint.

The Jazz Masters compilation is a quicker fix, but again a perfectly acceptable one, with the label's usual scrupulous detailing of sessions and previous releases. The Jazztime *Special* is an excellent and well-transferred sampler of non-Django material, covering the period from their post-war reunion to the great guitarist's death in 1953 and beyond. Grappelli once said somewhat wearily that he would rather play with lesser musicians than ever again have to suffer Django's 'monkey business'. There's enough evidence here to confirm both the violinist's independent stature as an improviser and the plentiful supply of like-minded players.

Half a dozen tracks locate Grappelli in harpist Spiers's fine, standards-based quartet. Earlier – 1954 – sets find him alongside the excellent pianist Dieval, yielding a lovely 'The World Is Waiting For The Sunrise', and the guitarist Henri Crolla, who plays in an idiom intriguingly removed from Django's. A single track from the immediately post-war Hot Four, which included Hot Club veterans Chaput and Django's brother, Joseph Reinhardt, marks it unmistakably as Grappelli's band, with a less ambitious improvisatory focus than the great original. 'Tea For Two' is a charmingly slight piano solo from Grappelli.

Anniversaire is a useful complement to the Verve set, containing a number of interesting sessions not included there. One, with Jean-Luc Ponty, points forward to a new style of jazz violin playing that was to develop out of Grappelli's example. Though there are only a couple of early tracks and some largish gaps in the selection, the pieces included are so consistently interesting and pleasurable that one stops worrying about the completeness or otherwise of the trawl.

*** **Meets Barney Kessel** Black Lion BLCD 760150
    Grappelli; Barney Kessel (*g*); Nino Rosso (*g*); Michel Gaudry (*b*); Jean-Louis Viale (*d*). 6/69.
(*) **Limehouse Blues Black Lion BLCD 760158
    As above.
It might have been better had they restricted both of these to a duo. The second guitar, though it follows a sanctified precedent, really adds nothing to the overall sound of the Black Lion, and Grappelli scarcely needs a drummer as prosy as Viale to keep him to the mark. Kessel, who is a disciple of Charlie Christian rather than a practising Djangologist, sounds bluesier than most of Grappelli's usual cohorts, but the combination works surprisingly well on a roster of unexceptional standards.

Limehouse Blues scrapes together more material from the same Paris studio sessions. There are previously unreleased readings of Kessel's 'Copa Cola' and 'Blues For Georges', 'I Got Rhythm', and a fine 'Perdido', together with an alternative take of 'Honeysuckle Rose'.

***(*) **To Django** Accord 401202
    Grappelli; Alan Clare, Marc Hemmeler (*p*); Ernie Cranenburgh, Lennie Bush (*b*); Chris Karan (*d*). 6/72.
*** **Joue George Gershwin Et Cole Porter** Accord 402052
    Grappelli; Marc Hemmeler, Maurice Vandair (*p*); Eddie Louiss (*org*); Jimmy Gourley, Ike Isaacs (*g*); Guy Pedersen, Luigi Trussardi (*b*); Daniel Humair (*d*).
The Gershwin/Porter material is fairly predictable and played with either jaunty insouciance or syrupy romanticism, neither of which does much credit to Grappelli or the composers he is honouring. Despite sounding as if it were recorded in a cathedral, *To Django* is much preferable. The opening version of 'Djangology' is one of the best available, and there are lovely versions of 'Manoir De Mes Rêves' and 'Nuages' (featuring Hemmeler and Clare respectively on electric piano). There's a warmth and richness to Grappelli's tone that suggest viola rather than orthodox fiddle. That's particularly noticeable on the longest track, an extended 'Blues' co-written with Django before the war, as was 'Minor Swing', which receives a particularly sensitive reading.

*** **Stéphane Grappelli / Jean-Luc Ponty** Accord 556552
    Grappelli; Jean-Luc Ponty (*vn*); Maurice Vander (*p*); Eddie Louiss (*org*); Philip Catherine, Jimmy Gourley (*g*); Marc Hemmeler (*p*); Tony Bonfils, Guy Pedersen (*b*); André Ceccarelli, Kenny Clarke (*d*). 11/72, 12/73.
This is not quite the 'Violin Summit' one of the tracks proclaims. Half the material is by Grappelli's own group, recorded a year earlier than the session with his most obvious heir, who in those days was touting a brand of jazz-rock that never quite shook off the Hot Club mannerisms. The 'Summit' itself is a showpiece. Better things lie in 'Golden Green' and 'Memorial Jam For Stuff Smith', which has the two fiddlers exchanging ideas at a furious pace. Both men also briefly switch to baritone violin, an unusually attractive sound that seems pitched somewhere in the viola-to-cello range. A novelty effect, perhaps, but not so much so that it dilutes Grappelli's musical personality.

*** **Stardust** Black Lion 760117
    Grappelli; Alan Clare (*p, cel*). 3/73.
There aren't too many 'alternate takes' of Grappelli performances available. The *Stardust* CD affords a valuable opportunity to study how the violinist thinks and rethinks his way through a theme, subtly roughening textures and sharpening the basic metre on a second take of 'Tournesol' (the original is also

sampled on a good label compilation, *Artistry In Jazz* – BLCD 760100) and rescuing two rather schmaltzy 'Greensleeves' with firm bow-work.

*** Just One Of Those Things Black Lion BLCD 760180
Grappelli; Marc Hemmeler (*p*); Jack Sewing (*b*); Daniel Humair (*d*). 7/73.
A great favourite at Montreux, Grappelli always rises to the occasion, as on this 65th birthday bash. Just when most men are looking forward to retirement, he is gearing up for another two decades of extremely active music-making. This wasn't the best band he had around this time (the group on *Parisian Thoroughfare*, below, is heaps better), but Hemmeler knows when to step in and when to lift his foot off the gas, and that's virtually all that's required of him. 'Misty' and 'All God's Chillun' are the highlights of a set that runs the emotional gamut from A to about D.

*** Sweet Georgia Brown Black Lion BLCD 7602
Grappelli; Alan Clare (*p, cel*); Roland Hanna (*p*); Diz Disley, Denny Wright (*g*); George Mraz, Len Skeat (*b*); Mel Lewis (*d*). 9 & 11/73.

***(*) Parisian Thoroughfare Black Lion 760132
Grappelli; Roland Hanna (*p, electric p*); George Mraz (*b*); Mel Lewis (*d*). 9/73.
A further counter to the persistent canard that Grappelli is an MOR entertainer with no real jazz credibility. Working with a first-class mainstream rhythm section, he sounds fantastically assured but also probingly sceptical about the broader and better-trodden melodic thoroughfares. Hanna's electric piano is a little over-bright and loses some of the firmness he invests in left-hand chords, but Mraz and Lewis combine superbly.

Sweet Georgia Brown contains more from the same session, and from a concert by the Hot Club of London in the Queen Elizabeth Hall. A certified Djangologist, Disley plays the parts with great expressiveness, though the medleys are a touch contrived.

*** Live In London Black Lion BLCD 760139
Grappelli; Diz Disley, Denny Wright (*g*); Len Skeat (*b*). 11/73.
'Not jazz', the promoters muttered; and Grappelli's ultimately successful 1972 British tour made a round of folk clubs and small theatres, thereby reinforcing a growing popular appeal (certainly much more effectively than if he had remained on the jazz circuit). The performances on *Live In London* aren't quite vintage, but they represent a more than useful documentation of the sensibly weighted nostalgia of the Hot Club of London. There's a fine 'Nuages', which Grappelli appears to have rationed since, and a lovely 'Manoir De Mes Rêves'.

***(*) La Grande Réunion Musidisc 557322
Grappelli; Baden Powell (*g*); Guy Pedersen (*b*); Pierre-Alain Dahan (*d*); Jorge G. Rezende, Clement De Waleyne (*perc*); orchestra conducted by Christian Chevallier. 74.
Grappelli and guitarist Powell were old jamming partners. They slide into this session, as old friends should, without missing a beat. It's standard-issue Latin jazz and bossa nova, with Grappelli fronting a string orchestra for half a dozen (mostly Beatles) tunes at the end of the set. There are more exciting Grappelli albums around, but few with quite this measure of laid-back enjoyment.

*** Stéphane Grappelli Meets Earl Hines Black Lion BLCD 760168
Grappelli; Earl Hines (*p*). 7/74.
If only Livingstone and Stanley had been jazz musicians. Black Lion have flogged the 'meets' formula to the brink of cruel and unusual punishment. Every now and then, though, it throws up something quite special. This is one of them. Temperamentally, Grappelli and Hines are just unalike enough for the chemistry to be right. They know each other's history well enough to have fun with it, Hines rolling off little Django flourishes with the left hand, Grappelli quoting Louis Armstrong fills in the upper register. Great fun.

***(*) Young Django MPS 815672
Grappelli; Philip Catherine, Larry Coryell (*g*); Niels-Henning Orsted-Pedersen (*b*). 1/79.
This is such a gift of a pairing that it's almost a surprise it works so well. Coryell is mannered and rather pretentious in places, but Catherine has this repertoire in his bloodstream and responds to the situation with alacrity, purring beautiful streams of notes and soft, chiming chords. The recording is very good indeed, but it might have been better expended on a slightly more adventurous programme of material. This one suffers slightly from obviousness.

**** Tivoli Gardens, Copenhagen, Denmark Original Jazz Classics OJC 441
Grappelli; Joe Pass (*g*); Niels-Henning Orsted-Pedersen (*b*). 7/79.
A superb set, marred only slightly by variable sound. Grappelli's interpretations of 'Paper Moon', 'I Can't Get Started', 'I'll Remember April', 'Crazy Rhythm', 'How Deep Is The Ocean', 'Let's Fall In Love', 'I Get A Kick Out Of You' reaffirm his genius as an improviser and also his ability to counter

slightly saccharine themes with the right hint of tartness. Pass, who occasionally errs on the side of sweetness, plays beautifully, and NHOP is, as always, both monumental and delicate.

*** **Satin Doll** Musidisc 440162
    Grappelli; Eddie Louiss (*org*); Marc Hemmeler (*p*); Jimmy Gourley (*g*); Guy Pedersen (*b*); Kenny Clarke (*d*).
This is so Gallic in conception you can almost taste the *aioli*. Louiss's playing will be a revelation to anyone who hasn't encountered it before, darkly sauced and salty, accented by Clarke and the greatly underrated Pedersen (what genetic trick makes such fine bass players of this clan?). There is, predictably, little innovation to report, but that will not perturb Grappelli fans at this stage in the story.

*** **At The Winery** Concord CCD 4139
    Grappelli; John Etheridge, Martin Taylor (*g*); Jack Sewing (*b*). 9/80.
*** **Vintage 1981** Concord CCD 4169
    Grappelli; Mike Gari, Martin Taylor (*g*); Jack Sewing (*b*). 7/81.
Taylor and Disley have been Grappelli's two most sympathetic latterday collaborators, and they complement each other near-perfectly on the live set recorded in the States a decade later. Taylor's amplified sound adds a little sting to Grappelli's playing, which is always more robust live than in an acoustically 'dead' and feedback-free studio situation.

    Better known as a jazz-rock player in one of the many later versions of the protean Soft Machine, Etheridge nevertheless fits in well with Grappelli's conception on *At The Winery*. Hard to choose between the two sets, though enthusiasts will want both.

*** **Stephanova** Concord CCD 4225
    Grappelli; Marc Fosset (*g*). 6/83.
The relatively unfamiliar material suggests either momentary impatience with his usual regimen of personalized standards or else a genuine desire to branch out into new areas. Fosset is a more interesting player in this more sharply focused context than in a group setting (see below), and the two trade a range of interesting and occasionally adventurous ideas.

(*) **In Tokyo Denon Compact Disc CY 77130
    Grappelli; Marc Fosset (*g*); Jean-Philippe Viret (*b*); Marcel Azzola (*acc*). 10/90.
*** **One On One** Milestone M 9181
    Grappelli; McCoy Tyner (*p*). 4/90.
At 82, some signs of ageing may well be inevitable. *In Tokyo* is a slightly jaded set, not so much in execution (Grappelli's playing is as zestful as ever) but in conception. Themes are medleyed rather too slickly and with occasional minor violence to taste. Azzola adds a little Gallic bounce (a shade too self-consciously?) to a rather static rhythm section.

    By contrast, the outwardly improbable duo with McCoy Tyner works astonishingly well, including Coltrane's 'Mr P. C.' and the Coltrane-associated 'I Want To Talk About You', alongside more familiar repertoire like 'I Got Rhythm' and 'St Louis Blues'. Ever the romantic stylist, Tyner plays with impeccable taste, never losing contact with the basic structure of a tune. Recommended.

***(*) **Stéphane Grappelli: 1992 Live** Birdology 517392
    Grappelli; Philip Catherine, Marc Fosset (*g*); Niels-Henning Orsted-Pedersen (*b*). 3/92.
And so it goes on, seemingly unstoppable. Grappelli's association with Catherine is now, remarkably, of longer standing than that with Reinhardt and, as one might expect, their understanding is considerable. This is a joyous disc, recorded in concert at Colombes. 'Oh, Lady Be Good' has the light bounce and unaffected grace that you'd expect, but there are unprecedented depths to 'Blues For Django And Stéphane', which Catherine brought forward for the session. For a live recording, the sound is very good indeed, though there are moments when Grappelli almost sounds detuned: a tape problem? heat?

**** **Reunion** Linn AKH 022
    Grappelli; Martin Taylor (*g*). 1/93.
One of the happiest new partnerships of more recent years was with the brilliant young British guitarist Taylor, whose solo career was taking off at the time of this utterly enjoyable record. It has the relaxed feel of something put down between lunch and dinner, but there is a steely precision behind the guitarist's relaxed mien and Grappelli is, of course, no pushover. 'Drop Me Off At Harlem' and 'La Dame Du Lac' are the most taxing workouts, but 'Paper Moon' takes the biscuit for sheer charm, if charm is indeed awarded with biscuits.

Milford Graves (born 1941) PERCUSSION

***(*) **Percussion Ensemble** ESP Disk ESP 105
    Graves; Sonny Morgan (d, perc). 7/65.

All the pieces are called 'Nothing', and there has always been a vague sense that Graves's musical conception begins with a blank page, a *tabula rasa*. He is one of the most forceful of the free drummers, less fiery than Sunny Murray (who some sources would have you believe is the percussionist here), not as traditionally orientated or polyrhythmic as Andrew Cyrille, with whom he recorded in 1983. The physicality of Graves's approach is partially explained by the fact that until his late teens he played congas, not kit. It is this that mitigates his determined abstraction and prevents it from becoming cold and antiseptic. Not much is ever said about Morgan, a very accomplished player in his own right who shows no sign of wanting to adhere to a groove.

Georg Gräwe PIANO, BANDLEADER, COMPOSER

(*) **Songs And Variations hat Art CD 6028
    Gräwe; Phil Minton (v); Horst Grabosch (t); Radu Malfatti (tb); Michael Reissler (cl); Roberto Ottaviano (as); Phil Wachsmann (vn); Dieter Manderscheid (b); Thomas Witzmann (vib); Achim Kramer (d). 12/88, 5/89.

Gräwe the composer may prove a little too hard-boiled for the average jazz enthusiast, though if *Songs And Variations* proves too daunting, the more approachable *Six Studies For Piano Solo* would be well worth hunting out. The long and rather fraught 'Variations For Chamber Ensemble', with which *Songs And Variations* ends, is Webernian not just in some of its structures but also in the refreshing directness of its articulation, a model for contemporary chamber and improvising players. Gräwe's GrubenKlangOrchester attempts a bold synthesis between the two idioms, and much of the time it succeeds.

    The two longish 'song' pieces are settings of T. S. Eliot's 'East Coker' – 'In my end is my beginning' and all that stuff – and of 'Lookin' For Work' by Manfred Karge, which develops the line of enquiry established in Gräwe's *Industrial Folk Songs* and Brecht scores. Phil Minton's voice is one of the most remarkable instruments in jazz but it's oddly querulous when confronted by an English text, and it's a rather strained version of Eliot's inherently musical measures that comes across. To be approached with (some) caution.

*** **Sonic Fiction** hat Art CD 6043
    Gräwe; Ernst Reijseger (clo); Gerry Hemingway (d, perc). 3/89.
***(*) **The View From Points West** Music & Arts CD 820
    As above. 6/91.
***(*) **Flex 27** Random Acoustics RA 007
    As above. 12/93.

In addition to a duo with the drummer, Willi Kellers, Gräwe has worked regularly with two very different improvising trios: well-received work with tubist Melvyn Poore and GrubenKlangOrchester member Phil Wachsmann (see below) and the trio captured in striking form on these discs. These are three players of markedly different temperament, united by a resistance to the fixed resolutions of both 'jazz' and 'New Music'. They play undogmatically and with great exactness, as if they have been rehearsing these pieces for years. Like Eddie Prévost, Hemingway manages to swing even when playing completely free, and his range of articulation is quite extraordinary.

    The long 'Fangled Talk' is slightly disappointing, a solitary lapse into what is usually called self-indulgence but which is probably merely inattention. Gräwe, one of the most enterprising of the post-Schlippenbach pianists, is apt to dissolve his own most acute observations in a flood of repetitions and curious evasions, but the ideas are strong enough to resist corrosion. Reijseger, by contrast, knows how to enjoy an idea and when to dispense with it. Thoroughly recommended.

    The Random Acoustics set is immensely detailed, full of exactitudes and tiny, outwardly meaningless gestures that seem to propel things forward to the next crux. The festival performances documented on *The View From Points West* are more relaxed and strung out and do tend to fall back on settled licks and patterns more often, especially on the long 'Lighthouse', nearly half an hour of concentrated music delivered without a hint of strain.

*** **Chamber Works** Random Acoustics 003
    Gräwe; Horst Grabosch (t); Melvyn Poore (tba); Michael Moore (cl, bcl); Philip Wachsmann (vn); Ernst Reijseger (clo); Anne LeBaron, Hans Schneider (hp); Gerry Hemingway (d); Phil Minton (v). 91–92.

Random Acoustics, Gräwe's own label, now has a rather impressive list of new music. This is the boss's day in court, a run-down of some of his more adventurous projects at the turn of the decade. The trio is represented again, but so, too, are some of Gräwe's more formal pieces and the celebrated trio with Poore and Wachsmann in which nothing sounds as one would expect it to and there is no obvious heading or trajectory for the music, just a concentrated sense of immediacy and presence as the players feed off one another.

Wardell Gray (1921–55) TENOR SAXOPHONE

**(*) One For Prez Black Lion BLCD 760106
> Gray; Dodo Marmarosa (*p*); Red Callender (*b*); Chuck Thompson or Doc West (*d*). 11/46.

**(*) Way Out Wardell Boplicity CDBOP 014
> Gray; Ernie Royal, Howard McGhee (*t*); Vic Dickenson (*tb*); Vido Musso (*ts*); Erroll Garner, Arnold Ross (*p*); Red Callender, Harry Babison (*b*); Irving Ashby, Barney Kessel (*g*); Jackie Mills, Don Lamond (*d*). 48.

**** Memorial: Volume 1 Original Jazz Classics OJC 050
> Gray; Frank Morgan (*as*); Sonny Clark, Al Haig, Phil Hill (*p*); Teddy Charles (*vib*); Dick Nivison, Tommy Potter, Johnny Richardson (*b*); Roy Haynes, Lawrence Marable, Art Mardigan (*d*). 11/49, 4/50, 2/53.

**** Memorial: Volume 2 Original Jazz Classics OJC 051
> Gray; Art Farmer, Clark Terry (*t*); Sonny Criss (*as*); Dexter Gordon (*ts*); Jimmy Bunn, Hampton Hawes (*p*); Harper Crosby, Billy Hadnott (*b*); Lawrence Marable, Chuck Thompson (*d*); Robert Collier (*perc*). 8/50, 1/52.

Like his friend and collaborator, Dexter Gordon, Wardell Gray often had to look to Europe for recognition. His first recordings, made just after the war, were not released in the United States. There were not to be very many more, for Gray died in rather mysterious circumstances in 1955, three months after Charlie Parker. The shadow cast by Bird's passing largely shrouded Gray's no less untimely departure.

Unlike Gordon, Gray was less than wholly convinced by orthodox bebop, and he continued to explore the swing style of bop's immediate ancestor, Lester Young. *One For Prez* is, as it sounds, an extended tribute to Young. Heavy on alternative takes, but sufficiently inventive to merit the inclusion of all but a few. Gray is in firm voice and Marmarosa, who has since vanished from sight, plays brilliantly.

The jams on *Way Out Wardell* were originally issued as a Crown LP. They're interesting but scarcely overwhelming. Gray is obviously in difficulties here and there, though the reason for this isn't clear. Several of his solo choruses resort to exactly identical ideas and/or mechanical inversions of them. He was capable of very much more.

The two-volume *Memorial* remains the best representation of his gifts. The earliest of the sessions is a quartet consisting of Haig, Potter and Haynes, and it includes 'Twisted', a wry blues since covered and vocalized by Annie Ross and, much later, by Joni Mitchell. Ross's version has tended to overshadow the original, which is a pefect place to gauge Gray's Prez-influenced style and his softly angular approach to the basic changes. The CDs include some alternative takes that are frankly pretty redundant both interpretatively and acoustically. Too often, Gray tries to reduplicate what he feels are successful ideas, rather than wiping the slate clean and trying again from scratch.

The best of the rest is a 1952 session with Hawes and Farmer, who do interesting things with 'Farmer's Market' and that Parker shibboleth, 'Lover Man'. The second volume is also notable for the first recorded performances by Frank Morgan, who copied not just Bird's articulation but also some of his offstage habits and found himself in San Quentin for his pains. It's still a thin haul for a player of Gray's class, but these should be considered the essential purchases.

*** Live At The Haig 1952 Fresh Sound FSR CD 157
> Gray; Art Farmer (*t*); Hampton Hawes, Amos Trice (*p*); Howard Roberts (*g*); Joe Mondragon (*b*); Shelly Manne (*d*). 9/52.

He was no less fortunate in having the gloriously expressive Hampton Hawes on all but one track of this fine 1952 date (one Amos Trice, better known for his work with Harold Land, plays on 'Lady Bird'). Gray had been working with Count Basie before these sessions and his conception is significantly pared down, even from the uncluttered approach of *One For Prez*. There is, though, a creeping weariness and inwardness in the voice, sadly reminiscent of Young's own rather paranoid decline, and it's left to Hawes and a pre-flugelhorn Art Farmer to keep spirits up. The mix of styles is just about right and the sound perfectly respectable for material over four decades old.

Bennie Green (1923–77) TROMBONE

*** **Blows His Horn** Original Jazz Classics OJC 1728
> Green; Charlie Rouse (*ts*); Cliff Smalls (*p*); Paul Chambers (*b*); Osie Johnson (*d*); Candido (*perc*). 6–9/55.

(*) **Walking Down Original Jazz Classics OJC 1752
> Green; Eric Dixon (*ts*); Lloyd Mayers (*p*); Sonny Wellesley (*b*); Bill English (*d*). 6/56.

*** **Bennie Green With Art Farmer** Original Jazz Classics OJC 1800-2
> Green; Art Farmer (*t*); Cliff Smalls (*p*); Addison Farmer (*b*); Philly Joe Jones (*d*). 4/56.

*** **Glidin' Along** Original Jazz Classics OJC 1869-2
> Green; Johnny Griffin (*ts*); Junior Mance (*p*); Paul Chambers (*b*); Larry Gales, Ben Riley (*d*). 3/61.

While these are good records, they rate some way below the excellent discs Green made for Blue Note in 1958–9. Albums for Time, Bethlehem and Jazzland, all from the early 1960s, would also be welcome in reissue form, though *Glidin' Along* has now reappeared: a good-natured blow with Griffin, with a set of scrappy originals betraying the lack of preparation. Although he was one of the first trombonists to fraternize with bop – as a teenager, he was in the Earl Hines orchestra that included Parker and Gillespie – Green's personal allegiance remained with a less demanding approach. The 1955 session highlights his singing tone and straightforward phrasing on attractive versions of 'Travellin' Light' and 'Body And Soul'. The band is a congenial one and Rouse's solos are an ounce more interesting than the leader's. *Walking Down* features a less impressive group and is slightly less interesting as a result, though Green is again in swinging form. Best of the four is the edition of the Prestige session which matched Green with Art Farmer, whose affable and calmly intense playing is a piquant complement to the somewhat more boisterous leader: compare their solos on Farmer's 'Skycoach', the trombonist a louche performer.

Benny Green (born 1965) PIANO

*** **Prelude** Criss Cross 1036
> Green; Terence Blanchard (*t*); Javon Jackson (*ts*); Peter Washington (*b*); Tony Reedus (*d*). 2/88

*** **In This Direction** Criss Cross 1038
> Green; Buster Williams (*b*); Lewis Nash (*d*). 12/88–1/89.

Green came to prominence as pianist with Betty Carter's group, and his mastery of bebop piano – particularly the chunky rhythms of Horace Silver – was leavened by an apparent interest in swing styles as well: Green hits the keyboard hard on up-tempo tunes, and his preference for beefy chords and straight-ahead swing can make him sound like a more 'modern' Dave McKenna. These albums for Criss Cross feature a lot of piano, but there's nothing particularly outstanding about them: the quintet date sounds too much like a mere blowing session for any of the players to make a distinctive mark, and the trio set seems hastily prepared, although the rhythm section lend impressive support.

***(*) **Lineage** Blue Note 793670-2
> Green; Ray Drummond (*b*); Victor Lewis (*d*). 1–2/90.

***(*) **Greens** Blue Note 796485-2
> Green; Christian McBride (*b*); Carl Allen (*d*). 3/91.

Handsomely recorded, impeccably organized and programmed, delivered with panache and full-blooded commitment, these are exemplars of the contemporary piano-trio record. Green has few pretences to innovation, and his composing is persuasive rather than absorbing, but these sessions are so full of brio and certainty of intention that such shortcomings are made to seem like mere details. *Lineage* is the more concentrated of the two, with a surprising list of compositions – from Monk, Ma Rainey, Neal Hefti and Bobby Timmons – dealt with in crisp, attacking terms; originals such as 'Debo's Theme' and the swinging 'Phoebe's Samba' introduce Green the composer almost shyly. He restricts himself to four credits on *Greens*, including the haunting title-blues, and allows the trio a greater freedom with form.

*** **Testifyin'! Live At The Village Vanguard** Blue Note 798171-2
> Green; Christian McBride (*b*); Carl Allen (*d*). 91.

*** **That's Right!** Blue Note 784467-2
> As above. 12/92.

*** **The Place To Be** Blue Note 829268-2
> Green; Byron Stripling (*t*); Delfeayo Marsalis (*tb*); John Clark (*frhn*); Jerry Dodgion (*f, af, as*); Gary Smulyan (*bs*); Herb Besson (*tba*); Christian McBride (*b*); Kenny Washington (*d*). 3/94.

Green's records continue to be cheerful, funky affairs, although some of his mannerisms pall over the long stretch and a certain cuteness invades a few of his tune choices and arrangements. The live record has real sparkle in the trio's interplay and, while some of the set-pieces such as 'Bu's March' are a bit wearying, Benny has plenty of fun with originals such as 'Don't Be 'Shamed'. No change with the next studio session, *That's Right!*: some entertaining revisions of standards, a couple of dreamy ballads, a helping of acoustic funk from the back pages of Ahmad Jamal or Red Garland. *The Place To Be* varies the palette just a shade by adding three of Bob Belden's characteristic horn arrangements – funky on 'Nice Pants', pretty on 'I Want To Talk About You'. Green likes to have fun at the piano, and the Petersonesque charge through 'Playmate' is typical – it might not lend the record much 'substance', but that's how he plays. In an age dominated by pianists hung up on Tyner or Hancock, Benny's playing is good to have around.

Bunky Green ALTO AND SOPRANO SAXOPHONES

*** **Healing The Pain** Delos D E 4020
    Green; Billy Childs (*p*); Ralph Penland (*b*); Art Davis (*d*). 12/89.
There's nothing in print from Green's earlier stint with Argo and Vanguard, which leaves about a dozen albums in the cold. This set for Delos concentrates on ballads and has a rather forlorn air (the title reflects on his own situation since both Green's parents were recently dead at the time of the session). 'Who Can I Turn To' and 'Goodbye' are particularly downcast. But Green's severe tone and legato phrasing give the melodies real power, and on an up-tempo piece like 'I Concentrate On You' he runs through the changes with a finely controlled abandon. The rhythm section are reserved but attentive.

Grant Green (1931–79) GUITAR

(*) **Reaching Out Black Lion B LCD 760129
    Green; Frank Haynes (*ts*); Billy Gardner (*org*); Ben Tucker (*b*); Dave Bailey (*d*). 3/61.
*** **Grantstand** Blue Note B21Y 46430
    Green; Yusef Lateef (*ts, f*); Jack McDuff (*org*); Al Harewood (*d*). 8/61.
***(*) **Born To Be Blue** Blue Note B21Y 84432
    Green; Ike Quebec (*ts*); Sonny Clark (*p*); Sam Jones (*b*); Louis Hayes (*d*). 12/61, 3/62.
*** **Street Funk & Jazz Grooves: The Best Of Grant Green** Blue Note 789622
    No personnel specified. 64–72.
(*) **His Majesty King Funk Verve 527 474
    Green; Harold Vick (*ts, f*); Larry Young (*org*); Ben Dixon (*d*); Candido Camero (*perc*). 5/65.
History has condemned Green to a fate accorded certain poets: that of the 'anthology' artist. The guitarist's marvellous output for Blue Note is now scattered over a series of bland thematic compilations, leaving collectors searching the second-hand and import bins for the marvellous *Solid*, which is *rara avis* nowadays. The 'best of' most certainly isn't, rather a collection of smooth grooves targeted, like the later Verve (which incidentally shares space with Donald Byrd's *Up, Up, Up*), on the acid jazz and club dance scene. Long, lazy tracks like 'Grantstand', 'Sookie Sookie' and 'Talkin' About J C' were ideal in that environment, but they offer only a partial impression of what he was about.

This is Green's most familiar setting. He started out in the early 1960s playing in organ groups led by Jack McDuff and others, an association that de-emphasized his remarkable delicacy (almost fragility) of tone and highlighted his harder, bluesier side. Recorded less than six months before his fine Blue Note debut, *Reaching Out* is a disappointing portent of the bland funk he chugged out in the post-detox early 1970s. Haynes, who plays beautifully on Kenny Dorham's *Osmosis*, sounds curiously messy here and certainly fogs some of Green's more thoughtful ideas. *Grantstand* is in every respect much better, though the format is still rather unsubtle and McDuff's swirling lines and sudden, choked-off probings are often too loud to hear Green's subtler movements. Lateef has a lovely flute tone and his straightforward tenor style, on 'Old Folks' and 'My Funny Valentine', sets up some of the best playing on the album.

The delicacy of Green's playing is highlighted on *Born To Be Blue* by Ike Quebec's booting tenor on 'Someday My Prince Will Come', but the very fact that Green is in evidence at all suggests that he's a tougher customer than at first appears. His solos on 'My One And Only Love' and 'If I Should Lose You' are among his most directly emotional on record, and 'Count Every Star', taken from a slightly earlier date, is judged to perfection, letting down just before it threatens to turn schmaltzy. Sonny Clark contributes enormously to the overall sound, a talent still in the throes of rediscovery.

Rediscovery, or initial discovery, is complicated by Blue Note's pretty shameful treatment of Green's back-catalogue, which has been plundered for a whole range of 'theme' records. Search out his best session for them, the excellent 1963 *Idle Moments*, which perfectly captured his laid-back, cross-legged style.

Burton Greene PIANO

(*) **Burton Greene Quartet ESP Disk ESP 1024
    Greene; Marion Brown (*as*); Frank Smith (*ts*); Henry Grimes (*b*); Dave Grant, Tom Price (*d*).
    12/65.

Subsequent history has eclipsed Greene pretty largely and the voice one tends to pick out of these sessions is Brown's frail, oddly pitched alto. Unlike label-mate Lowell Davidson, Greene lacked a really distinctive sound and tends to lapse into an ill-defined generic approach that harks back to Bud Powell, drawing something from the Cecil Taylor style of the time and a few other, less readily identifiable influences. If the recording were a little sharper and more vivid, it might be possible to feel more strongly but, as it stands, this comes across as nothing more than a slightly drab time-capsule item, unshakeably of its time.

Green Room GROUP

***(*) **Hidden Music** Leo LAB CD 007
    Chick Lyall (*p, elec, f*); David Baird (*vn, g, v, elec, perc*); David Garrett (*p, perc*). 7/94.

A new generation of improvisers on Leo's freshly radicalized Laboratory imprint, and these ones are from a line of latitude familiar to Leo-listeners of long standing. Green Room is a Scottish outfit. Whether the kind of improvisation they favour can be said to have a Celtic – or even a northern – dimension isn't immediately clear. The musical decks unmistakably are. Lyall in particular has thrown overboard almost all of the inflexions one might expect from one of Scotland's best straight jazz piano players. He anchors the sound, giving Baird and Garrett immense freedom to muse, embellish, and sometimes frankly experiment with sound.

    It all sounds cheerfully unrehearsed and uncluttered and, but for some drab moments on the long 'Flux' and 'Satellites', mercifully free of the usual improv clichés. The average length of track is about three and a half minutes, and this is certainly the group's most effective span at the moment. It would be tempting to suggest that what Green Room need more than anything is more exposure in live contexts, except that it may perversely be one of this group's strengths that their day-to-day situation offers few opportunities to work in this context.

Sonny Greenwich GUITAR

*** **Bird Of Paradise** Justin Time JUST 22-2
    Greenwich; Fred Henke (*p*); Ron Seguin (*b*); Andre White (*d*). 11/86.
(*) **Live At Sweet Basil Justin Time JUST 26-2
    As above. 9/87.

This Canadian guitarist's approach veers between guitar-driven jazz in a contemporary vein and an attempt to capture the sound of the late John Coltrane Quartet. This is not quite as misguided as it might sound, but it works only intermittently. The studio setting of *Bird Of Paradise* allows Greenwich more scope for experimentation and he produces some fascinating ideas on 'Of Stars And Strings' and the deeply felt 'Only One Earth' (which recalls his work with Paul Bley), only lapsing into sentiment on two out-of-place standards. He uses guitar synth sensitively and creatively, not just as a source of vague orchestral washes, and puts to shame most attempts to make something of this item of technology. The band, as will be seen above, is an established one, each member very responsive to the others. Most of the material on the live session, too, is original but without on this occasion being remotely innovative; the one attempt at a standard, 'You Go To My Head', misfires badly. 'Libra Ascending' is a heartfelt tribute to Coltrane but all the passion in the world doesn't make up for a wayward conception, and the recording is grim throughout, though Seguin can comfort himself with the realization that no one could ever hear Jimmy Garrison either. The drummer splashes about noisily, and should be made to play in cuffs for three months after what he does to Greenwich's best tune, 'The Sky's The Limit' (oddly, available only as a CD bonus track). Time, perhaps, for a decent studio recording. Greenwich clearly has a good deal to say for himself, but it will take a sensitive producer and engineer to make it happen.

Michael Gregory (Jackson) GUITAR, VOCAL, MARIMBA, BAMBOO FLUTE, PERCUSSION

** **Karmonic Suite** IAI 123857-2
    Gregory; Oliver Lake (*ss, as, f*). 5/78.

** **The Way We Used To Do** Tiptoe 888806

> Gregory (solo). 5/82.

Gregory is a talented guitarist without much luck on record. In the 1970s he secured an association with some of the music being made in New York lofts, and as Michael Gregory Jackson he made the IAI album, primarily a solo date but with Lake adding some remarks to a few of the tracks. The home-made feel and ascetic playing are redolent of loft-era experiments, and he and Lake make scrawking, jittery music out of 'We Have The Power', but it doesn't stand up well to more than a listen or two. The 1982 album highlights his unsure affiliations: an interesting fusion of rock, jazz and free styles on the guitar is augmented by a decent soul voice, yet he can't sustain a solo album like this, and his subsequent foray into soul fusion for Novus disappeared very quickly.

Al Grey (born 1925) TROMBONE

*** **Al Grey Featuring Arnett Cobb And Jimmy Forrest** Black & Blue 233143

> Grey; Xavier Chambon, Claude Gousset (*tb*); Michel Attenoux (*as*); Arnett Cobb, Jimmy Forrest, Hal Singer (*ts*); Ray Bryant, Tommy Flanagan (*p*); Stan Hunter (*b*); Clarence Gatemouth Brown (*g*); John Duke (*b*); J. C. Heard, Bobby Durham, Chris Columbo (*d*). 4/73–7/77.

***(*) **Truly Wonderful** Stash CT-CD-552

> Grey; Jimmy Forrest (*ts*); Shirley Scott (*p*); John Duke (*b*); Bobby Durham (*d*). 7/78.

*** **Al Grey–Jesper Thilo Quintet** Storyville STCD 4136

> Grey; Jesper Thilo (*ts*); Ole Kock Hansen (*p*); Hugo Rasmussen (*b*); Alex Riel (*d*). 8/86.

Al Grey will always be remembered as a Basie sideman, even though he spent more years away from the Count's band than with it. His humorous, fierce style of improvising is more in the tradition of such colleagues as saxophonist Lockjaw Davis than in the rather more restrained trombone lineage, although Grey is especially accomplished with the plunger mute. He has recorded as a leader only infrequently, but there are a number of good records now available again. The Black & Blue CD collects material from three different sessions, most of the tracks coming from a rousing meeting with the rambunctious Arnett Cobb: unambitious blues material, but it's impossible not to feel better after hearing the likes of 'Ain't That Funk For You'. Two tracks with a quintet including Forrest and Flanagan are gentler, and two more with a mostly French group are fillers. The Storyville session, made on another of his many European sojourns, is typical of his usual manner: brisk mainstream with some sterling blues playing, although Thilo and the rhythm section accommodate rather than compel Grey into his best form. The most splendid playing comes on the Stash CD, recorded over a three-day stint at Rick's, a club in Chicago. Scott has to contend with a rotten piano, and Forrest sometimes resorts to his hoariest blues licks, but the trombonist is in marvellous form: the blazing solo on 'Jumpin' Blues' and the sourly beautiful ballad style displayed on 'Summertime' and 'I Can't Get Started' are Grey at his inimitable best.

*** **The New Al Grey Quintet** Chiaroscuro CD 305

> Grey; Mike Grey (*tb*); Joe Cohn (*t, g*); J. J. Wiggins (*b*); Bobby Durham (*d*). 5/88.

***(*) **Al Meets Bjarne** Gemini GM 62

> Grey; Bjarne Nerem (*ts*); Norman Simmons (*p*); Paul West (*b*); Gerryck King (*d*). 8/88.

*** **Fab** Capri 74038-2

> Grey; Clark Terry (*t, flhn, v*); Don Sickler (*t*); Mike Grey, Delfeayo Marsalis (*tb*); Virginia Mayhew (*as*); Norman Simmons (*p*); Joe Cohn (*g*); J. J. Wiggins (*b*); Bobby Durham (*d*); Jon Hendricks (*v*). 2/90.

The quintet date for Chiaroscuro features a 'family band': Mike is Al's son, Joe is Al Cohn's son, and J. J. Wiggins is pianist Gerald's offspring. Although the group sound a little rough-and-ready at times, and the absence of a pianist is probably not quite as useful a freedom as it might have been, it works out to be a very entertaining record. Mike is almost as ripe a soloist as his father, and the sound of the two trombones together leads to a few agreeably toe-curling moments; but Joe Cohn's playing is equally spirited, and Wiggins and Durham sound fine. The set-list includes some standards and a few pleasingly obscure choices, such as Hank Mobley's 'Syrup And Bisquits' and Art Farmer's 'Rue Prevail'.

The session with Nerem was cut on a visit to Norway. The title-blues is almost indecently ripe, and 'I'm In The Mood For Love' is taken at surely the slowest tempo on record, but there are meaty blowing tunes as well and Nerem, a player in the kind of swaggering swing tradition which Grey enjoys, has the measure of the trombonist. Outstandingly good studio sound.

The Capri record is a bit self-consciously 'produced' around Grey, with a number of guessable routines in place – mumbling duet with Clark Terry, all-bones-together blues, and so on. Al still sounds robust and comfortably on top of the situation. Capri also have a seasonal album featuring Grey, *Christmas Stocking Stuffer* (Capri 74039-2 CD), for those with a taste for yuletide jazz.

*** **Centerpiece – Live At The Blue Note** Telarc CD-83379
> Grey; Harry 'Sweets' Edison (*t*); Jerome Richardson (*ts, f*); Junior Mance (*p*); Ben Brown (*b*); Bobby Durham (*d*). 3/95.

Another good-natured meeting, though Grey himself is still more than keen to play: check the torrid solos on 'Diz Related' and 'Homage To Norman'. Richardson also does well, though Edison is taking things easy. Vivid live sound.

Dick Griffin TROMBONE

*** **The Eighth Wonder & More** Konnex KCD 5059
> Griffin; Sam Rivers (*reeds, f*); Clifford Jordan, Bill Saxton (*ts*); Don Smith (*f, p*); Warren Smith (*vib*); Ron Burton, Hubert Eaves (*p*); Calvin Hill, Cecil McBee (*b*); Billy Hart, Freddie Waits (*d*); Lawrence Killian, Leopoldo F. Smith (*perc*); Geraldine Griffin (*v*). 79.

*** **A Dream for Rahsaan & More** Konnex KCD 5062
> Griffin; Gary Bartz (*as*); Clifford Jordan, Bill Saxton (*ts*); Stanley Cowell, Hubert Eaves (*p*); Calvin Hill, Cecil McBee (*b*); Billy Hart, Freddie Waits (*d*); Lawrence Killian (*perc*). 79, 85.

On an undersubscribed instrument in this modernist idiom, Griffin could hardly *not* sound individual. He is closer in spirit to Knepper than to ultra-modernists like Mangelsdorff, Lewis or Rutherford, and there is some soaring, Ellington- and Mingus-influenced orchestration on the 1979 date. It is a measure of his musicianship and standing in the jazz community that he can call on players of the quality of Bartz, Jordan, Rivers and McBee, and there is no mistaking that he feels completely at ease in such company. There is scarcely a moment of strain anywhere on these tracks and there are some – as on the original 'Oree Me' – which are both idiosyncratic and strangely graceful.

Johnny Griffin (born 1928) TENOR SAXOPHONE

*** **A Blowing Session** Blue Note 781559
> Griffin; Lee Morgan (*t*); John Coltrane, Hank Mobley (*ts*); Wynton Kelly (*p*); Paul Chambers (*b*); Art Blakey (*d*). 5/57.

This is the period when Griffin's youthful rep as the fastest tenor on the block was made official. In the company of Coltrane and Mobley, neither of them slouches, he rattles through 'The Way You Look Tonight' like some love-on-the-run hustler with his mates waiting out in the car. Only Trane seems inclined to serenade, and it's interesting to speculate how the track might have sounded had they taken it at conventional ballad tempo; 'All The Things You Are' begins with what sounds like Reveille from Wynton Kelly and then lopes off with almost adolescent awkwardness. This was a typical Griffin strategy. For much of his most productive period, Griffin more or less bypassed ballad-playing and only really adjusted his idiom to the medium and slower tempos as he aged; 'It's All Right With Me' is way over the speed limit, as if Griffin is trying to erase all memory of Sonny Rollins's magisterial reading of a deceptively difficult tune. *Blowing Session* is oddly unsettling and by no means the most appealing thing Griffin put his name to.

**** **Johnny Griffin Sextet** Original Jazz Classics OJC 1827
> Griffin; Donald Byrd (*t*); Pepper Adams (*bs*); Kenny Drew (*p*); Wilbur Ware (*b*); Philly Joe Jones (*d*). 58.

Despite the drummer's name, this was a Chicago group *par excellence*. Everything seems just a little magnified, and tunes like 'Stix' Trix' and 'Woody'N'You' are gloriously pumped-up and brazen. A pity that Griffin didn't record more with this line-up. They sound like they're just about to hit proper stride when the record ends. Ware is magnificent as always, and Kenny Drew stretches himself ambitiously.

*** **The Little Giant** Original Jazz Classics OJC 136
> Griffin; Blue Mitchell (*t*); Julian Priester (*tb*); Wynton Kelly (*p*); Sam Jones (*b*); Albert 'Tootie' Heath (*d*). 8/59.

This isn't the only album bearing this title (which refers to the diminutive saxophonist's nickname), so it might be worth checking that you're getting the right one. Heath finds it harder than Blakey to keep up, but the rhythm section get it just about right, opening up the throttle for Griffin and two rather underrated brass soloists with just the right amount of brassiness in their tone to match the leader's.

*** **The Big Soul-Band** Original Jazz Classics OJC 485
> Griffin; Clark Terry, Bob Bryant (*t*); Julian Priester, Matthew Gee (*tb*); Pat Patrick, Frank

Strozier, Edwin Williams, Charles Davis (*sax*); Harold Mabern, Bobby Timmons (*p*); Bob Cranshaw, Vic Sproles (*b*); Charli Persip (*d*). 60.

A little like standing out in a high wind. Griffin wasn't necessarily the most subtle of bandleaders but he knew how to make a group swing, and that's what he brings to this. An alternative version of 'Wade In The Water' on the CD suggests that this was a group always teetering on the brink of self-destruction, in the musical if not the personal sense. Griffin's frontmanship was pretty tenuous – but when it worked, it worked wonderfully.

*** Salt Peanuts Black Lion BLCD 760121

Griffin; Bud Powell (*p*); Guy Hyat (*b*); Jacques Gervais (*d*). 8/64.

Strictly speaking a Bud Powell set, recorded in France during the last productive period of his life. There's a lot of the old fire left, and he and Griffin trade powerful choruses on 'Wee', 'Hot House' and 'Straight, No Chaser'. Neither the piano nor the rhythm section is anything to write home about, but those were the settings in which Powell found himself towards the end, and Griffin seems to have decided. If it's good enough for him . . .

*** The Man I Love Black Lion BLCD 760107

Griffin; Kenny Drew (*p*); Niels-Henning Orsted-Pedersen (*b*); Albert 'Tootie' Heath (*d*). 3/67.

In the Black Lion catalogue, this immediately follows Wardell Gray's *One For Prez* (SLCD 60106), which includes three takes of 'The Man I Love'. There could hardly be a sharper contrast. Where Gray's tone and delivery drew heavily on Lester Young's pre-bop idiom, Griffin swoops on the same material with an almost delinquent energy that comes direct from Charlie Parker. It isn't the most settling of sounds, but the technical control is superb and only a rhythm section of the quality of this one could keep the tune on the road.

** Blues For Harvey Steeplechase SCCD 31004

Griffin; Kenny Drew (*p*); Mads Vinding (*b*); Ed Thigpen (*d*). 7/73.

** The Jamfs Are Coming Timeless SJP 121

Griffin; Rein De Graaff (*p*); Henk Haverhoek or Koos Serierse (*b*); Art Taylor (*d*). 12/75, 10/77.

Both these sessions mark something of a low point in Griffin's generally even output. There's something slightly numbed about the solos on *Blues For Harvey* (compare the title-track with the lovely version on *The Man I Love* (above)), and some questionable material, which includes a mercifully rare jazz reading of Gilbert O'Sullivan's 'Alone Again (Naturally)'. Griffin takes the theme at his natural clip but makes nothing significant of it. He constantly overshoots the measure on 'Rhythm-A-Ning', another slightly surprising choice which wrong-foots the band on a couple of measures. De Graaff is an interesting player with a steady supply of unhackneyed ideas, but he's only a questionable partner for Griffin and the two never catch light on *The Jamfs Are Coming*.

Griffin fans with some practice in mentally editing out dodgy backgrounds might well want to have both of these, but everyone else might as well hang on to their cash.

*** The Cat Verve 848 421

Griffin; Curtis Fuller (*tb*); Steve Nelson (*vib*); Michael Weiss (*p*); Dennis Irwin (*b*); Kenny Washington (*d*). 10/90.

At sixty-plus, Griffin has lifted his foot and eased back to cruising speed, revealing a tender balladeer beneath the furious munchkin of the 1950s and '60s. 'Hot Sake' still belts along, but '63rd Street Theme', dedicated to the clubs and bars of Chicago's South Side, has more of a melancholy ring these days (compare the version on *The Little Giant*, above, where he rampages through it like a latter-day Chicago Fire), its minor blues tonality milked shamelessly. Uncontroversial stuff, it's hard to imagine objecting violently, or being wildly converted to Griffin on the strength of it, but well worth the admission fee all the same.

*** Chicago, New York, Paris Verve 527 367

Griffin; Roy Hargrove (*t*); Kenny Barron, Peter Martin (*p*); Christian McBride, Rodney Whitaker (*b*); Rodney Hutchinson, Victor Lewis (*d*). 12/94.

Verve offers the wee man not one but two toughly professional contemporary groups. Martin, Whitaker and Hutchinson are not well known, but they stand up very well indeed in the same setting as their more illustrious colleagues. There are signs – expressive rather than acoustic – that a couple of solos here and there (on the opening 'The Jamfs Are Coming' and 'You Must Believe In Spring') might have been edited into place. If so, they're done seamlessly and with taste. There's certainly little now that reflects the player of old. After this, though, no one could say that Griffin, even on a cruising gear, couldn't keep up with the pace.

Henry Grimes (born 1935) DOUBLE BASS

*** **Henry Grimes Trio** ESP Disk ESP 1026

Grimes; Perry Robinson (*cl*); Tom Price (*d*). 12/65.

This should by rights be no more than the recording equivalent of a campaign medal, a routine acknowledgement of services rendered. Except that it's utterly unusual. Only Giuffre had been playing much clarinet in creative jazz around the early 1960s, and he had been soundly spanked for making it sound so buttoned-down. Robinson gets a big, dirty tone and plays gutsily throughout. Price is quite anonymous, except on 'Son Of Alfalfa', where he displays a belated relish for the weird swing and suddenly begins to have himself a good time. Worth checking out.

Tiny Grimes (1916–89) PIANO, VOCAL

*** **Tiny In Swingville** Original Jazz Classics OJC 1796

Grimes; Jerome Richardson (*ts, bs, f*); Ray Bryant (*p*); Wendell Marshall (*b*); Arthur Taylor (*d*). 8/59.

At one time Grimes's standing with fans and fellow-musicians utterly confounded his diminutive nick-name. One of the midwives of popular music, he attended bebop's first contractions (the earliest of the legendary Charlie Parker Savoy sessions were under Grimes's leadership) and then, in the early 1950s, slapped rock and roll firmly on the bottom with his bizarrely kilted (*sic*.!) Rockin' Highlanders, who can be heard on the now-deleted *Rock The House*.

In Swingville dispenses with the theatricals. Though there's still a novelty element to the music, which includes 'Annie Laurie' (hoots, mon!) and 'Frankie And Johnnie', front man Richardson is a completely convincing player, and Grimes himself glides through some parallel sections that would do Kenny Burrell proud. Though perhaps commanding no more than a substantial footnote in the history of modern jazz, he's an intriguing figure.

Don Grolnick (1947–96) PIANO, KEYBOARDS

*** **Hearts And Numbers** VeraBra 2016-2

Grolnick; Michael Brecker (*ts*); Jeff Mironov, Hiram Bullock, Bob Mann (*g*); Will Lee, Marcus Miller, Tom Kennedy (*b*); Peter Erskine, Steve Jordan (*d*). 86.

**** **Nighttown** Blue Note B21Z-98689

Grolnick; Randy Brecker (*t*); Steve Turre (*tb*); Joe Lovano (*ts*); Marty Ehrlich (*bcl*); Dave Holland (*b*); Bill Stewart (*d*). 92.

Grolnick's standing as producer/arranger/Svengali to some of the leading lights of the studio circuit has obscured his own music to some extent, but these very fine records ought to have a wider hearing. The VeraBra album (originally released on the tiny Hip Pocket label) is dominated by Brecker's character-istically muscular tenor solos, and Grolnick contents himself with small touches. The result is thought-ful, smart, flexible fusion. The Blue Note album (the earlier *Weaver Of Dreams* has gone) is on an altogether higher level, utilizing a starry personnel with exemplary finesse, sharing out duties with democratic insight but letting each man test the weight of the music. Grolnick might have been saving his best writing for the date, since the compelling 'Heart Of Darkness', for one, cuts anything on the previous records, good though they are, and the brilliant update on 'What Is This Thing Called Love' is a recurring surprise. Brecker, Turre and Lovano play to their best, but it's Ehrlich's bass clarinet which is the key voice in the ensemble. Grolnick himself plays shrewd composer's piano as the icing on a considerable cake. His recent death is a terrible loss.

Richard Grossman (died 1992) PIANO

**** **Trio In Real Time** Nine Winds NWCD 0134

Grossman; Ken Filiano (*b*); Alex Cline (*d*). 10/89–1/90.

**** **In The Air** Nine Winds NWCD 0146

As above, except add Vinny Golia (*sno, ss, bcl*), John Carter (*cl*). 10–12/89.

Grossman's death silenced a valuable piano voice too soon. He managed the rare feat of distilling structure and freedom, lyricism and astringency, in a tough yet profoundly sensitive way. His playing from moment to moment evokes most of the post-Taylor masters without ever sounding much like any of them, and he secures a very fine interplay with Filiano (who suffers a bit here and there on these recordings, all done at various concerts) and the superbly virtuosic Cline, who really does run the gamut from whispered skin-strokes to screaming clatter. The trio album revises piano-trio dimensions, taking in a pulsing, Evans-like quietness along with the more customary energetics, ideas appearing and evolving with formidable speed. Seventy minutes are sustained here without much trouble. The quintet date is even longer, and is cleverly programmed around one theme, an opening improvisation, a very long sequence of overlapping solos and a sardonic encore entitled 'Henny Youngman's Bird Imitation'. Golia and Carter are wonderfully loquacious in their playing, which acts as a neat contrast to the more rigorous piquancy of Grossman's manner: his solo passage on 'Everything Else Is Away' merits close attention. The vinyl-only '1-2-3-4' (Nine Winds 119) is also worth having, if you can find any surviving copies.

Steve Grossman (born 1951) SOPRANO AND TENOR SAXOPHONES

*** **Way Out East Vol. 1** Red 123176-2
    Grossman; Juni Booth (b); Joe Chambers (d). 7/84.
*** **Way Out East Vol. 2** Red 123183-2
    As above. 7/84.
*** **Love Is The Thing** Red 123189-2
    Grossman; Cedar Walton (p); David Williams (b); Billy Higgins (d). 5/85.
(*) **Standards DIW 803
    Grossman; Fred Henke (p); Walter Booker (b); Masahiro Yoshida (d). 11/85.
*** **Reflections** Musidisc 500212
    Grossman; Alby Cullaz (b); Simon Goubert (d). 9/90.

Grossman was working with Miles Davis when still only a teenager, and it's tempting to suggest that his career peaked too early. He has a prodigious command of the saxophone and a fearless energy, which puts him in the same class as Michael Brecker and Bill Evans. But Grossman's unlovely tone and sometimes faceless facility can also make him appear as just another Coltrane/Rollins disciple. The records under his own name make no attempt to evade the appropriate comparisons, since they all stand as quickly prepared blowing dates, Grossman peeling off suitably muscular solos against a conventional post-bop rhythm section. The two trio sessions for Red offer perhaps the most exciting music, since Grossman gets more space to work in, and *Vol. 1* provides some impressively characterized standards. *Love Is The Thing*, though, has the players setting themselves a few challenges by turning a ballad recital upside down in a couple of places with, for instance, an almost brutal 'I Didn't Know What Time It Was'. A later return to the trio format in *Reflections* is also a shade more interesting than the somewhat plain date for DIW. but Grossman's undoubted talent may work best either with another leader or with a firm producer.

*** **My Second Prime** Red 123246-2
    Grossman; Fred Henke (p); Gilbert Rovere (b); Charles Bellonzi (d). 12/90.
(*) **Live At Café Praga Timeless SJP 314
    As above. 12/90.

My Second Prime and *Live At Café Praga* were recorded on an Italian sojourn. The Red album is another grandstanding festival set, with the time of year marked by Grossman's choice of 'The Christmas Song' as one of the tunes. His tone has a dusky, almost chargrilled feel to it, and there are some improvisations of expansive power, but the rhythm section merely mark time. The *Café Praga* set is marred by indifferent sound, Bellonzi's snare having a tinny quality and Grossman seemingly too far back, though he plays with his customary authority.

*** **Do It** Dreyfus 191032-2
    Grossman; Barry Harris (p); Reggie Johnson (b); Art Taylor (d). 4/91.
***(*) **In New York** Dreyfus 1910867-2
    Grossman; McCoy Tyner (p); Avery Sharpe (b); Art Taylor (d). 9/91.
***(*) **A Small Hotel** Dreyfus FDM 36561-2
    Grossman; Cedar Walton (p); David Williams (b); Billy Higgins (d). 3/93.

Persistence is making Grossman into an impressive character. He still doesn't seem ambitious so far as record-making is concerned: *In New York* is live, the other two are both studio dates; but all three seem cursorily organized and find him reeling off standards and easily picked jazz themes, seemingly at a moment's notice. For consistency, he's hard to beat. But if the sheer strength of his playing usually transcends any banalities, he seldom goes for broke either. The difference with these three records is in the calibre of his accompanists. *Do It* is all heartland bebop – 'Cherokee', 'Dance Of The Infidels', 'Oblivion', 'Chi Chi' – possibly at Harris's request. The pianist doesn't seem quite at his best, though, and it's Taylor's incisive work that stimulates Grossman into his best moments. Though at times it suffers from club-set longueurs, the session with McCoy Tyner is on a more intense level: when they dig into 'Impressions', it's as if Tyner has found the man to replace his old boss after all this time. Some great playing here. *A Small Hotel* is more mediated, civilized by Walton's urbane playing and the more rounded feel to the performances; but again Grossman plays with real purpose and feel. If these are all, in the end, further chapters in a hard-bopper's blowing book and little more, it's still exhilarating jazz.

Marty Grosz (born 1930) GUITAR, BANJO, VOCAL

***(*) **Swing It!** Jazzology JCD-180
    Grosz; Peter Ecklund (*t*); Dan Barrett (*tb*); Bobby Gordon (*cl*); Loren Schoenberg (*ts*); Keith Ingham (*p*); Murray Wall (*b*); Hal Smith (*d*). 6–7/88.

*** **Extra!** Jazzology JCD-190
    Grosz; Peter Ecklund (*c*); Bobby Gordon (*cl, v*); Ken Peplowski (*cl, as*); Murray Wall, Greg Cohen (*b*). 8–9/89.

**** **Unsaturated Fats** Stomp Off CD1214
    Grosz; Peter Ecklund (*c*); Dan Barrett (*tb*); Joe Muranyi (*cl, ss*); Keith Ingham (*p*); Greg Cohen (*b*); Arnie Kinsella (*d*). 1–2/90.

*** **Songs I Learned At My Mother's Knee And Other Low Joints** Jazzology JCD-220
    Grosz; Randy Sandke (*t*); Peter Ecklund (*c*); Bob Pring, Joel Helleny (*tb*); Ken Peplowski (*as, cl*); Dick Meldonian (*cl, ts*); Keith Ingham (*p*); Greg Cohen (*b*); Chuck Riggs (*d*). 3–6/92.

*** **Live At The L.A. Classic** Jazzology JCD-230
    Grosz; Peter Ecklund (*c*); Bobby Gordon (*cl*); Greg Cohen (*b*); Hal Smith (*d*). 6/92.

*** **Thanks** J&M CD 502
    Grosz; Peter Ecklund (*c*); Dan Barrett (*tb*); Bobby Gordon (*cl*); Scott Robinson (*ts, bs, bsx*); Mark Shane, Keith Ingham (*p*); Murray Wall, Greg Cohen (*b*); Hal Smith (*d*). 4–5/93.

***(*) **Ring Dem Bells** Nagel-Heyer 022
    Grosz; Jon-Erik Kellso (*t*); Scott Robinson (*cl, ss, bs*); Martin Litton (*p*); Greg Cohen (*b*); Chuck Riggs (*d*). 2/95.

Grosz has been industriously documenting hot and sweet tunes of pre-war vintage on the basis that they don't write 'em like that any more, although anyone who's heard this transplanted Berliner in concert will know that these studio records are only half his story: a laconic, merciless wit, Grosz comes on like the spirit of Cliff Edwards inside a political satirist's shell. His genuine affection for this kind of music takes it out of the museum bracket and it is all performed with much aplomb. But some of the tunes sound as if they were best left with a layer of dust on them, and the philosophy that 'old-fashioned values were best' can often make him seem like another mouldy fygge in the box, even if he's the funniest of the bunch. The hot, wistful Ecklund, the charming Gordon and the ineffable Barrett save most of the days with playing that has freshness and bloom. The above discs are variously credited to the Orphan Newsboys, The Collectors Item Cats and Destiny's Tots; but the best of them is certainly *Unsaturated Fats*, by the Grosz–Ingham Paswonky Serenaders. This is dedicated entirely to Fats Waller tunes, all but one of them obscurities which Waller himself never recorded: Ingham's spry arrangements put new life into melodies unheard for decades, and there are some real discoveries such as 'Dixie Cinderella' and 'Asbestos'. Of the others, *Swing It!* is a shade hotter, and *Songs I Learned At My Mother's Knee* has the best title. The live album might have been the most fun but the sound is less than ideal and Grosz has suppressed all his between-song patter (probably so that he can recycle it at future gigs). But the latest in-concert set, *Ring Dem Bells*, is completely fired up from the opening 'Rose Of The Rio Grande'. The occasionally restrained Robinson really lets himself go on the likes of 'Old Man Blues', Kellso plays livelier horn than he ever has, and Grosz seems to relish every moment. His roguish light tenor usually sounds dry, and his rhythm guitar is now an accomplished stringsman's consolation.

Gigi Gryce (1927–83) ALTO SAXOPHONE, FLUTE

*** **Do It Yourself Jazz** Savoy SV 0130
    Gryce; Duke Jordan (*p*); Oscar Pettiford (*b*); Kenny Clarke (*d*). 3/55.

***(*) **Nica's Tempo** Savoy SV 0126
    Gryce; Art Farmer (*t*); Jimmy Cleveland, Gunther Schuller (*tb*); Bill Barber (*tba*); Danny Bank (*bs*); Horace Silver, Thelonious Monk (*p*); Percy Heath, Oscar Pettiford (*b*); Art Blakey (*d*); Ernestine Anderson (*v*). 10/55.

Gryce is one of those players – Herbie Nichols and Richard Twardzik are two more – who are known by a couple of compositions that have been taken up by others, but who are little recognized for their own playing. 'Nica's Tempo' and, to a lesser degree, 'Speculation' were favourite recording pieces in the later days of bebop. Gryce's own version of it is played by a group that includes Thelonious Monk and Art Blakey.

In the year of Bird's death, the pretenders were thrown into unusually high profile. Gryce was never a virtuosic player, but these sessions suggest he was more interesting than is often supposed, standing out with great definition in the larger ensemble, which is immaculately voiced and tightly rehearsed. The earlier quartet tracks are from a CD shared with pianist Hall Overton. While lacking something in energy terms, they're worthwhile additions to the gradually shifting discography of the mid-1950s, suggesting the breadth of talent at the time.

*** **Saying Somethin'!** Original Jazz Classics OJCCS 11851
      Gryce; Richard Williams (*t*); Richard Wyands (*p*); Reggie Workman (*b*); Mickey Roker (*d*). 3/60.
*** **The Rat Race Blues** Original Jazz Classics OJC 081
      Gryce; Richard Williams (*t*); Richard Wyands (*p*); Julian Euell (*b*); Mickey Roker (*d*). 6/60.
*** **And The Jazz Lab Quintet** Original Jazz Classics OJC 1774
      Gryce; Donald Byrd (*t*); Wade Legge (*p*); Wendell Marshall (*b*); Arthur Taylor (*d*).

Gryce's success as a writer – 'Capri' for J. J. Johnson, 'Nica's Tempo' for Art Farmer and the Jazz Messengers – rather overshadowed his abilities as a boppish altoist who, in all but instrumental timbre, sounds like a cross between Jackie McLean and Sonny Criss. The material used on *Saying Somethin'!* is, on balance, better than the playing. Gryce is often eclipsed by Williams, and the rhythm section boil away as if on their own private date. *The Rat Race Blues* is certainly his best album, full of vivid originals and marked by the distinctive phrasings of Williams and Wyands. The other set is more conventional, and one wonders a little at the title of the group, which is by no means as experimental as Gryce's earlier dates. He remained a quietly potent force, though, until his death.

Vince Guaraldi (1928–76) PIANO

(*) **Vince Guaraldi Trio Original Jazz Classics OJC 149
      Guaraldi; Eddie Duran (*g*); Dean Reilly (*b*). 4/56.
** **Jazz Impressions Of Black Orpheus** Original Jazz Classics OJC 437
      Guaraldi; Monty Budwig (*b*); Colin Bailey (*d*). 62.
*** **Greatest Hits** Fantasy FCD-7706-2
      Guaraldi; various groups as above.
*** **A Boy Named Charlie Brown** Fantasy FCD-8430-2
      Guaraldi; Monty Budwig (*b*); Colin Bailey (*d*).
** **A Charlie Brown Christmas** Fantasy FCD-8431-2
      As above.

Guaraldi was a harmless pop-jazz pianist, not as profound as Dave Brubeck, not as swinging as Ramsey Lewis, but capable of fashioning catchy tunes from favourite licks; the most famous example remains his Grammy-winning 'Cast Your Fate To The Wind'. If this kind of music appeals, the best way to sample it is through the *Greatest Hits* collection. The earlier trio dates offer mild, unambitious variations on standards, with Eddie Duran figuring rather more strongly than Guaraldi himself. The *Black Orpheus* set is marked by the seemingly relentless triviality of the material.

As a composer, though, Guaraldi is best represented by his music for the Charlie Brown TV-cartoon series. The first record in particular includes some charming miniatures, performed with surprising delicacy. The second is merely more of the same with less of the freshness.

Lars Gullin (1928–76) BARITONE SAXOPHONE, PIANO

*** **Lars Gullin Vol. 1 1955–56** Dragon DRCD 224
      Gullin; Chet Baker (*t*); George Olsson (*tb*); Arne Domnérus (*cl, as*); Rolf Berg, Bjarne Nerem (*ts*); Lennart Jansson (*bs*); Dick Twardzik, Gunnar Svensson (*p*); Georg Riedel, Jimmy Bond (*b*); Peter Littman, Bosse Stoor, Egil Johansen (*d*); Caterina Valente (*v*). 4/55–5/56.
**** **Lars Gullin Vol. 2 1953** Dragon DRCD 234
      Gullin; Weine Renliden, Conte Candoli (*t*); Frank Rosolino (*tb*); Lee Konitz (*as*); Zoot Sims (*ts*); Kettil Ohlsson (*bs*); Putte Lindblom, Bob Laine, Mats Olsson (*p*); Yngve Akerberg, Georg Riedel, Simon Brehm, Lars Petersson, Tauno Suojärvi, Don Bagley (*b*); Jack Norén, Bosse Stoor, Stan Levey (*d*); Rita Reys (*v*). 3–12/53.

It's a fine initiative by the Swedish company, Dragon, to reissue all of Gullin's most important recordings: five excellent LPs are (slowly) making their way to CD. After working in big bands as an alto player, he took up the baritone at the age of 21, and his utterly distinctive sound – delicate, wistful, pensively controlled – is the linchpin of his music: when he wrote for six or eight or more instruments he made the band sound like a direct extension of that big, tender tone. He seems like neither a bopper nor a swing stylist. The first volume includes a meeting with Baker's quartet, with a few precious glimpses of Twardzik, a very melancholy 'Lover Man' and Caterina Valente vocalizing on 'I'll Remember April'; there are also three charming octet scores. The second disc includes the superb tracks that were issued as a 10-inch album by Contemporary in the USA: Gullin sustains a steady, effortless flow of ideas on all his solos and plays alto on two tunes. The rest of the disc includes various studio sessions with other leaders, and three tracks with the visiting Americans, in which Gullin holds his own comfortably.

*** **1954/55 Vol. 3 Late Date** Dragon DRCD 244
> Gullin; Leppe Sundevall (*bt*); Kurt Jarnberg (*tb*); Rolf Billberg (*ts*); Jutta Hipp, Bengt Hallberg, Claes-Goran Fagerstadt (*p*); Rolf Berg (*g*); Georg Riedel, Simon Brehm (*b*); William Schiopffe, Bosse Stoor (*d*); The Moretone Singers (v). 9/54–6/55.

Lower marks only because the seven tracks with the cooing Moretone Singers may disenchant some supporters – even though Gullin's own playing remains impeccable (consult the fine improvisation on 'Lover Man' for one example). Four brief tracks with Hipp's trio are unremarkable, but two tracks by the Gullin sextet, 'Late Summer' and 'For F. J. Fans Only', are superb.

*** **Lars Gullin With Strings** Sonet (Swed) SLPCD 521458-2
> Gullin; Bengt Ernryd (*t*); Torgny Nilsson (*tb*); Rolf Billberg (*as*); Allan Lundstrom (*ts*); Lennart Malmer (*f*); Nils Lindberg (*p*); Bjorn Alke (*b*); Jan Carlsson (*d*); strings. 3/64.

***(*) **Portrait Of My Pals** EMI (Swed) 7924292
> Gullin; Jan Allan, Torgny Nilsson (*tb*); Rolf Billberg (*as*); Harry Backlund (*ts*); Lars Sjosten (*p*); Bjorn Alke, Kurt Lindgren (*b*); Bo Skoglund (*d*); strings. 6/64.

***(*) **Aeros Aromatic Atomica Suite** EMI (Swed) 4750752
> Gullin; Bertil Lovgren, Leif Hallden, Jan Allan, Maffy Falay (*t*); Hakan Nykqvist (*t, frhn*); Bertil Strandberg (*tb*); Sven Larsson (*btb, tba*); Arne Domnérus, Claes Rosendahl, Lennart Aberg, Erik Nilsson (*woodwinds*); Bengt Hallberg (*p*); Rune Gustafsson (*g*); Stefan Brolund, Georg Riedel (*b*); Egil Johansen (*d*). 72–73.

*** **Bluesport** EMI (Swed) 1364612
> Gullin; Maffy Falay (*t, flhn*); Bertil Strandberg (*tb*); Lennart Aberg (*ss*); Lennart Jansson (*as*); Bernt Rosengren (*ts*); Gunnar Lindqvist (*f*); Lars Sjosten (*p*); Amadeo Nicoletti (*g*); Jan Bergman, Bjorn Alke (*b*); Fredrik Norén, Rune Carlsson (*d*); Ahmadu Jarr, Okay Temiz (*perc*). 9/74.

Though released only in Sweden, these reissues are essential parts of the Gullin canon. The two albums from the 1960s feature some of Gullin's best-loved themes – there are contrasting versions of 'Prima Vera' (alias 'Manchester Fog'), 'Portrait Of My Pals', 'Decent Eyes' and 'Gabriella' – but the Sonet album comes from a Museum Of Modern Art concert and *Portrait Of My Pals* is all studio work. The looser textures of the concert and Billberg's more pronounced role may be less appealing to some tastes, but there is an exemplary quintet-only treatment of 'Chicarones'. *Portrait* includes some of Gullin's most skilful writing, with strings appended to six tracks; the versions of 'Prima Vera' and 'Decent Eyes' are among his best work, the timbres of the ensemble beautifully handled. Remastering hasn't helped the original sound, which was never very clear, and the presence of two basses in the rhythm section imparts a rather odd, off-centre feel to the rhythms. The CD includes three alternative takes and one newly issued tune.

Aeros Aromatica Atomica Suite was a project close to Gullin's heart, and this fine performance by a team of Swedish mainstays must be counted one of his strongest records. If one isn't always convinced that the composer truly has hold of the thematic thread running through the three parts, the textures and contrasts are still absorbing, and there is always the solo work by the horns (and the perennially undervalued Gustafsson). Excellent sound this time. *Bluesport*, though recorded later, has an inferior mix, and this time some of the music sounds only half-finished. But the vibrant title-track alone is compellingly done and Gullin's own powers as an improviser, if less sharp than in his youth, remained a notable force.

Peter Gullin BARITONE SAXOPHONE, TENOR SAXOPHONE

*** **Tenderness** Dragon DRCD 222
> Gullin; Jacob Fischer (*g*); Ole Rasmussen (*b*). 92.

***(*) **Transformed Evergreen** Dragopn DRCD 266

>   As above, except omit Fischer; add Morten Kaargard (g). 3/94.

Gullin himself likens the approach on these records to that of the Dutch national soccer team in the 1970s. They espoused 'total football', in which every player was expected to play – or be prepared to play – in every position, as need arose. There is certainly no distinction between 'front line' and 'rhythm' players. Some may feel that the likelier analogy lies closer to home with the Swedish national side: correct, polite, almost apologetic in the tackle. Not much aggression in these sides – but then aggression wasn't the calling-card of Gullin's father, the legendary Lars, who dedicated 'Peter Of April' to his offspring.

>   Unusual and brave for sons to follow on the same instrument, though young Coltranes have also done it. Peter has a broader, less wistful sound than the old man and takes a more direct, less thoughtful approach to solo construction. His baritone work is more than just a straight copy; there are original things going on there, and it is certainly less formulaic than on the smaller horn, where he often sounds like an off-duty Dexter Gordon. Working without a drummer makes perfect sense for him because, like his partners (Rasmussen most obviously), he has a flawless sense of metre and timing, laying notes at exactly the points where balance requires them. *Tenderness* is a lovely record, but the later record, which consists almost entirely of imaginative Gullin arrangements of standard material (Carl Nielsen's 'Snurretoppen' is a surprise inclusion), touches heights and depths the young man hasn't been inclined to reach for yet.

>   He's not an entirely confident writer. The three 'Fantasias' border on the pedestrian. 'The Hollow Clown' (or does he mean 'crown'?) suggests an acquaintance with Mingus. For the most part, though, he is content to work with given themes and received stylistic ideas. Not an innovator, but a very natural improviser with a deceptively relaxed approach.

Gully Low Jazz Band GROUP

*** **Down To Earth** GHB BCD-233

>   Dan Barrett (c, v); Joel Helleny (tb); Clarence Hutchenrider (cl); David Ostwald (tba); Frank Vignola (g, bj); Fred Stoll (d). 4/85.

David Ostwald's group plays happy, skilful, traditionally styled jazz. The band has a curious mix of players – Barrett is usually renowned as a trombonist, Vignola wasn't long out of college, and Hutchenrider, a veteran of the Casa Loma Orchestra, is in his eighties and played with Beiderbecke. But they work together with fine grace and aplomb. Barrett's cornet lead is as strong and flexible as it has to be, and Helleny and Hutchenrider play more idiosyncratic but no less authoritative solos. The others provide an unflappable, at times even velvety beat, a rarity in this kind of group. The live recording favours some instruments over others (Vignola's virtuoso banjo comes through loud and clear) but it falls easily on the ear.

John Gunther (born 1966) ALTO SAXOPHONE

*** **Big Lunage** Capri 74035

>   Gunther; Greg Gisbert (t); Eric Gunison (p); Mark Simon (b); Paul Romaine (d). 9/93.

This kicks off with a lot of promise, with four tracks (by Gunther, Gunnison, Gunther and Gunther again) that conspicuously avoid cliché. 'Beceeted' overturns the usual head and solos format in a fascinating contrapuntal setting which reflects the equal billing for the two horns. (Gisbert's solo work can be found under his own name.) 'An Old Haunt' is for saxophone and rhythm only, a mysterious theme that reflects the influence of Wayne Shorter, while 'Big Lunage' draws more conspicuously on Trane.

Trilok Gurtu (born 1951) TABLA, PERCUSSION

***(*) **Crazy Saints** CMP CD 66

>   Gurtu; Louis Sclavis (ss, cl, bcl); Pat Metheny (g); Ernst Reijseger (clo); Joe Zawinul (p, ky); Daniel Goyone (p); Marc Bertaux (b); Shobha Gurtu (v). 5 & 6/93.

*** **Believe** CMP CD 76

>   Gurtu; Daniel Goyone (p, ky); David Gilmore (g); Chris Minh Doky (b). 7/94.

*** **Bad Habits Die Hard** CMP CD 80

>   Gurtu; Bill Evans (ts, ss); Mark Feldman (vn); David Gilmore (g, v); Andy Emler (p, ky); Chris Minh Doky (b). 10/95.

Trilok's mother, Shobha Gurtu, is a distinguished singer in the Indian classical tradition, and his own background is in the demanding discipline of tabla playing. He was turned on to jazz by hearing John Coltrane, doubtless reacting to the Indian elements Trane had imported into his own modal conception, and after a period working in Europe Trilok moved to New York City.

It was, however, with the new European jazz, and particularly the ECM label, that he first came to prominence, recording with Don Cherry and Barre Phillips, as well as in Asiatically tinged groups fronted by saxophonist Charlie Mariano. Following the tragic death of Collin Walcott, he became percussionist with Oregon. A natural showman, he has not always seemed to fit comfortably into the group's slightly academic approach, and they have on occasion worked without him, while he has continued to develop a solo career.

Perhaps inevitably, neither of these records quite captures the vibrant spontaneity of a Gurtu performance. The first is certainly the more adventurous, experimenting with awkward time-signatures (awkward in a jazz context, at any rate) and an unusual instrumental palette. Varying the instrumentation from track to track, from a duo with Zawinul to the bones of what was to become his working ensemble on the title-track, gives the set a pick'n'mix quality. The outstanding tracks are those which feature Shobha Gurtu, and one would liked to have heard much more in this vein.

Trilok's own voice is foregrounded on *Believe*, which sounds more like a recording by a settled group. Goyone has clearly become the right-hand man, and there is a sense in which they complement each other in the way that Zawinul and Shorter did in Weather Report, rock-steady foundations from the keyboards, wackier stuff from the front man. The replacement of Reijseger with a bassist, even one of Chris Minh Doky's skill, points to the more conservative orientation of the later album, and this is reinforced on *Bad Habits Die Hard*, the most straight-ahead session yet from the percussionist. Emler is the key player here; his arrangements are crisp and thoughtful and, though the tracks still tend to outstay their welcome by a couple of minutes apiece, there is always enough going on in a freshly remixed instrumentation to hold the attention. Clearly, Gurtu thrives on association with the open-eared Kurt Renker and Walter Quintus at CMP. A major-label deal might utterly spoil this remarkable talent.

Barry Guy (born 1947) DOUBLE BASS, CHAMBER BASS

***(*) **Arcus** Maya MCD 9101
   Guy; Barre Phillips (*b*). 90.
*** **Elsie Jo** Maya MCD 9201
   Guy; Conrad Bauer (*tb*); Evan Parker (*sax*); Irene Scheweizer (*p*); Barre Phillips (*b*); Paul Lytton (*d*). 91.
**** **Fizzles** Maya MCD 9301
   Guy (*b, chamber b*). 9/91.
**** **Study – Witch Gong Game 11/10** Maya MCD 9402
   Guy; John Korsrud (*t*); Ralph Eppel (*tb*); Saul Berson (*as*); Coat Cooke (*ts, bs, f*); Graham Ord (*ts, ss, picc*); Bruce Freedman (*ss*); Paul Plimley (*p*); Ron Samworth (*g*); Peggy Lee (*clo*); Paul Blaney, Clyde Read (*b*); Dylan Van der Schyff (*d*); Kate Hammett-Vaughan (*v*). 2/94.

Guy's activities in recent years have been largely focused on composition for the London Jazz Composers Orchestra, which is listed separately. He has, however, kept up his improvisational work, and the items here are well worth pursuing, even if they prove difficult to track down.

Though recorded as if on the other side of the veil of Maya, *Arcus* is improvised music of the very highest order. Guy's productive trade-off of freedom against more formal structures is constantly in evidence, and there is enough music of straightforward, digestible beauty to sustain listeners who might otherwise find an hour and a quarter of contrabass duos more than a little taxing. It ends, appropriately enough, on the quiet majesty of 'New Earth', where Phillips's purged simplicity and dancer's grace sound out ahead of Guy's more formal and sculpted delivery. Twice wonderful, but may call for patience.

Fizzles is not so immediately appealing, but it has a quiet charm that reveals itself over repeated listenings and it is certainly better-recorded than its predecessor. Guy uses a conventional contrabass on only three tracks, switching for the others to a small chamber bass. In his liner-note, John Corbett relates this to Guy's stated desire to make his instrument as small as possible while he is improvising. One can hear this effect on 'Five Fizzles', a sequence dedicated to Samuel Beckett in which, using both his basses, Guy concentrates on the tiniest details with an almost hallucinatory intensity, much as Beckett would concentrate on a single word, sound or gesture. Pitched higher than a conventional bass, the concert instrument has a cello-like warmth of tone and speed of response that is very attractive, and the drone-like effects in 'Afar' and 'Tout Rouge' are reminiscent of devices in the work of cult Italian composer, Giacinto Scelsi. Significantly or not, the most compelling track is for double bass. Dedicated to a native American friend, 'She Took The Sacred Rattle And Used It' is one of Guy's finest moments as an instrumentalist.

It isn't immediately clear whether *Elsie Jo* should properly be credited to Guy or Schweizer, but it seems to us to carry his stamp so thoroughly as to belong in this listing. This is familiar company for the bass player, and he sounds comfortable but uncomplacent in a relatively free improvisational setting. The last of the group takes him back closer to the kind of formal-free experiment promulgated and sustained with the London Jazz Composers Orchestra. Recorded in Canada, *Witch Gong Game 11/10* is a musical realizaton of certain signs and symbols in paintings by Alan Davie, another of the visual artists to have provided Guy with a rich vein of inspiration in recent years. Guy reads Davie's work as a floating, by no means determinant, system of archetypes which can be interpreted so as to create dense polyphonies, lighter, more textural passages, or else entirely free improvisational areas. The music is as vividly present as Davie's curiously totemic images, and the young orchestra respond to it very openly and sympathetically.

Bobby Hackett (1915–76) CORNET, TRUMPET

*** 1943 World Broadcasting Jam Session Jazzology JCD 111
> Hackett; Ray Conniff (*tb*); John Pepper (*cl*); Nick Caizza (*ts*); Frank Signorelli (*p*); Eddie Condon (*g*); Bob Casey (*b*); Maurice Purtill (*d*). 12/43.

*** Dr Jazz: Volume 2 – 1951–1952 Storyville STCD 6042
> Hackett; Vic Dickenson (*tb*); Gene Sedric (*cl*); Teddy Roy (*p*); John Giuffrida, Irv Manning (*b*); Buzzy Drootin, Morey Feld, Kenny John (*d*). 2/52.

***(*) Off Minor Viper's Nest VN 162
> Hackett; Dick Oakley (*t*); Jack Teagarden (*tb*); Ernie Caceres (*cl, bs*); Tom Gwaltney (*cl, vib*); Dick Cary (*p, ahn*); Don Ewell (*p*); Stan Puls (*b*); John Dengler (*bb*); Buzzy Drootin, Ronnie Greb (*d*). 7/57, 7/58.

*** Milton Jazz Concert 1963 IAJRC CD 1004
> Hackett; Vic Dickenson (*tb*); Edmond Hall (*cl*); Evans Schwartz (*p*); Champlin Jones (*b*); Mickey Sheen (*d*). 4/63.

Louis Armstrong liked to keep the opposition under the closest observation and so, for much of the 1940s, Bobby Hackett played second cornet under the wing of the man who had influenced his style more than any other. That's evident on the 1943 jam, made by Milt Gabler for the World Broadcasting Systems Inc., which were originally for radio only. Though not a vintage band, the music is of high quality, though some will find the false starts and incompletes irritating. The Dr Jazz sessions were originally broadcast from Lou Terrasi's on West 47th Street as part of a WMGM series. It's very much Hackett's gig, though Dickenson is also a presence. The best of Hackett was yet to come, and with a still more substantial partner. His association in the 1950s with trombonist Jack Teagarden produced some of the best traditional/mainstream jazz of the post-war years, with Hackett's supremely elegant legato and deceptive force perfectly matched by the man who virtually patented modern jazz trombone.

The Viper's Nest disc brings together two live concerts exactly a year apart. The second is by Teagarden's sextet, with Hackett as the main soloist. The earlier includes some surprising material, alongside the more predictable 'Fidgety Feet' and 'Royal Garden Blues'. Hackett approaches Monk's 'Off Minor' with understanding and control and makes a profound contribution to it.

The Milton concert is released by the International Association of Jazz Record Collectors, which has done a great service to Hackett fans by making this Massachusetts gig available. The sound-reproduction isn't tip-top but is generally very good, and both Hackett and Dickenson play out of their skins in front of a workmanlike band. Despite equal billing, Hall has a quieter time of it.

**(*) Melody Is A Must: Live At The Roosevelt Grill Phontastic PHONT 7571
> Hackett; Vic Dickenson (*tb*); Dave McKenna (*p*); Jack Lesberg (*b*); Cliff Leeman (*d*). 3 & 4/69.

Switching from Jack Teagarden to Vic Dickenson must have felt a little like dating Liza Minnelli after Judy Garland. Unmistakable kinship, same eyes and voice, same raw edges, but somehow not quite, a little safer and more humane. Dickenson's very limited technique was carefully husbanded and put in the service of a warm, humorous approach which drew something from Dickie Wells but which worked most comfortably alongside someone like Hackett, who shared his untroubled preference for a quiet good time.

Melody Is A Must is a perfect example of Hackett's grace-without-pressure. There are no steam-valve emotional tantrums underlying a mixed and rather more contemporary repertoire than usual. Nor is there any casual verbosity. As Whitney Balliett relates, Duke Ellington once spoke, apparently approvingly, of Dickenson's 'three tones'. Like Dickenson, Hackett keeps his music simple and direct, remarkably uncluttered by ego.

Charlie Haden (born 1937) DOUBLE BASS

***(*) **The Golden Number** A&M 390 825
      Haden; Don Cherry (*pkt-t, f*); Ornette Coleman (*t*); Archie Shepp (*ts*); Hampton Hawes (*p*). 6, 8 & 12/76.
*** **Closeness** A&M 397000-2
      Haden; Ornette Coleman (*as*); Keith Jarrett (*p*); Alice Coltrane (*hp*) Paul Motian (*d*). 76.
*** **As Long As There's Music** Verve 513534
      Haden; Hampton Hawes (*p*). 1 & 8/76.

Haden is one of the great bass players, standing self-sufficiently in a line from Blanton through Wilbur Ware, Scott LaFaro and Jimmy Garrison. His deep, dark sound is innately musical. Duo playing has always had a special place in his career. *The Golden Number* and *Closeness* were its first major documentation, pairing him with artists for whom he had a special closeness and sympathy. The high points, predictably, are the duets with Ornette, and especially the title-piece of *Number*, which recalls their great partnership of the 1950s; note that the favoured instrument is trumpet rather than alto, lending the performance a stark, harmonically unadorned quality which leaves Haden very much as pilot. Interestingly, he is much less assertive with Alice Coltrane on 'For Turiya' (her Muslim name), allowing her to establish the terms of discourse.

Head to head with Archie Shepp, he is obliged to be a touch more forceful, setting up the sort of rising, chromatic figure the saxophonist loves to play, and then setting him loose on it to weave together ironic bebop flourishes with free passages and delicate upper-register trills. Jarrett and Motian, in their different ways, put him to the test, and Haden graduates with honours. The piece with Cherry, 'Out of Focus', makes use of double tracking and consequently has a richer, fuller sound than the others, ably captured by engineer Baker Bigsby. (Given the length of the original releases, it might have been possible to combine these into a single CD or mid-price double disc. No one will feel short-changed, though.)

The surprise element for newcomers may well be the duet on Ornette's 'Turnaround' with Hawes. In the last months of his life the pianist was again in transition and perhaps moving back towards a more radical conception, having exhausted his interest in fusion. An alternative version appears on *As Long As There's Music*. It was originally released on Ornette's Artists House label and bespeaks his strong current interest in harmonic bases and written pitch notes. Unlike the other collaborators on *The Golden Number*, Hawes is very much tied to the classical 88. Not having slurs and smeared notes at his disposal means that he has to take a rather different tack on this material. It would be interesting to hear what Ornette thinks about 'Turnaround' now.

Padding out the Haden/Hawes session are further alternatives of the pianist's own 'Irene' and the standard 'As Long As There's Music', out of which, on the issued take, Haden carves one of the best recorded solos of his career. The two wholly improvised pieces, the first of them based on the chords of 'What Is This Thing Called Love', are intuitively crafted and coherent. The pianist takes the lead on his own 'Rain Forest' and 'Irene', but elsewhere the two voices are democratically balanced.

***(*) **The Ballad Of The Fallen** ECM 1248
      Haden; Don Cherry (*pkt-t*); Michael Mantler (*t*); Gary Valente (*tb*); Sharon Freeman (*frhn*); Jack Jeffers (*tba*); Jim Pepper (*ts, ss, f*); Dewey Redman (*ts*); Steve Slagle (*as, ss, cl, f*); Mick Goodrick (*g*); Carla Bley (*p, glock*); Paul Motian (*d*). 11/82.
(*) **Dream Keeper Verve 847876
      Haden; Tom Harrell (*t, flhn*); Earl Gardner (*t*); Ray Anderson (*tb*); Sharon Freeman (*frhn*); Joe Daley (*tba*); Ken McIntyre (*as*); Joe Lovano (*ts, f*); Branford Marsalis, Dewey Redman (*ts*); Juan Lazaro Mendolas (*wooden f, pan pipes*); Mick Goodrick (*g*); Amina Claudine Myers (*p*); Paul Motian (*d*); Don Alias (*perc*); Carla Bley (*cond*); Oakland Youth Chorus. 4/90.

The inclusion of 'Hymn Of The Anarchist Women's Movement' on *Dream Keeper* may help explain the performance ethos of the revived Liberation Music Orchestra, whose live sets in 1982 and afterwards entirely confounded any expectations based on the excellent *Ballad Of The Fallen* or, more nostalgically, on the original 1970 record. No great arranger himself (his compositional talents are restricted to outwardly slight melodies of remarkable emotional power), Haden has relied heavily throughout on Carla Bley's fine structural sense, which deserts her only on the shambolic *Dream Keeper*.

Her efforts aside, the LMO remains essentially an augmented small group, centred on the insistently low-pitched voices of Haden, Bley and Redman, with one or more of the lower-register brasses, and with Motian keeping the surface textures variable and interesting. That basic foundation provides launching pads for stratospheric soloists like Barbieri.

Much of the material is drawn from songs of the Spanish Civil War (with a broader mix of liberationist anthems from the Latin Third World on the latter pair), but the classic cut was, of course, Haden's own 'Song For Che' on the original *Liberation Music Orchestra*, which is (temporarily, one hopes) out of circulation. One hopes that GRP, who now look after the Impulse! catalogue, aren't disturbed by the record's strident political elements.

'Dream Keeper' is a long suite by Carla Bley which intersperses the Latin-American and Spanish anarchist songs familiar from earlier Haden/LMO records with a poem by the Harlem Renaissance writer, Langston Hughes. Sung by the Oakland Youth Chorus, it has a sombre, almost apocalyptic quality, like a '*Dies Irae*', that matches Haden's own brooding statements, whose apparent hesitancy allows each note to resonate on into the silence. His introduction to a later track, 'Sandino', so strongly recalls 'Song For Che' that one wonders if Haden's melodic sense isn't beginning to recycle. There is a slightly too familiar aspect to much of the music on the album. Soloists like Dewey Redman and Mick Goodrick (who does a good Sam Brown impression on 'Sandino') seem to have less to say than their talents would suggest, and *Dream Keeper* as a whole is more surface than substance. Only the palimpsest of a (South African) choir and band on 'Nkosi Sikelel'i Afrika', the anthem of the African National Congress, reflects the passion Haden used to bring to this music. By contrast, Carla Bley's arrangement of the 'Hymn Of The Anarchist Women's Movement' sounds like tourist folk. Disappointing.

(*) **Duo Dreyfus Jazz Line 365052
Haden; Christian Escoude (*g*). 9/78.
Very predictable stuff indeed – 'Nuages', for God's sake – which almost any decent jobbing bass player could have handled. It does, however, serve to highlight the romantic side of Haden which is audible even in his fiercest and most committed work but which really came out only in the later Quartet West. Escoude plays prettily, but without drama.

*** **Magico** ECM 1151
Haden; Jan Garbarek (*ts, ss*); Egberto Gismonti (*g, p*). 6/79.
***(*) **Folk Songs** ECM 1170
As above. 11/79.
Though released under Haden's name, the dominant voice on both of these splendid albums is, perhaps inevitably, Garbarek's. The saxophonist swoops and wheels over Gismonti's rippling patterns (interesting to compare with Ralph Towner's more abstract approach) and the deep swell of Haden's rather sombre approach. The slightly later *Folk Songs* (usefully sampled on Garbarek's *Works* – ECM 823266) is a classic, one of the finest records of the late 1970s.

*** **Quartet West** Verve 831673
Haden; Ernie Watts (*ts, as, ss*); Alan Broadbent (*p*); Billy Higgins (*d*). 12/86.
(*) **In Angel City Verve 837031
As above, except omit Higgins; add Lawrence Marable, Alex Cline (*d*). 6/88.
*** **Haunted Heart** Verve 513078
As for *In Angel City*, except omit Cline; add Billie Holiday, Jeri Southern, Jo Stafford (*v* on records). 90.
The first of Haden's Quartet West records is still the best. In attempting to recapture the musical and emotional atmosphere of his childhood, he has relied more and more on 'atmospheric' devices, culminating in the flashback approach of *Haunted Heart*. On the first record, the same feelings were communicated quite simply by fine playing in the character of the 1940s. Watts and Broadbent were well-chosen partners in this exercise. Setting aside the sparkling quality of the recording and an occasional giveaway surge from the bassist, who would have been able to date 'Body And Soul' or 'My Foolish Heart' with any confidence? Haden's solo feature, 'Taney County', conjures up the days when he was part of a family radio show, and it contains some elegant string playing, too.

The sequel is by no means as appealing. Once again dedicated to the bassist's adopted home, the Chandlerish evocation of Los Angeles is more diffuse and the range of material less convincing. Watts is a surprisingly effective foil and Marable, who drums on all but one of the tracks, marvellously precise without being dogmatic about the exact count. Less than compelling, though.

Haunted Heart is a 'radio days' reconstruction, maintaining the group's nostalgic standpoint by using old recordings of singers: Billie Holiday and 'Deep Song', Jeri Southern on 'Every Time We Say Goodbye' and Jo Stafford's haunting title-piece. If it's a wallow, it's a remarkably disciplined one, with well-organized arrangements and some fine playing from all concerned. And hasn't just about every jazz player duetted with Billie in his mind, at some time or another?

***(*) **Charlie Haden's Private Collection: Volume 1** Naim CD 005
Haden; Ernie Watts (*ts*); Alan Broadbent (*p*); Billy Higgins (*d*). 8/87.
***(*) **Charlie Haden's Private Collection: Volume 2** Naim CD 006
As above, except replace Higgins with Paul Motian (*d*). 4/88.
Not a bad way to party on your fiftieth birthday. Your wife books the cake and the balloons, and asks pals Higgins, Watts and Broadbent round for a jam. The recording isn't studio quality but the 'exclusively for my friends' feel carries it through. The playing is pretty nifty, as well. It isn't clear who shouted the tunes, but they run through Pat Metheny's 'Hermitage' and 'Farmer's Trust' (a favourite of

Haden's that reappears on Volume 2), two Charlie Parker themes, 'Passport' and 'Segment', Miles's 'Nardis' and Tony Scott's 'Misery'.

There's a reasonable continuity with the later, concert set. Motian, as always, is right on the money, and he makes all the difference to the Metheny tune. There is a truly wonderful 'Lonely Woman' (surpassed only by the Montreal version, below), another Parker title ('Lisa', this time) and long versions of the bassist's own 'Bay City' and 'Silence'.

These discs have had only a rather limited currency – Naim is an audio company based in Salisbury, England – but they are still around and well worth hunting out.

** **Silence** Soul Note 121172
      Haden; Chet Baker (*t, v*); Enrico Pieranunzi (*p*); Billy Higgins (*d*). 11/87.
An oddity, really, which without the presence of Billy Higgins would be quite conscionably ignorable. Baker's chops were irreparably busted by this point (a fact which certainly isn't reflected in one of the most overcooked discographies of recent times) and the solos are incredibly enervated. Haden para-doxically thrives in that kind of environment – and it is, after all, his album. The little-known Pieranunzi has made some impressive records of his own, and if *Silence* has one overriding merit, it is that it might introduce an excellent pianist to listeners who haven't caught up with his previous work with Baker or with the Space Jazz Trio.

**** **The Montreal Tapes: Volume 1** Verve 523 260
      Haden; Don Cherry (*pkt-t*); Ed Blackwell (*d*). 7/89.
**** **The Montreal Tapes: Volume 2** Verve 523 295
      Haden; Paul Bley (*p*); Paul Motian (*d*). 7/89.
Another shining moment in the bassist's career, caught live at the Festival International de Jazz in the Canadian city. Over nine nights, Haden was honoured with inspirational partnerships from various stages of his career, climaxing with a Liberation Music Orchestra event. His long-standing affinity for Latin/Iberian players was marked by a duo with Egberto Gismonti and a trio with Gonzalo Rubalcaba and Paul Motian. He was partnered by Joe Henderson and Al Foster, Pat Metheny and Jack DeJohnette, and by the two groups documented here.

There's a touch of *Hamlet*-without-the-Prince to the first. Haden, Cherry and Blackwell had functioned – with saxophonist Dewey Redman – as Old and New Dreams, an outfit dedicated to the music of Ornette Coleman. In Redman's absence, recollection of the classic Atlantic quartets with Ornette himself seems paradoxicaly stronger. This is immensely stirring music. Long versions of 'The Sphinx', which opens the set, and 'Lonely Woman', which is the main item, are just about as well crafted as anyone could wish, and performances of other material – 'Art Deco', 'Mopti', 'The Blessing' and 'When Will The Blues Leave?' – are clearer and less ambiguous than when the composer has given them his own quirky spin.

The second volume might have been an anticlimax, were not this such a fantastic group in its own right. There is another airing for 'When . . .' and the set is bracketed by the definitive 'Turnaround'. Bley, on home turf, plays wonderfully, and Motian has so securely hitched his wagon to this music that it becomes his own as well.

*** **Dialogues** Polydor 843445
      Haden; Carlos Paredes (*Portuguese g*). 1/90.
Haden is something of a hero on the left in Portugal, having offered selfless support to the liberation and anti-colonial movement and after suffering arrest by the far from dismissive PIDE secret police (from whom one of the editors of the *Guide* bears intriguingly situated scars) for the political effrontery of 'Song For Ché'. During one of his visits to Portugal in the 1970s, Haden met the guitarist Carlos Paredes and arranged to jam with him. So successful was the encounter that a studio recording was arranged. On reflection, it might have been preferable to have had the original meeting, warts and all, instead of this rather stilted and unspontaneous re-enactment.

Almost all the material is by Paredes himself (one track is credited to his kinsmen, Artur and Gonçalo) and he plays with great passion on the wide-bodied instrument. The inclusion of 'Song For Ché' was inevitable, but it strikes a curiously false note here. Perhaps by now its subversive content has been largely exhausted, leaving only a rather slight, even irritating, tune.

*** **First Song** Soul Note 121222
      Haden; Enrico Pieranunzi (*p*); Billy Higgins (*d*). 4/90.
Credited to Haden, but interesting primarily for the stately lyricism Pieranunzi brings to the music. In approach, he is much like the bassist, combining a deep-toned, romantic approach with a clipped swing at faster tempos. Higgins has little to do on the quiet opening track, but he contributes crisp, uncount-able metres elsewhere, with his characteristic throbbing pulse. The session really gets into top gear only with the fourth track, Tristano's 'Lennie's Pennies', a thoughtful essay by the bassist, and it may be a little too understated for some tastes.

*** **Always Say Goodbye** Verve 521501
>   Haden; Ernie Watts (*ts*); Alan Broadbent (*p*); Stéphane Grappelli (*vn*); Larance Marable (*d*).
>   7–8/93.

Haden's insistence that Quartet West's music is about a 'dedication to beauty' is paying dividends, although many listeners will find the excerpts from his favourite records (this time: Hawkins, Django, Duke, Chet and Jo Stafford) as intrusive as they are beguiling. Besides, the quartet is playing well enough to merit a clear run of their own: Watts's tenor is enormously authoritative, Broadbent is a deferential master. Grappelli's walk-on cameo is a charmer.

***(*) **Steal Away: Spirituals, Hymns And Folk Songs** Verve 527 249
>   Haden; Hank Jones (*p*). 7/94.

Haden has never been afraid to wear his heart on his sleeve and, more than once in recent times, has consented to go walking with sheer sentiment. That's evident again on this lovely disc. There is, of course, a set of political agenda, a tribute to the unknown and unsung artists who created these traditional items, but behind the recording, one suspects, lies the recent loss of the woman from whom Haden learned much of his music, Virginia Day Haden. Most of the tunes will be familiar (to Americans, at least), but they are no less entrancing for that. Haden's and Jones's interpretations of the fifteenth-century French 'Amour de Moy', resurrected as an Arcadian folksong, and of the 'Londonderry Air' are quite magnificent. Perhaps lacking a little in exploratory edge; we look forward to hearing some of this material examined more quizzically in a live context.

Tim Hagans TRUMPET

*** **No Words** Blue Note 789680-2
>   Hagans; Joe Lovano (*ts*); Marc Copland (*p*); John Abercrombie (*g*); Scott Lee (*b*); Bill Stewart
>   (*d*). 12/93.
***(*) **Audible Architecture** Blue Note 831808-2
>   Hagans; Bob Belden (*ts*); Larry Grenadier (*b*); Billy Kilson (*d*). 12/94.

Hagans has become sought after for all kinds of work, and his own records for Blue Note expose a mercurial, accomplished trumpeter with a significant discography ahead of him. He has an elegant tone and a penchant for long, rococo lines which he seems able to deliver without undue strain. *No Words* is a rather cautious start in that he's a little crowded by the top-notch band, and none of the compositions makes a special mark (interestingly, his sleeve-notes to the second disc reveal that he wrote all the tunes here on piano, accounting for the harmonic rather than melodic interest, whereas the themes on disc two came straight off the horn). Lovano and Abercombie do their usual sterling work and, though Hagans sounds more like a bandsman than a leader, it's still an enjoyable record.

Audible Architecture is much more a trumpet showcase – he even sounds further forward in the mix. Two standards are thoughtfully done, but it's the snap and hustle of the up-tempo originals that one remembers, and when Belden sits in on four tracks the music takes on a cast that moves from bright free bop to a funky groove. Kilson plays as Hagans instructed him, as if the whole thing were a continuous drum solo, and, while he sometimes goes too far, it's an exciting response. The leader's own playing sounds sharper and riskier without trading in his fundamentally clam eloquence.

Jerry Hahn (born 1940) GUITAR

*** **Time Changes** Enja ENJ 9007
>   Hahn; Dave Liebman (*ss*); Art Lande, Phil Markowitz (*p*); Steve LaSpina (*b*); Jeff Hirshfield
>   (*d*). 10/93.

Though hardly a household name, Hahn is an extremely important figure in jazz guitar. He made his name with John Handy and Gary Burton. For many years thereafter, he devoted his time to teaching and writing a column for *Guitar Player*, but the compulsion to perform returned and Hahn moved to Oregon and then to Denver in pursuit of an active improvising scene. This record, which for many will be a first glimpse of the man, oozes maturity and, after 20 years without a record as leader, seems bursting with ideas. Perhaps because of this the trio tracks with LaSpina and Hirshfield are far and away the most interesting. Liebman adds next to nothing beyond curlicues and furbelows, and the piano players are both too quirky to make much sense of music that anticipates the work of 1980s/'90s icons, Abercrombie and Scofield. The arrangement of Dolphy's '245' is fascinating, as is the resolutely unmournful 'Goodbye Pork Pie Hat'. Hahn wrote 'Oregon' before moving to the North-West, and it doesn't seem to have any direct relation to the place; it is, though, one of his most moving pieces and, for once, Markowitz sounds like the right man for the job.

Al Haig (1924–82) PIANO

**** The Al Haig Trio Esoteric Fresh Sound FSR-CD 38
    Haig; Bill Crow (*b*); Lee Abrams (*d*). 3/54.
**** Al Haig Trio Fresh Sound FSR-CD 45
    As above. 3/54.
*** Al Haig Quartet Fresh Sound FSR CD 12
    Haig; Benny Weeks (*g*); Teddy Kotick (*b*); Phil Brown (*d*). 9/54.
*** Al Haig Today! Fresh Sound FSR-CD 6
    Haig; Eddie De Haas (*b*); Jim Kappes (*d*). 65.

Al Haig was deplorably served by records in the earlier part of his career, and as a result he is almost the forgotten man of bebop piano. Yet he was as great a figure as any of the bebop masters. If he denied himself the high passion of Bud Powell's music, he was still a force of eloquence and intensity, comparable to anyone in the movement. The first trio album, originally released on the Esoteric label, is a masterpiece that can stand with any of the work of Powell or Monk. Haig's elegance of touch and line, his virtually perfect delivery, links him with Teddy Wilson rather than with any of his immediate contemporaries, and certainly his delivery of an unlikely tune such as 'Mighty Like A Rose' (on FSR-CD 45) has a kinship with the language of Wilson's generation. Yet his complexity of tone and the occasionally cryptic delivery is unequivocally modern, absolutely of the bop lineage. Voicings and touch have a symmetry and refinement that other boppers, from Powell and Duke Jordan to Joe Albany and Dodo Marmarosa, seldom approached. The second *Trio* album, originally released on Period, dates from the same day of recording and is virtually as good – but it could just as easily have fitted on to the same CD as its companion-piece. Still, Haig's bittersweet reduction of 'Round Midnight', present here, is unmissable, even among the many versions of that tune.

The *Quartet* and *Today!* albums are flawed by their circumstances. On *Quartet*, his accompanists are no more than adequate, even though the pianist's subtle touch on a typical programme of standards is impeccable. The sound, though, is inadequate. *Today!* is a stray bulletin from the mid-1960s, originally very rare on vinyl, and several of the tunes sound foreshortened. 'Bluesette' and 'Polka Dots And Moonbeams' still show that Haig's powers were undimmed.

*** Ornithology Progressive PCD 7024
    Haig; Jamil Nasser (*b*); Frank Gant (*d*). 77.

Haig went through a burst of recording late in his life, and remained a marvellous musician to the end. So far, though, most of the vinyl has yet to make it to CD, outside of Japanese issues. This one is so-so. Nasser and Gant are no more than workmanlike, and Haig himself is sometimes content to take it easy, though his version of Strayhorn's 'Daydream' reminds us how he might have been the premier poet of bebop. Wait for Spotlite's beautiful *Invitation* to make it to general CD release.

Pat Halcox (born 1930) TRUMPET

**(*) There's Yes! Yes! In Your Eyes Jazzology JCD-186
    Halcox; John Beacham (*tb*); Bruce Turner (*cl*); Ray Smith (*p*); Jim Douglas (*g*); Vic Pitt (*b*);
    Geoff Downes (*d*). 6–7/89.

Halcox will for ever be associated with Chris Barber's band, and this is a rare example of a record under his nominal leadership. There's no notable grandstanding from the trumpeter, just a sensible and mildly persuasive set of performances on a group of mostly very old tunes, several of them exceptionally obscure even by trad standards. Unfortunately, the record works out as a little too polite, with the rhythm section clunking along and Halcox sounding too gentlemanly to take a serious lead. The recording (at the Bull's Head, Barnes) sounds authentically British and is no better for it.

Edmond Hall (1901–67) CLARINET

**** Edmond Hall 1936–1944 Classics 830
    Hall; Billy Hicks (*t, v*); Sidney De Paris, Emmett Berry (*t*); Vic Dickenson, Fernando Arbello
    (*tb*); Meade Lux Lewis (*cel*); Cyril Haynes, Teddy Wilson, Eddie Heywood, James P. Johnson
    (*p*); Red Norvo (*vib*); Leroy Jones, Jimmy Shirley, Al Casey, Carl Kress (*g*); Al Hall, Israel
    Crosby, Billy Taylor, Johnny Williams (*b*); Arnold Boling, Big Sid Catlett (*d*); Henry Nemo (*v*).
    6/37–1/44.
*** Edmond Hall With Alan Elsdon Jazzology JCD-240
    Hall; Alan Elsdon (*t*); Phil Rhodes (*tb*); Andy Cooper (*cl*); Colin Bates (*p*); John Barton (*g*);
    Mick Gilligan (*b*); Billy Law (*d*). 66.

*** **Edmond Hall Quartet** Jazzology JCD-207

  Hall; Colin Bates (*p*); Mick Gilligan (*b*); Billy Law (*d*). 11/66.

**** **Edmond Hall In Copenhagen** Storyville STCD 6022

  Hall; Finn Otto Hansen (*t*); Arne Bue Jensen (*tb*); Jørgen Svare (*cl*); Jørn Jensen (*p*); Bjarne
'Liller' Petersen (*bj*); Jens Sølund (*b*); Knud Ryskov Madsen (*d*). 12/66.

Hall was one of the most popular musicians in the Eddie Condon circle, but his experience – with big
bands in the 1920s and '30s and with Louis Armstrong's All Stars – was much wider than that. He
played in a driving manner that married the character of his New Orleans background with the more
fleet methods of the swing clarinettists. The Classics disc starts off with an obscure session by Billy
Hicks and his Sizzlin' Six, with Hall as a sideman, but the meat of it is in Hall's first three sessions for
Blue Note and a stray Commodore date. This is outstandingly fine midstream swing, with superb
contributions from de Paris, Berry, the incomparably refined Wilson, Lewis (on celeste), James P.
Johnson and, above all, the magnificent Dickenson whose solos on the blues are masterful statements of
jazz trombone. And there is Hall himself. Sound is mainly excellent, but the final Blue Note date is a bit
scruffy.

  Hall toured in the 1960s until he died, and the two Jazzology discs come from a British tour with
Elsdon's band: one with the horns, one without. The date with horns just has it for the better variety,
though this is in the main an average line-up of performers, and Hall's careful heat and elegant, supple
parts outclass his surroundings, even in his final year.

  The Copenhagen date makes the best memorial to him. 'I like to work in different contexts, but I can
only play one style': hot, fluent, swinging, pinching the odd note here and there, but mostly displaying a
remarkably clean and supple line, here is Ed Hall at his best, only a few weeks before he died. The Papa
Bue band play on two tracks, the rhythm section and Hall on most of the others and, while the Swedish
players are no great masters, they know how to respect a player who is. Hall even turns in a lovely *a
capella* treatment of 'It Ain't Necessarily So'. Splendid remastering of a beautiful record.

Jim Hall (born 1930) GUITAR

*** **Where Would I Be?** Original Jazz Classics OJC 649

  Hall; Ben Aronov (*p*); Malcolm Cecil (*b*); Airto Moreira (*d*). 7/71.

Hall's smooth, gentlemanly approach got seriously interesting only once he had passed his sixtieth
birthday and started to work with larger groups. The problem with these early sessions boils down, as
the title implies, to their unvarying niceness. Totally professional, Hall delivers reliably every time, with
no apparent difference in approach between live and studio sessions. He can certainly never be accused
of pointless redundancy, for his solos are always unimpeachably controlled.

(*) **Alone Together Original Jazz Classics OJC 467

  Hall; Ron Carter (*b*). 8/72.

A live set without a single rough edge or corner, and with almost no improvisational tension either. The
slight surprise of Rollins's 'St Thomas' quickly evaporates as Hall negotiates its contours with almost
cynical ease – is there really no more to it than that? The rest is more caressingly familiar. There are
moments of genuine beauty, notably on 'Softly As In A Morning Sunrise' and 'Autumn Leaves', but
there's something fatally lacking in the conception. All of which is just a curmudgeonly, jazz-critic way
of saying this is a lovely record which a lot of people are going to like.

*** **Circles** Concord CCD 4161

  Hall; Don Thompson (*p, b*); Rufus Reid (*b*); Terry Clarke (*d*). 3/81.

There's still a big gap in Hall's discography, accounting for much of the 1970s, an admittedly fallow
period for the guitarist. *Circles* finds him more conventionally swinging than for some time, but in a
rather oddly weighted group in which Thompson doubles on piano and bass (Reid's only in for the fine
'All Of A Sudden My Heart Sings' – did he show up late?). There's not a lot of substance to it, and it
would be as flat as a pancake if it weren't for Clarke's peppy drumming, a feature of most Hall records
from here on.

*** **Jim Hall's Three** Concord CCD 4298

  Hall; Steve LaSpina (*b*); Akira Tana (*d*). 1/86.

Ironically, Clarke isn't on hand for this rather drab standards session; but LaSpina, another regular, is
and he takes a fairly strong hold on things from the off. Tana's too busy and energetic for the general
pace of things and he tends to go round and round in pointless loops on 'All The Things You Are',
which might have benefited from a subtler approach.

  Hall himself isn't bad, but the jaded familiarity of a lot of his solos, now seemingly composed of strings
of favourite figures and runs, may put off some listeners.

(*) These Roots Denon C Y 30002 EX
    Hall; Tom Harrell (*t, flhn*); Steve LaSpina (*b*); Joey Baron (*d*). 2/88.
A solo 'All Too Soon', a couple of intriguing duos with Harrell and LaSpina respectively on 'Something Tells Me' and 'Darn That Dream', a trio 'My Funny Valentine' that draws all the remaining marrow out of the tune, and a generally effective quartet set hinged on 'Where Or When' and 'With A Song In My Heart'. Typically uncontroversial stuff from Hall, but Harrell is much too diffident in the group setting; it's a shame the duo format wasn't observed throughout.

***(*) All Across The City** Concord CCD 4384
    Hall; Gil Goldstein (*p, ky*); Steve LaSpina (*b*); Terry Clarke (*d*). 5/89.
This contains some of Hall's most innovatively 'contemporary' playing. Certainly, no one thrown into the deep end of 'R. E. M. Movement' – a Gil Goldstein composition with free passages from all the players – would suspect the provenance. Elsewhere the material is more familiar. 'Young One (For Debra)' consciously recalls Bill Evans and 'Waltz For Debbie'. Of the other originals, the gentle 'Jane' is dedicated to Mrs Hall, composer in turn of 'Something Tells Me'; 'Drop Shot' and 'Big Blues' are tougher but also more humorous in conception, the former featuring Goldstein's electronic keyboards to good effect, the latter an unexpected tribute to Stanley Turrentine. The title-track, a gentle and slightly wondering cityscape, also recalls Hall's association with Bill Evans.
    Hall, though, is much more than an impressionistic colourist. His reading of Monk's 'Bemsha Swing' confirms his stature as one of the most significant harmonic improvisers on his instrument. Good sound on all three formats. Strongly recommended.

*** **Live At Town Hall** Musicmasters 65066-2
    Hall; Gil Goldstein (*p, syn*); John Scofield, Mick Goodrick, John Abercrombie, Peter Bernstein (*g*); Gary Burton (*vib*); Steve LaSpina (*b*); Terry Clarke (*d*). 6/90.
A guitar summit in New York City to mark Hall's sixtieth birthday. It's perhaps a measure of his level of performance that the most striking track on the disc is a duo version of 'My Funny Valentine', performed by Goodrick and Abercrombie. Elsewhere, the main man is upstaged by Scofield and even by Bernstein, and Gary Burton briefly steals the show on 'Careful', where he has to contend with all five guitarists.
    It must have been a good night (and there was an earlier volume from the same session), but as a record it's not much more than an interesting souvenir for jazz guitar fans.

*** **Youkali** CTI 1001
    Hall; Chet Baker (*t posth.*); Lew Soloff, Byron Stripling (*t*); Bob Millikan (*t, flhn*); Larry Lunetta (*flhn*); Jim Pugh, Keith O'Quinn (*tb*); Dave Taylor (*btb*); John Clark (*frhn*); Matt Finders (*tba*); Grover Washington Jr (*ss, ts*); Donald Harrison (*ss*); Chuck Loeb (*g*); Kenny Barron, Sir Roland Hanna (*p*); Ted Rosenthal (*p, syn*); Francisco Centeno, Mark Egan (*b*); Jimmy Madison, Dave Weckl (*d*); Bashiri Johnson (*perc*); Carmen Cuesta (*v*). 91.
The nightmare scenario, that the already over-represented Chet Baker would start making records from beyond the grave, has come to pass. *Youkali* is an oddity, to be sure. Creed Taylor has taken solos recorded by Baker and Hall shortly before the trumpeter's death and set them in freshly recorded (and mostly very good) arrangements by Don Sebesky and Jim Pugh. There are actually only three Baker tracks, 'Django', 'Skylark' and 'All Blues', but they occupy a good chunk of the record.
    The other pieces reflect Hall's growing interest in working with horns again. Washington gives him a lovely, plangent sound and the brasses strike a middle course between big-band fullness and the delicacy of a smaller ensemble. One suspects that *Youkali* will be the sort of record that will appeal first and foremost to techno queens. Everyone else will remember it for the lovelier episodes: Chet's entry on 'Skylark' and Hall's response; Roland Hanna's chunky comping on the same track; Kenny Barron's magnificently humane electric-piano sound on 'Django', and so on.

*** **Subsequently** Musicmasters 65078-2
    Hall; Rasmus Lee (*ts*); Toots Thielemans (*hca*); Larry Goldings (*p, org*); Steve LaSpina (*b*); Terry Clarke (*d*). 92.
(*) Something Special Musicmasters 518 445
    Hall; Larry Goldings (*p*); Steve LaSpina (*b*). 3/93.
There are signs that, having passed the 60 mark, Hall shook himself down and tried to look at his playing and his repertoire afresh. Anchored by the regular rhythm section of LaSpina and Clarke, *Subsequently* is quite an adventurous record. Though outwardly a rather lightweight programme of mid-tempo themes, Hall's approach is quite different from his usual laid-back stroll, and Lee gives it a bit of unflustered pace, sounding a lot like Zoot Sims. Thielemans is an asset to any set, and one can imagine duets with Hall working well. Here, they're a bit cramped, but the combination yields some lovely moments.
    Just to prove or disprove our earlier point about drummers, *Something Special* dispenses with a percus-

sionist. There's probably more straightforward guitar playing on this than on any of the recent things, but it's neither inventive nor particularly well recorded, and the balance of the trio sounds all wrong; odd, because producer Gil Goldstein normally does these things exceptionally well.

***(*) **Dedications & Inspirations** Telarc Digital CD 8365
    Hall (*g* solo). 10/93.
. . . or not entirely solo, since on this fascinating record he experiments with a multi-playback system that allows him to overlay rich contrapuntal patterns and often surprisingly austere textures in a set that reflects his love of the visual arts as much as his lifelong passion for jazz. The telling thing is that at no point does the technology ever render it difficult to recognize Jim Hall in there. The voice is his from start to finish, and what he does with 'Bluesography' (which might have made a good alternative title for this session) and 'In A Sentimental Mood' could bear no other stylistic signature. It's perhaps a little too much sheer technical virtuosity to absorb at album length, but track by track it's hard to beat in this superb player's output.

Bengt Hallberg (born 1932) PIANO, ORGAN, ACCORDION

*** **Hallberg's Happiness** Phontastic PHONT 7544
    Hallberg (*p* solo). 3/77.
***(*) **The Hallberg Treasure Chest: A Bouquet From '78** Phontastic NCD 8828
    Hallberg (*p* solo). 8–10/78.
*** **The Hallberg Touch** Phontastic PHONT 7525
    Hallberg (*p* solo). 8/79.
Bengt Hallberg is a major part of Swedish jazz and has been active since the 1940s; not much of his earlier work is currently in print, though. The pianist made only a few albums under his own name in the 1960s and '70s, and most of those have disappeared; but these two solo sessions are engaging, if a little lightweight compared to some of his earlier discs. *Happiness* is a packed collection of miniatures, some dispatched in a few breaths, others lingered over: there is a measured look at 'Sophisticated Lady' as well as a couple of jolly, faintly ludicrous ragtime pieces. The presence of the traditional 'Herdesang' reminds that Hallberg looked into the possibilities of improvising on native Scandinavian tunes before many more publicized attempts. *Touch* is another mix of unpredictable choices – 'In A Little Spanish Town', 'Charleston' – but plays out with a more thoughtful élan overall. The 1978 *Treasure Chest* set includes an 'Erroll Garner Joke', some judiciously picked standards and a couple of particularly fine ballads – 'I Couldn't Sleep A Wink Last Night' is one.

** **Hallberg's Hot Accordeon** Phontastic PHONT 7553
    Hallberg; Arne Domnérus (*as, cl*); Rune Gustafsson (*g*); Georg Riedel (*b*). 5/80–6/81.
(*) **Kraftverk Phontastic PHONT 7553
    As above. 5/80–9/83.
Some of Hallberg's projects suggest an oddball streak that is perhaps more interesting for him than for anyone listening. The appeal of the *Accordeon* set hinges entirely on how much one likes the piano-accordion, since all involved play the Dixie-to-swing repertoire with charming commitment. *Kraftverk* finds Hallberg at the organ of the Stockholm Konserthus, abetted by Domnérus on alto (there are a couple of stray tracks with the quartet from the earlier record, this time with Hallberg on piano). There's a certain creaking grandeur about their readings of 'God Bless The Child' and 'Blood Count', but a few tune choices ('Just A-Sittin' And A Rockin''?) seem almost bizarre, and one is often reminded of Frank Zappa's decision to play 'Louie Louie' on the Albert Hall organ.

*** **Hallberg's Yellow Blues** Phontastic PHONT 7583
    Hallberg (*p* solo). 84.
***(*) **Hallberg's Surprise** Phontastic PHONT 7581
    Hallberg (*p* solo). 3–5/87.
Few would credit Hallberg with leading the march from jazz to any kind of 'world music'. Yet the sleeve-note author for *Surprise* opines that it 'is not a jazz record', and the other disc consists of traditional folk material. Hallberg has studied and composed in the European tradition, and he moves through non-jazz mediums with the same ease with which he slips from swing to bop and after. These records feature him improvising on music remote from conventional jazz repertory, but they sound unequivo-cally comfortable, the familiar songful touch brought to bear on a surprising range of themes. The folk pieces are dealt with a little more discreetly, and the pianist trusts the inner lights of the material rather than imposing too much of himself on it; but the *Surprise* record is considerably more adventurous, with 'Take The "A" Train' sandwiched between Paganini's 'Caprice No. 24' and Handel's 'Sarabande', and Neal Hefti lining up with Corelli and Chopin. Hallberg plays on and around each of the pieces, never

unduly respectful but sticking to his essential thriftiness and grace as an improviser: some pieces work superbly, others sound curiously abstracted, yet it's an altogether intriguing record.

*** **Spring On The Air** Phono Suecia PSCD 51
> Hallberg; Jan Allen, Gustavo Bergalli, Bertil Lövgren, Magnus Johansson (*t, flhn*); Lars Olofsson, Olle Holmqvist, Ulf Johansson (*tb*); Sven Larsson (*btb*); Arne Domnérus, Krister Andersson (*cl, as*); Lennart Aberg (*ss, ts, af*); Jan Kling (*ts, f*); Erik Nilsson (*bs, bcl, f*); Stefan Nilsson (*p*); Rune Gustafsson (*g*); Sture Akerberg (*b*); Egil Johansen (*d*). 5/87.

Hallberg's writing for big band hasn't been widely documented on record, which makes this CD the more welcome. Nearly an hour of music is devoted to a sequence of impressionist themes meant to evoke aspects of his country and, while it's hard to know if the sax writing for 'Göta River' is any kind of accurate picture, there's a vividness in the writing which the players respond to with the kind of sober relish that's characteristic of them. Old friends such as Jan Allen and Arne Domnérus are provided with features which suggest either Ellington or Gil Evans; but a piece such as 'Night In The Harbour', with its virtuoso trombone part by Ulf Johansson, sounds like Hallberg through and through. The recording lacks a little punch, but the clarity illuminates all the strands of the writing.

(***) **Skansen In Our Hearts** Aquila CD 3
> Hallberg; Gustaf Sjokvist (*p*); Gavleborg Symphony Orchestra. 91.

(***) **5 × 100** Improkomp IKCD 1
> Hallberg; Ad Libitum Choir. 6/94.

Two of Hallberg's 'outside' projects, touched by jazz but primary examples of how far afield he's explored. *Skansen In Our Hearts* collects five of his orchestral pieces, some concerto-like in form (he sees little reason to exclude himself from any of his own works) and all firmly in a Scandinavian symphonic tradition. Some might wish for some extra gravitas, but there's no questioning the sonority and inventiveness of the composer's writing. *5 × 100* features his writing for choir – psalm settings, Shakespeare, Schubert, Swedish folksong and something of himself. He can't resist the occasional bit of mischief, but some of the music is disarmingly lovely and admirers of his piano will be partial to the four solo interludes. Rather remote recording from the Linkoping Cathedral School.

*** **The Tapdancing Butterfly** Aquila CD 4
> Hallberg; Ronnie Gardiner (*b*); Sture Akerberg (*d*). 92.

Hallberg's trio music has an element of kitsch about it: he likes tempos and rhythms that suggest a kind of jazz vaudeville at times, and the queer setting chosen for 'Poor Butterfly', for instance, will raise either a smile or a wince of irritation. The butterfly theme drifts through these pieces, and the best of them are vintage Hallberg, but it's as well to be tuned in on his wavelength.

**** **Time On My Hands** Improkomp IKCD 2-3 2CD
> Hallberg (*p* solo). 2/94–4/95.

Hallberg played a radio concert in which he performed nothing but written requests from the audience, and he liked it so much that he repeated the method at two subsequent sessions. This two-disc set takes the pick of the three occasions. Non-Swedish speakers are denied the chance to savour the pianist's amusing introductions (his first number is the theme from *Dallas*!), but nobody will mistake the elegance, wit and lucidity on show in the playing itself. This is vintage Hallberg, and probably the ideal introduction to one of Europe's most eminent masters.

Rich Halley TENOR SAXOPHONE

*** **Saxophone Animals** Nine Winds NWCD 0139
> Halley; Rob Blakeslee (*t, flhn, perc*); Tom Hill (*tb*); Gary Harris (*as*); Geoff Lee (*p*); Phil Sparks (*b*); William Thomas (*d*). 7/88–8/90.

Halley, who lives and works in Portland, Oregon, has asserted a firm and engaging identity on his records. His band, The Lizard Brothers, perform his charts with great enthusiasm. But working in a straight-ahead context with the occasional nod towards freedom seems to be Halley's best routine, for he reaches further out on *Saxophone Animals* to somewhat lesser effect. While there are some striking things here – an interesting reworking of Miles Davis's 'The Serpent's Tooth', for instance – the long pieces struggle a little to balance the free and formal ingredients, and Hill and Harris sound less at ease than they were on an earlier record. Halley himself, though, remains a formidable improviser in the Rollins mould.

Lin Halliday (born 1936) TENOR SAXOPHONE

*** **Delayed Exposure** Delmark DE 449

> Halliday; Ira Sullivan (*t, flhn, f*); Jodie Christian (*p*); Dennis Carroll (*b*); George Fludas (*d*). 6/ 91.

*** **East Of The Sun** Delmark DE 458

> As above. 4/92.

The title of the first disc is suitably pointed, since this was Halliday's debut as a leader: 'An extremely likeable tenor saxophonist,' says the sleeve-note writer, and there's little here to make one disagree. Halliday emerges as a well-practised Rollins disciple. He's been living and working in Chicago for a little over a decade, and Delmark's minor crusade to record the city's less sensational but worthy constituents pays off with a muscular, well-fashioned blowing date. Some standards and a blues give everyone a chance to hold down some choruses and, if Sullivan's trumpet turns are the most distinctive things here, Halliday acquits himself with the comfortable assurance of a veteran player. The second album is a plain and simple second helping, but one can't expect fresh initiatives from a seasoned campaigner at this stage: just good, unfeigned jazz. Sullivan brings out his tenor for the final 'Will You Still be Mine', and it's a splendid joust that results. Both are extremely likeable.

Andy Hamilton (born 1918) TENOR SAXOPHONE

***(*) **Silvershine** World Circuit WCD 025

> Hamilton; Graeme Hamilton (*t*); Andy Sheppard, Jean Toussaint, Steve Williamson (*ts*); David Murray (*ts, bcl*); Sam Brown (*p*); Ralf DeCambre (*g*); Ray Pablo Brown (*b*); Johnny Hoo, Mark Mondesir (*d*). 1 & 3/91.

Hamilton formed his first band in Jamaica as long ago as 1936. He called it Silvershine, and the name has stuck with him. Just after the war, the movie actor Errol Flynn employed him as musical arranger on his floating seduction platform, the yacht *Zaka*. Hamilton composed a jazzed-up calypso signature-tune which he also called 'Silvershine'.

He's lived in Britain since 1949, mainly in Birmingham. Hamilton's unstinted kindness and generous, mellow saxophone-tone have turned him into a much-loved figure, both in the West Indian community and with visiting jazz players. The roster of guest stars on his World Circuit debut, recorded at the age of 72, bears witness to his almost legendary standing. Foremost among these is David Murray, bringing drive and the special intensity of his samba mode to 'Silvershine' and throaty bass clarinet to 'Old Folks'. (At press time, word was that Murray had rejoined Hamilton for an all-calypso album; no sign of it as yet.)

The opening 'Andy's Blues' has tenor men queueing up to pay tribute; no Murray on this one, but a trio of fine young Anglos: Andy Sheppard, Steve Williamson and (the Andy Hamilton of his generation?) Jean Toussaint. Fine as Hamilton's Blue Notes are, the six tracks ('Andy's Blues' included) with Mark Mondesir in for regular Blue Note Johnny Hoo on drums seem to move with greater purpose than the rest. Orphy Robinson turns in some of his best playing on record on two tracks, but the additional percussionists don't add very much.

Silvershine sold a few extra units on the strength of a vocal from Mick Hucknall of Simply Red. Orthodox jazz fans scoffed, but Hucknall's credentials as the blackest white voice around are more than confirmed by his performance of 'You Are Too Beautiful'. The follow-up record eschewed pop-crossover draws of this sort in favour of a rather straiter pulpit for the old fellow's characteristically spiritual philosophy: 'Play sweet and you can baptside anybody, wild animals included.' The most unaffected embodiment is 'Nobody Know The Trouble I've Seen' with Sam Brown, one of only two non-Hamilton numbers on *Jamaica By Night*, which tries to catch some of the atmosphere of his old bandleading days on the island. He called in a few young stallions and bears for the session, but they behave beautifully, deferential and supportive. The Coltrane tinge is slightly more overt this time in the construction of solos and, if one can manage to hear some of Trane's later ballad and spiritual forms played with the earlier, Getz-influenced voice, then you're getting close to how Hamilton sounds at 75.

Chico Hamilton (born 1921) DRUMS

*** **Gongs East** Discovery DSCD 831

> Hamilton; Eric Dolphy (*as, f, bcl*); Dennis Budimir (*g*); Nathan Gershman (*clo*); Wyatt Ruther (*b*). 12/58.

*** **Featuring Eric Dolphy** Fresh Sound FSCD 1004

> As above, except add Ralph Pena (*b*). 5/59.

Hamilton poses rather self-consciously on the cover like a pre-Charles Atlas, 110-lb weakling version of J. Arthur Rank's trademark gong-beater. By 1958, though, nobody was kicking sand in the face of this band, which was commercially one of the most successful modern-jazz units of its day. The recruitment of Dolphy in place of previous multi-reedmen Buddy Collette and Paul Horn came just in time for the Newport Jazz Festival appearances, captured in the evergreen movie, *Jazz on a Summer's Day*, and gave the album, his second with Hamilton, the kind of unexpectedly pointed resonance that has always characterized the drummer's slightly Europeanized chamber jazz.

Dolphy's later enthusiasm for cello in place of piano may have been inspired by Gershman's distinctive passage-work, but the album is now primarily of interest for his own increasingly confident soloing; check out 'Passion Flower'. His bass clarinet work on the title-track and the alto-led ensembles on 'Tuesday At Two' are particularly distinctive. Budimir makes a few successful interventions and Hamilton's drumming is as adventurous as always.

The May 1959 session – previously released as *That Hamilton Man* – is darker and more angular. On his last studio appearance with the Quintet, Dolphy chips in with his first recorded composition; the moody 'Lady E' largely avoids the folkish sentimentality of parts of *Gongs East* and helps sustain the later album's prevailing air of appealing melancholy.

*** **Man From Two Worlds** Impulse! GRP 11272
    Hamilton; George Bohanon (*tb*); Charles Lloyd (*ts, f*); Gabor Szabo (*g*); Albert Stinson (*d*). 62, 63.

(*) **The Dealer Impulse! MCAD 39137
    Hamilton; Arnie Lawrence (*as*); Ernie Hayes (*org*); Archie Shepp (*p*); Larry Coryell (*g*); Richard Davis (*b*). 66.

Hamilton's reputation as a one-man finishing school for promising young players was only enhanced by these 1960s groups, which brought on Lloyd and Coryell, and (more ambiguously) boosted the rather turgid Szabo to considerable commercial success. The earlier of the two is actually an uneven compilation of two LPs, of which *Passin' Thru* (perhaps a reference to the rapid turnover of personnel) is the better. On the brink of his own big breakthrough, Lloyd plays superbly, with imagination and a big, forceful tone, not yet blurred by the hippie hazifying that shrouds *The Dealer*.

This is an odd set, not least for Archie Shepp's piano role on his own 'For Mods Only'. Its main historical interest, other than as a historical snapshot, comes from Coryell's jazz debut; he brought along the atmospheric 'Larry Of Arabia'. *The Dealer* is big on atmos, a little deficient on sustainable ideas. One exception, Lawrence's alto solo on 'Thoughts', is worthy of comparison with Charlie Mariano's work for Mingus, but it stands apart. With titles like 'The Trip' and a dateline like that, you surely know what you're buying into.

*** **Reunion** Soul Note 121 191
    Hamilton; Buddy Collette (*f, cl, as*); Fred Katz (*clo*); John Pisano (*g*); Carson Smith (*b*). 6/89.

No longer 110 lb, the latter-day Hamilton packs a beefy and impressive punch. After spelling out the personnel – a brief album-and-tour reunion of the original Hamilton Quintet, with Pisano in for the otherwise-engaged Jim Hall – the liner-note announces rather enigmatically: 'Chico Hamilton plays [large blank space] drums'. Though a maker's name or logo has presumably dropped off the final proof, it's tempting to follow up the cue, for *Reunion* reveals Hamilton as one of the most underrated and possibly influential jazz percussionists of recent times. Rather than keeping up with any of the Joneses, he sustains a highly original idiom which is retrospectively reminiscent of Paul Motian's but is altogether more abstract. The spontaneously improvised 'Five Friends' might have worked better as a duet with Collette (like 'Brushing With B' and 'Conversation'), but the immediately preceding 'Dreams Of Youth', dedicated by its composer, Fred Katz, to the dead and betrayed of Tiananmen Square, is one of the most moving jazz pieces of recent years, drawing out Hamilton's non-Western accents.

By no means a cosy, 'old pals' act, *Reunion* is confidently exploratory and powerfully effective. Recommended.

***(*) **Arroyo** Soul Note 121241
    Hamilton; Eric Person (*as, ss*); Cary DeNigris (*g*); Reggie Washington (*b*). 12/90.

That Hamilton should christen his latest band Euphoria is testimony to his continued appetite for music-making. Though it's as far in style as it is in years from the 1950s Quintet, there are clear lines of continuity. Hamilton's preference for a guitarist over a piano player helps free up the drums, allowing Hamilton to experiment with melodic improvisation. Typically, DeNigris is given considerable prominence – much as Jim Hall, Larry Coryell and John Abercrombie were at different times – with Person assigned a colourist's role.

The long opening 'Alone Together' is a vibrantly inventive version of a wearying warhorse. Hamilton's polyrhythms open the tune to half a dozen new directions and Washington produces some of his best work of the set. The other standard, Lester Young's and Jon Hendricks's 'Tickle Toe', has the drummer scatting with the same relaxed abandon he applies to his kit. His writing on 'Sorta New', 'Cosa Succede?' and the intriguingly titled 'Taunts Of An Indian Maiden' is still full of ideas, exploiting band textures to the full. DeNigris and Person both claim at least one writing credit, and the guitarist's 'Stop' is ambitious and unsettling.

The mix doesn't favour the leader unduly, but Washington is slightly submerged on some of the up-tempo numbers. Hamilton's inventiveness seems unstinted; this is impressive stuff.

***(*) Trio! Soul Note 121 246

Hamilton; Eric Person (*as, ss, sno*); Cary DeNigris (*g*). 5/92.

At 71, Hamilton still produces a beefy sound and still refuses to stay rooted in the styles of his youth. The 'heavy metal' mannerisms of his late-'80s bands have mellowed a bit, though both Person and DeNigris let rip when the need arises. The trio had been around for some time when the record was cut, and they play as if they're used to one another. DeNigris and Hamilton combine effectively on 'C & C' but the outstanding track is Person's long '10th Vision', which calls in M-BASE mannerisms, the oozing funk of old-time organ trios, and hints of a free-ish idiom.

Hamilton simply can't stay still and has obviously decided to play until he drops. Be assured, there's plenty more to come.

***(*) My Panamanian Friend Soul Note 121265

As for *Arroyo*, except omit Washington, add Kenny Davis (*b*). 8/92.

To mark the thirtieth anniversary of the saxophonist's death, this is a tribute to former employee Eric Dolphy, whose tragically foreshortened career after leaving the Hamilton band is still one of the major, if unassimilated, achievements of contemporary jazz. Predictably, perhaps, Hamilton selects from among the least wiggy areas of Dolphy's output: 'South Street Exit', 'Springtime', the blues 'Serene', the inevitable 'Miss Ann' (perhaps Dolphy's best-known composition), 'Mandrake', 'Miss Movement' and, from *Out To Lunch*, 'Something Sweet, Something Tender'. Dolphy's young namesake plays decently, but a lot of the emphasis falls on Hamilton, whose rather enigmatic title relates to Dolphy's Panamanian ancestry, of which Eric Dolphy senior was so proud.

*** Dancing To A Different Drummer Soul Note 121291

Hamilton (solo *perc*). 3 & 4/93.

There haven't been many drummers who could sustain this level of interest unaccompanied. Hamilton has always been a highly melodic player and, though there are moments among these ten tracks when he seems to be striving *too* hard for that effect, there is no mistaking the innate musicality of his approach. Some of the tracks – like 'Dance Of The Tympanies' and 'The Snare Drum' – would be mere technical exercises in other hands, but Chico carries them through, logically, smilingly and lovingly. Not perhaps the most instantly accessible of his records, but certainly one for Hamilton enthusiasts.

Scott Hamilton (born 1954) TENOR SAXOPHONE

***(*) Scott Hamilton Is A Good Wind Who Is Blowing Us No Ill Concord CCD 4042

Hamilton; Bill Berry (*t*); Nat Pierce (*p*); Monty Budwig (*b*); Jake Hanna (*d*). 77.

*** Scott Hamilton 2 Concord CCD 4061

As above, except omit Berry; add Cal Collins (*g*). 1/78.

***(*) Tenorshoes Concord CCD 4127

Hamilton; Dave McKenna (*p*); Phil Flanigan (*b*); Jeff Hamilton (*d*). 12/79.

When the disturbingly young Scott Hamilton signed up with Concord in 1977, his arrival was greeted with much the same mixture of uncritical excitement and patronizing cavil as the boy Jesus's disputation with the Elders. The fact was that Hamilton was playing in an idiom two generations old, and playing so superbly as to render favourable comparison with his putative forebears – Coleman Hawkins, Chu Berry, Lester Young, Don Byas and Zoot Sims – more than mere rhetoric.

His Concord debut, named after Leonard Feather's enthusiastic imprimatur, wasn't perhaps quite forceful enough to describe in terms of wind (a commodity that had been cornered by the critics) but it was at very least a breath of fresh air. From the opening lines of 'That's All', it was clear that a special new talent was at work. At 22, Hamilton had the poise and patience of a much more experienced player, and there are only one or two instances of him coltishly rushing ahead of the group, who stick to a very medium groove throughout.

The follow-up was recorded with understandable promptness, given the enthusiasm for *Wind/Ill*, but perhaps too soon for Hamilton to have settled down again to think about directions and ideas. The absence of Berry was unfortunate, and the addition of guitar makes for a rather smoother and less pungent product. Hamilton's solo construction is rather formulaic and, though every track is executed with absolute professionalism, there is hardly one that jumps out with mnemonic urgency

The cover of *Tenorshoes* features a pair of basketball boots bronzed like a baby's first shoes, and beside them a dish of chocolates. However tired he was of references to his age – a veteran 25 in 1979 – he should certainly have sued over the sweets, for Hamilton's tenor playing is fat-free, low-cholesterol jazz of a very high order. However saccharine the themes – here 'I Should Care', 'The Shadow Of Your Smile' and 'The Nearness Of You' are perhaps the most filling-threatening – Hamilton explores the changes with a fine, probing intelligence that is every bit as satisfying intellectually as it is emotionally fulsome.

The unaccompanied intro to 'I Should Care' and an energetic reading of 'How High The Moon' bespeak considerable formal control which is fully matched by the band, with McKenna soloing beautifully and succinctly on both of the above. The album as a whole is brightly recorded, though the saxophone is occasionally a shade over-miked.

*** **Close Up** Concord CCD 4197
    Hamilton; John Bunch (*p*); Chris Flory (*g*); Phil Flanigan (*b*); Chuck Riggs (*d*). 2/82.
*** **In Concert** Concord CCD 4233
    As above, except add Eiji Kitamura (*cl*). 6/83.
*** **The Second Set** Concord CCD 4254
    As above, except omit Kitamura. 6/83.
*** **The Right Time** Concord CCD 4311
    As above.
***(*) **Plays Ballads** Concord CCD 4386
    As above. 3/89.

The early 1980s saw Hamilton consolidating his position as a leading exponent of mainstream jazz. 'Mr Big And Mr Modern' on *Close Up* might be read as a response to a press that dismissed him as a young fogey – a judgement relative, one supposes, to his contemporaries on the saxophone, almost all of whom seemed to be in thrall to John Coltrane. It's a strong record, with Bunch and Flory more prominent than they tended to be on tour.

Setting aside the irritation of a relentlessly self-congratulatory Japanese audience (who applaud themselves every time they recognize a standard), the two Tokyo sets are absolutely marvellous. It's not often that a label can cull two top-flight discs from a single concert, but there's nothing shop-soiled or second-rate about *The Second Set*, which opens with a reading of 'All The Things You Are' that within a few bars confirms Hamilton as a highly individual improviser and not just a mellow stylist. The band play briskly and intelligently. Guitarist Flory's contributions to big-band flag-wavers like Basie's 'Taps Miller' (*Second Set*) and 'One O'Clock Jump' (*In Concert*) are impeccably judged, and Bunch turns in half a dozen exceptional choruses between the two sets. The *In Concert* CD has a bonus encore featuring the Japanese clarinettist, Eiji Kitamura (who has a worthwhile album of his own on Concord CJ 152).

Ballads was Hamilton's best record to date; the recent *Race Point* just beats it to the line. Though he handles faster numbers with consummate skill and without an awkward excess of notes, this is his natural tempo. 'Round Midnight' and 'In A Sentimental Mood' are read with an intriguing slant which considerably mitigates the former's recent over-exposure. 'Two Eighteen', dedicated to Hamilton's wife, is his first recorded composition; it doesn't suggest a writing talent commensurate with his playing, but it's an engaging enough piece.

The Don Byas-associated 'Laura' and an oblique 'Body And Soul' are CD-only. If Byas and Coleman Hawkins have clubbed together in Jazz Heaven to buy a compact disc player, they'll like what they hear. Ballad albums are not as fashionable as they were. This is an impeccable example and certainly the best way to start a Hamilton collection (there are now 35 albums in the discography, as leader and sideman).

(*) **Major League Concord CCD 4305
    Hamilton; Dave McKenna (*p*); Jake Hanna (*d*). 5/86.

In comparison to Hamilton's consistently high standard, and more specifically in comparison to the same trio's earlier, baseball-inspired *No Bass Hit* (Concord CJ 97), this is slightly disappointing. Hanna is a more propulsive drummer than Riggs or Jeff Hamilton, and the extra bounce doesn't seem to suit the saxophonist, though Connie Kay's spring-wristed metre on *Radio City* (below) serves him very well indeed. Top credit really goes to Dave McKenna, the more-than-nominal leader on *No Bass Hit* as well. The pianist's solo on 'It All Depends On You' is masterly, with a powerful low-register left-hand line that, as on all the tracks, more than compensates for the absence of a string bassist. Disappointing, but only slightly.

***(*) **Radio City** Concord CCD 4428
    Hamilton; Gerald Wiggins (*p*); Dennis Irwin (*b*); Connie Kay (*d*). 2/90.

Excellent. The material is the usual mix of the familiar – 'Yesterdays', 'My Ideal', 'The Touch Of Your Lips' – and the less familiar – Duke and Mercer Ellington's lovely 'Tonight I Shall Sleep With A Smile

On My Face' and Woody Herman's 'Apple Honey' – together with a couple of originals. The title-track is the best of these to date, a vigorous, bouncing theme with an appealing rawness of tone. Wiggins is a superb piano player with a big, friendly delivery; right on top of Kay's rimshots and sharp cymbal accents, he pushes Hamilton up a further gear without the least hint of strain. The future is going to be interesting.

**** Race Point Concord CCD 4492
> Hamilton; Gerald Wiggins (*p*); Howard Alden (*g*); Andy Simpkins (*b*); Jeff Hamilton (*d*). 9/91.
*** Groovin' High Concord CCD 4509
> Hamilton; Ken Peplowski, Spike Robinson (*ts*); Howard Alden (*g*); Gerry Wiggins (*p*); Dave Stone (*b*); Jake Hanna (*d*). 9/91.

Carl Perkins's 'Groove Yard' is an intriguing choice of opener for *Race Point* and it sets the tone for Hamilton's best and most inventive set to date. Interspersed with the quartet tracks are four duets with guitarist Alden; 'Chelsea Bridge' is outstanding, and so is 'The Song Is You', which closes the set. Alden's bass figures and Hamilton's squeezed harmonics give the duos a tremendous range. Of the quartets, Hamilton's own 'Race Point' is notable; Wiggins opens up the middle section with a wild, intervallic ladder that feeds a storming solo. Jeff Hamilton plays immaculately, if a little stiffly in places. The sound is crisp but rather bunched towards the centre, which gives a good 'live' feel but tends to spoil some of the louder ensembles.

Sensibly, *Groovin' High* avoids the three-tenor front line for every track. Hamilton sits out 'What's New', Peplowski powders his nose during 'That Old Devil Called Love' and Robinson takes a powder for 'I'll See You In My Dreams'. It might have been good to let Peplowski air his clarinet, but that doesn't seem to have been part of the deal. They open, Musketeer fashion, with Sonny Stitt's 'Blues Up And Down', after which, nicely aerobicized, there's a fairly predictable round of exercises and solo spots, culminating in 'Body And Soul', which they manage to knock off with a solo each in 5½ minutes. There's certainly no hint of the kind of shapeless jamming that often takes over multiple-horn sessions. The heads are relaxed and bitty enough to suggest that there wasn't much time for advance preparation, but there's sufficient empathy and hands-on experience for that not to matter.

*** Scott Hamilton With Strings Concord CCD 4538
> Hamilton; Alan Broadbent (*p*); Bob Maize (*b*); Roy McCurdy (*d*); strings. 10/92.

Ah, the strings record. They all do one, those who are marketable enough to merit the investment, at any rate. They all sound much of a muchness, and few of them have enough wrinkles for a decent critical purchase. So, the usual drill: highly professional, good charts, somewhat unswinging, trio bits better, Scott fine out in front, ultimately a bit dull.

**** East Of The Sun Concord CCD 4583
> Hamilton; Brian Lemon (*p*); Dave Green (*b*); Allan Ganley (*d*). 8/93.
***(*) Live At Brecon Jazz Festival Concord CCD 4649
> As above. 8/94.

At this point in his career, Hamilton could make a living without ever setting foot back in the United States. It is quite possible that he could do it without leaving the United Kingdom, where he has built up a loyal following, and where he has found *simpatico* players who share his approach. Just to complicate the geography the tunes on *East Of The Sun* were the result of a readers' poll in the Japanese *Swing Journal*. Hamilton had apparently long wished to record with a British group, and one can see why. Lemon is one of the finest accompanists around, and he solos with a slightly bluff confidence that often masks the subtlety of what he is playing. Ganley and Green combine effectively, and both of them are accurately caught.

The live session from Brecon (a smallish festival in Wales which has nevertheless always managed to attract big and sometimes adventurous acts) is inevitably more relaxed and free-flowing, though there are hints here and there – 'Come Rain Or Come Shine', 'Blue Wales' – that Hamilton is working on autopilot and not thinking through his ideas. These are quibbles and cavils, though. The whole thing gives off an air of matey enjoyment, and the standard of musicianship from the trio suggests one more reason than English beer why Scott might yet settle here.

Just for the record (so to speak), the programme *SJ* readers wanted to hear from Hamilton went as follows: 'Autumn Leaves' (big-toned and romantic); 'Stardust'; 'It Could Happen To You'; 'It Never Entered My Mind' (perhaps the loveliest version recorded since Miles's classic); 'Bernie's Tune' (they *voted* for this?); 'East Of The Sun (And West Of The Moon)'; 'Time After Time'; Hamilton's own 'Setagaya Serenade'; 'That's All'; 'All The Things You Are'; and 'Indiana'. Full of surprises, the Japanese.

**** Organic Duke Concord CCD 4623
> Hamilton; Mike LeDonne (*org*); Dennis Irwin (*b*); Chuck Riggs (*d*). 5/94.

This instantly superseded *Ballads* as our favourite Hamilton disc to date. Needless to say, it helps that he is dealing with absolutely immaculate material, from robust swingers like 'Jump For Joy' and 'Castle Rock' (a favourite Hodges vehicle), to 'Moon Mist' and 'Isfahan', which Hamilton gives a strong Yankee accent. This is one of the last records supervised by Concord boss Carl Jefferson before his death and, all those years after that improbable debut, it must have given him considerable satisfaction. It also features one of the best bands Hamilton has assembled since then. The use of organ is a surprise, and a very effective one, but it might have been an idea to replace bass with a guitar and vary the textures a little. As it is, some tracks are just a shade dark and monochrome.

Atle Hammer TRUMPET AND FLUGELHORN

** **Joy Spring** Gemini GMCD 49
     Hammer; Harald Bergersen (ss, ts); Eivin Sannes (p); Terje Venaas (b); Egil Johansen (d). 6/85.
*** **Arizona Blue** Gemini GMCD 65
     Hammer; Jon Gordon (as); Red Holloway (ts); Egil Kapstad (p); Terje Venaas (b); Egil Johansen (d). 8/89.

Honest and workmanlike music fronted by a self-effacing brassman. Hammer's affection for Clifford Brown's music is evident, but he is a long way short of his model here. The first session, co-led with tenorman Bergersen, is decently enough done; but the material, an interesting set of jazz themes, is woefully under-characterized, and nobody seems eager to take advantage of the solo limelight. *Arizona Blue*, hurriedly organized to take advantage of the presence of Holloway on a visit to Oslo, works out much better. Kapstad contributes two memorable themes, with the 3/4 'Remembrance Of Eric Dolphy' particularly strong, and Hammer, though still no match for the other horns, makes his careful style sound appropriate to 'Stranger In Paradise' and 'Portrait Of Jenny'. Gordon's blues 'Rainbow Rabbit' is the other playing highlight.

Doug Hammond DRUMS, PERCUSSION

***(*) **Perspicuity** L+R CDLR 45031
     Hammond; Steve Coleman (as); Muneer Abdul Fatah (clo). 11/82.
***(*) **Spaces** DIW 359
     As above, except add Byard Lancaster (as, f); Kirk Lightsey (p). 82.

With their keening, insistent sound and free-jazz percussion, these might almost be an ESP session from the late '60s, rather than M-Base concepts. Hammond alternates fugitive, out-of-tempo passages with a hard, nervy swing that often recalls Kenny Clarke. Kirk Lightsey reinforces the bebop associations on *Spaces*, but it's the use of cello (an ESP staple) that most strongly conjures up the post-bop language of the mid- to late 1960s.

There's nothing on which to choose between the two. The trio is tight, plain and faintly hostile. Two cuts each of 'Lush Life' and the title-track demonstrate Hammond's ability to cross-cut rhythms at speed. Coleman responds with typical energy. The saxophonist is credited with four compositions on *Spaces* (three urban grooves, one busted tango), but it's Lancaster's gospelly wail and breathy flute which command the foreground. Hammond's recitation, 'To My Family', backed with soft Chico Hamilton patterns played with soft mallets on heavy-sounding (possibly de-tuned) toms, is quite effective and helps tie the whole disc, not just the three-part opening 'Space And Things', into a coherent suite.

Gunter Hampel (born 1937) COMPOSER, VIBRAPHONE, PIANO, REEDS

** **Music From Europe** ESP Disk 1042
     Hampel; Willem Breuker (cl, bcl, ss, as, ts, bs); Piet Veening (b); Pierre Courbois (d, perc). 12/66.
(*) **The 8th July 1969 Birth 001
     Hampel; Anthony Braxton (as, ss, sno, f, cbcl); Willem Breuker (ss, as, ts, b cl); Arjen Gorter (b); Steve McCall (d); Jeanne Lee (v). 7/69.

Virtually all of Hampel's work since 1969 has appeared on the fissiparous Birth label (and virtually the whole Birth catalogue consists of Hampel's work, in small groups and in various versions of his improvisation collective, the Galaxie Dream Band; the only two exceptions are duos nominally led by singer Jeanne Lee, who is Mrs Hampel, and by the alto saxophonist, Marion Brown). Birth has only just begun the process of transferring a substantial back-catalogue to CD, and this entry is perforce very much smaller than that of previous editions. Dedicated Hampel collectors can probably still find factory-condition LPs at specialist shops.

The main exception is the ESP Disk, made when he was almost thirty and already a determined individualist. One wonders what they made of it over in New York. Recorded in the Netherlands, this is one of the poorer ESP sessions. Swamped by Breuker's and, to a lesser extent, Hampel's own slightly unfocused multi-instrumentalism, this presents a long, very abstract 'Assemblage', consisting of mutually interchangeable elements and little or no defining structure. That the rhythm section is so obviously at sea doesn't help, but the disappointing thing is how inept and po-faced Breuker sounds. Since the deletion of FMP's vinyl, this is Hampel's only non-Birth recording, and it's a less than compelling one.

There are obvious and misleading parallels between Hampel's work and that of the similarly cosmically obsessed Sun Ra, but Hampel is typically saturnine rather than Saturnian and he lacks the ripping, swinging joy of Ra's various Intergalactic Arkestras. There is another obvious connection, another American one, which has the beauty of having a basis in this discography. However deeply absorbed he has appeared to be in Afro-American music, multi-instrumentalist composer Anthony Braxton learned a great deal from the European collective/free movement of the late 1960s, and particularly from Hampel, who has written pieces with numbered and coded titles reminiscent of Braxton's own later practice.

8th July 1969 was the first Birth disc to become available on CD. It isn't quite as time-warped as some of his work of the time, but nor is it quite as individual. Lee's voice is one of the most significant in contemporary improvisation; only Linda Sharrock, Diamanda Galas and Joan La Barbara match her for sheer strength and adaptability. Willem Breuker is already an imaginative and powerful soloist. Braxton, who in 1969 had just completed the epochal solo *For Alto* (which then had to wait three years for commercial release), still sounds as if he's fishing for a music commensurate with his remarkable talent. It's not at all clear that he found it with Hampel.

*** **Jubilation** Birth 0038
  Hampel; Manfred Schoof (*t*); Albert Mangelsdorff (*tb*); Perry Robinson (*cl*); Marion Brown (*as*); Thomas Keyserling (*as, f, af*); Barre Phillips (*b*); Steve McCall (*d*); Jeanne Lee (*v*). 11/83.
*** **Fresh Heat – Live At Sweet Basil** Birth CD 0039
  Hampel; Stephen Haynes, Vance R. Provey (*t*); Curtis Fowlkes (*tb*); Bob Stewart (*tba*); Perry Robinson (*cl*); Thomas Keyserling, Mark Whitecage (*as, f*); Bob Hanlon (*ts, f*); Lucky Ennett (*ts*); Bill Frisell (*g*); Kyoto Fujiwara (*b*); Marvin 'Smitty' Smith (*d*); Arthur Jenkins, Jeanne Lee (*v*). 2/85.
***(*) **Dialog – Live At The Eldena Jazz Festival, 1992** Birth CD 041
  Hampel; Matthias Schubert (*ts*). 7/92.
***(*) **Time Is Now – Live At The Eldena Jazz Festival, 1992** Birth CD 042
  Hampel; Mike Dietz (*g*); Jurgen Attig (*b*); Heinrich Kobberling (*d*). 7/92.
*** **Celestial glory – Live At The Knitting Factory** Birth CD 040
  Hampel; Perry Robinson (*cl*); Mark Whitecage (*as, ss*); Thomas Keyserling (*as, f*); Jeanne Lee (*v*). 9/91.

Promising signs that Hampel, now in his mid-fifties, is branching out in new directions and at the same time attracting a wider following. *Jubilation* is an excellent album – 'Little Bird' is particularly strong – which lacks some of the instinctive empathy of the Galaxie Dream Band but also some of its increasingly hermetic inwardness. The live New York City set smacks of no one more forcibly than Charles Mingus, who was at the very least a conscious presence in Hampel's thinking as far back as 1980 and the double reference of *All The Things You Could Be . . .* (Birth 0031). Mingus's legacy is still largely unexplored and Hampel, now that he has abandoned the more indulgent aspects of free music, may be the man to do it.

The Knitting Factory would seem on the face of it to be a potential home away from home for Hampel, the kind of place where his approach to improvisation meets with a ready acceptance and understanding. Unfortunately, the three pieces included on *Celestial Glory* are a bit drab and slabby. Robinson is always interesting, and his solo passages and duets with the leader provide much of the interest. Lee is recorded very close, which introduces some ugly pops and squawks, and there is an overall lack of good production which CD cruelly exposes.

The duos with Schubert at Eldena are very good indeed and 'After The Fact' is one of the best-documented performances by any of the Hampel 'family'. The other record, taped a day earlier at the same festival, has a less familiar line-up but is marked by 'Serenade For Marion Brown', a heartfelt tribute to a loyal ally who seems to have been ill with dental problems at the time. One wouldn't wish the same thing on Hampel but, at this stage in the game, it may be time for him to lay down the bass clarinet and concentrate his attention exclusively on vibes.

Collectors may be interested to note that there are also videos of some of Hampel's activities, also available from Birth, and that he has also published four books of music and interviews which offer important insights into one of Europe's most independent improvisers.

Lionel Hampton (born 1909) VIBES, PIANO, DRUMS, VOCAL

*** **Lionel Hampton 1929 To 1940** Jazz Classics In Digital Stereo RPCD 605
Hampton; Benny Carter (*t, as*); Ziggy Elman, George Orendorff, Jonah Jones, Cootie Williams,
Walter Fuller, Dizzy Gillespie, Henry 'Red' Allen (*t*); Bobby Hackett (*c*); J. C. Higginbotham,
Lawrence Brown, Vernon Brown (*tb*); Benny Goodman, Eddie Barefield, Pee Wee Russell,
Buster Bailey, Edmond Hall, Mezz Mezzrow (*cl*); Marshall Royal, Omer Simeon (*cl, as*); Vido
Musso (*cl, ts*); Johnny Hodges, Earl Bostic, Toots Mondello, Buff Estes, George Oldham (*as*);
Arthur Rollini, Paul Howard, Bud Freeman, Budd Johnson, Robert Crowder, Ben Webster, Chu
Berry, Coleman Hawkins, Jerry Jerome (*ts*); Edgar Sampson (*bs*); Jess Stacy, Joe Bushkin, Clyde
Hart, Harvey Brooks, Dudley Brooks, Sir Charles Thompson, Nat Cole, Spencer Odun (*p*); Ray
Perry (*vn*); Allan Reuss, Charlie Christian, Freddie Green, Ernest Ashley, Oscar Moore, Irving
Ashby, Eddie Condon (*g*); Thomas Valentine (*bj*); James Jackson (*bb*); Billy Taylor, Artie
Shapiro, Jesse Simpkins, Milt Hinton, Artie Bernstein, Vernon Alley, Mack Walker, Johnny
Miller, John Kirby, Wesley Prince (*b*); Cozy Cole, Alvin Burroughs, Big Sid Catlett, Zutty
Singleton, Sonny Greer, Gene Krupa, Lee Young, Nick Fatool, Al Spieldock (*d*). 4/29–12/40.

***(*) **Lionel Hampton 1937–1938** Classics 524
Hampton; Ziggy Elman, Cootie Williams, Jonah Jones (*t*); Lawrence Brown (*tb*); Vido Musso
(*cl, ts*); Mezz Mezzrow, Eddie Barefield (*cl*); Johnny Hodges, Hymie Schertzer, George Koenig
(*as*), Arthur Rollini (*ts*); Edgar Sampson (*bs*); Jess Stacy, Clyde Hart (*p*); Bobby Bennett (*g*)
Allan Reuss (*g*); Harry Goodman, John Kirby, Mack Walker, Johnny Miller, Billy Taylor (*b*);
Gene Krupa, Cozy Cole, Sonny Greer (*d*). 2/37–1/38.

***(*) **Lionel Hampton 1938–1939** Classics 534
Hampton; Cootie Williams, Harry James, Walter Fuller, Irving Randolph, Ziggy Elman (*t*); Rex
Stewart (*c*); Lawrence Brown (*tb*); Benny Carter, Omer Simeon (*cl, as*); Russell Procope (*ss, as*);
Hymie Schertzer (*as, bcl*); Johnny Hodges, Dave Matthews, George Oldham (*as*); Herschel
Evans, Babe Russin, Jerry Jerome, Chu Berry (*ts*); Edgar Sampson, Harry Carney (*bs*); Jess
Stacy, Billy Kyle, Spencer Odun, Clyde Hart (*p*); Allan Reuss, Danny Barker (*g*); Billy Taylor,
John Kirby, Jesse Simpkins, Milt Hinton (*b*); Sonny Greer, Jo Jones, Alvin Burroughs, Cozy
Cole (*d*). 1/38–6/39.

***(*) **Lionel Hampton 1939–1940** Classics 562
Hampton; Dizzy Gillespie, Henry 'Red' Allen, Ziggy Elman (*t*); Benny Carter (*t, as*); Rex
Stewart (*c*); Lawrence Brown, (*tb*); Edmond Hall (*cl*); Toots Mondello (*cl, as*); Earl Bostic, Buff
Estes (*as*); Coleman Hawkins, Ben Webster, Chu Berry, Jerry Jerome, Budd Johnson (*ts*); Harry
Carney (*bs*); Clyde Hart, Nat Cole, Joe Sullivan, Spencer Odun (*p*); Allan Reuss, Charlie
Christian, Al Casey, Ernest Ashley, Oscar Moore (*g*); Billy Taylor, Milt Hinton, Artie
Bernstein, Wesley Prince (*b*); Sonny Greer, Cozy Cole, Big Sid Catlett, Slick Jones, Zutty
Singleton, Nick Fatool, Al Spieldock (*d*). 6/39–5/40.

*** **Lionel Hampton 1940–1941** Classics 624
Hampton; Karl George, Ernie Royal, Joe Newman (*t*); Fred Beckett, Sonny Craven, Harry Sloan
(*tb*); Marshall Royal (*cl, as*); Ray Perry (*as, vn*); Dexter Gordon, Illinois Jacquet (*ts*); Jack McVea
(*bs*); Nat Cole, Sir Charles Thompson, Marlowe Morris, Milt Buckner (*p*); Oscar Moore, Teddy
Bunn, Irving Ashby (*g*); Douglas Daniels (*tiple, v*); Wesley Prince, Hayes Alvis, Vernon Alley
(*b*); Al Spieldock, Kaiser Marshall, Shadow Wilson, George Jenkins (*d*); Rubel Blakey, Evelyn
Myers (*v*). 7/40–12/41.

**** **Hot Mallets Vol. 1** Bluebird ND 86458
Personnel basically as above three records. 4/37–9/39.

***(*) **The Jumpin' Jive Vol. 2** Bluebird ND 82433
Personnel basically as above four records. 2/37–10/39.

**** **Tempo And Swing Vol. 3** Bluebird 74321 101612
Similar to above. 10/39–8/40.

Lionel Hampton's Victor sessions of the 1930s offer a glimpse of many of the finest big-band players of
the day away from their usual chores: Hampton creamed off the pick of whichever band was in town at
the time of the session and, although most of the tracks were hastily organized, the music is consistently
entertaining. If one has a reservation, it's to do with Hampton himself: if you don't enjoy what he does,
these discs are a write-off, because nobody at any of the dates can have been under any illusion as to who
the leader was; Hampton dominates everything. He'd already worked with Louis Armstrong in Les
Hite's band as far back as the late 1920s, and he came to New York in 1936, following an offer from
Benny Goodman. The Victor dates began at the same time, and Hampton cut a total of 23 sessions
between 1936 and 1941. The personnel varies substantially from date to date: some are like small-band
sessions drawn from the Ellington or Goodman or Basie orchestras, others – such as the extraordinary
1939 date with Gillespie, Carter, Berry, Webster and Hawkins – are genuine all-star jams. Carter wrote

the charts for one session, but mostly Hampton used head arrangements or sketchy frameworks. The bonding agent is his own enthusiasm: whether playing vibes – and incidentally establishing the dominant style on the instrument with his abrasive accents, percussive intensity and quickfire alternation of long and short lines – or piano or drums, or taking an amusing, Armstrong-influenced vocal, Hamp makes everything swing.

In the end, surprisingly few tracks stand out: what one remembers are individual solos and the general climate of hot, hip good humour which prevails. One might mention Benny Carter on 'I'm In The Mood For Swing', Chu Berry on 'Shufflin' At The Hollywood', Dizzy Gillespie on 'Hot Mallets', J. C. Higginbotham on 'I'm On My Way From You' or Buster Bailey on 'Rhythm, Rhythm'; but there are few disappointments amid an air of democratic enterprise. Hamp's drum and piano features are less than enthralling after one has heard them once, but they don't occupy a great deal of space. The availability of this fine jazz is less than outstanding at present. While the Classics CDs take a full chronological look up to December 1941 and the start of Hamp's own big band, the sound is inconsistent: some tracks field too much surface noise, others seem unnecessarily dull. Indifferent sound also bothers the original editions of the first two Bluebird CDs, but the third disc is handsomely remastered and includes some fine and comparatively little-known tracks, such as the swinging session with Nat Cole's trio, the tumultuous 'Gin For Christmas' and Benny Carter and Coleman Hawkins teaming up again on 'Dinah' and 'My Buddy'. The final disc in the Classics sequence includes the final 13 tracks for Victor which aren't on the Bluebird CDs and, while these are a shade less interesting than the earlier dates, it's useful to have them in sequence. The European label, Memoria, has also issued four discs covering the same material. Robert Parker's compilation starts with a few early tracks featuring Hampton as sideman, but then concentrates on his pick of the 1930s dates. The music is fine and vital enough to demand a general four-star rating for most of these compilations, but we would issue a caveat that collectors might wish to audition the various editions and judge for themselves as to the most preferred transfers.

*** Lionel Hampton 1942-1944 Classics 803

Hampton; Snooky Young, Wendell Culley, Joe Morris, Dave Page, Lamar Wright, Ernie Royal, Karl George, Joe Newman, Roy McCoy, Cat Anderson (*t*); Booty Wood, Vernon Porter, Andrew Penn, Fred Beckett, Sonny Craven, Allen Durham, Al Hayes, Harry Sloan, (*tb*); Herbie Fields, (*cl, as*); Gus Evans, George Dorsey, Ray Perry, Marshall Royal, Earl Bostic (*as*); Arnett Cobb, Fred Simon, Jay Peters, Dexter Gordon, Illinois Jacquet, Al Sears (*ts*); Charlie Fowlkes (*bs*); Milt Buckner (*p*); Billy Mackel, Irving Ashby, Eric Miller (*g*); Charles Harris, Ted Sinclair, Vernon King, Vernon Alley, Wendell Marshall (*b*); George Jenkins, Fred Radcliffe, Lee Young (*d*); Rubel Blakey (*v*). 3/42-10/44.

***(*) Midnight Sun MCA GRP 16252

Hampton; Joe Morris, Dave Page, Wendell Culley, Jimmy Nottingham, Lamar Wright, Joe Wilder, Duke Garrette, Leo Shepherd, Kenny Dorham, Snooky Young, Teddy Buckner, Walter Williams (*t*); Jimmy Wormick, Booty Wood, Andrew Penn, Al Hayes, Britt Woodman, Sonny Craven, James Robinson (*tb*); Jack Kelso (*cl, as*); Bobby Player, Ben Kynard (*as*); Arnett Cobb, Johnny Griffin, Morris Lane, John Sparrow (*ts*); Charlie Fowlkes (*bs*); Milt Buckner (*p*); Billy Mackel (*g*); Charles Harris, Ted Sinclair, Joe Comfort, Charles Mingus (*b*); George Jenkins, Curley Hamner, Fats Heard, Earl Walker (*d*). 1/46–11/47.

Hampton's big bands of the 1940s were relentlessly entertaining outfits, their live shows a feast of raving showstoppers which Hampton somehow found the energy to replenish time and again. He tended to rely on a repertoire – including 'Flying Home', 'Hamp's Boogie Woogie' and a few others – which he has stuck by to this day, but his ability to ignite both a band and an audience prevailed over any doubts concerning staleness. The studio sessions are inevitably a lot tamer than what happened on stage, but there's still some good, gritty playing, which opened the book on a blend of swing and R&B which other bandleaders followed with some interest. The Classics disc gets a bit stuck on some dull material – there are four different takes on 'Flying Home' in all, including a two-part V-Disc version – but there are also some strong charts by Clyde Hart and Milt Buckner.

Some of the best of the band's slightly later studio performances are on *Midnight Sun*, which offers 20 tracks covering some two years of work. The emphasis is mostly on the up-tempo tunes; Hamp's fondness for backbeats and the combative interplay of the sections makes the music occasionally exhausting rather than invigorating: routine can infect the records as much as the actual live shows. But there are some great things here, such as Arnett Cobb's filibustering 'Cobb's Idea', the nattering charts of 'Red Top' and 'Goldwyn Stomp', the swagger of 'Three Minutes On 52nd Street', Charles Mingus's dramatic composing debut with 'Mingus Fingers' and the lustrous treatment of 'Midnight Sun' itself, one of Hampton's best inspirations. The sound seems excessively dried out by the remastering and is rather glassy, but it's not disagreeable.

*** Real Crazy Vogue 74321 134092

Hampton; Walter Williams (*t*); Jimmy Cleveland, Al Hayes (*tb*); Mezz Mezzrow (*cl*); Clifford

Scott, Alix Combelle (ts); Claude Bolling (p); Billy Mackel (g); William Montgomery (b); Curley Hamner (d). 9/53.

Most of the tracks from a sort of jam session at the Salle Pleyel in Paris in 1953. Hamp gives himself all the limelight, but he deserves it: the long blues improvisation on 'Blues Panassie' is a marvel by itself. The band is an interesting mix, though they mostly have little to do but vamp till ready. Imperfect sound, but not too bad.

*** Oh, Rock! Natasha NI 4010

Hampton; Clifford Brown, Art Farmer, Quincy Jones, Walter Williams (t); Jimmy Cleveland, Buster Cooper, Al Hayse (tb); Gigi Gryce, Tony Ortega (as); Clifford Solomon, Clifford Scott (ts); Oscar Estell (bs); George Wallington (p); Billy Mackel (g); Monk Montgomery (b); Alan Dawson, Curley Hamner (d). 53.

*** Paris Session 1956 EMI Jazztime 251274-2

Hampton; Guy Lafitte (ts); Claude Bolling (p); Billy Mackel (g); Paul Rovere (b); Curley Hamner (d). 5/56.

Hampton's endless series of tours carried on through the 1950s, although there is some good material missing from the catalogue at present. *Oh, Rock!* is from a famous European sojourn with an amazingly star-studded ensemble, and it's very disappointing that there's so little solo space given to some of Hampton's sidemen; but that is the way with Hamp. Decent airshot sound-quality, though, and the punch of the orchestra comes through convincingly.

The later Paris studio session features the vibraphonist in very fluent form, perhaps too much so for the others: Lafitte sounds very stodgy and unswinging, and Bolling is blandly supportive. But Hamp's own playing carries the band.

** Hamp's Big Band RCA 74321 21821 2

Hampton; Ed Williams, Ed Mullens, Dave Gonzalez, Cat Anderson, Donald Byrd (t); Clarence Watson, Lou Blackburn, Wade Marcus (tb); Bobby Plater (as, f); Herman Green, Andrew McGhee (ts); Lonnie Shaw (bs); Wade Legge (p); Billy Mackel (g); Lawrence Burgan (b); Charli Persip, Wilbur Hogan (d). 4/59.

A dozen of Hamp's hits, one more time. The big RCA sound offers a glimpse of how a Hampton orchestra must have sounded at full throttle, but the foreshortened arrangements, rote solo features and utter predictability of it all are disheartening.

*** Reunion At Newport Bluebird 07863 66157 2

Hampton; Snooky Young, Jimmy Nottingham, Joe Newman, Wallace Davenport, Dave Gonzalez (t); Al Grey, Garnett Brown, Britt Woodman, Walter Morris (tb); Benny Powell (btb); Scoville Brown (cl); Ed Pazant (as, ts, f); George Dorsey, Bobby Plater (as); Frank Foster, Dave Young, Eddie Chamblee, Illinois Jacquet (ts); Jerome Richardson, Curtis Lowe (bs); Oscar Dennard, Tete Montoliu, John Spruill, Milt Buckner (p); Billy Mackel (g); George Duvivier, Peter Badie (b); June Gordner, Steve Little, Alan Dawson (d); Maria Angelica (perc). 6/56–7/67.

One of the best of Hamp's many in-concert albums returns to the catalogue (it was formerly known as *Newport Uproar*) with the bonus of six tracks from a session cut in Madrid some 11 years earlier. The Newport date features much of the expected rabble-rousing, but there are some pointed charts – a new treatment of Quincy Jones's 'Meet Benny Bailey' and the attractive ballad, 'Thai Silk', to name two – which feature the leader near his best, and Al Grey's barnstorming solo on the opening 'Turn Me Loose' is a great piece of theatre. The Spanish titles include much bustling percussion – Maria Angelica's castanets are, indeed, a bit too much – but there is the surprise appearance of the young Montoliu, whose rhapsodic course through 'Tenderly' is impressive.

**(*) Lionel Hampton And His Jazz Giants Black & Blue 59107-2

Hampton; Cat Anderson (t); Eddie Chamblee (as, ts); Paul Moen (ts); Milt Buckner (org); Billy Mackel (g); Barry Smith (b); Frankie Dunlop (d). 5/77.

Hamp carried on his exhaustive touring and playing regimen with undiminished energy as he entered his sixties. If he stuck mostly to his trusted routines with the big bands, occasional record dates in other circumstances produced entertaining if not enlightening music. The Black & Blue disc is patchy and sounds dull when the leader chooses to play drums rather than vibes, but there is some lovely interplay with Buckner on 'Limehouse Blues' especially, and Anderson gets off a couple of mocking muted solos.

*** Rare Recordings Vol. 1 Telarc CD-83318

Hampton; Woody Shaw, Clark Terry, Jack Walrath, Thad Jones (t); J. J. Johnson (tb); Lucky Thompson, Steve Marcus (ss); Ricky Ford, Dexter Gordon, Coleman Hawkins (ts); Gerry Mulligan (bs); Earl Hines, Hank Jones, Barry Kiener, Teddy Wilson, Bob Neloms (p); Bucky Pizzarelli (g); Tom Warrington, Arvell Shaw, Charles Mingus, Milt Hinton, George Duvivier (*b*); Oliver Jackson, Buddy Rich, Dannie Richmond, Teddy Wilson Jr, Grady Tate, Osie Johnson (*d*); Candido Camero, Sam Turner (*perc*). 4/65–11/77.

A peculiar set of tracks, mostly from the mid-'70s, but with a 'Stardust' from 1965 that includes Hawkins, Hines and others. Hampton stars with Mingus, Mulligan, Wilson and Hines in various small-to-medium group situations: the two tracks with Mingus, 'Slop' and 'So Long Eric', are dynamic workouts that Hampton fits right into, and the pairings with Hines and Wilson are effective. Less interesting are those with Mulligan and Gordon, and the 'Stardust' is a tail-dragger.

** Live At The Muzevaal Timeless SJP 120

Hampton; Joe Newman, Victor Paz (*t*); Eddie Chamblee (*as, ts*); Paul Moen (*ts*); Wild Bill Davis (*p, org*); Billy Mackel (*g*); Barry Smith (*b*); Frankie Dunlop (*d*). 5/78.

** All Star Band At Newport '78 Timeless SJP 142

Hampton; Cat Anderson, Jimmie Maxwell, Joe Newman (*t, flhn*); Doc Cheatham (*t*); Eddie Bert, John Gordon, Benny Powell (*tb*); Earle Warren (*cl, as, f*); Bob Wilber (*cl*); Charles McPherson (*as*); Arnett Cobb, Paul Moen (*ts*); Pepper Adams (*bs*); Ray Bryant (*p*); Billy Mackel (*g*); Chubby Jackson (*b*); Panama Francis (*d*). 7/78.

** Hamp In Harlem Timeless SJP 133

Hampton; Joe Newman, Wallace Davenport (*t*); Curtis Fuller (*tb*); Steve Slagle (*as*); Paul Moen (*ts*); Paul Jeffrey (*bs*); Wild Bill Davis (*p, org*); Billy Mackel (*g*); Gary Mazzaroppi (*b*); Richie Pratt (*d*). 5/79.

This is a disappointing batch of records. The three albums by smaller bands set only a functional setting for Hampton and, although there's some interesting material – 'Giant Steps', 'Moment's Notice' and Joe Henderson's 'No Me Esqueca' on *Muzevaal*, for instance – the arrangements are stolid and the playing routine. Nor is the recording very good, poor in balance and detail. It's worse on the *All Star Band* record, though, which is a weak souvenir of what must have been a fine tribute concert. Panama Francis is too far upfront – his hi-hat sounds louder than the brass section – and some instrumentalists disappear altogether, while the final 'Flying Home' is a mess. There are some good moments from the soloists – especially Cheatham's pointed improvisation on 'Stompin' At The Savoy' – but only hardcore Hampton enthusiasts will get much out of it.

*** Made In Japan Timeless SJP 175

Hampton; Vince Cutro, John Marshall, Barry Ries, Johnny Walker (*t*); John Gordon, Chris Gulhaugen, Charles Stephens (*tb*); Tom Chapin, Ricky Ford, Paul Jeffrey, Yoshi Malta, Glenn Wilson (*saxes*); John Colianni (*p*); Todd Coolman (*b*); Duffy Jackson (*d*); Sam Turner (*perc*). 6/82.

The opening charge through 'Air Mail Special' makes it clear that this was one of the best of Hampton's latter-day big bands: accurate, attacking section-work, a set of virile soloists and a hard-hitting rhythm section fronted by the useful Colianni. The choice of material spotlights the interesting paradox in the leader's direction – while he seems content at one moment to rely on the most familiar warhorses in his repertoire, uncompromising 'modern' scores such as Ricky Ford's 'Interpretations Opus 5' and James Williams's 'Minor Thesis' sit just as comfortably in the programme, and Hampton takes to them with the same enthusiasm. Ford stands out on his own tune, and there are worthy efforts from Jeffrey, Wilson and others. The sound is big and strong, although the vibes have a less attractive dryness in their timbre.

** Mostly Blues Musicmasters 65011-2

Hampton; Bobby Scott (*p*); Joe Beck (*g*); Bob Cranshaw, Anthony Jackson (*b*); Grady Tate, Chris Parker (*d*). 3–4/88.

*(*) Mostly Ballads Musicmasters 65044-2

Hampton; Lew Soloff (*t*); Harold Danko, John Colianni (*p*); Philip Markowitz, Richard Haynes (*ky*); Bill Moring, Milt Hinton (*b*); James Madison, James D. Ford (*d*). 9–11/89.

**(*) Two Generations Phontastic NCD 8807

Hampton; Lars Erstrand (*vib*); Kjell Ohman (*p, org*); Tommy Johnson (*b*); Leif Dahlberg (*d*). 3/91.

** Live At The Blue Note Telarc Jazz CD-83308

Hampton; Clark Terry (*t, flhn*); Harry 'Sweets' Edison (*t*); Al Grey (*tb*); James Moody, Buddy Tate (*ts*); Hank Jones (*p*); Milt Hinton (*b*); Grady Tate (*d*). 6/91.

** Just Jazz Telarc Jazz CD-83313

As above. 6/91.

** For The Love Of Music MoJazz 530554-2

Hampton; Wallace Roney, John Pendenza, Patrick Rickman, Jose Jerez Jr, Joseph Gollehon, Raymond Vega (*t*); Al Grey, Sam Burtis, Richard Trager Lewis Kahn (*tb*); Grover Washington (*as*); Ravi Coltrane, Joshua Redman, Jerry Weldon, Lance Bryant, Mitchell Forhman, Robert Porcelli, Mike Rubino (*ts*); Stevie Wonder (*hca*); Patrice Rushen, Yimoleon Regusis, Steve

Skinner (*ky*); Julian Mance, Roberta Piket, Elio Oscar, Kuni Mikami (*p*); Michael D. Campbell, Chris Taylor, Norman Brown, Chieli Minucci (*g*); Ron Carter, James Wood, Gary Haase, Ruben Rodriguez, Al McKibbon (*b*); Roy Haynes, Kenny Washington, Bernard Davis, Ndugu Chancler (*d*); Tito Puente, Jose Madera, Bashiri Johnson (*perc*); Chaka Khan, Johnny Kemp (*v*). 94.

Hampton's recent recordings are, with the best will in the world, echoes of a major talent. Since he isn't the kind of artist to indulge in autumnal reflections, one has to use his earlier records as a yardstick, and these sessions inevitably fall short in energy and invention. At this stage in his career, Hamp is taking things steady and, while no one can blame him for that, one can recommend these discs only to Hampton completists. The *Blues* and *Ballads* collections are both taken at an undemanding tempo throughout, and both – particularly the soporific *Ballads* – sound as if they'd prefer to stay well in the background. The session recorded at New York's Blue Note is an expansive all-star session by musicians whose best work is, frankly, some way behind them: only the seemingly ageless Terry and the exuberant Grey defy the circumstances and muster a sense of commitment. Everyone else, including Hampton, falls back on simple ideas and tempos which give no cause for alarm. The second volume, *Just Jazz*, is more of the same. The nicest record in this batch is the hastily organized meeting with the group led by fellow vibesman, Lars Erstrand: lots of chummy dialogue between the two musicians on harmless material. A pity that they didn't have enough time to get a better sound in the studio, though. Despite the blend of youth and experience (and stars and unknowns) on *For The Love Of Music*, this is another lemon. Redman and Roney get off a couple of shots, Hampton seems to be enjoying it, but it's all dunked in a pop production that might as well be playing in an elevator somewhere.

Slide Hampton (born 1932) TROMBONE

*** Slide! Fresh Sound FSR-CD 206

Hampton; Freddie Hubbard, Booker Little, Hobart Dotson, Willie Thomas, Burt Collins (*t*); Bernard McKinney (*euph*); George Coleman (*ts, cl*); Jay Cameron (*bs, bcl*); Eddie Kahn, George Tucker (*b*); Pete LaRocca, Lex Humphries, Charli Persip, Kenny Dennis (*d*). 59–61.

The personnel, with Hubbard, Little and Coleman, looks mouth-watering, but the horns have an ensemble role; Hampton gives himself most of the solos, which is fair enough: they were his dates, now usefully combined on to a single CD. The earlier date has a fine 'Newport', among some smart originals; the second mixes five tunes from *Porgy And Bess* with a dance suite called 'The Cloister'. Hampton depends mainly on brass sound, the reeds used for low tone colours, and the absence of piano gives unusual weight to the front lines. An interesting survival.

**(*) World Of Trombones Black Lion 60113

Hampton; Clifford Adams Jr, Clarence Banks, Curtis Fuller, Earl McIntyre, Douglas Purviance, Janice Robinson, Steve Turre, Papo Vasquez (*tb*); Albert Dailey (*p*); Ray Drummond (*b*); Leroy Williams (*d*). 1/79.

This kind of band is a logical development for Hampton, who has always loved trombone sound, has developed a rare fluency in his own playing, yet has made his significant mark as an arranger. An arranger's band featuring an all-trombone front line is, not surprisingly, long on texture and short on much excitement or flexibility. The massed horns gliding through 'Round Midnight' and 'Chorale' are impressive, but the record isn't very involving overall.

**** Roots Criss Cross Jazz Criss 1015

Hampton; Clifford Jordan (*ts*); Cedar Walton (*p*); David Williams (*b*); Billy Higgins (*d*). 4/85.

A session in which everything worked out right. Hampton and Jordan are perfectly paired, the trombonist fleet yet punchy, Jordan putting a hint of dishevelment into otherwise finely tailored improvisations; and Walton has seldom played with so much vitality, yet without surrendering his customary aristocratic touch. Williams and Higgins are asked to play hard throughout the four long titles, and they oblige without flagging. Although a very fast 'Solar' is arguably the highlight, it's a fine record altogether.

***(*) Dedicated To Diz Telarc Digital 83323

Hampton; Jon Faddis, Roy Hargrove, Claudio Roditi (*t, flhn*); Steve Turre (*tb, shells*); Douglas Purviance (*btb*); Antonio Hart (*as, ss*); Jimmy Heath (*ts*); David Sanchez (*ts, ss, f*); Danilo Perez (*p*); George Mraz (*b*); Lewis Nash (*d*). 2/93.

Having Faddis in a Gillespie tribute guarantees a certain authenticity of sound. The idea of founding the Jazz Masters, as this group is known, was to record larger-scale arrangements of work associated with the greats. A great charts-man as well as player, Hampton handles this one with entirely characteristic discretion and charm. Our only quibble is that it might have sounded better done in a studio than live at the Village Vanguard. There are moments when the sound is imperfect, and one or two of the ensembles could – and probably should – have been touched up.

Also the idea of weaving some of the themes into a more or less continuous suite doesn't altogether come off. The high points are 'Lover Man' and (surprise, surprise) 'A Night In Tunisia'. Faddis is quite properly the star, but Hargrove, Roditi and Turre, Heath and Sanchez also have their moments in the sun on this thoroughly sun-warmed date.

Herbie Hancock (born 1940) PIANO, KEYBOARDS

*** Takin' Off Blue Note 746506

Hancock; Freddie Hubbard (*t*); Dexter Gordon (*ts*); Butch Warren (*b*); Billy Higgins (*d*). 63.

Takin' Off was a pretty remarkable debut by any standards and lifted Hancock straight into the front rank of contemporary jazz pianists. It also established him as a composer with a God-given instinct for the line that separates good taste from kitsch. 'Watermelon Man' alone must have earned Hancock more in BMI copyright returns than most jazz composers see in a whole career.

Gordon – at the peak of his comeback powers – was the perfect collaborator, and the intimacy of the relationship was more than fleetingly reflected in the movie, *Round Midnight*, in which Hancock played accompanist to Gordon's ageing 'Dale Turner'.

**** Maiden Voyage Blue Note 746339

Hancock; Freddie Hubbard (*t, c*); George Coleman (*ts*); Ron Carter (*b*); Tony Williams (*d*). 64.

*** Empyrean Isles Blue Note 784175

As above, except omit Coleman. 6/64.

*** Cantaloupe Island Blue Note CDP 829331

As above, except add Donald Byrd (*t*); Grachan Moncur III (*tb*); George Coleman, Dexter Gordon (*ts*); Butch Warren (*b*); Billy Higgins (*d*). 5/62, 3/63, 6/64, 3/65.

Joachim Berendt likens the first pair to Debussy's *La Mer* and considers them to contain the best jazz tone-poems since Ellington. That is, as they say, a fairly heavy number to lay on anyone. *Maiden Voyage* is, though, by any standards one of the finest albums in post-war jazz, keeping its freshness through all the dramatic stylistic changes that the music has undergone (not least at Hancock's own nimble hands).

The playing, from a line-up that is effectively the Blue Note house band, is fleet and utterly confident, and the writing and arranging are sophisticated without sounding mannered or contrived. 'Maiden Voyage', the lovely 'Dolphin Dance' and 'Canteloupe Island' from *Empyrean Isles* have become highly successful repertoire pieces. The ensembles are both expansive and uncluttered (and thus well worthy of the Ellington parallel), and there's a fullness to Hancock's unpacking of the harmonic and melodic information that makes Berendt's even grander parallel not completely preposterous.

Maiden Voyage should be in every self-respecting collection. Most will want to find room for the slightly tauter *Empyrean Isles* as well. *Cantaloupe Island* is more of a grab-bag. The best (specifically, the title-track) is hard to fault. The rest is never less than pretty, occasionally more, but it shouldn't distract attention from the other pair.

*** Speak Like A Child Blue Note 746136

Hancock; Thad Jones (*flhn*); Jerry Dodgion (*af*); Peter Phillips (*btb*); Ron Carter (*b*); Mickey Roker (*d*). 3/68.

Hancock makes effective use of a trio of unusually pitched winds to create another almost suite-like album that, 'The Sorcerer' apart, conspicuously lacks the melodic spontaneity and immediacy of its predecessors. Not to be overlooked, though.

*** The Best Of Blue Note 791142

Hancock; Freddie Hubbard (*t*); Thad Jones (*flhn*); Peter Phillips (*btb*); Jerry Dodgion (*af*); George Coleman, Dexter Gordon (*ts*); Ron Carter, Butch Warren (*b*); Billy Higgins, Mickey Roker, Tony Williams (*d*). 5/62, 6/64, 3/65, 3/68.

'Watermelon Man' from *Takin' Off*, 'Dolphin Dance' and the eponymous 'Maiden Voyage', 'One Finger Snap' and 'Canteloupe Island' from *Empyrean Isles*, and 'Riot' and 'Speak Like A Child'. No complaints about the selection or old-fashioned VFM. Ideal for a tight budget or for the car.

***(*) Mwandishi: The Complete Warner Bros Recordings Warner 245732 2CD

Hancock; Johnny Coles, Eddie Henderson, Joe Newman, Ernie Royal (*t*); Garnett Brown, Bennie Powell, Julian Priester (*tb*); Ray Alonge (*frhn*); Bennie Maupin (*ss, bcl, picc, af, perc*); Joe Farrell (*as, ts*); Joe Henderson (*ts, af*); Arthur Clarke (*bs*); Patrick Gleason (*syn*); Billy Butler, Eric Gale, Ron Montrose (*g*); Jerry Jermott, Buster Williams (*b*); Billy Hart, Albert 'Tootie' Heath, Bernard Purdie (*d*); Ndugu Leon Chancler (*d, perc*); Jose Areas, George Devens, Victor

Pontojoa (*perc*); Candy Love, Sandra Stevens, Della Horne, Victoria Domagalski, Scott Beach (*v*). 10, 11 & 12/69, 12/70, 2/72.

After leaving Miles Davis, Hancock made a trio of electric albums for Warner Bros, very much along the lines of the band he had spent the previous half-decade with, but steered in his own direction. They were called *Fat Albert Rotunda*, *Mwandishi* (the name Hancock adopted at the time), and *Crossings*. The first was based on themes written for a television animation series fronted by Bill Cosby, and the music has a breezy cartoon quality that gets the best out of Hancock's often derided Fender Rhodes playing. After *Maiden Voyage*, it's perhaps a touch one-dimensional, but there is no mistaking the sheer drive and verve of this band.

Mwandishi is predictably more sombre and focused, stretching out over great expanses of musical time – 'Wandering Spirit Song' gives an unprecedented sense of sheer duration – and stylistically unlocatable. Henderson, who was known as Mganga at the time, does his own personal version of electro-Miles, and it is perhaps worth considering these dark-toned performances alongside Davis's notorious *Agharta* and *Pangaea* performances. Maupin is again the key element on the final disc, contributing 'Quasar' and 'Water Torture' and seeming to try out for his own, never quite successful, solo recording career.

*** **Man Child** Columbia 471235
  Hancock; Wilbur Brisbois, Jay DaVersa (*t*); Garnett Brown (*tb*); Dick Hyde (*btb, tba*); Ernie Watts, Jim Horn (*f, sax*); Wayne Shorter (*ss*); Bennie Maupin (*ts, ss, saxello, bcl, af*); Stevie Wonder (*hca*); Blackbird McKnight, David T. Walker (*g*); Paul Jackson, Henry Davis (*b*); Mike Clark, James Gadson (*d*); Bill Summers (*perc*).

 **** **Headhunters** Columbia 471239
  Hancock; Bennie Maupin (*ts, ss, saxello, bcl, f*); Paul Jackson (*b*); Harvey Mason (*d*); Bill Summers (*perc*). 73.

*** **Mr Hands** Columbia 471240
  Hancock; Bennie Maupin (*ts*); Wah Wah Watson (*g*); Paul Jackson, Ron Carter, Byron Miller, Jaco Pastorius (*b*); Harvey Mason, Ndugu, Tony Williams (*d*), Bill Summers, Sheila Escovedo (*perc*).

*** **Secrets** Columbia CK 34280
  Hancock; Bennie Maupin (*ts, ss, bcl, lyricon, perc*); Wah Wah Watson (*g, syn, v*); Ray Parker (*g*); Paul Jackson (*b*); James Levi (*d*); Kenneth Nash (*perc*). 76.

(*) **Sound-System Columbia 471236
  Hancock; Wayne Shorter (*lyricon*); Henry Kaiser, Nicky Skopelitis (*g*); Bill Laswell (*b, syn, elec*); Johnny St Cyr (*turntables*); Will Alexander, Bob Stevens (*elec*); Anton Fier (*d, perc*); Hamid Drake, Daniel Ponce (*perc*); Aiyb Dieng (*perc*); Jali Foday Musa Suso (*dusunguni, balafon*); Bernard Fowler, Toshinori Kondo (*v*). 84.

A little bit of history. *Headhunters* was the most successful jazz record of its time, selling in units that even pop acts would have been glad of. It's gloriously upbeat, funky music, the kind of thing that gave jazz-rock a good name. Compared to most of the lumbering, saurian fusion groups, Hancock and his team simply flew. Most of the emphasis falls on the leader, inevitably, but the rhythm section thud out a rich, shifting beat that makes all previous versions of 'Watermelon Man' sound rinky-dink.

Hancock provides most of the colours with his electric keyboards, but Maupin, who was schooled in Miles Davis's band, has the ability to invest just a few sounds on his various horns with a great deal of significance and effectiveness. Mason was the right drummer for the job. Where someone like Cobham would have overwhelmed the group, he had the relative simplicity of a rock player, coupled with several extra gears when power was required.

Hancock couldn't possibly have known what he had spawned. Though such things were staples of rock and soul music, it suddenly became possible for jazz acts to go out in spandex suits, big Afros and sci-fi album sleeves. Nothing else the pianist did in this vein was ever as successful, though 'Rockit' from the 1983 *Future Shock* album was a chart hit; some were downright bad, though all had at least a hint of the enormous energy of the original *Headhunters*.

Hancock's mid-1980s work has little of that freshness and impact, and the best of those that followed have now disappeared into CBS's roomy Dead Platter Office. *Sound-System* has its moments – notably 'Hardrock' and the title-track – but its synthesis of Afro-funk with New Wave gestures and relatively straight jazz voicings never quite gels.

(*) **An Evening With Herbie Hancock & Chick Corea Columbia 477296-2
  Hancock; Chick Corea (*p*). 2/78.

Not a *whole* evening, surely? It certainly feels like it. There's some exemplary playing from each of the participants (most often when the other is silent or comping quietly). Hancock comes out of the left channel and, since another selection from this concert has appeared on Polydor under Corea's name (and been reviewed there), the rating above relates specifically to Hancock. He seems a trifle uneasy with the setting and relies on a whole sequence of elaborate fakes and rolls to get himself out of situations that Corea seems to find stimulating rather than disconcerting. The version of his own 'Maiden Voyage' is very weak, even with the composer leading.

***(*) **Quartet** Columbia 465626

    Hancock; Wynton Marsalis (*t*); Ron Carter (*b*); Tony Williams (*d*). 82.

This looked very much like a – whisper it – *jazz* group again. Instead of funky electric beats, Hancock was back playing acoustically and running through stuff like 'I Fall In Love Too Easily' and 'Well You Needn't'. No Monkian, alas, he only really gets to grips with the un-Monkish 'Round Midnight', a tune that was to dominate the latter part of the decade for him as he got involved in Bernard Tavernier's moody biopic. Originals like 'The Eye Of The Hurricane' and 'The Sorcerer' still sound good, though the 21-year-old Marsalis tends to deal with the melodies as though they were flies to swat. Williams and Carter also contribute two tunes apiece.

*** **A Tribute To Miles** Qwest/Reprise 45059

    Hancock; Wallace Roney (*t*); Wayne Shorter (*ts*); Ron Carter (*b*); Tony Williams (*d*). 9/92.

The original VSOP Quintet was a wheeze to re-create the great Miles quintet. There were several festival bookings. It was thought or hoped that Miles would turn up. Perhaps predictably, he didn't, and someone else, usually Freddie Hubbard, took the trumpet role.

It would almost have been perverse enough of Miles to turn up for this one. The last, unfulfilled fantasy surrounding his career was that one day he would abandon all the electricals, the modish funk and rap, and join old friends onstage for a pure, acoustic set. Never happened.

This is as close as it's going to get, though Roney has a much more agile technique than the man whose career he is celebrating. 'So What' and 'All Blues' are both live and rather colourless. The studio tracks have a good deal more polish and drive, and it would be interesting to hear the rejected takes of something like 'Pinocchio', which is so smoothly executed it's hard to believe it wasn't fully written out. This isn't a great record. As a souvenir or a memorial, it has some value, but it plods a bit, even on those terms.

***(*) **The New Standard** Verve 527 715

    Hancock; Michael Brecker (*ts, ss*); John Scofield (*g, sitar*); Dave Holland (*b*); Jack DeJohnette (*d*); Don Alias (*perc*); woodwinds; brass. 96.

The notion of what constitutes a 'standard' is, like everything else, a relative one. For more than a generation we have been accustomed to think of certain songs – 'I Got Rhythm', 'How High The Moon', 'Body And Soul', 'On Green Dolphin Street', 'My Old Flame', 'Embraceable You' – as appropriate for changes-or melody-based jazz performance, but is there a need to replenish the stock? That is the premise of this record, part of Hancock's steady re-centring in the jazz midstream. The range of material covered is extraordinary, from British soul diva Sade's 'Love Is Stronger Than Pride' (a lush big-band interpretation), to the late Kurt Cobain's 'All Apologies', to Prince's irrepressibly funky 'Thieves In The Temple' and Peter Gabriel's 'Mercy Street'.

The approach is no different from any other standards recording, except that Hancock is clearly aware that some of these songs will not stand too much harmonic deconstruction at this stage in their histories. There are, as yet, no significant contrafacts, except for elements of the more familiar 'Scarborough Fair'; and the limitation of the record, excellently performed as it is, lies in the reliance on melodic variation of songs that in some cases are fairly cut and dried, and not susceptible to this treatment. Brecker clearly revels in the challenge and turns in some uncliché'd and fresh-voiced solos. Holland and Scofield (who switches to electric sitar for 'Norwegian Wood') are masterful, and it is only DeJohnette who shows signs of not quite understanding what is afoot.

Captain John Handy (1900-1971) ALTO SAXOPHONE, CLARINET

(*) **The Very First Recordings American Music AMCD-51

    Handy; Jimmy Clayton (*t*); Dave Williams, Louis Gallaud (*p*); George Guesnon (*g, bj*); Sylvester Handy, McNeal Breaux (*b*); Alfred Williams, Josiah Frazier (*d*). 7/60.

***(*) **Capt. John Handy & His New Orleans Stompers Vol. 1** GHB BCD-41

    Handy; Kid Thomas Valentine (*t*); Jim Robinson (*tb*); Sammy Rimington (*cl*); Bill Sinclair (*p*); Dick Griffith (*bj*); Dick McCarthy (*b*); Sammy Penn (*d*). 12/65.

*** **Capt. John Handy & His New Orleans Stompers Vol. 2** GHB BCD-42.

    As above. 12/65.

*** **Television Airshots 1968–1970** Jazz Crusade JCCD-3008

    Handy; Punch Miller, George 'Kid Sheik' Cola (*t, v*); Homer Eugene, Louis Nelson (*tb*); Andrew Morgan (*cl, ts*); Dick Wellstood, Bill Sinclair (*p*); Dave Duquette (*bj*); Sylvester Handy, Chester Zardis (*b*); Lester Alexis, Sammy Penn (*d*). 3/68–6/70.

At this remove, it seems strange that John Handy should have had so much flak from New Orleans purists for so long. He seldom worked very far from the city and had been a fixture in local bands since 1919. But because he preferred to play alto over clarinet – there is just a single track of the smaller horn on the American Music CD – and his style anticipated such R&B players as Earl Bostic, he was almost ostracized for many years. Yet he is always the most interesting player on all these records, and the bounce and wit of his playing can sometimes be phenomenal in the strict channels of New Orleans playing.

Actually, many listeners will be reminded of the alto playing of Earl Fouche with Sam Morgan. One can't hear Handy that well on the *First Recordings* disc since he seems to be at the back of the band, but when he breaks through – as on the animated 'Panama' – he makes the music bristle. Most of the disc consists of previously unreleased music, but the band is clumsy and the final three tracks, where Handy works with a different rhythm section, slightly disappointing. The two live shows from 1965 are much more like it and a strong document of the New Orleans movement at its most spirited. Valentine's jabbing trumpet spars with Handy's almost pirouetting lines, with Rimington the elegant voice in the middle. This is great stuff and, though raggedness sometimes takes over – more often on the second volume – these are records to play if one wants to sample how vibrant this kind of jazz can be.

The TV recordings are from two shows with different groups, though there's little between them in terms of either playing or sound, which is decent if flat. Miller and Kid Sheik divide honours about even and, though the presence of Wellstood on the first date is a surprise, neither pianist has much to do. Handy weathers all storms with soldierly fortitude and gets in some good blows on the way.

John Handy (born 1933) ALTO SAXOPHONE, FLUTE, OTHER REEDS

*** Two Originals: Karuna Supreme / Rainbow MPS 519195 2CD
     Handy; Ali Akbar Khan (*sarod*); L. Subramaniam (*vn*); Zakir Hussain, Shyam Kane (*tabla*); Mary Johnson, Yogish S. Sahota (*tambura*). 11/75, 9/80.

Not to be confused with the much older alto saxophonist, 'Captain' John Handy, the Texan is one of the few contemporary players who sounded as though he had listened carefully to Eric Dolphy, an enthusiasm that must have been encouraged during his association with Charles Mingus. He shares Dolphy's ability to adapt his multi-instrumentalism to almost any setting without losing its individuality and character and, like Dolphy, he has shown a particular interest in Indian music.

This is evident on *Musical Dreamland*, but its most idiomatic and effective expression comes on the MPS twofer, which brings together the 1975 LP *Karuna Supreme* with *Rainbow*, recorded five years later. Unlike John Mayer's much overpraised *Indo-Jazz Fusions*, rather more like some of Charlie Mariano's crossover experiments, Handy seems to have found a way to combine and blend jazz and Karnatic harmonic language and rhythms. The association with Ali Akbar Khan and, on the second record, Dr L. Subramaniam proved to be immensely fruitful, and Handy's playing always sounds secure and relaxed.

Jake Hanna (born 1931) DRUMS

*** Live At Concord Concord CCD 6011
     Hanna; Bill Berry (*t*); Carl Fontana (*tb*); Plas Johnson (*as, ts*); Dave McKenna (*p*); Herb Ellis (*g*); Herb Mickman (*b*). 75.

This imperturbable sessionman and late-swing veteran seldom heads up records of his own, but this reissue of one of the earliest Concord albums restores to the catalogue the band he co-led with Carl Fontana. It's what one would expect – simple charts taking a swinging route through a bunch of tunes anyone can whistle – but Hanna's resolute professionalism acts as a tonic on Berry and Johnson, who play with no suspicion of boredom. Full and crisp sound.

Roland Hanna (born 1932) PIANO

***(*) Perugia Freedom 741010
     Hanna (*p* solo). 7/74.
***(*) Duke Ellington Piano Solos Musicmasters 65045-2
     Hanna (*p* solo). 3/90.

Sir Roland Hanna, as he should more properly be addressed (he was knighted by the President of Liberia in 1970), is one of the finest living piano improvisers. Though Bud Powell remains the single most important influence on his playing style, he has also taken careful note of Tommy Flanagan and

Teddy Wilson. In these superb solo performances there are also echoes of Tatum's tightly pedalled, rapid-fire runs and crisply arpeggiated chords. *Perugia* begins with a superb rendition of Strayhorn's 'Take The "A" Train' and a clever 'I Got It Bad And That Ain't Good', before moving off into original material.

Anyone unfamiliar with Hanna's work should certainly begin with *Perugia* but equally certainly shouldn't overlook the excellent Ellington disc. Opening with 'In My Solitude', Hanna brings a calm, meditative quality to a gently paced programme. 'Isfahan' and 'Single Petal Of A Rose' mark the mid-point and a slight change of direction. By the end, Hanna seems to be taking more liberties (though they're probably there from the off), and 'Caravan' has a curiously remote air that defamiliarizes the theme.

*** **Impressions** Black & Blue 59.753 2
     Hanna; George Duvivier or Major Holley (*b*); Alan Dawson (*d*). 7/78, 7/79.
(*) **Glove Storyville STCD 4148
     Hanna; George Mraz (*b*); Motohiko Hino (*d*). 87.
(*) **Persia My Dear DIW 8015
     Hanna; Richard Davis (*b*); Freddie Waits (*d*). 8/87.
A brilliant accompanist – he worked for Sarah Vaughan from 1960 – Hanna has well-developed instincts for the dynamic of a rhythm section. He's content and able to let his left hand pick out a walking bass-line while the double-bass goes 'out' for a measure or two, or to punch in sharply damped tom-tom accents while the drummer concentrates on ride and splash cymbals, all the time developing a constantly shifting top line.

He sounds most obviously like Flanagan when duetting with the excellent Mraz. Formerly listed on Black Hawk, *Glove* is a set of tunes with 'love' in the title, a thematic approach more associated with another pianist, Dave McKenna. The sound is nothing like as exact as that on the DIW, also from Japan, and the drummer is all over the music, like a cheap suit. Surprisingly, perhaps, with Richard Davis, normally the most classically inclined of bassists, Hanna opts to groove. 'Persia My Dear' has a Monkish quality, but the stand-out tracks are 'Summer In Central Park' and 'Manhattan Safari', tributes to the city that has been the Detroit-born Hanna's working home for many years and focus of his long-standing New York Jazz Quartet.

(*) **This Time It's Real Storyville STCD 4145
     Hanna; Jesper Thilo (*ts*); Mads Vinding (*b*); Aage Tanggaard (*d*). 6/87.
Saxophonist Thilo gets equal billing and takes his full ration of solo space. Hard to begrudge him it, but he isn't the most terrifically interesting of players, lacking the harmonic sophistication of, say, Bernt Rosengren, whom he occasionally resembles. It's a safe programme for the Tivoli Gardens punters – 'Stella', 'Cherokee', 'Body And Soul', 'Star Eyes' – and the only really startling bit is Hanna's segue between the title-track and the last of these, a glimmer of pure invention on an otherwise rather overcast night.

***(*) **Maybeck Recital Hall Series: Volume 32** Concord CCD 4604
     Hanna (*p* solo). 8/93.
The Maybeck setting seems to reawaken Sir Roland's interest in the classics. There is a rich chromaticism, worthy of Debussy, and in its extreme form pointing on to Schoenberg, lurking behind more than a few of these solo performances. The opening 'Love Walked In' is a good example, though the more obvious sources for it are Monk and Garner. As Grover Sales notes in an appreciative liner-comment, it is Hanna's sense of structure that is so impressive. Not a single track carries on past its logical conclusion, and even the long, seemingly episodic Gershwin medley has a firm anchoring logic. Above all, too, it's a witty set. A charge through 'Oleo' and a technically brilliant coda to 'This Can't Be Love' are both done with a smile, which makes the romantic-tragic strains of 'Lush Life' all the more convincing.

(We have reviewed almost all the Maybeck recitals in this edition. This might be an opportune moment to register the contribution of Fred Allen, who keeps the Recital Hall's Yamaha S 400 B tuned and in such tip-top condition.)

Kip Hanrahan COMPOSER, ARRANGER, VOCAL, PERCUSSION

*** **Coup De Tete** American Clave AMCL 1007
     Hanrahan; Michael Mantler (*t*); John Clark (*frhn*); David Liebman (*ss*); Chico Freeman (*ts, cl*); Byard Lancaster (*ts, f*); John Stubblefield, Teo Macero (*ts*); George Cartwright (*as, picc, f*); Carlos Ward (*as*); Carla Bley (*p, v*); Orlando DiGirolamo (*acc*); Billy Bang (*vn*); Arto Lindsay, Bern Nix, Fred Frith, George Naha (*g*); Bill Laswell, Cecil McBee (*b*); Anton Fier, Victor Lewis,

Ignacio Berroa (*d*); Daniel Ponce, Nicky Marrero, Jerry Gonzalez, Dom Um Romao, Carlos Mestre, Angel Perez (*perc*); Lisa Herman (*v*). 7/79–1/80.

(*) Desire Develops An Edge American Clave AMCL 1008/9
Hanrahan; Dave Liebman (*ss*); Carlos Ward (*as*); George Cartwright (*as, f*); Chico Freeman (*ts*); Byard Lancaster (*ts, f*); John Clark (*frhn*); Orlando DiGirolamo (*acc*); Arto Lindsay, George Naha (*g*); Billy Bang (*vn*); Bill Laswell, Jamaaladeen Tacuma (*b*); Ignacio Berroa, Anton Fier (*d*); Daniel Ponce, Jerry Gonzalez, Angel Perez, Nicky Marrero (*perc*); Lisa Herman (*v*). 7–9/82.

*** **Conjure** American Clave AMCL 1006
Olu Dara (*t*); Lester Bowie (*t, v*); David Murray (*ts*); Allen Toussaint (*p, org*); Kenny Kirkland, Peter Scherer (*p*); Taj Mahal (*g, v*); Jean-Paul Bourelly, Elysee Pyronneau, Arto Lindsay (*g*); Steve Swallow, Jamaaladeen Tacuma, Sal Cuevas (*b*); Billy Hart (*d*); Puntilla Orlando Rios, Milton Cardona, Frisner Augustin, Olufemi Claudette Mitchell (*perc*); Ejaye Tracey, Don Jay, Ishmael Reed, Molly Farley, Brenda Norton, Robert Jason (*v*). 8–10/83.

*** **Vertical's Currency** American Clave AMCL 1010-2
Hanrahan; Lew Soloff, Richie Vitale (*t*); Ned Rothenberg, David Murray (*ts*); Mario Rovera (*bs*); Peter Scherer (*ky*); Arto Lindsay (*g*); Jack Bruce (*p, b, v*); Steve Swallow (*b*); Ignacio Berroa, Anton Fier (*d*), Frisner Augustin, Milton Cardona, Puntilla Orlando Rios (*perc*); Nancy Weiss (*v*). 2/84.

*** **Cab Calloway Stands In For The Moon** American Clave AMCL 1015
Olu Dara (*t, hca, v*); Eddie Harris, David Murray (*ts, v*); Lenny Pickett (*ts*); Hamiet Bluiett (*bs*); Allen Toussaint (*p*); Don Pullen (*org, v*); Leo Noventelli, Elysee Pyronneau, Johnny Watkins (*g*); Fernando Saunders (*b, v*); Steve Swallow (*b*); Ignacio Berroa (*d*); Milton Cardona, Manenquito Giovanni Hidalgo, Frisner Augustin (*perc*); Diahnne Abbott, Tennessee Reed, Shaunice Harris, Carla Blank, Ishmael Reed, Bobby Womack, Calire Bathe, Robert Jason, Grayson Hugh (*v*). 9/87–3/88.

*** **Tenderness** American Clave AMMCL 1016-2
Hanrahan; Alfredo Armenteros (*t*); Chico Freeman (*ts*); Don Pullen (*p*); Leo Nocentelli (*g*); Alfredo Triff (*vn*); Sting (*b, v*); Andrew Gonzales (*b*); Andrew Cyrille, Marvin 'Smitty' Smith, Robbie Ameen (*d*); Manenquito Hidalgo, Milton Cardona, Richie Flores, Cecilia Englehardt (*perc*); Carmen Lundy, Diahnne Abbott, Lucy Gabriella Penabaz (*v*). 88–90.

*** **Exotica** American Clave AMCL 1027-2
Similar to above, except omit Sting, Armenteros, Freeman, Lundy, Abbott, add Ralph Peterson, J. T. Lewis (*d*). 2–5/92.

The main mystery surrounding these records continues to be Kip Hanrahan's own contribution: though credited as chief composer, he seldom plays anything much, sings in a tired, half-speaking voice, and otherwise seems to 'direct' proceedings like some *auteur* of New York's avant-garde jazz and Latin communities. Luckily, formerly involved in record distribution himself, he founded his own record label to get these discs out. *Coup De Tete* has an amazing cast of players, scattered into disparate groupings: the music emerges as a prickly series of enigmatic songs set to Latinesque rhythms, offering a vague recall of *Escalator Over The Hill* – and, suitably enough, Carla Bley and Michael Mantler appear on a couple of tracks – yet energized by outbursts from such performers as Lancaster, Ward and Freeman.

Having set this pattern, Hanrahan's records have followed it ever since, with sundry variations on a dissolute theme. *Desire Develops An Edge* turned the singing duties over to Bruce, but the album (originally released as one LP and one EP) is too long for its own good. *Conjure*, the title of which came to be used for a Hanrahan touring group, found him slipping further into the background, directing music to texts by Ishmael Reed, with the addition of Taj Mahal involving another strain of roots music. In peculiar fusions such as 'Untitled II', played by a quartet of Mahal, Murray, Swallow and Hart, Hanrahan was certainly overseeing a departure, blending a blues set with a jazz one; despite greater use of the studio, the record again seemed too disparate to create a consistent impression. This, though, is probably Kip's goal. *Vertical's Currency* is a good title and has a lot of enigmatic bits and pieces, with Murray blowing hard on a few tracks, and the brass turning up for the closing 'Shadow Song'. *Cab Calloway Stands In For The Moon* includes the tracks 'The Author Reflects On His 35th Birthday' and 'Beware: Don't Listen To This Song', but at least there was another stellar cast of players. Hanrahan's interest in Latin percussion endures, and all his music musters a rhythmic thrust to carry it over the more pretentious spots. But it usually requires a sympathetic ear.

Latest bulletins don't bring about any revelation. *Tenderness* is almost all of a piece, and skulks around a sort of operatic design about family, journeying and misplaced alliances and affections. The band play with unlikely gusto. *Exotica* provides a couple of Kip's best titles in 'You Can Tell Someone Who'll Never Fulfill Their Potential By The Way They Measure The Evening' and 'The Last Song On The Album'. Devotees will flock; the rest of us might settle for a new and improbable *Anthology*, a two-disc set of highlights also on American Clave.

Wilbur Harden (born 1925) TRUMPET, FLUGELHORN

***(*) **Jazz Way Out** Savoy SV 0122
> Harden; John Coltrane (*ts*); Tommy Flanagan (*p*); Al Jackson (*b*); Art Taylor (*d*). 6/58.
*** **Tangyanika Strut** Savoy SV 0125
> Harden; Curtis Fuller (*tb*); John Coltrane (*ts*); Tommy Flanagan, Howard Williams (*p*); Al Jackson (*b*); Art Taylor (*d*). 5–6/58.
*** **The King And I** Savoy SV-0124
> Harden; Tommy Flanagan (*p*); George Duvivier (*b*); Granville T. Hogan (*d*). 9/58.

He made so few jazz recordings that Harden has been perpetually undervalued – it was both good luck and a misfortune that his important records all featured John Coltrane for, while they have kept the music in print, Coltrane's contributions have entirely overshadowed Harden's own. The sessions on *Tangyanika Strut* and *Jazz Way Out* are a little overstretched, with a long piece such as 'Gold Coast' failing to sustain interest; yet Harden's burnished tone (he was one of the first trumpeters to make extensive use of doubling on flugelhorn) and circumspect phrasing help him establish a quiet corner next to the massive sound of the saxophonist. While it's true that Coltrane does provide the principal interest – there is actually more imposing playing from him on the companion session that produced the mighty 'Countdown', not yet available in this series – Harden makes a tacit foil in the manner, if not quite the character, of Miles Davis. He takes the spotlight on the collection of tunes from *The King And I*, but being the sole horn doesn't suit him: he seems to be under orders to play the melodies very straight, and the ensuing solos sound thin rather than reserved. All three titles have been cleanly remastered.

Bill Hardman (1933–90) TRUMPET

*** **What's Up** Steeplechase SCCD 1254
> Hardman; Robin Eubanks (*tb*); Junior Cook (*ts*); Mickey Tucker (*p*); Paul Brown (*b*); Leroy Williams (*d*). 7/89.

Bill Hardman was a Jazz Messenger, a staunch sideman, and the long-time front-line partner of Junior Cook. A tough, no-nonsense hard bopper of the second division, he usually raised the temperature of whatever date he was on. This was his final album (three good Muse records languish in obscurity) and was made not long before his sudden death. It's a typically likeable statement. Eubanks, who can play in almost any kind of modern setting, fits in comfortably alongside Hardman's regular colleagues and, as well as the customary hard bop and blues, there are a couple of sober ballads in 'I Should Care' and 'Like Someone In Love' which, in the circumstances, enact a poignant farewell to the trumpeter's art. Exceptionally well recorded by the Steeplechase team: Hardman's sound was probably never captured better.

Roy Hargrove (born 1970) TRUMPET, FLUGELHORN

*** **Diamond In The Rough** Novus PD 90471
> Hargrove; Antonio Hart (*as*); Geoff Keezer, John Hicks (*p*); Charles Fambrough, Scott Colley (*b*); Ralph Peterson Jr, Al Foster (*d*). 12/89.
*** **Public Eye** Novus PD 83113
> Hargrove; Antonio Hart (*as*); Stephen Scott (*p*); Christian McBride (*b*); Billy Higgins (*d*). 10/90.
*** **The Vibe** Novus PD 90668
> As above, except Marc Cary (*p*), Rodney Whitaker (*b*) and Gregory Hutchinson (*d*) replace Scott, McBride and Higgins. 1/92.
*** **Of Kindred Souls** Novus PD 63154
> Hargrove; André Hayward (*tb*); Gary Bartz (*as*); Ron Blake (*ts, ss*); Marc Cary (*p*); Rodney Whitaker (*b*); Gregory Hutchinson (*d*). 93.
*** **The Tokyo Sessions** Novus 01241 63164-2
> Hargrove; Antonio Hart (*as*); Yutaka Shiina (*p*); Tomoyuki Shima (*b*); Masahiko Osaka (*d*). 12/91.
***(*) **With The Tenors Of Our Time** Verve 523019-2
> Hargrove; Ron Blake (*ss, ts*); Johnny Griffin, Joe Henderson, Branford Marsalis, Joshua Redman, Stanley Turrentine (*ts*); Cyrus Chestnut (*p*); Rodney Whitaker (*b*); Gregory Hutchinson (*d*). 1/94.

While much of the new jazz of the 1990s has attracted criticism for excessive orthodoxy or mere executive showmanship, it's less often remarked that many of today's younger players exhibit a rhythmic bravado and harmonic lucidity which are a natural step forward from (and within) the tradition. After the sideways evolutionary paths of fusion, the so-called 'neo-classicism' which players like Hargrove represent offers a dramatic refocusing, if not any particular radicalism. Hargrove is a highly gifted trumpeter whose facility and bright, sweet tone bring a sense of dancing fun to his music. But he is steadily working towards a gravitas that places him in the trumpet lineage as surely as Marsalis or Faddis. Antonio Hart, a friend and college colleague, is equally impressive, his searingly pure tone placed at the service of a canny understanding of bebop alto. Of the three early sets, *Diamond In The Rough* is slightly stronger for a couple of reasons: the two different groups involved create a greater variety, with Peterson's aggression a vigorous spur on the five tracks on which he appears, and the original material is superior – there are three satisfying themes by Geoff Keezer; whereas *Public Eye* relies on Hargrove for four of its tunes, and as yet he isn't a very telling composer. But the *Public Eye* band – all very young, apart from the comparatively ancient Higgins – is still very good, and there's a delightful reading of 'September In The Rain'. Hargrove takes a solo on his own 'Lada' which sums up his appeal: snappy, button-bright, and daring enough to suggest a man who wants to push himself hard. *The Vibe* is a solid rather than an exciting continuation, with some of the music sounding a bit self-conscious, though the title-tune and 'Caryisms' show how this band could make its own repertory. The live album loses some of the *joie de vivre* that the group could generate in concert, but still has plenty of fizz: Gary Bartz makes a magisterial appearance on one tune. *The Tokyo Sessions* sounds like a quota-filler, a session done with Hart and a Japanese rhythm section: the studio sound has an unglamorous resonance and, while both horn players go at the material with real gumption, it's an on-the-hoof blowing date in all but name. After five records there was still no classic on the shelves. *With The Tenors Of Our Time* isn't quite it, but the trumpeter rises to the challenge of having five grandmasters sit in on the different tunes – although Blake holds his own with real class on 'Once Forgotten' and with Redman on 'Mental Phrasing'. Branford gets off a good one on 'Valse Hot' and Hargrove and Turrentine enjoy themselves on 'Soppin' The Biscuit'; but the trumpeter plays with fresh resolve throughout, and his flugelhorn solo on 'Never Let Me Go' is a quiet showstopper.

*** **Family** Verve 527630-2
    Hargrove; Wynton Marsalis (*t*); Jesse Davis (*as*); David 'Fathead' Newman (*ts, f*); Ron Blake (*ts*); Stephen Scott, John Hicks, Ronnie Mathews (*p*); Rodney Whitaker, Walter Booker, Christian McBride (*b*); Gregory Hutchinson, Lewis Nash, Karriem Riggins (d). 1/95.

***(*) **Parker's Mood** Verve 527907-2
    Hargrove; Stephen Scott (*p*); Christian McBride (*b*). 4/95.

Family is a sequence of dedications to personal and spiritual kin that opens out into an interesting meditation on Hargrove's possible future course. Fats Navarro's 'Nostalgia', delivered as a duet with Marsalis, sounds like two parallel reflections on bebop tradition, and the ruminative pieces which open the disc include some of the trumpeter's most skilful and personalized playing. His regular band provides decisive support, but the line-up of guest stars rocks the record at some moments where it ought to be steady, and in the end this still feels like a transitional disc.

Recorded in Parker's 75th anniversary year, *Parker's Mood* is a delightful meeting of three young masters, improvising on 16 themes from Bird's repertoire. Hargrove's luminous treatment of 'Laura' provides further evidence that he may be turning into one of the music's pre-eminent ballad players, but it's the inventive interplay among the three men that takes the session to its high level: Scott, sometimes burdened by the weight of his conceptions on his own records, plays as freely as he ever has, and McBride is simply terrific.

Harlem Jazz Camels GROUP

*** **Drop Me Off In Harlem** Phontastic PHONTCD 8832
    Bent Persson (*t*); Jens Lindgren (*tb, v*); Goran Eriksson (*as*); Claes Brodda (*cl, ts, bs*); Ulf Lindberg (*p*); Goran Stachewsky (*g, bj*); Lars Lindbeck (*b*); Sigge Dellert (*d*). 1/93.

This Swedish repertory band, specializing in the small-group jazz of the 1930s, has been around long enough to have pre-dated the more fashionable interest in this area of jazz in America. The speciality of the day here is Ellington's small-unit music, which brings the likes of 'The Jeep Is Jumpin'', 'Love In My Heart', 'Back Room Romp' and 'Barney Going Easy' into the book. Persson's uncanny ability with bygone styles is becoming well known, but equally impressive here is Eriksson's stroll in Hodges' footsteps, and the congenial ensembles hit the bullseye.

Billy Harper (born 1943) TENOR SAXOPHONE, ALTO SAXOPHONE

***(*) **Capra Black** Strata East 660 51 022
  Harper; Jimmy Owens (*t*); Julian Priester, Dick Griffin (*tb*); George Cables (*p*); Reggie
  Workman (*b*); Warren Smith, Elvin Jones, Billy Cobham (*d*); Barbara Grant, Laveda Johnson,
  Gene McDaniels, Pat Robinson (*v*). 73.
***(*) **Black Saint** Black Saint 120001
  Harper; Virgil Jones (*t*); Joe Bonner (*p*); David Friesen (*b*); Malcolm Pinson (*d*). 7/75.
*** **In Europe** Soul Note 121001
  Harper; Everett Hollins (*t*); Fred Hersch (*p*); Louis Spears (*b*); Horace Arnold (*d*). 1/79.
(*) **Destiny Is Yours Steeplechase 1260
  Harper; Eddie Henderson (*t*); Francesca Tanksley (*p*); Clarence Seay (*b*); Newman Baker (*d*).
  12/89.
***(*) **Live On Tour In The Far East** Steeplechase SCCD 31311
  Harper; Eddie Henderson (*t*); Francesca Tanksley (*p*); Louis Spears (*b*); Newman T. Baker (*d*).
  4/91.
**** **Live On Tour In The Far East, Volume 2** Steeplechase SCCD 31321
  As above. 4/91.

'They told me all the hymns were born / Out of the saxophone,' Tim Buckley used to sing. Saxophonist
Billy Harper's very personal and distinctive style combines elements of bebop and of John Coltrane's
harmony with a passionate interest in gospel music. He creates on saxophone a highly emotional, almost
hymnic sound, and his compositions (such as 'Thoroughbred' and 'Priestess', which were recorded by
Gil Evans) are similarly rooted in big, strophic patterns.

The Harper discography is in better shape these days; a pity, though, that we can't cite anything released
since that's remained widely available. *Black Saint* remains the record of choice for most of his supporters (so good, they named a whole label after it), the later live stuff shouldn't be missed either.
Harper always sounds a little constrained in the studio, almost as if fearful of drifting off-mike, which
he does occasionally on the tour records; any technical quibbles are more than compensated by fiery,
intense playing.

Capra Black is very much of its time, putting much of the emphasis on experiment and on Harper's
emergence as a composer. The title-piece makes plentiful use of double time and skewed, left-field
bridges. By contrast, the other tunes are more broadly emotional. 'New Breed' is a blues which never
leaves the groove Cobham chisels out for it. 'Soulfully, I Love You' is a spiritual with voices which recalls
Andrew Hill's *Lift Every Voice And Sing*. 'Cry Of Hunger!' brings the session to a close with the leader
wailing righteously over Barbara Grant's urgent voice.

Harper kicked off not one but two important contemporary jazz labels. Joe Bonner is the key to *Black
Saint*'s success, constantly building up the fervour. The sound is excellent, a benchmark for the label as a
whole. By contrast, the Soul Note is slightly disappointing, albeit full of potential. The less than
generously exposed Everett Hollins, who has also recorded with Archie Shepp, lays joyous top lines over
Harper's Old Testament preaching and Latter-Day inflexions. There are three long tracks, of which
'Calvary' is outstanding.

As far as recording was concerned, the 1980s were a pretty quiet time for the saxophonist. Made a full
decade after *In Europe*, *Destiny Is Yours* is marred by an awkwardly mechanical rhythm section.
However, the excellent Henderson (who combines a musical career with work as a physician and a
psychiatric practice) co-operates with Harper in a way occasionally reminiscent of the Ayler brothers'
brief but intense relationship. By 1991 and the Far East tour documented on the two Steeplechases, the
band has settled down considerably. Spears is a more responsive bass player than Seay, and Tanksley has
gained hugely in confidence. Their version of 'Priestess' on *Volume 2* is definitive, and the cover of 'My
Funny Valentine' that follows it gives Henderson an opportunity to shine. Recorded a few days previously, *Volume 1* is more complex musically but far less engaging. Only 'Countdown', a tribute to John
Coltrane, seriously catches light.

Herbie Harper (born 1920) TROMBONE

*** **Five Brothers** VSOP 9
  Harper; Bob Enevoldsen (*vtb, ts*); Don Overburg (*g*); Red Mitchell (*b*); Frank Capp (*d*). 55.
*** **Two Brothers** VSOP 80
  Harper; Bill Perkins (*ts, bs, f*); Larry Koonse (*g*); John Leitham (*b*); Larance Marable (*d*). 9/89.

Harper's buttery high notes and mellifluous mid-register have been poured over countless Californian
record dates for 40 years and more. These rare excursions into the limelight are good to have in the
catalogue, though neither makes a pressing claim on the casual listener. The 1955 date is one of those

clipped West Coast schedule-fillers which succeeds in spite of itself: the two horns plait their lines together with beguiling finesse, though they don't give themselves much space – even with three alternative takes on the CD reissue, the music doesn't crack the 40-minute barrier.

A generation later, Harper revisited the same instrumentation. Koonse shares solo honours with the others, playing with great fluency, and Perkins sounds good, too. A couple of the arrangements – such as the misplaced funk of Neal Hefti's 'Fred' – are a strain. But Harper's lovely sound is a pleasure to hear all the same.

Philip Harper TRUMPET, FLUGELHORN

*** **Soulful Sin** Muse MCD 9505
> Harper; Jamal Haynes (*tb*); Javon Jackson (*ts*); Kevin Hays (*p*); Dwayne Burno (*b*); Nasheet Waits (*d*); Terry Harper (*v*). 2/93.

Never as interesting with the Harper Brothers as he proves to be as a solo artist, Philip draws on a variety of influences, from Fats to Wynton, with Clifford Brown prominent in the mix, and turns it into something refreshingly individual. These are fairly stock originals, mostly written in hard-bop clichés, but with some interesting melodic components and a constant supply of driving rhythmic material. 'Weaver Of Dreams', 'Blue Jay' and a handful more tracks benefit from the inclusion of a third horn. The rhythm section is either frantic or pipe-and-slippers, with not much modulation between the two. It would be good to hear Harper, who has had a big-label contract, working with senior players. One suspects they'd be the making of him.

Winard Harper DRUMS

*** **Be Yourself** Columbia 478197-2
> Harper; Eddie Henderson (*t*); Antonio Hart (*as*); Don Braden, David Fathead Newman (*ts*); Reuben Brown (*p*); Buster Williams (*b*). 94.

A drummer's album – though that needn't mean something bereft of writing. Some of the tunes here are unusually strong: Myron Walden's 'Night Watch' and any of the three Reuben Brown themes are good enough to stand comfortably next to Randy Weston's 'Hi Fly', and the band is very good – Henderson continues his great run, Braden's sardonic streak works well, and Hart has one of the sweetest sounds around. Newman contributes two avuncular cameos. But it's still a drummer's album: Harper's two tunes are nothing much and, though he resists the temptation to take many solos, he can't stop messing up a simple 4/4 with any number of oddball rolls and rushes. He doesn't have the authority and ingenuity of, say, Paul Motian or Joey Baron – the mix of insight and brio that would make that hyperactivity work for the music.

Tom Harrell (born 1946) TRUMPET, FLUGELHORN

*** **Moon Alley** Criss Cross 1018
> Harrell; Kenny Garrett (*as, f*); Kenny Barron (*p*); Ray Drummond (*b*); Ralph Peterson (*d*). 12/85.

(*) **Open Air Steeplechase SCCD 31220
> Harrell; Bob Rockwell (*ts*); Hal Galper (*p*); Steve Gilmore (*b*); Bill Goodwin (*d*). 5/86.

***(*) **Stories** Contemporary C 14043
> Harrell; Bob Berg (*ts*); Niels Lan Doky (*p*); John Scofield (*g*); Ray Drummond (*b*); Billy Hart (*d*). 1/88.

**** **Sail Away** Contemporary C 14054
> Harrell; Dave Liebman (*ss*); Joe Lovano (*ts*); John Abercrombie (*g, g syn*); James Williams (*p*); Ray Drummond (*b*); Adam Nussbaum (*d*). 3/89.

***(*) **Form** Contemporary C 14059
> Harrell; Joe Lovano (*ts*); Danilo Perez (*p*); Charlie Haden (*b*); Paul Motian (*d*). 4/90.

**** **Visions** Contemporary CCD 14063
> Harrell; George Robert (*as*); Joe Lovano (*ts, ss*); Bob Berg, Dave Liebman (*ss*); Cheryl Pyle (*f*); Niels Lan Doky, James Williams (*p*); John Abercrombie (*g syn*); Ray Drummond, Charlie Haden, Reggie Johnson (*b*); Bill Goodwin, Billy Hart, Paul Motian, Adam Nussbaum (*d*). 4/87, 1/88, 3/89, 4/90.

***(*) **Sail Away** Musidisc MU 500252
> Harrell; Kenny Werner (*p*); Paul Imm (*b*); André Ceccarelli (*d*). 4/91.

**** **Passages** Chesky J D 64
   Harrell; Joe Lovano (*as, ts, ss*); Danilo Perez (*p*); Peter Washington (*b*); Paul Motian (*d*); Cafe
   (*perc*). 10/91.
***(*) **Upswing** Chesky J D 103
   As above, except omit Cafe, replace Motian with Bill Goodwin (*d*); add Phil Woods (*as*). 6/93.
Though Harrell's output has been notoriously uneven, it is still difficult to pick one outstanding album
from the current catalogue. Persistent psychological problems of a more than incidental nature (though
why is it that self-doubt assails trumpeters more than almost any other musicians?) have sometimes led
him to cultivate an artificial evenness of tone which is rather off-putting. But it's worth listening hard to
Harrell for the tiny shifts of harmony and rhythmic emphasis with which he punctuates the eggshell
finish of a solo.
   Of the above, only *Open Air* falls more or less flat as an album, though it's worth hearing for the fine
lyrical interplay between the trumpeter and Galper. *Form* is an exceptionally fine album. With the
anchor of Haden and Motian – not one of your cut-price rhythm sections – Harrell sounds very secure.
   The earlier *Moon Alley* has a slightly morose quality in places, but it's probably the most rounded of the
performances, showing off Harrell's technical range to best advantage. On open trumpet, he sounds
most like Kenny Dorham, but, alongside Art Farmer and Freddie Hubbard, he is among the best
contemporary exponents of the reverse-action flugelhorn, avoiding the 'fat' sound many doubling players slip into. Harrell's natural sound has an almost keening quality that seems to come from somewhere
between Clifford Brown and Miles, two men who dealt with self-doubt in their own, very different ways.
Teamed with Kenny Garrett – one of the last of Miles's saxophone players – he sounds uncannily like a
younger Miles, slightly out of synch with the rapid progressions of 'Scrapple From The Apple'. Berg
comes from the same academy and comes across beefy and strong on *Stories*, with Scofield adding his
class to the three strongest tracks. 'Story' is a long minor-key campfire, round which all the soloists tell
their tales; Harrell's only solo is strikingly original.
   Confusingly titled, given the later Musidisc set, *Sail Away* is one of his strongest statements, revealing
Harrell to be much more than a floaty impressionist with a post-Chet grasp of ballad forms. The title-
piece, with Abercrombie in close support, and the visionary 'Glass Mystery' and tougher 'Buffalo
Wings' with Lovano are model performances.
   Visions is actually an assemblage of material from over quite a long span of time recording for
Contemporary, during which Harrell seemed to recover some of the snap and pointed delivery people
had noted during his sojourn with Horace Silver. He's on flugelhorn for much of this disc, sounding a
little distanced but never abject. Just occasionally, though, as on the otherwise atmospheric 'Visions Of
Gaudi' with Liebman and Abercrombie, there are phrases so exact and shrewd that their notes resemble
the facets of some hard stone, like those the architect studded his buildings with. 'April Mist', with
Lovano sharing the front line, is more conventional, but 'Suspended View', with Bob Berg on soprano
and Harrell back on the trumpet, restores the fleeting, uncertain quality one associates with him. A
compelling collection, beautifully selected and mastered.
   Lovano is on hand again to energize *Passages* and *Upswing* for Chesky (and who knows what personal
agony lies behind the latter title?). Woods is a revelation, too, on the later record, blending his boppish
lines with Harrell's, often scurrying in with an additional idea or a friendly gesture as the pace seems too
slow or diffuse. Motian seems the ideal drummer for this group, and he's rather missed second time
round. Against whatever odds, Harrell has demonstrated conclusively that he is one of the most gifted
and creative exponents of harmonic jazz at work today. This is now a substantial body of work, and
anyone concerned with contemporary jazz should get to grips with it.

Barry Harris (born 1929) PIANO

*** **At The Jazz Workshop** Original Jazz Classics OJC 208
   Harris; Sam Jones (*b*); Louis Hayes (*d*). 5/60.
*** **Preminado** Original Jazz Classics OJC 486
   Harris; Joe Benjamin (*b*); Elvin Jones (*d*). 12/60–1/61.
*** **Chasin' The Bird** Original Jazz Classics OJC 872
   Harris; Bob Cranshaw (*b*); Clifford Jarvis (*d*). 5/62.
The career of Barry Harris suggests a self-effacing man, for although he is among the most accom-
plished and authentic of second-generation bebop pianists, his name has never excited much more than
quiet respect among followers of the music. Musicians and students – Harris is a noted teacher – hold
him in higher esteem. One of the Detroit school of pianists, which includes Tommy Flanagan and Hank
Jones, Harris's style suggests Bud Powell as an original mentor, yet a slowed-down, considered version
of Powell's tumultuous manner. Despite the tempos, Harris gets the same dark timbres from the keyboard. He cut several records for Prestige and Riverside in the 1960s, but these are the only ones left in

the catalogue. The live date from 1960 finds him with the ebullient rhythm section of Cannonball Adderley, and the music is swinging if not especially absorbing. Rather better is the date with Elvin Jones, which features some fiery interplay between piano and drums, although the highlight is probably an uncommonly thoughtful solo reading of 'I Should Care'. *Chasin' The Bird* is a smart exercise in bebop piano, unfussy, unpretentious, but carried off with a distilled intensity that keeps the attention.

**** Live At Maybeck Recital Hall Vol. 12 Concord CCD 4476
    Harris (*p* solo). 3/90.
Very fine, and a prime example of why this series is working so well. Harris has sometimes sounded too hurried or too desultory on his solo records, but here he finds just the right pace and programme: a leisurely but not indolent stroll through bop and after, with Powell and Parker represented as composers and influences, and a lovely choice of tunes including 'Gone Again', 'Lucky Day' and 'Would You Like To Take A Walk'.

Beaver Harris (1936–91) DRUMS, PERCUSSION

**** Beautiful Africa Soul Note 121002
    Harris; Grachan Moncur III (*tb*); Ken McIntyre (*as, f, bsn*); Rahn Burton (*p*); Cameron Brown (*b*). 79.
*** Sound Compound yvp CD 3009
    Harris; Gijs Hendriks (*ts, ss, bs*); Charles Loos (*p*); Bert Van Erk (*b*). 3/86.
Harris called his group the 360° Music Experience, a title that refers to his search for a multi-perspectival and non-hierarchical approach that goes beyond styles and, to a degree, distinctions between leaders and sidemen. To a degree only, because his music is always focused on the drums, as in African performance.

    The opening track on *Beautiful Africa* is a statement of that ideal, a stately theme in 3/4 time with solo space for all the players. However, only this and a brief percussion solo, dedicated to the team at Soul Note in Milan, are written by Harris. Moncur, Burton and bassist Cameron Brown contribute material. Brown had never recorded his own work before. At the heart of his 'Baby Suite' is a wonderful duet for Moncur and McIntyre, two depressingly under-exposed musicians who demonstrate their pedigree in every bar.

    McIntyre's multi-instrumentalism is clearly in keeping with the ethos of 360° Experience. He is the only one without a composition credit, but the sheer range of sound he produces on his three horns makes him central to all the performances and recalls his own *Looking Ahead*. Moncur's fat, brassy sound is the perfect complement, and Burton moves around in modalities that are subtly shifting and uncertain, utterly consistent with Harris's own conception.

    However that might be defined, it is conspicuously missing on *Sound Compound*, which is jointly credited to the Dutch saxophonist. The disc is intermittently effective, but it has little of the hypnotic flow of *Beautiful Africa*. Anyone interested in Harris would do well to follow up his work with Archie Shepp and with the Albert Ayler ensemble which toured Europe in 1966 (see hat ART CD 6039).

Bill Harris (1916–73) TROMBONE

**** Bill Harris And Friends Original Jazz Classics OJC 083
    Harris; Ben Webster (*ts*); Jimmy Rowles (*p*); Red Mitchell (*b*); Stan Levey (*d*). 9/57.
Harris was always among the most distinctive and sometimes among the greatest of jazz trombonists. His style was based firmly on swing-era principles, yet he seemed to look both forward and back – his slurred notes and shouting phrases recalled a primitive jazz period, yet his knowing juxtapositions and almost macabre sense of humour were entirely modern. But he made few appearances on record away from Woody Herman's orchestra and is now a largely forgotten figure. This splendid session should be far more widely known. Both Harris and Webster are in admirable form and make a surprisingly effective partnership: Ben is at his ripest on 'I Surrender, Dear' and 'Where Are You', and Harris stops the show in solo after solo, whether playing short, bemused phrases or barking out high notes. A fairly hilarious reading of 'Just One More Chance' caps everything. The remastering favours the horns, but the sound is warmly effective.

Craig Harris (born 1954) TROMBONE

***(*) Black Bone Soul Note 121055
    Harris; George Adams (*ts*); Donald Smith (*p*); Fred Hopkins (*b*); Charli Persip (*d*). 1/83.

The trombone is by no means as prominent an instrument in contemporary jazz as it was in the 1940s. Nevertheless players as distinctive as Albert Mangelsdorff and Paul Rutherford in Europe, Ray Anderson, George Lewis and Craig Harris in the United States are keeping the tradition alive.

Harris plays in a strong, highly vocalized style which draws directly on the innovations of former Mingus sideman Jimmy Knepper and on players like Grachan Moncur III and Roswell Rudd who, in reaction to the trombone's recent desuetude, have gone back to the New Orleans and Dixieland traditions in an attempt to restore and revise the instrument's 'natural' idiom.

Adams is the perfect partner in any modern/traditional synthesis, and the rhythm section (Smith occasionally excepted) is rock-solid on such pieces as 'Conjure Man' and 'Song For Psychedelic Souls', which could almost have been by Roland Kirk. Excellent.

*** **Shelter** JMT 834408
> Harris; Tailgater's Tales: Eddie E. J. Allen (*t*); Don Byron (*c, bcl*); Rod Williams (*p*); Anthony Cox (*b*); Pheeroan akLaff (*d*); Tunde Samuel (*v*). 12/86.

(*) **Blackout In The Square Root Of Soul JMT 834415
> As above, except omit Williams; add Clyde Criner (*ky*); Jean-Paul Bourelly (*g*), Ralph Peterson (*d*). 11/87.

(*) **4 Play JMT 834444
> Harris; Cold Sweat: Eddie E. J. Allen (*t*); Sam Furnace (*as, bs, f*); George Adams, Booker T. Williams (*ts*); Brandon Ross, Fred Wells (*g*); Douglas Booth (*ky*); James Calloway, Melvin Gibbs (*b*); Damon Mendes (*d*); Kweyao Agyapon (*perc*); Andy Bey, Sekou Sundaita (*v*). 8/90.

The first two are credited to Harris's band, Tailgater's Tales, *4 Play* to a more recent and somewhat funkier line-up known as Cold Sweat, on which some tracks again feature George Adams's big, bawling tenor. 'Tailgating' was a trombone style popularized by Kid Ory and named after the fact that on a New Orleans bandwagon the trombonist had to sit on the back running-board to accommodate the extension of his slide. No longer limited to mere bass phrasing, Ory 'filled' round the other horns, often creating long, slithering runs up through the scale. Harris's latter-day revisions of that style take note of all sorts of other putative influences, from the European free movement to Fred Wesley's brass arrangements for James Brown.

Tailgater's Tales are a superb live band who have never quite lived up to promise on disc. AkLaff's drumming is as good as always, but there's a slight vagueness of conception (particularly on *Blackout*) which is hard to shake off.

***(*) **F-Stops** Soul Note 121255
> Harris; John Stubblefield (*ts*); Hamiet Bluiett (*bs*); Bill White (*g*); Darrell Grant (*p, ky*); Calvin Jones (*b*); Tony Lewis (*d*). 6/93.

A fascinating interconnected suite of themes and observations, realized by the best band Harris has had in a decade, if one leaves aside the more mainstream/crossover Tailgater's Tales. Using trombone and didjeridu, he conjures up dark, roiling shapes that confirm his growing interest in John Coltrane's music. Bluiett is the ideal partner in this enterprise and Stubblefield, having done some similar things as a dep with the World Saxophone Quartet and on his own account, seems absolutely across the music.

Eddie Harris (born 1934) TENOR SAX, KEYBOARDS, TRUMPET, VOCAL

*** **The Electrifying Eddie Harris / Plug Me In** Rhino/Atlantic R2 71516
> Harris; Melvin Lastie, Jimmy Owens, Joe Newman, James Bossy (*t*); Garnett Brown, Tom McIntosh (*tb*); King Curtis, David Newman (*ts*); Haywood Henry (*bs*); Jodie Christian (*p*); Chuck Rainey, Ron Carter, Melvin Jackson (*b*); Richard Smith, Grady Tate (*d*); Ray Barretto, Joe Wohletz (*perc*). 4/67–3/68.

***(*) **Artist's Choice: The Eddie Harris Anthology** Rhino/Atlantic R2 71514 2CD
> As above, except add Ray Codrington, Don Ellis, Benny Bailey (*t*); Willie Pickens, Cedar Walton, Muhal Richard Abrams, Milcho Leviev, Les McCann (*p*); Ronald Muldrow, Joe Diorio (*g*); Leroy Vinnegar, Rufus Reid, Bradley Bobo (*b*); Billy Higgins, Billy James, Billy Hart, Harold Jones, Donald Dean, Paul Humphrey (*d*); Felix Henry, Marshall Thompson (*perc*). 1/61–2/76.

There's nothing amiss with Harris's command of the tenor saxophone. But he spent most of his first ten years on record experimenting with electric saxes, trumpets played with sax mouthpieces and other gimmicks, with varying levels of success. The *Artist's Choice* compilation picks tracks from 16 albums, the best of them making a good case for Harris's eminence: he's no genius improviser, and many a solo seems to get too pooped to continue, but he had a knack for making simple licks and phrases fit on shuffling, boogaloo rhythms and have it all sound great. There's a surprisingly extravagant range to his music: the straight-ahead post-bop of 'Freedom Jazz Dance', pretty pop-jazz with 'The Shadow Of

Your Smile', a growling big-band chart in '1974 Blues', the knockout funk of 'Is It In' and the ragbag electric sax treatment of 'Giant Steps'. Much of it sounds hopelessly dated in the age of digital keyboards, but that only adds to the charm of Harris's futurism. The indivdial albums from the period are a patchy lot, evidenced by the two-in-one reissue on the second disc: the tracks from *The Electrifying Eddie Harris* are often hot stuff, especially the choogling 'Sham Time', but those from *Plug Me In* are more like a downright mess, the sax hollering against the brass to little purpose.

** People Get Funny . . . Timeless SJP 228
Harris; William S. Henderson III (*ky, perc*); Larry Gales (*b*); Carl Burnett (*d*).
** Eddie Who? Timeless SJP 244
Harris; Ralph Armstrong (*b, v*); Sherman Ferguson (*d, v*). 2/86.
Harris's career got off to such an explosive start in commercial terms – his 'Theme From Exodus' sold in the millions in 1961 – that the subtext of much of his later work seems to be of the order of why-can't-I-sell-more? At least on the title-track of *Eddie Who?* he gets some fun out of it. Both these records suffer from the leader's modest attention-span: on the earlier disc, he switches from alto to tenor to electric sax to piano to clavinet and then sings a little, and on the 1986 session he works through some strong material with the same diffuse results. Frankly, these are hardly worth bothering with.

*** There Was A Time (Echo Of Harlem) Enja 6068
Harris; Kenny Barron (*p*); Cecil McBee (*b*); Ben Riley (*d*). 5/90.
At last, Harris produces a concentrated tenor-and-rhythm date, and the results are good enough to make you wonder why he wastes his time on the other music. There's a courageous solo reading of 'The Song Is You', but the rest is adeptly supported by the no-nonsense rhythm team and, although Harris's rubbery tone and pinched expressiveness won't be to all tastes, there's no denying his energy.

**(*) For You, For Me, For Evermore Steeplechase SCCD 31322
Harris (*ts, p*). 10/92.
The idea was to do a duo session with another pianist but, when the second musician never turned up, Harris volunteered to set down his own piano parts first. While he's scarcely a dunce at the keyboard, having played professional piano in the past, the impromptu nature of the date forbade much preparation, too many of the pieces sound hesitant and the 'dialogue' is clumsily realized. There are some beguiling passages, and Harris's tenor tone is taking on a querulous, affecting frailty, but this is no solo masterwork.

**(*) Listen Here! Enja 7079-2
Harris; Ronald Muldrow (*g*); Ray Peterson (*b*); Norman Fearrington (*d*). 11/92.
Harris's brand of funky jazz still has plenty of potency in it, despite an apparent frailty of health. On record, the music loses much of its grit and snap: what endures is the easy-going intimacy of the Harris groove. It helps that old buddy Ronald Muldrow is back on the team here, and they remake 'Funkaroma' from the great *Is It In* (still unreissued by Atlantic) to start the session off. But too much of the music is merely OK.

Gene Harris (born 1933) PIANO

*** Gene Harris Trio Plus One Concord CCD 4303
Harris; Stanley Turrentine (*ts*); Ray Brown (*b*); Mickey Roker (*d*). 11–12/85.
*** Listen Here! Concord CCD 4385
Harris; Ron Eschete (*g*); Ray Brown (*b*); Jeff Hamilton (*d*). 3/89.
After many years with The Three Sounds, Gene Harris has assumed a wider reputation in the last ten years via his work for Concord, specifically with big bands. These small-band dates are good in their way – simply resolved light blues on the second record, a handful of standards on the first with Turrentine sitting in – but polish and good taste tend to stand in for genuine excitement. Brown, Tucker and Hamilton can certainly cover their tasks here without having to try very hard. But it's agreeable enough to service those moments when the last thing one wants on the sound-system is some monumental masterwork. Turrentine sounds like his now sensible, middle-aged self on *Trio Plus One*.

*** Tribute To Count Basie Concord CCD 4337
Harris; Jon Faddis, Snooky Young, Conte Candoli, Frank Szabo, Bobby Bryant (*t*); Charles Loper, Bill Watrous, Thurman Green, Garnett Brown (*tb*); Bill Reichenbach (*btb*); Marshall Royal, Bill Green, Jack Kelso (*as*); Bob Cooper, Plas Johnson (*ts*); Jack Nimitz (*bs*); Herb Ellis (*g*); James Leary III, Ray Brown (*b*); Jeff Hamilton (*d*). 3–6/87.
*** Live At Town Hall, N.Y.C. Concord CCD 4397
Harris; Joe Mosello, Harry 'Sweets' Edison, Michael Philip Mossman, Johnny Coles (*t*); Eddie

Bert, Urbie Green, James Morrison (*tb*); Paul Faulise (*btb*); Jerry Dodgion, Frank Wess (*as, f*); James Moody (*ts, cl, f*); Ralph Moore (*ts*); Herb Ellis (*g*); Ray Brown (*b*); Jeff Hamilton (*d*); Ernestine Anderson, Ernie Andrews (*v*). 9/89.

*** **World Tour 1990** Concord CCD 4443

Harris; Johnny Morrison (*t, flhn*); Harry 'Sweets' Edison, Joe Mosello, Glenn Drewes (*t*); Urbie Green, George Bohannon, Robin Eubanks (*tb*); Paul Faulise (*btb*); Jeff Clayton, Jerry Dodgion (*as, f*); Plas Johnson (*ts, f*); Ralph Moore (*ts*); Gary Smulyan (*bs*); Kenny Burrell (*g*); Ray Brown (*b*); Harold Jones (*d*). 10/90.

Like the latter-day records of such bandleaders as Basie and Herman, these discs tend to be enjoyable more for their gold-plated class and precision than for any special inventiveness. The first session, credited to Gene Harris and The All Star Big Band, is, in those circumstances, a very truthful kind of tribute to Basie's band, the eight charts offering a fair approximation of the familiar sound. The two discs by the later bands – now known as The Philip Morris Superband – are, we find, rather more entertaining. The *Town Hall* set boasts a vast digital presence, the brass particularly bright and all the soloists well catered for, but some may find its showbiz atmosphere less than ingratiating. Andrews and Anderson have some enjoyable vehicles and there are appropriately outgoing solos from Edison, Ellis, Dodgion and others. *World Tour 1990* reprises the situation, with a somewhat different cast but much the same atmosphere.

*** **At Last** Concord CCD 4434

Harris; Scott Hamilton (*ts*); Herb Ellis (*g*); Ray Brown (*b*); Harold Jones (*d*). 5/90.

*** **Black & Blue** Concord CCD 4482

Harris; Ron Eschete (*g*); Luther Hughes (*b*); Harold Jones (*d*). 6/91.

(*) **Like A Lover Concord CCD 4526

As above. 1/92.

*** **At Maybeck Recital Hall** Concord CCD 4536

Harris (*p* solo). 8/92.

*** **A Little Piece Of Heaven** Concord CCD 4578

Harris; Ron Eschete (*g*); Luther Hughes (*b*); Paul Humphrey (*d*). 7/93.

*** **Funky Gene's** Concord CCD 4609

As above. 5/94.

*** **Brotherhood** Concord CCD 4640

As above. 8/92.

Scott Hamilton's unwavering consistency is somewhat akin to Harris's own, but the tenorman has a slightly greater capacity to surprise and, while the material could have stood a couple of less familiar inclusions, the quintet plays with great gusto on *At Last*. Even 'You Are My Sunshine' is listenable. *Black & Blue* introduces a new Harris group: Eschete returns on guitar, but Hughes and Jones are first-timers, and they dig into the programme – dependent on traditional blues of the order of 'C C Rider' – with the same infectious enthusiasm as Harris. *Like A Lover* continues along the same path, but the ballads sound almost soppy in comparison with the upbeat tunes – Harris wasn't made to be tenderized. *A Little Piece Of Heaven* restores order by dropping the group into a live situation. This must be one of the most rollicking treatments of 'Take The "A" Train' on record, and there are somewhat bacchanalian treatments of 'Old Dog Blues' and 'Blues For Ste Chapelle' (appropriately, since this is one of Concord's live-at-the-winery dates). Harris is always going to end up making the same record, but so far it still sounds pretty good.

His entry in the Maybeck Recital Hall series is typically straight-ahead and without frills. There are four more blues in the programme, but this time the ballads don't seem quite so ponderously tender, and he is assuredly enjoying himself throughout.

The two latest Concords (*Brotherhood* apparently dates from 1992 but didn't get a release until '95) continue a solid if scarcely arresting run. *Funky Gene's* is comfortably in the usual pocket and, although 'Children Of Sanchez' is a mistaken choice, most of the tunes fit Harris like his favourite tuxedo. *Brotherhood* is pretty much the same. Eschete's solo on 'I Remember You' makes one sit up and wish that perhaps he had more space than he usually gets; Harris, on the other hand, has never sounded more swinging than he does on Frank Loesser's 'The Brotherhood Of Man'. If you have some Gene Harris albums already, you probably won't need this one, but it's still a very good place to start.

Kevin Bruce Harris BASS

(*) **Kevin Harris & Militia TipToe 807102

Harris; Rod Williamson (*ky*); David Gilmore (*g*); Victor Jones (*d, v*); David Silliman (*perc*); D. K. Dyson (*v*). 1/89.

*** **Folk Songs – Folk Tales** TipToe 888807-2
  Harris; Steve Wilson (*as, ss*); Uri Caine (*ky*); Ralph Peterson (*d*). 4/93.
Harris has frequently worked with Cassandra Wilson and Steve Coleman, and he sounds well versed in
the now-familiar M-Base genre which their early music represents. His own offering is an oddball
gathering of ideas and, like so many other such records, it is more a sampler of his interests than a
coherent set. But there are humorous, clever pieces such as 'Revenge Of The Elephants', along with
bruising funk and the kind of dreamy mood-pieces which end up as ballad substitutes. *Folk Songs – Folk
Tales* is altogether tougher and more 'played': Harris tends to be unsure whether he wants to play jazztime or funk rhythms, but Peterson just plays every kind of time anyway and, with Wilson tossing out
hot solos and the splendid Caine running the middle ground, this is the kind of band you'd like to see
anywhere.

Donald Harrison (born 1960) ALTO SAXOPHONE, SOPRANO SAXOPHONE, BASS CLARINET

*** **Full Circle** Sweet Basil 660 55 003
  Harrison; Cyrus Chestnut (*p*); Mark Whitfield (*g*); Dwayne Burno (*b*); Carl Allen (*d*). 5/90.
*** **For Art's Sake** Candid CCD 79501
  Harrison; Marlon Jordan (*t*); Cyrus Chestnut (*p*); Christian McBride (*b*); Carl Allen (*d*). 11/90.
Donald 'Duck' Harrison is part of that generation of young New Orleanians who grew up round
Wynton Marsalis but, in the young saxophonist's case, subsequently followed a rather more radical
path. Harrison studied under Ellis Marsalis and Alvin Batiste; but his playing is coloured by an
exposure to more modernist styles (see the Dolphy project with Terence Blanchard, below). He was a
notably radical influence in the Jazz Messengers, pushing that bastion of hard bop (probably) as far as it
has ever been in the direction of harmonic freedom. His 1982 piece, 'New York Second Line', was a
deliberate attempt to fuse contemporary sounds with the traditions of New Orleans jazz.
  Ironically then (unless that's what the title means) *Full Circle* is a much more traditionally-minded
album. Harrison's own playing is still pretty hot and occasionally wayward, but by and large he sticks to
a language that would be familiar to players of the bebop generation. As if to date-stamp the session,
Charlie Parker's 'My Little Suede Shoes' receives prominent attention at the top of the disc, coming
after Harrison's own warm-up, 'The Force'. Other standards include 'Bye, Bye Blackbird', 'Nature Boy'
and 'Good Morning Heartache'; all three show signs of having come right back round to the old style in
jazz. Carl Allen's 'Evidence Of Things Not Seen' is perhaps the most radical composition, written and
introduced in a resonant, slightly stark C minor. Chestnut, as always, gives a flawless performance, most
prominently on 'Nature Boy', where he sounds as though he's still backing a singer. Harrison's own
solos are less than completely satisfying and one or two of them sound a little foreshortened, as if
cosmetic editing has been done at the mixing stage. All in all, though, a satisfactory performance.
  For Art's Sake is a classic instance of a leader being upstaged by his sidemen. Harrison has assembled a
powerful young band (bassist McBride was only eighteen) who know the tradition inside out and are
ready to chip in with their own contributions. Chestnut's semi-eponymous 'Nut' follows on from the
opening 'So What'; the pianist turns in a beautifully sculpted and quite formal solo, prising apart the
rhythm (as Allen does in his short, staccato interlude) and laying out the workings to see. Harrison gives
most of the opening statements to the nineteen-year-old Jordan, a rawer version of Wynton Marsalis,
and really comes into his own only on his featured 'In A Sentimental Mood', which he gradually cranks
up from a melancholy ballad into a funky swinger. Offered as 'proof' that 'hard bop is the basis of '90s
jazz', *For Art's Sake* does no more than confirm that there are still lots of youngsters around who are
willing to take it on. Which isn't quite the same thing.

*** **Indian Blues** Candid CCD 79514
  Harrison; Cyrus Chestnut, Mac Rebennack (Dr John) (*p, v*); Phil Bowler (*b, v*); Carl Allen (*d, v*);
  Bruce Cox, Howard Smiley Ricks (*perc, v*); Donald Harrison Sr (*v*). 5/91.
A startling mixture of direct hard bop and Fat Tuesday vocal histrionics. Harrison Sr has been Big
Chief of four Mardi Gras Indian 'tribes' and is currently leader of Guardians of the Flame, who also
feature on the album. 'Hiko Hiko' and 'Two-Way-Pocky-Way' are traditional chants (the former is
credited to the legendary Black Johnny); 'Ja-Ki-Mo-Fi-Na-Hay' and the opening 'Hu-Ta-Nay' are
credited to the Harrisons. Dr John sings and plays piano on the two originals, sings on Professor
Longhair's 'Big Chief' and plays piano on 'Walkin' Home' and Big Chief Jolly's 'Shave 'Em Dry'.
  If it's part of Harrison's intention to reflect the continuity of the black music tradition, he does so very
convincingly, and there's no sense of a break between the densely rhythmic N'w'Orleans numbers with
their chattering percussion and the more orthodox 'jazz' tracks. He plays 'Indian Red' pretty much as a
straight alto feature, but then adds a rhythmic line to the prototypical standard 'Cherokee' that gives it
an entirely new dimension. His own 'Indian Blues' and 'Uptown Ruler' reflect a decision in 1989 to

'mask Indian' once again and joined the feathered throngs that march on Mardi Gras. In touching his roots, he's brought them something new as well.

Nancy Harrow VOCAL

**(*) Wild Women Don't Have The Blues Candid CCD 79008
 Harrow; Buck Clayton (*t*); Dicky Wells (*tb*); Tommy Gwaltney (*cl, as*); Buddy Tate (*ts*); Danny Bank (*bs*); Dick Wellstood (*p*); Kenny Burrell (*g*); Milt Hinton (*b*); Oliver Jackson (*d*). 11/60.
*** Secrets Soul Note 121233-2
 Harrow; Clark Terry (*t, flhn, v*); Dick Katz (*p*); Ray Drummond (*b*); Ben Riley (*d*). 11/90–1/91.
*** Lost Lady Soul Note 121263-2
 Harrow; Phil Woods (*cl, as*); Dick Katz (*p*); Ray Drummond (*b*); Ben Riley (*d*); Vernel Bagnaris (*v*). 6–11/93.

With her grown-up kewpie-doll voice, Harrow sounds like an improbable choice as 'wild woman', but the 1960 album is abetted by the excellent Buck Clayton group and the musicians play the blues even when Harrow herself doesn't quite approximate them. Thirty years on, and with many out-of-print records in between, she sounds much the same, but wiser, and wittier – five of the songs are her own, and she has a good eye for an irony or a romantic folly. Her voice remains something of an acquired taste, but Terry is as beguiling as usual – they do a pretty hilarious duet on 'Hit The Road Jack' – and the rhythm section are in great shape. Sample the duet between the singer and Ray Drummond on 'So Why Am I Surprised?' and you may find yourself hooked. *Lost Lady* is a repeat meeting with the rhythm section, but this time Phil Woods steps in for Terry. Harrow builds the record round a sequence of songs which follow the story of a novella by Willa Cather, *A Lost Lady*, with Bagneris as the male voice in the story. Whatever the concept, she continues in a vein of wistful but self-aware reflection which the musicians slip into very comfortably and, though Bagneris doesn't always sound at ease, it's effective in a low-key way.

Antonio Hart (born 1969) ALTO SAXOPHONE

*** For The First Time Novus PD 83120
 Hart; Roy Hargrove, Thomas Williams (*t*); Billy Pierce (*ts*); Mulgrew Miller (*p*); Christian McBride (*b*); Lewis Nash (*d*). 2–4/91.
**(*) Don't You Know I Care Novus 41631422
 Hart; Darren Barrett (*t*); Jamal Haynes (*tb*); Gary Bartz (*as*); Aaron Graves (*p*); Rodney Whitaker (*b*); Gregory Hutchinson (*d*); Kimati Dinizulu (*perc*). 92.
*** For Cannonball And Woody Novus 4131622
 Hart; Darren Barrett (*t*); Nat Adderley (*c*); Steve Turre, Robin Eubanks, Slide Hampton (*tb*); Mark Gross (*as*); Craig Handy (*ts*); Carlos McKinney, Mulgrew Miller (*p*); Omar Avital, Ray Drummond (*b*); Jimmy Cobb (*d*). 92.
**(*) It's All Good Novus 4163183
 Hart; Darren Barrett (*t, syn*); Robin Eubanks (*tb*); Gary Thomas (*ts*); Carlos McKinney (*p*); Steve Nelson (*vib*); Collin Barrett, Tassili Bond (*b*); Nasheet Waits (*d, bell*); Andrew Daniels (*perc*); strings. 95.

These are rather premature sets by a young player who still hasn't settled into a recognizable style of his own. Hart has sounded far better on other people's discs, not least those of label-mate Roy Hargrove, who at least has a distinctive, if rather obvious, signature. He takes one guest spot on the debut, which otherwise settles for the graceful if anonymous Thomas Williams on trumpet; Pierce plays some of his usual gutsy tenor, and the rhythm section is first class. There are some good blowing tunes, but Hart's own themes are unremarkable.

On *Don't You Know I Care* there's lots of energy but not much focus, and the band is uniformly drab. The one bright spot is Gary Bartz's guest appearance on 'At The Closet Inn'. In half a dozen bars he blows the young pretender out of the studio.

The two most recent records see Hart casting about for a context and a 'peg'. The tribute album gives him both and spurs him to some of his most thoughtful playing. The company of Cannonball's brother and several musicians associated with Woody Shaw seems to help, but there is still a rather intermittent focus, a sense that Hart is not equally engaged all the time, but is drifting in and out. *It's All Good* is his attempt to get down to street level and do something contemporary and relevant. All that emerges is a mish-mash of styles and a heavily over-produced gumbo of effects and overlays. Not a happy album, and a digression from this young developer's rather stop-start progress.

Billy Hart (born 1940) DRUMS

(*) Amethyst Arabesque AJ 01505
    Hart; John Stubblefield (*ts, ss*); David Kikoski (*p*); Marc Copland (*ky*); Mark Feldman (*vn*);
    David Fiuszynski (*g*); Santi Debriano (*b*). 93.

Like many drummers, Hart has a huge number of recording credits, but very few records of his own.
However, his solo career does go back almost 20 years to the mid-'70s *Enhance* on A & M, and it surely
isn't too much to expect something a little more adventurous than this drab, head-and-solos work-out.
There are redeeming features, including some of Hart's fills and solos but, by and large it's an extremely
forgettable piece of work.

Johnny Hartman (1923–83) VOCALS

***(*) I Just Dropped By To Say Hello** Impulse! IMP 11762
    Hartman; Illinois Jacquet (*ts*); Hank Jones (*p*); Kenny Burrell, Jim Hall (*g*); Milt Hinton (*b*); ·
    Elvin Jones (*d*). 10/63.
*** **The Voice That Is!** Impulse! GRP 11442
    Hartman; Dick Hafer (*reeds*); Phil Krauss (*mar*); Bob Hammer (*p*); Howard Collins, Barry
    Galbraith (*g*); Richard Davis (*b*); Osie Johnson (*d*); Willie Rodriguez (*perc*). 9/64.

Until recently, Hartman owed his small corner in the awareness of modern-jazz fans to his role in Bob
Thiele's attempt to prettify John Coltrane by having him work with a singer. It was a relatively successful
experiment on its own terms but it did tend to obscure Hartman's own achievement. Possessed of a rich,
full baritone, somewhere between Nat Cole and Al Hibbler, Hartman had the ability to caress even a
banal lyric into shape, infusing it not so much with emotion as with a sort of intelligence. He was a
graceful interpreter of ballads particularly, and both these albums succeed in direct ratio to the success
of the slower songs. The earlier of the pair is enhanced by the musicians, while on the second they fulfil a
pretty workmanlike function. Listen to Jones's accomaniment on 'Stairway To The Stars' and the
Sinatra-associated 'Wee Small Hours Of The Morning' for a sense of how invaluable he could be to a
singer. Nothing of that power on the later record, but both will appeal greatly to fans of vocal jazz, who
should take an opportunity to catch up with this neglected artist.

Mark Harvey Aardvark Jazz Orchestra GROUP

***(*) Aardvark Steps Out** Nine Winds NWCD 0155
    Mark Harvey (*t, p*); Mike Peipman, Frank London, Jeanne Snodgrass, Raj Mehta (*t*); Bob
    Pilkington, Jay Keyser, Jeff Marsanskis (*tb*); Marshall Sealy (*frhn*); Arni Cheatham, Peter
    Bloom, Tom Hall, Phil Scarff, Brad Jones, Vinny Golia (*reeds*); Rick Nelson (*g*); Diana Herold
    (*vib*); Ken Filiano, Joe Higgins, Brian McCree (*b*); Jerry Edwards (*b, v*); Harry Wellott (*d*); Craig
    Ellis (*perc*); Donna Hewitt-Didham (*v*). 4–8/91.
(***) **Paintings For Jazz Orchestra** Leo Lab 014
    As above, except add K. C. Dunbar (*t*), John Patton (*frhn*), Eric Hipp, Joel Springer (*reeds*),
    John Funkhauser (*b, p*); omit Peipman, London, Mehta, Golia, Herold, Higgins, McCree. 4/93–
    4/94.

Intriguing big-band music from the Boston underground, masterminded by Harvey who's been running
the group on and off for 20 years. His writing on *Aardvark Steps Out* ransacks various disciplines and
forms, with huge, prodigious pieces juxtaposed with single ideas: 'Mutant Trumpets' is a brief brass
feature, 'A Zippy Manifesto' is a 24-minute sprawl that is actually an episode from a work called
'American Zen', which Harvey describes as 'much larger'! Blues and impressionistic pieces touch base
with jazz scoring traditions, but the ideas are opened out by an adventurous team of soloists, and the
gospel chords and celebratory union of 'Blue Sequence' bring about a rousing climax. It's a pity that the
sometimes cloudy sound doesn't do the Orchestra full justice. That problem is exacerbated by *Paintings*,
which comes in fidelity that isn't much above bootleg quality. This is a critical weakness, since Harvey
and his team put so much into detail and texture – and it's pretty poor for a record made in the 1990s
anyway. Harvey's admiration for the twin poles of Ellington and Ives remains well served by the
Orchestra across two more sprawling works and, despite the numerous interesting solo contributions,
it's the band that counts. But next time someone should record them in a decent studio.

Michael Hashim ALTO AND SOPRANO SAXOPHONES

**** Lotus Blossom Stash ST-CD-533
> Hashim; Mike Le Donne (*p*); Dennis Irwin (*b*); Kenny Washington (*d*). 90.

*** A Blue Streak Stash ST-CD-546
> Hashim; Mike Le Donne (*org*); Peter Bernstein (*g*); Kenny Washington (*d*). 91.

*** Transatlantic Airs 33 Records 023
> Hashim; David Newton (*p*); Dave Green (*b*); Clark Tracey (*d*); Tina May (*v*). 11/94.

Hashim is that rarity, a passionate, humorous and quick-witted repertory player. His alto recalls Hodges, Carter and Willie Smith without placing himself entirely in anyone's debt, and his sound and phrasing have a mercurial, breezy assurance. From the opening measures of 'Grievin'', from *Lotus Blossom*, which is entirely dedicated to Billy Strayhorn themes, it's clear that the material is at Hashim's service rather than the other way around. He has often worked with the Widespread Depression/Jazz Orchestra and sounds entirely at home with pre-bop material: the excellently produced first record captures his rich timbre with eloquent clarity, and his quartet – especially the outstanding Washington – shadow him with exact aplomb. Since *Lotus Blossom* is so consistently delivered, honouring Strayhorn's familiar pieces and refurbishing such lesser-known ones as 'Juniflip' and 'Sunset And The Mockingbird', it's easily the superior record. *A Blue Streak* is slightly disappointing, with Hashim turning to more bop-directed music on some tracks: Le Donne's switch to organ, on which he doesn't have much to say, is another drawback, as is the somewhat bass-heavy sound. But tracks such as a fine soprano reading of 'Brother, Can You Spare A Dime?' are still substantial.

Transatlantic Airs catches him on one of his visits to England and in the context of a British rhythm section. Hashim sounds as good as ever, with a very fine meditation on 'Love Song' from Weill's *Threepenny Opera* as the standout. The local team aren't truly a match for the Americans, but it's a record that holds the attention.

*** Guys And Dolls Stash ST-CD-558
> As above, except Peter Washington (*b*) replaces Bernstein. 5/92.

The concept this time is Frank Loesser's musical. Hashim is on bumptious form on the up-tempo numbers and he plays the ballad, 'I'll Know', with great tenderness: unfussily done, it's closely reminiscent of countless similar projects that filled jazz recording dates in the late 1950s and early '60s. The one to start with, though, remains the Strayhorn album.

George Haslam BARITONE SAXOPHONE, TAROGATO

*** 1989 – And All That Slam CD 301
> Haslam; Paul Rutherford (*tb*). 4/89.

*** Level Two Slam CD 303
> Haslam; Paul Rutherford (*tb*); Howard Riley (*p*); Marcio Mattos (*b*); Tony Marsh (*d*); Liz Hodgson (*d*). 6/92.

A relatively late starter on the saxophone, Haslam was quick to see the potential of free or spontaneous music. The solos and duos on the record with Rutherford are, with the exception of a surprisingly subtle solo baritone version of Ellington's 'Come Sunday', improvised without predetermined structure. The record launched Haslam's own label, an operation which broadly reflects the range of his musical interests.

He has continued to play in a more conventional jazz context, concentrating largely on West Coast material and, like other British free players, has shown a strong awareness of folk forms. The name of his regular improvising group, Level Two, reflects an interest in performance that falls between the realization of scored compositions – level one – and complete abstraction – level three. If Riley introduces a strong compositional element, Rutherford is again on hand to prevent the music drifting into a settled groove or fixed direction. Mattos and Marsh impart a constantly unpredictable swing, while Haslam himself and (on two tracks only) singer Hodgson provide a vigorous melodic focus that cements the interplay of otherwise disparate elements.

Haslam's baritone has the husky uncertainty of pitch one expects of a folk instrument, and in some respects the tarogato (a Hungarian instrument of parallel antiquity to the saxophone) is the horn that provides his definitive voice. Its graininess is ideally suited to the open-ended songs and quasi-pastoral themes on *Level Two*.

***(*) Argentine Adventures Slam CD 304
> Haslam; Enrique Norris (*t*); Daniel Harari (*ts*); Ruben Ferrero (*p*); Quique Sinesi (*g*); Pablo Blasich, Mono Hurtado (*b*); Horacio López, Sergio Urtubei (*d*); Fernando Barragan, Tim Short, Horacio Straijer (*perc*); Mirta Insaurralde (*v*). 3 & 12/91, 8/93.

This is a fascinating document. Haslam was the first British jazz musician to play in Argentina (and, earlier, in Cuba) and he has kept up contacts and a working association with musicians there. When plans to take his regular quintet fell through, Haslam went as a single. The first track is an unaccompanied tarogato solo. Thereafter, however, the album consists of collaborations with Argentinian players, tracing Haslam's exploration of forms like the elegiac *vidala* – sung by Insaurralde – and rhythms like the *malambo* and *carnavalito*. The session ends with a remarkable trio performance of John Coltrane's 'Affirmation', for saxophones and bass, with Paulucci also adding a vocal component. Highly recommended.

Ake 'Stan' Hasselgård (1922–48) CLARINET

*** **At Click 1948** Dragon DRCD 183
        Hasselgård; Benny Goodman (*cl*); Wardell Gray (*ts*); Teddy Wilson (*p*); Billy Bauer (*g*); Arnold Fishkind (*b*); Mel Zelnick (*d*). 5–6/48.
***(*) **The Permanent Hasselgård** Phontastic NCD 8802
        As above, except add Tyree Glenn (*tb*), Red Norvo, Allen Johansson (*vib*), Thore Swanerud (*p, vib*), Hasse Eriksson, Lyman Gandee (*p*), Sten Carlberg (*g*), Rollo Garberg, Jud DeNaut (*b*), Uffe Baadh, Nick Fatool (*d*); Louise Tobin (*v*). 10/45–11/48.

Stan Hasselgård left only a handful of legitimate recordings at the time of his death – he was killed in a car accident while driving to California – but the diligence of Lars Westin of Dragon Records in Sweden has ensured that his legacy has been enriched by many airshots and private records. There is something like five CDs' worth of material to be issued. So far, Dragon has issued four LPs which have effectively disappeared from print, but the *At Click* CD begins a programme of CD transfers, and the Phontastic release covers the broad spectrum of the clarinettist's work.

His precocious talent and early death have made Hasselgård something of a folk hero in Swedish jazz circles, and the evidence of the surviving tracks is that he was an outstanding player. He worshipped Goodman and never tried to evade comparisons with his guru, but the traces of bebop in his playing hint at a stylistic truce which he never had the opportunity to develop further. The Goodman septet, which featured Hasselgård, is comprehensively covered on *At Click*, where the Swede worked with his idol in a two-week engagement. The contrast between the two players isn't as interesting as the similarity: often it's quite hard to tell them apart, and whatever Hasselgård is reputed to have taught Goodman about bop isn't clear from this music. In fact, Hasselgård often gets short shrift in these tracks, with Goodman getting the lion's share of the solos, and Gray and Wilson taking their share. But it's surprising to hear Goodman playing on the likes of 'Mary's Idea' and even 'Donna Lee'. The sound varies, but the meticulous remastering has done the best possible job.

Anyone wanting a one-disc primer on Hasselgård, though, is directed to the Phontastic compilation, which includes many of the tracks on the earlier Dragon releases as well as four fine quintet tracks led by the clarinettist (in excellent sound), a feature for Tyree Glenn and a sextet track with Red Norvo. A generously filled and respectful memorial to a fine player.

Fritz Hauser DRUMS, PERCUSSION

***(*) **Zwei** hat Art 6010
        Hauser; duos with Christy Doran (*g*); Stephan Grieder (*p*); Rob Kloet (*perc*); Rene Krebs (*stereo flhn, seashell*); Lauren Newton (*v*); Pauline Oliveros (*acc, elec environment*). 12/87.
*** **Die Trommel / Die Welle** hat Art 6017
        Hauser (*d* solo) and with: Michel Erni, Roli Fischer, Barbara Frey, Martin Andre Grutter, Fran Lorkovic, Cyril Lutzelschwab, Lukas Rohner, Severin Steinhauser, Hans Ulrich, Ruud Weiner (*perc*). 11/87, 11/88.
**** **Solodrumming** hat Art 6023 2CD
        Hauser (*d* solo). 4/85.
*** **The Mirror** hat Art 6037
        Hauser; Stephan Grieder (*org*). 3/89.
*** **Pensieri Bianchi** hat Art CD 6067
        Hauser (*perc* solo). 5/90.
(****) **2 2 1 3 2 4 3 4 1 4 1** sound aspects sas cd 053
        As above. 94.

Percussion-only and even percussion-led albums often make excessive demands on the listener. There are probably only a handful of drummer-percussionists active today – Andrew Cyrille, Edward Vesala, John Bergamo, Gerry Hemingway, Tony Oxley – who really are worth listening to on their own. Hauser is certainly one of that number.

His music is unapologetically abstract, but it is by no means undynamic. 'Dog's Night', his long duo with fellow-percussionist Rob Kloet on *Zwei*, is one of the most exciting improvisatory performances of recent years. Indeed, *Zwei* as a whole can't be recommended too strongly. Hauser has selected his partners with care. Guitarist Doran and flugelhorn-player Krebs are in places a little too light in touch, but in general all the participants are wonderfully complementary. Pauline Oliveros – along with the Australian Eric Gross the most significant composer of accordion music in the West – is at her very best on 'La Chambre Obscure', playing 'in' an electro-acoustic environment devised by Peter Ward.

The most conventional structures are those devised with pianist Grieder, whose church-organ figures on *The Mirror* would be more compelling had they been more sympathetically recorded. Otherwise an excellent album, and it should be listened to alongside the more relaxed *Pensieri Bianchi*, which is the most accessible of the unaccompanied discs.

Hauser's solo work is uniquely impressive. The massive double-CD, *Solodrumming*, is an exhausting experience but affords the best available representation of his technical range. Those unfamiliar with his work might do better to start with '*Die Trommel*' and its remarkable percussion-choir partner, '*Die Welle*' – 'The Drum' and 'The Wave'. The latter features timpani, cymbals and tam-tam in an extraordinary exploration of resonance that equals the best percussion pieces by 'serious' composers like Xenakis. Our only reason for qualifying enthusiasm for the oddly titled – or numbered – sound aspects disc is that it consists of composed pieces written for Hauser by a range of modernists including Bun-Ching Lam, John Cage, fellow-percussionists Joey Baron and Pierre Favre, Pauline Oliveros and Franz Koglmann, eleven in all.

Almost needless to repeat, Hauser comes highly recommended and shouldn't on any account be missed, especially if the account is some qualm about these not being jazz records in any strict sense.

Hampton Hawes (1928–77) PIANO

*** I Just Love Jazz Piano Savoy SV 0117
    Hawes; Joe Mondragon (*b*); Shelly Manne (*d*). 9/52.
Hampton Hawes's *Raise Up Off Me* is one of the most moving and authentic autobiographical documents ever written by a jazz musician, full of valuable insights into the bebop movement. In it he briefly mentions *The Challenge*, his first and only solo album, recorded in Tokyo as a result of a Japanese producer's enthusiasm for Hawes's music. This is currently out of circulation, meaning that there is no unaccompanied material by this remarkable stylist. He said of the session, 'There's a space between me and the piano.' There is, increasingly, a space between Hawes and a critical consensus. His early work, like the tracks on this attractive compilation shared with Herbie Nichols, Paul Mehegan and Paul Smith, are lyrically boppish, with an elegant two-handedness that was to become more of an obstacle than an asset as the years went by. It's a largish discography now and full of good things but, like many a club piano, it does have its dead spots.

**** The Trio Original Jazz Classics OJC 316
    Hawes; Red Mitchell (*b*); Chuck Thompson (*d*). 6/55.
**** The Trio Original Jazz Classics OJC 318
    As above. 12/55.
***(*) Everybody Likes Original Jazz Classics OJC 421
    As above. 1/56.
***(*) The Green Leaves Of Summer Original Jazz Classics OJC 476
    Hawes; Monk Montgomery (*b*); Steve Ellington (*d*). 2/64.
**(*) Here And Now Original Jazz Classics OJC 178
    Hawes; Chuck Israels (*b*); Donald Bailey (*d*). 5/65.
*** The Seance Original Jazz Classics OJC 455
    As above. 5/66.
**(*) Blues For Bud Black Lion BLCD 760126
    Hawes; Jimmy Woode (*b*); Art Taylor (*d*). 3/68.
**(*) Live In Montreux, '71 Fresh Sound FSR 133
    Hawes; Henry Franklin (*b*); Michael Carvin (*d*). 6/71.
**(*) Plays Movie Musicals Fresh Sound FSR 65
    Hawes; Bobby West (*b*); Larry Bunker (*d*); strings.
**(*) Live At The Jazz Showcase, Chicago: Volume 2 Enja 6028
    Hawes; Cecil McBee (*b*); Roy Haynes (*d*). 6/73.
If the trio was Hawes's natural territory, there are few better places to explore it than on the first three of these, which represent a reorganization of material from his first LP as leader and from subsequent Contemporary sessions with the same line-up. Brilliant up-tempo performances from an almost telepathic group who show a fine sensitivity in ballad playing as well.

The best of the rest are undoubtedly the sessions recorded, again with Mitchell, but with the slightly tougher Donald Bailey on the drum stool, in 1966, when the pianist had been back in circulation only a couple of years; the slightly earlier *Green Leaves Of Summer*, with Wes Montgomery's elder brother on bass, and *Here And Now* still betray occasional shades of the prison-house (Hawes spent the early 1960s in jail). On *The Seance*, 'Oleo' almost perfectly reconstructs the bridge between Parker's bebop and Miles Davis's cool, modal explorations; 'For Heaven's Sake' and 'My Romance' are classic performances.

Though he had always explored unusual melodic configurations and unfamiliar repertoire, later in his career Hawes tried to compensate for the roughening edges of his once instinctive lyricism by delving into some slightly questionable material; the forgettable *Plays Movie Musicals* was fortunately an aberration, the strings quietly murdering Hawes's songful lines.

Why only the poorer of the two Enja sets, with Hawes drifting into late Chet Baker mode, should have been transferred to CD is slightly mysterious, though it's useful and overdue recognition in that format. Unfortunately, the Fresh Sound performances don't match up to their sound-quality, verbose, over-long and strangely crude in execution, but the Black Lion sets suddenly lift his remarkable and very 'classical' touch back up into focus; it's ironic that a tribute album to Bud Powell should be the clearest testimony to how *little* Hawes was influenced by Powell's approach and seemed instead to anticipate – most noticeably on *The Trio* – some of Horace Silver's 'funky' blues approach.

** **Piano: East / West** Original Jazz Classics OJC 1705
    Hawes; Larry Bunker (*vib*); Clarence Jones (*b*); Lawrence Marable (*d*). 12/52.
***(*) **All Night Session: Volume 1** Original Jazz Classics OJC 638
    Hawes; Jim Hall (*g*); Red Mitchell (*b*); Bruz Freeman (*d*). 11/56.
***(*) **All Night Session: Volume 2** Original Jazz Classics OJC 639
    As above. 11/56.
*** **All Night Session: Volume 3** Original Jazz Classics OJC 640
    As above. 11/56.
(*) **Four! Original Jazz Classics OJC 165
    Hawes; Barney Kessel (*g*); Red Mitchell (*b*); Shelly Manne (*d*). 1/58.
Hawes's session of the night of 12/13 November 1956 remains one of his best. The material was mainly familiar bop fare – 'Groovin' High', 'I'll Remember April', 'Woody'n'You' – but cuts like 'Hampton's Pulpit' are a reminder of the pianist's church background and the curious underswell of gospel, Bach and Rachmaninov that keeps freshening the top-waters of his harmony. Hall is magnificent, comparing very favourably with Barney Kessel's more conventional approach on *Four!*. The combination of Mitchell (whose legato soloing was the most immediate influence on Scott LaFaro) with Manne was inspired, and it's no disgrace to Bruz Freeman that his Max Roach-influenced approach doesn't compare.

Piano: East/West was a double-header album shared with Freddie Redd, who represents the opposite seaboard on side two. Though Hawes gets off good solos on 'Hamp's Paws' and, again, 'I'll Remember April', the combination with vibraphonist Bunker isn't all that successful.

*** **Live At Memory Lane** Fresh Sound FSR CD 406
    Hawes; Harry 'Sweets' Edison (*t*); Sonny Criss (*as*); Teddy Edwards (*ts*); Leroy Vinnegar (*b*);
    Bobby Thompson (*d*); Joe Turner (*v*). 70.
Jazz has never been well served by television on either side of the Atlantic, but this record stands as a reminder of what could be done. Hawes and his group were captured at a beat-up old club in Los Angeles as part of a series of short films made by Jack Lewerke. The combination of Criss and Hawes is irresistible (see also the saxophonist's entry) and their blues interpretations are impeccable. The entry of Joe Turner dilutes the musical content a little, but the audience love it and the sound of cheering must have attracted Teddy Edwards, who sits in for a final extended blues jam on which only Edison is rather disappointing. Good, clubby sound.

***(*) **As Long As There's Music** Verve 513 534
    Hawes; Charlie Haden (*p*). 1/ 76.
This was released only after Hawes's death in 1977 and the CD has three alternates which bring it up to decent length as well as filling out the story of this unexpected collaboration, which dates from the same sessions as the *Closeness* and *The Golden Number* duets (see under Haden). The chemistry between the two is very evident, and Hawes plays wonderfully on what sounds like a big, resonant piano. His original 'Irene' is outstanding, as is the quasi-bossa nova 'Rain Forest', but the best thing in the session is a lope through Ornette Coleman's 'Turnaround'. Here the partnership could hardly be better balanced. An attractive record.

*** **Something Special** Contemporary CCD 14072
    Hawes; Denny Diaz (*g*); Leroy Vinnegar (*b*); Al Williams (*d*). 6/76.

Hawes kept super-busy almost to the end. There is certainly no deterioration and no sense of fated hurry about his work over the last year or two. This is a particularly relaxed session, recorded almost on the beach at a club in Half Moon Bay, California. He had been working in commercial settings for some time, and it was often only on occasions like this that he could afford to slip back into straight jazz, though 'Fly Me To The Moon' has a quasi-pop feel to it. Also on the date was Denny Diaz, who had been working with Steely Dan, and Al Williams, an undersubscribed player who eventually gave up peformance to manage Birdland West (now sadly defunct). Vinnegar, as ever, is poised and resourceful, and it is often he who provides the musical stimulus to the leader, prodding him on rhythmically (Williams is too accommodating) and throwing in fresh melodic or harmonic ideas. Not a classic, but meat and drink to Hawes fans.

Coleman Hawkins (1901–69) TENOR SAXOPHONE, VOCAL

**** Coleman Hawkins 1929–1934 Classics 587

Hawkins; Henry Allen, Jack Purvis (*t, v*); Russell Smith, Bobby Stark (*t*); Muggsy Spanier (*c*); Glenn Miller, J. C. Higginbotham, Claude Jones, Dicky Wells (*tb*); Russell Procope, Hilton Jefferson, Jimmy Dorsey (*cl, as*); Pee Wee Russell (*cl*); Adrian Rollini (*bsx*); Red McKenzie (*comb, v*); Frank Froeba, Jack Russin, Horace Henderson, Buck Washington (*p*); Bernard Addison, Jack Bland, Will Johnson (*g*); Pops Foster, Al Morgan, John Kirby (*b*); Gene Krupa, Charles Kegley, Josh Billings, Walter Johnson (*d*). 11/29–3/34.

The first great role model for all saxophonists began recording in 1922, but compilations of his earlier work usually start with his European sojourn in 1934. This valuable cross-section of the preceding five years shows Hawkins reaching an almost sudden maturity. He was taking solos with Fletcher Henderson in 1923, and was already recognizably Hawkins, but the big sound and freewheeling rhythmic command weren't really evident until later. By 1929 he was one of the star soloists in the Henderson band – which he remained faithful to for over ten years – and the blazing improvisation on the first track here, 'Hello Lola' by Red McKenzie's Mound City Blue Blowers, indicates the extent of his confidence. But he still sounds a little tied to the underlying beat, and it isn't until the octet session of September 1933 that Hawkins establishes the gliding but muscular manner of his 1930s music. The ensuing Horace Henderson date of October 1933 has a feast of great Hawkins, culminating in the astonishing extended solo on 'I've Got To Sing A Torch Song', with its baleful low honks and daring manipulation of the time. Three final duets with Buck Washington round out the disc, but an earlier session under the leadership of the trumpeter Jack Purvis must also be mentioned: in a curious line-up including Adrian Rollini and J. C. Higginbotham, Hawkins plays a dark, serious role. Fine transfers throughout.

*** The Hawk In Europe ASV AJA 5054

Hawkins; Arthur Briggs, Noel Chiboust, Pierre Allier, Jack Bulterman, George Van Helvoirt (*t*); Benny Carter (*t, as*); Guy Paquinet, Marcel Thielemans, George Chisholm (*tb*); André Ekyan, Charles Lisee, Alix Combelle, Wim Poppink, Sal Doof, Andre Van der Ouderaa, Jimmy Williams (*saxes*); Stanley Black, Stéphane Grappelli, Nico De Rooy, Freddy Johnson (*p*); Albert Harris, Django Reinhardt, Jacques Pet, Fritz Reinders, Ray Webb (*g*); Tiny Winters, Len Harrison, Eugene D'Hellemes, Toon Diepenbroek (*b*); Maurice Chaillou, Kees Kranenburg, Tommy Benford, Robert Montmarche (*d*). 11/34–5/37.

***(*) Coleman Hawkins 1934–1937 Classics 602

As above, except add Henk Hinrichs (*t*), Ernst Hoellerhagen (*cl, as*), Hugo Peritz, Omer De Cock (*ts*), Ernest Berner, Theo Uden Masman (*p*), Billy Toffel (*g*), James Gobalet (*b*), Benny Peritz (*d*), Annie De Reuver (*v*); omit Carter, Williams, Johnson and Webb. 11/34–37.

Hawkins arrived in England in March 1934 and stayed in the old world for five years. Most of his records from the period have him as featured soloist with otherwise strictly directed orchestras, and while this might have been occasionally discomforting – the routines on such as 'What Harlem Is To Me' with the Dutch group The Ramblers aren't much better than a suave variation on Armstrong's contemporary struggles – Hawkins was polishing a sophisticated, rhapsodic style into something as powerful as his more aggressive, earlier manner. Two sessions with Benny Carter, including the four tumultuous titles made by the All Star Jam Band, are included on the ASV set, while the Classics sticks to the chronology; but the ASV sound is much more mixed. Classics begin with four titles made in London with Stanley Black at the piano, continue with dates in The Hague, Paris and Laren, and add the little-known Zurich session which finds Hawkins singing on the fairly awful 'Love Cries'! A spirited 'Tiger Rag' makes amends, and there's a curiosity in an unidentified acetate (in very poor sound) to close the disc. 'I Wish I Were Twins', 'What A Difference A Day Made' and 'Netcha's Dream' are three examples of the lush but shrewdly handled and often risky solos which Hawkins creates on an instrument which had still only recently come of age.

**** Coleman Hawkins 1937–1939 Classics 613

Hawkins; Jack Bulterman, George Van Helvoirt (*t*); Benny Carter (*t, as*); Maurice Thielemans (*tb*); Wim Poppink (*cl, as*); Alix Combelle, Andre Van der Ouderaa (*cl, ts*); Sal Doof (*as*); Nico De Rooy, Stéphane Grappelli, Freddy Johnson (*p*); Fritz Reinders, Django Reinhardt (*g*); Jack Pet, Eugene D'Hellemes (*b*); Kees Kranenburg, Tommy Benford, Maurice Van Cleef (*d*). 4/37–6/38.

**** Coleman Hawkins In Europe Timeless CBC 1-006

As above discs. 11/34–5/39.

The last of Hawk's European recordings. The All Star Jam Band titles turn up here again, as well as a further session with The Ramblers, but otherwise the main interest is in ten titles with just Freddy Johnson (and Maurice van Cleef on the final six). 'Lamentation', 'Devotion' and 'Star Dust' are masterclasses in horn technique, Hawkins exploring the registers and feeling through the harmonies with complete control. The sound is good, although the engineers aren't bothered about surface hiss. Vinyl followers should be aware of *Dutch Treat* (Xanadu 189, LP), which includes all the tracks with Johnson and van Cleef (including two alternative takes) and the 1936 Zurich session, in respectable transfers.

The Timeless CD cherrypicks some of the best Hawkins of the 1930s: the London quartet session of 1934, four tracks with The Berries, one with Reinhardt, five with The Ramblers, and a London pair with Jack Hylton from 1939. The very fine remastering is by John R. T. Davies: enough said.

***(*) Coleman Hawkins 1939–1940 Classics 634

Hawkins; Tommy Lindsay, Joe Guy, Tommy Stevenson, Nelson Bryant (*t*); Benny Carter (*t, as*); Earl Hardy, J. C. Higginbotham, William Cato, Sandy Williams, Claude Jones (*tb*); Danny Polo (*cl*); Eustis Moore, Jackie Fields, Ernie Powell (*as*); Kermit Scott (*ts*); Gene Rodgers, Joe Sullivan (*p*); Ulysses Livingston (*g, v*); Lawrence Lucie, Bernard Addison, Gene Fields (*g*); William Oscar Smith, Artie Shapiro, Johnny Williams, Billy Taylor (*b*); Arthur Herbert, George Wettling, Walter Johnson, Big Sid Catlett, J. C. Heard (*d*); Thelma Carpenter, Jeanne Burns, Joe Turner, Gladys Madden (*v*). 10/39–8/40.

**** Body And Soul RCSA Bluebird ND 85717

As above, except omit Bryant, Cato, Williams, Powell, Scott, Fields, Taylor, Turner, Madden and Burns; add Fats Navarro, Jimmy Nottingham, Bernie Glow, Lou Oles, Ernie Royal, Charlie Shavers, Nick Travis (*t*); J. J. Johnson, Urbie Green, Jack Satterfield, Fred Ohms, Tom Mitchell, Chauncey Walsh (*tb*); Jimmy Buffington (*frhn*); Budd Johnson, Hal McKusick, Sam Marowitz (*as*); Zoot Sims, Al Cohn (*ts*); Marion De Veta, Sol Schlinger (*bs*); Phil Bodner (*ob*); Julius Baker, Sid Jekowsky (*f*); Hank Jones (*p*); Marty Wilson (*vib*); Chuck Wayne, Barry Galbraith (*g*); Jack Lesberg, Milt Hinton (*b*); Max Roach, Osie Johnson (*d*). 10/39–1/56.

**** April In Paris RCA Bluebird ND 90636

As above. 10/39–1/56.

*** Body And Soul Topaz TPZ 1022

As various discs above, plus tracks with McKinney's Cotton Pickers, Spike Hughes, Fletcher Henderson and Mound City Blue Blowers. 29–41.

Hawkins didn't exactly return to the USA in triumph, but his eminence was almost immediately re-established with the astounding 'Body And Soul', which still sounds like the most spontaneously perfect of all jazz records. Fitted into the session as an afterthought (they had already cut 12 previous takes of 'Fine Dinner' and eight of 'Meet Doctor Foo'), this one-take, two-chorus improvisation is so completely realized, every note meaningful, the tempo ideal, the rhapsodic swing irresistible, and the sense of rising drama sustained to the final coda, that it still has the capacity to amaze new listeners, just like Armstrong's 'West End Blues' or Parker's 'Bird Gets The Worm'. A later track on the Classics CD, the little-known 'Dedication', revisits the same setting; although masterful in its way, it points up how genuinely immediate the greatest jazz is: it can't finally compare to the original. If the same holds good for the many later versions of the tune which Hawkins set down – there is one from 1956 on *Body And Soul* – his enduring variations on the structure (and it's intriguing to note that he only refers to the original melody in the opening bars of the 1939 reading – which didn't stop it from becoming a huge hit) say something about his own powers of renewal.

The Classics CD is let down by dubbing from some very surfacey originals, even though it includes some strong material – two Varsity Seven sessions with Carter and Polo, the aforementioned 'Dedication' and a 1940 date for OKeh which features some excellent tenor on 'Rocky Comfort' and 'Passin' It Around' – and those who want a superior-sounding 'Body And Soul' should turn to either of the two Bluebird CDs. *Body And Soul* also includes the full, remarkable date with Fats Navarro and J. J. Johnson, who are superb on 'Half Step Down, Please' and 'Jumping For Jane', as well as the 1956 tracks, which suffer from schmaltz-driven arrangements but feature the Hawkins tone in the grand manner. *April In Paris* offers (at budget price) only ten of the tracks on the earlier set, and it misses the best of the Navarro/Johnson date, but it's a pleasing introduction, and the remastering (abjuring the

NoNoise system, though there's actually little to choose between the two discs) is very full and forward. Both deserve four stars on the basis of the best of the material included.

The Topaz disc offers a wide cross-section of Hawkins recordings through the 1930s but starting as far back as McKinney's Cotton Pickers in 1929. In the end it seems like a bit of a jumble, but the music sounds good enough.

**** The Complete Coleman Hawkins Mercury 830960-2 4CD
> Hawkins; Roy Eldridge, Joe Thomas, Buck Clayton, Charlie Shavers (*t*); Jack Teagarden, Trummy Young (*tb*); Hank D'Amico (*cl*); Tab Smith (*as*); Don Byas (*ts*); Harry Carney (*bs*); Teddy Wilson, Earl Hines, Johnny Guarnieri, Herman Chittison (*p*); Teddy Walters (*g*); Israel Crosby, Billy Taylor, John Kirby, Al Lucas, Slam Stewart (*b*); Cozy Cole, Denzil Best, Big Sid Catlett, George Wettling (*d*). 1–12/44.

***(*) Rainbow Mist Delmark DD-459
> Hawkins; Dizzy Gillespie, Vic Coulson, Ed Vandever (*t*); Leo Parker, Leonard Lowry (*as*); Georgie Auld, Ben Webster, Don Byas, Ray Abrams (*ts*); Budd Johnson (*ts, bs*); Clyde Hart, Bill Rowland (*p*); Hy White (*g*); Oscar Pettiford, Israel Crosby (*b*); Max Roach, Specs Powell (*d*). 2–5/44.

***(*) Coleman Hawkins 1943–1944 Classics 807
> As above, except add Cootie Williams, Roy Eldridge (*t*), Edmond Hall, Andy Fitzgerald (*cl*), Art Tatum, Ellis Larkins, Eddie Heywood (*p*), Al Casey, Jimmy Shirley (*g*), Shelly Manne, Max Roach (*d*). 12/43–2/44.

*** Coleman Hawkins 1944 Classics 842
> Similar to above discs. 2–5/44.

1944 was a busy year for Hawkins in the studios. His Keynote recordings have been reissued in various editions over the years, but the Mercury set includes the whole series and has no fewer than 27 alternative takes. The eight sessions have a number of all-star line-ups; particularly outstanding are two quartet dates with Wilson, the Sax Ensemble session with Smith, Carney and Byas and a Cozy Cole group with Earl Hines. Hawkins plays on a consistently high level and there is treasure on all four discs. Delmark's *Rainbow Mist* includes three sessions for Apollo. The first includes what's thought of as the first bop recording, 'Woody'N'You', which also features Gillespie's first modern solo, and 'Rainbow Mist' itself is a little-known but superb variation on the 'Body And Soul' chords. A sextet with Auld and Webster is the makeweight. Sound is quite good, though these weren't the liveliest of recordings.

The Classics discs cover similar territory, but Classics 807 includes some other, excellent material: an Esquire All Stars date with Tatum in imperious form, and three sessions for Signature, with Hawk outstanding on 'The Man I Love', 'Sweet Lorraine' and 'Lover Come Back To Me'.

**** Hollywood Stampede Capitol B21Y-92596-2
> Hawkins; Howard McGhee (*t*); Vic Dickenson (*tb*); Sir Charles Thompson (*p*); Allan Reuss (*g*); Oscar Pettiford, John Simmons (*b*); Denzil Best (*d*). 2–3/45.

These dates for Capitol contain some top-flight Hawk. *Hollywood Stampede* includes the results of a recording trip to Los Angeles, with McGhee an ebullient and *simpatico* partner: 'Rifftide' and 'Stuffy' show the older man relishing the challenge of McGhee's almost-bop pyrotechnics, although the sly intrusions of Vic Dickenson on four other titles are just as effective, and Pettiford and Best are a crackling rhythm section. The remastering makes the most of the dry but very immediate recording.

***(*) Jazz Tones Xanadu FDC 5156
> Hawkins; Emmett Berry (*t*); Eddie Bert (*tb*); Billy Taylor (*p*); Milt Hinton (*b*); Jo Jones (*d*). 11/54.

Hawkins didn't make many records under his own name in the early 1950s, and this date – originally isssued on Jazztone – is something of an exception. Nevertheless it finds him in good fettle: the opening 'Cheek To Cheek' features chorus after chorus of ideas, and the excellent rhythm section keep fast, flexible time. Berry and the boppish but still swing-directed trombone of Bert join in on six tracks. The only drawback is the original sound, which is heavily reverberant, somewhat in the manner of the Dial and Savoy sessions of the 1940s.

*** The Vogue Recordings Vogue 74321 115112
> Hawkins; Nat Peck (*tb*); Hubert Fol (*as*); Jean-Paul Mengeon (*p*); Pierre Michelot (*b*); Kenny Clarke (*d*). 53.

** The Hawk Returns Savoy SV-0182
> Hawkins; Buddy Smith (*org*); unknown *b, d, v*. 5/54.

***(*) Body And Soul Revisited MCA GRP 16272
> Hawkins; Benny Harris, Idrees Sulieman, Joe Wilder (*t*); Rex Stewart (*c*); Tyree Glenn, Matthew Gee, Jimmy Knepper (*tb*); Tony Scott, (*cl*); Cecil Payne (*bs*); Duke Jordan, Hank Jones, Sanford Gold, Tommy Flanagan, Claude Hopkins (*p*); Bill Doggett, Danny Mendelsohn (*ky*); Al

Casimenti, Billy Bauer, George Barnes (*g*); Wendell Marshall, Gene Casey, Conrad Henry, Arvell Shaw, Trigger Alpert (*b*); Arthur Taylor, Bunny Shawker, Jimmy Crawford, Cozy Cole, Shadow Wilson, Walter Bolden (*d*). 10/51–10/58.

The Vogue album offers only six brief tracks (the rest are by a Johnny Hodges group), but Hawkins sounds in top shape. The other horns play only a desultory role and sit out altogether on 'I Surrender Dear' and 'Sophisticated Lady', where the Hawkins rhapsody is in full flow. *The Hawk Returns*, by contrast, is a near-disaster: Hawk plays some spirited stuff, and there are some blues choruses worth saving, but the sickly organ of Buddy Smith and the cooing, boo-boo-boo voices dubbed in by Ozzie Cadrena virtually kill the record. The most interesting of these three is *Body And Soul Revisited*, which sweeps up miscellaneous Decca sessions of the 1950s. Hawk is here with strings, with small groups, at a live date, with an odd group featuring Cozy Cole, Rex Stewart and Tyree Glenn, playing a two-minute unaccompanied solo and delivering a final (previously unreleased) blues with Tony Scott. Some weaker things, but much excellent Hawkins.

***(*) **The Genius Of Coleman Hawkins** Verve 825673-2
    Hawkins; Oscar Peterson (*p*); Herb Ellis (*g*); Ray Brown (*b*); Alvin Stoller (*d*). 57.
**** **Coleman Hawkins Encounters Ben Webster** Verve 823120-2
    As above, except add Ben Webster (*ts*). 3/59.
*** **Coleman Hawkins & Confreres** Verve 835255-2
    As above, except add Roy Eldridge (*t*), Hank Jones (*p*), George Duvivier (*b*), Mickey Sheen (*d*). 10/57–2/58.
*** **At The Opera House** Verve 521641-2
    Hawkins; Roy Eldridge (*t*); J. J. Johnson (*tb*); Stan Getz, Lester Young (*ts*); John Lewis, Oscar Peterson (*p*); Percy Heath (*b*); Connie Kay (*d*). 9–10/57.
***(*) **Coleman Hawkins: Verve Jazz Masters 34** Verve 521586-2
    As above Verve discs, except add Cecil Payne (*bs*), Al Haig, Tommy Flanagan, Teddy Wilson (*p*), John Collins (*g*), Major Locke, John Kirby, Israel Crosby, Nelson Boyd (*b*), Big Sid Catlett, Buddy Rich, Eddie Locke, Shadow Wilson, Cozy Cole (*d*). 44–62.

Hawkins and Webster are some team. On some of these tracks they seem to be vying to see who could sound, first, more nasty and, second, more charming. But there's an undercurrent of mutual feeling that makes 'It Never Entered My Mind' as moving as anything in Hawkins's discography. Ben is alternately respectful and keen to make his own points, and the rhythm section play up to their names. The earlier disc is only marginally less appealing: too many ballads, perhaps, when a couple of stompers would have put some more beef in the session, but the playing is very fine. *And Confreres* takes a couple of tracks off those sessions and puts them with a studio date with Eldridge: not a classic encounter, and Hawkins's tone sounds like solid granite on 'Hanid', but some agreeable music. Their Opera House meeting was actually recorded at two shows, one in stereo and one in mono, and the horns are in jousting mood, with the imperturbable MJQ rhythm section as a bonus. A 15-minute jam on 'Stuffy', with Getz and Young, comes from another JATP show.

    The *Jazz Masters* disc rounds up Hawkins from various Verve and Keynote dates, with an especially valuable addition in the 'Picasso' *a capella* solo from 1947.

***(*) **Standards And Warhorses** Jass J-CD-2
    Hawkins; Henry 'Red' Allen (*t*); J. C. Higginbotham (*tb*); Sol Yaged, Earl Warren (*cl*); Lou Stein, Marty Napoleon (*p*); Milt Hinton, Chubby Jackson (*b*); Cozy Cole, George Wettling (*d*). 57.

These two sessions were – along with the Henry Allen date which produced *World On A String* (RCA Bluebird) – effectively Hawkins's final nod back to a 'traditional' jazz. The music here is a hectic, sometimes almost hysterical Dixieland, though such histrionics derive mostly from the backing group which accompany in such a one-dimensional way that they try to copy the more outlandish flights of Allen and end up sounding cartoonish. It's still a remarkable effort by both leading lights, with Allen's bludgeoning solos carrying their own peculiar elegance and Hawkins sounding as immediately explosive as he did in his Fletcher Henderson days.

**** **The Hawk Flies High** Original Jazz Classics OJC 027
    Hawkins; Idrees Sulieman (*t*); J. J. Johnson (*tb*); Hank Jones (*p*); Barry Galbraith (*g*); Oscar Pettiford (*b*); Jo Jones (*d*). 3/57.
***(*) **Soul** Original Jazz Classics OJC 096
    Hawkins; Ray Bryant (*p*); Kenny Burrell (*g*); Wendell Marshall (*b*); Osie Johnson (*d*). 1/58.
*** **Hawk Eyes** Original Jazz Classics OJC 294
    Hawkins; Charlie Shavers (*t*); Ray Bryant (*p*); Tiny Grimes (*g*); George Duvivier (*b*); Osie Johnson (*d*). 4/59.

***(*) **Coleman Hawkins With The Red Garland Trio** Original Jazz Classics OJC 418
    Hawkins; Red Garland (*p*); Doug Watkins (*b*); Charles 'Specs' Wright (*d*).
***(*) **At Ease With Coleman Hawkins** Original Jazz Classics OJC 181
    Hawkins; Tommy Flanagan (*p*); Wendell Marshall (*b*); Osie Johnson (*d*). 1/60.
*** **Night Hawk** Original Jazz Classics OJC 420
    Hawkins; Eddie 'Lockjaw' Davis (*ts*); Tommy Flanagan (*p*); Ron Carter (*b*); Gus Johnson (*d*).
    12/60.
*** **The Hawk Relaxes** Original Jazz Classics OJC 709
    Hawkins; Ronnell Bright (*p*); Kenny Burrell (*g*); Ron Carter (*b*); Andrew Cyrille (*d*). 2/61.
(*) **In A Mellow Tone Original Jazz Classics OJC 6001
    As above eight discs. 58–61.

Hawkins's records for Riverside and Prestige revived a career that was in decline and reasserted his authority at a time when many of the older tenor voices – Lester Young, Don Byas – were dying out or in eclipse. Hawkins could still feel at home with his immediate contemporaries – the same year he made *The Hawk Flies High*, he cut tracks with Henry 'Red' Allen and a Fletcher Henderson reunion band – but the younger players represented by J. J. Johnson and Idrees Sulieman on *Flies High* were a greater challenge; the tenorman responds, not by updating his style, but by shaping it to fit the context. The rhythm sections on these records are crucial, particularly the drummers: Jo Jones, Osie Johnson and Gus Johnson were men after Hawk's own heart when it came to the beat, and their bass-drum accents underscore the saxophonist's own rhythmical language.

Hawkins keeps abreast of the times, but he doesn't really change to suit them. *The Hawk Flies High* was an astonishingly intense beginning, almost a comeback record and one in which Hawkins plays with ferocious spirit. The notes claim that he picked all his companions on the date, and Sulieman and Johnson were intriguing choices: it brings out the bluesman in each of them rather than the bopper, and both seldom played with this kind of bite. 'Laura' is a peerless ballad, but it's the blues on 'Juicy Fruit' and 'Blue Light' which really dig in. *Soul*, though sometimes rattling uneasily over prototypical soul-jazz grooves courtesy of Burrell and Bryant, isn't much less intense, and 'Soul Blues' and the bewilderingly harsh 'I Hadn't Anyone Till You' are classic set-pieces. Unfortunately, the similar *Blues Groove* with Tiny Grimes is currently deleted, but *Hawk Eyes* brings in Grimes and Charlie Shavers, though to sometimes hysterical effect: Hawkins's opening solo on 'C'mon In' seems to be carved out of solid rock, but Shavers's preposterous bawling soon takes the pith out of the music. Still an exciting session overall, though.

The trio sessions with Garland and Flanagan are hot and cool respectively, and they prove that Hawkins could fill all the front-line space a producer could give him. The force he puts into his phrasing in this period sometimes undoes the flawless grip he once had over vibrato and line, but these are living sessions of improvised jazz. *Night Hawk* is a good-natured five-round contest with Lockjaw Davis, who was virtually suckled on the sound of Hawkins's tenor, and there's plenty of fun if no great revelations and little of the intuitive empathy with Webster (see above). *The Hawk Relaxes* puts him back with Kenny Burrell on a more peaceable programme, and there are no problems here. As a sequence of tenor albums, there aren't many this strong, in whatever jazz school one can name. But the best-of, *In A Mellow Tone*, gets only moderate marks for an imbalance of ballads: there are already two fine ballad records listed above, and a classic compilation from these seven discs has yet to be made.

(*) **The Hawk Swings Vol. 1 Fresh Sound FSR-CD 14
    Hawkins; Thad Jones (*t*); Eddie Costa (*p, vib*); Nat Pierce (*p*); George Duvivier (*b*); Osie
    Johnson (*d*). 60.
(*) **The Hawk Swings Vol. 2 Fresh Sound FSR-CD 15
    As above, except omit Pierce. 60.
*** **Coleman Hawkins & His All Stars** Fresh Sound FSR-CD 88
    Hawkins; Emmett Berry (*t*); Eddie Bert (*tb*); Billy Taylor (*p*); Milt Hinton (*b*); Jo Jones (*d*). n.d.
The two 1960 discs have been out on various labels in the past: Fresh Sound are docked a notch for spreading this 60-odd-minute session over two CDs, though. The band sound unfamiliar with the material but there is some fine playing, with Jones a compatible front-line partner for Hawkins and the mercurial Costa sounding good. The *All Stars* date comes in aircraft-hangar sound but, for all that, this is a swinging session, powered by Taylor, Hinton and Jones to terrific effect and with the undervalued Berry taking some strong solos. Hawkins is his consistent self.

*** **Just You, Just Me** Stash ST-CD 531
    Hawkins; Roy Eldridge (*t*); Don Wilson (*p*); Bob Decker (*b*); Buddy Dean (*d*). 59.
*** **Dali** Stash ST-CD-538
    Hawkins; Roy Eldridge (*t*); George Arvanitas, Don Wilson (*p*); Bob Decker, Jimmy Woode (*b*);
    Kansas Fields, Buddy Dean (*d*). 59–6/62.

*** **Bean Stalkin'** Pablo 2310-933

  Hawkins; Roy Eldridge (*t*); Benny Carter (*as*); Don Byas (*ts*); Lou Levy, Lalo Schifrin (*p*); Herb Ellis (*g*); Max Bennett, Art Davis (*b*); Gus Johnson, Jo Jones (*d*). 10-11/60.

***(*) **Hawkins! Eldridge! Hodges! Alive! At The Village Gate** Verve 513755-2

  Hawkins; Roy Eldridge (*t*); Johnny Hodges (*as*); Tommy Flanagan (*p*); Major Holley (*b*); Eddie Locke (*d*). 8/62.

*** **Masters Of Jazz Vol. 12: Coleman Hawkins** Storyville SL4112

  Hawkins; Billy Taylor, Bud Powell, Kenny Drew (*p*); Oscar Pettiford, Niels-Henning Orsted-Pedersen (*b*); Kenny Clarke, Albert 'Tootie' Heath, Jo Jones (*d*). 11/54–2/68.

Live recordings from this period find Hawkins in variable but usually imposing form. His tone had hardened and much of his old fluency had been traded for a hard-bitten, irascible delivery which placed force over finesse. But he was still Hawkins, and still a great improviser, weatherbeaten but defiant. The meeting with Bud Powell found him in flag-waving form (the rest of the Storyville album is made up of odds and ends), and the two European sets on *Bean Stalkin'* are strong sessions. Roy Eldridge was one of his favourite jamming partners and they made several sets together: *Just You, Just Me* comes from a Washington club date, and the remastering has been done well, leaving the music sounding clear and quite bright: a good set, though the material is sometimes a bit too well-thumbed. The Bandstand set is let down by poor sound, and Eldridge in any case sounds as if he can't think of anything interesting to play. *Dali* is much more valuable. There are three tracks from a 1959 date with Eldridge, but it's the quartet numbers from three years later that feature some important Hawkins. 'Riviera Blues' is a considered, skilful blues, and 'Dali' itself is one of his rare *a cappella* solos, a refining of his art that should have been captured more often by microphones. With Eldridge and Hodges at New York's Village Gate, Hawkins sounds in ripe good humour: four of the tracks are tenor-and-rhythm, and he bullies his way through 'Bean And The Boys'. 'Satin Doll' is a very slow warm-up, but 'Perdido' and 'The Rabbit In Jazz', a sprawling blues, get the best out of the horns; and one shouldn't forget Flanagan, unobtrusively in the pocket.

** **Hawk Talk** Fresh Sound FSR-CD 130

  Hawkins; Hank Jones, Dick Hyman (*p*); Milt Hinton, George Duvivier (*b*); Jimmie Crawford, Osie Johnson (*d*); Frank Hunter Orchestra. 3/63.

*** **Desafinado** MCA MCAD-33118

  Hawkins; Tommy Flanagan (*p*); Barry Galbraith, Howard Collins (*g*); Major Holley (*b*); Eddie Locke (*d*); Willie Rodriguez (*perc*). 10/62.

(*) **Wrapped Tight Impulse! GRP 11092

  Hawkins; Bill Berry, Snooky Young (*t*); Urbie Green (*tb*); Barry Harris (*p*); Buddy Catlett (*b*); Eddie Locke (*d*). 2–3/65.

There was probably a great Hawkins-with-strings album to be made, but *Hawk Talk* wasn't really it. The pieces are trimmed too short to give the tenorman much space to rhapsodize, and too many of them sound foreshortened. Nor are Hunter's strings particularly well handled. *Desafinado* and *Wrapped Tight* are also disappointing in their way. Manny Albam's arrangements for *Wrapped Tight* plod through the material, and Hawkins can't muster a great deal of interest. There's a readier warmth and lustre on *Desafinado*, where Hawkins gets a sympathetic setting and a sense of time passing at just the pace he wants; still, like most such records of the period, it's finally little more than an easy-listening set with the saxophonist adding a few characteristic doodles of his own.

*** **Supreme** Enja 9009-2

  Hawkins; Barry Harris (*p*); Gene Taylor (*b*); Roy Brooks (*d*). 9/66.

(*) **Sirius Original Jazz Classics OJC 861

  Hawkins; Barry Harris (*p*); Bob Cranshaw (*b*); Eddie Locke (*d*). 12/66.

There's no need to be sentimental about Hawkins's later recordings: it's not as if his life was a tragic spiral, the way Young's or Holiday's was, and if his playing was audibly impaired in his final years he was doing his best not to reveal it. *Supreme*, a live session released for the first time, finds him in Baltimore, still playing chorus after chorus on 'Lover Come Back To Me' to open with. If this 'Body And Soul' has only a halting majesty about it, the phrasing broken into pieces, majesty there still is. Harris comps with the utmost sensitivity, and by the time of the playful treatment of 'Ow!' at the close, it sounds as though the players have enjoyed it. *Sirius* is more hesitant still, and perhaps this isn't the way to wind up a Hawkins discography; but that is what it currently does.

Erskine Hawkins (1914–93) TRUMPET

*** **The Original Tuxedo Junction** Bluebird ND 90363

  Hawkins; Sammy Lowe, Wilbur Bascomb, Marcellus Green, James Harris, Charles Jones, Willie

Moore, Robert Johnson (*t*); Edward Sims, Robert Range, Richard Harris, Norman Greene, David James, Donald Cole (*tb*); William Johnson, Jimmy Mitchelle, Bobby Smith (*cl, as*); Julian Dash, Paul Bascomb, Aaron Maxwell (*ts*); Haywood Henry (*cl, bs*); Avery Parrish, Ace Harris (*p*); William McLemore, Leroy Kirkland (*g*); Leemie Stanfield (*b*); James Morrison, Edward McConney, Kelly Martin (*d*). 9/38–1/45.

*** **Erskine Hawkins 1936–1938** Classics 653
Similar to above. 7/36–9/38.

*** **Erskine Hawkins 1938–1939** Classics 667
Similar to above. 9/38–10/39.

*** **Erskine Hawkins 1939–1940** Classics 678
Similar to above. 10/39–11/40.

*** **Erskine Hawkins 1940–1941** Classics 701
Similar to above. 11/40–12/41.

They called him the 'Twentieth-century Gabriel' and, although Erskine Hawkins was at heart only a Louis Armstrong disciple, his big band's records stand up remarkably well, considering their comparative neglect since the orchestra's heyday. They were certainly very popular with black audiences in the 1930s and '40s, staying in residence at Harlem's Savoy Ballroom for close to ten years and delivering a smooth and gently swinging music that was ideal for dancing. Hawkins's rhapsodic high-note style has been criticized for excess, but his was a strain of black romanticism which, interestingly, predates the work of later Romeos such as Billy Eckstine, even if he did sing with his trumpet. Besides, the band had a number of good soloists, including Julian Dash, Paul Bascomb and Avery Parrish, who, with Sam Lowe, arranged most of the material. The 16 tracks on the Bluebird compilation are a valuable cross-section of the band's work, with swingers such as 'Rockin' Rollers' Jubilee' and 'Swing Out' balancing the sweetness of 'Nona' and 'Don't Cry Baby'. If the character of the music is comparatively bland, it was absolutely reliable. The transfers are, for the most part, clean and full-blooded, but a couple of tracks (notably the 1945 'Tippin' In') sound harsh.

Swing specialists may want to invest in the chronological series on Classics. The first CD documents Hawkins's sometimes uncertain but still swinging early sessions for Vocalion (as 'Erskine Hawkins And His 'Bama State Collegians') and goes up to his first session for Bluebird in 1938. Given the limited number of tracks on the Bluebird set, and the rare consistency of Hawkins's individual records, there are many fine tracks to discover, including 'Hot Platter' (Classics 667), 'Baltimore Bounce' and 'Uptown Shuffle' (Classics 678) and 'No Use Squawkin'' (Classics 701); but it's the high professionalism of the section playing and the crisp, no-waste arrangements which make one wonder why Hawkins has been neglected in favour of Jimmie Lunceford or even Basie. The certitude which is supposed to be a virtue of Basie's records is certainly here in abundance. The transfers are the usual mixture from Classics: mostly solid enough, some from less than perfect sources. The Bluebird disc remains a strong single choice, but any of the Classics records will please followers of this kind of jazz.

Edgar Hayes (1904–79) PIANO

*** **Edgar Hayes 1937–1938** Classics 730
Hayes; Bernie Flood (*t, v*); Henry Goodwin, Shelton Hemphill, Leonard Davis (*t*); Robert Horton, Clyde Bernhardt, John Haughton, David 'Jelly' James, Joe Britton (*tb*); Rudy Powell (*cl, as*); Roger Boyd, Stanley Palmer, Alfred Skerritt (*as*); Joe Garland (*ts, bs*); Crawford Wethington, William Mitchner (*ts*); Andy Jackson, Eddie Gibbs (*g*); Elmer James, Frank Darling (*b*); Kenny Clarke (*d, vib*); Orlando Roberson, Earlene Howell, Bill Darnell, Ruth Ellington (*v*). 3/37–1/38.

Hayes led a very good orchestra, following his stint with the Mills Blue Rhythm Band. They had a big hit with 'Star Dust' – ironically, not one of their best records – but that lies outside this first chronological volume in the Classics survey. There were good soloists: trombonist Robert Horton was exemplary on both muted and open horn, Joe Garland could play tenor, baritone and bass sax with equal facility, and Henry Goodwin's trumpet shines here and there. Garland was also a very capable arranger, and the rhythm section could boast the young Kenny Clarke, already restlessly trying to swing his way out of conventional big-band drumming: all of the band's records benefit from his presence. There are too many indifferent vocals, and some of the material is glum, but many of the 24 tracks here bear a close listen. The remastering might serve some of the records better, but it's not too bad.

Louis Hayes (born 1937) DRUMS

*** **Ichi-Ban** Timeless SJP 102

   Hayes; Woody Shaw (*t*); Junior Cook (*ts*); Ronnie Mathews (*p*); Stafford James (*b*); Guilherme Franco (*perc*). 5/76.

Having drummed for Cannonball Adderley throughout that leader's most successful period, Louis Hayes has gone on to become a leader of some authority himself. He plays hard and fast and without unnecessary complexities, but he likes to nudge a soloist along with surprising fills, and his partnership with Junior Cook – they co-led the group that made this Timeless album – was a brief but interesting one (Woody Shaw shared leadership duties when Cook left). In the end this is perhaps just another hard-bop record, but the quality of the playing means that it's a good one.

*** **Light And Lively** Steeplechase SCCD 31245

   Hayes; Charles Tolliver (*t*); Bobby Watson (*as*); Kenny Barron (*p*); Clint Houston (*b*). 4/89.

***(*) **Una Max** Steeplechase SCCD 31263

   Hayes; Charles Tolliver (*t*); Gerald Hayes (*as*); John Stubblefield (*ts*); Kenny Barron (*p*); Clint Houston (*b*). 12/89.

*** **The Crawl** Candid CCD 79045

   Hayes; Charles Tolliver (*t*); Gary Bartz (*as*); John Stubblefield (*ss, ts*); Mickey Tucker (*p*); Clint Houston (*b*). 10/89.

***(*) **Nightfall** Steeplechase SCCD 31285

   Hayes; Eddie Allen (*t*); Gerald Hayes (*as*); Larry Willis (*p*); Clint Houston (*b*). 1/91.

***(*) **Blue Lou** Steeplechase SCCD 31340

   Hayes; Eddie Allen (*t*); Gerald Hayes (*as*); Javon Jackson (*ts*); Ronnie Mathews (*p*); Clint Houston (*b*). 4/93.

*** **The Super Quartet** Timeless SJP 424

   Hayes; Javon Jackson (*ts*); Kirk Lightsey (*p*); Essiet Okun Essiet (*b*). 2/94.

These are good, hard-headed records which take time to unfold their virtues. Besides Hayes's own playing – and he is probably the star performer overall – the first point of interest is the return of Tolliver to active duty after a number of years away. He sounds in need of some further woodshedding on *Light And Lively*, but the two later records are better showcases for him. Watson sounds a shade too slick for the company on the first record, but *Una Max* is a record that grows in stature on repeated hearings: Stubblefield is in the mood for some grand oratory, Tolliver's spacious solos accumulate strength as they go forward, and the rougher, unpredictable alto of the younger Hayes is an interesting wild card. The Candid set, recorded live, could use some editing, but it's an atmospheric occasion and, although Bartz sounds a little sour at some moments, there is still some fiery hard bop in the programme. Going back into the studio for *Nightfall*, Hayes assembles a fresh front line: Allen's trumpet is less immediately distinctive than Tolliver's, but he has a very impressive solo on 'I Waited For You', and Hayes and Willis are in buoyant form. Besides that, the drummer's evolving command of the leader's role seems to be inspiring his own playing to new heights.

Blue Lou continues the exceptional run at Steeplechase. Still not quite in the absolute top bracket, but all three horns have some fine contributions to make, and what registers most strongly is the bustle and impetus of Hayes's group – a Blakey trademark which Louis seems intent on following through. 'Quiet Fire' is a classic example of what Hayes's bands can do, the soloists brimming with fire and excitement without surrendering the improviser's control. The distinguished Mathews is a valuable recruit to the team, too.

The Super Quartet is perhaps not quite as super as some of the preceding discs. With Jackson as sole horn, the date is more of a potboiler tenor-plus-rhythm affair – although the saxophonist is nobody's slouch. But the familiar material and relatively routine performances don't lift it above average.

Tubby Hayes (1935–73) TENOR SAXOPHONE, FLUTE

*** **Jazz Tête A Tête** Progressive PCD-7079

   Hayes; Les Condon (*t*); John Picard (*tb*); Tony Coe (*ts*); Mike Pyne, Colin Purbrook (*p*); Frank Evans (*g*); Ron Matthewson, Peter Ind (*b*); Jackie Dougan, Tony Levin (*d*). 11/66.

***(*) **For Members Only** Mastermix CDCHE 10

   Hayes; Mick Pyne (*p*); Ron Matthewson (*b*); Tony Levin (*d*). 1–10/67.

*** **Live 1969** Harlequin HQ CD 05

   As above, except Spike Wells (*d*) replaces Levin. 8–12/69.

Tubby Hayes has often been lionized as the greatest saxophonist Britain ever produced, and while his facility on the horn (and both soprano and vibes) is as formidable and muscular as that of, say, George

Coleman, there is a question mark over his ability to make his solos fall into place. Having put together a big, rumbustious tone and a delivery that features sixteenth notes spilling impetuously out of the horn, Hayes often left a solo full of brilliant loose ends and ingenious runs that led nowhere in particular. Most of his recordings, while highly entertaining as exhibitions of sustained energy, tend to wobble on the axis of Hayes's creative impasse: having got this facility together, he never seemed sure of what to do with it in the studio, which may be why his studio records (all currently missing in action) ultimately fall short of the masterpiece he never came to make. At present, these scrappy live records are the only examples of Tubby in print. *Jazz Tête A Tête* will be nostalgic for many British readers as a souvenir of one of the concerts promoter Peter Burman organized in the 1960s, this one at Bristol University, with groups led by Les Condon (with Tubby sitting in), Tony Coe and Frank Evans. Hayes followers will welcome his rhapsodic ballad, 'When My Baby Gets Mad'; the rest is more routine, but Coe's playing is a reminder that there was more than one great tenorman at work in Britain then. The recording quality – the original album was issued on Doug Dobell's 77 Records – is of documentary standard, but isn't too bad, and there is a previously unheard version of 'Tenderly' by Coe.

The Mastermix CD has some 70 minutes of music drawn from three broadcasts, with a couple of rare excursions on flute and plenty of rousing tenor, as well as a nice glimpse of Hayes the composer. The CD suffers from some occasional blinks and drop-outs, but nothing too distracting. *Live 1969* sounds pretty dusty, drawn from a couple of London gigs, and Hayes is too generous with everybody else's solo space. But the second date, with a tumbling reading of 'Where Am I Going' and a couple of Hayes originals, is a degree more intense.

Roy Haynes (born 1926) DRUMS

**(*) Transatlantic Meeting Vogue 2111512
    Haynes; Barney Wilen (*ts*); Jay Cameron (*bs*); Henri Renaud (p); Jimmy Gourley (*g*); Joe Benjamin (*d*). 10/54.
*** We Three Original Jazz Classics OJC 196
    Haynes; Phineas Newborn Jr (*p*); Paul Chambers (*b*). 11/58.
***(*) Out Of The Afternoon Impulse! IMP 11802
    Haynes; Roland Kirk (*ts, manzello, stritch, f*); Tommy Flanagan (*p*); Henry Grimes (*b*). 5/62.
*** Cracklin' Original Jazz Classics OJC 818
    Haynes; Booker Ervin (*ts*); Ronnie Mathews (*p*); Larry Ridley (*b*). 4/63.
*** Equipoise Mainstream MDCD 715
    Haynes; Marvin Peterson (*t*); George Adams (*ts, f*); Carl Schroeder (*p*); Marvin Bronson (*b*); Elwood Johnson, Lawrence Killian, Terud Nakamura (*perc*). 71, 74.
*** True Or False Freelance FRLCD 007
    Haynes; Ralph Moore (*ts*); David Kikoski (*p*); Ed Howard (*b*).
***(*) Te Vou! Dreyfus FDM 36569
    Haynes; Donald Harrison (*as*); Pat Metheny (*g*); David Kikoski (*g*); Christian McBride (*b*). 94.
Relative to his enormous contribution to post-war jazz, Haynes's output as leader has been disappointingly small. Few contemporary drummers have been so precise in execution, and what Haynes lacks in sheer power – he is a small man and has generally worked with a scaled-down kit – he gains in clarity, playing long, open lines that are deceptively relaxed but full of small rhythmic tensions.

The early material on Vogue is from an album shared by Kenny Clarke, who sits at the other end of the bebop axis. It's an interesting point of comparison, but the Haynes material is quite formulaic and hampered by the deficiences of the Renaud group, workmanlike but basically uninspired. Only on the 'Jordu' contrafact, 'Minor Encamp', does the leader really kick into life.

In 1958 his work still clearly bears the mark of stints with Thelonious Monk and Miles Davis. Bar lines shift confidently or else are dispensed with altogether, without violence to the underlying pulse. Phineas Newborn's recent association with Charles Mingus had helped pare down his slightly extravagant style; he plays very differently against Haynes's slightly staccato delivery than with, say, Elvin Jones much later in his career or Philly Joe Jones in 1961 where Chambers again provided the harmonic substructure. Haynes himself sounds wonderful on 'Sugar Ray' and the romping 'Our Delight', where he is almost tuneful.

The Impulse! record is a splendid one-off. After a big, dramatic opening on cymbals, Kirk blasts off on the Artie Shaw theme, 'Moon Ray', using both manzello and tenor (beautifully in tune), doubling his lines against a big reverb that makes him sound like a whole section. Haynes's solo is low, slow and dramatic, halving the basic tempo at one point. That is not Kirk's bent. On 'If I Should Lose You', he squalls his way through a magnificent stritch solo which pulls the standard apart. (The original liner-note by Stanley Dance was slightly misleading about Kirk's two non-canonical horns; any misconceptions are corrected on this otherwise intact reissue by Michel Cuscuna.) 'Snap Crackle' was an expression coined by bassist Al McKibbon to describe Haynes's sound. The drummer adopts it here as a song title and, coupled to Kirk's weird vocalized flute and nose-flute solo, it rather stands out from the rest of the album.

Cracklin' is more mainstream, but the fizz and pop are still very much there and Haynes's polyrhythms are all the more evident for not being eclipsed by such an idiosyncratic front man. Which isn't to say that Ervin is less than exemplary. His solo on 'Under Paris Skies' is first rate and Mathews's accompaniment pushes a rather slight vehicle to the limit.

The material on *Equipoise* shows some signs of having been affected by the rock-music of the late '60s when Haynes was still running his Hip Ensemble. Haynes was well able to accommodate new inputs, but he was never able to generate the sheer power that this style required, and he is awkwardly over-miked on a lot of this record. The most coherent performances, like George Adams's 'You Name It' and 'Lift Every Voice And Sing', which are medleyed, confirm his quality and that of the young Peterson, but it's an uneasy hotch-potch of a record, best left to fans of big drumming.

True Or False is a bright, breezy set, without much personality. Moore plays some interesting stuff but never sounds entirely relaxed. The mix is over-loud, with some distortion at the top end. The quite recent *Te Vou!* is absolutely consistent with past form. Haynes dares to play quietly and delicately, and his solo on 'Trigonometry' is exquisite. He has some interesting companions here, not least Metheny, who quite clearly revels more in this setting than in the bombast of Denardo Coleman on *Song X*. The guitarist features strongly on 'John McKee', a beautiful thing made out of perfectly balanced parts. The recording is flatteringly balanced and very true, with no artificial heightening of the soloists. A delightful latter-day set by an important musician.

Kevin Hays (born 1968) PIANO

***(*) **Sweet Ear** Steeplechase SCCD 31282
    Hays; Eddie Henderson (*t*); Vincent Herring (*ss, as*); James Genus (*b*); Joe Chambers (*d*). 1/ 91.
*** **Ugly Beauty** Steeplechase SCCD 31297
    Hays; Larry Grenadier (*b*); Jeff Williams (*d*). 8/91.
***(*) **Crossroad** Steeplechase SCCD 31324
    Hays; Scott Wendholt (*t, flhn*); Freddie Bryant (*g*); Dwayne Burno (*b*); Carl Allen (*d*). 11/92.
Hays is a gifted young American pianist whose three Steeplechase albums include a lot of satisfying jazz. The leader himself is sometimes a rather demure performer: his touch, if not exactly diffident, is a little reticent in making an impact on the keys and rhythmically he tends to organize solos around certain patterns – halving the tempo or working a sequence of arpeggios – which crop up often enough to hint at routine. But his writing offers some interesting situations and on, say, the trio reading of 'You And The Night And The Music' on the first album, he manages to create a logical and inventive development far away from the melody.

The first album is arguably the best by dint of some excellent teamwork: Henderson, still undervalued, takes some very fine solos, Herring manages to step out of his Adderley impersonation for most of the date, and Chambers is as eccentrically inventive as ever (sample his solo on 'Neptune'). The quintet with Wendholt is notable for the trumpeter's beautiful solos, expertly paced and tonally exquisite, as well as fine covers of Ray Bryant's 'P.S. The Blues' and Duke Pearson's 'Gaslight'. The trio record is inevitably less absorbing, given Hays's light grip, but is still worth hearing.

***(*) **7th Sense** Blue Note 789679-2
    Hays; Seamus Blake (*ss, ts*); Steve Nelson (*vib*); Doug Wiess (*b*); Brian Blade (*d*). 1/94.
*** **Go Round** Blue Note 832491-2
    Hays; Seamus Blake (*ss, ts*); Steve Hall (*ts*); Doug Wiess (*b*); Billy Hart (d); Daniel Sadownick (*perc*). 1/95.
Moving to Blue Note, Hays has expanded his horizons. *7th Sense* is a prototypical post-modern session, a clutch of standards and originals with a few modish underpinnings – an arrangement of a piece by Hindemith, for instance. But Hays and team play through it with a commitment that takes out any sense of dilettantism. Surprisingly, it's Nelson who emerges as the strongest soloist: content to shimmer in the background on many other records, he plays a genuinely urgent improviser's role here (ironically, he sits out on their treatment of Bobby Hutcherson's 'Little B's Poem'). Blake is effective if comparatively restrained, and it's the rhythm section as a whole that one finds oneself listening to. *Go Round* contains a few surprises. The title-piece sounds like a complete throwback to either early Weather Report or late Eddie Harris, a boogaloo piece where Hays moves to electric piano (and wah-wah attachment), a keyboard he returns to for 'The Run'. Hall and Blake find themselves working together on most tracks, but both go missing on the chunky, latinized treatment of 'Invitation'. 'Early Evening' is perhaps the

most interesting piece, an open-ended drift for quartet that grows hypnotically effective. But we are ambivalent about the strength of the album as a whole. What next from Hays?

Jon Hazilla DRUMS

*** The Bitten Moon Cadence CJR 1058
> Hazilla; James Williams (*p*); Ray Drummond (*b*). 3/94.

Hazilla's ingenuity sets the tone for this session. He likes to dominate but realizes that a domineering drummer can be a bore, so he plays intrusively rather than giving himself lots of solos. Williams and Drummond are personalities in their own right, and they hold their own, but it must have been Hazilla's decision to do a snappy, uptempo version of 'Naima', for one. There are two short but interesting solo pieces – one, 'Pancakes from Meductiv', is actually a cymbal solo – and the overall result is a sharp, out-of-the-ordinary rhythm-section record with some bite to it.

Jimmy Heath (born 1926) TENOR SAXOPHONE, ALTO SAXOPHONE, SOPRANO SAXOPHONE

**** The Thumper Original Jazz Classics OJC 1828
> Heath; Nat Adderley (*cl*); Curtis Fuller (*tb*); Wynton Kelly (*p*); Paul Chambers (*b*); Albert 'Tootie' Heath (*d*). 9/59.

*** Blue Soul Original Jazz Classics OJC 765
> As above. 9/59.

*** The Riverside Collection: Nice People Original Jazz Classics OJC 6006
> Heath; Donald Byrd, Freddie Hubbard, Clark Terry (*t*); Nat Adderley (*c*); Curtis Fuller, Tom McIntosh (*tb*); Dick Berg, Jimmy Buffington, Don Butterfield (*tba*); Julius Watkins (*frhn*); Cannonball Adderley (*as*); Pat Patrick (*bs*); Herbie Hancock, Wynton Kelly, Cedar Walton (*p*); Kenny Burrell (*g*); Paul Chambers, Percy Heath (*b*); Albert 'Tootie' Heath, Connie Kay (*d*). 12/ 59–64.

***(*) Really Big! Original Jazz Classics OJC 1799
> Heath; Clark Terry, Nat Adderley (*t*); Tom McIntosh, Dick Berg (*tb*); Cannonball Adderley, Pat Patrick (*sax*); Tommy Flanagan, Cedar Walton (*p*); Percy Heath (*b*); Albert 'Tootie' Heath (*d*). 60.

*** The Time And The Place Landmark LCD 1538
> Heath; Curtis Fuller (*tb*); Stanley Cowell (*p*); Pat Martino (*g*); Sam Jones (*b*); Billy Higgins (*d*); Mtume (*perc*). 6/74.

*** New Picture Landmark LM 1506
> Heath; Benny Powell (*tb*); Bob Boutch, John Clark (*frhn*); Howard Johnson (*tba*); Tommy Flanagan (*p, electric p*); Tony Purrone (*g*); Rufus Reid (*b*); Al Foster (*d*). 6/85.

**(*) Peer Pleasure Landmark LM 1514
> Heath; Tom Williams (*t, flhn*); Larry Willis (*p*); Tony Purrone (*g*); Stafford James (*b*); Akira Tana (*d*). 2/87.

*** You've Changed Steeplechase SSCD 31292
> Heath; Tony Purrone (*g*); Ben Brown (*b*); Albert 'Tootie' Heath (*d*). 8/91.

The middle of the three Heath brothers is perhaps and quite undeservedly now the least known. Jimmy Heath's reputation as a player has been partly overshadowed by his gifts as a composer ('C.T.A.', 'Gemini', 'Gingerbread Boy') and arranger. *The Thumper* was his debut recording. Unlike most of his peers, Heath had not hurried into the studio. He was already in his thirties and writing with great maturity; the session kicks off with 'For Minors Only', the first of his tunes to achieve near-classic standing. He also includes 'Nice People'. The Riverside compilation which bears that name was until recently the ideal introduction to the man who was once known as 'Little Bird' but who later largely abandoned alto saxophone and its associated Parkerisms in favour of a bold, confident tenor style that is immediately distinctive. Now that *The Thumper* is around again, the compilation album is a little less appealing.

Also well worth looking out for is the big-band set from 1960. Built around the three Heath and the two Adderley brothers, it's a unit with a great deal of personality and presence. Sun Ra's favourite bariton-ist, Pat Patrick, is in the line-up and contributes fulsomely to the ensembles. Bobby Timmons's 'Dat Dere', 'On Green Dolphin Street' and 'Picture Of Heath' are the outstanding tracks, and Orrin Keepnews' original sound is faithfully preserved in Phil De Lancie's conservative remastering.

Heath's arrangements often favour deep brass pedestals for the higher horns, which explains his emphasis on trombone and french horn parts. The earliest of these sessions, though, is a relatively stripped-down blowing session ('Nice People' and 'Who Needs It') for Nat Adderley, Curtis Fuller and a rhythm section anchored on youngest brother, Albert, who reappears with Percy Heath, the eldest of the three, on the ambitious 1960 'Picture Of Heath'. Like Connie Kay, who was to join Percy in the Modern Jazz Quartet, Albert is an unassuming player, combining Kay's subtlety with the drive of Kenny Clarke (original drummer for the MJQ).

More than once in these sessions (and most noticeably on the 1964 'All The Things You Are' with Kenny Burrell and the brilliant Wynton Kelly) it's Albert who fuels his brother's better solos. This is a fine set, though chronological balance occasionally dictates a less than ideal selection of material. Well worth investigating.

There isn't so very much middle-period stuff around, unfortunately. *The Time And The Place* is a welcome stop-gap, reuniting Heath with Fuller in a band that seldom sounds as if it comes from the generally arid mid-'70s, when electric pianos, bass guitars and fussy production afflicted jazz. Mtume is actually Jimmy's son James, an important figure in bringing aspects of jazz percussion into rock, not vice versa as often suggested. His African-influenced rhythms are an integral part of four tracks, including the title-piece and the very fine '13th House', which is about the strongest thing on the record.

Heath's playing career has been marked by a number of hiatuses, usually when he was busy writing and arranging. The sabbaticals have if anything increased his appetite for performance. He clearly relished the sibling challenges of the Heath Brothers, and in the later 1980s has produced some strong solo material. *New Picture* is beautifully conceived and arranged (french horns again), with sweetly deft piano lines from Tommy Flanagan (undimmed by the switch to a Fender instrument) and effective guitar by Purrone, who reappears among the younger line-up on *Peer Pleasure*, a less appealing album but testimony to Heath's resilience and adaptability.

In the early 1990s he was still playing with great character. The opening solo on *You've Changed* delivers 'Soul Eyes' at an easy lope that scarcely varies for the remainder of the set. Heath can now say more in half a dozen notes than most young players can in three choruses. He places accents so carefully that even straightforward theme statements become objects of considerable interest. The group – even Tootie on this occasion – is rather dull and sluggish, but Jimmy sails on regardless, often quite blatantly ignoring key shifts and rhythmic downshifts to follow an interesting thought to its destination.

*** **Little Man Big Band** Verve 513 956
    Heath; Lew Soloff, Bob Millikan, John Eckert, Virgil Jones, Claudio Roditi (*t*); John Mosca, Eddie Bert, Bennie Powell, Jack Jeffers (*tb*); Jerome Richardson, Ted Nash (*as*); Bill Easley, Loren Schoenberg, Billy Mitchell (*ts*); Danny Bank (*bs*); Sir Roland Hanna (*p*); Tony Purrone (*g*); Ben Brown (*b*); Lewis Nash (*d*); Steve Kroon (*perc*). 1 & 3/92.

This is the first opportunity to hear Heath out in front of a full-size band since the *Really Big* sessions. Compared to them, it sounds a bit of a set-up. Heath is the main soloist and sole composer (apart from 'Two Friends', co-written by producer Bill Cosby and Stu Gardner). That's probably more emphasis than the little guy's playing can support in this sort of context. His solos are never less than competent, but rarely more than mildly interesting. Even a well-mined vein like 'C.T.A.' doesn't inspire anything out of the ordinary, and it's Virgil Jones who makes the piece his own, with a bright, chiming statement. A good enough album, but one that could have been so much better with a little discipline in the booth.

Christoph Heberer (born 1965) TRUMPET

**** **Chicago Breakdown** Jazzhaus Musik JHM 38
    Heberer; Dieter Manderscheid (*b*). 10/89.

Heberer is an outstandingly gifted young trumpeter. He has been turning up in a wide variety of situations, and the curious should seek out some of the various-artists compilations on Jazzhaus Musik to hear him in contemporary and electronic settings. Under his own name there is still the essential *Chicago Breakdown*. An album of trumpet and bass duets sounds like a forbidding exercise, but the material puts everything on much more familiar ground: they perform variations on six Jelly Roll Morton themes. Miraculously, the music succeeds in honouring Morton and letting the identity of his melodies endure while at the same time deconstructing them entirely and subjecting the themes to the most outlandish of variations. Heberer can play anything he thinks of on the horn: freakish (and they do play 'Freakish' here) effects and tonal grotesqueries intermingle with lovely voluntaries and lip-splitting exercises in virtuosity. He sounds alert to all the free-playing innovations of the last 30 years yet brings insights and sensibilities which suggest a post-modern bite and snap. Manderscheid is by no means outclassed; though performing an essentially subsidiary role, he is a full duet partner, and comes up with voicings and counterweights of his own. Highly recommended.

Dick Heckstall-Smith (born 1934) TENOR SAXOPHONE, SOPRANO SAXOPHONE

(*) This That Atonal ACD 3017

    Heckstall-Smith; Jack Bruce (b); John Stevens (d). 6/93.

Heckstall-Smith's first record as leader was an opus entititled *Dust In The Air Suspended Marks The Place Where A Story Ended*, released in the mid-1970s. There was little follow-up. The lesson may be: never borrow an album title from T. S. Eliot, or a title so long that only Eng. Lit. postgraduates stand any chance of remembering it. Heckstall-Smith did return to recording in the early '90s, a studio set and some live material from Europe. The approach had changed remarkably little and is as distinctive as ever, combining a tough, bluesy distillation of Hank Mobley and Wayne Shorter with Roland Kirk's simul-instrumentalism (younger British players like Barbara Thompson took the notion of playing two saxophones at once from Heckstall-Smith). Some of his more extreme acoustic effects border on abstraction, but in a manner which recalls the Afro-tinged sector of the British avant-garde.

He's probably still best known for his role on Jack Bruce's first post-Cream records, leading the horns on 'Never Tell Your Mother She's Out of Tune', for instance. The association is revived on *This That*, a relatively unstructured and thoroughly laddish jam by three old mates. Nothing fancy, you understand, as track-titles like 'This Piece', 'That Piece', 'Next Piece' and 'Other Piece' might suggest. It all worked rather better in a festival context – they repeated the experience live later in the summer – than it does on disc. Bruce's yawing bass lines are pretty indigestible in this context (it's a long time since he played in a genuinely improvisational context) and the real action occurs between saxophonist and drummer Stevens, whose shockingly sudden death occurred less than a year later.

It was a fun idea, but not the sort of thing that has much staying power on CD. Avid collectors of British jazz and improv only.

Lucas Heidepriem TROMBONE

*** Voicings In + Out 7011**

    Heidepriem; Ulli Mock (p, ky); Karoline Hofler (b); Martin Hug (d).

Influenced primarily by Mangelsdorff, Heidepriem repays the debt in an elegant unaccompanied 'For Albert'. He has a big tone and a quite abrasive attack for a player who is essentially a melodist. 'Stella By Starlight' is fulsome and intact; 'When Elephants Fall In Love' pokes gentle fun at the trombone and its cumbersome grace; 'Voicings' is subtle, softly ironic modern jazz; but the most tradeable token of Heidepriem's talent is still that solo piece.

Mark Helias (born 1950) DOUBLE BASS, ELECTRIC BASS

(*) The Current Set Enja 5041

    Helias; Herb Robertson (t, c, flhn); Robin Eubanks (tb); Tim Berne (as); Greg Osby (ss); Victor
    Lewis (d); Nana Vasconcelos (perc, v). 3/87.

*** Desert Blue Enja 6016**

    Helias; Herb Robertson (t, c); Ray Anderson (tb); Marty Ehrlich (as, ts, cl, bcl); Anthony Davis
    (p, syn); Pheeroan akLaff (d). 4/89.

***(*) Attack The Future Enja 7019**

    Helias; Herb Robertson (t, flhn, c); Michael Moore (cl, bcl, as); David Lopato (p); Tom Rainey
    (d, perc). 3/90.

**** Loopin' The Cool Enja 9049**

    Helias; Ellery Eskelin (ts); Regina Carter (vn); Tom Rainey (d, perc); Epizo Bangoura (djembe,
    perc). 12/94.

There is now a fully fledged generation of jazz musicians for whom rock is a simple fact, part of the background of contemporary music, and not a hard place to be defiantly or submissively negotiated. Helias is one of the more influential of the Young Turks; as well as his own impressive work, he has recorded with Barry Altschul and with Ray Anderson, who makes a welcome appearance on *Desert Blue*.

Helias is capable of boiling intensity or an almost desolate abstraction. The currently deleted *Split Image* was the most tightly structured and arranged of Helias's records until *Attack The Future* was released, largely due to Hemingway's inspirational drumming. The combination of Tim Berne, who is much less effective on *The Current Set*, with the veteran Dewey Redman, currently enjoying a welcome rejuvenation, is particularly enjoyable.

Helias is rhythmically not the most sophisticated of players and he seems to rely quite heavily on his drummers. Lewis is in some respects too oblique and elided and it's akLaff's every-which-way explosions around a solid beat which lift *Desert Blue*. Helias is, though, constantly aware of texture and resonance, and of his own technical limitations, deploying instrumental voices with great subtlety. Regular cohort Robertson is a less than virtuosic player but makes up for any purely mechanical shortcomings with a clever disposition of brasses.

Attack The Future is committed and venturesome, benefiting hugely from the presence of Robertson and Moore. There are signs here, and even more clearly on *Loopin' the Cool*, that Helias is moving out into new territory, refining his own sound quite considerably and putting ever greater emphasis on highly dissonant ideas and unsettling rhythms. 'Loop the Cool' is a long line that sets Eskelin's wonderfully relaxed tenor against Regina Carter's violin; it's a compelling combination, and Carter is first to the punch again on the following 'One Time Only', which is the most rhythmically challenging thing on the session. Some of the ideas have resurfaced from other contexts, like the Ed Blackwell Project, but here they seem to have found their ideal expression. Helias has long been a respected sideman. This, though, lifts him up into the top league.

Paul Heller TENOR SAXOPHONE

***(*) **Paul Heller** Mons LC 6458
   Heller; Ack Van Rooyen (*flhn*); Roberto Di Gioia (*p*); Ingmar Heller (*b*); Wolfgang Haffner (*d*). 94.

Nothing wrong with this. Heller is a skilful, unselfconscious tenorman: he plays the opening blues with beguiling confidence, sidestepping cliché but standing foursquare in the Rollins lineage. Most of the date comes off around mid-tempo, which evades any hard-bop breathlessness, and Heller (with his brother, Ingmar, on bass) rings the changes throughout – each of the two horns has a ballad to itself, but both disappear on 'Song For Bea', and the drums are out on the suitably thoughtful 'Contemplation'. Ack van Rooyen was a good choice for front-line partner, mellow but incisive on the big brass horn. The writing is a shade lacking in any ambition, but the playing is full of rewarding things.

Gerry Hemingway (born 1955) DRUMS, PERCUSSION

(*) **Outerbridge Crossing sound aspects sas 017
   Hemingway; Ray Anderson (*tb, tba*); David Mott (*bs*); Ernst Reijseger (*clo*); Mark Helias (*b*). 9/85.
*** **Special Detail** hat Art 6084
   Hemingway; Don Byron (*reeds*); Wolter Wierbos (*tb*); Ernst Reijseger (*clo*). 10/90.
***(*) **Down To The Wire** hat ART CD 6121
   Hemingway; Wolter Wierbos (*tb*); Michael Moore (*as, cl, bcl*); Mark Dresser (*b*). 12/91.
**** **Slamadam** Random Acoustics RA 012
   As above, except add Ernst Reijseger (*clo*). 11/91, 2/93, 2/94.
**** **Demon Chaser** hat ART CD 6137
   As above. 3/93.
***(*) **The Marmalade King** hat ART CD 6164
   As above. 2/94.

Gerry Hemingway is still a little weighed down in critical terms by his part in what for a significant number of listeners remains *the* Anthony Braxton group, the 1985 quartet with Marilyn Crispell and Mark Dresser. A lot of water, as Sam Goldwyn used to say, has been passed since then. Hemingway has gone on to assert himself as a fine individual talent with a strong sense of tradition, incidentally revealing in the process, one suspects, that his attunement to Braxton's vibrational philosophy was an act of will rather than of instinct and conviction.

Despite Ray Anderson's typically exuberant contributions, *Outerbridge Crossing* is slightly disappointing – especially for anyone familiar with Hemingway's work for Anthony Braxton – and gives a less than ideal impression of Hemingway's consistent intelligence as a group player. *Special Detail* is much more representative of Hemingway's sophisticated harmonic awareness, and it's interesting how much more of the earlier album reveals itself in the context of the later one. Reijseger is superb on both, and if Wierbos isn't another Ray Anderson – and there's probably only room on the planet for one Ray Anderson at a time – he's still a wonderfully effective player.

With *Down To The Wire* and *Demon Chaser*, Hemingway breaks through to the premier division. The latter record is a pungent masterpiece. Featuring a rare standard, 'A Night In Tunisia', it never lets the pace drop from first to last. Hemingway fuels the other members, of whom Moore is the most significant addition, an admirable replacement for Byron – but as another instrumentalist, not just as a time-keeper. His playing on 'Demon Chaser' itself is a marvel. The earlier album inevitably palls by comparison, but it contains some of Moore's best recorded playing, on his own 'Debby Warden 2', and without Reijseger's cello it has a sparer, more open fabric that some may find preferable.

The Marmalade King is a loose suite modelled round a free-association story for children. Unfortunately, the music tends to drift off into oddities and mis-shapes, with Reijseger not quite keeping his natural instinct for the bizarre under rein. The three shorter tracks in the middle – titles too long to list here – are more effective in general, but the suite as a whole tends to the wearisome over 55 minutes and most listeners may prefer to take it a track at a time. Not so the spanking *Slamadam*, which appears on Georg Gräwe's ambitious small label. The disc brings together material over quite some time, but the bulk of the recording was done within days of *The Marmalade King*, and it's interesting to hear how different the group sounds in concert, a lot fresher and more immediate and with a fire that the studio discipline seems to bank down and even extinguish. The closing 'Pumbum' was a quartet performance because Reijseger was in hospital with a slipped disc, and if you ever saw the way he waves a cello around . . .

Julius Hemphill (1940–95) ALTO SAXOPHONE, SOPRANO SAXOPHONE

***(*) **Live In New New York** Red R R 123138
     Hemphill; Abdul Wadud (*clo*). 5/76.
**** **Flat-Out Jump Suite** Black Saint 120040
     Hemphill; Olu Dara (*t*); Abdul Wadud (*clo*); Warren Smith (*perc*). 6/80.
Hemphill was the chief composer for the World Saxophone Quartet, and his signature style was a lean – some said 'raw' when his Texas roots were showing – and often quite drastically pared-down style. Seemingly inspired by Dolphy's collaborations with Ron Carter, he favoured cello as an alternative harmony instrument, enjoying a fruitful relationship with Wadud. Like Dolphy, his alto sound was piercing and intensely vocalized, and always locked into very clear musical logics. Hemphill exerted a major influence on the following generation of American musicans – people like Tim Berne especially – and his premature death was a significant loss.

Initially a more abstract session than Hemphill's later output, the *Flat-Out Jump Suite* builds to a rousing funk climax on 'Body'. Hemphill intones the title to each part as it begins, starting with the soft, percussion-led figures of 'Ear', plunging into the complexities of 'Mind' (which is dominated by Wadud) and then picking up a more continuous rhythm with 'Heart', on which Hemphill begins to string together his light, slightly floating textures into a more continuous, jazz-based improvisation.

On the original LP, 'Mind, Part 2' opened the second side with a brief coda to the long central piece. It makes more sense as an integral drum solo, typically understated. It is, until the very end, a remarkably quiet album that requires some concentration. Dara uses his mute a good deal and otherwise plays quite softly. Hemphill seems to play a wooden flute and gives his saxophone a soft-edged quality that is very attractive. An excellent record, easily overlooked.

The duos are not so well recorded, a little too loud and indistinct (certainly not as faithfully rendered, even in the studio, as the 1992 concerts on *Oakland Duets*, covered below), but the long 'Echo 2 (Evening)' offers a clear sense of how Hemphill's ears worked, harmonically speaking. There are moments when his stark lines seem to be light years apart from Wadud's chocolatey chords and faster, more rhythmic devices. Then suddenly the whole improvisation clicks into focus as a whole. Ironically, it is these four pieces which, despite the limited personnel, offer the best introduction to Hemphill the composer, even in the context of the most basic personnel. Virtually all the later things, including his 'saxophone opera', *Long Tongues*, and his larger ensemble and big-band projects stem from this.

***(*) **Fat Man And The Hard Blues** Black Saint 120115
     Hemphill; Marty Ehrlich (*as, ss, f*); Carl Grubbs (*as, ss*); James Carter, Andrew White (*ts*); Sam Furnace (*bs, f*). 7/91.
*** **Live From The New Music Café** Music & Arts CD 731
     Hemphill; Abdul Wadud (*clo*); Joe Bonadio (*d, perc*). 9/91.
*** **Oakland Duets** Music & Arts CD 791
     As above; omit Bonadio. 11/92.
**** **Five Chord Stud** Black Saint 120140
     Tim Berne, James Carter (*as, ts*); Marty Ehrlich, Andrew White (*ss, as, ts*); Fred Ho, Sam Furnace (*ss, as, bs*). 11/93.
'The Hard Blues', the last and longest track on Hemphill's first post-WSQ recording, is an old tune which seemed finally to have found its appropriate setting in Hemphill's all-horn groups of the early '90s. The sextets were an obvious extension of his work with the Quartet, with the emphasis on Hemphill's composition and arranging, and on a distinctive variation on conventional theme-and-solo jazz; often the group will improvise round a theme stated quite simply and directly by the 'soloist'.

The same process can even be heard in the duos with Wadud, still going strong after more than a decade. What's different this time around, perhaps reflecting the wider change in Hemphill's self-definition, is that the pieces are shorter and more self-contained, and they obey a more obvious structural logic. Good to have a live version of one of the 'Dogon' pieces. The longest single item, significantly, is Wadud's dull 'Sigure'; Hemphill palpably loses interest, and blares his impatience. Bonadio isn't the most virtuosic drummer, but he's right for this music precisely because he doesn't want to plug every hole, fill every silence with sound.

This has a bearing on the music for the larger, horn groups, which do tend to become rather heavy round the middle. Hemphill avoids extremes of pitch, often building long passages on minor seconds and quasi-microtonal ideas, scoring in such a way that small variations of register and timbre take on considerable significance. That stands out on the sinuous 'Tendrils', one of the more linear themes and written chiefly for the two flautists. The piece actually seems to unravel, in contrast to the melting, blurry quality of most of the other tracks. Unwise to review an album by recourse to its sleeve, but the deceptively liquescent lines of ceramic artist Jeff Schlanger's blue stoneware saxophone suggests something of Hemphill's hard centre. *Fat Man And The Hard Blues* was both an intelligent continuation of the last decade's work and a challenging new departure.

Unfortunately, Hemphill's health subsequently deteriorated to the extent that he was no longer able to perform. There is no error in the personnel detailed for *Five Chord Stud*. Even in his absence as a player – he was recovering from open heart surgery (alas, not successful in the long term) – this is unmistakably Hemphill's group and Hemphill's music. The title-piece is fascinating not least for an apparent lack of interest in textural and timbral variation: two tenor solos, three alto solos, sopranos and baritones reserved for ensembles. There is strong evidence that Hemphill has been listening to Ornette on harmolodics; 'Mr Critical' is a tribute and there are frequent allusions to Ornette themes throughout the session. It isn't absolutely clear whether the composer/conductor is directing the two collective improvisations (in which Ehrlich for one cuts loose) but he certainly puts his stamp very firmly on the rest.

As with *Fat Man*, the back cover illustration is a ceramic figure: a saxophone player, languid but compact, dark, atavistic, and absolutely concentrated on his music; a portrait of an artist who will be greatly missed.

Eddie Henderson (born 1940) TRUMPET, FLUGELHORN

*** **Phantoms** Steeplechase SCCD 31250
> Henderson; Joe Locke (*vib*); Kenny Barron (*p*); Wayne Dockery (*b*); Victor Lewis (*d*). 4/89.
*** **Think On Me** Steeplechase SCCD 31264
> As above, except replace Lewis with Billy Hart (*d*). 12/89.
***(*) **Flight Of Mind** Steeplechase SCCD 31284
> Henderson; Larry Willis (*p*); Ed Howard (*b*); Victor Lewis (*d*). 1/91.
*** **Inspiration** Milestone MCD 9240
> Henderson; Grover Washington Jr (*ss*); Joe Locke (*vib*); Kevin Hays (*p*); Ed Howard (*b*); Lewis Nash (*d*). 7/94.

Blame Miles Davis that the world acquired one more trumpet player and one less physician. It was Miles who persuaded Eddie Henderson to make music rather than medicine his first priority. Five years after qualifying MD, and after a further internship in Herbie Hancock's group, Henderson made his first recordings, *Realization* and *Inside Out*, for the Capricorn label. A less goatish trumpet sound could scarcely be imagined. Henderson has a softly vocalized, slightly raw-edged delivery that is ideally suited to ballads but which woofs along in an odd, trombone-like way on faster-paced numbers. The end of the 1970s saw him dabbling in rock, but also resume medical work, and he has maintained a psychiatric practice to this day.

He must be the most accomplished part-timer around and, while his technique isn't always razor sharp (trumpet being a full-time avocation, and a notoriously cruel one), he always plays feelingly and with admirable intelligence. Quite how he found the equanimity to perform on *Flight Of Mind*, which was made just weeks after the death of his son, Ronnie, isn't clear, but it represents the clearest statement of his own virtues. There are obvious echoes of Miles Davis, particularly when muted, and one can imagine Miles responding to 'Un Bel Dì Vedremo' from *Madama Butterfly* with similar grace and constraint; perhaps here and in the Freddie Hubbard composition, 'Lament For Booker', Henderson was able to sublimate some of his feelings, for there is certainly no breast-beating anguish, just wonderfully mature, poised jazz. If this is what psychiatry does for you, we should all be on the couch.

Of the earlier Steeplechases, *Think On Me* is distinguished by great performances from vibist Joe Locke, who also brings Hutcherson's 'Little B's Poem' to the Milestone session. Henderson himself dips back into the Herbie Hancock catalogue and comes up with 'Revelation', a terse but ambitiously structured reading that it might have been better to keep separate from Locke's extended 'Seven Beauties' at the end of the CD. Locke actually dominates the credits with a long opening piece as well; for the rest, it's mostly repertory stuff, Duke's 'Come Sunday', Lee Morgan's 'Ceora', and a delicate restatement of 'Every Time We Say Goodbye'.

Phantoms for some reason isn't quite as compelling, though it's very hard to fault on any count whatsoever. The rhythm section is perhaps more aggessive, with Lewis constantly speeding up the pulse; this is not altogether to Henderson's advantage, though one isn't aware of any similar problems on *Flight Of Mind*, perhaps because Howard is less propulsive there. He's back for the recent *Inspiration*, a relaxed and relatively undemanding stroll through by now rather familiar territory. Nothing wrong with the choice of material – 'Phantoms' is back, and there are tunes by McCoy Tyner, Hancock again ('Oliloqui Valley' this time), sometime sidekick Billy Harper and Joe Henderson – but there is a certain predictability to the delivery which is disconcerting. Grover Washington is drafted in for the Hancock and, with less logic, 'I Remember Clifford' as well, but it needs a more forceful second voice. Locke plays quite beautifully but in his most laid-back mode. Most Henderson fans will find more to occupy them on the Steeplechases.

Fletcher Henderson (1897–1952) PIANO, BANDLEADER

(*) Fletcher Henderson 1921–1923 Classics 794
> Henderson; Elmer Chambers, Russell Smith, Joe Smith (*c*); George Brashear (*tb*); William Grant Still, Edgar Campbell, Ernest Elliott, Don Redman, Billy Fowler (*reeds*); Leroy Vanderveer, Charlie Dixon (*bj*); plus various unknowns. 6/21–6/23.

*** **Fletcher Henderson 1923** Classics 697
> Henderson; Elmer Chambers, Howard Scott (*c*); Teddy Nixon (*tb*); Don Redman (*cl, as*); Coleman Hawkins (*ts, bsx, cl*); Billy Fowler (*bsx*); Allie Ross (*vn*); Charlie Dixon (*bj*); Ralph Escudero (*bb*); Kaiser Marshall (*d*). 6/23–4/24.

*** **Fletcher Henderson 1923–1924** Classics 683
> As above, except omit Ross. 12/23–2/24.

*** **Fletcher Henderson 1924** Classics 673
> As above. 2–5/24.

(*) Fletcher Henderson 1924 Vol. 2 Classics 657
> As above, except add Charlie Green (*tb*), Lonnie Brown (*as*), Rosa Henderson (*v*). 5–8/24.

*** **Fletcher Henderson 1924 Vol. 3** Classics 647
> As above, except add Louis Armstrong (*c, v*), Buster Bailey (*cl, as*), omit Nixon, Brown, Rosa Henderson. 9–11/24.

*** **Fletcher Henderson 1924–1925** Classics 633
> Henderson; Louis Armstrong, Elmer Chambers, Howard Scott, Joe Smith, Russell Smith (*t, c*); Charlie Green (*tb*); Don Redman (*cl, as, v*); Buster Bailey (*cl, as*); Coleman Hawkins (*cl, Cmel, ts, bsx*); Charlie Dixon (*bj*); Ralph Escudero (*bb*); Kaiser Marshall (*d*); Billy Jones (*v*). 11/24–11/25.

**** **The Complete Louis Armstrong With Fletcher Henderson** Forte F38001/2/3 3CD
> As above. 24–25.

Henderson drifted into both music and bandleading after casually working for the Black Swan record label, and his first records as a leader are frequently no more than routine dance music. The arrival of Louis Armstrong – whom Henderson first heard in New Orleans at the turn of the decade – apparently galvanized everyone in the band and, eventually, every musician in New York. But it's hard to make assumptions about Henderson's band. He already had Don Redman and Coleman Hawkins working for him prior to Armstrong's arrival, and there are too many good records prior to Louis's first session of October 1924 to dismiss the group as jazz ignoramuses. The sequence of Classics CDs has now been expanded into a complete run of Henderson's recordings (though there remain a number of blues accompaniments yet to find their way to CD). These were skilful if not particularly outward-looking musicians, and even as early as 1923 – on 'Shake Your Feet' or '31st Street Blues' – there are fragments of solos which work out. The very first disc in the sequence is of no more than historical interest: only at the very end does the band begin to stir into life beyond the most ordinary dance music, though there are three interesting early solos by Henderson himself. Classics 697 includes Coleman Hawkins's first session, where he played what's an extraordinary solo for 1923 on the Vocalion version of 'Dirty Blues'. The next three CDs are inevitably mixed affairs: Henderson cut some songs in a completely straight manner, barely allowing the musicians any leeway, and he let them have their head on others. From session to session, though, there is usually something of interest. The weakest disc is probably Classics 657, which includes a preponderance of dull tracks – although even here there is Redman's interesting chart for 'The Gouge Of Armour Avenue', which features Green's rasping trombone, and two good versions of 'Hard Hearted Hannah'. Classics 647 goes up several gears with Armstrong's arrival and, while he doesn't exactly dominate, the music always catches fire when he takes a solo, even on an early piece like the Pathé version of 'Shanghai Shuffle'. He is present on most of Classics 633 and, luckily, gets a solo on most of the tracks. His cornet improvisations – often set against Marshall hitting the off-beat to heighten the dramatic effect – are breathtaking, especially on what would otherwise be dreary tunes, such as 'I'll See You In My Dreams' or the amazing 'I Miss My Swiss', where he electrifies the whole band. But some of the other musicians were getting into their stride, too: Redman delivers some strong early arrangements, Hawkins and Bailey sneak through some breaks, and the best of the material – 'TNT', 'Money Blues', 'Carolina Stomp', and above all, their hit version of 'Sugar Foot Stomp' – lets the best black band in New York play to their strengths.

Transfer quality is unfortunately often indifferent. Classics appear to have opted for a variety of sources and, while the original 78s differ strikingly in terms of their sound from label to label, the remastering is often less than ideal: the Vocalion originals sound a touch too heavy in the bass, and a comparison between the Classics Pathé tracks and those on Fountain's *The Henderson Pathés* (listed in our first edition but now out of print) shows a cleaner, lighter sound on the LP version. Classics, though, offer the only edition of many of the earlier tracks, which scholars should welcome.

For Henderson with Armstrong, the clear winner is the Forte three-disc collection: the 65 tracks include all known original and alternative takes, and the remastering by John R. T. Davies is of the very best.

*** Fletcher Henderson 1925–1926 Classics 610
  As above, except Rex Stewart (*c*) replaces Armstrong, Scott and Chambers. 11/25–4/26.
***(*) Fletcher Henderson 1926–1927 Classics 597
  As above, except add Tommy Ladnier (*t*), Jimmy Harrison (*tb*), Fats Waller (*p, org*), June Cole (*bb, v*), Evelyn Thompson (*v*). 4/26–1/27.
***(*) Fletcher Henderson 1927 Classics 580
  As above, except add Jerome Pasquall (*cl, as*); omit Escudero, Thompson. 1–5/27.
***(*) Fletcher Henderson 1927–1931 Classics 572
  Henderson; Bobby Stark, Tommy Ladnier, Russell Smith, Rex Stewart, Cootie Williams (*t, c*); Jimmy Harrison (*tb, v*); Charlie Green, Claude Jones, Benny Morton (*tb*); Jerome Pasquall, Benny Carter, Harvey Boone (*cl, as*); Coleman Hawkins (*cl, ts*); Charlie Dixon, Clarence Holiday (*bj, g*); John Kirby, June Cole (*bb, b*); Kaiser Marshall, Walter Thompson (*d*); Lois Deppe, Andy Razaf (*v*). 11/27–2/31.
**** Fletcher Henderson 1925–1929 JSP CD 311
  As above four discs. 25–29.
***(*) Fletcher Henderson & The Dixie Stompers 1925–1928 Disques Swing 8445/6 2CD
  As above. 11/25–4/28.

By the mid-1920s Henderson was leading the most consistently interesting big band on record. That doesn't mean all the records are of equal calibre, and the title of a famous earlier retrospective of Henderson's work – 'A Study In Frustration' – gives some idea of the inconsistencies and problems of a band that failed to secure any hit records and never sounded on record the way it could in person (at least, according to many witnesses). But Henderson's best records are classics of the period. Don Redman was coming into his own, and his scores assumed a quality which no other orchestral arranger was matching in 1926–7 (though it is tantalizing to ponder what Jelly Roll Morton could have done with the same band): 'The Stampede', 'The Chant', 'Henderson Stomp', the remarkable 'Tozo' and, above all, the truly astonishing 'Whiteman Stomp' find him using the colours of reeds and brass to complex yet swinging ends. Luckily Henderson had the players who could make the scores happen: though Armstrong had departed, Hawkins, Ladnier, Joe Smith, Jimmy Harrison and Buster Bailey all had the stature of major soloists as well as good section-players. The brass sections were, indeed, the best any band in New York could boast – the softer focus of Smith contrasting with the bluesy attack of Ladnier, the rasp of Rex Stewart, the lithe lines of Harrison – and any group with Hawkins (who was loyal enough to stay for ten years) had the man who created jazz saxophone. Henderson's own playing was capable rather than outstanding, and the rhythm section lumbered a bit, though string bass and guitar lightened up the feel from 1928 onwards. It took Henderson many records to attain a real consistency: in 1925, he was still making sides like 'Pensacola' (for Columbia, and on the JSP disc), which starts with a duet between Hawkins and Redman on bass sax and goofus! But there weren't many vocals, which let the band drive through their three-minute allocation without interruption, and if Henderson never figured out the best use of that time-span (unlike Ellington, who grew to be his most serious rival among New York's black bands) his team of players made sure that something interesting happens on almost every record.

Those who want to sample Henderson's music should go straight to the JSP CD. This collects all his records for Columbia (where he invariably received the best studio sound) and includes 'Jackass Blues', 'Tozo', 'Whiteman Stomp', 'A Rhythmic Dream', 'King Porter Stomp' and several other near-masterpieces. The remastering is mostly superbly done by John R. T. Davies, although there still seems to be a hint of distortion on some loud passages. The Classics CDs offer chronological surveys which Henderson specialists will welcome, although no alternative takes are included (there are actually relatively few in existence). We would single out the 1926–7 and 1927 discs as the most important, but there are so many fine moments scattered through even second-rate pieces that any who sample the series may well find that they want them all. Remastering is again variable: the tracks made under the name 'The Dixie Stompers' were made for Harmony, which continued to use acoustic recording even after most other companies had switched over to the electric process in 1925, and some may find these tracks a little archaic in timbre. Mostly, we find that the transfers are acceptable, though they don't measure up to the relentlessly high standards of JSP. The 1927–31 disc marks the departure of Redman, the first steps by Henderson himself as arranger, guest appearances by Fats Waller (who reportedly gave Henderson a dozen tunes in trade for a plate of hamburgers at a Harlem eatery) and Benny Carter, and the arrival of the fine and undervalued trumpeter, Bobby Stark, whose solos on 'Blazin'' and 'Sweet And Hot' find a lyrical streak somewhere between Joe Smith and Rex Stewart. But the band was already in decline, especially following Henderson's car accident in 1928, after which he was never the same man. They cut only three record dates in 1929 and three in 1930 (compared with 17 in 1927).

The Disques Swing double-CD collects all of the Dixie Stompers tracks for Harmony, and the sound suggests that the music has been dubbed straight from the two fine Parlophone LP editions of the late 1960s. As a collected edition, this is a very good one, though Harmony's acoustic recording may bother some ears.

*** **Fletcher Henderson 1931** Classics 555

As above, except add Sandy Williams (*tb*); Russell Procope (*cl, as*); Edgar Sampson (*cl, as, vn*); Horace Henderson (*p*); George Bias, Dick Robertson (*v*); omit Ladnier, Green, Pasquall, Dixon, Cole, Marshall, Deppe, Razaf. 2–7/31.

(*) **Fletcher Henderson 1931–1932 Classics 546

Henderson; Russell Smith, Bobby Stark (*t*); Rex Stewart (*c*); Sandy Williams, J. C. Higginbotham (*tb*); Russell Procope (*cl, ss, as*); Edgar Sampson (*cl, as, vn*); Coleman Hawkins (*cl, ts*); Clarence Holiday, Ikey Robinson (*bj, g*); John Kirby (*bb, b*); Walter Johnson (*d*); John Dickens, Harlan Lattimore, Baby Rose Marie, Les Reis, Dick Robertson (*v*). 7/31–3/32.

***(*) **Fletcher Henderson 1932–1934** Classics 535

As above, except add Henry Allen, Joe Thomas, Irving Randolph (*t*); Keg Johnson, Claude Jones, Dicky Wells (*tb*); Buster Bailey (*cl*); Hilton Jefferson (*cl, as*); Ben Webster (*ts*); Horace Henderson (*p*); Bernard Addison, Lawrence Lucie (*g*); Elmer James (*b*); Vic Engle (*d*); Charles Holland (*v*); omit Robinson, Holiday, Lattimore, Marie, Reis and Robertson. 12/32–9/34.

*** **Fletcher Henderson 1934–1937** Classics 527

Henderson; Russell Smith, Irving Randolph, Henry Allen, Dick Vance, Roy Eldridge, Joe Thomas, Emmett Berry (*t*); Ed Cuffee (*tb, v*); Keg Johnson, Claude Jones, Fernando Arbello, George Washington, J. C. Higginbotham (*tb*); Omer Simeon (*cl, as, bs*); Jerry Blake (*cl, as, v*); Buster Bailey, Hilton Jefferson, Russell Procope, Jerome Pasquall (*cl, as*); Benny Carter, Scoops Carey (*as*); Ben Webster, Elmer Williams, Chu Berry (*ts*); Horace Henderson (*p*); Bob Lessey, Lawrence Lucie (*g*); Elmer James, John Kirby, Israel Crosby (*b*); Walter Johnson, Big Sid Catlett (*d*); Teddy Lewis, Georgia Boy Simpkins, Dorothy Derrick (*v*). 9/34–3/37.

(*) **Under The Harlem Moon ASV 5067

As above two discs. 12/32–6/37.

** **Fletcher Henderson 1937–1938** Classics 519

Henderson; Russell Smith, Emmett Berry, Dick Vance (*t*); George Washington, Ed Cuffee, Milt Robinson, George Hunt, J. C. Higginbotham, Albert Wynn, John McConnell (*tb*); Jerry Blake (*cl, as, v*); Eddie Barefield (*cl, as*); Hilton Jefferson (*as*); Chu Berry, Elmer Williams, Ben Webster (*ts*); Lawrence Lucie (*g*); Israel Crosby (*b*); Walter Johnson, Cozy Cole, Pete Suggs (*d*); Chuck Richards (*v*). 3/37–5/38.

Henderson's music was already in decline when the 1930s began, and by the end of the decade – as illustrated on the rather sad final disc in the Classics sequence – the orchestra was a shadow of what it was in its glory days. Ironically, it was Henderson's own work as an arranger in this period which set off the swing era, via the charts he did for Benny Goodman. The 1931 and 1931–2 discs offer sometimes bewildering juxtapositions of corn (Henderson employed some excruciating singers at this time) and real jazz: the extraordinary 'Strangers', on Classics 546, includes an amazing Coleman Hawkins solo in the middle of an otherwise feeble record, while some of the tunes which the Hendersonians might have been expected to handle well – 'Casa Loma Stomp' (Classics 546) and 'Radio Rhythm' (Classics 555) – turn out poorly. Yet the band was still full of fine ensemble players and soloists alike, and some of the Horace Henderson arrangements from this time – especially 'Queer Notions', 'Yeah Man' and 'Wrappin' It Up' (all on Classics 535) – are as well managed as any band of the period could do. Besides, while players of the calibre of Hawkins, Allen and (subsequently) Webster, Berry and Eldridge were on hand, there can't help but be fine moments on many of the records. Classics 535 is certainly the pick of these later discs, with a dozen excellent tracks included. Classics 527 and 519, which were recorded mainly after Henderson temporarily disbanded for a while in 1934 and worked with Goodman, show the vitality of the band sagging, and the final dozen sides they made might have been done by any competent dance orchestra (as a PS, there are four nondescript 1941 tracks which wind up the Horace Henderson disc listed below). Transfers are usually reasonably good and clear, although as usual it's the later discs which sound cleaner and less prone to track-to-track fluctuations in quality. The ASV disc compiles 23 of the better tracks from the 1932–7 period, but the sound appears muddier than on the Classics issues.

*** **Fletcher Henderson & His Orchestra** Topaz TPZ 1004
      As appropriate discs above. 4/27–8/36.
***(*) **Tidal Wave** MCA GRP 16432
      As appropriate discs above. 4/31–9/34.
**** **A Study In Frustration: The Fletcher Henderson Story** Columbia 57596 3CD
      As appropriate discs above. 8/23–5/38.

The Topaz compilation is a sensible if sometimes arbitrary compilation of Henderson's later material, concentrating on the 1930s and missing out on most of his best early work. The remastering is respectable if rather bass-heavy, and it compares less than favourably with the sound on the fine MCA set. If a little thin in the lower frequencies, this disc nevertheless presents some of the best of the Decca tracks in startlingly clear and immediate sound. The reappearance of the famous Columbia set, though, is to be welcomed. Originally a four-LP set, it's been smartly remastered across three CDs. It misses very few of the best Henderson tracks from the crucial mid- to late-1920s period, and the choice of Vocalion sides from the 1930s is never less than sound. Remastering, while not quite as vivid as MCA's, is consistently clean and clear, and the packaging is splendid.

Horace Henderson (1904–1988) PIANO

**** **Horace Henderson 1940** Classics 648
      Henderson; Emmett Berry, Harry 'Pee Wee' Jackson, Gail Brockman, Nat Bates (*t*); Harold 'Money' Johnson (*t, v*); Ray Nance (*t, vn*); Edward Fant, Nat Atkins, Joe McLewis, Leo Williams, Archie Brown (*tb*); Dalbert Bright (*cl, as*); Willie Randall, Howard Johnson, Charles Q. Price (*as*); Elmer Williams, Dave Young, Mosey Gant, Bob Dorsey, Lee Pope (*ts*); Leonard Talley (*bs*); Hurley Ramey, Leroy Harris (*g*); Jesse Simpkins, Israel Crosby (*b*); Oliver Coleman, Debo Williams (*d*); Viola Jefferson (*v*). 2–10/40.

'One of the most talented yet most neglected and enigmatic figures in all of jazz' – Gunther Schuller's verdict on Horace Henderson sounds over-enthusiastic, but the 1940 tracks collected on this important CD go a long way towards bearing out his verdict. Fletcher's brother was a fine, Hines-like pianist, but it was his arranging that was outstanding: the 16 themes collected here include charts by both brothers, and the contrasts between Fletcher's stylized call-and-response figures and the fluid, overlapping ideas of Horace are remarkable. Horace's band was full of fine soloists who received sometimes unprecedented space: Nance has two full choruses of violin on the engaging 'Kitty On Toast', and Berry is generously featured throughout: his 'Ain't Misbehavin'' melody is beautifully sustained. But it's the section-work, the saxes full and rich, the brass outstandingly punchy, which brings complex charts to life: 'Shufflin' Joe', the very first track here, is a little masterpiece of varied dynamics and interwoven tone-colours. The rhythm players – including the young Israel Crosby on some of the later sides – are as good as their colleagues. This Classics CD displaces the Tax LP listed in our last edition and though the sound is, as so often with discs from this source, a little inconsistent, the CD remains a very good buy. There are four tracks by the 1941 Fletcher Henderson band tagged on at the end, but these are a somewhat doubtful bonus.

Joe Henderson (born 1937) TENOR SAXOPHONE

**** **Page One** Blue Note B21Y-84140
      Henderson; Kenny Dorham (*t*); McCoy Tyner (*p*); Butch Warren (*b*); Pete La Roca (*d*). 6/63.

Joe Henderson is always in the middle of a great solo. He's a thematic player, working his way round the structure of a composition with methodical intensity, but he's a masterful licks player too, with a seemingly limitless stock of phrases that he can turn to the advantage of any post-bop setting: this gives his best improvisations a balance of surprise, immediacy and coherence which few other saxophonists can surpass. His lovely tone, which combines softness and plangency in a similar way, is another pleasing aspect of his music. *Page One* was his first date as a leader, and it still stands as one of the most popular Blue Notes of the early 1960s. Henderson had not long since arrived in New York after being discharged from the army, and this six-theme set is very much the work of a new star on the scene. 'Recorda-Me', whose Latinate lilt has made it a staple blowing vehicle for hard-bop bands, had its debut here, and the very fine tenor solo on Dorham's 'Blue Bossa' explains much of why Henderson was creating excitement. But everything here, even the throwaway blues, 'Homestretch', is impressively handled. Tyner, Warren and La Roca are a rhythm section who seldom played together but they do very well here, as does the erratic Dorham.

**** Inner Urge Blue Note B21Y-84189
> Henderson; McCoy Tyner (*p*); Bob Cranshaw (*b*); Elvin Jones (*d*). 11/64.

***(*) Mode For Joe Blue Note B21Y-84227
> Henderson; Lee Morgan (*t*); Curtis Fuller (*tb*); Bobby Hutcherson (*vib, mar*); Cedar Walton (*p*); Ron Carter (*b*); Louis Hayes, Joe Chambers (*d*). 1/66.

Inner Urge, which features Henderson as sole horn, is dark and intense music. The title-tune, commemorating Henderson's experiences of trying to make a living in New York, is a blistering effort at a medium tempo, and it's interesting to compare Tyner and Jones as they are with Henderson rather than with Coltrane. While the atmosphere isn't as teeth-grittingly intense, it's scarcely less visceral music. Even the sunny reading of 'Night And Day' musters a terrific urgency via Jones's continuously glittering cymbals.

Mode For Joe plants Henderson in a bigger environment, and at times he sounds to be forcing his way out: the solos on the title-track and 'A Shade Of Jade' make a baroque contrast with the otherwise tempered surroundings. Chambers drums with pile-driving intensity in places, and, though the large number of players tends to constrict the soloists at a time when Henderson could handle all the stretching out he was given, it's still a fine record.

*** The Best Of Joe Henderson Blue Note CDP 7956272
> As above discs, plus Richard Davis, Ron Carter (*b*), Al Foster (*d*). 6/63–11/85.

An attractive compilation from the Blue Note period, with two tracks from the otherwise-unavailable *In 'N' Out* and one from the latter-day *State Of The Tenor Vol. One*. But there's so much good music on the originals that most will want to hear all of them.

**** The Blue Note Years Blue Note CDP 789287-2 4CD
> Henderson; Kenny Dorham, Lee Morgan, Carmell Jones, Donald Byrd, Woody Shaw, Snooky Young, Al Porcino, Denny Moore, Marvin Stamm (*t*); Freddie Hubbard (*c, t*); Thad Jones, Johnny Coles (*flhn*); Benny Powell, Garnett Brown, Jimmy Knepper, Bob Burgess, Julian Priester (*tb*); Tony Studd (*btb*); Jerome Richardson, James Spaulding, Hubert Laws, Jerry Dodgion, Eddie Daniels, Pepper Adams, Leo Wright (*reeds*); Herbie Hancock, McCoy Tyner, Barry Harris, Andrew Hill, Tommy Flanagan, Horace Silver, Duke Pearson, Cedar Walton, Steve Kuhn, Roland Hanna, Renée Rosnes (*p*); Freddie Roach, Larry Young (*org*); Grant Green, Eddie Wright (*g*); Richard Davis, Butch Warren, Gene Taylor, Bob Cranshaw, Teddy Smith, Steve Swallow, Ron Carter, Herbie Lewis, Buster Williams, Ira Coleman (*b*); Tony Williams, Al Foster, Ray Brooks, Pete La Roca, Al Harewood, Clarence Johnston, Roy Haynes, Billy Higgins, Elvin Jones, Albert 'Tootie' Heath, Roger Humphries, Joe Chambers, Mickey Roker, Mel Lewis, Billy Drummond (*d*). 4/63–2/90.

Henderson appeared on 34 different Blue Note albums, and this massive four-disc survey covers many rare moments as well as most of his classics. Expected milestones such as 'Blue Bossa', 'Recorda Me' and 'Isotope' are here; but so are two numbers from Pete La Roca's *Basra*, one from Freddie Roach's *Brown Sugar*, one where he guests with the Jones–Lewis Orchestra and a pair from Bobby Hutcherson's excellent *Stick Up!*. Points that emerge from a rich programme include his real mastery at very slow tempos – Blue Mitchell's 'Sweet And Lovely' includes a masterful solo, and the improvisation on Grant Green's 'Idle Moments' at a dead-slow pace is mesmerizing – as well as his pointed adaptability. He settles into the furious organ groove of Larry Young's Unity sessions as comfortably as the fierce abstractions of Andrew Hill's music. As off-centre as his phrasing sometimes is, there is already that sense of inner calm which pervades all his latter-day music, even in many of the earlier tracks here. Excellent sound and documentation in a very worthwhile package.

*** Four! Verve 523657-2
> Henderson; Wynton Kelly (*p*); Paul Chambers (*b*); Jimmy Cobb (*d*). 4/68.

A historical curiosity, brought to life courtesy of Henderson himself. He played this set with the old Miles Davis rhythm section at an unrehearsed show at Baltimore's Left Bank. The sound is sometimes muddy, without much top end, but listenable. The quartet work through six themes with a mix of intensity and doggedness, which leaves the music a bit colourless at times, yet the feeling of three old masters in conversation with a younger one comes through, and it's interesting to hear Henderson on standard material which he otherwise never plays.

*** The Milestone Years Milestone 4413-2 8CD

Henderson; Mike Lawrence, Woody Shaw, Oscar Brashear (*t*); Grachan Moncur III, Julian Priester, Curtis Fuller (*tb*); Jeremy Steig, Ernie Watts (*f*); Haldey Caliman (*ts, f*); Lee Konitz (*as*); Kenny Barron, Don Friedman, Joe Zawinul, Mark Levine, Joachim Kühn, Herbie Hancock, George Cables, Hideo Ichikawa, George Duke, Alice Coltrane, Patrick Gleason (*ky*); Michael White (*vn*); George Wadenius, James Blood Ulmer, Lee Ritenour (*g*); Ron Carter, Victor Gaskin, Stanley Clarke, Kunimitsu Inaba, Dave Holland, Charlie Haden, Jean-François Jenny-Clark, David Friesen, Ron Carter, Alphonso Johnson (*b*); Louis Hayes, Jack DeJohnette, Roy McCurdy, Lenny White, Motohiko Hino, Leon Chancler, Daniel Humair, Harvey Mason (*d*); Airto Moreira, Carmelo Garcia, Bill Summers (*perc*); Flora Purim (*v*). 67–76.

While there are many rewarding things in this exhaustive collection of Henderson's work for the Milestone operation, it's finally let down by the indifferent calibre of the early 1970s' sessions which he made for the label. Sessions such as *If You're Not Part Of The Solution*, *Live At The Lighthouse* and *In Japan* find him in sharp, creative form, adapting to rhythm sections that remained rooted in hard bop but which fed in the kind of groove playing that would lead to jazz-rock. Later sets like *Canyon Lady* find Joe fighting a losing battle with his backings, and the final set, *Black Miracle*, is close to disaster. Henderson fanatics will want this, and the packaging and annotation are exemplary, but there is too much driftwood to elicit a general recommendation. The discs listed below will be useful samplers of this period for most.

**(*) The Kicker Original Jazz Classics OJC 465

Henderson; Mike Lawrence (*t*); Grachan Moncur III (*tb*); Kenny Barron (*p*); Ron Carter (*b*); Louis Hayes (*d*). 8/67.

***(*) Tetragon / In Pursuit Of Blackness BGP CDBGPD 084

Henderson; Woody Shaw (*t, flhn*); Curtis Fuller (*tb*); Pete Yellin (*as, f, bcl*); Kenny Barron, Don Friedman, George Cables (*p*); Ron Carter, Ron McClure, Stanley Clarke (*b*); Louis Hayes, Jack DeJohnette, Lenny White (*d*). 9/67–5/71.

*** Multiple Original Jazz Classics OJC 776

Henderson; Larry Willis (*ky*); James Blood Ulmer, John Thomas (*g*); Dave Holland (*b*); Jack DeJohnette (*d*); Arthur Jenkins (*perc*). 1/73.

A disheartening step after the Blue Note albums, *The Kicker*, Henderson's debut for Milestone, is respectable but prosaic stuff, with Lawrence and Moncur adding little of interest and the tracks sounding short and 'produced'. BGP's coupling of two later albums on a single CD is a much better choice: the sessions for *Tetragon* offer some very hard-edged playing by the leader, with a riveting dissection of 'Invitation', and the four Henderson originals from the *Blackness* date are blown open over polyrhythmic bases that the horns meet head on. The sound and feel are sometimes a little more dated than the straight tenor-and-rhythm tracks – Cables uses a tinkly electric piano, and there are elements of fashionable freak-out in some of the ensembles – but it's a valuable CD. *Multiple* is another that has worn less well: Henderson doubles on soprano, flute and percussion (and even does some chanting), Willis plays electric keyboards, and the guitarists strum to no great purpose; yet the saxophonist still earns the stars for the surprising tenor solos.

**(*) Barcelona Enja 3037-2

Henderson; Wayne Darling (*b*); Ed Soph (*d*). 6/77–11/78.

Not bad – but, for Henderson, this is notably second-rate. The main piece is the title-cut, recorded live, and it presents a chance to hear him in the trio format he's favoured of late; there is some typically magisterial playing, but Darling and Soph can't centre the music the way the saxophonist's current groups can. Two brief studio pieces beef up the playing time.

***(*) Relaxin' At Camarillo Original Jazz Classics OJC 776

Henderson; Chick Corea (*p*); Tony Dumas, Richard Davis (*b*); Peter Erskine, Tony Williams (*d*). 8–12/79.

***(*) Mirror, Mirror MPS 519092-2

Henderson; Chick Corea (*p*); Ron Carter (*b*); Billy Higgins (*d*). 1/80.

Henderson and Corea made an improbable but productive team: Joe's doggedly unpredictable lines asked the pianist to concentrate, and a fundamentally lyrical bent is something they both share, even if Corea usually oversweetens his playing. The OJC reissue just has the edge for a long, firmly sustained treatment of 'Y Todavia La Quiero', one of the best of Henderson's Latin tunes – but there is excellent jazz on both discs.

**** The State Of The Tenor Volumes One And Two Blue Note CDP 828779-2 2CD
Henderson; Ron Carter (*b*); Al Foster (*d*). 11/85.

Although they had a mixed reception on their release, these records now sound as authoritative as their titles suggest. Henderson hadn't recorded as a leader for some time, and this was his return to the label where he commenced his career, but there is nothing hesitant or routine about the playing here. Carter and Foster provide detailed support – the dates were carefully prepared, the themes meticulously chosen and rehearsed, before the recordings were made at New York's Village Vanguard – and the bassist in particular is as inventive as the nominal leader. Henderson takes an occasional wrong turning, noted perhaps in a recourse to a favourite lick or two, but he mainly functions at the highest level. The intelligent choice of themes – from Silver, Monk, Mingus, Parker and others, none of them over-familiar – prises a rare multiplicity of phrase-shapes and rhythmical variations out of the tenorman: as a single instance, listen to his manipulations of the beat on Mingus's 'Portrait' (on *Volume Two*), with their accompanying subtleties of tone and attack. Both discs have now been coupled as a mid-price two-disc set.

*** An Evening With Joe Henderson Red 123215-2
Henderson; Charlie Haden (*b*); Al Foster (*d*). 7/87.

More of the same, with Haden substituting for Carter and the four longish tracks opening out a little further. The music isn't as comprehensively prepared, and Haden's flatter sound and less flexible rhythms make him no match for Carter; but Henderson himself plays with majestic power. Decent concert recording, from the Genoa Jazz Festival of 1987.

***(*) The Standard Joe Red RR 123248-2
Henderson; Rufus Reid (*b*); Al Foster (*d*). 3/91.
***(*) Lush Life Verve 511779-2
Henderson; Wynton Marsalis (*t*); Stephen Scott (*p*); Christian McBride (*b*); Gregory Hutchinson (*d*).

There is very little to choose between the two 1991 recordings, though they're very different from each other. The trio session for Red is an off-the-cuff blowing date, but it's obvious from the first measures of 'Blue Bossa' that all three players are in peak form, and the matching sonorities of Reid and Henderson create a startlingly close level of empathy. There is almost 70 minutes of music, including two long but quite different takes of 'Body And Soul', and the invention never flags. *Lush Life* is a programme of Billy Strayhorn compositions done as one solo ('Lush Life'), three duos (one with each member of the rhythm section), a lovely quartet reading of 'Blood Count' and three pieces with Marsalis joining the front line, of which 'Johnny Come Lately' is especially spirited. If Henderson's delivery sounds a fraction less assured than he does at his best, the quality of his thinking is as outstanding as always and, though there is the odd tiny blemish – Scott's treatment of 'Lotus Blossom' seems too irritatingly clever – it's a splendid record.

**** So Near, So Far (Musings For Miles) Verve 517674-2
Henderson; John Scofield (*g*); Dave Holland (*b*); Al Foster (*d*). 10/92.

Great music. Henderson's astonishing run continued with a tribute to Miles Davis from four former sidemen (Henderson played with Davis briefly in the mid-'60s) that stands as a masterclass of top-flight improvising. Impeccably prepared charts for the likes of 'Miles Ahead', boiled down from the original Gil Evans arrangement to a setting for four-piece, directed the players to a particularly acute yet heartfelt memorial. Many of the tunes associated with Davis as composer have scarcely been covered by other players, which adds a note of unusual freshness, but the scope and calibre of the improvising by all four men is what one remembers. Scofield's runs of melody are a match for Henderson's own, and Holland and Foster – the latter in some of his finest playing – are a dream team.

*** Double Rainbow Verve 527222-2
Henderson; Eliane Elias, Herbie Hancock (*p*); Oscar Castro-Neves (*g*); Christian McBride, Nico Assumpcao (*b*); Paul Braga, Jack DeJohnette (d). 95.

Though conceived as a collaboration with Antonio Carlos Jobim, this turned out to be a memorial to the composer after his death, a dozen tunes shared between one Brazilian and one all-American rhythm section. Everybody plays well and Henderson sounds supremely relaxed, but sometimes one longs for a really outstanding solo or for something to intrude on the general sunniness of the music: lush, charming, this is essentially high-calibre light-jazz.

Jon Hendricks (born 1921) VOCALS

***(*) Love Muse MCD 5258
Hendricks; Harry 'Sweets' Edison (*t*); Jerome Richardson (*ts*); David Hazeltine, Jimmy Smith

(*p*); Ray Scott (*g*); Jon Burr, James Leary III, John B. Williams (*b*); Marvin 'Smitty' Smith (*d*); Bob Gurland, Lesley Dorsey, Judith Hendricks, Michele Hendricks (*v*). 8, 9 & 11/81, 1 & 2/82.

*** **Freddie Freeloader** Denon CY 76302
Hendricks; Wynton Marsalis, Randy Sandke, Lew Soloff (*t*); Al Grey, Britt Woodman (*tb*); Jerome Richardson (*as*); Frank Foster, Stanley Turrentine (*ts*); Joe Temperley (*bs*); Tommy Flanagan, Larry Goldings (*p*); Al Rogers, Romero Lumbambo (*g*); Andy McCloud, Tyler Mitchell, George Mraz, Rufus Reid (*b*); Cliff Barbaro, Jimmy Cobb (*d*); Ron McBee (*perc*); Al Jarreau, George Benson, Bobby McFerrin, Judith Hendricks, Aria Hendricks, Kevin Fitzgerald Burke, Manhattan Transfer (*v*); Count Basie Orchestra; strings. 6/89–3/90.

Along with Dave Lambert and Annie Ross, he created some of the most remarkable and underrated jazz ever. Nothing ever quite added up to the sheer *esprit* of Lambert, Hendricks & Ross, but there are flashes on both these later records that allow one to gauge the size and scope of Hendricks's remarkable talent. It is a full, forceful voice, with near-perfect control right through its range and with a speed of articulation only matched by Ross in her heyday. Nonsensical too to suggest that he lacked either accuracy or expressiveness (these are common enough quibbles) when he bends notes with the same freedom as any saxophone player or trumpeter who would receive immoderate praise for what in Hendricks is considered to be uncertain technique. The Denon disc is a virtual summit conference, with superb guest soloists and an uncringey spot for the family group. The earlier disc is undoubtedly a more authentic representation of his art, but it lacks polish and its decidedly sloppy production may prove off-putting to some listeners.

Michele Hendricks VOCAL

(*) **Carryin' On Muse MCD 5336
Hendricks; Stan Getz, Ralph Moore (*ts*); David Leonhardt (*p*); Ray Drummond, Anthony Jackson (*b*); Marvin 'Smitty' Smith (*d*); Kenyate Rahman (*perc*).
(*) **Keepin' Me Satisfied Muse MCD 5363
Hendricks; Claudio Roditi (*t*); Slide Hampton (*tb*); David Newman (*ss, ts*); David Leonhardt (*p*); Anthony Jackson, Ray Drummond (*b*); Marvin 'Smitty' Smith (*d*); Jon Hendricks (*v*). 5/88.
*** **Me And My Shadow** Muse MCD 5404
Hendricks; James Williams, David Leonhardt (*p*); Ray Drummond (*b*); Marvin 'Smitty' Smith (*d*). 2/90.

Jon Hendricks's daughter has a powerful voice of her own, but these scrappy records present her in the endless search for context. Like every singer with mixed jazz and pop ambitions, she can't seem to settle down in either genre. The backings are consistently fine: Leonhardt is a rather moony pianist, but the rhythm sections are otherwise sharp and swinging, and Moore and Getz turn in useful guest-star spots on *Carryin' On*. The biggest problem is with the material: *Carryin' On* is respectably chosen, with a charming 'Dream A Little Dream Of Me' and a well-judged 'Old Devil Moon'; but the attempt at funking up 'I Feel The Earth Move' has few planetary virtues. *Keepin' Me Satisfied* is very erratic: Marvin Gaye's 'What's Going On' is a disastrous start, and the duet with her father is pure indulgence; but a virtuoso dash through 'Just In Time' is genuinely clever and exciting. *Me And My Shadow* is her best to date. James Williams comes in on some tracks and there are no horns to distract from the singer, who picks a more consistent programme this time. 'Na Na Na', a calypso, was a waste of time, but she makes the most of 'Almost Like Being In Love' and 'Misty' is good enough.

Ernie Henry (1926–57) ALTO SAX

*** **Seven Standards And A Blues** Original Jazz Classics OJC 1722
Henry; Kenny Dorham (*t*); Wynton Kelly (*p*); Wilbur Ware (*b*); Philly Joe Jones (*d*). 9/57.
Henry left few records in a very brief career, but those he did make reveal a limited but vividly creative post-Parker altoist. His intense tone points towards Jackie McLean, even as his phrasing mixes the wistfulness of Tadd Dameron (with whom he made some of his early records) and Parker's high drama. *Seven Standards And A Blues* is arguably his best record (two others are still not yet available on CD): not quite fast enough to stand next to the best boppers, Henry instead makes a mark through the plangency of his phrases. On these show-tunes (and the Dameron-like blues, 'Specific Gravity') he leaves a telling mark.

Peter Herbolzheimer (born 1935) BANDLEADER, ARRANGER, TROMBONE

*** Jazz Gala Concert '79 Rare Bid BID 156501 2CD

Herbolzheimer; Allan Botschinsky, Art Farmer, Chuck Findley, Palle Mikkelborg, Jan Oosthof (*t*); Erich Kleinschuster, Nat Peck, Bart Van Lier, Jiggs Whigham (*tb*); Herb Geller (*as, f*); Tony Coe, Don Menza, Ferdinand Povel (*ts*); Heinz Von Hermann (*bs*); Fritz Pauer (*p, electric p*); Eef Albers (*g*); Niels-Henning Orsted-Pedersen (*b*); Alex Riel, Grady Tate (*d*); Leata Galloway (*v*). 11/79.

**(*) Bandfire Koala Records Panda CD 1

Herbolzheimer; Rhythm Combination and Brass. 3 & 8/81.

** Fat Man Boogie Koala Records Panda CD 2

As above. 11/81.

** Fat Man 2: Tribute To Swing Koala Records Panda CD 3

As above. 1/82.

*** Bigband Bebop Koala Records Panda CD 4

As above. 10 & 12/83.

**(*) More Bebop Koala Records Panda CD 5

As above. 8/84.

*** Latin Groove Koala Records Panda 13

As above. 86.

*** Friends And Silhouettes Koala Music P25 / IRS 970.345

As above, except add Charlie Mariano (*as*); David Friedman (*vib, mar*). 11/91.

Peter Herbolzheimer's Rhythm Combination and Brass is a superbly schooled and utterly professional big band with a well-deserved reputation among musicians and fans alike. It has retained a remarkably consistent line-up throughout the 1980s and, perhaps as a result, can sound on occasions about as exciting as a well-tuned auto engine. On the other hand, Herbolzheimer's charts can generate intense excitment. His handling of trumpets is particularly vivid, and it's this aspect that lifts the heavily guest-starred *Jazz Gala Concert* of 1979 right out of the ordinary; alongside such intriguingly named originals as 'The Age Of Prominence' and 'The Mixolydian Highlander' (a reference to one of the modes of medieval music), there are superb readings of 'Giant Steps', 'Stormy Monday' and 'Bluesette'.

Much of the Koala catalogue (Herbolzheimer's own label) has now been transferred to CD. There are a lot of these records and not a great deal beyond the obvious generic targets to distinguish them. Again, the guest slots on *Friends And Silhouettes* sets it somewhat apart, but there should be no confusing the fact that Herbolzheimer's recruiting policy delivers a quality product time after time.

Peter Herborn ARRANGER, CONDUCTOR, TROMBONE, EUPHONIUM

*** Something Personal JMT 849156

Herborn; Auryn String Quartet: Matthias Lingenfelder, Jens Oppermann (*vn*); Steuart Eaton (*vla*); Andreas Arndt (*clo*); with Tim Berne (*as*); Django Bates (*p, thn*); Marc Ducret (*g*); Lindsey Horner (*b*). 5/91.

**** Traces Of Trane JMT 514002

Herborn; Robin Eubanks (*tb*); Gary Thomas (*as*); Marc Ducret (*g*); Mark Helias (*b*); Tom Rainey (*d*); WDR Big Band: Andy Haderer, John Marshall, Klaus Osterloh, Rick Kiefer, Bob Bruynen (*t, flhn*); Dave Horler, Ludwig Nuss, Bernd Laukamp, Edward Partyka (*tb*); Reiner Wiberny, Stefan Pfeiffer, Olivier Pieters, Rolf Römer, Paul Peucker (*reeds*); Frank Chastenier (*p*). 2/92.

The title of Herborn's first record – now unfortunately deleted – has it just about right: *Subtle Wildness*. Herborn's music habitually achieves a balancing act between academic formality and the improvisational freedom still largely demanded of jazz. Though it is on the surface a very 'European' sound, its roots are always to be found in American jazz (and rock) of the 1960s. Like another erstwhile trombonist-turned-composer, Mike Gibbs, he has a brilliant melodic instinct and a sure feel for unexpected voicings.

Is this what we should expect from Jazz Music Today, as the label's initials promise? Herborn is certainly in the line of mavericks like the Austrian Franz Koglmann in that his traditionalism is cool, ironic and largely detached from conventional expectations of virtuosity. In so far as he is a jazz musician at all (and his trombone playing has an almost classical tonality), he has moved one step beyond improvisation towards the idealized 'composition' the critic Jacques Attali suggested was the ideal terminus of the whole Western tradition.

On *Something Personal* Herborn took the bold, though not unprecedented, step of giving most of the work to a string quartet, using the other instruments for coloration or to highlight the interplay of rhythm and melody. The opening piece, 'The Last Objection', is for strings alone and might take its place in a straight programme of contemporary compositions. Most of the rest contain graphic flourishes from Ducret, whose 12-string sound is carefully woven into the lighter texture of the fiddles. The absence of percussion allows the rhythms to float ambiguously, but not without a firm pulse. The horns are used very sparingly; Berne hectic on 'Rush Hour', more nonchalant on 'Music For Forgotten Lovers' and 'Fallingwater'; Bates's tenor horn on a rewritten and un-Monkish 'Evidence' stands in for both Wheeler and Herborn himself, who might normally have been expected to fill this role. A version of 'All Along The Watchtower' in Hendrix mode is little more than a steal from the Kronos Quartet's 'Purple Haze' transcription.

Coltrane tributes came and went after 1987, the twentieth anniversary of the saxophonist's death. *Traces of Trane* is one of the best of them, largely because it sets aside sentimental homage in favour of a wholesale reappraisal of the mechanics of Coltrane's writing. The chaotic majesty of *Ascension* was the nearest the saxophonist came to big-band composition. Herborn manages to capture some of that clattering disorder (notably in the opening bars of 'Impressions') while giving the pieces – 'My Favorite Things', 'Naima', 'Acknowledgement' and 'Resolution' from *A Love Supreme* – a considerable architecture. A medley of 'Love', 'To Be' and 'The Drum Thing' is less successful, though it again attempts to emphasize internal consistencies rather than contrasts.

Solos serve a rather different function than they did in the originals. Gary Thomas is a curious actor for the Coltrane role, but the very inappropriateness of his tone and approach is part of the drama, centrally on 'Naima' and the closing 'Resolution'. Eubanks and Ducret both contribute significantly, but the main focus remains Herborn's detailed charts. By the end of the 1980s, Coltrane's influence, particularly on saxophone players, seemed to be on the verge of exhaustion. Along with Marilyn Crispell's examination of the saxophonist's rhythm, *Traces of Trane* points a way forward.

Heritage Hall Jazz Band GROUP

**(*) Cookin! GHB BCD-287
> Teddy Riley (t, v); Fred Lonzo (tb); Manuel Crusto (cl); Ellis Marsalis (p); Walter Payton Jr (b); Freddie Kohlman (d, v). 92.

Swinging new jazz from New Orleans in the old style, even if it was recorded in New York. The problem might be that, personable as these stylists are, they don't make up a convincing ensemble. Riley and Crusto are old-school players, with the trumpeter's powers in some decline, and their leads are sometimes a little overwhelmed by Marsalis's sweeping piano and Kohlman's spirited drums. Lonzo, one of the best of the younger New Orleans traditionalists, plays more of a cameo role. The material is old hat, even if these oldish heads have the right to wear it.

Woody Herman (1913–87) CLARINET, ALTO SAXOPHONE, VOCAL

*** **Blues On Parade** MCA GRP 16062
> Herman; Clarence Willard, Kermit Simmons, Steady Nelson, Mac MacQuordale, Bob Price, John Owens, Ray Linn, Cappy Lewis, George Seaberg, Billy Rogers, Charles Peterson (t); Joe Bishop (flhn); Neal Reid, Toby Tyler, Bud Smith, Vic Hamann, Tommy Farr, Walter Nimms (tb); Murray Williams, Don Watt, Joe Estrin, Ray Hopfner, Herb Tompkins, Joe Denton, Eddie Scalzi, Jimmy Horvath, Sam Rubinowich (as); Saxie Mansfield, Bruce Wilkins, Pete Johns, Ronnie Perry, Nick Caiazza, Sammy Armato, Mickey Folus, Herbie Haymer, Pete Mondello (ts); Skippy DeSair (bs); Horace Diaz, Tommy Linehan (p); Nick Hupfer (vn); Chick Reeves, Hy White (g); Walter Yoder (b); Frank Carlson (d). 4/37–7/42.

*** **At The Woodchoppers Ball** ASV AJA 5143
> Similar to above. 3/36–1/42.

Woody Herman didn't secure his principal fame until after these early tracks were made, but as an instrumentalist and vocalist he was already a characterful performer, and the pre-war sides – by a band that came together out of the Isham Jones Orchestra in 1936 – were centred mainly around him. There was some light pop fodder in among them but the MCA compilation concentrates on the better material, and while the band is short on strong soloists – trombonist Reid and flugelhorn player Bishop, who also contributed several of the charts, are about the best of them – the arrangements make the most of simple blues resources, one reason why the orchestra was called 'The Band That Plays The Blues'. By the 1940s, though, Herman was seeking out superior material and hiring sharper musicians. Lowell Martin contributed a fine 'Blues In The Night' to the band's book, and the final tune on this disc, 'Down Under', was penned by John Birks Gillespie. Woody himself was a clarinettist whose easy-going playing lacked the brilliance of Goodman or Shaw but made up in affable, on-the-beat timing. A few tracks are by the small band of The Four Chips and the immortal 'Woodchoppers' Ball' is here in its original version, a Joe Bishop head arrangement. The transfers here are mostly superior examples of the NoNoise system of remastering. They're a shade better than ASV's reproduction, although there's little in it and, if the ASV set is a tad more generous, it's less hardcore in jazz terms.

(*) At The Hollywood Palladium 1942–1944 RST 91536-2

> Herman; Cappy Lewis, George Seaberg, Chuck Peterson, Neal Hefti, Chuck Frankhauser, Ray Wetzel, Pete Candoli, Carl Warwick (*t*); Neal Reid, Tommy Farr, Walter Nimms, Bill Harris, Ralph Pfeffner, Ed Kiefer (*tb*); Sam Rubinowich, James Horvath, Mickey Folus, Pete Mondello, Skippy DeSair, Sam Marowitz, John LaPorta, Flip Phillips (*reeds*); Tommy Linehan, Ralph Burns (*p*); Marjorie Hyams (*vib*); Hy White, Billy Bauer (*g*); Chubby Jackson, Walter Yoder (*b*); Dave Tough, Frank Carlson (*d*); Carolyn Grey, Frances Wayne (*v*). 8/42–11/44.

A couple of broadcast shows, the first in quite good sound, the second very scrappy; and the pity is that the latter features the really interesting band. '125th Street Prophet' is a glimmer of what the band could do. Too many vocals, but the playing remains swinging.

**** **The V-Disc Years Vols 1 & 2** Hep CD2/3435 2CD

> Herman; Sonny Berman, Shorty Rogers, Cappy Lewis, Billy Rogers, Pete Candoli, Conte Candoli, Chuck Frankhauser, Carl Warwick, Ray Wetzel, Neal Hefti, Irv Lewis, Ray Linn, Marky Markowitz (*t*); Bill Harris, Ed Kiefer, Ralph Pfeffner, Neal Reid, Bob Swift, Rodney Ogle, Tommy Pederson (*tb*); Sam Marowitz, John LaPorta, Les Robinson, Jimmy Horvath (*as*); Mickey Folus, Flip Phillips, Pete Mondello, Vido Musso, Ben Webster (*ts*); Sam Rubinowich, Skippy DeSair (*bs*); Ralph Burns, Fred Otis, Tony Aless (*p*); Margie Hyams, Red Norvo (*vib*); Chuck Wayne, Billy Bauer, (*g*); Joe Mondragon, Chubby Jackson, Walt Yoder (*b*); Dave Tough, Don Lamond, Johnny Blowers (*d*); Martha Raye, Frances Wayne, Carolyn Grey (*v*). 2/45–12/47.

A brilliant rhythm section, a brass team that could top any big-band section on either coast and arrangements that crackled with spontaneity and wit: Herman's 1945 band was both a commercial and an artistic triumph. With Burns, Bauer, Tough and Jackson spurring the horns on, the band handled head arrangements and slicker charts such as Neal Hefti's 'Wild Root' with the same mixture of innate enthusiasm and craft. There was a modern edge to the group that suggested something of the transition from swing to bop, even though it was the Second Herd that threw in its lot with bop spirit if not letter.

Until Columbia do their Herman recordings justice in a full CD reissue, this collection of V-Discs will have to do. Impeccably restored by Jack Towers and John R. T. Davies, the music comes flag-waving through with most of its original punch intact. Showstoppers such as 'Red Top' and 'Apple Honey' still impress and, if the soloists don't always have the finesse of some of Woody's later section stars, there is still some superb playing from most hands, with rare glimpses of Berman, Burns, Bauer and others.

*** **Woodchoppers' Ball Live 1944 Vol. 1** Jass 621

> Herman; Neal Hefti, Billy Robbins, Ray Wetzel, Pete Candoli, Conte Candoli, Charlie Frankhauser, Carl 'Bama' Warwick (*t*); Ralph Pfeffner, Bill Harris, Ed Kiefer (*tb*); Sam Marowitz, Bill Shine, John LaPorta (*as*); Flip Phillips, Pete Mondello (*ts*); Skippy DeSair (*bs*); Ralph Burns (*p*); Margie Hyams (*vib*); Billy Bauer (*g*); Chubby Jackson (*b*); Dave Tough (*d*); Frances Wayne (*v*). 8–10/44.

***(*) **Northwest Passage Live 1945 Vol. 2** Jass 625

> As above, except add Sonny Berman, Ray Linn (*t*), Tony Aless (*p*); omit Robbins and Shine. 7–8/45.

Live material by Herman was reissued in a somewhat haphazard way in the LP era, and these two CDs sort out a few broadcasts with good sound and sensible programming. The first includes a V-Disc version of 'Flying Home' and two broadcast sessions. Herman, Harris, Phillips and Pete Candoli take the lion's share of the solo features and the band sound in exuberant form. But the second disc, with this edition of the Herd really getting into its stride, is even better: Frances Wayne has two of her best features in 'Saturday Night' and 'Happiness Is A Thing Called Joe' and the band rocket through 'Apple Honey', 'Bijou' and 'Red Top'. A valuable supplement to the studio sessions.

***(*) **Keeper Of The Flame** Capitol 984532-2

> Herman; Ernie Royal, Bernie Glow, Stan Fishelson, Red Rodney, Shorty Rogers, Charlie Walp, Al Porcino (*t*); Earl Swope, Bill Harris, Ollie Wilson, Bob Swift, Bart Varsalona (*tb*); Sam Marowitz (*as*); Al Cohn, Zoot Sims, Stan Getz, Herman Marowitz, Gene Ammons, Buddy Savitt, Jimmy Giuffre (*ts*); Serge Chaloff (*bs*); Lou Levy (*p*); Terry Gibbs (*vib*); Chubby Jackson, Joe Mondragon, Oscar Pettiford (*b*); Don Lamond, Shelly Manne (*d*); Mary Anne McCall (*v*). 12/48–7/49.

Finally a CD reissue for some of the best tracks by Herman's Second Herd. A look through the personnel reveals a formidable roll-call, and the obvious stand-out is the famous reading of 'Early Autumn' with Getz's immortal tenor solo. Chaloff is memorable in his outings, especially 'Lollipop', and 'That's Right' and 'Lemon Drop' are minor Herman classics; but there is some commercial chaff too, which reminds that this was a band that was looking for an audience as well as trying to swing.

*** **Early Autumn** Discovery DSCD-944

Herman; Don Fagerquist, John Howell, Roy Caton, Stu Williamson, Tommy DiCarlo, Joe Brunette, Ernie Royal, Bernie Glow, Harold Wegbreit, Bobby Styles, Doug Mettome, Chris Griffin, Phil Cook, Dick Collins, Al Porcino, Reuben McFall, Bill Gastagnino, Arno Marsh, Bill Perkins, Charlie Walp (*t*); Cy Touff (*bt*); Carl Fontana, Urbie Green, Jack Green, Will Bradley, Frank Rehak, Vernon Friley, Kai Winding, Dick Kenney, Keith Moon (*tb*); Arno Marsh, Dick Hafer, Bill Perkins, Bill Trujillo, Jerry Coker, Dave Madden (*ts*); Sam Staff (*bs, f*); Jack Nimitz (*bs*); Nat Pierce (*p, cel*); Chubby Jackson, Red Kelly (*b*); Sonny Igoe, Art Madigan, Chuck Flores (*d*); Candido Camero, Jose Mangual (*perc*). 5/52–7/54.

The 'Early Autumn' here is primarily a feature for Herman as a vocalist (and a fine one, too). This CD collects 17 performances by the Third Herd: it may have lacked the starry quality of the previous band, and in the aftermath of the big-band era charts such as 'Four Others' (a 'Four Brothers' revision for the trombone section) and the light hokum of 'Mother Goose Jumps' sound anachronistic at a time when, for instance, Shorty Rogers was streamlining big-band practice. But the orchestra still had a lot of very good players, and a piece such as 'Men From Mars' finds the Herd adjusting to cooler conditions with a fair degree of success. The remastering has been carefully done and the band sound big and strong.

*** **The Great Soloists 1945–1958** Blue Flame BFCD-1003

Personnels unlisted. 45–58.

A scattering of mostly heated big-band workouts covering a 15-year period, this has scrappy documentation but is full of great music. There are starring moments for Getz, Sims, Berman, Chaloff and many more, with the extraordinary workout on Shorty Rogers's chart, 'More Moon', hitting a pinnacle of big-band energy. Sound varies widely – several bright and clean tracks, but a lot suffer from hiss, surface noise or general wear and tear.

**** **Live Featuring Bill Harris Vol. 1** Status STCD 107

Herman; Bill Berry, John Cappola, Bill Castagnino, Andy Peele, Danny Styles (*t*); Bill Harris, Bobby Lamb, Willie Dennis (*tb*); Jay Migliori, Jimmie Cooke, Bob Newman (*ts*); Roger Pemberton (*bs*); John Bunch (*p*); Jimmy Gannon (*b*); Don Michaels (*d*). 6/57.

***(*) **Live Featuring Bill Harris Vol. 2** Status STCD 110

As above. 6/57.

*** **Live At Marion** Jazz Hour JH-1014

As above. 6–8/57.

***(*) **Live At Peacock Lane Hollywood 1958** Jazz Hour JH-1015

Herman; Danny Stiles, Bobby Clark, John Cappola, Andy Peele, Hal Posey (*t*); Bill Harris, Archie Martin, Roy Weigand (*tb*); Joe Romano, Jay Migliori, Arno Marsh (*ts*); Roger Pemberton (*bs*); Pete Jolly (*p*); Jimmy Gannon (*b*); Jake Hanna (*d*). 1/58.

***(*) **The Herd Rides Again** Evidence ECD 22010-2

Herman; Ernie Royal, Al Stewart, Bernie Glow, Nick Travis, Burt Collins, Marky Markowitz, Joe Ferrante, Willie Thomas (*t*); Bob Brookmeyer, Billy Byers, Frank Rehak (*tb*); Sam Marowitz (*as*); Al Cohn, Sam Donahue, Paul Quinichette (*ts*); Danny Blake (*bs*); Nat Pierce (*p*); Billy Bauer (*g*); Chubby Jackson (*b*); Don Lamond (*d*). 7–8/58.

*** **Herman's Heat And Puente's Beat** Evidence ECD 22008-2

Herman; Willie Thomas, Danny Stiles, Hal Posey, Al Forte, Bobby Clark, Ernie Royal, Steve Lipkins, Nick Travis, Marky Markowitz (*t*); Willie Dennis, Jimmy Guinn, Roger DeLilio, Bill Elton, Billy Byers, Frank Rehak (*tb*); Mart Flax, Joe Romano, Jay Migliore, Pete Mondello, Danny Bank, Al Cohn, Herman Marowitz, Paul Quinichette, Al Belletto (*reeds*); Al Planck (*p*); Major Holley, Robert Rodriguez (*b*); Jimmy Campbell (*d*); Tito Puente, Ray Barretto, Raymond Rodriguez, Gilbert Lopez (*perc*). 9/58.

Superbly remastered by Dave Kay, the Status CDs are wonderful souvenirs of the Herman band as it sounded on a typical dance date in Omaha in 1957. While Woody's records for Capitol and Verve from the 1950s have nearly all slipped from circulation, these live sets are a glowing testimony to how fine the band could be. The ballads have a smooth, perfectly cooked texture, the brass almost gliding from *piano* to *forte*, but the swingers hit home with astonishing precision, and the arrangements – mainly by Ralph Burns or Gene Roland – play to all the strengths of the band and give them enough to chew on to keep everybody interested. The simple notion of Roland's 'Stairway To The Blues' is almost a textbook exercise, but the band make it into a classic performance, finding just the right tempo and leavening with half a dozen solos that lead to Bill Harris's climactic statement. Harris had already been with Herman for many years, but only now was he genuinely asserting himself as the band's major soloist, his playing utterly unpredictable and individual from phrase to phrase. Both Status discs are full of great music, and so is the Peacock Lane session, which is also in fine sound: there is a spellbinding feature for Harris in Ralph Burns's arrangement of 'Gloomy Sunday', but the reeds have a very good night of it as well. Jazz Hour's *Marion* disc adds still more to the 1957 dates, with ten tunes from one concert and three more from another in September.

The Evidence reissues restore two more good Herman dates to the catalogue. Harris is replaced by Brookmeyer, and he brings his more ascetic wit to his features, while both reed and rhythm sections exude class. The programme on *The Herd Rides Again* is mostly remakes of old Herman hits, which are revised as frequently as the Ellington band's staples. Half of *Herman's Heat* is the band alone on six charts; the rest is a bang-up meeting with Tito Puente's percussion team, period stuff but engagingly done.

*** **1963 Summer Tour** Jazz Hour JH-1006
    Herman; Bill Hunt, Dave Gale, Bill Chase, Gerry Lamy, Paul Fontaine (*t*); Bob Rudolph, Phil Wilson, Henry Southall (*tb*); Sal Nistico, Carmen Leggio, Bobby Jones, Jack Stevens (*ts*); Frank Hittner (*bs*); Nat Pierce (*p*); Chuck Andrus (*b*); Jake Hanna (*d*). 63.

The Fourth Herd in action. The swinging delivery of 'The Preacher' sets a notable tone from the start and, though sound is indifferently mixed and the programme is still reliant on some Herman warhorses, this is a tough and hard-hiting edition which is an impressive curtain-raiser for the kind of playing heard on the next entry.

**** **Woody's Winners** Columbia 468454-2
    Herman; Bill Chase, Bob Shew, Don Rader, Dusko Goykovich, Gerald Lamy (*t*); Henry Southall, Frank Tesinsky, Donald Doane (*tb*); Gary Klein, Sal Nistico, Andy McGhee (*ts*); Tom Anastas (*bs*); Nat Pierce (*p*); Anthony Leonardi (*b*); Ronnie Zito (*d*). 6/65.

For sheer excitement this is in a class of its own, one of the greatest big-band records ever made. Cut live at San Francisco's Basin Street West, the band roar through a programme that includes some of the best writing Herman ever had – from Don Rader, Bill Chase, Dusko Goykovich and Nat Pierce – performed by one of his most enthusiastic and capable outfits. The opening showcase for the trumpet section, Chase's '23 Red', is a showstopper in itself, but the up-tempo revision of 'My Funny Valentine', Sal Nistico's burn-up on 'Northwest Passage' and Woody's own serene treatment of 'Poor Butterfly' maintain a standard that climaxes with a famous demolition of Horace Silver's 'Opus De Funk'. The sound was never in the highest of fidelity (even on original vinyl), but this CD is pretty good, and is one of the most welcome reissues of recent years.

(*) **The Raven Speaks Original Jazz Classics OJC 663
    Herman; Al Porcino, Charles Davis, John Thomas, Bill Stapleton (*t*); Bill Byrne, Bob Burgess, Rick Stepton, Harold Garrett (*tb*); Frank Tiberi, Greg Herbert, Steve Lederer, Tom Anastas (*reeds*); Harold Danko (*p*); Pat Martino (*g*); Al Johnson (*b*); Joe LaBarbera (*d*); John Pacheco (*perc*). 8/72.

Herman's 1970s bands were still impressive outfits, but their studio records tended towards a fashionable and ultimately pretty indifferent eclecticism. This one has a top-notch cast largely wasted on some dreary tunes and so-so charts, which just occasionally flicker or burst into life.

(*) **Live In Warsaw Storyville STCD 8207
    Herman; Jeffrey Davis, Nelson Hatt, John Hoffman, Dennis Dotson, William Byrne (*t*); Jim Pugh, Dale Kirkland (*tb*); Vaughan Wiester (*btb*); Frank Tiberi, Gary Anderson, Salvatore Spicola, John Oslawski (*reeds*); David Mays (*p*); Wilbur Stewart (*b*); Stephen Houghton (*d*). 2/76.

A typical late-period Herman concert, cut in Poland in 1976. The programme relies heavily on the Herman hits with an overblown 'McArthur Park' there to test the stamina of some. Amazing, really, that the band could attack what were very old charts and tunes with such spirit.

*** **Woody And Friends** Concord CCD 4170
    Herman; Dizzy Gillespie, Joe Rodriguez, Tim Burke, Kitt Reid, Jim Powell, Bill Byrne, Woody Shaw (*t*); Birch Johnson, Nelson Hinds, Larry Shunk, Slide Hampton (*tb*); Frank Tiberi (*ts, f, bsn*); Dick Mitchell (*ts, f, af, ob, picc*); Bob Belden, Stan Getz (*ts*); Gary Smulyan (*bs*); Dave Lalama (*p*); Dave LaRocca (*b*); Ed Soph (*d*). 9/79.

*** **Woody Herman Presents . . . Vol. 1: A Concord Jam** Conord CCD 4142
    Herman; Warren Vaché (*c*); Eiji Kitamura (*cl*); Dick Johnson (*as, f*); Scott Hamilton (*ts*); Dave McKenna (*p*); Cal Tjader (*vib*); Cal Collins (*g*); Bob Maize (*b*); Jake Hanna (*d*). 8/80.

*** **Woody Herman Presents . . . Vol. 2: Four Others** Concord CCD 4180
    Herman; Al Cohn, Sal Nistico, Flip Phillips, Bill Perkins (*ts*); John Bunch (*p*); George Duvivier (*b*); Don Lamond (*d*). 7/81.

(*) **Live At The Concord Jazz Festival Concord CCD 4191
> Herman; Brian O'Flaherty, Scott Wagstaff, Mark Lewis, George Rabbai, Bill Stapleton (*t, flhn*); Gene Smith, John Fedchock, Larry Shunk (*tb*); Bill Ross (*ts, f, af, picc*); Paul McGinley (*ts, f*); Randy Russell (*ts, f*); Al Cohn, Zoot Sims (*ts*); Nick Brignola (*bs, bcl*); John Oddo (*p*); Mike Hall (*b*); Dave Ratajczak (*d*). 8/81.

*** **Live In Chicago** Status 105
> As above. 3/81.

(*) **World Class Concord CCD 4240
> As above, except Bill Byrne (*t, flhn*), Randy Hawes (*tb*), Sal Nistico, Jim Carroll, Med Flory, Flip Phillips, Frank Tiberi (*ts*), Dave Shapiro (*b*), Jeff Hamilton (*perc*) replace Stapleton, Shunk, Ross, Russell, Sims and Hall. 9/82.

*** **50th Anniversary Tour** Concord CCD 4302
> Herman; Roger Ingram, Les Lovitt, Mark Lewis, Ron Stout, Bill Byrne (*t*); John Fedchock, Paul McKee (*tb*); Mark Lusk (*btb*); Dave Riekenberg (*ts, f*); Frank Tiberi, Jerry Pinter (*ts*); Nick Brignola (*bs*); Brad Williams (*p*); Lynn Seaton (*b*); Jim Rupp (*d*). 3/86.

(*) **Woody's Gold Star Concord CCD 4330
> As above, except George Baker, Jim Powell (*t, flhn*), Joe Barati (*btb*), Joel Weiskopf (*p*), Nick Carpenter (*b*), Dave Miller (*d*), Pete Escovedo, Poncho Sanchez, Ramon Banda (*perc*) replace Lovitt, Lewis, Lusk, Williams, Seaton and Rupp. 3/87.

Herman's final years were capably documented by Concord and, although there are no truly outstanding records in this stint, there are sound standards of big-band playing on the orchestral records and plenty of characteristic Herman dudgeon on the small-group discs. Though his final years were tragically marred by problems with the IRS, he somehow found the spirit to play jazz with much of his old fire. What had changed – as it did for Ellington, Basie and Goodman, his fellow survivors from a bygone era – was the traditional big band's place in the music. As a repertory orchestra, filled with good, idiomatic players but few real characters, Herman's last Herd had no more going for it than precision and automatic punch. *Woody And Friends* finds them at the 1979 Monterey Festival, with Gillespie, Hampton, Shaw and Getz (doing a lovely 'What Are You Doing The Rest Of Your Life') as guest stars, and the occasion is atmospherically recalled by the record. The *Concord Jam* session mixes young and older players and everyone is in strong voice, with features for everybody. *Four Others* lines up four tenor stalwarts to so-so effect. The remaining big-band records all have their moments without securing any serious candidacy for any collection that already has plenty of vintage Herman in it.

Vincent Herring (born 1964) ALTO AND SOPRANO SAXOPHONES

*** **American Experience** Musicmasters 5037-2
> Herring; Tex Allen, Dave Douglas (*t*); Clifford Adams (*tb*); John Hicks, Bruce Barth (*p*); James Genus, Marcus McLaurine (*b*); Mark Johnson, Beaver Harris (*d*). 4/86–12/89.

***(*) **Evidence** Landmark LCD 1527
> Herring; Wallace Roney (*t*); Mulgrew Miller (*p*); Ira Coleman (*b*); Carl Allen (*d*). 6–7/90.

***(*) **Dawnbird** Landmark LCD 1522
> As above, except add Scott Wendholt (*t*), Kevin Hays (*p*), Dwayne Burno (*b*), Carl Allen, Billy Drummond (*d*). 10/91–2/92.

*** **Secret Love** MusicMasters 65092
> Herring; Renée Rosnes (*p*); Ira Coleman (*b*); Billy Drummond (*d*). 92.

***(*) **Don't Let It Go** Music Masters 65121
> Herring; Scott Wendholt (*t*); Cyrus Chestnut (*p*); Jesse Yusef Murray (*b*); Carl Allen (*d*). 10/94.

All Herring's early press talked about Cannonball Adderley. It wasn't just that he was the main force in brother Nat's band; he sounded so close to the keening blues of Cannon that it seemed like he'd sprung from the man's own alto. These records don't tell a very different story, but they're a pretty fair résumé of a career on the move. It would be hard to top his solo on the opening 'The Athlolete' on *American Experience* as an example of here-I-am *brio* – firing through the changes with an attack that blows past any doubts about his experience. This is 'prentice work, all the same, and, though there is a youthful exuberance about the two sessions that make up the record, the bands are comparatively ordinary and Herring stands out like a beacon. *Evidence* is more like it: a great quintet and vintage hard bop on eight well-chosen pieces. Roney plays well and the rhythm section are blue-chip. *Dawnbird* is in some ways even better, most of the record cut by the same group (with Drummond in for Allen) but an extra edge lent by the last three tracks with the very keen Wendholt and Hays on the case. One can see why he wanted to make the more easy-going and ballad- or mid-tempo-orientated *Secret Love* – nobody wants to be seen as a mere speed merchant – but one misses Herring's quota of derring-do and the hint of dark deeds in his distinctive minor-key compositions.

Don't Let It Go is surely the best of the bunch to date, a beautifully crafted and unfussily executed session that ends on a 'Blueprint For a New Tomorrow' (still the same shadows, though). The combination with Wendholt has been proven before, but it is Chestnut who adds the necessary leaven on this occasion.

Fred Hersch PIANO

*** **Sarabande** Sunnyside SSC 1024
  Hersch; Charlie Haden (*b*); Joey Baron (*d*). 12/86.
***(*) **Etc** Red 123233-2
  Hersch; Steve LaSpina (*b*); Jeff Hirshfield (*d*). 5/88.
*** **Heartsongs** Sunnyside SSC 1047
  Hersch; Mike Formanek (*b*); Jeff Hirshfield (*d*). 12/89.
***(*) **Evanessence: A Tribute To Bill Evans** Jazz City 660.53.027
  Hersch; Gary Burton (*vib*); Toots Thielemans (*hca*); Marc Johnson, Michael Formanek (*b*); Jeff Hirshfield (*d*). 8/90.
*** **Forward Motion** Chesky JD 55
  Hersch; Richard Perry (*ts*); Erik Friedlander (*clo*); Scott Colley (*b*); Tom Rainey (*d*). 7/91.
*** **Dancing In The Dark** Chesky JD 90
  Hersch; Drew Gress (*b*); Tom Rainey (*d*). 12/92.

Even though he denies the closeness of the affinity, Fred Hersch is one of the guardians of Bill Evans's light. He's rhythmically more varied in his approach than Evans but, in terms of touch and harmonic sensibility, there's a very close parallel. Originals such as 'Lullabye' (*Heartsongs*) and 'Child's Song' (*Sarabande*) are close kin to Evans's ballads, too. But Hersch has an energy of his own, and all these records have something to commend them. *Heartsongs* is one of the best-integrated, since it's by a regular trio: Haden is a little too stodgy to make *Sarabande*'s liveliest tunes break out, and *Horizons* is good though a trifle routine. *Heartsongs* has the most individual approach to the material, and Hersch chooses good covers: Wayne Shorter's 'Fall' is done in *passacaglia* form, and Ornette Coleman's 'The Sphinx' casts the composer in an impish light. But a few of the freer pieces sound more effortful than they should: Hersch may be an impressive conservative, but he's a conservative all the same. *Etc* is a more straight-ahead date, and this time the music works out beautifully: a fine programme of jazz themes, with LaSpina and Hirshfield both constructive and challenging in support, the bassist in particular coming up with some quick ideas and agile lines.

Evanessence wears Hersch's affections on his sleeve, but he 'felt that this was the best way to exorcize the ghost' of being in a Bill Evans pigeonhole. Although it doesn't work to that end, Hersch's subtle variations on certain Evans favourites put a lot of himself into the project, Thielemans plays beautifully on his tracks, and even the normally pacific Gary Burton plays with unusual aggression – as if in the spirit of the exploratory, later Evans – on his three appearances. The two Chesky albums bask in the glowing studio sound that has become this label's speciality and, while both feature strong support for Hersch from the rhythm section, the music doesn't quite catch as much fire as *Etc* or the best of the Evans tribute. *Dancing In The Dark* has the edge for the attacking edge Hersch puts on the up-tempo tunes.

***(*) **At Maybeck Vol. 31** Concord CCD 4596
  Hersch (*p* solo). 10/93.

Hersch's turn at Maybeck might not be his finest hour, but it sets up a near-perfect balance of his meditative and argumentative sides. The percussive, almost stabbing treatment of Coleman's 'Ramblin'' and the breezy lyricism of his own 'Heartsong' are set beside a glowing 'If I Loved You' and a very ambitious approach to 'Haunted Heart' which opens the song out into a long *fantaisie*. As usual, impeccable sound.

**** **Last Night When We Were Young** Classical Action 1001
  Hersch; Jane Ira Bloom (*ss*); Bobby Watson, Craig Bailey (*as*); Phil Woods (*as*); Dan Faulk (*ts*); Toots Thielemans (*hca*); Andy Bey (*p, v*); George Shearing, Rob Schneiderman, Dave Catney (*p*); Oscar Castro-Neves (*g*); Gary Burton (*vib*); Drew Gress, Rufus Reid (*b*); Tom Whaley, Akira Tana (*d*); Leny Andrade, Mark Murphy, Janis Siegel (*v*). 94.

Recorded for the label set up by Performing Arts Against AIDS, this remarkable record was organized by Hersch and he plays on eight of the 13 tracks. As a sequence of ballad interpretations there can be few recent records to come even close to it, with some of the artists giving career performances: Leny Andrade on 'Quiet Nights', Jane Ira Bloom on 'Wee Small Hours Of The Morning', the Tana Reid group on 'Memories Of You'. Bobby Watson does a memorable one-take exploration of 'Soul Eyes', Janis Siegel eclipses most memories of 'More Than You Know', and Toots Thielemans is typically superb on 'Estate'. Fred, who is himself HIV-positive, has a very fine 'Somewhere' and he accompanies elsewhere with a sympathy that lifts everyone's game, with the closing duet with Mark Murphy leaving the listener very quiet. Despite the melancholy subtext, this is a superlative and ultimately uplifting record.

*** **Beautiful Love** Sunnyside SSC 1066
    Hersch; Jay Clayton (*v*). 5/94.
Rather different from Hersch's occasional collaboration with Janis Siegel, but no less rewarding in its way. Clayton's adventurous ways wih time and space lend occasionally over-startling timbres to some of these standards, and it's not an approach for all tastes. But any who admire the kind of sensibility that Betty Carter has brought to jazz will surely warm to this: try their version of 'Footprints' to start.

John Hicks (born 1941) PIANO

(*) **Steadfast Strata East 660.51.011
    Hicks (*p* solo). 5/75.
**** **Live At Maybeck Recital Hall, Volume 7** Concord CCD 4442
    As above. 8/90.
Hicks has been the pianist of choice on so many fine recordings that it's often overlooked how compressed his own career has been. With nothing in the catalogue between the two Strata Easts (*Hell's Bells* is considered with the other trios) and the first live session on Evidence in 1984, there is then a great rush of material from the '80s, perhaps too much from the casual collector's point of view.

As with many another pianist, there could be no better start than the Maybeck Hall concert. The opening 'Blue In Green' has a relaxed, untroubled quality and helps check out both the piano and a lovely acoustic. 'All Of You' is so bouncy that one isn't quite prepared for the fulsome sweep of 'After The Rain'. Hicks has shown a considerable understanding of and sympathy for Coltrane's harmonic ideas, and Coltrane compositions appear regularly throughout his work. His own composition, 'Naima's Love Song', has a strong Coltrane resonance, and echoes of the original 'Naima', heard on the duos with David Murray (below), frequently insinuate themselves into solos.

The set continues with an improvised 'Blues For Maybeck' and with material by Billy Childs, Kurt Weill, Monk, Mingus and Wayne Shorter. Bud Powell's 'Oblivion' is a long-standing favourite (also included on *In Concert*, below) and 'Straighten Up And Fly Right' has been Hicks's curtain-piece for some time.

By contrast, the Strata East session is almost callow. It is remarkable how much and how quickly Hicks developed as a soloist without changing his essential style. Mal Waldron's 'Soul Eyes' retains much of the moody romanticism Coltrane once poured into it, but the phrasing is slightly hesitant (again, compare the group version on *In Concert*) and an almost mawkish quality afflicts the record as a whole.

*** **Hell's Bells** Strata East 660.51.002
    Hicks; Clint Houston (*b*); Cliff Barbaro (*d*). 5/75.
***(*) **Inc.1** DIW 817
    Hicks; Walter Booker (*b*); Idris Muhammad (*d*). 4/85.
**** **In Concert** Evidence ECD 22048
    As above, but add Elise Wood (*f*); Bobby Hutcherson (*vib*). 8/84.
*** **Luminous** Evidence ECD 22033
    Hicks; Elise Wood (*f*); Clifford Jordan (*ts*); Walter Booker (*b*); Jimmy Cobb, Alvin Queen (*d*). 7/ 85, 9/88.
*** **I'll Give You Something To Remember Me By** Limetree MCD 0023
    Hicks; Curtis Lundy (*b*); Idris Muhammad (*d*). 3/87.
***(*) **East Side Blues** DIW 8028
    Hicks; Curtis Lundy (*b*); Victor Lewis (*d*). 4/88.
**** **Naima's Love Song** DIW 823
    As above, but add Bobby Watson (*as*). 4/88.
***(*) **Two Of A Kind** Evidence ECD 22017
    Hicks; Ray Drummond (*b*). 8/88.
***(*) **Is That So?** Timeless SJP 357
    Hicks; Ray Drummond (*b*); Idris Muhammad (*d*). 7/90.
The sentimentality that spoils *Steadfast* is much less in evidence on the trio session recorded for Strata East at the same time. This is probably Hicks's most natural setting. He favours bassists with a low, dark tone and straightforward delivery. Similarly, he looks to drummers for a firm, reliable count.

Even on ballads, Hicks enunciates very strongly and makes effective use of the damper pedal, trimming off chords tidily but with none of the staccato bite one hears from Bud Powell, one of his stylistic models and a more dominant one than Monk. The Monk themes on *Inc.1* are stretched out to an unfamiliar extent, something that happens to 'Rhythm-a-Ning' on the Maybeck set. Though the performances themselves are not long, Hicks seems determined to unpack the melody as much as possible. What seemed a vice on *Steadfast* quickly became the central thrust of his improvisational approach; though essentially a chordal player, he resembles Mal Waldron in his attention to melody.

After the still and inattentive Houston and Barbaro, Booker and Muhammad sound heaven-sent. The mid-'80s sessions with that trio on DIW and on Evidence were the most searching that Hicks ever made, though not necessarily always the most polished or satisfying. The partnership with Lundy and then with Lewis merely iced the cake. The bassist plays an understated but vital role on the Limetree, with lovely phrasing on Paul Arslanian's 'Pas De Trois' and big, bold sound on Rollins's 'Airegin'. The same combination occurs on *In Concert*, though this time the Rollins tune is 'Paul's Pal' and Hicks is pushed along by Bobby Hutcherson's often hectic vibes. Elise Wood sounds pretty, but hasn't much to say for herself, certainly not enough to sustain her role on the rather odd *Luminous*.

After *In Concert*, the real highspots are *East Side Blues* and the associated *Naima's Love Song*, which Bobby Watson nearly pinches with a display of flawlessly lyrical alto. Brightly recorded and balanced, these should be considered priority items, though it would be worth finding a space for the two sessions with Drummond which, for sheer beauty of playing, are hard to beat. The duos include Ellington's 'Take The Coltrane' (a favourite with the Booker/Muhammad axis) and a late-night 'Parisian Thoroughfare'; the trios work seasonal variations on a carefully limited palette.

**** Sketches Of Tokyo DIW 812
Hicks; David Murray (*ts, bcl*). 4/85.
This has, not surprisingly, been seen as another Murray album and, despite the saxophonist's respectful nods to past masters – Coltrane's 'Naima', Dolphy's bass clarinet version of 'God Bless The Child' – Hicks can equally claim it as a quiet exorcism of some of his own ghosts: Monk in 'Epistrophy', Bud Powell, and even Ellington. It's a superb record, but it's the pianist who impresses most on later hearings, once Murray's almost casual brilliance has been absorbed.

*** Friends Old And New Novus 41631412
Hicks; Clark Terry, Greg Tisbert (*t*); Al Grey (*tb*); Joshua Redman (*ts*); Ron Carter (*b*); Grady Tate (*d*). 1/92.
This is a bit of an oddity. Hicks has generally not sounded good in larger agglomerations, and here he is comprehensively eclipsed by the horns. His solos are all taken more loudly than usual and there are unexpected and unwelcome crudities in his choice of material. Even if he wanted an evening off from the more romantic stuff, 'Makin' Whoopee' and 'It Don't Mean A Thing . . .' really aren't his bag.

*** Crazy For You Red Baron AK 52761
Hicks; Wilbur Bascomb Jr (*b*); Kenny Washington (*d*). 4/92.
***(*) Beyond Expectations Reservoir RSR CD 130
Hicks; Ray Drummond (*b*); Marvin 'Smitty' Smith (*d*). 9/93.
Drummond's introduction to 'There Is No Greater Love' on the Reservoir disc captures in just a few bars what a valuable player he is and how much the competent but stolid Bascomb has to learn. Drummond's statement of the Isham Jones theme tees Hicks up for a firmly unsentimental set of variations that gains in stature (despite an uncertain beginning) with virtually every bar. The piano is recorded with a lot of presence and the recording as a whole has Rudy van Gelder stamped all over it: lively, resonant, utterly musical. By this point in his career, Hicks records come with all sorts of expectations attached (the actual reference is to a composition with Elise Wood), and this one confounds none of them, an utterly professional performance from a seasoned performer.

The Red Baron disc is a Gershwin songbook, nicely done for the most part. 'I Got Rhythm' is, of course, a cornerstone of modern jazz idiom, and Hicks pulls it apart to examine afresh its harmonic and rhythmic possibilities, though in no way to the detriment of the original song, which remains intact and unsullied at the end. 'K-ra-zy For You' (the original spelling) isn't a million miles behind for sheer originality and inventiveness; tackled in two parts, its bright downscale shifts and eager one-two two-two-three patterns inspire some notably upbeat playing from the trio as a whole.

***(*) In The Mix Landmark 1542
Hicks; Vincent Herring (*as, ss*); Elise Wood (*f*); Curtis Lundy (*b*); Cecil Brooks III (*d*). 11/94.
*** Single Petal Of A Rose Mapleshade 02532
Hicks; Jack Walrath (*t*); Elise Wood (*f*); Curtis Lundy (*b*). 94.
In the Mix is very much up to scratch and Hicks sounds good again in the context of a horns-based group. 'Yemenja' is the most significant item, a long piece written for the same Naima who inspired the 'Love Song'. Herring takes it thoughtfully on his soprano, a very different voice from the sharp, boyish alto he unveils on his own 'Elation'. There is a nice mix of quartet, quintet and trio material and, throughout, the pure-voiced Lundy and the unfussy Brooks (who also produces) can't be faulted on any count.

Wood is still an acquired taste, but she makes some pretty sounds here and there, and it might be that there's a bit more stuff to her playing of late. She's strongly featured on the Mapleshade session (Walrath has a guest role only) and there is considerable lyric invention in her statement on the title-piece. Working without percussion gives it all a very light, chamber-jazz feel, but there is enough substance to keep the level of interest high.

Billy Higgins (born 1936) DRUMS, VOCALS, GUITAR

*** **Soweto** Red RR 123141
>   Higgins; Bob Berg (*ts*); Cedar Walton (*p*); Tony Dumas (*b*). 1/79.
***(*) **The Soldier** Timeless SJP 145
>   Higgins; Monty Waters (*as*); Cedar Walton (*p*); Walter Booker (*b*); Roberta Davis (*v*). 12/79.
*** **Mr Billy Higgins** Evidence ECD 22061 2
>   Higgins; Gary Bias (*sax*); William Henderson (*p*); Tony Dumas (*b*). 4/84.
*** **3/4 For Peace** Red RR 123258
>   Higgins; Harold Land (*ts, ss*); Bill Henderson (*p*); Jeff Littleton (*b*). 1/93.

During the preparation of the first edition of the *Penguin Jazz Guide*, there was a book running on which artist would clock up most recording credits in the current catalogue. It was always going to be a rhythm-section man, and it turned out to be bassist Ray Brown. Billy Higgins ran him very close. Raised in LA, he started playing in his early teens and broke through professionally at 21 in Red Mitchell's quartet (see *Presenting*, OJC 158). Since then, Higgins has been a drummer of choice in a huge variety of playing contexts.

Like many busy rhythm players, he's had relatively few opportunities to record under his own name. Higgins generally doesn't compose his own material and the records are often only as good as the charts he's given to play. That's what holds back the Evidence set. Gary Bias has a lovely tone, but can't write for toffee. Only W. J. Lee's 'John Coltrane' gives the leader the push he needs. Otehwise, even in the signature solo on bassist Henderson's oddly famliar 'Dance of the Clones' he remains rather static.

The Red session opens on the powerful statement, 'Soweto', on which Higgins sings. His vocal skills are pretty limited, but the vocal has an unmistakable power, more so than the closing feature, 'Bahia Bahia Bahia', on which he's also credited with guitar, taking a leaf out of Elvin Jones's book. The rest of the session is given over to tunes by Cedar Walton, who was to become his most reliable co-conspirator, and by the oddly reticent Bob Berg, who has an off-day, not even rising to the attractive hook on his own 'Neptune'.

The Soldier is plagued by disappointing sound. One has to listen actively for Booker, one of those big, booming string players who sound good alongside Higgins, and the drummer's own sounds lacks the crispness and power one normally expects of him. However, the playing is uniformly good, particularly on 'Midnight Waltz' and 'Peace', where Walton excels himself.

The military theme returns, albeit negatively, in *3/4 For Peace*, which is interesting mainly for Land's rich, full-voiced tenor and the interplay between horn and drums. A subtle, insistent record that recalls aspects of Max Roach's association with Clifford Brownie, a perfect axis. The drum suite dedicated to Juno Lewis is one of Higgins's most personal statements on record, though it makes slightly uncomfortable listening at the second and third attempt.

Eddie Higgins PIANO

*** **By Request** Solo Art SACD-104
>   Higgins; Milt Hinton (*b*); Bobby Rosengarden (*d*). 8/86.
***(*) **Those Quiet Days** Sunnyside SSC 1052D
>   Higgins; Kevin Eubanks (*g*); Rufus Reid (*b*). 12/90.
***(*) **Zoot's Hymns** Sunnyside SSC 1064D
>   Higgins; John Doughten (*ts*); Phil Flanigan (*b*); Danny Burger (*d*). 2/94.

Higgins has been making occasional visits to the studio since the 1950s. *By Request* sticks to well-trodden paths, so far as material is concerned, though the pianist's approach has a verve that takes it out of routine: he has some of the rocking ebullience of the great Chicago pianists, and touches of stride and boogie are integrated into a wide-ranging taste. Hinton and Rosengarden provide flexible support, and a couple of original Higgins rags round out the picture. The irreproachable *Those Quiet Days* is one of his most recent records and surely one of his best. The interplay of piano, guitar and bass has a natural litheness and melodic and harmonic tang and, with Eubanks and Reid sounding both attentive and inventive throughout, the ideas have a seamless momentum. Higgins is no great original, with a style much indebted to the deceptively easy swing of Hank Jones, but he has a calm authority perfectly suited to this kind of date. Eubanks continues his double life as a traditional modernist and a fusioneer with another distinguished turn in the former category, and Reid hunkers down on all the bass lines.

Zoot's Hymns – the dedication is obvious – is another unassuming beauty. Doughten can't quite live up to the Sims and Getz comparisons that come in the sleeve-notes, but he's still darn good – easy swing, good head for melody and prototypical big tone. Higgins sounds more relaxed than ever, but he can't help coming up with ingenious turns in solos that never quite resolve into any of the clichés one expects in this setting. He also picks great tunes: three rare A. C. Jobim pieces are highlights to go with his pair of orignals.

Andrew Hill (born 1937) PIANO

*** Live At Montreux Freedom FCD 741023
  Hill (*p* solo). 7/75.
**(*) Faces Of Hope Soul Note 121010
  As above. 6/80.
***(*) Verona Rag Soul Note 121110
  As above. 7/86.

Hill's whole career has been marked by the silences that punctuate his compositions. Of the important bop and post-bop pianists – Bud Powell, Horace Silver, Mal Waldron, Paul Bley, Cecil Taylor – he is the least known and most erratically documented; even Herbie Nichols enjoys a certain posthumous cachet. And if Hill's primary influence is Thelonious Monk, the connection is more a matter of spirit and personality than of direct technical inheritance. He is in every respect an original.

Born in Chicago, Hill's work has been marked by the emotional and spiritual ambivalence of his Caribbean descent, torn between cultures. Marked by a forceful dissonance, unusual and unsettling harmonic intervals, Hill's dark, incantatory manner sometimes obscures a lighter, folksy side. Like Monk's, his gammy melodic patterns work better either solo or with horns; conventional trio playing represents only a surprisingly small proportion of his output.

Of the solo albums, the latest and best is *Verona Rag*, a gloriously joyous set full of romping vamps, gentle ballad interludes and Hill's characteristic harmonic ambiguities. Not recognized as a standards player, he invests 'Darn That Dream' with an almost troubling subtext in the bass that stops just short of reinventing the tune.

The Montreux set is marred by some unevenness of tone and *Faces Of Hope* by some of his least compelling charts. However, both are essential purchases for Hill enthusiasts and only disappoint relative to an astonishingly high career standard.

**** Point Of Departure Blue Note 81467
  Hill; Kenny Dorham (*t*); Eric Dolphy (*as, f, bcl*); Joe Henderson (*ts*); Richard Davis (*b*); Tony
  Williams (*d*). 3/64.

One of the very great jazz albums of the 1960s. Nowhere is Hill's determination to build on the example of Monk clearer than on the punningly titled 'New Monastery'. Hill's solo, like that on the long previous track, 'Refuge', is constructed out of literally dozens of subtle shifts in the time-signature, most of them too subliminal to be strictly counted. Typically, Hill is prepared to hold the basic beat himself and to allow Williams to range very freely. 'Spectrum' is the one disappointment, too self-conscious an attempt to run a gamut of emotions and instrumental colours; an extraordinary 5/4 passage for the horns almost saves the day. Henderson at first glance doesn't quite fit, but his solos on 'Spectrum' and 'Refuge' are exemplary and in the first case superior to Dolphy's rather insubstantial delivery. The mood of the session switches dramatically on the final 'Dedication', a dirge with a beautiful structure that represents the sharpest contrast to the rattling progress of the previous 'Flight 19' and brings the set full circle.

Hill's writing and arranging skills matured dramatically with *Point Of Departure*. Unfortunately, he had the opportunity to record with similar forces only occasionally in years to come and suffered long neglect, pigeon-holed with the awkward squad. The original sound was so good that little sweetening seems to have been required for the CD. Unfortunately, digital processing gives a rather brittle quality to Dolphy's and Hill's contributions, overstates the drums to a degree, and gives Davis's fine, almost pianistic lines a whumphing sonority that kills their subtlety. An essential purchase, even so.

*** Spiral Freedom FCD 741007
  Hill; Ted Curson (*t, flhn, picc t*); Robin Kenyatta (*as*); Lee Konitz (*as, ts, ss*); Stafford James,
  Cecil McBee (*b*); Barry Altschul, Art Lewis (*d*). 12/74, 1/75.

Spiral is a slightly mixed album, featuring two rather different bands. The sessions with Konitz, Curson, McBee and Lewis are smoother and outwardly less oblique, but without cost to the harmonic interest. The disposition of Curson's and Konitz's three horns apiece (it's often now forgotten how adept Konitz was on tenor and even baritone saxophones) invest 'Laverne', 'The Message' and the title-track with maximum variety, and the solos are extremely effective. By no means an afterthought on this session, there is a duo 'Invitation' by Hill and Konitz, spontaneously done and strongly recalling Hill's Waldron-like talents as an accompanist.

In contrast to the variety he achieves with Konitz, the sessions with alto saxophonist Robin Kenyatta, another adoptive New Yorker with a highly individual musical background, are much more direct and to the point, with less self-conscious manipulation of mood. Kenyatta is a fine and restless player who nevertheless prefers to get down to business, doing most of his soul-searching and experimentation on his own time.

*** **Invitation** Steeplechase SCCD 31026
  Hill; Chris White (b); Art Lewis (d). 10/74.
Like many of his contemporaries, Hill enjoyed greater visibility in Europe than in the USA during the 1970s. This was one of his consistently good performances for the Danish label, a studio session rather than one of Steeplechase's notoriously unselective club recordings. Hill is playing well, albeit with a rather stiff and foot-soldierish rhythm section who don't seem altogether easy with the material.

***(*) **Strange Serenade** Soul Note 121013
  Hill; Alan Silva (b); Freddie Waits (d). 80.
This is as dour and dark as anything Hill has committed to record. Silva and Waits are ideal partners in music that isn't so much minor-key as surpassingly ambiguous in its harmonic language. Hill seems on occasion to be exploring ideas that can be traced back to Bud Powell – not the straight bebop language so much as the more impressionistic things. There are curious little broken triplets and wide-interval phrases which seem to come straight from Bud's last recordings, and it would be interesting to know if Hill had been studying these at the time *Strange Serenade* was recorded.

**** **Shades** Soul Note 121113
  Hill; Clifford Jordan (ts); Rufus Reid (b); Ben Riley (d). 7/86.
Far from settling back into a comfortable accommodation with a 'personal style', Hill's work of the later 1980s was as adventurous as anything he had done since *Point Of Departure*. Reid and Riley create exactly the right background for him, taut but undogmatic, elastic around the end of phrases, constantly propulsive without becoming predictable. His kinship with Monk (whom Riley had accompanied) was always obvious, but it was increasingly clear that the differences were more important (some have suggested Herbie Nichols and Ellington as more fruitful sources) and that Hill was nobody's follower.

Shades is one of the very best jazz albums of the decade. The two trio tracks – that is, with the pungent Jordan absent – are probably the finest since his debut on *Black Fire*, one of the missing Blue Notes. Hill has been inclined to avoid the conventional trio format. Like Monk, he operates better either solo or with horns, but on 'Tripping' and 'Ball Square' he is absolutely on top of things, trading bass lines with Reid and constantly stabbing in alternative accents. 'Monk's Glimpse' pays not altogether submissive homage to Hill's spiritual ancestor. The one slight misgiving about the album is its sound, which is a trifle dark, even on CD.

Buck Hill (born 1928) TENOR SAXOPHONE

*** **This Is Buck Hill** Steeplechase SCCD 31095
  Hill; Kenny Barron (p); Buster Williams (b); Billy Hart (d). 3/78.
*** **Capitol Hill** Muse MCD 5384
  Hill; Barry Harris (p); Ray Drummond (b); Freddie Waits (d). 8/89.
*** **I'm Beginning To See The Light** Muse MCD 5449
  Hill; Jon Ozment (p); Carroll Dashiell (b); Warren Shadd (d). 6/91.
*** **The Buck Stops Here** Muse MCD 5416
  Hill; Johnny Coles (flhn); Barry Harris (p); Ray Drummond (b); Kenny Washington (d). 4/90.
*** **Impulse** Muse MCD 5483
  Hill; Jon Ozmont (p); Carroll Dashiell (b); Warren Schadd (d). 7/92.
Buck Hill is one of the most notable 'regional' jazzmen in America. Like Von Freeman, who has never strayed far from his Chicago base, Hill has spent the largest part of his career with local players on local bandstands, the locale in question being Washington, D.C. He has made relatively few records, but this handful reveals a tenorman soaked in the tradition. He has a big, Hawkins-like sound but says he prefers Lester Young, and inside a bluff manner is a certain elliptical way with phrasing a tune. The Steeplechase album, recently reissued on CD, was his 'discovery', and it still sounds effective, but the Muse albums offer the best documentation in front of three contrasting rhythm sections. Harris, Drummond and Waits offer classic line and length on *Capitol Hill*, though the programme of tunes

sounds a little offhand and Hill doesn't really stretch himself. *The Buck Stops Here* adds the somewhat frayed elegance of Johnny Coles, and this time Hill is more forthright, with a simmering treatment of 'Harlem Nocturne' especially fine. Perhaps the best of them, though, is *I'm Beginning To See The Light*, where Hill performs with his regular D.C. rhythm section. They swing as unaffectedly as if this was just another night at the club, and the lack of pretension takes any weight off Hill and gives his playing a lusty, trenchant sense of purpose. There's a return match on *Impulse*, which is unsurprisingly on just the same level: big, gutsy playing by all hands. The tunes are a less than inspiring bunch, though, with the frightful 'How Do You Keep The Music Playing' in the set-list.

Teddy Hill (1909–78) TENOR SAXOPHONE, BANDLEADER

*** Uptown Rhapsody Hep CD 1033
> Hill; Bill Dillard, Bill Coleman, Shad Collins, Roy Eldridge, Dizzy Gillespie, Frank Newton (*t*); Dicky Wells (*tb*); Russell Procope (*cl, as*); Howard Johnson (*as*); Chu Berry, Robert Carroll (*ts*); Cecil Scott (*ts, bs*); Sam Allen (*p*); John Smith (*g*); Richard Fullbright (*b*); Bill Beason (*d*); Beatrice Douglas (*v*). 2/35, 4 & 5/36, 3, 4 & 5/37.

**(*) Teddy Hill, 1935–1937 Classics 645
> As above.

Nowadays Hill is guaranteed his slight fingerhold on lasting celebrity for his custodianship of Minton's Playhouse in New York City, the most pungent crucible of the bebop movement. By that point in his career, his own musical career was pretty much over, but he had led a short-lived but quite significant big band which numbered among its most illustrious alumni Chu Berry, Bill Coleman, Roy Eldridge and Dizzy Gillespie.

These two items are in pretty direct competition, and it behoves us to say that the Hep, intelligently and very faithfully remastered by John R. T. Davies, is the only one to consider. The 26 tracks in question, from 'Lookie, Lookie, Lookie, Here Comes Cookie' in February 1926 to 'Blue Rhythm Fantasy' a decade and a few months later, are the entire output of the orchestra. The first track is dominated by a blistering Eldridge solo; the last session marks Diz's first recorded solo, on 'King Porter Stomp'. This may seem a by-way in the history of the music, but it is one worth exploring.

Earl Hines (1905–89) PIANO, VOCAL

***(*) Earl Hines 1928–1932 Classics 545
> Hines; Shirley Clay, George Mitchell, Charlie Allen, George Dixon, Walter Fuller (*t*); William Franklin (*tb, v*); Lester Boone, Omer Simeon (*cl, as, bs*); Darnell Howard (*cl, as, vn*); Toby Turner (*cl, as*); Cecil Irwin (*cl, ts*); Claude Roberts (*bj, g*); Lawrence Dixon (*g*); Quinn Wilson (*bb, b*); Hayes Alvis (*bb*); Wallace Bishop (*d*). 12/28–6/32.

**** Earl Hines 1932–1934 Classics 514
> As above, except add Louis Taylor, Trummy Young, Kenneth Stuart (*tb*); Jimmy Mundy (*cl, ts*); Herb Jeffries (*v*); omit Clay, Mitchell, Boone, Turner, Roberts and Alvis. 7/32–3/34.

***(*) Earl Hines 1934–1937 Classics 528
> As above, except add Milton Fletcher (*t*); Budd Johnson (*ts*); The Palmer Brothers, Ida Mae James (*v*); omit Franklin. 9/34–2/37.

**** Earl Hines Collection: Piano Solos 1928–1940 Collector's Classics COCD 11
> Hines (*p* solo). 12/28–2/40.

Earl Hines had already played on some of the greatest of all jazz records – with Louis Armstrong's Hot Five – before he made any sessions under his own name. The piano solos he made in Long Island and Chicago, one day apart in December 1928, are collected on the first Classics CD – a youthful display of brilliance which has seldom been surpassed. His ambidexterity, enabling him to finger runs and break up and supplant rhythms at will, is still breathtaking, and his range of pianistic devices is equalled only by Tatum and Taylor. But these dozen pieces were a preamble to a career which, in the 1930s, was concerned primarily with bandleading. The remainder of the first Classics disc is filled with the first recordings by the orchestra which Hines led at Chicago's Grand Terrace Club for ten years, from December 1928. Their 1929 sessions struggle to find an identity, and only the leader cuts any impressive figures.

The 1932–4 sessions on the second record are better played, better organized and full of brilliant Hines. The surprising thing may be Hines's relatively subordinate role within the band: he had few aspirations to compose or arrange, entrusting those duties to several other hands (including Fuller, Mundy, Johnson, Crowder and Wilson); he revelled instead in the role of star soloist within what were increasingly inventive frameworks. By 1934 the band was at its first peak, with fine Mundy arrangements like

'Cavernism' (including a startling violin solo by Darnell Howard) and 'Fat Babes' and Wilson's vigorous revisions of older material such as 'Maple Leaf Rag' and 'Wolverine Blues'. It's a pity that the chronology has split the 1934 sessions between the second and third Classics volumes. Hines is a wonder throughout, both in solo and in the commentaries with which he counters the arrangements. The other principal soloist is Walter Fuller, a spare, cool-to-hot stylist whose occasional vocals are agreeable copies of Armstrong. The 1934–7 disc shows an unfortunate decline in the consistency of the material, and their move to Vocalion to record coincided with a dissipation of the band's energy.

All three records feature transfers which are respectable rather than notably effervescent, which is disappointing – the sound of the original recordings is excellent, as John R. T. Davies had shown on some earlier LP transfers for Hep, currently yet to emerge on CD. However, Davies has also done the remastering for the piano solos collection on *Collector's Classics*, which covers all the 1928 pieces, five takes of two solos from 1932/3, and a pair of titles from 1940. Excellent sound and strongly recommended.

*** **Earl Hines 1937–1939** Classics 538
   Hines; Walter Fuller (*t, v*); Milton Fletcher, Charlie Allen, Freddy Webster, George Dixon, Edward Sims (*t*); Louis Taylor, Trummy Young, Kenneth Stuart, Joe McLewis, Ed Burke, John Ewing (*tb*); Omer Simeon (*cl, as, bs*); Leroy Harris (*cl, as, v*); Darnell Howard (*cl, as*); Budd Johnson (*cl, as, ts*); William Randall, Leon Washington (*cl, ts*); Robert Crowder (*ts*); Lawrence Dixon, Claude Roberts (*g*); Quinn Wilson (*b*); Wallace Bishop, Alvin Burroughs, Oliver Coleman (*d*); Ida Mae James (*v*). 37–39.

*** **Earl Hines 1939–1940** Classics 567
   As above, except add Shirley Clay, Harry Jackson, Rostelle Reese, Leroy White (*t*); Edward Fant (*tb*); Scoops Carey (*as*); Franz Jackson, Jimmy Mundy (*ts*); Hurley Ramey (*g*); Truck Parham (*b*); Billy Eckstine, Laura Rucker, Madeline Green (*v*); omit Allen, Taylor, Young, Stuart, Howard, Randall, Washington, Dixon, Bishop and James. 10/39–12/40.

*** **Earl Hines 1941** Classics 621
   Hines; Harry Jackson, Tommy Enoch, Benny Harris, Freddy Webster, Jesse Miller (*t*); Joe McLewis, George Hunt, Edward Fant, John Ewing, Nat Atkinson, Gerald Valentine (*tb*); Leroy Harris (*cl, as, v*); Scoops Carey (*cl, as*); William Randall, Budd Johnson, Robert Crowder, Franz Jackson (*ts*); Hurley Ramey (*g*); Truck Parham (*b*); Rudolph Taylor (*d*); Billy Eckstine, Madeline Greene, The Three Varieties (*v*). 4–11/41.

*** **Piano Man** RCA Bluebird ND 86750
   Similar to above. 10/37–3/42.

**** **Fatha** Topaz TPZ 1006
   Similar to above, except add Sidney Bechet (*ss*). 32–42.

*** **Piano Man!** ASV AJA 5131
   Similar to above. 28–40.

It wasn't until the emergence of Budd Johnson as an arranging force that the Hines band recovered some of its flair and spirit. The most renowned of the later pieces – 'Grand Terrace Shuffle' and 'G. T. Stomp' – are both on the 1937–9 CD, which follows the band as it tries to recapture its earlier zip. Johnson himself is a significant soloist, and Hines softens into a more amiable version of his daredevil self. The important thing about the 1940 tracks, on Classics 567, is the arrival of Billy Eckstine, who would influence the band's move towards modernism and first provide it with a couple of major hits, starting with the 1940 'Jelly, Jelly'. He is featured further on the final Classics CD in the sequence, which also features arrangements from several hands – Johnson, Benny Harris, Jackson – and which includes a couple of imposing Hines features in 'The Father Jumps' and 'The Earl'. These tracks haven't been reissued very often, and they deserve to be better known.

Some of these sides also turn up on the Bluebird compilation, which covers 1937–42. The best single-disc compilation of Hines in the 1930s comes with the new Topaz set, *Fatha*. An excellent choice of tracks by both the early and later bands comes in clear, lively sound, with only an occasional surface swish to betray their 78 origins. *Piano Man!* also sounds good for the most part, though some of the later Bluebird sides are inexplicably gritty, and the choice of tracks – including Armstrong Hot Fives and Bechet's 'Blues In Thirds', which is also on the *Fatha* set – concentrates more on Hines the soloist than on Hines the bandleader.

*** **Earl Hines And The Duke's Men** Delmark DD-470
   Hines; Rex Stewart (*c*); Cat Anderson, Lee Brown, Don Devilla, Archie Johnson, Joe Strand (*t*); Lawrence Brown, Joe Britton, Floyd Brady, LeRoy Hardison, George Stevenson (*tb*); Curby Alexander, Vince Royal, Johnny Hodges (*as*); Jimmy Hamilton (*cl, ts*); John Hartzfield, Vincent McCleary, Flip Phillips (*ts*); Harry Carney (*bs*); Marlowe Morris, Horatio Duran (*p*); Al Casey, Teddy Walters (*g*); Oscar Pettiford, Bob Paige (*b*); Sonny Greer, Big Sid Catlett, Bobby Donaldson (*d*); Betty Roche (*v*). 4/44–5/47.

An interesting hotchpotch of tracks from the Apollo label: there are six by a Hines-led sextet, but the other groups are led by either Sonny Greer or Cat Anderson (Anderson's mysterious line-up of unknowns may actually be pseudonymously hiding more famous names). Some of these are minor mixtures of swing and jump-band R&B, but there are many nice touches – from Hodges, Stewart, Nance and Hines himself, though Anderson's usual top notes are a bore – and it's a useful sweep through an otherwise obscure period for many of these players. Good transfers.

***(*) **Fine And Dandy** Vogue 74321 15082
    Hines; Buck Clayton (*t*); Barney Bigard (*cl*); Arvell Shaw (*b*); Wallace Bishop (*d*). 11/49.
Little-known tracks from a Paris session: three rather wistful solos, four swinging pieces with rhythm – 'Snappy Rhythm', cut to a fingersnap beat, features some outrageous piano – and a run of tunes with Clayton and Bigard sitting in. Rather crackly sound, but a rare glimpse of Hines in an otherwise not-much-documented period.

*** **Grand Reunion** Verve 528137-2
    Hines; Roy Eldridge (*t*); Coleman Hawkins (*ts*); George Tucker (*b*); Oliver Jackson (*d*). 3/65.
*** **Reunion In Brussels** Red Baron A K 48854
    Hines; Roland Haynes (*b*); Wallace Bishop (*d*). 3/65.
**** **Blues In Thirds** Black Lion CLCD 760120
    Hines (*p* solo). 4/65.
***(*) **A Night At Johnnie's** Black & Blue 59.300-2
    Hines; Budd Johnson (*ss, ts*); Bill Pemberton (*b*); Oliver Jackson (*d*). 11/68.
Hines's career on record is something of a mess, at least so far as his sessions from the 1950s onwards are concerned. He joined Louis Armstrong's All Stars in 1948, but he worked as a soloist or leader from 1951 until his death, and the host of records he made are now only spottily available. There is virtually nothing left from the 1950s – a couple of fine albums for Fantasy await CD reissue – and these 1960s albums are among the survivors from the next decade. Hines made a strong transition to the LP era, even though it happened rather slowly. He was able to unleash all the rococo elements in his methods at whatever length he chose, and the so-called 'trumpet style' – using tremolo to suggest a horn player's vibrato and taking a linear path even when playing an ensemble role – began to sound modern by dint of its individuality. Nobody played like Hines, as influential as he had been. He was more or less rediscovered in 1964, following New York concerts that were greeted as a sensation, and thereafter embarked on regular tours and records. For some reason, 1965 is particularly well represented at present. *Grand Reunion* effectively replaces an earlier issue on Xanadu. Eldridge and Hawkins are guests with Hines and they play on eight of the eleven tracks, while Hines elaborates on a stack of tunes via three medleys. Recording is less than ideal, with Jackson's cymbals sounding all too loudly in the mix, but it isn't too bad. There is better playing by all three masters on other records, but the meeting has plenty of charisma and some genuinely inspired playing in patches.

    Reunion In Brussels is a typical working night by a Hines trio, with several favourite tunes given handsome workouts: generous in playing time at over 70 minutes but not quite the finest Hines, given the sometimes too familiar material and a slight imbalance favouring the drums. The session with Budd Johnson, who remained a favourite partner of Hines's, works better. *A Night At Johnnie's* is a generously filled CD and opens with half an hour of Hines with bass and drums, before Johnson joins in for 'Body And Soul' and a whirlwind 'Lester Leaps In'. A number of tunes are duplicated among these records – 'Tea For Two' keeps turning up, as do 'Black Coffee' and 'Sweet Lorraine' – but the pianist's enthusiasm is undimmed. The best portrait is provided by, inevitably, the one solo set, *Blues In Thirds*, which adds three extra tracks to the original LP release. The 'Tea For Two' here is an overwhelming *tour de force* and the blues playing on 'Black Lion Blues' and 'Blues After Midnight' is even more luxuriant than Art Tatum's essays in the method.

***(*) **Spontaneous Explorations** Columbia/Red Baron J K 57331 2CD
    Hines; Richard Davis (*b*); Elvin Jones (*d*). 3/64–1/66.
(*) **Live! Aalborg, Denmark, 1965 Storyville STCD 8222
    Hines; Morten Hansen (*b*); Jorgen Kureer (*d*). 4/65.
(*) **Blues So Low (For Fats) Stash ST-C D-537
    Hines (*p* solo). 4/66.
*** **Live At The New School** Chiaroscuro C R D 157
    Hines (*p* solo). 3/73.
*** **Live** Black & Blue 59/305.2
    Hines (*p* solo). 7/74.
***(*) **Blues For Sale** Black & Blue B L E 233084
    Hines; Budd Johnson (*ts*); Jimmy Leary (*b*); Panama Francis (*d*). 7/74.
It's hard to go wrong with Hines on record, but one should be a trifle cautious in approaching some of

his live records: the fondness for medleys and a weakness for an over-extended right-hand tremolo betray a hankering for applause which, merited though it may be, occasionally tips his style into excess. *Spontaneous Explorations*, though unnecessarily reissued as a two-disc set (it runs less than 70 minutes), has much classic Hines. The first half is a solo date cut on the occasion of a famous 'comeback' concert in New York; the second matches him with Davis and Jones in a session that recalls the Ellington *Money Jungle* date. These are brimming performances which reach a climax of sorts in the trio version of 'Shoe Shine Boy', where the empathy in the trio is superb. The Danish concert is much less substantial and is compromised by the noisy recording. Medleys take up much of the set, and Hines's closing party piece of 'St Louis Blues' is best heard only once.

The 1966 concert has as much overcooked Hines mannerism as inspiration, and the Doctor Jazz album listed below is a much better Waller tribute. The 16-minute Fats Waller medley on *New School* and other flag-wavers let down the superior aspects of the set, while the Ellington medley on *Live* misses the intensity of the set listed below. But both still have a share of Hines in regal form: he liked to play for people, and some of the pyrotechnics are *echt*-Hines.

The return match with Budd Johnson, though, is characteristically splendid. The title-piece is a classic dissertation on the blues, but the interest level seldom drops, and three tracks by the trio alone also include some fine Hines.

*** **In Paris** Musidisc 500562
> Hines; Larry Richardson (*b*); Richie Goldberg (*d*). 12/70.

**** **Tour De Force** Black Lion BLCD 760140
> Hines (*p* solo). 11/72.

**** **Tour De Force Encore** Black Lion BLCD 760157
> Hines (*p* solo). 11/72.

***(*) **Plays George Gershwin** Musidisc 500563
> Hines (*p* solo). 10/73.

***(*) **One For My Baby** Black Lion BLCD 760198
> Hines (*p* solo). 3/74.

*** **Hines 74** Black & Blue 59.073.2
> Hines; Jimmy Leary (*b*); Panama Francis (*d*). 7/74.

***(*) **Mostly Fats** Doctor Jazz/EPM FDC 5017
> Hines; Ray Nance (*c, vn, v*). n.d.

***(*) **Masters Of Jazz Vol. 2** Storyville STCD 4102
> Hines (*p* solo). 3/74.

A spate of solo recording meant that, in his old age, Hines was being comprehensively documented at last, and he rose to the challenge with consistent inspirational force. The two *Tour De Force* discs are among his very best records, since the studio sound is fine, if a little hard, and Hines seems completely relaxed and under his own orders (although Stanley Dance's discreet supervision must have assisted). The CD versions include previously unheard tracks, but since alternative takes are spread across the pair of discs, most will choose one or the other. The single take of 'Mack The Knife' on each disc is, though, Hines at his most extraordinary: his variation of time, ranging from superfast stride to wholly unexpected suspensions, is bemusing enough, but the range of dynamics he pushes through each solo is more so. He seldom lingers in thought – one of the things he bequeathed to later players such as Oscar Peterson and Cecil Taylor was the bruising speed of the process by which ideas are executed – but the essentially tuneful stamp he puts on every improvisation (and the different takes underline his spontaneity) humanizes what might otherwise be a relentless, percussive attack. *One For My Baby* isn't too far behind the other Black Lion discs: the expected fireworks are ignited on the up-tempo pieces, but the most telling interpretation is arguably the slow and handsomely detailed 'Ill Wind', which distils a gravity unusual in Hines, who never forgot to be an entertainer. The Storyville disc strings together six standards, and again the playing is extravagantly strong and elaborate, with a couple of tunes that Hines seldom recorded ('As Long As I Live' and 'My Shining Hour') adding some spice.

The two Musidisc sets are both worthwhile. *In Paris* has a desultory rhythm section accompaniment and is merely very good, but the solo meditations on Gershwin tunes are more substantial. The two extravagances are long versions of 'Embraceable You' and 'They Can't Take That Away From Me', but there are also several tunes that Hines didn't cover elsewhere, such as a boisterous 'Let's Call The Whole Thing Off', and his opening and closing versions of 'Rhapsody In Blue' – which Gershwin himself once complimented Hines on – are a neat piece of dovetailing.

Mostly Fats is only just – there are five Waller tunes and one dedication out of the 12 tracks, of which half are Hines solos and the rest duets with the irrepressible Nance, who blows hot cornet, scrapes beguiling violin and howls through some vocals, too. Hines is mixed but sometimes magnificent on the solo pieces – 'Honeysuckle Rose', in which he scarcely refers to the melody at all, is outstanding – and both men have fun on their shared tunes.

**** **Earl Hines Plays Duke Ellington** New World NW 361/2 2CD
    Hines (*p* solo). 12/71–4/75.
Made over a period of four years, this is much more than a casual one-giant-nods-to-another record.
Hines was cajoled by Stanley Dance into looking into many unfamiliar Ellington tunes and creating a
memorial (Ellington died around the time of the final sessions) which is surely among the best tributes
to the composer on record. Since Hines's more aristocratic touches are close in feeling to Ellington's
own, there is an immediate affinity in such pieces as 'Love You Madly' and 'Black And Tan Fantasy'.
But Hines finds a wealth of new incident in warhorses such as 'Mood Indigo' and 'Sophisticated Lady'
and turns 'The Shepherd' and 'Black Butterfly' into extravagant fantasies which go far beyond any of
Ellington's own revisionist approaches. Even a simple piece such as 'C Jam Blues' receives a fascinating,
rhythmic treatment, and the voicings conjured up for 'I'm Beginning To See The Light' upset conventional wisdom about Ellingtonian interpretation. In his variety of resource, Hines also points up all
the devices he passed on to Powell, Monk and virtually every other post-swing pianist. A memorable
lesson, and a fine tribute to two great piano players, spread over two hours of music.

Motohiko Hino (born 1946) DRUMS

***(*) **Sailing Stone** Gramavision R2 79473
    Hino; Terumasa Hino (*c*); Dave Liebman (*ss, ts*); Karen Mantler (*org, hca*); Mike Stern, Marc
    Muller (*g*); Steve Swallow (*b*). 11/91.
'Satisfaction', 'Lady Jane', 'Angie' and 'Continental Drift' are the Stones tunes rolling through this
fetching set, helmed by the lesser-known of the Hino brothers (Terumasa turns 'Lady Jane' into a lovely,
cracked lament). The insistent drone of Mantler's organ and the buoyancy of Swallow's bass-lines give
the varying instrumentations a firm identity, and Liebman and Stern play up to their best: Stern's
'Satisfaction' is a winning revamp. Nor is the leader in the shadows: he plays with restraint but is always
varying the pace and density of the rhythms, and there are four good themes of his own.

***(*) **It's There** Enja 8030-2
    As above. 3/93.
Same again – same band, same concept, but different source, since Hino this time tackles (sharp intake
of breath) the Led Zeppelin songbook. He makes the likes of 'The Rain Song', 'The Ocean' and 'Thank
You' into lovely things, too, the guitarists setting the melodies all a-shimmer. 'Dazed And Confused' is
the rave-up, though whether Jimmy Page approves is a mystery. His own themes, 'Tok O' The Town' and
'Hangin' Out', are fine enough to hope for an all-original date next time. Or maybe he'll do Black
Sabbath next.

Terumasa Hino (born 1942) TRUMPET, CORNET

***(*) **Live At Warsaw Jazz Festival 1991** Jazzmen 660.50.004
    Hino; Roger Byam (*ts*); Onaje Allan Gumbs (*p*); John Hart (*g*); Jay Anderson (*b*); Michael
    Carvin (*d*). 10/91.
*** **Unforgettable** Blue Note 781191-2
    Hino; Cedar Walton (*p*); David Williams (*b*); Michael Carvin (*d*). 4/92.
*** **Spark** Blue Note 830450-2
    Hino; Tatsuya Satoh (*ts*); Jay Hoggard (*vib, mar*); Hiromasa Suzuki, Takeaki Sugiyama (*ky*);
    Benisuke Sakai, Kenji Hino (*b*); Motohiko Hino (*d*); Don Alias, Tatsuji Yokoyama, Mark
    DeRose (*perc*). 3/94.
*** **Acoustic Boogie** Blue Note 836259-2
    Hino; Greg Osby (*as*); Masabumi Kikuchi (*p*); James Genus (*b*); Billy Kilson (*d*). 3/95.
Japanese jazz musicians were still something of a novelty to Western audiences when Hino started
making waves in Europe and the US. Like so many of his classical contemporaries, he displayed a
terrific technique – faultless intonation and a fat, glossy tone – and his early albums (some for Enja and
Denon) are worth seeking out, despite some flawed conceptions. His albums for Blue Note of the 1980s
and early '90s are already in limbo, but this live snapshot of an imposing band includes some exciting
music. 'Kimiko' is a pleasing Hino original; 'Sweet Love Of Mine' thoughtfully remodels Woody Shaw's
songful mid-tempo ballad; 'Over The Rainbow' is a lavish reading of a Hino favourite, and Michel
Camilo's 'Why Not?' is a showstopping finale. Byam and Gumbs play with expert assurance but, aside
from the leader, the honours are taken by the fine and undervalued Hart, whose playing has a ringing
decisiveness about it.
    Three more recent entries for Blue Note show Hino trying out different situations. *Unforgettable* is a

ballad album, almost exclusively done at slow to mid-tempo, and while Hino can play this sort of thing well it's not really his speciality: he does the whole album on cornet, getting a whispery, idiosyncratic edge on the horn. Walton is a master at this kind of date, but it's an unobtrusive sort of mastery, and the record as a whole misses the last ounce of dedication from the team. *Spark* is a mix of straight hard bop, funkier stuff done on polyrhythmic bases and a couple of modish mood tunes with synthesizers in the background. 'Calcutta Cutie' reminds of Hino's powers as a bop repertory man, and it's a good, bouncy kind of set, if not quite any kind of classic. *Acoustic Boogie* credits him as co-leader with Kikuchi, but it's more the pianist's date, since he wrote most of the tunes and arranged the whole show. Hino and Osby put flickering improvisations over the stark rhythms of Genus (on electric bass) and Kilson, and Kikuchi sounds to be trying to get a simplified M-Base feel out of it. Patchily interesting, with some typically enigmatic solos by the pianist, though Hino himself seems like something of a bystander.

Milt Hinton (born 1910) DOUBLE BASS

*** **Old Man Time** Chiaroscuro CRD 310 2CD
> Hinton; Doc Cheatham (*t*); Eddie Barefield (*as, ts*); Buddy Tate (*ts*); Red Richards (*p*); Al Casey (*g*); Gus Johnson (*d*); Dizzy Gillespie (v).

*** **Laughing At Life** Columbia 478178
> Hinton; Jon Faddis (*t, flhn*); Harold Ashby (*ts*); Richard Wyands, Derek Smith (*p*); Lynn Seaton, Brian Torff, Santi Debriano, Rufus Reid (*b*); Alan Dawson, Dave Ratajczak, Terry Clarke (*d*). 95.

Hinton is a great entertainer, playing, singing and rapping about the good old days with undiminished vigour into his eighties. 'The Judge And The Jury' on *Laughing At Life* is a four-bass party piece that just about scores a home run, somewhat reminiscent of his role in 'Splanky' on young Christian McBride's first album. As there, Hinton is quite at ease working with players almost two generations below him. He has such an accumulated head of experience that he can pick – or, failing that, talk – his way out of almost any situation. Like a great many rhythm players, the discography is huge but very little is credited to him, so the slightly overcooked two-volume *Old Man Time* has to be seen as a kind of *This Is Your Life* accolade. The band, arranged and conducted by Buck Clayton, gives him plenty of room for his party pieces on the big bull fiddle, while the Mississippi voice spins its yarns. Entertaining but lightweight. The interesting music comes in the trios on the Columbia. Milt isn't ready to hang up his bow yet.

Erhard Hirt GUITAR

(****) **Gute Und Schlechte Zeiten** FMP OWN-90003
> Hirt (*g* solo). 12/91–5/93.

The bracketed qualification is only to warn any who might expect something in the tradition of Herb Ellis or Tal Farlow – or, indeed, of anyone who's played guitar before. Hirt's attitude seems to be to start from scratch and treat it as a new instrument. He gets a different sound on every one of 18 tracks, most of them over in three or four minutes. The sonic range seems inexhaustible, from bizarre dinosaur roars to radio static to feedback banshees to staccato blips and blats. His deadpan titles – 'Percussion', 'Drone', 'Flute', 'Axes' – give nothing away beyond a bare programmatic description. One is occasionally reminded of the work of Fred Frith or Hans Reichel, but only through casting around for comparisons: Hirt is after new sound-worlds, and it's a challenge keeping up with him. 'Please think of Magritte, Duchamp, Broodthaers,' sleeve-note writer, Markus Muller, pleads. Absolutely.

Jeff Hittman TENOR SAXOPHONE

*** **Mosaic** Soul Note 121 137
> Hittman; Valery Ponomarev (*t*); Larry Willis (*p*); Dennis Irwin (*b*); Yoshitaka Uematsu (*d*). 1/86.

Hittman is a Rollins-influenced New Yorker with broad, catholic tastes. Two of the tracks are originals, but it is the choice of material by Hank Mobley ('The Opener'), Steve Grossman ('New York Bossa') and two versions, quick and slow, of 'Cedar's Blues' by pianist Cedar Walton that underlines the saxophonist's versatility and taste. The performances have a relaxed, clubby feel, but they are expertly and sympathetically recorded. Uncontroversial, mainstream-modern jazz with just enough individuality to lift it above the mass.

Fred Ho (Houn) & Afro-Asian Music Ensemble BARITONE SAXOPHONE, CHINESE INSTRUMENTS, BANDLEADER

*** **Tomorrow Is Now** Soul Note 121117
> Fred Houn (*bs, leader*); Sam Furnace (*as, ts*); Sayyd Abdul Al-Khabyr, Al Givens (*ss, ts, f*); Richard Clements (*p*); Jon Jang (*p*); Kyoto Fujiwara (*b*); Taru Alexander (*d*); Carleen Robinson (*v*). 85.

(*) **We Refuse To Be Used And Abused Soul Note 1211167
> Fred Houn (*bs, ss, f*); Sam Furnace (*as, ss, f*); Hafez Modir (*ts, f*); Jon Jang (*p*); Kyoto Fujiwara (*b*); Royal Hartigan (*perc*). 11/87.

***(*) **The Underground Railway To My Heart** Soul Note 121267
> Ho; Martin Wehner (*tb*); Sam Furnace, James Norton (*as, ss*); David Bindman, Hafez Modirzadeh, Allen Won (*ts*); Francis Wong (*ts, f, picc*); Peter Madsen (*p*); Kiyoto Fujiwara, John Shifflet (*b*); Royal Hartigan (*d, perc*); Pei Sheng Shen (*sona, ob*); You Qun Fu (*erhu*); Pauline Hong (*san shuen*); Cindy Zuoxin Wang (*v*). 90–93.

This is powerfully advocated music from a 'rainbow coalition' of fine young players, Afro- and Asian-Americans in the main. Houn, who has more recently phoneticized his name to Ho, has a big, powerful sound reminiscent of Harry Carney, and this sets the tone for ensembles with a strongly Ellingtonian cast.

The title of the first album sets up all sorts of different expectations – from Ornette Coleman's *Tomorrow Is The Question* to Max Roach's *Freedom Now* suite – which are not so much confounded as skirted. There would seem to be little place for prettiness in music as aggressively programmatic as this, but the band plays with surprising delicacy and unfailing taste. CD transfer flatters Houn's skills as an orchestrator.

The second album is more bitty and has a much less coherent sound. There is also an unwonted and mostly unwelcome stridency. Unlike Charlie Haden and his Liberation Music Orchestra, Ho still hadn't quite found a way of synthesizing political urgency with lyricism. That's largely addressed in the excellent *Underground Railway*. It starts unpromisingly with a noodling ethnic jam featuring the double-reed *sona* over bass and drums. What follows is the title-piece: a long, elegantly communicated suite which Ho describes as 'anti-bourgeois boogie-woogie'. Here the Ellington (and Carney) influence is unmistakable and in character. Too much of the remainder is bland *chinoiserie*: full, unfamiliar sonorities used for their own sake. There is, though, an interesting 'revisit' to Billie Holiday's 'Strange Fruit' and a glorious reading of Tizol's 'Caravan'. They make it possible to forgive the multilingual 'Auld Lang Syne' (oh, go on, it's not that bad), or the two closing selections from an 'epic' score called *Journey Beyond The West: The New Adventures Of Monkey*. Nuts to that. Otherwise excellent.

Jim Hobbs (born 1968) ALTO SAXOPHONE

*** **Babadita** Silkheart SHCD 133
> Hobbs; Timo Shanko (*b*); Django Carranza (*d*). 1/93.

A sparky set of trio workouts. The group is more regularly known as the Fully Celebrated Orchestra, but the CD appears under Hobbs's name – he writes most of the material and hits a point somewhere between Ornette Coleman and (he claims) Willie Nelson. He squeaks his way through a lot of these brief vignettes (there are 15 in 70-odd minutes): interestingly, he claims to have been inspired more by Don Cherry than by the leader on the early Coleman recordings. Shanko and Carranza play boisterously in support and the music is fun, but it doesn't go anywhere particular – three guys in search of a context, which the deliberately quirky and jagged writing doesn't always allow for.

Paul Hock GUITAR, GUITAR SYNTHESIZER

*** **Fresh Fruit** Timeless SJP 343
> Hock; Ben Van den Dungen (*ts*); Harry Emmery (*b*); Kees Kranenburg (*d*). 2/91.

After two tracks it sounds as if the record will be nothing but a straight steal from John Scofield, with Hock affecting a carbon of Sco's tone and the rest of the group functioning much as the players on the Blue Note albums do. But then comes a spare and surprisingly evocative reading of Jacques Brel's 'Voir Un Ami Pleurer', and the music opens out and moves to a different plane. Hock's improvising still owes much to the American, although touches of guitar-synth add a further colour, and Van den Dungen's lines aren't notably individual, but a theme such as 'Samba For Johan Cruyff' creates a distinctive climate for improvisation, and bassist and drummer work with the same intensity as the front line. A name worth watching, though there's nothing new since our last edition.

Art Hodes (1904-93) PIANO

*** **Up In Volly's Room** Delmark DE 217
>   Hodes; Nappy Trottier (*t*); George Brunis (*tb*); Volly DeFaut (*cl*); Truck Parham (*b*); Barrett
>   Deems (*d*). 3 & 4/72.

***(*) **Pagin' Mr Jelly** Candid CCD 79037
>   As above. 11/88.

**** **Keepin' Out Of Mischief Now** Candid CACD 79717
>   As above. 11/88.

**** **The Parkwood Creative Concept Sessions: Volume 1** Parkwood PWCD 114
>   Hodes (*p* solo). 4 & 6/87, 3 & 7/89.

Born in Russia and raised in Chicago, Hodes combines a blues-drenched South Side piano style with a
passionate articulacy which turned him into one of jazz's most significant ambassadors and educators,
working as a disc jockey, journalist (on *The Jazz Record*) and lecturer.

If consistency and regularity are the keys to longevity, Hodes seems to have survived by *not* bending to
the winds of fashion. Though little of his hefty output is currently available, his records – solos in
particular – tend to be comfortably interchangeable, and only real enthusiasts for his rather throwaway
style or for the South Side pianists in general will want shelf-loads. *Real* enthusiasts will already have the
Mosaic box, *The Complete Art Hodes Blue Notes* (see Introduction), which remains the most important
single item in his catalogue.

Though often less interesting as a solo performer than in a group context, Hodes conjures some interesting variations on Jelly Roll Morton, his greatest single influence, on *Pagin' Mr Jelly*, and this, or the
remaining material from that session on *Mischief*, is perhaps the place for fans of either to start. Hodes's
only originals, the title-tune and the related 'Mr Jelly Blues', are virtually impossible to pick out from a
session that sticks to only the most sanctified of early jazz tunes: the march 'High Society', 'Wolverine
Blues', 'Mr Jelly Lord', 'Winin' Boy Blues', 'Buddy Bolden's Blues' and 'The Pearls'. What's wonderful
about Hodes's approach to this material, the Morton stuff in particular, is how *natural* he sounds.
There's no pressure or effort, no hint of pastiche, just straightforward playing of magnificent music. For
a change, he's playing on a really decent piano, and that is perversely disconcerting.

The Parkwood disc pulls together two sessions from the late 1970s, the second of which, *Art's Originals*,
has never been available on vinyl. The earlier of the pair, *Christmastime Jazz and Blues* (or *Joy To The
Jazz World*), is the sort of 'concept' package that makes many purists and even fans with more adulter-
ated tastes spit blood. Wrong on this count. The Christmas tunes are beautifully executed and jazzed up.
Hodes manages to turn 'Silent Night' into a softly swinging quasi-blues, and even 'Jingle Bells' works.
The originals set is less startling but of no less quality. 'Selections From The Gutter', 'Gipsy Man Blues'
and 'Russian Ragu' contain unusual harmonic elements that will throw off unwary blindfold listeners.
The remainder has Hodes's signature through it like a stick of rock. A second CD in the same series is
expected out at any time. Called *Moldy Fig/Dirty Bopper*, it features Hodes in company with the young
trumpeter, Marcus Belgrave, and in the second part with fellow-survivor Doc Cheatham and singer
Carrie Smith, reviving one of those staple 1920s vocal sessions with trumpet and piano. Watch out for it.

The Delmark works according to a similar principle. When it was recorded, back in 1972, the clarinet
was pretty much in abeyance as a jazz instrument. A great deal has happened since, of course – the
emergence of Don Byron and Michael Moore, Hamiet Bluiett's Clarinet Project, the renaissance of
Jimmy Giuffre – that reduces the impact of this record's special pleading. On its own terms, as relaxed
and matey old buzzards meet, it sounds pretty good. DeFaut is a decent player of the Dodds school,
with traces of Jimmie Noone and even of Goodman thrown in. He actually appears on only four tracks;
the rest are duets with Parham, and the whole thing is topped off like a rather wobbly sundae with two
pieces featuring the splendidly monikered Trottier and George Brunis. Poorly recorded, but well worth a
listen.

*** **Art Hodes Jazz Trio** Jazzology JCD 307
>   Hodes; Reimer Von Essen (*cl, as*); Trevor Richards (*d*). 86.

(*) **Art Hodes Trio Jazzology JCD 237
>   Hodes; Trevor Whiting (*reeds*); John Petters (*d*); Dave Bennett (*v*). 9/87.

*** **Art Hodes Blue Five And Six** Jazzology JCD 172
>   Hodes; Al Fairweather, Pat Halcox (*t*); Wally Fawkes (*cl*); Fapy Lapertin (*g*); Andy Brown (*b*);
>   Dave Evans, Stan Greig (*d*); Johnny Mars (*v*). 9 & 10/87.

Hodes's trip to Britain in 1987 was as a laying-on of hands, a chance to make contact with someone who
belonged to an apostolic line back to the origins of jazz. Traditional jazz players of all sorts made their
way to listen to and sit in with the great man. The results are pretty uniform, with most of the best music
coming in solo performances by Hodes himself. There is no apparent stylistic distinction between the
Trio and the Jazz Trio; the latter is simply better. The larger groups called on more seasoned and

experienced musicians and the playing is better in proportion, with some excellent moments from that Chris Barber stalwart, Pat Halcox. Fawkes is still underrated and Greig is as good in this style as one could hope to find.

(*) Live From Toronto's Café Des Copains Music & Arts 610
Hodes; Jim Galloway (ss, bs).

Music & Arts have a slightly odd approach to matchmaking on disc, alternating avant-garde couplings Anthony Braxton and Marilyn Crispell, Jane Bunnett and Don Pullen with the likes of this Odd Couple set. Galloway, like Davern, is an instinctive revivalist and seems blissfully unaware of the incongruity of much of the stuff he plays. Though the material doesn't always seem to suit Hodes, he responds imaginatively to some of the Scotsman's more probing cues and plays like a man on monkey glands.

Johnny Hodges (1907–70) ALTO SAXOPHONE, SOPRANO SAXOPHONE

*** **Classic Solos: 1928–1942** Topaz TPZ 1008
Hodges; Bunny Berigan, Freddy Jenkins, Bubber Miley, Ray Nance, Arthur Whetsol, Cootie Williams (t); Rex Stewart (c); Lawrence Brown, Joe 'Tricky Sam' Nanton, Juan Tizol (tb); Barney Bigard (cl, ts); Harry Carney (bs, as, cl); Otto Hardwick (as, bsx); Ben Webster (ts); Duke Ellington, Teddy Wilson (p); Fred Guy (bj); Fred Guy, Lawrence Lucie, Allan Reuss (g); Hayes Alvis, Jimmy Blanton, Wellman Braud, John Kirby, Grachan Moncur, Billy Taylor (b); Cozy Cole, Sonny Greer (d); Mildred Bailey (v). 10/28–7/41.

*** **His Greatest Recordings: 1928–1941** ASV CD AJA 5180
As above, except add Buck Clayton, Louis Metcalfe (t); Buster Bailey (cl); Lester Young (ts); Edgar Sampson (bs); Jess Stacy (p); Lionel Hampton (vib); Artie Bernstein, Harry Goodman (b); Gene Krupa (d); Billie Holiday (v). 6/28–6/41.

*** **Johnny Hodges And His Orchestra, 1937–1939** Black & Blue 59.239
Hodges; Cootie Williams (t); Lawrence Brown (tb); Harry Carney (bs); Duke Ellington, Billy Strayhorn (p); Billy Taylor, Jimmy Blanton (b); Sonny Greer (d). 3/38–10/39.

**** **Caravan** Prestige PRCD 24103
Hodges; Taft Jordan, Cat Anderson, Harold Baker (t); Lawrence Brown, Juan Tizol (tb); Willie Smith (as); Paul Gonsalves, Al Sears (ts); Jimmy Hamilton (ts, cl); Harry Carney (bs); Duke Ellington (p); Billy Strayhorn (p, org); Wendell Marshall, Oscar Pettiford (b); Wilbur De Paris, Louie Bellson, Sonny Greer (d). 6/47–6/51.

*** **The Vogue Recordings** Vogue 111511
Hodges; Harold Baker (t); Quentin Jackson (tb); Jimmy Hamilton (cl); Don Byas (ts); Raymond Fol (p); Wendell Marshall (b); Sonny Greer (d). 4 & 6/50.

**** **Jazz Masters 35: Johnny Hodges** Verve 521857
Hodges; Cat Anderson, Shorty Baker, Emmett Berry, Willie Cook, Roy Eldridge, Dizzy Gillespie, Eddie Mullens, Ernie Royal, Charlie Shavers, Clark Terry, Snooky Young (t); Ray Nance (t, v); Lawrence Brown, Chuck Connors, Vic Dickenson, Quentin Jackson, John Saunders, Britt Woodman (tb); Tony Studd (btb); Russell Procope, Jerome Richardson, Frank Wess (cl, as); Jimmy Hamilton (cl, ts); Danny Bank (cl, bs); Benny Carter, Charlie Parker (as); Paul Gonsalves, Flip Phillips, Al Sears, Ben Webster (ts); Harry Carney, Gerry Mulligan (bs); Earl Hines, Jimmie Jones, Hank Jones, Leroy Lovett, Junior Mance, Oscar Peterson, Billy Strayhorn, Claude Williamson (p); Everett Barksdale, Kenny Burrell, Barney Kessel, Les Spann (g); Aaron Bell, Ray Brown, Buddy Clark, Richard Davis, Milt Hinton, Sam Jones, Lloyd Trottman, Jimmy Woode (b); Sonny Greer, J. C. Heard, Lex Humphries, Mel Lewis, Joe Marshall, Grady Tate, Sam Woodyard (d). 2/51–8/67.

***(*) **Used To Be Duke** Verve 849 394
Hodges; Harold Shorty Baker (t); Lawrence Brown (tb); John Coltrane (ts); Jimmy Hamilton (ts, cl); Harry Carney (bs); Call Cobbs, Richard Powell (p); John Williams (b); Louie Bellson (d). 7 & 8/54.

(*) **Masters Of Jazz: Volume 9 Storyville STCD 4109
Hodges; Ray Nance (t); Lawrence Brown (tb); Harry Carney (bs); Ben Webster (ts); Herb Ellis (g); Lou Levy, Al Williams (p); Aaron Bell, Wilfred Middlebrooks (b); Gus Johnson, Sam Woodyard (d). 11/60, 3/61.

***(*) **Johnny Hodges At Sportpalast, Berlin** Pablo 2620 102 2CD
Hodges; Ray Nance (t); Lawrence Brown (tb); Harry Carney (bs); Al Williams (p); Aaron Bell (b); Sam Woodyard (d). 61.

**** **Everybody Knows Johnny Hodges** Impulse! GRP 11162
Hodges; Cat Anderson, Rolf Ericson, Herb Jones, Ray Nance (t); Lawrence Brown, Buster

Cooper, Britt Woodman (*tb*); Harry Carney, Paul Gonsalves, Jimmy Hamilton, Russell Procope (*reeds*); Jimmy Jones (*p*); Ernie Shepard (*b*); Grady Tate (*d*). 2/64.

*** **Johnny Hodges / Wild Bill Davis: Volume 1 – 1965–1966** RCA ND 89765 2CD

Hodges; Wild Bill Davis (*org*); Bob Brown (*ts, f*); Dickie Thompson, Mundell Lowe (*g*); George Duvivier, Milt Hinton (*b*); Bobby Durham, Osie Johnson (*d*). 1/65, 8/66.

When Johnny Hodges gave up playing like an angel and went to heaven in person, Adolphe Sax beat St Peter to a handshake at the gates. 'Thank you, my friend,' he cried. 'That is the way my saxophone was meant to sound.' There are still few voices in jazz more purely sensuous. Subtract Hodges's solos from Duke Ellington's recorded output and it shrinks disproportionately. He was a stalwart presence right from the Cotton Club Orchestra through the Webster–Blanton years and beyond. Sadly, perhaps, for all his pricklish dislike of sideman status in the Ellington orchestra (he frequently mimed counting bills in the Duke's direction when receiving his usual ovation for yet another perfectly crafted solo), Hodges was a rather unassertive leader, and his own recordings under-represent his extraordinary qualities, which began to dim only with the onset of the 1960s.

Perhaps the best-known of those records, the lovely *Everybody Knows Johnny Hodges*, has only recently reappeared, in a bright CD issue that captures the saxophonist's distinctive combination of tough jump tunes and aching ballads. Billy Strayhorn composed '310 Blues' specially for the session; Hodges is somewhat upstaged by both Gonsalves and the on-form Brown, but he has the final word. Strayhorn's other credit is the evergreen 'A Flower Is A Lovesome Thing', given a brief and tender reading. It's one of four small-group pieces from within the full band. 'Papa Knows' and 'Everybody Knows' represent a pair; the first is something of a ragbag of familiar Hodges materials, the latter a fine opening blues. Other tracks include a big-band 'Main Stem' and a medleyed 'I Let A Song Go Out Of My Heart'/-'Don't Get Around Much Anymore'.

The sessions on *Caravan* were originally recorded for the short-lived Mercer label. Long unavailable, they include some classics, like 'Charlotte Russe' (aka 'Lotus Blossom'), for which Hodges, Duke and Strayhorn all claimed some credit at varying times. Recorded in 1947, it is one of the most graceful of Hodges's solos. 'Caravan' itself is performed by a band that includes Duke Ellington and the composer, Juan Tizol, himself.

Otherwise, only Verve and Bluebird have done much to bring Hodges into the CD era, even if in the rather improbable company of organist Wild Bill Davis, a *mésalliance* of spectacular proportions that nevertheless survived half a dozen recorded encounters during the early 1960s. The inclusion of guitar, for which Hodges had contracted an inexplicable dependence and liking, on most of the tracks muddies the sound still further, though Mundell Lowe is a cut above the herd. RCA's Jazz Tribune series packages studio material from New York City in the first week of 1965 with an encounter the following August in Atlantic City. The August 1966 material used to be available as *In A Mellotone*, though it was given a later date by one month and contained some inconsistencies in respect of personnel. Whatever its date, the session included four fine Hodges originals (including 'Good Queen Bess' and 'Rockville') and good versions of 'It's Only A Paper Moon' and the co-written (with Ellington Jr) 'Belle Of The Belmont'. The sound is uneven, but Hodges comes across well.

Of the original Verves, *Used To Be Duke* is one of the very best. Repackaged with three further tracks from the same session – including the slightly poppy 'Skokiaan' – this is from the later stages of Hodges's solo foray from the Ellington band. Even when his own man, though, Duke was never far from his mind, and there is a strong Ellingtonian cast to the arrangements. In addition to the powerful title-number, there is a reading of Ellington's 'Warm Valley'. The bulk of the album is a long, beautifully modulated ballad medley which parcels out the solos and theme statements, with Carney and Richard Powell deservedly prominent. Baker plays beautifully, with more attention to the middle register than usual. Coltrane completists should be aware that he only fills out the backings on 'Used To Be Duke' and the additional 'All Of Me'; no solos.

Hodges's own modest diffidence and subtle mainstream approach failed to start any critical or contractual fires. In little over a year he was back with Ellington. As an instance of what he was capable of on his own account, *Used To Be Duke* is an essential acquisition. Surprisingly, Hodges and Tiny Grimes seem to get along famously; 'A Tiny Bit Of Blues' and the two parts of a gospel-laden 'Take 'Em Off, Take 'Em Off' are about the best things on an otherwise pretty average set.

From the other end of his career, the ASV and the Topaz do a fairly good job of compiling a representative profile and doing so with very little overlap. Probably the best guide to these is not personnel but session dates. Topaz ignore things like the 1940 'Good Queen Bess' and the slightly earlier 'Warm Valley', but material from the 1929 Cotton Club Orchestra *is* included, filling in an important gap in the transition from blues and jump to the lyrical majesty of later years. Hodges's alto (and occasionally soprano) stand out strongly wherever featured, and The Black & Blue selection (which overlaps only on half a dozen tracks, inevitably including 'The Jeep Is Jumping') is a good option, selecting the better material and skipping some of the fluff. Despite the date given in the title, the dates all come from 1938 and 1939. All this leaves room for a dozen tracks from 1939. Hodges switches to soprano again for 'Rent Party Blues' (Topaz) and 'Tired Socks' (ASV).

The Vogue Recordings suggest one of the Ellington bands, but after some mishap to Duke? That's very much the impression given by this Paris recording by an Ellingtonian splinter-group. Hodges is still prepared to dive back into his older jump style, though there are slower and more measured perform-ances as well. His reading of 'Perdido' is immaculate, and 'Mood Indigo', which follows shortly after, contains phrases which are as good as anything he put on record. However, the whole session has a slightly second-hand cast, and that piano player . . . it isn't really Duke, is it?

The Verve Jazz Masters compilation, which begins just after, is an ideal representation of later Hodges, at his most magisterial. Usually working with Ellingtonians, there is little to distinguish most of these settings from Ducal ones, except for the fact that Rabbit is even more generously featured than usual. It is wonderful to hear him in the company of a baritonist other than Carney on the 1959 session with Mulligan, and the compilation reprises the July 1952 Norman Granz jam which saw Hodges onstage with Benny Carter, Ben Webster and Charlie Parker.

A surprising dearth of live material makes the return of the 1961 Sportpalast recording doubly wel-come. Hodges was in magnificent voice on this occasion, playing with the moody grace that was his stock-in-trade. A few moments into 'Satin Doll' one realizes how wonderful it would have been to have seen this complex, rather difficult man perform as he does on these discs.

Jay Hoggard VIBRAPHONE

*** **Solo Vibraphone** India Navigation IN 1040
  Hoggard (*vib* solo). 11/78.
***(*) **Overview** Muse MCD 5383
  Hoggard; Geri Allen (*p*); Ed Rozie (*b*); Freddie Waits (*d*). 6/89.
*** **The Little Tiger** Muse MCD 5410
  Hoggard; Benny Green (*p*); Marcus McLaurine (*b*); Yoron Israel (*d*). 6/90.
***(*) **The Fountain** Muse MCD 5450
  Hoggard; James Weidman (*p*); Kenny Burrell (*g*); Marcus McLaurine (*b*); Yoron Israel (*d*). 7/91.
**** **In The Spirit** Muse MCD 5476
  Hoggard; James Newton (*f*); Dwight Andrews (*ss, af, bcl*); Mark Helias (*b*); Ed Blackwell (*d*). 5/92.

There's a fierceness about Hoggard – 'the little tiger' seems a perfect description – that communicates itself through almost everything he does, not just the more avant-garde aspects. His approach to stand-ards on *The Fountain* is consistently original and carefully thought out. 'Prelude To A Kiss' has a brittle and resonant edge that one rarely hears and, though 'Fables Of Faubus' and 'Epistrophy' on the same disc might seem to be closer to Hoggard's natural territory, the ballad is beautifully etched.

It's illuminating to compare the 1991 album with the solo India Navigation set. This is very much the other side of Hoggard's musical personality. Titles like 'May Those Who Love Apartheid Rot In Hell' give a sense of the burning intensity that fuels all his work, but even here it's worth noting that such pieces sit alongside 'Toe Dance For A Baby' and a markedly jovial reading of 'Air Mail Special'. Recorded live, the disc doesn't give the best representation of Hoggard's clean, exact delivery.

Technically, he sounds closer to Hamp than to Milt Jackson or Bobby Hutcherson. The partnership with Geri Allen on the excellent *Overview* works to mutual advantage. Allen's briskly accurate statement on 'Ruby My Dear' tees Hoggard up for one of his best recorded solos. By contrast, Green is a little too laddish and self-indulgent, and the emotional balance of the set never quite sorts itself out.

Wedged in between 'Epistrophy' and the closing 'My One And Only Love', the title-piece of *The Fountain* is in Hoggard's more abstract manner, with dark, rumbling sounds from McLaurine and randomly placed accents by Israel. It's a remarkable performance by a considerably undervalued player, but it is as nothing compared to the astonishing *In The Spirit*, a tribute to multi-instrumentalist Eric Dolphy, who had featured Bobby Hutcherson's vibes so prominently on *Out To Lunch*. Hoggard reprises one track – the flute-based 'Gazzeloni' – from that classic record, and includes an original written as a farewell and a benediction to the 'Peaceful Messenger Of God's Music'. There is no mistaking the heartfelt nature of the response, and the band Hoggard has assembled are more than sympathetic to his aims.

John Hogman (born 1953) TENOR AND BARITONE SAXOPHONES, SYNTHESIZER

***(*) **Good Night Sister** Sittel SITCD 9202

      Hogman; Ulf Johansson (*tb*); Knud Jorgensen (*p*); Thomas Arnesen (*g*); Nils-Erik Sparf (*vn, vla*); Bengt Hansson (*b*); Johan Dielemans (*d*). 10/92.

Hugely enjoyable. Hogman's opening tune, 'Theodore', is a Sonny Rollins dedication that makes clear his primary influence, but it's Rollins without the soul-searching and the inner demons: what one hears is a confident unfurling of fine melodic ideas, etched in a big, shapely sound. He plays baritone on two cuts, and that sounds just as impressive. 'Look For The Silver Lining' is another Theodore-like performance, but the exquisite ballad-work on the title-piece and the wry, ambivalent bounce of 'Hiccup' prove his range. Johansson and Arnesen take cameo roles; more important is Jorgensen, who plays very well but who sadly died only weeks after the session.

Billie Holiday (1915–59) VOCAL

*** **The Quintessential Billie Holiday Vol. 1 1933–35** Columbia 450987-2

      Holiday; Charlie Teagarden, Shirley Clay, Roy Eldridge, Dick Clark (*t*); Benny Morton, Jack Teagarden (*tb*); Cecil Scott, Benny Goodman, Tom Macey (*cl*); Johnny Hodges (*as*); Art Karle, Ben Webster, Chu Berry (*ts*); Joe Sullivan, Teddy Wilson (*p*); Dick McDonough, Lawrence Lucie, John Trueheart, Dave Barbour (*g*); Artie Bernstein, Grachan Moncur, John Kirby (*b*); Cozy Cole, Gene Krupa (*d*). 11/33–12/35.

***(*) **The Quintessential Billie Holiday Vol. 2 1936** Columbia 460060-2

      Holiday; Chris Griffin, Jonah Jones, Bunny Berigan, Irving Randolph (*t*); Rudy Powell, Artie Shaw, Irving Fazola, Vido Musso (*cl*); Harry Carney (*cl, bs*); Johnny Hodges (*as*); Ted McCrae, Ben Webster (*ts*); Teddy Wilson (*p*); John Trueheart, Allan Reuss, Dick McDonough (*g*); Grachan Moncur, John Kirby, Pete Peterson, Artie Bernstein, Milt Hinton (*b*); Cozy Cole, Gene Krupa (*d*). 1–10/36.

**** **The Quintessential Billie Holiday Vol. 3 1936–37** Columbia 460820-2

      Holiday; Irving Randolph, Jonah Jones, Buck Clayton, Henry 'Red' Allen (*t*); Vido Musso, Benny Goodman (*cl*); Cecil Scott (*cl, as, ts*); Edgar Sampson (*cl, as*); Ben Webster, Lester Young, Prince Robinson (*ts*); Teddy Wilson (*p*); Allan Reuss, Jimmy McLin (*g*); Milt Hinton, John Kirby, Walter Page (*b*); Gene Krupa, Cozy Cole, Jo Jones (*d*). 10/36–2/37.

*** **Billie Holiday 1933–37** Classics 582

      As above three discs. 33–37.

**** **The Quintessential Billie Holiday Vol. 4 1937** Columbia 463333-2

      Holiday; Cootie Williams, Eddie Tompkins, Buck Clayton (*t*); Buster Bailey, Edmond Hall (*cl*); Johnny Hodges (*as*); Joe Thomas, Lester Young (*ts*); Harry Carney (*bs*); Teddy Wilson, James Sherman (*p*); Carmen Mastren, Freddie Green, Allan Reuss (*g*); Artie Bernstein, Walter Page, John Kirby (*b*); Cozy Cole, Alphonse Steele, Jo Jones (*d*). 2–6/37.

***(*) **The Quintessential Billie Holiday Vol. 5 1937–38** Columbia 465190-2

      Holiday; Buck Clayton (*t*); Benny Morton (*tb*); Buster Bailey (*cl*); Prince Robinson, Vido Musso (*cl, ts*); Lester Young (*ts*); Claude Thornhill, Teddy Wilson (*p*); Allan Reuss, Freddie Green (*g*); Walter Page (*b*); Jo Jones (*d*). 6/37–1/38.

***(*) **The Quintessential Billie Holiday Vol. 6 1938** Columbia 466313-2

      Holiday; Bernard Anderson, Buck Clayton, Harry James (*t*); Dicky Wells, Benny Morton (*tb*); Buster Bailey (*cl*); Edgar Sampson, Benny Carter (*as*); Lester Young (*cl, ts*); Babe Russin, Herschel Evans (*ts*); Claude Thornhill, Margaret 'Queenie' Johnson, Teddy Wilson (*p*); Al Casey, Freddie Green (*g*); John Kirby, Walter Page (*b*); Cozy Cole, Jo Jones (*d*). 5–11/38.

(*) **The Quintessential Billie Holiday Vol. 7 1938–39 Columbia 466966-2

      Holiday; Charlie Shavers, Roy Eldridge, Hot Lips Page, Frankie Newton (*t*); Bobby Hackett (*c*); Trummy Young, Tyree Glenn (*tb*); Tab Smith (*ss, as*); Benny Carter, Toots Mondello (*cl, as*); Teddy Buckner (*as*); Kenneth Hollon, Ernie Powell, Bud Freeman, Chu Berry, Stanley Payne (*ts*); Teddy Wilson, Sonny Payne, Kenny Kersey (*p*); Danny Barker, Al Casey, Jimmy McLin, Bernard Addison (*g*); Milt Hinton, John Williams (*b*); Cozy Cole, Eddie Dougherty (*d*). 11/38–7/39.

*** **Billie Holiday 1937–1939** Classics 592

      As above four discs. 37–39.

*** **The Quintessential Billie Holiday Vol. 8 1939–1940** Columbia 467914-2

      Holiday; Charlie Shavers, Buck Clayton, Roy Eldridge, Harry 'Sweets' Edison (*t*); Tab Smith, Earl Warren, Jimmy Powell, Carl Frye, Don Redman, George Auld (*as*); Kenneth Hollon, Stanley Payne, Lester Young, Kermit Scott, Jimmy Hamilton, Don Byas (*ts*); Jack Washington (*bs*); Sonny White, Teddy Wilson, Joe Sullivan (*p*); Bernard Addison, Freddie Green, John Collins, Lawrence Lucie (*g*); John Williams, Walter Page, Al Hall (*b*); Eddie Dougherty, Jo Jones, Harold 'Doc' West, Kenny Clarke (*d*). 7/39–9/40.

*** **Billie Holiday 1939–1940** Classics 601
As above two Columbia discs. 39–40.

**** **Billie Holiday – The Voice Of Jazz: The Complete Recordings 1933–1940** Affinity AFS 1019 8CD
Collective personnel as above Columbia records. 11/33–10/40.

*** **The Quintessential Billie Holiday Vol. 9 1940–42** Columbia 467915-2
Holiday; Bill Coleman, Shad Collins, Emmett Berry, Roy Eldridge (*t*); Benny Morton (*tb*); Jimmy Hamilton (*cl*); Benny Carter (*cl, as*); Leslie Johnakins, Hymie Schertzer, Eddie Barefield, Ernie Powell, Lester Boone, Jimmy Powell (*as*); Lester Young, George Auld, Babe Russin (*ts*); Sonny White, Teddy Wilson, Eddie Heywood (*p*); Ulysses Livingston, John Collins, Paul Chapman, Gene Fields, Al Casey (*g*); Wilson Meyers, Grachan Moncur, John Williams, Ted Sturgis (*b*); Yank Porter, Kenny Clarke, J. C. Heard, Herbert Cowens (*d*). 10/40–2/42.

Billie Holiday has become so surrounded by hagiography that it's now almost impossible to hear and treat her music on its own terms: the legendary suffering and mythopoeic pain which countless admirers have sought out in her work make it difficult for the merely curious to warm to a singer who was uneven and sometimes content to coast. There is occasionally a troubling detachment in Holiday's singing which is quite the opposite of the living-every-line virtue which some have impressed on her records; and those that she made in her later years often demand a voyeuristic role of any listener determined to enjoy her interpretations. Nevertheless, Holiday was a singular and unrepeatable talent, whose finest hours are remarkably revealing and often surprisingly – given her generally morose reputation as an artist – joyful. New listeners may find the accumulated weight of the Holiday myth discouraging and they may be equally surprised at how much fun many of the earlier records are. Part of the difficulty in approaching her lies in the way her music has been repackaged. All of her pre-war music is now available on CD: the nine-record sequence on Columbia is perhaps the most desirable way to collect it, since the handsome packaging offers comprehensive documentation. The Affinity set includes many alternative takes and is lavishly spread across eight packed CDs. But both projects are let down by the transfers, which don't have much sparkle but homogenize the often superb accompaniments into a dull blend that lacks dynamics. Some of the dubbings sound crisp while others are beset by surface noise (this particularly applies to the alternative masters heard on the Affinity set). The sheer weight of both sets also tells against music which is best heard session by session: the casual nature of the original dates invites one to listen to a few songs at a time, and – as with many such reissue projects – some listeners may find the bulkiness of the presentation intimidating.

We must not, however, carp too much! The standard of these records – particularly considering how many tracks were made – is finally very high, and the best of them are as poised and finely crafted as any small-group jazz of the period. One of Holiday's innovations was to suggest a role for the singer which blended in with the rest of the musicians, improvising a line and taking a 'solo' which was as integrated as anything else on the record. On her earlier sides with Wilson as leader, she was still credited as responsible for the 'vocal refrain', but the later titles feature 'Billie Holiday and her Orchestra'. She starts some records and slips into the middle of others, but always there's a feeling of a musician at ease with the rest of the band and aware of the importance of fitting into the performance as a whole. Her tone, on the earliest sides, is still a little raw and unformed, and the trademark rasp at the edge of her voice – which she uses to canny effect on the later titles – is used less pointedly; but the unaffected styling is already present, and there are indications of her mastery of time even in the tracks on *Quintessential* Volume 1. While the most obvious characteristic of her singing is the lagging behind the beat, she seldom sounds tired or slow to respond, and the deeper impression is of a vocalist who knows exactly how much time she can take. She never scats, rarely drifts far from the melody, and respects structure and lyrical nuance, even where – as has often been remarked – the material is less than blue-chip. But her best singing invests the words with shades of meaning which vocalists until that point had barely looked at: she creates an ambiguity between what the words say and what she might be thinking which is very hard to distil. And that is the core of Holiday's mystique. Coupled with the foggy, baleful, sombre quality of her tone, it creates a vocal jazz which is as absorbing as it is enduring.

Like her fellow musicians, she had good and bad days, and that's one reason why it's difficult to pinpoint the best of the records listed above. Some may prefer to have those albums featuring the best-known songs; but one peculiarity of these sessions is that her attention seldom depends on the quality of the material: an otherwise forgotten Tin Pan Alley novelty may give rise to as great a performance as any of the best-known standards. The constantly changing personnel is also a variable. The tracks with Lester Young on tenor (and occasionally clarinet) have been acclaimed as the greatest of her collaborations, and those on Volumes 3 and 4 of the Columbia sequence are certainly among the best tracks: but some may find them occasionally lachrymose rather than moving. 'This Year's Kisses' (Volume 3), for instance, may be a serenely involving treatment of the song, with Holiday and Young seemingly reading each other's minds, but it points towards the bathos which blights much of her later work. Other accompanists do equally fine work in their way: Roy Eldridge, who suppresses his wildest side to surprisingly controlled effect on his appearances; Ben Webster, whose solo on 'With Thee I Swing' (Volume 2) is memorably sustained; Bunny Berigan, who plays superbly on Volume 2 and contributes (along with Artie Shaw) a classic solo to 'Billie's Blues', one of the greatest performances in the series; Irving Fazola, Buck Clayton, Tab Smith and Hot Lips Page, who all play with knowing insight; and, above all, Teddy Wilson, who organized many of the sessions, and who finesses his playing into little masterpieces of economy and apposite counterpoint, whether in solo or ensemble terms.

Holiday herself is at her freshest and most inspirational in these pre-war recordings and, whatever one may think about the later albums, these sessions surrender nothing in gravitas and communicate a good humour which is all their own. The session producers – John Hammond or Bernie Hanighen – encouraged an atmosphere of mutual creativity which the singer seldom fails to respond to and, even on the less immortal songs, Holiday makes something of the situation: there is no sense of her fighting against the material, as there often is with Armstrong or Waller in the same period. On some sessions she sounds less interested: much of the music on Volume 7 fails; and elsewhere she reacts against a tempo or simply lets her interest flag, sometimes within the parameters of a single tune. If we single out Volumes 3, 4 and 5 of the Columbia series, it's purely because some of the tracks – such as 'I Must Have That Man', 'My Last Affair' (3), 'Foolin' Myself', 'Mean To Me' (4), 'Trav'lin' All Alone' and 'I Can't Believe That You're In Love With Me' (5) – reach a special peak of creativity from all involved. The Classics CDs cover all the material which isn't also included on their Teddy Wilson series: a useful way to fill gaps if the other discs are already in the collection, but splitting the music between Wilson and Holiday separates much of the best material. The transfer quality is mixed. The Affinity set is at least comprehensive and, given the quality of the material, it would be churlish to award it fewer than four stars; only scholars will find the alternative-take material of much interest, though.

Other compilations from the period include: *The Early Classics 1935–40* (Flapper CD-9756), a decent cross-section in bright if sometimes thin sound; *The Essential* (Columbia 467149), an intelligently programmed 16 tracks; and the companion *16 Most Requested Songs* (Columbia 474401-2), an excellent choice.

*** The Legacy (1933–1958) Columbia 469049-2 3CD

As above Columbia discs, plus Duke Ellington Orchestra, Benny Goodman Orchestra, Martha Tilton, Johnny Mercer, Leo Watson (*v*). 33–58.

An unsatisfactory mixture of Columbia's pick from the nine-volume 'Quintessential' series and various obscure airshots, including 'Saddest Tale' with Ellington and two pieces with Goodman's band. There are 70 tracks, and most of them come from the 1936–41 period; only a few from her final years are here, and they sound wretched in comparison. Ornately packaged in an oversize box, this seems awkward and unnecessarily overbearing as a compilation, but the best of the music is, of course, splendid.

***(*) The Complete Original American Decca Recordings MCA GRP 26012 2CD

Holiday; Russ Case, Joe Guy, Gordon Griffin, Rostelle Reese, Billy Butterfield, Jimmy Nottingham, Emmett Berry, Buck Clayton, Bernie Privin, Tony Faso, Dick Vance, Shad Collins, Bobby Williams, Bobby Hackett (*t*); Dicky Wells, George Matthews, Henderson Chambers, Mort Bullman, George Stevenson (*tb*); Milter Yaner, Bill Stegmeyer (*cl, as*); Hymie Schertzer, Jack Cressey, Lem Davis, Toots Mondello, Al Klink, Rudy Powell, George Dorsey, Johnny Mince, Pete Clark, Sid Cooper (*as*); John Fulton (*ts, cl, f*); Dick Eckles (*ts, f*); Larry Binyon, Paul Ricci, Dave Harris, Hank Ross, Armand Camgros, Bob Dorsey, Art Drelinger, Lester Young, Joe Thomas, Budd Johnson, Freddie Williams, Pat Nizza (*ts*); Eddie Barefield (*bs, cl*); Stan Webb, Sol Moore, Dave McRae (*bs*); Dave Bowman, Sammy Benskin, Joe Springer, Charles LaVere, Bobby Tucker, Billy Kyle, Horace Henderson, Bernie Leighton (*p*); Carl Kress, Tony Mottola, Everett Barksdale, Bob Bain, Mundell Lowe, Tiny Grimes, Jimmy Shirley, Dan Perry (*g*); Haig Stephens, Bob Haggart, Billy Taylor, John Simmons, Thomas Barney, George Duvivier, Joe Benjamin, Jack Lesberg, Lou Butterman (*b*); Johnny Blowers, George Wettling, Specs Powell, Big Sid Catlett, Kelly Martin, Denzil Best, Kenny Clarke, Norris 'Bunny' Shawker, Shadow Wilson, Cozy Cole, Wallace Bishop, Jimmy Crawford, Nick Fatool (*d*); Louis Armstrong (*v*); strings and choir. 10/44–3/50.

*** Billie Holiday 1944 Classics 806

Similar to above, except add Roy Eldridge, Doc Cheatham, Freddy Webster (*t*), Vic Dickenson (*tb*), Barney Bigard (*cl*), Lem Davis (*as*), Al Casey, Teddy Walters (*g*), Oscar Pettiford (*b*). 3–11/44.

Holiday's Decca sessions have been impeccably presented here, in a double-CD set which has been remastered to make the music sound as big and clear as possible. Some may prefer a warmer and less boomy sound, but the timbre of the records is impressively full and strong. These sessions were made when Holiday had established a wider reputation, and their feel is very different from the Columbia records: carefully orchestrated by a multitude of hands, including Sy Oliver and Gordon Jenkins, the best of them are as good as anything Holiday did. Many listeners may, indeed, find this the single most entertaining set of Holiday reissues on the market, for the polish and class of the singing and playing – while less spontaneously improvisational in feel – is hard to deny. Her own songs 'Don't Explain' and 'God Bless The Child' are obvious highlights, even if they mark the beginning of Holiday's 'victim' image, and here is the original reading of the subsequently famous 'That Ole Devil Called Love', two duets with Louis Armstrong, slow and emotionally draining readings of 'Porgy' and 'My Man' (from the one session with the sole accompaniment of a rhythm section), and a lot of pleasing, brightly paced readings of superior standards. Few players stand out the way Young and Wilson do on the pre-war sides, but these aren't the same kind of records.

The Classics sequence continues with various 1944 tracks. It starts with three tracks from a Metropolitan Opera House show, with Eldridge and Tatum in the band, then goes through material with Eddie Heywood's Orchestra and finally reaches the first of the sessions on the MCA set. A useful in-between compilation.

***(*) **Solitude** Verve 519810-2
> Holiday; Charlie Shavers (t); Flip Phillips (ts); Oscar Peterson (p); Barney Kessel (g); Ray Brown (b); Alvin Stoller (d). 52.

*** **Recital By Billie Holiday** Verve 521868-2
> Holiday; Harry 'Sweets' Edison, Joe Newman, Charlie Shavers (t); Willie Smith (as); Paul Quinichette (ts); Oscar Peterson (p, org); Bobby Tucker (p); Herb Ellis, Freddie Green, Barney Kessel (g); Ray Brown, Red Callender (b); Chico Hamilton, Gus Johnson, Ed Shaughnessy (d). 7/52–9/54.

*** **Lady Sings The Blues** Verve 521429-2
> Holiday; Charlie Shavers (t); Tony Scott (cl, p); Budd Johnson, Paul Quinichette (ts); Wynton Kelly, Billy Taylor (p); Billy Bauer, Kenny Burrell (g); Aaron Bell, Leonard Gaskin (b); Cozy Cole, Lenny McBrowne (d). 2/55–6/56.

***(*) **Music For Torching** Verve 527455-2
> Holiday; similar to above. 8/56.

**** **All Or Nothing At All** Verve 529226-2
> Holiday; Harry 'Sweets' Edison (t); Ben Webster (ts); Jimmy Rowles (p); Barney Kessel (g); Joe Mondragon (b); Alvin Stoller (d). 8/56–1/57.

*** **Songs For Distingué Lovers** Verve 815055-2
> Holiday; Harry 'Sweets' Edison (t); Ben Webster (ts); Jimmy Rowles (p); Barney Kessel (g); Joe Mondragon (b); Alvin Stoller, Larry Bunker (d). 7/56.

***(*) **The Billie Holiday Songbook** Verve 823246-2
> Holiday; Joe Newman, Charlie Shavers, Roy Eldridge, Buck Clayton, Harry 'Sweets' Edison (t); Tony Scott (cl); Willie Smith (as); Paul Quinichette, Al Cohn, Coleman Hawkins (ts); Wynton Kelly, Carl Drinkard, Mal Waldron, Oscar Peterson, Bobby Tucker (p); Kenny Burrell, Herb Ellis, Freddie Green, Barney Kessel (g); Aaron Bell, Ray Brown, Carson Smith, Milt Hinton, Red Callender (b); Gus Johnson, Chico Hamilton, Ed Shaughnessy, Don Lamond, Lenny McBrowne (d). 7/52–9/58.

***(*) **Verve Jazz Masters: Billie Holiday** Verve 519825-2
> Holiday; various groups. 52–8/56.

*** **Jazz Masters 47: Sings Standards** Verve 527650-2
> As above. 2/45–3/59.

***(*) **Lady In Autumn** Verve 849434-2 2CD
> Holiday; Buck Clayton, Joe Guy, Charlie Shavers, Joe Newman, Harry 'Sweets' Edison, Roy Eldridge (t); Tommy Turk (tb); Tony Scott (cl); Romeo Penque (as, bcl); Willie Smith, Gene Quill, Benny Carter (as); Ben Webster, Lester Young, Coleman Hawkins, Al Cohn, Paul Quinichette, Budd Johnson (ts); Oscar Peterson (p, org); Milt Raskin, Bobby Tucker, Mal Waldron, Carl Drinkard, Jimmy Rowles, Hank Jones, Wynton Kelly (p); Irving Ashby, Barney Kessel, Kenny Burrell, Barry Galbraith, Freddie Green (g); Janet Putnam (hp); Milt Hinton, Carson Smith, Joe Mondragon, Red Mitchell, Red Callender, Aaron Bell, Leonard Gaskin, John Simmons, Ray Brown (b); Dave Coleman, Alvin Stoller, J. C. Heard, Ed Shaughnessy, Chico Hamilton, Larry Bunker, Lenny McBrowne, Osie Johnson (d); strings. 4/46–3/59.

**** **First Issue: The Great American Songbook** Verve 523003-2 2CD
> Similar to above. 52–59.

Holiday's last significant period in the studios was with Verve in the 1950s, and this is the best-known and most problematical music she made. Her voice has already lost most of its youthful shine and ebullience – even a genuine up-tempo piece like 'What A Little Moonlight Can Do', where Oscar Peterson does his best to rouse the singer, is something she only has the energy to glide over. Whether this makes her music more revealing or affecting or profound is something listeners will have to decide for themselves. There are songs where the pace and the timbre of her voice are so funereal as to induce nothing but acute depression; others have a persuasive inner lilt which insists that her greatness has endured. And the best of the interpretations, scattered as they are through all these records, show how compelling Holiday could be, even when apparently enfeebled by her own circumstances.

Although there is a complete edition available (see below), Verve have now released Holiday's output in seven separate sets (the last, *All Or Nothing At All*, is a two-disc set, while the live records are listed below). Preference among the discs depends mainly on song selection and accompanists: whatever her own physical well-being, Norman Granz always made sure there were top-flight bands behind her. *Solitude* has some lovely things: a classic 'These Foolish Things', a marvellous 'Moonglow'. *Recital* has some happy work, including 'What A Little Moonlight Can Do' and 'Too Marvellous For Words', but there are some sloppy pieces too. *Lady Sings The Blues* (which basically relaces the previous disc under that title) has three or four of her best-known heartache songs and includes the rehearsal tape with Tony Scott where they work up 'God Bless The Child' – intriguing, but probably for scholars only. *Music For Torching* is small-hours music of a high, troubling calibre. *All Or Nothing At All* rounds up seven long sessions across two discs and includes some magnificent work from Edison and Webster (there is even a warm-up instrumental cut while they were waiting for her to arrive at the studio on one date) as well as what is probably Holiday's most regal, instinctual late work. It all seems to come to a peak on the very last track on disc two, the definitive version of 'Gee Baby, Ain't I Good To You?'.

In the light of this sequence, the other discs – either compilations or, in the case of *Songs For Distingué Lovers*, 'proper' album reissues – are rendered superfluous except for those who prefer the odd Holiday record in their collection. Both discs in the Jazz Masters series would do fine for that, though the *Standards* selection rather inevitably comes off second-best. The *First Issue* two-disc set is, though, a beautifully chosen retrospective which eschews Holiday's tortured epics and lines up the choicest examples of Tin Pan Alley instead. Remastering has been done to a very high and meticulous standard.

(*) Masters Of Jazz Vol. 3: Billie Holiday Storyville 4103

    Holiday; Hot Lips Page, Roy Eldridge, Neal Hefti (*t*); Herbie Harper, Jack Teagarden (*tb*); Barney Bigard (*cl*); Herbie Steward (*cl, ts*); Coleman Hawkins (*ts*); Teddy Wilson, Jimmy Rowles, Art Tatum (*p*); Al Casey (*g*); Iggy Shevack, Oscar Pettiford (*b*); Blinkie Garner, Sid Catlett (*d*). 44/49.

** **The Complete 1951 Storyville Club Sessions** Fresh Sound FSR-CD 151

    Holiday; Stan Getz (*ts*); Buster Harding (*p*); John Fields (*b*); Marquis Foster (*d*). 10/51.

(*) At Storyville Black Lion BLCD 760921

    As above, except add Carl Drinkard (*p*); Jimmy Woode (*b*); Peter Littman (*d*). 10/51–10/53.

*** **Billie's Blues** Blue Note CDP 748786-2

    Holiday; Monty Kelly, Larry Neill, Don Waddilove (*t*); Skip Layton, Murray McEachern (*tb*); Buddy DeFranco (*cl*); Alvy West, Dan D'Andrea, Lennie Hartman (*reeds*); Haywood Henry (*ts, bs*); Carl Drinkard, Bobby Tucker, Buddy Weed, Sonny Clark, Beryl Booker (*p*); Jimmy Raney, Mike Pingitore, Tiny Grimes (*g*); Red Mitchell, Artie Shapiro (*b*); Elaine Leighton, Willie Rodriguez (*d*). 42–54.

*** **Jazz At The Philharmonic** Verve 521642-2

    Holiday; Buck Clayton, Roy Eldridge, Howard McGhee (*t*); Tony Scott (*cl*); Illinois Jacquet, Wardell Gray, Al Cohn, Coleman Hawkins, Lester Young (*ts*); Carl Drinkard (*p*); Kenny Burrell (*g*); Charles Mingus, Carson Smith (*b*); Dave Coleman, J. C. Heard, Chico Hamilton (*d*). 2/45–11/56.

*** **At Carnegie Hall** Verve 527777-2

    Holiday; Buck Clayton, Roy Eldridge (*t*); Al Cohn, Coleman Hawkins (*ts*); Tony Scott (*cl, p*); Carl Drinkard (*p*); Kenny Burrell (*g*); Carson Smith (*b*); Chico Hamilton (*d*). 11/56.

Holiday left a great number of live recordings, most of them unauthorized at the time, and they make a rather depressing lot to sort through. Unlike, say, Charlie Parker's live music, this presents a less than fascinating portrait, mostly of a musician in adversity. Club recordings such as the two Storyville discs find her in wildly varying voice, almost from song to song: truly affecting performances may sit next to ragged, throwaway ones. *Miss Brown To You* includes airshots with Count Basie and concert tracks with Louis Armstrong; however, all but the last few are in appalling sound, and this can't be recommended. The 'Masters Of Jazz' series disc includes some good material from the 1940s, but better is the Bandstand disc, which includes some excellent tracks with a trio and some surprisingly spirited blues singing with (of all people) Eddie Condon, from a 1949 TV show. Sound here is good for the period. *Billie's Blues* is an interesting cross-section of tracks: several from a European tour which was a mixed success, including three with Buddy DeFranco's group that feature some fine clarinet by the leader, and four from an obscure session for Aladdin with a group that puts the singer into a jump-band blues situation. She handles it unexpectedly well. Her JATP appearances are collected on the Verve album, situation. She handles it unexpectedly well. Her JATP appearances are collected on the Verve album, plus material from other (somewhat less inspiring) appearances from the 1950s. *At Carnegie Hall* is the record of one of her last great live performances. The notes reveal she was scarcely in any fit state to perform and, with the music interspersed with readings from her book, there is a macabre quality which her artistry somehow rises above.

**** The Complete Billie Holiday On Verve 1945–1959 Verve 517658-2 10CD
    Holiday; various groups as above. 45–59.
***(*) Billie's Best Verve 513943-2
    As above.
With the appearance of this set, the circle is closed on Holiday's career: the various multi-disc packages impose an order which allows anyone to follow her from the beginning to the end. There are rarities in this major collection which include what are often wryly funny rehearsal tapes with Jimmy Rowles (it seems strange to hear this famously tormented woman laugh and tell jokes), but its main purpose is to provide first-to-last coverage of her major studio years. There is splendid documentation to go with the records. *Billie's Best* is a useful pocket edition that samples the big box.

(***) Lady In Satin Columbia 450883-2
    Holiday; strings. 58.
(***) Last Recordings Verve 835370-2
    Holiday; Harry 'Sweets' Edison, Joe Wilder (*t*); Jimmy Cleveland, Bill Byers (*tb*); Romeo
    Penque (*as, ts, bcl*); Gene Quill (*as*); Al Cohn (*ts*); Danny Bank (*bs*); Hank Jones (*p*); Kenny
    Burrell, Barry Galbraith (*g*); Milt Hinton, Joe Benjamin (*b*); Osie Johnson (*d*); strings. 3/59.
A troubling farewell which, nevertheless, has a certain macabre fascination. The croaking voice which barely gets through *Lady In Satin* has its admirers, and there is arguably some of the tormented revelation which distinguishes such earlier works as Parker's 'Lover Man', but we suggest that it be approached with care. *Last Recordings* emerges in much the same way, if it is in sum rather less harrowing.

Dave Holland (born 1946) DOUBLE BASS, CELLO

*** Life Cycle ECM 1238
    Holland (*clo* solo). 11/82.
Miles smiled when he first saw and heard Holland. The premier British bass player of his generation has the quality, rare among rhythm players, of drawing attention to what he is doing, almost irrespective of whatever else is going on in the band. Even more remarkably, he does so entirely without histrionics; he is always a seamless part of any group of which he is a member. Even so, given his formidable technique on both cello and bass fiddle, solo recording was always likely.

Like its predecessor, *Emerald Tears*, *Life Cycle* is pretty demanding in its absolute concentration of resources, but not forbiddingly so. The cello phrasings conjure echoes of just about everyone from Bach to Zoltán Kodály, and then onward to Oscar Pettiford and Ron Carter. Solo recitals of this type (ECM have also recorded David Darling, Barre Phillips and Miroslav Vitous) are always demanding, on player, technicians and listeners alike; what's remarkable about Holland is how straightforwardly listenable he is.

**** Conference Of The Birds ECM 1027
    Holland; Anthony Braxton, Sam Rivers (*reeds, f*); Barry Altschul (*d, perc, mar*). 11/72.
More than 20 years old, and one of the classics of contemporary jazz. The title-track has less to do with Attar's great poem than with the dawn chorus outside Holland's London flat, and there's a shifting, edge-of-sleep quality to each of the bassist's six compositions. Braxton and Rivers intermesh more or less indistinguishably on flutes, but their saxophone voicings are almost antagonistic, which works fine. Time and again attention is quite properly diverted to Holland's astonishingly musical bass lines which illustrate his near-perfect tone and timing. Altschul is superb throughout, but his marimba figure on the title-piece is achingly beautiful, setting the listener up for the bite and bustle of 'Interception'. Indispensable.

***(*) Jumpin' In ECM 1269
    Holland; Kenny Wheeler (*t, pkt-t, c, flhn*); Julian Priester (*tb*); Robin Eubanks (*tb*); Steve
    Coleman (*as*); Steve Ellington (*d*). 10/83.
*** Seeds Of Time ECM 1292
    As above, except omit Ellington, add Marvin 'Smitty' Smith (*d*). 11/84.

*** **The Razor's Edge** ECM 1353
>As above, except omit Priester; add Robin Eubanks (*tb*). 2/87.

(*) **Triplicate ECM 1373
>Holland; Steve Coleman (*as*); Jack DeJohnette (*d*). 3/88.

*** **Extensions** ECM 1410
>Holland; Steve Coleman (*as*); Kevin Eubanks (*g*); Marvin 'Smitty' Smith (*d*). 9/89.

Hard to choose between them. State-of-the-art modern jazz pivoted on the interplay between Coleman (who miraculously combines the qualities of his two saxophonic namesakes) and Holland's beautifully tempered bass playing. As on *Conference*, the individuality of the music stems from a tension between modernist freedoms and old-fashioned melodic susceptibilities. 'Blues For C. M.' on *Razor's Edge* is a tribute to Charles Mingus, who may be a greater influence on Holland's theme-writing than on his actual playing, which hovers between Scott LaFaro and early Ron Carter. The ground-breaking *Jumpin' In* should be considered essential, but it's hard to envisage a well-rounded collection without at least one of the others.

Triplicate hovers uneasily between wonderful and galling, almost like a *nouvelle cuisine* meal that, dammit, looks too good to eat. One of the rare occasions when the much-blathered-about 'ECM sound' actually does seem a hindrance rather than a virtue. Much as you might scuttle out of a trendy restaurant and devour a hamburger at the corner, *Triplicate* creates a hunger for the sort of after-hours brilliance the trio could doubtless conjure up when a trifle less self-conscious than this.

***(*) **Dream Of The Elders** ECM 1572
>Holland; Eric Person (*as, ss*); Steve Nelson (*vib, mar*); Gene Jackson (*d*); Cassandra Wilson (*v*). 95.

Holland's first record for ECM in eight years does not disappoint, yet nor can it be said to be either startling or innovative. It is entirely consistent with a particular period in British jazz, a folkish melodic style of writing that is accurately reflected in spacious playing with lots of light and shade. Person is very much a version of Steve Coleman, but he shoulders the responsibility with some flair and actually manages to make his presence felt. Jackson has previously recorded with Michelle Rosewoman and others and sounds entirely comfortable with this sort of material. Wilson is used for a vocal version of 'Equality', to a lyric by Maya Angelou.

Rick Hollander (born 1956) DRUMS

*** **Private Ear** yvp music CD 3013
>Hollander; Tim Armacost (*ts, ss*); Walter Lang (*p*); Jos Machtel (*b*). 12/88.

*** **Out Here** Timeless SJP 309
>Hollander; Tim Armacost (*ts*); Walter Lang (*p*); Will Woodard (*b*). 6/91.

*** **Accidental Fortune** Concord CCD-4550
>As above. 9/92.

(*) **Once Upon A Time Concord CCD 4666
>As above. 4/94.

Midstream post-bop, served with all the usual accomplishments. The most interesting and effective item on both *Private Ear* and *Accidental Fortune* is a drum-and-bass-only version of 'Star Eyes'. As a performance, it suggests that Hollander, a forty-year-old native of Detroit who has worked with Woody Shaw and Warne Marsh, has also paid attention to the great bebop drummers, Clarke, Roach and, to a lesser extent, Blakey. He is, *rara avis*, a drummer who is interesting enough on his own account to sustain a whole record. His performance on 'My Old Flame' on the Concord is leerily satirical, though this time he is supported by a long-established group, which is undeniably capable; but there are sour touches that sit uncomfortably with the listener. When tackling standards, they seem to go for self-consciously different approaches: 'I've Grown Accustomed To Her Face' is almost torpedoed by Lang's preposterous introduction (on the Concord album). They treat the original material with far more respect, and Armacost's snaky lines often grab the limelight. *Once Upon A Time* is a programme of Hoagy Carmichael material, but this time it's Hollander's own playing that lets the group down, fussily working through what are often very slow tempos that don't suit either band or material very well.

Major Holley (1924–90) BASS, VOCAL

(*) **Mule Black & Blue 59.002
>Holley; Gerald Wiggins (*p*); Ed Thigpen, Oliver Jackson (*d*). 3/74–2/77.

*** **Major Step** Timeless SJP 364

    Holley; Joe Van Enkhuizen (*ts*); Rein De Graaff (*p*); Han Bennink (*d*). 7/90.

Plenty of high-spirited fun on both of these records. The Black & Blue album is really Major Holley's sole effort as a leader – he is basically sitting in with Joe van Enkhuizen's trio on the other date – and, although Gerald Wiggins provides much of the strictly musical interest, Holley's loping bass parts and singalong arco work (in the manner pioneered by Slam Stewart) give the likes of 'Mack The Knife' a fresh spirit. *Major Step*, though, is the preferable record, given van Enkhuizen's brawny solos and Holley's decision to restrain his singing to modest levels.

Red Holloway (born 1927) ALTO AND TENOR SAXOPHONE

*** **Brother Red** Prestige PRCD-24141-2

    Holloway; Alvin Red Tyler (*ts*); Brother Jack McDuff (*org*); George Benson (*g*); Wilfred
    Middlebrooks (*b*); Joe Dukes (*d*). 2/64.

*** **Nica's Dream** Steeplechase SCCD 31192

    Holloway; Horace Parlan (*p*); Jesper Lundgaard (*b*); Aage Tanggaard (*d*). 7/84.

(*) **Red Holloway & Company Concord CCD 4322

    Holloway; Cedar Walton (*p*); Richard Reid (*b*); Jimmie Smith (*d*). 1/87.

***(*) **Locksmith Blues** Concord CCD 4390

    Holloway; Clark Terry (*t, flhn, v*); Gerald Wiggins (*p*); Phil Upchurch (*g*); Richard Reid (*b*);
    Paul Humphrey (*d*). 6/89.

This Chicago alto and tenor veteran is still inadequately served by reissues: a bundle of Prestige albums from the early 1960s are waiting their turn for CD transfer, but at least *Brother Red* has appeared: basically the *Cookin' Together* collaboration with Jack McDuff, and a sturdy if unexceptional example of the sax/organ genre of the time. More recent records have been decidedly mixed. The Steeplechase session is another recent reissue, and here Holloway hits a swinging groove that hardly lets up for 40-odd minutes: since he likes the high parts of the tenor and the middle range of the alto, it often sounds like he's playing a hybrid of the two horns, lean, many-noted and decidedly cheerful – he plays blues as if they were fun, and ballads tend to be amiable rather than deeply felt. Parlan and the Scandinavians do well for him. Although the 1987 session is a pleasing enough collection, Holloway sounds perfunctory in the company of players who are content to perform to order. With nobody pushing him much and with a pro's pro like Walton at the piano, the music is just another set of standards and blues. But the meeting with Clark Terry is very different, suggesting that Holloway is always happier with another horn to joust with. The title-blues is lavishly done, 'Red Top' is a terrific swinger, and the Ellington tunes are delivered with a finesse which normally eludes Holloway's records. Catch him also with Norwegian tenorman Knut Riisnaes.

Ron Holloway TENOR SAXOPHONE

(*) **Slanted Milestone MCD-9219-2

    Holloway; Chris Battistone, Tom Williams (*t*); Reuben Brown, Bob Butta, George Colligan (*p*);
    Paul Bollenback, Larry Camp (*g*); Lennie Cuje (*vib*); Keter Betts, James King, Tommy Cecil,
    Pepe Gonzalez (*b*); Lenny Robinson, Steve Williams, John Zidar (*d*). 8–9/93.

*** **Struttin'** Milestone MCD-9238-2

    Holloway; Mac Gollehon (*t, flhn*); John Bell (*f, sitar*); Kenny Barron, Larry Willis (*p*); Lonnie
    Smith (*p*); Paul Bollenback, John Scofield, Marlon Graves, Ray Tilkens (*g*); David Williams,
    Gary Grainger, Lamar Brantley (*b*); Victor Lewis (*d*); Steve Berrios, Broto Roy (*perc*). 2/95.

Holloway's manifest authority on tenor is let down by a lack of purpose on the first record. He's played in countless situations in and out of jazz, a journeyman who's worked with everybody, from Dizzy Gillespie to Gil Scott-Heron, but that experience adds up to a faceless consistency on this date. Standards like 'Pent-up House' and 'Autumn Leaves' are loaded with calories but short on any kind of individuality.

Struttin' offers some improvement. Todd Barkan's production involves the band as something more than bystanders, and a few tracks – like the bare-bones treatment of 'Where Are You?' or the unusual choice of 'I've Found A New Baby' – stand aside from cliché. But Holloway still gives only modest evidence that he merits a leadership role – and the east–west fusion of 'Cobra' sounds like a cast-iron clinker.

Christopher Hollyday (born 1970) ALTO SAXOPHONE

*** **Christopher Hollyday** Novus PD 83055
    Hollyday; Wallace Roney (*t*); Cedar Walton (*p*); David Williams (*b*); Billy Higgins (*d*). 1/89.
(*) **On Course Novus PD 83087
    Hollyday; Larry Goldings (*p*); John Lockwood (*b*); Ron Savage (*d*). 1/90.
(*) **The Natural Moment Novus PD 83118
    Hollyday; Brad Mehldau (*p*); John Webber (*b*); Ron Savage (*d*). 1/91.

Hollyday emerged as a *wunderkind* some years before the debut record for Novus, which was actually his fourth album. He has a formidable technique, but the striking thing about him is his tone: he has the sour, fractious sound which is a stock-in-trade of his idol, Jackie McLean – so much so, in fact, that some have dismissed him as a McLean imitator. Since Hollyday recorded two McLean themes on *Christopher Hollyday*, it seemed as if he was scarcely trying to avoid the comparison. But that first session is a highly enjoyable slice of contemporary bop. The up-tempo charges through 'Bebop' and 'Ko-Ko' are so handsomely led by Hollyday that his more experienced sidemen have to play hard to keep up, and the McLean tunes, 'Omega' and 'Appointment In Ghana', are a refreshing change from the customary hard-bop fare of Silver, Shorter *et al*.

The subsequent records, unfortunately, emerge as rather less impressive. *On Course* offers eight originals by the leader plus one by Goldings, along with 'Memories Of You': it's all well played, and the group read each other's moves well enough, but the music misses the edge of excitement which distinguished the first record, and Hollyday's writing is all bits and pieces. He contributes five further tunes to *The Natural Moment*, and there are four pieces from other hands, including a reading of 'Every Time We Say Goodbye' which is so tart that it strikes a note of parody. This time the music seems over-intense, as if Hollyday were reacting to the usual charges of neo-conservatism by trying to prove how impolite he can be. He does sound more like McLean than ever, but the fierceness of the title-track, for instance, seems like a hurried miscalculation. Nevertheless, this is characterful work from a player who will surely do greater things.

*** **And I'll Sing Once More** Novus PD90685
    Hollyday; Earl Gardner, Joe Mosello (*t, flhn*); John Mosca, Ed Neumeister (*tb*); Douglas
    Purviance (*btb*); John Clark (*frhn*); Scott Robinson (*cl, bcl, ts, bs, f, af*); Mark Feldman (*vn*);
    Kenny Werner (*p*); Scott Colley (*b*); Ron Savage (*d*); Eric Cherry, Jamey Haddad (*perc*). 1/92.

Although there is an alleged parallel with *Miles Ahead*, this big-scale setting for Hollyday is really nothing like either a Gil Evans or a Miles Davis record. Werner's arrangements are interestingly varied around a diverse set of themes: 'Kate The Roommate' is a near-burlesque, 'Beyond The Barren Lands' is neurotically overwrought, but Werner keeps the ensemble in check and always gives Hollyday space as well as support. The result is curiously baroque, with tracks like the quasi-Eastern 'Chant', the battering 'Storm' and the oddball reworking of Wayne Shorter's 'Nefertiti' confounding expectations. Hollyday is absorbed in his playing, and the sour side of his music is far more manifest than the rhapsodic one.

Richard 'Groove' Holmes (1931–91) ORGAN

*** **Soul Message** Original Jazz Classics OJC 329
    Holmes; Gene Edwards (*g*); Jimmie Smith (*d*). 10/66.
** **Misty** Original Jazz Classics OJC 724
    Holmes; Gene Edwards (*g*); Jimmie Smith, George Randle (*d*). 4–7/66.
***(*) **Blues Groove** Prestige PRCD-24133-2
    Holmes; Blue Mitchell (*t*); Harold Vick, Teddy Edwards (*ts*); Pat Martino, Gene Edwards (*g*);
    Paul Chambers (*b*); George Randle, Freddie Waits, Billy Higgins (*d*). 3/66–5/67.

Holmes was one of the most swinging of organists. A sometime bassist, he liked earthy, elemental bass lines, and he decorated melodies with something like reluctance: he made the organ sound massive and implacable. He recorded most prolifically in the 1960s, but most of those records are now long out of print, although the OJC and Prestige reissues make a start. These discs give a fair idea of his music. *Soul Message* is a fat, funky album which opens on the blues workout 'Groove's Groove', seven minutes that just about sum up Holmes's entire style. *Misty* is a ballad-orientated collection and the kind of thing that organists were obliged to make as songs for sedentary lovers: purely on those terms, it's rather good, but the formula is still boring over the long haul. A better choice is *Blues Groove*, which doubles up two Prestige albums, *Get Up And Get It!* and *Soul Mist!*. The first offers Edwards a guest role which he makes the most of: there's a long, expansive treatment of the tenorman's set-piece, 'Body And Soul'. Mitchell and the unimpressive Vick sit in on two tracks of the second set, but this is Groove's show, and he's at his best on the light touch of 'Up Jumped Spring'.

** **Hot Tat** Muse MCD 5395
    Holmes; Cecil Bridgewater (*t*); Houston Person (*ts*); Jimmy Ponder (*g*); Wilbur Bascomb (*b*);
    Greg Bandy (*d*); Ralph Dorsey (*perc*). 9/89.

Groove passed away in 1991 and this might have been his last album. Sadly, it's not much good. Modish soul licks from Ponder and Person playing his umpteenth hollering blues solo don't give the organ man much company, and some of the tunes are feeble. Better to remember him via one of the reissues from the 1960s – which was, when all's said and done, his real era.

Adam Holzman KEYBOARDS

** **Overdrive** Lipstick LIP 890252
    Holzman; Hiram Bullock, David Phelps, Jimi Tunnell, Drew Zingg (*g*); Steve Logan (*b*); Van
    Romaine (*d*); Large Richard And The Rhythm Marines (*v*). 91–92.

This may be Holzman's idea of what the later Miles bands sounded like, or it's possible that he has made it all up out of his own head. Either way, it's a mess, overloaded with indifferent guitar playing (Bullock at least has energy on his side) and heavy-handed rhythm. Only Holzman himself escapes complete obloquy, playing with surprising exactitude and taste, but too little in evidence to rescue a dud.

Ged Hone TRUMPET, CORNET, GUITAR, PIANO, VOCAL

** **Throwing Stones At The Sun** Lake LACD28
    Hone; Chris Blount (*cl*); Spats Langham (*bj, g, mand, v*); Howard Washington (*b*); Stu Seton (*d, wbd*). 11/92.

Hone's band is called the New Orleans Boys but they're Britishers emulating the style, rather than natives. On the more unusual tunes – 'Montmartre', 'Blue Blood Blues' and 'Japansy' – they continue the trad movement's rehabilitation of the past with a pleasing mix of gumption and sprightliness. Blount, the most interesting player here, doesn't try too hard to sound like the obvious clarinet models and varies his methods from track to track. But a lot of the music sounds like formula trad, the vocals are as terrible as usual, and several tracks continue the bizarre British obsession with mixing trad and skiffle. Crisp sound, though the prominent banjo sometimes lends a tinny quality.

Bertha Hope PIANO

(*) **In Search Of . . . Hope Steeplechase SCCD 31276
    Hope; Walter Booker (*b*); Billy Higgins (*d*). 10/90.
*** **Elmo's Fire** Steeplechase SCCD 31289
    Hope; Eddie Henderson (*t*); Junior Cook, Dave Riekenberg (*ts*); Walter Booker (*b*); Leroy
    Williams (*d*). 1/91.
*** **Between Two Kings** Minor Music 801025
    Hope; Walter Booker (*b*); Jimmy Cobb (*d*). 92.

Elmo Hope's widow makes no attempt to disguise her fealty to his music: there are two of his tunes on the first album, four on the second, one on the third; and Bertha's own style is a gentle extrapolation of Elmo's off-centre lyricism. She is no great executant, happiest at a steady mid-tempo and unwilling to risk any flourishes in a solo, but her improvisations have a patient and rather beguiling beauty about them, a bebop vocabulary fragmented into very small pieces which she seems to turn over and over in her phrases. *In Search Of . . . Hope* is a little too tasteful and laid-back, Higgins as solid as ever, Booker quiescent, and it bows before the superior quintet date (Riekenberg appears on only one tune). Eddie Henderson, who's done little wrong on record of late, walks a measured line between elegance and real fire, with a remarkable improvisation on the blues 'Bai Tai'. Junior Cook is patchy, but Hope herself sounds convincing, and her treatment of Sonny Fortune's wistful 'For Duke And Cannon' is splendid. *Between Two Kings* returns her to the trio format and blends standards with her own writing, which comes out best on the charming 'Hokkaido Spring' and the inverted tribute to sardine salad, 'De La Senidras'. Booker and Cobb are in more lively form, too.

Elmo Hope (1923–67) PIANO

***(*) **Meditations** Original Jazz Classics OJC 1751
    Hope; John Ore (*b*); Willie Jones (*d*). 6/55.

*** **Hope Meets Foster** Original Jazz Classics OJC 1703

   Hope; Freeman Lee (*t*); Frank Foster (*ts*); John Ore (*b*); Art Taylor (*d*). 10/55.

*** **The All Star Sessions** Milestone M 47037

   Hope; Donald Byrd, Blue Mitchell (*t*); John Coltrane, Jimmy Heath, Hank Mobley, Frank Wess (*ts*); Paul Chambers, Percy Heath (*b*); Philly Joe Jones (*d*). 5/56, 6/61.

*** **Elmo Hope Trio** Original Jazz Classics OJC 477

   Hope; Jimmy Bond (*b*); Frank Butler (*d*). 2/59.

***(*) **Plays His Original Compositions** Fresh Sound FSR CD 181

   Hope; Paul Chambers, Butch Warren (*b*); Granville Hogan, Philly Joe Jones (*d*). 61.

***(*) **Homecoming** Original Jazz Classics OJC 1810

   Hope; Blue Mitchell (*t*); Jimmy Heath, Frank Foster (*ts*); Percy Heath (*b*); Philly Joe Jones (*d*). 6/61.

Hope managed to sound sufficiently different from both his main influences, Bud Powell (with whom he went to school) and Thelonious Monk, to retain a highly individual sound. His reputation as a composer is now surprisingly slight, but he had a strong gift for melody, enunciating themes very clearly, and was comfortable enough with classical and modern concert music to introduce elements of fugue and canon, though always with a firm blues underpinning.

   Like a good many pianists of his generation, he seems to have been uneasy about solo performance (though he duetted regularly with his wife Bertha) and is heard to greatest effect in trio settings. The early *Meditations* sounds remarkably Monk-like in places and John Ore's slightly limping lines confirm the resemblance (Ore was a long-standing member of the Thelonious Monk quartet and Jones was one of Monk's favourite drummers, a rating passed on to Charles Mingus). 'Elmo's Fire' and 'Blue Mo' are deft originals. The Blue Note sessions are taut and well disciplined, and the trios are generally better organized than the quintet tracks, where the sequence of solos begins to seem rather mechanical and Hope progressively loses interest in varying his accompaniments of others. Originals like 'Freffie' and 'Hot Sauce' come across well, though.

   Hope responded well to the challenge of Coltrane's developing harmonic language and the Milestone sessions contain some provocative indications of Trane's early willingness to deconstruct standard material, in this case a bold reading of 'Polka Dots And Moonbeams'. The sessions with Foster are rather more conventional, but 'Georgia On My Mind' demonstrates Hope's original and uncompromising approach to standard ballad material, and Foster is only able to embellish a very strong conception. The 1959 trio, which was for Contemporary, is rather disappointing, but Hope had by this stage moved to the West Coast (which he found professionally conducive – i.e. more gigs – but artistically a little sterile) and had become further involved in drugs, for which he was eventually gaoled. His fortunes were on a roller-coaster from then until his untimely death, aged only 43. The Fresh Sound is an excellent way of getting Hope's most interesting compositions on one disc, though the Blue Note should be the item of first choice. *The Final Sessions*, released in 1966 shortly before his death, are not in catalogue at present. However, the very fine *Homecoming* is back again, restoring material from the trio and sextet dates in June 1961 and unveiling another batch of intelligent arrangements. In the final analysis, it's a quite substantial legacy of material. Hope deserves still wider recognition.

Claude Hopkins (1903–84) PIANO

*** **Claude Hopkins 1932–1934** Classics 699

   Hopkins; Ovie Alston (*t, v*); Albert Snaer, Sylvester Lewis (*t*); Fred Norman (*tb, v*); Fernando Arbello, Henry Wells (*tb*); Ed Hall (*cl, as, bs*); Gene Johnson (*as*); Bobby Sands (*ts*); Walter Jones (*bj, g*); Henry Turner (*b*); Pete Jacobs (*d*); Orlando Roberson (*v*). 5/32–12/34.

*** **Claude Hopkins 1934–1935** Classics 716

   As above, except add Snub Mosley (*tb*), Hilton Jefferson (*cl, as*), omit Wells. 1/34–2/35.

(*) **Claude Hopkins 1937–1940 Classics 733

   Hopkins; Shirley Clay, Jabbo Smith, Lincoln Mills, Sylvester Lewis, Robert Cheek, Albert Snaer, Russell Jones, Herman Autrey (*t*); Floyd Brady, Fred Norman, Vic Dickenson, Ray Hogan, Norman Greene, Bernard Archer (*tb*); Gene Johnson, Chauncey Haughton, Ben Smith, Floyd Blakemore, Ben Richardson, Howard Johnson, Norman Thornton (*as*); Bobby Sands, Cliff Glover, Benny Waters (*ts*); Walter Jones, Rudolph Williams (*g*); Abe Bolar, Elmer James (*b*); Pete Jacobs, George Foster, Walter Johnson (*d*); Beverley White, Froshine Stewart, Orlando Roberson (*v*). 2/37–3/40.

Hopkins was a skilful pianist and he liked to get a lot of solos with his band – so much so that the demands of arranging around him may have told against the ambitions of the group. It certainly never worked as well as the Earl Hines orchestra and, though Hopkins had fewer imposing soloists – the brief stays by Smith and Dickenson in 1937 were wasted – the group's ensemble sound lacked character and the arrangements were often second-rate. These chronological CDs tell the story in decent if unexceptional transfers. Some of the music on the early disc promises more than is eventually delivered: 'Mad Moments', 'Shake Your Ashes', 'Hopkins Scream' and especially Jimmy Mundy's arrangement of 'Mush Mouth' are exciting and surprising pieces. But the two later discs, while interesting, never break very far out of swing-era clichés.

Johan Horlen (born 1967) ALTO AND SOPRANO SAXOPHONES

*** Dance Of Resistance Dragon DRCD 260
    Horlen; Torbjorn Gulz (*p*); Christian Spering (*b*); Jukkis Uotila (*d*). 6/94.
Playing alto on all but one of the seven themes, the young Swede is equal parts lyricism and passion here. The title-piece exemplifies this tightrope walk: continually skirling up towards a false note, he keeps pulling himself back in line before matters get out of hand. That reserve makes the still waters of 'To Miss', a lovely duet for soprano and piano, and the contrary position of 'The Best Things In Life Are Free', an argument for alto and drums, the more effective. But some of his ideas go nowhere, and the closing blow-out on 'Everything I Love' is perhaps a step too far. Another horn shouldering some responsibility might have balanced out the session better, though Horlen will be worth watching.

John Horler PIANO, KEYBOARDS

*** Lost Keys MasterMix CHECD 00109
    Horler; Jeff Clyne (*b*); Trevor Tomkins (*d*). 5/93.
The obvious influence is Bill Evans, though probably filtered through Evans student, Gordon Beck. Even playing 'Re: Person I Knew' or 'Blue In Green', Horler sounds indefinably English, and the more abstract pieces – so named – still manage to retain a folkish tonality that is immensely attractive.

Shirley Horn (born 1934) PIANO, VOCAL

*** Loads Of Love / Shirley Horn With Horns Mercury 843454-2
    Horn; Jimmy Cleveland (*tb*); Hank Jones, Bobby Scott (*p*); Kenny Burrell (*g*); Milt Hinton (*b*); Osie Johnson (*d*); rest unknown. 63.
A reissue of the two albums Horn made for Mercury in 1963. They're modest, pleasing records, much like many another light-jazz vocal record of the period and, while Horn's voice is transparently clear and warm, she was used to accompanying herself; placed in the studios with a stellar but unfamiliar band, she occasionally sounds stilted. Nor was she allowed to work at her favourite dead-slow tempos on ballads. Fine remastering.

***(*) Trav'lin' Light Impulse! GRP 11382
    Horn; Joe Newman (*t*); Frank Wess (*as, f*); Jerome Richardson (*f*); Kenny Burrell (*g*); Marshall Hawkins (*b*); Bernard Sweeney (*d*). 65.
The reissue of this hard-to-find album suggests something of the maverick performer that Horn already was. She talks her way through these songs as much as she sings them, and a tune such as 'Someone You've Loved' becomes a wry sort of meditation; even the Lennon–McCartney tune, 'And I Love Him', is made into something oddly cool and detached. The stock arrangements and song choices don't give her much free rein, but this is idiosyncratic stuff for 1965.

***(*) A Lazy Afternoon Steeplechase SCCD 1111
    Horn; Buster Williams (*b*); Billy Hart (*d*). 7/78.
***(*) All Night Long Steeplechase SCCD 1157
    Horn; Charles Ables (*b*); Billy Hart (*d*). 7/81.
*** Violets For Your Furs Steeplechase SCCD 1164 CDLP
    As above. 7/81.
*** The Garden Of The Blues Steeplechase SCCD 1203
    Horn; Charles Ables (*b*); Steve Williams (*d*). 11/84.
Horn's first Steeplechase set broke a long silence; if anything, it was effectively a debut album. The manner here, and throughout these four fine and under-recognized records, is reflective and sparsely evocative. Horn establishes her liking for intensely slow tempos with a compelling treatment of 'There's No You', but feels able to contrast that immediately with the hipsterish reading of 'New York's My Home', and the long trio instrumental on 'Gentle Rain' displays a piano method that works with the simplest materials and makes something distinctive. Williams and Hart – the latter an old friend who

might understand Horn's music better than anyone – play with complete empathy. If anything, the three remaining discs are a slight letdown after *A Lazy Afternoon*, since Horn had already made a nearly definitive statement in this context, although each has its valuable interpretations. *A Lazy Afternoon* is also available in an audiophile LP pressing.

*** **Softly** Audiophile 224
    Horn; Charles Ables (*b*); Steve Williams (*d*). 10/87.
*** **I Thought About You** Verve 833235-2
    As above. 87.
***(*) **Close Enough For Love** Verve 837933-2
    Horn; Buck Hill (*ts*); Charles Ables (*b*); Steve Williams (*d*). 11/88.
***(*) **You Won't Forget Me** Verve 847482-2
    Horn; Miles Davis, Wynton Marsalis (*t*); Buck Hill, Branford Marsalis (*ts*); Toots Thielemans (*hca, g*); Charles Ables (*b, g*); Buster Williams (*b*); Billy Hart, Steve Williams (*d*). 6–8/90.
*** **Here's To Life** Verve 511879-2
    Horn; Wynton Marsalis (*t*); Steve Kujala, James Walker (*f*); Alan Broadbent (*p*); John Chiodini (*g*); Charles Ables, Chuck Domanico (*b*); Steve Williams, Harvey Mason (*d*); strings. 91.
***(*) **Light Out Of Darkness** Verve 519703-2
    Horn; Gary Bartz (*as*); Charles Ables (*g, b*); Tyler Mitchell (*b*); Steve Williams (*d*). 4–5/93.
*** **I Love You, Paris** Verve 523486-2
    As above, except omit Bartz and Mitchell. 3/92.
***(*) **The Main Ingredient** Verve 529555-2
    As above, except add Roy Hargrove (*flhn*), Joe Henderson, Buck Hill (*ts*), Steve Novosel (*b*), Elvin Jones (*d*). 5–9/95.

What amounts to Horn's second comeback has been distinguished by a perfect touch and luxury-class production values. Actually, in terms of her own performances or those of her trio – Ables and Williams have been faithful and diligent disciples – there's no special advance on her Steeplechase albums, or on the single Audiophile set, which is an especially slow and thoughtful disc. The first two Verves continue to work at favourite standards, and Hill's presence adds a useful touch of salt to proceedings that may sound a little too sweetly sensuous for some listeners. But *You Won't Forget Me* is a step forward in its pristine attention to detail, awesome array of guest-star soloists – Davis was a great Horn admirer, and he sounds like himself, if well below his best – and the faithfulness with which Horn's voice is recorded. Marsalis turns up again on two tracks on *Here's To Life*, which is otherwise dedicated to arrangements by Johnny Mandel, and again there's a hint of overdoing the sentiment: some may find the title-track far too wobbly in its emotional appeal. But the particular qualities of Horn's singing – the eschewal of vibrato, the even dynamic weight – are given full rein. *Light Out Of Darkness* is pitched as a tribute to Ray Charles, and after the heavyweight emoting of the previous record Horn sounds almost carefree on the likes of 'Hit The Road Jack' and 'I Got A Man'. Bartz lends a few swinging obbligatos, but the emphasis here is on Horn's understading of the beat, her dry, almost elemental phrasing, and the intuitive touch of her regular group.

    I Love You, Paris comes from a French concert. Shirley makes no concessions to the occasion in terms of turning up her tempos, and 'It's Easy To Remember' is about as slow as it will ever get. But she has the art of making the time move, even at this kind of tempo: 'Wouldn't It be Luvverly' is luvverly indeed. The disc is perhaps overlong at almost 75 minutes, but the best of it is top-flight Horn. Same applies to *The Main Ingredient*, cut mainly at her home, with famous names sitting in to add variety to what's now a long string of similarly inclined dates. Buck Hill outdoes Joe Henderson, and Hargrove is untypically laid back on his flugelhorn feature. Yet the highlight is surely her gorgeous version of 'The Look Of Love', done alone with her regular team of Ables and Williams, which suggests that Shirley can probably play this way for ever and still make it sound good.

Lindsey Horner BASS

***(*) **Never No More** Open Minds 2401
    Horner; Herb Robertson (*t, flhn, c*); Marty Ehrlich (*ss, as, af*); Tim Berne (*as*); Gust William Tsilis (*vib*); Reggie Nicholson (*d*). 10/89.

This leadership debut by a bassman often encountered as a sideman in this kind of ensemble has a breezy, melodic feel that Horner has few qualms about sustaining over the whole record; only on the closing 'Mabinogion' is there any real rumpus. 'I'll Never Let It Rain Again' is a beautiful theme and the title-piece is powered by the unexpected drone of Jerry O'Sullivan's pipes. Tsilis, surprisingly, is the dominant soloist, turning in an intense ballad performance on 'No Diff'rence At All', although

Robertson has a few challenging moments too. Slightly introverted when it should be outgoing, but a very worthwhile effort.

Wayne Horvitz PIANO, KEYBOARDS

*** **Some Order, Long Understood** Black Saint 121159
    Horvitz; Butch Morris (*c*); William Parker (*b*). 2/82.
*** **The New Generation** Elektra Nonesuch 60759
    Horvitz; Robin Holcomb, Doug Wieselman (*ky*); Bill Frisell (*g*); Elliott Sharp (*g, b*); Jon Rose
    (*clo*); David Hofstra (*b, tba*); Bobby Previte (*d, ky*); Jim Mussen, Joey Peters (*elec d*); Chris
    Brown (*gazamba, wing*); Nica (*v*). 9/85.
*** **Nine Below Zero** sound aspects sas 014
    Horvitz; Lawrence Butch Morris (*c, mar, syn*); Bobby Previte (*d, mar, syn*). 1/86.
(*) **Todos Santos sound aspects sas 019
    As above. 1/88.
***(*) **Miracle Mile** Elektra Nonesuch 7559 79278 2
    Horvitz; J. A. Deane (*tb, elec*); Denny Goodhew (*sax*); Doug Wieselman (*ts, cl*); Stew Cutler,
    Bill Frisell, Elliott Sharp (*g*); Ben Steele (*g syn*); Kermit Driscoll (*b*); Bobby Previte (*d*). 91.

Horvitz got off to a brisk start with a clattery sound that wasn't too proud to make use of user-friendly electronics and pop-punk dynamics. *Some Order, Long Understood* consists of just two long tracks, spun out of seemingly nothing by a surprisingly lyrical trio. Morris is revelatory in his use of classic-jazz shapes and modernist accents and Parker's *arco* work is superb. It's possible to hear in this session embryonic intimation of everything that was to follow. *Nine Below Zero* is named after a Brett Easton Ellis novel, and it seems compounded of much the same volatile mix of sharply self-conscious style and furious, half-suppressed violence. Whether or not 'Three Places In Suburban California' is intended to echo Charles Ives's American classic *Three Places In New England*, the syncretism of high and low styles is very much the same in spirit. A marvellous, effective album.

Nothing is more fearsome than intelligence suffused with anger (or vice versa). These are the qualities Morris brings, a dramatic counterpoise to Previte's tranced drums-and-effects and Horvitz's tense, Gestalt-therapy keyboard patterns. The longer and more developed improvisational structures on *Some Order, Long Understood* cue some of the most interesting episodic material, but the album doesn't entirely cohere, and there's little of the compression that excites the shorter pieces on *Nine Below*. It's slightly difficult to set *Todos Santos* against the same measure, since the disc is shared with a group of fine duo performances from Doug Wieselman and Bill Frisell, which fans of the guitarist will want to have in any case; all the material, though, is written (or comprovised, to work changes on Butch Morris's macaronic 'conduction') by Horvitz's wife, Robin Holcomb, who has had a rough ride from jazz critics. She has a brief part on *The New Generation*, the disc that established Horvitz as a recording artist. It consists of 13 brief excusions with various permutations from the line-up shown. The best tend to be those with Frisell and Previte, and the duos with Wieselman are merely dull.

Miracle Mile offers moody and slightly threatening music from Horvitz's band, The President. Horvitz is an impressive melodist, but tunes are constantly set in front of rather sinister guitar and synth backgrounds as if to suggest that the 'kinder, gentler America' of George Bush, apostrophized in an interesting 'Open Letter', merely caps the kind of violence implied by the dramatic smoke-pall on the cover. The horns don't do much of interest, but Previte is absolutely superb, giving one of his best performances on record.

*** **Pigpen: V As In Victim** Avant AVAN 027
    Horvitz; Briggan Kraus (*as*); Fred Chalenor (*b*); Mike Stone (*d*). 5/93.

Pigpen is an extra-curricular project of Horvitz's, a band which tries to make associations between jazz, advanced rock and country music, often in near-unrecognizable forms. The 'Portrait Of Hank Williams Jr' and the long title-piece are the heart of a session which bears the A&R stamp of label guru John Zorn, who also has a hand in production. Not much to say about the other players, beyond the obvious point that they execute Horvitz's wishes competently and with an authentic lack of feeling.

Hot Stuff! GROUP

(*) **Hot Stuff! Lake LACD40
    Chez Chesterman (*c, v*); Mike Pointon (*tb*); Dick Charlesworth (*cl, ss, ts, v*); Barney Bates (*p*);
    Jim Forey (*g*); John Rodber (*b*); Graham Scriven (*d*). 2/94.

This is good fun, though one needs a tolerance for some of the nuttier aspects of British trad.

Charlesworth (senior readers may recall his group, The City Gents) seems to be the leader, but all seven men have records as long as your arm at this kind of thing and such misdemeanours are second nature to the lot of them. A lot of interesting obscurities among the 17 tracks, and there's actually some fine playing: Chesterman's gracious if slightly ashthmatic-sounding cornet on 'Will You Or Won't You Be My Babe', Pointon's brawling trombone on 'Sunset Café Stomp' and so on. But docked a notch for the sound, which has so little bottom-end it makes Bates sound like he's playing tack piano. And docked another for the vocals, which are a large side-order of ham.

François Houle CLARINET, SOPRANO SAXOPHONE

***(*) **Schizosphere** Red Toucan RT 9203
     Houle; Tony Wilson (*g, khaen, aktira*); Dylan Van der Schyff (*perc*). 8/94.
*** **Any Terrain Tumultuous** Red Toucan RT 9305
     Houle; Marilyn Crispell (*p*). 9/95.
Houle is a classically trained Canadian who has been turned on to improvised music by the likes of Evan Parker and Steve Lacy. In sound, he is immediately reminiscent of another latter-day clarinet master, Michael Moore, but Houle is perhaps less interested in structures and navigable harmonies. The trio on *Schizosphere* is beautifully balanced; Houle's richly grained sound blending perfectly with Wilson's sudden electrical storms and van der Schyff's Bennink-inspired drumming. There is a lot of gestural playing, passages of simul-instrumentalism *à la* Roland Kirk, and abstract effects from Wilson as he rubs the strings with his forearms while playing a Khmer mouth-organ.

    The record with Crispell is inevitably very different, and the pianist does tend to dominate. However, she does show her partner considerable respect, and as time goes by it is Houle's voice which commands attention. His sheer quality of sound, clean, unfailingly accurate at the register break (though as often as not played *chalumeau* in the Giuffre style), is highly attractive, but it is the quiet urgency of the ideas which increasingly comes across. One to watch, as is Red Toucan's Open Fields imprint.

Karsten Houmark GUITAR

(*) **Four Storyville STCD 4197
     Houmark; Thomas Clausen (*ky*); Lennart Ginman (*b*); Jonas Johansen (*d*). 9/94.
Excellent playing by a talented quartet: Houmark is a nimble improviser and unselfish enough to let his accomplished team have plenty of space, with the reliable Clausen in his usual thoughtful form. But the music fails to make any impact in the end. None of Houmark's nine originals impresses, his various guitar sounds are blandly derivative, and the faceless production closes off the inspiration.

Avery 'Kid' Howard (1908–66) TRUMPET, VOCAL

(***) **Prelude To The Revival Vol. 1** American Music AMCD-40
     Howard; Andrew Anderson, Punch Miller (*t, v*); Duke Derbigny (*t*); Joe 'Cornbread' Thomas (*cl, v*); Martin Cole (*ts*); ? Harris (*p, v*); Joe Robertson (*p*); Leonard Mitchell (*g, bj, v*); Frank Murray (*g*); Chester Zardis (*b*); Charles Sylvester, Junious Wilson, Clifford 'Snag' Jones (*d*); Matie Murray (*v*). 37–41.
So little jazz was recorded in New Orleans during the 1930s that any archive material from the period is valuable. Sam Charters, perhaps not the most reliable judge, reckoned that Kid Howard would have been the next King of New Orleans trumpet after Joe Oliver. He is only on the first four tracks here, in barely passable sound, but they show a mature, hard-hitting musician displaying the inevitable debt to Armstrong but resolutely going his own way. Anderson and Derbigny are less individual but they bridge the older and younger New Orleans traditions unselfconsciously enough. The sleeve-notes detail the detective work that went into finding and restoring the original acetates, and ears unused to prehistoric sound must beware. The five tracks by Miller are discussed under his name.

(*) **Kid Howard's La Vida Band American Music AMCD-54
     Howard; Eddie Sommers (*tb*); Israel Gorman (*cl*); Homer Eugene (*bj*); Louis James (*b*); Josiah Frazier (*d*). 8–9/61.
Recorded on the cusp of the oncoming revival of the 1960s, this date went some way to re-establishing Howard's standing. It's a pity, though, that there's some rustiness, not only in his playing, but with most of the band, too: fluffs and sloppiness are a distraction, even in the name of authenticity. But there are great moments, such as the tribute to Chris Kelly, Howard's early idol, in 'The Three Sixes', or the opening ensemble of 'Nelly Gray', and New Orleans scholars will welcome an important record on CD.

The sound has attracted some haziness in the digital remastering. Howard can also be heard on several records with George Lewis.

Noah Howard (born 1943) ALTO SAXOPHONE

***(*) **Noah Howard Quartet** ESP Disk 1031
    Howard; Ric Colbeck (*t*); Scotty Holt (*b*); Dave Grant (*d*). 1/66.
**** **At Judson Hall** ESP Disk 1064
    Howard; Ric Colbeck (*t*); Dave Burrell (*p*); Catherine Norris (*clo*); Norris Jones (*b*); Robert Kapp (*d*). 10/66.

Howard's playing in the 1970s bears the tribal scars of his association with Archie Shepp, a music that blends political and aesthetic radicalism with a straightforward desire to entertain – a split personality reflected in two good LPs from 1975 and 1977, *Berlin Concert* and *Schizophrenic Blues*, which have (temporarily at least) fallen foul of FMP's belated decision to delete their vinyl catalogue and switch to CD only. At press time, some copies of both were still in circulation.

Typically, a Howard concert was an almost too self-conscious alternation of styles, tempos and treatments, and there is something slightly formulaic about his approach. However, despite reservations about his improvisation, on form he could be a devastating performer, with the sour, slightly off-pitch tone one associates with Marion Brown. The Howard discography has been transformed by the reappearance of the ESP Disk catalogue. The Coleman-and-Cherry-influenced studio debut is a little ragged and tentative compared to the Judson Hall concert, recorded later the same year. Colbeck in particular has advanced by leaps and bounds over the summer, playing longer and more developed lines in place of his trademark staccato bugling. (Sadly, Colbeck was later to take his own life, having made a fine record of his own for Fontana in 1970, with the equally tragic Mike Osborne.) The other significant addition to the Judson Hall line-up is pianist Dave Burrell, who plays unpredictable thematic statements and vigorous off-centre vamps behind the front line. Catherine Jones plays a bit-part (and was perhaps significantly not included in the photo-call for the original sleeve).

Freddie Hubbard (born 1938) TRUMPET, FLUGELHORN

***(*) **Breaking Point** Blue Note B21Y-84172-2
    Hubbard; James Spaulding (*as*); Ronnie Mathews (*p*); Eddie Khan (*b*); Joe Chambers (*d*). 5/64.
**** **Hub-Tones** Blue Note B21Y-84115-2
    Hubbard; James Spaulding (*as, f*); Herbie Hancock (*p*); Reggie Workman (*b*); Clifford Jarvis (*d*). 10/62.

Freddie Hubbard's career on record has been a frustrating one, since his great technique and beautiful tone have so often been deployed in chanceless settings and on dismal material. As a young giant of hard bop, he was among the most admired and sought-after of musicians, The deletions axe has decimated his early work as a leader for Blue Note and there are some superb records either already gone or never put on to CD. If he wasn't quite as incendiary as his contemporary, Lee Morgan, there is a compensating logic and shapeliness to his phrases which makes his solos consistently satisfying. *Breaking Point* reflects some of Hubbard's adventures with the likes of Ornette Coleman and Eric Dolphy: the writing includes many shifting metres, unexpected harmonies and the like. If it is always going to sound like uncomfortable territory for the trumpeter, this record is one of his most convincing efforts at looking outside his normal hard-bop parameters. The long 'Far Away' is a complex yet smoothly delivered theme, and 'D Minor Mint' is an admirable bop swinger. James Spaulding, the unsung hero of many a Blue Note session, matches the leader's drive. Essentially, any record from this period by Hubbard is going to be worth hearing. The splendid *Hub-Tones* is a classic meeting with Spaulding, including an affecting tribute to Booker Little and a couple of strong originals in 'Hub-Tones' and 'Prophet Jennings'. Blue Note's usual excellent sound transfers well to the CD reissues. *The Best Of Freddie Hubbard* (Blue Note CDP 793202 CD) is a well-chosen compilation, mostly from his early Blue Note years.

*** **Minor Mishap** Black Lion BL 60122
    Hubbard; Willie Wilson (*tb*); Pepper Adams (*bs*); Duke Pearson (*p*); Thomas Howard (*b*); Lex Humphries (*d*). 8/61.

This doesn't burn as brightly as the contemporary Blue Notes, perhaps because the band is less enthusiastic than Hubbard, who plays well, if a little within himself. Extra takes of all but one of the seven titles pad it out to CD length, but to no special advantage.

*** **The Night Of The Cookers** Blue Note CDP 828882-2 2CD
> Hubbard; Lee Morgan (*t*); James Spaulding (*as, f*); Harold Mabern (*p*); Larry Ridley (*b*); Pete
> LaRoca (*d*); Big Black (*perc*). 4/65.

Essentially an exhaustive blow-out on four tunes by a Hubbard group in almost hysterical form on
'Jodo' and 'Breaking Point'. Morgan's muted parts on 'Pensativa' cool things off, and 'Walkin'' comes
in an easy-going if messy incarnation. Nobody's finest hour, but enjoyably chaotic if one is in the mood.

(*) **Backlash Atlantic 7567-90466-2
> Hubbard; James Spaulding (*as, f*); Albert Dailey (*p*); Bob Cunningham (*b*); Ray Appleton (*d*);
> Ray Barretto (*perc*). 10/66.

A good enough session, but the emphasis on backbeats, riff tunes and squared-off solos is a broad hint
at the lighter direction Hubbard was already looking towards, as jazz faced its slump in popularity.
Perhaps he can't be blamed. A likeable 'Up Jumped Spring', the most enduring of the trumpeter's
compositions, adds a little extra weight.

***(*) **The Artistry Of Freddie Hubbard** Impulse! 33111
> Hubbard; Curtis Fuller (*tb*); John Gilmore (*ts*); Tommy Flanagan (*p*); Art Davis (*b*); Louis
> Hayes (*d*). 7/62.

Hubbard made two appearances as a leader for Impulse!. The 1962 sextet session is unusual for
Gilmore's presence, one of the few small-group albums he made away from Sun Ra in the early 1960s.
The music offers a slightly more expansive setting than Hubbard was used to at Blue Note and, though
Fuller and Gilmore are perhaps at less than their best, the music has a forceful presence, with Flanagan
offering a dapper counterpoint to the horns.

***(*) **Red Clay** CTI EPC ZK 40809
> Hubbard; Joe Henderson (*ts, f*); Herbie Hancock (*p, org*); Ron Carter (*b*); Lenny White (*d*). 1/
> 70.

** **First Light** CTI EPC 450562
> Hubbard; George Marge (*cl, f*); Romeo Penque (*ob, c, f*); Walter Kane (*bsn, f*); Hubert Laws (*f*);
> Jane Taylor (*bsn*); Ray Alonge, Jimmy Buffington (*frhn*); Richard Wyands (*p*); Phil Kraus (*vib*);
> George Benson (*g*); Ron Carter (*b*); Jack DeJohnette (*d*); Airto Moreira (*perc*); strings arr. Don
> Sebesky. 9/71.

** **Sky Dive** CTI EPC 460838
> Hubbard; Alan Rubin, Marvin Stamm (*t, flhn*); Wayne Andre, Garnett Brown (*tb*); Paul Faulise
> (*btb*); Hubert Laws (*f*); Phil Bodner (*f, bcl, picc*); George Marge (*cl, bcl, f*); Wally Kane (*bcl,
> picc*); Romeo Penque (*cl, ob, c, f*); Keith Jarrett (*p*); George Benson (*g*); Ron Carter (*b*); Billy
> Cobham (*d*); Ray Barretto, Airto Moreira (*perc*). 10/72.

*** **In Concert Vol. 1 & 2** CTI ZGR 40688
> Hubbard; Stanley Turrentine (*ts*); Herbie Hancock (*p*); Eric Gale (*g*); Ron Carter (*b*); Jack
> DeJohnette (*d*). 3/73.

(*) **Keep Your Soul Together CTI EPC 460417
> Hubbard; Junior Cook (*ts*); George Cables (*p*); Aurell Ray (*g*); Kent Brinkley, Ron Carter (*b*);
> Ralph Penland (*d*); Juno Lewis (*perc*). 10/73.

These were successful albums for Hubbard, at a time when jazz trumpeters faced unpalatable artistic
and commercial choices, and they have worn perhaps slightly better than one might have imagined. *Red
Clay* is a fine instance of an updated blowing session, with everybody playing hard within a shiny-
sounding context that suggested a possible fresh direction for the traditional hard-bop mien. But CTI
production values instead stuck Hubbard in front of large orchestras and in the middle of ponderous
arrangements, where the only thing worth listening to is the beauty of Hubbard's tone. It's a tribute to
his innate powers that that is sometimes enough. *Keep Your Soul Together*, despite a less than perfect
rhythm section, takes on Cook as a useful partner, and the *In Concert* sessions, while no masterpieces, at
least reassert Hubbard in a relatively challenging situation, even if the similarly restrained Turrentine
isn't a very exciting partner. All the albums have been suitably remastered for CD, and there is some
unremarkable extra music on both *Red Clay* and *First Light*.

** **Born To Be Blue** Original Jazz Classics OJC 734
> Hubbard; Harold Land (*ts*); Billy Childs (*ky*); Larry Klein (*b*); Steve Houghton (*d*); Buck Clark
> (*perc*). 12/81.

*** **Outpost** Enja 3095-2
> Hubbard; Kenny Barron (*p*); Buster Williams (*b*); Al Foster (*d*). 2–3/81.

(*) **Face To Face Pablo 2310-876
> Hubbard; Oscar Peterson (*p*); Joe Pass (*g*); Niels-Henning Orsted-Pedersen (*b*); Martin Drew
> (*d*). 5/82.

All of Hubbard's 1970s albums for Columbia are currently out of print. These records for Pablo are a disappointing lot. The two earlier sessions were both recorded live on European tours and, while the leader plays with much of his old energy, neither group musters much distinction: Schnitter is a faceless foil and Land sounds largely uninterested, while Childs adds nothing special of his own. While there is the usual quota of virtuoso fireworks on the meeting with Peterson, the session is, like so many involving Peterson's group, built on technical bravura rather than specific communication. The quartet session for Enja, though, is much more worthwhile. Hubbard sometimes sounds bland and, talented though the rhythm section is, they don't ask him to be demonstrative; but there are some glowingly executed solos and a particularly rapt flugelhorn treatment of 'You Don't Know What Love Is'. Excellent recording.

*** **Keystone Bop: Sunday Night** Prestige 24146-2
    Hubbard; Joe Henderson (*ts*); Bobby Hutcherson (*vib*); Billy Childs (*p*); Larry Klein (*b*); Steve Houghton (*d*). 11/81.

A smoking live date, compiled from the LPs, *A Little Night Music* and *Keystone Bop*. Hubbard sets a cracking pace with his own blues, 'Birdlike', which leads to inspired solos from Henderson and Hutcherson too. Thereafter the pressure drops a little and the rest is merely very good, but it's a pleasure to hear three great improvisers, all on resolute form.

*** **Feel The Wind** Timeless SJP 307
    Hubbard; Javon Jackson (*ts*); Benny Green, Mulgrew Miller (*p*); Lonnie Plaxico, Leon Dorsey (*b*); Art Blakey (*d*). 11/88.

*** **Topsy** Enja 7025-2
    Hubbard; Kenny Garrett (*as*); Benny Green (*p*); Rufus Reid (*b*); Carl Allen (*d*). 12/89.

***(*) **Bolivia** Musicmasters 65063-2
    Hubbard; Ralph Moore (*ss, ts*); Vincent Herring (*ss, as*); Cedar Walton (*p*); David Williams (*b*); Billy Higgins (*d*); Giovanni Hidalgo (*perc*). 12/90–1/91.

*** **Live At Warsaw Jazz Festival 1991** Jazzmen/Bellaphon 660.50.001
    Hubbard; Donald Braden (*ts*); Ronnie Mathews (*p*); Michal Urbaniak (*vn*); Jeff Chambers (*b*); Ralph Penland (*d*). 10/91.

*** **Live At Fat Tuesday's** Musicmasters 65075-2 2CD
    Hubbard; Javon Jackson (*ts*); Benny Green (*p*); Christian McBride (*b*); Tony Reedus (*d*). 12/91.

Recent Hubbard sessions have been hit-and-miss, but there's always something interesting going on, even when the leader isn't at his peak. *Feel The Wind* breezes along without much happening, though Green and Jackson are always good value, and they're in sterling form on the live session from Fat Tuesday's, where Freddie manages some solid improvisations. The sound is a bit unfavourable, particularly to Jackson. *Topsy* is a batch of standards, beautifully recorded: Kenny Garrett comes in for three tracks, there is a 'Cherokee' which must be one of the fastest on record, and Hubbard keeps the mute in for the whole session, often a sign that he's a bit unsure about his tone that day. The Warsaw set starts with a good, noisy treatment of 'Bolivia', and Braden shows that Freddie usually knows how to pick his saxophonists; harmless stuff, perhaps, but when Urbaniak strolls on stage for an impromptu blues, it's nice to hear. All rather so-so for Freddie himself, but every so often Hubbard does a session like *Bolivia*, and all his old virtues fall back into place. The major props here are Cedar Walton and Billy Higgins, two men who've little time for frippery; they play with such class that it obliges Hubbard to work hard and return the favour. Moore is a little in shadow (and Herring makes only one appearance), but the weight rests on Hubbard, and he seems to be feeling good about it.

(*) **M.M.T.C. (Monk, Miles, Trane, Cannon) Musicmasters 65132-2
    Hubbard; Robin Eubanks (*tb*); Vincent Herring (*as*); Javon Jackson (*ts*); Gary Smulyan (*bs*); Stephen Scott (*p*); Peter Washington (*b*); Carl Allen (*d*). 8–12/94.

If Hubbard had been able to hold his own with this all-star assemblage, this could have been a classic encounter. As it is, it sounds like a contrived tribute concept covering the poor form of a man who by the sound of it can't play too well any longer. The five-horn front line gets in some good blows and the rhythm section is A-1. It seems a pointless exercise, nevertheless.

Peanuts Hucko (born 1918) CLARINET, TENOR SAXOPHONE, VOCALS

*** **Tribute To Louis Armstrong / Benny Goodman** Timeless TTD 512/3
    Hucko; Billy Butterfield (*t*); Trummy Young (*tb*); Marty Napoleon (*p*); Lars Erstrand (*vib*); Jack Lesberg (*b*); Gus Johnson (*d*); Louise Tobin (*v*). 10/83.

Hucko's association with both Armstrong and Goodman (for whom he tactically shifted to tenor saxophone) affords him the best possible background for this kind of material. In tone, he combines something of Goodman's sinuous grace with the blacker, biting sound of Edmond Hall. On the Armstrong numbers, notably 'Basin Street Blues' on TTD 512, he favours a grittier, grainier vibrato, but there's a slight tendency these days to squeal in the upper register. The smoother chalumeau appropriate for much of the Goodman material suits the seventy-plus Hucko a little better. These sides are a respectable introduction to the conspicuously under-recorded Hucko; there is, for instance, a fine (if slightly faded) version of Hucko's signature, 'Stealin' Apples', a classic of traditional jazz.

Spike Hughes (1908–87) BASS, PIANO, CELESTE, REED ORGAN

***(*) **Spike Hughes Vols 1 & 2** Kings Cross Music KCM 001/002 2CD
Hughes; Sylvester Ahola, Jack Jackson, Max Goldberg, Norman Payne, Bill Gaskin, Leslie Thompson, Arthur Niblo (*t*); Muggsy Spanier (*c*); Jock Fleming, Lew Davis, Bernard Tipping (*tb*); Danny Polo, Rex Owen (*cl*); Max Farley (*cl, as, f*); Jimmy Dorsey, Philip Buchel, Harry Hines (*cl, as*); Bobby Davis (*cl, bs*); Buddy Featherstonehaugh (*cl, ts*); Eddie Carroll, Claude Ivy, Gerry Moore(*p*); Stan Andrews, George Hurley (*vn*); Leslie Smith, Alan Ferguson (*g*); Val Rosing (*d, v*); Bill Harty (*d*). 3–12/30.

**** **Spike Hughes Vols 3 & 4** Kings Cross Music KCM 003/004 2CD
As above, except add Jimmy Macaffer, Chick Smith, Billy Higgs, Billy Smith, Bruts Gonella (*t*); Freddy Welsh, Don Macaffer, Bill Mulraney (*tb*); Billy Amstell (*cl, as*); Harry Hayes, Dave Shand (*as*); Billy Munn, Billy Mason (*p*); Ronnie Gubertini (*d*); Elsie Carlisle, Joey Shields (*v*); omit Ahola, Jackson, Goldberg, Spanier, Polo, Owen, Dorsey, Davis, Moore, Andrews, Hurley, Smith. 11/30–11/32.

**** **High Yellow** Largo 5129
As above, except add Henry 'Red' Allen, Leonard Davis, Shad Collins, Bill Dillard, Howard Scott (*t*), Dicky Wells, Wilbur De Paris, George Washington (*tb*), Benny Carter (*as, ss, cl*), Howard Johnson (*as, cl*), Wayman Carver (*as, cl, f*), Coleman Hawkins (*ts*), Chu Berry (*ts*), Luis Russell, Nicholas Rodriguez (*p*), Lawrence Lucie (*g*), Ernest Hill (*b*), Big Sid Catlett, Kaiser Marshall (*d*). 11/31–5/33.

Spike Hughes had a brief affair with jazz: 'I left jazz behind me at the moment when I was enjoying it most, the moment when all true love-affairs should end.' It was just after the sessions with the all-star American line-up which features on *High Yellow*. But he had already made an extraordinary mark on the music in Britain. His early 78s, handsomely collected on the four discs on the Kings Cross label, are intensely sought after and contain some of the best British music of the period. Even on the earliest sessions Hughes was looking for hot material to put in a dance context – 'Zonky', 'The Man From The South'. Soon enough he was on to 'The Mooche', 'Harlem Madness' and 'Blue Turning Grey Over You'. Jimmy Dorsey appears as guest soloist on one 1930 session and, as adept as he is, the best British horn-players aren't outclassed: there are fine moments for Payne, Davis, Farley and others. If British players had been under the sway of the Red Nichols school, Hughes's interest in Ellington especially was bringing in a new slant on playing hot, and when he *did* tackle a New York piece such as Joe Venuti's 'Doing Things', the results were rather different from those of some years before. The second set includes nuggets like 'A Harlem Symphony', 'Six Bells Stampede' and 'Blues In My Heart', and both collections, expertly remastered and neatly packaged, are outstanding bargains for anyone interested in the second age of British jazz. But the Largo disc, which sets ten tracks by the British groups next to the set of American recordings which Hughes made on a visit to New York, is indispensable. Though the band was really the Benny Carter orchestra, Hughes did the writing and arranging, and in pieces such as 'Donegal Cradle Song', a luminous feature for Hawkins, and 'Sweet Sorrow Blues', with superb Henry Allen, Hughes closed his jazz career on an amazing high note. Remastering on all three sets is by John R. T. Davies.

Daniel Humair (born 1938) DRUMS

**** **Daniel Humair Surrounded** Blue Flame 40322
Humair; Eric Dolphy (*as, bcl*); Phil Woods (*as*); Johnny Griffin (*ts*); Gerry Mulligan (*bs*); Jane Ira Bloom (*ss*); Kenny Drew, Michel Graillier, Joachim Kühn, Tete Montoliu, Martial Solal, Maurice Vander (*p*); Eddie Louiss (*org*); Dave Friedman (*vib*); René Thomas (*g*); Jean-François Jenny-Clark, Ron Mathewson, Gus Nemeth, Guy Pedersen, Mike Richmond, Gilbert Rovere, Henri Texier (*b*). 5/64, 4/70, 8 & 10/71, 2/77, 11/81, 10/82, 8/83, 6/85, 7/87.

It's often a little difficult when Gato Barbieri is playing in his characteristic hyperthyroid manner, to hear much else that is going on in the band. But sometime try to follow the drumming behind Barbieri on the classic *Last Tango In Paris*, for it illustrates in convenient miniature the qualities that have made Humair one of the finest European drummers. He has all the rhythmic subtlety and inventiveness one associates with Philly Joe Jones, but also some of the inherent tunefulness of Roy Haynes.

Surrounded is a superb introduction, documenting almost a quarter-century of sterling performance. The roster of names is testimony to Humair's pedigree as a drummer. The 1983 session with Johnny Griffin is not quite as hectic as earlier encounters, but 'Wee' is still taken at a respectable gallop. On Dolphy's blues, 'Serene', a session under Kenny Drew's leadership, he sounds appropriately thoughtful and never hurries the delivery. And so on, down the years, taking in the funky organ trio of Eddie Louiss (see below), the cool swing of Gerry Mulligan, and the abstract folkiness of Martial Solal. Appropriately, the most recent piece is a solo percussion work, 'L'Espace Sonore', a strongly constructed piece with scarcely a wasted gesture.

***(*) **Humair–Louiss–Ponty: Volume 1** Dreyfus 191018-2
Humair; Eddie Louiss (*org*); Jean-Luc Ponty (*vl*). 67.
*** **Humair–Louiss–Ponty: Volume 2** Dreyfus 191028-2
As above. 67.
Fascinating as much as anything for a glimpse of the 25-year-old Ponty, who takes the lead on a good few of these picturesque but undeniably swinging sessions. Louiss has an emphatic touch, with a lot of dissonance thrown in for sheer colour. Humair keeps things pretty neat, except on 'Bag's Groove' (*Volume 2*), which is a bit of a mess. The outstanding performances are all on the first set, with 'You've Changed', a shameless 'Summertime' and 'Round About Midnight', and a chipper 'So What' that manages to hang on to a thread of pure romance.

***(*) **Akagera** JMS 012-2
Humair; François Jeanneau (*ts, ss, f, bcl, syn*); Henri Texier (*b, oud, perc*); Gordon Beck (*p*). 10 & 11/80.
An African-inspired session (the title is an alternative or mythical name for the Nile), this eases Humair out of straight jazz playing and allows him to focus on more exotic rhythms. Jeanneau frequently sounds as if he's playing some exotic shawm or wood flute, and Texier's use of oud is both idiomatic and highly personal. Gordon Beck pops up for a brief outing on 'Nebbia'. A good idea to reserve him for that. The rest of the session is spacious, even sparse, and works all the better for light and air. One or two other Humair sessions for JMS, including a couple of early all-solo dates, have drifted in and out of circulation lately; admirers may like to keep their eyes peeled for them.

*** **Pépites** CELP C3
Humair; André Jaume (*reeds*). 4/87.
Like all duo records, this could just as easily have been listed under the other partner, except that here Humair does seem to be the driving force, increasing the energy levels on what might otherwise have been a rather stiffly filigreed session and adding his own wry awareness to pseudo-classical skits like 'Les oiseaux sont marteaux', which has nothing whatever to do with either Messiaen or Boulez. Jaume turns in a splendid solo version of Coltrane's 'Naima'. All the other tunes are originals, with both men putting up pieces.

**** **9–11 p.m. Town Hall** Label Bleu LBLC 6517
Humair; Michel Portal (*sax, bcl, bandoneon*); Joachim Kühn, Martial Solal (*p*); Jean-François Jenny-Clark (*b*). 6/88.
Humair's own records have the same thoroughgoing musicality that he brings to work with artists as different as Anthony Braxton, Stéphane Grappelli and Lee Konitz. *Town Hall* is a superb introduction to all the participants, and if the veteran Solal's part isn't as large as one might wish for, it's none the less significant as an exercise in the genealogy of the 'new' French jazz, whose roots actually strike a lot deeper than first appears. That is nowhere more evident than here and on . . .

*** **Up Date 3.3** Label Bleu LBLC 6530
Humair; François Jeanneau (*as, ss, ts, f*); Henri Texier (*b*). 2/90.
. . . where Humair teams up with Texier (a bassist with a more folkish and structured approach than the more freely orientated Jenny-Clark) in an album of looser compositions and improvisations. Jeanneau more than makes up for any slight technical shortcomings by an intelligent disposition of his four horns, but the real foundation of the music is the interaction in the bass and drums. Both come highly recommended.

***(*) **Edges** Label Bleu LBLC 6545
Humair; Jerry Bergonzi (*saxes*); Aydin Esen (*p*); Miroslav Vitous (*b*). 5/91.
Much of the interest here settles again on the interplay between Humair and another great European bassist. Vitous's own 'Monitor' is a strange stop–start theme that downplays Esen's rippling accompaniments and Bergonzi's full-ahead Coltranism in order to explore the complex times and sonorities that are meat and drink to both 'rhythm' players. Something of the same goes on throughout the very long 'Genevamalgame' (co-written by Joachim Kühn and the drummer, his only compositional credit on the album).

The title suggests a much more exploratory, risk-taking endeavour. Humair's out-of-tempo sequences and dramatic *rallentando* passages must be extremely challenging to his players. There may be a hint of compromise to the market in Bergonzi's and Esen's dramatic soloing, but they are both capable of abstraction, too, and the net effect of their more obvious strategies is to concentrate attention on the drummer and bassist. The mix is nicely horizontal, though Vitous could have done with a slight lift, particularly on the early tracks.

Helen Humes (1913–81) VOCAL

**** 'Tain't Nobody's Biz-ness If I Do Original Jazz Classics OJC 453
>   Humes; Benny Carter (*t*); Frank Rosolino (*tb*); Teddy Edwards (*ts*); André Previn (*p*); Leroy
>   Vinnegar (*b*); Shelly Manne, Mel Lewis (*d*). 1–2/59.
**** Songs I Like To Sing Original Jazz Classics OJC 171
>   Humes; Al Porcino, Ray Triscari, Stu Williamson, Jack Sheldon (*t*); Harry Betts, Bob
>   Fitzpatrick (*tb*); Art Pepper (*cl, as*); Ben Webster, Teddy Edwards (*ts*); Bill Hood (*bs*); André
>   Previn (*p*); Barney Kessel (*g*); Leroy Vinnegar (*b*); Shelly Manne (*d*). 9/60.
***(*) Swingin' With Helen Original Jazz Classics OJC 608
>   Humes; Joe Gordon (*t*); Teddy Edwards (*ts*); Wynton Kelly (*p*); Al Viola (*g*); Leroy Vinnegar
>   (*b*); Frank Butler (*d*). 7/61.

Helen Humes made her first records as far back as 1927, when she was fourteen, but her sessions with Count Basie in the 1930s established her career. Her three albums for Contemporary have luckily all been reissued in the OJC series, and they make a powerful argument for her standing as one of the finest – and most overlooked – jazz vocalists of the swing era and after. Recorded in stereo for the first time, her voice's natural mix of light, girlish timbre and hard-hitting attack creates a curiously exhilarating impact. She's like a less matronly Ella Fitzgerald, yet she can phrase and change dynamics with more inventiveness than Ella. The 1959 session, organized almost as a jam session by Benny Carter, has a rare grip and immediacy; although almost everything on it is fine, special mention should be made of a superbly structured 'Stardust' and 'I Got It Bad And That Ain't Good' and a perfectly paced 'You Can Depend On Me'. The band, a strange mix of players, work unexpectedly well together, with the rhythm section's modern grooving offsetting terrific solos by Carter, Rosolino and Edwards.

Swingin' With Helen is just a shade less impressive, but the 12 standards here are all delivered with great charm and aplomb. The pick of the three, though, is *Songs I Like To Sing*, which arranger Marty Paich built very specifically around Humes's talents. The singer has no problem dealing with scores which would have taxed such a modernist as Mel Torme, and these eight tracks define a modern approach to swing singing. But the other four, with Humes set against a rhythm section and the sole horn of Ben Webster, are equally beautiful, particularly a glorious reading of 'Imagination'. Although Humes's voice isn't as forward in the sound-balance as it might be, the remastering of all three records is very crisp and strong.

**(*) Sneakin' Around Black & Blue 233083
>   Humes; Arnett Cobb, Gerard Bardini (*ts*); Gerald Wiggins, Jay McShann (*p*); Milt Buckner
>   (*org*); Clarence Gatemouth Brown (*g*); Major Holley, Roland Lobligeois (*b*); Paul Gunther, Ed
>   Thigpen (*d*). 8/73–5/74.
*** 'Deed I Do Contemporary 14071-2
>   Humes; Don Abney (*p*); Dean Reilly (*b*); Benny Barth (*d*). 4/76.

Humes is in good voice on *Sneakin' Around*, and the band, although a motley bunch of players on both sessions, sounds enthusiastic. But the material is no more than a run-through of Helen's greatest hits, all available in better versions elsewhere. The more intimate *'Deed I Do*, with a plain old rhythm section for company, is a shade better, though the material is again only too familiar.

*** Helen Humes And The Muse All Stars Muse MCD 5473
>   Humes; Eddie Vinson (*as, v*); Arnett Cobb (*ts*); Buddy Tate (*ts, bs*); Gerald Wiggins (*p*); George
>   Duvivier, Lisle Atkinson (*b*); Ronnie Cole (*d*). 10/79.

Probably the best of Helen's later records, although a rough-and-ready atmosphere meant to convey authenticity probably works against this subtle singer. The three Texan saxophonists have a good time at their chores, Vinson chipping in with a duet on 'I'm Gonna Move To The Outskirts Of Town'; but it's the ballads that find Humes in her most sympathetic condition. The CD reissue includes two alternative takes of 'These Foolish Things' and 'I've Got A Crush On You'.

Percy Humphrey (1905–1995) TRUMPET

(*) Sounds Of New Orleans Vol. 1: Paul Barbarin & His Band / Percy Humphrey's Jam Session
Storyville SLP 6008
> Humphrey; Joe Avery (*tb*); Ray Burke (*cl*); Sweet Emma Barrett (*p*); Billy Huntington (*bj*);
> Ricard Alexis (*b*); Cie Frazier (*d*). 5/54.

* New Orleans The Living Legends: Percy Humphrey's Crescent City Joymakers** Original Jazz Classics
OJC 1834-2
> Humphrey; Louis Nelson (*tb*); Albert Burbank (*cl*); Emanuel Sayles (*g, bj*); Louis James (*b*);
> Josiah Frazier (*d*). 1/61.

* Percy Humphrey's Hot Six** GHB BCD-85
> Humphrey; Louis Nelson (*tb*); Albert Burbank (*cl*); Lars Edegran (*p*); Chester Zardis (*b*); Barry
> Martyn (*d*). 11/66.

The youngest of the three Humphrey brothers was a substantial figure in New Orleans jazz. His most significant playing was usually done with the city's brass bands, and he became leader of the Eureka Brass Band in the early 1950s until its disbandment some 20 years later. The 1954 jam session, one-half of a disc shared with a Paul Barbarin set, is relatively slight music, but Humphrey plays with the characteristically curt, short-breathed phrasing of the New Orleans brassman and makes all his notes count: his solo on 'Everybody Loves My Baby', decorated with the familiar wobble which is the New Orleans vibrato, sums up his style: a mixture of abrasiveness and raw melody. The sound is quite good, although Sweet Emma Barrett, a minor legend who wore bells on her hat and round her ankles, is almost inaudible at the piano.

Most of Humphrey's later records are hard to locate, but this 1961 date in Riverside's Living Legends series is worth remembering, recorded in far superior sound to that often granted this kind of jazz. Humphrey himself is rather overpowered by Albert Burbank, whose clarinet predominates with an eagerness that recalls Boyd Senter, and Frazier's drumming is crashingly resonant; but the band live up to their name at many points.

The 1966 date captured on the GHB CD is a memento of one of Barry Martyn's trips to New Orleans – though Humphrey is the nominal leader, the date was organized by the drummer. The front line may have been a little tired – Jim Asman's notes record that they'd been playing the previous night till seven a.m. – and the playing is ragged, though ably policed by Martyn's beat. The rough, open-hall ambience reeks of vintage New Orleans music and it's a charismatic disc.

Willie Humphrey (1900–1994) CLARINET

* Two Clarinets On The Porch** GHB BCD-308
> Humphrey; Brian O'Connell (*cl*); Les Muscutt (*g, bj*); Frank Fields (*b*); Ernie Elly (*d*). 8/91.

Only a few months younger than George Lewis, Willie Humphrey harked back to an ancient New Orleans tradition. He didn't start recording until 1926; here, a mere 65 years later, he pals up with another clarinet man 60 years his junior. Humphrey's phrasing and gargled tone are those of an old man, as much as he enjoys his music, and the other players walk a little gingerly round him: the seven trio pieces, which Willie and Ernie Elly sit out, probably account for the best music, deftly sprung round Muscutt's deferential banjo and O'Donnell's sweet-toned clarinet. But 'I Want To Be Happy' or 'China Boy' feature some amusing interplay, and it's pleasant to hear an unalloyed New Orleans legend raising his voice in the 1990s on what turned out to be a sprightly farewell.

Charlie Hunter GUITAR

(*) Bing, Bing, Bing! Blue Note CDP 831809
> Hunter; Jeff Cressman (*tb*); Ben Goldberg (*cl*); Dave Ellis (*ts*); David Phillips (*g*); Jay Lane (*d*);
> Scott Roberts (*perc*). 95.

Hunter was a charter member of the wonderfully named Disposable Heroes of Hiphoprisy but has turned to a more jazz-based – but no less eclectic – trio, in which his eight-string guitar, pitched against tenor saxophone and drums, cleaves to a radical, modernized version of bebop. Hunter has claimed his namesake and fellow-guitarist Christian as a model, which somehow has to be taken on trust rather than heard on *Bing, Bing, Bing!*. Stylistically it isn't quite fully achieved, but Hunter is unmistakably an energy-source and will surely make more of this intriguing approach.

Chris Hunter ALTO SAXOPHONE

*** **This Is Chris** Paddle Wheel K32Y 6261
>   Hunter; Gil Goldstein (*p, syn*); Emily Remler (*g*); Ratzo Harris (*b*); Terri Lyne Carrington (*d*).
>   6/88.
(*) **Scarborough Fair Paddle Wheel KICJ 5
>   Hunter; Chris Botti (*t*); Conrad Herwig (*tb*); John Clark (*frhn*); Joe Daley (*euph*); Alex Foster
>   (*f, picc, ss*); Howard Johnson (*bcl*); Chuck Loeb (*g*); Gil Goldstein (*p, syn*); Mike Richmond
>   (*b*); Adam Nussbaum (*d*). 8/89.
** **I Want You** Sweet Basil 660 55 004
>   Hunter; Chris Botti (*t*); Conrad Herwig (*tb*); David Taylor (*btb*); David Bargeron (*euph, tba*);
>   John Clark (*frhn*); Lawrence Feldman (*f, picc*); Alex Foster (*ts, ss*); Roger Rosenberg (*bcl*); Gil
>   Goldstein (*p, syn, arr*); Ross Traut (*g*); Mike Richmond (*b*); Adam Nussbaum (*d*); Mino Cinelu
>   (*perc*); Romeyn Nesbitt (*v*). 91.

Chris Hunter had to survive a long period of 'young, gifted and white' hype *and* the inevitable critical
backlash. His high, slightly sharp alto sound, bluesier than David Sanborn's, cooler and less frantic than
Richie Cole's, found favour with Gil Evans, and most of Hunter's best recorded solos are to be found on
Evans albums.

The saxophonist's solo record has been decidedly stop-start. These three sets vary enormously in quality. The big-band disc, with its pretentiously eclectic mix – 'Holiday For Strings', Villa-Lobos's
Bachianas Brasileiras, Lennon/McCartney, and Wayne Shorter's 'Nefertiti' – falls pretty flat, despite Gil
Goldstein's intelligent arrangements and a band whose clean, brassy bite can at least partly be attributed to the stripped-down saxophone section. Romeyn Nesbitt's contributions certainly don't help and
serve only as a distraction; her franglais lyrics on the Shorter tune are nothing but embarrassing and her
take on 'Fever' is bad enough to induce night sweats.

The other two discs are, mercifully, very much better. Hunter functions better with a smaller group, and
there are some fine moments on *This Is Chris*, particularly 'Here's That Rainy Day', where Emily
Remler extends the group to a quintet. Hunter's solos on 'Cherokee' and 'Lover Man' won't cause any
lost sleep up in jazz heaven. As so often, he sounds as if he's absorbed a big record collection without
having thought through how – or indeed why – the greats played the way they did. The result is just a
mish-mash of hat-doffing gestures with no real logic or purpose. Occasionally, though, on the quartet
record, he appears to get in touch with his own conception; 'Jail Blues' and 'Talk To The Wild' have
more than a whisper of originality.

Robert Hurst (born 1964) BASS

***(*) **Robert Hurst Presents Robert Hurst** DIW 873
>   Hurst; Marcus Belgrave (*t, flhn*); Branford Marsalis (*ss, as, ts, cl*); Ralph Miles Jones III (*bcl,
>   bsn*); Kenny Kirkland (*p*); Jeff Watts (*d*). 8–9/92.

Hurst is the bass-playing eminence in residence for the Marsalis clan, but he sounds better here than he
does on any Delfeayo Marsalis production, his broad, juicy tone standing clear in the sound-mix. The
record is a little objectified, a shade overworked, but there is some very fine music here. 'Aycrigg', 'The
Snake Charmer' and even the oversmart 'Devil's Night In Motown' are compellingly realized as melodic
and textural vehicles for the group: Marsalis plays with a refinement and concentration that he seldom
musters on his own, rather self-conscious records, Belgrave is a master of several different trumpet
styles, and Kirkland is an unobtrusive wonder: sample his perfect touch on the almost indecently
charming 'Joyce Faye'. Hurst sometimes over-indulges himself, as a bassist who has to be leader usually
does (his solo 'Evidence' isn't very interesting), but it's a creditable effort.

Bobby Hutcherson (born 1941) VIBRAPHONE, MARIMBA, PERCUSSION

*** **Solos / Quartet** Original Jazz Classics OJC 425
>   Hutcherson solo and with McCoy Tyner (*p*); Herbie Lewis (*b*); Billy Higgins (*d*); John Koenig
>   (*bells*). 9 & 10/81, 3/82.
***(*) **Farewell Keystone** Theresa TR 124
>   Hutcherson; Oscar Brashear (*t, flhn*); Harold Land (*ts*); Cedar Walton (*p*); Buster Williams (*b*);
>   Billy Higgins (*d*). 7/82.

If Bobby Hutcherson had been a horn player, or even a pianist, he would certainly be regarded as one of
the major figures of the past 25 years. Unfortunately, the vibraphone is still seen as something of a
novelty instrument, suitable for showbizzy histrionics (Lionel Hampton's doing) or else as too soft in

tone for serious improvisation. There is, of course, a lively tradition of vibraharp playing with both traditionalist and radical wings, but few have developed such a consistently challenging language for the instrument as Hutcherson. In the 1960s he made a series of superb albums for Blue Note, the equal of any of the classic dates from that label.Alas, all are now deleted, although some have recently returned fleetingly as limited editions.

The 1980s have seen something of a revival in his fortunes: uncompromised recording opportunities, sympathetic collaborators and, one suspects, a consequently renewed faith in his own abilities. *Farewell Keystone* reunites him with Harold Land, and the encounter still sounds pretty incisive more than ten years on, with a truly fantastic rhythm section propelling the front men. Hutcherson's multi-directional contrapuntal imagination, with melodic, harmonic and rhythmic parameters all intelligently controlled, makes solo performance more than commonly feasible, particularly with the use of multi-tracking; where Lionel Hampton required a great surfer's wave of chords and riffs piled up behind him, Hutcherson creates his own internal impetus. The tone is by no means as percussive as it was on *Out To Lunch*, though ironically Hutcherson has put increasing emphasis on xylorimbas at the same time as smoothing out his vibraphone lines in what looks like a degree of accommodation with Milt Jackson.

The quartet sessions, which include a sparkling 'Old Devil Moon' and 'My Foolish Heart', simply underline Tyner's astonishing eclecticism and adaptability. Those with longer memories will automatically track back to Hampton's interplay with Teddy Wilson in the classic Benny Goodman Quartets of 1936 and 1937. That good.

*** **Four Seasons** Timeless SJP 210
    Hutcherson; George Cables (*p*); Herbie Lewis (*b*); Philly Joe Jones (*d*). 12/83.
*** **Good Bait** Landmark LM 1501
    Hutcherson; Branford Marsalis (*ts, ss*); George Cables (*p*); Ray Drummond (*b*); Philly Joe Jones (*d*). 8/84.

The Dutch recording on Timeless has great sound, with vibes and piano carefully aligned in the mix. Cables is at his best and is constantly looking out for cues from Hutcherson. They make a very convincing partnership, and it's a shame this group couldn't have toured more.

Marsalis, B., doesn't seem right for the first of the Landmarks. He has a slithery, almost lackadaisical approach to phrasing, as if he'd try to get away with fewer notes if only he could be bothered riding the spaces. In the event, you get a lazy-man's-load of sound, bits falling off it all over the place. It's engaging stuff, though, and the rest of the band are great. By far the best track is a quartet 'Spring Is Here', with Hutcherson and Cables nudging slightly cautiously at one another, and explicit references to Miles's more emotional approach in the modes and voicings. Like almost all the Landmark catalogue, impressively well recorded, with just the right miking for the drumkit.

***(*) **Color Schemes** Landmark LM 1508
    Hutcherson; Mulgrew Miller (*p*); John Heard (*b*); Billy Higgins (*d*); Airto Moreira (*perc*). 10/85.

A marvellous record. The duos with Miller and Airto drift into occasional redundancies and embellishments, but Hutcherson sustains the overall direction with impressive ease. Miller really comes into his own on a quintet reading of 'Bemsha Swing' that dis-assembles the chord structure rather than merely improvising with it. Though Jones's contribution to *Good Bait* is enormous, Higgins would seem to be *the* drummer for Hutcherson. As on *Solos/Quartet* (above) and in marked contrast to Victor Lewis (below), who likes to play by the book, Higgins scythes through the bar-lines, keeping the pulse and the metre in view with the odd accurately placed accent or simply with the sheer impetus of his playing. Very highly recommended.

**** **In The Vanguard** Landmark LM 1513
    Hutcherson; Kenny Barron (*p*); Buster Williams (*b*); Al Foster (*d*). 12/86.

Take the title any way you like – it refers, of course, to the one in the Village – Hutcherson is still at the forefront of contemporary jazz. This, a surprisingly rare live recording, is one of the very best things he has ever committed to disc. The setting – with no horns – develops his interest in the interaction of piano and vibes, with the enormous harmonic and contrapuntal possibilities that implies. Standards-based, the emphasis is on improvisation, rather than on tightly organized charts (and producer Orrin Keepnews has described the album as a deliberate tactic in reaction to the very controlled, and occasionally contrived, feel of its predecessors).

As it turns out, the band's harmonic centre is the bassist; Buster Williams has a huge tone and, with his wonderfully controlled pedal passages on the likes of 'Some Day My Prince Will Come' (which needs to be compared with Miles's version), pushes the rest of the band in the direction of freedom; his introduction to Bruno Martino's 'Estate', an underexploited theme which has also caught Herbie Hancock's eye, is the perfect cue for Hutcherson at his most romantic. The set opens with Randy Weston's 'Little Niles', then blows the fluff off 'Young And Foolish' and 'Witchcraft', and tackles Monk's 'Well, You Needn't' like it was already overtime. Al Foster does the work of three men and Barron could almost be Hutcherson's third instrument. Superb; high in the top 50 albums of the decade.

***(*) Cruisin' The 'Bird Landmark LM 1517
Hutcherson; Ralph Moore (*ts, ss*); Buddy Montgomery (*p*); Rufus Reid (*b*); Victor Lewis (*d*). 4/88.

By no means just a straight-ahead blowing session and not, as one American reviewer glibly assumed (did he *listen* to it?), a tribute to Charlie Parker. The second apostrophe gives the game away; Hutcherson's 'Bird is a 1964 convertible the size of a swimming pool, and it makes a fair image of the classic aerodynamics and effortless acceleration that had reappeared in the vibist's playing two decades later.

Hutcherson's ability to work on several levels simultaneously opens up this fine set of originals. The three rhythm players (Montgomery, himself normally a vibist, here fulfils a largely supportive role) provide a footsure platform for some fine solo work from both Hutcherson and Moore, whose soprano figures on the ballad, 'Sierra', are noticeably individual; Hutcherson doubles marimba on the same track, and in a curious way it's the wooden instrument that now more often reflects his familiar, firmly struck style. *Cruisin' The 'Bird* is a deceptively demanding album; its immediate pay-off doesn't last long, but there's so much incident, so much evidence of pure improvisational *thinking*, that tracks – let alone sides – call for the repeat button.

**(*) Ambos Mundos (Both Worlds) Landmark LM 1522
Hutcherson; James Spaulding (*f*); Bruce Forman, Randy Vincent (*g*); Smith Dobson (*p*); Jeff Chambers (*b*); Eddie Marshall (*d*); Francisco Aguabella, Orestes Vilato, Roger Glenn (*perc*). 8–9/89.

Disappointing in the light of recent strides back to full performing and compositional form. The Latin structures and metres do clearly appeal to Hutcherson, but his treatment of them, and his obvious unwillingness to eschew the vibraharp for even one session, weakens the impact slightly; it's a little too light and floating. Bruce Forman plays well on 'Besame Mucho' and 'Tin Tin Deo', returning the compliment of his own *There Are Times* (Concord CJ 332) on which Hutcherson guested.

***(*) Mirage Landmark LM 1529
Hutcherson; Tommy Flanagan (*p*); Peter Washington (*b*); Billy Drummond (*d*). 2/91.

This doesn't quite reach the heights of the Village Vanguard sessions, but it's close. Hutcherson and Flanagan had never played together previously, so there's a certain tentative respect on the three originals. The set catches light with Monk once again. 'Pannonica' was Keepnews's idea and is played as a duet, as is 'Love Letters'. The latter illustrates once again Hutcherson's enthusiasm for taking the ribbon off unread standards. Antonio Carlos Jobim's 'Zingaro' is little performed in a jazz context and Cole Porter's 'I Am In Love' is a surprising rarity. Cedar Walton's 'Groundwork' becomes a feature for Billy Drummond; originally written for his namesake Higgins, the comparison by no means disgraces the younger man. Hutcherson enters another decade in the top flight.

Dick Hyman (born 1927) PIANO, ORGAN, VOCAL

***(*) Live At Michael's Pub JazzMania JCD-6007
Hyman; Roger Kellaway (*p*). 7/81.

**(*) They Got Rhythm! Jass J-CD-635
Hyman; Derek Smith (*p*). 2/83.

*** The Kingdom Of Swing And The Republic Of Oop Bop Sh'Bam Musicmasters CIJD 60200
Hyman; Joe Wilder (*t*); Warren Vaché (*c*); Urbie Green (*tb*); Buddy Tate (*cl, ts*); Derek Smith (*p*); Milt Hinton (*b*); Butch Miles (*d*). 7/87.

*** Plays Harold Arlen Musicmasters CIJD 60215
Hyman (*p* solo). 4/89.

*** 14 Jazz Piano Favourites Music & Arts CD 622
Hyman (*p* solo). 6/88.

*** Plays Fats Waller Reference RR-33
Hyman (*p* solo). 8/89.

***(*) Music Of 1937 Concord CCD 4415
Hyman (*p* solo). 2/90.

*** Stride Piano Summit Milestone 9189
Hyman; Harry 'Sweets' Edison (*t*); Ralph Sutton, Jay McShann, Mike Lipskin (*p*); Red Callender (*b*); Harold Jones (*d*). 6/90.

*** **Plays Duke Ellington** Reference R R-50
    Hyman (*p* solo). 90.
**** **All Through The Night** Musicmasters 5060-2
    Hyman (*p* solo). 91.
*** **Gershwin Songbook: Hyman Variations** Musicmasters 5094-2
    Hyman (*p* solo). 9/92.
*** **Concord Duo Series Vol. 6** Concord CCD 4603
    Hyman; Ralph Sutton (*p*). 11/93.

Dick Hyman has had a pretty paradoxical career in many ways. In the 1940s he was playing with both Charlie Parker and Benny Goodman. Working as a studio musician through much of the 1950s and '60s, he also recorded novelty tunes under various pseudonyms, as well as Scott Joplin's complete works. He loves early jazz, is an expert on the jazz-piano tradition, can re-create pit-band orchestrations or ragtime arrangements to order – yet he was also one of the first to record an album of tunes played on prototype synthesizers.

For a long time there was very little 'strict' jazz in the catalogue under Hyman's name, but recent times have found him busy on repertory albums of one sort or another. Most of these discs validate his findings with their exuberance as well as their attention to detail. The earlier records of piano duos find him with two different but sympathetic partners. The session with Derek Smith is impeccably played, but the consistently jolly tone is wearing after a couple of tunes: some of the music takes on a clock-work, parlour-piano feel. With Kellaway, a far more adventurous performer, they go to sometimes fantastical lengths to explode the tune: 'Swinging On A Star', for instance, is demolished and rebuilt over and over again, and there is a hilariously bizarre 'Chopsticks'. Yet 'Summertime' has real gravitas, too.

The Kingdom Of Swing provides a record of a New York show where Hyman enlisted various swing-era types (authentic and modernist) for an evening of good-hearted fun. Vaché is on good form and there is a charming duet between Hyman and Tate, on clarinet instead of his shakier tenor. The four-man *Stride Piano Summit* sets Hyman against two other masters (Lipskin is rather less of a giant) in another multi-combination show: he does his Fats Waller pipe-organ bit on 'Persian Rug' and roisters through 'Sunday' with McShann and Edison. Lightweight but good fun.

The solo albums are the best place to examine the range of Hyman's interests. He goes back as far as ragtime and Jelly Roll Morton on the Café des Copains recital for Music & Arts, making light of any rhythmical squareness in the likes of 'Frog-I-More Rag' and freshening up 'Blue Skies' until it sings. *Music Of 1937*, an early entry in the Maybeck Recital Hall series, concentrates on a single year in songwriting: by no means exceptional, but the best of these pre-war hits – 'The Folks Who Live On The Hill', 'Some Day My Prince Will Come', 'Thanks For The Memory' – tend to prove the subtext that they don't write 'em like that any more, which would be a curmudgeonly verdict if it weren't for the sprightly and glowing readings which Hyman gets. His five composer-dedicated records are unfailingly entertaining if mixed in their profundities. Hyman is an excellent mimic when he wants to be, and for the Arlen record he sounds like an urbane, less fulsome copy of Art Tatum, an impressive trick to be sure. When he sets 'Over The Rainbow' to a bossa rhythm, the humour is Tatumesque, too. This is a bright, ingenious collection, and it works out rather better than the Waller set: Hyman loves this music but sometimes even he must feel that it sounds a little dated and, since he has none of Waller's genial uproar in his bones, he can't always bring it to life. Ellington also eludes him to some extent, since Duke's intimacies are just as personal to himself; but both records still have a degree of sophistication and elegance that set them some way above everybody's routine tribute record.

The very best of this sequence, though, is *All Through The Night*, which is all Cole Porter. Hyman's delivery seems an exact match for Porter's own blend of sophistication and sardonicism, with the romantic undertow of his warmest music still on hand. The opening 'Easy To Love' seems like an encyclopedia of stride and swing piano in 18 choruses and ten minutes. 'Were Thine That Special Face' is as placid as motionless water. 'Brush Up Your Shakespeare' is the most light and swinging 3/4 time imaginable, and 'Let's Do It' is perky without once seeming cute. This is all Hyman at his best. Piano sound (from live shows in Cambridge Springs, Pennsylvania) is less than ideal, but not troublesome.

The Gershwin disc features Hyman playing 18 pieces of the composer straight off the sheet-music before adding his own variations to each. This kind of formal lesson is meat and drink to Hyman, but as a record it palls just a little over the long haul, despite his many ingenuities. The same could be said of his duets with Ralph Sutton, indomitably swinging but falling into patterns, if not routines, across a dozen tunes. Taken a couple of tracks at a time, this is delightful, but the earlier disc with Kellaway is just a fraction better.

Abdullah Ibrahim (formerly known as Dollar Brand) (born 1934) PIANO, SOPRANO
SAXOPHONE, CELLO, VOICE

*** **Reflections** Black Lion 760127
    Ibrahim (*p* solo). 3/65.
(*) **African Sketchbook Enja 2026
    As above. 5/69.
**** **African Piano** Japo 60002
    As above. 10/69.
*** **Anthem For The New Nations** Denon DC 8588
    As above. 6/78.
***(*) **African Dawn** Enja 4030
    As above. 6/82.

Ibrahim left his native South Africa in the aftermath of the Sharpeville massacre, settling first in Europe, latterly in the United States. He adopted his Islamic name on his conversion in 1968, but his given name, Dollar Brand, still has considerable currency and, however improperly, is apt to be used interchangeably.

Brand came to the attention of Duke Ellington in the United States and it was Ellington who gave him the opportunity to make his first American recordings. Ellington had been his greatest single influence, though there are perhaps stronger traces of black church music, African folk themes and hints of Thelonious Monk and the 1960s free movement in his solo performances. These have a hypnotic intensity and a surprising level of formality, which lends an often-repeated tune like 'Bra Joe From Kilimanjaro' (on the surviving Japo and *African Portraits*, for instance) an almost ritual quality.

African Piano is certainly still the best of the solo records, even though the CD robs the music of some of its full-hearted resonance. The later Enja (*Sketchbook* is as bitty as it sounds) offers valuable insights into some of Ibrahim's stylistic debts, with tributes to Ellington, Coltrane (just one of a rash of memorials marking the fifteenth anniversary of the saxophonist's death) and Monk. He plays 'A Flower Is A Lovesome Thing', 'Blue Monk' and an inventive, firmly contoured 'Round About Midnight' that strips the tune down to more authentically Monkish basics. The early *Reflections* develops a similar range of material, applying Brand's drumming lyricism to 'Don't Get Around Much Any More' (an astonishing performance), 'Mood Indigo', 'Take The "A" Train' and 'Monk's Mood'. The great thing about the Japo and the Enjas is that they're recorded in dramatic close-up, with a presence that's bleached out of the otherwise excellent Denon.

*** **Round Midnight At The Montmartre** Black Lion BLCD 760111
    Ibrahim; Johnny Gertze (*b*); Makaya Ntoshko (*d*). 1/65.
(*) **Anatomy Of A South African Village Black Lion BLCD 760172
    As above. 1/65.

'Round About Midnight' takes on a more conventional outline in the first of these trio performances, recorded at the Café Montmartre. There's a short version of 'Tintiyana', and two solo tracks, which are much jazzier than usual and don't initially sound typical of Brand's work of the time. Ntoshko plays in the post-Elvin Jones idiom favoured by Billy Higgins and Hart. Like his fellow-countryman, Louis Moholo, he has the ability to range between freedom and strict (but complex) time and can blur the line between polyrhythmic playing and complete abstraction so much that it often sounds as though Brand is keeping time for the drummer. The mix is rather uneven and the bass is often lost altogether, though what one can hear isn't that interesting.

Taken from the same set, *Anatomy* sounds perversely much more like a mainstream jazz album. With the exception of the title-track, Brand seems content to work his way through some mildly Africanized changes. The fact that he does so with fire doesn't quite eliminate the essential blandness of what he is doing. A disappointing follow-up, but a sure sign that they got the selection right first time.

*** **African Space Program** Enja 2032
    Ibrahim; Cecil Bridgewater, Enrico Rava, Charles Sullivan (*t*); Kiane Zawadi (*tb*); Sonny
    Fortune, Carlos Ward (*f, as*); Roland Alexander (*ts, hca*); John Stubblefield (*ts*); Hamiet Bluiett
    (*bs*); Cecil McBee (*b*); Roy Brooks (*d*). 11/73.

A rare opportunity to hear Ibrahim fronting a substantial, hand-picked band. Six months before Duke's death, the parallels are once again strongly evident, with Ward sounding like an Africanized Hodges and Hamiet Bluiett slipping easily into the Harry Carney role. 'Tintinyana' falls into two parts, its progress clarified by the leader's piano statements and percussive breaks. The sound is somewhat better on CD than on the original release, but it's still very bottom-heavy and leaden.

***(*) **Good News From Africa** Enja 2048
    Ibrahim; Johnny Mbizo Dyani (*b, bells, v*). 12/73.

**** **Echoes From Africa** Enja 3047
As above. 9/79.

Dyani towers on these fascinating and often moving duos, which move between a dark, almost tragic pessimism to a shouting, joyous climax. 'Saud' is a dedication to McCoy Tyner (the title reflects the other pianist's more briefly adopted Islamic name) and interestingly suggests how some of Ellington's modal explorations of the 1960s filtered into the vernacular via younger piano players. Ibrahim adds some flute colours to the earlier album and the two voices entwine in celebration of the homeland. *Echoes* was originally released as an audiophile direct-to-disc recording. CD makes the music even more immediate and penetrative.

*** **The Children Of Africa** Enja 2070
Ibrahim; Cecil McBee (*b*); Roy Brooks (*d*). 1/76.

A set of strongly coloured African themes, containing the germ of Ibrahim's 1980s work with Carlos Ward and Ekaya. In fact, what the set seems to call for is a full-time horn player. The pianist's limited contribution on soprano saxophone does little more than point to its lack elsewhere, and there's a touch of thinness to the overall sound that can't entirely be blamed on a poor mix, though McBee's middle register does collide awkwardly with the piano.

(*) **Duet Denon CD 8561
Ibrahim; Archie Shepp (*ts*). 6/78.

This is a record of dismal predictability, one of those occasions where Shepp's claims to omnicultural competence has to be severely questioned. It is a patent mismatch, and the more the two men try to discover a sound-alike common ground the more fatuous it becomes, like strangers insistent on speaking the other's language.

*** **Africa Tears And Laughter** Enja ENJ 3039
Ibrahim; Talib Qadr (*ts, ss*); Greg Brown (*b*); John Betsch (*d*). 3/79.
***(*) **African Marketplace** Discovery 71016
Ibrahim; Gary Chandler (*t*); Craig Harris, Malindi Blyth Mbityana (*tb*); Carlos Ward (*as, ss*); Dwayne Armstrong, Jeff Jawarrah King (*ts*); Kenny Rogers (*bs*); Lawrence Lucie (*bj*); Cecil McBee (*b*); Andre Strobert (*d, perc*); Miguel Pomier (*perc*). 12/79.

There were signs that at this point in his career Ibrahim wanted to take stock of his progress so far. The Enja date examines its Africanness almost clinically, holding itself up to the light in a way that he either couldn't or wouldn't do in the company of Johnny Dyani later that same year. This – along with the Shepp encounter – is one of the only points in Ibrahim's career when the relentlessness of his approach begins to sound like self-parody, or at least self-pastiche.

A little later again, *Marketplace* contains a pretty substantial reworking of much of his work since coming to America and, ending on 'Anthem For The New Nation', with its pounding, cyclical ostinati and another soaring statement from Ward, seems to look forward to the next stage and to a future for South Africa that in 1979 was still unimaginably distant. The title-piece is the most substantial, expressing a movement from African community – signalled by drums – through fragmentation and pain to re-integration. It contains one of Ibrahim's most significant saxophone solos of recent years.

There is plenty of unaffectedly raucous blowing. 'The Homecoming Song' is a throwback to the she-beens and clubs of his homeland; one almost expects to hear Kippy Moetketsi instead of Ward. 'Mamma' is a straight blowing theme with a gospelly chorus. A fine, if occasionally shambolic record.

***(*) **Montreux '80** Enja 3079
Ibrahim; Carlos Ward (*as, f*); Craig Harris (*tb*); Alonzo Gardner (*b*); Andre Strobert (*d*). 7/80.
*** **Zimbabwe** Enja 4056
Ibrahim; Carlos Ward (*f, as*); Essiet Okon Essiet (*b*); Don Mumford (*d*). 5/83.
*** **Abdullah Ibrahim / Dollar Brand** Enja 5007
As above, except add Johnny Classens (*v*). 7/83.
**** **Water From An Ancient Well** Tiptoe 88812
Ibrahim; Dick Griffin (*tb*); Carlos Ward (*as, f*); Ricky Ford (*ts*); Charles Davis (*bs*); David Williams (*b*); Ben Riley (*d*). 10/85.
***(*) **The Mountain** Kaz Records KAZ CD 7
As above, except omit Williams.

The association with Carlos Ward has been the most productive and sympathetic of Ibrahim's career. The saxophonist has a high, exotic tone (superficially reminiscent of Sonny Fortune's, but much less raucous) that is ideally suited to his leader's conception. Working with Ward has reinforced Ibrahim's preference for song-like forms built over harmonically unvarying ostinati but has allowed him to develop a more abstract, improvisational feel, which reaches its peak on *Water From An Ancient Well*.

This was made by Ibrahim's band Ekaya (the word means 'home'), who are also responsible for the live Kaz set; an earlier, eponymous disc on Black Hawk has disappeared. *Water* is a carefully structured album with something of the feel of Ellington's *Far East Suite*, and most of the drama comes from the interplay between Ibrahim and the horns. It includes another heartfelt tribute to Sathima Bea Benjamin, 'Daughter Of Cape Town'.

In their earlier encounters, Ward seemed willing to play Charlie Rouse to Ibrahim's Monk, but increasingly he develops his own approach, and by 1983 is putting his own stamp on the music. *Ibrahim/Brand* is the most self-consciously African of the group, an impression heightened by Classens's effective vocal contributions. *Zimbabwe* is less original in either content or treatment, but it contains some of Ibrahim's best group-work on record, and Essiet's bass-work (clearly drawn from the example of Johnny Dyani) is very fine.

*** Mindif Enja 5073
> Ibrahim; Benny Powell (*tb*); Ricky Ford (*ts, ss*); Craig Handy (*f, ts*); David Williams (*b*); Billy Higgins (*d, perc*). 3/88.

**** African River Enja 6018
> Ibrahim; Robin Eubanks (*tb*); John Stubblefield (*fl, ts*); Horace Alexander Young (*ss, as, picc*); Howard Johnson (*bs, tba*); Buster Williams (*b*); Brian Adams (*d*). 6/89.

Ward is immediately missed on *Mindif* (which was written as the soundtrack to Claire Denis's atmospheric film, *Chocolat*; see also below) but Powell and Handy are both exciting players, and Higgins's drumming is so imaginative as often to become the focus of a piece like 'African Market' or 'Thema [*sic.*] For Monk'. The later album is absolutely superb and a vivid extension of the kind of arrangements Ibrahim had attempted on *African Space Program*. 'The Wedding' reappears from 1980 (*Montreux* and *Duke's Memories*) and receives a definitive performance, with Eubanks to the fore. Stubblefield and Young more than make up for the departure of Ricky Ford, and Howard Johnson does his usual patented stuff in the bottom half of the chart. Williams is a rather significant addition, playing big, singing lines that are occasionally reminiscent of Ibrahim's own early experiments on cello. Anyone with the solo *African Piano* and *African River* in their possession (the titles are uniquely repetitive and rather unimaginative) can feel confident of a reasonable purchase on his best work.

***(*) No Fear, No Die / S'en fout la mort Tiptoe 88815
> Ibrahim; Frank Lacy (*tb*); Ricky Ford (*ts*); Horace Alexander Young III (*as, ss, f*); Jimmy Cozier (*bs, cl*); Buster Williams (*b*); Ben Riley (*d*). 7/90.

Where *Mindif* was intended to evoke the magnificent spaciousness of the African landscape which forms the backdrop to *Chocolat*, *No Fear, No Die* is a more brooding and troubled score. Claire Denis's film concerns cockfighting in France among the African community. Its edgy unease was immediately likened to Louis Malle's quasi-*vérité* thriller, *L'Ascenseur pour l'échafaud*, and to Miles Davis's score for that film. There are parallels (as there are to Duke's *Anatomy of a Murder* music) but they are more apparent than actual. Ibrahim's music is actually more effective on record than in the film because the individual pieces are better made, more carefully constructed than is usually considered either necessary or desirable for a film score. So where Miles's magnificent improvisations sound like snippets out of a longer continuum, *No Fear, No Die* behaves very much like a consciously produced album, programmed to work on its own and without images.

The group performs brilliantly, with Ford as always delivering far more on someone else's record than on his own. Williams and Riley keep Monk very much in the stylistic frame. One suspects that dedicated Ibrahim fans may reject the record as 'untypical' or a second-order project. The first it may be; the second it's not.

*** Mantra Mode Tiptoe 88810
> Ibrahim; Johnny Mekoa (*t*); Basil Coetzee (*ts*); Robbie Jansen (*as, bs, f*); Errol Dyers (*g*); Spencer Mbadu (*b*); Monty Weber (*d*). 1/91.

*** Desert Flowers Enja 7011
> Ibrahim (*p, ky* solo). 12/91.

These were meant to express a sort of homecoming to what was, even then, being hailed as the 'new' South Africa; Ibrahim had spent much of his creative life in exile. *Desert Flowers* is a very personal programme of music and there are moments when emotion (and the synthesizer) blur the focus badly. Ibrahim actually uses synth only on the first and last tracks, an uneasy welcome and farewell that completely belies the warmth radiating from the heart of the set. Significantly, middle position is occupied by Duke's 'Come Sunday', a gorgeous performance preceded by a breath of the past in 'Ancient Cape', followed by 'District Six', 'Sweet Devotion', and a passionate vocal tribute to John Coltrane. Though far from a classic Ibrahim album, it contains enough of real merit to lift it to the fringes of the first division.

Mantra Mode is less inward and more buoyant, but one can't quite ignore the feeling that these men don't play with the bounce and gusto one hears in South African recordings of the late 1950s, from

groups like the Jazz Epistles. The joy of playing appears to be assumed rather than completely spontaneous, and there is a thread of melancholy through even the upbeat numbers.

***(*) **Knysna Blue** Tiptoe 888816
> Ibrahim (*p* solo). 9 & 10/93.

Frankly celebratory, and intended as a mystical reconsecration of post-apartheid South Africa as a
country at the world's apex, between two great oceans and focusing the cultural energies of four
continents. All this is probably too much freight for one piano album, and sometimes one feels Ibrahim
is trying too hard to express the inexpressible, to catch the ineffable in a combination of heavy chords
and floating melody lines. There is, though, no mistaking the joy with which it comes and the total
identification in Ibrahim's mind of personal and political/cultural liberation. It is, very simply, an
extended love song, and the closing Monk cover, 'Ask Me Now', is as nakedly personal and unguarded
as Ibrahim has ever been.

**** **Yarona** Tiptoe 888820
> Ibrahim; Marcus McLaurine (*b*); George Johnson (*d*). 1/95.

A truly magisterial performance by the sixty-year-old, bringing the house down at Sweet Basil in New
York City. Ibrahim was on record around this time, reinforcing his conviction that the piano-trio format
permitted the most fundamental representation of the African source; and it is very hard to argue with
that on the basis of these performances. He still hits the piano very hard, using the bass almost as a
drone, alternating narrow intervals and often allowing the drummer considerable licence to range outside the metre. The left hand is relentless and, in the other sense, timeless, the melody lines stripped down
and ritualized. 'Duke 88' once again acknowledges a personal debt. 'Nisa' is an exclamatory hymn to
another, the womenfolk of South Africa. There is a reworking of 'African Marketplace' and a concert
outing for 'Stardance', one of the lovelier themes from the *Chocolat* soundtrack. The love song, 'Cherry'
(not, as one critic assumed, a tribute to the trumpeter), shows his more lyrical side.

ICP Orchestra GROUP

*** **Herbie Nichols / Thelonious Monk** BVhaast 026
> Toon De Gouw (*t*); Wolter Wierbos, George Lewis (*tb*); Steve Lacy (*ss*); Michael Moore (*cl, as*);
> Paul Termos (*as*); Ab Baars (*ts, ss, cl*); Sean Bergin (*ts*); Misha Mengelberg (*p*); Ernst Reijseger
> (*clo*); Maurice Horsthuis (*vla*); Larry Fishkind (*tba*); Han Bennink (*d*). 84–87.

A larger-scale version of the tributes which Mengelberg, Lacy and others recorded for Soul Note at
much the same time, this highly coloured and generous programme makes light of the difficulties in both
composers' work. Monk tributes have become commonplace, but Baars, Moore and Wierbos are soloists with an idiosyncratic accent, and Lewis appears on a few tracks for an extra brassiness. Mengelberg
and Bennink, the most practised of in-to-out rhythm sections, make Monk's rhythmic eccentricities
their own property, too. But the Nichols tracks are more interesting, since his tunes are less familiar, and
the larger group – which includes Termos, Horsthuis, Bergin and Lacy – lends a firmer substance to
music which is difficult to characterize.

Klaus Ignatzek PIANO

*** **Magic Secret** Nabel 4617
> Ignatzek (*p* solo). 1/85.

(*) **Gershwin Songs Nabel 4631
> As above. 7/88.

** **Plays Beatles Songs** Nabel 4643
> As above. 8/90.

Ignatzek has immersed himself so completely in the idiom (shouldn't that be idiom*s*?) of Horace Silver,
Bill Evans, Sonny Clark and Wynton Kelly as to claim almost apostolic understanding of the roots of
hard bop. Like some clairvoyant transcriber of 'posthumous' Mozart symphonies, he has produced a
steady stream of rather unconvincing pastiche that may sound good in a club setting but which seems a
thoroughly dull option when set against a random sample of late-1950s Blue Notes.

Technically, Ignatzek is hard to fault, but compositions like the ubiquitous 'Monk's Visit' (heard in its
most po-faced form on *Magic Secret*, the best of the solo albums) carry little more than a whisper of the
dedicatee's divine simplicity and humour. The Gershwin and Beatles sets seriously miscalculate the
robustness and durability of the original material. The average Lennon–McCartney song played
'straight' would sound much more impressive than these earnest stylings which flood the tunes with
irrelevance.

*** **The Spell** Nabel 4614
> Ignatzek; Dave Liebman (*ss*); Dieter Ilg (*b*); Uwe Ecker (*d*). 4 & 5/84.

(*) **Don't Stop It Timeless SJP 271
> Ignatzek; Claudio Roditi (*t, flhn*); Paulo Cardoso (*b*); Mario Gonzi (*d*). 5/87.

***(*) **Jacaranda** Timeless SJP 292
> As above. 5/87.

** **New Surprise** Timeless CD SJP 324
> Ignatzek; Claudio Roditi (*t, flhn*); Tim Armacost (*ts*); Paulo Cardoso (*b*); Mario Gonzi (*d*). 11/ 88.

(*) **The Klaus Ignatzek Trio yvp 3020
> Ignatzek; Jean-Louis Rassinfosse (*b*); John Engels (*d*). 7/89.

*** **Day For Night** Nabel 4639
> Ignatzek; Joe Henderson (*ts*); Jean-Louis Rassinfosse (*b*); Joris Dudli (*d*). 10/89.

*** **Today Is Tomorrow** Nabel 4654
> Ignatzek; Claudio Roditi, Gustavo Bergalli (*t*); Jean-Louis Rassinfosse (*b*); Joris Dudli (*d*). 10/ 91.

*** **Airballoon** Nabel 4651
> Ignatzek; Jean-Louis Rassinfosse (*b*); Anca Parghel (*v*). 3 & 4/92.

***(*) **The Answer!** Candid CCD 79534
> Ignatzek; Claudio Roditi, Gustavo Bergalli (*t*); Jean-Louis Rassinfosse (*b*); Jorge Rossy (*d*). 12/ 92.

Ignatzek has been singularly fortunate in his access to saxophone players of the quality of Dave Liebman, Joe Henderson and, on a deleted LP, Bobby Watson. Ignatzek's comping gives soloists of this quality little to work on. This is less of a problem for Liebman, who gives the music an uncharacteristically abstract cast. *The Spell* is rather good. Henderson, perhaps inevitably, treats the gig much more functionally and good-humouredly, with no obvious anxiety to get inside Ignatzek's bland modalities. 'Blue Energy' and 'Monk's Visit' are dispatched with untroubled understanding.

If the saxophonists are the measure of the group, then Ignatzek's regular band of the late 1980s was of very intermittent quality. *Jacaranda* is remarkably good, with trumpeter Roditi leading a Messengers line on standards such as 'Softly As In A Morning Sunrise' and 'There Is No Greater Love', along with an original 'Blues for Lee M.' and a take of 'Day For Night'. Neither the earlier *Don't Stop It* (with the same group) nor the ghastly *New Surprise*, which adds Tim Armacost's inept tenor, sounds like the same band at all, and the charges of bland revivalism, to which Ignatzek has always hotly replied, very definitely stick. The most recent sets show something of a consolidation, with Roditi giving the music a hint of sparkle and edge, but they still seem terribly rootless. Just as clichés are clichés because they communicate some pretty basic truths, standards are standards because they contain something over and above the normal run of songs. Even the most ambitious of the boppers knew that they had to negotiate the standards first.

The most recent of the records, *The Answer!*, is probably the best of all, a tight, well-disciplined set with a minimum of fuss, but with some sharp arrangements that make maximum use of the two horns and exploit the more percussive side of this saxophone-less band.

Keith Ingham (born 1942) PIANO

*** **Out Of The Past** Sackville SKCD 2-3047
> Ingham (*p* solo). 11–12/90.

***(*) **Donaldson Redux** Stomp Off CD 1237
> Ingham; Peter Ecklund (*c*); Dan Barrett (*tb*); Bobby Gordon, Billy Novick (*cl*); Loren Schoenberg (*ts*); Vince Giordano (*bsx, tba, b*); Marty Grosz (*g, bj, v*); Greg Cohen (*b*); Hall Smith, Arnie Kinsella (*d*). 6–11/91.

Ingham's playing is all too admirable. An Englishman in New York (though the solo album was cut mainly in Toronto), he plays a history of jazz piano with unflinching finesse, taste and skill, and unearths tunes that few would think of trying. The 18 tracks on *Out Of The Past* cover composers from Richard M. Jones to Barry Harris, and resuscitate such cadavers as 'Just Like A Butterfly' and Rube Bloom's 'Truckin' '. It is all beautifully played, the variations improvised with rag-like precision, but the unobtrusive nature of Ingham's talent is eventually frustrating. After a dozen tracks one wonders if there ought to be greater difference between such diverse sources than Ingham allows, and his version of, say, Jimmy Yancey's 'At The Window' is very pale next to the composer's own.

The Stomp Off album is another matter, since it documents the further adventures of Marty Grosz in hot dance music. The songs are all by Walter Donaldson, and some of this archaeology is almost preposterously rarefied. Grosz does his usual update of Ukulele Ike at the microphone, and the band play a lilting approximation of old-time hot music with a few knowing modern licks. Ingham is co-credited as leader and no doubt approves of all the fun.

*** **My Little Brown Book** Progressive PCD 7101
    Ingham; Harry Allen (*ts*); Chris Flory (*g*); Dennis Irwin (*b*); Chuck Riggs (*d*). 3/93.
***(*) **The Intimacy Of The Blues** Progressive PCD 7102
    As above. 3/93.
*** **Music From The Mauve Decades** Sackville SKCD2-2033
    Ingham; Bobby Gordon (*cl*); Hal Smith (*d*). 4/93.
*** **Just Imagine** . . . Stomp Off CD1285
    Ingham; Peter Ecklund (*c, t*); Dan Barrett (*tb*); Dan Levinson (*cl, Cmel*); Scott Robinson (*cl, ts, bs, bsx*); Marty Grosz (*g, v*); Greg Cohen (*b*); Joe Hanchrow (*tba*); Arnie Kinsella (*d*). 4/94.
*** **New York Nine Vol. 1** Jump JCD12-18
    Ingham; Randy Reinhart (*c, tb*); Dan Barrett (*t, tb*); Phil Bodner (*cl, as*); Scott Robinson (*ss, ts, bs*); James Chirillo (*g*); Vince Giordano (*bsx, b*); Murray Wall (*b*); Arnie Kinsella (*d*). 5/94.
*** **New York Nine Vol. 2** Jump JCD12-19
    As above. 5/94.
***(*) **The Back Room Romp** Sackville SKCD2-3059
    Ingham; Peter Ecklund (*t*); Scott Robinson (*cl, ss, bs*); Harry Allen (*ts*); James Chirillo (*g*); Murray Wall (*b*); Jackie Williams (*d*). 1/95.

Ingham has been busy in the studios of late. The two albums of Billy Strayhorn tunes on Progressive are a light, floating collaboration with the classically styled tenor of Harry Allen. This is Strayhorn done straight, the melodies softly enunciated, the improvisations taken only a few feline steps away from the melodies. Ingham varies the arrangements between groupings of musicians and plays a few tracks solo. Scarcely an adventurous approach to repertory, but satisfyingly done: the second disc just edges ahead since it has the less frequently encountered material.

    Music From The Mauve Decades covers 1900–1920 in terms of material. Some of it is a little too musty, and the normally reliable Smith doesn't always sound appropriate in some of the tunes: a simple duet between Gordon and Ingham might have worked better. But there are still some exquisite moments, such as the lulling 'Just A-Wearyin' For You'. The remaining discs are all by bigger ensembles, and whistle in several of the top repertory players in the field. *Just Imagine* . . . is mostly infectious fun though a shade below the Walter Donaldson set listed above. The two New York Nine albums slip between the 1920s and '30s without any pain, and though the band could still use a little more heat on the fiercer tunes the playing is impeccably crafted. Best of them is perhaps *The Back Room Romp*, which concentrates on the small-band swing repertory of the 1930s. They rescue a couple of Rex Stewart rarities in the title-piece and 'San Juan Hill', and Allen continues his progress from Ben Webster and Paul Gonsalves to something approaching an individual style. Ecklund, though, is irreproachable as usual. Ingham is often content to stay in the shadows on these records, but his calm hand on the arranging tiller seems rock-solid.

Cosmo Intini (born 1958) PIANO

(*) **My Favourite Roots Timeless SJP 339
    Intini; Paolo Fresu (*t, flhn*); Gary Bartz (*ss, as*); Carroll Dashiell (*b*); Victor Lewis (*d*). 5/89.
Intini is a strong if unambitious executant whose music suggests a player keen to make the most of a conservative setting. The Timeless session is clearly a pick-up date, with Bartz sounding prosaic and the rhythm section impersonally alert; yet one of the two originals, 'Powerful Warrior', is a striking theme, and a leisurely stroll through 'When Sunny Gets Blue' is sustained gracefully, with Fresu at his most Milesian. Well recorded, aside from Dashiell's bass, which has a disagreeably buzzing timbre.

Italian Instabile Orchestra ENSEMBLE

***(*) **Italian Instabile Orchestra** Leo CD LR 182
    Pino Minafra (*t, flhn, didjeridu*); Guido Mazzon (*t, flhn*); Alberto Mandarini (*t*); Giancarlo Schiaffini (*tb, tba*); Sebi Tramontana (*tb, v*); Lauro Rossi (*tb*); Martin Mayes (*frhn*); Mario Schiano (*as, v*); Eugenio Colombo (*as, ss, f*); Carlo Actis Dato (*ts, bs, bcl*); Daniele Cavallanti (*ts, bs*); Gianluigi Trovesi (*as, cl in A, bcl*); Renato Geremia (*vn*); Paolo Damiani (*clo, b, v*); Bruno Tommaso (*b*); Giorgio Gaslini (*p*); Vincenzo Mazzone, Tiziano Tononi (*d, perc*). 6/91, 1/92.
Uncategorizable. Founded in 1990 by trumpeter Pino Minafra and the poet Vittorino Curci, the Orchestra was an attempt to compress the whole spectrum of creative music in Italy. The aim was to

create an ensemble with the non-hierarchical range of the Vienna Art Orchestra, the Willem Breuker Kollektief or (no accident that this disc comes from Leo) one of the more theatrical of the Russian free-jazz groups of the 1980s.

Like ARFI in France (of which Louis Sclavis is an adherent) the Orchestra seeks to articulate an 'imaginary folklore', an improbable common ground between popular forms, formal composition and free improvisation. There shouldn't be a strong enough gravitational field to hold it all together but, miraculously, there is. All but one of the pieces were recorded at Radio France's international jazz festival at Rive-de-Gier. The exception is perhaps the key to the whole enterprise. Giorgio Gaslini's 'Pierrot Solaire' proposes a sunshine cure for the moonstruck icon of musical modernism. Relaxed, funny, joyous, you're meant to think it's a long way from Schoenberg, except, of course, he's in there too.

Eugenio Colombo's 'Ippopotami' is a typically amphibian theme; satirically cumbersome ashore, it shows considerable if improbable grace once in the freer element of improvisation. There's also an element of that in Giancarlo Schiaffini's 'La Czarda Dell'Aborigeno', which manages to graft a did-jeridu introduction on to a Hungarian dance and which features fine soloing from Carlo Actis Dato on baritone and transplanted Scot, Martin Mayes, on horn.

Pachyderms reappear in Minafra's 'Noci . . . Strani Frutti', a title that contains one of the Orchestra's carefully veiled allusions to jazz. This has less to do with Billie Holiday's 'Strange Fruit' than with the improbable pickings of surrealist art. Divided into 'African' and 'Indian' sections, it sets Afro-American jazz off against the other major improvisational tradition with a flute *raga* by Colombo. Dato (wearing rubber elephant ears, allegedly) rants a tale of Latin intrigue and passion.

The set opens with cellist Paolo Damiani's 'Detriti', a Noah's ark of musical and textual specimens rescued from the latter-day flood of genres and styles. It ends with 'I Virtuosi De Noci', a free-jazz piece reminiscent of Globe Unity or the Berlin Jazz Orchestra, and a powerful statement of belief in the stabilizing and cohesive power of improvisation.

Itchy Fingers GROUP

*** **Live** Enja 6076-2
> John Graham (*ss, as, ts*); Nigel Hitchcock (*as*); Mike Mower (*ts*); Howard Turner (*bs*). 4/88–6/89.

*** **Full English Breakfast** Enja 7085-2
> Matt Wates (*as*); Pete Long (*cl, as*); Andy Panayi (*ss, as, ts*); David O'Higgins (*ts*); Mike Mower (*ts, bs, cl, f*). 10/92.

The line-up has fluctuated over its existence, but Itchy Fingers are a sax quartet dedicated in the main to the composing of Mike Mower. His scores call for a virtuosity fierce enough to dismay most saxophonists: the originals are fantastically elaborate, and the revision of 'Invitation' on the live record unfolds with Byzantine complexity. The players are all up to it – Hitchcock, for instance, plays his parts with almost inhuman ease – but some may find the incessant brilliance a little wearying. *Live* is mostly fast and furious: the clarinet and flute pairing on 'Dakhut' is ridiculously helter-skelter, and knock-out set-pieces like 'Yuppieville Rodeo' bring cheers from the frequently intrusive audiences. But it's somewhat ironic that the single most memorable piece in the Fingers' repertoire is still John Graham's 'The Devil's Pulpit'.

The studio date is less frantic, but Mower listened back to some of the solos in the original pieces and overdubbed newly fashioned accompaniments. O'Higgins is the best improviser the group has had, and his tenor solo on 'The Dome' adds jazz distinction to Mower's ingenuity.

Cliff Jackson (1902–70) PIANO

*** **Carolina Shout** Black Lion BLCD 760194
> Jackson (*p* solo). 61–62.

He learned to walk – or to stride – by keeping pace with James P. Johnson and Fats Waller, and then he adapted his gait to suit the accelerated pace of swing and its later derivatives. Attempts to portray Jackson as a 'pure' branch of the primitive New York school are doomed to nonsense. What he offered was an engaging commercial hybrid, self-conscious, witty and often slyly clever. He quotes almost subliminally from the old masters and takes delight in hybridizing their and later styles. The whole is something more than its parts, but only a little more.

D. D. Jackson (born 1967) PIANO

***(*) Peace-Song Justin Time JUST 72
> Jackson; David Murray (ts); John Geggie (b); Jean Martin (d). 11/94.

He comes to the music with an intriguing pedigree. His father is an ,academic, specializing in Afro-Hispanic culture, and his mother is Chinese; 'didi' is Cantonese for something like 'bubba' or 'little brother'. Though he grew up in Canada, Jackson had lessons with Don Pullen and was quickly recruited for duties with compatriot Jane Bunnett (herself a student of Pullen's), and then with Billy Bang, Dewey Redman and David Murray.

The saxophonist returns the favour here but, typically, finds it difficult to cede the limelight, and his high-register solo on the opening 'Waltz For A New Life' (not to be confused with Pullen's 'Ode To Life') almost steals the show. Among current players, Jackson perhaps most recalls Jacky Terrasson for his sheer exuberance and vivacity, but there is a much darker and more sombre side to him that takes a moment or two to register. The dedication to a departed older brother ('Funerale') confirms that all has not been plain sailing. Monk is a major influence ('For Monk-Sake'), but the abrasive, minor-key Monk. On his main feature, 'Seasons', and the brief, intense 'Breakout', Jackson attacks the keyboard vigorously. He deserves a fuller sound; a Bösendorfer Imperial generally sounds a touch bigger than this. A very impressive debut, though, and one of the strongest things Justin Time have yet released from the burgeoning Canadian scene.

Duffy Jackson DRUMS, VOCAL

**(*) Swing! Swing! Swing! Milestone MCD-9233-2
> Jackson; Bill Prince, Ken Faulks, Luis Aquino, Jeff Kivit, Reilly Mullins, Barry Rios, John Bailey (t); Phil Gray, Dana Teboe, Greg Cox (tb); Billy Ross, Ed Calle, Chip McNeill, Ed Maina, Neil Bonsanti, Rob Scheps, Gary Campbell, Todd Del Giudice (reeds); Mike Levine, Larry Ham, Roger Wilder (p); Joe Cohn (g); Jay Leonhart, Jeff Grubbs (b); Robert Thomas (perc); Chubby Jackson (v). 95.

Duffy is Chubby Jackson's son, and he doesn't let us forget it – 'I'm Just A Son Of A Bass Player' is the second tune, and Jackson Senior steps up to scat on 'Lemon Drop'. This is showbiz jazz of a modestly entertaining mien. A few boppish scores get out from under Jackson's grasp and a few soloists have their say, which is about as far as it goes. Bob Weinstock continues a seemingly inauspicious second-time-around career as producer.

Ed Jackson (born 1959) ALTO SAXOPHONE

***(*) Wake Up Call New World CounterCurrents NW 80451
> Jackson; James Zoller (t, f); Clark Gayton (tb); Tom Varner (frhn); Jamie Baum (f); Rich Rothenberg (ts); John Stetch (p); Dave Jackson (b); Steve Johns (d). 94.

A member of the 29th Street Saxophone Quartet, Jackson stands in the same relationship to this group as the late Julius Hemphill did to the World Saxophone Quartet, its most disruptive element and, paradoxically, its most adventurous formal composer. Wake Up Call is Jackson's debut as leader and it is thoroughly impressive. The range of sounds is unusual, with excellent use of the inventive Varner, and there is a near-perfect balance between those same qualities, the subversive, centrifugal spin of impro-visation and the more centred, centripetal tug of Jackson's well-thought-out, somewhat Mingus-like compositions.

Franz Jackson (born 1912) CLARINET

*** Franz Jackson's Original Jass All-Stars OJC 1824-2
> Jackson; Bob Shoffner (t); John Thomas (tb); Rozelle Claxton (p); Lawrence Dixon (bj); Bill Oldham (tba); Bill Curry (d). 9/61.

One of the best in this series of revivals from the Riverside catalogue's 'Chicago Living Legends' sequence. Jackson was something of a modernist compared to the others – he worked with Earl Hines in the 1940s, playing mainly tenor sax – and he approaches the ten warhorses in this programme with gusto, thick-toned and hard-hitting. Shoffner and Thomas, much older hands, play with comparative reserve but, while Jackson is right up in the front of the mix, they seem to be at the back of the room. Nevertheless Shoffner, who was already in his sixties, sounds well, and Thomas plays better than he ever did with Louis Armstrong. The steady-rolling rhythm is maintained throughout by the other four, and they all kick their feet up on a spiffing 'King Porter Stomp'.

Javon Jackson TENOR SAXOPHONE

*** **Me And Mr Jones** Criss Cross CRISS 1053
    Jackson; James Williams (*p*); Christian McBride (*b*); Elvin Jones (*d*). 12/91.
***(*) **When The Time Is Right** Blue Note TOCJ 5924
    Jackson; Kenny Garrett (*as*); Jacky Terrasson (*p*); Chris Thomas, Peter Washington (*b*); Carl Allen, Clarence Penn (*d*); Dianne Reeves (*v*). 9 & 10/93.
***(*) **For One Who Knows** Blue Note CDP 8 30244
    Jackson; Jacky Terrasson (*p*); Fareed Haque (*g*); Peter Washington (*b*); Billy Drummond (*d*); Cyro Baptista (*perc*). 95.
Mr Jones is, of course, drummer Elvin, with whom Jackson worked a productive internship after his stint in the Messengers. Whatever else he learned from these luminaries, he has emerged as a leader of tremendous resourcefulness and self-confidence. Even if his soloing still doesn't sound completely mature, his sense of purpose is unmistakable.

The first disc leans heavily on a restricted range of ideas and tempos and could sound a little formulaic compared to the later Blue Notes. Here Jackson benefits from more thoughtful production – Betty Carter has a hand in *When The Time Is Right* – and a more relaxed approach to the material. His writing is quite blunt and unambiguous, sometimes a little too assertive, but that too will sort itself out when the time is right. The third album finds him, as it should, developing strongly and moving out into new areas of concern. There is a splendid trio version of Rollins's seldom-covered 'Paradox' which suggests another source for a young player who has done his utmost to steer clear of bargain-basement Traneism.

That the best of the tracks should be a trio is perhaps suggestive. For all Jackson's progress, the band on *For One Who Knows* simply isn't as good. Terrasson has his own ideas now and is unwilling to be held in check. Good as Drummond is, in a School of Blakey way, he doesn't quite suit the more lyrical and legato new style and is apt to chop up the time feel rather than letting it breathe. Hard to fault any of these on more serious counts, though. Jackson is a happening player who will make a substantial career for himself.

Milt Jackson (born 1923) VIBES, PIANO, VOCAL

(*) **In The Beginning Original Jazz Classics OJC-1771
    Jackson; Russell Jacquet (*t*); J. J. Johnson (*tb*); Sonny Stitt (*as*); Leo Parker (*bs*); Sir Charles Thompson, John Lewis (*p*); Al Jackson (*b*); Kenny Clarke (*d*); Chano Pozo (*perc*). 47–48.
Obscure beginnings, though Jackson had already made a remarkable debut with Dizzy Gillespie on the sextet session for Victor which produced the astonishing 'Anthropology'. But there is nothing primitive about the playing on the four quartet tracks with three-quarters of the MJQ, from 1948, where Jackson's ballad playing on 'In A Beautiful Mood' matches the title. An earlier sextet date is more conventional bebop.

*** **Roll 'Em Bags** Savoy SV-0110
    Jackson; Kenny Dorham (*t, p*); Julius Watkins (*frhn*); Lucky Thompson, Billy Mitchell (*ts*); Wade Legge (*p*); Curley Russell, Wendell Marshall (*b*); Kenny Clarke (*d*). 1/49–1/56.
*** **Meet Milt Jackson** Savoy SV-0172
    Jackson; Bill Massey (*t*); Henry Coker (*tb*); Julius Watkins (*frhn*); Frank Morgan (*as*); Walter Benton, Billy Mitchell, Lucky Thompson (*ts*); Charlie Fowlkes (*bs*); Walter Bishop Jr, Wade Legge, Gerald Wiggins (*p*); Nelson Boyd, Percy Heath, Eddie Jones, Wendell Marshall (*b*); Roy Haynes, Kenny Clarke (*d*). 2/49–1/56.
*** **Opus De Jazz** Savoy SV-0109
    Jackson; Frank Wess (*ts, f*); Hank Jones (*p*); Eddie Jones (*b*); Kenny Clarke (*d*). 10/55.
**** **The Jazz Skyline** Savoy SV-0173
    Jackson; Lucky Thompson (*ts*); Hank Jones (*p*); Wendell Marshall (*b*); Kenny Clarke (*d*). 1/56.
**** **Jackson's-Ville** Savoy SV-0175
    As above. 1/56.
Milt Jackson is one of those jazz musicians – like Jack Teagarden or Zoot Sims – whose consistency on record is peerless. He seldom if ever falls below a high level of execution, which means that all his records are worth hearing, though the price for that is a certain blandness: deprived of any direct or formal challenges to his great facility as a player, he's been stuck in a rut of mere excellence for 40 or so

years. He saw little real action in the studios during the bebop era, and the handful of late-'40s tracks on the two earlier Savoy sessions find him in an ancillary role; those on *Roll 'Em Bags*, for instance, seem to be peculiarly dominated by Julius Watkins. This is rote Savoy bebop. But the 1955-6 sessions are among his classic statements. *Opus De Jazz* is slightly less interesting, since Wess is less intriguing than Thompson and the tracks ramble on a bit: the two to have are *The Jazz Skyline* and *Jackson's-Ville*, since they find the leader and Lucky Thompson in perfect, memorable accord. Cut on two January days in 1956, with a near-ideal rhythm section (Hank Jones replaces Wade Legge on the later of the two), this is cool, reflective bebop, lightly shot through with the blues. Jackson's dexterity and fine understanding of his instrument's capabilities blend with the smooth yet questing improvisations by Thompson to a degree rarely matched in such impromptu situations. Since these reissues follow the original LP form, the sessions are somewhat irritatingly split between SV-0110, SV-0172, SV0173 and SV-0175, but the latter two at least are quite indispensable. The remastering seems very well done.

**** **Milt Jackson** Blue Note B21Y-81509
 Jackson; Lou Donaldson, Sahib Shihab (*as*); Thelonious Monk, John Lewis (*p*); Percy Heath,
 John Simmons, Al McKibbon (b); Shadow Wilson, Art Blakey, Kenny Clarke (*d*). 6/48–4/52.
Six of these tracks can also be found on records under Monk's name, while a quintet date with Donaldson and what was to become the MJQ was first issued as a 10-inch LP. The tracks with Monk are flawless classics, rising to their greatest height with the riveting version of 'I Mean You', while the other date, though at a less exalted level, finds Jackson quite at home with Donaldson's uncomplicated, bluesy bop. The CD is currently a US-only release.

*** **MJQ** Original Jazz Classics OJC 125
 Jackson; Henry Boozier (*t*); Horace Silver (*p*); Percy Heath (*b*); Kenny Clarke (*d*). 6/54.
*** **Milt Jackson** Original Jazz Classics OJC 001
 Jackson; Horace Silver (*p*); Percy Heath (*b*); Connie Kay (*d*). 5/55.
MJQ features four titles by the personnel listed (the remainder are by a first-generation MJQ). Though no more than a pick-up date, all concerned play well. *Milt Jackson* is more substantial, but the preponderance of slow tempos lends a rather sleepy air to the date: the exception is 'Stonewall', a blues with a 13-chorus vibes solo that effectively defines the principles of Jackson's art. Remastering up to the strong OJC standard.

*** **Bags Meets Trane** Atlantic 1553-2
 Jackson; John Coltrane *(ts)*; Hank Jones (*p*); Paul Chambers (*b*); Connie Kay (*d*). 1/59.
The surviving album from Jackson's Atlantic period is a solid if relatively unambitious meeting of giants. Always the most unprejudiced of collaborators, Milt simply goes ahead and blows, and though Coltrane is on the verge of his first great breakthroughs, he responds to the less fearsome blues situations with his usual majestic command.

*** **Bags' Opus** Blue Note B21Y 84458-2
 Jackson; Art Farmer (*t*); Benny Golson (*ts*); Tommy Flanagan (p); Paul Chambers (b); Connie
 Kay (d). 12/58.
**** **Bags Meets Wes** Original Jazz Classics OJC 240
 Jackson; Wynton Kelly (*p*); Wes Montgomery (*g*); Sam Jones (*b*); Philly Joe Jones (*d*). 12/61.
(*) **Invitation Original Jazz Classics OJC 260
 Jackson; Kenny Dorham, Virgil Jones (*t*); Jimmy Heath (*ts*); Tommy Flanagan (*p*); Ron Carter
 (*b*); Connie Kay (*d*). 8–11/62.
*** **Big Bags** Original Jazz Classics OJC 366
 Jackson; Clark Terry (*t, flhn*); Bernie Glow, Ernie Royal, Snooky Young, Doc Severinsen, Dave
 Burns (*t*); Jimmy Cleveland, Melba Liston, Paul Faulise, Tom McIntosh (*tb*); Willie Ruff (*frhn*);
 James Moody (*as, ts, f*); Earl Warren, George Dorsey, Jerome Richardson (*as*); Jimmy Heath
 (*ts*); Tate Houston, Arthur Clarke (*bs*); Hank Jones (*p*); Ron Carter (*b*); Connie Kay, Philly Joe
 Jones (*d*). 6–7/62.
*** **At The Village Gate** Original Jazz Classics OJC 309
 Jackson; Jimmy Heath (*ts*); Hank Jones (*p*); Bob Cranshaw (*b*); Albert 'Tootie' Heath (*d*). 12/
 63.
*** **For Someone I Love** Original Jazz Classics OJC 404
 Jackson; Clark Terry, Thad Jones, Dave Burns, Snooky Young, Bill Berry, Elmon Wright (*t*);
 Quentin Jackson, Jimmy Cleveland, Jack Rains, Tom McIntosh (*tb*); Bob Northern, Julius
 Watkins, Ray Alonge, Willie Ruff, Paul Ingraham (*frhn*); Hank Jones, Jimmy Jones (*p*); Major
 Holley (*tba*); Richard Davis (*b*); Connie Kay, Charli Persip (*d*). 3–8/63.
Jackson was firmly ensconced in the MJQ by this time, but occasional blowing dates were something he obviously enjoyed, and his association with Riverside led to some more challenging situations. The stray session reissued on Blue Note is agreeable if desultory, with Jackson intruding slightly on the established

front line of Farmer and Golson. *Invitation* is somewhat disappointing, given the personnel: some of the tunes are cut off short, and Dorham and Heath never quite get into it as they might. Heath fares better on the live date from the Village Gate, which works mostly from a blues base. *Big Bags* puts Jackson to work in some Ernie Wilkins arrangements for orchestra, and there is a puissant 'Round Midnight' among the charts (an alternative take is also included on the CD reissue), although the vibraphonist's impassive assurance isn't ideal for this situation. *For Someone I Love* is another try at the same sort of thing, though here the front lines are all brass, working from charts by Melba Liston. Jackson approaches it in just the same way, digging in hard on 'Extraordinary Blues', rhapsodic on 'Days Of Wine And Roses'. The best of this group is the meeting with Wes Montgomery. This time the tunes seem just the right length, even on a miniature like the ballad, 'Stairway To The Stars', and the quintet lock into an irresistible groove on the up-tempo themes. The CD includes three alternative takes, all worth having.

*** **Statements** Impulse! GRP 11302
        Jackson; Jimmy Heath (*ts*); Hank Jones, Tommy Flanagan (*p*); Paul Chambers, Richard Davis (*b*); Connie Kay (*d*). 12/61–8/64.
Jackson's associations with other pianists besides John Lewis have been insufficiently remarked on, and he secures a fine camaraderie with both Jones and Flanagan here. The CD is split between the original programme of eight quartet tracks and five by the quintet with Heath, but it's a pity that some strong ideas – the arrangement of Jackson's own 'Statement' or Flanagan's tantalizing introduction to 'I Got It Bad' – get lost in otherwise rote studio surroundings. Remastering is fairly good, although the cloudy bass on the first session doesn't do Chambers any favours.

** **Sunflower** CTI ZK-40800
        Jackson; Freddie Hubbard (*t, flhn*); Herbie Hancock (*p*); Jay Berliner (*g*); Ron Carter (*b*); Billy Cobham (*d*); Ralph MacDonald (*perc*); strings. 72.
A stray one from a brief association with Creed Taylor. Probably mercifully brief, since this promising line-up gets lost in soupy Don Sebesky orchestrations and runs aground on 'What Are You Doing The Rest Of Your Life'. Jackson salvages a few nice lines for posterity.

*** **The Big Three** Original Jazz Classics OJC 805
        Jackson; Joe Pass (*g*); Ray Brown (*b*). 8/75.
*** **Montreux '77** Original Jazz Classics OJC 375
        Jackson; Clark Terry (*t*); Eddie 'Lockjaw' Davis (*ts*); Monty Alexander (*p*); Ray Brown (*b*); Jimmie Smith (*d*). 7/77.
** **Feelings** Original Jazz Classics OJC 448
        Jackson; Hubert Laws, Jerome Richardson (*f*); Tommy Flanagan (*p*); Dennis Budimir (*g*); Ray Brown (*b*); Jimmie Smith (*d*); strings. 4/76.
*** **Soul Fusion** Original Jazz Classics OJC-731
        Jackson; Monty Alexander (*p*); John Clayton (*b*); Jeff Hamilton (*d*). 6/77.
***(*) **Milt Jackson + Count Basie + The Big Band Vol. 1** Original Jazz Classics OJC 740
        Jackson; Waymon Reed, Lyn Biviano, Sonny Cohn, Pete Minger (*t*); Bill Hughes, Mel Wanzo, Fred Wesley, Dennis Wilson (*tb*); Danny Turner, Bobby Plater (*as*); Eric Dixon (*ts, f*); Kenny Hing (*ts*); Charlie Fowlkes (*bs*); Count Basie (*p*); Freddie Green (*g*); John Clayton (*b*); Butch Miller (*d*). 1/78.
***(*) **Milt Jackson + Count Basie + The Big Band Vol. 2** Original Jazz Classics OJC 741
        As above. 1/78.
*** **All Too Soon** Original Jazz Classics OJC 450
        Jackson; Joe Pass (*g*); Ray Brown (*b*); Mickey Roker (*d*). 1/80.
*** **Night Mist** Original Jazz Classics OJC 827
        Jackson; Harry Edison (*t*); Eddie Cleanhead Vinson (*as*); Eddie 'Lockjaw' Davis (*ts*); Art Hillery (*p*); Ray Brown (*b*); Lawrence Marable (*d*). 4/80.
***(*) **Ain't But A Few Of Us Left** Original Jazz Classics OJC 785
        Jackson; Oscar Peterson (*p*); Ray Brown (*b*); Grady Tate (*d*). 11/81.
***(*) **It Don't Mean A Thing If You Can't Tap Your Foot To It** Original Jazz Classics OJC 601
        Jackson; Cedar Walton (*p*); Ray Brown (*b*); Mickey Roker (*d*). 7/84.
*(*) **Soul Believer** Original Jazz Classics OJC 686
        Jackson; Plas Johnson (*ts*); Cedar Walton (*p*); Dennis Budimir (*g*); Ray Brown (*b*); Billy Higgins (*d*). 9/78.
(*) **Bags' Bag Pablo 2310-842
        Jackson; Cedar Walton (*p*); Vaughan Andre, John Collins (*g*); Ray Brown (*b*); Billy Higgins, Frank Severino (*d*).

*** **Soul Route** Pablo 2310-900
>   Jackson; Gene Harris (*p*); Ray Brown (*b*); Mickey Roker (*d*). 11–12/83.
*** **Brother Jim** Pablo 2310-916
>   Jackson; Jimmy Heath, Harold Vick (*ss, ts*); Cedar Walton (*p*); Joe Pass (*g*); Bob Cranshaw (*b*);
>   Mickey Roker (*d*). 5/85.
*** **A London Bridge** Pablo 2310-932
>   Jackson; Monty Alexander (*p*); Ray Brown (*b*); Mickey Roker (*d*). 4/82.
*** **Mostly Duke** Pablo 2310-944
>   As above. 4/82.
*** **Memories Of Thelonious Sphere Monk** Pablo
>   As above. 4/82.
*** **The Best Of Milt Jackson** Pablo 2405-405
>   Compilation from the above. 77–82.

Jackson's signing to Pablo – which also snared the MJQ for a time – brought forth a flood of albums, nearly all of which are now available on CD. Just as he did with Count Basie, Granz basically set Milt up in the studio and let him go, which means that all these records are solidly entertaining without ever quite going the extra distance and becoming a classic.

One of the most obvious mix-and-match situations, though, proved to be a winner: the two albums with Basie, cut at a single session in 1978. Here are two kindred spirits, both in love with playing the blues, giving it their best shot, and with the orchestra in towering form behind them. There are a few small-group tracks, but it's mostly the big band with Jackson taking most of the solos, Basie restricting himself to the occasional rejoinder. The only disappointment must be that the material is nearly all Basie warhorses; but it gives Jackson the unshakeable platform which his previous records with a big band never finally secured.On 'Lil' Darlin'' he sounds gorgeous, and on a stomper like Ernie Wilkins's 'Basie' the studio nearly goes up in smoke, even if it's always a controlled explosion with this band.

Most of the other records keep to a high standard. *The Big Three*, a typical Granz set-up of masters, works pretty well – there is a lovely 'Nuages', and Pass digs in unusually strongly on a fast 'Blue Bossa' – without making a very deep impression. *Soul Believer*, where Jackson sings, is eminently avoidable, and the strings album, *Feelings*, is pretty but disposable. The Montreux jam session is slightly above par for this kind of course. Of the remainder, another standout is the quartet date on *It Don't Mean A Thing*. Cedar Walton and Jackson inspire each other to their best form, and an intensely swinging 'If I Were A Bell' and the Ellington near-title-track, taken at a daringly relaxed tempo, are marvels. *Soul Route*, with Gene Harris on piano, is another good one. *Ain't But A Few Of Us Left* is as swinging as the best Peterson records can be, and Jackson seems to have enjoyed his meeting with the great man: 'Body And Soul', set off with a bossa feel, is impressive, and they take a luxurious time over 'If I Should Lose You'. *All Too Soon* is a little too laid-back as an Ellington tribute and *Brother Jim* is merely very good. The rest of the band sometimes get in Jackson's way on *Night Mist*, an all-blues programme, but – pro that he is – Bags settles into the situation and takes some typically collected solos. *A London Bridge* and *Mostly Duke* were cut at the same engagement at Ronnie Scott's in London, and Alexander's carousing piano parts are an interesting foil for Jackson's imperturbable solos. *Memories Of Thelonious Sphere Monk*, from the same occasion, is also good, but in a sense a wasted opportunity. A full-scale meditation on Monk by Jackson, one of his canniest interpreters, should have been set down before now; here, though, three of the four themes are tossed to the other members of the quartet as features, and Bags tackles only the comparatively straightforward 'In Walked Bud'.

(*) **The Harem Musicmasters 5061-2
>   Jackson; Jimmy Heath (*ss, ts*); James Moody (*f*); Cedar Walton (*p*); Bob Cranshaw (*b*); Kenny
>   Washington (*d*). 12/90.

A largely disappointing meeting of some considerable talents. Heath's soprano and Moody's flute were an odd choice for a lead sound, and the arrangements seem beached by tempos that sound sluggish when they ought to wing. Nor does the thin studio sound help. But Jackson, as ever, has his moments, particularly on the title-track and 'Holy Land'.

(*) **Reverence And Compassion Qwest/Reprise 945204-2
>   Jackson; Oscar Brashear (*t*); George Bohannon (*tb*); Jeff Clayton (*as*); Gary Foster (*ts, f*);
>   Ronald Brown (*ts*); Jack Nimitz (*bs, bcl*); Cedar Walton (*p*); John Clayton (*b*); Billy Higgins (*d*);
>   strings. 92.

Hugely overproduced, with thunderous orchestral arrangements draped over and round the music, but Jackson and his rhythm section still manage to make worthwhile music when the smoke clears. 'Young And Foolish' and the dreaded 'How Do You Keep The Music Playing' may sound like high-class mood music, but when the quartet digs into 'Bullet Bag' and 'Reverence' it sounds like the real thing.

*** **The Prophet Speaks** Qwest/Reprise 945591-2
>   Jackson; Joshua Redman (*ts*); Cedar Walton (*p*); John Clayton (*b*); Billy Higgins (*d*); Joe
>   Williams (*v*). 93.

*** **Burnin' In The Woodhouse** Qwest/Reprise 945918-2
>   Jackson; Nicholas Payton (*t*); Jesse Davis (*as*); Joshua Redman (*ts*); Benny Green (*p*); Christian
>   McBride (*b*); Kenny Washington (*d*). 94.

Milt's tenure with Qwest/Reprise is offering him some nice opportunities to play, but these are still largely unremarkable records. *The Prophet Speaks* features guest Redman on several tracks, and when they take on Monk's 'Off Minor' the intensity goes up a notch. The magisterial Walton is also good value: try his sly blues deconstruction on 'Five O'Clock In The Morning'. But the music has no real fire, and Joe Williams sounds past it on his three features. The horns play on only three tracks of *Burnin' In The Woodhouse*, which is more like a slow simmer than anything with flames in it. Jackson's vibes sound different on all three of his records for this company, and they're notably muffled on the last two.

Ronald Shannon Jackson (born 1940) DRUMS, PERCUSSION, OTHER INSTRUMENTS

*** **Raven Roc** DIW 862
>   Jackson; Jef Lee Johnson, David Fiuczynski (*g*); Dom Richards (*b*). 2/92.

*** **What Spirit Say** DIW 895
>   Jackson; James Carter (*ts, ss*); Martin Atangana, Jef Lee Johnson (*g*); Ngolle Pokossi (*d*). 12/94.

The sound of Shannon Jackson's Decoding Society is characteristically an unsettling amalgam of dark, swampy vamps, huge, distorted chorales, and sudden outbursts of urban noise. Decoded, it yields up a huge range of putative influences, from Albert Ayler's increasingly abstract and fissile music (Shannon played with the saxophonist in the early 1960s), to Mingus's open-ended compositional style, to Ornette Coleman's harmolodics, to black and white thrash-metal music; it was James Blood Ulmer's brutal funk *Are You Glad To Be In America?* that established the drummer's reputation in Europe. He in turn has had a powerful impact on such currently fashionable outfits as Decoding Society guitarist Vernon Reid's Living Color and the Black Rock Coalition, while his work with the heavyweight Last Exit has spawned a shoal of imitators.

Though *Decode Yourself* enjoyed considerable popular success, it is not around at present. Jackson had spent much of the 1970s in obscurity and has had to suffer oversights and unimaginative marketing throughout his career. *The* drummer of the late 1980s looked like making only a slow and uneasy accommodation to the new decade, but *Raven Roc* found him in pleasingly murky and bad-tempered form, battering out themes of authentic unpleasantness like 'Sexual Drum Dance' and 'Hatched Spirit Blues'. The upgraded Decoding Society lacks some of its predecessors' metallic blare, but Jackson makes it clear that he doesn't need horns, and the guitarists demonstrate that they don't need optional extras like technique. A record to impress your Gothic niece with.

What Spirit Say is more from the same dark place, though the addition of saxophone in place of a second guitar gives the music a more vocalized and thus more humane sound. There is always a twinkle about Jackson, a slimmed-down, pawky version of the fat boy who 'wants to make yer flesh creep'. There's more sheer fun and soul food in his 'Sorcerer's Kitchen' than he'd like to pretend.

Willis Jackson (1928–87) TENOR SAXOPHONE

** **Call Of The Gators** Delmark DD-460
>   Jackson; Andrew Fats Ford, Bobby Johnson (*t*); Booty Wood, Bobby Range (*tb*); Haywood
>   Henry, Ben Kynard, Reuben Phillips (*bs*); Bill Doggett, Arnold Jarvis, Duke Anderson (*p*);
>   Leonard Swain, Lee Stanfield (*b*); Joe Murphy, Panama Francis (*d*). 1–5/50.

*** **Please Mr Jackson** Original Jazz Clasics OJC 321
>   Jackson; Jack McDuff (*org*); Bill Jennings (*g*); Tommy Potter (*b*); Alvin Johnson (*d*). 5/59.

*** **Willis Jackson With Pat Martino** Prestige 24161-2
>   Jackson; Frank Robinson (*p*); Carl Wilson (*b*); Joe Hadrick (*d*). 3/64.

(*) **Bar Wars Muse MCD 5162
>   Jackson; Charles Earland (*org*); Pat Martino (*g*); Idris Muhammed (*d*); Buddy Caldwell (*perc*).
>   12/77.

Willis 'Gator' Jackson made a lot of records for Prestige and Muse, most of them in the tenor-and-organ format, but there's not many of them around at present. Delmark have reminded us of where he began with a compilation of ancient R&B sides: leathery, honking solos coughed out over sloppy-joe rhythms, good fun provided you don't have to hear more than a couple of tracks at a time. His long stint as a soul-sax man at Prestige has lately been rewarded with a couple of reissues, one with the young Pat

Martino: reliably gritty playing by all hands, and – again – taken a few minutes at a time, this stuff can sound great. But don't expect a CD to have staying power.

Bar Wars, the sole survivor of his more recent albums, is at least one of the best: solid material, a hard-hitting band, and Jackson cheerfully blowing the blues. The CD includes some extra takes over the original LP issue.

C. W. Jacobi's Bottomland Orchestra GROUP

*** A Tribute To Clarence Williams Stomp Off CD1266

> Roland Pilz (*c, v*); René Hagmann (*tb*); Matthias Seuffert (*cl, as*); Claus Jacobi (*cl, as, ts*); Rurik Van Heys (*p*); Gunter Russel (*bj*); Dietrich Kleine-Horst (*tba*); Gunter Andernach (*wbd, perc*); Gaby 'Ottilie' Schulz (*v*). 3/93.

Despite Williams's widespread influence on early jazz, only three of the 18 tunes here – 'Baby Won't You Please Come Home', 'I Wish I Could Shimmy Like My Sister Kate' and 'Old Folks' Shuffle' – could be called standards. Yet the entire programme is played with easy panache and fluency by this splendid outfit of German connoisseurs. The remarkable Hagmann is on loan from The Dry Throat Fellows, playing trombone this time, and the reed players get very close to the warbling style of their 1920s counterparts; Pilz, too, makes a good fist of the Ed Allen cornet parts. The result is a bright, happy session which flirts with the novelty flavour that Williams himself traded on without succumbing to it: symbolic in this regard is the ferocious trashing of 'Anywhere Sweetie Goes (I'll Be There)', but almost anything here would have sounded just fine on an original Vocalion of 65 years earlier.

Illinois Jacquet (born 1922) TENOR SAXOPHONE, BASSOON, VOCALS

*** Flying Home Bluebird ND 90638

> Jacquet; Russell Jacquet (*t, v*); Joe Newman (*t*); J. J. Johnson (*tb*); Ray Perry (*as*); Leo Parker (*bs*); Maurice Simon (*bs*); Milt Buckner, Cedric Haywood, Sir Charles Thompson (*p*); Lionel Hampton (*vib*); John Collins (*g*); George Duvivier, Al Lucas (*b*); Alan Dawson, Jo Jones, Shadow Wilson (*d*). 12/47, 4/49, 5/50, 7/67.

***(*) Flying Home: The Best Of The Verve Years Verve 521644

> Jacquet; Roy Eldridge, Russell Jacquet, Joe Newman, Elmon Wright, Lamar Wright Jr (*t*); Henry Coker, Matthew Gee (*tb*); Ernie Henry, Earle Warren (*as*); Count Hastings, Ben Webster (*ts*); Cecil Payne (*bs*); Johnny Acea, Carl Perkins, Hank Jones, Jimmy Jones, Sir Charles Thompson (*p*); Count Basie, Wild Bill Davis, Gerry Wiggins (*org*); Irving Ashby, Kenny Burrell, John Collins, Herb Ellis, Freddie Green, Oscar Moore, Gene Ramey, Joe Sinacore (*g*); Ray Brown, Red Callender, Curtis Counce, Al Lucas (*b*); Al Bartee, Art Blakey, Jimmy Crawford, J. C. Heard, Osie Johnson, Jo Jones, Johnny Williams, Shadow Wilson (*d*); Chano Pozo (*perc*). 1 & 5/51, 3, 7 & 12/52, 12/53, 12/54, 11/55, 10/56, 4/58.

Born in Broussard, Louisiana, and raised in Houston, Texas, you somehow just know how Illinois Jacquet is going to sound. It's a big blues tone, edged with a kind of desperate loneliness that somehow underlines Jacquet's status as a permanent guest star, an unbreakable mustang of a player who was never really given either the right amount of room or genuinely sympathetic sidemen. He learned his showmanship in the Lionel Hampton band of the early 1940s, trading on his remarkable facility in the 'false' upper register and on sheer energy.

Jacquet seems permanently saddled with the largely meaningless 'Texas tenor' tag. In fact, his playing can show remarkable sensitivity (as on many of these late-1960s sessions) and he is one of the fastest thinkers in the business. His ability to take care of his own business was obvious from the shrewd self-management that kept him in the forefront of Norman Granz's Jazz At The Philharmonic, a story that has yet to be told in revealing detail. Jacquet's work for Verve is gathered on the later of two compilations here called *Flying Home*, named after the Benny Goodman–Lionel Hampton–Sid Robin tune that became his calling card. Brian Priestley has made an intelligent selection and sequence of the Granz recordings, placing quite a bit of emphasis on the 1951 and 1952 sessions that made up the two volumes of *Illinois Jacquet Collates*, which were issued on Verve's elder sibling, Clef, like all the other tracks on offer. It's a selection of big-band and small-group settings (the latter featuring a diversity of accompanists, covering the elegant Hank Jones and the eccentric Carl Perkins). Only 'No Sweet', from the 1958 *Cool Rage*, and some of the material from the less reflective organ groups disappoint.

Despite the apparent chronological spread, the Bluebird *Flying Home* is essentially a sampling of Jacquet's late-1940s work, with a single track, the concluding title-shot, from the Newport Festival in 1967 on which the tune's co-author Lionel Hampton is the main attraction. The rest of the material is typical high-energy Jacquet. Not much sophistication, compared to what he was capable of in other contexts, but jolly, soulful jazz all the same. The bands are always rather distanced in the mix (with the distinctive baritones too far back for proper effect), and there's a good deal of tape-hiss, but the sound-quality is generally very faithful to the original and there has been no obvious attempt to clear Jacquet's distinctive tone, which always sounds as if it should have Vick rubbed on it. For sheer grandstanding, it's hard to beat his manically repeated two-note figure on the opening 'Jet Propulsion'. It seems to go on for ever. With the exception of the above-mentioned title-piece, all the material is by Jacquet (Russell Jacquet sings and wins a co-credit on 'Try Me One More Time') and offers a valuable introduction to his less recognized talent.

Jacquet's style didn't really develop in the accepted sense. His great virtue was consistency and, while this is a plus in a gigging musician, it is somewhat at a discount in the studio, where surprises, new wrinkles and out-and-out rethinks are called for.

*** The Soul Explosion Original Jazz Classics OJC 674
Jacquet; Russell Jacquet, Joe Newman, Ernie Royal (*t*); Matthew Gee (*tb*); Frank Foster (*ts*); Cecil Payne (*bs*); Milt Buckner (*org*); Wally Richardson (*g*); Al Lucas (*b*); Al Foster (*d*). 3/69.

*** Bottoms Up Original Jazz Classics OJC 417
Jacquet; Barry Harris (*p*); Ben Tucker (*b*); Alan Dawson (*d*). 68.

*** The Blues, That's Me! Original Jazz Classics OJC 614
Jacquet; Wynton Kelly (*p*); Tiny Grimes (*g*); Buster Williams (*b*); Oliver Jackson (*d*). 9/69.

Jacquet seldom played the blues better than on these good sets, which were originally released on Prestige. Not much to be said about the music, except that the large-group material on *The Soul Explosion* is more sophisticated than might be supposed. Fine versions of 'Still King' and 'Round About Midnight' on *The Blues, That's Me!*, both of which demonstrate, in markedly different ways, the delicacy of Jacquet's touch. Neither will disappoint.

*** The Comeback Black Lion BLCD 760160
Jacquet; Milt Buckner (*org*); Tony Crombie (*d*). 4/71.

Of all the organists Jacquet worked with, it was Buckner with whom he worked up the closest rapport. Their exchanges on the two Ellington tunes that form the bulk of this Ronnie Scott's session from 1971 (not a comeback at all – that's the title of one of the pieces) are full of the sort of understanding that lifts this above the immediately apparent roar-and-rave. Recorded in the presence of Stan Getz, though not of Ella Fitzgerald, as Jacquet claims (the scat vocal on 'I Wanna Blow' is his own), it reflects little of Getz's legendary finesse, but it's undoubtedly energetic and entertaining stuff, and one shouldn't be too condescending about its more unsophisticated elements.

**(*) Illinois Jacquet And Wild Bill Davis Black & Blue 233044
Jacquet; Wild Bill Davis (*org*); Al Bartee. 1/73.

*** Jacquet's Street Black & Blue BLE 59.112
Jacquet; Francis Williams (*t*); Alfred Cobbs (*tb*); Milt Buckner (*p, org*); George Duvivier, Roland Lobligeois (*b*); Oliver Jackson, Jo Jones (*d*). 1/74, 7/76.

Typical of Black & Blue's rather jolly catalogue, these are friendly and pleasurable sessions, clearly and faithfully transferred to CD. The earlier has Jacquet in familiar organ-and-drums setting; not as sympathetic a collaboration as the very successful trio with Milt Buckner (a Black & Blue stalwart) and Jo Jones, but there are some rousing performances, notably 'Blue Skies (Trumpets No End)' and a gentler 'The Man I Love'.

Jean-Marc Jafet BASS, PERCUSSION

***(*) Agora JMS 18639
Jafet; Stéphane Belmondo (*t*); Denis Leloup (*tb*); Eric Seva (*ss*); Jean-Yves Candela (*p, syn*); Sylvain Luc (*g*); Marc Berthoumieux (*acc, syn*); Thierry Eliez (*syn*); Thierry Arpino, André Ceccarelli (*d*); François Constantin, François Laizeau (*perc*). 7/93, 9/94.

Jean-Marie Salhani's JMS label has been an important sponsor of new talent in France, giving players enough time and resources to develop ideas that might not otherwise see the light of day. Jafet is very much in the Henri Texier mould and there might be some doubt about the originality of some of his compositional ideas. However, his real skill, and Salhani's, is in collaging a wide range of sounds (and the synths expand the palette considerably) to create new entities that seem to be much larger than the basic band. Belmondo and Leloup are both gifted players, with an accent on sonority over straight harmonic blowing, and Jafet's devotion to Miles Davis and Jaco Pastorius opens up areas of contemporary non-jazz usage.

Andrzej Jagodzinski PIANO

**** **Chopin** Polonia CD 022
    Jagodzinski; Adam Cegielski (*b*); Czeslaw Bartkowski (*d*). 12/93.
Most attempts to jazz up classical composers are doomed to failure, but Jagodzinski manages to avoid the 'switched-on Bach' approach, listening out for those aspects of Chopin's celebrated pianism which are most jazz-like, rather than attempting to impose it from the outside. This is a convincing exploratory essay, containing some very beautiful and unaffected music. It may be hard to overcome initial scepticism, but it will be worth the suspension of disbelief.

Ahmad Jamal (born 1930) PIANO

*** **Ahmad's Blues** Chess GRP 18032
    Jamal; Israel Crosby (*b*); Vernell Fournier (*d*). 9/58.
*** **Freeflight** Impulse! GRP 1332
    Jamal; Jamil Nasser (*b*); Frank Gant (*d*). 7/71.
** **Night Song** Mojazz 530 303
    Jamal; Oscar Brashear, Robert O. Bryant Sr (*t*); Maurice Spears, Garnett Brown (*tb*); Pete Christlieb (*as*); Ernie Fields Jr (*bs*); Gil Askey, Dean Paul Gant (*ky*); Calvin Keys, Greg Poree (*g*); John Heard, Kenneth Burke (*b*); Chester Cortez Thompson (*d*). 10/80.
** **Digital Works** Atlantic 781258
    Jamal; Larry Ball (*b*); Herlin Riley (*d*); Iraj Lashkary (*perc*). 85.
** **Rossiter Road** Atlantic 781645
    Jamal; James Cammack (*b*); Herlin Riley (*d*); Manolo Badrena (*perc*). 85.
(*) **Live At The Montreux Jazz Festival Atlantic 781699
    As above, except Seldon Newton (*perc*) replaces Badrena. 2/86.
(*) **Crystal Atlantic 781793
    Jamal; James Cammack (*b*); David Bowler (*d*); Willie White (*perc*); orchestra.
*(*) **Pittsburgh** Atlantic 782029
    As above, except omit White, orchestra.
***(*) **Live In Paris '92** Birdology 849 408
    Jamal; James Cammack, Todd Coolman (*b*); David Bowler, Gordon Lane (*d*). 4/92.
**** **Chicago Revisited** Telarc CD 83327
    Jamal; John Heard (*b*); Yoron Israel (*d*). 11/92.
*** **The Essence: Part 1** Birdology 529 327
    Jamal; George Coleman, James Cammack, Jamil Nasser (*b*); Idris Muhammad (*d*); Manolo Badrena (*perc*).
But for his enormous influence on Miles Davis and especially on Miles's conception of rhythm, Ahmad Jamal might by now have fallen into the pit dug for him by tin-eared critics, dismissed as an inventive cocktail pianist or (still more invidiously) as an entertainer rather than an artist. As Brian Priestley has pointed out, pianists who achieve a modicum of commercial success tend to move closer to the entertainment mainstream than any other musicians, except possibly singers, who are often thought to belong there anyway. For many years, Jamal gave much of his attention to running a chi-chi club, the Alhambra, rather than to playing.

He is certainly not a studio-friendly pianist and almost always sounds better caught live, as on the early *Ahmad's Blues* or the two (*Freeflight* is the other) discs recorded at the Montreux Festival. The other interesting point about these is the extent to which they illustrate how little his style changed over the years. Only the dismal fusion experiment (of its time, of its time) documented on *Night Song* is a step outside the main current of his notably self-motivated, self-valorizing course, but even this, executed on electric keyboards, is unmistakably his, resisting admirably many of the resident clichés of the form.

His technique – which is probably closer to Erroll Garner than to anyone else – has remained absolutely pristine, concentrating on fragile textures and almost calligraphic melodic statements, rather than the propulsive logic of bebop piano. Sadly, the trio recordings of the late 1950s are not currently available and there is a slackness and repetitiousness in his soloing in the 1980s which quickly wear off the chrome-bright delivery. The addition of electric and electronic keyboards on *Digital Works* creates some interesting colorations, reminiscent of his better work with orchestras. *Pittsburgh*, alas, doesn't fall into that category. Most of the recent recordings sound as if they need a little cigarette smoke blown through the tape gates.

The *Montreux* set contains some fine moments. There is a fine version of Wayne Shorter's 'Footprints', which extends Jamal's reading on *Digital Works* in a way that suggests his jazz brain still functions when called upon. Equally, his reading of Roland Hanna's 'Perugia' on *Crystal* shows an imaginative approach to a challenging theme. On the other hand, the *Montreux* version of 'Rossiter Road' shows how readily the pianist lapses back into prefabricated figures and patterns.

The 1990s have seen a startling renaissance. Jazz piano has become fashionable again, and Jamal has started to play with something like the poise and brilliance of the 1950s. The Paris recordings (Jamal has not generally been enamoured of Europe) are very fine, despite some reservations about the band. Cammack plays bass guitar rather stiffly and Bowler is so robotic one wonders what purpose he serves. Coolman and Lane are credited with only a single track. The material is as varied as ever. 'The Tube' celebrates successful surgery rather than the London Underground; 'Acorn' is a witty exercise in harmonic development. Typically, though, Jamal looks to Garner ('Dreamy') and to the standards for inspiration. A medley of ballads puts together 'Alone Together', 'Laura' and the theme from an Anthony Quinn movie, 'Wild Is The Wind' – a performance that more than incidentally recalls Hampton Hawes's homage to the Glitter Factory. 'Easy Living' and Jerome Kern's 'Look For The Silver Lining' are so elegantly phrased as to sound almost like speech.

Half a year later, back in the States and with a flawless rhythm section, Jamal sounds better still. *Chicago Revisited* could hardly be bettered as an example of contemporary jazz piano. The elegance of his line on 'All The Things You Are', with which the set opens, is such that it could be balanced on a pin. Clifford Brown's 'Daahoud' recalls a whole era in just a few bars. The remainder of the set is typically eclectic, tunes by Irving Ashby, Harold Adamson and Jimmy McHugh, Nick Brodszky and Sammy Cahn, and John Handy, closing with a 'Lullaby Of Birdland' that is concentrated songfulness.

These days, he has the wise, thoughtful look of an African parliamentarian, and a measured, slightly unrevealing delivery, well represented on *The Essence*, which so obviously runs counter to the prevailing expectation that it is still easily dismissed as shallow and clinical, unemotional and even unexpressive. Nonsense; there are more things to be expressed than anguish and despair, or roaring delight. Jamal has chosen to refract a misunderstood band of the jazz spectrum, and the music would be poorer without him.

Harry James (1916–83) TRUMPET

*** Harry James And His Orchestra Featuring Frank Sinatra Columbia CK 66377-2

James; Jack Schaeffer, Claude Bowen, Tom Gonsoulin, Jack Palmer, Claude Lakey (*t*); Russell Brown, Truett Jones, Dalton Rizzotto, Bruce Squires (*tb*); Dave Matthews, Claude Lakey, Bill Luther, Drew Page (*saxes*); Jack Gardner (*p*); Brian Kent (*g*); Thurman Teague (*b*); Ralph Hawkins, Mickey Scrima (*d*); Frank Sinatra (*v*). 7–10/39.

(***) Best Of the Big Bands Columbia 466955-2

Personnel unlisted, includes some of above, plus Kitty Kallen, Betty Grable, Helen Forrest, Dick Haymes (*v*). 39–41.

Considering that he remains one of the major jazz players in terms of overall record sales, James has had a peculiarly hard time in the CD era. There is no comprehensive edition of his studio work, with these so-so Columbia compilations as a start, and the Capitol set of some of his 1950s work is out of print again. *Featuring Frank Sinatra* is a good set of the young crooner's vocals with James and, though jazz followers will be disappointed at the low temperature, it remains a classy edition of smooth playing and singing. Transfers are mostly good, though one or two masters sound inexplicably rough. *Best Of the Big Bands* has a notoriously variable transfer-quality but, with no other representation of James's studio work from this period, this is where to go for the originals of 'Ciribiribin', 'Music Makers', 'The Man With The Horn' and his other early hits.

*** James With Haymes – 1941 Circle CCD-5

James; Claude Bowen, Al Stearns (*t*); Hoyt Bohannon, Dalton Rizzotto, Harry Rogers (*tb*); Claude Lakey, Vido Musso, Sam Marowitz, Chuck Gentry (*saxes*); Al Lerner (*p*); Ben Heller (*g*); Thurman Teague (*b*); Mickey Scrima (*d*); Dick Haymes (*v*); strings. 41.

*** Jump Sauce Vipers Nest VNG-201

James; Jimmy Campbell, Nick Buono, Vincent Badale, Al Cuozzo (*t*); Murray McEachern, Don Boyd, Harry Rogers, Ray Heath (*tb*); Philip Palmer (*frhn*); Johnny McAfee, Sam Marowitz, Claude Lakey, Corky Corcoran, Hugo Lowenstein, King Guion, Sam Sachelle (*saxes*); Al Lerner (*p*); Ben Heller (*g*); Thurman Teague (*b*); Mickey Scrima (*d*); Helen Forrest, Buddy Moreno (*v*); strings. 6–12/43.

**(*) Spotlight Bands Broadcast 1946 Jazz Hour JH-1046

Personnel unlisted, but includes Willie Smith (*as*), Helen Forrest (*v*). 43–46.

*** 1948 Broadcasts Jazz Hour JH-1007

Personnel unlisted; 48.

***(*) **Bandstand Memories 1938–1948** Hindsight HBCD503 3CD
    As all discs above, probably with numerous others! 38–48.
The only way to get a feel for James's music at present is to listen to some of these numerous aircheck recordings. James seemed to remain popular on radio throughout the 1940s, and plenty of material has survived in pro-am recordings. The cleanest of the lot is certainly the *Jump Sauce* disc of two 1943 broadcasts, in very clear sound from acetates. Though there were no real stars in the band at this point other than James himself, they play with a crisp and surprisingly limber swing which – on the occasional interesting chart, like 'The Gravy Train' – musters a fair attack. The strings weren't used with anything like the imagination that Artie Shaw employed, but they still create some impressive effects, especially on a fine transformation of 'Chelsea Bridge'.
    The disc with Dick Haymes luxuriates in the singer's impeccable vocals – extraordinarily deep and resonant for a man of 21. Not much jazz here, but a beguiling disc. The 1946 Spotlight Bands disc is rougher and, though the band take a good romp through 'King Porter Stomp' and generally give the impression that they're waking up rather more often, the sound tells against it – even more so on six pretty horrible-sounding transcriptions from 1943, here as a dubious bonus. A better bet is the 1948 session. James seemed to get more rather than less adventurous as the big-band era wore down, and there are some fine charts here from Jimmy Mundy, Neal Hefti (who was playing trumpet in the band around this time) and others. Most of the tunes here weren't recorded in the studio and, though the sound varies rather alarmingly – some tunes are obviously put together from different sources – the disc has a buzz to it.
    First choice, though, must go to the handsomely boxed, three-disc set on Hindsight. This covers ten years of material and is as good a summary of James as we're likely to get for now. The first disc, with the earliest material, has many rough spots, but the next two range from good to excellent, and the third in particular is a strong manifesto for the band. James himself remained the main soloist, his style an idiosyncratic blend of schmaltz, practised routine and surprising twists. Some part of the young firebrand who started with Goodman remains, but the broad tone and sometimes broader taste of his later work is in there too.

*** **The Silver Collection** Verve 823229-2
    James; personnel unlisted. 59–64.
(*) **1964 Live! Holiday Ballroom, Chicago Jazz Hour JH-1001
    James; Buddy Rich (*d*); rest unlisted. 64.
A new Verve *Jazz Masters* compilation of James's MGM tracks arrived too late for this edition; *The Silver Collection* covers much the same ground, though. Harrry re-made some of his old hits and other swing-era staples here and, though the performances are rather curtailed, the trumpeter actually sounds pretty good, and without too much affectation. The 1964 show was obviously a happy occasion, with the band playing with real fire on some excellent charts and Rich firing everyone up from the drums. But the sound is very trebly, with a lot of top end that lends a shrillness to everything from the hi-hat downwards. Tune that out and anyone will enjoy.

Jon Jang PIANO

***(*) **Self Defense!** Soul Note 121203
    Jang; John Worley Jr (*t, flhn*); Jeff Cressman (*tb, perc*); Melecio Magdaluyo (*as, ss, f, perc*); Jim Norton (*bcl, ss, f, dizi*); Mark Izu (*bass, sheng*); Anthony Brown (*d, perc*); Susan Hayase, James Frank Holder (*perc*). 6/91.
***(*) **Tiananmen!** Soul Note 121223
    Jang; Liu Qi-Chao (*suona, erhu, sheng, v*); Zhang Yan (*guzheng*); John Worley Jr (*t, flhn*); Jeff Cressman (*tb*); James Newton (*f*); Melecio Magdaluyo (*as, ss, f*); Francis Wong (*ts, f*); Jim Norton (*cl, bcl, af*); Mark Izu (*b*); Anthony Brown (*perc*). 2/93.
A young Chinese-American who was first recognized when a member of Fred Houn's Afro-Asian Ensemble, Jang took up piano rather late. He still has a fairly limited range as an instrumentalist – but in any case his main strength lies elsewhere, in composition and cultural activism. In 1987 he co-founded AsianImprov Records, a label dedicated to what can realistically be called frontier music, a radical alternative to the stiff retro sound of traditionalists like Wynton Marsalis. Jang's own sets there (which may still be found) are slightly more tongue-in-cheek than his work for Soul Note, but the disciplines of working with an outside producer have clearly served him well.
    It was widely assumed that the title of Jang's ensemble was a reference to Sun Ra's intergalactic academy of musicians. In fact, it relates to the Pan African People's Arkestra, led by radical Californian composer, Horace Tapscott. Like Tapscott, Jang is an activist. The pieces on *Self Defense!* relate to issues such as anti-Japanese violence in America, the demand for reparations for Japanese-Americans

interned during the war, Jesse Jackson's pan-ethnic Rainbow Coalition. Even 'A Night In Tunisia' has a political resonance; Dizzy Gillespie was once put forward as a write-in candidate for the presidency. Jang gives it a huge programme that links it to 'The Butterfly Lovers Song' and Jang's own 'Never Give Up!'.

The original pieces may depend too heavily on exclamation marks, but 'Concerto For Jazz Ensemble And Taiko' demonstrates Jang's ability to give large-scale structures a quietly appealing directness that doesn't depend on either volume or a ready-to-wear outfit of worthy slogans. Even in live performance (and this is a recording of a festival appearance in Seattle), there is no tendency to hector. There are fewer actual references to Asian music on *Self Defense!* than on *Tiananmen!*, a magnificent suite of pieces dedicated to the activists and martyrs of the Chinese democracy movement. Jang repeats the 'Butterfly Lovers Song' and calls repeatedly on Chinese folk-tunes, but the main influences are Charles Mingus (for his integration of polemical ideas with jazz) and Duke Ellington (particularly the later 'world music' suites); 'Come Sunday, June 4, 1989' contains an explicit homage, when Ellington's tune is played in counterpoint to Jang's theme by James Newton, a long-time supporter of the Asian jazz movement.

Jang's use of Asian instruments like the *taiko* drums on 'Concerto', the *guzheng* zither, the double-reeded *suona*, the two-stringed *erhu* and harmonica-like *sheng* is never purely for local effect. Frequently, as in 'Come Sunday', he exploits them to highlight a dramatic contrast between East and West, or to effect an integration between jazz and non-Western styles and concerns. The effect is less shambolic, more carefully marshalled than Houn's collective, and ultimately more satisfying.

Guus Janssen PIANO, HARPSICHORD

*** **Pok** Geestgronden 3
    Janssen; Paul Termos (*as*); Wim Janssen (*d*). 1/88–7/89.
*** **Harpsichord** Geestgronden 7
    Janssen (*hpd* solo). 90.
(*) **Klankast Geestgronden 9
    Janssen (*p* solo). 6/87–8/91.
*** **Lighter** Geestgronden 11
    Janssen; Ernst Glerum (*b*); Wim Janssen (*d*). 11/92–4/95.

Janssen's music is funny and accomplished. *Pok*, which starts with a dedication to Sandy Nelson and moves on through nods to boogie-woogie and swing time, tends to crash around various points, suggesting free jazz but always tied to a quite strict, formal aesthetic. The pianist's playing incorporates many styles, and Wim Janssen's drums are similarly diverse, but Termos's rather spindly alto parts could use an ounce more determination. The recording is rather distant. *Harpsichord* is a possibly unique example of solo free music on a keyboard that scarcely ever enters into the field. As with the previous disc, Janssen's taste runs to odd, wide-ranging ideas within a distinct formal grasp, and there are perhaps unsurprising echoes of the baroque repertory within an otherwise unpredictable record.

Klankast does much the same for the piano, though in a piece like 'Hi-Hat' Janssen seems to be back to guying the swing tradition. Some of the tunes run out of steam before they're done and this set is perhaps not the one to try first. *Lighter*, on the other hand, might be his best to date. Though pieced together from sessions over a three-year period, this is a more throughgoing exploration of jazz and free playing and how the two might work together. Janssen's use of silences, long form and satire makes the most of these sketched frameworks and, when they get to a version of 'Lennie's Pennies', the connection between this kind of free playing and the Tristano-ite school suddenly seems clear. Glerum and the other Janssen add a merry accompaniment.

Lars Jansson PIANO, KEYBOARDS

*** **A Window Towards Being** Imogena IGCD 019
    Jansson; Brynjar Hoff (*ob*); Lars Danielsson (*b*); Anders Kjellberg (*d*). 2/91.
*** **Invisible Friends** Imogena IGCD 055
    As above, except omit Hoff. 1/95.

Jansson is an excellent post-bop pianist whose affection for Bill Evans's manner is wedded to an attractive way with melody in his writing: it means that his music comes out with a little more brightness than that of the typical Evans disciple. The fine *Trio 84* on Dragon is currently out of print, but the sensitive programme on *A Window Towards Being* is played with some flair by the trio: Danielsson is the most reliable of bassists, and Kjellberg has a very good touch. Hoff is used for instrumental colour on three atypically lightweight tracks; but the main interest is in the piano improvisations on Jansson's own originals. *Invisible Friends* picks up the thread four years on and continues in the same impeccable vein. Here and there Jansson drifts off a little, but his playing partners pilot a firm rhythmic course that admits of no rambling. The portentousness of some of the titles seems to be nicely deflated by the penultimate one: 'I Have Nothing To Say And I Am Saying It'.

Rolf Jardemark GUITAR

** **Jungle Crunch** Imogena IGCD 027
    Jardemark; David Wilczewski (*ss, ts*); Jan Zirk (*ky*); Fredrik Bergman (*b*); Terje Sundby (*d*). 5/ 91.
*** **Guitarland** Imogena IGCD 044
    Jardemark; Lars Danielsson (*b*); Anders Kjellberg (*d*). 5/93.
Jardemark started as if meaning to take on the GRP guitarists at their own game: *Soft Landing* (Liphone LiCD 3095) was a noisy and flavourless fusion bash. *Jungle Crunch* suffers from the hangover of that approach, with Zirk's keyboards spread over everything and Jardemark and Wilczewski getting in a few interesting points in spite of it all; 'Half Spanish' survives as a pleasing theme. But *Guitarland* is down-the-line guitar, bass and drums, and all the better for it. Danielsson is the ideal man to have on hand, firming up all the lines and feeding Jardemark with good cues, and Kjellberg fits right in. The leader leaves his fuzz and effects boxes at home and gets a cool, limpid sound that suits the tones of 'Freddie Freeloader' and a few decent tunes of his own, with nimble solos on top.

Joseph Jarman (born 1937) SAXOPHONES, OTHER REEDS, FLUTE

(*) **Song For Delmark DD 410
    Jarman; Bill Brimfield (*t*); Fred Anderson (*ts*); Christopher Gaddy (*p, mar*); Charles Clark (*b*); Thurman Barker, Steve McCall (*d*). 10 & 12/66.
Art Ensemble of Chicago fans are apt to regard record projects by Joseph Jarman or Roscoe Mitchell much as Rolling Stones fans might regard a new solo record by Mick Jagger or Charlie Watts: worthy of notice and support, but essentially a distraction from the main matter at hand. In the former case, at least, they're quite wrong. Whether or not the Art Ensemble members feel disinclined to record or tour together, there's no doubt that most of their interesting work since 1975 has been apart.

    This is particularly true of Jarman who, depending on your viewpoint, is either the quintessential voice of the AEC or else its squarest peg. The reissued *Song For* is relatively standard AACM fare, intercut with neo-Dada recitations and characterized by a lack of formal shape. The supporting performers, with the exception of the two drummers, are not always up to scratch, though Clark produces some wonderfully sonorous bass on 'Adam's Rib', which certainly benefits considerably from CD transfer. The long tracks – 'Non-Cognitive Aspects Of The City', 'Song For' and a second and longer unissued take of Fred Anderson's 'Little Fox Run' with its skittering marimba patterns – pall slightly on repeated hearings. Of great documentary and historical significance, it's unlikely to effect any dramatic conversions.

Keith Jarrett (born 1945) PIANO, ORGAN, SOPRANO SAXOPHONE, OTHER INSTRUMENTS

**** **Foundations: The Keith Jarrett Anthology** Rhino R2 71593
    Jarrett; Chuck Mangione (*t*); Joe Farrell, Hubert Laws, Charles Lloyd (*f*); Frank Mitchell, Jim Pepper, Dewey Redman (*ts*); George Benson, Sam Brown (*g*); Gary Burton (*vib*); Ron Carter, Charlie Haden, Reggie Johnson, Cecil McBee, Steve Swallow (*b*); Art Blakey, Bill Goodwin, Bob Moses, Paul Motian (*d*); Airto Moreira (*perc*). 66–75.
Having passed his half-century, Jarrett is now a senior figure, and some kind of revised perspective seems in order. Inevitably, for an artist of his range and ambition, he wildly divides critical opinion and is himself, as every great artist must be, wildly inconsistent. The sheer momentum of early success has allowed him to experiment freely, but it has also allowed an unusual and not always desirable licence to experiment in public. (Many artists might have attempted the material documented on *Spirits*, below; few would have expected to see it make the shops.)

    It's tempting to suggest that the essential Jarrett is to be found in the solo performances and that these are the place to begin. He has now, though, reached the position where there is more than one essential Jarrett, and it is worth while backtracking a little. The appearance of *Foundations* makes this possible. It's a remarkably modest selection, just two discs to cover the seven years from his tough New York apprenticeship to the much-underrated and very ambitious Atlantic session *El Juicio* with the Redman/ Haden/Motian quartet.

What is immediately striking, listening to Jarrett play a standard, 'Smoke Gets In Your Eyes', in Bob Moses' group behind the gruff, squally tenor of Jim Pepper, is how fully formed he already sounds. 'Love No 3', nominally a Charles Lloyd Quartet cut, is actually a Jarrett solo, played in front of a first-house crowd at the Fillmore West; again, it's the same voice, not even in embryo, but already working out its own priorities. Go back a further year (the tracks aren't in strict chronological order on the disc, either) and listen to the 21-year-old hold his own with Art Blakey, albeit in a non-vintage Messengers. It all reinforces the impression of a young man who came of age with his artistic and creative agenda already in place and who has spent the last quarter-century working through all of its ramifications and by-ways.

He is perhaps the most sophisticated technician working today outside the 'straight' repertoire (and he has, of course, crossed that boundary, too). The early piano style – the Lloyd group apart – is less obviously influenced by rock and country music than by the jazz mainstream, but then he was playing for other leaders at this stage and was required to do so in the idiom, a discipline that has paid colossal dividends in the recent 'Standards Trio'. Lloyd's influence and tolerance shouldn't be underestimated; that extraordinary group was clearly the catalyst. From 'Love No 3' to the closing selection on disc two, the improvised 'Pardon My Rags', there is plentiful evidence of Jarrett's gifts as an 'instant composer', an instinctive melodist who seems able to find a match and a harmonic logic for almost any musical given. As his premises become more searching, then with almost Wagnerian logic the improvisations grow proportionately longer and more intense. He's still capable, even at his most intense, of throwing in cheesy little songs or marking time with big, time-killing exercises straight out of h&c class at the conservatory. There is also a slightly fluffy track under Airto's leadership and some sub-standard material with Gary Burton, a partnership that might have been better represented.

There is an unavoidable problem with an output of this bulk – a cash problem if nothing else. ECM have arguably released too much material, more than 50 hours' worth in the present catalogue, of which perhaps only one-third has the stamp of greatness. It's a fascinating story, all the same and, for new-comers or seasoned enthusiasts alike, *Foundations* is an excellent way of getting up to speed.

***(*) **Facing You** ECM 1017
    Jarrett (*p* solo). 11/71.
***(*) **Solo Concerts** ECM 1035/6/7 2CD
    As above. 3 & 7/73.
**** **The Köln Concert** ECM 1064/5
    As above. 1/75.
*** **Spheres** ECM 1302
    Jarrett (*org* solo). 9/76.
(*) **Staircase ECM 1090/1
    Jarrett (*p* solo). 11/76.
** **Sacred Hymns Of G. I. Gurdjieff** ECM 1174
    As above. 11/79.
*** **Sun Bear Concerts** ECM 1100 6CD
    As above. 3/80.
** **Invocations** ECM 1201/2 2CD
    Jarrett (*p, pipe org, ss* solo). 7–10/80.
*** **Concerts** ECM 1227
    Jarrett (*p* solo). 5 & 6/81.
** **Book Of Ways** ECM 1344/5 2CD
    Jarrett (*clavichord* solo). 7/86.
* **Spirits** ECM 1333/4 2CD
    Jarrett (assorted instruments). 4/87.
** **Dark Intervals** ECM 1379
    Jarrett (*p* solo). 10/88.
** **Paris Concert** ECM 1401
    As above. 10/88.
***(*) **Vienna Concert** ECM 1481
    As above. 7/91.

There was an uneasy giantism in the work of the later 1970s, culminating in the release of the infamous *Sun Bear Concerts*, hours of densely personal piano improvisations in a ten-LP box, and only slightly less cumbersome on CD. It's clear that these episodically remarkable performances occupied a very significant, slightly chastened place in Jarrett's rather lonely and dogged self-exploration, but that doesn't automatically make for good music. Without being excessively Dr Johnsonish ('It is not done well; but you are surprised to find it done at all') about music so naked and questing, one wonders how much of the critical excitement it garnered was simply a response to its size and to Jarrett's brass neck in releasing product on a scale usually only accorded the great and the dead.

The jury needn't stay out quite so long on the preposterous *Spirits*, a double (of course) album of overdubs on a bizarre variety of ethnic insruments. For the record, the album has its serious proponents (including Jarrett's biographer, Ian Carr) but, for all its healing and restorative intent and putative impact on the music that followed, it occupies only a marginal place in Jarrett's output. Other offences to be taken briefly into consideration are the thin *Gurdjieff* essays, the jangly clavichord improvisations on *Book Of Ways* (which is also burdened by the fact that the clavichord is an inherently unpleasant instrument to listen to at any length) and the dismal *Invocations*, executed in part on the same organ as *Spheres* but lacking that album's extraordinary experimental intensity and concentration. *Spheres* derives from the double-LP set, *Hymns Spheres*. It is by no stretch of the imagination a jazz record, but it does belong to another great improvisatory tradition, and it may be significant that, in contrast to the critical spanking it received in the United States, the album was favourably reviewed in Europe, though without quite enough leverage to see it transferred in full to compact disc. A great shame. Jarrett's approach to the unfamiliar keyboards and their associated pedals and stops is quite remarkable and generates one of his finest ever performances, easily the equal in conception and intelligence of the best-selling *Köln Concert*.

This is perhaps Jarrett's best and certainly his most popular record. ECM has been dining out or, to be fairer, recording others on the proceeds for two decades. Made in conditions of exceptional difficulty – not least an audibly unsatisfactory piano – Jarrett not for the first time makes a virtue of adversity, carving out huge slabs of music with a rare intensity. His instrument does sound off-puttingly bad-tempered, but his concentration on the middle register throughout the performance has been a characteristic of his work throughout his career.

The Bremen and Lausanne sets on *Solo Concerts* are almost equally good. Jarrett's first multi-volume set was extraordinarily well received on its release and stands up particularly well now (by contrast, *Facing You* seems slightly time-locked for some reason). These are friendlier, less intense performances than the *Köln* sides, but no less inventive for that, exploring Jarrett's characteristic blend of popular and 'high' forms. The 1981 *Concerts* was also recorded in Germany and in slightly easier circumstances (Jarrett suffered agonizing back pain throughout the Bremen *Solo Concert*) and perhaps as a consequence there's far less tension in the music; this is the surviving half of a two-LP release from Germany, of which the Munich half was probably better.

That same quality of tension is noticeable on both *Facing You*, the earliest of the solo recordings and the best place to get a feel of Jarrett's characteristic method before tackling the multi-volume sets, and *Staircase*, where he seems to range across a multiplicity of idioms (many of them identifiably classical rather than popular) with no apparent urgency.

Much has been made of the cohesion and unity of Jarrett's solo performances. They are often likened to multi-movement suites rather than collections of discontinuous tunes or numbers. This is certainly true of *Facing You*, which shares with the *Köln Concert* a satisfying roundness; it certainly isn't true of *Staircase* or of the recent *Dark Intervals* and *Paris Concert*. The former is a moody, sonorous affair, recorded live in Tokyo and interspersed with thunderously disciplined applause. Apart from 'Fire Dance' – track titles are rare or *ex post facto* in the improvised performances – the music has a very formal, concertizing solemnity. The *Paris Concert*, by contrast, is lively at least but is also disturbingly predictable. The idiomatic shifts have become mannered almost to the point of self-parody, and there's a slightly cynical quality to Jarrett's apparent manipulation of audience expectations. The notorious grunting and moaning, with which he signals ecstasy and effort, have never been more intrusive.

By the turn of the 1990s Jarrett's solo concerts had their own terms of reference; it is hard to imagine where one might find a critical language larger than the music itself. The *Vienna Concert* is at once more formal and more coherent than the disappointing *Paris Concert*. If there is a dominant influence it is Bach, who is explicitly (though possibly unconsciously) quoted at a number of points, as is Shostakovich, whom Jarrett has also been recording. It opens with a quiet, almost hymnic theme which develops very slowly over sombre pedals for just over 20 minutes, before opening out into a broken-tempo country theme that still preserves the original material in inverted form. The second and third pieces seem to develop material from the first, but in such a way that one wonders if they have been released in the order of the original concert. Long-standing Jarrett fans will find all the required elements in place; newcomers may find this more approachable than *Köln* or *Sun Bear*, but only if they're not put off by the classical resonances of the opening movement.

(*) **Somewhere Before Atlantic 7567 81455
    Jarrett; Charlie Haden (*b*); Paul Motian (*d*). 8/68.
(*) **Fort Yawuh Impulse! 33122
    Jarrett; Dewey Redman (*ts, perc*); Charlie Haden (*b*); Paul Motian (*d*); Danny Johnson (*perc*). 2/73.

*** **Treasure Island** Impulse! 39106

Jarrett; Dewey Redman (*ts, perc*); Sam Brown (*g*); Charlie Haden (*b*); Paul Motian (*d*); Guilhermo Franco (*perc*); Danny Johnson (*perc*). 2/74.

*** **Death And The Flower** Impulse! 29406

As above, except omit Brown and Johnson. 10/74.

***(*) **The Survivor's Suite** ECM 1085

Jarrett; Dewey Redman (*ts, perc*); Charlie Haden (*b*); Paul Motian (*d*). 4/76.

*(*) **Eyes Of The Heart** ECM 1150

Jarrett; Dewey Redman (*ts, perc*); Charlie Haden (*b*); Paul Motian (*d*). 5/76.

Jarrett's American quartet probably never reached the heights or achieved the almost telepathic understanding of the European group responsible for the classic *Belonging*, below. The early *Somewhere Before* is for trio, reuniting the line-up that made *Life Between The Exit Signs*. Heavily rock-influenced and still reminiscent of the methodology of the Charles Lloyd Quartet, of which Jarrett had been a member, it includes a version of Bob Dylan's 'My Back Pages' and two delightfully cadenced rags. Recorded live and slightly rough in texture, it has a freshness of approach that Jarrett quickly lost and was slow to regain.

The addition of Dewey Redman on *Fort Yawuh* (another of Jarrett's irritating pun-anagrams, this time of 'Fourth Way') gives that album a dark power that re-emerges on *Treasure Island*. Recorded a matter of weeks before *Belonging*, *Treasure Island* has most of the virtues of the 'European' album in embryo, but there is little doubt that Haden and Motian were either uncertain of Jarrett's direction or else were simply too forceful to fall in with his increasingly eclectic approach.

With the appearance of *Belonging*, Jarrett was able to operate a highly creative trade-off between two working bands. *Death And The Flower* already shows how differently he conceived the two bands, and it brings a nicely creative tension to the American sessions. Indeed *Survivor's Suite*, two years further down the road, is a masterpiece, with the quartet pulling together on an ambitiously large-scale piece, each member contributing whole-heartedly and passionately. By the sharpest of contrasts, *Eyes Of The Heart*, a live exploration of much the same material, is a near-disaster. The original release was as a double LP with one blank side. What it documents – and the format is in every way symbolic – is the final break-up of a rather fissile band; Dewey Redman contributes scarcely anything, and the album ends with Jarrett playing alone.

**** **Expectations** Columbia 467902

Jarrett; Dewey Redman (*ts*); Sam Brown (*g*); Charlie Haden (*b*); Paul Motian (*d*); Airto Moreira (*perc*); strings and brass. 10/71.

Only recently restored from Columbia's capacious back-catalogue, this is one of Jarrett's best group-sessions and his only one for the label; predictably they claim it as his breakthrough, and it's possible to argue that line rather more disinterestedly by pointing to the pianist's increasingly confident synthesis of jazz ('Circular Letter'), rock ('Sundance'), gospel ('There Is A Road') and Latin ('Common Mama') themes into a passionate, occasionally ecstatic mix, which all comes together on the closing 'Nomads'. Some of the more extravagant freedoms relate closely to his work with a man who stayed with Columbia a while longer. Jarrett learned – or allowed himself – to play free on Miles Davis's *Live–Evil* and there is ample evidence of that here. Redman plays on only half the tracks, Brown on six; a piano-and-strings track has been dropped and the running order revised, but with perfect logic. Jarrett plays soprano saxophone in addition to piano, but also, and despite Columbia's silence on the matter, organ and percussion. A fine record from a vintage period.

*** **Silence** Impulse! GRP 11172

Jarrett; Dewey Redman (*ts*); Charlie Haden (*b*); Paul Motian (*d*). 75.

A sensible compilation of two previous Impulse! LPs, *Bop-Be* and *Byablue*, dropping 'Pyramids Moving' from the former and concentrating on those tracks on *Byablue* that featured the whole group, with the exception of a piano solo reading of 'Byablue' itself. This was the last of Jarrett's records for the label and it's a slightly uneasy affair, reflecting not just a measure of strain that had grown up within the group but also (a matter of months after the Cologne concert) Jarrett's increasing interest in solo performance. As such, it's of considerable historical importance, but it can't be considered one of the more important albums.

**** **Belonging** ECM 1050

Jarrett; Jan Garbarek (*ts, ss*); Palle Danielsson (*b*); Jon Christensen (*d*). 4/74.

***(*) **My Song** ECM 1115

As above. 1/77.

*** **Personal Mountains** ECM 1382

As above. 4/79.

*** **Nude Ants** ECM 1171/2
    As above. 5/79.

Both *Belonging* and *My Song* have also been covered in the entry on Jan Garbarek, because the saxophonist's contribution to both albums seems particularly significant. The 'European Quartet' was probably the most sympathetic grouping Jarrett ever assembled and *Belonging* in particular is a superb album, characterized by some of the pianist's most open and joyous playing on record; his double-time solo on 'The Windup' is almost Tatum-like in its exuberance and fluency. The country-blues feel of 'Long As You Know You're Living Yours' is a confident reflection of his music roots. The ballads 'Blossom', 'Solstice' and the title-piece – the first two powerfully extended, the last uncharacteristically brief – are remarkable by any standards; Garbarek's slightly out-of-tune opening statement on 'Solstice' and Danielsson's subsequent solo are masterful, while Jarrett's own split chords accentuate the mystery and ambiguity of the piece.

    Nude Ants is a live set from New York City (the title is a metathesis of the bouncing 'New Dance'). It's a valuable documentation of the European Quartet outside the studio, but the performances are somewhat below par and Garbarek (who admits dissatisfaction with the performances) sounds alternately forced and diffident. Recording quality is also disappointing and well below ECM's usual standard. *Personal Mountains* sounds very much better, but the playing has a sleepy, jet-lagged quality (it was taped in Tokyo) that blurs the impact of the title-piece and the momentarily beautiful 'Prism', 'Oasis' and 'Innovence'.

(*) **Rutya And Daitya ECM 1021
    Jarrett; Jack DeJohnette (*d*). 5/71.
***(*) **Standards: Volume 1** ECM 1255
    As above, except add Gary Peacock (*b*). 1/83.
*** **Changes** ECM 1276
    As above. 1/83.
**** **Standards: Volume 2** ECM 1289
    As above. 7/85.
*** **Standards Live** ECM 1317
    As above. 7/86.
***(*) **Still Live** ECM 1360/1 2CD
    As above. 10/86.
***(*) **Standards In Norway** ECM 1542
    As above. 10/89.
(*) **Tribute ECM 1420/1 2CD
    As above. 10/89.
***(*) **Changeless** ECM 1392
    As above. 4/90.
**** **The Cure** ECM 1440
    As above. 4/90.

One of the less fair subtexts to the widespread critical acclaim for Jarrett's 'Standards Trio' is the implication that he is at last toeing the line, conforming to an established repertoire, finally renouncing the extravagances of the *Köln Concert* and the other multi-volume sets.

    In practice, nothing could be much further from the truth. Jarrett's approach to standards is nothing if not individual; for all his obvious respect and affection for the material, he consistently goes his own way. The main difference from the solo performances is the obvious one: Peacock's firmly harmonic bass and DeJohnette's astonishingly imaginative drumming (which Jarrett failed fully to appreciate on the early and little-known *Rutya And Daitya*, now available on CD and worth hearing) adjust his improvisatory instincts to the degree that they simplify his articulation and attack and redirect his attention to the chords and the figuration of melody.

    It doesn't always come off. There are moments on *Standards: Volume 1* which are simply flat and uninspired, as on 'God Bless The Child'. *Volume 2* immediately feels more confident. The themes, which are less familiar anyway, are no longer an embarrassment; Jarrett clearly feels able to leave them implicit a little longer. That is even more obvious on the fine *Standards Live* and *Still Live*, though it's a pity – from the point of view of comparison – that Jarrett hasn't repeated any of the studio titles. The only occasion where this is possible is on the strangely patchy *Tribute*, which repeats 'All The Things You Are' from *Standards: Volume 1*. The later version is more oblique, but also simpler. Like the rest of the tracks, it is intended as a *hommage*, in this case to Sonny Rollins, which is pretty typical of the curious but doubtless very conscious matching of standards and dedicatees. Typically, perhaps, Jarrett adds two of his own compositions to an already rather overblown and diffuse set, as if to inscribe himself more legibly into the tradition he is exploring and rediscovering.

    In that same vein, the 'Standards Trio' hasn't limited itself to existing repertoire. *Changes* and

Changeless contain original material which is deeply subversive, though also respectfully aware, of the whole tradition of jazz as a system of improvisation on 'the changes'. Typically, Jarrett invests the term with quite new aesthetic and philosophical considerations. On *Changeless*, there are no chord progressions at all; the trio improvises each section in a single key, somewhat in the manner of an Indian *raga*. The results are impressive and thought-provoking, like everything Jarrett has attempted. Even his failures, of which two more are reviewed below, are never less than interesting.

(As a footnote, the same trio has also recorded under Gary Peacock's leadership. The fine *Tales Of Another* is reviewed more fully under the appropriate heading.)

***(*) **Bye Bye Blackbird** ECM 1467
    Jarrett; Gary Peacock (*b*); Jack DeJohnette (*d*). 10/91.
***(*) **At The Deer Head Inn** ECM 1531
    Jarrett; Gary Peacock (*b*); Paul Motian (*d*). 9/92.

Bye Bye Blackbird is Jarrett's tribute to the late Miles Davis, with whom he worked in the 1960s and about whom in later years he had made some decidedly snitty comments. It is certainly startling to hear him talk in a rare ECM liner-note about Miles's 'purity of desire' (the phrase, or a version of it, is repeated) when the burden of on- and off-stage comments in the 1980s had been that Miles had seriously compromised the music – to electricity, to mere fashion, and so on.

Taken on its own merits, *Bye Bye Blackbird* is a wonderful record. The choice of material is refreshingly unobvious (how often is Oliver Nelson's 'Butch And Butch' covered?) and immaculately played, as this group always does. The two originals, 'For Miles' and a coda 'Blackbird, Bye Bye', are as intensely felt as anything Jarrett has done in recent years, and the level of abstraction that has crept back into the music is well judged and unobtrusive. DeJohnette performs wonders, changing metre subtly with almost every bar on 'Straight No Chaser'. An excellent record, beautifully packaged. What one wouldn't have given for an LP-sized print of Catherine Pichonnier's magnificent silhouette cover-photo.

It's a recurrent craving of superstars that they should turn their backs on the big halls and all the paraphernalia of stardom and play small venues again. The Dear Head Inn in Allentown, Pennsylvania, was the scene of Keith Jarrett's first serious gig on piano. It has now sustained a jazz policy for more than 40 years, a dedication passed on by the original owners to their daughter and son-in-law. In order to re-launch the club in 1992, Jarrett agreed to play a gig there, taking along Paul Motian, with whom he had not worked since the time of *Silence*.

Motian brings a lighter and more flowing pulse to the music than DeJohnette. The obvious point of comparison is 'Bye Bye Blackbird', which glides along without wires or other obvious support for more than ten minutes, a beautiful, airborne performance. This might almost be a second tribute to Miles. It opens with a superb reading of 'Solar', but then follows with skilful readings of 'Basin Street Blues' and Jaki Byard's 'Chandra', two pieces which belong to an entirely different musical realm, but which take on a similar coloration to the Miles tune. As so often, Peacock is more forceful and less complex out of the studio. He drives 'You And The Night And The Music', giving it a pugnacious edge one doesn't normally hear. It seems unlikely that Jarrett will ever need to go back to bar-room gigs, but here he's demonstrated his ability to work a small audience with powerful, unpretentious jazz. Anyone who has never heard him could hardly be better advised than to start with one of these.

**** **At The Blue Note: The Complete Recordings** ECM 1575/6/7/8/9/0 6CD
    As above. 6/94.

This is an extraordinary piece of documentation, two sets from each of three consecutive nights at the New York club. It might be considered warts-and-all but for the fact that there are no warts. Nor is there any repetition or aimless noodling. It's fascinating, given sufficient time and attention, to hear Jarrett import ideas – harmonic resolutions, phrases, improbable interval jumps like elevenths and thirteenths – from one piece to another on different nights. As an insight into how spontaneously creative he can be, it is unparalleled even in this extraordinary discography.

It was played, one suspects, with the recording very much in mind. One might almost prefer more repetition of tunes, but he goes his own individual way, leaning a little more than previously on top-ten standards – 'Autumn Leaves', 'Alone Together', 'On Green Dolphin Street' – and on jazz repertory pieces like Rollins's 'Oleo'. There may ultimately be a scaled-down compilation from this, but if you can afford the cash and patience to get the full set, don't hesitate for a moment. One of the high points of jazz playing in the 1990s.

(*) **In The Light ECM 1033/4 2CD
    Jarrett; Ralph Towner (*g*); string quartet; brass quintet; strings. 73.
(*) **Luminessence ECM 1049
    Jarrett; Jan Garbarek (*ts, ss*); strings. 4/74.
(*) **Arbour Zena ECM 1070
    Jarrett; Jan Garbarek (*ts, ss*); Charlie Haden (*b*); strings. 10/75.

*(*) **The Celestial Hawk** ECM 1175
    Jarrett; symphony orchestra. 3/80.
If it's every jazzer's dream (it was certainly Charlie Parker's) to play with strings, then it seems hard to
deny Jarrett his moment. Hard, but not impossible. These mostly sound like the indulgences of a star
figure unchecked by sensible aesthetic criteria and doubtless encouraged by sheer bankability. And why
not? The *Köln Concert* is still shifting units like a life-jacket sale before the Flood.
    Jarrett would doubtless argue that critical sniffiness about these albums is the result of sheer prejudice,
the jazz community's snotty, elbows-out attitude to anything scored or on the grand scale and, on the
other hand, the sheer exclusivism of the 'straight' music cartel. *Arbour Zena* and *Luminessence* contain
some beautiful moments, but what an opportunity missed for a stripped-down duo with Garbarek. The
overall mood of *Arbour Zena* is elegiac and slightly lorn, and the strings melt like marshmallows over
some of the sharper flavours; the later album has simply been left cooking too long.
    The earlier *In The Light* was a composer's showcase and, as such, a forerunner of ECM's much-
admired New Series. The individual works struggle to stay in focus, but as a whole the album has
surprising consistency. *The Celestial Hawk* is pure tosh . . . with some nice bits.

** **Works** ECM 825425
    Jarrett (solo) and with Jan Garbarek (*ts*); Palle Danielsson (*b*); Jon Christensen (*d*); string
    quartet.
There was once a joke that in the year 2045 someone brought out a 'Best of Keith Jarrett' set in the
currently fashionable laser-hologram/virtual reality format. It consisted of 87 LHVR diskettes. (There
was an audiophile vinyl option, but you needed your own truck to take it home.) Selecting a Jarrett
compilation must have been a thankless task. The results – 'Ritooria' from *Facing You*, part of the
eponymous 'Staircase', 'Country' and 'Journey Home' from *My Song*, selections from the *Sun Bear
Concerts*, *Invocations* and *In The Light* – are anything but predictable; nothing from *Belonging*, not so
much as a quick edit-and-fade from the *Köln Concert*, too early in the shops for the 'Standards' stuff.
Taken cold as a first introduction to Jarrett, it's no more misleading than any other logistical sample, but
it's hardly an inspired choice.

Jayne Jarvis PIANO

*** **Cut Glass** Audiophile ACD-258
    Jarvis; Joe Beck (*g*); Jay Leonhart (*b*); Grady Tate (*d*). 85.
*** **The Jayne Jarvis L.A. Quartet** Audiophile ACD-248
    Jarvis; Tommy Newsom (*ts*); Monty Budwig (*b*); Jake Hanna (*d*). 2/88.
**** **Jayne Jarvis Jams** Arbos SRCD 19152
    Jarvis; Dan Barrett (*c, tb*); Bob Haggart (*b*); Grady Tate (*d*). 6/95.
Pretty good jazz for a former baseball-crowd organist and executive of the Muzak corporation. Jarvis's
style comes from the generous, big-handed swing stylists of Erroll Garner's generation, though when
she actually tackles a Garner theme ('One Good Turn' on *Cut Glass*) she sounds curiously unlike him.
Both Audiophile discs offer an assured programme of standards and a very occasional original: the title
blues on *Cut Glass* is a delightful one, and her funky modification of 'Bali Ha'i' on the same session is an
instance of how wittily she varies the pace. The quartet date (Beck sits in on only a single track of the
earlier disc, which is otherwise all trio) offers fewer surprises, but Newsom's romantic tenor flourishes
fit the bill very comfortably.
    There could hardly be a better example of four old pros enjoying themselves than *Jayne Jarvis Jams*
(even if Barrett isn't so old). The level of sheer good spirits in this programme of standards is completely infectious and, when coupled with Jarvis's skill at renewing fusty old tunes, it makes the record
irresistible. The pep and swing in 'Mountain Greenery' ('It's so clean that I feel like I've brushed my
teeth every time I play it'), 'Begin The Beguine' and 'Lady Be Good' is enough to rattle the floor, and
there are deep-toned treatments of 'For Jess' (for Jess Stacy), Haggart's own immortal 'What's New?'
and 'I Get Along Without You Very Well'. Barrett chimes in when he has to with some delicious
choruses, and Haggart and Tate are marvellous. As is the piano player.

Bobby Jaspar (1926–63) TENOR SAXOPHONE, FLUTE

*** **Bobby Jaspar With George Wallington, Idrees Sulieman** Original Jazz Classics OJC 1788
    Jaspar; Idrees Sulieman (*t*); George Wallington (*p*); Wilbur Little (*b*); Elvin Jones (*d*). 5/57.
*** **Bobby Jaspar With Friends** Fresh Sound FSRCD-166
    Jaspar; Mundell Lowe, René Thomas (*g*); George Duvivier, Monty Budwig, Jean Marie Ingrand
    (*b*); Ed Shaughnessy, Jean-Louis Viale (*d*). 58–62.

Jaspar, who was born in Liège, sounded like Lester Young might have done if Lester had been Belgian. His pale tone and amorphous phrasing on tenor were matched with an agile and exceptionally pointed flute style, abjuring the mere prettiness which normally attends that instrument. He has two flute features on the agreeable if unexceptional 1957 session: Sulieman sits out on four of the seven numbers, but Jaspar is quite confident enough to handle the front line by himself. *With Friends* is a motley but absorbing collection of mainly live tracks, most with a small group under Mundell Lowe's leadership, but two cut in Paris with René Thomas – excellent, sinuous bebop workouts. The tracks with Lowe are a mixed lot: Jaspar has a gorgeous flute feature on 'It Could Happen To You' and generally uses this horn over the tenor. Lowe's own work shouldn't be discounted: he has a fine improvisation on 'Gal In Calico'. There are a number of earlier sessions for Vogue, Barclay and Columbia that could stand CD reissue.

*** The Bobby Jaspar Quartet At Ronnie Scott's 1962 Mole 11

> Jaspar; René Thomas (*g*); Benoit Quersin (*b*); Daniel Humair (*d*). 1/62.

This private recording features a rather flat and grey sound, but the music has plenty of colour. Jaspar frequently takes second place to the exceptionally energetic Thomas: any hint that this might be like the Rollins–Jim Hall partnership, especially with three Rollins themes in the set, is dispelled by Thomas's sometimes helter-skelter playing. Jaspar performs well, although he sometimes falters in longer solos, and the set – while excellent value at 75 minutes in length – includes some lesser material. A charming flute version of 'Stella By Starlight', though, recalls Jaspar's other talent.

André Jaume (born 1940) TENOR SAXOPHONE, FLUTE, CLARINET, BASS CLARINET

*** L'Oc hat Art CD 6058

> Jaume; Jean-François Canape (*t, flhn*); Yves Robert (*tb*); Jacques Veille (*btb*); Michael Overhage, Heiner Thym (*clo*); François Mechali (*b*); Gérard Siracusa (*perc*). 10/81.

After beginning with Dixieland groups, Jaume sought out more modern company in the 1960s, and since then his work on record has been rather unpredictable, with solo and duo recordings (with Joe McPhee, a long-time associate) sequenced with more large-scale efforts. This 1981 session puts an octet through Jaume's paces for seven tunes, with a further two pieces rendered by smaller editions of the same band. What emerges is a rather crabby sort of impressionism. There are some good improvisers in the group – Robert is a master, full of unexpected sounds, and Jaume himself has filtered his experience into a lean and questing solo style – but the sometimes fragmentary nature of the music can distract the listener.

***(*) Pour Django CELP C1

> Jaume; Raymond Boni (*g*). 6/85.

*** Songs And Dances CELP C4

> As above, except add Joe McPhee (*t, ss*). 5/87.

**** Cinoche CELP C7

> Jaume; Remi Charmasson (*g*); François Mechali, Claude Tchamitchian (*b*); Daniel Humair (*d*). 1/84–3/88.

***(*) Piazza Di Luna CELP C10

> Jaume; Remi Charmasson (g); Jean-Marc Montera (*g-syn*); Claude Tchamitchian (*b*); Freddy Studer (*d*); Jackie Micaelli, Jean-Pierre Lanfranchini, Jean-Claude Albertini, Jean-Etienne Langianni, Francis Marcantei (*v*). 8–9/89.

*** Standards CELP C12

> Jaume; Jean-Sebastien Simonoviez (*p*); François Mechali (*b*); Olivier Clerc (*d*). 4/89.

**(*) Something . . . CELP C15

> Jaume; Joe McPhee (*ss, vtb*); Clyde Criner (*p*); Anthony Cox (*b*); Bill Stewart (*d*). 4/90.

***(*) Peace/Pace/Paix CELP C19

> Jaume; Charlie Haden (*b*); Olivier Clerc (*d*). 5/90.

***(*) Abbaye De L'Epau CELP C20

> Jaume; Charlie Mariano (*as, f*). 3/91.

**** Giacobazzi, Autour De La Rade CELP C25

> Jaume; Barre Phillips (*b*); Barry Altschul (*d*). 6/92.

Jaume's sequence of records for the French CELP company is a superb body of work that deserves to be far more widely known than it is. His own playing has acquired tremendous stature: the tenor is still his primary instrument, and he gets a granitic, almost gothic tone out of it when he wishes, though he's often content to play quietly, almost deferentially. The alto he picks up only occasionally, but his bass clarinet and flute work are also distinctive – lyrical but with a dark, sometimes misshapen side to them.

His tribute to Django casts only a sidelong look at Reinhardt's material: he and Boni play 'Mélodie Pour Julie' relatively straight, but there are also abstract originals here that honour the guitarist's spirit as well as the letter of his music. Boni's effects colour much of the festival set recorded on *Songs And Dances*, where they play Coleman's 'Blues Connotation' as well as Otis Redding's 'Dock Of The Bay', and play three solos in tribute to Jimmy Lyons. *Cinoche* is a masterful record, music for '*un film policier qui n'existe pas*': split between one group with Humair and Mechali and another with Charmasson and Tchamitchian, Jaume's playing has a Rollins-like authority on tenor, with the superb 'Ballade A Perdre Le Temps' outstanding. *Piazza Di Luna* documents a project with Tavagna, a group of Corsican polyphonic singers. An unlikely collaboration, with two of the vocalists reciting the words of Andrée Canavaggio as well as singing; but Jaume makes it work by choosing to create two contrasting vistas rather than a fusion.

The *Standards* collection seems to set Jaume off on a new midstream course. Aside from a single original, 'Escapade', the programme offers nine familiar songs to work with, and Jaume's querulous tone and slightly tortuous phrasing make deliberately unsettled work of the music. He takes out the bass clarinet as often as the tenor and soprano, and it lends a mooching air to 'Nancy'. Jaume's first recording with an American rhythm section is a little disappointing. Criner, Cox and Stewart play as if this were just another post-bop date, and that's how it ends up sounding: with compositions by Jackie McLean and Grachan Moncur in the programme, as well as four Jaume originals, the feel is reminiscent of Blue Note's experimental mid-1960s period. But Jaume and McPhee give the impression of being tranquillized by the setting. An austere reworking of Moncur's 'Love And Hate' is rather effective, and Jaume's terseness works well with the splashier playing of McPhee, but the record is slack overall.

On the next two records Jaume sounds as if he's growing ever more quiet and introspective. He seldom raises his saxophone voice on either one, yet both make a firmer impression than some of the earlier discs. The trio session establishes a line of descent from Ornette Coleman, which 'Peace' and 'Blue Connotation' make manifest, but Jaume's playing has little of Coleman in it: he's too quirkily himself, and the steady-rolling pulses devised by Haden and Clerc support what's now a very personal kind of melodic improvisation. *Abbaye De L'Epau* is more soberly reflective, a little akin to his programme of duets with Jimmy Giuffre (Eiffel), and the very even pacing of the music makes this sequence all-of-a-piece, with Mariano turning his own light down a little to remain in keeping with the occasion. Both discs are well recorded (the second is from a concert session) and gently absorbing.

Any fear that Jaume might be heading towards silence is dispelled by the most recent trio session, a series of dedications to painter Jean-Pierre Giacobazzi, performed in collaboration with the sombre, earth-solid bass of Phillips and the magnificent Altschul, whose exacting, intensely detailed playing is remarkable by itself. Jaume makes the most of all his horns, with the soprano and bass clarinet finding new depth, but his tenor continues to impress the most, and the best music here is as absorbing as Coleman's great Golden Circle sessions.

Jazz At The Philharmonic SUPERGROUP

*** **The First Concert** Verve 521 646
> Shorty Sherock (*t*); J. J. Johnson (*tb*); Illinois Jacquet, Jack McVea (*ts*); Nat Cole (*p*); Les Paul (*g*); Lee Young (*d*). 7/44.

*** **Norman Granz's Jazz At The Philharmonic, Hartford, 1953** Pablo 2308240
> Charlie Shavers, Roy Eldridge (*t*); Bill Harris (*tb*); Benny Carter, Willie Smith (*as*); Flip Phillips, Ben Webster (*ts*); Oscar Peterson (*p*); Herb Ellis (*g*); Ray Brown (*b*); Gene Krupa (*d*). 5/53.

***(*) **JATP In Tokyo** Pablo PACD 2620 104 2CD
> As above, except add Raymond Tunia (*p*); J.C. Heard (*d*); Ella Fitzgerald (*v*). 11/53.

*** **The Exciting Battle: JATP, Stockholm '55** Pablo 2310713
> Roy Eldridge, Dizzy Gillespie (*t*); Bill Harris (*tb*); Flip Phillips (*ts*); Oscar Peterson (*p*); Herb Ellis (*g*); Ray Brown (*b*); Louie Bellson (*d*). 2/55.

***(*) **JATP In London, 1969** Pablo 2620 119
> Dizzy Gillespie, Clark Terry (*t*); Benny Carter (*as*); Coleman Hawkins, Zoot Sims (*ts*); James Moody (*ts, f*); Teddy Wilson (*p*); T-Bone Walker (*g*); Bob Cranshaw (*b*); Louie Bellson (*d*). 3/69.

***(*) **JATP At The Montreux Festival, 1975** Pablo 2310748
> Clark Terry (*t, flhn*); Benny Carter (*as*); Zoot Sims (*ts*); Joe Pass (*g*); Tommy Flanagan (*p*); Keter Betts (*b*); Bobby Durham (*d*). 7/75.

*** **Return To Happiness: JATP At Yoyogi National Stadium, Tokyo** Pablo 2620117
> Harry 'Sweets' Edison, Clark Terry (*t*) J. J. Johnson, Al Grey (*tb*); Zoot Sims, Eddie 'Lockjaw' Davis (*ts*); Joe Pass (*g*); Oscar Peterson, Paul Smith, (*p*); Keter Betts, Niels-Henning Orsted-Pedersen (*b*); Louie Bellson, Bobby Durham (*d*); Ella Fitzgerald (*v*). 10/83.

Jazz At The Philharmonic dates from 2 July 1944 at the Philharmonic Auditorium in Los Angeles, when Norman Granz mounted a concert headlined by Nat Cole, Illinois Jacquet, Meade Lux Lewis and others who will probably sound slightly unfamiliar in this context at least. A decade later, when JATP had reached the peak of its international celebrity, there was a relatively fixed roster of stars, all from within Granz's recording empire, who took part in these events – part concerts, part public jams – which gained him such success and which lasted virtually uninterrupted over the span of these records and beyond.

Granz was a passionate believer in the racial integration of jazz. He was also shrewd enough to recognize that more very definitely meant more so far as marketing big jazz names was concerned. There is often a sense of 'never mind the quality, count the names' on a JATP record, and finesse and expressive sophistication were very often lost in polite cutting sessions which put high note playing and amicably fiery exchanges at a premium. There are many more records than these, but they offer a decent representation of JATP over nearly 20 years. Difficult to identify highs and lows or to make qualitative judgements about the playing. There are no bad or even disappointing records. The earlier Japanese session recommends itself on grounds of sheer length and also because there is a winning freshness to everybody's playing, but that might also be said of the 1969 London concert or the triumphant return to Japan (and 'to happiness') which neatly rounds off the 40-year span of these particular discs. There are others around, which collectors will have fun tracking down, but these seem to us to be the best and most representative.

An astonishing feat of organization, JATP also made great marketing sense, and Granz has to be complimented for keeping the music going during a period when in market terms it was more than embattled. Mainstream fans will love any of these.

Jazz Composers Orchestra (founded 1967) GROUP

***(*) **Communications** JCOA 1001/2

> Michael Mantler (*dir*); Don Cherry (*c*); Randy Brecker, Stephen Furtado, Lloyd Michels (*flhn*); Bob Northern, Julius Watkins (*frhn*); Jimmy Knepper, Roswell Rudd (*tb*); Jack Jeffers (*btb*); Howard Johnson (*tba*); Al Gibbons, Steve Lacy, Steve Marcus (*ss*); Bob Donovan, Gene Hull, Frank Wess (*as*); Gato Barbieri, George Barrow, Pharoah Sanders, Lew Tabackin (*ts*); Charles Davis (*bs*); Carla Bley, Cecil Taylor (*p*); Kent Carter, Ron Carter, Bob Cunningham, Richard Davis, Eddie Gomez, Charlie Haden, Reggie Johnson, Alan Silva, Steve Swallow, Reggie Workman (*b*); Andrew Cyrille, Beaver Harris (*d*). 1/68, 5/68, 6/68.

The JCO was formed to give improvising musicians an opportunity to play extended structures in larger formations than were normally considered either economic or artistically viable. Its best-known product is still the massive opera – or 'chronotransduction' – *Escalator Over The Hill*, remembered with affection by crossword puzzlers, proto-*Twin Peaks* fans and the odd adventurous rocker, but, alas, not in the current catalogue.

Communications is, if anything, a more ambitious work. It consists of four enormous slabs of orchestrated sound and a brief 'Preview' (which comes fourth of five), each with a featured soloist. Or, in the case of the opening 'Communications No. 8', two soloists: Don Cherry and Gato Barbieri. Mantler's scoring is interesting in itself. Cherry's squeaky cornet is the only high-pitched brass instrument; the sections are weighted towards french horns and trombones, with flugelhorn accents generally located in the middle register and the higher-pitched parts assigned to soprano saxophones. In addition, Mantler scores for five double basses on each track (perm from the list above), which gives each piece a complex tonal rootedness for the soloists' (mostly) unrestrained excursions.

Restraining Gato Barbieri would be pointless. He tends to begin a solo where most saxophonists climax. It's redundant to say he sounds strained on 'Communications No. 8' but, tone apart, he seems to be straining for ideas. By contrast, Pharoah Sanders has to squeeze everything into a brief 3½ minutes on 'Preview' and nearly achieves meltdown in the process.

On 'Communications No. 9' Larry Coryell is used as a sound-effects department. If Barbieri seems slightly short of ideas, Coryell is a *tabula rasa*. Fortunately, the best is still to come. Roswell Rudd's playing on the longer 'No. 10' is some of the best he has committed to record; Steve Swallow's bass introduction establishes its parameters with great exactness, and again the dark scoring works superbly.

The final two-part section fully justifies Cecil Taylor's top billing. His solo part is full of huge, keyboard-long runs and pounded chords and arpeggios that leave Andrew Cyrille sounding winded and concussed. Very much of its time, and betraying occasional signs of a dialogue of the deaf, *Communications* is still a vitally important historical document. However demanding its headlong progress may be on the intellect and the emotions, Mantler – like Barry Guy, who followed his example in the United Kingdom – has a considerable musical intelligence and shapes performances that have logic, form and a sort of chastening beauty.

Jazz Group Arkhangelsk GROUP

***(*) **Live In Japan** Ninety One CRCJ 9102
   Vladimir Rezitsky (*as, f, melodica, perc*); Vladimir Turov (*syn*); Nikolai Klishin (*b, vn, hca*); Oleg
   Yudanov (*d, perc*); Nikolai Yudanov (*perc*); Konstantin Sedovin (*v*). 11/91.
*** **Portrait** Leo CDLR 180
   As above, except omit Sedovin. 11/91.
On the downside of the 'liberation' of Eastern Europe and Russia is a dramatic change in the status of
creative artists in the former people's democracies. The Jazz Group Arkhangelsk is a perfect instance of
a creatively adventurous ensemble that won official sanction, playing regular 'workers' concerts' in and
around the northern port of Arkhangel. Typical of Russian new music – see entries on the Ganelin Trio
and Sergey Kuryokhin – the JGA combined an accelerated historiography of jazz (they include 'Afro
Blue' in the Tokyo concert) and a welter of native and imported popular musics.
   Leader Rezitsky is a deceptively smooth player, sounding almost as if he is still doing the restaurant gigs
that supported the band until they received State backing. That isn't quite the case on *Portrait*, recorded
at an impromptu concert at a community college in Leicester, with most of the band suffering from
viruses. Generally, though, the overall blend is headlong, buoyant and joyous. The huge 'Sound Of The
World' that makes up most of *Live In Japan* is the most characteristic performance currently on record.
Unfortunately, like the Art Ensemble of Chicago, the JGA are difficult to assess on record. Unlike the
Chicagoans, they have also been difficult for Westerners to see in the flesh.

The Jazz Members Big Band Of Chicago GROUP

***(*) **Diggin' In** Sea Breeze CDSB-2049
   Danny Barber, Steve Jensen, Dave Urban, Art Davis, Jeff Helgesen, Thomas Shabda Noor (*t,
   flhn*); Scott Bentall, Edwin Williams, Tom Kordus, Paul McKee (*tb*); Michael Young, Art
   Linsner (*btb*); Chris Lega, Steve Duke, Edward Petersen, Jerry DiMuzio, Eddie Johnson, Les
   Thimmig, Glenn Kostur (*reeds*); Greg Flint (*frhn*); Frank Mantooth (*p*); Charles Harrison (*g*);
   Tom Korda (*euph*); Dan Anderson (*tba*); Michael Barnett (*b*); Bob Chmel (*d*); Frieda Lee (*v*);
   Jeff Lindberg (*cond*). 6/92.
One of the better Sea Breeze 'occasional' big bands. This crack team of Chicago-based players sound as
formidable at their best as any big band working today. A difficult score such as Thomas Fredrickson's
'Deja Vu' is dispatched with seemingly effortless aplomb, and soloists deliver with real class: sample
Jerry DiMuzio's tenor on that arrangement, or Eddie Johnson's magisterial delivery of Ellington's
'Happy Reunion'. The tunes are an exceptionally well-chosen list, including Neal Hefti's 'Fauncy
Meeting You' and Billy Byers's 'Presidential Manor', along with some demanding originals, and the
intelligence of the scoring meets all requirements. The only weaker spots are the three vocal features for
Frieda Lee: they're all right but a distraction rather than a break from the class of the playing. As usual
from the label, splendid, full-blooded recording.

The Jazz Passengers GROUP

**** **Implement Yourself** New World/Countercurrents NW 398
   Curtis Fowlkes (*tb*); Roy Nathanson (*as, ts, ss*); Bill Ware (*vib*); Bill Nolet (*vn*); Marc Ribot (*g, E
   flat horn*); Bradley Jones (*b*); E. J. Rodriguez (*d, perc*); Waldwick High School Marching Band.
   3/90.
*** **Live At The Knitting Factory** Knitting Factory KFWCD 107
   As above, except omit Ribot, band; add Marcus Roja (*tba*); Dave Fuczinski (*g*); Dougie Bowne
   (*d*); Yuka Honda (*samples*). 1/91.
*** **Plain Old Joe** Knitting Factory KFWCD 139
   As above, except omit Ribot, Fuczinski, Roja, Bowne, Honda; add Michael Dorf (*hca*); Helen
   Wood (*v*).
**** **In Love** High Street Records 72902 10328
   As above, except omit Dorf and Wood; add Marc Ribot, David Tronzo (*g*); Anthony Coleman
   (*harm*); Mary Wooten (*clo*); Bob Dorough, Mavis Staples, Deborah Harry, Jimmy Scott,
   Elisheba Fowlkes, Abie Rodriguez, Jenni Muldaur, Freddy Johnston, Manuel Oliveras, D. K.
   Dyson, Leopoldine Core, Carter Spurier, Wilbur Pauley, Marc Bleeke, Kate Silverman, Laurie
   Gallucio (*v*). 94.
The original idea was a trombone/saxophone duo consisting of Curtis Fowlkes and Roy Nathanson, but
it has steadily expanded into a flexible ensemble that does what can only be described as a form of jazz

cabaret. Many of the vocal arrangments are reminiscent, weirdly, of Carla Bley's *Escalator Over The Hill*, or one of Frank Zappa's jazzier projects, which may or may not be enticing news. If one could imagine an avant-garde or post-modern Crusaders, that might be even nearer the mark. The drill is not to expect anything too much like the last track/album. Fortunately, it's all done with too much wit and intelligence to risk the charge of mere perversity, and the playing, from Fowlkes and Nathanson especially, is so good that one seldom pauses to wonder why? or even what?

With impeccable illogic, the Passengers' first recording appeared on the Crepuscule label, which hails from Belgium and enjoys a somewhat twilit reputation elsewhere. Since the turn of the 1990s, the group has had a fairly regular berth at the Knitting Factory in New York City and the first of these discs was recorded in concert there. It's by far the weakest of the available records and the only one to which the charge of self-indulgence sticks. Though they seem on the surface to be the quintessential live act, the Passengers are brilliant exponents of studio performance, and *Implement Yourself* manages to combine a relaxed 'live feel' with astonishing discipline and exactness. As befits a group that has grown organically, there is no obviously dominant voice, though Fowlkes and Nathanson are clearly the guiding personalities, somewhat like Zawinul and Shorter in Weather Report. Even so, Jones, Ware, Rodriguez and, somewhat episodically, Nolet add their two cents' worth, and it is difficult to conceive of the group (unlike the Report) other than as a unit. That being so, guests are absorbed into the unit quite seamlessly, rarely sticking out or intruding.

Implement Yourself has much less vocal material than most, but Ribot's vocalized guitar line intercutting with the vibes on the Dolphyish 'Peace In The Valley' takes the place of a conventional lyric. As a whole, it's a bruising but constantly fascinating listen. *Plain Old Joe* is somewhat closer to the group's music-theatre vein and doesn't come across so well on disc. There is a lack of presence, which certainly doesn't trouble the completely barking *In Love*, one of those records that demand complete surrender and a suspension of all normal generic expectations. It starts off with a chaotic dialogue between the Angels, Mr Strawhat and the Underground Man, before segueing into the Ellingtonish 'Imitation Of A Kiss', sung 'straight' in Billie Carter/Peggy Lee manner over a late-nite vibes accompaniment, before Nathanson takes it away in a gloriously distraught tenor solo. The guest singers are extraordinary: Mavis Staples, Jeff Buckley and Deborah Harry – perhaps the only person on the planet who could deliver with conviction lines like: 'Just this mornin' I met a strange old man / A distant cousin at a taxi stand / The half-blind stepson of my weird aunt Flo.' Uh huh.

They're not easy to categorize. They'll either irritate in half a minute, or you'll fall in love for ever, like a dog in sand. Unique.

Jazz Tribe GROUP

*** **The Jazz Tribe** Red R R 123254
>Jack Walrath (*t*); Bobby Watson (*as*); Steve Grossman (*ts*); Walter Bishop Jr (*p*); Charles Fambrough (*b*); Joe Chambers (*d*); Ray Mantilla (*perc*). 12/90.

This is just one of several seemingly *ad hoc* units fronted by Walrath, who has become a festival favourite in Europe, and particularly in Italy. This entertaining session was recorded at La Spezia. It's a fairly uncomplicated mix, with much of the emphasis given to Mantilla compositions, though there are two pieces by Bishop and one each by Walrath and Watson. Grossman guests on 'Star Eyes' and updates the Charlie Parker solo with some dazzling flourishes and turnarounds. This isn't a band that you would have put together on the back of an envelope, but it works very well in this context.

François Jeanneau (born 1935) SOPRANO AND TENOR SAXOPHONES

*** **Taxiway** Label Bleu L BLC 6518-2
>Jeanneau; Andy Elmer (*p*); Michel Benita (*b*); Aaron Scott (*d*). 5/88.
(*) **Maloya Transit Label Bleu L BLC 6546
>As above, except add Joel Allouche (*d*), Christian Daffreville, Nicolas Moucazambo, Gilbert Marapin (*perc*); omit Scott. 6/91.

These records scarcely convey the breadth of Jeanneau's experience and talents. He has been a force in French jazz for decades, and there are numerous appearances as both sideman and leader that are currently out of print. *Taxiway* is a pleasing if fairly unexceptional quartet date: the hard-hitting 'Wysiwyg' (a familiar acronym) lets everybody flex their muscles, and Jeanneau's thoughts on Coltrane are always worth a listen. But his small-group sessions for Owl, none of them as yet on CD, are more serious business. *Maloya Transit* blends his quartet with African percussion and voice, but the fusion sounds relatively half-hearted and lacks a pressing need to exist.

Eddie Jefferson (1918–79) VOCALS

*** **Letter From Home** Original Jazz Classics OJC 307
> Jefferson; Ernie Royal, Clark Terry (*t*); Jimmy Cleveland (*tb*); James Moody (*as, f*); Johnny Griffin (*ts*); Arthur Clarke (*bs*); Junior Mance, Joe Zawinul (*p*); Barry Galbraith (*b*); Louis Hayes, Osie Johnson, Sam Jones (*d*). 12/61.

***(*) **Body And Soul** Original Jazz Classics OJC 396
> Jefferson; Dave Burns (*t*); James Moody (*ts, f*); Barry Harris (*p*); Steve Davis (*b*); Bill English (*d*). 9/68.

***(*) **Come Along With Me** Original Jazz Classics OJC 613
> Jefferson; Bill Hardman (*t*); Charles McPherson (*as*); Barry Harris (*p*); Gene Taylor (*b*); Bill English (*d*). 8/69.

*** **Godfather Of Vocalese** Muse MCD 6013
> Jefferson; Waymon Reed (*t, flhn*); Richie Cole (*as*); Mickey Tucker (*ky*); Rick Laird (*b*); Eddie Gladden (*d*); Harold White (*perc*); Betsy Fesmire (*v*). 3 & 5/76.

A death sentence is a pretty harsh review, as Ralph Ellison wrote of Salman Rushdie. In 1979, the sixty-year-old Jefferson was shot dead outside the Detroit club in which he'd been appearing. Like most of the bebop vocalists – and despite a brief recent revival in the critical fortunes of King Pleasure, who successfully co-opted Jefferson's style – he is little known among younger jazz fans, and various attempts at revival in recent years have fallen rather flat. There is though a widespread belief that Pleasure wrote the lyrics to 'Moody's Mood For Love', a vocalized transcription of James Moody's alto saxophone solo on 'I'm In The Mood For Love'; Pleasure certainly made it a monster hit, but the song was Jefferson's. Perhaps his best track, an intelligent and inventive 'Body And Soul' (later revived by Manhattan Transfer as a tribute to Jefferson), is revived on the fine 1968 session, which also features Moody and a brilliant version of 'Filthy McNasty'.

Letter boasts a heavyweight line-up and some sure-footed – Jefferson was also a dancer – vocal arrangements. Four of the tracks are for sextet, but the better pieces use the full breadth of the band, with Jefferson high-wiring it over the 29-year-old Joe Zawinul's spry comping; check out Jefferson's version of the pianist's 'Mercy, Mercy, Mercy' on the 1968 *Body And Soul*. The singer's longest-standing partnership, with saxophonist Moody, is reflected in a dozen cuts, one of the best of which is a lively 'So What' (again on *Body And Soul*). Their relationship had rekindled in the 1960s, when Jefferson, who had been eclipsed by smoother talents like Jon Hendricks, staged something of a comeback; the later sessions (*Come Along With Me*) with Bill Hardman and Charles McPherson on staples like 'Yardbird Suite' and 'Dexter Digs In' are well worth catching, though the voice has lost some of its elasticity and bounce. Like King Pleasure, Jefferson improvised and wrote lyrics to some of the classic bop solos; precisely because they worked such similar turf, there was a constant risk of copyright wrangles, which explains why 'Body And Soul' is sometimes retitled 'I Feel So Good', 'Parker's Mood' and 'Bless My Soul'.

The Muse was recorded within a few years of Jefferson's death. He's far from a spent force, but 'Ornithology' sounds a bit earthbound and the other stuff has lost much of its spontaneity. Not to everyone's taste, but vocal jazz of Jefferson's sort is a significant and currently neglected aspect of jazz history that needs to be taken account of in any comprehensive collection.

Billy Jenkins (born 1954) GUITAR, PIANO, VOICE

**** **Scratches Of Spain** Babel BDV 9404
> Jenkins; Chris Batchelor, John Eacott, Skid Solo (*t*); Dave Jago (*tb*); Ashley Slater (*btb, tba, v*); Iain Ballamy, Steve Buckley, (*sax*); Dai Pritchard (*sax, cl*); Dave Cooke (*g*); Django Bates (*ky*); Jimmy Haycraft (*vib*); Jo Westcott (*clo*); Tim Matthewman, Simon Edwards (*b*); Steve Arguelles, Roy Dodds (*d, perc*); Dawson (*perc*). 87.

*** **Entertainment USA** Babel BDV 9401
> Jenkins; John Eacott (*t*); John Harborne (*tb*); Mark Lockheart (*ts*); Martin Speake (*as*); Django Bates (*ky*); Maria Lamburn (*vla*); Huw Warren (*acc, clo*); Steve Watts (*b*); Roy Dodds (*d*); Dawson, Martin France (*perc*); Lol Graves, Suzy M., Lindy Lou, Tina G., Tony Messenger (*v*). 94.

*** **Mayfest '94** Babel BDV 9502
> Jenkins; Rainer Brennecke (*t*); Jorg Huke (*tb*); Thomas Klemm (*ts, f*); Huw Warren (*p, acc, glockenspiel*); Steve Watts (*b*); Martin France (*d*). 5/94.

**** **First Aural Art Exhibition** VOTP VOCD 921
> Jenkins; John Eacott, Skid Solo (*t*); John Harborne, Dave Jago (*tb*); Ashley Slater (*btb, tba*); Iain Ballamy, Mark Ramsden, Martin Speake (*as*); Steve Buckley, Mark Lockheart (*ts*); Dai

Pritchard (*bs, bcl*); Stuart Hall, Andy McFarlane (*vn*); Jo Westcott (*clo*); Dave Cooke, Robin Aspland (*g*); Jim Haycraft (*vib*); Steve Berry, Winston Blissett, Tim Matthewman, Steve Watts (*b*); Roy Dodds, Martin France (*d*); Dawson (*perc*). 84, 85, 86, 87, 89, 90, 91.

Billy Jenkins is a musical anarchist. Notably resistant to ideology, he espouses a version of the kitchen-sink Situationism which lay behind the British punk movement. If music has become business (an equation he rejects), then the only refuge is a kind of unselfconscious anti-technique Jenkins has christened 'Spazz', which encourages the retention of 'wrong' notes and false starts, and the propagation of lo-fi recordings on the least sophisticated of formats.

Jenkins is uniquely concerned with the packaging of music, not just in the cardboard-and-laminate sense but in terms of its perceived contours and limits. His 'Big Fights' encounters restrict duo improvisation to 12 three-minute 'rounds', the antithesis of the open-ended approach of most 'free' improvisers, but which also levels pertinent comment at their tacit belief that sheer duration is an end in itself. More satirically, Jenkins has presented 'uncommercial' samples of his work in chocolate wrappers, a neat comment on music's consumable nature, and has mimicked ECM and Windham Hill colophons and the ubiquitous 'Nice Price' cover to Miles Davis's *Sketches Of Spain. Scratches of Spain* is, rightly, Jenkins' most celebrated single record, a frantic, un-Cool exposition of 'Spazz' technique and his deployment of a ragged army of co-religionists known as the Voice of God Collective. *Scratches*' arrival on CD doesn't for a moment diminish its brutal simplicity or its deceptive sophistication as a piece of 'product'. Jenkins's transfer to CD is not yet total, and a good deal of his work, including the 'Big Fights', may still be found on Voice of the People cassettes, but we have not listed these this time round.

Jenkins has been around on the British scene long enough now for pieces like 'Benidorm Motorway Services' and 'Cooking Oil' to have become minor classics, albeit harder to hum than the adagio from *Concierto de Aranjuez*. In place of the 'Spanish tinge', a pervasive greasy taste. In place of Gil Evans's limpid orchestration, the 'ensemble' sound of a dozen lager louts going home at two a.m., like the discoboats that used to compromise Jenkins's rest in his studio home at Greenwich. For all that, Jenkins is an able tone poet and one hopes that *Sounds Like Bromley* and *Greenwich* will soon be available on CD.

His gift for pastiche and even meta-pastiche is more evident still on the brilliant *Entertainment USA*, a collection of bilious and affectionate tributes to great American entertainers like Ronald Reagan, Oliver North, daffy-haired boxing promoter and philanthropist Don King and Charles Manson, to say nothing of weightier individuals like Doris Day, Elvis Presley and Johnny Cash.

Both the excellent *First Aural Art Exhibition* and the live Glasgow gig with the Fun Horns offer a chance to hear earlier Jenkins opus numbers on CD, in advance of some of the earlier vinyl and cassettes being reissued entire. The former includes 'Brilliant', 'Expensive Equipment', 'Fat People', 'The Blues', 'Sade's Lips', 'Discoboats At Two O'Clock', 'Cooking Oil', 'Donkey Droppings', and 'Elvis Presley', which – initiates will confirm – is a pretty fair representation. The Glasgow session has, *inter alia*, 'Arrival Of The Tourists', 'Greenwich One Way System' and 'Fat People', delivered in a rough-and-ready taping straight off the mixing desk at the old Renfrew Ferry.

As always, genres and the whole idea of 'genre' are turned upside down. It may be that Frank Zappa is the nearest measurable equivalent to Jenkins, but it seems unlikely that he would be flattered by the comparison and it may yet be that he is a more significant figure.

John Jenkins (born 1931) ALTO SAXOPHONE

(*) **Jazz Eyes Savoy SV 0230
    Jenkins; Donald Byrd (*t*); Curtis Fuller (*tb*); Tommy Flanagan (*p*); Doug Watkins (*b*); Arthur Taylor (*d*). 9/57.

This is a fairly skimpy (37 minutes) representation of the young Chicagoan, whose heart never seemed to be quite with his music-making. Jenkins has a stuttery, sometimes rather awkward delivery, and on *Jazz Eyes* he is blown away by both Byrd (then in his pomp as a straight jazz player) and the ever-professional Fuller. The original themes – 'Orpheus', 'Honkeylike' and 'Rockaway' – show why he was valued by some as a writer, but there is little to get excited about as regards his playing, and this one may safely be passed over by all but the most curious or dedicated.

Leroy Jenkins (born 1932) VIOLIN, VIOLA

*** **Lifelong Ambitions** Black Saint 120033
    Jenkins; Muhal Richard Abrams (*p*). 3/77.

*** **Urban Blues** Black Saint 120083
>   Jenkins; Terry Jenoure (*vn, v*); James Emery, Brandon Ross (*g*); Alonzo Gardner (*b*); Kamal
>   Sabir (*d*). 1/84.

***(*) **Live!** Black Saint 120122
>   Jenkins; Brandon Ross (*g*); Eric Johnson (*syn*); Hill Greene (*b*); Reggie Nicholson (*d*). 3/92.

Leroy Jenkins and George Lewis share one often-forgotten characteristic that makes them ideal improvising partners. Though both are given to very forceful and even violent gestures, they are also capable
of great lyricism; the same has to be said of Andrew Cyrille. In a period when Billy Bang is, rightly or
wrongly, the benchmark jazz violinist, critics have often missed the fact that Jenkins's percussive, rasping delivery rarely departs from an identifiable tonal centre or melodic logic. His preference is for
looping statements, punctuated by abrupt rhythmic snaps; the most obvious influence is Stuff Smith,
but there are also parallels with the way saxophonist Anthony Braxton used to deliver improvised lines.
Like pianist Anthony Davis, Jenkins has an almost 'legitimate' technique and a tone that one can
imagine negotiating with Bartók or Stravinsky.

   Jenkins released no commercial recordings between 1984 and 1992, and his back-catalogue is in a rather
threadbare state. Two Black Saints – *Mixed Quintet* and *Urban Blues* – have recently gone to the great
vinyl recycling plant in the sky, but with no hint yet of a shinier reincarnation for the former. Their
replacements could hardly be more different. Jenkins's working band, Sting, were capable of great
things in a live setting, but they're nothing compared to the new Computer Minds. The live session
completely merits the exclamation mark. It's a fierce, urgent session, recorded in a New York public
school, and sounds appropriately in contact with what's going on on the streets. To an extent, Jenkins is
a traditionalist rather than a radical. His interests, though, have always reached well beyond jazz, and
his band tackles a whole range of black musics.

   The duos with Abrams are also both traditionally minded and innovative. All the compositions are from
the violinist, even the closing 'The Father, The Son, The Holy Ghost', which clearly isn't the same as the
Albert Ayler piece. Like their titles – 'The Blues', 'Meditation', 'Happiness' – the pieces are kept pretty
abstract (and are all almost exactly the same length). There's a patient, almost schoolmasterly side to
Abrams's playing. Jenkins moves off into pan-tonality a few times but stays firmly anchored in an
identifiable key for most of the set, even when his partner has dissolved the normal ties of melody and
accompaniment. It's difficult to tell when they're improvising and when reading, and the abiding
impression is of formality rather than freedom.

   Urban Blues is a less-than-representative account of a band that on its night could be wildly exciting.
Recorded live in Sweet Basil in New York City (on 2 January, which might explain the liverish playing),
it comes across as muddled rather than waspy. Terry Jenoure's vocals were a luxury that Sting could
have dispensed with, and the twinned guitars (great players when on their own turf) are often repetitive
and unilluminating. The CD brightens up the sound considerably, but doubts remain.

Ingrid Jensen TRUMPET, FLUGELHORN

*** **Vernal Fields** Enja ENJ 9013
>   Jensen; Steve Silson (*as, ss*); George Garzone (*ts*); Bruce Barth (*p*); Larry Grenadier (*b*); Lenny
>   White (*d*) 10/94.

Like Rebecca Coupe Franks before her, Jensen wholly confounds the notion that 'girls' can't play
effective jazz horn. Coming to this, her debut recording, cold and without presuppositions, one would
guess at a considerably older and more road-tested player. Jensen has spent some time living in Vienna,
where she has benefited from association with Hal Galper and, on her own instrument, Art Farmer.

   She gives early notice of her intentions on the brisk opening 'Marsh Blues', one of four originals
contributed by Jensen and her sister, Christine. As elsewhere, there's no camouflage or spurious grandstanding; it's a muscular, contemporary blues that stands up well on its own. It also establishes a
powerful rapport between Jensen and drummer White which is sustained right through the set.

   The flugelhorn solo on 'Every Time We Say Goodbye' is the only point on the album where her
influences are overt, Farmer looking over her shoulder. Otherwise Jensen is entirely her own woman,
self-possessed enough to be cryptically brief, unabashed at more extended displays, as on 'By Myself',
which rounds things off with a clear statement of future intent.

   Garzone contributes intelligent and tasteful material and Bruce Barth is, as always, right where he's
needed. No complaints about the other participants, but this is unmistakably the leader's set.

Jeff Jerolamon (born 1955) DRUMS

*** **Introducing Jeff Jerolamon** Candid CCD 79522
    Jerolamon; George Cables (p); Javier Colin (b). 10/91.
*** **Swing Thing!** Candid CCD 79538
    Jerolamon; Randy Sandke (t); Doug Lawrence (ts); George Cables (p); Harvie Swartz (b). 7/93.
Jerolamon's heart is on his sleeve. His household gods are not Elvin Jones or even Klook, but the
drummers of the swing generation, guys like Gene Krupa, Buddy Rich and Louie Bellson. The second
record is much more obviously in that line and – retrospectively at least – one detects Jerolamon's slight
discomfort with some of the settings on *Introducing*; too far down the bebop road for this most mainstream of young drummers.
    Recorded in Valencia at the end of a highly successful Spanish tour, the debut set has a sun-warmed
spontaneity that has at least as much to do with Cables's confident swing as with the drummer's
undoubted skills. The pianist contributes two originals, 'Dark Side/Light Side' and 'Quiet Fire', which
sit very comfortably alongside such well-worn standards as 'Round Midnight', 'Straight, No Chaser', 'A
Night in Tunisia' and 'You Stepped Out Of A Dream'. It might have been better to have placed more
emphasis on original themes, for Jerolamon comes out of a tradition that isn't strictly jazz-based. It's
still possible to hear the narrow-gauge steadiness of a rock beat from time to time, and that sits slightly
awkwardly with the Monk tunes especially. He takes to Bobby Hutcherson's 'Little B's Poem' so
adroitly that you almost wish he could switch to vibes for the duration.
    Swing Thing! is less laid back, a little pushier, and it suits the rhythm section well. While the improbably
named Randy Sandke (featured on just three tracks, two Charlie Shavers tunes and the Goodman/
Christian 'Seven Come Eleven') contributes very little, Lawrence has the deceptively lazy swing and
dramatic bite of Paul Gonsalves. Cables is heroic throughout, and especially good on 'Nancy With The
Laughing Face' and the Monk medley, for our money the heart of an otherwise slightly directionless set.
Jerolamon is going to have to work to avoid slipping into the retread business.

Bjorn Johansen (born 1940) TENOR SAXOPHONE

*** **Dear Henrik** Gemini GMCD 52
    Johansen; Erling Aksdal (p); Carl Morten Iversen (b); Ole Jacob Hansen (d). 2–5/86.
*** **Take One** Odin 21
    Johansen; Cedar Walton (p); David Williams (b); Billy Higgins (d).
A Norwegian with much local experience but with little exposure overseas, Johansen is one of the many
cases of European jazz musicians who ought to be better known outside their local base. His leathery
tone and sometimes gnarled phrasing remind one of Clifford Jordan, and it's no surprise to find a tune
on the Gemini album dedicated to the American saxophonist. Johansen works a furrow which is much
like other post-bop – but, as conventional as it may be, the music never quite settles into cliché or
routine. 'Beside', on *Dear Henrik*, opens as a ballad yet gathers power and momentum in a surprising
way, with Aksdal proving a match for Walton on the 'American' session. Higgins gives an ounce or
two's extra lift to the Odin record, but there is really little to choose between them, although the Gemini
is recorded a little more modestly in terms of sonic punch.

Henrik Johansen (1935–92) CLARINET

*** **Og Det Var Sa Det!** Storyville STCD 5501
    Johansen; Gunnar Johnsson, Theis Egil Jensen (c); Al Fairweather, Chris Bateson, Jorn
    Thomsen, Valdemar Rasmussen (t); Peter Nyegaard, Arne Bue Jensen, John R. T. Davies, Ole
    Toft (tb); Sandy Brown (cl); Adrian Bentzon, Bent Eriksen, Hans Otto Jorgensen (p); Russell
    Quay (g, kz, v); Jack Elliott, Hylda Sims (g, v); Diz Disley (g); Knud Fryland (g, bj); Freddy
    Poulson, Anthony Buguet, Per Krogh (bj); Fridolin Bentzon (bj, b); Ole Christiansen, Major
    Holley, Jens Solund, Heinz Carstens, Hugo Rasmussen, Henrik Hartmann (b); Ole Karn,
    Henrik Eigil Jensen, Graham Burbidge, Niels Bodker, Poul Jensen, Ole Streenberg (d); Alan
    Sutton (wbd). 54–81.
A splendid memorial to a musician whose sympathies stretched well across the jazz spectrum. The
opening track, a 1954 version of 'Careless Love', sets the Danish clarinettist down as a classic-jazz
stylist, but the final tracks find him in more mainstream company and, though his strong tone and agile
phrasing show preference for the New Orleans masters, he holds his own with the maverick Sandy
Brown on four tracks where they cross liquorice sticks. There is a nice 'New Orleans Hop Scop Blues'
with Fairweather, Davies and Disley, a track with the City Ramblers Skiffle Group and a very fine 'Cool

Water' from a 1963 session with his own band. Johansen is always at least as good as the best man on the date, and he's usually better. Excellent sound throughout from diverse source material.

Jan Johansson (1931–68) PIANO, ORGAN, VIBES

**** 8 Bitar Johansson/Innertrio Heptagon HECD-005
Johansson; Gunnar Johnson, Georg Riedel (*b*); Ingvar Callmer, Egil Johansen (*d*). 2/61–7/62.
**** Folkvisor Heptagon HECD-000
As above, except add Bosse Broberg (*t*), Arne Domnérus (*cl*), Lennart Aberg (*ts*), omit Johnson and Callmer. 2/62–9/67.
***(*) Live In Tallinn Heptagon HECD-007
Johannson; Rune Gustafsson (*g*); Georg Riedel (*b*). 6/66.
*** Spelar Musik Pa Sitt Eget Vis Megafon MFCD-2021 2CD
Johansson; Andreas Skjold (*tb*); Arne Domnérus (*cl, as*); Claes Rosendahl (*cl*); Bjarne Nerem (*ts*); Rune Gustafsson (*g*); Georg Riedel, Sture Nordin, Sture Akerberg (*b*); Egil Johansen, Rupert Clemendore (*d*). 9/64–11/66.
**** Den Korta Fristen Heptagon HECD-001
Johansson; Bertil Lovgren, Rolf Ericson, Jan Allan, Bosse Broberg, Lars Samuelsson (*t*); Runo Ericksson (*btb*); Arne Domnérus, Claes Rosendahl, Lennart Aberg, Erik Nilsson, Rune Falk (*reeds*); Rune Gustafsson (*g*); Georg Riedel (*b*); Egil Johansen (*d*). 67–68.
*** 300,000 Heptagon HECD-006
Johansson; Lennart Aberg (*ts*); Georg Riedel (*b*); Egil Johansen, Rupert Clemendore (*d*); Gote Nilsson (*elecs*). 8/67–7/68.
*** Musik Genom Fyra Sekler Heptagon HECD-002 2CD
Johansson; Claes Rosendahl (*cl, f*); Sven Berger (*f, ob, bsn*); Rune Gustafsson (*g*); Georg Riedel (*b*); Arne Wilhelmsson, Sture Akerberg (*b*). 9–10/68.

Johansson has been badly neglected by CD reissue until recently – so much so that many outside Sweden may scarcely be aware of this pioneering composer-pianist, whose inquiring mind was extraordinary enough to demand a place for him among the modern masters of the music. Luckily, since our last edition the Heptagon label has done much to bring back several of Johansson's major albums. Though most of his recording was compressed into an eight-year period, he was prolific enough to have cut some 20 LPs, and some of the best are now back in circulation. Many may know him for his work with Stan Getz on some of the saxophonist's recordings in Scandinavia, but that seems like mere 'prentice-work compared with the two marvellous discs reissued on *8 Bitar Johansson/Innertrio*. Beautifully shaded between differing jazz styles, the music seems entirely fresh and unjaded, even after more than 30 years. The standards include a lovely 'She's Funny That Way' and a remarkable revision of Morton's 'The Chant', while the originals drift placidly between bebop and swing tempo, improvisations falling out of the set patterns, tamed by the lucidity of Johansson's touch and the variety of his voicings. *Folkvisor* is, if anything, even more impressive, bringing together the original albums *Jazz Pa Svenska* and *Jazz Pa Ryska*. The 12 variations on Swedish folksong, with only the solid Riedel for company, make up a heartfelt meditation that equals any fusion of jazz and folk music so far committed to disc and, if the Russian themes that make up the rest of the disc are less affecting, they're a delightful makeweight. Johansson's insights are uniquely valuable, and it's fitting that his own notes mention Jimmy Giuffre, since one is reminded of the American folklore which Giuffre inculcated into his own masterpiece, *The Jimmy Giuffre Clarinet*.

The live album suffers from indifferent sound but gains from the intense communication among the three men, Gustafsson sounding especially involved: sample the interplay on 'Blues For Lange', or the jaunty treatment given to Oscar Pettiford's 'Laverne Walk'. *Spelar Musik Pa Sitt Eget Vis* is comparatively disappointing, a hotch-potch of bits and pieces from various radio sessions: there's a fine 'Django' with strings and some other telling fragments, but some of the experiments take on an unappealing cast – a strange 'Camptown Races', for instance. This is completely outdone by the compelling scores for Radiojazz Gruppen on *Den Korta Fristen*, music of real power and originality that makes one realize why his fellow-musicians held Johansson in such high regard. The almost shocking revision of 'A Night In Tunisia', set up as a feature for Nilsson's superb baritone, is a revelation – but so is 'Hej Blues', a haunting feature for Domnérus, the sparse setting for Gustafsson on 'Samba Triste' and several of Johansson's own scores, crowded with ideas.

Another live album, *300,000*, is less essential: Johansson had a taste for flirting with the edges of the avant-garde, and the two pieces which involve electronics and radio static sound as dated as most such adventures of the period. *Musik Genom Fyra Sekler* is a curious coda to the rest, a double-CD covering further explorations into Swedish traditional music. Johansson handles his group like a chamber ensemble, the reed players switching between instruments from track to track, melodies given a poker-faced treatment or just slightly subverted by the leader's variations. 'Ack Varmeland Du Skona', which every Swedish jazzman has played at some point, is given a soberly attractive reading, but some of the other tunes run dangerously close to kitsch. An odd if intriguing end. Only weeks later, Johansson was killed in a car accident on the way to a concert.

Jan Johansson (born 1944) GUITAR

*** **Blaus** Dragon DRCD 272
    Johansson; Red Mitchell (*b, p, v*). 9/89.
Johansson is a music teacher and occasional performer who struck up a friendship with Red Mitchell that resulted in their working as a duo in the last years of the bassist's life. This disc of duets was cut at Red's Stockholm apartment and is the only souvenir of their work together. The easeful charm and sly intelligence which Mitchell injected into every date holds this one together: Johansson plays very capably, but his twangy sound and spidery inflexions are made to sound even thinner by Red's characteristically boomy parts. There is a lovely treatment of 'Lover Man' among the five standards on display, and 'In A Sentimental Mood' is nearly as good. Sound isn't bad, but it would have been good to have heard the duo in a proper studio situation.

Ulf Johansson (born 1957) PIANO, TROMBONE, VOCAL

(*) **Trackin' The Wulf Phontastic PHONT 8809
    Johansson (*p* solo); Kicki Werre-Johansson (*v*). 1/91.
***(*) **The Wobbling Woodwinds – Solo Flight** Phontastic NCD 8829
    Johansson; Tord Larsson, Peter Lindqvist, Jan Lundberg, Stefan Lindberg, Jan-Eric Sundqvist (*woodwinds*); Tor Holmstrom (*p*); Stefan Nordgaard (*g*); Stefan Karlsson (*b*); Ulf Degerman (*d*). 5/93.
*** **Hot Time In Umea** Phontastic NCD 8833
    Johansson; Antti Sarpila (*cl*); Ronnie Gardiner (*d*). 8/93.
Johansson plays good trombone, but he sticks to the piano on *Trackin' The Wulf* for a bright recital of swing-styled piano. Despite his comparative youth, it's the earlier generation of Wilson, Waller and perhaps Nat Cole that Johansson seems to admire, and he likes a striding left hand more than any bebop triplets. The 16 tracks include plenty of pre-war chestnuts as well as four originals of his own, and he usually has a fresh idea for most of them: listen to the way he sidles into 'Sweet Georgia Brown', for instance. Beautiful piano-sound, but docked a notch for the singing that he decides to contribute to four tracks. Ms Werre-Johansson sings only on 'Until The Real Thing Comes Along', nicely enough.
    Solo Flight offers a trim programme of swing-era settings for the very accomplished Swedish woodwind team. They open with seven Benny Carter tunes – none of them obvious choices, aside from 'When Lights Are Low' – and then work through 11 other charts with no concessions to cliché. The playing is uniformly impeccable, and Johansson, on trombone this time, peppers the ensemble with some splendidly agile solos. *Hot Time In Umea* is a festival set where Johansson returns to the piano and Finnish clarinet maestro Sarpila and drummer Gardiner dig into a bag of Benny Goodman chestnuts. This is skilful repertory playing and, though the musicians choose not to impose too much of themselves on the situation, it's beguiling stuff, and a useful blindfold test for swing-jazz pundits.

Budd Johnson (1910–84) TENOR, SOPRANO AND ALTO SAXOPHONE, CLARINET

***(*) **Let's Swing** Original Jazz Classics OJC 1720
    Johnson; Keg Johnson (*tb*); Tommy Flanagan (*p*); George Duvivier (*b*); Charli Persip (*d*). 12/60.
*** **The JPJ Quartet** Storyville STCD 8235
    Johnson; Dill Jones (*p*); Bill Pemberton (*b*); Oliver Jackson (*d*). 69 or 70, 6/71.
Budd Johnson was a jazz giant for over five decades, yet he made comparatively few recordings under his own leadership, and it's sad that fewer still are currently in circulation. This OJC reissue is a thin representation, but at least it restores a good record to wider availability. Johnson was already a veteran when he made these, having been an arranger for big bands throughout the 1930s and '40s, involving himself in many of the pioneering bebop gatherings and generally slotting comfortably into almost any setting. His tone was in the classic Hawkins mould: big, broad, soaked in blues feeling. 'Blues By Budd', on *Let's Swing*, is an inimitable example of Johnson at his best. There is a certain dry humour in his playing which never spills over into parody or flippancy: listen to the way he opens his solo on 'Uptown

Manhattan' on the quintet album, and hear how he intensifies his playing from that point. His brother Keg plays some cheerful solos, but it's Budd's record – try the lovely reading of 'Someone To Watch Over Me', in which the saxophonist composed a unison passage for himself and Duvivier.

The later quartet was recorded in the studio (exact date not reliably known) and at the Montreux Jazz Festival in 1971. Of the two, the live performances are immeasurably superior, and one wonders whether there wasn't more material from the same event to make the record a concert set without recourse to what could justifiably be dismissed as rehearsal material. The group has a seasoned, familiar sound, as if used to working together, and Johnson obviously thrives on a conducive harmonic environment.

Bunk Johnson (1889–1949) TRUMPET

*** **Bunk Johnson And His Superior Jazz Band** Good Time Jazz 12048
 Johnson; Jim Robinson (*tb*); George Lewis (*cl*); Walter Decou (*p*); Lawrence Marrero (*bj*);
 Austin Young (*b*); Ernest Rogers (*d*). 6/42.
*** **Bunk And Lou** Good Time Jazz 12024
 Johnson; Lu Watters, Bob Scobey (*c*); Turk Murphy (*tb*); Ellis Horne (*cl*); Wally Rose, Burt
 Bales (*p*); Clancy Hayes, Russ Bennett, Pat Patton (*bj*); Dick Lammi (*bb*); Squire Gersback (*b*);
 Bill Dart (*d*). 2/44.

A difficult and contentious man, Bunk Johnson remains mysterious and fascinating, still the figure-head of 'revivalist' jazz even though his records remain difficult to find and have been marginalized where those by, say, George Lewis have kept their reputation. Deceitful about his age – he was long thought to have been born in 1879, which would have made him even older than Buddy Bolden – Johnson was rediscovered in 1942 and, after being fitted out with new teeth, began making records. He had never recorded before, even though he'd played in Bolden's band, had moved on from New Orleans sometime in his mid-teens and gone on to play all over the South. But many records came out of the next five years. Those for Good Time Jazz were among the earliest. *Bunk Johnson And His Superior Jazz Band* establishes the best-remembered Johnson line-up, with fellow veterans Robinson, Lewis and Marrero, and the material is mostly New Orleans staples such as 'Down By The Riverside'. *Bunk And Lou* pits him against the Lu Watters band, who mix 'modern' items such as 'Ory's Creole Trombone' with a number of truly ancient ragtime pieces like 'Smokey Mokes', although frustratingly Johnson plays on only the more recent material. While neither is a really satisfactory record – Watters and company sound too slickly amateur to suit an original like Johnson, and the other record lacks the awareness which Johnson would quickly develop – both establish the tenets of his own trumpet style: a polished, almost courtly sort of phrasing, the elimination of 'hot' tricks such as growls or shakes or needless vibrato, a bright and optimistic open tone and a way of swinging which sounds like a development out of ragtime and older brass traditions than jazz. Something, perhaps, between swing and syncopation.

***(*) **Bunk Johnson In San Francisco** American Music AMCD-16
 Johnson; Mutt Carey (*t*); Jim Robinson, Kid Ory, Turk Murphy (*tb*); Wade Whaley, Ellis Horne
 (*cl*); George Lewis (*cl*); Buster Wilson, Burt Bales, Bertha Gonsoulin (*p*); Frank Pasley (*g*);
 Lawrence Marrero, Pat Patton (*bj*); Sidney Brown (*bb*); Ed Garland, Squire Gersback (*b*);
 Everett Walsh, Clancy Hayes, Edgar Moseley (*d*). 9/43–1/44.
*** **The King Of The Blues** American Music AMCD-1
 Johnson; Jim Robinson (*tb*); George Lewis (*cl*); Lawrence Marrero (*bj*); Sidney 'Jim Little'
 Brown (*b, bb*); Alcide 'Slow Drag' Pavageau (*b*); Baby Dodds (*d*). 44–45.
**** **Bunk Johnson 1944** American Music AMCD-3
 Johnson; Jim Robinson (*tb*); George Lewis (*cl*); Sidney Brown (*bb*); Lawrence Marrero (*bj*);
 Alcide 'Slow Drag' Pavageau (*b*); Baby Dodds (*d*). 8/44.
**** **Bunk Johnson 1944 (2nd Masters)** American Music AMCD-8
 As above. 8/44.
**** **Bunk's Brass Band And Dance Band 1945** American Music AMCD-6
 Johnson; Louis 'Kid Shots' Madison (*t*); Jim Robinson (*tb*); George Lewis (*cl*); Isidore Barbarin
 (*ahn*); Adolphe Alexander (*bhn*); Joe Clark (*bass hn*); Lawrence Marrero (*bj, d*); Alcide 'Slow
 Drag' Pavageau (*b*); Baby Dodds (*d*). 5/45.

Johnson's American Music recordings are his most substantial legacy, even if there is occasionally indifferent sound-quality and various incompatabilities with sidemen and material. Robinson and Lewis may have been New Orleans's finest, but Johnson didn't seem to like them all that much, and he frequently plays much better than Lewis on these sessions. Nevertheless *The King Of The Blues* and *1944* – as well as its subsequent CD of alternative takes on AMCD-8 – feature much fine music, the first all on blues themes, the second a mix of the obvious ('Panama' and so forth) and tunes which show Johnson's weakness for popular novelties, such as 'There's Yes Yes In Your Eyes'. It is mostly an ensemble music, leads being passed around the front line and small inflexions making each performance unique to itself; but there is a freshness and intensity here (Johnson had, after all, been waiting a long time to make serious records) which give the music a real cumulative power that grows with each listening. Any raggedness in the playing or flaw in the sound is made to seem insignificant by the surpassing rigour of Johnson's men and their fierce craftsmanship, especially on the 1944 discs (recorded on a hot day: a photo of the session shows everyone in their undershirts). Bill Russell's session notes make fascinating reading in the booklet with AMCD-8.

The other two discs are at least as interesting. *In San Francisco* includes a This Is Jazz broadcast with an all-star band including, intriguingly, Johnson's trumpet contemporary, Mutt Carey, and though Johnson sounds unhappy on 'Dipper Mouth Blues' it's absorbing music. Even better, though, are the six trumpet–piano duets with Bertha Gonsoulin. Nowhere else can one hear Johnson's silvery tone and proper phrasing so clearly. *Bunk's Brass Band And Dance Band* is a fine introduction to Johnson's music, since it features what would have been a regular parade band line-up on 11 tracks and a further nine by a typical Johnson dance group (recorded at George Lewis's home). Lewis sounds a little shrill on the *Brass Band* tracks, which makes one wonder about the pitching, though there is a credit for 'pitch rectification' on the CD. It is a pioneering record nevertheless, as the first authentic, New Orleans brass-band session. The 'dance' tracks are very sprightly and feature some fine Lewis, as well as some of Johnson's firmest lead and even some respectable solos. The sound is quite clean as these sessions go, though some of the *Brass Band* acetates are in less than perfect shape.

*** **Bunk & Leadbelly At New York Town Hall 1947** American Music AMCD-46
> Johnson; Jimmy Archey (*tb*); Omer Simeon, Edmond Hall (*cl*); Ralph Sutton (*p*); Huddie 'Leadbelly' Ledbetter (*g, v*); Danny Barker (*g, bj*); Cyrus St Clair (*bb*); Freddie Moore (*d, v*); Mama Price (*v*). 9/47.

*** **Bunk Johnson & Mutt Carey In New York 1947** American Music AMCD-45
> Johnson; Mutt Carey (*t*); Jerry Blumberg (*c*); Jimmy Archey, Bob Mielke (tb); Albert Nicholas, Jack Sohmer (*cl*); James P. Johnson, Dick Wellstood (*p*); Pops Foster, Charles Treager (*b*); Baby Dodds, Irv Kratka (*d*). 10/47.

Two souvenirs from Johnson's stay in New York during 1947. the *Town Hall* concert with an all-star group is sound, spirited Dixieland: Johnson isn't on his best form but he plays decently enough. Leadbelly's billing is a bit misleading since he sings for only four minutes on the entire record. The sound, drawn from previously bootlegged acetates, has been cleaned up very respectably.

The other disc finds Bunk at the Caravan Ballroom, once with a team of old hands, the other time with a very young group of white Dixielanders including the 20-year-old Wellstood. Mutt Carey replaces Bunk on four tracks, rather than sitting in with him. None of this counts as 'authentic' Johnson, but it shows that he was more adaptable than his roots following might wish to think, since there's nothing that disgraces him.

***(*) **Last Testament** Delmark DD 225
> Johnson; Ed Cuffee (*tb*); Garvin Bushell (*cl*); Don Kirkpatrick (*p*); Danny Barker (*g*); Wellman Braud (*b*); Alphonse Steele (*d*). 12/47.

Johnson's farewell was reportedly the only session in which he really got his own way, choosing both sidemen and material; and New Orleans purists must have been surprised on both counts: he lined up a team of players quite different from the American Music cronies, and he chose rags and pop tunes to perform. 'The Entertainer', 'Kinklets' and 'The Minstrel Man' have a rather wistful animation about them, while a tune such as 'Till We Meet Again' has a (perhaps inevitable) air of valediction about it. Cuffee and Bushell play with more fluency and zip than Robinson and Lewis ever did, but their slightly anonymous quality stops them from overwhelming Johnson himself, who sounds far from finished. He plays a firm lead and takes simple, bittersweet solos. The sound is a drawback: though recorded in the Carnegie Recital Hall, the quality is indifferent, often boxy and without much definition, and Jack Towers and Bob Koester haven't been able to do much with it in the remastering.

Charlie Johnson (1891–1959) PIANO

**** **The Complete Charlie Johnson Sessions** Hot 'N Sweet FDC 5110
> Johnson; Gus Aiken, Leroy Rutledge, Jabbo Smith, Thomas Morris, Sidney De Paris, Leonard Davis (*t*); Regis Hartman, Charlie Irvis, Jimmy Harrison, George Washington (*tb*); Ben Whittet, Benny Carter (*cl, as*); Benny Waters (*as, ts*); Edgar Sampson (*cl, as, vn*); Bobby Johnson (*bj*); Cyrus St Clair, Billy Taylor (*tba*); George Stafford (*d*); Monette Moore (*v*). 10/25–5/29.

Charlie Johnson was a major name in Harlem and he led a band at Small's Paradise Club until 1938, so it's mystifying that he recorded only 14 titles in all that time. All of them are collected here, along with 10 alternative takes, and the calibre of the music is strong enough to regret that Johnson didn't do more in the studios. He lured some top sidemen into the band, including Jimmy Harrison, Jabbo Smith and Sidney De Paris; Benny Carter contributed some arrangements and played on one date; Benny Waters, who was still recording 60 years later, made some of his earliest appearances here. If the earlier pieces such as 'Meddlin' With The Blues' sound like rough-and-ready examples of black dance music of the day, there is a greater polish by the time of the superb 1928–9 sessions. The rhythms are still a little old-fashioned, tied to St Clair and Taylor, but the music seems to have rocket fuel in it on the likes of 'Walk That Thing', and their farewell tracks, 'Harlem Drag' and 'Hot Bones And Rice', are front-rank examples of hard-swinging Harlem dance music. De Paris, Smith and Waters all have their moments, but Harrison stands out even more remarkably than he does with Fletcher Henderson. The remastering is inconsistent, some tracks being much louder than others, but no serious reservations on an important reissue.

Dick Johnson ALTO SAXOPHONE, CLARINET

*** **Dick Johnson Plays** Concord CCD 4106
Johnson; Dave McKenna (*p*); Bob Maize (*b*); Jake Hanna (*d*). 5/79.
Nice, plain title; nice, plain mainstream jazz from a musician whose absence of pretension and unaffected delivery are matched by a witty thematic approach which is similar in spirit to that of his pianist on this date. McKenna is, almost inevitably, the true star of the session, a rolling, fulsome approach that tempers the oddly sardonic character of Johnson's own solos.

Howard Johnson (born 1941) TUBA, BARITONE SAXOPHONE, FLUGELHORN

*** **Arrival** Verve 523985
Johnson; Sarah Seidel (*f, af, v*); Johannes Georg Baumann (*p*); Sabine Worthmann (*b, v*); Wolff Reichert (*d, perc*); Dumisani Mabaso, Kojo Samuels (*perc*). 7/94.
***(*) **Gravity!!!** Verve 531 021
Johnson; Dave Bargeron, Nedra Johnson, Carl Kleinsteuber, Tom Malone, Bob Stewart, Earl McIntyre, Joe Daley, Marcus Rojas (*tba*); Raymond Chew, Paul Shaffer, James Williams (*p*); George Wadenius (*g*); Bob Cranshaw, Melissa Slocum (*b*); Kenwood Dennard, Kenny Washington (*d*); Victor See Yuen (*perc*). 96.
The big Alabaman was for many years first-call tuba player, paving the way for later revivers of this wonderful precursor of string bass. Johnson had other strings to his bow, both the baritone saxophone, on which he has a rich, uncomplicated delivery very close to his brass playing, and also the flugelhorn, which he deployed to great effect with Gato Barbieri's excellent mid-'70s band. *Arrival* features his band, Nubia, a Euro-African outfit which never quite settles into an identifiable idiom but scoots back and forth between Euro-bop and an Afro-tinged avantist revivalism. One suspects these probably aren't the players Johnson should be working with at this stage in his career.

Gravity!!! marks a definite step forward. An attempt to highlight the tuba as a solo instrument, it probably replaces neglect with overkill. Anthony Braxton has written pieces for tuba ensemble more thoroughly idiomatic than these. Johnson, though, seems to have concentrated on getting the maximum range of sonority out of the big horns, and his choice of material, from Jackie McLean's 'Appointment In Ghana' to Wynton Kelly's 'Kelly Blue', to 'Yesterdays' and some originals are tailored to that end. The results are interesting enough, but the best of Johnson is still to be found on other people's records.

J. J. Johnson (born 1924) TROMBONE

*** **J. J. Johnson's Jazz Quintets** Savoy SV 0151
Johnson; Sonny Rollins (*ts*); Leo Parker, Cecil Payne (*bs*); Hank Jones, John Lewis, Bud Powell (*p*); Leonard Gaskin, Al Lucas, Gene Ramey (*b*); Max Roach, Shadow Wilson (*d*). 6/46, 12/47, 5/49.
***(*) **Jay And Kai** Savoy SV 0163
Johnson; Kai Winding (*tb*); Leo Parker (*bs*); Wally Cirillo, Hank Jones, Lou Stein (*p*); Billy Bauer (*g*); Al Lucas, Charles Mingus, Eddie Safranski (*b*); Kenny Clarke, Tiny Kahn, Shadow Wilson (*d*); Al Young (*perc*). 12/47, 3/52, 8/54.
***(*) **Trombone By Three** Original Jazz Classics OJC 091
Johnson; Kenny Dorham (*t*); Sonny Rollins (*ts*); John Lewis (*p*); Leonard Gaskin (*b*); Max Roach (*d*). 5/49.

**** **The Eminent Jay Jay Johnson: Volume 1** Blue Note B21Y 81505
**** **The Eminent Jay Jay Johnson: Volume 2** Blue Note B21Y 81506

> Johnson; Clifford Brown (*t*); Hank Mobley (*ts*); Jimmy Heath (*ts, bs*); Wynton Kelly, John Lewis, Horace Silver (*p*); Paul Chambers, Percy Heath, Charles Mingus (*b*); Kenny Clarke (*d*); Sabu Martinez (*perc*). 6/53, 9/54, 6/55.

J. J. Johnson is one of the most important figures in modern jazz. Once voguish, the trombone, like the clarinet, largely fell from favour with younger players with the faster articulations of bebop. Johnson's unworthily low standing nowadays (his partnership with Kai Winding, as 'Jay and Kai' was once resonantly popular) is largely due to a perceived absence of trombone players with whom to compare him. In fact, Johnson turned an occasionally unwieldy instrument into an agile and pure-toned bop voice; so good was his articulation that single-note runs in the higher register often sounded like trumpet. He frequently hung an old beret over the bell of his horn to soften his tone and bring it into line with the sound of the saxophones around him.

The two Savoys offer worthwhile if scrappy documentation of the early years. The June 1946 session with a heavy-handed Bud Powell and the rather one-dimensional Payne doesn't show the trombonist off in the best possible light. He sounds good with another baritone man, the ever-buoyant Parker, on Christmas Eve 1947 (there's an additional track from this on *Jay And Kai*), and the tracks with Rollins and Lewis are a delight. An often overlooked point about the Johnson/Winding partnership was its sheer imbalance in terms of playing skill. Johnson always sounds poised and affable when his sparring partner is casting about for ideas; there are a couple of tracks from Winding's own group, and they're pretty uninspired. That contrast is resoundingly reinforced on *Trombone By Three*, where the Johnson material is streets ahead of the Winding and Bennie Green tracks parcelled with it.

The first volume of the Blue Note set is one of the central documents of post-war jazz and should on no account be missed. Johnson – who was working as a blueprint checker at the time of the earliest sessions recorded, apparently dissatisfied with his output to date – sounds fleet and confident, and has a marvellous band round him, including a young Clifford Brown. 'Turnpike' and 'Capri' exist in two versions each and show Johnson's ability to rethink his phraseology, adjusting his attack on the original-release versions to accommodate Clarke's powerful but unemphatic swing (which is rather swamped on the sessions of September 1954 by Mingus's chiming bass and the slap-happy Martinez); even on the slow-tempo 'Turnpike', Clarke provides an irresistible moving force underneath the melody. 'Get Happy' is appropriately up-beat and joyous, with notes picked off like clay pipes at a shooting gallery. In contrast, 'Lover Man' is given a mournful, drawn-out statement that squeezes out every drop of emotion the melody has to offer. The 1954 session yields some fine exchanges between Johnson and Kelly, notably on 'It's You Or No One' and 'Too Marvellous For Words', where the leader's tone and attack are almost as perfect as on 'Turnpike'. Volume 2 is filled out with a less than inspiring 1955 date featuring Hank Mobley and Horace Silver, neither of whom seem attuned to Johnson's taxing idiom.

*** **Kai Winding And Jay Jay Johnson** Bethlehem BET 6026

> Johnson; Kai Winding (*tb*); Dick Katz (*p*); Milt Hinton, Wendell Marshall (*b*); Al Harewood (*d*). 1/55.

***(*) **Jay and Kai + 6** Columbia COL 480990

> Johnson; Kai Winding (*tb, trombonium*); Urbie Green, Bob Alexander, Eddie Bert, Jimmy Cleveland (*tb*); Bart Varsalona, Tom Mitchell (*btb*); Hank Jones (*p*); Milt Hinton, Ray Brown (*b*); Osie Johnson (*d*); Candido Camero (*perc*). 56.

***(*) **The Great Kai And J.J.** Impulse! MCAD 42012

> Johnson; Kai Winding (*tb*); Bill Evans (*p*); Paul Chambers, Tommy Williams (*b*); Roy Haynes, Art Taylor (*d*). 60.

The Impulse! recording was a commercially motivated reunion, some time after the partnership had been amicably dissolved. Perhaps because the band behind them was so good, J.J. and Kai very quickly rediscovered their old groove. The two horns are exactly in balance, and the vibrato, which in Winding's case was apt to get wider as he aged, is exactly co-ordinated. There is much good-natured four-bar swapping which might pall after a while, were it not so sweetly and tunefully done.

There is nothing like Bill Evans's brief but elegantly articulated solos on the first record, and he makes an enormous difference to the overall feel of the Impulse!, which sounds like a proper group project rather than a trombone feature with accompaniment. That's the problem with the Bethlehem, where even on CD the band sounds very far back.

The best point of comparison, before-and-after, is 'Going, Going, Gong', which refers back to the lively 'Gong Rock' on the 1955 Bethlehem session. If this is qualitatively representative, and we tend to feel it is, then the later sessions have gained considerably in sophistication and sheer class and, though dedicated J. J. and Kai fans will think the suggestion heretical, the Impulse! is the one to go for, though trombone nuts will find themselves drawn to the Columbia, which features eight – count 'em – of the sliding fellows, often in jubilant unison. The two frontmen vary the sound a bit on the self-explanatory 'Piece for Two Tromboniums', which is interesting enough to suggest that these admittedly less limber valved horns could have been developed a step further. The arrangments are very good indeed and the material (with the exception of 'Surrey With The Fringe on Top') highly original and exciting. George Avakian's production is, as always, faultless.

*** Four Trombones: The Debut Recordings Prestige PCD 24097

Johnson; Willie Dennis, Bennie Green, Kai Winding (*tb*); John Lewis (*p*); Charles Mingus (*b*); Art Taylor (*d*).

Originally recorded for the short-lived independent label co-run by Mingus and Max Roach, this suffers slightly from its own ungainly format, which buries Johnson a little. There are, though, fine and fresh performances all round, including a stirring account of 'Now's The Time'. Mingus takes charge more than once. The sound is a shade too bright on the transfer and the top notes are inclined to be a bit vinegary.

***(*) The Birdlanders Fresh Sound FSRCD 170

Johnson; Jerry Lloyd (*t*); Al Cohn (*ts*); Gigi Gryce (*bs*); Milt Jackson (*vib, p*); Henri Renaud (*p*); Percy Heath, Curley Russell (*b*); Walter Bolden, Charlie Smith (*d*). 2 & 3/54.

***(*) Live At The Café Bohemia Fresh Sound FSRCD 143

Johnson; Bobby Jaspar (*ts, f*); Tommy Flanagan (*p*); Wilbur Little (*b*); Elvin Jones (*d*). 2/57.

Among the best of the surviving albums, both are beautifully transferred to CD, avoiding the awkward chiming effect that plagues much trombone of the period, particularly on live recordings. The first is very nearly hi-jacked by the vibraharpist, whose soloing on another supposedly cumbersome instrument is dazzlingly self-confident. Cohn is actually rather muted, and the later sessions with Gryce and trumpeter Jerry Lloyd aren't up to standard. Despite Jaspar's shortcomings as a soloist (he's still a block ahead of Henri Renaud) and a degree of unease in the ensembles, the Café Bohemia sessions provide an ideal blowing context for Johnson; he lets go joyously on 'Angel Eyes', 'Old Devil Moon' (see also *Eminent*, Volume 1) and, a favourite, 'Solar'. Flanagan's chording and fills are as near perfect as they could be. A constant delight.

*** At The Opera House Verve 847340

Johnson; Stan Getz (*ts*); Oscar Peterson (*p*); Herb Ellis (*g*); Ray Brown (*b*); Connie Kay (*d*). 9 & 10/57.

Later the same year as the Café Bohemia session, Johnson and Stan Getz co-led a band at the Civic Opera in Chicago, and then again at the Shrine in LA. Someone had the nous to get the first one down in stereo, but the West Coast tracks, which are probably the better musically, are in very four-square mono. It's fascinating to be able to compare versions of 'Billie's Bounce' (which Getz doesn't really treat as a bebop tune either time), 'Crazy Rhythm', 'Blues In The Closet' and 'My Funny Valentine', though of course the variance in recording means that some of the apparent stylistic differences are artefacts.

One great beauty of the session is the opportunity to hear both front men playing songs not normally associated with them. As such, it has to be considered a footnote rather than a centrally important record. Even so, it's well worth the investment.

***(*) The Trombone Master Columbia 44443

Johnson; Nat Adderley (*c*); Victor Feldman (*p, vib*); Tommy Flanagan (*p*); Paul Chambers, Sam Jones, Wilbur Little (*b*); Louis Hayes, Albert 'Tootie' Heath, Max Roach (*d*). 4 & 5/57, 2/58, 12/60.

A marvellous compilation with the accent on ballads and easy-swinging numbers. It's interesting to compare Johnson's approach to Monk's 'Misterioso', the opening cut, with the version he recorded with Sonny Rollins on the saxophonist's eponymous 1957 Blue Note. It's smoother, but also more sophisticated rhythmically, with that wonderful french horn sound. On 'Laura', Johnson sticks to a slightly faster-than-usual tempo and builds a solo of near-perfect melodic invention. The long 'Blue Trombone' is gutsier and closer to an orthodox blowing theme, but 'My Old Flame' and 'Cry Me A River' stay very close to the basic song-form, and the closing 'Goodbye' is a small masterpiece of compression.

Perhaps a little too laid back to be completely representative of Johnson's skills, but a valuable introduction to his gentler side.

*** Proof Positive Impulse! GRP 11452

Johnson; Harold Mabern, McCoy Tyner (*p*); Toots Thielemans (*g*); Richard Davis, Arthur Harper (*b*); Frank Gant, Elvin Jones (*d*). 5/64.

Not the least valuable thing about this record is that it helps narrow a gap in the Johnson discography which, as will be judged from the dates above and below, is almost two decades long. Though the 1980s material has a very definite gravitas and it lacks the bounce and buoyancy of the earlier years – certainly of the J. J. and Kai project – there is a sombre quality to all of Johnson's work. It comes through very strongly on *Proof Positive*, most notably on 'My Funny Valentine', where he digresses from the final bars of the melody to reach away down (seemingly using an altered slide position) to a deep C that lends the song an almost tragic cast. He is the main solo voice here, working without another horn (which, curiously, he has always resisted) and with a slightly reticent group who push him ever forward into the daylight. For sheer musicianship, and an insight into his harmonic mastery, Miles Davis's composition 'Neo' (aka 'Teo') is instructive. It's a long track, rapidly paced in 3/4 and moving through a spectrum of chords that all veer to the darker end. Even starlit, with Stella, Johnson sounds a wry, philosophical note.

Mabern keeps the mood from getting too sombre, alternating his own chunky chordal style with quick-fingered single-note runs and stealing the boss's thunder on 'Blues Waltz', a Max Roach composition, with a great solo that exactly mirrors and inverts the harmonic contours of the trombone's earlier excursion.

The album also includes a single track from a session with the unlikely line-up of Thielemans (on guitar at this point rather than the more familiar harmonica), Tyner, Davis and Jones. It seems, according to Michael Cuscuna's reissue team, that this was part of a longer session; two other track titles are known and even an issue number, but no trace can be found of masters or pressings.

*** Concepts In Blue Original Jazz Classics OJC 735
> Johnson; Clark Terry (*t, flhn*); Ernie Watts (*ts, as*); Pete Jolly (*ky*); Victor Feldman (*vib, ky*); Ray Brown (*b*); Tony Dumas, Kevin Johnson (*d*). 9/80.

This wasn't exactly a comeback album, but it marks an end to a hole in the existing discography. What's obvious again, even before a note is played, is Johnson's ability to put together great bands. Despite a few 1970s giveaways (like electric keyboards) and a rather busy mix, it's a terrific disc. A saminess starts to creep in before the end, particularly from Watts, who seems to have only a handful of ideas in his bag, but Terry's clear upper-register notes and broad smears are an ideal complement to Johnson, and it might even have been possible to dispense with a saxophonist altogether. Recommended.

***(*) We'll Be Together Again Pablo 2310911
> Johnson; Joe Pass (*g*). 10/83.
*** Things Are Getting Better All The Time Pablo Today 2312141
> Johnson; Al Grey (*tb*); Kenny Barron (*p, ky*); Ray Brown (*b*); Mickey Roker (*d*). 11/83.

Johnson kept out of sight for most of the 1970s, composing and arranging for the movies and television. Within five weeks in 1983, however, he made two sterling albums that belied the full-stop some critics had put after his name. The sanguinely titled *Things* looks suspiciously like another attempt to reduplicate the Jay and Kai sound, but it comes across much more individually. Grey, a year younger than Johnson, is a more traditional stylist; a genius with the plunger mute, he has a big, belting tone that goes well with Johnson's increasingly delicate fills and recapitulations. 'Soft Winds', 'Paper Moon' and 'Softly As In A Morning Sunrise' are particularly good. Pianist Barron is contained and exact, but Brown and Roker are uncharacteristically listless, perhaps recognizing that the two principals (who shared the billing) play to their own inner metre. Good stuff.

Like Johnson, Joe Pass represents an extraordinary cross-section of modern jazz idiom, all carefully assimilated and absorbed. His constant lower-string pulse makes him particularly adaptable to solo and duo performance, and *Together Again* has the fullness of texture that might be expected of a larger group. The performances – 'Nature Boy', 'Bud's Blues', 'Solar', 'When Lights Are Low', six others – have a fresh-minted sparkle and immediate currency. Strongly recommended.

**** Live At The Village Vanguard Emarcy 848327
> Johnson; Ralph Moore (*ts, ss*); Stanley Cowell (*p*); Rufus Reid (*b*); Victor Lewis (*d*). 7/88.
***(*) Standards Emarcy 848328
> As above. 7/88.

Anyone who missed a chance to see Johnson with this band at the Village Vanguard in New York in the summer of 1988 must be kicking himself now. These are terrific discs, recorded with loads of atmosphere and a sensible attention to detail. The first of the pair is the more adventurous, not just in terms of material, but also in playing. Moore sounds a little more confident with the contemporary stuff (and trad chestnuts like 'Saints') than he does with the songbook material on *Standards*. Interestingly, so does the leader. The second record gives no sign of being an afterthought, but it lacks a bit of zip and one finds oneself listening to Cowell even when the front line's in action. Not a bad sign in itself, but an indication that maybe it lacks something. Johnson's solos on 'Nefertiti' (*Live*) and 'Misterioso' (*Standards*) are exemplary, and the rhythm section does him proud, with Reid sounding remarkably like Mingus back in the old days. He obviously liked this band and reassembled it for *Let's Hang Out* (below). They never played better than this, though, surely?

***(*) **Vivian** Concord CCD 4523

Johnson; Rob Schneiderman (*p*); Ted Dunbar (*g*); Rufus Reid (*b*); Akira Tana (*d*). 6/92.

A gentle ballad set, dedicated to the trombonist's late wife who succumbed to a stroke after more than 40 years of marriage. The band is just right for the job. Reid and Tana are almost telepathically linked, and Schneiderman and Dunbar strike up a rapport and a partnership that feeds Johnson a huge range of colours and dynamic variations, even within a gentle and slightly melancholy programme. A lovely record; for hopeful romantics everywhere.

***(*) **Let's Hang Out** Emarcy 514 454

Johnson; Terence Blanchard (*t*); Jimmy Heath (*ts*); Ralph Moore (*ts, ss*); Stanley Cowell, Renée Rosnes (*p*); Rufus Reid (*b*); Victor Lewis, Lewis Nash (*d*). 12/92.

Just four years on from the Village Vanguard sessions, and Johnson is maybe showing his years just a little; unless, of course, it's simply the studio that constrains him. Producer Jean-Philippe Allard goes for a very mellow tone and there's a slight anxiety that he has robbed the three front-line horns of their individuality. Blanchard and Moore have certainly had more muscle on other sessions.

Kicking off the set is the four-part 'Friendship Suite', which brings in the 'other' band of Heath (still playing like a cut-down Bird), Rosnes, Reid and Nash. As a composition, it's no big deal, and the whole thing doesn't occupy ten minutes. 'Kenyatta' in the middle of the programme has a bit more to chew on, but it's here that Moore and Blanchard are made to seem a little colourless. J. J. takes 'Beautiful Love' unaccompanied and then on the closing 'I Got It Bad' plays with just rhythm, something he's seemingly resisted throughout his career. A pity; it's a lovely ending.

*** **Tangence** Verve 526 588

Johnson; Nigel Carter, Ronnie Hughes, Derek Healey, Simon Gardner, Kenny Baker (*t*); Don Lusher, Gordon Campbell, Colin Sheen, Bill Geldard (*tb*); John Pignegny, Jeff Bryant, Nick Busch, Richard Watkins (*frhn*); Ray Swinfield, Tommy Whittle, Robin Kennard, Joseph Sanders, Ray Willox, Peter Hughes, Denis Walton (*saxes*); Laurie Holloway (*p, ky*); Louis Stewart (*g*); Hugh Webb (*hp*); Chris Laurence, Peter Cullington, Allen Walley (*b*); Terry Jenkins (*d*); Eric Allen (*perc*). 7/94.

Johnson was an able big-band composer, but there have been all too few opportunities to hear him in these contexts. This late disc demonstrates once again the pointlessness of the criticism that J. J. is a rather limited, one-dimensional player who lacks pep. He dominates a rather over-strung orchestra from the word go, and even when Wynton Marsalis makes his first guest appearance, on 'For Dancers Only', he's well up to the young guy's speed. That being said, there's nothing too hostile about any of the tracks on *Tangence*. J. J. still favours that easy-sounding swoop down to low C and still likes to elongate phrases that most of his imitators would try to compress.

The album was made in the United Kingdom, mainly with British players. Robert Farnon, an able but rather lush orchestrator, overcooks in the time-honoured British way, but there's nothing mushy about J. J.'s playing. He sounds masterful and poised, still at the top of his craft.

James P. Johnson (1894–1955) PIANO, COMPOSER

***(*) **Harlem Stride Piano, 1921–1929** Hot'N'Sweet 151032

Johnson; Louis Metcalf (*c*); King Oliver, David Nelson, Cootie Williams (*t*); James Archey, Geechie Fields (*tb*); Ernest Elliott (*cl*); Bobby Holmes (*cl, as*); Charles Frazier (*ts*); Fats Waller (*p*); Teddy Bunn, Bernard Addison (*bjo, g*); Harry Hull, Joe Watts (*b*); Edmund Jones, Fred Moore (*d*); Perry Bradford (*d, v*); other personnel unidentified. 8, 10 & 12/21, 6, 7 & 8/23, 6/25, 2 & 9/27, 6/28, 1, 3 & 11/29.

***(*) **James P. Johnson, 1921–1928** Classics 658

As above, except omit Oliver, Archey, Fields, Elliott, Jefferson, Frazier, Addison, Hull, Jones, Moore. 8, 10 & 12/21, 6, 7 & 8/23, 3 & 9/27, 3 & 6/28.

*** **James P. Johnson, 1928–1938** Classics 671

Johnson; restore the above; add Louis Metcalf (*c*); Joe 'Tricky Sam' Nanton (*tb*); Johnny Hodges (*as, ss*); Barney Bigard (*cl, ts*); Ernest Elliott (*cl*); Clarence Williams (*p, v*); Sonny Greer (*d*); Perry Bradford, Gus Horsley (*v*). 10/28, 1, 3 & 11/29, 1/30, 3/31, 8/38.

**** **Snowy Morning Blues** MCA/GRP 16042

Johnson (*p* solo), and with Eddie Dougherty (*d*). 30, 44.

*** **James P. Johnson, 1938–1942** Classics 711

Johnson; Henry 'Red' Allen (*t*); J. C. Higginbotham (*tb*); Pee Wee Russell (*cl*); Gene Sedric (*ts*); Albert Casey, Eugene Fields (*g*); Pops Foster, Johnny Williams (*b*); Big Sid Catlett, Zutty Singleton (*d*); Anna Robinson, Ruby Smith (*v*). 8/38, 3 & 6/39, 7/42.

*** **James P. Johnson, 1943–1944** Classics 824
    Johnson; Sidney De Paris (*t*); Vic Dickenson (*tb*); Ben Webster (*ts*); Jimmy Shirley (*g*); John
    Simmons (*b*); Big Sid Catlett (*d*). 7, 11 & 12/43, 3 & 4/44.
*** **James P. Johnson, 1944** Classics 835
    Johnson; Frank Newton, Sidney De Paris (*t*); Vic Dickenson (*tb*); Albert Casey, Jimmy Shirley
    (*g*); Pops Foster, John Simmons (*b*); Big Sid Catlett, Eddie Dougherty (*d*). 4 & 6/44.

Too little is known now about James P. Johnson's orchestral music (of which much has been lost) to make any settled judgement about his significance as a 'straight' composer. Ironically, though, his enormous importance as a synthesizer of many strands of black music – ragtime, blues, popular and sacred song – with his own stride style has been rather eclipsed by the tendency to see him first and only as Fats Waller's teacher.

Johnson was in almost every respect a better musician than Waller, and perhaps the main reason for his relative invisibility has been the dearth of reliable recorded material. As so often, the French Classics label has made up a considerable deficit. The early material overlaps at around the dates indicated with the Hot'N'Sweet compilation. This is as close as anyone is going to get to the sound of Harlem rent parties – if there were an additional quarter-star for quality of sound, *Harlem Stride Piano* might just nip it – and it's a pity that some of these sessions are not more fully documented. The group that recorded the autumn 1921 'Carolina Shout' (there is a solo version from the same period, different label) goes unidentified. Johnson is unmistakable from the first moments of 'Harlem Strut', a subtle, propulsive player with bags of ideas.

Classics omit a piano-roll 'Charleston (South Carolina)' from June 1925 but fill in with four Original Jazz Hounds numbers from March 1927 and March 1928. The second volume takes the story on a full decade, opening with a couple of numbers by the Gulf Coast Seven (an uncertain personnel but possibly including Ellingtonians Nanton and Hodges) before covering the overlap with Hot'N'Sweet. Among the highlights here are two duets and chirpy *kvelling* with Clarence Williams, together with three songs from 1931 with Andy Razaf (co-author of 'Honeysuckle Rose') as vocalist. As on *Volume 1*, Johnson tends to get buried in the group recordings. Ultimately it is the solo tracks, including little gems like 'You've Got To Be Modernistic' and the earlier 'Riffs', that are most significant. The disc ends with a session by Pee Wee Russell's Rhythmakers; Johnson solos on a second take of 'There'll Be Some Changes Made'.

The picture is getting steadily more patchy as the decade advances. *Volume 3* is significant because it contains a lot of band material which scarcely saw the light of day during the LP era and which is now heard for the first time since their first release. One of these features vocals by Ruby Smith, a niece of the great Bessie. The disc overlaps with *Volume 2* in the shape of a trio with Pee Wee Russell and Zutty Singleton, apparently recorded at the end of the August 1938 date. There are excellent solo performances from the following spring, made for Columbia.

The later Classics anthologies have filled in much of the rest of the picture, inevitably with some further overlap with earlier releases. GRP's release of the excellent American Decca sessions that make up *Snowy Morning Blues* had, until their release, filled in some of the gaps. There is an overlap with the *Chronological* second volume, but it is minor, and likewise with the third and fourth. Only the first four tracks come from 1930, but they include 'You've Got To Be Modernistic' and 'Jingles', which were originally released together as a Brunswick 78. Unfortunately, the version of the title 'Snowy Morning Blues', one of Johnson's most beautiful compositions, is a later one. Some of the 1944 cuts already betray signs of the ill-health that, as a series of mild but progressively debilitating cerebral haemorrhages, was to overtake Johnson later in the decade, finally incapacitating him in 1951.

The basic elements of the style are still in place, though. The subtly varied bass figures and forward motion of his sophisticated melodic variations place him closer to later jazz than to the increasingly basic syncopations and repetitions of ragtime. For that reason alone, and for his incorporation of jazz and blues tonalities, Johnson sounds much more 'modern' than many of his contemporaries, and a far more compelling musician than the overrated Waller.

These CD transfers are taken either from original metal masters, from safety copies (or, in the case of the four 1930 tracks, from shellac 78s) and remastered using the NoNoise system. Absolutely no complaints about the sound, though Dougherty's irritatingly under-recorded percussion does at faster tempi blur into a background crackle. It's worth looking out for *The Symphonic Jazz Of James P. Johnson* (Musicmasters 20066 LP), with an intelligent liner-note by Johnson scholar Willa Rouder.

Marc Johnson DOUBLE BASS, ELECTRIC BASS

*** **Bass Desires** ECM 1299
    Johnson; Bill Frisell (*g, g-syn*); John Scofield (*g*); Peter Erskine (*d*). 5/85.

** **Second Sight** ECM 1351
As above. 3/87.
(*) **2 × 4 Emarcy 842 233
Johnson; Toots Thielemans (*hca*); Makoto Ozone (*p*); Gary Burton (*vib*); Lucy Crane (*v*). 4/89.
(*) **Right Brain Patrol JMT 849 153
Johnson; Ben Monder (*g*); Arto Tunçboyaci (*perc, v*). 9 & 11/91.
***(*) **Magic Labyrinth** JMT 514 018
As above, except replace Monder with Wolfgang Muthspiel (*g*). 6/94.

The original *Bass Desires* was a vibrantly exciting album which used Bill Frisell's disciplined surrealism in an imaginative textural counterpoint to Scofield's more logically organized play. 'Samurai Hee-Haw' and the remarkable arrangement of 'Black Is The Color Of My True Love's Hair' (compare 'straight' composer Luciano Berio's version in *Folk Songs*) were among the freshest sounds heard in 1985–6. The backgrounds are all big and stately, perhaps too much influenced by the prevailing (deny it as they may) house style at ECM. By contrast, *Second Sight* is less than visonary, swapping the bite and humour of the first album for a wishy-washy product, alternating saccharine high-note twiddles with a sort of apologetic deutero-rock that sounds disconcertingly the way Sonny Sharrock might if he were put on probation.

Right Brain Patrol is prepared from time to time to rattle the bars, but Monder is a decidedly low-budget replacement for Frisell and the material he's given to work with doesn't encourage him to attempt anything out of the ordinary. Tunçboyaci is a splendid fellow on occasions like this, a sort of thinking man's David Moss.

The duos on *2 × 4* are equally mild-mannered, but there are some exceptional moments. While the partnership with Gary Burton on Bill Evans's 'Time Remembered' and, less probably, 'Monk's Dream' are exceptionally colourless, even by Burton's palish standard, the version of 'Goodbye Pork Pie Hat' with Thielemans is gorgeous. The album-title is possibly also intended as a pun, because one of the things Johnson is trying to do in it is break up the expected 4/4 beat into overlapping patterns of 3/4s and overlapping 2/4s and 4/4s, giving these stripped-down performances a much richer spectrum. It's very effective, but one keeps wishing he would move on to a more vivid page on the shade card . . .

. . . which is exactly what happens on *Magic Labyrinth*. Much of the credit has to go to Mutshpiel, who galvanizes the whole thing with his intelligent blend of hi-NRG amplification and delicate jazz lines. The opening 'Samurai Hee-Haw' (a Johnson favourite) offers some indication of what this would be like as a live band. They tackle 'Solar' and 'Ne Um Talvez' in due deference to Miles, but with a completely original focus. A very good album indeed – the record Johnson has long threatened to deliver.

Pete Johnson (1904–67) PIANO

**** **Pete Johnson 1938–1939** Classics 656
Johnson; Harry James, Hot Lips Page (*t*); Buster Smith (*as*); Albert Ammons, Meade Lux Lewis (*p*); Lawrence Lucie, Ulysses Livingston (*g*); Abe Bolar, Johnny Williams (*b*); Eddie Dougherty (*d*). 12/38–12/39.
***(*) **Pete Johnson 1939-1941** Classics 665
Johnson; Hot Lips Page (*t*); Eddie Barefield (*cl, as*); Don Stovall (*as*); Don Byas (*ts*); Albert Ammons (*p*); John Collins, Ulysses Livingston (*g*); Abe Bolar, Al Hall (*b*); A. G. Godley, Jimmy Hoskins (*d*). 12/39–6/41.
*** **Pete's Blues** Savoy SV-0193
Johnson; Hot Lips Page (*t*); J. C. Higginbotham, Clyde Bernhardt (*tb*); Albert Nicholas (*cl*); Don Stovall (*as*); Ben Webster, Budd Johnson (*ts*); Jimmy Shirley (*g*); Al Hall, Abe Bolar (*b*); J. C. Heard, Jack Parker (*d*); Etta Jones (*v*). 2/46.
*** **Central Avenue Boogie** Delmark DD-656
Johnson; Arnold Wiley (*p, v*); Charles Norris, Carl Lynch (*g*); Bill Davis, Al McKibbon (*b*); J. C. Heard, Jesse Price (*d*). 4–11/47.

Johnson's mastery of boogie woogie and blues piano is given a near-definitive airing on these four CDs. The chronological survey on Classics begins with the Kansas City pianist accompanying Joe Turner on the singer's first studio date before two quartet tracks with Harry James: 'Boo-Woo' is an outright classic. His complete 1939 date for Solo Art is another memorable occasion, nine solos that go from the Tatum-like elaborations on Leroy Carr's 'How Long, How Long Blues' to the furious 'Climbin' And Screamin'' and 'Shuffle Boogie'. The sound here is rather thin, but Johnson's energy and invention shine through. There are four more tracks with a small band including Page and Turner, a solo 'Boogie Woogie', two trio pieces and the first trio with Albert Ammons and Meade Lux Lewis on 'Café Society Rag'. There are shortcomings in the remastering but this is a marvellous disc.

His 1939 session for Blue Note is, unfortunately, split across the end of Classics 656 and the beginning of Classics 665, which opens on the stunning 'Holler Stomp', the most audacious of boogie showcases. 'You Don't Know My Mind', from the same date, is contrastingly dreamy and may remind blues aficionados of pianists such as Walter Davis and Lane Smith. Aside from another track with Joe Turner's Fly Cats and a small group with Page and others, the rest of the disc is made up of duets with Ammons; as elegant as these sometimes are, they also fall prey to routine from track to track. Savoy's 1946 sessions are a bit contrived, though good fun: the seven players on the first date introduce themselves with a knock on the studio door and sit in one by one. Page, Webster and Nicholas all sound fine. The second session, with a couple of vocals from the young Etta Jones, is much less interesting.

Delmark's compilation sets Johnson back in front of guitar, bass and drums, and includes several previously unheard takes. He still sounds best by himself, but there is some virtuoso stuff on 'Margie' and the several takes of 'Hollywood Boogie'.

Plas Johnson (born 1931) ALTO SAXOPHONE, TENOR SAXOPHONE

*** **The Blues** Concord CCD 4015
    Johnson; Mike Melvoin (*p*); Herb Ellis (*g*); Ray Brown (*b*); Jake Hanna (*d*); Bobbye Hall (*perc*). Johnson has an appealingly sharp and direct approach to the blues. His sole Concord disc benefits from the presence of a highly professional rhythm section which glosses over his more obvious deficiencies. Not a player for the over-extended solo, Johnson tends to make a few points forcefully, with a tendency to repeat ideas a little louder just to make sure they've sunk home. Not a classic, but entertaining enough in its limited way.

Philip Johnston ALTO SAXOPHONE, SOPRANO SAXOPHONE

***(*) **Philip Johnston's Big Trouble** Black Saint 120152-2
    Johnston; Bob DeBellis (*ss, bs, bcl*); Jim Leff (*tb*); Marcus Rojas (*tba*); Joe Ruddick (*ky, as*); Adam Rogers, David Tronzo (*g*); David Hofstra (*b, tba*); Kevin Norton (*d, perc, mar*); Richard Dworkin (*perc*). 6 & 7/92.
*** **The Unknown** Avant AVAN 037
    Johnston; Steve Swell (*tb*); Bob DeBellis (*f, af, bcl, bs*); Joe Ruddick (*p, syn*); David Hofstra (*b*); Kevin Norton (*d, perc, vib*).
Big Trouble was formed following the demise of the Microscopic Sextet, one of the more original of the saxophone-based 1980s bands. In the new band, Johnston has pushed even further his offbeat arranging skills. 'Chillbone' on the Black Saint is scored for soprano saxophone, tuba and marimba, set over a stark wind ostinato. The set also includes notably complex compositions by Steve Lacy (the brief but awkwardly structured 'Hemline') and by Herbie Nichols, who's credited with both 'Step Tempest' and 'Twelve Bars'. The addition of slide guitar gives the last of these and the closing 'Powerhouse' an entirely unexpected dimension.

Johnston uses space brilliantly, often leaving yawning gaps precisely where one expects to hear fills or returns to a head theme. The obvious comparison is with John Zorn, who is the mastermind behind Avant, except that Big Trouble play in a more structured and less ironic idiom. *The Unknown* is packed with strange Zornish titles and weird staccato music that never allows the listener more than a moment's complacent comfort before breezing on to the next idea. On this showing the prospects are good, and anyone who enjoyed what the Micros did should certainly check it out.

Randy Johnston (born 1957) GUITAR

(*) **Walk On Muse MCD 5432
    Johnston; Bill Easley (*ts*); Benny Green (*p*); Ray Drummond (*b*); Kenny Washington (*d*). 1/91.
*** **Jubilation** Muse MCD 5495
    Johnston; Eric Alexander (*ts*); Bruce Barth (*p*); Nat Reeves (*b*); Michael Carvin (*d*). 11/92.
*** **In A-Chord** Muse MCD 5512
    Johnston; Eric Alexander (*ts*); Joey DeFrancesco (*org*); Mickey Roker (*d*). 10/94.
Made to showcase the chops of guitarist Johnston, these are much like blowing sessions of 30 years ago: the only difference on the first disc lies in the feel of Ivory Joe Hunter's 'I Almost Lost My Mind' and Percy Mayfield's 'Please Send Me Someone To Love', which are more like straight blues pieces than a jazz group jamming on the blues. This is serviceable stuff that doesn't impress much beyond its constituents: Washington's playing is typically fine, Green is right at home, Easley unpeels a few choice bits of tenor preaching. But they never focus round Johnston, who sounds like a sideman on his own date.

Jubilation is just that bit better: Johnston is more the centre of attention this time, although baby-faced tenorman Alexander gets in some interesting shots on his three appearances. Things get better still on *In A-Chord*, which enlists DeFrancesco and turns the feel around into typical organ-combo jazz, something which Alexander (currently with Charles Earland) and Johnston seem to relish. Certainly the guitarist's improvisations on 'Sunday In New York' and the wing-footed 'The Philadelphians' are a fine display of chops. That said, there are a great many records in this genre, and this doesn't quite have the extra ounce to lift it into a higher bracket.

Joint Venture GROUP

***(*) **Joint Venture** Enja 5049
    Paul Smoker (*t*); Ellery Eskelin (*ts*); Drew Gress (*b*); Phil Haynes (*d*). 3/87.
*** **Ways** Enja 6052
    As above. 1/89.
*** **Mirrors** Enja ENJ 7049
    As above. 9/91.

Jointly fronted by Smoker and Eskelin, this group performs more straight-ahead material than either man does on solo records. 'Chorale And Descendance', which Smoker has also recorded on his own, is a choppy but curiously formal piece which takes up ideas that lie all over the place in contemporary jazz and weaves them all into a satisfyingly ironic shape. The second album is less successful, largely because it is too easy to hear Smoker and Eskelin working out ideas from their own projects, but also because Gress and Haynes seem to have settled into a predictable groove that does the front line no favours whatever. If there were hairs to split, *Mirrors* might be considered something of an advance. It is certainly a more polished and professional product, but the sheer intelligence and control required to drive music like this is not conducive to warm, uncomplicated expressiveness, and again the album is slightly forbidding.

Ed Jones TENOR SAXOPHONE, SOPRANO SAXOPHONE, FLUTES

(*) **Piper's Tales ASC CD2
    Jones; Jonathan Gee (*p*); Wayne Batchelor (*b*); Brian Abrahams (*d*). 7/91, 12/92.

Jones's place in a certain British jazz lineage is evident from his opening couple of bars on 'So The Story Goes'. And it does indeed, a little too predictably to sustain interest over the hour. Jones's compositions have a familiar, folk-tinged quality to which his slightly sharp, keening tone lends itself very well. He has an ideal group for material of this sort. Gee is a lovely, delicate player and a very sensitive accompanist, while the bassist and drummer are widely recognized for their facility in a wide range of contexts. Neither is expecially well recorded here, which is a pity; Abrahams's cymbal accents are far enough back in the mix to be irritatingly clicky, and Batchelor's resonant tone isn't sufficiently boosted.

    The recordings were made over quite a span of time, as will be seen. This may contribute to a slightly uneven quality in the playing. Without knowing what was done when, it isn't a theory we can test, but perhaps the more cohesive tracks – 'The Piper's Tale', 'The Long Days', 'Kindred Spirit' – were made when the band was a little more thoroughly played in.

Elvin Jones (born 1927) DRUMS

*** **Elvin!** Original Jazz Classics OJC 259
    Jones; Thad Jones (*c*); Frank Wess (*f*); Frank Foster (*ts*); Hank Jones (*p*); Art Davis (*b*). 7 & 12/61, 1/62.
***(*) **Live At The Village Vanguard** Enja 2036
    Jones; Hannibal Marvin Peterson (*t*); George Coleman (*ts*); Wilbur Little (*b*).

If one were to make a list of the dozen most influential jazz musicians in the period since 1945, Elvin Jones would *have* to be upsides with Miles Davis, Ornette Coleman and the drummer's former boss and mentor, John Coltrane. His whirlwind style and famous 'polyrhythmic' delivery (frequently name-checked but still not clearly understood) are of lasting significance and, if Coltrane lies across the history of saxophone playing like the Great Wall of China (as Keats said of Milton), then it's equally hard for drummers to avoid a confrontation with Elvin Jones.

    Elvin! is noisy, heated hard bop with some good interplay between Jones and a naughty-boy front rank that won't stay in line. The trio tracks with Jones and Davis are particularly good, but the best of the album can be had on an above-average drummers' sampler, *The Big Beat* (Milestone M 47016 CD/

2LP), which also includes Art Blakey, Max Roach and Philly Joe Jones (who's no blood kin, but a kind of artistic Dutch uncle to the Mr Jones under discussion).

Imagine the Coltrane Quartet as a (pianoless) trio, with the drummer playing 'chords' and counter-melodies behind the saxophone. That is approximately the effect of Jones's Village Vanguard sessions. At first blush George Coleman sounds unlikely to trouble John Coltrane's ghost, but he is a more sophisticated harmonic thinker than at first appears, let down only by a Brillo-pad tone. Much as in the 1960s when Jones and Coltrane seemed to be in astral communication to the virtual exclusion of Garrison or Workman and Tyner, the drums and saxophone leave little for bassist Little to do, and he contents himself with steady figuring and occasional keep-awake flurries. Hannibal Peterson gate-crashes on 'Mr Jones', taking the shine off another perfectly good trumpet. Good, enjoyable stuff all through.

*(*) Heavy Sounds Impulse MCAD 33114
Jones; Richard Davis (b); Frank Foster (ts); Billy Green (p). 68.

Heavy Sounds is a pretty horrible record. Billed as a Jones–Davis co-effort, it breaks down into a series of individual 'features' – like Davis's misconceived out-of-tempo breaks on the overlong opening 'Raunchy Rita' – stitched together with rather suspect ensemble play. Foster's compositions, 'Rita' and the classic 'Shiny Stockings', are actually rather good, and there's a good but unexploited number from pianist Green. Jones's one composition credit is the dismal 'Elvin's Guitar Blues', on which he strums the opening choruses like a teenager with a teach-yourself book. 'Summertime' is left an unrecognizable corpse, but 'Here's That Rainy Day' is quite nice. Too late, though.

**(*) Live In Japan Konnex 5041
Jones; Frank Foster (ts); Pat LaBarbera (ts, ss); Roland Prince (g); Andy McCloud (b). 4/78.
*** Very R.A.R.E. / Love & Peace Konnex 5036
Jones; Pharoah Sanders (ts); Art Pepper (as); Roland Hanna (p); Jean-Paul Bourelly (g); Richard Davis (b). 6/79, 4/82.

Around this time, Jones tried to beef up his bands (coals to Newcastle, one would have thought) with muscular young players, guitarists in particular. Prince – that's *Roland* Prince – won't win any poll nominations for Most Understated Artist, but the trouble is he doesn't really have anything to say; his own 'Antigua' is overlong and rambling. The two horns are mismatched, and a 26-minute re-run of 'A Love Supreme' is almost embarrassingly amateur.

Put the piano back into the mix and . . . it doesn't really work. The pairing on Konnex 5036 – *Love & Peace* is the same session as the old Black Hawk *Reunited* – puts the good, the bad and the ugly side by side. Hanna holds his own and cops a lovely feature right at the end of *Very R.A.R.E.* on his own 'The Witching Hour'. Tyner is such an adaptive musician that he can re-centre his idiom many times over without strain, but on *Love & Peace* one hears little more than one of the wobbles on the axle of the Coltrane Quartet, a slight but basic incompatibility of vision and timing. Bourelly seems extraneous and gets in the way of some of Davis's more inventive moves and progressions. 'Little Rock's Blues' is great; 'Sweet And Lovely' falls apart. Mercifully, Sanders by 1982 was over his Coltrane sound-alike stage and plays instead with a graciousness that sits ill with the rest.

*** When I Was At Aso-Mountain Enja 7081
Jones; Sonny Fortune (as, f); Takehisa Tanaka (p); Cecil McBee (b). 12/90.

A lovely record. It overcomes much of Elvin's chronic awkwardness and allows eight shortish tracks to flow lyrically and without undue elaboration. Fortune's an ideal voice for this sort of Eastern-tinged affair, and Tanaka (who's a highly respected fixture on the Japanese jazz scene) proves to be a more than competent soloist: a little wishy-washy on 'You Don't Know What Love Is' and 'Stella By Starlight', more robust on his own tunes. McBee plays his part like a professional, and is rewarded with a handful of compact solo spots that he puts to measured good use.

**(*) The Elvin Jones Jazz Machine In Europe Enja 7009 2
Jones; Sonny Fortune (ts, f); Ravi Coltrane (ts, ss); Willie Pickens (p); Chip Jackson (b). 6/91.

Lest anyone get overexcited at the thought of Jones playing with a Coltrane again, it has to be said that Ravi, born only a year before his father's death, is not an altogether convincing chip off the block. His tone is painfully uncertain and his solos virtually devoid of ideas. Almost all the emphasis falls on Fortune, a wonderfully atmospheric player who doesn't worry overmuch about complex harmonic relationships; his flute introduction to 'Doll Of The Bride', a traditional Japanese tune arranged by Jones's wife, Keiko, is one of the best things on a thinly recorded album that clocks in at just over an hour and feels like twice that.

**(*) Youngblood Enja 7051
Jones; Nicholas Payton (t); Javon Jackson, Joshua Redman (ts); George Mraz (b). 4/92.

*** **Going Home** Enja 7095
>Jones; Nicholas Payton (*t*); Javon Jackson (*ts*); Ravi Coltrane (*ts, ss*); Kent Jordan (*f, picc*);
>Willie Pickens (*p*); Brad Jones (*b*). 10/92.

These are pretty dull. Some of the excess of former years has been stripped away, but the awful truth is that, without all the drama and bluster, there isn't much going on with Jones musically. *Going Home* is halfway to being a big-band session and there are some quite good basic treatments. 'East Of The Sun' is peppy and imaginative; brother Thad's 'Cross Purpose' receives a rather cursory reading. Jones's own themes are more to the point than on some records, and Rudy van Gelder's engineering means you can actually hear a bit of detail. Coltrane junior has developed an interesting voice of his own, more personalized on soprano, but still serviceable on the bigger horn, though here he tends to defer to Jackson.

Ironically, though Jackson keeps his end up, the most interesting tracks on *Youngblood* are a pair of trios – 'Angel Eyes' and 'Body And Soul', nothing fancy, you understand – with just Redman and Mraz. The lack of a harmony instrument is pretty irrelevant when Jones is around, and he doesn't leave any white spaces on either one. A duo with Mraz is neither here nor there. Jones's solo feature, 'Ding-A-Ling-A-Ling', must be one of the most aptly titled things he's ever put his name to.

*** **It Don't Mean A Thing** Enja ENJ 8066
>Jones; Nicholas Payton (*t*); Delfeayo Marsalis (*tb*); Sonny Fortune (*ts, f*); Willie Pickens (*p*);
>Cecil McBee (*b*); Kevin Mahogany (*d*). 10/93.

A mixed band of Young Turks and the old guard, and a programme of material which, despite an emphasis on new themes, is constantly aware of the tradition, as reflected on the beautiful 'Lush Life'. Jones is not too upfront and self-important, and 'A Change Is Gonna Come' is delivered with becoming modesty and simplicity when the temptation must have been to turn it into a grand percussion epic.

Etta Jones (born 1928) VOCAL

***(*) **Don't Go To Strangers** Original Jazz Classics OJC 298
>Jones; Frank Wess (*ts, f*); Richard Wyands (*p*); Skeeter Best (*g*); George Duvivier (*b*); Roy
>Haynes (*d*). 6/60.
(*) **Something Nice Original Jazz Classics OJC 221
>Jones; Lem Winchester (*vib*); Richard Wyands, Jimmy Neely (*p*); George Duvivier, Michael
>Mulia (*b*); Roy Haynes, Rudy Lawless (*d*). 9/60–3/61.
*** **Lonely And Blue** Original Jazz Classics OJC 702
>Jones; Gene Ammons, Budd Johnson (*ts*); Patti Bown (*p*); Wally Richardson (*g*); George
>Duvivier (*b*); Ed Shaughnessy (*d*). 4–5/62.
*** **So Warm** Original Jazz Classics OJC 874
>Jones; Ray Alonge (*frhn*); Eric Dixon, Jerome Richardson, Phil Bodner, Arthur Clarke (*reeds*);
>Mal Waldron (*p*); George Duvivier (*b*); Charli Persip, Bill English (*d*); strings. 61.

Jones began recording as a teenager in the 1940s, and by the time she came to make *Don't Go To Strangers* she was already a veteran. But the title-song from the LP became a gold record, and she subsequently made several albums for Prestige. In its modest way the album remains a fine achievement, with Jones's heavy, blues-directed voice piling extra substance on to fluff such as 'Yes Sir, That's My Baby', with rolling support from an excellent band. The subsequent *Something Nice* is more quiescent, the 11 songs dispatched matter-of-factly, although Jones's regal delivery makes such as 'Through A Long And Sleepless Night' into sometimes heady stuff. *Lonely And Blue* was a prescient suggestion of the kind of albums she would make for Muse, a generation later: small-hours, lonesome music which is barely a step away from outright blues. Johnson handles most of the tenor chores (as Houston Person would later do), and his wry rejonders on 'Gee Baby Ain't I Good To You' are delightful. *So Warm* tips the scales towards MOR, but Etta's natural warmth heats up the string charts, and it's a beguiling result.

*** **I'll Be Seeing You** Muse M 5351
>Jones; Houston Person (*ts*); George Devens (*vib*); Stan Hope (*p*); Milt Hinton (*b*); Vernell
>Fournier (*b*); Ralph Dorsey (*d*). 9/87.
(*) **Sugar Muse M 5379
>Jones; Houston Person (*ts*); Horace Ott (*ky*); Stan Hope (*p*); Randy Johnson (*g*); Wilbur
>Bascomb, Peter Martin Weiss (*b*); Cecil Brooks III, Bertel Knox (*d*); Ralph Dorsey (*perc*); Della
>Griffin, Earl Coleman (*v*). 10/89.
(*) **Christmas With Etta Jones Muse M 5411
>Jones; Johnny Coles (*flhn*); Bill Easley (*ts, f*); Houston Person (*ts*); Horace Ott, Stan Hope (*p*);

Randy Johnson (*g*); Wilbur Bascomb, Peter Martin Weiss (*b*); Bertel Knox, Cecil Brooks III (*d*); Sammy Figueroa (*perc*). 6/90.

***(*) Reverse The Charges Muse MCD 5474

Jones; Philip Harper (*t*); Houston Person (*ts*); Benny Green (*p*); Christian McBride (*b*); Winard Harper (*d*); Sammy Figueroa (*perc*). 9/91–1/92.

Jones has been in considerable voice of late, and this fruitful sequence of albums is, taken a disc at a time, very enjoyable. Person has become her keeper of the flame, producing and playing on all these sessions with an authority that matches Etta's own singing, and while some of the albums strain a bit to stay together, they're finished with wise authority. *I'll Be Seeing You* is probably the best for the magisterial treatment of 'Jim' and 'Etta's Blues', but *Sugar* is nice enough, though the guest shots by Coleman and Griffin are decidedly hammy. The Christmas album is about as friendly as these things can be, but it ends on an unspeakably dreary 'I'll Be Home For Christmas', and tolerance will depend on how many seasonal greetings one is prepared to receive over the course of a CD. *Reverse The Charges* drops the average age of the band right down, but it works out fine since Green, McBride and the Harpers make a terrific band in their own right (and they make Person sound a bit weary by comparison). Etta sounds close to her best as a result, with a delicious 'Ma, He's Making Eyes At Me' and a deeply felt 'Say It Isn't So' worth the admission price by themselves.

Hank Jones (born 1918) PIANO

*** The Jazz Trio Of Hank Jones Savoy SV 0184

Jones; Wendell Marshall (*b*); Kenny Clarke (*d*). 8/55.

***(*) Quartet / Quintet Savoy 0147

Jones; Donald Byrd, Matty Dice (*t*); Eddie Jones (*b*); Kenny Clarke (*d*). 11/55.

*** Bluebird Savoy 0138

As above, except add Joe Wilder (*t*); Jerome Richardson (*ts, f*); Herbie Mann (*f*); Wendell Marshall (*b*). 8 & 11/55.

*** Hank Jones Trio / Quartet Savoy SV 0236

Jones; Bobby Jaspar (*ts, f*); Paul Chambers (*b*); Kenny Clarke (*d*). 8/56.

The eldest of the three brothers, Hank Jones is as quiet and unassuming as drummer Elvin is extrovert, but he shares something of the late Thad Jones's deceptive sophistication, often lost in outsize arrangements or group settings. The early Savoys are consistently attractive, though Jones now finds himself sharing the top billing with Klook. Well transferred, they represent an attractive investment in Jones's mid-1950s work. *Quartet/Quintet* is marginally ahead of the rest. Working without a saxophone and using the two trumpets (mostly in thirds on unison themes) gives the band a bright, hard-edged sound that is enhanced by a faithful, hiss-free reproduction. A hint of echo in the acoustic adds some depth to spacious, uncomplicated arrangements. The formula works best on the long 'An Evening At Papa Joe's', where the slow blues theme encourages Byrd to stretch out a bit, and introduces Dice for three good choruses. The young Newarkian has a slightly raucous tone that is an effective foil to Byrd's saxophone-influenced phrasing and roughens up the ensemble textures. 'Hank's Pranks' on *Bluebird* follows the same configuration but falls a little short.

Jones's interest in new and unusual textures is also evident on *Quartet*, and particularly 'Relaxin' At Camarillo', where he introduces the pale-toned Jaspar. On *Bluebird* he again relies quite heavily on flute in preference to saxophone, using either Jerome Richardson or the 25-year-old Herbie Mann, whose articulation on the title-track is typically beautiful and a salutary reminder of what he was capable of before fusion music overwhelmed his impeccable sound; the title-piece is another extended form, but this time it palls as it approaches a rather inconsequential conclusion. The earliest of the group is rather hissily recorded, with a lot of wobble in the piano sound.

**** Hank All Art AAJ 11003

Jones (*p* solo). 1/76.

***(*) 'Bop Redux Muse MCD 5444

Jones; George Duvivier (*b*); Ben Riley (*d*). 1/77.

*** Tiptoe Tapdance Original Jazz Classics OJC 719

As above. 6/77, 1/78.

**(*) Just For Fun Original Jazz Classics OJC 471

Jones; Howard Roberts (*g*); Ray Brown (*b*); Shelly Manne (*d*). 6/77.

*** I Remember You Black & Blue 233122

Jones; George Duvivier (*b*); Alan Dawson, Oliver Jackson (*d*). 7/77 & 7/78.

**(*) Jones–Brown–Smith Concord CCD 4032

Jones; Ray Brown (*b*); Jimmie Smith (*d*).

***(*) **Bluesette** Black & Blue 233168
>   Jones; George Duvivier (*b*); Alan Dawson. 7/78 & 7/79.

Like everyone else, Jones had a quiet time of it in the 1960s, but he re-emerges with a bang in the following decade, which really marks the beginning of his now substantial output of high-quality solo and trio jazz. Never much of a composer, a fact often adduced to downplay his significance, Jones is not given to wholesale reassessment of standard progressions but prefers to concentrate on the *sound* of a tune. *Hank* is certainly the place to start; the songs are all very brief – and there are 14 of them squeezed into less than 45 minutes – but it's worth listening closely to the way Jones colours every chord and fine-brushes his own solo contributions. His delicacy and balance, that tiptoeing, tapdancing feel, are among the qualities which have enhanced and prolonged his reputation as a great accompanist, but (unfairly) only a rather lightweight soloist. *Hank* is full of gospel and hymn tunes, which receive sensitive and sometimes quite oblique interpretations. There are some inconsistencies of sound, but nothing untoward.

For Jones's first Muse recording, he deliberately restricted himself to Charlie Parker and Thelonious Monk compositions. This became his normal practice in later years, but here it leaves him spoilt for choice. His approach to Monk is especially interesting, in that he tends to even out the jagged edges of the original themes and turn them into something altogether more polished and entire. 'Monk's Mood', treated rather briefly at the end, loses much of its lumpiness (and some of its blues tonality) and sounds like a different piece. The Parker pieces are more faithful to the originals, and work rather better in trio arrangements; the Monk material would almost all sound better as solo performances. Recording quality is reasonably good for the mid-1970s.

The Concord and *Just For Fun* are both growers, records that initially come across as rather superficial, but gradually yield up subtleties not audible first time around. Despite the presence of Manne (the players actually split into two – drummerless and guitarless respectively – trios) the results are slightly uncertain. Jones is too straightforward an executant to be able to rely on irony, and pieces like 'A Very Hip Rock And Roll Tune' and 'Kids Are Pretty People' fall flat on that account.

Though they perhaps lack the inventive fire of the Savoys, the 1970s sets are to be preferred for their almost magisterial calm and command.

*** **The Incredible Hank Jones** Stash ST CD 553
>   Jones; Jon Faddis (*t, flhn*); Ira Sullivan (*t, flhn, as, ts, f*); Bob Malach (*ts*); Bucky Pizzarelli (*g*);
>   Eddie Gomez, Milt Hinton (*b*); Louie Bellson, Duffy Jackson (*d*). 79, 5/80.

This became a Jones record only by sleight of hand. The material had formerly been released on two LPs under the names of Louie Bellson and the irritatingly eclectic Ira Sullivan. It isn't as if Jones is such a prominent soloist on either of them, and Bellson is certainly strongly favoured on the sound-mix. Taken on their merits, though, these are both highly desirable selections, and a worthy inclusion in any collection.

***(*) **Duo** Timeless SJP 283
>   Jones; Red Mitchell (*b*). 12/87.

Two master-craftsmen left to their own devices with a pile of music. Mitchell's singing tone fulfils the same function as Holland's slightly more robust approach. Jones works around and under the bassist's lines like the great accompanist he is. 'Wee' and 'I'll Remember April' are almost consciously mis-remembered returns to bebop, freshly and inventively conceived. 'Like Someone In Love' draws freely on Coltrane's reading. Gorgeous.

**** **The Oracle** Emarcy 846376
>   Jones; Dave Holland (*b*); Billy Higgins (*d*). 3 & 4/89.
**** **Lazy Afternoon** Concord CCD 4391
>   Jones; Ken Peplowski (*as, cl*); Dave Holland (*b*); Keith Copeland (*d*). 7/89.

The trio has not always been Jones's 'natural' format. He often sounds better with a whisper of brass or flute, as on *Lazy Afternoon*, with the classy Peplowski. Holland has worked comfortably with Jones for some time, with no sign that he finds the material too routine. Higgins, as always, is a wonder, pacy and lyrical. *The Oracle* is a small masterpiece, certainly Jones's most inventive and adventurous album for a great many years; they sound as well harmonized and individualized as a great vocal trio. 'Trane Connections' is certainly marked by Tommy Flanagan's approach to Coltrane, and there is enough elsewhere – 'Blood Count', 'Maya's Dance', 'Beautiful Love' – to suggest that Jones has kept his ears pinned back for new wrinkles. Old pianists don't die; they just get better.

Lazy Afternoon is a peach: warm, vibrant jazz with the modulation and pace of a good club date. Jones is generous with solo space for his sidemen, though his unusual approach to Kurt Weill's 'Speak Low', a striking choice for openers, is marred by an intrusive Copeland solo. Holland and Copeland had acted as the pianist's performing trio, with an evident empathy; quite properly, the bassist is strongly featured, with particularly fine excursions on the J. J. Johnson composition, 'Lament', and the succeeding

'Comin' Home Baby'. Jones's fine touch as a colourist is evident on the title-track, where a hint of Ellingtonish celeste under Ken Peplowski's smooth clarinet spices a slightly bland approach. Warmly recommended.

***(*) **Live At Maybeck Recital Hall, Volume 16** Concord CCD 4502
    Jones (*p* solo). 90.
***(*) **Jazzpar 91 Project** Storyville STCD 3091
    Jones; Mads Vinding (*b*); Al Foster (*d*). 3/91.
***(*) **Handful Of Keys** Emarcy 513 737
    Jones (*p* solo). 4/92.
**** **Upon Reflection** Verve 514 898
    Jones; George Mraz (*b*); Elvin Jones (*d*). 2/93.

Jones entered the 1990s one of the music's elder statesmen. His Maybeck recital was, predictably, one of the high points of the series, and his recent recording has all been of a tremendously high standard. There are inconsistencies in the discs from the Danish Jazzpar project (otherwise a signal moment of recognition) and the Waller songbook on Emarcy, where he simply doesn't know what to do with some of the songs but play them straight and then . . . play them straight again.

There is, however, a second masterwork to sit alongside the Maybeck. *Upon Reflection* is devoted to the music of his brother, Thad, who died in 1986. Quite properly, the drummer's job went to Elvin rather than to Foster or Higgins, who might have been more suitable musically. It's a tender, but by no means sentimental, record. However, if you can listen to 'A Child Is Born' without a tear, tear up your donor card. They can't transplant hearts of stone.

*** **Sarala** Verve 528 783
    Jones; Cheick-Tidiane Seck (*org, perc, v*); The Mandinkas. 4/95.

The result of Jones's desire to record an album of traditional African music, *Sarala* tends to marginalize him slightly, so powerful and compelling is the playing and sheer presence of Cheick-Tidiane Seck and his Mandinkas. Mixing flutes, guitars, other native instruments and intense vocalization, they generate textures of close, grainy detail that frequently capture the foreground from Jones. If one is looking for jazz 'roots' in the contemporary world, this is as close and as deep as it gets.

Jo Jones (1911–85) DRUMS

*** **Jo Jones Trio** Fresh Sounds FSR-CD 40
    Jones; Ray Bryant (*p*); Tommy Bryant (*b*). 5/59.
*(*) **Percussion And Bass** Fresh Sound FSR-CD 204
    Jones; Milt Hinton (*b*). 5/60.

The master drummer of the swing era became widely celebrated after he left Count Basie in 1948, but thereafter he seldom found the best contexts for his work, at least on record. His great sessions for Vanguard seem to be back in limbo for the moment. The Emarcy album is an anticlimax after those earlier discs: thinner, sometimes obscured sound, and the tracks are too short to allow the trio to stretch their legs on the material. Still plenty worth hearing, though. But don't bother with *Percussion And Bass*. The idea of a supposedly improvised duo record with Hinton was fascinating, but the results – Papa Jo noodling away on chimes, skins and even vibes at one point, while Milt booms alongside – are pretty laughable, and made worse by the ridiculous studio sound, which suggests that both men were recorded at the bottom of separate wells. Avoidable.

Oliver Jones (born 1934) PIANO

(*) **The Many Moods Of Oliver Jones Justin Time JUST 3
    Jones (*p* solo). 2–3/84.
** **Lights Of Burgundy** Justin Time JUST 6
    Jones; Fraser McPherson (*ts*); Reg Schwager (*g*); Michel Donato (*b*); Jim Hillman (*d*). 4/85.
(*) **Requestfully Yours Justin Time JUST 11
    Jones; Skip Beckwith (*b*); Anil Sharma (*d*). 11/85.
*** **Speak Low Swing Hard** Justin Time JUST 17
    Jones; Skip Beckwith (*b*); Jim Hillman (*d*). 7–9/85.
*** **Cookin' At Sweet Basil** Justin Time JUST 25
    Jones; Dave Young (*b*); Terry Clarke (*d*). 9/87.

(*) Just Friends Justin Time JUST 31
>   Jones; Clark Terry (*t*); Dave Young (*b*); Nasyr Abdul Al-Khabyyr (*d*). 1/89.

**** Northern Summit** Justin Time JUST 34/Enja 6086-2
>   Jones; Herb Ellis (*g*); Red Mitchell (*b*). 6–9/90.

***** A Class Act** Justin Time JUST 41
>   Jones; Steve Wallace (*b*); Ed Thigpen (*d*). 4–5/91.

Oliver Jones is destined to be always the second most famous piano export from Canada, after Oscar Peterson. His style is heavily indebted to Peterson's too, and his original tunes – such as 'Blues For Helene' (*Just Friends*) or 'Fulford Street Maul' (*Lights Of Burgundy*) – are exactly the kind of uptempo blues which Peterson himself writes. Jones is nevertheless a frequently engaging soloist, filling his records with good-hearted, swinging music. His ballads are glossy rather than introspective, but one listens to Jones for his generous virtuosity, not his tenderness. He worked away from any limelight as an accompanist until the 1980s, but since then he has recorded regularly for Justin Time.

Since his playing scarcely varies in intensity or prowess from record to record, preferred sessions are more a matter of the setting. The solo set is slightly less interesting since, like Peterson, Jones thrives on a propulsive rhythm section. Both *Speak Low Swing Hard* and the *Sweet Basil* concert set find everyone playing with huge enthusiasm, and the earlier of these sessions is distinguished by some interesting material, including Ferdie Grofé's 'On The Trail' and a reading of 'I'm An Old Cowhand' that sounds as if it was played on tiptoes. *Lights Of Burgundy* is let down by the unattractive studio-sound. Clark Terry sparks a few tracks on *Just Friends*, although he's not quite at his best; but the meeting with Mitchell and Ellis takes a ponderous course, with so much space allotted to each man that the music lacks Jones's usual ebullience. *A Class Act*, though, might be his best record to date, with two of his best originals in 'Mark My Time' and 'Peaceful Time', and a couple of mature embellishments on Kenny Wheeler's 'Everybody's Song But My Own' and Bill Evans's 'Very Early'. Thigpen and Wallace offer seamless support.

Philly Joe Jones (1923–85) DRUMS

**** Blues For Dracula** Original Jazz Classics OJC 230
>   Jones; Nat Adderley (*c*); Julian Priester (*tb*); Johnny Griffin (*ts*); Tommy Flanagan (*p*); Jimmy Garrison (*b*). 9/58.

**** Showcase** Original Jazz Classics OJC 484
>   Jones; Blue Mitchell (*t*); Julian Priester (*tb*); Bill Barron (*ts*); Pepper Adams (*bs*); Charles Coker (*p*); Jimmy Garrison (*b*). 11/59.

(*) Mo'Joe Black Lion BLCD 760154
>   Jones; Les Condon, Kenny Wheeler (*t*); Chris Pyne (*tb*); Pete King (*as*); Harold McNair (*ts, f*); Mike Pyne (*p*); John Hart, Ron Mathewson (*b*). 10/68.

These bracket a torrid decade in Philly Joe's personal life, but his most productive as a musician. *Blues For Dracula* was recorded towards the end of the drummer's main association with Miles Davis's touring band, a period in which he was much in demand musically, but also making absurd demands on himself by means of a well-developed habit. There are some signs of strain on a mainly good-natured blowing album, with Jones well up in the mix and his characteristic rimshots slightly overloud; 'Two Bass Hit', which inspired some of Philly Joe's best moments on Davis's *Milestones*, is particularly strong. The three horns were well chosen but sound ragged in some of the less frenetic ensembles. The 'European' sessions sound altogether less certain, though Wheeler and King in particular produce an acceptable synthesis of their own slightly abstract idiom with Jones's whacking verve and oblique intelligence. The middle album is notable for a multi-tracked trio, 'Gwen', on which Philly Joe plays piano, bass and drums and does so very swingingly. The other tracks are strongly coloured by the horn players, Mitchell's raw earth colours, Priester's slightly surreal tinge, Garrison's magnificently centred bass playing. By contrast, the drummer is something of a bit-player. None of these can be said to be absolutely essential to a good modern collection; nevertheless, Philly Joe was a significant presence for three decades, and his influence can be heard today in the likes of Andrew Cyrille.

**** Drums Around The World** Original Jazz Classics OJC 1792
>   Jones; Lee Morgan, Blue Mitchell (*t*); Curtis Fuller (*tb*); Cannonball Adderley (*as*); Benny Golson (*ts*); Herbie Mann (*f, picc*); Wynton Kelly (*p*); Jimmy Garrison, Sam Jones (*b*). 5/59.

Some of this material – 'Stablemates', 'El Tambores', and the solo percussion 'Tribal Message' from OJC 1792, which is subtitled 'Big Band Sounds' – may be familiar from a good Milestone compilation of drummers' bands called *The Big Beat*. It's all good stuff, with imaginative horn arrangements and carefully disciplined solo stretches from the leader. 'Cherokee' is a good example of how positively Jones responds to the challenge of overworked changes. Recording quality is still far short of what contemporary percussionists would expect as of right, but it's better than most.

Quincy Jones (born 1933) ARRANGER, BANDLEADER, TRUMPET

**** This Is How I Feel About Jazz Impulse! GRP 11152
Art Farmer, Bernie Glow, Ernie Royal, Joe Wilder (*t*); Jimmy Cleveland, Urbie Green, Frank Rehak (*tb*); Gene Quill, Phil Woods, Benny Carter, Art Pepper, Charlie Mariano (*as*); Herbie Mann, Jerome Richardson (*ts, f*); Bunny Beirach, Lucky Thompson, Zoot Sims, Buddy Collette, Bill Perkins, Walter Benton (*ts*); Jack Nimitz, Pepper Adams (*bs*); Hank Jones, Billy Taylor, Lou Levy, Carl Perkins (*p*); Milt Jackson (*vib*); Paul Chambers, Charles Mingus, Red Mitchell, Leroy Vinnegar (*b*); Charli Persip, Shelly Manne (*d*). 9/56–2/57.

*** Free And Easy Ancha ANC 9500-2
Jones; Lennie Johnson, Benny Bailey, Floyd Standifer, Clark Terry (*t, flhn*); Ake Persson, Melba Liston, Quentin Jackson, Jimmy Cleveland (*tb*); Julius Watkins (*frhn*); Porter Kilbert, Phil Woods, Jerome Richardson, Budd Johnson, Sahib Shihab (*reeds*); Patti Bown (*p*); Les Spann (*g, f*); Buddy Catlett (*b*); Joe Harris (*d*). 2/60.

*** Swiss Radio Days Jazz Series Vol. 1 TCB 02012
As above, except Roger Guérin, Clyde Reasinger (*t*), Harold McNair (*as*) replace Terry, Lennie Johnson and Budd Johnson. 6/60.

*** Strike Up The Band Mercury 830774-2
Joe Newman, Clark Terry, Ernie Royal, Snooky Young, James Nottingham, Al Perisi, Jimmy Maxwell, John Bello, Benny Bailey (*t*); Curtis Fuller, Urbie Green, Richard Hixson, Bill Byers, Quentin Jackson, Tony Studd, Paul Faulise, Jimmy Cleveland, Kai Winding, Thomas Mitchell, Santo Russo, Melba Liston (*tb*); Zoot Sims, Roland Kirk, Walter Levinsky, James Moody, Phil Woods, Frank Wess, Al Cohn, Jerome Richardson, Seldon Powell, Romeo Penque, Walter Kane, Sahib Shihab, Eric Dixon, Stanley Webb, Budd Johnson, Seldon Powell (*reeds*); Jimmy Buffington, Tony Miranda, Bob Northern, Ray Alonge, Julius Watkins, Earl Chapin, Bob Ingraham, Fred Klein, Willie Ruff (*frhn*); Charles McCoy (*hca, perc*); Toots Thielemans (*hca*); Lalo Schifrin, Bobby Scott, Patti Bown (*org, p*); Gary Burton (*vib*); Wayne Wright, Sam Herman, Kenny Burrell, Jim Hall, Vincent Bell, Mundell Lowe, Don Arnone (*g*); Bill Stanley, James McAllister (*tba*); Milt Hinton, Art Davis, George Duvivier, Major Holley, Ben Tucker, Chris White (*b*); Rudy Collins, Osie Johnson, Ed Shaughnessy, Stu Martin, Jimmy Crawford (*d*); Tito Puente, Potato Valdez, Mike Olatunji, Martin Grupp, Philip Kraus, James Johnson, Carlos Gomez, Jack Del Rio, Jose Paula, Bill Costa, George Devins (*perc*). 1/61–2/64.

**(*) Walking In Space A&M 396993-2
John Frosk, Freddie Hubbard, Lloyd Michaels, Marvin Stamm, Dick Williams, Snooky Young (*t, flhn*); Jimmy Cleveland, George Jeffers, J. J. Johnson, Norman Pride, Alan Ralph, Tony Studd, Kai Winding (*tb*); Joel Kaye, Roland Kirk, Hubert Laws, Jerome Richardson (*reeds*); Toots Thielemans (*hca, g*); Paul Griffin, Bob James (*p*); Eric Gale (*g*); Ray Brown, Chuck Rainey (*b*); Bernard Purdie, Grady Tate (*d*); Hilda Harris, Marilyn Jackson, Valerie Simpson, Maretha Stewart (*v*). 6/69.

Jones has been among the most charismatic figures in black music in the past 40 years. His specific jazz records have been few, since he's chosen to make his mark as a producer/Svengali to countless other artists, involving himself in some of the most successful recording projects of recent years with Michael Jackson and others. But his best music assuredly deserves a place in a comprehensive jazz collection. The pick of these is *This Is How I Feel About Jazz*, which combines the original album of that name with most of *Go West, Man*. The latter session was a variation on a typical West Coast date of the period, with scores by Giuffre, Mariano and Lennie Niehaus, and various sax combinations – four altos on three tracks, three tenors on another three – predominating. Jones seems to have done little more than produce. But the six earlier tracks, by a fantastically star-studded personnel, demonstrate how Jones was even then, at the age of 23, a master at assembling musicians and getting the best out of them. He seldom uses the big band as a source of weight and power here, preferring to let smaller groups within the orchestra take a lead; as a result the music is unusually light and airy. 'Walkin'' and 'Stockholm Sweetnin'' are vehicles for impressive solos, but Jones's own 'Evening In Paris', a lovely vehicle for Zoot Sims, shows the strength of his writing. A very fine record, excellently remastered.

Jones managed to tour Europe with some of his orchestras, and the two recent releases from their 1960 sojourn have some fine music. The earlier disc, recorded for Swedish Radio in Goteborg, is marginally more hi-fi, though the performances here sound more buttoned-up; the similar (and slightly longer) programme in Lausanne swings with greater abandon, though ensembles are paradoxically more secure. Interesting to compare solo spots between the two shows: Clark Terry and Benny Bailey each take a crack at 'I Remember Clifford' (Terry wins), while Melba Liston and Quentin Jackson go through 'The Phantom's Blues' (honours even).

Strike Up The Band is rather less impressive than the Impulse! CD, the tracks culled from various Mercury albums of a commercial bent, though Jones again assembles several remarkable orchestras and persuades them to make the most of 'Baby Elephant Walk' and 'Cast Your Fate To The Wind'. By the late '60s, Jones was leaving jazz to other hands, though he usually found room for soloists in his prolific film and TV scoring. Walking In Space was one of his last records in which jazz was the primary ingredient, and it's pretty glum: lumpen beats, soupy production, and the soloists (Kirk, Hubbard, Laws) hardly make an impact.

Sam Jones (1924–81) BASS, CELLO

*** The Riverside Collection: Sam Jones – Right Down Front Original Jazz Classics OJC 6008
> Jones; Blue Mitchell, Clark Terry, Snooky Young (t); Nat Adderley (c); Melba Liston, Jimmy Cleveland (tb); Cannonball Adderley, Frank Strozier (as); Jimmy Heath, Jimmy Smith (ts); Charles Davis, Tate Houston, Pat Patrick (bs); Bobby Timmons, Victor Feldman, Joe Zawinul, Wynton Kelly (p); Les Spann (g, f); Keter Betts, Ron Carter, Israel Crosby (b); Louis Hayes, Ben Riley, Vernell Fournier (d). 3/60–6/62.

*** The Soul Society Original Jazz Classics OJC 1789
> Jones; Nat Adderley (c); Blue Mitchell (t); Jimmy Heath (ts); Charles Davis (bs); Bobby Timmons (p); Keter Betts (b); Louis Hayes (d). 3/60.

*** The Chant Original Jazz Classics OJC 1839
> As above, except add Melba Liston (tb), Cannonball Adderley (as), Tate Houston (bs), Wynton Kelly (p), Victor Feldman (p, vib), Les Spann (g); omit Davis, Timmons. 1/61.

Sam Jones had a beautiful sound on bass – fat, resonant, fluid without any loss of body – and he was among the first to make the cello sound plausible in post-bop jazz. The compilation is chosen from five sessions he made during his time with Cannonball Adderley and, although the settings are mostly rather ordinary – two tracks by a big band with Melba Liston charts are more challenging – Jones's quiet good humour gives as much buoyancy as his bass to the music. A quintet reading of 'Round Midnight' with Jones on cello is a little fluffy, and 'Some Kinda Mean' gives a better idea of his powers on that instrument. That track is drawn from The Soul Society sessions, which has also been reissued as a single album. The cello tracks (there are four with Sam on that instrument, where Keter Betts takes over bass duties) are a little gimmicky in the fashion of the day, but the band is a rousing one, and the other session with Mitchell in for Adderley boils water on 'All Members' and 'The Old Country'.

The Chant is another good session. Cannonball takes a back-seat role, but most of the other horns get in a blow, and the studio sound gets a nice burnish on the section-work. Jones himself has a number of features, but what one remembers is his drive in the ensembles and alongside old partner, Louis Hayes.

**(*) Visitation Steeplechase SCCD 31097
> Jones; Terumasa Hino (c); Bob Berg (ts); Ronnie Mathews (p); Al Foster (d). 3/78.

Sam's few sessions as a leader in the 1970s found him pursuing a lyrical kind of hard bop. Visitation is dependable rather than especially exciting, although Hino's peculiar mix of rhapsody and restlessness is as engaging as usual.

Thad Jones (1923–86) TRUMPET, CORNET, FLUGELHORN, VALVE TROMBONE, BANDLEADER, ARRANGER

***(*) The Fabulous Thad Jones Original Jazz Classics OJC 625
> Jones; Frank Wess (ts, f); John Dennis, Hank Jones (p); Charles Mingus (b); Kenny Clarke, Max Roach (d). 54.

*** After Hours Original Jazz Classics OJC 1782
> Jones; Frank Wess (ts, f); Kenny Burrell (g); Mal Waldron (p); Paul Chambers (b); Arthur Taylor (d).

***(*) Mad Thad Fresh Sound FSR CD 117
> Jones; Henry Coker (tb); Frank Foster (ts); Frank Wess (ts, f); Tommy Flanagan, Jimmy Jones (p); Eddie Jones, Doug Watkins (b); Elvin Jones, Jo Jones (d). 12/56.

**(*) Mean What You Say Original Jazz Classics OJC 464
> Jones; Pepper Adams (bs); Duke Pearson (p); Ron Carter (b); Mel Lewis (d). 4 & 5/66.

*** Three And One Steeplechase SCS 1197
> Jones; Ole Kock Hansen (p); Jesper Lundgaard (b); Ed Thigpen (d). 10/84.

Though better known than the quiet Hank, the middle Jones brother has been consistently underrated as a soloist, recognized mainly as an arranger for the band he co-led with drummer Mel Lewis (see below). Not usually considered a small-group player, or even a soloist of any unusual interest, Jones's recorded output on this scale is disappointingly slight, relative to his significance as a composer. On the measure of *Three And One* alone, this is a pity. He's a subtle and vibrant player with a cornet tone reminiscent of Nat Adderley but able to sustain big transitions of pitch with absolute confidence, much as he demands of his big bands. 'But Not For Me' is marred by a slightly tentative accompaniment, but Thigpen splashes in sensuous slo-mo, almost tuneful. Recommended.

Mad Thad is even better. The trumpeter was signed to Basie for most of the late 1950s and early '60s, a period that firmed up his reputation as an arranger but afforded regrettably few solo flights. He'd recorded on Mingus's demanding *Jazz Experiment* and won the bassist's heart for ever with his bustling, opportunistic runs and confident entanglements in and around the theme. On *Mad Thad*, playing trumpet only, he sounds full-throated and sure of himself; there are what appear to be very minor articulation problems on a couple of tracks, but these are incidental stammers in some beautifully crafted ('Whisper Not' especially) solos.

The sessions done for Mingus's and Roach's Debut label are very good indeed; these are also to be found in the 12-CD Debut compilation. Mingus admired the trumpeter inordinately and Jones was the only artist to record twice under his own name for Debut. Their duo on 'I Can't Get Started' is interesting first of all for Mingus's restructuring of the harmony, but Jones's response to this bare-boned setting and to the quasi-modal 'Get Out Of Town' is full confirmation of his ability to improvise at the highest level. Wess's flute makes a fine contrast on 'Sombre Intrusion'. The slighter *After Hours* has nothing quite so daring, but it's a solidly inventive session nonetheless, and the CD sound on both is very good.

Mean What You Say comes just after the formation of the Jones–Lewis big band. Though it casts the trumpeter in what should be completely sympathetic company, it's a rather uncertain affair, with most of the honours going to baritonist Pepper Adams, named as co-leader on the session. The sound is exemplary, though, with a representation of bass and percussion that was better than average for the time, even on the very acceptable vinyl.

*** **Eclipse** Storyville STCD 4089
> Jones; Jan Glasesel, Tim Hagans, Egon Petersen, Lars Togeby, Erik Tschentscher (*t*); Richard Boone, Ture Larsen, Niels Neergaard, Bjarne Thanning, Axel Windfeld (*tb*); Michael Hove, Bent Jaedig, Ole Thoger Nielsen, Jorgen Nilsson, Sahib Shihab (*sax*); Horace Parlan (*p*); Jesper Lundgaard (*b*); Ed Thigpen (*d*). 9/79.

After leaving Mel Lewis in 1978, Jones spent most of his remaining years in Scandinavia, where he formed and led the Eclipse big band, an outfit which reflected some of the old partnership's combination of power and complexity. For all his virtues, Thigpen is no Lewis, but the band sounds well drilled and the charts are razor-sharp. In the late 1970s, Jones took up valve trombone as an alternative horn. It sounds fleet and subtle, and lends him a breadth of tone he could not have achieved with trumpet. The LP sound doesn't hold up to current digital standards, but it's big and warm and preserves enough of the grain in the ensembles to afford a hint of what this band was like in concert.

**** **Live At Montmartre** Storyville STCD 4172
> Jones; Benny Rosenfeld, Palle Bolvig, Idrees Sulieman, Allan Botschinsky, Perry Knudsen (*t*); Vincent Nilsson (*tb*); Erling Kroner, Richard Boone (*tb*); Ole Kurt Jensen (*btb*); Axel Windfeld (*btb, tba*); Jesper Thilo (*ss, as, cl, f*); Per Carsten Petersen (*ss, as, f*); Bent Jaedig (*ts, f*); Uffe Karsakov (*ts, as, f, cl*); Flemming Madsen (*bs, cl, bcl*); Ole Kock Hansen (*p*); Bo Sylven (*g*); Niels-Henning Orsted-Pedersen (*b*); Bjarne Rostvold (*d*); Ethan Weisgard (*perc*). 3/78.

One of the authors was present at the concert recorded here and can confirm that this is an authentic documentation of one of the very finest concerts of Jones's later career, made on the eve of his departure from the long-standing Jones/Lewis band, and the trumpeter (or, rather, cornetist) played his socks off. His tone on the ballad, 'Old Folks', on his own 'Tip Toe' and 'A Good Time Was Had By All' is pure and bell-like and the solos are relaxed enough to allow digressions into other themes and harmonic displacements without losing the thread.

The sound is considerably better than in the rather cramped acoustic of the Jazzhus Montmartre. Bass trombonist Jensen co-produced and gets the brasses sounding as shiny as Gabriel's. Completely enjoyable, and one of the best big-band records of recent times.

Herbert Joos (born 1940) TRUMPET, FLUGELHORN, ARRANGER

*** **Daybreak** Japo 60015
> Joos; strings. 10/76.

*** Cracked Mirrors ECM 1356

    Joos; Harry Pepl (*g, g synth*); Jon Christensen (*d*). 2/87.

***(*) Plays Billie Holiday Songs Emarcy 522634

    Joos; Nirjam Ernst (*eng hn*); Paul Schwarz (*p*); Joe Koinzer (*perc*). 4/94.

Joos has been a member of the Vienna Art Orchestra since the end of the 1970s, an association that reflects his equal interest in improvisation and more formal structures. The music of *Cracked Mirrors* offers back a splintered version of his Miles-influenced quasi-modality, but with a hard and brilliant tone that is all his own. Christensen is responsive to every parameter of the music, and the production establishes a fine balance between the three players, with Pepl's guitar synthesizer acting as colour and condiment in one. If *Daybreak* then reflects Joos's interest in Miles Davis, it is a Miles refracted by Gil Evans. The Stuttgart Radio Symphony strings sound slightly muffled in places, but Joos plays with a deceptively hard edge to his romanticism. This is a further intriguing example of the impact Miles has made on classically influenced European composers, to be set alongside the best of Palle Mikkelborg's work.

    The Billie Holiday session is fascinating. Essentially a trumpet, piano, percussion trio, with the addition of cor anglais (a much-undersubscribed jazz instrument) on five tracks, it has a cool reserve that may be typical of Joos and his peers but comes as something of a shock and revelation with this repertoire. 'God Bless The Child' is wholly revelatory, an exquisite performance.

Clifford Jordan (1931–93) TENOR SAXOPHONE

***(*) Bearcat Original Jazz Classics OJC 494

    Jordan; Cedar Walton (*p*); Teddy Smith (*b*); J. C. Moses (*d*).

**** Spellbound Original Jazz Classics OJC 766

    Jordan; Cedar Walton (*p*); Spanky De Brest (*b*); Albert 'Tootie' Heath (*d*). 8/60.

At first blush, Jordan is 'just' another Chicago tenor. That was very much the way he was perceived and marketed. His Blue Note debut, *Blowin' In From Chicago*, is currently in limbo. Thirty years ago his style was much closer to the tempestuous approach associated with such natives of the Windy City as Johnny Griffin (whom he momentarily resembles on 'Sunrise In Mexico' here) and – in timbre particularly – Von Freeman.

    Bearcat is the perfect characterization of Jordan's sound, sometimes growling, sometimes purring. This old Jazzland set isn't particularly well recorded and the bassist is prone to sudden surges towards the mike, but the music is fine and Jordan is in good voice on 'How Deep Is The Ocean?' and the original 'Middle Of The Block'. The old home town is eulogized in 'Dear Old Chicago', a performance that name-checks one or two distinguished ancestors. A word of praise is in order for Walton and Moses, both of whom play exceptionally well.

    Spellbound makes a welcome return, containing as it does one of Jordan's very finest recorded perform-ances, on 'Lush Life'. His understanding with Walton was only to grow and deepen with the years, but their level of communication here is most impressive and they hurtle through 'Au Privave' with almost cavalier abandon. The sound – originally a Riverside – is very full and authentic. A recommended purchase.

***(*) Glass Bead Games Strata East 660.51.017

    Jordan; Stanley Cowell, Cedar Walton (*p*); Bill Lee, Sam Jones (*b*); Billy Higgins (*d*). 73.

*** Glass Bead Games 2 Strata East 660.21.023

    As above. 10/73.

Strata East was the creation of Jordan, Cowell and trumpeter Charles Tolliver and has issued some powerful jazz over the years. Quite why it should have made such a monkey of one of the founders' better albums is a mystery. Rather than put together a single coherent CD, *Glass Bead Games* has been left at LP dimensions; questionable value for money, even given music of this quality. Jordan is blowing magnificently on the title-tune, 'Powerful Paul Robeson' and (Volume 2) 'Alias Buster Henry'. Cowell is a more demanding accompanist than Walton and he pulls the music in all sorts of exhilarating direc-tions at once. The arrangements are unfailingly tight and accurate, and the two different groups give the sessions a change of pace and of texture which is very welcome, preventing the second volume at least from becoming too one-dimensional. Even so, it would have made better artistic and commercial sense to have packaged these in a single box.

*** On Stage: Volume 1 Steeplechase SCS 1071

    Jordan; Cedar Walton (*p*); Teddy Smith (*b*); Billy Higgins (*d*). 3/75.

*** On Stage: Volume 2 Steeplechase SCCD 31092

    As above. 3/75.

*** **The Highest Mountain** Steeplechase SCS 1047
    As above. 4/75.
*** **Firm Roots** Steeplechase SCS 1033
    As above. 4/75.
It was having such firm roots that allowed Jordan to drift through a theme as cavalierly as he often did. Throughout the highly productive mid-1970s, he was probably playing more 'legitimately' than at any other time in his career, but there are constant reminders of his Mingus-influenced tendency to regard the note as a dartboard (which, of course, you don't always want to hit dead centre) and a progression as a series of mentally totted-up scores that always come out right in the end.

Though he had a fair change of pace, he was definitely more successful at a medium to slow clip. He was a consummate ballad-player (see 'Stella By Starlight' on *On Stage: Volume 2*), with the kind of articulation and presence that suggest unused gears. Throughout these sets, it is the romantic ballads which consistently score high points. Compared to, say, Griffin, he never quite convinces at a gallop.

In the 1970s, Jordan was playing regularly with Cedar Walton, Sam Jones and Billy Higgins under the name The Magic Triangle; *Firm Roots* was more prosaically designated, but the evocative title captures something like the equidistance and responsiveness that Jordan, a great arranger, achieved with his colleagues. They work hard for each other, creating spaces and textures, laying off chords that lead whoever is soloing out into new territory, then gently pulling on the strings.

It's very difficult to choose from among these records. The quality is consistently high, and none will disappoint.

***(*) **Highest Mountain** Muse MCD 5445
    Jordan; Cedar Walton (*p*); Sam Jones (*b*); Billy Higgins (*d*). 3/75.
A remarkable live set, recorded in France. The title-piece is a complex, irregular theme divided into two passages of 23 bars each. Walton takes a prominent solo, then Higgins, and the piece closes with a sequence of ambiguous resolutions that so closely recall those on 'Psalm' at the end of *A Love Supreme* that 'Highest Mountain' almost sounds like the culmination of a suite begun with the opening 'John Coltrane'. Written by Bill Lee, the father of movie director Spike Lee, this is a stately, multi-part theme which develops in a manner very similar to Coltrane's epic, and over very much the same kind of propulsive cymbal accent. Halfway through, as if to rubber-stamp the resemblance, the group chant 'John Coltrane, black spirit, first new-born' in an echo of the *Love Supreme* mantra.

After these two tracks, on which Jordan maintains a keening, restless tone, 'Blue Monk' seems quite conventional, and Jordan's delivery immediately simplifies, shedding the overtones and harmonics in favour of an orthodox blues shout. Walton's solo suddenly accelerates into double time, a bravura performance that confirms the responsiveness of the whole rhythm section. The pianist's 'Midnight Waltz' is one of his loveliest compositions and features low-register interplay between piano and bass. Jones again features strongly on his own composition, 'One For Amos', sharing the main statement with Jordan. Thoroughly recommended.

*** **Repetition** Soul Note 121084
    Jordan; Barry Harris (*p*); Walter Booker (*b*); Vernell Fournier (*d*). 2/84.
*** **Two Tenor Winner** Criss Cross Criss 1011
    Jordan; Junior Cook (*ts*); Kirk Lightsey (*p*); Cecil McBee (*b*); Eddie Gladden (*d*). 10/84.
***(*) **Royal Ballads** Criss Cross Criss 1025
    Jordan; Kevin O'Connell (*p*); Ed Howard (*b*); Vernell Fournier (*d*). 12/86.
In recent years Jordan has perfected a ballad style that is strikingly reminiscent of Wardell Gray's. *Royal Ballads* is a lovely record; if it steers close to easy listening on occasion, a more attentive hearing uncovers all manner of subtleties and harmonic shifts. The opening 'Lush Life' is almost lost in Fournier's constant cymbal-spray, but the drummer – who has worked to great effect with Ahmad Jamal – is a great ballad player and every bit as adept as Jordan at varying an apparently sleepy beat with odd, out-of-synch metres and quiet paradiddles. As Jordan quotes 'Goodbye Pork Pie Hat' on the original 'Royal Blues', Fournier squeezes the tempo almost subliminally, so that the reference evades identification as the mind subconsciously readjusts to the beat. Subtle and intelligent jazz, and a sure sign that ballads albums are not just the preserve of MOR acts.

The slightly earlier *Repetition* and *Two Tenor Winner* have more variation of pace (though no less inventive a trawl of material). Fournier doesn't seem quite so much at ease, but Harris is a much subtler player than O'Connell. Cook plays with a loose-limbed ease, but he lacks the chops to go head to head with Jordan in this way.

Once again, nothing to choose between them. Late-nighters might prefer the ballads.

***(*) **Four Play** DIW 836
    Jordan; James Williams (*p*); Richard Davis (*b*); Ronnie Burrage (*d*).
It's not quite clear who's supposed to be leader here. A companion DIW set, *sans* Jordan, and either

deliberately or misleadingly entitled *I Remember Clifford*, is reviewed under Richard Davis's name. Jordan contributes two fine compositions to *Four Play* and kicks off the session on his 'Tokyo Road' with a dark, Coltranish wail that lightens steadily as the set progresses. There's an excellent reading of Monk's 'I Mean You', one of the less exploited items in the canon, and a superb long version of Randy Weston's 'Hi-Fly', which leads in to Richard Davis's moving 'Misako – Beautiful Shore', a theme that brings back some of the sombre quality to Jordan's voice. Impeccably recorded, and laurels for the unsung Williams and the prodigious Burrage. Well worth what might seem a pricey investment.

**** **Masters From Different Worlds** Mapleshade 01732
> Jordan; Ran Blake (*p*); Julian Priester (*tb*); Steve Williams (*d*); Windmill Saxophone Quartet: Clayton Englar, Jesse Meman, Tom Monroe, Ken Plant (*sax*); Alfredo Mojica (*perc*); Claudia Polley (*v*). 12/89.

A most unusual record: Jordan in duo and in an assortment of slightly unlikely settings with composer and pianist Blake, one of the most analytical of contemporary players. Much of the material is Blake's, including the contemporary classic, 'Short Life Of Barbara Monk'; but there are also interpretations of 'Mood Indigo', Billy Strayhorn's 'Something To Live For' played as a moody duo, and even John Lennon's song to his mother, 'Julia'. There's nothing overtly 'Third Stream' about the set, except that Blake does seem to slide into occasional reveries and lets the rhythm go completely to pot. On 'Arline', Jordan makes a rare shift to soprano, sounding very polished indeed; with Priester beside him, the sound is wonderful. To what extent, and with what success, they've sunk their differences really isn't clear, but this is an extraordinary record nevertheless.

**** **Down Through The Years** Milestone MCD 9197
> Jordan; Dizzy Reece, Stephen Furtado, Dean Pratt, Don Sickler (*t*); Brad Shigeta (*tb*); Kiane Zawadi (*euph*); Jerome Richardson, Sue Terry (*as*); Lou Oresteen, Willie Williams (*ts*); Charles Davis (*bs*); Ronnie Mathews (*p*); David Williams (*b*); Vernell Fournier (*d*). 10/91.

For the time being, this has to stand as the last testament of a player who stuck to his guns to the very end and never compromised his own quietly dogged vision. Jordan rarely had an opportunity to play with a big band, and this hand-picked orchestra was the fulfilment of considerable planning and thorough rehearsal. Recorded at Condon's in New York City, the disc captures the sound of an excellent ensemble playing at full stretch. The programme includes such long-standing favourites as 'Highest Mountain', on which the saxophonist is, appropriately, the only soloist, singing away on his solitary eminence, 'Japanese Dream', which provides an outlet for Dizzy Reece, and the strangely moving 'Charlie Parker's Last Supper', which brings the set to a close.

Jordan has played better many times, but rarely in such a completely sympathetic setting. His phrasing is almost always right on the beat, but he manages to avoid sounding mechanical.

Duke Jordan (born 1922) PIANO

*** **Do It Yourself Jazz** Savoy SV 0130
> Jordan; Gigi Gryce (*as*); Oscar Pettiford (*b*); Kenny Clarke (*d*). 3/55.

**** **Duke Jordan** Savoy SV 0149
> Jordan; Cecil Payne (*bs*); Percy Heath (*b*); Art Blakey (*d*). 10 & 11/55.

Duke Jordan's career has an odd trajectory. At 25, with an apprenticeship under Coleman Hawkins behind him, he was thrust into the limelight with Charlie Parker and proved himself an able and frequently imaginative accompanist. Thereafter, though, his progress has been curiously elided, with long disappearances from the scene. Perhaps as a consequence, he is by far the least well-known of the bebop pianists, surprisingly diffident in performing manner and little given to solo performance. Though he is a fine standards player, he has from time to time preferred to rework a sizeable but tightly organized body of original compositions. These have been documented by the Danish Steeplechase label with a thoroughness which borders on redundancy and which seems quite inconsistent with the pianist's rather marginal reputation. There are very many recorded versions of some of the pianist's most successful themes. 'Jordu', in particular, has become a popular repertoire piece. A Jordan theme tends to be brief, tightly melodic rather than just a launching-pad of chords, and disconcertingly unmemorable, in the positive sense that they resist being hummed.

'Jordu' gets an early airing on *Do It Yourself Jazz*, which is shared with fellow-pianist Hall Overton. Even with a couple of standards as reference points, it's by no means easy to get a fix on Jordan's technique or his intentions. His long lines are essentially segments of melody, and his rhythm surprisingly staccato and uncountable, like a milder version of Thelonious Monk.

The trio tracks collected on *Duke Jordan* are as good as he has ever played. 'Summertime' and 'Night In Tunisia' recall his musical background and document his divergence from it. The sound is good and clear. It muddies a little with the addition of trombone and baritone saxophone, and Jordan himself tends to disappear, but 'Flight To Jordan' and 'Two Loves' – the latter has an imaginative structure – are particularly strong, and 'Yesterdays' is a rhapsodic swirl of chords and melodic fragments.

(*) **Flight To Denmark Steeplechase SCCD 31011
    Jordan; Mads Vinding (*b*); Ed Thigpen (*d*). 11/73.
*** **Two Loves** Steeplechase SCCD 31024
    As above. 12/73.
Unlike his later work for Steeplechase, these are essentially albums of standards, and in some sense an attempt to come to terms with the legacy of bebop. There are finely judged readings of 'Here's That Rainy Day', 'On Green Dolphin Street' and 'How Deep Is The Ocean' on *Flight*, 'I'll Remember April' and 'Embraceable You', 'Blue Monk' and 'My Old Flame' on *Two Loves*, which also includes the ubiquitous 'Jordu' and 'Lady Dingbat', an unaccountably popular original. Jordan's career had been rather stop-start since the mid-1950s and there are occasional rust-spots on his faster runs and a slight stiffness in his octaves. The CD transfers aren't perfect. There are alternative takes of several tracks; newcomers might find *Two Loves* preferable.

(*) **Misty Thursday Steeplechase SCCD 31053
    Jordan; Chuck Wayne (*g*); Sam Jones (*b*); Roy Haynes (*d*). 6/75.
*** **Lover Man** Steeplechase SCCD 31127
    Jordan; Sam Jones (*b*); Al Foster (*d*). 11/75.
*** **Live In Japan** Steeplechase SCCD 1063/4 2CD
    Jordan; Wilbur Little (*b*); Roy Haynes (*d*). 9/76.
*** **Osaka Concert: Volume 1** Steeplechase SCCD 31271
    As above.
*** **Osaka Concert: Volume 2** Steeplechase SCCD 31272
    As above.
*** **Duke's Artistry** Steeplechase SCCD 31103
    Jordan; Art Farmer (*flhn*); David Friesen (*b*); Philly Joe Jones (*d*). 6/78.
(*) **The Great Session Steeplechase SCCD 31150
    As above, except omit Farmer, add Paul Jeffrey (*bells*). 6/78.
(*) **Tivoli One Steeplechase SCCD 31189
    Jordan; Wilbur Little (*b*); Dannie Richmond (*d*). 11/78.
(*) **Wait And See Steeplechase SCCD 31211
    As above.
***(*) **Duke Jordan Solo Masterpieces Vol. One** Steeplechase SCCD 31299
    Jordan (*p* solo). 1 & 2/79.
***(*) **Duke Jordan Solo Masterpieces Vol. Two** Steeplechase SCCD 31300
    Jordan (*p* solo). 2–11/79.
*** **Thinking Of You** Steeplechase SCCD 31165
    Jordan; Niels-Henning Orsted-Pedersen (*b*); Billy Hart (*d*). 10/79.
(*) **Time On My Hands Steeplechase SCCD 31232
    Jordan; Jesper Lundgaard (*b*); Billy Hart (*d*). 79, 7/85.
(*) **As Time Goes By Steeplechase SCCD 31247
    As above. 7/85.
The late 1970s were a remarkably productive time for Jordan. In Billy Hart and Dannie Richmond he found drummers with the kind of rhythmic tension he required on which to sound his taut melodic figures. The mix of material is much as usual, but some mention should be made of 'Light Foot' and 'The Queen Is Home To Stay' on *Thinking Of You*, which averages out as one of the best of this group.

Compare the studio version of 'Night Train To Snekkersten', one of his best compositions, with the live versions recorded in Osaka 15 months later. Jones has a more contained approach and lacks Little's strength, but he is absolutely right for the lovely 'Hymn To Peace'. The sound is a little flat.

The *Tivoli* sessions with Richmond are again standards-based, with an accent on bebop-associated themes. Jordan's vocals on *Time On My Hands* and *As Ditto Goes By* can't be considered an advantage. Much as Ahmad Jamal is popularly supposed to, Jordan occasionally skirts a Vegas-style 'entertainment' approach that obscures his more interesting ideas to all but the most attentive listeners.

Jordan was warmly received in Japan. The Osaka concert is a confident and lively recording and, though *Volume One* possesses a snap and professionalism that seem to drift on the sequel, it amply justifies the double release. Since favourites like 'Misty Thursday', 'Jordu' and 'Flight To Jordan' are all included, it might make a sensible introduction to the pianist's work. The CD quality is excellent, with good atmosphere.

'Lady Bird' on *The Great Session* helpfully points to Tadd Dameron as a further factor in the development of Jordan's approach (Lennie Tristano, at the opposite pole from bebop, is another). These are unexceptionable sessions; Philly Joe plays with his incomparable verve and exactness, and Friesen sounds confident and aware.

What all this amounts to is very difficult to judge. Though there are later recordings from the mid-'80s on the CD of *Time On My Hands* and *As Time Goes By*, and the playing sounds as solid and untroubled as ever, Jordan's *annus mirabilis* had been and gone. This is an almost unprecedented body of work, with only the most obvious reference-points in the shape of oft-repeated themes and compositions. Doubtless there are aficionados who can speak with authority on the question of their respective merits. Since we are dealing with records and not tracks, though, only a rather impressionistic valuation is feasible. Perhaps the two *Masterpieces* discs offer the best music.

*** **One For The Library** Storyville STCD 4194
    Jordan (*p* solo). 10/93.
What an odd, perhaps even cynical title for a record. One does begin to wonder how much of the Jordan discography has been merely 'for the library', documentation for the sake of it. The galling thing is that this is a perfectly respectable record, swinging in the rather restrictive mode of solo piano records, packed with melody and invention (18 tracks in 65 minutes) and beautifully recorded in the studio on a responsive, big-hearted piano. But ask us to differentiate it blindfold from half a dozen others of Duke's records and we'd have to bow out.

Louis Jordan (1908–75) ALTO AND BARITONE SAXOPHONES, CLARINET, VOCAL

*** **At the Swing Cats' Ball** JSP CD 330
    Jordan; Mario Bauza, Bobby Stark, Taft Jordan, Courtney Williams (*t*); Sandy Williams, Nat Story (*tb*); Pete Clark (*cl, as, bs*); Lem Johnson (*cl, ts*); Ted McRae, Stafford 'Pazuza' Simon (*ts*); Wayman Carver (*ts, f*); Stafford Simon (*ts*); Tommy Fulford, Clarence Johnson (*p*); John Trueheart (*g*); Beverley Peer, Charlie Drayton (*b*); Chick Webb, Walter Martin (*d*); Rodney Sturgis (*v*). 1/37–11/39.

*** **Louis Jordan 1934–1940** Classics 636
    As above, except add Charlie Gaines (*t, v*); Ed Allen (*c*); Claude Jones (*tb*); Cecil Scott (*cl, as*); James P. Johnson (*p*); Cyrus St Clair (*bb*); Floyd Casey (*wbd*); Clarence Williams (*v*). 3/34–1/40.

*** **Louis Jordan 1940–1941** Classics 663
    Jordan; Courtney Williams, Freddy Webster, Eddie Roane (*t*); Stafford Simon (*cl, ts*); Kenneth Hollon (*ts*); Arnold Thomas (*p*); Charlie Drayton, Henry Turner, Dallas Bartley (*b*); Walter Martin (*d*); Mabel Robinson, Daisy Winchester (*v*). 3/40–11/41.

*** **Louis Jordan 1941–1943** Classics 741
    Jordan; Eddie Roane (*t*); Arnold Thomas (*p*); Dallas Bartley, Jesse Simpkins (*b*); Walter Martin, Shadow Wilson (*d*). 11/41–11/43.

***(*) **Best Of Louis Jordan** MCA MCAD-4079
    Jordan; Eddie Roane (*t*); Arnold Thomas (*p*); Dallas Bartley, Al Morgan (*b*); Walter Martin, Shadow Wilson (*d*). 42–45.
Jordan, who came from Arkansas and had a father in vaudeville, quit playing in big bands in the early 1940s to form his Tympany Five, one of the most successful small bands in jazz history: their hit records, 'Five Guys Named Moe', 'Choo Choo Ch'Boogie', 'Caldonia' and many more, established the idea of the jump band as a jiving, irrepressible outfit which persists to this day. Rightly so: Jordan was a pro's pro, tirelessly seeking out fresh songs and constantly touring. But, surprisingly, the music seldom suffered, which is why his best sides still sound fresh. Most of the hits – which mixed comic lyrics with spirited swing-style playing and paved the way for R&B – are collected on the MCA record. The JSP and Classics discs tell the beginning of the story: the JSP opens with three tracks with the Chick Webb band, but this is trumped by Classics 636 which starts with an obscure 1934 Clarence Williams date where Jordan croons 'I Can't Dance, I Got Ants In My Pants'. The usual Classics approach of chronological order is then followed through to the end of the 1941–3 disc and, though some of the material is just a tad strained – try 'Sam Jones Done Snagged His Britches' – there is some unbeatable jive here too. Classics 741 is probably the first choice, given that there are the first versions of some of Jordan's most enduring hits: 'Five Guys Named Moe' (also present in a V-Disc version), 'The Chicks I Pick Are Slender, Tender And Tall' and so on. JSP, as usual, have superior sound on their selection.

*** **Rock 'N' Roll** Mercury 838219-2
    Jordan; Ernie Royal (*t*); Jimmy Cleveland (*tb*); Budd Johnson (*ts, bs*); Sam 'The Man' Taylor (*ts*); Ernie Hayes (*p*); Jackie Davis (*org*); Mickey Baker, Irving Ashby (*g*); Wendell Marshall, Billy Hadnott (*b*); Charli Persip, Marvin Oliver (*d*); Francisco Pozo (*perc*); Dorothy Smith (*v*). 10/56–8/57.

*** No Moe! Verve 512523-2

    As above. 10/56–8/57.

**(*) I Believe In Music Black & Blue 59.059-2

    Jordan; Irv Cox (*ts*); Duke Burrell (*p*); Louis Myers (*g*); John Duke, Dave Myers (*b*); Archie
    Taylor, Fred Below (*d*). 11/73.

Jordan's later recordings were remakes of his old ones. On the Mercury sessions it worked out well, since
Quincy Jones's arrangements brought in some sterling instrumentalists and updated Jordan's sound just
enough without prettifying it too much. As a result, the likes of 'Is You Is Or Is You Ain't My Baby'
become rejuvenated, and Louis never sounded wilder than he did on 'Salt Pork, West Virginia'. The
Verve disc is almost the same: five fewer tracks, but three from a later small-group session which *Rock
'N' Roll* misses. The Black Lion album is another bunch of Louis's old hits, some standards and a few
blues, all done with few signs of Jordan slowing up. He sings with the same élan, if not quite with the old
abandonment, and his alto playing remains attractively greasy. Good fun.

** Louis Jordan And Chris Barber Black Lion BLCD 760156

    Jordan; Pat Halcox (*t*); Chris Barber (*tb, v*); Ian Wheeler, John Crocker (*cl, as*); Steve
    Hammond, Johnny McCallum (*g, bj*); John Slaughter (*g*); Eddie Smith (*bj*); Dick Smith, Jackie
    Flavelle (*b*); Graham Burbidge (*d*). 12/62–12/74.

Nine tracks with the 1962 Barber band and five more by Barber's men without Louis. Jordan does his
best but these Englishmen aren't much good at jiving.

Marlon Jordan (born 1970) TRUMPET

** The Undaunted Columbia CK 52409/473056-2

    Jordan; Tim Warfield Jr (*ts*); Eric Reed (*p*); Tarus Mateen (*b*); Troy Davis (*d*). 1/92.

It's not only Jordan, a young trumpeter from New Orleans, who's trying too hard here. Warfield strains
through his solos with an effort that's almost painful to hear, strangling himself on his own impetus on
the title-track and throwing in irrelevant distortions in most of his other solos. The interminable opening blues is followed by a piece called 'Confrontation' that goes nowhere on the basis of the improvisations. Jordan plays with plenty of brassy power but most of it sounds like so much hot air, and by the
time they get to the closing 'New Orleans Street Beat' the album seems dead. Reed, probably the most
gifted player in the group, threads his way through much of the music with thoughtful finesse, and it's he
who earns the stars.

Sheila Jordan (born 1928) VOICE

**** Portrait Of Sheila Blue Note CDP 789902

    Jordan; Barry Galbraith (*g*); Steve Swallow (*b*); Denzil Best (*d*). 9 & 10/62.

*** Sheila Steeplechase SCCD 31081

    Jordan; Arild Andersen (*b*). 8/77.

**(*) Old Time Feeling Muse MCD 5366

    Jordan; Harvie Swartz (*b*). 10/82.

**(**) Songs From Within M.A. Recordings M014A

    As above. 3/89.

*** The Very Thought Of Two M.A. Recordings M018

    As above. 93.

Sheila Jordan owes her stage name and something of her distinctive delivery to a marriage, since
dissolved, to the bebop pianist, Duke Jordan. She has all her former husband's concentration on the
melodic progress of a song (and pays notable attention to the semantics of a lyric) and much of his
intelligent, unhistrionic and almost diffident delivery. Like the truly great instrumentalists, Sheila Jordan
is content to explore all the potential of the middle register, where words are more likely to remain intact
(with lesser talent, prosaically so), rather than over-reach a range which is nevertheless greater than
sometimes appears. At the end of phrases, she deploys a superbly controlled vibrato.

    On *Portrait*, her most complete artistic statement, she ranges between the rapid and slightly alienating
'Let's Face The Music And Dance' (which anticipates the surrealism of her contributions to Roswell
Rudd's remarkable *Flexible Flyer* (Affinity/Freedom)) to the fragile beauty of 'I'm A Fool To Want You'
and 'When The World Was Young' with its extraordinary, ambiguous ending.

    The instrumentation is highly subtle. Bobby Timmons's 'Dat Dere' is given just to voice and bass (and
Swallow is superb), 'Who Can I Turn To?' to voice and guitar, while 'Hum Drum Blues' and 'Baltimore
Oriole' are set against rhythm only, as if she were a horn.

If one is looking for an exact instrumental analogy for Sheila Jordan's voice, it's probably the round, precariously controlled wobble of the reverse-action flugelhorn. Tom Harrell was an ideal foil on *The Crossing*, a fine Black Hawk record from 1984, since deleted but worth looking out for.

The sparser landscape of *Sheila* and *Old Time Feeling*, where she is accompanied only by double bass, suits her much better. Andersen is a much more interesting player, and appears more responsive, than Swartz, but the Muse is well worth having, and the later session with Swartz is a winner; that despite the 'acoustically unfriendly' heating system, put on in the Japanese hall where *Songs From Within* was recorded to counteract the effects of cold on Swartz's bass. The repertoire on both is good, but *Songs* has it by a head, with lovely versions of 'Waltz For Debby', 'St Thomas', 'A Child Is Born' and a work through the classic bop changes, 'I Got Rhythm/Anthropology'. (The disc also includes a bonus track by the Marty Krystall Spatial Quartet.) The connection is sustained on *Very Thought Of Two*, but, though technically fine, there are signs of archness and cuteness here, unbecoming to either musician.

Few singers have been as consistently inventive and challenging in an era dominated by horns and guitars; few, predictably, have been so little appreciated. Sheila Jordan is an essential figure in modern jazz and *Portrait* should be in every collection.

**** Lost And Found Muse 5390

> Jordan; Kenny Barron (*p*); Harvie Swartz (*b*); Ben Riley (*d*). 90.

*** One For Junior Muse MCD 5489

> Jordan; Mark Murphy (*v*); Kenny Barron (*p*); Bill Mays (*p, syn*); Harvie Swartz (*b*); Ben Riley (*d*). 9/91.

Lost And Found is the first product of Sheila Jordan's first mutually acceptable recording contract. To underline just how disgraceful the industry's default has been, it's her best record yet and a surprise winner in *The Wire* magazine's 1991 'album of the year' poll.

Her voice is in superb form and the band know what they're about. She's a daring performer, switching from 'Lost In The Stars' to the Jacobite plaint, 'The Water Is Wide', to 'My Shining Hour' and 'We'll Be Together Again'. The understanding with Barron is particularly close, but she likes the lift of bass and drums as well. Urgently recommended. If you 'don't like' jazz singing, this is as good a way as any to take the cure.

It is, however, perfectly possible to be shriven and forgiven for 'not liking' *One For Junior*. Jordan is as good as always, but Murphy is more of a problem (or at least he is a problem in the company of Ms Jordan). With his mortuary tan and streaked hair, he comes on like some parody of a club crooner. The truth is more complex. Murphy is a fairly daring improviser, scatting choruses like a tenor sax and then making up new lyrics with impressive speed of thought. The problem is that he just sounds all wrong in a setting geared almost exclusively towards Jordan's delicate and tremulous settings. Though he handles dynamics with a fair degree of sophistication, there's always an uncomfortable sense that he's blaring. It's off-putting and spoils what in other contexts would be a pleasurable record. Mismatch.

Theo Jorgensmann CLARINET

**(*) Aesthetic Direction Konnex KOCD 5054

> Jorgensmann; Rainald Schuckens (*bcl*); Albrecht Maurer (*vn*); Donja Eghbal (*clo*); Achim Kramer (*perc*). 3/93.

This is one of those improvising records which might just as easily be a set of written compositions in what now must be considered the 'old' atonal style. The Werkschau Ensemble is a fascinating variation on the horns/harmony/bass/drums format, but the gentle avoidance of a groove does tend to lead the music into rarefied regions that take some getting used to. Split decision: excellent on its own terms; peripheral to the main concerns of this *Guide*.

Anders Jormin (born 1957) BASS

*** Alone Dragon DRCD 207

> Jormin (*b* solo). 91.

*** Jord Dragon DRCD 243

> Jormin; Per Jorgensen (*t, perc, v*); Harald Svensson (*ky*); Severi Pyysalo (*vib*); Lisbeth Diers (*perc, v*). 10/94.

Two fine group records on Dragon await CD reissue, so this solo session is Jormin's earliest entry at present. He aimed for something 'naked, pure and lyrical', cutting the 40-odd minutes of music in a single evening with a DAT machine, and the unaffected qualities of the playing lend the music much charm – where most bass albums are deliberately cumbrous and sombre in texture, this one is songful and optimistic. Jormin plays only three brief tunes of his own: the rest are dominated by three burnished melodies by Silvio Rodriguez and the unforgettable melody of A. Ramirez's 'Alfonsina'. Those hoping for the kind of sumptuous bass sound which hallmarks studio bass albums may be disappointed in the relatively light and 'live' atmosphere here, but it emphasizes the calibre of the playing over any mere hi-fi experience.

Jord is a live-in-the-studio group record, carefully balanced among the four musicians. Svensson's keyboards provide melting electronic textures which Pyysalo's vibes dance gently over; Jorgenson comes on as principal soloist, and Diers and Jormin create elliptical rhythms. A bit shapeless but some exquisite passages.

Julian Joseph (born 1967) PIANO, KEYBOARDS, VOCAL

*** The Language Of Truth East West 75122-2

Joseph; Jean Toussaint (*ts*); Alec Dankworth (*b*); Mark Mondesir (*d*); Sharon Musgrave (*v*). 91.

**(*) Reality East West 4509-93024-2

Joseph; Peter King (*as*); Jean Toussaint (*ts*); Charnett Moffett, Wayne Batchelor (*b*); Mark Mondesir (*d*). n.d.

*** In Concert At Wigmore Hall East West 0630-11370-2

Joseph; Eddie Daniels (*cl*); Johnny Griffin (*ts*); Jason Rebello (*p*); Alec Dankworth (*b*). 1/94.

Joseph's assured and generous playing can be very satisfying, and his very sure touch at all tempos gives these records a consistency that sustains a lot of otherwise indifferent writing. The first album is played with an intensity that proposes the image of a young lion taking his chance at wider success and, although Musgrave's vocals introduce an unwonted 'commercial' element, it's the playing by Joseph and his quartet that one remembers. But *Reality* is a frequently misconceived follow-up. The reverberant studio sound puts the music out of focus, and some superior writing is let down by too many weaker tunes – 12 tracks and over 70 minutes is a bridge too far on this occasion. Nor does Joseph's singing merit exposure on record. It's a pity that this self-importance gets in the way of the best music, since a fine 'Body And Soul' and originals such as 'The Whispering Dome' would benefit from a clearer setting.

The live album has some very enjoyable music, the result of an invitation concert where Joseph brought in guests from the UK and the USA. Perhaps surprisingly, the best pieces are those with Daniels, whose virtuosity suits Joseph's own full-blooded style: 'Hard Cash', 'Soft Shoe For Thad' and the tranquil 'Soul Eyes' are glittering displays. Three pieces with Griffin are merely OK, while the duet with Rebello on 'Maiden Voyage' is an expansive display by both men. Dankworth keeps unobtrusive time throughout.

Christian Josi VOCALS

*** I Walked With My Feet Off The Ground Master Mix CHECD 00111

Josi; Harry Allen (*ts*); Tony Monte (*p*); Dave Green (*b*); Trevor Tomkins (*d*). 2/94.

Master Mix have made something of a speciality of unconventional vocal jazz within what might manage to masquerade as 'the mainstream'. Josi demonstrates the redundancy of the concept, offering tough, feeling performances of standard material delivered in an oddly insouciant, almost stoical style. The trio is splendid, rooted in Green's generous bass figures, and Allen convincingly cleaves to the vocal line when he can, musing speculatively when he can't.

Kamikaze Ground Crew GROUP

*** Madame Marie's Temple Of Knowledge New World 80138

Steven Bernstein (*t, slide t, c, flhn*); Jeff Crossman (*tb*); Bob Lipton (*tba*); Doug Weiselman (*ts, ss, bs, cl, perc*); Gina Leishman (*as, bcl, picc, p, toy p, v*); Ralph Carney (*as, ts, cl, toy p*); Danny Frankel (*d, perc, whistle*). 91–92.

This splendidly-titled San Francisco unit don't quite deliver on record. Exact navigation and precise steering may be at something of a discount in kamikaze circles, and the problem with this relatively long-standing group is that nobody – Weiselman's and Leishman's co-leadership notwithstanding – seems to be in charge. The result is that the music is defined more by its changeability and unpredictability than by any consistency of voice. In that sense, it's all rather reminiscent of fellow-Californian Peter Apfelbaum's Hieroglyphic Ensemble, which tended to deploy a different group for every track. Not so much variation with the Ground Crew but a diffidence about solo space nevertheless. The two nominal leaders are rather anonymous and the most ambitious soloist, trombone player Crossman, is granted little space to make his mark. The mixes are rather muddy and condensed, and one feels the need of either a crisp solo voice or a lighter and more innovative hand at the desk.

Richie Kamuca (1930–77) TENOR SAXOPHONE

***(*) **Jazz Erotica** Fresh Sound FSR 500
> Kamuca; Conte Candoli, Ed Leddy (*t*); Frank Rosolino (*tb*); Bill Holman (*bs*); Vince Guaraldi (*p*); Monty Budwig (*b*); Stan Levey (*d*). 59.

***(*) **West Coast Jazz In Hi-Fi** Original Jazz Classics OJC 1760
> As above.

The title of the Fresh Sound (not the 'Jazz' part) is perhaps a shade misleading, though Kamuca favoured an intimate, close-to-the-ear murmur which comes direct from Lester Young, seductive with little hint of Pres's native ambivalence. The 'jazz' part in the title is important because there isn't much sign either of the gimmicky Kenton approach in which much of the band was schooled. Kamuca's approach to standards – 'Star Eyes', 'Angel Eyes', 'Stella By Starlight' – is direct and unsentimental, and for combined impact and sophistication there's little to choose between the four quartet tracks and Holman's arrangements for the larger group. There are one or two minor technical quibbles about the transfer, and the identical OJC sounds a little brighter and cleaner, but, in the absence of three excellent Concords, *Drop Me Off In Harlem*, *Richie* and *Richie Kamuca's Charlie* (where he explores the Parker legacy), this makes for a highly desirable introduction to the saxophonist's work.

Egil Kapstad (born 1940) PIANO

***(*) **Cherokee** Gemini GMCD 61
> Kapstad; Terje Venaas (*b*); Egil Johansen (*d*). 11/88.

A beautiful and typically individual record by a modern master of Norwegian jazz. Kapstad's thoroughgoing absorption of the requisite piano influences lets him put a personal spin on what is actually his first-ever trio date: the nine standards all have a novel point of view, such as the piano/bass duet on 'Autumn Leaves' or the dreamily slow treatment of 'Cherokee' itself. His solo reading of 'Darn That Dream' is modelled out of a simple but detailed look at the harmonies, and the opening run through 'When You're Smiling' freshens even that tune. Venaas and the redoubtable Johansen are perfectly in step, and the only disappointment is that there isn't more of Kapstad's own writing. He restricts himself to a blues and the brief, charming 'Our Autumn Waltz'.

**** **Remembrance** Gemini GMCD 82
> As above. 10/93.

Even more remarkable. Kapstad's record is, in effect, a celebration of Norwegian jazz, since it draws from the work of eight native composers (including the members of the trio). The abiding factor is his meticulous technique: even in the middle of a fast piece such as 'Big Red' he displays a refinement of touch that elevates the composer without relinquishing his own stamp on the piece. If the overall feel of the session is romantic, even a trifle forlorn, the exacting lyricism which he gets out of most of the tunes is intensely satisfying. Venaas and Johansen take honours, too.

Jan Kaspersen PIANO

***(*) **Space And Rhythm Jazz** Olufsen DOCD 5060
> Kaspersen; Anders Bergcrantz (*t*); Simon Cato Spang-Hanssen (*ss, ts*); Frederik Lundin (*ss, ts*); Michael Hove (*as, bs*); Peter Danstrup (*b*); Ole Romer (*d*). 10/87.

*** **Ten By Two** Olufsen DOCD 5053
> Kaspersen; Simon Cato Spang-Hanssen (*ss, ts*). 7/87.

***(*) **Special Occasion** Olufsen DOCD 5111
> Kaspersen; Peter Danstrup (*b*); Ole Romer (*d*). 9/90.

**** **Live In Sofie's Cellar** Olufsen DOCD 5136
> Kaspersen; Anders Bergcrantz (*t*); Bob Rockwell (*ts*); Peter Danstrup (*b*); Ole Romer (*d*). 8/91.

Marvellous records from a Dane whose music is a beautifully personal, inventive and humorous response to the particular influence of Thelonious Monk. *Space And Rhythm Jazz* is a skilful, all-original programme that makes the music of a quirkily expressive cast of horn players and creates consistently absorbing ideas within what is broadly a post-bop framework. *Ten By Two* relies in the main on Monk and Ellington and is a bit po-faced, perhaps because Spang-Hanssen is a little stolid in places, but there are still some pleasing variations on the material. The pianist gets a fuller rein on the trio set, which has some mischievous originals ('Bird Goes Cuckoo') and a couple of nicely reflective ballads. Kaspersen's heavily rolling manner will strike a chord of recognition in British listeners who've heard Stan Tracey, but his sense of humour is a little more impish than our man's. The masterpiece here is the glorious live session: Bergcrantz reveals himself as a major (and so far shamefully under-recognized) soloist, Rockwell is only a beat behind, and Kaspersen directs with great exuberance from the piano. There is the third version of his favourite 'I Mean Monk' and this is surely the best.

*** **Joinin' Forces** Olufsen DOCD 5184
      Kaspersen; Horace Parlan (p). 4/94.
***(*) **Special Occasion Band Live In Copenhagen Jazzhouse** Olufsen DOCD 5303/4 2CD
      Kaspersen; Lars Vissing (t); Erling Kroner, Lis Wessberg (tb); Simon Spang-Hanssen (as); Bob
      Rockwell, Fredrik Lundin (ss, ts); Henrik Sveidahl-Hansen (ts, bs); Aske Jacoby (g); Peter
      Danstrup (b); Ole Romer (d); Jacob Andersen (perc). 9/94.
The duo with Parlan is an enjoyable if lightweight meeting where the two keyboards bump and jostle over some familiar ground. The big-band set is much more exciting. With seven horns in the front line, Kaspersen marshals a serious force to get the most out of his writing and, in what's almost a greatest-hits set of his own tunes, the band play with unquenchable enthusiasm and flair. Sound is just a little rough, but the ambience and enjoyment of the occasion – recorded when the band were flying at the end of a tour – comes right through.

Bruce Katz PIANO, ORGAN

*** **Transformation** Audioquest AQ CD 1026
      Katz; Tom Hall (ts); Kevin Barry (g); David Clark (b); Lorne Entress (d). 11/93.
This band's favoured groove is a medium funk shuffle, but with lots of unexpected elements – weird bent notes, busy little percussion outbreaks from co-founder Entress, top-line/bass-line swaps – that lift it a little out of the ordinary. Katz's piano and organ sound had been heard for a while in and around Boston (including recordings with Ronnie Earl and the Broadcasters) before he and the drummer unveiled this project of their own.

   The organ tracks, beginning with 'Boppin' Out Of The Abyss', are generally more energetic and force-ful, but it is Katz's piano playing that is the key to his sound. He's an active, multi-directional player, often building solo ideas out of fast, narrow-interval arpeggios, with occasional excursions out into free time, almost like the young Cecil Taylor. Sensibly, he seldom dwells on an idea past its due time, preferring to spin off in a new direction. Saxophonist Tom Hall is just a cut above the average bar-room honker and he turns in some very nifty solo work, as do the guitarist and super-solid bassist. The real axis of the group, though, are Katz and Entress, the latter contributing one composition to a set of lively, thoughtful originals.

Shake Keane (born 1927) FLUGELHORN

*** **Real Keen: Reggae Into Jazz** LKJ CD 001
      Keane; Henry Holder (ky); John Kpiaye (g); Dennis Bovell (b, ky, d machine); Jah Bunny, Angus
      Gaye (d); Geoffrey Scantlebury (perc). 91.
He was christened Ellsworth McGranahan Keane, and he derived his nickname from a passion for Shakespeare, which was reinforced during a spell at the University of London. Keane never acquired the legend that attached to his fellow West Indian, Joe Harriott, with whom he played in the Harlem All-Stars after leaving college. Quite simply, Keane survived and went off to work with various big bands in Europe, including the Clarke–Boland outfit and Kurt Edelhagen's. Not such a romantic story.

   This disc comes 30 years after his excellent Columbia session, *In My Condition*, which British jazz collectors greatly prize. The reggae grooves have become something of a cliché in recent years, but Keane's lyrical style and expansive musical understanding make something out of a rather restrictive set of formulae. On 'Gorby Gets Them Going' (one of several politically tinged titles) he moves outside the rhythm altogether, while on 'Prague 89' and the very differently paced 'Rift', he floats or bounces along on top of the basic metre, creating a curious tension that is resolved only in the melody. The youngish band plays this sort of stuff pretty much by-the-yard, professionally but hardly passionately; in the final count, it's hard to get over-excited about *Real Keen*.

Lewis Keel ALTO SAXOPHONE

**(*) Coming Out Swinging Muse MCD 5438

> Keel; Harold Mabern (*p*); Jimmy Ponder (*g*); Jamil Nasser (*b*); Leroy Williams (*d*); Buzz Hollie (*perc*). 8/90.

It's hard to dislike the music on this belated debut by a Memphis-born altoman who's been teaching music in New York public schools for the past 20 years. But as a leader he doesn't really get hold of it. Mabern and Ponder, workmanlike as they are, are more impressive improvisers and, though Keel has plenty of bebop licks to hand, they don't cohere into anything much beyond a nice imitation of the real thing. A clearer, more hard-edged studio sound might have helped.

Geoff Keezer (born 1970) PIANO

***(*) Waiting In The Wings Sunnyside SSC 1035D

> Keezer; Bill Mobley (*t*); Billy Pierce (*ss, ts*); Steve Nelson (*vib*); Rufus Reid (*b*); Tony Reedus (*d*). 9/88.

*** Curveball Sunnyside SSC 1045D

> Keezer; Steve Nelson (*vib*); Charnett Moffett (*b*); Victor Lewis (*d*). 6/89.

Geoff Keezer is a formidable young pianist, even in a generation in which youthful endeavour is nothing out of the ordinary. Both of these records were made before he was twenty. While he's a vivid executant, synthesizing such influences as Ahmad Jamal and Phineas Newborn into the kind of broad post-bop style which is the contemporary norm, he's also an unusually thoughtful composer, organizing a small band into a distinctive ensemble and building rhythmic licks into convincing melodies. Examples here include the title-tunes of *Waiting In The Wings* and *Curveball*, and 'Accra', a blistering waltz-tune; but Keezer's thoughtful programming of rare Ellington and Monk themes adds a piquant variety to his own writing. He greatly admires Steve Nelson's playing, and the vibes player in turn does some of his best work to date here. While there is an occasional shortfall of ideas and an inevitable assumption that Keezer has greater music in him still to come, these are all highly enjoyable records, with perhaps the first Sunnyside release edging through on the sheer enthusiasm displayed by all the players.

*** World Music DIW 609

> Keezer; James Genus (*b*); Tony Reedus (*d*); Rudy Bird (*perc*). 1/92.

*** Other Spheres DIW 871

> Keezer; Bill Mobley (*t, flhn*); Bill Pierce (*ss, ts*); Bill Easley (*as, f, af, cl, bcl*); Peter Bernstein (*g*); Steve Nelson (*vib, mar*); John Lockwood (*b*); Leon Parker (*d*); Rudy Bird (*perc*); Jeanie Bryson (*v*). 11/92.

These are ambitious records, the trio set no less demanding than the subsequent *Other Spheres*, and, while they're impressive in their way, they also suggest a leader overplaying his hand. *World Music* starts with an ingenious revision of 'It's Only A Paper Moon' and moves into an ominously bleak 'Black And Tan Fantasy', but Keezer's originals aren't quite as fresh as before and the trio tend to push too hard as a unit, Reedus piling on detail when a simpler, more directly swinging beat would do better. *Other Spheres* is an all-original programme that brims with complexity, the three Bills creating a continually shifting front line of horn sounds, Nelson meshing loyally with the leader's piano, and the studio used to add a few deft overdubs. But while it makes for some intriguing arranger's jazz, notably on 'Little Minu' and 'Serengeti Stampede', pieces such as 'Auntie Matter' and 'Event Horizon' sound overwritten, their energy a little stifled by their complexity.

***(*) Trio Sackville SKCD2-2039

> Keezer; Steve Nelson (*vib*); Neil Swainson (*b*). 11/93.

Recorded at Toronto's Montreal Bistro, this live set overflows with playing, and though Swainson is a useful anchor it's mainly about the prodigious outpouring of two men in full command. Keezer and Nelson run delighted rings round each other on tunes by Parker and Monk, settle into a mellifluous rendition of Nelson's 'There Are Many Angels In Florence' and end on a blow-out with 'Eternal Triangle'. Maybe not the most subtle or elevated record either man has been involved with, but basically a delight, in excellent location sound.

Roger Kellaway (born 1939) PIANO

**** A Portrait Of Roger Kellaway Fresh Sound FSR-CD 147

> Kellaway; Jim Hall (*g*); Steve Swallow, Ben Tucker (*b*); Dave Bailey, Tony Inzalaco (*d*). 63.

Kellaway made only four albums in the 1960s, and only this one has been restored to circulation. It's good enough to make one wish that he'd done much more in the studios. He has a scholar's approach to jazz history, bundling together stride, boogie and swing devices into a manner which is otherwise entirely modern. 'Double Fault' calls to mind such contemporaries as Andrew Hill, yet the off-centre lyricism and abstracting of melody mark Kellaway as very much his own man. Tucker and Bailey offer prime, swinging support on four tracks, which keeps the composer's ideas in accessible domain, while the trio of Hall, Swallow and Inzalaco create a contrapuntal music of sometimes bemusing intricacy to go with the pianist's work. Two solos are equally rich and detailed, and there is a brilliant transformation of 'Crazy She Calls Me'. Slightly brittle sound doesn't mar a very fine record.

*** **In Japan** All Art Jazz AAJ-11002
    Kellaway; Valery Ponomarev (*t*); John Goldsby (*b*); Terry Clarke (*d*). 6/86.
***(*) **Fifty-Fifty** Natasha NI-4014
    Kellaway; Red Mitchell (*b*); Brad Terry (*whistling*). 2/87.
*** **Alone Together** Dragon DRCD 168
    Kellaway; Red Mitchell (*b*). 7/88.
***(*) **Live At Maybeck Recital Hall Vol. 11** Concord CCD 4470
    Kellaway (*p* solo). 3/91.

Kellaway's career has kept him away from jazz more often than not, working in the classical and film-score fields, but he is a very fine and under-appreciated musician whose earlier records are all missing in action again. His scholar's approach to jazz history bundles together stride, boogie and swing devices when he feels like it, yet always in a manner that suggests a shrewd, modern mind. A number of more recent recordings show no loss of inspiration. The two earlier duos with Red Mitchell are very like the ideal of eavesdropping on a couple of old friends after hours. We were a little hard on the Dragon album in our last edition, but it sounds better all the time, though Mitchell's whimsical search for the lowest note a bass can produce may still irritate some listeners, and sometimes they ramble, as after-hours sessions will. But there are beautiful deconstructions of choice standards on both records, with the Natasha set edging ahead for a fantastical 'Gone With The Wind' and a funky 'St Thomas' to wrap things up. Brad Terry whistles on 'Doxy', for some reason. The solo set is a winner, far more satisfying. Perhaps the pianist is sometimes a little too relaxed, with three tunes running around nine minutes and the tempos more often stately than up, but there is much marvellous pianism here. He takes three minutes over the first chorus of 'How Deep Is The Ocean' before moving into an intense, labyrinthine exploration, and his bitonal ventures are so completely assimilated that the most outré gestures become a plausible part of his flow. Especially fine is the resplendent version of Hoagy Carmichael's 'New Orleans'. As with the rest of this series, impeccable sound and an attentive crowd. *In Japan* is mostly either solo or trio and works as a fine introduction to Kellaway. He might start a tune such as 'People Will Say We're In Love' as conventional piano-trio stuff and then take it far, far out; or he'll do 'We Kiss In A Shadow' as a grandly voiced solo, following an almost minimalist breakdown of 'I've Grown Accustomed To Her Face'. Ponomarev walks in for the last two tunes to no great purpose, since Kellaway smokes right past him on 'I Want To Be Happy'. The drum sound is very big and a little too strong on some of the trio tracks.

*** **That Was That** Dragon DRCD 201
    Kellaway; Jan Allan (*t*); Red Mitchell (*b*). 1/91.

While this is something of a re-run of the earlier session with Mitchell, the presence of Jan Allan seems to focus the music much more and, though most of the tracks run to seven or eight minutes in length, there's no sense of excessive meandering. Mitchell's amusing vocals on 'Leavin' Blues' and the title-track add to the fun and there are some very pleasing solos by Allan, whose unassuming and rather frail playing suits this context very well.

***(*) **Roger Kellaway Meets Gene Bertoncini And Michael Moore** Chiaroscuro CR(D) 315
    Kellaway; Gene Bertoncini (*g*); Michael Moore (*b*). 2/92.
***(*) **Life's A Take** Concord CCD-4551
    Kellaway; Red Mitchell (*b*). 5/92.

The trio session is a densely packed series of performances that can seem a bit much over CD length, given the high, concentrated interplay among the three men. On 'All The Things You Are' their contrapuntal thinking is astonishing. Yet their simple, songful treatment of Moore's sweet-natured 'Old New Waltz' is as charming as it is naggingly memorable. Kellaway continues to surprise, improvising on the melody or the chords just when one expects the opposite, turning the device of 'locked hands' into something ingenious. Bertoncini's acoustic guitar never sounds altogether right in the context, and Rudy van Gelder's somewhat eccentric studio sound might be the cause.

Life's A Take is another meeting with Red Mitchell, cut only months before the bassist's death. This concert session (the first in a new sequence of Maybeck Recital Hall duos for Concord) is merely more of the same: if you have either of the studio dates listed above, it's probably superfluous. But there's an extra sting with the live setting, and there are some beautiful introductions from both men that make an affecting memorial to Mitchell. Sound doesn't favour him as much as it does on the studio recordings, though.

Ed Kelly PIANO

*** **Ed Kelly And Pharoah Sanders** Evidence ECD 22056-2
>Kelly; Larry Jones, A. J. Johnson (*t*); Anthony Sidney (*tb*); Pharoah Sanders (*ss, ts*); Don Ramsey (*as*); Junius Simmons (*g*); Peter Barshay, Harley White (*b*); Eddie Marshall, Mark Lignell (*d*); strings. 12/78–12/92.

Kelly has spent many years teaching in Oakland, but this genial record is a pleasing documentation of his rolling, two-handed gospel style. Half of it was cut in 1978, the remainder 14 years later: some of the earlier tracks have some dubious pop leanings, but the entire disc rates three stars for the superb tenor-and-piano duet on Sam Cooke's 'You Send Me' alone, where Sanders sounds like a slowly boiling volcano. The 1992 tracks offer some local hard bop in unaffected good humour.

Wynton Kelly (1931–71) PIANO

(*) **Piano Interpretations Blue Note CDP 784456
>Kelly; Oscar Pettiford or Franklin Skeete (*b*); Lee Abrams (*d*). 7 & 8/51.
*** **Wynton Kelly – Piano** Original Jazz Classics OJC 401
>Kelly; Kenny Burrell (*g*); Paul Chambers (*b*); Philly Joe Jones (*d*). 1/58.
**** **Kelly Blue** Original Jazz Classics OJC 033
>Kelly; Nat Adderley (*c*); Bobby Jaspar (*f*); Benny Golson (*ts*); Paul Chambers (*b*); Jimmy Cobb (*d*). 2 & 3/59.

On the face of it, Kelly didn't seem the most obvious replacement for Bill Evans and Red Garland in the Miles Davis group, but he had a lyrical simplicity and uncomplicated touch that appealed enormously to the trumpeter, who hired him in 1959; Kelly played on only one track on the classic *Kind Of Blue*, but 'Freddie Freeloader' is enough to show what distinguished him from Evans's more earnestly romantic style and to establish his quality.

The gentle but dynamic bounce to his chording comes to the fore on the marvellous *Kelly Blue* (which also reunites the *Kind Of Blue* rhythm section). On the title-track and 'Keep It Moving', the addition of Adderley and Jaspar makes perfect sense, but Benny Golson's robust contributions tend to unbalance the delicate strength of Kelly's arrangements. The trio cuts are far superior.

This was Kelly's natural turf. *Piano Interpretations* catches the 20-year-old in transition from the blues and R&B network to the mature post-bop of *Kelly Blue*. In some respects it's a very callow album. Skeete and Abrams are inelastic, Pettiford impatient, and the accompaniment seldom flatters Kelly's liquid triplets and confident, Horace Silver-like vamps; two alternative takes, and particularly the second, slower attempt at 'Goodbye', discover him adjusting his ambitions downwards, squaring up the edges of the metre and disambiguating some of the progressions. The overall sound is unspoiled by a few gremlins. *Piano* is very much better, a full-voiced quartet which makes full use of Burrell's boppish grace.

Kelly's death at only 40 robbed jazz of one of its most inventive and hard-working figures. He deserves wider recognition.

Rodney Kendrick PIANO

***(*) **The Secrets Of Rodney Kendrick** Verve 517588
>Kendrick; Roy Hargrove (*t*); Graham Haynes (*c*); Kenny Garrett (*as*); Houston Person (*ts*); Tarus Mateen (*b*); Taru Alexander (*d*); Chi Sharpe (*perc*). 1/93.
**** **Dance World Dance** Verve 521 937
>Kendrick; Graham Haynes (*c*); Arthur Blythe (*as*); Bheki Mseleku (*ts*); Patience Higgins (*bs*); Sharron Mcleod (*f*); Michael Bowie, Tarus Mateen (*b*); Yoron Israel (*d*); Chi Sharpe, Aaron Walker (*perc*). 12/93.

A fascinating musician, Kendrick sounds like a cross between Abdullah Ibrahim or Randy Weston and the last piano player to try out for an Ornette Coleman group. He favours dark, interlocking chord shapes rather than strict melodies, and plays with a resonantly percussive attack that propels the music forward with intense momentum.

Verve have provided him with some wonderful musicians to play with, though it is nearly always

Kendrick who catches the ear, especially on the second record. *Secrets*, or at least the tracks featuring Hargrove and Garrett, sounds much more like a working band, though it is the rawer and less polished material with Person and the brilliant Graham Haynes which repays the most careful auditioning. Haynes rightly reappears on the second record, bringing his high, slightly sharp brass voice to an ensemble that could probably do with one more brass horn, ideally a trombone.

The later disc features a solitary solo track, which allows a glimpse of Kendrick at work close up. It's a very dense sound, unexpectedly voiced and weighted, a Weston composition played pretty much as found, once the melody is established. The prospect of hearing him duet with Bheki Mseleku is confounded by the small print; the South African plays tenor saxophone on three tracks, and no piano; perhaps as well, for Kendrick has his own unique voice and it would have been ill-advised to try to match it to Mseleku's rapt, rolling idiom.

The pianist's basic trio of Mateen and Alexander is heard only once without horns on *Secrets*, which is a pity; unfortunately, Alexander doesn't reappear for the December session. His replacement, however, is one of the undersung talents of recent times. Israel is an immensely gifted percussionist with a completely convincing musical understanding. A word, too, for the underachieving Blythe, who always plays more effctively on other people's records than on his own.

Stan Kenton (1911–79) PIANO, VOCAL, BANDLEADER

*** Stan Kenton 1941–1944 Classics 828
> Kenton; Frank Beach, Chico Alvarez, Earl Collier, Ray Borden, John Carroll, Buddy Childers, Karl George, Dick Morse, Mel Green, Gene Roland (*t*); Harry Forbes, Dick Cole, George Faye, Bart Varsalona, Bill Atkinson, Freddie Zito, Milt Kabak, Lory Aaron (*tb*); Jack Ordean, Ted Romersa, Eddie Meyers, Art Pepper, Boots Mussulli, Al Harding, Bill Lahey, Chester Ball (*as*); Red Dorris (*ts, v*); Maurice Beeson, Dave Matthews, Stan Getz, Emmet Carls (*ts*); Bob Gioga (*bs*); Bob Ahern, Ralph Leslie (*g*); Buddy Hayes, Clyde Singleton, Gene Englund, Bob Kesterson (*b*); Chauncey Farre, Jesse Price, John S. Bock, Joe Vernon (*d*); Anita O'Day, Gene Howard (*v*). 11/40–12/44.

*** Broadcast Transcriptions 1941–45 Music & Arts 883
> Similar to above; 41–45.

A vast band, a colossal legacy, and an outsize personality at the helm: Kenton's achievement is possibly the 'biggest' that jazz has ever seen or will see. How much of it is truly worth listening to is harder to evaluate. Kenton seemed to believe in principles which often had little to do with musical substance: volume, power, weight, noise. Nobody ever had bigger-sounding big bands, and nobody ever went to such pretentious lengths as Kenton could, with his espousal of 'progressive' ideas and arrangements which owed more to half-assimilated ideas of twentieth-century orchestral composition than to jazz scoring. Later editions of the band pilfered from rock and soul idioms without loosening the stiffness of Kenton's stays. Yet his best music swung mightily, was brilliantly played, and went to exhilarating extremes of both musicianship and showmanship.

The very early sessions for Decca and Capitol are collected on the Classics disc. 'Artistry In Rhythm', Kenton's theme, turns up in the fourth session, but otherwise these are often run-of-the-mill swing arrangements, and the main point of interest is the early vocal features for Anita O'Day. *Broadcast Transcriptions* is a livelier mix, with a teenage Getz taking a solo on 'Pizzicato' among other odds and ends of interest, and a very appreciative crowd on hand on some of the dates. Classics have fair if erratic sound, from unlisted sources; Music & Arts have the usual variable aircheck quality, but the band come through with plenty of spark.

*** Summer Of '51 Garland GRZ006
> Kenton; Maynard Ferguson, John Howell, Chico Alvarez, Ray Wetzel, Shorty Rogers (*t*); Milt Bernhart, Harry Betts, Bob Fitzpatrick, Dick Kenney, Bart Varsalona (*tb*); Bud Shank, Art Pepper (*as*); Bob Cooper, Bart Calderall (*ts*); Bob Gioga (*bs*); Ralph Blaze (*g*); Don Bagley (*b*); Shelly Manne (*d*); Jay Johnson (*v*). 51.

**(*) Live At Cornell University '51 Jazz Unlimited JUCD 2008
> As above, except add Conte Candoli, Stu Williamson, John Coppola (*t*), Bill Russo, George Roberts (*tb*), John Graas, Lloyd Otto, George Price (*frhn*), Stan Fletcher (*tba*), Abe Luboff (*b*), string section; omit Alvarez, Wetzel, Rogers, Bernhart, Varsalona. 10/51.

A glance at the personnels here will reveal the extent of Kenton's sidemen, and Cooper, Rogers, Ferguson and, especially, the unpredictable and volatile Milt Bernhart play some exciting solos on the Garland CD, on what are swing charts brassed over by blaring horn volleys. Highlights include a couple of Pete Rugolo charts, 'Minor Riff' and 'Collaboration', the Cuban feel accorded to 'Love For Sale' – Kenton was quick to endorse and follow up Dizzy Gillespie's experiments – and a frenetically overblown

'Lover' to end on. The sound is quite good, if occasionally scuffed by age and inclement broadcasting weather. Poorer fidelity on the next two: the Jazz Unlimited disc does feature Kenton's notorious 'Innovations' orchestra (which totalled 43 pieces, including the string section) and one only catches glimmers of what it must have been like with this concert material. Soloists wander on and off mike and textures are muddy, but there is still much fine playing, with features for Graas, Pepper, Cooper and Ferguson and an extract from Bob Graettinger's 'City Of Glass'.

***(*) **New Concepts Of Artistry In Rhythm** Capitol B21Y-92865-2
    Kenton; Conte Candoli, Buddy Childers, Maynard Ferguson, Don Dennis, Reuben McFall (*t*); Bob Fitzpatrick, Keith Moon, Frank Rosolino, Bill Russo (*tb*); George Roberts (*btb*); Lee Konitz, Vinnie Dean (*as*); Richie Kamuca, Bill Holman (*ts*); Bob Gioga (*bs*); Sal Salvador (*g*); Don Bagley (*b*); Stan Levey (*d*); Derek Walton (*perc*); Kay Brown (*v*). 9/52.
Laden with top-flight musicians, this was another of Kenton's best bands. There is one arrangement by Bill Holman – the intriguing 'Invention For Guitar And Trumpet' – but most of the scores were penned by Bill Russo, including the glorious kitsch of the opening 'Prologue: This Is An Orchestra!', a kind of Young Person's Guide with Kenton himself narrating and characterizing each member of the band (considering the personalities he's describing, it's both funny and oddly moving at this distance, especially when he calls Frank Rosolino – who would later take his own life – 'this fellow who has few if any moody moments'). The brass section is top-heavy and blows all else before it, but the rhythm section swings hard, and there are some wonderful interjections on almost every piece by the major soloists, especially Salvador on 'Invention', Konitz on 'Young Blood' and 'My Lady', Rosolino on 'Swing House'. The remastering is bright and just a little harsh in places, but it makes the band sound grandly impressive, which is as it should be.

***(*) **The Concerts In Miniature Broadcasts 1952–53** Artistry CD 001
    Kenton; Conte Candoli, Buddy Childers, Ernie Royal, Don Dennis, Don Smith, Maynard Ferguson, Reuben McFall, Vinnie Dean, Ziggy Minichelli (*t*); Frank Rosolino, Bill Russo, Keith Moon, Tommy Shepard, Milt Gold (*tb*); George Roberts, Bill Smiley (*btb*); Lee Konitz, Don Carone, Dave Schildkraut (*as*); Zoot Sims, Ed Wasserman, Richie Kamuca (*ts*); Tony Ferina (*bs*); Sal Salvador, Barry Galbraith (*g*); Don Bagley (*b*); Stan Levey (*d*).
*** **Stan Kenton Live!** Natasha 4017
    Similar to above, but with Chris Connor (*v*). 12/52–4/53.
Broadcast performances: sound is only reasonably good on the Artistry disc, although anyone accustomed to radio airshots from the period will find them quite listenable. There are good features for Konitz and Sims, and a few strong Holman scores: nothing that isn't handled at least as well on the studio dates, but the flavour of the period comes through. Chris Connor has several featured vocals on the Natasha disc, which again relies rather heavily on period flavour, given the announcements and repartee.

**** **City Of Glass** Capitol 832084-2
    Similar to above discs. 12/47–5/53.
The 16 pieces arranged by Bob Graettinger which make up this CD number among the most exacting works Kenton was ever responsible for. Graettinger's two major pieces, 'City Of Glass' and 'This Modern World', are extraordinary works – Ellingtonian in their concentration on individuals within the band, yet using the bigger resources of the orchestra to create its own sound-world. All of his 14 originals (there are two arrangements on standards) create their own kind of jazz, and its suitability to Kenton's orchestra might almost be likened to Strayhorn's music for Ellington – except Graettinger was by far the more original thinker. Splendidly remastered, this is an important memorial to a man often forgotten in the annals of jazz composition, and Max Harrison's typically elegant sleeve-note supplies the fine context.

*** **Festival Of Modern American Jazz** Status CD 101
    Kenton; Bobby Clark, Johnny Capolo, Sam Noto, Herb Pomeroy, Norman Prentice, Conte Candoli (*t*); Bob Fitzpatrick, Frank Rosolino, Kent Larsen, Frank Strong (*tb*); Norman Bartold (*btb*); Lennie Niehaus, Charlie Mariano (*as*); Boots Mussulli (*as, bs*); Bill Holman, Jack Montrose (*ts*); Ralph Blaze (*g*); Gene Englund (*tba*); Max Bennett (*b*); Mel Lewis (*d*). 9/54.
*** **Kenton '56** Artistry CD 002
    Kenton; Ed Leddy, Dennis Grillo, Lee Katzman, Phil Gilbert, Tom Slaney (*t*); Archie LeCocque, Kent Larsen, Jim Amlotte (*tb*); Ken Shroyer (*btb*); Irving Rosenthal, Joe Mariani (*frhn*); Lennie Niehaus (*as*); Bill Perkins, Richie Kamuca (*ts*); Pepper Adams (*bs*); Ralph Blaze (*g*); Jay McAllister (*tba*); Don Bagley (*b*); Mel Lewis (*d*). 11/56.
***(*) **Kenton In Hi-Fi** Capitol CDP 7984451-2
    Similar to above. 2/56–7/58.

(*) **Live At The Macumba Club Vol. 1 Magic DAWE 48
    As above. 11/56.
(*) **Live At The Macumba Club Vol. 2 Magic DAWE 49
    As above. 11/56.
*** **Rendezvous Of Standards And Classics** Music For Pleasure 833620-2 2CD
    Similar to above discs. 43–57.
*** **Cuban Fire** Capitol B21Y-96260-2
    Kenton; Ed Leddy, Sam Noto, Phil Gilbert, Al Mattaliano, Bud Brisbois, Dalton Smith, Bob
    Rolfe, John Audino, Steve Hofsteter (*t*); Bob Fitzpatrick, Carl Fontana, Kent Larsen, Don
    Kelly, Dick Hyde, Ray Sikora (*tb*); Jim Amlotte, Bob Knight (*btb*); Dwight Carver, Joe Burnett,
    Bill Horan, Tom Wirtel, Gene Roland (*mel*); Gabe Baltazar, Lennie Niehaus (*as*); Bill Perkins,
    Lucky Thompson, Sam Donahue, Paul Renzi (*ts*); Wayne Dunstan (*bs, bsx*); Billy Root, Marvin
    Holladay (*bs*); Ralph Blaze (*g*); Jay McAllister, Albert Pollan (*tba*); Curtis Counce, Pete Chivily
    (*b*); Mel Lewis, Art Anton (*d*); Saul Gubin, George Gaber, Tommy Lopez, George Laguna,
    Roger Mozian, Maro Alvarez, George Acevedo (*perc*). 5/56–9/60.

The mid-1950s found Kenton somewhat in transition, from the more stylized West Coast touches of the early-'50s band to another kind of progressive-orchestral music which he had tried in the 1940s with mixed results. Live sessions were customarily a blend of straight-ahead swing variations on standards, the Afro-Cuban element, and Kenton's penchant for orchestral bombast. All three turn up on *Festival Of Modern American Jazz*, an enjoyable live set in excellent sound (although there are a few balance problems with some of the soloists). Candoli features on two tracks (and makes a belated appearance while an embarrassed Kenton has to fill in!) but the main body of music is made up of charts by Holman and Russo; the latter's 'Improvisation' and 'A Theme Of Four Values' typify the kind of pop-complexity which Kenton seemed to admire. Excellent playing, though, and Niehaus and Mussulli make sure the brass don't have things all their own way. The 1956 albums are a patchy lot. The three discs from the Mocamba Club use some of the same material, and the best choice is probably the Artistry CD, which runs for over 70 minutes and includes some of the best music. A new trumpet section and Adams on baritone lend some variation to the sound, but otherwise it's standard Kenton fare, in respectable if not terrific sound.

    The two original studio albums are the most important. *Kenton In Hi Fi* was a hit album for the bandleader and offered a reworking (almost Ellingtonian in intent) of many of his early successes, seeking the crisper definition of LP-era sound. If hardly a dramatic improvement or a startling revision (Kenton kept many of the patterns intact), it reasserts the orchestra's clout on its staple themes. The CD is beefed up with three 1958 tracks. *Cuban Fire* chronicles the arrival of arranger Johnny Richards, who had been studying Latin rhythms and came up with a series of charts which incorporated a six-man percussion team. The results catch much of the undertow of explosive kitsch which Latin bands love, although how 'authentic' it is in other ways is harder to judge. The six later tracks, from 1960, document one of Kenton's so-called 'mellophonium' bands, with five men playing that instrument among what is incredibly a band with 16 brass. Much of it sounds like mood or movie music, taken at tempos which tend towards trudging. The remastering is strong on the brass, but the bass frequencies are less well handled and the percussion section is mixed well off-mike on the earlier session.

    Rendezvous Of Standards And Classics is a two-disc set (at bargain price) which collects no fewer than five Capitol albums: *Milestones*, *Sketches On Standards*, *Kenton Classics*, *Portraits On Standards* and *Rendezvous With Kenton*. Familar material and some of the hits dominate the first disc, but most of the rest offers often relatively subdued arrangements of songbook tunes. A nice package for fans, though one slight caveat on the remastering: very shrill on some tracks, with the brass deafening, and misty on others – the power of the band comes through, but not very subtly.

*** **Live At The Patio Gardens Ballroom Vol. 1** Magic DAWE 56
    Kenton; Ed Leddy, Sam Noto, Billy Catalano, Lee Katzman, Phil Gilbert (*t*); Kent Larsen,
    Archie LeCoque, Don Reed, Jim Amlotte (*tb*); Kenny Shroyer (*btb*); Lennie Niehaus, Bill
    Perkins, Bill Robinson, Wayne Dunstan, Steve Perlow (*reeds*); Red Kelly (*b*); Jerry McKenzie
    (*d*). 8/57.
(*) **Live At The Patio Gardens Ballroom Vol. 2 Magic DAWE 57
    As above. 8/57.
(*) **Live At The Patio Gardens Ballroom Vol. 3 Magic DAWE 58
    As above. 8/57.

Music from a two-night engagement in Salt Lake City. These are typical Kenton sets for a dancing audience, which means less ambitious programmes, many standards, brief interpretations, careful solos. Given all that, the playing is still pointed and skilful, and Niehaus, Perkins and Noto have many good moments. Sound isn't as good as on some of the Status CDs, but isn't bad. *Volume One* has the best material.

*** **At The Rendezvous Vol. 1** Status CD 106
> Kenton; Sam Noto, Jules Chaikin, Billy Catalano, Lee Katzman, Phil Gilbert (*t*); Kent Larsen, Archie LeCoque, Don Reed, Jim Amlotte (*tb*); Kenny Shroyer (*btb*); Lennie Niehaus (*as*); Bill Perkins, Wayne Dunstan (*ts*); Billy Robinson (*bs, as*); Steve Perlow (*bs*); Red Kelly (*b*); Jerry McKenzie (*d*); Ann Richards (*v*). 1/58.

*** **At The Rendezvous Vol. 2** Status STCD 108
> As above. 1/58.

***(*) **At Ukiah** Status STCD 109
> Kenton; Frank Huggins, Bud Brisbois, Rolf Ericson, Joe Burnett, Roger Middleton (*t*); Archie LeCocque, Kent Larsen, Jimmy Knepper (*tb*); Jim Amlotte, Bill Smiley (*btb*); Lennie Niehaus (*as*); Bill Trujillo, John Bonnie (*ts*); Billy Root, Sture Swenson (*bs*); Scott LaFaro (*b*); Jerry McKenzie (*d*). 2/59.

***(*) **In New Jersey** Status STCD 104
> As above, except add Bobby Knight (*btb*), Charlie Mariano (*as*), Jack Nimitz (*bs*), Carson Smith (*b*), Billy Stuart (*d*), Mike Pacheco (*perc*); omit Niehaus, Swenson, LaFaro, McKenzie and Smiley. 6/59.

(*) **Live In Biloxi Magic DAWE 30
> Kenton; Frank Huggins, Bud Brisbois, Jack Sheldon, Billy Catalano, Bob Ojeda (*t*); Archie LeCocque, Kent Larsen, Jim Amlotte (*tb*); Bob Olsen, Bill Smiley (*btb*); Lennie Niehaus (*as*); Bill Perkins, Bill Trujillo (*ts*); Bill Robinson, Steve Perlow (*bs*); Red Kelly (*b*); Jerry McKenzie (*d*). *c.* 60.

(*) **Return To Biloxi Magic DAWE 35
> As above. *c.* 60.

*** **Live At Barstow 1960** Status DSTS1001 qq
> Kenton; Bud Brisbois, Dalton Smith, Bill Chase, Rolf Ericson, Danny Nolan (*t*); Bob Fitzpatrick, Kent Larsen, Bill Smiley (*tb*); Jim Amlotte, Bob Knight (*btb*); Lennie Niehaus (*as*); Bill Trujillo, Ronnie Rubin (*ts*); Jack Nimitz, Marvin Holladay (*bs*); Pete Chivily (*b*); Jimmy Campbell (*d*); Mike Pacheco (*perc*). 1/60.

This recently issued crop of live CDs has given Kenton's 1958–9 period a comprehensive documentation. The Status CDs are superb feats of remastering, giving the band real presence and a transparent clarity on most of these discs. The two *Rendezvous* discs both feature programmes of standards – in person, Kenton was usually playing dance or dinner dates, and seldom got to fire out all his most progressive material – and display a top-class big band in a period when there weren't many of them left. The *Ukiah* and *New Jersey* discs are similarly inclined, and casual listeners might try the New Jersey performance as the best introduction: there are some immaculately crafted little variations on the likes of 'Bernie's Tune', 'Laura' and 'Frenesi', and Jimmy Knepper – not much remembered as a Kentonian – takes some splendid solos. Only Kenton himself sounds a bit grumpy in his introductions, and his piano is a little remote in the mix. *Ukiah* has an almost entirely different set, with good work from Ericson, Root and Niehaus and the surprise appearance of Scott LaFaro in the rhythm section. The two Biloxi sets – the first is the more progressive material, the second a more standards-orientated session – are recorded mistily and the orchestra comes over rather waywardly. *Live At Barstow* is nearly all standards, with many nice solo spots for Niehaus, Ericson and Trujillo, and the band sound strong on what must have been a dance date for the marine corps.

***(*) **Mellophonium Magic** Status CD 103
> Kenton; Dalton Smith, Bob Behrendt, Marvin Stamm, Bob Rolfe, Phil Grossman (*t*); Dwight Carver, Gene Roland, Carl Saunders, Keith LaMotte (*mel*); Bob Fitzpatrick, Jack Spurlock, Bud Parker (*tb*); Jim Amlotte (*btb*); Dave Wheeler (*btb, tba*); Gabe Baltazar (*as*); Sam Donahue, Paul Renzi (*ts*); Wayne Dunstan (*bs, bsx*); Marvin Holladay (*bs*); Pierre Josephs (*b*); Jerry McKenzie (*d*); George Acevedo (*perc*). 6/61.

***(*) **Mellophonium Moods** Status STCD 106
> Kenton; Dalton Smith, Marvin Stamm, Bob Behrendt, Keith Lamotte, Bob Rolfe (*t*); Gene Roland, Ray Starling, Dwight Carver, Carl Saunders (*mel*); Bob Fitzpatrick, Dee Barton, Bud Parker (*tb*); Jim Amlotte (*btb*); Dave Wheeler (*btb, tba*); Gabe Baltazar (*as*); Charlie Mariano, Ray Florian (*ts*); Allan Beutler (*bs*); Joel Kaye (*bsx*); Val Kolar (*b*); Jerry McKenzie (*d*). 3/62.

(*) **One Night Stand Magic DAWE 66
> Similar to above two discs. 9/61–7/62.

*** **More Mellophonium Moods** Status DSTS1010
> As above, except add Bill Briggs (*t*), Lou Gasca (*mel*), Tom Ringo (*tb*), Bucky Calabrese (*b*), Bill Blakkested (*d*), Jean Turner (*v*); omit Rolfe, Roland, Kolar, McKenzie. 8/62.

(*) **At The Holiday Ballroom, Northbrook, Chicago Status DSTS1018
> As above. 5/62.

Kenton's 'mellophonium' band took his fascination with brass to new lengths: there are 14 brass players in both of these bands. The leader's verdict was that the band represented 'the New Era in Modern American Music', but it actually sounds like a beefier, more metallic edition of the old Kentonian machine. By this time Kenton had become entirely *sui generis*, and the prevailing winds of jazz fashion had little effect on the orchestra's direction. But he was still usually on the dinner-dance circuit, and both these discs contain somewhat rueful admissions from the leader that they'll play something people can dance to, but he wouldn't mind if some people also wanted to listen. No false pride: this was a great, swinging band and, if Kenton had lost most of his best soloists, the features for Baltazar, Mariano and some of the brassmen are handled with great aplomb. The *Mellophonium Moods* set is the better one in terms of fidelity – the sound is quite superb for a supposedly private recording – and, with a higher degree of original material, including a number of Kenton rarities, it's marginally more interesting musically, too. But either disc will surprise even those who may think Kenton is merely bombastic and tedious. The two concerts on *One Night Stand* are from AFRS broadcasts from New Jersey, something of a throwback; while the band still sound well, the sound is far below that achieved on the Status CDs. *More Mellophonium Moods* doesn't quite have the hi-fi of the other two, but it still sounds pretty good, and there is some lovely playing: Ray Starling takes a perfectly poised solo on 'Misty', and 'Maria' is a resplendent treatment of Johnny Richards's arrangement. The comedy version of 'Tea For two' is a drawback, though. The same band took to the boards at Northbrook, Chicago, and this time the sound is muzzier and the programme a little lacking in lift. Nevertheless, Status should be congratulated for unearthing so much by this edition of the band.

** **At Fountain Street Church Part One** Status DSTS 1014
    Kenton; Mike Price, Jim Kartchner, Jay Daversa, Carl Leach, John Madrid (*t*); Dick Shearer, Tom Whittaker, Shelley Denny (*tb*); Joe Randazzo (*btb*); Bob Goodwin (*btb, tba*); Ray Reed (*as, f*); Mike Altschul, Bob Crosby (*ts*); Earle Dumler (*bs*); Bill Fritz (*bs, bsx*); John Worster (*b*); Dee Barton (*d*); Efrain Lorgreira (*perc*). 3/68.

** **At Fountain Street Church Part Two** Status DSTS 1015
    As above.

There are some good things here, particularly among the more shaded sections of the arrangements, which catch the band midway between its subtler middle period and the supposed populism of the 1970s. But for once Dave Kay's source material let him down: the sound isn't much better than an average bootleg, with balances off and the drums booming like an artillery range.

(*) **Live At Redlands University Creative World STD 1015
    Kenton; Joe Ellis (*t, v*); Mike Vax, Jim Kartchner, Dennis Noday, Warren Gale (*t*); Dick Shearer, Mike Jamieson, Fred Carter, Tom Bridges (*tb*); Graham Ellis (*btb, tba*); Quin Davis (*as*); Richard Torres, Norm Smith, Jim Timlin (*ts*); Willie Maiden (*bs*); Gary Todd (*b*); John Von Ohlen (*d*); Efraim Logreira (*perc*). 10/70.

(*) **Live At Brigham Young University Creative World STD 1039
    Kenton; Mike Vax, Gary Pack, Jay Saunders, Joe Marcinkiewicz (*t*); Dick Shearer, Fred Carter, Mike Jamieson, Mike Wallace, Graham Ellis (*tb*); Quin Davis, Kim Frizell (*as*); Willie Maiden (*ts, bs*); Richard Torres (*ts*); Chuck Carter (*bs*); Gary Todd (*b*); John Von Ohlen (*d*); Ramon Lopez (*perc*). 8/71.

** **Live At Butler University** Creative World STD 1059
    Kenton; Jay Saunders, Dennis Noday, Mike Vax, Mike Snustead, Raymond Brown (*t*); Dick Shearer, Mike Jamieson, Fred Carter, Mike Wallace (*tb*); Phil Herring (*btb, tba*); Quin Davis (*as, f*); Richard Torres, Chris Galuman (*ts, f*); Chuck Carter (*bs, ss, f*); Willie Maiden (*bs*); John Worster (*b*); Jerry McKenzie (*d*); The Four Freshmen (*v*). 6/72.

*** **Birthday In Britain** Creative World STD 1065
    Kenton; Dennis Noday, Paul Adamson, Frank Minear, Mike Snustead, Robert Winiker (*t*); Dick Shearer, Harvey Coonin, Lloyd Spoon (*tb*); John Park (*as*); Chris Galuman (*ts, f*); Richard Torres, Willie Maiden (*ts*); Roy Reynolds (*bs*); John Worster (*b*); Peter Erskine (*d*); Ramon Lopez (*perc*). 2/73.

(*) **At The Pavilion, Hemel Hempstead Status DTS1017
    As above. 2/73.

*** **Live At London Hilton 1973 Vol. I** Status DSTS1005
    As above. 2/73.

*** **Live At London Hilton Vol. II** Status DSTS1006
    As above. 2/73.

(*) **7.5 On The Richter Scale Creative World STD 1070
    As above, except add Mike Barrowman (*t*), Gary Pack, Dale Devoe, Bill Hartman, Mike Wallace (*tb*), Mary Fettig (*ts*), Kim Park (*ts, as*), Kirby Stewart (*b*); omit Minear, Winiker, Coonin, Maiden and Worster. 8/73.

*** **Live At Carthage College Vol. One** Magic DAW E 69

    Kenton; Mike Barrowman, Kevin Jordan, Glenn Stuart, John Harner, Mike Snustead (*t*); Dick Shearer, Lloyd Spoon, Brett Stamps (*tb*); Bill Hartman (*btb*); Mike Wallace (*btb, tba*); Terry Cooke (*as*); Richard Torres, Dick Wilkie (*ts*); Roy Reynolds, Rich Condit (*bs*); Kirby Stewart (*b*); Peter Erskine (*d*); Ramon Lopez (*perc*). 2/74.

(*) **Live At Carthage College Vol. Two Magic DAW E70

    As above. 2/74.

(*) **Plays Chicago Creative World STD 1072

    Kenton; John Harner, Dave Zeagler, Mike Barrowman, Mike Snustead, Kevin Jordan (*t*); Dick Shearer, Lloyd Spoon, Brett Stamps, Bill Hartman (*tb*); Tony Campise, Greg Smith, Rich Condit, Dick Wilkie, Roy Reynolds (*reeds*); Mike Wallace (*tba*); Mike Ross (*b*); Peter Erskine (*d*); Ramon Lopez (*perc*). 6/74.

***(*) **Fire, Fury & Fun** Creative World STD 1073

    As above, except Tim Hagans (*t*), Dave Keim, Greg Sorcsek, Mike Suter (*tb*), Dan Salmasian (*reeds*) replace Snustead, Stamps, Hartman and Wilkie. 9/74.

(*) **Kenton '76 Creative World STD 1076

    Kenton; John Harner, Jay Sollenberger, Steve Campos, Jim Oatts, Tim Hagans (*t*); Dick Shearer, Dave Keim, Mike Egan (*tb*); Alan Morrissey (*btb*); Douglas Purviance (*btb, tba*); Terry Layne (*as, f*); Roy Reynolds, Dan Salmasian (*ts, f*); Alan Yankee, Greg Smith (*bs, f*); Dave Stone (*b*); Gary Hobbs (*d*); Ramon Lopez (*perc*). 12/75.

(*) **Journey Into Capricorn Creative World STD 1077

    As above, except Dave Kennedy (*t*), Jeff Uusitalo (*tb*), Dave Sova (*ts*), Bill Fritz (*bs*), John Worster (*b*) replace Oatts, Keim, Salmasian, Smith and Stone. 8/76.

Like any bandleader working through this period, Kenton had to change and compromise to survive, and the orchestra he worked with through the 1970s became as modish and subject to fads as any big-band survivor. But at least Kenton had always stood by his 'progressivenes' and, as subject to trashy material and clockwork charts as many of the later records are, the orchestra is no less predictable or bombastic than, say, the Basie band in the same period. Kenton had no great array of soloists but, as with the Buddy Rich band, he valued precision and overall effect, and all the surviving records (on CD – presumably there is much more that will be reissued) have virtues of their own.

    The various university concerts (where Kenton was always in favour, it seems) are sometimes bizarre mixtures of old and new: at Redlands he plays 'Hey Jude' and 'Macarthur Park' alongside 'Here's That Rainy Day' and 'Artistry In Rhythm'. At Brigham Young, it's 'Theme From Love Story' and 'Rhapsody In Blue'. Most peculiar of all is the Butler University set, where the band play 'Surfer Girl' (in 1972?) and 'Brand New Key', and then have The Four Freshmen join them! But the usual assertiveness of the brass section introduces moments of both grandeur and genuine excitement into all of these sets. The best of them is *Fire, Fury And Fun*, which has splendid features for Reynolds ('Roy's Blues') and Erskine ('Pete Is A Four-Letter Word'), and is let down only by Campise's silly 'Hogfat Blues'. *Birthday In Britain* has a superior set of charts (with the young Peter Erskine driving them), and *7.5 On The Richter Scale*, despite opening with the theme from *Live And Let Die* and going on to 'It's Not Easy Being Green', isn't a bad set of punch-ups for the sections. *Plays Chicago* refers not to the town but to the group, a modish attempt at playing thin, rocked-up tunes – insulting to Kenton, really – and the fact that he and the band make as good a fist of it as they do is surprising. *'76*, with another new band, is merely OK big-band fare, and *Journey Into Capricorn* bogs down on the ponderous 'Celebration Suite', though 'Too Shy To Say' (also on *Street Of Dreams*, listed below) is a warm revision of a Stevie Wonder tune.

    More live material has appeared on Status and Magic. The British concerts from February 1973 appear in good sound on their respective discs, but since the programme at Hemel Hempstead is largely duplicated on the Hilton show, which is spread across two discs (with a lot of chat, banter and introductions), only fanatics would consider getting both. Each is a decent set, though, with some of Kenton's most jazz-directed charts and Park, Winiker and Torres all taking good turns – Park's feature on 'Street Of Dreams' at the Hilton is a gem. The Carthage College date also sounds full and vivid, with occasional bass-heaviness. The programme is a typically catholic mixture, with 'Peanut Vendor' sitting next to 'Macarthur Park'. Probably for hardcore fans only, well though the band play.

*** **Live At Sunset Ridge Country Club Chicago** Magic DAW E 59

    Kenton; Jay Sollenberger, Dave Kennedy, Steve Campos, Tim Hagans, Joe Casano (*t*); Dick Shearer, Dave Keim, Mike Egan (*tb*); Allan Morrisey (*btb*); Doug Purviance (*btb, tba*); Roy Reynolds, Dan Salmasian (*ts*); Terry Layne (*as*); Greg Smith, Alan Yankee (*bs*); John Worster (*b*); Gary Hobbs (*d*); Ramon Lopez (*perc*). 5/76.

(*) **Live In Cologne 1976 Vol. One Magic DAW E 64

    As above, except Jeff Uusitalo (*tb*), Teddy Andersen (*ts*), Greg Metcalf (*bs*) replace Keim, Salmasian and Smith. 9/76.

*** Live In Cologne 1976 Vol. Two Magic DAWE 65
    As above. 9/76.
Two concerts from towards the end of the band's life. Kenton is still reprising his remarks about music
for dancing versus music for listening at the start of the Chicago dance date, but he's humorous enough
about it, and the band sound very full and strong (though the sound-mix shoves Worster to the very
front). Terry Layne sounds good on alto and, though the tempos are easy-going, they don't get slack.
The Cologne date is more ambitious, though not necessarily more enjoyable: sound is a bit less palatable, and 'Intermission Riff' on the first disc is a bit of a never-ending story, but the band sound healthy
and Kenton enjoys it, even though his own health was in serious decline.

***(*) Street Of Dreams Creative World STD 1079
    As above discs. 73–76.
A rather good and well-chosen compilation from some of Stan's latter-day sessions. It's mostly ballads,
which lets the great sonority of the Kenton brass assert itself one final time, and Chuck Carter's
baritone on 'Rhapsody In Blue', Tim Hagans on 'My Funny Valentine' and John Park's exquisite alto
on 'Street Of Dreams' honour the arrangements.

Barney Kessel (born 1923) GUITAR

**(*) Easy Like Original Jazz Classics OJC 153
    Kessel; Bud Shank, Buddy Collette (*as, f*); Harold Ross, Claude Williamson (*p*); Harry Babasin
    (*b*); Shelly Manne (*d*). 11/53–2/56.
*** Plays Standards Original Jazz Classics OJC 238
    Kessel; Bob Cooper (*ts, ob*); Claude Williamson, Hampton Hawes (*p*); Monty Budwig, Red
    Mitchell (*b*); Shelly Manne, Chuck Thompson (*d*). 6–7/54.
*** To Swing Or Not To Swing Original Jazz Classics OJC 317
    Kessel; Harry 'Sweets' Edison (*t*); Georgie Auld, Bill Perkins (*ts*); Jimmy Rowles (*p*); Al
    Hendrickson (*g*); Red Mitchell (*b*); Irv Cottler (*d*). 6/55.
*** Music To Listen To Barney Kessel By Original Jazz Classics OJC 746
    Kessel; Buddy Collette, Jules Jacob, George Smith, Howard Terry, Justin Gordon, Ted Nash
    (*reeds*); André Previn, Jimmy Rowles, Claude Williamson (*p*); Buddy Clark, Red Mitchell (*b*);
    Shelly Manne (*d*). 8–12/56.
'The blues he heard as a boy in Oklahoma, the swing he learned on his first band job and the modern
sounds of the West Coast school': Nesuhi Ertegun's summary of Kessel, written in 1954, still holds as
good as any description. Kessel has been undervalued as a soloist in recent years: the smoothness and
accuracy of his playing tend to disguise the underlying weight of the blues which informs his improvising, and his albums from the 1950s endure with surprising consistency. *Easy Like*, with flute by Shank
and Collette, is a little too feathery, but the guitarist's clean lines spare little in attack, and the terrific
'Vicky's Dream' emerges as furious bop. The two subsequent albums suggest a firm truce between Basie-
like small-band swing – hardly surprising with Edison on hand – and the classic West Coast appraisal of
bop. The inclusion of such ancient themes as 'Louisiana', 'Twelfth Street Rag' and 'Indiana' suggests
the breadth of Kessel's interests and, although most of the tracks are short, nothing seems particularly
rushed. Lester Koenig's superb production has been faithfully maintained for the reissues: Manne,
especially, is well served by the engineering. *Music To Listen To Barney Kessel By* sweetens the mix by
sticking to cute woodwind and reed arrangements of familiar tunes while Kessel swings smilingly
through it; nothing demanding, but it's so breezily done that it cuts most of the so-called easy-listening
jazz of recent years.

*** The Poll Winners Original Jazz Classics OJC 156
    Kessel; Ray Brown (*b*); Shelly Manne (*d*). 3/57.
**(*) The Poll Winners Ride Again Original Jazz Classics OJC 607
    As above. 8/58.
*** Poll Winners Three Original Jazz Classics OJC 692
    As above. 11/59.
Since Kessel, Brown and Manne regularly scored high in jazz fans' polls of the day, Contemporary's
decision to record them as a trio was commercially impeccable. But they were a committed musical
group too. *The Poll Winners* includes jamming on 'Satin Doll' and 'Mean To Me' which is sophisticated
enough to imply a telepathy between Kessel and Manne. But the group push harder on the remaining
records, although *Ride Again* includes some weak material. The superb studio sound highlights inner
detail.

** **Plays Carmen** Original Jazz Classics OJC 269
>Kessel; Ray Linn (*t*); Harry Betts (*tb*); Buddy Collette (*cl, f*); Bill Smith (*cl, bcl*); Jules Jacobs (*cl, ob*); Pete Terry (*bcl, bsn*); Herb Geller (*as*); Justin Gordon (*ts, f*); Chuck Gentry (*bs*); André Previn (*p*); Victor Feldman (*vib*); Joe Mondragon (*b*); Shelly Manne (*d*). 12/58.

*** **Some Like It Hot** Original Jazz Classics OJC 168
>Kessel; Joe Gordon (*t*); Art Pepper (*cl, as, ts*); Jimmy Rowles (*p*); Jack Marshall (*g*); Monty Budwig (*b*); Shelly Manne (*d*). 3–4/59.

The *Carmen* album was a cute idea that might best have stayed as no more than that, although Kessel gives it enough dedication to create some typical swinging blues out of the likes of 'Carmen's Cool'. *Some Like It Hot* works much better, since this set of tunes from the then-hit film offered the kind of new-lamps-for-old which Kessel had already been trying on earlier records. Pepper shines on all three horns, Gordon contributes some acrid solos on one of his rare appearances on record, and Kessel experiments with three different guitars and a couple of duo-only tunes. 'Runnin' Wild', taken at a blistering pace, is a tiny gem.

(*) **Autumn Leaves Black Lion BL 60112
>Kessel; Teddy Edwards (*ts*); Jimmy Rowles (*p*); Kenny Napper (*b*); John Marshall (*d*). 10/68–9/69.

*** **Yesterday** Black Lion BLCD760183
>Kessel; Danny Moss (*ts*); Stéphane Grappelli (*vn*); Brian Lemon (*p*); Kenny Baldock (*b*); Johnny Richardson (*d*). 7/73.

*** **The Poll Winners / Straight Ahead** Original Jazz Classics OJC 409
>Kessel; Ray Brown (*b*); Shelly Manne (*d*). 7/75.

Kessel spent most of the 1960s as a studio session guitarist, but when he did return to a jazz setting his playing was scarcely impaired. Most of the music on *Autumn Leaves* is with the sole support of Napper and Marshall, who play perfunctorily, which leaves Kessel to toy with ideas; it's still a pretty record, with three odd tracks with Edwards and Rowles as makeweight. *Yesterday* replays Kessel's Montreux Festival appearance from 1973, with a guest appearance apiece by Moss and Grappelli, the latter on his patented sashay through 'Tea For Two'. 'Laura' and 'Old Devil Moon' are vintage Kessel, the former building from a featherdown exposition of the tune through progressively burning choruses. Moss sits in on a gruffly swinging blues and, though the music has the ad hoc feel of a typical festival set, it was worth keeping. *The Poll Winners* reunion is as good as their earlier records, yet looser, less drilled. 'Caravan' and 'Laura' become springboards for playing as freely as they ever could together.

** **Three Guitars** Concord CCD 6004
>Kessel; Herb Ellis, Charlie Byrd (*g*); Joe Byrd (*b*); Johnny Rae (*d*). 7/74.

** **Barney Plays Kessel** Concord CCD 6009
>Kessel; Herbie Steward (*ss, as, f*); Victor Feldman (*vib*); Jimmy Rowles (*p*); Chuck Domanico (*b*); Jake Hanna (*d*); Milt Holland (*perc*). 4/75.

** **Soaring** Concord CCD 6033
>Kessel; Monty Budwig (*b*); Jake Hanna (*d*). 77.

(*) **Live At Sometime Storyville STCD 4157
>Kessel; Kunimitsu Inaba (*b*); Tetsujirah Obara (*d*). 2/77.

Kessel doesn't sit very comfortably in Concord's cosy setting. The duos and trios with Byrd and Ellis offer only routine virtuosity, and his first programme of originals isn't much of an event when the accompanying band play them as politely as they do here. *Soaring* creates some pretty music, but is laid-back enough to raise itself barely above the horizontal. He fares better on his meeting with Monty Alexander, *Spontaneous Combustion*. The Storyville record catches him on a globe-trotting expedition to Japan, where two local players offer respectful support on a sometimes banal programme of ready-mades: Barney strolls through it.

Steve Khan (born 1947) GUITAR

** **Local Color** Denon 33CY-1840
>Khan; Rob Mounsey (*ky, v*). 4–5/87.

(*) **Public Access GRP GRD-9599
>Khan; Anthony Jackson (*b*); Dave Weckl (*d*); Manolo Badrena (*p, v*). 1/89.

A talented guitarist in search of a context, Steve Khan's earlier records succumb to introversion. He's far from the expected merchant of bombast which so many fusion-orientated guitarists become, his improvisations often interestingly fragmented and concerned with tonal variation as much as with racing up and down complex scales. He apprenticed as a rock session musician through most of the 1970s, but his interest in jazz playing led him to form Eyewitness, the band which is responsible for

Public Access. The album of duets, *Local Color*, is sensitively done, but dull: the seven tunes miss the melodic fillip which might compensate for the rhythmic languor, and Mounsey's playing is faceless. Eyewitness are inward-looking in another way: Khan seems reluctant to take command, and it's Weckl's irritatingly busy rhythms which dominate their work. When Khan gets to take charge – on the interesting 'Blue Zone 41', where he patiently builds a thoughtful solo in the midst of a torrent of other noise – matters look up. The best moment by far is his gentle reading of 'Dedicated To You', co-written by his father, Sammy Cahn; here Weckl plays relatively straight time and Khan's vibrant tone is distinctly affecting.

***(*) **Let's Call This** Polydor 849563-2
    Khan; Ron Carter (*b*); Al Foster (*d*). 91.
*** **Headline** Polydor 517690-2
    As above, except add Anthony Jackson (*b*); Dennis Chambers (*d*); Manolo Badrena (*perc*). 1/92.
*** **Crossings** Verve Forecast 523269-2
    As above, except add Michael Brecker (*ts*). 12/93.

These superior records build on the more thoughtful traits of the last two. The trio with Carter and Foster has a masterclass air about it: Khan goes for jazz-heartland material – Monk, Shorter, standards such as 'Street Of Dreams' – and sounds completely at home, the improvisations informed by his prodigious technique but not driven into overdrive, as so often happens with reformed fusioneers. *Headline* is arguably a notch less impressive, despite the sharing of credits among the same trio and a light-Latin group with Badrena, Chambers and Jackson. 'Turnaround' and 'The Blessing' are fine transformations of Ornette Coleman tunes, but some of the other pieces seem to drift off midway through. *Crossings* goes for another interesting programme of hard-bop nuggets, and the playing is uniformly confident, though again the results sound somewhat anodyne. Monk's 'Think Of One' comes out about as un-Monk-like as one can imagine, and Brecker's three cameos add little except extra weight. Best shot is the pretty, rippling treatment of Tony Williams's 'Pee Wee'.

Franklin Kiermyer (born 1956) DRUMS

*** **Break Down The Walls** Konnex KCD 50444
    Kiermyer; Chris Gekker (*t*); John Rojak (*tb*); Russ Rizner (*frhn*); Dave Braynard (*tba*); Peter Madsen (*p*); Tony Scherr (*b*).
***(*) **In The House Of My Fathers** Konnex KCD 5052
    As above, except omit Scherr; add Dave Douglas (*t*); John Stubblefield (*ts*); Anthony Cox (*b*).
***(*) **Solomon's Daughter** Evidence ECD 22083
    Kiermyer; Pharoah Sanders (*ts*); John Esposito (*p*); Drew Gress (*b*). 93.
***(*) **Kairos** Evidence ECD 22144
    Kiermyer; Eric Person (*as, ss*); Sam Rivers (*ss*); Michael Stuart (*ts, ss*); John Esposito (*p*); Drew Gress, Dom Richards (*b*). 2/95.

Someone listening to a late Coltrane group with Pharoah Sanders in the line-up said that they sounded as if they were trying to demolish Jericho; one hears the same Hebraic intensity in Albert Ayler's work. This is the musical birthright of a powerful young Canadian whose interests have broadened in recent years into ritual and shamanistic musics from around the world. *Kairos* is interspersed with such oddities (in jazz terms) as Angolan circumcision rituals, rainforest Pygmy chants, M'buti Congo drums, Native-American medicine chants and Pontic Greek pipes.

    The basic inspiration, however, remains the New Thing of the 1960s. The two Konnexes have the turbulent horn-and-drum sound of Coltrane projects like *Ascension*, though with a much more evident melodic edge. On *Solomon's Daughter* Sanders abandons the warm ballad tones he has adopted in recent times for the shrieking fury of his 1960s work with Coltrane. It's all rather ancestral and backward-looking until, on *Kairos* with what has become his regular band, Kiermyer begins to allow more straightforwardly expressive themes to assert themselves. Eric Person's soprano solo on 'In Your Presence I Behold' is a delight, topped only by Sam Rivers's sinuous and frenzied counter-statement on the following track, 'Basheret', where he sounds as if he's playing in a pool of muffled reverb. It is testimony to Kiermyer's standing that he is able to call in players of this calibre. His progress will be interesting to observe.

Masabumi Kikuchi PIANO

**** **Tethered Moon** Paddle Wheel KICJ 93
    Kikuchi; Gary Peacock (*b*); Paul Motian (*d*). 11/91.

*** **Triangle** Paddle Wheel KICJ 130
> As above. 11/91.

*** **Feel You** Paddle Wheel KICJ 141
> Kikuchi; James Genus (*b*); Victor Jones (*b*). 1/93.

The music of Tethered Moon, Kikuchi's acclaimed trio with Peacock and Motian, is spacious, abstract and unencumbered with any generic assumptions. 'Misterioso', on the first album, more or less defines the turf, so much so that the follow-up, recorded at the same time, sounds a little like the afterthought it may have been. There were things happening in the first group that Kikuchi could not possibly hope to replicate or imitate with any other player, but the later, more obviously jazz-based trio with Genus and Jones imports as much of the original conception as possible and inscribes it on a much tighter and funkier swing. Kikuchi still sounds like an abstractionist, but one who is capable of keeping things secured to the melody. Excursions like 'Free Stroll' offer the unvarnished version, while 'It Never Entered My Mind' suggests he may have been listening to Bill Evans as well as Ahmad Jamal.

Jonny King PIANO

***(*) **In From The Cold** Criss Cross CRISS 1093
> King; Vincent Herring (*as, ss*); Mark Turner (*ts*); Ira Coleman (*b*); Billy Drummond (*d*). 1/94.

King is the sort of chap who makes less talented mortals sour with envy. Only really a semi-professional musician, his day job is in a law practice specializing in intellectual property. Across his career to date has fallen the shadow of his girlfriend Rosanna Graham's premature death from cancer, and there is a sober maturity to King's writing and playing. 'Conundrum' was written for Rosanna and, though one can readily appreciate the mystery and puzzle that inspired him, the title more exactly refers to a piece that turns and twists, never quite revealing its secret: very subtle, unmannered, utterly contemporary. The opening 'El Jefe' is more of a straightforward blowing piece, but one suspects that King is easier with more demanding settings, as when the two saxes (both excellent, by the way) weave countermelodies or operate with a measure of harmonic tension.

King already asserts a modest moral right to his own voice. As a player, he's somewhat stiff-fingered and inflexible, but he writes with authority and will surely always find quality players willing to work with him. A class act.

Peter King (born 1940) ALTO SAXOPHONE, SOPRANO SAXOPHONE, CLARINET

*** **Brother Bernard** Miles Music MM CD 076
> King; Guy Barker (*t*); Alan Skidmore (*ts*); John Horler (*p*); Dave Green (*b*); Martin Drew, Tony Levin (*d*). 88–89.

*** **Tamburello** Miles Music MM CD 083
> King; Steve Melling (*p, ky*); James Hellawell (*ky*); Alec Dankworth (*b*); Stephen Keogh (*d, perc*). 10/94.

King remains Britain's most eminent keeper of the bebop alto flame, although his recent work has sought wider fields and a way out of perceived restrictions. In fact, the best and most convincing music on both of the available records under his own name remains broadly in the bebop idiom. *Brother Bernard* includes extended solos on 'Overjoyed' and 'But Beautiful' which offer intensely lucid thinking on fertile melodies, but the rhythm section contribute facelessly admirable support and the guest spots by Barker and Skidmore add little except extra weight. *Tamburello* is a deal more ambitious yet doesn't hang together very well as an album. Fine improvisations on Wayne Shorter's 'Yes And No' and McCoy Tyner's 'You Taught My Heart To Sing' sit alongside a couple of diffident King originals and arrangements on Bartók and Purcell, with the final four tracks standing as a linked meditation on the death of Ayrton Senna. Touchingly effective in parts, but too much of the music is compromised by the electric keyboards. It's not that their presence is disagreeably 'modern', but that they're just not recorded or mixed with any subtlety. When King gets clear space and plays, he still sounds terrific.

John Kirby (1908–52) DOUBLE BASS

***(*) **John Kirby, 1938–1939** Classics 750
> Kirby; Charlie Shavers (*t*); Buster Bailey (*cl*); Russell Procope (*as*); Billy Kyle (*p*); O'Neil Spencer (*d, v*). 10/38–10/39.

***(*) **John Kirby, 1939–1941** Classics 770
> As above. 10/39–1/41.

**** **The Biggest Little Band In The Land** Columbia 477635-2 2CD
    As above, except add Maxine Sullivan (*v*). 39–41.
*** **John Kirby, 1941–1943** Classics 792
    As above, except omit Sullivan; add George Johnson (*as*); Clyde Hart (*p*); Bill Beason, Specs
    Powell (*d*). 7/41–12/43.
*** **John Kirby, 1941–44** Tax CD 3714
    As above, except omit Powell, add Ben Webster (*ts*). 5 & 9/41, 11/43, 8/44.

A fascinating musician originally taught by Wellman Braud and Pops Foster, Kirby has rarely received due attention for his intricately woven, understated small-group swing with an emphasis on exact harmony rather than rapid improvisational counterpoint. They performed in white tails and very much sound that way: elegant, sophisticated, even slightly chill and distant. Given its prominence on radio and in recordings over the years covered by these Classics volumes, it is hard not to think the Sextet must have had a significant impact on later generations of musicians, not least the 'cool school', and there are moments on the more impressionistic cuts when one might almost be listening to some early Giuffre project.

The band began under Buster Bailey's leadership, but – a little like Andy Kirk – Kirby had a flair for leadership and was able to sustain a stable personnel. Many of the arrangements are credited to Charlie Shavers, and it is slightly surprising to find him so suavely well-mannered, both with pencil and horn, rarely raising his voice. Titles like 'Opus 5', 'Impromptu' and 'Nocturne' on the first Classics volume and on the excellent Columbia point to the classical sources for some of the material; the earlier 'Anitra's Dance' sounds like Grieg and there are borrowings from Schubert, Chopin ('The Minute Waltz', alas), and Dvořák elsewhere.

The Classics imprint is always a reliable source, if not acoustically impeccable. Fortunately, on this occasion, there is the option of the two-CD Columbia compilation, which offers the additional bonus – for fans of singing – of half a dozen Maxine Sullivan vocals. Their absence from the *Chronologicals* shouldn't put off anyone who is primarily interested in Kirby, however; of these, only the last volume, documenting a less skilful wartime band, might be thought surplus to strict requirements. For serious collectors, the Tax compilation factors in some radio transcriptions from the same period. The quality – of playing, if not of reproduction – remains very high and it is clear how much improvisation went on in what has often been dismissed as a rather stiff 'chamber jazz' group.

Andy Kirk (1898–1993) BANDLEADER, BASS SAXOPHONE, TUBA

*** **Andy Kirk, 1929–1931** Classics 655
    Kirk; Clouds of Joy (various personnel). 29–31.
**** **Andy Kirk, 1936–1937** Classics 573
    Kirk; Paul King, Harry Lawson, Earl Thomson, Clarence Trice (*t*); Ted Donnelly, Henry Wells
    (*tb*); John Harrington (*cl, as, bs*); John Williams (*as, bs*); Earl Miller (*as*); Dick Wilson (*ts*);
    Claude Williams (*vn*); Mary Lou Williams (*p*); Ted Brinson, Ted Robinson (*g*); Booker Collins
    (*b*); Ben Thigpen (*d*); O'Neil Spencer, Pha Terrell (*v*). 3–12/36.
***(*) **Andy Kirk, 1937** Classics 581
    As above. 2–12/37.
***(*) **Andy Kirk, 1937–1938** Classics 598
    As above. 2–12/38.
***(*) **Kansas City Bounce** Black & Blue 59.240
    As above, except add Harold Baker (*t*); Fred Robinson (*tb*); Edward Inge (*cl, ts*); Rudy Powell
    (*as*); Don Byas (*ts*); Floyd Smith (*g*); June Richmond (*v*). 11/39, 6 & 7/40.
*** **Mary's Idea** Decca GRC 622
    As above. 36–40.
*** **Andy Kirk, 1939–1940** Classics 640
    As above. 39–40.
*** **Andy Kirk, 1940–1942** Classics 681
    As above. 40–42.
*** **A Mellow Bit Of Rhythm** RCA 113028
    Kirk; Conte Candoli, Ray Copeland, Bernie Glow, Joe Newman, Ernie Royal (*t*); Jimmy
    Cleveland, Fred Ohms, Frank Rehak, Chauncey Welsh (*tb*); Tom Mitchell (*btb*); Sam Marowitz,
    Hal McKusick (*as*); Al Cohn, Ed Wasserman (*ts*); Al Epstein (*bs*); Kenny Kersey, Moe
    Wechler (*p*); Marty Wilson (*vib*); Freddie Green, Jimmy Raney (*g*); Milt Hinton, Buddy Jones
    (*b*); Osie Johnson (*d, v*). 3/56.

Though he was often out front for photo opportunities, Andy Kirk ran the Clouds of Joy strictly from the back row. The limelight was usually left to singer June Richmond or vocalist/conductor Pha Terrell;

the best of the arrangements were done by Mary Lou Williams, who left the band in 1942; as a bass saxophonist, Kirk wasn't called on to take a solo. All the same, he turned the Clouds of Joy – which he inherited bloodlessly from Terrence Holder's Dark Clouds of Joy in 1929 and ran successfully and then intermittently for the next five decades – into one of the most inventive swing bands. His disposition was sunny and practical and he was a competent organizer (who in later life ran a Harlem hotel, the legendary Theresa, and organized a Musicians' Union local in New York City).

Inevitably, given Kirk's low musical profile, critical attention is more usually directed to other members of the band. The classic Clouds of Joy cuts are those that feature Mary Lou Williams's arrangements and performances, and for these the three Classics compilations are essential, though many of the best tracks can be found on compilations under Williams's own name. The earlier material is still the best, with 'Moten Swing', 'Until The Real Thing Comes Along' and the hit 'Froggy Bottom' prominent. There are, though, fine performances from 1937 and 1938, most notably 'Mary's Idea' from December 1938. Sound-reproduction is reasonably good. Still missing from the catalogue are the sessions recorded between 1939 and Mary Lou Williams's departure, which include such classic tracks as 'Floyd's Guitar Blues', 'McGhee Special', a feature for young trumpeter Howard McGhee. This will be rectified in subsequent Classics releases.

Kansas City Bounce will answer most non-specialist needs. It offers a reasonable selection from arguably the most significant period of the Clouds' activity. The CEDAR noise-reduction process has made some of the louder passages a bit shrill and unnatural, but it's no worse than average for music of the period.

A Mellow Bit Of Rhythm dates from much later in the story and is far from compelling, despite the presence in the orchestra of some excellent ensemble and solo players. The title-track, 'Walkin' And Swingin'' and 'Little Joe From Chicago', all recorded within a few March days, convey something of the Kirk magic, compounded by a band which is packed with stars of the future.

Rahsaan Roland Kirk (1936–77) TENOR SAXOPHONE, MANZELLO, STRITCH, FLUTE, ASSORTED INSTRUMENTS

(*) **Third Dimension Bethlehem BET 6006
    Kirk; Booker Ervin (*ts*); Jimmy Madison (*p*); Carl Pruitt (*b*); Henry Duncan (*d*). 11/56.
Jazz purists were quick to dismiss Roland Kirk as a mere showman. Blinded as an infant, he built his music on a vivid dream-life, using false fingerings and one or two blatant tricks to enable him to play up to three saxophones at a time. The saxophones themselves were non-standard. In a music-shop basement Kirk discovered a manzello and a stritch, rare horns apparently used in Spanish marching bands. The manzello approximated the pitch of the soprano saxophone – close, as they said in the booths, but no cigar – and the stritch was an off-pitch alto saxophone. By playing them together and breezily circumventing some of the harmonic anomalies, Kirk could mimic a whole saxophone section. His flute was heavily vocalized and he punctuated performances with blasts from whistles and sirens.

This early record was listed in our last edition on Affinity as *Soulful Saxes*. It features Booker Ervin, another heterodox saxophonist who would catch Charles Mingus's eye. The sound is raw and slightly off-putting, and Kirk hasn't yet achieved the astonishing contrapuntal effects of later years. There is, indeed, some overdubbing of saxophone 'ensembles'. 'The Nearness Of You' offers some pointers to future greatness, and the Ervin tracks are well worth having, but this is pretty much a collector's disc.

(*) **Kirk's Work Original Jazz Classics OJC 459
    Kirk; Jack McDuff (*org*); Joe Benjamin (*b*); Art Taylor (*d*). 7/61.
'Skater's Waltz' is one of Kirk's best bits of surreal kitsch, combined with his familiar inventive ambiguity. He clearly enjoys the big, bruising sound of McDuff's electric organ and boots furiously on all three saxophones and flute. On 'Three For Dizzy' he executes difficult tempos with quite astonishing dexterity. A largely forgotten Kirk album, but one which generally deserves the classic reissue billing.

***(*) **We Free Kings** Mercury 826 455
    Kirk; Richard Wyands, Hank Jones (*p*); Art Davis, Wendell Marshall (*b*); Charli Persip (*d*). 61.
This is the first major Kirk record, and the opening 'Three For The Festival', a raucous blues, is the best evidence there is on record of his importance, even greatness. Kirk's playing is all over the place. He appears out of nowhere and stops just where you least expect him to. On 'You Did It, You Did It', he creates rhythmic patterns which defeat even Persip and moves across the chords with a bizarre crabwise motion. A wonderful record that every Kirk fan should have.

**** **Rahsaan** Mercury 846630 10CD + bonus
    Kirk; Nat Adderley, Al Derisi, Freddie Hubbard, Virgil Jones, Jimmie Maxwell, Joe Newman, Jimmy Nottingham, Ernie Royal, Clark Terry, Richard Williams, Snooky Young (*t*); Martin

Banks (*flhn*); Garnett Brown, Billy Byers, Jimmy Cleveland, Paul Faulise, Curtis Fuller, Charles Greenlea, Dick Hixon, Quentin Jackson, J. J. Johnson, Melba Liston, Tom McIntosh, Tom Mitchell, Santo Russo, Tony Studd, Kai Winding (*tb*); Ray Alonge, Jimmy Buffington, Earl Chapin, Paul Ingraham, Fred Klein, Tony Miranda, Bob Northern, Willie Ruff, Julius Watkins (*frhn*); Don Butterfield, Jay McAllister, Henry Phillips, Bill Stanley (*tba*); Benny Golson, Lucky Thompson (*ts*); Tubby Hayes (*ts, vib*); James Moody (*ts, f;* as 'Jimmy Gloomy'); Pepper Adams (*bs*); Al Cohn, Jerry Dodgion, Budd Johnson, Walt Levinsky, Romeo Penque, Seldon Powell, Jerome Richardson, Zoot Sims, Stan Webb, Frank Wess, Phil Woods (*reeds*); Walter Bishop Jr, Jaki Byard, Hank Jones, Wynton Kelly, Harold Mabern, Tete Montoliu, Bobby Scott, Horace Parlan, Richard Wyands (*p*); Andrew Hill (*p, cel*); Patti Brown, Lalo Schifrin, Bobby Scott (*p, org*); Eddie Baccus (*org*); Gary Burton, Milt Jackson, Bobby Moses (*vib*); Vincent Bell, Kenny Burrell, Mose Fowler, Jim Hall, Wayne Wright (*g*); Sonny Boy Williamson (*hca;* as 'Big Skol'); Charles McCoy (*hca*); Bob Cranshaw, Art Davis, Richard Davis, George Duvivier, Michael Fleming, Milt Hinton, Sam Jones, Wendell Marshall, Vernon Martin, Eddie Mathias, Don Moore, Niels-Henning Orsted-Pedersen, Major Holley, Abdullah Rafik, Ben Tucker, Chris White (*b*); Art Blakey, Sonny Brown, George Cook, Rudy Collins, Charles Crosby, Henry Duncan, Steve Ellington, Louis Hayes, Roy Haynes, Albert Heath, Osie Johnson, Elvin Jones, J. C. Moses, Walter Perkins, Charli Persip, Ed Shaughnessy (*d*); Bill Costa, Jack Del Rio, George Devens, Charles Gomez, Phil Kraus, Montego Joe, Jose Paula, Manuel Ramos (*perc*); Miss C. J. Albert (*v*); others unidentified. 61–64.

***(*) **Verve Jazz Masters 27** Verve 523 489
As above. 61–64.

*** **Does Your House Have Lions?** Rhino R2 71406 2CD
Kirk; Ron Burton, Jaki Byard, Hank Jones, Charles Mingus, Trudy Pitts, Lonnie Smith, Sonelius Smith, Richard Tee (*p*); Ron Carter, Major Holley, Vernon Martin, Steve Novosel, Henry Pearson, Henry Mathias Pearson, Bill Salter, Doug Watkins (*b*); Sonny Brown, Charles Crosby, Jimmy Hopps, Oliver Jackson, James Madison, Khalil Mhridri, Bernard Purdie, Robert Shy, Harold White (*d*); woodwinds, strings. 61–76.

Potential purchasers shouldn't be misled into thinking that *Rahsaan* is a 'Complete' or 'Collected' Kirk. It represents only the – admittedly marvellous – recordings he made for the Mercury label during five of his most productive years. Serious collectors will also want to have later material like *The Inflated Tear*, and a group of unpredictable Atlantics, *Volunteered Slavery*, *Rahsaan Rahsaan* (ATL 40127 LP), *Natural Black Invention: Roots Strata* (ATL 40185 LP), *Left And Right* (ATL 40235 LP) and *Here Comes The Whistleman* (ATL 40389 LP).

Disc 1 of the Mercury set is a repackaging of the popular *We Free Kings* with a good alternative take of Parker's 'Blues For Alice' and an unissued 'Spring Will Be A Little Late This Year'. This is roughly the pattern observed throughout the set: alternatives have been included on merit, not (as with some Parker compilations) merely for the sake of checking matrix numbers. The other original releases are *Domino* (MG 20748, now disc 2), *Reeds And Deeds* (MG 20800, discs 3–4), *The Roland Kirk Quartet Meets The Benny Golson Orchestra* (MG 20844, now 4) where Kirk sounds quite at home in Golson's rich, Gil Evans-like arrangements; there is the live *Kirk In Copenhagen* (MG 20894, now discs 5–6, with nine unissued tracks) featuring Sonny Boy Williamson, *Gifts And Messages* (MG 20939, now disc 7), *I Talk With The Spirits* (LM 82008, now disc 8), *Rip, Rig And Panic* (LM 82027, now disc 9 – but see below), and *Slightly Latin* (LM 82033, now disc 9). In addition to an uncredited and mostly unissued 1964 session on disc 7, there are also cuts made under the leadership of Tubby Hayes, organist Eddie Baccus (one track only) and Quincy Jones.

The Jones tracks bear much the same relation to the better material as the Bird-with-strings sessions to the classic Verve small groups. Jones's advocacy – like Ramsey Lewis's – was critical to the hornman's career and helped overcome a deadweight of industry suspicion, but the mid-market pitch was unfortunate. Eminently professional, the arrangements smooth out Kirk's eldritch sound in a way that Golson's imaginative charts don't.

Of the small groups, the *We Free Kings* session is still as fresh as paint; Kirk's mildly irreverent rework-ing of the Christmas carol sounds hokey at first hearing but makes increasing sense on repeated exposure, much like Thelonious Monk's 'straight' 'Abide With Me'. 'Three For The Festival' became one of his most frequently performed compositions. There are marvellous things, too, on the 1962 and 1963 sessions with Andrew Hill (his first working group) and Harold Mabern slip-anchoring sympa-thetic rhythm sections. Some of the real surprises come in the one-off collaboration with Tubby Hayes. Also featuring James Moody (under the contractual *nom de studio*, 'Jimmy Gloomy'), the pairing of flutes over Hayes's vibes on 'Lady "E"' is masterful. The tenor-chase effects recall 'Three For The Festival'. Elsewhere, Kirk and Moody play off against the visitor's less abstract bop style. During a superb ballad medley, Kirk attacks 'For Heaven's Sake' without a reed in his tenor saxophone; the sound is both startling and beautiful.

The live Copenhagen sessions with bluesman Williamson are credited with two bassists, Don Moore and the ubiquitous NHOP. They don't seem to play together, but it isn't always easy to pick detail out of a raucous, clubby recording which has Montoliu optimistically bashing an out-of-tune and tinny piano much as his model Bud Powell had to do in later years. Needless to say, Kirk remains triumphantly unfazed.

Inevitably expensive but beautifully packaged, and with an intelligently detailed booklet by critic Dan Morgenstern, *Rahsaan* nevertheless affords unparalleled detail on perhaps the most significant single phase of Kirk's career. Newcomers should certainly start elsewhere, ideally with the well-selected but inevitably very selective *Jazz Masters* set; but enthusiasts will find these ten discs (and the brief bonus 'Stritch In Time' from the 1962 Newport Festival) essential acquisitions.

The smaller *Does Your House Have Lions?* covers his recording for Atlantic and is both more selective and less richly funded in the first place. The label deliberately encouraged his more maverick side on the assumption that Kirk unfettered was the only Kirk anyone really wanted, when in fact he was an artist who, more than most, needed a sympathetic but steadying hand. As a result, these discs are patchy and sometimes downright disappointing. But Kirk is Kirk, and it would be a mistake to expect smoothly crafted mainstream jazz.

***(*) Rip, Rig And Panic / Now Please Don't You Cry, Beautiful Edith Emarcy 832164 IMS

Kirk; Lonnie Liston Smith, Jaki Byard (*p*); Ronnie Boykins, Richard Davis (*b*); Elvin Jones, Grady Tate (*d*). 1/65, 4/67.

Now included on the Emarcy CD twofer, *Now Please Don't You Cry, Beautiful Edith* revives one of Kirk's unaccountably least-known recordings; it was his only record for Verve, made between contracts. Kirk's usual approach to schmaltz was to pepper it furiously. Brief as it is, 'Alfie' is given a half-ironic, half-respectful reading that is genuinely moving, with a typically ambiguous coda. Elsewhere, Kirk ranges from big Ellingtonian themes to out-and-out rock'n'roll.

Rip, Rig And Panic justifies single-CD release in this packaging (it's also to be found in the *Rahsaan* compilation, above) by its sheer energy and popularity (a British-based funk band named themselves after the album). The opening 'No Tonic Pres' is a tribute to Lester Young developed without definite key resolution. Like the succeeding 'From Bechet, Fats And Byas', it underlines Kirk's allusive invention and ability to make music with the most attenuated materials. Both 'Slippery, Hippery, Flippery' and the furious title-track develop Kirk's interest in 'found' or chance effects; Byard's piano playing switches between Bud Powell, the rhythmic fractures of Monk and the uncentred tonality of Cecil Taylor. Elvin Jones's drum solo on 'Rip, Rig And Panic' is one of his very best on record. On the final 'Mystical Dream', Kirk plays stritch, tenor and, incredibly, oboe at the same time, posing articulation and harmonic problems that would have sunk a less complete musician.

Fine as it is, there seems little point in going for the vinyl *Now Please Don't You Cry* unless you've already invested in the ten-CD *Rahsaan*. If not, *Rip, Rig And Panic* is a must.

***(*) The Inflated Tear Atlantic 7567 81396

Kirk; Ron Burton (*p*); Steve Novosel (*b*); Jimmy Hopps (*d*). 5/68.

One of the finest of all Kirk's albums, it is also one of the most contained and straightforward, establishing his gifts as an improviser beyond all contradiction. The title-track relates to his blindness and conveys the dreamlike oddity and human passion of his music to perfection. The band are by no means top-drawer, but Kirk had a happy knack not just of getting the best out of players but also of subtly adapting his own delivery to the men round him. An ideal place to begin if you've never heard a note of Kirk; but prepare for surprises elsewhere. The CD sound is pretty good.

** The Case Of The Three-sided Dream In Audio Color Atlantic 1674

Kirk; Pat Patrick (*bs*); Cornell Dupree, Keith Loving, Hugh McCracken (*g*); Arthur Jenkins, Hilton Ruiz, Richard Tee (*ky*); Francisco Centeno, Henry Metathias Pearson, Bill Salter (*b*); Sonny Brown, Steve Gadd, John Goldsmith (*d*); Lawrence Killian; Ralph McDonald (*perc*).

This later album is disappointing. The much-hyped *Three-sided Dream* was a self-conscious bid to bring Kirk to the attention of rock audiences. The cover-art was a good match for his surrealist approach, but the arrangements are too flabby for the imaginative suite-like approach, and the performance as a whole tumbles between two stools. Given that Kirk could almost always levitate in exactly that position, its failure is all the more galling.

***(*) Volunteered Slavery Rhino R2 71407

Kirk; Charles McGhee (*t*); Dick Griffin (*tb*); Ron Burton (*p*); Vernon Martin (*b*); Charles Crosby, Sonny Brown, Jimmy Hopps (*d*); Joe Habao Texidor (*perc*); Roland Kirk Spirit Choir (*v*). 7/69.

***(*) Blacknuss Rhino R2 71408

Kirk; Charles McGhee (*t*); Dick Griffin (*tb*); Richard Tee, Sonelius Smith (*p*); Mickey Tucker (*org*); Cornell Dupree, Billy Butler, Keith Loving (*g*); Henry Metathias Pearson, Bill Salter (*b*);

Bernard Purdie, Khalil Mhridri (*d*); Richard Landrum, Joe Habao Texidor, Arthur Jenkins (*perc*); Cissy Houston, Princess Patience Burton (*v*). 8 & 9/71.

*** **Bright Moments** Rhino R2 71409 2CD

Kirk; Ron Burton (*p*); Todd Barkan (*syn, perc*); Henry Metathias Pearson (*b*); Robert Shy (*d*); Joe Habao Texidor (*perc*). 6/73.

These are the records which brought Kirk to a wider audience in the 1970s but which maintained a degree of creative integrity that was lost on nonsense like *The Case Of The Three-sided Dream*. There were signs of failing powers even before the debilitating stroke of 1975. *Bright Moments* is disconcertingly bland (and overlong, scarcely justifying two CDs-worth) and for the first time Kirk's multi-instrumentalism began to seem a mere gimmick. Ironically, the most obvious effect of the stroke was to throw him back into much straighter playing.

He is at his best on *Volunteered Slavery*: five powerful studio tracks, followed by a set from the 1968 Newport Festival, at which Kirk played a deeply felt and touching 'Tribute To John Coltrane', before finishing with his own 'Three For The Festival'. There is nothing quite so powerful on *Blacknuss*, but it holds up triumphantly as a record. Kirk was playing a lot of pop tunes at this point. On *Blacknuss* he includes Marvin Gaye's 'What's Goin' On' and 'Mercy Mercy Me'; on *Slavery*, Burt Bacharach's 'I Say A Little Prayer' and Stevie Wonder's 'My Cherie Amour'. Though doubtless under a certain amount of pressure from the label to do so, he sounds completely comfortable with the slight change of emphasis, and throws in old spirituals and hymn tunes as well. What it essentially does is reassert the continuity of Afro-American music; to give just one example, the Cissy Houston who sings on 'Never Can Say Goodbye' and 'Blacknuss' itself is the mother of present-day pop star Whitney Houston.

Some of the arrangements are a little guitar-heavy and the backbeats are decidedly uncouth, but Kirk can transcend difficulties of that sort. These are by no means peripheral to his main output.

Ryan Kisor (born 1973) TRUMPET, FLUGELHORN

*** **Minor Mutiny** Columbia CK 48796

Kisor; Ravi Coltrane (*ss, ts*); Michael Cain (*p*); Lonnie Plaxico (*b*); Jeff Siegel (*d*); Jack DeJohnette (*d, ky*). 92.

***(*) **On The One** Columbia CK 53563 / 473768-2

Kisor; Chris Potter (*as*); Mark Turner, David Sanchez (*ts*); Mulgrew Miller (*p*); Christian McBride (*b*); Lewis Nash (*d*). 93.

Kisor was the youthful winner of a 1990 trumpet competition, and at nineteen he made his first record, *Minor Mutiny*. It's an impressive start. He has no difficulties at any tempo, has a strong tone (and, unusually, an equally full sound on flugelhorn) and he plays a risky hand in many of his improvisations. The first disc drew some accusations of copying Miles Davis – and the first track is called 'One For Miles', even if it is a steal from 'Well You Needn't' – but Kisor doesn't seek any of Davis's idiosyncrasies. He's very schooled, which might take some of the edge off his playing, but in the context of these excellent bands he still makes a lot of exciting music. Ravi Coltrane has seldom sounded better on record so far, and the rhythm section play fiercely and accurately, though Siegel's drums are too busy by half on the likes of 'Little Nick' (DeJohnette, who drums on two tracks, produced the record).

On The One was produced by Bobby Watson, who chooses a less upfront sound. This session sites Kisor as more of a member of the band, with the admirable Potter, Turner and Sanchez in comparable roles. Not quite a cutting contest, but the horns work up some terrific blowing on 'Remembering Tomorrow' in particular, while Kisor shows his gift for a ballad on a charming 'Darn That Dream' duet with Miller.

Miriam Klein VOCAL

*** **Ladylike** MPS 523379-2

Klein; Roy Eldridge (*t*); Slide Hampton (*tb*); Dexter Gordon (*ts*); Vince Benedetti (*p*); Oscar Klein (*g*); Isla Eckinger (*b*); Billy Brooks (*d*). 5/73.

Klein's singing was almost irresponsibly close to that of Billie Holiday, and with this band and a set of Billie-associated tunes the illusion is close to complete. But this is still a good record. She has the dawdling phrasing, lazy vibrato and vague slur captured perfectly, but she misses the abject pathos – and many will welcome that, at least. This was a one-off for the MPS label and the reissue revives the excellent original sound. Eldridge, Hampton and Gordon were hired guns for the occasion and all played rather well, the trumpeter in particular forgoing much of the inconsistency that marred his later work.

Goran Klinghagen (born 1955) GUITAR

*** Time Again Dragon DRCD 247

> Klinghagen; David Wilczewski (*ss, ts*); Lars Jansson (*p*); Bruno Raberg (*b*); Magnus Gran (*d*).

The opening track, 'Include', is one of those set-pieces that linger long in the mind. After a rambling introduction, the music settles into a shifting groove in which Wilczewski's soprano picks out a melody against Klinghagen's lonesome guitar arpeggios. The record is never quite as haunting as this again, though it's an interesting showcase for the guitarist's range, from Hendrix licks to the kind of windswept impressionism that Terje Rypdal made his own 20 years earlier. Jansson guests on one track only.

Eric Kloss (born 1949) ALTO AND TENOR SAXOPHONES

***(*) Eric Kloss And The Rhythm Section Prestige PRCD-24125-2

> Kloss; Chick Corea (*ky*); Pat Martino (*g*); Dave Holland (*b*); Jack DeJohnette (*d*). 7/69–1/70.

Kloss caused ripples of excitement when he arrived on the American scene in the late 1960s, but most of his 10 Prestige albums have been in limbo for many years. This CD doubles up two of them, *To Hear Is To See!* (a discreet reference to Kloss's blindness) and *Consciousness!*, both faintly reminiscent of the beatific aspirations of the day but filled with hard-edged blowing that teeters on a line between bop and the oncoming explorations of Miles Davis's electric music. Given the rhythm-section personnel, this was hardly a surprise: Holland and DeJohnette lay down some of their funkiest parts (and they're recorded rather better than they were by Teo Macero with Miles), and Corea's almost minimalist electric piano cushions the harshness of Kloss's solos. Martino arrives for the second session, which opens on the bizarre choice of Donovan's 'Sunshine Superman'. No problem, though, since the quintet pile into it, Kloss lets go with some of his greasiest licks and they almost succeed in turning it into a blues. Most of the music rockets along on this path, and perhaps the insistent tightness palls a little in the way that some of Gene Ammons's record do, but it's a fine example of the style. Several other strong albums by Kloss – especially the terrific blow-out with Booker Ervin, *In The Land Of The Giants* – would still be welcome as reissues, but no sign of them since our last edition.

Kerry Kluner TRUMPET, FLUGELHORN

**(*) Live At The West End Cultural Centre Justin Time JTR 8436-2

> Kluner; David Jackson, David Lawton, David Dutka, Richard Boughton (*t, flhn*); Ray Egan, Hubert Grenier, Rob Browne (*tb*); Michael Joyce (*btb*); Paquito D'Rivera (*as, cl, EWI*); Ken Gold (*ss, as, f*); Ely Herscovitch (*as, f*); Brian Klowak, Bill Prouten (*ts, f*); Julie Husband (*bs, f*); Marilyn Lerner (*ky*); Tim Cummings (*g*); Gille Fournier (*b*); Tony Cyre (*d*); Paul Cerilli, Carlos Diaz (*perc*). 3/91.

Although there are a couple of real successes from this skilful Canadian orchestra – the 'Suite For Jazz Orchestra', which refines Kenton-like exaggerations into a convincing whole, and the hard-hitting but well-tempered 'Europa' – too much of this music stands as prepackaged big-band excitement, with the section-work regimentally precise and the arrangements fussily exact. This is meat and drink to the guest soloist, Paquito D'Rivera, whose insouciant solos are as overheated as usual, and will evoke either exhilaration or irritation according to taste. When he takes a back-seat role, as in the 'Suite', the band sound better, which suggests they might need a studio date on their own.

Jimmy Knepper (born 1927) TROMBONE

**(*) Cunningbird Steeplechase SCCD 31060

> Knepper; Al Cohn (*ts*); Roland Hanna (*p*); George Mraz (*b*); Dannie Richmond (*d*). 11/76.

*** Special Relationship Hep CD2012

> Knepper; Bobby Wellins (*ts*); Joe Temperley (*bs, ts*); Pete Jacobsen, Derek Smith (*p*); Dave Green, Michael Moore (*b*); Billy Hart, Ron Parry (*d*). 10/78, 11/80.

***(*) I Dream Too Much Soul Note 121092

> Knepper; John Eckert (*t*); John Clark (*frhn*); Roland Hanna (*p*); George Mraz (*b*); Billy Hart (*d*). 2 & 3/84.

*** Dream Dancing Criss Cross Jazz Criss 1024

> Knepper; Ralph Moore (*ts*); Dick Katz (*p*); George Mraz (*b*); Mel Lewis (*d*). 4/86.

Long associated with Charles Mingus, Knepper has an astonishingly agile technique (based on altered slide positions) which allows him to play extremely fast lines with considerable legato, more like a saxophonist than a brass player. Doing so has allowed him to avoid the dominant J. J. Johnson style and to develop the swing idiom in a direction that is thoroughly modern and contemporary, with a bright, punchy tone.

A dramatic contretemps with Mingus drove him out of active jazz performance for some time, and much of the next decade was spent in the relative obscurity of recording sections and theatre work. *Cunningbird* effectively marked his renaissance as a soloist and leader. It's a fine, strong album, though Knepper's tone isn't quite as assured here as it became in the 1980s, and Al Cohn is below par.

Mraz's firm melodic sense makes him the ideal accompanist, but Knepper has also been shrewd or lucky in his choice of drummers. Hart has the right kind of swing and Richmond is endlessly adaptable; an initial question mark about Lewis's big sound on *Dream Dancing* resolves into an ignorable quirk of the mix, which could be rectified on what would be a welcome CD transfer. It's not quite the best of the bunch, but it's still a fine album. Ralph Moore still had some growing to do, but he didn't make the mistake of doing it in the studio, concentrating on playing within his perfectly respectable limits.

The beautifully arranged brass tonalities of *I Dream Too Much* make it Knepper's most ambitious and fulfilling album. Hanna's comping is first rate throughout, though he isn't very generously placed in the mix on *Cunningbird*.

Special Relationship, as the name and personnel imply, is a transatlantic project, two quintets of respectively Americans and Brits, though Joe Temperley really falls into both categories. Bobby Wellins (strictly speaking, a Scot) is the star turn here. His tone is as airy as ever and his soloing on 'Round About Midnight' and 'Latterday Saint' underlines once again what a loss his absences from the scene always were. Knepper plays against him with great delicacy and control, reserving his more expansive gestures for the sessions with an engagingly gruff and even impatient-sounding Temperley.

Jonas Knutsson SOPRANO, ALTO, TENOR AND BARITONE SAXOPHONES

*** **Views** Caprice CAP 21426
> Knutsson; Lars Lindgren (*t, flhn*); Mikael Raberg (*tb*); Joakim Milder (*ss*); Jan Levander (*as*); Johan Soderqvist, Mats Oberg (*ky*); Anders Persson (*p*); Per Westerlund, Max Schultz, Hakan Wyoni (*g*); Olle Steinholtz, Christian Spering (*b*); Magnus Gran, Martin Löfgren, Michael Hedenquist (*d*); Bengt Berger, Rafael Sida (*perc*); Lena Willemark (*v*). 1–2/92.

*** **Lust** Caprice CAP 21459
> Knutsson; Mats Oberg (*ky, hca*); Hakan Wyoni (*g, perc*); Mikael Berglund (*b*); Michael Hedenquist (*d*); Rafael Sida (*perc*). 9/94.

Knutsson's is a kind of digital folk music. His themes and arrangements suggest an ancient Swedish strain – and there are three traditional tunes on the second record – but the timbre of the music is modern, electric and high on texture. His main instrument is soprano sax and he uses it as a piper might, chanting elegant melodies against a backdrop of keyboards, resonant electric bass and occasional other horns: the first track on *Views* finds him alongside Milder, Levander, Lindgren and Raberg in a bracing swirl of voices. But his own writing tends towards an impressionism that goes soft some of the time. The only other memorable piece on the first disc is the lovely duet with Oberg's piano and bubbling synthesizer on 'Vadring'; elsewhere, Knutsson relies heavily on programmatic effects.

The second set is more of a fusion-band session, even settling into a little gentle funk on 'Loff', although it's the more restrained and songful pieces, like the mildly affecting 'Hymn', which linger longest in the mind. Knutsson himself is an impeccable performer on soprano, and it would be interesting to hear him in a more straight-ahead situation.

Hans Koch TENOR AND SOPRANO SAXOPHONES, CLARINET, BASS CLARINET

** **Acceleration** ECM 1357
> Koch; Martin Schutz (*b, clo*); Marco Käppeli (*d*). 6/87.
**** **Uluru** Intakt CD 014
> Koch (solo). 1/89.
**** **Duets, Dithyrambisch** FMP CD 19/20
> Koch; Louis Sclavis (*ss, bcl*); Evan Parker (*ts*); Wolfgang Fuchs (*sno, cbcl*). 7/89.
(*) **The Art Of The Staccato sound aspects sas CD 033
> As for *Acceleration*. 1/90.

Until the appearance of the utterly marvellous *Uluru*, Koch was heard to best advantage on the FMP record, *Duets, Dithyrambisch*, with Evan Parker and Louis Sclavis, which has only recently been restored to the catalogue. The Englishman is, of course, a completely intuitive and sympathetic partner, but Sclavis also has things to say for himself, and Koch revels in the moment. On the 1989 record he creates a bewildering variety of voices with his three horns. 'Whirly Bird' and 'Tongue Salad' are both virtuosic, but there are more accessible things as well. There is some harsh, interesting music on both *Acceleration* (well named) and *Staccato* (likewise). Schutz and Käppeli play a subsidiary but highly interactive role: on the ECM album, against some ponderous improvising by Koch on a variety of horns, they work up a vivid rhythm partnership. But the programming of that album, with dreary interludes such as the clarinet solo on 'Loisada', lets it down. The sound aspects disc is rather better, the trio working more cohesively and Koch's improvisations breathing more freely in the air surrounding cello and drums, but finally nothing too special.

Franz Koglmann TRUMPET, FLUGELHORN

**** **Schlaf Schlemmer, Schlaf Magritte** hat Art CD 6108
 Koglmann; Rudolf Ruschel (*tb*); Erich Saufnauer (*frhn*); Raoul Herget (*tba*); Georg Lehner (*ob*); Theo Jorgensmann (*cl*); Roberto Ottaviano (*ss*); Robert Michael Weiss (*p*); Klaus Koch (*b*); Peter Barborik (*d*). 12/84.

*** **Ich** hat Art 6033
 Koglmann; Rudolf Ruschel (*tb*); Martin Mayes (*frhn*); Raoul Herget (*tba*); Mario Arcadi (*ob*); Martin Schelling (*cl*); Roberto Ottaviano (*ss*); Robert Michael Weiss (*p*); Klaus Koch (*b*); Peter Barborik (*d*). 10/86.

**** **About Yesterday's Ezzthetics** hat Art 6003
 Koglmann; Steve Lacy (*ss*); Mario Arcadi (*ob*); Klaus Koch (*b*); Fritz Hauser (*d, perc*). 4/87.

*** **Orte Der Geometrie** hat Art 6018
 Koglmann; Rudolf Ruschel (*tb*); Jean-Christoph Mastnak (*frhn*); Raoul Herget (*tba*); Mario Arcadi (*ob*); Martin Schelling (*cl*); Roberto Ottaviano (*ss*); Guillermo Gregorio (*as*); Ran Blake, Robert Michael Weiss (*p*); Burkhard Stangl (*g*); Klaus Koch (*b*); Fritz Hauser (*d*). 11/88.

**** **A White Line** hat Art 6048
 Koglmann; Jean-Christoph Mastnak (*frhn*); Raoul Herget (*tba*); Mario Arcadi (*ob*); Tony Coe (*cl, ts*); Helmut Federle (*acc*); Paul Bley (*p*); Burkhard Stangl (*g*); Klaus Koch (*b*); Gerry Hemingway (*d*); Gustav Bauer (*cond*). 11/89.

**** **The Use Of Memory** hat Art 6078
 Koglmann Pipetet. 90

**** **L'Heure Bleue** hat Art 6093
 Koglmann; Tony Coe (*cl, ts*); Burkhard Stangl (*g*); Klaus Koch (*b*); Misha Mengelberg (*p*). 4/91.

**** **Canto I–IV** hat Art CD 6123
 Koglmann; Richard Mitterer (*t*); Rudolf Ruschel (*tb*); Jean-Christoph Mastnak, Tom Varner (*frhn*); Raoul Herget (*tba*); Mario Arcari (*ob, eng hn*); Martin Schelling (*cl*); Roberto Ottaviano (*ss*); Guillermo Gregorio (*as*); Tony Coe (*ts, cl*); Hans Steiner (*bcl*); Robert Michael Weiss (*p, syn*); Burkhard Stangl (*g*); Klaus Koch (*b*); Gerry Hemingway (*d*); Karl Fischer (*perc, vib*). 10/92.

***(*) **We Thought About Duke** hat Art CD 6163
 Koglmann; Rudolf Ruschel (*tb*); Raoul Herget (*tba*); Lee Konitz (*as*); Tony Coe (*cl, ts*); Burkhard Stangl (*g*); Klaus Koch (*b*). 6/94.

With important recent recordings by Anthony Braxton, Steve Lacy, Cecil Taylor, David Murray, Georg Gräwe, Joe McPhee and the late Warne Marsh in its catalogue, the Swiss-based hat Art label has become the locus of one of the most comprehensive re-examinations of the jazz tradition currently in progress. In contrast to the others, Austrian flugelhorn player Franz Koglmann is a label discovery. He may yet turn out to be one of the most significant jazz revisionists of the 1990s.

 It's clear that he is undertaking that revision from outside the jazz tradition proper; given that, he almost inevitably picks on the work of jazz outsiders: Richard Twardzik on *A White Line*, George Russell extensively on the manifesto-like *About Yesterday's Ezzthetics*; he also makes frequent reference to literary and plastic artists, as in the title of the wonderful *Schlaff Schlemmer, Schlaff Magritte*. Koglmann is not primarily an improviser and his bleakly sentimental attachment to Bix is, on the face of it, rather strange. His charts are meticulously detailed and increasingly (a dead giveaway) scored without drums; Gerry Hemingway makes only sporadic and rather abstract contributions to *A White Line* and Koglmann doesn't seem to know what to do with Barborik or even with the splendidly inventive Hauser on earlier albums. His models are primarily 'cool' and 'progressive'; *White Line* – cited again because it seems to have been his breakthrough record – includes Shorty Rogers, Gerry Mulligan and Stan Kenton materials; earlier, Johnny Carisi's newborn-cool 'Israel' was included on *Orte Der Geometrie*. However, recent evidence is that he is working through from the almost Webernian sparseness and stillness of the earlier records to a richer (and, dare one say it, more humane) feel.

Any sense, though, that Koglmann started out as a desiccated desecrator of the jazz tradition can be dispelled by the reissued *Schlaff Schlemmer*, a dreamy and elusive set that remains the most purely emotional thing the trumpeter has recorded. The opening piece, 'The Moon Is Hiding In Her Hair', based on a poem by e. e. cummings, is a contemporary classic, full of tiny lower-case gestures.

Ich and *Orte Der Geometrie* are not quite satisfactory, marking a significant step backwards from the remarkable compression and intelligence of *About Yesterday's Ezzthetics* and the inventive early trio. Ran Blake, who has done similar work to Koglmann on the Gershwin songbook, appears as a guest on a new and yet more melancholy version of his own 'Short Life Of Barbara Monk'. There's much less overt standard material here, and a good deal of the music could be updated Third Stream. 'My Funny Valentine', with nods to both Chet Baker and Miles Davis, sets *Ich* back on a jazz parallel, but the cue isn't really followed and the record slowly evaporates in a series of precise but insubstantial meditations.

The Use Of Memory could have been put together only by a European of a particular age. A shoring of jazz fragments against the ruins of the European tradition, it begs the question, how some of the themes came to be broken in the first place. Listening to it is rather like sifting through a rich but chaotic archaeological dig or trying to solve two or three jigsaw puzzles whose pieces have been mixed in a single box. Koglmann's flugelhorn has an almost valedictory air, poised as if prepared to fade on any of the tiny thematic segments it handles. *L'Heure Bleue*, his finest record to date, to a large extent puts the pieces back together. New and old themes are recalled at twilight. Coe's clarinet carries the title-piece almost single-handed, and there are extraordinarily beautiful duet performances with Misha Mengelberg of 'My Old Flame', Tony Fruscella's 'Baite', and the originals, 'Slow Fox' and 'Nachts'. The guitarist's four-note encodement of the opening 'Leopard Lady' is the most obvious insight yet into Koglmann's method. Also included are 'Night And Day', Ellington's 'Black Beauty' and Ralph Richardson's 'It Ain't Easy'; and there is a further dedication 'For Bix', which gets ever closer to the spirit of thing.

With *Cantos*, Koglmann effectively bids jazz adieu and strikes out into new territory. Scored for the largest version of the Pipetet to date, it sweeps along in a grand, abstract manner that sounds like a triple distillation of all the music which has preceded it. There is no point picking out soloists, since the writing is so tight and individual passages so carefully integrated into the overall fabric. Recently, Koglmann has repeated his conviction that jazz, like film, is a phenomenon of the twentieth century and is unlikely to survive it. To those who regard this as fashionable apocalypticism, he points out that the great works in any genre – Baroque music, Elizabethan drama – are made when that genre appears to be exhausted. There seems little doubt that Koglmann will have his place in whatever music is being made in the new millennium.

The 'we' in the title of the Ellington tribute includes Lee Konitz, who is credited as joint leader. The saxophonist has worked in very similar territory – cool to abstract – over recent years and sounds like a soulmate, albeit better adjusted to the so-called Monoblue Quartet of Koglmann, Coe, Stangl and Koch than to the stripped-down Pipe Trio who're credited with the other five tracks. Koglmann contributes three original compositions under the generic heading, 'Thoughts About Duke', and otherwise explores the less familiar reaches of the ducal canon. 'Dirge' and 'Zweet Zurzday' bear the counter-signature of Billy Strayhorn and 'Pyramid' is a Tizol tune; otherwise, it's 'Lament For Javanette', 'Ko-Ko', 'Love In My Heart' and 'The Mooche'. All are beautifully played and atmospheric, as you'd expect by now.

Eero Koivistoinen (born 1941) TENOR SAXOPHONE

*** **Picture In Three Colors** Core Records/Line COCD 9.00515
 Koivistoinen; Tom Harrell (*t, flhn*); John Scofield (*g*); Jim McNeely (*p*); Ron McClure (*b*); Jack DeJohnette (*d*). 10/83.

*** **Altered Things** Timeless SJP CD 367
 Koivistoinen; Randy Brecker (*t*); Conrad Herwig (*tb*); John Scofield (*g*); David Kikoski (*p*); Bugge Wesseltoft (*syn*); Ron McClure (*b*); Jack DeJohnette (*b*). 9/91.

***(*) **Dialog** L + R CDLR 45094
 Koivistoinen; Anders Bergcrantz (*t*); Seppo Kantonen (*p*); Jesper Lundgaard (*b*); Leroy Lowe (*d*). 1/94.

Koivistoinen, who has yet to make much of a mark on the international scene, has a pungent, spicy tone that is deceptively 'American' in accent; certainly, his kinship with the dominant Garbarek approach is rather fleeting and he veers towards a free style that dispenses with orthodox changes.

The line-ups alone are a virtual guarantee of quality on these. DeJohnette is relaxed and attentive to the spaces in Koivistoinen's impressive charts, creating abstract figurations within the basic sequence. Harrell has rarely sounded more haunted than he does on *Picture* but is in excellent voice, and Brecker is only a rather one-dimensional replacement.

The only quibble is the co-presence of McNeely and Scofield. Given the nature of the music, it might have been preferable to dispense with a keyboard instrument and rely more heavily on the less formalized chording and high accents of the guitarist who is replacing John Abercrombie as the player of choice for this kind of gig. Sco makes a big impact on the second record, but without theatricals. He's rarely been so contained and subtle, and the whole set is very much lighter in touch than its predecessor, though this may also have something to do with the first-rate production.

On *Dialog*, Koivistoinen shares the honours with trumpeter Bergcrantz, an agile enough player whose real ace is a big rich tone that sits beautifully with saxophone. On the evidence of 'Home', 'Sinuhe' and 'All Those Dreams', he also writes well. The (nominal) leader takes a more relaxed attitude on this date, lying back a bit and easing into solos with a conversational quality that is as attractive as it is unexpected. The rhythm section, anchored on Lowe, who looks as though he might have considered pro basketball as an alternative, is solid through and through. The only problem is Kantonen's tendency to use every good idea at least three times, as if we might have misheard.

Hans Koller (born 1921) TENOR SAXOPHONE, SOPRANO SAXOPHONE, SOPRANINO SAXOPHONE

**(*) Out On The Rim In + Out 7014
  Koller; Wolfgang Puschnig (*as*); Martin Fuss, Warne Marsh (*ts*); Klaus Dickbauer (*ts, bs*);
  Bernd Konrad (*bsx, as*). 84, 3, 5 & 6/91.
One of the most remarkable figures in modern jazz, Koller's career began under the shadow of Nazism. Hitler's *Anschluss* had swallowed the saxophonist's native Austria and proscribed jazz as 'Judaeo–Negroid' degeneracy. Koller played on regardless and became one of the beacons of post-war American jazz, playing in a personalized Cool School manner that increasingly took on modernist inflexions, the most notable of which was John Coltrane's impact on Koller's tenor saxophone playing.

In 1993 Koller was the subject of a major three-day retrospective in his native Vienna. There's still next to nothing available on record. The L + R LPs are now all going or gone, and there is only this all-saxophone disc, some of which is admirably intelligent and well played, while some of the rest is a disagreeable racket. The title-piece runs through the record and consists of detailed variations on the same few ideas. It's a not uninteresting exercise but, unusually for Koller, it's almost entirely uninvolving. The album has one historical gem, an exercise in the 'All The Things You Are' changes with Warne Marsh, for whom it becomes a memorial, recorded in Luxemburg. More like that might have made a rescue plan.

Kolner Saxophon Mafia GROUP

**** Die Eiserne Nachtigall Jazz Haus Musik JHM 28
  Joachim Ullrich (*ts, cl, bcl*); Gerhard Veeck (*as, ss, bs, f*); Norbert Stein (*ts, ss*); Armin Tretter (*as, bs, cl, acl, f*); Wollie Kaiser (*ts, bcl, cbcl, picc*). 11/86.
*** Baboma Jazz Haus Musik JHM 33
  As above, except omit Tretter; add Roger Haenschel (*as, f, sno, v*); Stefan Bauer (*vib, mar, syn, v*);
  Christoph Heberer, Michael Peters (*d, perc, v*); Manzanza Tsakala, Pelo Yika, Monzali
  Yabusele, Ikonola Iko-Ja, Desa Jose (*perc, v*). 8/88.
***(*) Saxfiguren Jazz Haus Musik JHM 36
  As above, except add only Haenschel. 8/89.
*** Proudly Presents Jazz Haus Musik JHM 46
  As above; with guest musicians and groups. 90–91.
**** Mafia Years, 1982-1986 Jazz Haus Musik JHM 58
  As above. 82-92 [sic].
*** Go Commercial Jazz Haus Musk JHM 65
  As above. 9/93.
. . . which should of course read Kolner Saxophon Members of the Italian Business Community. These arch surrealists are the German equivalent of Willem Breuker's Kollekteif in the Netherlands, a mixture of theatre troupe and new music ensemble, with elements of circus, marching band and other stuff thrown in. The most multi-media of the records – and thus in a sense the most authentic – is the celebratory *Proudly Presents*. There is a useful, if oddly dated, compilation on *Mafia Years*, but the very best of the records musically is the first. 'The Iron Nightingale' and the 'Second Concerto for Five Instruments' (both titles translated) are a reasonable sampling of what the group is about: lots of sound up and down the scale, some polyphonic stuff, some roaring unisons, little in the way of conventional theme-plus-solo improvisation. A heady mix, but not for everybody.

Krzysztof Komeda (1931–69) PIANO

**** **Astigmatic** Power Bros 00125
Komeda; Tomasz Stańko (*t*); Zbigniew Namyslowski (*as*); Günter Lenz (*b*); Rune Carlsson (*d*). 12/65.
(***) **Live In Copenhagen** Polonia CDO 10/11 2CD
Komeda; Tomasz Stańko (*t*); Michal Urbaniak (*sax*); Bo Stief (*b*); Simon Kopel (*d*). 65.

Komeda is the Lost Leader of Polish jazz. A brilliant composer rather than a virtuosic player, he remains best known in the West for his film music; he wrote the scores for his friend and compatriot Roman Polanski's *Knife in the Water* and *Rosemary's Baby*, the latter a chillingly atmospheric piece of work that stands up surprisingly well as a soundtrack album.

Komeda was born Trzcinski and trained as an ear, nose and throat specialist. He changed his name to avoid the attentions of both the political and medical authorities, neither of whom would have taken kindly to his extracurricular activities; later, in America, he was to anglicize his first name to Christopher. In 1956 he made his musical debut at a small, semi-official jazz festival at the coastal town of Sopot in Poland, the forerunner to the now annual Jazz Jamboree in Warsaw. In 1960 he recorded a standards album with Adam Skorupka and Andrzej Zielinski.

The following year Komeda wrote the music for *Knife in the Water*, using the gifted Swedish saxophonist, Rosengren. 'Crazy Girl' became a favourite concert-piece and is included in a rather rambling version on the Copenhagen live set. It also includes disappointingly lax interpretations of themes from his masterpiece, *Astigmatic*, which in our view (now reinforced by expert remastering) is not just one of the best Polish or European jazz records, but quite simply one of the best jazz records, full stop. Komeda was at the height of his powers when he made the disc in 1965 and he had with him a sympathetic and highly gifted group of young Poles, including trumpeter Stańko, then making his professional debut. 'Kattorna' and 'Svantetic' are both highly original, combining jazz tonality with folk and classical idioms; however, it is 'Astigmatic' itself, a swirling, multi-part suite with a skewed, elusive quality, that represents his masterpiece. There is not so very much solo space devoted to Komeda himself and it is one of the ironies of his career that his importance is less as a performer than as a composer and catalyst.

The second soloist, Zbigniew Namyslowski, was replaced on the Scandinavian tour by Michal Urbaniak, who was then still playing saxophone. The Danish tapes were released by Komeda's widow for release to mark the 25th anniversary of his death. Unfortunately the tape quality is diabolical, with extraneous noise and unignorable dropouts. In addition, Urbaniak is playing poorly, leaving Stańko again to carry much of the weight of the music, which he does with characteristic fire.

Less than four years later, Komeda was brought home to Poland from the United States in a coma from which he never recovered. His death was a symbolic moment in the assimilation of jazz in Eastern Europe. Whether he would have succumbed to the lure of Hollywood or whether the embryo of another *Astigmatic* perished with him can never be known. What is certain is that he created one permanent masterwork.

Klaus Konig COMPOSER, CONDUCTOR

*** **Times Of Devastation / Poco A Poco** Enja ENJ 6014 2CD
Konig; Kenny Wheeler, Reiner Winterschladen (*t, flhn*); Ray Anderson, Bruce Collings (*tb*); Frank Struck (*frhn*); Michel Godard (*tba*); Marty Ehrlich (*cl, bcl, as*); Frank Gratkowski (*f, bcl, as, ss*); Matthias Schubert (*ts, ob*); Renato Cordovani, Michael Pilz (*bcl*); Simon Nabatov (*p*); Tim Wells (*b*); John Betsch, Frank Kollges (*d*). 6/89.
*** **At The End Of The Universe: Hommage A Douglas Adams** Enja ENJ 6078
Konig; Kenny Wheeler, Reiner Winterschladen (*t*); Conrad Bauer (*tb*); Horst Grabosch (*frhn*); Michel Massot (*tba*); Louis Sclavis (*cl*); Jane Ira Bloom (*ss*); Frank Gratkowski (*as, f*); Matthias Schubert (*ts, ob*); Wollie Kaiser (*bs*); Simon Nabatov (*p*); Dieter Manderscheid, Tim Wells (*b*); John Betsch, Tom Rainey (*d*). 3/91.
***(*) **Song Of Songs** Enja 7057
Konig; Herb Robertson (*t, flhn*); Reiner Winterschladen (*t*); Bruce Collings, Jorg Huke (*tb*); Michel Godard (*tba*); Jay Clayton, Phil Minton, Montreal Jubilation Gospel Choir (*v*); James Newton (*f*); Frank Gratkowski (*ss, as, f, bcl*); Michael Moore (*cl, as*); Matthias Schubert (*ts, ob*); Wollie Kaiser (*bsx, cbcl*); Marc Ducret (*g*); Simon Nabatov (*p*); Mark Dresser (*b*); Tom Rainey (*d*). 11/92.
**** **Time Fragments** Enja ENJ 8076
Konig; Reiner Winterschladen (*t*); Kenny Wheeler (*t, flhn*); Jorg Huke (*tb*); Michel Godard (*tba*); Frank Gratkowski (*as, ss, f*); Matthias Schubert (*ts, ob*); Wollie Kaiser (*ss, bcl*); Robert

Dick (*f, picc*); Mark Feldman (*vn*); Stefan Bauer (*mar*); Mark Dresser (*b*); Gerry Hemingway (*d*). 5/94.

The individual sections of *Time Fragments* are dedicated to some of Klaus Konig's heroes, past and present: Alban Berg and Charles Mingus, Thelonious Monk and Béla Bartók, Igor Stravinsky and Anthony Braxton, Duke Ellington and Charles Ives, Henry Threadgill and Gustav Mahler, Scott Joplin and Maurice Ravel. Pausing only to wonder what Threadgill and the Gloomy Gus of classical music might find to talk about, mix and serve.

These are remarkable records, conceived and confected by a genuine original. Konig's charts are multi-layered, poly-stylistic and densely detailed. The Braxton/Stravinsky/Ellington/Ives axes are probably the most helpful to an understanding of what is going on. There is a kind of neo-classical purity to the overall conception of what Konig describes as a cycle, to be completed by a piece called *Reviewed Reviews Revue*. There is also a hint of Braxton's open-ended jazz codes and of Ives's wonderful compression of tunes-from-unusual-angles. In terms of orchestration and *dramatis personae*, Duke is the significant forebear. Everything is written with a player in mind. The opening piece on *Time Fragments* has a wonderfully idiomatic solo for Michel Godard's tuba. It retrospectively establishes the parameters of the sound-world that is still chaotic and unshaped on *Times Of Devastation*. The first of the bunch is, properly, the weakest, an occasionally hesitant prolegomenon to the main action, though the hesitation is the players' and not the composer's.

At The End Of The Universe may be the weakest of the bunch, not because it is ostensibly tied to Douglas Adams's irritating stories or because the playing is off, which it isn't, but because the overall logic of the album fails to cohere as the others do with increasing confidence and definiteness. *Song Of Songs* also has an underlying programme, and the presence of a gospel choir gives the biblical subtext additional impact. The really successful piece, though, is *Time Fragments*, a marvellous (literally) romp through jazz and 'straight' styles. For once, a CD booklet actually turns out to be useful. A graphic schema of the piece really does help make sense of its overlapping layers, and it folds out to reveal a beautifully shot mini-poster of the band in action. The expression on Gerry Hemingway's face as he looks at the composer/conductor is worth a thousand words. And this is a man who played for Anthony Braxton night after night. Challenging, adventurous music; a little chill and formal for some tastes, but full of meat.

Lee Konitz (born 1927) ALTO SAXOPHONE, SOPRANO SAXOPHONE

***(*) **Lone-Lee** Steeplechase SCCD 31035
    Konitz solo. 8/74.

Most of the more casual generalizations about Lee Konitz – cool, abstract, passionless, untouched by bebop – were last relevant about 40 years ago. A stint in the Stan Kenton band, the musical equivalent of Marine Corps boot camp, toughened up his articulation and led him steadily away from the long, rather diffuse lines of his early years under the influence of Lennie Tristano, towards an altogether more pluralistic and emotionally cadenced approach.

Astonishingly, Konitz spent a good many of what should have been his most productive years in relative limbo, teaching when he should have been playing, unrecognized by critics, unsigned by all but small European labels (on which he is, admittedly, prodigal). Despite (or because of) his isolation, Konitz has routinely exposed himself over the years in the most ruthlessly unpredictable musical settings, thriving on any challenge, constantly modifying his direction.

Even three years after the release of Anthony Braxton's ground-breaking *For Alto*, solo saxophone performance was still considered a radical strategy. Konitz's unaccompanied treatment of just two standards – 'Cherokee' and 'The Song Is You' – contains some of his very best playing. Smooth legato passages are interspersed with harsher, almost percussive sections in which his pads snap down impatiently on the note. There are few if any hints of the free playing he essayed during a thoroughly unexpected collaboration with Derek Bailey's improvising collective Company in 1987; but there is a further dimension of freedom in his playing on the record that is rarely encountered elsewhere in his work. Even so, nowhere does he lose contact with the source material, which is transformed with a robust logic that never degenerates into pointless noodling. Recording quality is unexceptional and the CD sounds rather metallic.

***(*) **Subconscious-Lee** Original Jazz Classics OJC 186
    Konitz; Warne Marsh (*ts*); Sal Mosca, Lennie Tristano (*p*); Billy Bauer (*g*); Arnold Fishkin (*b*);
    Denzil Best, Shelly Manne, Jeff Morton (*d*). 1/49, 6/49, 9/49, 4/50.
***(*) **Quintets** Vogue 111503
    Konitz: Henri Renaud (*p*); Jimmy Gourley (*g*); Don Bagley (*b*); Stan Levey (*d*). 9/53.

*** **Jazz At Storyville** Black Lion BCD 760901
 Konitz; Ronnie Ball (*p*); Percy Heath (*b*); Al Leavitt (*d*). 1/54.
(*) **Konitz Black Lion BLCD 760922
 Konitz; Ronnie Ball (*p*); Peter Ind (*b*); Jeff Morton (*d*). 8/54.

Subconscious-Lee brings together material made under Lennie Tristano's leadership in January 1949, with quartet and quintet tracks made a few months later, featuring the wonderful Warne Marsh on the anything but redundant 'Tautology' and four other numbers. The remaining group material with Mosca and Bauer is less compelling (and certainly not as good as the 1951 sessions with Miles Davis on the deleted *Ezz-thetic*), but there is a fine duo with the guitarist on 'Rebecca' which anticipates some of the saxophonist's later intimacies.

The Paris sessions for Vogue are pretty good but have slightly more filler than meat. On a disc already shared with Bob Brookmeyer's five-in-hand group, Konitz is credited with 11 tracks, of which no fewer than six are alternative takes. There are four versions of 'I'll Remember April', three of 'All The Things You Are' and two of 'These Foolish Things'. Fascinating as they are, a more judicious selection might have trimmed them down a bit.

Konitz is a useful reminder of how the saxophonist sounded on demob from the Kenton orchestra. Multiple cuts of 'Mean To Me', 'Bop Goes The Leesel' (ouch!) and 'Nursery Rhyme' show to what extent he'd already reached an accommodation with some of the more intractable lessons of bebop and how far behind he'd left his initial thrall to Lennie Tristano. Morton and Ind are too mannerly even for this company. The *Storyville* band has some of the edge Konitz thrives on. 'Lee' puns abound in the track titles but 'These Foolish Things' and 'Foolin' Myself' are both first rate.

(There's an interesting Konitz track from the same period, but in the improbable company of Charles Mingus on an intriguing compilation called *Autobiography In Jazz*, Original Jazz Classics OJC 115; how self-revealing the saxophonist actually is remains a matter for conjecture.)

***(*) **Live At The Half Note** Verve 521 659 2CD
 Konitz; Warne Marsh (*ts*); Bill Evans (*p*); Jimmy Garrison (*b*); Paul Motian (*d*). 2 & 3/59.

Not released until 1994, these club tapes were made available on Verve's Discoveries imprint, dedicated to putting out previously unheard or rare material, irrespective of its acoustic polish. The music here is wonderful; the sound, you should be warned, is not, though no worse than many a classic club record.

The unfamiliar line-up is explained by Lennie Tristano's decision to reserve one night (Tuesday, for the record) as a teaching slot. Evans doesn't fit in all that comfortably and once or twice falls silent behind Konitz's choppy, enigmatic phrases; he does play magnificently on 'Subconscious-Lee', but often the group sounds like a trio, in anticipation of the hard-edged cool of *Motion*, Konitz's 1961 trio with Sonny Dallas and Elvin Jones. The other Motian plays well, in exactly the sort of multi-directional style that drew Konitz to Elvin a couple of years later.

Garrison, interestingly (and it must have something to do with the way the whole thing was miked up), is more audible on these cuts than on some of the 'classic' Coltrane material, where he was badly served. His bowed solo on 'Baby, Baby, All The Time' is a model of its sort. He seems as unlikely as Evans for this particular gig, but fits in well and adaptably.

Which leaves Warne Marsh. Unlike his fellow-saxophonist, he had remained loyal to the 'Tristano School' (Konitz was already a renegade) and plays here in a light, reflective manner that interestingly overlaps with Konitz's transitional idiom. It's one of those moments where stylistic changes can almost be heard happening, something musicians prefer to think critics only reconstruct, rationalize or plain invent later. There probably isn't really two CDs' worth of top-flight music here, but the historical importance of the moment justifies the extra length and (modest) cost.

***(*) **From Newport To Nice** Philology W 65
 Konitz; Warne Marsh (*ts*); Russ Freeman, Roland Kovac, Misha Mengelberg, Jimmy Rowles
 (*p*); Jimmy Raney, Johnny Smith, René Thomas, Attila Zoller (*g*); Frank Carroll, Bob Carter,
 Johnny Fischer, Henry Grimes, Rob Langereis, Red Mitchell, Barre Phillips (*b*); Han Bennink,
 Buzzy Drootin, Don Lamond, Ed Levinson, Shelly Manne, Stu Martin, Rudi Sehring (*d*). 7/55–
 7/80.

An odd but very valuable compilation of festival appearances from Newport in 1955 to the Grande Parade in the south of France 35 years later. The style has undergone some significant changes, of course, but it's less noticeable than one might expect. He's perfectly full-voiced on 'Two Not One' with Marsh at Newport, and he's perfectly capable of sounding dry and abstract when it suits his purpose in later years. Outstanding tracks? A long 'Lover Man' from Turin in 1978, with Jimmy Rowles in support, and a devilishly subtle and ironic 'All The Things You Are' with René Thomas, Misha Mengelberg and Han Bennink (the Low Countries Mafia) in 1965.

***(*) **The Lee Konitz Duets** Original Jazz Classics OJC 466
 Konitz, with Marshall Brown (*vtb, euph*); Joe Henderson, Richie Kamuca (*ts*); Dick Katz (*p*);

Karl Berger (*vib*); Jim Hall (*g*); Ray Nance (*vn*); Eddie Gomez (*b*); Elvin Jones (*d*). 9/67.
**** **I Concentrate On You** Steeplechase SCCD 1018
Konitz; Red Mitchell (*b, p*). 6/74.
***(*) **Windows** Steeplechase SCCD 31057
Konitz; Hal Galper (*p*). 77.
(*) **Once Upon A Line Musidisc 500162
Konitz; Harold Danko (*p*). 6/90.

Improvising duets fall somewhere between the intimacies of a private dinner and the disciplines of the boxing ring. If there are minor embarrassments in being overheard with, so to speak, the emotional gloves off, that's nothing to being caught out by a sudden rhythmic jab or harmonic cross from your partner; there's no band waiting in the corner. In a very real sense, the duo is Konitz's natural constituency. Perhaps only fellow alto saxophonist Marion Brown gets near him for sheer quality in a demanding setting that perfectly suits Konitz's balancing of almost conversational affability with a gimlet sharpness of thought.

On the 1967 record, Konitz comes on like a cross between an all-comers' booth boxer and a taxi dancer: a lover, not a fighter. The album pivots on five versions of the classic duo piece, 'Alone Together'; the first is solo, the next three duets with Karl Berger, Eddie Gomez, and with Elvin Jones (with whom he made the marvellous *Motion*), culminating in a fine quartet reading.

The pairings with saxophonists Joe Henderson ('You Don't Know What Love Is') and Richie Kamuca ('Tickle Toe'), and with trombonist Marshall Brown are astonishing, as far as possible from the comforting horn-plus-rhythm options, most of them refused, of the tracks with Dick Katz, Jim Hall, and even Ellingtonian Ray Nance (who plays his 'second' instrument). It all culminates in a fine, all-in nonet, an intriguing numerical anticipation of one of Konitz's best later bands.

Hal Galper's lush, velvety backgrounds inspire some of Konitz's most lapidary performances. There is very little harmonic tension in the pianist's approach, in contrast to Red Mitchell (on either double bass or piano), and the result is to focus Konitz very much on the tune rather than on its changes. That is particularly noticeable on 'Stella By Starlight'. Each man has one (improvised) solo slot; Konitz's 'Soliloquy' is a lean, un-self-indulgent exercise in low-fat improvisation and, as such, an illustration of the album's considerable strengths; Galper's 'Villainesque' is exactly the opposite, clotted like some multi-layered Viennese confection.

The duos with Harold Danko are more assured, but they suggest a polished concert performance rather than the more exploratory intrigues that Konitz foments with one-of partners, as if sounding them out and challenging them to try something different, come across to his bit of turf. 'Hi, Beck', based on the chords of 'Pennies From Heaven', has become an established set-opener, perhaps too familiar now to Konitz-watchers to reveal all the finessing he does on the top line. Danko is an adequate partner, but a desperately unexciting one; it's by no means the only instance of Konitz playing brilliantly in less than challenging contexts.

The Cole Porter readings with Red Mitchell explore equally familiar territory, but as if by night. Konitz clearly enjoys this kind of dead-reckoning performance and steers through the chords with finely tuned instinct. He also seems to like the extremes of pitch he gets opposite the notoriously straight-backed Mitchell, a man who prefers to play bass-as-bass, and it's a pity that the saxophonist wasn't currently toting a soprano instrument as well. Minor quibbles can't detract from the unfailing quality of the performances, which are absolutely top-notch. An essential Konitz album.

***(*) **Jazz A Juan** Steeplechase SCCD 1072
Konitz; Martial Solal (*p*); Niels-Henning Orsted- Pedersen (*b*); Daniel Humair (*d*). 7/74.
Top-of-the-range standards jazz by a marvellously Esperantist quartet. Solal is one of the great harmonists, with the ability to find anomalous areas of space within the most restrictively familiar themes; his statement and subsequent excursions on "Round About Midnight' are typical of his innate resistance to cliché. NHOP is the Terry Waite of jazz: big and bearded; willing to go anywhere; able to communicate in almost any company; a reconciler of opposites, gentle, but with a hard centre. His low notes behind 'Autumn Leaves' merit at least one listen with the 125-Hz slide on the graphic equalizer up at +10 and the rest zeroed. Konitz sounds relaxed and easy, flurrying breathy top notes and leaving space round the brighter middle register.

***(*) **Pyramid** Improvising Artists Inc 123845
Konitz; Paul Bley (*p*); Bill Connors (*g*). 77.
A welcome reissue from the influential IAI label, which specialized in this kind of Third Stream-ish abstraction. Konitz's dry, papery sound of the time blends well with the other two, both of whom use amplified instruments as well as acoustic. Konitz also doubles on soprano saxophone, most effectively on the duet with Connors, 'Tavia'. Cool, slightly academic music, of a sort one associates with Jimmy Giuffre, but with an unmistakable, deep-rooted swing. Connors is mainly used as a colourist. The sound is rather remote, but perfectly acceptable.

*** **Yes Yes Nonet** Steeplechase SCCD 31119
> Konitz; Tom Harrell (*t, flhn*); John Eckert (*t, picc t, flhn*); Jimmy Knepper (*tb*); Sam Burtis (*btb, tba*); Ronnie Cuber (*bs, cl*); Harold Danko (*p*); Buster Williams (*b*); Billy Hart (*d*). 8/79.

(*) **Live At Laren Soul Note 121069
> Konitz; Red Rodney (*t, flhn*); John Eckert (*t, picc t, flhn*); Jimmy Knepper (*tb*); Sam Burtis (*btb, tba*); Ronnie Cuber (*bs, cl*); Ben Aronov (*p, electric p*); Harold Danko (*p*); Ray Drummond (*b*); Billy Hart (*d*). 8/79.

The Nonet was one of Konitz's more successful larger groups. The brass settings were well ventilated and open-textured and Konitz soloed confidently, often oblivious to the constraints of metre. The Steeplechase is the better of the two (though the title is unforgivable), largely because Harrell sounds more sympathetic to Konitz's own conception; Wayne Shorter's 'Footprints' is the outstanding cut. On *Live At Laren*, generally a good concert rendering, the saxophonist rather too generously accommodates Rodney's rather backward-looking bop manner with what occasionally sound – on 'April' and 'Moon Dreams' – like pastiches of himself.

***(*) **Art Of The Duo** Enja ENJ 5059
> Konitz; Albert Mangelsdorff (*tb*). 6/83.

It's a pity that Konitz hadn't made the soprano saxophone a routine part of his travel-kit at this point. There's a slight lack of variation in pitching on these fascinating tracks, and there is certainly a tendency for Mangelsdorff to cleave to the same range as his partner. The pieces range from brief, song-form duets to more antagonistic and searching confrontations in which Konitz's acerbic wit and the trombonist's dry romanticism clash fruitfully.

***(*) **Dedicated To Lee** Dragon DRCD 250
> Konitz; Jan Allan (*t*); Gustavo Bergalli (*t, flhn*); Torgny Nilsson (*tb*); Hector Bingert (*ts*); Gunnar Bergsten (*bs*); Lars Sjosten (*p*); Lars Lundstrom (*b*); Egil Johansen (*d*). 11/83.

A decade before this session, Konitz had played on one of the last studio sessions by Lars Gullin. Though the great Swedish baritonist, who died in 1976, is widely acknowledged as one of the best European players of his day, his compositional output is still very little known. Hence the happy idea of putting Konitz together with Lars Sjosten's octet and a group of Gullin pieces.

Sjosten was Gullin's regular accompanist during the last decade and a half of his career, and he knows this material inside out. 'Dedicated To Lee' and 'Late Date' had actually been written for Konitz 30 years before, when the two saxophonists recorded in Stockholm; the originals are included on a Gullin composition issued by Dragon.

The immediate reaction to these tracks is that Gullin was a deceptively simple melodist. Pieces like 'Fine Together' and 'Happy Again' may be generic, and might have been written by any one of a dozen American song-writers, but 'Peter Of April' (dedicated to his son) is a subtle and masterful conception that is very difficult to reduce to its essential parts. A couple of pieces have been reconstructed from piano scores, which partly explains the inclusion of Jan Allan, a guest spot in thanks for bringing in the chart for 'Peter Of April'. Anyone who hasn't made Lars Gullin's acquaintance would be well advised to start sampling the Dragon discs (see above), but this is a very worthwhile piece on its own account, and the combination of Gullin and Konitz is, as ever, irresistible.

*** **Ideal Scene** Soul Note SN 1119
> Konitz; Harold Danko (*p*); Rufus Reid (*b*); Al Harewood (*d*). 7/86.

*** **The New York Album** Soul Note SN 1169
> Konitz; Harold Danko (*p*); Marc Johnson (*b*); Adam Nussbaum (*d*). 8/87.

Danko's exact chording and fine grasp of durations on *Ideal Scene* open up the challenging spaces of George Russell's 'Ezz-thetic' and the more familiar, but inexhaustible, 'Stella By Starlight'. He is more conventional but no less inventive on *The New York Album*. Constant duo performance tended to reinforce Konitz's early preference for very long, unpunctuated lines. Working with a band as closely attentive as both of these allows him to break up his development and give it an emotional directness which is reminiscent – in mood if not always in tonality – of the blues. Johnson's and Reid's moody delivery, and Nussbaum's almost casual two-fours on the later album, reinforce the slightly darker sound – 'Limehouse Blues' included! Hard to choose between them.

*** **Medium Rare** Label Bleu LBLC 6501
> Konitz; Dominique Cravic (*g*); Francis Varis (*acc*); Hélène Labarrière (*b*); Jean-Claude Jouy (*d*). 86.

Positively undercooked in places, but there's enough juicy substance from the mid-point 'Monk's Mood' onwards to keep eyes on the plate. 'Ezz-thetic' is marvellous again, one of the most imaginative covers the piece has ever received; 'Chick Came Round' also reappears from *Ideal Scene* (and is worth a brief comparison); and Dominique Cravic's three originals (notably the name-checking 'Blue Label', with its fine intro from Hélène Labarrière), are all excellent. The accordion functions very differently from a piano or even a vibraphone in the mix, keeping the harmonies from tightening up, laying on areas of colour, accentuating a softly shuffling rhythm. Konitz ranges between alto and soprano saxophones, with a tight clarinet sound in the higher registers which is exactly right for this company. Unusual and fine.

***(*) Round And Round Musicmasters 820804
Konitz; Fred Hersch (*p*); Mike Richmond (*b*); Adam Nussbaum (*d*). 88.
At sixty-plus, Konitz sounds relaxed and confident, using a broader embouchure for dramatic contrast, touching icons like Miles ('Someday My Prince Will Come') and Coltrane ('Giant Steps') with sureness and a hint of wry humour. With the exception of a fine 'Bluesette', there still isn't enough variation of tone; this would have seemed an ideal opportunity for some of Konitz's still-undervalued soprano saxophone.

***(*) 12 Gershwin In 12 Keys Philology W 312
Konitz; Franco D'Andrea (*p*). 12/88.
Exactly what it says it is. A round dozen Gershwin tunes in all the keys from A round to A &musflat; again with, tacked on, another Gershwin medley also recorded live, this time at Massalombarda. The Vicenza concert is utterly fascinating. Apparently the format was decided (by Konitz) at a pre-gig meal. Listening to Konitz drill his way through the familiar melodies, it's clearly the piano player who is having to think ahead, and he doesn't seem to know 'Our Love Is Here To Stay' or 'Love Walked In' as well as the rest, but D'Andrea has a secure technique and doesn't sound fazed. Something funny happens in 'But Not For Me'. Nominally in E &musflat;, it starts somewhere else and finishes up nowhere in particular, in an odd version of the atonal exercises Konitz must have done all those years ago with Lennie Tristano. A splendid disc, all the same.

*** Blew Philology W 26
Konitz; Enrico Pieranunzi (*p*); Enzo Pietropaoli (*b*); Alfred Kramer (*d*). 3/88.
A studio recording by the have-sax-will-travel Konitz and the highly professional Space Jazz Trio. The set has the feel of one put together in rather a hurry, though it seems to have followed a short residency at Rome's Big Mama club. Pieranunzi's 'From E To C' sounds a little like a back-of-envelope run-down (though the pianist plays it with great conviction and development) and the two standards at the end sound as if they have been tacked on *faute de mieux*. Konitz's tone is sharp and resonant, and very well captured by producer Piangiarelli.

*** Solitudes Philology W 28
Konitz; Enrico Pieranunzi (*p*).
In contrast with his earlier performances with Pieranunzi's Space Jazz Trio, Konitz plays with a rather thin detachment that doesn't quite fit in with the Italian's very proper phrasing and tight rhythmic control. Konitz almost sounds as if he has gone back to a version of the Lester Young-influenced cool he espoused at the beginning of his career. It would be interesting to hear him do it in a rather more promising context than this.

**** Zounds Soul Note 121219
Konitz: Kenny Werner (*p, ky*); Ron McClure (*b*); Bill Stewart (*d*). 5/90.
Konitz continues to surprise with three remarkable free improvisations on which he abandons chord changes, conventional melody and straightforward rhythmic computations in favour of an exploration of pure sound. These tracks are interspersed with two staple items ('Prelude To A Kiss' and 'Taking A Chance On Love'), an original samba and the astonishing 14-minute 'All Things Considered', which sounds like a summation of what Konitz has been doing for the last 25 years. The whole set has a freewheeling, spontaneous feel that confirms the saxophonist's status as one of the most original players on the scene.

As a free player, Konitz has well-attested credentials, having worked in unscripted formats with Lennie Tristano, four decades before his surprise inclusion in Derek Bailey's Company collective for 1987. 'Synthesthetics' is a set of duets over Werner's highly individual synthesizer lines (an individual player, he brings a doom-laden atmosphere even to the Ellington tune); Konitz vocalizes with surprising self-confidence. His soprano saxophone playing on 'Soft Lee' is probably the best he's yet committed to record. Werner and McClure are both magnificent, but there has to be a slight hesitation over Bill Stewart, who seems to fall in and out of synch with the music, overcompensating furiously when a more regular groove is re-established. Otherwise absolutely sterling.

**(*) S'Nice Nabel 4641
Konitz; Frank Wunsch (*p*); Gunnar Plumer (*b*); Christoph Heberer (*d*). 9/90.
Just before this was recorded, a British cabinet minister, hostile to the idea of European union, opined that the Germans were constitutionally bent on world domination. On this showing, it won't be with their native rhythm sections. Konitz plays with typical grace and detachment, largely ignoring the awkward lockstep behind him. A very middling album, again only for real enthusiasts.

***(*) Lullaby Of Birdland Candid CCD 79709
     Konitz; Barry Harris (*p*); Calvin Hill (*b*); Leroy Williams (*d*). 9/91.
As with *Jazz Nocturne*, below, this is valuable for showing Konitz on home turf and with a front-rank *jazz* accompanist. Harris plays the changes immaculately, eschewing fancy modulations and non-canonical key-changes. If it sounds boringly conventional, it ain't. Both men are at the top of their craft, and the solos on a totally standards-based programme are packed with invention. Konitz's solo on 'Cherokee' even manages to squeeze in a couple of Ornette phrases, just as he inverts a Parker idea, stretching out its metre in the process, on 'Anthropology'. The only quibbles about *Lullaby Of Birdland* concern the rhythm section, who are either playing too loud or else have been badly balanced in Mark Morganelli's final mix. Otherwise, hard to fault.

*** Friends Dragon DRCD 240
     Konitz; Gunnar Bergsten (*bs*); Lars Sjosten (*p*); Peter Soderblom (*b*); Nils Danell (*d*). 12/91.
The performances of two Lars Gullin compositions – 'Lars Meets Jeff' and 'Happy Again' – suggest that Konitz may have been studying the great Swede's records, since he quotes from original solos in a couple of places. This sort of gig is now pretty run-of-the-mill for him, but there's never a moment when the attention seems to flag or waver. Sjosten's quartet is highly professional and very musical, and the permutation of alto/soprano with baritone saxophone works delightfully.

*** Lunasea Soul Note 121249
     Konitz; Peggy Stern (*p*); Vic Juris (*g*); Harvie Swartz (*b*); Jeff Williams (*d*); Guilherme Franco (*perc*). 1/92.
Stern's a gutsy, uncomplicated player with a very individual delivery that somehow recalls Tommy Flanagan. Konitz clearly enjoys the settings Stern and Juris lay out, for he plays with great freedom and relaxation, compressing ideas into short, slightly enigmatic, solo statements that frequently drift outside the confines of the song in question. Swartz and Williams keep things securely moored, but Franco is mixed up way too loud and his busy percussion intrudes more than once.

*** Leewise Storyville STCD 4181
     Konitz; Jeff Davis (*t*); Allan Botschinsky (*t, flhn*); Erling Kroner (*tb*); Niels Gerhardt (*btb, tba*); Jens Sondergaard (*ss, as, bs*); Peter Gullin (*ts, bs*); Butch Lacy, Peggy Stern (*p*); Jesper Lundgaard (*b*); Svend-Erik Norregaard (*d*); Brigitte Frieboe (*v*). 3/92.
Konitz was the 1992 winner of the prestigious Jazzpar Prize, an accolade which brings with it the opportunity to record with a hand-picked Danish group. Only the first three tracks – 'Partout', 'Alone Together' and 'Body And Soul' – were recorded at the Jazzpar concert. The All-Star Nonet, directed by Jens Sondergaard, is exemplarily professional but lacks a little in relaxed expressiveness. As probably befits a celebratory event, the emphasis is on playing rather than on ground-breaking new material. There are a couple of more improvisatory duets, with saxophonist Sondergaard and with Botschinsky, but these are less focused than usual, even a little casual and bland.

**** Jazz Nocturne Evidence ECD 22085
     Konitz; Kenny Barron (*p*); James Genus (*b*); Kenny Washington (*d*). 10/92.
Great to hear Konitz in a straight jazz context and in such a good band. Though his younger European collaborators deserve every credit and respect for their musicianship, these are the saxophonist's peers – Barron at least – and this is the kind of music where his gifts are best deployed. It's entirely a standards session: 'Misty', 'Body And Soul', 'You'd Be So Nice To Come Home To', 'Everything Happens To Me', 'Alone Together', 'In A Sentimental Mood'. Impeccably played and engineered with taste and discretion by Peter Beckerman, who's managed to iron out some shaky moments with discreet edits (or so it sounds on a very careful listen). All of the material was laid down in a day, but it does sound as if the studio was rearranged at least once; Genus certainly moves in the mix.

***(*) So Many Stars Philology W 45
     Konitz; Stefano Battaglia (*p*); Tiziana Ghiglioni (*v*). 11/92.
Chet Baker's spirit rests heavily on this strangely intense vocal set. Much care has been taken in the *construction* of the record – much more, certainly, than on the average small-label session. The saxophonist's second-take solos on the title-track and 'O Cantador' have been grafted on to the first complete takes, making composite pieces. There are two gorgeous takes of 'My Funny Valentine' (a jazz anthem in Italy), with totally different inflexions by Ghiglioni and Battaglia, and a superb reading of 'It Never Entered My Mind' which in addition pays homage to Miles. Konitz sounds brassier than usual, leaving the floatier lines to Ghiglioni, who gets better every time she records.

*** The Jobim Collection Philology W 68
     Konitz; Peggy Stern (*p, syn*). 1/93.
Elegantly crafted and typically individual readings of 14 Jobim songs, of which the majority are likely to be unfamiliar to all but bossa nova collectors. 'Corcovado', 'How Insensitive' and 'The Girl From

Ipanema' are all included and given just enough spin to rescue them from banality. The saxophonist's attachment to Stern makes more sense each time they record, but she is still a rather enigmatic player, as likely as he is to throw something unexpected into the mix. Her synth work is very expressive.

*** **A Venezia** Philology W 53

Konitz; Paolo Fazio, Marlon Nather, Davide Boato (*t*); Giuseppe Calamosca, Dario Prisco, Umberto De Nigris, Roberto Rossi (*tb*); Massimiliano Tonello (*tba*); Piero Cozzi, Euro Michelazzi (*as*); Massimo Spiro, Massimo Parpagiola (*ts*); Michele Magnifichi (*bs*); Tatiana Marian, Carolina Casciani (*cl*); Roberto Rossetti (*bcl*); Stefano Benini, Loris Trevisan, Margherita Mesirca, Giuliana Cravin (*f*); Paolo Birro (*p*); Walter Lucano, Sandro Gibellini (*g*); Lello Gnesutta (*b*); Davide Ragazzoni (*d*); Renzo Zulian (*v*). 3/93.

*** **Free With Lee** Philology W 46

Konitz; Augusto Mancinelli, Donovan Mixon (*g*). 3/93.

The first finds Konitz in a Venetian television studio with the Suono Improvviso big band and a hatful of originals by director Giannantonio De Vicenzo, Marco Castelli and Paolo Birro. It's very much an honoured-guest role (he solos on all but three of the tracks) and he doesn't sound as comfortably across the charts as some of the young Italians, who play with uniform precision. Trombonist Rossi establishes his presence from the word go, and he is perhaps the most compelling voice on the set, though Castelli's soprano (on the opening number again and on De Vicenzo's 'Eros Detritus') has a quiet forcefulness that recalls the younger Steve Lacy. A great deal of emphasis is placed on the flutes and Benini has a prominent part, coming in behind Konitz on the long 'Solo Sogni'.

Not strictly part of Lee's own discography, but it's always good to see him working with musicians of a generation he helped to foster. His sponsorship of Mancinelli and Mixon on this stage in their respective careers is also interesting. Working as a trio and as two duos, they run down some demanding and unexpected stuff, and the existence of alternatives for Wayne Shorter's 'Nefertiti', Bruno Martino's 'Estate' and the improvised original 'Free With Lee' permits a glimpse of the two younger players learning from the master on the spot. Certainly guitar players will want to study this one, not least for the difference between Mixon's Wes-influence octaves and the Italian's floatier, less anchored approach.

**** **Rhapsody** Paddle Wheel KICJ 174

Konitz; Clark Terry (*flhn, v*); Gerry Mulligan (*bs*); Joe Lovano (*ts, ss, acl*); Jimmy Giuffre (*cl*); Paul Bley, Peggy Stern (*p*); Bill Frisell, Jean François Prins (*g*); Ben Allison, Gary Peacock (*b*); Paul Motian, Jeff Williams (*d*); Jay Clayton, Helen Merrill, Judy Niemack (*v*). 6–9/93.

*** **Rhapsody 2** Paddle Wheel KICJ 210

As above, except omit Frisell, Giuffre, Lovano, Merrill, Peacock, Williams; add Toots Thielemans (*hca*); Kenny Werner (*p, syn*); Yuko Fujiyama, Frank Wunsch (*p*); John Scofield (*g*); Mark Feldman (*vn*); Harvie Swartz (*b*). 7–9/93.

These are the definitive Lee Konitz records of recent times, and an excellent introduction to the way he works with different players and in different styles. As befits the title, the music is mostly lyrical, in ballad forms, soft-voiced and generally slow; but there are exceptions (such as 'Mumbles' with Clark Terry) and there is no slackening of invention.

He takes two full choruses to make himself known at the start of the first volume, following Helen Merrill's exquisite vocal with a solo of such delicate mastery that one immediately wants to cue it up again. The long 'Exposition' with the Giuffre/Bley/Peacock group (note: *not* Swallow on this occasion) is exacting and wonderful, an extended essay full of textures and sly wisdoms. 'Lo-Ko-Mo and Frizz', with the eponymous Lovano, Motian and Frisell, is clearly improvised and sees Lee move from soprano to alto and tenor in pace with music that reinvents itself comfortably, a conversation among intelligent friends, conducted at a high level of abstraction.

These are the high points. There is nothing half as powerful on *Rhapsody 2*, though it opens with huge promise – Toots Thielemans and Kenny Werner completing the trio for 'Body And Soul' – continues with a brief, wry duo with violinist Feldman, another with Sco and then, magnificently, 'Lover Man' with Mulligan; piano-less, no bass or drums either. From there, it's downhill. The material with Terry is pretty irritating this time around, and Peggy Stern, prettily as she plays, seldom sustains attention for longer than a couple of minutes. *Rhapsody*, volume one, should be on all shopping lists, however.

*** **Haiku** Nabel 4664

Konitz; Rudi Mahall (*bcl*); Andreas Schmidt (*p, v*); Jerry Granelli (*d, perc, v*); Sayumi Yoshida (*v*). 11/94.

Beyond its confirmation of Konitz's openness to new sounds and ideas, it's difficult to say where this one fits. Modernist trappings like Mahall's occasional turntable scratches neither fit comfortably nor meld with Konitz's sound; he simply moves through these sessions under his own star. Mostly original material, most of it rather beautifully played. Collectors will not be disappointed; others can afford to pass it over.

Peter Kowald (born 1944) DOUBLE BASS

**** **Duos: Europa America Japan** FMP CD 21
    Kowald; with Derek Bailey, Conrad Bauer, Han Bennink, Peter Brötzmann, Tom Cora, Andrew
    Cyrille, Danny Davis, Floris Floridis, Diamanda Galas, Junko Handa, Masahiko Kono, Jeanne
    Lee, Joëlle Léandre, Seizan Matsuda, Keiki Midorikawa, Akira Sakata, Irene Schweizer, Tadao
    Sawai, Evan Parker. 86–90.
**** **When The Sun Is Out You Don't See The Stars** FMP CD 38
    Kowald; Butch Morris (*c*); Werner Ludi (*as, bs*); Sainkho Namtchylak (*v*). 11/90, 7/91.
  **** **Was Da Ist** FMP CD 62
    Kowald (*b* solo). 94.

Kowald is one of the finest and most accessible of the European free players, combining the firm
rhythmic awareness of conventional jazz bass with a strong musical philosophy of his own that
encompasses classical and non-European musics. He is widely cited as an influence and a great catalyst,
bringing together individuals and styles and creating contexts in which genuinely exploratory music can
be made.

    Kowald's discography took a pasting with the demise of FMP's vinyl catalogue. Indeed, three geo-
graphically divided LPs containing material from the *Duos* were the last to be issued by the German
label. Though it contains different material and is *not* a compilation, the CD is a marvellous record and
an ideal introduction to contemporary improvised music. There isn't a piece of more than seven minutes' length, and many of them are very much shorter than that. By no means all of them are purely
spontaneous free improvisation; the pieces with Evan Parker, Conny Bauer, Andrew Cyrille, Akira
Sakata, Peter Brötzmann and some others were developed on the basis of a predetermined idea. Nor is
the usual improvising convention of absolute democracy and equality among instruments strictly
observed. In quite a number of cases, Kowald takes an accompanist's role, backing Diamanda Galas's
typically fraught vocal with doomy pedals, Andrew Cyrille's increasingly complex body language with
quite conventional octaves and a vocal drone.

    The instrumental combinations are of particular interest and it's fascinating to hear Kowald adapt his
attack accordingly. He takes a more prominent role with the horn players, building counter-melodies
and little retrograde progressions. This works fine with the Westerners, but there are inevitable difficulties with the Japanese performances. The problem isn't by any means one of sonority (Derek Bailey's
guitar frequently sounds like *shamisen* or *biwa*) but of basic aesthetic philosophies. Though Sakata and
Kondo are well versed in jazz and formal harmony from the West (and they play orthodox improvising
instruments), most of the others espouse a kind of violent synthesis between great formality of diction
and very disruptive abstraction. Though this is also typical of Bailey's music, the poles are reversed with
attention diverted to the *form* rather than the aural substance of the piece. This is a remarkable sequence
of music which deserves careful study as much as it invites repeated enjoyment. Find the LPs, though.

    Readers may have raised eyebrows at the very high ratings for this relatively little-known musician (as far
as straight jazz is concerned, at any rate), but they should be reassured that such marks do accurately
reflect Kowald's historical importance in the development of European free music. Only Derek Bailey
and Evan Parker command similar respect. Full five-star rating for a record of solo contrabass improvisations may stretch credibility too far, however. The only solution is to ask your dealer to provide a
quiet corner and sample the first three or four parts of a 72-minute recording – ten minutes out of your
life that may well transform your listening habits in future. It is the sheer quantity and quality of sound
that Kowald produces which is impressive. At no point in the 23 separate pieces that make up *Was Da Ist*
does one waste a second thinking about the instrumentation, yet everything is entirely idiomatic, even
when 'extended' techniques are being employed. Neither an abstract technical exercise nor an autobiographical inscape, but a passionate documentation of a relationship: man and instrument, and their
mutual absorption of experience.

    The group tracks on *When The Sun Is Out . . .* are less concentrated but no less compelling. Some doubts
persist about Namtchylak's voice. Once its sheer strangeness has been registered, there is little more to
say about it and it becomes decreasingly communicative. Between Morris and the 'Europeans' (as
Namtchylak must now be considered) there is a hint of the friendly incomprehension that often marks
such encounters, but it's overcome for the most part, and the later sessions recorded in Berlin – those
from November 1990 have a Lucerne byline – are much closer in spirit.

Krakatau GROUP

*** **Volition** ECM 511983
    Raoul Bjorkenheim (*g, shekere*); Jone Takamaki (*ts, krakaphone, toppophone, whirlpipe*); Uffe
    Krokfors (*b*); Alf Forsman (*d*).

Krakatau is essentially guitarist Bjorkenheim's band, hived off from percussionist Edward Vesala's Sound & Fury collective in the mid-1980s. Where Vesala mixed free playing with '60s psychedelia, tangos and straight composition, Bjorkenheim has a declared interest in Hendrix, Cream, Zappa, and a line of post-bop jazz that takes in Coltrane, Eric Dolphy, and the Miles of *Agharta*.

Volition is a cheerfully noisy record with remarkably little of the big-biceps nonsense that often comes with guitar-fronted groups. In Sound & Fury, Vesala had used Bjorkenheim a little aside from the main thrust of a composition, often asking him for explosively abstract sound-shapes that encouraged non-standard techniques: bowed and scrabbled strings, electronic distortion, 10+ volume readings. A dedicated instrument-hunter, like Vesala, saxophonist Takamaki supplies his own fair share of unusual sonorities, most notably the 'krakaphone', a copper organ pipe two feet taller than the performer and fitted with a baritone saxophone mouthpiece and reed. It lends its bulk most effectively to 'Little Big Horn', a title that's also been used by Gerry Mulligan.

It's a not entirely absurd parallel, for there is a softer and more lyrical side to Krakatau, most obviously heard on the soothingly oriental 'Changgo' and the folkish 'Nai', but clearly audible too on the closing ballad, 'Dalens Ande', which has a cool modality far removed from the all-out impact of the title-track.

Diana Krall VOCALS, PIANO

*** **Stepping Out** Enja ENJ 8042
    Krall; John Clayton (b); Jeff Hamilton (d). 93.
***(*) **Only Trust Your Heart** GRP 98102
    Krall; Stanley Turrentine (ts); Ray Brown, Christian McBride (b); Lewis Nash (d). 94.
*** **All For You** Impulse! IMP 11642
    Krall; Benny Green (p); Russell Malone (g); Paul Keller (b); Steve Kroon (perc). 10/95.

Vocally and stylistically, Krall sounds a generation older than her chronological age, which is still shy of thirty. She has a rich, resonant contralto and a preference for standard repertoire. The most obvious influences on her singing are Carmen McRae and Shirley Horn, who has also doubled vocals and piano. As 'Straighten Up And Fly Right' and 'Frim Fram Sauce' on the first of these suggests, Krall has also listened attentively to Nat Cole, and the second album is intended as a tribute to his great trio, hence the basic instrumentation of piano, guitar and bass, with just a touch of percussion thrown in on 'Boulevard Of Broken Dreams'. What the third album lacks, inevitably, is musicianship of the sort guaranteed by Brown, McBride and Nash. Turrentine does more than just show up, contributing hugely on his three tracks. Our preference for the GRP disc is based solely on their roles; Krall's singing is impeccable throughout and clearly the young Canadian is going places fast.

Wayne Krantz GUITAR

*** **Signals** Enja 6048-2
    Krantz; Jim Beard (ky); Leni Stern (g); Hiram Bullock, Anthony Jackson (b); Dennis Chambers (d); Don Alias (perc). 5–6/90.
***(*) **Long To Be Loose** Enja 7099-2
    Krantz; Lincoln Goines (b); Zach Danziger (d). 3/93.
***(*) **2 Drink Minimum** Enja 9043-2
    As above. 2–4/95.

Krantz works an interesting furrow somewhere between Frisell's displaced ruralisms and a bluesier improvisation that sounds plausible as either jazz-rock or, well, rock-jazz. In other words, another good guitar player who's hard to slot in. What he enjoys is the resonant sound of strong lead guitar: he's not much interested in FX, delay, fuzz, or whatever. The starry cast on the first record suggests a typical fusion slugging match, but the support team is used rather sparingly (drums and percussion on only five out of ten tracks) and, though the pieces are rather short and curtailed, they're an entertaining bunch. The trio-orientated records put Krantz in a setting that plays tight or loose as he pleases and has a lot of fine, unassumingly accomplished guitar. The studio set is structured piece-by-piece, even though the titles tell a story if you read them end-to-end, but to get a handle on what this group is about, the live *2 Drink Minimum* is an even better choice. Though spliced together from various shows at New York's 55 Bar, the disc plays like a single, well-paced, explosive concert set: the cumulative intensity of 'Whippersnapper' and the lyricism of 'Isabelle' work despite (or because of) their rough edges, the occasion adding a pinch of seasoning to music that a studio might have dried out a little. The fine, interlocking work of Goines and Danziger comes over with the same power as Krantz's.

Ernie Krivda (born 1945) TENOR SAXOPHONE

*** Ernie Krivda Jazz Cadence CJR 1049
> Krivda; Dennis Reynolds, Mike Hazlett (*t*); Pat Hallaran (*tb*); Joe Hunter (*p*); Pete Selvaggio (*acc*); Jeff Halsey, Gary Aprile, Roger Hines, Chris Berger (*b*); Paul Samuels, Scott Davis (*d*). 1–8/91.

*** So Nice To Meet You Cadence CJR 1056
> Krivda; Joe Hunter (*p*); Bill Plavan, Chris Berger (*b*); Val Kent, Mark Gondor (*d*). 6/93–1/94.

*** Sarah's Theme CIMP 102
> Krivda; Bob Fraser (*g*); Jeff Halsey (*b*). 9/95.

Krivda has a markedly individual approach to the tenor: wildly elongated lines with barely a pause for breath, a hiccupy kind of rhythm that abjures conventional hard-bop phrasing, and a tone that evades obvious comparison, though he sometimes gets a scuffling sound that is rather like Warne Marsh. The ingredients tend to make his music exciting but unresolved. On *Ernie Krivda Jazz*, the three duets with bassist Halsey are the most interesting things: two pieces with accordionist Selvaggio are unusual but not terribly involving, 'The Bozo' is a more complicated chart involving the two trumpeters, and the final quartet/quintet tracks are lively but let down slightly by the modest support. The album is further compromised by the scrawny, indifferent production. The pairing with singer Paula Owen is even stranger: Owen's basically straightforward style is embellished by Krivda's jawbreaking solos, everything pitched in double-time, each solo a blitz on its surroundings. It's oddly exhilarating stuff, but over a CD's duration a little exhausting. One could say the same about *Sarah's Theme*: the title-track runs just over 20 minutes and, aside from the three subsequent interludes, each of the tracks seems obsessively long. Halsey and Fraser play a shadowy role, but Krivda himself is actually in comparatively restrained mood on this set. CIMP's two-track digital sound, designed for 'realism', tends to sound rather dry and unappealing, but in some ways it suits Krivda's tough and uncompromising approach.

Karin Krog (born 1937) VOCALS

**** Jubilee: The Best of 30 Years Verve 527316 2CD
> Krog; Don Ellis, Bob Harman, Palle Mikkelborg, Glenn Stuart, Ed Warren, Alan Weight (*t*); David Sanchez, Terry Woodson (*tb*); Per Carsten, Tom Scott, Ira Schulman, Ron Starr, Ruben Leon, John Magruder (*f, sax*); Dexter Gordon, Bjorn Johansen, Warne Marsh, Archie Shepp (*ts*); John Surman (*bs, ss, syn*); Bent Larsen (*f, as, bf*); Niels Peters (*ob*); Kenny Drew (*p, org*); Jon Balke, Bengt Hallberg, Ole Koch-Hansen, Egil Kapstad, Roger Kellaway, Mike Lang, Arild Wickstrom (*p*); Jan Berger, Philip Catherine (*g*); Arild Andersen, Niels-Henning Orsted-Pedersen, Kurt Lindgren, Per Loberg, Red Mitchell, Ray Neapolitan, Frank De La Rosa (*b*); Jon Christensen, Beaver Harris, Alex Riel, Epsen Rud (*d*); Steve Bohannon, Mark Stevens, Chino Valdes, Kasper Vinding (*perc*); strings. 3/64–6/94.

***(*) Some Other Spring Storyville STCD 4045
> Krog; Dexter Gordon (*ts*); Kenny Drew (*p*); Niels-Henning Orsted-Pedersen (*b*); Epsen Rud (*d*). 5/70.

***(*) Gershwin With Karin Krog Meantime MR4
> Krog; Egil Kapstad (*p*); Arild Andersen (*b*); Jon Christensen (*d*). 74, 89.

*** You Must Believe In Spring Meantime MR5
> Krog; Palle Mikkelborg (*t*); Per Carsten (*as, f*); Bent Larsen (*f, af, bf*); Niels Peters (*ob*); Ole Koch-Hansen (*p*); Philip Catherine (*g*); Niels-Henning Orsted-Pedersen (*b*); Alex Riel (*d*); Kasper Vinding (*perc*); strings. 5/74.

*** Hi-Fly Meantime MR3
> Krog; Archie Shepp (*ts*); Charles Greenlea (*tb*); Jon Balke (*p*); Arild Andersen, Cameron Brown (*b*); Beaver Harris (*d*). 6/76.

***(*) Two Of A Kind Meantime MR1
> Krog; Bengt Hallberg (*p*). 4/82.

**** Freestyle Odin NJ 4017
> Krog; John Surman (*ss, syn, perc*); Brynjar Hoff (*ob*). 8/85, 4/86.

*** Something Borrowed . . . Something New Meantime MR2
> Krog; Kenny Drew (*p*); Niels-Henning Orsted-Pedersen (*b*); Alex Riel (*d*). 6/89.

Turned on to jazz very largely by seeing Billie Holiday sing at a matinee performance in Oslo, Krog has developed into one of Europe's most stylish and significant jazz singers. The early work documented on the capacious *Jubilee* finds her working an idiosyncratic swing vein, with strong intimations of bebop, perhaps of Annie Ross's vocalise. Her first recordings are with Arild Wikstrom's group, professional, swinging and sufficiently offbeat to seem individual. There is a significant shift at the time of the first

American recording, made in LA with Don Ellis's eclectic orchestra. Perhaps the bandleader's open-mindedness encouraged Krog's folkish-classical vein, for there is a very different approach to basic changes on 'In Your Arms' and 'Spring Affair'. Her work with Dexter Gordon, with the refiguring of bop that entailed, is also documented on the Storyville; most listeners would be satisfied to have the well-packaged and -documented Verve.

It takes the story forward, overlapping with a good deal of the stuff also available separately on other labels, the association with Shepp and Hallberg, for instance. Much of Krog's best work has been with her companion, John Surman. However, her own catalogue has undergone a significant boost over the last two years, largely as a result of her own initiative in releasing material on the Meantime imprint which is usually quite easy to track down.

A fine technician, Krog doesn't allow an impressive understanding of 'extended technique' to over-reach itself, keeping the words and their attendant emotions in view. Perhaps because of this, she sounds best in small-scale and rather intimate surroundings. The session with Surman is quite exotic in sonority, with overdubbing and electronic treatments on some tracks, unusual percussion and synth patterns on the original material. The repertoire is pretty ambitious, even including 'Raga Variations' by the com-poser, Arne Nordheim, who writes brilliantly for voice. A Fran Landesman medley strongly recalls the work of the late Radka Toneff, a Norwegian compatriot of Krog's, but is even more musical in conception.

Something Borrowed is more straightforwardly jazz-orientated, as is the Gershwin record. A gap of 15 years between them (or the contrast between the 1974 and 1989 material on *Gershwin With Karin Krog*) demonstrates how completely the singer has absorbed the basic repertoire and made it her own. Krog's versions of well-tramped turf like 'Summertime' and 'Someone To Watch Over Me' (*Gershwin*, later sessions) or 'I Get A Kick Out Of You' and 'Everytime We Say Goodbye' (*Borrowed*) are entirely her own.

Hallberg is a graceful accompanist who gives her a softly insistent beat as a springboard into her vocal and there isn't a track that one wouldn't want to listen through again, so subtle is some of her phrasing and her awareness of harmony. That's at more of a premium in the Legrand session, *You Must Believe In Spring*, where the outstanding track is 'Once Upon A Summertime' (also on the Verve). She's a little swamped here by Mikkelborg's dense orchestration but mostly manages to rise above the waves.

She's under a different sort of pressure on the session with Shepp, a player who turned himself from a screamer into a (relatively) sensitive balladeer rather later in the day. Krog adds lyrics to Carla Bley's 'Sing Me Softly Of The Blues' and makes an impressive job of Mal Waldron's 'Soul Eyes' (a singer's tune if there ever was one) and Randy Weston's affirmative 'Hi-Fly'. The horns are too dominant and Harris is slightly overpowering in places; Krog also sounds uncomfortable on Shepp's own 'Steam', though their duet, 'Solitude', suggests that there was more than enough common ground.

The group on *Borrowed* is much better attuned to what Krog is doing. NHOP emerges as the dominant voice, easing aside a rather lacklustre and uncharacteristically heavy-handed Drew. The sound is far from ideal, pinching some of the top notes, but the vocal performances are generally of a very high standard. Excellent as all these records are, we would emphasise that *Jubilee* will answer all but the most dedicated requirements.

Gene Krupa (1909–73) DRUMS

***(*) **Gene Krupa 1935–1938** Classics 754
Krupa; Tom Di Carlo, Tom Gonsoulin, Dave Schultze, Roy Eldridge, Nate Kazebier (*t*); Chuck Evans, Joe Harris, Charles McCamish, Bruce Squires (*tb*); Benny Goodman (*cl*); Murray Williams, George Siravo (*as*); Chu Berry, Dick Clark, Vido Musso, Carl Bleisacker (*ts*); Milton Raskin, Jess Stacy (*p*); Ray Biondi, Allan Reuss (*g*); Israel Crosby, Horace Rollins (*b*); Helen Ward, Jerry Kruger (*v*). 11/35–7/38.

*** **Gene Krupa, 1938** Classics 767
Krupa; Tom Di Carlo, Ray Cameron, Tom Gonsoulin, Nick Prospero, Dave Schultze (*t*); Charles McCamish, Bruce Squires, Toby Tyler, Chuck Evans (*tb*); Murray Williams, Mascagni Ruffo, George Siravo (*as*); Vido Musso, Carl Bleisacker, Sam Musiker, Sam Donahue (*ts*); Milton Raskin (*p*); Ray Biondi (*g*); Horace Rollins (*b*); Irene Daye, Leo Watson (*v*). 7–12/38.

*** **Gene Krupa, 1939** Classics 799
Krupa; Ray Cameron, Charles Frankhauser, Tom Gonsoulin (*t*); Toby Tyler, Bruce Squires, Dalton Rizzotto (*tb*); Bob Snyder, Mascagni Ruffo (*as*); Sam Musiker, Sam Donahue (*ts*); Milton Raskin (*p*); Ray Biondi (*g*); Horace Rollins (*b*); Irene Daye (*v*). 2–7/39.

***(*) **Gene Krupa, 1939–1940** Classics 834
Krupa; Johnny Martel, Corky Cornelius, Torger Halten, Nate Kazebier, Johnny Napton, Shorty Sherock (*t*); Al Sherman, Floyd O'Brien, Red Ogle, Al Jordan, Sid Brantley (*tb*); Bob Snyder,

Clint Neagley (*as*); Sam Donahue (*ts*); Sam Musiker (*cl, ts*); Tony D'Amore, Milt Raskin (*p*); Ray Biondi (*g*); Buddy Bastien (*b*); Irene Day, Howard Dulany (*v*). 7/39–2/40.

*** **Drum Boogie** Columbia Legacy 473659
Krupa; Norman Murphy, Torger Halten, Rudy Novack, Shorty Sherock (*t*); Pat Virgadamo, Jay Kelliher, Babe Wagner (*tb*); Clint Neagley, Musky Ruffo (*as*); Walter Bates (*ts*); Sam Musiker (*cl, ts*); Bob Kitsis (*p*); Ray Biondi (*g*); Buddy Bastien (*b*); Irene Day (*v*). 40–41.

*** **1946 Live!** Jazz Hour JH 1039
Krupa; Red Rodney, Ziggy Elman, Don Fagerquist (*t*); Charlie Ventura (*ts*); Anita O'Day, Buddy Stewart (*v*); other personnel not specified. 1, 3 & 9/46.

*** **Krupa And Rich** Verve 521 643
Krupa; Roy Eldridge, Dizzy Gillespie (*t*); Illinois Jacquet, Flip Phillips (*ts*); Oscar Peterson (*p*); Herb Ellis (*g*); Ray Brown (*b*); Buddy Rich (*d*). 5 & 11/55.

There is a memorable photograph of the young Gene Krupa at the kit, hair slick, tux sleeves and collar soaked with sweat, mouth and eyes wide and hungry, his brushes blurred to smoke with the pace of his playing. Received wisdom has Krupa down as a showman who traded in subtlety for histrionic power. George T. Simon, in the hopped-up prose that was almost *de rigueur* in the *Metronome* of the late 1930s, referred to the drummer's 'quadruple "f" musical attacks'; it's interesting to speculate how many people read that as 4F (that is, unfit for military service) rather than as some battering dynamic above *molto fortissimo*, for there is no doubt that Krupa's film-star looks and superb technique also made him a target. During the war, which he spent as a very combative non-combatant, he was twice set up for police arrest and spent part of his thirty-fifth year waiting on remand until a witness contracted amnesia. The critics have taken much the same route, sniping, then forgetting.

Even in neglect, Krupa's impact on the jazz rhythm section is incalculable. He himself said, 'I made the drummer a high-priced guy.' Though black percussionists who had worked for years in the shadow of the front men had some cause to be resentful, Krupa's respectful investigation of the African and Afro-American drumming tradition was of tremendous significance, opening the way for later figures as diverse as Max Roach, Elvin Jones, Andrew Cyrille and Milford Graves.

The documentation is in much better shape these days with the issue of Classics' typically detailed job. Krupa joined the Benny Goodman band in 1934 and stayed till 1938, when his boss finally decided there was room for only one of them on stage. The drummer recorded under his own name only twice during the Goodman years. The sessions of November 1935 (made for Parlophone UK) and February 1936 kick off the first Classics volume on a high. Being able to call on Goodman, Jess Stacy and the remarkable Israel Crosby offered some guarantee of quality, and 'Three Little Words' and Krupa's own 'Blues For Israel' are spanking performances, driven along by that dynamic drumming. The following session included Chu Berry and Roy Eldridge, an established double act in the Fletcher Henderson outfit and always ready to try something new. Berry cheekily weaves in and out of Goodman's line, while Eldridge dive-bombs from above. Great stuff.

There is then a chronological hiatus until Krupa's break with Goodman and the chance to capitalize on his own rising stardom. The April 1938 Brunswicks also signalled a move to New York City, which seems to have put a slight brake on Krupa's invention for a while, unless it was the new burden of managing his own orchestra. Not yet the banked strings of the later band but a slightly cumbersome feel nevertheless, and the fourth item ('The Madam Swings It') of an uninspired session was eventually rejected. Singers Helen Ward, Jerry Kruger and Irene Day fail to add very much, but vocals were commercially essential and these discs did big business right through 1938, with the band averaging a session a month. Leo Watson's scats were lively and often very musical, but Krupa must have felt partly inhibited by the formula and there's an audible sense of relaxation and renewed vigour about the sessions recorded back in Chicago in October, when he is able to lay down a couple of fine instrumentals, including the excellent 'Walkin' And Swingin''. November and December saw the band on the West Coast, where a new audience was conquered and three excellent recording sessions laid down. Watson's 'Do You Wanna Jump, Children?' brought the year to a happy close.

The following year was no less busy and there is a strong sense of consolidation in the band, which begins to sound like a more solidly integrated unit. Krupa's leadership is tight and very musical. A new version of 'The Madam Swings It' is cut and this time passes muster. Nate Kazebier returns to the fold and Floyd O'Brien signs up to stiffen the brasses. Apart from a couple of novelty instrumentals made for dancing ('Dracula' and 'Foo For Two') the standard is very high and Krupa can increasingly be heard to experiment with rhythmic embellishments, off-accent notes, single beats on the edge of his cymbals, and with the dynamics. Even with such a powerful group, he was always prepared on occasion to play quietly and to contrast *fff* and *pp* passages within a single song, relatively unusual at that time when up was up and a ballad was a ballad.

The last (for now) of the Classics volumes takes the story up to the first months of 1940. It's pretty much a question of steady as she goes, even with the inevitable personnel changes. By this point Krupa can be heard to be shaping the band to his new requirements, which were much more musicianly and much less histrionic. The Benny Carter piece, 'Symphony In Riffs', recorded for Columbia in September 1939, and the majestic two-part 'Blue Rhythm Fantasy' (nearly seven minutes in total) stand out as representative masterpieces, making this, along with the first volume, essential buys.

It would be hard to ignore the Columbia compilation, which affords a glimpse of the band in a somewhat more reflective mood. Jimmy Mundy's arrangements often cleave to a rather mechanical shuffle-beat that doesn't suit a group of this size or inclination, but the horns are nicely voiced and there is a lot more space round the music than in earlier days. Irene Day is still the singer, still leaning on ballads rather than faster numbers. She was soon (in 1941) to be replaced by one of the great presences in the band. Anita O'Day refused to wear a spangly frock and turned out in a band jacket like the rest of them, emphasizing that she was part of things and not just a walk-on. (Re)joining with her was Eldridge, who helped transform the group yet again, into a less poppy, more jazz-based and improvisational unit. The 1946 live material on Jazz Hour is not significantly enlivened and is all pitched 'for your listening and dancing pleasure', as the MC ritually intones. These airshots are no worse than others of their type, though there is considerable dropout at the bass end. Personnel are not fully identified, but O'Day, the young Red Rodney, Charlie Ventura and Ziggy Elman (not 'Elmer', as given) were all in the orchestra, and some of the arrangements were contributed by a clever 19-year-old called Gerry Mulligan.

Krupa and Rich shouldn't be confused with an earlier Compact Jazz compilation on Verve which included some of the material. This record documents a typical Norman Granz summit, bringing together the younger Rich and probably the only man who could properly be said to have influenced his own fiercely swinging style. Given the nature of the occasion, this wasn't nearly as arid and tiresome as the majority of contemporary 'drum battles'. Each takes a big solo spot – 'Gene's Blues', 'Buddy's Blues' – and, for the rest, it's a matter of trading fours and eights until the customers are satisfied. Fortunately the band is good enough to assert itself and nobody will feel percussed out of countenance when they hear Oscar Peterson's sweepingly elaborate accompaniments or Dizzy poking gentle fun at the vanities of drummers.

Marty Krystall TENOR SAXOPHONE, BASS CLARINET

***(*) Seeing Unknown Colors MA M015A
Krystall; Hugo Schick (t); Takumi Iino (b); Yasushi Yoneki (d). 5/90.

Krystall's earlier records with Buel Neidlinger on K2B2 are still awaited on CD; for now, this thoughtful set, recorded on a visit to Japan, will have to do. Krystall's favoured mode is a light, open-ended free bop, rarely resorting to extremes of register or dynamics: there is Monk and Ellington here (including a nicely bleak 'Prelude To A Kiss') as well as some melodically attractive originals. But the most striking music comes in three tunes borrowed from the Native American Papago tradition, especially the haunting, gently insistent 'Song Of Elder Brother After He Had Created The Wind And The Clouds'. Schick plays a Don Cherry-like role and, though bassist and drummer could use a touch more sensitivity, it's fine music.

Tom Kubis SAXOPHONES

*** Slightly Off The Ground Sea Breeze SB 109
Kubis; Jack Sheldon (t, v); George Graham, Wayne Bergeron, Dan McGurn, Stan Martin, Charlie Peterson (t); Charlie Moralis, Andy Martin, Alex Iles, Rich Bullock, Bill Watrous (tb); Dan Higgins, Greg Huckins, Gordon Goodwin, Bill Liston, Paul Baker (saxes); Matt Catingub (p, as); Mike Higgins (g); Kevin Axt (b); Matt Johnson (d). 1/89.

Southern California is full of skilful big-band players, and this ensemble headed by Kubis is accomplished enough to make his demanding charts seem like simplicity itself. The style is late Basie in terms of the section-work, with drilled brass trading licks with the reed section over the kind of clipped rhythms that dominate modern mainstream orchestras, but there's enough good humour to give it an extra fillip. Sheldon's vocal on 'Play It Again, Sam' will become tiresome after a few listens, but he takes a couple of superior solos elsewhere, and Watrous plays a trombone part on the title-track which will have most trombonists in despair. The material is a mix of derivative originals – 'Purple Porpoise Parkway' is 'On Green Dolphin Street', 'Exactly Like This' is 'Exactly Like You', and so on – and a handful of standards.

Joachim Kühn (born 1944) PIANO, KEYBOARDS

*** **Distance** CMP CD 26
. Kühn (*p* solo). 5/84.
*** **Wandlungen / Transformations** CMP CD 29
As above. 5/86.
(*) **Ambiance AMB 1
Kühn; Walter Quintus (*digital sound-board*). 88.
***(*) **Get Up Early** Ambiance AMB 2
As above. 91.
(*) **Kiel / Stuttgart Live! Inak 868
Kühn; Jan Akkerman (*g, el g, syn*). 79.
***(*) **Nightline New York** Inak 869
Kühn; Michael Brecker, Bob Mintzer (*ts*); Eddie Gomez (*b*); Billy Hart (*d*); Mark Nauseef
(*perc*); collective personnel. 4/81.
**** **From Time To Time Free** CMP 35
Kühn; Jean-François Jenny-Clark (*b*); Daniel Humair (*d*). 4/88.
*** **Live: Théâtre De La Ville, Paris, 1989** CMP 43
As above. 11/89.
***(*) **Let's Be Generous** CMP CD 53
Kühn; Miroslav Tadic (*g*); Tony Newton (*b*); Mark Nauseef (*d, perc*). 8/90.
Joachim Kühn has a prodigious, rather 'legitimate' technique that reflects a solid grounding in classical practices and sometimes cramps his improvisational instincts. These, though, are considerable and they're perhaps better heard in a group or duo context than in solo performance. *Distance* is a beautifully inflected album, as is the subsequent solo *Transformations*, and much of the credit for their success goes to CMP supremo, Walter Quintus, who also figures as live electronics man on the experimental *Ambiance* and its rather better and more achieved sequel, *Get Up Early*. This is not strictly a duo performance at all. Quintus operates a digital soundboard which transforms the sound of Kühn's piano (huge, Weather Report-like gongs at the start of *Get Up Early*, harpsichord trills, thunder, massed strings); despite a set-up which allows each man to react to the movements of the other, Quintus's acoustic environments on the first album do not sound particularly responsive.

Nor, unfortunately, are Jan Akkerman's. Star of the once-fashionable progressive rock band, Focus, Akkerman manages to sound both fleet and stiff, not at all an instinctive improviser, and is best at colouring backdrops for Kühn's lavishly voiced chord-structures and thoughtful lines.

To gauge Kühn as an improviser in the Euro-American contemporary mainstream, one needs to turn to *Nightline New York*, where he sounds quite at ease with a quick-witted two-tenor front line, and in particular to the superb trios with Jenny-Clark and Humair. These are of the highest quality. There is a rawness of texture which balances Kühn very well indeed, and which is evident again in the choice of material on the later set, where 'India' and 'Spy Vs Spy' are the outstanding tracks.

The recent *Let's Be Generous* is a powerful – and, judging by the chatter of studio noise at the beginning, largely improvised – set that brings a heavy, Mahavishnu Orchestra sound largely compounded of guitar, synthesizer and drums to Eric Dolphy's 'The Prophet' and 'Something Sweet, Something Tender', and to some fine Kühn originals. The final track is wholly improvised and points a new way forward for Kühn, perhaps into the territory softened up by Last Exit.

*** **Carambolage** CMP 58
Kühn; Rob Bruynen, Andreas Hederer, Rick Kiefer, Jon Eardley, Bob Coassin, Ruud Bruells, Klaus Osterloh (*t*); David Horler, Peter Feil, Bernd Laukamp, Roy Deuvall, Dan Gotschall, Ludwig Nuss (*tb*); Heiner Wiberny, Harald Rosenstein, Olivier Peters, Rolf Römer, Steffen Schorn, Claudio Püntin (*reeds*); Jean-François Jenny-Clark (*b*); Daniel Humair (*d*). 2, 3 & 9/91.
Something of a jump for Kühn, whose records hitherto have all been notably small-scale and intimate. The writing lets him down a bit over this range, but there is plenty of ambition in evidence and some basis for future work. The WDR Big Band give it plenty of oomph as usual.

Rolf Kühn (born 1929) CLARINET, SYNTHESIZER

***(*) **Rolf Kühn** Blue Flame 40162
Kühn; Joachim Kühn (*p, syn*); Klaus Blodau, Larry Elam, Paul Kubatsch, Mannie Moch (*t*); Wolfgang Ahlers, Egon Christmann (*tb*); Ronald Piesarkiewicz (*tba*); Herb Geller, Charlie Mariano (*reeds*); Klaus-Robert Kruse, Thilo Von Westernhagen (*ky*); Philip Catherine, Peter Weihe (*g*); Niels-Henning Orsted-Pedersen (*b*); Alphonse Mouzon (*d*); strings. 78, 80.

*** **Don't Split** L + R 40016
    Kühn; Bob Mintzer (*ts*); Joachim Kühn (*p*); Peter Wiehe (*g*); Detlev Beier (*b*); Mark Nauseef
    (*d, perc*). 6/82.
***(*) **As Time Goes By** Blue Flame 40292
    Kühn; Joachim Kühn (*p*); Detlev Beier (*b*). 4/89.

Clarinet is still sufficiently rare an item in contemporary jazz to render exact location of Rolf Kühn's style rather difficult. Leonard Feather, though, was in no doubt when he called the young German the 'new Benny Goodman'. Like his pianist brother, Joachim Kühn, who makes intelligent contributions to all three albums, and, of course, much like Goodman, Rolf Kühn has a well-schooled and sophisticated approach that suits both small groups and larger orchestral settings. In 1959 he played some memorable sessions with the great American bassist Oscar Pettiford, and they can still be found on a good Jazzline CD called *Jazz Legacy – Baden-Baden Unreleased Radio Tape*.

    The fusion impulse that underlines much of the music on *Don't Split* and the earlier big-band album is handled with considerable intelligence and a fine grasp of dynamics and textures, but it's encouraging to find Kühn making a more direct approach to jazz in the late 1980s. *As Time Goes By* is a fine combination of standard material – 'When I Fall In Love' and the title-track – with originals and some elements of free-form playing. Not plugging in his once-ubiquitous synthesizer allows him to develop a much more direct discourse, which is extremely impressive and well worth the effort of discovery.

Steve Kuhn (born 1938) PIANO, KEYBOARDS

***(*) **Looking Back** Concord CCD 4446
    Kuhn; David Finck (*b*); Lewis Nash (*d*). 10/90.
***(*) **Live At Maybeck Recital Hall: Volume 13** Concord CCD 4484
    Kuhn (*p* solo). 11/90.
*** **Remembering Tomorrow** ECM 1573
    Kuhn; David Finck (*b*); Joey Baron (*d*). 3/95.

Unrelated to Rolf and Joachim Kühn – though occasionally confused with the latter – Steve Kuhn is an older and more traditionally minded player whose roots reach back as far as Tatum and Waller, but who most immediately recalls Bill Evans. Kuhn has worked with Kenny Dorham, Stan Getz and Sheila Jordan, and is often at his best comping for a very lyrical player or singer. With a left hand that is less than sturdy, he is more than usually dependent on a strong bass player and has tended to recruit very dominant bass fiddlers to his trios; his solo work can sound a little ungrounded and introspective. Recorded a month after *Looking Back*, the Maybeck recital underlines once again the differences between Kuhn's solo and trio work. Where the latter is increasingly a partnership of equals, the solo work opens up a remarkable amount of space in the middle of the music. The Maybeck Hall series, recorded in a warm but uncomplicated acoustic in Berkeley, California, has tended to feature meditative and/or lyrical piano music rather than the wilder shores of improv, and this is no exception.

    Kuhn's sometimes extreme opposition of left and right hands (if you like, the exact antithesis of Keith Jarrett's normal strategy) still betrays a certain crudity towards the bass end. The marvellous, Bird-influenced melodic figures on 'Old Folks', the opening cut, are made over an almost childishly simple left-hand alternation that very quickly palls (if it isn't intended to make a satirical comment about the song). Much the same happens on an otherwise beautiful and very thoughtful 'I Remember You', where a rumbling bass-line suddenly and disconcertingly gives way to an abstract passage over the basic chords.

    Of the available trios – the fine *Trance* with Steve Swallow and Jack DeJohnette is deleted – by far the best is *Looking Back* where, perhaps ironically, the pianist is working with a much less dominant rhythm section and gives signs of having broadened his own intonation and sharpened his attack. Finck is not a bass player one hears much about, but he clearly provides Kuhn with what he needs and, in company with a drummer of Baron's wit and acumen, he can sound very good indeed. The most recent record is just a little lacking in spark and variety. The pianist sounds thoughtful and relaxed but, despite Baron's playfulness, it never quite catches light.

Akemi Kuniyoshi (born 1953) PIANO

*** **ARP Music** Leo Lab CD 004
    Kuniyoshi; Paul Moss (*sax, t, tb, g, f, cl, etc.*); Russell Lambert (*perc, etc.*).

Kuniyoshi grew up in Japan, where she received a classical training, then worked as an entertainer, singing Elton John songs in sushi restaurants. She has no jazz background whatsoever, and her previous improvisations for Leo (both now deleted) occupied a middle ground with formal composition. She was also a member of the improvisation group, Coherents, now sadly in abeyance.

The new disc, her first on CD, is a much freer and more adventurous setting for this exceptionally talented performer. While Moss and Lambert create interesting textures, it is the pianist's intense concentration that insists on capturing the attention. Leo Lab is a new imprint of cutting-edge music from a label that has undergone an enormous transformation since its inception in the 1970s. On the strength of this release, it is looking in the right direction.

Sergey Kuryokhin (1954–96) PIANO, OTHER INSTRUMENTS

***(*) **Some Combinations Of Fingers And Passion** Leo LRCD 178
    Kuryokhin (*p* solo). 91.

Classically trained, and capable of playing quite legitimately in the midst of an otherwise chaotic performance, Kuryokhin is easily the most charismatic of the younger Russian players. He fronts his own 'Pop Mechanics' performances, mixed-media pieces that ape Western forms in a deliberately exaggerated, 'Martian' fashion that is not so much satirical as clownishly respectful. *An Introduction To Pop Mechanics* and *Pop Mechanics No. 17*, a performance of the variable piece, may still be found on Leo, and Kuryokhin can also be heard on his own *Piano Zoological Elements*, with guitarist Boris Grebenschchikov, the first of the Russian new wave to be accorded major-label status in the West, on *Mad Nightingales In The Russian Forest* and the double *Subway Culture*, and with Grebenshchikov and saxophonist Vladimir Chekasin on *Exercises*. However, Leo's vinyl stocks are running down and it is in any case as a piano player that Kuryokhin is most interesting on record. (The 'Pop Mechanics' projects, recently sampled on Leo Feigin's television documentaries about the new Russian music, were probably best heard and seen live and translate to record only partially.)

Kuryokhin is more likely to refer to Rachmaninov than to Art Tatum in his solo performances, and he seems to make it a point of principle to avoid direct reference from the jazz tradition. 'Blue Rondo A La Russ – A Tribute to Dave Brubeck' on *Some Combinations* is an apparent exception; Brubeck is perceived in a very different way in Russia than in his native United States, and enjoys honorific status as one of the first major jazzmen to appear there, but Kuryokhin's tribute is typically oblique.

Technically, his technique is interesting largely for its avoidance of the usual jazz-piano dichotomy between the left hand, with its rhythmic chording, and the right, which carries the melody and the subsequent improvisation. In addition, Kuryokhin is a virtuosic user of the pedals (a sharp contrast to Cecil Taylor, who uses them very sparingly indeed), creating some quite remarkable two-piano illusions. Rapidly pedalling also creates an occasional sense, as on the long 'Passion And Feelings' section of the later session, that tiny segments of music are being edited together at very high speed, creating the studied artificiality of tone one hears throughout his earlier work, an apparent refutation of conventional pianistic 'passion', whether of the Horowitz or Taylor variety.

Kuryokhin's is very difficult music to characterize, because it consistently undermines its own premises. These are quite alien to Western ears in any case. Kuryokhin is on record as believing that the end of State suppression of improvised music is an aesthetic disaster on a par with the death of Satan. There is certainly a slackness of purpose to the later record which one does not associate with Kuryokhin and which dilutes its considerable technical achievements.

Charles Kynard ORGAN

(*) **Reelin' With The Feelin' / Wa-Ta-Wa-Zui BGP CDBGPD 055
    Kynard; Virgil Jones (*t*); Wilton Felder, Rusty Bryant (*ts*); Joe Pass, Melvin Sparks (*g*); Carol
    Kaye, Jimmy Lewis (*b*); Paul Humphrey, Idris Muhammed, Bernard Purdie (*d*). 8/69–71.

Kynard, who is from Kansas City, was perhaps the last of the jazz organists to emerge in the 1960s. This British reissue doubles up two of his five Prestige albums. The first session is sagging with organ-combo clichés and Humphrey is a pedestrian drummer; the second adds electric piano to Kynard's instrument-list and is a bit brighter, thanks to the reliable Jones and Bryant, who can play the legs off a blues when they feel like it. Nothing fancy, but a good one to cheer up a traffic jam with the in-car stereo. We still await the reissue of *Afro-Disiac*, with Grant Green and Houston Person, which is surely Kynard's best record.

L.A.4 GROUP

(*) **Just Friends Concord CCD 4199
    Bud Shank (*as, f*); Laurindo Almeida (*g*); Ray Brown (*b*); Jeff Hamilton (*d*). 78.

*** **The L.A.4** Concord CCD 4018
    As above, except Shelly Manne (*d*) replaces Hamilton.
(*) **The L.A.4 Scores! Concord CCD 6008
    As above.
*** **Watch What Happens** Concord CCD 4063
    As above, except Jeff Hamilton (*d*) replaces Manne.
*** **Zaca** Concord CCD 4131
    As above. 6/80.
*** **Montage** Concord CCD 4156
    As above. 4/81.

Though with a broader palette and dynamic range, the L.A.4 shares something of the Modern Jazz Quartet's intelligent conflation of jazz with classical forms. Almeida's presence also guarantees a hefty infusion of Latin-American themes and rhythms, and the two influences come together on CCD 4018 with a fine excerpt from Rodrigo's *Concierto De Aranjuez*, a piece which it is now difficult to hear unmediated by either Segovia or Miles Davis and Gil Evans, but which is performed with intelligence and some fire. Some of these experiments, like 'Prelude Opus 28, No. 4' on *The L.A.4 Scores!* and 'Nouveau Bach' on *Just Friends*, the two most disappointing of the albums, drift towards pretentiousness. By and large, though, the quartet has a strong jazz feel and is capable of playing, as on the excellent *Montreux* set, with a robust swing; the Ellington medley – or 'melange' – is beautifully done.

As well as a few residual Parkerisms, Shank has something of the tendency of his next model, Art Pepper, to float free of the rhythm section, which in this context permits some interesting counterpoint with Almeida. Shank's flute playing is usually more challenging but tends to accentuate a vapidity which overtakes Almeida on slower ballads, as on his (mostly forgettable) Concord albums with Charlie Byrd. The rhythm section are unimpeachable and, though Manne was a more interesting drummer, Hamilton is a better blend with the overall sound. *Watch What Happens* is a good alternative to a currently deleted *Montreux* set, with sensitive readings of 'Summertime', 'Mona Lisa', 'Nuages' and 'Misty'.

Of the two recent reappearances, there is not much to say except: steady as she goes. *Montage* is perhaps the drier and more academic of the pair, with its snatch of Villa-Lobos and the reedy chromaticism of 'Syrinx'. Brown plays out of his skin on this record and is, by some ironic contrast, rather far back on *Zaca*. As often, it is his contribution that anchors the group. To make up the deficit, Shank is masterful on the 1980 record.

Pat LaBarbera (born 1944) SOPRANO AND TENOR SAXOPHONE

*** **JMOG** Sackville SKCD2-2301
    LaBarbera; Don Thompson (*p*); Neil Swainson (*b*); Greg Joe LaBarbera (*d*). 4/87.

Though he grew up in New York State, LaBarbera moved to Canada many years ago and is now seldom heard from on record. His most renowned stint was with Buddy Rich in the 1960s and '70s. *JMOG* is an acronym for Jazz Men On The Go, with brother Joe at the drums and the experienced team of Thompson and Swainson handling the middle row. It's not a rote blowing date since the seven originals all come from the pens of LaBarbera, Swainson or Thompson and, though there's nothing fancy in the construction, the lack of standard melodies asks a little more than usual from such seasoned pros. Swainson's nocturne, 'Dark Ocean', and Thompson's thoughtful tunes are the best. But LaBarbera's tenor blows along too many familiar paths to make the record transcend the usual tenor-and-rhythm virtues.

Steve Lacy (born 1934) SOPRANO SAXOPHONE

*** **Axieme** Red R R 123120
    Lacy (*ss* solo). 9/75.
***(*) **Only Monk** Soul Note 121160
    As above. 7/85.
(*) **Solo In Situ 590051
    As above. 85.
**** **More Monk** Soul Note 121210
    As above. 4/89.
***(*) **Remains** hat ART CD 6102
    As above. 4/91.

There are, at a (now very) conservative estimate, more than 100 recordings in the Lacy discography, with a substantial proportion of those as leader or solo performer. His prolific output anticipates that of

Anthony Braxton, consisting as it does of group performances with a relatively conventional – if Thelonious Monk can ever be considered conventional – 'standards' repertoire, large-scale compositions for ensembles and mixed-media groups, right down to solo improvisation. In one significant respect, though, the two part company utterly. Where Braxton has been promiscuously eclectic in his multi-instrumentalism, tackling all the saxophones from sopranino to contrabass, and all the clarinets as well, Lacy has concentrated his considerable energies throughout his career on the soprano saxophone.

Drawing his initial inspiration from Sidney Bechet, he has combined a profound interest in Dixieland jazz with an occasionally extreme modernism. In a typical performance there may be short, almost abecedarian melodic episodes, repeated many times with minimal variation; there will be passages of free, abstract sound, often produced by sucking through the reed; there may even be strange, onomatopoeic effects, bird-calls and toneless shouts. The 1975 *Axieme* is probably the best available example of his more abstract style; the recent *Remains*, with its 'Tao' suite, reflects a more meditative and structured style that has been developing since then.

Lacy also favours tremendously long lines with no obvious developmental logic – which might be reminiscent of Lee Konitz's work, but for Lacy's insistence on long, sustained notes and modestly paced whole-note series. The weakness of *Solo*, caught live in the mid-1980s and perhaps best left in the vaults, is that such devices do untypically seem to be in default of anything larger. A melodist rather than an orthodox changes player – those unfamiliar with his music can find it deceptively simplistic, almost naïve, on first exposure – Lacy has been obsessed with the compositions of Thelonious Monk for more than 30 years and has become perhaps the foremost interpreter of Monk's music.

The two solo Monk albums are among the finest of Lacy's multifarious and often interchangeable recordings. If the earlier of the pair is less immediately appealing, it is also more challenging and requires a closer acquaintance with the source material; with the exception of 'Pannonica' and 'Misterioso', the pieces are less well known than those established favourites on *More Monk*: 'Ruby My Dear', 'Straight No Chaser', 'Trinkle Tinkle', 'Crepuscule With Nellie'. 'Epistrophy', which was the pianist's theme-tune, turns up again on *Remains* as a sort of encore.

Lacy has turned to Monk's music many times during his career. (There is more of it, alongside work by fellow-Monastics, on DIW's four-CD *Interpretations Of Monk*.) It represents a source of inexhaustible inspiration for him. However, Lacy also draws on many other musics, both formal and popular. In his solo improvisations he often accelerates essentially simple 12-tone figures to the point of disintegration, allowing each piece to end unresolved. The antithesis of bebop expressionism or the huge inscapes of John Coltrane (whose use of soprano saxophone was directly inspired by Lacy's example), the solos are cold and impersonal but not without a certain broad humour that skirts burlesque. There are perhaps more completely achieved recordings than these, but there's no better place to make acquaintance with one – or perhaps two – of the music's great originals.

*** **Soprano Sax** Original Jazz Classics OJC 130
    Lacy; Wynton Kelly (*p*); Buell Neidlinger (*b*); Dennis Charles (*d*). 11/57.
**** **Reflections** Original Jazz Classics OJC 063
    Lacy; Mal Waldron (*p*); Buell Neidlinger (*b*); Elvin Jones (*d*). 10/58.
As with *The Straight Horn*, below, there was some attempt at the end of the 1950s to market Lacy as the soprano saxophone specialist, trading on the instrument's relative unfamiliarity. *Soprano Sax* is somewhat atypical in that it consists of rather more developed harmonic improvisations on open-ended standards. Kelly's time-feel and exuberant chording aren't obviously suited to Lacy's method, and 'Rockin' In Rhythm' sounds much as if a lion were playing see-saw with a swan. There is, though, an excellent, slightly off-beat reading of 'Alone Together'. Some hints still of the problems recording engineers faced in miking Lacy's horn.

Reflections was the first of Lacy's all-Monk recordings. Waldron was one of the few piano players who understood how such intractable material could be approached, and there are hints already of what he and Lacy were capable of in duo performance. Neidlinger has an attractively firm sound on both records, but Jones sounds slightly out of place, reinforcing Lacy's characteristic tendency to ignore the explicit metre. The sound is not altogether well balanced, and Neidlinger's lower-register fills are lost on the vinyl format. Lacy, on the other hand, sounds rather acid on the CD, but the performances more than make up for minor cosmetic defects.

*** **The Straight Horn Of Steve Lacy** Candid 9007
    Lacy; Charles Davis (*bs*); John Ore (*b*); Roy Haynes (*d*). 60.
One of the best-known and certainly most accessible of Lacy's records, *The Straight Horn* sounds rather muted and tentative after the passage of three decades. In conception it marks a bridge between bebop (which was never Lacy's natural constituency) to the New Thing, as represented by two Cecil Taylor compositions. Monk again provides the keystone, but whereas the saxophonist sounds in complete sympathy with this material – 'Introspection', 'Played Twice' and 'Criss Cross' – his approach to Charlie

Parker's 'Donna Lee' sounds remarkably hesitant, all the more so given Roy Haynes's palpable delight in the accelerated metre. Nor is it certain that Lacy or his sidemen have got a firm purchase on Taylor's 'Louise' and 'Air'; compare Archie Shepp's handling of the latter on *The World Of Cecil Taylor*, also Candid.

Nevertheless, this is a significant and not unattractive record. Davis's throaty baritone fulfils much the same timbral function as Roswell Rudd's or George Lewis's trombone on later recordings, and the piano-less rhythm section generates a more sympathetic context than Elvin Jones's wilder rush. Recommended, but with reservations.

***(*) Evidence Original Jazz Classics OJC 1755

Lacy; Don Cherry (*t*); Carl Brown (*b*); Billy Higgins (*d*). 11/61.

Lacy's associations with Monk and Cecil Taylor are well known, and there was an intriguing attraction-of-opposites in his impact on John Coltrane. Rarely, though, is he ever mentioned in the same breath as the other great modernist, Ornette Coleman. In part, this is because they worked on parallel tracks, rarely intersecting but concentrating on a similar redistribution of melody and rhythm. *Evidence* is the closest Lacy comes to the sound if not the substance of Coleman's great quartets. On 'The Mystery Song' and 'Evidence', he achieves something like Ornette's lonely stillness. Cherry, on trumpet rather than one of his squeaky miniatures, provides a strong tonal contrast (but wouldn't it have been interesting to pair Lacy's soprano with cornet or pocket trumpet?) and the rhythm section, piano-less again and with the little-known Carl Brown standing as acceptable substitute for Charlie Haden, plays with good understanding.

**** Schooldays hat ART CD 6140

Lacy; Roswell Rudd (*tb*); Henry Grimes (*b*); Dennis Charles (*d*). 3/63.

A most welcome revival, this, plugging a long-standing gap in the Lacy discography. *Schooldays* is a live recording from the New York coffee-house scene that helped support so much of the New Thing; Phase Two was a favourite haunt of many of the ESP Disk crowd (see below). The music was previously available on Emanem and Qed LPs, but not much has been seen of either for years and they are now seriously collectable.

With characteristic scrupulousness, Werner Uehlinger of hat ART adds a brief *caveat* about recording quality. Though there's certainly more hiss and distortion than would have been acceptable in a studio recording of the time, the band as a whole is surprisingly well registered. *Not* surprisingly, the programme consists entirely of variations on Monk tunes. These are not approached as if they were open-ended 'standards'. Lacy remains very loyal to the basic conception of each piece, playing it straight before embellishing the structure with new features. It's interesting to hear how full-voiced he sounds in a live setting at this period; there's certainly a contrast with the studio recordings.

Rudd is magnificent as always, moving between bleakly trumpeting lines and long, richly coloured slides round Lacy's figure. Grimes suffers most from the recording, as bassists do, alas; but he also sits out the first and last tracks, 'Bye-Ya' and 'Pannonica', and it's obvious that Charles is the real engine-room. He's a pawky, satirical drummer, whacking away at the tail end of 'Monk's Mood' until Lacy's solo unravels. Watch out for him again on *The Flame* nearly 20 years later.

Though it would be valuable merely as a historical document, this is an excellent record in its own right.

**** The Forest And The Zoo ESP Disk 1060

Lacy; Enrico Rava (*t*); Johnny Dyani (*b*); Louis Moholo (d). 10/66.

A saxophonist from the Big Apple, a trumpeter from Trieste, and a rhythm section from East London, SA, and Cape Town. Lest anyone thought jazz *still* wasn't truly international, they recorded in Buenos Aires. Like *Schooldays*, Lacy's one album for ESP plugs a gap in his output.

The Forest And The Zoo consists of two long tracks (so named) and a free-floating, improvisational style that is rather different from anything else Lacy has recorded. Though he doesn't always sound entirely comfortable, the album itself is lifted into the first division by the performances of the other three. Rava positively crackles and Dyani plays long, ravelling bass lines with the singing passion he virtually cornered, reserving his clipped upper register for dialogues with the drums. His compatriot, typically, plays inside and outside almost simultaneously. Of its time, but in its way less dated than most of the ESP catalogue.

**** Weal & Woe Emanem 4004

Lacy; Steve Potts (*as, ss*); Irène Aëbi (*v, vl, clo*); Kent Carter (*b*); Oliver Johnson (*d*). 72, 73.

Two important components to this very valuable reissue of Emanem and Quark LP material. The earlier recording is a document of Lacy's first ever solo soprano saxophone concerts, made in Avignon. Just four years after Anthony Braxton's pioneering *For Alto*, it is fascinating to hear Lacy take a very different course, sinuously melodic, less antagonistic in attack than Braxton but no less percussive and definite, and no less willing to superimpose different rhythmic shapes over a pretty basic line.

The Woe was Lacy's anti-war suite, a powerfully advocated protest that gave this classic group something to get their teeth into. The recording is a little unfriendly to Aëbi and to some of the quieter soprano saxophone parts, but there is so much meat and meaning to the performances that one hardly notices any such shortcomings.

*** **Trickles** Black Saint 120008
    Lacy; Roswell Rudd (*tb, chimes*); Kent Carter (*b*); Beaver Harris (*d*). 3/76.
With his brief substantive titles, Lacy almost seems to be attempting a new generic definition with each succeeding album. There is certainly a sense in which *Trickles* works by the slowest accumulation, like the slow accretions of limestone. There is also, unfortunately, an obduracy and resistance in this music that one doesn't often find elsewhere. The fault is not with the band. Rudd plays wonderfully, carving big, abstract shapes that are shaded in by Carter and Harris, coaxing a more intense sound from the saxophonist. It's Lacy who seems unyielding. On sabbatical from his lifelong study of Monk, he seems at something of a loss, stating ideas without rationale or conviction, redeeming them only by the absolute consistency of his playing. Utterly fascinating, like all of Lacy's work, and perhaps all the more significant for being less entire and achieved, but certainly not his most successful recording.

(*) **Sidelines Improvising Artists Inc I A I 123847
    Lacy; Michael Smith (*p*). 9/76.
Recorded for Paul Bley's I A I at the zenith of its short life, this is respectably recorded but rather half-heartedly played, with Smith sounding as if he's drifted in from another session, and Lacy constantly battling to keep the whole thing within bounds. A disappointment – but, hey, who's going to buy all this stuff anyway?

*** **High, Low And Order** hat Art 6069
    Lacy; Maarten Altena (*b*). 12/77.
**** **Chirps** F M P CD 29
    Lacy; Evan Parker (*ss*). 7/85.
By the turn of the 1980s, Lacy appears to have regarded total improvisational abstraction as a way-station rather than a long-term direction in his work. Nevertheless, in *Chirps* he and fellow soprano saxophonist Evan Parker produced one of the best and most significant free albums of the decade. Concentrating on high, brief sounds that are more like insect-twitter than bird-song, the two players interleave minimalist episodes with a level of concentration that seems almost superhuman. Endlessly demanding – and a quarter of an hour longer on CD reissue – it's unlikely to appeal to anyone primed for hummable melody or more than usually susceptible to sounds at the dog-whistle end of the spectrum. It is, though, curiously involving and has considerably more accessible charm than the sere whisperings of the now-deleted duos with British guitarist Derek Bailey.

    The Altena duos are recorded in an intimate close-up. At first hearing, the spectrum seems altogether wider, ranging from the total abstraction of 'Inconsistent Shuffle' (on which Lacy doesn't blow a single note) to freely harmonic passages with a discernible beat. This good-quality CD reissue puts back together what sounds like an altogether less fragmented performance, a relationship whose moods may seem initially paradoxical to outsiders, while remaining perfectly logical to the participants.

    Lacy doesn't sound like any of these any more, but all three open up significant aspects of his technique and musical vision, and *Chirps* at least shouldn't be ignored.

(*) **Troubles Black Saint 120035
    Lacy; Steve Potts (*as, ss*); Kent Carter (*clo, b*); Oliver Johnson (*d*); Irène Aëbi (*v, vl, clo*). 5/79.
*** **The Way** hat Art 2 6154
    As above. 79.
This was the period when Lacy characterized his music as 'poly-free', an attempt to categorize his still rather ramshackle combination of unfettered group improvisation with scored or predetermined passages. One of the problems with the album is that it sounds precisely like that: uneasy alternations with little coherence or flow other than the sidewinding motion of Lacy's own lines.

    The group sounds a little more unhinged on *The Way*, a live recording from the Stadttheatre in Basle, but the open-endedness is as appealing as the more buttoned-up and shapely studio material.

***(*) **Songs** hat Art 6045
    Lacy; Steve Potts (*as, ss*); Bobby Few (*p*); Irène Aëbi (*vn, v*); Jean-Jacques Avenel (*b*); Oliver Johnson (*d*); Brion Gysin (*v*). 1/81.
**** **Futurities** hat Art 6031/2 2CD
    Lacy; George Lewis (*tb*); Steve Potts (*as, ss*); Gyde Knebusch (*hp*); Barry Wedgle (*g*); Jeff Gardner (*p*); Jean-Jacques Avenel (*b*); Oliver Johnson (*d*); Irène Aëbi (*v*). 11/84, 1/85.
Two relatively ambitious examples of Lacy's interest in multi-media encounters (the latter embraces abstract plastic images and movement, in addition to text). Robert Creeley's verse has the same fractured immediacy as Lacy's music; like all the Black Mountain poets, his work is much concerned with

'rhymes', not in the sense of precise aural consonance, but rather sympathetic semantic vibrations which lead the reader out of the text. In much the same way, Lacy has composed a group of what he was to call 'instant standards': brief, unflustered patterns which are not so much melodies as potentialities of melody and certainly a strong invitation to improvisation other than on chord progressions. The earlier *Songs*, to texts by the late Brion Gysin, co-inventor of the 'cut-up' method associated with William Burroughs, is less successful, largely because Gysin's words are too forthright to remain part of the musical fabric. Irène Aëbi's voice has a flat, almost discursive quality that is far removed from conventional jazz singing and which takes some getting used to, but her expressive range is considerable. George Lewis plays beautifully as always on *Futurities* and, like Roswell Rudd (see above) would seem a perfect duo partner for Lacy, should the opportunity present itself again. Though full marks are awarded to both albums for sheer adventurousness, it's the later set that commands attention.

***(*) **The Flame** Soul Note 121035-2
      Lacy; Bobby Few (*p*); Dennis Charles (*d*). 1/82.
Whenever he plays, Few emerges as the fulcrum of Lacy's groups. His composition, 'Wet Spot', is the briefest and the only non-Lacy number on the album, but it's a particularly clear example of how Lacy and his loyal group of collaborators have rationalized the stretched-out improvisations of Cecil Taylor and the tautness of Monk. In timbre and tonality these sessions strongly resemble Taylor's 'bass-less' trios, but with the emphasis switched unequivocally to the saxophone. Lacy's four compositions form part of an ongoing series of dedications to 'eminent source figures', or what Lacy calls his 'Luminaries'; 'The Match' is for the surrealist Man Ray, 'Gusts', 'Licks' and 'The Flame' for an assortment of instrumentalists from around the world whose music has inspired him.

   In the trio context, Lacy sounds much more rhythmic than usual and appears to adapt his line to the drummer's beat, punching his own little toneless accents at appropriate moments.

*** **The Condor** Soul Note 121135
      Lacy; as for *Songs*, but without Gysin. 6/85.
**** **Morning Joy: Live At Sunset Paris** hat Art 6014
      Lacy; Steve Potts (*as, ss*); Jean-Jacques Avenel (*b*); Oliver Johnson (*d*). 2/86.
***(*) **Flim-Flam** hat Art 6087
      Lacy; Steve Potts (*as, ss*). 12/86.
***(*) **The Window** Soul Note 121185
      Lacy; Jean-Jacques Avenel (*b*); Oliver Johnson (*d*). 7/87.
Morning Joy is perhaps the best single Lacy album, and certainly one of the most straightforward; like much of his recorded work of this period, it reworks material to be found on the excellent *Blinks*, which hat ART have unfortunately deleted. The line-up on *Morning Joy* is a stripped-down version of his long-standing sextet (pianist Bobby Few and Lacy's cellist wife, Irène Aëbi, weren't on the gig) for a one-night club date. As always, the material is a mixture of originals and Monk tunes, with 'In Walked Bud' receiving a notably bouncy reading which contrasts sharply with the slightly melancholy version on *More Monk*, above. Throughout, Lacy pitches himself against Potts's throatier and more expressive delivery, as he does in duo performance.

   The channel separation on *Flim-Flam* is a little too complete and exact to allow the two voices to merge and interact. A long track like '3 Points' begins to sound like a chance overlap rather than a coherent performance, certainly the opposite effect to the developed discourse of 'Wickets' (all 16 minutes of it) on *Morning Joy*, which ranks as one of the finest jazz performances of the later 1980s.

   'Morning Joy' also kicks off the fine 1985 *The Condor*, where the balance of written-out passages and freer improvisation seems almost ideal; it also features some of the best interplay between the two saxophones, with Potts in exceptionally good form. If one of the great pleasures of investigating Lacy's mammoth output is the comparison of (sometimes drastically, sometimes only minimally) different versions of the same repertoire piece or 'instant standard' (his term), then these are critical performances for an understanding of how unconventionally he relates to a 'rhythm section'.

   Stripped down to just saxophone, bass and drums on *The Window*, he reveals just how unconventional a player he actually is, refusing all the obvious rhythmic and chordal clues, playing lines so oblique as almost to belong to another piece altogether. 'Flakes' is another of those apparently self-descriptive compositions that resist all external reference. Again, very fine.

***(*) **One Fell Swoop** Silkheart SHCD 103
      Lacy; Charles Tyler (*as, bs*); Jean-Jacques Avenel (*b*); Oliver Johnson (*d*). 6/86.
*** **The Gleam** Silkheart SHCD 102
      As above, except omit Tyler, add Steve Potts (*as, ss*). 7/86.
Lacy's two Silkheart recordings throw up some interesting contrasts. It's fascinating to hear him working with a lower horn, as he had with Charles Davis way back. There are signs on *One Fell Swoop* that he is looking back and rerunning some ideas from his own bottom drawer, reviving that Dixieland coun-

terpoint which had tended to get unravelled and spun out at unrecognizable length in more recent years. The title-track (two vesions) and 'Ode To Lady Day' are splendid performances. Nothing quite as striking on *The Gleam*, but it's another perfectly acceptable quartet performance for enthusiasts, and the two takes of 'Napping' provide much to think about.

**(*) Image Ah Um 001
  Lacy; Steve Arguëlles (*d*). 10/87.
Arguëlles may be outclassed; Lacy may have done just one gig too many of this sort. The effect is of two players conversing politely over slightly too great a distance, like friends spotting each other by chance at opposite corners of a restaurant and refusing to get up and walk over to the other's table, thus spending the evening mouthing deafly over the gap. Lacy generally takes the lead, easing his way through Monk's 'Evidence' with almost magisterial calm, leaving the drummer to patter out completely autonomous lines and figures (how might Steve Noble have faced the same challenge?). Only towards the end of the set, which goes up a gear after the second track and then over-revs in it until almost too late, is there any real dialectic. Lacy has some fine moments, like the solo intro to 'Art', but it's not a classic.

***(*) Deadline sound aspects sas 013
  Lacy; Ulrich Gumpert (*p*). 3/85.
Gumpert is a classically schooled player with an instinctive understanding of the whole range of modern piano repertoire from Schoenberg through Satie to Cage and beyond. *Deadline* is lighter in touch than one might expect, with an intellectually playful approach to fixed intervals. By way of homage, it includes one early version of 'I Feel A Draft' (orchestrated on *Itinerary*, below; there are other versions on deleted records), a rippling theme dedicated to Lacy's long-time associate, Mal Waldron. It's by far the most affecting piece on a notably cool album, which nevertheless repays careful and repeated attention.

**** Sempre Amore Soul Note 121170
  Lacy; Mal Waldron (*p*). 2/86.
***(*) Let's Call This . . . Esteem Slam CD 501
  As above. 5/93.
The dedication to Waldron signals one of the most productive partnerships in Lacy's career. The pianist's name comes first on the wonderful *Sempre Amore*, but the honours are strictly shared. Waldron's big, dark left-hand chords and single-note statements take some of the acid out of Lacy's frail and thinly voiced takes on a bag of Ellington and Strayhorn themes. The opening 'Johnny Come Lately' is appealingly off-centre and 'Prelude To A Kiss' sounds at the edge of sleep. It's worth comparing 'A Flower Is A Lovesome Thing' to the version Waldron recorded with Marion Brown the previous year on *Songs Of Love And Regret*, where his accompaniment is little more than a sequence of moodily recessed pedals. With the undemonstrative Lacy, he's all over the place, arpeggiating and trilling furiously, like Wordsworth trying to explain to Newton what a flower really is.

 Let's Call This . . . Esteem shouldn't be confused with the hat ART *Let's Call This*, which still hasn't made it to CD. The Slam disc was recorded during a concert at Oxford Playhouse, compered by another soprano specialist, Lol Coxhill. The sound is oddly cavernous but the performances are uniformly excellent. Another version of 'Johnny Come Lately' suggests how much they've grown into the partnership. The Monk tunes – 'Let's Call This', 'Monk's Dream', 'Evidence' and the inevitable 'Epistrophy' – are expertly co-ordinated and by no means soulless. Waldron's own 'Snake Out' sounds great without a larger band, and the pianist has his moment again on 'In A Sentimental Mood'. Good stuff.

***(*) The Door RCA/Novus 83049
  Lacy; collective personnel as for *Songs*, but without Gysin; and add Sam Woodyard (*d*). 7/88.
A marvellously concentrated set of performances from internal permutations of Lacy's (by now almost telepathically responsive) regular band. The addition of a second drummer on 'Virgin Jungle' follows no obvious rationale but works remarkably well, and there are intriguing Ellington touches in the distribution of voices. The duos and trio with Few, Avenel, and Avenel and Johnson are completely confident, highlighting Lacy's searching ricercars and 'found' melodies. 'Clichés' – again from *Blinks* – sets him against Avenel on African thumb piano, odd but quite beautiful and far from hackneyed.

**(*) Itinerary hat Art 6079
  Lacy; Klaus Peham (*t*); Franz Koglmann (*flhn*); Glenn Ferris, Radu Malfatti (*tb*); Raoul Herget (*tba*); Andreas Kolbe (*f, picc*); Steve Potts (*as, ss*); Urs Leimgruber (*ss, ts*); Hans Steiner (*bcl*); Bobby Few (*p*); Burkhard Stangl (*g*); Gyde Knebusch (*hp*); Irène Aëbi (*clo, vn, v*); Jean-Jacques Avenel (*b*); John Betsch (*d*); Sam Kelly (*perc*). 11/90.
Surprise that this is Steve Lacy's first recording with a large group of his own may be tempered somewhat by the recognition that some of the material is more than 20 years old. (The liner art is lovingly produced, but might have gone with a free-jazz record *c*. 1975.) The second track, 'Cloudy'

(part of a triptych called 'Precipitation Suite' which has been played by the Rova Saxophone Quartet and the Kronos String Quartet), and the later 'Moon' both appear in solo performance on the 1975 album, *Stabs*. It's not immediately clear what the music gains from orchestration, for its essence remains as simple as raindrops, and it's tempting to see the tune's history as a piece of reverse-action natural history, a bright condensation reversing course and turning into a murky cloud.

Itinerary as a whole is dedicated to Gil Evans and betrays more than a few touches of the master's hand, notably in the handling of the saxophones. Individual items are also dedicated: 'I Feel A Draft' (which was previewed on *Deadline*, above) to Mal Waldron, 'Cloudy' to the conceptualist Giuseppe Chiari, 'Rain' to Cecil Taylor (who provides its informing scale) and the title-track to 'Juan Louis Borges' (who might have enjoyed being told of the mistaken version of his name). Through-composed, the pieces seem a little stiff, but in the way that Borges's prose is stiff, resistant to critical inquiry. But there's little flexibility in the playing, which sounds like a sight-read rehearsal. It's easy to be put off by surfaces: Irène Aëbi's flat recitation of a Buckminster Fuller text on 'Sun' is calculatedly odd and not intended to sound lyrical. Some of the voicings are deliberately wayward. The problems lie deeper. This does not sound like music that was written for these forces. Working outside his natural territory, Lacy looks to have 'worked up' existing material with very little sense of the inherent problems of idiom and scale. With all the 'anxiety of influence', he seems to have misread Gil Evans's example.

***(*) **Remains** hat Art CD 6102
Lacy (*ss* solo). 4/91.

Dominated by two long pieces, this is Lacy's most accomplished solo performance for some time, and a close-up, attentive recording catches every gritty little resonance and breath noise. This is particularly appropriate to the opening piece, actually a suite of shorter tracks inspired by the *Tao Te Ching* and very much concerned with what might be thought of as the interface between the physical and the spiritual: 'Bone', 'The Breath', 'Name', 'Life On Its Way'. This is an abiding concern of Lacy's and it comes through again in the 18-minute 'Remains', a piece inspired by Belgian artist James Ensor's bizarre 1880 self-portrait of his own skeleton as it would appear in 1960. Originally a dance piece, it explores ideas of decay and disintegration by making virtuosic use of repetitions with a progressively diminished body of material. Largely scored, it also includes three improvised sections.

Lacy's work is often thought to be desiccated and intellectual, fatally unfunky. As if to quash that one, Lacy follows 'Tao' and 'Remains' with a Kansas City blues, 'Afterglow', dedicated to Jay McShann, and a brief take of Monk's 'Epistrophy', which is typically quite unlike any other performance he has recorded.

***(*) **Clangs** hat ART CD 6116
Lacy; Hans Kennel (*t*); Glenn Ferris (*tb*); Steve Potts (*as, ss*); Bobby Few, Eric Watson (*p*); Sonhando Estwick (*vib*); Jean- Jacques Avenel (*b*); John Betsch (*d*); Sam Kelly (*perc*); Irène Aëbi, Nicholas Isherwood (*v*). 3/92.

**** **We See** hat ART CD 6127
As above, except omit Ferris, Few, Watson, Kelly, Isherwood, Aëbi. 9/92.

This is a band working at its peak. The doubling of the Sextet on *Clangs* causes some undesirable complications without really adding anything to the texture, though individually Ferris and the widely separated pianists contribute a good deal to its success. Much better is the new Monk album; 1992 vintage, Lacy tackles 'Evidence' and 'Misterioso' as if he had heard them only yesterday. Potts has grown hugely in stature and Kennel brings a throaty bark to the slower tracks that is curiously moving. Strongly recommended both, but don't on any account miss *We See*.

***(*) **Revenue** Soul Note 121234
Lacy; Steve Potts (*as, ss*); Jean-Jacques Avenel (*b*); John Betsch (*d*). 2/93.

**** **Vespers** Soul Note 121260
As above, except add Ricky Ford (*ts*); Tom Varner (*frhn*); Bobby Few (*p*); Irène Aëbi (*v*). 7/93.

Betsch's arrival on board gave the Lacy group a less raw, slightly more delicate rhythmic feel. Even so, as he proves, on 'The Rent' and the title-track, the new drummer is no slouch when it comes to sticking his foot in the door and demanding a hearing. He powers these tracks along very crisply and, on 'Gospel', subtly stretches and compresses the time exactly in keeping with Lacy's own elastic pulse. Potts more than ever brings in ideas of his own and a range of contributions that might be likened to Don Cherry's in the classic Ornette quartet: responsive, aware of the leader's intentions and requirements, but still absolutely individual and effortlessly taking up point on 'The Uh Uh Uh'.

Now in the middle of a long, purple patch, Lacy seems incapable of making an indifferent album. Where the previous pair were instrumental (*Clangs* especially, even in its treatment of voices), *Vespers* is focused on Blaga Dimitrova's lyrics for Aëbi. The songs are softly melancholy farewells and remembrances of departed friends and idols: Miles Davis, Corrado Costa, the artists Arshile Gorky (whose 1946 abstract graces the cover) and Keith Haring (whose bold, stark lines had something in common with Lacy's saxophone sound), clarinettist John Carter, John Coltrane, Charles Mingus and Stan Getz. This is perhaps the most personal music we've heard from Lacy, and it is all the more affecting in coming from a man normally so reticent about inward states. Aëbi is magnificent, as is Ricky Ford, who now notoriously plays better on other people's records than on his own.

Guy Lafitte (born 1927) TENOR SAXOPHONE

***(*) **Joue Charles Trenet** Black & Blue 59 190
>   Lafitte; Marc Hemmeler, Hank Jones (*p*); Milt Buckner (*org*); George Duvivier, Jack Sewing
>   (*b*); Philippe Combelle, J. C. Heard, Sam Woodyard (*d*). 77–84.

If the name Trenet is not familiar, you can rely on having heard 'La Mer' on the radio at some point in your life. He is not a songwriter who has frequently invited jazz musicians, and Lafitte, who is a part-time player in essence, has always had the luxury of following his own star. Stylistically, he is a Websterian with just a few pre-boppish hints of Don Byas sewn like sequins on the warm, velvety contours of his solos. These are basically trio sessions recorded over the better part of a decade. The organ tracks are dispensable, but Jones is a near-ideal foil. 'I Wish You Love' is everything a jazz ballad should be, without a single jazz-ballad cliché. A gorgeous record by a much-underrated stylist.

Bireli Lagrene (born 1966) GUITAR

*** **Routes To Django** Jazzpoint JP 1003
>   Lagrene; Jorg Reiter (*p*); Wolfgang Lackerschmidt (*vib*); Gaiti Lagrene, Tschirglo Loeffler (*g*);
>   Scmitto Kling (*vn*); Jan Jankeje (*b*). 5/80.
*** **Bireli Swing '81** Jazzpoint JP 1009
>   As above, except omit Reiter, Lackerschmidt and Kling; add Bernd Rabe (*ss*), Allen Blairman
>   (*d*). 4/81.

If Django Reinhardt were to have a spiritual heir, it would surely be Lagrene, who emerged from a gypsy community in the 1980s to stun European and American audiences with his virtuosity. Both of the above were recorded in concert, with Lagrene's electrifying improvisations (all done on acoustic guitar) conducted on a range of material which includes swing, blues, bop and original themes, all of it mastered with effortless aplomb, even when it sounds as if the guitarist isn't sure of his ground.

  That hint of flying blind gives the greatest excitement to the debut album, *Routes To Django*, which includes a nerve-racking romp through the tune identified as 'Night And Day' (actually 'Don't Worry 'Bout Me'). The 1981 session is nearly as good, although Rabe is an irrelevance; but from this point Lagrene began to fall foul of seeming like a novelty act.

(*) **Stuttgart Aria Jazzpoint JP 1019
>   Lagrene; Vladislaw Sendecki (*ky*); Jaco Pastorius (*b, p, v*); Jan Jankeje (*syn, v*); Peter Lubke (*d*);
>   Serge Bringolf (*perc, v*). 3/86.

Lagrene meets Pastorius. This souvenir of a European tour is good-humoured but tends to go the way of all live fusion albums: a noisy dead-end. Salvaged by flashes of brilliance by both frontmen, including a ferocious 'Donna Lee', it doesn't amount to very much. Lagrene's subsequent Blue Note albums all seem to be missing in action at present.

Oliver Lake (born 1944) ALTO SAXOPHONE, OTHER SAXOPHONES, FLUTE

**** **Zaki** hat ART CD 6113
>   Lake; Michael Gregory Jackson (*g*); Pheeroan akLaff (*d*). 9/79.
*** **Prophet** Black Saint BSR 0044
>   Lake; Baikida Carroll (*t, flhn*); Donald Smith (*p*); Jerry Harris (*b*); Pheeroan akLaff (*d*). 8/80.
***(*) **Gallery** Gramavision GR 8609
>   As above, except add Rasul Siddik (*t*). 6/86.
**** **Compilation** Gramavision GV 79458
>   Lake; Frank Abel, Geri Allen (*p*); Anthony Peterson, Alphonia Tims (*g*); Santi Debriano, Billy
>   Grant, Fred Hopkins (*b*); Andrew Cyrille, Pheeroan akLaff, Gene Lake, Brandon Ross (*d*);
>   Jawara (*perc*). 82, 86, 87, 88.
*** **Boston Duets** Music & Arts CD 732
>   Lake; Donal Leonellis Fox (*p*). 8/89.

***(*) **Again And Again** Gramavision GRV 74682
     Lake; John Hicks (*p*); Reggie Workman (*b*); Pheeroan akLaff (*d*). 4/91.
*** **Edge-ing** Black Saint 120104
     Lake; Charles Eubanks (*p*); Reggie Workman (*b*); Andrew Cyrille (*d*). 6/93.
*** **Dedicated To Dolphy** Black Saint 120144
     Lake; Russell Gunn (*t*); Charles Eubanks (*p*); Belden Bullock (*b*); Cecil Brooks (*d*). 11/94.

A founding member of the pioneering World Saxophone Quartet, Lake has been rather neglected in the rush to sanctify his WSQ partner, David Murray. A player of great power who touches bases in funk and free improvisation, Lake is also capable of great sophistication and a sort of convulsive beauty that requires a little time to assimilate.

The trio Lake brought to the Willisau Jazz Festival in 1979 was unquestionably ahead of its time, and it took a long while for *Zaki*, a recording of that event, to emerge on disc. In retrospect, it's one of the best of Lake's records, free-flowing, tough and uncompromising from start to finish. Lake has never quite returned to this style, though there are echoes of it, paradoxically, in the slightly formal setting of the duos with Donal Fox.

Gallery is the later and better of two impressive sets involving pianist Geri Allen (who has since largely dissociated herself from this aesthetic). Less imposing than *Otherside*, it nevertheless remains an impressive performance. Siddik's contributions to 'The Sport Suite' add a further dimension to Lake's multi-instrumentalism. The tunes are all compact and rather intense, and much is required of the three rhythm players.

Lake shares with Allen a powerful enthusiasm for the work of Eric Dolphy and, on *Prophet*, includes two of Dolphy's most vibrant compositions, 'Hat and Beard' and 'Something Sweet, Something Tender', both from the classic *Out to Lunch!*. They're imaginative re-readings, not just pastiches, and certainly a good deal more inventive than the very straight versions of those same two tracks (plus 'Miss Ann', 'G.W.', '245' and Mal Waldron's 'Fire Waltz') on *Dedicated To Dolphy*, which is in every way a disappointment. The one quantifiable plus is the trumpet-work of Russell Gunn from St Louis, sounding brisk and bright and very like the young Freddie Hubbard.

Gallery may be a more coherent piece of work than its predecessors, but the earlier album is better representative of Lake's able synthesis of styles. To some extent, though, it is rendered redundant by *Compilation*, which preserves the best of it alongside material from the no-longer-available *Impala* and *Otherside*, and a solitary track from the much earlier *Jump Up*. It hangs together well, with the bands organized like latter-day Dolphy units. Lake's keening intensity somehow never palls, and Geri Allen comps and solos with imagination and grace.

Again And Again offers an uncommonly lyrical and mainstream performance from Lake. Only 'Aztec' and 'Re-cre-ate' approach the angularity one normally expects of his soloing. There's no doubt that Hicks contributes substantially to the romantic atmosphere, and the closing 'M.I.L.D.' (apparently Lake's wife's initials) is the most nakedly emotional he has allowed himself to be on record.

He veers towards lyricism again on *Edge-ing*, rejigging 'Zaki' for a fuller-voiced band and bringing in material like John Hicks's almost schmaltzy 'Peanut Butter' and Curtis Clark's unexpected 'Verve Nerve'. Lake's bluesy tone is eloquent enough to sustain some rather bland arrangements, and the bass and drum interactions are consistently interesting. Which leaves the finger pointing at Eubanks, a rather dull accompanist who doesn't quite have the Hicks trick of playing spikily *and* lyrically off pat.

Ralph Lalama (born 1951) TENOR SAXOPHONE

***(*) **Feelin' And Dealin'** Criss Cross 1046
     Lalama; Tom Harrell (*t, flhn*); Barry Harris (*p*); Peter Washington (*b*); Kenny Washington (*d*).
     11/90.
*** **Momentum** Criss Cross 1063
     Lalama; Kenny Barron (*p*); Dennis Irwin (*b*); Kenny Washington (*d*). 12/91.
*** **You Know What I Mean** Criss Cross 1097
     Lalama; George Cables (*p*); Dennis Irwin (*b*); Leroy Williams (*d*). 12/93.

A former section-player with the Jones–Lewis big band, Lalama plays with iron in his tone. His choice of composer credits gives his idols away – Rollins, Dexter, Mobley – and though he sometimes falls prey to the habitual anonymity of the great section-man, his improvising has real class and substance from moment to moment. A very fine solo on Mobley's 'Third Time Around' on the first record shows what he can do: the way he masters the rhythmic suspensions in the tune, throws in a couple of unexpected, whistling high notes and takes in a timbral exploration along the way suggests technical and conceptual mastery. The record isn't consistently good, and Harrell doesn't seem quite at his best, but there is a lot to enjoy. *Momentum* is a degree more ordinary: Lalama handles the casting as sole horn with aplomb, but the session ends up as merely decent hard bop. *You Know What I Mean* follows a similar pattern, although Lalama's playing continues to give much pleasure: his persuasive handling of 'This Love Of Mine', where his solo manages to get all over the horn without any apparent effort, is very beguiling, and nearly every track has its own satisfactions.

Lambert, Hendricks & Ross GROUP

***(*) **Sing A Song Of Basie** Impulse GRP 11122
     Dave Lambert, Jon Hendricks, Annie Ross (*v*); Freddie Green (*g*); Nat Pierce (*p*); Eddie Jones (*b*); Sonny Payne (*d*). 8 & 9/57.

Stanley Dance's liner-note (originally written in 1965) provides some useful background to the relatively brief fashion of jazz vocalese. One thing that he doesn't make clear is an important distinction with a classical technique known as *vocalise*, whereby the singer fits wordless syllables and phonemes to the music, sometimes ad lib., often in accordance with a strict score. Jazz vocalese, which may have begun as a version of the classical form with the Mills Brothers' vocal mimicry of brass and saxophone sections, developed along very different lines when Eddie Jefferson and then King Pleasure and Annie Ross began to fit words to famous jazz solos; Jefferson's vocalization of James Moody's solo on 'I'm In The Mood For Love' was perhaps better known in the King Pleasure version; Ross's virtuoso interpretation of Wardell Gray's 'Twisted' was a huge hit (and was revived nearly 40 years later by soul singer Crystal Waters on a chart album). Perhaps the finest exponent of vocalese, though, was Jon Hendricks, who seemed to have an unfailing facility for words to fit particular instrumental effects and for glib rhymes to link lines together. Whatever the weather.

On *Sing A Song Of Basie* Creed Taylor and Irv Greenbaum used multi-tracking, enabling the vocal trio to mimic with extraordinary precision the instrumental parts in 10 Basie big-band arrangements. The liner-notes reproduce the words used and the sections and solos copied. Ross had a particular genius for the timbre of trumpets. Her section-work is remarkable, full of growls, 'shakes' and sudden, percussive blasts; her versions of Buck Clayton's solo on 'Fiesta In Blue' and Joe Newman's on 'Blues Backstage' are quite remarkable, as is her 'tenor saxophone' duet with Hendricks on 'Two For The Blues' (which had originally featured Frank Foster and Frank Wess).

Though a relatively short-lived phenomenon in this (with due apology to Hendricks) 'white' form, vocalese called on a long-standing black tradition of rapid-fire, hip improvisation, and it reappears in its purest form in contemporary rap, perhaps the most influential popular music of the late 1980s and early '90s.

Lammas GROUP

*** **This Morning** EFZ 1008
     Tim Garland (*sax, f, syn*); Don Paterson (*g*); Jason Rebello (*p*); Steafan Hannigan (*uileann pipes, bodhran*); Mark Fletcher (*d*); Christine Tobin (*v*). 94.

Lammas are not strictly a jazz group, but they follow on in the line of outfits like Ken Hyder's Talisker (with which the excellent Paterson was associated) in trying to combine Celtic melodies with blues-based improvisation. Garland and Paterson are intelligent enough as musicians to recognize where this is and isn't possible, and there is little sign of them trying to put a kilt or a shamrock on everything. Most of the material is allowed to find its own direction and geographical location, and only Tobin's slightly mannered vocals tend to force things into 'ethnic' pigeonholes.

Harold Land (born 1928) TENOR SAXOPHONE, FLUTE, OBOE

*** **Harold In The Land Of Jazz** Original Jazz Classics OJC 162
     Land; Rolf Ericson (*t*); Carl Perkins (*p*); Leroy Vinnegar (*b*); Frank Butler (*d*). 1/58.

Made towards the end of his stint with bassist Curtis Counce's band, this is the first of a series of fine Land records. A still underrated player, hampered by a rather dour tone, Land favoured – or happened across – unusual piano players, giving more than one of his albums a harmonic unease that is more disconcerting than genuinely attractive. Perkins's crab-wise gait across the keyboard is mitigated by the vibrant rhythm work of Vinnegar and Butler, and the best track on the album is the quartet 'You Don't Know What Love Is', which the showy Ericson sits out (Land made some interesting brass appointments as well).

***(*) **The Fox** Original Jazz Classics OJC 343
     Land; Dupree Bolton (*t*); Elmo Hope (*p*); Herbie Lewis (*b*); Frank Butler (*d*). 8/59.

Jazz history has drawn something of a veil over the subsequent career of trumpeter Dupree Bolton.

Though this is his solitary appearance in the current catalogue, he plays with confidence and some fire, seemingly at ease at the accelerated tempo of 'The Fox' and the easier flow of 'Mirror-Mind Rose'. If Carl Perkins recalls a crab, then Elmo Hope has to be, yes, a butterfly. His touch was as light as his ideas and colours were fleeting. One of the least dynamic of players (and singularly dependent on drummers of Butler's kidney), he was nevertheless able to keep track with a rhythm line he wasn't actually playing, laying out astonishing melody figures on 'One Down' in what is probably his best recorded performance, certainly a step ahead of *Harold In The Land Of Jazz*.

Land is an underrated composer with a deep feeling for the blues, who never quite translated his most compelling ideas into practice. *The Fox*, tricky and fugitive as much of it is, must be thought his finest moment.

(*) Eastward Ho! Original Jazz Classics OJC 493
    Land; Kenny Dorham (*t*); Amos Trice (*p*); Joe Peters (*d*). 7/60.
Pianist Trice was briefly known for his work with Wardell Gray and, heard blindfold, this rather unusual session might well suggest Gray's work. Land and Dorham are both in fine voice but rarely seem to be thinking along the same lines. 'Slowly' and 'On A Little Street In Singapore' (the latter well known to Glenn Miller fans) are both engagingly handled. Not one of Land's best records, though.

***(*) Xocia's Dance** Muse M 5272
    Land; Oscar Brashear (*t, flhn*); George Cables (*p*); Bobby Hutcherson (*vib*); John Heard (*b*);
    Billy Higgins (*d*); Ray Armando (*perc*). 10/81.
*** **Mapanzi** Concord 4044
    Land; Blue Mitchell (*t, flhn*); Kirk Lightsey (*p*); Reggie Johnson (*b*); Albert 'Tootie' Heath (*d*).
    77.
The association with Hutcherson was a much-needed shot in the arm for Land. The two-decade gap in the current catalogue sees the saxophonist emerging from a long and not always coherent examination of John Coltrane's harmonics with a new, mature style that retains much of the temper of his late-1950s work, but with added strength in the upper register. The cuts with Hutcherson are more interesting than those with Cables alone; the pianist is apt to be a rather stultifying player in groups of this size but, pitched against the vibes, he damps notes more sharply and cleans up the edges of his chords. Brashear has a lovely tone, with an unapologetic wobble round the 'break'. The overall sound is very good indeed.

The earlier *Mapanzi* is *almost* a terrific record, but Mitchell seems ill at ease with the saxophonist's new-found modernism and catches light only on his own 'Blue Silver'. Land and Lightsey work well together, and the leader's 'Rapture' is a finely etched confessional that pitches his adapted 'sheets of sound' approach against the pianist's highly wrought but never overwrought chords.

*** **A Lazy Afternoon** Postcards POST 1008
    Land; Bill Henderson (*p*); Alan Pasqua (*syn*); James Leary (*b*); Billy Higgins (*d*); orchestra
    conducted by Ray Ellis. 12/94.
Comfy, pipe-and-slippers settings for the old chap. Ellis's arrangements are lush and uncomplicated, and Land responds with some of his most soulful playing in years. All the themes are standards and one only wonders how it would have panned out if the saxophonist had worked with rhythm section alone. There are intermittent question marks about his intonation, and the pacing of some of the songs is a little odd, though mostly on the fast side. A lovely record, though, if you have an appetite for strings dates.

Art Lande (born 1947) PIANO, PERCUSSION

*** **Rubisa Patrol** ECM 1081
    Lande; Mark Isham (*t, flhn, ss*); Bill Douglas (*b, f*); Glenn Cronkhite (*d*). 5/76.
The first of Lande's two albums for ECM with this band (the second record is deleted) has now been reissued on CD. Renewed acquaintance with the music suggests that it is rather more durable than we had previously allowed. Isham, who has spent most of his time subsequently in film music, plays with a steely elegance and contributes two of the best themes, 'Many Chinas' (which opens the record after Douglas's remarkable bamboo flute solo) and 'For Nancy'. Although Lande's improvising is unremark-able, his own music displays a sense of nocturnal quiet that the group distil with great skill. The sound remains limpidly beautiful on CD.

*** **Skylight** ECM 1208
    Lande; Paul McCandless (*ss, cor, ob, bcl, f*); David Samuels (*vib, mar, perc*). 5/81.
Another charming record, though more of a co-operative venture: Lande contributes two tunes, and one of them, 'Dance Of The Silver Skeezix', is pure floss. It's McCandless's pair of compositions that

suit the trio best. But the music as a whole is unaffectedly sweet: a bright summer's day after the cool evening of *Rubisa Patrol*.

Landes Jugend Jazz Orchester Hessen GROUP

*** **Magic Morning** Mons CD 1905
> Ralph Himmler, Norbert Kuner, Joachim Losch, Christoph Schopsdau, Randy Brecker (*t*); Jurgen Neudert, Chris Perschke, Mario Cimiotti, Michael Grun, Gunter Bollmann (*tb*); Ed Partyka (*btb*); André Cimiotti, Christian Weidner, Felix Petry, Karen Schafer, Jens Hunstein, Oliver Leicht, Wolfgang Deifenbach, Thomas Bachmann (*reeds*), Markus Horn (*p*); Christian Muller (*g*); Andreas Buchmann (*b*); Simon Zimbardo, Roman Beilharz (*d*); Christof Wettich (*perc*); Dee Daniels (*v*). 4-5/93.

Agreeable if unmilitant big-band music, staffed mainly by capable German session-players. Aside from a couple of standards, the music is penned by the likes of Bob Florence and John Clayton, which suggests the kind of lucid though unadventurous fare on offer. Dee Daniels contributes a couple of spirited vocals, but the most welcome guest is Randy Brecker, whose own chart for 'Guaraja' and incisive trumpet part makes for the best track on the record.

Eddie Lang (1904–33) GUITAR

***(*) **A Handful Of Riffs** ASV AJA 5061
> Lang; King Oliver (*c*); Leo McConville, Andy Secrest, Bill Margulis (*t*); Tommy Dorsey, Bill Rank (*tb*); Jimmy Dorsey (*cl, as*); Charlie Strickfadden, Bernard Daly (*as*); Izzy Friedman (*cl, ts*); J. C. Johnson, Frank Signorelli, Arthur Schutt (*p*); Hoagy Carmichael (*p, cel*); Henry Whiteman (*vn*); Lonnie Johnson (*g*); Joe Tarto, Mike Trafficante (*b*); George Marsh, Stan King (*d*); Justin Ring (*perc*). 4/27–10/29.
*** **Jazz Guitar Virtuoso** Yazoo 1059
> Lang; Frank Signorelli, Rube Bloom, Arthur Schutt (*p*); Lonnie Johnson, Carl Kress (*g*); Justin Ring (*chimes*). 27–29.

Eddie Lang was the first guitarist to make a major impact on jazz away from the blues, and even there he took a hand by recording many duets with the 'authentic' bluesman, Lonnie Johnson. Lang's polished, civilized art was worked out in dance bands and as an accompanist – after joining Paul Whiteman in the late 1920s, the guitarist struck up a professional kinship with Bing Crosby, who hired him until his early death. He was an important member of the white New York school of the period and can be found on records by Beiderbecke, Joe Venuti and the Dorseys, but the sides made under his own name were also plentiful. We still await a truly comprehensive CD collection, but the two discs above provide a useful if finally inadequate representation of his work.

Exasperatingly, eight of the Yazoo tracks are also included on the ASV set. Yazoo concentrate on Lang the soloist, including all eight of the sides he made in that context, plus two tracks with Carl Kress and three with Johnson. There isn't much jazz in Rachmaninov's 'Prelude' or 'April Kisses', but showpieces like 'Eddie's Twister' and the luxuriant duet with Johnson on 'Blue Guitars' show all of Lang's beauty of touch, harmonic shrewdness and rhythmical dexterity. A couple more spirited tracks wouldn't have come amiss here, and the ration of 14 tracks is somewhat short measure.

The ASV issue offers a wider choice of 21 pieces, including the famous session with King Oliver on cornet and the five tracks by an orchestra led nominally by Lang. Sound on both issues is generally very good: the Yazoo is a little livelier but has a higher level of surface hiss. A comprehensive edition of Lang's solo and duet work is still awaited in a single CD package. His tracks with violinist Joe Venuti are discussed under Venuti's name.

Don Lanphere (born 1928) TENOR SAXOPHONE, SOPRANO SAXOPHONE

*** **First Sessions 1949/50** Prestige PCD 24114
> Lanphere; Fats Navarro (*t*); Al Haig, Duke Jordan (*p*); Tubby Phillips, Tommy Potter (*b*); Roy Hall, Max Roach (*d*). 7 & 9/49.

Hailing from the far north-west of the United States, Lanphere made a momentous decision in 1947 when he moved to New York rather than down the long coast to Los Angeles. His fiddly, off-beat phrasing and inimitable tone might well have been rationalized away in warmer climes and among cooler jazz; on the other hand, his playing career might have been more continuous. In 1948 and 1949 he recorded promising sets with trumpeter Fats Navarro and some debut sides with his own quartet, which featured Duke Jordan. The Navarro cuts are better, largely because the rhythm section of Haig, Potter and Roach is more accomplished than Lanphere's own.

It's interesting to listen to the saxophonist in close proximity to sessions from Cool exponents Lennie Tristano and Lee Konitz; the kinship is immediately evident, even amid the boppish phrases. *First Sessions* is not simply a chronicle of early promise; more than one of the tyros featured on it came to a sticky end. Lanphere's at least wasn't terminal. Introduced to heroin in New York, he was charged with possession and fled home to Washington State, where he sold rather than made records for most of the next 20 years, playing rather intermittently. He managed to outride the nightmare, though, and re-emerged, with a robust, Born Again faith, in the 1980s.

***(*) **Go . . . Again** Hep 2040
    Lanphere; Jon Pugh (*t*); Jeff Hay (*tb*); Marc Seales (*p, syn*); Chuck Deardorf (*b*); Dean Hodges (*d*); Jay Clayton (*v*). 1/87 & 3/88.
***(*) **Don Lanphere / Larry Coryell** Hep 2048
    As above, except omit Pugh, Clayton; add Larry Coryell (*g*). 4/90.

Go . . . Again harks back to Lanphere's 1949 sessions with Fats Navarro, a free blow round the chords of 'The Way You Look Tonight'. Trumpet and trombone accompany the saxophone at opposite ends of the register. 'What Are You Doing The Rest Of Your Life' is for soprano saxophone and synthesizer; Lanphere plays it straight, with a delivery reminiscent of Ronnie Scott. Jay Clayton's vocal on 'Darn That Dream' is pitched somewhere between Sheila Jordan and Carmen McRae. A beautiful album, resolutely performed.

It's a pity there isn't more duo material with Coryell. Horace Silver's 'Peace' was chosen as a brief 'Amen' to the 1990 session, a scant minute that retrospectively promises much. At the opposite end, the opening 'Dragon Gate' leaves Lanphere on the outskirts of a trombone–guitar unison statement until he comes in with a smoothly burnished soprano solo. Bill Evans's 'Very Early' has him shift to a less familiar or effective alto. Coryell takes the lead on a duet 'Spring Can Really Hang You Up The Most' with keyboard man Seales, who's an impressive writer too on the strength of 'Ascending Truth'. Coryell's busy action and pure diction fit remarkably well with Lanphere's, and the album has an engaging sweetness of tone. Recommended.

Ellis Larkins (born 1923) PIANO

(*) **Duologue Black Lion BLCD 760911
    Larkins (*p* solo). 54.
(*) **A Smooth One Black & Blue 591232
    Larkins; George Duvivier (*b*); J. C. Heard (*d*). 7/77.
***(*) **At Maybeck Recital Hall** Concord CCD 4533
    Larkins (*p* solo). 3/92.

Larkins's mastery is so understated that his reputation lags some way behind his abilities. Although he has been active for over half a century – he was a child prodigy in his native Baltimore and worked in New York clubs through the 1940s – there are very few records under his own name, since he's worked most prolifically as an accompanist to singers. *Duologue* offers four brief solos from 1954 (the rest of the record features Lee Wiley with a Ruby Braff group). *A Smooth One* is Larkins's only available trio date. Several of the eight pieces remind one of his judgement that with some songs 'you just play them and get out'; but there are some bewitching moments hidden behind his professional excellence.

The Maybeck recital finds him back in the spotlight at last, and seemingly bemused by it: the monochrome photograph on the front sleeve looks like an old blues daguerrotype, with Larkins posing in his old-fashioned suit and wide tie. The music exists in a state of old-world elegance, too. He chose a rarefied selection of songs – 'Howdja Like To Love Me', 'I Don't Want To Cry Any More', 'Leave Me Alone' – as well as some Ellington and a tune of his own, 'Perfume And Rain', that really does sound like raindrops on the keys. His proper technique, off-kilter humour and very slow, stately swing make up a kind of jazz that has almost vanished; here is a reminder of it.

Prince Lasha (born 1929) ALTO SAXOPHONE, FLUTE

***(*) **Firebirds** Original Jazz Classics OJC 1822
    Lasha; Sonny Simmons (*as*); Bobby Hutcherson (*vib*); Buster Williams (*b*); Charles Moffett (*d*). 65.

Lasha – pronounced 'Lashay' – was in the same Fort Worth high school band as Ornette Coleman and King Curtis. There are elements of both in his playing, should you wish to look for them, but the dominant influence is Eric Dolphy, with whom Lasha played on *Iron Man*. That session also featured Hutcherson and Simmons, who both appear on the one surviving record.

Lasha has a frail, slightly thin tone on alto saxophone, explained in part by his choice of a plastic instrument (this was inspired not so much by Ornette Coleman as by Charlie Parker's use of a bakelite horn at the famous Massey Hall concert); as a result, he often sounds as if he may be playing a North African or Asian wind instrument of variable pitch. Following the same instinct for unusual colours, he also uses a wooden flute, which gives a softer, slightly 'dead' timbre; though again influenced by Dolphy, it is a markedly individual sound which anticipates the later work of multi-instrumentalists like Oliver Lake, Douglas Ewart and, above all, Henry Threadgill. *Firebirds* is enough to suggest that Lasha is a figure who deserves wider acknowledgement.

Steve LaSpina (born 1954) BASS

*** **New Horizon** Steeplechase SCCD 31313
    LaSpina; Billy Drewes (*ss, ts*); Marc Copland (*p*); Jeff Hirshfield (*d*). 4/92.
This is distinguished by persistently inventive writing by the leader. LaSpina is best known on record for his association wih Jim Hall, and he shares something of the guitarist's wryly expressive streak when it comes to composing: check the very slow but funky 'You Can't Go Back'. The ballads, especially 'Socks', a dedication to Bobby Scott, are very pleasant, and Drewes is a tenorman who has something of the fluidity and soft-edged articulation of late-period Getz. If there's a weakness, it's Copland, whose playing is undeniably deft but can sound pretentiously pleased with itself. LaSpina himself plays very songful lines.

Last Exit GROUP

**** **Last Exit** Enemy EMY 101
    Peter Brötzmann (*reeds*); Sonny Sharrock (*g*); Bill Laswell (*b*); Ronald Shannon Jackson (*d, v*). 2/86.
**** **The Noise Of Trouble** Enemy EMY 103
    As above, plus Akira Sakata (*cl, as*); Herbie Hancock (*p*). 10/86.
Some may feel that the above are generous evaluations for a group which some have dismissed as a noisy rock-jazz band, but the sheer exhilaration which Last Exit can create when they hit their stride is almost incomparable. The group is a meeting of four particularly cussed spirits whose tastes for sonic extremes are competitive: at their wildest, these recordings suggest four men all trying to outdo one another in volume and extravagance. While Jackson's polyrhythmic parts establish a single, ever-evolving drum solo, Laswell anchors the pieces with huge, juddering bass-lines decorated by the wailing Brötzmann and Sharrock, whose guitar parts bridge heavy metal rock and free jazz more cogently than anyone else has ever done.

All the above are live recordings, aside from the Venture set. The mixes inevitably leave much to be desired, but for bludgeoning force there is little to choose between them. Pieces such as 'Discharge' establish an outpouring of sound with few equals among the records in this book, but there are elements of the blues as well as a canny sensitivity to how far to push things, which both vary and intensify the flow. *The Noise Of Trouble* adds the maverick element of guest star Sakata duelling crazily with Brötzmann on 'Blind Willie', as well as a bewildering appearance by Hancock on 'Help Me Mo, I'm Blind'.

Yusef Lateef (born 1921) TENOR SAXOPHONE, OBOE, FLUTE, OTHER SAXOPHONES, COR ANGLAIS, OTHER INSTRUMENTS, VOCALS

*** **Jazz Moods** Savoy SV-0237
    Lateef; Curtis Fuller (*tb*); Hugh Lawson (*p*); Ernie Farrow (*b*); Louis Hayes (*d*); Doug Watkins (*perc*). 4/57.
*** **Prayer To The East** Savoy SV-0210
    Lateef; Wilbur Harden (*t*); Hugh Lawson (*p*); Ernie Farrow (*b*); Oliver Jackson (*d*). 10/57.
*** **Cry! – Tender** Original Jazz Classics OJC 482
    Lateef; Lonnie Hillyer (*t*); Wilbur Harden (*flhn*); Hugh Lawson (*p*); Ernie Farrow, Herman Wright (*b*); Frank Gant, Oliver Jackson (*d*). 10/59.

***(*) **The Centaur And The Phoenix** Original Jazz Classics OJC 712
    Lateef; Clark Terry, Richard Williams (*t*); Curtis Fuller (*tb*); Tate Houston (*bs*); Josea Taylor
    (*bsn*); Barry Harris, Joe Zawinul (*p*); Ernie Farrow, Ben Tucker (*b*); Lex Humphries (*d*); Roger
    Sanders (*perc*). 10/60, 6/61.

***(*) **Eastern Sounds** Original Jazz Classics OJC 612
    Lateef; Barry Harris (*p*); Ernie Farrow (*b*); Lex Humphries (*d*). 9/61.

***(*) **Live At Pep's** Impulse! GRP 11342
    Lateef; Richard Williams (*t*); Mike Nock (*p*); Ernie Farrow (*b*); James Black (*d*). 6/64.

*** **The Blue Yusef Lateef** Atlantic 82270
    Lateef; Blue Mitchell (*t*); Sonny Red (*as*); Buddy Lucas (*hca*); Hugh Lawson (*p*); Kenny Burrell
    (*g*); Cecil McBee, Bob Cranshaw (*b*); Roy Brooks (*d*); Selwart Clarke, James Tryon (*vn*); Alfred
    Brown (*vla*); Kermit Moore (*clo*); Sweet Inspirations (*v*). 4/68.

(*) **The Diverse Yusef Lateef / Suite 16 Rhino Atlantic R2 71552
    Lateef; Richard Tee, Joe Zawinul, Hugh Lawson, Barry Harris (*p*); Neil Boyar (*vib*); Eric Gale
    (*g*); Chuck Rainey, Bob Cunningham (*b*); Albert 'Tootie' Heath, Roy Brooks, Bernard Purdie,
    Jimmy Johnson, Ray Lucas (*d*); Ray Barretto (*perc*); strings, voices. 5/69–4/70.

*** **The Gentle Giant** Atlantic 1602
    Lateef; Bill Campbell (*as*); Ray Bryant (*p*); Kenny Barron (*electric p*); Eric Gale (*g*); Neal Boyer
    (*vib, chimes*); Sam Jones, Chuck Rainey (*b*); Bob Cunningham, Bill Salter (*b*); Albert 'Tootie'
    Heath, Jimmy Johnson (*d*); Sweet Inspirations (*v*). 74.

Born plain Bill Evans, Lateef avoided the confusion of yet another Evans boy in the catalogue by
adopting a Muslim name in response to his growing and eventually life-long infatuation with the musics
of the Levant and Asia. One of the few convincing oboists in jazz and an ancestor of East-West outfits
like Oregon (whose Paul McCandless has, consciously or unconsciously, adopted some of Lateef's tonal
devices), he has suffered something of Rahsaan Roland Kirk's fate in finding himself dismissed or
marginalized as a 'speciality act', working apart from the central dramas of modern jazz. Like Kirk's,
Lateef's music was cartoonized when he came under Atlantic's wing, making albums that were enthusiastically promoted and received, but which rarely represented the best of his work.

    The two early Savoy reissues find him blowing rough, burly tenor alongside two solid, hard-bop rhythm
sections, together with the elegant Harden on one album and the bluff Fuller on the other. Already,
though, there are the exotic touches: 'A Night In Tunisia' gets off to a suitably authentic start with the
muezzin-like wail of the *argol*, and the same thing happens with 'Metaphor' on *Jazz Moods*. The OJC
records are consistently interesting, with relatively unfussy arrangements leavened by unusual timbres
and instrumental colours. *The Centaur And The Phoenix* isn't well known, despite the presence of
critically OK names like Terry and Fuller. The vocal 'Jungle Fantasy' is dire, but the large-group pieces
are as good as anything on the earlier *Cry! Tender*, and 'Summer Song' is among the most straightforwardly lyrical things in Lateef's whole output. One of two good Impulse! concert recordings, *Live At
Pep's* (originally *Pep's Lounge*), has returned to the catalogue relatively recently, and it stands up
extremely well, substantiating Lateef's often queried jazz credentials. His oboe solo on 'See See Rider'
might almost be soprano saxophone, were it not for the slightly dry reediness of the tone. Throughout
the record (which contains three pieces – one, a Williams composition, not on the original LP) he plays
with great spirit and an authentically bluesy drive that makes the exact choice of instrument (oboe,
saxophone, shenai, flute) pretty much irrelevant.

    Like Kirk though, the tenor saxophone is Lateef's 'natural' horn, but in his best period he made jazz
whatever he was playing. In approach, he is somewhat reminiscent of the pre-bop aspect of Sun Ra's
long-time associate, John Gilmore, working in a strong, extended swing idiom rather than with the more
complex figurations of bebop. Just occasionally, this spilled over into something schmaltzier. The
Eastern Sounds session also included film music from *The Robe* and *Spartacus*, on flute and oboe
respectively, that borders on kitsch, but the tenor-led 'Snafu', a thoroughly Occidental expression of
fatalism, has a surging energy that has Lateef's very good band panting.

    There are good things on *Blue*, with an orchestra fronted by Lateef, Mitchell and Lucas and anchored
on two basses (upright and electric) and the power drumming of Brooks. However, the vocal tracks and
the string arrangements on 'Like It Is' are pretty shallow, or only rather shallowly pretty in a *Summer Of
Love*-ish way, and the album as a whole lacks focus. Matters worsen with the terribly mixed double-
reissue of *The Diverse Yusef Lateef/Suite 16*: the first album is a strange blend of funk, a lot of Lateef
flute, some pseudo-gospel singing, and oddball string charts, ending on a blowsily exotic 'When A Man
Loves A Woman'. *Suite 16* is an extended concerto for Lateef that veers wildly from passionate improvising to mere pretentiousness and exposes some of his wider ambitions as fatally dilettantish: there is
much of interest in the writing which is sunk by the wrong-headed parts.

    Lateef's vocal contributions on some of the earlier records merely anticipate the grosser insult of 'Hey,
Jude' on *The Gentle Giant*. In turning Lateef into a marketable crossover performer, Atlantic took most

of the bite out of his playing. There are four good tracks on the mid-1970s album, most notably 'Nubian Lady', but there was an awful thinness to much of the rest that boded ill for the future.

**(*) Heart Vision YAL 900
>Lateef; Everett Haffner (*syn*); Christopher Newland (*g*); Adam Rudolph (*perc*); Nnenna Freelon, Tsidii Le Loka, Richard Ross, Mount Nebo Baptist Church Choir (*v*). 1/92.

**** Tenors YAL 977
>Lateef; Archie Shepp (*ts*); Tom McLung (*p*); Avery Sharpe (*b*); Steve McCraven (*d*); Adam Rudolph, Mulazimuddin Razool, Tony Vacca (*perc*). 1/92.

*** Plays Ballads YAL 333
>As above, except omit Razol and Vacca. 12/92.

***(*) Tenors YAL 911
>Lateef; Von Freeman (*ts*); John Young (*p*); John Whitfield (*b*); Terry Morrisette (*d*). 7/92.

***(*) Tenors YAL 019
>Lateef; René McLean (*ts*); Andrew Hollander (*p*); Avery Sharpe (*b*); Kamal Sabir (*d*). 5/93.

***(*) Metamorphosis YAL 100
>As above, except omit McLean and Hollander. 12/93.

*** Woodwinds YAL 005
>Lateef; Ralph M. Jones (*ts, ss, f, bf, hirchirki*); Andrew Hollander (*p*); Avery Sharpe (*b*); Adam Rudolph (*d*). 7/93.

*** Tenors YAL 105
>Lateef; Ricky Ford (*ts*); Avery Sharpe (*b*); Kamal Sabir (*d*). 94.

**(*) Suite Life YAL 111
>Lateef; Andrew Hollander (*p*); Marcie Brown (*clo*). 94.

*** In Nigeria YAL 707
>Lateef; Shittu Iskyaku (*d*); P. Adegboyega, Salisu I. Mashi, Awwalu Adamu (*perc*); voices. 7/83.

In his seventies, Lateef's energy and commitment are astonishing. He has now formed his own label, has released a stack of records in four years, and has expunged much of the new-age fluff which was sinking his output for other companies. They are a fascinating sequence. *Heart Vision* has the closest links with Lateef's recent work: the use of voices and choir, the shimmering electronics and Lateef's occasional bursts of tenor flirt with pretension but as often return to planet earth. The next four discs, though, are all about the tenor saxophone. *Ballads* is a slow, almost ritual unpeeling of the ballad form, with the rhythm players seemingly itching to get at the kernel but Lateef consistently holding them back: a tense, sometimes strange session, but the saxophonist has some imperious improvising on what are all original themes. The four meetings with other tenormen are all remarkable in their way. He challenges Shepp into his best form: there's little of the bleariness which has tarnished all of Archie's later music, just irascible, grouchy saxophone playing: Lateef with his eyes on higher things, Shepp always dragging matters back to worldly affairs. It's like a sour re-run of a Hawkins/Webster date, and it's splendid music. With McLean, all taut, biting lines, Lateef sounds sagacious; with Freeman, whose ragged phrasing and streetfighter tone crowd into the microphone like a swelling bruise, he ducks and weaves in what sometimes sounds like a punch-drunk cutting contest. But the extraordinary thing about all three encounters is that all the material is new, abstract, almost no more than a few sketchy lines: this is anchorless free playing much of the time, and the gutsy performances by all the rhythm players are compelling too. *Metamorphosis* is also much about rhythm: stripping the cast back to himself, Sharpe and Sabir, Lateef looks for a free kind of funk, the pulse staggered across an indeterminate time. Lateef rails away on tenor but adds a chorus of murmuring flutes as well: a workshop date, perhaps, but full of energy and surprise.

The *Tenors* meeting with Ricky Ford is another good blow-out, as basically formless and free-flowing as the others. *In Nigeria* is an archive piece from an African visit, a slowly simmering backdrop of percussion and voices framing the leader's improvisations, some simple, some deceptively complex. *Suite Life* is a sequence of chamberish pieces of no great weight or import, while *Woodwinds* is more about the hushed whisper of confiding flutes than reeds: only on the closing 'Brother Man' do Jones and Lateef get stuck into a tenor duel. An effective set. YAL has its share of indulgences, but overall this is an absorbing body of work from a man who clearly has a lot of music in him.

Christof Lauer (born 1953) TENOR SAXOPHONE

***(*) Christof Lauer CMP 39
>Lauer; Joachim Kühn (*p*); Palle Danielsson (*b*); Peter Erskine (*d*). 4/89.

***(*) Bluebells CMP CD 56
>Lauer; Wolfgang Puschnig (*as*); Bob Stewart (*tba*); Thomas Alkier (*d*). 4/92.

One of the younger generation of European players who have stepped beyond the overpowering influence of John Coltrane, Lauer has assimilated such a range of styles – from Stan Getz's smooth *legato* to Albert Ayler's all-out fury – that he seems derivative only episodically. Taken over the length of this sterling set of originals, he is very much his own man. The emotional range is impressive, covering the adventurous up-tempo post-bop of 'Descent' to the backward glances of 'Harlem Nocturne'. If 'Eva' records a romantic affair, it must have been a doozy; half-way through, after a sensitive interlude from Kühn, Lauer breaks into an upper-register scream that is almost as impressively controlled as it is emotionally fraught. Danielsson and Erskine are as splendid as ever. Too early yet to make categorical judgements about Lauer's progress, but this is a most striking record.

Bluebells sustains the high quality. Kicking off with 'Screwbirds' from the last record was a slightly unusual decision. Was it meant to suggest continuity or dissatisfaction? Either way, the new version is very different, with the two saxophones squalling away in intermittent unison, and Stewart's tuba pumping out the bass line. He plays a big role on the record, surfacing as a solo voice only occasionally (notably on his own 'Tunk') but anchoring almost every track. Alkier is slightly heavy-handed compared to Erskine, but he does a good job on what is ultimately a much tougher and more individual record. The collectively composed 'Ann-Charlotte' is perhaps the high point, but Lauer and Puschnig are no slouches, and almost everything they do commands attention. Nice recording, as always from the label.

Andy LaVerne (born 1948) KEYBOARDS

** Another World Steeplechase SCCD 31086
  LaVerne; Mike Richmond (*b*); Billy Hart (*d*). 9/77.
**(*) Frozen Music Steeplechase SCCD 31244
  LaVerne; Rick Margitza (*ss, ts*); Marc Johnson (*b*); Danny Gottlieb (*d*). 4/89.
** Fountainhead Steeplechase SCCD 31261
  LaVerne; Dave Samuels (*vib*). 6/89.
**(*) Standard Eyes Steeplechase SCCD 31280
  LaVerne; Steve LaSpina (*b*); Anton Fig (*d*). 10/90.

LaVerne is a dedicated, accomplished player whose records sound either underdone or overplayed.. There's no gainsaying his technique, but his music tends to run aground on its own thoughtfulness: rhythmically he can be a little four-square, and he plays so many notes that his solos can get hung up on a rush to reharmonize. His Steeplechase albums tend to be worthy rather than exciting sessions. *Frozen Music* offers a glimpse of the useful young Margitza, but the LaVerne originals are disappointingly unmemorable. The meeting with Samuels creates a lot of pretty music and not much more, while the session of standards at least affords the trio something strong to work with.

** Natural Living Musidisc 500092
  LaVerne; John Abercrombie (*g*). 11/89.
*** Nosmo King Steeplechase SCCD 31301
  As above. 12/91.
** Pleasure Seekers Triloka 320186
  LaVerne; Bob Sheppard (*ss, ts, cl, f*); John Patitucci (*b*); Dave Weckl (*d*). 1/91.
** Buy One Get One Free Steeplechase SCCD 31319
  LaVerne (*p* solo). 4/92.
**(*) Double Standard Triloka 320198
  LaVerne; Billy Drewes (*ss, ts*); Steve LaSpina (*b*); Greg Hutchinson (*d*). 1/93.
*** Plays Bud Powell Steeplechase SCCD 31342
  LaVerne (*p* solo). 2/93.
**(*) At Maybeck Recital Hall Vol. 28 Concord CCD 4577
  LaVerne (*p* solo). 4/93.
***(*) First Tango In New York Musidisc 500472
  LaVerne; Joe Lovano (*ss, ts*); Steve LaSpina (*b*); Bill Stewart (*d*). 5/93.

LaVerne and Abercrombie work well together, and *Natural Living* should have been a promising collection of standards and originals. But the bass-heavy sound smudges detail and sensitivity, and one tune soon comes to sound like another. Only on the title-piece, where Abercrombie switches to acoustic guitar, does the music become fully expressive. *Nosmo King* is a good deal better, sensibly varied in pace; but several of the pieces meander past their natural climax and LaVerne's heavy voicings make one wish for a lighter touch. The main highlight is the rarefied treatment of 'I Loves You Porgy'. *Pleasure Seekers* is a competent, dull, reeds-and-rhythm date, and the more interesting *Double Standard*, where LaVerne takes his penchant for reharmonizing standards to the extreme of adding a new melody to go with them, doesn't benefit much from Walter Becker's big-screen production.

The solo albums only seem to indulge the pianist's temptations to overdo things. *Buy One Get One Free* double-tracks him with piano parts recorded earlier on a Disklavier, and it all gets fulsome beyond words on the endless glisses of 'Fine Tune'. His contribution to the Maybeck series is similarly ponderous: this is impressive pianism, and some of the pieces make a more substantial showing, but too often one longs for a more filigree touch. *Plays Bud Powell* is a smart idea, since Powell is still surprisingly neglected as a composer, and for once LaVerne says his piece on each of the tunes briskly and without undue ornamentation: probably the best of his solo sessions to date.

LaVerne has top billing on *First Tango In New York* but, as usual, the session is dominated by Lovano's splendid playing. Six good standards are topped off with two LaVerne originals, but the material takes second place to the playing, which is primed by Lovano's furry tone and circuitous lines.

John Law PIANO

**** Exploded On Impact Slam CD 204
    Law; Alan Wilkinson (*as, bs*); Roberto Bellatalla (*b*); Mark Sanders (*d*). 2 & 7/92.
**(*) Talitha Cumi FMR CD06 081994
    Law (*p* solo). 8/93.
***(*) The Boat Is Sinking, Apartheid Is Sinking Impetus IMP CD 19322
    Law; Louis Moholo (*d*). 11 & 12/93.

Law is an improviser whose background in and understanding of classical piano language alternately fuels and haunts him. His harmonics and sense of structure are unexceptionable, but there are moments on *Talitha Cumi*, a set of meditations on the *Dies irae*, when he sounds much too correct and self-absorbed. Compared to the group and duo work, it is a disappointing appearance, given the powerful music he has played elsewhere.

Law first emerged as a force to be reckoned with in 1989 as one-third of Atlas, a group that also featured Mark Sanders. *Exploded On Impact* is a huge step on from the earlier group's *Trio Improvisations*. Law is still carrying much of the weight on shoulders that also support an unseasonally wise head. His writing breathes intelligence through and through, and is distinguished by a firm architecture seldom encountered in free bop of this type. It's often difficult to discern what is predetermined and what is spontaneously improvised, particularly on the two main statements, 'Mothers' Lament' (a threnody for Yugoslavia), and the punning 'A Pissed-Off Tree', which nods in the direction of a 'felonious monk'.

Bellatalla is a less percussive and somewhat less energetic player than Rogers, and much of the harder-edged stuff has been consigned to Wilkinson, one of the unsung heroes of new music in Britain. Sanders plays briskly and with humour, as he does with Jon Lloyd's similarly disposed group. Law himself develops relatively small harmonic areas with great intensity, building up climaxes which are as logical as they are explosive.

The association with Moholo might seem surprising at first glance, but it is a happy combination of opposites: the pianist's careful sense of order providing a solid, provocative base for Moholo's fierce, highly directed drumming. The South African is a model improviser, pushing on forcefully with the sort of deceptive intelligence that marked the 'Freedom Tour' documented on *Boat/Apartheid*. The recording is somewhat off-balance: the drums peaking too high and the piano overloading at the top end. Such shortcomings are incidental, though; this is a very worthwhile modern record from an unexpectedly fruitful pairing.

Hugh Lawson (born 1935) PIANO

*** Colours Soul Note 121052
    Lawson; Calvin Hill (*b*); Louis Hayes (*d*). 1/83.

Better known as a sideman with George Adams–Dannie Richmond, Turk Mauro and Yusef Lateef, Lawson has a strong, slightly dry delivery that lends itself better to the ironies of 'Pictures At An Exhibition' and 'If' than to the more conventional changes of '23rd Street Blues'. Hayes raises the temperature and Hill, who has also recorded with Max Roach and McCoy Tyner, keeps the multilinear feel going. Worth checking out.

Yank Lawson (1911–95) TRUMPET

**** Something Old, Something New, Something Borrowed, Something Blue Audiophile APCD-240
    Lawson; George Masso (*tb*); Johnny Mince (*cl*); Lou Stein (*p*); Bucky Pizzarelli (*g*); Bob Haggart (*b*); Nick Fatool (*d*). 3/88.

*** **Jazz At Its Best** Jazzology JCD-183
>   Lawson; George Masso (*tb*); Kenny Davern (*cl*); Al Klink (*ts*); John Bunch (*p*); Bucky Pizzarelli (*g*); Bob Haggart (*b*); Jake Hanna (*d*). 2/89.

***(*) **Singin' The Blues** Jazzology JCD-193
>   As above, except Joe Muranyi (*cl, ss*) replaces Davern; omit Klink; add Barbara Lea (*v*). 3/90.

*** **With A Southern Accent** Jazzology JCD-203
>   As above, except Davern returns; omit Muranyi and Lea. 3/91.

Yank Lawson and Bob Haggart played together for almost 60 years. Their Lawson–Haggart Jazz Band of the 1950s was one of the best Dixieland outfits of its kind; their World's Greatest Jazz Band repeated the trick in the 1960s and '70s. Their recent records for Audiophile and Jazzology maintain a formidable standard: Yank Lawson's tough, growling solos have a bite and pungency which he retained, even into his eighties, and Haggart's steady propulsion hasn't faltered at all. This is a splendid group of discs and only the relatively tame repertoire on the latter three keep them out of the top bracket: the mostly recent material on the first disc is so fresh and is played so enjoyably that one wishes the group would stick to originals over warhorses. A lovely 'Blues For Louise', a Spanish-sounding 'Bumps', played by a trio of Lawson, Stein and Fatool, and a swaggering 'Come Back, Sweet Papa' are only three highlights from a very fine set. The next three all rely for the most part on Dixieland and traditional staples and, though all are played with gusto and panache, there's a trace of weariness here and there in tunes that might be laid to a comfortable rest. *Jazz At Its Best* dispatches its tunes capably, with extended explorations of 'Willow Weep For Me' and 'Mandy Make Up Your Mind', as well as a memorial to Maxine Sullivan, 'Lonesome Yank'. *Singin' The Blues* finds Yank in tremendous form on the title-song, on a slow, sturdy 'Tin Roof Blues' and a fine 'Blue, Turning Grey Over You'. *With A Southern Accent* peaks on an intensely felt 'Creole Love Call'. This and *Jazz At Its Best* are somewhat pointlessly padded out with a couple of alternative takes. Masso, Davern and Bunch play strongly throughout these dates, but it's always Lawson himself who makes the most striking impression. Excellent, lively sound on all four.

Nguyen Lê GUITAR, DANH TRANH, GUITAR SYNTHESIZER

***(*) **Miracles** Musidisc 500102
>   Lê; Art Lande (*p*); Marc Johnson (*b*); Peter Erskine (*d, perc*) 11/89.

*** **Zanzibar** Musidisc MU 500352
>   Lê; Paul McCandless (*ss, ob, eng hn, bcl*); Art Lande (*p, thumb p*); Dean Johnson (*b*); Joël Allouche (*d*). 5/92.

*** **Million Waves** ACT 9221
>   Le; Dieter Ilg (*b, v*); Danny Gottlieb (*d, perc*). 12/94.

Something about the overall packaging leads one to expect a hybrid of rock and world music from these records. The reality is quite otherwise. Lê favours soft, clean-picked lines and delicately arpeggiated chords, often using a nylon-strung electric guitar to get a rich 'acoustic' sound that is quite squarely in the jazz tradition. The synths are reserved for delicate background traceries or gently insistent ostinati.

If this is world music, it is unusually well focused and assimilated. The presence of Oregon's Paul McCandless on the later and more diffuse *Zanzibar* gives a reasonable impression of its provenance; the spontaneously improvised 'Sarugaku' might almost have been an early Oregon piece. Much of the material is credited to assistant producer Dominique Borker, who also turns up as co-writer on the earlier and better *Miracles*, a surprisingly tight and jazzy set that recalls Joe Zawinul's stronger post-Weather Report projects.

Lê's habit of alternating longer and more developed tracks with short impressionistic sketches (the dread term *haiku* turns up towards the end of *Miracles*) runs a risk of becoming too mannered. The brief 'Cerf Volant', for Vietnamese zither or dulcimer, is too slight to have been worth including, leading one to wonder why the guitarist hadn't been tempted to use the *danh tranh* more extensively. One obvious answer is that his guitar-sound is attractive enough in itself. Lande, Marc Johnson and Erskine prove to be sympathetic interpreters, and McCandless produces moments of chilling beauty on the later disc.

Lê seemed to have gone as far as he could with this approach after two albums. *Million Waves* is both more of the same and very different. It isn't quite a conventional jazz trio, but the rudiments are quite definitely there and the long, spontaneously improvised 'Trilogy', the only track not recorded at Walter Quintus's state-of-the-art CMP studios, opens up sufficient files for a decade's-worth of experimentation; excellent stuff. The high gloss that Quintus brings occasionally diverts attention away from less than stirring material. 'Butterflies And Zebras' is a short gloss on Jimi Hendrix's 'Little Wing', which follows it, without adding much to the original. Dominique Borker is co-credited again on the attractive 'Moonshine', confirming the fruitfulness of that relationship. Surprisingly, Lê plays out on James Brown's 'I Feel Good'; perhaps the jazz-funk album is just around the corner.

The Leaders GROUP

***(*) **Out Here Like This** Black Saint 120119
> Lester Bowie (*t*); Arthur Blythe (*as*); Chico Freeman (*ts, bcl*); Kirk Lightsey (*p*); Cecil McBee (*b*); Famoudou Don Moye (*d*). 6/86.
*** **Slipping And Sliding** Sound Hills SSCD 8054
> As above. 6/93.

Occupying a mid-point between the now almost parodic anarchy of the Art Ensemble of Chicago and the more professional musical showmanship of Lester Bowie's Brass Fantasy, and offering a left-of-centre balance between Chico Freeman's freer style and the soul-funk of his Brainstorm band, The Leaders also helped redeem Arthur Blythe's skidding career. Never as impressive on record as they have been live, *Out Here Like This* is nevertheless a powerful and varied sampling of contemporary styles. There's a better balance of sound between the front-row voices and a more prominent role for McBee, who shares some of Ron Carter's ability to style-shift while maintaining a basic consistency of tone. Bowie's theatrical approach manages to compress a huge acreage of jazz history, calling in references to Armstrong, Bix Beiderbecke and Miles Davis.

   The more recent *Slipping And Sliding* reinforces the Art Ensemble analogy more than we might have expected, with an emphasis on showmanship and pure theatre that might dismay some listeners. However, the sheer range of musicianship is what sustains this band and there is enough quality playing from just about every position to satisfy even the most finicky.

The Leaders Trio

***(*) **Heaven Dance** Sunnyside SSC 1034
> Kirk Lightsey (*p*); Cecil McBee (*b*); Famoudou Don Moye (*d*). 5/88.

Not the least of *Heaven Dance*'s merits is that it sends us back to the original Leaders sets with a heightened awareness of what was going on in the warp-factor engine-room. Which is not to say that *Heaven Dance* is not a substantial achievement on its own terms. Though it may masquerade as a conventional piano trio, the balance of emphasis favours McBee (particularly) and Don Moye. The title-track is an intriguing pattern of melorhythms with some fine piano; 'Cecil To Cecil' and a tribute to the great bassist, Wilbur Ware, also catch the eye. Recommended.

Joelle Léandre (born 1951) DOUBLE BASS, VOICE

*** **Urban Bass** Adda 581254
> Léandre; Sylvie Altenburger (*vla*). 90.
*** **Ecritures** Adda 590038
> Léandre; Carlos Zingaro (*v*).
*** **Palimpseste** hat Art CD 6103
> Léandre; Eric Watson (*p*). 9/81.
***(*) **L'Histoire De Mme Tasco** hat Art CD6122
> Léandre; Rüdiger Carl (*acc, cl*); Carlos Zingaro (*v*). 3 & 4/92
***(*) **Blue Goo Park** FMP CD 52
> As above, except omit Zingaro. 7/92.

A good proportion of Léandre's concert and recorded output consists of new music. She has either commissioned or received dedication of speciality pieces for double bass from composers such as Betsy Jolas, Jacob Druckman, Sylvano Bussotti and especially Giacinto Scelsi, and has adapted other materials, including John Cage's song, 'The Wonderful Widow of Eighteen Springs' for bass and voice; all of these are on Adda 581043. This work apart, though, Léandre is a formidable improviser. She has appeared as part of Derek Bailey's Company project and has a number of improvisation-based recordings to her credit.

   Violinist Zingaro (another occasional Company shareholder) is a sympathetic collaborator, offering the same wild and unrestrained string-playing she experienced with maverick Australian fiddler/inventor, Jon Rose. On a single track from the *Urban Bass* session, she looks to Altenburger for a rich viola sound. Zingaro's musical conception is perfectly compatible with Carl's, and the trio has an atmospheric – and undeniably Gallic – quality which lends itself most effectively to the 'Mme Tasco' suite. Léandre and Watson explore the idea of palimpsest improvisation, overlaying composed structures with freehand materials, much as she does with Carl on the FMP session, which is probably her most concentrated to date. Consisting of 23 tracks, at just over an hour's tracking time, it emphasizes Léandre's interest in brief, almost song-like forms. Only rarely does she turn away from that impacted approach, but the longer tracks on *Palimpseste* lapse into imprecision and discursiveness.

Anne LeBaron (born 1953) HARP, ELECTRONICS

*** **Phantom Orchestra** Ear-Rational ECD 1035
    LeBaron; Frank London (*t, c, perc*); Marcus Rojas (*tba*); Davey Williams (*g*); Gregg Bendian (*d, vib, perc*). 3/91.

LeBaron is known in the United States primarily as a straight composer. More than a narrowly focused or 'hyphenate' composer-performer, writing exclusively for her own instrument, she has produced a substantial body of compositions, many of them haunted by the subject of Orpheus. Her second opera, *The E & O Line*, is a blues re-telling of the myth. Blues and jazz as such have played only an incidental role in her work, but LeBaron has a parallel career as an improviser, working with her own band in a free but not entirely abstract idiom.

On *Phantom Orchestra* she's heard closely paired with the excellent Davey Williams, one of the best guitar improvisers around, and with two bright and buoyant wind players who give the group sound its humanized, breathing elements. 'Superstrings And Curved Space' indicates her interest in scientific ideas, a concern that runs all through her work, a tightly woven, structurally anomalous piece that shouldn't make sense, but somehow does. 'Bouquet For A Phantom Orchestra' is more impressionistic. 'Top Hat On A Locomotive' confirms the element of humour in LeBaron's own conception of things.

There's nothing forbidding about LeBaron's music, but it requires (and repays) a slight adjustment of expectations.

LeeAnn Ledgerwood PIANO

*** **You Wish** Triloka 187
    Ledgerwood; Bill Evans (*ts, ss*); Jeremy Steig (*f*); Eddie Gomez, Steve LaSpina (*b*); Danny Gottlieb (*d*). 1/91.

LeeAnn Ledgerwood was first noticed by Marian McPartland and received enthusiastic acclaim for her role on McPartland's 'Piano Jazz' broadcasts in 1990. Buoyed up by that success, Ledgerwood recorded her debut record with a degree more haste and enthusiasm than judgement. There's a nervy edge to *You Wish* that a more interventionist producer (Walter Becker is an avowed fan) might have tried to temper. She solos on every track but seems to play the same solo at least four times over. The record also leans rather heavily on Evans and Steig, neither of whom is a charismatic soloist. Better, surely, to have essayed a modest trio album with Gomez (for whom she had already recorded) and the estimable Gottlieb, who stands out like a beacon in this.

Mike LeDonne PIANO

*** **'Bout Time** Criss Cross Jazz Criss 1033
    LeDonne; Tom Harrell (*t, flhn*); Gary Smulyan (*bs*); Dennis Irwin (*b*); Kenny Washington (*d*). 1/88.
(*) **The Feeling Of Jazz Criss Cross Jazz Criss 1041
    As above. 1/90.
(*) **Common Ground Criss Cross 1058
    As above, except omit Harrell and Smulyan. 12/90.
***(*) **Soulmates** Criss Cross 1074
    LeDonne; Ryan Kisor (*t*); Joshua Redman (*ts*); Jon Gordon (*as*); Peter Washington (*b*); Lewis Nash (*d*). 1/93.

LeDonne leads some very capable groups here. The first two discs are typical, consistent, slightly soft Criss Cross dates, despite the skilful team involved. Tunes, charts and solos all bespeak an unflagging but rather charmless dedication to hard-bop routine. Four of the themes on the second record are handled by the rhythm section alone, but otherwise there's little to tell the two records apart. *Common Ground* gives LeDonne the spotlight with only bass and drums in support; though the tunes are way out of the ordinary – Wes Montgomery, some rare Ellington – they sound as if they were meant to show off his ingenuity. The newest disc, *Soulmates*, is a different matter. Kisor and Redman are an indecently talented front line and they finesse the material to a degree that takes this out of the usual neat-and-tidy sessionman bag. Come to that, Gordon is quite up to their level. LeDonne himself doesn't do anything awesomely different from the other records, but it all sounds very accomplished.

Phil Lee GUITAR

***(*) **Twice Upon A Time** Cadillac SGCASCD 1
    Lee; Jeff Clyne (*b*). 12/86–1/87.
Quiet, often subliminal guitar and bass music. Both men light on points of harmonic detail rather than pushing for a rhythmic result, and the consequence is a series of improvisations of delicate, exacting finesse. The tunes are very well chosen, with composers from Mercer Ellington to Steve Swallow in the list.

Soren Lee GUITAR

*** **Soren Lee Quartet** L + R CDLR 45073
    Lee; Thomas Clausen (*p*); Ray Brown (*b*); Alvin Queen (*d*). 2/90.
***(*) **Soren Lee Trio** L + R CDLR 45072
    Lee; Jesper Lundgaard (*b*); Adam Nussbaum (*d*). 2 & 4/92.
Nothing fancy, nothing spare or wasted; just excellent guitar jazz, with fleet, horn-inflected lines and a generous harmonic range, many of the tunes cast in keys which don't sit entirely comfortably for the instrument. Lee calls on top-flight sidemen for both these sessions. Having Ray Brown in the studio is a bit of luxury and the great man is mixed a little high, as is drummer Queen. On purely acoustic grounds, the live sessions are preferable – compare 'Dr Jeckyll' for confirmation – though some of the sharper guitar attacks come through a little harshly. Lee sticks in the main to familiar material – 'My Favourite Things', 'Bemsha Swing', 'All The Things You Are' – and it is easy to be caught napping by this, for there is some thoughtful music-making going on, especially again in the numbers recorded at the Jazzhus Montmartre, where he is a much-admired regular.

Michel Legrand (born 1932) PIANO, ORGAN, VOCAL

**** **Legrand Jazz** Philips 830074-2
    Legrand; Miles Davis, Ernie Royal, Art Farmer, Donald Byrd, Joe Wilder (*t*); Frank Rehak, Billy Byers, Jimmy Cleveland, Eddie Bert (*tb*); James Buffington (*frhn*); Gene Quill, Phil Woods (*as*); Ben Webster, John Coltrane, Seldon Powell (*ts*); Jerome Richardson (*bs, bcl*); Teo Macero (*bs*); Herbie Mann (*f*); Bill Evans, Hank Jones, Nat Pierce (*p*); Eddie Costa, Don Elliot (*vib*); Betty Glamann (*hp*); Major Holley (*b, tba*); Paul Chambers, George Duvivier, Milt Hinton (*b*); Don Lamond, Kenny Dennis, Osie Johnson (*d*). 6/58.
*** **Le Jazz Grand** Castle PACD 027
    Legrand; Joe Shepley, Burt Collins, John Gatchell, John Clark, Albert Richmond, Jon Faddis, Brooks Tillotson, Tony Price (*t*); Phil Woods (*as*); Gerry Mulligan (*bs*); Bernie Leighton, Tom Pierson (*ky*); Harry Leahey (*g*); Ron Carter, Don Elliot (*b*); Jimmy Madison, Grady Tate (*d*). 78.
***(*) **After The Rain** Original Jazz Classics OJC 803-2
    Legrand; Joe Wilder (*t, flhn*); Phil Woods (*as, cl*); Zoot Sims (*ts*); Gene Bertoncini (*g*); Ron Carter (*b*); Grady Tate (*d*). 5/82.
*** **Live At Fat Tuesday's** Verve 843444-2
    Legrand; Jean-Loup Longnon (*t*); Denis Leloup (*tb*); Marc Michel (*b*); François Laizeau (*d*). 1/85.
Legrand's name is so widely known as a pop composer that his jazz leanings are largely ignored. But this small discography is worth much more than a passing look. The sessions for the *Legrand Jazz* album are uniquely star-studded, and the quality of the writing matches up to the cast-list. Legrand chose many unexpected tunes – including ancient history such as 'Wild Man Blues', as well as the more predictable 'Nuages' and 'Django' – and recast each one in a challenging way. 'Night In Tunisia' is a controlled fiesta of trumpets, ''Round Midnight' a glittering set-piece for Davis, 'Nuages' a sensuous vehicle for Webster. The latter is placed alongside a trombone section in one of the three groupings devised by the arranger; another is dominated by a four-man trumpet group. The third has the remarkable situation of having Davis, Coltrane and Evans as sidemen, playing Fats Waller and Louis Armstrong tunes. Many of the arrangements are tellingly compact, seven not even breaking the four-minute barrier, and it ends on a *fast* treatment of Beiderbecke's 'In A Mist'.
    The 1978 *Le Jazz Grand* is comparatively lightweight, with Woods, Faddis and Mulligan as featured soloists: interesting, and the brass writing is carefully worked-through, though it's hardly on a par with its predecessor. *After The Rain* was done almost off the cuff and stands as a ballad album, the group working casually through six lesser-known Legrand tunes – yet the playing by the three front-liners is so

exquisitely done that the music glows. 'Nobody Knows', in which Sims and Woods luxuriate through the lovely chords as if taking a bath in them, is an impromptu classic.

If Legrand's name hadn't been on the boards outside, it's doubtful whether New Yorkers would have filled up even the tiny Fat Tuesday's club to hear a French band. Still, Longnon and Leloup are no slouches, and even Legrand himself plays nicely quirky composer's piano. His singing may be an acquired taste, but it has some of the quavery charm of Antonio Carlos Jobim.

Johan Leijonhufvud (born 1971) GUITAR

***(*) **Speaks The Local Bebop** Sittel SITCD 9215
> Leijonhufvud; Anders Bergcrantz (*t*); Mattias Hjorth (*b*); Kristofer Johansson (*d*); Sofia Pettersson (*v*). 11/93–5/94.

A winner. Leijonhufvud gets a huge sound out of his (untreated) electric instrument and, as the title suggests, he prefers the rules and language of hardcore bop – without sounding encumbered by any of it. The result is a fresh, excitable session that has the trio playing as if they're just discovering this new music. Bergcrantz sits in on four tunes and he sounds terrific on 'Vals', the pairing of trumpet and guitar emerging as sonorously beautiful. Some of the tunes are on the glib side but, if the playing ever strays in that direction, their enthusiasm sees them through it. Pettersson takes a cameo role on one tune and sounds a little uneasy with the lyrics.

Urs Leimgruber TENOR SAXOPHONE, SOPRANO SAXOPHONE, BASS SAXOPHONE, FLUTE

*** **Reflexionen Live** Timeless SJP 234
> Leimgruber; Don Friedman (*p*); Bobby Burri (*b*); Joel Allouche (*d*). 11/85.
*** **Reflexionen** Enja 5057
> Leimgruber; Don Friedman (*p*); Palle Danielsson (*b*); Joel Allouche (*d*). 2/87.
***(*) **Statement Of An Antirider** hat ART 6015
> Leimgruber (solo). 3/88.
*** **Ungleich** hat Art CD 6049
> Leimgruber; Adelhard Roidinger (*b*). 1/90.
***(*) **Lines** hat Art CD 6149
> As above, except add Fritz Hauser (*d, perc*). 5/90.
*** **L'Enigmatique** hat Art CD 6091
> Leimgruber; Fritz Hauser (*d, perc*). 5/91.

In tonal range and diversity of concerns, Leimgruber somewhat resembles Briton John Surman. Surman, though, has only rarely ventured into total freedom and utilizes extremes of pitch rather sparingly. Leimgruber's Reflexionen is far from being a conventional horn-and-rhythm unit. The Timeless session, recorded live in Switzerland, finds him working with space and extended structures like the 'Rotsee Suite'. The three later recordings document a shift towards a more abstract and gestural approach, still with occasional folk or traditional references (much as he has developed in duo with John Wolf Brennan).

The solo *Statement* is a quite remarkable performance and has to be seen as the quintessence of Leimgruber's work to date. Even when working with a highly sophisticated band and with players of the calibre of Danielsson and Friedman, he always sounds slightly detached and self-involved, much as Surman frequently sounds alone at the centre of the music. To that extent, solo performance is a logical progression for both of them.

It is tempting to dismiss *L'Enigmatique* as merely that, except that its short, compacted tracks do seem to develop quite logically, preparing the way for two more substantial statements, 'The Commuter' and 'Long Forgotten Night', in which the partnership really clicks.

The partnership with Roidinger proves to be especially fruitful, a genuine meeting of minds. In company with the polystylistic Hauser, the mix is even more potent, not intoxicating in the more obvious swinging way, but endlessly surprising and packed with ideas.

Peter Leitch GUITAR

***(*) **Red Zone** Reservoir RSR CD 103
> Leitch; Pepper Adams (*bs*); Kirk Lightsey (*p*); Ray Drummond (*b*); Marvin 'Smitty' Smith (*d*). 11/84, 11/85, 7/88.

*** **Exhilaration** Reservoir RSR CD 118
> Leitch; Pepper Adams (*bs*); John Hicks (*p*); Ray Drummond (*b*); Billy Hart (*d*). 11/84, 12/88.
*** **On A Misty Night** Criss Cross CRISS 1026
> Leitch; Neil Swainson (*b*); Mickey Roker (*d*). 11/86.
***(*) **Portraits And Dedications** Criss Cross Criss 1039
> Leitch; Bobby Watson (*as*); Jed Levy (*afl*); James Williams (*p*); Ray Drummond (*b*); Marvin
> 'Smitty' Smith (*d*). 12/88, 1/89.
*** **Mean What You Say** Concord CCD 4417
> Leitch; John Hicks (*p*); Ray Drummond (*b*); Marvin 'Smitty' Smith (*d*). 1/90.
***(*) **Trio / Quartet '91** Concord CCD 4480
> Leitch; John Swana (*t, flhn*); Neil Swainson (*b*); Marvin 'Smitty' Smith (*d*). 2/91.
***(*) **From Another Perspective** Concord CCD 4535
> Leitch; Gary Bartz (*as*); Jed Levy (*afl, ts, ss*); John Hicks (*p*); Ray Drummond (*b*); Marvin
> 'Smitty' Smith (*d*). 6/92.

A glance at the personnel on Leitch's records gives a quick summary of his standing in the jazz community. One moment the young guitarist was hacking a living in his native Canada, the next – or so it seemed – he was pumping out a steady flow of top-flight jazz albums. In a recording career stretching back just a decade, Leitch has evolved from an essentially horn-based style to a much more (his own word) guitaristic approach. The tracks with Pepper Adams on the November 1984 session worked because of the degree of separation between the baritone and Leitch's own lines. A couple of duos with Drummond explore a similar contrast. Hicks and Lightsey are both quite dominant, dark-toned piano players, and that contributed to the overall feel of these sessions.

When he came to Criss Cross, Gerry Teekens gave him the breadth and leeway he wanted to make swinging but intelligent records which refused to sit neatly in any currently agreed niche. *On A Misty Night* betrays some signs of having been his debut. Leitch tries to pack in too much and falls rather flat, caught between opposites rather than using them to fuel one another. Leitch has, though, always known what he wants. The change of emphasis on *Portraits And Dedications* was quite striking. It would be difficult to imagine a saxophonist who sounds less like Pepper Adams than Bobby Watson, and the switch to James Williams marked a clear recognition that Leitch was increasingly capable of sustaining a broader, self-accompanied sound, the very thing that seemed lacking on the first Reservoir's solo tracks. Jed Levy's alto flute is used very sparingly on *Portraits*, for the softly romantic 'Visage De Cathryn' and 'Portrait Of Sylvia'. His moment was to come later.

The three Concords are uniformly excellent. *Mean What You Say* pared the sound down again. Leitch plays ringingly on 'Blues On The East Side' and 'Stairway To The Stars', but he's always prepared to step aside for Hicks. On the *Trio/Quartet* record, he brings in a horn for three tracks and modernizes the material considerably; Joe Henderson's 'Inner Urge' and Chick Corea's 'Tones For Joans Bones' present new challenges. Leitch has devised a new way of playing chords which also allows him to pick off clean top-string lines; as a technique, it comes down through Jim Hall and Joe Pass, but Leitch makes it his own, and in the absence of piano it serves him wonderfully well. Smitty Smith's presence is an important factor throughout the decade, but this is his best moment. His sheer control at low tempi and softer volumes is exemplary.

The most recent release is very much a re-run of the *Portraits* concept. Bartz is magnificent and Jed Levy gets to show off his considerable skill. The charts are perhaps tighter than before, and original material like 'For Elmo, Sonny And Freddie' and '91-1' is well organized and unfussy. Leitch clearly hasn't run out of ideas yet. For relatively straight-ahead guitar jazz, his work has been remarkably unpredictable and always fresh. Leitch is clearly going places.

John Leitham BASS

*** **Leitham Up** USA CD-725
> Leitham; Tom Ranier (*ts, bcl, p*); Jake Hanna (*d*). 5/89.
*** **The Southpaw** USA CD-765
> Leitham; Buddy Childers (*t, flhn*); Bob Cooper (*ts*); Tom Ranier, Milcho Leviev (*p*); Roy
> McCurdy (*d*). 9/92.

A lightning-fast left-hander, John Leitham would probably have been a first call in the West Coast studios of 30 or 40 years earlier. He leads these two Los Angeles sessions with good humour and much aplomb: nothing stirs the coals of innovation, but it's good, sunny, swinging jazz, the kind of thing that comes naturally to the area. The trio album sometimes stalls on Leitham's virtuosity: he can play awfully fast, and rapid-fire bass solos can get boring all too quickly; but the on-the-toes gumption of his companions keeps the music from growing mundane. Ranier plays piano for most of the date, but his two horn features – including, oddly, 'Moose The Mooche' on bass clarinet – are respectable enough.

The Southpaw is mostly trio, too (Leviev takes the piano stool on three tracks), though Childers and the great Bob Cooper sit in for four affable numbers. 'Scrapple From The Apple' is a fine slug of straightforward bebop, and Leitham has the front to play the melody of 'Jitterbug Waltz' on bass. Nice.

Peter Lemer (born 1942) PIANO, KEYBOARDS

*** **Local Color** ESP Disk ESP 1057
Lemer; Nisar Ahmad Khan (*ts*); John Surman (*bs, ss, bcl*); Tony Reeves (*b*); Jon Hiseman (*d*). 66.

Lemer's music was infused with that most British of qualities: irony. As a result, it went down awkwardly in the United States, and the immense promise of *Local Color* was not fulfilled. The only comparable Americans were Annette Peacock, with whom he later worked, and Richard Twardzik, composer of 'Yellow Waltz'.

'Ictus' is British free jazz of its period, but the five other compositions, each terse and pointed, are more difficult to pin down. Surmanophiles will be delighted with material from a decade in which the saxophonist laid the foundations for everything he's done since. His bass-clarinet work and his contributions to 'Flowville' contain in embryo what came to flower 20 years later in the solo records. Hiseman isn't obviously the right man for the occasion, but Eddie Kramer engineered an appropriately big sound that rescues Lemer from sounding too introverted.

Lemer went on to work with the art-rock band, Gong, and with the Gnaoua musicians of North Africa. He also ran his own group, E, an initial which still hadn't acquired its sub-cultural resonance. Listening to *Local Color*, it's hard not to wonder why Lemer didn't break through to bigger things.

Brian Lemon (born 1937) PIANO

*** **But Beautiful** Zephyr ZECD1
Lemon; Dave Cliff (*g*); Dave Green (*b*); Allan Ganley (*d*). 1 & 3/95.
(*) **A Beautiful Friendship Zephyr ZECD4
Lemon; Warren Vaché (*c*); Roy Williams (*tb*); Dave Cliff (*g*); Dave Green (*b*); Martin Drew, Allan Ganley (*d*). 2/95.
*** **How Long Has This Been Going On?** Zephyr ZECD5
As above, except omit Vaché, Drew; add Scott Hamilton (*ts*). 8/95.

Lemon is a stalwart of the British mainstream scene. His career began in the mid-1950s with Freddy Randall and Betty Smith, before he became the (often unacknowledged) kingpin of clarinettist Sandy Brown's and trumpeter Al Fairweather's group. Like John Taylor a generation later, he has often been more properly appreciated by visiting American players than at home in the UK.

Recording opportunities under his own name have been relatively rare, and the appearance of these discs on the Portsmouth-based Zephyr are very welcome. These days Lemon plays with consummate taste and restraint, nothing left to prove. His solos on 'Just Friends' (*Beautiful Friendship*) and the title-track of *But Beautiful* are models for any player in this idiom; a reading of Sonny Rollins's 'St Thomas' is more unexpected, and Lemon's easy swing is seductive from first to last. The session with horns is a touch too matey and relaxed, but there is some adroit playing from all three principals; Williams and Vaché receive equal billing.

Tenor saxophonist Hamilton is a considerable anglophile and has called on some of these guys for his own recordings with Concord. His presence lends a touch of class to *How Long*, which is billed as Lemon and Williams with 'The Supreme Sidemen'. It's clear, though, that this isn't his gig, and there are odd sloppy moments when he lapses unwontedly into formula playing, bland licks and odd, uneasy resolutions.

As small-label recordings go, these aren't all bad, at very least providing a worthy calling-card for a hard-working, much respected musician who still isn't much known by the record-buying public.

Harlan Leonard (1905–83) CLARINET, ALTO AND BARITONE SAXOPHONES, BANDLEADER

***(*) **Harlan Leonard And His Rockets 1940** Classics 670
Leonard; James Ross (*t*); Edward Johnson, William H. Smith (*t*); Fred Beckett, Walter Monroe, Richmond Henderson (*tb*); Darwin Jones (*as, v*); Henry Bridges (*cl, ts*); Jimmy Keith (*ts*); William Smith (*p*); Effergee Ware, Stan Morgan (*g*); Winston Williams, Billy Hadnott (*b*); Jesse Price (*d*); Myra Taylor, Ernie Williams (*v*). 1–11/40.

The forgotten men of Kansas City jazz. Leonard had previously worked in the Bennie Moten band and, when Basie left for New York, Leonard's orchestra took over many of the Count's local engagements. But he didn't make many records; all 23 surviving tracks are here, in quite good transfers. It was a good, rather than a great, band, lacking something in individuality – some of the tracks are built round the kind of devices which Basie was personalizing to a much greater degree, the section work is occasionally suspect, and the KC rocking rhythm is something they fall back on time and again. But something good is to be found in nearly all these tracks, and some fine soloists, too – Henry Bridges is an outstanding tenorman, Fred Beckett (whom J. J. Johnson admired) a surprisingly agile trombonist, and the trumpets hit the spot whenever they have to. Scholars will prize the six early arrangements by the young Tadd Dameron, an intriguing hint of things to come, and one shouldn't miss the blues-inflected vocals of Ernie Williams, a lighter Jimmy Rushing.

Billy Lester PIANO

***(*) Captivatin' Rhythm Zinnia 108
    Lester; Frank Canino, Joe Solomon (*b*); Ed Ornowski, Tim Pleasant (*d*). 85–95.
A New Yorker, one-time fan of Bud Powell and Fats Domino, a former student of Sal Mosca, Lester comes straight out of left field with a record like this, one that confounds most of the stereotypes in contemporary jazz piano. Though he plays slow as often as fast, and never at the hurricane tempo of original bebop, he sounds more closely attuned to bop's lexicon than many a more fêted contemporary player. Whatever he learned from Mosca has been thoroughly absorbed, and the Tristano-ite approach of disguised chord sequences, plain-speaking rhythm sections and labyrinthine investigations of a particular structure has become integral within his style. Some of the tracks were cut as far back as 1985, while others are more recent; but the record unfolds as all of a piece, six solos and six with bass and drums. Lester manages to suggest the fleetness of right-hand bop lines while never neglecting his left hand, and the result is a music full of dark sonorities, swinging without surrendering a certain inner reserve. The sound is a little home-made, but it concentrates the ear on Lester's methods. A very interesting discovery.

Lou Levy (born 1928) PIANO

*** Jazz in Four Colours RCA ND 74401
    Levy; Larry Bunker (*vib*); Leroy Vinnegar (*b*); Stan Levey (*d*). 3/56.
***(*) Lunarcy Emarcy 512 436
    Levy; Pete Christlieb (*ts, af*); Eric Von Essen (*b, clo*); Ralph Penland (*d, perc*). 2/92.
**** Ya Know Verve 519 700
    Levy; Eric Von Essen (*b, clo*); Pierre Michelot (*b*); Alvin Queen (*d*). 3 & 4/93.
*** By Myself Verve 522 510
    Levy (*p* solo). 3 & 11/94.
Just over a decade ago, Lou Levy released an album on the Jazzis label that quickly became a prized collectable among jazz piano fans. It was called *The Kid's Got Ears*, a judgement of Levy subscribed to by almost all the singers he ever worked for, and they included Ella Fitzgerald, Sarah Vaughan, Peggy Lee and Frank Sinatra. The odd thing about the ears is that they were never quite aligned in the normal way. Levy was always looking for angles, tinkering with the changes just far enough to make things interesting, never to the detriment of the song.

    The earliest (by far) of the bunch is testimony that Levy's maverick approach wasn't cooked up the day before yesterday. The final track, 'Indiana', for trio only, uses a spectrum of altered harmonies that take the tune far away from its original sense of direction. Bunker has his moment in the sun on 'Imagination' and takes the opportunity to craft an elegant solo that quotes a couple of favoured Red Norvo phrases as well as a couple of passing references to Hamp. There's an original, 'The Gray Fox', which is more than just a blowing theme but which is intended here to give everyone a brisk work-out. It doesn't sit quite well in the middle of the session, but it's an engaging piece all the same.

    The passing years have done nothing to dampen Levy's instincts for experiment and the unobvious. *By Myself* is a series of elegant contrafacts, not so much variations and changes on old tunes as pretty drastic reworkings. Often he'll slide diagonally from one mode to the next, too quickly and seamlessly for any change to be superficially evident. 'Embraceable You' and, a long-standing favourite, 'How High The Moon' end up in places that even Charlie Parker could not have anticipated.

    So why did all this take so long to come out? Did an extra three or four decades under his belt and his own name on the studio board really make such a difference? One suspects it must. 'How High' emerges again in 'Lunarcy', which is derived from it, bebop style. It's less difficult than many of Levy's tunes, certainly than 'Pathetique', an adaptation of the 'I'm Old Fashioned' chords, with a snippet from Tchaikovsky's Sixth Symphony; it's a boggler.

The other distinctive thing about *Lunarcy* is the use of cello, which becomes an even more important factor on *Ya Know*, where the two bass players are given horn parts. Though Christlieb makes a convincing job of some difficult exchanges on the earlier album, the sheer originality of the voicings on the 1993 disc puts it in front. There's a sequel to 'Lunarcy', logically entitled 'Lunartique', on which von Essen plays the melody line, as he does on 'Paradise'. Michelot, who fulfils his usual, absolutely solid role, drops out for 'Dancing In The Dark', but all the other tracks feature twinned basses, and very effective it is, too. The Frenchman contributes an intriguingly original 'Quarte's Fever', which he has also recorded with his own group. His lead line is absolutely magnificent, with von Essen staying in reserve and Levy feeding delinquent chords in the background. Michelot also finishes off the title-piece, written by classical musician Joe Emley. Queen has his moment on an old Charlie Parker tune, 'The Hymn', soloing with authority and admirable control.

George Lewis (1900–68) CLARINET

***(*) **And His New Orleans Stompers: Volume 1** American Music AMCD 100
    Lewis; Avery 'Kid' Howard (*t*); Jim Robinson (*tb*); Lawrence Marrero (*bj*); Sidney Brown (*bb*); Chester Zardis (*b*); Edgar Moseley (*d*). 5/43.

**** **And His New Orleans Stompers: Volume 2** American Music AMCD 101
    As above, except omit Brown. 5/43.

**** **George Lewis With Kid Shots** American Music AMCD 2
    Lewis; Bunk Johnson, Louis 'Kid Shots' Madison (*t*); Jim Robinson (*tb*); Lawrence Marrero (*bj*); Alcide 'Slow Drag' Pavageau (*b*); Baby Dodds (*d*). 7 & 8/44.

**** **Trios And Bands** American Music AMCD 4
    Lewis; Avery 'Kid' Howard, Louis 'Kid Shots' Madison (*t*); Jim Robinson (*tb*); Lawrence Marrero (*bj*); Ricard Alexis, Alcide 'Slow Drag' Pavageau, Chester Zardis (*b*); Baby Dodds, Edgar Moseley (*d*). 5/45.

*** **At Herbert Otto's Party** American Music AMCD 74
    Lewis; Herb Morand (*t*); Jim Robinson (*tb*); Albert Burbank (*cl*); Lawrence Marrero (*bj*); Alcide 'Slow Drag' Pavageau (*b*); Albert Jiles, Bob Matthews, Joe Watkins (*d*). 11/49.

Rarely has a traditional jazz musician been documented on record in so concentrated a way as clarinettist George Lewis was in the early 1950s. American Music's patient documentation, which now extends beyond the capacity of this listing, even gives street numbers and times of day for the earliest material here. Having been coaxed out of a 'retirement' working as a dockhand at the start of the war, Lewis was by the mid-'50s the surviving pillar of 'serious' revivalism, which he'd helped kick off with Bunk Johnson, working what looked like a politician's itinerary across the United States; Johnson is featured on three tracks of the early *With Kid Shots* compilation.

The early material is absolutely pristine and comes across on CD with remarkable freshness. The first tracks on Volume One of the 1943 material were recorded in the drummer's house and, though they're more raggedy than the later sessions at the Gypsy Tea Room (high point: two takes each of 'Climax Rag' and 'Careless Love'), they provide an excellent starting point for serious examination of this remarkable musician. Lewis's solo breaks are oddly pitched (and there are a couple where this might be down to tape yaw) but the pitching remains consistent relative to other players so it has to be considered an idiosyncrasy rather than poor articulation. The *Trios & Bands* compilation includes some second takes from the group sessions with 'Shots' (including a marvellous second try on 'San Jacinto Blues' and the first, presumably rejected, take of 'High Society'). He was apparently unhappy about the quality of some of the performances and asked to make some more discs with just banjo and bass. These contain some of his best-ever improvisations, all delivered in that plaintive, singing style that is among the most imitated of jazz sounds. The bounce and economy of 'Ice Cream' and the brief, gentle optimism of 'Life Will Be Sweeter' contain in four minutes the essence of Lewis's music: clear melodic statement, rhythmic simplicity and straightforward emotion.

*** **Jazz Band Ball** Good Time Jazz GTCD 12005
    Lewis; Elmer Talbert (*t*); Jim Robinson (*tb*); Alton Purnell (*p*); Lawrence Marrero (*bj*); Alcide 'Slow Drag' Pavageau (*b*); Joe Watkins (*d*). 6/50.

Not strictly a Lewis record, and not, as sometimes hinted, documentation of a single evening's moment. Nevertheless, this affords a valuable opportunity to hear Lewis in company with bands led by trombonists Turk Murphy and Kid Ory, and cornetist Pete Daily, thus providing a clear diagnostic section of what was going on in revivalist jazz between the end of the war and 1950, when the Lewis tracks were recorded. Talbert is a surprise, a little-recorded player with a fine individual tone and some interesting ideas to contribute on 'Willie The Weeper', where he keeps his main influence firmly in view.

***(*) **George Lewis With Red Allen** American Music AMCD 71
>   Lewis; Alvin Alcorn (*t*); Henry 'Red' Allen (*t, v*); Bill Matthews, Jim Robinson (*tb*); Lester
>   Santiago (*p*); Lawrence Marrero (*bj*); Alcide 'Slow Drag' Pavageau (*b*); Paul Barbarin (*d*). 8/51.
It's very rare that anyone catches American Music out in an error, but the Alcide Marrero playing bass
on these tracks has to be old 'Slow Drag' Pavageau who is listed for one session and garbled for the
other. Nor would we accuse the label of short measure, but Allen fans should be aware that he appears
on only five tracks, albeit five excellent ones. 'Hindustan' and the two versions of 'St James Infirmary'
are up with the trumpeter's best recorded work and, if Lewis sounds a little shadowed, he makes up for
it later (presumably) that same day with Alcorn. These are studio recordings, a little boxy but not
unpleasantly so, and the quality of the music – other highlights include 'Bourbon Street Parade' and
'Who's Sorry Now', taped a fortnight later – more than makes up for any technical deficit.

***(*) **The George Lewis Ragtime Band Of New Orleans: The Oxford Series – Volume 1** American Music
AMCD 21
>   Lewis; Percy G. Humphrey (*t*); Jim Robinson (*tb*); Alton Purnell (*p*); Lawrence Marrero (*bj*);
>   Alcide 'Slow Drag' Pavageau (*b*); Joe Watkins (*d*). 52.
***(*) **The George Lewis Ragtime Band Of New Orleans: The Oxford Series – Volume 2 (Concert, First
Half)** American Music AMCD 22
>   As above. 52.
***(*) **The George Lewis Ragtime Band Of New Orleans: The Oxford Series – Volume 3 (Concert,
Second Half)** American Music AMCD 23
>   As above. 52.
*** **The George Lewis Ragtime Band Of New Orleans: The Oxford Series – Volume 4 (Recording Session)**
American Music AMCD 24
>   As above. 3/53.
**(*) **The George Lewis Ragtime Band Of New Orleans: The Oxford Series – Volume 5 (Concert, First
Half)** American Music AMCD 25
>   As above. 3/53.
*** **The George Lewis Ragtime Band Of New Orleans: The Oxford Series – Volume 6 (Concert, Second
Half)** American Music AMCD 26
>   As above. 3/53.
*** **The George Lewis Ragtime Band Of New Orleans: The Oxford Series – Volume 7 (Concert, First
Half)** American Music AMCD 27
>   As above. 3/53.
*** **The George Lewis Ragtime Jazz Band Of New Orleans: The Oxford Series – Volume 8 (Concert,
Second Half)** American Music AMCD 28
>   As above. 3/53.
**(*) **The George Lewis Ragtime Jazz Band Of New Orleans: The Oxford Series – Volume 9 (Church
Service, Rehearsal And Party)** American Music AMCD 29
>   As above. 3/53.
(*) **The George Lewis Ragtime Jazz Band Of New Orleans: The Oxford Series – Volume 10 (Party)
American Music AMCD 30
>   As above. 3/53.
In 1952, Lewis was recorded by the American Folklore Group of the English department at Miami
University, an institution rather confusingly situated in Oxford, Ohio. The 'Oxford Series' CDs are well
mastered and sound amazingly fresh for recordings four decades old. Lewis made a studio recording of
seven quite extended pieces, including a long 'Tin Roof Blues' (on which Humphrey makes his presence
felt) and a rousing 'Saint' to finish. The subsequent concert discs are better still, with excellent performances of Lewis staples like 'Over The Waves', 'Darktown Strutters' Ball' and 'Careless Love', closing
with a vintage 'Sheikh Of Araby'.

  It seems unlikely that anyone other than stoneground experts will want to have the later rehearsal and
party volumes, though these contain some of the most unfettered playing in the set. The concert of 21
March on Volumes Seven and Eight is superior to that of the day before only because the band now
sounds played in and relaxed. Lewis is soloing well and Howard plays with great dexterity on 'Glad
When You're Dead, You Rascal You'. The sound may also be a shade brighter in places, though that is
probably a function of Lewis lifting his enunciation to compensate for a generally more buoyant
ensemble.

  Purely as an experiment, it's fascinating to listen to this material continuously from start to finish. There
are literally dozens of tiny changes of inflexion and emphasis (countless fluffs and missed cues, too,
which might be overlooked on a more casual listen), but also a growing sense that the presumed
spontaneity and freshness of this music are actually much less than its advocates might like to think.
Lewis is prone to fall back on a set of stock phrases (though Howard is not) and there are very few real

surprises. A double-CD of the very best performances would be welcome, particularly now that the series has been extended further, though discs one to three will already suffice for most tastes.

**** The Beverley Caverns Sessions Good Time Jazz GTCD 12058
 Lewis; Avery 'Kid' Howard (*t, v*); Jim Robinson (*tb*); Alton Purnell (*p*); Lawrence Marrero (*bj*); Alcide 'Slow Drag' Pavageau (*b*). 5/53.

***(*) Jazz At Vespers Original Jazz Classics OJC 1721
 As above. 2/54.

***(*) Jass At Ohio Union Storyville STCD 6020/1 2CD
 As above. 3/54.

*** Sounds Of New Orleans: Volume 7 Storyville SLP 6014
 Lewis; Kid Howard (*t*); Jim Robinson (*tb*); Alton Purnell (*p*); Lawrence Marrero (*bj*); Alcide 'Slow Drag' Pavageau (*b*); Joe Watkins (*d*); Lizzie Miles (*v*). 12/53 & 1/54.

*** Jazz In The Classic New Orleans Tradition Original Jazz Classics OJC 1736
 Lewis; Alvin Alcorn (*t*); Bill Matthews (*tb*); Alton Purnell, Lester Santiago (*p*); Lawrence Marrero (*bj*); Alcide 'Slow Drag' Pavageau (*b*); Paul Barbarin (*d*).

*** George Lewis Of New Orleans Original Jazz Classics OJC 1739
 Lewis; Kid Howard, Peter Bocage (*t*); Jim Robinson, Harrison Barnes, Joe Howard (*tb*); Alcide 'Slow Drag' Pavageau (*b*); Baby Dodds (*d*); Sister Berenice Phillips (*v*).

*** George Lewis In Stockholm, 1959 Dragon DRCD 221
 Lewis; Kid Howard (*t*); Jim Robinson (*tb*); Joe Robichaux (*p*); Alcide 'Slow Drag' Pavageau (*b*); Joe Watkins (*d, v*). 2/59.

*** The Spirit Of New Orleans: Volume 1 Music Mecca CD 1014
 Lewis; Kid Howard (*t, v*); Jim Robinson (*tb*); Charlie Hamilton (*p*); Alcide 'Slow Drag' Pavageau (*b*); Emanuel Sayles (*bjo*); Joe Watkins (*d, v*). 61.

*** George Lewis And The Barry Martyn Band GHB BCD 37
 Lewis; Cuff Bilett (*t*); Pete Dyer (*tb*); Graham Paterson (*p*); John Coles (*bjo*); Terry Knight (*b*); Barry Martyn (*d*). 3/65.

*** Classic New Orleans Jazz: Volume 1 Biograph BCD 127
 Lewis; George Blod (*t*); Jay Brackett (*tb*); J. R. Smith (*tba*); Ronnie Bill (*bjo*); Alex Bigard (*d*). 4/65.

*** George Lewis With Ken Colyer's Jazzmen Lake LACD 27
 Lewis; Ken Colyer (*t, v*); Geoff Cole (*tb*); Tony Pyke (*cl*); Johnny Bastable (*bj*); Bill Cole (*b*); Ryan Hetherington (*d*). 9/66.

In later life, Lewis was a celebrity, a living link back to the prehistory of the music. As such he toured Japan and Europe, turning up in such unlikely places as the White Horse Inn, Willesden, and the Dancing Slipper, Nottingham, both occasions documented on the GHB set, above. By contrast, the Stockholm visit of 1959 looked like part of an imperial progress.

 Lewis's almost studied primitivism and simplicity of tone were curiously beguiling and he had the disconcerting ability to invest almost subliminal changes of emphasis or diction with a disproportionate significance, which is one reason not so much why there are so many live discs available as why so many of them are valuable acquisitions. The Beverley Caverns record, made in Hollywood, is a good case in point. A now familiar band, hardly a surprise in the set list, and yet something to listen to and ponder in virtually every chorus. This is easily the most desirable of all the later sessions, and it should be a high priority for anyone who wants to get to grips with Lewis and his music.

 His appearance with Ken Colyer's Jazzmen in Manchester 30 years ago must have seemed a little like the Road to Emmaus for these very purist believers and their fans. It is perhaps ironic that clubs and concert halls in the British midlands and north should have become the last bastions of strict constructionism while players back in New Orleans were beginning to tinker with rock and roll. With that in mind, it's easy to see why Lewis became the icon and his work the sacred texts of the revivalist movement, susceptible as both are to myth-making and picayune analysis. Are occasional bent notes the result of carelessness or a gesture of experiment from a seemingly conservative man whose putative conservatism was what made him famous? Were rephrased licks the result of new ideas or, as appears to be the case on 'Walk Through The Streets Of The City' at Beverley Caverns, a combination of faulty memory and fast reflexes? The *Times-Picayune* in his native city became inclined to harshness about Lewis's technical shortcomings in succeeding years, and there is no doubt that constant performance of a severely limited repertoire seriously overstretched his abilities. The life, in a curious way, was always more interesting than the music. Lewis's residency at the Hangover Club in San Francisco was the high-water mark of revivalism, and the many recordings from this period have a joyous optimism which it is hard not to like; even so, it's equally hard to get over-excited about them. Lewis's fame largely depends on his willingness to be cast in a particular role. The *Tradition* OJC introduces bandleader and drummer, Paul Barbarin, a nearly exact New Orleans contemporary of Lewis. Utterly obsessed, where Lewis was innocently untroubled (and thus manipulable), about the status of black musicians, Barbarin dropped dead on his first appearance at the hitherto segregated Proteus parade; Lewis beat him to the farm by a mere two months.

George Lewis (born 1952) TROMBONES, SOUSAPHONE, TUBA, COMPUTER

**** **Shadowgraph, 5 (Sextet)** Black Saint 120016
    Lewis; Roscoe Mitchell (*as, ss, bs, cassette recorder*); Douglas Ewart (*cl, bcl, sno, f, bsn, cassette recorder, perc*); Muhal Richard Abrams, Anthony Davis (*p*); Leroy Jenkins (*vn, vla*); Abdul Wadud (*clo*). 77.
*** **Jila – Save! Mon – The Imaginary Suite** Black Saint 120026
    Lewis; Douglas Ewart (*as, f, perc*). 78.
  **** **Homage To Charles Parker** Black Saint 120029
    As above, except add Anthony Davis (*p*); Richard Teitelbaum (*syn*). 79.
It is significant that, as a trombonist growing up in a period marked by the dominance of the saxophone, George Lewis should have taken saxophone players as his primary models. His rather emotional legato is reminiscent of both Lester Young and, depending on context, virtually all the evolutionary stages of John Coltrane's style. Context is of considerable importance because Lewis has played in a bewildering variety of musical settings, from relatively conventional section-playing (a brief stint with the mid-1970s Basie band) to technically adventurous free playing. Lewis habitually plays either with intense and surprisingly gentle lyricism or with a deconstructive fury that has led him to dismantle his trombone in mid-performance, producing non-tempered and abstract tones on mouthpiece and slide. He has also taken a close interest in electronics, using computers with increasing technical assurance to provide backgrounds and to create a much-needed dialectical tension in improvised performances.

Lewis's discography as leader is scandalously thin, but the quality is very high indeed. *Shadowgraph* and the duos with Ewart are characteristic of the free abstract jazz that emerged out of AACM's explorations in the 1960s and early '70s. Listening to them, one is aware how little of this music has been assimilated into the mainstream of either jazz or improvisation. 'Monads' is almost a philosophical primer for free players, an oblique and sometimes violent outburst of sound in which ideas fly around almost too fast to be absorbed. One wonders how it would ever have been possible to assimilate this music in live performance.

'Triple Slow Mix' is a more spacious and accommodating piece, with Abrams and Davis (in opposite channels) suggesting different points of focus for Lewis's gloriously flatulent sousaphone. 'Cycle' recalls the duos, but the real meat of the record is the title-track, part of a series of compositions written by Lewis under a grant from the National Endowment for the Arts. Though the sonic landscape is much more exotic, 'Shadowgraph' is identifiably in the line of one of Ellington's noise pieces. The main soloists are Mitchell and Abrams, with Lewis himself eschewing his synths in favour of an exotic selection of brasses, including Wagner tuba. The tension is almost palpable as potential grooves rise up and are systematically extinguished in a mass of sound that includes cassette players and (from Ewart) incidental percussion of the home-made variety favoured at the time. It's a wonderful record to have back in the lists, but it scarcely reaches the heights of what was to follow.

Ewart is Jamaican-born and 'Save! Mon' is his dedication to the poeple of his homeland. It features him on alto, which is more immediately appealing but less idiomatic and challening than his work on flute and 'Ewart flutes'. 'Jila' is a more straightforward and expressive piece, indeed unexpectedly so, written as a posy for his daughter. Lewis is much more obviously in command on the two parts of *The Imaginary Suite* included on the record. These are inspired by figures or icons of ancient mythology and some of their modern counterparts; Anthony Braxton may or may not be pleased to learn that 'Charon' is dedicated to him. The addition of electronics greatly expands the available sound-palette and the playing is more expansive and sustained, rather than the staccato, pointillistic approach of the other two pieces. It is in this sense much closer to the blues-tinged world of Lewis's best work, *Homage To Charles Parker*.

It represents a further triumphant extension and synthesis of the same basic language premises, combining improvisation with predetermined structures – rather in the manner of Lawrence 'Butch' Morris or pianist-composer Anthony Davis, who plays on the date – and reintroducing a strong programmatic element to abstract music. As he shows in the fine duets with Ewart, using predetermined structures in indeterminate juxtapositions and dynamics can create a music of considerable resonance. 'Homage To Charles Parker' and 'Blues', the two long sides that made up the original LP, are among the most profound and beautiful performances of recent times and certainly rank in the top dozen or so jazz/improvised records made since 1960.

Lewis's rather stilted liner-notes somewhat undersell the emotional impact of both pieces. 'Blues' consists of four independent diatonic 'choruses' of absolute simplicity which are played in shifting configurations by the four musicians. Despite the fact that there are no conventional resolutions and no predictable coincidence of material, the piece evokes order as much as freedom. Although none of the material conforms to the blues, its 'feel' is absolutely unmistakable and authentic.

If 'Blues' is a triumphant extension of the black tradition in music, 'Homage To Charles Parker' concerns itself intimately with the saxophonist's putative afterlife and musical real-presence. There is a long opening section on electronics, synthesizers and cymbals which evoke Parker's 'reality'. Reminiscent of evocations of primeval Chaos by Marilyn Crispell on *Gaia* (Leo Records) and the electronic composer Bernard Parmegiani, it gradually yields place to a series of apparently discontinuous solos on saxophone, piano and finally with no ensemble backing beyond the synthesizer sounds, which recast and project Parker's life and language. There are no explicit bebop references and, indeed, the piece seems to serve as a healing response to the fractures that separated bop from the earlier history of black American music, of which it was also the apotheosis. The music is calm and almost stately, occasionally suggesting a chorale. Lewis's concluding statements are unbearably plangent but also forceful and intelligent. In their refusal of tragedy, they also have to be seen as political statements. This is an essential modern record.

***(*) Voyager Avant AVAN 014
Lewis; Roscoe Mitchell (*ss, as*). 2/93.

Fine musician though Douglas Ewart is, he seems a beginner compared to the mighty Roscoe Mitchell, who comprehensively outclasses even the nominal leader here. There is a sense in which this is intended as a musical autobiography of the trombonist. Enthusiasts will hear lots of references to earlier work, including the Ewart duos, and will wonder, on occasion, why it wasn't tackled as an entirely solo project, with or without electronic enhancements. The eight parts of 'Voyager' and the single-part 'Homecoming' are by far the most accessible things Lewis has attempted in years, and it is Mitchell who introduces a level of complexity that on occasion really does prompt one to stop and rethink what is going on. Not necessarily a good sign with music of this type.

*** Changing With The Times New World NW 80434
Lewis; Douglas Ewart (*as, cl, bcl, shakuhachi, didjeridu, perc*); Jeannie Cheatham (*p, org, v*); Daniel Koppelman, Ruth Neville (*p*); Mary Oliver (*vn, vla*); Peter Gonzales III (*perc*); Bernard Mixon, Ned Rothenberg, Quincy Troupe (*v*). 3/93.

Recorded just a month later, this music-and-poetry session with its unlikely-looking participants (Jeannie Cheatham?) is a most untypical Lewis record, unless of course it signals a move – 'changing with the times' – in this rather mild-mannered direction. Lewis has always been concerned with the dramatic dimension of what he is doing, and the trombone is a highly dramatic instrument; but there is a flimsiness here and a lack of focus which will disconcert those who have been turned on by the above.

John Lewis (born 1920) PIANO

*** Grand Encounter Blue Note B21Y-46859
Lewis; Bill Perkins (*ts*); Jim Hall (*g*); Percy Heath (*b*); Chico Hamilton (*d*). 2/56.
***(*) The Wonderful World Of Jazz Atlantic 90979-2
Lewis; Herb Pomeroy (*t*); Gunther Schuller (*frhn*); Eric Dolphy (*as, f*); Benny Golson, Paul Gonsalves (*ts*); Jimmy Giuffre (*bs*); Jim Hall (*g*); George Duvivier (*b*); Connie Kay (*d*). 7–9/60.

John Lewis's greatest preoccupation has been with the MJQ, but he has been making occasional discs under his own name since the mid-1950s, and this is one of the earliest. Hall and Perkins quickly grasp the refined but deep-set bluesiness of Lewis's preferred settings, and the result is a West Coast album of unusual intimacy and quiet feeling. '2 Degrees East, 3 Degrees West' is the track to remember, but it's a very pretty record. Unfortunately, many of Lewis's later records have yet to make it to CD. But *The Wonderful World Of Jazz* has recently been remastered. It opens with a superb Gonsalves solo on a 15-minute 'Body And Soul' and then works through a short programme of jazz standards, including a new '2 Degrees East, 3 Degres West'. Newly available on the CD are 'The Stranger', precious for Eric Dolphy's solo, and a long quartet version of 'If You Could See Me Now'; but the whole disc is a thoughtful reflection on the jazz tradition as it was standing in 1960.

***(*) Afternoon In Paris Dreyfus 849234-2
Lewis (*p* solo). 11/79.
*** Kansas City Breaks DRG Disques Swing 8430
Lewis; Frank Wess (*f*); Howard Collins (*g*); Joe Kennedy Jr (*vn*); Marc Johnson (*b*); Shelly Manne (*d*). 5/82.
**** Private Concert Emarcy 848267-2
Lewis (*p* solo). 9/90.

Regrettably few of Lewis's own-name projects are currently in print. The 1982 session features an unlikely combination of players, though the music has some beautiful touches: Lewis has pursued an amalgam of jazz and chamber music on many levels, and this instrumentation is one more example, even if Kennedy's almost bluegrass violin and Wess's pretty flute make strange bedfellows. Manne is as swinging as usual, and there is a fine 'Milano', a smooth 'Django'. The sound is rather clattery.

Lewis's solo albums are never alike. The 1979 session is a very short, almost clipped recital, his favourite themes skimmed through, a series of lightning sketches rather than the full oils of the Emarcy date. Yet there are fascinating revisions, the almost perky 'Django' for one, and a reverent take of Ellington's 'Come Sunday'. Eleven years later, with the Lewis Steinway shipped into New York's Church of the Ascension for the occasion, the pianist created one of the most refined and memorable piano records of recent times. The programme is much the same as always, with some particular favourites from his own book, yet each interpretation sounds different: his latest thoughts on 'Round Midnight' shed new light on that faded masterpiece, while 'Milano', 'Afternoon In Paris' and 'Midnight In Paris' bring European elegance and charm into a direct fusion with the blues that Lewis has always loved. Superlative sound.

Meade Lux Lewis (1905–1964) PIANO, CELESTE, HARPSICHORD

**** Meade Lux Lewis 1927–1939 Classics 722
> Lewis; Albert Ammons, Pete Johnson (*p*). 12/27–1/39.

***(*) Meade Lux Lewis 1939–1941 Classics 743
> Lewis; J. C. Higginbotham (*tb*); Albert Ammons (*p*); Teddy Bunn (*g*); Johnny Williams (*b*); Big Sid Catlett (*d*). 1/39–9/41.

*** Meade Lux Lewis 1941–1944 Classics 841
> Lewis (*p, cel, hpd* solo). 4/41–8/44.

**(*) The Blues Piano Artistry Of Meade Lux Lewis Original Jazz Classics OJC 1759
> Lewis (*p* solo). 11/61.

Lewis encapsulated his contribution to jazz in his first three minutes as a soloist with his 1927 Paramount record of 'Honky Tonk Train Blues'. He recorded it again at his second session, and again at his fourth. All three are on the Classics CD, along with 15 other variations on the blues and boogie woogie. His signature-piece remains a marvellous evocation of a locomotive rhythm, perfectly balanced through all its variations, and if he became tired of it his listeners never did. It's a pity, though, that it's about the only piece he's much remembered for, since there is plenty of other excellent music among his various sessions, and the first Classics CD brings together much of it. His 1936 session for Decca includes two extraordinary pieces on celeste, 'I'm In The Mood For Love' and 'Celeste Blues', and his 1939 session for Blue Note – which supplied the first Blue Note issue, 'Melancholy' and 'Solitude' – opens with a five-part investigation of 'The Blues', all rejected at the time but a remarkable sequence, at least as personal and imaginative as his train pieces. The sound on the CD is frequently muffled, sloppily remastered or otherwise imperfect, but the music is marvellous. There's a modest decline on Classics 743: the 1940 version of 'Honky Tonk Train Blues' goes off at a faintly ludicrous tempo, and some of Lewis's boogie pieces end up as all the same. But three duets with Ammons and the rest of the Blue Note session tracks offer rewards, while the 1939 Solo Art session is mostly at a slow tempo and spotlights Lewis the bluesman to stunning effect. Sound here is far less than ideal once again, though the Blue Note tracks (from an unidentified source) are better, if brittle.

That disc ends on two rather nutty harpsichord solos, and the next one starts with the other two from the same session. A single V-Disc finds Lewis playing piano and celeste simultaneously on 'Doll House Boogie' before nine tracks cut at a date for the Asch label. Again, the fast pieces suggest a sinking into boogie clichés, but there are still some startling things, notably 'Denapas Parade' and above all the previously rejected 'Special No. One', with its melody carried in the left hand. There is yet another 'Honky Tonk Train', and this one is taken at a farcical pace. He must have been fed up with it.

His 1961 Riverside session, now reissued in the OJC series, wasn't a milestone or a major rediscovery. Lewis had clearly grown tired of his own work over the years, and this group of remakes is done professionally, without much joy. He died three years later, following a car accident.

Mel Lewis (1929–90) DRUMS

*** Got'cha Fresh Sound FSR-CD 73
> Lewis; Ed Leddy (*t*); Richie Kamuca, Jerry Coker (*ts*); Pepper Adams (*bs*); Johnny Marabuto (*p*); Dean Reilly (*b*). 11/56.

(*) Naturally! Telarc 83301

> Lewis; Earl Gardner, Ron Tooley, Larry Moses, John Marshall (*t*); John Mosca, Lee Robertson, Lolie Bienenfeld (*tb*); Jim Daniels (*btb*); Dick Oatts, Steve Coleman (*ss, as, f*); Bob Rockwell, Richard Perry (*ts, f*); Gary Brown (*bs*); Jim McNeely (*p*); Bob Bowman (*b*). 3/79.

Lewis was a master of big-band drumming, less relentlessly driving than Buddy Rich but as capable of swinging a big ensemble from the kit. His enduring achievements in that respect were with the band he led for many years with Thad Jones; yet little from their (admittedly rather sparse) discography is currently available. These two sessions, almost a generation apart, show some of his mettle. *Got'cha*, cut in San Francisco, is characteristic of certain aspects of West Coast jazz of the day without capitulating to the clichés of the style: Bill Perkins's arrangement of 'In A Mellowtone', for instance, is interestingly lugubrious, even sour; and with Coker and Leddy – otherwise neglected players – often in the solo limelight, this is a refreshing cut above several such sessions.

Naturally! is distinguished by the excellent reed section, with Oatts and Coleman sounding young and hungry, and the lacerating punch of the brass is undeniable; but the degree of flair that Jones could interpolate is missed.

***(*) The Definitive Thad Jones Vol. 1** Musicmasters 5024-2

> Lewis; Earl Gardner, Joe Mosello, Glenn Drewes, Jim Powell (*t, flhn*); John Mosca, Ed Neumeister (*tb*); Douglas Purviance, Earl McIntyre (*btb*); Stephanie Fauber (*frhn*); Dick Oatts, Ted Nash, Joe Lovano, Ralph Lalama, Gary Smulyan (*reeds*); Kenny Werner (*p*); Dennis Irwin (*b*). 2/88.

*** **The Definitive Thad Jones Vol. 2** Musicmasters 5046-2

> As above. 2/88.

A double tribute to Thad, with the Lewis band breezing through a selection of the trumpeter's tunes at a Village Vanguard engagement. Lewis's band sounded friendlier than many a big ensemble, with the reed section having a wide range of tones and the horns securing a fine attack without undue brassiness. They sound in top fettle on both discs: the first has a very good 'Three In One' and, though the second is a mite more ordinary, they finesse the material rather than bang it about.

***(*) The Lost Art** Musicmasters 6022-2

> Lewis; Jim Powell (*flhn*); John Mosca (*tb*); Dick Oatts (*ss, as, ts*); Gary Smulyan (*bs*); Kenny Werner (*p*); Dennis Irwin (*b*). 4/89.

The sextet date was one of Lewis's final recordings. The music is skilfully arrranged by the idiosyncratic Werner – who cites such influences here as Andrew Hill and Bob Brookmeyer – into a rounded portrait of the options for small-group jazz in the aftermath of hard bop. On the face of it, Lewis is an unlikely choice as drummer for such an occasion, but he never played better, embellishing march or 4/4 or intensely slow pieces with the same assiduous craft and subtlety. 'The Lost Art' itself refers to his use of the brushes. Mosca is too bland, but Oatts, Smulyan and Werner are an absorbing team of improvisers, and they were all masterfully recorded by producer John Snyder. A fine farewell for Lewis in the studios.

Ramsey Lewis (born 1935) PIANO, KEYBOARDS

***(*) Live** Stereo JHR 73524

> Lewis; Eldee Young (*b*); Isaac Red Holt (*d*). 65.

*** **Maiden Voyage (and more)** GRP Chess 18042

> Lewis; Cleveland Eaton (*b*); Maurice White (*d*) Minnie Riperton (*v*); orchestra. 4 & 12/68.

** **Sky Islands** GRP 97452

> Lewis; Art Porter (*as*); Henry Johnson (*g*); Mike Logan (*ky*); Chuck Webb (*b*); Steve Cobb (*d, perc*); Tony Carpenter, Eve Cornelious, Carl Griffin, Brenda Stewart (*v*).

(*) Ivory Island GRP 96882

> Lewis; Mike Logan (*ky*); Henry Johnson (*g*); Charles Webb (*b*); Steve Cobb (*d, perc*). 92.

Failure to include Ramsey in previous editions has been interpreted as snobbery on the editors' part. Not a bit of it. We are as convinced as any of his greatness. His million-seller, *The In-Crowd*, was a great record, and those parts of it included on *Live* (a slight misnomer) are still very listenable. One suspects that Lewis had been listening to it when he decided to turn legit and return to acoustic piano in the 1980s. Unfortunately, most of his latter-day material is drab, formulaic funk, sounding like a Herbie Hancock project gone disastrously wrong. He tackles a Hancock tune at the top of the best of these discs, *Maiden Voyage*, and throws in a rather lovely version of Mike Gibbs's 'Sweet Rain', but the trio is no more than functional, the strings overpowering, and Minnie Riperton's voice belongs on another record entirely. The 'and more' component of this CD is an LP called *Mother Nature's Son*, on which Lewis tackled – late, and with studs showing – a batch of Beatles tunes. These are uniquely horrible, jazzed-up and orchestrated in the most contrived way; but they have the interesting effect of pointing to some of the merits of *Maiden Voyage*, Lewis's own deceptively simple keyboard touch, which has a lot of variation, his exact sense of time and how to bend it a shade.

The 1990s 'revival' and 'return to mainstream' are very much in the ear of the behearer. Lewis is still a fleet and effective piano player, but he has spent far too much time in discotheques to understand the fundamental differences between jazz and pop, and *Sky Islands* in particular is a macaronic mish-mash of styles. However, in keeping with our earlier endorsement, we are convinced that the giant is merely dozing . . .

Ted Lewis (1890–1971) VOCAL, CLARINET, C-MELODY SAXOPHONE

*** **Classic Sessions 1928–1929** JSP CD 326
> Lewis; Dave Klein, Walter Klein (*t*); Muggsy Spanier (*c*); George Brunies, Harry Raderman (*tb*); Don Murray (*cl, as, ts, bs*); Frank Teschemacher (*cl, ts*); Frank Ross, Jack Aronson (*p*); Sol Klein, Sam Shapiro (*vn*); Tony Girardi (*g*); Bob Escamilla, Harry Barth (*bb*); John Lucas (*d*). 2/28–8/29.

Lewis was a vaudevillian rather than a jazzman, and his capabilities as a clarinettist were of dubious value: when he takes a solo, he plays in the gaspipe manner which musicians such as Boyd Senter turned into masterpieces of low art. He recognized better players though (he had Benny Goodman in his band for a time, and, on one record, he has the cheek to call out 'Play it, Ted!' during one of Goodman's solos) and many strong players turn in solos on Lewis's records. The leader had actually begun recording as far back as 1917, with Earl Fuller's Famous Jazz Band, but this compilation takes in one of the peaks of the Lewis band, with Spanier, Murray (who was killed in a car accident in the period between the final two recording sessions here) and Brunies all on hand. The 23 tracks vary fairly wildly in quality, and the determining factor seems to be how much Lewis himself is involved. His egregious vocal style will be enough to send many listeners to the track-skip facility, but even a feeble entry like 'Oh, Baby!' features a fine solo by Murray. The straight-ahead jazz titles – including 'Farewell Blues', 'Wabash Blues', 'Clarinet Marmalade' and 'Limehouse Blues', all of which are free of vocals – inevitably emerge as the best, and here the band shows it could play as well as the best of the white New York dance bands of the day. A useful collection, and the sound has been beautifully remastered by John R. T. Davies.

Vic Lewis (born 1919) BANDLEADER and
West Coast All Stars (founded 1963)

** **Play Bill Holman** Candid CCD 79535
> Conte Candoli, Jack Sheldon (*t*); Andy Martin, Rob McConnell (*tb*); Ron Loofbourrow (*frhn*); Lanny Morgan, Lennie Niehaus, Bud Shank (*as*); Bob Cooper (*ts, cl, f*); Bill Perkins (*bs, ss, f, as, bcl*); Alan Broadbent, Mike Lang, Dudley Moore (*p*); John Clayton (*b*); Jeff Hamilton (*d*); Ruth Price (*v*). 8/89, 3/93.
*** **Shake Down The Stars** Candid CCD79526
> Andy Martin (*tb*); Bob Cooper (*ts*); Bill Perkins (*ts, bs, ss, cl, f*); Mike Lang (*p*); Joel Di Bartolo (*b*); Paul Kreibach (*d*). 4/92.
*** **A Celebration Of West Coast Jazz** Candid CCD 7971/2
> Steve Huffsteter (*t, flhn*); Andy Martin, Charlie Lopez, Alex Eyles, Bob McCheskie (*tb*); Don Shelton (*as, cl, picc, f*); Bill Perkins (*f, cl, as, ts, bs*); Bob Cooper (*ts, cl, f*); Bob Efford (*bs, ob, ts, cl*); Jack Nimitz (*bs, bcl*); Clare Fischer, Christian Jacob, Frank Strazzeri (*p*); John Leitham, Tom Worthington (*b*); Paul Kreibach, Bob Leatherbarrow (*d*); Sue Raney (*v*). 4/93, 2/94.

Short, on the round side, and with hair even blacker than near-contemporary Ronald Reagan's, Lewis cuts an improbable figure in the jazz world. He grew up in London, gravitating to jazz as a banjo player, later spieling his way into gigs with Django Reinhardt, Tommy Dorsey and Louis Armstrong. During the war he played in an assortment of RAF bands before co-leading a group with Jack Parnell. In the late 1940s he unveiled a progressive 'Music for Moderns' project and managed to have his picture taken standing alongside Stan Kenton, just in case anyone failed to see the connection.

In the 1960s he turned to management, became involved in the company out of which Brian Epstein managed the Beatles and Cilla Black, and still managed to keep a few jazz strings to his bow. The most prominent of them has been the West Coast All Stars, who have previously recorded for Candid. As always, his role on this project – beyond having his picture taken standing alongside featured trombonist Martin – seems to have been purely fiscal. Even joint arranging (with Lang) and co-production credits with the reliably sharp-eared Perkins have to be regarded with some scepticism. He does, though, manage to persuade top-flight players to turn out and record for the same rates as session men, which implies a gift of the gab if nothing else.

So what of the records themselves? *Shake Down The Stars* is attributed to Lewis's favourite songwriter, Jimmy Van Heusen. Among the tracks: 'But Beautiful', 'Here's That Rainy Day', the warhorse 'Polka Dots and Moonbeams', 'I Thought About You' and the title-track. Lewis had himself once turned to trombone, so featuring Martin on every track except 'I'll Only Miss Her' (a welcome outing for the stalwart Cooper, who is the only ever-present All-Star) smacks of surrogacy or wishful thinking. Martin has a nice old-fashioned tone and isn't troubled by too many fancy ideas, and there it really ends. As Miss Brodie used to say, one that will appeal to people who like that sort of thing.

The Bill Holman set is pretty messy, padded out with an alternative version of 'Oleo' and a re-recorded vocal by Ruth Price. It sounds as if not one of them cares even remotely about what they're playing, and the solos, such as they are, fail to register. Dudley Moore has played better solos off the cuff in the middle of comedy programmes, but at least he sounds as if he's enjoying himself.

The *Celebration* was also a fly way of marking Lewis's own 75th birthday. The box actually contains two sessions, recorded almost a year apart. Given that the band on the very first All Stars date included Shorty Rogers, Bud Shank, Laurindo Almeida, Victor Feldman and Shelly Manne, it might be thought that we have drifted into a Silver Age. The silvery quality of Perkins's flute playing only serves to underline that. Everything is bright and polished, very clean-edged and not very involving. Martin's solos are increasingly routine, and it is really only Perkins who continues to put some emotion into the playing; his 'Waltz For Coop' on disc two is lovely. But where are the trumpet-players of yesteryear?

Victor Lewis DRUMS

*** **Family Portrait** Audioquest 1010
Lewis; John Stubblefield (*ss, ts*); Eduardo Simon (*p*); Cecil McBee (*b*); Don Alias, Jumma Santos (*perc*); Pamela Watson, Bobby Watson, Yvonne Hatchet, Shani Phillpotts, Michael Moses, Melissa Thomas, Raymond Cruz (*v*). 11–12/92.

***(*) **Know It Today, Know It Tomorrow** Red 123255-2
Lewis; Eddie Henderson (*t, flhn*); Seamus Blake (*ts*); Eduardo Simon (*p*); Christian McBride (*b*). 4/92.

Lewis is one of the leading drummers of today, but his recent showing as a composer has been confined to a few themes turning up on other people's dates. These two sessions give him a better opportunity, and some of the material is interesting enough to suggest that Lewis could be as involved in writing as, say, Joe Chambers. The Audioquest album is sometimes obscured by an ambitious gameplan, with massed voices used on three tracks (offering a slight recall of Max Roach's work in this area) and the percussionists building over rather than especially complementing Lewis's own work. Stubblefield, though, is as authoritative as always and Simon's Herbie Hancock touches make modest waves. *Know It Today, Know It Tomorrow* is less self-consciously striving but more detailed and meticulous. It's as much a showcase for the youthful Blake as it is for Lewis: aside from the slow crescendo at the climax of 'Swamp Dog', there is very little grandstanding from the drums. Blake's diffident, slightly hollow sound can be very affecting on slow pieces such as 'The Loss Of A Moment', a scrupulous, Shorterish ballad by Lewis, or 'The Truce', but he has no trouble keeping up a flow of ideas at quicker tempos, and the long melody lines of his own tune, 'Gotta Start Somewhere', are intriguing. The only gripe would be that Henderson, going through a memorable patch of playing, appears only occasionally on the date. The phenomenal McBride gels perfectly with Lewis, as ever.

David Liebman (born 1946) TENOR SAXOPHONE, SOPRANO SAXOPHONE, FLUTES

(*) **One Of A Kind Core/Line COCD 9.00887
Liebman (*ss* solo). 81–84.
** **The Loneliness Of A Long Distance Runner** CMP 24
As above. 11 & 12/85.
*** **The Tree** Soul Note 121195
As above. 4/90.

It's one of the paradoxes of David Liebman's career that an improviser who has put such emphasis (in bands such as Lookout Farm and Quest) on collective improvisation and non-hierarchical musical tradition should so frequently evoke solitariness. In 1980 Liebman, perhaps tired of reading about the 'dominant Coltrane influence' on his work, decided to give up tenor saxophone and flute in order to concentrate on the horn that best expressed his individuality. It's interesting that the soprano saxophone (which was always the least Coltrane-accented of his horns) should also be associated, via John Surman and Steve Lacy, with solo performance.

One Of A Kind is a curious act of self-restitution. Multi-tracked, like some of Surman's or Alfred 23

Harth's solo projects or Keith Jarrett's restorative *Spirits*, it has something of the same self-probing intensity; track-titles like 'Ethnic Suite: The Semites', 'Real Self', 'Relentless', 'Words', 'Spirit', 'The Power Of The Cross', and even the Satie 'Trois Gnossiennes', give some sense of Liebman's curiously referential approach to improvisation.

That is even clearer in the 1985 *Loneliness Of A Long Distance Runner*, a 'concept album' of the oddest sort which evokes with surprising literalism the frequent agonies and occasional ecstasies of marathon competition. The album's demerits and joys occur in roughly those proportions, and most listeners will feel cramp setting in before the second half.

In contrast, *The Tree* is for unaugmented soprano saxophone, with none of the overdubs of the previous pair. Liebman solemnly intones, 'Roots – take one,' gradually building up his image of jazz tradition as a vegetative organism with taproots and trunk representing origins and mainstays, giving way to branches and twigs of lesser structural or more individual significance, and finally the transitory leaves of fashion. Palindromic in structure, the second takes occur in mirror order, leading back to the roots. In its lonely oddity and *faux-naïf* simplicities, it's reminiscent of Joyce Kilmer's great-awful poem about trees. In sharp contrast to the creeping pretentiousness of the earlier sets, it's simple and direct, and the mimetic references – wind, mainly – are logical and unintrusive.

Far removed from either Coltrane or Lacy, Liebman's sound is vocalized in a much more straight-forwardly humane way, and one can easily reconstruct the impact it has had on the French saxophonist and clarinettist, Louis Sclavis. Remarkable as these albums may be, they're probably best approached via Liebman's more conventional group work.

*** The Dave Liebman Quartet in Australia Enja ENJ 3065

Liebman; Mike Nock (*p*); Ron McClure (*b*); Ed Soph (*d*). 2/79.

And why should the Antipodes be denied the multi-active Liebman? At least some of the material is site-specific: 'The Opal Hearted Aborigine' and 'Down Under' must have set the beer glasses rattling in appreciation. A pretty decent set from a more than workmanlike band who could have done with just another couple of notches on the dials. Everything sounds a bit far away . . . Yes, we know it is.

***(*) Doin' It Again Timeless SJP 140

Liebman; Terumasa Hino (*t, flhn*); John Scofield (*g*); Ron McClure (*b*); Adam Nussbaum (*d*). 80.

*** If They Only Knew Timeless SJP 151

As above. 80.

This was Liebman's touring band of the late 1970s, and one of his very best. Some of the rhythmic energy of his early rock experience (with the otherwise forgettable Ten Wheel Drive and in Miles Davis's fusion experiment) had crept back into his work, and he seems liberated by the absence of piano, playing off and against the high-energy pairing of Hino and Scofield. The first of the CDs is marginally the better, but both are worth having; the writing and playing are of high quality and there's one great standard on each, 'Stardust' and a wholly unexpected 'Autumn In New York'.

**** Double Edge Storyville STCD 4091

Liebman; Richard Beirach (*p*). 4/85.

**(*) Chant CMP CD 401

As above. 7/89.

*** Nine Again Red RR 123234

Liebman; Franco D'Andrea (*p*). 89.

At first glance, not at all the kind of set one would expect to find on the rather traditionalist Storyville. At second, Liebman's approach to an obvious-looking set of standards – 'Naima', 'Lover Man', ''Round Midnight', 'On Green Dolphin Street' – is even less likely to attract conservatives.

It's the very lushness of Beirach's chording and the frequent but almost subliminal displacements of the rhythmic pattern that cue Liebman for his more adventurous explorations. On 'Naima', which became a pianist's tune in any case, he moves outside the chords; on 'Green Dolphin Street' he all but ignores them. Throughout, he sounds quizzical, as if reading from an early and much-revised manuscript of the tune. Liebman at his best.

Chant is a bit like listening to a private conversation, fascinating to the outside precisely because of its impenetrable freemasonry. In freer mode – there are only two tracks, 'Incantation' and 'Invocation' – Liebman and Beirach know each other too well to avoid cancelling out some of the more interesting ideas from each. Improvisation requires a degree of tension, perhaps even antagonism, to work well. This conspicuously lacks both and, though Walter Quintus's admirable production presents the music crisply and balanced well, CD seems a very mixed blessing and not much more than an encouragement to be prolix.

D'Andrea is a less troubled romantic than Richie Beirach, but he's well up to Liebman's by now almost routine respraying of standards. 'Autumn Leaves', a tune that creaks with the weight of bad interpretations, sounds as if it was written yesterday. Repertoire pieces, like the once fashionable 'Freedom Jazz Dance', are given a fresh gloss. The problem is that these brightened-up covers contain absolutely no suggestion of depth. With Beirach, Liebman seemed to reach down into a tune; with D'Andrea, it's all brushwork and no perspective or dimensionality. A lot more interesting than just watching paint dry, all the same.

*** Quest II Storyville STCD 4132
Liebman; Richard Beirach (*p*); Ron McClure (*b*); Billy Hart (*d*). 4/86.

The liner image of four intensely staring and mustachioed figures gives away something about the music inside, which is almost too intense and inward. Certainly less dynamic than other Quest sets, this one has a pervasive melancholy quality, even a touch of bleakness. It isn't unattractive – there's an unmistakable edge of humour to the opening 'Gargoyles', but it palls a bit after half an hour. The shortest track, 'The Hollow Men', is one of the toughest things Liebman has written for this line-up, and it's a pity that it wasn't developed further.

***(*) Trio + One Owl 051
Liebman; Caris Visentin (*ob*); Dave Holland (*b, clo*); Jack DeJohnette (*d*). 5/88.
***(*) Quest / Natural Selection Core/Line 9.00748
Liebman; Richard Beirach (*p*); Ron McClure (*b*); Billy Hart (*d*). 6/88.

The slightly calculated eccentricity of Liebman's standards playing surfaces only peripherally on *Trio + One* with the ironic 'All The Things That . . . '. For the most part, this is an intelligent set of straight-forwardly conceived originals, given flesh and complexion by the top-flight rhythm section and a height-ened emotional profile by the interplay of the horns. (Ms Visentin is Mrs Liebman in private life.) DeJohnette is in powerful form, but it's odd that other leaders don't find room for his outstanding synthesizer work.

Liebman's band, Quest, a more settled outfit with a more exploratory ethos, steered an unsteady course between starchy music logics and inspired nonsense. At their best, as on most of *Natural Selection*, they seemed able to find a reasonable middle ground with a configuration that represented an at least partial return to conventional horn–piano–rhythm hierarchy, with which Liebman – no instinctive radical, one suspects – seems happiest.

*** Plays The Music Of Cole Porter Red R R 123236
Liebman; Steve Gilmore (*b*); Bill Godwin (*d*). 88.

This is a very sparse setting for Porter. Without a piano, Liebman is required to play very melodically and to spin new lines out of the songs. This is the sort of thing he can do standing on his head, and unfortunately, after about 25 minutes, one begins to hope that he will stand on his head, just to vary the pace and timbre a bit. Beautifully done, but decidedly passionless, a Porter flaw which most of his more intelligent interpreters have managed to work around.

***(*) Classic Ballads Candid CCD 79512
Liebman; Vic Juris (*g*); Steve Gilmore (*b*). 12/90, 1/91.
**** Setting The Standard Red R R 123253
Liebman; Mulgrew Miller (*p*); Rufus Reid (*b*); Victor Lewis (*d*). 5/92.

The ballads album is dedicated to Liebman's mother-in-law, Natalie Visentin. She chose the material from the songs that she loved in her teens. Liebman plays them pretty straight but is still willing to introduce material from outside the basic sequence in a romantic version of bebop technique. It's a pity there isn't a track in common with the Red recording, which is more rhythmic and changes-based. Juris is used as a second lead as well as a harmony instrument, which means that Gilmore is also called into play as an accompanist. That's clearly the case on 'Angel Eyes' and 'If I Should Lose You', the two most developed tracks.

Setting The Standard is probably the straightest recording Liebman's made in years, and it suits him. Miller has the same rolling, harmonically dense quality that McCoy Tyner brought to the Coltrane quartet ('Grand Central Station' is a nod in that direction) and he pulls Liebman along more insistently than Beirach, say, or d'Andrea. Liebman's tendency to play in rather fixed metres is less evident with a rhythm section as probing as this, and on several of the tracks the pace changes quite dramatically, forcing the saxophonist to vary his phrasing and often his dynamics accordingly. The studio sound is full but not especially flattering.

***(*) Joy Candid CCD 79531
Liebman; Gregory Oaks, Donna Ott, Brian Garland, Christopher Breault, Kevin Lewis (*t*); Tom McKenzie, Michael Mosley, Kim Zitlau (*tb*); Steve Coonly (*btb*); Bill Schnepper, Mike Fansler (*as, bcl*); Jed Hackett, Kenny Flester (*ts, bcl*); Jim Wingo (*bs*); Kristi Blalock, Mary Kay Adams, Margaret Ross, Tracie Vies, Melinda Gryder, Kerry O'Connor, Jen Kuk, Dawn Rhinehart, Jennifer McQueen, Mandy Harris, Grace P. Manuel, Elisabeth L. Boivin, Susan L. Walker,

Carrie Scattergod, Miranda Hopkins, Christine Fry (*f*); Butch Taylor (*p*); Michael Souders
(*ky*); Jim Roller, Pete Spaar (*b*); Mike Nichols (*d*); R. J. Geger (*perc*). 3/92.

In the later 1980s, Liebman became much obsessed with the legacy of Coltrane. He'd already made one
tribute album. *Joy* was recorded just after what would have been Coltrane's 65th birthday. It's an
altogether more positive and coherent session, backed by a forward-looking and utterly competent
campus jazz orchestra (from James Madison U. in Harrisonburg, Virginia) under the directorship of the
impressive Mossblad, who solos himself on 'Alabama' and 'India'. On the latter, both he and Liebman
switch to ethnic flutes, Mayan and Indian respectively. They collaborate on an astonishing arrangement
of 'After The Rain' which uses the university flute choir, a strange but stirring sound. 'Alabama' is the
only small-group track, and it exposes Spaar and Curtis a little, though Taylor is an exceptional accompanist, capable of a thoughtful solo, as he proves on 'Naima', 'Untitled Original' and 'Joy/Selflessness'.

   Liebman more or less surrenders himself to the music, playing unaffectedly in a lower register than
normal. The recording, made (catch this) by the Multitrack Recording Class, is first rate and puts a
good many so-called professional efforts to shame.

*** **The Seasons** Soul Note 121245
   Liebman; Cecil McBee (*b*); Billy Hart (*d*). 12/92.

Big on the concepts, is Liebman. This interweaves some Vivaldi quotes, some pretty straight-ahead jazz
and some free-form impressionism, with a few compositional ideas that have floated around for years in
the Liebman canon. His dry, almost Lacy-like delivery suits this line-up very well indeed, though the
fullness of accompaniment sometimes overpowers his lighter passages.

(*) **Besame Mucho Red R R 123260
   Liebman; Danilo Perez (*p*); Tony Marino (*b*); Bill Goodwin (*d*); Mark Holen, Scott Cutshall
   (*perc*). 3/93.

The Latin Album. Had to happen eventually, and of course Liebman handles it with consummate
professionalism. It isn't the most inspiring group he's ever recruited, and they let him down a bit. Not
much in the way of atmosphere, which may be the result of doing a south-of-the-border record in
Saylorsburg, Pennsylvania, where they can't even pronounce *jalapena*, and probably think 'Insensatez' is
an ointment for poison ivy. What we're trying to say is: no.

*** **Songs For My Daughter** Soul Note 121295
   Liebman; Vic Juris (*g*); Phil Markowitz (*p*); Tony Marino (*b*); Jamey Haddad (*d*); Scott
   Cutshall (*perc*).

Very much better, but still oddly focused and amazingly sloppy in execution here and there. Liebman's
flute playing is the main revelation, and there is some nice interplay between it and Juris's smoothly
articulate guitar. A very enjoyable record, but still down the list of priorities for this artist.

Terry Lightfoot (born 1935) CLARINET, ALTO SAXOPHONE, VOCAL

*(*) **When The Saints Go Marching In! / Varied Jazz** C5 MCD 566
   Lightfoot; Ian Hunter-Randall (*t*); Mickey Cooke (*tb*); Paddy Lightfoot (*bj, v*); Peter Skivington
   (*b*); Ian Castle (*d*). 71–75.
(*) **Down On Bourbon Street Timeless TTD 581
   Lightfoot; Ian Hunter-Randall (*t*); Phil Rhodes (*tb*); Bruce Boardman (*p*); Tony Pitt (*g, bj*);
   Andy Lawrence (*sou, b*); Johnny Armatage (*d*). 8/93.

Lightfoot is an also-ran in British trad. A few years younger than the Ball/Barber/Bilk axis, he never had
the same impact and has never quite won the authenticity which those groups have marked out for
themselves. The C5 compilation is a frightful set of crusty trad staples and indifferent originals, played
as if everyone in the group was on buttoned-down best behaviour. Lightfoot's prim vocals don't help.

   Down On Bourbon Street isn't too bad. 'Grandpa's Spells' is an attempted carbon of Morton's original
and was ill-advised. 'Bourbon Street Parade' itself sounds more like a march down Wandsworth High
Street. But 'Closer Walk With Thee', taken apart by Rhodes's comically over-the-top trombone, and
Lightfoot's gentle examination of 'Petite Fleur' are more encouraging, and Hunter-Randall usually has
some decent points to make, even after 25 years with the band.

Kirk Lightsey (born 1937) PIANO

***(*) **Lightsey Live** Sunnyside 1014 D
   Lightsey (*p* solo). 6/85.

*** **Shorter By Two** Sunnyside 1004 D
> Lightsey (*p* solo) and with Harold Danko (*p*). 7/83.

Beginning, middle and end: Lightsey's compositions and solo performances have a well-made, almost narrative quality that is the antithesis of free-form 'blowing'. It's a characteristic he shares with Wayne Shorter, and Lightsey has long shown an interest in the saxophonist's unusually gnomic small-group compositions (which Miles Davis once likened to short stories).

Transcribing Shorter pieces for solo piano presents quite particular difficulties. These are partially overcome in the duos with Danko, whose rich articulation is a softer version of Lightsey's, but a good many of these pieces are over-egged and compare rather poorly with the wonderful 'Fee Fi Fo Fum' on *Live*. The solo album also takes in Monk – a finger-bending 'Trinkle Tinkle' – Cole Porter, Rodgers and Hart, and Tony Williams, whose 'Pee Wee' (from the drummer's 1988 *Angel Street*, Blue Note 748494 CD) gets the album off to a deceptively stately start. Lightsey's delivery is quite formal, and improvisations unfold with an absence of histrionics, which means that tracks often make their full impact only on subsequent hearings.

***(*) **Isotope** Criss Cross Criss 1003
> Lightsey; Jesper Lundgaard (*b*); Eddie Gladden (*d*); Jerry Gonzalez (*perc*). 2/83.

*** **Everything Happens To Me** Timeless SJP 176
> Lightsey; Chet Baker (*t, v*); David Eubanks (*b*); Eddie Gladden (*d*). 3/83.

*** **First Affairs** Limetree MCD 0015
> As above, except add Santi Debriano (*b*); omit Gladden. 4/86.

*** **Everything Is Changed** Sunnyside SSC 1020
> As above, except add Jerry Gonzalez (*t, flhn*); Jerry Routch (*frhn*); Chico Freeman, Famoudou Don Moye (*perc*). 6/86.

*** **Temptation** Timeless SJP 257
> Lightsey; Freddie Hubbard (*t*); Santi Debriano (*b*); Eddie Gladden, Jerry Gonzalez (*perc*). 5 & 6/87.

*** **From Kirk To Nat** Criss Cross Criss 1050
> Lightsey; Kevin Eubanks (*g*); Rufus Reid (*b*). 11/90.

Only deceptively in opposition to Lightsey's interest in Shorter is a liking for broad vamps over repeated figures, a device strongly reminiscent of Abdullah Ibrahim (Dollar Brand), who has something of Shorter's enigmatic brevity. On *First Affairs*, 'Habiba' (given a superior reading on the *Live* solo record) counters a strong African flavour with imaginative Bartók progressions and dramatic shifts of pace.

The quartet version reduces it to rather more of a head-and-solo piece, but the other tracks are, perhaps oddly, much stronger. 'For Albert' has a greater emotional range than the pianist normally strives for, but at the partial expense of accuracy. The group functions equally well on the near-contemporary *Everything Is Changed*, but the significant addition of Jerry Gonzalez further restricts Lightsey's multilinear instincts. Gonzalez's brass lead flatters 'Blues On The Corner' (arranged for piano trio on *First Affairs*) but tends to muffle Lightsey elsewhere. There are, though, interesting experiments in tonecolour, notably the french horn on 'Nandi' and the augmented percussion (featuring, of all people, Chico Freeman, *sans* saxophone, and, another Leader, Don Moye).

Debriano and Gladden serve the pianist no less well than Moye and McBee in the hived-off Leaders Trio (*q.v.*) but with less emphasis on a democracy of voices; the bassist is often a shade recessed and his role is certainly more functional than McBee's. The earlier and excellent *Isotope* has transferred predictably well to CD, gaining in resolution as a result; the performances are very fine indeed, with an unexpected 'Oleo', some more Monk stylings, and another fine version of Williams's 'Pee Wee' (the CD has 'I'll Never Stop Loving You' as a bonus track). *Everything Happens To Me* was recorded a month later. The Chet Baker tracks – 'Ray's Idea' and 'Everything' – are worth having for Lightsey's beautifully judged responses, but it's on the trio versions of Shorter tunes that he really gets going.

The band on *Temptation* is responsive and obviously familiar with Lightsey's requirements. Hubbard plays muted more often than usual, to great effect on 'Evidence' and on his own 'Brigitte', which he plays pretty straight this time around. Though he's the main writer and claims 'featured' billing on the disc, he defers to the pianist throughout the session. They're exactly on a wavelength for the long 'Temptation' (Hubbard again muted) and 'Love Is A Many Splendored Thing', perhaps the outstanding track.

The immediate inspiration for *From Kirk To Nat* is Nat Cole's wartime piano–guitar–bass trio with Oscar Moore and Johnny Miller (see *The Early Forties*, Fresh Sound FSR CD 139). One of the most copied of piano and vocal stylists, Cole has rarely been imitated successfully, and Lightsey steers well clear of pastiche. His singing on 'Never Let Me Go' and 'Close Enough For Love' is growly and soft, almost spoken, and it draws something from late Chet Baker. On piano he is already individual enough not to risk unconscious echo, and his firm touch on the opening 'You And The Night And The Music' sets the tone for the whole album.

Guitarist Eubanks, always more impressive on other people's albums, presents a useful latter-day version of Oscar Moore's single-note runs and softly strummed counter-melodies; it's Rufus Reid who dominates the longest single track, a subtle 'Sophisticated Lady', with a resonant solo that is mixed too loud but which is as purposeful and strongly outlined as anything by Jimmy Blanton.

Abbey Lincoln (born 1930) VOCALS

(*) Straight Ahead Candid CCD 79015
> Lincoln; Booker Little (*t*); Julian Priester (*tb*); Eric Dolphy (*as, b cl, f*); Walter Benton, Coleman Hawkins (*ts*); Mal Waldron (*p*); Art Davis (*b*); Max Roach (*d*); Roger Sanders, Robert Whitley (*perc*). 2/61.

It would be quite wrong – and at worst deeply patronizing – to suggest that Abbey Lincoln owes her career to her association and marriage with Max Roach. However, it's true that her oddly persistent reputation has been built on her part in Roach's powerful *We Insist! Freedom Now Suite*, which helped complete her transformation from a rather *ersatz* club 'shan-tooze' into a figure closely associated with the new Black consciousness, and perceived in some quarters as Billie Holiday's matrilineal heir. Lincoln herself has paid tribute to Roach's part in her self-discovery.

Straight Ahead was recorded with basically the same players as *We Insist!*, but with the notable addition of Eric Dolphy, whose dance card for 1961 was almost absurdly over-subscribed. In the event, it's Dolphy's friend and associate, Booker Little, and the slightly raw-toned Coleman Hawkins who take the majority of the solo slots. The arrangements are mostly excellent and the recording quality stands up very well.

The received wisdom is that Roach allowed Abbey Lincoln to become a more 'natural' and a more feeling singer, but the immediate impression of these tracks is a self-absorption which, however respectful of the words, is seldom responsive to the music. There is certainly nothing legitimate about her delivery, but 'expressive' flatting of notes has to be handled with scrupulous care if it isn't to look like incompetence. Three tracks stand out: 'When Malindy Sings', based on a Paul Lawrence Dunbar poem, a vocalization of 'Blue Monk' (with the composer's blessing), and the closing 'Retribution', co-written with Julian Priester, which is forceful in the extreme. Here at least, Lincoln seems willing to confront the music rather than stand upstage of it.

*** **That's Him!** Original Jazz Classics OJC 085
> Lincoln; Kenny Dorham (*t*); Sonny Rollins (*ts*); Wynton Kelly (*p*); Paul Chambers (*b*); Max Roach (*d*). 10/57.
*** **It's Magic** Original Jazz Classics OJC 205
> Lincoln; Kenny Dorham, Art Farmer (*t*); Curtis Fuller (*tb*); Benny Golson (*ts*); Jerome Richardson, Sahib Shihab (*f, bs*); Wynton Kelly (*p*); Paul Chambers, Sam Jones (*b*); Philly Joe Jones (*d*). 8/58.
***(*) **Abbey Is Blue** Original Jazz Classics OJC 069
> Lincoln; Kenny Dorham, Tommy Turrentine (*t*); Julian Priester (*tb*); Stanley Turrentine (*ts*); Les Spann (*g, f*); Wynton Kelly, Cedar Walton, Philip Wright (*p*); Bobby Boswell, Sam Jones (*b*); Philly Joe Jones, Max Roach (*d*). 59.

If Billie Holiday suggested two diverging means of expressing the black woman's place in American society – the surreal anger of 'Strange Fruit' and the weary-but-assertive deconstructions of conventional romantic modes – Abbey Lincoln made a brave attempt to combine the two; see also Enja 6012, below. It's noticeable, though, that in the late 1950s she was more or less content to work within the available tradition of jazz-show tunes, subverting their original content by shifts of emphasis, displacements of metre and meaning, and downright distortions of intent. It's very much the same method John Coltrane was to bring to 'My Favorite Things' and 'Chim Chim Cheree'.

'Afro Blue', with the Max Roach Sextet on *Abbey Is Blue*, is as powerful a performance as anything she recorded, but not without indications of later defaults. The unaccompanied 'Tender As A Rose' on *That's Him!* is rather mannered but very nearly succeeds. Dorham's trumpet is one of the most vocal of the bop trumpeters, and as such an ideal partner. However, it's Kelly's rhythmic approach that always seems to carry the day, and it's a shame there are no duo performances in the catalogue.

** **People In Me** Verve 515246
> Lincoln; David Liebman (*ts, ss, f*); Hiromasa Suzuki (*p*); Kunimitsu Inaba (*b*); Al Foster (*d*); James Mtume (*perc*). 6/73.

Lincoln's attempt to recolonize the border regions of pop and soul have consistently foundered on her ultra-self-conscious *négritude* and patent unwillingness to sing a lyric plainly. The 'people in me' might be anyone from Bessie Smith to Diana Ross, which is fine as far as it goes, except that they seem to be jostling for the spotlight. There are two fine tracks on this 1973 album. One, significantly by Max Roach, is 'Living Room', which evokes a convincing response; the other is the opening 'You And Me Love' with Lincoln's words to a tune by Johnny Rotalla. A similar job on Coltrane's 'India' is preposterous, and it's fair to ask if her lack of trust in an improvisatory vocalise is less an emotional-political insistence on significant statement than a tacit recognition of technical shortcomings.

** Talking To The Sun Enja 4060
Lincoln; Steve Coleman (*as*); James Weidman (*p*); Bill Johnson (*b*); Mark Johnson (*d*); Jerry Gonzalez (*perc*); Bemshee Shirer, Naima Williams (*v*). 11/83.

A largely empty display of technical prowess in a marketably 'contemporary' setting. Lincoln follows the stage directions scrupulously but has rarely sounded more passionless. Coleman plays very nicely, as members of the extended Coleman tribe carrying saxes invariably do.

*** A Tribute To Billie Holiday Enja 6012
Lincoln; Harold Vick (*ts*); James Widman (*p*); Tarik Shah (*b*); Mark Johnson (*d*). 11/87.
*** Abbey Sings Billie: Volume 2 Enja 7037
As above. 11/87.

The band here really aren't up to the task, but Lincoln herself seems to be awash with ambivalence, tackling 'Strange Fruit' with a pitch of emotion that sounds almost sarcastic, giving 'Lover Man' the back of her hand. It's a fine, un-obvious set that, generally speaking, works well. The recording quality isn't too exciting, but it lends a smoky authenticity to what on second hearing sound like slightly fudged settings. *Volume 2* might even just have the edge. There's a lovely off-centre reading of 'God Bless The Child', in among some less obvious or familiar material. There's probably one spanking album to be drawn from the pair.

*** The World Is Falling Down Verve 843476
Lincoln; Clark Terry (*t, flhn*); Jerry Dodgion, Jackie McLean (*as*); Alain Jean-Marie (*p*); Charlie Haden (*b*); Billy Higgins (*d*). 2/90.

A whole new audience got a handle on Abbey Lincoln via her title-track vocal on Steve Williamson's Verve debut, *A Waltz For Grace*. Her own 1990 set draws on similar stylistic roots but melds them rather better. With a finely tuned band and an intelligent book of songs, she does better than for several years. 'How High The Moon' gives the answer almost astronomically, but without losing the romance; 'Hi Fly', still the only universally known composition by her *Straight Ahead* ('African Lady') collaborator, is vibrant and tough. Fine performances all round.

***(*) You Gotta Pay The Band Verve Gitanes 511 110
Lincoln; Stan Getz (*ts*); Hank Jones (*p*); Charlie Haden (*b*); Maxine Roach (*vla*); Mark Johnson (*d*). 2/91.

This is a marked improvement on recent sets. Lincoln still sounds a little too involved in the seen-it-all persona at the expense of straightforward singing, and she's still inclined to chop the sense of a lyric. However, she has a band worthy of her talents and the material (with the exception of 'Bird Alone') is immeasurably better than on *People In Me*. The set will be valued every bit as much for a curtain-call from Stan Getz, who played with lyrical grace and feeling to the very end. The best track is undoubtedly 'A Time For Love', where the metre seems to fall just right for that slightly lazy delivery.

**(*) Devil's Got Your Tongue Verve 513 574
Lincoln; J. J. Johnson (*tb*); Stanley Turrentine (*ts*); Rodney Kendrick (*p*); Maxine Roach (*vla*); Marcus McLaurine (*b*); Grady Tate, Yoron Israel (*d*); Babatunde Olatunji, Kehinde O'Uhuru, Sule O'Uhuru, Gordy Ryan (*perc*); The Staple Singers, The Noel Singers (*v*). 2/92.
*** When There Is Love Verve 519697
Lincoln; Hank Jones (*p*). 10/92.
**** A Turtle's Dream Verve Gitanes 527 382
Lincoln; Roy Hargrove (*t*); Julien Lourau (*ts, ss*); Kenny Barron, Rodney Kendrick (*p*); Pat Metheny, Lucky Peterson (*g, v*); Charlie Haden, Christian McBride (*b*); Victor Lewis (*d*); strings. 5, 8 & 11/94.

A collection of very personal songs, *Devil's Got Your Tongue* goes in too many directions at once and calls on too many different musical strands to make a consistent impact. Lincoln's lyrics are impassioned, faintly surreal and, rather too often, embarrassingly banal. Her 'Story Of My Father' is undoubtedly deeply felt, but it founders on ponderous rhymes and bathetic repetitions. Another family story, 'Evelina Coffey (The Legend Of)', fares very much better, perhaps because it doesn't have the Staple Singers wallpapering the arrangement. 'People In Me' and 'Rainbow' have both been heard before, but again these versions are disturbingly sentimental. Only when Lincoln switches to Thad Jones's 'A Child Is Born' and Alex Wilder's lyric does she allow herself to sing more naturally and without emoting so pointedly. There, for the first time on the record, one hears her true voice.

To our surprise, the duets with Hank Jones are by no means as effective as we would have expected.

'C'est Si Bon' was a grotesque misjudgement, but the main objection is to the rather mannered way the set has been put together: showbizzy segues, big shouters followed by torchy ballads. Jones is as great as ever, but this somehow isn't Abbey's gig. She is altogether more focused on *A Turtle's Dream*, which re-establishes a continuity with the earlier Verves. It would have been lovely to have had Nina Simone herself accompany her on 'Hey Lorda Mama', but Kendrick, one of the many Verve stars featured, does an excellent job. This is one of those albums where fans can flick through to find dream permutations like Metheny and Kendrick or Metheny and Barron with Haden and Lewis; but listen to it without the notes to hand, find yourself enchanted by the saxophone on 'A Turtle's Dream' or 'Not To Worry' and discover later that it isn't some guest superstar but the relatively little-known Lourau. Like Betty Carter, Abbey has a gift for bringing on players, and it would be great at this stage in her distinguished career to see her put together a regular working band, mould it to her requirements, and let its potentialities and limitations mould *her* next step.

Lincoln Center Jazz Orchestra GROUP

**(*) Portraits By Ellington Columbia 472814-2

> Marcus Belgrave (*t, flhn*); Wynton Marsalis, Umar Sharif, Lew Soloff, John Longo (*t*); Art Baron, Britt Woodman, Wycliffe Gordon (*tb*); Chuck Connors (*btb*); Michael White (*cl*); Bill Easley (*cl, ts*); Frank Wess, Norris Turney (*as*); Todd Williams (*ts*); Joe Temperley (*bs*); Sir Roland Hanna (*p*); Steve Nelson (*vib*); Andy Stein (*vn*); Paul Meyers (*g*); Reginald Veal (*b*); Kenny Washington (*d*); Milt Grayson (*v*). 8/91.

While this must be an exhilarating experience in a concert situation (where it was recorded), on CD it emerges as a sometimes pointless exercise in re-creating some eventful Ellington scores. Whatever sleevenote-writer Stanley Crouch claims, too much of the music here sounds like slavish duplication, especially the three themes from 'New Orleans Suite'. The sound may be better engineered than on most Ellington albums, and the best things happen when the orchestra musters a resonant grandeur of delivery, but there are no new insights into Ellington's music. Among the soloists, Todd Williams tries to come on as both Paul Gonsalves and Coleman Hawkins and succeeds in sounding like nobody in particular, while Wynton does a credible Cootie Williams on 'Portrait Of Louis Armstrong'. The best music comes in the 'Liberian Suite', where vocalist Grayson's sonorous baritone is startling. Overall, though, this is nothing like as good as the American Jazz Orchestra's Ellington tribute.

*** The Fire Of The Fundamentals Columbia 474348-2

> Wynton Marsalis, Joe Wilder, Marcus Belgrave, Umar Sharif (*t*); Britt Woodman, Wycliffe Gordon, Freddie Lonzo (*tb*); Michael White (*cl*); Jimmy Heath (*ss*); Charles McPherson, Norris Turney, Wessell Anderson, Jerry Dodgion (*as*); Todd Williams, Frank Wess, Bill Easley (*ts*); Joe Temperley (*bs*); Marcus Roberts, Cyrus Chestnut, Kenny Barron, Mulgrew Miller (*p*); Don Vappie (*g*); Reginald Veal, Curtis Lundy, Chris Thomas (*b*); Herlin Riley, Lewis Nash, Clarence Penn, Kenny Washington (*d*); Betty Carter, Milt Grayson (*v*). 7/92–2/93.

*** They Came To Swing Columbia 477284-2

> As above, except add Lew Soloff, Jon Faddis, Nicholas Payton, Marcus Printup, Ryan Kisor, Russell Gunn, Roger Ingram (*t*); Art Baron, Jamal Haynes, Ronald Westray (*tb*), Herb Harris (*ss*); Jesse Davis (*as*); Joshua Redman, Victor Goines, Robert Stewart, Walter Blanding Jr (*ts*), James Carter (*bs*); Kent Jordan (*picc*); Sir Roland Hanna, Eric Reed (*p*); Billy Higgins (*d*); omit Wilder, Sharif, Lonzo, White, Heath, McPherson, Turney, Wess, Chestnut, Barron, Miller, Vappie, Lundy, Penn, Washington, Carter. 10/92–4/94.

Though the 'official' Orchestra is responsible for much of the music on these two discs, they're really various-artists albums accredited to 'Jazz At Lincoln Center', with material culled from a number of shows, some of them by the Orchestra on tour. *Fire Of The Fundamentals* stretches from piano solos to big-band episodes. Kenny Barron's 'Trinkle Tinkle' is terrific and Marcus Roberts does all right by 'Bolivar Blues', but his version of Morton's 'The Crave' is a massacre. Betty Carter's group follow her through her gorgeous set-piece, 'You're Mine You', and Michael White leads the New Orleans homies on 'Jungle Blues'. The Marsalis group tackle two chunks of classic repertory and Wynton just gets away with his Miles parts on 'Flamenco Sketches', while the Orchestra close on a rare piece of Strayhorn, 'Multi-Colored Blue'. An entertaining mixed bag. *They Came To Swing* is more consistently about the big band, though some of the repertory is ponderous: a hugely overheated 'Black And Tan Fantasy' at a tempo Ellington would never have allowed, and a similarly melodramatic 'Things To Come'. Better is Marsalis's fast, funny locomotion sketch, 'Express Crossing', and Grayson does his Eckstine bit in 'Jelly, Jelly'. Rich and sonorous at its best, the Orchestra is quite something, but these are more like show souvenirs.

Ove Lind (1926–91) CLARINET

***(*) **One Morning In May** Phontastic PHONTCD 7501
 Lind; Bengt Hallberg (*p*); Lars Erstrand (*vib*); Staffan Broms (*g*); Arne Wilhelmsson (*b*); Egil
 Johansen (*d*). 4/75–5/76.
**** **Summer Night** Phontastic PHONTCD 7503
 As above. 4/75–5/76.

There was something of a revival of swing-styled jazz in Sweden in the 1970s, a rehabilitation of a
manner that Swedish musicians had helped to pioneer in Europe the first time around, and these records
– the very first Phontastic LPs, now transferred to CD – are mildly historic in their way. They're also
very fine, irresistibly swinging small-group sessions. Lind was cast entirely in Benny Goodman's image
and was proud of it. There are obvious echoes of the Goodman small-band records, but an extra degree
of inventiveness takes this well beyond any copycat concept. Hallberg and Erstrand are inspired
throughout, thinking almost telepathically when their improvisations run together, and the utterly
relaxed pulse of the rhythm section is both unobtrusive and indispensable. Little to choose between the
two records, but *One Morning In May* has a slight edge for the freshness of the material as it features
standards of a less familiar stripe.

John Lindberg (born 1959) DOUBLE BASS

***(*) **The East Side Suite** sound aspects sas 001
 Lindberg; John Carter (*cl*); Eric Watson (*p*). 7/83.
**** **Dodging Bullets** Black Saint 120108
 Lindberg; Albert Mangelsdorff (*tb*); Eric Watson (*p*). 6/92.

It's disappointing that John Lindberg's recording career should have straddled the vinyl/CD divide so
squarely. Some of his best material has been on Cecma (a small vinyl label which appears to deal only in
the highest-quality performance), and two very good Black Saints have not yet made the transition. It
isn't just the outer shadows of Lindberg's dark tone that are lost on vinyl but, more critically, some of
the smaller motions of the music itself. Untypically of a bassist, Lindberg is a miniaturist, working best
with a restricted canvas and tiny, almost calligraphic, musical gestures.

 Though he seems generally better disposed to brass players than to the more legato diction of the reeds,
the bassist responds superbly to Carter's fragmented lines on *East Side Suite*, which dispenses with a
drummer altogether, developing a long-form piece with a forceful interior logic. If 'give and take' is the
key to improvisation at any length, that may be why.

 Given the holes that have sprung in Lindberg's list, it's good to see a new disc. *Dodging Bullets* once
again demonstrates his preference for open, uncluttered settings, and also for working with trombone
players, as he had on the deleted *Give And Take* with George Lewis. The new record is bright, unfussy
and clear-spoken, with an almost folksy quality that recalls Jimmy Giuffre's trio with Bob Brookmeyer
and Jim Hall. Mangelsdorff is a master of understatement, and Watson (who has worked with Steve
Lacy) relishes the challenge of playing an independent line rather than an accompaniment. Thoroughly
recommended.

Nils Lindberg (born 1933) PIANO

**** **Sax Appeal & Trisection** Dragon DRCD220
 Lindberg; Jan Allan, Idrees Sulieman, Lars Samuelsson (*t*); Sven-Olof Walldoff, Eje Thelin (*tb*);
 Rolf Billberg (*as*); Harry Backlund, Allan Lundstrom (*ts*); Lars Gullin (*bs*); Sture Nordin (*b*);
 Olle Holmqvist (*tba*); Sture Kallin, Conny Svensson (*d*). 2/60–1/63.
***(*) **Saxes Galore / Brass Galore** Bluebell ABCD 3004
 Lindberg; Jan Allan, Allan Botschinsky, Markku Johansson (*t, flhn*); Torgny Nilsson (*tb*); Sven
 Larsson (*btb, tba*); Herb Geller (*as, ss, f*); Claes Rosendahl (*ts, f*); Bernt Rosengren (*ts, as, f*);
 Lennart Aberg, Erik Nilsson (*bs, f*); Mads Vinding, Red Mitchell (*b*); Rune Carlsson (*d*). 5/79–5/
 81.
***(*) **Melody In Blue** Dragon DRCD 245
 Lindberg; Anders Paulson (*ss, ts*); Johan Horlen (*as*); Joakim Milder, Krister Andersson (*ts*);
 Charlie Malmberg (*bs*); Jan Adefeldt (*b*); Bengt Stark (*d*). 5/93.
*** **Alone With My Melodies** Dragon DRCD 277
 Lindberg (*p* solo). 4/95.

Nils Lindberg plays piano, but what he loves to do is write for horns, especially saxophones. His current

CD listing has a rather unique distinction in that he has written saxophone records for three generations of Swedish reed players. The first, *Sax Appeal*, has been reissued in tandem with the slightly later *Trisection* on a single Dragon CD. In Jan Olsson's words, Lindberg's sound is 'the sound of Swedish summer nights and 52nd Street at the same time' – although, more accurately, it's the timbre of West Coast saxes that he gets here and on the later *Saxes Galore*. There are superb sequences not only for the whole section but also for Gullin and Billberg, and the subsequent *Trisection* brings in brass for a Gil Evans-like exploration of timbre.

The first track, 'Curbits', turns up again as the first on *Saxes Galore*, where Lindberg repeated his formula with another all-sax team, and this time inveigled a genuine West Coast man (Herb Geller) to participate. The sound he gets out of the section is a haunting drift that seems to float between traditions, with solos emerging from the ensemble like smoke drifting through clear, cold air. *Brass Galore* is coupled with this session on the Bluebell reissue: not quite as impressive, but there are still some inventive charts here, especially the 3/4 ballad, 'Waltz For Anne-Marie'.

Melody In Blue puts together a third reed team made up of the latest generation of Swedish saxophonists and, if anything, this sounds like the best of the three, given a modern studio mix and vivid, energetic playing from all hands. One or two of the pieces sound comparatively ordinary and Lindberg doesn't always set out to have the band swing; but 'Blue Bop' defies that judgement, and in the extraordinary miniature of 'Polska With All My Love' – once a student work of Lindberg's – the poise of the playing is breathtaking.

His solo piano album is a slow and reflective set, a bit ponderous in parts, and perhaps one of those records which means more to the maker than to his audience. Worth hearing, though, for his deeply felt 'In Memoriam', the piece he wrote on the untimely death of Rolf Billberg in 1966 – which brings this discography full circle for now.

François Lindemann PIANO

**** Different Masks Plainisphare 1267-47

    Lindemann; Matthieu Michel (*t, flhn*); Robin Eubanks (*tb*); Yvan Ischer (*as*); Maurice Magnoni (*ss, ts*); Olivier Rogg (*ky*); Ivor Malherbe (*b*); Marc Erbetta (*d*). 10/89.

This ingeniously prepared and brilliantly executed record is an exemplar of what's currently happening in European jazz. Lindemann's themes manage to be tuneful, funny and deeply felt, using familiar harmonic language yet whirling together new ensemble colours and a rare vitality of improvisation. It's some indication of the quality of the playing that the admirable Eubanks, a famous visitor from New York, has to take his place with the other soloists, all of whom are excellent. The maddeningly catchy lines of 'Ghost Train', lavish textures of 'Forgotten Faces' and 'Different Masks' and the far-from-lugubrious requiem for Woody Shaw, 'Song For Woody', are highlights of a programme that is enormously satisfying. Well recorded and highly recommended.

*** Montreux Jazz & Swiss Movement Live In U.S.A. Evasion ECD 92211

    As above, except add Pascal Schaer (*alphorn, tb*), Robert Morgenthaler (*tb*), Erik Truffat, Jan Gordon-Lennox (*alphorn, buchel*), Jean-Jacques Pedretti (*alphorn*), omit Eubanks. 8/91.

The alphorn quartet who join with Lindemann for this Detroit concert bring the usual problems of eccentric instrumentation: wayward intonation, dubious key centres, all the authenticities that tend to foul up meaningful fusions of jazz with so-called folk traditions. That said, the bizarre bellowing of the horns has a certain demonic charm that provides a rollicking backdrop for some of Lindemann's ideas. On two fine studio tracks he also continues the characterful arranging of the previous record.

**(*) Solo TCB 01022

    Lindemann (*p, perc* solo). 4–6/94.

Lindemann's solo album is beautifully recorded and the piano parts are embellished by a deft use of percussion, mostly Javanese gongs that add resonance to the keyboard tones. But they also introduce a note of solemnity that goes with a somewhat becalmed set of themes. Some of the music approximates Jarrett at his prettiest, but an episode for prepared piano is dead meat and in the end the record goes nowhere.

Lasse Lindgren TRUMPET

*** To My Friends Dragon DRCD 227

    Lindgren; Mikael Raberg (*tb*); Esbjorn Svensson (*ky*); Jan Adefeldt (*b*); Raymond Karlsson (*d*). 4/92.

Walking a line between post-bop and something like abstruse jazz-funk on some tracks, Lindgren's group keep their options attractively open. The leader has a good tone – which even comes through on the couple of points when he uses a little electronic alteration – and in tandem with the splendidly forceful Raberg he creates an all-brass front line that bounces off the rather hard rhythms of the trio. Svensson's lyrical side comes out to good effect on the slow tunes, and in 'Two Bass Fishers Walking Down The Line' and 'Ice Eyes' they fashion some plausible impressionism.

Lines GROUP

*** **Lines** Odin 4026
> Tore Brunborg (*ts*); Vigleik Storaas (*p*); Olaf Kamfjord (*b*); Tron Kopperud (*d*). 9/88.

Brunborg is one of the best post-Garbarek saxophonists to emerge from Norway, and away from Masqualero, the group he's best known in, his delivery takes on a more playful, if no less intense, edge. This free-speaking band somehow suggests a very loose gait without surrendering structural power: hear 'Penn' for a fine, multifarious tune that is full of incident and somehow spontaneous in feeling. Brilliantly engineered by the redoubtable Jan Erik Kongshaug.

Rudy Linka (born 1960) GUITAR

*** **Czech It Out** Enja 9001
> Linka: George Mraz (*b*); Marvin 'Smitty' Smith (*d*). 1/94.

Historical circumstance dictated that Linka had to come of age outside his native Czechoslovakia. Moving to Scandinavia at the age of 21, he was enthusiastically sponsored by the late Red Mitchell, and from there he managed to study with both Jim Hall and John Abercrombie. Those are perhaps the most obvious stylistic imprints on this, by no means his first recording as leader. There are few folkish or ethnic mannerisms, even on the so-called 'Folk Song', and only the most disciplined and self-aware foray into the quasi-abstract territory Abercrombie and Ralph Towner have made their own at ECM.

A good deal of credit has to go to Linka's countryman, George Mraz, and to Smitty, for keeping the pace brisk and uncluttered without ever losing the contour of a song like 'How Deep Is The Ocean' or 'Love Letters'. There's just a hint of electronic impressionism on 'Traveler', a tune that declares its kinship to the Zawinul/Vitous partnership in early Weather Report. For the most part, though, this is absolutely of the jazz guitar mainstream and good enough to be able to forgive him that awful pun in the title.

Jukka Linkola (born 1955) PIANO

*** **Pegasos** Imogena IGCD 050
> Linkola; Lars Lindgren, Jan Eliasson, Hildegunn Oiseth, Jan Anders Berger (*t, flhn*); Mikael Raberg, Christer Olofsson, Ralph Soovik (*tb*); Niclas Rydh (*btb*); Miklas Robertsson, Sven Fridolfsson, Erik Norstrom, Michael Karlsson, Janne Forslund (*reeds*); Jan Zirk (*ky*); Steffan William-Olsson (*g*); Yasuhito Mori, Fredrik Bergman (*b*); Marko Timonen (*d*). 11/93.

Linkola's sympathies aren't only with jazz: he's written operas, ballet and chamber music, and this set of charts for the Bohuslan Big Band – something of a co- operative between Swedish and Finnish musicians – is an extension of his work for his touring eight- and ten-piece groups. The round dozen arrangements are performed with great enthusiasm by the orchestra, and it's a pity there isn't more going on inside them. Linkola's melodies are a bit thin and he tends to let his guard down when leaving space for a soloist: several of the themes are no more than a tissue surrounding whoever steps out of the ensemble. He's interested in the texture of electric keyboards, so Zirk's parts are important, and on a few tunes – 'Boogie Woogie Waltz' and 'Syrene' – the music assumes more substance.

Staffan Linton (born 1916) PIANO

*** **Unfinished Affair** Dragon DRCD 193
> Linton; Yasuhito Mori (*b*); Christian Jormin (*d*). 3/90.

Linton spent some of his formative years in London and actually broadcast for the BBC in the 1940s, cutting a few sides for Decca in 1948. He didn't make another record, though, until *Nevergreen* in 1984, which is still awaited on CD. That album had some problems, but they were overcome on the engaging *Unfinished Affair*. Jormin provides just the right balance of drive and sensitivity, and the session is beautifully recorded. The youthful gaiety of 'Song For Judith' belies Linton's age, and the trio even concoct a reggae-like syncopation for 'Heart Beat'. The leader composes plain but often affecting minor-key melodies, and the music is a refreshing antidote to the busy, overwrought attack of many contemporary pianists.

Booker Little (1938–61) TRUMPET

*** **Booker Little 4 And Max Roach** Blue Note CDP 784457
    Little; Louis Smith (*t*); Frank Strozier (*as*); George Coleman (*ts*); Tommy Flanagan, Phineas Newborn (*p*); Calvin Newborn (*g*); Art Davis, George Joyner (Jamil Nasser) (*b*); Charles Crosby, Max Roach (*d*). 58.

***(*) **Out Front** Candid 9027
    Little; Julian Priester (*tb*); Eric Dolphy (*as, b cl, f*); Don Friedman (*p*); Ron Carter, Art Davis (*b*); Max Roach (*d, tim, vib*). 3 & 4/61.

The arithmetic is depressingly straightforward – 23 scant years. It's very difficult to assess Little's output, for he was only just shaking off the husk of a then-dominant Clifford Brown influence and drying his wings in the early sun of a partnership with Eric Dolphy when he died of uraemia. His tone was bright and resonant, but there were already ambiguities inscribed in his playing which can't be put down to youthful uncertainty but point forward to a new configuration he was never able to articulate.

In face of dearth, small survivals become more valuable. The slightly shapeless jams on 'Blue'n'Boogie' and 'Things Ain't What They Used to Be' (the latter marred by outbreaks of static) on the Blue Note would probably not be considered worth releasing if there were more Little around (like the 1960 group with another doomed youth, Scott LaFaro, which has appeared as *The Legendary Quartet Album* on Island and as a valuable Time CD, with the same material covered in a limited-edition live series on Jazz View). As it is, out-takes assume an even more considerable significance. Little had emerged under Max Roach's patronage, playing on the classic Candid LPs *Freedom Now Suite* and *Straight Ahead*, the latter by Roach's then wife, Abbey Lincoln. The Blue Note reissue pairs him with fellow Memphisite George Coleman in a state-of-the-art '50s front line that on tracks like 'Dungeon Waltz' and 'Jewel's Tempo' – both Little compositions – suggests a development independent of and parallel to Ornette Coleman's voicing experiments. Flanagan's piano, which is rather poorly recorded and inaudible *vis-à-vis* the drums, scarcely gets a look in, and there are moments when the two horns seem to break free of the chords.

The larger group that recorded the Ellington and Gillespie jams is inevitably much less inventive, but there are fine moments from Little (who makes the unrated Smith's trumpet sound positively verdigrised) and from both Coleman again and alto player Frank Strozier, who has enough of a foretaste of Dolphy's imaginative harmonics to satisfy.

Out Front is one of the best albums of the early 1960s. The opening 'We Speak' serves straightforwardly as an introduction to the players. The balance of tonalities, consonant and dissonant harmonies evokes a faint reflection of Ornette's *Free Jazz* experiment, recorded a bare four months before, but the direction is unmistakably Little's and Roach's. The drummer adds timpani and vibraharp to the overall sound, making up for some of the shortcomings of Friedman's piano playing, but tending to interfere with Davis and Carter, who alternated bass duties. The shifting signature of 'Moods In Free Time' stretches Little's phrasing and 'Hazy Hues' explores his interest in tone-colour; there are valuable alternative takes of both tracks, and of 'Quiet, Please' on the *Candid Dolphy* compilation. The closing 'A New Day', with its inbuilt freedoms and fanfare-like annunciations, acquires a certain retrospective irony, given the trumpeter's fate, but is still a wonderfully positive note on which to end.

Charles Lloyd (born 1938) TENOR SAXOPHONE, FLUTE

*** **Forest Flower / Soundtrack** Atlantic/Rhino 8122 71746
    Lloyd; Keith Jarrett (*p*); Cecil McBee, Ron McClure (*b*); Jack DeJohnette (*d*). 2/67, 1/69.

*** **Fish Out Of Water** ECM 1398
    Lloyd; Bobo Stenson (*p*); Palle Danielsson (*b*); Jon Christensen (*d*). 7/89.

***(*) **Notes From Big Sur** ECM 1465
    Lloyd; Bobo Stenson (*p*); Anders Jormin (*b*); Ralph Peterson (*d*). 11/91.

(*) **The Call ECM 1522
    Lloyd; Bobo Stenson (*p*); Anders Jormin (*b*); Billy Hart (*d*). 7/93.

*** **All My Relations** ECM 1557
    As above. 7/94.

Any man who discovers both Keith Jarrett *and* Michel Petrucciani can't be more than half bad. The story and the statistics of Charles Lloyd's astonishing rise to fame as the token jazz presence of the

Haight-Ashbury and the Love Generation (a stereotype that pretended to no understanding of the kind of music he was playing) has been told often enough elsewhere. There isn't much of the '60s stuff left in the catalogue, but the two LPs telescoped on *Forest Flower/Soundtrack* give a pretty good sense of what he was about. This material was so thoroughly laughed out of countenance that the revival was very slow in coming. Even without benefit of hindsight, the Lloyd quartets were pretty exceptional. In 1967, Jarrett was bursting with promise, as was DeJohnette. Neither exactly explodes on *Forest Flower*, which remains unmistakably the leader's gig, but there is enough of both on show to suggest important things to come; Jarrett's composer credit on 'Sorcery' is an early foretaste and McBee is the only other band member to get his name under the line. The two-part title-piece remained a favourite, almost a signature tune, until the band broke up. It's much more robust and much less impressionistic than one remembers. Never thought of as a standards player, Lloyd does have a crack at 'East Of The Sun' and shows off something of the blues coloration that crept into his more idiomatic work.

Despite the kind of 'demographics' then enjoyed only by pop musicians, Lloyd turned his back on jazz performance (more gradually than is sometimes supposed) after the end of the 1960s. By the end of the following decade, the sabbatical was judged to be permanent and Lloyd was largely forgotten. His return to performance came in 1982, when he made a much-trumpeted but slightly under-saxed appearance at the Montreux Jazz Festival, playing in a diffidently mystical style which owed something to the 'Eastern' Coltrane. The latter-day Lloyd is rather more pastel than he ever was with the '60s quartet, but he still has an attractive tone and smooth phrasing.

The comeback inevitably set tape-machines whirring. The first indication of Lloyd's renewed creativity was the studio album, *Fish Out Of Water*. Lloyd takes six new but rather samey compositions at an easy pace, unhurried by the ECM house rhythm section, who can do this stuff with pyjamas on. Though there are flashes of increased intensity, it's mostly a rather enervated affair. Lloyd's tone, digitalized, has lost none of its soft burnish and mild Traneisms; his flute-sound on 'Haghia Sophia' is deep and tremulous enough to be an alto instrument. Low-key and late-night.

Notes From Big Sur is a more varied and enterprising set, still dominated by Coltraneisms but with a bedrock of solid invention underneath the rather melancholy delivery. It might have been preferable to start with the jolly 'Monk In Paris'. 'Requiem' is probably the weakest thing on the album and certainly shouldn't have come first. 'Sister', which follows, is alarmingly similar in theme and it's only really with Jormin's plangent introduction to 'Persevere', part one of 'Pilgrimage To The Mountain', that interesting things start to happen. 'Sam Song' is a medium-tempo swinger underpinned by Peterson's gentle but unmistakably firm drumming (he's a more percussive player than Christensen and pushes Lloyd along proportionately harder) and Stenson's impeccable accompaniment. Jormin introduces 'Takur' with horn-like harmonics down near the bridge, but the piece doesn't travel beyond its own opening bars. 'When Miss Jessye Sings', a tribute to opera singer Jessye Norman, begins disconcertingly close to Coltrane's most famous intro and, in the light of 'Pilgrimage To The Mountain: Persevere/Surrender', one almost wonders if Lloyd intends this album to be his *Love Supreme*, a passionate personal statement in suite form rather than a collection of discontinuous pieces. If so, he falls inevitably short, but he has created something rather lovely in the attempt.

Inside *The Call* is a photograph of four rather depressed-looking men, apparently listening to a play-back. You guessed it . . . This really is full circle, back to the wishy-washy stuff that was just about OK in 1967 but really won't do now. The follow-up *All My Relations* is more satisfactory in every way, suggesting that in Stenson, Jormin and Hart, Lloyd has assembled a like-minded and responsive group who will grow together. The 'Cape To Cairo Suite' is a tribute to Nelson Mandela, overlong and fuzzy in conception. The shorter cuts – 'Thelonious Theonlyus', 'Little Peace' and 'Hymne To The Mother' – are very much better, played with a snap and crispness one would not have expected of Lloyd. An Indian summer, perhaps?

Jon Lloyd (born 1958) ALTO SAXOPHONE, SOPRANO SAXOPHONE

***(*) **Syzygy** Leo CDLR 173
　　　Lloyd; John Law (*p*); Paul Rogers (*b*); Mark Sanders (*d*). 1 & 5/90.
**** **Head** Leo CDLR 186
　　　As above. 1/93.

Lloyd didn't take up the saxophone until he was 23. His previous interest in rock led him through a brief 'ECM' period with the duo, Confluence, in which he played an impressionistic quasi-jazz which can be heard on his self-produced and -published cassette, *Pentimento*. With the turn of the 1990s, though, Lloyd toughened up his act and began to devise the angular momentum that takes him through *Syzygy*. Here he is still leaning quite heavily on the supporting players, notably Rogers and the rapidly maturing Sanders. On *Head*, which was recorded live during an Arts Council tour that gave Lloyd his greatest public exposure to date, the emphasis has shifted a little to the the leader and to Law, who is the group's other composer (though none of his pieces appear on the live record). They make a formidable partnership. 'Fragment 92 & 93' reappears briefly from the first record, and there are two versions of the fine 'Audax Drop'. Lloyd remains a player to watch.

Joe Locke (born 1959) VIBRAPHONE

*** **Restless Dreams** Chief CD1
    Locke; Phil Markowitz (*p*); Eddie Gomez (*b*); Keith Copeland (*d*). 6/83.
*** **Present Tense** Steeplechase SCCD 31257
    Locke; Larry Schneider (*ts*); Kenny Werner (*p*); Ron McClure (*b*); Ronnie Burrage (*d*). 7/89.
***(*) **Longing** Steeplechase SCCD 31281
    Locke; Mark Ledford (*t, v*); Johannes Enders (*ss, ts*); George Cables (*p*); Jeff Andrews (*b*);
    Ronnie Burrage (*d*). 10/90.
**** **But Beautiful** Steeplechase SCCD 31295
    Locke; Kenny Barron (*p*). 8/91.
**** **Wire Walker** Steeplechase SCCD 31332
    Locke; Danny Walsh (*as, ts*); David Kikoski (*p*); Ed Howard (*b*); Marvin 'Smitty' Smith (*d*). 11/92.

In the select group of contemporary vibes players, Locke has claims to head the list. While he can easily assert the kind of virtuosity associated with Gary Burton, it's Bobby Hutcherson's asymmetrical lines and dark, eruptive solos to which he sounds most in debt. Tonally, he gets an idiosyncratic sound from the notoriously faceless instrument – he keeps the sparkle of the vibes but loses their glassiness. As an improviser, he weaves very long lines out of open harmonic situations, maintaining a momentum over short or long distances – he can send up resonant clouds of notes or pare a trail back to its sparsest origins. He can also make the most of slow tempos: the duo album with Barron strikes a meditative pose that is remarkably well sustained for the 70-plus minutes it lasts.

The album co-led with Phil Markowitz is a strong if conventional vibes-and-rhythm date, but the Steeplechase discs are more adventurous. *Present Tense* is dominated by the interplay of Locke and the rhythm section (Schneider makes three somewhat cursory appearances), and Werner's probing accompaniments are particularly acute, although the sometimes inconclusive air of the music suggests that more preparation might have yielded a better result. *Longing* exchanges Werner for Cables, who's equally involved (Ledford and Enders are on only three tracks between them): 'The Double Up' and a profoundly felt 'A Child Is Born' offer very effective music. *But Beautiful*, as noted, is impeccably done, with Barron's felicities as telling as Locke's: this version of 'My Foolish Heart' is on a par with Hutcherson's classic set-piece. *Wire Walker* continues a memorable run: Smith stokes the fires on the burning title-track, Kikoski has seldom played with more point, and the leader's solos on 'A New Blue', 'A Time For Love' and the mesmerizingly complex introduction to 'Young And Foolish' figure among his best work. It scarcely matters that Walsh is little more than a bystander. A strongly recommended sequence.

**** **Very Early** Steeplechase SCCD 31364
    Locke; Ron McClure (*b*); Adam Nussbaum (*d*). 10/94.
***(*) **Moment To Moment** Milestone MCD 9243-2
    Locke; Billy Childs (*p*); Eddie Gomez (*b*); Gene Jackson (*d*). 11/94.

Joe is still in great form here. The trio date with Nussbaum and McClure is another perfectly paced session, with the swinging tempo for 'You Don't Know What Love Is' giving way to a rapt 'I Loves You Porgy', a dramatic 'Nature Boy' and on through eight tunes. McClure's bass lines are the ideal melodic/rhythmic counterweight, indecently rich but always on the right part of the chord, and Nussbaum is at his most subtle. *Moment To Moment* is really only a shade behind, starting with a terrific workout on 'Slow Hot Wind' and making the best of an ingenious choice of standards and connoisseur's pop. After McClure, Gomez can sound unnecessarily busy, and sometimes one wants to stop and revel in Locke's sound more, but this is basically another good 'un.

Mornington Lockett TENOR SAXOPHONE, PIANO, BASS

*** **Mornington Lockett** EFZ 1006
    Lockett; Jonathan Gee (*p*); Jim Mullen (*g*); Laurence Cottle (*b*); Ian Thomas (*d*); Sarah Jane
    Morris (*v*). 94.

Lockett came to notice with club owner/saxophonist Ronnie Scott's band, but he was immediately identified as a man who would go his own way. On the evidence of the more ambitious things on this debut disc, the complex 'P2C2E', and the deceptively straight-ahead 'Red Shift II' and 'Forca Al Canut', he is going to be a significant writer. He tackles the standard 'Lush Life' with conviction and a warmth of feeling. It comes two tracks after 'Laphraoig', the name of a wry, sardonic malt whisky whose distinctive flavour – iodine, seaweed, salt, smoke – seems to have found its way into Lockett's sound. Guitarist Jim Mullen guests on 'Lush Life' and one other track and fills out the harmony considerably; a pity he couldn't have been on hand for the whole session. Less enthusiasm for Sarah Jane Morris's vocal on the Etta James groaner, 'Don't Go To Strangers', which may have been a bid for airplay but fell flat if it was. A promising, thoughtful debut, perhaps too determined to show off a spectrum of ideas and styles rather than concentrating on good, straightforward playing, of which Lockett is demonstrably capable.

Didier Lockwood (born 1956) VIOLIN

**** Out Of The Blue JMS 037
    Lockwood; Gordon Beck (*p*); Cecil McBee (*b*); Billy Hart (*d*). 4/85.
**(*) 1 2 3 4 JMS 041
    Lockwood; Thierry Eliez (*ky, v*); Jean-Michel Kajdan (*g*); Tom Kennedy (*b*); André Ceccarelli (*d*); Abdou M'Boup (*perc*); Nicole Croisille, Toure Kunda, Alex Ligertwood (*v*). 87.
***(*) New York Rendezvous JMS 075
    Lockwood; Dave Liebman (*ss*); David Kikoski (*p, ky*); Dave Holland (*b*); Gil Goldstein (*acc*); Mike Stern (*g*); Peter Erskine (*d*). 1/95.

Lockwood is an immensely gifted player, combining a virtuosic technique with an attractive musicality. His association with Gordon Beck has been particularly fruitful. The earliest of the three JMS discs sees the two Europeans holding their own admirably in the company of two brilliant American rhythm players. Beck is in particularly good form and contributes the lovely 'November Song' to an exquisite session, revealing himself again as one of the finest accompanists Europe can provide.

Unlike Michal Urbaniak or his fellow countryman, Zbigniew Seifert, Lockwood shows no desire to make the violin sound like a saxophone and is happy to explore the legacy of Stéphane Grappelli, albeit in a much updated form. It's hard to fault *Out Of The Blue* on any count, but the 1987 follow-up really is rather dull. The attempt to divide the album into four distinct 'chapters' simply doesn't make sense of the music, and the players are resolutely uninspired, with the exception of Ceccarelli and his occasional percussion partner, Abdou M'Boup, who make 'Aquamarine' a winning idea.

The New York session marks a welcome return to form. Holland and Erskine provide the solid foundation Lockwood thrives on, and the guests chip in with folksy melodic contributions that help mitigate the slightly monotonous sound of the violin as a front-line instrument. It's odd, given how good he is at it, that Lockwood hasn't capitalized more on his dazzling pizziccato work. He tried it on *Out Of The Blue* but has made precious little use of it since.

All three records, it should be said, are expertly and feelingly engineered by the (almost) eponymous Jean-Marie Salhani of JMS, one of the unsung heroes of European jazz music.

Claudio Lodati GUITAR

*** Chance Splasc(h) H 306-2
    Lodati; Maurizio Brunod (*g*); Laura Culver (*clo*); Enrico Fazio (*b*); Fiorenzo Sordini (*d, marim*). 1/90.

Lodati has toyed with far more avant-garde music than he provides here – as a member of the Italian Art Studio, he would have played in much less ordered settings – but this is a likeable fusion of a number of guitar-driven ideas. He favours a thick, almost chewy tone that glues the other instruments together into a dense, small-group music, rather than looking for open solo space. Culver appears on three tracks as a textural agent, Brunod plays second fiddle and, together with Fazio's big sound and nimble lines, they suggest something of an Eberhard Weber or a Terje Rypdal group. Two weepy, reverberant features, 'Gulls' and 'Maria G', are a bit of an indulgence, but Lodati just about earns it.

Giuseppi Logan (born 1935) TENOR SAXOPHONE, ALTO SAXOPHONE, CLARINET, FLUTE, PAKISTANI OBOE, PIANO

**** Giuseppi Logan Quartet ESP Disk ESP 1007
    Logan; Don Pullen (*p*); Eddie Gomez (*b*); Milford Graves (*d*). 11/64.

(*) More ESP Disk ESP 1013
    As above, but Reggie Johnson (*b*) replaces Gomez. 5/65.
Though he has not been active in music for many years, Logan is still spoken of with respect and affection by members of the 1960s avant-garde. If for no other reason, his debut record on ESP Disk would be remembered for the exposure it afforded such up-and-coming talents as Pullen, Gomez and Graves. In practice, all three significantly upstaged the session leader. *Quartet* sounds like a hot trio session with horns rather superfluously overlaid. Pullen's weighty, R&B-influenced approach was a little too earthbound for Logan, who plays somewhat like the later, less jazz-orientated Yusef Lateef. Gomez is very much a bottom-end player, content to play *bass* lines, rather than acting like a frustrated horn player. He is as central to 'Bleecker Partita' as Graves is to 'Dance Of Satan'.

    It was always said of the drummer that on record he never sounded anything like as powerful as he did in person. (His own ESP Disk recording (*q.v.*) was a major disappointment.) Graves's 'disappearance' in the later 1970s, by no means as final as Logan's, was in fact only a disappearance from the studios. The percussionist has continued to exert the same powerful influence, documented by Valerie Wilmer in her study of the new jazz, *As Serious As Your Life*, offering a viable alternative to the knitting-pattern antics of Elvin Jones and Sunny Murray. Graves has recorded again in recent years, with David Murray (*q.v.*) and others.

    Logan's second record was a serious disappointment, suggesting that the first had been a bit of a one-off. The original B-side consisted of 'Curve Eleven', which was little more than sub-Cecil Taylor noodling on a slightly wonky studio piano. Though the two survivors from *Quartet* reach their usual high quality on 'Mantu' and 'Shebar', it's a pretty thin diet. The only other Logan material available is on a record by singer Patty Waters [ESP Disk ESP 1025 CD], but this is for avid collectors only.

Michael Logan BASS

(*) Night Out Muse MCD5458
    Logan; Joe Ford (*ss, as*); Houston Person (*ts*); Benny Green (*p*); Cecil Brooks III (*d*). 8/90.
This one sat on the shelf for four years before issue, and it's not hard to see why: pleasant enough midstream hard bop, but no pressing reason for it to exist, and even the normally reliable Green sounds bored. Logan's title-piece is a nice line, Person does his customary big breathy ballad on 'Cry Me A River' and Ford does decently by Lionel Richie's unpromising 'Hello'. But Brooks, who produced (and not very well), is far too fussy.

London Jazz Composers Orchestra (founded 1970) GROUP

**** **Ode** Intakt CD 041
    Barry Guy (*b, ldr*); Harry Beckett, Dave Holdsworth, (*t*); Marc Charig (*c*); Paul Rutherford, Mike Gibbs, Paul Nieman (*tb*); Dick Hart (*tba*); Trevor Watts (*as, ss*); Mike Osborne, Bernard Living (*as*); Alan Wakeman, Evan Parker (*ts, ss*); Bob Downes (*ts, f*); Karl Jenkins (*bs, ob*); Howard Riley (*p*); Derek Bailey (*g*); Jeff Clyne, Chris Laurence (*b*); Tony Oxley, Paul Lytton (*d, perc*); Buxton Orr (*cond*). 4/72.
**** **Harmos** Intakt 013
    Barry Guy (*b, ldr*); Jon Corbett, Henry Lowther (*t*); Marc Charig (*c*); Radu Malfatti, Paul Rutherford, Alan Tomlinson (*tb*); Steve Wick (*tba*); Paul Dunmall, Peter McPhail, Evan Parker, Simon Picard, Trevor Watts (*reeds*); Phil Wachsmann (*vn*); Howard Riley (*p*); Barre Phillips (*b*); Paul Lytton (*d*). 4/89, 4/89.
***(*) **Double Trouble** Intakt 019
    As above. 4/89.
**** **Theoria** Intakt CD 024
    As above, but Irène Schweizer (*p*) replaces Riley; Conrad Bauer (*tb*) replaces Rutherford. 2/91.
**** **Portraits** Intakt CD 035 2CD
    As above, except Paul Rutherford (*tb*) replaces Bauer. 3/93.
In an age of hyper-specialization and carefully compartmentalized musical styles, it's encouraging to find someone like Barry Guy. Classically trained in both composition and double bass, Guy has combined a passionate commitment to free improvisation with a long-standing interest in large-scale composition for improvising ensembles, and a far from incidental interest in Baroque music, an area of music-making which, for a time at least, he considered every bit as radical and experimental as free improvisation. Needless to say, eclecticism as untroubled as this has tended to alienate those of his more dogmatic brethren who regard anything older than yesterday as dead and buried and who subject anything as authoritarian as a score to the purest anathema.

What unites these apparently disparate interests is Guy's concern for the articulation of musical language, learning how it is that music speaks to us. In recent years Guy has been concentrating on improvisation and on writing for and directing the London Jazz Composers Orchestra, the remarkable group he first formed two decades ago.

The orchestra was inspired by the example of the American trumpeter and composer Michael Mantler's Jazz Composers' Orchestra, which afforded improvising players a rare opportunity to work outside the small-group circuit and to experiment with enlarged structures that went a little beyond the 8- and 16-bar tunes that were the basic jazz staple. Inevitably, given the European commitment to collective improvisation, the LJCO quickly developed a more radical – some thought chaotic – language which was most clearly represented in a hefty piece called *Ode*.

This was conceived as a 'social framework' for improvising musicians, a brilliant response to the difficulty of combining what were thought to be almost antagonistic musical philosophies. Initially inspired by Olivier Messiaen's *Chronochromie*, Guy devised and disguised structures, a series of philosophical quiddities to which the orchestra both as a collective and as a sum of expressive individuals were asked to respond. The result is, as John Corbett suggests, not dense in the way that orchestral *tutti* are dense. It is dense in that the level of musical communication is such that every statement implies more than it states, creates networks of interaction between players, between constituent instrumental and personal groups, and between types of musical response. This is exactly what Guy was to do later in *Portraits*, where the orchestra, having served on the European free scene for a quarter of a century, was found to be made up of several pre-existing and (in some cases) concurrent groups – Paul Rutherford's Iskra 1903, Evan Parker's Trio, John Corbett's Doppler – and thus to be in a sense a confederation rather than a vertically organized 'orchestra' at all. This posed fascinating problems/possibilities for Guy, most of which can be traced right back to the earliest projects.

Ode proved to be a little hard-boiled for most of the critics, and for some of the players, and represented something of a blind alley in Guy's attempt to maximize soloists' freedom in such a way as not to blur or compromise an overall and very coherent musical argument. Reissued now, it is revealed as a grand triumph, in some respects a more satisfying work than the more exploratory and sophisticated compositions that have followed in recent years. Unheard for some time, it has been possible to think of it as a 'prentice essay. It is, in fact, one of the masterpieces of European improvisation.

In the years that followed, the LJCO changed somewhat in ethos, opening up its repertoire to compositions other than those by Guy. These included challenging graphic scores by drummer Tony Oxley, intricately structured pieces by pianist Howard Riley, looser structures from trombonist Paul Rutherford and, from outside the band, challenging works from 'straight' composers with an interest in improvisation. *Harmos* marks what Guy considers a third stage in the band's progress. Guy intends the title to be understood in its original sense of a coming together. It opens sharply enough with a kind of broken fanfare from the trombones that has the jagged authority typical of the best of British improvisation, followed by a stately chorale that calls to mind Guy's other enthusiasms. But if the piece has a centre, it is the long, winding melody played by saxophonist Trevor Watts, a veteran of the band and in this composition its First Mate and pilot. Coming quite early (it's a long piece), Watts's solo nevertheless shapes the whole composition around itself and marks Guy's reawakened and always adventurous interest in harmonic language. Everyone in the 17-strong line-up has at least some solo space, so *Harmos* fits very closely Guy's ideal of a large-scale musical argument which nevertheless leaves its participants considerable personal freedom. Even if 45 minutes isn't considered tip-top value on CD, *Harmos* should be in every serious contemporary-jazz collection.

Double Trouble is a slightly tougher nut. Originally intended as a two-piano project for Howard Riley and Alex Von Schlippenbach, the recorded version is anchored on Riley alone, with a sequence of carefully marshalled instrumental groupings (notably two trios, the first consisting of Guy, Evan Parker and Paul Lytton, and the second of Riley, Marc Charig and Barre Phillips) not so much following in his wake as orbiting. As a whole the piece has a strong centrifugal coherence that balances the apparently anarchic, but often tightly scored, behaviour of soloists and section players. If it's down a degree of stellar magnitude on *Harmos*, that's simply because it seems much less immediately accessible. On the other hand, it may pay a longer dividend.

Harmos is effectively a piano concerto for Irène Schweizer, a player who had close contacts with the British avant-garde of the 1960s. The difficulty presented was that of balancing individual and ensemble elements in a work of this scale and complexity; neither Guy nor Schweizer would have welcomed anything as fixed and definitive as a classical or Romantic concerto, yet clearly it would be undesirable to have a soloist improvise completely freely for nearly an hour against a fixed orchestral score. The solution, which subsequently became even more important in *Portraits*, is to demarcate very precisely the starting and finishing points for individual soloists and for internal sub-divisions of the orchestra, allowing the players a paradoxical degree of freedom within the basic structure. Guy attempts not to juxtapose blandly different styles of playing but to overlap them creatively, and it is this which gives *Theoria* its great power. In an orchestra of soloists, Schweizer stands out clearly but does not dominate;

what happens is that her improvisations become the constituent elements of other musicians' activity, a process parallel to but obviously very different from jazz musicians' reliance on chord sequences or standard tunes. It is a formidable achievement, and seen alongside *Portraits*, it will become clear that Guy's work, and that of the LJCO, has entered a new and creative phase.

Portraits, as we have suggested, sits more than comfortably alongside *Ode*. It is of its time – as was its predecessor – but most obviously in the decision to allow the inclusion of some quite explicitly melodic material (which did seemingly confuse and antagonize some of the more dogmatic improvisers). In the fifth of the main sections, which are interspersed by portrait subsections, there is a ballad, written for Simon Picard. Alan Tomlinson is given a blues (words by Paul Rutherford, recited by the players), and there are other identifiable generic outlines. However, because of the internal configuration of languages and of personnels, none of these insists on anything like generic autonomy. They all function as part of this triumphant whole. Along with Guy himself, Evan Parker is the player who sustains the networks making up the piece, communicating at one point with several of the players around him, maintaining associations that would seem to be dispersed in time. It is a remarkable achievement. *Ode* has a greater historical resonance, but *Portraits* is a work of masterful control and profundity.

London Jazz Orchestra GROUP

*** **Dance For Human Folk** Hot House HHCD 1016/7 2CD
        Noel Langley, Andy Bush, Henry Lowther, Ian Carr, Sid Gould (*t, flhn*); Scott Stroman, Paul Nieman, Brian Archer, Richard Edwards (*tb*); Dave Stewart, Andy Lester (*btb*); Stan Sulzmann, Martin Hathaway, Tim Garland, Pete Hurt, Jamie Talbot, Mark Lockhart, Alan Barnes (*reeds*); Pete Saberton (*p*); Phil Lee (*g*); Alec Dankworth (*b*); Paul Clarvis (*d*). 1/94.

A 'mingling of generations' among London's jazz community, the LJO has Stroman as its MD and he wrote the four-part 'The Tradition' which takes up the first disc. The second features scores by Sulzmann, Hathaway, Hurt, Saberton, Lowther and Garland, which takes in a fair sweep of several of the major voices on the local scene from the past 25 years. The music is rather discouragingly ordinary at times, and as an orchestra the players don't really create a singular entity. But there are some lucid and worthwhile solos which emerge from the scores, and of the 12 pieces Stan Sulzmann's pair of charts show an interestingly cluttered vision.

Jean-Loup Longnon TRUMPET

***(*) **Cyclades** JMS 18637
        Longnon; Tony Russo, Eric Giausserand, Michael Delakian, Christian Martinez, Philippe Slominski, Patrick Artero (*t*); Jacques Bolognesi, Denis Leloup, Jean-Louis Pommier, Jean-Marc Welch (*tb*); Patrice Petitdidier, Jacques Peillon (*frhn*); Didier Havet (*tba*); Lionel Belmondo, Christophe Laborde, Nicholas Montioer, Guillaume Naturel, Pierre Schirrer, André Villeger (*sax*); Pierre Mimran(*f*); Robert Persi (*ky*); Jean-Michel Pilc (*whistle*); Stéphane Grappelli (*vn*); Hervé Sellin (*p*); Jeorgino Amorim, Khalil Chahine (*g*); Jean-Marc Jafet, Carlinho Verneck (*b*); Luis Augusto Cavani, François Laizeau (*d*); Americo Pintinho Da Silva (*perc*); Zabele Pidner (*v*); orchestra. 11/92.

Epic, and satisfyingly naïve, a little like a Tintin story, translated and transposed on to a grand musical stage. The piece is actually subtitled '*Les Extraordinaires aventures de Barnabe, le petit cochon voyageur*', the details of which need not detain us here. However, anything that ends with a booming, jazzy arrangement of the 'Marseillaise' can't be bad. There is just a hint of Maynard Ferguson about Longnon, but MF with a Gauloise in his mouth; he even has a four-valve flugelhorn to cement the parallel. The most surprising guest artist is Grappelli, who solos on 'Paros' with customary grace and enthusiasm, but without the slightest indication that he knows what the hell is going on. *Cyclades* is the kind of eclectic, non-generic, boundary-squelching thing that the French have become extremely good at. What it's about and how to describe it is beyond our critical capacity, but the noise it makes is terrific and hugely enjoyable. Do try.

Louisiana Repertory Jazz Ensemble GROUP

***(*) **Uptown Jazz** Stomp Off CD 1055
        Eddie Bayard (*c*); Leroy Jones Jr (*t*); Eddie Lonzo (*vtb*); Fred Starr (*cl, ss, ts, Cmel*); John Royen (*p*); John Chaffe (*bj, g, mand*); Curtis Jerde (*helicon*); Sherwood Mangiapane (*b*); Walter Payton Jr (*sou*); John Joyce (*d*). 6/82–6/83.

**** Hot & Sweet Sounds Of Lost New Orleans Stomp Off CD 1140

>Roy Tate (*t, c*); Charlie Fardella (*c*); Tom Ebbert (*tb*); Jacques Gauthe (*cl, ss, as*); Henry Duckham (*cl, as*); Fred Starr (*cl, Cmel, ts, bs*); Vince Giordano (*bsx*); John Royen (*p*); John Chaffe (*g, bj*); Walter Payton Jr (*b, E-flat helicon*); John Joyce (*d, wbd*). 6/86.

The vogue for authentic performance which has dominated the classical world in recent years has scarcely entered into jazz interpretation as yet, since trad groups the world over are content to savage the old repertoire to their own ends. This remarkable ensemble instead takes a purist's hand to original 1920s' material. They use old instruments – the notes to CD 1140 reveal that six different cornets, made between 1895 and 1922, were used by Tate and Fardella – and arrangements taken straight from original records. Solos are probably patterned on routines, but it hardly matters since this is basically an ensemble approach to the music. On these terms it's an extraordinary success. There are infinite variations in light and shade: on *Hot And Sweet Sounds* the players appear in ten different combinations across the 17 tracks, and they sound as comfortable in Jelly Roll Morton's music as in Freddie Keppard's or Richard M. Jones's. More important, they understand the differences among all the styles. On the key issue of tempo they consistently make it sound right: a very slow pace for 'Smoke House Blues', perfectly sprung rhythms (even without a bass instrument) on 'Original Dixieland One-Step' and 'Stockyards Strut'. The earlier record is perhaps just slightly the more static, and consequently more at the mercy of history, though the concept – to differentiate the pulse of Uptown as opposed to Downtown New Orleans classicism – is an intriguing one. But both discs are marvellously entertaining, as well as the most enjoyable kind of history lesson.

Joe Lovano (born 1952) TENOR SAXOPHONE, ALTO SAXOPHONE, ALTO CLARINET

*** Tones, Shapes And Colors Soul Note 121132

>Lovano; Ken Werner (*p*); Dennis Irwin (*b*); Mel Lewis (*d*). 11/85.

**** One Time Out Soul Note 121224

>Lovano; Bill Frisell (*g*); Paul Motian (*d*). 9/87.

*** Village Rhythm Soul Note 121182

>Lovano; Tom Harrell (*t*); Ken Werner (*p*); Marc Johnson (*b*); Paul Motian (*d*). 6/88.

In a club setting, the Lovano–Frisell–Motian trio generated tile-melting excitement. On record, there are more subtleties, more opportunities for sophisticated interplay. Lovano started out a relatively straightforward technician, often relying on others to embellish his slightly throaty but plain-speaking lines. Long association with Motian has accustomed him to a very strong pulse embedded in a vibrant surface; he gets much the same thing from the late Mel Lewis, who is surprisingly reminiscent of Krupa in a small-group setting, and also from guitarist Frisell, whose chords and single-note figures are ever more clearly enunciated as his delay-and-distort effects become more dominant.

Experience, however, has turned him into perhaps the most distinctive tenor player at work today, and a hectic recording schedule has greatly added to his discography. It must be said that Lovano is one of the few artists that Blue Note have handled with sympathetic intelligence in recent years, allowing him to work with an impressive cross-section of contemporary players, but with no sense that they're just ticking off the A-list. What's become obvious since the turn of the 1990s is how much of Lovano's mature style was present in germ in his earlier work.

Village Rhythm is as impressive for the writing as for the playing, and reveals Lovano to be a surprisingly accomplished bop melodist. 'Sleepy Giant' is particularly memorable. On a couple of tracks the saxophonist overdubs his own rather World Music-al drumming. An indulgence? No more so than the ghastly poem to his father on 'Twas To Me'.

Bearish and slightly withdrawn of aspect, Lovano hadn't yet made a completely individual impact, but all three of these are worthwhile efforts, steering clear of clichéd effects and overworked material.

***(*) Ten Tales Owl CD 053

>Lovano; Aldo Romano (*d*). 5/89.

Almost unknown, this is an unusual sidebar on Lovano's discography, a one-off session with the veteran drummer, recorded in Paris with what sounds like a minimum of preparation and advance planning. Taken for what it is, a fairly spontaneous head-to-head, it works remarkably well. What is startling is how much like his old friend and sparring partner, Jim Pepper, Lovano sounds. A lot of the pieces have a folksy, chanting sound that's attractive over the short haul but which palls a bit by tale number 7. 'Autumn In New York' sounds as if it was tacked on to fill up the tape. It's not actually very well done but, like the album as a whole, is full of suggestive promise. Worth checking out.

**** Landmarks Blue Note CDP 796108

>Lovano; John Abercrombie (*g*); Ken Werner (*p*); Marc Johnson (*b*); Bill Stewart (*d*). 8/90.

This is Lovano's breakthrough record, a wholly satisfying set that shouts for the repeat button before the last raucous notes of 'Dig This' (with its curious, Monkish interruptions) have died away. Stylistically it's poised midway between Monk and Coltrane, but with a pungent sauce of latter-day urban funk poured over the top, as on the mid-point 'Here And Now', with Abercrombie's uncharacteristically vocalized guitar well to the fore. The (impeccable) production is by John Scofield, who might have been a more obvious choice for the guitarist's role, but Abercrombie seems to take in Scofield's virtues as well as his own, absolutely howling through 'Dig This'.

Lovano's ballad-playing, as on the tribute to Elvin Jones, is increasingly impressive, with a virile focus that belies the slightly tremulous delivery. One of the finest jazz albums of 1991 and a pointer for the decade to come.

**** Sounds Of Joy Enja CD 7013 2
Lovano; Anthony Cox (*b*); Ed Blackwell (*d*). 1/91.

Working without a harmony instrument still places considerable demands on a horn player. The opening 'Sounds Of Joy' immediately recalls the stark, melodic approach of the classic Ornette Coleman Atlantics, a jolting, unpredictable saxophone sound that seems to select notes from all over the scale without reference to anything other than the simplest sequences of melody. There are clear signs that Lovano is anxious to broaden his sound as much as possible. In addition to tenor and soprano (the latter given its most thorough and demanding workout to date on the dedication 'This One's For Lacy'), he has also taken on the alto saxophone (giving it a sonority somewhere between Bird and Ornette) and the seldom-used alto clarinet, which he unveils on Judith Silverman's free-tonal 'Bass Space', an almost formal theme executed over a tense 7/8 beat from Blackwell (the actual count varies considerably) and huge, *arco* effects from the fine Cox, who solos magnificently on 'Strength And Courage'.

*** Universal Language Blue Note 799830
Lovano; Tim Hagans (*t*); Ken Werner (*p*); Scott Lee, Steve Swallow, Charlie Haden (*b*); Jack DeJohnette (*d*); Judi Silvano (*v*). 6/92.

Whereas *Sounds Of Joy* seemed like a genuine attempt on Lovano's part to push himself out into rather edgier territory, *Universal Language* is rather self-consciously eclectic, an attempt to broaden the sound by bringing in all sorts of world-music touchstones and shifting the emphasis over heavily to Lovano the composer, an individual still much less resourceful than Lovano the player. Even the latter is somewhat compromised by the shift to a multi-instrumental approach that lacks the logic it undoubtedly had on the Enja session. 'Lost Nations', in memory of the late Jim Pepper, features him on both soprano and alto clarinet. 'Cleveland Circle' has him moving off into Coltrane harmonics; but, significantly, the most effective piece on the record is the ballad, 'The Dawn Of Time', on which Jack DeJohnette is magnificent.

The rhythm section isn't quite as ambitiously constructed as might appear. Haden and Lee don't appear on the same tracks, and Swallow is used essentially as a guitarist, weaving lines round Werner's ramrod comping.

**** From The Soul Blue Note 798363
Lovano; Michel Petrucciani (*p*); Dave Holland (*b*); Ed Blackwell (*d*). 12/91.

This is much more like it, a definitive jazz record for the 1990s. Lovano's 'Body And Soul' wins him lifetime membership of the tenor club. Interestingly, though, he takes John Coltrane's rarely covered 'Central Park West' on alto, as if doing it on the bigger horn were unpardonable arrogance. What's wonderful about the record – aside from the playing, which is gilt-edged all round – is how beautifully modulated the tracks are. There's not a cliché in sight. Lovano's own writing – 'Evolution', 'Lines & Spaces', 'Modern Man', 'Fort Worth', and the closing waltz, 'His Dreams' – has a clean muscular edge and, from the opening fanfare of 'Evolution' onwards, it's clear that the album is going to be something special.

Petrucciani has established such a presence as a recording artist in his own right that it's easy to forget how superb an accompanist he can be. The Frenchman's responses on 'Left Behind', unfamiliar territory for him, are startling. He sits 'Fort Worth' out, leaving Holland and Blackwell to steer a markedly abrasive theme. Though ailing and by no means as dynamic as in former years, the drummer still sounds completely masterful. His delicate mallet figures on 'Portrait Of Jenny' are one of the instrumental high points of a thoroughly compelling record.

***(*) Tenor Legacy Blue Note CDP 827014
Lovano; Joshua Redman (*ts*); Mulgrew Miller (*p*); Christian McBride (*b*); Lewis Nash (*d*); Don Alias (*perc*). 6/93.

Even given the impossibility of topping *From The Soul*, this is a slightly muted set, with a tentative quality that hasn't been evident in Lovano's work before. Redman had been garnering a huge amount of press before this was recorded, and it may be that both men felt that reputations were at stake. Certainly Lovano sounds edgy and over-assertive, making a decidedly strange fist of 'Love Is A Many-Splendored Thing'.

The two-tenor front line gives the music a rather old-fashioned aspect that is accentuated by probably the straightest rhythm section Lovano's worked with in years. The centre-piece is a version of Monk's 'Introspection', delivered with few frills and patient development by all the soloists. Nothing else quite comes up to that standard, though, and the long ballad, 'To Her Ladyship', has a cloyingly soft centre.

At this stage in his career, Lovano's entitled to lay a couple of eggs. This isn't, but in the context of its predecessors, it's a bit of a disappointment.

***(*) **Quartets** Blue Note CDP 829125 2CD
    Lovano; Tom Harrell (*t, flhn*); Mulgrew Miller (*p*); Anthony Cox, Christian McBride (*b*); Billy Hart, Lewis Nash (*d*). 95.

A slightly worrying development, albeit a highly accomplished record. Why should either Blue Note or Lovano feel it was necessary at this juncture to confirm his bona fides in avant/progressive and mainstream jazz, with these differently constituted quartets at the Village Vanguard? That he functions well in both realms has been beyond doubt for so long, who remains to be convinced? This initiative smacks of label unease, a lack of clear thinking about what to do with a major artist. Blue Note have been down this path before. Let's hope that with Lovano they don't drop the ball.

Allen Lowe TENOR SAXOPHONE

**** **Dark Was The Night** Music & Arts CD 811
    Lowe; Robert Rumboltz (*t*); Roswell Rudd (*tb*); Paul Austerlitz (*cl, bcl*); Stacy Phillips (*g*); Jeff Fuller (*b*); Ray Kaczynski (*d*). 4, 4, 7 & 11/93.
***(*) **Woyzeck's Death** Enja ENJ 9005
    Lowe; Roswell Rudd (*tb*); Randy Sandke (*t*); Ben Goldberg (*cl, bcl*); Andy Shapiro (*p, syn*); Jeff Fuller (*b*); Ray Kaczynski (*d*). 5/94.

Most of the attention devoted to these on release focused on the role of new wave trombonist Rudd, effectively co-leader on both sessions, who has spent much of the last decade well away from the scene. Both projects are, however, essentially Lowe's concept, with just two Rudd compositions (albeit fascinating ones) tacked on at the end of *Woyzeck's Death*.

The 'American Song Project' that yields *Dark Was The Night* is an intriguing business, the result of Lowe's fascination with an art form which is at the heart of jazz – all those standards – but which nonetheless is largely overlooked; lots of guys know the chords to 'Body And Soul', not so many nowadays could sing you the words and proper melody. This isn't however a collection of Americana. Most of the material is by Lowe himself, an impressive melodist with a dry, slightly acidulous character, and is intended as a tribute to Louis Armstrong, Blind Willie Johnson, Elvis Presley and other neglected (*sic.*) American masters. Some of Lowe's own playing is imprecise, a problem he puts down to a broken finger on the July session in Providence, but audible elsewhere as well. Rudd plays magnificently and the bit parts, touches of clarinet, National guitar and trumpet, are all handled professionally.

The other is a different kind of concept album, inspired by Georg Büchner's two plays, *Woyzeck* and *Dantons Tod*. Once the liner-notes and the relevant contexts have been absorbed the exact programme scarcely matters. Suffice it to say that Lowe has captured something of the brittle gaiety and bleak despair that oscillate through Büchner. His saxophone sound, on the opening 'Cold As Ice', 'Hard Gray Sky' and the climactic 'Woyzeck's Death' itself, has a kind of muscular melancholy that recalls no earlier player, other than perhaps Chu Berry in darker mood.

Mood is the weasel word here, for there is no ECM-ish picture-painting; every episode is carefully shaped and logically constructed. Rudd is the anarchic element, breaking across Lowe's argument, Goldberg's atmospheric reed sound, and even Sandke's patiently built solos, with abrupt, ironic intensity. On his own 'Bonehead' and 'Concentration Suite', which closes the album, the trombonist shows again how solidly grounded he still is in classic jazz idiom and how exciting a performer he can be in a straight blowing context. However, he shouldn't be allowed to steal more than his fair share of Lowe's thunder. This is a fascinating contemporary record but *Dark Was The Night* probably offers more lasting satisfaction.

Frank Lowe (born 1943) TENOR SAXOPHONE

**** **Black Beeings** ESP Disk ESP 3013
    Lowe; Joseph Jarman (*as, ss*); The Wizard (*vn*); William Parker (*b*); Rashid Sinan (*d, perc*). 3/72.
**** **Exotic Heartbreak** Soul Note 1211032
    Lowe; Lawrence Butch Morris (*c*); Amina Claudine Myers (*p*); Wilber Morris (*b*); Tim Pleasant (*d*). 10/81.

**** Decision In Paradise Soul Note 1211082

>Lowe; Don Cherry (*t*); Grachan Moncur III (*tb*); Geri Allen (*p*); Charnett Moffett (*b*); Charles Moffett (*d*). 9/84.

Memphis-born Lowe has the big, abrasive tone of his fellow-townsman George Coleman, tempered with a once-unfashionable interest in classic swing players like Chu Berry and, from slightly later, Don Byas. The ESP is as hectic as most of the label's output, but Jarman is a steadying influence and Lowe's understanding of earlier idiom makes a big difference. 'In Trane's Name' is a fairly routine memorial, distinguished by the fact that neither saxophonist seems to have been much influenced by him. Nor is there much bop residue in Lowe's harmonic thinking, and a cover like 'Cherryco' on *Decision In Paradise*, doubtless suggested by the trumpeter's presence on the session, isn't immediately suited to his approach. A heavyweight rhythm section, led off by Allen's no less forcefully eclectic chords and runs, keeps the energy-level high; Moncur, as always, plays superbly, varying his slide positions and embouchure to stay just this side of multiphonics. *Exotic Heartbreak* makes good use of Lawrence Butch Morris and Amina Claudine Myers, both of whom are in excellent form. One Black Saint disc remains in the limbo file: *The Flam*, with Leo Smith and Joe Bowie. It would be well worth reviving.

*** Inappropriate Choices ITM Pacific ITM 970062

>Lowe; James Carter, Michael Marcus, Carlos Ward (*saxes*); Phillip Wilson (*d*).

When the World Saxophone Quartet invited drummers to the party, they at least had the grace to give them something to do. Wilson, a fine technician, is left without a job description on this boldly interesting but ultimately unsatisfactory sax quartet-plus set. Future releases should be well worth hearing. On this, though, a raincheck.

**** Bodies & Souls CIMP 104

>Lowe; Tim Flood (*b*); Charles Moffett (*d*). 11/95.

As spare and stern as the great Ornette Coleman Trio, which Moffett also graced, this is the Lowe disc of choice, for all its technical oddities. The Cadence Improvised Music Project is dedicated to raw, unprocessed, slice-of-life veritism when it comes to recording spontaneous music. Fair enough, but may we respectfully suggest that a little tidying up does no more than throw the musicians into the best possible light and in no way compromises their performances; Lowe's breath-sounds and pad-clicks may be construed as integral to the music, but they could comfortably be dispensed with.

A long set, with the usual intensity, *Bodies & Souls* mixes four originals with material by Pharoah Sanders, Don Cherry (who is also the dedicatee of two joyous, complex numbers by Lowe himself), Ornette ('Happy House') and, on the stirring opening 'Impressions', John Coltrane. It stands first, one feels, because Lowe wants to demonstrate both his respect for and distance from Coltrane's and, later, Coleman's language. By placing 'Body And Soul' last, he demonstrates more clearly than ever before how much he sees himself standing on the shoulders of earlier giants. It's a delicate performance, lighter-toned than Lowe often is, and slightly more elaborate. Flood tends to come into his own at this tempo and Moffett can be heard working on ever smaller areas of his kit.

(To be fair to CIMP, their 'statement of purpose' provides a very useful practical guide to setting controls for this kind of music. Set the levels so that the loudest peaks are comfortable, while resisting the temptation to bung up the volume on very quiet passages; after all, that was the way they were played.)

Werner Ludi (born 1936) ALTO AND BARITONE SAXOPHONES

**(*) Grand Bazaar Creative Works CW 1012-2

>Ludi; Burhan Ocal (*darbuka drums, dawul, tanbur, perc*). 1/88.

*** The Bird Who Makes The Cloud Sing As He Drums It – Live At Montreux Creative Works CW 1019-2

>As above. 7/89.

***(*) Brain Drain Unit UTR 4051

>Ludi; Wadi Gysi (*g*); Mich Gerber (*b*); Mani Neumeier (*d*). 6/92.

Ludi is a veteran Swiss free player who has drifted in and out of the music. His group, Sunnymoon, made records in the 1980s which are not yet on CD. The duo with Ocal is an interesting blend of skirling alto playing and Turkish drumming which makes no pretensions to 'world music' – it's two skilful musicians from different backgrounds playing as freely as they feel. *Grand Bazaar* sounds a little anaemic in its studio environment, and the various duo performances are a little stunted, despite scattered fine moments. Captured live, they generate much more heat and real passion, with 'Lisa Mona Overdrive' and 'Flow Motion' both generating a swinging interplay of drum tattoos and serpentine alto lines.

Brain Drain is by Blauer Hirsch, Ludi's riposte to the likes of Last Exit. It's a pretty marvellous record:

Gysi and Gerber are in charge of a steadily bubbling volcano of noise, Neumeier provides rather proper drum parts as the anchor, and Ludi just blows his heart out over the top.

Tony Lujan TRUMPET, FLUGELHORN

*** **Magic Circle** Capri 74023-2
　　Lujan; Bob Sheppard (*ss, ts*); George Cables (*p*); John Patitucci (*b*); Tom Brechtlein (*d*). 90.
(*) **Zulu Capri 7441-2
　　Lujan; Rob Lockart (*ts, f*); Kei Akagi (*p*); Ken Filiano (*b*); Billy Mintz (*d*). 1/92.

Lujan plays like the professional that he is – a section player of wide experience, a skilled executant but perhaps not a terribly characterful leader. None of the themes on *Magic Circle* lingers long in the mind, though the improvising includes many handsome and detailed passages from all the players. Sheppard's big, bullying delivery is just right for the front line, and Lujan's long, tight lines and pin-bright tone are impressive. Patitucci, on acoustic bass for once, has a capable feature on 'Space Bass'. At 43 minutes, it's just the right length, too.

　　Zulu is a lot longer, and it lacks the balance of the earlier group: Lockart is merely fast where Sheppard had an underlying concentration. There are some smart variations on a Latin-jazz pulse, but by the time they get to 'Gingerbread Boy' the record seems worn out.

Jimmie Lunceford (1902–47) ALTO SAXOPHONE, BANDLEADER

**** **Jimmie Lunceford 1930–1934** Classics 501
　　Lunceford; Sy Oliver, Eddie Tompkins, Tommy Stevenson, William 'Sleepy' Tomlin (*t*); Henry Wells (*tb, v*); Russell Bowles (*tb*); Willie Smith, Earl Carruthers (*cl, as, bs*); LaForest Dent (*as*); Joe Thomas (*cl, ts*); Edwin Wilcox (*p, cel*); Al Norris (*g*); Moses Allen (*bb, b*); Jimmy Crawford (*d, vib*). 6/30–11/34.
***(*) **Jimmie Lunceford 1934–1935** Classics 505
　　As above, except add Paul Webster (*t*), Elmer Crumbley, Eddie Durham (*tb, g*), Dan Grissom (*cl, as, v*), omit Tomlin. 11/34–9/35.
*** **Jimmie Lunceford 1935–1937** Classics 510
　　As above, except add Ed Brown (*as*), omit Stevenson, Wells. 9/35–6/37.
***(*) **Jimmie Lunceford 1937–1939** Classics 520
　　As above, except add Trummy Young (*tb*), Ted Buckner (*as*). 6/37–1/39.
***(*) **Jimmie Lunceford 1939** Classics 532
　　As above, except omit Durham, add Gerald Wilson (*t*). 1–9/39.
*** **Jimmie Lunceford 1939–1940** Classics 565
　　As above, except add Snooky Young (*t*), The Dandridge Sisters (*v*), omit Tompkins. 12/39–6/40.
(*) **Jimmie Lunceford 1940–1941 Classics 622
　　As above, except omit Dandridge Sisters. 7/40–12/41.

Lunceford's orchestra is doomed always to be remembered behind Ellington and Basie as the great also-ran big band of its day. Part of the reason for that is its sheer class: there were no special idiosyncrasies which lifted the Lunceford orchestra away from the consistent excellence which it aspired to. Its principal arrangers – Sy Oliver in particular, but also Edwin Wilcox (in the earlier days) and Willie Smith – built the section-sounds into superbly polished, interlocking parts which made their records exude a high professional elan. Soloists stepped naturally out of and back into this precision machine, and there was never much danger of a Rex Stewart or a Lester Young breaking any rule. Lunceford's virtues were very different to those of the rough-and-ready (early) Basie band, or to Ellington's unique cast of characters. Still, the records endure very well, even though – as so often with the big bands of the period – the later sides show a dramatic falling-off. The first volume of the Classics chronological survey shows the band coming together – there is a single 1930 session in the discography, followed by an incongruous jump to 1934 – but the important hit coupling of 'Jazznocracy' and 'White Heat' is here, as well as the remarkably nonconformist versions of 'Mood Indigo' and 'Sophisticated Lady'; once under way in earnest, Lunceford turned out some very fine records. The first two CDs feature some of the best of Oliver and Wilcox – there is even the very rare instance of two Ellington compositions, 'Rhapsody Junior' and 'Bird Of Paradise', which were never recorded by Duke, on the 1934–35 disc – and the 1935–37 session includes one of Oliver's masterpieces, the chart for 'Organ Grinder's Swing'. But a certain staleness sets in to the band from about 1936 onwards, with the Lunceford precision taking on a formulaic feel that fast tempos and good soloists – Smith was a rival to Hodges and Carter as one of the great alto stylists of the day, and Joe Thomas and Eddie Tompkins were excellent half-chorus players – never quite overcame.

The band continued to develop in minor ways: new players such as Trummy Young and Snooky Young were given tasks which raise the overall game on several of the tracks. Young's extraordinary playing (and singing) on 'Annie Laurie' and 'Margie' (Classics 520) is enough to make one wonder if this is the same man who was such a dullard with Louis Armstrong's All Stars. Nevertheless, the band's records started to sound as if they were being churned out by the end of 1939, although considered track by track there is still much eloquent and occasionally surprising music here. The departure of first Oliver and then Smith (the latter in 1942, after the last of the records here) was a blow that Lunceford's orchestra never recovered from, though to its last records it still sounds like a skilful band, a tribute to Lunceford's meticulous preparations and admiration for Paul Whiteman. There is some dreary material on the last two discs, particularly the 1940–41 set, but even here there are a couple of interesting arrangements by new arrival Gerald Wilson ('Hi Spook' and 'Yard Dog Mazurka') and the closing two-part 'Blues In The Night', though laden with kitsch, is effective in its way. Overall, on musical standards, we recommend the first two discs as the near-essential Lunceford, with the next three still full of interesting music. Transfers are, as usual from this source, rather variable: some of the earliest sides sound scratchy, and some of the later ones have a reverberant feel which suggests dubbings from tape copies at times. For the most part, though, it's been cleanly done.

**** Stomp It Off MCA GRP 16082
As appropriate discs above. 9/34–5/35.
The start of MCA/Decca's own chronological series of Lunceford reissues. They have to miss out the two 1934 sessions for Victor, but the 21 tracks here (including an alternative take of 'Rhythm Is Our Business') make a strong grouping and the NoNoise restoration has made the music come through very cleanly. A fine way to make Lunceford's acquaintance.

Jan Lundgren (born 1966) PIANO

*** Conclusion Four Leaf Clover FLC CD 136
Lundgren; Jesper Lundgaard (b); Alex Riel (d). 5–6/94.
Lundgren does what he does so well – 'a mainstream modern style', says Bertil Sundin in the sleeve-note – that it seems churlish to criticize an unambitious record. Five engaging originals, four standards and two jazz tunes are wrapped up in just over an hour. Lundgren likes the deftness and clarity of mainstream jazz and just occasionally tosses in an unlikely wrinkle: Elmo Hope's 'So Nice' makes a surprise appearance, and there is a quickfire pirouette through 'Oleo'. Otherwise the pianist makes light of his moods and his inspirations and leaves us pleased if not quite stirred. Lundgaard and Riel, that most reliable of teams, groove knowingly alongside.

Claude Luter (born 1923) CLARINET, SOPRANO SAXOPHONE

*** Red Hot Reeds GHB BCD-219
Luter; Jacques Gauthe (cl, ss); Steve Pistorius, David Boeddinghaus (p); Neil Unterseher (g, bj); Amy Sharpe (bj); Tom Saunders (tba, b); Rick Elmore (tba); Ernie Elly, Dicky Taylor (d). 4/86.
Not much survives of Luter's discography at present but he was one of the leading forces in French traditional jazz for decades, and this 1986 date, co-led with Jacques Gauthe, is more like a postscript to a ubiquitous career. The horns play in a manner that offers an inevitable echo of Luter's records with Sidney Bechet in the 1950s, and the setlist covers Morton, Handy, Bechet and Jimmy Blythe. Recorded on consecutive days in New Orleans, with entirely different accompanists each day, and performed with much brio and enjoyment by the two front-line veterans.

Brian Lynch (born 1955) TRUMPET, FLUGELHORN

***(*) Peer Pressure Criss Cross Criss 1029
Lynch; Ralph Moore (ts); Jim Snidero (as); Kirk Lightsey (p); Jay Anderson (b); Victor Lewis (d). 12/86.
**(*) Back Room Blues Criss Cross Criss 1042
Lynch; Javon Jackson (ts); David Hazeltine (p); Peter Washington (b); Lewis Nash (d). 12/89.
Peer pressure, indeed. One of the occupational horrors of the jazz musician's life is 'going single', travelling from town to town, playing with local rhythm sections. Eric Dolphy suffered profoundly by it, Lee Konitz seems to thrive on it; *Back Room Blues* would seem to put Brian Lynch squarely with the Dolphys. There's nothing amiss about the leader's playing. His bright, brassy sound – particularly vivid

on the often smudgy flugelhorn – is well up to scratch. But the band seems entirely devoid of ideas and the sound might just as well be live.

The line-up on *Peer Pressure* makes weight-for-weight comparison of the two albums as uneven as a Don King boxing bill. Where Jackson is sophomoric, the British-born, Berklee-graduated Ralph Moore is right on the case, responding to Lynch's unpretentious hard bop with a mixture of fire and intelligence. Jim Snidero has less to say but says it with unapologetic verve; his own *Mixed Bag* (Criss Cross Criss 1032 – the label's titles are always curiously self-revealing!) also features Lynch and is worth checking out.

Tommy Turrentine's roistering 'Thomasville' gets everybody in and warmed up for the subtler cadence of Benny Golson's 'Park Avenue Petite'. Horace Silver's 'The Outlaw' gets a slightly camp reading but, apart from the low-key CD bonus, 'I Concentrate On You', the rest of the material is by the trumpeter and is generally very impressive, both in conception and in execution. Amazing what a bit of peer pressure can do.

*** **At The Main Event** Criss Cross Criss 1070
    Lynch; Ralph Moore (*ts*); Mel Rhyne (*org*); Peter Bernstein (*g*); Kenny Washington (*d*); Jose Alexis Diaz (*perc*). 12/91.

A good-hearted, expansive, blowin'-in-from-Milwaukee date, which celebrates local club, The Main Event. There's plenty of playing to enjoy, even if Lynch acts as not much more than the genial host, and the round-robin of solos on the seven tracks elicits nothing knockout from any of the musicians. Mel Rhyne fans may welcome another one of his rare appearances.

Jimmy Lyons (1932–86) ALTO SAXOPHONE, FLUTE

**** **Jump Up** hat Art CD 6139
    Lyons; John Lindberg (*b*); Sunny Murray (*d*). 8/80.
***(*) **Something In Return** Black Saint 120125
    Lyons; Andrew Cyrille (*perc*). 81.
***(*) **Give It Up** Black Saint 120087
    Lyons; Enrico Rava (*t, flhn*); Karen Borca (*bsn*); Jay Oliver (*b*); Paul Murphy (*d*). 3/85.

If Charlie Parker had a true heir – in the sense of someone interested in getting interest on the inheritance, rather than merely preserving the principal – it was Jimmy Lyons. Compared to his light-fingered onrush, most of the bop *epigoni* sound deeply conservative. He didn't have the greatest tone in the world, though it seems rather odd to describe a saxophonist's tone as 'reedy' as if that were an insult. Lyons's delivery was always light and remarkably without ego. Years of playing beside Cecil Taylor, in addition to accelerating his hand-speed, probably encouraged a certain self-effacement as well.

The live session on *Jump Up*, recorded at the 1980 Willisau Festival, is a vintage performance, and one is grateful for a bonus track, 'Tortuga', for which there was no room on the original LP. Murray and Lyons understood each other well, and a lot of the action consists of duets between them, while Lindberg patiently colours in the spaces. The title-track is a little masterpiece.

On *Give It Up*, Lyons seems quite content to remain within the confines of the group. Significantly piano-less and with only a rather secondary role for the bassist and drummer, it resolves into a series of high, intermeshed lines from the saxophone and horn, with the bassoon tracing a sombre counterpoint. Karen Borca's role might have been clearer were she not so close in timbre to Jay Oliver's bass, but it's worth concentrating for a moment on what she is doing; the effect is broadly similar to what Dewey Redman used to do behind Ornette Coleman and Don Cherry; she also appears to great effect on the earlier and deleted *Wee Sneezawee*, which also merits reissue. Only on the brief, uncharacteristic 'Ballada', with which the album ends, does Lyons occupy the foreground. It's immediately clear that his fey, slightly detached tone doesn't entail an absence of feeling; the closing track is a sad monument to an undervalued career that had little more than a year left to run.

Among the most fruitful encounters of Lyons's sadly under-documented career were his duos with Cyrille, a fellow-alumnus of Cecil Taylor Academy. Cyrille is a one-man orchestra, conjuring layered energies that make a sax-and-drums 'Take The "A" Train' seem anything but absurd. One of the great modern drummers, Cyrille can play at astonishing volume (at one point almost sounding as if he were trying to re-create a Cecil Taylor trio *à deux*), but also with considerable subtlety and a user-friendly reliability of beat. 'Exotique', on the later session, is a superbly structured and emotionally committed performance.

Johnny Lytle (1932–96) VIBES

(*) The Loop / New & Groovy BGP CDBGPD 961
> Lytle; unknown *p, b* and *d*. 65.

If there is a classic record by this Ohio-born drummer-turned-vibesman, it's surely *The Village Caller*, where he lives out all the clichés of organ–vibes rhythm combos and delivers a perfectly cooked slice of soul-jazz in the title-tune. But the album, though a Vinyl OJC release some years ago, is still not yet on CD. The BGP CD couples two very rare albums from the same period, originally issued on Tuba with no personnel details, and the music is even slighter (typical titles include 'The Snapper' and 'Screamin' Loud'). The formula wears thin after a number of tracks but, taken a few at a time, they certainly stir the feet. The pianist sounds very like Wynton Kelly here and there, and the remastering is good if a little overbright. Lytle's subsequent Muse albums are awaited on CD, aside from the recent *Moonchild* (Muse MCD 5431), which is scarcely worth bothering with. Nor is the equally feeble *Possum Grease* (Muse MCD 5482). Lytle's passing leaves his status sadly unrealized.

Humphrey Lyttelton (born 1921) TRUMPET, CORNET, CLARINET, VOCAL

*** **Movin' And Groovin'** Black Lion BL 760504
> Lyttelton; Roy Williams (*tb*); Bruce Turner (*as*); Kathy Stobart, John Barnes (*ts, bs*); Mick Pyne (*p*); Dave Green (*b*); Adrian Macintosh (*d*). 1/83.

Broadcaster, quizmaster, media wit and unrivalled keeper of the flame, Lyttelton has secured a place that few trumpeters – few jazz musicians – could aspire to. His purely musical achievements, though, shouldn't be undervalued. In his seventies, he remains a remarkably creative figure, never content with trad or swing clichés and exceptionally aware of the continuing vibrancy of the jazz tradition. Unfortunately, with nothing available of his earlier work on CD, there's a huge gap at present in Humph's discography, and we must hope that the many fine records listed in our first edition will make their way to the current format soon. For now, we have to start with this date, cut at the tail-end of a Black Lion contract. Another bridge between trad ('Basin Street Blues', 'Aunt Hagar's Blues') and mainstream ('Never No Lament', 'One For Buck'), this shows Lyttelton had kept faith with a catholic philosophy which few others – anywhere in the music – have cared to maintain. His own chops also sound little weathered by the years: a bright, middleweight sound, coloured by his affections for players from Armstrong to Clayton.

***(*) **Beano Boogie** Calligraph CLG 021
> Lyttelton; Pete Strange (*tb*); John Barnes (*cl, ss, ts, bs*); Alan Barnes (*cl, ss, as*); Stan Greig (*p*); Paul Bridge (*b*); Adrian Macintosh (*d*). 3/89.

*** **Rock Me Gently** Calligraph CLG 026
> As above, except Kathy Stobart (*cl, ss, ts, bs*) replaces John Barnes, add Dave Cliff (*g*). 7/91.

The formation of Calligraph, his own label, has produced a steady stream of new records from Humph, and they maintain a standard which many jazz musicians should envy. Some fine records from the early 1980s, including *At The Bull's Head* and *Gigs*, have yet to acquire CD transfer, though there may still be some LP stocks in circulation. *Beano Boogie* is notable for the arrival of Alan Barnes whose alto turns add fresh fizz to a well-established front line. Though the record gets off to a slow start, when it reaches 'Apple Honey', a nearly explosive reading of the Woody Herman tune, it lifts off. The elder Barnes departed with *Rock Me Gently*, but Kathy Stobart's return to the fold (35 years after they recorded 'Kath Meets Humph') means there is no drop in authority, and she delivers a grippingly unsentimental version of 'My Funny Valentine' on what's a generously filled CD.

***(*) **At Sundown** Calligraph CLG 027
> Lyttelton; Acker Bilk (*cl, v*); Dave Cliff (*g*); Dave Green (*b*); Bobby Worth (*d*). 1/92.

It seems little short of amazing that these two veterans had never recorded together before, but apparently not! The result is a warmly amiable meeting which holds up throughout CD length. Humph's own interest in the clarinet – there's at least one clarinet feature for him on most of the Calligraphs listed above – makes him a fine match for Bilk here on 'Just A Little While To Stay Here', but it's the easy give-and-take between trumpet and clarinet, over an almost lissom rhythm section, which gives the record its class; even Acker's vocals sound sunny enough, and his clarinet has become as idiosyncratic and engaging as Pee Wee Russell's.

*** **Rent Party** Stomp Off CD1238
> Lyttelton; Keith Nichols (*tb, tba*); John Beecham (*tb*); Wally Fawkes (*cl*); Stan Greig (*p*); Paul Sealey (*bj, g*); Jack Fallon, Annie Hawkins (*b*); Colin Bowden (*d*). 8/91–1/92.

***(*) **Hear Me Talkin' To Ya** Calligraph CLG CD 029
>   Lyttelton; Pete Strange (*tb*); Jimmy Hastings (*cl, as, f*); Kathy Stobart (*cl, ts, bs*); Stan Greig (*p*);
>   Paul Bridge (*b*); Adrian Macintosh (*d*). 5/93.

These bulletins from Humph make a neatly contrasting illustration of the breadth of his interests. *Rent Party* is straight out of the traditional pocket, with ancient material such as 'Texas Moaner' and 'Viper Mad' given a lusty work-out. Fawkes, who goes, as they say, way back with Lyttelton, gets as close to Bechet-like authority as he ever has, and the banjo-driven rhythm sections find the necessary feel without resorting to caricature. *Hear Me Talkin' To Ya* is a pleasing jazz-history lesson, with obscure Ellington (one of Humph's specialities), Carla Bley and Buck Clayton in the set-list as well as carefully revised treatments of 'Beale Street Blues' and 'St James Infirmary'. Jimmy Hastings comes on board for the first time and makes a keen addition to what is now a very commanding front line. The joints may creak a bit here and there, but this is still excellent jazz.

*** **Three In The Morning** Calligraph CLG 30
>   Lyttelton; Acker Bilk (*cl, v*); John Barnes (*cl, as, bs*); Dave Cliff (*g*); Dave Green (*b*); Bobby
>   Worth (*d*). 9/93–4/94.

After-hours with Humph and Acker. The newly established old firm sound fine again here, though the session droops a little in places, possibly because of the absence of the late Bruce Turner, who fell ill before he could play the parts which ultimately fell to John Barnes. As usual, Lyttelton has done some inspired work in choosing material: 'I'd Climb The Highest Mountain', Al Fairweather's 'Ludo' and Ida Cox's 'Last Smile Blues' are among the nuggets that nobody else would have thought of.

Harold Mabern (born 1936) PIANO

*** **Wailin'** Prestige PRCD 24134
>   Mabern; Virgil Jones (*t, flhn*); Lee Morgan (*t*); George Coleman (*ts*); Hubert Laws (*ts, f*);
>   Boogaloo Joe Jones (*g*); Buster Williams (*b*); Idris Muhammad (*d*). 6/69, 1/70.

**** **Straight Street** DIW 608
>   Mabern; Ron Carter (*b*); Jack DeJohnette (*d*). 12/89.

*** **Philadelphia Bound** Sackville SKCD 23051
>   Mabern; Kieran Overs (*b*). 4/91, 2/92.

**** **Lookin' On The Bright Side** DIW 614
>   Mabern; Christian McBride (*b*); Jack DeJohnette (*d*). 2 & 3/93.

*** **The Leading Man** Columbia 477288
>   As above, except add Bill Mobley (*t*); Bill Easley (*as*); Kevin Eubanks (*g*); Ron Carter (*b*). 11/92,
>   1, 3 & 4/93.

There is something about Harold Mabern that just breathes Memphis. Few jazz pianists have come so close to the essence of the blues, yet there is nothing crude or revivalist about his playing, which also indicates a heavy debt to Ahmad Jamal and Phineas Newborn Jr, both pianists who made a distinctive use of space.

Even when Philadelphia bound, as on the duos with that marvellous accompanist, Kieran Overs, he sounds like a man happily locked into his own corner of the world. There is much that can be learnt about Mabern from this record, not least his awesome flexibility and awareness within his chosen stylistic field. Being in Philly (they were actually in Toronto, but the mood-setting number was Ray Bryant's 'Philadelphia Bound'), he touches on Coltrane ('Dear Lord' and 'Lazybird') and plays a solo version of 'The Cry of My People', written by Trane's friend, Cal Massey. There are also two Benny Golson numbers ('Are You Real' and 'Whisper Not') which take him back to the kind of material he was doing a couple of decades earlier.

Wailin' brings together two Prestige sessions from the late 1960s. The electric piano dates it a bit on 'Blues For Phineas'; however, like Kenny Barron, Mabern invests the instrument with a bit of character. *Wailin'* also traces his development as a composer of original themes, still largely blues-based but forward-looking and surprisingly memorable (surprising only in that they seem to be covered so rarely); 'Greasy Kid Stuff' and 'Waltzing Westward' sit up and ask to be played. Morgan is an essential component of the 1970 group and Mabern was to return the compliment in the trumpeter's last group before his untimely death. One of the better tunes on the 1969 record, 'Too Busy Thinking About My Baby', has been held out but is promised on a further compilation, which may well include a greater variety of standards. On OJC, *Rakin' And Scrapin'* hasn't yet made it on to CD.

The DIWs establish Mabern as one of the most imaginative current players of repertoire material. His ability to invest a tune with new lights and shades and to transform relatively banal material into substantial music is deeply impressive. Working with sidemen of the quality of DeJohnette and Carter has undoubtedly made a difference, but on each of these records it is Mabern's commanding voice which makes the final difference. In addition to writing new themes – 'Too Late Fall Back Baby' on *Bright Side*, 'Seminole' and 'Mr Stitt' on *Straight Street* – the pianist has also begun to turn his attention to more recent jazz composition. Both records attest to his interest in John Coltrane, and there is a Wayne Shorter tune (the far from obvious 'Yes Or No'). These are flawless records.

The chap who wrote the sleeve-notes for the Columbia record suggests that Mabern resembles 'an aging offensive lineman', which is apparently a compliment in the United States. We'd suggest that he's much more like a mature dancing master, a little thicker in girth than of yore, but still with that pungently graceful approach to the blues. As we've said, recent years have seen him experiment with more adventurous material, and there are tunes by Wayne Shorter, Parker ('Au Privave'), Wes Montgomery and Coltrane again ('Moment's Notice') on this record. The only drawback to it can be inferred from the session dates. Neither expressively nor acoustically does it hang together as a package. There are effectively two groups represented with a very different stance on the material. No serious problem with this, but it does demand a certain internal readjustment. *The Leading Man* appears as part of Columbia's Legendary Masters of Jazz series. No arguments with that.

Teo Macero (born 1925) TENOR SAXOPHONE

*** **Teo Macero With The Prestige Jazz Quartet** Original Jazz Classics OJC 1715
    Macero; Teddy Charles (*vib*); Mal Waldron (*p*); Addison Farmer (*b*); Jerry Segal (*d*). 4/57.
Prior to his involvement with Third-Stream composition and his long tenure as a record producer for Columbia, Macero made a handful of mildly interesting albums as a saxophonist-leader. As a soloist, he stands as a somewhat pale version of Warne Marsh and, since the music seeks out the off-centre lyricism which suggests Lennie Tristano's groups – they even do a version of Marsh's favourite 'Star Eyes' – the echo at times seems complete. Waldron's typically dark-hearted hard bop strengthens the sound and Charles's quizzical lines add further interest to the five originals, which are unclichéd yet hard to remember. Macero returned to the studios in the 1980s, but the results are already hard to find.

Vanessa Mackness VOICE

***(*) **Respiritus** Incus CD014
    Mackness; John Butcher (*ss, ts*). 4–12/94.
A long-awaited debut from the British improvising vocalist, here with frequent partner Butcher, recorded at two concerts in 1994. This is funny, serious music, and the two musicians strike up a brilliant empathy at many moments. An operatic bark might come from Mackness in response to some entirely different gesture by Butcher, and yet the juxtaposition can sound exactly right. The singer's range is wide, if not quite as awesome as, say, Diamanda Galas's, and it's her acute grasp of dynamics which makes these ten duets sound vital and vivid. Mouth, glottal and dialect effects are used sparingly and effectively. Butcher, in many ways as vocal a performer himself, is sensitive but never submissive in the dialogues. A splendid encounter session.

Fraser MacPherson (1928–93) TENOR SAXOPHONE

*** **Indian Summer** Concord CCD 4224
    MacPherson; Oliver Gannon (*g*); Steve Wallace (*b*); Jake Hanna (*d*). 6/83.
*** **Honey And Spice** Justin Time Just 23
    MacPherson; Oliver Gannon (*g*); Steve Wallace (*b*); John Sumner (*d*). 3/87.
(*) **Encore Justin Time 8420
    As above. 4/90.
He might have been the Canadian Getz, or Sims, or another Lestorian pupil; but Fraser MacPherson's name was seldom kept before the wider jazz public, and his decent, graceful sound and sure-footed delivery must be accounted as merely the work of another accomplished tenorman with a couple of records to his name. Anyone checking him out with no greater expectations will find these records good value. The Concord album is a little more refined in studio terms (there are two other deleted albums on the label) but the Justin Time discs benefit from complete understanding between MacPherson and his rhythm team, and *Honey And Spice*'s considered mixture of ballads and swingers is probably his best memorial.

Peter Madsen PIANO

*** Snuggling Snakes Minor Music 801030
> Madsen; Chris Potter (*as, ts, ss*); Toninha Horta (*g, v*); Anthony Cox (*b*); Lewis Nash (*d*). 12/92.
*** Three Of A Kind Minor Music 801039
> Madsen; Dwayne Dolphin (*b*); Bruce Cox (*d*). 93.
**(*) Three Of A Kind Meets Mr T Minor Music 801043
> As above, except add Stanley Turrentine (*ts*).

Madsen is the kind of piano player who will always get gigs. Tremendously adaptable and eclectic, he sounds quite at ease in a mainstream jazz setting, as in *Three Of A Kind*, can push out the envelope a little bit, as in the more contemporary-sounding 1992 group, or he can function in the avant garde, having recorded with Franklin Kiermyer. Whether one likes the third of these really depends on having or lacking a settled view of Turrentine, who comes in very much like Mr T on *The A Team* and dominates things. Madsen is a forceful enough player and a clear-sighted leader, and he manages to put his personal stamp even on this one. *Snuggling Snakes* is diluted a bit by having Horta on two tracks, but it is still a very effective modern-jazz record and, set alongside the trios, suggests that Madsen is going places as long as he can sustain both strands without compromise.

The Magnolia Jazz Band GROUP

**(*) The Magnolia Jazz Band And Art Hodes Vol. 1 GHB BCD-171
> Jim Borkenhagen (*t*); Jim Klippert (*tb*); Bill Carter (*cl*); Art Hodes (*p*); Danny Ruedger (*bj, v*); Robbie Schlosser (*b*); Jeff Hamilton (*d*). 1/83.
**(*) The Magnolia Jazz Band And Art Hodes Vol. 2 GHB BCD-172
> As above. 1/83.

The Magnolias are from Stanford, California, and they play upright, big-sounding trad, which comes swaggering off this session (somewhat inconveniently split over two CDs). Art Hodes knew them and sat in for this studio date which finds him suitably prominent in the mix and sounding in superior form. The material sticks to familiar staples of the trad book and a few blues and, while it's not hard to live without it, this won't disappoint fans of either Hodes or local American trad. Docked a notch for the singing, which is pretty awful.

Maurice Magnoni TENOR, SOPRANO AND BARITONE SAXOPHONES, BASS CLARINET, FLUTE

** Baby Call Plainisphare PL 1267-48
> Magnoni; Olivier Rogg (*ky*); Dusan Roch (*b*); Marc Erbetta (*d*). 90.
*** L'Etat Des Sons Plainisphare PL 1237-36
> Magnoni; Jan Gordon-Lennox, Carlos Baumann, Daniele Verdesca (*t*); Yves Massy (*tb*); Didier Hatt (*euph*); Pete Ehrnrooth, Philippe Ehinger (*cl*); Maurizio Bionda (*as*); Jacques Demierre (*p*); Pavel Pesta (*b*); Marc Erbetta (*d*). 4/88.
***(*) New York Suite L&R CDLR 45077
> Magnoni; Matthieu Michel, Carlos Baumann, Erik Truffaz (*t, flhn*); Jan Gordon-Lennox (*t, euph, tba*); Pascal Schaer, Robert Morgenthaler (*tb*); Maurizio Bionda (*cl, as*); Antonio De Rosa (*bs*); Pierre-Luc Vallet (*ky*); Olivier Rogg (*p*); Jean-Philippe Zwahlen (*g*); Ivor Malherbe (*b*); Marc Erbetta (*d*); François Bauer (*perc*). 11/92.

Magnoni is an interesting European voice on the saxophone, though it's as a writer that he makes his mark with the two records by L'Etat des Sons, his modestly big band. The eponymous 1988 album sews six themes together into an unbroken piece that runs a few seconds under 60 minutes. Dedicated to Mingus, Ellington and Gil Evans, the music is an eventful collage, strewn with absorbing moments which perhaps never impress as an entire piece. Given the mildly unusual instrumentation, one might expect results more idiosyncratic than the often conventional if well-played modern big-band textures on offer. Magnoni is himself the most vivid improviser, yet on the *New York Suite* he plays a much less substantial instrumental role. This is a better record, though. While it doesn't say very much about New York, the suite has passages of cleverly staged excitement, and the frameworks for soloists in 'Elisabethstreet' and the concluding 'Electric Babyland' have a subtle cumulative power that assists minor if effective players such as Schaer and Bionda. Magnoni aside, Truffaz is otherwise the most capable soloist, but the achievement is in the way the group finesses the scores, delivering a palpable European impression of an outsider's view of America. The rather dry and punchy recording helps further in making an impact.

Baby Call gives Magnoni more space to solo in, but his electric quartet settle for a kind of super-smart fusion that too often falls into rhetoric or chilly modal blowing. Although Rogg has a sensitive touch with the electric keyboards, the brittle sound and meandering themes are less attractive.

Mahavishnu Orchestra GROUP

**** The Inner Mounting Flame Columbia CK 31067
    John McLaughlin; Jan Hammer (*p, syn*); Jerry Goodman (*vn*); Rick Laird (*b*); Billy Cobham (*d*). 71–73.
***(*) Birds Of Fire Columbia 468224
    As above.
*** Between Nothingness And Eternity Columbia 468225
    As above.
** Apocalypse Columbia 467092
    John McLaughlin; Jean-Luc Ponty (*vn*); Gayle Moran (*ky, v*); Carol Shive (*vn, v*); Marsha Westbrook (*vla*); Philip Hirschi (*clo, v*); Ralph Armstrong (*b, v*); Narada Michael Walden (*d*); Michael Gibbs (*arr*); London Symphony Orchestra, Michael Tilson Thomas (cond). 3/74.
** Visions Of The Emerald Beyond Columbia 467904
    John McLaughlin; other personnel unidentified. 75.
*** Best Of The Mahavishnu Orchestra Columbia 468226
    As above.
One of the few jazz-rock bands of the early 1970s whose (early) work is guaranteed to survive, the Mahavishnu Orchestra combined sophisticated time-signatures and chord structures with drum and guitar riffs of surpassing heaviness. Wielding a huge double-neck incorporating 6- and 12-string guitars, McLaughlin produced chains of blistering high notes, influenced by Hendrix and by earlier R&B, but still essentially in a jazz idiom. Less obviously dominant than on *Extrapolation*, McLaughlin works his group collectively, like an orchestra, rather than a theme-and-solo outfit. Billy Cobham's whirlwind drumming was and remains the key to the group's success, underpinning and embellishing McLaughlin's and Hammer's often quite simple lines. His opening press-roll and subsequent accents on (the still incorrectly titled) 'One Word' (*Birds Of Fire*) clear the way for Rick Laird's finest moment on record. Even where he is poorly recorded on the live album, he is still dominant. Goodman came from the American 'progressive' band Flock, and is used largely for embellishment, but his rather scratchy sound contributed a great deal to the overall impact of *Inner Mounting Flame*, still the group's best album, and he has no apparent difficulty playing in 13/8.

The first Mahavishnu album was one of the essential fusion records, largely because it was more generously promoted and more obviously rock-derived than *Extrapolation*. Ironically, just as he was pushing the iconic guitar solo to new heights of amplification and creative abandon, McLaughlin was also working against the dominance of electricity and setting a new standard for 'acoustic' performance. 'Thousand Island Park' and 'Open Country Joy' on *Birds Of Fire* recalls the beautiful acoustic 'A Lotus On Irish Streams' from the first album. They ought to have done more in that vein, and McLaughlin's subsequent work with Shakti strongly suggested that it was far from exhausted. Unfortunately Columbia have not drawn the Great Veil of Kindly Oblivion over the expanded Orchestra's subsequent recordings, *Apocalypse* and *Visions Of The Emerald Beyond*; apart from flashes of quality from replacement violinist Jean-Luc Ponty, these were as drearily directionless as the three quintet albums were forceful, developing the line McLaughlin had begun with *Extrapolation* and *Where Fortune Smiles*. The *Best Of* compilation is, therefore, very nearly that, though most people would have swapped the live tracks for more from *Inner Mounting Flame*.

Kevin Mahogany VOCALS

*** Double Rainbow Enja ENJ 7097
    Mahogany; Ralph Moore (*ts*); Kenny Barron (*p*); Ray Drummond (*b*); Lewis Nash (*d*). 93.
**(*) Songs And Moments Enja ENJ 8072
    Mahogany; Michael Philip Mossman (*t*); Robin Eubanks (*tb*); Arthur Blythe (*as*); Steve Wilson (*as, cl*); Willie Williams (*ts, cl*); Phil Brenner (*ss, af*); Gary Smulyan (*bs, bcl*); John Hicks (*p*); Ray Drummond (*b*); Marvin 'Smitty' Smith (*d*); backing vocalists. 3/94.
What a splendid name for a jazz singer! We'd say the voice was closer to ripe cherry wood, with a bright, slightly splintery grain and the ability to turn to almost anything. Enja obviously consider Mahogany something of a discovery and have thrown some top-ranking players at him. The earlier album is obviously intended as a technical showcase, while the second, with a much bigger orchestra, is more

relaxed and expressive. Ironically, Mahogany is less convincing in the latter mode. Unlike a lot of fast, scatty singers, he does know how to pull down the tempo without sounding flabby; purely as a matter of pacing and balance, however, he does better on the former. The highlights include tongue-twisting versions of Parker's 'Confirmation', 'Dat Dere' and a very moving performance of 'Duke Ellington's Sound Of Love'. He also does a James Baldwin recitation which suggests some more challenging musical areas that he might productively move into.

The next record is fussier and more obviously 'produced', with arrangements that once or twice threaten to swamp even an over-miked singer. It's worth it for 'My Foolish Heart' alone, and the take on both 'Caravan' and the '"A" Train' is joyous and provocative. A precious talent which will be hard to manage, one suspects, in an industry that still has weirdly fixed ideas about what singers are meant to do.

Adam Makowicz (born 1940) PIANO

***(*) **The Solo Album: Adam In Stockholm** Verve 517 888
    Makowicz (*p* solo). 3/86.
*** **Live At Maybeck Recital Hall Series, Volume 24** Concord CCD 4541
    As above. 7/92.
**** **The Music Of Jerome Kern** Concord CCD 4575
    Makowicz; George Mraz (*b*); Alan Dawson (*d*). 9/92.
***(*) **My Favorite Things: The Music Of Richard Rodgers** Concord CCD 4631
    As above. 9/93.
*** **Adam Makowicz / George Mraz: Concord Duo Series – Volume 5** Concord CCD 4597
    Makowicz; George Mraz (*b*). 5/93.

It has become almost a cliché to characterize Adam Makowicz's style as a hybrid of Tatum and Chopin. Technically at least, it's pretty near the mark, and there is a persistent romantic (even tragic) tinge to even his most exuberant playing that makes the parallel with his (adoptive) compatriot a reasonable one. Born in Czechoslovakia, Makowicz studied at the Chopin School of Music in Warsaw and subsequently settled there. His first jazz partnership was with the trumpeter, Tomasz Stańko. Together they explored modal forms and free jazz but, whereas Stańko was a wild, instinctual risk-taker, Makowicz approached the music in a more orderly and conceptual way. In the 1970s he wrote perceptive music criticism while he was working with both Michal Urbaniak and his then wife, Urszula Dudziak, in a number of fusion projects.

It's unfortunate that there should be nothing available from before Makowicz's 46th year. By the time of his solo Verve session, recorded in Sweden (where much of his best work has been done), the pianist had settled into an elegantly stylized manner in which his two great influences have merged. There are moments on 'I Surrender Dear' and 'Body And Soul' when he sounds disconcertingly like Oscar Peterson. The originals, however, are absolutely distinctive and unmistakable. There is nothing essentially 'Polish' or 'Eastern European' about 'Snowflower'. Its harmonic sequence is a familiar enough one; Makowicz brings to it, though, a touch and presence which are very different from what would be expected of an American musician. The same is true even of the opening 'Blues For Stockholm' and 'Scandinavia'.

In the formal surroundings of the Maybeck Hall, his more classical leanings are in greater evidence. He opens, heart on sleeve, with 'Tatum On My Mind' but gives the theme a precise, rather stiff enunciation one hasn't heard in it from him before. The Cole Porter material that makes up the rest of the set has a convincingly *soigné* air but it's sustained too resolutely, and the final couple of numbers are rather dull. Some of this spills over into the duos with Mraz, which again are rather academic, not quite swinging enough to sustain interest over the full stretch. There are, to be sure, very beautiful things, such as the long originals 'Mito', 'Culebra', 'Concordance' and '400 West D-Flat', but much of the rest is a little drab and best sampled in smallish doses.

Mraz sounds a great deal more comfortable in the trio with Dawson. The drummer has an easy-sounding but very exact swing which never lets him down and he gives the familiar material a lot of pep and sparkle which rubs off on Makowicz. We like the Kern selection better. No special reason; it just seems to work more coherently as an album.

Raphe Malik TRUMPET

***(*) **21st Century Texts** FMP CD 43
    Malik; Brian King Nelson (*Cmel*); Glenn Spearman (*ts*); Larry Roland (*b*); Dennis Warren (*d*).
    6/91.

Malik is a sometime Cecil Taylor sideman who has managed to derive something from the pianist's style without being swamped by it. On the only disc so far available, he marshals a tight little posse of like-minded improvisers (Spearman inevitably dominant, as he is wherever he plays) in the sort of session ESP Disk used to have a corner in. Nelson's C-melody sax has a strikingly unfamiliar tonality but, with no piano or guitar as a reference point, it's able to find its own territory, often coming in under Malik in a series of call-and-response passages that are both alien and highly traditional. The sound is pretty good (though the horns all seem to be clustered together) and there is bags of bass, which does the rather anonymous Roland a favour.

Russell Malone (born 1963) GUITAR, VOCAL

*** **Russell Malone** Columbia 472261-2
    Malone; Donald Brown, Harry Connick Jr (*p*); Milt Hinton, Robert Hurst (*b*); Yoron Israel, Shannon Powell (*d*). 8/91–3/92.
*** **Black Butterfly** Columbia 474805-2
    Malone; Gary Motley (*p*); Steve Nelson (*vib*); Paul Keller (*b*); Peter Siers (*d*). 3–4/93.
Malone's career has been abetted by his featuring as a Harry Connick sideman (the pianist returns the favour with a few appearances on the first album), but these two records are slickly achieved through his own virtuosity rather than by any mere association. The first finds him chopping between acoustic and electric; the second is by a tight quartet with Nelson sitting in on two tracks. While neither is any breakthrough for jazz guitar, Malone makes few compromises to anyone's idea of a popular audience. The superfast chops on 'Jingles' (*Black Butterfly*) will impress anybody, and there are some surprising tunes in both programmes: Duke Pearson's 'Gaslight', Georgia Tom Dorsey's 'Precious Lord', Enrico Pieranunzi's 'Dee's Song'. While Malone tends to play entertaining licks rather than congruous solos, it would take a curmudgeon not to enjoy his music.

Junior Mance (born 1928) PIANO

*** **Live At The Village Vanguard** Original Jazz Classics OJC 204
    Mance; Larry Gales (*b*); Ben Riley (*d*). 61.
***(*) **Smokey Blues** JSP CD 219
    Mance; Marty Rivera (*b*); Walter Bolden (*d*). 6/80.
*** **Junior Mance Special** Sackville CD 3043
    Mance (*p* solo). 9/86, 11/88.
***(*) **Softly As In A Morning Sunrise** Enja ENJ 8080
    Mance; Jimmy Woode (*b*); Bobby Durham (*d*). 7/94.
Unmistakable from a random sample of half a dozen bars as a Chicago man, Mance can be a maddeningly predictable player on record, resorting to exactly the figure one expects him to play rather too often to leave any interest for his often adventurous variations and resolutions. That's certainly evident on the live OJC, a rare available example of pre-1980 Mance. It's a notably self-confident performance and it will be obvious to anyone who has hitherto heard only the recent stuff that Mance's expert chops and obvious awareness of the earlier literature did not appear magically on his fiftieth birthday. It's a fairly representative programme, with the favoured 'Smokey Blues' (see below) prominent, and a slot for Basie's '9.20 Special'. There's an immediate lift to the five live tracks on *Special*, recorded at Toronto's intimate and much-documented Café des Copains, which suggests that studio performance really isn't Mance's strong suit. Certainly the opening 'Yancey Special', done on a better-tempered studio piano, is remarkably flat and unvaried; the long interpretations of 'Careless Love', Billy Taylor's 'I Wish I Knew How It Would Feel To Be Free' (a theme familiar to British fans as the sig to a well-known TV movie programme) and Ivory Joe Hunter's 'Since I Lost My Baby I Almost Lost My Mind' are characteristically bluesy but also rather tentative, and it's only among the live tracks – which include 'Blue Monk', Golson's 'Whisper Not' and two Ellington numbers – that Mance really seems to let go, working towards those knotted climaxes for which he is rightly admired.

    Rivera is a bassist who fits snugly into the pianist's conception of how the blues should be played: strongly, but with considerable harmonic subtlety. The trio album is perhaps the best of the recent recordings, despite a rather uncertain sound-mix. Mance's ability to suffuse relatively banal ballad material with genuine blues feeling (a characteristic noted by the late Charles Fox in a typically perceptive liner-note) is nowhere more obvious than on 'Georgia On My Mind', a melody that can sound footling and drab but which acquires something close to grandeur here. Bolden's 'Deep' is basically a feature for the rhythm players and doesn't add very much to the total impact, but the closing 'Ease On Down The Road' and 'Smokey Blues' are authentic Mance performances.

    The recent *Softly* is just about everything one could ask for in a record of this sort (and that is an assessment that also acknowledges its limitations). Mance has predictably become less assertive, more thoughtful, but he is still capable of swinging out on an up-tempo theme. It is just that he takes more care and time over the ballads. The title-track positively sparkles with freshness and optimism. Excellent stuff.

Augusto Mancinelli GUITAR

***(*) **Extreme** Splasc(h) H 303-2
  Mancinelli; Roberto Rossi (*tb, shells*); Valerio Signetto (*cl*); Pietro Tonolo (*ts*); Mario Arcari (*ob*); Giulio Visibelli (*f*); Piero Leveratto (*b*); Tony Oxley (*d*). 10/88–3/90.

A fascinating set which will appeal to anyone interested in improvisation. Mancinelli includes three very precise and hair-fine compositions, 'Poiesis' consisting of 23 sounds and a dodecaphonic series, written for oboe, flute and clarinet and designed to go with a display of electronic art. The other 29 tracks are all free improvisations, some lasting less than a minute, none more than five. Some are guitar solos – Mancinelli uses everything from wide, Frisell-like sweeps to hectic fingerpicking and strangled-tone twangs – while others involve Oxley, Leveratto, Rossi and Arcari (but not Tonolo or Signetto) in various combinations. As fragmented as it all is, the even dynamic of the music binds the various pieces together, and several of the improvisations sound so whole and finished that they might as well be compositions in any case. Mancinelli clearly has a challenging mind, and one hopes there will be much more forthcoming from this source.

Albert Mangelsdorff (born 1928) TROMBONE

***(*) **Purity** Mood 33631
  Mangelsdorff (*tb* solo).
*** **Tension** L + R CDLR 71002
  Mangelsdorff; Gunther Kronberg (*as, bs*); Heinz Sauer (*ts*); Gunter Lenz (*b*); Ralf Hubner (*d*). 7/63.
(*) **Now Jazz Ramwong L + R CDLR 71001
  Mangelsdorff; Heinz Sauer (*ts, ss*); Gunther Kronberg (*as*); Gunter Lenz (*b*); Ralf Hubner (*d*). 6/64.
*** **Room 1220** Konnex LC 8718
  Mangelsdorff; John Surman (*bs*); Eddy Louis (*p, org*); Niels-Henning Orsted-Pedersen (*b*); Daniel Humair (*d*). 10/70.
*** **Live In Tokyo** Enja 2006
  As above, except omit Kronberg. 2/71.
**** **Three Originals: Never Let It End / A Jazz Tune I Hope I Triple Entente** MPS 529090 2CD
  Mangelsdorff; Heinz Sauer (*ts, as*); Wolfgang Dauner (*p*); Gunter Lenz, Eddie Gomez (*b*); Ralf Hubner, Elvin Jones (*d*). 3/70, 8/78, 3/82.
**** **Three Originals: The Wide Point / Trilogue / Albert Live In Montreux** MPS 519 213 2CD
  Mangelsdorff; Palle Danielsson, Jean-François Jenny-Clark, Jaco Pastorius (*b*); Ronald Shannon Jackson, Elvin Jones, Alphonse Mouzon (*d*). 5/75, 11/76, 7/80.
*** **Spontaneous** Enja 2064
  Mangelsdorff; Masahiko Hito (*p, ring modulator*); Peter Warren (*b*); Allen Blairman (*d*).
*** **Internationales Jazzfestival Münster** Tutu 88110
  Mangelsdorff; John Scofield (*g*). 6/88.
*** **Lanaya** Plainisphare CH 1267
  Mangelsdorff; Reto Weber, Nana Twum Knketia, Djamchid Chemirani, Adama Drame (*perc*). 11/93.

The younger Mangelsdorff brother is the virtual inventor of modern German jazz. Only with his post-war recordings is it possible to trace the emergence of a distinctive idiom, rather than a mere copy of British and American models. Even relative to his importance, there is still too little of Mangelsdorff's work available. One of the least egocentric of musicians, Mangelsdorff has been a model proponent of collectivist improvisation, both in smaller units nominally under his leadership and in larger combinations like the Globe Unity Orchestra and the United Jazz and Rock Ensemble, with whom he has produced some of his most striking work. He has worked with everyone from Lee Konitz to Barbara Thompson and Jaco Pastorius, who appears on the middle third of the sets collected on the second set of *Three Originals* listed. Alphonse Mouzon isn't any more likely as a partner, but a relationship forged for the 1976 Berliner Jazztage works suprisingly well. In addition to *Trilogue*, which documents that occasion, *Three Originals* also includes *The Wide Point*, a 1975 trio with Danielsson and Jones, and the later and rather better *Albert Live In Montreux* with Jenny-Clark and Jackson, both of whom are in powerful form on the closing 'Rip Off'.

The highpoint of the other MPS compilation (and what an excellent initiative this was) is the quartet with Wolfgang Dauner, Eddie Gomez and Elvin Jones, in whose company the trombonist sounds confidently swinging and lyrical; the association with Gomez is particularly fruitful and it's a shame there is so little of it. The later trio that recorded *Triple Entente* is rather less inspiring; the early group with Sauer and a German rhythm section is a boilingly fierce outfit which demonstrates Mangelsdorff's early interest in drones, vocalized didjeridu effects interspersed with sweet solo passages of quite unexpected delicacy.

The more aggressive side can be sampled on the 1970 session with Surman, which incidentally offers an interesting sample of the saxophonist's baritone work, before he put it away for its long sabbatical. He isn't playing at full stretch for most of the disc, tending to work in flashes that never seem to go anywhere. Mangelsdorff is more concentrated and constructs a beautifully balanced solo on 'My Kind Of Beauty'.

Whatever the context, Mangelsdorff always manages to sound both absolutely responsive and absolutely himself. The duo with Scofield, which is only part of a live recording from the 1988 Münster junket – a vintage year – works much better than it probably ought to; the version of 'Gray And Visceral' is a good deal more appealing than on Scofield's earlier *Live*.

Even of the much-improved current offering, the unaccompanied *Purity* still stands out. Few trombonists of any period could sustain interest over this length, but Mangelsdorff has such a range at his disposal, from caressing, saxophone-like sounds to hard, blatting snaps and vicious, stiletto-thin harmonics, that it is like listening to a whole group of players. He can also play prettily and with considerable control and sophistication, as he demonstrates on the 1962 session with MJQ-man Lewis, who's one of the great composers in the field.

At the opposite end of the list chronologically is the trombone and percussion project *Lanaya*, admirable evidence that Mangelsdorff is still experimenting, still pushing at the boundaries of what he knows. It is actually worth while listening to this record in the context of the very earliest things, because the basic language hasn't changed a bit, merely the questions that he asks with it. The recording could have been a little more professional, but these are difficult permutations to register exactly, with instruments like zarb and djembe calling for close, accurate studio miking, rather than the haphazard live mix that Plainisphare are offering. Fascinating nonetheless.

Emil Mangelsdorff (born 1925) SAXOPHONES, FLUTE

*** This Side Up L + R 45065

Mangelsdorff; Thilo Wagner (*p*); Gerhard Bitter (*b*); Janusz Stefanski (*d*). 9/92.
***(*) Meditation L + R CDLR 45088

Mangelsdorff; Jo Flinner, Bob Degen (*p*); Attila Zoller (*g*); Gerhard Bitter; Janusz Stefanski (*d*). 6/86, 8/94.

The suppression of jazz in both Germany and Japan before and during the Second World War resulted in a dramatic acceleration of interest as soon as the war ended. In Germany there was a particularly strong underground jazz movement during the war years; Frankfurt was the main centre, a detail which some observers have attributed to its being in the American zone of occupation, though groups like the Hot Club of Frankfurt were active during the war years. Emil Mangelsdorff and his younger brother, Albert, came through in this environment, sharing a broad grounding in the swing movement, followed by rapid exposure to bebop and the beginnings of free jazz. Emil retained more of the earlier style but achieved a highly intelligent synthesis of older and new techniques.

Like Lee Konitz, whom he sometimes resembles, he has a cooler approach than the average bebop player, but he is also capable of sustaining quite extended passages of dissonance, and complex rhythms. The solo tracks on *Meditation*, recorded in Italy as Mangelsdorff approached his seventieth birthday, are squarely in the Konitz mould, without surrendering a scrap of their originality.

Little of Mangelsdorff's recorded output is available (though the recent appearance of material from a Hessischer Rundfunk ensemble makes a welcome difference). Neither of these records offers an entirely rounded picture, though the second does change the picture considerably. The duos with Zoller and the rather anonymous Degen are full of interesting things, and the group-tracks, with their emphasis on flute and soprano saxophone, open up another aspect; but it's the unaccompanied improvisations which catch the attention. As for the other record, the raw lyricism one associates with the younger Mangelsdorff is present in a much-diluted form. Unfortunately, the original material sounds like any one of an identikit procession of European mavericks. A pity; the earlier records really are much better.

Chuck Mangione (born 1940) TRUMPET, FLUGELHORN

*** **Hey Baby!** Original Jazz Classics OJC 668
>   Mangione; Sal Nistico (*ts*); Gap Mangione (*p*); Steve Davis (*b*); Roy McCurdy (*d*). 3/61.

*** **Spring Fever** Original Jazz Classics OJC 767
>   As above, except Frank Pullara (*b*) and Vinnie Ruggieri (*d*) replace Davis and McCurdy. 11/61.

(*) **Recuerdo Original Jazz Classics OJC 495
>   Mangione; Joe Romano (*ts*); Wynton Kelly (*p*); Sam Jones (*b*); Louis Hayes (*d*). 7/62.

** **Love Notes** Columbia FC 38101
>   Mangione; Chris Vadala (*ss, ts, f, picc*); Peter Harris (*g*); Gordon Johnson (*b*); Everett Silver (*d*). 82.

Mangione worked his way out of small-time hard bop to big-band section-playing before settling for easy-listening jazz with a series of hugely successful albums in the 1970s (*Feels So Good* sold in the millions). None of this later music is worth listing here, although it's no more offensive than a typical lite fusion date of today; *Love Notes* is still in American print for the curious. Back at the beginning, though, are some serviceable (and sometimes excitable) sessions for Riverside, now back in the racks as OJC reissues. The two albums with brother Gap offer a genial reworking of some of the boppish trends of the day, but in each case the album is stolen from under the brothers' noses by Sal Nistico, whose tenor tear-ups are just the kind of thing he would do with Woody Herman on some of the best of Herman's '60s dates. A similar situation occurs on the pick-up date, *Recuerdo*, where Joe Romano's irascible solos undercut Mangione's efforts at fronting the action. The leader has a rather thin tone on trumpet, which hints at why he later switched to flugelhorn as his sole instrument; but his best solos are bright enough.

Manhattan Jazz Quintet GROUP

*** **Manhattan Jazz Quintet** Paddle Wheel K28P 6313
>   Lew Soloff (*t*); George Young (*ts*); David Matthews (*p*); Eddie Gomez (*b*); Steve Gadd (*d*). 7/84.

*** **Autumn Leaves** Paddle Wheel K28P 6350
>   As above. 3/85.

*** **My Funny Valentine** Paddle Wheel K28P 6410
>   As above. 11/85.

*** **Live At Pit Inn** Paddle Wheel K28P 6429/30 2CD/2LP
>   As above. 4/86.

*** **The Sidewinder** Paddle Wheel K28P 6452
>   As above. 10/86.

*** **My Favourite Things** Paddle Wheel K28P 6465
>   As above. 4/87.

*** **Plays Blue Note** Paddle Wheel K28P 6480
>   As above, except John Patitucci (*b*) and Dave Weckl (*d*) replace Gomez and Gadd. 1/88.

*** **Caravan** Paddle Wheel 292 E 6002
>   As above. 12/88.

*** **Face To Face** Paddle Wheel 292 E 6032
>   As above. 5/88–3/89.

It may seem over-cautious to award the above records with an identical rating throughout, but such is the consistency of this studio-supergroup that there genuinely is almost nothing to choose among the discs on overall merit. This brand of contemporary jazz is of a sort that creates a love-it-or-hate-it polarity among listeners: the quintet plays a perfectionist hard bop, seamless in its arrangements – rhythmic, harmonic or merely structural – and flawless in its pacing and solo contributions. Whether this strikes one as exciting or tediously conformist will depend upon one's own tastes. There is no edge-of-the-seat excitement such as one might get from a vintage Jazz Messengers record: all here is polish and control. But the skin-tight virtuosity of the band offers its own rewards: there's none of the empty showmanship that often turns up in fusion, and the variations of approach often display a more inquiring bent than many a more 'authentic' hard-bop session.

Although he provides the group arrangements, Matthews is the weak link as a player, his piano parts a characterless blend of hard-bop references. Soloff and Young, though, are consistently enterprising and graceful, the trumpeter a lean, affable soloist, the tenorman a prodigious aggressor who can turn surprisingly harsh when he wants to. Gomez and Gadd play with magisterial authority, as befits their status as pros' pros, and, while their precision tends to streamline rather than propel the horns, it creates the kind of blue-chip ambience which acts as context. Patitucci and Weckl, their replacements on the later records, are a little less interesting but, as the other three have grown even more confident, one scarcely notices.

Most of the music is drawn from the familiar hard-bop repertoire, with only a handful of Matthews originals spread through the records. The live double-set is no less polished than the studio material, although a little more elongated. *Plays Blue Note* offers the band exploring the repertory of the most famous of hard-bop labels, and it's gratifying to note that they choose less obvious tunes, such as 'Cleopatra's Dream' and 'Cheese Cake'. The part-live, part-studio *Face To Face* is a strong introduction to the current edition of the band, with a powerfully sustained version of 'Moanin'', while the six pieces on *Autumn Leaves* characterize the earlier group with perhaps the best distinction. All the discs are recorded with sometimes glaring digital clarity.

(*) **Manhattan Blues Sweet Basil 660.55.001
Lew Soloff (*t*); George Young (*ts*); David Matthews (*p*); John Scofield (*g*); Eddie Gomez (*b*); Steve Gadd (*d*). 2/90.
Billed as a reunion of the original band, with Scofield guesting on three tracks to add a little fresh flavour, the MJQ carry on as if nothing had intervened. Scofield's wry solos on 'Blues March' and 'St Louis Blues' inculcate a little hip insouciance into the music, but otherwise it is the same brew as before. In the pantheon of MJQ albums, though, it's a low-level achievement: most of the tunes are taken too easy.

Manhattan New Music Project GROUP

*** **Mood Swing** Soul Note 121207
Jack Walrath (*t, flhn*); Ron Tooley (*t*); Tom Varner (*frhn*); David Taylor (*btb, tba*); Bruce Williamson (*as, f, cl, bcl*); Chuck Clark (*ss, ts, f*); Tim Reis (*bs*); Neal Kirkwood (*p*); Paul Nash (*g*); Jeffrey Carney (*b*); Jamey Haddad (*d*). 9/92.
Directed by guitarist Nash, the Project is a tightly marshalled, rather wry and tongue-in-cheek outfit, as one would expect with prankster Walrath in the front row. Not to be confused with the Manhattan Project *tout court*, this outfit makes a little more of the reference to America's A-bomb programme, blasting out megaton arrangements that always suggest a much bigger band. In part, the intention is to highlight each of the main soloists, with Walrath prominent on his own 'Depressions of Eastern Europe', Nash on the weird 'Queen Of Din's New Religion' and 'Shadow', Varner on 'Shovel Man'. *Mood Swing* is the perfect title, because there is no real continuity from one track to the next and it's a record probably best sampled a track at a time, on a whim and as mood dictates.

Herbie Mann (born 1930) FLUTE, ALTO FLUTE, SAXOPHONE

*** **Flamingo: Volume 2** Bethlehem BET 6007
Mann; Joe Puma (*g*); Charles Andrus (*b*); Harold Cranowsky (*d*). 6/55.
*** **Herbie Mann With The Sam Most Quintet** Bethlehem BET 6008
Mann; Sam Most (*f*); Joe Puma (*g*); Jimmy Gannon (*b*); Lee Kleimann (*d*). 10/55.
(*) **Love And The Weather Bethlehem BET 6009
Mann; Joe Puma (*g*); Milt Hinton, Whitney Mitchell (*b*); Herb Wassermann (*d*); strings. 3/56.
***(*) **Herbie Mann Plays** Bethlehem BET 6010
Mann; Joe Puma, Benny Weeks (*g*); Keith Hodgson, Whitney Mitchell (*b*); Lee Rockey, Herb Wassermann (*d*). 12/54, 56.
*** **The Epitome Of Jazz** Bethlehem BET 6011
As above four items.
Mann occupies a similar position to Charles Lloyd in recent jazz history. Influential, but cursed by commercial success and an unfashionable choice of instrument, both have been subject to knee-jerk critical put-down. Where Lloyd's flute was his 'double', Mann's concentration slowly evolved a powerful and adaptable technique which gave him access to virtually every mood from a breathy etherealism, down through a smooth, semi-vocalized tone that sounded remarkably like clarinet (his first instrument), to a tough, metallic ring that ideally suited the funk contexts he explored in the late 1960s.

The best news for Mann fans since our last edition is the return of these early recordings for Bethlehem, It is a little hard to draw exact distinctions between them. Mann has not yet devised his favourite flute-plus-vibes sound and relies on Puma's softly ringing guitar to temper his own whistly, almost reed-like sound, most obviously on *Flamingo*, whose first volume doesn't seem to have made it back from the void. The two-flute front line of the record with Most is quite attractive, though it is clear which of the two has all the ideas. *Love And The Weather* calls for sou'westers and gumboots, and undoubtedly the best is the plain-spoken *Plays*, which puts the emphasis on Mann's attempts to adapt stray elements of contemporary idiom to a smoothed-out and mellifluous context. *Epitome* is useful as a sampler for this period.

*** **Flute Soufflé** Original Jazz Classics OJC 760
> Mann; Bobby Jaspar (*f, ts*); Tommy Flanagan (*p*); Joe Puma (*g*); Wendell Marshall (*b*); Bobby Donaldson (*d*). 3/57.

***(*) **Yardbird Suite** Savoy SV 0193
> Mann; Phil Woods (*as*); Eddie Costa (*vib*); Joe Puma (*g*); Wendell Marshall (*b*); Bobby Donaldson (*d*). 5/57.

*** **The Jazz We Heard Last Summer** Savoy SV 0228
> As above, except replace Marshall and Donaldson with Wilbur Ware (*b*), Jerry Segal (*d*). 5/57.

***(*) **At The Village Gate** Atlantic 7567 81350
> Mann; Hagood Hardy (*vib*); Ahmed Abdul-Malik (*b*); Rudy Collins (*d*); Chief Bey, Ray Mantilla (*perc*). 11/61.

*** **Memphis Underground** Atlantic 7567 81364
> Mann; Roy Ayers (*vib, perc*); Bobby Emmons (*org*); Larry Coryell, Sonny Sharrock, Reggie Young (*g*); Bobby Wood (*p, electric p*); Tommy Coghill, Mike Leach, Miroslav Vitous (*b*); Gene Christman (*d*). 68.

*** **The Best Of Herbie Mann** Atlantic 7567 81369
> Mann; Marky Markowitz, Joe Newman (*t*); Jack Hitchcock, Mark Weinstein (*tb*); Quentin Jackson (*tb, btb*); King Curtis (*ts*); Pepper Adams (*bs*); Chick Corea, Charlie Palmieri, Bobby Wood (*p*); Bobby Emmons (*org*); Larry Coryell, Al Gorgoni, Charlie Macey, Sonny Sharrock (*g*); Roy Ayers, Hagood Hardy, Dave Pike (*vib*); Tommy Coghill, Juan Garcia, Mike Leach, Joe Macko, Ahmed Abdul-Malik, Knobby Totah, Ben Tucker (*b*); Bruno Carr, Gene Christman, Rudy Collins, Pretty Purdie (*d*); Chief Bey, Ray Mantilla, Warren Smith, Carlos Valdez (*perc*); Tamiko Jones (*v*). 4/61–8/68.

Flute Soufflé is unusual in not having a vibes player on the strength. Mann found that soft metallic chime an ideal complement to the flute and, for the most part, one would have to agree with him. Flanagan does a similar job on the early disc, moving out into pentatonic scales on 'Tel Aviv', pattering through 'Let's March' and controlling the tempo on 'Chasing The Bird', obliging his colleagues to bring the beat back a notch in the last chorus. The Parker material on *Yardbird Suite* reveals Mann to be, at best, a second-string bebopper. There is no doubting his capacity to work at these speeds and in the music's complex harmonic dialact. It simply isn't, as they say, where he's at. The live performances on the early Atlantic are much more what we've come to expect of the flautist and, all prejudice aside, they're jolly good. His reading of 'Summertime' echoes some of Coltrane's trills and grace notes, and there are some telling moments on 'It Ain't Necessarily So'. Have a good look at the line-ups. Mann was playing with some interesting people. The association with Woods was as uncertain in its way as the rather crowded front line on *Soufflé*, and things go better when they move aside for one another. Hardy and Abdul-Malik are both interesting players – a pity the bassist wasn't persuaded to bring along his *oud* – and the vibist is clued in to this music in a way that Roy Ayers never was.

Though most of the Atlantics remain out of catalogue, the perennial *Memphis Underground*, one of the founding documents of the fusion movement, has made a successful transfer to CD. Though the recording quality would scarcely pass current muster, the music has survived unexpectedly well. The interplay of three guitarists, notably the Cain and Abel opposition of Sonny Sharrock and Larry Coryell, gives it a flavour that from moment to moment gives off a whiff of Ornette Coleman's *Prime Time*; the addition of Roy Ayers's vibes and Bobby Emmons's organ gives the backgrounds a seething quality that adds depth to Mann's slightly unemotional virtuosity. The presence of one-time Weather Report bassist, Miroslav Vitous, on a single track, the excellent 'Hold On, I'm Comin'', may also attract notice. Head and shoulders with Lloyd above most of the crossover experimenters of the time, Mann deserves to be heard, and it's a pity there isn't more around. A solitary example of his earlier approach, in the 'Californians' band that included Jack Sheldon, Jimmy Rowles and Mel Lewis, can be found on the compilation *Blues For Tomorrow* (Original Jazz Classics OJC 030 2LP). Otherwise, it's the second-hand racks.

*** **Caminho De Casa** Chesky JD 40
> Mann; Eduardo Simon or Mark Soskin (*p*); Romero Lubambo (*g*); Paul Socolow (*b*); Ricky Sebastian (*d*); Cafe (*perc*). 3/90.

Mann calls his current bossa-influenced band Jasil Brazz; fortunately the synthesis is slightly more elegant than the nomenclature. Like Gato Barbieri's more obviously Latin 'Chapters', this is pan-American music with a vigorous improvisational component, not just a collection of exotic 'stylings'. Guitarist Lubambo is particularly impressive, but it's the drummer who keeps the music rooted in jazz tradition, leaving most of the colour work to percussionist Cafe. Mann himself is in fine voice, particularly on the beautifully toned alto flute. Only one of the nine tracks – the rather weak 'Yesterday's Kisses' – is credited to him; the rest are substantial enough. Recommended.

** **Opalescence** Kokopelli KOKO 1298
    Mann; Mark Soskin (*ky*); Robben Ford, Romero Lubambo, Ricardo Silveira (*g*); Paul Socolow (*b*); Cyro Baptista (*perc*). 91.
(*) **Deep Pocket Kokopelli KOKO 1296
    Mann; David 'Fathead' Newman (*ts*); Les McCann (*p, v*); Richard Tee (*p, org*); Cornell Dupree (*g*); Chuck Rainey (*b*); Buddy Williams (*d, perc*). 4, 5 & 7/92.

These are for the most part drab slices of Latinized fusion, played with absolute authority and professionalism but lacking more than an occasional spark of imaginative improvisation. Most of these, to be fair, come from Mann himself, who does still occasionally throw in an unexpected element, as in his response to Newman on 'Moanin''. But such moments are too rare and widely spaced out for most needs.

Shelly Manne (1920–84) DRUMS

***(*) **Deep People** Savoy SV 0186
    Manne; Conte Candoli, Shorty Rogers (*t*); Bill Russo (*tb*); Art Pepper (*as*); Bob Cooper, Jimmy Giuffre (*ts*); Bob Gordon (*bs*); Gene Esposito, Frank Patchen (*p*); Don Bagley, Joe Mondragon (*b*). 11/51, 1/52.
***(*) **The Three And The Two** Original Jazz Classics OJC 172
    Manne; Shorty Rogers (*t*); Jimmy Giuffre (*cl, ts, bs*); Russ Freeman (*d*). 9/54.
*** **The West Coast Sound** Original Jazz Classics OJC 152
    Manne; Bob Enevoldsen (*vtb*); Joe Maini (*as*); Bob Cooper (*ts*); Jimmy Giuffre (*bs*); Russ Freeman (*p*); Ralph Pena (*b*). 9/55.

One of the finest – and shrewdest – musicians in modern jazz, Manne is also one of the most fully documented, playing with everyone from Charlie Parker and Coleman Hawkins to modernists like Ornette Coleman. (A useful wrong-footer for a jazz Trivial Pursuit is: Who played drums on *Tomorrow Is The Question*? Answer on OJC 342.) He combines the classic qualities of reliability and adaptable time with a much more inventive side that has more to do with the *sound* of the drums, an ability to play melodically, than with self-conscious fractures and complications of the basic four-in-a-bar. In the same way, Manne's solos could hardly have been more different from those of important predecessors like Gene Krupa. Where Krupa made the drummer a 'high-price guy', giving him a prominence from which Manne benefited, Manne draws attention to himself not by showmanship but by the sophistication of his playing.

The early material on Savoy – the album is shared with trombonist Bill Russo's lush orchestra – is only early in the sense of being earliest currently available. Unlike Krupa again, Manne was a relatively slow developer. By this point in his life he sounds completely poised and mature and a fascinating writer. The opening 'Princess Of Evil' is a *tour de force* and the writing for Russo on the big-band tracks is thoughtful, idiomatic and quite unlike by-the-yard West Coast jazz.

The trios with Rogers and Giuffre find the players working in parallel, not in a horns-and-rhythm hierarchy. On 'Flip', Manne plays in counterpoint with his colleagues. On 'Autumn In New York', the horns diverge almost entirely, giving the standard the same rather abstract feel that pianist Freeman brings to a notably unsentimental duo reading of 'With A Song In My Heart'. 'Three In A Row' is an experiment in serial jazz, giving a tone-row the same status as a 'head' or standard. Cool and almost disengaged it may be, but it's also compellingly inventive.

The duos with Freeman have survived rather less well, but broadly the same instincts are at work. On 'The Sound Effects Manne', Freeman plays a sharply percussive line alongside Manne's 'theme statement'. 'Billie's Bounce' is compact, bluesy and very intense. Strongly recommended.

The mid-1950s saw Manne turning his back slightly on the experimentalism still evident on *The West Coast Sound* in favour of a more direct idiom which nevertheless incorporated quietly subversive harmonic devices and a much enhanced role for the drummer. The material may be interesting, but there's that almost academic quality to the delivery which one associates with some of Giuffre's work of the time. 'Grasshopper' and 'Spring Is Here' are worth the money on their own, though.

*** **More Swinging Sounds** Original Jazz Classics OJC 320
    Manne; Stu Williamson (*t, vtb*); Charlie Mariano (*as*); Russ Freeman (*p*); Leroy Vinnegar (*b*). 7 & 8/56.

'More' just about covers it. This has the slightly anonymous, kit-built feel of a hundred contemporary West Coast discs. The playing is fine, of course, and Williamson's valve trombone mixes richly with Mariano's more acid saxophone tonality to create an attractive sweet-and-sour front line on 'Quartet'.

The remaining material is less distinctive. Like Rogers, Williamson wasn't an agile and virtuosic player so much as a tasteful colourman with a good sense of the broader structure. Manne shows no signs of wanting to go further in the direction of polyrhythms than he had previously, but he is unmistakably calling the shots, and the shots are by no means routine.

***(*) **Shelly Manne And His Friends: Volume 1** Original Jazz Classics OJC 240
    Manne; André Previn (*p*); Leroy Vinnegar (*b*). 2/56.
***(*) **My Fair Lady** Original Jazz Classics OJC 336
    As above. 8/56.
***(*) **My Fair Lady / West Side Story** Contemporary CDCOPCD 942
    As above. 8/56.
The first and probably the best of these Contemporary reissues (now on OJC) establishes firmly what a fine trio this was. The two-piano *Double Play*, co-led by André Previn and Russ Freeman, with Manne on drums, and also on OJC, is well worth catching, as are Previn's *West Side Story* covers, now reissued as a twofer with Manne's outwardly less promising *My Fair Lady*. It has taken on a life of its own. The Original Master Recording CD was, inevitably, preferred when there was only a vinyl option, but the bonus of the Previn tracks could outweigh the slightly less vivid sound on the Contemporary double-set. Manne's handling of 'Get Me To The Church On Time' and the surprisingly swinging 'I Could Have Danced All Night' is no surprise, but he works a kind of magic on 'Ascot Gavotte', and the reading of the standard 'I've Grown Accustomed To Her Face' is exemplary.

    **** **At The Blackhawk** Original Jazz Classics OJC 656–660 5CD (separately available)
    Manne; Joe Gordon (*t*); Richie Kamuca (*ts*); Victor Feldman (*p*); Monty Budwig (*b*). 9/59.
One of the finest and swingingest mainstream recordings ever made, *At The Blackhawk* benefits immeasurably from CD transfer. Feldman's slightly dark piano sound is lightened, Gordon and Kamuca lose a little of the crackle round the edges, and Budwig reappears out of the vinyl gloom. From the opening 'Our Delight' to the previously unissued material on Volume Five, and taking in a definitive performance of Golson's 'Whisper Not' along the way, this is club jazz at its very best. 'A Gem From Tiffany', heard on *Swinging Sounds*, above, had become Manne's signature theme and is rather indifferently played and repeated. Otherwise, everything sounds as fresh as paint, even the previously rejected 'Wonder Why' and 'Eclipse In Spain'. Utterly enjoyable . . . nay, essential.

**** **Live At The Manne Hole, Volume 1** Original Jazz Classics OJC 714
    Manne; Conte Candoli (*t*); Richie Kamuca (*ts*); Russ Freeman (*p*); Chuck Berghofer (*b*). 5/61.
***(*) **Live At The Manne Hole, Volume 2** Original Jazz Classics OJC 715
    As above. 5/61.
Nothing matches up to the Black Hawk sessions, but these come pretty close, confirming past doubt Manne's quality and staying power in the toughest gig of all, regular club work. This was his home turf, the joint he opened a year earlier as a hedge against failing chops and capricious bookers. That may be why he sounds more relaxed, even a little lazy, breaking out of a pleasant reverie only for one or two rather contrived solos. Again, though, as with the similar band on *Jazz Gunn*, below, it's the quality of the group as a whole that registers. Even on warhorses like 'Softly As In A Morning Sunrise' (*Volume 1*) and 'Green Dolphin Street' (the sequel), they have original and incisive points to make. Both discs have a place on the shelf alongside the Black Hawk stuff.

*** **2-3-4** Impulse! GRP 11492
    Manne; Coleman Hawkins (*ts*); Hank Jones (*p*); Eddie Costa (*p, vib*); George Duvivier (*b*). 2/62.
A magisterial encounter between the great tenorist and the most adaptable drummer on the scene. They do 'Me And Some Drums' as a duo, and Bean appears again on 'Take The "A" Train', 'Cherokee' and 'Avalon'. The only other tracks are trios with Costa and Duvivier, and these are essentially spot features for Manne, playing with a soft insistence that makes you realize there really was an Impulse! house style for recording drummers, up close and generously miked.

***(*) **Jazz Gunn** Atlantic 7567 82271
    Manne; Conte Candoli (*t, flhn*); Frank Strozier (*ts, f*); Mike Wofford (*p*); Monty Budwig (*b*). 6/67.
Dah dah dah-dah dit dah, dah dah dah-dah dit dah. Manne's version of 'Peter Gunn' is the kind of thing you whistle all day. This was a fine group, with a much more acute approach than the 'West Coast' line-up might at first glance suggest. Candoli in particular gets his jacket off and works up something of a lather. It's a very mixed book they work through and Wofford keeps the changes very tight and exact, just now and again over-elaborating the codas as if he's unwilling to let them go. Manne is not well recorded (Atlantic had problems with drummers) and sounds very muffled down at the bass end.

Ironically, he isn't playing at full stretch, but it's the quality of the band as a whole that puts this one in the play-offs.

***(*) **Alive In London** Original Jazz Classics OJC 773
> Manne; Gary Barone (*t, flhn*); John Gross (*ts*); Mike Wofford (*p*); John Morrell (*g*); Roland Haynes (*d*). 7/70.

Recorded during a fondly remembered residency at Ronnie Scott's club, this saw Manne experimenting in a slightly freer idiom, relaxing the usually watertight rhythms, exploring areas of pure sound. With the exception of Wofford (who plays an electric instrument throughout), the band are not particularly well known, but they play with great vigour and application, and Manne's original production job gives them all a decent representation. A branch line, perhaps, in view of what went before and what ensued, but an interesting and thoroughly enjoyable set nevertheless.

Wingy Manone (1900–82) TRUMPET, CORNET, VOCAL

(*) **The Wingy Manone Collection Vol. 1 1927–1930 Collector's Classics COCD-3
> Manone; Bob Price, Ed Camden (*t*); Orville Haynes (*tb*); Hal Jordy (*cl, as*); Wade Foster, Benny Goodman, Frank Teschemacher, George Walters (*cl*); Bob Sacks, Bud Freeman, George Snurpus, Joe Dunn (*ts*); Frank Melrose (*p, acc*); Johnny Miller, Jack Gardner, Art Hodes, Joe Sullivan, Maynard Spencer (*p*); Steve Brou, Ray Biondi (*g*); Miff Frink (*bj, tb*); Herman Foster (*bj*); Arnold Loyacano, Orville Haynes (*b*); John Ryan, Gene Krupa, Augie Schellange, Bob Conselman, Dash Burkis, George Wettling (*d*); Earl Warner (*v*). 4/27–9/30.

***(*) **The Wingy Manone Collection Vol. 2 1934** Collector's Classics COCD-4
> Manone; George Brunies, Santo Pecora, Dicky Wells (*tb*); Matty Matlock, Sidney Arodin (*cl*); Eddie Miller, Bud Freeman (*ts*); Gil Bowers, Jelly Roll Morton, Teddy Wilson, Terry Shand (*p*); Nappy Lamare (*g, v*); Frank Victor (*g*); Harry Goodman, John Kirby, Benny Pottle (*b*); Ray Bauduc, Bob White, Kaiser Marshall (*d*). 5–9/34.

*** **The Wingy Manone Collection Vol. 3 1934–1935** Collector's Classics COCD-5
> Manone; Russ Case, Phil Capicotta, Harry Gluck (*t*); Santo Pecora, Will Bradley, Charlie Butterfield (*tb*); Toots Mondello, Sid Trucker (*cl, as*); Matty Matlock, Sidney Arodin (*cl*); Eddie Miller (*cl, ts*); Arthur Rollini, Paul Ricci (*ts*); Terry Shand, Gil Blowers, Claude Thornhill (*p*); Joe Venuti, Nick Pisani, Tony Alongi (*vn*); Nappy Lamare (*g, v*); Jimmy Lewis (*g*); Benny Pottle, Harry Goodman, Charlie Barber (*b*); Bob White, Ray Bauduc, Chauncey Morehouse (*d*). 10/34–5/35.

Joseph Manone – the 'Wingy' came from his missing arm which he lost in a streetcar accident – was a New Orleans man, much in thrall to Louis Armstrong as both trumpeter and vocalist, and the leader of a great stack of records made in the 1930s. These three CDs take his story up to the beginning of his contract with Bluebird, which unfortunately isn't represented on CD at present. The first disc is very rough-and-ready, with the small groups offering glimpses of precocious youngsters such as Bud Freeman, Benny Goodman and Gene Krupa, yet stumbling on the scrappy recording quality, off-the-peg arrangements and other, second-rate sidemen. For those whose taste runs to the offbeat music of the day, this is worthwhile – it also features the famous first appearance of the 'In The Mood' riff on 'Tar Paper Stomp' – but non-specialists should start with the fine second record. Manone's derivative playing has grown in stature, his singing has a hip, fast-talking swagger about it, and the bands – with Miller, Matlock, Brunies and the excellent Arodin extensively featured – set a useful standard of small-group playing in the immediate pre-swing era. One remarkable session even has Teddy Wilson and Jelly Roll Morton sharing keyboard duties.

Volume Three has three more sessions in the same mode before the one that produced 'The Isle Of Capri', Wingy's big hit. By this time the run of material was shifting away from jazz and into novelty pop, and it's ironic that Manone's 'Capri' vocal sent up the genre, only to secure a hit (a previously unissued non-vocal version is also included). Even so, the group often mustered a surprisingly hard-bitten treatment on a tune such as 'March Winds And April Showers'. The transfers throughout are lifelike and vivid: some scratch, and some of the early records (from Champion and Gennett masters) will always sound harsh, but otherwise entirely listenable. True to form, the Classics label has commenced its own survey of Manone material, which more or less follows the same sequence as these discs. Transfers, from unlisted sources, are certainly no improvement on these, and there seems little reason for this sequence to be displaced.

** **Trumpet Jive!** Prestige PCD-24119-2
> Manone; Ward Silloway, Frank Orchard (*tb*); Joe Marsala, Hank D'Amico (*cl*); Nick Ciazza (*ts*); Conrad Lanoue, Dave Bowman (*p*); Chuck Wayne (*g*); Irv Lang, Bob Haggart (*b*); George Wettling (*d*). 12/44–7/45.

Wingy shares this record with a couple of Rex Stewart sessions. His eight titles aren't up to much: feeble novelty material ('Where Can I Find A Cherry?' is pretty lamentable) and scruffy recording. But when the band starts to swing, they manage to squeeze some life out of the situation, and Joe Marsala especially is always worth hearing.

Ray Mantilla PERCUSSION

*** **Synergy** Red 123198
>Mantilla; Dick Oatts (*sax, f*); Steve Grossman (*ts*); Eddie Martinez (*p*); Guillermo Edgehill (*b*); Steve Berrios (*d, perc*); Vivien Ara Martinez (*v*). 2/86.
*** **Dark Powers** Red 123221
>Mantilla; Bobby Watson (*as*); Dick Oatts (*ts, ss, f*); Eddie Martinez (*p*); Ruben Rodriguez (*b*); Steve Berrios (*d, perc*); Vivien Ara Martinez (*v*). 2/88.

Mantilla is a fine percussionist who has worked with Art Blakey, Herbie Mann, Richie Cole, and as a member of Max Roach's M'Boom. His own records with Space Station are a mixture of Latinized bebop (in the line of Parker's south of the border recordings) and a smoother, more impressionistic approach. *Synergy* is well crafted and acutely played. There is no mistaking the change in quality when guest star Grossman is playing, as he does on 'Star Eyes', Monk's 'Eronel' and pianist Martinez's rather catchy original, 'Laye'.

Karen Mantler HARMONICA, ORGAN, VOICE

(*) **My Cat Arnold XtraWatt 3
>Mantler; Steven Bernstein (*t*); Pablo Calogero (*bs, f*); Marc Muller (*g*); Steve Weisberg (*ky, syn*); Jonathan Sanborn (*b*); Ethan Winogrand (*d*); Eric Mingus (*v*). Spring 88.
*** **Karen Mantler And Her Cat Arnold Get The Flu** XtraWatt 5
>As above, except add Michael Mantler (*t*); Steve Swallow (*flhn*); Carla Bley (*Cmel*). Summer 90.

One of the most evocative sounds on Carla Bley's superb *Fleur Carnivore* (Watt/21 839 662) was daughter Karen's floating harmonica solo on 'Song Of The Sadness Of Canute'. As yet, it's an under-exploited voice. Her solo albums are basically song collections, alternately reminiscent of Laurie Anderson's half-spoken narratives and Carla Bley's own free-associating surrealism on *Escalator Over The Hill*, but influenced by 1930s popular song and basic rock rhythms.

The most obviously Anderson-like of the songs is the nightmarish 'Flu', spoken with a wry lack of expression. 'Mean To Me' is pure pastiche, featuring Mom and Dad and 'Uncle' Steve Swallow on decidedly unfamiliar instruments. The instrumental 'Au Lait', which appears to have been recorded live, is the most obviously jazz-based, with beautiful harmonica and trumpet parts.

Otherwise, this is no-category music that stands very sturdily on its own merits. It would only show bad breeding to mention the slightly dodgy liner pictures of Ms Mantler *en déshabille*. We have to note with regret that Arnold has since passed away.

Michael Mantler (born 1943) TRUMPET, COMPOSER

*** **The Hapless Child** Watt 4
>Mantler; Terje Rypdal (*g*); Carla Bley (*ky*); Steve Swallow (*b*); Jack DeJohnette (*d*); Alfreda Benge, Albert Caulder, Nick Mason, Robert Wyatt (*v*). 7/75 & 1/76.
*** **Silence** Watt 5
>Mantler; Carla Bley (*p, org*); Chris Spedding (*g*); Ron McClure (*b*); Clare Maher (*clo*); Robert Wyatt (*perc, v*); Kevin Coyne (*v*); strings. 1/76.
***(*) **Movies** Watt 7
>Mantler; Larry Coryell (*g*); Carla Bley (*p, syn, ts*); Steve Swallow (*b*); Tony Williams (*d*). 11/77.
*** **Something There** Watt 13
>Mantler; Carla Bley (*p*); Mike Stern (*g*); Steve Swallow (*b*); Nick Mason (*d*); London Symphony Orchestra. 6 & 7/82.
(*) **Alien Watt 15
>Mantler; Don Preston (*syn*). 3 & 7/85.
**** **Live** Watt 18
>Mantler; Rick Fenn (*g*); Don Preston (*syn*); John Greaves (*b, p*); Nick Mason (*d*); Jack Bruce (*v*). 2/87.

***(*) **Many Have No Speech** Watt 19
> Mantler; Rick Fenn (*g*); Jack Bruce, Marianne Faithfull, Robert Wyatt (*v*); orchestra. 5–12/87.

*** **Folly Seeing All This** ECM 1485
> Mantler; Wolfgang Puschnig (*af*); Rick Fenn (*g*); Karen Mantler (*p, v*); Dave Adams (*vib*); Balanescu Quartet: Alexander Balanescu, Clare Connors (*vn*); Bill Hawkes (*vla*); Jane Fenton (*clo*); Jack Bruce (*v*). 6/92.

***(*) **Cerco un paese innocente** ECM 1556
> Mantler; Bjarne Roupe (*g*); Marianne Sorensen (*vn*); Mette Winther, Gunary Lychou (*vla*); Helle Sorensen (*clo*); Kim Kristensen (*p*); Mona Larsen (*v*); Danish Radio Big Band. 1/94.

If Michael Mantler's world-view can be inferred from the texts he has chosen for setting, it is a dark and occasionally whimsical vista. His improvisational credentials have always been in some doubt and, were it not for the magnificent 'Communications' for his Jazz Composers Orchestra – and particularly No. 11, which featured Cecil Taylor – he might be consignable to an awkward limbo between jazz and art music. Born and raised in Vienna, Mantler appears to have swallowed the elephant of serialism whole, while straining at a 'simple' blues. His avant-gardism is tempered (or else confirmed) by an equal and opposite dependence on the raw, off-key quality of Austrian café music, and his songs hinge on an enervated drone that is deeply unsettling.

The surprisingly excellent *Live* (which is the place to begin) sums up the best of Mantler's music of the preceding decade. By no means a sampler or greatest hits (though it does repeat some of the Edward Gorey material from *The Hapless Child*), it demonstrates his use of a favoured instrumentation: Fenn's souped-up guitar, Preston's 'orchestral' synth programmes, Mason's rock-influenced drumming and, over it all, a voice that combines thorough illegitimacy of tone and diction with enormous emotional resonance.

Orchestral ambitions took over on *Something There*, a surprisingly successful collaboration with Michael Gibbs and the London Symphony, turning all those embarrassing rock-group and orchestra projects into something valid and worthwhile, and often very moving, as is the moody inscape of the later *Cerco un paese innocente*, on which Mantler emulates Berio by setting a group of poems by Giuseppe Ungaretti, and makes a very powerful fist of it, too. The key there, as in so much of Mantler's work, is the quality of the vocalist. Larsen is huskily beautiful and totally unaffected, delivering the words like a folk singer and not a diva.

Bruce, by contrast, emotes in overdrive. Like Robert Wyatt, Kevin Coyne and Marianne Faithfull elsewhere, he skins a lyric till it shows the nerves and sinews beneath. Grossly overrated as a bass player (and still sheet-anchored by the stresses of supergroup membership with Cream), he makes a remarkable virtue of his glaring technical faults. Whereas on *No Answer* (one of a number of Mantler LPs that may still be around in very small numbers) he is scouringly nihilistic in his articulation of Samuel Beckett's words from *How It Is*, the more recent Beckett settings of *Folly Seeing All This* are a bit more accommodating. The music is no less bare-boned than before, but Bruce's voice has acquired a mellower timbre and the strings give the disc a humane warmth which may or may not conform with Mantler's intentions. The Balanescus perform with the loose-limbed quality that 'classical' groups once notoriously lacked. Whether, again, such a virtue is what is required here is a moot point; but at least it's pleasant to listen to. Puschnig was another successful recruitment.

Bruce comes into his own again on the wonderful *Many Have No Speech*, which adds Philippe Soupault and Ernst Meister to the lyricists' roster and the gravelly Marianne Faithfull to the singers. Robert Wyatt, for many years Mantler's other vocal standby, is disappointingly little used here but is reserved for homier roles like the Harold Pinter settings on *Silence* and the Gorey whimsies of *The Hapless Child*, which is musically and lyrically one of Mantler's more accessible works. Without histrionics, Wyatt *lives* every word and every line. By contrast, Coyne and Faithfull seem to be contriving vocal or interpretative eccentricities, and Faithfull's French pronunciation on *Many Have No Speech* is truly awful.

Of the non-vocal records, *Alien* comes across like the work of a man who hasn't seen daylight for 20 years. Mantler has a strong but anti-virtuosic voice on his instrument and is capable of moments of rather bleak beauty. He is even more focused and lacerating on *Movies*, which showcases Coryell's OTT guitar-playing of the time and is powered along by Williams's torrential drumming. The other revival from that period is the vocal-based (?) *Silence* on which Kevin Coyne (once famous for a suicide anthem called 'Marjory Razorblade') overheats that wonderfully strangled voice.

Editorial disclaimer: if you are receiving medication or any other treatment for a depressive condition, you should consult a physician before buying any of these records.

Frank Mantooth KEYBOARDS, ARRANGER

*** **Suite Tooth** Sea Breeze SB 2055
> Mantooth; Bobby Shew, Danny Barber, Art Davis, Mike Steinel (*t*); Art Farmer (*flhn*); Scott

Bentall, Tom Garling, Mark Bettcher, Mike Young (*tb*); Howie Smith (*as, ss*); Bill Sears (*as, f*); Ed Petersen, Jim Massoth (*ts*); Scott Robinson (*bs, f*); Sam LiPuma (*g*); Kelly Sill, Curt Bley (*b*); Louie Bellson, Steve Houghton (*d*); Tim Kitsos (*perc*). 11/87.

*** **Persevere** Sea Breeze S B 2062

As above, except add Clark Terry (*t, flhn, v*), Steve Wiest (*tb*), Pete Christlieb (*ts*), Jerry DiMuzio (*bs, f, cl*), Steve Erquiaga (*g*), Bob Bowman (*b*), Alejo Poveda (*perc*); omit Farmer, Massoth, Robinson, LiPuma, Sill, Bellson, Kitsos. 10/89.

*** **Dangerous Precedent** Sea Breeze S B 2046

As above, except add Jeff Jarvis (*t*), Paul McKee, Leland Gause (*tb*), Kim Park, Scott Robinson (*reeds*), Matt Harris, Ramsey Lewis (*ky*), Danny Embrey (*g*), Kelly Sill (*b*), Kevin Mahogany (*v*); omit Christlieb, Bentall, Sears. 12/91.

*** **Sophisticated Lady** Sea Breeze S B 2074

As above, except add Roger Ingram, Marvin Stamm, Randy Brecker (*t*), Tom Matta (*tb*), Pat LaBarbera, Pete Christlieb, Nick Brignola (*reeds*); omit Terry, Jarvis, Steinel, Gause, Petersen, Robinson, Lewis, Embrey, Sill, DiMuzio, Erquiaga. 94.

More mighty big-band music from the West Coast, charted by the genial Mantooth, whose arrangements bristle with energy and sometimes hit a note of invention that carries them past the often rote nature of this kind of jazz. The first three albums all trade in fusion-based licks to some extent, though Mantooth finds a surprisingly provocative balance between that kind of jazz-lite and a more demanding arranger's taste. The three-part title-piece on *Suite Tooth* has some terrific playing and writing alike, especially in the mini-concerto for Shew which opens the disc, and the vim and vigour of 'Scam And Eggs' goes well enough with the mood-jazz feel of 'Lauralisa'. *Persevere* goes much the same way: Terry has a bumptious 'Mean To Me' mostly to himself, but four other standards are shrewdly arranged and there are good spots for Shew, Christlieb and Steinel. Terry and Shew have some more good moments on *Dangerous Precedent*, and Mahogany comes on like a young Joe Williams on his two appearances; but again it's the crackle of the band that overcomes any sense of muzak which could have overtaken relatively conventional scores such as 'Imagination'. *Sophisticated Lady* is in some ways the most traditional of the four discs, with Mantooth sticking to piano, the bassist staying acoustic and the charts hewing close to, say, the Jones–Lewis style of delivery. Excitements nevertheless exist in the knockout tribute to Woody Shaw, 'The Messenger', three more very able vocals by Mahogany and Brignola's authoritative solo on the title-piece. Little to choose among the discs, though we might pick *Dangerous Precedent* as the best sampler, if pressed.

Guido Manusardi (born 1935) PIANO

(*) **Downtown Soul Note S N 121131-2

Manusardi; Isla Eckinger (*b*); Ed Thigpen (*d*). 5–6/85.

Guido Manusardi is one of the major names in Italian post-bop jazz, and he has led very many albums, many of which have not made it to compact disc reissue so far. The few that are currently available give a comparatively indifferent account of his powers: he has a clear, decisive touch and, although given to rambling when left to his own devices, he leads a piano trio with much authority. *Downtown* should have been the ideal introduction to Manusardi's music, with four originals, two good standards, a fine rhythm section and good Soul Note recording. But some of the material isn't his best: 'Alexandria' is a merely doleful ballad, and only the Red Garland-like manoeuvres of 'Downtown' find the pianist at his most resourceful, although the up-tempo chosen for 'My Romance' is at least unusual.

*** **Together Again** Soul Note 121181

Manusardi; Red Mitchell (*b*). 11/88.

*** **So That** Splasc(h) H 328-2

Manusardi; Eddie Gomez (*b*); Gianni Cazzola (*d*). 10/90.

Manusardi meets two distinguished bassists. There's a greater compatibility with Mitchell, though the bassist is as wilful as ever, eccentrically dawdling over figures but doing so in such a charming way that the music picks up an idiosyncratic lilt which the pianist also takes note of; 'But Not For Me' is a delightful game of cat and mouse. *So That* is more obviously open-handed, the trio barrelling through most of the tunes at a rapid-fire tempo; but Gomez crowds out Manusardi at times and it's the sly interjections of Cazzola (listen to his fours on 'There Is No Greater Love') which referee the playing. Gomez's singalong bass is irritatingly picked up by the microphones, but recording is otherwise excellent.

*** **Colored Passages** Ram CD4504

Manusardi; George Garzone (*ss, ts*); John Lockwood (*b*); Bob Gullotti (*d*). 3/93.

The encounter this time is with the trio known as The Fringe. Manusardi brought some fine compositions to the session, with the catchy 'The Winding Road' leaping out of the gates and two pretty ballads in 'Engadina Valley' and 'Anytime, Anywhere'. His three compatriots don't quite let go the way they do on their own, and there are a couple of tracks too many – no need for the second take of 'The Touch Of Your Lips', perhaps. Otherwise well worth hearing.

*** **Concerto** Splasc(h) 437
    Manusardi (*p* solo). 6/90–6/92.
Excerpts from some recent solo concerts. Manusardi isn't one for doodling to himself in solo recitals: he plays for the audience, and there is some very energetic variation on his favourite standards here, though the prettiest moments come on originals like 'Velvet Sunset' and 'The Ruins Of Piuro'. Warm and good-natured piano.

Nancy Marano VOCALS

(*) **A Perfect Match Denon CY 79407
    Marano; Eddie Monteiro (*acc, v*); Claudio Roditi (*flhn*); Gerry Mulligan (*bs*); Roger Kellaway (*p*). 5 & 6/91.
The draw here is of course the three guest players, each of whom brings something distinctive and fresh to these slightly mechanical vocal-and-accordion duets, all of which could do with a bit more pep and swing. Roditi's contribution to 'Love Dance' is the most significant, lifting it from banality with a few well-picked notes. Mulligan and Kellaway are less focused but seem to enjoy their spots. Marano's voice manages to be unclassifiable and strangely anonymous at the same time, but these tracks will doubtless appeal to some Latin jazz fans.

Rita Marcotulli PIANO

***(*) **Night Caller** Label Bleu LBLC 6551
    Marcotulli; Nils Petter Molvaer (*t*); Tore Brunborg (*sax*); Michael Benita (*b*); Anders Kjellberg, Jon Christensen (*d, perc*). 92.
This is the sort of thing that ECM might have liked to get hold of. Marcotulli's writing is intelligent and atmospheric and isn't easy to boil down to its putative influences. The opening 'Night Caller' is a mysterious, echo-y thing that opens on plangent horns over Christensen's delicate cymbals and quickly establishes the Mediterranean/Middle Eastern tonality that dominates this fine record. Marcotulli herself is heard only deep in the background for quite some time, considerably processed, and it is clear that her importance is as a writer and arranger, rather than as a front-rank soloist. When she does emerge, it is in a musing, slightly detached way, a cross between Paul Bley in his minimalist phase and Marilyn Crispell in unwontedly tonal, single-note mode. An unfussy, unvirtuosic performance.

Michael Marcus (born 1952) SOPRANO SAXOPHONE, MANZELLO, STRITCH, CONN-O-SAX, CLARINETS

*** **Under The Wire** Enja ENJ 6064
    Marcus; Ted Daniel (*t*); Joseph Bowie (*tb*); William Parker (*b*); Reggie Nicholson (*d*). 5/90.
***(*) **Here At!** Soul Note 121243
    Marcus; Ted Daniel (*t*); Steve Swell (*tb*); Fred Hopkins, William Parker (*b*); Dennis Charles, Sadiq Abdu Shahid (*d*). 9/93.
Marcus was turned on to the more *outré* members of the saxophone family not so much by Roland Kirk as by George Braith, a Kirk disciple who had a brief fling with Blue Note in the later 1960s. Not to be confused with soprano saxophone specialist, Steve Marcus, who has worked with Buddy Rich and latter-day Stan Kenton outfits, this clan-member is an unreconstructed modernist with a full-tilt delivery and an unexpected gift for the tender moment. He delivers one on *Here At!* when he switches to the weirdly pitched conn-o-sax (in F) for the ballad, 'Hidden Springs'. Elsewhere on the Soul Note record he sticks to Kirk favourites: manzello in B&musflat; and stritch in E&musflat;. It isn't always possible to determine what key Marcus is working in, especially when he employs two horns simultaneously. The Enja session is more conventional and a good deal drabber than his work with modernists Sonny Simmons and Frank Lowe. It's only on the later record that he lets rip and really allows himself the leeway to blow freely. With twinned basses on 'Ithem' and double bass and drums on 'Here At', the sound is very full. Swell's trombone augments three tracks much as Bowie does on the earlier record, fulfilling the approximate role of a piano player without being restricted to orthodox key-changes. It's a

very effective mix, if a touch old-fashioned in conception. Anyone who retains an affection for the free jazz of the 1970s will enjoy these latter-day echoes enormously.

Rick Margitza (born 1963) TENOR AMD SOPRANO SAXOPHONES

**** Work It Steeplechase SCCD 31358
   Margitza; James Williams (*p*); George Mraz (*b*); Billy Hart (*d*). 4/94.
***(*) Hands Of Time Challenge 70021
   Margitza; Kevin Hays (*p*); George Mraz (*b*); Al Foster (*d*). 12/94.

Margitza's recordings have missed the attention they deserve: three earlier Blue Notes are already gone. But these two are filled with such exemplary work that one wonders at his apparent neglect. On the other hand, he's hardly a fashionable player: he takes a long, thoughtful time over his solos, resists any excess of double-time or scalar exhibitionism, and presents a sonorous yet rather oblique tone which puts an ambivalent edge on his improvising. The long, Rollinish cadenza on 'My Foolish Heart', the compelling circles cast through 'Widows Walk', the neo-blues shapes of 'Steppin' Out' and the unexpectedly jaunty revision of 'It Could Happen To You' are four highlights of the Steeplechase disc; but there really isn't a bad passage on it, and with Williams in top form and Mraz and Hart perfectly comfortable this is leagues ahead of the typical tenor-plus-rhythm date. If the Challenge album is just a shade behind, it's still very fine: more emphasis on his own writing here, with six out of the seven tunes, and an unpredictable set they make – 'Hip Bop' turns organ-band clichés inside out and 'Forty Five Pound Hound' does the same for the blues. 'Embraceable You' gets one of its bleakest treatments since Coleman's famous rendition. These are very strong entries from an outstanding saxophonist.

Charlie Mariano (born 1923) ALTO SAXOPHONE, SOPRANO SAXOPHONE, FLUTE, NAGASWARAM

*** Boston All Stars / New Sound From Boston Original Jazz Classics OJC 1745
   Mariano; Joe Gordon, Herb Pomeroy (*t*); Sonny Truitt (*tb*); Jim Clark (*ts*); George Myers (*bs*);
   Roy Frazee, Richard Twardzik (*p*); Bernie Griggs, Jack Lawlor (*b*); Gene Glennon, Carl
   Goodwin, Jimmy Weiner (*d*); Ira Gitler (*bells*). 12/51, 1/53.
*** Boston Days Fresh Sound FSRCD 207
   Mariano; Herb Pomeroy (*t*); Jaki Byard (*p*); Jack Carter (b); Peter Littman (*d*). 11/53.
**(*) Charlie Mariano Plays Fresh Sound FSR CD 115
   As above, except add John Williams (*p*). 7/54.
***(*) Alto Sax For Young Moderns Bethlehem BET 6013
   Mariano; John Williams (*p*); Max Bennett (*b*); Mel Lewis (*d*). 7/55.

Critics were quick to locate the much-underrated Mariano in the gaggle of post-Bird alto players. It's true as far as it goes. Mariano was born only three years after Parker, and his first and greatest influence remains Johnny Hodges. His studies in Indian music, and on the wooden, oboe-like *nagaswaram*, have helped emphasize the exotic overtones he absorbed from Hodges and which are already evident in the early, bop-inspired sessions on OJC.

The wrenching intensity of later years is not yet apparent, though Mariano invests 'Stella By Starlight' on *New Sound From Boston* with entirely convincing and personal feeling. It's interesting to compare this performance with that on the Fresh Sound *It's Standard Time* (below), made after a long break from standards repertoire. In the 1950s, Mariano is still playing in a very linear way, without the three-dimensional solidity and textural variation that he developed later; he was also still more or less rooted in conventional bop harmony, an attachment that weakened as he came to understand Indian music.

New Sound From Boston is excellent, if a little raw. *Boston Days* is good, too, though many will find it more useful for its insights into the under-recorded Pomeroy; he very nearly steals the show, and his solo on 'Sweet And Lovely' is definitive. Byard, who reappears on a later Mariano session, is in highly inventive form as well. Even in a couple of years, Mariano advanced considerably, and in the year of Charlie Parker's death *Alto Sax For Young Moderns* already has him looking forward to something new and different, playing good developmental lines, but ones which now have a less obvious destination. Williams, as before, is an understanding partner.

*** A Jazz Portrait of Charlie Mariano Fresh Sound FSRCD 176
   Mariano; Bernie Glow, Himmy Sedler, Jimmy Nottingham, Marvin Stamm (*t*); Wayne Andre,
   Bob Brookmeyer, Joe Ciarvadone, Paul Faulise (*tb*); Bob Abernathy, Dick Berg, Dave
   Clevenger, Aubrey Facenda (*frhn*); Don Butterfield (*tba*); Phil Bodner (*reeds*); Roger Kellaway

(*p*); Bob Phillips (*p, cel, vib*); Jim Hall (*g*); Art Davis, Richard Davis (*b*); Albert 'Tootie' Heath, Mel Lewis (*d*); Ed Shaughnessy (*perc*). 7/63.

This helps to fill the yawning gap in the Mariano discography a little. One doesn't usually think of him as a big-band player, though he had worked with Pomeroy's outfit (see him, above) and, of course, he had the closest association with Toshiko Akiyoshi, one of the best arrangers and band composers in America at the time.

This was recorded after the couple had flitted to Japan. The saxophonist was back in America to teach at campus jazz clinics, and these sessions were put together over two days during a slack spell in the summer. 'To Taoho' shows the most obvious oriental influence. A modal theme, like much of the stuff he was doing at this time, it uses some unexpected intervals, and again Mariano is slightly upstaged by one of his playing partners. Marvin Stamm's contributions are consistently excellent; this was billed as his coming-out gig and he certainly made best use of the opportunity. Don Sebesky's writing for the larger group is limited to 'Portrait Of An Artist', which sits for Charlie the way Mingus's 'Portrait Of Jackie' sat for McLean, a perfect opportunity to be at their best. The other stuff is nicely balanced, though the three tracks with Jim Hall, strings, harp and celeste err on the side of mush. Leaving Mariano as the only woodwind against trumpets and an array of French horns was a slightly risky strategy but it works, and the small-group material nicely modulates the session as a whole.

*** **Jyothi** ECM 1256
    Mariano; Karnataka College of Percussion: R. A. Ramamani (*v, tamboura, konakkol*); T. A. S. Mani (*mridamgam*); R. A. Rajagopal (*ghantam, morsing, konnakol*); T. N. Shashikumar (*kanjira, konakkol*). 2/83.

*** **Live** VeraBra 2034
    As above, except omit Rajagopal, add Ramesh Shotam (*chatam, morsing, tavil*). 2/89.

Only fans of a certain age remember Joe Harriott's and John Mayer's *Indo-Jazz Fusions*, released by Columbia in 1966 and 1967, hailed as the Next Big Thing, and then consigned to collector status. With a tonal approach not unlike Harriott's and with a similar awareness of the boundaries of tonality and abstraction, Mariano's albums with the Karnataka College of Percussion make a perfectly valid comparison. The saxophone is paired with R. A. Ramamani's expressive voice, and it's unfortunately easy to ignore the intricate rhythmic canvas being stretched behind them by the other players; the live session is a little more even-handed in this regard, but on *Jyothi* (with the close-miked and lapidary sound typical of ECM), most of the emphasis is on Mariano's fervid upper-register playing.

*** **It's Standard Time: Volume 1** Fresh Sound FSR 97
    Mariano; Tete Montoliu (*p*); Horacio Fumero (*b*); Peer Wyboris (*d*). 4/89.
***(*) **It's Standard Time: Volume 2** Fresh Sound FSR 98
    As above. 4/89.

Mariano has not been closely associated with standards jazz in recent years. Like Miles Davis (and only those who haven't heard the saxophonist play would consider the analogy absurd), he believes in confronting the 'music of today' rather than endlessly reworking changes. However, on the basis of a performance at the Kenton Festival in Oldham, Lancashire, where Mariano had played 'Stella By Starlight', producer Jordi Pujol persuaded him to cut a standards album in Barcelona with Catalan pianist Tete Montoliu and two other local players.

Mariano is in perfect voice. On Volume 1, 'Stella' is wonderful, given a harmonically 'flatter' but more resonant reading than Lee Konitz tends to. He misfires briefly on 'Billie's Bounce' and makes a bit of a nonsense of 'Poor Butterfly', but it's a highly appealing album nevertheless, ideal for anyone who hasn't previously made contact with the saxophonist's work or who has a constitutional aversion to the *konakkol* or the *kanjira*.

Unusually, the follow-up volume, drawn from the same two nights, is even better. The songs are no more demanding, though 'I Thought About You' and a second take of 'Billie's Bounce' include some stretching harmonic notions. Perhaps it's taken a CD's worth to get used to the idea of Mariano back playing this kind of material; neither volume will disappoint.

***(*) **Mariano** Intuition INT 3002
    Mariano; Paul Shigihara (*g*); Michael Hertin (*p, ky*). 87.
*** **Innuendo** Lipstick LIP 890082
    Mariano; Jasper Van't Hof (*p, ky*); Marilyn Mazur (*d, perc*). 7 & 9/91.
***(*) **Adagio** Lipstick LIP 890242
    As for *Mariano*. 93.

Like Lee Konitz, Mariano has increasingly moved back towards a mainstream jazz position. Mazur's uncomplicated drumming leads *Innuendo* into a more orthodox jazz groove. Like the standards sessions above, it takes a moment to adjust, but there's no doubting his competence in this idiom. Mariano relies heavily on high wails and big portamento effects and, while initially these are wearing, they also camouflage some fascinating harmonic activity that takes time to get across.

The drummerless trio on *Mariano* delivers a surprisingly focused and exact recording, and the music performed (which includes a version of Ravel's 'Pavane pour une infante défunte', previously tackled only by Larry Coryell) steers well clear of the drab New Age waffle such a programme might suggest. The follow-up on Lipstick is reminiscent of *Sleep, My Lovely*, a record for CMP recorded with guitarist Philip Cathering and Jasper van't Hof on keyboards. Shigihara and Herting are not so distinctive, but this is much more emphatically the saxophonist's date. At first glance, his choice of classical themes is questionable – can you really jazz up Dvořák's 'New World' *Adagio*, or the *Pathétique* or Villa-Lobos's *Bachianas Brasileiras*? The short answer is no, but that isn't really what Mariano is trying to do. His interpretations are admirably straight and unfussy, and no more alien to the language of jazz than 'My Romance' or Indian classical music.

**(*) Warum Bist Du Traurig B & W BW019
>   Mariano; Gregor Josephs (*p, ky*); Riccardo Del Fra (*b*); Gerd Breuer (*d*). 94.

A further step in the direction of classicism, and a less happy one. Josephs is also a straight composer, and a very good one, but his style really doesn't suit Mariano's slightly wild tonality. Some of the tunes, including the title-piece ('Why are you so sad?'), might have sounded better for just piano and bass. Del Fra seems to intuit much of what is going on, and he provides his own elaborately uncomplicated responses to the main theme. Interesting, inevitably, but of limited interest.

Sherrie Maricle (born 1963) DRUMS

*** Cookin' On All Burners Stash ST-CD-24
>   Maricle; John Mastroianni (*as*); Roger Kellaway (*p*); Peter Appleyard (*vib*); Michael Moore (*b*).
>   1/89.
** (*) The Time Being Jazz Alliance TJA-10019
>   Maricle; John Mastroianni (*ss, as*); Ted Rosenthal (*p*); Harvie Swartz (*b*). 8/92.

Sherrie Maricle co-leads these groups with John Mastroianni. The music takes a bright and energetic course through the lighter end of New York's current scene – hard bop with the occasional twist. There's nothing amiss with either group, but the music can't quite find a personal touch. *Cookin' On All Burners* is ahead for the interesting presence of Appleyard's vibes and the rousing work by Kellaway: every time he appears as a hired hand on a session he throws in a provocative or even an alarming performance, and this one features a hair-raising solo on the already superfast 'Scrapple From The Apple'. *The Time Being* throws more weight on to Mastroianni's alto playing, a skilful variation on the Phil Woods manner, but the writing here is merely serviceable on the eight originals, and nothing much lingers in the mind.

Dodo Marmarosa (born 1925) PIANO

*** On Dial: The Complete Sessions Spotlite SPJ-128
>   Marmarosa; Howard McGhee, Miles Davis (*t*); Teddy Edwards, Lucky Thompson (*ts*); Arvin
>   Garrison (*g*); Harry Babasin (*clo*); Bob Kesterson (*b*); Roy Porter, Jackie Mills (*d*). 46–12/47.
*** Dodo's Bounce Fresh Sound FSCD-1019
>   As above, except add Barney Kessel (*g*), Gene Englund, Red Callender (*b*); omit Davis,
>   McGhee, Edwards, Garrison, Kesterson, Porter. 46–47.

A bebop enigma. Marmarosa played an important minor role in bop's hothouse days, recording with Parker in Los Angeles, but less than two years later he was back in his native Pittsburgh and heading for an obscurity and silence that has seldom been broken since. He had a foot in swing as well as the modern camp, and his precise articulation and sweeping lines make one think of Tatum as much as any of his immediate contemporaries: a pair of solos from 1946, 'Deep Purple' and 'Tea For Two', are strikingly akin to the older man's conception. But he had a gentle, even rhapsodic side which colours the trio tracks on both of these discs and, while he flirts with an even more audacious conception – hinted at on the two 'Tone Paintings' solos from 1947 – one feels he never satisfactorily resolved the different strands of his playing. Much of his best playing is to be found on Parker's Dials (a solitary example, 'Bird Lore', is on the Spotlite CD), but the solo, trio and sextet (with Howard McGhee) tracks on *On Dial* include much absorbing piano jazz. The Fresh Sounds CD duplicates 14 of the 22 tracks on the Spotlite disc, but also includes ten tracks cut for the Atomic label prior to the Dials, plus six quartet sides with Lucky Thompson. Neither disc solves the problem of the indifferent sound of the originals, and both feature an atrocious speed wobble on the two 'Tone Paintings' solos (which originally were privately recorded in any case). Marmarosa has excited much admiration over the years, but he is beginning to fade into jazz history now; his 1961 date for Argo, *Dodo's Back!*, has yet to appear on CD.

Sal Marquez TRUMPET, FLUGELHORN

*** **One For Dewey** GRP 96782

Marquez; Doug Webb (*ts, ss*); John Beasley, Kenny Kirkland, Mike Lang (*p*); Dave Carpenter (*b*); Joe LaBarbera, Joel Taylor, Jeff 'Tain' Watts (*d*).

Having a name like a character in a Kerouac novel may be a problematic destiny. Marquez solos almost always sound off-the-cuff, unrehearsed and unmannered, but they do also tend to waffle a bit. With a bright, emphatic tone coupled to a soft-focus attack that confirms the debt to Miles, he is never less than pleasant to listen to, even when in mid-drift. The overall sound is much what one might expect for this label, a shade over-produced and lacking air and light.

Joe Marsala (1907–78) CLARINET

***(*) **Joe Marsala, 1936–42** Classics 763

Marsala; Pee Wee Erwin, Max Kaminsky, Marty Marsala (*t*); Bill Coleman (*t, v*); George Brunies (*tb*); Ben Glassman, Pete Brown (*as*); John Smith (*ts*); Dave Bowman, Joe Bushkin, Dick Cary, Frank Signorelli (*p*); Ray Biondi (*vn*); Adele Girard (*hp*); Eddie Condon, Carmen Mastren (*g*); Jack LeMaire (*g, v*); Jack Kelleher, Artie Shapiro, Haig Stephens, Gene Traxler (*b*); Danny Alvin, Stan King, Shelly Manne, Buddy Rich, Zutty Singleton (*d*); Dell St John (*v*). 1/36–7/42.

Joe's clarinet playing had a dark, winey quality that sounded wonderful in a small-group setting. Though he also dabbled with big bands, it was the group that retained a residency at the Hickory House on 52nd Street which made his reputation. These sides represent almost all of his recorded output, with the addition of an early pair made for Decca under the name, The Six Blue Chips; Pee Wee Erwin was the leading light. In 1937 Joe married harpist Adele Girard, who was already part of his regular line-up, adding an attractive sound to the front line of clarinet, trumpet and violin.

Armed with solid good looks of the Robert Wagner variety, he was a tough, uncompromising individual, much admired by Leonard Feather (who wrote all of the material for the April 1940 session) as a man who had battled to break down the race divide in jazz. There is no doubting the authenticity of the jazz he played, which swings furiously from first to last. Especially good are the cuts by his Chicagoans, a band that included brother Marty and the great Eddie Condon on guitar. There is more from Marsala to come on the Classics imprint, but for the time being this is an excellent introduction. He is often accorded a place in the history books for having given both Buddy Rich and Shelly Manne their first jazz gigs, in March 1938 and April 1941 respectively. On this showing, he is a much more significant figure in his own right.

Branford Marsalis (born 1960) TENOR AND SOPRANO SAXOPHONES

*** **Scenes In The City** Columbia 468458-2

Marsalis; John Longo (*t*); Robin Eubanks (*tb*); Mulgrew Miller (*p*); Ray Drummond, Ron Carter, Charnett Moffett, Phil Bowler (*b*); Marvin 'Smitty' Smith, Jeff Tain Watts (*d*). 4–11/83.

(*) **Royal Garden Blues Columbia 468704-2

Marsalis; Ellis Marsalis, Kenny Kirkland, Herbie Hancock, Larry Willis (*p*); Ron Carter, Charnett Moffett, Ira Coleman (*b*); Ralph Peterson, Marvin 'Smitty' Smith, Al Foster, Jeff Tain Watts (*d*). 3–7/86.

*** **Renaissance** Columbia 40711

Marsalis; Kenny Kirkland (*p*); Charnett Moffett (*b*); Jeff Tain Watts (*d*).

(*) **Random Abstract Columbia 468707-2

Marsalis; Kenny Kirkland (*p*); Delbert Felix (*b*); Lewis Nash (*d*). 8/87.

Articulate, hip, funny, the eldest of the Marsalis brothers has often seemed like the most likely to succeed. He started with Art Blakey's Jazz Messengers on alto; but his tenor playing is stonily powerful in the Rollins tradition, and he has stuck by the bigger horn on most of his solo records, with soprano – granted a sometimes reedy but usually impressive full tone – as second instrument. *Scenes In The City* was an entertaining debut, with a wry version of the Mingus title-tune (complete with dialogue), and the storming manifesto of 'No Backstage Pass' to show what he could do: but it's a bit of a jumble. *Royal Garden Blues* is a step down, the playing messy and subdivided among a bewildering variety of rhythm sections. *Renaissance* and *Random Abstract* emerge as accomplished but undecided sessions. On *Random Abstract* he seems to explore the mannerisms of a number of preceding tenor influences – Coltrane, Shorter, Coleman, even Ben Webster, whose celebration in a bathetic reading of 'I Thought About You' seems more of a parody than a tribute. The chief problem with all these sessions, though, is that Marsalis promises more than he delivers, both conceptually and in the heft and weight of his playing. While still sounding imaginative and technically top-line, he can't seem to focus an eloquent battery of remarks into a proper speech. Delfeayo Marsalis's production is idiosyncratic: his interest in 'more bass wood' tends to make the lower frequencies sound woolly and unclear.

*** **Trio Jeepy** Columbia 465134-2 2CD
    Marsalis; Milt Hinton, Delbert Felix (*b*); Jeff Tain Watts (*d*). 1/88.
A rambling jam session, illuminated by some brilliant moments. 'The Nearness Of You' is a mature ballad reading, 'Doxy' a convincing nod to Rollins, and 'Random Abstract' features the Marsalis/Felix/ Watts trio in full, exhilarating flight (the amazingly durable Hinton plays on most of the other tracks). While hailed (mystifyingly) as a breakthrough masterpiece in some quarters, it's actually a lightweight, fun record.

*** **Crazy People Music** Columbia 466870-2
    Marsalis; Kenny Kirkland (*p*); Robert Hurst (*b*); Jeff Tain Watts (*d*). 1–3/90.
*** **The Beautyful Ones Are Not Yet Born** Columbia 468896-2
    Marsalis; Wynton Marsalis (*t*); Robert Hurst (*b*); Jeff Tain Watts (*d*). 5/91.
Hurst and Watts are musicians of resolute power and high craft, and they provide Marsalis with the bedrock he needs to contextualize his playing. *Crazy People Music* is a solidly realized tenor-and-rhythm date, full of elegant playing, but the music on *The Beautyful Ones Are Not Yet Born* is better yet: the recording sounds warmer and more specifically focused, and the long, stretched-out improvisations insist that Marsalis has his perfect, singular setting in the trio with Hurst and Watts (brother Wynton makes a brief cameo appearance on one track). 'Citizen Tain', which has some of the wit of Sonny Rollins working against Philly Joe Jones on *Newk's Time*, 'Gilligan's Isle' and the steeply driven title-tune are aristocratic improvisations in which the leader finds a path away from merely discursive blowing. His soprano sounds pretty good, too. Recommended.

*** **I Heard You Twice The First Time** Columbia 472169-2
    Marsalis; Wynton Marsalis, Earl Gardner (*t*); Delfeayo Marsalis, David Sager (*tb*); Wessell Anderson (*as*); Kenny Kirkland (*p*); B. B. King, John Lee Hooker (*g, v*); Russell Malone, Joe Louis Walker (*g*); Reginald Veal, Robert Hurst (*b*); Jeff Tain Watts, Herlin Riley, Bernard Purdie (*d*); Thomas Hollis, Roscoe Carroll, Carl Gordon, Charles Dutton, Linda Hopkins (*v*). n.d.

***(*) **Bloomington** Columbia 473771-2
    Marsalis; Robert Hurst (*b*); Jeff Tain Watts (*d*). 9/91.
Branford's blues album is somewhat lighter than Wynton's three-volume dissertation, but there's still a tendency to ramble: the crackling 'Rib Tip Johnson', with superb guitar by Russell Malone, would have been better at five minutes rather than nine, and B. B. King's feature also runs into flab. 'Sidney In Da Haus' is an impeccably arranged small-group piece, 'Mabel' hires John Lee Hooker for one of his show-stealing cameos, and the rest is good Branford, swinging hard, often connecting. *Bloomington*, though, is his least adorned and best record. A snapshot of a live date from Indiana with his regular partners, the music makes a virtue of its open-ended situation: away from studio microphones, one can hear the terrific heat and tumbling spontaneity that this group can put out in a live situation. There is a treatment of 'Everything Happens To Me' that wipes out the song itself, all stark corners and cold stares; a bumping 'Friday The Thirteenth'; a vast 'Xavier's Lair'. Dead spots, too, and Delfeayo Marsalis's sound is as questionable as usual, but a fine record.

*** **Buckshot La Fonque** Columbia 476352-2
    Marsalis; Roy Hargrove, Chuck Findley (*t*); Matt Finders (*tb*); Delfeayo Marsalis (*tb, p*); Greg Phillinganes (*ky*); Kenny Kirkland (*p*); David Barry, Kevin Eubanks, Ray Fuller, Nils Lofgren, Albert Collins (*g*); Robert Hurst, Darryl Jones, Larry Kimpel (*b*); Jeff Tain Watts, Chuck Morris (*d*); Mino Cinelu, Vicki Randle (*perc*). 94.
Branford's hip hop album. Wacky, ironic, full of in-jokes, sardonic, embracing the idiom and rising over it at the same time, these are fragments from a busy man's workbook, and chips off an old block: black music from streets, clubs and concert halls. Marsalis doesn't suggest that he has any real faith or interest in hip hop, but he likes the style and he's interested in a piece of it. There is some inventive use of sampling, cut-ups, whatever, and some great playing. But it never seems like anything more than an ingenious bag of filed-down pieces.

Delfeayo Marsalis (born 1965) TROMBONE

*** **Pontius Pilate's Decision** Novus PD 90669.
>   Marsalis; Wynton Marsalis, Scotty Barnhart (*t*); Branford Marsalis (*ss*); Wessell Anderson (*as, sno*); Mark Gross (*as*); Nat Turner (*ts*); Victor Atkins (*p*); Reginald Veal, Bob Hurst (*b*); Jason Marsalis, Jeff Tain Watts (*d*); Kimati (*perc*). 5/91–3/92.

The first requirement is to get past the insufferable sleeve-notes, the portentous biblical concept and the wearying sense that this is a vastly important piece of work. All that set aside, there is some impressive and absorbing playing here. One of the younger of the Marsalis brothers (though not the youngest: drummer Jason, only fourteen when this disc was made, takes that honour) is a chameleonic trombonist, sounding at various points like several of the scores of 'bone men he lists in the acknowledgements column and seldom like himself, whoever that may be. But there are some witty and individual reductions of post-bop language here, some great improvisations, some glittering ensemble conversations. The trumpet-playing Marsalis has at least two magnificent solos on the title-track and 'The Weary Ways Of Mary Magdalene'; Branford plays some of his coolest soprano; the rhythm sections keep time with steely finesse. If only there wasn't so much surrounding persiflage.

Ellis Marsalis (born 1934) PIANO

*** **The Classic Ellis Marsalis** Boplicity CD BOP 016
>   Marsalis; Nat Perrilliat (*ts*); Marshall Smith (*b*); James Black (*d*). 1–3/63.
*** **Piano In E** Rounder 2100
>   Marsalis (*p* solo). 84.
*** **Ellis Marsalis Trio** Blue Note B21S-96107-2
>   Marsalis; Bob Hurst (*b*); Jeff Tain Watts (*d*). 3/90.
*** **Heart Of Gold** Columbia CK 47509
>   Marsalis; Ray Brown, Reginald Veal (*b*); Billy Higgins, Herlin Riley, Jason Marsalis (*d*). 2–6/91.
*** **Whistle Stop** Columbia 474555-2
>   Marsalis; Branford Marsalis (*ss, ts*); Robert Hurst (*b*); Jeff Tain Watts, Jason Marsalis (*d*). 3–6/93.

The founder of the Marsalis dynasty is no mean player himself. One can hear where Wynton got his even-handed delineation of melody from and where Branford's aristocratic elegance of line is rooted. Marsalis *père* isn't beyond tossing in the occasional surprise, such as a sudden right-hand rip in 'Just Squeeze Me' on the Blue Note album, but mostly he favours careful interpretations of standards, sparsely harmonized and delicately spelt out, with a few simple but cleverly hooked originals to lend a little extra personality. *The Classic Marsalis* is a surprising rarity, a quartet date from the early 1960s in which the pianist leads a group featuring the Coltrane follower, Nat Perrilliat, and the jittery, post-Elvin Jones drums of James Black, whose unsettling beats keep the group teetering on the brink of a chaos that the others carefully navigate. The recording is monochromatic, but it's a surprising period-piece. Of the contemporary sessions, the two trio records are the strongest, since Marsalis can leave rhythmic duties to bass and drums and concentrate on the path of the song; and on the first Columbia album there are two lions in magisterial form. *Whistle Stop* is one of the Marsalis family affairs, and this is impressive playing – perhaps a degree too impressive. The sleeve-notes belabour the point that the group are actually playing in 5 on some tunes, even though this is hardly the revolution the author suggests, and the quartet's resolve to make it all sound so easy gives the music a steeliness that detracts from the writing, much of which comes from former Marsalis sidemen, Black and Perrilliat: five of the tunes were previously covered on *The Classic Marsalis*.

Wynton Marsalis (born 1961) TRUMPET

**** **Wynton Marsalis** Columbia 468708
>   Marsalis; Branford Marsalis (*ts, ss*); Herbie Hancock, Kenny Kirkland (*p*); Ron Carter, Charles Fambrough, Clarence Seay (*b*); Jeff Watts, Tony Williams (*d*). 81.
*** **Think Of One** Columbia 468709
>   Marsalis; Branford Marsalis (*ts, ss*); Kenny Kirkland (*p*); Phil Bowler (*b*); Jeff Tain Watts (*d*). 83.
***(*) **Hothouse Flowers** Columbia 468710
>   Marsalis; Branford Marsalis (*ts, ss*); Kent Jordan (*af*); Kenny Kirkland (*p*); Ron Carter (*b*); Jeff Watts (*d*). 5/84.

**** **Black Codes (From The Underground)** Columbia 468711
     Marsalis; Kenny Kirkland (*p*); Ron Carter, Charnett Moffett (*b*); Jeff Tain Watts (*d*). 1/85.
**** **J Mood** Columbia 468712
     Marsalis; Marcus Roberts (*p*); Robert Leslie Hurst III (*b*); Jeff Tain Watts (*d*). 12/85.
'Wynton is good for jazz. End of conversation.' Branford Marsalis is not, perhaps, an entirely impartial
source of comment on his brother's worth, but the statement, quoted in *The Wire* magazine, has just the
right mixture of self-assured arrogance and respect. Wynton Marsalis's purity of conception has made
for good editorial copy. The earliest recordings, made at Bubba's in Fort Lauderdale in 1980, came a
year after his recruitment to the Jazz Messengers, and they suggest that he did, in embryo at least.
Though released on only relatively small labels, they bespeak a remarkable talent. Marsalis comes from
a virtual dynasty of musicians (his father, Ellis, is a fine pianist – see above – and brother Delfeayo has
produced albums for him) and it's tempting to see them as a jazz equivalent of the Kennedy clan:
glitteringly gifted, with a combination of radicalism and deep cultural conservatism, given to assertion
over argument, humane but often chillingly detached, and inevitably a target for every critical loner with
a grudge who resents their remarkable success.
    In 1981 he took leave of absence from the Messengers to tour and record with a top-drawer quartet
consisting of Tony Williams, Ron Carter and Herbie Hancock, all of whom appear with him on the first
of the Columbias. The opening 'Father Time', recorded by the trumpeter's 'own' band, which included
Branford and Kenny Kirkland, is an astonishing major-label debut, a beautifully structured piece with
inventive contrapuntal exchanges between the two horns and a marvellous sequencing of very different
rhythmic profiles. Listen to the way Marsalis subtly adjusts his delivery for the shift into common time.
Inevitably, though, most critical attention was directed towards the tracks with Williams, Carter and
Hancock. The bassist's 'RJ' and Williams's slightly melancholic 'Sister Cheryl' bracket a furious stop-
action Marsalis composition called 'Hesitation', which is actually a neo-bop variation on 'I Got
Rhythm'; together these are the nub of a record which is programmed with unusual care and intelligence, closing on the lovely 'Twilight'. The trumpeter's solos lack the declamatory mannerisms that
crept into some of his later records.
    Hothouse Flowers was a slightly unfortunate title. By this stage in Marsalis's career, there was already
considerable pressure on him to produce works of magisterial finish and almost classical perfection. His
sound on the 1984 album is less forced and overheated than it is simply detached. Marsalis sounds
increasingly as if he is playing under a bell jar. The tone-colours are almost astonishingly bright on
'Stardust', and 'When You Wish Upon A Star' is brilliantly confected out of nothing. Branford is much
less effective here and, though he gets ample solo space, he seems to be used increasingly for backgrounds, much as Jordan is. Watts, however, is integral to the sound: crisp, subtle and able to vary
furiously impacted rhythms with soft, almost melodic passages in Afro-waltz time. On *Black Codes
(From The Underground)* he is absolutely essential to the tight, tense sound of the trumpeter's best work
to date. *Black Codes* is a highly committed record, not just in its references to the slave laws of the
nineteenth century, but also in the sheer commitment of Marsalis's playing on the title-piece,
'Phryzzinian Man' and 'Chambers Of Tain' (a Kirkland composition dedicated to drummer Watts). On
'Black Codes' he sounds sorrowful but intense, anticipating the preaching style of *Majesty Of The
Blues*; on 'Phryzzinian Man' he attempts variations which almost sound 'classical', diametrically
opposed to the snarling fury of the drummer's feature, a track that recalls Miles's classic recordings. A
thoroughly marvellous album and, along with the Columbia debut, the best place to start with
Marsalis's work.
    Marsalis popped up out of a generation supposedly conditioned by funk and anti-musicianship very
nearly fully formed. His tone, forged in the hot press of the Messengers, is bright and scalpel-sharp, and
not above dipping down into dissonances that recall anyone you like between Bubber Miley and Leo
Smith. On 'Later' (*Think Of One*), he is as 'contemporary' as anyone might ask; on 'Much Later' (*J
Mood*; can these be references to Mr Davis's celebrated exit-line?) he is much more consciously in the
tradition. He also sounds much better without a second horn, laying out the theme with the same
thoughtful intensity that he brought to the still-underrated *Standard Time*, which featured the same
band as *J Mood*.
    The underlying proposition would seem to be that jazz is not an entity but a particular way of approach-
ing musical performance, embellishing past musics with that same mixture of arrogant 'originality' and
respect. To that extent, *J Mood* is philosophically very much in line with all three standards projects.
'Skain's Domain' and 'Presence That Lament Brings' touch the opposite boundaries of Marsalis's
emotional range and illustrate that his greatest and most lasting virtue is not virtuosic flash and fire but
his handling of the band as a whole. Though this is relatively conventional theme-and-solos jazz, it's the
overall direction of each piece (and of the over-familiar staples on *Standard Time*) that evokes the most
positive response, stimulating comparisons with the similarly aged Ellington, who achieved the same
productive balance of individual and collective creative responsibility.

*** **Fathers And Sons** Columbia CK 37574
> Marsalis; Branford Marsalis (ts); Ellis Marsalis (p); Charles Fambrough (b); James Black (d). 82.

A nice concept, bringing together the Marsalises with (on the second side) Chicagoan saxophonists Von and Chico Freeman, whose contributions are reviewed separately. For once, Wynton is almost entirely upstaged by his elder brother, who plays one solo on 'A Joy Forever' that makes one wonder why the saxophonist doesn't do it more often. Ellis is calmly authoritative throughout, playing with delicate sophistication on 'Lush Life'. Wynton's own finest moment comes on 'Nostalgic Impressions', which anticipates the quiet interchanges of *Standard Time: Volume 3*, below. Not an essential item in the Marsalis canon, but worth having for both family gatherings.

***(*) **Marsalis Standard Time: Volume 1** Columbia 468713
> Marsalis; Marcus Roberts (p); Robert Leslie Hurst III (b); Jeff Tain Watts (d). 5 & 9/86.
***(*) **Standard Time: Volume 2 – Intimacy Calling** Columbia 468273
> Marsalis; Wes Anderson (as); Todd Williams (ts); Marcus Roberts (p); Robert Hurst, Reginald Veal (b); Herlin Riley, Jeff Tain Watts (d). 9/87–8/90.
*** **Standard Time: Volume 3 – The Resolution Of Romance** Columbia 466871
> Marsalis; Ellis Marsalis (p); Reginald Veal (b); Herlin Riley (d).

These were long anticipated by fans and sceptics alike, by the latter in order to see whether Marsalis really could cut it with a standards repertoire or whether the much-discussed vices of fussy formality and unswinging delivery would trip him up. The first of the series found himself establishing his own time-zone out of the pell-mell revisionist rush of the modernists, but by no means moving over into the fogeyish plains of the neo-traditionalists. *Marsalis Standard Time* still hasn't lost its burnish and, though there is a suspicion that the trumpeter is thinking through his strategies too far ahead of time to let them come across with spontaneity and freshness, the ideas are bright and individual. Two versions of 'Cherokee' particularly catch the ear; Marsalis's muted solo on the first is one of the finest things he has done on record and the piece is left in mid-flight, as if in anticipation of the more formal version which brings the album to a close.

Marsalis, bass and drums sit out 'Memories Of You', a fitting recognition that Roberts's sterling qualities are not just limited to accompaniment. The trumpeter also isn't heard on 'East Of The Sun (West Of The Moon)' on *Intimacy Calling*. The two later *Standard Time*s are less immediately impressive than the original, but the second volume is a deceptively simple record that constantly reveals new facets. Ellis Marsalis is a warm, unhurried player and the settings he lays out for his son are comfortable rather than challenging. Perhaps sensing that, Wynton relies on a larger-than-usual battery of muted effects, most notably the frail Harmon effects of 'Bona And Paul' and the wobbly wah-wah of 'The Seductress' (both actually originals). Ultimately, *The Resolution Of Romance* is rather forgettable, pretty but uninvolving, and certainly a lot less interesting than the Marsalis segment of *Fathers And Sons*.

***(*) **Live At Blues Alley** Columbia 461109 2CD
> Marsalis; Marcus Roberts (p); Robert Leslie Hurst III (b); Jeff Tain Watts (d). 12/86.

Next question up was whether, after all the big-label attention and all the classical gigs in black-tie halls, Marsalis could still hack it in your standard-issue smoky club. Recorded shortly after the first volume of *Standard Time*, these Washington, D.C., performances are among Marsalis's best and clearly establish him as the heir of Fats Navarro, Clifford Brown, Freddie Hubbard and maybe even the uptight little cat who'd just frosted him off a stage in Vancouver. His tone ranges from bright clarions that seem to come from Roy Eldridge or Harry 'Sweets' Edison, right through to tightly pinched notes that don't settle comfortably into the harmony, a sure sign that he has recognized some continuity between the occasional and untroubled use of atonality in classic jazz and the doctrinaire abandonment of harmony by the 1960s avant-garde, which he rejected so vehemently.

Virtually all the material is familiar from earlier CBS sessions. 'Knozz-Moe-King', from *Think Of One*, gets the set off to a ripping start and is reiterated as a band theme throughout. A reading of 'Au Privave' recalls the Messengers, but the real highlights are scalding performances of 'Skain's Domain', 'Delfeayo's Dilemma' and 'Chambers Of Tain' on which Marsalis's intensity is matched by a fine formal balance. His elaborations on 'Do You Know What It Means To Miss New Orleans' are also greatly inventive and conspicuously lack the slight self-consciousness that has occasionally crept into his embellishments of standard and traditional material.

The band is now thoroughly familiar to Marsalis-watchers, enough to register slight disappointment with the way Jeff Watts plays or has been recorded, making him sound blustery. Roberts is his usual tasteful self, but Hurst excels himself, cutting through a rather sibilant background with lovely rounded phrases and big, tantalizing harmonic ideas.

*** **The Majesty Of The Blues** Columbia 465129
> Marsalis; Teddy Riley (t); Freddie Lonzo (tb); Dr Michael White (cl); Wes Anderson (as); Todd

Williams (*ts, ss*); Marcus Roberts (*p*); Reginald Veal (*b*); Herlin Riley (*d*); Rev. Jeremiah Wright Jr (*v*). 10/88.

Wynton's tribute to the music of his native New Orleans combines inventive arrangements with a rather two-dimensional construction of his own role, which is largely limited to mimicking the growls, smears and vocalized tones of his artistic forebears. It's wrong to call *Majesty* a revivalist album; despite the presence of the clarinettist and scholar, Dr Michael White, on the 'New Orleans Function' suite, the music feels quite contemporary, certainly more so than on the later *Standard Time* sessions. Roberts's use of bop harmonies is on the title-track (also known as 'The Puheeman Strut'), and 'Hickory Dickory Dock' helps draw attention to Marsalis's restorative concern for the continuity of jazz music, which he believes was betrayed in the 1960s by a combination of scorched-earth experimentalism and commercial pop.

The long suite is essentially a funeral procession for 'The Death Of Jazz' and is dominated by a 17-minute sermon, 'Premature Autopsies', written by Stanley Crouch (who writes all of Marsalis's liner-notes, or the same liner-note umpteen times, depending on how persuasive you find him) and delivered by the Rev. Jeremiah Wright over an instrumental backing that deserves to be listened to carefully. Crouch's tribute to the nobility of jazz, and in particular the example of Duke Ellington, is surprisingly moving and shouldn't be dismissed as an uncomfortable distraction from the music. Interpreted discursively, it isn't up to much, written in the slightly breathless vein of liner-notes; as performed, though, it has a convincing majesty, even if it sounds closer to William Bradford Huie than to Martin Luther King Jr.

As 'concept' albums go, this is better than most, but it will disappoint anyone who wants to hear Marsalis in good blowing form; he is almost relegated to the status of guest artist, playing second trumpet to Teddy Riley on 'The New Orleans Function'.

*** Crescent City Christmas Card Columbia CK 45287

Marsalis; Wycliffe Gordon (*tb*); Wes Anderson (*as*); Todd Williams (*ts, ss, cl*); Alvin Batiste (*cl*); Joe Temperley (*bcl, bs*); Marcus Roberts (*p*); Reginald Veal (*b*); Herlin Riley (*d*); Kathleen Battle, Jon Hendricks (*v*). 89.

A pleasing enough confection and one that ties in very closely to the thinking of *Majesty Of The Blues*. If anything, the use of New Orleans devices and tonalities is *more* successful here than on the more serious *Majesty*, and there are moments of genuine beauty. Marsalis's attempt to combine the awe and sheer fun of Christmas works surprisingly well and the arrangements are very inventive. 'Hark! The Herald Angels Sing' is conceived as a dialogue between European harmony and a jazz groove, but it's 'The Little Drummer Boy' that really takes the breath away. Vocal features for Jon Hendricks (wonderful on 'Sleigh Ride') and soprano Kathleen Battle (upstaged by Wynton's own muted solo on 'Silent Night') and guest appearances by Todd Williams, Alvin Batiste and the evergreen Joe Temperley. Marcus Roberts devotes the usual solo piano slot to 'O Come All Ye Faithful'.

*** Thick In The South Columbia 468659

Marsalis; Joe Henderson (*ts*); Marcus Roberts (*p*); Bob Hurst (*b*); Elvin Jones, Jeff Tain Watts (*d*).

*** Uptown Ruler Columbia 468660

Marsalis; Todd Williams (*ts*); Marcus Roberts (*p*); Reginald Veal (*b*); Herlin Riley (*d*).

***(*) Levee Low Moan Columbia 468658

Marsalis; Wessell Anderson (*as*); Todd Williams (*ts*); Marcus Roberts (*p*); Reginald Veal (*b*); Herlin Riley (*d*).

Three simultaneous 1991 releases from Columbia's capacious vault, issued under the more or less meaningless rubric 'Soul Gestures in Southern Blue'. *Thick In The South* is the closest to the earlier quartet sessions, with Watts more than making up for Roberts's apparent lack of interest in the rhythmic progress of pieces and Joe Henderson checking in with some magisterial pronouncements from down the generations (by contrast, Elvin Jones's two guest slots are pretty pointless). *Uptown Ruler* is a tighter but less incisive album, with a thin overall sound, and far more of the emphasis falls on the leader's wonderfully contained and unruffled blues playing; 'Down Home With Homey' is particularly good (and you have to be aware of the ambiguity of 'home' and 'homey' in black parlance).

The final session, though, is the best. Marsalis is able to let his sound trickle out through the rich, Delta mud voicings of the saxophones (and the ever-present Roberts), and the leader's contribution on 'Jig's Jig' has a startling flavour like a freshet of river water welling up through the salt.

***(*) Blue Interlude Columbia 471635

Marsalis; Wycliffe Gordon (*tb*); Wessell Anderson (*as*); Todd Williams (*ts, ss, cl*); Marcus Roberts (*p*); Reginald Veal (*b*); Herlin Riley (*d*). 92.

This was the record that established Marsalis's new septet as a force to be reckoned with in contemporary music. Marsalis increasingly sees himself in a composite role as teacher/griot/*auteur*, placing less emphasis on composition and/or improvisation in themselves, more and more on both as they relate to wider patterns of thought. A tendency on the part of the critical establishment to see only part of the picture led many to dismiss him as a cold technician in thrall to corporate values, when in fact this record and those that followed it were among the most significant recordings in creative Afro-American music since Duke Ellington.

That said, *Blue Interlude* is curiously muted and even uncertain in places, its real significance becoming evident only when it is placed alongside the Septet's subsequent live performances. Marsalis's long monologue of 'Sugar Cane And Sweetie Pie' sets up the title-piece's very Ellingtonian opposition of motifs, moods and harmonic atmospheres, out of which develops one of the trumpeter's most flowing improvisations.

The remainder of the album is inevitably an anticlimax. Wycliffe Gordon's 'And The Band Played On' has moments of distinct promise, but the 'Jubilee Suite', for which Todd Williams takes credit, has little shape or substance, and the final section sounds oddly forced.

**** **Citi Movement (Griot New York)** Columbia 473055 2CD
> As for *Blue Interlude*, except omit Roberts; add Eric Reed (*p*).

Citi Movement was written for the brilliant choreographer, Garth Fagan, whose approach to the dance balances traditional and contemporary values in very much the same way as Marsalis's music. As so often, a specifically targeted project allows a musician to work at a rate of development very much faster than if he were writing more 'purely' or 'absolutely'. By this point, the Septet is playing with a greased precision of movement that is only mechanical in the most positive sense. The first section, 'Cityscape', has an energy and drive that are close to Mingus's Jazz Workshop period – and surely Stanley Crouch's sudden invocation of Mingus is no coincidence? – for this whole piece has the layered, kinetic quality that Mingus's larger-scale pieces almost always gave off.

A further interesting dimension of the score is Marsalis's new interest in the African components of Afro-American culture. 'Transatlantic Echoes' is searching and thoughtful and resolutely refuses to lean on bland anthropological borrowings. Instead, Marsalis has created his own sense of Africanism, one that is entirely conditioned by his personal circumstances and ideas, rather than being adopted like fancy dress. The final movement, 'Some Present Moments Of The Future', sketches out in ever more lifelike outline his vision of a viable jazz tradition.

If it has always seemed inevitable that Marsalis would one day produce a work of authentic greatness, *Citi Movement* comes very close to being it.

*** **In This House, On This Morning** Columbia C2K 53220 2CD
> As above, except add Marion Williams (*v*). 5/92.

The first Sacred Concert? Marsalis is now stalked by Ellingtonian parallels, whatever he does. Plunging back into church music and the homely liturgy of the Afro-American communion gave the trumpeter a new principle of organization to match that in *Majesty Of The Blues*.

Double CDs have now become the order of the day – unfortunately so, for there simply isn't enough music to justify the length of performance. The ritual slowness of 'Call To Prayer' and 'Recessional' is doubtless entirely deliberate, but it smacks of hesitancy and, for the first time in his career, Marsalis sounds as though he's relying on formulae and pat resolutions. The band as a whole creaks through the sermon which opens the second disc and it's only when the Sunday business is over and the 'Uptempo Postlude' and 'Pot Blessed Dinner' re-establish secular communion that the music regains something of its impetus.

There have, of course, been many attempts to marry jazz and church ritual, Ellington's only the grandest of them. One suspects that here, exceptionally, Marsalis really isn't sufficiently engaged (that hoary old charge) in what he's writing about, that the rituals he observes and reproduces remain only as abstract 'pieties' not as genuinely held beliefs. That may sound incidental but, given the claims made for this music at its first performance and thereafter, its credibility would be further undermined.

Warne Marsh (1927–87) TENOR SAXOPHONE

**** **Ne Plus Ultra** hat Art 6063
> Marsh; Gary Foster (*as*); Dave Parlato (*b*); John Tirabasso (*d*). 69.

*** **Warne Marsh / Lee Konitz: Volume 1** Storyville STCD 4094
> Marsh; Lee Konitz (*as*); Ole Kock Hansen (*p*); Niels-Henning Orsted-Pedersen (*b*); Svend Erik Norregaard (*d*). 12/75.

*** **Warne Marsh / Lee Konitz: Volume 2** Storyville STCD 4095
> As above. 12/75.

*** **Warne Marsh / Lee Konitz: Volume 3** Storyville STCD 4096
    As above. 12/75.
***(*) **Star Highs** Criss Cross Criss 1002
    Marsh; Hank Jones (*p*); George Mraz (*b*); Mel Lewis (*d*). 8/82.
*** **A Ballad Album** Criss Cross Criss 1007
    Marsh; Lou Levy (*p*); Jesper Lundgaard (*b*); James Martin (*d*). 4/83.
*** **Newly Warne** Storyville STCD 4162
    Marsh; Susan Chen (*p*); George Mraz (*b*); Akira Tana (*d*). 3/85.
*** **Back Home** Criss Cross Criss 1023
    Marsh; Jimmy Halperin (*ts*); Barry Harris (*p*); David Williams (*b*); Albert 'Tootie' Heath (*d*). 3/86.
*** **Two Days In The Life Of . . .** Storyville STCD 4165
    Marsh; Ron Eschete (*g*); Jim Hughart (*b*); Sherman Ferguson (*d*). 87.

By far the most loyal and literal of the Tristano disciples, Warne Marsh sedulously avoided the 'jazz life', cleaving to an improvisatory philosophy that was almost chilling in its purity. Anthony Braxton called him the 'greatest vertical improviser' in the music, and a typical Marsh solo was discursive and rhythmically subtle, full of coded tonalities and oblique resolutions. He cultivated a glacial tone (somewhat derived from Lester Young) that splintered awkwardly in the higher register and which can be off-putting for listeners conditioned by Bird and Coltrane.

Marsh's reputation still falls far short of that of his exact contemporary, Lee Konitz, with whom he interlocks gracefully like dancing master and pupil on the live sessions from Fasching in Stockholm. Where Konitz changed down the years, Marsh remained a dogged strict-constructionist, perhaps the last major exponent of Tristano's 'Cool School'. He is disappointingly served on record, and his best work is so far mostly unavailable on CD. The reissued *Ne Plus Ultra* is certainly the most important thing currently available. With a less assertive group, the Tristano influence bounces back with a vengeance. Marsh plays with considerable energy, stretching out his line on 'Lennie's Pennies' and ducking away from the obvious resolutions the band would seem to prefer. The Criss Crosses are also good, with *Star Highs* definitely the one to plump for (listen to the straightened-out 'Moose The Mooche'), though Barry Harris and Albert 'Tootie' Heath are highly responsive on *Back Home*, with the pianist playing in a boppish blues idiom similar to that of Hawes 30 years before, and Halperin contributing a second tenor on 'Two, Not One'.

Marsh needs to be listened to patiently and carefully – not always possible, given the state the discography is in and the quality of the live discs that are available. Fans may conclude that it's better to persist with vinyl's shortcomings than to risk distorting one of the genuinely unique voices in jazz. Just before Christmas 1987, Marsh collapsed and died at Donte's; he was playing 'Out Of Nowhere'.

Claire Martin (born 1967) VOCALS

*** **The Waiting Game** Linn AKD 018
    Martin; Jim Mullen (*g*); Jonathan Gee (*p*); Arnie Somogyi (*b*); Clark Tracey (*d*). 12/91.
***(*) **Devil May Care** Linn AKD 021
    As above, except add Rick Taylor (*tb, perc*), Nigel Hitchcock (*as*); Iain Ballamy (*ts, ss*). 2/93.
***(*) **Old Boyfriends** Linn AKD 028
    As for *The Waiting Game* except replace Gee with Steve Melling (*p*). 5/94.
***(*) **Offbeat** Linn AKD 049
    Martin; Mark Nightingale (*tb*); Gareth Williams (*p*); Martin Taylor (*g*); Anthony Kerr (*vib*); Arnie Somogyi (*b*); Clark Tracey (*d*). 8/95.

Martin's star potential was recognized at once and it has been patiently nurtured on these records. Her voice matures noticeably and broadens in range across the two-year gap between the first two, so that when she turns to material like Bob Dorough's 'Devil May Care' it sounds convincingly offhand and not just flip; similarly, her reading of Coward's 'If Love Were All'. The originals are most impressive, tautly constructed, unsentimental lyrics very much in the tradition of the great songwriters. 'On Thin Ice' will stand her in good stead for many years, as will her contribution to David Newton's 'Victim Of Circumstance'.

Martin's best albums to date came next. *Old Boyfriends* has a richness and experience that weren't in evidence before. The voice has acquired a lived-in quality which allows the illusion that she is not singing but merely conversing. At the same time, its harmonic subtleties make it as musically satisfying as it is personally involving. The closer, 'Killing Time', is indeed a killer but there is scarcely a slack moment throughout. *Offbeat* is inevitably a bit less polished. Recorded in Ronnie Scott's club, it is both more spontaneous and in some respects more ambitious and unpredictable. The addition of 'Wishful Thinking', a song with words by *Old Boyfriends*' producer Joel E. Siegel, brings a touch of danger and invention to a record that never seems in danger of falling back on easy options but is occasionally a touch formulaic. The duo with Taylor on 'Some Other Time' is almost perfect and the other guests, Kerr and Nightingale, contribute their mite to this fine session.

Pat Martino (born 1944) GUITAR

(*) El Hombre Original Jazz Classics OJC 195
    Martino; Danny Turner (*f*); Trudy Pitts (*org*); Mitch Fine (*d*); Abdu Johnson, Vance Anderson (*perc*). 5/67.
*** **Strings!** Original Jazz Classics OJC 223
    Martino; Joe Farrell (*ts, f*); Cedar Walton (*p*); Ben Tucker (*b*); Walter Perkins (*d*); Ray Appleton, Dave Levine (*perc*). 10/67.
*** **East!** Original Jazz Classics OJC 248
    Martino; Eddie Green (*p*); Tyrone Brown, Ben Tucker (*b*); Lenny McBrowne (*d*). 1/68.
** **Baiyina (The Clear Evidence)** Original Jazz Classics OJC 355
    Martino; Gregory Herbert (*as, f*); Bobby Rose (*g*); Richard Davis (*b*); Charli Persip (*d*); Reggie Ferguson (*perc*); Balakrishna (*tamboura*). 6/68.
*** **Desperado** Original Jazz Classics OJC 397
    Martino; Eric Kloss (*ss*); Eddie Green (*p*); Tyrone Brown (*b*); Sherman Ferguson (*d*). 3/70.
After graduating from soul-jazz organ combos and the John Handy group, Martino led his own bands on a series of records for Prestige, all of which have now been reissued in the OJC series. Both *El Hombre* and *Strings!* depend on blues-based formulas and are typical of the genre; but Martino's maturing style – heavily indebted to Grant Green and Wes Montgomery, but built for bigger speed than either of those masters – is good enough to transcend the settings. *Strings!* is noteworthy for a long, burning treatment of Gigi Gryce's 'Minority', where Farrell's thunderous tenor solo is matched by equally flying statements by Martino and Walton. Aside from the prophetically 'mystical' title-track, *East* offers some of Martino's clearest and most articulate soloing against a straightforward rhythm section. *Baiyina* nodded towards incense and peppermints with its noodling rhythm parts, but Martino's own playing remained tough underneath, and the rambling themes sometimes dissolved in the face of his improvising. *Desperado* is a little-known stab at fusion: Martino plays electric 12-string against rumbling electric piano and bass, and the results are akin to a tighter, less violent Lifetime. 'Express' and 'Desperado' hit a particularly compelling movement, although Green isn't a very stimulating partner (Kloss plays on only one track, 'Blackjack'). All the OJC remastering is good, although *Desperado*'s original production betrays how engineers didn't really know how to deal with that sort of music at the time.

***(*) **Live!** Muse MCD 5026
    Martino; Ron Thomas (*p*); Tyrone Brown (*b*); Sherman Ferguson (*d*). 9/72.
*** **Consciousness** Muse MCD 5039
    As above, except Eddie Green (*p*) replaces Thomas. 10/74.
*** **Exit** Muse MCD 5075
    Martino; Gil Goldstein (*p*); Richard Davis (*b*); Billy Hart (*d*). 2/76.
Martino spent the early 1970s with Muse, producing another strong and undervalued series of records. *Live!* consists of three long, rocking workouts which show how the guitarist can rework simple material into sustained improvisations of elegant and accessible fire: even when he plays licks, they sound plausibly exciting. Both *Consciousness* and *Exit* are a little more ballad-orientated, although the new quartet on the latter backs the leader with some intensity.

*** **The Return** Muse M 5328
    Martino; Steve LaSpina (*b*); Joey Baron (*d*). 2/87.
After signing for Warners in 1976, the results of which are now out of print, in 1980 Martino became ill and had to work his way back following a bout of amnesia. This live set shows all his old fluency intact on four long tunes, closely matched by LaSpina and Baron. If it seems a little less exciting than before, that may be because Martino's technique can seem more commonplace – or even more classical – in an age when guitars are more likely to be used as deadly weapons.

*** **Interchange** Muse MCD 5529
    Martino; James Ridl (*p*); Marc Johnson (*b*); Sherman Ferguson (*d*). 3/94.
***(*) **Nightwings** Muse MCD 5552
    As above, except add Bob Kenmotsu (*ts*); Bill Stewart (*d*) replaces Ferguson. 5/94
***(*) **The Maker** Paddlewheel KICJ 229
    As above, except Joe Bonadio (*d*) replaces Stewart, omit Kenmotsu. 9/94.

Martino's latest outings confirm his eminence. The flowing single-note lines have never sounded more fluent, and as a composer he's starting to amass a considerable library of tunes which other guitarists might look to for source material. Almost anything off *Nightwings* in particular would enhance a set-list: 'Draw Me Down' is a melodic gem, 'Portrait' a shimmering example of playing old-style soul-jazz in the 1990s. For these, and for Kenmotsu's quicksilver playing, this album has the edge, but the two quartet dates are almost as appealing, resting all the main responsibility on Martino's shoulders to no ill effect. Though Johnson is almost invisible at times – the mixes tend to fold him into the harmonic background – it suits the empathy of the groups and underscores the logic of Martino's conception.

Barry Martyn (born 1941) DRUMS, VOCAL

** On Tour 1969 GHB BCD-255
> Martyn; Clive Wilson (*t*); Frank Naundorf (*tb*); Dick Douthwaite (*cl, as*); Jon Marks (*p*); Brian Turnock (*b*). 68.

**(*) Legends Of Jazz & Barney Bigard GHB BCD-338
> Martyn; Andrew Blakeney (*t, v*); Louis Nelson (*tb*); Barney Bigard, Joe Darensbourg (*cl*); Alton Purnell (*p, v*); Ed Garland (*b*). 5/74.

*** Barry Martyn's Down Home Boys Sackville KCD2-3056
> Martyn; Wendell Eugene (*tb*); Chris Burke (*cl*); Ron Simpson (*g*). 10/93.

This cigar-chomping Londoner went to New Orleans in 1961 and became an unlikely champion of the city's traditional jazz. Basing his own style around that of the New Orleans masters, he not only sought out his heroes but played with them, recorded them and conducted interviews that have become integral to the archives on the music. At the moment only a few of his many records are available on CD, and this handful is rather unrepresentative. The 1968 set features a band of Brits whose enthusiasm doesn't wholly make up for the lack of finesse on ancient history such as 'Dardanella'; the recording sounds rusty, too. Martyn formed his Legends Of Jazz with a crew of venerable old-timers in 1973, and they became something of a festival attraction. This is quite a spirited recording, with guest Bigard sounding much stronger than he does on the *Pelican Trio* sessions (listed under Bigard's name). Some of the pieces shake along rather than swing, and Purnell's two vocals sound like pure sandpaper, but somehow Martyn (who was some 40 years junior to all the others) makes the whole thing work. His playing is strong enough to lift the band but never rough enough to knock the players about.

The recent Sackville CD is a good-natured jazz beano and, though the interesting instrumentation is never used to any surprising ends, the way that the players seem to blend agility with amiable sloppiness is rather engaging. Bonus marks for playing 'Blue Hawaii', 'Sail Along Silvery Moon' and 'Dolores' instead of the usual old scrolls.

Greg Marvin TENOR SAXOPHONE

*** I'll Get By Timeless SJP 347
> Marvin; Hank Jones, Susan Chen (*p*); George Mraz (*b*); Billy Higgins, Akira Tana (*d*). 12/86–3/87.

**(*) Taking Off! Timeless SJP 348
> Marvin; Tom Harrell (*flhn*); Joe Locke (*vib*); George Cables (*p*); Eric Von Essen (*b*); Sherman Ferguson (*d*). 11/89.

The callow, impassive sound which Marvin finds in the tenor's upper register is a clue to his inspiration, Warne Marsh; and his improvisations have much of the lean, endlessly unspooling quality which Marsh bequeathed to modern saxophone. Marvin also likes to keep things on a steady simmer, which suits the situation on both records listed here. *I'll Get By* is a reissue of a couple of small-label LPs; with Jones, Mraz and Higgins at their professional best, it's a date full of felicities: Marvin sustains the very long ballad form of 'Our Angel' with real insight and, while some of his quicker solos seem like mere exercises, he obviously loves to play. Three tracks feature him with fellow Marshite Susan Chen on piano. But the relatively plain *Taking Off!* suggests that Marvin could already use a change of pace, at least in the studios: it's agreeable but blander than the earlier sets.

Keshavan Maslak aka Kenny Millions ALTO SAXOPHONE, BASS CLARINET, SYNTHESIZERS, OTHER INSTRUMENTS

*** Loved By Millions Leo CD LR 105
> Maslak; John Lindberg (*b*); Sunny Murray (*d*). 10/80.

*** **Mother Russia** Leo CD LR 177
    Maslak (solo) and with Misha Alperin (*p*); Anatoly Vapirov (*ts*); Vladimir Tarasov (*d*). 89.
*** **Not To Be A Star** Black Saint 120149
    Maslak; Paul Bley (*p*). 10/92.
***(*) **Romance In The Big City** Leo CD LR 104
    As above. 2/93.
*** **Excuse Me, Mr Satie** Leo CD LR 199
    Maslak; Katsuyuki Itakura (*p*). 5/94.
A talented but slightly enigmatic figure, Maslak cultivates a broadly satirical tone, as in the rock-influenced fantasies of another disc called *Loved By Millions* (formerly on ITM, but not to be confused with the fierce free-bop session listed above) and in 'Kenny Meets Misha Meets Hieronymus Bosch' on *Mother Russia*. The second Leo set was recorded during a tour of Lithuania and Maslak's ancestral Ukraine (he was born in New York). His technique is boppish, but with elements of abstraction; the satire in no way deflects or compromises his virtuosity. An extraordinarily overblown passage in the duet with pianist Alperin is sustained over nearly a minute by circular breathing, punctuating a folksy romp, some funeral music and a couple of cheesy dance tunes. The duets with Vapirov, 'One/Two/Three/Four Million Little Russians', are more intense but sound very dated. The real core of the album, and best confirmation of Maslak's quality, is the long duet with percussionist Tarasov, recorded on the same remarkable tour of the then Soviet Union. Considerably more accessible than most native Russian improvisation, Maslak's work is worth a look, and *Mother Russia* is the ideal place.

    The duos with Bley are extraordinary. All freely improvised – sometimes over lyrics written by Maslak in his Kenny Millions guise – they are some of the most intense and abstract performances the pianist has ever recorded, surprisingly so now at a time when he seemed to have rediscovered the jazz heartland. Access to a 24-track studio allowed the saxophonist to multi-track himself on clarinet at a couple of points on *Not To Be A Star*, a slightly gimmicky date that has less sheer impact than the less crisply recorded *Romance In The Big City*. Reissue of the 1980 record shows how little Maslak's basic approach has changed in the interim. Murray pushes him further than usual in the direction of abstraction, but the saxophonist tends to stick to a fairly linear programme nevertheless, creating an impression throughout that he is accompanying his own rhythm section. As on the other records, the music remains difficult to categorize: 'everyday magic / very deep / almost impossible to understand'.

    The Satie session combines straight performances of 'Gnossiennes', 'Le Piège de Méduse' and other compositions by the maverick Frenchman, with interpolated 'excuse mes', executed in the Kenny Millions persona. As usual, the range of stylistic registers is sufficiently bewildering to suggest that passive acceptance is the best stratagem. A clever, funny show, it loses a little on record.

Phil Mason CORNET

(*) **You Do Something To Me! Lake LACD33
    Mason; Martin Bennett (*tb, v*); James Evans (*cl, ts*); Jim McIntosh (*bj*); Trefor Williams (*b*); Colin Bowden, Pete Cotterill (*d*); Christine Tyrrell (*v*). 8/93.
Methodical trad from a band given to no frills and not much licence. Mason's lead is decent enough but it's Bennett's rather less predictable trombone parts that stand out in the ensembles. The foot-dragging tempos don't assist much, though.

Rod Mason CLARINET, CORNET, VALVE TROMBONE, ALTO SAXOPHONE

*** **Struttin' With Some Barbecue** Black Lion BLCD 760511
    Mason; Pete Allen (*cl, ts, bs*); Jonny Withers (*bj, g*); Chris Haskins (*b, v*); Jimmy Garforth (*d*). 1/77.
(*) **Hot Five Timeless TTD 538
    Mason; Joe Wulf (*tb*); Engelbert Wrobel (*cl, as*); Rainer Oeding (*tba*); Ray Smith (*p*); Udo Jaegers (*bj, g*). 12/86.
(*) **Rod Mason's Hot Music Timeless TTD 550/551
    Mason; Achim Sturm, Uwe Schmidt, Karl-Heinz Weinz (*t*); Joe Wulf (*tb, v*); Engelbert Wrobel (*cl, as*); Hans Zaehringer (*cl, ts, bs*); Gerhard Muller (*cl, ts*); Ralph-Michel Peyer (*p*); Udo Jaegers (*bj, g*); Rainer Oeding (*b, tba, p*); Marcel Van Maele (*perc*). 7/88.
An unreconstructed traditionalist, Mason often manages to sound like a computer-generated model of what traditionl jazz is supposed to sound like. His bands often sound stiffly correct and only rather mechanically swinging. There is doubtless a large market for material of this sort, and we could not in conscience suggest that any of these are less than professionally done, in either playing or performing

terms; but they will prove to be thin pickings for anyone who knows anything of the originals, Mason's sources.

Masqualero GROUP

***(*) **Bande A Part** ECM 1319
    Nils Petter Molvaer (*t*); Tore Brunborg (*ts, ss*); Jon Balke (*p, ky*); Arild Andersen (*b*); Jon Christensen (*d*). 8 & 12/85.
*** **Areo** ECM 1367
    As above, except Frode Alnaes (*g*) replaces Balke. 11/87.
***(*) **Re-Enter** ECM 1437
    As for *Bande A Part*, except omit Balke. 12/90.

Rooted on one of the finest rhythm sections in Europe, Masqualero occasionally sound like a self-conscious pastiche of the ECM sound: bleak, atonal passages grafted on to rippling polyrhythms, interspersed with sound-for-sound's-sake patterns from the horns, and quiet, folksy melodies. What is interesting about the group's development over three albums is the abandonment (tactical or enforced) of harmony instruments in favour of a very stripped-down melodic approach that casts the bassist and drummer into appropriately high profile. It's routine to say that the two young frontmen are not up to the quality of the 'rhythm section', but Molvaer and Brunborg sound fresh and unaffected on the first album and have matured considerably in the five years since then. Their contributions to 'Li'l Lisa', 'Re-Enter' and 'Gaia' on the most recent album are quite adventurous and certainly far in advance of anything attempted on the atmospheric *Bande A Part*.

It's still probably the best of the three. *Areo* is not so good, for indefinable reasons that don't have anything obvious to do with the change in personnel. *Re-Enter* sounds a little tentative again, but it does sketch out some promising ways forward. Needless to say, recording quality on all three is absolutely top-notch.

Cal Massey (1928–72) TRUMPET

*** **Blues To Coltrane** Candid 9029
    Massey; Julius Watkins (*frhn*); Hugh Brodie (*ts*); Patti Brown (*p*); Jimmy Garrison (*b*); G. T. Hogan (*d*). 1/61.

Massey arranged 'The Damned Don't Cry' for his friend John Coltrane's May 1961 session and then promptly disappeared again. Though he was widely respected as a writer, and co-wrote Archie Shepp's *Lady Day* for the Brooklyn Academy of Music, he recorded only once under his own name, and that was thanks to Nat Hentoff's generosity. For years the only part of the January 1961 session to be made available was an excerpt (*Jazz Life*, on Candid) of the long 'Father And Son', with which *Blues To Coltrane* closes.

Its overdue release does nothing to reshape the jazz or even the trumpet pantheon, but it does confirm Massey as an impressive composer whose performing range is no narrower than many a player who went on to rack up a dozen albums. The opening 'Blues To Coltrane' is a slightly raggy tribute, with Massey sounding somewhat like Wilbur Harden and Brodie reading out the Trane times in a rather flat, announcer's diction. 'Bakai' was originally written for the great saxophonist and recorded in 1957, with trumpeter Johnny Splawn and baritonist Sahib Shihab on the eponymous *Coltrane*. Massey's own version is far less smooth, but possibly closer to its keening clamour, implied by the Arabic title.

'These Are Soulful Days' was written for Lee Morgan's *Leeway*. Again, the composer's own version has more unplaned edges. The rhythm section, here and throughout, really isn't up to much, with Garrison curiously disappointing on his double-time solo. Only with 'Father And Son', which extends to 11 minutes, does the band start to gel, by which time it's all over. Not a classic, but a valuable solitary glimpse of a briefly influential and slightly tragic figure.

Mark Masters (born 1958) ARRANGER

*** **Priestess** Capri 74031-2
    Louis Fasman, Carl Saunders, Les Lovitt, Clay Jenkins (*t*); Rick Culver, Dave Woodley, Fred Simmons, Jimmy Knepper (*tb*); Clint Sandusky, Allan Morrissey (*btb*); Danny House (*as, f*); Jerry Pinter (*ts, f*); Terry Federoff (*ts, f, af*); Bill Harper (*ts*); Mike Turre (*bs, bcl, f*); Tommy Gill (*p*); Dean Taba (*b*); Randy Drake (*d*).

Conservative but not humdrum, this is a finely honed and smartly played record that speaks of only a modest ambition for Masters. Knepper and Harper are cast as the two principal soloists and both play with gusto and charm, although Harper is matched by Jerry Pinter on 'Naima'. Only Gill is a less than strong soloist. The material, unusually, has no composing by Masters (Harper himself contributes four tunes, including the minor classic 'Priestess' itself): he is content to do the arranging, which is skilful but unwilling to draw attention to itself. Both 'Naima' and 'Giant Steps' throw a little fresh light on Coltrane by concentrating on the themes themselves and, although the title-composition was handled more vividly by Gil Evans, it's a failsafe tune to have in the band's book.

Ronnie Mathews (born 1935) PIANO

***(*) **Selena's Dance** Timeless SJP 304
    Mathews; Stafford James (b); Tony Reedus (d). 1/88.
***(*) **Dark Before The Dawn** DIW 604
    Mathews; Ray Drummond (b); Billy Higgins (d). 10/90.
*** **Lament For Love** DIW 612
    Mathews; David Williams (b); Frank Gant (d). 6/92.

A venerable sideman, Mathews has made only rare excursions as a leader. He's an exemplar of the skilful and self-effacing modal pianists who came in the wake of McCoy Tyner's eminence in the 1960s. While there's nothing to pull listeners out of their seats on either of the first two of these records, each says much about the dedication and craft of the five men involved. Mathews likes generously voiced chords and momentous rhythmic drive, and his partners on both discs complement his playing with great insight. Yet they are very different recitals. With James – an old friend and playing companion – and Reedus, Mathews tries a wide variety of settings: 'Stella By Starlight' becomes a bass feature after a lovely out-of-tempo intro by James, 'My Funny Valentine' is an unexpectedly hard-hitting swinger, 'Body And Soul' starts with an improvisation on the verse, and the title-track is built on locomotive rather than dance rhythms, sustained with terrific power by all three men. *Dark Before The Dawn* is less variegated but, if anything, even more accomplished, in part because Higgins – whose work on cymbals is particularly well caught by the sumptuous sound – is so masterful. This time Mathews builds 'Theme From M*A*S*H' on to a Tynerish vamp, starts a reading of 'You Don't Know What Love Is' with a solo section from 'Don't Explain' and freshens up two infrequently visited standards in 'The End Of A Love Affair' and 'You Leave Me Breathless', which open and close the record with decisive authority. Two very satisfying records.

If *Lament For Love* is a fraction less satisfying, that's no disgrace: it's just that the nine themes here receive a treatment that relies more on solid, gracious routine than on the careful preparation which distinguished the earlier discs. 'Gee Baby Ain't I Good To You', a singer's vehicle and a rare one for the piano, touches a fine vein of wistful lyricism.

Bill Mays (born 1944) PIANO

*** **Kaleidoscope** Jazz Alliance TJA-10013
    Mays; Dick Oatts (ss, ts, f); Peter Sprague (g); Harvie Swartz (b); Jeff Hirshfield (d). 10/89.
*** **At Maybeck Volume 26** Concord CCD 4567
    Mays (p solo). 9/92.
*** **Bill Mays / Ed Bickert: Concord Duo Series Vol 7** Concord CCD 4626
    Mays; Ed Bickert (g). 3/94.
*** **An Ellington Affair** Concord CCD 4651
    Mays; John Goldsby (b); Lewis Nash (d). 7/94.

Though he subsequently settled on the East Coast, Mays is a Californian whose dynamics and even-tempered skills suggest a natural disciple of the tradition of Lou Levy, Pete Jolly, Claude Williamson and Marty Paich. *Kaleidoscope* bustles through some clever arrangements, the centrepiece being the pretty if ultimately rather bland 'Adirondack': Sprague shows more muscle than he does on his own records, and the reliable Oatts puts in some pungent playing, but the record is still sunnily polite rather than passionate. Mays's contribution to the Maybeck series turns out in much the same way: there are some imaginative standards, such as a neatly embroidered 'Nightingale Sang In Berkeley Square' and 'Guess I'll Hang My Tears Out To Dry', but 'Jitterbug Waltz' is done prissily, and 'Grandpa's Spells', delivered as a party-piece encore, misses the gravity that Marcus Roberts can bring to a similar chestnut. The meeting with Bickert is a charmer, the guitarist's old-fashioned elegance settling nicely alongside Mays's rather more inquiring parts, and while nothing here really makes one sit up and listen there are moments – especially the almost luminous ballad improvising of 'Quietly' – which run deep.

The Ellington album has its share of ingenuities – 'Satin Doll' is a revisionist treatment to end them all, finding a vein of melancholy which the song has scarcely sustained in the past – without making one sure that Mays has an agenda of any conviction beyond impressing the listener. He approaches almost every theme with an unexpected idea, but the chosen path – such as the boogie undertow of 'I'm Just A Lucky So And So' – can seem as gimmicky as it is genuine. Goldsby and Nash lend pristine support, all the same.

Marilyn Mazur PERCUSSION, DRUMS, VOICE

*** **Future Song** VeraBra 2105
> Mazur; Nils Petter Molvaer (*t*); Elvira Plenar (*p, ky*); Klaus Hovman (*b*); Audun Klieve (*d*); Aina Kemanis (*v*). 7/90.

Mazur works an area mid-way between rock and jazz, seemingly without entering into the predictable mannerisms of 'fusion'. The songs themselves are well structured and lyrically sound. 'First Dream' is a mini-cycle punctuated with Schubert references. Kemanis's high, strong voice and Mazur's backing vocals and percussion establish the basic framework round which the other players, Molvaer especially, are free to elaborate. The recording is bold and pointed, with a heavy bass, and the two drummers are well defined.

Giovanni Mazzarino (born 1965) PIANO

*** **Silence, Please!** Splasc(h) H 375-2
> Mazzarino; Flavio Boltro (*t, flhn*); Benedetto Modica (*tb*); Orazio Maugeri (*as*); Marcello Szocol (*vib*); Lello Panico (*g*); Riccardo Lo Bue (*b*); Paolo Mappa (*d*). 1/91.

An engaging, cheerful atmosphere surrounds this melodious and unpretentious session, with the sunny version of Horace Silver's 'Barbara' typifying the good humour of the date. The other five compositions are by Mazzarino and, though nothing makes a resounding impression, the music benefits from the contrasts in the cast: Panico's wishfully rocking guitar is countered by Boltro's imperturbably cool trumpet and flugelhorn, and Maugeri has a nicely bluesy tone. The leader does nothing extraordinary at the piano, but it doesn't detract.

Guido Mazzon TRUMPET, FLUGELHORN, VOICE, ELECTRONICS

***(*) **Other Line** Splasc(h) H 317
> Mazzon; Umberto Petrin (*p*); Tiziano Tononi (*d*). 4–5/90.
** **Il Profumo Della Liberta** Splasc(h) H 377-2
> As above, except add Renato Geremia (*vn, cl*); Eleonora Nervi (*tba*); Ellen Christi (*v*). 4/92.

Guido Mazzon has been seeking new forms for jazz trumpet for many years. He recorded an all-solo record as far back as 1975 and another with the sole support of vocalist Marco Magrini in 1979; but none of his albums has been much distributed outside Italy. All the more cause to welcome *Other Line*, a fine trio session for Splasc(h). While there is some studio doctoring – the multiple-horns effect on 'Secret Music' and a stern reading of Ornette Coleman's 'Lonely Woman' – it's mostly the highly detailed interplay among the three musicians which the album relies on to make its mark. Mazzon never comes on as a great virtuoso and prefers a more circumspect approach, picking over melodic fragments and using the false areas of the horn very sparingly. Petrin responds with a similarly restrained style, allusively hinting at tonalities in some pieces and taking a linear course in others; Tononi plays time-keeper and colourist with marvellously adept touches. A couple of the slower pieces perhaps outstay their welcome, but otherwise a fine encounter.

It's a pity that the augmented group on *Il Profumo Della Liberta* adds little but pretentious weight to Mazzon's music. Christi's vocalizations range from complementary to glaringly inappropriate, and the lyrics to 'Old Tales And New Songs' are insufferable. Nervi's tuba and Geremia's primitive violin also get in the way more than they help the music. Very disappointing.

M-Base Collective GROUP

*** **Anatomy Of A Groove** DIW 864
> Graham Haynes (*t*); Greg Osby (*as*); Steve Coleman (*as*); Jimmy Cozier (*bs*); David Gilmore (*g*); Andy Milne, James Weidman (*ky*); Reggie Washington (*b*); Marvin 'Smitty' Smith (*d*); Cassandra Wilson, Mark Ledford (*v*). 12/91–1/92.

'Current Structural Developments in 21st Century Creative Black Music'? Leave it out, guys. This is lively, sometimes pugnacious New York jazz-funk, salted with a few technological fillips. It's certainly not frontier music. The idiom is firmly rooted in the 1980s, and none the worse for that.

The collective nature of the project is reflected in writing credits, with Coleman (the dominant personality, one suspects), Milne, Gilmore, Osby, Weidman, Wilson and Washington all represented. The Coleman–Osby axis takes a fair chunk of the solo space, as predicted, and how one feels the need of a touch of brass to add a little bite and edge. That want is answered on the final track, the aptly titled 'Hormones', where Graham Haynes joins the two saxophonists for some testosterone-laden exchanges. Following immediately on from the Cassandra Wilson feature, 'One Bright Morning', it illustrates the potential range of the group. Unfortunately, for the most part *Anatomy Of A Groove* runs the gamut from A to B.

Christian McBride (born 1972) DOUBLE BASS

***(*) **Gettin' To It** Verve 523 989
>   McBride; Roy Hargrove (*t*); Steve Turre (*tb*); Joshua Redman (*ts*); Cyrus Chestnut (*p*); Ray Brown, Milt Hinton (*b*); Lewis Nash (*d*). 8 & 9/94.
***(*) **Number Two Express** Verve 529 585
>   McBride; Gary Bartz, Kenny Garrett (*as*); Kenny Barron, Chick Corea (*p*); Steve Nelson (*vib*); Jack DeJohnette (*d*); Mino Cinelu (*perc*). 11/95.

At just 24, McBride has the potential to become one of the legends on his instrument, up with the likes of Ray Brown and Milt Hinton. By the time he signed his deal with Verve, he was already a first-call sideman for a huge variety of sessions, and to date he has appeared on something like 60 or 70 records, preferred for his big woody tone and fluent delivery. He is one of the few mainstream bass players who is *always* interesting to listen to and who always has things to say rather than merely changes to negotiate.

Brown and Hinton join him on the first record for a remarkable three-bass version of Nefti's 'Splanky', but for the most part the date is unreconstructed and unapologetic hard bop with very few self-consciously contemporary references. *Gettin' To It* might almost be a Blue Note disc of a previous generation, something by Paul Chambers perhaps, except that McBride's approach goes back a half-generation beyond Mr P. C. for its sources and influences. One of those most frequently adduced when the album was released was Oscar Pettiford, and there is something of that in the riveting track, 'In A Hurry', with Josh Redman and Steve Turre in support. McBride works a number of variations on the basic quintet, and for 'Sitting On A Cloud' and 'Stars Fell On Alabama' he dispenses with horns altogether and substantially re-jigs piano-trio idiom with Chestnut and Nash. The last track of all is a pretty emphatic statement of intent, an unaccompanied trip on Jimmy Forrest's 'Night Train', with a magnificent bowed passage that makes one wish to hear more of his *arco* work.

The second album suffers only from the fact that McBride's quality is now so well attested that it is no longer a surprise. Again, he varies the line-ups, duetting with Barron on the Wayne Shorter tune, 'Mikayo', and with Cinelu (and using electric bass) on the closing 'Little Sunflower', another nod in the direction of Freddie Hubbard. Barron and Corea share piano duties, memorably on the latter's 'Tones For Joan's Bones' and, with Barron, on Ornette's 'Jayne'. Barron has always been a fine exponent of the Fender Rhodes; 'A Morning Story' is written for amplified instruments, a persuasive expansion of the language. The hornmen are not so much superfluous as something of a luxury in this company, and there are moments when one wonders whether they mightn't have been saved for another day, or whether a brass instrument mightn't have been a good idea. Bartz is, however, well up to his fine recent form and Garrett's uncluttered, bluesy lines are most attractive.

Production by Richard Seidel and Don Sickler is absolutely top-drawer, with McBride placed centre and left and the others ranged round him very naturally. The bass is very full, but never tiresomely dominant, as so often on gigs like this.

Les McCann (born 1935) PIANO, VOCAL

*** **Much Les** Rhino/Atlantic R2 71281
>   McCann; Leroy Vinnegar (*b*); Donald Dean (*d*); Willie Bobo, Victor Pantoja (*perc*); strings. 7/68.
(*) **Swiss Movement Atlantic 781 365-2
>   McCann; Benny Bailey (*t*); Eddie Harris (*ts*); Leroy Vinnegar (*b*); Donald Dean (*d*). 6/69.
*(*) **Layers** Rhino/Atlantic R2 71280
>   McCann; Jimmy Rowser (*b*); Donald Dean (*d*); Ralph MacDonald, Buck Clarke (*perc*). 11/72.

Although he has recorded dozens of albums, very little of Les McCann's output is currently in print –

fortunately for his reputation, since far too much of his production has been disfigured by faddish vocals and arrangements and by feeble material. *Much Les* is about the best of these three survivors. There are some fairly unintrusive strings on some tracks, but McCann sets up some grooving tempos that Vinnegar and Dean help him to keep moving, and it's as good as any soul-jazz of the decade. There's also a pleasing version of his charming ballad, 'With These Hands'. A hit album in its time, the appeal of *Swiss Movement* has faded fairly drastically. Cut live at Montreux, it's a ragged set of soul-jazz vamps, with a probably definitive version of McCann's 'Compared To What', but the excitement is mitigated by what remains atrocious sound, even for a live session. Bailey's solo on 'You Got It In Your Soulness' offers the best moment, but overall the revival of interest in soul-jazz has uncovered many better records than this. *Layers* is a trashy relic of thin, early-'70s soul-jazz, barely worth reviving.

*** **On The Soul Side** Musicmasters 65112-2
        McCann; Jeff Elliott (*t, flhn*); Keith Anderson, Eddie Harris (*ts*); Abraham Laboriel, John B.
        Williams (*b*); John Robinson, Tony St James (*d*); Lou Rawls (*v*). 1/94.

McCann has been in great live form of late, and this return to recording is sharp enough to warrant a listen. His fellow players here – apart from the wonderful Harris, whose double-act with Les on the road is a must – lean towards sessionman super-competence, but the old man's piano is sounding funkier than it has for a while. He persuades Lou Rawls to sing 'God Bless America' here, though it's not quite clear why.

Ron McClure (born 1941) DOUBLE BASS

**** **Descendants** Ken 660 56 007
        McClure; Tom Harrell (*flhn*); John Scofield (*g*); Mark Gray (*p*); Jimmy Madison (*d*). 7/80.
*** **Yesterday's Tomorrow** EPC 884
        McClure; John Abercrombie (*g*); Aldo Romano (*d*). 7/89.
***(*) **McJolt** Steeplechase SCCD 31262
        McClure; John Abercrombie (*g*); Richard Beirach (*p*); Adam Nussbaum (*d*). 12/89.
*** **Never Forget** Steeplechase SCCD 31279
        McClure; Eddie Henderson (*t*); Vincent Herring (*as*); Kevin Hayes (*p*); Bill Stewart (*d*). 10/90.
*** **For Tonite Only** Steeplechase SCCD 31288
        McClure; Randy Brecker (*t, flhn*); John Abercrombie (*g*); Adam Nussbaum (*d*). 3/91.
***(*) **Sunburst** Steeplechase SCCD 31306
        McClure; Tim Hagans (*t*); Conrad Herwig (*tb*); Joe Gordon (*as, ss*); Lee Ann Ledgerwood (*p*);
        Jeff Hirshfield (*d*). 12/91.
***(*) **Inner Account** Steeplechase SCCD 31329
        McClure; Rich Perry (*ts*); Kenny Drew Jr (*p*); Vic Juris (*g*); Sylvia Cuenca (*d*). 11/92.

McClure's fusion group, Fourth Way, extended the jazz-rock idiom he had helped create with Blood, Sweat and Tears and the Charles Lloyd Quartet into more adventurous compositional territory. A fine bassist, with an excellent *arco* technique (see 'Tainted Rose' on *Yesterday's Tomorrow*), he is also an exceptional composer who draws on non-jazz tonalities with great confidence.

The material on *Descendants* was written in 1980 for the group that recorded it. It opens brightly on 'Boat People', a deceptively funky theme that allows McClure to show how inventive he can be at the lower end of the bass without sounding glum or sententious. His line on 'Descendants' and 'Sunny Day' strongly recalls Scott LaFaro, who pioneered the rapid, multi-note approach McClure has adapted to a more straightforward rhythmic context. Like Eddie Henderson on the later and rather disappointing *Never Forget*, Tom Harrell has a rich, dark-edged tone that always sounds as if it ought to be registering a fifth down from what is actually being played. As such, it's the ideal complement to McClure.

The bassist sounds less persuasive in a conventional horn-led quintet, though, and Herring has an uneasy time of it on the 1990 session. McClure's preferred instrumentation is one that trickily pairs guitar and piano, usually allowing the keyboard player long, developed lines, while the guitarist plays 'free' over the top. That's essentially what Abercrobie does on *For Tonite Only*. The unstructured lines of 'Life Isn't Everything' on *Descendants* are a tongue-in-cheek version of open-form experiments McClure had participated in with Lloyd, and the guitar's role is made quite explicit here. He's also very interested in the way Miles Davis extended the language of modern jazz but constraining it harmonically, and uses both Abercrombie and Scofield (who played with Miles) in ambitious combinations with the rhythm line. Madison's drumming is a feature of the 1980s album that deserves to be highlighted. Madison has played with Carmen McRae, Jack Walrath and Roland Kirk, as well as with Harrell in the inventive Michael Cochrane quintet; like his leader, he's also a good pianist and adjusts his articulation very exactly to changes of key.

McClure's preference for players with a similar sound is obvious from the trio session with Romano and

Abercrombie (whose guitar synthesizer takes the place of an electric piano). This is more abstract, impressionistic music, and very different from the standards approach of *McJolt*, where McClure develops the LaFaro sound very impressively on tracks like 'Nardis', 'Stella By Starlight' and 'Once I Had A Secret Love'. The trio set, released on the Montpellier-based EPC, is slightly short on conventional jazz virtues but features some of McClure's best writing and some of his best arco work since 'Line' on *Descendants*. 'Midi Evil' presumably refers to the south of France rather than to MIDI technology. The set *is* rather dominated in places (on 'Panchito' to a great extent) by Abercrombie's effects, sometimes at the expense of McClure's and Romano's more delicate interchanges. The sound is also a bit overcooked.

That's two reasons why *Sunburst* registers so strongly. The recording is very bright and detailed, without too much rumble from the bass, and the playing is straightforward and to the point. McClure has rarely sounded better. This purple streak continues on the fine *Inner Account*. Decisively articulated and full of melody, the originals have splendid character, and journeymen like Perry and Juris play up to their best form.

Rob McConnell (born 1935) TROMBONE, VALVE TROMBONE

*** Live In Digital Sea Breeze CDSB 105

> McConnell; Arnie Chycoski, Erich Traugott, Guido Basso, Sam Noto, Dave Woods (*t, flhn*); Ian McDougall, Bob Livingston, Dave McMurdo (*tb*); Ron Hughes (*btb*); George Simpson, Brad Warnaar (*frhn*); Moe Koffman (*ss, as, f*); Jerry Toth (*as, f cl*); Eugene Amaro (*ts, f*); Rick Wilkins (*ts, cl*); Bob Leonard (*bs, bcl*); James Dale (*p*); Ed Bickert (*g*); Don Thompson (*b*); Terry Clarke (*d*); Marty Morell (*perc*). 12/80.

**(*) All In Good Time Sea Breeze CDSB 106

> As above, except John McLeod (*t, flhn*); Jim McDonald (*frhn*), Brian Leonard (*perc*) replace Warnaar, Bickert and Morell. 82.

Despite the accepted wisdom that a big band is a broke band, McConnell, a veteran of the Canadian dance-band scene of the 1950s and '60s, has kept his Boss Brass together on and off for 25 years. Initially they did without any kind of sax section, but by the time of these records the band had grown bigger. McConnell's charts suggest expansiveness as the band's signifying element: although the leader worked with Maynard Ferguson for a spell, the brassiness of the BB is exploited for sonority rather than clout, and there's a kind of reluctance to even their toughest arrangements. The music is skilfully handled, and the various editions of the orchestra never seem to marshal the kind of players to set light to the charts. Even where McConnell seeks to evade cliché, he can't altogether shrug off the MOR atmosphere which hangs round most of their records. The live disc is arguably their best, if only because the setting gives them a pinch of adrenalin which their studio records (there are several on Canadian labels) tend to miss. *All In Good Time* was a Grammy winner, but that tends to prove the even-tempered pitch of a band that ought to show a few more claws.

** The Rob McConnell Jive 5 Concord CCD 4437

> McConnell; Rick Wilkins (*ts*); Ed Bickert (*g*); Neil Swainson (*b*); Jerry Fuller (*d*). 8/90.

Away from the big band, McConnell reveals himself as a merely workmanlike soloist, and Wilkins is a carbon copy of Zoot Sims on an indifferent day.

** The Brass Is Back Concord CCD 4458

> McConnell; Arnie Chycoski, Steve McDade, John MacLeod, Guido Basso, Dave Woods (*t, flhn*); Ian McDougall, Bob Livingston, Jerry Johnson (*tb*); Ernie Pattison (*btb*); Gary Pattison, Jim McDonald (*frhn*); Moe Koffman, John Johnson (*ss, as, f, cl*); Eugene Amaro (*ts, cl, f*); Rick Wilkins (*ts, cl*); Bob Leonard (*bs, bcl, cl, f*); Don Thompson (*p*); Ed Bickert (*g*); Steve Wallace (*b*); Terry Clarke (*d*); Brian Leonard (*perc*). 1/91.

**(*) Brassy And Sassy Concord CCD 4508

> As above. 2/92.

The 'return' album by the Boss Brass is as accomplished as before, but there's too much lingering over detail and texture for a band in which details tend to disperse its impact. Most of the scores unfold at far too languorous a pace, each track clocking in between seven and eleven minutes. Moe Koffman's vigorous (in Boss Brass terms, splenetic) alto feature on 'All The Things You Are' is the most interesting event. *Brassy And Sassy* comes in at a slightly higher level: the notion of a 19-minute piece, 'Blue Serge Suit(e)', sounds frightening, but the band play with some aplomb here, and the opening 'Strike Up The Band' is about as sassy as this brassy lot will ever get.

*** Our 25th Year Concord CCD 4559

> As above, except Alistair Kay (*tb*) replaces McDougall. 93.

*** **Overtime** Concord CCD 4618

    As above, except Alex Dean (*cl, f, ts*), David Restivo (*p*), Jim Vivian (*b*) and Ted Warren (*d*)
replace Amaro, Thompson, Wallace, Clarke and Brian Leonard. 5/94.

(*) **Don't Get Around Much Any More Concord CCD 4661

    As above, except Judy Kay (*frhn*) and Lorne Lofsky (*g*) replace Pattison and Bickert. 4/95.

** **Trio Sketches** Concord CCD 4591

    McConnell; Ed Bickert (*g*); Neil Swainson (*b*). 5/93.

In and of themselves these are all plausible entries in McConnell's chosen genre – *Overtime* in particular
will probably be as close as the band will ever come to making a top-flight record. It starts with the lip-
busting title-track that takes off via Restivo's quirky solo and Johnson's hair-raising alto escapade, and
moves on through a lovely 'Stella By Starlight' for Basso and a two-tenor beanfest called 'This May Be
Your Lucky Day'. The rest is no more than the usual. So is *Our 25th Year*, which is more businesslike
than celebratory, and by the time of *Don't Get Around Much Any More*, which really starts to roll out the
clichés, one feels that the band might be ready for its collective pension. There's always the fire-power of
the section-work to enjoy, but even that is missing on McConnell's small-band starring role, *Trio
Sketches*. This is just plain dull.

Susannah McCorkle VOCAL

**** **The Quality Of Mercer** Jazz Alliance TJA-10031

    McCorkle; Digby Fairweather (*t, c*); Danny Moss (*ts*); Keith Ingham (*p*); Ron Rubin (*b*); Derek
Hogg (*d*). 9/77.

***(*) **No More Blues** Concord CCD 4370

    McCorkle; Ken Peplowski (*cl, ts*); Dave Frishberg (*p*); Emily Remler (*g*); John Goldsby (*b*);
Terry Clarke (*d*). 11/88.

***(*) **Sabia** Concord CCD 4418

    McCorkle; Scott Hamilton (*ts*); Lee Musiker (*p*); Emily Remler (*g*); Dennis Irwin (*b*); Duduka
Fonseca (*d*); Cafe (*perc*). 2/90.

*** **I'll Take Romance** Concord CCD 4491

    McCorkle; Frank Wess (*ts, f*); Allen Farnham (*p*); Howard Alden (*g*); Dennis Irwin (*b*); Keith
Copeland (*d*). 9/91.

McCorkle's records in the 1970s – mostly missing in action – established her as a major songbook
interpreter, uncovering rarities and seldom-heard verses from some of the best American composers.
But they did her few commercial favours. One at least has made it back to CD, and it's an absolute gem:
14 choice Johnny Mercer songs done with wit, feeling and guile in perfect balance, the charm of 'Love's
Got Me In A lazy Mood' matched to the wistfulness of 'Skylark'. A peerless session, with deft support
from Ingham, Fairweather and the rhapsodic Moss.

    Her current tenure with Concord has pointed her in a more successful direction, though the material is
often less challenging. *No More Blues* benefits from a superbly integrated band, with Peplowski and
Remler chiming in with pithy solos and Frishberg adding the most alert and gracious of accompaniments: McCorkle's big, courageous voice, which has been compared to Doris Day but will remind more
listeners of Julie London, is huskily entreating on the ballads and assuredly swinging on the faster tunes.
She's an interpreter rather than an improviser, which sees her through the Brazilian songs on *Sabia*: the
task here is to drift through the coolly appealing melodies rather than swinging them to pieces, and
McCorkle does it with perfect aplomb. A couple of the ballads sound too stretched, but her take on
Astrud Gilberto on 'So Danço Samba' is wholly beguiling, and Hamilton (in the Stan Getz role) and
Remler (in her final studio date) are marvellous.

    I'll Take Romance is perhaps a shade disappointing as a follow-up. Nothing wrong with the arrange-
ments and the players, with Wess defining his role as strong-but-tender tenorman. But the material – all
of it very well known, and excessively so in the case of 'Lover Man' and 'That Old Feeling' – seems like a
deliberate attempt to play down McCorkle's knack for discovering forgotten gems, and some of her
interpretations sound like false trails towards 'new' transformations. 'My Foolish Heart' and 'I
Concentrate On You' are studied enough to suggest caricature, although occasionally – as on a wonderfully sustained 'It Never Entered My Mind' – it works out, and the faster pieces are magical. All three
discs are recorded with fine lustre.

***(*) **From Bessie To Brazil** Concord CCD 4547

    McCorkle; Randy Sandke (*t, flhn*); Robert Trowers (*tb*); Dick Oatts (*as, f*); Ken Peplowski (*ts,
cl*); Allen Farnham (*p*); Howard Alden (*g*); Kiyoshi Kitagawa (*b*); Chuck Redd (*d*). 2/93.

Almost a classic – what holds it back, as always seems to happen with this tremendously gifted singer, is
the odd, strange lapse of judgement as to the kind of song she can get away with. The flaws this time are

an embarrassing 'My Sweetie Went Away', done as a misplaced tribute to Bessie Smith, and a wincingly cavalier 'Still Crazy After All These Years'. On the plus side are a dozen gorgeous interpretations. Her second attempt at 'The People That You Never Get To Love', Rupert Holmes's only memorable song, is as wryly affecting as Jobim's 'The Waters Of March' is coolly hypnotic, and she does Dave Frishberg ('Quality Time') and Mercer and Arlen as well as anyone today. Sound backing from one of the Concord repertory teams, with Allen Farnham directing.

*** From Broadway To Bebop Concord CCD 4615
 As above, except add Frank Vignola (*g*), Richard De Rosa (*d*); omit Alden and Redd. 4/94.
It will take tolerance to get through the aged kitsch of 'Chica Chica Boom Chic', and if she can do Broadway, then bebop isn't really her thing. But there are some great ones here: a Nancy Wilson-type drama called 'One Of The Good Girls', a fine 'Guys And Dolls'. And the husk in her voice is getting the more attractive, the older she gets. Farnham's group offer gold-plated support.

Jack McDuff (born 1926) ORGAN

*** Tough 'Duff Original Jazz Classics OJC 324
 McDuff; Jimmy Forrest (*ts*); Lem Winchester (*vib*); Bill Elliot (*d*). 7/60.
*** Brother Jack Meets The Boss Original Jazz Classics OJC 326
 McDuff; Harold Vick, Gene Ammons (*ts*); Eddie Diehl (*g*); Joe Dukes (*d*). 1/62.
*** Live! Prestige 24147-2
 McDuff; Red Holloway, Harold Vick (*ts*); George Benson (*g*); Joe Dukes (*d*). 6–10/63.
*** The Re-Entry Muse MCD 5361
 McDuff; Cecil Bridgewater (*t*); Houston Person, Ron Bridgewater (*ts*); John Hart (*g*); Grady Tate (*d*). 3/88.
*** Another Real Good 'Un Muse MCD 5374
 As above, except add Randy Johnston (*g*), Buddy Williams, Cecil Brooks III (*d*); omit Tate. 3/89–7/90.
**(*) Color Me Blue Concord CCD 4516
 McDuff; Red Holloway (*as, ts*); George Benson, Phil Upchurch, Ron Eschete (*g*); Kevin Axt (*b*); Joe Dukes (*d*); Denise Perrier (*v*). 5/91.
*** Write On, Cap'n Concord CCD 4568
 McDuff; Byron Stripling, Joe Magnarelli (*t*); Herb Besson (*tb*); Andrew Beals (*as*); Jerry Weldon (*ts*); John Hart (*g*); Winston Roye (*b*); Van Romaine, Rudy Petschauer (*d*); Johnnie Lambert (*v*). 6/93.
Titles like 'The Honeydripper', 'Whap!' and 'I Want A Little Girl' don't offer much promise of a delicate and subtle sensibility. However, 'Brother' Jack McDuff managed to shake loose from a basic Jimmy Smith influence to explore a subtler and less heavy-handed approach to organ jazz. The earlier stuff picked up by OJC has begun to reappear on CD and the three discs will be welcomed into the library of any collector who feels they have sufficient Smith albums by now. Little to choose between the two studio dates, though Harold Vick is rather unfairly made to play second fiddle to Ammons on *Brother Jack Meets The Boss*: his feature on 'Strollin'' is as good as anything the other tenorman comes up with. *Live!* gets the nod for an extra ounce of excitement, with the likes of 'Rock Candy' and 'Sanctified Samba' digging deep without losing sight of McDuff's inventiveness and willingness to pace himself through both a solo and a set. There are also interesting glimpses of the young George Benson at work.

 McDuff's career – or mission – has revived in the 1980s and '90s, and there are several recent sets to savour. The musical equivalent of soul food, they're undemanding and curiously satisfying. There's more musical fibre on the two Muses, with Person – who set the whole thing up – having a party to himself on 'Walking The Dog' and 'Electric Surfboard' (a young person's term for guitar, apparently) on the earlier date. Organist and tenorman do a nice duet on 'Summertime' on the second one. The Concords are a bit smoother and sometimes run ashore on dud material but McDuff is a genial host, and the horns lend muscle to *Write On, Cap'n*.

Bernie McGann ALTO SAXOPHONE

*** Ugly Beauty Spiral Scratch 0010
 McGann; Lloyd Swanton (*b*); John Pochee (*d*). 1/91.
*** McGann McGann Rufus R F011
 As above, except add James Greening (*tb*). 8/94.
McGann's base in Sydney isolates him from a wider awareness, but he's a powerful, surprising, indi-

vidual player whose work deserves wider currency. By working without a piano he opens these sessions up harmonically, yet he's a relatively conservative player: he sounds more in debt to the hard-bop masters than to Dolphy or Coleman. The weight and heft of his playing make him sound like a tenor player who's picked up the alto almost by chance, and since his closest cohort on these sessions is Pochee, they sometimes approximate the feel and timbre of the Sonny Rollins/Elvin Jones Vanguard battles (especially on the extended rumpus created out of 'Without A Song', on *Ugly Beauty*). For all its heat and light, though, the trio session could use a centre of gravity: here and there the music seems to be grinding forward, and there's a lot of weight on McGann's shoulders.

Some of that is solved by *McGann McGann* and the recruitment of Greening, who actually takes the first solo on the record. With a Brookmeyer-like sense of humour and a big, vocal (rather than vocalized) sound, he's an apposite foil to the altoman. Some of the tunes have a bucolic charm about them, such as 'Brownsville' and 'June Bug', which makes one think of some of Jimmy Giuffre's more spirited music. But the whimsicality doesn't always work to the music's advantage, and it sometimes comes out slight.

Howard McGhee (1918–87) TRUMPET

**** Howard McGhee & Milt Jackson Savoy SV 0167
     McGhee; Billy Eckstine (*vtb*); Kenny Mann (*ts*); Jimmy Heath (*as, bs*); Milt Jackson (*vib*); Will Davis, Hank Jones (*p*); Ray Brown, Percy Heath (*b*); Joe Harris, J. C. Heard (*d*). 2/48.
*** Maggie's Back In Town! Original Jazz Classics OJC 693
     McGhee; Phineas Newborn (*p*); Leroy Vinnegar (*b*); Shelly Manne (*d*). 6/61.
***(*) Sharp Edge Black Lion BLCD 760110
     McGhee; George Coleman (*ts*); Junior Mance (*p*); George Tucker (*b*); Jimmy Cobb (*d*). 12/61.
**(*) Just Be There Steeplechase SCCD 31204
     McGhee; Per Goldschmidt (*t*); Horace Parlan (*p*); Mads Vinding (*b*); Kenny Clarke (*d*). 12/76.
The relentlessly self-destructive McGhee helped shape a convincing synthesis between swing and bop, much as Roy Eldridge was to do. Fats Navarro, a colleague in the Andy Kirk band, was his first and most important model, and the two can be heard together on *The Fabulous Fats Navarro*. McGhee never achieved anything like Navarro's astonishing poise at speed (nor Gillespie's pure energy), settling instead for Eldridge's sharply toned medium tempo without the roof-lifting high notes. A firebrand when a younger man (he wrote the show-stopping 'McGhee Special' while with Andy Kirk), he developed into a thoughtful and rather inward player who could be banal or unorthodoxly brilliant in successive tracks. McGhee isn't well represented on CD, but the reappearance of the early Savoy is a welcome addition, even if it catches the trumpeter at a particularly tempestuous time, when music was taking a back seat to other imperatives. The partnership with Milt Jackson (another man slightly short on inner tranquillity) is unexpectedly calm and centred, and there are half a dozen breathtaking moments from the trumpeter.

On *Maggie's Back In Town!* McGhee sounds straightened out and clear-headed, tackling 'Softly As In A Morning Sunrise' and 'Summertime' at a hurtling pace that sounds good in the ensembles but flags a little when McGhee is soloing. The opening 'Demon Chase', dedicated to Teddy Edwards's son, is similarly hectic, but is good-natured enough. 'Brownie Speaks', included in homage to Clifford Brown, stretches him a little more convincingly, but by then the set is over. There is really only one ballad, and 'Willow Weep For Me' takes a slightly hysterical edge (as do one or two of the other tracks) from Newborn's very tensed-up accompaniment.

It's an uncomfortably thin legacy from (on his day) one of the finest trumpeters of the period.

Ladd McIntosh ARRANGER, COMPOSER

*** Bulbous Garlic Blues Sea Breeze CDSB-2042
     R. C. Bob Clark, Wayne Bergeron, Louise Baranger, Bob Summers, Peter Olstad, Doug Scharf, George Stone (*t*); Eric Jorgensen, Bruce Fowler, Alex Iles, Ken Foberg, Rich Bullock (*tb*); Glen Garrett, Jon Crosse, Steve Fowler, Jim Snodgrass, Ray Reed, Kurt McGettrick (*reeds*); Geoff Stradling (*p*); Jerry Watts (*b*); Rod Harbour (*d*); Billy Hulting (*perc*); Cheryl Bentyne (*v*). 10–11/91.
A studio orchestra and occasional vehicle for McIntosh's writing, this big big band packs a wallop that the exemplary Sea Breeze engineering makes the most of, with the reeds and brass positioned in delicious contrast. McIntosh musters some charts that go beyond the merely engaging – 'Moonrise' is an especially picturesque ballad, with Snodgrass's tenor as the jewel at its centre – but a perhaps inevitable

fondness for precision over looseness, in the West Coast big-band tradition, prevents the record from really cutting loose. There are still some ear-grabbing solos, especially the splendidly vociferous Jorgensen on a clever revision of 'Mack The Knife', and McIntosh pays tribute to another great modern arranger with a strongly coloured treatment of Duke Pearson's 'Jeannine'.

Randy McKean ALTO SAXOPHONE, BASS CLARINET

*** **So Dig This Big Crux** Rastascan BR D-012
    McKean; Paul Smoker (*t*); Drew Gress (*b*); Phil Haynes (*d*). 4/91.

The rest of the group are familiar from Smoker's Joint Venture band, but McKean is the leader, and he's a vigorous altoist in the post-Chicago manner of the American avant-garde. Since the record is dedicated to Anthony Braxton, it's appropriate that he has something of that great Chicagoan's fiercely deliberate phrasing and scalded tone at intense moments. But passages such as the bass clarinet and trumpet dialogue of 'Quilt' are also in the spirit, if not quite the manner, of Eric Dolphy with Booker Little. Some tracks, such as the 12-minute 'Marchling', don't justify their length, but the satirical gospel strokes of 'Wholly Roller' and disrespectful reading of Roscoe Mitchell's 'Line Fine Lyon Seven' show that all four know their onions. Besides, Smoker is always worth hearing.

Dave McKenna (born 1930) PIANO

**** **Giant Strides** Concord CCD 4099
    McKenna (*p* solo). 5/79.
*** **No Bass Hit** Concord CCD 4097
    McKenna; Scott Hamilton (*ts*); Jake Hanna (*d*). 3/79.
***(*) **Left Handed Complement** Concord CCD 4123
    McKenna (*p* solo). 12/79.
*** **My Friend The Piano** Concord CCD 4313
    As above.
*** **A Celebration Of Hoagy Carmichael** Concord CCD 4223
    As above. 5/83.
***(*) **Dancing In The Dark** Concord CCD 4292
    As above. 8/85.
***(*) **Live At Maybeck Recital Hall: Volume 2** Concord CCD 4410
    As above. 11/89.
*** **No More Ouzo For Puzo** Concord CCD 4365
    McKenna; Gray Sargent (*p*); Monty Budwig (*b*); Jimmie Smith (*d*). 6/88.
***(*) **Shadows And Dreams** Concord CCD 4467
    McKenna (*p* solo). 3/90.
***(*) **A Handful Of Stars** Concord Ccd 4580
    As above. 6/92.
*** **Concord Duo Series: Volume 2** Concord CCD 4552
    McKenna; Gray Sargent (*g*). 6/92.

Dave McKenna hulks over the keyboard; *Giant Strides* it is. He is one of the most dominant mainstream players on the scene, with an immense reach and an extraordinary two-handed style which distributes theme statements across the width of the piano. That's particularly evident on the good 1979 *Left Handed Complement*, a mixture of moody ballads and sharp, attacking modern themes (there's also an original 'Splendid Splinter') which keeps turning up fresh ideas. He doesn't threaten, he just plays, and on the earliest of these he plays up a storm. Long a 'players' player', he has grown in popularity and stature in recent years, not least through his association with the young Scott Hamilton, who plays a forceful but unquestionably secondary role on *One Bass Hit*.

McKenna is that rare phenomenon, a pianist who actually sounds better on his own. Though he is sensitive and responsive in group playing, and the association with Hamilton proves that, he has quite enough to say on his own account not to need anyone else to hold his jacket. The Hoagy tribute, recorded at the Second Story Club and the Tubaranch in Bloomington, Indiana, demonstrates his ability to tame an audience, and illuminate some turgid material in the process. No such problems (the former, at any rate) at Maybeck Hall, where the audiences are famously well behaved and attentive. McKenna's first Berkeley recital – *Handful Of Stars* was also played on that warm-hearted piano – is among the latest and best of McKenna's solo performances. He medleys – a frequently tiresome practice – with considerable ingenuity and absolute logic, switching hands, reversing the direction of the new theme and carefully disguising the welds. The 'Knowledge Medley' sounds odd and contrived on paper

– 'Apple For The Teacher', 'I Didn't Know What Time It Was', 'I Wish I Knew', 'You'll Never Know', but you get the idea? – and works superbly in performance. The final 'Limehouse Blues' is archetypal.

Jazz players owe Arthur Schwartz an enormous debt. There are well over 50 versions of 'Alone Together' in the current catalogue, a record that approaches old warhorses like 'Body And Soul' and 'All The Things You Are'. McKenna treats the tunes with considerable respect, preserving their shape rather than just winkling out the meat of the chords. 'A Gal In Calico' and 'I See Your Face Before Me', both routinely sentimentalized, are played with exemplary taste, and 'Dancing In The Dark' has almost as much innate energy as a much later composition of the same name by a Bruce Springbok or Springstream, something like that. *My Friend* is the weakest of the bunch. The two medleys – 'Summer' and 'Always' – are slacker, and McKenna's very physical relationship with his instrument is slightly off-balance. (Normally he sounds as if he might be able to pick it up and put it in his pocket.) The 1990 solo disc ends a bit that way. It's a 'Dreams' and 'Shadows' medley, but McKenna is as distinct and wide-awake as ever. One of his best.

The quartet might just as well be a solo performance. Gray Sargent isn't quite the death's head the opening number suggests, but *rigor* has set in somewhere. Budwig is as loose and flowing as ever, and Smith clatters along with more enthusiasm than finesse. There's a 'Talk' medley this time, but you'll have to guess what's in that.

Sargent reappears on an early Concord duo Maybeck ('Maybeck' has almost become generic) and this is altogether more satisfactory. The sound is as good as you could possibly hope for and the twosome are ideally matched on 'letter' and 'time' medleys which tax Sargent's harmonic abilities more than a little but out of which he emerges with the appropriate three stripes and a hearty round of applause.

McKinney's Cotton Pickers GROUP

**** The Band Don Redman Built (1928–1930) Bluebird N D 90517
John Nesbitt, Langston Curl, Joe Smith, Leonard Davis, Sidney De Paris, George 'Buddy' Lee (*t*); Rex Stewart (*c*); Claude Jones, Ed Cuffee (*tb*); Don Redman, George Thomas (*reeds, v*); Milton Senior, Prince Robinson, Jimmy Dudley, Benny Carter, Coleman Hawkins, Ted McCord (*reeds*); Todd Rhodes, LeRoy Tibbs, Fats Waller (*p*); Dave Wilborn (*bj, g, v*); Ralph Escudero, Billy Taylor (*tba*); Cuba Austin, Kaiser Marshall (*d*); Jean Napier (*v*). 6/28–11/30.
***(*) McKinney's Cotton Pickers 1928–29 Classics 609
As above. 6/28–11/29.
***(*) McKinney's Cotton Pickers 1929–1930 Classics 623
As above, except add James P. Johnson (*p*). 11/29–11/30.
Despite the title of the Bluebird compilation, it was primarily John Nesbitt who built McKinney's Cotton Pickers (although Jean Goldkette, who booked the band into his Graystone Ballroom in 1927, gave them their name). Redman's arrival in 1928 brought his distinctive touch as arranger to the band's book – there are 12 of his charts on the Bluebird disc – but Nesbitt's driving and almost seamless charts were as impressive, and they remain so, more than 60 years later. Bluebird have compiled a 22-track set which works well as a sampler of the band. McKinney's Cotton Pickers were among the most forward-looking of the large bands of their era: while the section-work retains all the timbral qualities of the 1920s, and the rhythm section still depends on brass bass and banjo, the drive and measure of the arrangements and the gleaming momentum of their best records both suggest the direction that big bands would take in the next decade.

On the later, New York sides, guest soloists include Coleman Hawkins, Rex Stewart and Fats Waller, and Benny Carter has one of his sharpest early outings on 'I'd Love It'. But Nesbitt, Robinson and Redman himself are significant players on the earlier sides, and the precision and verve of the band *in toto* is the main point of most of these tracks. Some of the vocals are banal, but most of the sides worst affected by that malaise of the period have been left off the Bluebird set at least, while the Classics pair of CDs cover twice as much ground – though there are no alternative takes (several exist), and it also includes all the weaker material. As a one-disc representation, the Bluebird set works well. The sound is a mixed bag. Most of the tracks come across in a full-bodied way, but one or two have some surface whistling and others blast at loud points. The Classics CDs are also variable – smooth and clear on some tracks, less gratifying on others. It's good that the complete set of the band's individual titles is available on CD, but one feels that there may be a better job to be done yet.

Hal McKusick (born 1924) ALTO SAXOPHONE

*** Triple Exposure Original Jazz Classics OJC 1811
McKusick; Billy Byers (*tb*); Eddie Costa (*p*); Paul Chambers (*b*); Charli Persip (*d*). 12/57.

A careful, swing-influenced stylist, McKusick took a thoughtful, melodic approach to soloing, keeping the tune in view at all times, rarely straying off into vertical fantasies. He's perhaps best known for his clarinet work with Charlie Parker and for the fine *Cross Section Saxes*, where he mixes ballad standards, 'Now's The Time' and 'Stratusphunk' by George Russell, a composer with whom he had a close relationship.

Some material from *Triple Exposure* was around for a while on the *Bird Feathers* compilation. McKusick stands up pretty well on an album of his own and manages to play in his own style, which is actually quite a long way from Bird in the final analysis. Byers is an excellent player with a big dynamic range. The two horns are particularly good on 'Con Alma', which is the archetypal McKusick performance.

John McLaughlin (born 1942) GUITARS, GUITAR SYNTHESIZER

**** Extrapolation Polydor 841598
  McLaughlin; John Surman (*bs, ss*); Brian Odges (*b*); Tony Oxley (*d*). 1/69.
**** Where Fortune Smiles BGO 1006
  McLaughlin; John Surman (*bs, ss*); Karl Berger (*vib*); Dave Holland (*b*); Stu Martin (*d*). 71.
Extrapolation is one of the finest jazz records ever made in Europe. Ranging between gently meditative runs, as on 'Peace Piece', and furious 13/8 scrabbles, it combines all of McLaughlin's virtues (accuracy, power, vision) on a single disc. It has transferred to CD reasonably well, though Odges and some of McLaughlin's lower runs sound slightly artificial.

The band was state-of-the-art for 1969. Oxley's drumming has the firmness of a rock beat, even when the count is extremely irregular, and Surman's playing is cast midway between folksy melodizing and complete abstraction. Tie to a chair any British jazz fan who came of age between 1967 and 1972, and a substantial number will confess that 'Binky's Beam' is their favourite track of all time. Those who attempt to deny Mclaughlin's *bona fides* as an improviser almost always refer to *Shakti*, pseudo-classical pieces like the *Mediterranean Concerto* or one of the duff Mahavishnu Orchestra records like *Visions Of The Emerald Beyond*. They generally keep stumm about *Extrapolation*. This is essential and timeless.

If anyone wants to trace back the lineage of the Orchestra, then the reissued *Where Fortune Smiles* is the place to look. Anticipations of Jan Hammer's rippling arpeggiations and electronic soars can be heard in Berger's vibes and Surman's deceptively plain-spoken saxophone lines. It would be stretching it a bit to suggest that Dave Holland fulfilled the violin part, except that he does play genuine counter-melodies and does so in a rich, stringy tone that was so different from the amplified bass playing of the time. When this record came along, a new idiom seemed securely in place. Later, as we've said, it became fashionable to deride it, but even after 25 years the musicianship is immediately impressive and the overall conception still valid. *Extrapolation* is still the masterwork, but its successor repays attention as well. Catch it while it's still around.

*** Shakti Columbia 467905-2
  McLaughlin; L. Shankar (*vn*); R. Raghavan (*mridangam*); T. S. Vinayakaram (*perc*); Zakir
  Hussain (*tabla*). 75.
Sweetly complex acoustic music that was initially hard to absorb after the fantastic energy of the original Mahavishnu Orchestra, but which was infinitely more impressive than the OTT gestures and uneasy syntheses of Mk II. Shankar quickly went on to personal stardom, but the real drama of this set (which is much superior to the later *Handful Of Beauty*) is the interplay between McLaughlin and the tabla and clay pot percussion. Though it appeared to many fans that McLaughlin had simply gone native, it's easier in hindsight to see the continuity of all his work, in bop-influenced advanced rock, fusion, flamenco and Eastern forms, rather than its apparent breaks and changes of direction.

*** Johnny McLaughlin: Electric Guitarist Columbia 467093
  McLaughlin; David Sanborn (*as*); Patrice Rushen (*p*); Chick Corea (*p, syn*); Stu Goldberg
  (*electric p, org, syn*); Tom Coster (*org*); Carlos Santana (*g*); Jerry Goodman (*vn*); Stanley
  Clarke, Jack Bruce, Neil Jason, Fernando Saunders (*b*); Alphonso Johnson (*b, b pedals*); Billy
  Cobham, Jack DeJohnette, Tony Smith, Narada Michael Walden, Tony Williams (*d*); Alyrio
  Lima, Armando Peraza (*perc*). 78.
To some extent, *Electric Guitarist* was an attempt to distance McLaughlin from the Mahavishnu image of a rather intense, mystically inclined artist in white cheesecloth and sandals, plugging direct into the Godhead. The original album-cover featured a hand-tinted school photo with pinned to it a cod business-card as if McLaughlin were a jobbing guitarist: weddings, functions, recording sessions – competitive rates. Here, it seemed to be saying, is an ordinary bloke playing with a selection of his mates, none of your metaphysical fannying about.

Unfortunately, the musical content was very much a case of steady as you go, and more than one reviewer mistook this star-studded session for a compilation of out-takes from previous bands. There is a neo-Mahavishnu track, 'New York On My Mind' with Goodman, Cobham and draftees Goldberg and Saunders; a 'Friendship' is co-fronted with 'Devadip' Carlos Santana, in recollection of the now unfairly sneered-at *Love, Devotion & Surrender* album (*two* cheesecloth shirts, *four* sandals); while 'Every Tear From Every Eye' brings in David Sanborn for a single hot solo, much like the one on Gil Evans's *Priestess*.

There is a Coltrane tribute, 'Do You Hear The Voices That You Left Behind?', with Corea, Clarke and DeJohnette, and the record reaches its peak with a superb duet with Cobham. In between, 'Are You The One? Are You The One?' reunites three-quarters of the second version of Lifetime only to prove how essential Larry Young was to the sound. Bruce's yawing bass might almost have been supplied by a machine at this point in his career, so unimaginative was his playing, and McLaughlin is reduced to big wah-wah shapes like a child's paper cutouts. The closing 'My Foolish Heart' is a rare chance to hear McLaughlin tackle a standard. Like the rest of the album, a split decision.

**(*) Adventures In Radioland Verve 519 397

> McLaughlin; Bill Evans (*sax, ky*); Mitchell Forman (*ky*); Abraham Wechter (*g*); Jonas Hellborg (*b*); Danny Gottlieb (*d, perc*). 1 & 2/86.

Confusingly, McLaughlin revived the Mahavishnu name for this project which bears no discernible relation to the early-'70s group. Dropping the 'Orchestra' tag was a little ironic, because all the synclavier digital equipment and Sycologic PSP drum interfaces and synths give the band a b-i-g expensive sound that conjures up adjectives like 'orchestral' willy nilly, but not without some irony. It seems that these recordings lay in the vault for some time before release. If so, one can easily relate to the marketing problem. Having done the stratospheric electric god bit, McLaughlin had recolonized a corner of the acoustic empire, and it must have been difficult to know how this testosterone-dripping sound would take.

The problem lies not so much with the playing as with the writing, which is uniformly drab and unconvincingly macho. Evans's squawking solos flap through chicken-coop effects from Forman's keyboards, while Hellborg and Evans plug away humourlessly in the background. There are flashes of the old McLaughlin on 'Reincarnation' (not just the title) and 'Florianapolis', but generally this is bankrupt stock, and the much-heralded return to electricity goes nowhere fast.

*** Live At The Royal Festival Hall JMT 834436

> McLaughlin; Kai Eckhardt (*b*); Trilok Gurtu (*perc*). 11/89.

Twenty years on, with Lifetime, the Mahavishnu Orchestra(s), Shakti, the One Truth Band, and a wobbly 1980s mostly behind him, McLaughlin again sounds on good form, punching out rows of notes which are almost as impressive for their accuracy as for their power. Eckhardt is a subtler and more involving player than his predecessor, Jonas Hellborg, and Gurtu, as with the revivified Oregon, gives excellent value. The themes are no longer as obviously visionary and Eastern-influenced and the guitarist seems content to re-run many of the stylistic devices he had adopted from the days with Miles Davis through the ringing harmonics of Shakti and back out into a more obviously jazz-grounded idiom. These days, though, they have a clear organic function in the music. Less indulgent than formerly, McLaughlin can afford to let his strengths show through.

**** Qué Alegría Verve 837280 2

> McLaughlin; Kai Eckhardt, Dominique De Piazza (*b*); Trilok Gurtu (*d*). 11 & 12/91.

Designer stubble on the liner-photo and the most robust set from McLaughlin in a long time. Gurtu has always been a pulse-driven percussionist, rarely content merely to provide exotic colours round the edges of the music, and he and the bassists (Eckhardt appears on 'Reincarnation' and '1 Nite Stand', the two most forceful tracks) push McLaughlin's acoustic but subtly MIDI'd lines almost to the limits. Very little sign of the rather soft-centred flamenco approach and Indo-fusions that have dominated his work for many years. Excellent.

**(*) Time Remembered Verve 519 861

> McLaughlin; Aighetta Guitar Quartet: François Szonyi, Pascal Rabatti, Alexandre Del Fa, Philippe Loli (*g*); Yan Maresz (*b*). 3/93.

McLaughlin's equation of Bill Evans = romanticism = guitars is the first and most serious thing wrong with this record. The Aighetta Quartet have performed many of the finest works for guitar ensemble, including, trivia collectors, one by the late British novelist and composer *manqué*, Anthony Burgess. Though there is nothing inherently wrong with having an essentially classical group play Evans's music (after all, the Kronos Quartet had done it), this is just not the group. In a brief personal memoir of Evans, McLaughlin remembers the pianist performing at the Village Vanguard and going into what he, very perceptively, describes as a 'state of grace'. The point was that Evans's trances were hard-won, the result of a profound dialectical approach to his material, not just an on/off mysticism.

Time Remembered drifts all too readily into such a state. The music (familiar and beautiful themes like 'Turn Out The Stars' and, of course, 'Waltz For Debby') has no tension. Lacking drama, it ultimately lacks interest, and a rather short set is beset with *longueurs* which eventually torpedo it.

*** **Tokyo Live** Verve 521 870
    McLaughlin; Joey De Francesco (*org, t*); Dennis Chambers (*d*). 12/93.
***(*) **After The Rain** Verve 527 467
    As above, except replace Chambers with Elvin Jones (*d*). 10/94.
McLaughlin calls this new group the Free Spirits. The organ/guitar/drums line-up has become modestly fashionable again; John Abercrombie has experimented with it, and McLaughlin really sounds as if he's having *fun* for the first time in a long while. He extends the big, chunky sound he was exploring again in the mid-'80s, throwing in Wes Montgomery octave-runs and some of his own old wobbly chords. 'JuJu At The Crossroads' is terrific, though it has to be said that some tracks, notoriously the closing 'Mattinale', drag their feet unconscionably in a way they couldn't have been allowed to do in a studio. Positive sign, though: wanting to play as long as that.

Still Free Spirited, but darker and more serious in tone and with one significant change of personnel, *After The Rain* is a set of Coltrane and Coltrane-associated pieces, with a couple of McLaughlin originals thrown in. The immediate reaction on hearing those organ bass-lines and every-which-way cymbal patterns is that this is some forgotten item from the McLaughlin–Larry Young–Tony Williams terror trio, Lifetime. Too cleanly recorded, though, and McLaughlin's guitar has a plainer, quasi-acoustic ring, not the full-choke distortion of earlier years. Like his predecessor, but with less competition, Jones is almost too much in this context. The opening workout on 'Take The Coltrane' very nearly damps enthusiasm for what's to come, except that 'My Favorite Things' and 'Sing Me Softly Of The Blues' and then 'Naima' (in which Jones dramatically switches to big palpitating tattoos on his skins) are so damn beautiful that you'd forgive him anything.

The mood is more sombre in the second half, and the drummer is less dominant, as if satisfied by his spot on McLaughlin's 'Tones For Elvin Jones'. On the face of it, 'Crescent' and 'After The Rain' aren't the likeliest items for this treatment, but they are exquisitely re-imagined, and demand to be heard again and again. A lovely record; shame about the rock album fades, though.

*** **The Promise** Verve 529 828
    McLaughlin; David Sanborn (*as*); Michael Brecker (*ts*); Jeff Beck, Philippe Loli, Paco De Lucia, Al DiMeola (*g*); Joey DeFrancesco (*org, t*); Jim Beard, Tony Hymas (*ky*); Nishat Khan (*sitar, v*); Pino Palladino, James Genus, Yan Maresz, Sting (*b*); Dennis Chambers, Vinnie Colaiuta, Mark Mondesir (*d*); Don Alias, Trilok Gurtu (*perc*); Zakir Hussain (*tabla*); Susana Beatrix, Stephania Bimbi, Mariko Takahashi (*v*). 95.
What is 'the promise'? The notion perhaps that, just as there are always new fields to explore, so too the past is never quite shut off, that there are always places to go, forward or back. McLaughlin has always been a restless explorer of his own past, unusually conscious of his own back-catalogue. In a sense, this record is a re-run of *Electric Guitarist*, a sampling of tracks by half a dozen different line-ups, collaged with readings from Dante, Lorca and *haiku*. The effect is bitty and slightly bewildering, but there are treasures to be found.

The Free Spirits trio is convened for 'Thelonious Melodius'. It immediately follows a guitar workout on John Lewis's 'Django', with Jeff Beck – of all people – as second guitar. An even less likely personnel credit is Sting, who joins McLaughlin and Vinnie Colaiuta for one minute and twelve seconds of head-down jamming; wonder if he kept the cab waiting. Another long-standing trio, with de Lucia and DiMeola, reappears for 'El Ciego', a slightly routine dip into their emotive contrapuntal bag. The really substantial stuff (and the bulk of the album) is contained in two saxophone-led tracks: 'Shin Jin Rui' with the guest performer *par excellence*, David Sanborn; and the long, long 'Jazz Jungle', with the even more ubiquitous Michael Brecker up front. The latter degenerates into a bit of a jam but, with saxophone and guitar swapping ideas at ever higher altitudes, it's sustained by sheer excitement and pace, even over 14 minutes.

One fascinating oddity is 'No Return' (which is presumably not McLaughlin's philosophy). Here he swaps places with DeFrancesco, who gets out his trumpet while the boss doubles on keyboards. Most of the ideas have been heard before, but never in this configuration, and it might have been more effective to leave it to the end of the record, which concludes on an ultra-mellow acoustic reading of Jimmie Rowles's 'The Peacocks'. Though this is a minor miscall, what comes across throughout the album is the extent of McLaughlin's fascination with the studio and its potentialities. He clearly wants to create an integrated and emotionally supple product that cancels out the item-by-item approach. He hasn't quite succeeded, but with continued major-label backing he has the opportunity to experiment further. A valid experiment by a major artist.

Jackie McLean (born 1932) ALTO SAXOPHONE

***(*) **Lights Out** Original Jazz Classics OJC 426
    McLean; Donald Byrd (*t*); Elmo Hope (*p*); Doug Watkins (*b*); Art Taylor (*d*). 1/56.
*** **4, 5 And 6** Original Jazz Classics OJC 056
    McLean; Donald Byrd (*t*); Hank Mobley (*ts*); Mal Waldron (*p*); Doug Watkins (*b*); Art Taylor (*d*). 7/56.
*** **McLean's Scene** Original Jazz Classics OJC 098
    McLean; Bill Hardman (*t*); Red Garland, Mal Waldron (*p*); Paul Chambers, Arthur Phipps (*b*); Art Taylor (*d*). 12/56, 2/57.
*** **Jackie's Pal** Original Jazz Classics OJC 1714
    McLean; Bill Hardman (*t*); Paul Chambers (*b*); Philly Joe Jones (*d*). 56.
*** **Alto Madness** Original Jazz Classics OJC 1733
    McLean; John Jenkins (*as*); Wade Legge (*p*); Doug Watkins (*b*); Art Taylor (*d*). 57.
*** **Makin' The Changes** Original Jazz Classics OJC 197
    McLean; Webster Young (*t*); Curtis Fuller (*tb*); Gil Coggins, Mal Waldron (*p*); Paul Chambers, Arthur Phipps (*b*); Louis Hayes, Art Taylor (*d*). 2/57.
*** **A Long Drink Of The Blues** Original Jazz Classics OJC 253
    As above. 8/57.
*** **Strange Blues** Original Jazz Classics OJC 354
(*) **Jackie McLean & Co. Original Jazz Classics OJC 074
    McLean; Bill Hardman (*t*); Ray Draper (*tba*); Mal Waldron (*p*); Doug Watkins (*b*); Art Taylor (*d*). 2/57.
*** **Fat Jazz** Fresh Sound FSR CD 18
    McLean; Webster Young (*t*); Ray Draper (*tba*) Gil Coggins (*p*); George Tucker (*b*); Larry Richie (*d*). 12/57.

Charlie Parker once invited Jackie McLean to kick him in the ass as pay-off for some typically selfish transgression. There were those who felt that McLean in turn could have used similarly robust encouragement in the 1950s, when his life and career teetered towards the edge.

These come from a turbulent but productive period in McLean's career. The OJCs mine almost to exhaustion the mid-1956 and early-1957 sessions with Waldron, filling in with other Prestige and New Jazz materials. McLean's pure, emotive blues tone, characteristically taking off with a wail at the break, has already become a manner, but there is a searching, troubled quality to his work on 'Abstraction' (*4, 5 And 6*), 'Flickers' and 'Help' (& *Co*), and the two takes of 'Long Drink Of The Blues' (OJC 253, which also includes desirable versions of 'I Cover The Waterfront', 'Embraceable You' and 'These Foolish Things'). Given the range and familiarity of material, this might seem a good place to start, but *Scene* ('Mean To Me' and 'Old Folks') and *Changes* ('I Hear A Rhapsody' and 'Chasin' The Bird') are more challenging, pointing a way out of the still-dominant Parker influence.

Perhaps the best of the group is the earliest. *Lights Out* has a directness and simplicity of diction that are not so evident elsewhere; where McLean does attempt something more adventurous, as in the 'bagpipe' introduction and carefully harmonized final chorus of 'A Foggy Day', he does so with taste and precision. As on *4, 5 And 6*, Byrd is a fine collaborator, soloing in a sweet, Dorham-influenced tone on the ballad 'Lorraine' and 'Kerplunk', both of which were written by the trumpeter. Hardman, a 'pal' from the *Hard Bop*-vintage Jazz Messengers, is almost equally good and Philly Joe cooks up an accompaniment very nearly as forceful as Blakey's.

The Fresh Sound is desirable not least because of the CD format but also for freshly minted charts, and the inventive brass interplay of Young and Draper (who led his own session with John Coltrane a year later – *A Tuba Jazz*, Fresh Sound CD 20). 'Tune Up' is one of McLean's leanest and most daring performances of the period.

**** **New Soil** Blue Note CDP 784013
    McLean; Donald Byrd (*t*); Walter Davis Jr (*p*); Paul Chambers (*b*); Pete LaRoca (*d*). 5/59.

Transitional and challenging, *New Soil* seems reasonably tame by present-day standards. McLean had passed through difficult times and was visibly reassessing his career and direction. The extended 'Hip Strut' is perhaps the most conventional thing on the album, but the saxophonist is straining a little at the boundaries of the blues, still pushing from the inside, but definitely looking from a new synthesis. 'Minor Apprehension' has elements of freedom which are slightly startling for the period and wholly untypical of McLean's previous work. Davis contributes a number of compositions, including the previously unreleased 'Formidable' (which isn't). Byrd is still a more than viable player. The transfer isn't as good as usual, with a lot of mess on the drummer's tracks, but the music is important enough to be labelled historic.

***(*) **Bluesnik** Blue Note B21Y 84067
    McLean; Freddie Hubbard (*t*); Kenny Drew (*p*); Doug Watkins (*b*); Pete LaRoca (*d*). 1/61.
Tough, unreconstructed modern blues that reveal considerable depths on subsequent hearings. That's particularly noticeable on the outwardly conventional title-track, on which McLean's solo has a formidably unexpected logic. The other soloists tend to take up space that one might prefer to have seen left to the on-form leader, but Hubbard is dashing and Drew affectingly lyrical. A word, too, for the seldom-discussed Watkins, who gives his lines a lazy-sounding drag that nevertheless holds the beat solidly together. An excellent record, that should be a high priority for anyone interested in McLean's music.

**** **Let Freedom Ring** Blue Note 7465272
    McLean; Walter Davis Jr (*p*); Herbie Lewis (*b*); Billy Higgins (*d*). 63.
A classic. Influenced by Ornette Coleman – with whom he was to record for Blue Note on *Old And New Gospel* – McLean shrugged off the last fetter of bop harmony and pushed through to a more ruggedly individual post-bop that in important regards anticipated the avant-garde of the later 1960s. McLean's phenomenally beautiful tone rings out on 'Melody For Melonae', 'I'll Keep Loving You', 'Rene' and 'Omega'. Higgins's bright, cross-grained drumming is exemplary and the band is generously recorded, with plenty of bass.

***(*) **Dr Jackle** Steeplechase SCCD 36005
    McLean; Lamont Johnson (*p*); Scott Holt (*b*); Billy Higgins (*d*). 12/66.
The later 1960s were a somewhat dead time for McLean, and it looked as though the huge strides he had taken at the beginning of the decade led nowhere. He acted in Jack Gelber's *The Connection*, and played some of the script for real. His playing of the time has a slightly tired edge, and a hesitancy that comes not from lack of confidence but from a seeming lack of motivation to develop ideas. *Dr Jackle* includes a take of 'Melody For Melonae' which is quite discouraging in its diffidence and defensive show; McLean clearly isn't helped by the rhythm section, but Higgins alone should have been enough to spur him to better things.

**** **Live At Montmartre** Steeplechase SCS 1001
    McLean; Kenny Drew (*p*); Bo Stief (*b*); Alex Riel (*d*). 8/72.
*** **A Ghetto Lullaby** Steeplechase SCCD 31013
    As above; replace Stief with Niels-Henning Orsted-Pedersen (*b*). 7/73.
For sheer *joie de vivre*, albeit with a chastened edge, *Live At Montmartre* is hard to beat. Full-voiced and endlessly inventive, McLean romps through 'Smile', adding the 'shave-and-a-haircut-*bay-rum*' cadence to the end of his first statement with an almost arrogant flourish. 'Parker's Mood' is perhaps the best of his later bebop essays, shifting out of synch with Drew's excellent chording for a couple of measures. *Lullaby* is less immediately appealing, though NHOP adds a significant element to the group's harmonic output, and he is a much solider player than Stief. 'Mode For Jay Mac' is interesting, and the title-track calls up some of McLean's most purely emotive playing.

(*) **Ode To Super Steeplechase SCCD 31009
    McLean; Gary Bartz (*as*); Thomas Clausen (*p*); Bo Stief (*b*); Alex Riel (*d*). 7/73.
A disappointing confrontation that recalls the *Alto Madness* session with John Jenkins from 1957. Bartz already sounds as if he has set his sights on a rock/fusion future and McLean battles against Clausen's apparent insistence on closing up the harmonies. 'Monk's Dance' makes a promising but unfulfilled opening, and 'Great Rainstreet Blues' bogs down rather too quickly.

*** **The Meeting** Steeplechase SCCD 31006
    McLean; Dexter Gordon (*ts*); Kenny Drew (*p*); Niels-Henning Orsted-Pedersen (*b*); Alex Riel (*d*). 7/73.
*** **The Source** Steeplechase SCCD 31020
    As above.
For once, Steeplechase's obsessive over-documentation makes sense. Recorded over two nights, this isn't a good album and a makeweight, but a 'double' of genuine quality. Gordon and McLean were poles apart stylistically, but temperament and geography suggested such a meeting was inevitable. The first volume is darker and more sensitive, and the opening 'All Clean' hits close to home. McLean is usually quicker to the punch, but Gordon spins out his ideas (particularly on the standards) with confidence and some in reserve. 'Half Nelson' and 'I Can't Get Started' (*The Source*) depend to a large extent on Drew's teasing out of the chords. The sound isn't spectacularly good, with a tendency to fragment round the edges; no better on the CD unfortunately, but the playing makes up for it.

*** **New York Calling** Steeplechase SCCD 31023
    McLean; Billy Skinner (*t*); René McLean (*ts, ss*); Billy Gault (*p*); James Benjamin (*b*); Michael Carvin (*d*). 10/74.

New York Calling is a respectable performance from a band capable of better. The Cosmic Brotherhood featured McLean's talented and indoctrinated-from-the-cradle son, René. Far from sounding like a chip, he shows considerable individuality on both his horns, carving out intriguing counter-melodies and straightforward responses, neither over-respectful nor wilfully defiant. The charts are impressively varied, but *New York Calling* isn't a first choice for CD transfer. The sound is unaccountably flat. McLean *père* takes his best solo early, on the title-track, and finds little to add to it. Skinner sounds as if he could do with a bottle of valve oil and has intonation problems throughout (unless he intends some of his middle-register notes to be flatted). Once again, it's the drummer who attracts positive attention. A couple of months before, McLean and Carvin had recorded a duo album, *Antiquity*, perhaps the most far-out thing the saxophonist has ever done, but, alas, no longer around.

**** Dynasty Triloka 181 2
   McLean; René McLean (*ts, as, ss, f*); Hotep Idris Galeta (*p*); Nat Reeves (*b*); Carl Allen (*d*). 11/88.
***(*) Rites Of Passage Triloka 188 2
   As above, except add Lenny Castro (*perc*). 1/91.

Both sessions start with McLean originals, but responsibility for producing new material for the Dynasty band has largely fallen on René and South African-born pianist Galeta. Their work introduces a range of altered changes and curious tonalities that are drawn from African and Asian musics ('Zimbabwe', 'Muti-Woman', Stanley Wiley's 'Third World Express' on *Dynasty*, 'Naima's Love Poem' and 'Destiny's Romance' on *Rites*), and to which McLean responds very positively, confirming how much on the outside of conventional bop language he always was. The unmistakable tone is still very much intact and infuses even a rather bland vehicle like Bacharach's 'A House Is Not A Home' with considerable feeling.

His son simply can't match him for either speed or articulation or beauty of tone, having a rather vinegary sound on his two main horns and a bleary version of Richie Cole's reedy whine on the alto. He is, though, a fine flute player and it would be good to hear him more often on that horn. Both albums are a must for McLean fans and the first (recorded in front of a studio audience) can be confidently recommended to anyone interested in the finest modern jazz.

***(*) The Jackie Mac Attack: Live Birdology 519 270
   Mclean; Hotep Idris Galeta (*p*); Nat Reeves (*b*); Carl Allan (*d*). 4/91.
*** Rhythm Of The Earth Birdology 513 916
   McLean; Roy Hargrove (*t*); Steve Davis (*tb*); Steve Nelson (*vib*); Alan Jay Palmer (*p*); Nat Reeves (*b*); Eric McPherson (*d*). 3/92.

These usefully illustrate a split which has haunted McLean's career almost from the off. While he's totally reliable as a live performer (and, by extension, on live discs), his studio projects have often been too deliberate and contrived. It's this which trips up *Rhythm Of The Earth*, an extended exploration of Dogon science and mythology. The compositions – by Mclean, Davis and Palmer – simply get in the way of some very fine playing. Hargrove is in excellent form, bitingly sharp on 'Rhythm Of The Earth' and 'The Collective Expression'. Davis turns out to be a better player than writer; well schooled in the Jazz Messengers, he has a knack of squeezing a great deal into a single chorus. Jackie himself only really lets go on the romantic ballad, 'For Hofsa', and with a fluid lyricism that recalls 'Profile Of Jackie' on Mingus's *Pithecanthropus Erectus*.

It's clear that he is still a great blowing player. For all its technical shortcomings – a narrow DAT recording of a concert in Belgium – *Jackie Mac Attack* is a winner. He blasts through the pianist's 'Cyclical' and 'Song For My Queen', downshifts a touch for René's 'Dance Little Mandissa', and rounds off what must have been a memorable set with his own 'Minor March' and 'Round Midnight'. For anyone who doesn't have a box of sneaky C90s of the man in action, this is the next best thing.

René McLean (born 1947) SAXOPHONES, FLUTE

*** Watch Out Steeplechase SCCD 31037
   McLean; Danny Coleman (*t, flhn*); Nathan Page (*g*); Hubert Eaves (*p*); Buster Williams (*b*); Freddie Waits (*d*). 7/75.
***(*) In African Eyes Triloka 203 195
   McLean; Hugh Masekela, Prince Lengoasa (*flhn*); Moses Molelekwa, Themba Mkhize, Rashid Lanie (*p*); Jonny Khumalo, Jonny Chancho, Prof. Themba Mokoena, Bheki Khasa (*g*); Bakhiti Khumalo, Fana Zulu, Victor Masondo (*b*); Sello Montwedi, Ian Herman, Lulu Gontsana (*d*); Jon Hassan, Papa Kouyate, Bill Summers, Zamo Mbuto (*perc*). 92.

Second generation in the family business, young René famously was given one of dad's old mouthpieces as a comforter. The early start (and lessons with Sonny Rollins) notwithstanding, he seemed slow to develop a genuinely individual voice on the saxophone. Not to mince it unduly, heredity doesn't always work and, while he has probably languished in the old fellow's shadow for many years, he simply doesn't have Jackie's basic chops.

Though he was working and recording with his father for several years beforehand, Rene didn't make a record of his own until 1975. *Watch Out* is a lively, often very impressive session, wisely mixing Young Turk enthusiasm up front with a solidly experienced back line. There are already intimations of the African interests that have become dominant more recently; 'Bilad As Sudan' makes for an arresting opening, and the pace doesn't slacken much before the close, though by then, one feels, Coleman is long out of ideas. Fielding as pianist and guitarist wasn't an entirely happy notion and there are moments when the accompaniments become unnecessarily cluttered.

Clutter is in a curious way the rationale of *In African Eyes*. René allows the sound to build up in bright, inexactly matched layers, a patchwork effect that is often very rewarding. The record was actually made in South Africa, hence his access to Masekela and the other rather lesser lights of the new Azanian jazz. It's a joyous sound, as befits a country and culture in rapid change. McLean might have thought of adding another saxophone to keep the symmetry and fill out his parts in ensembles. As it is, he can sound a little thin and boosting his volume doesn't entirely address this. Impressive nonetheless, and a sure sign of what he can achieve when the conditions are right.

Dave McMurdo TROMBONE

(*) The Dave McMurdo Jazz Orchestra Jazz Alliance TJA-10001
McMurdo; Arnie Chycoski, Chase Sanborn, Steve McDade, Mike Malone, Neil Christofferson (*t, flhn*); Rob Somerville, Terry Lukiwski, Ted Bohn (*tb*); Bob Hamper (*btb*); Mark Promane (*ss, as, cl, f*); Don Englert (*ss, as, f*); Pat Labarbera, Michael Stuart (*ts, cl, f*); Bob Leonard (*bs, bcl, f*); Don Thompson (*p*); Reg Schwager (*g*); George Mitchell (*b*); Kevin Dempsey (*d*). 10/89.
*** **Live At The Montreal Bistro** Sackville SKCD2-2029
As above, except Sandy Barter (*t, flhn*), Kevin Turcotte (*t, flhn*) and Perry White (*bs, bcl, f*) replace Chycoski, McDade and Leonard. 4/92.
*** **Different Paths** Sackville SKCD2-2034
As above, except Paul Novotny (*b*) replaces Mitchell. 6/93.
McMurdo's Canadian big band features many exemplars of a largely unsung (in international terms) scene and, though the music is often content to stay within the parameters of a well-drilled big band blowing conscientious arrangements, they are very good at their tasks. The first record is a little too precise and buttoned-down: a long, complex reworking of '(All Of A Sudden) My Heart Sings' is a fine opening, but some of the other scores are faceless, and the programme could use an all-stops-out snorter. The live session opens with just that, a rollicking treatment of 'Straight No Chaser', and the upfront punch of the live sound and a strongly contrasting choice of scores makes this the best album of the three, with McMurdo's own playing on 'A Nightingale Sang In Berkeley Square' and a terse arrangement of Wayne Shorter's 'Black Nile' among the standouts.

Different Paths is more of a writer's showcase. Since the orchestra uses several arrangers and propagates an ensemble sound of impeccable balance, it seldom aspires to a particular character, but Don Thompson's charts are some of its best: the sprawling 'Don't/Wintermist', 'a true concert piece', as McMurdo notes, is their most ambitious undertaking. The rest is interesting rather than outstanding.

Jim McNeely (born 1949) PIANO, KEYBOARDS

*** **The Plot Thickens** Muse MCD 5378
McNeely; John Scofield (*g*); Mike Richmond (*b*); Adam Nussbaum (*d*). 79.
*** **Winds Of Change** Steeplechase SCCD 1256
McNeely; Mike Richmond (*b*); Kenny Washington (*d*). 7/89.
Having worked with Mel Lewis, Stan Getz and Joe Henderson, McNeely has acquired a substantial reputation which these albums confirm in their unfussy way. A clever writer and a mercurial though restrained soloist, McNeely likes a lot of space to develop ideas in: the unfolding of, say, 'Chelsea Litany/Feng Liu' on *The Plot Thickens* takes some 13 minutes, and the Steeplechase session includes five originals that fill most of the record without any sense of time-wasting. The Muse session includes some good early Scofield on the two longest tracks, his lines running in close parallel with McNeely's, but better is *Winds Of Change*. Each of the five originals has a specific turn of phrase, while 'Bye-Ya' is a particularly fluent reading of a Monk piece that not many tackle. Richmond, whose voluble yet lightly weighted lines are entirely apt, is certainly his ideal bass partner.

*** **East Coast Blow Out** Lipstick LIP 89007-2

McNeely; John Scofield (*g*); Marc Johnson (*b*); Adam Nussbaum (*d*). 9/89.

As a big-band commission this seems like only a half-hearted exercise by McNeely. His scores for the WDR Big Band are more like interpolations into what is fundamentally a tightly arranged sequence for the quartet: Scofield has a marvellous, concerto-like feature on 'Do You Really Think ...?' and McNeely's own piano improvisations on 'Skittish' are impeccable, yet the orchestra always sounds as if it's trying to nudge its way in, rather than playing a full role. For the quality of the individual playing, though, it merits a recommendation.

**** **Live At Maybeck Recital Hall Vol. 20** Concord CCD 4522

McNeely (*p* solo). 1/92.

McNeely's entry in this quietly compelling series is one of the most 'modern' in the sequence. If these concerts offer no more than a mere snapshot of a pianist at work, their knack of creating an individual and vivid picture is exemplified by McNeely's brilliant playing, oddly diffident in its tone yet achieved with the greatest finesse and inventiveness. On the opening 'There Will Never Be Another You', for instance, he calmly plays the tune in all 12 keys, batting the melody and development alike between his two hands and completing the task with a shoulder-shrug ending. There are readings of Jobim, Monk and Powell that honour each composer by transforming them, and there are two fine themes of his own. Always one is conscious of a two-handed player: for all the clarity of his touch, he takes in more of the keyboard in each improvisation than many do over a whole recital. Highly recommended.

Jimmy McPartland (1907–91) CORNET, VOCAL

(*) **That Happy Dixieland Jazz RCA Victor 74321 18518-2

McPartland; Charlie Shavers (*t, v*); Cutty Cutshall (*tb*); Bob Wilber (*cl, ts*); Ernie Caceres (*cl, bs*); Dicky Cary (*ahn, t, p*); George Barnes (*g*); Harvey Phillips (*tba*); Joe Burriesce (*b*); George Wettling (*d*). 5/59.

The only disc under McPartland's name is a poor showing for one of the great names in Chicagoan jazz. Recorded in reverberant 'Living Stereo', which doesn't suit the music, this might have turned out well, with Cary's arrangements on a pack of what were already very tired warhorses. But the delivery seems consistently shrill and only the closing 'Farewell Blues' finds an interesting touch. McPartland, one of the brassiest and most passionate of the Chicagoan cornetists, has to compete with Shavers, yet he still gets enough good moments to make the record worth having despite it all. Check the index or wait for the best of some good 1950s albums from Columbia to make it to CD.

Marian McPartland (born 1920) PIANO

*** **Great Britain's** Savoy SV-0160

McPartland; Max Wayne, Eddie Safranski (*b*); Mel Zelnick, Don Lamond (*d*). 4–12/52.

*** **In Concert** Savoy SV-0202

McPartland; Eddie Safranski, Vinnie Burke (*b*); Don Lamond, Joe Morello (*d*). 6/51–10/53.

A welcome return for some of Marian McPartland's earlier recordings. *Great Britain's* is shared with George Shearing, but it's McPartland's deftly lyrical and unassumingly swinging music that has lasted better. The seven standards she tackles are all dispatched in short order, but they all have some particular felicity – a reharmonization or a melodic twist, perhaps – that keeps catching the ear. *In Concert* is split between two sessions. The first, noisily recorded, offers only four brief tracks from Boston's Storyville Club; but the second, cut at her favourite New York haunt, The Hickory Club, with frequent partner Joe Morello, sounds much better. Listen to the long lines of 'I've Got The World On A String' or the quickfire reworking of 'Four Brothers'. Some irritating introductions survive the CD transfer.

***(*) **A Sentimental Journey** Jazz Alliance TJA-10025

McPartland; Jimmy McPartland (*c, v*); Vic Dickenson, Hank Berger (*tb*); Jack Maheu (*cl*); Buddy Tate (*ts, bs*); Rusty Gilder (*b*); Gus Johnson, Larry Bell, Mike Berger (*d*). 11/72–6/73.

A lovely memento of two engagements by bands led by Jimmy, with Marian on piano and two entertaining front lines. Jack Maheu blends a spiralling virtuosity with Pee Wee-type licks, Tate is reliable (and picks up the baritone here and there), Dickenson is absolutely himself (his 'When You Wish Upon A Star' is priceless) and Jimmy leads with typical aplomb. The piano sounds a bit difficult here and there, but the pianist is obviously enjoying herself, and she contributes a delightful sleeve-note.

**** **Plays The Music Of Alec Wilder** Jazz Alliance TJA-10016

McPartland; Michael Moore, Rusty Gilder (*b*); Joe Corsello (*d*). 6/73.

This is one of the great single-composer recitals and it should be far better known than it is. McPartland has been intensely involved in Alec Wilder's difficult, bittersweet music for decades and she gets closer to the heart of it than any jazz player ever has. 'Jazz Waltz For A Friend', the first track, was written for her, and several of the other pieces have scarcely been touched by other improvisers. The five pieces with the lone support of Michael Moore are wonderfully lyrical and searching and, though the remaining five with Gilder and Corsello are a shade less involving, it is a memorable occasion which has been long overdue for CD release. The only regret must be that she didn't play Wilder's unforgettable 'Where Do You Go?' at the date.

*** **From This Moment On** Concord CCD 4086
    McPartland; Brian Torff (*b*); Jake Hanna (*d*). 12/78.
**** **Portrait Of Marian McPartland** Concord CCD 4101
    As above, plus Jerry Dodgion (*as, f*). 5/79.
***(*) **Personal Choice** Concord CCD 4202
    McPartland; Steve LaSpina (*b*); Jake Hanna (*d*). 6/82.
*** **Willow Creek And Other Ballads** Concord CCD 4272
    McPartland (*p* solo). 1/85.

McPartland's playing and composing have remained amazingly fresh and interested. Besides performing, she has hosted a long-running American radio series which features her with a different jazz pianist on every edition; and, perhaps as a result, her own playing seems sensitive to all the possible directions in contemporary jazz piano. Even though this would be classed by most as ostensibly 'mainstream jazz', there are inflexions in it which would be unknown to most of McPartland's immediate contemporaries. *From This Moment On* offers a tight, generous reading of familiar standards, but *Portrait* goes a notch higher by adding Dodgion's bristling alto and beautifully articulated flute to the mix. An incisive version of Herbie Hancock's 'Tell Me A Bedtime Story', a tart Dodgion blues called 'No Trumps' and an ideal treatment of the pianist's gorgeous 'Time And Time Again' are the highlights. *Personal Choice* is another catholic programme, with tunes by Jobim, Brubeck and Pettiford, but a surprisingly tough 'I'm Old-Fashioned' and a reflective solo 'Melancholy Mood' turn out the best. If the solo set is a shade behind the others, it's only because McPartland uses the resources of a trio so intelligently that she seems relatively quiescent by herself. While her treatments of the likes of 'Someday I'll Find You' are typically original, it would be agreeable to hear her tackle an entire set of her own compositions.

*** **Plays The Music Of Billy Strayhorn** Concord CCD 4326
    McPartland; Jerry Dodgion (*as*); Steve LaSpina (*b*); Joey Baron (*d*). 3/87.
***(*) **Plays The Benny Carter Songbook** Concord CCD 4412
    McPartland; Benny Carter (*as*); John Clayton (*b*); Harold Jones (*d*). 1/90.

Two fine excursions into repertory by McPartland. Strayhorn's suave impressionism is hard to evoke, let alone sustain for an entire album, but this is at least as successful as any similar homage. Despite a couple of less successful entries – 'A Flower Is A Lovesome Thing', for instance, is a little too doleful – the quartet have the measure of this deceptive music. There is a witty, unpredictable revision of 'Take The "A" Train', a springy 'Intimacy Of The Blues' and a purposefully crafted 'Lush Life' by the trio without Dodgion. The meeting with Carter, who plays on six of the 11 tunes chosen from his book, is flawlessly paced. Though his technique is still astonishing for a man in his eighties, Carter's sound and delivery are rather old-world compared to McPartland's astute command. Trio versions of 'When Lights Are Low', the beautiful 'Key Largo' and 'Summer Serenade' are probably the most distinguished moments on the record. Both sessions are recorded excellently.

***(*) **Live At Maybeck Recital Hall Vol. 9** Concord CCD 4460
    McPartland (*p* solo). 1/91.

Her latest solo recital finds the pianist in characteristically adventurous mood. The composers represented here include Alec Wilder, Ornette Coleman, Mercer Ellington and Dave Brubeck; there are her latest reflections on the tune she startled Ellington himself with, 'Clothed Woman', and one of the most affecting of her own themes, 'Twilight World'. Each interpretation contains nothing unnecessary in the way of embellishment, yet they all seem ideally paced, properly finished. She makes it sound very easy. Ripe, in-concert recording, typical of this series from Concord.

**** **In My Life** Concord CCD 4561
    McPartland; Chris Potter (*as, ts*); Gary Mazzaroppi (*b*); Glenn Davis (*d*). 1/93.

A marvellous record. This time Marian sets Coltrane and Ornette alongside Lennon and McCartney, quietly introduces a couple of her own tunes, and invites one of the sharpest new saxophonists on the scene to sit in. The result is as catholic and accomplished a jazz record as one can find among modern releases. Chris Potter's unfussy virtuosity is a serenely appropriate match for the pianist's diverse tastes, and he is as purposeful and convincing on 'Close Your Eyes' as he is on 'Naima'. To close, there is a deeply affecting solo treatment of 'Singin' The Blues', done as a memorial to Marian's late husband Jimmy. Essential.

***(*) **Plays The Music Of Mary Lou Williams** Concord CCD 4605
    McPartland; Bill Douglass (*b*); Omar Clay (*d*). 1/94.
This must have been a project close to Marian's heart, and she does this still-little-known songbook fine justice. One of the striking things about the playing is how Marian has an unerring instinct for the right tempo on a particular piece: 'Easy Blues' and 'It's A Grand Night For Swinging' hit an ideal pace from the start, and 'Cloudy', probably the most famous of Williams's tunes, is a beauty. If the disc has a weakness, it's that Marian doesn't always convince the listener that Williams's themes are as strong as they might be: her own composition 'Threnody', a delightful tune in three, actually outclasses several of the pieces here.

There are now more than 20 releases on Jazz Alliance drawn from editions of Marian's Piano Jazz series for NPR and, while some of them are perhaps more of documentary and historical interest, all feature some fine piano playing. We have listed many of them separately under the heading of Marian's guest in each case.

Joe McPhee (born 1939) TENOR SAXOPHONE, POCKET-CORNET, FLUGELHORN, ELECTRONICS

***(*) **Old Eyes & Mysteries** hat Art 6047
    McPhee; Urs Leimgruber (*ss, ts*); André Jaume (*bcl, ts*); Jean-Charles Capon (*clo*); Raymond
    Boni, Steve Gnitka (*g*); Pierre-Yves Sorin (*b*); Milo Fine (*p, d*); Fritz Hauser (*d, perc*). 5/79.
*** **Topology** hat Art 6027
    McPhee; Radu Malfatti (*tb, elec*); Irene Schweizer (*p*); André Jaume (*as, bcl*); Daniel Bourquin
    (*as, bs*); François Mechali (*b*); Michael Overhage (*clo*); Raymond Boni (*g*); Pierre Favre (*perc*);
    Tamia (*v*). 3/81.
**** **Oleo & A Future Retrospective** hat Art 6097
    McPhee; André Jaume (*cl, bcl, as*); Raymond Boni (*g*); François Mechali (*b*). 8/82.
**** **Linear B** hat Art 6057
    McPhee; André Jaume, Urs Leimgruber (*ss, ts*); Raymond Boni, Christy Doran (*g*); Léon
    Francioli (*b*); Fritz Hauser (*perc*). 1/90.
**** **Sweet Freedom – Now What?** hat Art 6162
    McPhee; Paul Plimley (*p*); Lisle Ellis (*b*). 7/94.
Time may have softened some of the anger in McPhee's playing, but it has not eliminated it. He is one of the most consistently impressive and adventurous composer/instrumentalists in the music. He bridges 'straight', thematic improvisation and total freedom, acoustic and electronic sound-sources in a way that is reminiscent of fellow-radicals George Lewis and Anthony Braxton (who are also, of course, likeminded traditionalists when the spirit moves them). The very important *Oleo & A Future Retrospective* has recently reappeared, accompanied by an unreleased suite of pieces, dedicated to Eric Dolphy and named after the words spoken by Dolphy at the end of 'Miss Ann' on his *Last Date*. The performance of Rollins's 'Oleo' suggests how thoroughly McPhee is versed in the saxophone literature and how intuitive is his grasp of basic jazz and bop tonality. There is no question, as some critics have suggested, that his technique is insecure and that his angularity is a form of disguise. Boni, who plays on all but the Dolphy tribute, is a marvellous partner and Jaume complements the leader's rather drier voice perfectly. They join him again for the utterly enjoyable and completely unexpected *Impressions Of Jimmy Giuffre*.

Over the past decade, McPhee has been involved with the creation of a large-scale cycle of works: *Topology*, *Linear B* and the latter's companion piece, *Old Eyes & Mysteries*, with which it shares a linernote. McPhee's aesthetic is based on the notion of 'provocation' as a source of improvisational cues, but it's interesting that its most common metaphoric underpinning relates to codes, mysteries, secrets, hidden languages (Linear B is an ancient Minoan language, which proved as tough to crack as the Second World War Enigma code). Listening to the music on all three albums is a little like encountering a private language, initially off-putting, but increasingly logical and self-consistent as time passes until it forms an entire, self-sufficient system that lacks for nothing but some point of reference outside of itself.

Perhaps the most confusing aspect of McPhee's work has been his willingness to combine total improvisation with 'standards' and progressive jazz repertoire. *Topology* is a surprisingly 'cool' confrontation with some impressive European modern/free players. The take of Charles Mingus's 'Pithecanthropus Erectus' develops the more abstract features of Mingus's original conception in ways that anticipate McPhee's own 'Topology', a two-part performance which sees Malfatti switch from trombone to a computer, another sign of the way McPhee is always looking for new musical codes that go beyond 'instrumentalism'. 'Blues For New Chicago' is more straightforward but is still a challenging variation on traditional values.

Linear B is less dense and much more theatrical in direction, a token of the way McPhee's work as a whole has been developing during the 1980s. The 13 tracks are taken from a total of nearly 60 recorded over a three-day session. The record centres on a long performance of Wayne Shorter's 'Footprints', played with considerable lyricism, as is 'Here's That Rainy Day', which is dedicated to the late Chet Baker. The music here and on *Eyes/Mysteries* is credited to Po Music, not as in 'po' white', but as in the popular psychologist Edward De Bono's hypothesis of a realm of thought 'beyond yes and no' and predicated on the **po**ssible, the **po**sitive, the **po**etic and the hy**po**thetical. McPhee's 'compositions' are thus no more than poetic hypotheses, blueprints of what the players might possibly play, but in no way restrictively so. The result is a kind of orderly freedom which is perhaps best heard in the series of 'Little Pieces', duos with percussionist Hauser, which follow 'Footprints' and serve as a kind of mid-point primer or résumé.

The most recent of these is largely given over to the compositions of Max Roach, as the album-title suggests. All three trio members are responsible for arranging Roach themes and material associated with him. With the exception of the drummer's 'Garvey's Ghost', 'Self Portrait' and an original 'The Persistence Of Rosewood', most of the tracks are short, some even to the extent of being enigmatic, but open-minded listeners will find much to ponder and enjoy.

McPhee is a major figure, and hat Art (who are also responsible for recording maverick traditionalists like Franz Koglmann) have performed a valuable service in documenting one of the most intriguing extended improvisations of recent times.

**** **Impressions Of Jimmy Giuffre** Celp C 21
McPhee; André Jaume (*ts, bcl*); Raymond Boni (*g*). 4/91.
This stands a little apart from McPhee's normal line of work (a bit like Braxton's Warne Marsh record), but there is no mistaking how much pleasure he took in making it. The trio kicks off with a glorious version of 'The Train And The River', with McPhee in the Brookmeyer role, and carries on with a mixture of Giuffre originals and specially written pieces which might have been laid down by the clarinettist's slightly wacky brother. There's even a posy for Juanita Giuffre, who has been a substantial influence on her husband's recent career. A sundae to balance the meatier side of McPhee's output.

Charles McPherson (born 1939) ALTO SAXOPHONE

*** **Be Bop Revisited** Original Jazz Classics OJC 710
McPherson; Carmell Jones (*t*); Barry Harris (*p*); Nelson Boyd (*b*); Albert 'Tootie' Heath (*d*). 64.
*** **The Quintet Live!** Original Jazz Classics OJC 1804
McPherson; Lonnie Hillyer (*t*); Barry Harris (*p*); Ray McKinney (*b*); Billy Higgins (*d*). 66.
*** **Live At The Five Spot** Prestige PRCD 24135
As above.
***(*) **First Flight Out** Arabesque AJ 0113
McPherson; Tom Harrell (*t, flhn*); Michael Weiss (*p*); Peter Washington (*b*); Victor Lewis (*d*). 1/94.

McPherson credits the relatively unsung Barry Harris, present on the first three albums above, for his schooling in bebop, but it's clear that Parker has marked his saxophone playing so deeply that he will always be identified as a faithful disciple. The straightforward bop covers on *Revisited* and the slightly more individualized live material have an energy and clarity of tone that are completely missing from the later, overproduced sessions once reissued on Mainstream.

First Flight Out is a good example of McPherson's more recent style. He still does a lot of Mingus material, which he presumably knows like the back of his hand, and there is a version of Monk's 'Well You Needn't' which suggests he's spent a bit of time on that fruitful source as well. The playing is lighter in touch but fuller in tone than it used to be and here it sits perfectly with Harrell's lyrical flugelhorn.

Carmen McRae (1922–94) VOCAL

*** **Sings Great American Songwriters** MCA GRP16312
McRae; with groups led by Ray Bryant, Mat Mathews, Ralph Burns, Tadd Dameron, Fred Katz, Jack Pleis, Frank Hunter and Luther Henderson. 6/55–3/59.
***(*) **Here To Stay** MCA GRP 16102
McRae; Jimmy Maxwell, Richard Williams, Al Stewart, Lennie Johnson, Ernie Royal (*t*); Jimmy Cleveland, Bill Byers, Mickey Gravine (*tb*); Paul Faulise (*btb*); Phil Woods, Vinnie Dean, Porter

Kilbert (*as*); Zoot Sims, Budd Johnson (*ts*); Sol Schlinger (*bs*); Herbie Mann (*f*); Dick Katz, Billy Strayhorn (*p*); Mat Mathews (*acc*); Mundell Lowe (*g*); Wendell Marshall, Tommy Williams (*b*); Kenny Clarke, Floyd Williams (*d*). 6/55–11/59.

*** **You'd Be So Easy To Love** Bethlehem 6018-2

McRrae; small groups led by Tony Scott (*cl*), Mat Mathews (*p*).

An accomplished pianist, Carmen McRae was something of a late starter as a featured vocalist, not recording a vocal session under her own name until 1954. Her fame has always lagged behind that of her close contemporaries, Sarah Vaughan and Billie Holiday, but in her senior years she has finally achieved something like the honour she deserves, and her commitment to jazz singing has been unflinching. Thus far, her early work has been unjustly ignored by CD reissues: until recently, virtually nothing was available from her Decca period of the 1950s, which means that great records like *Torchy* and *Carmen For Cool Ones* must languish as collectors' items. But *Here To Stay* at least brings back two albums, *Something To Swing About* and *By Special Request*, to the catalogue. One is a small-group session, the other is with a big band and charts by Ernie Wilkins; but both display McRae's muscular phrasing, aggressive timbre and impeccable timing to high effect. There's always a tigerish feel to her best vocals – no woman has ever sung in the jazz idiom with quite such beguiling surliness as McRae – and on, say, 'Just One Of Those Things' she gets closer to the tough spirit implied by the lyrics than anyone else ever has. The remastering is very good. *Sings Great American Songwriters* pulls together 20 tracks from ten different sessions, ranging from a full-orchestra backing to small groups led by Ray Bryant and Mat Mathews; though some of the interpretations are no more than perfunctory, she gets a temperamental sultriness out of 'Summertime' and makes 'When I Fall In Love' improbably cool. The Bethelehm album is something of a filler: a sequence of ballads sung at a very low flame, with backings under orders to play it down. Only on Tony Scott's ballad, 'Misery', with Scott himself behind her, does the music move up a notch.

***(*) **The Great American Songbook** Atlantic 781323-2

McRae; Jimmy Rowles (*p*); Joe Pass (*g*); Chuck Domanico (*b*); Chuck Flores (*d*). 72.

A couple of the songs are only questionably 'great', and some of the treatments seem surprisingly hurried or perfunctory. Otherwise this is blue-chip material, a top band, and Carmen in excellent voice, cut live at Donte's in Los Angeles. There are too few such occasions in the McRae discography, so it's a welcome reissue.

** **Heat Wave** Concord CCD 4189

McRae; Al Bent, Mike Heathman (*tb*); Mark Levine, Marshall Otwell (*p*); Cal Tjader (*vib*); Rob Fisher (*b*); Vince Lateano (*d*); Poncho Sanchez, Ramon Banda (*perc*). 1/82.

*** **You're Lookin' At Me** Concord CCD 4235

McRae; Marshall Otwell (*p*); John Collins (*g*); John Leftwich (*b*); Donald Bailey (*d*). 11/83.

(*) **Fine And Mellow Concord CCD 4342

McRae; Red Holloway (*ts*); Phil Upchurch (*g*); Jack McDuff (*org*); John Clayton Jr (*b*); Paul Humphrey (*d*). 12/87.

While none of her records for Concord is outstanding, these three albums have enough good McRae to make them all worth hearing. The session with Tjader is blemished by the vibesman's usual flavourless Latin-jazz stylings, which offer no backbone to the singer's efforts, and the Stevie Wonder tunes on the record scarcely suit a vocal personality which has a pronounced streak of cussedness when she warms up. Yet *Fine And Mellow* goes to the other extreme without much more conviction: McRae is too sophisticated a stylist to convince as an earthy R&B singer, which this programme and these accompanists are tailored for. The other record is a tribute to Nat Cole and, while she doesn't sound very taken with the likes of 'I'm An Errand Girl For Rhythm', the ballads and the more subtle lyrics garner her full attention, with a cool, attentive rhythm section in support.

***(*) **Any Old Time** Denon 33CY-1216

McRae; Clifford Jordan (*ts*); Eric Gunnison (*p*); John Collins (*g*); Scott Colley (*b*); Mark Pulice (*d*). 6/86.

As her voice grew heavier, McRae hung back on the beat more often, but in at least two instances here – 'Tulip Or Turnip', an Ellington rarity hardly ever done by a singer, and 'I Hear Music' – one can hear how fast tempos can be handled by a singer who wants to take her time: it's a masterful display. This is probably the best of her latter-day sessions, with a tuned-in rhythm section, two excellent soloists in Collins and Jordan (both used sparingly), impeccable programming and sympathetic production. 'Love Me Tender' and 'This Is Always' are slow and graceful yet expunged of mush, while 'Prelude To A Kiss' embodies the idea of a musician spontaneously recasting a song she's probably sung throughout her whole career.

***(*) **The Carmen McRae–Betty Carter Duets** Verve 529579-2

McRae; Eric Gunnison (*p*); Jim Hughart (*b*); Winard Harper (*d*). 1–2/87.

A one-off meeting inspired by an impromptu partnership at a club engagement, this is great fun and, though Carter remains the consummate bebop gymnast, McRae isn't outclassed once. What she does is bring her great gravitas to bear on a session that could have been mere frivolity. The opening 'What's New' sets an amiable tone, but there is some serious and superb singing in 'Glad To Be Unhappy', a virtuoso 'Sometimes I'm Happy', a lovely arrangement of 'Stolen Moments' where the two voices hit perfect accord, and the suitably climactic 'It Don't Mean A Thing'. Three bonus tracks feature Carmen by herself. The recording is rather remote and needs a bit extra on the volume switch.

*** **Carmen Sings Monk** Novus 83086
> McRae; Clifford Jordan (*ss, ts*); Charlie Rouse (*ts*); Eric Gunnison, Larry Willis (*p*); George Mraz (*b*); Al Foster (*d*). 1–4/88.

***(*) **Sarah – Dedicated To You** Novus 90546
> McRae; Shirley Horn (*p*); Charles Ables (*b*); Steve Williams (*d*). 10/90.

The singer worked very hard on the Monk collection, perhaps too much so, for some of the life seems to have been smothered out of it. While the familiar 'Round Midnight' sits up straight, too many of the other tracks suffer from the awkwardness of the lyric fitting into Monk's music and, with her own voice less limber than it once was, McRae makes heavy weather of some of them. But the two different quartets involved play well (Rouse on what was almost his farewell appearance), and a sense of commitment shines through.

The tribute to Sarah Vaughan, though, is better. It's far more about McRae herself than it is about Vaughan. In what might be a valedictory record, she muses through 'I've Got The World On A String' and 'Poor Butterfly' with a strikingly improvised air, and her 'Send In The Clowns' is as personal as any reading without betraying any of the gushing sentiment which the song is wont to bring out in most interpreters. The voice is frayed but resolutely defiant: no *Lady In Satin* nonsense here. And Horn's accompaniments are perfectly sympathetic.

*** **For Lady** Novus 01241 63163 2
> McRae; Zoot Sims (*ts*); Marshall Otwell (*p*); John Leftwich (*b*); Donald Bailey (*d*). 12/83.

Recorded on New Year's Eve 1983, this concert of Billie Holiday material is a pleasing discovery. McRae's friendship and kinship with Billie ran deep and, though this is a sometimes contrived show, the singing is heartfelt – not that she surrenders much of her characteristic toughness. 'Good Morning Heartache' is wry rather than defeated, and 'Lover Man' (with a beautiful Zoot Sims solo) is impassioned, not forlorn. She's in great voice.

Jay McShann (born 1916) PIANO, VOCAL, BANDLEADER

***(*) **Blues From Kansas City** MCA GRD-614
> McShann; Harold Bruce, Orville Minor, Bernard Anderson, Bob Merrill (*t*); Joe Baird (*tb*); Charlie Parker, John Jackson (*as*); Bob Mabane, Harry Ferguson, Fred Culliver, Paul Quinichette (*ts*); Leonard Enois (*g*); Gene Ramey (*b*); Gus Johnson, Harold West (*d*); Al Hibbler, Walter Brown (*v*). 4/41–1/43.

***(*) **Jay McShann, 1941–1943** Classics 740
> As above, except add Willie Cook, Dave Mitchell, Jesse Jones (*t*); Alonzo Pettiford, Alonso Fook, Rudy Morrison (*tb*); Rudolf Dennis (*as*); Bill Goodson (*ts*); Rae Brodely (*bs*); Dan Graves (*d*); Bob Merrill (*d*). 4/41–12/43.

Historically, McShann's swing band will always be remembered as the incubator for Charlie Parker's raw talent to start to blossom. He gets five solos on this set, but the main attraction is the band and McShann himself, especially since 11 of the tracks are by either a trio or a quartet built round the leader's piano. The orchestra pack a Kansas City punch that stands squarely as second-generation Basie, and the blues performances on 'Hootie Blues', 'Swingmatism' and 'Dexter Blues' still have an authentic tang of KC brio. Excellent remastering on a long-awaited reissue.

The Classics alternative adds material from December 1943, three tracks of no special consequence, not least in not including Parker, who had already taken the next step in his career. McShann, who was considered a footnote in that story ever since, scarcely sounds it here, chugging away at his own thing without a shred of anxiety about what might be going on elsewhere in New York City.

*** **With Kansas City In Mind** Swaggie CD 401
> McShann; Buddy Tate (*ts, cl*); Julian Dash (*ts*); Gene Ramey (*b*); Gus Johnson (*d*). 6/69–3/72.

*** **Going To Kansas City** New World 80358-2
> As above. 3/72.

Just as Dollar Brand records routinely figure 'Africa(n)' in the title and there are umpteen Django reissues working permutations on 'Paris' and 'swing', so McShann has found it hard to shake off the

KC tag, even though by this stage he is no longer strictly a Kansas City player, but one who draws much more freely on a wide range of traditional and contemporary idioms. It is, nevertheless, a fine vintage. On the Swaggie, there are eight piano solos from two sessions, three years apart, and a small group featuring McShann with the two tenors of Tate and Dash, larruping through seven indolent blues or game swingers. Nothing terribly fancy and certainly nothing wrong.

The New World (unexpected label for this kind of thing) re-orders the March 1972 material with a truer and more convincing sound, but one feels the lack of the solo material, so it's pretty much a matter of preference which to go for.

** **Roll 'Em** Black & Blue 233022
> McShann; Candy Johnson (*ts*); Claude Williams (*g, v*); T-Bone Walker (*g*); Roland Lobligeois, Gene Ramey (*b*); Paul Gunther, Gus Johnson (*d*). 3/69–3/77.

(*) **Kansas City Memories Black & Blue 590572
> McShann; Arnett Cobb (*ts*); Milt Buckner (*org*); Al Casey, Clarence Gatemouth Brown (*g*); Roland Lobligeois (*b*); Paul Gunther (*d*). 11/70–7/73.

McShann has worked and recorded prodigiously enough in recent years to have finally overcome a mere notoriety as the man who gave Bird his start. These reissues are rather slight, jam-sessionish stuff and, although a meeting of McShann, Cobb and Buckner could hardly fail to create a few sparks, the material offers only slim pickings from a scattering of sessions. Better is to come.

*** **Vine Street Boogie** Black Lion BLCD 760187
> McShann (*p, v*). 7/74.

Rising sixty, McShann could still put on a show, as he proved at the 1974 Montreux Festival. It was a vivid, highly personal accomplishment, marked by sharply defined performances of 'Satin Doll' and 'Yardbird Waltz'. McShann hits the piano with absolute confidence and resolve, several times elegantly manoeuvring out of difficult corners and fluffed passages. The voice isn't much to write home about on this occasion, but there is no mistaking the rapport with the crowd or the warmth of the reception.

** **Best Of Friends** JSP CD 224
> McShann; Al Casey (*g*); Kenny Baldock (*b*); Robin Jones (*d*). 4/82.

*** **Swingmatism** Sackville 2-3046
> McShann; Don Thompson (*b*); Archie Alleyne (*d*). 10/82.

(*) **Airmail Special Sackville 2-3040
> McShann; Neil Swainson (*b*); Terry Clarke (*d*). 8/85.

*** **At Café Des Copains** Sackville 2-2024
> McShann (*p* solo). 8/83–9/89.

McShann has recorded many albums for Sackville and they are starting to reappear on CD. At his best, he blends a wide variety of mannerisms into a personal kind of swing-stride-blues piano; at anything less than that, he can sound like a less than profound and overly eclectic performer. Most of these records feature moments when he's caught between both positions. The meeting with Al Casey is jolly, unprepossessing stuff, both men jogging along to no great end except to have a bit of fun. *Swingmatism* is rather better: focused by a decent rhythm section, McShann sets his mind to a programme that depends heavily on Ellington for source material, and 'The Jeep is Jumpin'' and 'The Mooche' are good accounts of less frequently heard tunes. *Airmail Special* is all right, if a bit uneventful, but the best disc is probably the solo set. McShann thinks through a wide spectrum of material – going as far back as Ferde Grofé's 'On The Trail' and ending up with Michel LeGrand – and the good piano and live atmosphere elicit a sound series of interpretations, recorded during several visits over a period of six years.

*** **A Tribute To Charlie Parker** Music Masters 5052
> McShann; Clark Terry (*t, flhn*); Terence Blanchard, Carmell Jones, Tony Russo (*t*); Al Grey, Jimmy Wilkins (*tb*); Marc Steckar (*btb*); Benny Carter, Phil Woods (*as*); Jimmy Heath, Hal Singer (*ts*); James Moody (*ts, v*); Sahib Shihab (*bs*); Jimmy Woode (*b*); Mel Lewis (*d*); Ernie Andrews (*v*). 6/89.

In later years McShann found himself in the anomalous and ironic position of having survived his most famous pupil and employee by decades. Apart from 'Parker's Mood', this tribute album features very little Bird-associated material and remains very much McShann's own gig. As will be seen from the line-up, it's a more than decent band, but one which illustrates the alternatives to Bird's style rather than that particular line. Historically, there's a lot to be said for this, though it sets up ironies that can't quite be reconciled here.

The presence of Terence Blanchard in the trumpet section may suggest that this is a cross-generational affair. Not so; he stands out very prominently as the only real representative of the younger tendency, fizzing with testosterone and change-the-world enthusiasm, while his elders simply remember the way it was. Interesting, but odd.

(*) Some Blues Chiaroscuro CR(D) 320
>   McShann; Clark Terry (*t, v*); Al Grey (*tb*); Major Holley (*b, v*); Milt Hinton (*b*); Ben Riley,
>   Bobby Durham (*d*). 2/90–9/92.

*** The Missouri Connection Reservoir RSR CD 124
>   McShann; John Hicks (*p*). 9/92.

Now into his eighties, McShann remains amazingly spirited. His meeting with John Hicks is a discussion about the blues over two keyboards and, while it hardly says anything new about the form, it's a genial encounter, neither man having to compromise his ground to any extent. *Some Blues* is a hotchpotch that starts with half an album of duos cut with Major Holley and two sessions with Terry, Grey and the others. The bass and piano tracks hit a characteristic McShann note of rough good humour, but the band titles are a bit thin. There's also a bonus track of the leader reminiscing for the microphone.

Medeski, Martin & Wood GROUP

*** It's A Jungle In Here Gramavision R2 79495
>   John Medeski (*org, p*); Billy Martin (*d, perc*); Chris Wood (*b*); Steven Bernstein (*t, flhn*); Josh
>   Roseman (*tb*); Jay Rodrigues (*ts, as*); Dave Binney (*as*); Marc Ribot (*g*). 8/93.

(*) Friday Afternoon In The Universe Gramavision GCD 79503
>   As above, except omit Bernstein, Roseman, Rodrigues, Binney, Ribot. 94.

. . . and in that jungle called Noo Yawk strange cries and rhythms proliferate like orchids. Where else would anyone put Monk's 'Bemsha Swing' in on top of Bob Marley's 'Lively Up Yourself' and make it work? Or follow it with King Sunny Ade's 'Moti Mo', and make that seem like a perfectly sensible juxtaposition? The basic organ trio is steaming enough not to require the assistance of horns (though Ribot's guitar is a definite fillip, abstract and funky by turns). This is probably a band to see live, preferably in CBGB's, but as a reasonable second best the debut album is more than acceptable. The second is disappointing, too, though largely because the organ trio clichés, albeit treated post-modernly, pall very quickly. They're guaranteed a certain modest success, but nothing to write home about.

John Mehegan PIANO

*** Reflections Savoy SV-0204
>   Mehegan; Kenny Clarke (*d*). 9/55.

** A Pair Of Pianos Savoy SV-0206
>   Mehegan; Eddie Costa (*p*); Vinnie Burke (*b*). 11/55.

Mehegan is an interesting theorist who has largely been relegated to footnote status in anyone's jazz history. This Savoy album restores something of his work to circulation (there is a session with Chuck Wayne and another with Clarke and Charles Mingus on *I Just Love Jazz Piano*, Savoy SV-0117). These ten tracks are evenly split between solos and duets: losing a bassist frees up Mehegan, but only to impose his own formal structures on the tunes. Each of the ten standards is methodically reharmonized, while Mehegan's rhythms have a clockwork quality that suggests more of transplanted Bach than revisionist swing. It has its tiresome side, but as 'experimentalism' this wears rather better than some such records, and it takes a strongly alternative course to either Bud Powell or Lennie Tristano. The meeting with Eddie Costa on *A Pair Of Pianos* is, though, mostly bizarre. Mehegan insists that they play standards in a way that blends classical counterpoint with 'modern jazz'. So 'I'll Remember April' comes out sounding like something a long-haired composer such as Beethoven might appreciate. Worth having for the sleeve-notes, by the mysterious 'Uncus', who speculates on how it would have sounded if Bach and Handel had 'blown on a set of changes'.

Brad Mehldau PIANO

**** Introducing Brad Mehldau Warner Bros 945997-2
>   Mehldau; Larry Grenadier, Christian McBride (*b*); Jorge Rossy, Brian Blade (*d*). 3–4/95.

There is some superb playing here by a man who has already made a name for himself in the crowded New York scene. Mehldau approaches this set of five standards and four originals with a rare kind of freedom. Though his playing is structured in a familiar post-bop mode, it's as if he were aware of jazz tradition but entirely unencumbered by it. That lends such freshness to, say, the opening 'It Might As Well Be Spring' that he seems to be uncovering a previously overlooked but brilliant piano interpretation. On Coltrane's 'Countdown' he creates a logical solo out of phrases and whole passages that seem superficially disparate from one another. His slow playing is distinguished by an exquisitely light touch –

'My Romance' is made to glow – and it's lightness that characterizes his manner. He shies away from dense voicings and will leave a daring amount of space in even a fast improvisation. His own writing fits in with the rest of his style: sample the unexpectedly jaunty 'Angst'. Two different rhythm sections shadow him very gracefully. An outstanding debut.

Dick Meldonian (born 1930) TENOR AND SOPRANO SAXOPHONES, CLARINET

*** You've Changed Progressive PCD-7052
    Meldonian; Derek Smith (*p*); Milt Hinton (*b*); Ronnie Bedford (*d*). 8/78.
*** 'S Wonderful Circle CCD-150
    Meldonian; Paul Cohen, Phil Sunkel, John Eckert, Johnny Glasel (*t*); Bob Pring (*tb*); Gary Klein, Cliff Hoff, Arthur Sharp, Chuck Fisher (*ts*); Dick Bagni (*bs, bcl*); Derek Smith (*p*); Marty Grosz (*g*); Frank Tate (*b*); Fred Stoll (*d*). 3/82.
*** It's A Wonderful World Jazzology JCD-164
    Meldonian; Marty Grosz (*g, v*); Pete Compo (*b*). 3/83.

A veteran of many big bands – Barnet, Kenton, Russo – Meldonian typifies the sax section pro: adept and at home on tenor and soprano, reliable solos, fluent delivery. There's no special distinction to the small-group date, *You've Changed*, which, surprisingly, has the leader taking out his soprano more often than the tenor; but it's very sure-footed in its demeanour. Smith and Hinton are about as solid as you can get for this situation, and Smith plays very wittily on the big-band date too (try his solo on 'Lullaby Of Birdland'). Here Meldonian leads a crack team through 14 charts by Gene Roland, some originals, some based on standards: if the music sometimes sounds like anonymous big-band greenstuff, Roland's charts throw in a little pepper just when blandness sets in. *It's A Wonderful World* pares things back to a trio, Meldonian sticking mostly to soprano but bringing out the clarinet for one tune. The three chaps chug through a set of old-timers with much fun, though if you don't care for the guitarist's singing style, be warned that much of it is subject to Grosz-out. Beefed up to CD length with eight alternative takes, though this tends to detract from rather than abet the show.

Myra Melford PIANO

*** Jump Enemy 115-2
    Melford; Lindsey Horner (*b*); Reggie Nicholson (*d*). 6/90.
*** Now & Now Enemy 131-2
    As above. 8/91.
***(*) Alive In The House Of Saints hat ART 6136
    As above. 2/93.
**** Even The Sounds Shine hat ART 6161
    As above, except add Dave Douglas (*t*); Marty Ehrlich (*cl, bcl, as*). 5/94.

By herself, Melford is an impressive pianist whose synthesis of 'out' playing with surprisingly infectious melodic hooks and harmonic rigour makes her music inviting and challenging at the same moment. With Horner and Nicholson, she makes up one-third of a terrifically swinging trio, since bassist and drummer play with compelling attack and authority. The resulting records are an absorbing blend of methods. Perhaps the two Enemy albums (both cut in the studio) are a little too effortful in bridging forms, which results in a studied air creeping in to some tracks; the first sounds more composed, the second more spontaneous, and it's a matter of taste as to which one sounds better. The live session for hat ART, though, is well ahead. The new versions of 'Frank Lloyd Wright Goes West To West' and 'Live Jump', both of which started out on *Jump*, secure an epic sweep and grandeur without sacrificing detail or the close-knit intimacy of the trio. Melford relishes her tunes, and Horner and Nicholson swing them off the bandstand.

    Even The Sounds Shine goes one better. Cut on a European visit, with Douglas and Ehrlich augmenting the trio, this is a superb sequence of pieces, the balance of composition and improvisation handled with engrossing aplomb: the extended 'La Mezquita Suite' is the obvious standout, but the title-theme, with a stunning solo by Douglas, is just as fine, and a revised look at 'Frank Lloyd Wright' is equally effective. Douglas and Ehrlich, who can play outside and in with equal facility, were ideal choices for the front line, and Melford's own piano takes the highest ground in melodic free playing. Excellent live sound.

Mike Melillo (born 1939) PIANO

*** **Moonlight On The Gange** (sic.) Red 123264-2
    Melillo; Michael Moore (*b*); Ben Riley (*d*). 5/94.
Melillo's interesting earlier records haven't so far made it to the current format. This forthright trio set would make a useful companion-piece to *Alternate Choices* (Red NS 211). Melillo's idiosyncratic take on bebop piano has a stuttering bounce to it, but he swings through his material, and Moore and Riley are in good shape alongside. Highlight: the nutty variations on Ornette Coleman's 'Humpty Dumpty'.

Marcello Melis BASS, VOCALS

*** **Free To Dance** Black Saint 120023
    Melis; Lester Bowie, Enrico Rava (*t*); George Lewis, Gary Valente (*tb*); Don Pullen (*p*); Fred Hopkins (*b*); Famoudou Don Moye, Nana Vasconcelos (*perc*); Jeanne Lee, Sheila Jordan (*v*). 76.
Sardinians are no more Italian than the Scots are English, and Melis takes a very serious view of his cultural ancestry. Several works – notably another, later, Black Saint, *Angedras* (a mirror-form of 'Sardegna') – draw directly on the folk traditions and poetry of his native island. *Free To Dance* was also recorded there, with some of the American players who have been associated with Melis and his music; the late Don Pullen was a loyal friend and supporter. Like the pianist, Melis sees himself working at the tail-end of the jazz tradition; in the past, and on *Angedras*, he actually imports snatches of recorded or radio jazz to underline the differences in what he is doing. Here, on his most completely satisfying record, he merely refers obliquely to aspects of jazz playing and improvisation, intermingling slap lines and off-beat 'walking' effects with huge, orchestral sounds recalling Richard Davis.

    There are, typically, only three tracks on the session, each of them patiently constructed and flawlessly crafted. All the instruments are doubled, creating cross-patterns of musical activity that allow Melis to build complex music out of essentially simple materials. The problem, and the rather unenthusiastic rating above, is that little of this music communicates freely. There is always a sense of observing something from the outside, picking out solo voices – Bowie's, Rava's, Lewis's – or concentrating on the vocals. However interesting, it signally fails to be involving. Why music so passionate in conception should seem so cool and abstract in fact is hard to explain, but that is our impression and our conclusion.

Gil Melle BARITONE SAXOPHONE, KEYBOARDS

**** **Primitive Modern / Quadrama** Original Jazz Classics OJC 1712
    Melle; Joe Cinderella (*g*); Bill Phillips (*b*); Ed Thigpen, Shadow Wilson (*d*). 4–6/56.
**** **Gil's Guests** Original Jazz Classics OJC 1753
    Melle; Art Farmer, Kenny Dorham (*t*); Hal McKusick (*as, f*); Julius Watkins (*frhn*); Don Butterfield (*tba*); Joe Cinderella (*g*); Vinnie Burke (*b*); Ed Thigpen (*d*). 8/56.
Melle's original sleeve-note for *Primitive Modern* suggests that 'modern jazz at its best is a wedding of the classics with the more modern developments native to jazz'; while that implies third-stream dogma, at least Melle put the notion to very striking use. Anyone who lists Bartók, Varèse and Herbie Nichols as major influences is going to do something more than hard bop, and the leader's attempts at shifting the parameters of standard jazz form remain surprising and invigorating. The fast-moving complexities of 'Ironworks', the mysterious dirge, 'Dominica', and the Russell-like 'Adventure Swing' mark out a path very different from most other developments of the time. Cinderella reveals himself as a fine soloist and perceptive interpreter of Melle's needs, and the rhythm section are also fine; while Melle himself is content to play an often reserved role, although his improvisations are melodically as strong as those of Lars Gullin, the baritone player he admits to admiring most. There are a couple of drawbacks – the original studio sound is rather flat, with the leader a little remote in the mix, and some of the structures are delivered a little stiffly by the quartet – but otherwise this is a significant and too little-known record. The new CD edition is greatly welcomed, especially since it includes the entire *Quadrama* album as a bonus on the original programme, another remarkable quartet date with two exceptional Ellington transformations and the fine original 'Rush Hour In Hong Kong'.

    If anything, *Gil's Guests* is even better, thanks to Rudy van Gelder's superior engineering and the opportunities which a bigger ensemble permits for Melle to create heightened colours, more vivid texture and counterpoint, and a smoother transition between his classically inspired ideas and a jazz execution. Even a conventional feature such as 'Sixpence', written for Kenny Dorham, has an ingenious arrangement for tuba and guitar at the beginning. 'Ghengis' is a direct borrowing from Bartók, and the shifting voicings of 'Block Island' merge brilliantly into a theme that works just as well as a blowing vehicle. An outstanding record, well remastered.

Misha Mengelberg (born 1935) PIANO, COMPOSER

***(*) **Change Of Season** Soul Note 101104
   Mengelberg; George Lewis (tb); Steve Lacy (ss); Arjen Gorter (b); Han Bennink (d). 7/84.
**** **Impromptus** FMP 7
   Mengelberg (p solo). 6/88.
**** **Mix** ICP 030
   As above. 4 & 5/94.
**** **Who's Bridge** Avant AVAN 038
   Mengelberg; Brad Jones (b); Joey Baron (d). 94.

Robert Frost once characterized free verse as 'playing tennis with the net down'. Improvisers like Dutchmen Mengelberg and Bennink have been very largely concerned with putting the net back, sometimes up to badminton height, searching for ways of combining the freedoms of improvisation with traditional jazz and even more formal structures.

Mengelberg is also a 'legitimate' composer, albeit one in the Louis Andriessen mould, with a very strong jazz influence in his work. The collectivism that was so strong a component of the Dutch 1960s avant-garde is evident in the autonomy granted to the performers (all of them expert players) on *Change Of Season*. Lewis seems most comfortable in the mixed idiom, though Lacy (a purist's purist) sounds a little glacial. Bennink whips up little rhythmic storms, but he plays with unwonted reserve and an often unrecognized sensitivity.

Mengelberg plays with great assurance and a graceful disposition of apparently self-contained and discontinuous ideas that are more reminiscent of the Swiss Irene Schweizer than of his compatriots, Fred Van Hove and Leo Cuypers. Interesting, if for no other reason than that there are other directions for 'free' piano than the one taken and dominated by Cecil Taylor.

Impromptus makes a generic nod to a (minor) classical form. The 13 individual pieces aren't obviously linked by theme or as variations, but they follow a barely discernible logic that can be picked up via Mengelberg's untutored vocalise, which is of the Bud Powell/Keith Jarrett/Cecil Taylor persuasion. *Mix*, recorded at a couple of live solo concerts in Amsterdam and The Hague, is very much in the same territory: huge, quasi-tonal shapes and structures jumbled together in what at first glance seems disorder but which is suddenly pierced by light, a simple melodic line that pulls the whole 'mix' into symmetry; perhaps the effect of a magnet on iron filings would be a more effective analogy.

Who's Bridge is intriguing in that it takes Melgelberg much closer to jazz idiom than he normally attempts. He has two very adept sidemen, and Baron is, when one thinks of it, the only younger-generation American who might remind listeners of Bennink. There are even songs here: the Monkish 'Romantic Jump Of Hares', the skittish, Morton-influenced 'Rumbone' and the real surprise, 'Peer's Counting Song', which finds Mengelberg in unwontedly lyrical and expressive mood.

Helen Merrill (born 1930) VOCAL

**** **Helen Merrill With Clifford Brown And Gil Evans** Emarcy 838292-2
   Merrill; Clifford Brown, Art Farmer, Louis Mucci (t); Jimmy Cleveland, Joe Bennett (tb); John LaPorta (cl, as); Jerome Richardson (as, ts, f); Danny Bank (f); Hank Jones, Jimmy Jones (p); Barry Galbraith (g); Oscar Pettiford, Milt Hinton (b); Joe Morello, Osie Johnson, Bobby Donaldson (d); strings, horns. 12/54–6/56.
***(*) **Dream Of You** Emarcy 514074-2
   As above, except omit Brown, Bank, Jimmy Jones, Hinton and Johnson. 6/56.

The kind of singer who makes strong men and intellectuals go weak at the knees – and any doubts about that should be dispelled by the sleeve-notes to either this compilation of her records for Mercury or Piero Umiliani's notes on the Liuto disc listed below. Merrill sings at a consistently slow pace, unfolding melodies as if imparting a particularly difficult confidence, and she understands the harmonies of the songs as completely as she trusts her way with time. That gives these lingering performances a sensuality which is less of a come-hither come-on than the similarly inclined work of a singer such as Julie London. Merrill thinks about the words, but she improvises on the music too. Her treatment of 'Don't Explain' is cooler yet no less troubling than Billie Holiday's exaggerated pathos, and 'What's New' is a masterpiece. Brown's accompaniments on seven tracks make an absorbing contrast to his work with Sarah Vaughan, and Evans's arrangements on the other eight songs are some of his most lucid work in this area. *Dream Of You* restores that entire session to the catalogue, with a couple of alternative takes for good measure.

***(*) **Helen Merrill In Italy** Liuto LRS 0063/5
> Merrill; Nino Culasso, Nino Rosso (*t*); Dino Piana (*tb*); Gianni Basso (*ts*); Gino Marinacci (*f*); Piero Umiliani, Renato Sellani (*p*); Enzo Grillini (*g*); Berto Pisano, Giorgio Azzolini (*b*); Sergio Conti, Ralph Ferraro, Franco Tonani (*d*); strings. 59–62.

This is flawed by the sometimes unlovely sound, but it's an otherwise compelling collection of all the pieces Merrill recorded on various trips to Italy. Three songs by Umiliani for film scores have lyrics by the singer, and those for 'My Only Man' and 'Dreaming Of The Past' are original and hard to forget. Most of the others are standards, again treated to the most rarefied of ballad settings – 'The More I See You' is almost impossibly slow – but the four closing tracks, sung in Italian with an orchestra conducted by Ennio Morricone, have a *Lieder*-like quality that's disarmingly direct.

*** **Collaboration** Emarcy 834205-2
> Merrill; Shunzo Ono (*t, flhn*); Lew Soloff (*t*); Jimmy Knepper (*tb*); Dave Taylor (*btb*); Chris Hunter (*ss, as, f, cl, ob, picc*); Jerry Dodgion (*ss, f*); Steve Lacy (*ss*); Danny Bank (*bs, f, bcl*); Phil Bodner (*bcl, f, af*); Wally Kane (*bcl, bsn*); Roger Rosenberg (*bcl*); Gil Goldstein (*ky*); Harry Lookofsky, Lamar Alsop (*vn*); Theodore Israel, Harold Colletta (*vla*); Jesse Levy (*clo*); Joe Beck, Jay Berliner (*g*); Buster Williams (*b*); Mel Lewis (*d*); Gil Evans (*cond*). 8/87.

One of the strangest singer-and-orchestra records ever made. Merrill's voice has grown weightier over the years, and she casts it very slowly on the waters of Gil Evans's arrangements here, the charts laying down thick, barely moving textures which suggest a mildewing romanticism. Her favourite slow tempos recur throughout, and it's Evans's often magical way with three different ensembles (one with strings, one with trombone and woodwinds, another led by brass) which stop the music from trudging to a stop. Lacy appears for a tart commentary on two tracks, but otherwise it's the long, carefully held tones of the vocalist which act on the music. Sometimes, as in an arrangement of 'Summertime' which harks back directly to *Porgy And Bess*, Evans seems to be reminiscing on his own past, too.

*** **Just Friends** Emarcy 842007-2
> Merrill; Stan Getz (*ts*); Joachim Kühn, Torrie Zito (*p*); Jean-François Jenny-Clark (*b*); Daniel Humair (*d*). 89.

Merrill's return to a small-group format brings forth some quietly resolute performances, their autumnal feel heightened by the appearance of Getz in his twilight phase. 'Cavatina' and 'It's Not Easy Being Green' were questionable choices of material, though.

**** **Clear Out Of This World** Emarcy 510691-2
> Merrill; Tom Harrell (*t, flhn*); Wayne Shorter (*ss, ts*); Roger Kellaway (*p*); Red Mitchell (*b*); Terry Clarke (*d*). 6–9/91.

One of the finest vocal records of recent years – although integral to the success is the superlative playing by the instrumentalists. Kellaway, Mitchell and Clarke are ideally sensitive and supportive, and Kellaway's playing in particular is extraordinary: his one-man accompaniment on 'Maybe', one of three good contemporary songs on the disc, is a textbook example of saying a lot while playing a little. Harrell's pristine control is in evidence on a luminous 'When I Grow Too Old To Dream', and the last 30 seconds of this track are reason enough to acquire the record. Shorter contributes eccentric soprano to one tune, strange tenor to another, and there's even a comic duet between Merrill and Mitchell on 'Some Of These Days' that actually works. The singer herself delivers some of her best latter-day performances, with her technique of holding very low notes close to the microphone used to expose telling detail in the songs.

*** **Blossom Of Stars** Emarcy 514652-2
> Merrill; personnel drawn from above Emarcy discs. 54–89.

A compilation of episodes from both ends of Merrill's career on record, culminating in the new 'We Are Not Alone', a film soundtrack song. Very worthwhile, of course, but the albums above are the place to start.

**** **Brownie** Verve 522363-2
> Merrill; Roy Hargrove, Tom Harrell (*t, flhn*); Lew Soloff, Wallace Roney (*t*); Kenny Barron (*p*); Torrie Zito (*ky*); Rufus Reid (*b*); Victor Lewis (*d*). 2/94.

Another extraordinary record, which works perfectly both as a homage to Clifford Brown and as a vehicle for Merrill's intensely refined approach to time. No matter how slow the tempo, she makes the line flow, the words mulled over but always sung, not talked through. Any frailties of tone are used for dramatic effect, and on a piece such as 'Born To Be Blue' it can be devastating. The stellar gathering of trumpeters evokes Brown's own ghost, with some electrifying unison passages and memorable individual turns for each of the four players; Barron, as ever, follows and fills in spaces with imperturbable grace.

Pat Metheny (born 1954) GUITAR

*** Bright Size Life ECM 1073
  Metheny; Jaco Pastorius (*b*); Bob Moses (*d*). 12/75.
*** Watercolours ECM 1097
  Metheny; Lyle Mays (*p*); Eberhard Weber (*b*); Danny Gottlieb (*d*). 2/77.
** Pat Metheny Group ECM 1114
  As above, except Mark Egan (*b*) replaces Weber. 1/78.
**(*) New Chautauqua ECM 1131
  Metheny (*g* solo). 8/78.
**(*) American Garage ECM 1155
  Metheny; Lyle Mays (*ky*); Mark Egan (*b*); Danny Gottlieb (*d*). 6/79.

Metheny emerged as a cool, limpid-toned guitarist at just the moment when the world seemed to want such a player. His first two ECM albums are a little untypical – each depends more on its respective star bassist to give it some clout – but, like the ones that follow, they are pleasant, hummable records with a degree of fine playing which the high-grade production values and sometimes over-sensitive musicianship can occasionally block out with sheer amiability. At this time Metheny favoured a clean, open tone with just enough electronic damping to take the music out of 'classic' jazz-guitar feeling, but he clearly owed a great debt to such urban pastoralists as Jim Hall and Jimmy Raney, even if he seldom moved back to bebop licks.

The Metheny Group albums settled the guitarist's music into the niche which he still works from: light, easily digested settings that let him play long, noodling solos which can as often as not work up a surprising intensity. His companions, Mays especially, can seem like much-too-nice influences on a player whose inclinations (as in the album with Ornette Coleman) may be far more interesting than most of his records allow.

*** 80 / 81 ECM 1180/1 2CD
  Metheny; Dewey Redman, Michael Brecker (*ts*); Charlie Haden (*b*); Jack DeJohnette (*d*). 5/80.
At the time this sounded like an almost shocking departure, but Brecker and Redman adapt themselves to Metheny's aesthetic without undue compromise and Haden and DeJohnette play with great purpose. There's too much music here and many dreary spots, but some excellent moments too.

**(*) As Falls Witchita, So Falls Witchita Falls ECM 1190
  Metheny; Lyle Mays (*ky*); Nana Vasconcelos (*perc*). 9/80.
** Offramp ECM 1216
  As above, except add Steve Rodby (*b*), Danny Gottlieb (*d*). 10/81.
*** Travels ECM 1252/3 2CD
  As above. 7–11/82.
The Metheny band was by now an international concert institution. The two studio albums suggested a drying up of ideas and, though the impish Vasconcelos added a little extra gumption to it all, Mays's relentlessly uninteresting parts continued to be a source of aggravation. *Travels*, though, summed up the band's tenure with ECM with a studious and densely packed live set that will do for those who want a single set from the period.

***(*) Rejoicing ECM 1271
  Metheny; Charlie Haden (*b*); Billy Higgins (*d*). 11/83.
It might seem conservative to pull out such a traditional record as Metheny's best up to this point, but he finds a loneliness in Horace Silver's 'Lonely Woman' and a happiness in Ornette Coleman's 'Rejoicing' which more severe interpreters of those composers don't seem to have time or room for. By itself the playing isn't so remarkable, but pairing him with Haden and Higgins, on a programme of mostly Coleman and Metheny originals, sheds new lustre both on himself and on music that's often somewhat neglected.

**(*) First Circle ECM 1278
  Metheny; Lyle Mays (*ky*); Steve Rodby (*b*); Paul Wertico (*d*); Pedro Aznar (*perc, v*). 2/84.
*** Works ECM 823270-2
  As records above.
The last ECM album is nothing much, a retread of paths already foot-hollowed enough. The collection is a decent introduction.

**** Song X Geffen 924096
  Metheny; Ornette Coleman (*as, vn*); Charlie Haden (*b*); Jack DeJohnette, Denardo Coleman (*d*). 12/85.
About the only problems with this record are DeJohnette – a great drummer, but perhaps not the right

one for Ornette Coleman – and the sense that some of the best and most extreme material was left off the record (which Metheny has subsequently confirmed). Otherwise it's the most astonishing move ever made by any musician perceived as a middle-of-the-road jazz artist. Not only does the guitarist power his way through Coleman's itinerary with utter conviction, he sets up opportunities for the saxophonist to resolve and he creates a fusion which Coleman's often impenetrable Prime Time bands have failed to come to terms with. Melody still has a place here, which suggests that Metheny's interest in the original Coleman legacy may be carrying forward in his own work more intently than it is in the composer's. Either way, on many of the more raving episodes here, both men sound exultant with the possibilities. Highly recommended.

(*) Still Life (Talking) Geffen GED 24145
    Metheny; Lyle Mays (*ky*); Steve Rodby (*b*); Paul Weryico (*d*); Armando Marcal (*perc, v*); David Blamires, Mark Ledford (*v*). 3–4/87.
*** **Question And Answer** Geffen GED 24293
    Metheny; Dave Holland (*b*); Roy Haynes (*d*). 12/89.
** **Secret Story** Geffen GED 24468
    Metheny; Gil Goldstein (*p, acc*); Lyle Mays (*ky*); Toots Thielemans (*hca*); Charlie Haden, Steve Rodby, Will Lee (*b*); Steve Ferrone, Paul Wertico, Sammy Merendino (*d*); Nana Vasconcelos, Armando Marcal (*perc*); Mark Ledford (*v*); strings and brass. 91–92.
*** **The Road To You** Geffen GED 24601
    Metheny; Pedro Aznar (*sax, vib, mar, perc, g, v*); Lyle Mays (*ky*); Steve Rodby (*b*); Paul Wertico (*d*); Armando Marcal (*perc, v*). 92–93.

Metheny's subsequent albums for Geffen have taken on even more of a light-rock feel than previously. *Still Life (Talking)* is an exemplar of the style, which peaks on the infectious 'Last Train Home'; but there's an awful lot of fluff that goes with it, often courtesy of Mays's noodling keyboards. *Question And Answer* – which seems to be the kind of periodic vacation that Metheny takes from his regular band, and may it continue – finds the guitarist, bassist and, especially, the drummer playing with great brio and suppleness. The tunes are another mix of standards, Coleman and Metheny tunes; and if some of the charm of the ECM trio date is missing and a few tunes seem to end up nowhere, it's well worth hearing. *Secret Story* is hopelessly overblown and would feel intolerably pompous were Metheny himself not so likeable: he always salvages something interesting to play, even when the music's weighed down with strings, brass and whatever. *The Road To You*, a concert album, is much livelier and is one of the best records by the regular group since the last live set.

*** **Zero Tolerance For Silence** Geffen GED 24626
    Metheny (*g* solo).

Has a major commercial artist ever conducted such a schizophrenic career? While the Metheny Group seems intent on mere pleasantry, the man himself seeks to peer over the edge and into the abyss with this one, a riot of electronic howling. Hardcore souls might sniff at the pretensions here, and it's scarcely on a par with a Sonny Sharrock or Hans Reichel solo record. But Metheny earns stars for doing something other hit-makers pay lip service to: going for the hard stuff and insisting it gets released.

*** **We Live Here** Geffen GED 24729
    Metheny; Mark Ledford (*t, flhn, v*); Lyle Mays (*ky*); Steve Rodby (*b*); Paul Wertico (*d*); Luis Conte (*perc*); David Blamires (*v*). 94.

Back on undeadly ground. A few tracks work off programmed drum beats, and Metheny gets to do a Bensonesque bit here and there, but by the middle of the disc he's returned to his favourite platform, the soft cadences of Brazilian beat. Once there, he actually sounds in very good form, confirming that, with the rotten *Secret Story* behind him, this is a good period for the man who must be the most popular guitarist in jazz.

Henrik Metz (born 1948) PIANO

***(*) **Henrik Metz** Music Mecca 1024-2
    Metz; Fredrik Lundin (*ss, ts*); Niels-Henning Orsted-Pedersen (*b*). 8/92.

Taken at an almost uniformly slow pace, this programme of 15 trio pieces creates a peculiar truce between wistfulness and a harsh melancholy. Metz lays down and expands all the harmonic bases, which Lundin and Pedersen roam across with two wholly opposite approaches: where the bassist delivers nimble, scampering, many-noted lines, Lundin is almost unflinchingly hard, dark and monosyllabic. Compare, to take one example, their different takes on 'I Fall In Love Too Easily'. After six American standards, the trio move into a series of meditations on themes by Scandinavian composers or traditional airs, a striking change of direction and a distinct success in the annals of jazz going native. The recording is suitably intimate and full-bodied.

Hendrik Meurkens VIBRAPHONE, HARMONICA

*** **Sambahia** Concord CCD 4474
> Meurkens; Claudio Roditi (*t, flhn*); Paquito D'Rivera (*as, cl*); Tim Armacost (*ts*); Lito Tabora (*p*); Jacare (*b*); Cesar Machado (*d*); Reginaldo Vargas (*perc*). 12/90.

(*) **Clear Of Clouds Concord CCD 4531
> Meurkens; Claudio Roditi (*t, flhn*); Osmar Milito (*p*); Fernando Merlino (*p, ky*); Claudio Jorge (*g*); Alceu Maria (*cavaquinho*); Jacare (*b*); Pascoal Meirelles (*d*); Dom Chacal (*perc*). 2 & 6/92.

*** **A View From Manhattan** Concord CCD 4585
> Meurkens; Jay Ashby (*tb, perc*); Dick Oatts (*af, as, ts, ss*); Mark Soskin (*p*); Harvie Swartz, Leonard D. Traversa (*b*); Carl Allen (*d*); Thelmo Martins Porto Pinho (*d, perc*). 7/93.

*** **Slidin'** Concord CCD 4628
> Meurkens; Peter Bernstein (*g*); Dado Moroni, Mark Soskin (*p*); David Finck, Harvie Swartz (*b*); Tim Horner (*d*). 6/94.

His name would hardly lead you to expect smoothly flowing Latin grooves, but that is what Meurkens delivers. Despite his Dutch ancestry, he was born in Hamburg, a seaport initiation that somehow always holds out the promise of eclectic enthusiasms to come. His Rio-Samba Jazz Group has been around for some time, delivering consistent product without ever having sparked much excitement. A little like Klaus Ignatzek, Meurkens responds very favourably to close attention; otherwise he is apt to pass the casual listener by on the assumption that the calm surface conceals shallowness rather than music of some depth and thought.

The latest of the group is the exception; no vibraphone, no Roditi, but an obvious attempt to move into the jazz mainstream with elegant portrayals of 'Have You Met Miss Jones?' and 'Come Rain Or Come Shine'. Bernstein is the key element here, a very underrated player whose sweeping arpeggiations and clean, accurate runs offer an ideal foil to Meurkens's plangent mouth harp.

Mezz Mezzrow (1899–1972) CLARINET, SAXOPHONES

*** **Mezz Mezzrow, 1928–1936** Classics 713
> Mezzrow; Muggsy Spanier (*c*); Max Kaminsky, Frank Newton, Freddie Goodman, Ben Gusick, Reunald Jones, Chelsea Quealey (*t*); Benny Carter (*t, as, v*); Floyd O'Brien (*tb*); Frank Teschemacher (*cl, as*); Rod Cless (*as*); Bud Freeman, Art Karle, Johnny Russell (*ts*); Joe Bushkin, Teddy Wilson, Willie 'The Lion' Smith, Joe Sullivan (*p*); Eddie Condon (*bjo*); Albert Casey, Clayton Sunshine Duerr, Ted Tonison (*g*); Wellman Braud, Pops Foster, John Kirby, Louis Thompson (*b*); Jim Lannigan (*bb*); Gene Krupa, Jack Maisel, George Stafford, Chick Webb (*d*); Chick Bullock, Elinor Charier, Red McKenzie, Lucille Stewart (*v*). 4/28–3/36.

*** **Mezz Mezzrow, 1936–1939** Classics 694
> Similar to above. 36–39.

*** **Masters Of Jazz: Sidney Bechet** Storyville STCD 4104
> Mezzrow; Sidney Bechet (*ss*); Hot Lips Page (*t, v*); Sammy Price, Fitz Weston, Sox Wilson (*p*); Danny Barker (*g*); Wellman Braud, Pops Foster (*b*); Big Sid Catlett, Baby Dodds, Kaiser Marshall (*d*); Douglas Daniels, Coot Grant, Pleasant Joe (*v*); other personnel unidentified. 7/45–12/47.

***(*) **Mezz Mezzrow In Paris, 1955** Jazz Time 252 712
> Mezzrow; Peanuts Holland, Guy Longnon (*t*); Maxim Saury (*cl*); Milton Sealey (*p*); Eddie De Haas (*b*); Kansas Fields (*d*). 5 & 7/55.

Nobody came closer to living the life of Norman Mailer's 'White Negro' than Milton 'Mezz' Mezzrow. Eddie Condon nicknamed him 'Southmouth' in ironic recognition of his obsessive self-identification with Black musicians and self-consciously disenchanted and unironic pursuit of a 'negro' lifestyle. (He claims to have insisted on being put in the black cells of a segregated police block, on the grounds that he was only 'passing for white'.)

His nickname also carries an echo of Louis Armstrong's soubriquet, 'Satchelmouth'. Mezzrow idolized the trumpeter and once worked for him as factotum and grass distributor (this was a *long* time before 'Hello, Dolly' and 'Wonderful World'). His music was considerably more 'authentic' than his personal manners: sinuous if slightly repetitive lines, a dry, sharp tone (compare George Lewis's) and a flow of ideas which, if not endless, were always imaginatively permed and varied. The pre-war *Panassié*

Sessions, made with Bechet and Tommy Ladnier for RCA, are sadly no longer available, but the immediate post-war material from the King Jazz label is very nearly as good.

The Bechet compilation consists largely of reorganized material from the series; the band was known as the Mezzrow–Bechet Xtet, depending on numbers, and, though Mezzrow largely called the shots music-ally, it's Bechet who is now (properly) identified as the more significant musician. Classics like 'The Sheikh Of Araby', 'Minor Swoon', 'Jelly Roll', 'Revolutionary Blues', 'Perdido Street Stomp' are all included (the middle pair with alternative takes). Musically, it's pure pleasure, but it's important to recognize Mezzrow's contribution, and that's best heard on the complete sequence.

For the time being, the best sources for Mezzrow are the Classics discs, which exclude material made under Bechet's leadership. There's nothing here that requires a wholesale revision of Mezzrow's oddly unbalanced reputation. Many of those who praise him to the skies like the *idea* of him, and would be dismayed if they were presented with a Mezzrow solo blindfold; by the same token, many of those who dismiss his playing out of hand do so because they have chosen to believe he is merely an ofay dabbler, indulging a species of *nostalgie de la boue*.

The legendary *A La Schola Cantorum* sessions were made in 1955 with a multiracial Franco-American band. Essentially, the May sessions consist of two long takes each of the first (slow) and second (fast) parts of 'Blues Aven Un Pont'. Mezzrow's improvisations on the bridge are as clearly enunciated as any he was to record and the later, July sessions are nowhere near as interesting, despite some exciting solos. If the music appeals, try to take in Mezzrow's ghosted and at least partly fictional 'autobiography', *Really The Blues*. It's an absolute gas.

Palle Mikkelborg (born 1941) TRUMPET, FLUGELHORN, COMPOSER

***(*) **Heart To Heart** Storyville STCD 4114
    Mikkelborg; Kenneth Knudsen (*ky*); Niels-Henning Orsted-Pedersen (*b*). 86.
A player of enormous technical capability and lyrical strength, Mikkelborg has always worn his influ-ences on his sleeve. The 1984 composition *Aura* was a harmonically coded dedication to Miles Davis (on which Davis was to play a guest role). Much of Mikkelborg's most important work in the late 1970s and '80s has been for large-scale conventional forces, much like his sometime collaborator, the guitarist-composer Terje Rypdal, but he remains more deeply rooted in jazz than the Norwegian, having served an impressively documented apprenticeship with the exiled Dexter Gordon.

Mikkelborg is one of the few convincing exponents of electric trumpet, which he uses, unlike Don Ellis, to produce great sheets of harmonic colour against which he dabs acoustic notes of surprising purity. *Aura* underlined the Miles influence to the apparent exclusion of any other; but he is perhaps closer in conception to Chet Baker and, even on an impressionistic set like *Heart To Heart*, he can sound astonishingly like both Clifford Brown and Howard McGhee.

The opening track is an unashamed Miles rip-off, though played with a clear, brassy resonance that is Mikkelborg's own. Fortunately, perhaps, it doesn't set a tone for the set, which is quite varied in temper, though mainly in a meditative mood. Knudsen's keyboard structures are always highly effective, and NHOP is far better recorded than usual. Recommended.

Joakim Milder TENOR SAXOPHONE

***(*) **Still In Motion** Dragon DRCD 188
    Milder; Steve Dobrogosz (*p*); Christian Spering (*b*); Rune Carlsson (*d*). 9/89.
***(*) **Consensus** Opus 3 CD 9201
    Milder; Johan Hölén (*as*); Anders Persson (*p*); Christian Spering (*b*); Magnus Gran (*d*). 2/92.
Milder sounds like one of the most adventurous and least conformist of players to emerge from the Swedish scene in the 1980s. As an improviser he eschews both easy licks and long, heavily elaborate lines, preferring a scratchy tone to the open-voiced timbre of most tenor players and fragmenting his lines with silences, rushes and retards, anything he can think of that varies the attack. Yet there is Rollins-like logic to some of his melodic paths, and on some standards he keeps the sense of the song to hand even as he takes it crabbily apart. The all-original *Still In Motion* was a tiny disappointment after the memorable debut LP, *Life In Life*, which is still on vinyl only: a more unified but fractionally less compelling session, since nothing quite aspires to the interplay with Palle Danielsson and Carlsson on the earlier set. *Consensus* returns to standards – there are 12 of them here – and refuses to take any obvious routes. 'My Funny Valentine', for instance, hints only obliquely at its melody, 'Some Day My Prince Will Come' gets a notably sour treatment – the tune almost exploded by Gran's crackling toms – and the use of a second saxophone to counterpoint some of the tenor parts is always different from what might be expected. Milder's own playing sounds more sewn-up than before, suggesting that he may be

losing some of his interesting rough edges; but this is still a fine continuation of a very impressive discography.

*** **Ways** Dragon DRCD 231
> Milder; Lasse Lindgren (*flhn*); Hakan Nykqvist (*frhn*); Staffan Martensson (*cl*); Steve Dobrogosz (*p*); Henrik Frendin (*vla*); Bertil Strandberg (*euph*); Christian Spering (*b*); Rune Carlsson (*d*); Peter Ostlund (*perc*); string section. 12/90–8/92.

Milder has been turning up on other records, but his own discography as leader is progressing slowly, carefully and with absorbing results. That said, this album of low-key, chamber-like music will be a distraction for those more interested in Milder's straight-ahead saxophone. The 11 originals are directed by their textural and tonal qualities rather than anything rhythmic, and only 'Apart' and 'Where Do Pies Go When They Die' push Milder into his most effective improvising form. Otherwise it's the contrasting brass and string sections that drive the content: lyrical and desolate in the almost typecast manner of Scandinavian jazz, it's a meritorious record but one for reflective tastes.

***(*) **Sister Majs Blouse** Mirrors MICD 002
> Milder; Bobo Stenson (*p*); Palle Danielsson (*b*); Fredrik Norén (*d*). 1/93.

*** **Remains** Dragon DRCD 285
> Milder; Steve Dobrogosz (*p*); Max Schultz (*g*); Henrik Frendin (*vn, vla*); Mats Rondin (*clo*); Christian Spering (*b*); Peter Ostlund (*perc*). 10/94–3/95.

*** **Ord Pa Golvet** LJ LJCD 5210
> Milder; Tobias Sjogren (*g*); Johannes Lundberg (*b*); Gunnar Ekelof (*v*). 1/95.

Three interesting records, but no masterpiece, and Milder's work seems to be slipping into a love of texture and sonic intricacy which may disappoint those who admire his saxophone playing. The *Sister Majs Blouse* project is dedicated to the music of the late Swedish saxman, Borje Fredriksson, with his original rhythm section standing in behind Milder. Fredriksson's tunes are a fascinating lot, from mood pieces to a wedding waltz, and the quartet characterize them with superb skill: Stenson, Danielsson and Norén have seldom sounded better. Ironically, Milder himself doesn't quite get hold of some of the tunes; but as a quartet disc this is very fine. *Remains* is distilled from woodwind, piano and strings: bountiful in terms of texture and variation, but not terribly vital to listen to. A theme like 'Simply Drift' shows how skilled Milder has become at fashioning themes out of fragments (and harmonic hooks), but his own playing here sounds relatively becalmed. Much the same could be said of the trio project, *Ord Pa Golvet*, but this is rather more mysterious, pieces of *audio vérité* passing into the music via traffic sounds and the enigmatic spoken commentary of Gunnar Ekelof. The most striking player here is actually Sjogren, whose wide vocabulary of sounds and influences creates the palette which most of the music is drawn from.

John Miles TENOR SAXOPHONE, FLUTE

*** **The Enchanter** Miles Music MMCD 082
> Miles; Neil Angilley (*p*); Phil Hudson (*g*); Julian Crampton (*b, d*); Laura Fairhurst (*clo*); Winston Clifford, Marc Meader, Dave Ohm (*d*). 93.

The technical details note that some of these tracks were made in Julian's bedroom; that, plus the family tie-up, might lead some to suspect a shabbily amateur effort. Not a bit of it. Like much of his generation, Miles wears his Coltrane influence very prominently, but he has turned it into a quite personal voice. The title-track, which opens, is very distinctive with its cello colours and, though there is nothing quite as arresting later on (except perhaps a duet with Crampton, done in the self-same bedroom studio), it establishes a tone and a standard which the record does not relinquish. One would like to hear the same music rather better recorded. There are some problems of audibility, and at one or two spots what sound like awkward edits or tape flaws. Otherwise very acceptable indeed.

Marcus Miller BASS, BASS CLARINET, KEYBOARDS, GUITAR

*** **The Sun Don't Lie** Dreyfus FDM 36560-2
> Miller; Miles Davis, Michael Stewart, Sal Marquez (*t*); David Sanborn, Kenny Garrett (*as*); Everette Harp (*ss, as*); Kirk Whalum, Wayne Shorter (*ts*); Joe Sample (*p*); Christian Wicht, Philippe Saisse (*ky*); Jonathan Butler, Vernon Reid, Paul Jackson Jr, Dean Brown, Hiram Bullock (*g*); Poogie Bell, Michael White, Tony Williams, Andy Narell, Steve Ferrone, Omar Hakim, William Calhoun, Lenny White (*d*); Don Alias, Paulinho Da Costa, Steve Thornton (*perc*). 90–92.

**(*) Tales Dreyfus FDM 36571-2

> Miller; Michael Stewart (*t*); Kenny Garrett (*as*); Joshua Redman (*ts*); Bernard Wright (*ky*); Hiram Bullock, Dean Brown (*g*); Poogie Bell, Lenny White (*d*); Lalah Hathaway, Me'Shell Ndege Ocello (*v*). 94–95.

Miller is the hippest, cleverest musician in contemporary black music, though that doesn't always mean he makes great records. Scientific and punctilious in the studio, as likely to get out his bass clarinet as his bass guitar, he masterminded most of the final Miles Davis studio records, and there are some notes from Miles on one track here, along with bits and pieces from some of the most famous session names in the business. Typically, it ends up being an album of brilliant fragments that, for all its skill, has a peculiarly unfinished feel to it, shards of jazz, rock, funk and film music flying in all directions. The ghost of Jaco Pastorius also haunts Miller's work – 'Mr Pastorius' is a simple solo tribute on bass, but so is the note-for-note re-creation of Weather Report's 'Teen Town'. If there's such a thing as post-modernist jazz-funk, it surely sounds like this. *Tales*, though strung around some sort of concept, works in much the same way: Garrett, Stewart and Redman toss in some jazz content, but some of the zing has also slipped away since the last record. Discouraging.

Mulgrew Miller (born 1955) PIANO

*** Keys To The City Landmark LCD 1507

> Miller; Ira Coleman (*b*); Marvin 'Smitty' Smith (*d*). 6/85.

*** Work! Landmark LCD 1511

> Miller; Charnett Moffett (*b*); Terri Lyne Carrington (*d*). 4/86.

*** Wingspan Landmark LCD 1515

> Miller; Kenny Garrett (*as*); Steve Nelson (*vib*); Charnett Moffett (*b*); Tony Reedus (*d*). 87.

*** The Countdown Landmark LCD 1519

> Miller; Joe Henderson (*ts*); Ron Carter (*b*); Tony Williams (*d*). 8/88.

*** From Day To Day Landmark LCD 1525

> Miller; Robert Leslie Hurst III (*b*); Kenny Washington (*d*). 3/90.

*** Landmarks Landmark LCD 1311-2

> As above discs.

Miller's sonorous touch and pensive improvising lend him great dignity, if not always great distinction: like so many other modern pianists, he is a marvellous executant and a sometimes indifferent personality, at least in the studio. He's a valuable sideman and accompanist and turns up on countless other dates, but the early records under his own leadership achieve a rather fleeting excellence: a few of his originals, such as 'The Countdown' or 'Sublimity' (*Work!*), stand out, and the rest are functional settings for a technique that has enough virtuosity to handle most situations.

His early experience, with Mercer Ellington, Betty Carter and Art Blakey, was comparatively diverse, but hard bop is Miller's natural métier, and most of this music could as easily stand as the trio sections of a Blakey record. Smith, Carrington and Washington all support him on exactly those lines, although Williams, who makes at least as much noise as Blakey would have done, is in other respects the least like him, and *The Countdown* is certainly the most individual of these records, with Henderson following his own private path and the trio combusting behind him. There is little to choose between the others; *Work!*, though, has a particularly pleasing programme of themes. Orrin Keepnews's production is unobtrusive and faithful to the music. *Landmarks* is a thoughtful selection from the five discs.

***(*) Time And Again Landmark LCD 1532-2

> Miller; Peter Washington (*b*); Tony Reedus (*d*). 8/91.

A degree of extra class makes itself felt with this imposing continuation of Miller's trio albums. Washington and Reedus make an exemplary team, not least for the way they vary their strokes: there's a marvellously grooving accompaniment for 'You And The Night And The Music', but a sensitive reading of Bud Powell's 'I'll Keep Loving You' is just as effective. Miller plays with authority and fresh lyricism: his two solo pieces, especially the gospel calm of 'Lord, In The Morning Thou Shalt Hear', are perfectly prepared and delivered.

**** Hand In Hand Novus 01241 63153 2

> Miller; Eddie Henderson (*t, flhn*); Kenny Garrett (*ss, as*); Joe Henderson (*ts*); Steve Nelson (*vib*); Christian McBride (*b*); Lewis Nash (*d*). 92.

A label change seems to have done Miller a power of good: this is his grandest, most commanding session to date, and an exemplar of what riches an all-star session can provide. The saxophonists are masterful, but it's the still-underrated Eddie Henderson who plays the best horn, and Nelson's marvellous vibes provide an eloquent subtext for Miller's harmonies. The leader responds with some of his best writing: 'Grew's Tune' is a natural as a theme song; 'Like The Morning' is his most handsome ballad, and everything else makes a point or two above the needs of any mere blowing vehicle. Excellent studio sound and a winner all round.

**** With Our Own Eyes Novus 01241 63171-2
    Miller; Richie Goods (*b*); Tony Reedus (*d*). 12/93.
*** Getting To Know You Novus 01241 63188-2
    Miller; Richie Goods (*b*); Karriem Riggins (*d*); Big Black, Steven Kroon (*perc*). 3/95.

Miller's purple patch continues with the beautifully conceived and programmed *With Our Own Eyes*. More than ever, he seems like McCoy Tyner's natural successor: less dependent on rolling bass figures, but the seigneurial touch and open-hearted romanticism are very close to Tyner's. His writing secures an extra ounce of melodic zest in the likes of the opener, 'Somewhere Else', and there are one or two surprising paths followed, such as the almost Tristano-like 'New Wheels'. A pensive 'Body And Soul' can stand with the great treatments of the song, and 'Summer Me, Winter Me' is definitive balladry. Goods and Reedus are with him all the way, and the studio sound is very fine.

After that, the mixed bag of *Getting To Know You* is a slight bringdown. The two extra percussionists make a lot of noise to no special purpose on their five tracks, and the sudden dependence on pop standards – Miller himself brings only three tunes to the date – is disappointing. Still, many lovely moments, but this is certainly a drop after the last two.

Punch Miller (1894–1971) TRUMPET, VOCAL

*** Prelude To The Revival Vol. 1 American Music AMCD-40
    Miller; – Harris (*p, v*); Clifford 'Snag' Jones (*d*). 1/41.

There are five tracks by this group on the CD (the rest are covered under Kid Howard's entry). It's a fascinating glimpse of a fine New Orleans hornman (Punch wasn't a native of the city, but he is closely associated with its music) in mid-life, following plenty of sideman appearances in the 1920s. Miller's quick-fingered lines and excitable attack are unencumbered by other horns on these rough but quite listenable recordings, made at the H&T Tavern in Chicago. Harris and Jones offer knockabout support to what are really trumpet and vocal showcases, an idiosyncratic adaptation of the Armstrong method.

** 1960 American Music AMCD-52
    Miller; Eddie Morris (*tb*); John Handy (*cl*); Louis Gallaud (*p*); Emanuel Sayles (*bj*); Sylvester Handy (*b*); Alex Bigard (*d*). 7/60.
** Punch Miller And Louis Gallaud American Music AMCD-68
    As above, except add Emanuel Paul (*cl*), omit Morris, Handy, Handy and Bigard. 5–7/61.

It's hard to know how good a player Miller really was: he wasn't recorded very often in what should have been his prime, and by the time of these informal tracks he was clearly wavering. The *1960* disc suffers from a somewhat chaotic personnel – John Handy was unused to playing clarinet, Miller struggles at the often too-fast tempos, and Morris drifts in and out of focus – and a pinched, dry sound. The second disc sounds better, but Gallaud's stentorian piano is a lumbering partner for Punch – he sounds better in the oddball duet with Sayles, 'I Never Had A Chance' – and the trumpeter veers between lovely singing notes and fumbling lines that are barely linked together. Approach with caution.

Vladimir Miller PIANO

*** Frontiers Leo LAB CD 016
    Miller; Vitas Pilibavicius (*tb*); V. Tarasov (*d*). 2/95.

Miller is also included below as composer/conductor of the Moscow Composers Orchestra, but this Ganelin-influenced trio affords a chance to hear him as a performer. He is generally romantic in a spare sort of way and, though this live recording from a theatre in Vilnius does not flatter him any more than the piano did, he comes across as a strong, assertive stylist with a very definite sense of direction. Tarasov was, of course, in the original Ganelin Trio. His starbursts of sound and unexpected silences are still very effective and against the rough-edged Pilibavicius (unknown to us until this record) he performs very cleverly indeed.

Lucky Millinder (1900–1966) BANDLEADER, VOCAL

*** Lucky Millinder 1941–1942 Classics 712
    Millinder; William Scott, Archie Johnson, Nelson Bryant, Freddy Webster, William Scott, Dizzy Gillespie (*t*); George Stevenson, Eli Robinson, Donald Cole, Edward Morant, Sandy Williams,

Joe Britton, Floyd Brady (*tb*); Billy Bowen, George James, Ted Barnett, Tab Smith (*as*); Buster Bailey (*cl, ts*); Stafford 'Pazuza' Simon, Dave Young (*ts*); Ernest Purce (*bs*); Bill Doggett, Clyde Hart (*p*); Trevor Bacon, Sister Rosetta Tharpe (*g, v*); Sterling Marlowe (*g*); Abe Bolar, George Duvivier, Nick Fenton (*b*); Panama Francis (*d*). 6/41–7/42.

Millinder went bankrupt in 1939 after nursing the Mills Blue Rhythm Band through its last days, but he fought his way back to bandleading and began recording with this new orchestra in 1941. By the time of the last session here, from July 1942, it was a top-class outfit. The earlier sessions, though, tend to rely on riff tunes and look towards the kind of R&B that would dominate black music a decade later: Doggett, who would later have some huge hits in the 1950s, must have been listening carefully from the piano chair. Rosetta Tharpe has some interesting features, but it's relatively unimaginative stuff until the likes of 'Let Me Off Uptown' (where Duvivier takes a Blanton-like role). Although the February 1942 session has some mediocre propaganda, the final date is memorable: Tab Smith's alto and chart for 'Mason Flyer' are inspiring, but everything changes with the brilliant final track, 'Little John Special', where Dizzy Gillespie steps forward and delivers a towering solo that tells of the revolution ahead. Mostly good transfers.

Steve Million PIANO

***(*) **Million To One** Palmetto PM-2014

Million; Randy Brecker (*t, flhn*); Chris Potter (*ts, ss*); Michael Moore (*b*); Ron Vincent (*d*). 2/95. Impeccably prepared, Million's leadership debut has real class and substance. His six originals are each deftly characterized while leaving enough space for Brecker and Potter, two very individual soloists, to impose ideas and mouldings of their own. Brecker especially sounds renewed by material of this calibre, after the many deadbeat sessions he's played on: consult the gorgeous flugelhorn solo on 'Missing Page' for evidence. Potter's status as a coming man is enhanced further by every solo and, with Moore at his usual beguiling best, the rhythms have a rubbery drive to them. Million himself is self-effacing as a soloist but as alert as everyone else to the way the music breathes and develops. Admirable contemporary jazz.

Mills Blue Rhythm Band GROUP

*** **Blue Rhythm** Hep CD 1008

Wardell Jones, Shelton Hemphill, Ed Anderson (*t*); Harry White, Henry Hicks (*tb*); Crawford Wethington (*cl, as, bs*); Charlie Holmes (*cl, as*); Ted McCord, Castor McCord (*cl, ts*); Edgar Hayes (*p*); Benny James (*bj, g*); Hayes Alvis (*bb, b*); Willie Lynch (*d*); Dick Roberston, Chick Bullock, George Morton (*v*). 1–6/31.

*** **Mills Blue Rhythm Band 1931** Classics 660

As above. 1–6/31.

***(*) **Rhythm Spasm** Hep CD 1015

As above, except add George Washington (*tb*), Gene Mikell (*cl, as*), Joe Garland (*cl, ts, bs*), O'Neil Spencer (*d*), Billy Banks (*v*). 8/31–8/32.

*** **Mills Blue Rhythm Band 1931–1932** Classics 676

As above. 7/31–9/32.

**** **Mills Blue Rhythm Band 1933–1934** Classics 686

Wardell Jones, Shelton Hemphill, Ed Anderson, Eddie Mallory, Henry Allen (*t*); George Washington, Henry Hicks, J. C. Higginbotham (*tb*); Crawford Wethington, Gene Mikell, Joe Garland, Buster Bailey (*reeds*); Edgar Hayes (*p*); Benny James (*bj, g*); Lawrence Lucie (*g*); Hayes Alvis, Elmer James (*b*); O'Neil Spencer (*d*); Lucky Millinder, Chuck Richards, Adelaide Hall (*v*). 3/33–11/34.

***(*) **Mills Blue Rhythm Band 1935–1936** Classics 710

As above, except add Tab Smith (*cl, as*); omit Anderson, Mallory, Hicks, James and Alvis. 1/35–8/36.

Although it lacked any solo stars in its early years, the Mills Blue Rhythm Band – the name derived from manager Irving Mills – was a very hot outfit when the first of these records were made, even though it was originally used by Mills as a substitute band for either Ellington or Calloway. The lack of a regular front-man and a rag-tag sequence of arrangers prevented the band from ever establishing a very clear identity of its own, but it still mustered a kind of fighting collectivism which comes through clearly on its best records. These chronological CDs tell the first part of the band's story. Cover versions of Ellington ('Black And Tan Fantasy') and Calloway ('Minnie The Moocher') reveal what the band's purpose was to start with, and the most interesting thing about the earlier tracks is usually the soloists' role, particularly the impassioned and badly undervalued trumpeter, Ed Anderson. But by the time the music on *Rhythm Spasm* was made, the band was energizing itself in splendid charts such as 'The Growl' and the overwhelmingly swinging 'White Lightning', which reveals the dynamism of Hayes Alvis and O'Neil Spencer in the rhythm section. There are some cringingly awful vocals from such experts as Billy Banks and Chick Bullock, but those used to music of the period will know what to expect. John R. T. Davies remasters with his usual care and attentiveness to the music on the Hep discs; the Classics counterparts are, as usual, more mixed, but mostly fine.

The 1933–6 material shows a steady if unspectacular growth in the band's abilities, the personnel remaining surprisingly stable over the period, although the arrival of Henry Allen, Buster Bailey and J. C. Higginbotham, all from Fletcher Henderson's band, gave the orchestra a new team of star soloists. Classics 686 is one of the best of the series, with swinging scores in 'Kokey Joe', 'The Growl', the terrific 'The Stuff Is Here (And It's Mellow)' and Allen's debut with 'Swingin' In E Flat'. There is also Adelaide Hall's extraordinary treatment of Ellington's 'Drop Me Off In Harlem', although the Classics remastering seems to be faulty here. There are more vital pieces on the next disc – the superb 'Harlem Heat' is one of Will Hudson's best scores, and 'Cotton', 'Truckin'' and 'Congo Caravan' aren't far behind – but the occasional show of routine and Chuck Richards's consistently unappealing vocals let matters down. As a sequence of records, though, an important portrait of a great Harlem orchestra.

Pino Minafra TRUMPET, BUGLE, DIDJERIDOO, OCARINA, PERCUSSION, VOCAL ETC.

*** **Noci . . . Strani Frutti** Leo LR 176
    Minafra; Ernst Reijseger (*clo*); Han Bennink (*d*). 7/90.
**** **Sudori** Victo CD034
    Minafra; Lauro Rossi (*tb, perc, v*); Carlo Actis Dato (*ts, bs, perc, v*); Giorgio Occhipinti (*ky, perc, v*); Daniele Patui (*perc*); Vincenzo Mazzone (*d*). 1/95.

Look out: genius at work. Minafra's early LPs for Splasc(h) were enjoyable post-bop outings of a comparatively conventional bent, but these are something else. The Leo disc catches him on the hoof at a late-night festival set with Reijseger and Bennink: his confiding, sputtering sound reminds one at different moments of Miles Davis, Ted Curson and Donald Ayler; but it's a very personal manner, and it fits well over the tumbling dialogue of the other two. Forty-five minutes of strong improvisation.

Sudori is entirely different. Meticulously arranged yet spontaneously exciting, Minafra's Sud Ensemble must be among the smartest outfits in European jazz today. With daredevil spirits like Dato and Rossi on hand, matters could have descended into chaos, given Minafra's own taste for excitement. Yet everything is perfectly realized, from the mounting movie-score drama of 'Exorcism' to the astonishing blues fantasy of 'Au Fond Je Suis Un Africain Du Nord'. The ensemble playing is as impeccable as the solos are rich and detailed, and in meltingly beautiful pieces like the gorgeous 'Tango', dedicated to Federico Fellini, one can hardly credit that this is the same band responsible for the uproarious stuff. A major piece of work that deserves the widest attention.

Pete Minger FLUGELHORN, TRUMPET

*** **Minger Painting** Jazz Alliance 10005
    Minger; Dolph Castellano (*p*); Keter Betts (*b*); Bobby Durham (*d*). 10/83.
*** **Look To The Sky** Concord CCD 4555
    Minger; John Campbell (*p*); Kiyoshi Kitagawa (*b*); Ben Riley (*d*). 8/92.

Though cut almost ten years apart, there's little to choose between these dates: Minger, a long-time Basie sideman in the 1970s, turns to the flugelhorn more often than the trumpet and secures the big, warm, comfortable sound that is almost a cliché in brass playing. The earlier date is livelier, the second takes more of a bath in the handsome Concord engineering and benefits from Campbell's useful commentaries. Minger always takes his time, flowing over fast tempos with a relaxed assurance, and the consequence is a fundamentally tranquil but satisfying jazz.

Charles Mingus (1922–79) DOUBLE BASS, PIANO, COMPOSER

**** **The Complete Debut Recordings** Debut 12DCD 4402 12CD
    Mingus; Miles Davis, Dizzy Gillespie, Louis Mucci, Thad Jones, Clarence Shaw (*t*); Eddie Bert, Willie Dennis, Bennie Green, J. J. Johnson, Jimmy Knepper, Kai Winding, Britt Woodman (*tb*); Julius Watkins (*frhn*); Charlie Parker, Lee Konitz, Joe Maini (*as*); Paige Brook, Eddie Caine (*as, f*); George Barrow, Phil Urso (*ts*); Frank Wess, Shafti Hadi, Teo Macero (*ts, f*); Danny Bank,

Pepper Adams (*bs*); John LaPorta, Julius Baker (*woodwinds*); Spaulding Givens, Hank Jones, Wynton Kelly, Wade Legge, John Lewis, John Mehegan, Phyllis Pinkerton, Bill Triglia, Mal Waldron, Hazel Scott (*p*); Teddy Charles (*vib*); George Koutzen, Jackson Wiley (*clo*); Fred Zimmerman (*b*); Elvin Jones, Kenny Clarke, Al Levitt, Joe Morello, Dannie Richmond, Max Roach, Art Taylor (*d*); Phineas Newborn Jr, Horace Parlan (*perc*); Bob Benton, George Gordon, George Gordon Jr, Honey Gordon, Richard Gordon, Jackie Paris (*v*). 4/51–9/57.

*** **Debut Rarities: Volume 1** Original Jazz Classics OJC 1807
Mingus; Ernie Royal (*t*); Willie Dennis, Jimmy Knepper (*tb*); Joe Maini (*as*); Eddie Caine (*as, f*); Teo Macero (*ts, f*); John Lewis, Bill Triglia (*p*); Jackson Wiley (*clo*); Kenny Clarke, Dannie Richmond (*d*). 10/53, 6/57.

***(*) **Debut Rarities: Volume 2** Original Jazz Classics OJC 1808
Mingus; Spaulding Givens (*p*); Max Roach (*d*). 4/51, 4/53.

*** **Debut Rarities: Volume 3** Original Jazz Classics OJC 1821
Mingus; Clarence Shaw (*t*); Shafti Hadi (*as, f*); Pepper Adams (*bs*); Wade Legge, Wynton Kelly (*p*); Henry Grimes (*b*); Dannie Richmond (*d*). 9?/57.

(*) **Debut Rarities: Volume 4 Original Jazz Classics OJC 1829
Mingus; Lee Konitz (*as*); Paige Brook (*as, f*); John Mehegan, Hank Jones, Phyllis Pinkerton (*p*); George Koutzen, Jackson Wiley (*clo*); Al Levitt, Max Roach (*d*); Bob Benton, Jackie Paris, The Gordons (*v*). 4/52, 4/53.

*** **Jazz Composers Workshop** Savoy SV 0171
Mingus; John LaPorta (*cl, as*); George Barrow, Teo Macero (*ts, bs*); Mal Waldron (*p*); Rudy Nichols (*d*). 10/54.

(*) **Jazzical Moods Fresh Sound CD 62
Mingus; Thad Jones (*t*); John LaPorta (*cl, as*); Teo Macero (*ts, bs*); Jackson Wiley (*clo*); Clem De Rosa (*d*). 12/54.

(*) **The Jazz Experiments Of Charlie Mingus Bethlehem BET 6016
As above. 12/54.

Huge, paradoxical and immensely influential, Mingus's true significance has taken a long time to be recognized, though most of his innovations have long since been absorbed by the modern/avant-garde movement. In that regard, he is very different from the broadly comparable Monk, whose work is still not fully assimilated and understood but who has been almost casually canonized. In addition to pioneering modern bass-playing, Mingus is responsible for some of the greatest large-scale composi-tions in modern 'jazz', beside which overblown efforts like Ornette Coleman's *Skies Of America* look positively sophomoric; Mingus also transformed the conception of collective improvisation, restoring the energies and occasionally the sound of early jazz to an identifiably modern idiom. He pioneered overdubbing and editing, thereby paving the way for Miles Davis and Teo Macero, who appears on these curiously lifeless, virtually identical compilations from two albums recorded for Period.

These can really only be mined for pointers to more impressive work later. 'Four Hands' experiments with overdubbed piano (not quite like Claude Williamson's two-piano essays on the same label), and there are out-of-tempo sections that anticipate later, more radical experiments. 'What Is This Thing Called Love' undergoes interesting transformations, in keeping with Mingus's palimpsest approach to standards and new composition, and the use of cello (one of Mingus's first instruments) is intriguing.

The problem lies in the playing. Macero – later to achieve his apotheosis as producer/arranger for Miles Davis – is unpalatably dry, and the drummer tackles his part with no discernible enthusiasm. The Fresh Sound and overlapping Bethlehem (which was formerly issued under the name *Abstractions*) also con-tains Macero's Third Streamish 'Abstractions', but that's a fairly minor plus. For serious Mingus scholars only.

The Savoy session is more appealing, though a substantial chunk of the record is devoted to a session by now-forgotten piano man, Wally Cirillo (with Mingus on bass). The Workshop sides are strong but endearingly gentle, with Mingus's more romantic side showing through rather more strongly than one might expect. 'Purple Heart' and 'Gregarian Chant' are outstanding. A valuable document, albeit for *very* serious collectors only, this fills in some of the gaps left in the inevitably pricey Debut set, which covers the period 1951 to 1957; it's a completist's dream. The musician-owned Debut was started by Mingus and Max Roach as a way of getting their own adventurous music recorded, and was briefly influential. With nearly 170 individual tracks under 19 nominal leaderships, and including many alter-native takes, it's an exhaustive and occasionally exhausting compilation, well out of the range and probable requirements of the average fan, who may have some of the material elsewhere. One example might well be Mingus's own tape-recording of the famous Massey Hall, Toronto, 'Quintet Of The Year' gig of 15 May 1953, and it's good to know that even some of the lesser material remains in circulation. The four *Rarities* abstracts may well be enough for most people, particularly those who have other, more accessible stuff on LP. The duos with Givens on *Volume 2* are well worth dusting down, as are the 1957 Workshop pieces on *Volume 4*, which point the way forward to Mingus's 1960s masterpieces.

*** **Mingus At The Bohemia** Original Jazz Classics OJC 045
  Mingus; Eddie Bert (*tb*); George Barrow (*ts*); Mal Waldron (*p*); Willie Jones, Max Roach (*d*).
  12/55.
*** **Plus Max Roach** Original Jazz Classics OJC 440
  As above. 12/55.
The Jazz Workshop in fine, searching form. Jones, who was to figure on the classic *Pithecanthropus Erectus* but who nowadays is little regarded, came to Mingus at Thelonious Monk's behest. The opening theme on *At The Bohemia* is a Monk dedication (with Waldron re-creating an authentic cadence) that underlines Mingus's increasing emphasis on the rhythm section as a pro-active element in improvisation.

'Septemberly' is a characteristic hybrid of 'Tenderly' and 'September In The Rain', and 'Percussion Discussion' a duet between Mingus, on bass and cello, and Max Roach, just one of a long line of challenging duos set up by or for the great drummer. The rest of the material from this session was issued on a Prestige album called simply *Charles Mingus* (HB 6042), not to be confused with the Denon set reviewed below.

**** **Pithecanthropus Erectus** Atlantic 81456
  Mingus; Jackie McLean (*as*); J. R. Monterose (*ts*); Mal Waldron (*p*); Willie Jones (*d*). 1/56.
One of the truly great modern jazz albums. Underrated at the time, *Pithecanthropus Erectus* is now recognized as an important step in the direction of a new, freer synthesis in jazz. To some extent, the basic thematic conception (the story of mankind's struggle out of chaos, up and down the Freytag's Triangle of hubris and destruction, back to chaos) was the watered-down Spenglerism which was still fashionable at the time. Technically, though, the all-in ensemble work on the violent C section, which is really B, a modified version of the harmonically static second section, was absolutely crucial to the development of free collective improvisation in the following decade.

The brief 'Profile Of Jackie' is altogether different. Fronted by McLean's menthol-sharp alto, with Monterose (a late appointee who wasn't altogether happy with the music) and Mingus working on a shadowy counter-melody, it's one of the most appealing tracks Mingus ever committed to record, and the most generous of his 'portraits'. McLean still carried a torch for orthodox bebop and soon came to (literal) blows with Mingus; the chemistry worked just long enough. 'Love Chant' is a more basic modal exploration, and 'A Foggy Day' – re-subtitled 'In San Francisco' – is an impressionistic reworking of the Gershwin standard, with Chandleresque sound-effects. Superficially jokey, it's no less significant an effort to expand the available range of jazz performance, and the fact that it's done via a standard rather than a long-form composition like 'Pithecanthropus' gives a sense of Mingus's Janus-faced approach to the music.

*** **The Clown** Atlantic 790142
  Mingus; Jimmy Knepper (*tb*); Shafi Hadi (*as, ts*); Wade Legge (*p*); Dannie Richmond (*d*); Jean
  Shepherd (*v*). 2 & 3/57.
With the first appearance of 'Reincarnation Of A Lovebird' and the *mano a mano* simplicities of 'Haitian Fight Song' (which saw Mingus build a huge, swinging performance out of the simplest thematic material), this is not a negligible record. It has never, though, been a great favourite.

'Blue Cee' is a dedication to Mingus's wife and has an almost gloomy cast. Throughout the album, the bassist grunts and hollers encouragement to himself and his players; perhaps he was still thinking about Bud Powell, who was apt to vocalize over his solos, because he had planned a 'portrait' of Powell before these sessions. The title-track is a reminder of Mingus's obsession with words and texts; Jean Shepherd's narration is fine, but one quickly longs for the instrumental versions that Mingus included in club sets thereafter. This is one of the few quality albums of Mingus's which is routinely neglected. That seems a pity.

***(*) **New Tijuana Moods** Bluebird ND 85644
  Mingus; Clarence Shaw (*t*); Jimmy Knepper (*tb*); Shafi Hadi (*as*); Bill Triglia (*p*); Dannie
  Richmond (*d*); Frankie Dunlop (*perc*); Ysabel Morel (*castanets*); Lonnie Elder (*v*). 7 & 8/57.
***(*) **East Coasting** Bethlehem BET 6014
  As above, except omit Triglia, Morel, Dunlop, Elder; add Bill Evans, (*p*). 8/57.
*** **A Modern Jazz Symposium Of Music And Poetry** Bethlehem 6015
  As above, except omit Evans; add Bill Hardman (*t*); Bob Hammer, Horace Parlan (*p*); Melvin
  Stewart (*v*). 10/57.
New Tijuana Moods combines the original release with the complete (that is, unedited) performances from which the label not always successfully spliced together LP-length tracks. 'Ysabel's Table Dance'/-'Tijuana Table Dance' is the classic track, with Mingus's structures constantly erupting into group improvisations. Nothing else quite compares with that track, though 'Dizzy Mood' is also very fine, and 'Los Mariachos' is an impressive piece of writing.

There is inevitably a bit more room on the longer versions for the soloists to stretch out; but, apart from that, most seasoned listeners will probably still want to cue the original releases on their CD players rather than the restored versions. What *Tijuana Moods* called for was better editing, not no editing.

The atmospheric *East Coasting* and the similarly constituted *Symposium* are part of the same cycle of pieces and bear strong similarities, in construction, material and of course personnel. 'Conversation' and 'West Coast Ghost' and the gloriously expressive 'Celia' are brilliantly realized collective performances and, while none of the pieces is quite as ambitious as the *Tijuana* structures, they all pay tribute to Mingus's growing stature as a grand synthesizer of blues, bop and swing, with the shadow of something entirely new hovering on the music's inner horizons.

The *Symposium* – and how extraordinary that title now seems – was an opportunity for Mingus to experiment with texts and with pure sound. 'Scenes In The City' reworks some of the ideas he had sketched in 'Foggy Day' on *Pithecanthropus Erectus*, but with a much greater degree of finish. The 'New York Sketchbook' is a parallel piece, finely drawn and performed, with Shaw rising above himself and playing some of the best trumpet heard on a Mingus album for some time before or since.

***(*) Jazz Portraits: Mingus In Wonderland Blue Note CDP 827325

Mingus; John Handy (*as*); Booker Ervin (*ts*); Richard Wyands (*p*); Dannie Richmond (*d*). 1/59.
Mingus's appearance as part of the Nonagon Art Gallery Composers' Showcase series in 1959 was a significant moment of recognition for a man whose life was passed in resistance to the 'jazz musician' tag. Previous composers showcased there had been Virgil Thomson, Aaron Copland and Carlos Chavez, and in addition there had been notable appearances by the MJQ and Cecil Taylor.

Working with something of a scratch band (the all-important Horace Parlan wasn't available), more emphasis than usual fell on Mingus's bass playing, which is consistently marvellous from the opening moody strains of 'Nostalgia In Times Square', written as part of the soundtrack to John Cassavetes' movie, *Shadows*, to the closing 'Alice's Wonderland', which gave the record its first release title. 'I Can't Get Started' had become one of his favourite standards, indeed the only non-original that seemed to fire him up to the heights of invention audible here, fiery double-stops and intense lyrical passages alternating with softer, almost guitar-like strums. Until recently, this has been one of the less well-known Mingus records (and on a label not normally associated with him). It's a welcome addition to the catalogue.

***(*) Blues And Roots Atlantic 781336

Mingus; Willie Dennis, Jimmy Knepper (*tb*); John Handy, Jackie McLean (*as*); Booker Ervin (*ts*); Pepper Adams (*bs*); Horace Parlan, Mal Waldron (*p*); Dannie Richmond (*d*). 2/59.
**** Mingus Ah Um Columbia 450436
As above, except omit Waldron, McLean; add Shafi Hadi (*ts*). 5/59.
A classic period. This was the point where, rising forty in just a couple of years and aware of the encroachment of younger and perhaps more accommodating musicians, he began to show his absolute understanding of the African-American musical tradition. *Ah Um* is an extended tribute to ancestors, cemented by the gospellish 'Better Git It In Your Soul', a mood that is also present on *Blues And Roots* with the well-loved 'Wednesday Night Prayer Meeting' in its doubled-up 6/4 time. Everything here has its place. The shouts and yells, the magnificently harmonized ostinati which fuel 'Tensions' and the almost jolly swing of 'My Jelly Roll Soul' (*Blues And Roots*), the often obvious edits and obsessive recycling of his own previous output, all contribute to records which are entire unto themselves and hard to fault on any count. Extra material from the *Ah Um* session was made available on a Columbia disc called *Nostalgia In Times Square*, but it would be sacrilegious to tamper now with something as perfectly balanced; three-quarters of an hour of sheer genius.

*** Mingus Dynasty Columbia 71440

Mingus; Don Ellis, Richard Williams (*t*); Jimmy Knepper (*tb*); Jerome Richardson (*f, bs*); John Handy (*as*); Booker Ervin, Benny Golson (*ts*); Teddy Charles (*vib*); Roland Hanna, Nico Bunink (*p*); Maurice Brown, Seymour Barab (*clo*); Dannie Richmond (*d*); Honey Gordon (*v*). 11/59.
Often, mistakenly but understandably, thought to refer to a posthumous album, *Mingus Dynasty* is a pretty obvious pun when looked at twice. It wraps up a period of activity that seems to catch Mingus in mid-mood-swing between fired up and confident and way down low. 'Strollin'' is a version of 'Nostalgia On Times Square' and the music written for the (mostly improvised) John Cassavetes film *Shadows*, in which jazz almost takes the place of orderly narrative dialogue. There is also a version of 'Gunslinging Bird', a take each of 'Song With Orange', 'Far Wells, Mill Valley', 'Slop' and, memorably, 'Mood Indigo'. As with so many other Mingus albums, this is somehow better and more coherent than it ought to be. Though not intended to be put together in this form, it works as an entity, and one wouldn't want the original sessions to be reconstructed in any other way.

**** **Mingus At Antibes** Atlantic 90532 2CD
   Mingus; Ted Curson (*t*); Eric Dolphy (*as, bcl*); Booker Ervin (*ts*); Bud Powell (*p*); Dannie
   Richmond (*d*). 7/60.
Charles Delaunay memorably likened Mingus's performance in the mellow warmth of Juan les Pins to a
'cold shower'. Certainly in comparison with the rest of the Antibes line-up, the 1960s band was intellectually recherché and somewhat forceful. Unreleased until after Mingus's death – the tapes had lain,
unexamined, in Atlantic's vault – the set contains a valuable preview of some of the material to be
recorded that autumn for Candid, below, and for a thumping 'I'll Remember April' with the exiled Bud
Powell guesting. Mingus himself gets behind the piano on a number of occasions, perhaps trying to give
the slightly chaotic ensembles more shape. The essence of the performance lies in the solos. Ervin is fine
on 'Better Git Hit In Your Soul', as is Dolphy, still sounding like a renegade Parker disciple, on a first
version of the gospelly 'Folk Forms', which reappears on *Presents*, below. The bass/bass-clarinet sparring on 'What Love' isn't quite as over the top as the later, studio version, but it shows how far Dolphy
was prepared to move in the direction of Ornette Coleman's new synthesis.
   Not just another 'previously unreleased' money-spinner, the *Antibes* set contains genuinely important
material. The chance to hear a Mingus concert in its entirety offers valuable clues to his methods at the
time.

**** **Charles Mingus Presents Charles Mingus** Candid CCD 79005
   Mingus; Ted Curson (*t*); Eric Dolphy (*as, bcl*); Dannie Richmond (*d*). 10/60.
***(*) **Charles Mingus** Candid CCD 79021
   As above, except add Lonnie Hillyer (*t*); Jimmy Knepper, Britt Woodman (*tb*); Booker Ervin
   (*ts*); Paul Bley, Nico Bunink (*p*). 10/60.
*** **Reincarnation Of A Love Bird** Candid CCD 79026
   As above, except omit Woodman, Bunink; add Roy Eldridge (*t*); Tommy Flanagan (*p*); Jo Jones
   (*d*). 11/60.
(*) **Mysterious Blues Candid CCD 79042
   As above. 10 & 11/60.
Mingus's association with Candid was brief (though no briefer than the label's first existence) and
highly successful. His long club residency in 1960 (interrupted only by festival appearances) gave him an
unwontedly stable and played-in band to take into the studio (he recorded a fake – and uncommonly
polite – night-club intro for the set), and the larger-scale arrangement of 'MDM' negatively reflects the
solidity of the core band. *Presents* is for piano-less quartet and centres on the extraordinary vocalized
interplay between Dolphy and Mingus; on 'What Love' they carry on a long conversation in near-
comprehensible dialect. 'Folk Forms' is wonderfully pared down and features a superb Mingus solo. 'All
The Things You Could Be By Now If Sigmund Freud's Wife Was Your Mother' has a wry fury (Mingus
once said that it had been written in the psych ward at Bellevue) which is more than incidentally
suggestive of 'harmolodic' and 'punk' procedures of the 1980s. The 'Original Faubus Fables' was a
further experiment in the use of texts, here a furious rant against what Mingus later called 'Nazi USA',
and his later '60s brothers 'Amerika'. It's powerfully felt but less well integrated in its blend of polemic
and music than Max Roach's *Freedom Now Suite* on the same label (Candid CS 9002 CD/LP).
   If *Presents* is a classic, *Charles Mingus* falls slightly short. The augmented band on 'MDM' sounds
uninspired, either unfamiliar or unhappy with the material (which isn't exceptionally demanding).
'Stormy Weather', also released on *Candid Dolphy*, below, features a monster introduction by the
saxophonist. Like 'ATTYCBBNISFWWYM' above, 'Lock 'Em Up' makes some reference to
Bellevue (or to Charlie Parker's 'holiday' in Camarillo), if only because it's taken at the same hare-
brained pace, and Mingus bellows instruction to his troops in a voice that sounds on the brink.
   At producer Nat Hentoff's suggestion, he had attempted to vary the existing band and re-create the
energy of the 'Newport rebels' anti-festival by bringing in past associates. The most notable of these was
Roy Eldridge, who is featured (with Knepper, Flanagan and Jo Jones also guesting, as the Jazz Artists
guild) on the long 'R & R', a superb 'Body And Soul', and a previously unreleased 'Wrap Your Troubles
In Dreams'.
   'Reincarnation Of A Love Bird' and 'Bugs' are both Parker-inspired. The title-track features Hillyer,
McPherson and Ervin over Dolphy's uncredited bass clarinet (Curson isn't listed either, and is men-
tioned only in Brian Priestley's characteristically detailed liner-note). By no means a classic Mingus
album, it restores some fascinating performances and alternatives from a critical period in his career.
Needless to say, worth having (and enthusiasts should take note of another 'Reincarnation' along with
the Dolphy-led 'Stormy Weather' on the label compilation, *Candid Dolphy* (CCD 9033)).
   The descending order of stars gives a fair account of *Mysterious Blues*' place in this sequence. Not much
more than a collection of bin-ends and alternatives, it's likely to appeal only to serious Mingus collectors. Taking up 9½ minutes with a drum solo by Richmond (who was never an inspiring soloist) is the
main symptom of padding. The rejected 'Body And Soul' has some nice Dolphy and Flanagan, but still
isn't particularly compelling.

*** **Oh Yeah** Atlantic 90667
>   Mingus; Jimmy Knepper (*tb*); Rahsaan Roland Kirk (*ts, manzello, stritch, f, siren*); Booker Ervin (*ts*); Doug Watkins (*b*); Dannie Richmond (*d*). 11/61.

The addition of Rahsaan Roland Kirk gave the Mingus band the kind of surreality evident on the spaced-out blues 'Ecclusiastics', which Mingus leads from the piano. Kirk is also the main attraction on 'Wham Bam, Thank You Ma'am', a typically de-romanticized standard. On the closing 'Passions Of A Man' Mingus overdubbed a bizarre, associative rap, which is rather more effective than the instrumental backing. Odd. Damned odd, even; but a significant instance of Mingus's often desperate conflation of music and words in the search for some higher synthesis.

*** **The Complete Town Hall Concert** Blue Note CDP 8 28353
>   Mingus; Snooky Young, Ernie Royal, Richard Williams, Clark Terry, Lonnie Hillyer, Ed Armour, Rolf Ericson (*t*); Britt Woodman, Quentin Jackson, Willie Dennis, Eddie Bert, Jimmy Cleveland (*tb*); Don Butterfield (*tba*); Charles McPherson, Charlie Mariano (as); Buddy Collette (*as, ts, f*); Eric Dolphy (*as, bcl, f*); Booker Ervin, Zoot Sims (*ts*); Dick Hafer (*ts, cl, f, ob*); Pepper Adams (*bs*); Jerome Richardson (*bs, ss, f*); Teddy Charles (*vib*); Toshiko Akiyoshi, Jaki Byard (*p*); Les Spann (*g*); Milt Hinton (*b*); Dannie Richmond (*d, tim*). 10/62.

An object case in the extraordinary performance history of Mingus's music. These ambitious charts, which were related to the huge *Epitaph* suite only performed after his death, were being prepared for a recording or concert-recording (the ambiguity was never quite settled) at New York's Town Hall. (This shouldn't be confused with the later occasion listed and discussed below.) Preparations were chaotic and there was no proper run-through on the night, leaving a body of material which was significantly flawed and in some cases considered unreleasable. The original LP lasted only 36 minutes. This reissue, digitally remixed from the original three-track tapes and produced by biographer Brian Priestley, restores the whole extraordinary occasion with one minor re-ordering of tracks.

'Clark In The Dark', a feature for trumpeter Terry, is marred by a completely skew-whiff mix; the engineer still apparently hadn't managed to effect a proper balance. The next piece, 'Osmotin', breaks off, much like some of the internal sections on *Blues And Roots* and *Ah Um*.

The opening part of 'Epitaph' features a glorious solo from Dolphy, communicating with the leader on a level far beyond any of the other soloists. There are versions of 'Peggy's Blue Skylight', more from 'Epitaph' and a new contrafact, 'My Search', on 'I Can't Get Started'. With time marching on, and the audience – presumably unused to the disciplines of recording – becoming restive, Mingus was signalled to stop towards the end of 'Please Don't You Come Back From The Moon', one of the previously unissued tracks. At this point, with the leader heading offstage and many of the players winding up, Terry, who'd kicked the whole thing off, went into 'In A Mellotone', and brought the band together again. It was, to be sure, something of a shambles, but a magnificent shambles. The reconstructed evening has its rough edges and unresolved parts, but it is an essential document in Mingus's progress, and who can say what might have happened had the record company been more accommodating and smart enough to realize that it was virtually impossible and also undesirable to tape so much brand-new music, some of it being (re)written on the spot in front of an audience. For all its frustrations and its rather shambolic feel, this is essential Mingus.

**** **The Black Saint And The Sinner Lady** MCA MCAD 5649
>   Mingus; Rolf Ericson, Richard Williams (*t*); Quentin Jackson, Don Butterfield (*tba*); Jerome Richardson (*as, bs, f*); Booker Ervin (*ts*); Dick Hafer (*ts, f*); Charlie Mariano (*as*); Jaki Byard (*p*); Dannie Richmond (*d*). 1/63.

***(*) **Mingus Mingus Mingus Mingus Mingus** MCA MCAD 39119
>   As above, except add Britt Woodman (*tb*); Jay Berliner (*g*). 1 & 9/63.

Black Saint is Mingus's masterpiece. Almost everything about it was distinctive: the long form, the use of dubbing, the liner-note by Mingus's psychiatrist. On its release, they altered its usual slogan, 'The new wave of jazz is on Impulse!', to read 'folk', in line with Mingus's decision to call the group the Charles Mingus New Folk Band. Ellingtonian in ambition and scope, and in the disposition of horns, the piece has a majestic, dancing presence, and Charlie Mariano's alto solos and overdubs on 'Mode D/ E/F' are unbelievably intense. There is evidence that Mingus's desire to make a single continuous performance (and it should be remembered that even Ellington's large-scale compositions were relatively brief) failed to meet favour with label executives; but there is an underlying logic even to the separate tracks which makes it difficult to separate them other than for the convenience of track listing. Absolutely essential.

Mingus etc. comes from the same and one later session. It includes 'Celia' and 'I X Love', both older pieces, both distinguished by great Mariano performances, with 'Theme For Lester Young', which is a variant on 'Goodbye, Pork Pie Hat', and 'Better Git Hit In Your Soul'. Nothing comes close to *Black*

Saint, but the pair give an even better account of Mingus's thinking at the time. Whatever the compromises forced upon him in the past by musicians (or now by his label), he is creating music of classic scope and lasting value.

**** **Town Hall Concert 1964** Original Jazz Classics OJC 042
    Mingus; Johnny Coles (*t*); Eric Dolphy (*as, fl, bcl*); Clifford Jordan (*ts*); Jaki Byard (*p*); Dannie Richmond (*d*). 4/64.
*** **Mingus In Europe: Volume 1** Enja 3049
    As above. 4/64.
*** **Mingus In Europe: Volume 2** Enja 3077
    As above. 4/64.
*** **Live In Amsterdam: Volume 1** Aroc 1204
    As above. 4/64.
*** **Live In Amsterdam: Volume 2** Aroc 1205 Cd
    As above. 4/64.
***(*) **The Great Concert, Paris 1964** Musidisc 500072 2CD
    As above, except add Johnny Coles (*t*). 4/64.
This is undoubtedly the most heavily documented period of Mingus's career. The Town Hall concert predated the European tour, and this set consists of two long tracks which strongly feature Dolphy (the dedicatee) on each of his three horns. The release shouldn't be confused with a 1962 Blue Note recording of the same name, which contains entirely different material.

There is a vast amount of bootleg material from the European tour of April 1964. We have omitted all but respectably licensed releases. Dedicated collectors may want to check dates and itinerary in our previous edition and argue about the respective merits of individual performances, for the repertoire overlaps very considerably. 'Peggy's Blue Skylight' is ubiquitous, only omitted on *Great Concert*; other staples include 'Orange Was The Color Of Her Dress, Then Blue Silk' and 'Fables Of Faubus'. 'So Long, Eric' is sometimes described as a threnody or epitaph to the multi-instrumentalist, who died on 29 June of that year, but there he is playing it; the piece was actually supposed to be a reminder to Dolphy (who'd decided to try his luck in Europe for a while) not to stay 'over there' too long. Sadly, it was all too soon to become a memorial.

A bonus on the Enjas (which were recorded in Wuppertal at the opposite end of the month to the Amsterdam material which was taped on the 10th) is a flute–bass duo credited to Dolphy as 'Started', but actually based on 'I Can't Get Started'. 'Fables' was awkwardly split on the LP format, and is very much better for being heard entire.

*** **Right Now** Original Jazz Classics OJC 237
    Mingus; John Handy (*as*); Clifford Jordan (*ts*); Jane Getz (*p*); Dannie Richmond (*d*). 6/64.
Two long cuts – 'Meditation (On A Pair Of Wire Cutters)' and a revised 'Fables Of Faubus' – which were originally released on Fantasy, featuring Mingus's Californian band of that summer. Handy comes in only on 'New Fables' but sounds funky and a lot more abrasive than McPherson. Jane Getz is by no means well known, and is certainly less individual than the otherwise-engaged Byard, but she acquits her piano duties more than adequately.

*** **Charles Mingus In Paris, 1970** DIW 326/7 2CD
    Mingus; Eddie Preston (*t*); Charles McPherson (*as*); Bobby Jones (*ts*); Jaki Byard (*p, arr*); Dannie Richmond (*d*). 10/70.
** **Charles Mingus** Denon DC 8565
    As above, except omit McPherson; add Toshiyuki Miyama (*cond*); Shigeo Suzuki, Hiroshi Takamu (*as*); Masahiko Sato (*p*); Yoshisaburo Toyozumi (*d*); other personnel unknown. 1/71.
In Paris is a rather straightforward, almost bland, concert recording from the city and country where Mingus had some of his more torrid moments. (The Musidisc, with its curious but persistent misspelling of the title-suite, is a useful enough condensation but has no other obvious advantage over the well-presented DIW, beyond the fact that the notes are in a species of English.) The repertoire combines recent arrangements with the well-worn but constantly evolving Ellington medley, and yet another version of 'Orange Was The Color ... ' In addition to the title-piece, played rather stodgily, *Pithecanthropus Erectus* includes the staples, 'Reincarnation Of A Lovebird' and 'Peggy's Blue Skylight', with a fine version of Parker's 'Blue Bird'.

The eponymous Denon is a rather dreary recording, made in Tokyo with a typically well-coached but utterly uninspired Japanese band. They follow Byard's charts – 'The Man Who Never Sleeps', the Oscar Pettiford dedication 'OPOP' (which also appear on *In Paris* and *Portrait*) – to the letter, leaving Mingus and his small touring group to inject what energy they can. Dispensable.

*** **Let My Children Hear Music** Columbia 471247
    Mingus; Snooky Young, Jimmy Nottingham, Lonnie Hillyer, Joe Wilder (*t*); Jimmy Knepper

(*tb*); Julius Watkins (*frhn*); Charles McPherson, Jerry Dodgion (*as*); Bobby Jones, James Moody (*ts*); Roland Hanna (*p*); Charles McCracken (*clo*); Milt Hinton, Richard Davis (*b*); Dannie Richmond (*d*); other personnel unknown. 9/71.

A strange hodge-podge of material, but in many ways a turning point in Mingus's later career, following a long melancholic lay-off and marking a return to realistic application of some of his large-scale orchestral ideas. Even though much of the material was 'dictated' to paid arrangers like Sy Johnson, Bobby Johnson and Alan Raph, it all has Mingus's unmistakable stamp.

The date arose from a plan to record 'The Chill Of Death', a recitation with an important place in the Mingus canon, but Columbia suggested a full session would be more cost-effective, so Mingus brought in some new material and set about preparing – or 'dictating' – new arrangements of work from the previous decade. 'Adagio Non Troppo' is a Byard rendition of 'Myself When I Am Real', played very straight, perhaps (Brian Priestley suggests) using the original Mingus piano recording and featuring a cello solo by McCracken and six bowed basses. The wonderfully titled 'The Shoes Of The Fisherman's Wife Are Some Jive Ass Slippers' with which the album opens is also a revival and re-orchestration, as is 'Don't Be Afraid, The Clown's Afraid, Too'. Of the new pieces, 'Hobo Ho' is pretty much a James Moody feature spot which calls up memories of a lot of work that went before, an extended tribute from soloist to composer.

Production was handled by Teo Macero, and he and Mingus wove together a dense, complex collage of sound (only 'The I Of Hurricane Sue' sounds straight-ahead) using existing material, overdubs and sound effects. It's a powerful, often heady mix, but 'The Chill Of Death', with its comic-bleak message, is still, ironically, the outstanding track.

***(*) **Changes One** Rhino R2 71403
     Mingus; Jack Walrath (*t*); George Adams (*ts*); Don Pullen (*p*); Dannie Richmond (*d*). 12/74.
***(*) **Changes Two** Rhino R2 71404
     As above, except add Jackie Paris (*v*), Marcus Belgrave (*t*). 12/74.

Long out of print, these are among the best of Mingus's later works. Recorded in a single session, they represent definitive performances by a group that had played and gradually transformed this material – 'Orange Was The Color Of Her Dress', 'Devil Blues', two versions of 'Duke Ellington's Sound Of Love', one instrumental, one vocal – over a longer period than almost any previous Mingus unit. Some of the fire has definitely gone, and there is a hint of studio polish which was never evident on the band's live dates; but they are powerful records nevertheless and essential documents for Mingus enthusiasts.

**** **Thirteen Pictures: The Charles Mingus Anthology** Rhino R2 71402 3CD
     Mingus; Jack Walrath, Marcus Belgrave, Hobart Dotson, Clark Terry, Bobby Bryant, Lonnie Hillyer, Melvin Moore, Eddie Preston, Richard Williams (*t*); Lou Blackburn, Jimmy Knepper, Eddie Bert, Jimmy Greenlee, Slide Hampton, Britt Woodman (*tb*); Don Butterfield, Red Callender (*tba*); Mauricio Smith (*as, ss, f, picc*); John Handy (*as, ts*); Eric Dolphy (*as, f, bcl*); Lee Konitz, Jackie McLean, John LaPorta, Charles McPherson (*as*); Buddy Collette (*as, f, picc*); Booker Ervin, Dick Hafer, Shafi Hadi, Roland Kirk, J. R. Monterose, George Barrow, Bill Barron, Joe Farrell, Ricky Ford (*ts*); Paul Jeffrey (*ts, ob*); Yusef Lateef (*ts, f*); Danny Bank (*bs*); Bob DiDomenica (*f*); Harry Schulman (*ob*); Jerome Richardson, Jack Nimitz (*bs, bcl*); Gary Anderson (*bcl, cbcl*); Gene Scholtes (*bsn*); Jaki Byard, Phyllis Pinkerton, Roland Hanna, Wade Legge, Mal Waldron, Horace Parlan, Duke Ellington, Bob Neloms (*p*); George Koutzen, Charles McCracken (*clo*); Doug Watkins (*b*); Willie Jones, Al Levitt, Walter Perkins, Sticks Evans, Dannie Richmond, Max Roach (*d*); Candido Camero, Alfredo Ramirez, Bradley Cunningham (*perc*); Jackie Paris (*v*). 52, 1/56, 12/55, 3/57, 5/59, 5/60, 4 & 9/62, 7 & 9/63, 9/64, 5/77.

An excellent compilation of Mingus's work for Atlantic, beautifully packaged in a box with a booklet of photographs. It contains material from *Pre-Bird*, *Chazz!*/*At The Bohemia*, *Plays Piano*, *Cumbia And Jazz Fusion*, *The Clown*, the immortal *Ah Um*, *Oh Yeah* and *Mingus Mingus Mingus Mingus Mingus*, *Pithecanthropus Erectus*, *Money Jungle*, *At Monterey* and a rare Debut single from 1952 with Jackie Paris as vocalist. The packaging and accompanying documentation are immaculate; the music is, of course, brilliant. One can hardly imagine a nicer present for someone who hasn't got all this stuff already.

*** **Three Or Four Shades Of Blues** Atlantic 7567 81403
     Mingus; Jack Walrath (*t*); Sonny Fortune (*as*); George Coleman (*ss, ts*); Ricky Ford (*ts*); Bob Neloms, Jimmy Rowles (*p*); Philip Catherine, Larry Coryell, John Scofield (*g*); Ron Carter, George Mraz (*b*); Dannie Richmond (*d*). 3/77.

Despite Mingus's deep and vocal reservations, this was one of his most successful albums commercially. The addition of guitarists clearly pitched it in the direction of the younger rock-buying audience that Atlantic had targeted, and the record also included staples like 'Goodbye, Pork Pie Hat' and 'Better Git

Hit In Your Soul' (presumably with a view to initiating that younger audience). The title-track, though, is rather too broad in its catch-all approach and sounds almost self-parodic. Mingus's health was beginning to break down in 1977, and there are signs of querulousness throughout, not least on 'Nobody Knows The Trouble I've Seen'.

(*) Cumbia And Jazz Fusion Atlantic 1039
> Mingus; Jack Walrath (*t, perc*); Dino Piana (*tb*); Jimmy Knepper (*tb, btb*); Mauricio Smith (*f, picc, as, ss*); Quarto Maltoni (*as*); George Adams (*ts, f*); Ricky Ford (*ts, perc*); Paul Jeffrey (*ts, ob*); Gary Anderson, Roberto Laneri (*bcl*); Anastasio Del Bono (*ob, eng hn*); Pasquale Sabatelli, Gene Scholtes (*bsn*); Bob Neloms (*p*); Danny Mixon (*p, org*); Dannie Richmond (*d*); Candido Camero, Daniel Gonzalez, Ray Mantilla, Alfredo Ramirez, Bradley Cunningham (*perc*). 3 & 4/76, 3/77.

'Cumbia And Jazz Fusion' is a slightly messy piece that levels some doubts at Mingus's remaining talents as arranger and instrumentator. The ensembles are all rather congested, which mars a fine and vibrant piece that ranks as one of his best late compositions. There is a regularity to the basic metre and a simplicity of conception which make the rather opaque surface all the more disappointing. The fault doesn't seem to lie with the recording, which is well transferred.

'Music for *Todo Modo*' was written (sight unseen) as soundtrack to the film by Elio Petri. The ten-piece Italo-American band works a typically volatile score, which includes a variant on 'Peggy's Blue Skylight' and some fine blues.

*** **Mingus Plays Piano** Mobile Fidelity MFCD 783
> Mingus (*p* solo). 7/63.

Mingus played something more than 'composer's piano' throughout his career. His touch and harmonic sense were so secure that, though hardly virtuosic, he more than passes muster on a very resonant and richly toned instrument with what sounds like a very brisk action. It's interesting to hear themes like 'Orange Was The Color Of Her Dress, Then Blue Silk' reduced to their essentials in this way, though the true highlights are 'When I Am Real' and a thoroughly unabashed 'Body And Soul'. Not in the front rank of Mingus albums, but certainly not just for collectors.

Mingus Dynasty / Big Band Charlie Mingus / Mingus Big Band
93 GROUP

***(*) **Reincarnation** Soul Note 121042
> Richard Williams (*t*); Jimmy Knepper (*tb*); Ricky Ford (*ts*); Sir Roland Hanna (*p*); Reggie Johnson (*b*); Kenny Washington (*d*). 4/82.

*** **Mingus's Sounds Of Love** Soul Note 121142
> Randy Brecker (*t*); Jimmy Knepper (*tb*); James Newton (*f*); Craig Handy (*ts*); Sir Roland Hanna (*p*); Reggie Johnson (*b*); Kenny Washington (*d*). 9/87.

*** **The Next Generation** Columbia 468387
> Jack Walrath (*t*); Craig Handy (*ts, f*); George Adams (*ts, v*); Alex Foster (*ts, ss, cl, picc*); John Hicks, Benny Green (*p*); Ray Drummond (*b*); Victor Lewis (*d*); Charles Mingus, Eric Mingus (*v*). 91.

There have always been 'ghost bands', orchestras which continued trading after the leader's death, like *Hamlet*s without the prince or, as *The Next Generation* may call to mind, *Star Trek* without Kirk and Spock. The best-known of these bands in jazz are the Duke Ellington and Count Basie orchestras, their posthumous life justified by the perfectly reasonable feeling that what makes a group distinctive is the bandbook and the soloists, not the physical presence of the leader. It's a view that can be pushed to absurdity; but, in the case of Charles Mingus, a man who regarded composition as a discipline which allowed others to discover their own musical language, it has a special significance.

After Mingus's death, conscious that his artistic legacy required careful investment, his widow, Sue Graham, formed Mingus Dynasty in the hope of seeing the music continuing to develop. To sustain an element of apostolic succession, at least one or two members of each line-up were to be musicians who had either worked with or studied under Mingus; the bassist's son, Eric Mingus, appears as a singer on the third record – so, too, rather more bizarrely does Mingus himself. Towards the end of his life, he was able to compose only by singing themes into a tape recorder; 'Harlene' and 'Sketch Four' on *The Next Generation* are examples. On the latter, Mingus sings the theme over a metronome count (he was no longer able even to beat time); Smitty Smith picks up the metre and the band come in. Craig Handy takes the main solo on that track, but the main featured voice on the record is that of George Adams, fiery as always on 'Opus Three', 'Opus Four' and 'Wham Bam', rapping a narration based on Mingus's autobiography, *Beneath The Underdog*, on 'Bad Cops'. Oddly, Jack Walrath, who MD'd this version of the band, takes no solos of his own, leaving the whole record extremely saxophone-heavy and somewhat unrelieved. The balance was rather better on earlier sets.

The studio version of 'Sue's Changes' on *Sound Of Love* gives Reggie Johnson one of his most forthright parts. 'The I Of Hurricane Sue' and 'Ysabel's Table Dance' are both outstandingly good. The band on *Reincarnation* is, if anything, even better and the choice of material aimed to please, with 'Wednesday Night Prayer Meeting', 'East Coasting' and 'Duke Ellington's Sound Of Love' all featured. Williams solos with great pointedness.

***(*) **Big Band Charlie Mingus: Live At The Théâtre Boulogne-Billancourt, Volume 1** Soul Note 121192
 Randy Brecker (*t*); Jon Faddis (*c*); Mike Zwerin, Jimmy Knepper (*tb*); John Handy (*as*); Clifford Jordan (*ts, ss*); David Murray (*ts, bcl*); Nick Brignola (*bs*); Jaki Byard (*p*); Reggie Johnson (*b*); Billy Hart (*d*). 6/88.

**** **Big Band Charlie Mingus: Live At The Théâtre Boulogne-Billancourt, Volume 2** Soul Note 121193
 As above. 6/88.

A related project, Big Band Charlie Mingus mercifully stopped short of all-out 'orchestral' arranging that would have taken the sting out of much of Mingus's music. As it is, this group is just an augmented version of the Dynasty groups. There are good things on *Volume 1*, 'Jump Monk' and 'E's Flat, Ah's Flat Too', but 'The Shoes Of The Fisherman's Wife Are Some Jive-Ass Slippers' doesn't give the band much to work on and it sounds very uncentred. For some reason, most of the really good stuff is on the second disc. Faddis and Murray solo pungently on 'My Jelly Roll Soul', and Murray returns on bass clarinet for the third of the wind solos on 'Goodbye Pork Pie Hat', giving ground to the superb Byard. 'Boogie Stop Shuffle' is aired again; this time Murray, obviously relishing the occasion, jumps in after Cliff Jordan with three rasping, joyous choruses that exactly capture the spirit of the man they all came to honour.

*** **Nostalgia In Times Square** Dreyfus FDM 369552
 Randy Brecker, Christopher Kase, Ryan Kisor, Lew Soloff, Jack Walrath (*t*); Art Baron, Sam Burtis, Frank Lacy (*tb*); Dave Taylor (*btb, tba*); Alex Foster, Steve Slagle (*as*); Chris Potter (*as, ts*); John Stubblefield, Craig Handy (*ts*); Ronnie Cuber, Roger Rosenberg (*bs*); Joe Locke (*vib*); Kenny Drew Jr (*p*); Michael Formanek, Andy McKee (*b*); Victor Jones, Marvin 'Smitty' Smith (*d*); Ray Mantilla (*perc*). 3/93.

*** **Gunslinging Birds** Dreyfus FDM 36575
 As above, except omit Kase, Walrath, Baron, Burtis, Taylor, Cuber, Rosenberg, Formanek, Jones, Smith, Mantilla; add Philip Harper (*t*); Jamal Haynes, Earl McIntyre (*tb*); Gary Smulyan (*bs*); David Lee Jones (*as*); Chris Potter (*ts*); Adam Cruz (*d*). 95.

The sleeve of *Gunslinging Birds* is misprinted Mingus Big Bang, which is just about right. Both records deliver with ferocious power and, when required, some delicacy as well. As usual, the material is taken from throughout the Mingus archive. *Nostalgia* is probably more interesting in terms of material – 'Don't Be Afraid, The Clown's Afraid, Too', 'Weird Nightmare', the title-piece – but the playing and the recording are sharper and more exact on the later album, which centres on a superb reading of 'Fables Of Faubus'. The fact that the group has been able to stay together, working a regular weekly residency/workshop, means that the material is thoroughly under their belts; no nasty surprises in these demanding scores.

The Minstrels Of Annie Street GROUP

*** **Original Tuxedo Rag** Stomp Off STCD1272
 Bob Schulz (*c*); Chris Tyle (*t*); John Gill (*tb, v*); Phil Howe (*cl, ss*); Ray Skjelbred (*p*); Carl Lunsford (*bj*); Bill Carroll (*tba*); Hal Smith (*d*). 7/93.

Led by Gill, this is a sextet (Tyle and Smith sit in as guests) dedicated to San Francisco repertory, and therefore heavily in debt to the Lu Watters revivalists. They take the more nimble rhythmic approach of today, though, which leavens the music and gives an extra lift to tunes that might otherwise tend towards flat-footed thunder. Nice touches include Tom T. Hall's country song, 'The Day Clayton Delaney Died', and a couple of ancient rags. Neat solos, but the band's the thing.

Phil Minton (born 1940) VOICE, TRUMPET

*** **Songs From A Prison Diary** Leo CDLR 196
 Minton; Veryan Weston (*p*). 10/91.

*** **Dada Da** Leo CDLR 192
    Minton; Roger Turner (*d, perc*). 1/93.

Minton is perhaps the most powerful vocal performer working in Europe today, and singing has virtually overtaken his trumpet playing. Associated with Mike Westbrook on a number of text-based projects, he is also a stunning vocal improviser, with a tonal and timbral range that seems quite uncanny.

The duos with Weston seem much more formalized than Minton's improvised work with Peter
Brötzmann and others on a deleted FMP album, and they lack the sheer power of the slightly earlier
work with Roger Turner on *AMMO*, but they are compelling all the same. The Ho Chi Minh texts on
Songs From A Prison Diary are intensely moving and Minton brings to them a natural actor's ability to
deliver apparently banal lines with a weight of experience that far exceeds their ostensible meaning.

The duos with Turner are initially rather baffling but they repay time and attention, confirming how
carefully and intuitively Minton navigates the rhythm of a piece. These are probably best heard first as
percussion duos. You even get the soundcheck as a bonus.

Bob Mintzer (born 1953) TENOR SAXOPHONE, BASS CLARINET

*** **Departure** DMP CD-493
    Mintzer; Marvin Stamm, Laurie Frink, Tim Hagans, Bob Millikan, Michael Mossman (*t, flhn*);
    Dave Bargeron, Mike Davis, Keith O'Quinn, Dave Taylor (*tb*); Lawrence Feldman, Bob Malach,
    Roger Rosenberg, Peter Yellin (*reeds*); Phil Markowitz, Jim McNeely (*p*); Michael Formanek,
    Lincoln Goines (*b*); Peter Erskine, John Riley (*d*); Sammy Figueroa (*perc*). 92.

*** **Only In New York** DMP CD-501
    As above, except Ron Tooley (*t, flhn*), Dave Panichi (*tb*), Jay Anderson (*b*) replace Mossman,
    Bargeron, McNeely, Formanek, Goines, Erskine and Figueroa. 11/93.

Mintzer is an accomplished soloist and arranger who's been recording big-band albums for almost a
decade. Earlier albums have been hit-and-miss affairs, with too much piling on of effects and a certain
cuteness standing in for wit or ingenuity. But the two most recent discs are more coherent, more
integrated, better. There is still some irritating stuff on *Departure*, such as 'The Big Show'; but some
more genuine material includes 'Horns Alone', a mildly arresting feature for the front line minus the
rhythm section, and with a superb team of players the sheer chutzpah of the musicianship is rewarding.
Only In New York is probably a shade better yet. We could have done without Mintzer's vocal on 'TV
Blues' – although the lyrics will probably raise a grin – but otherwise this is almost foot-perfect as skilful
big-band dates go. The oddly appealing sound of electric bass clarinet colours 'Modern Day Tuba', the
stop-go 'I Want To Be Happy' is an interesting revision, and so it goes through the ten tracks. Soloists
include the surpassingly fine Hagans as a standout and, though Mintzer himself is more agile than
profound, he has a good feature on 'What Might Have Been'. Both discs feature DMP's 20-Bit High
Resolution recording and they sound awfully strong. Still in the catalogue is the small-group date, *One
Music* (DMP CD-488), but it still barely passes muster.

Blue Mitchell (1930–79) TRUMPET, CORNET

**** **Big Six** Original Jazz Classics OJC 615
    Mitchell; Curtis Fuller (*tb*); Johnny Griffin (*ts*); Wynton Kelly (*p*); Wilbur Ware (*b*); Philly Joe
    Jones (*d*). 7/58.

***(*) **Out Of The Blue** Original Jazz Classics OJC 667
    Mitchell; Benny Golson (*ts*); Cedar Walton, Wynton Kelly (*p*); Paul Chambers, Sam Jones (*b*);
    Art Blakey (*d*). 1/59.

**** **Blue Soul** Original Jazz Classics OJC 765
    Mitchell; Curtis Fuller (*tb*); Jimmy Heath (*ts*); Wynton Kelly (*p*); Sam Jones (*b*); Philly Joe
    Jones (*d*). 59.

***(*) **Blues On My Mind** Original Jazz Classics OJC 6009
    Mitchell; Curtis Fuller (*tb*); Benny Golson, Johnny Griffin, Jimmy Heath (*ts*); Wynton Kelly
    (*p*); Paul Chambers, Sam Jones, Wilbur Ware (*b*); Art Blakey, Philly Joe Jones (*d*). 7/58, 1/59, 9/
    59.

*** **Smooth As The Wind** Original Jazz Classics OJC 871
    Mitchell; Burt Collins, Bernie Glow, Clark Terry (*t*); Jimmy Cleveland, Urbie Green, Britt
    Woodman, Julian Priester (*tb*); Willie Ruff (*frhn*); Tommy Flanagan (*p*); Tommy Williams (*b*);
    Philly Joe Jones, Charli Persip (*d*); strings. 12/60, 3/61.

***(*) **A Sure Thing** Original Jazz Classics OJC 837
> Mitchell; Clark Terry (*t*); Julius Watkins (*frhn*); Jerome Richardson (*as, f*); Jimmy Heath (*ts*);
> Pepper Adams, Pat Patrick (*bs*); Wynton Kelly (*p*); Sam Jones (*b*); Albert 'Tootie' Heath (*d*). 3/
> 62.
*** **The Cup Bearers** Original Jazz Classics OJC 797
> Mitchell; Junior Cook (*ts*); Cedar Walton (*p*); Gene Taylor (*b*); Roy Brooks (*d*). 63.

A stalwart of the Horace Silver band, Mitchell took it over in 1964, replacing the former leader with the young Chick Corea. The debut recording isn't particularly memorable; though Corea has a fine grasp of the required idiom, which is blues- and gospel-drenched hard bop of the kind Silver pioneered, it never quite ignites. The heavy-duty line-up on the Riverside reissues on OJC is much more satisfactory and *Big Six* is unquestionably the trumpeter's finest achievement. Griffin and Golson sound to have paid *lots* more dues than Cook. Mitchell shows that he can be sensitive, too, with a lovely quartet 'Blue Soul', ranging with unusual freedom over Kelly's blues lines. The *Blues On My Mind* compilation is, for most casual purchasers, a good buy, bringing together 'Brother Ball' and 'There Will Never Be Another You' from OJC 615 and 'It Could Happen To You' and a rousing 'Saints' from *Out Of The Blue*.

In many respects, *Blue Soul* is the best of the bunch, though here Mitchell is occasionally outclassed by his band; Henderson in particular sounds as if he's trying not to muscle in and one or two of his solos are curtailed rather suddenly, perhaps lest he outstay his welcome. Jimmy Heath resurfaces to equally good effect on *A Sure Thing*, especially on 'Gone With The Wind', which is arranged for just trumpet, saxophone and rhythm, a welcome variation on the big-band material but rather wastefully tucked away at the end. The two baritones and french horn provide a solid bottom for Heath's arrangements.

The *Cup Bearers* is a bit of a disappointment. Unlike the urbane Henderson on the earlier record, Cook is forever in a tearing rush to get back and have a further say, not quite knowing how to get out of what he's set up for himself. What it palpably needs is someone of Heath's intelligence to tie up the loose ends.

Like many of his contemporaries, Mitchell long nursed a desire to work with strings. *Smooth As The Wind* is the result, an on-again, off-again mish-mash of terse big-band jazz arranged by Tadd Dameron and Benny Golson with oddly distanced orchestral washes that neither add nor significantly detract but which over the entire session pall rather badly.

Red Mitchell (1927–92) DOUBLE BASS, PIANO

***(*) **Presenting Red Mitchell** Original Jazz Classics OJC 158
> Mitchell; James Clay (*ts, f*); Lorraine Geller (*p*); Billy Higgins (*d*). 3/57.
(*) **Chocolate Cadillac Steeplechase SCCCD 1161
> Mitchell; Idrees Sulieman (*t*); Nisse Sandstrom (*ts*); Horace Parlan (*p*); Rune Carlsson (*d*). 12/
> 76.
*** **Red'N'Me** Dreyfus Jazz Line 365042
> Mitchell; Jimmy Rowles (*p*). 7/78.
*** **Simple Isn't Easy** Sunnyside SSC 1016
> Mitchell (*p* solo). 9/83.
*** **The Red–Barron Duo** Storyville STCD 4137
> Mitchell; Kenny Barron (*p*). 8/86.

Known for a fluent improvising style in which pulled-off (rather than plucked) notes in a typically low register (Mitchell uses a retuned bass) suggest a baritone saxophone rather than a stringed instrument; Scott LaFaro was later sanctified for a broadly similar technique. Mitchell is also an accomplished pianist, with a hint of the romantic approach of his former colleague, Hampton Hawes. The early stuff on OJC with the short-lived Geller instead of Hawes is decent, boppish jazz consistently lifted by Mitchell's singing lines. 'Scrapple From The Apple' is a joy and a delight. The Sunnyside originals – with titles like 'I'm A Homeboy' and 'It's Time To Emulate The Japanese' – quash any notion that Mitchell is merely a standards hack, though he is more approachable in that territory. *Simple Isn't Easy* is entirely for piano and voice, and to that extent isn't typical; even so, it suggests that most of the elements of Mitchell's shaping intelligence are at work: harmonically limber, melodically sophisticated and rhythmically just dynamic enough to be listenable. Mitchell's really interesting work lies mostly in the past, and it's a great pity that the 1957 Contemporary *Presenting Red Mitchell* (now on OJC) is quoted only as an LP.

On *Chocolate Cadillac* the writing is good and Mitchell is playing well (top form on a couple of tracks). Unfortunately, the band simply isn't behind him. Parlan, normally a stylistic chameleon, seems to have his mind on something else, and the two horns lock only infrequently. Disappointing.

The *Red–Barron Duo* is the closest Mitchell came to duetting with himself. The pianist shares Mitchell's harmonic and rhythmic preoccupations to a productive degree, and their exploration of quite basic themes ('Oleo', 'The Sunny Side Of The Street') is compellingly inventive. So, too, is the collaboration with Rowles, except that here there is an entirely surprising element of tension, most of it generated by Mitchell's taut ostinati and a fresh set-list, in which only 'There Is No Greater Love' sounds like a chestnut.

Roscoe Mitchell (born 1940) REEDS, PERCUSSION

*** **Roscoe Mitchell** Chief CD 4

> Mitchell; Leo Smith (*t, pkt-t, flhn*); George Lewis (*tb, sou, tba*); Thurman Barker, Anthony Braxton, Don Moye, Douglas Ewart, Joseph Jarman, Henry Threadgill, Malachi Favors (*perc*). 7–8/78.

Several of Mitchell's crucial recordings have disappeared with the apparent demise of Chicago's Nessa label, but the above reissue of one of them returns some of his most significant 1970s' work to the catalogue. Away from the Art Ensemble Of Chicago, this dedicated reed theoretician and experimenter has sought out some very rarefied terrain. There are three long pieces here: a trio for woodwinds, high brass and low brass, with Smith and Lewis; a phantasmagoria for eight percussionists, 'The Maze'; and almost 18 minutes of Mitchell blowing as softly as he can through the soprano sax, 'S II Examples', drifting through a world of shadowy microtones. A remarkable programme, but there are drawbacks: the 'L-R-G' trio is full of fascinating juxtapositions and echoes of countless other composers, yet its deliberately piecemeal nature seems laboured next to the spontaneous structures conceived as a matter of course by European improvisers. 'The Maze' has a burnished, glistening quality, but the fact that only two 'genuine' drummers are among the percussionists makes one wonder what Mitchell could have achieved with the involvement of eight full-time drum exponents. As it stands, the piece is a matter of shifting textures, when it might have transcended that. 'S II Examples', too, is more of an intriguing idea than a valuable musical one – or, at least, one more important to Mitchell than to the listener. All that said, it's a rather bewitching set altogether, and a useful notebook on what Chicago's playing elite were looking into at the period. The equally significant *Nonaah* from the same period has yet to appear on CD.

*** **3 × 4 Eye** Black Saint 120050-2

> Mitchell; Hugh Ragin (*t, picc t, flhn*); Spencer Barefield (*g*); Jaribu Shahid (*b*); Tani Tabbal (*d*). 2/81.

**** **Roscoe Mitchell And The Sound And Space Ensembles** Black Saint 120070-2

> Mitchell; Mike Mossman (*t, flhn*); Gerald Oshita (*ts, bs, Conn-o sax, contrabass srpn*); Spencer Barefield (*g, v*); Jaribu Shahid (*b, v*); Tani Tabbal (*d, v*); Tom Buckner (*v*). 6/83.

** **The Flow Of Things** Black Saint BSR 0090

> Mitchell; Jodie Christian (*p*); Malachi Favors (*b*); Steve McCall (*d*). 6–9/86.

*** **Live At The Knitting Factory** Black Saint 120120-2

> Mitchell; Hugh Ragin (*t, picc t, flhn*); Spencer Barefield (*g*); Jaribu Shahid (*b*); Tani Tabbal (*d*). 11/87.

Two of the best of Mitchell's Black Saint records have emerged as CDs since our last edition. *3 × 4 Eye* features a picked team tiptoeing around a number of themes, including his tribute to Jarman, 'Jo Jar', and the ironic 'Variations On A Folk Song Written In The Sixties'. Improvisation becomes almost ritualized, yet the leader's idiosyncratic deployment of sound and space renders the sequence of events as something extraordinary. The subsequent *Sound And Space Ensembles* is completely *sui generis*. The trio of Mitchell, Oshita – on some of the oddest reed instruments ever made – and the classical tenor Tom Buckner perform an eerie mixture of Kurt Schwitters and Wilton Crawley, before a pseudo-funk rave-up by the whole ensemble, which features probably the only recorded solo on the contrabass sarrusophone. The two ensembles go on to blend again in two long, beautiful tracks, the needle-fine 'Linefine Lyons Seven' and the scuttling-drifting 'Variations On Sketches From Bamboo'.

In the latter part of the 1980s, though, Mitchell seemed to lose his way. While a colleague such as Anthony Braxton worked out many directions through obsessive recording, Mitchell scarcely recorded at all. The only studio date, *The Flow Of Things*, is a static and tamely conventional reeds-and-rhythm date which yields little advance on his earlier experiments. *Live At The Knitting Factory* replaces the live album from 1988 on Cecma, which so far is not on CD. The group is in good shape but Mitchell's notebook-like approach to recording tends to make for a fragmented listening experience: the short pieces and the two cut-out solos break up the impact of the powerful 'Almost Like Raindrops' and the blow-out memorial, 'The Reverend Frank Wright'. Ragin's impassioned yet curiously selfless playing is as effective as Mitchell's own.

*** **After Fallen Leaves** Silkheart SHCD 126

> Mitchell; Arne Forsén (*p*); Ulf Akerheim (*b*); Gilbert Matthews (*d*). 10/89.

(*) **Songs In The Wind Victo 011
>   Mitchell; Vartan Manoogian (*vn*); Vincent Davis, Richard Davis (*d*); Steve Sylvester (*bullroarers, windwands*). 6–8/90.

The haphazardness of Mitchell's recording regimen has made it difficult to take a balanced view of a musician whose work, had it been documented more extensively, might have had a far more profound impact on the new music of the 1980s and '90s. As it is, Mitchell's marginalization has made records like these latest two seem like hurried odds and ends from his workshop. *After Fallen Leaves* features him with the Swedish Brus Trio, and there are many good moments – the boiling alto solo on 'Mr Freddie' and the long patchwork improvisation, 'Come Gather Some Things' – without the session really making a coherent impact, since the trio seem eager but too unfamiliar with Mitchell's methods. *Songs In The Wind* is even more fragmented, the 13 pieces ranging through solo, duo and trio explorations of mood and form: Mitchell is at his most unflinchingly austere here, and the oddball contributions of Sylvester seem like nothing more than a textural distraction. Hopefully, if Mitchell's plans to create a large repertory ensemble come to fruition, there'll be more opportunities to hear him at length on record in future.

** **Duets And Solos** Black Saint 120133-2
>   Mitchell; Muhal Richard Abrams (*p*). 3/90.

(*) **This Dance Is For Steve McCall Black Saint 120150-2
>   Mitchell; Matthew Shipp (*p*); William Parker (*b, perc*); Jaribu Shihad (*b*); Tani Tabbal, Vincent Davis (*d*). 5/92.

The meeting with Abrams is a terrible disappointment. Each man's solo section rambles dutifully along to no great purpose, Abrams constructing a rolling but directionless panorama of piano styles, Mitchell practising some of his minimalist licks. Together they provide a few felicitous moments, but Abrams's decision to use a synthesizer for most of these passages pushes the music towards routine impressionism. *This Dance Is For Steve McCall* debuts a new group, The Note Factory, though not very auspiciously; aside from a thoughtful new treatment of Jarman's 'Ericka', several of the nine pieces sound half-realized or foreshortened, with the bass and percussion textures unclear. 'The Rodney King Affair', a stew of disquiet, is suitably blunt political art.

(*) **Hey Donald Delmark DE-475
>   Mitchell; Jodie Christian (*p*); Malachi Favors (*b*); Albert 'Tootie' Heath (*d*). 5/94.

Another largely disappointing affair. When the rhythm section are playing straight time and setting up a groove underneath, Mitchell's honking and mordant saxophone often sounds frankly ludicrous. On the Tab Smith-styled smoocher, 'Walking In The Moonlight', it's close to absurd. Yet there are still felicitous moments – the simple, sweet flute piece, 'Jeremy' – and four duets with Favors evoke some of the mystery of the old days. But this is, in sum, not much of a record.

Hank Mobley (1930–86) TENOR SAXOPHONE

*** **The Jazz Message Of Hank Mobley** Savoy SV-0133
>   Mobley; Donald Byrd (*t*); John LaPorta (*as*); Ronnie Ball, Horace Silver (*p*); Doug Watkins, Wendell Marshall (*b*); Kenny Clarke (*d*). 1–2/56.

(*) **The Jazz Message Of Hank Mobley Vol. 2 Savoy SV-0158
>   Mobley; Lee Morgan, Donald Byrd (*t*); Hank Jones, Barry Harris (*p*); Doug Watkins (*b*); Art Taylor, Kenny Clarke (*d*). 7–11/56.

Mobley's early records are customarily ignored, but these two discs for Savoy are probably as strongly delivered as anything he did in the 1950s. The first four tracks on the first *Jazz Message* (he doesn't play on the final three, which feature LaPorta) are played with great feeling and sensitivity, with 'Madeline' being an especially worthwhile ballad; even Byrd plays slightly above his usual faceless competence. The second *Message* sounds less forthright, with the programme clearly thrown together and the players sometimes watching the clock, but there are still some sinuous declamations on the blues from the leader. The remastering is good.

*** **Peckin' Time** Blue Note B21Y-81574
>   Mobley; Lee Morgan (*t*); Wynton Kelly (*p*); Paul Chambers (*b*); Charli Persip (*d*). 2/58.

**** **Soul Station** Blue Note B21Y-46528
>   Mobley; Wynton Kelly (*p*); Paul Chambers (*b*); Art Blakey (*d*). 2/60.

***(*) **Workout** Blue Note 84080-2
>   Mobley; Wynton Kelly (*p*); Grant Green (*g*); Paul Chambers (*b*); Philly Joe Jones (*d*). 3/61.

***(*) **No Room For Squares** Blue Note B21Y-84149
>   Mobley; Lee Morgan (*t*); Andrew Hill (*p*); John Ore (*b*); Philly Joe Jones (*d*). 10/63.

*** **Dippin'** Blue Note B21Y-46511

    Mobley; Lee Morgan (*t*); Harold Mabern (*p*); Larry Ridley (*b*); Billy Higgins (*d*). 6/65.

*** **A Caddy For Daddy** Blue Note B21Y-84230

    Mobley; Lee Morgan (*t*); Curtis Fuller (*tb*); McCoy Tyner (*p*); Bob Cranshaw (*b*); Billy Higgins (*d*). 12/65.

Mobley's catalogue has been hit by the deletions axe of late. Aside from *Workout*, there is nothing at all on Blue Note available in the UK, and these American editions are the only survivors, with the classic *Roll Call* a scandalous casualty. Still, this remains a good representation of a prolific tenorman on the label. *Peckin' Time* is an early one, with Morgan as much in the driving seat as Mobley. *Soul Station* is the one Mobley album that should be in every collection: his rhythmic subtlety, accenting unexpected beats and planting emphases in places which take his phrasing far from the realism of hard bop cliché, is his strongest suit. But his slightly foggy undertone is often what people remember about him. His interplay with Blakey on *Soul Station* is superbly effective, especially on 'This I Dig Of You', while his ballad playing on 'If I Should Lose You', played at a slightly hopped-up tempo which always suits the saxophonist, is entirely sugar-free. *Workout* is a notch behind, on account of the thinner material. *No Room For Squares* has a terrific Mobley solo on 'Three Way Split' and includes Andrew Hill on four tracks. *Dippin'* might have been sharper, and the intriguing personnel on *A Caddy For Daddy* doesn't quite live up to expectations: with scores of Blue Note sessions behind him, Mobley might have been feeling his age at the label a little. The slightly earlier Blue Notes remain the best place to get acquainted with Mobley's beguiling playing.

Modern Jazz Quartet GROUP

John Lewis (*p*); Milt Jackson (*vib*); Percy Heath (*b*); Connie Kay (*d*); Kenny Clarke (*d*; pre-1955).

***(*) **The Artistry Of The Modern Jazz Quartet** Prestige 60 016

    With Kenny Clarke (*d*), Sonny Rollins (*ts*). 12/52–7/55.

***(*) **Django** Original Jazz Classics OJC 057

    6/53–1/55.

***(*) **MJQ** Original Jazz Classics OJC 125

    With Henry Boozier (*t*), Horace Silver (*p*). 6/54, 12/56.

The group which – viewed from an unfamiliar angle – graces our cover is something of an enigma. Frequently dismissed – as unexciting, pretentious, bland, Europeanized, pat – they have been hugely popular for much of the last 30 years, filling halls and consistently outselling most other jazz acts (who else's catalogue has made such a comprehensive transition to CD?). So, they're commercial, then, MOR entertainers in tuxes with no real jazz credentials?

    The enigma lies in that epithet 'Modern' for, inasmuch as the MJQ shift more product than anyone else, they are also radicals (or maybe nowadays that American hybrid, radical-conservatives) who have done more than most barnstorming revolutionaries to change the nature and form of jazz performance, to free it from its changes-based theme-and-solos clichés. Leader/composer John Lewis has a firm grounding in European classical music, particularly the Baroque, and was a leading light in both Third Stream music and the *Birth Of The Cool* sessions with Gerry Mulligan and Miles Davis. From the outset he attempted to infuse jazz performance with a consciousness of form, using elements of through-composition, counterpoint, melodic variation and, above all, fugue to multiply the trajectories of improvisation. And just as people still, even now, like stories with a beginning, middle and end, people have liked the well-made quality of MJQ performances which, on their night, don't lack for old-fashioned excitement.

    The Modern Jazz Quartet was born viviparously out of the post-war Dizzy Gillespie band. The fact that it had been Gillespie's rhythm section (with Ray Brown on bass originally and Kenny Clarke on drums, both soon replaced) led people to question the group's viability as an independent performing unit. The early recordings more than resolve that doubt.

    Lewis has never been an exciting performer (in contrast to Jackson, who is one of the great soloists in jazz), but his brilliant grasp of structure is evident from the beginning. Of the classic MJQ pieces – 'One Bass Hit', 'The Golden Striker', 'Bags' Groove' – none characterizes the group more completely than Lewis's 'Django', first recorded in the session of December 1954. The Prestige is a useful CD history of the early days of the band, but it's probably better to hear the constituent sessions in their entirety. Some of the material on the original two-disc vinyl format has been removed to make way for a Sonny Rollins/MJQ set ('No Moe', 'The Stopper', 'In A Sentimental Mood', 'Almost Like Being In Love'), which is a pity, for this material was long available elsewhere.

*** **Concorde** Original Jazz Classics OJC 002

    7/55.

*** **Fontessa** Atlantic 781329
    1 & 2/56.
***(*) **Pyramid** Atlantic 781340
    8 & 12/59, 1/60.
  **** **Dedicated To Connie** Atlantic 82763 2CD
    5/60.
***(*) **Lonely Woman** Atlantic 780665
    62.
*** **Comedy** Atlantic 1390 2
    With Diahann Carroll (*v*). 10/60, 1/62.
(*) **Blues On Bach Atlantic 7831393
    11/73.
***(*) **The Last Concert** Atlantic 81976 2CD
    11/74.
(*) **Together Again Pablo Live 2308344
    7/82.
*** **Together Again – Echoes** Pablo 2312142
    3/84.
*** **Topsy – This One's For Basie** Pablo 2310917
    6/85.
*** **Three Windows** Atlantic 254833
    With New York Chamber Symphony. 87.
*** **For Ellington** East West 790926
    2/88.
*** **A Celebration** Atlantic 782538
    With Wynton Marsalis, Harry 'Sweets' Edison (*t*); Freddie Hubbard (*flhn*); Phil Woods (*as*); Nino Tempo, Illinois Jacquet (*ts*); Branford Marsalis (*ts, ss*); Mickey Roker (*d*); Bobby McFerrin (*v*). 6/92, 4/93.
(*) **The Best Of The Modern Jazz Quartet Pablo 2405 423
    80s.

Connie Kay slipped into the band without a ripple; sadly, his ill-health and death were the only circumstances in the next 40 years of activity necessitating a personnel change. His cooler approach, less overwhelming than Clarke's could be, was ideal, and he sounds right from the word go. His debut was on the fine *Concorde*, which sees Lewis trying to blend jazz improvisation with European counterpoint. It combines a swing, that would have sounded brighter if recording quality had been better, with some superb fugal writing. Though the integration is by no means always complete, it's more appealing in its very roughness than the slick Bach-chat that turns up on some of the Atlantics.

The label didn't quite know what to do with the MJQ, but the Erteguns were always alert to the demographics and, to be fair, they knew good music when they heard it. One of the problems the group had in this, arguably their most creatively consistent phase, was that everything appeared to need conceptual packaging, even when the music suggested no such thing. Chance associations, like the celebrated version of Ornette's 'Lonely Woman', were doubtless encouraged by the fact that they shared a label, and this was all to the good; there are, though, signs that in later years, as rock began to swallow up a bigger and bigger market share, the group began to suffer from the inappropriate packaging.

Though home-grown compositions reappear throughout the band's history (there's a particularly good 'Django' on *Pyramid*), there are also constant references to standard repertoire: 'How High The Moon' on the same album, 'Nature Boy' on the late, post-reunion Basie tribute.

By the same inverted snobbery that demands standards rather than 'pretentious classical rubbish', it's long been a useful cop-out to profess admiration only for those MJQ albums featuring right-on guests. The earlier Silver collaboration isn't as well known as a justly famous encounter with Sonny Rollins at Music Inn, reprising their encounters of 1951, 1952 and 1953, which were really the saxophonist's gig, and though there is a certain perversity in its disappearance from the catalogue, it may help reinforce our conviction – one widely shared by MJQ fans – that the group did not require the services of horn players to produce legitimate, creative jazz.

Lewis's first exploration of characters from the *commedia dell'arte* came in *Fontessa*, an appropriately chill and stately record that can seem a little enigmatic, even off-putting. He develops these interests considerably in the simply titled *Comedy*, which largely consists of dulcet character-sketches with unexpected twists and quietly violent dissonances. The themes of *commedia* are remarkably appropriate to a group who have always presented themselves in sharply etched silhouette, playing a music that is deceptively smooth and untroubled but which harbours considerable jazz feeling and, as on both *Fontessa* and *Comedy*, considerable disruption to conventional harmonic progression.

Given Lewis's interests and accomplishments as an orchestrator, there have been surprisingly few jazz-group-with-orchestra experiments. More typical, perhaps, than the 1987 *Three Windows* (a project that significantly included music written for a Roger Vadim film 30 years earlier and including the classic 'Golden Striker' in a magnificent triple fugue, also 'Django') is what Lewis does on *Lonely Woman*. One of the very finest of the group's albums, this opens with a breathtaking arrangement of Ornette Coleman's haunting dirge and then proceeds with small-group performances of three works – 'Animal Dance', 'Lamb, Leopard' and 'Fugato' – which were originally conceived for orchestral performance. Remarkably, Lewis's small-group arrangements still manage to give an impression of symphonic voicings.

There is little question that the energy and inventiveness of the band was diluted by time. By the early 1970s the MJQ had become stylists first and improvisers only then. They disbanded in 1974, after a final flourish, but got together again and were still producing vital music (once again largely composed) in the 1980s. Lewis's explorations into the wider ramifications of jazz composition have drawn him closer and closer to Ellington, and the Ducal tribute on East West combines the original title-track and 'Maestro E.K.E.' – standing for Edward Kennedy Ellington – with classics like 'Ko-Ko', 'Jack The Bear', 'Prelude To A Kiss' and 'Rockin' In Rhythm'. Invigorated by that contact, the MJQ sound as if they could go on for ever.

The 40th anniversary celebrations had to continue without Connie Kay and with Mickey Roker standing in. The guest-star formula works as well as ever on the most recent disc, and the MJQ machine moved smoothly along, the Cadillac of jazz groups, only halted when Kay's ill-health finally overcame him in December 1994. The following February, the MJQ issued in his memory a concert from 1960, recorded in what was then Yugoslavia and a relatively innocuous destination on the international tour. Whatever its historical resonance, it inspired (as John Lewis discovered when he auditioned these old tapes and has asserted ever since) one of the truly great MJQ performances, certainly one of the very best available to us on disc. It knocks into a cocked hat even the new edition of the so-called *Last Concert*. Jackson's playing is almost transcendentally wonderful on 'Bags' Groove' and 'I Remember Clifford', and the conception of Lewis's opening *commedia* sequence could hardly be clearer or more satisfying. It is a very special record, and we have given it our top rating despite some misgivings about the recording.

***(*) **MJQ 40** Atlantic 7 82330 2 4CD
    With Bernie Glow, Joe Newman, Ernie Royal, Clark Terry, Snooky Young (*t*); Jimmy Cleveland, Garnett Brown, Tony Studd, Kai Winding (*tb*); Jimmy Giuffre, Bill McColl (*cl*); Bob Di Domenica (*f*); Manny Zeigler (*bsn*); Paul Desmond, Charlie Mariano, Phil Woods (*as*); Richie Kamuca, Seldon Powell (*ts*); Wally Kane (*bs*); Laurindo Almeida, Howard Collins (*g*); Joe Tekula (*clo*); Betty Glauman (*hp*); The Swingle Singers (*v*). 52–88.

A magnificently packaged ruby-anniversary celebration which draws on all stages and aspects of the group's career. Fifty-four tracks on four CDs taking in music from such records as *Plastic Dreams*, *Live At The Lighthouse*, *Third Stream Music*, and from the fine 1966 concert in Japan. As an introduction to the group's music, the accompanying booklet (which includes a complete discography) could hardly be bettered.

Charles Moffett (born 1929) DRUMS, TRUMPET, VIBRAPHONE

*** **The Gift** Savoy SV 0217
    Moffett; Paul Jeffrey (*ts, acl*); Wilbur Ware (*b*); Dennis O'Toole, Cody Moffett (*d*). 69.

Moffett started his career playing trumpet with Jimmy Witherspoon, but he owes his place in jazz history to a switch to percussion and a place in Ornette Coleman's most incendiary small group, the trio that recorded the Gyldencirkeln sessions for Blue Note. Moffett is barely represented as a leader, though he has led groups featuring his children and drawn from his students; teaching has often put his own playing at a discount. His trumpet playing is disconcertingly similar to Coleman's: raw, sharp and unevenly pitched, but with boundless energy and an exclamatory directness. Likewise his vibes playing, which is much more recognizable as the man who skittered and thrashed his way through those legendary Scandinavian sessions. Something of a curiosity, this record; but anyone interested in the development and ramifications of Ornette's art should certainly try to find it.

Cody Moffett DRUMS

***(*) **Evidence** Telarc CD-83343
    Moffett; Wallace Roney (*t*); Kenny Garrett (*as*); Ravi Coltrane (*ss, ts*); Antoine Roney (*ts*); Charnett Moffett (*b*). 3/93.

The third famous Moffett – son of Charles, brother of Charnett – makes a pleasing debut as leader. The provocative element here is Moffett's reluctance to tie his flag to one mast: there are nods to Coltrane ('Equinox'), Coleman ('Blues Connotation'), bebop ('Salt Peanuts'), Monk ('Evidence'), midstream hard bop ('Bolivia') and even Freddie Hubbard ('Red Clay'). Surprisingly, most of it works very well. Each of the horns makes a fist of their differing assignments – Garrett does an interesting take on Ornette, and Roney's spin through 'Salt Peanuts' is good fun – and the drummer's enthusiasm carries them over any bumpy spots.

Anders Mogenson DRUMS

*** **Taking Off** Storyville STCD 4198
>   Mogenson; Rick Margitza (*ss, ts*); Gary Thomas(*ts*); Niels Lan Doky (*p*); Ron McClure (*b*). 10/94.

Good drummer, great band, five originals, one Monk, one standard. The complementary energies of Margitza and Thomas are smartly filtered through the session, each man having a ballad apiece, and Margitza just wins out with the tart soprano brooding on 'Lonely'. Lan Doky, who also produced, is in top fettle, and Mogenson drives without overpowering. Typical modern blowing, and typically impressive.

Louis Moholo (born 1940) DRUMS, PERCUSSION

*** **Exile** Ogun OGCD 003
>   Moholo; Sean Bergin, Steve Williamson (*reeds*); Paul Rogers (*b*). 90.
*** **Freedom Tour: Live In South Afrika, 1993** Ogun OGCD 006
>   Moholo; Claude Deppa (*t, flhn, v*); Sean Bergin (*ts, f, concertina, v*); Toby Delius (*ts, v*); Jason Yarde (*as, ss, v*); Pule Pheto (*p*); Roberto Bellatalla (*b*); Thebe Lipere (*perc*). 93.

In the 1960s, radical American improvisers (with separatist agenda firmly in mind) renewed their interest in African percussion. What was quickly evident was that traditional African musics frequently anticipated the methodologies of free jazz and that the sometimes anarchic energies of contemporary African jazz were already more abstract than the prevailing American models. In Europe, for a variety of reasons, this was perceived much more readily, and there was a quicker and less ideological trade-off between African jazz and popular music on the one hand, and free music.

Louis Moholo, more than most of the South African exiles active on the jazz scene in Britain (but much like the late Johnny Dyani and the late Dudu Pukwana), was able to make the transition without undue strain. His own bands – Spirits Rejoice, Viva La Black, the African Drum Ensemble – have always contained free or abstract elements, and Moholo has always been in demand as a more experimental improviser, where his drive and intensity are comparable to that of Americans Milford Graves and Andrew Cyrille.

Exile is a hot, dangerous session, with Bergin's ferocious statements in constant opposition to Williamson's much cooler delivery, and with Rogers and Moholo working independently of the horns most of the time. 'Wathinta Amododa' is the main piece, but most of its initial power is thrown away in an overlong development-cum-denouement.

Viva La Black's tour and roving workshop for young South African musicians was, inevitably, a powerfully moving experience for Moholo and much of that comes across on the live record, fighting through a not very good recording which resists even Steve Beresford's skill at the final mix. Many of the tracks are short song-forms, some of them traditional; only the opening 'Woza' is substantially longer than five minutes, but the whole thing has the feel of a long, continuous suite, mostly celebratory in nature but with a few, entirely expected, dark corners and ambiguities.

Lello Molinari BASS

*** **No More Mr Nice Guy** Accurate QAC-4501
>   Molinari; George Garzone (*ss, ts*); Douglas Yates (*as, bcl*); Luigi Tessarollo (*g*); Matt Wilson (*d*). 9/91.
*** **On A Boston Night** Accurate AC-4502
>   As above, except Rick Peckham (*g*) and Bob Gullotti (*d*) replace Tessarollo and Wilson. 3/94.

Molinari is an Italian who's hooked up with some of the interesting local voices on the Boston scene. The first album is a studio date and runs through a gamut of styles: clever post-bop on 'C'era Chi?', flat-out storming on 'Stunt Cars'. Yates (who, along with Wilson, comes from the Either/Orchestra) and the dependable Garzone make a useful, gregarious front line, with their four horns alternated for piquant contrast; Tessarollo is impressive but sometimes predictably noisy. The subsequent live album is looser, less frenetic in its uptempo pieces, but sometimes dull: Garzone's attempted tone-poem, 'Echoes Of Rome', is a washout. Peckham plays a more modulated role, and the leader plays with terrific propulsion without stealing too much limelight on both records. An interesting note on Boston's fertile and under-appreciated jazz community.

Lars Møller (born 1967) TENOR SAXOPHONE

***(*) **Copenhagen Groove** Stunt STUCD 18902
      Møller; Thomas Clausen (p); Niels-Henning Orsted-Pedersen (b); Jimmy Cobb (d). 5/88.
**** **Pyramid** Stunt STUCD 19302
      Møller; Thomas Clausen (p); Jesper Lundgaard (b); Billy Hart (d). 5/89.
'Ingen Mas' – no sweat – gives some sense of Møller's astonishing gifts, which seem to be conveyed almost effortlessly. In fact, as Dave Liebman points out in an admiring liner-note, the young Dane is a serious-minded and dedicated student of the music and takes a uniquely thoughtful line on performance that prevents him from accepting ready solutions.

   Perhaps inevitably, Coltrane is the dominant influence. Møller's version of 'The Night Has A Thousand Eyes' is immediately identifiable as a gloss on the original version on *Coltrane's Sound*, but the youngster has imposed his own rhythmic framework and ventures a couple of harmonic ideas towards the middle of a carefully wrought solo. The five originals on *Copenhagen Groove* are all patiently and rather modestly worked out, in which enterprise the experienced Clausen is an ideal partner, and NHOP and Cobb the kind of rhythm section young players dream of, astonishingly trumped on the second record.

   It was, however, an odd notion to kick off *Pyramid* with a relatively mild and uncontroversial reading of 'Autumn Leaves', when the next track, the title-piece, is so completely arresting. Møller's solo has a majestic progress, reworking and reharmonizing the basic three-note cell before zooming off into an impassioned altissimo reminiscent of Christoph Lauer's. Hart provides tireless accompaniment and Lundgaard is simply one of the best players in Europe. Ironically, the most arresting single moment on the whole record occurs while he is sitting out with Clausen, a fierce dialogue between the leader and Hart on the intense 'Bismillah', a by-product of Møller's period of study in India which also induced him to add *shenai* (though not on this record) to the high, pure soprano sound heard to best effect on 'Song For Joe'. There are five strong originals in all, and a closing workout on Chick Corea's 'Matrix'. Utterly satisfying and recommended unreservedly.

Ben Monder GUITAR

***(*) **Flux** Songlines 1509-2
      Monder; Drew Gress (b); Jim Black (d). 1–6/95.
Beautifully shaped and recorded, this is an absorbing trio record which makes a good case for demand-ing more of the so far relatively unexposed Monder. He gets a liquid (though not quite underwater) tone on the guitar that he chooses not to vary very much – the thrashy 'Lactophobia' is about the only tune where he puts on the fuzzbox. The rest is long, patiently unspooling lines which bleed into the firm commentary by Gress. Black's drum parts are splendidly tough and propulsive, rattling around unexplored parts of the kit but never surrendering a beatmaster's taste for velocity. To counter the hard-hitting parts, Monder includes three meditative solos, ending on the slow whirl of 'Propane Dream'.

T. S. Monk (born 1949) DRUMS

** **Take One** Blue Note CDP 7 99614 2
      Monk; Don Sickler (t); Bobby Porcelli (as); Willie Williams (ts); Ronnie Mathews (p); James Genus (b). 10/91.
*** **The Changing Of The Guard** Blue Note CDP 789050
      As above, except replace Genus with Scott Colley (b). 2/93.
Crude hard bop from Thelonious Monk Jr, who on his well-named debut murders a trio of dad's tunes with the kind of blunt insouciance that might be forgivable were he no older than Denardo Coleman was when *he* entered the family trade. The parallel isn't entirely incidental. They both have a clubbing, broom-handle sound, derived from R&B.

The arrangements are largely the work of Don Sickler, who also turns up on the second record. Covers of Hank Mobley's 'Infra-Rae', Clifford Jordan's 'Bear Cat' and two Kenny Dorham tunes all go the same way as a double-, then quadruple-time ''Round Midnight'. Monk Sr had a subtle and often overlooked instinct for dynamic modulation; Jr hectors. That might make sense of Tommy Turrentine's 'Shoutin'', but the band sounds ragged and under-rehearsed, and Rudy van Gelder's engineering skills can't make up the deficit.

Van Gelder had also been on hand 38 years earlier when the three-year-old T. S. Monk shouted out take numbers as his dad recorded 'Think Of One' with Sonny Rollins (see OJC 016) in November 1953. It might have been a nice touch to have included that little bit of studio business at the head of T. S.'s 1991 version.

For the record, no rating in the last edition caused as much dismay as a lowly two stars for *Take One*. It's encouraging to be able to note, also for the record, that take two is a signal improvement. Same band, but an altogether subtler approach for *The Changing Of The Guard*. Monk resists the urge to thrash, and the soloists – Sickler in particular – play with urgency *and* taste. The Monk Sr material is done with thought and some imaginative flair. Good news all round.

Thelonious Monk (1917–82) PIANO

**** Genius Of Modern Music: Volume 1 Blue Note 781510
  Monk; Kenny Dorham, Idrees Sulieman, George Taitt (*t*); Lou Donaldson, Sahib Shihab, Danny Quebec West (*as*); Billy Smith, Lucky Thompson (*ts*); Milt Jackson (*vib*); Nelson Boyd, Al McKibbon, Bob Paige, Gene Ramey, John Simmons (*b*); Art Blakey, Max Roach, Shadow Wilson (*d*). 10 & 11/47, 7/48.
**** Genius Of Modern Music: Volume 2 Blue Note 781511
  As above, except add John Coltrane (*ts*). 10/47–5/52.
 The Complete Blue Note Recordings Blue Note CDP 830363 4CD
  As above, except add Ahmed Abdul-Malik (*b*); Kenny Hagood (*v*). 47–58.
**** The Best Of Thelonious Monk: The Blue Note Years Blue Note CDP 795636
  As above. 47–51.

Monk is one of the giants of modern American music, whose output ranks with that of Morton and Ellington, as *composition* of the highest order. Though no one questions his skills as a pianist (they were compounded of stride, blues and a more romantic strain derived from Teddy Wilson and filtered through Monk's wonderfully lateral intelligence), it is as a composer that he has made the greatest impact on subsequent jazz music. Even so, it is vital to recognize that the music and the playing style are necessary to each other and precisely complementary. Though he has attracted more dedicated interpreters since his death than almost any musician (Ornette Coleman and John Coltrane perhaps approach his standing with other players, but from very different perspectives), Monk tunes played by anyone else always seem to lack a certain conclusive authenticity.

Frequently misunderstood by critics and fans (and also by the less discerning of his fellow musicians), he received due public recognition only quite late in his career, by which time younger pianists originally encouraged by him and his example (Bud Powell is the foremost) had recorded and died and been canonized. It's now questioned whether Monk was ever, as he once appeared, a founding father of bop. Though some of his work, like 'In Walked Bud' on *Genius Of Modern Music*, utilized a straightforward chord sequence, and though 'Eronel', one of the additional tracks from the critical July 1951 session with Milt Jackson, is relatively orthodox bop, Monk's interest in tough, pianistic melody, displaced rhythm and often extreme harmonic distortion (as in his treatment of 'Carolina Moon') rather sets him apart from the bop mainstream.

The Blue Notes are essential Monk recordings, no less achieved and magisterial for being his first as a leader. It isn't often that we demote a coronetted item, but the appearance of *The Complete Blue Note Recordings*, which takes in a rediscovered live recording with John Coltrane at the Five Spot in New York City (far from pristine but musical gold-dust) inevitably changes the picture slightly. It is tempting to say that all the newcomer needs is here, expensive as it is. For those who can't quite stretch to it or who need convincing, the *Best Of* set is very acceptable indeed, with 'Epistrophy', 'Misterioso', ''Round About Midnight', 'Evidence' , 'Ruby My Dear' and 'Straight No Chaser' all included from the classic performances.

Monk recorded only intermittently over the next ten years, which makes them particularly valuable. Thwarted first by an American Federation of Musicians recording ban and later by a prison sentence and a blacklisting, Monk took time to regain the highs of these remarkable sides. The earliest of the sessions, with Sulieman, Danny Quebec West and Billy Smith, is not particularly inspired, though the pianist's contribution is instantly identifiable; his solo on 'Thelonious', built up out of minimal thematic potential, is emotionally powerful and restlessly allusive. A month later he was working with a more enterprising group (the difference in Blakey's response between the two sessions is remarkable) and producing his first classic recordings – of 'In Walked Bud' and ''Round About Midnight'.

The addition of Milt Jackson exactly a year later for the session that yielded 'Epistrophy' and 'Misterioso' was a turning point in his music, enormously extending its rhythmic potential and harmonic complexity. Jackson who, because of his association with the Modern Jazz Quartet, is now rather apt to be dismissed as a player lacking in improvisational excitement, makes an incalculable contribution to the music, here and on the session of July 1951 which yielded the classic 'Straight, No Chaser'. The later recordings on the set are much more conventionally arranged and lack the excitement and sheer imaginative power of the earlier cuts, but they do help overturn the received image of Monk as a man who wrote one beautiful ballad and then so dedicated the rest of his career to intractable dissonance as to set him apart entirely from the main currents of modern jazz.

Between 1952 and 1955, when he contracted to Riverside Records, Monk's career was relatively in the doldrums. However, he had already recorded enough material to guarantee him a place in any significant canon. No jazz fan should be without these records.

**** Thelonious Monk Trio / Blue Monk: Volume 2 Prestige CDJZD 009
   Monk; Ray Copeland (*t*); Frank Foster (*ts*); Percy Heath, Gary Mapp, Curley Russell (*b*); Art Blakey, Max Roach (*d*). 10 & 12/52, 5 & 9/54.
***(*) Thelonious Monk Original Jazz Classics OJC 010
   Monk; Percy Heath, Gary Mapp (*p*); Art Blakey, Max Roach (*d*). 10 & 12/52, 9/54.
***(*) Thelonious Monk / Sonny Rollins Original Jazz Classics OJC 059
   Monk; Sonny Rollins (*ts*); Julius Watkins (*frhn*); Percy Heath, Tommy Potter (*b*); Art Blakey, Willie Jones, Art Taylor (*d*). 11/53, 9 & 10/54.
***(*) MONK Original Jazz Classics OJC 016
   Monk; Ray Copeland (*t*); Julius Watkins (*frhn*); Sonny Rollins, Frank Foster (*ts*); Percy Heath, Curley Russell (*b*); Art Blakey, Willie Jones (*d*). 11/53, 5/54.

The end of Monk's Prestige period included some remarkably inventive and adventurous music, which isn't always played as well as it deserves. The trios with Heath and Blakey remain among the best performances of his career, however, and should on no account be missed.

The first of this group is a valuable twofer reissue of Prestige P 7027 and 7848, with original liner-notes in each case; though it involves repetition with the OJCs, it's a useful way of getting the best of the material on a single CD. OJC 010 repeats all the material save for four quintet tracks from May 1954 featuring Copeland and Foster on 'We See', 'Smoke Gets In Your Eyes', 'Locomotive' and the too-little-played 'Hackensack', all of which are taken from *MONK*. The latter album also includes additional material from the November 1953 recordings with Sonny Rollins which yielded OJC 059. That date was marked by the astonishing 'Friday The 13th', a brilliant use of simultaneous thematic statements which doesn't quite come off in this performance but which sufficiently survives the group's uncertainty to mark it out as daring.

The September 1954 session with Heath and Blakey was originally the basis of the Prestige *Monk's Moods* and it's good to have it filled out with the additional 'Work' and 'Nutty', which are also on *Monk/Rollins*. Even with a repeat of 'Blue Monk' (*the* definitive version) and the solo slot, 'Just A Gigolo', the Prestige is unbeatable value, clocking in at nearly 78 minutes.

Monk's treatment of standards is remarkable. When Monk strips a tune down, he arranges the constituent parts by the numbers, like a rifleman at boot camp, with the overall shape and function always evident. On 'These Foolish Things' and 'Sweet And Lovely' he never for a moment loses sight of the melody, and, as with the originals, builds a carefully crafted performance that is light-years away from the conventional theme-solo-theme format into which even relatively adventurous jazz performance seemed to be locked. A vital episode in modern jazz; the precise format chosen will depend on level of interest and budget, for it's almost impossible to go wrong.

***(*) Solo 1954 Vogue 111502
   Monk (*p* solo). 6/54.

There is now, of course, very little left in the chest for 'rediscovery'. These unaccompanied sides are a welcome exception. Claude Carrière's claim that these are the only solo pieces he 'ever' recorded is of course incorrect. However, they are rare enough to merit careful attention now. It's a fairly straightforward roster of compositions, with 'Smoke Gets In Your Eyes', a standard the pianist very much liked to play and had just recorded with his quintet, thrown in for good measure. 'Evidence' and 'Off Minor' are played chunkily, with ironic trills round the end of the melody, and there are moments when one might be forgiven for thinking that Monk was sending the whole thing up. The last phrases of 'Hackensack' are certainly intended to be ironic, as he stomps round the key changes.

There is no information about the studio set-up or the piano Monk was given. On the strength of this, it sounds rather boxy, but there are oddities with the recording in places, which may suggest that the original tape-speed was uncertain. This doesn't mar a thoroughly enjoyable and historically important reissue, however.

*** Plays Duke Ellington Original Jazz Classics OJC 024
    Monk; Oscar Pettiford (*b*); Kenny Clarke (*d*). 7/55.
*** The Unique Thelonious Monk Original Jazz Classics OJC 064
    Monk; Oscar Pettiford (*b*); Art Blakey (*d*). 3–4/56.

A curious start at Riverside. Orrin Keepnews remembers that Monk spent an age simply picking out the Ellington tunes at the piano and trying to get them straight. It's a respectful nod from one master to another, but not much more. *The Unique* is a standards album which doesn't quite go to the extremes of demolition which Monk chose when dropping a standard into one of his otherwise original dates, and Pettiford doesn't seem like the best choice for bassist.

**** Brilliant Corners Original Jazz Classics OJC 026
    Monk; Clark Terry (*t*); Ernie Henry (*as*); Sonny Rollins (*ts*); Oscar Pettiford (*b*); Max Roach (*d*). 12/56.

A staggering record, imperfect and patched together after the sessions, but one of the most vivid insights into Monk's music. The title-tune was so difficult that no single perfect take was finished (after 25 tries), and what we hear is a spliced-together piece of music. Full of tensions within the band, the record somehow delivers utterly compelling accounts of 'Pannonica', 'Bemsha Swing', 'Ba-Lue Bolivar Ba-lues Are' as well as the title-piece, and Monk ties it up with a one-take reading of 'I Surrender Dear'.

**** Thelonious Himself Original Jazz Classics OJC 254
    Monk; John Coltrane (*ts*); Wilbur Ware (*b*). 4/57.
**** Thelonious Monk With John Coltrane Original Jazz Classics OJC 039
    Monk; Ray Copeland (*t*); Gigi Gryce (*as*); Coleman Hawkins, John Coltrane (*ts*); Wilbur Ware (*b*); Shadow Wilson, Art Blakey (*d*). 4–6/57.
**** Monk's Music Original Jazz Classics OJC 084
    Monk; Ray Copeland (*t*); Gigi Gryce (*as*); Coleman Hawkins, John Coltrane (*ts*); Wilbur Ware (*b*); Art Blakey (*d*). 6/57.

Thelonious Himself is a first solo album, and one of his definitive statements up to this point. Alone at last, Monk's prevarications on his own pieces begin to sound definitive as each progresses: he unpicks them and lays them out again with an almost scientific precision, but the immediacy of each interpretation is anything but detached. 'Functional' was probably never given a better reading than here, and his accompanying interpretations of standards are scarcely less compelling, melody and rhythm placed under new lights in each one. Capping it is the trio version of 'Monk's Mood' with Coltrane and Ware, and again, even with all the many versions of this tune which are extant, this one is unlike any other.

The sessions which made up *Thelonious Monk With John Coltrane* and *Monk's Music* are arguably the most compelling records with horns that he ever made. The first is actually by the quartet with Coltrane, Ware and Wilson on three tracks (frustratingly, the only ones the quartet made, despite working together for no less than six months at a New York residency), which include a lovely reading of 'Ruby, My Dear', and throughout Coltrane seems to play humbly, in almost complete deference to the leader. This contrasts pretty strikingly with Hawkins on the second session, of which two alternative takes are also on OJC 039. The sonorous qualities of the horns make this one of the most beautiful-sounding of Monk sessions, and his inspired idea to start the record with an *a capella* arrangement of 'Abide With Me' sets an extraordinary atmosphere at the very start. There are still problems: the group play stiffly on these rhythms, Hawkins comes in wrongly a couple of times and, as fiercely as everyone is trying, it often sounds more like six men playing at Monk rather than with him. But the flavour of the session is fascinating, and Monk himself sounds wholly authoritative.

(****) Live At The Five Spot: Discovery! Blue Note CDP 799786
    Monk; John Coltrane (*ts*); Ahmed Abdul-Malik (*b*); Roy Haynes (*d*). summer 57.

On atmosphere, it can't be faulted. The music's pretty amazing, too. These tapes were made by Juanita Coltrane (better known to posterity as Naima) during the band's residency at the Five Spot. The track order has been altered only slightly from the original performance, putting 'Crepuscule With Nellie' at the end of the disc in order to give the opening a rather more cosmetic quality.

Predictably the quality of sound is thoroughly archaeological. The tapes were made on a portable machine with a single mike. The wonder is that so much does actually register. From the prominence of Abdul-Malik's bass it has to be assumed that Mrs Coltrane was in front of him, to her husband's left and at some distance from the piano, which actually registers most poorly of all the instruments, sounding like an out-of-tune clavichord. Collectors of Coltrane solos will be transfixed by his opening statement on 'Trinkle Tinkle', where Monk drops out to let him play with just bass and drums, a practice that is repeated later. This is still in the 'sheets of sound' period and that much-misapplied concept may well become clearer after a listen to this record.

There are many electrical and mechanical noises on the tape, a huge dropout during 'Epistrophy', where a portion was accidentally over-recorded (imagine having done that!) and an odd, dissociated feel to the whole thing, not unlike the effect of listening to a sold-out gig through a fire-escape door or side window. A discovery, indeed. However, a remastered version of the tape, with a speed correction, is now available on the complete Blue Note edition listed above.

***(*) **Thelonious In Action** Original Jazz Classics OJC 103
  Monk; Johnny Griffin (ts); Ahmed Abdul-Malik (b); Roy Haynes (d). 8/58.
***(*) **Misterioso** Original Jazz Classics OJC 206
  Monk; Johnny Griffin (ts); Ahmed Abdul-Malik (b); Roy Haynes (d). 8/58.

It might, on the face of it, seem improbable that such a headstrong and unmysterious character as Johnny Griffin could be such a masterful interpreter of Monk. But their partnership was an inspiring one, the tenorman unperturbed by any idea that Monk's music was difficult, and the quartet is on blistering form on these dates, recorded live at New York's lamented Five Spot.

***(*) **At Town Hall** Original Jazz Classics OJC 135
  Monk; Donald Byrd (t); Eddie Bert (tb); Bob Northern (frhn); Phil Woods (as); Charlie Rouse (ts); Pepper Adams (bs); Jay McAllister (tba); Sam Jones (b); Art Taylor (d). 2/59.

Although Monk regarded this Town Hall concert as a triumph, the results seem rather mixed now. The long and suitably grand attempt at 'Monk's Mood' sounds rather lugubrious, and in general the ensemble catches only elements of Monk's intentions: his peculiar truce between a sober gaiety, bleak humour and thunderous intensity is a difficult thing for a big band to realize and, while there is some fine playing – by Woods and Rouse in particular – the band could probably have used a lot more time to figure out the composer's vision. Still, it's a valuable document of Monk's one personal involvement on a large-scale reading of his music.

*** **5 By Monk By 5** Original Jazz Classics OJC 362
  Monk; Thad Jones (t); Charlie Rouse (ts); Sam Jones (b); Arthur Taylor (d). 6/59.

A relatively little-known Monk session, but a very good one. Jones is another not much thought of as a Monk interpreter, but he carries himself very capably and commits a brilliant improvisation to 'Jackie-Ing', even though (as Orrin Keepnews remembers) he had to struggle with what was then a new piece that Monk attempted to teach everybody by humming it. The CD includes the first two (rejected) takes of 'Played Twice', another new tune.

**** **Thelonious Alone In San Francisco** Original Jazz Classics OJC 231
  Monk (p solo). 10/59.

Another ruminative solo masterwork. Besides six originals, here is Monk elevating (or destroying, depending on one's point of view) 'There's Danger In Your Eyes, Cherie' and 'You Took The Words Right Out Of My Heart'. As a primer for understanding his piano playing, there is probably no better introduction than this one.

*** **At The Blackhawk** Original Jazz Classics OJC 305
  Monk; Joe Gordon (t); Charlie Rouse, Harold Land (ts); John Ore (b); Billy Higgins (d). 4/60.

Live in San Francisco. Land and Gordon were late additions to the band, but both men play well. It's not a classic Monk date by any means – despite another tune making its debut, 'San Francisco Holiday' – but there seems to be a good spirit in the playing and the leader sounds at his most genial.

***(*) **Live In Stockholm** DIW 315/6 2CD
  Monk; Charlie Rouse (ts); John Ore (b); Frankie Dunlop (d). 5/61.

The 1961 European tour and the subsequent Columbia contract put the seal on Monk's critical reputation. It's arguable that the end of his great association with Riverside marked the watershed in his creativity and that nothing he did after 1962 had the inventiveness and authority of the Blue Note, Prestige and Riverside years. Certainly the concert recordings from the 1961 tour (and there have been others in circulation, from both sides of the contractual blanket) have a strange *fin de siècle* quality, with a more than usually repetitive carry-over of ideas and very little sign of the pianist's usual ability to re-invent songs night after night. It's ironic that he should have been so warmly received in Europe, for Monk's compositional sense and his playing style were largely overdetermined by American models, rarely (as was the case with Bud Powell) by direct or ironic reference to the European classical tradition. What may have appealed to European audiences, even Swedes weaned on marathon blowing sessions by American exiles, was precisely his emphasis on *compositions*, rather than schematic chord progressions, as the basis of improvisation.

As so often, Rouse is the bellwether, uneasy and aggressive by turns in the presence of a rather diffident Monk on the first of the records (see 'Off Minor') but finding his feet with a vengeance in Bern and Stockholm. The DIW sound is very clear and pristine, but it lacks the warmth and sheer 'feel' of the two-disc Dragon, and those who already have that needn't feel they have to update urgently. Of the group, the Bern concert is perhaps the most rounded, with a wonderful, spiky-romantic version of 'I'm Getting Sentimental Over You' and the staple 'Blue Monk'. The Swedish date offers welcome performances of 'Ba-Lue Bolivar Ba-Lues Are' from *Brilliant Corners*, and a fine 'Body And Soul'. 'Just a Gigolo' is a solo performance, played in a self-consciously distracted manner, as if saying It's a *hell* of a job, but someone has to do it.

*** Monk's Dream Columbia 40786
Monk; Charlie Rouse (*ts*); John Ore (*b*); Frankie Dunlop (*d*). 10 & 11/62.
This was Monk's first album for CBS and, as Peter Keepnews points out in the reissue notes, it established the pattern for those that followed. Each contained a mixture of originals – most of them now getting quite long in the tooth – and standards, and marked a slight softening of Monk's once rather alien attack. The standards performances – 'Body And Soul', 'Just A Gigolo', 'Sweet And Lovely' – are not always immediately identifiable with the brittle, lateral-thinking genius of the Blue Notes and Riversides and are increasingly dependent on rather formulaic solutions. 'Monk's Dream' and 'Bye-Ya' are slightly tame and the changes of title on 'Bolivar Blues' (weirdly phoneticized in its first version) and 'Five Spot Blues' (originally 'Blues Five Spot') suggest how much Monk was unconsciously and partially moving towards the mainstream.
  No one seems to have told Charlie Rouse, who really takes over on some of these tracks. The saxophonist sounds jagged and angular where the rhythm has been somewhat rationalized, intensely bluesy where the harmony begins to sound legitimate. Worthy of three stars for Rouse alone.

*** The Composer Columbia 463338
Monk; Charlie Rouse (*ts*); Larry Gales, John Ore, Butch Warren (*b*); Frankie Dunlop, Ben Riley (*d*); unidentified band conducted by Oliver Nelson. 11/62, 2, 3 & 5/63, 10/64, 3/65, 11/68.
A reasonable sampling of mostly live material from relatively late in Monk's active life. There's a previously unreleased version of 'Blue Monk', arranged for big band and conducted by Oliver Nelson, and two other tracks ('Brilliant Corners' and 'Reflections') from the same session. As Lee Jeske points out in his liner-note, Monk was often criticized for performing the same material over and over again, and this does represent something of a problem for the collector, who may well lose track of how many solo performances of 'Round Midnight' or 'Ruby, My Dear' he or she actually owns. Though these performances all date from the mid-1960s, all the compositions are from the immediate post-war decade, a further sign of the way Monk's genius as a composer diminished after the mid-'50s. Obviously pitched at newcomers as a useful compilation of the most important themes, this is a slightly muted introduction to Monk. Almost everything is available in a better and more varied form elsewhere.

*** Criss Cross Columbia 469184
Monk; Charlie Rouse (*ts*); John Ore (*b*); Frankie Dunlop (*d*). 63.
One of the drabbest of the Columbias, *Criss Cross* nevertheless contains two sterling tracks: a vibrant 'Don't Blame Me' and a subtly varied 'Eronel'. The rhythm section are slightly better recorded than on some of the sessions, as if to make up for Monk's occasional lack of enterprise.

***(*) Big Band / Quartet In Concert Columbia 476898 2CD
Monk; Thad Jones (*c*); Nick Travis (*t*); Eddie Bert (*tb*); Charlie Rouse (*ts*); Steve Lacy (*ss*); Phil Woods (*as, cl*); Gene Allen (*bs, cl, bcl*); Butch Warren (*b*); Frank Dunlop (*d*). 12/63.
The original LP release trimmed this important document in an irritatingly Procrustean manner, lopping off two long orchestral numbers, 'Bye-Ya' and 'Light Blue', a tiny quartet version of 'Epistrophy' and a long, magisterial 'Misterioso', also by Monk, Rouse, Warren and Dunlop. The sound has also been tweaked into something like acceptable form, reducing the cavernous boom of the Philharmonic Hall at Lincoln Center, where the concert was recorded the day before New Year's Eve 1963. Monk himself sounds very relaxed, and one can't help comparing his almost Zen-like calm on occasions like this with Charles Mingus's torrential outpourings. The pianist's exchanges with Rouse on 'Misterioso' are some of his gentlest on record, and his re-invention of the obscure 'When It's Darkness On The Delta', a pop song from 1932, is redolent of great predecessors like Tatum, Waller and, at one point near the end, usually unnoticed, Earl Hines.
  The orchestra plays vigorously and well, seemingly well acquainted with Hall Overton's charts and able to handle some of the quicker turns on 'I Mean You' and 'Oska T', neither of them unchallenging charts, with great aplomb. Fascinating to see (and occasionally hear) that most resolute Monkian, Steve Lacy, in the ensemble; what this must have meant to him. This is a valuable recording, long overdue for reissue and rehabilitation.

*** Solo Monk Columbia 471248
Monk (*p* solo). 1 & 10/64, 2 & 3/65.
A rather lacklustre collection of unaccompanied performances, this doesn't compare with earlier, more focused endeavours. Monk's solos always seem to work better in the wider context of group albums, but it may prove useful now and again to concentrate on the bare bones and, from that perspective, this is a useful introduction to Monk's still underrated piano style.

*** **1963: In Japan** Prestige PRCD SP 202

    Monk; Charlie Rouse (*ts*); Butch Warren (*b*); Frankie Dunlop (*d*). 5/63.

*** **Tokyo Concerts** Columbia 466552

    As above.

Monk's reputation in Japan was cemented much more quickly even than in Europe, and these document his first successful visit. The first of the pair was recorded at the TBS television studios. The group initially sound wary and uninspired, but almost every track catches light at some point. The standout performances on *Tokyo Concerts* are 'Pannonica' and a marvellous 'Hackensack'. By his own high standard, Rouse is rather anonymous and plays surprisingly little of consequence, but the set as a whole is well worth hearing.

***(*) **It's Monk's Time** Columbia 468405

    Monk; Charlie Rouse (*ts*); Butch Warren (*b*); Ben Riley (*d*). 64.

One of the best sessions of the period, recorded at the height of Monk's critical standing. In 1964 he was the subject of a cover story in *Time* magazine, one of only three jazz artists (all piano players, but no more clues) to have been accorded that accolade. There's certainly nothing compromised or middle-market about this tough, abrasive set. Monk's sound had softened considerably over the past decade, partly as a result of playing on better instruments, partly because of more sensitive recording set-ups. He still sounds angular and oblique, but he does so without the percussive edge he was wont to bring to theme statements like 'Lulu's Back In Town', 'Stuffy Turkey' and 'Shuffle Boil', which stand out from the rest for the piquancy of the melodic invention.

*** **Live At The It Club** Columbia 4691862

    Monk; Charlie Rouse (*ts*); Larry Gales (*b*); Ben Riley (*d*). 10/64.

*** **Live At The Jazz Workshop** Columbia 4691832

    As above. 11/64.

Established connoisseurs of live Monk material will value the latter of these for a fizzing performance of the challenging 'Hackensack' and for a rhythmically adroit 'Bright Mississippi', on which Monk calls the shots to his rhythm section. The earlier session is more convincing all round, though, with particularly fine readings of 'Misterioso', 'Blue Monk' and 'Ba-Lu Bolivar Ba-Lues Are'. As with several of these reissues, the sound reveals significantly more of the bass and drums than on earlier sessions. Good, but it would be hard to argue Monk's greatness on the strength of these alone.

*** **Straight, No Chaser** Columbia 468409

    Monk; Charlie Rouse (*ts*); Larry Gales (*b*); Frankie Dunlop (*d*). 66.

Includes the intriguing 'Japanese Folk Song' and a spanking version of 'We See', but this is as late as Monk gets really interesting. There are already *longueurs*, and too many of the eccentricities seem carefully studied. Much of the material is derived from a film made about Monk that further raised his critical standing without contributing substantially to awareness of what truly made him distinctive.

(*) **Monk Underground Columbia 460066

    Monk; Charlie Rouse (*ts*); Larry Gales (*b*); Ben Riley (*d*). 12/67, 2 & 12/68.

The contrived surrealism of the cover, with Monk seated at the piano in an overstuffed junk basement, a machine-pistol slung over his shoulder, may have been intended to appeal to a younger, rock audience. The music within is equally ersatz, perfectly straightforward interpretations lent a modicum of credibility by angular, out-of-tempo theme statements, bizarre shifts of metre and key, and a lazy, self-defeating approach to the solos that replaces Monk's usual careful craftsmanship with a loose, unsteady approach to chord changes.

*** **Monk's Blues** Columbia 475698

    Monk; Robert Bryant, Frederick Hill, Conte Candoli, Bob Brookmeyer (*t*); Bill Byers, Mike
    Wimberley (*tb*); Ernie Small, Tom Scott, Gene Cipriano, Ernie Watts, Charlie Rouse (*sax*);
    Howard Roberts (*g*); Larry Gales (*b*); Ben Riley (*d*); John Guerin (*perc*). 11/68.

For some reason, this one was credited to Thelonious Sphere Monk, his full name. Given the cost of this Oliver Nelson-arranged and -produced session, perhaps Columbia wanted it to sound as black-tie as possible. Monk came out to the Coast to do the session and to pick up a few side-gigs at the same time. It had apparently been impossible for Nelson, who was a busy television and film music writer and arranger, to get over to New York. What isn't clear is whether the pianist was attracted first and foremost by Nelson or by the chance to work in the sunshine for a while.

    Nelson certainly gives the complex tunes highly convincing arrangements. The horn players have some lip-busting parts to negotiate on 'Little Rootie Tootie' and 'Brilliant Corners', but they seem to manage. There was only one non-Monk tune on the list, Teo Macero's wryly titled 'Consecutive Seconds', and it stands out very prominently. The CD is filled out with about ten minutes of new material, including a rather slushy 'Round Midnight' which was quite properly omitted from the original release.

***(*) **The London Collection: Volume 1** Black Lion BLCD 760101
    Monk; Al McKibbon (*b*); Art Blakey (*d*). 11/71.
*** **The London Collection: Volume 2** Black Lion BLCD 760116
    As above. 11/71.
*** **The London Collection: Volume 3** Black Lion BLCD 760142
    As above. 11/71.
The solo performances on *Volume 1* offer a fair impression of how Monk's ability to invest improvisations on self-written or standard ('Lover Man', 'Darn That Dream') themes with the same logical
development and sense of overall form that one might look for in a notated piece. It isn't clear that
Blakey was an entirely sympathetic accompanist, and some of the faster-paced numbers sound a little
overpowered. Certainly, McKibbon is difficult to hear over clustered accents on the bass drum. There is
a wonderful improvisation, mockingly called 'Chordially' on *Volume 3*, which is presumably meant to
refute the charge that Monk's apparent indifference to conventional changes playing was a token of
limited technique rather than a conscious strategy. Useful and often enjoyable sessions, these are still
rather late in the day for genuine fireworks.

*** **Monk In Italy** Original Jazz Classics OJC 488
    Monk; Charlie Rouse (*ts*); John Ore (*b*); Frankie Dunlop (*d*).
*** **Monk In France** Original Jazz Classics OJC 670
    Monk; Charlie Rouse (*ts*); John Ore (*b*); Frankie Dunlop (*d*).
A couple of European tour dates which Riverside released as contract-closers with Monk. Both feature
the quartet in quite sunny mood, but both also contain the seeds of routine which would trouble many
of the 1960s recordings.

***(*) **The Thelonious Monk Memorial Album** Milestone 47064
***(*) **Thelonious Monk And The Jazz Giants** Riverside 60-018
    **** **The Complete Riverside Recordings** Riverside 022 15CD
    As above OJC discs.
The two compilations are perfectly adequate snapshots of Monk's Riverside period, though casual
listeners would be better off zeroing in on the four-star records listed above. *The Complete Riverside
Recordings* is another monument for the shelves, but there is so little flab and so much music in this set
that it defies criticism. Superbly annotated by producer Keepnews, and including many out-takes and
extras absent from the original records (though many of those have now been restored to the CD
reissues of the appropriate albums), this is enough for a lifetime's study. On that basis alone we award it
our (becoming coveted) crown.

J. R. Monterose (1927–93) TENOR SAXOPHONE, SOPRANO SAXOPHONE

**** **Straight Ahead** Xanadu 1233
    Monterose; Tommy Flanagan (*p*); Paul Chambers (*b*); Pete LaRoca (*d*). 11/59.
***(*) **The Message** Fresh Sound FSRCD 201
    As above, except replace Chambers with Jimmy Garrison (*b*). 11/59.
*** **Live At The Tender Trap** Fresh Sound FSCD 1023
    Monterose; Dale Oehler (*p*); Dick Vanizel (*b*); Joe Abodeely (*d*); Al Jarreau (*v*). 63.
*** **In Action** Bainbridge BCD 503
    As above, except replace Vanizel with Gary Allen (*b*). 64.
*** **A Little Pleasure** Reservoir RSR CD 109
    Monterose; Tommy Flanagan (*p*). 4/81.
Monterose made a considerable impression on Charles Mingus's *Pithecanthropus Erectus*, but he did
not record much on his own account. The Xanadu is exceptional (and all the more so on CD), owing a
great deal of its success to the tirelessly lyrical Flanagan, who also appears on *The Message* and on the
later record.
    Monterose experimented for many years with an amplified saxophone. One can understand its appeal.
He has a rather quiet and understated voice, somewhat similar to Warne Marsh, though less bleached.
On parts of *The Message* the parallel is almost uncanny, even down to specific phrases on 'Violets For
Your Furs' and 'I Remember Clifford', where he uses simple arch shapes with altered harmonics to
create a strange, slightly distanced quality. Garrison, as was his fate, remains poorly audible, but LaRoca
is again very good and totally musical.
    The two early-'60s sessions feature J. R.'s regular band, an able if slightly colourless unit, based at The
Tender Trap in Cedar Rapids, Iowa. *In Action* is widely regarded as his best record, but it has been
available only as a limited-edition vinyl record and has acquired semi-legendary status among collectors.
Most of the material is original. Themes like 'Waltz For Claire' and 'Herky Hawks' confirm

Monterose's abrasively witty but also romantic turn of thought, as well as the highly distinctive, attract-ively underpowered saxophone style. The group (with minor variants) enjoyed a long residency at The Tender Trap. Occasional guest players were David Sanborn and the young Al Jarreau, who studied psychology at the University of Iowa. His vocals are a must for collectors, as an earnest of the subtle stylist he was to become in later years. Alas, no glimpse of the young Sanborn, who went on to make more money per record than J. R. did in his entire career.

A Little Pleasure is Monterose's recording debut with soprano saxophone and it casts him in mostly reflective mood. There are two good originals: the 3/4 'Pain And Suffering . . . And A Little Pleasure' and the less satisfying 'Vinnie's Pad'. Monterose stays with the straight horn for 'A Nightingale Sang In Berkeley Square' (with Flanagan playing the verse) and on 'Central Park West', whose solo underlines just how little dependent on Coltrane Monterose has been down the years. It's very intimately miked, and Monterose's breathing is very audible. None of these discs is technically A1 but, as examples of a very gifted musician who never achieved major label success, all are valuable.

Wes Montgomery (1925–68) GUITAR, BASS GUITAR

*** **A Dynamic New Jazz Sound** Original Jazz Classics OJC 034
　　Montgomery; Mel Rhyne (*org*); Paul Parker (*d*). 10/59.
**** **Incredible Jazz Guitar** Original Jazz Classics OJC 036
　　Montgomery; Tommy Flanagan (*p*); Percy Heath (*b*); Albert 'Tootie' Heath (*d*). 1/60.
***(*) **Movin' Along** Original Jazz Classics OJC 089
　　Montgomery; James Clay (*ts, f*); Victor Feldman (*p*); Sam Jones (*b*); Louis Hayes (*d*). 10/60.
***(*) **So Much Guitar** Original Jazz Classics OJC 233
　　Montgomery; Hank Jones (*p*); Ron Carter (*b*); Lex Humphries (*d*); Ray Barretto (*perc*). 8/61.
***(*) **Full House** Original Jazz Classics OJC 106
　　Montgomery; Johnny Griffin (*ts*); Wynton Kelly (*p*); Paul Chambers (*b*); Jimmy Cobb (*d*). 6/62.
(*) **Boss Guitar Original Jazz Classics OJC 261
　　As for *Dynamic*, except replace Parker with Jimmy Cobb (*d*). 4/63.
*** **Portrait Of Wes** Original Jazz Classics OJC 144
　　As for *Full House*, except replace Cobb with George Brown (*d*). 10/63.
*** **Fusion!** Original Jazz Classics OJC 368
　　Montgomery; Phil Bodner (*sax, f*); Dick Hyman (*p, cel*); Hank Jones (*p*); Kenny Burrell (*g*);
　　Milt Hinton (*b*); Osie Johnson (*d*); strings. 4/63.
**** **The Complete Riverside Recordings** Riverside 12 RCD 4408 12CD
　　As for the above, except add Nat Adderley (*c*); Joe Gordon (*t*); Cannonball Adderley (*as*);
　　Johnny Griffin, Harold Land (*ts*); Barry Harris, George Shearing, Bobby Timmons (*p*); Victor
　　Feldman, Milt Jackson, Buddy Montgomery (*vib*); Ray Brown, Monk Montgomery (*b*); Walter
　　Perkins (*d*); woodwinds; strings. 59–63.

Wes Montgomery gave off that sense of effortlessness that is always bad karma in jazz. A little *sweat* and preferably some pain are almost considered *de rigueur*. But Montgomery used to loose off solos as if he was sitting on his back porch talking to friends. He used a homely, thumb-picking technique, rather than a plectrum or the faster finger-picking approach. Stylistically, he copied Charlie Christian's Ur-bop and added elements of Django Reinhardt's harmonic conception. It's interesting and ironic that Montgomery's most prominent latterday disciple, George Benson, should have made almost exactly the same career move, trading off a magnificent improvisational sense against commercial success.

In career terms, Montgomery really did seem to prefer his back porch. During the 1950s, which should have been his big decade, he hung around his native Indianapolis, playing part time. When his recording career got going again, he was still capable of great things. The massive Riverside box, including everything he did under the auspices of the label, has turned this entry on its head. Though much of the best material was and still is available separately, access to it in this bulk, and with a huge range of material recorded for other leaders – the Adderleys, Shearing, Land – and with the Montgomery Brothers makes a substantial difference to our view of the guitarist, highlighting his awesome consist-ency, pointing a slightly accusing finger at his tendency to settle for the obvious and familiar on occasion, rarely pushing out into the more experimental mode that he had flirted with early on.

The boxed set has a price-tag commensurate with its size, and many listeners will feel the need to pick one or more of the individual discs instead. Guitar–organ trios take a little getting used to nowadays, but *New Sound* and *Boss Guitar* contain some of the guitarist's most vibrant recordings. While some of the best of the material – ''Round Midnight', 'Fried Pies', and so on – has been sampled on the Milestone sets, below, these are worth hearing and having in their entirety. For no readily discernible reason, *Boss Guitar* sounds flatter than the others.

Incredible Jazz Guitar is probably the best Montgomery record currently available. His solo on 'West

Coast Blues' is very nearly incredible, though there are hints of banality even there, in his trademark octave runs, which he borrowed from Django. Flanagan may have slipped the engineer a sawbuck, for he's caught beautifully, and nicely forward in the mix. His lines on Sonny Rollins's buoyant 'Airegin' are exactly complementary to the guitarist's. There's a 'D-natural Blues' and covers of 'In Your Own Sweet Way' and 'Polka Dots And Moonbeams', which further hint at Montgomery's eventual artistic inertia, but for the moment he sounds like a master, and this is the one to go for if you aren't investing in the big box .

On *So Much*, Montgomery's smooth and uncannily fluent lines and Jones's elegant two-handedness lift 'Cotton Tail' out of the ordinary. Never a blindingly fast player, Montgomery specialized in sweeping oppositions of register that lend an illusion of pace to relatively stately passages.

***(*) Far Wes Pacific Jazz 94475
Montgomery; Pony Poindexter (*as*); Harold Land (*ts*); Buddy Montgomery (*p*); Monk Montgomery (*b*); Tony Bazley, Louis Hayes (*d*); collective personnel. 4/58, 10/59.

A welcome reissue (of the better 1958 sessions particularly). Montgomery plays fluently if a trifle dispassionately but emerges here as a composer of some substance. The title-track is in relatively conventional bop idiom but has an attractive melodic contour (which Land largely ignores) and a well-judged 'turn' towards the end of the main statement. The later sessions are a trifle disappointing, though the great Louis Hayes weighs in at the drum kit with characteristic confidence. It's worth buying for the first half-dozen tracks alone.

*** The Alternative Wes Montgomery Milestone M 47065
Montgomery; Johnny Griffin (*ts*); James Clay (*f*); Victor Feldman, Wynton Kelly, Buddy Montgomery (*p*); Mel Rhyne (*org*); Milt Jackson (*vib*); Paul Chambers, Sam Jones, Monk Montgomery (*b*); George Brown, Jimmy Cobb, Louis Hayes, Philly Joe Jones, Bobby Thomas (*d*); orchestra. 10/60–11/63.

A mass of material, and no maps. Some of Montgomery's better later performances were buried away on rather unselective, buffet-table Milestone LPs, but the cumulative impression is of incipient commercial *longueur*; certainly the extra takes on *Alternative* don't contain any real revelations.

Montgomery himself claimed to have been at his best a full decade before, but he spent most of the 1950s out of the limelight. He still sounds much more authoritative in the small groups, and *Movin' Along* is a fine record. There is some intelligent interplay with Feldman, who slotted into the guitarist's conception without a blink, and Clay has just enough acid in his tone to save the overall effect from becoming too bland and sugary.

It's hard to think that any but the most dogged of fans would want all the alternatives if the original releases were freely available on CD. For the time being, though, they represent a decent purchase.

The title *Fusion* is interesting because in a sense Wes was one of the figures who lay behind later attempts to integrate rock rhythm and energy with jazz harmonies. Ironically, there isn't much trace of that here. Jimmy Jones's arrangements are engagingly tight and spare – one has to admire the sheer workmanship of 'Baubles, Bangles And Beads' – but the one thing these sessions lack is energy. Wes sounds positively pipe-and-slippers and, but for 'God Bless The Child', rather detached and disengaged. As with all these later recordings, though, remastering significantly improves the overall balance of sound.

**** Impressions: The Verve Jazz Sides Verve 521 690 2CD
Montgomery; Donald Byrd, Mel Davis, Bernie Glow, Danny Moore, Joe Newman, Jimmy Nottingham, Ernie Royal, Clark Terry, Snooky Young (*t*); Wayne Andre, Jimmy Cleveland, Urbie Green, Quentin Jackson, Melba Liston, John Messner, Tony Studd, Bill Watrous, Chauncey Welsh (*tb*); James Buffington (*frhn*); Don Butterfield, Harvey Phillips (*tba*); Jerome Richardson (*ts, ss, f*); Stan Webb (*as, bs, cl*); Ray Beckenstein (*as*); Bob Ashton, Jerry Dodgion, Romeo Penque (*reeds*); Danny Bank (*bs, af, f, bcl*); Walter Kane (*bs, cl*); Herbie Hancock, Roger Kellaway, Wynton Kelly, Bobby Scott (*p*); Jimmy Smith (*org*); Jack Jennings (*vib*); Al Casamenti, Bucky Pizzarelli (*g*); Paul Chambers, Bob Cranshaw, George Duvivier (*b*); Jimmy Cobb, Sol Gubin, Grady Tate (*d*); Ray Barretto, Willie Bobo (*perc*). 11/64, 6, 11 & 12/65, 3, 9 & 11/66.

*** Movin' Wes Verve 810 045
Montgomery; Ernie Royal, Clark Terry, Snooky Young (*t*); Jimmy Cleveland, Urbie Green, Quentin Jackson, Chauncey Welsh (*tb*); Don Butterfield (*tba*); Jerome Richardson (*sax, f*); Bobby Scott (*p*); Bob Cranshaw (*b*); Grady Tate (*d*); Willie Bobo (*perc*). 11/64.

**(*) Tequila Verve 831671
Montgomery; George Devens (*vib*); Ron Carter (*b*); Grady Tate (*d*); Ray Barreto (*perc*); Bernard Eichem, Arnold Eidus, Paul Gershman, Emmanuel Green, Julius Held, Harry Lookofsky, Joe Malin, Gene Orloff (*vn*); Abe Kessler, Charles McCracken, George Ricci, Harvey Shapiro (*clo*). 3 & 5/66.

The 'jazz' in the title of the two-CD set is a careful hedge, in recognition of the unreconstructed commerciality of much that Wes was doing at the time. Just as the Riversides have realigned the pre-1963 material, this elegantly packaged compilation brings together the best of albums like *Willow Weep For Me*, *The Small Group Recordings*, *Just Walkin'*, *Smokin' At The Half Note*, *California Dreaming*, *Goin' Out Of My Head* and *Movin' Wes*, which remains available in its own right.

As an entity, it has a lot more presence than the majority of the later discs; remastering brings guitar and band into better balance than on the original release. The only soloist on the date, Wes is playing very smoothly indeed. Tunes like 'The Phoenix Love Theme', 'Moca Flor' and 'Theodora' are little more than beefed-up elevator music. The title-tune (which comes in two parts), 'Born To Be Blue' and 'People', are a bit more focused, but there still isn't much excitement.

Tequila is one of the sessions that Verve have plundered in order to reposition Wes as a founding father of both acid jazz and a smooth, ambient saloon funk. It finds Montgomery rather wearily putting in his time with the Claus Ogerman Orchestra. 'Bumpin' on Sunset' is of course a long-standing favourite (subsequently revived by Brian Auger's Oblivion Express in the jazz equivalent of minimalist trance music). Montgomery is still harmonically inventive, but the arrangements are too pre-packaged for very much in the way of surprises.

Montgomery Brothers GROUP

*** **Groove Yard** Original Jazz Classics OJC 139
   Buddy Montgomery (*vib, p*); Monk Montgomery (*b*); Bobby Thomas (*d*). 1/61.
A little like the Jackson Five, it can be a bit difficult to maintain an even focus on all the members of this once rather successful group. Monk and Buddy doubtless gained considerably from their association with Wes, but he also gained a sympathetic, supportive group which never quite attained its full potential in the midst of Wes's Riverside period. This record (and another recorded in Canada, still not on CD) represent the group's best output. Buddy's vibes playing was not quite in the Milt Jackson class but it was more than workmanlike, and his piano playing, which developed in years to come, is bright and rhythmic, with a slightly melancholy quality which suits the group very well. Monk has always been overshadowed, but the CD transfer allows him to come through quite strongly and his passage-work on 'If I Should Lose You' and 'Groove Yard' is quite impressive.

Tete Montoliu (born 1933) PIANO

***(*) **Songs For Love** Enja 2040
   Montoliu (*p* solo). 9/71.
*** **That's All** Steeplechase SCCD 31199
   Montoliu (*p* solo). 9/71.
Montoliu is, along with Martial Solal, Giorgio Gaslini, Alex Schlippenbach and Howard Riley, one of the reasons why Europe has a jazz piano tradition of its own in post-bop jazz. Dazzlingly fast in execution, his improvisations are mostly based on a standard bebop repertoire, yet at his best he seems driven to making his music fresh and new from record to record. From moment to moment he might suggest Tatum, Powell or Garner, and his feeling for blues playing is particularly sharp. He began recording in 1958, but until recently most of his '60s sessions as a leader were hidden on obscure, out-of-print Spanish labels (for contemporaneous work as a sideman, see under Dexter Gordon's entry). Frustratingly, a live set for Impulse! at the Village Vanguard in 1967, with Richard Davis and Elvin Jones, has never been released.

Montoliu opened a prolific decade of recording (there are plenty of obscure earlier sessions still to come on CD) with a single session in Munich, half of which was released at the time by Enja, the remainder turning up many years later on two Steeplechase albums, of which *Lush Life* has since been deleted. Little to choose among the three discs, but the first has a few originals by Tete and a thoughtful improvisation on 'Two Catalan Songs'. The question of Montoliu's employment of his Catalan roots in a jazz environment is an interesting one: his oft-quoted remark, 'Basically, all Catalans are blacks', isn't very helpful, but there's little doubt that he is exceptionally responsive to using his native music in a post-bop setting.

*** **Temas Brasilenos** Ensayo ENY-CD-3951
   Montoliu; Alberto Moraleda (*b*); Miguel Angel Lizandra (*d*). 11/73.
*** **Catalonian Fire** Steeplechase SCCD 31017
   Montoliu; Niels-Henning Orsted-Pedersen (*b*); Albert 'Tootie' Heath (*d*). 5/74.

***(*) **Tete!** Steeplechase SCCD 31029
    As above. 5/74.
*** **Music For Perla** Steeplechase SCCD 31021
    Montoliu (*p* solo). 5/74.
*** **Boleros** Ensayo ENY-CD-3473
    Montoliu; Manuel Elias (*b*); Peer Wyboris (*d*); Rogelio Juarez (*perc*).
***(*) **Tete A Tete** Steeplechase SCCD 31054
    As above. 2/76.
***(*) **Tootie's Tempo** Steeplechase SCCD 31108
    As above. 2/76.
*** **Yellow Dolphin Street / Catalonian Folk Songs** Timeless SJP 107/116
    Montoliu (*p* solo). 2–12/77.
*** **Blues For Myself** Ensayo ENY-CD-3954
    Montoliu; Eric Peter (*b*); Peer Wyboris (*d*). 1/77.

Montoliu seemed to release a lot of records in the 1970s, but actually had only a few concentrated bursts of recording. The four albums by the trio with NHOP and Heath remain his most impressive offerings: played with both elegance and fire, his improvisations on favourite themes – Montoliu is seldom very adventurous in his choice of material, preferring the same clutch of harmonically interesting standards and bebop themes – have a poise and dash which make one overlook the frequent appearance of many familiar runs and manipulations of the beat. Pedersen, who loves to play with a pianist of outsize technique, holds nothing back in his own playing, while Heath's rather gruff and unfussy drumming makes him a nearly ideal timekeeper for the situation. Of the Steeplechases, *Tootie's Tempo* and *Tete!* are particularly good, but any one is highly entertaining. The solo records are slightly less interesting, though the Timeless session – combining an LP of standards and one of Catalonian tunes – has some thoughtful moments.

The Ensayo albums, all recorded in Barcelona, feature Tete in congenial local company and offer some of his most relaxed playing. *Temas Brasilenos* is based around four long medleys of choice material by Jobim, Barroso and others, and there are unusual touches on well-worn tunes like 'La Chica De Ipanema' and 'Desafinado' to refresh jaded ears. *Boleros* is a set of Spanish compositions and as such is a rarity in Montoliu's discography. But the problem with both discs is the unimaginative rhythm section in each case, and neither is especially well recorded. *Blues For Myself*, a set of five blues and two standards, is marginally ahead, with Peter and Wyboris reading Montoliu's moves ably enough, though again the Steeplechase sets offer better work.

*** **Catalonian Nights: Volume 1** Steeplechase SCCD 31148
    Montoliu; John Heard (*b*); Albert 'Tootie' Heath (*d*). 5/80.
*** **Catalonian Nights: Volume 2** Steeplechase SCCD 31241
    As above. 5/80.

A very exciting meeting, this one, but it's let down by an indifferent balance – Montoliu is almost drowned out by Heath at times – and a suspiciously battered piano. The second disc is worth having for the almost ecstatically driving 'I'll Remember April', but the music maintains a high standard throughout.

*** **The Music I Like To Play: Volume 1** Soul Note 121180-2
    Montoliu (*p* solo). 12/86.
*** **The Music I Like To Play: Volume 2** Soul Note 121200-2
    As above. 12/86.
*** **The Music I Like To Play: Volume 3** Soul Note 121230-2
    As above. 1/90.
*** **The Music I Like To Play: Volume 4** Soul Note 121250-2
    As above. 1/90.

Montoliu has tended throughout his career to get maximum mileage from each session. It should be noted here, though, that the two later volumes are from a later date. The difference is immediately apparent, not so much qualitatively as in the nature of his playing, which is much more percussive and direct. The earlier Soul Notes number among the most finished of Montoliu's albums, with a superior studio sound and one or two unexpected choices: Bobby Hutcherson's 'Little B's Poem', for instance, on the first record. But some routine improvisations betray that the pianist can defer to familiar patterns on some tunes that he knows a little too well. There's a nice smattering of Monk tunes on the latter pair and some ballads that have not previously figured in the Catalan's discography. Though it might seem a hefty investment to spring for all four, these are better value than most.

*** **Sweet 'N' Lovely: Volume 1** Fresh Sound FSR-CD 161
    Montoliu; Mundell Lowe (*g*). 9/89.

*** **Sweet 'N' Lovely: Volume 2** Fresh Sound FSR-CD 162
    As above. 9/89.
The clean and persuasive interplay here suggests a friendly empathy that makes this unlikely combination work out very well: Lowe keeps to his unassumingly skilful, swing-based style, and the ease with which it slips alongside Montoliu's playing suggests that the pianist is more of a conservative than his more ferocious moments suggest. Both discs were recorded on the same day and, as pleasing as they are, one will be enough for most listeners.

*** **The Man From Barcelona** Timeless SJP 368
    Montoliu; George Mraz (*b*); Lewis Nash (*d*). 10/90.
*** **A Spanish Treasure** Concord CCD 4493
    Montoliu; Rufus Reid (*b*); Akira Tana (*d*). 6/91.
Up-to-scratch trio dates: Reid and Tana sound a bit too boisterous for Montoliu's sprightly lines to cut through as they should, and the more reserved Mraz and Nash work out better. As capable as the playing here is, though, one wishes Montoliu would seek out a new format for his studio dates, which are sounding very much the same. The quintet session with Peter King and Gerard Presencer on *Morning '89* (Fresh Sound FRS-117, 2LP; still awaited on CD!) was a nice blast of fresh air.

*** **Music For Anna** Mas I Mas 002
    Montoliu; Hein Van der Geyn (*b*); Idris Muhammed (*d*). 10/92.
Montoliu has surfaced only rarely in the 1990s, but this fairly recent club set suggests that his playing has lost little of its flash or surprise. The dramatic deconstruction of 'I'll Remember April' is a single example, but it's something he does at some point on most of the tunes on offer. As with Solal, the pianist's uncommon syntax has become a commonplace with the wider currency of his work via recordings, yet the impact of his most vivid improvising remains startling, and it's good to have this recent reminder. Sound is decent – Van der Geyn comes through strongly – though the piano itself sounds like a sometimes unresponsive instrument.

Jack Montrose (born 1928) TENOR SAXOPHONE

*** **The Horn's Full** RCA Victor 74321 18521 2
    Montrose; Red Norvo (*vib*); Jim Hall, Barney Kessel (*g*); Max Bennett, Larry Wooten (*b*); Bill Dolney, Mel Lewis (*d*). 9–12/57.
Montrose cut four good albums as a leader, when the West Coast was still hot, and this reissue is a timely reminder of a player who was drastically sidelined by the decline of the music in the 1960s. Two different quintets – Norvo is common to both – handle this programme, and the notes show how Montrose was at pains to create counterpoint and contrast between sax, vibes and guitar almost throughout. The result is a set that flows into a single piece, and the manner suits the leader's own playing: he nudges his solos along an even line, but there's a sense of invention which has survived the years. Some of the arranging is on the cute side, and a few of the uptempo pieces seem a little gauche, but otherwise it's a worthwhile souvenir from a vanished part of jazz.

James Moody (born 1925) TENOR SAXOPHONE, ALTO SAXOPHONE, SOPRANO SAXOPHONE, FLUTE, VOCALS

*** **New Sounds** Blue Note CDP 784436
    Moody; Dave Burns, Elmon Wright (*t*); Ernie Henry (*as*); Cecil Payne (*bs*); James Forman (*p*); Nelson Boyd (*b*); Teddy Stewart (*d*). 10/48.
*** **Sax Talk** Vogue 113410
    Moody; Roger Guérin (*t*); Raymond Fol (*p*); Pierre Michelot (*b*); Pierre Lemarchand (*d*); Pepito Riebe (*perc*); unknown woodwinds and strings. 7/51.
***(*) **Moody's Mood For Blues** Original Jazz Classics OJC 1837
    Moody; Dave Burns (*t*); William Shepherd (*tb*); Pee Wee Moore (*bs*); Sadik Hakim, Jimmy Boyd (*p*); John Latham (*b*); Joe Harris, Clarence Johnson (*d*); Eddie Jefferson, Iona Wade (*v*). 1, 4 & 9/54, 1/55.
***(*) **Hi Fi Party** Original Jazz Classics OJC 1780
    Moody; Dave Burns (*t*); Bill Shepherd (*tb*); Numa Moore (*bs*); Jimmy Boyd (*p*); John Latham (*b*); Clarence Johnson (*d*); Eddie Jefferson (*v*). 9/54.
***(*) **Wail, Moody, Wail** Original Jazz Classics OJC 1791
    As above, except omit Jefferson. 1, 8 & 12/55.
Moody's affability and slightly zany vocals have led some to dismiss him as a lightweight. Even on the

song with which he is now inextricably associated he demonstrates fine if unorthodox improvisational skills. His debut, 'I'm In The Mood For Love', recorded with a Scandinavian group in 1949, was a big hit, establishing him as a bopper with a quirky sensibility and a sombre, tense side; this is confirmed on the Modernists' session for Blue Note, the earliest of the recordings above. Moody's distinctive sinuousness became even more obvious when he added soprano saxophone to his kit a little later in his career.

He's also joined on *Hi Fi Party* and on the extra 'I Got The Blues' on *Moods* by Eddie Jefferson, who reworked a vocal version of the hit, thereby (allegedly) giving King Pleasure the idea for adding his own lyrics to bebop tunes. Moody has a strongly vocalized tone and frequently appears to shape a solo to the lyric of a tune rather than simply to the chords or the written melody, and that vocalized sound is perhaps more evident on his alto playing, though he even adapts it later in his career to flute, using a 'legitimate' version of Roland Kirk's vocalization. The saxophonist was off the scene for much of the 1970s, certainly as far as significant recording was concerned, and his reputation went into something of a decline. Without star names, though, both *Hi Fi Party* and the rather less gimmicky and straight-ahead *Wail* establish a strong, individual sound that deserves to be more widely known and which certainly stands up very strongly alongside later works.

Moody's work for French Vogue at the turn of the 1950s was sharp and stylish, even in front of a rather curdled string-section. The quintet tracks are top-drawer, with 'Lover Come Back To Me' outstanding. The disc is shared with half a dozen tracks by Frank Foster from 1954: an agreeable and logical pairing.

*** Return From Overbrook GRP Chess 18102

Moody; John Moore, Flip Richard, Earl Turner (*t*); John Avant, William Shepherd (*tb*); Lenny Druss, Bill Atkins (*as*); Vito Price, Eddie Johnson, Sandy Mosse (*ts*); Pee Wee Moore, Pat Patrick (*bs*); Floyd Morris, Junior Mance (p); Jimmy Boyd (*p, peckhorn*); John Gray (*g*); Johnny Pate (*b, tba*); John Latham (*b*); Clarence Johnston (*d*); Eddie Jefferson, Red Holt (*d*). 56, 9/58.

There was a dark strain underneath Moody's joviality. In 1958 he spent a period in a sanatorium called Overbrook in New Jersey, using his time there to write arrangements for a larger band than usual. Producer Dave Usher decided to record him on his release and these tracks are the result, originally issued as *Last Train From Overbrook*, paired with the earlier *Flute 'N The Blues*, on which he concentrated to some extent on that instrument.

Moody never looked back after he left the Big House. The parallel with Charlie Parker and Camarillo wasn't lost on observers, and there is no mistaking the sheer exuberance and intensity of his playing on 'All The Things You Are', the wire-happy 'Last Train' and 'Tico-Tico'. Even 'The Moody One', preceded by a false start that stands as a parallel to Bird's 'Famous Alto Break' is an upbeat swinger.

The other session perhaps isn't quite so compelling, but there are wonderful things there as well, notably Eddie Jefferson's hipper-than-thou narrative on 'Birdland Story', 'I Cover The Waterfront' and 'Parker's Mood'. It all goes to make up a splendid record with, for a change in this music, an unambiguously happy ending.

**(*) Sweet And Lovely Novus PD 83063

Moody; Dizzy Gillespie (*t, v*); Marc Cohen (*p, syn*); Todd Coolman (*b*); Akira Tana (*d*). 3/89.

On the sleeve, Moody mock-complains that people are still shouting for 'Moody's Mood For Love': 'I love It!' *Sweet And Lovely* is just a shade too mellowed and saccharin and Cohen's organ-like synth accompaniments are horrible, but this is the best of a pretty drab bunch on Novus, the rest having been deleted since our last edition. Dizzy's singing takes some handling, though he plays with great wit and the elder-statesman act carries the whole thing. Unlike his old teacher, Moody sat it out as long as rock seemed to be the only thing anyone wanted. He proves here that he could still play when he wanted to, and live appearances in the 1990s consolidated the rehab.

Jemeel Moondoc ALTO SAXOPHONE

*** Konstanze's Delight Soul Note 121041

Moondoc; Roy Campbell (*t*); Khan Jamal (*vib*); William Parker (*b*); Dennis Charles (*d*); Ellen Christi (*v*). 10/81.

**(*) Nostalgia In Times Square Soul Note 121141

Moondoc; Bern Nix (*g*); Ron Burton (*p*); William Parker (*b*); Dennis Charles (*d*). 11/85.

Musically, Moondoc belongs to an earlier age, in one of his mate Cecil Taylor's '60s groups, perhaps. His button-holing argument and raw, untutored approach certainly don't sound like an '80s product. The earlier of these consists of just three tracks of dramatically decreasing size. At half an hour, 'Konstanze's Delight' (she is the lady who took the cover shot) is well into stoppage time, and vocalist Ellen Christi has long since run out of significant things to do. For all its limitations, it does have much to recommend it, not least Jamal's tireless attempts to thread together the two out-of-sync horn-lines. A broadly similar group is weakened by the replacement of vibes with piano and the addition of Nix's Ornette-influenced chugging on guitar.

Moondoc comes across as a man absolutely convinced of his own mission and thus difficult to ignore, but with a tendency to reach conclusions some time after everyone else. One might recommend a long structured course of listening, except that half-way through he'd undoubtedly be back up on his feet again, arguing the toss.

Brew Moore (1924–73) TENOR SAXOPHONE

***(*) **Svinget 14** Black Lion BLCD 760164
> Moore; Sahib Shihab (*as*); Lars Gullin (*bs*); Louis Hjulmand (*vib*); Bent Axen (*p*); Niels-Henning Orsted-Pedersen (*b*); William Schiopffe (*d*). 9/62.
*** **I Should Care** Steeplechase SCCD 36019
> Moore; Atli Bjorn (*p*); Benny Nielsen (*b*); William Schioppfe (*d*). 4/65.

Moore was a terrific but star-crossed tenor player, at his best as good as Getz and Sims but never able to get a career together as they did. He left only a small number of records behind him, and only two are on CD so far. The Black Lion disc originally appeared on Debut and is full of fine blowing: 'Ergo' and the title-piece are superb improvisations with Moore at full stretch, his lightly foggy tone rounding all the corners and easing through problems without a murmur, while two duets with Gullin and a fierce blow with Shihab on 'The Monster' are outstandingly fine. The only problem is with the sound, which seems to break up into distortion quite often. The Steeplechase album is a surviving memento from a stay in Copenhagen: solid, but not quite Brew at his best. The city turned out to be his nemesis: Moore died when he fell down some stairs in Copenhagen in 1973.

Glen Moore (born 1941) DOUBLE BASS, PIANO

(*) **Dragonetti's Dream veraBra 2154
> Moore (*b, p* solo). 7/95.

This gifted bassist spent his early years with Ted Curson and Jake Hanna, plus a stint in Paul Bley's Synthesiser Show, before joining the Paul Winter Consort and taking the step that would ultimately lead to the formation of Oregon. His duets with the other string players in the group, guitarist Ralph Towner and sitarist Collin Walcott, were always a feature of Oregon's live performance, and the former pairing also recorded together outside the group. In recent times Moore has made records with singer Nancy King (they fall outside our remit) and as a solo performer. *Dragonetti's Dream* is a very mixed bag. There are fast, jazzy pieces, played with the fingers, slow sonorous *arco* chants, like 'Red And Black', and some thoroughly dismal New Age material. Unlike Towner, Moore is no piano player and most of his attempts to do so result in nothing more than indulgent noodling. That being said, there is much to admire here (including a wry dedication to skater Tanya Harding) and much of straightforward beauty.

Michael Moore CLARINET, BASS CLARINET, ALTO SAXOPHONE, ETC.

***(*) **Négligé** Ramboy 04
> Moore; Alex Maguire (*p*); Ernst Reijseger (*clo*); Michael Vatcher (*perc*). 12/89, 5/92.

Probably best known from Gerry Hemingway's Quintet, where he replaced the rather more mainstream Don Byron, Moore has moved his base of operations to Europe, where he has found a more sympathetic outlet for his demanding music. A brilliant composer as well as instrumentalist, he mixes structural elements with passages of complete freedom, and he is not afraid to use non-tempered sounds (or sheer noise) for dramatic effect.

On *Négligé* he has assembled a like-minded group. Maguire is completely at ease in environments like these, and his own 'Sparky' and 'Epigram' sit at the heart of the disc. There are 15 tracks, offering a good initial sample of Moore's music.

Ralph Moore (born 1956) TENOR SAXOPHONE, SOPRANO SAXOPHONE

*** **Round Trip** Reservoir RSR CD 104
> Moore; Brian Lynch (*t, flhn*); Kevin Eubanks (*g*); Benny Green (*p*); Rufus Reid (*b*); Kenny Washington (*d*). 12/85.

***(*) **623 C Street** Criss Cross Criss 1028
>   Moore; David Kikoski (*p*); Buster Williams (*b*); Billy Hart (*d*). 2/87.

**** **Rejuvenate!** Criss Cross Criss 1035
>   Moore; Steve Turre (*tb, conch*); Mulgrew Miller (*p*); Peter Washington (*b*); Marvin 'Smitty' Smith (*d*). 2/88.

*** **Images** Landmark LCD 1520
>   Moore; Terence Blanchard (*t*); Benny Green (*p*); Peter Washington (*b*); Kenny Washington (*d*); Victor See Yuen (*perc*). 12/88.

***(*) **Furthermore** Landmark LCD 1526
>   Moore; Roy Hargrove (*t*); Benny Green (*p*); Peter Washington (*b*); Victor Lewis, Kenny Washington (*d*). 3/90.

***(*) **Who Is It That You Are** Denon CY 75778
>   Moore; Benny Green (*p*); Peter Washington (*b*); Billy Higgins (*d*). 4/93.

London-born Moore has a muscular and very distinctive tone that renders the title of the recent Denon entirely rhetorical. Moore has always known who he is and where he is going, even if in the early days his self-confidence was not yet accompanied by much profundity. A hard bopper in the approved retro style, he has demonstrated that there is still plenty of good music to squeeze out of the idiom. Moore does nothing to ironize it or spice it up with contemporary references (other, perhaps, than Kevin Eubanks's soupy guitar on parts of *Round Trip*, for which he also wrote the final track).

Rudy van Gelder has been engineering this kind of material for longer than even he cares to remember, and all the records are technically flawless. The performances are equally unexceptional but may prove a little cool. Though his writing skills have sharpened considerably ('Hopscotch' on *Furthermore*, 'Josephine', 'C. R. M.' and 'Song For Soweto' on *Rejuvenate!*), he draws much of his material from piano-centred late bop – Bud Powell's 'Un Poco Loco' on *623 C Street*, 'Monk's Dream' on *Furthermore* – though rarely anything as ambitious as Elmo Hope's inventively Monkish 'One Second, Please', which appears on Moore's *Images*. This is a fine set, often lifted by Blanchard's contribution and often sounding like his album rather than Moore's. The quartet tracks are perfectly self-sufficient, though, and Moore's solos on 'Enigma' and 'Morning Star' are deftly constructed in such a way as to include choruses up in the trumpet range.

His soprano playing, restricted to 'Cecilia' and 'Christina' on *623 C Street*, still needs thinking out, and he seems to have some intonation and breath-control problems, neither of which are remotely evident in his supremely confident tenor playing. One to watch, not so much because he promises to shake the foundations, but simply because he's so consistently good.

The Denon marks a slight change of direction in certain indefinable ways that must have something to do with the change of label. Green and Washington have worked with him before and, though he has generally preferred another horn, there's no sign that he is remotely fazed by its absence. What has crept in is a certain thoughtful diffidence, a tendency to pause and mull over an idea and reject it quite brusquely if it does not fit, whereas in the old days he would have toyed with it laddishly. It's rather engaging and not at all downbeat. One suspects that we are seeing Moore preparing to mount to the next phase in his extraordinary career, and it will be interesting to be there with him.

Tony Moore CELLO

***(*) **Observations** Matchless MRCD 22
>   Moore (*clo* solo). 8/93.

***(*) **Assessments And Translations** Matchless MRCD 28
>   Moore; Josep Vallribera (*gesto-grafia*). 5/95.

According to the liner-note, the apparently abstract cover art is a detail of a portrait of Moore by the Catalan artist, Josep Vallribera. Putting together these sixteen improvised 'observations' is a little like doing a jigsaw without the lid, and doing a jigsaw of late Jackson Pollock at that. There is a strongly marked personality in every gesture, but even the longest and most discursive sections (only two exceed five minutes, four are less than two minutes) manage to be both lucid and elusive.

Moore's use of extended techniques is less overt than Marie-France Uitti's, closer perhaps to another classically literate improviser with ties to Matchless, Rohan de Saram. As label founder Eddie Prévost perceptively suggests in his introduction, Moore's main focus of observation is the cello itself, which is observed historically, dialectically, and sometimes even subversively. Set these pieces alongside any of David Darling's ECM albums and the difference will immediately be evident. The results may, however, be less readily palatable and, though the performances were in many cases continuous, some listeners will want a little space round individual tracks.

Vallribera's contribution to the second album requires a tiny gloss: 'gesto-grafia' appears to be a method of non-notational scoring in which graphic gestures (Pollock again) are assessed and then translated into the extra temporal dimension that music demands. These are very much longer and more developed pieces, just four of them on the CD. It may be that some listeners will find it easier to get a purchase on this second disc. Not that there is any commercial compromise on either.

Herb Morand (1905–52) TRUMPET, VOCAL

*** **Herb Morand 1949** American Music AMCD-9
> Morand; Louis Nelson (*tb*); Andrew Morgan (*ts, cl*); Albert Burbank (*cl, v*); Johnny St Cyr, Raymond Glapion (*g*); Austin Young, Eddie Dawson (*b*); Albert Jiles, Andrew Jefferson (*d*). 5–7/49.

Morand wasn't a typical New Orleans brassman. He is best remembered as the trumpeter with The Harlem Hamfats in Chicago, and these recordings were done following his return to his native city in the 1940s. He sounds a little out of place with these old-school players, but his firm lead and terse solos give the music an extra ounce of assertiveness. Most of the music comes from a session recorded by Bill Russell, a large part of it too long for 78s and heretofore unreleased, but there are four rough and exciting tracks recorded at a dance at Mama Lou's Lounge two months earlier. The sound is a little muffled throughout but all the players come through clearly enough.

Claudio Morenghi TENOR SAXOPHONE

(*) **Sky Gates Splasc(h) H 347-2
> Morenghi; Pampa Pavesi (*p*); Raimondo Meli Lupi (*g*); Gianmarco Scaglia, Otello Savoia (*b*); Paolo Mozzoni (*d*). 5/90–3/91.

Jazz from Brescello, in southern Italy. Morenghi is a skilful player, but not one to stand out in a crowd of tenormen: he writes most of the tunes himself, and there are a couple of pretty themes in 'Children Turnaround' and 'One Year, A Theme For You'; but the playing is really no more than serviceable in a post-bop mould. The pick is a quite intense reading of Mal Waldron's 'Soul Eyes'.

Frank Morgan (born 1933) ALTO SAXOPHONE

***(*) **Gene Norman Presents Frank Morgan** Fresh Sound FSR CD 71
> Morgan; Conte Candoli (*t*); Wardell Gray (*ts*); Carl Perkins (*p*); Wild Bill Davis (*org*); Howard Roberts (*g*); Bobby Rodriguez, Leroy Vinnegar (*b*); Jose Mangual, Lawrence Marable (*d*); Ralph Miranda, Uba Nieto (*perc*). 55.

Frank Morgan's story is not just about paid dues. He also had to serve a stretch in San Quentin, after years of barely controllable drug abuse. Debts paid to society, he reappeared in the mid-1980s, purveying a brand of chastened bop, his initially bright and Bird-feathered style only slightly dulled by a spell in the cage.

In the mid-1950s, he was one of a group of saxophonists who hung on Charlie Parker's coat-tails. The currently deleted Savoy sessions aren't the best place to pick up on what Morgan was doing at the time, partly because the material is relatively unfamiliar and because the dominant figure on the session is Milt Jackson, who is already thinking in new directions. The Fresh Sound CD is a much better place to begin, though the septet tracks with Wild Bill Davis and three Latin percussionists are a touch crude; 'I'll Remember April' succumbs almost completely. Wardell Gray lends his easy swing to 'My Old Flame', 'The Nearness of You' and four other tracks, and Carl Perkins's bouncy clatter at the piano keeps the textures attractively ruffled.

***(*) **Lament** Contemporary C 14021
> As above, except Buster Williams (*b*) replaces Dumas. 4/86.
***(*) **Double Image** Contemporary C 14035
> Morgan; George Cables (*p*). 5/86.
***(*) **Bebop Lives!** Contemporary C 14026
> Morgan; Johnny Coles (*flhn*); Cedar Walton (*p*); Buster Williams (*b*); Billy Higgins (*d*). 12/86.
*** **Quiet Fire** Contemporary CCD 14064
> Morgan; Bud Shank (*as*); George Cables (*p*); John Heard (*b*); Jimmy Cobb (*d*). 3/87.
***(*) **Major Changes** Contemporary C 14039
> Morgan; McCoy Tyner (*p*); Avery Sharpe (*b*); Louis Hayes (*d*). 4/87.
*** **Yardbird Suite** Contemporary C 14045
> Morgan; Mulgrew Miller (*p*); Ron Carter (*b*); Al Foster (*d*). 11/88.

***(*) **Reflections** Contemporary 14052
>   Morgan; Joe Henderson (*ts*); Bobby Hutcherson (*vib*); Mulgrew Miller (*p*); Ron Carter (*b*); Al Foster (*d*). 89.
*** **A Lovesome Thing** Antilles 848213
>   Morgan; Roy Hargrove (*t*); George Cables (*p*); David Williams (*b*); Lewis Nash (*d*); Abbey Lincoln (*v*). 9/90.
*** **Listen To The Dawn** Antilles 518 979
>   Morgan; Kenny Burrell (*g*); Ron Carter (*b*); Grady Tate (*d*). 93.

San Quentin must have been a rough woodshed. Outwardly, there's no immediate sign of change. Modern recording makes his sound more intimate – grainier, anyway – so there's no reason to suppose that occasional huskiness is especially significant. Nor has Morgan forgotten where he came from. Almost the first thing he did on his comeback in 1985 was a brightly intelligent 'Now's The Time' (it's also excerpted on *Bird Lives!* (Milestone M 9166)), and there's a trawl of Parker-associated material on *Yardbird Suite*, with Jackie McLean's 'Little Melonae' thrown in on *Bebop Lives!*.

What *is* noticeable, even with these closely focused recordings, is that he has grown quieter and more reflective. The Antilles sessions hover on the edge of being mood pieces and are often rescued by the quality of the other players: guest star Marsalis, trumpet prodigy Hargrove, the redoubtable Buster Williams (who earns an unaccompanied track on *A Lovesome Thing* and is the lynchpin of *Bebop Lives!*), and George Cables, with whom Morgan enjoys a sympathetic playing relationship.

He seems rather hung up on Cables's 'Lullaby', which gets played with the group on *Mood Indigo* and then twice as a duo on *A Lovesome Thing*. Some of that softness comes through on the duo *Double Image*, which is reminiscent of Marion Brown's collaborations with Mal Waldron; Cables lacks the broad harmonic grasp of a McCoy Tyner, who provides the focus of *Major Changes*.

By far the best of the comeback albums is the complex *Reflections* on Contemporary. The straight-shooting thing Morgan does with Joe Henderson there is also part of the recipe on *Quiet Fire*, with Shank sounding more rasping than of yore. Their exchanges on 'The Night Has A Thousand Eyes' are terrific.

Of all the pianists Morgan has worked with since his return, Miller is the least sympathetic, ironically because he is not forceful enough. He sounds much too respectful on *Yardbird Suite*; at this point in time, isn't it legitimate to interrogate that material a bit more vigorously? That's broadly what Tyner and Walton do on their respective albums, and they're all the better for it.

Morgan in turn is treated very respectfully by all concerned on the Antilles dates, and the effect is emotionally fulsome (there is an icky spoken thanks at the end; 'kiss the kids', 'smile at your neighbours', 'let's work for world harmony', what, now?) to the point where the tunes lack all internal tension, merely providing vehicles for Morgan's floating lines. In the same way, Abbey Lincoln's take on the Chris Connor staple 'Ten Cents A Dance' sounds unlived-in and *ersatz*, which in the circumstances is rather ironic. *Listen To The Dawn* continues in the same vein and, though Morgan is accurately pitched and expressive, there seems less and less to say, however ably. The duos with Burrell are still tasteful, but at least here there is a bit of action. On the remaining tracks one feels there is nothing to do but admire technique, which is a short-term satisfaction.

Lee Morgan (1938–72) TRUMPET

***(*) **Introducing Lee Morgan** Savoy SV 0116
>   Morgan; Hank Mobley (*ts*); Hank Jones (*p*); Doug Watkins (*b*); Art Taylor (*d*). 11/56.
*** **Candy** Blue Note 746508
>   Morgan; Sonny Clark (*p*); Doug Watkins (*b*); Art Taylor (*d*). 2/58.
***(*) **Take Twelve** Original Jazz Classics OJC 310
>   Morgan; Clifford Jordan (*ts*); Barry Harris (*p*); Bob Cranshaw (*b*); Louis Hayes (*d*). 1/62.
**** **The Sidewinder** Blue Note 784157
>   Morgan; Joe Henderson (*ts*); Barry Harris (*p*); Bob Cranshaw (*b*); Billy Higgins (*d*). 12/63.
*** **Tom Cat** Blue Note 784446
>   Morgan; Curtis Fuller (*tb*); Jackie McLean (*as*); McCoy Tyner (*p*); Bob Cranshaw (*b*); Art Blakey (*d*). 8/64.
*** **Cornbread** Blue Note 784222
>   Morgan; Jackie McLean (*as*); Hank Mobley (*ts*); Herbie Hancock (*p*); Larry Ridley (*b*); Billy Higgins (*d*). 66.
*** **Dizzy Atmosphere** Original Jazz Classics OJC 1762
>   Morgan; Al Grey (*tb*); Billy Mitchell (*as, ts*); Billy Root (*bs, ts*); Paul West (*b*); Charli Persip (*d*).

***(*) **Live In Baltimore, 1968** Fresh Sound FSRCD 1037
    Morgan; Clifford Jordan (*ts*); John Hicks (*p*); Reggie Workman (*b*); Ed Blackwell (*d*). 7/68.
*** **Live At The Lighthouse** Fresh Sound FSR CD 140/2 2CD
    Morgan; Bennie Maupin (*ts*); Harold Mabern (*p*); Jymie Merritt (*b*); Mickey Roker (*d*). 7/70.
***(*) **We Remember You** Fresh Sound FSR CD 1024
    Morgan; Jimmy Heath (*ts*); Billy Harper (*ts, f*); Barry Harris, Harold Mabern (*p*); Spanky De
    Brest, Jymie Merritt (*b*); Albert 'Tootie' Heath, Freddie Waits (*d*). 11/62, 1/72.

Morgan was a member of a vintage Jazz Messengers, cutting two – *Moanin'* and *A Night In Tunisia* – of
Art Blakey's vintage performances. He had a punchy, bluesy tone that sounded a generation old but
which yet proved adaptable to contemporary requirements. To some extent he dined out for a long time
on a hit with 'The Sidewinder', but he was stretching the bounds of what he had learnt from Clifford
Brown before and after that.

On the early Savoy, Morgan still sounds like an unreconstructed Brownie-ite, but there are occasional
glimpses of the embellished, off-centre phrases which became his stock-in-trade. Alongside Mobley, in
places he sounds surprisingly delicate – but almost anything, from a foghorn to an enraged pachyderm,
could have managed to sound delicate alongside Mobley.

Recorded around the time the youthful Morgan graduated from section player with Dizzy Gillespie to
featured soloist with the Messengers, *Candy* has a frosting of arrogant self-confidence which is rather
attractive. Sonny Clark is a current rediscovery from the hard-bop era, as is Mabern, both of whom were
eclipsed by Herbie Hancock and, to a lesser extent, Wynton Kelly, who gives a fine bluesy texture to
Indestructible. On *Candy*, Clark works his call-and-response style into something really quite substantial, feeding new ideas back to Morgan and Henderson.

Take Twelve was the first post-Messengers album. Hayes is a less dominant drummer than the trumpeter's ex-boss, and he leaves a lot more room for Morgan to develop his blues phrasing asymmetrically and
with added notes that hint (distantly) at polytonality. Compositions like Elmo Hope's title-track suggest
that Morgan was looking for something more challenging than straightforward hard bop. Ironically,
The Sidewinder nearly foreclosed on further experimentation by being a resounding hit. Funky and
danceable, the title-track has become a staple, known to people who think a Blue Note is a kind of
aerogram. Unfortunately it has obscured some other good material on the album ('Totem Pole', 'Hocus
Pocus', 'Gary's Notebook' and 'Boy, What A Night') and reinforced the notion that Morgan took a
commercial route in 1963, never again to be a serious contender.

Unfortunately, that opening up of the chorus-structure did tempt Morgan towards a more sterile,
grandstanding approach, heard on *Cornbread* and *Tom Cat*. These are entertaining enough, and
McLean is hot, but they represent a step back towards a middle-of-the-road approach that Morgan was
easily capable of transcending. His ability to arrange effectively for a more substantial horn front-line is
evident on *Dizzy Atmsophere*, which includes valuable alternatives of 'Whisper Not' and 'Over The
Rainbow', both of which run a spectrum from sentimental to hard-edged.

A great pity that the Morgan/Jordan group documented on the Baltimore disc never made it into the
studio. This, however, is plenty to be going on with, and there are hints that there might be more
material from the same source. It's a dream band, securely anchored by Blackwell and Workman and
benefiting from Hicks's still muscular lyricism. Morgan's solos on 'Like Someone In Love' and Miles
Davis's 'Solar' make use of unfamiliar intervals and phrasing that suggest he was trying out a new,
quasi-modal approach, but not quite getting there. Fascinating, all the same.

Live At The Lighthouse is an incendiary confrontation with next-generation players, who seem bent on
pushing the leader to the limit. The sound is all over the place on CD, but the excitement is palpable and
it's a generous length. *We Remember You* puts together two very good sessions, one from 1962 with
Jimmy Heath and Barry Harris, the second a decade later, with Billy Harper and Harold Mabern,
featuring a superb latter-day cover of 'The Sidewinder'. A matter of weeks after it was recorded,
Morgan was shot dead at Slugs club in New York City, after a fight with a ladyfriend.

Sam Morgan (1887–1936) CORNET, VOCAL

**** **Papa Celestin & Sam Morgan** Azure AZ-CD-12
    Morgan; Ike Morgan (*c*); Jim Robinson (*tb*); Earl Fouche (*as*); Andrew Morgan (*cl, ts*); Tink
    Baptiste, O. C. Blancher (*p*); Johnny Davis (*bj*); Sidney Brown (*b*); Nolan Williams, Roy Evans
    (*d*). 4–10/27.

The eight titles by Morgan's band are among the classics of 1920s jazz. They are a very rare example of
a New Orleans group recorded in the city during this period, and it's been claimed that these are the
most truthful recordings of how such a band sounded in its prime. Morgan's music is ensemble-based,
solos and breaks threaded into the overall fabric, the playing driven by the gusty slap-bass of Sidney
Brown. Fouche might be the outstanding player, with his mile-wide vibrato, but it's as a band that these

players have endured. There are few more exhilarating records from the period than 'Steppin' On The Gas' or 'Mobile Stomp'. Together with the Celestin tracks, this makes up one of the most essential reissues of early jazz, in outstandingly fine sound.

Joe Morris (born 1955) GUITAR

*** **Symbolic Gesture** Soul Note 121204
    Morris; Nate McBride (*b*); Curt Newton (*d*). 6/93.
*** **Illuminate** Leo Lab CD 008
    Morris; Rob Brown (*as*); William Parker (*b*); Jackson Krall (*d*). 95.
**** **No Vertigo** Leo CD LR 226
    Morris (*g, mand, banjouke* solo). 4/95.

A charter member of the Boston Improvisers' Group, Morris was an actively eclectic sideman and local star before he made it big as a recording artist. He has a facility for straight blues and fusion playing, but he works in a pumped-up free style that doesn't just put the emphasis on dynamics but also works in quite stark, abstract ways. The Soul Note is not a debut because Morris has put material out on his own Riti label for some time – though, alas, distribution is not exactly universal. As a first point of contact, it is slightly soft-centred, and it might be as well to move quickly on to *Illuminate* on Leo's radical Lab imprint, before coming to any settled conclusion. The quartet there is fresh and unclichéd, but comes off the back of saxophonist Brown's Riti session with Morris and other associations for different labels. A clangorous, unfussy record, it will appeal not just to guitar-trio fans (who may feel more comfortable with *Symbolic Gesture*) but also to those who don't like their free jazz too vegetarian and mild.

The best record of the three is the solo *No Vertigo*. Morris has obviously been influenced by British improviser Derek Bailey. His acoustic work is very reminiscent of Bailey's 1970s work but with a hint of a jazz groove always hovering in the background, which Bailey seldom permits. He also includes tracks on an electric instrument (the long, very detailed 'For Adolphus Mica'), banjouke ('Long Carry') and even mandolin (a sequence called 'The Edges'). There is nothing slipshod about this music. Morris is a stern self-disciplinarian, and the defining characteristic of the music on *Illuminate* is the responsiveness of the players to one another, a listening quality that extends not just to pitching but also to dynamics, rhythmic and para-rhythmic properties, even the use of space and (relative) silence.

Lawrence Butch Morris (born 1947) CORNET, CONDUCTOR

**** **Current Trends In Racism In Modern America** sound aspects sas 4010
    Morris; John Zorn (*as, game calls*); Frank Lowe (*ts*); Brandon Ross (*g*); Eli Fountain (*vib*); Zeena Parkins (*hp*); Curtis Clark (*p*); Tom Cora (*clo*); Christian Marclay (*turntables*); Thurman Barker (*d, mar, perc*); Yasunao Tone (*v*). 2/85.
***(*) **Homeing** sound aspects sas 4015
    Morris; J. A. Deane (*tb, elec*); Vincent Chauncey (*frhn*); Daniel Werts (*ob*); Eli Fountain (*vib*); Zeena Parkins (*hp*); Curtis Clark (*p*); Pierre Dørge (*g*); Jason Hwang (*vn*); Tom Cora (*clo*); Jean-Jacques Avenel (*b*); Oliver Johnson (*d*); David Weinstein (*elec*); Shelley Hirsch (*v*). 11/87.
*** **Dust To Dust** New World/Countercurrents 80408-2
    Morris; J. A. Deane (*tb, elec*); Marty Ehrlich (*cl*); John Purcell (*ob*); Janet Grice (*bsn*); Vicki Bodner (*cor*); Myra Melford (*p*); Jason Hwang (*vn*); Jean-Paul Bourelly (*g*); Bryan Carrott (*vib*); Wayne Horvitz (*ky*); Zeena Parkins (*hp*); Andrew Cyrille (*d*). 11/90.

Most visible lately as the *éminence grise* behind some of saxophonist David Murray's most challenging music, Morris is an exponent of what he calls 'conduction', a kind of directed improvisation by which improvising players respond moment to moment to the conductor's signals.

Current Trends may sound like a Ph.D. topic but is in fact a turbulent and often disturbing piece whose subtitle, 'A Work In Progress', is as much a polemical comment as a formal disclaimer. It certainly isn't 'finished' music and the surface is kept in a state of considerable flux, but there is a logic to it which is reflected in individual performances. Zorn's anarchic duck-calls and honks camouflage a sophisticated bop-player with a fine structural sense; Lowe's Coltrane-derived screams are combined with an easy swing that comes from Don Byas and Chu Berry.

Morris's interest in non-standard instrumentations is more obvious on *Homeing*, which dispenses with saxophones. Zeena Parkins overturns most of the usual associations of harp-playing, as does Cora with his cello. *Homeing* has a more settled surface and a gentler timbre, but it's still extremely forceful music.

Dust To Dust is the first proper documentation of a Morris 'conduction', examined in much greater detail by the set listed below. In small, shapely episodes, this is a very approachable proposition, and a good taster for the feast which followed next.

***(*) **Testament: A Conduction Collection** New World/Countercurrents 80479-2/80488-2 10CD
    Morris; Hugh Ragin (*t*); J. A. Deane (*tb, elec*); Wolter Wierbos, Daniel Raney, David Tatro (*tb*);
    Vincent Chauncey (*frhn*); Jon Raskin, Larry Ochs, Dave Barrett, Dietmar Diesner, Kizan
    Daiyoshi, Bruce Ackley, Arthur Blythe, Kazutoki Umezu, Marion Brandis, Jemeel Moondoc,
    Yukihiro Isso, Shonosuke Okura, Makiko Sakurai, Jesse Canterbury, Mimi Patterson, Scott
    Deeter, Michel Titlebaum, Philip Gelb, Michael Barker, Peter Van Bergen, Michihiro Sato, Janet
    Grice, Hans Koch (*reeds, woodwinds*); Jon Jang, Guillaume Dostaler, Curtis Clark, Steve
    Colson, Steve Beresford, Haruna Miyake, Michiel Sheen, Myra Melford (*p*); Christian Marclay,
    Yoshihide Otomo (*turntables*); Chris Brown (*ky*); BlK Lion, Bill Horvitz, Brandon Ross, Hans
    Reichel, Wiek Hijmans, Elliott Sharp, Chris Cunningham, Gregor Harvey, Ethan Schaffner (*g*);
    Elizabeth Panzer, Zeena Parkins (*hp*); Pierre Dube, Bryan Carrott, Damon Ra Choice, Reggie
    Nicholson (*vib*); Hikaro Sawai (*koto*); Ayuo Takahashi (*zheng*); Yumiko Tanaka (*gidayu*); Kash
    Killion, Martin Schutz, Eric Longsworth, Tom Cora, Tristan Honsinger, Michelle Kinney, Ken
    Butler, Dierdre Murray, Martine Altenburger (*clo*); Edgar Laubscher (*vla*); Helmut Lipsky,
    Kaila Flexer, Hal Hughes, Yuji Katsui, Alison Isadora, Gregor Kitzis, Dana Friedli (*vn*); Mike
    Milligan, Keizo Mizoiri, Peter Kowald, Motoharo Yoshizawa, William Parker, Mark Helias,
    Fred Hopkins (*b*); William Winant, Han Bennink, Thurman Barker, Taylor McLean, Gunter
    Muller, Ikue Mori, Sachiko Nagata, Le Quan Ninh, Michael Vatcher (*perc*); Catherine
    Jauniaux, Asuka Kaneko, Jannie Pranger, Elisabeth King, Tomomi Adachi (*v*); Shuichi Chino
    (*computer*); The Suleyman Erguner Ensemble. 88–95.
Morris's steady evolution of his 'conduction' – in two words, conducted improvisation – has been
documented in fine detail by this handsomely prepared ten-disc set. Morris outlines all the principles in
the accompanying notes, which are a useful guide, since the music across this vast spread is difficult and
challenging and not without its share of obfuscatory passages. While some of the individual pieces are
only a few minutes long, others stretch to nearly an hour in length. There are groupings from America,
Europe, Japan and (a memorable one) Turkey. In the main Morris favours large ensembles, but there is
one group of no more than five players. This kind of thing needs to be superbly recorded, and most of
the sets come in excellent fidelity, though the earliest isn't quite so clear.

If we withhold our highest recommendation, it's because the music isn't quite as satisfying as it might be
to witness. The textures seem to aspire to a density which makes it difficult to hear what precisely may be
going on and, if Morris appears to favour orchestral weight and gravity, he can't always sustain the kind
of argument which would be second nature to a 'straight' composer. Some of the pieces follow surprisingly predictable forms of rise and fall, call and response; though soloists emerge from the ensembles
with sometimes electrifying effectiveness, there is an innate sense of balance which a more free-flowing
improvisation wouldn't admit. But perhaps that is the point.

Even so, there is much fascinating and rewarding music. Occasionally, as in the Tokyo set, which also
involved Butoh dancers, nothing truly seems to communicate across. Other pieces have the vivacity and
crackle of the best improvising. Others aspire to slow-moving sound-mountains. An accompanying
video would be a useful source of further enlightenment, but for now the booklet will have to do. The
individual CDs are to be made available separately, and we will cover each on a solo basis in our next
edition.

Sonny Morris TRUMPET, VOCAL

*** **The Spirit Lives On** Lake LACD46
    Morris; Bob Ward (*tb, v*); Terry Giles (*cl*); Ben Marshall (*bj*); John Sirett (*b*); Colin Bowden (*d*).
    9/94.
The spirit in question is that of the Johnson/Lewis American Music groups of the 1940s, and this
congenial group of veterans pay a likeable homage on this set. Morris and Marshall have their own
authenticity in spades, both being founder-members of the Crane River Jazz Band alongside Ken
Colyer, and the rest of the group hardly put a foot wrong. The anti-virtuosic solos are scarcely the point
of this music. What counts is the steady beat, the *simpatico* ensembles and the irresistible sense of
inevitability about it all. Crucially, the rhythm section are exactly right, with Bowden particularly
outstanding in the Baby Dodds manner. Excellent choice of material, and docked a notch only for the
occasional shakiness and the vocals, dispensable as usual.

Thomas Morris (1898–date unknown) CORNET

*** **When A 'Gator Hollers** . . . Frog DGF-1
    Morris; Rex Stewart, Jabbo Smith (*c*); Geechie Fields, Joe Nanton, Charlie Irvis (*tb*); Ernest

Elliott (*cl, ts, bs*); Happy Caldwell (*cl, ts*); Bob Fuller (*cl, ss*); Mike Jackson (*p, v*); Phil Worde (*p*); Buddy Christian (*g, bj*); Lee Blair (*bj*); Bill Benford (*tba*); Wellman Braud (*b*); Helen Baxter, Margaret Johnson (*v*). 7–11/26.

Hardcore collectors will welcome this lovingly assembled set of early-jazz rarities; everybody else should be warned that this is second-rate music, for all its undoubted charm and savvy at this great distance. Morris – peculiarly little is known about his life – was a frequent accompanist to singers, but the sides made under his own leadership for Victor are more notable for the sidemen than for his own distinctly average playing. The best moment on the whole record is Rex Stewart's thrilling solo on 'Charleston Stampede', and that's even more thrilling on the Fletcher Henderson original. Elsewhere there are some interesting fragments from names usually consigned to the lumber-room of jazz history. Some typical hokum – 'Who's Dis Heah Stranger' or 'Jackass Blues', again not a patch on the Henderson version – mingles with the title-piece, sung by Margaret Johnson, and some later tracks that feature Joe Nanton just before he joined Henderson. The remastering is superbly done and every known take is here.

Wilber Morris BASS

*** Wilber Force DIW 809
Morris; David Murray (*ts, bcl*); Dennis Charles (*d*). 2/83.

While flawed – there are too many bass solos for Morris to sustain with comfort and the material is repetitive – this concert set has a fine intensity of spirit. The best piece is the opening number, 'Randy', which features some superb interplay among the three musicians over a series of shifting metres. Murray's characteristically rambling improvisations muster their usual ornery temperament and his bass clarinet showcase on 'Afro-Amer. Ind' is marvellously articulated. The sound is rather restricted but not too distracting from the music.

Jelly Roll Morton (1890–1941) PIANO, VOCAL

*** Blues And Stomps From Rare Piano Rolls Biograph BCD111
Morton (*p roll*). 24–26.

Piano rolls tend to make all pianists sound the same, no matter what their stylistic differences, and Morton's nine original rolls don't offer any exception to a rule that blunts rhythmic and dynamic subtleties and neuters touch and voicings. But Morton's music survives better in this context than does Fats Waller's: the refinement and complexity of his compositions can be heard with crystal clarity in these performances, and if it tends to isolate some aspects of his art, it doesn't destroy it. And there are interesting variations with his solo playing on record, the gentler reading of 'Grandpa's Spells', for instance. One or two pieces are rarer matters, too, such as 'Tom Cat Blues', which was only recorded as a duet with King Oliver (even if it is a development of 'Mr Jelly Lord'). Purely on its own terms, this is a very enjoyable disc, and the player-piano sound is fine.

**** Jelly Roll Morton 1923–1924 Classics 584
Morton; Tommy Ladnier, Natty Dominique (*c*); Zue Robertson (*tb*); Wilson Townes, Boyd Senter, Horace Eubanks (*cl*); Arville Harris (*as*); W. E. Burton (*d, kazoo*); Jasper Taylor (*d*). 6/23–6/24.

**** Piano Solos Retrieval RTR 79002
Morton (*p solo*). 7/23–4/26.

The self-styled originator of jazz and stomps started on record here, and showed the door to all other pretenders. The old, discredited idea was that the piano solos cut in 1923–4 were sketches for the band sessions he recorded for Victor, but Morton's all-embracing mastery of the keyboard makes these 19 solos a sublimation of everything jazz had done up to this point. He combines the formal precision of ragtime with a steady melodic flow and a portfolio of rhythms that are tirelessly varied: if Louis Armstrong finally liberated jazz rhythms, Morton had already set out the possibilities to do so. As a series of compositions, this was a storehouse of ideas which has yet to be exhausted: here are the first versions of two of jazz's most enduring masterworks, 'King Porter Stomp' and 'Wolverine Blues', as well as such definitive Morton portraits as 'The Pearls' and the brilliantly delivered 'Shreveport Stomp'. His timing is ambitious yet miraculously secure: listen to the poetic elegance of 'New Orleans (Blues) Joys', or the famous 'Spanish Tinge' in 'Tia Juana'. Considering the roughness of the original record-ings, the fact that the music remains utterly compelling is testament to Morton's greatness. The piano-sound is still pretty awful to modern ears, and some of the (often very rare) originals are clearly in less-than-perfect shape, but this is essential music. The Classics CD scarcely improves on the earlier Fountain/Retrieval LP, now on CD although the individual tracks have not been remastered from their

1972 incarnation. Admittedly, it adds what were really some false starts in Morton's career – two very cloudy 1923 tracks for Paramount, with a band that may or may not include Tommy Ladnier, a not-much-better session for OKeh with the feeble Dominique, Robertson and Eubanks and a fairly disastrous 'Mr Jelly Lord', where he's buried behind Boyd Senter and some kazoo playing – but some may feel that it simply devalues the consistency of the solos.

Retrieval's reissue now also includes the four solos for Vocalion from 1926, and this is certainly our first choice.

**** **The Complete Jelly Roll Morton 1926–1930** RCA Bluebird ND82361 5CD
Morton; Ward Pinkett, Edward Anderson, Edwin Swayzee, David Richards, Boyd 'Red' Rosser, Henry 'Red' Allen, Bubber Miley, Sidney De Paris (*t*); George Mitchell (*c*); Kid Ory, Gerald Reeves, Geechie Fields, William Cato, Charlie Irvis, J. C. Higginbotham, Wilbur De Paris, Claude Jones (*tb*); Sidney Bechet, Paul Barnes (*ss*); Omer Simeon, Ernie Bullock (*cl, bcl*); Barney Bigard, Darnell Howard, Johnny Dodds, George Baquet, Albert Nicholas (*cl*); Russell Procope (*cl, as*); Walter Thomas (*as, bs*); Stump Evans (*as*); Joe Thomas (*cl, ts*); Joe Garland, Happy Caldwell (*ts*); Rod Rodriguez (*p*); J. Wright Smith, Clarence Black (*vn*); Howard Hill, Bernard Addison, Bud Scott, Lawrence Lucie, Will Johnson (*g*); Johnny St Cyr, Lee Blair (*bj, g*); Barney Alexander (*bj*); Bill Benford, Billy Taylor (*bb, b*); Pete Biggs, Harry Prather, Bill Moore, Quinn Wilson (*tba*); Pops Foster, Wellman Braud, John Lindsay (*b*); Andrew Hilaire, Tommy Benford, Baby Dodds, Manzie Johnson, William Laws, Cozy Cole, Paul Barbarin, Bill Beason, Zutty Singleton (*d*). 9/26–9/39.

  **** **Jelly Roll Morton Volume One** JSP CD 321
Morton; George Mitchell (*c*); Gerald Reeves, Kid Ory (*tb*); Omer Simeon, Darnell Howard, Barney Bigard, Johnny Dodds (*cl*); Stump Evans (*as*); Clarence Black, J. Wright Smith (*vn*); Johnny St Cyr (*bj, g*); Bud Scott (*g*); Quinn Wilson (*bb*); John Lindsay (*b*); Andrew Hilaire, Baby Dodds (*d*). 9/26–6/27.

**** **Jelly Roll Morton Volume Two** JSP CD 322
Morton; Ed Anderson, Ed Swayzee, Boyd Rosser, Walter Briscoe, Henry 'Red' Allen (*t*); William Cato, Charlie Irvis, J. C. Higginbotham (*tb*); Albert Nicholas, Barney Bigard (*cl*); Russell Procope, Walter Thomas, Paul Barnes, Joe Garland, Joe Thomas (*reeds*); Rod Rodriguez (*p*); Barney Alexander, Lee Blair (*bj*); Will Johnson (*g*); Henry Prather, Bill Moore (*bb*); Pops Foster (*b*); Manzie Johnson, Paul Barbarin, William Laws, Zutty Singleton (*d*). 12/28–12/29.

**** **Jelly Roll Morton Volume Three** JSP CD 323
Morton; Ward Pinkett, Bubber Miley (*t*); Geechie Fields, Wilbur De Paris (*tb*); Albert Nicholas (*cl*); Happy Caldwell, Joe Thomas, Walter Thomas (*reeds*); Bernard Addison, Howard Hill (*g*); Lee Blair (*bj*); Billy Taylor (*bb, b*); Bill Benford, Pete Biggs (*bb*); Cozy Cole, Tommy Benford (*d*). 3–10/30.

**** **Jelly Roll Morton Volume Four** JSP CD 324
As Volumes One and Two, above.

**** **Jelly Roll Morton Volume Five** JSP CD 325
As Volumes Two and Three, above.

**** **Jelly Roll Morton Vol. 1 1926–27 'Doctor Jazz'** Black & Blue 59.227-2
As JSP Volume One, above. 26–27.

**** **Jelly Roll Morton Vol. 2 1928–39 'Didn't He Ramble'** Black & Blue 59.228-2
As appropriate discs above. 28–39.

*** **Jelly Roll Morton 1924–1926** Classics 599
Morton; Lee Collins, King Oliver, George Mitchell (*c*); Roy Palmer, Kid Ory, Ray Bowling (*tb*); Omer Simeon (*cl, bcl*); Barney Bigard (*cl, ts*); Balls Ball, Volly De Faut, Darnell Howard (*cl*); Alex Poole (*as*); W. E. Burton (*kazoo*); Clarence Black, J. Wright Smith (*vn*); Johnny St Cyr (*bj, g*); John Lindsay (*b*); Clay Jefferson, Andrew Hilaire (*d*); Edmonia Henderson (*v*). 9/24–12/26.

**** **Jelly Roll Morton 1926–1928** Classics 612
Morton; Ward Pinkett (*t*); George Mitchell (*c*); Kid Ory, Gerald Reeves, Geechie Fields (*tb*); Omer Simeon, Johnny Dodds (*cl*); Stump Evans (*as*); Bud Scott, Johnny St Cyr (*g*); Lee Blair (*bj*); Bill Benford, Quinn Wilson (*tba*); John Lindsay (*b*); Andrew Hilaire, Tommy Benford, Baby Dodds (*d*). 12/26–6/28.

**** **Jelly Roll Morton 1928–1929** Classics 627
Morton; Ed Anderson, Edwin Swayzee, Boyd 'Red' Rosser, Walter Briscoe, Henry 'Red' Allen, Freddy Jenkins (*t*); William Cato, Charlie Irvis, J. C. Higginbotham (*tb*); Russell Procope, Albert Nicholas, Wilton Crawley, George Baquet (*cl*); Paul Barnes (*ss*); Joe Thomas, Johnny Hodges (*as*); Joe Garland, Walter Thomas (*ts*); Luis Russell, Rod Rodriguez (*p*); Lee Blair, Will Johnson (*g*); Barney Alexander (*bj*); Bill Moore, Harry Prather (*tba*); Pops Foster (*b*); Manzie Johnson, William Laws, Paul Barbarin, Sonny Greer (*d*). 12/28–12/29.

*** **Jelly Roll Morton 1929–1930** Classics 642

> Morton; Ward Pinkett, Bubber Miley (*t*); Geechie Fields, Wilbur De Paris (*tb*); Albert Nicholas, Barney Bigard, Ernie Bullock (*cl*); Bernard Addison, Howard Hill (*g*); Lee Blair (*bj*); Billy Taylor, Bill Benford, Pete Biggs (*tba*); Zutty Singleton, Tommy Benford, Cozy Cole (*d*). 12/29–7/30.

*** **Jelly Roll Morton 1930–1939** Classics 654

> Morton; Ward Pinkett, Sidney De Paris (*t*); Geechie Fields, Claude Jones, Fred Robinson (*tb*); Sidney Bechet (*ss*); Albert Nicholas, Eddie Scarpa (*cl*); Happy Caldwell (*ts*); Bernard Addison, Lawrence Lucie (*g*); Billy Taylor (*tba*); Wellman Braud (*b*); Bill Beason, Zutty Singleton (*d*). 10/30–12/39.

We should deal first with the three earlier Classics CDs, which include material that the Bluebird and JSP discs have ignored. Classics 599 starts with a 1924 date with Morton's (so-called) Kings Of Jazz, and horrible it sounds too, poorly transferred from grim originals and featuring diabolical clarinet from the suitably named 'Balls' Ball and even worse alto by Alex Poole. Trio versions of 'My Gal' and 'Wolverine Blues' with Volly De Faut aren't much better, but a fine 1926 solo date for Vocalion *is* included, and these tracks (unavailable elsewhere) must make the disc attractive to Morton specialists. Two sides with (allegedly) King Oliver and Edmonia Henderson are a further bonus. They then go into the Victor sequence, which continues through Classics 612 and 627, although the latter adds an unremarkable session at the end under Wilton Crawley's leadership, with (somewhat mystifyingly) a number of Ellingtonians present.

Morton's recordings for Victor are a magnificent body of work which has been done splendid but frustratingly mixed justice by some of the various reissues now available. His Red Hot Peppers band sides, particularly those cut at the three incredible sessions of 1926, are masterpieces which have endured as well as anything by Armstrong, Parker or any comparable figure at the top end of the jazz pantheon. Morton seemed to know exactly what he wanted: having honed and orchestrated compositions like 'Grandpa's Spells' at the piano for many years, his realization of the music for a band was flawless and brimful of jubilation at his getting the music down on record. Mitchell, Simeon and the others all took crackling solos, but it was the way they were contextualized by the leader which makes the music so close to perfection. The 1926–7 dates were a summary of what jazz had achieved up to that time: as a development out of the New Orleans tradition, it eschewed the soloistic grandeur which Armstrong was establishing and preferred an almost classical poise and shapeliness. If a few other voices (Ellington, Redman) were already looking towards a more modern kind of group jazz, Morton was distilling what he considered to be the heart of hot music, 'sweet, soft, plenty rhythm', as he later put it.

While the earliest sessions are his greatest achievements, it's wrong to regard the later work as a decline. There are the two trio tracks with the Dodds brothers, with Morton tearing into 'Wolverine Blues'. The 1928 sessions feature his ten-piece touring band on the fine 'Deep Creek' and a small group handling the beautiful 'Mournful Serenade', while 1929 saw a memorable solo session which produced 'Pep', 'Fat Frances' and 'Freakish', and an exuberant band date that uncorked swinging performances in 'Burnin' The Iceberg' and 'New Orleans Bump'. But the sessions from 1930 onwards suffer from personnel problems and a vague feeling that Morton was already becoming a man out of time, with New York and territory bands moving into a smoother, less consciously hot music. His own playing remains jauntily commanding, but sidemen become sloppy and a piece like the complex 'Low Gravy', from July 1930, never reaches its potential on record. His last session for Victor until 1939 produced a final shaft of Mortonian genius in 'Fickle Fay Creep'; but a feeling was now deep-set that the pianist was a declining force, and he didn't record for Victor again until the end of the decade.

The 1939 tracks show the old master in good spirits, singing 'I Thought I Heard Buddy Bolden Say' and 'Winin' Boy Blues' with his old panache and directing an authentic New Orleans band with resilient aplomb. It is very old-time music for 1939, but it's still very different from the early Peppers sides and none the worse for either. Classics 654 covers these sessions and also includes four titles from an excellent solo date from 1938.

Morton's music is fine enough to demand a comprehensive representation in all collections, and the current choices on disc are somewhat confusing. The most convenient method is to acquire the Bluebird set, which is handsomely documented and pretty well remastered; but there are problems with some of the tracks, which are from imperfect sources, and a couple of mistakes let down the project to some extent. Some may prefer to have the alternative takes – which are, frankly, revealing only in that Morton had a firm idea of what he wanted by the time take one was recorded each time – set apart, as the JSP series does, rather than on top of one another, as here. Nevertheless, it makes an impressive package. For sheer quality of transfers, though, the JSP sequence is clearly superior. John R. T. Davies's painstaking work from top-quality originals outfaces that secured by the Bluebird engineers, which even use latterday tape transfers in some cases. The first volume, which includes the early Peppers dates, is unequivocally a five-star record. There are a couple of chronology problems, though, with the JSP series, since the 11 June 1928 session doesn't appear until Volume 4, along with the various alternative takes on the 1926–30 sessions complete. JSP also omit the 1939 tracks. But the first three volumes, which otherwise include all the master takes of the 1926–30 material, are our strong first recommendation. The Classics CDs follow the company's customary chronological path but also suffer from patchy sound and, while the music remains outstanding, they can only be a secondary choice. The CDs from Black & Blue cover all the important Red Hot Peppers dates but, on Volume 2, jump rather suddenly from 1929 to the last Victor sessions of 1939. So many important tracks are missing; but the remastering is mostly very good. To add to the glut of issues, there are also sets available from Memoria (*The Complete Jelly Roll Morton, 1926–1930*, two CDs), EPM (*Creole Genius*, three CDs) and Fremaux (*The Quintessence*, two CDs) which go over the same ground. *Sweet And Hot* (Topaz TPZ 1003) is another good single-disc collection in the Topaz series of compilations. We still feel that there are now enough issues available to provide a lasting choice!

**** Kansas City Stomp Rounder CD1091
>   Morton (*p, v*). 5–6/38.
***(*) Anamule Dance Rounder CD1092
>   Morton (*p, v*). 5–6/38.
**** The Pearls Rounder CD1093
>   Morton (*p, v*). 5–6/38.
**** Winin' Boy Blues Rounder CD1094
>   Morton (*p, v*). 5–6/38.
***(*) The Library Of Congress Recordings Affinity AFS 1010-3 3CD
>   Morton (*p, v*). 5–6/38.

In the summer of 1938, broke and almost finished, Morton was recorded – almost by chance at first – by Alan Lomax at the Library Of Congress, and when Lomax realized the opportunity he had on his hands, he got Morton to deliver a virtual history of the birth pangs of jazz as it happened in the New Orleans of the turn of the century. His memory was unimpaired, although he chose to tell things as he preferred to remember them, perhaps; and his hands were still in complete command of the keyboard. The results have the quality of a long, drifting dream, as if Morton were talking to himself. He demonstrates every kind of music which he heard or played in the city, re-creates all his greatest compositions in long versions unhindered by 78 playing time, remembers other pianists who were never recorded, spins yarns, and generally sets down the most distinctive document we have on the origins of the music. The sessions were made on an acetate recorder and, while the sound may be uncomfortably one-dimensional to modern ears, everything he says comes through clearly enough, and the best of the piano solos sound as invigorating as they have to be. The new remastering achieved by Rounder is the best attempt to date to reproduce the music in correct pitch and speed; while much talk has been omitted from the four CDs, it is a wonderfully illustrated lecture on Morton's music by the man who created it. Of the four discs, only Volume Two is slightly less than essential, with the final disc offering perhaps the best selection of solos, including his astonishing extended treatment of 'Creepy Feeling'. Indispensable records for anyone interested in jazz history.

The Affinity set, although it has many of the virtues of the Rounder edition, is finally a bit disappointing. There is an hour's worth of material missing in order to squeeze the rest on to three CDs, and the use of the CEDAR process for remastering has blurred the piano-tone and put a light fog over the sound, even if it has taken some of the rasp out of the tone of previous transfers.

***(*) Jelly Roll Morton 1939–1940 Classics 668
>   Morton; Henry Allen (*t*); Joe Britton, Claude Jones (*tb*); Albert Nicholas (*cl*); Eddie Williams (*as*); Wellman Braud (*b*); Zutty Singleton (*d*). 12/39–1/40.

Morton's final recordings are relatively little-known, cut originally for General and later appearing on Commodore. The tracks by the Morton Six and Seven find him back with several sons of New Orleans, but the music lacks the authority of his great days; a couple of solo sessions from 1939 do, though, reassert his enduring powers at the keyboard, with several favourite pieces still sounding like pieces of jazz legend.

Mosaic Sextet GROUP

*** Today, This Moment Konnex KCD 5058
>   Dave Douglas (*t*); Michael Rabinowitz (*bsn*); Michael Jefry Stevens (*p*); Mark Feldman (*vn*); Joe Fonda (*b*); Harvey Sorgen (*d*). 1/88, 2/89, 3/90.

No surprise at all to find another group fronted by the ubiquitous Douglas or to see that existing commitments dictate they're only able to record at 13-month intervals. The slightly unusual instrumentation, with the little-used bassoon given a quite prominent role in the front line, occasionally detracts or distracts attention from the sheer quality of the compositions, which are shared out. 'Gang

Wars For Sexter' is distinctive, as are 'Superconductor' and 'In Process', the better material coming, significantly or not, from the most recent of the three sessions. No indication whether this group has recorded since or, indeed, whether it is still a going concern. One has to imagine that Douglas's availability is the stumbling-block these days.

Sal Mosca (born 1927) PIANO

***(*) **A Concert** Jazz Records JR-8
> Mosca (*p* solo). 6/79.

Belatedly released in 1990, this is a rare example of one of the leading followers of Lennie Tristano in a solo situation. Because Mosca has made so few recordings, his appearances always seem eventful and, despite the dour atmosphere of the CD – which settles for the grimmest monochrome packaging and presentation, a characteristic refusal to distract from the music's inner qualities – it is played electrically. Though most of the tunes are 'originals', they usually follow the standard Tristano-ite practice of an abstruse variation on a standard. Mosca's approach is formidably varied, both from piece to piece and within individual treatments. 'Co-Play', which starts as a relatively simple variation on 'Sweet And Lovely', becomes a labyrinthine investigation of the properties of the song, and 'That Time' turns 'That Old Feeling' into a fantasy on a number of kinds of jazz rhythm. Sometimes he plays it straight, but unexpectedly so: 'Prelude To A Kiss' has voicings more dense than in any authentic Ellington version. Always he is prodigiously inventive: while the music sometimes takes on a painstaking quality, Mosca's spontaneity is genuine enough to pack the programme with surprises. An important record, docked a notch only for the sound quality: it's clear enough, but the piano's tone is scarcely ingratiating, and there's a lot of tape hiss.

*** **Sal Mosca / Warne Marsh Quartet Vol. 1** Zinnia 103
> Mosca; Warne Marsh (*ts*); Frank Canino (*b*); Skip Scott (*d*). 81.
*** **Sal Mosca / Warne Marsh Quartet Vol. 2** Zinnia 104
> As above. 81.

More problems with sound-quality here. Mosca taped these Village Vanguard sessions himself and, for a recording dating from the 1980s, it's pretty shabby, though Tristano-ites and other scholars will have their ears used to this sort of thing by now. Still, it does detract from music that is as refined and impeccable as chords-based improvising with no emotional agenda can get. Marsh's streaming elegance matches Mosca's slightly more fanciful playing to the expected 't'. As always, they are working on old staples such as '317 East 32nd' and the usual, thinly disguised standards, and as always their inventiveness on material they'd mused on countless times already is enough to provoke disbelief. Canino and Scott are no more than functional, though that is presumably how the principals wanted it.

Moscow Composers Orchestra ENSEMBLE

*** **Kings And Cabbages** Leo Lab CD 005
> Vladimir Miller (*p, cond*); Yuri Parfyonov, Vyacheslav Guyvoronsky (*t*); Andrew Solovyov (*t, flhn*); Arkady Shilkloper (*frhn, flhn*); Oleg Ruvinov (*tba*); Alexander Voronin (*ss, f*); Edward Sivkov (*as*); Sergey Batov (*ts*); Sergei Letov (*bs, bcl, f*); Bram Groothoff (*bs*); Alexey Levin (*p*); Alexander Kostikov (*g*); Vladislav Makarov (*clo*); Vladimir Volkov, Victor Melnikov (*b*); Valentin Sokolov (*d*); Mikhail Zhukov (*perc*). 1/93.

A slightly misleading designation, since the MCO is fronted by an Englishman (albeit of Russian extraction) and the orchestra includes players from outwith Muscovy, and even as far afield as the Netherlands. Musically, it's an intriguing session, though a little chewy for some tastes.

The new music scene in post-Soviet Russia has had its ups and downs, and the survival of creative music has been largely due to dedicated promoters and broadcasters like Nick Dmitriev and Dmitri Ukhov, both of whom are loyal supporters of radical experimentation. A good deal of Leo's output has an unmistakable theatrical component and *Kings And Cabbages* is no exception, a latter-day fairy tale suspended in ironic narrative space which denies conventional beginnings and endings. There are whispers of Rimsky-Korsakov (the fairy tale operas most obviously) in some places, but these may be accidental; they're certainly incidental to the main progress of the four long pieces. Miller gives his oneiric method a clear musical equivalence in titles like 'Theme No Theme Yet A Re-occurring Dream', but his airily shifting, restlessly ambiguous approach is best encountered on the title-track, which is worth playing first, before running the set through as a whole.

A beautifully drilled band, recorded in an unusually reverberant and responsive studio acoustic. Given the situation in present-day Russia, it seems unlikely that the MCO will be convened very often; all the more reason to value this interesting disc.

Bob Moses (born 1948) DRUMS

***(*) **Visit With The Great Spirit** Gramavision GR 8307
>Moses; Tiger Okoshi (*t, flhn, electric t*); John D'Earth (*electric t*); Michael Gibbs (*tb*); David Sanborn (*as*); David Liebman (*ss*); David Gross (*as, f*); George Garzone (*ts, ss*); Bob Mintzer (*ts, b*); Tony Coe (*ts*); Howard Johnson (*bs, tba, b*); Steve Kuhn (*p*); Delmar Brown, Cliff Korman (*syn*); Bill Frisell (*g*); Eddie Gomez, Lincoln Goines, Jerome Harris (*b*); Ron DeFrancesco, Janet Levatin, Bill Martin, Manoel Montero, Claudio Silva (*perc*); Kyoki Baker, Hiroshi Hieda, Rayko Shiota (*v*). 83.

*** **Wheels Of Colored Light** Open Minds OM 2412
>Moses; Terumasa Hino (*c, wood f, perc*); Dave Liebman (*ts, ss, as, wood f, musette*); Jeanne Lee (*v*).

A somewhat aggressive populist, Moses is also a superb arranger with an unfailing instinct for tone-colours that resembles Mike Gibbs's. The drummer's former boss is persuaded to blow his rarely seen trombone on 'Macchu Picchu', a dark piece heavily laden with bass guitars, and 'Carinho'. Moses's slightly mystical bent tinges only a couple of the tracks. His Latin effects have the brooding ambiguity and repressed violence which the Spanish call *duende*. There are big, structural references to Miles Davis and to Monk.

If *Visit* is forceful, imaginative and resonant, *Wheels Of Colored Light* is much lighter and more spacious; it's no less imaginative but leaves more for the individual players to contribute of their own. Together with the earlier album, it again raises the question of what Moses might have done had his career been more focused.

Danny Moss (born 1927) TENOR SAXOPHONE

(*) **The Good Life Progressive PCD 7018
>Moss; Ted Ambrose (*t, v*); Mike Collier (*tb*); Jack Jacobs (*as*); Terry Whitney (*p*); Alan Kennington (*b*); Derek Middleton (*d*). 10/68.

*** **Weaver Of Dreams** Nagel-Heyer 017
>Moss; Brian Lemon (*p*); Len Skeat (*b*); Butch Miles (*d*). 11/94.

Moss has often been hidden by his surroundings on record, usually in sections or anonymous groups, and he's had only a few opportunities of clear space. These discs, almost a generation apart, give a decent idea of his powers. The Hawkins/Webster tradition is what he sticks closest to, and it comes out mainly on slow and medium tempos: the big, beefy tenderness on the two takes of 'The Good Life' itself, from the 1968 session, is enduringly impressive and affecting. Much of this date is taken up with time-wasting by the mixed British talents on hand: Ambrose insists on singing on some tracks, Jacobs's Willie Smith-styled alto falls into routine, and Moss simply doesn't get enough space, though he also has a Hawkins-like 'Star Dust' to himself.

Weaver Of Dreams finds him in Hamburg, delivering a faithful set of tenorman's staples – '9.20 Special', 'Smoke Gets In Your Eyes', 'Blue Lou' and a small number of choice ballads. Utterly reliable playing, though some of the old facility has been worn away, and one regrets that Moss wasn't featured more in his prime.

Michael Mossman (born 1959) TRUMPET, PICCOLO TRUMPET, FLUGELHORN

*** **Granulat** Red 123240-2
>Mossman; Daniel Schnyder (*ss, ts, f*); Wladislaw Sendecki (*p*); Hami Hammerli (*b*); Guido Parini (*d*). 4/90.

Mossman has done time in many worthwhile European bands, and this group – which he co-leads with Schnyder – gives him a little more space than usual. The compositions are nearly all by Schnyder (the sole exception is Mossman's own 'Cage Of Ice') and display his brainy method as capably as the records under his own name, with the quicksilver lines of the title-track and 'Bifurcat' posing difficult tasks for the players which all five solve with impressive assurance. The rhythm section set down usefully straight-forward grooves while the horns follow the pirouetting lines of Schnyder's melodies: some of them, such as 'Blue Tinjokes', have a crackpot demeanour which can seem slightly too cute, but they're mastered so smartly that it usually works. Mossman's bright tone and crisply accurate attack thrive in a situation like this.

Bennie Moten (1894–1935) PIANO, BANDLEADER

**(*) Bennie Moten 1923–1927 Classics 549

Moten; Lamar Wright, Harry Cooper, Ed Lewis, Paul Webster (c); Thamon Hayes (tb, v); Harlan Leonard (cl, ss, as); Woody Walder (cl, ts); Jack Washington (cl, as, bs); LaForest Dent (as, bs, bj); Sam Tall, Leroy Berry (bj); Vernon Page (tba); Willie Hall, Willie McWashington (d). 9/23–6/27.

Moten's band was the most important group to record in the American southwest in the period, and luckily it made a large number of sides for OKeh and Victor: but the quality of the music is very inconsistent, and much of the earlier material is of historical rather than musical interest. This first CD in the complete edition on Classics couples the band's 14 sides for OKeh from 1923–5 with the first recordings for Victor. The OKeh tracks are a curious mixture: the very first two, 'Elephant's Wobble' and 'Crawdad Blues', are little more than strings of solos, while the subsequent 'South' and 'Goofy Dust' are driving, rag-orientated tunes which emphasize the ensemble. Wright is the only really interesting soloist from the period, and Walder, the apparent star, indulges in some idiotic antics on the clarinet, but, even so, the lumpy rhythms and clattery ensembles yield some strong, hard-hitting performances, sometimes redolent of Sam Morgan's New Orleans band of a few years later. The early Victors don't show a very great advance, despite electrical recording, and one must wait for the later sides for Moten's band to really shine. Decent remastering of what are very rare originals, although not superior to the old Parlophone LP which first collected the OKeh tracks.

**(*) Bennie Moten 1927–1929 Classics 558

As above, except omit Wright, Cooper, Tall and Hall; add Booker Washington (c), Buster Moten (p, acc), James Taylor, Bob Clemmons (v). 6/27–6/2

*** Bennie Moten 1929–30 Classics 578

As above, except Count Basie (p) replaces Buster Moten; add Hot Lips Page (t), Eddie Durham (tb, g), Jimmy Rushing (v). 7/29–10/30.

Moten's band progressed rather slowly, handicapped by an absence of both truly outstanding soloists and an arranger of real talent. The surprisingly static personnel did the best they could with the material, but most of the tunes work from a heavy off-beat. Walder has barely improved, and the arrival of Bennie's brother, Buster, with his dreaded piano-accordion, was enough to root the band in novelty status. The second Classics CD still has some good moments – in such as 'The New Tulsa Blues' or 'Kansas City Breakdown' – but sugary saxes and pedestrian charts spoil many promising moments. Matters take an immediate upward turn with the joint arrival of Basie and Durham in 1929. 'Jones Law Blues', 'Band Box Shuffle' and 'Small Black' all show the band with fresh ideas under Basie's inspirational leadership (and soloing – here with his Earl Hines influence still intact). 'Sweetheart Of Yesterday' even softens the two-beat rhythm.

**** Bennie Moten 1930–1932 Classics 591

Moten; Ed Lewis, Booker Washington (c); Hot Lips Page, Joe Keyes, Dee Stewart (t); Thamon Hayes, Dan Minor (tb); Eddie Durham (tb, g); Harlan Leonard, Jack Washington, Woody Walder, Eddie Barefield, Ben Webster (reeds); Count Basie (p); Buster Moten (acc); Leroy Berry (bj, g); Vernon Page (tba); Walter Page (b); Willie McWashington (d); Jimmy Rushing (v). 30-32.

Under Basie's effective leadership, the Moten orchestra finally took wing, and its final sessions were memorable. There were still problems, such as the presence of Buster Moten, the reliance on a tuba prior to the arrival of Page, and a general feeling of transition between old and new; but, by the magnificent session of December 1932, where the band created at least four masterpieces in 'Toby', 'Prince Of Wails', 'Milenberg Joys' and 'Moten Swing', it was a unit that could have taken on the best of American bands. Page, Rushing, Webster, Durham and especially Basie himself all have key solo and ensemble roles, and the sound of the band on 'Prince Of Wails' and 'Toby' is pile-driving. Ironically, this modernism cost Moten much of his local audience, which he was only recovering at the time of his death in 1935. Fair remastering, though one feels better could have been done with a set of mint originals.

Paul Motian (born 1931) DRUMS, PERCUSSION

*** Conception Vessel ECM 1028

Motian; Becky Friend (f); Sam Brown (g); Leroy Jenkins (vn); Keith Jarrett (p); Charlie Haden (b). 11/72.

**** Tribute ECM 1048

Motian; Carlos Ward (as); Sam Brown, Paul Metzke (g); Charlie Haden (b). 5/74.

**** **Dance** ECM 1108
    Motian; Charles Brackeen (*ts*); David Izenzon (*b*). 9/77.
*** **Le Voyage** ECM 1138
    Motian; Charles Brackeen (*ts, ss*); Jean-François Jenny-Clark (*b*). 3/79.

Not a conventionally swinging drummer, Motian spins a shimmering web of cymbal lines and soft, delicately placed accents. He belongs to the Max Roach school of musical, almost melodic drummers, but is wholly undemonstrative in his commitment to group performance, with a built-in resistance to the grandstanding solo.

There is one unaccompanied track on *Conception Vessel*, the thoughtful 'Ch'i Energy', and much of the album is devoted to showcasing the drummer in a variety of carefully contoured partnerships; the title-track and 'American Indian: Song Of Sitting Bull' are duos with Keith Jarrett (who plays flute on the latter). There are two trios with Haden and Brown, and the set closes with 'Inspiration From A Vietnamese Lullaby', which uses Friend and Jenkins. With no horn, it's a deliberately low-key session and, along with its immediate successors, provides a good, if slightly ethereal, introduction to Motian's folksy angularity.

The 1974 album with its twinned guitars and keening saxophone (though Ward is used sparingly) remains one of the most beautiful things Motian has done. Metzke is a grossly underrated performer on the electric guitar and should be investigated without delay. It's certainly worth remembering that Motian was featuring a guitarist of this type long before Bill Frisell came on the scene. The session consists of three Motian tunes, of which 'Sod House' and 'Victoria' are the best-known, together with Ornette's 'War Orphans' and Haden's 'Song For Ché'. On *Le Voyage* and the more recently reissued *Dance*, he's supported by a 'strong' saxophone player and two bassists of considerable tonal range. These are fine sessions in their own right, full of fascinating material like the tersely generic tracks on the latter, but their main interest lies in the way they look forward to the trio with Joe Lovano and Bill Frisell.

*** **Psalm** ECM 1222
    Motian; Joe Lovano (*ts*); Billy Drewes (*ts, as*); Bill Frisell (*g*); Ed Schuller (*b*). 12/81.
*** **The Story Of Maryam** Soul Note 121074
    Motian; Jim Pepper (*ts, ss*); Joe Lovano (*ts*); Bill Frisell (*g*); Ed Schuller (*b*). 7/83.
***(*) **Jack Of Clubs** Soul Note 121124
    As above. 3/84.
**** **Misterioso** Soul Note 121174
    As above. 7/86.

Motian has generally preferred to work with familiar and sympathetic players than to mix and match bands. In the 1980s, his most frequent collaborators have been tenor saxophonist Joe Lovano and post-Hendrix guitarist Bill Frisell, first as members of a larger group, subsequently as a stripped-down trio.

The addition of a more driving horn-sound fuels Motian's more boppish side, one that wasn't to come out explicitly until the early 1990s. Nevertheless it's clear from these sessions that the drummer is no mere water-colourist, but swings a band with considerable power and, where necessary, with aggression, too. 'Drum Music' on *Jack Of Clubs* and 'Folk Song For Rosie' on *Misterioso* reappear from *Le Voyage* and have meanwhile acquired a riper self-confidence, accentuated by the combination of Lovano with Jim Pepper, a North American Indian who played with a distinctive yodelling vibrato and shared Motian's interest in non-Western resolutions. *Psalm*, on which the little-known Billy Drewes played second saxophone, now seems an interim album, a proving-ground for Frisell and Lovano.

***(*) **It Should've Happened A Long Time Ago** ECM 1283
    Motian; Joe Lovano (*ts*); Bill Frisell (*g, syn*). 7/84.
*** **One Time Out** Soul Note 1211224
    As above. 9/87.
***(*) **Monk In Motian** JMT 834421
    Motian; Joe Lovano, Dewey Redman (*ts*); Geri Allen (*p*); Bill Frisell (*g*). 3/88.
***(*) **Motian In Tokyo** JMT 849 154
    As for *It Should've Happened*. 3/91.
**** **Trioism** JMT 514 012
    As above, except add Dewey Redman (*ts*). 6/93.

Where the earlier Motian albums had been slightly one-dimensional and lulling, the trio was a roller-coaster ride. A retake of 'Conception Vessel' on *Should've* gives some sense of how far the drummer had come in a decade. He was also at this time beginning to reintroduce standards. The Soul Note covers 'The Man I Love', 'If I Should Lose You' and 'My Funny Valentine' in versions that give the songs a rhythmic configuration which comes straight out of Monk. No surprise, then, that 1988 should have thrown up a Monk tribute. Motian also drafts in pianist Geri Allen (for 'Ruby My Dear' and 'Off Minor') and a thoroughly ineffectual Dewey Redman for 'Straight No Chaser' and 'Epistrophy'. He's miles better on *Trioism* but, gallingly, is restricted to just one track. That being said, the basic trio's in great shape. Individual songs are punchier than before; 'Play', 'Congestion' and 'Endgame' are quite clipped and the writing's no longer kinda Monkish, but starts to push out into territory of its own.

The 1988 record wasn't of course the first time Motian had tackled Monk tunes; consider 'Monk's Mood' on the earlier *One Time Out* or 'Pannonica' on *Misterioso*. However, this is the first time that he gets right inside them and allows them to work for him. He's magnificent on 'Crepuscule With Nellie' and 'Ugly Beauty'. Showing no desire to dominate, he drops into the background more often than not, and on several occasions drops out altogether, but for the softest tick on a cymbal to indicate the measure.

*** **Paul Motian On Broadway: Volume 1** JMT 834430
    Motian; Joe Lovano (*ts*); Bill Frisell (*g*); Charlie Haden (*b*). 11/88.
*** **Paul Motian On Broadway: Volume 2** JMT 834440
    As above. 9/89.
***(*) **Paul Motian On Broadway: Volume 3** JMT 849157
    As above, except add Lee Konitz (*as, ss*). 8/91.
'Ugly Beauty' is a fair description of the Broadway treatments. Of the quartet, only Frisell wasn't obviously raised on the standards. Lovano, for all his tearing at the pages, certainly was, and the bassist and drummer have been coming across this repertoire for years. With Haden at hand, there are signs that Motian might be content to slip into conventional patterns – noticeably on 'Someone To Watch Over Me' (*Volume 1*), more insidiously on 'But Not For Me' and the creaking gate 'Body And Soul' (both *Volume 2*). Nevertheless these are very beautiful records and highly original in their approach to far-from-virginal territory.

The addition of Konitz on *Volume 3* was a surprise – but there are few more surprising players than Konitz around, and it works admirably. Ironically, perhaps, Konitz is a less romantic player than Lovano. The older man brings a wry nostalgia to themes like 'Just One Of Those Things' and 'The Way You Look Tonight', keeping both his horns up in a light, deliberately colourless register that makes an effective contrast. He also plays comfortably across the beat, appropriately on 'Crazy She Calls Me' and 'Weaver Of Dreams', which are perhaps the best things in the whole three-volume programme.

**** **Bill Evans** JMT 834445
    Motian; Joe Lovano (*ts*); Bill Frisell (*g*); Marc Johnson (*b*). 5/90.
Between 1959 and 1964, Motian played with the enormously influential Bill Evans trio, an association that subordinated time-keeping to a more subtle semi-harmonic role, and that steered Motian in his own music towards a fragile blend of orthodox harmony with atonality, jazz with folk or classical themes, freedom and restraint. In their common tendency to mix delicacy with unbridled power, they make a superficially unlikely combination for a tribute album of Bill Evans tunes, but the chemistry works and it's testimony both to Evans's durable writing and to Motian's taste and control that Frisell's guitar effects on the classic 'Re: Person I Knew' sound perfectly apposite (which is doubly remarkable in that they also have to stand in for a piano part).

Typically nonlinear in focus, there's no more conventional time-keeping on *Bill Evans* than on the Monk tribute. Perhaps if anything unites the two great pianists, it's the sense that their rather different conceptions of swing shared the common characteristic of being rooted in the melody rather than being tacked on underneath.

***(*) **And The Electric Bebop Band** JMT 514004
    Motian; Joshua Redman (*ts*); Brad Schoeppach, Kurt Rosenwinkel (*g*); Stomu Takeishi (*b*). 6/92.
Even given Motian's absorption in standard repertoire during the 1980s, this was a bit of a surprise. Disappointing as the band often was in the flesh, it works phenomenally well on disc. The twinned guitars and Motian's much-simplified and very forward drum-sound suggest echos of Ornette Coleman's Prime Time band. The music, however, is all straight out of the bebop book: 'Shaw Nuff', 'I Waited For You', 'Dance Of The Infidels', 'Scrapple For the Apple', a searing 'Monk's Dream' and a couple more, all played with brisk intensity.

Redman Jr is one of the most discussed young horn-players of the past decade, combining intelligence with vigorous attack and a clear, slightly impersonal sound. It's not impossible to imagine Lovano and Frisell fitting into this setting (again, it's important to recognize the essential continuity of Motian's project), but they are both perhaps slightly too expressive for what Motian has in mind. What hindered the Electric Bebop Band's first live appearances was the players' tendency to kick over the traces and emote when something more restrained seemed to be called for.

***(*) **Reincarnation Of A Love Bird** JMT 514 016
    Motian; Chris Potter (*as, ts*); Chris Cheek (*ts*); Wolfgang Muthspiel, Kurt Rosenwinkel (*g*);
    Steve Swallow (*b*); Don Alias (*perc*). 6/94.

Wedged in between two versions of his own 'Split Decision', eight modern-jazz staples handled in a way that, though duly respectful, confirms how unchallengeable is Motian's right to consider himself at the heart of all of it, from Parker, Dizzy and Miles ('Ornithology', 'Be-Bop' and 'Half Nelson') to Monk ('Skippy' and 'Round Midnight') and Mingus (the title-track). Motian's supremely musical personality is now etched on every track and every moment; there is nothing here that could conceivably have been performed and recorded by anyone else. Why the tiny quibble in the bracketed rating, then? A small one, to be sure, but somehow serious enough to register. There is just a sense that these performances are a touch *too* personalized, a little idiosyncratic and mannered. Stefan F. Winter's expert production and Joe Ferla's intuitive engineering give the drummer exactly the sound he deserves, easily as good as the much-vaunted ECM product, but there is something slightly too smooth and perfect about the whole, and it fails to deliver as fulsomely on second and subsequent hearings, which may be an issue in choosing a record to purchase by this now well-documented artist.

The group perform superbly, with Rosenwinkel and Muthspiel nicely defined and well separated in the stereo picture. The two horns are not quite so well integrated and tend to be decorative rather than functional, but one wouldn't want them not to be there.

**** You Took The Words Right Out Of My Heart JMT 514 028
Motian; Joe Lovano (*ts*); Bill Frisell (g). 7/95.

Tsss tsss tsss; para pa da wee DAH; braang-a-lang brang brang brang. This is a group with an instantly recognizable signature and an absolute sense of purpose. Good to hear Motian revert to his own material after a period of time devoted largely to repertoire material. Of these, 'Abacus' and 'Folk Song For Rosie' are the most substantial, tender and abstract by turns, tuneful and veering towards abstraction. Lovano takes a different role from previous recordings, often playing quite simple harmonic parallels to Frisell before veering off again into areas of his own. Motian is flawless from start to finish; what a joy it must be to work in front of him!

Bheki Mseleku (born 1955) PIANO, ALTO AND TENOR SAXOPHONE, GUITAR, VOCAL

*** Celebration World Circuit WC 019
Mseleku; Steve Williamson, Courtney Pine (*ss*); Jean Toussaint (*ts*); Eddie Parker (*f*); Michael Bowie (*b*); Marvin 'Smitty' Smith (*d*); Thebe Lipere (*perc*). 91.

***(*) Timelessness Verve 521306-2
Mseleku; Joe Henderson, Pharoah Sanders (*ts*); Kent Jordan (*f*); Rodney Kendrick (*p*); Michael Bowie (*b*); Marvin 'Smitty' Smith (*d*); Abbey Lincoln (*v*). 8/93.

**(*) Meditations Verve 521337-2
Mseleku (*p, ts, v* solo). 92.

*** Star Seeding Verve 529142-2
Mseleku; Charlie Haden (*b*); Billy Higgins (*d*). 3/95.

The South African-born Mseleku waited a long time for his debut record. It's a positive and big-hearted set, full of grand major themes and impassioned playing from a distinguished local cast, although overall Mseleku added little to the firm base established by SA expatriates such as Louis Moholo and Dudu Pukwana. His piano playing owes its weight and impetus to McCoy Tyner – 'Blues For Afrika' might have come off any of Tyner's Milestone albums of the 1970s – and his tunes are full of the call-and-response ingredients of such writers as Abdullah Ibrahim and Randy Weston. Not that the music lacks inner conviction: Bowie and Smith lend transatlantic muscle which raises the temperature several degrees on the faster pieces, and Jean Toussaint comes off best among the sax stars, with a measured improvisation on 'The Age Of Inner Knowing'. The debut record for Verve, though, was pitched at a higher level, with an extraordinary gallery of guest players. It's impressive enough that Mseleku stands as tall as any of them, but the quality of his writing here is exceptional, with the title-track a towering feature for Henderson and Smith, and such themes as 'Yanini' and 'Ntuli Street' given extra weight by the calibre of the players. Flawed, arguably, by its undue length and one or two lesser efforts (notably Lincoln's appearance), the record augurs well for a renewed affiliation of South African jazz with American currents.

Meditations captures Bheki live at the Bath Festival on a solo excursion. The record is well named since the two long tracks have the quality of a man musing gently to himself. Listeners outside may find it difficult finding a way in: without structural limitations, he does tend to ramble. *Star Seeding* goes back to the studio with some more heavyweight friends. Some of this has as much Hank Jones in it as anything, with the bluesy licks of 'Ballad For The Saints' getting the record off to a good start. Mseleku's forays into tenor and guitar are rather less appealing: since his pianism is so strong, it seems a distraction. But his supply of hymnal melodies looks to have a long way to go yet.

Gerry Mulligan (1927–96) BARITONE SAXOPHONE, PIANO, SOPRANO SAXOPHONE

*** Mulligan Plays Mulligan Original Jazz Classics OJC 003
Mulligan; Jerry Hurwitz, Nick Travis (*t*); Ollie Wilson (*tb*); Allen Eager (*ts*); Max McElroy (*bs*); George Wallington (*p*); Phil Leshin (*b*); Walter Bolden (*d*); Gail Madden (*perc*). 8/51.

The most important baritone saxophonist in contemporary jazz, Mulligan took the turbulent Serge Chaloff as his model, but blended his fast, slightly pugnacious delivery with the elegance of Johnny Hodges and Lester Young. This produced an agile, *legato* sound which became instinct with the cool West Coast style, the flipside of bebop. Mulligan's – and Claude Thornhill's – major role in what became known as Miles Davis's *Birth Of The Cool* is now increasingly acknowledged, as is his genius as a composer/arranger. On the model of the *Birth Of The Cool* nonet, his big bands have the intimacy and spaciousness of much smaller groups, preferring subtlety to blasting power. His small groups, conversely, work with a depth of harmonic focus that suggests a much larger outfit.

In his short story, 'Entropy', the novelist Thomas Pynchon takes Mulligan's early-1950s piano-less quartets with Chet Baker as a crux of post-modernism, improvisation without the safety net of predictable chords. The revisionist argument was that Mulligan attempted the experiment simply because he had to work in a club with no piano. The true version is that there was a piano, albeit an inadequate one, but that he was already experimenting with a much more arranged sound for small groups (to which the baritone saxophone was peculiarly adaptable) and that the absence of a decent keyboard was merely an additional spur.

These early sessions already demonstrate what a fine composer and arranger the saxophonist was (he arranged 'Disc Jockey Jump' for Gene Krupa when he was only twenty). In comparison to later work, they're slightly featureless and Mulligan's playing is very callow. It's perhaps best to come back to this stuff.

***(*) The Best Of The Gerry Mulligan Quartet With Chet Baker Pacific Jazz CDP 7 95481 2
Mulligan; Chet Baker (*t*); Henry Grimes, Carson Smith, Bobby Whitlock (*b*); Dave Bailey, Larry Bunker, Chico Hamilton (*d*). 8 & 10/52, 2, 4 & 5/53, 12/57.

Let's face it. We are all, deep down, suckers for 'My Funny Valentine', just as Miles Davis fans play 'Time After Time' a good deal more often than they do *Agharta*. Don't be misled by the line-up details on *Quartet*. This *isn't* the Chet Baker version (a live version with Chet can be found on *The Best Of*) but one led, after the trumpeter's departure, by Bob Brookmeyer, who makes a much brisker, folksy job of it, a little like having your valentine written by the village scribe. The two Baker tracks – 'Lady Bird' and 'Half Nelson' – are quickly recognizable.

The Pacific Jazz compilation, drawn from singles (including the classic 'Soft Shoe'/'Walkin' Shoes' combination) and subsequent 10-inch LPs, is an excellent sampling of Mulligan's 11-month association with Chet, with a single item, 'Festive Minor', from the same December 1957 sessions that yielded *Reunion*. It's fair (to Chet, at least) to record that it was Mulligan, not the famously unreliable trumpeter, who brought the line-up to an end. In June 1953, Mulligan was gaoled for several months on a drugs offence. It is perhaps as well that the group was folded at its peak. Generously recorded in a warm close-up, the sessions convey all of Mulligan's skill as a writer and arranger, with the saxophone and a very foregrounded bass filling in the space normally occupied by piano. Chet's own 'Freeway', Carson Smith's 'Carson City Stage' and Mulligan's own 'Jeru' and 'Swinghouse' are largely upstaged by the standards, with 'My Old Flame' receiving its finest reading since Parker recorded it for Dial.

***(*) Pleyel Concerts 54: Volume 1 Vogue 113411
Mulligan; Bob Brookmeyer (*vtb*); Red Mitchell (*b*); Frank Isola (*d*). 6/54.
***(*) Pleyel Concerts 54: Volume 2 Vogue 113412
As above. 6/54.

Post-Chet. As far as French fans and critics were concerned, this was how young America looked and sounded. Sunny, cooled-out, elaborated but determinedly un-profound, it smacks very strongly of a time and place. No less than the slightly epicene Baker, the crew-cut, square-jawed Mulligan became a kind of icon, in sharp counter-definition to the long-hair, goatee and beret image of jazz. Early in 1954, following Mulligan's release from gaol, a version of the group with Bob Brookmeyer out front had played a series of gigs at the Salle Pleyel in Paris. The two discs are a little repetitive, punctuated by the 'Utter Chaos' signature theme, but Mulligan's playing is so subtly inflected that it's possible to listen to his solos back to back and hear him working through all the implicit chord variants. The 3 June version of 'Makin' Whoopee' is joyous, as is Giuffre's 'Five Brothers' (or 'Mothers', according to some versions). That vintage gig spills over on to Volume Two, but the two discs are worth having anyway. This issue largely supersedes Vogue 655616, which also included material with Chet, recorded in LA in May 1953.

***(*) **Monk Meets Mulligan** Original Jazz Classics OJC 301
    Mulligan; Thelonious Monk (*p*); Wilbur Ware (*b*); Shadow Wilson (*d*). 8/57.
Not an entirely probable encounter, but Mulligan more than keeps afloat on the Monk tunes, sounding least at ease on 'Rhythm-a-Ning', but absolutely confident on 'Straight, No Chaser' and, of course, 'Round About Midnight'.

    The dark, heavy sound of Wilbur Ware's bass is sufficiently 'below' Mulligan's horn and his intervals sufficiently broad to tempt the saxophonist to some unusual whole-note progressions. Monk darts in and out like a tailor's needle, cross-stitching countermelodies and neatly abstract figures.

***(*) **Gerry Mulligan–Paul Desmond Quartet** Verve 519850
    Mulligan; Paul Desmond (*as*); Joe Benjamin (*b*); Dave Bailey (*d*). 8/57.
Another of Verve's summit conferences – and a felicitous one. There has probably never been a saxophone sound as finely blended as this, and our only quibble – 'Body And Soul' notwithstanding – is that the material is not really up to the playing. Some of the tunes are obscure enough to suggest that it wasn't just run down on the spot, but there is a lack of anything to get one's teeth into. The best moments are, as in 'Body And Soul', when Desmond moves to the front and Mulligan plays what are effectively piano chord-shapes behind him. Glorious.

******* **What Is There To Say** Columbia 475699
    Mulligan; Art Farmer (*t*); Bill Crow (*b*); Dave Bailey (*d*). 12/58, 1/59.
*** **Americans In Sweden** Tax CD 3711
    As above. 5/59.
Farmer doesn't quite have the lyrical authority of Chet Baker in this setting, but he has a full, deep-chested tone (soon to be transferred wholesale and exclusively to flugelhorn) which combines well with Mulligan's baritone. *What Is There To Say* was Mulligan's first recording for Columbia. It's very direct, very unfussy, very focused on the leader, but with the same skills in evidence as on the earlier *The Arranger*, which was a dry run for the label. The first album proper is a small masterpiece of controlled invention. Mulligan's solos fit into the structure of 'As Catch Can' and 'Festive Minor' as if they were machine-tooled. Farmer responds in kind, with smooth *legato* solos and delicate fills.

    The Swedish gig is just one of many taken legitimately or otherwise around this time. Browsers will find several more of the same vintage, but this is one of the best. Farmer is not Chet Baker, but he does have his own things to offer, notably a solid attack and a very full, broad sound which can make Chet's sound decidedly underpowered.

***(*) **Gerry Mulligan Meets Ben Webster** Verve 841661
    Mulligan; Ben Webster (*ts*); Jimmy Rowles (*p*); Leroy Vinnegar (*b*); Mel Lewis (*d*). 11 & 12/59.
(*) **The Silver Collection: Gerry Mulligan Meets The Saxophonists Verve 827436
    Mulligan; Conte Candoli, Don Ferrara, Nick Travis (*t*); Bob Brookmeyer (*vtb, p*); Wayne Andre, Alan Ralph (*tb*); Paul Desmond, Johnny Hodges, Dick Meldonian, Gene Quill (*as*); Stan Getz, Zoot Sims, Ben Webster (*ts*); Gene Allen (*bcl, bs*); Lou Levy, Jimmy Rowles, Claude Williamson (*p*); Joe Benjamin, Ray Brown, Buddy Clark, Leroy Vinnegar (*b*); Dave Bailey, Stan Levey, Mel Lewis (*d*). 57–60.
*** **Verve Jazz Masters 36** Verve 523 342
    Mulligan; Conte Candoli, Don Ferrara, Doc Severinsen, Clark Terry, Nick Travis (*t*); Willie Dennis (*tb*); Bob Brookmeyer (*vtb*); Alan Ralph (*btb*); Gene Quill (*as, cl*); Bob Donovan, Dick Meldonian (*as*); Jim Reider, Zoot Sims (*ts*); Gene Allen (*bs*); Buddy Clark, Bill Crow (*b*); Gus Johnson, Mel Lewis (*d*). 7/60–12/62.
In Mulligan's book, everyone (by which he presumably means soloists as well as punters) profits from the 'good bath of overtones' you get standing in front of a big band. The great saxophonists lined up on *The Silver Collection* sound mostly constrained rather than inspired by the small- to medium-scale arrangements, steered in the direction of Mulligan's recitalist's cool rather than towards any new improvisational heights. Webster is magisterial on the sessions of November and December 1959 ('Chelsea Bridge' and 'Tell Me When' are excerpted on *The Silver Collection*), and the two saxophones blend gloriously in the lower register; something wrong with the balance on the rhythm section, though. Hodges probably sounds the happiest of the lot on the compilation, but then he was used to quite reasonable arrangements; these tracks were originally issued backed by the Paul Desmond sessions, which made perfect sense all round.

    The *Jazz Masters* collection is an excellent buy, but relatively limited in scope. Drawn in the main from *The Concert Jazz Band* discs, *Gerry Mulligan '63* (albeit recorded a year earlier) and *A Concert In Jazz*, it nevertheless gives full measure from these and fills in an important stage in Jeru's progress.

*** **Gerry Mulligan And The Concert Jazz Band** RTE Europe 1 710382/83 2CD
    As for *Jazz Masters*. 60.
This is one of a pair of live airshots recorded and issued by RTE. The Concert Jazz Band was an

extraordinary outfit, perhaps the best representation there was of Mulligan's music. Unfortunately, this recording is not especially good, muddy and indistinct in important areas, lacking in pep and definition at exactly the moment when one senses the music taking flight. The performances are mostly long and designed to give maximum exposure to the soloists, but there is enough tight ensemble work to confirm that, even in this environment, Mulligan was absolutely in the driving seat.

**** **The Age Of Steam** A&M 396996-2

Mulligan; Harry 'Sweets' Edison (*t*); Bob Brookmeyer (*vtb*); Jimmy Cleveland, Kenny Shroyer (*tb*); Bud Shank (*as, f*); Tom Scott (*ts, ss*); Ernie Watts (*reeds*); Roger Kellaway (*p*); Howard Roberts (*g*); Chuck Domanico (*b*); John Guerin (*d*); Joe Porcaro (*d, perc*). 2–7/71.

Almost unrecognizably long-haired and bearded, posed in denims in front of one of the locomotives that were his other great passion, Mulligan might almost be a footplateman on some lonely Mid-West branch line. In 1971 he hadn't recorded on his own account for nearly seven years, and so *The Age Of Steam* was awaited with considerable anticipation by those who had followed Mulligan's career, and with delight by many who were coming to him for the first time. The instrumentation (and Stephan Goldman's fine production job) are both identifiably modern, with Mulligan making extensive use of electric piano and guitar. Both 'Country Beaver' and 'A Weed In Disneyland' include strong rock elements (notably Roberts's strong solo on the latter) and there's a strong dash of country swing to the opening 'One To Ten In Ohio', which reunites him with Brookmeyer. The two finest tracks, though, are the long 'Over The Hill And Out Of The Woods', which Mulligan opens on piano, comping for an extensive range of horns out of which Harry 'Sweets' Edison emerges for a strong solo, and the hauntingly beautiful 'Grand Tour'. The latter must be counted among the saxophonist's most beautiful compositions, its meditative theme and misty timbre explored by Mulligan and Bud Shank. 'Golden Notebooks' is a further statement of Mulligan's long-sustained feminism. It's a light, almost floating piece from the yin side of his imagination.

Even allowing for the rather static dynamics of both tracks, the most striking characteristic of *The Age Of Steam* is its strongly rhythmic cast. Even when playing solidly on the beat, Mulligan's is an unmistakable voice and this is an important return to form after awkward years in the creative wilderness.

*** **Little Big Horn** GRP 95032

Mulligan; Alan Rubin (*t*); Keith O'Quinn (*tb*); Lou Marini (*as*); Michael Brecker (*ts*); Marvin Stamm (*t*); Dave Grusin (*electric p, syn*); Richard Tee (*p*); Jay Leonhart, Anthony Jackson (*b*); Buddy Williams (*d*).

Mulligan's hostility to (over-)amplification hasn't prevented him using electric instruments when the need arises. Few electric piano players have given the instrument the grace and sophistication Dave Grusin brings to it on 'I Never Was A Young Man' and 'Under A Star'. Doubled with Richard Tee on 'Bright Angel Falls', he sounds less spacious, but one sees what Mulligan is doing, trying to invest a small group with the breadth and harmonic range of a big band (as he had tried to do, ironically, with the piano-less quartets of the 1950s). The addition of brass on the title-track makes this even clearer, but it also underlines how much better it would have sounded with a full-size band.

** **Gerry Mulligan / Astor Piazzolla 1974** Accord 556642

Mulligan; Astor Piazzolla (*bandoneon*); Angel Pocho Gatti (*pipe org*); Alberto Baldan, Gianni Zilolli (*mar*); Filippo Dacci (*g*); Umberto Benedetti Michelangeli (*vn*); Renato Riccio (*vla*); Ennio Morelli (*clo*); Giuseppe Prestipino (*b*); Tullio Di Piscopo (*d*). 74.

A nice idea that doesn't quite happen. The problem is not with the instrumentation or the arrangements, nor that Mulligan is not in sympathy with Piazzolla's *nueva tango* approach. It's simply that the performances are so drably uninflected (certainly in comparison to what the two principals do on their own account) as to render the experiment non-consequential.

*** **Soft Lights And Sweet Music** Concord CCD 4300

Mulligan; Scott Hamilton (*ts*); Mike Renzi (*p*); Jay Leonhart (*b*); Grady Tate (*d*). 1/86.

What a session this might have been with Dave McKenna at the piano. As it is, Mulligan is left to carry too much of the harmonic weight, and his solo excursions seem cautious in consequence, rarely straying far from the most logical progression. There is also a tendency for the next phrase to be exactly the one you thought he was going to play. Hamilton shows off, but with forgivable charm and adroitness.

(***) **Symphonic Dreams** Sion 18130

Mulligan; Houston Symphony Orchestra. 2/87.

In recent years Mulligan has devoted considerable time to concert music. These are not the most interesting things he has done, consisting largely of softly jazzed-up versions of orchestral pieces like the 'Sacre Du Printemps', bits of Brahms, Richard Strauss, Bach and Debussy. Ironically, the most successful piece musically is a brief 'Song For Strayhorn'. Not really a jazz record at all. Interesting insights on offer for the established Mulligan fan; not much for anyone else.

***(*) Lonesome Boulevard A & M 397061
Mulligan; Bill Charlap (*p*); Dean Johnson (*b*); Richie De Rosa (*d*). 3 & 9/89.

Tonally sparse, but immensely suggestive of Mulligan's magisterial achievement as a writer/arranger. 'Flying Scotsman' is a small-group version of a piece reflecting Mulligan's affection for steam locomotives and commissioned for the 1988 Glasgow Jazz Festival. Far from lacking the impact of the big-band version, this account exposes the workings of the piece far more clearly, like a cut-away illustration in *Popular Railways*, and the subtlety of Mulligan's conception shows up.

The playing is softer, but also more varied, than the rather discursive voice of the 1950s. Mulligan's soprano saxophone isn't in evidence, which is a pity on the title-track and 'Splendor In The Grass', but his higher-register work on both is quite compelling. He may be spending more time on his orchestral work these days, but he can still produce deeply compelling jazz when the opportunities arise.

*** Re-Birth Of The Cool GRPGRD 9679
Mulligan; Wallace Roney (*t*); Dave Bargeron (*tb*); John Clark (*frhn*); Bill Barber (*tba*); Phil Woods (*as*); John Lewis (*p*); Dean Johnson (*b*); Ron Vincent (*d*); Mel Torme (*v*). 1/92.

There has been some rewriting of the history books over the past year or two on behalf of Mulligan and pianist/arranger John Lewis *vis-à-vis* the original *Birth Of The Cool*. Mulligan is on record as feeling that the project was subsequently hijacked in Miles Davis's name. Though Miles 'cracked the whip', it was Lewis, Gil Evans and Mulligan who gave the music its distinctive profile. In 1991, Mulligan approached Miles regarding a plan to re-record the famous numbers, which were originally released as 78s and only afterwards given their famous title. Unfortunately, Miles died before the plan could be taken any further, and the eventual session featured regular stand-in Roney in the trumpet part.

With Phil Woods in for Lee Konitz, the latter-day sessions have a crispness and boppish force that the original cuts rather lacked. Dave Grusin's and Larry Rosen's production is ultra-sharp and is perhaps too respectful of individual horns on 'Deception' and 'Budo', where a degree less separation might have been more effective (unless this is an impression based entirely on folk-memories of the original LP). The mix works rather better on the boppish 'Move' and 'Boplicity', and on the vocal 'Darn That Dream'. An interesting retake on a still-misunderstood experiment, *Re-Birth* (not to be confused with a funk-rap album of the same name, issued some time previously) sounds perfectly valid on its own terms.

*** Paraiso: Jazz Brazil Telarc Digital CD 83361
Mulligan; Emanuel Moreira (*g*); Charlie Ernst, Cliff Korman (*p*); Rogerio Maio, Leonard D. Traversa (*b*); Duduka Da Fonseca, Peter Grant (*d*); Waltinho Anastacio, Norberto Goldberg (*perc*); Jane Duboc (*v*). 7/93.

Mulligan towers head and shoulders above all the other musicians in this slightly cheesy Latin-American date. Jane Duboc's vocals are actually rather winning and grow with familiarity, but the arrangements lack the subtlety and depth of focus for which one always looked to Mulligan in the old days.

***(*) Dream A Little Dream Telarc Digital CD 83364
Mulligan; Bill Mays, Ted Rosenthal (*p*); Dean Johnson (*b*); Ron Vincent (*d*). 4/94.

His last album. There had been rumours for some time about Mulligan's health and most of them proved to be premature. Certainly there is no lapse in quality on this gloriously recorded session. Some of the best moments are the most intimate, a duo version with Rosenthal of Alec Wilder's 'I'll Be Around' and duet versions of 'My Funny Valentine' and 'As Close As Pages In A Book' with guest pianist Bill Mays, who had been a regular performer with the quartet. The closing 'Song For Strayhorn' pays tribute to one of the saxophonist's great friends and idols and the man who, perhaps more than any other – more than Ellington, arguably – influenced his approach to the jazz orchestra. But then, of course, Mulligan always thought of a small group, even a duo, as an orchestra in miniature, so the piece has the bigness of spirit and sound one would expect.

Mark Murphy (born 1932) VOCAL

***(*) Rah Original Jazz Classics OJC 141
Murphy; Ernie Wilkins Orchestra. 9–10/61.

*** That's How I Love The Blues Original Jazz Classics OJC 367
Murphy; Nick Travis, Snooky Young, Clark Terry (*t*); Bernie Leighton, Dick Hyman (*org*); Roger Kellaway (*p*); Jim Hall (*g*); Ben Tucker (*b*); Dave Bailey (*d*); Willie Rodriguez (*perc*). 62.

Mark Murphy's been hip all his professional life. His earliest records, of which these are two, found him looking to emulate Eddie Jefferson rather than Frank Sinatra (or Bobby Darin – Murphy looked a little like a bobbysoxer himself back then) and, while his delivery is sometimes self-consciously cool in its use of dynamics and bent notes, he's always an impassioned singer – sometimes too much so, such as on an overwrought 'Blues In My Heart' on the *Blues* collection. That record may annoy some with its showmanlike approach to a set of downbeat material, but Murphy is no more overbearing than Billy Eckstine or Al Hibbler. *Rah*, pitched as a college man's text of hipsterism, is marginally more enjoyable, but both records benefit from the singer's strong, flexible tenor – he's enough his own man never to shoot for black pronunciation – and canny arrangements by Ernie Wilkins and (on *Blues*) Al Cohn.

*** **Bop For Kerouac** Muse MCD 5253
> Murphy; Richie Cole (*as, ts*); Bill Mays (*p*); Bruce Forman (*g*); Bob Magnusson, Luther Hughes (*b*); Roy McCurdy, Jeff Hamilton (*d*); Michael Spiro (*perc*). 81.

***(*) **Sings Nat's Choice** Muse MCD 6001
> Murphy; Gary Schunk (*ky*); Joe Lo Duca (*g*); Bob Magnusson (*b*). 10–11/83.

*** **Beauty And The Beast** Muse M 5355
> Murphy; Brian Lynch (*t, flhn*); Bill Mays (*ky*); Lou Lausche (*vn*); Michael Formanek, Steve LaSpina (*b*); Joey Baron (*d*). 85–86.

(*) **Night Mood Milestone MCD-9145
> Murphy; Claudio Roditi (*t*); Frank Morgan (*as*); Jose Bertrami (*ky*); Alex Malheiros (*b*); Ivan Conti (*d*). 86.

*** **Kerouac Then And Now** Muse MCD 5359
> Murphy; Bill Mays (*ky*); Steve LaSpina (*b*); Adam Nussbaum (*d*). 11/86.

*** **September Ballads** Milestone MCD 9154-2
> Murphy; Art Farmer (*t*); Larry Dunlap (*ky*); Oscar Castro-Nueves (*g*); David Belove, Jeff Carney (*b*); Donald Bailey (*d*); John Santos, Vince Lateano (*perc*). 87.

*** **What A Way To Go** Muse MCD 5419
> Murphy; Danny Wilensky (*ts*); Pat Rebillot (*p*); John Cobert, Larry Fallon (*ky*); David Spinozza (*g*); Francisco Centeno (*b*); Alan Schwartzberg, Chris Parker (*d*); John Kaye, Sammy Figueroa (*perc*). 11/90.

(*) **I'll Close My Eyes Muse MCD 5436
> Murphy; Claudio Roditi (*t*); Cliff Carter (*ky*); Pat Rebillot (*p*); John Basile (*g*); Dave Finck (*b*); Peter Grant (*d*); Sammy Figueroa (*perc*). 12/91.

*** **Another Vision** September 5113
> Murphy; Ack Van Rooyen (*flhn*); Turk Mauro (*ts*); Jack Poll (*p*); Martin Wind (*b*); Hans Van Ossterhout (*d*). 7/92.

Many Murphy albums are still awaited on CD. These latter-day records offer a useful round-up of his interests and techniques. *Beauty And The Beast* is almost a sampler of his recent work, with a poem read as an accompaniment to Wayne Shorter's title-theme, a fine 'I Can't Get Started' and an example of his mastery of bebop singing on Sonny Rollins's 'Doxy'. A useful cast of players are on hand in support. His fascination with Kerouac opens with *Bop For Kerouac*, in which he intersperses song choices with a reading from *On the Road* and a version of 'Boplicity' that is a tribute to boppers of all stripes. It continues on *Then And Now*, where there are tunes chosen to suggest the writer's tastes, episodes from some of his works read to music, and even a re-creation of a Lord Buckley routine. If neither disc always works – Murphy can't help but sound self-conscious, even if he has a passion for this kind of thing – it's an interesting attempt at updating or rekindling beat repertory for an audience that would otherwise find this stuff quaintly hipsterish. But they may be more likely to warm to the after-hours ambience of his Nat Cole tribute, probably his best latter-day album. It's worth having for the charming treatment of 'I Keep Going Back To Joe's', but the whole programme is an appealing, graceful set of well-chosen tunes.

Night Mood and September Ballads both set him up with a light fusion of jazz and Latin rhythms (the group Azymuth back him on the former) and, although his singing is as accomplished as usual, the thin material on *Night Mood* is discouraging; and nothing really stands out on the pleasing but muted *September Ballads*. *What A Way To Go* returns to a mixture of standards and jazz tunes: Murphy has started to exaggerate some of his bent notes and rhythmic risks to compensate for a voice that is starting to turn grey at the edges, and some may dislike what he does with 'I Fall In Love Too Easily', to pick one. But he still sets himself the most inventive of programmes – Lee Morgan's 'Ceora', Ray Brown's 'Clown In My Window' – and makes them happen. *I'll Close My Eyes* is tarnished by the overlit production and middle-aged pop arrangements, but Mark still sounds affecting on the gentler tunes. *Another Vision* is distinguished by a fine team of players, a gentle production and some useful solos by guests Mauro and van Rooyen. Murphy's scatting and fast pace can sound affected on the swingers, and his voice has lost a lot of its bloom, but the more quiescent music still has an evocative streak.

Turk Murphy (1915–87) TROMBONE

*** **Turk Murphy's Jazz Band Favourites** Good Time Jazz 60-011
    Murphy; Don Kinch, Bob Scobey (*t*); Bill Napier, Skippy Anderson, Bob Helm (*cl*); Burt Bales,
    Wally Rose (*p*); Bill Newman (*g, bj*); Pat Patton, Dick Lammi, Harry Mordecai (*bj*); Squire
    Gersback, George Bruns (*b, tba*); Stan Ward, Johnny Brent (*d*). 49–51.

** **Turk Murphy And His San Francisco Jazz Band Vol. 1** GHB 091
    Murphy; Leon Oakley (*c*); Jim Maichak (*tb*); Phil Howe (*cl*); Pete Clute (*p*); Carl Lunsford (*bj*).
    4/72.

** **Turk Murphy And His San Francisco Jazz Band Vol. 2** GHB 092
    As above. 4/72.

Murphy's music would be a little more credible if he hadn't gone on making it for so long. At the time of
his earliest recordings, when he was a member of the Lu Watters circle, the Californian traditional jazz
movement had some nous as revivalists of music which had lain, unjustly neglected, for many years. In
that light, the Good Time Jazz compilation, hammy though much of the playing is, and often painfully
(as opposed to authentically) untutored, is both an interesting and an enjoyable one. But after more
than 20 years of this kind of thing, Murphy's one-track traditionalism sounds tiresome and soulless on
the two GHB CDs, taken from a single 1972 session. It might be cheerful and boisterous enough, and
Murphy's own playing has achieved a ready constituency, but there are many better arguments for
revivalism than this music. Murphy's legacy is better handled by some of the superior outfits now
recording for GHB and Stomp Off.

David Murray (born 1955) TENOR SAXOPHONE, BASS CLARINET

*** **Live At The Lower Manhattan Ocean Club** India Navigation IN 1032
    Murray; Lester Bowie (*t*); Fred Hopkins (*b*); Phillip Wilson (*d*). 12/77.

Over the last decade David Murray would seem to have confirmed Ornette Coleman's famous claim that
the soul of black Americans is best expressed through the tenor saxophone. A pivotal figure in contemporary jazz (and one of the most comprehensively documented), Murray has patiently created a
synthesis of the radical experimentation of John Coltrane and (particularly) Albert Ayler with the
classic jazz tradition. As such, his music is virtually uncategorizable, exploring freedom one moment,
locked in bright swing structures the next, moving without strain from astonishing aggression to openly
romantic expression (much of it dedicated to his wife, Ming).

He has worked with the World Saxophone Quartet and the Music Revelation Ensemble, but since 1976
has released more than 30 albums under his own name, some of which are already accorded classic
status. He has an expansive tone that is readily adaptable to fast, aggressive cross-cutting and slower,
more expressive ballad performance. *Ocean Club* introduces material – 'Bechet's Bounce' and 'Santa
Barbara And Crenshaw's Follies' – that typically reappears later, very much transformed; remastered
from the LPs, it has Murray doubling rather unconvincingly on soprano saxophone, though Bowie is on
top form. Stanley Crouch, who has cornered the market in liner-notes for young traditionalists like
Murray and Wynton Marsalis, has been one of the central personal influences on the saxophonist's
career, as is the superb Fred Hopkins.

*** **Interboogieology** Black Saint 120018
    Murray; Lawrence Butch Morris (*c*); Johnny Dyani (*b*); Oliver Johnson (*d*); Marta Contreras
    (*v*). 2/78.

Two compositions each by Murray and his most significant collaborator, Butch Morris. The opening
'Namthini's Song' is a stately procession, marked by Morris's typically unpredictable voicings. Marta
Contreras sings wordlessly, somewhere up near the cornet's register; it's certainly a more convincing use
of her voice than the Abbey Lincoln mannerisms of the title-track. 'Home' is a huge duet from Murray
and Dyani, with the bassist's solid chant underpinning a free-flowing improvisation. 'Blues For David' is
uncharacteristically direct for Morris, a fine blowing number with the leader's most shaped solo contributions of the set.

This album probably set the pattern for Murray's subsequent and now very substantial output. A
tireless experimenter, he also has a strong and canny urge to communicate, and there is a thread of
populism running through his music that belies the easy critical association with Ayler and makes a
nonsense of many critics' professed surprise at his rejection of unmediated avant-gardism in favour of a
'back to the future' examination of the whole sequence of black musical tradition.

*** **3D Family** hat Art 6020
    Murray; Johnny Dyani (*b*); Andrew Cyrille (*d*). 8/78.

Murray's solitary album on hat Art is a curious mixture of fantastic potential in some directions and overachieved mastery in other, less promising ones. As a collaborative trio, it's absolutely sussed, but the material doesn't always do any more than trip up what sound like excitingly spontaneous ideas. Cyrille is a whirlwind, and a duo performance would be worth arranging. '3D Family', which reappears on *Home*, is among the saxophonist's best charts, and Dyani gives it a vibrant surge that recalls their duet on the *Interboogieology* version of 'Home'. (By this time, the permutation of tunes and performances has become quite bewildering.)

**** **Sweet Lovely** Black Saint 120039
    Murray; Fred Hopkins (*b*); Steve McCall (*d*). 12/79.
Stripped down to basics, this anticipates *The Hill*. The first version of 'Hope/Scope', which has a slightly odd subsequent history, is the clearest, pivoted on Hopkins's booming bass. 'Coney Island' and 'The Hill' are at opposite ends of Murray's repertoire, but the trio gives them an unexpected coherence.

**** **Ming** Black Saint 120045
    Murray; Olu Dara (*t*); Lawrence Butch Morris (*c*); George Lewis (*tb*); Henry Threadgill (*as*); Anthony Davis (*p*); Wilber Morris (*b*); Steve McCall (*d, perc*). 7/80.
***(*) **Home** Black Saint 120055
    As above. 11/81.
For many fans, *the* jazz album of the 1980s was recorded before the decade was properly under way. *Ming* is an astonishing record, a virtual compression of three generations of improvised music into 40 minutes of entirely original jazz. The opening 'Fast Life' has a hectic quality reminiscent of another of Murray's household gods, Charles Mingus. 'Jasvan' is a swirling 'Boston' waltz that gives most of the band, led off by the marvellous Lewis, ample solo space. 'Ming' is a sweet ballad which follows on from the troubling, almost schizophrenic 'The Hill', a piece that occupies a central place in Murray's output, perhaps an image of the jazz *gradus ad Parnassum* that he is so studiously and passionately scaling.

    Recorded by the same octet, *Home* is very nearly the better album. The slow opening title-piece is a delicately layered ballad with gorgeous horn voicings. 'Last Of The Hipmen' is one of his best pieces, and the Anthony Davis vamp that leads out of Steve McCall's intelligent and exuberant solo is a reminder of how close to Ellington's bandleading philosophy Murray has come by instinct rather than design.

*** **Murray's Steps** Black Saint 120065
    Murray; Bobby Bradford (*t*); Lawrence Butch Morris (*c*); Craig Harris (*tb*); Henry Threadgill (*as, f*); Curtis Clark (*p*); Wilber Morris (*b*); Steve McCall (*d, perc*). 7/82.
This hasn't quite the sharpness of Murray's other octets and has to be considered, absurd as this will sound to anyone who has heard the disc, an off-day. The retake of 'Flowers For Albert' is an important index of how unwilling Murray has always been to leave his own output alone; there are more convincing versions; but, if the dedicatee represents some sort of magnetic north for Murray, then the piece is a good navigational aid.

***(*) **Morning Song** Black Saint 120075
    Murray; John Hicks (*p*); Reggie Workman, Ray Drummond (*b*); Ed Blackwell (*d*). 9/83.
Compare the version of 'Body And Soul' – the tenor saxophonist's shibboleth – here with the unaccompanied one on the first item, above. It is more assured, less willed and less concerned with deconstructing a piece that has been rendered virtually abstract by countless hundreds of improvisations. Note how Murray restores the tune in segments during his later statements of a freely arrived-at counter-theme.

    Hicks is a wonderfully supportive and sensitive partner, particularly on the standard (enthusiasts should check out their duo, *Sketches Of Tokyo*, DIW 8006 CD, which features a – then surprisingly rare, but now more frequent – take on Coltrane by the saxophonist, and Blackwell's drumming touches all the right bases. A pity they haven't done more together.

*** **Live At Sweet Basil: Volume 1** Black Saint 120085
    Murray; Olu Dara (*c*); Baikida Carroll, Craig Harris (*t*); Bob Stewart (*tba*); Vincent Chauncey (*frhn*); Steve Coleman (*ss, as*); John Purcell (*as, cl*); Rod Williams (*p*); Fred Hopkins (*b*); Billy Higgins (*d*); Lawrence Butch Morris (*cond*). 8/84.
*** **Live At Sweet Basil: Volume 2** Black Saint 120095
    As above. 8/84.
Volume 2 kicks off with a version of the wonderfully cheesy 'Dewey's Circle' from *Ming*, one of those compositions of Murray's that many listeners swear they have heard somewhere before. It's not quite the best piece on the set, but it's the one where most of the constituent elements are coming together. 'Bechet's Bounce' and 'Silence' on the first volume redirect some of Murray's increasingly familiar obsessions in quite new ways. The final track is a brief dedication to Marvin Gaye; by this stage in his career Murray is name-checking at an impressive rate.

The live context, with a hefty band pushing from behind, makes for some inventive conjunctions, but Murray's tone is uncharacteristically acid. There's no obvious explanation for it; the production is well up to Black Saint's careful standard.

*** Children Black Saint 120089

Murray; Don Pullen (*p*); James Blood Ulmer (*g*); Lonnie Plaxico (*b*); Marvin 'Smitty' Smith (*d*). 10 & 11/84.

Rededicated to his son, David Mingus Murray, this is one of the poorer 1980s albums. Smith and Plaxico dominate unnecessarily, and Ulmer and Pullen consistently get in each other's way. That's another two bankable modern names to tick off against Murray's list, with 'All The Things You Are' for anyone who's bird-watching the standards.

*** Recording NYC 1986 DIW 802

Murray; James Blood Ulmer (*g*); Fred Hopkins (*b*); Sonny Murray (*d*). 86.

***(*) I Want To Talk About You Black Saint 120105

Murray; John Hicks (*p*); Ray Drummond (*b*); Ralph Peterson Jr (*d*). 3/86.

Those who were disturbed by Murray's apparent abandonment of the avant-garde might have been reassured by his firm rejection of the backward-looking stance of Wynton Marsalis and others. It's clear from the live *I Want To Talk About You* that, while the saxophonist is looking increasingly to an earlier generation of saxophone players, Sonny Rollins pre-eminently, but also synthesizers like the fated Ellingtonian Paul Gonsalves, he is doing so with instincts very explicitly conditioned by Coltrane and Ayler. His reading of 'I Want To Talk About You' has to be heard in the context of Coltrane's own version; as a ballad player, Murray is vibrant and expansive and 'Heart To Heart' (written by Hicks) is one of his most nakedly emotional recorded performances.

'Morning Song' reappears, its robust R&B stretched out into something altogether stronger than the album version. 'Red Car', from *Recording NYC*, has him switch to bass clarinet; if the technique ultimately derives from Dolphy, Murray has managed to extend his great predecessor's somewhat predictable upper-register devices, making use of more of the horn.

Ulmer is another to have apparently turned his back on the avant-garde in pursuit of a more marketable neo-populism. In practice, of course, the more conservative Ulmer is also the one who digs deepest into black tradition, and so it turns out to be with Murray.

*** In Our Style DIW 819

Murray; Fred Hopkins (*b*); Jack DeJohnette (*d, p*). 9/86.

Murray played in DeJohnette's Special Edition band, notably on *Album Album* (ECM 1280), but their duo confrontation feels slightly uncomfortable, as if they're doing no more than sounding one another out. DeJohnette's piano backgrounds, though uncharacteristically basic, are more effective foils than the drummed tracks, where DeJohnette seems to restrict himself to a disappointingly narrow range of devices, some of them overpoweringly recorded. It all makes a bit more sense when Fred Hopkins comes in on the title-track and 'Your Dice'.

**** The Hill Black Saint 120110

Murray; Richard Davis (*b*); Joe Chambers (*d*). 11/86.

One of the peaks of Murray's career. The title-piece, pared down from eight voices to three, doesn't fall apart but retains its rather mysterious and troubling presence. Murray has significantly toned down his delivery from the immediately previous sessions and sounds altogether more thoughtful. The material, by now, is quite self-consciously programmed, with 'Chelsea Bridge' and 'Take The Coltrane' mixed in with the originals. 'Herbie Miller' contains Murray's best-recorded bass clarinet solo; pitched against Richard Davis's rich *arco*, he develops an intense thematic discourse that takes enough time to vary its accents in keeping with the changing emotional climate of the piece. By contrast, 'Fling' is exactly as throwaway as it sounds.

This is an essential modern album.

*** Hope Scope Black Saint 120139

Murray; Hugh Ragin, Rasul Siddik (*t*); Craig Harris (*tb*); James Spaulding (*as*); Dave Burrell (*p*); Wilber Morris (*b*); Ralph Peterson (*d*). 5/87.

Only released in 1991 (by which time Murray was recording for DIW), this is a bright, exuberant album, full of the band's palpable delight in what they're doing. This version of 'Hope/Scope' is much less convoluted than the one on *Special Quartet*, below, but it inspires some raggedly spirited ensemble improvisations. The tributes to Lester Young and Ben Webster are closer to pastiche than usual (see also DIW 851, below), reflecting a rather lightweight side to the album that is initially appealing but increasingly puzzling as the layers come off it.

*** The Healers Black Saint 120118

Murray; Randy Weston (*p*). 9/87.

Though Weston's sense of structure is much like Murray's, which turns out to be inhibiting rather than particularly productive, he tends to conceive developments in discontinuous units rather than in Murray's uninterrupted flow. Several times the pianist falls back on set licks, which make him sound a less sophisticated player than he is. 'Mbizo' is a further version of a dedication to Johnny Dyani, who died the previous year. A by-way on Murray's increasingly determined course, *The Healers* takes Murray down a road he has seemed disinclined to pursue. Which is a pity.

*** **Lucky Four** Tutu 888108
    Murray; Dave Burrell (*p*); Wilber Morris (*b*); Victor Lewis (*d, perc*). 9/88.
Moonlighting under the alias of Lucky Four, Murray and two long-standing collaborators turn in a slightly lacklustre session that, despite interesting variants on both 'Valley Talk' and 'As I Woke', never seems to grab the attention firmly. 'Chazz', dedicated to Mingus, and 'Strollin'', to Michel Basquiat, are both slightly woolly.

**** **Deep River** DIW 830
    Murray; Dave Burrell (*p*); Fred Hopkins (*b*); Ralph Peterson Jr (*d*). 1/88.
**** **Ballads** DIW 840
    As above.
***(*) **Spirituals** DIW 841
    As above.
**** **Special Quartet** DIW 843
    Murray; McCoy Tyner (*p*); Fred Hopkins (*b*); Elvin Jones (*d*). 90.
Murray's move away from the Italian-based Black Saint (who had generously supported his work in the absence of any major-label bites) to the Japan-based DIW did nothing to stem the flow of material. Releasing records in threes quickly became the norm. These albums, with their explicitly traditionalist agenda, all come from a single New York session and are not quite as varied as the 1991 batch. *Ballads* has become one of the most popular of the saxophonist's albums, with *Spirituals* also touching a popular nerve; but spare a moment for *Deep River*, with 'Dakar's Dance' and 'Mr P.C.'. The latter is topped only by a riveting version of another Coltrane track on the 1990 album. *Special Quartet*? It certainly is, and a fine piece of arrogance on Murray's part to put half the classic Coltrane band back together, but it's no better than the 1988 group, even if Tyner is in sparkling form.

***(*) **Tea For Two** Fresh Sound FSRCD 164
    Murray; George Arvanitas (*p*). 5/90.
Headed 'George Arvanitas Presents: The ballad artistry of . . . David Murray', there's a rabbit-out-of-hat quality to the ellipsis. Though no one's surprised any more to find Murray playing 'in the tradition', it's still rare to find him doing it quite this uncomplicatedly. The menu of standards doesn't really stretch him technically and there's a hint of a more mannered approach in his takes of past giants, almost as if he's over-anxious to inscribe himself into the history of jazz saxophone before the fortieth birthday comes up. For the record (this is a relatively undiscovered Murray album), the track listing is 'Chelsea Bridge', 'Polka Dots And Moonbeams', 'Star Eyes', 'Body And Soul' again, 'Tea For Two', 'I'm In The Mood For Love', an original 'Blues For Two', and 'La Vie En Rose'.

**** **Remembrances** DIW 849
    Murray; Hugh Ragin (*t*); Dave Burrell (*p*); Wilber Morris (*b*); Tani Tabbal (*d*). 7/90.
On the cover a tiny child kneels, a toy saxophone pressed to its lips, the bell raised in exact mimicry of, yes! Albert Ayler at his most impassioned (or of Murray himself on the cover of *Deep River*). *Remembrances* digs down into the same influences that conditioned Murray's great predecessor. Much of this material is in the spirit of the black church (and thus of *Spirituals* and *Deep River*), its abstractions emerging out of impassioned witness, its resolutions an expression of acceptance rather than of will.

The tonal integrity of Ragin and Burrell is extraordinarily beautiful, with the trumpeter pealing away with a much fuller sound than he often uses and Burrell laying fat, rolling chords over the rhythmic pattern. Very lovely, very accomplished, and absolutely of its time and place.

***(*) **Shakill's Warrior** DIW 850
    Murray; Don Pullen (*org*); Stanley Franks (*g*); Andrew Cyrille (*d*). 3/91.
*** **Shakill's II** DIW 884
    Murray; Don Pullen (*org*); Bill White (*g*); J. T. Lewis (*d*). 93.
A much more personal dredge of the past. *Shakill's Warrior* plugs Don Pullen into a Hammond B3 and Murray into his R&B roots. He even looked up his old pal, Stanley Franks, from their teenage band, Notations of Soul. Franks does damn-all on the album, but the remaining trio is red-hot. Pullen, working to a broadly similar concept, goes back virtually all the way with Murray; Cyrille is a new

factor and, if he doesn't at first seem ideally suited to this line-up, it's the drummer's 'High Priest' which dominates the album.

The sequel is fairly dismal, Pullen apart. Murray waffles from one theme to the next, rarely sounding properly engaged, often falling back on staringly obvious ideas. A disappointing follow-up to a steaming record.

*** David Murray Big Band DIW 851

Murray; Graham Haynes, Hugh Ragin, Rasul Siddik, James Zollar (*t*); Craig Harris, Frank Lacy, Al Patterson (*tb*); Vincent Chauncey (*frhn*); Bob Stewart (*tba*); Khalil Henry (*f, picc*); John Purcell (*as*); James Spaulding (*as, f*); Patience Higgins (*ts, ss*); Don Byron (*bs, cl*); Sonelius Smith (*p*); Fred Hopkins (*b*); Tani Tabbal (*d*); Joel A. Brandon (*whistle*); Andy Bey (*v*); Lawrence Butch Morris (*cond*). 3/91.

There are further versions of 'Lester' and 'Ben' from *Hope/Scope* and a dedication to Paul Gonsalves, acknowledged as an influence on Murray. The former pair are given an altogether more complex and detailed reading but, by and large, the performances on this album are disappointingly trite, and certainly lacking in the multi-layered obliqueness one expects from Morris (who, significantly or not, doesn't contribute as a composer, other than the shared credit on 'Calling Steve McCall').

The band is impressively constructed, on a scale Murray hasn't attempted before, but it seems a pity to have got them all together and fired up and then to give them so little of consequence to play.

*** The Jazzpar Prize Enja CD 7031

Murray; New Jungle Orchestra: Pierre Dørge (*g*); Per Jörgensen (*t*); Harry Beckett (*t, flhn*); Jörg Huke (*tb*); Jesper Zeuthen (*as, bcl*); Jacob Mygind (*ts, ss*); Horace Parlan (*p*); Irene Becker (*ky*); Jens Skov Olsen (*b*); Audun Klieve (*d*); Donald Murray (*v*). 3/91.

In the spring of 1991 Murray was awarded the third annual Jazzpar Prize, perhaps the only major international jazz award in the world. It was a significant accolade for a man not yet forty. During the course of the prize project, Murray recorded with Pierre Dørge's New Jungle Orchestra. The two men share an interest in Ellingtonian composition and sounds, and Murray fitted into the band with his usual ease. The two opening pieces are by the guitarist; there follows a gospel medley, with vocals from Donald Murray, a beautifully constructed version of 'In A Sentimental Mood', finishing with full-throated performances of 'Shakil's Warrior' and 'Song For Doni'.

Murray's solo is more restrained than usual, and in this context his kinship with Paul Gonsalves becomes entirely unambiguous. Though he varies the melody of the Ellington tune to spark off his solo, ironically it's one of the straightest and most respectful repertoire performances to be found anywhere in his recorded output.

*** Death Of A Sideman DIW 866

Murray; Bobby Bradford (*c*); Dave Burrell (*p*); Fred Hopkins (*b*); Ed Blackwell (*d*). 10/91.

Death Of A Sideman is a suite of pieces dedicated to the late clarinettist and educator, John Carter. It's relatively unusual for Murray to play quite so much work by another composer. He remains constantly open to Bradford's ideas, but his solos on this occasion are often little more than sets of alternative scalar structures which never seem to develop satisfactorily. Only on 'Woodshedetude' does he build up enough momentum to burst out of the confines of the written chart and play imaginatively. Bradford's post-Cherry sound, tight, small, almost folkish, presents such a startling contrast to Murray's broad vibrato that the pairing works quite well. The rhythm section never falters for a moment, but Blackwell, who was in very indifferent health at the time, sounds unusually robotic.

*** Black & Black Red Baron 451577

Murray; Marcus Belgrave (*t*); Kirk Lightsey (*p*); Santi Debriano (*b*); Roy Haynes (*d*). 10 & 11/91.

A matter of days later, Murray was recording this session for a new label. He'd made a record with Teresa Brewer earlier in the year, but this was the first under his own name. He's done this often enough to sound completely unfazed. Duke's 'C Jam Blues' is eaten up like warm toast, and the Ellington shadow, which lay heavily across the Jazzpar project, is still visible here. Murray's horn seems to be miked slightly differently, eliminating much of the gentle buzz he often gets down below G. It's a cleaner sound, but it may be that the saxophonist himself didn't warm to it, because later Red Baron releases don't sound quite the same.

**** Fast Life DIW 861

Murray; Branford Marsalis (*ts*); John Hicks (*p*); Ray Drummond (*b*); Idris Muhammad (*d*). 10/91.

Just to round out an extraordinarily productive month, this beautiful album by the quartet-plus-one. Branford's contributions to Dave Burrell's 'Crucificado' and the title-piece are astonishingly close in conception and execution to Murray's own work, suggesting an unsuspectedly large area of common ground. Murray himself is as definite as a shark, moving ever forward and laying off lyrical ideas at a rate that almost defies belief. It would be tempting to think that at least some of the solos had been pre-formed, but for the objection that Hicks so obviously throws curves. Drummond is as expansive as his own waistline, and the underrated Muhammad does a great job.

**** Ballads For Bass Clarinet DIW 880
  Murray; John Hicks (*p*); Ray Drummond (*b*); Idris Muhammad (*d*). 10/91.
It was logical that one day Murray would record exclusively on bass clarinet. The wonder is how effective an album it turns out to be, and how close his phrasing on the big, cumbersome horn is to his tenor work. The opening 'Waltz To Heaven' has a glowing warmth and presence, as does 'New Life'. 'Portrait Of A Black Woman' introduces a note of anguish, but only briefly.

**** Real Deal DIW 867
  Murray; Milford Graves (*d, perc*). 11/91.
*** A Sanctuary Within Black Saint 120145
  Murray; Tony Overwater (*b*); Sunny Murray (*d*); Kahil El'Zabar (*perc, v*). 12/91.
This might almost have come from a decade previously, when Murray was firmly locked into his avant-garde phase. Yet he has become much more varied in his choice of sounds, plumbing not just the stoical moods of 'Ballad For The Blackman' but also the more buoyant and affirmative 'Waltz To Heaven', a theme that was to reappear over the succeeding couple of years in a number of playing contexts, not least the bass clarinet album, above.

El'Zabar, a founding member of the Ethnic Heritage Ensemble, creates a whirl of exotic tinges round the fringes of each piece, but he doesn't feel integral to the project and a couple of tracks would certainly be improved if he simply weren't there.

Perversely, it would be fascinating to hear Murray work in duo with the percussionist for an entire session, as he does with the completely wonderful Graves on *Real Deal*. One of the pioneering musicians of the 1960s avant-garde, Graves largely disappeared from the recording scene and has come back to attention only quite recently. His encounter with Murray is as titanic as might have been supposed. Working in structures that might be called indefinite rather than abstract, they weave great loops of music on which first one, then the other, is able to improvise more freely. It's marvellously tight and wholly effective. An essential purchase for Murray admirers.

***(*) Live '93 Acoustic Octfunk Sound Hills SSCD 8051
  Murray; Fred Hopkins (*b*); Andrew Cyrille (*d*). 7/93.
This was a very successful tour for Murray, artistically if not always at the box office. Trio playing encouraged him to play simply, in bold strokes and relatively unadorned. His solos, as here on 'Mr P.C.' and 'Flowers For Albert', are intense, but it is the interplay among the three members of the group that is so impressive, and it communicates itself even across a rather unforgiving recording that booms and thuds away awkwardly. Hopkins plays superbly, and Cyrille's fills and solo spots are packed with ideas.

**** Tenors DIW 881
  Murray; Dave Burrell (*p*); Fred Hopkins (*b*); Ralph Peterson Jr (*d*). 1/88.
*** Picasso DIW 879
  Murray; Hugh Ragin, Rasul Siddik (*t*); Craig Harris (*tb*); James Spaulding (*as, f*); Dave Burrell (*p*); Wilber Morris (*b*); Tani Tabbal (*d*). 92.
**** Body And Soul Black Saint 120155
  Murray; Sonelius Smith (*p*); Wilber Morris (*b*); Rashied Ali (*d*); Taana Running (*v*). 2/93.
***(*) MX Red Baron 496534
  Murray; Bobby Bradford (*t*); Ravi Coltrane (*ts, ss*); John Hicks (*p*); Fred Hopkins (*b*); Victor Lewis (*d*).
***(*) Saxmen Red Baron JK 57758
  Murray; John Hicks (*p*); Ray Drummond (*b*); Andrew Cyrille (*d*). 8/93.
***(*) Jazzosaurus Rex Red Baron JK 57336
  As above, except add G'Ar (*v*). 8/93.
By the end of the 1980s, Murray's traditionalism was expressing itself in unambiguously literal form. Time and again, he plunged back into the history of the music, dredging up performances that fell somewhere between wholesale revision and an oddly uncertain faithfulness to the originals. Because it always sounded like Murray, nobody minded; but much of that was superficial, disguising how little he was prepared to disturb ancestral ghosts.

It's worthwhile looking at *Tenors* and *Saxmen* together. Recorded nearly five years apart, they trace the development of just that trend in Murray's playing. Both consist of tributes to the great tenormen; but the earlier addresses a much spikier pantheon: Coltrane, Ayler and Ornette, the second a more accom-modating bunch: Coltrane again, but this time the gentler 'Central Park West', Sonny Stitt, Charlie Rouse, Prez and Bird. Usefully, both discs include performances of Sonny Rollins's patented calypso, 'St

Thomas', a piece that has made a big impact on Murray's own approach to such material. Strayhorn's 'Chelsea Bridge', played so magnificently on *Tenors*, is also featured on *Jazzosaurus Rex*, turned into a quietly seductive love-song. There's nothing dull or compromised about the performances on *Saxmen* or *Jazzosaurus*, but there is, to repeat, a failure to interrogate history in the way that Murray had been doing just a few years previously. For all the fury he puts into 'Lester Leaps In', there's a strong sense of a man working well within known limits. At least on the earlier record there was a feeling that he was pushing at the boundaries.

It was odds on that Murray would one day record an album called *Body And Soul*. His understanding of Hawkins's classic solo is obvious from the outset of his own interpretation, which works a very specific, palindromic variation on the opening phrases. However, Murray's solo has only a rather artificial shape, not the almost organic unity of Hawkins, and the unity comes largely from Taana Running's vocal. In *Picasso*, a loose suite of tunes in which the great painter and Hawkins again are put within a single abstract frame, Bean's great unaccompanied meditation on 'Picasso' has become one of the most influential performances in jazz, as significant to the present generation as 'Body And Soul' was to previous cohorts. As before, Murray has absorbed it wholly. The question is whether he is able to do anything with it. The suite itself is little more than a sequence of faintly incompatible elements blended together by artificial means. It certainly lacks vision. The band on *Picasso* is a good one, but that on *Body And Soul* is superlative, always just poised to take the music one stage higher.

It's difficult to gauge whether and to what extent all of these reflect the commitment to endless inquiry that was always part of Murray's project when he was starting out. Whether they do or not, they are all supremely enjoyable.

***(*) South Of The Border DIW 897

Murray; Hugh Ragin, Rasul Siddik, James Zollar (*t*); Graham Haynes (*c*); Craig Harris, Frank Lacy, Al Patterson (*tb*); Vincent Chauncey (*frhn*); Khalil Henry (*f*); John Purcell (*as*); James Spaulding (*as, f*); Patience Higgins (*ts, ss*); Don Byron (*cl, bs*); Sonelius Smith (*p*); Fred Hopkins (*b*); Tani Tabbal (*d*); Larry McDonald (*perc*); Butch Morris (*cond*). 5/92.

This seems to have been held back for a while in DIW's release programme, leapfrogged for no discernible reason by more recent recordings. In some respects, this is a backward glance, a swing-derived session ('Happy Birthday, Wayne Jr', especially) that doesn't entirely square with either Murray's free-floating improvisation or Morris's 'comprovised' approach. The conductor's one writing credit is a big romantic blurt that will startle those who look to him for something altogether more tight-lipped and abstract.

The real strength of this album is the solo work by an excellent line-up. Murray features himself relatively sparingly. The Morris ballad, 'Fling', is a showcase, but he devolves Sonelius Smith's 'World Of The Children' to Haynes, and he is happy to join the line with Ragin and Harris on yet another re-run of 'Flowers For Albert'. Spaulding, Byron, the omnicompetent Lacy and Higgins all feature strongly, the last of these in duet with Murray on the opening 'St Thomas', a version that gives Sonny Rollins's theme a tersely jolly reading.

***(*) The Tip DIW 891

Murray; Bobby Broom (*g*); Robert Irving III (*org, syn*); Darryl Jones (*b*); Toby Williams (*d*); Kahil El'Zabar (*perc*); G'Ra (*poetry*). 5/94.

It keeps being said; it remains the case. Murray plays with magisterial calm and exactness, shows an intelligent awareness of the jazz tradition (*passim*), of the continuum of African-American music ('Sex Machine') and of his own back-catalogue ('Flowers For Albert'). This is an altogether funkier, more plugged-in project than he has previously seen fit to release, and it divided critical opinion somewhat: on the one hand, the 'sell-out' crowd bayed and barked in dismay; others found it a logical step along a long-established course.

It's not the best Murray album, of course; some of the Miles-derived electronic settings are pretty drab or drably pretty, but there is no mistaking the sheer intensity and individuality of Murray's own role. Like strong players before him – Parker, Coltrane, Miles – he simply breezes through uncertain accompaniments and contexts, transforming them in the process into something grander and more timeless. Quite a talent to have in this business. (Do note that it is Toby, not Tony, Williams at the kit; *caveat emptor*.)

Dierdre Murray CELLO

***(*) Firestorm Victo CD 020

Murray; Fred Hopkins (*b, sticks*). 7/92.

*** **Stringology** Black Saint 120143
     As above, except add Marvin Sewell (*g, dobro*); Newman Baker (*d, spoons*); Ray Mantilla (*perc*).
     9/93.
One of a small group of improvisers who have specialized in the cello, Murray is a player who probably
still functions best in the context of rather larger groups, bringing in new colours and identities. This is
not to say that her duos with the effervescent Hopkins are not interesting, or that there are no merits in
the larger group. It is simply that one feels she trades too heavily on certain rather limited ideas and
these, especially on the skittish second album, can't quite be made to last the pace.

Music Improvisation Company GROUP

***(*) **The Music Improvisation Company 1968–1971** Incus CD12
     Evan Parker (*ss, autoharp*); Hugh Davies (*org, elec*); Derek Bailey (*g*); Jamie Muir (*perc*). 68–71.
British improvisers were already a determined if small and embattled community by the time these
recordings had been made. As documentary pieces, culled from years of occasional work, they are in
some ways charming, with Davies's fiercely primitive electronics countering Bailey's resolutely un-
guitar-like guitar playing, an ongoing dialogue that will seem nostalgic of a vanished era to some
older listeners. Parker's soprano is years away from his major developments and discoveries, yet still
sounds startlingly original: like Bailey, he was set on searching out a new way to play. Muir's contributions are arguably the least impressive, at least when set beside what free percussionists have done
both before and since, and he isn't so well served by the recording; yet the six pieces are in the main
about a quartet thinking and speaking as freely with one another as they possibly could. CD transfer
has brought up some of the detail lost in ageing vinyl pressings, and the chamber-like quality of much
of the music is unsettled by harshness and strangeness. But it remains rather beautiful, too. A welcome return, to be set alongside Spontaneous Music Ensemble's roughly contemporary *Karyobin*, also
recently reissued.

Music Revelation Ensemble GROUP

*** **No Wave** Moers 01072
     David Murray (*ts*); James Blood Ulmer (*g*); Amin Ali (*b*); Jamaaladeen Tacuma (*b*); Ronald
     Shannon Jackson (*d*). 6/80.
(*) **Music Revelation Ensemble DIW 825
     As above. 88.
*** **Elec. Jazz** DIW 841
     As above, except omit Tacuma, Jackson; add Cornell Rochester (*d*). 2/90.
*** **After Dark** DIW 855
     As above. 92.
***(*) **In The Name Of . . .** DIW 885
     As above, except add Sam Rivers (*ss, ts*); Arthur Blythe (*as*); Hamiet Bluiett (*bs*). 94.
***(*) **Knights Of Power** DIW 905
     As above, except omit Rivers. 4/95.
Music Revelation Ensemble bears out Bill Shankly's famous dictum about football being played on
grass, not on paper. *Music Revelation Ensemble*, on paper the most impressive-looking of the three
earliest, is actually a rather dismal supergroup session that takes an inordinately long time to catch light.
Murray enters very late – and with some diffidence – on the opening 'Bodytalk', and throughout the
album he sounds as if he's just sitting in on someone else's date. Only with the third track, 'Nisa', do
things get moving, by which time more than 20 tedious minutes of abstract noodling have already gone
by. 'Blues For David', like all the tracks, is an Ulmer composition, and not the Butch Morris tune of the
same name on Murray's *Interboogieology* on Black Saint; the saxophonist plays a melancholy intro and
then takes the front over a surprisingly bland accompaniment. The closing 'Burn!' is a silly pile-up.
Prime Time and Last Exit (and Murray) fans may be tempted, but would be advised to leave well alone.
    With a change of personnel in the engine-room, *Elec. Jazz* is rather better and sounds more like the
product of a working group. Organized almost like a suite, with two parts each to 'Exit' and 'Big Top', it
has far more shape than the first album and affords a better balance of ensemble and solo work. The
musicians too are arrayed more logically in the mix, with Murray and Ulmer front and centre, bass and
drums nicely divided across the near background. (In contrast, *MRE* sounded as if all four players –
stars to a man – were queueing or jostling for a single spotlight.) *No Wave* is the rawest and most directly
to-the-point, which may well recommend it; the sound, though, is often very wayward.
    The more recent records keep up the standard, though it is the presence of Blythe and the huge, dark-

toned Bluiett that lifts *Knights Of Power* and its predecessor up a notch. Without them, one suspects, these would not have sustained the quality or the frantic pace of this fine contemporary band.

Michael Musillami GUITAR

***(*) **The Young Child** Stash ST-CD-556
    Musillami; Thomas Chapin (*as, f*); Kent Hewitt (*p*); Nat Reeves (*b*); Steve Johns (*d*). 12/90.
**** **Glass Art** Evidence ECD 22060-2
    Musillami; Randy Brecker (*t, flhn*); Thomas Chapin (*as, f*); Kent Hewitt (*p*); Ray Drummond
    (*b*); Steve Johns (*d*). 12/92.

Musillami works with an interesting blend of tonal and harmonic orthodoxy while encouraging the music to extend itself: that makes the tempestuous Chapin the key element in these records, since his taste for paint-stripping solos sets fire to what would otherwise be tastefully controlled post-bop. One interesting influence that the guitarist claims is Bill Barron, and his themes certainly manage to revise conventional forms in the way that Barron's compositions often would. The intricacies of 'Beijing' and 'Mohawk Mountain' on the first record typify his intentions. Both discs brim with strong improvising and there's little to choose between them, with Chapin's generously featured flute another reason to listen: he plays with a sweetness that is turned around by the fierceness of his articulation. Brecker sustains his recent good form, and the leader's straight-ahead execution makes all his ideas come through with fine clarity.

Christian Muthspiel TROMBONE

*** **Duo Due (Tre)** Amadeo 837 950
    Muthspiel; Wolfgang Muthspiel (*g, g syn*). 5 & 12/88.
*** **Octet Ost** Amadeo 513 329
    Muthspiel; Tomasz Stańko (*t*); Anatoly Vapirov (*ts, as, ss*); Nicolas Simion (*ts, ss, bcl*); Klaus
    Koch (*b*); Vladimir Tarasov (*d*); Anca Parghel, Sainkho Namtchylak (*v*). 5/90.
**** **Indirect View Of Beauty** Amadeo 521 823
    Muthspiel; Tomasz Stańko (*t*); Bela Szakoly (*tb, bt*); Arkady Shilkloper (*frhn, flhn*); Anatoly
    Vapirov (*ts, ss*); Petras Vysniauskias (*as, ss*); Mikulas Skuta (*p*); Vladimir Tarasov (*d, perc*). 6/92.
**** **Muthspiel – Peacock – Muthspiel – Motian** Amadeo 519676
    Muthspiel; Wolfgang Muthspiel (*g*); Gary Peacock (*b*); Paul Motian (*d*). 3/93.

More obviously outside-edge than his guitar-playing brother, Christian Muthspiel is nevertheless closer to the fractured romanticism of Albert Mangelsdorff or George Lewis than to free-form trombone players like Paul Rutherford. The duo pieces with his brother are strongly reminiscent of some of Mangelsdorff's more experimental projects, though perhaps a little callow in execution. Muthspiel has a broad, spacious tone, most often deployed in a generous *legato*. However, he is also able to integrate bendy, 'experimental' effects with tongue and slide, and it is these which give the excellent 1993 record (quite properly credited to all four musicians) its character.

    Octet Ost is rather more of a cactus, a somewhat unapproachable suite of pieces played out of numerical sequence for no apparent reason and linked by a series of vocal interludes from the extraordinary Tuvan throat singer, Namtchylak. Stańko's playing is magnificent but doesn't really sit comfortably with the other horns. It would be wonderful to hear him with the band on the fourth record, which is dazzling. Brother Wolfgang is typically polished, and rather more interesting than on the duo record, which has him floundering a bit. Motian and Peacock accommodate everything, from the more cutting funk of 'Chill Out Honey Pie' and 'Gnome's Run' to the floatier 'One For Igor' and '(Grand) Canon', which closes the set on a questioning, optimistic note that whets the appetite for Muthspiel's next.

    Though recorded earlier than the quartet, *Indirect View Of Beauty* has been rather slow in filtering through. It's a much richer sound, but at the same time closer to a jazz idiom. There are two unnamed parts, comprising shorter sub-sections, with an intermezzo called 'Song Nine'. As before, Stańko is the most dynamic soloist, but this time the young Lithuanian Vysniauskias brings an almost boppish attack to bear, and Tarasov seems to have taken on board some of Andrew Cyrille's African-inspired devices. The introduction of a piano player in lieu of a bass is interesting. To a degree it normalizes the music, suggesting tonalities, even when they aren't strictly adhered to. Additionally, though, it heightens the percussive effect of Muthspiel's arrangements.

Wolfgang Muthspiel (born 1965) GUITAR, GUITAR SYNTHESIZER, VIOLIN

*** **The Promise** Amadeo 847 023
> Muthspiel; Bob Berg (*ts*); Richie Beirach (*p*); John Patitucci (*b*); Peter Erskine (*d*).

***(*) **Black And Blue** Amadeo 517 653
> Muthspiel; Tom Harrell (*t, flhn*); George Garzone (*sax*); Larry Grenadier (*b*); Alex Deutsch (*d*); Don Alias (*perc*). 7/92.

***(*) **In And Out** Amadeo 521 385
> Muthspiel; Tom Harrell (*flhn*); Chris Cheek (*sax*); Larry Grenadier (*b*); Jeff Ballard (*d*). 7/93.

***(*) **Loaded, Like New** Amadeo 527 727
> Muthspiel; Tony Scherr (*b*); Kenny Wolleson (*d*); Don Alias (*perc*). 4/95.

The elegant complexities of Muthspiel's music are partly explained by his classical training. The young Austrian came to jazz only after a solid grounding in violin and then classical guitar at the conservatory in his native Graz; subsequently he studied on the jazz programme at the New England Conservatory and Berklee College. Any suspicion that such a route could result only in hidebound formality was dispelled instantly by his first Polygram release, *Timezones*, which was gloriously tuneful and swinging, and also jammed with intriguing compositional ideas.

The Promise is only slightly disappointing because it is so smoothed out. The rhythm section is so highly burnished and Gary Burton's production so watertight technically that, but for Bob Berg's unfettered soloing, the whole package might have been a little bland. *Black And Blue* featured a more promising band. Harrell plays at the top of his always considerable form, and Garzone brings a cooler, more methodical voice than his predecessor. 'Dance (4 Prince)' points to a rather unexpected enthusiasm; but the major statement here is 'Miles', easily the most substantial thing Muthspiel has yet to record. His own playing is a little more raw and less finished than on the earlier records.

That's even more obviously true of the live *In And Out*, recorded at Sweet Basil during a highly successful tour. Interspersed with synth shapes and occasional violin passages (which strongly recall the late Zbigniew Seifert's romantic aura), the guitar has a pungency one hasn't heard from Muthspiel's studio recordings. The promise looked ready to be delivered and the stripped-down, very direct approach works perfectly on *Loaded, Like New*. Muthspiel isn't afraid to throw in a pop tune like 'With A Little Help From My Friends', and he makes perfect sense of it within his own conception. What extra colours he needs come from his guitar synthesizer, and the band stand foursquare behind him every step of the way. An excellent new step in a burgeoning career.

Simon Nabatov PIANO

*** **Locomotion** ASP 11988
> Nabatov (*p* solo). 4/88.

***(*) **For All The Marbles** Suite ASP 31990
> Nabatov; Mark Helias (*b*); Barry Altschul (*d*). 3/90.

**** **Tough Customer** Enja 7063-2
> As above, except Tom Rainey (*d*) replaces Altschul. 1/92.

Nabatov is a displaced Muscovite, now based in Cologne, and his classical studies and ongoing experimentation with metre are some of the trademarks of a complex, two-handed pianism. The best introduction to what he can do is *Tough Customer*, which has some electrifying improvisation on themes that can turn labyrinthine when he wants them to: the opening 'Puzzled' takes off from a dissonant figure into a wonderland of devices that Nabatov clearly has complete mastery over. 'Simple Simon', at the other end of the disc, mixes Chinese chords with a lovely sing-song melody. This is a fine blend of form and freedom, and what takes it into the top bracket is the superbly responsive work of Helias and Rainey: the bounce of the bass lines and the high detail and free time that the drummer creates bolster everything that Nabatov does. The earlier date with Altschul is fine too, if a little more episodic, while the solo album has a show-off aspect (check the overpowering 'Linear') that takes an edge off Nabatov's undeniable skills. But this is altogether very impressive piano jazz.

Alberto Nacci TENOR SAXOPHONE

** **Isola Lontana** Splasc(h) H 310-2
> Nacci; Fabrizio Garofoli (*ky*); Giuliano Vezzoli (*b*); Stefano Bertoli (*d*). 1.90.

(*) **Colours Splasc(h) H 387-2
> Nacci; Davide Ghidoni (*t, flhn*); Stefano Colpi (*b*); Stefano Bertoli (*d*). 5/92.

Nacci's compressed tone and slurred phrasing suit his impressionistic aims, but the music on *Isola*

Lontana has nothing profound about it. The compositions fail to get below any surface prettiness – 'Van Gogh' has nothing in it that makes one think of the dedicatee – and Garofoli's pretentious solos are a wrong ingredient, along with the soft-focus production that suggests European film music. *Colours* is much better, with Colpi and Bertoli laying down a thoughtfully shifting base for the two horns. Ghidoni is a bit too reserved, but that makes the leader's improvisations take a firmer hold. The sound is still too soft round the edges, but at least the two long pieces, 'Danza Araba' (with a fine bass solo) and 'Nuvole', keep the attention.

Max Nagl SAXOPHONES, OTHER INSTRUMENTS, VOCALS

*** **Ohlsdorf 18** Rude Noises 001
    Nagl (solo). 89–92.
**** **Lunatic Fringe** ExtraPlatte EX 153
    Nagl; Burkhard Stangl (*g*); Josef Novotny (*syn*). 11/91.
*** **Wumm! Zack!** ExtraPlatte EX 181
    Nagl; Dan Froot (*sax, v*); Patrice Heral (*perc, v*). 11/92.

Nagl claims Briton Lol Coxhill as one of his chief inspirations, and there is enough on these three discs to suggest that the connection has been securely made. The young Austrian saxophonist clowns and mugs, to be sure, but there is an improvisational sense at work every bit as secure as Lol's. The solo CD (dedicated to film-maker Derek Jarman, incidentally) is the most obvious point of contact. Like all his work, it consists of short bursts of sound – there are 49 tracks on the three CDs listed above – which take their cues from initial gestures or from some particular areas of sound, or, as often, from verbal cues. The most coherent (though coherence isn't strictly the point) is the trio with Novotny and that most intelligent of modernists, Burkhard Stangl. The record begins startlingly with a sampled version of an Olivier Messiaen organ-piece; from then onwards the strangeness tends to compound. *Wumm! Zack!* was conceived for a multi-media event, and it does seem to lack an element which the sheer variety of sound doesn't ever entirely fulfil.

Naked City GROUP

*** **Naked City** Nonesuch 79238
    John Zorn (*as*); Bill Frisell (*g*); Wayne Horvitz (*ky*); Fred Frith (*b*); Joey Baron (*d*); Yamatsuka Eye (*v*). 91.
*** **Heretic: Jeux Des Dames Cruelles** Avant AVAN 001
    As above.
***(*) **Grand Guignol** Avant AVAN 002
    As above, except add Bob Dorough (*v*). 92.
(*) **Radio Avant AVAN 003
    As above. 93.
(*) **Absinthe Avant AVAN 004
    As above, except omit Eye. 93.

One British music journalist, having watched Naked City on their first visit to Britain, concluded, 'just a bunch of musos having fun'. It's hard to disagree, but it's pretty robust fun. The group have patented a stylish musical terrorism, favouring short explosions of sound that rarely last longer than a couple of minutes (there are 41 tracks on *Grand Guignol*). More controversially, these are coupled with porno-graphic and sado-masochistic imagery, drawn from a variety of sources; *Grand Guignol*'s cover features a pathology photograph of a severed foot and a cadaver's trepanned skull. Coupled with track-titles like 'Perfume Of A Critic's Burning Flesh' (cheers, lads), this has prompted a small measure of moral panic around the group.

    Much of the group's confrontational stance can be dismissed as an ironic tactic. It is undoubtedly both ear- and eye-opening, and *de facto* leader John Zorn (who runs the Avant imprint) is intelligent enough to realize that shock is effective only when juxtaposed to something else. *Grand Guignol* – to make it something of a test case – also includes a swooningly romantic interpretation of 'Louange pour l'éter-nité de Jésus' from Olivier Messiaen's *Quatuor pour la fin du temps*.

    For Zorn fans, the most approachable is *Heretic*, which poses as the soundtrack to a dominatrix film, *Jeux des dames cruelles*, and is dedicated to the visionary film-maker, Harry Smith; *Grand Guignol* is dedicated to another fantasy director, his namesake, Jack Smith, who succumbed to the AIDS virus in 1989. *Radio* is the least appealing. Like the others, it's a complex, slightly self-indulgent package, but it seems to have lost even an ironic rationale and, though both musically and visually the least aggressive of the discs, nevertheless it shocks by virtue of its sheer persistence. By the time we reach *Absinthe*, the packaging, which is eerily glamorous, has become more important than the music which, for its part, is uniformly dull. There are not, alas, a million tunes in the *Naked City*.

Zbigniew Namyslowski (born 1936) ALTO SAXOPHONE, SOPRANO SAXOPHONE, CELLO

*** **Zbigniew Namyslowski Quartet** Power Bros 33861
     Namyslowski; Adam Makowicz (*p*); Janusz Koslowski (*b*); Czeslaw Bartkowski (*d*). 1/66.
**** **Winobranie** Power Bros 00121
     Namyslowski; Stanislaw Cieslak (*tb, perc*); Tomasz Szukalski (*ts, bcl*); Pawel Jarzebski (*b*);
     Kazimierz Jonkisz (*d*). 2/73.
***(*) **Kujaviak Goes Funky** Power Bros 33859
     Namyslowski; Tomasz Szukalski (*ts, as*); Wojciech Karolak (*p*); Pawel Jarzebski (*b*); Czeslaw
     Bartkowski (*d*). 75.
***(*) **The Last Concert** Polonia CD 002
     Namyslowski; Janusz Skowron (*p*); Maciej Strzelczyk (*vn*); Zbigniew Wegehaupt (*b*); Cezary
     Konrad (*d*). 10/91.
If the highly compressed history of Polish jazz seems littered with significant 'firsts', then Namyslowski managed to be present at a good few of them. In 1964 in London, he and his quartet became the first Polish jazz musicians to make a record in the West, the elegant and often startling *Lola*, which was released on Decca. The following year he played on Krzysztof Komeda's epochal *Astigmatic*, one of the most important European jazz records of the period.

Temperamentally, Namyslowski resembled Komeda rather than someone like the pianist's colleague, Andrzej Trzaskowski, whose approach to the music was first and foremost intellectual. Where Komeda was only a rather limited performer, though, Namyslowski had an instinctive facility that made him an exciting soloist from the first. His debut in 1957 was as a cellist. Thereafter, he switched to trombone and thence to saxophones, though his cello can still be heard on the 1973 *Winobranie* – 'Wine Feast' – a glorious record only recently restored to circulation thanks to Power Bros' enlightened programme of reissue. This is one of Namyslowski's major statements and, though it lacks the weird brilliance of Komeda's *Astigmatic*, it is still very listenable and at moments quite profound.

From the start Namyslowski was interested in unusual sounds and metres and, like Jan Ptaszyn Wroblewski, he drew considerable inspiration from Polish music. The 1966 band with Adam Matyskowicz (later Makowicz) has him hopping around in 7/4 and 5/8; as late as 'Kujaviak Goes Funky' and 'Appenzeller's Dance', on the third of the reissued discs, where he was absorbing elements of American pop and R&B, he is still resistant to basic fours.

Though subsequent to *Kujaviak* Namyslowski went into something of a creative decline, he comes back with a bang on *The Last Concert*, a live recording from the closing night of the Warsaw Jazz Jamboree in 1991. The polyrhythms are still there in 'Half Done Chicken' and the aggressive 'Total Incompetence'. Violin has played a major role in Polish jazz, and Maciej Strzelczyk's contributions to 'Five In One', another metrical maze, and the long, dancing 'What's In Yemikoy' are highly idiomatic. One feels that Namyslowski doesn't play with quite the attack of yore, but in Skowron he has one of the best accompanists in Eastern Europe, and the standard of playing throughout the set is very high indeed.

Lewis Nash (born 1958) DRUMS

***(*) **Rhythm Is My Business** Evidence ECD 22041
     Nash; Mulgrew Miller (*p*); Steve Nelson (*vib*); Peter Washington, Ron Carter (*b*); Steve Kroon
     (*perc*); Teresa Nash (*v*). 10/89.
... and business would seem to be booming for the young Arizonan, who won his spurs with Betty Carter and still claims the enthusiastic support of his old boss. On this debut solo recording, Nash opens with a rolling, Afro-tinged theme by Roland Hanna, cast in double waltz time. His own '106 Nix' is just a blowing head but it offers some attractive possibilities to both vibes and piano, and Washington gives the blues line an interesting twist; he does well generally, only briefly upstaged by Ron Carter's walk-on piccolo bass feature on 'Omelette'. Don Pullen's 'Sing Me A Song Everlasting' was played at Dannie Richmond's funeral. It's one of the pianist's loveliest compositions, and Miller (who plays out of his skin from start to finish) rounds it off to perfection. Nash switches to brushes for 'My Shining Hour'; it might have been nice to do this one as a vocal instead of the rather stolid 'When You Return'. Ms Nash – who presumably got the gig on merit alone – is too beefy a singer for this material and she makes a bit of a stew of it. A promising debut, though, from a road-tested musician who's performed well over difficult terrain and finds his own routes through things.

National Youth Jazz Orchestra GROUP

*** **Maltese Cross** NYJO 08

Noel Langley, Lance Kelly, Richard Sidwell, Pat Fradgley, Gerard Presencer, Paul Edmonds, Ian Wood, Mark White, Peter Cooper, Paul Cooper, Martin Shaw, Russell Cook, Andy Mitchell, Paul Higgs, Steve Sidwell, Mike O'Gorman, Andy Gibson, Guy Barker, John Hinch, Steve Titchener, Mark Cumberland, Oliver Preece (*t*); Mark Nightingale, Colin Hill, Mark Bassey, Andy Hutchinson, Tibor Hartmann, Dennis Rollins, Alastair Sinclair, Adrian Lane, Nigel Barr, Fayyaz Virji, Steve Aitken, Mark Da Silva, Phil Neil, Dave Stewart (*tb*); Liz Price, Claire Lintott, Jonathon Jaggard, Simon Thomas, Justin Mansell-Short (*frhn*); Clifford Tracy, Nigel Hitchcock, Adrian Revell, Alan Ladds, Scott Garland, Alison Brown, Clive Hitchcock, Simon Currie, Dave O'Higgins, Andy Schofield, Steve Cadd, Julie Davis, Paula Borrell, Pete Long, Scott Garland, Adam Talbot, Andy Panayi, Pete Long, Richard Symons, Sarah Garbe (*reeds, flutes*); John R. W. G. Smith, Peter Murray, Paul Honey, Jim Osborne (*ky*); Paul Hart (*vn*); Paul Stacey, Malcolm Macfarlane, Mike Eaves (*g*); Phil Mulford, Don Richardson, Dave Hage, Neil Williams (*b*); Chris Dagley, Mike Bradley, Mike Smith, Ian Thomas (*d*); Keith Fairbairn, Bill Pamplin, Ian Thomas, Gareth Roberts (*perc*); Lorraine Craig (*v*). 2/86–3/89.

*** **Remembrance** NYJO 011

Similar to above, except add Fred Maxwell (*t*), Winston Rollins, Tracy Holloway, Richard Henry, Brian Archer (*tb*); Howard McGill, Melanie Bush, Nigel Crane (*bs*), Clive Dunstall, Steve Hill (*p*), James Longworth (*g*), Mark Ong (*b*). 2/86–7/90.

(*) **Cookin' With Gas NYJO 010

Ian Wood, Mark Cumberland, Olly Preece, Gerard Presencer, Fred Maxwell, Neil Yates, Paul Cooper, Martin Shaw, Graham Russell, Mark White (*t*); Dennis Rollins, Pat Hartley, Winston Rollins, Tracy Holloway, Richard Henry, Mark Nightingale, Brian Archer (*tb*); Claire Lintott (*frhn*); Michael Smith, Howard McGill, Scott Garland, Adrian Revell, Pete Long, Melanie Bush, Richard Williams, Nigel Crane (*reeds*); Julie Davis (*f*); Steve Hill, Clive Dunstall (*p*); Paul Hudson, James Longworth (*g*); Mark Ong (*b*); Chris Dagley (*d*); Steve Smith, John Robinson (*perc*); Jacqui Hicks (*v, f*). 90.

** **Looking Forward – Looking Back** NYJO 012

As above, except add Dave Peers, Jon Scott (*t*), Colin Philpott, Steve Sanders, Keith Hutton (*tb*), Lisa Grahame (*f*), Julian Siegel, Ben Waghorn (*reeds*), Phil Robson, Andy Jones (*g*), Darrin Mooney, David May, James Mack (*perc*); omit Maxwell, Yates, Cooper, Russell, Rollins, Rollins, Henry, Nightingale, Bush, Davis, Williams, Dunstall, Longworth, Smith and Robinson. 9/91.

*** **These Are The Jokes** Jazz House JHCD 024

As above, except omit White, Presencer, Peers, Scott, Holloway, Hutton, Siegel, Waghorn, Garland, Robson, Jones, Mooney, May and Mack. 3/91.

(*) **In Control Jazz House JHCD 037

Andy Cuss, Jim Lynch, Bard Mason, Olly Preece, Neil Yates (*t*); Malcolm Smith, Jeremy Price, Elliot Mason, Mark Penny (*tb*); Adrian Hallowell (*btb*); Howard McGill, Lisa Grahame, Jim Tomlinson, James Hunt, Mick Foster (*reeds*); Simon Carter (*p*); Andy Jones (*g*); Mark Ong (*b*); Chris Dagley (*d*); James Mack (*perc*); Jenny Howe (*v*). 3/94.

(*) **Cottoning On NYJO 016

As above, except add Mick Ball, Mike Thomas, Pat White (*t*), Ashley Horton, Andy Rogers, Mark Nightingale (*tb*), Ben Castle, Jon Halton (*reeds*), Phil Robson (*g*), Neil Williams (*b*), James Langton (*v*). 3/94–3/95.

A glance at the personnel will reveal how many young musicians have been through the ranks of this British jazz institution, run with boundless enthusiasm by venerable bede, Bill Ashton, for a quarter of a century – and these are only the more recent names. NYJO has been the breeding ground for countless young players, many of whom have gone on to individual fame if not fortune; and though the aims of the group are resolutely conservative – precision and tightness over adventure, virtuoso complexity over profundity – the impact of the Orchestra remains impressive, both live and on record. Ashton has been documenting their work regularly (there is a lot of vinyl in the back-catalogue, as well as these CDs) and, though the records seldom vary in intent, some highlights stand out. *Maltese Cross* and *Remembrance* collect tracks from various editions of the band, and the former includes some of the happiest playing the group has done. When players such as Gerard Presencer, Mark Nightingale, Fayyaz Virji and Scott Garland have the spotlight, there's some characterful improvising to go with the slam of the section-work. *Cookin' With Gas* highlights one of the sponsors the Orchestra has had ('Swonderfuel'?), and this kind of cornball kitsch perhaps doesn't do them too many favours. *Looking Forward – Looking Back* is a showcase for Jacqui Hicks, a decent band singer, but she's let down by the colourless original material. All the themes on *These Are The Jokes* are named after quips by proprietor

Ronnie Scott; despite that, this is one of the best sets the Orchestra has done, punchily recorded at Scott's club. *In Control* is another live session from Scott's and a few leftovers turn up on *Cottoning On*, which marks their 1995 stay at the club. Virtually nothing to choose among these, but if detractors wish to point to the fourth-form humour of the titles, the soporific predictability of the arrangements and the clear lack of soloists of any independent spirit, we wouldn't wish to make a case for the defence.

Fats Navarro (1923–50) TRUMPET

*** Memorial Savoy SV 0181 2CD
> Navarro; Kenny Dorham (*t*); Ernie Henry, Sonny Stitt (*as*); Morris Lane (*ts*); Eddie De Verteuil (*bs*); Bud Powell (*p*); Al Hall, Curley Russell (*b*); Kenny Clarke (*d*); Gil Fuller (*arr*). 9/46, 10/47.

**** The Complete Fats Navarro On Blue Note And Capitol Blue Note CDP 798684 2CD
> Navarro; Howard McGhee (*t*); Ernie Henry (*as*); Allen Eager, Wardell Gray, Sonny Rollins, Charlie Rouse (*ts*); Tadd Dameron, Bud Powell (*p*); Milt Jackson (*p, vib*); Nelson Boyd, Tommy Potter, Curley Russell (*b*); Kenny Clarke, Roy Haynes, Shadow Wilson (*d*); Chano Pozo (*perc*). 9/47, 9 & 10/48, 8/49.

***(*) Nostalgia Savoy SV 0123
> Navarro; Eddie 'Lockjaw' Davis, Dexter Gordon, Charlie Rouse (*ts*); Tadd Dameron, Al Haig (*p*); Huey Long (*g*); Nelson Boyd, Gene Ramey (*b*); Denzil Best, Art Blakey, Art Mardigan (*d*). 12/46, 12/47.

***(*) Fats Navarro Featured With The Tadd Dameron Band Milestone M 47041
> Navarro; Tadd Dameron (*p*); Rudy Williams (*as*); Allen Eager (*ts*); Milt Jackson (*vib*); Curley Russell (*b*); Kenny Clarke (*d*). 48.

*** Bird & Fats – Live At Birdland Cool & Blue C&B CD 103
> Navarro; Charlie Parker (*as*); Walter Bishop Jr, Bud Powell (*p*); Tommy Potter, Curley Russell (*b*); Art Blakey, Roy Haynes (*d*); Chubby Newsome (*v*). 6/50.

Like Howard McGhee, Navarro came up through the Andy Kirk band, having already worked with Snookum Russell. Overweight, with a high, rather effeminate voice (and nicknamed either 'Fat Boy' or 'Fat Girl'), he had by 1945, when he replaced Dizzy Gillespie in the Billy Eckstine orchestra, developed a trumpet style which replaced Gillespie's burp-gun lines with a more elegantly shaped approach that emphasized a bright, burnished tone. The open texture of his solos was altogether better suited to the Tadd Dameron band, which became his most effective setting. Dameron is the accompanist on the best of the *Nostalgia* material, which provides an additional 20 minutes' top-flight Navarro, with four dispensable tracks from a drab December 1946 session alongside Lockjaw Davis and Al Haig. There's also a slice of pre-Dameron work on *Memorial*, credited to Gil Fuller's Modernists, together with later stuff by an equally good band (Henry, Dameron, Russell, Clarke) and marred only slightly by Kay Penton's inconsequential vocals.

The Blue Note sessions are one of the peaks of the bebop movement and one of the essential modern-jazz records. Navarro's tone and solo approach were honed in big-band settings and he has the remarkable ability to maintain a graceful poise even when playing loudly and at speed. The contrast with McGhee (it seems extraordinary that some of their performances together have been misattributed) is very striking. Their duelling choruses on 'Double Talk' from a marvellous October 1948 session are some of the highpoints of the record; there is, as with several other tracks, an alternative take, which shows how thoughtful and self-critical an improviser the young trumpeter was, constantly refining, occasionally wholly rethinking his approach to a chord progression, but more frequently taking over whole segments of his solo and re-ordering them into a more satisfying outline. Navarro is rhythmically quite conservative, but he plays with great containment and manages to create an illusion, most obvious on 'Boperation', from the same session, that he is floating just above the beat; by contrast, McGhee sounds hasty and anxious. One hears the same effect rather more subtly on both takes of 'Symphonette' and on an alternative take of 'The Squirrel'.

There is an excellent version of 'Symphonette', also from 1948, on the Milestone Navarro/Dameron compilation. Milt Jackson is again present, but these performances, which also include 'The Squirrel', 'Dameronia' and two fine versions of 'Anthropology', are not up to the standard of the Blue Notes.

It's worth looking out for the unfortunately named *Fat Girl* and *Fat Again* on Savoy/Vogue. There are problems with both (including a degree of uncertainty whether Navarro or Dorham is playing on some cuts and the known fact that some of Navarro's solos were spliced in), but the quality of his playing shines through time and again on these earlier cuts. That talent dimmed only slightly towards the end. The tracks on *Live At Birdland*, one with his own quartet and 15 more with Bird's group, document his last public appearance. They find him still poised and lyrical, but lacking the dramatic edge of the classic sessions, and unmistakably weary.

Navarro died a week later of tuberculosis exacerbated by drug abuse. As an artist he was already astonishingly mature, and it's slightly ironic that many of the stylistic innovations and developments attributed to Clifford Brown were actually instigated by Navarro. Small as his legacy is, it is one of the finest in all of jazz.

Don Neely's Royal Society Jazz Orchestra GROUP

*** **Ain't That A Grand And Glorious Feeling** Stomp Off CD1208
    Frank Davis (*t, c*); Kent Mikasa (*c*); Jon Schermer (*tb*); Don Neely (*reeds, v*); Mark Warren, Lin Patch (*reeds*); Frederick Hodges (*p, bells, v*); Dix Bruce (*g*); Jeff Wells (*tba, b*); Steve Apple (*d*); Carla Normand, The Jesters (*v*). 4/90.
*** **Don't Bring Lulu** Stomp Off CD1250
    As above, except add Bob Schulz (*c*), Jeremy Cohen (*vn*), omit The Jesters. 4/92.
*** **Roll Up The Carpet** Circle CCD 147
    As above, except Brent Bergman (*tb*) replaces Schermer, omit Schulz and Cohen. 10/94.
Done with so much affection and enthusiasm that it's hard to dislike. This is the heart of hot dance music, original arrangements transcribed from records as often as not, with Neely's talented team of throwbacks playing in note-perfect re-creations of the best of such bandleaders as Paul Ash, Ted Weems, Paul Whiteman and Isham Jones. While they put in the occasional Henderson or McKinney's Cotton Pickers chart, this is mainly about the New York society bands of the 1920s. They sidestep some of the novelty element and concentrate on the gaiety of a style that takes its virtues from drollery and nuance rather than any camp affectation. Normand and The Jesters hit the right note in their vocal spots, but it's Neely's own half-spoken vocals that just about take the biscuit. Soloists seldom take any real limelight, yet here and there is a fine eight- or sixteen-bar interlude. Little to choose between the three records – period connoisseurs may wish to compare song-titles, but then they'll probably want all three anyway – though, if pressed, we pick the first for its marginally punchier sound.

Buell Neidlinger DOUBLE BASS

***(*) **Locomotive** Soul Note 1161
    Neidlinger; Marty Krystall (*ts*); Brenton Banks (*vn*); John Kurnick (*mand*); Billy Osborne (*d*). 6/87.
***(*) **Big Drum** K²B² Records K2B2 3069
    Neidlinger; Hugo Schick (*t*); Marty Krystall (*ts*); Vinny Colaiuta (*d*). 6/90.
***(*) **Rear View Mirror** K²B² Records K2B2 2969
    Neidlinger; Warren Gale (*t*); Marty Krystall (*ts*); Peter Ivers (*hca*); Jeremy Peters (*org*); Andy Statman (*mand*); Richard Greene (*vn*); John Beasley, Peter Erskine, Billy Higgins (*d*).
Neidlinger was an essential component of Cecil Taylor's vital 1960 band (and he features prominently on a rash of Candid reissues from that time). In later years he has developed in individual and unexpected directions, delving back into jump and swing, and even leading a bluegrass outfit.

At first glance, *Locomotive* is closer to what he was doing with Buellgrass (as he called it) than to his work with Taylor; but a closer comparative look at 'Jumpin' Punkins' here and on the Candid Taylor compilation of that name suggests much about the well-springs of the pianist's work at that time, and also about Neidlinger's contribution to it. A strong, uncomplicated player, he drives this unusually shaped band through a roster of Monk and Ellington tunes in a manner that emphasizes the two composers' similarities rather than their differences. Though the pace is as abrupt as on a John Zorn record, there are few obvious modernist concessions. Banks plays like a folk fiddler, not in the scratchy, microtonal style of Leroy Jenkins or Billy Bang, and, if there are already very few mandolin players, none of them bears useful comparison with what Kurnick is doing. Wholly original and absolutely riveting.

Big Drum is not quite so startlingly unusual, but it is a spanking good record. Recorded live by saxophonist Krystall, who again plays a highly significant role, it has loads of atmosphere. Neidlinger dedicates the set to Herbie Nichols but unfortunately doesn't include any of the pianist's compositions. There's a taut and compact reading of Monk's 'Brilliant Corners', on which Colaiuta shines. The remainder are originals, written by Neidlinger and Krystall. 'Ming's Last Visit', a torrid 14-bar blues, pays tribute to another great bassist. 'Tienanmen Bop' is a response to the massacre of pro-democracy students in Beijing. It sound as if it might have been written at any point since the early 1960s, but for the most part Neidlinger's ideas are very contemporary.

The retrospective on *Rear View Mirror* is the closest one gets to a rapid summation of the bassist's career. All of the material has been released previously on LP. Thus compiled, though, it gives a vivid sense of a player who has been through the mill, from straight repertoire to Monk and beyond. There

are versions of 'Little Rootie Tootie', 'Crepuscule With Nellie' and 'Jumpin' Punkins', a wonderfully
countrified version of the latter that points forward to concerns which were to develop beyond the
slightly uncertain focus of the last three tracks here.

'Big Eye' Louis Nelson (1902–90) CLARINET

*** **Big Eye Louis Nelson Delisle** American Music AMCD-7
    Nelson; Wooden Joe Nicholas (*t, v*); Charles Love (*t*); Louis Nelson (*tb*); Louis Gallaud (*p*);
    Johnny St Cyr, Louis Keppard (*g*); Austin Young, Albert Glenny (*b*); Ernest Rogers, Albert Jiles
    (*d*); William Tircuit (*v*). 5–7/49.
The only record under the nominal leadership of a man who taught Bechet and was an acknowledged
inspiration of Dodds and Noone. The CD consists of three informal studio or home sessions and
seven tracks from a dance-hall date in New Orleans; 10 tracks appear for the first time. Whatever the
credentials outlined above, Nelson sounds like a man content to coast through his working life: the
clarinet playing ambles along, mixing fluffs and good notes. The live tracks are a bit more animated,
played over a very steady beat, and, though Love and Nicholas provide firm leads, the horns (the
other Louis Nelson, on trombone, is no relation) play things very straight. Worth hearing by New
Orleans scholars, but of limited appeal otherwise. The sound is able-bodied but muffled on most of
the tracks.

Oliver Nelson (1932–75) ALTO SAXOPHONE, SOPRANO SAXOPHONE, TENOR SAXOPHONE, CLARINET, COMPOSER, ARRANGER

*** **Meet Oliver Nelson. Featuring Kenny Dorham** Original Jazz Classics OJC 227
    Nelson; Kenny Dorham (*t*); Ray Bryant (*p*); Wendell Marshall (*b*); Art Taylor (*d*). 10/59.
*** **Taking Care Of Business** Original Jazz Classics OJC 1784
    Nelson; Lem Winchester (*vib*); Johnny Hammond Smith (*org*); George Tucker (*b*); Roy Haynes
    (*d*). 3/60.
*** **Screamin' The Blues** Original Jazz Classics OJC 080
    Nelson; Richard Williams (*t*); Eric Dolphy (*as, bcl, f*); Richard Wyands (*p*); George Duvivier
    (*b*); Roy Haynes (*d*). 5/60.
(*) **Soul Battle Original Jazz Classics OJC 325
    Nelson; King Curtis, Jimmy Forrest (*ts*); Gene Casey (*p*); George Duvivier (*b*); Roy Haynes (*d*).
    9/60.
*** **Nocturne** Original Jazz Classics OJC 1795
    Nelson; Richard Wyands (*p*); George Duvivier (*b*); Roy Haynes (*d*). 60.
***(*) **Straight Ahead** Original Jazz Classics OJC 099
    As above, except add Eric Dolphy (*as, bcl, f*). 3/61.
*** **Main Stem** Original Jazz Classics OJC 1803
    Nelson; Hank Jones (*p*); George Duvivier (*b*); Charli Persip (*d*); Ray Barretto (*d*). 61.
**** **Blues And The Abstract Truth** Impulse! IMP 11542
    Nelson; Freddie Hubbard (*t*); Eric Dolphy (*as, f*); George Barrow (*bs*); Bill Evans (*p*); Paul
    Chambers (*b*); Roy Haynes (*d*). 2/61.
*** **Afro / American Sketches** Original Jazz Classics OJC 1819
    Nelson; Billy Byers, Ernie Royal, Joe Newman, Jerry Kail (*t*); Paul Faulise, Urbie Green, Britt
    Woodman, Melba Liston (*tb*); Don Butterfield (*tba*); Julius Watkins, Ray Alonge, Jim
    Buffington (*frhn*); Arthur Babe Clark, Bob Ashton, Eric Dixon, Jerry Dodgion, Charles
    McCracken (*sax*); Peter Makis (*p*); Art Davis (*b*); Ed Shaughnessy (*d*); Ray Barretto (*perc*). 62.
Nelson did apprenticeship with Louis Jordan and with the Erskine Hawkins and Quincy Jones big
bands. In style he was probably closer to Jones than to anyone else (liking to combine sophisticated
intervals with a raw, bluesy feel) and eventually drifted off in the same direction, wasting his last few
years on cop-show themes (and 'The Six Million Dollar Man'). One might almost say Nelson played
'arranger's sax', a slightly backhanded term usually reserved for piano players. His alto solos were direct
and to the point, and with the original theme very much in view. They contrasted sharply and well with
Eric Dolphy's more adventurous approach, though it's immediately evident from both *Screamin'* and
Straight Ahead that Dolphy also prefers to explore the inner space of a tune rather than take the path of
least resistance and go 'out'.

    Like *Soul Battle* and the reassuringly down-home *Taking Care Of Business*, these are slightly misleading
titles, accentuating Nelson's forcefulness over his undoubted subtlety as an arranger and composer. The
leader's alto solo on 'Six And Four' (*Straight Ahead*) is usefully representative of what he does; the two

horn players indulge in some instrumental banter on the long 'Ralph's New Blues' (reminiscent of the kind of thing Dolphy did with Mingus) with Nelson switching briefly to tenor.

Through his contributions to *Screamin'* Williams isn't altogether missed on the later album, perhaps underlining Nelson's greater enthusiasm for saxophone writing. Dorham, on the earlier OJC, is used largely as a guest soloist, floating over Nelson's tight blues arrangements. Though more than capable of shaping an exciting solo, Williams isn't up to the standard of the great bopper or of his descendant, Freddie Hubbard, who'd worked with Nelson a month before *Straight Ahead* on what was to be his best record.

Blues And The Abstract Truth is a wonderful set, and nothing else Nelson did came close to it. Again featuring Dolphy, with Bill Evans and Paul Chambers joining the redoubtable Haynes in the rhythm section, it has a broader harmonic spectrum than the OJC pair, though it remains based on the 12-bar blues and the changes of 'I Got Rhythm', which were so significant in the development of bebop. It also contains Nelson's two best compositions, 'Hoe Down' and 'Stolen Moments', the former a theme based on 44 bars and developed from the opening two notes, the second a minor blues with challenging internal divisions. 'Stolen Moments' features Dolphy on his flute and a fine tenor solo from Nelson. 'Teenie's Blues', dedicated to his sister, is an attempt to reduce the harmonic range to just three progressions, with transpositions in the two altos to give the piece the required tension and release. (The later *More Blues And The Abstract Truth* (Impulse! AS 75) is frankly a disappointment.)

The two tenors on *Soul Battle* aren't known for thoughtful abstraction, but Nelson seems able to steer them to a degree of imaginative sophistication, much as later in his *Swiss Suite* (on Flying Dutchman) he managed to put such drastically different horn players as Eddie Cleanhead Vinson and Argentinian screamer, Gato Barbieri, on stage together.

*** **Taking Care Of Business** Original Jazz Classics OJC 1784
    Nelson; Lem Winchester (*vib*); Johnny Hammond Smith (*org*); George Tucker (*d*); Roy Haynes (*d*). 3/60.
*** **Nocturne** Orginal Jazz Classics OJC 1795
    Nelson; Lem Winchester (*vib*); Richard Wyands (*p*); George Duvivier (*b*); Roy Haynes (*d*). 8/60.
Nelson's writing and arranging are consistently impressive, but these are rather drab sessions. Winchester is prominently featured on both but isn't an entirely convincing soloist, with a tendency to repeat ideas he likes. 'Trane Whistle' (*Taking Care*) is a little-known tribute to the great saxophonist in his *Blue Train* uniform, and Nelson continues to work new changes on the basic blues sequence. *Nocturne* is a nice album, but a little hyper-subtle to make it into the front rank.

*** **Sound Pieces** Impulse! GRD 103
    Nelson; Gabe Baltazar, Bill Green, Plas Johnson, Jack Nimitz, Bill Perkins (*reeds*); John Audino, Bobby Bryant, Conte Candoli, Ollie Mitchell, Al Porcino (*t*); Mike Barone, Billy Byers, Richard Leith, Dick Noel, Ernie Tack (*tb*); Bill Hinshaw, Richard Perissi (*frhn*); Red Callender (*tba*); Steve Kuhn, Mike Melvoin (*p*); Ray Brown, Ron Carter (*b*); Grady Tate (*d*); collective personnel. 9/66.
Like Toshiko Akiyoshi, Nelson tended to 'think high' as an arranger, and to some extent his personal switch to soprano saxophone was quite predictable. Even with the stern example of John Coltrane on the same label, Nelson sounds relaxed and surprisingly original, with a tight, hard-edged sound and no sign of intonation problems, except perhaps among the top notes on 'The Shadow Of Your Smile'. The five small-group tracks – with Kuhn, Carter and Tate – are not hard to place as Nelson's work, even allowing for the unfamiliarity of the instrument, but they're not entirely successful. 'Straight No Chaser' and the interesting original 'Example 78' were first released on *Three Dimensions*.

The first of the large-scale pieces, 'Sound Piece For Jazz Orchestra', was written for a German radio big band and covered by Stan Kenton's Newophonic Orchestra. With the solo part transposed up from his more usual horn, it has a vibrant, dramatic property, that doesn't carry over into the brief and skittish 'Flute Salad' (which is distinguished by a good Candoli solo), or 'The Lady From Girl Talk', which lacks Nelson's usual coherence of arrangement. Altogether rather disappointing.

Steve Nelson (born 1956) VIBES

*** **Live Session One** Red RR 123231
    Nelson; Bobby Watson (*as*); Donald Brown (*p*); Curtis Lundy (*b*); Victor Lewis (*d*). 7/89.
*** **Live Session Two** Red RR 123235
    As above. 7/89.
** **Full Nelson** Sunnyside SSC 1044D
    Nelson; Kirk Lightsey (*p*); Ray Drummond (*b*). 8/89.

(*) Communications Criss Cross Jazz Criss 1034

> Nelson; Mulgrew Miller (*p*); Ray Drummond (*b*); Tony Reedus (*d*). 10/89.

Nelson is a late starter as a leader but, since these four records were issued almost simultaneously, he may be making up for lost time. Unfortunately, the two studio dates don't show this strong and much-admired player in a very appealing light. *Communications* suffers from a dislikeable sound-mix, with the vibes poorly focused and Reedus obscuring too much detail; while the material, aside from the attractive 'Blues For Bob', is rather tepid and lacking in sparkle. *Full Nelson* is a ballad session that unreels at a snail's pace and, by the time of the concluding 14-minute ramble through 'Chelsea Bridge', most of the interest has trickled away. Lightsey tends to chime too closely with Nelson's lines to create enough contrast, and the thoughtful ballad, 'There Are Many Angels In Florence', is lost in the otherwise somnolent programme.

The live material is a different matter. While there are jam-session *longueurs* here and there – 'Afro Blue' on *One* runs for over 20 minutes, for instance – the rhythm section has energy in abundance and Nelson and Watson both take extravagant, mercurial solos on both records. Recording, while not ideal, isn't too distracting.

Neugebauer Groenewald Nine Piece Band GROUP

*** **Nude** West & East 220023-2

> Oliver Groenewald, Christof Wundrak (*t, flhn*); Michael Bergbauer (*t*); Jan Hupe (*ss, as, f*); Klemens Pliem (*ts*); Thomas Rottleuner (*bs, bcl*); Chris Geissler (*ky, bs, bcl*); Herwig Neugebauer (*b*); Michael Nagel (*d*). 93.

A crossover between modern mainstream and something a little more *outré*, the music here is a shade too unassuming to make a real mark, but it's played with much style by the youthful ensemble. Neugebauer and Groenewald share the credits for eight of the nine originals, with Geissler chipping in with one tune, and though there's nothing especially memorable the material suits the group. None of the soloists is strong enough to really buttonhole a listener, but Pliem's thoughtful soliloquy on the title-tune and Rottleutner's aggressive baritone catch the attention. Only on the deliberately *lumpen* funk of 'Bouncing Bubbles' does the music take a false turn.

Roger Neumann TENOR SAX

*** **Introducing Roger Neumann's Rather Large Band** Sea Breeze SBD 102

> Neumann; Gary Grant, Rick Baptist, Jack Coan, Larry Lunetta, Jack Trott (*t, flhn*); Alan Kaplan, Bob Enevoldsen, Herbie Harper, Morris Repass (*tb*); Dave Edwards, Eric Marienthal, Herman Riley, Bob Enevoldsen, Lee Callet (*reeds*); Tom Ranier (*p*); John Heard (*b*); John Perrett (*d*); Terry Schonig (*perc*). 4–6/83.

*** **Instant Heat!** Sea Breeze CDSB-2053

> Neumann; Frank Szabo, Wayne Bergeron, Hal Espinosa, Jack Coan, Bob Summers, Jack Trott, Ron Stout (*t*); Alan Kaplan, Andy Martin, Herbie Harper (*tb*); Bob Enevoldsen (*vtb*); Morris Repass (*btb, tba*); Sal Lozano, Brian Scanlon, Herman Riley, Bob Hardaway, Lee Callet, Jennifer Vaccaro (*woodwinds*); Tom Ranier, Carol Anderson, Sydney Jill Lehman (*p*); Kirk Smith (*b*); John Perrett (*perc*). 11/93.

Bright and entertaining big-band music by an orchestra that manages to let professional gloss vie with enthusiastic playing. Neumann likes to let the band rip and varies the section writing with intelligent craft rather than quirky individuality. The band on both dates is a mix of old familiars and younger pros, with an assertive team of soloists. For the 1983 session, Trott shines on the fast, funny 'Flintstones Theme', Rainer has a couple of good moments in the long piece conceived for Blue Mitchell, 'Blue', and everybody dispatches a flag-waving 'Cherokee' with great aplomb. The return visit took ten years to realize, but it's basically more of the same. Here and there Neumann lets a few novelties get in the way: hard to warm to the cute voicing of piccolo and tuba for 'Good Bait', for instance. Lee Callet's fine baritone tear-up on 'Straight Ahead And Strive For Tone' is compensation, and a score such as the pretty 'Sweden In The Rain' is more than worthwhile. Typically big and powerful sound from Sea Breeze.

Phineas Newborn (1931–90) PIANO

***(*) **Stockholm Jam Session** Steeplechase SCCD 36025

> Newborn; Benny Bailey (*t*); Oscar Pettiford (*b*); Rune Carlsson (*d*); unidentified (*tb*) and (*bs*). 9/

58.
*** **Stockholm Jam Session** Steeplechase SCCD 36026
    As above. 9/58.
***(*) **A World Of Piano!** Original Jazz Classics OJC 175
    Newborn; Paul Chambers (*b*); Louis Hayes, Philly Joe Jones (*d*). 61.
*** **The Great Jazz Piano Of Phineas Newborn Jr** Original Jazz Classics OJC 388
    Newborn; Sam Jones, Milt Turner, Leroy Vinnegar (*b*); Louis Hayes (*d*).
***(*) **The Newborn Touch** Original Jazz Classics OJC 270
    Newborn; Leroy Vinnegar (*b*); Frank Butler (*d*). 64.
***(*) **Harlem Blues** Original Jazz Classics OJC 662
    Newborn; Ray Brown (*b*); Elvin Jones (*d*). 2/69.

A player of tremendous technical ability, often likened to Oscar Peterson (who had come on to the East Coast scene with similar suddenness and plaudits), the younger Newborn was flashy, hyped-up and explosive, eating up themes like Clifford Brown's 'Daahoud' and Rollins's 'Oleo' as if they were buttered toast. Underneath the super-confident exterior of *A World Of Piano!* and *The Newborn Touch*, though, there was a troubled young man who was acutely sensitive to criticism, particularly the charge that he was no more than a cold technician.

Newborn suffered a serious nervous collapse from which he only partially recovered, and the remainder of his career was interspersed with periods of ill-health. His later recording output is spasmodic to say the least, marked by a chastened blues sound which contrasts sharply – in style and quality – with the early work.

Fortunately, it transpired in 1992 that tapes of Newborn's 1958 visit to Stockholm had survived, unheard, for 34 years. Expertly cleaned up by Nils Winther, they sound fresh and bright enough to counterbalance the vagaries of a single-mike recording and a ropy piano. The music is of an unexpectedly high quality for a spontaneous session. Some other instruments can be heard during the ensembles, but these did not play a major role and the individuals cannot be identified. Newborn's opening solo on the first session (Volume One) is patient and unhurried, growing in expressiveness as he moves outside the basic chords. It's perhaps his most complete statement of the evening. Elsewhere, he solos with great clarity and occasional glimpses of irony, as on Dizzy Gillespie's 'Woody 'N' You' where, with Bailey sitting out, he mimics the punchy attack of the original trumpet line.

Though badly recorded, Oscar Pettiford nearly makes the session his own. The bass solos on 'Ladybird' (Volume One) and 'It's You Or No One' (Two) are equally valuable additions to the Pettiford canon, and Bailey's luminous account of 'Confirmation' (Two) deserves a star or two. Local man Carlsson does his thing politely and professionally.

The New Jazz Wizards GROUP

*** **Good Stuff, Hot And Ready** Stomp Off CD1244
    Peter Ecklund (*c*); Jim Snyder (*tb*); Reimer Von Essen (*cl*); Billy Novick (*cl, as*); Butch
    Thompson (*p*); Peter Bullis (*bj*); Vince Giordano (*tba, bsx*); Pam Pameijer (*d*). 1/92.
*** **Golden Lily** Stomp Off CD1281
    As above, except John Otto (*cl, as*), Robin Verdier (*p*), Mike Walbridge (*tba*) replace Essen,
    Thompson, Giordano; add Dick Wetmore (*vn*). 3/94.

Excellent repertory, arranged and recorded with much panache by Pam Pameijer's group of revivalists. The first disc is dedicated to the music of Richard M. Jones; the second, to that of Tiny Parham. It presents two different faces of classic jazz in the 1920s – whereas Jones was a comparatively simple, blues-based, small-group man, Parham's more elaborate music hinted at an alternative to the arranged styles of Morton and Ellington. Oddly, the Wizards sound more formal and strait-laced on the Jones music, where the highly structured Parham tracks go off with more of a bang. Ted des Plantes (whose own disc of Parham interpretations has yet to make it to CD) describes the big man's music as 'stodgy and stompy rather than streamlined', yet the Wizards whistle it along. *Good Stuff, Hot And Ready* has much meticulously detailed hot playing but can't quite evade a certain stiffness. In their sincerity in dealing with both composers, the group makes no attempt at hiding the music's weakness as well as its strengths and, despite the fine solos by Ecklund and the others, their attention to the nuts-and-bolts of it holds a certain exuberance in check.

David 'Fathead' Newman (born 1933) TENOR, ALTO AND SOPRANO SAXOPHONES, FLUTE

*** **Bigger And Better / The Many Facets Of David Newman** Rhino/Atlantic R2 71453
    Newman; orchestra. 3/68–2/69.
***(*) **House Of David** Rhino/Atlantic R2 71452 2CD
    Newman; various groups. 52–89.
** **Back To Basics** Milestone 9188
    Newman; Wilbur Bascomb, Jimmy Owens, Milt Ward (*t*); Earl McIntyre (*tb*); Babe Clark (*ts*);
    Clarence Thomas (*bs*); Kenneth Harris (*f*); Pat Rebillot, George Cables, Hilton Ruiz (*ky*);
    George Davis, Lee Ritenour, Jay Graydon (*g*); Abraham Laboriel (*b*); Idris Muhammed (*d*); Bill
    Summers (*perc*); strings. 5–11/77.
*** **Still Hard Times** Muse M 5283
    Newman; Charlie Miller (*t*); Hank Crawford (*as*); Howard Johnson (*bs*); Steve Nelson (*vib*);
    Larry Willis (*p*); Walter Booker (*b*); Jimmy Cobb (*d*). 4/82.

Fathead by name, but not by nature: Newman is an ornery, driving saxophonist whose R&B background – including 12 years with Ray Charles – has left him with a consummate knowledge in the use of riffs and licks in a soul-to-jazz context. He always swings, and his unmistakable Texan sound is highly authoritative, but like so many musicians of a similar background he's had trouble finding a fruitful context. His early Atlantic albums have been filleted to produce the excellent *House Of David* compilation, which starts with a date by Texas bluesman Zuzu Bollinand and goes through to the late 1980s with Aretha Franklin, Dr John and others, taking in the years with Charles and the crossover albums of the 1960s along the way. Newman plays it all with consummate heart, and there is a share of real classics: the irresistible theme of his own piece of jazz immortality, 'Hard Times'; the straight-ahead bop of 'Holy Land'; the suaveness and grit of 'The Clincher'. But the miscellany does tend to prove Newman's second-fiddle status: he's a fine sideman, seldom a leader. The other Rhino disc is a double-header featuring Newman fronting a couple of albums of nice tunes and smoochy ballads, usually with a good rhythm section at bottom but the whole always papered over with strings and brass. Newman's playing salvages the music time and again, but a little can go a long way.

   The Milestone album is the same, and a waste of his time: puling backings, strings and horns sweeten up already saccharine material, and Newman's surviving solos are the only reason to listen. The Muse album, sympathetically produced by Michael Cuscuna, is much more like it. *Still Hard Times* reunites Newman with his old Ray Charles colleague Crawford, and they simply lay back and dig into the blues. Newman's solo on the opening 'Shana', a steadily mounting chorus of wails, is typical of the musician at his best, and also shows why Newman's records seldom sustain interest: he hasn't enough to say as a leader to keep a record's momentum going.

** **Blue Greens And Beans** Timeless SJP 351
    Newman; Marchel Ivery (*ts*); Rein De Graaff (*p*); Koos Serierse (*b*); Eric Ineke (*d*). 5/90.
(*) **Blue Head Candid CCD 79041
    Newman; Clifford Jordan (*ss, ts*); Buddy Montgomery (*p*); Ted Dunbar (*g*); Todd Coolman (*b*);
    Marvin 'Smitty' Smith (*d*). 9/89.

Solid records, but they lack some vital spark to make them come alive. *Blue Greens And Beans* is a two-tenor quintet which lacks all of the punch one has come to expect in the aftermath of the Lockjaw–Griffin records. *Blue Head* is much better, thanks to Jordan's energetic solos, Montgomery's dextrous piano, and the tremendously shifting rhythms laid down by Coolman and Smith. But six very long jam tunes is probably at least one too many.

Joe Newman (1922–92) TRUMPET

**** **The Count's Men** Fresh Sound FSR CD 135
    Newman; Benny Powell (*tb*); Frank Foster (*ts*); Frank Wess (*f, ts*); Sir Charles Thompson (*p*);
    Eddie Jones (*b*); Shadow Wilson (*d*). 9/55.
***(*) **I Feel Like A New Man** Black Lion BLCD 760905
    As above, except add Bill Byers (*tb*); Gene Quill (*as*); John Lewis (*p*); Freddie Green (*g*); Milt
    Hinton (*b*); Osie Johnson (*d*). 9/55, 4/56.
*** **Jazz For Playboys** Savoy SV 0191
    Newman; Frank Wess (*ts, f*); Kenny Burrell, Freddie Green (*g*); Eddie Jones (*b*); Ed Thigpen
    (*d*). 12/56.
*** **Good'n'Groovy** Original Jazz Classics OJC 185
    Newman; Frank Foster (*ts*); Tommy Flanagan (*p*); Eddie Jones (*b*); Bill English (*d*). 3/61.
***(*) **Jive At Five** Original Jazz Classics OJC 419
    Newman; Frank Wess (*ts*); Tommy Flanagan (*p*); Eddie Jones (*b*); Oliver Jackson (*d*).

*** **At The Atlantic** Phontastic NCD 8810

Newman; Ove Lind (*cl*); Lars Erstrand (*vib*); Staffan Broms (*g*); Arne Wilhelmsson (*b*); Robert Edman (*d*). 8/77.

***(*) **Hangin' Out** Concord CCCD 4462

Newman; Joe Wilder (*t, flhn*); Hank Jones (*p*); Rufus Reid (*b*); Marvin 'Smitty' Smith (*d*). 5/84. Newman was never a whole-hearted modernist. His sharp attack and bright sound were derived almost entirely from Louis Armstrong and, though he was chief cadre of the 'Basie Moderns' in the 1950s, he maintained allegiance to the Count's music over any other. *Good'n'Groovy* was recorded at about the time of his departure from the Basie band (and *Jive At Five* has very much the same feel). Newman always sounds good round Frank Foster, and the album bounces with enough vigour to cut through a rather flat mix.

Better to start with the Black Lion and Fresh Sound CDs from a pair of mid-1950s sessions, recorded while Newman was still Basie's trumpet star. 'East Of The Sun' on *New Man* is touched by Parker, but 'Difugality', with the larger Byers/Quill/Foster front line, seems to be hamstrung between two idioms, offering a slightly ironic slant to Leonard Feather's famous characterization of the trumpeter as 'neutralist modern'.

As a useful compare-and-contrast exercise, try 'A.M. Romp' on *The Count's Men* with the same tune on *Good'n'Groovy*. The later version is slightly wilder, but it's the tighter version with Sir Charles Thompson that really impresses, and newcomers to Newman's entertaining sound would do well to begin with the mid-1950s stuff, and especially the very good Savoy, which is shared with some tracks by Wess, who uses essentially the same band.

The Phontastic record, recorded live in one of Stockholm's leading restaurants, is essentially an Ove Lind disc with a prominent guest slot by Newman and, as such, isn't absolutely central to the story. The other newish one, though, is a must for fans of the trumpeter. His partnership with Wilder proved to be one of the most fruitful of his career. Though they share an approach, each is idiosyncratic and individual enough to stand out as a stylist, and what one gets is a clever dialogue between two wise heads.

A canny and enterprising musician (who represents a 'positive' counter-image to many of the musicians of his generation), Newman headed the educational/promotional Jazz Interactions trust in the later 1960s, a thin time for the music, and expanded his interests to include large-scale composition (a direction that reflected more of his New Orleans background than it did the turbulent classicism of his exact contemporary, Charles Mingus).

New Orchestra Workshop GROUP

***(*) **The Future Is N.O.W.** Nine Winds NWCD 0131

Daniel Lapp, Bill Clark (*t*); Graham Ord, Coat Cooke, Bruce Freedman, Roy Stiffe (*reeds*); Paul Plimley (*p*); Clyde Reed, Paul Blaney, Ken Lister (*b*); Claude Ranger, Gregg Simpson, Roger Baird, Stan Taylor (*d*). 90.

*** **NOW You Hear It** Nine Winds NWCD 0151

Bruce Freedman (*as*); Graham Ord (*ts, ss*); Coat Cooke (*ts*); Joseph Danza (*shakuhachi*); Paul Plimley (*p*); Ron Samworth (*g*); Lisle Ellis, Clyde Reed, Paul Blaney (*b*); Gregg Simpson, Roger Baird, Buff Allen (*d*); Jack Duncan (*perc*); Kate Hammett-Vaughan (*v*). 5–11/91.

Vancouver's New Orchestra Workshop is a co-operative venture inspired by Chicago's AACM. *The Future Is N.O.W.* offers the chance to sample the work of five different bands which have grown out of NOW. The outstanding piece is the opening track by Plimley's Octet, a swirling, compelling montage of rhythmic and melodic figures that is gripping throughout its nine-minute length; but there isn't a bad track among the six here. The harmolodically inspired quartet, Lunar Adventures, contribute two tracks; Chief Feature is a quartet that brews up a long, blustering workout reminiscent of early Archie Shepp; and Unity purvey a vivacious free improvisation, with excellent work by Lapp, Blaney, Ord and Baird. Only the muddled piece by Turnaround is in any way disappointing.

Their second report on *NOW You Hear It* is mildly disappointing: much of interest, but nothing that really stands out. The Plimley/Reed duo contribute three interactive duets, and MuseArt, a trio with Plimley, Ellis and Baird, offers a long abstraction of the blues. Lunar Adventures make brainy jazz-rock, Garbo's Hat are a chamberish trio featuring the singing of Kate Hammett-Vaughan, and the closing 'jam' by a group featuring Ord, Blaney and Baird, with Danza's shakuhachi hanging around the perimeter, isn't bad.

New Orleans Classic Jazz Orchestra GROUP

**** Blowin' Off Steam Stomp Off CD1223

     Eddie Bayard (*c*); Bob Havens (*tb*); Tom Fischer (*cl, as*); Steve Pistorius (*p*); John Gill (*bj*);
     Hank Greve (*tba*); Hal Smith (*d*). 8/90.

When jazz scholarship is carried off with this degree of skill, good humour and sheer aplomb, it stops being a history lesson and stands as great, timeless music. Bayard's group – several of the names will be familiar to followers of other Stomp Off productions – tackle 20 nuggets from the golden age with an élan that is quite unselfconscious, even when they're following 70-year-old arrangements. Their treatment of Morton's 'The Chant', for instance, makes light work of a classic difficult enough to be absent from almost everybody else's trad repertoire; even comparatively well-known chestnuts like 'Shim-Me-Sha-Wabble' come out as evergreens. At the heart of the disc are four tunes from the book of The Halfway House Orchestra and six from that of The New Orleans Owls, rarities that fan out into a joyful celebration of the less familiar side of old New Orleans. Bayard and Fischer are exemplary soloists, Pistorius is his usual accomplished self, and the lilt and swing of the ensemble is ideally caught by the dry, no-frills recording.

New Orleans Rhythm Kings GROUP

**** The New Orleans Rhythm Kings And Jelly Roll Morton Milestone 47020-2

     Paul Mares (*c*); Georg Brunies, Santo Pecora (*tb*); Leon Roppolo (*cl*); Don Murray (*cl, as*);
     Charlie Cordella (*cl, ts*); Jack Pettis (*Cmel, ts*); Elmer Schoebel, Mel Stitzel, Jelly Roll Morton,
     Kyle Pierce, Red Long (*p*); Lou Black, Bob Gillett, Bill Eastwood (*bj*); Arnold Loyacano, Chink
     Martin (*b*); Frank Snyder, Ben Pollack, Leo Adde (*d*). 8/22–3/25.

One of the major groups of jazz records, from the first stirrings of the music in recording studios, the New Orleans Rhythm Kings sessions still sound astonishingly lively and vital 70 years later. The band recorded in Chicago but had come from New Orleans: Mares was already a disciple of King Oliver (who hadn't yet recorded at the time of the first session here), Roppolo played fluent, blue clarinet, and even Brunies made more of the trombone – at that time an irresponsibly comical instrument in jazz terms – than most players of the day. The rhythms tend towards the chunky, exacerbated by the acoustic recording, but the band's almost visionary drive is brought home to stunning effect on the likes of 'Bugle Call Blues' (from their very first session, in August 1922), the relentlessly swinging 'Tiger Rag' and the knockabout 'That's A Plenty'. On two later sessions they took the opportunity to have Jelly Roll Morton sit in, and his partnership with Roppolo on 'Clarinet Marmalade' and 'Mr Jelly Lord' – something of a sketch for Morton's own later version – invigorates the whole band. 'London Blues' and 'Milenberg Joys' find Morton more or less taking over the band in terms of conception. The two final sessions they made, early in 1925, are slightly less impressive because of Brunies's absence, and there are moments of weakness elsewhere in the original records: the use of saxes sometimes swamps the initiative, Mares isn't always sure of himself, and the beats are occasionally unhelpfully overdriven. But this is still extraordinarily far-sighted and powerful music for its time, with a band of young white players building on black precepts the way that, say, Nick LaRocca of the ODJB refused to acknowledge.

    The Milestone CD is decent enough, though it's about time someone assembled a set of mint originals and did the best possible job of remastering: the music deserves it, historically and aesthetically.

Sam Newsome (born 1965) TENOR SAXOPHONE

***(*) Sam I Am Criss Cross Jazz 1056

     Newsome; Marcus Miller (*p*); Steve Nelson (*vib*); James Genus (*b*); Billy Drummond (*d*). 11/90.

Newsome is a tenorman of unpretentious authority. He courts trouble by framing tributes to both Coltrane and Rollins here, but 'In The Vein Of Trane', basically a simple F minor vamp, manages to reflect on Coltrane without slavishly copying him, and 'Pent-up House' settles for the brazen confidence rather than the delivery of the young Sonny. Actually, Newsome takes his time in his improvising, building solos methodically, savouring his best phrases and going for tonal extremes only when he sees their logical point. A rich, dark tenor tone and a penchant for fitting in with the band rather than dominating them give this record much bonhomie as well as a lot of rigorous playing. Nelson is in his most attacking form, throwing off some dazzling solos in single lines rather than multiple-mallet chords, and the rhythm section is as impressive as always on Criss Cross dates.

David Newton (born 1958) PIANO

*** Eyewitness Linn AKD 015
> Newton; Dave Green (*p*); Allan Ganley (*d*). 2/90.
*** Victim Of Circumstance Linn AKD 013
> Newton; Alec Dankworth, Dave Green (*b*); Clark Tracey, Allan Ganley (*d*). 2/90, 5/90.
***(*) Return Journey Linn AKD 025
> Newton (*p* solo). 2/92.
***(*) In Good Company Candid CACD 79714
> Newton; Dave Green (*b*); Allan Ganley (*d*). 9/94.

Like John Taylor before him, Newton established a considerable reputation as an accompanist to visiting American musicians before he launched his own solo career. The young Glaswegian served a gruelling apprenticeship in the theatre, and as singer and label-mate Carol Kidd's musical director. It has given him the precise – occasionally too precise – technique and clean-lined approach to solo performance that was evident on his first record, *Given Time*. It's audible, too, throughout these polished sets from the recording end of the Linn audio concern.

Newton worked with Dankworth and Tracey on a Buddy DeFranco record. There's a faint sense throughout *Victim Of Circumstance* that a horn player is just about to emerge. By the close, it's very much a felt need. Where Green and Ganley are paced and unhurried on the earlier disc (and on one track on *Victim*), the other pair seem to push the music to one false climax after another. This is a besetting vice of Newton's own work. The solo *Return Journey*, admirable as it is, falls prey to the same self-dramatizing instinct. There's a touch of flabbiness about some of the freer improvisations.

It's marvellous that, at this point in his steadily developing career, Newton should have been able to release so much professionally produced music. The switch to Candid for *In Good Company* is a shrewd one in that it might seem to open new horizons. Typical, though, of his loyalty to the home scene, he does not use the opportunity to work with overseas players but teams up with two of Britain's best rhythm men for a tightly organized and thoroughly enjoyable standards set.

Frankie Newton (1906–54) TRUMPET

***(*) Frankie Newton 1937–1939 Classics 643
> Newton; Cecil Scott (*cl, ts*); Edmond Hall (*cl, bs*); Mezz Mezzrow (*cl*); Pete Brown, Russell Procope, Tab Smith, Stanley Payne, Gene Johnson (*as*); Kenneth Hollon (*ts*); Don Frye, James P. Johnson, Kenny Kersey, Albert Ammons, Meade Lux Lewis (*p*); Frank Rice, Al Casey, Ulysses Livingston, Teddy Bunn (*g*); Richard Fullbright, John Kirby, Johnny Williams (*b*); Cozy Cole, O'Neil Spencer, Eddie Dougherty, Big Sid Catlett (*d*); Clarence Palmer, Slim Gaillard, Leon LaFell (*v*). 3/37–8/39.

Newton was an intriguing, unguessable player whose small number of recordings represents the rare strain of swing-era small groups at their most interesting. In some ways he was an old-fashioned hot player, using a terminal vibrato borrowed directly from Armstrong and turning in oblique, poetic solos on otherwise slight material. He worked extensively at New York's Onyx Club in the late 1930s, when the tracks on these two records were made. 'Who's Sorry Now' features a Newton solo which summarizes his style: the quirky lyricism and sudden bursts of heat make him exhilaratingly hard to predict. But it's his four choruses on 'The Blues My Baby Gave To Me' which are close to perfection, beautifully controlled and achingly lyrical reflections on the blues. There are other good solos from Brown and Hall scattered through these sides; Johnson is in fine form on the 1939 Bluebird session, and there are one or two strikingly unusual tunes, including 'Vamp' and the odd 'Parallel Fifths' from the final (1939) date. Classics take their material from unlisted sources and the sound is unfortunately very variable.

James Newton (born 1953) FLUTE

**** Axum ECM 1214
> Newton (*f* solo). 81.
*** James Newton Gramavision GR 8205
> Newton; Slide Hampton (*tb*); Jay Hoggard (*vib*); John Blake (*vn*); Anthony Davis (*p*); Cecil McBee (*b*); Billy Hart (*d*). 10/82.
***(*) Luella Gramavision GR 8304
> Newton; Jay Hoggard (*vib*); Kenny Kirkland (*p*); John Blake, Gayle Dixon (*vn*); Abdul Wadud (*clo*); Cecil McBee (*b*); Billy Hart (*d*). 83.

***(*) **Water Mystery** Gramavision GR 8407

    Newton; John Carter (*cl*); Greg Martin (*ob*); John Nunez (*bsn*); Charles Owens (*eng hn, ss*); Red Callender (*tba*); Alan Iwohara (*koto*); April Aoki (*hp*); Roberto Miguel Miranda (*b*); Anthony Brown (*perc*). 1/85.

*** **Suite For Frida Kahlo** Audioquest AQ 1023

    Newton; George Lewis, George McMullen (*tb*); Pedro Eustache (*f, bf, bcl, ts*); Julie Feves (*bsn*); Kei Akagi (*p*); Darek Oleszkiewicz (*b*); Sonship Theus (*d, perc*). 8/94.

One of the relatively few contemporary players to own to a direct Eric Dolphy influence, Newton started out as a Dolphyish multi-instrumentalist but gave up alto saxophone and bass clarinet towards the end of the 1970s in order to concentrate on the least developed aspect of the Dolphy legacy. As a virtuoso flautist, he too has worked in both formal and improvised contexts and has developed a wholly original means of vocalizing while he plays. This is by no means new (Roland Kirk was exceptionally proficient at it), but Newton has taken the technique far beyond unisons and harmonies to a point where he can sing contrapuntally against his own flute line. The results are frequently dazzling, as on the African-influenced *Axum*. Newton's vocalizations allow his pieces to develop with unprecedented depth, and his tone is quite remarkable.

    Newton's recording career is an odd one, divided almost exactly between smaller independent or border-line 'classical' labels (India Navigation, BvHaast) and the top-ranking jazz labels of the last couple of decades, who may have found his uncompromising artistic nature a difficult trade-off for his undoubted virtuosity and imagination. In 1985 he made a remarkable group recording with Blue Note. *African Flower* is a more obviously accessible work than the solo venture (partly because the bulk of the material is by Ellington) but is no less successful as a synthesis of Afro-American musics; unfortunately, Blue Note have not seen fit to keep it or the later *Romance And Revolution* in print. As on *Luella*, it featured a typically non-standard line-up, with John Blake's violin constantly undermining its own references to the European classical tradition. Blythe and Dara are both excellent, and Newton, though inevitably less prominent in a group setting, runs his flutes through some wildly unfamiliar harmonic intervals and 'false' notes.

    Luella is still identifiably a jazz album, and 'Mr Dolphy' puts Newton's heart throbbingly on his sleeve. However, the line-up also refers to a more formal tradition. Later Gramavision sessions were more obviously 'sheet-driven' and it's significant that the jazz tribute on *Water Mystery* should be to Billy Strayhorn. As a set of contemporary chamber pieces, it's hard to fault and the orchestration of winds and (unconventional) strings is quite beautiful; like his colleague, Anthony Davis, with whom he duets on the fine Moers set, Newton is pushing hard at the boundaries dividing musical traditions. If, like Davis, he has been accused of desiccation, he's still capable of living with a swinging player like Slide Hampton (on the 1982 *James Newton*) and coming out just ahead.

    The *Suite For Frida Kahlo* is an odd work which catches Newton once again in a sort of no-man's land. The dedication is to one of the honoured figures of feminist art history, but precisely what Newton *does* draw from Kahlo's surreally honest canvases isn't entirely clear. Though the best of the non-suite pieces on the record – 'Elliptical' is essentially a duet with the marvellous Lewis – still shows something of the Strayhorn influence, the sequence devoted to the painter is much closer in spirit and conception to Mingus's work. It is there in the voicing of the horns, the twinned flutes and trombones, the expressive part given to bassoon, the unexpected dance movements of 'The Broken Column' and the awkward spiritual breakthrough of 'The Love Embrace Of The Universe' which provides the climax.

    Newton himself notes classical composers Heitor Villa-Lobos and Toru Takemitsu as sources (rather than influences) for elements of the suite, and concedes that its creation was greatly affected by the recent death of clarinettist and composer John Carter, one of the few contemporary musicians to have taken up the challenge of Mingus's large-scale approach. The warm, analogue recording captures Newton's own playing more truthfully than anything in recent years, just as the album's range of styles reflects his ambition. A good, if challenging, place to make this undersung master's acquaintance.

New York Art Quartet GROUP

***(*) **New York Art Quartet** ESP Disk ESP 1004

    Roswell Rudd (*tb*); John Tchicai (*as*); Lewis Worrell (*b*); Milford Graves (*d*); Leroi Jones (*v*). 11/64.

According to recent rumours, Roswell Rudd is currently appearing with a hotel band in the Catskills. In 1964, he was *the* radical trombone player in America (only Albert Mangelsdorff challenged him for the world crown), working out rough-edged and spiky alternatives to the prevailing J. J. Johnson style. On 'Rosmosis' he puts his blurting, vocalized tone through its paces, consigning Tchicai to a back seat for the only time on the disc.

    Perhaps because he didn't succumb to the lure of New York for long, the Danish saxophonist has never received his full due. On 'No. 6' and 'Short' he builds up short, intense phrases into longer and longer solo lines which seem to revolve round tonal centres even when they don't make complete sense harmonically. ESP Disk was one of the few labels where Milford Graves's genius was preserved on record, and it is immensely valuable to have him back in such profusion. He and Worrell benefit greatly from CD transfer; it's possible at last to hear how controlled and exact Graves could be, even when playing at full tilt, and Worrell is not as anonymous as on the original release.

The final component is black radical poet and New Thing propagandist, Leroi Jones, who recites 'Black Dada Nihilismus' over an appropriately anarchic background played by the quartet. The title alone gives a good account of Jones's creative and political orientation at the time.

New York Composers Orchestra GROUP

*** **First Program In Standard Time** New World CounterCurrents 80418
    Eddie Allen, Jack Walrath (*t*); Steven Bernstein (*t, flhn*); Butch Morris (*c*); Ray Anderson, Art Baron (*tb*); Vincent Chauncey (*frhn*); Cleave E. Guyton Jr (*as, f*); Robert DeBellis (*as, ss*); Doug Wieselman (*ts, cl*); Marty Ehrlich (*ts, as, ss, cl, bcl*); Sam Furnace (*bs*); Robin Holcomb (*p*); Wayne Horvitz (*p*); Lindsey Horner (*b*); Bobby Previte (*d, mar*). 1/90, 1/92.

*** **Music By Marty Ehrlich, Robin Holcomb, Wayne Horvitz and Doug Wieselman** New World NW 397
    As above. 93.

These are the work of a more or less regular big band dedicated, as the title suggests, to new, large-scale composition for creative orchestra. The composers represented on the first disc – Braxton, Holcomb, Horvitz, Lenny Pickett, Previte and Elliott Sharp – are all cutting-edge representatives of a movement that no longer takes 'jazz' as its baseline but moves out into the wider reaches of contemporary music in search of inspiration. Ironically, perhaps, Braxton's numbered palimpsests are the most jazz-like things in the entire set until one comes to Previte's 'Valerie, Explain Pollock', a slightly mysterious piece for ensemble which is just about the only thing on the record not intended to highlight individual voices. This is its shortcoming, ironically. One would like to hear more ensemble work, and yet what springs out and insists on attention is solo material, by Ray Anderson on Pickett's 'Dance Music' and Horvitz's 'Nica's Day', and Wieselman (a little-appreciated writer and soloist) on Holcomb's title-piece and throughout the programme.

The other record is for some reason slightly less geared to soloistic play, but with almost wilful perversity the compositions are not nearly so strong and the effect is rather bland and unstimulating. On a good night, the NYCO generates a formidable noise. Even in the relative formality of the studio they manage to sound good.

Wooden Joe Nicholas (1883–1957) TRUMPET, CLARINET

*** **Wooden Joe Nicholas** American Music AMCD-5
    Nicholas; Jim Robinson, Louis Nelson, Joe Petit (*tb*); Albert Burbank (*cl*); Johnny St Cyr (*g*); Lawrence Marrero (*bj*); Austin Young, Alcide 'Slow Drag' Pavageau (*b*); Josiah Frazier, Baby Dodds, Albert Jiles (*d*). 5/45–7/49.

A legendary name. Wooden Joe's main idol was Buddy Bolden, and hearing him play may offer us the best idea of what Bolden himself might have sounded like. Nicholas blew a very powerful open horn, and was famous for dominating a dance-hall sound. These were his only recordings, and they are clustered together from a session at the Artesian Hall and two later dates. A lot of New Orleans history is tied up here: the fearsome blues singer, Ann Cook, is on one track, the legendary trombonist, Joe Petit, on another. Nicholas and Burbank are the main voices on all the tracks (Wooden Joe also played clarinet, and does so on two numbers): compared with the clarinettist's weaving lines, Nicholas is reserved in his phrasing and takes only a few breaks and solos. But much of his power and stately delivery was intact. The music has been remastered from acetates and, though the fidelity isn't as good as in some of the American Music series, the history still comes alive.

Herbie Nichols (1919–63) PIANO

*** **I Just Love Jazz Piano** Savoy SV 0117
    Nichols; Danny Barker (*g*); Chocolate Williams (*b, v*); Shadow Wilson (*d*); probable personnel. 3/52.

Despite being (posthumously) included in A. B. Spellman's important book, *Four Lives In The Bebop Business*, and despite the more practical advocacy of younger piano players like Geri Allen, Herbie

Nichols has remained a strangely marginal figure. Less obviously offbeat in technique than either Richard Twardzik or Carl Perkins, he is most immediately likened to Thelonious Monk (with whom he formerly shared the Savoy compilation, now divided among Nichols, Hampton Hawes, Paul Smith and John Mehegan – less stellar but, more importantly, less logical company). Nichols's distinctive approach might also usefully be compared to Eric Dolphy's, particularly with regard to the way both men used fixed keys and conventional thematic structures. Whereas Dolphy pushed out the harmonic envelope, however, Nichols preferred to concentrate on motivic and thematic variation, with considerable rhythmic innovation. His was a more engaging, less alienating sound than Monk's and much less stressed than the later Bud Powell's, though the sudden interpolation of a 6- or 10-bar measure in the middle of a song is as unsettling for the listener as it must have been for his fellow players.

Nichols's Blue Note recordings are again out of print, rendering the Mosaic box (see Introduction) more or less indispensable for serious collectors. His compositions are dazzlingly fresh. No one else was doing stuff like '23 Skidoo', 'Shuffle Montgomery', 'Cro-Magnon Nights' or 'Riff Primitif' (though the French title of the last might lead some to suspect Martial Solal as the composer). 'Hangover Triangle' is a perfect instance of the obliqueness of Nichols's imagination, and 'Lady Sings The Blues', with McKibbon and Roach in sympathetic attendance, is just lovely. The recording quality is excellent for the time, and there's no reason why these sides shouldn't be better known than they are. Nichols died of leukaemia in 1963, having spent his last few years accompanying singers, most notably Sheila Jordan.

Keith Nichols (born 1945) PIANO, VOCALS

*** **I Like To Do Things For You** Stomp Off CD1242
> Nichols; Guy Barker (*c*); Gordon Blundy (*tb*); Mac White (*cl, bcl, ss, as*); Randy Colville (*cl, as, ts*); Mike Piggott (*vn*); Mike French (*p*); Martin Wheatley (*g, bj*); Graham Read (*bsx, tba, sou, b*); Barry Tyler (*d*); Janice Day, Johnny M, The Happidrome Trio (*v*). 6–7/91.

*** **Syncopated Jamboree** Stomp Off CD 1234
> Nichols; Bent Persson, Mike Henry (*t*); Alistair Allan (*tb*); Claus Jacobi, Mac White, Mark Allway, Randy Colville, Robert Fowler (*reeds*); Mike Piggott (*vn*); Martin Wheatley (*g, bj*); Graham Read (*sou*); Richard Pite (*d*); Janice Day, Johnny M, Tony Jacobs (*v*). 9/91.

**** **Henderson Stomp** Stomp Off CD 1275
> Nichols; René Hagmann (*c, tb*); Bent Persson, Guy Barker, Mike Henry, Rolf Koschorrok (*t*); Alistair Allan (*tb*); Claus Jacobi (*ss, as, bsx, cl*); Nik Payton (*as, cl*); Michel Bard (*ts, cl*); Martin Wheatley (*bj*); Graham Read (*sou*); Richard Pite (*d*). 11/93.

Nichols is a British specialist in American repertory: ragtime, hot dance music, New York jazz of the 1920s, Blake, Morton, Berlin, whatever. His piano playing and Hoagy Carmichael-like singing are less important than the mastery of old form that he successfully displays on both these records. *I Like To Do Things For You* is more of a chamber-jazz session: the instrumentation varies, but the largest group has eight players, while 'I'm Nobody's Baby' cuts the cast to three. Familiarity with any Nichols/Mole session or even the Bix and Trumbauer dates will give the idea. Janice Day's rather plummy contralto is much featured and may be an acquired taste. There are plenty of tunes among the 20 tracks that have probably been unrecorded since the 1920s, and the irony of having a brilliant modernist like Barker on hand goes almost unnoticed (he is at least as good as Wynton Marsalis at this kind of thing). Recorded in a dry acoustic, but it has a very appropriate sound.

Syncopated Jamboree is by a bigger band and is more of a piece: Read, who moves between various bass instruments on the other record, plays strict brass bass here, and the section-work would surely have been good enough for Roger Wolfe Kahn. Another stack of obscurities, expertly reworked in a little over an hour of music. Sometimes it all seems like a pointless exercise – Nichols isn't trying to bring anything new to this music, he just loves to play it – but sympathetic ears will be rewarded.

Henderson Stomp, though, is surely his finest hour and one of the most convincing pieces of authentic-performance jazz ever set down. Twenty-two of Fletcher Henderson's most effective pieces – from several hands, though many of Don Redman's somewhat familiar charts are bypassed in favour of other arrangements – are re-created by a picked team of some of the most talented repertory players and revivalists in Europe: the brass team alone is gold-plated, with the amazingly versatile Persson and Barker set alongside the brilliant Hagmann. The reed section sounds totally schooled in the appropriate section-sound of the period, and each of the tunes emerges with the kind of rocking swing that sounds properly flavoursome of the era. With such a strong team of soloists, the various breaks and carefully fashioned improvisations have the nous needed to transcend any scripted mustiness. Dave Bennett engineers an ideal soundmix. Result: modern work of art wearing old-fashioned duds.

Red Nichols (1905–66) CORNET, TRUMPET

(*) Rhythm Of The Day ASV AJA 5025

Nichols; Manny Klein, Leo McConville, Donald Lindley, James Kozak, Charlie Teagarden, Wingy Manone, Johnny Davis (*t*), Miff Mole, Glenn Miller, Will Bradley (*tb*), Dudley Fosdick (*mel*); Ross Gorman (*cl, as, bs*), Alfie Evans (*cl, as, vn*), Harold Noble (*cl, as, ts*), Jimmy Dorsey, Benny Goodman (*cl, as*); Billy McGill, Fud Livingston (*cl, ts*); Pee Wee Russell (*cl*); Babe Russin (*ts*); Adrian Rollini, Barney Acquelina (*bsx*), Nick Koupoukis (*f, picc*), Murray Kellner, Joe Venuti, Jack Harris, Saul Sharrow (*vn*), Milton Susskind, Arthur Schutt, Edgar Fairchild, Jack Russin, Fulton McGrath (*p*), Eddie Lang, Tony Colicchio, Carl Kress (*g*), Tony Starr (*bj*), Artie Bernstein, Art Miller (*b*), Victor Engle, Chauncey Morehouse, Vic Berton, David Grupp (*d*). 10/25–2/32.

*** Original 1929 Recordings Tax CD5

Nichols; Leo McConville, Manny Klein, Tommy Thunen, John Egan, Mickey Bloom (*t*); Jack Teagarden, Glenn Miller, Herb Taylor, Bill Trone (*tb*); Alfie Evans, Arnold Brilhart (*cl, as, bsn, f*); Benny Goodman (*cl, as, bs*); Jimmy Dorsey (*cl, as*); Pee Wee Russell (*cl*); Jimmy Crossan (*ts, bsn, f*); Babe Russin, Bud Freeman, Fud Livingston (*ts*); Murray Kellner, Joe Raymond, Lou Raderman, Henry Whiteman, Maurice Goffin (*vn*); Arthur Schutt, Rube Bloom, Irving Brodsky, Joe Sullivan (*p*); Carl Kress (*g*); Tommy Felline (*bj*); Joe Tarto (*bb*); Jack Hansen, Art Miller (*b*); Gene Krupa, Vic Berton, George Beebe, Dave Tough (*d*); Scrappy Lambert, Red McKenzie, Dick Robertson (*v*). 4–10/29.

** Red Nichols And His Orchestra 1936 Circle CCD-110

Nichols; rest unknown. 11/36.

Nichols has been a maligned figure since the popular heyday of the white New York school of the 1920s, and it's true that his music has worn less well than much of the jazz of that decade. His own precise, lightly dancing work on either cornet or trumpet might seem to glance off the best of Beiderbecke's playing, and the scrupulous ensembles and pallid timbre of the Five Pennies or whatever he chose to call a group on its day in the studios now seems less appealing. But it is unique jazz and, in its truce between cool expression and hot dance music, surprisingly enjoyable when taken a few tracks at a time.

Peculiarly, we are still waiting for any proper representation of Nichols on CD: hundreds of tracks have yet to be remastered for the format, both under his own name and in countless hot dance situations. The ASV CD is something of a missed opportunity, since it purports to be a Five Pennies compilation yet includes two tracks by Mole's Molers and one by Ross Gorman's dance band, as well as including several of the later, lesser records. At least the 1925–7 selections – including 'Alabama Stomp', 'Buddy's Habits' and 'Cornfed' – are among the best of the Pennies.

Tax's compilation covers Nichols's 1929 sessions in chronological order. He was leaving the '20s with his best work already behind him, even though he wasn't yet 25 years old, and these sessions, studded with several future stars, are a little poignant because of that. Yet Nichols still sounds good when he emerges from what were good dance-band arrangements for a group larger than the early Pennies, and Teagarden and Goodman are there, too. Excellent remastering by John R. T. Davies.

None of Nichols's many records of Dixieland for Capitol have so far made it to CD, and from the 1930s we have only the Circle CD, WBS transcriptions which are shared with a nondescript dance session by Will Bradley's orchestra. Not that Nichols's titles are much better: the music is so anonymous that this was long thought to be a session by the Ray Noble band. Red has a meagre number of solo spots and the rest of the group are capable but unexceptional on routine arrangements. Good remastering, though, of what's a mere 28 minutes of music.

Giancarlo Nicolai (born 1957) CLARINET

**** Capo I Greco E Elle Leo LAB CD 006

Nicolai; Berner Klarinettensemble (*cl*); Pascal Flammer, Bruno Knurr, Xa Schuppisser (*g*); Regula Neuhaus (*vib, v*). 12/93.

Though born in Berne, Switzerland, Nicolai is as Italian as his name suggests. This extraordinary record is the result of a collaboration with Sylvia Schwarzenbach's wonderful clarinet ensemble, a group which generates a rich, complex sound which always seems to be bathed in overtones and woody timbres. The compositions are dense but not unexpressive, and Nicolai on this occasion is pretty much absorbed into the group, so he is not so very generously featured as an individualist. Like Clarinet Summit in the USA, the Berner Klarinettensemble trade quite heavily on new methods of playing, though they are somewhat more conventional in technical terms than the Americans.

Maggie Nicols (born 1948) VOCALS, ASSORTED INSTRUMENTS

***(*) **Nicols 'N' Nu** Leo CDLR 127
    Nicols; Pete Nu (*p*). 6/85.

A remarkable vocal performer, Scottish-born Nicols (who has French and Berber forebears) works in a personal style that combines orthodox singing with a homely *Sprechstimme* which is dramatic, moving and very funny within a generously undoctrinaire feminist agenda. The duets with Nu explore some of the territory mapped out by her earlier vocal groups, Okuren, Voice, and Loverly, frequently moving into abstract territory but constantly reasserting the lyrical potential of personal experience. She combines the avant-garde techniques of Cathy Berberian with the simplicity and directness of a folk singer, and she deserves much wider recognition. Nu is scarcely known either, and this is a valuable documentation of his brusque romanticism.

Lennie Niehaus (born 1929) ALTO SAXOPHONE

**** **The Octet No. 2: Volume 3** Original Jazz Classics OJC 1767
    Niehaus; Bill Holman (*t*); Stu Williamson (*t, vtb*); Bob Enevoldsen (*tb*); Jimmy Giuffre (*reeds*); Pete Jolly (*p*); Monty Budwig (*b*); Shelly Manne (*d*).

*** **Patterns** Fresh Sound FSR CD 100
    Niehaus; Bill Perkins (*ts, bs, ss, bcl*); Frank Strazzeri (*p*); Tom Warrington (*b*); Joe LaBarbera (*d*). 8/89.

Over-ripe for reassessment, Niehaus is a fine altoist with a smooth West Coast veneer that tends to belie his imaginative compositions and standards arrangements. *The Octet* is excellent, full of inventive and sophisticated arrangements that make up for a hint of blandness and propriety in the performances. Sadly, these fine sessions coincided with the beginning of a second stint with the Stan Kenton band. Niehaus also appears on a wilderness of Kenton albums (though there's little point looking for him there), after which he turned his music into a day job, writing and arranging for television and the movies. A loss and a lack.

    The Fresh Sound is a welcome addition to this skimpy list. As ever, Perkins does the work of ten men, but the revelation here is Warrington, a huge-voiced bass player with an inexhaustible stock of ideas. Very impressive indeed, and of a stature to steal the thunder of his employers.

Judy Niemack VOCAL

(*) **Blue Bop Freelance FRL CD 009
    Niemack; Curtis Fuller (*tb*); Cedar Walton (*p*); Ray Drummond (*b*); Joey Baron (*d*). 9/88.

Judy Niemack is a strong presence, but she also performs like a member of the band, which justly elevates her accompanists – Fuller (who appears on only three tracks), Walton, Drummond and Baron all play with superb authority. It's a strong programme, with some jazz themes as well as a sound mix of standards: Niemack turns 'Dizzy Atmosphere' into an all-scat vehicle, reshapes King Pleasure's take on 'Parker's Mood' and swings through a duet with Drummond on 'Softly As In A Morning Sunrise'. But while she exudes confidence, some of her approaches don't always ring true: she has a sometimes breathy, overblown way with her phrasing, and a certain light-opera plumminess detracts from her intensity. 'Gentle Rain', for instance, is mishandled: some lines rushed, others sounding too ripe. She's best on the tunes where she's most integrated with the band, such as Walton's memorable 'Bolivia'. The recording is clear if a little resonant.

*** **Long As You're Living** Freelance FRL-CD 014
    Niemack; Joe Lovano (*ts*); Fred Hersch (*p*); Scott Colley (*b*); Billy Hart (*d*). 8/90.

*** **Heart's Desire** Stash ST-CD-548
    Niemack; Kenny Barron (*p*); Erik Friedlander (*clo*). 91.

Long As You're Living is a set of jazz standards and a challenging programme: 'Daahoud', 'Infant Eyes', 'Monk's Dream', even Ornette Coleman's 'To Welcome The Day'. Niemack handles them all with breezy assurance. Any who found her earlier record a little overbearing, though, will probably feel the same about this. 'Waltz For Debby' comes out as merely sticky, and Cedar Walton's embarrassing 'The Maestro', a dedication to Ellington, doesn't transcend its feeble lyric. But there is superb accompaniment from the band, with Lovano taking some choice solos and Billy Hart playing with brilliant touch: at times, as on the title-track, he seems to be duetting with the singer, finding all sorts of ingenious strokes. *Heart's Desire* is a reflective series of duets with Barron (Friedlander underscores on only three tracks). Mostly standards, with a couple of pop tunes from Joni Mitchell and Stevie Wonder. Niemack sings with a little more restraint and Barron is his customarily masterful self: nothing hits any special heights, but it's a pleasing record.

(*) Straight Up Freelance 018
> Niemack; Toots Thielemans (*hca*); Kenny Werner (*ky*); Jean-François Prins (*g*); Scott Colley (*b*); Mark Feldman (*vn*); Adam Nussbaum (*d*); Cafe (*perc*); Peter Eldridge, Theo Bleckmann (*v*). 8/92.

A disappointment after two good records. Niemack longs to cross over, at least on the evidence of a song-list that features Sting and her own co-composing along with 'You Don't Know What Love Is'; and her big, breezy voice gusts through some of these lyrics with a personality that at least steps aside from the lonesome cabaret persona such material often dictates. It's just not a terribly appealing session, for all the commitment that the singer puts in and the artful accompaniment from the reliable Werner (Thielemans gets in a couple of nice turns in the spotlight, too).

*** Mingus, Monk & Mal Freelance CDFRL 45637
> Niemack; Mal Waldron (*p*). 93.

Whatever else, Waldron knows his singers, and this is an elegantly balanced combination of two very distinctive voices and some top-flight material. The pianist is as gently responsive as Niemack is adventurous, attempting things with her phrasing that we have not heard before. A fine record, marred only by an odd, rather tinny sound.

Bern Nix GUITAR

**** Alarms And Excursions New World 80437
> Nix; Fred Hopkins (*b*); Newman Baker (*d*). 1/93.

After a dozen years with Ornette Coleman's Prime Time band, Nix is well versed in the philosophy and practice of harmolodics. The final track on *Alarms And Excursions* is an exceedingly useful point of reference for anyone who still hasn't come to terms with Ornette's rather circular logic. On 'Boundaries', Nix dispenses with conventional tonality and blurs bar-lines to the point where the music, though still intensely propulsive, has none of the expected reference points.

Very different from the abstract, pulseless approach of the avant-garde, Nix's strategy may be one of the first successful expressions of harmolodic ideas since Ronald Shannon Jackson's *Decode Yourself*. It's a great deal more listenable, an exciting, headlong set that constantly refers back to earlier jazz, as on 'Z Jam Blues', the standard transcription 'Just Friends', or the boppish 'Acuity', which is played as a duet with the magnificent Baker. At the opposite extreme is 'Ballad For L', on which Hopkins takes a leading part, gradually withdrawing as Nix reconstructs the theme at an ever higher register.

This is essential listening for anyone who has followed Ornette's recent progress with interest or puzzlement. Nix's vivid extensions of guitar technique, most of them without the use of electronic technology, are an additional dimension, contributing to a very fine record indeed.

Steve Noble PERCUSSION

**** Ya Boo, Reel And Rumble Incus CD06
> Noble; Alex Ward (*cl, as*). 3/89, 7/90.

*** Bad Gleichenberg Festival Edition: Volume 3 Jazz Live n/n
> Noble; Oren Marshall (*tba*); Steve Buckley (*as, bcl, whistle*). 94.

Steve Noble came to wider notice during the 'Company Week' of 1987, when he joined one of Derek Bailey's most adventurous collectives for a week of improvisation. At the same time, Noble and his occasional partner, Alex Maguire, were winning a reputation in the London free-music community for improvised performances that combined intense, sometimes ferocious interplay with a rare infusion of wit.

Another partner, reeds player Alex Ward, was only in his mid-teens when the first of the performances of *Ya Boo, Reel And Rumble* were recorded. A virtuosic player with a strong background in modernist formal repertoire, he plays with considerable authority, matched move for move by Noble's quick-witted percussion. The opening '8th And How' may still be Noble's best performance on record. The only other CD around at the moment is a live concert from the Bad Gleichenberg Festival of 1994. Much of the record is taken up with solo material, which means that the two others demand equal billing, but it really is Noble's session. He energizes it and brings it a focus and intelligence that his partners cannot quite muster.

Mike Nock (born 1940) PIANO

*** **Almanac** Improvising Artists Inc 123851
    Nock; Bennie Maupin (*ts, bcl*); Cecil McBee (*b*); Eddie Marshall (*d*). 77.
(*) **In Out And Around Timeless SJP 119
    Nock; Michael Brecker (*ts*); George Mraz (*b*); Al Foster (*d*). 7/78.
** **Ondas** ECM 1220
    Nock; Eddie Gomez (*b*); Jon Christensen (*d*). 11/81.

A New Zealander by birth, Nock came to the USA in the 1960s and stayed until 1985: he is on some records by Yusef Lateef and John Handy from the 1960s, and tried jazz-rock before reverting to acoustic music in the '70s. The IAI session, made for Paul Bley's eclectic label, is both of its time and very individual; were it not for the sound-quality, it would be a very difficult record to date. His earlier hard-bop style is eschewed on the trio record for a much windier, overcooked method which seeks to feel every note and succeeds in communicating very little. Gomez sounds bemused, and it's left to the reliable Christensen to find a line to earth for Nock's airy meanderings. Brecker gets off some good solos on *In Out And Around*. In a subsidiary role, Nock sounds fine: like many a journeyman pianist, he's vulnerable only when exposed to a solo spotlight.

(*) **Dark & Curious VeraBra vBR 2074
    Nock; Tim Hopkins (*ts, rec*); Cameron Undy (*b*); Andrew Dickeson (*d*). 90.
*** **Touch** Birdland BL001
    Nock (*p* solo). 7/93.

Two bulletins from Nock's Antipodean base. Hopkins sounds like an accomplished saxophonist, with a sanded, morose tone and a way of undulating long lines through the rhythm section, but there's something wearisome about the way the quartet plays: it's too ponderous, too full of portent, even when worthwhile ideas – as on a steady, well-turned piece like 'Resurrection' – are clearly there. Nock's own improvisations suggest that he remains a little too hung-up on his delivery. Yet the solo album shows a clearing-away of some of his affectations. He still plays with an effortful tread, and rhythmically these pieces seem lame, but for once his seeking out of the essence of the tune sounds effective. The stiffly elegiac 'Django', and the rolling lyricism of (ahem) 'The Sibylline Fragrance Of Gardenias' are personal and absorbing.

Jimmie Noone (1895–1944) CLARINET

*** **Jimmie Noone, 1923–1928** Classics 604
    Noone; various groups. 23–28.
***(*) **Apex Blues** MCA GRP 16332
    Noone; George Mitchell (*c*); Fayette Williams (*tb*); Lawson Buford, Bill Newton (*tba*); Joe Poston (*cl, as*); Eddie Pollack (*as, bs*); Zinky Cohn, Alex Hill, Earl Hines (*p*); Junie Cobb, Wilbur Gorham, Bud Scott (*bj, g*); Johnny Wells (*d*). 28–30.
*** **Jimmie Noone, 1928–1929** Classics 611
    Similar to *Apex Blues*. 28–29.
*** **Jimmie Noone, 1929–1930** Classics 632
    Similar to *Apex Blues*. 29–30.
*** **Jimmie Noone 1930–1934** Classics 641
    Noone; Jimmy Cobb (*t*); Eddie Pollack (*as, bs, v*); Earl Hines, Zinky Cohn (*p*); Wilbur Gorham (*g, bj*); John Henley (*g*); Quinn Wilson, John Lindsay (*b*); Bill Newton (*bb*); Johnny Wells, Benny Washington (*d*); Georgia White, Elmo Tanner, Art Jarrett, Mildred Bailey (*v*).
*** **Jimmie Noone 1934–1940** Classics 651
    As above, except add Guy Kelly, Charlie Shavers (*t*); Natty Dominique (*c*); Preston Jackson (*tb*), Pete Brown (*as*); Richard M. Jones, Gideon Honore (*p*); Teddy Bunn (*g*); Henry Fort, Israel Crosby, Wellman Braud (*b*); O'Neil Spencer, Tubby Hall (*d*); Ed Thompson, Teddy Simmons (*v*); omit Hines, Newton, Bailey, White, Wells, Jarrett, Wilson. 11/34–12/40.

Noone has long been reckoned as one of the premier jazz clarinettists, but his records have fallen out of wide renown. Much of his output was spoiled by weak material, unsuitable arrangements, poor sidemen or a sentimental streak which eventually came to dominate the playing. These are all familiar character-istics of the period, but Noone seemed oblivious to the excessive sweetness which overpowered so many of the records with his Apex Club band, named after his resident gig in Chicago. He had a mellifluous, rather sad-sounding tone and preferred his solos to be insinuating rather than fierce: where Johnny Dodds, the other great New Orleans player of the day, was comparatively harsh, Noone sought to caress melodies. But the plunking rhythm sections, still dominated by banjos even in 1928–9, and the unsuitable front-line partners failed to give Noone the kind of sympathetic settings which would have made his romantic approach more feasible. Poston tarnishes many of the tracks, and his replacement, Pollack, is even worse; even Earl Hines, who plays on 18 tracks on the first disc, can provide only flashes of inspiration. Mitchell arrives for a single session, and even that is ruined by some awful vocals, a final burden which afflicts far too many of these tracks.

For most collectors, *Apex Blues* will be a perfectly acceptable sampling, avoiding some of the redundant detail of the Classics sets, which are also rather poorly transferred. The MCA, which features things like 'I Know That You Know', 'My Monday Date' and 'El Rado Scuffle', has the additional merit of being comfortably audible at all registers. There are examples of the great musician Noone could be. The ballad-playing on 'Sweet Lorraine' and 'Blues My Naughty Sweetie Gives To Me' is of a very high order and investigates a rare, cool vein in the Chicago jazz of the period. 'Oh, Sister! Ain't That Hot?', 'El Rado Scuffle', 'It's Tight Like That' and 'Chicago Rhythm' are further isolated successes, but otherwise one has to pick out Noone amidst an otherwise discouraging backdrop.

Noone's questionable judgement pervades much of the rest of his legacy. Classics 641 has some dreary material and vocals, and Hines's brief reappearance has little impact. But Noone had two great sessions left in him with the small-group swing tracks recorded in 1936–7 and featured on Classics 651. 'Blues Jumped A Rabbit' is the track most remembered, but all four from this session are impressive, and so are the tracks made with Charlie Shavers in New York the following year. The sound is mostly quite decent.

Caecilie Norby VOCAL

**** Caecilie Norby Blue Note 832222-2

Norby; Randy Brecker (*t*); Rick Margitza (*ss*); Scott Robinson (*ts*); Ben Besiakov (*p, org*); Lars Jansson, Niels Lan Doky (*p*); Jakob Foscher (*g*); Lennart Ginman (*b*); Billy Hart (*d*). 9/94.

The Danish singer's international debut is distinguished by a brilliant production by Niels Lan Doky. He chooses an ingenious setting for almost every tune, deploying a crack team of players with spontaneous assurance, and the rich detail of the studio sound is a further embellishment. Inside all this, Norby isn't once intimidated. She has a big, rather awkward voice that she can use with great dramatic force, and on ballads she finds a low-key but steely power, with nothing downcast entering the interpretation. The songs are a fascinating lot, with initially unpromising things like Rod McKuen's 'I've Been Town' and Jimmy Webb's 'By The Time I Get To Phoenix' surprising successes, and a couple of oblique originals adding a further dimension. Something of a European alternative to Cassandra Wilson's *New Moon Daughter*, and a superior record.

Fredrik Norén DRUMS

*** City Sounds Mirrors MICD 001

Norén; Magnus Broo (*t*); Robert Nordermark (*ts*); Torbjorn Gulz (*p*); Dan Berglund (*b*). 12/91.

Norén's band have become a byword for Swedish hard bop, and this Mirrors release updates his line-up once again, the team completely different from that on *To Mr J* (Sonet), which we listed in our last edition. Cut live at Stockholm's enduring Jazzclub Fashing, this is a typical Noren set – smart but sparse arrangements, usually set aside in favour of meat-and-potatoes blowing. Much depends on the horns to keep the interest going, especially through a disc that runs for 70-odd minutes, but Broo and Nordermark have plenty to say, if not quite enough to keep one riveted. Some of the best music comes on Gulz's 'I'm Ready', where the two horns are chased into their best work after the oddball out-of-tempo opening. As usual, the old man at the kit doesn't let anyone sleep. Excellent live sound.

Charlie Norman PIANO

*** Papa Piano Phontastic NCD 8830

Norman; Arne Wilhelmsson (*b*); Ronnie Gardiner (*d*); Johan Lofcrantz (*perc*). 6/93.

Another senior member of Sweden's mainstream school takes the lead. Norman's spry good humour and sense of mischief inform all of the 16 miniatures on display here: he has 'Anything Goes' teetering on a locomotive stride rhythm, for instance, and has it over and done with in less than a minute and a half. 'The Eternal Three' and 'Tribute To Swais' are interesting originals, 'March Of The Dalecarlian Grooms' is a silly one, and he acknowledges his debt to Erroll Garner's records with a good-natured 'Misty'. Recorded on the superb piano at the Royal Swedish Academy of Music, though the concert-hall ambience robs the session of some of its intimacy.

Norrbotten Big Band GROUP

*** Animations Phono Suecia PSCD 75

Bo Strandberg, Dan Johansson, Magnus Ekholm, Magnus Plumppu (*t, flhn*); P. O. Svanstrom, Magnus Puls, Tony Andersson, Anders Wiborg, Bjorn Hjangsel (*tb*); Hakan Brostrom, Christer Johnsson (*ss, as*); Jan Thelin (*as, cl*); Mats Garberg (*ts, f*); Bengt Ek (*ts*); Per Moberg (*bs*); Hans Andersson (*ky*); Hans-Ola Ericsson (*org*); Johan Granstrom (*b*); Christer Sjostrom, Lennart Gruvstedt (*d*); Kjell Westerberg (*perc*); Orjan Dahlstrom (*cond, arr, ky*). 9/92–2/93.

*** Norrbotten Big Band Featuring Nils Landgren Caprice CAP 21494

As above, except add Tapio Maunuvaara (*t, flhn*), Nils Landgren (*tb, v*), Hans Delander (*ky*), Johan Norberg (*g*). 2/93–2/95.

Demanding big-band charts played with panache and fastidious clarity by this typically impressive Swedish orchestra. Orjan Dahlstrom leads and does most of the writing. *Animations* features two long works, a series of pieces to go with the silent film, *Witchcraft Through The Ages*, and the title-work, a full-scale concerto for pipe organ and big band. It's a little hard to see how the film scores really fit with Benjamin Christensen's startling old film, since they actually sound like an unlinked sequence of charts, but there's no denying the impact. 'Animations' is an impressive if finally improbable blending of the organ and the band: Klas Persson cleverly mixes the two factors, but the music is more a matter of competition than integration. The Caprice disc (which also includes a single left-over track from the previous sessions) is a sometimes unconvincing mixture, with a few rhythms straying towards rock. Landgren is the main soloist but his singing on 'Stone Free' and 'Ticket To Ride' wasn't the smartest of ideas, and the best music is on the more thoughtful scores: a big, punchy 'Impressions', a sonorous Philip Catherine tune, 'Twice A Week', and Landgren's mellifluous trip through 'The Midnight Sun Never Sets'.

Walter Norris PIANO

**** Drifting Enja 2044

Norris; George Mraz, Aladar Pege (*b*). 8/74, 5/78.

***(*) Live At Maybeck Recital Hall, Volume 4 Concord CCD 4425

Norris (*p* solo). 4/90.

A fine and sensitive pianist, who worked with Ornette Coleman in the days when the saxophonist still had a use for piano players, Norris has a moody, intense delivery best suited to introspection. His favoured recording format – without drummer – heightens a sense of almost static harmony, though Norris can swing when he chooses. Stylistically, he is probably closest to George Mraz's better-known piano partner, Tommy Flanagan.

A CD reissue brings together the original *Drifting* with a slightly later album, *Synchronicity*, another duo session but featuring Aladar Pege in place of the wonderful George Mraz. It's Mraz who really lifts the earliest of these sessions, subtly adumbrating Norris's occasional uncertainties. The versions of 'Spacemaker' and 'A Child Is Born', both Norris originals, are more clearly articulated than the performances on *Synchronicity* and the LP-only *Winter Rose*, which has now drifted (so to speak) out of catalogue. Mraz's inside-out familiarity with a standard like 'Spring Can Really Hang You Up The Most' gives it a singing confidence. Pege's virtuosity (impressive enough to win him the late Charles Mingus's role in the Mingus Dynasty) sometimes clutters essentially simple themes and is in marked contrast to Mraz's clearness of line.

Norris's Maybeck recital is further out than most in the series. His reworkings of 'The Song Is You', with its softly ambiguous introduction, and of 'Body And Soul', which Norris claims was influenced by Teddy Edwards's version, are strikingly original. On his own 'Scrambled' and 'Modus Vivendi' he has the Maybeck Yamaha singing in unfamiliar accents. A delightful record.

*** Lush Life Concord CCD 4457

Norris; Neil Swainson (*b*); Harold Jones (*d*). 9/90.

**** Sunburst Concord CCD 4486

Norris; Joe Henderson (*ts*); Larry Grenadier (*b*); Mike Hyman (*d*). 8/91.

Henderson is one of the few saxophone players around who shares Norris's fragile and very thoughtful lyricism. They do a masterful 'Naima' together, one that avoids all the dreary clichés which have attached themselves to Coltrane's love-theme. It's not at all clear that the two rhythm players are necessary to this music, but they have the good sense to maintain a lowish profile, accenting choruses and rounding off each number. It would have been intriguing to have had just one track as a duet between saxophone and piano.

Swainson is such a gifted and tasteful player (very much in the line of Mraz and Pege) that by contrast he seems essential to the success of *Lush Life*. The problem here, ironically, is Norris, playing well below his best and resorting to pat and generalized forms rather than his usual incisive structures. Disappointing.

Northern Arizona University Jazz Ensemble GROUP

*** **The Year Of The Cow** Walrus CDWR-4506
> James Gregg, Matt Walsh, Ralph Cuda, Nick Cooper, Bob Woosley (*t*); Steve McAllister, Danny McQuillin, Mike Hilditch, Fred Krueger, Jesse Ribyat, Peter Vivona (*tb*); Jason Collins, Jim Hughens, Jason Kerr, Jeff Kay (*saxes*); Stephanie Galloway (*p*); Rob Hutchinson (*b*); Frank Rosaly (*d*); Barb Burzynski (*perc*). 5/93.

*** **Herding Cats** Sea Breeze SBV-4508
> As above, except David Reed, Chris Ecklund (*t*), Coln Mason, Kenson Nishino, Joshua Cook (*saxes*), Jorg Brosemann (*p*), Geoffrey Miller (*g*), Louis Presti (*b*) and Dan Smithiger (*perc*) replace Gregg, Woosley, Ribyat, Collins, Hughens, Kerr, Galloway, Hutchinson and Burzynski. 5/94.

The NAU Ensemble play their jazz with great spirit and panache and, while this kind of music ends up as something of an exercise in muscle-building, at least these records have some spit along with the polish. None of the soloists stand out, yet all of them impress; none of the charts is genuinely memorable, yet each holds the attention while it's being played. The penmanship is by genre favourites like Bob Florence, Tom Kubis and Matt Catingub, and there is a degree of inspiration along with the mere ingenuity: try Florence's explosive (yet carefully controlled) 'BBC' on the second disc, or the peppery section interplay on Kubis's 'Slauson Cutoff' on the earlier set. Each is recorded and mixed with pristine clarity.

Red Norvo (born 1908) XYLOPHONE, VIBRAPHONE

***(*) **Dance Of The Octopus** Hep CD 1044
> Norvo; Stewart Pletcher (*t*); Eddie Sauter, Jack Jenney (*tb*); Jimmy Dorsey, Donald McCook, Artie Shaw (*cl*); Benny Goodman (*bcl*); Charlie Barnet (*ts*); Bobby Johnson, Dick McDonough, George Van Eps (*g*); Fulton McGrath, Teddy Wilson (*p*); Artie Bernstein, Hank Hayland, Pet Peterson (*b*); Billy Gussak, Gene Krupa, Bob White, Maurice Purtill (*d*); Mae Questal (*v*). 4/33–3/36.

*** **Jivin' The Jeep** Hep CD 1019
> Norvo; Bill Hyland, Stewart Pletcher, Louis Mucci, George Wendt (*t*); Leo Moran, Eddie Sauter (*tb*); Frank Simeone (*as*); Slats Long, Hank D'Amico (*cl, as*); Len Goldstein (*as*); Charles Lanphere (*as, ts*); Herbie Haymer (*ts*); Joe Liss, Bill Miller (*p*); Dave Barbour, Red McGarvey (*g*); Pete Robinson (*b*); Mo Purtill (*d*); Mildred Bailey, Lew Hurst (*v*). 36–37.

***(*) **Red Norvo On Dial** Spotlite SPJ 127
> Norvo; Dizzy Gillespie (*t*); Charlie Parker (*as*); Flip Phillips (*ts*); Teddy Wilson (*p*); Slam Stewart (*b*); J. C. Heard, Specs Powell (*d*). 6/45.

*** **Move!** Savoy SV 0168 2CD
> Norvo; Tal Farlow (*g*); Charles Mingus (*b*). 5 & 10/50, 4/51.

***(*) **Red Norvo Trio** Original Jazz Classics OJC 641
> Norvo; Jimmy Raney (*g*); Red Mitchell (*b*). 53, 54.

*** **Red Plays The Blues** RCA 2113034
> Norvo; Harry 'Sweets' Edison, Don Fagerquist, Ed Leddy, Ray Linn, Don Paladino (*t*); Ray Sims (*tb*); Willie Smith (*as*); Harold Land, Ben Webster (*ts*); Chuck Gentry (*bs*); Jimmy Rowles (*p*); Jimmy Wyble (*g*); Bob Carter, Red Wootten (*b*); Bill Douglas, Mel Lewis (*d*); Helen Humes (*v*). 55.

*** **Live From The Blue Gardens** Musicmasters 65090
> Norvo; Jimmy Saiko, Bob Kennedy, Jack King (*t*); Eddie Bert, Abe Noel, Leo Conners (*tb*); Freddy Artzberger (*as*); Sal Dettore (*as, cl*); Johnny Mazet (*ts*); Sam Spumberg (*ts, ob, eng hn*); Jimmy Gemus (*bs, f*); Bob Kitsis (*p*); Joe Kawchak (*b*); Frank Vesley (*d*); Helen Ward, Kay Allen, Fran Snyder (*v*). 8/89.

Norvo's early recorded work, before he made the switch from xylophone to vibraharp, illustrates the problem of placing so self-effacing an instrument in a conventional jazz line-up; it's sometimes difficult to separate technical limitations and compromises from conscious dynamic strategies in Norvo's recorded work. The material on the xylophonic Heps (there used to be an Affinity compilation with the self-explanatory title *Knock On Wood*) is generally pretty good, though inevitably much of the interest stems from the fantastic line-ups Norvo commanded as a youngster; compare the rather drab arrangements and unconvincing soloing on *Live From The Blue Gardens*. The last year of the war was a good one for Norvo. The super-session with the young Gillespie and Parker from 1945 is a significant moment in the development of bebop and the music that came after it. Though as ragged as any jam session, it is full of life and energy.

In those early, 'hands-off' days, Norvo frequently encountered engineers who would unilaterally boost the sound on quieter numbers or adjust the balances to accord with conventional expectations. Most of those were overturned in the 1950–51 trio in which Charles Mingus was the outwardly unlikely replacement for Red Kelly. Just as Norvo made a pioneering contribution to the use of vibraphone in jazz, so too did the early trios contribute enormously to the development of a style of 'cool' or 'chamber' jazz that became dominant much later in the decade. One of the more significant aspects of the early trio (it may also reflect the bassist's personality to some extent, particularly in the context of an otherwise white group) is the unprecedentedly prominent role assigned to Mingus.

The later trios with Raney and Mitchell are much less obviously adventurous, though again it's the bassist's singing lines that carry much of the interest. Sooner or later when dealing with so-called 'chamber jazz', the question of its supposed 'pretentiousness' is bound to come into play. Norvo's 1954 quintet with Buddy Collette on flute and Tal Farlow on guitar strongly recalls fellow-member Chico Hamilton's sophisticated chamber jazz, with its soft, 'classical' textures and non-blues material. Titles like 'Divertimento In Four Movements' on (now vinyl-only and scarce) *Music To Listen To Red Norvo By* are apt to be seen as red rags by hard-nosed boppers. It's clear, though, from the album title if not immediately from the music itself, that there is a hefty dose of humour in Norvo's work. Structurally, the 'Divertimento' is unexceptionable, with a beautiful division of parts and as lightweight as the genre demands. Other tracks, like 'Red Sails' and the boppish thematic puns of 'Rubricity', suggest a 'different' side to Norvo which is actually present throughout his work, even in his sixties.

Though by no means a one-dimensional figure, Norvo has held to a steady course from the early days of bebop to the beginnings of a swing revival in the 1960s and '70s. His technique is superb and prefigures much of Milt Jackson's best MJQ passage-work. The early trios are unquestionably the place to begin, but there's plenty of good music later and newcomers shouldn't be prejudiced by the instrumentation. Norvo plays modern jazz of a high order.

Hod O'Brien PIANO

*** **Opalessence** Criss Cross Criss 1012
    O'Brien; Tom Harrell (*t, flhn*); Pepper Adams (*bs*); Ray Drummond (*b*); Kenny Washington (*d*); Stephanie Nakasan (*v*). 9/84.
(*) **Ridin' High Reservoir RSR CD 116
    O'Brien; Ray Drummond (*b*); Kenny Washington (*d*). 8/90.
Thirty years ago, Hod O'Brien made an impressive contribution to Belgian guitarist René Thomas's *Guitar Groove*, playing alongside mavericks like J. R. Monterose and Albert 'Tootie' Heath. Recent years have seen him associated with Chet Baker (on the Criss Cross *Blues For A Reason*) and with saxophonist Ted Brown, strong bop credentials with a label not exactly short of respectable pianists.

Unfortunately his work as leader hasn't matched up to his sterling reliability and propulsive strength as a sideman. His solos seem studied to the point of predictability and he suffers from an irritating odd-handedness that sees him switching almost on cue from 'rhythm' to 'lead' like an electric guitarist. With players of Harrell's elegance and with Adams beefing up the arrangements, *Opalessence* is the more interesting of the two albums but, like the semi-precious sheen of the title, it seems all surface and no depth or durability. The trio album reintroduces standards material. 'You And The Night And The Music' reflects O'Brien's innate romanticism, but at opposite extremes 'Willow Weep For Me' and 'Yardbird Suite' simply expose his limitations.

Giorgio Occhipinti PIANO

**** **The Kaos Legend** Leo LAB CD 012
    Occhipinti; Alberto Mandarini (*t, flhn*); Lauro Rossi (*tb*); Gianni Gebbia (*as, ss*); Eugenio Colombo (*as, ss, f*); Carlo Actis Dato (*bcl, bs*); Renato Geremia (*vn*); Giovanni Macioci (*clo*); Giuseppe Guarella (*b*); Vincenzo Mazzone (*d, perc*). 10/93, 10/94.
Take our word for it, there is no need to be aware of or be distracted by the legend of primeval *kaos* to appreciate this remarkable record. It is, in any case, not a continuous performance, but two pieces from the studio and two from the Ibleo Festival. That two are live merely underlines what a thoroughly competent band this is and what excellent improvisers it includes. Of their number only Gebbia and

Dato are otherwise discussed in these pages, and our enthusiasm for both speaks for itself. Occhipinti himself is not a dramatic soloist, though he does often generate considerable volume against the full ensemble. His style is difficult to pin down – which is probably a good thing. Do try *The Kaos Legend*. It is one of a kind.

Bill O'Connell DRUMS

(*) Jazz Alive Sea Breeze CDSB-2056
    O'Connell; Chuck Kininmouth, Rex Richardson, Yerry Connell, Jared Brame (*t*); David Gross, Edwin Williams, Dan Snyderman, Bill Curran (*tb*); Dave Creighton, John Schmitt, Michael Finnerty, Paul Kober, Ken Bender (*saxes*); Eric Scott (*ky*); Andy Meachum (*g*); Joe Bonadonna (*b*); Mike Marotta (*perc*); Sherrilyn Riley (*v*). 11/93.

* **Unfinished Business** Sea Breeze CDSB-2063
    O'Connell; Kirk Garrison, Jim Peterson, Steve O'Brien, Rex Richardson, Jared Brame (*t*); Mark Corey, Edwin Williams, Rich Lapka, Craig Kaucher (*tb*); Dave Creighton, Jim Johnson, Mark Tuttle, Mike Knauf, Kenny Bender (*saxes*); Eric Scott (*p*); John Elmquist (*d*); Sherrilyn Riley (*v*). 9/94.

A Chicago-based outfit helmed by O'Connell, this big band seems to be made up of whichever local session players are available on the day – hence the dramatically different personnels in records only a year apart – yet their similarity says something about the generic path that contemporary big bands follow. There's nothing very striking or original about the first disc, and some of the scores sound glumly by-the-numbers, but the band hits a useful stride here and there and could (on this date) boast some interesting soloists – notably trombonist Gross, whose oddball turns on 'All Of Me' and 'I Get The Blues When It Rains' are refreshingly out of kilter. The second disc is a shade tighter, faster and more exciting, and some of the charts have an independent life: solid filler for ears that can't get enough big-band sound.

Anita O'Day (born 1919) VOCALS

*(*) Swings Cole Porter With Billy May Verve 849 266
    O'Day; main tracks with Billy May Orchestra, unknown personnel; other tracks include Conte Candoli, Roy Eldridge, Lee Katzman, Al Porcino, Jack Sheldon, Ray Triscari, Stu Williamson (*t*); Milt Bernhart, Bob Edmundson, Lloyd Elliot, Bill Harris, Joe Howard, Lou McCreary, Frank Rosolino, Simon Zentner (*tb*); Kenny Shroyer (*btb*); Al Pollan (*tba*); Charlie Kennedy, Joe Maini (*as*); Budd Johnson, Richie Kamuca, Bill Perkins (*ts*); Jimmy Giuffre (*reeds, arr*); Jack Nimitz, Cecil Payne (*bs*); Ralph Burns, Lou Levy, Jimmy Rowles, Paul Smith (*p*); Tal Farlow, Al Hendrickson, Barney Kessel (*g*); Monty Budwig, Buddy Clark, Al McKibbon, Joe Mondragon, Leroy Vinnegar (*b*); Larry Bunker, Don Lamond, Mel Lewis, Lawrence Marable, Jackie Mills, Alvin Stoller (*d*); Buddy Bregman, Bill Holman (*arr*). 1/52–4/59.

*(*) Verve Jazz Masters 49 Verve 517 954
    O'Day; Conte Candoli, Lee Katzman, Jack Sheldon, Al Porcino, Ray Triscari, Stu Williamson, Roy Eldridge, Joe Ferrante, Bernie Glow, Herb Pomeroy, Doc Severinsen, Ernie Royal, Nick Travis (*t*); Milt Bernhart, Jimmy Cleveland, Bob Edmondson, Lew McCreary, Frank Rosolino, Billy Byers, Bill Harris, Joe Howard, Willie Dennis, J. J. Johnson, Fred Ohms, Kai Winding, Lloyd Ulyate, Simon Zentner (*tb*); Bob Brookmeyer (*vtb*); Kenny Shroyer (*btb*); Al Pollan (*tba*); Richie Kamuca, Jerome Richardson, Zoot Sims, Bill Perkins, Budd Johnson, Eddie Shu (*ts*); Sam Marowitz, Hal McKusick, Charlie Kennedy, Joe Maini, Phil Woods (*as*); Walt Levinsky (*as, cl*); Aaron Sachs, Jimmy Giuffre (*ts, cl*); Bud Shank (*as, f*); Danny Bank, Jack Nimitz, Cecil Payne (*bs*); Dave McKenna, Joe Masters, Oscar Peterson, Bob Corwin, Lonnie Hewitt, Hank Jones, Arnold Ross, Jimmy Rowles, Paul Smith (*p*); Barry Galbraith, Herb Ellis, Barney Kessel (*g*); Morty Cobb, George Duvivier, John Drew, Ray Brown, Buddy Clark, Monty Budwig, Larry Woods, Al McKibbon, Joe Mondragon (*b*); Corky Hale (*hp*); Jo Jones, Gene Krupa, Mel Lewis, Don Lamond, Jackie Mills, Lawrence Marable, John Poole, Alvin Stoller (*d*); and as for *Sings The Winners* and *Pick Yourself Up*. 4/54–2/62.

*(*) Pick Yourself Up Verve 517329
    O'Day; Conte Candoli, Pete Candoli, Harry 'Sweets' Edison, Conrad Gozzo, Ray Linn (*t*); Milt Bernhart, Lloyd Elliot, Frank Rosolino, George Roberts (*tb*); Herb Geller (*as*); Georgie Auld, Bob Cooper (*ts*); Jimmy Giuffre (*bs*); Larry Bunker (*vib*); Paul Smith (*p*); Barney Kessel, Al Hendrickson (*g*); Joe Mondragon (*b*); Alvin Stoller (*d*); Buddy Bregman (*cond*); other personnels unknown. 1–12/56.

*** **Sings The Winners** Verve 837 939
  As above, except add Bill Catalano, Jules Chaikin, Phil Gilbert, Lee Katzman, Sam Noto (*t*);
  Bob Enevoldsen, Jim Amlotte, Kent Larsen, Archie LeCoque, Ken Shroyer (*tb*); Lennie
  Niehaus, Bud Shank (*as*); Richie Kamuca, Bill Perkins (*ts*); Jack Dulong (*bs*); Gene Harris,
  Lonnie Hewitt, Joe Masters, Marty Paich (*p*); Cal Tjader (*vib*); Red Kelly, Freddie Schreiber,
  Andy Simpkins, Larry Woods (*b*); Bill Dowdy, Mel Lewis, John Poole, Johnny Rae (*d*). 9/56–10/
  62.

***(*) **At Vine St Live** Disques Swing 8435
  O'Day; Gordon Brisker (*ts, f*); Pete Jolly (*p*); Steve Homan (*g*); Bob Maize (*b*); Danny
  D'Imperio (*d*). 8/91.

Anita O'Day lived the jazz life. She tells about it in *High Times, Hard Times* (1983). As a young woman
she worked as a singing waitress and in punishing dance marathons. And she shot horse until her heart
began to give out in the 1960s and she was forced to battle her demons cold. As is immediately obvious
from her combative, sharply punctuated scatting and her line in stage patter, O'Day was a fighter. As a
'chirper' with the Gene Krupa band in 1941, she refused to turn out in ball-gown and gloves, and
appeared instead in band jacket and short skirt, an unheard-of practice that underlined her instinctive
feminism. With Stan Kenton, she gave a humane edge to a sometimes pretentiously modernist repertoire. O'Day's demanding style had few successful imitators, but she is the most immediate source for
June Christy and Chris Connor, who followed her into the Kenton band.

   The most familiar image of O'Day is at the Newport Festival in 1958, a set preserved in the movie *Jazz
on a Summer's Day*. In a spectacular black dress and a hat that must have accounted for half the egrets
in Louisiana, she resembles one of those subtly ball-breaking heroines in a Truman Capote story. The
voice even then is unreliably pitched, but there's no mistaking the inventiveness of 'Tea For Two' and
'Sweet Georgia Brown'. The woman who sang 'The *Boy* From Ipanema' with a sarcastic elision of the
'aahhs' was every bit as capable as Betty Carter of turning Tin Pan Alley tat into a feminist statement.

   O'Day never sounds quite as effective with a full band, and May's beefy arrangements tend to overpower her subtler rhythmic skills. Fortunately, the reissue of the Cole Porter set includes six bonus
tracks, including band arrangements by Buddy Bregman and Bill Holman, together with a magnificent
small-group 'From This Moment On', a second, rather smoothed-out version of 'Love For Sale' to
compare with May's, and Jimmy Giuffre's superb, throbbing arrangement of 'My Heart Belongs To
Daddy'. The May tracks are virtually all at accelerated tempos (in contrast to the Rodgers and Hart
sequel) but varied with Latin ('I Get A Kick Out Of You') or 'Eastern' ('Night And Day') settings. Even
so, one would much prefer to hear O'Day swing Porter to the basic accompaniment of bass and drums.
She sounds unusually husky at extremes of pitch, as if from the effort of projecting over the band, but
these are still more than worthwhile performances, and a great deal wittier and more stimulating than
most of the 'songbook' sessions that were rife at the time.

   The 1956 sessions with Bregman's orchestra amount to a survivor's testament, a hard-assed, driving
gesture of defiance that is still completely musical. The version of 'Sweet Georgia Brown', which she was
to include in the Newport programme, is buoyant and lightfooted like all the Bregman arrangements,
but the best of the record surely has to be among the small-group tracks with Sweets Edison. An
alternative take of 'Let's Face The Music And Dance' is much broader than the released version; O'Day
was nothing if not subtle and rarely attempted to nudge her audience. The 1958 performances are well
above average and perfect examples of O'Day's wittily daring rhythmic sense. From the mid-1950s, her
closest musical associate was drummer John Poole, who anchors the bonus 'Star Eyes' on *Winners*; she
sticks close by him, leaving the pitched instruments to do their own thing, and, but for the words, she
might almost be involved in a percussion duet. *Winners* is a useful compilation of material from the
Verve catalogue and complementary to the excellent *Jazz Masters*, which is probably the best disc for an
introduction to O'Day. It includes 'Sweet Georgia Brown' with Bregman's band, a duo 'God Bless The
Child' with Barney Kessel from *Trav'lin' Light*, Giuffre's 'Four Brothers' chart from *Sings The Winners*
and the marvellous 'I've Got the World On A String' from *Sings The Most*, one of her best records.

   The 1970s sessions are rather low-key, with a definite loss of exuberance and stamina. Elsewhere there
are scattered performances with Oscar Peterson, but the pianist tends to overpower her. It's to be hoped
that the excellent trio-backed *Once Upon A Summertime* on Jasmine, featuring live European and
American studio sessions, will return from limbo.

   The pitching is more than a little uncertain in places on the Vine Street CD, but O'Day was never a
singer who depended on beauty of tone. She begins with a daringly off-balance 'You'd Be So Nice To
Come Home To', leaning into the rhythm of the song, as far ahead of the beat as she can be. It's a
remarkable performance, unmistakable and individual. Her accompanists are slick, perhaps a little
bland, but Brisker and Jolly seem to understand her requirements pretty well, and the live sound is well
balanced and resonant. It's an attractive programme, mixing old standards ('Old Devil Moon',
'S'posin'', 'It Don't Mean A Thing') with less-familiar material like the Earl Hines, Melvin Dunlap,
Charles Carpenter croon, 'You Can Depend On Me', Leon Russell's 'A Song For You' and Lennon/

McCartney's 'Yesterday', cleverly segued into 'Yesterdays'. Professional vocal jazz that bursts with personality.

***(*) **Rules Of The Road** Pablo CD 2310 950

O'Day; Jack Sheldon, Wayne Bergeron, Ron King, Ron Stout, Stan Martin (*t*); Andy Martin, Bob McChesney, Bob Enevoldsen, Bob Sanders, Alex Iles (*tb*); Sal Lozano, Danny House (*sax, f, cl*); Pete Christlieb, Jerry Pinter, Brian Williams (*sax, cl*); Christian Jacob (*p*); Trey Henry (*b*); Ray Brinker (*d*). 3/93.

She's in great shape, and there's none of Billie's morose self-pity in this nicely structured and immaculately played saga of life on the road. The great thing about O'Day is the fact that she's survived without turning hard. She sings gamily and with wit on material like 'Here's That Rainy Day', 'Soon It's Gonna Rain' and the title-song, still pumping out that beat like she's always done. The band is absolutely Rolls-Royce, two generations of players who combine verve and expertise in almost equal proportions. The only quibble: a rather flat and unresponsive sound and a positioning that sets O'Day way out in front, not where she needs to be and always used to be – in among the guys.

Dave O'Higgins (born 1963) TENOR, SOPRANO & ALTO SAXOPHONES

*** **All Good Things** EFZ 1002

O'Higgins; Robin Aspland (*p*); Alec Dankworth (*bass*); Jeremy Stacey (*d*). 8/92.

***(*) **Beats Working For A Living** EFZ 1009

O'Higgins; Joe Locke (*vib*); Joey Calderazzo (*p*); James Genus (*b*); Adam Nussbaum (*d*). 94.

*** **Under The Stone** EFZ 1016

As for *All Good Things*, except add Gerard Presencer (*t*); replace Stacey with Gene Calderazzo (*d*). 95.

Unlike several of the younger British jazz players, who seemed to make the leap from nowhere at all to 'exciting new recording star' in a matter of weeks, O'Higgins is a time-served performer with an already impressive track-record. A graduate of NYJO, he was spotted and then recruited by the hard-to-fool John Dankworth and Cleo Laine (the Dankworths' son is an effective presence on *All Good Things*), before making a partial breakthrough with the much-touted Roadside Picnic, for whom O'Higgins wrote much of the better material. Since then, he's played a part in Sax Appeal, Gang of Three, the prizewinning Itchy Fingers, and in the Pizza Express Modern Jaz Sextet.

Backing singers is an excellent discipline for a horn man. A typical O'Higgins solo is crisp, direct and to the point, and rarely lasts longer than two or three nicely balanced choruses. The material on *All Good Things* is more obviously jazzy than anything written for Roadside Picnic and the band oozes unfussy professionalism, honed for the occasion on a week's residency at Ronnie Scott's. Dankworth and Stacey impress throughout. All the tunes are by O'Higgins, with the exception of 'Every Time We Say Goodbye' and, following it, Colrane's 'Dear Lord', a pairing which ironically serves only to underline the saxophonist's slight unease with more romantic or emotive stuff.

The second album saw him take the plunge and record with top-flight New Yorkers, a move that had tripped up another promising young Brit, the Scot Tommy Smith. Locke turned out to be the key to the session; in conjunction with the fiery Calderazzo, whose London-based brother turns up on the third album, the vibist soars and thunders, throwing out fast melodic lines with seeming ease. O'Higgins sounds well within himself and plays magnificently on 'Duke Ellington's Sound Of Love', a Mingus composition that requires delicacy as well as strength. The third album might have been a cautious consolidation, but O'Higgins (and here the parallel with Smith holds up) decides to push out the envelope a little and try some new things in his writing. These charts are much more detailed and complex, and the addition of a second horn in places adds a wonderful new dimension . . . but largely in potential. There is an odd unpreparedness to parts of the record, mistimed cues and entrances, ensembles which are not quite clicking. At 70 minutes, too, there is probably just a touch too much material. A more tightly structured hour would have been quite satisfactory.

Tiger Okoshi (born 1950) TRUMPET

*** **Two Sides To Every Story** JVC 2039

Okoshi; Mike Stern (*g*); Gil Goldstein (*p*); Dave Holland (*b*); Jack DeJohnette (*d*). 94.

Okoshi came of age, and came to America. A hard-hitting, pungent trumpeter with an uncompromising approach, he paradoxically took Miles Davis's groups as the model for his own and made his breakthrough working for the equally understated and unaggressive Gary Burton.

His reputation allowed him to recruit top-flight players but obliged him to work very largely on their turf rather than in his own, essentially fusion, style. His attack and phrasing on 'Finders Keepers' recalls no one more strongly than Lee Morgan, and the group hits a hard-bop groove from the off, without a hint of irony. Occasionally Okoshi will let his guard drop and play in a more restrainedly lyrical style, as on 'Yuki No Furu Machi O' here, which draws something, one feels, from the association with Burton. A vivid individualist who works in primary colours, he could do with trying a few more things in this gentler, middle-register vein. There are, after all, two sides . . .

Old And New Dreams GROUP

***(*) **Old And New Dreams** ECM 1154
    Don Cherry (*t, p*); Dewey Redman (*ts, musette*); Charlie Haden (*b*); Ed Blackwell (*d*). 8/79.
*** **Playing** ECM 1205
    As above. 6/80.
***(*) **One For Blackwell** Black Saint 120113
    As above. 11/87.

One wonders if this is how the classic Ornette Coleman Quartet might have sounded with modern recording techniques and a more democratic sound-balance. Now that Coleman is concentrating largely on his electric Prime Time band and on large-scale projects, Old and New Dreams are perhaps the foremost interpreters of his acoustic small-group music. The dirges – 'Lonely Woman' on the first album and 'Broken Shadows' on *Playing* – are by no means as dark as the composer made them, and Redman adheres much more closely to a tonal centre on all the pieces, a role he performed in the Coleman quintet of the late 1960s/early 1970s (see *Crisis*). Cherry also seems to be using orthodox concert trumpet on at least the majority of the tracks, and its fuller tone sits more comfortably alongside Redman than the squeaky pocket cornet. Redman's eldritch musette, a two-reed oboe with a sound not unlike a shawm, gives 'Song Of La-Ba' (*OND*) a mysterious timbre.

    Ed Blackwell has always been prominently featured with the band; the tribute album, recorded live at a Blackwell festival in Atlanta, Georgia, is entirely appropriate, given his multifarious commitment to New Orleans music, modern free jazz and, of course, the work of Ornette Coleman, to which he often stood as *il miglior fabbro*. The live versions of Ornette's 'Happy House' (from *Playing*) and the Ghanaian theme, 'Togo' (from the first album), are slightly rawer and more extended but show no significant differences over the studio versions. Indeed, the main difference between the live album and the others is the extent to which the drummer solos. It's in his work that the 'old' and 'new' of the band title truly resonates. Drawn to the rough second-line drumming of the marching bands, he adds the sibilant accents familiar from bebop, and also a strong element of African talking drum. His rhythmic patterns are dense, coded and allusive but, taken whole, refreshingly entire and self-sufficient. Altogether, these three albums are a monument to a crucially important figure on the modern-jazz scene, who kept out of the critical pantheon by a mixture of chance (circumstances dictated that he didn't play on the early Coleman records, whose music he had done so much to create) and persistent ill-health.

Joe 'King' Oliver (1885–1939) CORNET, TRUMPET

**** **King Oliver Volume One 1923 To 1929** Jazz Classics in Digital Stereo RPCD 607
    Oliver; Louis Armstrong (*c*); Tommy Dorsey, Bob Shoffner (*t*); Honoré Dutrey, Kid Ory, Ed Atkins (*tb*); Johnny Dodds (*cl*); Albert Nicholas (*cl, ss, as*); Billy Paige, Darnell Howard (*cl, as*); Barney Bigard (*cl, ts*); Stump Evans (*ss, as*); Charlie Jackson (*bsx*); Lil Hardin, Jelly Roll Morton, Luis Russell (*p*); Arthur Schutt (*harm*); Eddie Lang, Lonnie Johnson (*g*); Bud Scott, Bill Johnson (*bj, v*); Bert Cobb (*bb*); Jimmy Williams (*b*); Baby Dodds, Paul Barbarin, Stan King (*d*). 4/23–5/29.
**** **King Oliver 1923** Classics 650
    Similar to above. 4–10/23.
***(*) **King Oliver 1923–1926** Classics 639
    Similar to above two discs, except add Teddy Peters, Irene Scruggs (*v*). 10/23–7/26.

The third King of New Orleans, after Buddy Bolden and Freddie Keppard, remains among the most stately and distinguished of jazz musicians, although newer listeners may wonder whether Oliver's records are really so important in the light of what his protégé, Louis Armstrong, would do in the years after the Oliver Jazz Band records of 1923. Joe Oliver was in at the inception of jazz and it's our misfortune that his group wasn't recorded until 1923, when its greatest years may have been behind it: accounts of the band in live performance paint vivid images of creativity which the constricted records barely sustain. Yet they remain magnificent examples of black music at an early peak: the interplay between Oliver and Armstrong, the beautifully balanced ensembles, the development of polyphony, the blues-drenched colours of Dodds, the formal but driving rhythms. If the music is caught somewhere between eras – summing up the aftermath of ragtime and the move towards improvisation and individual identity represented by Armstrong – its absolute assurance is riveting, and presents a leader who knew exactly what he wanted. Oliver's subsequent band, the Dixie Syncopators, was far less successful, troubled by a feeble reed section and cluttered arrangements, but its best sides – such as the furiously paced 'Wa Wa Wa' – are as good as anything from their period.

There are 37 surviving sides by the Oliver (Creole) Jazz Band, although only ten of them appear on the first volume of Robert Parker's compilation. Yet Parker's work here is astonishingly good. If these primitive recordings have been transferred many times, none has appeared in such fine sound as here: Parker's search for only the finest originals pays off handsomely, and as he gathers the missing discs he will surely proceed until the Oliver story is complete. In the meantime, here are 'Dippermouth Blues' (the Gennett version), 'Riverside Blues', 'Sweet Lovin' Man' and other records which pace out the first distinctive steps of black jazz on record. Parker adds one of the duets with Jelly Roll Morton, 'King Porter'; seven sides by the Dixie Syncopators; the pair of tracks by 'Blind Willie Dunn's Gin Bottle Four', a session with Eddie Lang and Lonnie Johnson where Oliver's presence is in some doubt; and a track with Tommy Dorsey on trumpet which allows scholars to compare his work with that of the hornman on the previous session. This is a model reissue in almost every way.

For those who want the 1923 sessions on a single disc, the Classics survey is good enough, though remastering seems only average next to Parker's painstaking work. Classics 639 takes off from the end of the Creole Jazz Band sessions and includes both of the Oliver/Morton duets, seven titles by the Dixie Syncopators and three tracks where the King accompanies blues singers Teddy Peters and Irene Scruggs.

***(*) **King Oliver Volume Two 1927 To 1930** Jazz Classics in Digital Stereo RPCD 608
   Oliver; Tick Gray, Ed Allen (*c*); Dave Nelson, Henry 'Red' Allen (*t*); Jimmy Archey, Kid Ory, Ed Cuffee (*tb*); Omer Simeon, Arville Harris, Ernest Elliott, Barney Bigard, Benny Waters, Buster Bailey, Bobby Holmes, Glyn Paque, Hilton Jefferson, Charles Frazier, Walter Wheeler, Paul Barnes (*reeds*); Clarence Williams (*p, cel, v*); Luis Russell, Don Frye, Norman Lester, Henry Duncan, Eric Franker (*p*); Eddie Lang (*g, vn*); Bud Scott, Leroy Harris, Arthur Taylor (*bj*); Bert Cobb, Cyrus St Clair, Clinton Walker, Lionel Nipton (*bb*); Paul Barbarin, Edmund Jones, Fred Moore (*d*); Justin Ring (*perc*); Texas Alexander (*v*). 4/27–9/30.

*** **1926–1931 Complete Vocalion/Brunswick Recordings** Affinity AFS 1025-2 2CD
   Oliver; Bob Shoffner, Ed Anderson (*c*); Ward Pinkett (*t, v*); Tick Gray, Dave Nelson, Bill Dillard, Louis Metcalf (*t*); Kid Ory, Jimmy Archey, Ed Cuffee, J. C. Higginbotham, Ferdinand Arbello (*tb*); Buster Bailey, Johnny Dodds (*cl*); Albert Nicholas, Barney Bigard, Billy Paige, Omer Simeon, Stump Evans, Ernest Elliott, Arville Harris, Henry L. Jones, Bingie Madison, Fred Skerritt, Teddy Hill, Charlie Holmes (*reeds*); Luis Russell, Leroy Tibbs, Gene Rogers (*p*); Bud Scott, Leroy Harris, Will Johnson (*bj*); Goldie Lucas (*g, v*); Cyrus St Clair, Lawson Buford, Richard Fulbright (*tba*); Paul Barbarin, Bill Beason (*d*); Andy Pendelton, Willie Jackson (*v*). 3/26–4/31.

*** **King Oliver 1926–1928** Classics 618
   As appropriate records above. 3/26–6/28.

*** **King Oliver 1928-1930** Classics 607
   Oliver; Dave Nelson, Henry 'Red' Allen (*t*); Jimmy Archey (*tb*); Bobby Holmes, Glyn Paque, Charles Frazier, Hilton Jefferson, Walter Wheeler (*reeds*); Don Frye, James P. Johnson, Hank Duncan, Eric Franker, Norman Lester (*p*); Roy Smeck (*st-g, hca*); Arthur Taylor (*bj, g*); Clinton Walker (*bb*); Fred Moore, Edmund Jones (*d*). 6/28–3/30.

*** **King Oliver Volume One 1929–1930** JSP CD 348
   As above. 1/29–9/30.

*** **King Oliver Volume Two 1929–1930** JSP CD 348
   As above. 1/29–9/30.

*** **King Oliver And His Orchestra 1930–1931** Classics 594
   As above, except omit Frye, Johnson, Smeck and Jones; add Ward Pinkett (*t, v*), Bill Dillard (*t*); Ferdinand Arbello (*tb*) Buster Bailey (*cl*), Henry L. Jones, Bingie Madison, Fred Skerritt (*reeds*), Gene Rodgers (*p*); Goldie Lucas (*g, v*); Richard Fullbright (*bb*), Bill Beason (*d*). 4/30–4/31.

Oliver's later recordings are a muddle in several ways. Illness and problems with his teeth steadily cut down his instrumental powers, and some celebrated career errors – such as turning down a New York engagement which subsequently went to Duke Ellington – ruined his eminence. The first 13 tracks on the second Jazz Classics compilation trace his decline in fortunes, with nine underrated tracks by the Dixie Syncopators to start, two obscure blues accompaniments with Sara Martin and Texas Alexander to follow, and a session with Clarence Williams and Eddie Lang to complete the picture. Oliver could still play very well: his phrasing is usually simple and unadorned, a very different tale from Armstrong's vaulting mastery, but the quality of his tone and the starkness of his ideas can be both affecting and exhilarating. Parker concludes the disc with seven tracks from the King's Victor sessions. The Classics series takes a chronological route from the first Dixie Syncopators sides to the final Vocalion session of 1931, while the Affinity double-CD includes all the Dixie Syncopators tracks, three obscure blues accompaniments which are unavailable elsewhere, and the three final Vocalion sessions from 1931. The two JSP discs cover the Victor sessions, though alternative takes are evenly split across the pair of CDs, which are in themselves chronological. A complex situation!

The Victor sessions were often plodding and routine orchestral jazz that ran aground on some inept material ('Everybody Does It In Hawaii' features a bizarre appearance by steel guitarist Roy Smeck), and Oliver's own contributions are in much doubt: it's very hard to know where and when he plays, for he may even have asked some of his trumpeters to play in his own style. Nevertheless there are still many records with interesting passages and a few genuinely progressive items, such as 'Freakish Light Blues' and 'Nelson Stomp'. On a piece such as 'New Orleans Shout', where the soloist does sound like Oliver, he shows he can still play with the kind of sombre authority which befits a King. We primarily recommend the second Jazz Classics compilation as an introduction to this period of Oliver's work. The JSP discs offer very fine remastering by John R. T. Davies of all the various original and alternative takes, and for Oliver specialists this will be a first buy. For less committed completists, the Classics series can be safely recommended, although reproduction is, as usual, varied.

*** **King Oliver 1926–1931** Topaz TPZ 1009
    As appropriate discs above. 26–31.
*** **King Oliver & His Orchestra 1929–1930** RCA ND 89770 2CD
    As appropriate discs above. 29–30.

A pair of plausible if inessential compilations of Oliver's later work. RCA's two-disc set covers virtually all his latter-day Victors and makes a useful choice for any who want to study this period. Topaz offer a blend of Dixie Syncopators and Victor material, in clean and acceptable sound. By themselves these don't make up definitive portraits of the third King of New Orleans trumpet, but in their choice of coverage they do a decent job.

Peter O'Mara GUITAR

*** **Avenue 'C'** Enja 6046
    O'Mara; Joe Lovano (ts); Roberto Di Gioia (p); Dave Holland (b); Adam Nussbaum (d). 10/89.
O'Mara has made a couple of rockier records, but this intelligently paced set seems more like a dry run for John Scofield's albums with Joe Lovano. The saxophonist is probably the most interesting soloist here, with his dry tone and broken-up phrasing characteristically in place, but the guitarist takes plenty of well-utilized space for himself, his improvisations comfortably sustained. Holland is as marvellous as always but Nussbaum doesn't sound like the right man for the drum seat: he makes too much noise, and the straight rock beat for 'Uptown' sets the wrong metre at the start. A worthwhile listen.

*** **Stairway** Enja CD 7077-2
    O'Mara; Alex Lakatos (ts); Russell Ferrante (ky); Anthony Jackson (b); Tom Brechtlein (d). 1/ 92.
Another agreeable record, though again one that finds no great profundities. O'Mara continues to sound like a Scofield follower – the title-track resembles a direct extension of Scofield's 'Still Warm' theme – and he doesn't personalize the kind of international fusion sound secured by the group. But there is still some inventive playing within those limits, the music much more tuneful than most fusion, and O'Mara and Lakatos display a thoughtful grip on the material.

Junko Onishi (born 1967) PIANO

*** **Cruisin'** Blue Note 828447-2
    Onishi; Rodney Whitaker (b); Billy Higgins (d). 4/93.
*** **Live At The Village Vanguard** Blue Note 831886-2
    Onishi; Reginald Veal (b); Herlin Riley (d). 5/94.
Onishi plays catholic modern piano: she can do bebop or swing, and make it fit to either Ornette Coleman or John Lewis tunes. She also likes Ellington: there is a sweet version of 'The Shepherd' and a funny one of 'Caravan' on the studio disc. Her own writing is only cautiously allowed space – two tunes on the first session, one on the second – so it's not easy to pass judgement on this aspect of her work. But she performs with much enjoyment, and her respective rhythm sections play a swinging yet oddly subservient role on each disc. Certainly Veal and Riley play much more respectfully (and effectively)

here than they do with Marcus Roberts. The live date includes a version of 'Blue Skies' that expands into an extravagant fantasy on the melody; but just as effective is a rare piano version of Mingus's 'So Long Eric' and Lewis's tolling ballad, 'Concorde'. Interesting to hear her next either with horns or by herself.

Orange Then Blue GROUP

*** Orange Then Blue GM 3006
Roy Okutani, Tommy Smith, Tim Hagans, Kerry MacKillop (*t, flhn*); Swami Harisharan, Gary Valente (*tb*); Peter Cirelli (*btb, euph*); Matt Dariau, Adam Kolker, Dave Mann (*reeds*); Bruce Barth (*ky*); Dave Clark (*b*); George Schuller (*d*); Pat Hollenbeck (*perc*). 12/85–3/86.

*** Jumpin' In The Future GM 3010
Roy Okutani, Andy Gravish, Ken Cervenka, Greg Hopkins, Richard Given (*t, flhn*); Rick Stepton, Curtis Hasselbring, Kenny Wenzel, Peter Cirelli (*tb*); Krista Smith, Mark Taylor (*frhn*); Robert Carriker (*tba*); Howard Johnson (*tba, bcl*); Matt Dariau, Allan Chase, Dave Finucane, Adam Kolker, George Garzone, Bob Zung (*reeds*); Katharine Halvorsen (*ob*); Andrew Strasmich (*f*); Bevan Manson (*p*); Ben Sher (*g*); Dave Clark (*b*); George Schuller (*d*); Gunther Schuller (*cond*). 3–5/88.

**(*) Where Were You? GM 3012
As above, except Matt Simon (*t, flhn*) replaces Given; omit Wenzel, Smith, Taylor, Carriker, Chase, Zung, Halvorsen, Strasmich and Sher; add George Adams (*ts*), Bruce Barth (*p*), Russ Gold (*perc*). 5/87–3/88.

*** Funkallero GM 3023
Roy Okutani, Andy Gravish, Ken Cervenka, Diego Urcola, John Allmark (*t, flhn*); Rick Stepton (*tb*); Peter Cirelli (*btb*); Matt Darriau, Stan Strickland, Allan Chase, Adam Kolker, Dave Finucane (*reeds*); Tim Ray (*ky*); Paul Del Nero (*b*); George Schuller (*d*); Russ Gold, Bob Weiner, Alain Mallet (*perc*). 8–11/89.

The band is led by George Schuller, son of Gunther, and is based in the Boston area. Their three records should tempt anyone interested in the development of post-bop jazz, since they consist of 'historical' material as translated through a contemporary set of inflexions. *Orange Then Blue* includes Mingus's 'Nostalgia In Times Square' and Monk's 'Think Of One', along with originals such as 'Ornette's Music'; *Jumpin' In The Future* is a set of Gunther Schuller's charts dating from the mid-1940s to the mid-1960s, conducted by the arranger himself. Both records strike a sometimes uneasy but often revealing alliance between the essential period quality of the music and the freedoms of a more modern jazz vocabulary. Schuller's scores especially show a concern with form which tends to override individual contributions, but the slow and peculiarly bleak reading of 'When The Saints Go Marching In' and the misty voicings of 'Summertime' provide their own rewards.

The third record is in some ways less successful, drawn from three live concerts by the band: although the choice of material includes pieces culled from the books of Miles Davis and Paul Motian as well as Monk and Mingus, the band play a little stiffly, and the presence of George Adams on three tracks tends to show up the other soloists as merely workmanlike. But when the music takes off, as on Garzone's 'New York', it makes an impressive sound. *Funkallero* restores some of their qualities: the title-piece is a vivid revision of the Bill Evans tune, strung out over a hypnotic bass-vamp, with a terrific, brawling tenor solo by Finucane; there's a strange, almost eerie 'Moose The Mooche' and a sharp expansion of Jack DeJohnette's 'Ahmad The Terrible'. Some of the other pieces are still rather overworked, and solos are variable; but a good introduction to the band overall.

Orchestra National Du Jazz GROUP

***(*) 86 Label Bleu 6503
Christian Martinez, Eric Mula, Michel Delakian, François Chassagnite (*t, flhn*); Denis Leloup, Yves Robert, Jean-Louis Damant (*tb*); François Jeanneau, Jean-Louis Chautemps, Eric Barret, Richard Foy, Pierre-Olivier Govin, Bruno Rousselet (*reeds*); Andy Emler, Denis Badault (*ky*); Marc Ducret, John Scofield (*g*); Didier Havet (*tba*); Michel Benita (*b*); Aaron Scott (*d*); François Verly (*perc, vib*). 86.

*** African Dream Label Bleu 6521
Antoine Illuz, Michel Delakian, Christian Martinez, Philippe Slominski (*t, bug*); Patrice Petitdidier (*c*); Bernard Camoin, Jacques Bolognesi, Denis Leloup, Glenn Ferris, Didier Havet (*tb*); Laurent Dehors, Pierre-Olivier Govin, Gilbert Dall'Anese, Jean-Pierre Solves, Francis Bourrec, Alain Hatat (*reeds*); Philippe Guez (*ky*); Antoine Hervé (*p*); Nguyen Le (*g*); François Moutin (*b*); Mokhtar Samba (*d*); Pierre-Michel Balthazar (*perc*). 88-89.

*** **Claire** Label Bleu 6529

> Jean-François Canape, Patrick Fabert (*t, bug*); Yves Favre, Luca Bonvini (*tb*); Robert Rangell, Michael Riessler (*as, cl, f*); Michel Godard (*tba*); Nissim Mico (*p*); Jean-Louis Matinier (*acc*); Claude Barthélemy, Gérard Pansanel, Serge Lazarevitch (*g*); Jean-Luc Ponthieux, Renaud Garcia-Fons (*b*); Christian Lete, Manuel Denizet (*d*). 12/89.

*** **Jack-Line** Label Bleu 6538

> As above, except add Claire Fargier-Lagrange (*clo*), Xavier Garcia (*elec*), Gérard Siracusa (*body music*). 91.

*** **A Plus Tard** Label Bleu 6554

> Claude Egea, Claus Stotter (*t, bug*); Geoffroy De Masure, Jean-Louis Pommier (*tb*); Philippe Selam, Simon Spang-Hanssen, Remi Biet (*reeds*); Denis Badault (*p*); Nedim Nalbantoglu (*vn*); Laurent Hoevenaers (*clo*); Lionel Benhamou (*g*); Didier Havet (*tba*); Heiri Kaenzig (*b*); François Laizeau (*d*); Xavier Desandre-Navarre (*perc*); Elise Caron (*v*). 7–8/92.

The ONJ is a loose-knit big band sponsored by France's Ministry of Culture, with a revolving person-nel based round French musicians but often featuring a number of guests. Each recording is master-minded by a single MD: Jeanneau (*86*), Hervé (*African Dream*), Barthélemy (both *Claire* and *Jack-Line*) and Badault (*A Plus Tard*). Although the nature of the music is subject to inevitable change, the Orchestra's approach is to take big-band conventions about as far out as they'll go: contrast, call-and-response, massed power and multicoloured textures are familiar ingredients for any such outfit, but the ONJ seem to get wilder and less predictable as they go on. Jeanneau's turn in the driving seat is marked by his assurance: big scores like 'Jazz Lacrymogène' or the Afrocentric 'Kalimba' are packed with incident yet smoothly flowing. There is an especially witty arrangement of Coltrane's 'Syeeda's Song Flute'. *African Dream* finds Hervé pursuing a similar line: grand use of the Orchestra's sonic weight, with Le's guitar cutting through as a major soloist. Barthélemy takes a more combative view of the ensemble, and with a nearly delirious treatment of 'Airegin' on *Jack-Line*, he delivers a sound that's entirely different from Jeanneau's. Stripping down the reed section and strapping in more guitarists turns the Orchestra into an electrified fusion playground of sorts, but Barthélemy treats the situation with enough humour (one of the tunes is called 'Ivan Lendl') to avoid the worst consequences.

Denis Badault contributed some scores to Jeanneau's album, and his own turn out front returns the Orchestra to a more orthodox big-band situation with a completely new personnel. There are a few awkward spots, with a few nods to rock and a sometimes undecided use of polyrhythms turning out wrong, but Badault's brass writing is adept – he gets the best out of the excellent Stotter, who takes some strong solos – and a score like the opening dedication to Kenny Wheeler, 'For K.W.', is impressively sonorous.

Oregon GROUP

**** **Music Of Another Present Era** Vanguard VSD 79326

> Ralph Towner (*g, 12-string g, p, syn, c, mellophone, frhn*); Paul McCandless (*ob, eng hn, ss, bcl, tin f, musette*); Glen Moore (*b, cl, vla, p, f*); Collin Walcott (*tabla, perc, sitar, dulc, cl, v*). 73.

**** **Distant Hills** Vanguard VSD 79341

> As above. 73.

***(*) **Winter Light** Vanguard VSD 79350

> As above. 74.

***(*) **The Essential Oregon** Vanguard VSD 109/110

> As above, except add Zbigniew Seifert (*vn*); David Earle Johnson (*perc*).

(*) **Out Of The Woods Discovery 71004

> As above, except omit Seifert and Johnson. 4/78.

(*) **Roots In The Sky Discovery 71005

> As above. 12/78, 4/79.

*** **Oregon** ECM 1258

> As above. 2/83.

(*) **Crossing ECM 1291

> As above. 10/84.

Hugely talented and *sui generis*, Oregon have always managed to stay just a step ahead of critical prejudice. The band was formed in 1970, an offshoot of the Paul Winter Consort, at a point of low commercial ebb for jazz. By the time jazz had come to seem viably marketable again, the group had evolved far enough beyond their filigree'd chamber-music origins and towards much more forcefully pulsed instrumental combinations to avoid the (still occasionally registered) charge that they were 'merely' a Modern Jazz Quartet for the 1970s. In much the same way, their assimilation of ethnic sources from Asian and native American music was complete long before 'world music' became a marketing niche and a critical sneer.

The early records were largely, but not exclusively, devoted to Towner compositions and were characterized by delicate interplay between his 12-string guitar and Paul McCandless's equally 'classical' oboe. The music on *Music Of Another Present Era* and *Distant Hills* was widely perceived as ethereal and impressionistic, and there was a tendency (perhaps encouraged by intermittent sound-balance on the original vinyl releases) to underestimate the significance of Glen Moore's firm bass-lines (see 'Spring Is Really Coming' on *Present Era*) or the forcefulness of Collin Walcott's tablas. The music combined evocative thematic writing ('Aurora' on *Present Era*, recently re-recorded on the last item below; the classic 'Silence Of A Candle' and McCandless's 'The Swan' on *Distant Hills*) with abstract, collectively improvised pieces (like the 'Mi Chirita Suite' on *Distant Hills*; a neglected aspect of the band's career), and forcefully rhythmic tunes like 'Sail' (*Present Era*) which should have confounded a lingering belief that the band were too professorial to rock.

Winter Light was in some respects a transitional album. Simpler in outline and in its commitment to song forms, it is nevertheless curiously muted, lifted only by 'Deer Path' and by a version of Jim Pepper's 'Witchi-Tai-To', an item that has remained a staple of Oregon performances ever since. The album is also interesting for its (relative) avoidance of so-called ethnic elements in favour of native American elements; Pepper is a North American Indian.

The *Essential Oregon* compilation tends to highlight this side of the band's work, certainly at the expense of more abstract treatments, but offers a much less balanced picture of the band's work than the original releases; the additional tracks featuring Johnson and Seifert are something of a distraction.

Oregon went through something of a slump in the later 1970s. Two studio albums, originally for Elektra, *Out Of The Woods* and *Roots In The Sky*, represent perhaps their weakest moments on record, though a live double-album contained some excellent individual work and a further sample of the group's free mode. The way forward had, however, been plotted by an astonishing collaboration with drummer Elvin Jones, also in Vanguard's back-catalogue, an unlikely combination of forces that in retrospect seemed perfectly logical. Though received wisdom has it that Jones taught them how to swing, it's clear that his polyrhythmic method was *already* part of the group's language. During this same period, the most obvious changes of focus were a gradual subordination of Towner's guitar playing in favour of piano (and later synthesizer) and McCandless's decision to double on the much more forceful soprano saxophone.

Oregon represents a partial return to form in the new, upbeat manner. Clearly, too, the group sound benefited enormously from ECM's state-of-the-art production. However, the writing seems remarkably tame and formulaic, a tendency reinforced on its successor. *Crossing* has acquired a slightly sentimental aura, since it is the last Oregon record on which Walcott appeared; between recording and release, he and the group's road manager were killed in an auto accident while on tour in Europe. It is, though, a very unsatisfactory record with few compelling themes and some of the group's most banal playing.

**(*) Ecotopia ECM 1354
    As above, but Trilok Gurtu (*tabla, perc*) replaces the late Collin Walcott.
*** 45th Parallel VeraBra CDVBR 2048
    As above, except add Nancy King (*v*). 8 & 9/88.
*** Always, Never And Forever VeraBra CDVBR 2073
    As for *Ectopia*. 90.

It is, of course, idle to speculate what might have happened had Walcott survived. A hugely talented musician, with a recording career of his own (*q.v.*), he was in some senses the most wayward of the group's members. To some extent, the range of his skills was at a premium in the 'new' Oregon. However, he was a vital component of the group's sound, and his death was a shattering blow which almost sundered the band permanently. Trilok Gurtu was recruited only after much heart-searching and because he combined many of Walcott's strengths with an individuality of voice and technique. His group debut on *Ecotopia* is uncertain, though the album's flaws can hardly be laid to his account. The group were still in personal and artistic shock, and there is a nostalgic rootlessness inscribed in every aspect of the album, from the title onwards. *45th Parallel* is better and more firmly demarcated, with some swinging piano from Towner (and a partial return to form on guitar) and a better balance of material. It's marred by Nancy King's preposterous vocal on 'Chihuahua Dreams', but there's a clear sense that the band has re-established contact with its own past output (that is made clear in the brief 'Epilogue') and with its own sense of development. Whether that is signalled equally successsfully in the new version of 'Aurora' on the second VeraBra album is a matter of conjecture; but the turn of the group's third decade does seem to represent a promising new dawn.

***(*) Troika veraBra 2078
    Ralph Towner (*g, syn*); Paul McCandless (*ob, eng hn*); Glen Moore (*b*). 1–11/93.

The experiment with Gurtu seemed to founder despite successful tours. Whether this was as a result of artistic incompatibility or as a result of his own burgeoning solo career is difficult to judge. *Troika* would seem to find Oregon in their natural state again. The absence of a percussionist is partially compensated by Towner's increasingly inventive touch on the Korg synth, and Moore seems to have devised ways of playing in a much more accented and forceful style. There are a couple of free pieces which hark back to the early days, but most of the tracks are short songs that concentrate on particular harmonic and textural areas. Only the longer 'Mariella' and 'Celeste' and, to a degree, 'Gekko' and 'Tower' show much emphasis on structure as a guiding principle. There is no mistaking Oregon's viability as a creative force. This isn't one of their classics, but it is a cracking good album.

Original Dixieland Jazz Band GROUP

***(*) **Sensation!** ASV AJA 5023R
> Nick LaRocca (c); Emil Christian, Eddie Edwards (tb); Larry Shields (cl); Bennie Krueger (as), · J. Russel Robinson, Billy Jones, Henry Ragas (p); Tony Sbarbaro (d). 2/17–11/20.

***(*) **In England** EMI France Jazztime 252716-2
> As above. 4/19–5/20.

(****) **The 75th Anniversary** RCA Bluebird ND 90650
> As above. 2/17–12/21.

**** **The Original Dixieland Jazz Band 1917–1921** Timeless CBC 1-009
> As above. 2/17–12/21.

***(*) **The Complete Original Dixieland Jazz Band 1917–1936** RCA ND 90026 2CD
> As above, except add Earle Ison, George Walters, George Johnson (t), Charles Harris, Alex Polascay (tb), Joe Hunkler, Buddy Saffer (as), George Dessinger (ts), Chris Fletcher (g), Boyd Bennett (b), Chris Fletcher (v). 2/17–9/36.

Whatever effects time has had on this music, its historical importance is undeniable: the first jazz band to make records *may* have been less exciting than, say, the group that King Oliver was leading in the same year, but since no such records by Oliver or any comparable bandleader were made until much later, the ODJB assume a primal role. Harsh, full of tension, rattling with excitement, the best records by the band have weathered the years surprisingly well. Although the novelty effects of 'Barnyard Blues' may seem excessively quaint today, the ensemble patterns which the group created – traceable to any number of ragtime or march strains – have remained amazingly stable in determining the identity of 'traditional' jazz groups ever since. The blazing runs executed by Shields, the crashing, urgent rhythms of Sbarbaro and LaRocca's thin but commanding lead cornet cut through the ancient recordings. Although the band were at the mercy of their material, which subsequently declined into sentimental pap as their early excitement subsided, a high proportion of their legacy is of more than historical interest.

Fifty-four of their recordings between 1917 and 1922 have survived, but there is no comprehensive edition currently available. Their 1917 sessions for Aeolian Vocalion, very rare records, have yet to make it to CD. The ASV CD includes 18 tracks and offers a good cross-section of their work, although a couple of undistinguished later pieces might have been dropped in favour of the absent and excellent 'Mournin' Blues' or 'Skeleton Jangle'. The EMI France CD duplicates nine tracks with the other disc and has some weak closing items, but it also includes five rare tracks by other jazz-influenced bands from the London scene of the same period, including the black groups, Ciro's Club Coon Orchestra (doing perhaps the first-ever version of 'St Louis Blues' on record) and Dan and Harvey's Jazz Band. Each disc varies in its remastering almost from track to track, with some items obviously dubbed from poorer copies than others, although we find that the EMI France disc is overall a shade livelier in its reproduction, as well as offering some 15 minutes' more music.

The appearance of the Timeless CD sweeps the board, since it covers all of their Victor sessions up to the end of 1921, a perfect duplication of the Bluebird CD – but in much livelier and more enjoyable sound, which gives the best idea of the sensation this remarkable group must have caused. The *75th Anniversary* CD remains a decent alternative, but Timeless's remastering is clearly superior.

The appearance of the two-disc set in RCA's Tribune series is a complication. It includes all their Victor masters and goes on to cover the slightly odd and anachronistic sessions which LaRocca led in 1936, with the old team reunited and with an augmented, near-big band on two dates covering some of the now-ancient favourites. A band out of their time, these were hardly successful re-creations. But they're interesting to hear, and they make a useful pendant to the old material, which sounds fair enough in these transfers.

Original Memphis Five GROUP

*** Original Memphis Five Collection Vol. 1 Collectors Classics COCD-16

Phil Napoleon (*c, t*); Charles Panelli, Miff Mole (*tb*); Doc Behrendsen, Jimmy Lytell, Sam Lanin (*cl*); Rudy Wiedoeft (*as*); Frank Signorelli (*p*); Ray Kitchingman (*bj*); Jack Roth (*d*). 4/22–12/23.

With the Ladd's Black Aces LPs on Fountain/Retrieval now out of print, this is the only disc dedicated to the work of the group that came to be, usually, the Original Memphis Five, although many of the tracks here are credited to Jazbo's Carolina Serenaders or The Southland Six. Napoleon is on every track, Mole on most of them, and together they make one of the best front lines of the day: Mole's flexibility shines through even the early tracks, and Napoleon's steady, unflashy lead is a thread that runs through all 23 tunes. Improvisation is done more in breaks than in solos, but this is primarily an ensemble music, still edging away from the ODJB. It would be admirable to see this huge group of titles (more than 400 78-r.p.m. masters) given a proper reissue: this is a good start! Remastering is excellent but younger ears should beware: this is ancient-sounding music, even off the cleanest transfer.

The Original Victoria Jazz Band GROUP

** Plays Chicago Classics London Jazz LMJ 024B

Alan Snook (*t, c*); David Chandler (*tb*); Pete Bennetto (*cl, ts*); Billy Boston (*bsx*); Colin Good (*p*); Greg Potter (*bj*); Steve Wick (*sou*); Arthur Fryatt (*d, wbd*). 3–5/90.

**(*) More Chicago Classics London Jazz LMJ 025B

As above, except omit Wick. 3/92.

Trad from London. The material is all straight out of the Chicago repertory, and the trouble is that you can hear better versions of any of the tunes elsewhere, without trying very hard. The earlier disc is all too polite and tasteful – their 'Sheikh Of Araby' is flat out and taking forty winks. But there's a smidgeon of extra bounce and vim in the second CD, which is really more of the same only a little hotter. None of the soloists has much to say, and the rhythm section could use some rocket assist. Best moment: an agreeably tousled 'See See Rider'.

Niels-Henning Orsted-Pedersen (born 1946) DOUBLE BASS

***(*) Jaywalkin' Steeplechase SCCD 31041

Orsted-Pedersen; Philip Catherine (*g*); Ole Kock Hansen (*p*); Billy Higgins (*d*). 9 & 12/75.

**** Double Bass Steeplechase SCCD 31055

Orsted-Pedersen; Sam Jones (*b*); Philip Catherine (*g*); Albert 'Tootie' Heath, Billy Higgins (*d, perc*). 2/76.

**** Live At Montmartre: Volume 1 Steeplechase 51083

Orsted-Pedersen; Philip Catherine (*g*); Billy Hart (*d*). 10/77.

***(*) Live At Montmartre: Volume 2 Steeplechase 51093

As above. 10/77.

**** Dancing On The Tables Steeplechase SCCD 31125

Orsted-Pedersen; Dave Liebman (*ts, ss, af*); John Scofield (*g*); Billy Hart (*d*). 7 & 8/79.

**** The Viking Pablo 2310894

Orsted-Pedersen; Philip Catherine (*g*). 5/83.

NHOP's credits as a sideman almost defy belief. He plays on something over 150 currently available CDs and LPs, backing the likes of Chet Baker, Kenny Drew, Lee Konitz, Ben Webster and (crucially) Dexter Gordon and Oscar Peterson. He has recorded with younger-generation players as far apart in style as Niels Lan Doky and Anthony Braxton. If his playing on the two Steeplechases from the Club Montmartre in Copenhagen sounds particularly confident, that is because he spent much of his later twenties as house bassist there. His technique as a young man was staggering, combining forceful swing with great melodic and harmonic sense and a sure-fingeredness that gave his big, sonorous tone an almost horn-like quality. While still in his teens, he was invited to join the Basie band, but decided against it.

Equally consistent as a leader, NHOP probably hasn't received his due of praise for his own records. They are all broadly of a piece, largely standards-based, with the group sessions placing greater emphasis on swing, and the duos on a more musing, intimate quality, and the ratings above give a reasonable sense of their respective merits.

The bassist has enjoyed a particularly fruitful relationship with guitarist Philip Catherine, who shares many of his virtues; the two in combination are responsible for some formidably beautiful music, notably on *The Viking*. The punning *Double Bass* is an interesting experiment that almost falters when a second drummer joins the group, doubling not just the bass lines but the whole rhythm section; Catherine is left with an unenviable continuity job, but 'Au Privave' (Oscar Peterson's favourite Charlie Parker theme) and Coltrane's 'Giant Steps' fare remarkably well. *Dancing On The Tables* explores less familiar materials and tonalities. Liebman's saxophone playing is sufficiently light and spacious not to swamp the foreground, and NHOP produces some intriguing rapid-fire counterpoints to the guitarist.

Few modern players have developed mainstream bass to anything like this extent and Orsted-Pedersen is overdue a comprehensive assessment.

Anthony Ortega (born 1928) ALTO AND SOPRANO SAXOPHONES, FLUTE

***(*) **New Dance** hat Art 6065
    Ortega; Chuck Domanico, Bobby West (*b*); Bill Goodwin (*d*). 10/66–1/67.
Ortega's earlier records as a leader – he apprenticed with Lionel Hampton in the early 1950s – are obscure, and the two sessions included here would be too if it hadn't been for a very enterprising reissue by Werner Uehlinger's hat Hut operation. The leader was an untypical West Coast saxman in that he chose to move some way beyond the customary neat, quicksilver playing of his peers and began instead to investigate what there was in the new music of Ornette Coleman for him. Like Art Pepper, Ortega blended elements of that freedom into a style that still depended on bebop shapes and symmetries. When he strays too far into open space, as at the end of 'New Dance' itself, his tonal distortions begin to sound affected. Most of this material is based on standards, though, and with a flicker of a sequence in the background Ortega sounds completely confident. Several tracks are open-ended duets with Domanico (two bass solos from the original Revelation albums have been omitted here) which are like coiled lines slowly drawn into straightness: 'The Shadow Of Your Smile' does it with the ballad form, while the pell-mell pace of 'I Love You' does it at full tilt. The trio tracks with West and Goodwin are less dramatic, yet Ortega's sinuous lines and startlingly pure tone sound utterly distinctive in both settings. The original recordings were rather cloudy but the remastering does the music no disservice.

***(*) **Anthony Ortega On Evidence** Evidence EVCD 213
    Ortega; Sylvain Kassap (*bcl*); Manuel Rocheman (*p*); Didier Levallet (*b*); Jacques Mahieux (*d*). 4/92.
Ortega has lost none of his adventurousness. This welcome return to the studios finds him in ruminative rather than urgent mood: the tempos are often dreamily slow, the melodies (all originals by Ortega or his wife, bar Mal Waldron's 'Warm Canto') poignantly caressed, and his previously astringent tone has softened a little. But there are still improvisations of absorbing skill and cumulative power: he's again a trifle unconvincing on the 'out' moments of 'Gone Again', yet the spiralling trails of 'Avignon' or 'Norge' are bewitching in their quiet intensity, with a new interest in soprano offering a change of timbre. The rhythm section are fine, even if Rocheman is occasionally a shade too flowery in some of his solos, and Kassap appears only on the closing 'Warm Canto', a sparse, almost elemental treatment.

Kid Ory (1886–1973) TROMBONE, VOCALS

**** **Ory's Creole Trombone** ASV CD AJA 5148
    Ory; Mutt Carey, George Mitchell, King Oliver, Bob Shoffner (*c*); Louis Armstrong (*c, v*); Johnny Dodds, Dink Johnson, Omer Simeon (*cl*); Stump Evans, Albert Nicholas, Billy Paige (*cl, as, ss*); Darnell Howard (*cl, as*); Barney Bigard (*cl, ts, ss*); Joe Clarke (*as*); Lil Armstrong, Jelly Roll Morton, Luis Russell, Fred Washington (*p*); Bud Scott, Johnny St Cyr (*bj*); Ed Garland, John Lindsay (*b*); Bert Cobb (*bb*); Paul Barbarin, Ben Borders, Andrew Hilaire (*d*). 6/22–4/44.
**** **Kid Ory's Creole Jazz Band** GHB BCD 10
    Ory; Mutt Carey (*t*); Darnell Howard, Omer Simeon (*cl*); Buster Wilson (*p*); Bud Scott (*bjo, v*); Ed Garland (*b*); Minor Ram Hall, Alton Redd (*d*). 8/44–11/45.
*** **New Orleans Legends** Vogue 655603
    Ory; Teddy Buckner, Mutt Carey (*t*); Joe Darensbourg, Jimmie Noone (*cl*); Lloyd Glenn, Buster Wilson (*p*); Bud Scott (*g*); Ed Garland (*b*); Minor Ram Hall, Zutty Singleton (*d*). 4 & 10/44.
***(*) **Kid Ory: '44–'46** American Music AMCD 19
    Ory; Mutt Carey (*t*); Barney Bigard, Albert Nicholas, Joe Darensbourg, Wade Whaley (*u*); L. Z. Cooper, Buster Wilson (*p*); Huddie Leadbetter, Bud Scott (*g, v*); Edward Garland (*b*); Charlie Blackwell, Minor Ram Hall, Zutty Singleton (*d*). 1/44–5/46.
*** **At The Green Room: Volume 1** American Music AMCD 42
    As above, except omit Bigard, Nicholas, Whaley, Leadbetter, Singleton, Blackwell. 2/47.

*** **At The Green Room: Volume 2** American Music AMCD 43
As above. 2/47.
*** **King Of The Tailgate Trombone** American Music AMCD 20
As above, except add Andrew Blakeney, Teddy Buckner (*t*). 48, 49.
***(*) **New Orleans Jazz** Sony 462954
Ory; Teddy Buckner, Mutt Carey (*t*); Barney Bigard (*cl*); Joe Darensbourg (*cl, v*); Lloyd Glenn, Buster Wilson (*p*); Julian Davidson (*g*); Bud Scott (*g, v*); Morty Cobb, Ed Garland (*b*); Minor Ram Hall (*d*); Helen Andrews, Lee Sapphire (*v*). 6/50, 10/66.
***(*) **This Kid's The Greatest** Good Time Jazz GTCD 12045
Ory; Teddy Buckner (*c*); Pud Brown, Phil Gomez, Bob McCracken, George Probert (*cl*); Don Ewell, Cedric Haywood, Lloyd Glenn (*p*); Julian Davidson, Barney Kessel (*g*); Wellman Braud, Morty Cobb, Ed Garland (*b*); Minor Ram Hall (*d*). 7/53–6/56.
***(*) **Kid Ory's Creole Jazz Band, 1954** Good Time Jazz GTJ 12004
Ory; Alvin Alcorn (*t*); George Probert (*cl*); Don Ewell (*p*); Bill Newman (*g, bj*); Ed Garland (*b*); Minor Ram Hall (*d*). 8/54.
*** **Sounds Of New Orleans: Volume 9** Storyville STCD 6016
Ory; Alvin Alcorn (*t*); Albert Burbank, Phil Gomez, George Probert (*cl*); Don Ewell (*p*); Ed Garland (*b*); Minor Ram Hall (*d*). 5/54–2/55.
*** **Kid Ory's Creole Jazz Band** Good Time Jazz GTJ 12008
Ory; Alvin Alcorn (*t*); George Probert (*cl*); Don Ewell (*p*); Barney Kessel (*g*); Ed Garland (*b*); Minor Ram Hall (*d*). 12/55.
***(*) **The Legendary Kid** Good Time Jazz 12016
Ory; Alvin Alcorn (*t*); Phil Gomez (*cl*); Lionel Reason (*p*); Julian Davidson (*g*); Wellman Braud (*b*); Minor Ram Hall (*d*). 11/55.
*** **Favorites!** Good Time Jazz 60-009
Ory; Alvin Alcorn (*t*); Phil Gomez (*cl*); Cedric Haywood (*p*); Julian Davidson (*g*); Wellman Braud (*b*); Minor Ram Hall (*d*).

Kid Ory's 1940s albums (on Good Time Jazz) had Creole cooking tips printed on the sleeves. On his comeback, after nearly a decade out of music fattening up chickens, the trombonist's rhythmic tailgating style was still as salty as blackened kingfish and as spicy as good gumbo. Ironically, he spent much of his life away from Louisiana, going to California for his health just after the First World War, where he recorded the first ever sides by an all-black group, 'Ory's Creole Trombone' and 'Society Blues', in 1922. For some purists, these – collected on the ASV compilation, *Ory's Creole Trombone* – and not the Original Dixieland Jazz Band's earlier discs, mark the real start of jazz recording.

A man can learn a lot watching chickens forage. Ory's comeback coincided with the big Dixieland revival, and he turned an instinct for self-marketing to lucrative effect. Notoriously difficult to work for, he was particularly demanding of his trumpet players. When Mutt Carey died in 1948, Ory used the equally brilliant Teddy Buckner and later Alvin Alcorn in what was to be one of the best and most authentic of the revivalist bands. Kid Ory's Creole Jazz Band lasted until the 1960s, by which time his exemplary stamina was failing and the big glissandi and slurs were sounding slightly breathless. Ory was a fine technician who cultivated a sloppy, 'rough' effect and a loud, forthright delivery that led some listeners to dub him a primitive. Like all the great Delta players, though, he thought of the whole group as a single instrument into which his own voice slotted perfectly.

The ASV also includes some important sides from 1926 with King Oliver and Louis Armstrong, and a group called the New Orleans Wanderers which was effectively the Hot Five without Pops. There is also material from later that year with Jelly Roll Morton and a jump forward in time to the revivalist band of 1944. A very valuable collection indeed.

The Good Time Jazz catalogue is now pretty much up to date, and frankly there's very little to choose between individual items. The titles are confusingly unvaried but the GHB disc has all of the legendary Crescent recording sessions, excellent readings of 'Maple Leaf Rag', 'Ory's Creole Trombone', 'Careless Love Blues' and 'Oh, Didn't He Ramble', though not, unfortunately, Ory's own 'Muskrat Ramble', which was one of the revival hits of the mid-1950s. It's to be found on the good Storyville, with Alvin Alcorn's trumpet going sharp as a tack in and out of the melody, and also on *1954*, which was unfortunately misnumbered in the last edition. There are also a couple of good tracks on the Vogue compilation, and the earlier material on *New Orleans Jazz*; despite the presence of Bigard and Carey, the later stuff is pretty tired.

The first American Music disc is mostly airshot material from Standard Oil-sponsored broadcasts in the first half of 1946. There is a brief, fascinating encounter with Huddie Leadbetter, better known as Leadbelly, on 'Bye'N'Bye' and 'Swing Low, Sweet Chariot', but for the most part it's the group with Carey or Joe Darensbourg, with four studio tracks showing Albert Nicholas in particularly good lip. There is some excellent material from the Green Room in San Francisco; content-wise nothing out of the ordinary except for a rather moving version of the 'Rifle Rangers (1919 March)' which must have pleased any old soldiers in the room. *King Of The Tailgate Trombone* is less individual, Blakeney and Buckner (on this 1949 occasion) rather indistinct and waffly. Sound-quality varies on all these but isn't significantly better or worse than the norm for the period, and Ory himself always took care to come through at the front, loud and firm, just in case anyone forgot his name.

Mary Osborne (1921–92) GUITAR

*** **A Memorial** Stash ST-CD-550
> Osborne; Tommy Flanagan (*p*); Danny Barker (*g*); Steve LaSpina, Tommy Potter (*b*); Charli Persip, Jo Jones (*d*). 59–81.

A pleasing tribute to an unsung pioneer of swing-to-bop guitar. Mary Osborne was a Christian disciple, but her gender probably kept her out of enough of the right circles to make much headway or many recordings: an appearance with Coleman Hawkins in the 1940s is all many collectors will remember. This CD collects two sessions 22 years apart. The 1959 date finds Mary with a fine quintet, including Flanagan and Jones, although the tracks are rather short; the sound suffers from a mysteriously crackly source and a sometimes disagreeable reverb. No problems, though, with the six elegant tracks cut with LaSpina and Persip in 1981. On this evidence, Osborne remained true to her roots: simple, unfussy lines of chords and single-string melodies, unadventurous but always swinging.

Mike Osborne (born 1941) ALTO SAXOPHONE

**** **Outback** Future Music FMR CD 07
> Osborne; Harry Beckett (*t, flhn*); Chris McGregor (*p*); Harry Miller (*b*); Louis Moholo (*d*). 70.

For the past 15 years illness has silenced one of the most powerful and emotionally stirring voices in British jazz. A Mike Osborne gig, with whatever line-up, was a furious dance of disparate parts: simple hymnic tunes, wild staccato runs, sweet ballad formations and raw blues, all stitched together into a continuous fabric that left most listeners exhausted, and none unmoved.

Osborne's early album, *Outback*, was until recently rarely seen and highly collectable in its original LP issue on Turtle. With the Ogun catalogue, *All Night Long*, *Border Crossing*, *Tandem* and *Marcel's Muse* out of print, this is a more than worthwhile reissue. Readers of *Wire* magazine voted *Outback* one of the records they would most like to see on CD, and one can immediately hear why. Ossie's wailing, turbulent voice fills up the room. He was probably always heard to greater advantage in the pianoless trio with Louis Moholo and the late Harry Miller, but before this session he invited friends Harry Beckett and Chris McGregor (who has also since passed away) to join in. Beckett lightens the sound with blinks of pure sunshine, but he's capable of a darker, freer tonality as well.

There are just two long tracks, the title-piece and the more sanguine 'So It Is'. On the original LP they occupied opposite sides. Here, though, it's possible to hear them as two sides of a single musical personality, undoubtedly troubled, fiercely questing, but full of quiet humour as well. What's now impossible is to judge what Osborne might have gone on to do. All that's left is to hear his music and wish him well.

Greg Osby (born 1960) ALTO AND SOPRANO SAXOPHONES, FLUTE, KEYBOARDS

(*) **Greg Osby And Sound Theatre JMT 834411
> Osby; Michele Rosewoman (*p*); Fusako Yoshida (*koto*); Kevin McNeal (*g*); Lonnie Plaxico (*b*); Paul Samuels, Terri Lyne Carrington (*d*). 6/87.

*** **Mindgames** JMT 834422
> Osby; Geri Allen, Edward Simon (*ky*); Kevin McNeal (*g*); Lonnie Plaxico (*b*); Paul Samuels (*d*). 5/88.

(*) **Season Of Renewal JMT 834435
> Osby; Edward Simon, Renée Rosnes (*ky*); Kevin Eubanks, Kevin McNeal (*g, g-syn*); Lonnie Plaxico (*b*); Paul Samuels (*d*); Steve Thornton (*perc*); Cassandra Wilson, Amina Claudine Myers (*v*). 7/89.

** **Man Talk For Moderns Vol. X** Blue Note CDP 795414-2
> Osby; Steve Coleman (*as*); Gary Thomas (*ts, f*); Edward Simon, Michael Cain (*ky*); David Gilmour (*g, g-syn*); Chan Johnson (*g*); James Genus, Lonnie Plaxico (*b*); Billy Kilson (*d*); Steve Moss (*perc*); Hochmad Ali Akkbar (*v*). 10–11/90.

** **3-D Lifestyles** Blue Note CDP 798635-2
> Osby; Darrell Grant, Geri Allen (*p*); Cassandra Wilson (*v*). 92.

*** **Black Book** Blue Note 7243 8 29266-2
> Osby; Mulgrew Miller (*p*); Calvin Jones (*b*); Bill McClellan (*d*); Sha-Key, Mustafo, Markita
> Morris, Taj McCoy, Riva Parker, Bernard Collins Jr (*v*). 94.

Osby is a hip, creative mind in search of a context that can do something worthwhile with a talent that gets wasted on most of these records. He plays alto sax in the sharp, coolly incisive manner which has become a standard among many of the younger New York-based players, and his agility and rhythmic acuity on the horn is unanswerable: he can move in the most complex time and make it sound effective, and the impassive tartness of his tone serves to harden the edge of his improvising. But too much of the music here seems to stand as a mere creative exercise for skilful players; and, at its most rarefied, Osby's composing suggests a kind of intellectual fusion which comes dressed in unyielding funk rhythms. The debut album for JMT is one of the best under his own name, since it forges a genuine creative partner-ship – with pianist Michele Rosewoman, whose improvisations make Osby's tunes sound stronger than they are – and works through a range of options, from romantic ballads to tight, flat-out blowing. *Mindgames* moves the keyboards to a more textural role, and Osby turns up the guitar: there's also less variation in pulse and delivery. *Season Of Renewal* runs aground on some heartless material – five of the tracks are sung as songs, and Osby is no great songwriter – but his own playing sounds exactingly up to the mark. A move to Blue Note doesn't seem to have done him any artistic favours, though. *Man Talk For Moderns Vol. X* is so modish that it ought to have a sell-by date on it, and the record is compromised by some tracks which sound like a direct bid at American jazz-radio crossover. *3-D Lifestyles* goes further by aiming for an all-out fusion of rap, hip-hop and jazz creativity; mostly, though, it seems to emphasize the incompatibilities of the forms rather than their potential for blending. There is still some incisive playing, and Osby's swagger cuts through in several places, but it's a mess, and seldom an exciting one.

Black Book, though, suggests that Osby has much more development in him yet. Instead of going for a mishmash fusion of jazz/hiphop, he pares it back to a simple joining of spare hiphop beats with his own alto improvisations. All the polyrhythmic jolt of his earlier music is traded in for a thoughtful, almost sorrowing music: some of the tracks succumb to the usual motormouth bravado of rap, but others engender a wistfulness which Osby's sax parts underline – he's never had such a refined sound on record. Miller contributes some magisterial piano which adds to the gravitas of the music.

Oslo 13 GROUP

**** **Off-Balance** Odin NJ 4022-2
> Nils Petter Molvaer (*t*); Torbjørn Sunde, Dag Einar Eilertsen (*tb*); Erik Balke (*as, bs*); Tore
> Brunborg (*ts*); Arne Frang (*ts, bsx*); Olave Dale (*bs*); Jon Balke (*ky*); Carl Morten Iversen (*b*);
> Audun Klieve (*d*). 8/87.

The sound of a Norwegian sax section is surely a unique one in contemporary music, with the mournful vibrato and wind-chilled timbre seemingly a national characteristic. Jon Balke, who arranges and com-poses most of the music for this band, first formed in 1980 as a forum for young Oslo-based jazzmen, makes the most of that sound. Much of their music is based on the textural possibilities of the reeds, either skirling in opposition to the brass and rhythm or drifting in still, barren space. *Off-Balance* is a superb effort: Balke's scores offer something different in every track, the soloists are uniformly excellent, the balance of the band – trombones in tart opposition to the reeds, Molvaer a strong lone voice on trumpet, and Klieve's drum parts never content with playing time – is radically out of synch with any other contemporary large ensemble. They are also served with brilliant recording by Jan Erik Kongshaug.

*** **Nonsentration** ECM 1445
> Per Jørgensen, Nils Petter Molvaer (*t*); Torbjørn Sunde (*tb*); Morten Halle (*as*); Tore Brunborg,
> Arne Frang (*ts*); Jon Balke (*ky*); Audun Klieve, Jon Christensen (*d*); Finn Sletten, Miki N'Doye
> (*perc*). 9/90.

Both livelier and more inert than the previous record, this is a vaguely disappointing continuation. Balke's interest in texture and line continues to create some fascinating music, and the group again plays with real finesse and cumulative intensity, but the addition of funkier percussion on several tracks contrasts uneasily with the motionless mood-pieces which still take up a lot of the record.

*** **Oslo 13 Live** Curling Legs CD07
> Jens Petter Antonsen, Staffan Svennson (*t*); Torbjørn Sunde (*tb*); Morten Halle (*as*); Thomas
> Gustavsson (*ss, ts*); Trygve Seim (*ts*); Jon Balke (*ky*); Carl Morten Iversen (*b*); Audun Klieve,
> Jon Christensen (*d*). 5/92.

Something of a stopgap live album, though much of the music here is strong and there's nothing less than interesting. Balke's opening 'Taraf' and Halle's finale, 'Hvit Vei', are the best pieces, sounding somewhat like slow Nordic marches: Svennson is superb in the first, and the intense ensemble colours run right through the second. Much of what comes in between seems slight, though. Impeccable playing, and Balke's exacting awareness of what the group can do is impressive, but one feels more could have been made of a rather brief live record. Very fine concert sound.

Roberto Ottaviano SOPRANO AND ALTO SAXOPHONE, MANZANO

*** **Sotto Il Sole Giaguro** Solstice SOLCD 1000
    Ottaviano; Stefano Battaglia (*p*); Piero Leveratto (*b*); Ettore Fioravanti (*d*). 5/89.
***(*) **Items From The Old Earth** Splasc(h) H 332
    Ottaviano; Roberto Rossi (*tb*); Mario Arcari (*ss, ob, cor*); Martin Mayes (*frhn*); Sandro Cerino (*cl, bcl, f, bf*); Fiorenzo Gualandris (*tba*). 12/90.

He has done significant work as a sideman with Ran Blake, Franz Koglmann and Tiziana Ghiglioni among others, but Ottaviano's albums as a leader offer some of the best indication of his powers. He sticks to the soprano for the well-sustained quartet record for Solstice. He's clearly worked very hard on his tone, for he gets an unusually pure and unaffected sound on the horn, rarely going for a squawk or anything remotely expressionist, and it lends his improvisations a clear if somewhat terse intensity. Six of the nine themes are by him – the other players have one writing credit each – and although some are less impressive, such as the fractured freebop of 'Our Kind Of Wabi', others work splendidly. 'Feu De Glui' concentrates the quartet into a single voice, 'Freaks' has an ingeniously jabbing theme which sets up some pithy improvising, while Leveratto's 'Memories Memories' has a soprano solo of lucid beauty over walking bass and brushes. Excellent digital sound.

   Items From The Old Earth is by Ottaviano's all-horns group, Six Mobiles. The sonorities are hard to predict, brassy at some points, woody at others, and the compositions are crowded (perhaps excessively so at times) with both ideas and techniques, some of which beg comparison with European composition rather than jazz. But Ottaviano's own solos add a sudden brightness at moments when the ensemble threatens to turn wholly academic.

*** **Above Us** Splasc(h) H 330-2
    Ottaviano; Stefano Battaglia (*p*); Piero Leveratto (*b*); Ettore Fioravanti (*d*). 11/90.
** **Otto** Splasc(h) H 340-2
    Ottaviano (*ss* solo). 1/91.

Ottaviano returns to more conventional ground on the quartet record, which matches him with the gifted Battaglia: loose modal blowing seems to be the mainstay of the date, and it's done with aplomb, although some of the music lacks anchor and compass. *Otto* takes a stab at a solo album but seems a mite too cleverly conceived: reverb and overdubs distract from the point of Ottaviano's improvising, and some of the solos seem like mere technical points-winners. A pretty record, though, when the saxophonist locates an attractive line.

Tony Oxley (born 1938) DRUMS, PERCUSSION

**** **The Tony Oxley Quartet** Incus CD15
    Oxley; Pat Thomas (*ky, elec*); Derek Bailey (*g*); Matt Wand (*drum machine, tape switchboard*). 4/92.

Tony Oxley is a major figure in free music's evolution in Europe, but infrequent appearances on record (and in his native land – he lives in Germany) have sometimes marginalized his contribution. A surprising involvement with Cecil Taylor has been famously successful in recent years, and this quartet session (recorded by WDR, Cologne) is a memorable reunion with Bailey as well as a meeting with two talented younger members of British improv. There are three quartet pieces, one trio (minus Oxley) and a duet between each of the four players. The opening quartet is a mesmerizing feeling-the-way performance, the soundscape wide open, with every man vital, nobody overplaying, each sound of interest. Thomas varies between analogue-synth wheezes and crisp digital arpeggios, while Wand's bricolage of found sounds and drumbeats redefines notions of minimalism. Bailey remains imperturbably himself, and his duet with Oxley is a superb co-operative battle of wits. The leader, if such he be here, continues to make free rhythm and pulse out of crashings and bangings that in other hands would be, well, unmusical. A magnificent and important (as well as enjoyable) modern document.

Hot Lips Page (1908–54) TRUMPET, MELLOPHONE

*** Hot Lips Page, 1938–1940 Classics 561

Page; Bobby Moore, Eddie Mullens (*t*); George Stevenson, Harry White (*tb*); Ben Smith, Buster Smith (*cl, as*); Jimmy Powell, Ulysses Scott, Don Stovall (*as*); Ben Williams (*as, ts*); Don Byas, Sam Davis, Ernie Powell, Sam Simmons, Benny Waters (*ts*); Pete Johnson, Jimmy Reynolds (*p*); John Collins, Connie Wainwright (*g*); Abe Bolar, Wellman Braud (*b*); A. G. Godley, Ed McConney, Alfred Taylor (*d*); Romayne Jackson, Bea Morton, Delores Payne, Ben Powers, The Harlem Highlanders (*v*). 3/38–12/40.

***(*) Hot Lips Page, 1940–1944 Classics 809

Page; Jesse Brown, Joe Keyes (*t*); Vic Dickenson, Benny Morton (*tb*); Earl Bostic, Benjamin Hammond, George Johnson, Floyd Horsecollar Williams (*as*); Don Byas, Ike Quebec, Ben Webster, Lem Johnson, Lucky Thompson (*ts*); Ace Harris, Leonard Feather, Clyde Hart, Hank Jones (*p*); Sam Christopher Allen (*g*); Teddy Bunn (*g, v*); Al Lucas, John Simmons, Carl Flat Top Wilson (*b*); Ernest Bass Hill (*b, bb*); Big Sid Catlett, Jack Parker, Jesse Price (*d*). 12/40–11/44.

An Armstrong imitator who never quite made it out of that constricting sack, Page has always hovered just below the threshold of most fans' attention. Realistically, he is a much less accomplished player who wasted much of his considerable talent on pointless jamming and dismal but lucrative rhythm and blues. The material recorded for Bluebird in April 1938 features a band that might have gone places had Page not had to disband it. At the beginning of 1940 he was recording with the remarkable Buster Smith, a Texan out of Ellis County (Page was from Dallas), who became a mainstay of the Kansas City sound during the war years and after. These are fine sides, not altogether improved by some very odd remastering wobbles, but they're surpassed by the four cuts made for Decca towards the end of the year with Pete Johnson and Don Byas, which (leaving aside an indifferent vocal by Bea Morton) are among the best of the period and unjustly neglected.

The title of the second Classics volume is slightly misleading. There is, to be sure, material from 1940 and from 1944, but nothing in between. Some of the interim period is covered in various bootlegged jam sessions which may be available. The drummerless 1940 group with Feather, Bunn and Hill is very good indeed, with Hill a considerable surprise for a bass player of his day. Page also shows off his touch on the now seldom-used mellophone. The real treat on this volume, though, is the later material featuring Byas. As Anatol Schenker's informative liner-notes suggest, 'These Foolish Things' is one of the high points of 1940s saxophone jazz, worth playing to unsuspecting experts for a guess at the saxophonist involved. There are giveaway phrases here and there, but at these sessions for Commodore Byas excelled himself. There is some Savoy material from June 1944, a bigger group in which Byas has to give ground to the great Ben Webster; but it is the two dates for Milt Gabler's label which stand out. Even the quasi-novelty items like 'The Blues Jumped A Rabbit' are excellent. It wouldn't be a Classics volume without an early appearance from a star of the future. On the last session, from November 1944, Hank Jones makes his recording debut backing Page, Dickenson and the very fine Thompson on 'The Lady In Bed' and 'Gee, Baby, Ain't I Good For You?'.

**(*) Dr Jazz: Volume 6 – 1951–1952 Storyville STCD 6046

Page; Wild Bill Davison (*c*); Lou McGarity, Sandy Williams (*tb*); Eddie Barefield, Peanuts Hucko, Pee Wee Russell, Cecil Scott, Bob Wilber (*cl*); Dick Cary, Charlie Queener, Red Richards, Joe Sullivan (*p*); Eddie Safranski, Jim Thorpe (*b*); George Wettling (*d*). 12/51–3/52.

These late airshots were broadcast from Stuyvesant Casino at Second and Ninth in New York City, under the auspices of drummer Wettling's group. There is one great session here, featuring Page with Wild Bill Davison and Lou McGarity on what occasionally sounds like an alto trombone, a sharp, puncturing sound that sits wonderfully with the two trumpets. Otherwise, it's fairly run-of-the-mill. To a large extent Page was yesterday's man; he can only occasionally, as on 'St Louis Blues' from February 1952, summon up the old fire. A valuable addition for dedicated collectors, but pretty marginal stuff compared to the above.

Marty Paich (1925–95) PIANO, ARRANGER

**(*) The Picasso Of Big Band Jazz Candid CCD 79031

Paich; Pete Candoli, Buddy Childers, Jack Sheldon (*t*); Bob Enevoldsen (*vtb, cl*); Herbie Harper (*tb*); Vince DeRosa (*frhn*); Herb Geller (*as*); Bob Cooper, Bill Perkins (*ts*); Marty Berman (*bs*); Joe Mondragon (*b*); Mel Lewis (*d*). 6/57.

Paich is widely admired as an arranger, particularly for the honeyed settings he made for Mel Torme in the mid-'50s. *Picasso* comes from that period and is pretty much by-the-book West Coast cool. If the soubriquet applies at all, then it's a Rose Period we're talking about, rather than one of the more angular styles. Despite Cubists like Sheldon and Blue-Period romantics like Geller in the band, there's not much to get excited about.

Willie Pajeaud TRUMPET, VOCAL

*(*) Willie Pajeaud's New Orleans Band 1955 504 LP31
    Pajeaud; Raymond Burke (*cl*); Danny Barker (*g, bj, v*); Len Ferguson (*d*); Blue Lu Barker (*v*).
    55.

Pajeaud is best known as a principal in the Eureka Brass Band, but this memento of a jam session on Bourbon Street in 1955 finds him leading a small group of New Orleans stalwarts. Frankly, it's more of historical interest than anything else: Danny and Blue Lu Barker take three of the numbers virtually by themselves, and the remainder are enthusiastic but ragged accounts of the kind of tunes these men must have played every night of their professional lives. The recording is an amateur one and, unfortunately, sounds it.

Papa Bue's Viking Jazz Band GROUP

*** On Stage Timeless CD TTD 511
    Arne Bue Jensen; Ole Stolle (*t, v*); Jorgen Svare (*cl*); Jorn Jensen (*p*); Jens Sjølund (*b*); Soren
    Houlind (*d, v*). 4 & 9/82.
**(*) Everybody Loves Saturday Night Timeless CD TTD 580
    As above, except add John Defferary (*cl*); replace Sjølund with Ole Olsen (*b*), Houlind with
    Didier Geers (*d, v*). 12/92.

The Viking empire once stretched as far south as the Mediterranean, and considerable ingenuity has been expended in attempting to prove that a Norseman beat Christopher Columbus across the Atlantic. Arne Bue Jensen represents circumstantial evidence that the Vikings made it not just to a slippery rock off Newfoundland, but all the way down to New Orleans.

Nonsense about 'authenticity' apart, Papa Bue's long-running band is one of the finest revival outfits ever to emerge north of the Mason–Dixon line. The emphasis, inevitably, is on ensemble playing rather than soloing, and these are as confidently relaxed as anyone might wish for, with none of the stiffness that creeps into more studied revivalism. The rhythm players have a particularly good feel, the giveaway with most such bands.

Under the eponymous Jensen's leadership, the band became a tireless gigging unit, establishing a big reputation in Eastern Europe, as had Chris Barber.

The 1992 studio recording is a rather lacklustre introduction compared to what one knows the band can do at a regular gig. There are other things around on Music Mecca and Storyville, but *On Stage* is probably the best available disc. It was recorded on the familiar turf of Copenhagen, and before a home crowd the Vikings play like they're all bound for Valhalla, with a rousing 'Tiger Rag' and genuinely affecting 'Just A Closer Walk With Thee'. Erik the Blue would have been very proud.

Paramount Jazz Band Of Boston GROUP

**(*) Ain't Cha Glad? Stomp Off CD1205
    Jeff Hughes (*c*); Gary Rodberg (*cl, ss, as*); Steve Wright (*cl, bcl, ss, as, ts, bs, c*); Robein Verdier
    (*p*); Jimmy Mazzy (*bj, v*); Chuck Stewart (*tba*); Ray Smith (*d*). 5–6/89.
*** . . . And They Called It Dixieland Stomp Off CD1247
    As above. 4/90-11/91.

Skilful if not very involving playing from another group of American revivalists. They avoid carbon-copying original arrangements on the first disc, preferring to try some new twists on Ellington, Dodds, Doc Cook and others, but the playing lacks much individuality and the ensemble work is too polite to muster any of the heat of hot dance. When they try a faded rose such as 'Yearning And Blue', it just sounds old. The second disc, recorded at two live shows, is a lot more energetic, if still a bit short on a style of their own, and the sound is a mixed bag – Mazzy's banjo often seems like the loudest instrument in the group.

Tony Parenti (1900–1972) CLARINET

**** Tony Parenti & His New Orleanians Jazzology JCD-1
> Parenti; Wild Bill Davison (*c*); Jimmy Archey (*tb*); Art Hodes (*p*); Pops Foster (*b*); Arthur
> Trappier (*d*). 8/49.

*** Parenti–Davison All Stars Vol. 1 Jazzology JCD-91
> Parenti; Wild Bill Davison (*c*); Lou McGarity (*tb*); Eustis Tompkins, Ernie Carson (*p*); Jerry
> Rousseau (*b*); Bob Dean (*d*). n.d.

*** Parenti–Davison All Stars Vol. 2 Jazzology JCD-92
> As above. n.d.

A New Orleans man who left the city in 1927, Parenti made many records but has been frequently overlooked. Never an original, he could still play with a ferocious intensity; though he approached the gaspipe manner at times, there was no little sophistication in an approach that seldom strayed far from Dixieland ideology. The first CD above was the one that started the Jazzology operation in 1949, and it still sounds hard-nosed and terrific: Davison was at his most vituperative-sounding, Parenti weaves his way round the front line with much invention, Hodes stomps through everything, and Foster slaps his strings harder than ever. Rough old recording, though that doesn't matter, and rather unnecessarily padded out with extra takes.

The All Stars session is of indeterminate date but was cut at a club in Atlanta. The balance is all off, the drums louder than everyone else, the other players are relatively undistinguished and Parenti himself sometimes sounds like he's playing on another stage. But the spirit comes through, and Wild Bill stops at nothing.

Tiny Parham (1900–1943) PIANO

***(*) Tiny Parham 1926–1929 Classics 661
> Parham; B. T. Wingfield, Punch Miller, Roy Hobson (*c*); Charles Lawson (*tb*); Junie Cobb (*ss,
> as, cl*); Charles Johnson (*cl, as*); Leroy Pickett, Elliott Washington (*vn*); Charlie Jackson (*bj, v*);
> Mike McKendrick (*bj*); Quinn Wilson (*bb*); Jimmy Bertrand, Ernie Marrero (*d*). 12/26–7/29.

***(*) Tiny Parham 1929–1940 Classics 691
> As above, except add Dalbert Bright (*cl, ss, as, ts*), Ike Covington (*tb*), Darnell Howard (*cl, as*),
> Jimmy Hutchens (*cl, ts*), John Henley (*g*), Milt Hinton (*bb*), Bob Slaughter (*d*), Sam Theard,
> Tommy Brookins (*v*); omit Wingfield, Cobb, Pickett and Jackson. 10/29–6/40.

Parham's jazz was an idiosyncratic, almost eccentric brand of Chicago music: his queer, off-centre arrangements tread a line between hot music, novelty strains and schmaltz. The latter is supplied by the violinists and the occasional (and mercifully infrequent) singing – but not by the tuba, which is used with surprising shrewdness by the leader. Some of his arrangements are among the more striking things to come out of the city at that time – 'Cathedral Blues', 'Voodoo' and 'Pigs Feet And Slaw' don't sound like anybody else's group, except perhaps Morton's Red Hot Peppers, although Parham preferred a less flamboyant music to Jelly's. The 'exotic' elements, which led to titles such as 'The Head Hunter's Dream' or 'Jungle Crawl', always seem to be used for a purpose rather than merely for novelty effect and, with soloists like Miller, Hobson and the erratic Cobb, Parham had players who could play inside and out of his arrangements. The two-beat rhythms he leans on create a sort of continuous vamping effect that's oddly appropriate, and Tiny's own piano shows he was no slouch himself. There is a lot of surprising music on these two discs, even when it doesn't work out for the best. The transfers are good. The final two tracks on Classics 691 date from 1940, by which time he was playing the electric organ; it was at a smart hotel engagement where he was the organist that this enormous man died of a heart attack in 1943.

Paris Washboard GROUP

*** . . . Waiting For The Sunrise Stomp Off CD1261
> Daniel Barda (*tb*); Alain Marquet (*cl*); Louis Mazetier (*p*); Gérard Bagot (*wbd, perc*); Michel
> Marcheteau (*sou*). 8/92.

*** California Here We Come Stomp Off CD1280
> As above, except Gérard Gervois (*tba*) replaces Marcheteau. 11/93.

Not since The Louisiana Five (in 1919!) has a group relied on a clarinet/trombone front line, and though the group is basically a quartet – Marcheteau and Gervois are guests – they tackle repertoire that's not dissimilar to The L5's output. There the comparisons stop. Mazetier is a play-anything stylist who can do Waller, James P., Morton or anybody, while Barda and Marquet are superbly lively on their horns, whether in ensemble, counterpoint or quickfire solos. Each of the two discs is a smart mix of old-time classics and a sprinkle of rarities, with Mazetier helping himself to a couple of solos and originals. Yet the most important member may be Bagot: never has there been a washboard player this nimble and light with his fingers, working up a scurrying kind of rhythm that's light-years from the mistreatment this instrument received in skiffle bands or wherever. Perhaps a certain sameness creeps into each disc as it goes on, and the general cheeriness may irritate some; but both CDs are really tremendous fun.

Charlie Parker (1920–55) ALTO SAXOPHONE, TENOR SAXOPHONE

**** The Complete Dean Benedetti Recordings Mosaic MD7-129 7CD
> Parker solos, with Miles Davis, Howard McGhee (*t*); Hampton Hawes, Duke Jordan,
> Thelonious Monk (*p*); Addison Farmer, Tommy Potter (*b*); Roy Porter, Max Roach (*d*); Earl
> Coleman, Kenny Hagood, Carmen McRae (*v*); other unknown personnel. 3/47–7/48.

Parker's innovation – improvising a new melody line off the top, rather than from the middle, of the informing chord – was a logical extension of everything that had been happening in jazz over the previous decade. However, even though the simultaneous inscription of bebop by different hands – Dizzy Gillespie, Charlie Christian and Thelonious Monk all have their propagandists – suggests that it was an evolutionary inevitability, any artistic innovation requires quite specific and usually conscious interventions. With its emphasis on extreme harmonic virtuosity, bop has become the dominant idiom of modern jazz and Parker's genetic fingerprint is the clearest.

The British saxophone virtuoso, John Harle, has spoken of the remarkable *clarity* of Parker's music, and in particular his solo development. Even at his most dazzlingly virtuosic, Parker always sounds logical, making light of asymmetrical phrases, idiosyncratically translated bar-lines, surefooted alternation of whole-note passages and flurries of semiquavers, tampering with almost every other parameter of the music – dynamic, attack, timbre – with a kind of joyous arrogance. Dying at thirty-five, he was spared the indignity of a middle age given over to formulaic repetition.

Because, in theory at least, he never repeated himself, there has been a degree of fetishization of many of Parker's solos, like 'The Famous Alto Break' from the Dial recordings, below, or some of the later Verve material, in which a solo is either preserved out of the fullest context on an incomplete take or executed with insouciant disregard for bland or faulty accompaniments. There is, though, an explanation that usefully combines mythology with sheer pragmatism. In his faulty biography of Parker, *Bird Lives!*, Ross Russell introduced a composite figure called Dean Benedetti (the Kerouac resonance was inescapable) who follows Bird throughout the United States capturing his solos (and the solos only) on a primitive wire-recorder. Though unreleased until 1990, the Dean Benedetti archive has enjoyed cult reputation with Parker fans, the Dead Sea Scrolls of bebop, fragmentary and patinized, inaccessible to all but adepts and insiders, but containing the Word in its purest and most unadulterated form.

The real Benedetti, routinely characterized by Russell as a saxophonist *manqué*, remained a practising player, and these remarkable recordings fall into place ever more clearly if one starts towards the end, with Benedetti's amateurishly dubbed attempts to play along with Parker records, and then accepts the absoluteness of his identification with his idol. Dean Benedetti died of *myasthenia gravis* (a progressive atrophying of the musculature) two years after Bird. Benedetti was already fatally ill when he heard of Charlie Parker's death. He wrote: '*Povero C. P. anche tu. Dove ci troveremmo?*' (Poor Bird. You too. Where will we meet again?) The answer is: here. Benedetti's archive was left in the care of his brother, Rick, who in turn died just too soon to witness the release of these astonishing records.

The Mosaic set, lovingly restored and annotated by Phil Schaap, consists of 278 tracks and a boggling 461 recordings of Charlie Parker, made between 1 March 1947 and 11 July 1948 in Los Angeles and New York (a much smaller span of time and geography than legend finds comfortable). The famous wire-recorder certainly existed but was not used for recording Bird. Benedetti worked with 78-r.p.m. acetate discs, and only later with paper-based recording tape. A good many of the recordings are vitiated or distorted by swarf from the cutting needle (which an assistant was supposed to brush away as a recording progressed) getting in the way; since the cutter moved from the outer edge of the disc towards the centre, there was also a problem with torque, and the inner grooves are often rather strained and indistinct. The sound-quality throughout is far from impressive. What is remarkable, though, is the utter dedication and concentration Benedetti brought to his task. Some of the tracks offer fully developed solos occupying several choruses; others, to take two examples only from a recording made in March 1947 at the Hi-De-Ho Club in Los Angeles, last as little as three ('Night And Day'!!) or seven (possibly 'I Surrender Dear') *seconds*.

As an insight into how Parker approached the same tune with the same group on successive nights (there are six separate solos from 'Big Noise' / 'Wee' between 1 and 8 March 1947) or how he continued to tackle less familiar material associated with pre-bop figures like Coleman Hawkins (three helpings of

'Bean Soup' in the same period), it is an unparalleled resource. There is also valuable documentation of a rare meeting with Thelonious Monk, recorded on 52nd Street in July 1948. The density of background material (titles, durations, key-signatures, in some cases transcriptions) is awesome, and though some of the material has been available for some time as *Bird On 52nd Street* (Original Jazz Classics OJC 114 LP) the vast bulk of it has not been in the public domain. As such, *The Dean Benedetti Recordings* represent the last step in the consolidation of Parker's once inchoate and shambolic discography. Though there is a vast muddle of live material and airshots, there is a surprisingly small corpus of authorized studio material. Parker's recording career really lasts only a decade, from 1944 to 1953, and is enshrined in three main blocks of material, for Savoy (1944–8), for Dial (1946 to December 1947) and for Norman Granz's Verve (1948–53); throw in the significant Royal Roost live sessions and, but for the Benedetti archive, the main pillars of Parker's reputation are in place.

The painter, Barnett Newman, once said that aesthetics was for artists like ornithology was for the birds, and the unintended reference can usefully be appropriated in this context. Though essentially for specialists (and rather well-heeled experts at that) who are untroubled by the abruptly decontextualized nature of these performances, the Benedetti material represents a quite remarkable auditory experience. The initially exasperating sequence of sound-bites gives way to an illusion of almost telepathic insight, a key to the inner mystery of who and what Parker was.

*** **Early Bird** Stash STCD 642
> Parker; Jay McShann Orchestra; other personnel unknown. 40-44.

The archaeology and pre-history of bebop is a subject of intense fascination. These sides afford a chance to hear the young Parker, working with McShann in 1940 and already sounding remarkably like the giant of the post-war years. The articulation and the unique, asymmmetrical but perfectly balanced phrasing are already in place, though there are no hints yet of the dizzying (no pun intended) harmonic swoops that took him a huge step on from his Lester Young-derived approach.

This is an eminently collectable set, with decent sound, given the circumstances. It should be clear, though, that quite a number of tracks do not feature Parker at all, even in embryo.

***(*) **The Immortal Charlie Parker** Savoy SV 0102
> Parker; Miles Davis, Dizzy Gillespie (*t*); Clyde Hart, John Lewis, Bud Powell (*p*); Tiny Grimes (*g*); Nelson Boyd, Jimmy Butts, Tommy Potter, Curley Russell (*b*); Max Roach, Harold Doc West (*d*). 9/44, 11/45, 5 & 8/47, 9/48.

**** **The Charlie Parker Story** Savoy SV 0105
> Parker; Miles Davis (*t*); Dizzy Gillespie (*p, t*); Bud Powell (*p*); Curley Russell (*b*); Max Roach (*d*). 11/45.

**** **Charlie Parker Memorial: Volume 1** Savoy SV 0101
> Parker; Miles Davis (*t*); Duke Jordan, John Lewis, Bud Powell (*p*); Nelson Boyd, Tommy Potter, Curley Russell (*b*); Max Roach (*d*). 12/47.

**** **Charlie Parker Memorial: Volume 2** Savoy SV 0103
> As above. 5/47, 9/48.

**** **The Genius Of Charlie Parker** Savoy SV 0104
> As above; also Jack McVea (*ts*); Tiny Brown (*bs*); Sadik Hakim, Dodo Marmarosa (*p*); Slim Gaillard (*p, g, v*); Zutty Singleton (*d*). 12/45, 5 & 12/47, 9/48.

The sides Parker cut on 26 November 1945 were billed by Savoy on the later microgroove release as 'The greatest recording session made in modern jazz'. There's some merit in that. The kitchen-sink reproduction of fluffs, false starts and breakdowns gives a rather chaotic impression. Miles Davis, who never entirely came to terms with Parker's harmonic or rhythmic requirements, doesn't play particularly well (there is even a theory that some of the trumpet choruses – notably one on a third take of 'Billie's Bounce' – were played by Dizzy Gillespie in imitation of Miles's rather uncertain style), and some of Bud Powell's intros and solos are positively bizarre; step forward, pianist Argonne Thornton, who remembers (though he's the only one who does) being at the sessions. Despite all that, and Parker's continuing problems with a recalcitrant reed, the session includes 'Billie's Bounce', 'Now's The Time' and 'Ko-Ko'. The last of these is perhaps the high-water mark of Parker's improvisational genius and the justification for a five-star rating.

Though this is undoubtedly the zenith of Parker's compositional skill as well (in later years he seems to have created fewer and fewer original themes), it is noticeable that virtually all of the material on these sessions draws either on a basic 12-bar blues or on the chord sequence of 'I Got Rhythm', the Ur-text of bebop. 'Ko-Ko' is based on the chords of 'Cherokee', as is the generic 'Warming Up A Riff', which was intended only as a run-through after Parker had carried out running repairs on his squeaking horn. The remainder of Parker's material was drawn, conventionally enough, from show tunes; 'Meandering', a one-off ballad performance on the November 1945 session, unaccountably elided after superb solos from Parker and Powell, bears some relationship to 'Embraceable You'. What is striking about Parker's playing, here and subsequently, is the emphasis on rhythmic invention, often at the expense of harmonic creativity (in that department, as he shows in miniature on 'Ko-Ko', Dizzy Gillespie was certainly his superior).

Availability on programmable CD means that listeners who find the staccato progression of incomplete takes disconcerting are able to ignore all but the final, released versions. Unfortunately, though these are usually the best *band* performances, they do not always reflect Bird's best solo playing. A good example comes on 'Now's The Time', a supposedly original theme, but one which may retain the outline of an old Kansas City blowing blues (or may have been composed – that is, played – by tenor saxophonist Rocky Boyd). There is no doubt that Parker's solo on the third take is superior in its slashing self-confidence to that on the fourth, which is slightly duller; Miles Davis plays without conviction on both.

None of the other three volumes contains a single recording session, nor do any of the constituent sessions match up to the erratic brilliance of 26 November 1945. There are seven other dates represented, notably intermittent in quality. The sessions with Slim Gaillard, creator of 'Vout', an irritating hipster argot apparently still used by Ronald and Nancy Reagan in affectionate moments (if such a situation can be visualized with equanimity), are pretty corny and time-bound; a bare month after 'Ko-Ko', Parker seems to have come down to earth. An early session with guitarist Tiny Grimes and an unusual August 1947 date (under Miles Davis's control) on which Bird played tenor saxophone have been excluded from this CD reissue. Of the remaining dates, that of 8 May 1947, a rather uneasy affair, nevertheless yielded 'Donna Lee' and 'Chasing The Bird'; by contrast, on 21 December 1947, Parker seems utterly confident and lays down the ferocious 'Bird Gets The Worm' and 'Klaunstance'; the sessions of 18 and 24 September 1948 yielded the classic 'Parker's Mood' (original take 3 is suffused with incomparable blues feeling) and 'Marmaduke' respectively.

The other key figures on these recordings are Max Roach, barely out of his teens but already playing in the kind of advanced rhythmic count that Parker required, and Dizzy Gillespie. Miles Davis was demonstrably unhappy with some of the faster themes and lacked Parker's ability to think afresh take after take; by the time of the 'Parker's Mood' date, though, he had matured significantly (he was, after all, only nineteen when 'Ko-Ko' and 'Now's The Time' were recorded). A word, too, for Curley Russell and Tommy Potter, whose contribution to this music has not yet been fully appreciated and who were rather sorely used on past releases, often muffled to the point of inaudibility.

The Genius Of Charlie Parker brings together original masters only from the six sessions, with an introduction by Al 'Jazzbeau' Collins. It's an attractive package, ideal for those who find the archaeology of recording sessions less than inspiriting. But for sheer majesty of performance and the best available representation of Parker's ability to pack the inner space of his phraseology with musical information, listeners should try to ignore the naff cover-art (one side features an unrecognizable portrait that makes him look like a hip dentist from Barksdale) and go for *The Charlie Parker Story*. *The Immortal* takes us into the anoraky world of the alternative take. Was matrix X better than matrix Y? Did you hear that reed squeak at the turnaround in the fourth chorus? Was that Bud's piano stool squeaking? It does no harm to have these on a separate disc. There's enough awesome music-making on it to have established three more reputations, but at least it's now possible to listen to the classic performances uncluttered and as the artists themselves originally intended.

**** **Charlie Parker On Dial: The Complete Sessions** Spotlite/Dial SPJ CD 4 4101 4CD
    Parker; Miles Davis, Dizzy Gillespie, Howard McGhee (*t*); J. J. Johnson (*tb*); Flip Phillips,
    Lucky Thompson, Wardell Gray (*ts*); Jimmy Bunn, Duke Jordan, Russ Freeman, Erroll Garner,
    George Handy, Dodo Marmarosa (*p*); Red Norvo (*vib*); Arvin Garrison, Barney Kessel (*g*);
    Ray Brown, Red Callender, Arnold Fishkind, Bob Kesterson, Vic McMillan, Tommy Potter,
    Slam Stewart (*b*); Don Lamond, Specs Powell, Jimmy Pratt, Stan Levey, Roy Porter, Max
    Roach, Harold Doc West (*d*), Teddy Wilson, Earl Coleman (*b*). 6/45, 2, 3 & 7/46, 2, 10, 11, & 12/
    47.
**** **The Legendary Dial Masters: Volume 1** Stash ST CD 23
    As above.
**** **The Legendary Dial Masters: Volume 2** Stash ST CD 25
    As above.

On 26 February 1946, Parker signed what was intended to be an exclusive recording contract with Dial Records, an outgrowth of the Tempo Music Shop on Hollywood Boulevard in Los Angeles. The co-signatory was Tempo owner Ross Russell, subsequently author of *Bird Lives!* and disseminator of some of the more lasting myths about Parker.

A contemporary headline declared rather enigmatically: 'West Coast Jazz Center Enters Shellac Derby With Be-Bop Biscuits'. Russell's original intention to specialize in classic jazz (largely ignoring swing, in other words) had been confounded by an unanticipated demand for bop 78s. With typical perspicacity, he lined up Parker, Gillespie and others, gave them unprecedented free rein in the studio and backed his commitment with the best engineers available. The investment predictably took some time to recoup. Parker's Dial period straddles a near-catastrophic personal crisis and a subsequent period of almost

Buddhist calm, when his playing takes on a serene logic and untroubled simplicity which in later years was to give way to a blander sophistication and chastened professionalism.

On Volume 1 of the Spotlite Dial, a solitary February 1946 cut ('Diggin' Diz') under Gillespie's leadership predates the remarkable session seven weeks later which yielded 'Moose The Mooche', 'Yardbird Suite', 'Ornithology' and 'A Night In Tunisia', four of his classic performances. Parker's solo on the third take of 'Ornithology' is completely masterful, by turns climbing fiercely and soaring effortlessly, always on the point of stalling but never for a moment losing momentum; close study reveals the daring placement of accents and a compelling alternation of chromatic runs (first refuge of beginners or those suffering temporary harmonic amnesia, but never handled with such grace) and dazzling intervallic leaps. Multiple takes of virtually every item (the six Spotlite volumes take in 39 tunes but 88 separate performances) demonstrate the extent to which Parker was prepared to re-take at constantly shifting tempi, never wrong-footing himself but often having to pull some of the rhythm players along in his wake. The 'Famous Alto Break', 46 seconds of pure invention on the saxophone, is all that remains of a first take of 'A Night In Tunisia'; before the Benedetti materials were made available, 'The Famous Alto Break' was Parker's best-known cameo solo.

In contrast to Curley Russell and Max Roach, Vic McMillan and Roy Porter can sound a little stiff, but Dodo Marmarosa (an undervalued player whose present whereabouts are unknown) has a bright, sharp-edged angularity which suits Parker perfectly and which is picked up generously by good digital remastering. On 29 July 1946, Parker was in the C. P. Macgregor Studios, Hollywood, with Howard McGhee, a fellow addict, in for Miles Davis or Dizzy Gillespie. Bird was practically comatose during the recording of 'Lover Man' (but nevertheless managed a brutal, convoluted solo that is a rare converse to his usual formal clarity) and collapsed shortly after the session, setting off a train of disasters that landed him in the State Hospital at Camarillo.

Heroin addiction permits surprisingly extended activity at a high level, but usually at a high rate of interest. There has been a tendency again to festishize work born out of appalling physical and psychological anguish at the expense of less troubled performances. In the summer of 1946 Parker was writing cheques that his body and normally indomitable spirit could no longer cash. 'Lover Man', like so many club and concert solos from the preceding years, was done on autopilot. Bird's headlong flight was briefly halted.

He emerged healthier than he had been for a decade. Rest (as in 'Relaxin' At Camarillo'), detoxification and the occasional salad had done him more good than any amount of largactil. A rehearsal session held at Chuck Kopely's house on 1 February 1947 is included, but the recording is very poor (Howard McGhee allegedly kept a hand-held mike pointing at Bird throughout); there are two more tracks from the same occasion on Stash ST CD 25, below. Parker's first post-release recording for Dial cast him in the unlikely company of Erroll Garner and the singer, Earl Coleman. Garner's intriguing two-handedness, offering apparent independence in the bass and melody lines, was a valuable prop for Parker, and he sounds remarkably composed. Coleman's singing on 'This Is Always' and 'Dark Shadows' is uncomplicated and rather appealing. The meat of the sessions comes with 'Bird's Nest' and the marvellous 'Cool Blues', again attempted at very different tempi. The fourth – or 'D' – take of 'Cool Blues' is positively lugubrious. The soloing is limpid and logical, and not much circumstantial knowledge is required to hear the difference between these tracks and the tortured 'Lover Man' of six months before.

A week later, Parker returned to the studio with McGhee and Marmarosa. 'Relaxin' At Camarillo' was allegedly written in the back of a cab en route to the date; it was cast in familiar blues form but with an intriguing tonality that suggested Bird was beginning to exercise greater inventiveness along the other, relatively neglected, axis of his work. Unfortunately, the 26 February performances are rather cluttered (Wardell Gray's tenor adds nothing very much; Barney Kessel sounds rather blocky) and the sound isn't up to previous standards.

Parker's last West Coast recording for Dial came towards the end of 1947. The selections from 28 October and 4 November are some of the most lyrical in Parker's entire output. 'Bird Of Paradise' is based on the sequence of 'All The Things You Are', with an introduction (Bird and Miles) that was to become one of the thumbprints of bebop. Parker reinvents his solo from take to take, never exhausting his own resources, never losing contact with the basic material. 'Embraceable You' and the gentle 'Dewey Square' (October; Volume 4), 'Out Of Nowhere' and single takes of 'My Old Flame' and 'Don't Blame Me' (November; Volume 5) don't reach quite the same heights, but the third (unissued) take of 'Out Of Nowhere' is further demonstration of how much magnificent music had to be picked off the editing-room floor. The November session also included two of Parker's finest originals, 'Scrapple From The Apple' and the bizarrely entitled 'Klact-oveeseds-tene' (apparently a quasi-phonetic transcription of *Klage, Auf Wiedersehen* – some give it as 'Klact', meaning 'bad noise' – which could be taken to mean something like 'Farewell To The Blues'), which is a raw and slightly neurotic theme played entirely out of kilter.

Roach's grasp of Bird's requirements was by now completely intuitive. Only he seems to have been entirely in tune with the saxophonist's often weirdly dislocated entries, and there is a story that Roach had to shout to Duke Jordan not to elide or add beats or half-bars, knowing that Parker would navigate a course back to the basic metre before the end of his solo choruses. This intuitive brilliance is particularly easy to trace on the slower ballad numbers, where the saxophone's entry is often breathtakingly unexpected and dramatic, underlined by Miles Davis's increasingly confident ability to work across the beat, especially at lower tempi.

Bird's final recording session for Dial and with the great quintet was held in New York City on 17 December 1947, with the addition of trombonist J. J. Johnson. 'Crazeology' is fast and furious and Parker's solos on both the 'C' and (released) 'D' takes are impeccable; he was allegedly playing with a new horn and his tone is more than usually full and precise. Johnson was certainly the first trombone player to understand bop completely enough to make a meaningful contribution to it. His solos on 'Crazeology' and 'Bird Feathers' are excellent, rhythmically much more daring than anyone had previously dared to be on slide trombone.

The Parker Dials, though perhaps of less concentrated brilliance than the Savoys, are among the greatest small-group jazz of all time; masters were cut in October 1949 and the album released shortly thereafter. They are also of considerable significance in that *Bird Blows The Blues*, formerly available as a separate LP, was the first long-playing record devoted to jazz performance. It was distinctive in two regards. In the first place, Russell favoured the 12-inch format, which maintained its hegemony (until the rise of tape cassette and the compact disc) over the more usual 10-inch format, which was the record dealers' preference. Dial later bowed to market pressure, but subsequent 10-inch releases were pressed on a poor-quality vinyl mix that created a great deal of background noise. In the second place, Russell began to include alternative takes of many tracks, setting in motion a discographical mania that has haunted Parker fans ever since. Solos are sipped like vintages and too often spat into a bucketful of matrix numbers rather than fully savoured and absorbed.

For those who have problems on both counts, the availability of master performances on good-quality CD and without the distraction of multiple takes may well be a godsend, and the first volume of the Stash compilation should perhaps be considered essential to anyone building up a non-vinyl jazz collection from scratch. However, the fully documented Spotlite Dials are still theoretically available separately in the old format, as well as in a six-volume boxed set, and it may be possible to find copies of these still, if vinyl is your poison. There are, in the Dial documentation, a large number of alternatives, of which the following seem to be the most important and merit the closest attention: 'Yardbird Suite', 'The Famous Alto Break', 'Cool Blues', 'Relaxin' At Camarillo', 'Bird Of Paradise', 'Scrapple From The Apple', 'Out Of Nowhere', 'Drifting On A Reed' (another of Parker's themeless improvisations) and 'Bongo Beep' (a December 1947 track that shouldn't be confused with the slightly earlier 'Bongo Bop'). Volume 2 also takes in two themeless blues recorded at the same home rehearsal at Chuck Kopely's that yielded 'Home Cooking', three versions in all. The Stash also includes some other material that has already appeared elsewhere; the trumpeters (McGhee, Rogers, Broiles) are scarcely audible and sit it out on the Spotlite title-track. If listeners went no further down this entry, they could be assured of having the very best work that Parker did, the tracks that made him unequivocally great. They would, of course, also miss some wonderful music . . .

**** **Bird: The Complete Charlie Parker On Verve** Verve 837141 10CD
    Parker; Mario Bauza, Buck Clayton, Paquito Davilla, Kenny Dorham, Harry Edison, Roy Eldridge, Dizzy Gillespie, Chris Griffin, Benny Harris, Al Killian, Howard McGhee, Jimmy Maxwell, Doug Mettome, Carl Poole, Al Porcino, Bernie Privin, Rod Rodney, Charlie Shavers, Al Stewart, Ray Wetzel, Bobby Woodlen (*t*); Will Bradley, Bill Harris, Lou McGarity, Tommy Turk, Bart Varsalona (*tb*); Vinnie Jacobs (*frhn*); Hal McKusick, John LaPorta (*cl*); Benny Carter, Johnny Hodges, Gene Johnson, Toots Mondello, Sonny Salad, Freddie Skerritt, Willie Smith, Harry Terrill, Murray Williams (*as*); Coleman Hawkins, Jose Madera, Pete Mondello, Flip Phillips, Hank Ross, Sol Rabinowitz, Ben Webster, Lester Young (*ts*); Manny Albam, Danny Bank, Leslie Johnakins, Stan Webb (*bs*); Artie Drelinger (*reeds*); Walter Bishop Jr, Al Haig, Rene Hernandez, Hank Jones, Ken Kersey, John Lewis, Thelonious Monk, Oscar Peterson, Mel Powell, Arnold Ross (*p*); Irving Ashby, Billy Bauer, Jerome Darr, Freddie Green, Barney Kessel (*g*); Ray Brown, Billy Hadnott, Percy Heath, Teddy Kotick, Charles Mingus, Tommy Potter, Roberto Rodriguez, Curley Russell (*b*); Kenny Clarke, Roy Haynes, J. C. Heard, Don Lamond, Shelly Manne, Buddy Rich, Max Roach, Art Taylor, Lee Young (*d*); Machito, Jose Mangual, Luis Miranda, Umberto Nieto, Chano Pozo, Carlos Vidal (*perc*); Ella Fitzgerald, Dave Lambert Singers (*v*); woodwinds; strings. 1/46–12/54.

After the extraordinary Savoys and Dials, the sessions for Norman Granz's label mark an inevitable diminuendo. However, it must never be forgotten that Granz was a passionate and practical advocate of better treatment for black American musicians, and it was he who brought Parker to the attention of the wider audience he craved. For the saxophonist, to be allowed to record with strings was a final rubber-stamp of artistic legitimacy. Just as his association with Granz's Jazz At The Philharmonic jamborees are still thought to have turned him into a circus performer, the Parker With Strings sessions (fully documented here and on the special single CD noted below) have attracted a mixture of outright opprobrium and predictable insistence that Bird's solos be preserved and evaluated out of context; the point, though, would seem to be that Parker himself, out of naïvety, a wakening sense of self-advancement, or a genuine wish to break the mould of 'jazz' performance, was every bit as concerned with the context as he was with his own place in it. There is a fair amount of saccharin in the first strings performances, but Parker is superb on 'April In Paris' and 'I Didn't Know What Time It Was', and the release of the material in January 1950 propelled Parker on to a new national stage. From February he toured with strings opposite Stan Getz. These experiments weren't always a perceived success. A vocal set to Gil Evans arrangements foundered after 15 takes of just four numbers; there are major problems with balances (and Schaap has fulfilled Evans's wish by re-weighting the rhythm section), but the performances are by no means the disaster they're commononly thought to be.

Parker's signing with Verve almost coincided with a recording strike that was called by the AFM for 1 January 1948. Verve boss Norman Granz managed to fit in two hasty recordings before that time, both of which were for a compilation album called *The Jazz Scene*, but neither of them did Parker much justice. There is some controversy as to the exact circumstances of his recording 'Repetition' with Neal Hefti's orchestra. Some sources suggest that Bird is overdubbed; he sounds merely overpowered by a lush arrangement, but manages to throw in a quote from *The Rite Of Spring* (Stravinsky was currently high on his playlist). 'The Bird' was recorded by a scratch quartet (Hank Jones, Ray Brown, Shelly Manne) and apparently done at speed. Parker fluffs a couple of times and the rhythm section accelerate and stutter like courtiers trying to keep an even 10 paces behind the king.

The same group (with the unsuitable Buddy Rich in for the elegant Manne) sounded much better two and a half years later. On 'Star Eyes', 'I'm In The Mood For Love' and 'Blues (Fast)' Parker plays remarkably straight and with little of the jagged angularity of earlier recordings. The CD compilation adds no new material or alternatives, in sharp contrast to a session recorded two months later, in June 1950, for which Granz, ever on the look-out for eye-catching combinations, brought together Dizzy Gillespie, Thelonious Monk (their solitary studio encounter), Curley Russell (Bird's most sympathetic partner on bass) and, again, the wholly unsuitable Buddy Rich, who thrashes away to distraction. The new material consists of little more than tiny canapés of studio noise, false starts and run-downs, but there are previously undiscovered or unreleased takes of 'Leap Frog' and 'Relaxin' With Lee', tunes Parker is said to have composed spontaneously when it was discovered that he had forgotten to bring sheets with him. 'Ballade', apparently recorded for use in a film by Gjon Mili, partners Bird with Coleman Hawkins, their only known studio recordings together.

The most substantial single item uncovered by Phil Schaap in his painstaking trawl through the vaults is an acceptable master of Chico O'Farrill's 'Afro-Cuban Jazz Suite', recorded in December 1950 with Machito. Less adept at Latin rhythms than Dizzy Gillespie, Parker had nevertheless experimented with 'south of the border' sessions (there's a fine 1952 session with Benny Harris, co-composer of 'Ornithology') and solos with great flourish on the 17-minute 'Suite'.

There are more Latin numbers on disc 6, which encapsulates Parker's finest studio performances for Granz. It covers three sessions recorded in January, March and August 1951. The earliest, with Miles, Walter Bishop Jr, Teddy Kotick and Max Roach, featured the classic original 'Au Privave', 'She Rote', 'K. C. Blues', and 'Star Eyes'. The 'Au Privave' solos (two takes) are rapid-fire, joyous Bird, deliberately contrasting with Miles's soft touch; on the alternative, Parker really pushes the boat out and Miles cheekily responds with mimicry of the last couple of bars. The tune is now an influential bebop staple, but it was originally issued as the B-side to 'Star Eyes' which, like the later 'My Little Suede Shoes', recorded in March with a Latin beat, enjoyed enormous success as a single. The August sessions featured a racially integrated line-up fronted by Parker and the young white trumpeter, Red Rodney, whose fiery playing reflected his nickname and hair coloration much more than it did his race, which presented a problem to some 'authenticity'-obsessed critics. The most poignant moment is a re-run, played at first with great correctness but with a bubbling eagerness coming up from underneath, of 'Lover Man', which had been the on-mike flashpoint of Parker's disastrous collapse in 1946. It is said that Bird was upset that the Dial performance was ever released; five years later, he gets his own back with an airy, problem-free reading (he even anticipates his own entry) and a snook-cocking 'Country Gardens' coda, a device Parker used frequently but which he intended here to be deflationary.

Swedish Schnapps (which covers the original LP of that name, the wonderful January 'Au Privave' sessions, and three alternatives from the May 1949 sessions with Kenny Dorham) is available as a separate CD and is an excellent buy for anyone not yet ready or not well-enough-funded for the kitchen-sink approach of the 10-CD set.

The small-group material thins after this point. There is a good December 1952/January 1953 quartet recording ('The Song Is You', 'Laird Baird', 'Cosmic Rays', 'Kim') with Jones, Kotick and Roach, and two late flourishes from an increasingly erratic Parker in July 1953 and March and December 1954. The latter sessions, which were to be the last studio recordings of his life, were devoted to Cole Porter themes. Parker plays much more within the beat than previously and, but for a near perfection of tone, some of these later performances could safely be relegated. Schaap has found a long alternative of 'Love For Sale', however, which suggests how thoroughly Parker could still rethink his own strategies. It also conveniently brings the whole extraordinary package full circle.

Bird will already have superseded the eight-volume vinyl *Definitive Charlie Parker* in most serious collections. The most important additional material, apart from a couple of genuinely valuable alternatives and the restored 'Afro-Cuban Jazz Suite', is a substantial amount of live performance recorded under the umbrella of Granz's JATP. The earliest item in the collection is a live jam from January 1946 at which Parker encountered (and, on 'Lady Be Good', totally wiped out) his great role-model, Lester Young, then already in his post-war doldrums. The two men met once again at Carnegie Hall in 1949, but it's the earlier encounter that conveys the drama of Bird's precarious grasp on the highest perch. Absent at the beginning of the performance, he comes onstage to thunderous applause and tosses something on to Bud Powell's piano strings, creating a weird jangle. It may be his reed guard, but Phil Schaap suggests (rather improbably, one would have thought) that it was a hypodermic and spoon. The beauty of the 1946 concert lies in its spontaneity. The later, June 1952, 'alto summit' with Johnny Hodges and the veteran Benny Carter is by contrast rather stilted, with an 'after you' succession of solo appearances. (Oscar Peterson, being groomed for stardom by Granz, is also present.)

Pricey and perhaps a little overcooked for non-specialists, *Bird* is nevertheless a model of discographical punctiliousness. The sound is excellent, the notes detailed and fascinating (often backed by anecdotal material from interviews Schaap has conducted with surviving participants) and the packaging very attractive.

**** Confirmation Verve 527 815 2CD
    As above. 2/49–7/53.
**** Bird's Best Bop Verve 527 452
    Parker; Miles Davis, Kenny Dorham, Dizzy Gillespie, Red Rodney (*t*); Walter Bishop Jr, Al
    Haig, Hank Jones, John Lewis, Thelonious Monk (*p*); Ray Brown, Percy Heath, Teddy Kotick,
    Tommy Potter, Curley Russell (*b*); Kenny Clarke, Buddy Rich, Max Roach (*d*). 5/49–7/53.
*** Jazz Masters 15: Charlie Parker Verve 519827
    As above. 47–53.
**** Swedish Schnapps Verve 849 393
    Parker; Miles Davis, Kenny Dorham, Red Rodney (*t*); John Lewis, Walter Bishop Jr, Al Haig
    (*p*); Ray Brown, Teddy Kotick, Tommy Potter (*b*); Kenny Clarke, Max Roach (*d*). 49–51.
**** Bird: The Original Recordings Of Charlie Parker Verve 837 176
    As above. 2/49–7/53.
**** Now's The Time Verve 825 671
    Parker; Hank Jones (*p*); Percy Heath, Teddy Kotick (*b*); Max Roach (*d*). 12/52, 8/53.
***(*) Gitanes Jazz – Round Midnight: Charlie Parker Verve 847 911
    As above; various dates.

So humungous and expensive is the 10-CD set that all but the very well-heeled would be advised to pick and choose among these wallet-friendly repackagings of the Verve Parkers. Most of the titles are self-explanatory or have been glossed in some way above. *Confirmation* attempts a distillation of the whole shebang, which is quixotic but admirable and done with excellent taste and sense of balance. The *Jazz Masters* series is irreproachably accurate and well documented, but the boxes are unattractive and the by-the-numbers approach to Verve's back-catalogue is a touch off-putting. More casual listeners might find it a helpful, if ultimately misleading way of building a library. *Swedish Schnapps* we have already commented on, and it should perhaps be a priority purchase. For the car stereo, mobile disc-player or the *pied-à-terre*, *Bird's Best Bop* would be a sensible investment, covering the strongest of the Verve tracks ('Now's The Time', 'Confirmation', 'Swedish Schnapps', 'She Rote' and the glorious 'Au Privave'); romantics will find the *Gitanes Jazz – Round Midnight* compilation a little more amenable.

***(*) The Cole Porter Songbook Verve 823250
    Parker; drawn from *Bird: The Complete Charlie Parker On Verve*. 7/50–12/54.
Parker was very drawn to Cole Porter's music and was contemplating another all-Porter session at the time of his death. The slightly dry, pure melodism gave him the perfect springboard for some of his most unfettered solos. A lovely record and an ideal purchase for Parker or Porter addicts.

*** South Of The Border Verve 527 779
    Parker; Machito Afro Cuban Orchestra; Roy Haynes, Buddy Rich, Max Roach (*d*). 48–52.
*** Charlie Parker With Strings – The Master Takes Verve 523 984
    Parker; Tony Aless, Al Haig, Bernie Leighton (*p*); Art Ryerson (*g*); Ray Brown, Bob Haggart,

Tommy Potter, Curley Russell (*b*); Roy Haynes, Don Lamond, Shelly Manne, Buddy Rich (*d*). 12/47–1/52.

There is still some pointless controversy as to the merits of Parker's With Strings projects. Pointless, because it is clear from a single chorus of 'Repetition', from 1947 (made for *The Jazz Scene*) or 'Stella by Starlight' in 1952 that here is a master at work. Bird's solo construction is poised and tasteful, and much of the talk about his 'impatience' with these smooth settings is a sort of wishful thinking. He basked in them and if on occasion he anticipates the beat, that's no more than he did with Al Haig or Thelonious Monk.

We find more to question among the Machito sessions on *South Of The Border*, but this aspect of Parker is hugely popular, too, and there is no mistaking his own pleasure in these rhythms, which challenged him to widen his phrasing and open up his tone a touch. Time, surely, to put paid to snobbery about these lovely records.

**** The Bird Returns Savoy SV 0155
Parker; Miles Davis, Kenny Dorham (*t*); Lucky Thompson (*ts*); Milt Jackson (*vib*); Al Haig (*p*); Tommy Potter (*b*); Max Roach (*d*). 9/48–3/49.

***(*) Newly Discovered Sides By The Immortal Charlie Parker Savoy SV 0156
As above. 9/48–3/49.

Anyone in possession of the Savoys, Dials, Verves, the Dean Benedetti collection (if they can afford it) and the Royal Roost recordings can reasonably feel they have a purchase on the major outcrops of Parker's career. Of the very many live sessions and airshots in circulation, only these should be considered absolutely essential. These CD reissues mark one significant advance over earlier vinyl issues in reducing to a minimum the announcements of 'Symphony Sid' Torin, who always manages to sound like an alternative comedian mimicking an American radio presenter. This may have the negative effect of spoiling the 'live atmosphere' of the LPs; atmospherics, though, represent a serious problem on vinyl, and the CDs deliver the music in a much cleaner signal, if a little sharply in places.

What are missing from these are the dates from May 1950, also at the Roost, when Parker recorded the astounding 'Street Beat' with Fats Navarro, on which the ill-fated trumpeter, who died shortly thereafter, put together perhaps the most balanced solo of his whole career. This is now available on the very useful Cool & Blue. Dorham is much less convincing and sounds very jaded indeed in places on the early-1949 sessions (though a rocky sound-balance doesn't favour his middle-register work, which is more subtle than first appears), tending to play formulaically and in rather staccato, predetermined bites. At this period Miles Davis plays very much more consistently in club situations than under the stop–start discipline of the recording studio.

Parker, of course, is sublime. His career was powerfully in the ascendant at this point, whatever 'personal problems' skulked around the edges; the recording ban was lifted and the substantial backing he was getting from Norman Granz allowed him to think ever more expansively. In a club context, too, he was able to freewheel in a way that wasn't possible in the studio and, though few of the individual performances are very long (the norm is still 3–5 minutes, perhaps a concession to commercial times), there is a palpable sense of relaxation about his playing that comes through even on these rather one-dimensional recordings.

*** Live Performances: Volume 1 ESP Disk ESP 3000
Parker; Kenny Dorham, Dizzy Gillespie (*t*); John LaPorta (*cl*); Billy Bauer (*b*); Al Haig, Lennie Tristano (*p*); Ray Brown, Tommy Potter (*b*); Max Roach (*d*). 9/47, 12/48.

*** Broadcast Performances: Volume 2 ESP Disk ESP 3001
Parker; Miles Davis (*t*); Tadd Dameron, Al Haig (*p*); Tommy Potter, Curley Russell (*b*); Joe Harris, Max Roach (*d*). 6 & 8/49.

Most of this material is already well known, though it's startling to find it on ESP Disk, a label more commonly associated with the 1960s avant-garde. Like Blue Note, though, ESP were anxious to cash in – artistically, if not commercially – on the greatest figure of the preceding generation. The 1947 material on Volume 1 is prized for an opportunity to hear Bird playing with the pianist who seemingly represented the opposite tendency in modern jazz, Lennie Tristano. It is immediately obvious on 'Tiger Rag', the solitary cut, that the differences between them were not entirely irreconcilable.

The Christmas night 1948 material is also well known from the LP era. 'White Christmas' is a piece of pure hokum but it shows how readily Bird could be triggered by the slightest piece of musical fluff. His solo is breathtaking. The Royal Roost recordings included on Volume 2 have had a rather chequered discographical history, but they are very well documented here, sounding clean and remarkably noise-free, particularly given that this is not a label normally much concerned with the niceties of hi-fi. Parker tackles his solo on 'Groovin' High' with ferocious application, trying out ideas that don't turn up elsewhere in the discography. He's more relaxed on 'East Of The Sun', which features a lovely statement from Dorham.

***(*) **1949 Jazz At The Philharmonic** Verve 519 803
 Parker; Roy Eldridge (*t*); Tommy Turk (*tb*); Flip Phillips, Lester Young (*ts*); Hank Jones (*p*);
 Ray Brown (*b*); Buddy Rich (*d*); Ella Fitzgerald (*v*). 9/49.
***(*) **Charlie Parker Jam Session** Verve 833 564
 Parker; Charlie Shavers (*t*); Benny Carter, Johnny Hodges (*as*); Flip Phillips, Ben Webster (*ts*);
 Oscar Peterson (*p*); Barney Kessel (*g*); Ray Brown (*b*); J. C. Heard (*d*). 7/52.

The symbolic importance of these two jams was Parker's appearance on the same stage as fellow-saxophonists, Lester Young (in 1949) and Benny Carter, Johnny Hodges and Ben Webster on the later session. Prez and Bird nose round each other for a bit on 'The Opener', a routine B-flat blues, but things get a little tougher on 'Lester Leaps In', where the tenor master with the sound that made Bird's possible lets everybody know that he's still in charge and still able to cut it. Parker doesn't show as strongly again until 'How High The Moon'.

 Norman Granz's *Jam Session* of July 1952 was more of a processional and, though there are some extremely fine moments, from Bird, Shavers (who has refined the Eldridge style) and the stalwart Phillips, the confrontation with Carter and Hodges is pretty anticlimactic, a dialogue of the deaf rather than a significant joust. Each plays completely in character, Hodges with the walk-on walk-off shrug he was prone to. The biggest summit since Yalta was every bit as much a diplomatic window-display. The future of the world – or of modern music – had been decided elsewhere.

***(*) **'Bird' Charlie Parker** Forlane UCD 19009
 Parker; Dizzy Gillespie, Fats Navarro, Red Rodney (*t*); Al Haig, Bud Powell (*p*); Tommy Potter
 (*b*); Roy Haynes, Max Roach (*d*). 12/49, 5/50, 3/51.
*** **Live At Carnegie Hall** Bandstand BD 1518
 As above; also Walter Bishop Jr (*p*); Walter Yost (*b*); Candido (*perc*); woodwinds; strings. 12/49,
 11/52.

The sleeve omits personnel for the first five (1949) items, but these feature concert performances (presumably not continuous, given the variation in sound from 'Ornithology' to 'Cheryl') featuring Rodney, Haig, Potter and Haynes. Parker's skiddling solo on 'Ko-Ko' and his varied opening to 'Bird Of Paradise' are worth the price on their own, but there are plenty of good things from the later sessions with Navarro (from the Royal Roost period) and Gillespie. The discographical documentation is untrustworthy (Haynes and Blakey seem to be transposed) but the music is excellent and the stereo reprocessing acceptably unobtrusive and natural.

 The 1949 materials are also available on the Bandstand with a Parker With Strings concert from 1952. Nothing to write home about on the latter count, and the Forlane seems a better bet in every respect.

***(*) **Charlie Parker In Sweden, 1950** Storyville STCD 4031
 Parker; Rolf Ericson, Rowland Greenberg (*t*); Lennart Nilsson, Gosta Theselius (*ts, p*); Thore
 Jederby (*b*); Jack Noren (*d*). 1/50.

Record of a hectic week during Parker's second visit to Europe. He had had great success at the Paris Jazz Festival the previous year and was revered in Scandinavia, where bebop took deep and lasting root. A measure of that is the quality of the local musicians, who more than hold their own (Rolf Ericson, of course, acquired a substantial American reputation later in his career). Though Parker also played in Stockholm and Gothenburg, the materials are taken from sets in the southern towns of Hälsingborg and Malmö, plus a remarkable restaurant jam session at an unknown location. This last yielded the most notable single track, a long version of 'Body And Soul', more usually a tenor saxophonist's shibboleth but given a reading of great composure. This item was previously known in an edited form (which dispensed with solos by Theselius, who plays piano on the other selections, and Greenberg); but the restored version is very much more impressive, again by virtue of relocating Parker's improvisation in the wider context of a group performance.

 The remaining material is pretty much a 'greatest hits' package, with two versions each of 'Anthropology' and 'Cool Blues'. Worthwhile, but not essential.

*** **An Evening At Home With Bird** Savoy SV 0154
 Parker; Claude McLin (*ts*); Chris Anderson (*p*); George Freeman (*g*); Leroy Jackson (*b*); Bruz
 Freeman (*d*). 50.

Crumbs from the master's table. It's hard to begrudge McLin and Anderson their 15 minutes of fame, but there's not much more to this than a casual blow in a Chicago dance hall (only ironically 'at home'). Bird spins out a couple of effortless solos on 'There's A Small Hotel' and 'Hot House', while McLin puffs in his wake. And that's about it. Doubtless five sets of feet didn't touch ground on the way home. Collectors only.

***(*) **Bird At St Nick's** Original Jazz Classics OJC 041
 Parker; Red Rodney (*t*); Al Haig (*p*); Tommy Potter (*b*); Roy Haynes (*d*). 2/50.

An attractively varied package of material (including 'Visa', 'What's New', 'Smoke Gets In Your Eyes' and other, more familiar themes) from a tight and very professional band who sound as if they've been together for some time. Haynes is no Max Roach, even at this period, but his count is increasingly subtle and deceptive, and he cues some of Rodney's better releases brilliantly. Worth watching out for, and much more compelling than the rag-bag of material on *Bird's Eyes: Volume 1*.

***(*) Charlie Parker Live; February 14, 1950 EPM Musique FCD 5710
Parker; Red Rodney (*t*); J. J. Johnson (*tb*); Al Haig (*p*); Tommy Potter (*b*); Roy Haynes (*d*). 2/50.
A Valentine's Night airshot from a rather jaded and uncertain band. Bird is playing well, though there are reed problems and a constant mis-hitting of the octave button, but the two brass players sound remote and uncommunicative, and the rhythm section is much more sluggish than on the other recordings of the period.

**** Bird And Fats – Live At Birdland Cool & Blue C&B CD 103
Parker; Fats Navarro (*t*); Walter Bishop Jr, Bud Powell (*p*); Tommy Potter, Curley Russell (*b*); Art Blakey, Roy Haynes (*d*); Chubby Newsome (*v*). 6/50.
There are moments on these when Parker is very nearly eclipsed by Fats Navarro, whose death was not far away when they recorded the astounding 'Street Beat'. Somebody calls out, 'Blow, Girl!' (Navarro's nickname was Fat Girl) as he burns through an absolutely astonishing solo that combines fire and attack with near-perfect balance. On his day, there was no one to touch him. Unfortunately, there were very few days left. Elsewhere, he is superb on 'Ornithology' and 'Cool Blues'. A marvellous moment, captured with lots of atmosphere and not too much extraneous noise.

*** Inglewood Jam Fresh Sound FSRCD 17
Parker; Chet Baker (*t*); Sonny Criss (*as*); Russ Freeman (*p*); Harry Babasin (*b*); Lawrence Marable (*d*). 6/52.
A historic encounter, Parker playing with two hornmen who in dramatically different ways (but with equally tragic repercussions) would take his legacy forward into the next generation. Baker sounds a modestly accomplished bebopper, much like the young and hesitant Miles Davis, in fact; but Criss is much more individual and distinctive than all the Bird-and-water copy might suggest. There are moments of marvellous tension in this, as when Baker throws Gillespie phrases at Bird during 'Donna Lee'. Parker appears to ignore them, but during his final chorus stuffs them all together into a single hectic phrase and heaves them back. Fifteen-all.

**** The Quintet / Jazz At Massey Hall Original Jazz Classics OJC 044
Parker; Dizzy Gillespie (*t*); Bud Powell (*p*); Charles Mingus (*b*); Max Roach (*d*). 5/53.
Perhaps the most hyped jazz concert ever, to an extent that the actuality is almost inevitably something of a disappointment. Originally released on Debut (a musician-run label started by Mingus and Roach), the sound, taken from Mingus's own tape-recording, is rather poor and the bassist subsequently had to overdub his part. However, Parker (playing a plastic saxophone and billed on the Debut release as 'Charlie Chan' to avoid contractual problems with Mercury, Norman Granz's parent company) and Gillespie are both at the peak of their powers. They may even have fed off the conflict that had developed between them, for their interchanges on the opening 'Perdido' crackle with controlled aggression, like two middleweights checking each other out in the first round. There is a story that they didn't want to go on stage, preferring to sulk in front of a televised big game in the dressing-room. Parker's solo on 'Hot House', three-quarters of the way through the set, is a masterpiece of containment and release, like his work on 'A Night In Tunisia' (introduced by the saxophonist in rather weird French, in deference to the Canadian – but the wrong city, surely? – audience). Perhaps because the game was showing, or perhaps just because Toronto wasn't hip to bebop, the house was by no means full, but it's clear that those who were there sensed something exceptional was happening.

Powell and Roach are the star turns on 'Wee'. The pianist builds a marvellous solo out of Dameron's chords and Roach holds the whole thing together with a performance that almost matches the melodic and rhythmic enterprise of the front men. The Massey Hall concert is a remarkable experience, not to be missed. (A cassette version of the full concert, with Bud Powell's trio set, is still advertised.)

**** Charlie Parker At Storyville Blue Note CDP 785108
Parker; Herb Pomeroy (*t*); Red Garland, Sir Charles Thompson (*p*); Bernie Griggs, Jimmy Woode (*b*); Kenny Clarke, Roy Haynes (*d*). 3/53, 9/53.
First released in 1985, these Boston club dates are the only Parker performances on Blue Note. The tapes, made on a Rube Goldberg home-made system by John Fitch (aka John McLellan, the compère), have been magically reprocessed by Jack Towers and are among the most faithful live recordings of Parker from the period. Of the performances it is necessary only to say that Parker is magisterial. Pomeroy strives manfully but seems to be caught more than once in awkward whole-note progressions which start well but then lapse back into cliché. Local bassist Griggs (who appears again on Stash's compilation of rarities, below) chugs along manfully on the March sessions, but Roy Haynes is a heavy-

handed disappointment. The September quintets are generally less enterprising, and there are even signs that Parker may be repeating himself. In an interview recorded in June of the same year, McLellan pointed to an increasingly noticeable tendency for Parker to play old and established compositions. By the turn of the 1950s, the flow of new variations on the basic blues or on standards had virtually dried up. Despite that, Parker's ability to find new things to say on tunes as well-worn as 'Moose The Mooche', 'Ornithology' and 'Out Of Nowhere' (March) or 'Now's The Time', 'Cool Blues' and 'Groovin' High' (September) is completely impressive. The addition of relatively unfamiliar pieces like 'I'll Walk Alone' and 'Dancing On The Ceiling' contributes to a highly attractive set.

The McLellan interview concludes with one of Parker's most quoted articles of faith: 'You can never tell what you'll be thinking tomorrow. But I can definitely say that music won't stop. It will continue to go forward.'

*** Bird In Boston: Live At The Hi Hat, 1953/54 Fresh Sound FSCD 1006
Parker; Herb Pomeroy, Herbert J. Williams (*t*); Dean Earle, Rollins Griffith (*p*); Bernie Griggs, Jimmy Woode (*b*); Marquis Foster, Billy Graham (*d*); Symphony Sid Torin (*v*). 6/53, 1/54.
*** Bird At The High Hat Blue Note 799787
As above, except omit Pomeroy, Earle, Graham. 12/53, 1/54.

One gets so used to hearing Parker with Miles, Gillespie, Navarro or Dorham that the immediate reaction to this is to ask, 'Who the hell's that?' as Pomeroy starts to play on 'Cool Blues'. These were game professional bands who had spent hours listening to the classic Parker recordings. Griffith in particular cops riffs and runs from Bud Powell, and the two trumpeters have their own respective allegiances. The Blue Note corrals material from the same club on a different date, though there is doubt about precisely what dates are involved. Bird himself sounds tired but surprisingly focused, leaning into one or two choruses as if the clock had gone back half a dozen years. There is no mistaking the change in quality, though. There was a man called Billy Graham at the drumkit. Bird was already much nearer to God.

***(*) The Complete Birth Of The Bebop: Bird On Tenor, 1943 Stash STCD 535
Parker; Chet Baker, Miles Davis, Billy Eckstine, Dizzy Gillespie (*t*); Jimmy Rowles, Hazel Scott (*p*); Milt Jackson (*vib*); Red Callender, Oscar Pettiford, Carson Smith (*b*); Hurley Ramey, Effergee Ware (*g*); Roy Haynes, Shelly Manne, Harold Doc West (*d*); Bob Redcross (*brushes*); Benny Goodman Trio and Quartet on record; other personnel unidentified. 5/40, 9/42, 2/43, 12/45, ?50, 11/53.
(***(*)) The Bird You Never Heard Stash ST-280
Parker; Herb Pomeroy, Bud Powell (*p*); Charles Mingus (*b*); Art Taylor (*d*); Candido (*perc*); other personnel unidentified. 8/50.

Barrel-scrapings, perhaps, but with Parker there was valid music to record every time he put a reed between his lips. Among the earliest items on *Birth Of The Bebop* are two examples of Bird's rare use of tenor saxophone; his only 'official' tenor recording was on a Miles Davis Prestige date, where he appeared as 'Charlie Chan' for contractual reasons. The first is a jammed 'Sweet Georgia Brown' with Dizzy Gillespie and Oscar Pettiford, the second a fascinating hotel-room recording with Gillespie and Billy Eckstine on trumpets and the rhythm shuffled out on a suitcase lid. Of the remaining material, by far the most interesting are the solo 'Body And Soul' and 'Honeysuckle Rose' (which Stash date from May 1940), two sets of duos with guitarists Ware (Bird on alto) and Hurley Ramey (tenor), and remarkable recordings of Parker improvising over Benny Goodman 78s of 'Avalon' and 'China Boy'. The original LP included tracks from 1953 with the 24-year-old Chet Baker on 'Ornithology', 'Barbados' and 'Cool Blues', but this has not been carried over.

Both these Stashes are marred by very poor airshot sound. *The Bird You Never Heard* is the poorer, but the performances are all first class. Four tunes ('Ornithology', 'Out Of Nowhere', 'My Funny Valentine', 'Cool Blues') come from Parker's January 1954 residency at the Hi-Hat in Boston (local trumpeter Pomeroy figures on the Blue Note *At Storyville* – see above – from the previous year, and obviously enjoyed Parker's confidence).

The anonymous author of the liner-notes offers an interesting sidelight on Parker's behaviour during such performances, pointing to his joshing and 'kvelling' with MCs and implying that the image of Bird as a lonely genius who refused to don motley and clown for his audience is not borne out by the recorded facts. A point to ponder.

***(*) Bird's Eyes: Last Unissued – Volume 1 Philology W 5/18
Parker; Miles Davis (*t*); Walter Bishop Jr, Duke Jordan (*p*); Tommy Potter (*b*); Roy Haynes, Max Roach (*d*); Candido (*perc*). 40, 48, 11/52.
***(*) Bird's Eyes: Last Unissued – Volumes 2 & 3 Philology W 12/15
Parker; Red Rodney (*t*); Al Haig (*p*); Tommy Potter (*b*); Max Roach (*d*). 11/49.

. . .

*** **Bird's Eyes: Last Unissued – Volume 10** Philology W 200
  Parker; Kenny Dorham (*t*); Al Haig (*p*); Tommy Potter (*b*); Max Roach, Roy Haynes (*d*); strings. 5/49.

***(*) **Bird's Eyes: Last Unissued – Volume 11** Philology W 622
  As above, except omit Haynes and strings. 5/49.

*** **Bird's Eyes: Last Unissued – Volume 12** Philology W 842
  As above; add Aimé Barelli, Norma Carson, Bill Coleman, Miles Davis, Jon Eardley, George Jouvin Fassin, Roger Guérin, Hot Lips Page (*t*); Big Chief Russell Moore, Maurice Gladieu, Jimmy Knepper, André Paquinet (*tb*); Hubert Rostaing (*cl*); Joe Maini (*as*); Robert Merchez, Sidney Bechet (*ss*); Don Byas, Don Lanphere, James Moody, Bob Newman, Roger Simon, Gers Yowell (*ts*); Honoré True (*bs*); Robert Cambier, Gers Williams (*p*); Hazy Osterwald (*vib*); Buddy Jones, Henri Karen (*b*); Buddy Bridgeford, Roy Haynes, Pierre Loteguy (*d*). 5/49, 6 & 11/50.

***(*) **Bird's Eyes: Last Unissued – Volume 14** Philology W 844
  Parker; Miles Davis, Dizzy Gillespie, Fats Navarro, Red Rodney (*t*); J. J. Johnson, Kai Winding (*tb*); Buddy DeFranco (*cl*); Charlie Ventura (*ts*); Ernie Caceres (*bs*); Lennie Tristano, Al Haig, Duke Jordan (*p*); Billy Bauer (*g*); Tommy Potter, Eddie Safranski (*b*); Shelly Manne, Max Roach (*d*). 1/46, 11/47, 1 & 11/48, 1 & 11/49.

(*) **Bird's Eyes: Last Unissued – Volume 15 Philology W 845
  Parker; Marty Bell, Don Ferrara, Dizzy Gillespie, Don Joseph, Jon Nielson, Al Porcino, Sonny Rich, Red Rodney, Neil Friez (*t*); Frank Orchard (*vtb*); Eddie Bert, Porky Cohen, Jimmy Knepper, Paul Seldon (*tb*); Joe Maini (*as*); Al Cohn, Don Lanphere, Tommy Mackagon, Flip Phillips, Zoot Sims (*ts*); Marty Flax, Bob Newman (*bs*); Harry Biss, Teddy Wilson (*p*); Sam Herman (*g*); Red Norvo (*vib*); Buddy Jones, Slam Stewart (*b*); Phil Arabia, Sam Gruber, Don Manning, Specs Powell, J. C. Heard (*d*). 6/45, 4/50.

*** **Bird's Eyes: Last Unissued – Volume 16** Philology W 846
  Parker; Kenny Dorham, Benny Harris (*t*); Lucky Thompson (*ts*); Milt Jackson (*vib*); Al Haig (*p*); Tommy Potter, Teddy Kotick (*b*); Roy Haynes, Max Roach (*d*). 3/49, 6/51.

. . .

*** **Bird's Eyes: Last Unissued – Volume 19** Philology W 849
  Parker; Dizzy Gillespie (*t*); Trummy Young, Clyde Bernhardt (*tb, v*); Don Byas, Flip Phillips (*ts*); Clyde Hart, Nat Jaffe, Tadd Dameron, Jay McShann (*p*); Bill De Arango, Mike Bryan (*g*); Al Hall, Gene Ramey, Curley Russell (*b*); Gus Johnson, Specs Powell, Max Roach (*d*); Sarah Vaughan, Rubberlegs Williams (*v*). 1 & 5/45.

*** **Bird's Eyes: Last Unissued – Volume 20** Philology W 850
  Parker; Red Rodney, Jon Nielson? (*t*); Charlie Kennedy? (*as*); Al Haig (*p*); Tommy Potter (*b*); Freddie Gruber, Roy Haynes (*d*); other personnel unknown. 2/50, 52 or 53.

Bird's Eyes – Last Unissued is the general title of one of the most extraordinary jazz documentations of recent times. It now stretches to 20 volumes of extremely mixed but, for Parker completists, absolutely essential material. We have noted some of the most valuable CDs but must leave it to dedicated collectors to follow up the remainder, should they feel so moved (and they should be warned that availability is sporadic in some territories).

The most startling items on this collection are two unaccompanied recordings of 'Body And Soul' and 'Honeysuckle Rose', apparently made in a booth. Both are also included on Stash STCD 535, above, where they are improbably dated 1937; Philology's suggestion of May 1940 seems much more realistic. Parker had recently heard Art Tatum playing in New York City and had experienced the much-discussed epiphany while playing 'Cherokee' which led him to improvise on the higher intervals of the chord. Though the voice on these crude recordings is still unmistakably Parker's, the music (a fairly basic set of harmonic variations) is still unsophisticated and rhythmically unenterprising; of course solo performance was not the norm, and it's unrealistic to expect more from what was probably a very casual self-documentation.

The 1948 live material with the great quintet is well up to scratch, with Miles producing some distinctively fragile solos and Roach, when he is clearly audible, steadily elaborating the rhythmic vocabulary he had limned on the Dial sessions. The later Parker With Strings tracks (two takes of 'Just Friends' and a theme) are pretty forgettable.

The second volume is something of a rag-bag of long and short edits. Rodney had joined Parker only rather diffidently, uncertain of his own abilities. He was frequently ill during their earlier association but allowed himself to become addicted to narcotics (perhaps in a misguided gesture of identification). There's a degree of strain in these early sets that is much less evident on the Jazz Anthology and *At St Nick's* sessions, above.

Volume 10, where we pick up the run again, mixes some rather good quintet material from the Salle

Pleyel in Paris, May 1949, with another strings project at the Apollo the following August. Sound-quality in both cases is average to somewhat below, but there are valuable choruses in both sessions from Parker and some very crisp playing from Dorham, who sounds immensely relaxed and poised in Paris. The French trip also forms the substance of Volume 11 and the better part of 12. The first of these brings together more stuff from the Pleyel with material from a side-trip to Roubaix. On the latter, the quintet is generously augmented by fellow-visitors, a sprawling jam featuring Miles, Hot Lips Page, Bill Coleman, Don Byas, James Moody, and (a valuable encounter) Sidney Bechet. The quality of the music is, frankly, nothing to write home about, but it's marvellous to have all these names together in the one space.

There is more jam material on 12, Parker with Maurice Moufflard's well-drilled but uninspired orchestra. The more interesting material is recorded back home in New York, at the home of saxophonists Joe Maini and Don Lanphere, where a regular jam seems on occasion to have been recorded. Bird is the dominant voice but there are lots of others clamouring for attention, and it's hard to keep the attention riveted.

The next volume can be skipped on the thin grounds that all the material is under Dizzy Gillespie's name. Fourteen, though, is back to the small groups and a single take from the Metronome All Stars in January 1949. The next volume is perhaps the weakest of the latter bunch from a documentary point of view; the Red Norvo material is available elsewhere, and the big-band material under Gene Roland's leadership finds Parker somewhat under the weather, misfingering a couple of times.

Anyone who is interested in this music more than casually should, however, attempt to have a listen to the next volume. It includes a nine-minute lecture or lesson from Parker with a fascinating insight into his work on scales, all recorded in Dick Meldonian's apartment. Beside this, all the other tracks melt into relative insignificance, though the pair from the Waldorf Astoria with Dorham and Thompson from 1951 are very good indeed, if a little early in the evening for fireworks. In the lecture, one hears very little speech from Parker, but one audible fragment contains the nugget 'all music is harmony, melody and rhythm'. Harmony with who? someone asks. Parker informs him he's a fool, presumably because of the grammar.

Milt Jackson is on hand at the Waldorf Astoria for a version of 'Anthropology' which runs some minor variations on previously familiar versions. By this point in the series, producer Paolo Piangiarelli is adding material from other musicians. Volume 16 is filled out with Louis Armstrong material. Nineteen has some tracks from 1949 by a Miles/Dameron group, but this volume also has reconstruction of four legendary glass-based acetates by blues singer and trombonist, Clyde Bernhardt, who had been in the Jay McShann band at around the same time as Parker. It had long been believed that these discs, which were in the possession of Frank Driggs, were unplayable. Rough and ready as they are, and containing only homoeopathic amounts of recognizable Parker, they fill in an important part in the story. The Clyde Hart material is lacklustre but there are flashes of brilliance from all the horn players, and the Sarah Vaughan material from May 1945, with Parker in the octet, is worth checking out.

The last item (in the current run of releases, at least) is subtitled 'The Great Lie', an item included in a previously unissued 1952 or 1953 jam session about which there is little definite information. There is an Art Pepper recording of the tune but, so far as is known, Parker had not played it before. The identity of the second altoist is a matter for speculation. He is a disciple of sorts, but not in the premier league; someone has suggested Charlie Kennedy. Nor is the identification of Jon Nielson as trumpeter entirely secure, though this does seem like a good bet. There is a re-run of the St Nicks material from 1950, sounding well mastered and very musical, and, as with recent issues, a batch of tracks by the Tadd Dameron Tentet which help fill out that rather intermittent discography.

Much as the discovery of Shakespeare's rough notes would be a major discovery, there is a place in the overall picture for almost all the Philology material; the ratings given are intended to reflect its historical significance. Casual buyers are counselled to save their money for more highly finished product and to leave these admirable releases to those who make Parker and his immediate environment their special study and passion.

Errol Parker (born 1930) DRUMS

*** **A Night In Tunisia** Sahara 1015
        Parker; Philip Harper, Michael Thomas (*t*); Tyrone Jefferson (*tb*); Doug Harris (*ss*); Donald Harrison (*as*); Bill Saxton (*ts*); Patience Higgins (*bs*); Cary De Nigris (*g*); Reggie Washington (*b*). 4/91.

*** **Remembering Billy Strayhorn** Sahara 1016
        As above, except Kenny Sheffield (*t*) and David Lee Jones (*as*) replace Harper and Harrison, add Jimmy Cozier (*bs*). 9/94.

Parker has had a rather extraordinary career, often as a drummer, which he became after many years as a pianist. But he's seldom had the opportunity to record. His own label, Sahara Records, has had some earlier vinyl releases and can now boast these two CDs. Parker's 'A Night In Tunisia' is dramatically different from almost any other version: he breaks down both the melody and the rhythm (his drumming uses a modified kit in which the snare is replaced by a conga and there are more tom toms and fewer cymbals in use) to make it more like a bouncing, dishevelled fantasy on the original theme. Since Parker is Algerian-born, it can scarcely be a more authentic re-creation, though. Originals such as 'Daydream At Noon' and 'The Rai' move to rhythms and grooves unfamiliar to the contemporary mainstream, most of them drawn from Parker's African background, and it places a compelling new context on the otherwise familiar solos of Harrison, Harper and Jefferson. The unglamorous sound, with the drums mixed right at the front, will knock out its appeal for many; but in a way this rough-and-ready mix suits what is a deliberately non-conformist session from a leader who deserves respect and attention.

   Remembering Billy Strayhorn pretty much picks up where he left off three years earlier. The band is almost the same horn-heavy aggregation as before, the brass and reeds not so much acting as sections as working as a talking-in-tongues ensemble that rumbles over and round Parker's themes. With typical audacity, the disc includes not a single Strayhorn composition, despite the title: instead, it opens with two pieces which were written at Duke Ellington's request, some 30 years before, as a souvenir for Strayhorn of a Paris visit. Parker coaxes a powerhouse performance out of his group and, though there are some failures – 'Reggae' is a wrong 'un, and 'Autumn In New York' seems unnecessarily sour – they end on a tumultuous thrashing of 'Straight No Chaser'. Along the way, a heap of good solos and Parker's own inimitable propulsion from his unique drum set-up. Enigmatic.

Evan Parker (born 1944) SOPRANO SAXOPHONE, TENOR SAXOPHONE

*** **Three Other Stories (1971–1974)** Emanem 4002
   Parker; Paul Lytton (*d, perc, harm, elec*). 6/71, 6/73, 7/74.
**** **Saxophone Solos** Chronoscope CPE 2002
   Parker (*ss* solo). 6 & 9/75.
There's a certain irony in the fact that Evan Parker, now almost universally acknowledged as one of the finest and most virtuosic instrumentalists working in improvised music today, should at one crucial stage in his career have rejected instrumentalism altogether. In the late 1960s improvisers became concerned that 'the instrument' (with its apparently fixed repertoire of pitches and timbres) had become too narrow and restrictive for the free-flowing, spontaneous music they wished to create. The alternative was to devise *ad hoc* sound-sources (inevitably, most of them were percussive), never allowing them or their users the comfort of 'technique'. Enthusiasts for improvised music (and its detractors, who had always suspected something of the sort) became used to seeing the kitchen cupboard and tool-shed raided for sound-producing objects – bicycle pumps, pot lids, squeaking hinges, off-station radios – which were untouched by the formal, canonical, hierarchical properties associated with concert instruments.

   Since the early 1970s, Parker's work has been a sustained rejection of that approach he once flirted with. Taking what is perhaps the only genuinely new musical instrument of the last 150 years, Parker has vastly increased its potential range. By means of circular breathing (a technique which allows a wind player to inhale while maintaining air pressure on the reed), he is able to improvise uninterrupted for astonishingly long periods. An early LP was called *The Topography Of The Lungs*. So rapid and constant is his articulation that sceptical listeners have been moved to suggest that some of his purportedly solo recordings 'must' be the result of overdubbing; it was more than a little ironic when, on *Process And Reality* (see below), he did just that.

   In addition to eliminating the need to improvise in breath-groups, Parker has confronted the treacherous pitching of the soprano saxophone as a positive resource to be exploited rather than a technical difficulty to be overcome. Parker has created a unique repertoire of multiphonic effects and split notes which allows him to make progressive microtonal adjustments to a melodic cell, often working in very high harmonics. The effect of his music is of organic change over considerable durations. Though his music is now almost wholly abstract, it is clear that among its fundamental inspirations are the immensely long para-harmonic improvisations created by John Coltrane during his final years, and Parker's tenor saxophone playing is still often reminiscent of Coltrane's use of 'wrong' or 'ugly' notes. Though not a single-minded soprano specialist like Steve Lacy, the straight horn has figured increasingly largely in Parker's work, often at the expense of his wonderful tenor playing.

   The Parker discography is now very large and widely scattered, presenting a challenge to Francesco Martinelli, the man who has dedicated considerable time and patience to documenting it. The best news for Parker enthusiasts since our last edition, and the proper place for newcomers to start, is the reissued *Saxophone Solos*, restored to circulation by the estimable Trevor Manwaring and his Chronoscope label. These pieces are fascinating to compare to later solo performances on record because they are, for all their initially forbidding aspect, still tentative. Parker calls them 'Aerobatics' and appends subtitles drawn from his favourite writer, Samuel Beckett. They share a concern with the points at which 'language' in one or other of its conventional aspects (which include musical language) cedes to silence, non-communication and sheer physicality. Parker can be heard experimenting with sustained notes, often changing the colour progressively through time, or else giving a particular tone successively different attacks. Instead of ranging between registers, as his predecessors did, he uses multiphonics to collapse vertical organization in favour of simultaneity and co-presence. With hindsight these pieces serve as a prolegomenon to the next 20 years of activity. They are an essential modernist document.

The slightly earlier duos with percussionist Lytton also have their place in the story, half a step back again in historical terms. The most obvious antecedent for these is Coltrane's late work with Rashied Ali, except that the saxophonist has stripped out the last vestiges of harmonic exploration and Lytton cleaves to a non-pulse or anti-pulse which denies any illusion of 'development'. The three 'stories' are determinedly non-linear and Duchampian. Parker adds *sheng* and invented aerophones to his armoury and overlays cassette versions of earlier performances; Lytton's kit, by all accounts, was huge. Notwithstanding which, the sound is remarkably detailed, controlled and spacious. A less compelling record than *Saxophone Solos*, but a significant moment nevertheless.

*** **4,4,4** Konnex KCD 5049
    Parker; Paul Rutherford (*tb, euph*); Barry Guy (*b, elec*); John Stevens (*d, v*). 8/79.
Anachronistically sharing the space with a single long performance by the latter-day Spontaneous Music Ensemble, this finds Parker at a stage in his career when the last ties to jazz had been undone but without an alternative faith. The music is chaotic, sometimes rambling and – but for Rutherford and Guy – on occasion would seem to be coming apart at the seams. For once Stevens doesn't keep on the case, and his clattery ramblings are irritating. Parker plays with typical definiteness of purpose, but there is little support for what he is doing and the record tends to sound like horns and rhythm again.

**** **Atlanta** Impulse IMP 18617
    Parker; Barry Guy (*b*); Paul Lytton (*d, perc*). 12/86.
**** **Conic Projections** Ah Um 015
    Parker (*ss* solo). 6/89.
(*) **Duets: Dithyrambisch FMP CD 19/20
    Parker; Louis Sclavis (*bcl, ss*); Wolfgang Fuchs (*bcl, cbcl*); Hans Koch (*ss, ts*). 7/89.
*** **Hall Of Mirrors** MM&T 01
    Parker; Walter Prati (*elec*). 2/90.
*** **Process And Reality** FMP CD 37
    Parker (*ts, ss* solo and with multitracking). 91.
**** **Corner To Corner** Ogun OGCD 005
    Parker; John Stevens (*d, t*). 6/93.
Conic Sections catches Parker at a point when his solo soprano recitals still held an element of surprise, even shock. A few years later they had begun to seem a little repetitive and predictable, an almost inevitable problem with unaccompanied performance. Better recorded than the earlier sessions, the 1989 album is probably the definitive solo disc.

Unfortunately, that's the case only because most of his remarkable solo works for Incus (the improvised-music label he co-founded with Derek Bailey and Tony Oxley in 1970) are no longer available. A limited-edition box which includes masterworks like *Monoceros* and *The Snake Decides* sold out rapidly (and no one in his or her right mind is going to trade it in second-hand).

A long-standing partnership with Barry Guy is revived on *Atlanta*, a much more open and accessible performance than previous encounters on FMP and one that heralds an unprecedented user-friendliness in Parker's work. Where previously he might have entered at an absurd altitude and pace and continued from there, perhaps alienating as many unprepared listeners as impressing converts, here he seems content to build up the level of energy and complexity of interplay more slowly, approaching the summit from foothills mapped and contoured by the free-jazz movement of the late 1960s and early '70s rather than simply overflying. Lytton's contribution can't be underestimated; he is one of Europe's most inventive percussionists and a master in this context.

Hall Of Mirrors and *Process And Reality* might almost have swapped titles. It's the solo multi-tracked album that suggests the *mise-en-abîme* effects of a mirror gallery, while Walter Prati's delicate acoustic environments perform a function closer to West Coast composer Morton Subotnick's electronic 'ghost scores', suggesting a numinous significance lying underneath Parker's surprisingly vocalized lines. The pieces on *Process And Reality* are much briefer (there are 16 of them) and melodically coherent than has been typical of his work. 'Diary Of A Mnemonist' is perhaps the most reachable and humane thing Parker has yet to commit to record. As such, it stands at an opposite pole to the remarkable duos with Lacy on *Chirps*, which are the ten-minute egg of hard-boiled abstraction and a tough breakfast for the uninitiated. By contrast, the duos with Fuchs, Koch and Sclavis are untypically vague and unfocused, suggesting *mésalliance*. In context they may have been wonderful performances, but they are uncommunicative on disc.

Corner To Corner revives a much more fruitful association. In 1977 Parker and John Stevens recorded a much-admired two-LP set called *The Longest Night* for the Ogun label. Fifteen years later their dialogue has by no means been blunted but is certainly less hostile. The titles – 'Acute', 'Incidence', 'Angles', 'Reflections' – self-mockingly suggest that cliché'd honorific: angularity; but there is also mutuality, a desire to find common ground, which wasn't always there before, and it's significant they should have called the final and most beautiful cut 'Each/Other'. This would be an excellent place to start listening to either man.

**** Imaginary Values Maya MCD 9401
    Parker; Barry Guy (*b*); Paul Lytton (*d, perc*). 3/93.
**** 50th Birthday Concert Leo CD LR 212/213 2CD
    As above, except add Alex von Schlippenbach (*p*); Paul Lovens (*d, perc*). 4/94.
***(*) Breaths And Heartbeats Rastascan BRD 019
    As above, except omit von Schlippenbach and Lovens. 12/94.
*** Obliquities Maya MCD 9501
    As above, except omit Lytton. 12/94.
***(*) The Redwood Sessions CIMP 101
    As above, except add Joe McPhee (*t*); Paul Lytton (*d, perc*). 6/95.

The association with both Guy and Lytton goes back a long way and there is absolute *trust* in these trio recordings. To look at the music from Parker's point of view alone (though clearly all of it is collaborative), one becomes aware of the extent to which he is willing to submerge his 'solo-personality', if such a concept suffices, to the interests of the group, allowing the other performers to establish their place in the continuum. *Breaths And Heartbeats* is a less comfortable performance than the earlier set. As on *Process And Reality*, Parker allows a certain level of manipulation and resequencing. Between each section there are percussion passages – 'breaths' – which restore the music's red-cell count at each stage. Unfortunately, for the most part the results are uninvolving and the pace of the record is wrong.

The duos with Guy are immensely accomplished, but again there is a sense in which this music has turned inward. It doesn't project, even as the trios on *Imaginary Values* managed to project despite themselves, and it is never clear what the informing logic is: a conversation between friends which obstinately refuses to identify external referents. *The Redwood Sessions* were made by the same trio (McPhee guests on just one track) in a notably relaxed and amiable atmosphere in which birdsong (an American robin and some kind of babbler, we can note with reasonable ornithological authority) is audible through the open windows of the Spirit Room at Rossie, New York, where this recording for *Cadence* magazine's own label was made. McPhee had toured in Europe with Parker and was induced to join in for the final item. It's a lovely session, as usual for this new imprint recorded with almost naïve simplicity.

The *50th Birthday Concert*, held at Dingwalls in north London, was a high point in every respect. Grouping Parker with two very different trios was a happy notion and makes for a fascinating record. The Schlippenbach Trio has been responsible for some of the finest free-jazz records ever made, and the term is chosen advisedly, for the language here is clearly a derivative of jazz. Not so the well-documented '90s trio which, despite Guy's appetite for structures, obeys no normative logic of any sort, but hews to a fearsomely unsettling improvisational discipline that time and time again on 'In Exultation' appears to demand some sort of resolution yet continues unabated and unchecked for a full 20 minutes. As a representation of Parker's career range, the two-CD Leo is hard to pass over, but the others ought to be sampled, too, for what they show of a major artist in his pomp.

Leo Parker (1925–62) BARITONE SAXOPHONE, ALTO SAXOPHONE

*** Prestige First Sessions: Volume 1 Prestige PCD 24114
    Parker; Al Haig (*p*); Oscar Pettiford (*b*); Max Roach, Jack Parker (*d*). 7/50.

Like Zeppo Marx, Leo is the saxophone-playing Parker whom people tend to forget. Like Zeppo, too, he quit the scene early, dying of a heart attack aged only 37. His best-known recordings were with Fats Navarro and Illinois Jacquet, having switched under Billy Eckstine from alto to baritone; he plays both on an early Prestige compilation. Just as the Eckstine Orchestra was always known, *tout court*, as 'The Band', so Leo was 'The Kid' or 'Lad'; themes like 'Mad Lad Returns' on the Prestige debut compilation (which is shared with his accompanist, Al Haig, and Don Lanphere) were meant to show off the jollier side of his personality, often at the cost of turning Leo into a novelty act; the two cuts (alternatives of 'Mad Lad Returns') with Jack 'The Bear' Parker fall into that trap. At this stage, though, Leo was playing some useful alto as well as baritone, but comparisons with another Parker probably put him off and he tended to concentrate on the bigger horn thereafter.

Though fate didn't give him much personal leeway, there's a sense in which he never entirely grew up musically. Either way, his modest Blue Note discography is currently back in limbo.

Maceo Parker ALTO SAXOPHONE

*** Roots Revisited Minor Music 1015
      Parker; Fred Wesley (*tb*); Vince Henry (*as*); Pee Wee Ellis (*ts*); Don Pullen (*org*); Rodney Jones
      (*g*); Bootsy Collins (*b*); Bill Stewart (*d*).
*** Mo' Roots Minor Music 801018
      As above, except omit Pullen, Collins, Henry; add Larry Goldings (*org, ky*). 3/91.
***(*) Live On Planet Groove Minor Music 801023
      Parker; Fred Wesley (*tb*); Candy Dulfer (*as*); Vincent Henry (*as, b*); Pee Wee Ellis (*ts*); Larry
      Goldings (*prog*); Rodney Jones (*g*); Kenwood Dennard (*d*); Kim Mazelle (*v*). 92.
*** Southern Exposure Minor Music 801033
      Parker; Kermit Ruffins, Derek Shezbie (*t*); Stafford Agee, Fred Wesley (*tb*); Philip Frazier (*tba*);
      Pee Wee Ellis, Roderick Paulin (*ts*); Will Boulware (*org*); Rodney Jones, Leo Nocentelli (*g*);
      George Porter Jr (*b*); Herman Ernest III, Ajay Mallory, Keith Frazier, Bill Stewart (*d*); Michael
      Ward (*perc*). 93.
*** Maceo Minor Music 801046
      Parker; Fred Wesley (*tb*); Pee Wee Ellis (*ts*); Will Boulware (*org*); Bruno Speight (*g*); Jerry
      Preston (*b*); Jamal Thomas (*d*); Rebirth Brass Band; George Clinton, Kim Mazelle (*v*). 4/94.
Just what the world needs, another saxophone-playing Parker. All things considered, though, this one may turn out to be the most widely exposed of all. As a member of soul godfather James Brown's backing group, he created an instrumental sound – hard, funky, tight as a nut – that has been immensely influential in popular music.

During Brown's, ahem, *difficulties* of the late '80s, various members of the J B Horns made records on their own account. The jazziest was probably trombonist and musical director Fred Wesley, who also appears here; but Parker's discs for Minor Music are certainly worthy of their place as well, and the live missive from *Planet Groove* just gets the nod because this is what Parker, Wesley and Ellis do best: getting down and having a ball in the process.

Qualitatively, the others are almost impossible to set apart. The first has a brash, almost unrehearsed immediacy that suggests (correctly or not) that the band simply set up and got going. Pullen, whose involvement in R&B predates his avant-garde activities, throws in some readily identifiable shapes, and guest star Collins does some brilliant slap bass guitar. The remainder are more polished and trimmed at the edges. *Southern Exposure* and the recent *Maceo* (which also bears the enigmatic word 'Soundtrack' on its front cover, and is also – regrettably – sponsored by a tobacco company) feature members of the Rebirth Brass Band sounding not too revivalist. All these discs are beautifully packaged in laminate cases by the German label, who are probably very pleased with their investment.

Horace Parlan (born 1931) PIANO

*** Arrival Steeplechase SCCD 31012
      Parlan; Idrees Sulieman (*flhn*); Bent Jaedig (*ts*); Hugo Rasmussen (*b*); Ed Thigpen (*d*). 12/73.
*** No Blues Steeplechase SCCD 31056
      Parlan; Niels-Henning Orsted-Pedersen (*b*); Tony Inzalaco (*d*). 12/75.
**** Blue Parlan Steeplechase SCCD 31124
      Parlan; Wilbur Little (*b*); Dannie Richmond (*d*). 11/78.
*** Musically Yours Steeplechase SCCD 31141
      Parlan (*p* solo). 11/79.
*** Pannonica Enja 4076
      Parlan; Reggie Johnson (*b*); Alvin Queen (*d*). 2/81.
***(*) Glad I Found You Steeplechase SCCD 31194
      Parlan; Thad Jones (*flhn*); Eddie Harris (*ts*); Jesper Lundgaard (*b*); Aage Tanggaard (*d*). 7/84.
**(*) Little Esther Soul Note 121145
      Parlan; Per Goldschmidt (*bs*); Klaus Hovman (*b*); Massimo De Majo (*d*). 3/87.
Parlan's most moving single performance is arguably the unaccompanied 'Lament For Booker Ervin', posthumously tacked on to the Ervin album of that title. None of his other solo recordings evinces that much intensity or attention to detail. A middle-order bop pianist in a highly oversubscribed field, Parlan

only catches the attention for his tough bass chords and highly restricted melody figures (an attack of infantile paralysis crabbed his right hand) which contributed substantially to *Mingus Ah Um* and accorded closely with the bassist/composer's preference for highly rhythmic and unorthodox pianists.

Parlan has developed a blues-influenced repertoire, marked by a substantial inclusion of Thelonious Monk themes, heavily left-handed melodies like 'Lullaby Of The Leaves' and throbbing swingers like Randy Weston's 'Hi-Fly', both of which recur throughout his recorded work, and in particular a wilderness of minimally differentiated Steeplechase sessions, of which only the best, below, have survived into CD-hood.

Perhaps the best of Parlan's group work was made for Blue Note in the 1960s. The best of those, *Happy Frame Of Mind*, which featured his friend Ervin, was briefly available on CD (CDP 784134 CD) but has subsequently disappeared again. The excellent 1960 sessions with the Turrentine brothers are no longer available. Like other American players of the time, facing a slackening demand for jazz recording, Parlan emigrated to Scandinavia where he has pursued a workmanlike and unspectacular career, documented by Steeplechase from *Arrival* onwards with almost redundant thoroughness. The only highspots that call for separate treatment are the fine 1978 trio with Wilbur Little and Dannie Richmond (also, of course, a Mingus man) and the much later *Glad I Found You*, where Parlan and the late Thad Jones shrug off a rather diffident setting to produce some sparkling performances. For the rest, cautious sampling is perhaps the best bet. One of the least cliché-bound of players, Parlan is still somewhat repetitive in the structuring of his solos, and he's rarely as challenging as like-minded figures such as Roland Hanna, Jaki Byard or even Duke Jordan (whose Steeplechase discography marches on to the crack of doom).

Rob Parton's Jazztech Big Band GROUP

*** Rob Parton's Jazztech Big Band Featuring Conte Candoli Sea Breeze CDSB-112
    Rob Parton, Conte Candoli, Mike McGrath, Steve Smyth, Tom Reed, Al Hood (*t*); Russ Phillips, Brian Jacobi, Jim Martin, Scott Bentall, Tony Garcia (*tb*); Mike Young (*btb*); Bob Frankich, Ian Nevins (*as*); Tony Vacca, Greg Mostovoy (*ts*); Kurt Berg (*bs*); Larry Harris (*p*); John Moran (*g*); Stewart Miller (*b*); Bob Rummage, Bob Chmel (*d*); Bill Elliot (*perc*). 91.

*** The Count Is In! Sea Breeze CDSB-2047
    As above, except add Mark Thompson (*t*), Jack Schmidt (*tb*), Mark Colby (*ss, ts*), Brian Budzik (*ts, bs*), Eric Montzka (*d*), omit Candoli, Phillips, Bentall, Garcia, Vacca, Berg, Moran and Chmel. 7/92.

*** What Are We Here For? Sea Breeze CDSB-2067
    Rob Parton, Mike McGrath, Scott Wagstaff, Art Davis, Corey Deadman (*t*); Jack Schmidt, Brian Jacobi, Dan Jonson, Antonio J. Garcia (*tb*); Mike Meyers (*btb*); Bob Frankich, Ian Nevins (*as*); Mark Colby, Brian Budzik (*ts*); Kurt Berg (*bs*); Karl Montzka (*p*); Jeff Hill (*b*); Mark Walker (*d*); Kristy Smith (*v*). 11/94.

Big-band music comfortably dispatched by a likeable if not markedly individual orchestra. Parton likes to lead the trumpet section rather than compose or arrange, and most of the charts for the band follow familiar routes of punchy brass contrasting with sinewy reeds. Candoli is named as the featured man on the first album, but he actually solos on only three numbers; the other soloists rarely rise above the workmanlike, but there's a nice contrast between the effortful playing of Phillips and Frankich on 'Sentimental Journey' and the smooth reworking of the melody. *The Count Is In!* adds the brusquely authoritative tenor of Mark Colby, and his impact suggests that the band could use a few more soloists of this calibre. *What Are We Here For?* is a little better still. Colby has a couple of good turns once again; Parton treats himself to a feature on 'My Romance', and the band have gained a fine vocalist in Kristy Smith, with a very swinging 'Deed I Do' as one result. Garcia's trombone feature on 'Loved One (To Maria)' is a neat departure. Their best calling-card to date.

Alan Pasqua (born 1954) PIANO

**** Milagro Postcards POST1002
    Pasqua; Willie Olenick (*t, flhn*); Jack Schatz (*tb, btb*); John Clark (*frhn*); Michael Brecker (*ts*); Roger Rosenberg (*af*); Dave Tofani (*bcl*); Dave Holland (*b*); Jack DeJohnette (*d*). 10/93.

**** Dedications Postcards POST1012
    Pasqua; Randy Brecker (*t*); Gary Bartz (*as*); Michael Brecker (*ts*); Dave Holland (*b*); Paul Motian (*d*). 12/95.

Pasqua started late as a leader, but this pair of albums make such good listening that one wonders where he's been. His own playing as an improviser is comparatively unexceptional, but the compositions on

Milagro stick in the mind on one hearing, and the arrangements are absolutely gorgeous. Pasqua varies the pace between trio tracks, features for Brecker, and arrangements where the brass glower in the background as the rhythm section works through a lush harmonic sequence ('Heartland') or a luminous melody ('Milagro'). The opening 'Acoma' is transcendentally beautiful, and Brecker, Holland and DeJohnette give unstintingly of their own talents throughout.

Dedications is marginally more conventional, the disc divided between trios and tracks where the horns join in; but again it's the quality of the writing that elevates the situations and brings out the best in Bartz and the Breckers. 'Ellingtonia', taken at a daringly slow pace, is among the most intelligent of tributes; 'Mr Softee' is a clever vamp; 'Homage' is a darkly fiery manifesto to open the album. Throughout, Pasqua holds his own in the kind of band that most dream about fronting. There is the odd indulgence on both records, but the results are so fine overall – and so well recorded – that it would be churlish to hold back a top recommendation.

Joe Pass (1929–94) GUITAR

**** Virtuoso Pablo 2310-708
    Pass (*g* solo). 12/73.
*** Portraits Of Duke Ellington Pablo 2310-716
    Pass; Ray Brown (*b*); Bobby Durham (*d*). 6/74.
***(*) Virtuoso No. 2 Pablo 2310-788
    Pass (*g* solo). 10/76.
*** Virtuoso No. 3 Original Jazz Classics OJC 684
    Pass (*g* solo). 5–6/77.
*** Montreux '77 Original Jazz Classics OJC 382.
    Pass (*g* solo). 7/77.
**(*) Tudo Bem! Original Jazz Classics OJC 685
    Pass; Don Grusin (*p*); Oscar Castro Neves (*g*); Octavio Bailly (*b*); Claudio Slon (*d*); Paulinho
    Da Costa (*perc*). 5/78.
***(*) Chops Original Jazz Classics OJC 686
    Pass; Niels-Henning Orsted-Pedersen (*b*). 11/78.
*** I Remember Charlie Parker Original Jazz Classics OJC 602
    Pass (*g* solo). 2/79.
*** Ira, George And Joe Original Jazz Classics OJC 828
    Pass; John Pisano (*g*); Jim Hughart (*b*); Shelly Manne (*d*). 11/81.
*** We'll Be Together Again Pablo 2310-911
    Pass; J. J. Johnson (*tb*). 10/83.
** Whitestone Pablo 2310-912
    Pass; Don Grusin, John Pisano (*g*); Abe Laboriel, Nathaniel West, Harvey Mason (*d*); Paulinho
    Da Costa (*perc*); Armando Compean (*v*). 2–3/85.
*** University Of Akron Concert Pablo 2308-249
    Pass (*g* solo). 85.
*** Blues For Fred Pablo 2310-931
    Pass (*g* solo). 2/88.
*** One For My Baby Pablo 2310-936
    Pass; Plas Johnson (*ts*); Gerald Wiggins (*p, org*); Andrew Simpkins (*b*); Albert 'Tootie' Heath
    (*d*). 4/88.
*** Summer Nights Pablo 2310-939
    Pass; John Pisano (*g*); Jim Hughart (*b*); Colin Bailey (*d*). 12/89.
*** Appassionato Pablo 2310-946
    Pass; Jim Hughart (*b*); Colin Bailey (*d*).
*** Virtuoso Live! Pablo 2310-948
    Pass (*g* solo).
*** Live At Yoshi's Pablo 2310-951
    Pass; John Pisano (*g*); Monty Budwig (*b*); Colin Bailey (*d*). 1/92.
***(*) Finally Emarcy 512603-2
    Pass; Red Mitchell (*b*). 2/92.
*** Songs For Ellen Pablo 2310-955
    Pass (*g* solo). 8/92.
*** My Song Telarc CD-83326
    Pass; John Pisano (*g*); Tom Ranier (*p*); Jim Hughart (*b*); Colin Bailey (*d*). 2/93.
Taste, refinement and an unflappable rhythmic poise are the hallmarks of a style which made Joe Pass

the benchmark player for mainstream jazz guitar. Pass smooths away the nervousness of bop yet counters the plain talk of swing with a complexity that remains completely accessible. An improvisation on a standard may range far and wide, but there's no sense of him going into territory which he doesn't already know well. There's nothing hidden in his music, everything is absolutely on display, and he cherishes good tunes without sanctifying them. His tone isn't distinctive but it is reliably mellifluous, and he can make every note in a melody shine. Compared with Tal Farlow or Jimmy Raney, Pass took few risks and set himself fewer genuine challenges, but any guitarist will recognize a performer who has a total command over the instrument. His career went through a muddled phase in the 1960s – he first recorded as a member of a Synanon Rehabilitation Centre house-band – but the string of albums he made for Pacific Jazz during the decade are all currently out of general circulation. On signing for Pablo in the 1970s, Pass effectively became the house guitarist, and a steady flow of albums under his own name was supplemented by many guest appearances with Oscar Peterson, Milt Jackson and the rest of the company stable.

One could complain that Pass made too many records, but even taking a few deletions into account it only amounts to about one a year under his own name. The problem is more that his favourite context tended to be quiet, reflective and insufficiently various to make one want to own more than one or two of them. *Virtuoso*, his debut for Pablo, remains the obvious place to start: at a time when traditional jazz guitar playing was being sidelined by the gradual onset of fusion, this seemed to reaffirm the deathless virtues of the straight-ahead instrument, and Pass never sounded sharper or warmer on a set of standards, played with all the expertise which the title suggests. The three subsequent volumes (number four is deleted) are replays with lightly diminishing returns. Concert situations don't seem to affect Pass's concentration: he played with the same careful diligence as in the studio, so the live solo albums sound much alike. *Blues For Fred* is a particularly attractive set of tunes in tribute to Fred Astaire, and although the Parker album could have been a bit more exciting than it turned out – Pass's first allegiance is certainly to bebop – it may be because it set him to work on the sort of standards which Bird covered during his Verve era, rather than bop originals. *Chops* is plenty of fun for the sheer expertise on display, Pass and NHOP basically doing little more than showing off how well they can play, but with enough nous to make it sound good. The meeting with J. J. Johnson on *We'll Be Together Again* is a little sleepy, but these are two sly old dogs, and you can almost hear them kidding each other on the blues 'Naked As A Jaybird'. Johnson deadpans his way through it and for once Pass sounds like the assertive one; still, it's hard to think of a more sheerly mellifluous partnership. Shelly Manne is a useful presence on *Ira, George And Joe*, and this set of Gershwin tunes is nicely varied: Pass almost twangs his way through 'Bidin' My Time' and 'It Ain't Necessarily So', makes a waltz out of 'Love Is Here To Stay' and does a beautifully slow take on 'Lady Be Good'.

Of the trio sets, the Ellington album with Ray Brown and Bobby Durham is a shade disappointing. *Summer Nights* is something of a tribute to Django Reinhardt, and Pass sounds contented and thoughtful, while the recent *Appassionato*, which benefits from a wider and more modern sound on CD, chooses terser material than usual – 'Grooveyard', 'Relaxin'' At Camarillo', 'Nica's Dream' – and finds a cutting edge which some of Pass's records pass by. *Live At Yoshi's* is a solid club set, recorded in California, with a boppish tinge that gets a little extra juice out of 'Doxy' and 'Oleo'. The odd records out are *One For My Baby*, which sets the guitarist up in a sort of down-home kind of roadhouse band with mixed success, although Johnson contributes a few lively solos; and the two Latin-styled albums, both of which are gently scuppered by Don Grusin's penchant for light-music triviality, as prettily as everyone plays.

There is some poignancy about *Finally*, given that it's among the last recordings by both Pass and Mitchell, but the sheer good humour and craftiness of the playing makes it a special item in the Pass list. Mitchell's knack of elevating an ordinary playing situation brings out the best in both men, and there's an extra twist in such staples as 'Blue Moon' and 'Have You Met Miss Jones?'. 'I Thought About You', done at a tempo which approximates syrup dripping off a spoon, is very fine.

Virtuoso Live! is in most respects just another solo album, but the pieces chosen reflect Pass's concern to try and wriggle free of his own routines. 'Mack The Knife' appears as a ballad, delivered with a superb touch, and the chopped rhythms of 'Stompin'' At The Savoy' show how he can find a new tone, even in such a warhorse as that. His first for Telarc reunited him with old sparring partner, John Pisano, and the rhythm section generate some civilized heat. It's still a bit restrained, but a couple more records by this group might have seen them reaching beyond the norm. But Pass's passing closed the chapter.

*** **The Best Of Joe Pass** Pablo 2405-419

    As Pablo albums, above.

A respectable cross-section from the Pablo albums, though almost any one of the three- or four-star recommendations above will do at least as good a job for the casual listener.

Jaco Pastorius (1951–87) BASS GUITAR

***(*) **Jaco** DIW 312
> Pastorius; Paul Bley (*p*); Pat Metheny (*g*); Bruce Ditmas (*d*). 6/74.

***(*) **Pastorius Metheny Ditmas Bley** Improvising Artists Inc IAI 123846
> As above. 6/74.

***(*) **Jaco Pastorius** Epic CDEPC 81453
> Pastorius; Randy Brecker, Ron Tooley (*t*); Peter Graves (*btb*); Peter Gordon (*frhn*); Hubert
> Laws (*picc*); Wayne Shorter (*ss*); David Sanborn (*as*); Michael Brecker (*ts*); Howard Johnson
> (*bs*); Herbie Hancock, Alex Darqui (*p, ky*); Richard Davis, Homer Mensch (*b*); Narada Michael
> Walden, Lenny White, Bobby Oeconomy (*d*); Don Alias (*perc*); Othello Molineaux, Leroy
> Williams (*steel d*); Sam And Dave (*v*); strings. 75.

**** **Holiday For Pans** Sound Hills SSCD 8001
> Pastorius; Peter Graves (*tb*); Wayne Shorter (*ss*); Toots Thielemans (*hca*); Mike Gerber (*p*); Ted
> Lewand (*g*); Craig Thayler (*vn*); Kenwood Dennard (*d*); Bobby Oeconomy (*d, perc*); Don Alias
> (*perc*); Othello Molineaux, Leroy Williams (*steel d*); Michael Gibbs Orchestra. 80–82.

*** **PDB** DIW 827
> Pastorius; Hiram Bullock (*g, ky*); Kenwood Dennard (*d*). 2/86.

***(*) **Punk Jazz** Big World Music BW 1001
> Pastorius; Jerry Gonzalez (*t, perc*); Alex Foster, Butch Thomas (*sax*); Michael Gerber (*p*);
> Delmar Brown (*ky*); Hiram Bullock (*g*); Kenwood Dennard (*d*).

(*) **Honestly Jazzpoint JP 1032
> Pastorius (*b* solo). 3/86.

***(*) **Live In Italy** Jazzpoint JP 1037
> Pastorius; Bireli Lagrene (*g*); Thomas Borocz (*d*). 3/86.

*** **Heavy 'N Jazz** Jazzpoint JP 1036
> Pastorius; Bireli Lagrene (*g*); Serge Bringolf (*d*). 12/86.

*** **Jazz Street** Timeless SJP 258
> Pastorius; Brian Melvin (*d, perc, d prog*); Rick Smith (*sax, d prog*); Jan Davis (*p, syn*); Paul
> Mousavizadeh (*g*); Keith Jones (*b*); Bill Keaney (*perc, syn*). 10 & 11/86.

A recent biography of the tragic Pastorius does little more than compound the mystery of this vastly
talented musician. It takes something extraordinary to get the public to part with hard-won cash for
somewhat over an hour of solo bass guitar playing. There is absolutely no doubt that Pastorius was a
remarkable player, but (to use Max Roach's valid distinction) how good a *musician* was he? The untitled
improvisations on *Honestly* frequently seem no more than a Sears catalogue of exotic harmonics and
effects, put together with diminishing logic and questionable taste. Needless to say, the Italian crowd
cheer it to the echo, though they don't respond at all to an early quote from 'My Favorite Things'; but
they don't rise to 'America The Beautiful' or the riff from 'Purple Haze' either, so what does that suggest
about their musical expectations?

Put Pastorius in a group context, however, and he is transformed. The Epic CD sees him working on an
appropriately epic scale and demonstrating with the tiniest gestures how completely in command he
was, not just of his own instrument but of an entire musical conception. But for oddities like the vocal
contribution of soulmen Sam and Dave, which doesn't really work, and an understandable desire to
show off as many different facets of his musical personality as possible, this might stand as Pastorius's
best memorial. Unfortunately, something about it doesn't quite add up. For his enthusiasts, such considerations never seem to have computed. Before his sanctification as the Hendrix of the bass guitar
(followed by near-canonization when he was killed in 1987), he had lent his considerable lyricism and
power to Weather Report and to the ever more self-consciously jazzy Joni Mitchell; he is also increasingly recognized and covered as a composer. The quartet with Metheny and Paul Bley is pretty much
how you'd expect it to sound at that vintage. Metheny's playing is articulate but not profound, and a
great pianist (even on an electric instrument) is lost in a sound-mix that resonates in all the wrong places.

With a larger group, *Punk Jazz* is more impressive. Pastorius's wish to be considered a jazz man (albeit a
punk jazz man) prompts an athletic, snappy 'Donna Lee', dedicated by Charlie Parker to the only
substantial woman bassist of the bebop era (and by all accounts a very courageous one). The remainder
of the set is good, hot-sauce electric jazz, surprisingly conventional when set alongside the 'punk'
aesthetic of Zorn, Lindsay, Marclay and company.

PDB is considerably more subtle and tasteful than the ingredients might lead you to expect. Pastorius's
lines sing and throb without any serious aspiration to lead-guitar status, preferring to explore the
curious hammered-on steel drum effects that have always peppered his solos. Bullock in turn plays with
great restraint and considerable jazz finesse. Only Kenwood Dennard tends to mix it, blatting out coarse
rock figures at inopportune moments. They do 'Dolphin Dance', but they also do 'Ode To Billy Joe',
and who's to say it's any less viable? The sound is good, though Dennard might have been eased back in
the mix a smidgeon. Make that a *big* smidgeon.

Live In Italy is almost the guitarist's album, as is *Heavy 'N Jazz* on the same label. In contrast to Metheny's Wes Montgomery fixation, Lagrene is in thrall to his countryman, Django Reinhardt. His opening improvisaton more or less focuses the mind on what he's doing thereafter, to the virtual exclusion of a slightly subdued and acoustically recessed Pastorius. They do creditable versions of 'Satin Doll', Joe Zawinul's Weather Report theme 'Black Market' and Bob Marley's pop-reggae 'I Shot The Sheriff', which underlines Pastorius's childhood closeness to Caribbean music of all sorts.

Holiday For Pans is an oddity, but a rather marvellous one. The imaginative use of steel drums is a throw-back to the bassist's Florida upbringing. The set opens with a fragment of Alan Hovhaness's symphony, *Mysterious Mountain*, and develops rapidly into mid-period Weather Report sound-alike on 'Elegant People', soft calypso-reggae on 'Good Morning Annya' and from there into any number of stylistic sidetracks. Though idiosyncratic in the extreme, it's by far the most imaginative project Pastorius ever undertook.

Honestly is very much more for specialized tastes, but the group albums should be sampled before writing Pastorius off as just another histrionic showman. A sincere and troubled artist, he was prey to alcoholism and bouts of clinical depression towards the end of his life. His death has been rewritten many times to imply a form of martyrdom; drunk and disordered, he was beaten by a club manager who had several times banned Pastorius from his premises, and died of his injuries several days later.

Pat Brothers GROUP

***(*) **The Pat Brothers** Moers Music 02052
 Wolfgang Puschnig (*as, f, ky*); Wolfgang Mitterer (*elec*); Wolfgang Reisinger (*d*); Linda
 Sharrock (*v*). 3/86.
A great one-shot record, though there is more of this sort of thing under Puschnig's entry. He scatters thin-toned, squealing alto and flute lines over Reisinger's mixture of backbeats and looser time, but the key man in the group is Mitterer, who uses electronics and samples in an ingenious, non-stop cut-up of ideas that pinball around the sound-mix until everything seems to be spinning; yet it's a very melodic, songful, almost tender record at times. Linda Sharrock's cool, sung-spoken words only occasionally veer off into the gymnastics she once essayed with former partner Sonny, and the larger impression is of a band that combines songs, funky immediacy and improvisational flair with a far higher success rate than anything the M-Base collective have so far come up with.

Big John Patton (born 1935) ORGAN

*** **Boogaloo** Blue Note CDP 831878-2
 Patton; Vincent McEwan (*t*); Harold Alexander (*ts, f*); George Edward Brown (*d*); Pablo
 Landrum (*perc*). 8/68.
*** **Understanding** Blue Note CDP 831223-2
 Patton; Harold Alexander (*ts, f*); Hugh Walker (*d*). 10/68.
*** **The Organization! The Best Of Big John Patton** Blue Note 830728-2
 Patton; Blue Mitchell, Tommy Turrentine (*t*); George Braith (*ss, stritch*); Harold Alexander,
 Marvin Cabell (*ts, f*); Fred Jackson, Harold Vick (*ts*); Richard Williams (*bs*); Bobby Hutcherson
 (*vib*); James Blood Ulmer, Grant Green (*g*); Ben Dixon, Hugh Walker, Larry Hancock, Otis
 Finch (*d*); Pablo Landrum (*perc*). 63–70.
*** **Blue Planet Man** Paddlewheel K ICJ 168
 Patton; Bill Saxton (*ss, ts*); John Zorn (*as*); Pete Chavez (*ts*); Ed Cherry (*g*); Eddie Gladden (*d*);
 Lawrence Killian (*perc*); Rorie Nichols (*v*). 4/93.
Patton has had a patchy time of it so far as reissues are concerned. Some albums have been intermittently available, but this seems to be the roll-call for the moment. He was one of the most entertaining of the players who followed in Jimmy Smith's footsteps, and a pile of Blue Note albums became his principal legacy. *Boogaloo* is a previously unreleased date; *Understanding* was the last of his sessions for the label. Coming at the far end of his tenure, they catch him on the cusp of greater things which never materialized, either commercially or aesthetically. The febrile 4/4 beat and ominous pedal lines that distinguished the best Hammond jazz offered a cycle of diminishing returns that Patton seemed stuck with. There are hints of wider ambition on *Understanding*, with Alexander's raw, wriggling tenor making the best of bringing the avant-garde down home, but a listen to Patton's dead-end improvisation on his own 'Congo Chant' suggests that he didn't know how to make it work, and he sounds a lot happier with 'Chittlins Con Carne'. *Boogaloo* is more in his usual bag: Alexander does some interesting things, but McEwan isn't a lot of help.

Inevitably, perhaps, the compilation is certainly the one to get, collecting tracks off nine different sessions – although, at nearly 80 minutes, it's probably too much of a good thing. 'Silver Meter', the archetypal boogaloo beat, still sounds terrific, and the funky treatment of Hank Mobley's 'The Turnaround' doesn't miss. Patton has enjoyed a revival of his old appeal in the 1980s and '90s, and John Zorn's enthusiastic patronage helped get *Blue Planet Man* realized as a sort of comeback. A set of favourites is benignly despatched by the old man with help from a few old friends and Zorn himself; not bad.

Bruce Paulson TROMBONE

*** **Minnesota** Sea Breeze S B-3017
> Paulson; Bob Sheppard (*ss, ts*); Bill Cunliffe (*p*); Tom Warrington (*b*); Joe LaBarbera (*d*). 3–4/ 93.

The title is a reference to Paulson's home-town, but the music is spawned from the Los Angeles session scene, which remains a potent if unrecognized part of the jazz lineage, 40 years after 'West Coast Jazz' made its mark. The music strikes that rare balance of virtuosity and modesty which has hallmarked this kind of jazz: all five men have tremendous chops, but their penchant is always to keep something in reserve. Paulson, who spent 20 years in the Tonight Show band but who makes his leadership debut here, takes an authoritative role, even if he makes only a middling impression as a soloist; Sheppard is the classic West Coast tenor, agile and forceful but unwilling to take even a step too far; the rhythm section are never less than warmed up. There are some pleasing originals, especially Cunliffe's title-tune, as well as genial takes on 'Stablemates' and 'I Hear A Rhpasody', but it's the sense of camaraderie that makes the disc very enjoyable without really lifting it into the first division. As usual with Sea Breeze, studio sound is exemplary.

La Pause Del Silenzio VOCAL GROUP

*** **Freedom Jazz Dance** Soul Note 121247
> Lucia Pinetti, Michela Martelli, Paola Lorenzi, Gabriella Rolandi, Laura Conti (*v*); Giorgio Gaslini (*p*); Roberto Bonati (*b*); Giampiero Prina (*d*). 3 & 4/92.

Forget the Swingles and Manhattan Transfer. This is a jazz vocal group with imagination and, what's more, with jazz. Giorgio Gaslini directs with his usual precision and imagination, arranging the title-tune as if the voices were horns, peeling off one at a time to solo. He does the same on Bessie Smith's 'Hard Time Blues' and Sy Oliver's 'Opus One', but on each occasion adds a dark, brooding introduction, reminiscent of Monk. Elsewhere, it's Bonati's full-voiced bass that provides both counterpoint and shading to the female voices.

Not unexpectedly, given Gaslini's own eclectic repertoire, there is a diversity of material. The Lennon/McCartney song, 'Here, There, And Everywhere', is systematically deconstructed, as is Dave Brubeck's 'In Your Own Sweet Way'. There are two pieces by Gino Paoli, 'Dormi' and 'Sassi'; jazz players would do well to look at them closely. There's a fine version of Horace Silver's 'Peace' and of 'Mean To Me'. Interestingly, given the harmonic bias of the set, there's also a group of tunes associated with John Coltrane: 'Softly As In A Morning Sunrise', 'Nature Boy', and his own 'Spiritual'.

This is fine stuff, far in advance of the average vocal-jazz set. Very strongly recommended.

Mario Pavone DOUBLE BASS

*** **Toulon Days** New World 80420
> Pavone; Steve Davis (*tb*); Thomas Chapin (*as, f*); Marty Ehrlich (*cl, f*); Joshua Redman (*ts*); Hotep Idris Galatea (*p*); Steve Johns (*d*). 11/91.
***(*) **Song For (Septet)** New World 80452
> Pavone; Peter McEachern (*tb*); Thomas Chapin (*as, f*); Marty Ehrlich (*as, cl, bcl*); Peter Madsen (*p*); Bill Ware (*vib*); Steve Johns (*d*). 3/93.

Two strong statements from a very able player with great presence and an admirable grasp of harmonics. Pavone's work with Thomas Chapin has been much admired and the saxophonist returns the favour admirably, partnered by the seemingly omnicompetent Ehrlich. The inclusion of Josh Redman on the earlier of the pair guaranteed it a sympathetic hearing, but it is a mistake to judge these solely on the strength of the band and it is on *Song For* that Pavone begins to emerge as a distinctive stylist on his own account. His complex, singing style is reflected in the decision to give prominence to trombone in the ensembles and solos; McEachern is a less fluent but a much more engaging player, and he tucks in tight behind his boss.

Comparisons with Mingus are obviously both premature and risky, but there are moments during 'George On Avenue A' and 'Song For M' when they spring to mind unbidden. Both records are beautifully recorded, giving the leader and partner Johns due prominence but affording the horns lots of breadth as well. There will be more from the same source, but it might be as well to jump the crowd and get involved now.

Cecil Payne (born 1922) BARITONE SAXOPHONE, FLUTE

*** **Patterns Of Jazz** Savoy SV 0135
> Payne; Kenny Dorham (*t*); Duke Jordan (*p*); Tommy Potter (*b*); Arthur Taylor (*d*). 5/56.
*** **Stop And Listen To . . .** Fresh Sound FSR CD 193
> Payne; Clark Terry (*t*); Bennie Green (*tb*); Duke Jordan (*p*); Ron Carter (*b*); Charli Persip (*d*). 61, 3/62.
*** **Casbah** Stash CD 572
> Payne; Richard Wyands (*p*); Joe Carter (*g*); Stafford James (*b*). 2/85.

Payne cut his teeth as a soloist with Dizzy Gillespie's late-1940s Cuban-bop big band. Along with the lighter-sounding Leo Parker (*q.v.*), he did much to adapt the hefty baritone to the rapid transitions and tonal extremities of bebop. Charlie Parker was his main influence, but in 1956, with Parker gone, he was beginning a fruitful association with pianist Randy Weston, who contributes two of the most interesting compositions on *Patterns Of Jazz*. Payne has not recorded prolifically under his own name, and this is a welcome and overdue reissue.

Weston's 'Chessman's Delight' is a dark, minor theme geared to Payne's lower register. As on the preceding ballad, 'How Deep Is The Ocean?', the solo is stately and fluid, with no sign of Leo Parker's rather slack embouchure. Dorham lifts the second Weston composition considerably; 'Saucer Eyes' has an engaging two-part melody-line, alternating a soft, four-note glide with a rhythmic bounce; and once again Payne is meditative rather than forceful in his solo. At this point at least, his own writing isn't up to Weston's scratch. 'Arnetta', dedicated to his mother, is an attractive, rhythmic theme, but both 'Bringing Up Father' and the collaborative 'Man Of Moods', co-written with the excellent Jordan, are rather derivative. Just to acknowledge the source of the derivation, the set ends on a rousing 'Groovin' High', from Dizzy Gillespie's book.

Compared to Serge Chaloff, Gerry Mulligan and the affectionately remembered Leo Parker, Payne is still known to the record-buying public only as a useful sideman. *Patterns Of Jazz* suggests a more substantial, albeit transitional, figure in the development of bebop. *Stop And Listen To . . .* does little more than confirm his authority and demonstrate how comfortably he could function in company as demanding as this. Both are New York City sessions, recorded at a time when Payne seemed to be bent on proving that Charlie Parker's music *could* be played convincingly on the big horn. You want him to be right, but there are moments when it all falls apart rather badly. The Kenny Drew material on the 1962 date is more his speed, but of course it lacks that whirling intensity one gets from Parker.

Payne was still playing comfortably, though not with any noticeable intensity, in the 1980s. The Stash record features a drummerless group, and the leader very much dictates the pace of things. Joe Henderson's 'Carney' and his own 'Bosco' are the key tracks.

Nicholas Payton TRUMPET

*** **From This Moment** Verve 527 073
> Payton; Mark Whitfield (*g*); Mulgrew Miller (*p*); Monte Croft (*vib*); Reginald Veal (*b*); Lewis Nash (*d*). 95.
*** **Gumbo Nouveau** Verve 531 199
> Payton; Jesse Davis (*as*); Tim Warfield (*ts*); Anthony Wonsey (*p*); Reuben Rogers (*b*); Adonis Rose (*d*). 96.

Produced by Delfeayo Marsalis, this young Polygram discovery couldn't help but sound a *little* like Wynton. He's a traditionalist who, in addition to developing his own book of songs, has shown a deep interest in classic jazz, as witness the material on *Gumbo Nouveau*. Interestingly, by the time he gets into the swing (and swing is the word) of both these crisp, uncomplicated sets, one has forgotten all about the Marsalis connection and begun to concentrate on the young man's bright, storytelling voice. He makes no demands on himself that he can't comfortably fulfil, and his best solos occupy that middle register which so many younger players seem to think is either dull or sissy. The material is all carefully thought out and, having seen service with Elvin Jones, he has a brilliant grasp of how to pace a set, one of Elvin's less well-publicized gifts. The band are pretty familiar now and go about their business with precision and enthusiasm. Needless to say, the recordings are absolutely up to standard.

Gary Peacock (born 1935) DOUBLE BASS

**** **Tales Of Another** ECM 1101
    Peacock; Keith Jarrett (*p*); Jack DeJohnette (*d*). 2/77.
(*) **Shift In The Wind ECM 1165
    Peacock; Art Lande (*p*); Eliot Zigmund (*d*). 2/80.
*** **Voice From The Past / Paradigm** ECM 1210
    Peacock; Tomasz Stańko (*t*); Jan Garbarek (*ts, ss*); Jack DeJohnette (*d*). 8/81.
(*) **Guamba ECM 1352
    Peacock; Palle Mikkelborg (*t, flhn*); Jan Garbarek (*ts, ss*); Peter Erskine (*d, d syn*). 3/87.
*** **Oracle** ECM 1490
    Peacock; Ralph Towner (*g*). 5/93.
Set any of Gary Peacock's solos alongside those of slightly younger players like Glen Moore and it's immediately obvious how much more rooted Peacock is in the jazz tradition. Pouncing on a minor programmatic coincidence, it may be instructive to compare Peacock's 'Pleiades Skirt' with Moore's 'Belt Of Asteroids' and trace his careful negotiation of a balance between formal progression and abstraction.

Peacock's career has rarely hewn to the centre. After a brief apprenticeship in Europe, he moved to the West Coast and worked with the likes of Bud Shank and Shorty Rogers, before absorbing himself in the challenging formal structures of Don Ellis, Bill Evans, Jimmy Giuffre and George Russell, maintaining the while a powerful involvement in avant-garde transformations of early jazz, notably with Albert Ayler, Roland Kirk and Steve Lacy. His playing style combines elements of Jimmy Blanton's and Wilbur Ware's sonority with something of Oscar Pettiford's rapid disposition of wide intervals.

Peacock's own records have been rather mixed and can't be taken as representative of his abilities. The earliest, *Tales Of Another*, is performed by the band that was to become known as Keith Jarrett's 'Standards Trio' six years later. In the late 1960s, Peacock had turned his back on the music scene and gone to Japan to study macrobiotics. However uncertain he may have been about a return to bass playing (and he may have been persuaded by ECM chief, Manfred Eicher), there is a wonderful coherence to his solo work on 'Vignette' (with piano rippling underneath) and on 'Trilogy I/II/III' that quashes any suggestion that this is another Jarrett album, politely or generously reattributed; it is, in fact, his last appearance but one as a sideman. Even so, the pianist is clearly at home with Peacock's music and there is a level of intuition at work which became the basis of their later standards performances, but it is unmistakably Peacock's record.

Sadly, he never sounds quite so poised or concentrated again. *Shift In The Wind* is merely enigmatic, and there seems to be little positive understanding (beyond, that is, an agreement not to tread on one another's toes) among the trio. The later quartets further obscure Peacock's playing, and though *Voice From The Past* is particularly good, it is chiefly memorable for the atmospheric interplay of Garbarek and Stańko. Mikkelborg's hyperactive style dissipates much of the concentration of Peacock's writing on *Guamba*, and Erskine seems a poor substitute for DeJohnette's brilliant out-of-tempo colorations.

The comparison with Moore rises again with *Oracle*, which some listeners may find reminiscent of Towner's *Trios/Solos* project with his fellow Oregonian. And the contrast holds again. Peacock is driven and propulsive where Moore is happy to dwell on particular areas of sound. This isn't a criticism but a description. Where one might criticize *Oracle* is in its rather haphazard alternation of moods and its rather indistinct programme. There is a floaty, New Age quality to some parts, and then the duo throws in something almost violent as if to offer a sufficient contrast. This isn't an effective way to make records, and the final verdict has to be that, good as *Oracle* is in parts, it doesn't cohere.

Duke Pearson (1932–80) PIANO

*** **Sweet Honey Bee** Blue Note CDP789792
    Pearson; Freddie Hubbard (*t*); James Spaulding (*as, f*); Joe Henderson (*ts*); Ron Carter (*b*); Mickey Roker (*d*). 12/66.
*** **The Right Touch** Blue Note CDP 828269
    Pearson; Freddie Hubbard (*t*); Garnett Brown (*tb*); James Spaulding (*as*); Jerry Dodgion (*as, f*); Stanley Turrentine (*ts*); Gene Taylor (*b*); Grady Tate (*d*). 9/67.
Pearson seemed for a time to be one of those artists consigned to the permanent limbo of Blue Note 'theme' compilations. His natural life was uncomfortably fated as well. As a young man he was thwarted

in his ambitions to become a trumpeter by dental problems. His activities in the 1970s were curtailed by multiple sclerosis. What remains, though, is bright and fizzingly aware. The addition of Henderson on the first of these records probably ought to lift it a notch, but *The Right Touch* is the place to observe Pearson the technician, a clever pianist relatively free of Bud Powell mannerisms, who was also a superb arranger, with an affection for the flute in large or small ensembles. Time to pull him back out of obscurity.

Wayne Peet ORGAN

**** Fully Engulfed Nine Winds NWCD 0165
Peet; G. E. Stinson (*g*); Lance Lee (*d, v*). 3/94.
Peet's previous listing (in our first edition) was for an acoustic solo piano record, and there could hardly be a greater contrast with this release. It's a power trio in the hallowed tradition of Lifetime. Peet's organ is matched blow for blow with Stinson's guitar, with Lee playing the Tony Williams part, and it's as exhilarating as any record cut in the wake of that original typhoon. Where other efforts at reviving this feel have floundered in the face of modern recording's cleanliness, Peet's group are mired in fuzz, feedback and a bottom-heavy studio mix that restores this ultimate kind of jazz-rock to its proper purgatory. Peet's only concession to modern times is to use a synth bass as well as the organ pedals, which adds some useful bandwidth in the lower frequencies; otherwise it's a torrid show of sound, washes of chords flowing over each other, Stinson piling licks over the top while Lee thrashes out a relatively straightforward beat. In some ways, Lee's part is critical: where someone like Dennis Chambers would be filling up every available space with polyrhythms, Lee's simplicity is marvellously effective. It's for sure that John McLaughlin's Free Spirits band have come nowhere near this in building on the feel and excitement of Lifetime's old music, and it's fitting that Peet both dedicates the album to Larry Young and delivers a fine, sinister cover of Young's 'Visions' in the tracklist.

Harry Pepl GUITAR, GUITAR SYNTHESIZER, PIANO

***(*) Cracked Mirrors ECM 1356
Pepl; Herbert Joos (*flhn*); Jon Christensen (*d*). 2/87.
Pepl's characteristically melancholy style is tempered by a firmness and concision that make him an ideal group-player. His is one of the more impressive contributions on Adelhard Roidinger's *Schattseite* (ECM 1221 LP) and he has also worked with bandoneon player, Dino Saluzzi, another ECM artist. His own recordings of the late 1980s tend to overplay a rather limited imagination, and Pepl resorts over and over again to a restricted code of octave runs, out-of-tempo scales with electronically divided pitches, and clusters of grace notes that obscure interesting melodic ideas. But for the presence of the subtly swinging Christensen, the very fine *Cracked Mirrors* might almost be one of Austrian flugelhorn player Franz Koglmann's meditative essays on the jazz literature. The interplay between Pepl and Joos recalls some of Koglmann's work with guitarist Burkhard Stangl. Even without conscious reference to standards, Pepl's work is closer to orthodox jazz but draws on a wide stylistic spectrum as if to suggest that post-Schoenbergian music really is a cracked mirror, giving back a creatively splintered image of harmony.

Ken Peplowski CLARINET, ALTO SAXOPHONE, TENOR SAXOPHONE

**(*) Double Exposure Concord CCD 4344
Peplowski; Ed Bickert (*g*); John Bunch (*p*); John Goldsby (*b*); Terry Clarke (*d*). 12/87.
*** Sunny Side Concord CCD 4376
Peplowski; Howard Alden (*g*); David Frishberg (*p*); John Goldsby (*b*); Terry Clarke (*d*). 1/89.
*** Mr Gentle And Mr Cool Concord CCD 4419
Peplowski; Scott Hamilton (*ts*); Bucky Pizzarelli (*g*); Hank Jones (*p*); Frank Tate (*b*); Alan Dawson (*d*). 2/90.
*** Illuminations Concord CCD 4449
Peplowski; Howard Alden (*g*); Junior Mance (*p*); Dennis Irwin (*b*); Alan Dawson (*d*). 90.
*** The Natural Touch Concord CCD 4517
Peplowski; Frank Vignola (*g*); Ben Aronov (*p*); Murray Wall (*b*); Tom Melito (*d*). 1/92.
There was once a *Punch* cartoon of a balding pipe-and-slippers man drowsing in front of the fire and telly while his wife and a friend look on: 'Oh, yes, Ken *does* have another side, but it's exactly the same as this one.' Pure coincidence, of course, but there is something slightly one-dimensional about Peplowski's

sweetly elegant saxophone and clarinet playing. Certainly in comparison with Scott Hamilton, doyen of the young fogey swing revivalist boom, he is a very limited technician, who relies on rather meretricious cosmetic effects.

Mr Gentle And Mr Cool emphasizes just how much he could do with a little of Dr Jekyll's elixir. The two sextet tracks with Hamilton lift the album two notches. There's nothing comparable to lift *Illuminations* (from later the same year), though Junior Mance's piano playing impresses, as does the impeccable Hank Jones. A clarinettist first, with a method half-way between Benny Goodman and the great swing saxophonists, he seems locked on to a single dynamic wavelength.

The two earlier albums show slight leanings towards the harmonic upsets of bop, but Peplowski's solos are the musical equivalent of what used, disgustingly, to be called heavy petting, ending just when he seems to be getting somewhere. That's nowhere truer than on *Natural Touch*, which is even more reticent and uncommunicative than usual. There's a ready market for material like this, but it's by no means up to Concord's usual high scratch.

***(*) Concord Duo Series: Volume 3 Concord CCD 4556
Peplowski; Howard Alden (*g*). 12/92.
After the solos, the duos, and presumably still to come the trios as well. This is a heaven-made partnership, of course, friendly and fruitful, and the quality of playing is just about out of this world. Like heaven, though, there is a risk of it becoming just a little boring over the long haul, and by the end one is almost longing for Concord to start the trios here and now and wheel in another star guest.

*** Steppin' With Peps Concord CCD 4569
Peplowski; Randy Sandke, Joe Wilder (*t*); Howard Alden, Bucky Pizzarelli (*g*); Ben Aronov (*p*); John Goldsby (*b*); Alan Dawson (*d*). 3/93.
By this stage in his career, it's clear that what turns Peplowski on is to be challenged by new partners and new contexts. One can hear that happening only intermittently here, with Sandke throwing down the gauntlet a few times. It's an '& friends' date and the rivalry has an easy, joshing feel that doesn't really lend itself to fiery playing.

*** Live At Ambassador Auditorium Concord CCD 4610
Peplowski; Harry 'Sweets' Edison (*t*); Howard Alden (*g*); Ben Aronov (*p*); Murray Wall (*b*); Tom Melito (*d*). 2/94.
A lively, beautifully paced concert from the Ambassador in Pasadena, California. The ambassadorial figure from Columbus, Ohio, brings his trumpet on at just the right moment – like comedy, diplomacy is all about timing – and transforms what threatens to become a run-of-the-mill Peplowski Quintet workout into a rather special occasion. The old chap only plays on 'With You', 'The Best Things In Life Are Free' and 'Exactly Like You', but these stand head and shoulders above the rest.

The sound isn't bad for a hall believed to have acoustic problems, and the group is often more evenly distributed than on the studio discs.

Art Pepper (1925–82) ALTO AND TENOR SAXOPHONES, CLARINET

**(*) Surf Ride Savoy SV-0115
Pepper; Jack Montrose (*ts*); Russ Freeman, Hampton Hawes, Claude Williamson (*p*); Bob Whitlock, Joe Mondragon, Monty Budwig (*b*); Bobby White, Larry Bunker (*d*). 2/52–12/53.
*** The Late Show / A Night At The Surf Club Vol. 1 Xanadu 117
Pepper; Hampton Hawes (*p*); Joe Mondragon (*b*); Larry Bunker (*d, vib*). 2/52.
*** The Early Show / A Night At The Surf Club Vol. 2 Xanadu 108
As above. 2/52.
**(*) Two Altos Savoy SV-0161
Pepper; Jack Montrose (*ts*); Claude Williamson, Hampton Hawes, Russ Freeman (*p*); Bobby Whitlock, Joe Mondragon, Monty Budwig (*b*); Larry Bunker, Bobby White (*d*). 3/52–8/54.
*** The Art Pepper Quartet Original Jazz Classics OJC 816
Pepper; Russ Freeman (*p*); Ben Tucker (*b*); Gary Frommer (*d*). 8/56.
Pepper's remains one of the most immediately identifiable alto sax styles in post-war jazz. If he was a Parker disciple, like every other modern saxophonist in the 1940s and '50s, he tempered Bird's slashing attack with a pointed elegance that recalled something of Benny Carter and Willie Smith. He was a passionate musician, having little of the studious intensity of a Lee Konitz, and his tone – which could come out as pinched and jittery as well as softly melodious – suggested something of the duplicitous, cursed romanticism which seems to lie at the heart of his music. After a brief period with Californian big bands, he began recording as a leader and sideman on the Hollywood studio scene of the early 1950s. *Surf Ride* includes his earliest tracks as a leader: these clipped, rather brittle records find him a

little wound up, and the six tracks with Jack Montrose in the front line – who sounds untypically hesitant on a couple of his solos – are standard West Coast fare. There are some leftovers on *Two Altos*, which is otherwise shared with some tracks led by Sonny Red, and aside from a characteristically engaging trip through 'Everything Happens To Me' (a favourite throughout Pepper's career) this is slight stuff. A better glimpse of the early Pepper is offered by the club recordings on the two Xanadu discs. Hawes and Pepper hit it off with superb élan, and their various attempts at standards and the blues suggest a rare balance between professional expertise and quizzical, exploratory music-making. The problem lies with the recording, which was made by a fan and does the pianist in particular a disservice, his tone sounding frankly awful in places. It's a comment on the quality of the music that it nevertheless remains very listenable. The recent OJC release is drawn from a session for the Tampa label, with five alternative takes beefing up the playing time. This is Pepper entering his greatest period, and the quality of his thinking and playing is already nearing that of the remarkable Contemporary sessions, though the rather brief tracks clip the wings of some of the solos.

*** **The Artistry Of Pepper** Pacific Jazz B21Y-797194-2
    Pepper; Don Fagerquist (*t*); Stu Williamson (*vtb*); Bill Perkins, Bill Holman (*ts*); Bud Shank (*bs*); Jimmy Rowles, Russ Freeman (*p*); Red Callender (*tba*); Monty Budwig, Ben Tucker (*b*); Mel Lewis, Shelly Manne (*d*). 12/56–8/57.

*** **The Return Of Art Pepper** Blue Note B21Y-746863-2
    Pepper; Jack Sheldon (*t*); Red Norvo (*vib*); Gerald Wiggins, Russ Freeman (*p*); Leroy Vinnegar, Ben Tucker (*b*); Shelly Manne, Joe Morello (*d*). 8/56–1/57.

**** **Modern Art** Blue Note B21Y-746848-2
    Pepper; Russ Freeman, Carl Perkins (*p*); Ben Tucker (*b*); Chick Flores (*d*). 12/56–4/57.

**** **The Art Of Pepper** Blue Note B21Y-746853-2
    As above, except omit Freeman. 4/57.

Pepper's sessions for Aladdin, collected on the three Blue Note albums, have been overshadowed by his records for Contemporary (below). *The Return Of Art Pepper* (the altoist had been in prison for narcotics offences, a problem that would plague his career) puts together a fair if patchy quintet session with Jack Sheldon – the two ballad features without Sheldon, 'You Go To My Head' and 'Patricia', are easily the best things – with a set originally led by Joe Morello, with Red Norvo in the front line. *Artistry* couples a pleasing quintet date with Bill Perkins with a nonet playing Shorty Rogers arrangements and featuring Pepper as principal soloist: rather stylized in the West Coast manner, but the altoist plays impeccably. The really valuable records, though, are the two quartet discs. *Modern Art* is a deceptively quiet and tempered session: the opening 'Blues In' is a seemingly hesitant, improvised blues which typifies the staunchless flow of Pepper's ideas, and the following 'Bewitched' and a quite exceptional reworking of 'Stompin' At The Savoy' are so full of ideas that Pepper seems transformed. Freeman responds with superbly insightful support. Yet the succeeding *Art Of Pepper* is even better, with bigger and more upfront sound and with Carl Perkins spinning along in accompaniment. 'Begin The Beguine' is both beguiling and forceful, the dizzying lines of 'Webb City' are an entirely convincing tribute to Bud Powell, and the melodies unravelled from 'Too Close For Comfort' and 'Long Ago And Far Away' – which Pepper returns to on the Contemporary sessions – show a lyrical invention which few players of the day could have matched.

***(*) **The Way It Was!** Original Jazz Classics OJC 389
    Pepper; Warne Marsh (*ts*); Ronnie Ball, Red Garland, Dolo Coker, Wynton Kelly (*p*); Ben Tucker, Paul Chambers, Jimmy Bond (*b*); Philly Joe Jones, Gary Frommer, Frank Butler, Jimmy Cobb (*d*). 11/56–11/60.

**** **Meets The Rhythm Section** Original Jazz Classics OJC 338
    Pepper; Red Garland (*p*); Paul Chambers (*b*); Philly Joe Jones (*d*). 1/57.

**** **Modern Jazz Classics** Original Jazz Classics OJC 341
    Pepper; Pete Candoli, Jack Sheldon, Al Porcino (*t*); Dick Nash (*tb*); Bob Enevoldsen (*vtb, ts*); Vince DeRosa (*frhn*); Herb Geller, Bud Shank (*as*); Charlie Kennedy (*ts, as*); Bill Perkins, Richie Kamuca (*ts*); Med Flory (*bs*); Russ Freeman (*p*); Joe Mondragon (*b*); Mel Lewis (*d*). 3–5/59.

***(*) **Gettin' Together** Original Jazz Classics OJC 169
    Pepper; Conte Candoli (*t*); Wynton Kelly (*p*); Paul Chambers (*b*); Jimmy Cobb (*d*). 2/60.

**** **Smack Up** Original Jazz Classics OJC 176
    Pepper; Jack Sheldon (*t*); Pete Jolly (*p*); Jimmy Bond (*b*); Frank Butler (*d*). 10/60.

**** **Intensity** Original Jazz Classics OJC 387
    Pepper; Dolo Coker (*p*); Jimmy Bond (*b*); Frank Butler (*d*). 11/60.

Pepper's records for Contemporary, all of which have been reissued in the OJC series, make up a superlative sequence. *The Way It Was!* remained unissued until the 1970s, but the first half of it – a session with Warne Marsh, which secures a brilliant interplay on 'Tickle Toe' and exposes all

Pepper's lyricism on 'What's New' – is as good as anything in the series (the other tracks are out-takes from the succeeding sessions). The playing of the quartet on *Meets The Rhythm Section* beggars belief when the circumstances are considered: Pepper wasn't even aware of the session till the morning of the date, hadn't played in two weeks, was going through difficult times with his narcotics problem and didn't know any of the material they played. Yet it emerges as a poetic, burning date, with all four men playing above themselves. *Modern Jazz Classics* is in some ways more prosaic, with Marty Paich's arrangements of Monk, Gillespie, Giuffre, Mulligan and more working from the by now over-familiar West Coast glibness, yet the sound of the ensemble is beautifully rich, Paich conjures new things out of 'Bernie's Tune' and 'Anthropology', and Pepper – who also brings out his clarinet and tenor – alternately glides through the charts and dances his way out of them. There isn't a great deal to choose between the three remaining sessions: *Smack Up* finds Pepper playing Ornette on 'Tears Inside' as well as a memorable version of Duane Tatro's haunting 'Maybe Next Year', and the appropriately titled *Intensity* is a wistful series of ballads and standards in which Pepper, a peculiarly astringent romantic, seems to brood on the words of the songs as well as their melodies and changes: 'Long Ago And Far Away', for instance, seems a perfect transliteration of the song's message. Throughout these records, the saxophonist's phrasing, with its carefully delivered hesitations and sudden flurries, and his tone, which sometimes resembles a long, crying ache, communicate matters of enormous emotional impact. They demand to be heard. Remastering of all of them is well up to the fine OJC standards.

(*) Art Pepper Quartet '64 In San Francisco Fresh Sound FSCD-1005
  Pepper; Frank Strazzeri (*p*); Hersh Hamel (*b*); Bill Goodwin (*d*). 5–6/64.
Devastated by his personal problems, Pepper didn't make another studio record (aside from a Buddy Rich session) until 1973. These tracks come from a 1964 TV appearance and another at a San Francisco club. Not long released from prison, his style had changed dramatically: hung up on Coltrane and a fear that his older style would be out of touch, he sounds in a bizarre transition from the former, lyrically confident Pepper to a new, darker, often incoherent style based round tonal investigations and timbral distortions as much as anything. It's a trait he would rationalize with his 'normal' self in the 1970s, but here he's finding his way. He's still musician enough to make it an intriguing document, too, with the first version of 'The Trip' and a long 'Sonnymoon For Two'. The sound is rough, not much better than an average bootleg, but Pepperphiles will want to hear it. There is also an interview track with presenter Ralph Gleason.

** **I'll Remember April** Storyville STCD 4130
  Pepper; Tommy Gumina (*polychord*); Fred Atwood (*b*); Jimmie Smith (*d*). 2/75.
***(*) **Living Legend** Original Jazz Classics OJC 408
  Pepper; Hampton Hawes (*p*); Charlie Haden (*b*); Shelly Manne (*d*). 8/75.
*** **The Trip** Original Jazz Classics OJC 410
  Pepper; George Cables (*p*); David Williams (*b*); Elvin Jones (*d*). 9/76.
(*) **A Night In Tunisia Storyville STCD 4146
  Pepper; Smith Dobson (*p*); Jim Nichols (*b*); Brad Bilhorn (*d*). 1/77.
(*) **No Limit Original Jazz Classics OJC 411
  Pepper; George Cables (*p*); Tony Dumas (*b*); Carl Burnett (*d*). 3/77.
*** **Tokyo Debut** Galaxy GCD-4201-2
  Pepper; Clare Fischer (*p*); Cal Tjader (*vib*); Bob Redfield (*g*); Rob Fisher (*b*); Peter Riso (*d*); Poncho Sanchez (*perc*). 5/77.
Pepper's re-emergence blossomed into the most remarkable comeback of its kind. He became a symbol of jazz triumph-over-adversity, and though in the end it didn't last very long, there was a stubborn, furious eloquence about his later playing that makes all his records worth hearing, even when he struggles to articulate a ballad or has to fight to get his up-tempo lines in shape. The earlier sessions, following the *Living Legend* set, continue his struggle to digest Coltrane and reconcile that influence with his honourable past achievements: on both *The Trip* and *No Limit* he gets there some of the time, and the former at least includes his haunting blues line, 'Red Car'. But *Living Legend* itself is the one to hear first. 'Lost Life' is one of his gentle-harrowing ballads, a self-portrait rigorously chewed out, and the whole session seems imbued with a mixture of nerves, relief and pent-up inspiration which the other players – an inspiring team – channel as best they can. The two Storyville discs chronicle a couple of live dates with local players in the rhythm sections. *I'll Remember April* is marred by a gymnasium sound and Gumina's odd-sounding polychord, but Pepper blows very hard throughout. *A Night In Tunisia* is better – Dobson is a useful player, and there is another strong version of 'Lost Life' – but the studio albums merit prior attention.

  Tokyo Debut documents Pepper's first tour of Japan, which started with the utmost trepidation and ended in triumph. The Cal Tjader group is the unlikely support, with Fischer playing an ugly-sounding electric piano; but Pepper, who was honoured by every audience throughout the trip, pours himself into the music. 'Cherokee' is chorus after chorus of ideas and, when Tjader joins in for three numbers, the altoist fits comfortably with the lite-bossa grooves.

***(*) **Thursday Night At The Village Vanguard** Original Jazz Classics OJC 694
    Pepper; George Cables (*p*); George Mraz (*b*); Elvin Jones (*d*). 7/77.
*** **Friday Night At The Village Vanguard** Original Jazz Classics OJC 695
    As above. 7/77.
*** **Saturday Night At The Village Vanguard** Original Jazz Classics OJC 696
    As above. 7/77.
*** **More For Les: At The Village Vanguard Vol. 4** Original Jazz Classics OJC 697
    As above. 7/77.
***(*) **The Complete Village Vanguard Sessions** Contemporary CCD-4417-2 9CD
    As above. 7/77.

Pepper's four nights at New York's Village Vanguard were filleted down to four single LPs (and, subsequently, CDs) in the past but, since our last edition, Contemporary have gone for broke and brought together every note of the engagement in a single nine-disc set. This provides more than five hours of extra music. The new material includes alternative versions of tunes played in other sets plus three entirely fresh pieces: a jangling 'Stella By Starlight', a notably impressive blues called 'Vanguard Max' and 'Live At The Vanguard'. Pepper specialists can compare the different versions of 'Goodbye', 'Blues For Heard' and 'For Freddie' at their leisure, but the main point of the set is the way it documents one of the major performers of the era with unflagging candour. Pepper was always a fascinating man to see and hear in concert – his sometimes obsessive talking with audiences gets full rein with some of the announcements here – and playing through these discs will remind all who saw him of his enduring struggle with his own demons, as well as the sometimes cruel beauty of his music-making. Besides him, there is the blue-chip rhythm section to listen to. The less committed will settle for the remaining single discs, of which the first is probably the single best. Excellent location recording.

*** **Live In Japan Vol. 1** Storyville STCD 4128
    Pepper; Milcho Leviev (*p*); Bob Magnusson (*b*); Carl Burnett (*d*). 3/78.
*** **Live In Japan Vol. 2** Storyville STCD 4129
    As above. 3/78.
*** **Art Pepper Today** Original Jazz Classics OJC 474
    Pepper; Stanley Cowell, Cecil McBee (*b*); Roy Haynes (*d*); Kenneth Nash (*perc*). 12/78.
*** **Landscape** Original Jazz Classics OJC 676
    Pepper; George Cables (*p*); Tony Dumas (*b*); Billy Higgins (*d*). 7/79.
***(*) **Straight Life** Original Jazz Classics OJC 475
    Pepper; Tommy Flanagan (*p*); Red Mitchell (*b*); Billy Higgins (*d*); Kenneth Nash (*perc*). 9/79.
**** **Winter Moon** Original Jazz Classics OJC 677
    Pepper; Stanley Cowell (*p*); Howard Roberts (*g*); Cecil McBee (*b*); Carl Burnett (*d*); strings. 9/80.
*** **One September Afternoon** Original Jazz Classics OJC 678
    As above, except omit strings. 9/80.
*** **Art 'N' Zoot** Pablo 2310-957-2
    Pepper; Zoot Sims (*ts*); Victor Feldman (*p*); Barney Kessel (*g*); Ray Brown, Charlie Haden (*b*); Billy Higgins (*d*). 9/81.
*** **Arthur's Blues** Original Jazz Classics OJC 680
    Pepper; George Cables (*p*); David Williams (*b*); Carl Burnett (*d*). 8/81.
*** **Goin' Home** Original Jazz Classics OJC 679
    Pepper; George Cables (*p*). 5/82.
*** **Tete-A-Tete** Original Jazz Classics OJC 843
    As above. 4-5/82.

The later records for Galaxy are in some ways all of a piece, and it's rather appropriate that the Fantasy group have chosen to issue a colossal boxed set of the whole output (see below). Pepper remained in fragile health, however robustly he played and carried himself, and the sense of time running out for him imparted an urgency to almost everything he played: ballads become racked with intensity, up-tempo tunes spill over with notes and cries. Studio and live dates are the same in that respect. Of these many late albums, the best should be in all general collections: *Straight Life*, with another fine quartet; *Landscape*, a sharp set by the band Pepper worked with most frequently in his last years; and above all the profoundly beautiful *Winter Moon*, a strings album which far surpasses the norm for this kind of record, Pepper uncorking one of his greatest solos against the rhapsodic sweep of Bill Holman's arrangement on 'Our Song'. The two Japanese live albums are also well worth seeking out.

    The meeting with Zoot Sims is an oddity, a UCLA concert in which Zoot had three features, Art one, and they jammed together on a pair of tunes. Pepper's 'Over The Rainbow' is one of his typical slowburns on a ballad, while Zoot breezes affably through 'In The Middle Of A Kiss' and digs in surprisingly hard on 'The Girl From Ipanema'; but the main point of interest is hearing them together on the old bebop jam, 'Wee'. It's good. The sound is much better than it was on an unauthorized European release.

Arthur's Blues is a distillation of nearly an hour of previously unreleased music, taken from the complete Galaxy set listed below. Like so much later Pepper, it's full of interesting music while falling short of essential, although the gripping title-track is a prototypical blues workout by a man desperate to play his soul out in the time he had left. The two duo sessions with Cables, his favourite accompanist, are neither more nor less 'naked' than the quartet music, since Pepper never spared himself or his listeners from his versions of the truth. 'Over The Rainbow' (*Tete-A-Tete*) and 'Don't Let The Sun Catch You Cryin'' (*Goin' Home*) are among his final ballads, and set down the closing thoughts of an unbowed spirit.

**** The Complete Galaxy Recordings Galaxy 1016 16CD
    As above OJC/Galaxy albums. 77–82.
A vast and surprisingly playable archive – most such monuments seldom come off the shelf, but Pepper's resilience, febrile invention and consistency of commitment make this music endure far beyond expectations. There are dead spots, inevitably, and it's a costly undertaking, but there is also a lot of music unavailable elsewhere, including many alternative takes, out-takes and Japanese-only issues. Sumptuous packaging and a fine essay by Gary Giddins are included.

Jim Pepper (died 1992) TENOR SAXOPHONE

*** Dakota Sound Enja 5043
    Pepper; Kirk Lightsey (*p*); Santi Wilson Debriano (*b*); John Betsch (*d*). 1/87.
***(*) The Path Enja 5087
    As above, except add Stanton Davis (*t*); Arto Tuncboyaci (*perc*); Caren Knight (*v*). 3/88.
*** West End Avenue Nabel 4633
    Pepper; Christoph Spendel (*p*); Ron McClure (*b*); Reuben Hoch (*d*). 2/89.
*** Camargue Pan PMC 1106
    Pepper; Claudine François (*p*); Ed Schuller (*b*); John Betsch (*d*); Kendra Shank (*v*). 5/89.
*** Remembrance Live Tutu 888152
    Pepper; Bill Bickford (*g*); Ed Schuller (*b*); John Betsch (*d*). 5/90.
Pepper is best known as the composer of 'Witchi-Tai-To', a jauntily haunting theme reflecting his Native-American roots and turned into an album and concert hit by Oregon. A melodic player with a strong roots feel and a resistance to abstraction, Pepper performs best against a highly lyrical background with a firm pulse. Lightsey seems an ideal accompanist and *The Path* (which includes 'Witchi-Tai-To' as well as the pianist's 'Habiba') is his most accomplished album. The later pair, on smaller labels, lack the emotional urgency that Pepper frequently brings to his work, audible throughout the Münster set on *Remembrance* with his band, Eagle Wing. Pepper's untimely death was a great loss to the music.

Perfect Houseplants GROUP

*** Perfect Houseplants Ah Um 014 ·
    Mark Lockheart (*sax*); Huw Warren (*p, acc, clo*); Dudley Phillips (*b*); Martin France (*d*). 93.
*** Clec EFZ 016
    As above. 94.
This imaginative British group has never quite managed to dig itself out of the hole that yawns for intelligent 'name' bands (one thinks of Roadside Picnic and Itchy Fingers). They certainly deserve to. All four players are gifted craftsmen and, if Lockheart and Warren are the main writers, the balance of responsibilities seems very evenly shared around. In common with many of their contemporaries, they have introduced a folk element – sometimes almost subliminally – into a jazz context. Because it *is* almost subliminal, it works very well indeed.

Bill Perkins (born 1924) TENOR AND BARITONE SAXOPHONE, FLUTE, BASS CLARINET

*** Quietly There Original Jazz Classics OJC 1776
    Perkins; Victor Feldman (*p, org, vib*); John Pisano (*g*); Red Mitchell (*b*); Larry Bunker (*d*). 11/66.

This was one of only two sessions that Perkins, a veteran West Coast reedman, made under his own name in the 1960s. Gentle, pretty, but closely thought-out, this is easy-listening jazz as it could be at its best. The nine tracks are all Johnny Mandel compositions, and Perkins devises a different setting for each one, some decidedly odd: baritone sax and organ for 'Groover Wailin'', for instance, which mainly proves that Feldman was no good as an organist. But Perkins's grey, marshy tone makes a charming matter of 'The Shining Sea', the flute-and-vibes treatment of 'A Time For Love' is ideal, and tempos and textures are subtly varied throughout. A welcome reissue of a little-known record.

*** **The Front Line** Storyville STCD 4166
>Perkins; Gordon Goodwin (ss, ts); Pepper Adams (bs); Lou Levy (p); Bob Magnusson (b); Carl Burnett (d). 11/78.

Perkins plays tenor, flute and baritone here, with another baritone expert in attendance in the shape of Adams. The latter's memorable 'Civilization And Its Discontents' gets a stringent reading here, but space is otherwise evenly split between the horns, and one could use more of Perkins's own playing.

***(*) **Remembrance Of Dino's** Interplay IPCD-8606-2
>Perkins; Alan Broadbent (p); Putter Smith, Gene Cherico (b); John Tirabasso (d). 86.

*** **The Right Chemistry** Jazz Mark 108
>Perkins; James Clay (ts); Frank Strazzeri (p); Joel Di Bartolo (b); Billy Mintz (d). 8/87.

*** **I Wished On The Moon** Candid CCD79524
>Perkins; Metropole Orchestra. 11/89–4/90.

***(*) **Warm Moods** Fresh Sound FSR-CD 191
>Perkins; Frank Strazzeri (p). 11/91.

After long periods away from the studios, Perkins is almost ubiquitous again. The album recorded over various sessions at the Pasadena club, Dino's, is drawn from Perkins's own tapes of many nights' playing, and he has put together a relaxed but very swinging collection: Cedar Walton's 'Bolivia' is taken at a fantastic tempo, 'Naima' is as thoughtful and mature a reading as we've had in recent years, and bop from Monk and Bird is suitably hard-hitting. The sound is very immediate, if lacking in some finesse. The meeting with James Clay is slightly troubled by Clay's cloudy, unconvincing phrasing, and only on 'Take The Coltrane' is there real empathy; but Perkins and Strazzeri both sound very good. Rob Pronk's arrangements for *I Wished On The Moon* give Bill his chance at a big band/strings album and, though the arrangements have more mush than backbone, the saxophonist breezes through the charts with an old pro's ease. The *Warm Moods* session is altogether tougher. Perkins chooses to use baritone for most of the record (with two forays into bass clarinet and a single clarinet reading of 'Sweet Lorraine') and his faintly peevish sound on the horn sits nicely with Strazzeri's energetic bop lines. When they get to a ballad like 'You Know I Care' the leathery sound unravels into tenderness. Warmly recommended.

*** **Our Man Woody** Jazz Mark 110
>Perkins; Rick Baptist, Joe Davis, Wayne Bergeron, Bob Summers, Clay Jenkins (t); Charlie Loper, Andy Martin, Rich Bullock (tb); Bob Cooper (ts); Brian Nimitz (as, ts); Jack Nimitz (bs); Frank Strazzeri (p); Dave Stone (b); Paul Kreibach (d). 1/91.

*** **Frame Of Mind** Interplay IP 8612
>Perkins; Clay Jenkins (t); Frank Strazzeri (p); Bob Leatherbarrow (vib); Tom Warrington, Ken Filiano (b); Bill Berg (d). 5/93.

Perkins was a Herman sideman, and his tribute to Woody's band is a genuine and sometimes scintillating one. The swingers come off at a terrific clip – though brass-laden, the band's real colour is provided by the reed section, dominated by Perkins and Cooper – and the ballads are played with great aplomb. Soloists pop in and out of the ensemble in the finest West Coast tradition, and the sound is a proper update on the classic California texture.

Frame Of Mind, according to Perkins's own sleeve-note, granted him more control than he's ever had over a record. With a picked band, old compadre Strazzeri on hand and an intriguing programme – Strazzeri, Duke Pearson, Monk, Jimmy Heath – the band play with gusto and excellent chops, though in the final analysis nobody quite has the character of Perkins himself to take it into the top bracket. The leader's solos, with just a hint of tonal quirkiness, are still the most arresting thing.

Carl Perkins (1928–58) PIANO

*** **Introducing Carl Perkins** Fresh Sound FSRCD 10
>Perkins; Leroy Vinnegar (b); Lawrence Marable (d). 7/55.

Perkins was famous for playing with his left hand turned an extra 90 degrees to the keyboard, a position that allowed him to punch out extra bass notes with his elbow. He was also famous for dying young. In a short career that began with Tiny Bradshaw's band in 1948 and ended a round decade later, he played with everyone from Big Jay McNeely to Curtis Counce, taking in Miles Davis, Chet Baker, Pepper Adams, Harold Land, Art Pepper and Victor Feldman *en route*. More than a journeyman player, it seems certain that he would have recorded much more had he survived. What remains is still slightly tentative, though the four originals – 'Way Cross Town', 'Marblehead', 'Westside' and 'Carl's Blues' – strongly suggest that he was going places as a composer, too.

Originally issued on the Dooto label, this trio was recorded around the time of Carl's association with tenor giant, Dexter Gordon, and some of the big man's laid-back bop can be heard throughout the session. There are moments when one wonders if what it needs is a horn – though perhaps a trumpet rather than a woodwind to counteract the young pianist's fashionably saxophone-influenced phrasing and timbre. Vinnegar is on very good form and takes some nice solo choruses here and there, often carrying an improvisational melody while Carl varies the chords on top.

Rich Perry TENOR SAXOPHONE

*** **To Start Again** Steeplechase SCCD 31331
     Perry; Harold Danko (*p*); Scott Colley (*b*); Jeff Hirshfield (*d*). 4/93.
Perry has been hidden in big-band sections and sideman roles for some 20 years, and this is his first date as a leader. Like many such projects, it's pleasant, polished music that misses the last degree of individuality which would take it out of the ordinary. Perry's improvising has a reticent, almost circumspect quality at times, as if he's reluctant to take a particular lead – which at least makes a change from some of his peers. But the principal here is Danko, whose charming 'Candlelight Shadows' is the best theme in the programme and who solos and accompanies with his customary insights.

Charli Persip (born 1929) DRUMS, PERCUSSION

*** **In Case You Missed It** Soul Note 121079
     Persip; Eddie E. J. Allen, Frank Gordon, Ambrose Jackson, Ron Tooley, Jack Walrath (*t*);
     Clarence Banks, Jason Forsythe, David Graf (*tb*); Carl Kleinsteuber (*tba*); Bobby Watson (*as*);
     Monty Waters (*as*); Orpheus Gaitanopoulos, Alan Givens, Bill Saxton (*ts*); Fred Houn (*bs*);
     Richard Clements (*p*); Anthony Cox (*b*); Eli Fountain (*perc*). 9/84.
***(*) **No Dummies Allowed** Soul Note 121179
     Persip; Tony Barrero, Ambrose Jackson, Genghis Nor, Jack Walrath (*t*); Nathan Duncan, Jason
     Forsythe, Matt Haviland, Herb Huvel (*tb*); Sue Terry, Sayyd Abdul Al-Khabyyr (*as, f*); Orpheus
     Gaitanopoulos, Craig Rivers (*ts, f*); Pablo Calajero (*bs*); Darrell Grant (*p*); Melissa Slocum (*b*);
     Eli Fountain (*perc*). 11/87.
Drummer Persip and his Superband have attempted to maintain a collectivist, internationalist and (intermittently) non-sexist approach without any of the pomposity and attitudinizing that have marred some otherwise excellent work by the Afro-Asian Ensemble, a broadly similar outfit co-led by baritonist Fred Houn. Houn also appears on the brawling *In Case You Missed It*.

Persip's track record is quite extraordinary and his technique is now honed to perfection. He's something of a hybrid of Blakey and Big Sid Catlett, but he has also paid attention to Cozy Cole and Shadow Wilson. They're all performance players, big sounds but with sufficient sense of space (compare Rich or Krupa) to let things happen around them. Persip's inspirational qualities (mustn't say leadership) are evident in *No Dummies Allowed*, a dumb title for such a spanking set of big-band arrangements. Alto saxophonist Sue Terry's work on the Billie Holiday medley, 'Strange Crazy Heartache', suggests that she has a formidable musical intelligence; her solo statement catches something of Lady's voice, and Jack Walrath does some terrific back-of-the-stand stuff.

'Vital Seconds' and 'Desert Ship' are both composed by saxophonist Orpheus Gaitanopoulos, a robust player who occasionally disrupts the band's surprising finesse. Both albums are worth finding, but the later set is the better by some distance.

Eric Person (born 1964) ALTO SAXOPHONE, SOPRANO SAXOPHONE

*** **Arrival** Soul Note 121237
     Person; Michael Cain (*p, ky*); Cary DeNigris (*g*); Kenny Davis (*b*); Ronnie Burrage (*d*). 93.
*** **Prophecy** Soul Note 121287
     As above, except omit Cain and Burrage. 3/92.
Like the great majority of young St Louis players, Person manages to touch a great many stylistic bases

without sounding mannered or trite. Like his father Thomas (a well-respected figure in their home town), he has a strong blues inflexion, but his experience with funk bands, and more recently with the rejuvenated Chico Hamilton, attests to his range.

Burrage (another Missourian) is the ideal drummer for the first session. He has a big sound, but manages to avoid undue busyness. The same is true of another Hamilton employee, guitarist DeNigris. He guests on just two tracks, but his duet with Person on 'Every Time I Smile' is one of the highlights.

There are rough edges aplenty, but almost all of them come out of boldness rather than lack of technique. Person recalls no one more than the young 'Black' Arthur Blythe. If he can steer clear of the lucrative but unrewarding distractions that held Blythe back, he has the makings of a very considerable contender. (None of the reviewers failed to note that, a generation before, Chico Hamilton had recruited another saxophone-playing Eric.)

Disappointingly at first glance, instead of rising to that challenge in his second record, Person chooses to backtrack the well-trodden path opened up by John Coltrane. There are two Coltrane pieces on the record, 'Up Against The Wall' and parts of 'Interstellar Space'; but what Person is attempting to do is to give his own sound a recognizable shape within the confines of long-form or relatively open-ended improvisational pieces, and that above all is the function the Coltrane pieces serve. In terms of sound pure and simple, he is emphatically not a Trane disciple. The inclusion of Wayne Shorter's 'Delores', and the arrangement of it for this drummerless group, suggests that his interests lie mainly in certain aspects of post-bop writing that have still not been fully explored. A promising follow-up that has yet to be sustained.

Houston Person (born 1934) TENOR SAXOPHONE

*** **The Talk Of The Town** Muse MCD 5331
> Person; Cecil Bridgewater (*t*); Stan Hope (*p*); Buster Williams (*b*); Grady Tate (*d*); Ralph Dorsey (*perc*). 1/87.

*** **Basics** Muse MCD 5344
> Person; Stan Hope (*p*); Peter Martin Weiss (*b*); Cecil Brooks III (*d*); Ralph Dorsey (*perc*). 10/87.

*** **The Party** Muse MCD 5451
> Person; Randy Johnston (*g*); Joey DeFrancesco (*org*); Bertel Knox (*d*); Sammy Figueroa (*perc*). 11/89.

***(*) **Why Not!** Muse MCD 5433
> Person; Philip Harper (*t*); Joey DeFrancesco (*org*); Randy Johnston (*g*); Winard Harper (*d*); Sammy Figueroa (*perc*). 10/90.

Squarely in the soul–jazz mould. Person sounds like a latter-day Ike Quebec. The records are absolutely consistent. One either goes for this aural equivalent of soul food or one doesn't, though sceptics shouldn't remain misled about the level of sophistication of Person's playing. He is a more conscious artist and a subtler technician than may at first appear. Bridgewater is a fine accomplice on the first of these records, and the only thing that *Basics* lacks is the counterpoint and timbral variation of another horn.

The best of the bunch by the narrowest of whiskers is the more recent *Party*, which finds him wailing with unabashed self-indulgence over a thick Hammond stew from boy wonder DeFrancesco, who could be Jimmy McGriff reborn. The opening two tracks, 'Love Me Tender' and 'Blue Velvet', serve much the same function as the old Blue Note juke numbers. The rest is rather more interesting: a fine version of Lee Morgan's 'Ceora', which successfully negotiated the soul–jazz / mainstream–modern divide; a really excellent reading of Betty Comden, Adolph Green and Jules Styne's 'The Party's Over'; and a knocked-together curtain-piece called 'True Blues', which is no more than a blowing session but which tempts both Person and DeFrancesco into some of their most unhackneyed playing. For a party, cranked up loud and with lots of bottom, it could hardly be better.

Ably abetted by the Harper brothers, Person turns in a more reflective and inventive set on *Why Not!*, bringing his unique timbre to the hokey 'As Time Goes By' and an unexpected bustle to Gene DePaul's 'Namely You'. DeFrancesco's organ and Figueroa's rippling percussion effects may be a little obtrusive for some tastes, but the basic ingredients are as wholesome as cornbread.

*** **Something In Common** Muse MCD 5371
> Person; Ron Carter (*b*). 89.

***(*) **Now's The Time** Muse MCD 5421
> As above. 90.

The duets with Carter are an unexpected delight. It has often been said that the big bassist plays horn lines, and there are moments here when Person chugs out a low-register accompaniment to Ron's almost vocalized improvisations. He has the habit of tackling some of the themes in unexpected keys and then modulating back to something more comfortable, not because he can't find the places on the neck of the big fiddle, but simply to keep the thing moving along. As it does, they do, triumphantly.

Bent Persson (born 1947) TRUMPET

*** **Swinging Straight** Sittel SITCD 9218
> Persson; Dicken Hedrenius (*tb*); John Hogman (*ts*); Ulf Johansson (*p*); Goran Lind (*b*); Ronnie Gardiner (*d*). 12/94.

Persson can sound like any bygone trumpeter he cares to – and he's been asked to play in just that way, on a number of revivalist projects – and perhaps that tells against his own session having a character of its own. Instead, this is purely pleasurable mainstream, buoyed up by a sense of enjoyment that is often hard to find on equivalent American dates. Persson here comes on like one of the great Basie trumpeters, and Hedrenius's rascally trombone and Hogman's burly tenor merely add to the fun.

Edward Petersen TENOR SAXOPHONE

*** **Upward Spiral** Delmark 445
> Petersen; Brad Williams (*p*); Fareed Haque (*g*); Rob Amster (*b*); Jeff Stitely (*d*). 6/89.
***(*) **The Haint** Delmark 474
> Petersen; Odies Williams III, Billy Brimfield (*t*); Willie Pickens (*p*); Brian Sandstrom (*b*); Robert Shy (*d*). 94.

Upward Spiral is a part-studio, part-live account of a band that has worked regularly on the contemporary Chicago scene. Petersen is the dominant voice, walking the line between bop form and a freer conception with an unfussy confidence, and his solos contrast with the cloudier effects of Haque. Williams, Amster and Stitely provide competent support, but the extra grit and swing of the first four tracks – which were cut live in Chicago – suggest that the band has yet to find its feet in the studio. Since comparatively little is heard of Chicago's newer jazz, a welcome document.

So is *The Haint*. Though Petersen has apparently moved to New Orleans, this is still a Chicago band, and they play with a gutsy finesse that is different from the slick virtuosity of contemporary New York. Not that the playing sounds rough: Petersen has toughened his personal sound, and he has a fierce grip on material ranging from 'Jitterbug Waltz' to the near-free piece, 'Walking In The Sky'. Brimfield and Williams bring contrasting trumpet styles, and Pickens plays with fine authority.

Oscar Peterson (born 1925) PIANO, ORGAN, ELECTRIC PIANO, CLAVICHORD

*** **Jazz Masters 37: Oscar Peterson Plays Broadway** Verve 516893
> Peterson; Clark Terry (*t*); Irving Ashby, Herb Ellis, Barney Kessel (*g*); Ray Brown (*b*); Gene Gammage, Alvin Stoller, Ed Thigpen (*d*). 3 & 8/50, 1, 2 & 12/52, 12/53, 11/54, 11/58, 5 & 7/59, 1/60, 1 & 9/62, 8/64.
***(*) **Jazz Masters 16: Oscar Peterson** Verve 516320
> Peterson; Roy Eldridge (*t*); Sonny Stitt (*as*); Stan Getz, Flip Phillips, Ben Webster, Lester Young (*ts*); Lionel Hampton (*vib*); Milt Jackson (*vib*); Herb Ellis, Barney Kessel (*g*); Ray Brown (*b*); J. C. Heard, John Poole, Buddy Rich, Alvin Stoller, Ed Thigpen (*d*); Fred Astaire, Ella Fitzgerald, Anita O'Day (*v*). 1952–61.
*** **Jazz At The Philharmonic, Hartford 1953** Pablo Live 2308240
> Peterson; Roy Eldridge, Charlie Shavers (*t*); Bill Harris (*tb*); Benny Carter, Willie Smith (*as*); Flip Phillips, Ben Webster, Lester Young (*ts*); Herb Ellis (*g*); Ray Brown (*b*); J. C. Heard, Gene Krupa (*d*). 5/53.
***(*) **At Zardi's** Pablo Live 2620118
> Peterson; Herb Ellis (*g*); Ray Brown (*b*). 55.

No single moment ever gave a clearer impression of Oscar Peterson's fabled technique than a tiny incident on one of those all-star Jazz At The Philharmonic events released in rafts by the Pablo label. Count Basie has just stated the opening notes of a theme in his inimitable elided style when there is a pause and then, presto! showers of sparkling notes. Any suspicions about what the Count might have ingested in his few bars of silence are allayed by the liner-note. What had happened, quite simply, was that Basie had spotted Oscar Peterson standing in the wings and had dragged him on for an unscheduled 'spot'.

Peterson has been almost as prolific as he is effusive at the piano. He appears on literally dozens of albums in solo and trio setting, but also with horn-led groups and orchestras. He is one of the finest accompanists in swing-orientated jazz, despite which he served no real apprenticeship as a sideman, being introduced to an American audience (he was born and raised in Canada) by impresario and record producer Norman Granz in 1949. He has ridden on the extraordinary momentum of that debut ever since, recording almost exclusively for Granz's labels, Verve and, later, Pablo. The earliest material available here suggests how complete he was as an artist, even at the very beginning. He quickly became a favourite at JATP events and the *Hartford 1953* sessions anticipate the walk-on/walk-off sensation he was to become in the 1970s.

Peterson is perhaps best as a trio performer. During the 1950s these tended to be drummerless, and with a guitarist. Barney Kessel sounds rather colourless and Herb Ellis is much more responsive to Peterson's technique, as was his much later replacement, Joe Pass. After 1960, the stalwart Ray Brown was joined by a drummer, first by Ed Thigpen then by Louis Hayes. This coincided with Peterson's consolidation as a major concert and recording star and his early work, influenced primarily by Nat Cole, is now rather less well known. Of the mid-1950s sets, *At Zardi's* and the excellent *Jazz Masters* compilation (which covers the early years of the later trio as well) are certainly the best.

There has long been a critical knee-jerk about Peterson's Tatum influence. This was very much a later development. Tatum died in 1956 and only then does Peterson seem to have taken a close interest in his work. Even then it overlay the smoothed-out, ambidextrous quality he had found in Cole. The vocal record is a not entirely successful experiment in the Cole manner; there has been no great appetite for a repeat performance. With the turn of the 1960s and international stardom, Peterson's style changes only in accordance with the context of specific performances, particularly between the big, grandstanding 'all star' events and more intimate occasions with his own trio, where he demonstrates an occasional resemblance to Hampton Hawes and, more contentiously, to Bill Evans. Peterson's powerfully swinging style does tend on occasion to overpower his melodic sense and he is apt to become repetitious and, less often, banal. After four decades in the business, though, he understands its workings better than anyone. Above all, Peterson *delivers*.

***(*) **At The Stratford Shakespearean Festival** Verve 513 752
    Peterson; Herb Ellis (*g*); Ray Brown (*d*). 8/56.
***(*) **At The Concertgebouw** Verve 521 649
    As above. 9 & 10/57.
Unlike the Ahmad Jamal and Nat Cole trios, which also dispensed with drummers in favour of piano, guitar and bass, the Peterson group never sounded spacious or open-textured – the pianist's hyperactive fingers saw to that. Here, though, for once Peterson seemed able to lie back a little and let the music flow under its own weight, rather than constantly pushing it along. Peterson has described how during the daytime Brown and Ellis sat and practised all the harmonic variables that might come up during a performance. A sensible precaution, one might have thought, given a player with Peterson's hand-speed. The irony is that his vertical mobility, in and out of key, was never as rapid as all that, and there are occasions here, as on 'How High The Moon' and the closing 'Daisy's Dream' (both from Stratford), where it appears that Ellis and Brown manage to anticipate his moves and push him into configurations he hadn't apparently thought of.

The other concert is augmented with material from Los Angeles a fortnight later, suggesting a quick return to the United States. However, the 'Concertgebouw' material was actually recorded in Chicago. The Dutch concert given by the trio earlier in 1957 was never actually taped, but presumably it sounded classier on the sleeve to pretend that it had. One other mistake has been corrected from the CD. The track originally labelled 'Bags Groove' clearly wasn't and has now been retitled 'Bluesology'.

***(*) **Plays My Fair Lady & The Music From Fiorello** Verve 521 677
    Peterson; Ray Brown (*b*); Gene Gammage (*d*). 11/58, 1/60.
***(*) **A Jazz Portrait Of Frank Sinatra** Verve 825 769
    Peterson; Ray Brown (*b*); Ed Thigpen (*d*). 5/59.
*** **Plays The Cole Porter Songbook** Verve 821 987
    As above. 7 & 8/59.
**** **Plays Porgy & Bess** Verve 519 807
    As above. 10/59.
Not to be confused with the later duo intepretation featuring Joe Pass, the Gershwin set is brilliantly spontaneous jazz, apparently recorded after the sketchiest of run-throughs. Peterson has played 'I Wants To Stay Here' (or 'I Loves You Porgy', as it is more commonly known) many times in his career (see *Tristeza*, below), but nowhere with the pure feeling and simplicity that he gives it on this disc. The two apostrophes to Bess at the end are heartfelt and utterly compelling, with liquid left-hand figures and an unstoppable flow of melody ideas. As pianist (Benny Green indicates in a special introductory note to the reissue), Ray Brown gets less solo space here than on many of the trio's records, unlikely to be a symptom of unfamiliarity with the material, more probably because Peterson makes the session so

forcibly his own. Brown's contribution to the fiery 'There's A Boat Dat's Leavin' Soon For New York' is beyond reproach, however, and his intro to 'I Got Plenty O' Nuttin'' is masterful.

With Peterson, nothing fundamental rests on the quality of the material he has to work with. His almost alchemical transformation of the songs from *Fiorello* beggars belief. *My Fair Lady* offers more familiar melodies and the element of surprise is proportionately less. However, these are some of his most lyrical and melody-centred interpretations, often sticking quite close to the line.

The Porter and Sinatra records are slightly odd in that Peterson does very little more than run through the songs, chorus by chorus, adding very little in the way of improvisational embellishment. The shortest track on the Sinatra is under two minutes, the longest on either just three and a half, the average about two minutes forty-five. This gives the performances a slightly abrupt air that's only partly mitigated by the sheer empathy the pianist feels with the tunes. Though Peterson's admiration for Sinatra comes through strongly, the Porter tribute isn't a great record, and there are signs that it was made to order as part of a burgeoning catalogue of 'songbook' projects; but its value lies precisely in its terseness, Peterson's brilliant feel for song form.

(A Gershwin songbook, noted in the first edition, is currently out of favour, but will presumably be reissued at some future juncture.)

*** **En Concert Avec Europe 1** RTE 1002
    Peterson; Roy Eldridge (*t*); Sam Jones (*b*); Bobby Durham, Louis Hayes, Ed Thigpen (*d*). 2/61,
    3/63, 4/64, 3/65, 11/69.
A rather oddly spaced-out compilation of radio sessions. The opening 'Daahoud' is masterful and the two tracks with Eldridge are worth adding to their other confrontations, particularly 'Mainstem'. For the most part, though, this is a collector's item only.

*** **The Silver Collection** Verve 823447
    Peterson; Ray Brown (*b*); Ed Thigpen (*d*); Nelson Riddle Orchestra. 8/59 & 63.
*** **The Trio – Live From Chicago** Verve 823008
    As above, except omit orchestra. 9 & 10/61.
***(*) **Very Tall** Verve 827821
    As above, except add Milt Jackson (*vib*). 9/61.
*** **West Side Story** Verve 821 575
    As above. 1/62.
**** **Night Train** Verve 821724
    As above. 12/62.
*** **Plus One** Emarcy 818 840
    As above, except add Clark Terry (*t, flhn*). 8/64.
*** **We Get Requests** Verve 810047
    As above. 10 & 11/64.
After 30 years, *Night Train* is well established as a hardy perennial and is certainly Peterson's best-known record. Dedicated to his father, who was a sleeping-car attendant on Canadian Pacific Railways, it isn't the dark and moody suite of nocturnal blues many listeners expect but a lively and varied programme of material covering 'C-Jam Blues', 'Georgia On My Mind', 'Bag's Groove', 'Honey Dripper', 'Things Ain't What They Used To Be', 'Band Call', 'Hymn To Freedom', and a couple of others. Though by no means a 'concept album', it's one of the best-constructed long-players of the period and its durability is testimony to that as much as to the quality of Peterson's playing, which is tight and uncharacteristically emotional.

We Get Requests and *Live* reverse the polarity totally. Cool but technically effusive, Peterson gets all over two sets of (mostly) romantic ballads, played with a portrait of Nat Cole perched on the soundboard in front of him. *The Silver Collection* has four excellent trio tracks fighting for their lives among nine syrupy orchestrations that might have worked for another pianist but which are emphatically not in Peterson's line of sight.

The *West Side Story* covers are interesting because they put the weight of emphasis on all the unlikeliest tunes. The 'Jet Song' receives the most developed interpretation but, while 'Maria' and 'Somewhere' are both consummately polished performances, they lack the commitment and graceful intelligence Peterson normally brings to romantic ballads. As a whole the record is a little lightweight and uninvolving.

So different is Peterson from John Lewis's unemphatic keyboard approach that there's not the remotest chance that *Very Tall* might be mistaken for an MJQ record. One of the great improvisers in modern jazz, Jackson is the undoubted star of the session, finessing 'On Green Dolphin Street' with a subtle counterpoint and adding a tripping bounce to 'A Wonderful Guy'. Excellent stuff. Watch out for *Reunion Blues*, listed below, which saw Peterson and the vibist get together again.

Plus One is aptly named. Terry never gets more involved than his guest star role would imply, and there are occasions when (to be frank) he sounds more like a revelling gatecrasher. He slides into a sombre, almost remorseful mood on 'They Didn't Believe Me', giving his flugelhorn that celebrated bone china fragility, before bouncing back with a second wind on a Peterson original (averaging one or two per disc around this time) called 'Squakay's Blues', dedicated to the redoubtable Joanie Spears, who managed the big man's career at about this time.

**** Exclusively For My Friends MPS 513 830 4CD
    Peterson; Ray Brown, Sam Jones (*b*); Bobby Durham, Louis Hayes, Ed Thigpen (*d*). 63–68.
*** Exclusively For My Friends: The Lost Tapes MPS 529 096
    As above, except omit Hayes. 5/65, 11/67, 10/68.
Between 1963 and 1968, Peterson recorded a series of six LPs for the MPS label in the Villingen home of German producer, Hans Georg Brunner-Schwer. It's not quite the same sort of relationship as existed between Bud Powell and François Paudrais. Peterson was successful, fit and hip to the realities of the music business. What is different about these recordings is the degree of relaxation (and, to a certain degree, of risk) in the performances.

'Love Is Here To Stay' on Volume 2 is one of the most interesting performances Peterson ever put on disc. Essentially a tribute to Tatum, it is full of harmonic ambiguities and stretched-out metres, and there is more musical meat in it than in the over-long 'I'm In The Mood For Love' on the first volume, which at 17 minutes begins to pall slightly. The highlight there is 'Like Someone In Love', which Peterson turns into a grand romantic concerto, closing with quotes from *Rhapsody In Blue*.

The sessions were played before a small invited audience of friends and admirers, and the recordings are clearly aimed at connoisseurs, offering the nearest thing to a candid portrayal of Peterson musing on his art. There are unexpected touches of modernity, as in 'Nica's Dream' with Sam Jones and Bobby Durham on Volume 2, and there are perhaps too many knowing quotes (mostly from Ellington, but also from Basie's single-finger intros and even, less obviously, from Monk on 'Lulu's Back In Town'). The piano sounds big and resonant and the recordings are immediate and appropriately intimate.

By 1968, the magic of these sessions had perhaps worn a little thin and the *Lost Tapes* material suggests that it may be possible to have too much of a good thing. The solo pieces on Volumes 3 and 4 are rarely as acute as the group tracks, and there are signs that Peterson is simply not concentrating on 'Someone To Watch Over Me', which opens the last disc. A hint of self-indulgence at last?

It should be noted that the six MPS LPs were: *Action, Girl Talk, The Way I Really Play, My Favourite Instrument, Mellow Mood* and *Travelin' On*. The reappearance of the missing tapes wasn't quite drama of Watergate proportions and doesn't add significantly to the tally on this handsome compilation. Peterson aficionados will be delighted with an 11-minute version of 'Tenderly', played with Brown and Thigpen, and with an unexpected run-through of Bobby Timmons's 'Moanin'' from a later session with Jones and Durham. For the most part, though, this is an item for completists, though of course it stands up on its own quite respectably as a Peterson record. If there were fewer of them around, it would be most desirable.

**(*) Motions And Emotions MPS821 289
    Peterson; Claus Ogerman (*cond*). 69.
*** Hello Herbie MPS 821 846
    As above, except add Herb Ellis (*g*); Ray Brown (*b*); Bobby Durham (*d*). 11/69.
*** Tristeza On Piano MPS 817 489
    As above, but omit Ellis. 70.
*** Three Originals MPS 521 059 2CD
    As above. 69–70.
*** Tracks MPS 523498
    Peterson (*p* solo). 11/70.
Later sessions for Brunner-Schwer, though *Tristeza* was recorded in a New York studio. What's lost there, and in the others to an extent, is the gentle experimentalism of the private sessions. Peterson sounds as if he's on auto-pilot, and it's probably no coincidence that the track-listing veers strongly away from the earthbound, 'Down Here On The Ground' notwithstanding. 'Nightingale' is a rare self-written piece; 'Tristeza' and 'You Stepped Out Of A Dream' are equally moody.

Motions And Emotions is disappointing because the repertoire is so bland. The mixture of Lennon–McCartney, Mancini, Jim Webb, Bobby Gentry and Bacharach needs more leavening than even Peterson can give it; though professionally rehearsed and recorded, the strings are as gooey as always. As such, it represents a serious stumbling block to any unqualified recommendation for the two-CD compilation, *Three Originals*. Most listeners might be prepared for two, rather better, originals. *Hello Herbie* is certainly worth having, if only for Peterson's great reading of Hampton Hawes's 'Hamp's Blues' and the Wes Montgomery tune, 'Naptown Blues', both of which catch him at his best. The reunion with Ellis is also a happy one; their interplay on 'Seven Come Eleven', a theme associated with Benny Goodman and Charlie Christian, is spot on.

The solo performances on the oddly titled *Tracks* have the musing, unselfconscious quality that was the other side of Peterson's prodigious keyboard showmanship. Things like 'A Little Jazz Exercise' and the reworkings of 'Basin Street Blues' and 'Honeysuckle Rose' are so chock-full of ideas that any aspirant jazz pianist will want to study them. For more casual listeners, these are valuable as solo perform-ances, of which there are surprisingly few, relative to the huge mass of issued trios.

(*) Oscar Peterson–Stéphane Grappelli Quartet Accord 403292
>   Peterson; Stéphane Grappelli (*vn*); Niels-Henning Orsted-Pedersen (*b*); Kenny Clarke (*d*). 2/72, 2/73.

Likeable, uncomplicated, undemanding; what more can one say? The duo 'Them There Eyes' was just one of a whole batch of such encounters that Grappelli (and Peterson) logged during the 1970s. It's no better or worse than the rest of them. Unfortuntely, the recording quality on this one isn't up to scratch, with a very poor balance in the rhythm section. This is particularly dismaying because Clarke is one of the session's unambiguous assets.

*** **History Of An Artist** Pablo 2625702 2CD
>   Peterson; Irving Ashby, Herb Ellis, Barney Kessel, Joe Pass (*g*); Ray Brown, Sam Jones, George Mraz, Niels-Henning Orsted-Pedersen (*b*); Bobby Durham, Louis Hayes (*d*). 12/72, 2 & 5/73, 5/74.

Actually Volume Two of this compilation set, now augmented with some extra material. It won't be of much use to those who collect Peterson avidly but, as an introduction to his small group playing over this period, it's not bad.

*** **The Trio** Pablo 2310701
>   Peterson; Joe Pass (*g*); Niels-Henning Orsted- Pedersen (*b*). 73.
*** **The Good Life** Original Jazz Classics OJC 627
>   As above. 73.

For some fans this is Peterson's best vintage and most effective partnerships. *The Trio* concentrates largely on blues material, with a withers-wringing 'Secret Love' as a curtain-piece. On the other album, 'Wheatland' needs the rhythmic drive that Ed Thigpen brought to the tune on *Compact Jazz*, above; but by and large the drummer-less trio is a setting that suits Peterson's Tatumesque delivery. Only five tracks, and little sense of significant development on any of them as Peterson's technique becomes increasingly pleased with itself.

*** **Oscar Peterson In Russia** Pablo 2625711
>   Peterson; Niels-Henning Orsted-Pedersen (*b*); Jake Hanna (*d*). 11/74.

The real meat of this journey was the duos with NHOP. Their trip down Green Dolphin Street is a revelation, one of the partnership's genuinely shining moments. Hanna is a rather pushy, forceful drummer for this context, but he has his strengths and, with temperatures outside doubtless plummet-ing, his push through 'Take The "A" Train' and 'Do You Know What It Means To Miss New Orleans' must surely have been welcome. Oscar redresses the balance with lovely readings of 'Someone To Watch Over Me' (solo) and 'Georgia On My Mind' (trio).

*** **Oscar Peterson & Dizzy Gillespie** Pablo 2310740
>   Peterson; Dizzy Gillespie (*t*). 11/74.
***(*) **Oscar Peterson & Roy Eldridge** Original Jazz Classics OJC 727
>   Peterson; Roy Eldridge (*t*). 12/74.
***(*) **Oscar Peterson & Harry Edison** Original Jazz Classics OJC 738
>   Peterson; Harry 'Sweets' Edison (*t*). 12/74.

This instrumentation goes all the way back to 1928, when Louis Armstrong and Earl Hines recorded 'Weather Bird'. There are, inevitably, hints of a later Bird in Gillespie's blues style, but there is also a slackness of conception similar to what overtook Armstrong in later years, and Peterson's overblown accompaniments don't help. The ballads are better, but only because they're prettier.

   Eldridge pushes a little harder (and, incidentally, sounds prettier than Diz), and the slightly later session is on balance the more compelling. There is still a feeling of Buggins's turn and mix-and-match about a lot of these sessions, but the two players' artistry does show through. Peterson's switch to organ was a happy stroke and might have been usefully extended to the album as a whole, rather than to selected tracks. The closing 'Blues For Chu' is a small master-stroke.

   Of the three, Sweets is closest in conception to Armstrong, and the opening 'Easy Living' reverberates back and forth across almost half a century of the music. There are some lovely things later on in the set as well: 'Willow Weep For Me', where Sweets squeezes low, throaty tones out of his trumpet, and 'The Man I Love', a straight, unabashed performance.

***(*) **At The Montreux Jazz Festival 1975** Pablo 2310747
>   Peterson; Milt Jackson (*vib*); Toots Thielemans (*hca*); Joe Pass (*g*); Niels-Henning Orsted-Pedersen (*b*); Louie Bellson (*d*). 7/75.

Notable for the inclusion of Parker's 'Au Privave', a bebop classic that has been a favourite of the pianist's but which still sits rather awkwardly alongside Peterson's usual diet of blues and swing. In the event, it's an effective enough performance, though the logic of his solo is rather lost in the showers of notes he plays. Thielemans underlines how good an improviser he can be, but Pass is very muted.

*** Porgy And Bess Pablo 2310779
Peterson; Joe Pass (*g*). 1/76.

Peterson's choice of clavichord for the *Porgy And Bess* session looked initially promising but ultimately suggests nothing more than a way of freshening up rather stale performances. It's perhaps the least known of the keyboard family, covering between three and five octaves (Peterson seems to be using the larger model) and distinguished from the piano and harpsichord by the fact that the strings are struck (rather than plucked, as with the harpsichord) by metal tangents which can be left in contact with the string rather than rebounding, altering its distinctive vibrato. Peterson certainly hasn't mastered that aspect of the instrument and plays it with a pianist's 'clean' touch that loses him the delicious, bluesy wavers and bends it could have brought to these rather stolid Gershwin interpretations.

*** Montreux '77 Original Jazz Classics OJC 383
Peterson; Ray Brown, Niels-Henning Orsted-Pedersen (*b*). 7/77.
*** Montreux '77 Original Jazz Classics OJC 378
Peterson; Dizzy Gillespie, Clark Terry (*t*); Eddie 'Lockjaw' Davis (*ts*); Niels-Henning Orsted-Pedersen (*b*); Bobby Durham (*d*). 7/77.

The first of these is an intriguing two-bass experiment from the much-documented 1977 festival, where Peterson had become a recognized draw. Brown tends to take on some of the responsibilities of a guitarist, alternating his familiar 'walk' with clipped strums reminiscent of Herb Ellis's guitar and leaving the darker sonorities to the great Dane. The material, with the exception of 'There Is No Greater Love', is perhaps not ideally suited to the two string-players and they're often left with a rather subsidiary role. Peterson was just about blown out of sight by Tommy Flanagan's excellent performance earlier in the weekend, but he's generally in good if undemanding form. He can also be heard on other sets from the same event: with Roy Eldridge (OJC 373), Eddie 'Lockjaw' Davis (OJC 384) and on an *All-Star Jam* (OJC 380); there are festival highlights on OJC 385.

*** The Paris Concert Pablo Live 2620112
Peterson; Niels-Henning Orsted-Pedersen (*b*); Joe Pass (*g*). 10/78.

Again, much of the interest focuses on two Parker tracks, 'Donna Lee' and 'Ornithology', both of which receive the kind of scalping treatment meted out by the army barber at boot camp. There's a 'who's next?' feel to the succession of tracks that makes you wish someone had shouted out, 'Excursion On A Wobbly Rail' or 'Three Blind Mice' . . . *anything* to wrong-foot the man. Playing without drums, as he did a lot around this time, Peterson seems rhythmically yet more commanding, but he also opens up his phrasing quite noticeably, highlighting the stresses and accents.

***(*) Skol Original Jazz Classics OJC 496
Peterson; Stéphane Grappelli (*vn*); Joe Pass (*g*); Niels-Henning Orsted-Pedersen (*b*); Mickey Roker (*d*). 7/79.

Peterson as group player. He defers more than usual to his colleagues – 'Nuages' and 'Making Whoopee' have Grappelli's thumbprint on them, after all – and contributes to a surprisingly rounded performance. The music is still on the soft side, but Peterson is as unfailingly sensitive as an accompanist as he is as a leader, and his solo spots are all the more striking for being tightly marshalled. A good choice for anyone who prefers the pianist in smaller doses, or who enjoys Grappelli. The fiddler suffers broadly similar critical problems. A player of consummate skill and considerable improvisational gifts, he has been somewhat hijacked by television and has come (quite wrongly) to seem a middle-of-the-road entertainer rather than a 'legitimate' jazz man. There is still probably more thought and enterprise in just one Grappelli solo than in a whole raft of albums by Young Turk tenor saxophone players.

**(*) Digital At Montreux Pablo Live 2308224
Peterson; Niels-Henning Orsted-Pedersen (*b*). 7/79.

Very much a middle-market package for the hi-fi enthusiast who wants to watch the dials glow and twitch. This is a rather dead spell in Peterson's career, and listening to him negotiate 'Caravan' or 'Satin Doll' for the umpteenth time is a little like watching a snooker professional clear the table according to the book. One longs for a few near-misses. Collectors and dial-twitchers only.

**(*) The Personal Touch Pablo Today 2312135
Peterson; Clark Terry (*t, flhn*); Ed Bickert, Peter Leitch (*g*); Dave Young (*b*); Jerry Fuller (*d*); orchestra conducted by Rick Wilkins. 1 & 2/80.

Rick Wilkins's orchestrations aren't as drowningly fulsome as one might have feared, and both Peterson and Clark Terry are forceful enough players to rise above them. All the same, it's hard to see how a fairly unenterprising set would have been much different for quintet alone. Peterson's brief switch to electric piano (see 'The World Is Waiting For The Sunrise' for a quick sample) underlines the instrument's limitations rather than the player's.

*** Live At The Northsea Jazz Festival Pablo 2620115

Peterson; Toots Thielemans (*hca*); Joe Pass (*g*); Niels-Henning Orsted-Pedersen (*b*). 7/80.
The sprawling Northsea Festival has some of the chaotic glamour of the old JATP packages. Though not a pianist who generally sounds good around horns, Peterson gives Thielemans a lot of space and respect, weaving counterlines round his plangent figures on 'Like Someone In Love' and 'Caravan' (a gorgeously exotic performance). It's a quieter, less dynamic set than many of the festival albums from the period (which suits Thielemans) but isn't particularly reflective. The Nat Cole references are well to the forefront if you care to look for them.

***(*) Nigerian Marketplace Pablo Live 2308231

Peterson; Niels-Henning Orsted-Pedersen (*b*); Terry Clark (*d*). 7/81.
The title-track has a vivid 'live from Lagos' bustle about it that carries on into 'Au Privave', by now established as Peterson's favourite Charlie Parker item. The middle of the programme is on much more familiar turf with 'Nancy', 'Misty' and, perhaps more surprisingly, Bill Evans's lovely 'Waltz For Debby'. Peterson hasn't shown a great deal of interest in Evans's book (and it's difficult to judge whether his occasional Hawes and Evans touches show a direct influence), but he handles this theme with characteristic amplitude and not too much depth. Newcomer Clark performs well if rather busily.

*** Freedom Song Pablo 26401001

Peterson; Joe Pass (*g*); Niels-Henning Orsted-Pedersen (*b*); Martin Drew (*d*). 2/82.
There are few places in the world where Peterson has not recorded, but there are no fans more vociferous in their support than the Japanese. These dates were recorded in Tokyo and they find him in cracking good form. 'Now's The Time' reinforces his attachment to bebop and the medley 'Hymn To Freedom'/-'The Fallen Warrior'/'Nigerian Marketplace' is one of his grandest conceptions. Reservations? Two. The sound is not all it might be, a little muffled and indistinct, and the band is not playing anything like as well as the leader's performance requires. Two cheers.

**(*) A Tribute To My Friends Pablo 2310902

Peterson; Joe Pass (*g*); Niels-Henning Orsted- Pedersen (*b*); Martin Drew (*d*). 11/83.
*** If You Could See Me Now Pablo 2310918
As above. 11/83.
The tribute album nods in the direction of Fats Domino, Dizzy Gillespie, Ella and others who've crossed the big man's path over the years. There's a slight air of the end-of-contract, A&R meeting about it: how do we find a new wrinkle? *If You Could See Me Now* includes 'Limehouse Blues' and the bassist's feature, 'On Danish Shore'. These are about the best things on offer, but it's a thin set altogether.

**(*) Oscar Peterson Live! Pablo 2310940

Peterson; Joe Pass (*g*); David Young (*b*); Martin Drew (*d*). 11/86.
***(*) Time After Time Pablo 2310947
As above.
*** Oscar Peterson + Harry Edison + Eddie Cleanhead Vinson Pablo 2310927
As above, except add Harry 'Sweets' Edison (*t*); Eddie Cleanhead Vinson (*as*). 11/86.
The first of these related sessions consists largely of the deutero-classical 'Bach Suite', a more gainly and authentic pastiche than anything of Jacques Loussier's, but with an awful predictability about it as well. 'City Lights', 'Perdido' and 'Caravan' are tacked on at the end to keep the strict-constructionists happy. Better on harpsichord?

Time After Time restores the balance considerably. An original 'Love Ballade' revives Peterson's reputation as a melodist, and the closing 'On The Trail' allays any doubts about failing stamina. The material with Edison and Vinson fails to live up to past encounters with the trumpeter and there are odd occasions when Vinson seems to get in the way. It is, though, a hard session to fault on any more serious ground, and the 'Stuffy' and 'Satin Doll' work-outs are top class.

***(*) Live At The Blue Note Telarc CD 83304

Peterson; Herb Ellis (*g*); Ray Brown (*b*); Bobby Durham (*d*). 3/90.
*** Saturday Night At The Blue Note Telarc CD 83306
As above. 3/90.
*** At The Blue Note: Last Call Telarc CD 83314
As above. 3/90.

*** **Encore At The Blue Note** Telarc CD 83356
> As above. 3/90.

Whatever stiffness has crept into Peterson's fingers over the last few years has served only to increase the feeling he injects into his playing. It's hard to relate 'Peace For South Africa' on the first volume to the torrents of sound he conjured up in his big-hall Pablo days. This is quieter, more intimate and more thoughtful, and the ballad medley at its centre shows genuine melodic inventiveness. A must for Peterson fans, and 'Honeysuckle Rose' offers a good – albeit second-gear – impression of the Tatum-derived technique which overlaid his earlier commitment to Nat Cole.

The second volume was recorded the following night. It's a more varied, less familiar programme, but the playing is pretty much by the numbers. The 'final' visit and the almost invevitable *Encore* are even more subdued and formal. The elegance of Peterson's segues begins to pall long before the end. Fans will value 'It Never Entered My Mind' on the last but one, but more casual purchasers might want to plump for the first volume and leave it at that, even if it means missing the *Encore* performance of 'I Wished On The Moon' which, though brief, is exquisite.

Ralph Peterson (born 1962) DRUMS

***(*) **Art** Blue Note 827645-2
> Peterson; Graham Haynes (*c*); Frank Lacy (*tb*); Steve Wilson (*ss, as*); Craig Handy (*ts*); Michele Rosewoman (*p*); Phil Bowler (*b*). 3/92.
*** **The Reclamation Project** Evidence 22113
> Peterson; Steve Wilson (*ss*); Bryan Carrott (*vib*); Belden Bulloch (*b*). 11/94.

Five earlier albums by this exceptional drummer/leader have already been deleted, which gives a somewhat foreshortened view of his progress. Five minutes of any record that he's on will impress his powers on any listener, though: stunningly energetic, never content to let a simple 4/4 stand, always overplaying his hand, yet delivering his accents with razor-sharp finesse and choking his cymbals with pinpoint precision.

Art is in some ways his most conventional record to date, perhaps deliberately cast as an 'inside' hard-bop session with few distracting frills. If so, it succeeds at a high level: Haynes has seldom played with such clarity and flowing inventiveness, Wilson is amiably fluent, Rosewoman summons all the energy she needs to keep pace with the fierce rhythm section (Lacy and Handy are on one track only). Peterson's tunes continue to be melodically fertile and his playing is as combustible as usual, an eloquent homage to the man mentioned in the title.

Reclamation Project takes the sombre theme of recovery from substance abuse and turns it into a thematic thread. Peterson is back in his more demanding groove here, delivering tunes in 9/8 and 14/8, setting Carrott and Wilson hugely difficult rhythmic tasks as improvisers – and somehow making it click. His innate sense of swing sees him through even the most potentially awkward situations. That said, this is a dark and sometimes introverted record and some may find it hard to find a way inside.

Umberto Petrin PIANO

*** **Ooze** Splasc(h) CDH 384.2
> Petrin; Guido Mazzon (*t*); Tiziano Tononi (*d*). 4–5/92.

Petrin has taken a long hard look at jazz piano history and synthesized a very idiosyncratic method. Many of these 15 tracks are miniatures, several last only a minute or two, but the opening treatment of Ornette Coleman's 'Street Woman' – which sounds like Earl Hines playing a Coleman tune – or the bleak, ghostly farewell of Donald Ayler's 'Our Prayer', with Mazzon making a guest appearance, display real understated authority. Though there are avant-garde flourishes here and there, Petrin has more conservative manners and, in reflective, almost rhapsodic pieces such as 'Mesty' or the slow but incisive look at ''Round Midnight', he approaches the serene radicalism of Paul Bley. Tononi adds very spare percussion parts to four tracks. The record has a disjointed and sometimes half-realized feel, but how many pianists making their debut would offer such an uncompromising programme?

Michel Petrucciani (born 1962) PIANO

**** **100 Hearts** Concord CCD 43001
> Petrucciani (*p* solo). 83.
**** **Live At The Village Vanguard** Concord CCD 43006 2CD
> Petrucciani; Palle Danielsson (*b*); Eliot Zigmund (*d*). 3/84.

There's a freshness and quicksilver virtuosity about Michel Petrucciani's early records which is entirely captivating. While he is an adoring admirer of Bill Evans – 'Call me Bill,' he once suggested to Jim Hall, who demurred – his extrovert attack places Evans's harmonic profundity in a setting that will energize listeners who find Evans too slow and quiet to respond to. Petrucciani was already a formidable talent when he began recording for Owl and, while some of these discs have been criticized for being the work of a pasticheur, that seems a curmudgeonly verdict on someone who enjoys the keyboard so much. *100 Hearts* is arguably the best of the early sessions, if only for the marvellous title-tune which skips and leaps around its tone centre: in themes like this, Petrucciani stakes a claim as one of the great romantic virtuosos in contemporary jazz. *Live At The Village Vanguard* captures a typically rumbustious concert set by Petrucciani's trio of the day: 'Nardis' and 'Oleo' offer fresh annotations on well-worn classics, and there are sparkling revisions of his own originals, 'To Erlinda' and 'Three Forgotten Magic Words'.

*** **Pianism** Blue Note CDP 746295-2
    Petrucciani; Palle Danielsson (*b*); Eliot Zigmund (*d*). 12/85.
***(*) **Power Of Three** Blue Note B21Y-46427-2
    Petrucciani; Wayne Shorter (*ss, ts*); Jim Hall (*g*). 7/86.
*** **Michel Plays Petrucciani** Blue Note B21Y-48679-2
    Petrucciani; John Abercrombie (*g*); Gary Peacock, Eddie Gomez (*b*); Roy Haynes, Al Foster (*d*); Steve Thornton (*perc*). 9–12/87.
Petrucciani's move to Blue Note gave him a bigger sound, courtesy of Blue Note's engineering; and the first three albums provided a variety of challenges. *Pianism* is another excellent batch of six work-outs by the trio who made the earlier live album, and if Zigmund and Danielsson sometimes sound a little perfunctory, that's partly due to the leader's brimming improvisations. *Power Of Three* is a slightly fragmented but absorbing concert meeting of three masters, skittish on 'Bimini' and solemnly appealing on 'In A Sentimental Mood'.

Plays Petrucciani is an all-original set which lines the pianist up against two magisterial rhythm sections, with Abercrombie adding some spruce counterpoint to two pieces. The smart hooks of 'She Did It Again' suggest that the pianist has a good living as a pop writer if he decides to quit the piano, but the more considered pieces show no drop in imagination, even if some of the themes seem to be curtailed before the improvisations really start moving.

*** **Promenade With Duke** Blue Note CDP 780590-2
    Petrucciani (*p* solo).
*** **Marvellous** Dreyfus FDM 36564-2
    Petrucciani; Dave Holland (*b*); Tony Williams (*d*); Graffiti String Quartet. n.d.
Michel's promenade is more with Strayhorn and Petrucciani than Ellington. Beautifully played and recorded, but it's rather sombre after the elated feel of his earlier sessions. *Marvellous* matches him with the formidable team of Holland and Williams, who play up the music's dramatic qualities to the hilt: a graceful tune like the 3/4 'Even Mice Dance' gets thumped open by Williams's awesome drumming. The pianist revels in the situation, though, and produces some of his most joyful playing. Yet it hardly squares with the string quartet parts, arranged by Petrucciani but more of a distraction than an integral part of such fierce playing.

*** **Conference De Presse** Dreyfus FDM 36568-2
    Petrucciani; Eddie Louiss (*org*). 94.
*** **Conference De Presse Vol. 2** Dreyfus FDM 36573-2
    As above. 94.
An enjoyable romp. Petrucciani duels with Hammond man Louiss on some standards, bebop, swing and whatever takes their fancy. Lots of tremolos, call-and-response joshing and so forth. It gets a bit much over two CDs, but they enjoyed themselves and so did the crowd at Petit Journal Montparnasse.

John Petters DRUMS

*** **Mixed Salad** Jazzology JCD-176
    Petters; Ben Cohen (*t*); Len Baldwin (*tb*); Wally Fawkes (*cl, ss*); Martin Litton (*p*); Paul Sealey (*g*); Annie Hawkins (*b*). 11/85–7/86.
(*) **Boogie Woogie And All That Jazz Rose RRCD003
    Petters; Neville Dickie (*p*); Mickey Ashman (*b*). 7/93.
There's nothing very 'authentic' about these records, but how much authenticity can a chubby young drummer from Harlow give to traditional jazz? In fact Petters brings a great sense of fun to these sessions, and it's disappointing that both should be let down by their circumstances. The Jazzology date features some memorable playing on both 'Shim-Me-Sha-Wabble' and 'Out Of The Galleon', with the

veteran Cohen sounding wonderfully lyrical, and Fawkes and Baldwin playing their part. The music never seems to hit quite the same high after those two tracks, and Litton's 'Wolverine Blues' is perfunctory; but the music is excellent trad, and it's a pity that the tinny sound and poor balance detract. *Boogie Woogie And All That Jazz* is a session of rag, boogie and novelty piano in which Dickie does all the playing and Ashman and Petters keep straight, simple time. Some of it sounds more like B Bumble And The Stingers than James P. Johnson, and the tunes are often ones that many will never want to hear again, but it's righteous. Recorded in Eastleigh.

Oscar Pettiford (1922–60) BASS, CELLO

***(*) **Discoveries** Savoy 0142

Pettiford; Gene Roland (*t*); Paul Quinichette (*ts*); Herbie Mann (*f*); Chasey Dean (*bcl*); Eddie Costa, Hank Jones, Nat Pierce, Billy Taylor (*p*); Joe Roland (*vib*); Doyle Salathiel (*g*); Mat Mathews (*acc*); Charles Mingus (*b*); Osie Johnson, Charlie Smith, Ed Thigpen (*d*). 2/52, 8/56, 10/57.

*** **Deep Passion** Impulse! GRP 11432

Pettiford; Ernie Royal, Art Farmer, Ray Copeland, Kenny Dorham (*t*); Jimmy Cleveland; Al Grey (*tb*); Julius Watkins, David Amram (*frhn*); Gigi Gryce, Lucky Thompson, Jerome Richardson, Benny Golson, Sahib Shihab, Danny Bank (*reeds*); Janet Putnam, Betty Glamann (*hp*); Tommy Flanagan, Dick Katz (*p*); Whitney Mitchell (*b*); Osie Johnson (*d*). 6/56–9/57.

*** **Vienna Blues: The Complete Session** Black Lion BLCD 760104

Pettiford; Hans Koller (*ts*); Attila Zoller (*g, b*); Jimmy Pratt (*d*). 1/59.

***(*) **Montmartre Blues** Black Lion BLCD 760124

Pettiford; Allan Botschinsky (*t*); Erik Nordstrom (*ts*); Louis Hjulmand (*vib*); Jan Johansson (*p*); Jorn Elniff (*d*). 8/59, 7/60.

Like Charlie Haden's, Pettiford's playing career began in a family orchestra, under the tutelage of his father, Harry 'Doc' Pettiford. Like another great bassist, Charles Mingus, he never quite outgrew the turbulences of his early upbringing, and there was an undercurrent of anger and frustration just below the surface of Pettiford's wonderfully propulsive bass-playing. In terms of jazz history, he marks a middle point between Jimmy Blanton and his exact contemporary, Mingus; had he lived longer and closer to the centre, he might well now be acknowledged the more influential player.

As it is, he didn't live to see forty and spent his last years as a European exile. As a musical environment, it suited him rather well, encouraging his underlying classicism and allowing him to experiment with more flexible contexts. Only Ron Carter among bassists has shown a commensurate interest in the cello, and Carter very much followed Pettiford's example. There are a number of cello features on *Deep Passion*, which is otherwise dominated by Gryce's arrangements and Thompson's solos, luminous and mysterious by turn. The Impulse! reissue brings together two original ABC albums on a single disc. As a front-line voice, the cello sounds good, but the basis of its success is the close interplay with the other horns, and Thompson's title track and one of the earliest recordings of 'I Remember Clifford' are among the standouts.

Discoveries demonstrates the extent to which Pettiford was experimenting with the basic jazz ensemble at the end of the 1950s. One track has him playing bass alongside flute, bass clarinet, vibraphone, accordion and drums, elsewhere using accordion in place of piano or guitar. Austrian saxophonist Koller features prominently on *Vienna Blues*.

Pettiford's work with Monk and Ellington (who recognized both the break and the continuity with Blanton) survives on disc, and it's worth concentrating on the bassist's performances. It should also be noted that, though credited to Bud Powell, Black Lion's *The Complete Essen Jazz Festival Concert* documents a performance by the Oscar Pettiford Trio and (with Coleman Hawkins) Quartet from April 1960. The material on *Montmartre Blues* is every bit as good, suggesting that Pettiford's decline was not an artistic one, whatever else it was. Only weeks later, Pettiford died in his adoptive city of Copenhagen of what was then still called 'infantile paralysis'.

Barre Phillips (born 1934) DOUBLE BASS, ELECTRONICS

**** **Mountainscapes** ECM 1076

Phillips; John Surman (*bs, ss, bcl, syn*); John Abercrombie (*g*); Dieter Feichtener (*syn*); Stu Martin (*d*). 3/76.

**** **Three Day Moon** ECM 1123

Philips; Terje Rypdal (*g, g syn, org*); Dieter Feichtener (*syn*); Trilok Gurtu (*perc*). 3/78.

*** **Journal Violone II** ECM 1149
> Phillips; John Surman (*ss, bs, bcl, syn*); Aina Kemanis (*v*). 6/79.

***(*) **Camouflage** Victo 08
> Phillips solo. 5/89.

*** **Aquarian Rain** ECM 1451
> Phillips; Alain Joule (*perc*). 5/91.

***(*) **Uzu** PSF CD 75
> Phillips; Yoshizawa Motoharu (*b*). 96.

Phillips made the first-ever album of solo bass improvisations as long ago as 1968. At the time, as Steve Lake relates in the liner-note to *Aquarian Rain*, he believed he was providing material for an electronic score, but composer Max Schubel thought the bass parts stood more than adequately on their own, and *Unaccompanied Barre* was eventually released. Nearly 25 years later, Phillips produced an album which does make significant use of electronic processing of instrumental performance. The effect suggests that Schubel's instincts were sound, for *Aquarian Rain* is the most diffuse and least focused album the bassist has released. Phillips's own description of the process of 'collective composition', by which tapes were sent back and forth between his French home in Puget-Ville and the Studio Grame in Lyon where Jean-François Estager and James Giroudon worked the filters and gates, may have yielded exemplary music for live performance (a suite called 'Brick On Brick' was created, incorporating pieces like 'Inbetween I And E' and 'Promenade De Mémoire') but it sounds rather stilted and contrived when digitalized and fixed. Enthusiasts for the bassist's work will find much of value but, compared to the duos with Guy, these interchanges with percussionist Joule lack even that tiny spark of electricity which rescues processed improvisation of this sort from becoming acoustic set-dressing.

It's galling to note that Phillips's very best record is *still* out of catalogue. The solo *Call Me When You Get There* (ECM 1257 LP) from 1983, with its lyrical journeyings and unfussy philosophical musings, covers similar musical territory to the much earlier but almost equally fine *Mountainscapes*, a suite of subliminally interrelated pieces which demonstrate the astonishing transformations visited on basic musical perspectives by very slight changes in the angle of vision. Almost all of Phillips's output operates in that way. Whatever is being hidden on the recent solo *Camouflage*, it can scarcely be the artist himself. Recorded in almost disturbing close-up (an effect necessarily heightened by CD reproduction), one can almost hear the bassist thinking as he investigates the sometimes fugitive tonalities of his instrument. Something of the same relationship between *Call Me* and *Mountainscapes* applies (recognizing the lapse in time) between *Camouflage* and *Journal Violone II*. The 1979 trio again makes use of Surman's melancholy soliloquizing, but in a rather more colouristic way that is reminiscent of *Three Day Moon*. This is Phillips's most accessible work on record but is by no means unrepresentative. Rypdal is an intelligent partner, and Feichtener adds (as he had on *Mountainscapes*) some highly individual flourishes. One questions Gurtu's role, though: too effusive and individual a player, surely, for this selfless idiom.

Looking at Phillips's career only in the context of his recent solo work or of his improvisational activities with Derek Bailey's Company collective tends to cast it as something rarefied and dauntingly inward of gaze (the duo *Figuring* with Bailey (*q.v.*), Incus CD05, might attract that charge) but it's as well to remember that Phillips was Archie Shepp's bass player at the 1965 Newport Festival and that, with Surman and the late Stu Martin, also on *Mountainscapes*, he was a member of The Trio, one of the most dynamic free jazz units of the late 1960s. There is a dancer's grace and concentration in Phillips's playing, an internal balance and rhythm that, as on *Camouflage*'s 'You And Me', makes it virtually impossible to separate man and instrument.

There are problems on *Uzu*. Motoharu has so thoroughly wired himself up to what is described as a 'homemade electric vertical five string bass' that it is genuinely difficult to work out what one is listening to. This is only a problem if you take a close interest in the technical dimensions of music like this. For most people, the album will be a vivid, arresting experience, well worth a bit of patience.

Flip Phillips (born 1915) TENOR SAXOPHONE

***(*) **Flip Wails: The Best Of The Verve Years** Verve 521645-2
> Phillips; Howard McGhee, Harry Edison, Allen Smith, Al Porcino, Al Derisi, Bernie Glow, Roy Eldridge, Lou Oles, Charlie Shavers (*t*); Bill Harris, Chuck Etter (*tb*); Charlie Kennedy, Sam Marowitz, Hal McKusick (*as*); Al Cohn (*ts*); Cecil Payne, Jerome Richardson, Danny Bank (*bs*); Hank Jones, Oscar Peterson, Dick Hyman, Richard Wyands, Mickey Crane, Ronnie Ball (*p*); Herb Ellis, Billy Bauer, Freddie Green (*g*); Ray Brown, Gene Ramey, Vernon Alley, Clyde Lombardi, Peter Ind (*b*); J. C. Heard, Buddy Rich, Jo Jones, Max Roach, Alvin Stoller, Louis Bellson (*d*). 10/47–1/58.

A stalwart of Jazz At The Philharmonic and a mainstay of many a tenor battle, the spotlight has seldom been turned on this accomplished tenorman in more reflective mood. Recent years have seen him assume a comfortable elder-statesman role, but in his original prime he was only rarely recorded as a leader. This useful disc draws in the pick of a number of sessions for Norman Granz, mostly from the 1950s – although the opening 'Znarg Blues', with Howard McGhee in 1947, shows how near Phillips came to being a charter bebopper. More characteristic is the beefy tenderness of 'If I Had You', the nod to Bix and Trumbauer in 'Singin' The Blues' and the vigorous bounce of 'Three Little Words', almost a signature-tune for this school of players. Bill Harris turns in sterling work on his several appearances and the set winds up with a live quartet date featuring Buddy Rich as leader. There are no real masterpieces here but a lot of strong, swinging jazz. Consistently fine remastering.

(*) **A Sound Investment Concord CCD 4334
> Phillips; Scott Hamilton (*ts*); John Bunch (*p*); Chris Flory (*g*); Phil Flanigan (*b*); Chuck Riggs (*d*). 3/87.

*** **A Real Swinger** Concord CCD 4358
> Phillips; Dick Hyman (*p*); Howard Alden, Wayne Wright (*g*); Jack Lesberg (*b*); Butch Morris (*d*). 5–6/88.

In what's been an Indian summer for him, Phillips sounds warmly charismatic, pacing his solos with some flair and digging in just when he has to: the session in which he is the sole horn sounds fine, with 'September Song' and 'Poor Butterfly' to remind one of his authoritative ballad playing. The set with Hamilton is sometimes too much of a good thing, with both tenors thickening the romantic broth a little over-generously at times, but one can't deny the heartiness of it all.

(*) **The Claw Chiaroscuro CR(D) 314
> Phillips; Clark Terry (*t*); Buddy Tate, Al Cohn, Scott Hamilton (*ts*); John Bunch (*p*); Chris Flory (*g*); Major Holley (*b*); Chuck Riggs (*d*). 10/86.

*** **Try A Little Tenderness** Chiaroscuro CR(D) 321
> Phillips; Dick Hyman (*p*); Howard Alden, Bucky Pizzarelli (*g*); Bob Haggart (*b*); Ronnie Traxler (*d*); strings. 6–7/92.

Flip is in good spirits for both these disparate sessions for Chiaroscuro. *The Claw* is a tenors-all-out jam session on board the SS *Norway* during the 1986 Floating Jazz Festival: they didn't look too far afield for the material ('Topsy', 'Flying Home' and so forth) and in the end it sounds too much like a parade of tenor solos to make for a satisfying record. But Flip and Al Cohn especially come up with a few remarks that evade the rules of the tenor extravaganza. Phillips gets to make his strings album on *Try A Little Tenderness* and, with canny arrangements by Dick Hyman and the saxophonist in his ripest form, the music is sly enough to sidestep most of the clichés of the situation – or, at least, to make them enjoyable anyway. A nice indulgence for the old warrior.

Enrico Pieranunzi (born 1949) PIANO

**** **Isis** Soul Note 121021
> Pieranunzi; Art Farmer (*flhn*); Massimo Urbani (*as*); Furio Di Castri (*b*); Roberto Gatto (*d*). 81.

*** **New Lands** Timeless SJP 211
> Pieranunzi; Marc Johnson (*b*); Joey Baron (*d*). 2/84.

*** **Autumn Song** Enja 4094 LP
> Pieranunzi; Massimo Urbani (*as*); Enzo Pietropaoli (*b*); Fabrizio Sferra (*d*). 11/84.

*** **Deep Down** Soul Note SN 1121
> Pieranunzi; Marc Johnson (*b*); Joey Baron (*d*). 2/86.

*** **What's What** yvp 3006
> Pieranunzi (*p* solo). 6/85.

(*) **Moon Pie yvp 3011
> Pieranunzi; Enzo Pietropaoli (*b*); Roberto Gatto (*d*). 5–6/87.

*** **No Man's Land** Soul Note SN 1221
> Pieranunzi; Marc Johnson (*b*); Steve Houghton (*d*). 5/89.

*** **Trioscape** yvp 3050
> Pieranunzi; Piero Leveratto (*b*); Mauro Beggio (*d*); Francesco Petrini (*d, perc*). 2 & 5/95.

**** **Flux And Change** Soul Note 121242
> Pieranunzi; Paul Motian (*d*). 95.

Pieranunzi's music is a persuasive and accomplished indexing of some of the options thrown open to pianists in the aftermath of Tyner, Hancock, Taylor and – to cite one source away from Afro-America – Martial Solal. Pieranunzi is not a virtuoso in the manner of any of those players – though his rather self-effacing manner recalls something of Hancock – but he uses their ground-breaking discoveries in modality, rhythm and the broadening of pianistic devices to his own ends. As with the Space Jazz trio, which he apparently leads with bassist Pietropaoli, this is convincingly post-modern jazz, in which the pianist sounds perfectly self-aware yet concerned to introduce elements of abstraction and emotional flow alike. Perhaps the two discs to seek out are the ruminative but pointedly argued solo set, *What's What*, and the excellent trio session, *No Man's Land*, though the earlier *New Lands* and *Deep Down* are both very good too. Urbani's winsome bop manner adds some variation to the Enja album, though not enough to make a compelling difference; and *Moon Pie* sounds a little under-baked.

The reappearance of *Isis*, which is lifted immeasurably by Farmer and by a couple of gorgeous solos from the ill-fated Urbani, changes the picture somewhat, as does the emergence of a fine set of duos with Paul Motian, no fewer than 23 standard and original songs arranged into two long suites. Persuasive and elegant.

Billie Pierce (1907–74) PIANO, VOCAL and
De De Pierce (1904–73) CORNET

** **With Kid Thomas Valentine 1960** 504 CD 36
    Pierce; Pierce; Kid Thomas Valentine (*t*). 60.
(*) **In Binghamton, N.Y. Vol. 2 American Music AMCD-81
    Pierce; Pierce; Albert Warner (*tb*); Willie Humphrey (*cl*); Cie Frazier (*d*). 10/62.
(*) **In Binghamton, N.Y. Vol. 3 American Music AMCD-82
    As above. 10/62.
*** **New Orleans: The Living Legends** Original Blues Classics OBC 534
    Pierce; Pierce; Albert Jiles (*d*). 1/61.

The Pierces were a familiar husband-and-wife team in New Orleans dance-halls for many years. Though De De also worked in the Preservation Hall Jazz Band, it's his recordings with Billie that remain his best legacy; so far, these have made it to CD. The session with Kid Thomas sitting in as guest is very ramshackle-sounding, but the spirit abides, and it's a curiously moving document even with all the fluffs and effortful playing. The two Binghamton discs were cut at a college concert (the first two volumes are duet recordings, yet to appear on CD). The music is often all over the place, and De De is so unpredictable that Willie Humphrey seems to be trying to watch him all the time; but, for all the rackety playing, it becomes oddly exhilarating after a while.

On the OBC, the programme is nearly all simple, slow blues, taken at a stately tempo by Billie's piano, with cornet elaborations by De De that are modestly ambitious: he plays a much more improvised line than the standard New Orleans lead horns and, though he cracks a lot of notes and sometimes loses his way, he works hard at his playing. Billie's high vocals are sometimes hard to take, since she hardly varies her delivery (she once accompanied Bessie Smith, but sounds more like Clara Smith). This is deep New Orleans music.

Billy Pierce (born 1948) TENOR AND SOPRANO SAXOPHONES

(*) **The Complete William The Conqueror Sessions Sunnyside SSC 9013D
    Pierce; James Williams, James 'Sid' Simmons (*p*); John Lockwood (*b*); Keith Copeland (*d*). 5/85.
** **Give And Take** Sunnyside SSC 1026 D
    Pierce; Terence Blanchard (*t*); Mulgrew Miller (*p*); Ira Coleman (*b*); Tony Reedus (*d*). 6-10/87.
*** **Equilateral** Sunnyside SSC 1037 D
    Pierce; Hank Jones (*p*); Roy Haynes (*d*). 1/88.

Another Jazz Messengers tenorman steps out on his own, with characteristically mixed results. Pierce is as easily tempted by bland competence as the next saxophonist, and nothing memorable happens on either of the two earlier discs: it's especially disappointing with regard to *Give And Take*, which from moment to moment suggests a genuinely heavyweight encounter but over the long stretch delivers nothing much at all. *Equilateral* starts out with two advantages: the presence of Jones and Haynes, still among the best props a young musician could hope to find alongside him, and the unusual bass-less instrumentation, which isn't intrusive but at least proposes a different balance from the usual. The programme is nearly all standards, and on some of them – particularly 'You Don't Know What Love Is' and 'Come Rain Or Come Shine' – Pierce summons the gravitas of greater players without surrendering too much of himself.

*** **One For Chuck** Sunnyside 1053
    Pierce; Bill Mobley (*t, flhn*); Mulgrew Miller (*p*); Ira Coleman (*b*); Alan Dawson (*d*). 4/91.

*** **Rolling Monk** Paddle Wheel K I C J 154
> Pierce; Donald Brown (*p*); Christian McBride (*b*); Billy Drummond (*d*). 12/92.

One For Chuck sets Pierce in front of another top-flight rhythm section, and with the useful if undemonstrative Mobley beside him he shoulders the weight of the session impressively enough, even dismissing the others for a couple of *a cappella* solos. In the end, though, it makes no deeper impression than the other Sunnyside dates.

On Paddle Wheel, Pierce meets Monk and Rollins, at least in terms of paying homage. He starts with 'I'm An Old Cow Hand', not quite as swaggering as Sonny's treatment, but it perambulates along nicely enough. 'Bye-Ya', with a fine tenor essay at its heart, is probably the best of the four Monk tunes here, while Brown's original 'In Walked Toot' is an obvious nod to the master; 'Pent-Up House' returns to Rollins at close of play, and Pierce still has plenty of licks left in him. This is a good, filling programme of tenor and rhythm, even if it does nothing more than mark time for the leader.

Dave Pike (born 1938) VIBES, MARIMBA

(*) **Pike's Groove Criss Cross 1021
> Pike; Cedar Walton (*p*); David Williams (*b*); Billy Higgins (*d*). 2/86.

*** **Bluebird** Timeless S J P 302
> Pike; Charles McPherson (*as*); Rein De Graaff (*p*); Koos Serierse (*b*); Eric Ineke (*d*). 10–11/88.

Pike is another musician whose several recordings have suffered at the hands of the deletions axe. Although he once worked with Paul Bley in the late 1950s, Pike's main interests are more conservative than that association might suggest: both the above records are light and undeniably skilful bebop sessions. *Pike's Groove* matches him with the most propulsive of rhythm sections and, thanks to Walton's craft and sensitivity to tone-colours, vibes and piano don't cancel each other out as they often do in such situations. Seven familiar pieces, but everyone is crisply on top of them.

The Timeless set features eight Charlie Parker themes, three by Pike and the rhythm section, four by the quintet, and one by the rhythm section alone. While the music is entirely regressive – the Dutch players are content to be model executants and Pike's own playing isn't characterful enough to transcend bop routine – the themes are at least covered with great finesse, and McPherson, one of the premier exponents of bop repertory, is marvellously agile. Sharp, full sound.

Courtney Pine (born 1964) TENOR, ALTO AND SOPRANO SAXOPHONES, BASS CLARINET, FLUTE, ALTO FLUTE, KEYBOARDS

(*) **Journey To The Urge Within Island 842687
> Pine; Kevin Robinson (*t*); Ray Carless (*bs*); Julian Joseph (*p*); Roy Carter (*ky*); Orphy Robinson (*vib*); Martin Taylor (*g*); Gary Crosby (*b*); Mark Mondesir (*d*); Ian Mussington (*perc*); Susaye Greene, Cleveland Watkiss (*v*). 7–8/86.

*** **Destiny's Song And The Image Of Pursuance** Island 842772
> Pine; Julian Joseph, Joe Bashorun (*p*); Paul Hunt, Gary Crosby (*b*); Mark Mondesir (*d*).

*** **The Vision's Tale** Island 842373
> Pine; Ellis Marsalis (*p*); Delbert Felix (*b*); Jeff Tain Watts (*d*). 1/89.

** **Closer To Home** Island 510769
> Pine; Ian Fraser (*bs*); Robbie Lynn (*ky*); Cameron Pierre (*g*); Danny Browne, Delroy Donaldson (*b*); Cleavie (*d*); Pam Hall, Carroll Thompson (*v*).

*** **Within The Realms Of Our Dreams** Island 848244
> Pine; Kenny Kirkland (*p*); Charnett Moffett (*b*); Jeff Tain Watts (*d*). 1/90.

*** **To The Eyes Of Creation** Island 514044
> Pine; Dennis Rollins (*tb*); Keith Waite (*f, perc*); Bheki Mseleku (*p*); Julian Joseph (*ky*); Tony Remy, Cameron Pierre (*g*); Wayne Batchelor (*b*); Mark Mondesir, Frank Tontoh, Brian Abrahams (*d*); Thomas Dyani, Mamadi Kamara (*perc*); Cleveland Watkiss, Linda Muriel (*v*). 92.

*** **Modern Day Jazz Stories** Antilles/Talkin' Loud 529 428
> Pine; Eddie Henderson (*t*); Geri Allen (*p, org*); Mark Whitfield (*g*); Charnett Moffett (*b*); Ronnie Burrage (*d, perc*); D. J. Pogo (*turntables*); Cassandra Wilson (*v*). 95.

British readers will have had a difficult time of it separating Pine the musician from Pine the marketing phenomenon since, starting around the time of the first record above, he was fruitfully presented as the face of young British jazz in the 1980s. It was a move that brought unprecedented attention to the music in the UK, but the fallout has been a certain suspicion among many who are wary of media hype, as well as a problem in evaluating the records purely on their musical worth. Fortunately, Pine himself is a saxophonist of clear and outstanding capabilities: whatever flaws these records may have, his own contributions are of a consistently high standard. *Journey To The Urge Within*, his hit debut, emerges as a sampler for young British talent, with Joseph, Mondesir, Crosby, Robinson and Watkiss all making interesting debut appearances and Pine leading the pack. There are good moments, and the sense of a group of players seizing their time is palpable, but inexperience and fragmentation take their toll on the record's impact and it tends to work out as a series of half-fulfilled gestures. *Destiny's Song* was a strong follow-up: tunes such as 'Sacrifice' show that Pine has a knack for turning catchy riffs into feasible melodies, and an emerging dialogue with Mondesir (Pine's Dannie Richmond, if not quite his Elvin Jones) gave the session real clout. But both this and the subsequent *The Vision's Tale* hint at a talent that is taking a long time to work out what it wants to do: too many of the double-time solos and pyro-technics smack of pointless virtuosity, and several improvisations sound like sketches for real achieve-ments that have to be left unfinished. *The Vision's Tale* (a penchant for obfuscatory titles shouldn't put listeners off) put Pine in the hands of an American rhythm section, with Marsalis at his wiliest in accompaniment, and if a reading of 'I'm An Old Cowhand' seems to be asking for trouble – Pine has often been accused of balling together a host of unassimilated influences, though Coltrane rather than Rollins is the leading name involved – it's dealt with in enough good humour to lend a self-deprecatory note.

Closer To Home returns Pine to roots which no American jazz musician can really claim: like so many young black British musicians, he started in reggae and funk bands, and this lightly shuffling reggae set is a very pleasant if finally inconsequential disc. It has the merit, though, of reminding that Pine's records never sound like American jazz albums, for all his leaning towards familiar role-models: rhyth-mically, tonally, harmonically, all his music – and that of many of his British sidemen – is informed by sources (Jamaican reggae being a prime example) which seldom filter through to the post-bop main-stream of American jazz. *Within The Realms Of Our Dreams* puts him back with a formidable American rhythm section, and there's no hint of difficulty for the leader. Originals such as 'Zaire', which features a double-time passage on soprano which is quite breathtaking in its technical aplomb, and 'The Sepia Love Song' show a maturing sense of detail as a composer, and 'Una Muy Bonita' and 'Donna Lee' sweep through Coleman and Parker with ferocious accomplishment. There are still too many notes, and too few ideas channelled down a single route to resolution, but this multifariousness of idea and delivery is clearly Pine's way.

To The Eyes Of Creation marks another change – Pine must be among the most restless talents of his generation – by bringing in a fresh interest in electronics, texture and timeless folk arcana, as in the bells, flutes and shakers of the closing 'The Holy Grail'. This set is something of a pan-global journey, taking in Africa, ska ('Eastern Standard Time'), a universal soul ballad ('Children Hold On'), bridging inter-ludes, and a fair amount of intense saxophone. With a widescreen-soul production, the music sounds big and impressive but, like most travelogues, it's more a patchwork of interesting sights and sounds than a convincingly resolved statement.

Modern Day Jazz Stories finds Pine consolidating and developing this strain. He has the experience of Geri Allen to guide him and 'hook up the chords' and, with guest contributions from Eddie Henderson and Mark Whitfield and the ferocious bass of Charnett Moffett to root the whole session, it has a powerfully evocative quality. Pine keeps the turntable manipulations relatively far back in the mix, and places himself just left of centre. Interestingly, the most effective single track on the album is a setting of Langston Hughes's poem, 'The Negro Speaks Of Rivers', which Pine originally heard on a Gary Bartz album of the early 1970s. He has made something very contemporary and immediate out of Hughes's timeless lines.

Armand Piron (1888–1943) VIOLIN, VOCAL, BANDLEADER

*** Piron's New Orleans Orchestra Azure AZ-CD-13

Piron; Peter Bocage (*t*); John Lindsay (*tb*); Lorenzo Tio Jr (*cl, ts*); Louis Warnecke (*as*); Steve Lewis (*p*); Charles Bocage (*bj, v*); Bob Ysaguirre (*tba*); Louis Cottrell (*d*); Esther Bigeou, Ida G. Brown, Lela Bolden, Willie Lewis (*v*). 12/23–4/26.

For the most part they were recorded in New York, but Piron's band was a New Orleans outfit and as such were one of the few to be documented in the 1920s. This splendid reissue is a model of its kind: the sleeve-notes sum up years of research into the performers' activities, and the remastering of a set of terrifically rare originals is excellent, though a few of the 78s were obviously rather beaten up. That said, the disc isn't a revelation on a par with Azure's Papa Celestin/Sam Morgan disc. Piron's group was a more genteel, proper orchestra, pitching itself somewhere between ragtime, society music and the glim-mers of early jazz: though 1923 is early in jazz recording history, they still sound a much less modern band next to Oliver or Fletcher Henderson from the same year (one should compare their treatment of 'Doo Doodle Oom' with Henderson's 1923 Vocalion version). A few tracks, including the very first,

'Bouncing Around', brew up a potent mix of syncopation, with Tio's wriggling clarinet-breaks and Bocage's urbane lead making their mark over an ensemble rhythm that is almost swinging. But there is surprisingly little development between the earliest and the latest tracks by the orchestra. The CD is beefed up with four tracks in which pianist Lewis accompanies blues singer Willie Jackson, and it closes on the charming discovery of a Lewis piano-roll of a title from their second session, 'Mama's Gone, Goodbye'.

Steve Pistorius (born 1954) PIANO, VOCAL

***(*) T'Ain't No Sin GHB BCD-289
>   Pistorius; Scott Black (c, v); Jacques Gauthe (cl, as); John Gill (bsx, bj, v); Chris Tyle (d, v). 89.
***(*) Kiss Me Sweet Stomp Off CD-1221
>   Pistorius; Chris Tyle (c, v); Tom Fischer (cl, as); Tim Laughlin (cl); Hal Smith (d); Suzy Malone (v). 7/90.

In addition to his records with Tyle and Smith as leaders, Steve Pistorius has made these two excellent small-group records of his own. The quintet of the GHB record has a thinnish sound and some of the rhythms get close to the clockwork beat that trad parodists deploy, but much of the music is hot, affectionate, oddly lyrical. There are perhaps too many vocals, shared around the band, although Pistorius's own voice is a likeable one, something akin to a Leon Redbone minus the mumbling. The material is a fascinating stack of 1920s' arcana, with items from the repertoires of Louis Armstrong, New Orleans Willie Jackson, Natty Dominique, Don Redman and Jelly Roll Morton, and the horn-playing – Black plays a sweetly strong lead, and Gauthe is all over the clarinet, with a whinnying alto as second string – is perfectly apposite. *Kiss Me Sweet* mixes trio, quartet and quintet tracks on another cheering programme of oddities and faithful trad vehicles. Pistorius himself is a frisky player, clearly out to enjoy himself but aware that this is delicate as well as rude music.

Bucky Pizzarelli (born 1926) GUITAR

**** The Complete Guitar Duos (The Stash Sessions) Stash ST CD 536
>   Pizzarelli; John Pizzarelli (g). 80, 84.

Pizzarelli's finest recording of recent years remains the unfortunately deleted solo, *Love Songs*, a set of gentle swing improvisations on his favoured seven-string guitar (which nevertheless sounds quite conventionally tuned). Pizzarelli maintained a highly successful swing duo with George Barnes until the latter died in 1977, since when he has worked with his son, John Pizzarelli Jr, an excellent family act reminiscent of the Raneys but untouched by their bop leanings. John Pizzarelli was still developing an individual style over the period covered by the two sessions; on the earlier tracks he sounds like an able accompanist but rarely stamps any real personality on a piece. The later sessions sound much more like an equally balanced duo, and the material is marginally more challenging in response, with a wonderfully shuffling 'Four Brothers' and a near-perfect 'Lush Life'. Highly recommended.

John Pizzarelli (born 1960) GUITAR, VOCAL

**(*) Hit That Jive Jack! Stash STB 2508
>   Pizzarelli; Dave McKenna (p); Bucky Pizzarelli (g); Hugh McCracken (hca); Jerry Bruno, Gary Hasse (b); Butch Miles, Steven Ferrera (d). 6/85.
*** My Blue Heaven Chesky JD38
>   Pizzarelli; Clark Terry (t, v); Dave McKenna (p); Bucky Pizzarelli (g); Milt Hinton (b); Connie Kay (d). 2/90.
*** All Of Me Novus PD 90619
>   Pizzarelli; Randy Sandke, John Frosk, Anthony Kadleck, Michael Ponella (t); Jim Pugh, Rock Ciccarone, Michael Davis (tb); Paul Faulise (btb); Walt Levinsky, Phil Bodner (as); Scott Robinson (ss, ts, f); Frank Griffith (ts); Sol Schlinger (bs); William Kerr, Lawrence Feldman (f); Ken Levinsky (p); Bucky Pizzarelli (g); Martin Pizzarelli (b); Joe Cocuzzo (d); Gordon Gottlieb (perc, vib); strings. 91.
***(*) Naturally Novus 63151-2
>   As above, except add Clark Terry (t, flhn), Jim Hynes (t), Bob Alexander, Mark Patterson, Wayne Andre (tb), Frank Wess, Harry Allen (ts), Jack Stuckey (bs), Dominic Cortese (acc); omit Sandke, Pugh, Ciccarone, Davis, Bodner, Schlinger, Kerr, Feldman and Gottlieb. 92.

***(*) **New Standards** Novus 63172-2
> Pizzarelli; Ted Nash (*ts*); Ray Kennedy (*p, org*); Bucky Pizzarelli (*g*); Jim Saporito (*vib, perc*);
> Martin Pizzarelli (*b*); Tony Corbiscello, Joe Cocuzzo (*d*); horns, strings, voices. 93.

*** **Dear Mr Cole** Novus 63182-2
> Pizzarelli; Benny Green, Ray Kennedy (*p*); Christian McBride, Martin Pizzarelli (*b*); John
> Guerin (*d*). 94.

*** **After Hours** Novus 63191-2
> Pizzarelli; Randy Sandke (*t*); Harry Allen (*ts*); Ray Kennedy (*p*); Bucky Pizzarelli (*g*); Martin
> Pizzarelli (*b*); Joe Cocuzzo (*d*). 95.

John Pizzarelli follows in father's footsteps by using a guitar style that owes an obvious debt to paternal influence: quick, clean picking, a Django-like tone and a penchant for the humorous aside in the middle of otherwise terse improvisations. While this makes for solid, gratifying mainstream, Pizzarelli isn't really a young fogey: there's a coolness about his manner which detaches him a little from the material and, while some of his song choices are as neo-classic as one could get, he sounds a little dreamier than the Concord crew of mainstreamers. Besides, he sings – and this is what has determined his career in recent years. Pizzarelli was doing this sort of thing long before the likes of Harry Connick, and his singing and playing is accomplished in its own right; but the tenor of the later records is unmistakably tuned to Connick's huge audience, at least to start with.

The Stash album is a reissue of an early vocal outing. Pizzarelli and the band have fun with the likes of 'The Frim Fram Sauce' but the manner and production sound elementary next to the sophistication of the Novus records. *My Blue Heaven* is beautifully recorded and shrewdly programmed, with Clark Terry tossing in some characteristic obbligatos and the instrumental pieces – including a very sharp-witted 'Don't Get Around Much Any More' – finding a real, spontaneous zest. *All Of Me* is Pizzarelli's initial stab at the big time: cleverly pitched between the big-band charts and the nucleus of the singer and the rhythm section, it's artfully realized but a legitimate musical success by dint of Pizzarelli's trust of the material. His three original songs are, though, no special achievement. The recording and mix are superbly full and wide-bodied. *Naturally* continues the run with splendid results. An unlikely choice such as 'When I Grow Too Old To Dream' is beautifully pitched, 'I'm Confessin'' is as delicate a ballad as one could wish for, and 'Nuages' receives a clever update. Pizzarelli still sounds self-effacing instead of self-satisfied. But his originals are still a long way behind the standards.

That problem is solved in part on *New Standards*, where Pizzarelli elects to base a programme around new or unfamiliar songs. His own pieces are only so-so, but the others – especially 'Fools Fall In Love', 'I'm Your Guy' (which he at least had a hand in), 'I'm Alright Now' and 'Look At Us' – suit his persona to a tee: smart, hip, but an easy-going romantic under the skin. The arrangements are again nicely poised between small groups and horn and string embellishments, and the warm but not too foggy studio sound is ideal. Probably his best record.

Dear Mr Cole looks promising: with the nucleus of Green, McBride and Pizzarelli himself as a dream trio, Nat Cole tunes as the repertoire, and a perfectly intimate studio mix, this was set up to be a classic. But the opening 'Style Is Coming Back In Style' with the other rhythm section is so blissful that the rest is almost a disappointment and, as cleverly as the trio plays, it's just a shade too neo-classic to wholly convince, despite some lovely moments.

After Hours moves the concept to a full-fledged ballad album. Sandke and Allen blow sweetly apposite obbligatos and John's working trio play with intuitive rightness: on a couple of less obvious choices such as 'Coquette' and 'Mam'selle', the pitch is flawlessly right. Because he's singing so quietly and without undue emphasis, it's easy to miss how effective Pizzarelli has become at this music, too. Yet the album still fails to make a significant mark – by its very nature, perhaps. If some of these gradings look harsh, it should be noted that in many ways this is the best sequence of vocal records of recent times, even though the individual albums have yet to attain masterpiece status.

King Pleasure (born 1922) VOCALS

*** **King Pleasure Sings** Original Jazz Classics OJC 217
> Pleasure; Ed Lewis (*t*); J. J. Johnson, Kai Winding (*tb*); Charles Ferguson, Lucky Thompson
> (*ts*); Danny Banks (*bs*); Jimmy Jones, John Lewis, Ed Swanston (*p*); Paul Chambers, Percy
> Heath, Peck Morrison (*b*); Kenny Clarke, Joe Harris, Herbie Lovelle (*d*); Betty Carter, Jon
> Hendricks, Eddie Jefferson, The Dave Lambert Singers, The Three Riffs (*v*). 12/52, 9/53, 12/54.

Born plain Clarence Beeks, in plain old Oakdale, Tennessee, Pleasure won an amateur night at the Apollo in 1951 and went on to scoop enormous success with 'Moody's Mood For Love', a vocalese version of James Moody's saxophone solo on 'I'm In The Mood For Love', and later with 'Red Top'. Eddie Jefferson claimed to have invented the practice of fitting lyrics to bop solos, but it was Pleasure who garnered the praise and what cash was going. (Just to confirm Jefferson's luck, he was blown away outside a Detroit club in 1979, just as his career was reviving; Jefferson, Jon Hendricks and The Three Riffs all feature on two 1954 tracks from *Sings*.)

The disc is shared with Annie Ross, who sings the classic vocalization of Wardell Gray's 'Twisted', along with 'Moody's Mood For Love' and Pleasure's 'Parker's Mood' the best-known vocalese performance. Pleasure has something of Ross's honeyed smoothness of tone but combines it with a more biting articulation that can sound remarkably like Charlie Parker's alto saxophone (or, more frequently, the smooth tenor sound of Teddy Edwards and Lucky Thompson). Using less sophisticated arrangements and generally less witty lyrics than Jon Hendricks's for Lambert, Hendricks and Ross, Pleasure more often relies on the quality of the voice alone. The accompaniments are generally good, but the Quincy Jones backings to 'Don't Get Scared' and 'I'm Gone' are exceptional. Something of an acquired taste, though this by-way of jazz has assumed greater retrospective significance in recent years.

Paul Plimley PIANO, MARIMBA

*** Both Sides Of The Same Mirror Nine Winds 0135
 Plimley; Lisle Ellis (*b*). 11/89.
Although the tune titles ('Moving The Twin Entrances Of Light', 'Reflections Of A Persistent Mirage') suggest a trip into New Age wonderland, Plimley's music – he is a veteran of Canada's free-jazz movement – is a good deal thornier than that. He and Ellis have worked together for many years, and a thread of experience runs through all the playing here. Plimley's employment of clusters suggests Cecil Taylor or Don Pullen without really bowing to either man, and when he picks up the marimba mallets for 'Mirage' he expands on the percussiveness of his approach with a fine understanding of his own strengths. Ellis counterpoints with *arco* of guitar-like lines, and on a version of Jimi Hendrix's 'Third Stone From The Sun' he sounds as impressive a soloist as Plimley. The CD seems a little long at almost an hour – a concentrated 40 minutes might have made a better impression – but it's a solid introduction to these players.

**** Kaleidoscopes hat ART CD 6117
 As above. 4/92.
A masterpiece. The most remarkable raid on the Ornette Coleman songbook yet, and all the more extraordinary considering that keyboards have always seemed alien to Coleman's music. Plimley and Ellis honour the melodic beauty of Coleman's tunes but otherwise go entirely their own way, and each of the 11 tracks (there are two versions of 'Kaleidoscope') is as various and passionate as many an entire record of free playing. There are dramatic interpretations ('Beauty Is A Rare Thing', 'Dancing In Your Head') as well as passages such as those in 'Poise' where the interplay of bass and piano is so delicate as to seem fragile; always, though, the music sounds brilliantly new. Ellis favours blunt, elemental lines when plucking the strings, but his *arco* work is ethereal or grave as the music demands; Plimley seems to see some of the tunes right to the end from his first notes, and there's the kind of inevitability about each of the improvisations which is the hallmark of great free playing.

***(*) Noir Victo CD 022
 As above, except add Bruce Freedman (*ss, as*), Gregg Bendian (*d*). 10/92.
A bristling contrast to the previous set, but hardly less absorbing. Basically a trio record – Freedman adds lyrical alto to one track, harsher soprano to another – the music is driven as much by Bendian as by the other two: his disruptive attacks on 'Noir' and 'Jill Cyborg' shatter any introversion between piano and bass. But all three fashion a free-thinking trio music that climaxes with the intense eloquence of the closing 'Fade To Grey Then Blue'. Plimley's music continues to demand a wider audience.

**** Density Of The Lovestruck Demons Music & Arts CD 9906
 Plimley; Lisle Ellis (*b*); Donald Robinson (*d*). 6/94.
***(*) Everything In Stages Songlines SGL 1503-2
 Plimley (*p* solo). 4/95.
Plimley continues to create a formidable body of work. the trio set is a very accomplished manifesto from another Plimley group: besides the usual crop of originals, there are new meditations on Coleman's music, and the level of interaction among the three men is astonishingly vivid and sophisticated, from the quietest moment to the loudest. *Everything In Stages* is another contrast: 17 pieces, many very brief episodes, many examining one, often minute aspect of the piano – technique, vocabulary, structure. Plimley makes one think about the whole nature of the instrument here, its physicality and resonances, and though it can be tough going it's many times more absorbing than the typical piano record.

Jimmy Ponder (born 1946) GUITAR

** **Jimmy Ponder** LRC CDC 9031
> Ponder; Jon Faddis, Marvin Stamm (*t*); Barry Rogers, Urbie Green (*tb*); Eddie Daniels, David Tofani (*reeds*); Bobby Rose, Jeff Maelen (*g*); Pat Rebillot, Rob Mounsey (*ky*); Jimmy McGriff (*org*); Ron Carter (*b*); Richard Crooks, Jim Young (*d*); Gwen Guthrie, Diva Gray, Jocelyn Brown, Jonathan Grody (*v*); strings. 78.

*** **Mean Streets, No Bridges** Muse MCD 5324
> Ponder; Bill Saxton (*ts, f*); Big John Patton (*org*); Geary Moore (*g*); Greg Bandy (*d*). 6/87.

*** **Jump** Muse MCD 5347
> Ponder; Jimmy Anderson (*ts*); Big John Patton (*org*); Geary Moore (*g*); Eddie Gladden (*perc*); Lawrence Killian (*perc*). 3/88.

***(*) **To Reach A Dream** Muse MCD 5394
> Ponder; Lonnie Smith (*org*); Geary Moore (*g*); Greg Bandy (*d*); Lawrence Killian (*perc*). 7/89.

*** **Come On Down** Muse MCD 5375
> Ponder; Houston Person (*ts*); Lonnie Smith (*org*); Winard Harper (*d*); Sammy Figuera (*perc*). 90.

The Pittsburgh-born Ponder makes his guitar sound like viola or cello, picking out lines with a soft vibrato that is much mellower and more delicately resonant than almost any other guitarist in the field. Ponder spent enough time working in testosterone organ trios and sax bands to know how to blow (the version of 'Oleo' on *To Reach A Dream* bears that out), but on his own records he generally prefers a more yielding sound.

There really isn't much to separate these. The big-band session on LRC is the only out-and-out dud, but in amongst the soggy string settings there are three powerful quintet tracks with McGriff and Carter which are much closer to the kind of thing he does so well with Patton on *Mean Streets* and *Jump*, and the little-known Smith (not to be confused with fusioneer Lonnie Liston Smith) on *To Reach A Dream*. The latter scores higher, largely because the band has managed to find a steady groove. One misses Patton's beefy organ-lines, but Smith is in many ways closer to Ponder temperamentally. The Wes tribute, 'Bumpin' On Sunset', has them in complete synch, with Moore's rhythm guitar keeping pace in the left channel. It's a lush performance, completely unvogue-ish but irresistibly pretty.

Even when the context is more straight-ahead and funky, as on the unappetizing-sounding *Come On Down*, Jimmy retains his wish to play pretty lines, albeit at higher volume. This 1990 set cooks along without a beat missed and for fans of Houston Person will provide hours of harmless and slightly deafened delight. One for party night.

Valery Ponomarev (born 1943) TRUMPET

*** **Trip To Moscow** Reservoir RSR CD 107
> Ponomarev; Ralph Moore (*ts*); Hideki Tadao (*p*); Dennis Irwin (*b*); Kenny Washington (*d*). 4/85.

***(*) **Profile** Reservoir RSR CD 117
> Ponomarev; Joe Henderson (*ts*); Kenny Barron (*p*); Essiet Essiet (*b*); Victor Jones (*d*). 5/91.

Valery Ponomarev left Russia in 1973, when pre-*glasnost* winds were still blowing chill. From 1977 to 1980 he held the trumpet chair in the Jazz Messengers and has adopted the idiom with unabashed aplomb.

The stint taught him how to juggle changes. Blakey used to let him loose nightly on 'I Remember Clifford' (acknowledging the obvious stylistic influence) and there's a marvellous version on Ponomarev's own *Means Of Identification*, which is scheduled for CD transfer during the life of this book. The same combination of sinew and tenderness on 'For You Only' here underlines the fact that he isn't just a fast-valve showman but has absorbed the subtler cadence of Brown's approach. British-born Ralph Moore is in fine form, as is the drafted-in pianist, who had to read a projected guitar part and pulls it off with great credit.

Henderson makes a huge difference to *Profile*, as you'd expect. Ponomarev seems to respond with a bigger tone and a longer line in his improvisations, especially on 'I Concentrate On You', which is one of his best recorded performances. The rhythm section are impeccable and the sound much better than on the earlier record, where it's a bit unresponsive.

Jean-Luc Ponty (born 1942) VIOLIN, ELECTRIC VIOLIN, KEYBOARDS

*** **Aurora** Atlantic 19158-2
> Ponty; Patrice Rushen (*ky*); Daryl Stuermer (*g*); Tom Fowler (*b*); Norman Fearrington (*d*). 12/75.

*** **Imaginary Voyage** Atlantic 19136-2
> Ponty; Allan Zavod (*ky*); Daryl Stuermer (*g*); Tom Fowler (*b*); Mark Craney (*d*). 7–8/76.

** **Enigmatic Ocean** Atlantic 19110-2
> Ponty; Allan Zavod (*ky*); Allan Holdsworth, Daryl Stuermer (*g*); Ralph Armstrong (*b*); Steve Smith (*d*). 6–7/77.

*** **Cosmic Messenger** Atlantic 19189-2
> Ponty; Allan Zavod (*ky*); Peter Maunu, Joaquin Lievano (*g*); Ralph Armstrong (*b*); Casey Scheuerell (*d*). 78.

(*) **Mystical Adventures Atlantic 19333-2
> Ponty; Chris Ryne (*p*); Jamie Glaser (*g*); Randy Jackson (*b*); Rayford Griffin (*d*); Paulinho Da Costa (*perc*). 8–9/81.

** **Individual Choice** Atlantic 80098-2
> Ponty; George Duke (*ky*); Allan Holdsworth (*g*); Randy Jackson (*b*); Rayford Griffin (*d*). 3–5/83.

** **Open Mind** Atlantic 80185-2
> Ponty; Chick Corea (*ky*); George Benson (*g*); Casey Scheuerell, Rayford Griffin (*d*). 6/84.

** **Fables** Atlantic 81276-2
> Ponty; Scott Henderson (*g*); Baron Browne (*b*); Rayford Griffin (*d*). 7–8/85.

(*) **Tchokola Columbia 468522-2
> Ponty; Yves Ndjock (*g*); Guy Nsangue (*b*); Brice Wassy (*d*); Abdou Mboup (*perc, v*). 91.

***(*) **No Absolute Time** Atlantic 82500
> Ponty; Wally Minko (*ky*); Martin Atangana, Kevin Eubanks (*g*); Guy Nsangue (*b*); Mokhtar Samba (*d*); Abdou Mboup, Sydney Thiam (*perc*). 12/92–3/93.

***(*) **Le Voyage** Rhino/Atlantic 72155-2 2CD
> As Atlantic albums above. 75–85.

Ponty had always amplified his violin, but by the 1970s he was making it a major part of his aesthetic, trying out echo and other effects to colour an approach which had fundamentally changed little since his earliest recordings, none of which are currently available. He had recorded a session with Frank Zappa, *King Kong*, in 1969, and Zappa's punishingly difficult kind of instrumental rock was a significant influence on the sort of fusion which Ponty recorded once he signed with Atlantic in 1975. Tunes were built out of complicated riffs or trance-like harmonic patterns, with modal solos played at blistering speed to create the excitement. Unusually, though, the music is more interesting than the average fusion band of the period allows, since the lyrical tang of the leader's violin sustains the mood of most of the records.

The earlier records, especially *Aurora* and *Imaginary Voyage*, are the best, if only because the sound of the group is at its freshest. Players like Stuermer and Zavod are capable technicians, but it's always Ponty whose fire ignites the music. Some of the Atlantics from this period are currently out of print, and after *Mystical Adventures* the music grew a little stale: *Individual Choice* and *Open Mind* are almost solo albums by the leader, with Duke, Holdsworth and Benson turning up only in guest spots, and the music lacks much sense of interplay. *Fables* returns to a quartet format, but Ponty seems uninterested in the overall sound. A label switch brought him to Columbia, with mixed consequences: *Tchokola* was an attempt at a new kind of fusion, with Afropop players from different schools, and the results were an interesting but uneasy alliance. *No Absolute Time*, though, is his best record for years. Jazz-rock is cast aside in favour of a glittering kind of electric world-music: all the tracks simmer over a polyrhythmic base, drawn equally from human hands and drum machines, and Ponty's violin and keyboard effects are hummably rich and pleasing.

Atlantic have gone back to their vaults and compiled *Le Voyage*, an excellent two-disc set with several of the highlights from his many albums for the label. Hard to better this for a cross-section of Ponty's particular kind of fusion over the years.

Odean Pope (born 1938) TENOR SAXOPHONE

***(*) **The Saxophone Choir** Soul Note 1129
> Pope; Robert Landham, Julian Pressley, Sam Reed (*as*); Bootsie Barnes, Arthur Daniel, Bob Howell (*ts*); Joe Sudler (*bs*); Eddie Green (*p*); Gerald Veasley (*b*); Dave Gibson (*d*). 10/85.

**** The Ponderer Soul Note 1229

    Pope; Byard Lancaster, Julian Pressley, Sam Reed (*as*); Glenn Guidone, Bob Howell, Middy Middleton, John Simon (*ts*); Joe Sudler (*bs*); Eddie Green (*p*); Tyrone Brown, Gerald Veasley (*b*); Cornell Rochester (*d*). 3/90.

*** Epitome Soul Note 121279

    As above, except omit Lancaster, Veasley, Rochester; add Robert Landham (*as*); Dave Burrell (*p*); Craig McIver (*d*). 10/93.

Pope is a mystically inclined Philadelphian, whose inspiration in music is the pianist, Ibn Hassan Ali, who seems to have considered John Coltrane's music some species of divine communication. Pope gave notice of interesting things to come in his work with Catalyst, a toughly modern, under-recorded outfit who received far less than their fair share of critical attention. A sophisticated composer and arranger, Pope has turned the Saxophone Choir into an exciting studio group which responds gamely to rather intricate charts. The whole ensemble plays 'I Wish I Knew' on *The Ponderer* (the album's only standard) with a snap and finesse that recalls the Ellington horn section. Many of Pope's voicings seem to derive from Duke's late suites, with their 'oriental' scales and off-centre rhythms. As with Ellington albums, though, much of the drama derives from the alternation of solo and ensemble sections. Pope has a powerful tone, somewhat reminiscent in phrasing of Charlie Rouse, but drawing elements from John Coltrane, Sam Rivers and from funk and soul.

    The earlier of the Choir albums is still a little ragged, but the opening 'Saxophone Shop' is done with a light, almost ironic touch that makes up for some technical shortcomings, and 'Elixir' is one of the best things in Pope's book to date. The two parts of 'Out For A Walk' on *The Ponderer* have a strong Latin feel, and direct attention to Pope's characteristic latticing of rhythm lines, doubling two electric bassists (one upright, one on guitar) with the powerful drumming of trio colleague Cornell Rochester, who is also a much more robust large-group player than Gibson. The Ellington influence is strongly evident on 'Phrygian Love Theme', which has a minor feel and a strong 'Spanish tinge'. As elsewhere, it's the bass lines that carry the code, and Pope characteristically plays in a lower register, closer to the saxophone's 'cello' tones, rather than an octave-plus above the accompaniment.

    Epitome carries forward the same basic conception, though this is a more ambitious record on any number of counts. The inclusion of Burrell in the rhythm section offers a gospelly roll and a distinctive tonality which Pope makes use of at several points on his own 'Zanzibar Blue'. Pope and Pressley are the two most prominent soloists, but Howell, Guidone, Landham and Brown all get generous space. The only track played as a straight arrangement without solos is 'Coltranetime', a dedication to the man who perhaps most thoroughly suffuses these sessions. No *Ascension*, *Epitome* nevertheless gets to places few other large-scale jazz ensembles have attempted to reach.

Michel Portal (born 1935) TENOR SAXOPHONE, BASS CLARINET

***(*) ¡Dejarme Solo! Dreyfus Jazz Line 849231

    Portal (*solo saxophones, clarinets, percussion, accordion*). 79.

*** Arrivederci Le Chouartse hat Art CD 6022

    Portal; Leon Francioli (*b*); Pierre Favre (*d*). 10/80.

*** Turbulence Harmonia Mundi HMC 905186

    Portal; Claude Barthelemy, Harry Pepl (*g*); Richard Galliano (*acc*); Andy Emler, Bernard Lubat (*syn*); Jean-François Jenny-Clark, Yannick Top (*b*); André Ceccarelli, Daniel Humair (*d*); Mino Cinelu (*perc*); Jean Schwarz (*elec*). 86.

Portal is a highly accomplished instrumentalist who has taken in modern and free jazz, as well as avant-garde 'straight' music. In 1970 he was working with John Surman, and a decade later he was still exploring that idiom. The hat Art is more structured and large-scale than any of Surman's work with The Trio, but the improvisational configuration is broadly the same, with a forceful, all-in feel. The earlier solo record will certainly recall some of Surman's work, not least in its confident incorporation of folk themes, but there is a jaggedness and angularity to Portal's attack that are very different from the Englishman's softer and more accommodating accents. As with much of Portal's work, it would be difficult to distinguish *Turbulence* from a good deal of scored, formal music. That is not to say that it does not 'swing', but it does seem to belong to an idiom very far removed from jazz.

Chris Potter (born 1970) TENOR, ALTO AND SOPRANO SAXOPHONES, BASS CLARINET, ALTO FLUTE

**** Presenting Chris Potter Criss Cross Jazz 1067

    Potter; John Swana (*t, flhn*); Kevin Hays (*p*); Christian McBride (*b*); Lewis Nash (*d*). 12/92.

***(*) **Sundiata** Criss Cross Jazz 1107
>> Potter; Kevin Hays (*p*); Doug Weiss (*b*); Al Foster (*d*). 12/93.
*** **Concentric Circles** Concord CCD 4595
>> Potter; Kenny Werner (*p*); John Hart (*g*); Scott Colley (*b*); Bill Stewart (*d*). 12/93.
*** **Pure** Concord CCD 4637
>> Potter; Larry Goldings (*p, org*); John Hart (*g*); Larry Grenadier (*b*); Al Foster (*d*). 6/94.

Potter is surely a major saxophonist in the making. The astonishingly confident and full-blooded debut shows his prowess with any one of his chosen horns – there's amazingly little to choose between his alto and tenor playing, both of them muscular in the post-bop manner but full of surprising stylistic twists that make one think of the artists of both Parker's generation and the elegant elaborations of a Benny Carter or a Hodges. The breakneck opener, 'Juggernaut', is a typical young man's manifesto, but just as impressive are the various approaches to Monk's 'Reflections', Davis's 'Solar' and the five other originals by the leader. One could single out Potter's consistently powerful tone, his reluctance to go too far out for effect or the thematic weight applied to all of his improvisations; it's the way that all this is combined which is impressive. He also gets the best out of the sometimes little to choose Swana as a front-line partner, and Hays, McBride and Nash are a superb team. *Sundiata* is a shade behind: a little of Potter's playing exuberance seems to have been held back, and on a set-piece like 'Body And Soul' his lines of thinking are a mite too calculated to convince. That said, there's still plenty of terrific music. Foster, Weiss and Hays don't miss any tricks, and when the group take on another immortal tenor situation by tackling Rollins's 'Airegin' there's a sense of new adventure along with Potter's insistent classicism.

The Concord albums are, though, a disappointment. Despite Potter's best intentions and obvious hard work, both seem over-produced and smothered. Good compositions like 'Lonely Moon' and 'Bad Guys' suffer from surroundings in which the arrangements and tempos sound airless and effortful. Where Potter gives himself some space, as on the opener on *Concentric Circles*, 'El Morocco', the fluency and detail of his playing are still a marvel, and both discs are worth hearing just for his own good spots. But the doubled-up horns, doubtful tunes (there's a particularly unfortunate take on 'Fool On The Hill' on *Pure*) and general feeling of weightiness tell against both discs. One longs to hear Potter in an unencumbered *Newk's Time* sort of setting.

Bud Powell (1924–66) PIANO

**** **The Complete Bud Powell on Verve** Verve 521 669 5CD
>> Powell; Ray Brown, George Duvivier, Percy Heath, Curley Russell, Lloyd Trotman (*b*); Art Blakey, Kenny Clarke, Osie Johnson, Max Roach, Art Taylor (*d*). 5/49–2/51.

Bud Powell was probably the most important jazz pianist between Art Tatum and Cecil Taylor. He appropriated the former's improvising style to a large extent and anticipated the latter's pianistic ferocity (the frequent suggestion that Powell played like a saxophonist is patently absurd). His life was almost archetypally tragic, and the parallel path of his downfall and death with Charlie Parker's has perhaps clouded the pianist's independence of resource and development.

Powell was committed in 1951, suffering from variously diagnosed mental disorders. The brilliance of his Blue Note recordings has tended to cloud the remarkable work that Powell did for Norman Granz. The Verve documents his solo playing just before that catastrophic breakdown, and takes him through to rather calmer waters. There is no indication that neglect was ever part of Powell's problem. He was well looked after by Verve and they have done him proud with this magnificent five-CD package.

Powell's virtuosity shines through the bustling 'Parisian Thoroughfare' (a piece which, like 'Un Poco Loco', always precisely reflects his mood at the moment of playing) and 'A Nightingale Sang In Berkeley Square', which draws heavily on a Tatum influence. No single sesssion on this disc really outweighs the Blue Notes below, but cumulatively and collectively this sits beside them, one of the pillars of this most complex man's life-work.

**** **The Amazing Bud Powell: Volume 1** Blue Note 781503
>> Powell; Fats Navarro (*t*); Sonny Rollins (*ts*); Tommy Potter (*b*); Roy Haynes (*d*). 8/49, 5/51.
**** **The Amazing Bud Powell: Volume 2** Blue Note 781504
>> Powell (*p* solo), and with George Duvivier, Curley Russell (*b*); Max Roach, Art Taylor (*d*). 5/51 & 8/53.
*** **Birdland '53** Fresh Sound FSCD 1017
>> Powell; Oscar Pettiford, Frank Skeete, Charles Mingus (*b*); Sonny Payne, Roy Haynes (*d*). 2 & 3/53.
***(*) **Jazz At Massey Hall** Original Jazz Classics OJC 111
>> Powell; Charles Mingus (*b*); Max Roach (*d*). 5/53.

**** Swingin' With Bud RCA 13041
    Powell; George Duvivier (*b*); Art Taylor (*d*). 2/57.
**** The Complete Blue Note And Roost Recordings Blue Note CDP 830083 4CD
    Powell; Fats Navarro (*t*); Curtis Fuller (*tb*); Sonny Rollins (*ts*); Curley Russell, Tommy Potter,
    George Duvivier, Paul Chambers, Sam Jones, Pierre Michelot (*b*); Max Roach, Roy Haynes, Art
    Taylor, Philly Joe Jones, Kenny Clarke (*d*). 47–63.

Despite the linking name and numbered format, the four Blue Note CD transfers can quite comfortably be bought separately; indeed *Volume One* – with its multiple takes of 'Bouncing With Bud' (one of which was previously on *The Fabulous Fats Navarro: Volume 1*), the bebop classic 'Ornithology' and Powell's own barometric 'Un Poco Loco' – was out of print for some time, and the fourth volume was issued only in 1987, after which the whole series was made available again at a very acceptable mid-price. *Three* and *Four* have now disappeared again, but they have to some extent been superseded by the magnificent *Complete* which is a must for every Powell enthusiast in the land and is denied a coronet only because it does have its dark and troublous moments and isn't perhaps the kind of thing you'd want to spend extended periods of time with. The multiple takes of 'Un Poco Loco' are perhaps the best place for more detailed study of Powell's restless pursuit of an increasingly fugitive musical epiphany. 'Parisian Thoroughfare' contrasts sharply with the unaccompanied version, above, and is much tighter; Powell had a more-than-adequate left hand; however, since he conceived of his music in a complex, multi-linear way, bass and drums were usually required – not for support, but to help proliferate lines of attack. The quintet tracks are harshly tempered, but with hints of both joy and melancholy from all three frontmen; Navarro's almost hysterical edge is at its most effective, and Powell plays as if possessed.

    Volume 2 contains one of the most famous Powell performances: the bizarre, self-penned 'Glass Enclosure', a brief but almost schizophrenically changeable piece. There are also alternative takes of 'A Night In Tunisia', 'It Could Happen To You', 'Reets And I' and 'Collard Greens And Black Eyed Peas' (better known as 'Blues In The Closet', see below). *Jazz At Massey Hall* is the rhythm section's spot from the classic Parker/Gillespie concert in Toronto, which has become a trig point for bop fans. (Any lucky dog who owns the 12-CD compilation of Mingus on Debut will already have it.) If for no other reason, these tracks redirect attention to the enormous influence all three players had on bebop. Powell's schizophrenic opposition of delicate, high-register lines and thudding chords is most obvious on 'Cherokee'. He displaces 'Embraceable You' entirely, losing his two colleagues in the middle choruses as he works out his own romantic agony.

    The RCA recordings with Duvivier and Taylor are, by contrast, much lighter, less inward and, as the title rightly claims, more swinging. For anyone who looks to Powell for bleak and unyielding intensity, these may turn out to be a disappointment, but 'Almost Like Being In Love' and 'In The Blue Of The Evening' suggest the kind of artist he might have been, had the shadows not crowded him. There's even a lighter edge to 'Oblivion' and 'Another Dozen', both of which are peppered with tiny, mock-classical quotes.

*** Bud Powell: Spring Broadcasts 1953 ESP Disk 3022
    Powell; Charles Mingus, Oscar Pettiford (*b*); Roy Haynes (*d*). 3/53.
*** Bud Powell: Summer Broadcast 1953 ESP Disk 3023
    Powell; Charlie Parker (*as*); Charles Mingus (*b*); Art Taylor (*d*); Candido Camero (*perc*). 53.
*** Bud Powell: Autumn Broadcast 1953 ESP Disk 3024
    Powell; George Duvivier, Curley Russell (*b*); Art Taylor (*d*). 9/53.

A good deal of this material has also been circulated in cheap and sometimes suspect packaging, apparently recorded off these discs. Powell isn't an artist you'd normally associate with an avant-garde label like ESP, but he was, of course, an idol to the generation of piano players that followed, the so-called Taylor generation. These are actually rather disappointing records. Mingus and Haynes don't deliver as we know they could and, though the Parker tracks – just 'Moose The Mooche' and 'Cheryl' – are precious, they don't quite lift these discs out of the B-list.

**** Inner Fires Discovery 71007
    Powell; Charles Mingus (*b*); Roy Haynes (*d*). 53.

A better bet all round. These tapes, made at Club Kavakos in Washington, D.C., were in the private collection of Bill Potts until 1982, when they were released on Elektra Musician. The great bonus of the CD set is a brief five-minute interview with Bud, but it doesn't need that to make it a compelling session. He plays out of his skin for most of the hour, and the long versions of 'Little Willie Leaps' and 'Salt Peanuts' are simply masterful, a genius at the office.

*** The Complete Essen Jazz Festival Concert Black Lion BLCD 760105 .
    Powell; Coleman Hawkins (*ts*); Oscar Pettiford (*p*); Kenny Clarke (*d*). 4/60.

Announced by MC Joachim Berendt as the Oscar Pettiford Trio, it's not until the third track and Pettiford's superb introduction to 'Willow Weep For Me' that the nominal leader begins to assert himself. Powell has already got in two brisk solos, with only a couple of misfingerings on the hectic 'Shaw Nuff'. A few minutes later, the bassist is referring to Powell, putative composer of 'John's Abbey', as 'your favourite'.

Hawkins (the other claimant for that credit) comes in for the last three tracks. He'd played 'Stuffy' many times before, but it's rare to hear him on 'All The Things You Are', which gets an unusually jaunty reading and some nice stretching of tempo on later choruses, closing with the familiar bop arrangement. The sound is well balanced and clean, and Powell seems to have lucked out on a decent instrument for a change.

***(*) Blue Note Café, Paris 1961 ESP Disk ESP 1066
Powell; Pierre Michelot (*b*); Kenny Clarke (*d*). 61.

***(*) Round About Midnight At The Blue Note Dreyfus Jazz Line 849227
As above.

One doesn't normally think of Powell as an avant-gardist or of ESP Disk as handling anything so conventionally boppish. However, the chemistry seems to be pretty effective, and the reissue turns another page on Bud's happy-sad European sojourn. Michelot and fellow-exile Clarke are as attentive as courtiers, and Bud himself sounds unusually focused and responsive to what they in turn are doing, frequently making space for Michelot's miniature counter-melodies. The Dreyfus option works a couple of changes on the same material, but there honestly isn't much to choose between them. Lovely stuff.

**(*) At The Golden Circle: Volume 1 Steeplechase SCCD 36001
Powell; Torbjörn Hultcranz (*b*); Sune Spangberg (*d*). 4/62.

**(*) At The Golden Circle: Volume 2 Steeplechase SCCD 36002
As above.

**(*) At The Golden Circle: Volume 3 Steeplechase SCCD 36009
As above.

** At The Golden Circle: Volume 4 Steeplechase SCCD 36014
As above.

*** Budism Steeplechase SCCD 30007/9 3CD
As above. 4 & 9/62.

We're now firmly in the era of an important discographical sub-genre: the Bud Powell-live-in-Europe album. There are a great many of these. Some are good, others awful, but the majority don't really stand up on their own terms. Steeplechase have long been guilty of excessive documentation. One sharply edited disc from the 19 April 1962 gig would have been more than adequate. The Copenhagen session finds Powell wavering between the hesitant and the near-brilliant, without ever quite capturing the quality of the previous decade. The rhythm section play about as much part in the music as Rosencrantz and Guildenstern do in *Hamlet*, though, like most Scandinavian players, they seem well enough versed in the idiom.

Volume 3 has a second version of 'I Remember Clifford' from later in the residency; the last three all come from 23 April and are of more than passing interest, but by this stage the whole exercise seems rather redundant. Four volumes of Powell at his *best* would still call for stamina. There is no certainty about the dating of the material on *Budism*. With the exception of ten tracks which are known to come from the autumn residency, there is no firm dating. However, listening to the tracks one by one, instinct suggests that they may well all come from the later period. There are a few small rhythmic devices which don't seem to be audible on the earlier sessions, most notably a sharp trill near the start of 'Dance Of The Infidels' on disc three (one of the definite September tracks), which crops up again on 'Epistrophy' and 'Off Minor' on the uncertainly provenanced disc one. Amorphous as the changes are, one might fudge it by saying that *Budism* is a more 'Monkish' selection, stylistically speaking, than the earlier Steeplechases. That may well recommend it.

*** Bouncing With Bud Storyville STCD 4113
Powell; Niels-Henning Orsted-Pedersen (*b*); William Schiopffe (*d*). 4/62.

Recorded three days after the later Golden Circle session, this has the pianist nosing again at 'I Remember Clifford', apparently dissatisfied with something in the theme. Otherwise it's quite predictable fare, played with discipline but not much passion.

***(*) Salt Peanuts Black Lion BLCD 760121
Powell; Johnny Griffin (*ts*); Guy Hayat (*b*); Jacques Gervais (*d*). 8/64.

You can almost smell the garlic and the sweat. Wonderfully authentic club jazz from the latter end of Powell's career, with Johnny Griffin doing his familiar unexpected sit-in on 'Wee', 'Hot House' and 'Straight, No Chaser'. Powell has an awful piano to play and the rhythm section isn't up to much, but (odd though the analogy may sound) much like Keith Jarrett in years to come, Powell always played best at moments of greatest adversity, and here he sounds supercharged. The title-track, 'Move' and '52nd

Street Theme', for trio, bring France to Harlem. If 'Bean And The Boys' is familiar, the reason is explained above, apropos *Time Waits*. Wonderful, but don't expect audiophile sound.

(*) Blues For Bouffemont Black Lion BLCD 760135
    Powell; Michel Gaudry, Guy Hayat (*b*); Jacques Gervais, Art Taylor (*d*). 7/64, 8/64.
Johnny Griffin doesn't sweep in like the 7th Cavalry to rescue *Bouffemont* and Powell is left to plod his lonely course on the July session. Bouffemont was the convalescent equivalent of Charlie Parker's Camarillo, but there's nothing very relaxed about these tracks. Further material from the *Salt Peanuts* line-up is enough to convince anyone that Black Lion got it right first time. Second rank, even by the rather relative standards of late Powell recordings.

***(*) Early Bud Powell** Mythic Sound MS 6001-6010 10CD
    consists of:
***(*) Early Years Of A Genius, 44–48** Mythic Sound MS 6001
    Powell; Benny Harris, Ermit Perry, Tommy Stevenson, George Treadwell, Cootie Williams, Lamar Wright (*t*); Ed Burke, Ed Glover, Bob Horton, J. J. Johnson (*tb*); Buddy DeFranco (*cl*); Eddie Cleanhead Vinson (*as, v*); Frank Powell (*as*); Eddie 'Lockjaw' Davis, Budd Johnson, Lee Pope, Sam Taylor (*ts*); Eddie Deverteuil, Cecil Payne (*bs*); Leroy Kirkland, Chuck Wayne (*g*); Nelson Boy, Norman Keenan, Carl Pruitt (*b*); Vess Payne, Max Roach (*d*); Ella Fitzgerald (*v*). 1 & 7/44, 12/48.
****Burning In USA, 53–55** Mythic Sound MS 6002
    Powell; Dizzy Gillespie (*t*); Charles Mingus, Oscar Pettiford, Franklin Skeete (*b*); Art Blakey, Roy Haynes, Sonny Payne, Max Roach (*d*). 2, 3 & 5/53, 55.
***(*) Cookin' At Saint Germain, 57–59** Mythic Sound MS 6003
    Powell; Clark Terry (*t*); Barney Wilen (*ts*); Pierre Michelot (*b*); Kenny Clarke (*d*). 57, 11/59.
*** Relaxin' At Home, 61–64** Mythic Sound MS 6004
    Powell; Michel Gaudry (*b*); Francis Paudras (*brushes*). 61–64.
***(*) Groovin' At The Blue Note, 59–61** Mythic Sound MS 6005
    Powell; Dizzy Gillespie (*t*); Zoot Sims, Barney Wilen (*ts*); Jean-Marie Ingrand, Pierre Michelot (*b*); Kenny Clarke (*d*). 57?, 5 & 6/60, 1/61.
*** Writin' For Duke, 63** Mythic Sound MS 6006
    Powell; Gilbert Rovère (*b*); Kansas Fields (*d*). 2/63.
(*) Tribute To Thelonious, 64 Mythic Sound MS 6007
    Powell; John Ore (*b*); J. C. Moses (*d*); Francis Paudras (*brushes*). 2/64.
****Holidays In Edenville, 64** Mythic Sound MS 6008
    Powell; Johnny Griffin (*ts*); Guy Hayat (*b*); Jacques Gervais (*d*). 8/64.
****Return To Birdland, 64** Mythic Sound MS 6009
    Powell; John Ore (*b*); J. C. Moses (*d*). 9/64.
***(*) Award At Birdland, 64** Mythic Sound MS 6010
    As above. 10/64.
Here, then, is the basic story-board for *Round Midnight*, the almost obsessional but unmistakably sincere attachment of a young French fan and musician *manqué* to an ageing and disturbed American jazzman whose talent and emotions alike are as brilliant and as fragile as light bulbs. Francis Paudras lovingly recorded Bud Powell in performance at clubs like the Paris Blue Note, at home, and on recuperative holiday at Edenville. The story of his association with Powell is told in Paudras's book, *Dance of the Infidels*, on which Bernard Tavernier's movie was based.

    In 1979, Paudras willed his archive of private recordings of Bud Powell to the pianist's daughter, Cecilia Barnes Powell, who subsequently permitted their release. The material is patchy in the extreme and shouldn't be seen as a comprehensive compilation of Powell material between 1944 and 1964. Given the circumstances of recording, the quality is not always up to scratch, and some of Powell's later performances are unbearably weary. The earliest material suggests an able accompanist with some skill as an arranger. Powell's version of Mary Lou Williams's 'Roll 'Em' underlines his skill in juxtaposing areas of dissonance (something he did constantly on the keyboard) while preserving the continuity of harmonic development. The early-1950s tracks include material from the legendary Massey Hall concert, and also excellent versions of 'Star Eyes', 'Like Someone In Love' and Pettiford's 'Blues In The Closet' from Birdland in September of that same year. The French sessions on *Cookin' At Saint Germain* are almost equally fine, though the rhythm sections lack the robust challenge posed by Pettiford and Roach. The later Blue Note (club, not label) recordings are alternately more abrupt and rather elided. Aesthetically, the effect is a little like taking the sound-board off the piano to expose the strings, for the workings of Powell's increasingly troubled mind are sometimes painfully evident.

    Thanks to the generosity of Frank Sinatra, Powell was able to record a rare studio session in Paris in 1963, to be made under the supervision of Duke Ellington. Resources clearly didn't stretch to a reasonable rhythm section – both Rovère and Kansas Fields are pretty dire – but this supplement to the released *Bud In Paris* is of more than historical value, and Bud's performance of 'Satin Doll', whistled to him by its composer as he sat at the keyboard, is one of his most remarkable.

Much of the rest of the material is rather more ephemeral. The home recordings of Powell working through half a dozen Monk compositions are neatly balanced by five similarly focused tracks from autumn 1964, during his emotional return to Birdland. After his release from the sanatorium in the summer, Paudras had taken a convalescent Powell on holiday to Edenville on the Normandy coast, where he played now legendary sessions with a ropy local rhythm section and a piano that was one stage beyond clapped out. Johnny Griffin sat in, and the music has a strangely evocative quality, more redolent of a time long gone and of a man no longer living than many a professional recording.

A month or two later, a fitter, chubbier Powell received an ecstatic reception at Birdland, playing the last great sessions of his life (and receiving the Schaeffer award; Paudras notes his disappointment that Schaeffer was a brand of beer rather than a musical foundation) with the workmanlike support of Ore and Moses. The playing is full of familiarly unexpected dissonances – intentional here – but also a kind of quiet joy, exactly the quality that comes through on *Relaxin' At Home*, where Paudras scuffs out a brush rhythm over Powell's unselfconscious improvisations.

The ten albums are available separately and should perhaps be sampled one at a time. Paudras's extensive liner-notes are fulsome and occasionally mawkish – and the music often tells a different story – but the pictures are wonderful, and Powellites will treasure the set.

André Previn (born 1929) PIANO

*** **Previn At Sunset** Black Lion BLCD 760189
    Previn; Buddy Childers, Howard McGhee (*t*); Willie Smith (*as*); Vido Musso (*ts*); Dave Barbour, Irving Ashby (*g*); Red Callender, Eddie Safranski, John Simmons (*b*); Lee Young (*d*). 10 & 11/45, 3 & 5/46.
*** **Double Play** Original Jazz Classics OJC 157
    Previn; Russ Freeman (*p*); Shelly Manne (*d*). 4 & 5/57.
*** **Pal Joey** Original Jazz Classics OJC 637
    Previn; Red Mitchell (*b*); Shelly Manne (*d*). 10/57.
*** **Gigi** Original Jazz Classics OJC 407
    As above. 4/58.
*** **Andre Previn And His Pals** Fresh Sound FSR CD 106
    As above, except add Leroy Vinnegar (*b*), Frank Capp (*d*). 6 & 8/58.
*** **Plays Songs By Vernon Duke** Original Jazz Classics OJC 1769
    Previn (*p* solo). 8/58.
*** **King Size!** Original Jazz Classics OJC 691
    Previn; Red Mitchell (*b*); Frank Capp (*d*). 11/58.
*** **Plays Songs By Jerome Kern** Original Jazz Classics OJC 1787
    Previn (*p* solo). 2 & 3/59.
*** **West Side Story** Original Jazz Classics OJC 422
    As for *Pal Joey*. 8/59.
***(*) **Plays Songs By Harold Arlen** Original Jazz Classics OJC 1840
    Previn (*p* solo). 5/60.
*** **After Hours** Telarc Digital 83002
    Previn; Joe Pass (*g*); Ray Brown (*b*). 3/89.
(*) **Uptown Telarc Digital 83303
    As above, except Mundell Lowe (*g*) replaces Pass. 3/90.
(*) **Old Friends Telarc Digital 83309
    As above, except omit Lowe. 8/91.

André Previn likes to tell the story of how, while working as a cinema accompanist, he so lost himself in a piece of improvisation that he looked up some time later to see that he had vamped 'Tiger Rag' right through the Crucifixion scene in D. W. Griffiths's *Intolerance*. It's often forgotten that Previn, now a highly popular orchestral conductor and media personality, began his professional life as a jazz pianist, once considered hip enough (by Hollywood standards, anyway) to appear as the stage band in a film adaptation of Jack Kerouac's *The Subterraneans*.

Previn first recorded as a teenager, and the sessions on *At Sunset* find him confident and accomplished, certainly showing no signs of being overawed by the horns on 'All The Things You Are' and 'I Found A New Baby'. The unaccompanied tracks are a little lacking in meat and substance, but they're still creditable. The show-tune sessions with Mitchell and Manne are much more successful. Previn's minimal opening statements on 'Something's Coming' on *West Side Story* give way to a brash and tightly belted solo which exactly suits the emotional temper. Typically, though, it degenerates into rather technical figuring, octave jumps and altered chords which are impressive without being very involving. The CD pairs the Bernstein sessions with Shelly Manne's *My Fair Lady*, which also features Previn, with Leroy Vinnegar instead of the sonorous Mitchell. *Pal Joey* and *Gigi* have a more dated charm, but there are signs even here that Previn was more than just a dabbler, and the Kern, Duke and (especially) Arlen sessions are not just polished, but often quite imaginative in their re-intepretation of the melodies. The Arlens have a quiet intimacy, reinforced by solo performance; a high point.

Like Dudley Moore (but with ideas remaining), Previn has recently returned to his first love. At sixty, he lacks the range and emotional complexity of his earlier work, but he is still a formidable technician who will appeal to fans of laid-back piano-trio jazz.

Bobby Previte DRUMS, PERCUSSION

*** **Bump The Renaissance** sound aspects sas 08
Previte; Tom Varner (*frhn*); Lenny Pickett (*ts, bcl*); Richard Shulman (*p*); David Hofstra (*d*). 6/ 85.
*** **Claude's Late Morning** Gramavision R2 79448
Previte; Ray Anderson (*tb, tba*); Wayne Horvitz (*p, org, hca*); Bill Frisell (*g, bjo*); Josh Dubin (*pedal steel g*); Guy Klucevesek (*acc*); Carol Emmanuel (*hp*); Joey Baron (*d*); Jim Mussen (*elec*). 88.
**** **Empty Suits** Gramavision GV 79447
Previte; Robin Eubanks (*tb*); Marty Ehrlich (*as*); Steve Gaboury (*ky*); Allan Jafee, Elliott Sharp (*g*); Skip Krevens (*pedal steel g*); Jerome Harris (*b, g, lap steel g, v*); Carol Emmanuel (*hp*); Roberta Baum (*v*); David Shea (*turntables*). 5/90.
**** **Weather Clear, Track Fast** Enja 6082
Previte; Graham Haynes (*c*); Robin Eubanks (*tb*); Don Byron (*cl, bcl*); Marty Ehrlich (*as, f, cl, bcl*); Anthony Davis, Steve Gaboury (*p*); Anthony Cox (*b*). 1/91.
(*) **Music Of The Moscow Circus Gramavision GRV 74662
Previte; Herb Robertson (*t, c*); Steve Gaboury (*p, org, ky*); Jerome Harris (*g*); Mark Feldman (*vn*); Carol Emmanuel (*hp*); Mark Helias (*b, v*); Roger Squitero (*perc*); Saint Pancras Choristers, Elaine Zarate, Matthew Brosky (*v*). 8/91.
***(*) **Hue And Cry** Enja ENJ 8064
Previte; Eddie E. J. Allen (*t*); Robin Eubanks (*tb*); Don Byron (*cl, bs*); Marty Ehrlich (*as, ss, f, cl*); Anthony Davis (*p*); Larry Goldings (*org*); Anthony Cox (*b*). 12/94.

Previte's drumming has a strangely loose, unfettered quality that sometimes camouflages very effectively the absolute steadiness of the beat he is laying down. In the decade since he started recording under his own name, he has shown an ability to function in all sorts of contexts, drawing on musics outside jazz, stamping everything with a wry, slightly mischievous personality.

The records often sound like soundtracks to an imaginary movie, with a multiplicity of characters, an enigmatic story-line, and no particular axe to grind. Moody reprises loom out of nowhere and disappear again. Despite the richness and diversity of its materials, *Claude's Late Morning* has a tremendous unity of feel that marks it out very distinctly. Frisell's guitar is an important element but, as with Tim Berne (for whom Previte has regularly played), there are no hot solos or featured spots as such, just a continuous flow of music, out of which performers emerge briefly before being drawn back into the fabric again.

Empty Suits is a joyous, all-in set that touches all the bases. Previte's compositions and arrangements are absolutely spot on (as they are on the smaller acoustic canvas of *Bump The Renaissance*) and the guitars are used to maximum effect. 'Great Wall' is a dedication to the minimalist composer John Adams, who may well have had an impact on Previte's repetitive but shifting structures.

As a drummer, he combines the swing era with latter-day power *à la* Ronald Shannon Jackson, but he never overpowers an intelligently balanced mix. On the jazzier *Weather Clear, Track Fast* (significantly *not* on Gramavision), the tunes are more stretched out and developed, leaving more space than usual for improvised passages. Don Byron plays an expansive role, but he's slightly overshadowed by the always resourceful Ehrlich, who has a bewildering array of voices at his disposal, and always manages to sound like a 40-a-day man, ranging from raw bop saxophone to bronchial bass clarinet and breathless flute. Haynes and Eubanks complete a most impressive front line. Davis is a bit stiff and there's a big difference when Steve Gaboury, regular pianist with the Empty Suits band, comes in to play the speciality 'Quinella'.

Music Of The Moscow Circus is an attractive failure, a series of impressionistic miniatures intended to evoke staged rather than traditional ring acts. Without visuals, there really isn't anything to get one's teeth into, and that's very frustrating because all the music is sharply and precisely imprinted. *Hue And Cry* is a welcome return to form and one of the most satisfyingly rounded Previte albums. As more and more solo space is devolved to sidemen, he works ever harder to imprint himself on the music. The result is some of the rhythmically most subtle and fluent music of the 1990s.

Eddie Prévost (born 1942) DRUMS, PERCUSSION

**** Live Matchless MRCD 01/02
> Prévost; Gerry Gold (*t*); Geoff Hawkins (*ts*); Marcio Mattos (*b*). 79.

***(*) Supersession Matchless MR 17
> Prévost; Evan Parker (*ss, ts*); Keith Rowe (*g, elec*); Barry Guy (*b, elec*). 9/84.

Like his exact contemporary, Han Bennink, Prévost is a free player who understands how to swing. Influenced primarily by Max Roach, but by Ed Blackwell too, he can also play with the stark simplicity of the early jazz drummers or with the ritualized freedoms of a Korean court musician. Like Bennink again, he is very much a kit drummer and, though the early days of AMM (the influential improvising ensemble of which Prévost is a founding member) demanded a very radical diversification of sound-producing technics, he has shown remarkably little interest in exotic or 'ethnic' percussion.

Prévost's own groups have tended to remain within the British free-jazz tradition, governed to some degree by structures, but never constrained by them. The 1979 albums are a joy, veering dramatically between moments of austere fury and jovial rave-ups fuelled by Prévost's tireless invention. (That an album called *Live* should have a skull on the cover is a token of Prévost's refusal to treat even quite abstract music-making with deathly seriousness.) Trumpeter Gerry Gold (who has also played with the radical improvising group, Coherents) is one of the buried treasures of British jazz. He has a bright, generous tone, which he can turn on the instant into a thin, acidulous stream of off-pitch comments. Mattos has an enormous, dramatic sound. *Live* kicked off Prévost's own cottage-industry label, and it's good to have a CD reissue. Since 1980, Matchless has built up a remarkable body of material within the free-jazz-to-free spectrum.

Supersession isn't strictly Prévost's band. The whole ethos of the group is opposed to the idea of leadership and can be laid to his credit only because he is the organizer and provides in the liner-note an admirably brief and cogent discussion of the differences that prevail between the bland, self-exhausting alienation strategies of the avant-garde and an improvisational approach which 'supersedes' such ideologies and approaches music-making with confidence, mutual regard and without undue triumphalism.

It is, of course, a 'supersession' in another sense, bringing together the backbone of AMM and two of the most distinguished improvisers and composers on the British scene. The music – a single continuous performance – is rather better value for money than its meagre duration might suggest. It's typically difficult, and pointless, to separate individual performers, but it's Parker's chirping soprano harmonics and Prévost's exuberant battering outbreaks that one remembers.

Sam Price (1908–92) PIANO, VOCAL

*** Sam Price 1929–1941 Classics 696
> Price; Douglas Finnell, Joe Brown, Eddie 'Moon' Mullens, Shad Collins, Bill Johnston, Chester Boone, Emmett Berry (*t*); Bert Johnson, Floyd Brady, Ray Hogan (*tb*); Fess Williams (*cl, as*); Lem Fowler (*cl, v*); Don Stovall (*as*); Ray Hill, Lester Young, Skippy Williams (*ts*); Percy Darensbourg (*bj*); Duke Jones, Ernest 'Bass' Hill, Billy Taylor (*b*); Wilbert Kirk, Harold 'Doc' West, Herb Cowens, J. C. Heard (*d*); Yack Taylor, Ruby Smith, Jack Meredith (*v*). 9/29–12/41.

Aside from two 1929 tracks, all this material dates from 1940–41, when Price was recording regularly for Decca with his 'Texas Bluesicians'. It might have been recorded in New York, but the music is authentic southern swing, fronted by the pianist from Honey Grove, Texas. Many of the 24 tracks are features for his simple, blues-to-boogie playing and amiable vocals, which tend to predominate as the sessions go by, but there's also some fine playing from the horns. 'Sweepin' The Blues Away' includes excellent work by Brown and Stovall, and a 1941 session actually features the Lester Young band, though Young himself has only a few bars here and there in the limelight. Remastering is quite good, though the two 1929 tracks are noisy and some surface hiss is intrusive on a couple of later tracks.

** Midnight Boogie Black & Blue 59.025-2
> Price (*p* solo). 11/69.

** Fire Black & Blue 59.079-2
> Price; Doc Cheatham (*t*); Gene Connors (*tb*); Ted Buckner (*as*); Carl Pruitt (*b*); J. C. Heard (*d*). 5/75.

** **Boogie And Jazz Classics** Black & Blue 59.111-2
    As above. 5/75.

Sam Price's recordings for King Jazz are scattered through the Storyville albums discussed under Mezz Mezzrow and Sidney Bechet. Although he remained active as a player almost to the end of his life, his records have been few in number and were often made for minor labels in inauspicious situations. The Black & Blue CDs are, along with the fine duo session with Doc Cheatham on Sackville, the most representative of his later records. But they're finally rather dull. *Midnight Boogie* is an entirely straight-forward selection of boogie and blues, played with a slow momentum which sounds weary rather than intense. Price's pieces are full of routine configurations and tend to prop up the theory that boogie piano is tediously one-dimensional in its impact. All 15 tracks are virtually interchangeable and, while any one of them makes a plausible performance, it's hard to see why anyone would want to work through an entire CD's worth of this sort of playing. The full band plays on eight of the 15 tracks on *Fire* and on only two on *Boogie And Jazz Classics*, and they bring a little more spirit to the proceedings, even if all three horn players sound ragged at times. The trio tracks, though, are distinctly plain. Price plays his boogie with a steadily rocking pulse, but it tends to pall rather than become hypnotic, as the best boogie piano should. Pruitt and Heard play the most functional of rhythm roles and the tunes are mostly one-paced originals.

*** **Barrelhouse And Blues** Black Lion BLCD 760159
    Price; Keith Smith (*t*); Roy Williams (*tb*); Sandy Brown (*cl*); Ruan O'Lochlainn (*g*); Harvey
    Weston (*b*); Lennie Hastings (*d*). 12/69.

Price is rather better served by this enjoyable occasion, on which he was recorded in London with a British band. The music is split between solo and ensemble tracks and, although the pianist is rather less glib than usual on the reflective 'Honey Grove Blues', the numbers with the full band turn out rather better: O'Lochlainn's oddball solos are a neat touch of local colour, and the lamented Brown contributes deep-set solos to each of two takes of Leroy Carr's 'In the Evening'. The CD runs to nearly 73 minutes and the remastering is fine.

Brian Priestley (born 1946) PIANO

*** **You Taught My Heart To Sing** Spirit of Jazz CD09-0995
    Priestley; Don Rendell (*ss, ts, f*). 7/94.

A connoisseur's recital. Priestley, by now a veteran commentator and performer on the British scene, knows jazz piano history inside out, and this series of dedications to 15 keyboard masters eschews the obvious at almost every turn – only Bill Evans's 'Waltz For Debby' could be called over-familiar. His Ellington is 'Heaven', his Monk is 'In Walked Bud' and his Bud is 'Dance Of The Infidels', and each has a personal wrinkle in it. Priestley's delivery isn't exactly springheeled but his measured approach lets him map out ideas with a useful clarity, and the thick voicings add density rather than excess weight. He's also meticulous about avoiding bathos on the slower pieces. The presence of Don Rendell, who contributes a rather faded presence on several tracks, isn't a great bonus.

Marcus Printup TRUMPET

*** **Song For The Beautiful Woman** Blue Note CDP 830790-2
    Printup; Walter Blanding (*ts*); Eric Reed (*p*); Reuben Rogers (*b*); Brian Blade (*d*). 12/94.

The first track is unexceptional, but the trumpet solo on the second, a sanguine treatment of 'I'll Remember April', is so genuine and songful that one suddenly warms to Printup's manner. He has a broad, generous vibrato that gives a romantic buff to music that's otherwise in the hard, modern manner of the day. Much is made in the sleeve-notes of how he came to write the title-piece, but it makes no profound impression, which goes for most of the original composing here. He plays a tight, crisp 'Speak Low' with the mute in, and the band finishes with Coltrane's 'Dahomey Dance': Blanding plays respectable second fiddle throughout, and Reed performs with less flash than he does in some other sideman situations. A solid start for a man of promise.

Dudu Pukwana (1938–90) ALTO SAXOPHONE, SOPRANO SAXOPHONE, VOCALS

(*) **Cosmics Chapter 90 Ah Um 05
    Pukwana; Lucky Ranku (*g*); Roland Perrin (*ky*); Eric Richards (*b*); Steve Arguëlles (*d*); Fats
    Ramobo Mogoboya (*perc*); Pinise Saul (*v*). 11/89.

Whatever Yeats feared, the best can also be full of passionate intensity. Larger than life, Dudu Pukwana was a much-loved presence on the British music scene. A South African exile, he had been a member of Chris McGregor's multi-racial Blue Notes (which also included Mongezi Feza and Louis Moholo, and which was barred from performing in the Republic of South Africa) and later the pianist's Brotherhood of Breath. An able composer with a heated alto (and, later, soprano) saxophone style, Pukwana was able to work in African, mainstream and free/abstract settings with equal ease; as with Moholo, he tended to bring the virtues and techniques of each to the others, playing *kwela* music with considerable harmonic and thematic latitude, free music with the kind of fire normally heard only in the shebeens.

If exile and rootlessness were corrosive, it rarely showed in Pukwana's stage manner, which was unboundedly joyous. Towards the end of his life, though, his music took on a more inward character and was increasingly abstract in manner. This development was reflected in his turn to soprano saxophone, which is strongly featured on the rather disappointing *Cosmics Chapter 90*. Though Pukwana is still able to generate considerable excitement, there is a tiredness in his playing, and much of the emphasis of his band – now known as Zila – rests with vocalist Pinise Saul and guitarist Lucky Ranku.

Don Pullen (1944–95) PIANO, ORGAN, COMPOSER

*** **Capricorn Rising** Black Saint 120004
    Pullen; Sam Rivers (*ts, ss, f*); Alex Blake (*b*); Bobby Battle (*d*). 10/75.
*** **Healing Force** Black Saint 120010
    Pullen (*p* solo). 76.
***(*) **Warriors** Black Saint 120019
    Pullen; Chico Freeman (*ts*); Fred Hopkins (*b*); Bobby Battle (*d*). 4/78.
*** **Milano Strut** Black Saint 120028
    Pullen; Famoudou Don Moye (*d, perc*). 12/78.
**** **Evidence Of Things Unseen** Black Saint 120080
    Pullen (*p* solo). 9/83.
(*) **Plays Monk Paddle Wheel K28P 6368
    As above. 11/84.
***(*) **The Sixth Sense** Black Saint 120088
    Pullen; Olu Dara (*t*); Donald Harrison (*as*); Fred Hopkins (*b*); Bobby Battle (*d*). 6/85.
**** **New Beginnings** Blue Note 791785
    Pullen; Gary Peacock (*b*); Tony Williams (*d*). 12/88.
**** **Random Thoughts** Blue Note 794347
    Pullen; James Genus (*b*); Lewis Nash (*d*). 3/90.
*** **Kele Mou Bana** Blue Note CDP 798166
    Pullen; Carlos Ward (*as*); Nilson Matta (*b*); Mor Thiam, Guilherme Franco (*perc*); Keith
    Pullen, Taneka Pullen (*v*). 9/91.
**** **Ode To Life** Blue Note CDP 789233
    As above, except omit Keith and Taneka Pullen. 2/93.
*** **Sacred Common Ground** Blue Note CDP 832800
    Pullen; Joseph Bowie (*tb*); Carlos Ward (*as*); Santi Debriano (*b*); J. T. Lewis (*d*); Mor Thiam
    (*perc*); Chief Cliff Singers. 95.

Don Pullen's solo records demand comparison with Cecil Taylor's. Pullen's traditionalism is more obvious, but the apparent structural conservatism is more appearance than fact, a function of his interest in boogie rather than Bartók, and he routinely subverts expected patterns. Some of the earlier solo discs are no longer available, but they tend to reinforce an impression of Pullen as a performer interested in large masses of sound, sometimes to the detriment of forward progress. That in turn has led him back to the organ, on which he can create huge, sustained chords and swirling textures, as on the duo record with Moye. *Evidence Of Things Unseen* is by far the best of the solo discs, though the recently reissued *Healing Force* will have its supporters as well. *Evidence* bespeaks the same dark-and-light opposition as Andrew Hill or Ran Blake, though Pullen is more of a free player than either, and certainly less of an ironist than Blake.

He favours exotic dissonances within relatively conventional chordal progressions and, to that extent, is a descendant of Monk. His tribute album is very uneven, with completely wrong-headed effects on ''Round Midnight' and some of the aimlessness that creeps into his duos with George Adams.

Of the groups with horns, the best are those fronted by Freeman and Dara, where Pullen develops spiky, almost spasmodic graph-lines of improvisational material in the midst of inventive and often rather Ivesian structures; the technique is reminiscent of Mingus, with whom Pullen played in the mid-1970s. Rivers is too floaty and ethereal to be entirely effective in this context, though he noticeably tailors his approach to Pullen's cues.

The best work of all is in the two late-1980s trios. The first, with its big-name rhythm section, explodes in the fury of 'Reap The Whirlwind', where Williams's scything cymbal-lines and almost military patterns give a very fair taste of apocalypse. Though less revelatory than *Evidence*, Pullen's piano-playing seems trance-like, rooted in voodoo, pentecostalism and the Old Religion. By contrast, *Random Thoughts*, with its less experienced bass player and drummer, is calmer and less intense (though Pullen's right-hand swirls on 'Andre's Ups And Downs' and 'Endangered Species: African American Youth', which makes its thematic point by systematically eliding beats, are absolutely characteristic). The closing 'Ode To Life' is unaccompanied and almost child-like, with echoes of 'Falling In Love Again' and 'Lili Marlene' in the first and second halves of the brief phrase out of which it's constructed.

Both *Kele Mou Bana* and *Ode To Life* are credited to Pullen's Afro-Brazilian Connection, a highly rhythmic unit that has prompted some of the pianist's more full-hearted and light-toned playing. The later of the records is by far the more pleasing. The title-piece becomes a memorial to the late George Adams, a gorgeous chorale that builds steadily into a set of complex variations. Ward's distinctive, soaring voice is an important component of the overall sound. The vocal elements on *Kele Mou Bana* are not sufficiently well done to be very interesting, and the later record scores again, but it is also uncluttered and direct.

One might wish for a better send-off for Pullen than *Sacred Common Ground*. His desire to find ever broader bases for the Afro-American music that is jazz was immensely laudable, but in casting about for new roots he dissipates much of the energy that made him such a distinctive presence on the scene. Pullen's death at the age of 51 left a hole, and one has to wonder what his state of health was when he completed this final record. Such considerations ought to be illegitimate, but it is such a strange piece of work in so many ways that an explanation is desirable. Only two of the longer tracks seem to cohere in any organic way, and these, significantly enough, are the tracks on which Pullen himself is dominant. For the rest, the record is a curious mish-mash of influences, with little imaginative centre. An ambiguous legacy.

Alton Purnell (1911–87) PIANO, VOCAL

*** **Alton Purnell In Japan 1976** GHB BCD-243
   Purnell; Yoshio Toyama (*t*); Yoshizaku Yokomizo (*tb*); Masahiro Gotah (*cl*); Keiko Toyama (*bj*); Akio Tada (*b*); Yoshizo Nakajima (*d*). 7/76.
This veteran of the Bunk Johnson and George Lewis bands was born in a room over Preservation Hall, so New Orleans music came naturally to him. There is very little under his own nominal leadership on record, but this cheerful, noisy live date from 1976 catches him in good fettle. Purnell's clattery, strange piano isn't well served by the sound-mix, but his singing comes through well enough – he is surprisingly affecting on 'You've Changed', for example – and the Japanese team with him carry off their parts with enthusiasm and a fair amount of panache. Trumpeter Toyama is especially fine at playing a Louisiana-via-Tokyo lead, and Gotah is very nimble. Rough-and-ready sound, but it doesn't spoil the fun.

Nick Purnell COMPOSER, ARRANGER

***(*) **onetwothree** ah um 006
   Purnell; Kenny Wheeler, Paul Edmonds (*t, flhn*); Mike Gibbs (*tb*); Ashley Slater (*btb, tba*); Ken Stubbs, Julian Arguëlles (*sax*); John Taylor (*p*); Django Bates (*ky*); Mike Walker (*g*); Mick Hutton, Laurence Cottle (*b*); Peter Erskine (*d, perc*); Dave Adams (*perc*). 9/90.
ah um is Purnell's own label, but there is no hint of vanity publishing on this excellent compositional debut. He has assembled a superb cast of soloists and a set of themes sufficiently limber and flexible to bring the best out of them. From Julian Arguëlles's haunting opening solo on 'Helena' the attention is held fast. At first the saxophonist looks as if he might be about to hi-jack the record, but John Taylor, Kenny Wheeler and Django Bates all contribute prominently, and there are extremely impressive contributions from guitarist Mike Walker and from altoist Ken Stubbs, the first of whom will not be widely known to record buyers. Purnell's writing and arranging are unfussy and to the point, and he produces sensibly, allowing the solo voice to project forward more than might normally be considered acceptable. And that's very much in the spirit of the project.

Wolfgang Puschnig ALTO SAXOPHONE, PICCOLO

*** **Pieces Of The Dream** Amadeo 837322-2
   Puschnig; Hans Koller (*ts*); Uli Scherer, Carla Bley (*p*); Charlie Krachler, Harry Pepl, Hiram Bullock (*g*); Jamaaladeen Tacuma, Heiri Kaenzig (*b*); Linda Sharrock (*v*); choir. 4/88.

Puschnig is perhaps best known as a stalwart with both Carla Bley and the Vienna Art Orchestra. This is the earliest record under his own name currently available. It sets a pattern which he has broadly stuck to since: almost obsessively eclectic, rootsy and post-modern from beat to beat, the music can be extraordinarily moving – as on the opening, gospellified 'A Long Way From Home' – or emerge as knowing pastiche. Structured mainly as a sequence of duets, this is like a skeleton-plan of the later stuff. It also highlights Puschnig's wounded alto style.

***(*) **Alpine Aspects** Amadeo 511 204
Puschnig; Rudolf Pilz, Bumi Fian, Josef Burcharts (*t*); Hans Schaupp, Franz Rappersberger (*flhn*); Günter Innerlohinger, Leopold Libal (*tb*); Herbert Klaus (*tba*); Hermann Berger (*thn*); John Sass, Herbert Klaus (*tba*); Oskar Eder (*f*); Ingrid Schaupp, Robert Pussecker (*cl*); Johan Leonhartsberger (*cl, as*); Raimund Aichinger (*cl, ts*); Jamaaladeen Tacuma (*b*); Wolfgang Schneider, Thomas Alkier (*d*); Linda Sharrock (*v*). 5/91.

Puschnig is understandably anxious not to let this fine disc be pigeonholed misleadingly; not 'modern folk', not crossover, not anything the industry's going to put a label on. Which, of course, presents the reviewer with a problem.

Essentially, *Alpine Aspects* draws on the bubbly but also curiously melancholy sound of German and Swiss brass bands. Puschnig lists band and soloists separately, and there's a definite split (more so than in the Vienna Art Orchestra, say) between the ensembles and the improvised passages. Themes like 'Strange March', which includes a chilling vocal by Linda Sharrock, are written by Puschnig and arranged by Pussecker. A couple of others are adaptations of traditional band material.

Relative to the VAO, Puschnig doesn't offer quite such a convincing synthesis of his materials. There's a prevailing bittiness – here comes a folksy bit, here comes a 'jazz' bit – and the inclusion of 'Looney Tune' at the end runs a mild risk of sending the whole thing up. Undoubtedly interesting and often compelling, though; for those who feel that the only true measure of this music is in the solos, there's plenty of incident and invention in that department.

*** **Mixed Metaphors** Amadeo 527266-2
Puschnig; Rick Iannacone, Andy Manndorff (*g*); Jamaaladeen Tacuma (*b*); Ahmir Thompson (*d*); Milton Cardona (*perc*); Linda Sharrock, Antoine Green (*v*). 8/94.

A group record, heavily involved with poetry – whether rapped, by Green, or sung, by Sharrock – and the kind of fractured funk customarily peddled by Tacuma and James Blood Ulmer, this is all right, but in the end lacking in the surprise of the previous disc. More adventurous tastes may prefer to seek out Puschnig's collaboration with Korean drumming group Red Sun SamulNori (Amadeo 841222-2).

Ike Quebec (1918–63) TENOR SAXOPHONE

*** **Blue And Sentimental** Blue Note 784098
Quebec; Sonny Clark (*p*); Grant Green (*g*); Paul Chambers (*b*); Philly Joe Jones (*d*). 12/61.

Blue Note's last recording date in Hackensack and first in its new headquarters at Englewood Cliffs were both by Ike Quebec. Little known to younger fans, the saxophonist was nevertheless a figure of considerable influence at the label, acting as musical director, A&R man and talent scout (Dexter Gordon and Leo Parker were two of his 'finds'). He was also an important Blue Note recording artist, producing some marvellous sessions for the label just after the war and steering the label in the direction of a more contemporary repertoire. Mosaic had already issued a compilation of mid-1940s work by Quebec and John Hardee. *The Complete Blue Note 45 Sessions* brought together 27 popular sides Quebec made for the thriving juke-box market. By no means wholly organ-dominated, as such 45s tended to be, the sessions strongly featured Quebec's still-underrated tenor style, which sounds like a cross between Wardell Gray and Dexter Gordon.

Quebec has several times teetered on the brink of major rediscovery, but each time interest has flagged. He is, admittedly, a rather limited performer when set beside Gordon or any of the other younger tenor players emerging at the time, but he has a beautiful, sinuous tone and an innate melodic sense that negotiates standards with a simplicity and lack of arrogance that are refreshing and even therapeutic. *Blue And Sentimental*, with fine performances on 'Minor Impulse', 'Don't Take Your Love From Me' and 'Count Every Star', is an excellent place to start.

John Rae (born 1934) VIBES

*** **Opus De Jazz No. 2** Savoy S V-0179
Rae; Bobby Jaspar (*f*); Steve Kuhn (*p*); John Neves (*b*); Jake Hanna (*d*). 12/60.

This sequel to Milt Jackson's earlier Savoy session might be less obviously swinging than the previous record, but the canny collaboration between Rae, the sweet/sour Jaspar and the enquiring Kuhn makes for some compelling interplay. Their 'Ah-Leu-Cha' is a fascinating attempt at cooling out a classic Parker theme. But the rest of the date relies too heavily on the blues, suggesting that there was little time for preparation. Rae isn't a major voice on vibes – he worked with George Shearing's quintet in the 1950s – but his solos are pleasingly swinging and a neat counterpoint to the more substantial Jaspar, who again proves the possibilities of flute as a hard-bop instrument.

Boyd Raeburn (1913–66) BASS SAXOPHONE, TENOR SAXOPHONE, BARITONE SAXOPHONE, BANDLEADER

*** **More 1944–1945** Circle CCD 113
    Louis Cles, Ewell Payne, Pincus Stavitt, Benny Harris, Stan Fishillsen, T. D. Allison, J. B. Gillespie (*t*); Earl Swope, Pullman Pederson, Bob Swift, Trummy Young, J. K. Corman, O. C. Wilson, W. C. Robertson (*tb*); John Bothwell, Hal McKusick (*as*); Angelo Tompros, Joe Megro, Al Cohn (*ts*); Serge Chaloff (*bs*); George Handy, George Hendelman, Ike Carpenter (*p*); Dennis Sandole, John Payuo, Steve P. Jordan (*g*); Andy Delmar, Mort Oliver, Oscar Pettiford (*b*); Don Lamond, Shelly Manne (*d*); Don Darcy, Marjorie Wood Hoffman (*v*). 6 & 8/44, 1/45.

***(*) **Boyd Meets Stravinsky** Savoy SV 0185
    Raeburn; Dale Pierce, Ray Linn, Carl Groesn, Nelson Shelladay, Dizzy Gillespie, Barry Harris, Tommy Allison, Stan Fishelson, Carl Berg, Allan Jeffreys, Frank Beach (*t*); Ollie Wilson, Britt Woodman, Trummy Young, Jack Carmen, Walt Robertson, Hal Smith, Fred Zito (*tb*); Lloyd Otto, Evan Vail (*frhn*); Harry Klee, Wilbur Schwartz, Ralph Lee, Gus McReynolds, Hy Mandel, Johnny Bothwell, Hal McKusick, Lennie Green, Serge Chaloff, Al Cohn, Joe Magro, Frank Socolow, Stu Anderson, Julie Jacobs (*reeds*); Dodo Marmarosa, Hal Schaefer, Ike Carpenter (*p*); Harry Babasin, Joe Beris, Oscar Pettiford (*b*); Steve Jordan, Dave Barbour, Tony Rizzi (*g*); Gale Laughton (*hp*); Irv Kluger, Shelly Manne, Jackie Mills (*d*); Margie Wood, Ginny Powell, David Allyn (*v*). 45, 46, 47.

In 1944 an unexplained fire at the Palisades Pleasure Park in New Jersey destroyed the instruments and music of one of the most challenging big bands of the period. Typically of Boyd Raeburn, his re-formed band and new book were even more adventurous than what had gone before. Musically, the Circle material from the apocalyptic year is typical of the leader's adventurous spirit and of the willingness of his players to push out the boat a little and take risks. Often exhilarating stuff. Raeburn's was a musicians' band, held in the highest esteem by his peers, regarded with some suspicion by those who believed that bands were for dancing.

Raeburn had an intelligent awareness of classical and twentieth-century forms – 'Boyd Meets Stravinsky' gives a sense of his range – and was as comfortable with Bartók and Debussy as he was with Ellington and Basie. The bands were clangorous, neither 'sweet' nor 'hot', but a curious admixture of the two, and arrangements were full of awkward time-signatures and tonalities. Tunes such as 'Tonsilectomy', 'Rip Van Winkle' and 'Yerxa', from earlier and (as yet) not reissued sessions, are among the most remarkable of modern-band pieces. Hal McKusick was a featured soloist and the Raeburn bands of the time (like Kirk's or McShann's) are well worth scouring for the early work of prominent modernists. From these sessions, in addition to McKusick, one might list Shelly Manne, Serge Chaloff, Al Cohn, Jimmy Giuffre, Dodo Marmarosa, Conte Candoli, Buddy DeFranco and Charles Mingus's buddy and inspiration, Britt Woodman; the Circle CD notes with laconic literalism a trumpeter called 'J. B. Gillespie'. Would that be Jim Brown Gillespie, perhaps?

It may be that simple market forces pushed Raeburn back in the direction of the swing mainstream. The latest of the Savoy selections, from the summer of 1947, are 'Body And Soul' and 'Over The Rainbow', still intelligently and uncompromisingly arranged (by Johnny Richards), but less immediately powerful than earlier sessions.

Ane Ramlose VOICE

*** **Days Without Makeup** Storyville STCD 4195
    Ramlose; Flemming Agerskov (*t*); Fredrik Lundin (*ss, ts, bf*); Hans Ulrik (*ss, ts*); Thomas Clausen (*p*); Hans Anderson (*b*); Peter Danemo (*d*). 12/92–5/93.
Ramlose's small voice and soft articulation set the tone for this chamberish and not unpleasing set of dreamy modal themes. With Agerskov coming on like a Kenny Wheeler disciple and Clausen's smoothly lyrical piano underneath, the music offers an inevitable variation on Azimuth, though Ramlose is

scarcely a match for Norma Winstone. Lundin and Ulrik put in harsher notes with some quite terse and involved improvising on their appearances. One for an autumn afternoon.

Enzo Randisi VIBES

*** Ten Years After Splasc(h) H 346-2
> Randisi; Salvatore Bonafede (*p*); Giuseppe Costa (*b*); Mimmo Cafiero (*d*). 12/90.

Enzo Randisi is a veteran Italian vibes player who hasn't recorded much: the title refers to the date of his last record prior to this one. He has nothing out of the ordinary to say and ambles through most of this session at a slow to medium tempo, working through a series of familiar ballads. Yet it all works out very well. Bonafede sees through the problems of making piano work with vibes, Costa and Cafiero play patiently and unemphatically, and Randisi is left to concentrate on his lines, which sidestep the kind of overplaying that vibes players tend to be tempted into and seek out clear, ringing melodies instead. He can pick up gears when he wants to – the gathering power of his solo on 'Poor Butterfly' is particularly well handled – but most of the time he doesn't have to, and he sounds the better for it.

Doug Raney (born 1957) GUITAR

*** Cuttin' Loose Steeplechase SCCD 31105
> Raney; Bernt Rosengren (*ts*); Horace Parlan (*p*); Niels-Henning Orsted-Pedersen (*b*); Billy Hart (*d*). 8/78.

*** Listen Steeplechase SCCD 31144
> As above, except omit Parlan; replace NHOP with Jesper Lundgaard (*b*). 12/80.

*** Meeting The Tenors Criss Cross Criss 1006
> Raney; Bernt Rosengren (*ts, f*); Ferdinand Povel (*ts*); Horace Parlan (*p*); Jesper Lundgaard (*b*); Ole Jacob Hansen (*d*). 4/83.

*** Lazy Bird Steeplechase SCCD 31200
> Raney; Bernt Rosengren (*ts*); Ben Besiakov (*p*); Jesper Lundgaard (*b*); Ole Jacob Hansen (*d*). 4/84.

***(*) Something's Up Steeplechase SCCD 31235
> As above, except omit Rosengren; replace Hansen with Billy Hart (*d*). 2/88.

*** Guitar Guitar Guitar Steeplechase SCCD 31212
> Raney; Mads Vinding (*b*); Billy Hart (*d*). 7/85.

**** The Doug Raney Quintet Steeplechase SCCD 31249
> Raney; Tomas Franck (*as*); Bernt Rosengren (*ts*); Jesper Lundgaard (*b*); Jukkis Uotila (*d*). 8/88.

Raised to the family craft, Doug Raney quickly established his own identity and a more contemporary idiom that also seemed to draw on swing guitar (missing out, that is, much of the bebop influence his father has sustained). Less robust rhythmically than his father, Raney slots more conventionally into a horn-and-rhythm set-up. His trio, *Guitar Guitar Guitar*, is highly accomplished but it has a one-dimensional quality, noticeable on more familiar material like 'Solar' and 'My Old Flame'. CD doesn't flatter his technique, which sounds slightly scratchy and lacks Jimmy Raney's smooth, Jim Hall-like legato.

The closing 'Moment's Notice' (also by Coltrane) on *Listen* is one of Raney's best performances on record. There is a steady modal shift on his theme statements, and the soloing is robust without losing the tune's innate romanticism. Rosengren's Coltraneisms are reasonably well assimilated, and he modulates well, as on *Cuttin' Loose* and *Lazy Bird*, between a smooth swing and a more aggressive modernism. Things pick up sharply again, after an early-'80s slump, with the 1988 album. Besiakov is nowhere near as commanding a player as Parlan, but he has sharpened considerably over the four years since his last recording with Raney and lends a genuine presence to 'Good Morning Heartache' and 'Upper Manhattan Medical Group'.

The '88 quintet album is excellent in every department. There is another fine version of 'Speedy Recovery' (also on *Something's Up*). The extra horn and absence of piano restores certain harmonic responsibilities to the guitar, but it also generates a very different texture through which he has to play with just a little more force than usual. It's difficult to know where else to start with Raney. The late-1980s albums are completely accomplished, but one misses the freshness of the earlier material. Follow the stars.

Jimmy Raney (1927–95) GUITAR

**** A Original Jazz Classics OJC 1706
  Raney; John Wilson (*t*); Hall Overton (*p*); Teddy Kotick (*b*); Art Mardigan, Nick Stabulas (*d*). 5/
54–3/55.

Of the bop-inspired guitarists Raney perhaps best combined lyricism with great underlying strength. Essentially a group player, he sounds good at almost any tempo but is most immediately appealing on ballads. *A*, which contains some of his loveliest performances, is overdue for CD transfer. Overton anticipates some of the harmonic devices employed by Hank Jones (below) and bebop bassist Kotick plays with a firm authority that synchronizes nicely with Raney's rather spacious and elided lower string work. Wilson adds a dimension to the lovely 'For The Mode' and to four more romantic numbers, including 'A Foggy Day' and 'Someone To Watch Over Me'.

***(*) The Complete Jimmy Raney In Tokyo Xanadu FDC 5157
  Raney; Charles McPherson (*as*); Barry Harris (*p*); Sam Jones (*b*); Leroy Williams (*d*). 4/76.

They may not be able to pronounce the band members' names with any certainty, but the Japanese are warmly appreciative of Raney's work. This was a bit of a purple patch for the guitarist, and the guest appearance of Charles McPherson for 'Groovin' High' and 'Blue'N'Boogie' was a sincere homage from a player whose route out of bebop has been rather thornier. This must be one of the best groups Raney ever assembled. Jones is towering and Leroy Williams (a bit of a shibboleth for Japanese announcers) never puts a foot wrong. Don Schlitten's production delivers a clean and full sound, almost as good as many studio recordings.

**** Here's That Raney Day Black & Blue 59.756
  Raney; Hank Jones (*p*); Pierre Michelot (*b*); Jimmy Cobb (*d*). 7/80.
***(*) Raney '81 Criss Cross Criss 1001
  Raney; Doug Raney (*g*); Jesper Lundgaard (*b*); Eric Ineke (*d*). 2/81.
**** The Master Criss Cross Criss 1009
  Raney; Kirk Lightsey (*p*); Jesper Lundgaard (*b*); Eddie Gladden (*d*). 2/83.
**** Wisteria Criss Cross Criss 1019
  Raney; Tommy Flanagan (*p*); George Mraz (*b*). 12/85.

The early 1980s saw some vintage Raney on record. The quartet with Hank Jones is valuable largely for the inclusion of alternative takes that give a clearer idea of how subtly the guitarist can shift the dynamic of a piece by holding or eliding notes, shuffling the rhythm and increasing the metrical stress. *'81* includes some rejected takes, of 'Sweet And Lovely', 'If I Should Lose You' and 'My Shining Hour' most obviously, which offer convincing demonstration of his speed of thought and suggest once again what an underrated player he was by all except jazz guitar groupies, who presumably know their way round this stuff already.

 Raney Day is distinguished by a couple of bebop staples, 'Au Privave' and 'Scrapple From The Apple', which are taken medium-fast but with great control. Jones is bettered as an accompanist only by Flanagan and, at moments, Lightsey, both of whom are more elaborate and romantic players.

 The Master offers second takes of 'The Song Is You' and 'Tangerine' (but not, unfortunately, the vibrant 'Billie's Bounce'), revealing how thoughtful an accompanist Lightsey is. The rhythm players are slightly too stiff for him, but he compensates by breaking up their less elastic figures with single-note stabs and scurrying runs at the next bar-line.

 Flanagan's right hand is lost in a rather woolly mix, but the material on this marvellous album more than makes up for any purely technical shortcomings. From the opening 'Hassan's Dream', with its big, dramatic gestures, to 'I Could Write A Book', the drummer-less group plays at the highest level and 'Out Of The Past' is very special indeed.

**** Duets Steeplechase SCCD 31134
  Raney; Doug Raney (*g*). 4/79.
*** Stolen Moments Steeplechase SCCD 31118
  Raney; Doug Raney (*g*); Michael Moore (*b*); Billy Hart (*d*). 4/79.

If you can't hire 'em, breed 'em. Raney's partnership with his son, Doug, has been one of the most productive and sympathetic of his career. Their duos are masterpieces of guitar interplay, free of the dismal call-and-response clichés that afflict such pairings, and often unexpectedly sophisticated in direction. Generally, the repertoire is restricted to standards, but Raney is also an impressive composer and frequently surprises with an unfamiliar melody.

 Duets is probably still the best available performance and is obtainable on all formats. The closing 'My Funny Valentine' would melt a heart of stone, and Doug Raney, with the lighter, less strongly accented style that was so responsive to Chet Baker's needs, is particularly good on 'My One And Only Love' and 'Have You Met Miss Jones'. The addition of rhythm doesn't alter the basic conformation of the music, but it does increase the tempo and spices up the slightly unlikely samba. The curtain number is that old duo warhorse, 'Alone Together'.

***(*) **But Beautiful** Criss Cross Criss 1065
>   Raney; George Mraz (*b*); Lewis Nash (*d*). 12/90.

This is the master at work, to be sure. Raney plays with consummate ease and elegance, as perfectly balanced and utterly tasteful as ever. It's a great pity that he hasn't recorded more in this format. Mraz and Nash are both excellent, as ever, and contribute considerably to the direction of Raney's solos, which do still have a tendency to drift and turn hazy at the edges. Mraz is formidably disciplined without losing expressiveness. The recording is very close and soft, picking up all the overtones in both sets of strings. By contrast, Nash is a little recessed.

John Rapson TROMBONE

***(*) **Bing** Sound Aspects SAS CD 036
>   Rapson; John Fumo (*t, flhn*); Kim Richmond (*cl, as, f*); Vinny Golia (*ts, bs, bcl, af*); Tom Lackner (*vib, d, perc*); Bill Hoper (*tba*); Chris Symer (*b*); Alex Cline (*d*). 1/89.

Rapson is a member of the Californian avant-garde whose records are more usually found on Nine Winds; several of the usual suspects are in this octet, which does a superlative job of bringing his complex scores to life. The achievement is to take difficult ideas and free thinking into structures that remain swinging and easily digested. The title-piece is a brilliant example of free and structured playing in seamless sympathy, and that can be contrasted with the 'power tune', 'Real Reality', or the enigmatic ballad, 'E.A.R. Mark No. 10'. Rapson takes a relatively modest role as soloist: the most striking improvisations come from Richmond, Golia and Fumo. But it's as an ensemble record that it makes an impact. The closing Monk medley is a tiresome bit of mock-comic revisionism which jazz has probably had enough of by now; everything else is very fine.

Enrico Rava (born 1943) TRUMPET, FLUGELHORN

**** **The Pilgrim And The Stars** ECM 1063
>   Rava; John Abercrombie (*g*); Palle Danielsson (*b*); Jon Christensen (*d*). 6/75.
***(*) **The Plot** ECM 1078
>   As above. 8/76.
**** **Enrico Rava Quartet** ECM 1122
>   Rava; Roswell Rudd (*tb*); Jean-François Jenny-Clark (*b*); Aldo Romano (*d*). 3/78.
*** **Rava String Band** Soul Note 121114
>   Rava; Augusto Mancinelli (*g*); Giovanni Tommaso (*b*); Tony Oxley (*d*); Nana Vasconcelos (*perc*); string quartet. 4/84.
***(*) **Secrets** Soul Note SN 1164
>   Rava; Augusto Mancinelli (*g, g syn*); John Taylor (*p*); Furio Di Castri (*b*); Bruce Ditmas (*d*). 7/86.
*** **Volver** ECM 1343
>   Rava; Dino Saluzzi (*bandoneon*); Harry Pepl (*g*); Furio Di Castri (*b*); Bruce Ditmas (*d*). 10/86.
*** **Enrico Rava Quintet** Nabel 4632
>   Rava; Ullmann Gebhard (*ts, ss, bf*); Andreas Willers (*g*); Martin Willichy (*b*); Nikolas Schauble (*d*). 3/89.
***(*) **Bella** Philology W 64
>   Rava; Enrico Pieranunzi (*p*); Enzo Pietropaoli (*b*); Roberto Gatto (*d*). 5/90.

Born in the 'international city' of Trieste, Rava evolved a richly esperantist style (originally but not slavishly influenced by Miles Davis) which allows him access to a broad range of musics from the highly formal to the near-free. The best news regarding this underrated artist is that ECM have at last seen fit to reissue on CD Rava's three finest recordings, all dating from the later 1970s and including the eerily beautiful *The Pilgrim And The Stars*.

Rava's distinctive manner is a combination of sustained, curving notes, unmistakably coloured, with sudden rhythmic tangents. In combination with Abercrombie's guitar and the top-flight Scandinavian rhythm section, he creates a sound-world all his own. Reconvening the same band two years later yielded a more subtle album, structurally and compositionally, but *The Plot*'s narrative sophistication ('Amici', 'The Plot' itself) consistently yields to the sheer pictorial poetry evident on 'Foto Di Famiglia', a Rava/Abercrombie collaboration that might have come from the same sessions as the earlier record. Anyone interested in the progress of European jazz should take notice of it at least.

The eponymous Quartet album paired him – often literally – with the waywardly brilliant Rudd. Their unison lines on the upbeat 'The Fearless Five' would be useful evidence for anyone wanting to disprove the old canard about ECM's supposed New Ageist failings. Both men are in cracking form, but they save their most expressive and lyrical statements for the long 'Lavori Casalinghi', co-written with Graciela Rava, which opens the set. There are strong things on 'Tramps' as well, but here it's the remarkable rhythm section of Jenny-Clark and Romano which catches the ear; their interaction could hardly be bettered on either side of the Atlantic, and the bassist in particular is given a lot to do, covering for the absence of a harmony instrument. 'Round About Midnight' is a hokey party piece for the two horns on their own.

In the early 1980s, Rava worked with (mainly) Italian bands, relying heavily on Maricinelli's Abercrombie-derived guitar. Tony Oxley's recorded contribution is restricted to the less than wholly successful *String Band* project, which reflects Rava's growing interest in formal composition for orchestral groups. *Secrets* gains immeasurably from the presence of another Englishman, John Taylor, whose cultured accompaniments and understated soloing are probably more widely recognized outside the British Isles.

The recent Nabel underlines how much a player of Rava's warmth and sensitivity owes to CD. The band is less interesting than any he has previously mustered (and Gebhard is a rather bland colourist), but the leader's tone and invention on two takes of 'Fourteen Days' are impressive indeed. *Bella* is a small gem. The chemistry between Rava and Pieranunzi, that most sensitive of accompanists, is enrapturing on 'My Funny Valentine' and, if the session as a whole rests a little heavily on Chet references, they're done with enough imagination for it not to matter. The 1986 record with Saluzzi is pleasant enough, but it belongs to the bandoneon maestro rather than to Rava, who doesn't find much room for movement in it.

Much of Rava's best work is on other people's records. Nevertheless, he's an individual stylist who completely transcends his stylistic roots and has created a consistently interesting and appealing body of work.

Jason Rebello (born 1970) PIANO, KEYBOARDS, VOCALS

(*) A Clearer View Novus PD 74805
>   Rebello; David O'Higgins (ss, ts); Julian Crampton, Laurence Cottle (b); Jeremy Stacey (d); Karl Van den Bosch (perc). 90.

** **Keeping Time** Novus 74321 129042
>   Rebello; Patrick Clahar (reeds); Tony Remy (g); Mike Mondesir (b); Darren Abraham (d); Thomas Dyani Akuru (perc); Marianne Jean Baptiste, Jocelyn Brown (v). 92.

Rebello made a considerable impact with his signing to Novus, with a reputation as one of the most interesting younger British jazzmen already in the bag. But his two albums for Novus are less encouraging. The first has some striking moments and Rebello's own pianism suggests that he's already moved past his immediate influences. He also provides a sharp focus for the contributions of others such as O'Higgins, a talented saxophonist who has one of his best solos on the chattering 'Tone Row'. But the modish production values distracted from the results rather than firming them up, and matters grew worse with the subsequent *Keeping Time*. There are good things here, but the vocal tracks sound as if they've drifted in from some bland soul project, and a worthwhile composition such as 'The Stream' is lost amidst a lot of fusion fluff. Rebello's subsequent *Last Dance* (All That), co-credited with the vocalist Joy Rose, was a further disappointment.

Freddie Redd (born 1927) PIANO

*** **Piano: East / West** Original Jazz Classics OJC 1705
>   Redd; John Ore (b); Ron Jefferson (d). 2/55.

*** **San Francisco Suite** Original Jazz Classics OJC 1748
>   Redd; George Tucker (b); Al Dreares (d). 10/57.

**** **The Music From 'The Connection'** Blue Note CDP 789392
>   Redd; Jackie McLean (as); Michael Mattos (b); Larry Ritchie (d). 2/60.

*** **Live At The Studio Grill** Triloka 182 2
>   Redd; Al McKibbon (b); Billy Higgins (d). 5/88.

*** **Everybody Loves A Winner** Milestone MCD 9187
>   Redd; Curtis Peagler (as); Teddy Edwards (ts); Phil Ranelin (tb); Bill Langlois (b); Larry Hancock (d). 90.

Redd's amiable West Coast bop soundtracks an unscripted (but you've seen it) Bay Area movie: bustling streetcars, pretty girls flashing their legs, sudden fogs and alarms, an apology for a narrative. The *San Francisco Suite* is cliché from start to finish but, like the very much later *Winner* (Redd has been only a sporadic recorder in recent years), the hackneyed moods are unpretentiously and engagingly done.

He was a lot more coherent when there was a real narrative to deal with. Redd was one of several jazzmen drawn to Jack Gelber's drugs drama, *The Connection*, and in Jackie McLean he had a player who knew both the music and the life inside out, the one illuminating and shadowing the other. It's still a splendid record. For long enough it was available, with the other good Blue Note, *Shades of Redd*, only as a limited-edition double-CD on Mosaic (see Introduction). It's good to have the better even of these two available on its own. It's a stunning performance, which Redd later tried and failed to reduplicate. Despite that apparent apotheosis, his career has been largely static since the late 1950s.

He is a player who hasn't been able to fall back on an absolutely secure playing technique. The younger Redd certainly gave Hampton Hawes no frights on the double-header *Piano: East/West* disc, and his biggest strength has always been the kind of terse writing the Gelber play inspired and which the San Francisco skyline unfortunately didn't. The Studio Grill sessions document a career-reviving residency in the Santa Monica Boulevard restaurant. 'I'll Remember April' has a vivid bounce that contrasts well with the blunt block chords Redd favours in his own compositions. It and the closing 'All The Things You Are' are the two longest cuts of the set, suggesting perhaps a degree of Redd's frustration at the lack of sympathetic recording opportunities over the years. 'Waltzin' In' is the best of the originals, a bright, hummable melody that, like 'Don't Lose The Blues', sounds as if it ought to be a long-serving standard. 'Round Midnight' (credited to Monk, Bernice Hanighan and Cootie Williams) is beautifully executed, with just a hint of Redd's impressionism creeping back in.

Everybody Loves A Winner again highlights his talent as a composer (and some of his limitations as a performer). The addition of horns gives him some room for experiment, certainly more than with a conventional piano trio, but only Curtis Peagler's youthful alto in any way attempts to break the mould. An interesting figure, but by no means a 'neglected genius'. His critical standing is just about right.

Dewey Redman (born 1931) TENOR SAXOPHONE, CLARINET, MUSETTE, ALTO SAXOPHONE

*** **Redman And Blackwell In Willisau** Black Saint 120093
    Redman; Ed Blackwell (*d*). 8/80.
***(*) **Living On The Edge** Black Saint 120123
    Redman; Geri Allen (*p*); Cameron Brown (*b*); Eddie Moore (*d*). 9/89.
***(*) **Choices** Enja 7073
    Redman; Joshua Redman (*ts*); Cameron Brown (*b*); Leon Parker (*d*). 7/92.

Redman's career has been notably erratic and, though he recorded classic solo albums as far back as 1966 (*Look For The Black Star*, Arista Freedom) and 1973 (*Ear Of The Behearer*, Impulse), he has attained proper recognition as a performer in his own right only in the 1980s, from which decade all his surviving material derives. Alternately volatile and magisterial, Redman is a difficult player to characterize. For much of his career, his critical visibility was limited by his role in Charlie Haden's Liberation Music Orchestra and by his ultimately self-destructive behaviour in Keith Jarrett's American band; *The Survivor's Suite* (ECM 1085) was a masterpiece, *Eyes Of The Heart* (ECM 1150) an unmitigated disaster. He acted as an almost normative presence in Ornette Coleman's inflammable 1970s quintet, and, as Ornette's 'double' in the band Old and New Dreams (*q.v.*), has since become perhaps the most significant explorer on saxophone of the elder Texan's compositional output.

There are few direct traces of Ornette's approach in Redman's recent work, yet they demonstrably come from a single source. To the hard-toned 'Texas tenor' style, Redman has brought a strong Middle Eastern influence, most noticeable on the fine duos with Blackwell, where he also uses the twin-reed musette, exploring almost microtonal territory a long way removed from the blues. Blackwell's chiming, resonant sound is one of the redeeming aspects of *The Struggle Continues*, an awkward, aesthetically shapeless album that renewed doubts about Redman's contradictory personality. (It seems there are still stocks of the LP, and no immediate plans to transfer it.)

By the end of the 1980s he appeared to have achieved some sort of psychological and artistic breakthrough. *Living On The Edge* preserves much of the menace Redman can generate, but with a new simplicity of emotion and with a tone notably less forced than on previous outings. Allen is an ideal partner, in that she is willing to examine intervals that fall outside the usual geometry of blues and bebop, but she also has an unfailing rhythmic awareness that keeps Redman within bounds. Strongly recommended (and *Dark Star* and *Behearer* should be looked out for as well).

Choices got more than usual attention because of Redman Jr who, having graduated from Harvard, was being wooed by most of the major labels and profiled in almost all the music papers. He grew up apart from Dad and doesn't sound remotely like him. Dewey stays with alto for all but 'Everything Happens To Me', a big, soft ballad of the kind Pharoah Sanders has been playing of late. Joshua sits it out and, with just Dewey and rhythm, it sounds cool and spare, well this side of mawkishness. Joshua takes his turn with the slow stuff on 'Imagination' and cuts an elegant solo. He gets some room again on 'O'Besso', when Dewey switches to musette. It's one of the less successful of his Eastern things and goes on way too long at 14 minutes. The final track, an original dedicated to the late Eddie Moore (who drummed with Dewey's early-'70s group), is a stormer, with an expansive free section in the middle that pits the Redmen against one another in what initially sounds like a stand-off and develops steadily into a shoulder-to-shoulder surge. Impressive stuff, and the old guy wins out by a whisker. Just as it should be.

Don Redman (1900–64) ALTO SAXOPHONE, SOPRANO SAXOPHONE, OTHER INSTRUMENTS, BANDLEADER

*** **Don Redman, 1931–1933** Classics 543
Redman; Henry Allen, Shirley Clay, Bill Coleman, Langston Curl, Reunald Jones, Sidney De Paris (*t*); Claude Jones, Benny Morton, Fred Robinson, Gene Simon (*tb*); Jerry Blake (*cl, as, bs*); Robert Cole, Edward Inge (*cl, as*); Harvey Boone (*as, bs*); Robert Carroll (*ts*); Horace Henderson, Don Kirkpatrick (*p*); Talcott Reeves (*bj, g*); Bob Ysaguirre (*bb, b*); Manzie Johnson (*d, vib*); Chick Bullock, Cab Calloway, Harlan Lattimore, The Mills Brothers (*v*); Bill Robinson (tap dancing). 9/31–5/36.
*** **Don Redman, 1933–1936** Classics 553
As above.
*** **Chant Of The Weed** Topaz TPZ 1043
As above, except add Tom Stevenson, Robert Williams, Sidney De Paris (*t*); Quentin Jackson, Gene Simon (*tb*); Carl Frye, Ed Inge (*cl, as, bs*); Eddie Williams, Gene Sedric (*ts*). 28–38.

He was small, compact, well loved. He played a mean alto and sang in a soft, almost ethereal whisper. He arranged and composed. And he conducted with his left hand.

Redman's reputation has been in progressive eclipse since the war, but he remains one of the essential figures of the big-band era. He started out as lead saxophonist and staff arranger with Fletcher Henderson's band, infusing the charts with a breathtaking simplicity and confidence, eventually leaving in 1928 to front the highly successful McKinney's Cotton Pickers. Redman quickly moved on to form a 'name' band. The material on *Chronological* is the core of Redman's output. The earlier of the pair features the band's remarkable theme-tune, 'Chant Of The Weed', Redman's brilliant and justly celebrated arrangement of 'I Got Rhythm' and two cuts of the title-track. The band at this time also featured Harlan Lattimore, one of the few genuinely challenging singers of the era, who was once described by George T. Simon as sounding like a rather hip Bing Crosby; one man or the other is spinning in his coffin even now. The arrangements are well up to scratch, and there is more impressive work from Lattimore. Bojangles Robinson tip-taps on one version of the title-piece, but the better cut features the Mills Brothers and Cab Calloway.

The Topaz compilation is, as they always are, a useful fast run-through of the career, without much depth in focus at any point. The obvious things are there – 'Chant Of The Weed', 'Shakin' The African', 'Nagasaki' – and there aren't any glaring chronological gaps. A very worthwhile purchase.

Redman's bandleading career effectively ended with America's entry into the Second World War. He became a professional arranger and writer, working freelance for Harry James and others. He did, though, have one significant fling in 1946, when he led the first American band to visit Europe since peace broke out, a period not yet documented on CD.

Joshua Redman (born 1969) TENOR SAXOPHONE

**** **Joshua Redman** Warner Bros 945242-2
Redman; Kevin Hays, Mike LeDonne (*p*); Christian McBride, Paul LaDuca (*b*); Gregory Hutchinson, Clarence Penn, Kenny Washington (*d*). 5–9/92.
**** **Wish** Warner Bros 945365-2
Redman; Pat Metheny (*g*); Charlie Haden (*b*); Billy Higgins (*d*). 93.
***(*) **Mood Swing** Warner Bros 9362-45643-2
Redman; Brad Mehldau (*p*); Christian McBride (*b*); Brian Blade (*d*). 3/94.
*** **Spirit Of The Moment – Live At The Village Vanguard** Warner Bros 945923-2 2CD
Redman; Peter Martin (*p*); Christopher Thomas (*b*); Brian Blade (*d*). 3/95.

Joshua Redman's albums have caused a sensation, and their commercial success is deserved: few albums in recent years have communicated such sheer joy in playing as these. Although he had already made some interesting sideman appearances, the saxophonist's eponymous set was a stunning debut: a canny blend of bop, standards, the odd tricky choice (Monk's 'Trinkle Tinkle') and young man's fancy (James Brown's 'I Got You (I Feel Good)'), all of it buoyed up on the kind of playing that suggests an instant maturity. His lean tone turned out to be as limber or as weighty as he wished, his phrasing had plenty of spaces but could cruise at any bebop height, and his invention sounded unquenchable. The euphoric but controlled feeling extends to his sidemen, Hays, McBride and Hutchinson (two odd tracks were drafted in from other sessions). Beautifully recorded, too.

Wish was an equally splendid follow-up: a little more self-conscious with the starry support group, and a couple of the tunes (Eric Clapton's 'Tears In Heaven'?) seemed a little too modish; but the more open harmonics of Metheny's guitar and the gravitas of Haden and Higgins framed the younger man's improvisations with great eloquence. The bonus live versions of 'Wish' (from the first album) and a roughly sketched 'Blues For Pat' add a further dimension and extend the joyousness of Redman's playing.

After such a start, *Mood Swing* had huge expectations to live up to. It's still a very impressive record, but it's just arguable that the sheer *joie de vivre* of the playing on the first two records has been suspended in favour of a more considered, careful methodology. Not that Redman holds much back in his solos, or that his group are any less imposing. Mehldau, in fact, gives notice that he is a star in the making himself: his contributions, allusive, mischievous and profound by turns, are as substantial as the leader's own. And McBride and Blade are superfine. But here and there are traces of a self-conscious eloquence that suggest a spirit in transition.

Spirit Of The Moment might also be a snapshot analysis of work in progress. There are inevitable recalls of the great Rollins records of nearly 40 years before, especially when Redman tackles 'My One And Only Love' and 'St Thomas'. But this is more exhaustive – two CDs of close to 80 minutes apiece – and more prone to longueurs. As good as the group is, it doesn't really match either the quartet on *Mood Swing* or Redman's previous touring band of McBride, Blade and Eric Reed. Perhaps, too, the days of a new voice setting down an instantaneous great document, as Rollins once did, are as long gone for jazz as is, say, the idea of rock giants cutting their debut set in an afternoon (cf. the Beatles). Gripes aside – and when a man makes a start as powerful as Redman's, one can't help but be anticipatory – there's still much great jazz here.

Dizzy Reece (born 1931) TRUMPET

*** **Blues In Trinity** Blue Note CDP 832093
Reece; Tubby Hayes (*ts*); Terry Shannon (*p*); Lloyd Thompson (*b*); Art Taylor (*d*). 58.
***(*) **Asia Minor** Original Jazz Classics OJC 1806
Reece; Joe Farrell (*ts, f*); Cecil Payne (*bs*); Hank Jones (*p*); Ron Carter (*b*); Charli Persip (*d*). 62.
Born in Jamaica, Reece established his base of operations in Europe for a long while and became a regular partner of British players like Tubby Hayes and Victor Feldman. The Blue Note was recorded a decade after his arrival in England as a teenager and it's still a boisterously brash and confident set, offset a little by Tubbs' own more maturely centred soloing. Even at a somewhat later stage, Reece is slightly difficult to pin down stylistically. Though he can play skyrocketing top-note lines, there's something curiously melancholy about his work on *Asia Minor*, an all-too-rare solo recording which recalls some of the South African players. His trump card here is, of course, the marvellous band he has round him, all of whom contribute to this very welcome calling-card from a dedicated practitioner who has been unjustly neglected in recent years.

Eric Reed (born 1970) PIANO

(*) **Soldier's Hymn Candid CCD 79511
Reed; Dwayne Burno (*b*); Gregory Hutchinson (*d*). 11/90.
***(*) **It's All Right To Swing** MoJazz 530255-2
Reed; E. Dankworth (*t*); Wessell Anderson (*as*); Rodney Whitaker (*b*); Gregory Hutchinson (*d*); Carolyn Johnson-White (*v*). 4/93.
*** **The Swing And I** MoJazz 530468-2
Redd; Ben Wolfe, Rodney Whitaker (*b*); Greg Hutchinson (*d*); voices. 8/94.
Although intended as a showcase debut for Reed, *Soldier's Hymn* is much more of a trio record. Originals like the title-piece (present in two different versions) and 'Coup De Cone' are conscious evaluations of the manner of a Jazz Messengers rhythm section (Art Blakey is the album's dedicatee), and elsewhere Reed's chord-based solos and call-and-response interplay suggest the influence of Ahmad Jamal or even Ramsey Lewis. This works out well on the less ambitious pieces – 'Soft Winds' is an impressive update of the old Benny Goodman tune – but on the more portentous tracks, such as 'Things

Hoped For' or the half-baked medley which Reed does as a solo turn, the music sounds more like a demo session than a finished record. *It's All Right To Swing*, though, is a real step forward. The choice of material and the pianist's gospel-inspired delivery build on the Jamal/Lewis/Mance lineage and suggest a re-evaluation of sanctified piano in the context of the modal jazz of the Marsalis generation. Certainly Reed's funky treatment of 'Wade In The Water' has an undertow of reverence that makes a surprising contrast to the secular manners such pieces normally evoke. The ensuing 'In A Lonely Place' and 'You Don't Know What Love Is' are different again, and by the time of the first quintet tune (with fine solos by Anderson and famous-name-in-disguise Dankworth) the record has real stature. 'Come Sunday', with a vocal by Johnson-White, closes the record on a suitably grand note.

Perhaps *The Swing And I* doesn't quite stand up to its immediate predecessor. This time, Reed sets out to make a full-fledged trio music, with solos and group dialogue relatively interchangeable. While this pays off over perhaps half the record, with some superbly responsive playing by all hands, one ironically hankers after Reed himself stepping forward and directing the group through a personal statement. The closing gospel tune is a rousing hosannah to finish the music.

Tony Reedus (born 1959) DRUMS

***(*) **The Far Side** Jazz City 660.53.016
    Reedus; Bill Evans (*ss, ts*); Mulgrew Miller (*p*); Charnett Moffett (*b*). 11/88.
***(*) **Incognito** Enja 6058
    Reedus; Gary Thomas (*ts, f*); Steve Nelson (*vib*); Dave Holland (*b*). 12/89.
That these two outstanding records are very different from each other says something about the itch to diversify which attends virtually all young jazz musicians nowadays. Reedus is typical of the masterful generation of young virtuosos who are directing the music in America today: his drumming is big and intense, but he plays for his bands, and he's no more egocentric than, say, Max Roach when it comes to directing the music. The Jazz City CD is the more concentrated set: despite a couple of distractions, such as a straight reading of Michael Jackson's 'I Just Can't Stop Loving You', the playing has elegant rigour and a passionate harshness in equal measure, with the undervalued Evans taking a few inspired solos – his Coltraneisms on the title-piece are especially exciting – and Miller anchoring matters when they threaten to slip into abstraction. *Incognito* is more considered, less of a blow-out, and the choice of players is ingenious: Nelson's delicate pointers, Holland's wiry lyricism and Thomas's stone-faced urgency (on tenor – his flute is surprisingly sweet and cultured) concoct a heady brew among them.

Hans Reichel GUITAR, PREPARED GUITAR, DAXOPHONE/DACHSOPHON, OTHER INSTRUMENTS

**** **The Death Of The Rare Bird Ymir / Bonobo Beach** FMP CD 54
    Reichel (*g* solo). 2/79, 4/81.
*** **Angel Carver** FMP CD 15
    Reichel; Tom Cora (*clo, cellodax*). 10/88.
*** **Coco Bolo Nights** FMP CD 10
    Reichel (*g* solo). 12/88.
***(*) **Stop Complaining / Sundown** FMP CD 36
    Reichel; Fred Frith, Kazuhisa Uchihashi (*g*). 6/90, 1/91.
***(*) **Shanghaied On Tor Road** FMP CD 46
    Reichel (*daxophone* solo). 2 & 3/92.
*** **The Dawn Of Dachsmann (Plus)** FMP 60
    Reichel (*g, daxophone* solo). 5 & 7/87.
**** **Lower Lurum** CD BRD 016
    As above. 94.
Riveting free-form guitar with a strong narrative flavour and a complete absence of the 'I've suffered for my art, now it's your turn' aggression of much solo improvised music. Reichel clearly desires to communicate and to convey a story, however notionally and abstractly. His playing is unfussy and uncluttered and he's generally best heard solo, though Cora offers stimulating support. The 'prepared' effects on some of the earlier records (which have disappeared with FMP's vinyl catalogue) are less effective than his admirably disciplined real-time performances, though he coaxes intriguing sounds from a group of personalized instruments which have some connection to the life and life-philosophy of Herr Dachsmann.

The marvellous *Death Of The Rare Bird Ymir* (now slightly edited and paired on CD with *Bonobo Beach*) is probably the best of the albums. Recorded in real time, it features Reichel using such challenging devices as playing two guitars simultaneously (something Derek Bailey had done on Gavin Bryars's piece, *The Squirrel And The Rickety-Rackety Bridge*), playing fretless guitars and picking below the bridge on an electric instrument. Reichel has also pioneered a group of instruments associated with Dachsmann, his imaginary version of Adolphe Sax. *Shanghaied* is devoted entirely to one of these, and a pretty strange sound it makes, too.

The long duet with Frith is curiously jazzy in places, almost as if he and Reichel were spoofing those chummy two-guitar sessions the catalogue is littered with. The Japanese is an interesting player and the live set from Kobe is starkly involving. Later material begins to sound rather similar, but a great deal depends from which end you are approaching this original and offbeat entertainer. Anyone stumbling across *Lower Lurum* (billed as an 'operetta' for guitar and daxophone) will be bowled over. Those who have followed Reichel's course over the years may need the aural equivalent of a sorbet before appreciating yet another weirdly rich course.

Django Reinhardt (1910–53) GUITAR, VIOLIN

***(*) Django Reinhardt, 1934–1935** Classics 703
Reinhardt; Pierre Allier, Gaston Lapeyronnie, Alphonse Cox, Maurice Moufflard, Alex Renard (*t*); Marcel Dumont, Isidore Bassard, Pierre Deck, René Weiss, Guy Paquinet (*tb*); André Ekyan (*cl, as*); Amédée Charles (*as*); Charles Lisée (*as, bs*); Andy Foster (*as, cl, bsx*); Maurice Cizeron (*as, cl, f*); Noël Chiboust, Alix Combelle (*ts*); Stéphane Grappelli (*vn, p*); Michel Warlop (*vn*); Jean Chabaud (*p*); Roger Chaput, Joseph Reinhardt (*g*); Roger Chomer (*vib*); Juan Fernandez, Roger Graset, Louis Pecqueux, Louis Vola (*b*); Maurice Chaillou (*d, v*); Bert Marshall (*v*). 3/ 34–3/35.

**** Django Reinhardt, 1935–1936** Classics 739
Reinhardt; Bill Coleman, Alex Renard (*t*); George Johnson (*cl*); Maurice Cizeron (*as, f*); Alix Combelle (*ts*); Garnet Clark (*p*); Stéphane Grappelli (*vn*); Pierre Feret, Joseph Reinhardt (*g*); June Cole, Lucien Simoens, Louis Vola (*b*); Freddy Taylor (*v*). 9/35–10/36.

**** Swing From Paris** ASV CD AJA 5070
Reinhardt; Stéphane Grappelli (*vn*); Roger Chaput, Pierre Ferret, Joseph Reinhardt, Eugène Vées (*g*); Robert Grassnet, Tony Rovira, Emmanuel Soudieux, Louis Vola (*b*). 9/35–8/39.

*** Swingin' With Django** Pro Arte CDD 549
Reinhardt; Stéphane Grappelli (*vn*); Joseph Reinhardt, Pierre Ferret, Marcel Bianchi, Eugène Vées (*g*); Louis Vola (*b*). 35–43.

*** Welcome To Jazz: Django Reinhardt** Koch 322 074
As above.

*** Django Reinhardt, 1937** Classics 748
Reinhardt; Stéphane Grappelli (*vn*); André Ekyan (*as*); Marcel Bianchi, Pierre Ferret (*g*); Louis Vola (*b*). 4 & 7/37.

***(*) Django Reinhardt, 1937: Volume 2** Classics 762
Reinhardt; Stéphane Grappelli, Paul Bartel, Josef Schwetsin, Michel Warlop (*vn*); Philippe Brun, Gus Deloof, André Cornille, André Pico (*t*); Guy Paquinet, Josse Breyère (*tb*); Jean Magnien (*cl*); Charles Blanc, Max Lisée, André Lamory (*as*); Charles Shaaf (*ts*); Maurice Cizeron (*f*); Georges Paquay (*f, d*); Pierre Zepilli (*p*); Louis Gaste, Joseph Reinhardt, Eugène Vées (*g*); Eugène D'Hellemes (*b*); Maurice Chaillou (*d*). 9–12/37.

***(*) Django Reinhardt, 1937–1938** Classics 777
Similar (i.e. Hot Club de France) to Classics above, except add Jean-Louis Jeanson (*tb, vn*); André Lluis (*as, cl*); John Arslanian (*cl, bcl, ts, bs*); Adrien Mareze, Noel Chiboust (*ts*); Larry Adler (*hca*); Roger Pirenet, Roger Du Hautbourg (*vn*); Bob Vaz (*p*); André Taylor (*d*); Gregoire Coco Aslan (*perc*); André Dassary (*v*). 12/37–6/38.

***(*) Jazz Masters 38: Django Reinhardt** Verve 516393
Similar to above. 38–53.

**** Bruxelles / Paris** Musidisc 403222
As above, except add Raymond Fol (*p*).

*** Django Reinhardt, 1938–1939** Classics 793
Similar to above, except add Bob Stewart (*c*); Barney Bigard (*cl, d*); Billy Taylor (*b*). 6/38–4/39.

***(*) Django Reinhardt, 1939–1940** Classics 813
Similar to above, except add Frank Big Boy Goudie (*t*); André Ekyan (*as*); Charles Lewis, Joe Turner (*p*); Marceau Sarbib, Lucien Simoens (*b*); Tommy Benford, Charles Delaunay (*d*). 5/39–8/40.

*** Django Reinhardt, 1940 Classics 831

> Reinhardt; Philippe Brun, Pierre Allier, Aimé Barelli, Christian Bellest, Alex Renard, Al Piguillem (*t*); Guy Paquinet, Gaston Moat, Pierre Deck (*tb*); Hubert Rostaing (*cl, ts*); Alix Combelle (*bs*); André Ekyan (*as*); Charles Lewis, Raymond Wraskoff (*p*); Pierre Ferret, Joseph Reinhardt (*g*); Emmanuel Soudieux, Francis Luca (*b*); Pierre Fouad (*d*). 2–10/40.

***(*) Swing De Paris Arco 3 ARC 110

> Reinhardt; Gerard Leveque, Maurice Meunier, Hubert Rostaing (*cl*); Joseph Reinhardt, Eugène Vées (*g*); Eddie Bernard (*p*); Ladislas Czabancyk, Emmanuel Soudieux (*b*); André Jourdan, Jacques Martinon (*d*). 7–11/47.

One of the Christian-name-only mythical figures of jazz, Django embodies much of the nonsense that surrounds the physically and emotionally damaged who nevertheless manage to parlay their disabilities and irresponsibilities into great music. Django's technical compass, apparently unhampered by loss of movement in two fingers of his left hand (result of a burn which had ended his apprenticeship as a violinist), was colossal, ranging from dazzling high-speed runs to ballad-playing of aching intensity.

There are a number of good-value CDs available. Classics have done their usual thorough job on the early material, and there can be no artist more fully documented by the French label. The coverage for 1937 alone is staggering, with virtually a whole CD devoted to one month. Unusually for this label, there is quite a bit of material which strictly belongs to other artists, prominently trumpeter Brun, but which features significant amounts of Django and so is included. The series begins with Django's first recordings with the Michel Warlop orchestra in 1934, reaching on into the classic Hot Club sessions over the next couple of years. In bulk, though, the music begins to sound slightly tired and dated, and Django's astonishing technique almost *too* perfect.

The later Classics are no less exhaustive, and the 1938/39 volume, with its roster of guests, is a most valuable indicator of his standing *vis-à-vis* the original begetters of a music he had graced for several years not fully appreciated outside Europe. Other curiosities in the run include four tracks with harmonica genius, Larry Adler (who's still around to tell the stories of that day in May 1938). The war years obviously brought a certain non-musical poignancy to the story, but the coldest and most detached audition still reveals a shift in Django's playing towards something altogether more inward, secretive, less joyous, and, even when there are no obvious shadows gathering, there is a hint of darkness and doubt. Again there is a good deal of non-Django (or non-lead) material included, largely stuff by Ekyan and Brun; and the latter's session from February 1940, recorded in Paris, has the fascinating discographical footnote of a playing role for Charles Delaunay, who was operating under the aka of H. P. Chadel.

With the war in progress, Django was cut off from many of his greatest sources of inspiration, Grappelli only most obviously. The last volume (to date) finds him artificially self-reliant. Lacking the usual feed of ideas, he is thrown back on his own resources, that inwardness again, and some of it makes for melancholy listening. The Classics project will obviously continue and doubtless with the same attention to detail. For collectors, it is an appetizing prospect. For the less committed, it may be preferable to look elsewhere and for a slightly more cursory approach.

The Verve is valuable for the breadth of its coverage. Some will quibble at the lack of earlier material, but the fact that it carries the story right up to the year of Django's death gives the picture a certain valuable symmetry, and the music is, of course, quite wonderful. The Hot Club reunion of 1946 in London is well represented, and some care has been taken to give a reasonable balance of material over the final years, including the poignant 'Night And Day' of March 1953, when the shadows were beginning to draw in.

The ASV is beautifully remastered by Colin Brown, an example of how historical recordings can be restored without intrusive sweetening or inauthentic balances. At 66 minutes, it's also excellent value. It's good to be reminded how extraordinarily forceful the drummer-less Hot Club could sound. Even with the chugging background, 'Appel Direct' is remarkably modern, and it's easy to see why Django continues to exert such an influence on guitarists of later, technically more sophisticated generations. The titles are confusingly similar, but this is the best single-volume option.

The Musidisc offers a more extensive sample of the important sessions of 21 May 1947 (with Hubert Rostaing and the reconstituted Hot Club; the albums share 'Just One Of Those Things') and of 8 April 1953, the month before his death (with Martial Solal; they share a marvellous 'I Cover The Waterfront'), as well as good-quality material from 1951: 'Nuits De St Germain-Des-Prés', 'Crazy Rhythm', 'Fine And Dandy'.

Bruxelles/Paris has a marginally tougher version of 'Nuages'. In 1947, Django was battling with amplification (not always successfully), coping with the repercussions of a not entirely ecstatic reception with Ellington in the USA (ditto), and slipping backwards into the moral vagrancy that undoubtedly shortened his life. On the better tracks, on 'Blues For Barclay', 'Manoir De Mes Rêves', 'Mélodie Du Crépuscule', and 'Nuages', his instincts seem to be intact. He picks off clusters of notes with tremendous compression, holds and bends top notes like a singer and keeps a deep, insistent throb on the bottom string that, when it makes it up through the lo-fi hiss and drop-out, is hugely effective.

*** **Swing Guitar** Jass J CD 628

> Reinhardt; Herb Bass, Robin Gould, Jerry Stephan, Lonnie Wilfong (*t*); Bill Decker, Don Gardner, Shelton Heath, John Kirkpatrick (*tb*); Jim Hayes (*cl, as*); Joe Moser (*as*); Bernie Calaliere, Bill Zickenfoose (*ts*); Ken Lowther (*bs*); Larry Mann (*p*); Bob Decker (*b*); Red Lacky (*d*). 10/45–3/46.

Django and the European Division Band of the Air Transport Command recorded from the American Forces Network *Bandstand* and *Beaucoup De Music* (*sic.*) broadcasts, in rehearsal and live at the Salle Pleyel in the months immediately following the end of the war in Europe. Eric Bogart likens the ATC band to one of the 'scrapping, blues-heavy' territory bands of the interwar years, of which only Basie's made it to the big time. They certainly have a tougher feel than one normally associates with such outfits, and the opening 'Djangology' gets more than a run for its money, with an altered bridge by arranger Lonnie Wilfong. There is a fine interpretation of 'Belleville', with the first really classy guitar solo. Django excels himself on the unaccompanied 'Improvisation No. 6', taken from a slightly later small-group session, after which the group returns for rather more routine runs through 'Honeysuckle Rose' and 'Sweet Sue', the latter featuring a surprisingly effective penny-whistle solo by Lieber. There's a second 'Djangology' and, rounding out the session, six cuts without the guitarist but including spirited readings of 'Swing Guitars' and 'Manoir De Mes Rêves' and other tunes not immediately associated with Django, of which 'Perdido' and Strayhorn's 'Midriff' are the most impressive. As Django sessions go, this is about beta-plus, but the ATC outfit are consistently impressive and are well worth checking out. Jack Towers's 'audio restoration' has been done with common sense and good taste.

***(*) **Pêche A La Mouche** Verve 835 419

> Reinhardt; Vincent Casino, Jo Boyer, Louis Menardi, Rex Stewart (*t*); André Lafosse, Guy Paquinet (*tb*); Michel De Villers (*as, cl*); Hubert Rostaing (*cl*); Jean-Claude Forenbach (*ts*); Eddie Bernard, Maurice Vander (*p*); Joseph Reinhardt, Eugène Vées (*g*); Will Lockwood, Ladislas Czabanyck, Pierre Michelot, Emmanuel Soudieux (*b*); Al Craig, Ted Curry, André Jourdan, Jean-Louis Viale (*d*). 4, 7, 10 & 12/47, 3/53.

Django's visit to the United States made a big impact on him, both positive and negative. It certainly reinforced the feeling of isolation and aggressive independence that increasingly became part of his character. It may also have reminded him that jazz was, after all, an American music. However, it did expose him to a whole raft of new influences – not least bebop – which henceforward were to play a part in his music.

Prefaced by a track each – 'Pêche A La Mouche' and 'Minor Blues' – from Django's quintet and orchestra, the 1947 sessions for Blue Star with the re-formed Hot Club are not classics like the great sides of the previous decade, but they have a spontaneity and ease that are both attractive and aesthetically satisfying. Producer Eddie Barclay gave Django a free hand to play what he wanted, and the music that emerged was bright, flowing and often thoughtful, with a rough edge that is only partially explained by the technical limitations of the recording.

There is one further session from 1947, under the leadership of Rex Stewart, which again might have served to remind Django of the huge cultural distance between him and the Americans. He plays with immense elegance on 'Night And Day' but never sounds as though he's on top of what Stewart is doing harmonically.

The later recording, which was issued as a 10-inch LP, not as 78s, saw the shadows move a little closer round the guitarist, but Django's solo on 'Brazil' is, as noted by Pierre Michelot, quite astonishing in its fiery grace, and he seems to have overcome some of the amplification problems he had been having since the war. He tackles 'Night And Day' again, on his own terms this time, and there are beautiful versions of 'Nuages' and 'Manoir De Mes Rêves'. He isn't a musician whose work divides easily into 'early' and 'late', but it's clear that the period between these two recordings was one of personal and artistic change and, in some respects, retrenchment. Django had made a great many miscalculations and had to spend too much time compensating for them.

***(*) **Djangology 1949** Bluebird/BMG ND90448

> Reinhardt; Stéphane Grappelli (*vn*); Gianni Safred (*p*); Carlo Recori (*b*); Aurelio De Carolis (*d*). 1 & 2/49.

A final opportunity to hear Reinhardt and Grappelli playing together, albeit with a dud rhythm section. In an intelligent sleeve-note (which includes useful track-by-track comments on all 20 CD items), guitarist Frank Vignola warns against making comparisons between these rather edgy and competitive sessions and the great days of the pre-war Quintette du Hot Club. The most evident token of changing musical times, and a legacy of Django's relatively unsuccessful American trip, is a boppish cast to several of the tracks, most significantly the Ur-text of bebop, 'I Got Rhythm'.

Fortunately for the session, both Django and Grappelli got rhythm to spare, for the local musicians are a positive hindrance. On 'All The Things You Are' Safred chords morosely in the background while Recori and de Carolis go off for a *grappa*. Django's frustration comes through in places, but it's clear that at least some of the aggression is directed at his one-time junior partner who now claims his full share of the foreground. For all its shortcomings, this is a worthwhile addition to the discography.

***(*) **The Indispensable Django Reinhardt (1949–1950)** RCA ND 70929 2CD
    Reinhardt; Stéphane Grappelli (*vn*); André Ekyan (*as, cl*); Gianni Safred, Ralph Schecroun (*p*); Alf Messelier, Carlo Pecori (*b*); Aurelio De Carolis, Roger Paraboschi (*d*). 1 & 2/49, 4 & 5/50.

Djangologists might quibble that this period is 'indispensable' relative to some of the earlier material, but it is doubtlessly of very high quality and it sees Django back with some – or at least two – of his most creative partners, Grappelli and Ekyan. The 1949 sessions were an attempt to reconstitute the Hot Club. Like the later grouping, they were recorded in Rome, which couldn't have helped when recruiting players. It isn't clear why RCA, with two CDs to play with, should have chosen to mix the sessions so pointlessly, unless the thought that having 'Manoir De Mes Rêves' and 'Nuages' on the first disc might make a faintly humdrum and second-order programme more palatable. It doesn't really work. Both are excellent performances, with Ekyan playing well, but it sits oddly with the Grappelli stuff, which is rather better recorded.

Emily Remler (1957–91) GUITAR

*** **Firefly** Concord CCD 4162
    Remler; Hank Jones (*p*); Bob Maize (*b*); Jake Hanna (*d*). 4/81.
*** **Take Two** Concord CCD 4195
    Remler; James Williams (*p*); Don Thompson (*b*); Terry Clarke (*d*). 6/82.
*** **Transitions** Concord CCD 4236
    Remler; John D'Earth (*t*); Eddie Gomez (*b*); Bob Moses (*d*). 10/83.
*** **Catwalk** Concord CCD 4265
    Remler; John D'Earth (*t*); Eddie Gomez (*b*); Bob Moses (*d*). 8/84.
**** **East To Wes** Concord CCD 4356
    Remler; Hank Jones (*p*); Buster Williams (*b*); Marvin 'Smitty' Smith (*d*). 5/88.

Remler's senseless early death (from heart failure while on tour in Australia) deprived us of a talent that seemed on the point of breakthrough. While her early role-models were conservative ones in terms of her instrument – Christian and Montgomery, specifically – her tough-minded improvising and affinity with hard-hitting rhythm sections let her push a mainstream style to its logical limits. *Firefly* was her debut for the label and is fluent if a little anonymous, although she handles the diversity of 'Strollin'' and 'In A Sentimental Mood' without any hesitation. *Take Two* puts on an extra layer of assurance: Williams is a sympathetic pianist, and the improvising on 'In Your Own Sweet Way' and 'For Regulars Only' shows new resource. *Transitions* and *Catwalk* were made in a somewhat unusual partnership with D'Earth, whose crisp, pinchy solos make an interesting foil to the leader's more expansive lines. The best single disc, though, is the impeccable Montgomery tribute, *East To Wes*. Smith proves to be an ideal drummer for the guitarist, his busy cymbals and polyrhythmic variations on the bebop pulse perfectly cast to push Remler into her best form: 'Daahoud' and 'Hot House' are unbeatable updates of each tune. Jones, imperturbable as ever, takes a cool middle course. While conceived as a Montgomery homage, Remler's playing actually shows how unlike Wes she really was: harder of tone, her solos more fragmented yet equally lucid.

**** **Retrospective, Vol. One: Standards** Concord CCD 4453
*** **Retrospective, Vol. Two: Compositions** Concord CCD 4463
    As above records, except add Larry Coryell (*g*), James Williams (*p*), Don Thompson (*b*), Terry Clarke (*d*). 81–88.

Two excellent compilations of Remler's Concord years. The first volume is superior, with an intelligent choice of standards, two beautiful duets with Larry Coryell and an unaccompanied solo on 'Afro Blue'. Her original themes are rather less memorable, but the playing on the second volume remains enticing throughout.

Don Rendell (born 1926) SOPRANO AND TENOR SAXOPHONES, CLARINET AND FLUTE

** **If I Should Lose You** Spotlite SPJ-146
    Rendell; Martin Shaw (*t, flhn*); Richard Edwards (*tb*); John Burch, Brian Dee (*p*); Peter Morgan, Mario Castronari (*b*); Robin Jones, Bobby Worth (*d*). 6/90–5/91.

None of Don Rendell's records from the 1950s and '60s have yet been reissued, which has conspired against this excellent saxophonist acquiring a wider following among younger listeners – unlike, say, the much-talked-of Tubby Hayes and Joe Harriott. Rendell broadened a swing-to-bop vocabulary with what he learnt from Coltrane and Rollins, and by the 1970s he was a masterful all-round stylist. This recent record is, alas, rather sorry stuff. Rendell's improvisations still show much imagination, but there are serious intonation problems on both clarinet and saxes which make for less than happy listening.

Arthur Rhames (1957–89) TENOR SAXOPHONE

*** **Live From Soundscape** DIW 401
     Rhames; Jeff Esposito (*p*); Jeff Siegel (*d*). 10/81.
The facts first, then the legend. Arthur Rhames grew up in Brooklyn, came out as a gay man around the time he was coming out as one of the most talked-about multi-instrumentalists of his generation, and then died of an AIDS-related illness just after Christmas 1989. Despite never having been signed by any record company, Rhames had an almost mythical reputation on the New York music scene. In addition to saxophone playing that seemed to take Coltrane-derived harmonics way past the far-out busking of Charles Gayle, he was a brilliant pianist in a version of McCoy Tyner's idiom, and he played scorching electric guitar.

How great was he? How much was promise? How much was delivered? Many musicians claim him as an important influence, young as he was, and there is much eloquent testimony (ironic in the circumstances) regarding Rhames's disciplined business sense (so why no deal?) and obsession with health and fitness – the other question asks itself. In the absence of studio records, this is all we have to go on for the moment, and it cannot be considered properly representative of what Rhames was about, except in its unabashed fixation on the Coltrane legacy.

A club session, recorded on a reel-to-reel machine with just two mikes, *Live From Soundscape* is a pretty raw document of a raw blowing gig. Sticking to tenor (an insert picture shows him playing soprano on the subway), Rhames provides exhaustive readings of both 'Giant Steps' and 'Moment's Notice', as well as a slightly terser rendition of 'Bessie's Blues'. That he had mastered Coltrane's language there can be no doubt; that he managed to take it even a modest step onward is more questionable. 'I Got Rhythm' underlines the surefootedness of his vertical improvisation, but there is nothing here that would cause a second-generation bebopper to blush. 'I Want Jesus To Walk With Me' suggests an additional kinship to Ayler. The remaining track, '42nd Street', is essentially a feature for Esposito, who acquits himself very well when fully audible over a drummer who is clearly trying to out-do his ancestors Elvin and Rashied.

Any ultimate judgement, of course, has to be suspended. It is important to recognize not just the technical limitations of this disc but also the fact that it consists of performances made when Rhames was only 24, with almost another decade of his short life to go. Where had he gone by the summer of 1989, when his health failed irrevocably? Without a sense of that, he may have to rest with those, like Buddy Bolden, whose legends are larger than the surviving record.

Melvin Rhyne (born 1936) ORGAN

*** **The Legend** Criss Cross Criss 1059
     Rhyne; Brian Lynch (*t*); Don Braden (*ts*); Peter Bernstein (*g*); Kenny Washington (*d*). 12/91.
*** **Boss Organ** Criss Cross Criss 1080
     Rhyne; Joshua Redman (*ts*); Peter Bernstein (*g*); Kenny Washington (*d*). 1/93.
Best known for his part in the Wes Montgomery trios on Riverside, this is Rhyne's first recording as a leader, done impromptu after the organist had finished a Criss Cross session for trumpeter Brian Lynch.

Rhyne immediately sounds different from the prevailing Jimmy Smith school of organ players. Instead of swirling, bluesy chords, he favours sharp, almost staccato figures and lyrical single-note runs that often don't go quite where expected. The format for the session is the same as that for the classic Montgomery recordings, and Kenny Washington makes a particularly strong impact.

The set opens with Eddie 'Lockjaw' Davis's 'Licks A-Plenty', kicks along with 'Stompin' At The Savoy', Wes Montgomery's 'The Trick Bag' and Dizzy Gillespie's 'Groovin' High'; there are two evocative ballads, 'Serenata' and 'Old Folks', and the session closes with a long 'Blues For Wes', with Lynch and saxophonist Braden sitting in.

Another young horn player makes a vital contribution to the later *Boss Organ*. Few saxophonists have been more comprehensively hyped than Joshua Redman. He lives pretty much up to billing on this set, swanking through tunes by Stevie Wonder and Wes Montgomery as if he grew up playing them. Rhyne sounds relaxed and laid back – almost too unhurried since, as the set advances, it begins to drag ever so slightly. Enjoyable, though, and a convincing consolidation of the fine form of *The Legend*.

Buddy Rich (1917–87) DRUMS, VOCAL

*** His Legendary 1947–48 Orchestra Hep CD 12
Rich; Tommy Allison, Stan Fischelson, Phil Gilbert, Charlie Shavers, Charlie Walp, Dale Pearce, Frank Le Pinto, Doug Mettome (*t*); Mario Daone, Bob Ascher, Chunky Koenigsberger, Rob Swope, Jack Carmen, Lou McGarity (*tb*); Peanuts Hucko (*cl*); Hal McKusick, Eddie Caine, Jerry Therkeld (*as*); Allen Eager, Mickey Rich, Ben Larry, Warne Marsh, Al Sears, Jimmy Giuffre (*ts*); Harvey Levine (*bs*); Harvey Leonard, Jerry Schwarz, Buddy Weed (*p*); Joe Mooney (*acc*); Terry Gibbs (*vib*); Gene Dell, Remo Palmieri (*g*); Trigger Alpert, Tubby Phillips, Charlie Leeds, Nick Stagg (*b*); Stan Kay, Big Sid Catlett (*d*); Ella Fitzgerald (*v*). 10/45–10/48.

Rich, probably the most renowned big-band drummer of all time, had a rough time as a bandleader in the late 1940s, but somehow he held on until 1949. This set of airshots, V-Discs and the like finds various editions of the group in vigorous form. Some of the charts are routine, but others make the most of the impressive sections, and there are some fine soloists, particularly Allen Eager on 'Daily Double' and 'Nellie's Nightmare'. There is one small-group track with Charlie Shavers on trumpet and a fairly hilarious 'Blue Skies' where Rich scats along with Ella Fitzgerald. The sound is seldom better than fair, but the clout of the orchestra still comes through.

*** Swingin' New Big Band / Keep The Customer Satisfied BGO BGOCD169
Rich; Bobby Shew, John Sottile, Yoshito Murakami, Walter Battagello, John Giorgani, John Madrid, Mike Price, George Zonce (*t*); Jim Trimble, John Boice, Rick Stepton, Tony Lada (*tb*); Larry Fisher, Mike Waverley (*btb*); Gene Quill (*cl, as*); Richie Cole, Jimmy Mosher, Pete Yellin (*as, f*); Jay Corre, Marty Flax (*cl, ts, f*); Pat LaBarbera (*ss, ts, f*); Don Englert (*ts, f*); Steve Perlow (*bs, bcl*); Bob Suchoski (*bs*); John Bunch, Meredith McClain (*p*); Barry Zweig (*g*); Rick Laird, Carson Smith (*b*). 9/66–2/70.

*** Swingin' New Big Band Pacific Jazz 835232-2
Similar to above. 9/66.

Two solid rather than great Rich albums, remastered for a single CD. For all his belief in the virtue of a driving big band, Rich probably had a sneaking liking for the kind of kitsch he'd dealt with in the big-band era. The medleys from *West Side Story* and *Midnight Cowboy* are prime examples of his penchant for the epic touch. While he might have disdained rock simplicity, that didn't stop him having Stevie Wonder's 'Uptight' in the 1966 band book or Paul Simon's 'Keep The Customer Satisfied' in the 1970 set. Both editions of the orchestra play with characteristic tightness, and the scores – Bill Holman's 1970 charts are the best of them – are swept clean by the section-work. The Pacific Jazz reissue of *Swingin' New Big Band* alone includes nine extra, previously unissued tracks from those sessions, which creates something of a problem choice for Rich collectors.

*** Buddy And Soul BGO BGOCD 23
Rich; Sal Marquez, Nat Pavone, Dave Culp, Bob Yance, Mike Price, Darryl Eaton, Ken Faulks, Oliver Mitchell (*t*); Rick Stepton, Vince Diaz, Don Switzer (*tb*); Ernie Watts, Joe Romano, Richie Cole, Don Menza, Pat LaBarbera, Joe Calo, Don Englert (*reeds*); Dave Lahm (*ky*); Herb Ellis, Dave Dana, Freddie Robinson (*g*); Bob Magnusson (*b*); Victor Feldman (*perc*). 1–6/69.

Live or in the studio, Rich's band hit very hard. Anachronistic in the age of Hendrix and Jefferson Airplane (Rich's choice of a tune called 'Love And Peace' probably didn't express what he thought about rock's ascendance), they made up in personal firepower what they lacked in stage amplification. There's some dreadful, modish material and some things which Rich made into valid vehicles through sheer force of will. Big-band jazz out of its time, and presumably for ever.

** Ease On Down The Road LRC CDC 8511
Rich; Greg Hopkins, Charlie Davis, John Hoffman, Larry Hall, Lloyd Michaels, Richard Hurwitz, Ross Konikoff, Danny Hayes, Charles Camilleri (*t*); Alan Kaplan, Keith O'Quinn, Barry Maur, Gerald Chamberlain (*tb*); Anthony Salvatori, John Leys (*btb*); Joe Romano, Bob Martin, Pat LaBarbera, Pete Yellin, Bill Blaut, Steve Marcus, Bob Mintzer, Bob Crea, Roger Rosenberg, John Laws (*reeds*); Buddy Budson, Greg Kogan (*p*); Joe Beck, Wayne Wright, Cornell Dupree, Cliff Morris (*g*); Tony Levin, Ben Brown (*b*); Sam Woodyard, Ray Armando (*perc*). 10/73–6/74.

Although the two main sessions on *Ease On Down The Road* were recorded less than a year apart, they feature two big bands with entirely different personnel from each other, aside from Rich – and he manages to make them sound virtually identical. Not bad, but only dedicated Rich admirers will warm to the session as a whole.

**(*) Lionel Hampton Presents Buddy Rich Kingdom GATE 7011
Rich; Steve Marcus (*ss, ts*); Gary Pribek, Paul Moen (*ts*); Barry Kiener (*p*); Lionel Hampton (*vib*); Tom Warrington (*b*); Candido Camero (*perc*). 77.

An engaging reunion for Hampton and Rich, with Marcus and Pribek coming from Rich's big band and Moen arriving from Hamp's. Two Coltrane themes give the tenors a chance to smoke, and the vibes and rhythm section trade plenty of fours. Nothing surprising happens, but all concerned seemed to enjoy the date.

Jerome Richardson (born 1920) SAXOPHONES, WOODWINDS, FLUTES

***(*) **Roamin' With Richardson** Original Jazz Classics OJC 1849
    Richardson; Richard Wyands (*p*); George Tucker (*b*); Charli Persip (*d*). 11/59.
*** **Midnight Oil** Original Jazz Classics OJC 1815
    Richardson; Jimmy Cleveland (*tb*); Hank Jones (*p*); Kenny Burrell (*g*); Joe Benjamin (*b*); Charli Persip (*d*). 63.

The quiet Texan was always more than a journeyman multi-instrumentalist. It took him some time to assert himself in his own voice. He only became a leader on moving to New York City in 1953, having served an apprenticeship with Jimmy Lunceford, Lionel Hampton and Earl Hines. There was an earlier session on New Jazz, predating *Roamin'* by a few months, but it is as rare as hen's teeth and so far hasn't been reissued. The interesting thing about the 1959 band is that all four are individualists, and each is encouraged to bring something to the session. Wyands in particular asserts himself on tracks like 'Warm Valley' and 'Poinciana', the latter a solitary outing on flute, the former with his very distinctive, Mulligan-influenced baritone. His only other horn this time out is tenor saxophone ('Friar Tuck' and 'Candied Sweets').

In the last edition, we argued Richardson's one great stock-in-trade has been the simple variety of his resources. Certainly on both records he can rely on an absolutely solid band and indulge a little decorative work here and there. Further acquaintance, though, confirms that he is an able, often thoughtful soloist, and his traded lines with Cleveland and the more boppish Burrell will be a revelation to those who have heard him only as a utility band player.

Dannie Richmond (1935–88) DRUMS

*** **Plays Charles Mingus** Timeless SJP 148
    Richmond; Jack Walrath (*t*); Ricky Ford (*ts*); Bob Neloms (*p*); Cameron Brown (*b*). 8/80.
*** **The Last Mingus Band A.D.** Landmark LCD 1537
    As above. 9/80.
*** **Three Or Four Shades Of Dannie Richmond** Tutu 888120
    As above, except replace Ford with Kenny Garrett (*as*). 7/81.

There probably wasn't a closer relationship in jazz than that between Charles Mingus and Dannie Richmond. Richmond's ability to anticipate Mingus's sudden shifts of tempo made them seem like two aspects of a single turbulent personality and, when Mingus died in 1979, it looked very much as though Richmond's legacy was merely to answer questions from journalists and to trim the flame.

Unfortunately, the surviving Richmond albums tend to reinforce that view. It's usually forgotten that the drummer had a lively and productive career as an independent leader and co-leader. The fine 1980 *Dannie Richmond Quintet* on Gatemouth is no longer available, and *Dionysius* on Red has also disappeared. Collectors of vinyl would do well to look out for these.

The current issues are well worth having, but only genuine fanatics will find room for all three. *Plays* is by no means a straightforward 'Greatest Hits', but Mingus's ghost hangs heavily over it. 'Goodbye, Pork Pie Hat' was perhaps inevitable, but 'Wee' (which you can *almost* hear Mingus playing on recordings of the infamous Massey Hall concert) was an inspired choice, opening up the band for some genuinely inventive improvisation. The spirited Walrath doesn't combine particularly well with Ford's rather callow sound, but, much as Mingus might, Richmond makes a virtue of any shortcomings.

There are two interesting versions of that late masterpiece, 'Cumbia And Jazz Fusion', on the Landmark. Walrath is the key player on this session, and his flugelhorn solos are especially good, with a richness and range of colour that mitigate the antagonistic edge of his trumpet playing. Neloms has always seemed content to do his job competently rather than express himself with any great force. For whatever reason, there are moments on this record where he does shine and, in the process, he highlights the contours of Mingus's music.

The sound still isn't that hot, but the live session on *Three Or Four Shades* is actually quite respectably balanced and offers a pretty accurate representation of the Richmond group on the road. Like all drummers, he had to contend with mikes that made him sound as though he was lagged in asbestos. A pity. Richmond is one of the great modern drummers and, though his work with Mingus is deathless, there ought to be more to say on his own account.

Kim Richmond ALTO SAX

*** **Looking In Looking Out** USA 630
>   Richmond; Mike Fahn (*vtb*); John Gross (*ts, f*); Tad Weed, Wayne Peet (*p*); Ken Filiano (*b*);
>   Billy Mintz (*d*). 6–11/88.

**** **Passages** Sea Breeze CDSB-2043
>   Richmond; Wayne Bergeron, Ron King, Clay Jenkins, Dave Scott (*t*); Rick Culver, George
>   McMullen, Charlie Morillas, Morris Repass (*tb*); Suzette Moriority, John Dickson (*frhn*); Sal
>   Lonzano, Phil Feather, Glen Berger, John Yoakum, John Mitchell, Bob Carr, John Gross
>   (*reeds*); Bill Cunliffe (*p*); Tom Hynes (*g*); Bill Roper (*tba*); Trey Henry (*b*); Ralph Razze (*d*);
>   Mike Turner, Dave Johnson (*perc*). 5/92.

***(*) **Range** Nine Winds NWCD 0172
>   Richmond; Clay Jenkins (*t*); Joey Sellars (*tb*); Dave Scott (*p*); Trey Henry (*b*); Joe LaBarbera
>   (*d*). 9/94.

Richmond has performed in many jazz and rock settings, and his debut as a leader reflects catholic and
well-informed preferences. There are six good originals on *The Best*, with flavoursome tone-colours and
a harried rhythmic undertow that won't let the music settle into mere mainstream blowing. Try the
clever use of valve-trombone against flute in 'Specifico Americano' or the straggling, vaguely inebriated
treatment of 'Nardis'. Richmond takes some acerbic solos but is smart enough to give Fahn, Gross and
Weed – all interesting soloists – the same measure of space. The leader's sleeve-note speaks of 'simultaneous improvisation' and, while this is of a comparatively ordered nature, it brings off a fine record.
Moving up to the scale of a big band seems to have held no terrors for him: *Passages* is a gutsy, songful
record that makes the most of the sleek power of an orchestra without turning to mere glibness. There
are excellent soloists – Gross, Cunliffe, McMullen and the leader's own alto – but what matters is the
sonority of the orchestra as a unit. Richmond makes 'My Funny Valentine' lush and uplifting instead of
wounded and sad (and still introduces an unexpected dissonance at the climax), writes a vast fantasy out
of 'Street Of Dreams' and pours an awful lot into the two minutes or so of 'Image And Likeness'. Sea
Breeze have made a speciality of recording this kind of album, and the studio sound is superb.

   Range continues an impressive sequence. Back in a small-group format, Richmond co-leads this
ensemble with Jenkins, and the music is an inquiring update on various West Coast traditions. The
music's essential reserve – as freely as the musicians play, underlying harmonic/rhythmic principles
remain firm – serves to underline the virtues of each man's improvisational thinking and, with the
excellent Sellars contributing just as much as the other two horns, the eight themes unfold with a sort of
compelling inevitability.

Mike Richmond (born 1948) BASS

*** **On The Edge** Steeplechase SCCD 31237
>   Richmond; Larry Schneider (*ss, ts, f*); Adam Nussbaum (*d*). 88.

***(*) **Dance For Andy** Steeplechase SCCD 31267
>   Richmond; Larry Schneider (*ss, ts*); Jim McNeely (*p*); Keith Copeland (*d*). 89.

The title-track which opens *On The Edge* is a superb trio improvisation that has Schneider and
Richmond almost locking horns before Nussbaum's resolving solo. The rest of the record doesn't quite
match up, but the leader – whose wide experience with leaders such as DeJohnette, Getz and Silver has
granted him a steadfast mainstream-modern reputation – pilots the trio with great enthusiasm. *Dance
For Andy* is one of those rare CDs which sustain interest through a 70-minute-plus duration.
Richmond's four originals are nothing special – aside, perhaps, from the witty, sanctified licks of
'Gospel' – but there is a serene trio reading of 'I Remember Clifford', a fast and swinging 'You And The
Night And The Music' and a reading of Jim Pepper's 'Witchi-Tai-To' which manages to supplant Jan
Garbarek's glorious version in the memory. Schneider deploys his Brecker influence to gripping effect
on both records.

*** **Blue In Green** Steeplechase SCCD 31296
>   Richmond; Larry Schneider (*ts*); Richie Beirach (*p*); Jeff Williams (*d*). 8/91.

A bit disappointing, perhaps, after the last two. Schneider sounds a little more diffident this time and,
though Beirach compensates by being more driving than he sometimes is, there's comparatively little of
the freewheeling energy that made 'On The Edge' exciting. It's still a solid and enjoyable traversal of
some good jazz and show tunes by four expert players.

Larry Ridley (born 1937) DOUBLE BASS

*** Sum Of The Parts Strata East 660.51.013
> Ridley; Sonny Fortune (*as*); Onaje Allan Gumbs (*p, ky*); Cornell Dupree (*g*); Grady Tate (*d*); Erroll Bennett (*perc*). 75.

***(*) Live At Rutgers University Strata East 660.51.020
> Ridley; Virgil Jones (*t*); Larry McClellan (*tb*); Doug Miller (*ts*); Ed Stoute (*p*); Charli Persip (*d*); Jann Parker (*v*). 4/89.

A highly experienced bassist, originally inspired by Ray Brown, Ridley has worked with a huge variety of players and styles, spending three years with Thelonious Monk and even stepping into Charlie Haden's shoes in the Ornette/Cherry quartet. His own work as leader is largely unknown, but the Jazz Legacy Ensemble has been a regular outlet for his snappingly forceful approach, both as player and leader.

Though acoustically it's a more appealing proposition than the later Strata East, *Sum Of The Parts* is very much a record of its time, fuzzy with keyboards and electric guitar, and hooked into an unrelieved, whacking beat. The later Rutgers session finds him on home territory (Ridley is head of the jazz programme there) and, though the band is slightly anonymous, its claim on that legacy is very assured. Perhaps the best thing is a Monk composition, 'Ugly Beauty', played at an unfamiliar pace. Persip is a key element in the overall sound and makes the whole session swing furiously.

Yannick Rieu TENOR SAXOPHONE

*** In The Myth Amplitude JACD-4011
> Rieu; Paul Bley (*p*); Normand Guilbeault (*b*); Michel Ratte (*d*). 90.

***(*) Sweet Geom Victo CD030
> Rieu; Frederik Alarie (*b*); Paul Leger (*d*). 5/94.

The Canadian tenorman makes a powerful if enigmatic mark on these two discs. The first is basically a trio date – Bley sits in on three brief improvisations – which is centred by the leader's stoic phrasing and hard, almost stony sound. Even when Guilbeault (superb) and Ratte stoke up the heat, Rieu seems unmoved by his surroundings: he's as likely to play slowly and solidly as he is to get worked up. The thunderous tenor-drums duet, 'Fusion', is all the more remarkable in that, even when Ratte is coming on like the son of Elvin Jones, Rieu refuses to sound like Coltrane. But this indifference to models also has its drawbacks: the session seems formless at times.

The festival set captured on the Victo CD is at least a notch ahead. The sheer audacity of doing a full-scale treatment of Rollins's 'Freedom Suite' is mitigated by the thoughtful, unflashy interpretation. Rieu *does* sound more like Rollins here and throughout, but his own themes – the title-piece, itself a three-part suite, spreads across a 25-minute span – have a shape which was missing on the earlier record. Good though the other players were, this trio is a more integrated unit too, and Rieu's generous allowance of space to the others pays off in a music that works its tension-and-release with real intelligence and the proper intensity. A fine document and one that demands that Rieu return to the studios.

Knut Riisnaes (born 1945) TENOR AND SOPRANO SAX

***(*) Confessin' The Blues Gemini GMCD 63
> Riisnaes; Red Holloway (*as, ts*); Kjell Ohman (*p, org*); Terje Venaas (*b*); Egil Johansen (*d*). 8/89.

*** The Gemini Twins Gemini GMCD 75
> As above. 1/92.

*** Knut Riisnaes / Jon Christensen Odin 4040
> Riisnaes; John Scofield (*g*); Palle Danielsson (*b*); Jon Christensen (*d*). 10/91–5/92.

Gifted with a huskily rich and weighty tone, Riisnaes is an Oslo-born jazzman who, like so many musicians from northern Europe, deserves a far wider reputation than he has (his brother, Odd, is also a fine tenorman). His celebrated *Flukt* LP won a Norwegian Grammy award but it's currently out of print. *Confessin' The Blues* is a fine place to start, though. The session was organized to document Red Holloway's visit to the Oslo Jazz Festival in 1989, and the sympathetic interplay among all five men belies the hasty circumstances of the occasion. While there are some straightforward blowing tracks, such as an ebullient 'Billie's Bounce', the highlight is probably the almost indecently languorous stroll through 'All Blues' at the beginning, which is paced out by both tenormen to sumptuous effect. If Holloway is the more perkily bluesy of the two saxophonists, Riisnaes emerges at least his equal, taking a solo 'My Romance' which methodically opens out the melody to superb effect. The rhythm section, with Ohman playing mostly organ, is absolutely on top of things, and the digital sound is excellent. They have a return match on *The Gemini Twins*, which is a mild disappointment since nothing hits the peaks of the previous record. Riisnaes's solo ballad treatment of 'Tribute To Melvin' and the ultra-slow 'Yesterdays' still make the record substantial.

The quartet with Scofield, Danielsson and Christensen puts Riisnaes into a more contemporary context and, while Scofield's status as a top hired gun means that his sound has become a commonplace in this setting, Riisnaes and Christensen carry on a serious dialogue of their own. No standards, but ten interesting originals, firmly if not definitively characterized.

Odd Riisnaes (born 1953) TENOR AND SOPRANO SAXOPHONES, PIANO

*** **Thoughts** Taurus TRCD 828
    Riisnaes; Dag Arnesen (*ky*); Kare Garnes (*b*); Tom Olstad (*d*). 8/89.
*** **Another Version** Taurus TRCD 831
    Riisnaes; Iver Kleive (*org*); Steinar Larsen (*g*); Terje Gewelt (*b*); Tom Olstad (*d*). 10/93.
Odd Riisnaes manages to be powerful and self-effacing at the same time. His rounded, full tone carries over from tenor to soprano, and he's fond of measuring out a melody, giving weight to every part of the line. But he seems reticent about asserting his own personality on the music, which is still an absorbing essay on the various options for sax and rhythm section. *Thoughts* has a number of mood pieces resolved in the partnership with Arnesen (on synthesizer as often as not): improvisation takes a back seat, but there's compensation in the brisk 'Somehow' and 'Modern And Larsen'. *Another Version* changes tack again. Several pieces were recorded in the Helgerud church in Baerum, Kleive playing the organ and Riisnaes standing in the nave; as meditative sketches they carry plenty of substance. But one misses the brighter moments of some of Riisnaes's earlier playing: only Gewelt's 'One Side' impresses as a jazz piece.

Howard Riley (born 1943) PIANO

***(*) **Flight** Future Music FMR CD 26
    Riley (*p* solo). 3/71.
**** **Procession** Wondrous WM 0101
    As above. 4/90.
***(*) **The Heat Of Moments** Wondrous WM 0103
    As above. 4/91, 4/92.
*** **Beyond Category** Wondrous WM 0104
    As above. 2/93.
***(*) **The Bern Concert** Future Music FMR CD 08
    Riley; Keith Tippett (*p*). 8/93.
***(*) **Wishing On The Moon** Future Music FMR CD 14
    Riley; Mario Castronari (*b*); Tony Marsh (*d*). 95.
Riley is indeed 'beyond category'. He has worked on the free scene for more than two decades but is also, like his one-time trio partner, Barry Guy, a gifted 'straight' composer. Unlike Guy, though, he still turns to jazz standards with relish, as on the 1993 Monk and Ellington set. Riley doesn't wish *Beyond Category* to be seen as a bland 'tribute' set, and what is interesting about the recording is that the pieces, the majority of them very brief by improvising standards, are mostly straightforward though by no means literal interpretations of the original melody.

This is a thread that runs through Riley's work. The individual titles on *Flight* have a jizz and sense of direction that is immediately recognizable, even when it is difficult to describe analytically what is going on. Even on the more abstract, spontaneously improvised *Procession* and *The Heat Of Moments*, there is always an implicit core of melody. Riley was relatively slow to come to solo improvisation, and nowadays it seems to represent part of a yin–yang balance with his group work, which tends to be more assertive and forceful. Working on his own, Riley tends to be meditative and inward-looking, but without ever losing sight of the particular direction he is exploring.

Though the reappearance of *Flight*, an intense, often quiet and completely centred solo piano essay, is more than welcome, the non-availability of a substantial back-catalogue is a major loss to British music. The 1970 trio, *The Day Will Come*, a three-LP Impetus set called *Facets*, and an astonishing two-piano duo at the Royal Festival Hall with Jaki Byard, originally released on Leo, all currently languish, though the last of these has been promised for reissue and was awaited at time of writing.

Sammy Rimington (born 1942) CLARINET, ALTO AND TENOR SAXOPHONES

*** The Exciting Sax Of Sammy Rimington Progressive PCD-7077

Rimington; David Paquette (*p, v*); Walter Payton (*b*); Placide Adams, Stanley Stephens, Ernest Elly (*d*). 4/86–4/91.

**(*) One Swiss Night Music Mecca 1021-2

Rimington; Freddy John (*tb*); Jon Marks (*p*); Koen De Cauter (*g, bj*); Karl-Ake Kronquist (*b*); Sven Stahlberg (*d*). 11/91.

*** More Exciting Sax Of Sammy Rimington Progressive PCD 7088

Rimington; Phamous Lambert (*p*); Lloyd Lambert (*b*); Ernie Elly (*d*). 5/94.

**(*) Watering The Roots Jazz Crusade JCCD-3011

Rimington; Big Bill Bissonnette (*tb*); Sarah Bissonnette (*ts*); Eric Webster (*bj*); Ken Matthews (*b*); Colin Bowden (*d*). 1/95.

A Londoner whose music earned him a New Orleans adoption, Rimington has had a strange career: a stalwart with Ken Colyer, a transplantation to Louisiana where he became a bosom friend of Capt. John Handy, a flirtation with jazz-rock and now occasional sightings in sundry pick-up groups, like these. The two Progressive albums feature him exclusively on alto, where he sounds like Handy but phrases as if he were brother to Johnny Hodges: the result is a queer hybrid, soaked in a woozy kind of romanticism. Engagingly done, although the sound-mix (with the piano in the distance, the drums right up front) doesn't assist on the earlier disc. The second sounds better, and goes along at a jollier pace, with Rimington this time sounding more like a jump-band hornman on a featured night of his own. *One Swiss Night* catches him with a second-rate band (John's trombone is especially unhealthy) on dull material, but there is one real surprise, a very Websterish reading of 'My Funny Valentine' on tenor. *Watering The Roots* finds Sammy back in England. Bissonnette organized and sponsored the recording, and it's fair enough that he plays on it, but he can't summon the authority to stand in the front line, and is painfully outclassed by the clarinettist. The material this time goes back to New Orleans purism, and the only one earning stars is Rimington. He deserves a break in better company, and on a proper budget.

Per Ringkjobing FLUGELHORN, TRUMPET

***(*) Everything Happens To Me Olufsen DOCD 5166

Ringkjobing; Erling Kroner (*tb*); Lennart Wallin (*p*); Jens Melgaard (*b*); George Cole (*d*). 3/92.

A Danish villager making a belated stab at his own record, Ringkjobing has been around – a two-year gig at a US Air Force base in Iceland was 'the top of the iceberg', he notes – and knows his jazz. If he's a Dixieland veteran, you'd hardly know it from the long lines, serpentine melodic sense and lovely, mellifluous tone he gets from the flugelhorn, which he uses as his first instrument. The wry, Dickenson-like trombone of Kroner is an ideal sparring-partner on this programme of standards. If it's reminiscent of the Hackett–Dickenson team, that makes it a rare strain indeed among today's records. Melgaard is stunningly quick and fluent in his solos, but Wallin is a bit clunky and Cole a little four-square. Otherwise, an exceptional brew of contemporary mainstream.

*** An Individual Thing Olufsen DOCD 5181

Ringkjobing; Erling Kroner (*tb*); Morten Hojring (*g*); Ole Skipper Mosgaard (*b*); Lars Beijbom (*d*); Helene Johnsson (*v*); strings and woodwinds. 3/93.

Ringkjobing was ill, recuperating from a car accident, when he made this record, and it shows in some involuntary frailties – but that makes the fine ballad treatment of the title-track all the more impressive, and throughout this gentle programme the playing has a blush of sincerity that draws the listener in. Kroner sounds a bit offhand here and there but has a splendid feature of his own on 'Chelsea Bridge', and Johnsson – otherwise booked as one of the string players – does a decent job on 'Day Dream'.

Sam Rivers (born 1930) TENOR SAXOPHONE, SOPRANO SAXOPHONE, FLUTE, PIANO, VOCAL

***(*) Colors Black Saint 120064

Rivers; Marvin Blackman (*f, ts, ss*); Talib Kibwe (*f, cl, ss, ts*); Chris Roberts (*f, ss*); Steve Coleman (*f, as*); Bobby Watson (*f, as*); Nat Dixon (*f, cl, ts*); Bill Cody (*ob, ts*); Eddie Alex (*picc, ts*); Jimmy Cozier, Patience Higgins (*f, bs*). 9/82.

*** Lazuli Timeless CD SJP 291

Rivers; Darryll Thompson (*g*); Rael Wesley Grant (*b*); Steve McCraven (*d*). 10/89.

Rivers's significance to Black American music is scarcely reflected by his current catalogue; two important Blue Notes – *Fuchsia Swing Song* (871044) and *Dimensions And Extensions* (84261) – and an excellent ECM – *Contrasts* (1162) – are currently out of print. Though none matches these three, what is left is of consistently challenging quality. Rivers's association with Dave Holland, as on the bassist's marvellous *Conference Of The Birds* (ECM 1027) and the item below, helped foster his growing interest in piano playing and afforded him the kind of regular and sensitive partnership he had lacked since the end of the 1960s.

As he often shows (except on the more conventionally structured *Lazuli*), Rivers pays little attention to a fixed rhythmic pattern, preferring to build his Coltrane-influenced lines in a kind of gravity-defying isolation that, spider-like, seems to bridge space with a web of ideas that reveals its structure only at the final juncture.

The excellent rhythmless Winds of Manhattan project, *Colors*, with its flute-dominated orchestra, takes this technique beyond small-group confines and on to a much larger scale. It's broadly successful but slightly dry.

Until Rivers's classic sets are reissued on well-balanced CD, he is likely to remain an unworthily marginalized figure on the current scene, universally admired by players and by his students, but increasingly unknown to younger fans.

***(*) **Dave Holland / Sam Rivers** Improvising Artists Inc 123843
    Rivers (*ts, ss*); Dave Holland (*b*). 2/76.
Awarded to Rivers purely on grounds of seniority (and because he takes the composition credits), this is a finely balanced duo performance which reunites the more interesting axis of Holland's *Conference Of The Birds* quartet. Composition students are always warned to be wary of verse-settings which will tempt them into predictable descending scales on words like 'Waterfall'. Rivers and Holland tackle the idea – following up with 'Cascade', the only other track – with no obvious desire to create a literal tone-poem. The music is too sharply focused to be impressionistic, and the broader intervals of the first piece, on which Rivers plays soprano, are deployed in a manner which is both highly abstract and movingly lyrical, a characteristic of Holland's work. The tenor lines on 'Casacade' become muddied when Holland is working in a parallel register, and it's unfortunate that the most interesting parts of the longer track come when the two players separate, either working solo or with minimal accompaniment. A pity, too, that Holland doesn't use his cello on the session. Paul Bley's production is predictably intimate. An intriguing album, strongly recommended for anyone who found the ECM quartet compelling.

Max Roach (born 1924) DRUMS, PERCUSSION

*** **Max Roach** Original Jazz Classics OJC 202
    Roach; Idrees Sulieman (*t*); Leon Comeghys (*tb*); Gigi Gryce (*as*); Hank Mobley (*ts*); Walter Davis Jr (*p*); Frank Skeete (*b*). 4 & 10/53.
***(*) **Brownie Lives!** Fresh Sound FSRCD 1012
    Roach; Clifford Brown (*t*); Sonny Rollins (*ts*); Richie Powell (*p*); George Morrow (*b*). 4 & 5/56.
A great educator and activist as well as a consummate musician, Roach was the most complete of the bebop drummers. Stylistically he stands mid-way between swing drummers like Dave Tough, Jo Jones, Gene Krupa and Big Sid Catlett and the avant-garde of the 1960s. His most immediate influence was the transitional Kenny Clarke, whose ideas he developed and carried forward. He was Charlie Parker's best drummer bar none, and Sonny Rollins owes more to Roach than to any other player. In the 1970s he became a tutelary genius of the new wave, almost reversing one-time collaborator Cecil Taylor's definition of the piano as 88 tuned drums.

Roach frequently made the drum kit (and he has tended to play a relatively conventional set-up) sound as tuneful and harmonically rich as a keyboard instrument. His on- and off-beat alternations and dense contrapuntal narratives have taken him close to his own ambition to transmit Bach's achievement in jazz terms. Some of Roach's most interesting solo performances have to be dug out of samplers; there are characteristic solo drum 'Conversations' on the intriguing and valuable *Autobiography In Jazz*, on *At Last!* and on *The Big Beat*. Most drum samplers of any pretension have something by him.

Roach began leading bands 40 years ago. The early sessions, like those on *Max Roach*, convey much promise but little real sense of the grandeurs to follow. The 1953 dates are unpretentious and bop-dominated, but with flashes of originality and the beginnings of Roach's characteristic emphasis on darkling themes and timbral density from the horns. In later years, rather than view a band as immutable, he liked to break it up into smaller units; there's some evidence of that happening here (though the rider 'collective personnel' doesn't indicate anything other than that six of the tracks were for quartet – Mobley and rhythm only – and without the brass and second saxophone that made 'Sfax' and 'Orientation' so vibrant).

Roach's career as leader really took flight only when he formed a tragically short-lived quintet with trumpeter Clifford Brown. While the other personnel changed, Brown and Roach established a rapport only briefly matched by that with the fated Booker Little, a few years later. Roach missed the road accident which killed Brown and Richie Powell, but his career faltered and nearly succumbed.

The live *Brownie Lives!* comes from a residency at Basin Street in New York, just six weeks before the tragic deaths of Brown and Powell. The record is, quite properly, billed as a memorial to the trumpeter – one of many – but what catches the attention more than anything is again Roach's ability to swing a band and to turn it in unfamiliar directions by subtly re-calibrating the rhythm or by implying a variation on the basic melody. He does it twice in 'I Get A Kick Out Of You' and briefly tries to re-write his young colleague's masterpiece 'Daahoud', before the trumpeter stamps his signature on it again.

***(*) **Jazz In 3/4 Time** Mercury 826 456
> Roach; Kenny Dorham (*t*); Sonny Rollins (*ts*); Bill Wallace, Ray Bryant (*p*); George Morrow (*b*). 9/56, 3/57.

***(*) **Max Roach + 4** Emarcy 822673
> As above. 9/56, 3/57.

**** **Alone Together** Verve 526 373
> Roach; Kenny Dorham, Booker Little, Tommy Turrentine (*t*); Julian Priester (*tb*); Ray Draper (*tba*); George Coleman, Harold Land, Hank Mobley, Paul Quinichette, Sonny Rollins, Stanley Turrentine (*ts*); Herbie Mann (*f*); Ray Bryant, Jimmy Jones, Richie Powell, Bill Wallace (*p*); Barry Galbraith (*g*); Joe Benjamin, Bob Boswell, Nelson Boyd, Art Davis, Milt Hinton, George Morrow (*b*); Boston Percussion Ensemble (*perc*); Abbey Lincoln (*v*). 9/56–10/60.

A cliché now, of course, but there was a time when the idea of breaking the basic 4/4 common time of jazz was considered to be a pretty radical departure. Roach's 'Blues Waltz' and Rollins's 'Valse Hot' set off a mostly quiet, even subdued, set of originals and standard interpretations that were to have a significant impact on the music of the following generation. Roach is well forward in the CD remastering, and his precise but swinging division of the beat is a joy to listen to.

The second record is equally easy on the ear, though rather less focused than the first choice of material from these sessions. The band plays wonderfully on George Russell's 'Ezz-thetic', and Roach's division of the beat in the middle section is a quiet object-lesson for young drummers.

Alone Together is a double-CD compilation of Roach material, both with and, later, without Clifford Brown. The whole of the second disc is taken from the time after the deaths of Brownie and Richie Powell, who were replaced by the likes of Dorham, the equally short-lived Booker Little and Tommy Turrentine, Ray Bryant and Bill Wallace. On balance of emphasis, this is probably more successful as a Roach compilation than one for cut-and-dried Browniephiles. There are two tracks from *Max Roach + 4* and just one from *3/4 Time*. Most of the rest is later, some of it from less well-known records like *The Many Sides Of Max* (1959, with Little, Priester and Coleman) and *Quiet As It's Kept* (1960, with the Turrentines and Priester again). 'Max's Variations' is based on 'Pop Goes The Weasel' and performed with the Boston Percussion Ensemble, a foreshadowing of later drum orchestra projects like M'Boom. A valuable selection from the work of an artist who will one day require careful discographical exploration and re-evaluation.

***(*) **Plays Charlie Parker** Verve 512 448
> Roach; Kenny Dorham (*t*); George Coleman, Hank Mobley (*ts*); Nelson Boyd, George Morrow (*b*). 12/57, 4/58.

No one had more right to claim a share in the Parker legacy, and Roach leads two groups through the material with consummate skill and exactness. The Coleman/Dorham front line is consistently more interesting than the April 1958 replacement on which Mobley sounds blustery and sometimes poorly rehearsed, taking a long time to settle on 'Parker's Mood', but there is enough excellent musicianship around to make up any slight deficit. Four previously unissued tracks turned up in 1984, and are included on the CD. Nothing of earth-shaking importance, but 'Raoul' and 'This Time The Dream's On Me' are well worth having.

**** **Deeds Not Words** Original Jazz Classics OJC 304
> Roach; Booker Little (*t*); Ray Draper (*tba*); George Coleman (*ts*); Art Davis (*b*). 9/58.

It's tempting to draw a moral from the title of this superb album and simply say: go out and buy it. Coleman was by far the most bruising of Roach's tenor players, but he was harmonically exacting in a way that Hank Mobley was not, and the drummer didn't find a saxophonist with the same balance of sheer power and finesse till the advent of Odean Pope in the late 1970s. Set against Draper's chesty valvings and Davis's accurate bass, drummer and young trumpeter weave intricate lines that were among the most ambitious in contemporary 'hard bop'. Whatever that unsatisfactory label really serves, this is it.

***(*) **Drum Conversation** Enja ENJ 4074
> Roach; Tommy Turrentine (*t*); Julian Priester (*tb*); Bobby Boswell (*b*). 60.

This may – and, indeed, we think it does – come slightly later than the details suggest, but stylistically it does have a lot more in common with the work of the previous few years than what came immediately after. The reedless front line gave Roach a lot of different sounds to work with, though Priester plays what could almost be legato saxophone lines on 'Lotus Blossom' and 'A Night In Tunisia'. Boswell is very anonymous, not really essential to the overall sound, even without a piano; a couple of decades further on, and this group would probably have had someone like John Abercrombie or John Scofield to touch in some of the harmonies and fill out the sound a little.

***(*) **Speak, Brother, Speak** Original Jazz Classics OJC 646
    Roach; Clifford Jordan (*ts*); Mal Waldron (*p*); Eddie Khan (*b*). 62.
Another extensive improvisatory composition with Roach in spectacular form. Some slight misgivings about Mal Waldron's rather nay-saying and reticent approach, though rhythmically it fits the drummer's conception surprisingly well. The sound is better than on the original Fantasy album.

**** **We Insist!: Freedom Now Suite** Candid CCD 79002
    Roach; Booker Little (*t*); Julian Priester (*tb*); Walter Benton, Coleman Hawkins (*ts*); James
    Schenck (*b*); Ray Mantilla, Olatunji, Thomas Du Vall (*perc*); Abbey Lincoln (*v*). 8 & 9/60.
***(*) **Percussion Bitter Sweet** Impulse! GRP 11222
    Roach; Booker Little (*t*); Julian Priester (*tb*); Eric Dolphy (*as, bcl, f*); Clifford Jordan (*ts*); Mal
    Waldron (*p*); Art Davies (*b*); Carlos Vaeler, Carlos Eugenio (*perc*); Abbey Lincoln (*v*). 8/61.
Overtaken by the furies of the Black Power movement (and the associated New Thing in jazz), *We Insist!* has a slightly corny feel today which utterly belies its significance as an American cultural document. The album made a major composer of Roach (though one mustn't forget the lyrical contributions of Oscar Brown Jr) and it transformed the drummer's then wife, Abbey Lincoln, from a night-club 'shantooze' of limited credibility into one of the most convincing vehicles of Black American experience since Billie Holiday.

The opening 'Driva' Man' is wry and almost sarcastic, enunciated over Roach's work-rhythms and Coleman Hawkins's blearily proud solo. It's followed by 'Freedom Day' which, with 'All Africa', was to be part of a large choral work targeted on the centenary of the Emancipation Proclamation. 'Freedom Day' follows Roach's typically swinging address, but is distinguished by a Booker Little solo of bursting, youthful emotion, and a contribution from the little-regarded Walter Benton that matches Hawkins's for sheer simplicity of diction.

The central 'Triptych' – originally conceived as a dance piece – is a duo for Roach and Lincoln. 'Prayer', 'Protest' and 'Peace' was not a trajectory acceptable to later militants, but there is more than enough power in Lincoln's inchoate roars of rage in the central part, and more than enough ambiguity in the ensuing 'Peace', to allay fears that her or Roach's politics were blandly liberal. The closing 'Tears For Johannesburg' has more classic Little, and also good things from Priester and Benton. It follows 'All Africa', which begins in a vein remarkably close to Billie Holiday, briefly degenerates into a litany of tribal names and slogans, but hinges on a 'middle passage' of drum music embodying the three main Black drum traditions of the West: African, Afro-Cuban and Afro-American. Its influence on subsequent jazz percussion is incalculable, and it remains listenable even across three decades of outwardly far more radical experimentation.

The *Freedom Now Suite* is one of the classic modern albums; its slightly dated feel (there are moments when it sounds closer in spirit to the Harlem Renaissance than to the era of Sharpeville and Watts) is no more than incidental. *Percussion Bitter Sweet* is another fine album from a purple patch in Roach's career. 'Garvey's Ghost' and 'Tender Warriors' are both exceptional, but Roach has written a convincing set of politically engaged themes and shapes that certainly long outlive their purely ephemeral or tactical significance. He was blessed in the musicians who surrounded him at this time. Dolphy and Dorham both sound extraordinarily in tune with the project, and Abbey Lincoln again adds a lyrical dimension that the music, unlike most jazz performance, somehow seems to welcome rather than resist.

**** **It's Time** Impulse! IMP 11852
    Roach; Richard Williams (*t*); Julian Priester (*tb*); Clifford Jordan (*ts*); Mal Waldron (*p*); Art
    Davis (*b*). 62.
A splendid record, by one of the best of the post-Brownie Roach groups. The key instrumentalist turns out to be Priester. His long A minor/A major solo on 'Another Valley' deserves to be listened to again and again. Waldron's accompaniment is spiky, ambiguous and full of stealth and art. The leader is more discursive and his feature might have been tightened up a bit. It would have been interesting to have heard the rhythm section working independently as a trio; as usual the record has lots of space, light and shade, but the horn quite properly demands a lot of the foreground and often there are more interesting things happening behind. Roach is mixed well up but, even on CD, it's sometimes hard to pick out Davis, and Waldron is in his quieter, more thoughtful mood.

*** **The Max Roach Trio Featuring The Legendary Hasaan** Atlantic 82273
    Roach; Hasaan (*p*); Art Davis (*d*). 12/64.

The pianist's legend hasn't stretched a great deal further than this record and the testimony of those who played with him in the 1960s. The disc opens with variations on the 3/4 and 6/8 patterns, but it doesn't really take them anywhere, and Hasaan (or Ibn Ali, as he was also known) offers little more than the odd exotic scale and a decidedly odd time conception that doesn't quite fit in with Roach's.

***(*) **Drums Unlimited** Atlantic 7567 81361
    Roach (*d* solo) and with Freddie Hubbard (*t*); Roland Alexander (*ss*); James Spaulding (*as*); Ronnie Mathews (*p*); Jymie Merritt (*b*). 10/65, 4/66.

Three mildly disappointing group tracks (though 'St Louis Blues' with Hubbard and the two saxophones is excellent) are more than made up for by Roach's three solo features. The title-track is a meticulously structured and executed essay in rhythmic polyvalence that puts Sunny Murray's and Andrew Cyrille's more ambitious works in context; the second is an exploration of Roach's characteristic waltz-time figurings; the last a heart-felt tribute to Big Sid Catlett.

    Roach's Catlett-like reflexes and responses are evidenced on countless recordings. On 'In The Red' here, he uses his own composition as the basis for a remarkably free but beautifully cadenced embellishment of the slow central theme. The band don't seem to be up to the task, though Hubbard – familiar with an autonomous rhythm section from work with Eric Dolphy and others – sounds assured. Marvellous – and particularly good on CD, which recovers some of Roach's more fugitive effects.

**** **Birth And Rebirth** Black Saint 120024
    Roach; Anthony Braxton (*as, ss, sno, f, cl, cbcl*). 9/78.
*** **One In Two – Two In One** hat Art 6030
    As above. 8/79.

In their anxiety, critics couldn't decide who was climbing into who's pigeon-hole on these. Did *Birth And Rebirth* illustrate '*avant-gardist*' Braxton's accommodation to the mainstream, or did it prove what a radical old Roach actually was? The answer, of course, made nonsense of the question. Few supposed radicals have been so firmly rooted 'in the tradition' as the multi-instrumentalist Braxton, and few hard-boppers have been so cerebrally adventurous as the veteran drummer.

    Together, they made music of a very high and challenging order, comparable to Roach's historic duos with Cecil Taylor at Columbia University in 1979 (Soul Note SN 1100 2LP). Braxton's references to bop have tended to be both respectful and subversive; with Roach, he pushes their harmonic ambiguity to the limits, constantly 'breaking down' into dissonances that are as sharply percussive in attack as Roach's melorhythms are legato-smooth.

    The later album gives off a far greater impression of contrivance than the inspired spontaneity the two players achieve on the Black Saint. A suite of four notionally connected arguments, used as the basis for extended improvisation, the prevailing tone is argumentative and divisive rather than the unity-in-diversity suggested by the title. Braxton's wider range of instruments – he adds flute, his least successful horn, and the still-unassimilated contrabass clarinet – helps out in places, but only cosmetically. It was a great idea, but it didn't last.

*** **Pictures In A Frame** Soul Note 121003
    Roach; Cecil Bridgewater (*t, flhn*); Odean Pope (*ts, f, ob*); Calvin Hill (*b*). 1 & 9/79.
*** **In The Light** Soul Note 121053
    As above. 7/82.

But for the bassist, this is Roach's 1980s working band just before the point when the drummer began to turn slightly away from his own compositional output and towards a re-engagement with jazz history. The writing is strong, if a little sombre, and the drums are 'featured' even when someone else is purportedly soloing. Pope's doubling on oboe and flute varies the textures. Good-quality performances all around, but with an underlying sense of change in the air; much of the music is for fractions of the basic band, and not always simply duets with the leader. The next decade found Roach facing in a quite different direction, and anyone who caught up with him only in the 1980s may find this a useful benchmark.

    In The Light already sounds more stripped-down and less tentative. Pope concentrates on tenor, Bridgewater clarifies his lines, and the fulcrum of the session is a pair of Monk readings – 'Ruby, My Dear' and 'Straight, No Chaser' – with Roach repositioning the rhythmic commas like the master he is.

**** **Historic Concerts** Soul Note 121100 2CD
    Roach; Cecil Taylor (*p*). 12/79.

Recorded at the McMillin Theatre, Columbia University, these summit encounters are as exhilarating now as they must have been on the night. Both men take a solo spot, very much warm-up stuff, before launching into a huge, 40-minute phantasy that sees neither surrendering a whit of individuality or idiosyncrasy. As was noted at the time, this was a perfect occasion to test the routine categorization of Roach as a melodic percussionist, and Taylor as a percussive pianist; like all successful sound-bites, this is both useful and misleading. For much of the opening duet, Roach fulfils a conventional drummer's role, sustaining a time-feel, accelerating and arresting the pace of development, filling and embellishing, and it is Taylor who creates the grandly insane melodies that spring away for whole minutes at a time. Part two of the duets is less compelling; something has unravelled and there is much more emphasis on solo space and shorter-term structure. The remainder of the set consists of interviews with these two masters. A fascinating record on every count.

*** **Swish** New Artists NA1001
Roach; Connie Crothers (*p*). 2/82.

No liner-note to explain how this unlikely collaboration came about, but it was presumably Crothers' idea, to help launch the New Artists imprint with a star name. Inevitably, it lacks the sheer drama and magisterial quality of the Roach/Taylor encounters. There is much less evidence of interaction and some of the pieces border on the inconsequential, with Roach trying hard to make things happen, and Crothers struggling to keep up. The second track, 'Let 'Em Roll', has a touch of drama and tension, but it falls away again from here.

Both are credited as producers, which makes one ask why Roach was happy to hear himself represented quite as unattractively as this: a hissy, imprecise sound that does him no favours at all. It doesn't sound as if the microphones used were suitable for percussion.

(*) **Collage Soul Note 121059
Roach; Kenyatte Abdur-Rahman (*xy, cabasa, perc*); Eddie Allen (*woodblocks, perc, cym*); Roy Brooks (*steel d, slapstick, musical saw, perc*); Joe Chambers (*xy, mar, vib, b mar*); Eli Fountain (*cowbell, xy, crotales, orchestral bells*); Fred King (*tim, concert bells, vib*); Ray Mantilla (*bells, chimes, perc*); Warren Smith (*b mar, perc*); Freddie Waits (*concert tom-toms, gongs, bass d, shaker*). 10/84.

Credited to the percussion collective, M'Boom, which Roach formed in the 1970s, this is a slightly chaotic and rackety affair, more interesting episodically than in its entirety. Roach plays a relatively limited, honoured-patron's role, playing bass and snare drums and marimba, and the music lacks his sterling discipline and formal control.

*** **Live At Vielharmonie Munich** Soul Note 121073
Roach; Cecil Bridgewater (*t, flhn*); Dwayne Armstrong (*ts*); Phil Bower (*b*); string quartet. 11/83.
***(*) **Easy Winners** Soul Note 121109
Roach; Cecil Bridgewater (*t, flhn*); Odean Pope (*ts*); Tyrone Brown (*b*); Ray Mantilla (*perc*); string quartet. 1/85.

Two of several experiments in 'doubling' the basic jazz quartet with strings. Typical of much of his 1980s work, the 1983 German concert is a retrospective homage to two of the drummer's most stimulating artistic partnerships. 'Booker Little' recalls the brilliant young trumpeter who died in 1961 after recording several classic sides with Roach; 'Bird Says' is an altogether more complex and angular work, exploring the Parker legacy.

The sound isn't always absolutely up to scratch and there are problems in the balance of the strings. Armstrong has a rather wearying tone, and Bower's electric bass sits rather awkwardly in front of the 'acoustic' fiddles, robbing them of some of their punch; why not an upright bass? or none at all, leaving the lower-register figures to the cello and to Roach's right foot? Intriguing, and as challenging as ever, but by no means a great record.

The drummer's daughter, Maxine Roach, a talented violist, plays with the Uptown String Quartet on *Easy Winners*. The album contains a further snippet of Roach's memorialization of Booker Little and a further, tougher reading of 'Bird Says'. The reappearance of percussionist Mantilla (who'd appeared on *We Insist*) for the latter adds nothing of any great substance, but the sound is better, the string players have considerably more rosin on their bows and grease in their elbows, and the album as a whole is to be preferred to the earlier one, which sounds almost academic in comparison.

*** **Scott Free** Soul Note 121103
Roach; Cecil Bridgewater (*t, flhn*); Odean Pope (*ts*); Tyrone Brown (*b*). 5/84.
*** **It's Christmas Again** Soul Note 121153
As above, except add Lee Konitz (*as*); Tony Scott (*cl*); Tommaso Lana (*g*). 6/84.

Scott Free is a hefty two-part suite dedicated to the brilliant young bassist, Scott LaFaro, who died in a motor accident in 1961, within four months of Booker Little (see above). Roach's ability to sustain interest over the length of the piece is traceable not just to the seamless cymbal-beat which gave the classic bebop sessions their fantastic excitement but also to a mathematically complex interference with common time. Roach's variations on a basic 4/4 metre give the characteristically sombre themes a vividness and motion they might otherwise lack. This is the same band as featured on *Easy Winners*, but they sound more clean-lined without the strings; as before, the band breaks down into challenging duos. As a unit they work within more basic codes, but Bridgewater and Pope have good contrapuntal instincts and play with considerable dash and eloquence (the former with more than a whiff of Roach's beloved Clifford Brown, whose death left the biggest hole in his artistic life). Not a classic, but further evidence of Roach's extraordinary inventiveness.

This was a very good year for Roach and *It's Christmas Again* stands up very well. Recorded in Italy, it includes a one-off track with Konitz, Scott and Lama, a makeweight track in some respects, but a vauable indication – if more were needed – of how adaptable and responsive a player the drummer is. The title suite is punctuated by ideas from elsewhere, and anyone familiar with this period or who takes the time to listen to these Soul Notes in a structured way will find a good deal of cross-fertilization going on.

***(*) **Survivors** Soul Note 121093
    Roach; Guillermo Figueroa, Donald Bauch (*vn*); Louise Schulman (*vla*); Christopher Finckel
    (*clo*). 10/84.
***(*) **Bright Moments** Soul Note 121159
    Roach; Odean Pope (*ts*); Tyrone Brown (*b*); Uptown String Quartet: Diane Monroe, Lesa Terry
    (*vn*), Maxine Roach (*vla*), Zela Terry (*clo*). 10/86.

A further extension of the strings experiment, *Survivors* dispenses with the conventional jazz group altogether and launches into the kind of territory the Kronos Quartet were claiming as their sole preserve only a couple of years later. 'The Drum Also Waltzes' reappears from way back when, but the best of the material is the vibrant 'Billy The Kid' and the African-influenced 'Smoke That Thunders'.

Roach alternates dotted rhythms and more conventional string sweeps to build up music of remarkable depth and texture. The effect may still be a little academic for some, but, even aimed at the head rather than the gut or feet, it's unquestionably exciting.

Bright Moments is perhaps more of a compromise, a step back in the direction of a more conventional jazz line-up. There are places where the parts simply don't integrate successfully, but in general it's a successful experiment.

**** **To The Max!** Enja 7021 22 2CD
    Roach; Cecil Bridgewater (*t*); Odean Pope (*ts*); George Cables, Tyrone Brown (*b*); Uptown
    String Quartet: Diane Monroe, Lesa Terry (*vn*); Maxine Roach (*vla*); Eileen Folson (*clo*);
    M'Boom: Roy Brooks, Joe Chambers, Omar Clay, Eli Fountain, Fred King, Ray Mantilla,
    Francisco Mora, Warren Smith (*perc*); The John Motley Singers: Priscilla Baskerville, Florence
    Jackson, Karen Jackson, Lucille J. Jacobsen, Sarah Ann Rodgers, Robbin L. Balfour, Brenda Lee
    Taub, Christopher Pickens, Abraham Shelton, Thomas Young, Games Gainer, Greg Jones, T.
    Ray Lawrence, John Motley, Ronnel Bey (*v*). 11/90, 4 & 6/91.

A massive celebration of Roach's recent career. Disc 1 is dominated by the three-part 'Ghost Dance', scored for orchestra and chorus, with an extraordinary central section by M'Boom, and recommendable to anyone who found Philip Glass's Amerindian-inspired *Koyaanisqatsi* excessively bland and pretentious. The piece has an almost formal elegance, but it is still deeply rooted in the blues; the closing section, marked by a speaker-threatening recording of an atomic blast, balances choral passages and steamingly intense passages from both Pope and Cables.

The very beautiful 'A Quiet Place' (played by M'Boom) almost comes in too quickly. Characterized by soft chimes and a swaying marimba pulse, it conjures up images of a drowned church, its bells pealing in the tides and currents. 'The Profit' is the first of four quartet tracks. Roach's jazz drumming is as inventive and propulsive as ever, pushing along Bridgewater's Clifford Brown-derived solo. The later 'Tricotism' is an Oscar Pettiford tune and appropriately a feature for Tyrone Brown, who continues to grow in stature. 'Tears' is an instrumental version of an Abbey Lincoln performance from *Freedom Now Suite*, while the long 'A Little Booker' brings on Maxine Roach and the Uptown strings for a superb double quartet.

Roach takes two solo slots, 'Self Portrait' and 'Drums Unlimited'. The latter was first recorded in 1966 and is every bit as fresh. Roach's technique has remained pristine, and even these live recordings reflect more of its subtlety than the badly miked studio originals.

For anyone who hasn't yet approached Roach's solo and leader work, this is an essential purchase, full of extraordinary riches.

George Robert ALTO AND SOPRANO SAXOPHONES, CLARINET

(*) **Live In Switzerland 1987–89 Jazz helvet JH 04
    Robert; Tom Harrell (*t, flhn*); Dado Moroni (*p*); Reggie Johnson (*b*); Bill Goodwin (*d*). 4/87–4/
    89.
*** **Featuring Mr Clark Terry** TCB 90802
    Robert; Clark Terry (*flhn, v*); Dado Moroni (*p*); Isla Eckinger (*b*); Peter Schmidlin (*d*). 12/90.

(*) Youngbloods Mons CD 1987
    Robert; Dado Moroni (*p*). 10/92.
* **Tribute** Jazz Focus JFCD004
    Robert; Dado Moroni (*p*); Oliver Gannon (*g*); Reggie Johnson (*b*); George Ursan (*d*). 7/94.
(*) Voyage TCB 95102
    Robert; Dado Moroni (*p*); Isla Eckinger (*b*); Peter Schmidlin (*d*). 12/94.
Robert plays bebop alto, pure and straight-ahead. His solos are collections of licks which he can reel off at impressive speed, and as an executant he's completely at ease with whatever tune is on the book. He likes the classic repertoire, and though he doesn't write that much, he sometimes comes up with a pleasing line: 'Remembering Henri', a requiem for his brother, turns up in two strong versions on *Tribute* and *Voyage*. Moroni is clearly a favourite partner, and the groups on these various records seem to enjoy having him in the front line. Yet none of the discs really cuts a very deep impression. The live set with Harrell covers two festival appearances two years apart and, if the trumpeter plays well, he can be heard to better advantage in many another situation. Clark Terry has plenty of fun on his guest appearance, which includes one of the most surreal versions of 'Mumbles' yet put on record, and the enthusiasm is infectious. *Youngbloods* is all right, but Moroni's heavyweight manner seems to crowd Robert for a lot of the time, and the very upfront piano sound doesn't assist.

    Tribute was recorded straight after a brief tour, and the band are well on their toes: 'The Village' has some genuinely impassioned alto, and Gannon's tart playing is a nice contrast. This is probably Robert's best record. *Voyage* re-runs some of this material with a different band at a club set in Lausanne: accomplished as usual, but there are predictable longueurs and *Tribute* is a better bet.

Yves Robert TROMBONE

*(*) Tout Court deux Z ZZ 84103
    Robert; Philippe Deschepper (*g*); Claude Tchamitchian (*b*); Xavier Desandre (*d*). 6/91.
Twenty-six tracks in just 50 intriguing minutes and, given that eight items have durations of over three minutes, it's obvious that *tout court* is exactly what he means. Robert is now a well-seasoned sideman, a first-call player on an undersubscribed instrument; but never previously has he shown himself to be quite so unpredictably original. Group tracks are interspersed with brief solos, not just from Robert but from the others as well. Deschepper's metallic noise guitar is particularly effective, but after a while one stops trying to work out who does what. The remarkable thing is that this set works almost as a continuous suite. It's fun to reprogramme the track listings (and with 26 items the permutations are mathematically impressive), but it works pretty well as it stands. Future outings will be worth watching out for.

Hank Roberts CELLO, FIDDLE, 12-STRING GUITAR, VOICE

* **Black Pastels** JMT 834417
    Roberts; Ray Anderson, Robin Eubanks (*tb*); Dave Taylor (*btb*); Tim Berne (*as*); Bill Frisell (*g, bjo*); Mark Dresser (*b*); Joey Baron (*d, perc*). 11 & 12/87.
** Birds Of Prey JMT 834437
    Roberts; Mark Lampariello (*g, v*); Jerome Harris (*b, v*); Vinnie Johnson (*d, v*); D. K. Dyson (*v*). 1 & 2/90.
*(*) Little Motor People JMT 514 005
    Roberts; Django Bates (*p, syn, thn*); Arto Tuncboyaci (*perc, v*). 12/92.
Though somewhat removed from the scratch-and-scrabble of more *avant* improvising cellists, Roberts has a style that identifiably owes something to post-Hendrix guitarists like Bill Frisell (with whom he played on *Lookout For Hope* (ECM 1350 CD/LP) and who returns the compliment on the excellent *Black Pastels*) and several generations of play-or-die country and bluegrass fiddlers. As middle man on the Arcado totem pole, he gave the music much of its harmonic oomph, and that's evident too on the albums as leader.

    Black Pastels treads the same splintery boards as Frisell's cracked C&W, but the brasses give the music an almost medieval darkness that is quite unsettling. 'Granpappy's Barn Dance Death Dance' and 'Scarecrow Shakedown' are both superb, while 'Lucky's Lament' (which may contain a reference to Coltrane's folksy 'Lonnie's Lament') draws an emotional resonance from the one-track-only addition of Arcado bass-man Dresser.

    Birds of Prey is inferior in almost every conceivable direction; a disappointing drift into lacklustre soul-funk with too much emphasis on Dyson's strictly limited vocal powers.

    In between all the tongue-in-cheek stuff, including sarky covers of 'Over The Rainbow', 'My Favourite

Things', 'Donna Lee' and 'Autumn Leaves', there's some spanking music on *Little Motor People*. The 'Saturday / Sunday' suite consists largely of the kind of miniatures Django Bates is also good at. The title-piece is more extended and gives full rein to Roberts's cello playing for the first time on the record. Whenever the squealy stuff takes a back seat, a little sunshine comes in and warms the cockles of an otherwise rather cool and sophomoric session.

Luckey Roberts (1887–1968) PIANO

***(*) **The Circle Recordings** Solo Art SACD-10
    Roberts (*p solo*). 5/46.
*** **Luckey & the Lion – Harlem Piano** Good Time Jazz GTJCD-10035
    Roberts; Willie 'The Lion' Smith (*p*). 58.

Charles Luckeyeth Roberts was a giant of Harlem stride piano, and he was also one of its least-documented performers, at least so far as records are concerned. One of the titles on the Circle session, 'Shy And Sly', was cut for Columbia as far back as 1916 but was never issued; aside from a few cameo appearances, it wasn't until the 1940s that he got himself properly on record. The six tracks on the Solo Art CD sound like a man making up for lost time: they explode with sheer bravado, rhythms taken at a helter-skelter pace, trills and runs and horn-like outbursts folded into each of the pieces. 'Pork And Beans', which Willie The Lion Smith also liked to play, is the one to try first. But this is all there is of Roberts on this CD: the rest is devoted to early tracks by Ralph Sutton.

Luckey joined forces with The Lion for the 1958 album: they share the date rather than playing together. It's a piquant contrast. Roberts was already an old man, but much of his particular flair is intact on the splendid locomotive piece 'Railroad Blues', and 'Complainin'' is a chuckle. Not much evidence, in sum, for a piano legend but, given the extravagances of Luckey's style, maybe that's all for the best.

Marcus Roberts PIANO

(*) **The Truth Is Spoken Here Novus 3051
    Roberts; Wynton Marsalis (*t*); Charlie Rouse, Todd Williams (*ts*); Reginald Veal (*b*); Elvin Jones (*d*). 7/88.
*** **Deep In The Shed** Novus PD 83078
    Roberts; E. Dankworth, Scotty Barnhart (*t*); Wycliffe Gordon (*tb*); Wessell Anderson (*as*); Todd Williams, Herb Harris (*ts*); Reginald Veal, Chris Thomas (*b*); Herlin Riley, Maurice Carnes (*d*). 8–12/89.

Despite an almost obsessive sobriety and respectfulness to his own idea of 'the tradition', Roberts's records are impressive statements. As a composer, he packs the themes with technical detail which his different groups negotiate without hesitation, and his own playing is marked by a pensive assurance. He has listened to and learned from Monk, Ellington and many others. But one can't help longing for a more direct melody or a less weighty construction even as the music makes its absorbing points. Marsalis, who was Roberts's boss in the four years leading up to the 1988 album, plays imperiously (he is almost certainly the mysterious 'E. Dankworth', too) and the solos by Rouse are a moving farewell to a musician who died not long after the record was made. *Deep In The Shed* investigates blues tonality with five-, six- and seven-strong groups, and its masterclass air is more frequently undercut by smart use of ensemble colour than was the debut. But the music will either captivate or induce boredom, depending on one's taste.

(*) **Alone With Three Giants Novus PD 83109
    Roberts (*p* solo). 6–9/90.
** **Prayer For Peace** Novus PD 63124-2
    Roberts (*p* solo).
*** **As Serenity Approaches** Novus PD 63130-2
    Roberts; Nicholas Payton, Wynton Marsalis, Scotty Barnhart (*t*); Ronald Westray (*tb*); Todd Williams (*cl, ts*); Ellis Marsalis (*p*). 6–11/91.
*** **If I Could Be With You** Novus 63149-2
    Roberts (*p* solo). 92.

Alone With Three Giants is an audacious recital, uniting six tunes each by Monk and Ellington and three by Jelly Roll Morton. Roberts is good with Monk, his primary influence, and his Ellington choices are interesting: 'Shout 'Em Aunt Tillie' and 'Black And Tan Fantasy' aren't in anybody else's solo piano repertoire. But he seems less sure with Morton: 'The Crave' entirely misses the loose-limbed courtliness of the composer's own. Engaging, but a certain didacticism hovers over it. The Christmas collection,

Prayer For Peace, is as well done as any such records, but Roberts isn't exactly a great humorist, and we prefer Ramsey Lewis's 'Rudolph The Red Nosed Reindeer' to the one here.

He is back on the track with the next two records. Perhaps it is pointless to grumble about Roberts's pedagogic air, since he's set himself an agenda that embraces jazz piano history as an all-encompassing knowledge, whether we care to follow him or not. For *As Serenity Approaches*, he brings in other instrumentalists for eight of the 19 tracks, but only one at a time: hence Wynton Marsalis tries to replicate King Oliver's steps with Jelly Roll Morton on 'King Porter Stomp' while the others blend with varying degrees into the Roberts revisionism. It works splendidly with Payton on the terrific 'Preach, Reverend, Preach', one of the best tunes Roberts has come up with so far; and Williams and the elder Marsalis do well, too, though Wynton's playing takes on the strangulated air that he sometimes adopts when trying to sound like an old master. At the piano, on themes as diverse as 'Jitterbug Waltz' and 'Cherokee', Roberts distils a sometimes cranky, often compelling vision. The all-solo *If I Could Be With You* is his best calling-card to date, though again one wonders if this recasting of jazz history has to sound as stiff as it does on, say, 'Maple Leaf Rag' (an audacious attempt to, allegedly, play it as Jelly Roll Morton might have done, though it sounds nothing like Morton's piano-roll) or the arthritically ponderous 'Moonlight In Vermont'. When Roberts relaxes, as he does on another version of 'Preach, Reverend, Preach', or when he settles into a sweet-toned miniature, such as 'Rippling Waters', he sounds something like the giant his sleevenote-writer cracks him up to be.

(*) Gershwin For Lovers Columbia 477752-2
    Roberts; Reginald Veal (*b*); Herlin Riley (*d*). 93.
Roberts's first for Columbia is 'intended to be part of a romantic evening', says the artist, but there's an awful lot of foreplay here. While there may be some of the pianist's best work – in a fine solo on 'They Can't Take That Away From Me' and a closing trot through 'But Not For Me', where the tempo finally picks up – there's some terribly serious music to get through as well. The intractably slow delivery of the earlier tunes on the record isn't just a matter of ballad tempos. It's a conceptual trudge, too. For all the interesting touches here and there, the bald reality is that Roberts and company don't even swing for much of the time.

Jim Robinson (1892–1976) TROMBONE

*** **Jim Robinson's New Orleans Band** Original Jazz Classics OJC 1844
    Robinson; Ernest Cagnalotti (*t*); Louis Cottrell (*cl*); George Guesnon (*g*); Alcide 'Slow Drag' Pavageau (*b*); Alfred Williams (*d*). 1/61.
*** **Plays Spirituals And Blues** Original Jazz Classics OJC 1846
    As above, except add Annie Pavageau (*v*). 1/61.
*** **Classic New Orleans Jazz Vol. 2** Biograph BCD 128
    Robinson; Kid Thomas Valentine, Ernest Cagnalotti, Tony Fougerat (*t*); John Handy (*as*); Sammy Rimington, Albert Burbank, Orange Kellin (*cl*); Dick Griffith, George Guesnon, Al Lewis (*bj*); Dick McCarthy, Alcide 'Slow Drag' Pavageau, James Prevost (*b*); Sammy Penn, Cie Frazier, Louis Barbarin (*d*). 8/64–12/74.
*** **Birthday Memorial Session** GHB BCD-276
    Robinson; Yoshio Toyama (*t*); Paul 'Polo' Barnes (*cl*); James Miller (*p, v*); Keiko Toyama (*bj*); Chester Zardis (*b*); Cie Frazier (*d*). 73.
The doyen of New Orleans trombonists – along with Louis Nelson – Robinson had turned eighty by the time the last of these records was made, but his simple, perfectly appropriate playing wasn't too bothered by the passing of time, and he performs much as he did on all of the sessions he appeared on over a space of some 35 years. The two OJCs were originally a part of Riverside's New Orleans Living Legends series, and were among the first occasions when Robinson had been asked to perform as a leader. Cagnalotti and Cottrell weren't much more interested than Jim in taking a lead, and as a result the front line sounds reserved here and there, but the two discs – neatly split between NO standards on the first and gospel and blues tunes on the second – are as tough and genuine as most such sessions from this period. The Biograph disc puts together three sessions stretching across ten years. The first is a noisy and quite exciting gathering of generations – Valentine and Robinson on one side, Rimington and Handy on another – with boisterous music resulting, and the four tracks from the following year are in the same mould; but it's on the closing 'Gasket Street Blues', which features one of Robinson's rare, unaffected solos, that the man himself stands out most clearly.

On *Birthday Memorial* the band play with undimmed enjoyment of the occasion. The presence of the Toyamas, the Japanese couple who lived and worked on Bourbon Street for a spell in the late 1960s, invigorates the other old-timers involved on the date, with Yoshio's admiration for Bunk Johnson letting him fit into the group without any sense of strain.

Perry Robinson (born 1938) CLARINET

**** Funk Dumpling Savoy SV 0255

Robinson; Kenny Barron (*p*); Henry Grimes (*b*); Paul Motian (*d*). *c*. 62.

*** Kundalini IAI 123856

Robinson; Badal Roy (*tabla*); Nana Vasconcelos (*perc, berimbau*). 2/78.

Long – and apparently apron-stringed – association with Gunther Hampel and the Galaxie Dream Band tended to blur Robinson's critical reputation. A formidable technician on a still-unfashionable instrument (he is a collateral descendant of Tony Scott and Jimmy Giuffre, but with a pronounced rock influence), Robinson inherited a fine structural sense from his composer father and builds solos out of daring architectural swoops and apparently unsupported harmony, much like Sonny Rollins.

The Savoy recording has only recently surfaced again, and it is an unexpected gem, fine contemporary clarinet playing of a vintage only really surpassed by Giuffre. Robinson is, of course, blessed with an exceptional band, even if the younger Kenny Barron offers only occasional earnests of the master he was to become. The Grimes/Motian axis is absolutely solid, setting Robinson loose on 'Moon Over Moscow' and the witty 'Farmer Alfalfa'. The only slight drawback is the recording, which is very dry and shrill, with the clarinet miked too close and the rhythm section somewhat recessed.

The duos with Badal Roy on *Kundalini* are pretty much of a piece with Paul Bley's resolutely experimental output on his IAI imprint. There are some interesting oriental touches, but the disc somehow manages to combine short measure (a mere 33 minutes) with pronounced longueurs – no mean feat.

Reginald R. Robinson (born 1973) PIANO

*** The Strongman Delmark DE-662

Robinson (*p* solo). 93.

*** Sounds In Silhouette Delmark DE-670

Robinson (*p* solo). 94.

His name even sounds like that of a ragtime composer. Yet Robinson was born in Chicago in the early 1970s and, though he wrote 40 of the 43 compositions on these two discs, he is a self-taught prodigy who only found out about ragtime from his local library. 'Ragtime seems mysterious to me,' he says, and it's the enigmatic, allusive strain in the music which Robinson fastens on and develops. He also likes Chopin, and some of his writing suggests a dignified balance of that composer with Joplin and Charles L. Johnson. The only non-originals he plays are 'Maple Leaf Rag' and a medley of three tunes by Johnson, but these fit alongside his own vignettes without any awkwardness. Whether suggesting a waltz or a cakewalk, the rhythms of his playing seem to light on exactly the syncopation which provided the heartbeat of a typical rag: what one hears isn't quite swing, it's the jauntiness of ragtime movement. He is well recorded (though his sprightly right hand is sometimes overlit in the studio mix) and apparently without any self-consciousness about his art. Rare and fascinating music.

Spike Robinson (born 1930) TENOR SAXOPHONE

***(*) At Chesters Vol. 1 Hep CD 2028

Robinson; Eddie Thompson (*p*); Len Skeat (*b*); James Hall (*d*). 7/84.

*** At Chesters Vol. 2 Hep CD 2031

As above. 7/84.

Robinson is an American who has made a secure reputation for himself in Britain, having first arrived here on a Navy posting. Although he plays tenor now, he was an altoman entirely under Parker's spell when he made these tracks in London in 1951. Robinson's switch to tenor may have deprived us of a fine Bird-man, but his command of the bigger horn is scarcely less impressive on what were comeback recordings. His models now are Getz, Sims and – at the insistence of some – Brew Moore, but Robinson is deft enough to make the comparisons sound fully absorbed. These two live records, made in Southend on a 1984 British visit, are wonderfully light and swinging, as if the tenor were an alto in his hands. *Volume 1* has the edge for a couple of ethereal ballads and the swing which is piled into 'Please Don't Talk About Me When I'm Gone'. Vivid location recording.

*** In Town Hep CD 2035 C

Robinson; Brian Lemon (*p*); Len Skeat (*b*); Allan Ganley (*d*); Elaine Delmar (*v*). 10/86.

*** The Odd Couple Capri 74008 C

Robinson; Rob Mullins (*ky*); Fred Hamilton (*b*); Jill Fredericsen (*d*). 8/88.

*** **Jusa Bit O'Blues** Capri 74012
>   Robinson; Harry 'Sweets' Edison (*t*); Ross Tompkins (*p*); Monty Budwig (*b*); Paul Humphrey
>   (*d*). 9/88.
*** **Jusa Bit O'Blues Vol. 2** Capri 74013
>   As above. 9/88.

The Capri records provide Robinson with some of his most encouraging settings. All three find Robinson drifting through a clutch of standards with carefree ease, and any preference among them might depend on the choice of songs on each. Edison is reliably lyrical, and both rhythm sections play their part without complaint; the only qualm might be the essential sameness which accompanies such seasoned and professional music-making. In other words, they're more satisfying than exciting.

*** **Three For The Road** Hep CD 2045
>   Robinson; Janusz Carmello (*t*); David Newton (*p*); Louis Stewart (*g*); Paul Morgan (*b*); Mark
>   Taylor (*d*). 7/89.
(*) **Stairway To The Stars Hep CD 2049
>   Robinson; Brian Kellock (*p*); Ronnie Rae (*b*); John Rae (*d*). 10/90.

Robinson continues on his steady way. *Three For The Road* makes for an amiable blowing match between a seasoned cast: nothing fancy, and nothing untoward. *Stairway To The Stars*, though, is a trifle dull – Robinson never plays with less than a professional commitment, but on this occasion he sounds as though he might have been a bit tired. What he may be in need of now is context and a producer: there are enough off-the-cuff live dates in his discography already.

*** **Reminiscin'** Capri 74029 C
>   Robinson; Mundell Lowe (*g*); Monty Budwig (*b*); Jake Hanna (*d*). 12/91.

Here's another off-the-cuff live date. But at least it presents Spike back in his local town of Denver and playing with three knowing veterans (it was one of Monty Budwig's last dates). A bit special: 'Dream Dancing', which floats like smoke over water, and its unspoken companion-piece, 'Dancing In The Dark'.

*** **Spike Robinson And George Masso Play Arlen** Hep CD 2053
>   Robinson; George Masso (*tb*); Ken Peplowski (*cl, ts*); John Pearce (*p*); Dave Green (*b*); Martin
>   Drew (*d*). 10/91.

Consistency has become Robinson's most obvious virtue: this is another dependable, likeable record, with Masso and Peplowski (who's on only two tracks) as foils. The trombonist plays quirkily enough to make one think of Bill Harris, and it's a strong counterpoint to Spike's gentlemanly playing. 'This Time The Dream's On Me' and 'My Shining Hour' work particularly well. But the snug, tasteful rhythm section keep dragging the music back into formulaic mainstream.

*** **Plays Harry Warren** Hep 2056
>   Robinson; Victor Feldman, Pete Jolly (*p*); Ray Brown, John Leitham (*b*); John Guerin, Paul
>   Kreibach (*d*). 12/81–8/93.

Spike's 'modern' career comes full circle with this release, which couples a reissue of his 1981 set for Discovery with a new date made in 1993 with a different American rhythm section. There's an almost seamless transition between the two dates and the playing is as handsome as one might expect – though, without another horn out front, Robinson sometimes lets himself drift off – as charmingly as ever. At nearly 80 minutes, another overloaded CD.

Betty Roche (born 1920) VOCAL

*** **Singin' And Swingin'** Original Jazz Classics OJC 1718
>   Roche; Jimmy Forrest (*ts*); Jack McDuff (*org*); Bill Jennings (*g*); Wendell Marshall (*b*); Roy
>   Haynes (*d*). 1/61.
*** **Lightly And Politely** Original Jazz Classics OJC 1802-2
>   Roche; Jimmy Neeley (*p*); Wally Richardson (*g*); Michael Mulia (*b*); Rudy Lawless (*d*). 1/61.

Roche had two separate spells with Duke Ellington, in the 1940s and again in the early '50s, but she made only a handful of sides with the orchestra: her set-piece was a version of 'Take The "A" Train' which incorporated a long scat episode. Duke liked her style: 'she had a soul inflexion in a bop state of intrigue'. Her Bethlehem records of the 1950s have been available but are now out of print; these 1961 sessions are a modest but enjoyable memento of her art. Bop appears on *Singin' And Swingin'* with 'Billie's Bounce', but her huskier ballad delivery takes some of the slush out of 'When I Fall In Love', and her Anita O'Day influence shows through in a certain wry sidelong-delivery of some of the lyrics. That trait is more exposed on the cooler, slower *Lightly And Politely*. Some of the lyrics she seems to phrase in abruptly chopped sections, a little like Abbey Lincoln, and it lends a curious detachment to heartbroken stuff like 'Jim'. By the end of the record, however, one feels she has made the songs her own in an odd sort of way.

Bob Rockwell (born 1945) TENOR AND SOPRANO SAXOPHONES

(*) **No Rush Steeplechase SCCD 1219
    Rockwell; Butch Lacy (*p*); Jesper Lundgaard (*b*); Jukkis Uotila (*d*). 11/85–2/86.
*** **On The Natch** Steeplechase SCCD 1229
    As above. 87.
*** **The Bob Rockwell Trio** Steeplechase SCCD 1242
    Rockwell; Rufus Reid (*b*); Victor Lewis (*d*). 1/89.
*** **Reconstruction** Steeplechase SCCD 31270
    Rockwell; Joe Locke (*vib*); Rufus Reid (*b*); Victor Lewis (*d*). 3/90.

An American who's relocated to Copenhagen, Rockwell is an assured player who can create exciting music without suggesting a singular vision. He touches on freedom and tonal exploration in the manner of Sonny Rollins – and he seldom goes further than touching – but there's no special adherence to the Rollins sound, or to any slavish worship of Coltrane, though Rockwell's facility (particularly on soprano) again recalls that towering influence. His solos are often about momentum rather than melody, and he can get knotted up in the twists and turns of a theme, but it makes it more interesting to see how he'll extricate himself. Which he usually does. *No Rush* is a composite of various sessions at the Café Montmartre, and the similarly constructed *On The Natch* goes off at the same pitch, although the later session seems slightly more energetic. Aside from a ballad on each disc, the material is all originals by Rockwell and Lacy, and they run into the familiar problem of faceless modal themes, useful enough as lift-off points but not very absorbing for a listener. At its best – on 'Nightrider' from *On The Natch* – the quartet push and challenge one another into a dense and plausible group music, but in isolation the improvising sounds a trifle introverted and uptight.

The two later records give Rockwell a better chance to shine. The trio set has some notably powerful tenor, the leader pacing himself over the long haul with fine assurance and winding up with the feeling that he has more to say yet; Reid and Lewis, two outstanding talents in themselves, add to the lustre. *Reconstruction* brings in the vibes of Joe Locke on a rarely encountered instrumentation, faintly reminiscent of the Milt Jackson–Lucky Thompson sessions of the 1950s, and while the playing here is much more studied in its intensity, all four men avoid meaningless blowing for most of the date.

***(*) **Light Blue** Steeplechase SCCD 31326
    Rockwell; Jesper Lundgaard (*b*). 1–12/92.
*** **Ballads And Cocktails** Olufsen DOCD 5156
    Rockwell; Jan Kaspersen (*p*). 1/92.

Rockwell in dialogue with two Danish homeboys. With Lundgaard, he's amiable, conciliatory: without drums or keyboards the leanness of the sound suggests the interplay of two horns and, with the bassist's wide range yet traditional inflexions, there's a classic feel to the improvising. They start with a rare Parker blues, 'Bird Feathers', stroll on through a neat range of standards and jazz themes, and end on a whipcrack treatment of 'After You've Gone'. Most of the tunes are despatched tightly enough – only 'Sweet Lorraine' ambles up to nearly eight minutes – and the saxophonist's tone warms all the melody lines a treat.

With the mercurial and slightly zany Kaspersen, the music is rather different. There are five originals by the pianist as well as new thoughts on his beloved Monk, and it is really much more his record than Rockwell's, since the saxophonist tends to comment a little distractedly on the galumphing rhythms and blocked-out chords, a Charlie Rouse to Kaspersen's eccentric chief. Engaging, nevertheless.

*** **Born To Be Blue** Steeplechase SCCD 31333
    Rockwell; Andy LaVerne (*p*); Jesper Lundgaard (*b*). 2/93.

Another good one, though a little compromised by material and context. Rockwell has preferred to be in dialogue with pianists rather than drummers of late, and it doesn't always suit him: some of the tracks, notably Charlie Haden's 'The First Song' and 'A Nightingale Sang In Berkeley Square', lumber along a bit and could use some propulsion. But the title-piece is a thoughtful meditation, assertively done, and Monk's 'Bye-Ya' is excellent. The trio do well in close-knit situations and, if Laverne is never as impressive as his reputation, he plays well.

Claudio Roditi (born 1946) TRUMPET, FLUGELHORN, VOCAL

(*) **Gemini Man Milestone M 9158
    Roditi; Daniel Freiberg (*ky*); Roger Kellaway (*p*); Nilson Matta (*b*); Ignacio Berroa, Akira Tana
    (*d*); Rafael Cruz (*perc*). 3/88.
(*) **Slow Fire Milestone M 9175
    Roditi; Jay Ashby (*tb*); Ralph Moore (*ts*); Danilo Perez (*p*); David Finck (*b*); Akira Tana,
    Ignacio Berroa (*d*); Rafael Cruz (*perc*). 89.
Roditi's bright tone and fizzing delivery have served him well in several bands, and these dates of his
own are intermittently exciting. His Brazilian roots turn up in the various samba-derived rhythmic bases
which account for several of the tunes but, like so many of the current wave of Latin-American jazz
musicians, he owes a great stylistic debt to Dizzy Gillespie. Neither date has perhaps quite the final
ounce of weight that would make it outstanding, but the first has Kellaway's astute comping and the
second adds Ashby and Moore to beef up the sound of the band, which otherwise tends to resolve itself
in the percussion section.

** **Two Of Swords** Candid CCD 79504
    Roditi; Jay Ashby (*tb*); Edward Simon, Danilo Perez (*p*); Nilson Matta, David Finck (*b*);
    Duduka Fonseca, Akira Tana (*d*). 9/90.
Not bad, but this is a bit of a potboiler. Roditi splits the session between a 'jazz' and a 'Brazilian' group,
and both perform in much the same direction, although the Brazilian band has Ashby in the front line to
add some tonal colour. Roditi's fat-toned flugelhorn gets a little more exposure than usual but the music
lacks much character. Another CD which doesn't really justify its 72-minute length.

(*) **Milestones Candid CCD 79515
    Roditi; Paquito D'Rivera (*cl, as*); Kenny Barron (*p*); Ray Drummond (*b*); Ben Riley (*d*). 11/90.
An absolutely top-class band with everybody feeling fine and playing hard – yet the results are, as with
the records above, vaguely disappointing. One can't fault the virtuosity of either of the horn players –
D'Rivera, especially, gets off some breathtaking flights on both alto and clarinet – but the final impression is of too many notes and too much said. The jam-session material doesn't assist matters much – the
ballad 'Brussels In The Rain' is the only departure from familiarity – and with playing time at almost 70
minutes it does start to sound like too much of a good thing. The live recording is clear if a little dry.

***(*) **Free Wheelin'** Reservoir RSRCD 136
    Roditi; Andres Boiarsky (*ss, ts*); Nick Brignola (*ss, bs*); Mark Soskin (*p*); Buster Williams (*b*);
    Chip White (*d*). 7/94.
*** **Samba – Manhattan Style** Reservoir RSRCD 139
    Roditi; Jay Ashby (*tb*); Greg Abate (*as*); Andres Boiarsky (*ss, ts*); Helio Alves (*p*); John Lee (*b*);
    Duduka Fonseca (*d*). 5/95.
Roditi doing a tribute to Lee Morgan sounds like a recipe for overcooking it. Yet *Free Wheelin'* comes
close to being exactly the classic album the trumpeter must have in him. This is the best band he's had in
the studio: Boiarsky is a heavyweight, and the rhythm section, especially the inimitable Williams, are
right there with the horns. But it's Roditi's concentration of his own powers that impresses here.
Without trading in any of his fire, he keeps all his solos tight and impeccable, which makes flare-ups like
those on 'Trapped' and 'The Joker' all the more exciting. 'The Sidewinder' follows the original arrangement – in his notes Roditi confesses that he couldn't see any point in messing around with the original
charts – and still sounds entirely different from Morgan's original. Nine of the ten tunes are from
Morgan's own pen, but the new twist on 'A Night In Tunisia' – with trumpet overdubs and a two-
soprano section – is a startling departure. Brignola guests on three and is a welcome visitor. Still slightly
exhausting at 70 minutes, but a good one.
    Samba – Manhattan Style is a notch lower, with a less impressive cast and a more modest programme,
but Roditi again gives notice that he's running into his best form in the studio.

Red Rodney (1927–94) TRUMPET

*** **First Sessions: Volume 3** Prestige PCD 24116
    Rodney; Jimmy Ford (*as*); Phil Raphael (*p*); Phil Leshin (*b*); Phil Brown (*d*). 9/51.
**** **Fiery** Savoy SV 0148
    Rodney; Ira Sullivan (*t, as, ts*); Tommy Flanagan (*p*); Oscar Pettiford (*b*); Philly Joe Jones (*d*).
    11/57.
Rodney was the red-haired Jewish boy in Charlie Parker's happiest band. Though diffident about his
own talents, the young Philadelphian had done his learning up on the stand, playing with the likes of

Jimmy Dorsey while still a teenager. Rodney was perhaps the first white trumpeter to take up the challenge of bebop, which he played with a crackling, slightly nervy quality. It sat well with Parker's, and Rodney was an integral part of Bird's quintet in 1950 and 1951, having first worked with him slightly earlier than that.

Not a prolific recording artist, Rodney's career succumbed from time to time to one of the more common jeopardies of life on the road, but there is some excellent stuff on disc. The early Prestige material dates from Rodney's time in the Parker band, and it has the nervy exuberance you'd expect. Ford is a very average player, and each number seems to mark time when he solos. Rodney's best work, the 1955 *Modern Music From Chicago*, is now available only on vinyl and is increasingly scarce. Ira Sullivan turns up again on *Fiery*, a mostly excellent but slightly patchy set of bop themes and variations on which Rodney works a few signature changes of his own. Sullivan is a remarkable player. From the 1960s he has restricted his field of operations largely to South Florida, where he enjoys legendary status. He and Rodney got together again at the end of the 1970s, but they've never again sounded as good as on these early encounters.

***(*) Bird Lives! Muse 5371
Rodney; Charles McPherson (*as*); Barry Harris (*p*); Sam Jones (*b*); Roy Brooks (*d*). 7/73.
... and, for a moment or two, it's possible to believe that he actually does. McPherson carries the Bird part with the alternate confidence and anxiety of a typecast actor. Here, he sounds perfectly convincing, though his solo structure is often telegraphed several measures ahead (as on 'I'll Remember April' and 'Donna Lee') and there are occasional eccentricities of intonation.

This is an unashamedly nostalgic record, one of the first Rodney made after a long, drug-haunted lay-off in commercial session-work. It came at a time when it was ideologically OK to discuss bebop again, and the trumpeter seems content to butterfly-net the original raptures of the music rather than dig any deeper into it. So far as it goes, that's fine, but it became a manner, and a respectably marketable one, which Rodney wasn't able to set aside. Listening to this and later albums, one always suspects him capable of something more than he wants to deliver. But beautiful.

***(*) Red Giant Steeplechase SCCD 31233
Rodney; Butch Lacy (*p*); Hugo Rasmussen (*b*); Aage Tanggaard (*d*). 4/88.
**(*) No Turn On Red Denon CY 73 149
Rodney; Dick Oatts (*as*); Gary Dial (*p*); Jay Anderson (*b*); Joey Baron (*d*). 8/86.
*** One For Bird Steeplechase SCCD 31238
As above, except John Riley (*d*) replaces Baron. 7/88.
**(*) Red Snapper Steeplechase SCCD 31252
As above.
Nowhere was bebop accorded higher sentimental status than in Scandinavia. House bands and rhythm sections have excellent chops (the same is true of Japanese players) but with a strongly authentic 'feel' as well. Of these 1988 sessions *Red Giant* is undoubtedly the best, with Rasmussen, Tanggaard and the rough-diamond Lacy all contributing substantially. Compare the versions of 'Greensleeves' and a curiously but effectively tempoed 'Giant Steps' with those on *Red Snapper*, which seem merely curious. Steeplechase has long been notorious for indiscriminate and prodigal release of marginally differentiated material. The sessions of 11 and 12 July 1988 have been used for one Bird and one non-Bird release, which may not make absolute artistic sense but may clarify matters for potential purchasers (who should nevertheless be warned that this is no pastiche band but a revisionist and quite challenging outfit with ideas of its own about the bop heritage). The original material on *Red Snapper* and *No Turn On Red* is perhaps more interesting, but there's very little doubt where Rodney's heart lies. At sixty-plus, he sounds chastened but undeterred, and his playing reveals a depth of reference that wasn't there previously.

*** Then And Now Chesky JD 79
Rodney; Chris Potter (*as, ts*); Gary Dial (*p*); Jay Anderson (*b*); Jimmy Madison (*d*). 5/92.
Flugelhorn soaks all the individuality out of Rodney's playing and, were it not for an able and committed young band, this would be little more than an exercise in nostalgic re-creation. The disc also includes an interview, which will be of interest to anyone who follows the trumpeter or the original bebop movement.

Shorty Rogers (1924–94) TRUMPET, FLUGELHORN

**** The Big Shorty Rogers Express RCA 218519
Rogers; Conte Candoli, Pete Candoli, Harry 'Sweets' Edison, Maynard Ferguson, Conrad Gozzo, John Howell (*t*); Harry Betts, John Haliburton, Frank Rosolino (*tb*); Bob Enevoldsen (*vtb*); John Graas (*frhn*); George Roberts (*btb*); Gene Englund, Paul Sarmento (*tba*); Charlie

Mariano (*as*); Art Pepper (*as, ts, bs*); Bill Holman, Jack Montrose (*ts*); Jimmy Giuffre (*ts, bs, cl*); Bob Cooper (*ts, bs*); Lou Levy, Marty Paich (*p*); Curtis Counce, Ralph Pena (*b*); Stan Levey, Shelly Manne (*d*). 53–56.

*** **A Portrait Of Shorty** RCA 2121822
Rogers; Conte Candoli, Don Fagerquist, Conrad Gozzo, Al Porcino (*t*); Harry Betts, Bob Enevoldsen, George Roberts, Frank Rosolino (*tb*); Herb Geller (*as*); Richie Kamuca, Jack Montrose (*ts*); Bill Holman (*ts, bs*); Pepper Adams (*bs*); Lou Levy (*p*); Monty Budwig (*b*); Stan Levey (*d*). 7/57.

***(*) **America The Beautiful** Candid CCD 79510
Rogers; Bud Shank (*as*); Conte Candoli (*t*); Bill Perkins (*bs, ts, ss*); Bob Cooper (*ts*); Pete Jolly (*p*): Monty Budwig (*b*); Lawrence Marable (*d*). 8/91.

Much influenced by the Davis–Mulligan–Lewis *Birth Of The Cool*, and even claiming a revisionist role in the creation of that movement, Shorty Rogers turned its basic instrumentation and lapidary arranging into a vehicle for relaxedly swinging jazz of a high order. *Express* includes all the material from the classic 1953 date, *Cool And Crazy*.

The material on *Express* and *Portrait* is consistently dramatic and varied, though after a while one does begin to wonder whether Rogers's talent isn't being spread a little too thinly. The cover photograph of the former has him sitting on the cow-catcher of a locomotive (Gerry Mulligan could have given us all the technical details) and again there is the suspicion that sheer momentum and steam-power carry these discs forward, a long way past subtlety or the more refined modulations of mood. Rogers himself was never a memorable soloist. His arrangements, though, are among the best of the time. If they lack the gelid precision that Lewis and Mulligan brought to *Birth Of The Cool*, Rogers charts combine the same intricate texture with an altogether looser jazz feel; 'Boar-Jibu' exactly bridges the distance between Giuffre's 'Four Brothers' for Woody Herman and *Birth*.

There is then something of a hiatus. For much of the intervening period, Rogers concentrated on film music. His 1980s comeback found him in strong voice and, alongside Bud Shank, in musically con-ducive company. Shank takes 'Lotus Bud' on alto saxophone rather than alto flute this time. The solo intro is huskily beautiful (with grace-notes and colours that make you wonder who has been listening to whom: Bud Shank or Bobby Watson?), and surpassed only by Bill Perkins's eerily cadenced soprano solo on another Bud's 'Un Poco Loco'.

'Here's That Old Martian Again' continues a series of similar conceits, done in reassuringly un-alien blue rather than green, but with a hint of 'Blue In Green' in the shift across the line. The Lighthouse All Stars play beyond themselves, with big credits to drummer Marable. Recommended.

*** **Yesterday Today And Forever** Concord CCD 4223
Rogers; Bud Shank (*as, f*); George Cables (*p*); Bob Magnusson (*b*); Roy McCurdy (*d*). 6/83.
*** **Eight Brothers** Candid CCD 79521
Rogers; Conte Candoli (*t, flhn*); Bud Shank (*as*); Bill Perkins (*ts, ss, bs*); Bob Cooper (*ts*); Pete Jolly (*p*); Monty Budwig (*b*); Lawrence Marable (*d*). 1/92.

Rogers still doesn't sound a naturally confident player alongside the other Lighthouse chapter members, and his solos on these latter-day recordings sound very much by the numbers. Better, perhaps, to look on both as Bud Shank discs (he shares top billing) and concentrate on his terse expressions instead.

Adrian Rollini (1904–56) BASS SAXOPHONE, GOOFUS, VIBES, KAZOO, PIANO, DRUMS

*** **Bouncin' In Rhythm** Topaz TPZ 1027
Rollini; Wingy Manone (*t, v*); Manny Klein, Dave Klein, Roy Johnson, Chelsea Quealey, Freddy Jenkins (*t*); Bix Beiderbecke, Bobby Hackett, Red Nichols (*c*); Jack Teagarden, Abe Lincoln, Bill Rank, Miff Mole (*tb*); Benny Goodman, Paul Ricci, Pee Wee Russell, Albert Nicholas (*cl*); Jimmy Dorsey (*cl, as, t*); Joe Marsala (*cl, as*); Fud Livingston (*cl, ts*); Don Murray (*cl, bs*); Arthur Rollini, Sam Ruby (*ts*); Putney Dandridge (*p, v*); Howard Smith, Fulton McGrath, Jack Russin, Frank Signorelli, Joe Turner (*p*); Joe Venuti (*vn*); Eddie Lang, George Van Eps, Dick McDonough, Carmen Mastren, Bernard Addison (*g*); Tommy Felline (*bj*); Artie Bernstein, Sid Weiss, Joe Watts (*b*); Vic Berton, Herb Weil, Stan King, Sam Weiss, Chauncey Morehouse (*d*). 10/34–1/38.

There are few instruments which can claim a single performer as their undisputed master, but it's true of the bass saxophone and Adrian Rollini. He played bass and melody lines with equal facility, could move through an ensemble with disarming ease, and never gave the impression that the instrument was anything but light and easy in his hands. Still, it remained a sound rooted in the 1920s, and with the onset of the swing era Rollini found himself more gainfully employed on vibes and – on the last session here, with a Freddy Jenkins group – drums. With the disappearance of an Affinity CD featuring

Rollini's own bands, all that remains is this hotchpotch of sessions with various masters – Beiderbecke, Trumbauer, Venuti and Lang, Mole and Jenkins – plus six from the few sessions under Rollini's leadership. It's a decent sampler of his methods, though any who collect jazz from the 1920s will probably have many of the tracks already. Remastering is cleanly done.

Sonny Rollins (born 1930) TENOR AND SOPRANO SAXOPHONE

(*) Sonny Rollins With The Modern Jazz Quartet Original Jazz Classics OJC 011
   Rollins; Miles Davis, Kenny Drew, John Lewis (*p*); Percy Heath (*b*); Art Blakey, Kenny Clarke, Roy Haynes (*d*). 1/51–10/53.
*** **Moving Out** Original Jazz Classics OJC 058
   Rollins; Kenny Dorham (*t*); Thelonious Monk, Elmo Hope (*p*); Percy Heath, Tommy Potter (*b*); Art Blakey, Art Taylor (*d*). 8–10/54.

Rollins's most important early session is with Miles Davis on *Bags' Groove* (OJC 245). The nine 1951 tracks on OJC 011 are cursory bop singles, and the MJQ – despite the headline billing – appear on only three tracks, in a meeting that took place a second time on an Atlantic album some years later. One track, 'I Know', has the novelty of Miles Davis on piano. *Moving Out* is more substantial, though it still stands as a stereotypical blowing date, even with a single track – 'More Than You Know' – from a session with Monk. The most interesting contributor here is probably Hope, whose off-centre lyricism still turns heads.

***(*) **Work Time** Original Jazz Classics OJC 007
   Rollins; Ray Bryant (*p*); George Morrow (*b*); Max Roach (*d*). 12/55.
***(*) **Sonny Rollins Plus 4** Original Jazz Classics OJC 243
   Rollins; Clifford Brown (*t*); Richie Powell (*p*); George Morrow (*b*); Max Roach (*d*). 3/56.
**** **Tenor Madness** Original Jazz Classics OJC 124
   Rollins; John Coltrane (*ts*); Red Garland (*p*); Paul Chambers (*b*); Philly Joe Jones (*d*). 5/56.
   **** **Saxophone Colossus** Original Jazz Classics OJC 291
   Rollins; Tommy Flanagan (*p*); Doug Watkins (*b*); Max Roach (*d*).
***(*) **Sonny Rollins Plays For Bird** Original Jazz Classics OJC 214
   Rollins; Kenny Dorham (*t*); Wade Legge (*p*); George Morrow (*b*); Max Roach (*d*). 10/56.
**** **Tour De Force** Original Jazz Classics OJC 095
   Rollins; Kenny Drew (*p*); George Morrow (*b*); Max Roach (*d*); Earl Coleman (*v*). 12/56.
*** **Sonny Rollins Volume 1** Blue Note B21Y-81542-2
   Rollins; Donald Byrd (*t*); Wynton Kelly (*p*); Gene Ramey (*b*); Max Roach (*d*). 12/56.

An astounding year's work on record. Rollins was still a new and relatively unheralded star when he was working through this series of sessions, and – in the aftermath of Parker's death – jazz itself had an open throne. There was a vast distance between Rollins and the tenorman who was winning most of the polls of the period, Stan Getz, but though Sonny evaded the open-faced romanticism and woozy melancholy associated with the Lester Young school, he wasn't much of a Parkerite, either. Rollins used the headlong virtuosity of bop to more detached, ironical ends. The opening track on *Work Time* is a blast through 'There's No Business Like Show Business', which prefigures many of his future choices of material. Parker would have smiled, but he'd never have played it this way. Still, Rollins's mastery of the tenor was already complete by this time, with a wide range of tones and half-tones, a confident variation of dynamics, and an ability to phrase with equal strength of line in any part of a solo. If he is often tense, as if in witness to the power of his own creative flow, then the force of the music is multiplied by this tension. The most notable thing about the records is how dependent they are on Rollins himself: Roach aside, whose magnificent drum parts offer a pre-echo of what Elvin Jones would start to develop with John Coltrane, the sidemen are often almost dispensable. It is Rollins who has to be heard.

If *Worktime* is just a little sketchy in parts, that is only in comparison with what follows. *Plus 4* is one of Rollins's happiest sessions. With both horn players in mercurial form, and Roach sensing the greatness of the band he is basically in charge of, the music unfolds at a terrific clip but has a sense of relaxation which the tenorman would seldom approach later in the decade. His own piece, 'Pent-Up House', has an improvisation which sets the stage for some of his next advances: unhurried, thoughtful, he nevertheless plays it with biting immediacy. *Tenor Madness* features Coltrane on, alas, only one track, the title-tune, and it isn't quite the grand encounter one might have wished for: but the rest of the record, with Miles Davis's rhythm section, includes surging Rollins on 'Paul's Pal' and 'The Most Beautiful Girl In The World'. The undisputed masterpiece from this period is *Saxophone Colossus* and, although Rollins plays with brilliant invention throughout these albums, he's at his most consistent on this disc. 'St Thomas', his irresistible calypso melody, appears here for the first time, and there is a ballad of unusual bleakness in 'You Don't Know What Love Is', as well as a rather sardonic walk through 'Moritat' (alias 'Mack

The Knife'). But 'Blue Seven', as analysed in a contemporary piece by Gunther Schuller, became celebrated as a thematic masterpiece, where all the joints and moving parts of a spontaneous improvisation attain the pristine logic of a composition. If the actual performance is much less forbidding than it sounds, thanks in part to the simplicity of the theme, it surely justifies Schuller's acclaim. *Plays For Bird*, though it includes a medley of tunes associated with Parker, is no more Bird-like than the other records, and a reading of 'I've Grown Accustomed To Her Face' establishes Rollins's oddly reluctant penchant for a tender ballad. *Sonny Rollins* ended the year in somewhat more desultory fashion – the session seems to return to more conventional horns-and-rhythm bebop – but *Tour De Force*, recorded two weeks earlier, is almost as good as *Colossus*, with the ferocious abstractions of 'B Swift' and 'B Quick' contrasting with the methodical, almost surgical destruction of 'Sonny Boy'. The OJC reissues are all remastered in splendid sound, even if it's not especially superior to the original vinyl.

***(*) **Way Out West** Original Jazz Classics OJC 337
    Rollins; Ray Brown (*b*); Shelly Manne (*d*). 3/57.
***(*) **Sonny Rollins Vol. 2** Blue Note B21Y-81558-2
    Rollins; J. J. Johnson (*tb*); Horace Silver, Thelonious Monk (*p*); Percy Heath (*b*); Art Blakey (*d*).
    4/57.
***(*) **The Sound Of Sonny** Original Jazz Classics OJC 029
    Rollins; Sonny Clark (*p*); Percy Heath (*b*); Roy Haynes (*d*). 6/57.
**** **Newk's Time** Blue Note B21Y-84001-2
    Rollins; Wynton Kelly (*p*); Doug Watkins (*b*); Philly Joe Jones (*d*). 9/57.
**** **A Night At The Village Vanguard Vol. 1** Blue Note B21Y-7465172
    Rollins; Donald Bailey, Wilbur Ware (*b*); Pete LaRoca, Elvin Jones (*d*). 11/57.
**** **A Night At The Village Vanguard Vol. 2** Blue Note B21Y-7465182
    As above. 11/57.

Rollins continued his astonishing run of records with scarcely a pause for breath. A visit to Los Angeles paired him with Brown and Manne on a session which, if it occasionally dips into a kind of arch cleverness, features some superb interplay between the three men, with Rollins turning 'I'm An Old Cowhand' into a jovial invention. The CD edition includes three alternative takes, which are also available on the *Alternate Takes* album listed below. One of the compelling things about this sequence is the difference in drummer from session to session: Blakey's inimitable pattern of rolls and giant cymbal strokes sounds, for once, a little inappropriate, with Philly Joe Jones using the same kind of drama to far more effect on *Newk's Time*. Jones, still in his formative phase, matches all of Rollins's most imperial gestures, and 'Striver's Row' and 'Sonnymoon For Two' become tenor–drums dialogues which must have directed the drummer towards his later confrontations with Coltrane. The undervalued player here, though, is Haynes, whose playing on *The Sound Of Sonny* is ingeniously poised and crisp. The Blue Note *Vol. 2* finds Rollins a little cramped by his surroundings, but Johnson's sober playing is a far more apposite accompaniment than Byrd's was, its deadpan line a wry rejoinder to the tenor parts. *The Sound Of Sonny* is unexpectedly cursory in its treatment of some of the themes: after the longer disquisitions which Rollins had accustomed himself to making, these three- and four-minute tracks sound bitten off. But the grandeur of Rollins's improvisations on 'Just In Time' and 'Toot-Toot-Tootsie' is compressed rather than reduced, and a solo 'It Could Happen To You', though a little snatched at, celebrates the breadth of his sound. We are somewhat divided on the merits of *Newk's Time* and the *Village Vanguard* sessions. If Rollins is arguably self-absorbed on some of the studio session, the extraordinary motivic development of 'Surrey With The Fringe On Top' is one of his most powerful creations and 'Blues For Philly Joe' takes the work done on 'Blue Seven' a step further. The live material, originally cherry-picked for a single peerless LP, has been stretched across two CDs with a certain diminution of impact, yet the leader is again in rampant form, and working with only bass and drums throughout leads him into areas of freedom which bop never allowed. If Rollins's free-spiritedness is checked by his ruthless self-examination, its rigour makes his music uniquely powerful in jazz. On the two versions of 'Softly As In A Morning Sunrise' or in the muscular exuberance of 'Old Devil Moon', traditional bop-orientated improvising reaches a peak of expressive power and imagination. Overall, these are records which demand a place in any collection. The remastering is mostly fine, although some of the Blue Notes seem a trifle recessed compared with original vinyl.

*** **The Essential Sonny Rollins On Riverside** Riverside FCD-60-020
    Rollins; Kenny Dorham (*t*); Ernie Henry (*as*); Sonny Clark, Thelonious Monk, Hank Jones,
    Wynton Kelly (*p*); Percy Heath, Paul Chambers, Oscar Pettiford (*b*); Max Roach, Roy Haynes
    (*d*); Abbey Lincoln (*v*). 56–58.
**** **The Complete Prestige Recordings** Prestige 4407 7CD
    As appropriate discs above. 51–56.

This best-of scores lower marks only because the original albums are indispensable. But it does include tracks which are otherwise under the leadership of Dorham or Monk. The *Complete Prestige* set, on the other hand, is an abundant feast for those who'd prefer to have the nine original albums compressed to a seven-disc edition.

***(*) **The Freedom Suite** Original Jazz Classics OJC 067
    Rollins; Oscar Pettiford (*b*); Max Roach (*d*). 2/58.
***(*) **The Sound Of Sonny / Freedom Suite** Riverside CDJZD 008
    Rollins; Sonny Clark (*p*); Percy Heath, Paul Chambers, Oscar Pettiford (*b*); Roy Haynes, Max Roach (*d*). 6/57–2/58.
*** **Sonny Rollins And The Contemporary Leaders** Original Jazz Classics OJC 340
    Rollins; Hampton Hawes (*p*); Victor Feldman (*vib*); Barney Kessel (*g*); Leroy Vinnegar (*b*); Shelly Manne (*d*). 10/58.
***(*) **In Sweden 1959** DIW
    Rollins; Henry Grimes (*b*); Pete LaRoca (*d*). 3/59.

Rollins hasn't shown much interest in composition – the early 'Airegin' and 'Oleo' remain in jazz repertory, and that's about all – but his piece 'The Freedom Suite' takes a stab at an extended work, although its simple structure makes it more of a sketch for an improvisation than anything else. The engineers caught his sound with particular immediacy on this date, and it's more a celebration of his tone and dynamic variation than a coherent, programmatic statement (Orrin Keepnews's sleeve-notes seem deliberately to fudge the directness of whatever Rollins was trying to say about black freedom). The (British) Riverside CD usefully couples both *The Freedom Suite* and *The Sound Of Sonny*. Despite a self-conscious clustering of stars for the Contemporary 'Leaders' date, Rollins takes a determined path through one of his most bizarre programmes: 'Rock-A-Bye Your Baby', 'In The Chapel In The Moonlight', 'I've Told Ev'ry Little Star'. Following this, he departed for Europe, where some live recordings have survived. The DIW set is the best, although the studio programme which makes up most of the record isn't quite up to the storming concert recording of 'St Thomas' which opens it. Throughout these records, though, is a feeling that Rollins is coming to the end of a great period, having balanced his own achievements within a straight bop milieu and realized that, as a singular figure, he is remote from the ideas of interplay within a group (and particularly between horns) which almost everyone else in jazz was pursuing.

***(*) **The Quartets** RCA Bluebird ND 85643
    Rollins; Jim Hall (*g*); Bob Cranshaw (*b*); Mickey Roker, Ben Riley, Harry T. Saunders (*d*). 1–5/62.
*** **The Bridge** Bluebird ND 90633
    As above. 62.
*** **On The Outside** RCA Bluebird ND 82496
    Rollins; Don Cherry (*t*); Bob Cranshaw, Henry Grimes (*b*); Billy Higgins (*d*). 7/62–2/63.
*** **All The Things You Are** RCA Bluebird ND 82179
    Rollins; Coleman Hawkins (*ts*); Paul Bley, Herbie Hancock (*p*); Jim Hall (*g*); Bob Cranshaw, Teddy Smith, Ron Carter, David Izenzon, Henry Grimes (*b*); Roy McCurdy, Stu Martin, Mickey Roker (*d*). 7/63–7/64.
***(*) **Alternatives** RCA Bluebird ND 61124
    Rollins; Thad Jones (*c*); Herbie Hancock (*p*); Ron Carter, Bob Cranshaw (*b*); Roy McCurdy (*d*); Candido (*perc*). 5/62–4/64.
***(*) **Sonny Rollins & Co** Bluebird 66530
    As above, except add Jim Hall (*g*), Mickey Roker (*d*), omit Jones and Candido. 64.

The saxophonist disappeared for two years, before returning to the studio for the sessions reissued on *The Quartets*, originally issued on albums called *The Bridge* and *What's New?*. On the face of it, little had changed: though Ornette Coleman's revolution had taken place in the interim, the music sounded much like the old Rollins. But this is his most troubled and troubling period on record. The first track on *The Quartets* is a reading of 'God Bless The Child' which is starkly desolate in feeling; although there are lighter moments in such as a shuffle-beat version of 'If Ever I Would Leave You', Rollins plays with a puzzling melancholy throughout. Hall, though, is an unexpectedly fine partner, moving between rhythm and front-line duties with great aplomb and actually finding ways to communicate with the most lofty of soloists. It's an often compelling record as a result. *The Bridge* has now reappeared in its original form, with the original sleeve art. The meetings with Cherry and Hawkins are much less successful. *On The Outside* was hailed as Rollins's head-on collision with the new thing, as exemplified by Cherry, but hardly anything the two men play bears any relation to the other's music: recorded live, they might as well be on separate stages. On an exhaustively long 'Oleo', the tenorman's pent-up outburst could almost be an expression of rage at the situation. Cherry, peculiarly, sounds like a pre-echo of the older Rollins in his crabby, buzzing solo on 'Doxy'. Three brief studio tracks at the end are a feeble postscript. But the subsequent Paris concert recording suggests a more peaceful co-existence: 'On Green Dolphin Street' and 'Sonnymoon For Two' are rambling, sometimes tortuous workouts that find Cherry in his most lyrical form, while Rollins pushes towards all the barriers he can reach, short of complete abstraction. The concert sound is surprisingly good. The encounter with Hawkins, which takes up half of *All The Things You Are*, is much more respectful, even if Rollins seems to be satirizing the older man at some points, notably in his weirdly trilling solo on 'Yesterdays'. Again, though, there's relatively little real interplay, aside from a beautifully modulated 'Summertime'. The rest of the record consists of quartet sessions with Herbie Hancock: aimless, encumbered by his own genius, Rollins sounds bored with whatever tune he's playing but can't help throwing in the occasional brilliant stroke. It's a fascinating if frustrating experience to hear, and there's more of it on *Alternatives*, which pools a series of fragments and offcuts from the workbench: Rollins plugs through impromptu cadenzas, wrecks some tunes, elevates others, while Hancock and the others gamely try to read what he's doing. For Rollins fanatics only, perhaps, but packed with fascinating moments. *Sonny Rollins & Co* plugs the remaining gaps in these sessions. It includes all of the original *The Standard Sonny Rollins* along with remaining alternative takes and oddments: a brief look at 'Three Little Words' explodes the tune, for instance. A contrasting 'Now's The Time' is elongated into a 16-minute essay where the bruised, broken-up style of the 'new' Rollins takes apart the old bebop blues. As always, a compelling insight into a master's methods.

***(*) **On Impulse!** Impulse! MCA 5655
    Rollins; Ray Bryant (*p*); Walter Booker (*b*); Mickey Roker (*d*). 7/65.
(*) **East Broadway Rundown Impulse! MCA 33120
    Rollins; Freddie Hubbard (*t*); Jimmy Garrison (*b*); Elvin Jones (*d*). 5/66.
Another problem period. 'Three Little Words', from *On Impulse!*, showed that when he had a mind to, Rollins could still outplay any other saxophonist, with a superbly driving and witty development out of the melody. But the inconclusive treatment of the other themes continued to suggest a dissatisfaction. *East Broadway Rundown* is spoilt by the incompatible rhythm section, and the long title-track spends a lot of time going nowhere: only a gnarled 'We Kiss In A Shadow' approaches the real Rollins.

*** **Next Album** Original Jazz Classics OJC 312
    Rollins; George Cables (*p*); Bob Cranshaw (*b*); David Lee (*d*); Arthur Jenkins (*perc*). 7/72.
** **Horn Culture** Original Jazz Classics OJC 314
    Rollins; Walter Davis Jr (*p*); Yoshiaki Masuo (*g*); Bob Cranshaw (*b*); David Lee (*d*); James Mtume (*perc*). 6–7/73.
(*) **The Cutting Edge Original Jazz Classics OJC 468
    Rollins; Rufus Harley (*bagpipes*); Stanley Cowell (*p*); Yoshiaki Masuo (*g*); Bob Cranshaw (*b*); David Lee (*d*); James Mtume (*perc*). 7/74.
** **Nucleus** Original Jazz Classics OJC 620
    Rollins; Raoul De Souza (*tb*); Bennie Maupin (*ts, bcl, lyr*); George Duke (*p*); Bob Cranshaw, Chuck Rainey (*b*); Roy McCurdy, Eddie Moore (*d*); James Mtume (*perc*). 9/75.
*(*) **The Way I Feel** Original Jazz Classics OJC 666
    Rollins; Oscar Brashear, Chuck Findley, Gene Coe (*t*); George Bohannon, Lew McCreary (*tb*); Marilyn Robinson, Alan Robinson (*frhn*); Bill Green (*ss, f, picc*); Patrice Rushen (*ky*); Lee Ritenour (*g*); Don Waldrop (*tba*); Alex Blake, Charles Meeks (*b*); Billy Cobham (*d*); Bill Summers (*perc*). 8–10/76.
(*) **Don't Stop The Carnival Milestone 55005
    Rollins; Donald Byrd (*t, flhn*); Mark Soskin (*p*); Aurell Ray (*g*); Jerry Harris (*b*); Tony Williams (*d*). 4/78.
(*) **Milestone Jazzstars In Concert Milestone 55006
    Rollins; McCoy Tyner (*p*); Ron Carter (*b*); Al Foster (*d*). 9–10/78.
Rollins returned to action with *Next Album*, a very happy album which sounded much more contented than anything he'd recorded in over a decade. 'Playin' In The Yard' and 'The Everywhere Calypso' were taken at a joyous swagger, 'Poinciana' showcased his debut on soprano, and 'Skylark' was the tenor *tour de force* of the record, the saxophonist locking into a persuasively argued cadenza which shook the melody hard. But at root the album lacks the sheer nerve of his early music. This reining-in of his darker side affects all of his 1970s records to some degree. *Horn Culture* makes a more oppressive use of the electric rhythm section, none of whom plays to Rollins's level, and while the two ballads are pleasing, elsewhere the music gets either pointlessly ugly ('Sais') or messy with overdubs and overblowing ('Pictures In The Reflection Of A Golden Horn'). *The Cutting Edge*, recorded at Montreux, is a muddle, with only a lovely reading of 'To A Wild Rose' to save it. *Nucleus* and *The Way I Feel* both court outright disaster. The former has at least some interesting material, and Rollins's very slow path through 'My Reverie' is perversely compelling, but the band have his feet chained, and none of the tracks takes off. The latter, with its dubbed-in horn section, is plain feeble.

    Don't Stop The Carnival has two great set-pieces, a ravishing 'Autumn Nocturne' and a fine display of virtuosity on 'Silver City', but the mismatched band – Williams tends towards extravagance, and Byrd prefigures his astonishing total decline of the 1980s – let him down. The *Jazzstars* live session is another disappointment, with the all-star group playing well but to no special purpose and with nothing to show at the end of the record. The almost sublime frustration of this period was provided by reports of (unrecorded) concerts where Rollins was reputedly playing better than ever.

*** **Love At First Sight** Original Jazz Classics OJC 753
  Rollins; George Duke (*p*); Stanley Clarke (*b*); Al Foster (*d*); Bill Summers (*perc*).
*** **Sunny Days, Starry Nights** Milestone 9122
  Rollins; Clifton Anderson (*tb*); Mark Soskin (*p*); Russel Blake (*b*); Tommy Campbell (*d*). 1/84.

Rollins began the 1980s with a session that intercut some of his old philosophies with supposed modernists like Duke and Clarke, though both are called on to perform in neo-traditional roles. The result is a diffident rather than a genuinely contrary record: not bad, with a nice 'The Very Thought Of You' and a sweet original called 'Little Lu', but the perfunctory retread of the ancient Rollins classic 'Strode Rode' shows up the lightweight cast and situation. *Sunny Days And Starry Nights* features the nucleus of the band he kept for many years, built around Soskin and Anderson. Nobody else is remotely on Rollins's level, and he seems to prefer it that way: certainly his best performances have arisen out of a certain creative isolation. This is another good-humoured date, with the melody of 'I'll See You Again' coming in waves of overdubbed tenor and jolly themes such as 'Kilauea' and 'Mava Mava' tempting the leader out of himself; it's as enjoyable as any of his later records.

***(*) **G Man** Milestone 9150
  Rollins; Clifton Anderson (*tb*); Mark Soskin (*p*); Bob Cranshaw (*b*); Marvin 'Smitty' Smith (*d*). 8/86–4/87.
*** **Dancing In The Dark** Milestone 9155
  As above, except Jerome Harris (*b, g*) replaces Cranshaw. 9/87.
*** **Falling In Love With Jazz** Milestone 9179
  As above, except add Branford Marsalis (*ts*); Tommy Flanagan (*p*); Bob Cranshaw (*b*); Jeff Watts, Jack DeJohnette (*d*); omit Smith. 6–9/89.
*** **Here's To The People** Milestone 9194
  As above, except add Roy Hargrove (*t*), Al Foster (*d*), Steve Jordan (*perc*), omit Marsalis and Flanagan. 91.

The live show which produced the title-track of *G Man* caught Rollins on his most communicative form: it might not be his most profound playing, but the sheer exuberance and tumbling impetus of his improvising sweeps the listener along. *Dancing In The Dark* seems tame in comparison, though the leader plays with plenty of bite: tracks such as 'Just Once', though, seem to have been designed more for radio-play than anything else, and the band's snappy delivery of 'Duke Of Iron' is a well-crafted routine, not a spontaneous flourish. The two studio sessions follow a similar pattern, with the guest horn player on each date doing no more than blowing a few gratuitous notes. *Falling In Love With Jazz* has a quite irresistible version of 'Tennessee Waltz', and there are two Rollins flights through 'Why Was I Born?' and 'I Wish I Knew' on *Here's To The People*, where his tone seems grouchier and less tractable than ever before. Both discs, though, sound excessively studio-bound, suggesting that Rollins could use a change of scene here. In his sixties, though, he is probably content to work at his own whim, which – on the basis of the extraordinary catalogue listed above – he has surely earned.

*** **Old Flames** Milestone MCD-9215-2
  Rollins; Jon Faddis, Byron Sterling (*flhn*); Clifton Anderson (*tb*); Alex Brofsky (*frhn*); Tommy Flanagan (*p*); Bob Stewart (*tba*); Bob Cranshaw (*b*); Jack DeJohnette (*d*). 7–8/93.

This is a sombre record after the sequence of mostly cheerful Milestones that Rollins has delivered in the past 10 years or so. The only upbeat piece is 'Times Slimes', a title directed at corporate greed and its effect on the environment; the major set-pieces, 'I See Your Face Before Me' and Franz Lehár's 'Delia', are wrenchingly slow, tragic laments. Rollins is in magisterial voice, his tone veering between exasperation and wistfulness; but the session still lacks the urgency and incisiveness he once brought to even his most wayward playing. He is a different musician now. Jimmy Heath's stentorian brass charts on two tracks lend a little variation, and Flanagan's thoughtful presence is an unobtrusive bonus.

*** **+ 3** Milestone 9250
  Rollins; Tommy Flanagan, Stephen Scott (*p*); Bob Cranshaw (*b*); Jack DeJohnette, Al Foster (*d*). 8–10/95.

Another strange one. Sonny's tone has never been grainier or more fogbound, he uses repetitions obsessively, cracks some notes as wilfully as Miles Davis, and states a written melody with a seemingly intentional cruelty. The two different rhythm sections – Cranshaw is common to both – adopt a mediatory role, yet both manage to sound relatively faceless, imposing though these players are. Rollins turns 'Cabin In The Sky' into one of his tragic vehicles, complete with roving cadenza, and he defaces 'Mona

Lisa'; but some of these pieces sound merely charmless – especially the two originals, which purport to be funky in an elephantine way. The most enigmatic figure in jazz continues to go his own way.

Aldo Romano (born 1941) DRUMS

***(*) **Non Dimenticar** MLP 518264-2
> Romano; Paolo Fresu (*t*); Franco D'Andrea (*p*); Furio Di Castri (*b*). 2/93.
*** **Prosodie** Verve 526 854
> Romano; Paolo Fresu (*t, flhn*); Stefano Di Battista (*as, ss*); Olivier Ker Ourio (*hca*); Franco D'Andrea (*p*); Jean-Michel Pilc (*p, whistle*); Michel Benita, Furio Di Castri (*b*). 1/95.

This Italian-born musician moved to France in childhood and began his musical career as a guitar player, switching to drums at the end of his teens and playing with a raw insouciance that has reminded some people of Denardo, though without Coleman Jr's relentless beat. Romano's stylistic development has been, by some standards, back to front, beginning with free drumming and only later adopting the more mainstream, time-keeping role that can be sampled on this record, a belated recognition of his gifts by a major label.

The compositions are certainly not mainstream, except in the sense that there is now a recognizable Franco-Italian style in jazz, compounded of bebop elements with a folk strain, dance and formal concert music. 'Nat Eyes' and the pugnacious 'Folk Off' are pretty clear examples, but these are mixed in with less pulse-driven items, including some featuring Romano reciting lyric poems by his wife. The relaxed, insouciant swing that made him such a favourite with players like Enrico Rava and Michel Petrucciani is in evidence throughout.

The slightly earlier *Non Dimenticar* is a dreamily beautiful exploration of ten favourite Italian songs. Lucio Dalla's 'Caruso', done at a wonderful dead-slow tempo, and a gorgeous 'Estate' stand out, with Fresu milking his Miles allegiance to superb effect. D'Andrea sounds in good fettle, and Di Castri and Romano play as if feeling every measure of their homeland's weepy romanticism – but who cares, when it sounds this good?

Furio Romano ALTO SAXOPHONE

*** **Danza Delle Streghe** Splasc(h) H 318-2
> Romano; Rudy Migliardi (*tb, tba*); Donato Scolese (*vib*); Piero Di Rienzo (*b*); Massimo Pintori (*d*). 6/90.
***(*) **Inside Out** Splasc(h) H 362-2
> As above, except Roberto Della Grotta (*b*) replaces Di Rienzo, add Tom Harrell (*t, flhn*). 9/91.

Romano rings many changes on hard bop expectations with his remarkable quintet. The four long tracks straggle through continuously evolving shapes and colours: there are conversations between instruments rather than themes and solos, and when they play 'Goodbye Pork Pie Hat' it only emerges after a fanciful dialogue between alto sax and tuba. Scolese's vibes are a key element, replacing the firm ground of a piano with an allusive shimmer that tends to evade harmonic ties. Rhythmically, Romano also eludes anything very boppish: if anything, Pintori is more inclined to choose a rock-orientated beat, which is certainly what drives 'Ombre Di Luna'. The second record is just as challenging, and is improved with the addition of the versatile Harrell, whose vigorous playing is always tempered by the feeling that fundamentally he's a cool stylist. There's a marvellous revision of Monk's 'Epistrophy', but they don't really get rude enough with another Mingus tune, 'Jelly Roll'. 'Iter', though, begins with a superb discussion between the horns before turning on a boogaloo beat. The leader's own playing is rather spiny and raw at times, but it suits the balance of the music. More intriguing new Italian jazz.

Antoine Roney (born 1961) TENOR SAXOPHONE

*** **Taking Off** Muse MCD5469
> Roney; Wallace Roney (*t*); James Spaulding (*ss, as, f*); Jacky Terrasson (*p*); Dwayne Burno (*b*); Louis Hayes (*d*). 2/92.

The sax-playing Roney brother is a great admirer of Wayne Shorter, and his record could almost pass for one of Shorter's earlier Blue Notes at times: originals like 'Chief Rahab' have a familiar blend of forlorn modality and off-kilter horn unisons. Roney is his own man, but he doesn't pervade the date with anything exceptionally memorable: the last four tracks, which are done as tenor and rhythm alone, make the best impression, with a dead slow treatment of 'Estate' particularly effective, though the oddly moping version of 'Bean And The Boys' is at least an interesting choice.

Wallace Roney (born 1960) TRUMPET

***(*) **Verses** Muse MCD 5335
> Roney; Gary Thomas (*ts*); Mulgrew Miller (*p*); Charnett Moffett (*b*); Tony Williams (*d*). 2/87.

***(*) **Intuition** Muse MCD 5346
> Roney; Kenny Garrett (*as*); Gary Thomas (*ts*); Mulgrew Miller (*p*); Ron Carter (*b*); Cindy Blackman (*d*); collective personnel. 1/88.

*** **The Standard Bearer** Muse MCD 5371
> Roney; Gary Thomas (*ts*); Mulgrew Miller (*p*); Charnett Moffett (*b*); Cindy Blackman (*d*); Steve Berrios (*perc*). 3/89.

**** **Obsession** Muse MCD 5423
> Roney; Gary Thomas (*ts, f*); Donald Brown (*p*); Christian McBride (*b*); Cindy Blackman (*d*). 90.

***(*) **Seth Air** Muse MCD 5441
> Roney; Antoine Roney (*ts*); Jacky Terrasson (*p*); Peter Washington (*b*); Eric Allen (*d*). 9/91.

*** **Misterios** Warner Bros 245641
> Roney; Ravi Coltrane, Antoine Roney (*ts*); Geri Allen (*p*); Gil Goldstein (*ky*); Clarence Seay (*b*); Eric Allen (*d*); Steve Barrios, Steve Thornton, Valtinho Anastacio (*perc*); strings; woodwinds. 93.

Wallace Roney brought a brief touch of edgy subtlety to the Jazz Messengers, a willingness to drift obliquely across and behind the beat which elicited knee-jerk and quite misleading comparisons with Miles Davis. While the open, modal charts and strong, independent rhythm of *Intuition* recall the Davis bands of the early 1960s (Ron Carter confirms the lineage), Roney has a far more dynamic approach to phrasing than His Unpleasantness, recalling Fats Navarro and, at rather slower tempi, Howard McGhee, rather than Miles. Only on 'Willow Weep For Me', arranged for quartet with no reeds, does the comparison really hold. 'Blue In Green' on *Verses* is a clearly stated tribute that almost makes explicit the younger man's point of departure from Miles's influence.

Elsewhere on *Intuition*, Roney lays his deceptively discontinuous statements at an angle to the powerful rhythm section (Cindy Blackman is an impressive simulacrum of Tony Williams, who contributes enormously to the success of *Verses*). The trumpeter sounds particularly good on the generously constructed 'For Duke', where the full sextet sounds like twice the band, an effect co-producers Williams and Michael Cuscuna achieve on the earlier album. 'Intuition' and 'Opus One Point Five' (minus Thomas) sound a little more pinched, with Garrett in acidulous form, keeping his blues tones deliberately flat and elided.

Verses is an album that gets better as it goes along, and it gains immeasurably from repeated hearings. Roney's variations on 'Blue In Green' at the close of the first half are very subtle, and the second side of the original LP is brilliantly constructed, lifting the pace again with Cindy Blackman's 'Topaz', followed by Williams's harmonically subtle 'Lawra', closing with a long blowing blues called 'Slaves', on which Roney produces some of his finest touches.

The (George) Coleman sound-alike Thomas can't match Kenny Garrett's dry, funky delivery, but he is a more impressive performer on other people's albums than he is on his own increasingly funk-derived releases. 'The Way You Look Tonight' and 'Con Alma' on *Standard Bearer* suggest a greater interest in exploring standard material, which Roney develops impressively on *Obsession*. On the earlier album, 'Giant Steps' pushes the quintet into a more demanding format than orthodox hard bop. Thomas sits it out on 'Don't Blame Me' and 'When Your Lover Has Gone' and on the intriguing trumpet plus two percussion of 'Loose'. A fine album, but not up to the thoughtful presence of *Intuition*.

Obsession is the best of the bunch to date, and in some respects the most conventional. Roney seems to have settled for a more direct and expressive approach, reaching back to Navarro's balance of virtuosity and lyricism. The set includes a breakneck version of the bop staple, 'Donna Lee', and a far from creaking version of the overworked 'Alone Together', on which Thomas respectfully emulates Eric Dolphy's flute playing. An impressively mature record from Thomas, who has only just turned thirty.

There's an air of consolidation if not retrenchment about the most recent discs. On neither occasion is brother Antoine Roney up to speed, and on *Seth Air* the rhythm section sounds unusually cautious. All this leaves the leader with a lot to do, and the trumpet seems unusually prominent, even a bit toppy, on some tracks. Maybe in response, he drowns track after track on *Misterios* in superfluous sound, either from the orchestra or from Goldstein's keyboard. It does him no favours and only swamps what sounds like a very adept and professional set.

Room GROUP

*** Hall Of Mirrors Music & Arts 700
> Larry Ochs (*sno, ts*); Chris Brown (*p, elec*); William Winant (*vib, perc*); Scott Gresham-Lancaster (*elec*). 5–8/91.

Room's second album (there is an earlier record for Sound Aspects) offers an ambiguous set of compositions that sound like almost total improvisations. If Ochs is the dominant voice, casting typically intense tenor and sopranino solos over the music, then Brown is the likely Svengali, playing piano like a percussion instrument and introducing samples and keyboard programmes seamlessly into the mix. Gresham-Lancaster also plays somewhere in the shadows: unlike George Lewis or Richard Teitelbaum, he seems to want electronics to simulate natural sounds, or at least to behave 'naturally'. Winant's ghostly vibes and pattering drums complete a chamberish line-up. Two long pieces and two fillers, and it might say something about the looseness of the group that it's the two briefer pieces which sound the most interesting.

Bernt Rosengren (born 1937) TENOR AND ALTO SAXOPHONES, FLUTE, TAROGATO, PIANO

*** Stockholm Dues EMI 792428-2 (Swed.)
> Rosengren; Lalle Svensson (*t*); Claes-Goran Fagerstadt, Lars Sjosten (*p*); Bjorn Alke, Torbjørn Hultcrantz (*b*); Bo Skoglund (*d*); Nannie Porres (*v*). 3–4/65.

**** Notes From Underground EMI 136462-2 (Swed.)
> Rosengren; Maffy Falay (*t, darbuka*); Bertil Strandberg (*tb*); Tommy Koverhult (*ss, ts, f*); Gunnar Bergsten (*bs*); Bobo Stenson (*p*); Torbjørn Hultcrantz, Bjorn Alke (b); Leif Wennerstrom (*d*); Okay Temiz, Bengt Berger (*perc*); Salih Baysal (*v, vn*). 9/73.

*** The Hug Dragon DRCD 211
> Rosengren; Carl Fredrik Orrje (*p*); Anders Ullberg (*g*); Torbjørn Hultcrantz (*b*); Leif Wennerstrom (*d*). 5/92.

***(*) Full Of Life Dragon DRCD 205
> Rosengren; Krister Andersson (*ts, cl*); Goran Lindberg (*p*); Sture Nordin (*b*); Bengt Stark (*d*). 3/91.

***(*) Bent's Jump: Summit Meeting Live At Bent J Dragon DRCD 233
> As above. 7/93.

At last two of Rosengren's earlier records are on CD – though both are Swedish-only issues. He has been a force in Swedish jazz for almost 40 years. *Stockholm Dues* is a decent approximation of a genre hard-bop record but it's let down by the thick, clattery sound and some occasionally scrappy playing; Porres' singing on some tracks is also an uneasily acquired taste. But Rosengren's muscular, assured playing stands out when he takes centre stage, with Svensson a solid partner. There are several tracks added to what was the original LP issue.

Notes From Underground is far superior and stands as an important record of its time. Rosengren varies the tracks from 11 pieces down to quartet, with the members of the Turkish-Swedish group Sevda also on hand – an early example of a jazz-world fusion that retains its potency. The big group plays with enormous gusto on Rosengren's charts, the rhythms roiling underneath, and the points of reference – Coltrane/Sanders and the McCoy Tyner groups of the early '70s – are subsumed in the force of Rosengren's delivery. Crucial is his partnership with Koverhult, now entirely neglected but a tenorman capable of the force and intensity of the leader's own best playing. The Rachmaninoff arrangement which opened the original double-album has been lost, but that means all the music can now be fitted on to a single CD. Splendid remastering, and the title is a somewhat ironic comment on the state of live jazz in Stockholm at the time.

The one recent disc under Rosengren's nominal leadership, *The Hug*, is an agreeable, lightly swinging programme of standards and a few originals which all involved take easily enough, though scrutiny of any passage reveals that nobody's asleep. Rosengren's tone and phrasing are a nice balance of strength and a certain vulnerability, which can sometimes give his solos a dozing quality they don't deserve. He is in more commanding form on the two albums by Summit Meeting. *Full Of Life* is a studio date, while *Bent's Jump* was recorded at the establishment squired by Bent J. Jensen, one of the great jazz-club owners. The live session has an ounce more snap to it, although the sound is somewhat documentary-standard. The music is a sinewy variation on midstream hard bop, and the two saxophonists – neither exactly a pugilist – forge an amicable front line that transcends jam-session clichés.

Ted Rosenthal PIANO

*** **New Tunes New Traditions** Ken 660.56.003
    Rosenthal; Tom Harrell (*t*); Ron Carter (*b*); Billy Higgins (*d*). 10/89.
*** **Images Of Monk** Jazz Alliance TJA-10023
    Rosenthal; Brian Lynch (*t*); Dick Oatts (*ss, as*); Mark Feldman (*vn*); Scott Colley (*b*); Marvin
    'Smitty' Smith (*d*). 12/92.
*** **At Maybeck Recital Hall Vol. 38** Concord CCD 4648
    Rosenthal (*p* solo). 10/94.

Rosenthal, a winner of the Monk Piano Competition in 1988, is very much under Thelonious's spell: the first two albums bed down in Monk repertory. *New Tunes New Traditions* shares the credits equally between Monk and Rosenthal originals: 'Roll Down, Roll On' is a particularly pleasing theme by the pianist, and his 'San Francisco Holiday' is a fine tribute to his mentor, although the perennially over-exposed 'Round Midnight' sounds no better than usual here. Carter and Higgins are their customary marvellous selves, and Harrell has some worthwhile solos. *Images Of Monk* is even more closely tied to the master, basing the material round half a dozen Monk tunes, with the horns and rhythm section otherwise standing tall as a fierce hard-bop outfit. Rosenthal himself suffers a little from the duties of leadership: he imposes only a modest amount of himself on the music. Lynch and Oatts make more impression.

   His turn in the Maybeck spotlight is slightly marred by a tendency to show off. Since he has a go at everything from 'Jesu Joy Of Man's Desiring' to 'You've Got To Be Modernistic', there's no denying the catholicity of his taste, but some of the treatments sound a bit pleased with themselves. His own tunes, where our familiarity is less taken for granted, tend to turn out the best.

Michele Rosewoman (born 1953) PIANO

**** **Quintessence** Enja 5039
    Rosewoman; Steve Coleman (*as*); Greg Osby (*as, ss*); Anthony Cox (*b*); Terri Lyne Carrington
    (*d*). 1/87.
*** **Contrast High** Enja 5091
    Rosewoman; Greg Osby (*as, ss*); Gary Thomas (*ts, f*); Lonnie Plaxico (*b*); Cecil Brooks III (*d*). 7/
    88.
*** **Harvest** Enja 7069
    Rosewoman; Steve Wilson (*as, ss*); Gary Thomas (*ts, f*); Kenny Davis (*b*); Gene Jackson (*d*);
    Eddie Bobe (*perc*). 93.

Like Geri Allen's, Michele Rosewoman's music is deeply marked by an intensive study not just of the jazz tradition in its widest construction but of a huge range of other musics. Though she now rarely plays in a straightforward 'Latin' context, the propulsive rhythms of Caribbean – and particularly Cuban – music are always evident, almost casually intermingled with an angular approach synthesized from Monk and Cecil Taylor. Less fêted than either Allen or Marilyn Crispell, she is a player and composer of consummate skill.

   Quintessence is the better of the first two albums and the more representative of the range of her skills. The opening 'For Now And Forever' has a stop-start theme which is momentarily reminiscent of the early-1970s Ornette Coleman. 'Lyons', a twin-alto tribute to the late Jimmy Lyons, is cast in a robust late-bop mode that paves the way for the more adventurous Taylorisms of 'Springular And Springle'; after that, the ironic ballad, 'The Thrill-of-Real-Love', comes as rather less of a shock. Osby sounds better with Coleman than with the occasionally wayward Gary Thomas on *Contrast High*, and the *Quintessence* rhythm section is much better attuned to Rosewoman's unpredictable metre.

   The later album swings with all of Rosewoman's characteristic exuberance but sounds more of an artefact, a great deal less adventurous and dangerous. *Quintessence* communicates the kind of imaginative range and adaptability she shares with Geri Allen and which has allowed her to work successfully in almost every setting, from conventional piano trio up to the New Yoruba big band, which she leads. One of the best jazz albums of the late 1980s.

   The strong African component on 'Warriors', the major statement on *Harvest*, leads one to suppose that Rosewoman desires deeper roots and a broader alternative to the jazz language she has inherited. On this most recent album she sounds both poised and uncertain, confident in her new language and prepared to take the forward step that will yield a new configuration of language.

Renée Rosnes (born 1962) PIANO, KEYBOARDS

*** **Without Words** Blue Note 798168-2
>   Rosnes; Buster Williams (*b*); Billy Drummond (*d*). 1/92.
*** **Ancestors** Blue Note 834634-2
>   Rosnes; Nicholas Payton (*t*); Chris Potter (*ss, ts, af*); Peter Washington (*b*); Al Foster (*d*); Don
>   Alias (*perc*). 10/95.

Rosnes is a Canadian who came to early attention in Joe Henderson's touring group. She has a sensitive touch and her classical background persuades her into offering hints of some study-composers in her voicings, and she can swing very hard, too. Two earlier Blue Notes have gone. *Without Words* is bedecked with string arrangements by Robert Freedman, which seems to be an attempt to make this music more palatable; in spite of that, it works out as Rosnes's most personal record. The orchestral backdrop is distracting, but against that the pianist offers some of her most intense and imaginative playing: the variations on 'You And The Night And The Music' and 'Estate' are reminiscent of McCoy Tyner's full-blooded romanticism. *Ancestors* is a fine follow-up, although with two such powerful horn players in the front line it's sometimes difficult for Rosnes to assert herself. Five original pieces have an inquiring and quite tough edge to them, and her version of Alec Wilder's 'The Sounds Around The House' has a radiant lyricism about it. If this is less immediately identifiable as a Rosnes record, it's still excellent jazz.

Frank Rosolino (1926–78) TROMBONE

*** **Swing . . . Nor Spring!** Savoy SV 0188
>   Rosolino; Barry Harris (*p*); Billy Christ (*b*); Stan Levey (*d*). 9/52.
**** **Free For All** Original Jazz Classics OJC 1763
>   Rosolino; Harold Land (*ts*); Victor Feldman (*p*); Leroy Vinnegar (*b*); Stan Levey (*d*).

Coming of age in Gene Krupa's post-war band, Rosolino developed a style that seemed to combine elements of bop harmony with the more durable virtues of swing. A wonderfully agile player with a tone that could be broad and humane, almost vocalized one moment, thinly abstract the next, Rosolino brings a twist of humour to almost everything he plays. The Savoy compilation (it also includes Terry Gibbs and Billy Mitchell tracks) catches him at his most ebullient, carving a path through 'Take Me Out To The Ballgame' and giving 'Sweet And Lovely' a glorious bounce. The OJC rounds out a fine session done for the Speciality label with some valuable alternative takes ('There Is No Greater Love', 'Chrisdee' and 'Don't Take Your Love From Me') and some great performances from the band that belie the undisciplined mood suggested by the title. Rosolino's end could hardly have been grimmer or more bitterly ironic for a man who had played on a record called *The Most Happy Fella*. In the autumn of 1978, suffering from depression, he murdered his children then took his own life.

Billy Ross TENOR, ALTO AND SOPRANO SAXOPHONES, CLARINET

(*) **The Sound Milestone MCD-9227-2
>   Ross; Roger Ingram (*t*); Dana Teboe (*tb*); Nick Brignola (*bs*); Mike Levine (*p*); Don Coffman
>   (*b*); Duffy Jackson, Archie Pena (*d*); Nelson Pedron (*perc*); Wendy Peterson (*v*). 6/94.

Conceived as a tribute to Stan Getz, this struggles to come to life. Ross is an able and sincere player, but he can't do much more than try and emulate Getz's high cry – quite effective on the title-track, but earthbound elsewhere. There is a redundant xeroxing of 'Four Brothers', with Ross overdubbing all but the baritone part, and when they get to the clip-clop rhythm of 'My Old Flame' it sounds more like Getz's fusion phase than anything. A few other nice spots, but otherwise a less than distinguished return for producer Bob Weinstock, back in the studios after a 35-year break.

Ned Rothenberg ALTO SAXOPHONE, BASS CLARINET, SHAKUHACHI

***(*) **Overlays** Moers CD 02074
>   Rothenberg; Thomas Chapin (*as*); Jerome Harris (*b, g*); Kermit Driscoll (*b*); Billy Martin (*d*);
>   Adam Rudolph (*perc*). 5/91.
**** **The Crux: Selected Solo Wind Works (1989–1992)** Leo CD LR 187
>   Rothenberg. 12/91, 6 & 8/92.

A member of the 29th Street Saxophone Quartet and of the advanced ensemble New Winds, Rothenberg is a player of incomparable technical range. The Double Band, which features on *Overlays*, is an interesting experiment, demonstrating Rothenberg's Ornette- and possibly M-Base-derived interest in using the saxophone not just as a melodic instrument but also as a rhythmic generator. The twinned line-up may most immediately recall Ornette's *Free Jazz* experiment but, in terms of sheer impact, it is surely far closer to the more recent Prime Time. It's a formula that allows individual players to express their creativity within a quite tightly controlled structure, and repeated listenings betray what may not at first be obvious: the sheer density of musical detail. *Overlays* is a marvellous record, but it demands patience.

The Crux is not the first solo record Rothenberg has released. During the 1980s unaccompanied performance became what he himself calls 'home base', the *crux* at which he reassessed both technique and philosophy. His alto saxophone playing – particularly unaccompanied – bears some comparison with Anthony Braxton's, but is much more precise in articulation, just as its content is rather more diffuse. By the same token, his solo bass clarinet performances have to be compared to Eric Dolphy's, and much the same judgements apply. At the centre of this recital is a meditative piece for shakuhachi, an instrument on which linear development is rather difficult, and sound colours, which vary with the pitches, are of paramount importance. Beautiful as it is, the significance of 'Do Omoi' lies in the extent to which these factors have influenced Rothenberg's saxophone work. The long closing item, 'Sokaku Reibo', is performed on alto and strongly suggests new approaches to the instrument.

In sharp contrast, 'Maceo' is dedicated to soul singer James Brown's longstanding partner and is as brief and punchy as 'Sokaku Reibo' (which means 'the cranes in their nest') is ethereal and impressionistic. The most jazz-orientated of the pieces is 'Epistrophical Notions', dedicated to Thelonious Monk and clearly inspired by his deliberately lumpish harmonies and spasmodic rhythms.

This is a fine record that should be pursued by anyone interested in contemporary saxophone playing and related disciplines.

Charlie Rouse (1924–88) TENOR SAXOPHONE

***(*) **Takin' Care Of Business** Original Jazz Classics OJC 491
    Rouse; Blue Mitchell (*t*); Walter Bishop (*p*); Earl May (*b*); Art Taylor (*d*). 5/60.
*** **Two Is One** Strata East 660.51.012
    Rouse; George Davis, Paul Metzke (*g*); Calo Scott (*clo*); Stanley Clarke, Martin Rivera (*b*); David Lee (*d*); Airto Moreira, Azzedin Weston (*perc*). 74.
**** **Epistrophy** Landmark 1521
    Rouse; Don Cherry (*t*); George Cables (*p*); Buddy Montgomery (*vib*); Jeff Chambers (*b*); Ralph Penland (*d*); Jessica Williams (*v*). 10/88.

Rouse always played saxophone as if he had a cold in the head. There were those who questioned whether his slightly adenoidal, wuffling tone was ever appropriate to Thelonious Monk's music. However, Rouse became one of Monk's most loyal and stalwart supporters, and an essential part of some of Monk's finest quartet recordings. Rouse also carried the banner posthumously in his band, Sphere, and in such tribute recordings as the not entirely successful *Epistrophy*, recorded just a month before his death.

Two Is One is a pretty startling performance, and most listeners would be hard pressed to identify the source. Using two guitars and the pungent timbre of Calo Scott's cello, Rouse creates a most unusual background for solos that are weighted differently and contain fewer overt bebop references. It's a difficult performance to locate within Rouse's overall output, but there is no denying its effectiveness.

Even without undue hindsight, *Epistrophy* sounds like a final throw. He runs through the songbook – 'Nutty', 'Ruby, My Dear', 'Blue Monk', 'Round Midnight', 'Epistrophy' and (a CD bonus) 'In Walked Bud' – with magisterial calm; much of the interest comes from the still-undiscovered Jessica Williams, a fine piano player and singer, and from Buddy Montgomery's spiky vibes. Rouse invests each of the numbers with the kind of rhythmic slant that is inalienably bound up with Monk's legacy. 'Pretty Strange', 'Weirdo' and 'Upptankt' on *Takin' Care Of Business* show how well Rouse anticipated Monk's approach and appreciated the level of resistance to it. A communicator rather than a pioneer, he must have found it strange and galling to be pushed out of view with the rest of the 'avant-garde'. On the strength of each of these, Rouse was 'in the tradition', centrally and majestically.

ROVA GROUP

*** **Saxophone Diplomacy** hat Art CD 6068
    Larry Ochs, Bruce Ackley, Andrew Voight, Jon Raskin (*reeds*). 6/83.

ROVA's first five albums were cut over a period of 12 months, but all are currently missing in action. Along with the World Saxophone Quartet, they pioneered the all-sax ensemble as a regular and conceptually wide-ranging unit. Whereas WSQ were more concerned with updating the swinging vitality of the big-band sax section, though, ROVA sought out remoter climes, specifically building on the discoveries of the Chicago avant-garde and claiming such composer-performers as Steve Lacy and Roscoe Mitchell as major influences. Their work can be rather hard-going: deliberately eschewing conventional notions about swing, prodding at the boundaries of sound and space, their records are notebooks which frequently throw up as many failures as successes. Their 1983 tour of the Soviet Union resulted in this concert set, easily the most vivid evidence of their work up to that point. It includes two of their Steve Lacy arrangements, an extended revision of 'Flamingo Horizons' from the Moers album, and one long piece – 'Paint Another Take Of The Shootpop' – which personifies their virtues, starting with a methodically intense tenor solo by Ochs and marching into a complex development from there. The section on the original vinyl release which also featured two Russian musicians has been omitted from the CD issue. The concert recordings are of mixed quality, but there are no distracting shortcomings.

*** **Favourite Street** Black Saint 120076-2
    As above. 11/83.
***(*) **Beat Kennel** Black Saint 120176-2
    As above. 4/87.

Steve Lacy has been belatedly recognized as a major patrician influence on a wide spectrum of modern players, and ROVA's homage to him on *Favourite Street* pays overdue tribute. The bony rigour of Lacy's themes focuses ROVA's meandering, no matter how adventurous their earlier trips had been: Lacy's music is a good way to clear the head of distractions, either as listener or as performer, and in their thoughtful elaborations on seven favourite themes they clear away some of the more baroque elements of their work. The subsequent *Beat Kennel* appears to build on this: in 'The Aggregate' and 'Sportspeak', their assured rhythms and tone-colours pull them closer to a jazz tradition, and in their vibrant reading of a Braxton composition (superior to anything on their disappointing collaboration with the saxophonist himself, listed under Braxton's name) they create distinctive jazz repertory. It's the best record they've made so far.

*** **Long On Logic** Sound Aspects SAS CD 037
    As above, except Steve Adams (*reeds*) replaces Voight. 3/89.
*** **For The Bureau Of Both** Black Saint 120135-2
    As above. 2–9/92.

Steve Adams has replaced Andrew Voight, but otherwise ROVA's universe remains constant: a teeming cosmos of saxophone sounds. It's still a sometimes unfriendly place, and these two programmes offer little respite: the Sound Aspects session starts with tunes by Fred Frith and Henry Kaiser, but the four originals by members of the group are the most concentrated offerings, hard and effortful exercises in saxophone oratory. *For The Bureau Of Both* is a shade lighter, with pieces like 'Streak' taking off from energetic riffs, but again one feels that their hearts are more involved in an epic work like the 18-minute 'The Floater'.

***(*) **The Works Vol. 1** Soul Note 120176-2
    As above.

Their best? Close to it, certainly. Like any group of long-standing experience, ROVA know themselves well enough by now to discover new things in old chapters. There are just three compositions here, each a lengthy exploration, and each concerned with both minutiae – of timbre, tempo, texture – and long-form considerations, such as the progressive weight of a piece, its sustainable intensities and its capacity to decay. Ochs's 'When The Nation Was Sound' is both one of their most ambitious and most approachable pieces, while the themes by Jack DeJohnette and John Carter are exemplary pieces of repertory and revisionism, ROVA-style. A good one.

Jimmy Rowles (1918–96) PIANO, VOCAL

**** **The Peacocks** Columbia 475697-2
    Rowles; Stan Getz (*ts*); Buster Williams (*b*); Elvin Jones (*d*); Jon Hendricks, Judy Hendricks, Michele Hendricks, Beverly Getz (*v*).
*** **Profile** Columbia 474556-2
    Rowles; Michael Moore (*b*). 6/81.

His vast experience with both big bands and vocalists gave Rowles a matchless repertoire of songs, and since the early 1970s he appeared as a significant figure in his own right. A number of albums have disappeared from print, including his early sessions as a leader from the 1950s, but those still available provide a fine portrait of this humorous, profound musician. *The Peacocks* was billed as a 'Stan Getz presents' album, but the pianist is the mastermind behind it: there is the definitive version of his lovely tune, 'The Peacocks', itself, a series of duets with Getz and trios with Elvin Jones added, which all work beautifully, a somewhat unlikely version of Wayne Shorter's 'The Chess Players' where Hendricks and family chime in, and a final stroll through 'Would You Like To Take A Walk' by Jimmy alone at the piano. French in spirit, but actually cut in New York, the album with Michael Moore is a ruminative amble through nine pieces by Henry Renaud – a little under-characterized, perhaps, as if the music wasn't too familiar to the players, but delightful anyway.

** **Looking Back** Delos DE 4009
> Rowles; Stacy Rowles (*t, flhn, v*); Eric Von Essen (*b*); Donald Bailey (*d*). 6/88.
*** **Sometimes I'm Happy, Sometimes I'm Blue** Orange Blue 003
> Rowles; Harry 'Sweets' Edison (*t*); Stacy Rowles (*t, flhn*); Ray Brown (*b*); Donald Bailey (*d*); Clementine (*v*). 6/88.
*** **Trio** Capri 74009
> Rowles; Red Mitchell (*b*); Donald Bailey (*d*). 8/89.
*** **Remember When** Mastermix CHECD 11
> Rowles; Eric Von Essen (*b*). 89.
*** **Lilac Time** Koko 1297
> As above. 4/94.

Rowles recorded through the 1980s and, while none of these records is less than good, it must be said that the energy level on some of them is occasionally negligible. The pianist's talent for reordering tunes and imparting felicities hadn't diminished, but he took things much easier. His trumpet-playing daughter, Stacy, takes a useful guest-role on some sessions, playing agreeable solos which recall a more boppish Harry 'Sweets' Edison, whose own appearance on the Orange Blue CD underlines the comparison, although the two never play together. The Delos record is sluggish, the players becoming so ruminative that the music slows to a tepid pace. But *Trio* restores some of the impishness which is an essential in Rowles's best music, as he investigates such hoary themes as 'Dreamer's Lullaby' and 'You People Need Music'. Red Mitchell, who plays on three of the above sessions, was a favourite companion, and his voluminous sound is a wry partner for Rowles's particular tale-spinning; Bailey, though, is less in tune and occasionally sounds indifferent to the conversation.

Remember When has some delightful music. The forgotten gem this time is 'Just Like A Butterfly'; the voice comes out on 'Looking Back', and there is a version of Carl Perkins's 'Grooveyard' which is an object-lesson in swinging at a slow tempo. It's mostly just Jimmy browsing through some old memories, and making them worth remembering. Despite indifferent health, he continued to play into the 1990s, and *Lilac Time* is a typical Rowles date: gentle, reflective, with a little iron running through it and a nostalgic's taste for buried treasure.

Gonzalo Rubalcaba (born 1963) PIANO, KEYBOARDS

(*) **Live In Havana Messidor 15960
> Rubalcaba; Lazaro Cruz (*t, flhn*); Rafael Carrasco (*ts, f*); Manuel Varela (*ts*); Felipe Cabrera (*b*); Horacio Hernandez (*d*). 2/86.
** **Mi Gran Pasion** Messidor 15999-2
> As above, except add Roberto Vizcaino (*perc*). 7/87.
** **Giraldilla** Messidor 15801-2
> Rubalcaba; Reynaldo Melian (*t*); Mario Garcia (*g*); Felipe Cabrera (*b*); Horacio Hernandez (*d*); Roberto Vizcaino (*perc*). 89.
(*) **Discovery: Live At Montreux Blue Note 795478-2
> Rubalcaba; Charlie Haden (*b*); Paul Motian (*d*). 7/90.
**** **The Blessing** Blue Note 797197-2
> As above, except Jack DeJohnette (*d*) replaces Motian. 5/91.
***(*) **Suite 4 Y 20** Blue Note 780054-2
> Rubalcaba; Reynaldo Melian (*t*); Felipe Cabrera, Charlie Haden (*b*); Julio Barreto (*d*). 5/92.
(*) **Rapsodia Blue Note 828264-2
> As above, except omit Haden. 11/92.
*** **Diz** Blue Note 830490-2
> Rubalcaba; Ron Carter (*b*); Julio Barreto (*d*). 12/93.

Rubalcaba is the most recent and perhaps the most singular of those Cuban musicians who have made an impact on the American jazz scene of late. While he plays with as much grandstanding power as his countrymen, there is also a compensating lightness of touch which one sometimes misses in the perpetually ebullient tone of most Cuban jazz. It's not very apparent on the three Messidor records, most of which mix Latin-jazz ebullience with fusion gymnastics to dispiriting effect: a solitary solo, 'Cuatro

Veinte', on *Mi Gran Pasion*, tells of better things. *Discovery*, a record of his sensational debut appearance at the Montreux Festival of 1990, suffers from an excess of tumult which finally makes the record wearisome, impressively played though it all is. From the first terrifically overheated workout on Monk's 'Well You Needn't', it sounds as if Rubalcaba is out to impress at any cost, and Motian and Haden can only anchor him as best they can. Much exhilaration, but not a record to play often.

The subsequent studio record, *The Blessing*, is a huge step forward. The pianist rations his outbursts to a handful and instead negotiates a thoughtful but no less compelling way through a delightful programme: Haden's 'Sandino' emerges with just the right note of troubled dignity, 'Giant Steps' is reharmonized and made new through brilliant use of repetition, DeJohnette's charming 'Silver Hollow' rivals the composer's own version, and 'The Blessing' and 'Blue In Green' remodel Coleman and Evans. Best of all, perhaps, is a beautifully chiselled treatment of 'Besame Mucho' which eliminates all sense of kitsch that the tune may possess, suggesting instead a flinty sort of romanticism. Rubalcaba's touch and finesse are marvellous throughout, and DeJohnette is clearly the ideal drummer for the situation, his unassuming virtuosity meeting all the challenges head on.

Suite 4 Y 20 reunites Rubalcaba with his Cuban group, and the results are fine: on a fundamentally reflective record it's the restraint which is most effective. Haden performs on five tracks, earthing the pulse with just the right amount of sobriety, but Rubalcaba also finds a lovely lyricism on McCartney's 'Here There And Everywhere', while Melian plays with a degree of resilience beyond the usual firecracker clichés. *Rapsodia*, though, plunges all back into the fusion carnival, with most of the music wildly overpowering (Rubalcaba adds some electric keyboards on this one). The speed-freak treatment of 'Moose The Mooche' is as preposterous as the preceding 'Santo Canto' is charming. An unpredictable artist.

Diz is his 'pure' bebop album, nine themes from the heartland of the repertory done partly as a tribute to Dizzy Gillespie. Appropriately enough, perhaps, it is not much like any traditional bebop record, infused with suggestions of Latin polyrhythms even when those rhythms aren't always directly stated. The dark colours of, say, 'Bouncing With Bud' are the elements which dominate. Yet this is all too knowing a record: Carter's elegant lines work well, but Barreto's drumming is aggravatingly ingenious, and it spurs the pianist on to some pointlessly clever improvising. For all his dazzle, Rubalcaba can be hard to warm to.

Roy Rubenstein TROMBONE

*** **Shout 'Em!** Delmark DE-227
    Rubenstein; Bob Nabors (*c*); Norrie Cox (*cl*); Jack Kuncl (*bj*); Dick Pierre (*b*); Ken Lowenstine
    (*d*); Katherine Davis (*v*). 12/93–1/94.
Somehow this expatriate English 'bone man has ended up leading his Chicago Hot 6 on that city's most eminent local label. Traditional music played without a trace of selfconsciousness, though not necessarily the better for it: the dynamic is unvaryingly even and some of the tempos are a bit too gentlemanly. 'Shout 'Em Aunt Tillie', a choice piece of early Ellington, gets a splendid treatment, and 'Pontchartrain Blues' counts as rarely-heard Jelly Roll Morton. Katherine Davis sings on four numbers and her surprisingly small, intimate voice suits the situation. Excellent recording.

Roswell Rudd (born 1935) TROMBONE

***(*) **Regeneration** Soul Note 121054
    Rudd; Steve Lacy (*ss*); Misha Mengelberg (*p*); Kent Carter (*b*); Han Bennink (*d*). 6/82.
It's been a matter of intense frustration that Rudd has made so few records since his work with the New York Art Quartet and Archie Shepp in the 1960s announced a marvellously vivid and unpredictable spirit in the new jazz of the period. Rudd, like Ayler, suggested a return to primordial jazz roots while remaining entirely modern. His trombone style recalled the more expressionist methods of an earlier age – slurs and growls, blustering swing, a big, sultry tone – while remaining aware of the technical sophistry of the few boppers who'd taken to the horn. Yet he has led fewer than ten albums over a long, interrupted career.

This one, at least, is very satisfying although, for a demonstration of Rudd's latter-day style, Enrico Rava's *Quartet* album for ECM is a more comprehensive example. *Regeneration* is a tribute to the pianist-composer Herbie Nichols, whom Rudd worked with in the early 1960s. The trombonist has campaigned against Nichols's neglect ever since; and with the similarly inclined Lacy – who also once worked with Rudd, in a band which played only Thelonious Monk tunes – he devised a tribute programme which includes three pieces by each composer. The Nichols tunes are the most absorbing, if only because they're much less familiar than 'Monk's Mood', 'Friday The 13th' and 'Epistrophy'.

Adam Rudolph PERCUSSION, OTHER INSTRUMENTS

** Skyway Soul Note 121269
>   Rudolph; Ralph Jones (*ts, ss, f, af, bcl*); Kevin Eubanks (*g*); Susan Allen (*hp, kayagum*); Jihad Racy (*f, oud, vn*). 3/94.

Very, *very* Californian. There's no mistaking Rudolph's talent or his dedication to the music, but *Dancing To The Skyway* is far too personal in focus to make much sense to any but the most dedicated listener. Actually finding the enthusiasm to give this music the attention it probably deserves may also prove to be a problem. Rudolph deploys a battery of ethnic percussion, overtone flute, kalimba and voice; his wife Hanna provides recitations; Racy wibbles away to himself, as do Jones and Allen; and Eubanks freaks out, albeit more quietly than usual. Not much to report on the jazz front, and only rather occasional signs that the whole thing was ever thought through properly.

Hilton Ruiz (born 1952) PIANO

**** Piano Man Steeplechase SCCD 31036
>   Ruiz; Buster Williams (*b*); Billy Higgins (*d*). 7/75.
*** New York Hilton Steeplechase SCCD 31094
>   Ruiz; Hakim Jamil, Steve Solder (*d*). 2/77.
*** Strut Novus PD 83053
>   Ruiz; Lew Soloff (*t*); Dick Griffin (*tb*); Sam Rivers (*ts, ss*); Rodney Jones (*g*); Francisco Centeno (*b*); Robert Ameen (*d, perc*); Steve Berrios, Mongo Santamaria (*perc*). 11 & 12/88.
*** Doin' It Right Novus PD 83085
>   Ruiz; Don Cherry (*t*); Jimmy Ronson, Ruben Rodriguez (*b*); Steve Berrios (*d, perc*); Daniel Ponce (*perc*). 11/89.
**** A Moment's Notice Novus PD 83123
>   Ruiz; George Coleman (*ts*); Kenny Garrett (*as*); Dave Valentin (*f*); Andy Gonzalez, Joe Santiago (*b*); Steve Berrios (*d, perc*); Endel Dweno, Daniel Ponce (*perc*). 2 & 3/91.
*** Manhattan Mambo Telarc Digital CD 83322
>   Ruiz; Charlie Sepulveda (*t*); Papo Vazquez (*tb*); David Sanchez (*ts, perc*); Andy Gonzalez (*b, bell*); Ignacio Berroa (*d, perc*); Joe Gonzalez, Manuel Giovanni Hidalgo (*perc*). 4/92.
*** Live At Birdland Candid CCD 79532
>   Ruiz; David Sanchez, Peter Brainin (*ts*); Andy Gonzalez (*b*); Steve Berrios (*d*); Giovanni Hidalgo (*perc*). 6/92.

Ruiz's desire to give jazz a Latin accent runs a little deeper than the usual South-of-the-Border trimmings. Born in Puerto Rico, he has a profound understanding of an impressive range of popular forms – samba, *soca, clave* – and makes them an integral element in his writing and reworking of standards and classics. *Piano Man* is perhaps Ruiz's best album; it's certainly his most impressive group, with Williams's singing bass and Higgins's tuneful drums complementing his own two-handed style. 'Straight Street' and 'Giant Steps' are the most ambitious (and successful) tracks. Strongly recommended.

There is a bit of a hiatus in the middle of the story here, because Ruiz's generally good if understated recordings for Steeplechase are not available on CD. Ruiz's attempt to Latinize the standards repertoire picked up again in the later 1980s with renewed confidence. 'Lush Life' has long been susceptible to Latin readings, but the version on *Strut* is more convincing and integral than most. The *soca*-flavoured 'Serenade' is slightly wishy-washy, but 'The Sidewinder' has some of the bite one associates with Ruiz's better work. Top-ranking talent in the brass, reeds and percussion, and a convincing fusion exercise all told.

More self-consciously eclectic (as Cherry's brief presence may indicate) than either its predecessors or successors, *Doin' It Right* is a more demanding package than most of Ruiz's 1980s recordings. Beautifully recorded and balanced, its immediate accessibility peels away to reveal a well-structured exploration of post-Bud piano styles. Shedding his occasional dips into modal blandness, Ruiz plays with considerable fire at the far right of the keyboard. 'Stella By Starlight' conjures up one of his most evocative and technically impressive solos, and the other material – 'The Blessing', 'Scottish Blues', 'I Didn't Know What Time It Was' foremost – is expertly sequenced with something close to Ahmad Jamal's genius for putting together a coherent and emotionally satisfying set. Somehow it's the *feel* of the group as a whole that lets this one down.

A Moment's Notice is a superb set that takes in Coltrane, Kenny Dorham's 'Una Mas' and Jimmy Van Heusen's 'Like Someone In Love'. The concluding 'Naima' sounds slightly odd over the neurotic voodoo percussion, but the romantic urgency of Kenny Garrett's fine solo is focused rather than blunted by it; turning the spotlight on the alto helps re-centre the piece. 'Moment's Notice' is more readily re-cast in Ruiz's now familiar mode, but the two horns find less to say. 'Jose' is a generous but questionable solo feature for bassist Joe Santiago. Forgivable at less than a minute and a half, and perfectly OK in a club or concert context, it seems rather out of place here, interrupting a finely judged and flowing set that shows Ruiz at the height of his considerable powers.

What the band on *Live At Birdland* cries out for is a brass player to replace one of the two rather anonymous saxophones. They are really effective only on the last two tunes, 'On Green Dolphin Street' and Wayne Shorter's 'Footprints'. Even the specially written 'Blues For Two Tenors' doesn't have much punch. Ruiz himself is playing very well, with lots of fire, and the recording is very expertly balanced.

Gosta Rundqvist PIANO

*** **Until We Have Faces** Sittel SITCD 9212
Rundqvist; Krister Andersson (*ts*); Sture Akerberg, Yasuhito Mori (*b*); Peter Ostlund (*d*). 5/94.
Rundqvist's playing is a gracious synthesis of modern styles – Evans, Jarrett, Corea – touched by a vein of introspection that sounds like his own, best heard here on his pensive original 'Northern Light', done as a piano solo. The long programme is divided between solos, duo with bass, trios and the rhythm section with Andersson, nicely varied and unpretentiously delivered. Sometimes the music ambles along without much consequence; but an interpretation like 'Tenderly', shimmeringly delivered at a very slow tempo, ought to delight anyone with ears. Impeccable studio sound.

Jimmy Rushing (1903–72) VOCAL

*** **Mr Five By Five** Topaz TPZ 1019
Rushing; orchestras of Walter Page, Bennie Moten and Count Basie. 11/29-4/42.
Jimmy Rushing began recording in 1929, with Bennie Moten, and carried on for 40 years. Many of his finest performances are with Count Basie and are listed under the bandleader's name, but this collection creams off some of his best features for Bennie Moten and Basie. It's useful to have the original takes of Rushing favourites like 'Sent For You Yesterday' and 'Harvard Blues' all in one place. That said, the remastering is erratic – not one of the best discs in the usually solid Topaz series – and the formulaic nature of his Basie discs makes an unbroken sequence less appetizing. With his Vanguard recordings back out in the cold, though, this is as good a place as any to start hearing this great blues-jazz man.

***(*) **The You And Me That Used To Be** Bluebird ND 86460
Rushing; Ray Nance (*c, vn*); Budd Johnson (*ss*); Zoot Sims, Al Cohn (*ts*); Dave Frishberg (*p*); Milt Hinton (*b*); Mel Lewis (*d*). 4/71.
Jimmy's last record. His own voice sounds bruised after four decades of blues shouting, but his spirit is undimmed, and the two groups involved – one with Sims and Nance, the other with Cohn and Johnson – work magnificently. Frishberg (who also did the arrangements) plays quirky piano against Hinton and Lewis at their most swinging, and Nance is simply extraordinary – his violin introduction to 'When I Grow Too Old To Dream' is enough to make the record essential, and his cornet solos are as good as anything he did with Ellington. Rushing and Frishberg go on to perform a duet version of 'I Surrender Dear' which is a moving farewell to a great jazz singer.

George Russell (born 1923) COMPOSER, BANDLEADER, PIANO, ORGAN

**** **Ezz-thetics** Original Jazz Classics OJC 070
Russell; Don Ellis (*t*); Dave Baker (*tb*); Eric Dolphy (*as, bcl*); Steve Swallow (*b*); Joe Hunt (*d*). 5/61.
***(*) **The Stratus Seekers** Original Jazz Classics OJC 365
Russell; Dave Baker, Don Ellis (*t*); John Pierce (*as*); Paul Plummer (*ts*); Steve Swallow (*b*); Joe Hunt (*d*).
*** **The Outer View** Original Jazz Classics OJC 616
Russell; Garnett Brown (*tb*); Paul Plummer (*ts*); Steve Swallow (*b*); Pete LaRoca (*d*); Sheila Jordan (*v*).
It would be difficult to overstate George Russell's significance within jazz or the degree to which he has been marginalized by the critical and commercial establishment. Russell is responsible for what remains the most significant single theoretical treatise written about the music. *The Lydian Chromatic Concept of Tonal Organization*, completed in the early 1950s, was the direct source of the modal or scalar experiments of John Coltrane and Miles Davis. Sometimes falsely identified with the original Greek Lydian mode, it is not in fact the same at all. In diatonic terms, it represents the progression F to F on the

piano's white keys; it also confronts the diabolic tritone, the *diabolus in musica*, which had haunted Western composers from Bach to Beethoven.

Russell's conception assimilated modal writing to the extreme chromaticism of modern music. By converting chords into scales, and overlaying one scale on another, it allowed improvisers to work in the hard-to-define area between non-tonality and polytonality. Like all great theoreticians, Russell worked analytically rather than synthetically, basing his ideas on how jazz *actually was*, not on how it could be made to conform with traditional principles of Western harmony. Working from within jazz's often tacit organizational principles, Russell's fundamental concern was the relationship between formal scoring and improvisation, giving the first the freedom of the second, freeing the second from being literally esoteric, 'outside' some supposed norm.

Russell's theories also influenced his own composition. 'A Bird In Igor's Yard' was a (rather too) self-conscious attempt to ally bebop and Stravinsky – it was also a young and slightly immature work – but it pointed the way forward. Russell's music always sounds both familiar and unsettlingly alien. His versions of staples like Charlie Parker's 'Au Privave', Thelonious Monk's equally precocious 'Round Midnight', and Miles Davis's almost oriental 'Nardis' on *Ezz-thetics* create new areas for the soloists to explore; in Don Ellis and Eric Dolphy he has players particularly responsive to expansions of the harmonic language (Dolphy in particular preferred to work the inner space of a piece, rather than to go 'out'). 'Ezz-thetic' first appeared on the classic 1956 *Jazz Workshop* sessions, now disgracefully deleted again. As a very good start to a Russell collection there's a strong case to be made for *Ezz-thetics*, with its fine Dolphy contributions. Coincidentally or not, the year of the saxophonist's death also marked the beginning of Russell's long exile in Europe and a mutual alienation from the American scene.

(*) Othello Ballet Suite / Electronic Organ Sonata No. 1 Soul Note 121014
> Russell; Rolf Ericson (*t*); Arne Domnérus (*as*); Bernt Rosengren (*ts*); Jan Garbarek (*ts*); Jon Christensen (*d*); others unknown. 1/67.

Conducting the exuberant big bands of the 1980s, Russell bore a striking physical resemblance to the choreographer, Merce Cunningham. There was a dancemaster's precision to his gestures that was communicated through his music as well. Russell's conception of harmonic space is somewhat like a modern choreographer's. The *Othello Ballet Suite* is only the most obvious example of how his imagination turns on movement – in this case, the curiously inward movements of Shakespeare's play – and on the formation of black identity in the West.

The music is more stately than passionate, with an almost ritualistic quality to its development. Russell's orchestration is curiously reminiscent of Ravel, and cloys in consequence; the saxophones sound slightly out of pitch. The *Electronic Organ Sonata* is rather superficial, too obvious an essay in Russell's harmonic and structural ideas to be entirely involving. The sound on both pieces, though, is good, and both are highly significant in his development of a non-canonical but systematic musical language.

***(*) The Essence Of George Russell** Soul Note 121044/5
> Russell; Maffy Falay, Bertil Lovgren, Palle Mikkelborg, Palle Boldtvig, Jan Allan, Lars Samuelsson, Stanton Davis (*t*); Georg Vernon, Gunnar Medberg (*tb*); Runo Ericksson, Olle Lind (*btb*); Arne Domnérus (*as, cl*); Claes Rosendahl (*ts, ss, as, f*); Lennart Aberg (*ts, ss, f*); Bernt Rosengren (*ts*); Erik Nilson (*bs, bcl*); Bengt Egerblad (*vib*); Rune Gustafsson, Terje Rypdal (*g*); Bengt Hallberg (*p*); Arild Andersen, Roman Dylag (*b*); Jon Christensen (*d*); Rupert Clemendore (*perc*). 66, 67.

*** **Electronic Sonata For Souls Loved By Nature** Soul Note 121034
> Russell; Manfred Schoof (*t*); Jan Garbarek (*ts*); Terje Rypdal (*g*); Red Mitchell (*b*); Jon Christensen (*d*). 4/69.

*** **Electronic Sonata For Souls Loved By Nature 1980** Soul Note SN 1009
> Russell; Lew Soloff (*t*); Robert Moore (*ts, ss*); Victor Gomer (*g*); Jean-François Jenny-Clark (*b*); Keith Copeland (*d, perc*). 6/80.

(*) Trip To Prillargui Soul Note SN 1029
> Russell; Stanton Davis (*t*); Jan Garbarek (*ts*); Terje Rypdal (*g*); Arild Andersen (*b*); Jon Christensen (*d*). 3/70.

For all the quality of the performances, these are conceptually woolly and rather abstract works that add no more than grace-notes to Russell's remarkable compositional output. In the triumvirate of great arrangers, Russell is closer to the open texture of Gil Evans than to Quincy Jones's lacquered surface. There is a sense, though, with these performances that surface is all that matters. The original *Electronic Sonata*, which is included on the big-band *Essence* as well as on the self-titled small-group recording, has a depth of perspective and firmness of execution that the still-puzzling 1980 revision totally lacks. Conceived for tapes and ensemble, the piece is again chiefly concerned with the relationship between scored and improvised materials. *Trip To Prillargui* is beautifully played but sounds curiously emptied of significance, and it yields no more on repeated hearings; the transfer to CD has made a big difference, but it's still less than compelling.

(*) **Vertical Form VI Soul Note SN 1019

> Russell; Americo Bellotto, Bertil Lovgren (*t, flhn*); Hakan Hyquist (*t, flhn, frhn*); Jan Allan (*t, frhn*); Ivar Olsen (*frhn*); Bengt Edvarsson, Jorgen Johansson, Lars Olofsson (*tb*); Sven Larsson (*btb, tba*); Arne Domnérus (*cl, as, ss*); Jan Uling (*f, as, ts*); Lennart Aberg, Bernt Rosengren (*f, as, ts, ss*); Erik Nilsson (*f, bcl, bs*); Rune Gustafsson (*g*); Bjorn Lind (*electric p*); Vlodek Gulgowski (*electric p, syn*); Monica Dominique (*electric p, cel, org, clavinet*); Stefan Brolund, Bronislaw Suchanek, Lars-Urban Helje (*b*); Lars Beijbom, Leroy Lowe (*d*); Sabu Martinez (*perc*). 3/77.

If we're looking for appropriate visual analogies, *Vertical Form VI* is less like an upright menhir than another kind of standing stone. The dolmen has a huge, slabby top perched on unfeasibly skinny supports. By that analogy Russell's piece has considerable mass and gravitational force, but seems to rest on nothing more than the bare uprights of theory, with little or no emotional engagement. The band is well drilled and produces a big, generous sound that might well benefit from CD transfer. Once encountered, though, the music seems just to sit there, much involved with its own enigma and a few intelligent guesses about its origins. Towards the end of the 1970s and during the following decade, Russell began to receive some of the attention he had long deserved.

***(*) **New York Big Band** Soul Note SN 1039

> Russell; as above, plus: Stanton Davis, Terumasa Hino, Lew Soloff (*t*); Gary Valente (*tb*); Dave Taylor (*btb*); John Clark (*frhn*); Marty Ehrlich (*as*); Ricky Ford (*ts*); Roger Rosenberg (*ts*); Carl Atkins (*bs, bcl*); Mark Slifstein (*g*); Stanley Cowell, Gotz Tangerding (*p*); Ricky Martinez (*electric p, org*); Cameron Brown (*b*); Warren Smith (*d*); Babafumi Akunyon (*perc*); Lee Genesis (*v*). 77–78.

***(*) **Live In An American Time Spiral** Soul Note SN 1049

> Russell; Stanton Davis, Tom Harrell, Brian Leach, Ron Tooley (*t*); Ray Anderson, Earl McIntyre (*tb*); Marty Ehrlich (*as, f*); Doug Miller (*ts, f*); Bob Hanlon (*bs*); Jerome Harris (*g*); Jack Reilly, Mark Soskin (*ky*); Ron McClure (*b*); Victor Lewis (*d*). 7/82.

New York Big Band includes a vital (in every sense) performance of the epochal 'Cubana Be, Cubana Bop', written in collaboration with Dizzy Gillespie and first performed in 1947. With its structural and not just decorative use of African and Caribbean metres, the piece opened out a whole new direction for jazz writing, paving the way for *The African Game* 25 years later. *Big Band* also includes two sections from *Listen To The Silence* and a wonderful and unexpected 'God Bless The Child' that derives something from Dolphy's long engagement with the piece.

The main piece on *Live* is a concert performance of 'Time Spiral' from *So What*. Concerned again with the larger, almost meta-historical movements of human life, the charts have a slightly dense philosophical feel on the studio album, but open up considerably in a live setting. The album also includes a fine reading of 'Ezz-thetic' and the faintly ironic 'D. C. Divertimento', given force by a (mostly) young and enthusiastic band.

*** **The London Concerts** Stash STCD 560/61

> Russell; Stuart Brooks, Ian Carr, Mark Chandler (*t*); Pete Beachill, Ashley Slater (*tb*); Andy Sheppard, Chris Biscoe, Pete Hurt (*reeds*); Brad Hatfield, Steve Lodder (*ky*); David Fiuczynski (*g*); Bill Urmson (*b*); Steve Johns (*d*). 89.

Somehat as he had in Scandinavia two decades earlier, Russell found young British players (and some of their elders) hanging on his every compositional idea, and more than willing to work with him. These recordings were the first discs since the early part of the decade, a bizarre neglect of the man some would consider one of the half-dozen most important composers to have graced the music. Whether that valuation stands up to these oddly confected discs, which contain another performance of the 'Electronic Sonata', is very much a matter of personal judgement. We tend to think rather not. The band is absolutely on the case, but the material sounds either diffuse or ridiculously knotty, needing something of the looseness and relaxation that Gil Evans got out of British players.

Hal Russell (1926–92) SAXOPHONES, TRUMPET, VIBRAPHONE, DRUMS, BANDLEADER

*** **Generation** Chief 5

> Russell; Chuck Burdelik (*cl, as, ts*); Charles Tyler (*as, cl, bs*); Brian Sandstrom (*g, b, t*); Curt Bley (*b*); Steve Hunt (*d, vib*). 9/82.

***(*) **Conserving NRG** Principally Jazz PJP CD 02

> Russell; Brian Sandstrom (*t, g, b, perc*); Chuck Burdelik (*ts, as, perc*); Curt Bley (*b*); Steve Hunt (*d, vib, perc*). 3/84.

***(*) **The Finnish / Swiss Tour** ECM 1455
    Russell; Mars Williams (*ts, ss, didgeridoo*); Brian Sandstrom (*b, t, g*); Kent Kessler (*b, didgeridoo*); Steve Hunt (*d, vib, didgeridoo*). 11/90.
*** **Naked Colours** Silkheart SHCD 135
    Russell; Joel Futterman (*p, rec*); Jay Oliver (*b*); Robert Adkins (*d*). 91.
*** **Hal's Bells** ECM 1484
    Russell (*all instruments*). 5/92.
***(*) **The Hal Russell Story** ECM 1498
    Russell; Mars Williams (*ts, as, bsx, f, didgeridoo, bells, v*); Brian Sandstrom (*b, g, t, toys, perc*); Kent Kessler (*b, tb*); Steve Hunt (*d, tim, vib, perc*). 7/92.

There is nothing else in contemporary jazz quite like Hal Russell's NRG Ensemble. Playing just one instrument is considered rather wimpish, especially when the old man drifts back and forth between vibes, cornet and high-register, Ayler-influenced saxophone. Russell actually set out as a drummer; he was recruited by Miles Davis in 1950 and by the radical Chicagoan, Joe Daley (now little known outside free-jazz circles in the United States), a decade later. Towards the end of the 1970s he took up trumpet again for the first time since his student days and learned to play the saxophone.

In its blend of forceful, rock-inflected ostinati, extreme dynamics and broadly satirical approach, the NRG Ensemble bears some kinship to Frank Zappa's Mothers of Invention; in his liner-note to *The Finnish/Swiss Tour*, Steve Lake also notes Russell's physical resemblance to Charles Ives, which isn't so far away, either. A record of the Ensemble's first and rather surreal European itinerary, the leader quotes from Keith Jarrett, and for 'Linda's Rock Vamp' dons Prince of Darkness shades over his prescription specs, as the liner-booklet shows, in dubious homage to his former employer. The band have the huge, dark sound of the mid-1970s Miles Davis units, the days when Miles was Abstract Expressionist rather than Neo-Figurative. 'Compositions' are treated as reference points, and performances frequently develop into all-out jams which nevertheless give off a strong aura of control. The sheer *size* of the sound suggests a much larger outfit. Sandstrom's stripped guitar-playing, Steve Hunt's ferocious time-keeping and the occasional use of twinned basses generate astonishing volume, with Mars Williams (formerly of the rock band, Psychedelic Furs) overblowing furiously beside the leader on the powerful 'Temporarily'. 'For MC' is for didgeridoos, electric guitar and cornet; the Zappa-sounding 'Hal The Weenie' is also an Aylerish invocation of ghosts and spirits.

Generation and *Conserving NRG* are slightly disappointing, sounding forced where *Tour* appears spontaneous, disorderly where the later things conform to some logic. Nevertheless it's powerful stuff, the sound is better, and there isn't that much of Russell available. Watch out for 'Generation' itself, and the scissorhands 'Poodle Cut'. Sadly, Russell was only beginning to receive proper recognition when he died.

His final legacy was two quite extraordinary 'concept' albums for ECM, the first a multi-tracked solo effort, the second a potted autobiography in music and cartoon narrations shouted through a paper megaphone. The tunes on both are a mixture of reworked standards and themes worked out on the spot for the session. Those in *Hal's Bells* range from vibraphone solos – the lovely 'I Need You Know' – to 'group' pieces like 'Kenny G', a curious name-check for Bill Clinton's favourite saxophonist, arranged for tenor, vibes and drums, to the more radical 'For Free' (saxophones, trumpets, vibes and drums) which harks back to his days with the Joe Daley group. Some of these tracks plod a little. Certainly, few of them have the all-out energy of the material on *Story*, a record which compresses 40 years of music-making into a standard-length CD. Russell's biography is no more linear and sequential than anything else Russell ever did, but it takes him from childhood fantasies right through to middle-aged fantasies of moving 'beyond the varlines / beyond the changes / beyond the time / tiptoeing in some wild and lonely space'. Underneath all the clamour, it is the loneliness and isolation that show through. Though the NRG ensemble had become Russell's mouthpiece, it is on the solo session that his curiously vulnerable personality emerges with greatest clarity. It comes through again on the quartet co-led with Futterman, a loyal supporter and interpreter who provides all the compositional material for the session, though Russell wholly dominates it. A figure to put alongside Ives and Ruggles, Nancarrow and Moondog and Harry Partch, Russell is a genuine American original.

Luis Russell (1902–63) PIANO, BANDLEADER

**** **Savoy Shout** JSP CD 308
    Russell; Louis Metcalf, Henry Allen, Bill Coleman, Otis Johnson (*t*); J. C. Higginbotham, Vic Dickenson (*tb*); Albert Nicholas (*cl, ss, as*); Charlie Holmes (*ss, as*); Teddy Hill, Greely Walton (*ts*); Will Johnson (*g, bj*); Bass Moore (*tba*); Pops Foster (*b*); Paul Barbarin (*d, vib*); Walter Pichon (*v*). 1/29–12/30.

**** The Luis Russell Collection, 1926–1934 Collector's Classics COCD-7
> As above, except add George Mitchell, Bob Shoffner (c); Leonard Davis, Gus Aiken (t); Kid
> Ory, Preston Jackson, Dicky Wells, Nathaniel Story, Jimmy Archey (tb); Darnell Howard,
> Henry Jones (cl, as); Bingie Madison (cl, ts); Barney Bigard (ts); Lee Blair (g); Johnny St Cyr
> (bj); Sonny Woods, Chick Bullock, Palmer Brothers (v). 3/26–8/34.

(****) Luis Russell 1926–1929 Classics 588
> Similar to above. 3/26–12/29.

(****) Luis Russell 1930–1931 Classics 606
> Similar to above. 1/30–8/31.

**** Luis Russell & His Orchestra Topaz TPZ 1039
> As above discs, except add Louis Armstrong (t, v), Eddie Condon (bj), Lonnie Johnson (g). 1/
> 29–8/34.

Russell was an indifferent pianist, but he led one of the great orchestras of its period, having originally
put it together in New Orleans in 1927, with such young local stars as Allen, Nicholas and Barbarin in
attendance. *Savoy Shout* collects their 18 essential sides from seven remarkable sessions in New York,
where the band had secured a prime Harlem residency at the Saratoga Club (they also backed Louis
Armstrong on some of his contemporaneous dates). This was a sophisticated band: first, in its soloists,
with Higginbotham dominating the earlier sides and Allen, Nicholas and Holmes adding their own
variations to the later ones; and, secondly, in its increasing stature as an ensemble. 'Louisiana Swing',
'High Tension', 'Panama' and 'Case On Dawn' all show the orchestra swinging through the more
advanced new ideas of counterpoint and unison variation while still offering chances for Allen and the
others to shine as soloists.

The Collector's Classics CD fills in all the gaps in the Russell discography. There are two small-group
sessions from 1926, the first having a Mortonesque sound through the presence of Mitchell, Ory and
Nicholas in the front line, the second a fine example of Chicago music moving out of the barrelhouse
and into the front parlour. 'Broadway Rhythm' and two takes of 'The Way He Loves Is Just Too Bad'
come from a Banner session of 1929 featuring the full band, and the final two sessions for Victor (1931)
and Banner (1934) appear in full: if the ten tracks suggest Russell's hard-bitten swing was softening a
little with the era of smooth big bands just around the corner, there is still some memorable playing on
the likes of 'Hokus Pokus'. There are only three duplications with the JSP issue, and both discs have
been given a superlative remastering by John R. T. Davies. Each is very highly recommended, especially
to any who feel this era of jazz is too far away for them.

The two Classics CDs cover all the same material, but they're superfluous in the light of the other two
discs. Topaz's compilation cherrypicks the best of Russell's orchestral sides but stirs in two tracks when
the band backed Louis Armstrong and also adds Armstrong's Savoy Ballroom Five classic, 'Mahogany
Hall Stomp'. A strong single disc, but the remastering is no improvement on Davies's work and first
recommendations lie with the JSP and Collector's Classics discs.

Pee Wee Russell (1906–69) CLARINET, TENOR SAXOPHONE

*** The Land Of Jazz Topaz TPZ 1018
> Russell; Red Nichols, Leo McConville, Manny Klein, Henry 'Red' Allen, Max Kaminsky, Marty
> Marsala (t); Red Nichols, Bobby Hackett (c); Miff Mole, Tommy Dorsey, George Brunies,
> Vernon Brown (tb); Brad Gowans (vtb); Fud Livingston (cl, ts); Jimmy Lord (cl); Happy
> Caldwell, Bud Freeman, Gene Sedric (ts); Adrian Rollini (bsx); Lennie Hayton, Fats Waller,
> Arthur Schutt, Jess Stacy, Joe Bushkin, Teddy Wilson, Frank Froeba (p); Jack Bland, Eddie
> Condon, Allan Reuss, Dick McDonough, Eddie Lang (g); Al Morgan, Pops Foster, Artie
> Shapiro, Sid Weiss (b); Vic Berton, Zutty Singleton, George Wettling, Johnny Blowers, Lionel
> Hampton (d); Billy Banks (v). 8/27–9/44.

*** Jack Teagarden / Pee Wee Russell Original Jazz Classics OJC 1708
> Russell; Max Kaminsky (t); Dicky Wells (tb); Al Gold (ts); James P. Johnson (p); Freddie Green
> (g); Wellman Braud (b); Zutty Singleton (d, v). 8/38.

He might have been a Dickensian grotesque, with his mile-long face and shopworn demeanour, and his
clarinet playing had a raddled, asthmatic tone that tended to conceal most of the creativity which had
gone into it. Yet Russell's music is a connoisseur's jazz, transcending schools and securing a personal
voice that can stand with any of the most idiosyncratic spirits in the music. There's a danger in patronizing his home-made approach to playing, and he *was* inconsistent, but his best music is exceptional. He
began with the New York players of the 1920s – Nichols, Mole, Beiderbecke – but was more readily
linked with Condon's Chicagoans in the 1930s and '40s. The Topaz compilation starts with Nichols,
adds four tracks with Billy Banks, including the immortal 'Oh Peter', but bulks up with various Condon
line-ups for Commodore from 1938. Pee Wee sounds fine on 'Tappin' The Commodore Till' and a lovely

slow solo on 'Sunday'. But the four outstanding items are by a quartet with Russell, Jess Stacy, Sid Weiss and George Wettling, culminating in the almost gargled 'D.A. Blues'. Sound is variable – some of the Commodores have a low-fi resonance – but mostly good.

The 1938 session (the rest of the CD features a Teagarden-led group) features a surprising line-up on five standards and a blues, two tracks featuring Russell and the rhythm section alone. Kaminsky and Wells are the most confident-sounding voices but it's Russell's queer sense of line and wobbly pitch that take the ear. His partnership with Johnson is just one of a series of unlikely alliances he formed with pianists on record, which would later include George Wein and Thelonious Monk.

***(*) **We're In The Money** Black Lion BLCD 760909
  Russell; Doc Cheatham, Wild Bill Davison (*t*); Vic Dickenson (*tb*); George Wein (*p*); John Field, Stan Wheeler (*b*); Buzzy Drootin (*d*); Al Bandini (*v*). 53–54.

***(*) **Jazz Reunion** Candid CS 9020
  Russell; Emmett Berry (*t*); Bob Brookmeyer (*vtb*); Coleman Hawkins (*ts*); Nat Pierce (*p*); Milt Hinton (*b*); Jo Jones (*d*). 2/61.

There probably isn't a single definitive Pee Wee Russell record: he turned up in unlikely settings and played improbable material until the end of his life. But these three dates give a splendid account of what he could do. *We're In The Money* includes two dates by basically the same band, although the substitution of Davison for Cheatham lends a different feel: the former's irascible, barking playing is a startling contrast to Cheatham's politely hot phrasing. Russell listens to each man and pitches his remarks for due contrast himself. Dickenson, a kindred spirit, kibitzes from the sidelines and the recording is fine. The *Reunion* was with Hawkins – one of the tracks, 'If I Could Be With You One Hour Tonight', they'd recorded together as far back as 1929 – and it caught both men in excellent form, Hawkins's solos delivered in his most leathery, autumnal manner which makes Russell's nagging at notes sound minimalist. Jones, in particular, reads everybody's moves superbly, although Berry and Brookmeyer especially seem rather irrelevant.

Charles Rutherford Jazz Pacific Orchestra GROUP

*** **Reunion** Sea Breeze CDSB-2044
  Joe Davis, Bob Bennett, Kevin Mayes, Tim Wendt, Charlie Peterson, Kai Palmer, Gary Roll, Bob Allen, Ron Stout (*t, flhn*); Regan Wickman, Mike Johnson, Corey Wicks, Mike Fahn (*tb*); Everett Carroll, Tom Smith, Chris Abernathy, Larry Jagiello, Dave Arrollado, Eric Marienthal, Doug Webb, Tom Kubic, Brian Williams (*saxes*); Alan Rowe (*p*); Todd Oliver (*g*); Eric Stiller, Ernie Nunez (*b*); Ray Price (*d*); Christine Rosander (*v*). 9/91.

*** **Groovin' Hard** Sea Breeze CDSB-2050
  Joe Davis, Gary Roll, Ron Stout, Kai Palmer, Matt Fronke (*t, flhn*); Regan Wickman, Mike Fahn, Corey Wicks, John Ward, Len Wicks (*tb*); Everett Carroll, Paul Bastin, Jeff Jorgenson, Jerry Pinter, Brian Williams (*saxes*); Alan Rowe (*p*); Todd Oliver (*g*); Ernie Nunez (*b*); Ray Price (*d*). n.d.

*** **Note Walker** Sea Breeze CDSB-2064
  As above, except Don Clark, Bob Bennett (*t*), Benjamin Olariu, Jim Boltinghouse, Mike Zelazo, Francisco Torres (*tb*); Bob Swaaley, Sy Eubank (*p*), Eric Stiller, Vakerie Sullivan (*b*) replace Davis, Roll, Wickman, Fahn, Ward, Rowe, Oliver and Nunez; add Christine Rosander (*v*). n.d.

Three irreproachable releases by a varying team of West Coasters. Rutherford leads, directs and produces but doesn't play and leaves most of the arranging to other hands, most notably Don Menza, to whom the third CD is dedicated. There's little enough between the three records that some of the routines crop up more than once: the flag-waver 'Shaw Nuff' on *Reunion* is a showcase for the trumpet section, and just the same thing happens with 'Ornithology' on *Note Walker*. But they're good routines, proficiently despatched. Certain guest soloists – Marienthal, Kubic – liven up the first disc somewhat; the second settles around the excellent reed section, while the third rises on its absorbing sequence of scores by Menza, notably the title-piece, 'Tenor Time' and the Latin bustle of 'Sambiana'. Each of them also has a share of rote passages and mere cliché. Hard to fault them, but difficult to see anyone wanting more than one.

Paul Rutherford (born 1940) TROMBONE

***(*) **Rogues** Emanem 4007
  Rutherford; Paul Rogers (*b*). 11/88.

***(*) **ISKRA / NCKPA 1903** Maya MCD 9502
    Rutherford; Phil Wachsmann (*vn*); Barry Guy (*b*). 10/92.
Schooled, like a lot of British players, in the RAF, and then more formally at the Guildhall, Rutherford has been one of the most uncompromising improvisers on the scene, a purist's purist with an enormous reputation among fellow players. He has had the courage to record unaccompanied, under such typically wry titles as *The Gentle Harm Of The Bourgeoisie* and *Old Moers Almanac*. Much of his best and most distinctive work, though, was with a mixed acoustic/electric trio named after Lenin's newspaper, *Iskra 1903*. Originally, it included Derek Bailey on guitar but in recent years has called on the uncompromising sound of Wachsmann's amplified violin, an instrument capable of a huge range of sounds and of expressive mood, from antagonistic to grass-rustlingly delicate. This live performance from Vancouver finds the trio in exceptionally nimble and positive form. If there is not quite an absolute democracy of sound, that has more to do with the recording and the relative loudness of the instruments concerned than with the actual emphases of the music, in which any subordination of 'rhythm' to 'lead' instrumentation is rendered null. Rutherford's leadership would seem to consist of his ability to throw up cues and build contexts for the others to inhabit and develop according to their own lights. It is a listening idiom, and it requires concentrated attention.
    Rutherford has also run a trio with a more familiar configuration: another bassist, Paul Rogers, but this time a drummer, Nigel Morris. His absence on *Rogues* allows the two to engage in an intense musical dialogue. The patrons of the pub where it was recorded provide their own percussion but it does not seem to affect the Pauls one whit, and the opening improvisation clocks in at a staggering 40 minutes, all of it absolutely valid and unformulaic. There are moments here, as on *1989 – And All That*, a duo with saxophonist George Haslam and reviewed under his name, when Rutherford almost seems to steer close to a jazz idiom, and it may be that certain trombone sounds reinforce that impression. Unlike George Lewis or fellow-Briton Alan Tomlinson, he has no apparent desire to deconstruct his instrument, literally or idiomatically, but there should be no doubt about how radical his language base is and how uncompromising his improvisational approach.

Niels Ryde BASS

** **Traffic Jam** Olufsen DOC 5113
    Ryde; Mikael Sloth (*ss, ts*); John Tchicai (*ts*); Morten Elbek (*as*); Johannes Grønager (*bs, sitar*); Kaev Glimann (*ky*); Uffe Steen (*g*); Jesper Bo Knudsen (*d*); Claus Rahuage (*perc*). 11/90.
A modish and fragmented record which suggests interesting ideas without realizing them. Ryde crams a lot of twists and turns into compositions that never take a coherent form, and guest-star turns by Tchicai and Steen embellish but don't transform the modal settings and thin jazz-funk gestures. The leader noodles on bass in the Pastorius fashion: 'Blues For Jaco' pays the obvious dues.

Terje Rypdal (born 1947) ELECTRIC GUITAR, GUITAR, SOPRANO SAXOPHONE, FLUTE, OTHER INSTRUMENTS AND EFFECTS

(*) **What Comes After ECM 1031
    Rypdal; Erik Niord Larsen (*ob, eng hn*); Sveinung Hovensjo, Barre Phillips (*b*); Jon Christensen (*perc, org*). 8/73.
(*) **Whenever I Seem To Be Far Away ECM 1045
    Rypdal; Odd Ulleberg (*frhn*); Erik Niord Larsen (*ob*); Pete Knutsen (*p, mellotron*); Sveinung Hovensjo (*b*); Jon Christensen (*perc*); Helmut Geiger (*vn*); Christian Hedrich (*vla*); strings of Südfunk Symphony Orchestra, conducted by Mladen Gutesha. 74.
*** **Odyssey** ECM 1067/8
    Rypdal; Torbjorn Sunde (*tb*); Brynjulf Blix (*b*); Svein Christiansen (*d*). 8/75.
*** **After The Rain** ECM 1083
    Rypdal; Inger Lise Rypdal (*v*). 76.
*** **Waves** ECM 1110
    Rypdal; Palle Mikkelborg (*t, flhn, elec*); Sveinung Hovensjo (*b*); Jon Christensen (*d, perc*). 9/77.
In the later 1980s, Terje Rypdal was increasingly seen at the head of an impressive train of opus numbers. 'Straight' composition was, in fact, his third string. His professional career had begun as a rock performer, in the pit band at a Scandinavian production of *Hair!* (chilblains were doubtless a problem) and as accompanist to his sister, Inger Lise Rypdal (who added soft vocal colours to the otherwise solo *After The Rain*). In the 1970s, under the influence of George Russell (directly) and of Jimi Hendrix (less so), Rypdal made a series of highly atmospheric guitar-led albums which combined elements of classical form with a distinctive high-register sound and an improvisational approach that

drew more from rock music than from orthodox jazz technique. (It's worth noting that *After The Rain* refers to a Rypdal composition, not Coltrane's.)

If there is an 'ECM sound', in either a positive or a more sceptical sense, it may be found in the echo-y passages of these albums. Rypdal's music is highly textural and harmonically static, its imagery kaleido-scopic rather than cinematic. At worst, Rypdal's solo excursions sound merely vacuous. The title and mood of 'Silver Bird Is Heading For The Sun' on ECM 1045 are reminiscent of Pink Floyd's woollier moments; the long title-track (which Rypdal calls an 'image', a useful generic description of his work) is, on the other hand, highly effective in its balance of winds, guitar and strings. ('Live' strings are more effective than the cumbersome and now outmoded mellotrons and 'string ensembles' that the guitarist uses elsewhere.)

Waves and *Odyssey* are the most interesting of this group. Rypdal favours brass with an almost medieval quality and, despite Mikkelborg's baroque embellishments, the trumpeter fits that prescription surpris-ingly well. Hovensjo and Christensen don't play as an orthodox rhythm section but as a shifting backdrop of tones and pulses; the bassist doubles on a 6-string instrument which is effectively a rhythm guitar.

Popular in their day, all these albums now sound a shade dated. Nevertheless they are still well worth hearing.

***(*) **Descendere** ECM 1144
    Rypdal; Palle Mikkelborg (*t, flhn, ky*); Jon Christensen (*d, perc*). 3/79.
***(*) **Terje Rypdal / Miroslav Vitous / Jack DeJohnette** ECM 1125
    Rypdal; Miroslav Vitous (*b, p*); Jack DeJohnette (*d*). 6/78.
*** **To Be Continued** ECM 1192
    As above. 1/81.

There have always been charges that Rypdal is not 'really' an improviser, just a high-powered effects man. At the root of the misconception is a prevailing belief that improvisation takes place only on a vertical axis, up and down through chord progressions and changes. Rypdal's genius is for juxtaposi-tions of textures, overlays of sound that act as polarizing lenses to what his companions are doing. A broad, open chord laid close over a drum pattern takes the 'percussive' stringency out of DeJohnette's line, making him sound as if he were playing piano (as in other and later company he might well be) or adding harmonics to Vitous's huge bass notes. There is also, of course, a great deal of straightforward interplay which in itself helps refute the charge that Rypdal is a mere techno-freak.

The other trio is less conventional in format, though Mikkelborg's palette-knife keyboard effects mean that there's very little sense of 'missing' piano or bass. The trumpeter, who has an approach broadly similar to Rypdal's, tends to lay it on a little thick, and there is a suspicion of either muddle or overkill on a couple of tracks. That apart, *Descendere* still sounds fresh and vital and stands out as a high point in Rypdal's output.

***(*) **Works** ECM 825428
    Rypdal; Palle Mikkelborg (*t, ky*); Olle Ulleberg (*frhn*); Jan Garbarek (*f*); Eckehart Fintl (*ob*);
    Brynjulf Blix (*org*); Pete Knutsen (*mellotron*); Arild Andersen, Sveinung Hovensjo, Miroslav
    Vitous (*b*); Jon Christensen, Jack DeJohnette (*d*). 74–81.

Whether or not this represents a 'best of' Rypdal's pre-1980s work, it does provide a useful sample for newcomers. The tracks with Mikkelborg, and with Vitous and DeJohnette inevitably stand ahead of the rest and, though there's little sense of how Rypdal operates on long-form pieces, these offer convincing testimony of his sometimes queried improvising credentials. Recommended.

*** **Eos** ECM 1263
    Rypdal; David Darling (*clo, 8-string electric clo*). 5/83.

The scorching power chords of the opening 'Laser' tend to mislead, for this is a remarkably subtle and sophisticated record, making the fullest use of the players' astonishing range of tone-colours and effects. Darling conjures anything from Vitous-like bass strums to high, wailing lines that are remark-ably close in timbre to Rypdal's souped-up guitar. He is still mostly reliant on rock-influenced figures played with maximum sustain and distortion, but his rhythm counts are consistently challenging, and the pairing of instruments sets up an often ambiguous bitonality. The title-track wavers a bit at over 14 minutes, but the two closing numbers, 'Mirage' and 'Adagietto', are particularly beautiful.

* **Chaser** ECM 1303
    Rypdal; Bjorn Kjellemyr (*b*); Audun Klieve (*d*). 5/85.
** **Blue** ECM 1346
    As above. 11/86.
(*) **The Singles Collection ECM 1383
    As above, plus Allan Dangerfield (*ky*). 8/88.

It may say something about Rypdal's psychic economy that, at a time when his scored, formal music was achieving new heights of sophistication and beauty, he should have gone on the road and on record with a power trio of minimum finesse. *Chaser* is a harsh, clunking slice of nonsense that does Rypdal very little credit. *Blue* at least shows signs of thought, notably on 'The Curse' and 'Om Bare'.

How many people have been thrown by the ironically titled *Singles Collection*? It's not utterly improbable that Rypdal might have been sneaking out the odd seven-incher over the years, but this is a wholly new album of wry, generic samples. Basically, it's a tissue of rock guitar styles, with the changing of stylistic season marked by Dangerfield's progress from apoplectic Hammond to a rather underprogrammed synth. Rypdal has expressed interest in Prince's music (and 'U.'N.I.' is presumably a reference to the Small One's trademark elision of titles) but it isn't clear whether he is drawn more to Paisley Park production techniques or to Prince's Carlos Santana-derived (rather than Hendrixderived) guitar playing. Rypdal emerges as a surprisingly good *pasticheur*, and there is plenty to think about in this slightly odd, deliberately regressive set. It's certainly his best work since forming the Chasers.

(It's worth noting that Rypdal's orchestral work has also been recorded by ECM. Watch out for *Undisonus* and *Q.E.D.*, beautifully conceived and performed modern music, and not very far from what he was doing on the more impressionistic of the 1970s records.)

Stefano Sabatini PIANO

(*) **Wonderland Splasc(h) H 360-2
    Sabatini; Flavio Boltro (*t*); Stefano Di Battista (*ss, as*); Maurizio Giammarco (*ts*); Francesco
    Puglisi, Furio Di Castri (*b*); Maurizio Dei Lazzaretti, Roberto Gatto (*d*). 4/91.
Sabatini's graceful music comes and goes, leaving barely a trace. His lyrical kind of midstream bop is nicely unpretentious but it also tends to be featherlight in impact and, as charming as the themes and solos are, they don't have any kind of impact, least of all his deferential piano solos. The best improvising comes from the reliable if occasionally sleepy Giammarco.

Helmut Joe Sachse GUITAR, FLUTE

***(*) **Berlin Tango** ITM 1448
    Sachse; George Lewis (*tb*); David Moss (*d, perc, elec, v*). 12/86, 10/87.
***(*) **European House** FMP CD41
    Sachse solo. 90.
Sachse thinks nothing of cutting across a chaotically abstract passage with a sudden rock riff or Wes Montgomery-style octave run. An eclectic of a fairly radical sort, he has synthesized whole tracts of modern and contemporary guitar playing. The earlier solo record is rather thinly recorded and misses much of Sachse's quieter gestures.

An earlier solo record on FMP had included a modestly reconstructed standard, 'Round About Midnight'; *European House* is rather less respectful of 'Epistrophy' and Coltrane's 'Impressions'. It's this element one misses on the anarchic *Berlin Tango*; 'Lover Man' may mislead, for it's actually a bizarre parody of all-stops-out soul, with Moss's surreal falsetto scats alternated with sexy murmurs and Sachse's lead guitarist posturing. Lewis plays a rather diffident role throughout and was presumably present on only one or other of the dates. The best of the group is undoubtedly the later FMP solo set; without Moss's clatteringly intrusive effects, Sachse improvises percussion on the guitar body and carrying case.

Johnny St Cyr (1890–1966) GUITAR, BANJO

*** **Johnny St Cyr** American Music AMCD-78
    St Cyr; Thomas Jefferson (*t, v*); Percy Humphrey (*t*); Jim Robinson, Joe Avery (*tb*); George
    Lewis (*cl*); Jeanette Kimball (*p, v*); Leo Thompson (*p*); Ernest McLean (*g*); Richard McLean,
    Fran Fields (*b*); Paul Barbarin, Sidney Montague (*d*); Jack Delany, Sister Elizabeth Eustis (*v*). 7/
    54–5/55.
The doyen of New Orleans rhythm guitarists was seldom noted as a group leader, but American Music have pieced together a CD's worth of material. The first two tracks are rather dowdy treatments of 'Someday You'll Be Sorry' by a band with Percy Humphrey, Lewis and Robinson; but more interesting are the five previously unheard pieces by a quintet in which protégé Ernest McLean is featured rather more generously than Johnny himself, both men playing electric. The rest of the disc is jovial New

Orleans music, fronted by the hearty Jefferson and the imperturbable Willie Humphrey. St Cyr, as always, is no more inclined to take any limelight than Freddie Green ever was, so it's nice to have a disc under his name. Remastering is from sources that were a lot cleaner than AM often have access to, so sound is good.

St Louis Ragtimers GROUP

*** **Full Steam Ahead And Loaded Up!** Stomp Off CD1267
>   Bill Mason (*c, hca, jaw hp, wbd*); Eric Sager (*cl, ss*); Trebor Tichenor (*p*); Al Strickler (*bj, v*); Don Franz (*tba, jaw hp*). 12/92.

More good fun from the Stomp Off stable of revivalists, this time an ensemble who don't stop at the 1920s but go right back to nineteenth-century ragtime and minstrelsy. Trebor Tichenor's superb notes identify such pieces of arcana as 'Blind Boone's Southern Rag Medley No. 2 – Strains From The Flat Branch' and, though some of these ancient cakewalks, rags and intermezzos are probably deservedly forgotten, the high spirits and vivacity of this little group bring it all back to life. A few fruity vocals by Al Strickler and a fine show of multi-instrumentalism by Mason complete the circle.

Salty Dogs Jazz Band GROUP

*** **Long, Deep And Wide** GHB BCD-237
>   Lew Green (*c*); Tom Bartlett (*tb*); Kim Cusack (*cl, as*); John Cooper (*p*); Mike Walbridge (*tba*); Jack Kuncl (*bj, g*); Wayne Jones (*d*); Carol Leigh (*v*). 6/89.

*** **Joy, Joy, Joy** Stomp Off CD1233
>   As above, except add John Otto (*as, cl, v*). 12/89–2/92.

This traditional outfit, originally from Lafayette, Indiana, has been around long enough – since 1947 – to create its own dynasty. John Cooper, who has been with them since 1953, is the longest-serving member, but even Carol Leigh has sung with them for 20 years, and they're hardly troubled by questions of 'authenticity'. There have been many records over the years, but these two CDs show their current form. Given their experience, it's a pity that the Salty Dogs don't take a few more chances with some of their treatments. The GHB disc is a very obvious gathering of warhorses, while *Joy, Joy, Joy* is a fascinating collection of material by or associated with Banjo Ikey Robinson, much of it unrecorded for decades. Yet there's little to choose between either record in terms of their persuasively chugging beat, the tight, neat solos and Leigh's engaging vocals, which are on the matronly side of bawdy. The second record is probably the more worthwhile, but their version of, say, 'Alexander's Ragtime Band' on the earlier set has a fine zest. They enjoy their jazz.

Dino Saluzzi BANDONEON, FLUTE, PERCUSSION, VOICE

*** **Kultrum** ECM 1251
>   Saluzzi solo. 11/82.

***(*) **Andina** ECM 1375
>   As above. 5/88.

*** **Argentina** West Wind WW 2201
>   As above. 90.

***(*) **Once Upon A Time . . . Far Away In The South** ECM 1309
>   Saluzzi; Palle Mikkelborg (*t, flhn*); Charlie Haden (*b*); Pierre Favre (*d*). 7/85.

*** **Volver** ECM 1343
>   Saluzzi; Enrico Rava (*t*); Harry Pepl (*g*); Furio Di Castri (*b*); Bruce Ditmas (*d*). 10/86.

*** **Mojotoro** ECM 1447
>   Saluzzi; Celso Saluzzi (*bandoneon, perc, v*); Felix Cuchara Saluzzi (*ts, ss, cl*); Armando Alonso (*g, v*); Guillermo Vadalá (*b, v*); José Maria Saluzzi (*d, perc, v*); Arto Tuncboyaci (*perc, v*). 5/91.

Though it was the Argentinian *nueva tango* master, Astor Piazzolla, who sparked the recent revival of interest in bandoneon and accordion, it has been Dino Saluzzi who has performed some of the most significant new music on an instrument that always held a peculiar fascination for the avant-garde; this partly because of its slightly kitsch image, but also because it permits an astonishing range of harmonic and extra-harmonic devices (wheezes, clicks, terminal rattles) that lend themselves very readily to improvisational contexts.

Saluzzi's compositions and performances (and he is usually best heard solo) cover a wide spectrum of styles, from sombre, almost sacred pieces (like 'Choral' on *Andina*, his best record), to a semi-abstract tone-poem like 'Winter' on the same album, which takes him much closer to the exploratory work of radical accordionist, Pauline Oliveros. While both *Kultrum* and the later *Argentina* are well worth hearing, *Andina* is the one to plump for; richly and intimately recorded, although doubtless less authentic in idiom, it has infinitely greater presence than the later album.

Saluzzi tends to recede a little in a group setting, perhaps because European ears have not been conditioned to listen to button accordion as anything other than a bland portable organ useful for dancing and local colour. Both Rava and (especially) Mikkelborg are rather dominant players and occupy more than their fair share of the foreground. *Once Upon A Time* is better because Haden and Favre are so responsive; *Volver* takes a bit of getting used to.

At first hearing remarkably similar to one of Edward Vesala's accordion-led pieces, 'Mojotoro' is dedicated to the universalization of musical culture. It draws on tango, Bolivian *Andina* music, Uruguayan *Candombe* and other folk forms, travelling between deceptively spacious but highly intricate bandoneon figures and passionate saxophone outcries which suggest a hybrid of Gato Barbieri with another ECM alumnus, Jan Garbarek. The multi-part 'Mundos' is less effective than the title-piece, and the strongest performances are on the more conventionally structured pieces, 'Tango A Mi Padre' and Pintin Castellanos's wonderful *milonga*, 'La Punalada'. Instrumental colours are expertly handled, but the main drama comes from the interaction between Saluzzi and his kinsman, 'Cuchara', who is a marvellously evocative clarinettist.

Perico Sambeat (born 1962) ALTO SAXOPHONE, FLUTE

*** Uptown Dance EGT 565
> Sambeat; Michael Philip Mossman (*t, picc t, tb*); David Kikoski (*p*); Bill Morning (*b*); Keith Copeland (*d*). 5/92.
*** Dual Force Jazz House JHCD 031
> Sambeat; Steve Melling (*p*); Dave Green (*b*); Stephen Keogh (*d*). 12/93.

The Spaniard plays with unstinting energy. He loves the sound of bebop alto to the extent that he could have stepped on to a bandstand with Stitt or Cannonball and come off just fine. The tightly packed solo on 'The Menace', on the earlier of these two sessions, shows what he can do. But the context, on this date in particular, is more modern and prickly than that: the compositions by the underrated Mossman establish a lean, angular world of unusual shapes and harmonies, and Sambeat seems to thrive on them. The brassman is in excellent voice himself, Kikoski is bright and alert, and the result is a cut above the average. The Jazz House disc, recorded during a season at Ronnie Scott's, is more cursory: as sole horn, Sambeat carries it and, though his colleagues play well, it's no more than a workmanlike result.

Dave Samuels (born 1948) VIBES, MARIMBA

** Natural Selection GRP 9656-2
> Samuels; Jeff Beal (*t, flhn, ky*); Jay Beckenstein (*reeds*); Russell Ferrante (*ky*); Bruce Hornsby (*p*); Julio Fernandez (*g*); Jimmy Haslip (*b*); William Kennedy (*d*); Marc Quinones (*perc*). 90.
** Del Sol GRP 9696-2
> Samuels; Danilo Perez, Javier Carizzo (*p*); Jorge Strunz (*g*); Lincoln Goines, Eliseo Borrero (*b*); Richie Morales, Walfredo Reyes (*d*); Andy Narell (*steel d*); Sammy Figueroa, Long John Oliva (*perc*). 12/92.

Joining the hugely successful pop-jazz group, Spyro Gyra, was either the making or the undoing of Samuels. He is as much interested in the vibes as a source of rhythm and percussive power as in their melodic capabilities. But it must have been his ability to play pretty which won his spurs with Spyro Gyra, and pretty is the best thing one can say about these GRP albums. The least one can ask from such records is a set of good, hummable tunes but Samuels isn't that kind of writer and his originals are staccato, jumpy affairs at up-tempo, hard and unripe at slow. *Natural Selection* has a couple of worthwhile tunes, but the best was written by guest trumpeter Jeff Beal, who contributes to only one track. *Del Sol* is marginally stronger through the occasional participation of Perez, who has some substance to add to the surface gloss. Not much, though.

David Sanborn (born 1945) ALTO AND SOPRANO SAXOPHONE

**(*) Taking Off Warner Bros 927295-2
> Sanborn; Randy Brecker (*t*); Tom Malone (*tb*); Peter Gordon, John Clark (*frhn*); Michael

Brecker (*ts*); Howard Johnson (*bs, tba*); Don Grolnick (*ky*); Steve Khan, Buzzy Feiten, Joe Beck (*g*); Will Lee (*b*); Chris Parker, Rick Marotta (*d*); Ralph Macdonald (*perc*); strings. 75.

** Heart To Heart Warner Bros 3189-2
Sanborn; Jon Faddis, Lew Soloff, Randy Brecker (*t*); Michael Brecker (*ts*); Mike Mainieri (*vib*). 1/78.

*** Voyeur Warner Bros 256900
Sanborn; Tom Scott (*ts, f*); Michael Colina (*ky*); Hiram Bullock, Buzzy Feiten (*g*); Marcus Miller (*b, g, ky, d*); Buddy Williams, Steve Gadd (*d*); Lenny Castro, Ralph Macdonald (*perc*). 81.

** As We Speak Warner Bros 923650-2
Sanborn; Bill Evans (*ss*); Bob Mintzer (*bcl*); Robert Martin (*frhn*); Don Freeman, Lance Ong, George Duke (*ky*); James Skelton (*org*); Michael Sembello (*g, v*); Buzzy Feiten (*g*); Marcus Miller (*b*); Omar Hakim (*d*); Paulinho Da Costa (*perc*). 82.

Whatever palatable, easy-listening trimmings are applied to David Sanborn's records, his own contributions always cut deeper than that. For someone who originally took up sax playing as a therapeutic exercise (he was affected by polio as a child), Sanborn has made the most of his medicine. He already had a signature sound by the time of *Taking Off*, his solo debut, having already worked in rock and blues bands for ten years, and while he is shy of jazz as a basis for his own music, his high, skirling tone and succinct phrasing have inspired countless other players. The problem with *Taking Off* and *Heart To Heart* (as well as the deleted *Sanborn* and *Promise Me The Moon*) is context: other than delivering vague funky instrumentals, there's little for Sanborn to bite on here, and the original tunes aren't much more than 1970s funk clichés. *Voyeur* is the album that raises the game a notch: the sound assumes a hard gleam, and a tightness which would be constricting for most players replaces any sense of a loose gait. The altoman thrives in the context, cutting sharp circular patterns like a skater on ice, with the prettiness of 'It's You' and 'All I Need Is You' balancing the bright, airless funk of 'Wake Me When It's Over'. *As We Speak*, though, was a disappointing repeat run, with sentimental fluff courtesy of guitarist-singer Sembello taking up too much room.

*** Backstreet Warner Bros 923906-2
Sanborn; Marcus Miller (*ky, g, b, perc*); Michael Colina (*ky*); Hiram Bullock (*ky, g*); Buzzy Feiten (*g*); Steve Gadd (*d*); Ralph Macdonald (*perc*). 83.

*** Straight To The Heart Warner Bros 925150-2
Sanborn; Randy Brecker, Jon Faddis (*t*); Michael Brecker (*ts*); Don Grolnick (*ky*); Hiram Bullock (*g*); Marcus Miller (*b, ky*); Buddy Williams (*d*); Erroll Bennett (*perc*). 84.

** A Change Of Heart Warner Bros 925479-2
Sanborn; Michael Brecker (*EWI*); Marcus Miller (*ky, g, b*); Don Grolnick, Rob Mounsey, Michael Colina, John Mahoney, Michael Sembello, Bernard Wright, Philippe Saisse, Ronnie Foster, Randy Waldman (*ky*); Mac Rebennack (*p*); Hiram Bullock, Hugh McCracken, Nicky Moroch, Carlos Rios (*g*); Anthony Jackson (*b*); Mickey Curry, John Robinson (*d*); Paulinho Da Costa, Mino Cinelu (*perc*). 87.

***(*) Close-Up Reprise 925715-2
Sanborn; Marcus Miller (*ky, g, b*); Richard Tee, Ricky Peterson (*p*); Hiram Bullock, Nile Rodgers, Steve Jordan, Jeff Mironov, G. E. Smith, Paul Jackson (*g*); Andy Newmark, Vinnie Colaiuta, William House (*d*); Paulinho Da Costa, Don Alias (*perc*); Michael Ruff (*v*). 88.

Marcus Miller had been playing and composing for Sanborn's records before, but with *Backstreet* he began producing as well, intensifying further the almost abstract neo-funk which the saxophonist had behind him. *Backstreet* featured some agreeable tunes as well as the beat, though, and in the title-piece, 'A Tear For Crystal' and 'Blue Beach' Sanborn wrung the most out of each situation. His sound was sometimes almost frozen in the still space of the studio, but his tone remained uniquely capable of emoting in this context. Cut before a studio audience, *A Change Of Heart* simulated one of Sanborn's live shows and, while it has some tedious features, it's a rare chance to hear the leader in more extended solos than usual, which are strong enough to belie his insistence that a jazz context is inappropriate for him.

A Change Of Heart was a false step. Four different producers handle the eight tracks and the result is a mishmash of styles where each man tries to affix Sanborn's trademark wail in his own setting. Only Miller's work is truly effective, although Michael Sembello gave Sanborn one of his most insistently catchy melodies in 'The Dream'; the rest is over-produced pop-jazz at its least amiable. *Close-Up*, however, was a brilliant return to form. This time Miller handled the whole project and turned in tunes and arrangements which took Sanborn to the very limit of this direction. Having experimented with different keyboard and drum-programme sounds on the earlier records, Miller built backing tracks of enormous complexity which barely gave the saxophonist room to breathe, yet the exciting riff-tune 'Slam', sweet melodies of 'So Far Away' and 'Lesley Ann' and staccato snap of 'Tough' squeezed Sanborn into delivering some of his smartest ideas. It's a little like a modernization of West Coast jazz,

where soloists were required to put a personal stamp on 16 bars in the middle of a skin-tight arrangement. The sound is artificially brilliant but entirely suitable for the music.

*** **Another Hand** Elektra Musician 7559-61088-2
>   Sanborn; Art Baron (*tb, btb*); Lenny Pickett (*cl, ts*); Terry Adams, Mulgrew Miller (*p*); Leon
>   Pendarvis (*org*); Bill Frisell, Marc Ribot, Al Anderson, Dave Tronzo (*g*); Greg Cohen, Charlie
>   Haden, Marcus Miller (*b*); Joey Baron, Steve Jordan, Jack DeJohnette (*d*); Don Alias (*perc*);
>   Syd Straw (*v*). 90.

A striking if sometimes uneasy change of direction. After working with a wide range of players on his
American TV series, *Night Music*, Sanborn (and producer Hal Willner) sought out less familiar territory and came up with this curious fusion of jazz, R&B and the kind of instrumental impressionism
which participants Frisell and Ribot have been associated with. Sanborn sounds interested but not
entirely sure of himself at some points, and happiest on the less rhythmically taxing pieces such as the
infectious lope of 'Hobbies' and two tracks with the Millers and DeJohnette. The film-music medley
arranged by Greg Cohen emerges as a queer pastiche. Possibly more important to its maker than to his
audience, but well worth hearing.

***(*) **Upfront** Elektra 7559-61272
>   Sanborn; Earl Gardner, Laurie Frink, Randy Brecker, Paul Litteral, Herb Roberston (*t*); Dave
>   Bargeron, Art Baron (*tb*); Stan Harrison (*as*); Lenny Pickett, Arno Hecht (*ts*); Crispin Cioe (*bs*);
>   Richard Tee (*org*); John Purcell (*ts, saxello*); William Patterson, Eric Clapton (*g*); Marcus Miller
>   (*b, ky, g, bcl*); Steve Jordan (*d*); Don Alias, Nana Vasconcelos (*perc*). 91.

Looser, funkier, free-flowing where the last one was bound up in itself, this is Sanborn sounding better
than he has for a while. His own playing doesn't change so much from record to record, but he sounds a
lot more comfortable back here in Marcus Miller's grooves than he did on Hal Willner's on the
previous disc – and a lot happier than Miles Davis ever did, too. The hip, updated treatment of
Ornette's 'Ramblin'' works out a treat, with Herb Robertson adding squittery trumpet, but the whole
record has a lot of fine playing – in a live-in-the-studio atmosphere – that stands up to plenty of
listening.

*** **Hearsay** Elektra 7559-61620-2
>   Sanborn; Earl Gardner, Michael Stewart (*t*); John Purcell, Lenny Pickett (*ts*); Marcus Miller
>   (*bcl, ky, g, b*); Ricky Peterson (*org, p*); William Patterson, Dean Brown, Robben Ford (*g*); Steve
>   Jordan (*d*); Don Alias (*perc*). 93.

Still seeking a live-in-the-studio sound, Miller produces a great set of grooves here for Sanborn to blow
over; a revision of Marvin Gaye's 'Got To Give It Up' and a gorgeous 'The Long Goodbye' are two
highlights among many. But the man himself sounds merely capable. One longs for a single killer solo,
or for one of the other horns to step up and push him into his best form.

*** **Pearls** Elektra 7559-61759-2
>   Sanborn; Don Grolnick (*ky*); Kenny Barron (*p*); Marcus Miller, Christian McBride, Mark Egan
>   (*b*); Steve Gadd (*d*); Don Alias (*perc*); Oleta Adams, Jimmy Scott (*v*); strings. 94.

Sanborn's strings album is an elegant vehicle for his sound. The choice of material is safe rather than
surprising, but it's interesting that the old-fashioned pieces – 'Willow Weep For Me' or 'Come Rain Or
Come Shine' – don't suit him nearly as well as the 'mature' modern pop of Sade's title-tune – where he
gets a nice note of menace in – or Leon Russell's 'Superstar'. Scott and Adams take a vocal apiece, to no
great effect, and the sound is glassy rather than warm, but the overall effect is pleasing enough.

*** **The Best Of David Sanborn** Warner Bros 9362-45768-2
Sanborn's hits collection covers seven of his eleven Warners albums and is a neat survey of his most
commercially successful years. As a pocket primer on the most copied and insidiously influential sax
sound of its era, very effective.

David Sanchez (born 1969) TENOR SAXOPHONE

*** **Sketches Of Dreams** Columbia 480236
>   Sanchez; Roy Hargrove (*t*); Danilo Perez, David Kikoski (*p*); Larry Grenadier (*b*); Adam Cruz
>   (*d*); Milton Cardona, Jerry Gonzalez, Leon Parker (*perc*). 94.

Like its Columbia predecessor, *The Departure*, which was the debut disc by this gifted young Puerto
Rican, *Sketches Of Dreams* was greeted with wild excitement that may have left some purchasers a mite
disappointed. Is Sanchez really the genius he was cracked up to be? On the evidence of this disc, that
may be pushing it a bit far. He has a big, broad, old-fashioned sound that some have likened to Johnny
Griffin but which in approach borrows much from Rollins and very little from Coltrane, unusually for a

player of his generation. What makes this album is the sterling support from Perez, Grenadier and Cruz, who turn what might have been an exercise in individualist showmanship into a jazz album.

Tommy Sancton CLARINET, VOCAL

***(*) **New Orleans Reunion** GHB BC-283
  Sancton; David Paquette (*p, v*); Cornelis 'Pam' Pameijer (*d*). 10/89.
The title suggests a homecoming of ancients, but these not-so-old veterans have a wonderful time on this almost impromptu studio date. All three men worked in New Orleans in revivalist outfits in the 1970s, but here they touch on an intimacy and unaffected warmth rare in much of this kind of music. Sancton is a careful, unflashy player, stately in the manner of the old masters of New Orleans clarinet but gifted with a smooth, beguiling tone that graces all of his lines. He seldom plays in the high register and that gives his solos a flowing ease of delivery on ballads and stompers alike. Paquette is a cheerful, two-fisted player, a fine partner, and Pameijer is as proper as a New Orleans drummer should be. Although most of the tunes are familiar enough, they picked some lovely rarities in Claude Hopkins's 'Crying My Eyes Out Over You' and Ellington's 'A Lull At Dawn'. The recording is very close-miked and friendly.

Pharoah Sanders (born 1940) TENOR SAXOPHONE

*** **Pharoah's First** ESP Disk ESP 1003
  Sanders; Stan Foster (*t*); Jane Getz (*p*); William Bennett (*b*); Marvin Patillo (*d, perc*). 9/64.
***(*) **Tauhid** Impulse! GRP 11292
  Sanders; Sonny Sharrock (*g*); Dave Burrell (*p*); Henry Grimes (*b*); Roger Blank (*d*); Nat Bettis (*perc*). 11/66.
(*) **Journey To The One Evidence ECD 22016
  Sanders; Eddie Henderson (*flhn*); Joe Bonner, John Hicks (*p*); Paul Arslanian, Bedria Sanders (*harm*); Mark Isham (*syn*); Chris Hayes, Carl Lockett (*g*); James Pomerantz (*sitar*); Yoko Ito Gates (*koto*); Ray Drummond, Joy Julks (*b*); Randy Merrit, Idris Muhammad (*d*); Phil Ford (*tabla*); Babatunde (*perc*); Claudette Allen, Donna Dickerson, Bobby McFerrin, Vicki Randle, Ngoh Spencer (*v*).
*** **Rejoice** Evidence ECD 22020
  Sanders; Danny Moore (*t*); Steve Turre (*tb*); Bobby Hutcherson (*vib*); John Hicks (*p*); Joe Bonner (*p, v*); Peter Fujii (*g, v*); Lois Colin (*hp*); Art Davis (*b*); Jorge Pomar (*b, v*); Billy Higgins, Elvin Jones (*d*); Babatunde, Big Black (*perc*); Flame Braithwaite, William S. Fischer, B. Kazuko Ishida, Bobby London, Sakinah Muhammad, Carol Wilson Scott, Yvette S. Vanterpool (*v*).
*** **Heart Is A Melody** Evidence ECD 22063
  Sanders; William Henderson (*p*); John Heard (*b*); Idris Muhammad (*d*); Paul Arslanian (*bells, whistle*); Andy Bey, Flame Braithwaite, Cort Cheek, Janie Cook, William S. Fischer, Mira Hadar, Debra McGriffe, Jes Muir, Kris Wyn (*v*). 1/82.
*** **Shukuru** Evidence ECD 22022
  Sanders; William Henderson (*syn*); Ray Drummond (*b*); Idris Muhammad (*d*); Leon Thomas (*v*).
***(*) **Africa** Timeless SJP 253
  Sanders; John Hicks (*p*); Curtis Lundy (*b*); Idris Muhammad (*d*). 3/87.
*** **A Prayer Before Dawn** Evidence ECD 22047
  Sanders; William Henderson (*p, syn*); John Hicks (*p*); Lynn Taussig (*sarod, chandrasarang*); Alvin Queen (*d*); Brian McLaughlin (*tabla*). 9/87.
*** **Moon Child** Timeless SJP 326
  Sanders; William Henderson (*p*); Stafford James (*b*); Eddie Moore (*d*); Cheikh Tidiane Fale (*perc*). 10/89.
***(*) **Welcome To Love** Timeless SJP 358
  Sanders; William Henderson (*p*); Stafford James (*b*); Ecclestone W. Wainwright (*d*). 7/90.
Learning that Pharoah Sanders had made an album of standards was a little like learning that Marvin Hagler gives flower-arranging classes. In the 1960s, Sanders was easily the most fearsome tenor sax-ophonist on the scene. Born in Little Rock, Arkansas, in 1940, and thus at the very intersection of every contradictory impulse facing young black males in America, he developed a tone of oxyacetylene heat, much influenced by Albert Ayler, but far harsher. He played on most of the late Coltrane albums and, rootless after Coltrane's death, made the obligatory ESP Disk record (now reissued on CD) and two shockers for Impulse!, of which the better is now available again. Unlike the ESP, which is terrorist

grunge with a shake of mysticism, *Tauhid* has worn quite well, certainly more gracefully than the awful *Thembi* which followed. Nowadays it's valued as much for Sonny Sharrock's contributions as for Sanders himself; but the album does demonstrate the ways in which the saxophonist was already poised for a move beyond extreme noise terror and into a more lyrical and melodic style. Both the long tracks, 'Upper Egypt & Lower Egypt' and a zodiacal suite, tend to oversauce intelligent improvisations with pointless 'ethnic' effects and chants, but the intelligence, and the improvisation, are still there, and still eminently listenable.

The saxophonist remained largely silent for the rest of the 1970s. His return wasn't anything like the grotesque flabby-middleweight comeback that everyone feared. Sanders had, perhaps inevitably, toned down the desperate inarticulacy which stood in place of conventional harmonic or melodic development (and was quite appropriate in the context of Coltrane's *Ascension*); what emerged in its place was a dry, philosophical voice that sought to persuade by logic and rhetoric rather than sheer power.

During the 1980s, Sanders regularly returned to Coltrane material: 'After The Rain' on both *Journey To The One* and *A Prayer Before Dawn*, the weakest of the recent sets, 'Moment's Notice' and 'Central Park West' on *Rejoice*, 'Ole' on *Heart Is A Melody*, 'Naima' on *Africa*, and a decidedly Coltraneish 'Night Has A Thousand Eyes' on *Moon Child*. Sanders has also been increasingly interested in standard material – with the tenor saxophonist's shibboleth 'Body And Soul' on *Shukuru* – which may represent a belated recognition that composing is not his trump.

Only a hardened cynic would suggest that dotting Coltrane themes throughout a rather densely packed programme of releases was a shrewd commercial tactic. They've certainly done well since their original release on Teresa. It's clear that Sanders feels the music deeply, from the inside, and he is arguably the most authentic and thoughtful interpreter of this material on the scene today.

At the back of the mind of course is the nudging recognition that this *is* Pharoah Sanders (a little like the dilemma confronting fans of the Visigothic Peter Brötzmann when he released a record called *Fourteen Love Poems*). The cover of *A Prayer Before Dawn* shows the middle-aged Sanders with white fringe beard and anomalously black hair framing a benevolently owlish expression far removed from the contorted scowl of former years. With accommodation has come productivity. There are now too many Sanders albums from too short a period. *Journey To The One* was a shaky start (though it apparently achieved considerable popularity in the clubs). Certainly there are still too many meandering, Afro-mystical themes and Nilotic fantasies, and too many ill-thought-out instrumental combinations. In Bonner, Henderson and Hicks though, luck, label politics or good judgement has delivered up to the saxophonist three players who understand his chastened romanticism, and there are genuinely touching moments on the recent *Welcome To Love*, where Sanders pays tribute to another fallen comrade, the late percussionist, Eddy Moore. (The disc also provides a calling card for Ecclestone W. Wainwright who, with a name like that, ought to be vice-president of his own corporation.)

*** **Message From Home** Verve 529 578
> Sanders; Michael White (*vn*); William Henderson (*p, ky, v*); Bernie Worrell (*ky, v*); Jeff Bova (*ky*); Dominic Kanza (*g*); Charnett Moffett (*b*); Steve Neil (*b*); Hamid Drake (*d, perc*); Aiyb Dieng (*perc*). 95.

Very much in the same dance-orientated mode of recent years. It will take older readers a moment or two to convince themselves that this bears any resemblance to the Pharoah Sanders who worked with Coltrane. Overcome that prejudice, though, and this is a fine record, a little overloaded with electronic sound but still viable and very strongly played.

Randy Sandke TRUMPET, CORNET, GUITAR

*** **The Sandke Brothers** Stash ST-CD-575
> Sandke; Jordan Sandke (*t, c*); Joel Helleny (*tb*); Michael Brecker, Tad Shull (*ts*); Jaki Byard, Jim McNeely (*p*); John Goldsby, Milt Hinton (*b*); Charles Braugham, Kenny Washington (*d*). 5–6/85.

*** **Stampede** Jazzology JCD-211
> Sandke; Dan Barrett (*tb, c*); Ken Peplowski (*cl*); Scott Robinson (*bsx, c*); Ray Kennedy (*p*); Marty Grosz (*g*); Linc Milliman (*tba*); Dave Ratajczak (*d*). 12/90.

*** **Wild Cats** Jazzology JCD-222
> As above, except Mark Shane (*p*), James Chirillo (*g*) and Jack Lesberg (*b*) replace Robinson, Kennedy, Grosz and Milliman. 7/92.

*** **The Bix Beiderbecke Era** Nagel-Heyer CD 002
> As above, except Scott Robinson (*Cmel, bsx, c*), Marty Grosz (*g, v*) and Linc Milliman (*tba*) replace Chirillo and Lesberg. 5/93.

*** **Broadway** Nagel-Heyer CD 003
>   As above, except omit Peplowski. 5/93.
*** **I Hear Music** Concord CCD-4566
>   Sandke; Ken Peplowski (*ts, cl*); Ray Kennedy (*p*); John Goldsby (*b*); Terry Clarke (*d*). 2/93.
***(*) **Get Happy** Concord CCD-4598
>   As above, except Kenny Barron (*p*) replaces Kennedy, add Robert Trowers (*tb*). 9/93.
***(*) **The Chase** Concord CCD-4642
>   Sandke; Ray Anderson (*tb*); Chris Potter (*as, ts, ss*); Michael Brecker (*ts*); Ted Rosenthal (*p*); John Goldsby (*b*); Marvin 'Smitty' Smith (*d*). 3/94.

When it comes to versatility, Sandke's the man, and it lines him up alongside Guy Barker, Wynton Marsalis and a select few in a trumpet section that could play more or less anything in pretty much any style. As ever, the problem with that skill lies in how to sound like yourself. Sandke is getting there, but on some of these records his accomplishments can sound hollow. The Stash CD reissues two LPs, one under the leadership of each Sandke brother: there's little to choose between them in terms of the improvising, but Randy's tunes have a more interesting bent – 'Bix's Place' is very pretty, and so is the ballad, 'Brownstones'. Jordan plays well, but he seems to have faded from the scene somewhat. Sandke's New Yorkers account for the next four discs. This is a repertory group in the manner of those helmed by Marty Grosz and Keith Ingham, and with a similar cast of performers, so there's little to surprise anyone who's heard the many records in this burgeoning genre. *Stampede* is a bit brisker than *Wild Cats*, but the latter gives the soloists some extra room and Sandke sounds more relaxed: he constructs a very fetching solo out of 'Wild Cat' itself, for instance. *The Bix Beiderbecke Era* is a concert in Hamburg on the occasion of Bix's ninetieth birthday and, though the sound isn't ideal, Sandke's team punch through the Beiderbecke repertoire with plenty of fizz. *Broadway* is a studio date, cut the next day: it was hot, the group were tired, and the material is an unpromising set of warhorses. That it still sounds good is some tribute to a jazzman's professionalism and, though there are a couple of duds, the band play with an unexpected attack that actually surpasses the Jazzology discs at some points. On all four discs there is first-class support from both Peplowski and Barrett, spirits in close kinship to the leader. Sandke himself is rather variable: some of his solos sound almost pernickety in their attempts to please period feel, others better their environment.

The Concords are more ambitious. *I Hear Music* mixes old songs with six originals by Sandke, and if his tunes aren't so impressive here they serve as sound vehicles for a deepening mastery of the trumpet: his high notes are cleaner and tougher, and his fast lines have a hard-bitten confidence. *Get Happy*, though, introduces an intriguing set-list: Monk's 'Humph', Ellington's 'Black Beauty' (done as an exquisite trio for trumpet, clarinet and piano), Miles Davis's 'Deception' and Mingus's 'Boogie Stop Shuffle'. There's also a somewhat odd affection for Al Jolson's repertoire. Barron's expert accompaniment is a further bonus, and Trowers adds extra colour to five tracks, while Sandke excels on a winsome arrangement of Fauré's 'Sicilienne'. *The Chase* continues what's by now an impressive sequence. Anderson and the splendid Potter add muscle and élan to the front line, while Robinson and Brecker lend further gravitas. The material stretches from Don Redman to Duke Jordan, and Sandke sounds in control of all of it.

Arturo Sandoval (born 1949) TRUMPET, FLUGELHORN, KEYBOARDS, PERCUSSION, VOCAL

(*) **No Problem Jazz House JHCD 001
>   Sandoval; Hilario Duran Torres (*p*); Jorge Chicoy (*g*); Jorge Reyes Hernandes (*b*); Bernardo Garcia Carreras (*d*); Reinaldo Valera Del Monte (*perc*). 8/86.
(*) **Straight Ahead Jazz House JHCD 007
>   Sandoval; Chucho Valdes (*p*); Ron Matthewson (*b*); Martin Drew (*d*). 8/88.
(*) **Just Music Jazz House JHCD 008
>   Sandoval; Hilario Duran Torres (*ky*); Jorge Chicoy (*g*); Jorge Reyes Hernandes (*b*); Bernardo Garcia Carreras (*d*); Reinaldo Valera Del Monte (*perc*). 8/88.
** **Flight To Freedom** GRP GRD-9634
>   Sandoval; Ed Calle (*ts, f*); Chick Corea, Mike Orta, Danilo Perez, Richard Eddy (*ky*); Rene Luis Toledo (*g*); Anthony Jackson, Nicky Orta (*b*); Dave Weckl, Orlando Hernandez (*d*); Long John, Portinho (*perc*). 91.

In person, Sandoval is one of the most ebullient trumpet ambassadors since Dizzy Gillespie, his great mentor. On record, this Cuban exile and scintillating virtuoso is a less convincing figure, though that may be due to overheated expectations. The live record is a fair sample of the kind of music he serves up at Ronnie Scott's on his regular visits, and while the playing bubbles with Latin fire and brilliance, battle fatigue tends to overtake the listener. Sandoval may be a great technician, but it's often hard to detect any reason for the galloping runs other than a love of showmanship. The band provide zesty accompaniment. In the studio, with Valdes and a British rhythm section, the atmosphere seems calmer until they go into the trumpet machismo of 'Mambo Influenciado', which shows that Sandoval doesn't need a live audience to prod him into going over the top. *Just Music* was recorded around the same time and is another mixed bag of kitsch and genuine music-making. The GRP set was his first 'American' statement after defecting to the USA, and the irony is that it often falls into international muzak: GRP house-bands provide faceless backing tracks which the trumpeter dances over with a sometimes light but more often crashingly heavy footfall. If Sandoval is going to make significant records, he'll need to think carefully about material, musicians and producers alike.

*** I Remember Clifford GRP GRP-96682

Sandoval; Ernie Watts, David Sanchez, Ed Calle (*ts*); Felix Gomez (*ky*); Kenny Kirkland (*p*); Charnett Moffett (*b*); Kenny Washington (*d*). 91.

Tribute albums are becoming a bore, but this is easily the best record under Sandoval's name to date. The material is all in dedication to Clifford Brown, and most of it emanates from Brownie's own repertoire, including 'Joy Spring', 'Daahoud' and the like. The up-tempo pieces are as thrilling as Sandoval can make them: 'Cherokee' is taken at a preposterously fast tempo, and the trumpeter still pulls off a solo which outpaces everybody else. Watts and Sanchez also fire off some exciting solos of their own, and the rhythm section is absolutely on top of it, with Kirkland at his most dazzling. Yet there remains a gloss of routine on the music, which can sound utterly unyielding, and the production decision to create some trumpet parts by feeding them through a harmonizer only adds to the sense of a spirit tamed by the demands of making successful records.

** Dreams Come True GRP GRD 9701

Sandoval; Bill Watrous (*tb*); Ernie Watts (*ts*); Michel Legrand, Otmaro Ruiz (*ky*); Brian Bromberg (*b*); Peter Erskine, Aaron Sefarty (*d*); Carlos Gomez, Mitchell Sanchez (*perc*); strings. 93.

** The Latin Train GRP GRD 9820

Sandoval; Dana Teboe (*tb*); Ed Calle (*ts, bs, f*); Kenny Anderson (*as*); Otmaro Ruiz (*p*); Rene Toledo (*g*); David Enos (*b*); Aaron Sefarty (*d*); Manuel Castrillo, Luis Enrique, Edwin Bonilla, Carl Valldejuli (*perc*); Joe Williams, Celia Cruz, Oscar D'Leon, Luis Enrique, Vicente Rojas, Laura Pifferrer, Cheito Quinones (*v*). 1/95.

Gimcracked around Sandoval's prodigious but exhausting talents, these albums are a stifling bore, and they show Sandoval already with nowhere interesting to go. *Dreams Come True* just about gets by on the basis of 'Dahomey Dance', which at least gives Watts and Watrous something useful to do; the rest, heavingly arranged by Legrand, is charmless. So is most of *The Latin Train*, which seems about as feelingful and sincere as a Las Vegas wedding. The frantic high-note playing and souped-up arrangements go nowhere fast. For diehard fans only.

Eivin Sannes PIANO

*** Sandu Gemini GMCD 67

Sannes; Sture Janson (*b*); Ronnie Gardiner (*d*). 5/90.

Sannes comes from, in his own words, 'the generation that will always be grateful to the great composers – Duke Ellington, Van Heusen, Benny Golson and many others'. The veteran Norwegian pianist plays 15 standards here with a lot of engaging sparkle. His manner is poised between swing and the cooler end of bebop – one of his early inspirations was Pete Jolly – and, while there's nothing to startle a casual listener here, the tracks are delivered with fine, unassuming candour. A duet with Janson on 'Lulu's Back In Town' is particularly crisp and witty, but there's something good in all the tracks and, though he can be a little too fond of arpeggios and the occasional commonplace, some unusual tunes – Buster Bailey's 'Peruvian Nights' and Victor Feldman's 'Azule Serape', which bookend the record – add fresh interest.

Mongo Santamaria (born 1922) PERCUSSION

***(*) Mongo Explodes / Watermelon Man! Beat Goes Public CDBGPD 062

Santamaria; Marty Sheller (*t*); Nat Adderley (*c*); Mauricio Smith (*f*); Robert Capers, Pat Patrick (*sax*); Hubert Laws (*ts, f, picc*); Rodgers Grant (*p*); Victor Venegas (*b*); Ray Lucas (*d*); Carmelo Garcia, F. Hernandez, Kako, Osvaldo Martinez, Joseph Gorgas, Osvaldo Chihuahua Martinez, Wito Kortwright (*perc*). 7/62, 64.

***(*) Skins Milestone 47038

Santamaria; Paul Serrano, Marty Sheller (*t*); Nat Adderley (*c*); Hubert Laws (*f, picc, ts*); Al Abreu, Pat Patrick (*f, sax*); Bob Capers (*as, bs*); Chick Corea, Rodgers Grant (*p*); Jose De Paulo (*g, perc*); Victor Venegas (*b*); Ray Lucas (*d*); Julio Collazo, Carmelo Garcia, Wito Kortwright, Osvaldo Chihuahua Martinez, To-Tiko (*perc*); Carmen Costa, Marcellina Guerra, Elliott Romero (*v*); chorus. 64, 7/72.

***(*) **Mongo At The Village Gate** Original Jazz Classics OJC 490
Santamaria; Marty Sheller (*t*); Pat Patrick (*f, sax*); Bob Capers (*as, bs*); Rodgers Grant (*p*); Victor Venegas (*b*); Frank Hernanadez, Osvaldo Chihuahua Martinez, Julian Cabrera (*perc*).

***(*) **Summertime** Original Jazz Classics OJC 626
Santamaria; Dizzy Gillespie (*t*); Doug Harris (*f, ts*); Allen Hoist (*f, bs, clo*); Toots Thielemans (*hca*); Milton Hamilton (*p*); Lee Smith (*b*); Steve Berrios (*perc*). 7/80.

(*) **Soy Yo Concord CCD 4327
Santamaria; Eddie E. J. Allen (*t*); Sam Furnace (*as, bs, f*); Tony Hinson (*ts, f*); Bob Quaranta (*p, ky*); Ray Martinez (*b*); John Andrews (*d, perc*); Pablo Rosario, Steve Thornton, Valentino (*perc*); Ada Chabrier, Denice Nortez Wiener (*v*). 4/87.

(*) **Soca Me Nice Concord CCD 4362
Santamaria; Ray Vega (*t, flhn*); Bobby Porcelli (*as, bs, f*); Mitch Frohman (*ts, f*); Bob Quaranta (*p*); Ray Martinez (*b*); Johnny Almendra Andreu, Humberto Nengue Hernandez (*perc*); Angelo-Mark Pagen (*v*). 5/88.

*** **Ole Ola** Concord CCD 4387
Santamaria; Ray Vega (*t, flhn*); Bobby Porcelli (*as, bs, f*); Mitch Frohman (*ts, f*); Bob Quaranta (*p*); Bernie Minoso (*b*); Johnny Almendra Andreu, Humberto Nengue Hernandez (*perc*); Jil Armsbury, Bobbi Cespedes, Claudia Gomez (*v*). 5/89.

*** **Live At Jazz Alley** Concord CCD 4427
Santamaria; Ray Vega (*t, flhn*); Bobby Porcelli (*as, bs, f*); Mitch Frohman (*ts, ss, f*); Bob Quaranta (*p*); Bernie Minoso (*b*); Johnny Almendra Andreu, Eddie Rodriguez (*perc*). 3/90.

Born in Cuba, Santamaria moved to the United States in 1950. Originally an orthodox *charanga* player, leading a group fronted by violin and flute, he introduced trumpets and saxophones and experimented with jazz voicings. Despite a resurgence of activity in the later 1980s, and two fine sessions for Concord, his reputation is now much less than it was in the 1960s and early '70s, when he was seen as largely responsible for the introduction of Latin-jazz and soul elements into the mainstream, developments which had a profound impact on players like Chick Corea and Hubert Laws, both of whom play on *Skins*, a compilation of sessions nearly a decade apart, and certainly the best place to begin. The once popular *Watermelon Man*, originally on Battle Records, has now reappeared on a useful twofer with the appropriately titled *Mongo Explodes*.

The percussionist's version of the Herbie Hancock tune is an Afro-Cuban classic, but there are other interesting things on both sessions. Long-time Sun Ra Arkestra member Pat Patrick chips in with 'Bayou Roots' and 'Boogie Cha Cha Blues', while fellow saxophonist Bobby Capers signs several compositions on both sessions, most notably 'Fatback' and 'Corn Bread Guajira' (*Explodes*) and 'Don't Bother Me No More' and 'Go Git It!' (*Watermelon Man*). Hubert Laws is the other featured writer. The best of the material is also available on *Skins* (which includes some additional tracks) and, in live versions, *At The Village Gate*. These and the *Summertime* OJC are lively club and concert recordings and give a good sense (though neither is particularly well registered) of the high level of excitement Santamaria can generate. The latter is properly co-credited to Dizzy Gillespie, whose Afro-Cuban experiments owe a good deal to the percussionist's influence. Santamaria fans will tell you that only the live records give a true representation of what he is about. That's largely the case; the studio stuff is pretty stilted, but there is an awful sameness about the club recordings that the studio arrangements manage to steer clear of. *Live At Jazz Alley* catches the old boy still doing his stuff as he approaches threescore and ten. It's a new and largely unfamiliar band and a completely predictable set-list, with a shuffling rendition of 'Afro Blue' that will be of interest to those who heard John Coltrane do the same tune, also in Seattle, a quarter of a century earlier.

Michel Sardaby PIANO

**** **Night Cap** Sound Hills SCCD 8004
Sardaby; Percy Heath (*b*); Connie Kay (*d*). 70.

***(*) **Straight On** Sound Hills SCD 8003
Sardaby; Louis Smith (*t*); Ralph Moore (*ts*); Peter Washington (*b*); Tony Reedus (*d*). 5/92.

For most listeners, these two widely spaced sessions will be a first introduction to the Frenchman's work. An artist and architect by training, Sardaby has the structural awareness one associates with Martial Solal or John Lewis, allied to a resonant left hand. Melody lines tend to be quite fast and detailed, with few non-functional notes.

The 1970 trios are a revelation. The presence of Heath and Kay is a reminder of the Lewis connection, and several of Sardaby's originals could almost have been by the great American. There are, however, signature devices and favourite chord progressions which give the game away. The originality of Sardaby's style is premised on a relatively small set of idiosyncrasies, but they are followed through so elegantly and unabashedly that they acquire considerable charm from their very repetition.

All the material on *Night Cap* and *Straight On* is by Sardaby, except for 'Satin Doll', which concludes the trios. The band seem comfortable with the charts. Moore is unflappable and exact, Smith more edgy and intense, but they combine very effectively and, with Sardaby chording more heavily than in the past, give the ensembles the weight of a much larger group. Two themes stand out: the appropriately elegant 'Smoothie', which has touches of Ahmad Jamal, and the slighter but no less beautiful 'Ballad For Roni', which initiates the leader's best solo. It's a pity there's no overlap between the two sessions to check Sardaby's progress. He's made 11 albums (no others currently available outside France, we believe) and it would be good to see him more generously exposed.

Akio Sasajima (born 1952) GUITAR

*** **Humpty Dumpty** Enja 8032-2
    Sasajima; Joe Henderson (*ts*); Renée Rosnes (*p*); Dave Gordon (*syn*); Kelly Sill, Thomas Kini (*b*); Joel Spencer (*d*); Marlene Alden (*v*). 8/88.
***(*) **Time Remembered** Muse MCD5417
    Sasajima; Harvie Swartz (*b*); Victor Lewis (*d*). 4/89.
*** **Akioustically Sound** Muse MCD 5448
    Sasajima; Ron Carter (*b*). 3/91.

Sasajima's songful tone and graceful phrasing make these records very playable. If he springs from the tradition of Jim Hall and Wes Montgomery, he plays with enough spirit to make an old-fashioned sound into something contemporary, and the picked teams of accompanists are strong enough to step away from neo-classicism. *Humpty Dumpty* is his second appearance with Henderson (an earlier date for Muse hasn't made it to CD) and, rather inevitably, is hijacked by the tenorman and Rosnes, both in good form and pushing the guitarist's contributions into second place (Gordon and Alden intrude on one track only). *Time Remembered* is a rather better showcase: Sasajima records himself with an agreeably muzzy guitar-sound, Swartz is beautifully nimble and in tune with the leader, and Lewis locks in perfectly, using brushes more often than sticks. Hardly an aggressive piece of music-making, but it swings hard. *Akiostically Sound* is a very pretty date, with Sasajima and Carter ambling along mutually compatible paths. The bassist doesn't seem to be putting himself out too much – he certainly sounds less involved than he was with Jim Hall on their duet sessions – but the guitarist's charming way of delivering a melody sustains the music.

Satchmo Legacy Band GROUP

*** **Salute to Pops: Volume 1** Soul Note 121 116
    Freddie Hubbard (*t, flhn, v*); Curtis Fuller (*tb, v*); Alvin Batiste (*cl, v*); Al Casey (*g, v*); Kirk Lightsey (*p, v*); Red Callender (*b, tba, v*); Alan Dawson (*d, v*). 6/87.
***(*) **Salute to Pops: Volume 2** Soul Note 121 166
    As above. 6/87.

The right-hand picture on the front of *Volume 1* is, remarkably, Freddie Hubbard rather than Louis Armstrong. Whether the resemblance stretches any further is a moot point. It's also a rather irrelevant one, since the purpose of the Satchmo Legacy (put together by Hubbard for a European tour) was not to produce identikit versions of the Hot Fives and Sevens but to give some of the classic Armstrong repertoire and associated material a respectful but thoroughly contemporary airing.

That's immediately evident in the boppish inflexion Hubbard gives to 'Struttin' With Some Barbecue', originally recorded before Christmas 1927 and credited to both Armstrongs, Louis and Lil; like all the tour material, it was transcribed and arranged by the Swiss-based Vince Benedetti. Lightsey's contribution to this opening track on *Volume 1* is thoroughly distinctive, and in a curious way the pianist dominates the session, constantly pushing familiar themes and progressions off in unexpected directions. The combination of Lightsey, Hubbard and Fuller acts as a guarantee against revivalist pastiche. One suspects that, left to their own devices, Batiste and Dawson in particular would play it a lot straighter, though Callender seems happy with an augmented role.

The bassist is featured on tuba for 'Ellingtonia Interlude', a segue of 'In A Sentimental Mood' and 'Sophisticated Lady', which is placed early in the session not just to give the rhythm players a more positive role but to underline that point that it is the Armstrong *legacy* that is under scrutiny. Batiste's 'Blues For Pops' is heartfelt but essentially undemanding, setting up a relaxed but slightly shambolic ending that takes in 'Ory's Creole Trombone' (a feature for Fuller), 'Stardust', 'Wild Man Blues' and 'Saints'. Though everyone is credited with a vocal role, it is Hubbard and Lightsey who dominate, the pianist with a slightly nutty take on Armstrong's still vocal approach.

Volume 2 is, if anything, stronger, with just enough focus to shave an extra half-star. If you're disinclined to shell out on both, this is certainly the one to go for. The opening 'Muskrat Ramble' is the best thing on the session and the most interesting with regard to the continuity between Armstrong and the bebop style which dominates the brass solos; Fuller takes his in the style of the tune's composer, Kid Ory, but tips his hat to J. J. Johnson as well. Batiste's reaction is slightly eccentric: low-toned and almost gloomy; but there is nothing to match the sheer oddity of Lightsey's vocal antics.

Much closer to the original performances are '12th Street Rag' (Satchmo's version was released only in 1941) and 'West End Blues'. The latter has always (and properly) been seen as the performance that made the June 1928 Fives so devastatingly epochal. Hubbard fudges the opening cadenza – as well he might – and ducks out of the original's vocal chorus. Nevertheless he turns in a strong and thoroughly idiomatic performance that makes up for the bland original, 'Blues For Duane', that follows, all 12 minutes of it.

Beautifully engineered at the BBC Studios in London, technically these sessions can't be faulted: Pete Briggs and Baby Dodds would have killed for the sound that Callender and Dawson get. If anything, the registration is a little too precise, throwing into distracting relief minor points of detail that don't really detract from a thoroughly enjoyable set of performances.

Savannah Jazz Band GROUP

(*) Savannah Jazz Band Lake LACD29
    Tony Smith (*t, v*); Brian Ellis (*tb*); Martin Fox (*cl*); Jack Cooper (*bj*); Tony Pollitt (*b*); John Meehan (*d*). 6/92–1/93.
(*) It's Only A Beautiful Picture . . . Lake LACD51
    As above. 1/95.

Based in Huddersfield, which is some way from Savannah, the SJB play unreconstructed trad in the Ken Colyer tradition: absolutely no frills, not many solos, and no shame about the vocals. Smith cracks too many notes to provide a really purposeful lead, and it's left to the bustling clarinet of Fox to make the biggest impression. These aren't bad records, but they sound pretty ramshackle when compared with the best of the new American traditionalists. The first has a more acidic sound-mix, but at least that has some life, which the second is a little short on.

Jarmo Savolainen (born 1961) PIANO

***(*) Songs For Solo Piano Beta BECD 4023
    Savolainen (*p* solo). 12/89, 6/90.
*** First Sight Timeless CD SJP 380
    Savolainen; Wallace Roney (*t*); Rick Margitza (*as*); Ron McClure (*b*); Billy Hart (*d*). 5/91.
**** True Image A Records AL 73031
    As above, except omit Roney and Margitza; add Tim Hagans (*t*); Dave Liebman (*ss*); Kari Heinila (*ts*). 3/94.

There's none of your copywriter's 'Nordic chill' about this debut set by the Finn. Brought up, like Edward Vesala, in the east of the country, Savolainen brings a range of languages to his keyboard but is much more obviously steeped in jazz than Vesala. The solo record, which came our way after the previous edition, actually pre-dates *First Sight*. It's a very different set, obviously, more introspective and ironic, but also a chance to hear this gifted player at close quarters. The two improvisations and 'Song No. 1' recall a spectrum of American players from Chick Corea to Keith Jarrett; but it is the standard 'Somewhere' that clinches a harmonic kinship with the latter. 'Lowlands', 'The Word' and the opening 'Ode For Opportunists' are all well-crafted originals. The piano – a model D Steinway – is super and has been given the sort of presence a classical player would ask for. A nicely constructed product.

Savolainen seems totally at home with the Americans on the New York session for Timeless. The writing is broadly conceived, not too busy, and always directed towards maximizing solo space. The pianist yields precedence to the hornmen, restricting himself to brisk and uncluttered interventions that always concentrate on reasserting the basic structure of the tune.

Rhythmically, he stays pretty much inside but has the kind of time feel that implies all manner of alternative counts, freeing his colleagues from slavish 4/4s. McClure's solo on 'The Word' is a good case in point. A couple of tracks later on, 'Inner Modes' and 'Thoughts' drift towards a Garbarek conception, but Margitza's bluesy sound and a raw mix (supervised by Jan Erik Kongshaug at the Oslo studio favoured by ECM, ironically) prevent it from taking over. Almost as a corrective, at this point Savolainen chips in with the one standard of the set, 'How My Heart Sings'.

The more recent of the NY sessions is better still, a long set packed with solid, four-square music-making. Essentially, there are two groups, fronted by Hagans and Heinila for the first half-dozen tracks, and by Liebman for the remainder. This was the first time that he had played with old Quest colleagues Hart and McClure since 1991, and it works wonderfully ('smooth as glass' in his own estimation). The soprano tracks coax the pianist out of his relative reserve as an accompanist, and there are some lovely exchanges on the cleverly constructed 'Things Are The Way They Are'.

It'll take another couple of albums, and a bit more solo exposure, to gain a clear fix on the young Finn, but the signs are nothing but positive.

Derek Saw SAXOPHONES

*** Step Up! Division DIVCD 1
    Saw; Martin Jones (*t*); Simon Pugsley (*tb*); Dave Wilkinson (*b*); Paul Hession (*d*). 10/93.
The most accurate measure of Saw's musical intelligence is 'Terra Firma', an original composition with which he has always ended sets, with whatever outfit he is leading. Rhythm Division is the latest of a series of groups active since the mid-1980s, and it is by far the best. It is also the most obviously jazz-influenced, in a clattery freebop idiom that is quintessentially British.

For *Step Up!* Saw draws on the considerable experience of Dave Wilkinson and Paul Hession, both of whom are free improvisers but who sound perfectly at ease with a more settled time feel. The choice of Butch Morris's 'Spooning' for an opening track is particularly bold, but it is the writing on 'Mr Mystery' (a memorial to the late Sun Ra) that really confirms Saw's originality and talent. It would be interesting to hear further coverage of standard and repertoire material; a saxophone and trombone duet on Strayhorn's 'Johnny Come Lately' suggests it could be highly successful.

Elsewhere, there are touches of R&B ('B.D. Blues') which draw on the leader's background in that idiom. Characteristically, though, it's given a thoroughly original slant by an able technician (alto, tenor and sopranino saxophones) who's sure to become more widely known.

Stefan Scaggiari PIANO

**(*) That's Ska-Jar-E Concord CCD 4510
    Scaggiari; John Lockwood (*b*); Colin Bailey (*d*). 9/91.
**(*) Stefanitely Concord CCD 4570
    As above. 4/93.
** Stefan Out Concord CCD 4659
    As above, except Jim Hughart (*b*) replaces Lockwood. 12/94.
The albums are presented like the work of a new man on the block, but Scaggiari is a veteran of the Washington D.C. scene and sounds like a local hero: these sets would sound fine in an unfamiliar bar on a quiet night when you're not expecting any surprises. Beyond that, they're rather less than absorbing. The pianist is a conservative – 'The melody should come first,' he says – whose bounciness and general bonhomie can be tiresome after two or three fast numbers, since he drives his points home. But there are some felicities that are likeable enough, and he swings, if a little too insistently. The second album has two interesting choices in Ralph Towner's 'Icarus' (wrong-headed) and Sam Jones's 'Bitter Sweet' (overcooked, but fun). *Stefan Out* (we've had enough of these titles, thank you) is docked a notch for going nowhere: for all his facility, he follows the same paths and makes the same points every time.

Antonio Scarano GUITAR

** Apreslude Splasc(h) H 356-2
    Scarano; Sandro Cerino (*bcl, cbcl*); Amerigo Daveri (*clo*); Loredana Gintoli (*hp*); Roberta Gambarini (*v*). 5–6/91.
Scarano's earlier and more interesting *Hot Blend* isn't available on CD as yet. Gambarini took a subdued role there; but *Apreslude* is basically a voice-and-guitar duo record, with the other players chipping in on only two tracks. It's a challenge to the two principals and one which Gambarini is frankly not up to yet: her scat readings of Ornette Coleman's 'Ramblin'' and Miles Davis's 'Nefertiti' are pretty but featherweight, and her voice is best used as a colour rather than a lead instrument. Scarano fills in behind her with honest toil, but the record doesn't amount to much.

Mario Schiano ALTO AND SOPRANO SAXOPHONES, SHEKERE

*** Original Sins Splasc(h) H 502-2
>   Schiano; Giancarlo Schiaffini (*tb*); Franco D'Andrea (*p*); Marcello Melis, Bruno Tommaso (*b*);
>   Franco Pecori, Paul Goldfield, Franco Tonani, Marco Cristofolini (*d*). 3/67–4/70.

***(*) Sud Splasc(h) H 501-2
>   Schiano; Massimo Bartoletti, Roberto Antinolfi, Gaitano Delfini (*t*); Guido Anelli, Ruggero
>   Pastore (*tb*); Eugenio Colombo, Tommaso Vittorini, Massimo Urbani, Maurizio Giammarco,
>   Toni Formichella (*reeds*); Domenico Guaccero (*ky*); Bruno Tommaso, Roberto Della Grotta
>   (*b*); Alfonso Alcantara Vieira, Michele Iannacone (*d*); Mandrake (*perc*). 1/73–5/78.

***(*) Unlike Splasc(h) H 309-2
>   Schiano; Co Strieff (*as*); Evan Parker (*ts*); Alex Von Schlippenbach (*p*); Maarten Altena, Joelle
>   Leandre (*b*); Jean-Marc Montera (*g*); Paul Lovens (*d*). 3/90.

***(*) Uncaged Splasc(h) H 357-2
>   Schiano; Giancarlo Schiaffini (*tb*); Marcello Melis (*b*); Famoudou Don Moye (*d*); Mauro Orselli
>   (*bells*). 4/91.

*** And So On Splasc(h) H 368-2
>   Schiano; Paul Rutherford (*tb*); Ernst Reijseger (*clo*); Leon Francioli (*b*); Gunter Sommer (*d,
>   etc.*). 10/91.

Schiano is a weathered veteran of Italy's tiny and often nearly invisible free-jazz movement. His
uncompromising but fundamentally lyrical and persuasive alto playing is relatively unstartling, but the
trials he has gone through in getting his music documented suggest an anti-establishment radical of the
first order. Actually, the recent sessions *Uncaged* and *And So On*, while entirely improvised, find fragments of melody and rhythmic formulas sometimes coalescing into regular jazz material: 'Lover Man'
invades the finale of the second half of 'And So On'. The two earlier CDs are of mixed historical and
musical interest, part of a Splasc(h) series to document milestones of Italian jazz, and while the earlier
date is an interesting patchwork of bits and pieces – 'Beat Suite' is the best excerpt, a dynamically varied
trio work-out by Schiano, Tommaso and Pecori – *Sud* is of more consistent quality. A mix of quick-fire
quintet pieces and rolling, blustering sketches for a big band, the record finds a fine and spontaneous
balance between its elements, uses the synthesizer with rare integrity for the period, and is a valuable
glimpse of some important players (apart from Schiano, there are major contributions by Vittorini and
Giammarco) from a largely 'unavailable' period of Italian jazz.

   The three later records each have their merits. *Uncaged* and *And So On* are full-length sessions by groups
assembled for the occasion, with old friend Moye in usefully alert form on his date, binding together the
memorable interplay between Schiano and the perennially undervalued Schiaffini, whose mix of trombone grotesqueries and hard-bitten commentary is something to treasure. The live date, recorded at
Rome's Alpheus Club, features a sober but intensely active group with Reijseger and Sommer the wild
cards, countering the more meditative work of the two horns (Reijseger gets a suitably demented solo
piece as an encore). *Unlike* finds Schiano in three group-settings: there are two brief duets with Strieff
and two numbers apiece with a quartet and a quintet, the latter the Von Schlippenbach Trio with
Leandre as a further guest. Perhaps surprisingly, it's the quintet pieces which turn out for the best:
Altena's brilliant yet discreet responses to Schiano and Lovens mitigate the more glaring noises made by
Montera on guitar. The group with Leandre, Parker, Von Schlippenbach and Lovens follows the vocabulary laid down by the nucleus of that group, and Schiano has a harder time making himself felt. But all
of these records have points of absorbing interest, and Splasc(h) have done a fine job in affording the
opportunity to hear this internationally neglected pioneer.

Lalo Schifrin (born 1932) PIANO, ARRANGER

*** Jazz Meets The Symphony Atlantic 782506-2
>   Schifrin; Ray Brown (*b*); Grady Tate (*d*); London Philharmonic Orchestra. 11/92.

*** More Jazz Meets The Symphony East West/Atlantic 95589-2
>   As above, except add Jon Faddis, James Morrison (*t*), Paquito D'Rivera (*as*). 12/93.

Schifrin has spent most of his career in Hollywood, but his arrangements have made a mark on some
fine albums, none more so than Dizzy Gillespie's *Gillespiana*. These engaging records aren't so much any
kind of Third Stream as sumptuous examples of high-grade jazz schmaltz. The LPO gamely play their
way through charts that won't tax any intellects, while Schifrin and the wily team of Brown and Tate
noodle over the top. The second disc is a little more high-powered, with two long suites in dedication to
Miles Davis and Louis Armstrong and the noted guest soloists in attendance, but it's really more of the
same – impeccably recorded, feather-bedded easy listening.

Alexander Von Schlippenbach (born 1938) PIANO

**** Smoke FMP CD 23
   Schlippenbach; Sunny Murray (*d*). 10/89.
**** Elf Bagatellen FMP CD 27
   Schlippenbach; Evan Parker (*ss, ts*); Paul Lovens (*d*). 5/90.
***(*) Physics FMP CD 50
   As above. 6/91.

Schlippenbach's clean, atonal lines are far more reminiscent of Thelonious Monk than of Cecil Taylor, the figure who is usually adduced as ancestor for this kind of free music. By 1970 Schlippenbach had to some extent turned away from total abstraction and was showing an interest not only in formal compositional principles (serialism, orthodox sonata form, aspects of *ricercare*) but in renewing his own initial contact with early and modern jazz, blues and boogie-woogie. These interests were still obvious even underneath the radical freedoms of his influential collective, Globe Unity Orchestra, but they became much clearer in his work with the later Berlin Contemporary Jazz Orchestra, where he uses the conventionally swinging drummer, Ed Thigpen, and trumpeter, Benny Bailey, in among the free men. Schlippenbach's conception of freedom has nearly always resulted in densely layered explorations of tonality, with a pronounced rhythmic slant. It's this which renders him surprisingly accessible as a performer.

Schlippenbach's catalogue has slumped with the disappearance of FMP's vinyl catalogue; two other great records, *Detto Fra Di Noi* and *Das Höhe Lied*, were released on Paul Lovens's small Po Torch label, which may now be difficult to find, and have not been on CD. Missing and mourned is the magnificent *Pakistani Pomade*, garlanded with top rating in our first edition. *Elf Bagatellen* almost merits *Pakistani Pomade*'s crown, not just for its markedly improved sound-quality, but also for the sheer untrifling intensity of the trio's performances, which are unsurpassed in latter, quieter days. Like the earlier record, this is a studio performance rather than a live set, and it acts as a very conscious summation of the trio's near-two-decade career. It is, inevitably, rather more predetermined than a more spontaneous performance, and there are shards of melody scattered throughout. 'Sun-Luck: Revisited' refers to 'Sun-Luck Night-Rain', one of the finest pieces on the 1972 album, while 'Yarak: Reforged' provides a similar gloss on a piece from *Payan*, a rare recording for a label other than FMP, in this case Enja. Parker and Lovens have rarely played better together and, if Schlippenbach seems a trifle mild-mannered in places, the richness of the sound more than compensates for a slight drop in pulse-rate. Tremendous stuff.

The more recent *Physics* by the same trio doesn't quite rise to the heights of its predecessors, but it is a dramatic performance all the same. Taped at the 1991 free-music workshops at the Akademie der Künst in Berlin, it has a freewheeling, exploratory quality which is one of the graces of European improvised music. Schlippenbach structures 'The Coefficient Of Linear Expansion' with magisterial control. At nearly 45 minutes, it has the compression and exactitude of a work a tenth that length, and yet it seems to imply all sorts of realities that lie outside the confines of the work.

Despite being tossed with insulting casualness into that overstuffed category, Schlippenbach is a very different kind of player from Cecil Taylor. By the same token, Sunny Murray is a very different kind of player *now* from what he was when he played with Taylor back in 1960. *Smoke* is an intriguing collaboration, in which both men hang up their 'free music' armour and get down to what sounds like a set of phantom standards. There are a dozen or more teasing echoes, more elusive than allusive, but only one outwardly identifiable theme, Monk's 'Trinkle Tinkle'. Beautifully recorded and superbly played, it warms slowly from a rather misterioso opening. Only on 'Down The Mission' does the Taylor parallel make complete sense. Elsewhere, Monk and even Herbie Nichols seem more valid points of reference. Murray's 'Angel Voice' uses material that he has developed over two decades; cymbal overtones create an illusion of choral effects, studded by tight accents and the familiar poly-directional lines.

***(*) The Morlocks FMP CD 61
   Schlippenbach; Henry Lowther, Thomas Heberer, Axel Dörner (*t*); Jörg Huke, Marc Boukoya, Sören Fischer (*tb*); Utz Zimmermann (*btb*); Tilman Denhard (*ts, f, picc*); Darcy Hepner (*as*); Evan Parker (*ts, ss*); Walter Gauchel (*ts*); Claas Willecke (*bs, f*); Aki Takase (*p*); Nobuyoshi Ino (*b*); Paul Lovens (*d, perc*). 7/93.

This is perhaps more strictly a Berlin Contemporary Jazz Orchestra record but, since it consists entirely of Schlippenbach pieces and bears his signature all over it, there is some justification for covering it here.

Unlike many of his contemporaries, Schlippenbach has never let go of the term 'free jazz', and it is interesting to compare the harmonic language of many of the pieces here, not least the opening dedication to his companion, Aki Takase, with the work of Ornette Coleman. There are moments in 'The Morlocks' itself when he seems to be playing with the parameters of pitch, duration and attack in a way that is very similar to Ornette's. Elsewhere, as on 'Rigaudon Nr 2 Aus Der Wassertoffmusik', he uses graphic scores and a much more gestural approach that now sounds slightly old-fashioned. On the magnificent 'Marcia Di Saturno', though, he constructs a dense landscape that is much closer to the neo-tonality of his American contemporaries; bassist Nobuyoshi Ino introduces it with a brooding grace before saxophonist Gauchel develops the difficult central elements.

This record establishes Schlippenbach much more clearly as a composer. It is worth comparing its language to that of the London Jazz Composers Orchestra under Barry Guy, which is simultaneously more abstract but also more orthodoxly jazz-centred.

Larry Schneider (born 1950) TENOR AND SOPRANO SAXOPHONES

*** So Easy Label Bleu LBLC 6516
   Schneider; David Friedman (vib); Marc Ducret (g); Henri Texier (b); Daniel Humair (d). 3/88.
***(*) Just Cole Porter Steeplechase SCCD 31291
   Schneider; Andy Laverne (p); Mike Richmond (b); Keith Copeland (d). 8/91.
***(*) Blind Date Steeplechase SCCD 31317
   As above. 4/92.

Schneider has played a sideman role in many situations, and these albums are perhaps a slightly belated recognition of an accomplished saxophonist. He is firmly emblematic of a generation of hard-bop tenor players who came of age in the 1970s, before the fashionable new interest in the form, which leaves his playing untainted by technical strivings and nicely weathered by his experience. So Easy finds him in a slightly less convincing situation, with Friedman's vibes an unusual partner and the rhythm section going their own way at times, fine though that often is. It's the Steeplechase albums, with long-time cohort Laverne, that feature him best. The album of Cole Porter tunes is close to being a definitive gallery of standards, with Schneider in riveting voice on 'What Is This Thing Called Love?', knowingly tender on 'Every Time We Say Goodbye'. Blind Date brings the quartet together again on four standards, two originals by Laverne and Charles Mingus's 'Peggy's Blue Skylight'. Schneider likes long improvisations and, more often than not, makes them work: the best solos here, such as the grand, sprawling oratory on the title-tune and the flaring urgency that grows out of 'Autumn Leaves', are usefully anchored by a rhythm section that hears him very clearly, with Laverne a comparably mature voice.

Rob Schneiderman (born 1957) PIANO

**(*) New Outlook Reservoir RSR 106
   Schneiderman; Slide Hampton (tb); Rufus Reid (b); Akira Tana (d). 1/88.
*** Smooth Sailing Reservoir 114
   As above, except add Billy Higgins (d), omit Hampton and Tana. 2/90.
*** Radio Waves Reservoir 120
   Schneiderman; Brian Lynch (t); Ralph Moore (ts); Gary Smulyan (bs); Todd Coolman (b); Jeff Hirshfield (d). 5/91.
*** Standards Reservoir 126
   Schneiderman; Rufus Reid (b); Ben Riley (d). 3–8/92.
*** Dark Blue Reservoir 132
   Schneiderman; Brian Lynch (t); Ralph Moore (ss, ts); Peter Washington (b); Lewis Nash (d). 5/94.

Solid, contemporary hard bop. Slide Hampton is an unusual choice as the sole horn on New Outlook, and his mild-mannered fluency suits Schneiderman's approach perhaps a little too well: the music tends to settle down into blandishments of the kind that have been committed to record many times before. Despite a couple of interesting ideas – such as the prickly waltz tempo chosen for Alec Wilder's 'While We're Young' – the music never quite lifts off the ground. Maybe the pianist just prefers the kind of knowing, grooving accompaniment that's second nature to Reid and Higgins, because they all sound much happier on Smooth Sailing, a blithe mix of standards and new tunes. On the other hand, good spirits prevail on the next date, with three horns in the front line. Lynch is a little overwhelmed by the beguiling Moore and the big, tough sound of Smulyan's baritone, but Schneiderman resolves any difficulties with intelligent if sketchy arrangements. But then it's back to the trio for the rather aristocratic treatment of Standards, in which Schneiderman gives up on his own writing for a day at least. Riley is such a wily drummer – very different from Higgins – that he's often barely there, but it suits the occasion. Schneiderman plays interesting things, as he does on all these records, without making one think it's of much consequence. Dark Blue is soundly professional without generating much excitement, and the preponderance of themes based on blues doesn't lift it out of routine; Lynch and Moore, though, guarantee good value. A beguiling 'People Will Say We're In Love' is the highlight.

Daniel Schnyder TENOR AND SOPRANO SAXOPHONES

*** **Secret Cosmos** Enja 5055-2
> Schnyder; Max Helfenstein (*t*); Hugo Helfenstein (*tb*); Hans Peter Hass (*btb*); Han Bergstrom
> (*frhn*); Matthias Ziegler (*f*); Urs Hammerli (*b*).

*** **The City** Enja 6002-2
> Schnyder; Lew Soloff, Michael Philip Mossman (*t*); Ray Anderson (*tb*); Vladislaw Sendecki (*p*);
> Michael Formanek (*b*); Ronnie Burrage (*d*). 9/88.

*** **Decoding The Message** Enja 6036
> As above, except add Matthias Ziegler (*f*), Daniel Pezzotti (*clo*), Robert Mark (*perc*). 5/89.

*** **Mythology** Enja 7003
> As above, except add Mark Feldman, Mary Rowell (*vn*), Lois Martin (*vla*), Erik Friedlander
> (*clo*), Jeff Hirshfield (*d*); omit Anderson, Sendecki, Burrage, Ziegler, Pezzotti and Mark. 4/91.

(*) **Nucleus Enja 8068-2
> Schnyder; Michael Philip Mossman (*t, flhn, picc t, tb*); Kenny Drew Jr (*p*); Michael Formanek
> (*b*); Marvin 'Smitty' Smith (*d*). 1/94.

A fluent player, Schnyder's real interest is in composing and arranging, and he's attracted some imposing names for his Enja albums. Post-bop orthodoxy is ignored in favour of a wide-ranging approach which is often as close to contemporary European composition as it is to jazz: Schnyder tinkers with textures and lines, tries tone rows and motivic variations as bases for themes, and generally asks a lot of his musicians. There's something good on all the earlier records, and perhaps the third, with a couple of impeccably scored pieces in 'The Sound Of The Desert' and 'A Call From Outer Space', is the best. But nothing ever quite manifests itself as a genuinely heavyweight piece, and the substance of some of the themes is dissipated by what might be a low boredom threshold: the shortness of several of the pieces isn't so much a refreshing brevity as a hint that Schnyder could be a bit of a gadfly. He brings in a string quartet for *Mythology*, which adds textural variation – though not so much that the surfaces of his writing are especially disturbed. No real change or improvement with *Nucleus*: in some ways, with titles like 'The Mystified Churchgoer' and throwaway, almost soundbite-like episodes such as 'Retrogradus Ex Machina', Schnyder is getting more arch and less tractable. There is still some good playing and some funny music here. But Mossman, who also plays a fair amount of trombone on this date, sounds like the interesting half of the duo.

Ed Schuller DOUBLE BASS

*** **The Eleventh Hour** Tutu CD 888 124
> Schuller; Greg Osby (*as, ss*); Gary Valente (*tb*); Bill Bickford (*g*); Victor Jones (*d*); Arto
> Tuncboyaci (*perc*). 2/91.

The son of composer/critic Gunther Schuller, the young bassist already had an impressive track-record before recording his first solo project. 'PM In The AM' is a tribute to his time with Paul Motian, and there's a slight sense that for *The Eleventh Hour* he was trying to put together something like that mid--'80s line-up which included Joe Lovano, the late Jim Pepper and Bill Frisell.

Former Defunkt guitarist Bill Bickford is no Frisell but he has a stronger melodic sense, as was evident when he joined Schuller on Pepper's gruff *Beartracks* in 1989. The strong horn-lines on this occasion are provided not so much by Osby, who sounds remarkably restrained, as by the huge-toned Valente, one of the loudest brass men in the business.

Schuller limits solo bass experiments to the very last track, a multi-tracked poem to a friend called 'For Dodo'. It's a surprisingly affecting piece and it gives some opportunity to assess Schuller's approach, which is influenced severally by Mingus (most prominently), rock guitar and Eastern drones. Two other obvious inputs are Charlie Haden and Scott LaFaro and, by extension, Ornette Coleman, who once baby-sat young Ed. Whether or not he sang harmolodic lullabies, something rubbed off. The opening 'O-Zone' is a straightforward tribute and provides Osby with a perfect launching pad (to which he rather diffidently returns as the set progresses).

The two-part title-piece has the same urgent impetus but tries to cram too much cleverness (no less than a miniature history of the world) into too short a space. 'Keeping Still/Mountain' is essentially a rhythmic exercise, pushed just a little too far; the material doesn't really stand up to the pasting it receives. The long 'Shamal' leads the group into promising overtone territory, but gets rather stranded there.

Irène Schweizer (born 1941) PIANO

*** **Irene Schweizer & Pierre Favre** Intakt CD 009
  Schweizer; Pierre Favre (*d, perc*). 2/90.
**** **Piano Solo: Volume 1** Intakt 020
  Schweizer (*p* solo). 5/90.
**** **Piano Solo: Volume 2** Intakt 021
  As above.

Almost inevitably saddled with a 'female Cecil Taylor' tag, Schweizer is nevertheless a highly distinctive player whose premises diverge quite sharply from Taylor's essentially percussive approach. Like Marilyn Crispell (with whom she has recently duetted on record) and Geri Allen, though earlier than the rather younger Americans, she has proved her worth in almost aggressively masculine company and emerged with an aesthetic which is unmistakably and uncompromisingly female, fulfilling Mary Lou Williams's assertion that 'working with men . . . you automatically become strong, though this doesn't mean you're not feminine'.

Like Crispell (but again much earlier), Schweizer has turned that initial and superficial Cecil Taylor influence into a combatively romantic approach to free playing. She is probably best heard solo, though the wholesale disappearance of the FMP vinyl catalogue means that, for the moment at least, there's not much opportunity to hear her in any other context. The duos with Favre are all right but aren't a patch on earlier pairings with Rudiger Carl, Louis Moholo, Baby Sommer and others.

The two solo records, made in 1990 in her native Switzerland, are excellent. The sonority of CD recording suits her touch very well, and the ambience – or ambiences, since one of the records is made in front of an invited audience – is warmer than on most of the FMPs. Brief and apparently inconsequential structures are delivered without elaboration and there is a meditative stillness about 'The Ballad Of The Sad Café' (a title derived from Carson McCullers's soft-tough story) that is unlike anything on the earlier work, but which is clearly derived wholly from it.

'Sisterhood Of Spit' (the name relates to an all-female collective of the 1970s) is dedicated to the late Dudu Pukwana, and to the late Chris McGregor, whose Brotherhood Of Breath was a lasting example of the possibility of reconciling lyrical expressiveness and improvisational freedom. As the title suggests, Schweizer has taken her own route to that end.

Despite her avowed feminism, Schweizer doesn't belong in the neutral enclave of 'women's music', but in the mainstream of European improvisation, a fact duly recognized by Barry Guy's *Theoria* (see under the London Jazz Composers Orchestra), a fiftieth-birthday dedication in which two generations of mostly male European improvisers pay overdue court to her.

Louis Sclavis BASS CLARINET, TENOR SAXOPHONE, SOPRANO SAXOPHONE

**** **Clarinettes** IDA 004
  Sclavis solo, and with Christian Rollet, Christian Ville (*perc*). 9/84, 1/85.
***(*) **Chine** IDA 012
  Sclavis; François Raulin (*p, syn, perc*); Dominique Pifarély (*vn*); Bruno Chevillon (*b*); Christian Ville (*d, perc*). 7 & 9/87.
***(*) **Chamber Music** IDA 022
  Sclavis; Yves Robert (*tb*); Michel Godard (*tba*); Dominique Pifarély (*vn*); Philippe De Schepper (*g*); François Raulin (*p, syn*); Bruno Chevillon (*b*). 7 & 9/89.
***(*) **Rouge** ECM 1458
  Sclavis; Dominique Pifarély (*vn*); François Raulin (*p, syn*); Bruno Chevillon (*b*); Christian Ville (*d*). 9/91.
**** **Ellington On The Air** IDA 032
  As for *Chamber Music*, except omit de Schepper; add Francis Lassus (*d, perc*). 12/91, 2/92.
***(*) **Acoustic Quartet** ECM 1526
  As for *Rouge*, except omit Raulin, Ville; add Marc Ducret (*g*). 93.

Potentially the most important French jazz musician since Django Reinhardt, Louis Sclavis has attempted to create an 'imaginary folklore' that combines familiar jazz procedures with North African and Mediterranean music, French folk themes and music from the *bal musette*. He is not yet an absolutely convincing recording artist and is best heard in concert. Nevertheless, early exposure on the mostly solo *Clarinettes* confirmed word-of-mouth reports from France that he was a performer to be reckoned with.

Unlike Sidney Bechet, who may have been a dim ancestral influence, his clarinet work is a great deal more forceful than his soprano saxophone playing, and Sclavis is one of the foremost of a growing number of younger jazz musicians who have rescued the clarinet from desuetude as an improvising instrument. His bass clarinet work is particularly original, drawing little or nothing from the obvious model and condensing most of Sclavis's virtues: melodic invention, timbral variation, rhythmic sophistication. Perhaps the most striking track on *Clarinettes* is 'Le Chien Aboie Et La Clarinette Basse' a husky duo with percussionist Ville which puns on a French gypsy saying: the dog barks *'et le caravane passe'*.

For all his interest in European folk and popular themes, Sclavis considers himself unequivocally a jazz musician. A duo version of 'Black And Tan Fantasy' on the same album suggests he has much to contribute to standards playing. Most of his work, however, has been original and this, coupled with his obvious straining at the conventions of the orthodox jazz ensemble (particularly as regards the drummer, whom Sclavis considers to be excessively dominant), has temporarily held back his development as a soloist. *Chine* is a fine and original set of pieces, but its unfamiliar tonal components only partially mitigate an overall lack of development. *Chamber Music*, as the title implies, throws still more weight on compositional values, but there are signs that Sclavis is working through his dilemmas. In Chevillon he has an understanding and highly effective foil whose rhythmic awareness makes light of settings without a part for a drummer or percussionist.

Sclavis's ECM debut is a challenging and surprisingly abstract set that rarely allows itself to settle into a jazz groove. *Rouge* establishes Sclavis as an enterprising and thought-provoking composer. If it does so at the expense of rhythmic energy (a strategy consistent with his ambivalence about jazz percussion), it doesn't short-change in other departments. The first four tracks are moodily atmospheric, with a strong suggestion of North African music; 'Nacht' is particularly effective, with dissonant flashes of multi-tracked clarinet echoed by the softly bouncing thunder of Ville's bass drum, before giving way to an evocative solo by Chevillon. Pifarély comes into his own on 'Reeves', teasing out a long unison statement with Sclavis and then soloing on his own 'Moment Donné'. Several tracks sound as if they are through-composed and, apart from the later stages of 'Les Bouteilles' and a delicious waltz tag on the title-piece, the emphasis is all on textures and rather brooding melodic outlines rather than on linear development. The longest track, 'Face Nord', echoes 'Reflet' in the way it suspends Sclavis's high, swooping clarinet lines over a dense chordal background (that on 'Face Nord' suddenly erupts into a convincing simulacrum of a flat-out electric guitar solo, all done on Raulin's imaginatively programmed synth).

The ECM follow-up is once again impressionistic rather than dynamic. The drummerless *Acoustic Quartet* is listed as co-led by Pifarély, and he certainly plays an increasingly prominent role in the music, as does Chevillon, another long-standing accomplice. Ducret has a less functional role and is used for broad (and not always very subtle) background effects, where a more adventurous leader and/or producer might have preferred a starker profile.

Pifarély contributes three compositions, including the long 'Seconde', and the violinist's writing has matured very quickly. However, Sclavis's touch on 'Sensible' and 'Rhinoceros' is flawless, and the brief 'Beata' is incomparably lovely. Attractive as it all is, one misses the edgy, improvisational sound that energizes the Ellington session. The interplay between Sclavis and the very promising Robert adds a dimension that has been missing for some time. The programme is an imaginative exercise in re-creation. Ellington themes are interleaved with associated originals by Sclavis, Chevillon, Raulin and others. 'Jubilee Stomp' yields 'J'Oublie'; though not itself included, 'Mood Indigo' suggests Chevillon's 'Indigofera Tinctoria' and Andy Emler's 'Mode Andy Go'; a snatch of 'Caravan' introduces 'Caravalse'; and so on. The verbal puns aren't screamingly witty, but the music is always intelligently allusive and manages to suggest new angles on Ellington without lapsing into pastiche. Indeed, it's very clear that Sclavis has picked precisely those themes which most emphatically suit his own compositional style. Which is precisely as it should be.

John Scofield (born 1951) GUITAR

**(*) Live Enja 3013
> Scofield; Richard Beirach (*p*); George Mraz (*b*); Joe LaBarbera (*d*). 11/77.
*** Rough House Enja 3033
> Scofield; Hal Galper (*p*); Stafford James (*b*); Adam Nussbaum (*d*). 11/78.

John Scofield was perhaps the last of Miles Davis's sidemen to break through to a major career, but the records listed above, all made prior to his joining Davis in 1982, bespeak a substantial talent already making waves. He had played with a diverse group of leaders – Charles Mingus, Lee Konitz, Gary Burton, Billy Cobham – before forming the band that made the 1977 live album. Beirach is a little too cool to suit Scofield's needs and Gomez is all tight virtuosity rather than loosely funky, but the music is still impressive, since the leader's own playing is an intriguing mix of a classic, open-toned bop style and a blues-rock affiliation. He gets the same sound on the studio date with Galper, but this is a tougher record, with the pianist flying directly alongside the guitarist on tunes which unreel at a uniformly fast tempo: Nussbaum gives them both plenty of push.

***(*) **Shinola** Enja 4004
    Scofield; Steve Swallow (*b*); Adam Nussbaum (*d*). 12/81.
***(*) **Out Like A Light** Enja 4038
    As above. 12/81.

Scofield's final Enja albums were recorded at a live date in Munich. Good though the earlier records are, these loose, exploratory tracks are his most interesting so far: the trio functions as a single probing unit, Swallow's fat sound counterpointing the guitar, and the space and drift of such as 'Yawn' from *Shinola* opens Scofield's horizon. With pianists, he was putting in as many notes as Coltrane on occasion, but here – with Nussbaum restlessly decorating the pulse – the guitarist sounds as if he doesn't see the need to cover every harmonic area. Good digital sound.

** **Electric Outlet** Gramavision GR 8045
    Scofield; Ray Anderson (*tb*); David Sanborn (*as*); Pete Levin (*ky*); Steve Jordan (*d*). 4–5/84.
**** **Still Warm** Gramavision GR 8508
    Scofield; Don Grolnick (*ky*); Darryl Jones (*b*); Omar Hakim (*d*). 6/85.
*** **Blue Matter** Gramavision 18-8702
    Scofield; Mitch Forman (*ky*); Hiram Bullock (*g*); Gary Grainger (*b*); Dennis Chambers (*d*); Don Alias (*perc*). 9/86.
*** **Loud Jazz** Gramavision 18-8801
    As above, except Robert Aries, George Duke (*ky*) replace Forman; Bullock omitted. 12/87.
*** **Pick Hits Live** Gramavision 18-8805
    As above, except omit Duke and Alias. 10/87.
***(*) **Flat Out** Gramavision 18-8903
    Scofield; Don Grolnick (*org*); Anthony Cox (*b*); Johnny Vidacovich, Terri Lyne Carrington (*d*). 12/88.

Scofield's six Gramavision albums are a coherent and highly enjoyable body of work. *Electric Outlet* was a false start: the band seems gimcracked around a dubious idea of highbrow pop-jazz, Sanborn and Anderson are there only for colour, and the attempted grooves are stiff and unyielding. But *Still Warm* solved matters at a stroke. Steve Swallow's production calorified the sound without overpowering the fluidity of Scofield's arrangements, Grolnick added thoughtful keyboard textures, and Jones and Hakim (colleagues from the Miles Davis band) were tight and funky without being relentlessly so. Scofield's own playing here assumes a new authority: tones are richer, the hint of fuzz and sustain is perfectly integrated, and his solos are unflaggingly inventive: for a single sample, listen to the sharp, hotly articulated solo on 'Picks And Pans'.

    The band which the guitarist then formed with Grainger and Chambers bolstered the funk-fusion side of his playing: the drummer, especially, is a thunderous virtuoso in the manner of Billy Cobham, and the next three albums are all fired up with his rhythms. Scofield's writing revolves around ear-catching melodic hooks and a favourite device of a riff repeated over a shifting harmonic base, and the two studio albums are full of naggingly memorable themes. But the music was formulaic in the end: the live record is a feast of hard-nut jazz-funk showmanship, but it starts to sound clenched by the end. *Flat Out* comes as a welcome change of pace: Vidacovich and Carrington, who split chores between them through the record, are swinging but no less busy drummers: hear the consummately controlled rave-up on 'The Boss's Car' (a cheeky rip-off of Bruce Springsteen's 'Pink Cadillac'). Two standards, a Meters tune and a rollicking turn through 'Rockin' Pneumonia' also lighten the programme.

**** **Time On My Hands** Blue Note B21Y-792894-2
    Scofield; Joe Lovano (*ts*); Charlie Haden (*b*); Jack DeJohnette (*d*). 11/89.
***(*) **Meant To Be** Blue Note B21Y-795479-2
    Scofield; Joe Lovano (*ts, cl*); Marc Johnson (*b*); Bill Stewart (*d*). 12/90.

Scofield's move to Blue Note has moved his career and his music substantially forward. Lovano is an inspired choice of front-line partner, renegotiating the jazz roots of Sco's approach without surrendering the feisty attack which he amplified through his Gramavision records. *Time On My Hands* provides some of his best writing, including the lovely ballad of 'Let's Say We Did' and the twining melodies of 'Since You Asked'. 'Fat Lip' is acoustic jazz-rock which Haden and DeJohnette jump on with brilliant ferocity. Superb studio sound throughout. If *Meant To Be* seems a shade less invigorating, it's only because it seems like a second run through the same territory. Both are very highly recommended.

***(*) **Grace Under Pressure** Blue Note B21Y-7981672
    Scofield; Randy Brecker (*flhn*); Jim Pugh (*tb*); John Clark (*frhn*); Bill Frisell (*g*); Charlie Haden (*b*); Joey Baron (*d*). 12/91.

Though given a mixed reception on its release, this is a strong and thoughtfully realized continuation of Scofield's work for Blue Note. If he's starting to seem over-exposed as a player, turning up in countless guest roles as well as on his own records, the ten themes here display a consistent strength as a writer:

variations on the blues, slow modal ballads, riffs worked into melodies, Scofield makes them all come up fresh, and he creates situations where the rhythm players can line the music with intensities and colours of their own. There are hard, swinging solos on the title-track and 'Twang', and if the interplay with Frisell can sometimes seem more like cheese and chalk, there are piquant contrasts which sometimes blend with surprising effectiveness: 'Honest I Do' is the kind of haunting, downbeat melody which Scofield has made his own. The brass are used very sparingly to underscore a few tracks.

*** **What We Do** Blue Note B21Y-799586-2
    Scofield; Joe Lovano (*ss, ts*); Dennis Irwin (*b*); Bill Stewart (*d*). 5/92.
***(*) **I Can See Your House From Here** Blue Note CDP 827765-2
    Scofield; Pat Metheny (*g*); Steve Swallow (*b*); Bill Stewart (*d*). 12/93.
From anyone else these would be outstanding records; by Scofield's own high standards they're comparatively ordinary. *What We Do* re-runs the earlier quartet dates with no loss of authority or class: perhaps the tunes are just a touch less memorable, or the playing more likely to settle for routine. For his second meeting with another leading guitarist, Scofield uncorked some more of his best writing: the title-piece and 'No Matter What' are typically serpentine, elegant, feelingful tunes to which the slick playing only adds. This is far more collaborative than the record with Frisell, with Metheny taking several writing credits himself, and while it occasionally softens in the face of Pat's tendency to turn to marshmallow, it's good.

*** **Hand Jive** Blue Note 827327-2
    Scofield; Eddie Harris (*ts*); Larry Goldings (*p, org*); Dennis Irwin (*b*); Bill Stewart (*d*); Don Alias (*perc*). 10/93.
***(*) **Groove Elation** Blue Note 832801-2
    Scofield; Randy Brecker (*t, flhn*); Steve Turre (*tb*); Billy Drewes (*ts, f*); Howard Johnson (*bs, bcl, tba*); Larry Goldings (*org, p*); Dennis Irwin (*b*); Idris Muhammed (*d*); Don Alias (*perc*). 94.
Scofield's final Blue Note albums (he has since signed to Verve) round off the most enjoyable run of guitar records in recent years. Perhaps no genuinely fresh ground is broken here but, just by shuffling his options, the guitarist finds new ways of walking over old paths. The fashion to turn back to the guitar/organ combos of the 1960s has already grown stale, but Scofield's take on the genre turns the emphasis around: unsurprisingly, it's the guitar player who takes the limelight rather than a licks-bound organist, and in any case Goldings is the most interesting new organ man on the scene. *Hand Jive* blends the chugging groove beloved of the old school with the leaner rhythms of Irwin and Stewart, Sco's pop-tune sensibility, Goldings's feel for line and colour and the surprise choice of maverick tenorman Harris. The result is excellent fun. But it's probably surpassed by the more formal though no less vibrant *Groove Elation*, which stirs in some deft horn arrangements by Bob Belden and varies pace and texture from track to track. Any who fear that Scofield's chops might be fading may like to check out the focused, rippling solo he scores with on the title-tune.

Ronnie Scott (born 1927) TENOR SAXOPHONE

***(*) **Never Pat A Burning Dog** Ronnie Scott's Jazz House JC 012
    Scott; Dick Pearce (*t*); Mornington Lockett (*ts*); John Critchinson (*p*); Ron Mathewson (*b*); Martin Drew (*d*). 10 & 11/90.
Club owner, philosopher and wit (he asked us to say), Ronnie Scott has long been recognized as one of the most authentic and blues-rinsed of the European saxophonists. An active performer, Scott has recorded only sparingly and *Never Pat A Burning Dog* (seems obvious, but you never know) will appeal to those who have worn out their copy of *Serious Gold*, his late-1970s Pye album, though they may also be surprised at how far his harmonic thinking has developed since then. A muted, almost elegiac set (recorded live at Ronnie Scott's Club in Soho) begins with a stunning version of McCoy Tyner's 'Contemplation', full of glassy harmonies and tender, dissonant flourishes. Scott's choice of material is typically adventurous and tasteful: Jimmy Dorsey's 'I'm Glad There Is You', David Sanborn's 'White Caps', Cedar Walton's 'When Love Is New', a slightly unsatisfactory reading of Freddie Hubbard's 'Little Sunflower' with the less than inspiring Lockett in for Pearce, and two standards, 'All The Things You Are' and the still-under-recorded 'This Love Of Mine'.

    Scott's tone is deep and subtly modulated and his phrasing has the kind of relaxed precision and inner heat one associates with Paul Gonsalves or Zoot Sims. Despite the variety of material, it's a remarkably consistent set, perhaps even a little unvaried in treatment.

Shirley Scott (born 1934) ORGAN, PIANO

*** **Workin'** Prestige PRCD 24126-2
> Scott; Eddie 'Lockjaw' Davis (*ts*); Ronnell Bright (*p*); Wally Richardson (*g*); George Duvivier, Peck Morrison (*b*); Arthur Edgehill, Roy Haynes (*d*); Ray Barretto (*perc*). 5/58–3/61.

***(*) **Soul Shoutin'** Prestige PRCD-24142-2
> Scott; Stanley Turrentine (*ts*); Major Holley, Earl May (*b*); Grassella Oliphant (*d*). 1–10/63.

*** **Queen Of The Organ** Impulse! GRP 11232
> Scott; Stanley Turrentine (*ts*); Bob Cranshaw (*b*); Otis Finch (*d*). 9/64.

*** **Blue Flames** Original Jazz Classics OJC 328
> As above. 8/65.

*** **Roll 'Em** Impulse! GRP 11472
> Scott; Thad Jones, Joe Newman, Jimmy Nottingham, Ernie Royal, Clark Terry (*t*); Paul Faulise, Quentin Jackson, Melba Liston, Tom McIntosh (*tb*); Phil Woods, Jerry Dodgion (*as*); Bob Ashton, Jerome Richardson (*ts*); Danny Bank (*bs*); Attila Zoller (*g*); George Duvivier, Richard Davis (*b*); Grady Tate, Ed Shaughnessy (*d*). 4/66.

Scott was no slouch when it came to mixing in heavy company: in 1955, in her native Philadelphia, she was working in a trio with John Coltrane. But it was her association with Eddie 'Lockjaw' Davis which made her name and led to dozens of albums for Prestige, Impulse!, Atlantic and Cadet through the 1970s. Many of them have disappeared from print, but the above have returned to CD. Scott wasn't a knockabout swinger like Jimmy Smith and didn't have the bebop attack of Don Patterson, but there's an authority and an unusual sense of power in reserve which keep her music simmering somewhere near the boil. She is a strong blues player and a fine accompanist, and her right-hand lines have a percussive feel that utilizes space more than most organ players ever did. She was also married to Stanley Turrentine, and they made a number of records together: *Soul Shoutin'* brings together the contents of the original albums *The Soul Is Willing* and *Soul Shoutin'*, and this one gets the nod as the pick of the reissues. The title-track off *The Soul Is Willing* is the near-perfect example of what this combination could do, a fuming Turrentine solo followed by a deftly swinging one by Scott. In comparison, *Blue Flames* seems like short measure, but this kind of jazz is perhaps best sampled a few tracks at a time in any case, including these two – nothing more nor less than some cooking tenor and organ on some blues and a ballad or two. *Workin'* is a compilation of four sessions that cover some of Shirley's earlier dates and includes one bruiser with Lockjaw Davis – good stuff, if a notch below *Soul Shoutin'*. Decent remastering on the OJC and Prestige reissues, but they have to be played very loud to approximate the impact which the group must have had live. One gets more of a feel for that from *Queen Of The Organ*, which is indeed live, at The Front Room in Newark. Despite already submitting to pop material – this must be one of the earliest covers of 'Can't Buy Me Love' – the music swings, and it boils on 'Rapid Shave' at least. *Roll 'Em* mixes trio tracks with four charts for big band penned by Oliver Nelson, though they seem to be bolted on rather than integrated into Scott's own playing. Solid, though the uncommitted should go for the other discs.

*** **Oasis** Muse M 5388
> Scott; Virgil Jones (*t*); Charles Davis, Houston Person (*ts*); Arthur Harper (*b*); Mickey Roker (*d*). 8/89.

After a long absence from the studios, Scott returned with a record as good as any she's made. Producer Houston Person, who plays on only one track, gets a smooth sound which suits the band, since the music is less about solos and more to do with ensemble timbre and the gently rocking grooves which Scott, Harper and Roker seem to relish. The title-track and 'Basie In Mind' are delectable slow swingers, but Scott's set-piece treatment of J. J. Johnson's 'Oasis' is the standout.

*** **Blues Everywhere** Candid CCD79525
> Scott; Arthur Harper (*b*); Mickey Roker (*d*). 11/91.

*** **Skylark** Candid CCD 79705-2
> As above. 11/91.

For once Scotty handles the acoustic keyboard for an entire date, and what comes out is a fat, funky, authoritative trio date somewhat in the style of Red Garland. Harper and Roker can sleepwalk through this kind of music and, since it keeps on swinging for nearly an hour, it's a tribute to Shirley that they stayed awake. The second set is set down on the subsequent *Skylark*, and one can safely say it's more of the same: two enjoyable records, but only a relative will need both of them. Fine live recording from Birdland in New York.

Stephen Scott (born 1969) PIANO

***(*) **Something To Consider** Verve 849 557

    Scott; Roy Hargrove (*t*); Justin Robinson (*as*); Joe Henderson (*ts*); Craig Handy (*ts, ss*);
    Christian McBride, Peter Washington (*b*); Lewis Nash, Jeff Tain Watts (*d*). 1 & 3/91.

**** **Aminah's Dream** Verve 517 996

    Scott; Terell Stafford (*t*); Jamal Haynes (*tb*); Bob Stewart (*tba*); Justin Robinson (*as*); Don
    Braden (*ts*); Ron Carter (*b*); Elvin Jones (*d*). 10/92.

The young New Yorker has matured fast. An apprenticeship in Betty Carter's backing band gave him
good ears and a tasteful approach to dynamics. He can stomp and roll and blues with the best of them.
Less commonly for a younger player, he can also play a ballad with exquisite judgement, and he's
emerging as a competent composer as well.

    Scott avoided the perils of a recording debut overstaffed with great names. Henderson's avuncular
presence does him no harm at all, and the saxophonist sounds great on both 'Steps, Paths And Journeys'
and a kicking version of 'Pent Up House'. However, it's with the younger guys that Scott clicks most
comfortably. Hargrove's sharp, slightly frail sound and Justin Robinson's clear, Bird-influenced alto set
the agenda on 'In The Beginning'. Craig Handy comes into his own on 'Something To Consider', when
he switches to soprano for one of three quartet sessions (two of the others are with Henderson). Scott
and producer Eulis Cathey have used the players at their disposal with considerable intelligence, mixing
the quartets in with sextets, a brief solo outing on 'Everything I Have Is Yours' and a trio with just
Washington and Nash.

    This comes closer to the sound the pianist gets on *Aminah's Dream*, which alternates trios with Carter
and Jones and larger-group arrangements. The kind of tough, bluesy – utterly contemporary in focus –
approach which Scott brought to 'Au Privave' on the first album is all over its successor. He picks the
meat out of Woody Shaw's 'Moontrane' with appetite. Jones is as overbearing as ever, but even he fails
to dull the sheer beauty of 'Aminah's Dream' itself and the thoughtful 'Positive Images (Mother,
Father)'. Carter never puts a foot wrong. Among the horns, only school-mate Robinson is back from the
last outing, but Stafford and Braden do their stuff for Verve with vim and, indeed, vigour. The addition
of tubist Bob Stewart on the opening track was a fine stroke, and it's a pity he didn't hang around for a
couple more tracks, because Haynes is a bit lightweight in the ensembles.

***(*) **Renaissance Suite** Verve 523863-2

    Scott; Michael Bowie (*b*); Clarence Penn, Karriem Riggins (*d*). 8/94.

Scott's third entry puts its trust in an unadorned trio format, with Bowie and Penn performing with
great empathy (Riggins takes over the drumstool only on the closing version of 'Maiden Voyage'). The
disc is split slightly uncomfortably between seven standards and the four-part title-suite. Scott continues
to surprise: this 'Solitude' must be one of the jauntiest on record, and the following 'Tenderly' is darkly
mysterious rather than introverted. But the extended original work carries the signs of someone trying a
bit too hard to write a masterpiece, and the attacking swing of the first two episodes isn't wholly
sustained. All the same, this affirms Scott's impressive progress to date.

Tony Scott (born 1921) CLARINET, BARITONE SAXOPHONE, PIANO, ELECTRONICS

**** **A Day In New York** Fresh Sound FSR CD 160/2 2CD

    Scott; Bill Evans (*p*); Clark Terry (*t*); Jimmy Knepper (*tb*); Sahib Shihab (*bs*); Henry Grimes,
    Milt Hinton (*b*); Paul Motian (*d*). 11/57.

***(*) **Dedications** Core COCD 9.00803

    Scott; Bill Evans, Horst Jankowski (*p*); Juan Suastre (*g*); Shinichi Yuize (*koto*); Scott LaFaro,
    Peter Witte (*b*); Paul Motian, Herman Mutschler (*d*). 57–59.

***(*) **Sung Heroes** Sunnyside SSC 1015

    As above, except omit Jankowski, Witte, Mutschler, Yuize. 10/59.

In 1959 Tony Scott turned his back on America, wounded by the death of several friends (Hot Lips
Page, Billie Holiday, Charlie Parker, Lester Young) and by what he considered the 'death' of the clarinet
in jazz terms. Since then he has been a wanderer, exploring the culture and music of the East, trading in
the sometimes aggressive assertions of bebop for a meditative approach to harmony that at its best is
deeply moving, at its least disciplined a weak ambient decoration.

    These beautiful *Dedications* (some of which were available under the title *Sung Heroes* on Sunnyside and
may still be found in that format) record Scott's reactions to a group who have figured iconically in his
life: Billie Holiday (the dedicatee of a delicate quartet, 'Misery'); Anne Frank (an overdubbed duet with
himself on clarinet and baritone saxophone that might seem inept were it not so moving); Art Tatum;
Hot Lips Page; an unnamed African friend; the Schoenbergian composer, Stefan Wolpe (who receives

the homage of an atonal blues); his father; Israel; the bullfighter, Manolete; and Charlie Parker. There are also Japanese-influenced pieces, based on traditional verse and images.

The high clarinet protestations of 'Blues For An African Friend' and the succeeding 'Atonal Ad Lib Blues' suggest what a remarkable talent Scott's was, giving the instrument the power and immediacy of soprano saxophone without sacrificing its distinctive timbre. Influenced primarily by Ben Webster, he seems to condense and process an enormous acreage of jazz history in his enticingly miniaturist structures.

Scott enjoyed a close and fruitful relationship with Bill Evans, and perhaps his best recorded work is the session of 16 November 1957 with the Evans trio and guests, tackling a copious roster of originals and well-worn standards (including a lovely 'Lullaby Of The Leaves' with Knepper). The clarinettist's opening statements on Evans's 'Five' are almost neurotically brilliant and a perfect illustration of how loud Scott could play. 'Portrait Of Ravi' and 'The Explorer' are Scott originals, directed towards the concerns that were increasingly to occupy him. Evans's light touch and immense harmonic sophistication suited his approach ideally. Scott was at the top of his professional tree and enjoyed great critical acclaim. More recent years have found him a relatively forgotten figure. But he is unmistakably an original.

** **Music For Zen Meditation** Verve 817209
>   Scott; Hozan Yamamoto (*shakuhachi*); Shinichi Yuize (*koto*). 2/64.

Scott's absorption in Buddhist thinking ultimately resulted in some intriguing cross-cultural experiments like this one. His interest in Indian *raga* (as in his ahead-of-the-pack dedication to Ravi Shankar on the Fresh Sound, above) and in African musics, below, bespeaks certain philosophical premises which are rather difficult to judge on purely artistic grounds. How efficacious *Music For Zen Meditation* may be for its professed purpose is beyond the scope of this book to determine, but it's slightly disappointing to note how quickly Scott seemed prepared to abandon the taut harmonic arguments of his work with Evans, LaFaro and Motian in favour of the bland affirmations here.

***(*) **African Bird** Soul Note 121083
>   Scott; Glenn Ferris (*tb*); Giancarlo Barigozzi (*f, bf*); Chris Hunter (*as, f*); Duncan Kinnel (*mar*); Rex Reason (*kalimba*); Robin Jones, Karl Potter (*perc*); Jacqui Benar (*v*). 81, 5/84.

Conceived and performed before 'World Music' had become a sneer, *African Bird* is a largely convincing synthesis of Scott's African and Afro-American concerns into a suite of songs with an impressive level of coherence and developmental logic. To all intents and purposes it is a solo record, with largely incidental colorations from all but Barigozzi and Kinnel, who both play beautifully. For a flavour of where Scott has been since 1960, this is ideal.

*** **Lush Life: Volume 1** Core COCD 9.00666
>   Scott; Bill Frisell (*g*); Ed Schuller (*b*); Tony D'Arco (*d*); Billy Strayhorn (*p, v*); Monica Sciacca (*v*). 81–4.
*** **Lush Life: Volume 2** Core COCD 9.00667
>   As above.

First blows in a promised seven-part dissection of Billy Strayhorn's great song, which has haunted his career. One can hear it almost subliminally quoted in umpteen Scott solos, most notably in 'Misery (To Lady Day)' on *Dedications*, above. This is far from a classical theme-with-variations. Scott provides a rap version; a recitation delivered over some heavily treated Frisell guitar; a quartet piece that stands in the same relation to the tune as a hangover to a great night out; solo piano, baritone saxophone, and clarinet performances; he has his young daughter (Sciacca is the family name) sing it; and he even includes an imperfect Strayhorn performance. Though there have been 'Round Midnight' albums by divers hands, rarely has a tune been subjected to such microscopic attention and loving deconstruction by a single individual. The effect is bizarre, kaleidoscopic and unsettlingly hypnotic.

(***) **Astral Meditation: Voyage Into A Black Hole 1** Core COCD 9.00590
>   Scott (solo instrumental and electronic treatments). 88.
(**) **Astral Meditation: Voyage Into A Black Hole 2** Core COCD 9.00591
>   As above.
(**) **Astral Meditation: Voyage Into A Black Hole 3** Core COCD 9.00592
>   As above.

It is, let's face it, none too difficult to dismiss projects of this New Age kind sight unseen. There is a certain conventional wisdom about their musical (if not their spiritual and therapeutic) worth that has critics reaching for their typewriters before the cellophane is off the record. In keeping with everything else he has ever done, Scott's exploration of electronics is maverick, highly personal, alternately riveting and galling. For him, synthesizers have opened up whole new harmonic territories that help draw together his interest in trance and process musics in the context of more conventional post-bop harmony. On the debit side, he shows no firm command of electronic processes and only a dull perception of the possibilities of *musique concrète*. The fundamental problem with *Astral Meditation* is that the music is largely insufficient to support the cosmic architecture Scott has erected around it; Parts 2 and 3, 'Astrala' and 'Astrobo', pall rapidly. In the context of this book, it's rather difficult to make a settled judgement; Scott's work is *sui generis*, but if the New Age is going to sound like this it may not be as boring as we'd feared.

*** **The Clarinet Album** Philology W 113
    Scott; Massimo Farao (*p*); Aldo Zunino (*b*); Giulio Capiozzo (*d*). 4/93.
The clarinet began to stage a bit of a comeback in the early 1990s and Scott's star rose again. Not far enough above the horizon for a Blue Note contract, but certainly high enough to earn him a couple of sympathetic magazine articles and a general reawakening of interest. *The Clarinet Album* sticks to a very conventional and unambitious repertoire, and Scott plays remarkably straight for a man who, a few years earlier, had boldly gone where only Sun Ra had gone before. His quirky phrasing and wedding-band tone are obvious from the opening choruses of 'My Funny Valentine'. An hour and a quarter later, these have begun to grate slightly, but the album's deficiencies are largely down to the band. Like a lot of Scott's natural countrymen, it's difficult to tell whether Farao, Zunino and Capiozzo are interestingly off-beat or just lazily incompetent: metres drift, passages go out of key for no very obvious reason, dynamics are all over the place. It's enjoyable enough, but when you think that the man last recorded 'I Can't Get Started' with Bill Evans, Milt Hinton, Jimmy Knepper and Paul Motian, you simply have to wonder how it might sound with a similar line-up now.

Jim Self TUBA

*** **Tricky Lix** Concord CCD 4430
    Self; Warren Luening (*t, flhn*); Bill Booth (*tb*); Gary Foster (*as, f, cl*); John Kurnick (*g*); Joel Hamilton (*b*); Alan Estes (*d, perc*). 6/90.
Jazz tubists are now few and far between, but a glance at the line-up of Jim Self's one and only extant recording helpfully rules out what he ain't. Self isn't merely a brass bass player of a sort once common, then almost extinct, now beginning to be fashionable again (Bob Stewart being the player of choice); nor does he merely offer a ponderous valve version of trombone lines.

    Self understands his instrument's intrinsic qualities (a slightly mournful sonority, with big, resonant overtones) and plays them to the hilt on a ballad-heavy set that also scores on bouncier numbers like 'Somebody's Samba' and 'Heather On The Hill'. A solitary quibble might be the role of saxophonist Foster; accomplished though he undoubtedly is, it might have been more satisfactory to focus on the brasses alone, a recipe that has served Lester Bowie unexpectedly well. The title-track is a bit of a test-piece but, once that's out of the way, this is a thoroughly musical set without novelty interest or arch jokiness. And 'My Funny Valentine' will make your eyes sting.

Joey Sellars TROMBONE

*** **Something For Nothing** Nine Winds NWCD 136
    Sellars; Greg Varlotta, Clay Jenkins (*t, flhn*); Alex Iles, Bruce Fowler (*tb*); Danny Hemwall (*btb*); Kim Richmond (*ss, as, cl, f*); John Schroeder (*ss, ts, cl, f*); Rob Verdi (*bs, bcl, f*); Kei Akagi (*p*); Ken Filiano (*b*); Billy Mintz (*d*). 2/89.
Although some of the big-band music on Nine Winds has been of a free-spirited nature, Sellars here leads a band of pros who could sit comfortably with any studio chores on the Los Angeles session-scene. The one cursory nod to any kind of dissembled structure on 'American Standard' is the least convincing moment on the record: the rest is sharply drilled and punchily phrased, modern big-band music, with Sellars throwing opportunities to soloists who can eat up changes and modal settings alike. His own trombone improvisations are as strong as anybody's, but a special mention to the splendid baritone of Verdi on the title-tune. Some measure of the success of the arrangements comes in the point that, although only five themes stretch across some 70 minutes of music, no track runs right out of steam.

**** **Pastels, Ashes** Nine Winds NWCD 0153
    Sellers; Clay Jenkins, Ron King (*t, flhn*); Bruce Fowler, Alex Iles (*tb*); Dan Hemwall (*btb*); Kim Richmond (*ss, as, cl, f*); Jerry Pinter (*ss, ts, cl, f*); Rob Verdi (*bs, bcl, f*); Kei Akagi (*p*); Ken Filiano (*b*); Billy Mintz (*d*). 10/91.
Cut live to two-track in a single day in the studio, this is a brilliant effort by Sellars. Again there are only six tunes, covering 70 minutes of music, but the brimming arrangements make use of every musician almost continuously, there are superb improvisations from Pinter, Jenkins and Fowler in particular, and Sellars blends structure and surprise with a deftness that should have other arrangers genuflecting.

Rather than recycling patterns or mixing together clichés, his scores actually develop and press ideas into new shapes, and he's one of the few current composers to require a long form to be at his most effective. Required listening for those wanting to know how the big band can survive.

Doug Sertl TROMBONE

***(*) **Joy Spring** Stash STCD-565
Sertl; Nick Brignola (*bs*); Roger Kellaway (*p*); John Lockwood (*b*); Adam Nussbaum (*d*). 5/90.
Sertl is a stalwart of the contemporary East Coast scene, runs a useful big band (with, unfortunately, no records in print) and has frequently worked with Brignola. For this off-the-cuff studio date they worked up a rare head of steam on mostly bop material, though Ornette's blues variation, 'Tears Inside', and the ancient 'I Cried For You' are a shrewd change of colour. The opening gallop through Clifford Brown's 'Blues Walk' is an astonishing display of chops from everybody, and the momentum seldom lets up from there: germane to all of this is the inspirational Kellaway, who refuses to take anything except a risk on solos and comping alike. His strange improvisation on 'Tears Inside' is just one example. A great blowing date.

Bud Shank (born 1926) ALTO SAXOPHONE, FLUTE; ALSO PENNY WHISTLE

*** **Bud Shank Quartet** Fresh Sound FSR CD 129
Shank; Claude Williamson (*p*); Don Prell (*b*); Chuck Flores, Jimmy Pratt (*d*). 11/56, 4/58.
*** **Sunshine Express** Concord CCD 6020
Shank; Bobby Shew (*t, flhn, c*); Mike Wofford (*p*); Fred Atwood (*b*); Larry Bunker (*d*). 1/76.
*** **At Jazz Alley** JVC/Fantasy VDJ 1120
Shank; Dave Peck (*p*); Chuck Deardorf (*b*); Jeff Hamilton (*d*). 10/86.
*** **Serious Swingers** Contemporary C 14031
Shank; Bill Perkins (*ts*); Alan Broadbent (*p*); John Heard (*b*); Sherman Ferguson (*d*). 12/86.
*** **Tomorrow's Rainbow** Contemporary C 14048
Shank; Marco Silva (*ky*); Ricardo Peixoto (*g*); Gary Brown (*b*); Michael Spiro (*d*).
**** **Lost In The Stars** Fresh Sound FSRCD 183
Shank; Lou Levy (*p*). 12/90.
*** **The Doctor Is In!** Concord CCD 79520
Shank; Mike Wofford (*p*); Bob Magnusson (*b*); Sherman Ferguson (*d*). 9/91.
***(*) **I Told You So!** Candid CCD 79533
Shank; Kenny Barron (*p*); Lonnie Plaxico (*b*); Victor Lewis (*d*). 6/92.
***(*) **New Gold!** Candid CCD 79707
Shank; Conte Candoli (*t*); Bill Perkins (*ts, ss*); Jack Nimitz (*bs*); John Clayton (*b*); Sherman Ferguson (*d*). 12/93.
Somewhat like Lee Konitz, Shank cast off a slightly wimpish initial reputation as a bland cocktail of Charlie Parker, Benny Carter and Johnny Hodges, to re-emerge with the tougher and more abrasive approach. The earlier style is in evidence on the Fresh Sound, which includes material from a TV show and was recorded in South Africa, where Shank shows off his skill with the penny whistle. The more abrasive approach that came along later is reflected in *I Told You So!* and some of the performances of the mid- to late '80s. *At Jazz Alley* is slightly rough and ready, certainly in comparison to *Serious Swingers*, co-led with Perkins a couple of months later; with the exception of Hamilton, the Jazz Alley group rarely finds a comfortable groove behind the leader.

Like Shorty Rogers, Shank spent much of his middle years as a session player. Perhaps ironically, the experience made him a more complete jazz musician. His work with the highly successful L.A.4 and, to a lesser extent, with the Lighthouse All Stars is inclined to be over-processed and self-consciously crowd-pleasing, but, as with the Modern Jazz Quartet, a superficial blandness masks formidable musicianship.

Tomorrow's Rainbow teams him with Marco Silva's fusion group, Intersection, for a lively Latin set that keeps the temperature well up. There are valuable glimpses of Shank's early work on a Jazzline airshot compilation called *Hello Baden-Baden*, where he plays with European luminaries Albert Mangelsdorff and Joe Zawinul. There is, though, little else of his pre-MOR, soft-bop phase, and (despite some good flute and a *tour de force* 'Tribute To The African Penny Whistle') *Misty Eyes* is a disappointingly thin offering, by no means as good a sample as the (also deleted) *Live At The Haig*, recorded in 1956 with Williamson, Prell and drummer Chuck Flores.

Lost In The Stars is a Sinatra songbook, marked by the quirky brilliance of Levy (an accompanist's accompanist) and by Shank's attractive alto sound which sounds as if it's been in and out of retirement as often as the man himself. 'This Love Of Mine', a much-overlooked standard, is played masterfully, with just the right balance of sentiment and cynicism.

The recent *New Gold!* sees him steering comfortably towards his seventieth birthday. Shank's own playing is exemplary, but it is Perkins who shapes the music round himself on this date and, though the varied package of songs suits Shank perfectly, he doesn't shine as he had on *The Doctor Is In!*.

(***) Explorations: 1980 Concord CCD 42001
    Shank; Bill Mays (*p*). 10/79.

This is from the Concord equivalent of ECM's New Series, a mainly classical programme (and an original suite from Mays), scored or arranged for flute and piano. Shank plays beautifully, if not quite classically. Not a jazz record, of course, but it could be worth exploring.

Lakshminarayana Shankar (born 1950) VIOLIN, DOUBLE VIOLIN

*** Who's To Know (M.R.C.S.) ECM 1195
    Shankar; Umayalpuram K. Sivaraman (*mridangam*); Zakir Hussain (*tabla*);
    V. Lakshminarayana (*tala keeping*). 11/80.
*** Vision ECM 1261
    Shankar; Jan Garbarek (*ts, ss, bsx, perc*); Palle Mikkelborg (*t, flhn*). 4/83.
*** Song For Everyone ECM 1286
    Shankar; Jan Garbarek (*ts, ss*); Zakir Hussain, Trilok Gurtu (*perc*). 84.
**(*) The Epidemics ECM 1308
    Shankar; Caroline (*syn, tamboura, v*); Steve Vai (*g*); Gilbert Kaufman (*syn*); Percy Jones (*b*). 85.
***(*) Nobody Told Me ECM 1397
    Shankar; V. Lakshminarayana (*vn, v*); Zakir Hussain (*tabla*); Vikku Vinayakram (*ghatam*);
    Ganam Rao, Caroline (*v*). 87.
*** M.R.C.S. ECM 1403
    Shankar; Zakir Hussain (*tabla*); Vikku Vinayakram (*ghatam*); Jon Christensen (*d*). 88.
*** Pancha Nadal Pallavi ECM 1407
    Shankar; Zakir Hussain (*tabla*); Vikku Vinayakram (*ghatam*); Caroline (*talam, sruthi*). 7/89.

Subheaded 'Indian classical music' (a designation that has caused some controversy in quarters unamused by Shankar's syncretism of subcontinental idioms), *Who's To Know* poses a sly challenge to the Western listener. Is this 'authentic' Indian music? How would we know even if it wasn't? ECM's initial resistance to liner-notes and tendency to throw uncontextualized music at purchasers has changed in recent years (not least with the advent of the classically orientated New Series), but if Shankar's extraordinary music is to be saved from a reductive categorization with 'ethnic', 'World Music' or 'New Age' materials, then more needs to be known about its rhythmic and harmonic premises than is usually forthcoming.

Shankar's performing style is clearly not authentic in the sense that it is not constrained by traditional formulae and proscriptions. Shankar has played with saxophonist Jan Garbarek, and with Eastward-stepping guitarist John McLaughlin, in Shakti, the group that introduced him to a wider European audience. The association with Garbarek and Mikkelborg was a particularly fruitful one, demonstrating how readily Shankar's idiosyncratic ten-string double violin (whose twin necks can be played separately or simultaneously) and largely microtonal language translate to a Western improvisational idiom. There is nothing floatingly 'ethnic' about the music on *Vision*, which contains unprecedented bass saxophone work from Garbarek; it is a thoroughly contemporary and extremely intense performance from all three participants. The enigmatically titled *M.R.C.S.* is a re-recording of a solo project, with tabla master Zakir Hussain more than taking the place of the original rhythm box, and the other musicians helping to create a taut rhythmic web that trades up Shankar's almost pedestrian melodic notions into music of extravagant dimensions.

Pancha Nadal Pallavi is very much closer to Indian classical idiom and is consequently less penetrable from a Western point of view. Like the excellent *Nobody Told Me*, these are American sessions centred on the interplay between Shankar's remarkable double-necked instrument (dimly reminiscent of John McLaughlin's trademark double-neck guitar in Mahavishnu days) and Zakir Hussain's virtuosic tabla. The singing is intricate and insistently rhythmic. The Music album also features the acoustic violin of Shankar's father, V. Lakshminarayana, and the drones (a technical device, no slur intended) of his wife Caroline (who seems to have shed a surname). She also appears on *The Epidemics*, a title used for Shankar's touring band, albeit with different personnel. This is the weakest of the albums, too far removed from the tradition that nourishes the best of them.

Jack Sharpe BARITONE SAXOPHONE

(*) **Roarin' Jazz House JHCD 016
  Sharpe; Derek Watkins, Jimmy Deuchar, Mark Chandler, Stuart Brooks, Simon Gardner (*t*);
  Geoff Wright, Chris Pyne, Pete Beachill, Dave Stewart (*tb*); Andy Mackintosh (*as*); Jamie
  Talbot, Dave Bishop (*ts*); Dave Hartley (*p*); Chris Laurence (*b*); Harold Fisher (*d*). 5/89.

Although the sleevenote-writer's claim that this 'may be the best big band ever put together outside America' is pretty laughable, it is actually an impressive outfit, creaming off some of the most proficient of British players to execute a sequence of tough and forceful scores. Mackintosh and Bishop are the two major soloists and they have virtuoso features on 'Old Folks' and Tubby Hayes's '100% Proof' respectively; while Mackintosh, in particular, may aspire to the kind of thing Chris Hunter or David Sanborn would do with the Gil Evans orchestra, it sounds more like routine pyrotechnics here. The only soloist who makes any real impression is Jimmy Deuchar, who sounds halting and imprecise on 'I'm Beginning To See The Light' beside the others, yet still seems to be more his own man than any of them. The band sound as if they need to relax more: only the closing 'J And B', a Deuchar theme, achieves a less forced take-off. Recorded live at Ronnie Scott's Club, the sound is constricted but clear enough.

Sonny Sharrock (1940–94) GUITAR

**** **Guitar** Enemy EMY 102
  Sharrock. 86.

Sharrock might have remained a lost legend if Bill Laswell hadn't provided him with a new context in Last Exit and egged him into this solo album, which shatters a former reputation for avant-garde 'weirdness'. His subsequent rise has completed the circle for a man who began by singing in a doo-wop group in the 1950s and spent seven years with Herbie Mann. *Guitar* is a textbook of what the electric instrument can be made to do in the hand of a master: Sharrock eschews fast picking in favour of blizzards of chords, walls of noise on the edge of feedback, drones that create a sort of violent timelessness and the first serious use of slide guitar in a 'jazz' context. 'Blind Willie', a dark nod to blues'n'-gospel masters Johnson and McTell, is as severe as 'Like Voices Of Sleeping Birds' is beautiful.

(*) **Seize The Rainbow Enemy EMY 104
  Sharrock; Melvin Gibbs, Bill Laswell (*b*); Abe Speller, Pheeroan akLaff (*d*). 5/87.
*** **Live In New York** Enemy EMY 108
  Sharrock; Dave Snyder (*ky*); Melvin Gibbs (*b*); Pheeroan akLaff (*d*); Ron 'The Burglar' Cartel
  (*v*). 7/89.
*** **Highlife** Enemy EMY 119
  Sharrock; Dave Snyder (*ky*); Charles Baldwin (*b*); Abe Speller, Lance Carter (*d*). 10/90.

After the opening-round knockout of *Guitar*, these band albums are a mite disappointing. *Seize The Rainbow* rationalizes rather than extends Sharrock's ideas within a brawny blues-rock format with hints of exotica. The live album unleashes a little more ferocity, without surrendering Sharrock's oft-obscured romantic streak, which peeks through on 'My Song'. Gibbs and akLaff play relatively straight but concentrated rhythms behind him. *Highlife* returns to polish rather than spit for its nine tracks – the guitarist is never one for rambling, unending solos – but gruff, clenched workouts like 'Chumpy' suggest that Sharrock's kind of fusion is good for many more records yet. Bass-heavy recordings on all these records, but crystalline clarity isn't what one should be looking for with music like this.

*** **Faith Moves** CMP CD 52
  Sharrock; Nicky Skopelitis (*g, b, sitar etc.*). 90.
**** **Ask The Ages** Axiom 848957-2
  Sharrock; Pharoah Sanders (*ss, ts*); Charnett Moffett (*b*); Elvin Jones (*d*). 91.

There is some charming, sparkly music on *Faith Moves*, which depends on the folk-like interaction of Sharrock and the uncategorizable guitarist Skopelitis (who also uses 'world' instruments such as the Iranian *tar* and the Turkish *saz* on the session). Much shimmering and interweaving of lines and, though it's scarcely a riveting record compared with what Sharrock's already done, it's an agreeable alternative.

Ask The Ages, though, is of a different order. Here Sharrock uncorks some of his most ecstatic playing, and there are no more suitable players to accompany such a flight than Sanders and Jones, who quickly move in on the guitarist's space and both exalt and liberate his electric waving and crying. Moffett is a bit of a helpless bystander but the interplay of the other three men is magnificently evocative of some kind of bliss.

Artie Shaw (born 1910) CLARINET

*** Artie Shaw And His Rhythm Makers 1938 Tax 3709-2

> Shaw; John Best, Malcolm Crain, Tom Di Carlo (*t*); Harry Rogers, George Arus (*tb*); Les
> Robinson, Harry Freeman (*as*); Tony Pastor, Jules Rubin (*ts*); Les Burness (*p*); Al Avola (*g*);
> Ben Ginsberg (*b*); Cliff Leeman (*d*); Nita Bradley (*v*). 2/38.

(**) Thou Swell ASV AJA 5056

> As above, except add Willis Kelly, Lee Castaldo, Dave Wade, Zeke Zarchey (*t*); Mark Bennett,
> Mike Michaels, Buddy Morrow (*tb*); Tony Pastor (*ts*); Joe Lippman, Fulton McGrath (*p*); Julie
> Schechter, Lou Klayman, Jerry Gray, Frank Siegfeld (*vn*); Sam Persoff (*vla*); Jimmy Oderich,
> Bill Schumann (*clo*); Wes Vaughan, Gene Stultz (*g*); Hank Wayland, Ben Ginsberg (*b*); Sam
> Weiss, George Wettling (*d*); Peg La Centra, Leo Watson (*v*). 6/36–12/37.

*** In The Beginning Hep CD 1024

> Similar to above. 6–12/36.

Anyone familiar with the facts of his extraordinary life – with its sensational marriages and vast range
of interests, overseen by a shrewd, restless mind – may find Artie Shaw's records a little lacking in fire.
Yet he remains one of the most outstanding of instrumentalists, playing clarinet with a piercing mastery
that outdoes any player of his day, and a musician whose search for superior settings has left an
intriguing body of work behind him. He was the first swing bandleader to make much use of strings, and
the 1936 sides collected on the ASV reissue chart his early interest in the projection of strings against
the other sections (although Glenn Miller had already tried this sort of thing). The problem with all of
Shaw's 1936–7 sessions, though, is a peculiarly old-fashioned feel to the rhythm section. Though his own
solos were already close to impeccable, the bands lacked singular voices and the beat stuck close to a
pulse that other rhythm sections were already streamlining into the smoother manner of the swing era.
The ASV disc we must discount because of the very poor transfers, which are muddy and reverberant.
The Tax disc covers a single day's recording of radio transcriptions and is perhaps the best representation of what Shaw's band could do: not a great deal. In character with its backward feel, one of the
strongest tracks is a version of the oddball tune of some years earlier, 'The Call Of The Freaks'.
Excellent transfers. As far as the studio tracks are concerned, the best single disc of this period is Hep's
In The Beginning. For once the transfers are less than ideal from this source, but this chronological
survey of Shaw's first important year as a bandleader is set down clearly. It also includes what is
probably the only known treatment of 'Dipper Mouth Blues' with a string section.

***(*) Begin The Beguine RCA Bluebird ND 82432

> Shaw; Chuck Peterson, John Best, Claude Bowen, Bernie Privin, Charlie Margulis, Manny
> Klein, George Thow, Billy Butterfield, George Wendt, J. Cathcart, Harry Geller (*t*); Jace Cave
> (*flhn*); George Arus, Les Jenkins, Harry Rogers, Randall Miller, Bill Rank, Babe Bowman, Ray
> Conniff, Jack Jenney, Vernon Brown (*tb*); George Koenig, Hank Freeman, Les Robinson, Blake
> Reynolds, Bud Carlton, Jack Stacey, Bus Bassey, Neely Plumb (*as*); Tony Pastor, Ronnie Perry,
> Georgie Auld, Dick Clark, Les Robinson, Jerry Jerome (*ts*); Joe Krechter (*bcl*); Morton
> Ruderman (*f*); Phil Nemoli (*ob*); Johnny Guarnieri (*p, hpd*); Les Burness, Bob Kitsis, Stan
> Wrightsman (*p*); Bobby Sherwood, Al Avola, Al Hendrickson, Dave Barbour (*g*); Sid Weiss, Jud
> DeNaut (*b*); Cliff Leeman, Buddy Rich, Carl Maus, Nick Fatool (*d*); Helen Forrest, Billie
> Holiday (*v*); strings. 7/38–1/41.

Although 'Begin The Beguine' made him a success – Shaw switched the original beguine beat to a
modified 4/4, and its lilting pulse was irresistible – the huge hit he scored with it was greeted with
loathing when it dawned on him what it meant in terms of fawning fans and general notoriety. He never
seemed satisfied with his bands, and the four different orchestras on this compilation played through a
series of breakdowns and disbandments by the leader. The second band, with arrangements by Jerry
Gray and with Buddy Rich powering the rhythm section, was a far harder-hitting outfit than the old
Shaw 'New Music'. But their best sides are still scattered. *Begin The Beguine* includes such hits as the
title-piece, 'Nightmare' (Shaw's first theme), 'Any Old Time' (the one title Billie Holiday recorded with
Shaw), 'Traffic Jam' and 'Frenesi', as well as sides with Helen Forrest handling vocals and two tracks by
the Gramercy Five, which has another CD to itself. The 1940 band includes Billy Butterfield and
Johnny Guarnieri, and 'Star Dust' and 'Moonglow' hint at Shaw's romantic-symphonic aspirations,
which troubled him at a time when listeners might have preferred to jitterbug. The remastering has been
smartly done, though the NoNoise system is, as usual, not to all tastes.

*** Live In 1938–39 Vol. One Phontastic CD 7609

> Shaw; Chuck Peterson, Claude Bowen, Johnny Best, Bernie Privin (*t*); George Arus, Russell
> Brown, Harry Rodgers, Les Jenkins (*tb*); Les Robinson, Hank Freeman, Tony Pastor, Ronnie
> Perry, Georgie Auld (*reeds*); Les Burness, Bob Kitsis (*p*); Al Avola (*g*); Sid Weiss (*b*); Cliff
> Leeman, Buddy Rich, George Wettling (*d*); Helen Forrest (*v*). 11/38–1/39.

*** **Live In 1938–39 Vol. Two** Phontastic CD 7613
    As above, except omit Bowen, Brown, Burness, Perry, Wettling and Leeman. 1–3/39.
*** **Live In 1939 Vol. Three** Phontastic CD 7628
    As above. 2–5/39.
***(*) **In The Blue Room / In The Café Rouge** RCA Victor 74321 18527-2 2CD
    As above, except add Harry Geller (*t*), Dave Barbour (*g*). 11/38–11/39.
***(*) **King Of The Clarinet 1938–39** Hindsight HBCD-502 3CD
    As above discs. 11/38–11/39.
*** **1938–39 Old Gold Shows** Jazz Hour 1009
    Probably as above discs. 38–39.
Airshots by the 1938–9 band. The Phontastics offer a broad survey. Like all such ancient history, there is period charm (the announcements, the hysterical applause) as well as period dross and even a decent amount of good music. Some of the tracks are too short to have much impact, but there are some more extended pieces that show the band at full stretch: a fast and sassy 'Carioca' and a long treatment of 'The Chant' that prefigures something of 'Concerto For Clarinet'. These are both on *Volume Three*, but there are interesting things on the first two discs as well, notably otherwise unrecorded items such as 'The Yam' (*Volume One*), Shaw playing Ellington with 'Diga Diga Doo' (*Volume Two*) and some alternative versions of hits like 'Back Bay Shuffle' (also *Volume Two*). The sound is very mixed: quite sharp and clear on some pieces, very fusty on others. Mostly these are for Shaw specialists. RCA's own *Blue Room/Café Rouge* set is a little more appealing since the sound is fine and the performances are of a more consistent standard. Shaw adds a little spoken introduction himself (recorded in the 1950s, when the LPs were originally released) and the live versions of the band's hits are played with great enthusiasm. Most notable, though, is the finesse Shaw could get from his musicians on even regular radio and dancing engagements. His own solos have their usual steely calm as well as an extra bite for the occasion. Hindsight's three-disc set may be a first choice for those wanting a generous survey: splendidly packaged and annotated, with interesting comments on most of these versions by Shaw himself, they underline how this band's airshots throw a strikingly different light on how a big band worked outside the studios. The sound isn't as bright as on some of these reissues, but there's a lot to enjoy across the three discs. Jazz Hour's compilation is another good one, if a notch behind Victor's, and it has some more strong material: 'In The Mood', 'Back Bay Shuffle' and 'Copenhagen', among others. Very clean sound for the period.

*** **The Complete Gramercy Five Sessions** RCA Bluebird ND 87637
    Shaw; Billy Butterfield, Roy Eldridge (*t*); Johnny Guarnieri (*hpd*); Dodo Marmarosa (*p*); Al Hendrickson, Barney Kessel (*g*); Jud DeNaut, Morris Rayman (*b*); Nick Fatool, Lou Fromm (*d*). 9/40–8/45.
Shaw's small group let him work off some more of his chamber-jazz hankerings, and though there are kitsch elements which outdo even Benny Goodman's 'Bach Goes To Town' – such as the very sound of Guarnieri's harpsichord and bouncing-ball tunes like 'Special Delivery Stomp' – the best of the Gramercy Five sounds surprisingly fresh, thanks mainly to the leader's unflinching dexterity and the heat generated by Butterfield (who sounds much like Cootie Williams in Goodman's small groups) and Eldridge. Youngsters like Marmarosa and Kessel also squeeze in solo parts. But the sense of a band working on artifice alone tends to drain off what excitement the group produces. The transfers sound rather thin.

*** **Mixed Bag** Musicmasters 65119-2
    Shaw; Roy Eldridge, Stan Fishelson, Bernie Glow, George Schwartz, Manny Klein, Ray Linn, Clyde Harley (*t*); Harry Rogers, Gus Dixon, Ollie Wilson, Bob Swift, Si Zentner (*tb*); Rudy Tanza, Lou Prisby, Skeets Herfurt (*as*); Herbie Steward, Jon Walon (*ts*); Chuck Gentry (*bs*); Dodo Marmarosa, Milt Raskin, Hank Jones (*p*); Barney Kessel, Tal Farlow, Dave Barbour (*g*); Morris Rayman, Artie Shapiro, Tommy Potter (*b*); Lou Fromm, Nick Fatool, Irv Kluger (*d*); Mel Torme, The Mel-Tones, Lillian Lane, Ralph Blane, Kitty Kallen (*v*). 8/45–3/54.
What it says – sessions for Musicraft from the mid-'40s, plus a stray Gramercy Five track with Hank Jones and Tal Farlow from 1954. Shaw admits in the notes that this was a comparatively unadventurous period for him, with the band sticking to simple charts and lusher frameworks than he might have liked. The Shaw trademark of precision remains a given. As smooth big-band music from an era on the wane, this serves well and, though some of the masters sound a bit scratchy, sound is mostly clean enough.

***(*) **The Last Recordings** Musicmasters 65071-2 2CD
    Shaw; Hank Jones (*p*); Tal Farlow (*g*); Joe Roland (*vib*); Tommy Potter (*b*); Irv Kluger (*d*). 54.
This was Shaw's last document and it's valuable to have it back in circulation, with ten new tracks. The music is poised somewhere between the swing principles which Shaw remained faithful to and the faintest wisp of bop-styled modernism which such fellow crossovers as Farlow and Jones also make the

most of. Lithe, piercing, but fundamentally relaxed and even-tempered, this is high-calibre chamber-jazz which leaves the Shaw story tantalizingly unfinished, even if the man himself is still sporadically active as a conductor.

Woody Shaw (1944–89) TRUMPET

**** **Cassandranite** Muse MCD 6007
> Shaw; Garnett Brown (*tb*); Joe Henderson (*ts*); Harold Vick (*ts, f*); George Cables, Herbie Hancock, Larry Young (*p*); Ron Carter, Paul Chambers, Cecil McBee (*b*); Joe Chambers (*d*). 12/65, 2/71.

**** **The Moontrane** Muse MCD 5472
> Shaw; Steve Turre (*tb*); Azar Lawrence (*ts, ss*); Onaje Allan Gumbs (*p*); Cecil McBee, Buster Williams (*b*); Victor Lewis (*d*); Guilherme Franco, Tony Waters (*perc*). 12/74.

*** **Lotus Flower** Enja ENJ 4018
> Shaw; Steve Turre (*tb, perc*); Mulgrew Miller (*p*); Stafford James (*b*); Tony Reedus (*d*). 1/82.

*** **Time Is Right** Red RR 123168
> Shaw; Steve Turre (*tb, shell*); Mulgrew Miller (*p*); Stafford James (*b*); Tony Reedus (*d*). 1/83.

*** **Woody Shaw With The Tone Jansa Quartet** Timeless SJP 221
> Shaw; Tone Jansa (*ts, ss, fl*); Renato Chicco (*p*); Peter Herbert (*b*); Dragan Gajic (*d*). 4/85.

***(*) **Solid** Muse MCD 5329
> Shaw; Kenny Garrett (*as*); Peter Leitch (*g*); Kenny Barron (*p*); Neil Swainson (*b*); Victor Jones (*d*). 3/86.

***(*) **Imagination** Muse MCD 5338
> Shaw; Steve Turre (*tb*); Kirk Lightsey (*p*); Ray Drummond (*b*); Carl Allen (*d*). 6/87.

**** **In My Own Sweet Way** In + Out 7003
> Shaw; Fred Henke (*p*); Neil Swainson (*b*); Alex Deutsch (*d*). 2/87.

Woody Shaw's career judgement was almost as clouded as his actual vision. A classic under-achiever, his relatively lowly critical standing is a function partly of his musical purism (which was thoroughgoing and admirable) but also more largely of his refusal or inability to get his long-term act together. A sufferer from *retinitis pigmentosa* (which severely restricted his sight-reading), he fell under a subway train in the spring of 1989 and died of his injuries.

It was Eric Dolphy who taught Shaw to play 'inside and outside at the same time', but it was listening to the classics that awakened a player with perfect pitch to the subtler nuances of harmony. Like all imaginative Americans, Shaw was violently stretched between opposites and inexorably drawn to the things and the places that would destroy him. Europe drew him for all the usual extramusical reasons, but there is a sense, too, that Shaw's foreshortened career represented a sustained fugue from the racially constrained job-description of the 'jazz musician'.

However hardly won, Shaw's technique sounded effortless, which disguised the awful disquiet at the root of his music. His influences were not settling ones: at the one extreme Debussy, the most inside-and-outside of the pre-Schoenberg composers; at the other his Newark friend, the organist Larry Young, with whom he recorded the superb *Unity* and who taught him, across the grain of the earlier Hubbardly aggression and linearity, the value of accepting a measure of chaos in music. Young appears (less familiarly playing piano) on the early Muse compilation, and the typically skewed and unpredictable 'The Organ Grinder' on *In My Own Sweet Way* is dedicated to Young.

The first recorded version of Shaw's best-known composition, 'The Moontrane', was on *Unity*. The 1974 Muse which bears its name has now been revived on CD, padded with a couple of alternative takes; 'Tapscott's Blues' is the more interesting of these, an Azar Lawrence composition that ought to be picked up by other players. Shaw is in good voice, and the partnership with Turre is already cemented, with 'Sanyas' and 'Are They Only Dreams' the outstanding collaborations. *Cassandranite* is a valuable glimpse of what made him distinctive,the title-piece built up of unexpected intervals in a deceptively innocuous setting. Henderson is a revelation, as ever, soloing majestically on his own clever 'Tetragon' and never sounding less than wholly in charge. There are actually two line-ups here from Christmas 1965, and a single track from a 1971 session with trombonist Garnett Brown.

Almost all the 1980s albums are worth having. Shaw's bands of the period were either the product of good luck, sympathetic label handling, or else they belie the received image of a guy perpetually nodding out on the practicalities, lost in a world of immaterial musical purity. (The only place he ever *sounded* that other-worldly was in his heavily Echoplexed work on *Zawinul*, the Weather Report keyboard man's Atlantic solo.) The Red *Time Is Right* is a concert recording from Bologna. Turre is disappointingly muffled during a couple of his solos and there is not much definition to the rhythm section. The two originals are strongly played, though, and the set ends with a very powerful reading of 'We'll Be Together Again'. *Solid* is a good indication of how successfully he'd translated the freedoms of the early years and the pure-sound effects he offered Zawinul into straight but carefully arranged jazz on the changes. 'There Will Never Be Another You' and 'You Stepped Out Of A Dream' are both fresh as paint. The long 'It Might As Well Be Spring' adds a substantial footnote to Miles Davis's treatment, while at the opposite end of the scale 'The Woody Woodpecker Song' is taken at a manic, chucklehead pace.

Turre proves again on *Imagination* how good a partner he was, with the ability to counterpoise Shaw's inward examinations with bounce and fire. Their exchanges on 'Dat Dere' and Turre's down-home replies on 'Stormy Weather' are absolutely marvellous. *In My Own Sweet Way* features a good working band (by contrast, the Jansa sessions aren't nearly as coherent) working an imaginatively varied book of tunes. Even the Brubeck plodder of the title gains an exceptional lyricism and depth of focus.

Michael Shea PIANO

***(*) **Last Night While You Slept** Accurate AC-5007
    Shea; Bryan Steele (*ts*); Mark Taylor (*frhn*); John Pineda (*b*); Steve Altenberg (*d*). 6/93.
An exemplary record, full of accomplished playing and writing which still announces itself quietly. Shea's quartet – Taylor is a guest on five tracks – create a fluid series of interpretations in which the ensemble is always involved while leaving plenty of space for the leader and Steele to create telling improvisations. Pieces such as 'Rafter Mammals', where the solos are pitched alongside the melodic line, or 'Water Exits', beautifully varied between two distinct tempos, make the most of post-bop structure yet sound unfettered and new. 'Kiely On The Moor' is an affectionate variation on an Irish march, 'When I See You Again' a deft lyrical line. Steele's expansive sound and Shea's own economical playing impress, but it's Taylor's admirable solos which are the cherry on top.

George Shearing (born 1919) PIANO, ACCORDION

*** **The London Years** Hep CD 1042
    Shearing; Leonard Feather (*p*); Carlo Krahmer (*d*). 3/39–12/43.
*** **Great Britain's** Savoy SV-0160
    Shearing; Gene Ramey, Curley Russell (*b*); Cozy Cole, Denzil Best (*d*). 2–12/47.
*** **Midnight On Cloud 69** Savoy 0208
    Shearing; Red Norvo, Marjorie Hyams (*vib*); Tal Farlow, Chuck Wayne (*g*); John Levy, Charles Mingus (*b*); Denzil Best (*d*). 1/49–3/50.
Shearing's early recordings are in some ways slight, given that he glossed over bop's passion with a tinkling kind of manner that suggested a clever pianist toying with the music. But the occasional parallels with Lennie Tristano suggest the more profound direction Shearing could have gone in; that he chose a more temperate kind of commercial climate leaves one of those might-have-beens that jazz is full of. His very earliest records are in any case a showcase of swing piano, recorded in London in the early years of the war. The Hep CD collects 25 tracks and is an enjoyable, witty sequence of solos (there are two early tracks with Krahmer and one with Feather on piano, where Shearing squeezes a few dolorous blues chords out of the accordion). There are many entertaining bits of Tatum, Waller and Wilson in the pianist's style and these tracks might surprise anyone unfamiliar with his first period. *Great Britain's* is shared with some tracks by Marian McPartland, who's rather more interesting, but the polished bounce of the music has some of the fine clip of a good Nat Cole session. *Midnight On Cloud 69* sets him alongside two different groups, one with Hyams, Wayne, Levy and Best, playing in the manner that brought him hits such as 'Lullaby Of Birdland', the other in the more demanding company of Norvo, Farlow and Mingus, although it's hardly a cutting contest. Titles such as 'Cotton Top', 'Be Bop's Fables' and 'Night And Day' still sound coolly pleasant.

*** **Three Originals** MPS 523522-2 2CD
    Shearing; Sigi Schwab, Louis Stewart (*g*); Herbert Thusek (*vib*); Andy Simpkins, Niels-Henning Orsted-Pedersen (*b*); Rusty Jones, Stix Hooper (*d*); Chino Valdes, Carmelo Garcia (*perc*). 10/73–9/79.
The contents of three original MPS albums – *Light, Airy And Swinging, Continental Experience* and *On Target* – in a two-disc package. The first is the best, eight tunes with the smart rhythm section of Simpkins and Hooper, and nothing outdoes the opening skip through 'Love Walked In'. The second gets bogged down in sluggish Latin percussion. The third is soaked in Robert Farnon's strings – nice, though the Telarc album, below, sounds better.

(*) **Blues Alley Jazz Concord CCD 4110
    Shearing; Brian Torff (*b*). 10/79.

*** **Two For The Road** Concord CCD 4128
    Shearing; Carmen McRae (*v*). 80.
*** **Alone Together** Concord CCD 4171
    Shearing; Marian McPartland (*p*). 3/81.
*** **First Edition** Concord CCD 4177
    Shearing; Jim Hall (*g*). 9/81.
** **Live At The Café Carlyle** Concord CCD 4246
    Shearing; Don Thompson (*b*). 1/84.
** **Grand Piano** Concord CCD 4281
    Shearing (*p* solo). 5/85.
** **Plays The Music Of Cole Porter** Concord CCD 42010
    Shearing; Barry Tuckwell (*frhn*); strings. 1/86.
(*) **More Grand Piano Concord CCD 4318
    Shearing (*p* solo). 10/86.
*** **Breakin' Out** Concord CCD 4335
    Shearing; Ray Brown (*b*); Marvin 'Smitty' Smith (*d*). 5/87.
(*) **Dexterity Concord CCD 4346
    Shearing; Neil Swainson (*b*); Ernestine Anderson (*v*). 11/87.
(*) **A Perfect Match Concord CCD 4357
    Shearing; Neil Swainson (*b*); Jeff Hamilton (*d*); Ernestine Anderson (*v*). 5/88.
*** **The Spirit Of '76** Concord CCD 4371
    Shearing; Hank Jones (*p*). 3/88.
(*) **George Shearing In Dixieland Concord CCD 4388
    Shearing; Warren Vaché (*c*); George Masso (*tb*); Kenny Davern (*cl*); Ken Peplowski (*ts*); Neil
    Swainson (*b*); Jerry Fuller (*d*). 2/89.
*** **Piano** Concord CCD 4400
    Shearing (*p* solo). 5/89.

Shearing has always been on the periphery of jazz rather than anywhere inside it, even when he's been making records with genuine jazz musicians. Many of his MGM sides, tinkerings with a kind of cocktail bop, have yet to make it to CD – earlier records for Capitol have been reissued, but they are entirely made up of middle-of-the-road albums with strings and, though fine in their class, they scarcely belong in this book. In the 1980s his many records for Concord have put some focus on his work and have drummed up a few more worthwhile situations. Some of his best work will be found on records under Mel Torme's name, but a few others listed here are also worth hearing. When Shearing sets aside his incessant borrowings from other players and eschews middlebrow ideas of what's tasteful to play in the jazz idiom, he can come up with some nice ideas: the partnerships with McPartland and Jones find him adapting to the far greater range of both those players with some success, and he even holds his own with the trio with Brown and Smith. Carmen McRae's recital finds her in good, typically grouchy form, and Shearing accompanies with deference and good humour. The meeting with Ernestine Anderson is all right, but Anderson isn't the singer that McRae is. One of the best discs, with Jim Hall, who can make any situation interesting, has unfortunately yet to make it to CD. The albums which lose their way are those where he has to provide most of the musical interest himself: the solo sets and duos with bassists usually have one or two clever or gracious reworkings of standards, but they don't really sustain or repay close attention. Having said that, the most recent solo disc, *Piano*, finds him in an unusually effective, ruminative mood. The 'Dixieland' album is routine but pleasing enough, while the Cole Porter set is MOR prettiness.

*** **I Hear A Rhapsody** Telarc 83310
    Shearing; Neil Swainson (*b*); Grady Tate (*d*). 2/92.

A new label and a live album from New York's Blue Note must have galvanized the expatriate Englishman a little. The bop he essays on 'Birdfeathers' and 'Wail' are some of his most convincing moments in years. Swainson and Tate are right there with him, too.

*** **Walkin'** Telarc 83333
    As above. 2/92.
*** **How Beautiful Is Night** Telarc 83325
    Shearing; Robert Farnon Orchestra. 93.
*** **That Shearing Sound** Telarc 83347
    Shearing; Steve Nelson (*vib*); Louis Stewart (*g*); Neil Swainson (*b*); Dennis Mackrel (*d*). 2/94.

It seems almost impertinent to say it, but Shearing seems to be getting better, at least as far as the calibre of his records is concerned. Certainly Telarc are eliciting some of his most enjoyable music in years. None of these is a masterpiece exactly, but each shows the man's persuasive craftsmanship at its best. *Walkin'* is a second helping from the Blue Note engagement which produced the earlier disc, and the programme is intriguing – 'That's Earl Brother', 'Pensativa', 'Celia' and, above all, 'Subconscious-Lee', which is dark enough to be genuinely Tristanoesque. Measure for measure, this must be one of his best records. *How Beautiful Is Night* recalls his Capitol days, although Farnon's arrangements are so luxuri-ous and so sumptuously recorded that one surrenders to the sheer comfort. *That Shearing Sound* debuts a new band, and with Nelson and Stewart in the line-up it looks very promising. That said, they both bow amiably enough to Shearing's sometimes tyrannical arrangements, which in the main elongate the style of his 1940s quintet to double-length tunes. On its own terms, smartly enjoyable.

Jack Sheldon (born 1931) TRUMPET, VOCAL

(*) **Hollywood Heroes Concord CCD 4339
    Sheldon; Ray Sherman (*p*); Doug McDonald (*g*); Dave Stone (*b*); Gene Estes (*d*). 9/87.
(*) **On My Own Concord CCD 4529
    Sheldon; Ross Tompkins (*p*). 8–9/91.

Sheldon has been something of a polymath: an ingenious comedian, a very hot cool-school trumpeter, a slight but charming vocalist – and for two of those attributes he owes something to Chet Baker. But he works best with a straight man, or at least a foil – in the Curtis Counce group of the 1950s, or on an early Jimmy Giuffre LP, he fires up on the challenge of the other horns. Here, with a useful rhythm section behind him, the results are pleasant rather than exciting, although Sheldon is probably taking it a bit easier these days anyway. *Hollywood Heroes* is lively, yet Sheldon has no real context, and the result sounds too much like a nice trumpet–voice–rhythm section date to make any deep impression. He is in talespinning mood in *On My Own*, though it's done with trumpet and singing rather than with one of his deadpan routines. Well, all right.

Archie Shepp (born 1937) TENOR SAXOPHONE, SOPRANO SAXOPHONE, ALTO SAXOPHONE, PIANO, VOICE

*** **The House I Live In** Steeplechase SCC 6013
    Shepp; Lars Gullin (*bs*); Tete Montoliu (*p*); Niels-Henning Orsted-Pedersen (*b*); Alex Riel (*d*). 11/63.
***(*) **Fire Music** MCA MCAD 39121
    Shepp; Ted Curson (*t*); Joseph Orange (*tb*); Marion Brown (*as*); David Izenzon, Reggie Johnson (*b*); Joe Chambers, J. C. Moses (*d*). 2 & 3/65.
***(*) **On This Night** Impulse! GRP 11252
    Shepp; Bobby Hutcherson (*vib*); Henry Grimes, David Izenzon (*b*); Rashied Ali, Joe Chambers, J. C. Moses (*d*); Ed Blackwell (*perc*); Christine Spencer (*v*). 3 & 8/65.

Archie Shepp once declared himself something 'worse than a romantic, I'm a sentimentalist'. Shepp has tended to be a theoretician of his own work, often expressing his intentions and motivations in off-puttingly glib and aphoristic language. He has, though, consistently seen himself as an educator and communicator rather than an entertainer (or even an Artist) and is one of the few Afro-American artists who has effected any sort of convincing synthesis between black music (with its tendency to be depoliticized and repackaged for a white audience) and the less comfortable verbal experiments of poets like LeRoi Jones (Imamu Amiri Baraka). The dialectic between sentiment and protest in Shepp's work is matched by an interplay between music and words which, though more obvious, is also harder to assess. A playwright who also wrote a good deal of influential stage music, Shepp devised a musical style that might be called dramatic or, at worst and later in his career, histrionic.

    Though strongly associated in most people's minds with John Coltrane (he worked on the augmented *Love Supreme* sessions and on *Ascension*), Shepp's most potent influence among the modernists was the radical populism of Ornette Coleman. Unlike Coltrane, the Texan saw no need to dismantle or subvert the tradition in order to use it, and Shepp was much affected by Ornette's rediscovery of the freedoms inherent in earlier forms. Unfortunately, early work with The New York Contemporary Five (which grew out of a Coleman-influenced quartet co-led with trumpeter Bill Dixon) is not available on CD; its absence has reinforced a whole set of mistaken assumptions about the origins of what might be called Shepp's mature style.

    Certainly the tenor on *The House I Live In* is very different from what people normally think of as the Shepp of the 1960s. Pre-radical, though, he sounds like a player long steeped in swing and blues. Though primarily of historical interest, this hasn't made the much-needed transition to CD in step with a Gullin rediscovery or a comprehensive reassessment of Shepp's career, and may therefore sound like a rather enigmatic one-off. The opening 'You Stepped Out Of A Dream' is perhaps the best of the set, the closing 'Sweet Georgia Brown' giving off the air of a hastily agreed encore. Shepp and NHOP met again on record in 1980, below.

One of the best of Shepp's albums (though sounding rather brittle on CD), *Fire Music* is the saxophonist's most balanced synthesis of *agitprop* and lyricism, avant-gardism and traditionalist deference. 'Hambone', the long opening track, is a blues-rooted but unconventional theme, cast in irregular time-signatures, tough and citified. At the opposite extreme, there is a slightly kitsch 'Girl From Ipanema' with a reworked bridge; Shepp's colonization of pop tunes is less subversive than Coltrane's (for the most obvious comparison, see 'My Favorite Things' on *New Thing*, below) because he always remains half sold on the sentiments therein, but he makes a persuasive job of the Jobim tune. 'Los Olvidados' is dedicated to the youthful underclass of the city, the 'forgotten ones', those who will not be beguiled by Sandy Becker's 'Hambone' television character. The main focus of the piece is on Marion Brown's desolate middle passage, conjuring up thwarted promise in a hectic but unheeding environment; Shepp's own solo, as became his norm, is a rather pat summing-up, musical Method-acting, that slightly detracts from the sophistication of the composition. 'Malcolm, Malcolm – Semper Malcolm', scored for just Shepp, Izenzon and Moses and dominated by Shepp's sonorous recitation, is a brief foretaste of the later but no more convincing 'Poem For Malcolm', below. Clipped and re-dedicated from a longer and more ambitious work, it runs a slight risk of being ironized by 'Prelude To A Kiss' and the Jobim tune that follow; Shepp's ironies, though, are maintained not just between but also within compositions.

It's interesting to note that the trajectory of the album is (roughly) from populist experimentalism to a kind of experimental populism. The absence of piano is significant because it prevents the music (and particularly the two familiar themes) from sinking into comfortable tone-centres, thus maintaining its ambiguous, questing nature.

On This Night has a slightly complicated discographical history, explained by a laudable desire to get Impulse! releases back into some semblance of chronological order. 'Malcolm' is repeated from *Fire Music*, a slightly unnecessary duplication; two takes of 'The Chase' and the alternative take of 'The Mac Man' were originally released on a sequel called *Further Fire Music*; a further take of 'The Chase' was around for some time on a compilation called *The Definitive Jazz Scene: Volume Three*. Anyone who has a vinyl copy of *On This Night* will now look in vain for 'Gingerbread, Gingerbread Boy', which has been moved, quite logically, to the *New Thing at Newport* document (again, below).

So much for the background. Having the March and August 1965 sessions together on one CD makes good sense, even though they are presented in reverse chronological order. It's a big, brawling record, announced by Shepp's out-of-kilter piano and Christine Spencer's churchy voice on the opening 'On This Night (If That Great Day Would Come)'. As well as those items mentioned above, there is a brief excursion on Ellington's 'In A Sentimental Mood', a fine 'The Original Mr Sonny Boy Williamson' and, one of Shepp's quirkily poetic titles, 'The Pickaninny (Picked Clean – No More – Or Can You Back Back Doodlebug)' . . . and your guess is probably as good as ours.

Hutcherson makes an important contribution, as do the various drummers, with Moses making his presence felt very strongly on the five trio tracks with Izenzon from the March session which yielded the classic 'Malcolm'. The sound-quality is much improved from LP, with due weight given to the sidemen, but some of Shepp's high-register stuff sounds brittle and harsh to no obvious purpose. Mostly, though, this can be tempered on a home hi-fi, so no permanent damage done.

*** **New Thing At Newport** Impulse! GRP 11052
    Shepp; Bobby Hutcherson (*vib*); Barre Phillips (*b*); Joe Chambers (*d*). 7/65.
With the classic Coltrane Quartet on the other side of the original album, this gave an explicit and, in the circumstances, slightly ironic blessing to Shepp's emergence as one of the leading lights of the New Thing. Again, the balance of apparently contradictory motivations is just about right, with a less than wholly subversive 'My Favorite Things' set against the inner furies of 'Call Me By My Rightful Name' and 'Skag', and the surreal 'Rufus (Swung His Face To The Wind . . .)' from *Four For Trane*. On the whole, though, the music is far from radical in impact, and Shepp's spoken interpolations serve, as throughout his career, to mitigate any slight shift towards abstraction at this stage. Perhaps because of the circumstances and the eventual packaging of the music, Shepp's Newport performance has been somewhat overrated.

Again piano-less, the quartet takes a sharp, percussive edge from Hutcherson's tightly pedalled vibes. Phillips fares deservedly better on the CD and can be heard for the remarkable influence he was on the group. Shepp sounds quite self-consciously like a latter-day descendant of Webster and Hawkins, aggravating swing rhythms and phraseology with devices borrowed from R&B and early rock (and, more immediately, from the unabashed populist radicalism of Ornette Coleman). On the other side, Coltrane already sounds tired, but with the understandable weariness of a man whose path would be hard to follow.

***(*) **Steam** Enja 2076
    Shepp; Cameron Brown (*b*); Philly Joe Jones (*d*). 76.

Perhaps the last point in his career at which Shepp can truly be considered a contender. The heavyweight 'Message For Trane' almost sounds like a gesture of farewell, a turning back once again from the trailing edge of the avant-garde to explore the roots, but also a slightly sorrowful recognition that the astral channels have grown too congested for many more such messages to get through. 'Steam' is brash and open, infinitely better here than the awful vocal version on the deleted *Attica Blues*, one of Shepp's worst and most ill-judged albums. 'Solitude' has the romantic quietly closing the door on the sentimentalist. Shepp doubles on piano but, given the space to develop his ideas (there are only those three tracks), the album is notable for the unwonted coherence of his saxophone solos.

**(*) The Rising Sun Collection: Volume 5 Rising Sun Collection RSC 005
    Shepp; Dave Burrell (*p*); Cameron Brown (*b*); Charli Persip (*d*). 4/77.
Be not afraid: there aren't four earlier volumes of Shepp at the Montreal club waiting in the wings. The rest of the series is basically blues, and the saxophonist is something of an odd catch. The repertoire is pretty much as per normal for this period, awkwardly balanced between fire and lyricism, bebop and something beyond: 'Steam', 'Girl From Ipanema', 'Donna Lee', 'Crucificado'. The big plus is Burrell on piano, consistently interesting and inventive from start to finish.

**(*) Ballads For Trane Denon DC 8570
    Shepp; Albert Dailey (*p*); Reggie Workman (*b*); Charli Persip (*d*). 5/77.
First and most inevitable of a series of tributes to the great players. Shepp's desire to write himself into the tradition rapidly became overweening and rather tiresome. With Coltrane, though, he could claim a degree of discipleship. Whether one chooses to hear or to dismiss the phantom 'second tenor' at the end of Coltrane's masterpiece, *A Love Supreme*, depends somewhat on a desire to see Shepp pick up the fallen torch and carry it onward. On *Four For Trane* he showed some sign of doing just that. On this, coinciding neatly with the tenth anniversary of Coltrane's death and with Shepp's own *crise de quarante*, he sounds like a man going through all sorts of elaborate motions in order to conjure up an emotion commensurate with the occasion. It doesn't work. 'Soul Eyes', written by Mal Waldron and immortalized by Coltrane, is a mess, with Dailey making a hash of the piano part and only Workman and Persip working at anything like a thoughtful level.

**(*) Day Dream Denon DC 8547
    Shepp; Walter Davis (*p*); Earl May (*b*); Philly Joe Jones (*d*). 6/77.
*** On Green Dolphin Street Denon DC 8587
    Shepp; Walter Bishop Jr (*p*); Sam Jones (*b*); Joe Chambers (*d*). 11/77.
Day Dream is the least satisfying of the Denon tribute records. In later years Shepp was to return to Ellington material many times, usually with more feeling and application than on any of these tracks. His solos on 'Caravan' and 'Prelude To A Kiss' are almost oily in their effort to invest the tunes with some of the emotion missing from a lacklustre band.

    The November session has an autumnal melancholy and niggling uncertainty that aren't unattractive but which don't seem to relate either to anything in the themes – standard fodder – or to particular interpretations. A look at the calendar hints at one possible, if rather psychologized, explanation: 1937, 1977, is this the *crise de quarante* we keep reading about?

*** Duet Denon DC 8561
    Shepp; Abdullah Ibrahim (*p*). 6/78.
Fine things in this head-to-head with the South African composer whose rolling piano lines give Shepp lots of freedom. The memorial to trumpeter Mongezi Feza, 'Barefoot Boy From Queenstown', is actually very moving: Shepp for once manages to avoid overdoing the emotion. The recording was made in Japan and is characteristically crisp and direct. Fans of Ibrahim will be interested to hear him as upfront and unalloyed as this.

***(*) Lady Bird Denon DC 8546
    Shepp; Jaki Byard (*p*); Cecil McBee (*b*); Roy Haynes (*d*). 12/78.
***(*) Looking At Bird Steeplechase SCCD 31149
    Shepp; Niels-Henning Orsted-Pedersen (*b*). 2/80.
Never short of a handy phrase and ever mindful of a need to resist the condescending nomenclature of 'jazz', Shepp prefers to consider bebop as the Baroque period of Afro-American classical music. Given the brutal accretions of his approach, it's an accurate but still slightly misleading designation. His Parker readings are irregular pearls with a raw, slightly meretricious beauty but with only questionable currency as serious re-examinations of the tradition. There is a rather better version of 'Now's The Time' (one of Parker's most traditionally rooted tunes and the one to which Shepp seems to be drawn) on the later *I Didn't Know About You*.

    The Denon session (one of a group of tribute discs; see elsewhere in this section) is marred by a long and rambling intepretation of 'Flamingo' at the end of the disc. Otherwise the readings of 'Donna Lee',

'Now's The Time' and 'Relaxin' At Camarillo' are first rate, with Byard and McBee barrelling through the changes at a furious lick, and Haynes crowding the saxophonist through each of his choruses.

The great NHOP cut his teeth on this repertoire and sounds completely at home with it, bouncing and singing through a more or less predictable roster of bebop anthems. It's probably easier for bass players who don't have to negotiate a dense and anxiety-inducing archaeology of previous readings to make their own statements, but the Dane does seem to encourage Shepp to some of his most relaxed and probing performances in the bebop canon. (It's worth listening to this in the context of two saxophone–bass duo takes of 'Davis' with Buell Neidlinger on Cecil Taylor's *Cell Walk For Celeste*, Candid 9034.)

***(*) Goin' Home Steeplechase SCCD 31079
Shepp; Horace Parlan (*p*). 4/77.
***(*) Trouble In Mind Steeplechase SCCD 31139
As above. 2/80.
Parlan's slightly raw, bluesy style suits Shepp almost perfectly. The earlier of these, a moving compilation of gospel tunes, is by far the best and most concentrated. *Trouble In Mind*, which takes the same line on 11 blues staples, is perhaps a little too earnest in its pursuit of authenticity but achieves a chastened dignity.

*** Things Have Got To Change: Live At The Totem, Volume 1 EPM Musique 152172
Shepp; Siegfried Kessler (*p*); Bob Cunningham (*b*); Clifford Jarvis (*d*); Cheikh Tidiane-Seck (*perc*). 1/79.
*** Round About Midnight: Live At The Totem, Volume 2 EPM Musique 152202
As above, except omit Tidiane-Seck. 1/79.
Somewhat run-of-the-mill live material from the Paris club. Kessler sounds willing but under-rehearsed, and it's left to Cunningham and Jarvis to spur the leader on. Dedicated Shepp-watchers will doubtless find interesting things in 'Donna Lee' (Volume 2) and a not quite accurate but none the less courageous run-through of 'Giant Steps' (Volume 1). Less committed listeners can safely pass over these, secure in the conviction that a single CD would have been perfectly adequate as a document.

*** Tray Of Silver Denon DC 8548
Shepp; Howard Johnson (*bs, tba*); Mickey Tucker (*p*); Takahashi Mizuhashi (*b*); Roy Brooks (*d*). 4/79.
A breezy, funked-up run through a set of Horace Silver tunes (and one long piece by Tadd Dameron). There's a slight sense that individual performances have been stretched out longer than is strictly necessary, especially on 'Cookin' At The Continental' and Dameron's 'If You Could See Me Now', and the group passages start to take on a certain chugging inevitability. Pleasant, though, and a further insight into some of Shepp's less obvious enthusiasms.

***(*) The Long March, Part 1 hat Art CD 6041/2 2CD
Shepp; Max Roach (*d*). 8/79.
This is a fine live document, recorded in Switzerland. Roach has made many important duo records – with Braxton, Cecil Taylor and others – but this is one of the most committed and engaging. His own 'Drums Unlimited' is a bit of a bore and occupies more space than it strictly merits, to the extent that one feels this could have been boiled down to a single disc. However, there is enough good playing on the other tracks, including an encore 'Sophisticated Lady' that is Shepp's best recorded performance of the theme.

**(*) I Know About The Life Sackville SK 3062
Shepp; Ken Werner (*p*); Santi Wilson Debriano (*b*); John Betsch (*d*). 2/81.
*** Soul Song Enja 4050
Shepp; Ken Werner (*p*); Santi Wilson Debriano (*b*); Marvin 'Smitty' Smith (*d*). 12/82.
**(*) Down Home New York Soul Note 121102
Shepp; Charles McGhee (*t, v*); Ken Werner (*p, v*); Saheb Sarbib (*b*); Marvin 'Smitty' Smith (*d, v*); Bartholomew Gray (*v*). 2/84.
**(*) Live On Broadway Soul Note 121122
Shepp; George Cables (*p*); Herbie Lewis (*b*); Eddie Marshall (*d*); Royal Blue (*v*). 5/85.
After about 1975, Shepp's reputation held up more robustly in Europe than in the USA, in part because it may have been easier to sustain the mien of cool, magisterial fury when removed from the company of younger black Americans who either did it better or who rejected the premisses and methodology. Smith takes a more pragmatic line on American racism, and he plays on *Down Home New York* (as on the earlier *Soul Song*) with a brisk self-confidence that rather shames the leader's dull rhythmic sense and increasingly formulaic phrasing. On both albums, it's the group rather than the leader that impresses.

Perhaps because the rhythm section is less ebullient, Shepp plays better on *Live On Broadway*, but 'My

Romance', 'A Night In Tunisia', 'Giant Steps' and a vocal 'St James Infirmary' still leave the residual impression of an illustrated lecture. *I Know About The Life*, the earliest of the group, is simply drab.

** Mama Rose Steeplechase SCCD 31169
    Shepp; Jasper van't Hof (*ky*). 2/82.
**(*) The Fifth Of May L + R Records LR 45004
    As above. 5/87.
Successive recordings of 'Mama Rose' (and there seem to be droves of them) are probably the most useful gauge of Shepp's progress or decline. The version with van't Hof is vulgarly overblown and recorded in horrible close-up. *The Fifth Of May* is rather better; the pianist limits himself to synthesizer and a slightly hollow-sounding grand, and there's a respectable though hardly inspired 'Naima'. Nothing, though, on a par with Shepp's longer-standing partnership with Horace Parlan.

** Lover Man Timeless SJP 287
    Shepp; Dave Burrell (*p*); Herman Wright (*b*); Steve McCraven (*d*); Annette Lowman (*v*). 1/88.
Shepp's previous approaches to the song give no hint of the tragic associations that still hover round 'Lover Man' as a result of Charlie Parker's catastrophic breakdown while attempting to record it. Here, he simply manages to sound inept. 'Lover Man' and 'Lush Life' are robbed of all pathos (and, what's worse, dignity), while 'My Funny Valentine' is full-choked sentimentality of a no longer appealing sort. Avoid.

*** Art Of The Duo Enja 7007
    Shepp; Richard Davis (*p*). 10/89.
Both Shepp and Davis are experienced duo performers. They know the tricks and the pitfalls, and both are able to work their way out of difficulties with considerable aplomb. Both 'Body And Soul' and 'Round Midnight' are models of seat-of-the-pants jazz playing – but this is where the problems also begin. There's a prevailing sense of observing two guys playing one-on-one, doing it for real but without much respect for rules, taste or onlookers. Recorded in a Boston club, the sound is rather messy. A pity there wasn't a studio available the following morning.

***(*) I Didn't Know About You Timeless CD SJP 370
    Shepp; Horace Parlan (*p*); Wayne Dockery (*b*); George Brown (*d*). 11/90.
**(*) Black Ballad Timeless CD SJP 386
    As above, except replace Brown with Steve McCraven (*d*). 1/92.
There have long been signs that Shepp regards himself as one of the last surviving heirs of the bop tradition. He switches to alto here for 'Hot House' and the title-track, sounding rather closer to Hodges than to Charlie Parker but not, at first hearing of these tracks, instantly recognizable as himself. He opens, after a brief historical excursus, with 'Go Down Moses (Let My People Go)', vocalizing through his horn before singing the verse with quiet passion. Shepp has always had problems coming to terms with Monk's output, but Parlan (here, as on their duo encounters) coaches him along; this time it's 'Ask Me Now', one of their very best recordings. The sound is bright and closely recorded, favouring saxophone and piano, and the album represents an encouraging return to form.

    Temporary, alas, since *Black Ballad* is little more than a weary plod through one of those 'in the tradition' sets that allow contemporary players to work out of character without significantly rethinking the source material. Shepp doesn't have anything to say on 'Do You Know What It Means To Miss New Orleans' or 'Ain't Misbehavin'', and both sound rather stiff and professorial. In contrast, on 'Lush Life' he whips out an onion and emotes shamelessly. It might have been OK in a club setting but, done like this, it comes across very forced and contrived.

Andy Sheppard (born 1957) TENOR SAXOPHONE, SOPRANO SAXOPHONE, FLUTE

***(*) Andy Sheppard Antilles ANCD 8720
    Sheppard; Dave Buxton (*ky*); Pete Maxfield (*b*); Simon Gore (*d*); Mamadi Kamara (*perc*). 87.
*** Introductions In The Dark Antilles ANCD 8742
    As above, except add Orphy Robinson (*vib*); Steve Lodder (*ky*); Chris Watson (*g*); Dave Adams (*perc*). 88.
By no means the precocious youngster the music press liked to think he was, Sheppard had actually been around for some time when he made his first album for Antilles. It's an assured and vividly executed debut, dominated by Coltranisms (as everything else was that year), but seen from a more individual perspective that anticipated the formal restlessness which was to be typical of Sheppard's subsequent career, which has taken in large-scale composition for his regular ensemble and for big-band, Miles-tinged rock–jazz, and (with his West Country friend, Keith Tippett, *q.v.*) an album of free improvisations disconcertingly entitled *66 Shades Of Lipstick*.

First indications that Sheppard would not be satisfied with transferring straightforward blowing gigs to record came with *Introductions In The Dark*. The album is dominated by the optimistically Ellingtonian 'Romantic Conversations (Between A Dancer And A Drum)', a huge two-part composition built out of attractively modest materials and then just slightly overcooked. Sheppard plays some engaging flute on Part One, but the later tenor work bogs down in an endless 'ethnic' vamp that is really rather dull and makeweight, redeemed only by vibraharpist Orphy Robinson's surprisingly pungent swing. There are signs that *Introductions*, produced with mixed success by Steve Swallow, was intended as an all-bases-touched presentation of Sheppard as a 'complete' musician. 'Optics' is a rather obvious Garbarek take-off, done in a bargain version of ECM's glacial acoustic. 'Where The Spirit Takes You' (CD only) loops along danceably, and only 'Rebecca's Glass Slippers' approaches anything like the fierce blowing of the first record.

***(*) Soft On The Inside Antilles ANCD 8751

As for *Andy Sheppard*, but add Claude Deppa (*t*); Kevin Robinson (*t, flhn*); Gary Valente (*tb*); Chris Biscoe (*as, ts, ss*); Pete Hurt (*ts, bcl*); Steve Lodder (*ky*); Orphy Robinson (*vib, mar*); Mano Ventura (*g*); Ernst Reijseger (*clo*); Han Bennink (*d*). 11/89.

Sheppard's best album is boldly arranged, with many of the instruments 'paired' with a self-conscious opposite, bringing the univocal immediacy and rhythmic suppleness of his basic sextet to his first venture in big-band scoring. Sheppard had worked with both George Russell and Carla Bley European bands and draws elements of his scoring and a new melodic obliqueness from the experience. 'Carla Carla Carla Carla' makes one debt clear, calling on Lodder for a wry, accordion-like synth solo. 'Rebecca's Silk Stockings' turns a Morse message from the brass into another freewheeling rave (shudder to think how 'Rebecca's Suspender Belt' – she sounds the kind of woman who'd wear one – is going to sound) that is topped only by the percussive batter of 'Adventures In The Rave Trade', another whole-side two-parter that is much more finely conceived and scored than 'Conversation' on the earlier record. Outstanding among the soloists are Robinson ('Carla' and 'Rave Trade'), Reijseger (the opening 'Soft On The Inside'), Deppa ('Silk Stockings') and Valente, another Bley man, on the opening episode of 'Rave Trade'. The sound is big but rather compressed towards the middle. Enthusiasts might like to note that a video is also available, on Island Visual Arts IVA 047.

*** In Co-Motion Antilles ANCD 8766

Sheppard; Claude Deppa (*t, flhn*); Steve Lodder (*ky*); Sylvan Richardson (*g, b*); Dave Adams (*d, perc, tb*). 2/91.

The clipped tracks' titles ('A.S.A.P.', 'Movies', 'Upstage', 'Circles', and nary a glimpse of Rebecca's underwear) immediately suggest a change of direction. The opening 'A.S.A.P.', with Deppa muzzled and dangerous, comes on like Miles's *Live-Evil* (Ydna Drappesh?), but there's too much again of *Introductions*' run-through feel of moods and styles. 'Eargliding' bears a disconcerting resemblance to 'The Girl From Ipanema', and there are satirical elements to both 'Let's Lounge', a sexy blur that provokes Sheppard's best solo, and 'Pinky', a co-credit with Lodder, who often sounds as if he's marbling Sheppard's scores with oil paint. The introduction of Richardson's six-string bass does nothing but smooth out the lower registers.

*** Rhythm Method Blue Note 827798

Sheppard; Claude Deppa (*t*); Kevin Robinson (*t, flhn*); Ashley Slater, Gary Valente (*tb*); Jerry Underwood (*ts*); Julian Arguëlles (*bs*); Steve Lodder (*ky*); Sylvan Richardson (*b*); Dave Adams (*d*). 5/93.

***(*) Delivery Suite Blue Note 828719

As above. 6/93.

Hints of new parenthood on these discs, with titles like 'Perambulator' and 'Gas And Air' on the second (and live) record. Sheppard is himself still breathing and pushing in all the right places, but there's something slightly too antiseptic about both albums. Compared to the rough-edged home delivery that Steve Swallow brought to the sound of *In Co-Motion*, Sheppard and right-hand man Lodder give *Rhythm Method* a finish that's as smooth as a baby's . . . you see the point.

The one live track on the studio record, 'Well Kept Secret' (there's also a live version of 'So' on *Delivery Suite*), has a lot more presence. This has nothing to do with 'live feel' or 'atmosphere'. Technically there's little to choose between them, and the rattle of applause at the end comes as something of a surprise. It has a lot to do with the way the band is playing. There's no need for music of this sort to be so tightly marshalled. A few stray threads would actually make it more rather than less interesting. As it is, the first of these at least is troublingly bland.

*** Inclassifiable Label Bleu LBLC 6583

Sheppard; Steve Lodder (*syn*); Nana Vasconcelos (*perc*). 10/84.

Sheppard lasted no longer with Blue Note than most of his European contemporaries, but one has to pause to wonder whether they are perhaps right. This is a troublingly diffuse record by an artist too mature to speak about in terms of 'promise'. Anyone who has heard a version of the group in concert will realize that the record is no more than a shadowy version of the live act, and should perhaps be comforted by that. This might have been an ideal occasion for a festival or concert recording. In the studio it sounds thin and stilted.

Sahib Shihab (born 1925) SOPRANO, ALTO AND BARITONE SAX, FLUTE

*** **Jazz Sahib** Savoy SV-0141
 Shihab; Phil Woods (*as*); Benny Golson (*ts*); Hank Jones, Bill Evans (*p*); Paul Chambers, Oscar Pettiford (*b*); Art Taylor (*d*). 9–11/57.
(*) **The Jazz We Heard Last Summer Savoy SV-0228
 Shihab; John Jenkins (*as*); Clifford Jordan (*ts*); Hank Jones (*p*); Addison Farmer (*b*); Dannie Richmond (*d*). 6/57.

The former Edmund Gregory is probably still best remembered for his work on some of Thelonious Monk's Blue Note sessions. Since relocating to Europe in the 1960s, though, he has turned up on many a continental big-band date. Shihab played alto with Monk some years earlier but had switched to baritone as his first instrument by the time he made this session for Savoy: bop certainly needed no more altomen, and Woods could probably have smoked the leader if he'd got his alto out on this date anyway. As it is, the programme provides a good-natured blow on the blues via some fairly undemanding Shihab originals: all three hornmen take gratifying solos, and the two rhythm sections make sure the rhythms are well sprung. *The Jazz We Heard Last Summer* is more routine, with Jordan and Jenkins playing lightweight roles: Shihab himself probably gets in the best solo on the ballad 'The Things We Did Last Summer'. Two Herbie Mann tracks fill up the disc.

Travis Shook (born 1971) PIANO

*** **Travis Shook** Columbia CK 53138/473770-2
 Shook; Bunky Green (*as*); Ira Coleman (*b*); Tony Williams (*d*). 93.

A youthful piano competition-winner from Washington, Shook stands at least a little apart from many younger pianists. Most of this programme consists of standards – the one Shook original, 'Dewey North', is unremarkable – and he seeks out challenging settings for the tunes, with 'Broadway' evolving into an elaborate series of variations and 'Witchcraft' arranged as a piano–bass duo. Green, an unlikely confrère, appears on only two tracks, one of which is his own 'Little Girl I'll Miss You', but most of them are dominated by Williams, who gives his usual no quarter to anybody else in the group. With so much noise coming from the drums it's sometimes hard to hear what Shook is doing, but he's clearly an inventive mind, though some of his improvisations come bolstered with irritating devices.

Wayne Shorter (born 1933) TENOR SAXOPHONE, SOPRANO SAXOPHONE

***(*) **Night Dreamer** Blue Note BCT 84173
 Shorter; Lee Morgan (*t*); McCoy Tyner (*p*); Reggie Workman (*b*); Elvin Jones (*d*). 4/64.
***(*) **Juju** Blue Note 746514
 As above, except omit Morgan.
**** **Speak No Evil** Blue Note 746509
 Shorter; Freddie Hubbard (*t*); Herbie Hancock (*p*); Ron Carter (*b*); Elvin Jones (*d*). 12/64.
**** **Adam's Apple** Blue Note 746403
 Shorter; Herbie Hancock (*p*); Reggie Workman (*b*); Joe Chambers (*d*). 2/66.
*** **Super Nova** Blue Note B21Y 84332
 Shorter; Walter Booker, John McLaughlin, Sonny Sharrock (*g*); Miroslav Vitous (*b*); Chick Corea (*vib, d*); Jack DeJohnette (*d, perc*); Airto Moreira (*perc*); Maria Booker (*v*). 9/69.
*** **The Best Of Wayne Shorter** Blue Note 791141
 Shorter; Freddie Hubbard (*t*); Curtis Fuller (*tb*); James Spaulding (*as*); Herbie Hancock (*p*); Ron Carter, Reggie Workman (*b*); Joe Chambers, Elvin Jones, Tony Williams (*d*); collective personnel. 12/64–3/67.

Anyone who has encountered Shorter only as co-leader of Weather Report will know him primarily as a colourist, contributing short and often enigmatic brushstrokes to the group's carefully textured canvases. They may not recognize him as the formidable heir of Rollins and Coltrane (scale up and repitch those brief soprano saxophone statements and the lineage becomes clear). They will emphatically not know him as a composer. As Weather Report's musical identity consolidated, Joe Zawinul largely took over as writer. However, much as Shorter's elided 'solos' (in a group that didn't really believe in solos) still retained the imprint of a more developed idiom, so his compositions for the early records – 'Tears' and 'Eurydice' in particular – convey in essence the virtues that make him one of the most significant composers in modern jazz, whose merits have been recognized by fellow-players as far apart as Art Blakey, Miles Davis ('ESP', 'Dolores', 'Pee Wee', 'Nefertiti') and Kirk Lightsey (a challenging tribute album).

Known as 'Mr Weird' in high school, Shorter cultivated an oblique and typically asymmetrical approach to the bop idiom. His five years with the Jazz Messengers are marked by an aggressive synthesis of his two main models, but with an increasingly noticeable tendency to break down his phrasing and solo construction into unfamiliar mathematical subdivisions. Working with Miles Davis between 1964 and 1970 (a period that coincides with his most productive phase as a solo recording artist), he moved towards a more meditative and melancholy style – with an increasing dependence on the soprano saxophone – which is consolidated on the fine *Super Nova*, where he also makes unusually inventive use of the Jekyll–Hyde guitar partnership of McLaughlin and Sharrock. Shorter's recordings at this time relate directly to his work on Miles's *In A Silent Way* and to his work with Weather Report over the following decade.

Shorter's most individual work, however, remains the group of albums made for Blue Note in the mid-1960s, ending in 1970 with the low-key *Odyssey Of Iska*. The *Best Of* selection reproduces the enigmatic valuation Blue Note have placed on Shorter's output, completely ignoring the early *Juju*, which, like the undervalued and compositionally daring *Night Dreamer*, pits him with one version of the classic Coltrane quartet and has him playing at his most Coltrane-like. Fortunately it is currently available on CD, along with *Adam's Apple* (also for quartet) and the excellent *Speak No Evil*, which is Shorter's most completely satisfying work (albeit one that has exerted a baleful influence on a generation of imitators).

There has always been some controversy about Freddie Hubbard's role on the session, with detractors claiming that, unlike Shorter, the trumpeter was still working the hand dealt him in the Messengers and was too hot and urgent to suit Shorter's growing structural sophistication. In fact, the two blend astonishingly well, combining Hubbard's own instinctive exuberance on 'Fee-Fi-Fo-Fum' with something of the leader's own darker conception; interestingly, Shorter responds in kind, adding curious timbral effects to one of his most straight-ahead solos on the record.

As with *Adam's Apple* (which includes the classic 'Footprints'), much of the interest lies in the writing. Shorter has suggested that 'Dance Cadaverous' was suggested by Sibelius's 'Valse Triste'; 'Infant Eyes' is compounded of disconcerting nine-measure phrases that suggest a fractured nursery rhyme; the title-piece pushes the soloists into degrees of harmonic and rhythmic freedom that would not normally have been tolerated in a hard-bop context. Set *Speak No Evil* alongside Eric Dolphy's more obviously 'revolutionary' *Out To Lunch!*, recorded by Blue Note earlier the same year, and it's clear that Shorter claims the same freedoms, giving his rhythm section licence to work counter to the line of the melody and freeing the melodic Hancock from merely chordal duties. It's harder to reconstruct how alien some of Shorter's procedures were, because by and large he does remain within the bounds of post-bop harmony, but it's still clear that *Speak No Evil* is one of the most important jazz records of the period.

** **Native Dancer** Columbia 467095
>   Shorter; Milton Nascimento (*g, v*); Herbie Hancock (*p*); Airto Moreira (*perc*); with Dave McDaniel, Roberto Silva, Wagner Tiso, Jay Graydon, Dave Amaro (instrumentation not listed). 12/74.

A decade to the month after *Speak No Evil* finds Shorter in a bland samba setting which does more to highlight Nascimento's vague and uncommitted vocal delivery than the leader's saxophone playing. There is a hint of the old Shorter in the oblique introduction to 'Lilia' and some fine tenor work on 'Miracle Of The Fishes', but much of the rest could have been put together by a competent session *pasticheur*. Reviewers tended to go one way or the other on *Native Dancer*, but the consensus was that it was a 'surprise' and a 'new departure'. In fact, Shorter had long shown an interest in Latin-American rhythms and progressions; 'El Gaucho' on *Adam's Apple*, above, is one of his finest compositions and *Native Dancer* is almost exactly contemporary with Weather Report's Pan-American *Tale Spinnin'*. The 'surprise' lay in the lush, choking arrangements and unnecessary verbiage. Shorter encountered similar resistance when his 1980s band flirted with discofied funk-jazz, stripped-down settings that pushed his distinctive tenor sound to the forefront again.

*** **High Life** Verve 529224-2
>   Shorter; Rachel Z (*ky*); David Gilmore (*g*); Marcus Miller (*b, bcl*); Will Calhoun, Terri Lyne Carrington (*d*); Lenny Castro, Airto Moreira, Munyungo Jackson, Kevin Ricard (*perc*); brass and strings. 95.

Shorter's return to active duty is a solid, colourful, gregarious session. Marcus Miller's production is characteristically multi-textured and inventive, and there are plenty of spots for Shorter the soloist to make a mark on what are generally more flexible fusion settings than he's enjoyed for some years. But the lack of either compositional depth or attention-grabbing melodies tells against the record making a deeper impact, and there's nothing here to challenge the best of the Weather Report era – which, consciously or not, Shorter seems intent on keeping faithful to.

Michael Shrieve DRUMS

*** **Fascination** CMP CD 67
  Shrieve; Bill Frisell (g); Wayne Horvitz (org). 11/93.
***(*) **Two Doors** CMP CD 74
  As above, except add Shawn Lane (g, v); Jonas Hellborg (b). 11/93, 5/95.
Shrieve strikes a blow for Lifetime revivalists everywhere with these steamy but not unsubtle trios. On the basis that anything with Frisell on it will be interesting and will probably also sell, these are a shrewd confection, and one suspects that Shrieve is a clever showman as well as a well-disguised drummer, whose lack of variety is almost a strength. Like Tony Williams, he can do a certain amount on sheer power, but he also has some interesting compositional devices, most noticeable on the recent trios with Lane and Hellborg, which keep the interest level topped up. He will probably have to diversify as time goes on, but for the time being these are very welcome sets.

Tad Shull (born 1955) TENOR SAXOPHONE

***(*) **Deep Passion** Criss Cross Criss 1047
  Shull; Irvin Stokes (t); Mike LeDonne (p); Dennis Irwin (b); Kenny Washington (d). 11/90.
*** **In The Land Of The Tenor** Criss Cross Criss 1071
  As above, except omit Stokes. 12/91.
Shull is a big-toned tenor specialist out of Norwalk, Connecticut. His first models were Don Byas and Coleman Hawkins, moving on to Johnny Griffin and Lockjaw Davis. Having taken the trouble to get himself a decent sound and to learn the changes inside out, he's not afraid to tackle ungarnished D flat blues. 'The Eldorado Shuffle' brings *Deep Passion* to a rambunctious, shouting close and *In The Land Of The Tenor* ends in much the same way, with another elastic blues, Lucky Thompson's little-heard 'Prey-loot'.

 Thompson also makes his mark on the quieter side of Shull's playing, but he's shown no sign of picking up the soprano, even for tunes which might seem to lie comfortably for the small horn. There's plenty of evidence that Shull keeps his ears open. Though an unabashed traditionalist, he doesn't look the kind of guy who's going to be prepared to grind out 'Body And Soul' every night. On *Deep Passion* (the title-track is another Thompson song) he digs out Mary Lou Williams's 'Why' and Babs Gonzales's 'Soul Stirrin''. A year later he's working equally enterprising material: Kurt Weill's lovely 'This Is New', Hank Jones's 'Angel Face' and Ellington's 'Portrait Of Bojangles'.

 The band fits him like an old jacket. LeDonne's a great player who also writes a decent tune; 'Tadpole' and 'Big Ears' on the first record are down to him. Irwin and Washington can't be faulted. It's a pity, though, that Stokes was dropped, or couldn't make it to the 1991 session. Despite a tendency to drift into a Wynton-as-Pops mode at inopportune moments, he adds a dimension that's missed the second time around.

Janis Siegel VOCAL

*** **Slow Hot Wind** Varese Sarabande VSD-5552
  Siegel; Fred Hersch (p); Tony Dumas (b); Ralph Penland (d). 95.
Siegel's fresh, open, unaffected singing makes this duet record (Dumas and Penland assist on four of the twelve tracks) a disarming confection. She sounds more like a Broadway singer, or at least a cabaret stylist, than an out-and-out jazz performer: lyrics are granted a steady, respectful delivery and her uncomplicated phrasing and sunny timbre give the lyrics a clear-headed beauty that is the hallmark of a performer with few pretensions. It's Hersch who supplies the ornamentation, the textural weight, and he's in good form. One or two dislikeable choices of song let the disc down here and there, but the whole is good enough to have one awaiting the reissue of Siegel and Hersch's *Short Stories* (Atlantic, currently out of print).

Alan Silva (born 1939) DOUBLE BASS, VIOLIN, CELLO, PIANO

*** **Alan Silva** ESP Disk ESP 1091

Silva; Becky Friend (*f*); Dave Burrell (*p*); Mike Ephron (*p, org*); Karl Berger (*vib*); Lawrence Cooke (*d, perc*); Barry Altschul (*perc*). 11/68.

Silva's CV is a relatively unusual one. He was born in Bermuda and raised in New York, where as a child he took 'straight' music lessons in piano and violin before showing an interest in jazz trumpet. He got his lead into jazz from Donald Byrd. However, he didn't take up his main instrument, the double bass, until he was 23 (by which age, be it noted, Scott LaFaro's life was almost over).

Silva's fresh and uncompromised approach to music led him into free jazz. In 1966, after only five years of bass playing, Cecil Taylor signed him for the *Unit Structures* session. In the years that followed, Silva played for Albert Ayler and Sun Ra, and has recorded with Archie Shepp and Sunny Murray. He subsequently formed his own Celestial Communication Orchestra as a free-jazz ensemble. Some of the orchestra's work can be found on old BYG LPs, but they are increasingly rare, even in specialist second-hand racks.

It's ironic that Silva's one and only current recording doesn't feature him as a double bass player, but on violin, cello and piano. As time went by, Silva became increasingly ambivalent about his main instrument, frequently claiming that he had exhausted his own interest in it. When he returned to active playing in the mid-'80s, he had abandoned it altogether in favour of keyboards. Its absence underlines the distinctive sound of the ESP session, which is best characterized by the qualifiying adjective applied to Barry Altschul's percussion: 'light'. With higher strings, flute, vibes and piano(s) as the main instruments, the ensemble generates light-fingered and intricate patterns, very different from the prevailing sound of the time.

There are two pieces only (a total of less than 40 minutes' music). The first, 'Skillfullness', is the longer and more diffuse, seemingly broken down into sets of exercises for different instrumental combinations. The second part, 'Solestrial Communications No. 1', might just be mistaken (by anyone who heard the title first) for one of Sun Ra's more delicate conceptions, but it's far less jazz-based than any of the Arkestra recordings, even at this period. One of the impressive things about the record is the extent to which Silva has submerged his personality in the ensemble. Conventional soloing is not really part of this music and the leader makes no exceptions for himself.

It's to be hoped that some of Silva's other records (and examples of his bass playing) will see the light of day again. In the vaults, and aside from work by his Orchestra, there are imaginative albums like *Lunar Surface*, as well as duos with Frank Wright and collaborations with the British percussionist, Roger Turner.

Horace Silver (born 1928) PIANO

*** **Horace Silver Trio** Blue Note B21Y-81520

Silver; Percy Heath (*b*); Art Blakey (*d*). 10/53.

***(*) **Horace Silver And The Jazz Messengers** Blue Note B21Y-46140

Silver; Kenny Dorham (*t*); Hank Mobley (*ts*); Doug Watkins (*b*); Art Blakey (*d*). 11/54.

Horace Silver's records present the quintessence of hard bop. He not only defined the first steps in the style, he also wrote several of its most durable staples, ran bands that both embodied and transcended the idiom and perfected a piano manner which summed up hard bop's wit and trenchancy and popular appeal. Yet he has recorded comparatively little in the last 20 years, and his back-catalogue is in general disrepair so far as current availability is concerned.

The Blue Note *Jazz Messengers* album might be the one that started it all: two sessions, originally issued as a brace of ten-inch LPs, with a definitive hard-bop cast. While the finest music by this edition of the original Jazz Messengers was probably recorded at the Café Bohemia the following year (listed in Art Blakey's entry), this one is still fresh, smart but properly versed in the new language (or, rather, the new setting for the old language). The trio album sets out Silver's own expertise: a crisp, chipper but slightly wayward style, idiosyncratic enough to take him out of the increasingly stratified realms of bebop piano. Blues and gospel-tinged devices and percussive attacks give his methods a more colourful feel, and a generous good humour gives all his records an upbeat feel.

*** **Blowin' The Blues Away** Blue Note B21Y-46526

As above. 8/59.

*** **Horace-Scope** Blue Note B21Y-84042-2

Silver; Blue Mitchell (*t*); Junior Cook (*ts*); Gene Taylor (*b*); Roy Brooks (*d*). 7/60.

**** **Song For My Father** Blue Note CDP 784185-2

As above, except add Carmell Jones (*t*); Joe Henderson (*ts*); Teddy Smith (*b*); Roger Humphries (*d*). 10/64.

***(*) **Cape Verdean Blues** Blue Note B21Y-84220-2
> Silver; Woody Shaw (*t*); J. J. Johnson (*tb*); Joe Henderson (*ts*); Bob Cranshaw (*b*); Roger
> Humphries (*d*). 10/65.

**** **The Jody Grind** Blue Note B21Y-84250-2
> Silver; Woody Shaw (*t*); James Spaulding (*as, f*); Tyrone Washington (*ts*); Larry Ridley (*b*);
> Roger Humphries (*d*). 11/66.

Although Silver went on to record some 25 further albums for Blue Note, only the above are currently available as CD reissues. It's hard to pick the best of the albums since Silver's consistency is unarguable: each album yields one or two themes which haunt the mind, each usually has a particularly pretty ballad, and they all lay back on a deep pile of solid riffs and intensely worked solos. Silver's own are strong enough, but he was good at choosing sidemen who weren't so characterful that the band would overbalance: Cook, Mitchell, Mobley, Shaw, Jones and Spaulding are all typical Silver horns, and only Johnson (who was guesting anyway) and Henderson on the above records threaten to be something rather more special. The two choicest records, though, are surely *Song For My Father*, with its memorable title-tune, the superb interplay of Jones and Henderson, and the exceptionally fine trio ballad, 'Lonely Woman', and *The Jody Grind*, which hits some sort of apex of finger-snapping intensity on the title-tune and 'Mexican Hip Dance'. *Blowin' The Blues Away* includes the soul–jazz classic, 'Sister Sadie', and *The Cape Verdean Blues* presents Henderson, Shaw and Johnson on three tracks for one of Silver's most full-bodied front lines.

(*) **It's Got To Be Funky Columbia 473877-2
> Silver; Oscar Brashear, Bob Summers, Ron Stout (*t, flhn*); Bob McChesney (*tb*); Maurice Spears
> (*btb*); Suzette Moriarty (*frhn*); Red Holloway (*as, ts*); Eddie Harris, Branford Marsalis (*ts*); Bob
> Maize (*b*); Carl Burnett (*d*); Andy Bey (*v*). 2/93.

*** **Pencil Packin' Papa** Columbia 476979-2
> As above except Jeff Bernell (*t*), George Bohannon (*tb*), James Moody (*ts*), Rickey Woodard (*ts*)
> and O. C. Smith (*v*) replace Summers, McChesney, Marsalis and Bey. 10–11/94.

Very disappointing. Silver has at last returned to a major label, but the over-produced, impersonal set of brass-dominated charts on *It's Got To Be Funky* sounds like a designer's idea of the man's funky language. Andy Bey's overripe vocals on four tunes ('The Hillbilly Bebopper' is a bit much, even for Silver) are rotten, and it's the more frustrating because the music does sometimes really work out: 'Funky Bunky' is smart, the leader's own piano is still worth a taste, and Harris takes solo honours by simply sounding like himself in an otherwise colourless ensemble. There's a slight upswing on *Pencil Packin' Papa*. Old soulman Smith is a respectable replacement for Bey, and the brass team sound looser and more in keeping with the Silver ethos. That said, this is still no more than a competent set of tunes, the new 'Senor Blues' is no match for the old, and only the tenormen make the most of their solo chances.

Sonny Simmons (born 1933) ALTO SAXOPHONE, COR ANGLAIS

*** **Staying On The Watch** ESP 1030
> Simmons; John Hicks (*p*); Teddy Smith (*b*); Marvin Patillo (*d*). 8/66.

*** **Music From The Spheres** ESP 1043
> Simmons; Barbara Donald (*t*); Bert Wilson (*ts*); Michael Cohen (*p*); Juni Booth (*b*); James
> Zitro (*d*). 12/66.

Isolated from the main currents of the music, Sonny Simmons has never built on the interest he created with a handful of records in the 1960s and '70s, which revealed a liaison between Ornette Coleman's freedoms and a terse, bop-orientated lyricism. There are two excellent albums for Arhoolie and Contemporary which have been missing for years, but these early ESPs have been reissued along with the rest of the catalogue. Hicks makes an early appearance on record on *Staying On The Watch*, but it's Simmons's trenchant delivery and hard, blues-inflected tone that make the impression. A West-Coaster who sounds as if he might have been at home in Texan R&B bands, Simmons sometimes blows as if oblivious to the accompaniment, but the duet with Smith on one track proves his sensitivity. The subsequent *Music From The Spheres* assembles a sort of ESP All Stars group and, though the feel of the record suggests a jumbled hard-bop/free fusion, the plangency of Simmons, Donald and Wilson has an agreeably unaffected quality.

***(*) **Ancient Ritual** Qwest/Reprise 945623-2
> Simmons; Charnett Moffett (*b*); Zarak Simmons (*d*). 12/92.

Really a marvellous comeback for Simmons, and a surprisingly uncompromised record from a major label. The old authority remains, coupled with a skirling fluency that makes simple themes like 'Country

Parson' and 'Theme For Linda' resonate with a master's eloquence. He manages to make reiterative statements hypnotic without sounding repetitive, and when the music ignites behind him he refuses to resort to hyperbole. The studio sound catches an embattled but lyrical alto tone beautifully, but it does no favours at all to either Moffett (almost inaudible at times) or Zarak Simmons. The bassist is, in any case, hardly the right man for this situation, his excessive ornamentation a distraction when you can hear it.

Ralph Simon TENOR, ALTO AND SOPRANO SAXOPHONES

*** As Postcards 1004
> Simon; Gene Adler (*p, kalimba*); Jeff Berman (*vib*); Dan Rose (*g*); Marc Johnson, David Dunaway (*b*); Billy Hart, Chip White (*d*); Tom Beyer (*perc*). 5/81.

Recorded in 1981 but unreleased until 1994, Simon's album is a colourful session, rich with the sound of kalimba, vibes and percussion, over which the saxophonist and Adler (who died in 1992 and is the dedicatee) float attractive modal improvisations. Each tune tends to find its own level, so 'Gepetto' and 'Julie And Julius' are brief episodes while 'Skin On Skin' drifts on for 20 minutes. Though it sometimes evaporates into high-calibre background music, Simon's playing brings it round when he asserts himself. He has a new disc scheduled for autumn 1996.

Zoot Sims (1925–85) TENOR, ALTO, SOPRANO AND BARITONE SAXOPHONES, VOCAL

*** Tenorly RCA Vogue 74321 13413 2
> Sims; Frank Rosolino (*tb*); Gerry Wiggins, Henri Renaud (*p*); Jimmy Gourley (*g*); Pierre Michelot, Don Bagley (*b*); Kenny Clarke, Jean-Louis Viale (*d*). 6/50–9/53.

*** Quartets Original Jazz Classics OJC 242
> Sims; John Lewis, Harry Biss (*p*); Curley Russell, Clyde Lombardi (*b*); Don Lamond, Art Blakey (*d*). 9/50–8/51.

***(*) Zoot! Original Jazz Classics OJC 228
> Sims; Nick Travis (*t*); George Handy (*p*); Wilbur Ware (*b*); Osie Johnson (*d*). 12/56.

Like Jack Teagarden, Zoot Sims started out mature and hardly ever wavered from a plateau of excellence throughout a long and prolific career (oddly enough, Sims's singing voice sounded much like Teagarden's). As one of Woody Herman's 'Four Brothers' sax section, he didn't quite secure the early acclaim of Stan Getz, but by the time of these sessions he was completely himself: a rich tone emboldened by a sense of swing which didn't falter at any tempo. He sounded as if he enjoyed every solo, and if he really was much influenced by Lester Young – as was the norm for the 'light' tenors of the day – it was at a far remove in emotional terms. *Tenorly* catches Zoot in Paris on two separate occasions; the 1950 tracks, with a heap of alternative takes, find him strolling through some themeless chord changes along with 'Night And Day' and a couple of other standards, with a French rhythm section in tow, all in rather scratchy sound. But the 1953 tracks offer a fine glimpse of the excellent Rosolino, as well as Jimmy Gourley, in improved sound. *Quartets* sets up the kind of session Sims would record for the next 35 years: standards, a couple of ballads, and the blues, all comprehensively negotiated with a rhythm section that strolls alongside the leader: neither side ever masters the other. 'Zoot Swings The Blues' has Sims peeling off one chorus after another in top gear, while a seemingly endless 'East Of The Sun' shares the solos around without losing impetus. The original Prestige recording is grainy. *Zoot!* goes up a notch for the inspirational pairing of Sims and Travis, a minor figure who probably never played as well on record as he does here: 'Taking A Chance On Love' is a near-masterpiece, and Ware and Johnson play superb bass and drums.

*** Tonite's Music Today Black Lion BLCD 760907
> Sims; Bob Brookmeyer (*vtb*); Hank Jones (*p*); Wyatt Ruther (*b*); Gus Johnson (*d*). 1/56.

***(*) Morning Fun Black Lion BLCD 760914
> As above, except Bill Crow (*b*) and Jo Jones (*d*) replace Ruther and Johnson. 8/56.

***(*) Zoot Sims In Paris EMI/Pathé Jazztime 794125
> Sims; Jon Eardley (*t*); Henri Renaud (*p*); Eddie De Hass, Benoit Quersin (*b*); Charles Saudrais (*d*). 3/56.

The albums with Brookmeyer and Eardley were recorded while they were in Gerry Mulligan's Sextet: 'Lullaby Of The Leaves', included on *Morning Fun*, was one of the staples in Mulligan's repertoire, and the mood here (and throughout the sessions with Brookmeyer) owes much to him. But the atmosphere on both dates is of an utterly relaxed, good-pals jam session, refereed by the eternally sweet-natured Jones. *Morning Fun* just has the edge, perhaps, for the knockout tempo of 'The King' and a couple of lovely ballads (Zoot also sings 'I Can't Get Started'). The session in Paris is even more informal, but Sims here sounds magisterial, partly because the microphones catch his sound very close up: Eardley, in comparison, is a bit recessed, and the drums are clattery on the first half of the date. A splendidly virile blowing date, nevertheless.

*** **The Rare Dawn Sessions** Biograph 131
> Sims; Jerry Lloyd (*t*); Bob Brookmeyer (*vtb*); John Williams (*p*); Milt Hinton, Bill Anthony, Knobby Totah (*b*); Gus Johnson (*d*). 1–9/56.

***(*) **That Old Feeling** Chess GRP 18072
> Sims; John Williams (*p*); Knobby Totah (*b*); Gus Johnson (*d*). 10–11/56.

*** **Down Home** Bethlehem BET 6022-2
> Sims; Dave McKenna (*p*); George Tucker (*b*); Dannie Richmond (*d*). 7/60.

The Rare Dawn Sessions compiles two sessions, one with the little-known Lloyd, one with Brookmeyer. Zoot plays alto on one track, and a surprise choice is Monk's 'Bye-Ya'. The session with Brookmeyer is effortless stuff, the two horns perfectly *simpatico*, though it's unambitiously delivered. Respectable sound, unlike the cavernous mix on *The Art Of Jazz* (Fresh Sound FSR-CD 25), which is another edition of the Brookmeyer tracks. *That Old Feeling* collects two sessions originally released on Argo and ABC-Paramount, including a date where Zoot overdubbed alto and baritone to make a one-man sax section. Unlike other such experiments, this one worked out well: Zoot's utter professionalism, coupled with his easy-going style, seems to have transcended the artifice of the situation, and a couple of tunes – 'Minor Minor' and 'Pegasus' – are lucid gems. But there is also a sumptuous ballad feature on 'The Trouble With Me Is You'. *Down Home* sets him up with a very interesting rhythm section, but Zoot doesn't quite have enough space: McKenna gets equal time in the front line, and he hadn't yet secured the authority of his later work.

*** **Either Way** Evidence ECD 22007-2
> Sims; Al Cohn (*ts*); Mose Allison (*p*); Bill Crow (*b*); Gus Johnson (*d*); Cecil 'Kid Haffey' Collier (*v*). 2/61.

*** **Live At Ronnie Scott's 1961** Fresh Sound FSR-CD 134
> Sims; Stan Tracey (*p*); Kenny Napper (*b*); Jackie Dougan (*d*). 11/61.

One of the earlier collaborations between these two tenor masters, *Either Way* suffers from a foggy sound-mix and the less-than-desirable presence of Collier, whose singing on three tunes wastes valuable saxophone time (on what is a short CD anyway). But there is still some great duelling on 'The Thing', 'I'm Tellin' Ya' and a honeyed 'Autumn Leaves', plus the bonus of Allison at the piano. The session at Scott's was originally released on a fondly remembered Fontana LP. Sims sweeps through the occasion and delivers an object lesson in blowing on the blues on the formidable 'Blues In E Flat'.

*** **Recado Bossa Nova** Fresh Sound FSR-CD 198
> Sims; Spencer Sinatra (*f, picc*); Phil Woods (*cl*); Gene Quill (*cl, bcl*); Sol Schlinger (*bcl*); Ronnie Odrich, Phil Bodner, Jerry Sanfino (*reeds, f*); Jim Hall, Kenny Burrell, Barry Galbraith (*g*); Milt Hinton, Art Davis (*b*); Sol Gubin (*d*); Ted Sommer, Willie Rodriguez, Tommy Lopez (*perc*). 8/62–63.

Zoot's entry in the bossa nova craze. Al Cohn and Manny Albam did a perfect pro's job in arranging everything from 'Bernie's Tune' to 'Cano Canoe' for Sims to blow on, and the results are finely manicured without encumbering the saxophonist. He takes some typically swinging, unruffled solos.

*** **Zoot Sims In Copenhagen** Storyville STCD 8244
> Sims; Kenny Drew (*p*); Niels-Henning Orsted-Pedersen (*b*); Ed Thigpen (*d*). 8/78.

A characteristic club date with Zoot. Drawbacks: the rhythm section play well but are too generously featured; the material is stuff Zoot did many times over; the sound is a bit rough here and there. The plus is that Sims is playing close to the top of his latter-day game, which ought to be good enough for anybody.

**** **Zoot Sims And The Gershwin Brothers** Original Jazz Classics OJC 444
> Sims; Oscar Peterson (*p*); Joe Pass (*g*); George Mraz (*b*); Grady Tate (*d*). 6/75.

(*) **Hawthorne Nights Original Jazz Classics OJC 830
> Sims; Oscar Brashear (*t*); Snooky Young (*t, flhn*); Frank Rosolino (*tb*); Bill Hood, Richie Kamuca, Jerome Richardson (*reeds*); Ross Tompkins (*p*); Monty Budwig (*b*); Nick Ceroli (*d*); Bill Holman (*arr*). 9/76.

**** **If I'm Lucky** Original Jazz Classics OJC 683
> Sims; Jimmy Rowles (*p*); George Mraz (*b*); Mousie Alexander (*d*). 10/77.

***(*) **Warm Tenor** Pablo 2310-831
> As above. 9/78.

***(*) **For Lady Day** Pablo 2310-942
   As above, except Jackie Williams (*d*) replaces Alexander. 4/78.
*** **Just Friends** Original Jazz Classics OJC 499
   Sims; Harry 'Sweets' Edison (*t*); Roger Kellaway (*p*); John Heard (*b*); Jimmie Smith (*d*). 12/78.
*** **The Swinger** Original Jazz Classics OJC 855
   Sims; Ray Sims (*tb, v*); Jimmy Rowles (*p*); John Heard, Michael Moore (*b*); Shelly Manne, John Clay (*d*). 11/79–5/80.
*** **Blues For Two** Original Jazz Classics OJC 635
   Sims; Joe Pass (*g*). 3–6/82.
*** **On The Korner** Pablo 2310-953
   Sims; Frank Colett (*p*); Monty Budwig (*b*); Shelly Manne (*d*). 3/83.
***(*) **Suddenly It's Spring** Original Jazz Classics OJC 742-2
   Sims; Jimmy Rowles (*p*); George Mraz (*b*); Akira Tana (*d*). 5/83.
*** **Quietly There** Original Jazz Classics OJC 787
   Sims; Mike Wofford (*p*); Chuck Berghofer (*b*); Nick Ceroli (*d*); Victor Feldman (*perc*). 3/84.
** **The Best Of Zoot Sims** Pablo 2405-406
   As above Pablo albums.

When Sims signed to Norman Granz's Pablo operation, he wasn't so much at a crossroads as contentedly strolling down an uneventful path. For a man who could fit effortlessly into any situation he chose – admittedly, he never chose a situation that might cause trouble – Sims could have spent his final years as a nebulous figure. But his Pablo albums set the seal on his stature, sympathetically produced, thoughtfully programmed and with enough challenge to prod Zoot into his best form. *Gershwin Brothers* is a glorious sparring match with Peterson, rising to an almost overpowering charge through 'I Got Rhythm' via a simmering 'Embraceable You' and a variation on Coltrane's approach to 'Summertime'. It's the ravishing tone which makes the session with Pass so attractive: with drums and bass cleared away, the tenor sound is swooningly beautiful. A pity, though, that Pass sounds so perfunctory throughout. The sessions with Jimmy Rowles at the piano, though, are indispensable examples of Zoot at his best. *If I'm Lucky* is, narrowly, the pick, for its ingenious choice of material – '(I Wonder Where) Our Love Has Gone' counts as one of Sims's most affecting performances – and the uncanny communication between saxophonist and pianist throughout. *Warm Tenor* is only a shade behind, and the recently discovered set of tunes associated with Billie Holiday, *For Lady Day*, is another plum choice, with an amble through 'You Go To My Head' that dispels the happy-sad clouds of Holiday's *œuvre* with a smouldering lyricism. *Suddenly It's Spring* is another that betrays Rowles's affection for unlikely material – 'In The Middle Of A Kiss', 'Emaline', even Woody Guthrie's 'So Long' – and, though the playing seems a shade too relaxed in parts, it's still delightful music. *The Swinger* reunites Zoot with brother Ray and they make a joshing, harmless team: 'Now I Lay Me Down To Dream Of You' is sweetness personified. Another session with Rowles, *I Wish I Were Twins*, is still awaited on CD.

The only disappointing disc is *Hawthorne Nights*, which finds Zoot a tad perfunctory for once on a generally uninspiring set of Bill Holman charts. *On the Korner* finds him in a San Francisco club, still enjoying himself, with 'Dream Dancing' and the surprisingly urgent soprano rendition of 'Tonight I Shall Sleep' of special interest; Frank Colett plays fine supporting piano. Although only a year away from his death when he made *Quietly There*, a set of Johnny Mandel themes, Sims was still in absolute command. Feldman's percussion adds a little extra fillip to the likes of 'Cinnamon And Clove', although Sims himself sounds undistracted by anything: his winding, tactile improvisation on the melody of 'A Time For Love', to pick a single instance, speaks of a lifetime's preparation. The *Best Of* is a mysteriously ill-chosen retrospective: better to pick any one of the albums with Rowles if a single disc is all that's required.

Jae Sinnett DRUMS

*** **House And Sinnett** Positive PMD78020-2
   Sinnett; Steve Wilson (*ss, as*); Cyrus Chestnut (*p*); Clarence Seay (*b*). 8/93.
A light, swinging slice of modern jazz, tailored by the leader to fit this quartet and achieving its modest aim. Sinnett is a bright but never overpowering drummer, and he's content to let Wilson and Chestnut take the major space: the pianist confirms his growing reputation, though Wilson doesn't have a great deal to say. Average writing, sound playing.

The Six Winds (Die Zes Winden) GROUP

*** Man Met Muts Bvhaast 9004

> Mariette Rouppe Van der Voort (*sno*); Dies Le Duc (*ss*); Frans Vermeerssen (*as*); John Tchicai (*ts*); Ad Peijnenburg (*bs*); Klaas Hekman (*bsx*). 10/89.

*** Anger Dance Bvhaast 9305

> As above. 10/91–12/92.

These Dutch sax specialists (along with Tchicai, still roaming Europe's avant-garde) make up a sober, highly refined team. Much of their music is ensemble-based; solos are comparatively brief and carefully tempered by the requirements of the tune; and they like to explore particular stretches of saxophone sound within the span of each composition. 'Fluitketel' and 'Kies Van Tien', both on the first record, are examples of how they seem to mull over the chords and harmonic variations they create in small areas of saxophone timbre. Since each of the six sticks to one horn, and none of them expresses particularly disparate personalities as improvisers, they establish an unusually solid, thoughtful music that acquires a dusky, hypnotic quality over the course of a whole record. *Man Met Muts* suffers from a drab sound-mix that spoils some of the subtleties of their approach, but *Anger Dance* is altogether brighter and displays lushness as well as depth. A valuable initiative in the all-sax area.

Lars Sjøsten (born 1941) PIANO

*** In Confidence Dragon DRCD 197

> Sjøsten; Jan Kohlin (*t*); Bertil Strandberg (*tb*); Dave Castle (*as*); Krister Andersson (*ts*); Gunnar Bergsten (*bs*); Petter Carlsson (*frhn*); Oystein Baadsvik (*tba*); Patrik Boman (*b*); Nils Danell (*d*). 11–12/90.

Sjøsten is a deft, economical pianist, conservative as a composer – he might build an idea round a rhythmic oddity or an unusual tonality – but good with groups of any size. He's been recording as a leader since 1971 but this is his only CD in print. These are pleasing, good-natured compositions, deftly arranged, without hidden depths but not short on imagination. The ten pieces are arranged for trio, quartet (with Bergsten), sextet and a ten-piece band and, while the theme statements by the horns could be tighter, the casual complexion suits the music rather well. Bergsten, Strandberg and Castle are the most inventive soloists, and Sjøsten rounds matters off with a thoughtful trio version of 'You'd Be So Nice To Come Home To'.

Alan Skidmore (born 1942) TENOR SAXOPHONE

***(*) Tribute To 'Trane Miles Music CDMM075

> Skidmore; Jason Rebello (*p*); Dave Green (*b*); Stephen Keogh (*d*). 2/88.

Like his saxophonist father, Jimmy, who was a stalwart of the British mainstream scene in the 1950s and early '60s, Alan Skidmore is much less well known than he ought to be. In a wilderness of clones, he stands out – admittedly older and therefore wiser – as one of the few who have submitted the Coltrane legacy to thoughtful consideration, rather than taking it as licence for frenzied harmonic activity and emotional streaking. Skidmore is rather poorly represented in the current catalogue, though he can also be heard on the eponymous *S.O.S.* with fellow-saxophonists Mike Osborne and John Surman; two records by the challenging SOH (Skidmore, drummer Tony Oxley and bassist Ali Haurand) are also well worth looking out for.

The first of these – released on the small, German-based view label – featured a majestic interpretation of Coltrane's 'Lonnie's Lament', a theme he returns to on *Tribute To 'Trane*. With typical self-effacement, Skidmore asks that the album, one of a flood marking the twentieth anniversary of the great saxophonist's death, be regarded as a 'thank you' rather than as another god-bothering ritual by a disciple. The choice of material is interesting. 'Naima' and 'Mr P.C.' represent a more predictable closing sequence, but 'Resolution', 'Bessie's Blues', 'Crescent' and 'Dear Lord', together with the outstanding 'Lonnie's Lament' (on which Rebello and Keogh are both superb, incidentally), suggest the depth of Skidmore's understanding of the music. The performances are not in themselves self-consciously *de profundis*, and there are no overpowering histrionics. Well recorded in medium close-up, this takes its place behind McCoy Tyner *et al.*'s *Blues For 'Trane* as the best of the twentieth-anniversary votes of thanks.

*** East To West Miles Music MMCD 081

> Skidmore; Stan Tracey, Steve Melling (*p*); Mick Hutton, Roy Babbington (*b*); Clark Tracey, Bryan Spring (*d*). 11/89–2/92.

A solid continuation of the work documented on the previous disc. There are three tracks from a Hong Kong club date of 1989, with Tracey's trio in support, and three more from the Scott club in 1992. Skidmore's tenor oratory is as mighty and full-blooded as before, with even Tracey's own 'Funky Day In Tiger Bay' transformed into a thunderous outpouring of saxophone. The later session brings further gifts to the Coltrane shrine with 'Crescent', 'Wise One' and as thumping a take on 'Mr P.C.' as you'll find outside the master's own work. But docked a notch for the indifferent sound, which isn't much above bootleg quality on the Hong Kong material.

Billy Skinner TRUMPET, FLUGELHORN

*** **Kosen Rufu** Accurate 3333
    Skinner; Henry Cook (as, f); Salim Washington (ts, f); Ichi Takato (b); Bobby Ward (d). 7/88.
Alternately breezy and wistful, this is a very attractive record with elements of free bop and more traditional playing mixed confidently together. Skinner writes simple but hauntingly effective melodies and seasons the programme with some favourite covers, including 'Mood Indigo' and a cleverly melded bebop sequence. His own playing has something of the free elegance of Bobby Bradford, though occasionally he seems a little too caught up in the music to make a decisive point, and Cook and Washington are good if relatively undemonstrative players.

Steve Slagle ALTO AND SOPRANO SAXOPHONES

*** **The Steve Slagle Quartet** Steeplechase SCCD 31323
    Slagle; Tim Hagans (t); Scott Colley (b); Jeff Hirshfield (d). 11/92.
***(*) **Spread The Word** Steepelchase SCCD 31354
    As above. 4/94.
***(*) **Reincarnation** Steeplechase SCCD 31367
    Slagle; Kenny Drew Jr (p); Cameron Brown (b); Jeff Hirshfield (d). 10/94.
Slagle is a fine, New York-based altoist whose playing has been only sparsely documented under his own name. The Steeplechase albums deserve a wider audience than they have so far received. *Quartet* features some difficult writing by the leader: 'Leadbelly Sez' is a tricky eight-bar blues, and 'Mondo' might suggest a leaning towards the original Ornette Coleman quartet. Colley and Hirshfield work very capably behind the horns, and Hagans plays thoughtfully. The quartet returns for *Spread The Word* and this time they manage to suggest an eloquent kind of free playing that actually owes little to Coleman's quartet. The improvising has an air of long-breathed virtuosity about it, the many-noted solos rooted in bebop but coloured by the freedoms of what came after. If the leader's convolutions suggest a struggle with form, Hagans's calm and lucid playing reconciles structure with freedom, and the contrast between the two styles makes the music compelling and rounded at the same time.

    Slagle's own work suggests a link between hard-bop stylists and the free players of a generation later, which some of his own sleeve-notes on *Reincarnation* also allude to. The opening track here is a long, sinewy extemporisation on Charles Mingus's 'Reincarnation Of A Lovebird', and Slagle recalls how it struck him as a link between Parker and Dolphy. If you add Jackie McLean to the mixture, it could almost come up as Slagle himself, and this twisting solo is certainly one of the best things he's done on record. There are fine ballads in 'Soultrane' and 'Bess You Is My Woman Now' and, though one misses some of the interaction which Hagans created on the other discs, Slagle takes the weight on his own shoulders very convincingly. In the circumstances, Drew's excellent work is something of a bonus.

Slickaphonics GROUP

*** **Slickaphonics** Enja 4024
    Ray Anderson (tb); Steve Elson (ts, syn, perc, v); Mark Helias (b, v); Allan Jaffe (g, v); Jim Payne (d, perc, v). 3/82.
*** **Modern Life** Enja 4062
    As above, except Daniel Wilensky (ts, v) replaces Elson. 11/83.
This is Anderson's Saturday night band. They're best heard live, and the records certainly don't give more than an approximation of the energy the group generates. Themes like 'Electro Plasma' and 'Red Planet' on the earlier of the pair draw on urban funk, an influence that's less overt on *Modern Life*. Hard to pick between them, though Anderson himself probably shows up more strongly in the latter, when he has a less effusive saxophonist to contend with.

Cees Slinger PIANO

*** **Sling Shot** Timeless SJP 225

   Slinger; Clifford Jordan (*ts*); Isla Eckinger (*b*); Philly Joe Jones (*d*). 4/85.

A stalwart among Dutch boppers, Slinger's rare records as a leader are usually worth a listen, and this one worked out fine. Clifford Jordan plays with gregarious enjoyment (the quartet had just wound up a European tour) which Slinger's knowing compositions are just the right setting for. As a bonus, Jordan's own witty 'Eye-Witness Blues' also makes it on to their set-list. This was Philly Joe's last record date and he sounds a little tired here and there, which robs the music of some of its vigour; but Jordan and Slinger are excellent.

Hal Smith DRUMS

*** **Milneburg Joys** GHB BCD-277

   Smith; Chris Tyle (*c*); David Sager (*tb*); Jacques Gauthe (*cl, ss*); Steve Pistorius (*p*); Amy Sharpe
   (*bj*); Bernie Attridge (*b*). 6/89.

Smith and Tyle are co-leaders of the Frisco Syncopators, one of the several fine American trad groups currently revisiting the classic repertoire with unusual aplomb. Though they take their cue from Bob Scobey's original Frisco Jazz Band, the group is actually New Orleans-based, and their approach seasons chestnuts such as 'Skid-Dat-De-Dat' and 'Panama' with enough sharpness to lend a fresh point of view. The rhythm of the group attains a nice blend of sleekness and ragged drive, and in the clean-toned Tyle and the adept Pistorius they have two excellent soloists. The studio sound eschews the accustomed murk of trad recordings in favour of a crisp and punchy attack that gives the record an extra zip, although most of the vocals are the usual acquired taste in this setting.

Jabbo Smith (1908–90) TRUMPET, VOCAL

**** **Jabbo Smith 1929–1938** Classics 669

   Smith; Omer Simeon, Willard Brown (*cl, as*); Leslie Johnakins, Ben Smith (*as*); Sam Simmons
   (*ts*); Millard Robins (*bsx*); Cassino Simpson, Kenneth Anderson, Alex Hill, William Barbee,
   James Reynolds (*p*); Ikey Robinson (*bj*); Connie Wainwright (*g*); Hayes Alvis, Lawson Buford
   (*tba*); Elmer James (*b*); Alfred Taylor (*d*). 1/29–2/38.

Until his rediscovery in the 1960s, Smith was legendary as Armstrong's most significant rival in the 1920s, a reputation built mainly on the records reissued on this CD. He had already made a name for himself with Charlie Johnson's orchestra, but it was the 20 sides he cut with his Rhythm Aces which have endured as Smith's contribution to jazz. This CD includes all of them, together with four tracks from a single 1938 session by Smith's then eight-strong group. Smith's style is like a thinner, wilder variation on Armstrong's. He takes even more risks in his solos – or, at least, makes it seem that way, since he's less assured at pulling them off than Louis was.

   Some passages he seems to play entirely in his highest register; others are composed of handfuls of notes, phrased in such a scattershot way that he seems to have snatched them out of the air. If it makes the music something of a mess, it's a consistently exciting one. Organized round Smith's own stop-time solos and dialogue with the rhythm, with the occasional vocal – a quizzical mix of Armstrong and Don Redman – thrown in too, the records seem like a conscious attempt at duplicating the Hot Five sessions, although in the event they sold poorly. Simeon is curiously reticent, much as Dodds was on the Hot Fives, and alto players Brown and James do no more than behave themselves. The livewire foil is, instead, the extraordinary Robinson, whose tireless strumming and rare, knockout solo (as on 'Michigander Blues') keep everything simmering. Shrill and half focused, these are still lively and brilliant reminders of a poorly documented talent (who reappeared in his seventies as a festival and stage performer). The CD follows the pattern of the pair of Retrieval albums listed in our first edition, and the transfers are fine; but the LP editions are worth seeking out, since they also include nine earlier tracks also featuring Smith.

Jimmy Smith (born 1925) ORGAN

*** **The Champ (A New Sound A New Star)** Blue Note 789391-2

   Smith; Thornel Schwartz (*g*); Bay Perry, Donald Bailey (*d*). 56.

*** **The Sermon** Blue Note B21Y-46097

   Smith; Lee Morgan (*t*); Curtis Fuller (*tb*); George Coleman, Lou Donaldson (*as*); Tina Brooks
   (*ts*); Eddie McFadden, Kenny Burrell (*g*); Donald Bailey, Art Blakey (*d*). 8/57–2/58.

** **Crazy Baby** Blue Note B21Y-84030
    Smith; Quentin Warren (*g*); Donald Bailey (*d*). 3/60.
***(*) **Open House / Plain Talk** Blue Note CDP 784269-2
    Smith; Blue Mitchell (*t*); Jackie McLean (*as*); Ike Quebec (*ts*); Quentin Warren (*g*); Donald
    Bailey (*d*). 3/60.
(*) **Midnight Special Blue Note B21Y-84078
    Smith; Stanley Turrentine (*ts*); Kenny Burrell (*g*); Donald Bailey (*d*). 4/60.
(*) **Back At The Chicken Shack Blue Note B21Y-46402
    As above. 4/60.
*** **I'm Movin' On** Blue Note 832750-2
    Smith; Grant Green (*g*); Donald Bailey (*d*). 1/63.
*** **Prayer Meetin'** Blue Note B21Y-84164
    Smith; Stanley Turrentine (*ts*); Quentin Warren (*g*); Donald Bailey (*d*). 2/63.

As Coleman Hawkins is to the tenor saxophone, so James Oscar Smith is to the Hammond organ. Amazingly, he didn't even touch the instrument until he was 28, but he quickly established and personified a jazz vocabulary for the instrument: tireless walking bass in the pedals, thick chords with the left hand, quick-fire melodic lines with the right. It was a formula almost from the start, and Smith has never strayed from it, but he so completely mastered the approach that he is inimitable. At his best he creates a peerless excitement, which is seldom sustained across an entire album but which makes every record he's on something to be reckoned with.

Smith made a great stack of albums for Blue Note, but there are now few left in print, and fanatics haunt second-hand racks in an effort to track down the rarest. The reissue of his first date, now apparently titled *The Champ*, is very welcome, since it catches much of the raw excitement that Smith was after. Pet licks and his familar great flourishes, delighting in the noise-making capacity of the organ, still sound at their most fresh and swinging here. Otherwise *The Sermon* isn't a bad place to start, a studio session at an only slightly lower flame than a typical Smith live set, with fine contributions from all the horns. *Open House/Plain Talk* doubles up two albums from a smoking group with an unbeatable front line – Mitchell, McLean and Quebec – although the three of them are together on only four tracks. *Back At The Chicken Shack* has Turrentine confronting Smith to somewhat lesser effect, although the title blues blows very warmly. They have a rematch on *Prayer Meetin'*, which is a salad of the secular ('Red Top') and the sacred (of a sort – 'When The Saints' and the title-tune).

Midnight Special and *Crazy Baby* are still available as US releases. The former was recorded at the same session as *Chicken Shack* and is more of the same, while the latter is a more prosaic studio set devoted to standards that don't really get Smith started. *I'm Movin' On* is the most recent reclamation, and it's notable mainly for the sole recorded appearance of Smith with guitarist Grant Green – though the programme never quite gets off the ground, and what should have been the big steamer, 'Back Talk', resolves itself into a series of clichés. There are two extra tracks added to the original LP's list.

*** **The Cat** Verve 810046-2
    Smith; Ernie Royal, Bernie Glow, Jimmy Maxwell, Marky Markowitz, Snooky Young, Thad
    Jones (*t*); Bill Byers, Jimmy Cleveland, Urbie Green (*tb*); Ray Alonge, Jimmy Buffington, Earl
    Chapin, Bill Correa (*frhn*); Tony Studd (*btb*); Kenny Burrell (*g*); George Duvivier (*b*); Don
    Butterfield (*tba*); Grady Tate (*d*); Phil Kraus (*perc*). 4/64.
(*) **Christmas Cookin' Verve 513711-2
    Smith; Quentin Warren, Kenny Burrell, Wes Montgomery (*g*); Bill Hart, Grady Tate (*d*);
    orchestra directed by Bill Byers. 6/64–9/66.
*** **Further Adventures Of Jimmy And Wes** Verve 519802-2
    Smith; Wes Montgomery (*g*); Grady Tate (*d*); Ray Barretto (*perc*). 9/66.
***(*) **Walk On The Wild Side: The Best Of The Verve Years** Verve 527950-2 2CD
    As above discs, plus Steve Williams (*hca*), George Benson, Arthur Adams, Quentin Warren, Eric
    Gale, Thornel Schwartz, Vince Gambella (*g*), Wilton Felder, Ron Carter, Bob Bushnell (*b*),
    Buck Clarke (*perc*), Paul Humphrey, Billy Hart, Bernard Purdie, Mel Lewis (*d*), orchestras
    directed by Oliver Nelson, Johnny Pate and Thad Jones, strings. 3/62–2/73.

Smith's Verve catalogue is also in disrepair, but a few original albums are currently in catalogue. *The Cat* sets him up in front of a big band, a favourite situation for him in the period, with Lalo Schifrin arrangements (very heavy on the brass) to nestle down in. A trusted formula, but Smith makes it exciting. The Christmas album is one of the best in a hapless genre: great cover-art, and the music isn't too hopeless. Smith's meeting with Montgomery isn't so much a battle of the giants as a genial bit of backslapping: thin material holds them back, but the sound of the group, Montgomery's funky lyricism matched with Smith's extravagant blues, is a delight. Verve's two-disc best-of is a very useful sweep through what is a very mixed catalogue, and as far as this period is concerned this should satisfy all but the most obsessive Smith devotee. Aside from obvious choices like the title-tune, the compilers choose a smart mix of small groups and big bands. One or two nuggets will tempt collectors, such as an alternative take of 'OGD' from the date with Montgomery, and there are a few rescued obscurities: two tracks from the orchestral collaboration with Thad Jones, *Portuguese Soul*; a live blues from 1972, 'Sagg Shootin' His Arrow', with a band including Arthur Adams and Wilton Felder; the title-track off Johnny Pate's set of charts, *Groove Drops*; and 'The Boss' with George Benson and Donald Bailey.

*** **Live At Salle Pleyel 1965** RTE 710379-380 2CD
    Smith; Quentin Warren (*g*); Billy Hart (*d*). 65.
With the many live sets for Blue Note mostly out of print, Smith acolytes will welcome this concert, recorded by French radio, which features nearly two hours of the man's stage show of the period. Loud, noisy and ineffably vigorous, this is how Smith will probably be best remembered, and though one disc might be enough for most tastes, it's useful to have a complete show in one package.

** **Go For Whatcha Know** Blue Note 846297-2
    Smith; Stanley Turrentine (*ts*); Monty Alexander (*p*); Kenny Burrell (*g*); Buster Williams (*b*);
    Grady Tate, Kenny Washington (*d*); Erroll Bennett (*perc*). 1/86.
*** **Prime Time** Milestone M 9176
    Smith; Curtis Peagler (*as, ts*); Herman Riley, Rickey Woodard (*ts*); Phil Upchurch, Terry Evans
    (*g*); Andy Simpkins (*b*); Michael Baker, Frank Wilson (*d*); Barbara Morrison (*v*). 8/89.
*** **Fourmost** Milestone MCD 9184-2
    Smith; Stanley Turrentine (*ts*); Kenny Burrell (*g*); Grady Tate (*d, v*). 11/90.
(*) **Sum Serious Blues Milestone MCD-9207-2
    Smith; Oscar Brashear (*t*); George Bohannon (*tb*); Maurice Spears (*btb*); Buddy Collette (*as*);
    Herman Riley (*ts*); Ernie Fields (*bs*); Mick Martin (*hca*); Phil Upchurch (*g*); Andy Simpkins
    (*b*); Michael Baker (*d*); Marlena Shaw, Bernard Ighner (*v*). 1/93.
***(*) **The Master** Blue Note 830451-2
    Smith; Kenny Burrell (*g*); Jimmie Smith (*d*). 12/93.
*** **Damn!** Verve 527631-2
    Smith; Roy Hargrove, Nicholas Payton (*t*); Abraham Burton (*as*); Tim Warfield, Mark Turner,
    Ron Blake (*ts*); Mark Whitfield (*g*); Christian McBride (*b*); Bernard Purdie, Art Taylor (*d*). 1/
    95.
Smith has adapted rather cautiously to changing times. He still sticks to straight-ahead Hammond, but he or his producers vary the other ground-rules, with varying results. The first Blue Note, *Go For Whatcha Know*, was a near-disaster: Turrentine played with prepackaged vigour, and the material seemed at odds with the title, including a missable version of Michael Jackson's 'She's Out Of My Life'. *Prime Time* and *Fourmost* are simple blowing records with muscular solos by the horns on the former and a rather more stately contribution from Turrentine on the latter. *Sum Serious Blues* is produced by Johnny Pate as a throwback to some of Smith's Verve sessions of the 1960s – some blues, a new version of 'The Sermon', a couple of vocals from Shaw and Ighner. Probably no more systematized than any of the older records, but it doesn't sound as spontaneous, either.

   The Master is another matter, and this one has been a little overlooked in Smith's recent work. Cut in Japan at Christmas 1993, Smith works through several of his old favourites with the sole support of Burrell and Jimmie Smith and, rather than taking the most routine way out, the playing is actually unexpectedly fresh, involved and spontaneous. There's a notably fine 'Back At The Chicken Shack'; but all the tracks feature some felicities and none outstays its welcome. Having gone back to Blue Note, Smith then returned to Verve with *Damn!*, an enjoyable if finally somewhat programmed session, where the old man spars alongside rather than with a bulging personnel of young Turks. The chosen themes blend bebop and funk, but it's a little stiff in the joints.

*** **The Best Of Jimmy Smith** Blue Note 791140-2
A serviceable compilation which includes 'Back At The Chicken Shack' and 'The Sermon' as well as a couple of lesser items: concessions to being 'representative' have perhaps told against the final choice here.

Leo Smith (born 1941) TRUMPET, FLUGELHORN, PERCUSSION, VOICE

***(*) **Go In Numbers** Black Saint 120053
    Smith; Dwight Andrews (*ts, ss, f*); Bobby Naughton (*vib*); Wes Brown (*b, odurgyaba f*). 1/80.
**** **Procession Of The Great Ancestry** Chief CD6
    Smith; Joe Powell (*ts*); Bobby Naughton (*vib*); Louis Myers (*g*); Mchaka Uba, Joe Fonda (*b*);
    Kahil El Zabar (*d, perc*). 2/83.

*** **Kulture Jazz** ECM 1507
    Smith solo. 10/92.
Smith is one of the few jazz musicians to have embraced Rastafarianism. That he has done so from a fastness in Iceland seems even more extraordinary. It isn't really possible to divide his career into earlier and later phases, since his concerns are remarkably consistent. He plays trumpet and flugelhorn with a strong Miles Davis influence (particularly when muted), but he has also absorbed other swing and bop players. The magnificent *Procession Of The Great Ancestry*, accompanied by 'seven mystical poems of jahzz in 17 links', is a series of tributes to models like Miles, Booker Little, Roy Eldridge, Dizzy Gillespie and the Rev. Martin Luther King Jr. Less pastiche than sincere invocation, the individual pieces follow the ritual character of the title-track. The dominant combination, as so often in Smith's career, is of trumpet and Bobby Naughton's post-Hutcherson vibes.

    Earlier rituals, like *The Mass On The World* and *Budding Of A Rose*, both on Moers, have not appeared on CD. Nor has the more improvisational *Touch The Earth* on FMP, though some vinyl may still be around. *Go In Numbers* is credited to the New Dalta Ahkri (who have also recorded on Smith's own Kabell imprint) and is performed in Smith's rapt, prophetic manner. Without a drummer, Naughton's vibes become the focal point, but, as with *The Mass On The World*, Andrews's multi-instrumentalism creates an important dimension.

    Kulture Jazz is actually Smith's second record for ECM, though its predecessor is long deleted. Here, he dispenses with a group in favour of overdubbed invocations to the ancestors (Billie Holiday, John Coltrane, Albert Ayler, Louis Armstrong) and to friends. As with Cecil Taylor, Smith's texts have become an integral part of the music. Indeed, here the words seem, if anything, more important than the instrumental sounds, which are rather thin and not always registered very precisely. One holds out for more of Smith's full-voiced trumpet and flugelhorn playing, but it's in disappointingly short supply.

Louis Smith (born 1931) TRUMPET, FLUGELHORN

(*) **Just Friends Steeplechase SCCD 31096
    Smith; George Coleman (*ts*); Harold Mabern (*p*); Jamil Nasser (*b*); Ray Mosca Jr (*d*). 3/78.
** **Prancin'** Steeplechase SCCD 31121
    Smith; Junior Cook (*ts*); Roland Hanna (*p*); Sam Jones (*b*); Billy Hart (*d*). 6/79.
** **Ballads For Lulu** Steeplechase SCCD 31268
    Smith; Jim McNeely (*p*); Bob Cranshaw (*b*); Keith Copeland (*d*). 3/90.
(*) **Strike Up The Band Steeplechase SCCD 31294
    Smith; Vincent Herring (*as*); Junior Cook (*ts*); Kevin Hays (*p*); Steve LaSpina (*b*); Leroy Williams (*d*). 91.
*** **Silvering** Steeplechase SCCD 31336
    Smith; Von Freeman (*ts*); Jodie Christian (*p*); Eddie De Haas (*b*); Wilbur Campbell (*d*). 4/93
Fondly remembered for two impressive Blue Note albums made in 1958, Smith's more recent work is much less exciting. His first records for 20 years were hesitant and lacking in conviction so far as his own playing was concerned: both teams of musicians outplay him on *Just Friends* and *Prancin'*, with the redoubtable Coleman surging through on the earlier disc. The third record is a collection of ballads, which Smith plays with exaggerated care: his tone is clear and strong but the phrasing seems indolent, and McNeely's accompaniment and sweeping solos are the principal attraction in a set which is rather too generous at 70 minutes in length. *Strike Up The Band* is by a youth-and-experience band that tends to put Smith in the shadows. Vincent Herring dominates much in the way he does in the Nat Adderley band, tearing to the front whenever the music needs a wake-up call; Cook, on one of his last dates, sounds sober and measured in comparison. The rhythm team are fine, but Smith himself is no more than solid. *Silvering* is a title in reminiscent dedication to the trumpeter's years with Horace Silver, and he sounds in good spirits throughout this date. The uncompromising tempo for 'Au Privave' was a big risk and his articulation still blurs at most velocities, but the calibre of the rest of the band raises the game. Freeman reaffirms his position as a great original: his tenor solos, such as the incorrigibly manic one on 'Roadies', really do sound like nobody else's. Christian is another Chicago veteran who has this music down cold, and his solo on 'Au Privave' is a killer. Again, rather too much music at close to 70 minutes, but a date worth keeping.

Marvin 'Smitty' Smith (born 1961) DRUMS

*** **Keeper Of The Drums** Concord CCD 4325
    Smith; Wallace Roney (*t*); Robin Eubanks (*tb*); Steve Coleman (*as*); Ralph Moore (*ts*); Mulgrew Miller (*p*); Lonnie Plaxico (*b*). 3/87.

*** The Road Less Travelled Concord CCD 4379

> As above, except James Williams (*p*) and Robert Hurst (*b*) replace Miller and Plaxico; add Kenyatte Abdur-Rahman (*perc*). 2/89.

One wonders if this is how Max Roach or Philly Joe Jones might have sounded on their own albums if recording techniques in the 1950s had been up to present-day standards. Drummer albums, even by some of the masters, used to be vulnerable to the Tedious Solo Syndrome, overlong and overmiked excursions that rattled the fillings. In a sense, Smitty Smith never stops soloing. His is the most insistent voice throughout almost every track, a maelstrom of furiously paced percussion that seems out of all proportion to the relatively modest bop-to-M-BASE foregrounds.

The debut *Keeper Of The Drums* is marginally the better of the two because the themes seem fresher. 'Miss Ann', not the Dolphy classic of that name, works a variation on the classic Spanish interval. 'Just Have Fun' and 'Song Of Joy' are directly reminiscent of 1950s models, and most people, offered a sample of 'The Creeper', will claim they've got it on a Blue Note somewhere.

The writing is less varied and more predictable on *The Road Less Travelled*. There's no significant difference between the line-ups, except that Miller and Plaxico are marginally more sensitive, but the later set is brittle where the earlier album bends and moulds to the context. Smith's off-beats and compressed rolls are technically impressive but ultimately rather wearing. In his backwash one tends to lose sight of some excellent work from Moore and Roney in particular.

Smith may yet be acknowledged as the Max Roach of his day. Or maybe just the Art Blakey. His sideman credits are impressive. But it will take something a little more distinctive than these to put him on a par with his role models.

Mike Smith ALTO AND SOPRANO SAXOPHONES

**(*) Unit 7 A Tribute To Cannonball Adderley Delmark DE 444

> Smith; Ron Friedman (*t, flhn*); Jodie Christian (*p*); John Whitfield (*b*); Robert Shy (*d*). 90.

*** On A Cool Night Delmark DE 448

> As above, except Jim Ryan (*p*) and Bob Rummage (*d*) replace Christian and Shy. 91.

*** The Traveler Delmark DE-462

> Smith; Ron Friedman (*flhn*); Jim Ryan (*p*); John Whitfield (*b*); Julian Smith, Bob Rummage (*d*). 92.

*** Sinatra Songbook Delmark DE-480

> As above, except omit Friedman and Julian Smith. n.d.

Hard bop from contemporary Chicago. Smith is frankly under the spell of Cannonball Adderley: he doesn't have the rasping, bluesy timbre down as well as Vincent Herring does, but the line of descent is clear from a few bars of any solo, and *Unit 7* is a proper genuflection in the direction of Cannon's work. But this young altoman looks a little further out, too: he organizes his bands with pithy discretion and seeks contrast in his choice and arrangement of material. 'Don't Scare Me None', for instance, the opening track on *On A Cool Night*, is a nicely measured bebop variation with a cunning tempo change to keep everyone awake. The first record begs direct comparison with the source of inspiration, and it takes only a goodish second place as a result, but *On A Cool Night* is more personal and hints at an emerging voice. Friedman is the more unusual player, though, if only for his curiously ingested tone – as if he were an avant-gardist trying to play it relatively straight. A useful reminder that New York doesn't have it all its own way as regards new American talent. Smith shows an increasing penchant for the soprano on *The Traveler*, and the band seem to be growing in confidence as a unit, with Ryan's sparely searching accompaniments and the compatibility of the horns lending further assurance. This is hardly a ground-breaking band, but it plays decent jazz. Smith has been earning his keep playing lead alto in Sinatra's backing orchestra, so his *Songbook* features material he must know well, and there are a couple of tunes jazz players rarely touch – 'Only The Lonely' especially. Otherwise this is another unsurprising but enjoyable blow from Mike.

Stuff Smith (1909–67) VIOLIN, VOCALS

***(*) Stuff Smith & His Onyx Club Boys Classics 706

> Smith; Jonah Jones (*t, v*); Buster Bailey (*cl*); George Clark (*ts*); Sam Allen, James Sherman, Clyde Hart, Raymond Smith (*p*); Bernard Addison, Bobby Bennett (*g*); John Brown, Mack Walker (*b*); Cozy Cole, Herbert Cowens, John Washington (*d*). 2/36.

***(*) Stuff Smith / Dizzy Gillespie / Oscar Peterson Verve 521 676 2CD

> Smith; Dizzy Gillespie (*t*); Wynton Kelly, Carl Perkins, Oscar Peterson (*p*); Red Callender, Curtis Counce, Paul West (*b*); Oscar Bradley, Frank Butler, J. C. Heard, Alvin Stoller (*d*); Gordon Family (*v*). 1–4/57.

***(*) **Live At The Montmartre** Storyville STCD 4142
>   Smith; Kenny Drew (*p*); Niels-Henning Orsted-Pedersen (*b*); Alex Riel (*d*). 3/65.
*** **Hot Violins** Storyville STCD 4170
>   Smith; Poul Olsen (*vn*); Svend Asmussen (*vn, v*); Kenny Drew, Jorgen Borch (*p*); Erik Molbak,
>   Niels-Henning Orsted-Pedersen (*b*); Makaya Ntoshko, Alex Riel, Bjarne Rostvold (*d*). 3/65, 1/
>   66, 2/67.

It's hard to imagine how Billy Bang's or Leroy Jenkins's mordant new-wave fiddling would have come about had it not been for the example of Stuff Smith. Initially influenced by Joe Venuti, Smith devised a style based on heavy bow-weight, with sharply percussive semiquaver runs up towards the top end of his range. Like many 1920s players, Smith found himself overtaken by the swing era and re-emerged as a recording and concert artist (though he had a thriving club career in the meantime) only after the war, when his upfront style and comic stage persona attracted renewed attention.

The Classics disc covers some important early material. This is when Smith's talent was at its most buoyant. 'I'se A Muggin'' and the associated musical numbers game are pretty corny, but they retain their appeal over five decades like all the Vocalion sides, and Smith's astonishing fiddle technique lifts them up out of the mere novelty class. Jones makes a big impact, with a slithery, burping style that's hard to categorize and which shouldn't fit these sessions as well as it seems to. Sensibly, Classics have restricted this first volume to things Smith made under his own name. Future releases will include sessions for Alphonso Trent which are much less typical.

Verve have, of course, always had a gift for picking up artists relatively late in their career and injecting new life into them. The sessions with Diz and Oscar are beautifully recorded, if not sublimely musical, and one values the record – a generously filled two-CD set – for the glimpses of the under-recorded Perkins as much as anything.

The later European sessions, recorded within a couple of years of Smith's death in Munich, are very much better. *Hot Violins* was made shortly before 'the cat that took the apron strings off the fiddle' was taken back into the fold. They're pretty tired, and it gets a bit dispiriting listening to Smith being cut by guys who're doing no more than playing his licks back at him. Asmussen does a party piece with a tenor violin on 'Caravan'; pitched somewhere between viola and cello, it makes a pretty noise, but it's hard not to feel so-what-ish about it.

Tab Smith (1909–71) ALTO AND TENOR SAXOPHONES

*** **Jump Time** Delmark DD-447
>   Smith; Sonny Cohn (*t*); Leon Washington (*ts*); Lavern Dillon, Teddy Brannon (*p*); Wilfred
>   Middlebrooks (*b*); Walter Johnson (*d*); Louis Blackwell (*v*). 8/51–2/52.
*** **Ace High** Delmark DD-455
>   As above, except add Irving Woods (*t*), Charlie Wright (*ts*). 2/52–4/53.

Smith jobbed around the Harlem big bands of the 1930s and eventually found a niche with Count Basie. But he won his wider fame as an R&B soloist in the 1950s, and for a while jockeyed with Earl Bostic on the nation's jukeboxes. This pair of CDs collects a stack of such performances, offering a chronological survey of his output for the United label. Backed by an unobtrusive small group, Smith works through ballads, the blues and more roisterous outings. His sound is more graceful than Bostic's: he always seems to have something in reserve, and the hollow sound he sometimes gets in the alto's upper register reminds that he often made use of the soprano, too, although not here. Given the sameness of the format and the repetitive formulas Smith had to apply, these are surprisingly engaging CDs, although one or other will be more than enough for all but the most devout followers. Very clean remastering.

Tommy Smith (born 1967) TENOR SAXOPHONE

***(*) **Reminiscence** Linn AKD 204
>   Smith; Terje Gewelt (*b*); Ian Froman (*d*). 7/93.
***(*) **Misty Morning And No Time** Linn AKD 040
>   Smith; Guy Barker (*t, monette*); Julian Arguëlles (*sax*); Steve Hamilton (*p*); Terje Gewelt (*b*);
>   Ian Froman (*d*). 12/94.

Saddled with quite unreasonable expectations as a fifteen-year-old, the young Scot's recording history has been an uncomfortable mixture of unreasonably inflated expectation and neglected achievement. His Blue Note debut, *Step By Step*, had a stellar rhythm section and a nervous, hasty quality that suggested Smith was trying to show off all his (by now considerable) talents in one brief session. In contrast to the two small-label sessions, *Taking Off* and *Giant Strides*, it was a remarkably callow performance, and Smith's insistence on using his own material didn't help his cause. At Berklee, Smith had been taken up by vibraharpist and composer Gary Burton, and he played in Burton's *Whiz Kids* band. The experience simplified and straightened out his playing, stripping it of some of the Coltrane clichés and homing in on essentials. Though the opening 'Ally The Wallygator' and 'Ghosts' are admirably well argued, Smith sounds overpowered by the company he's keeping, and the production is decidedly foggy; though the sound hardly accords with ECM standards, Smith seems increasingly inclined to withdraw (as on 'Ghosts') into a tentative and watered-down version of Jan Garbarek's demanding and deceptively imitable style.

Exasperatingly, all four of Smith's Blue Notes have been deleted. His new contract with Linn has revealed a fully mature talent. *Reminiscence* might seem to be a curious title for a young man of 27, but his first disc for Linn is in every sense a stocktaking exercise, though by no means a regressive one. Reunited with Gewelt and Froman in a stripped-down Forward Motion, he undertakes a more reflective and less thrusting programme. 'Ally' contains echoes of earlier pieces, as do 'Memoir' and Gewelt's 'Is Really This It?' (*sic.*). A folksong arrangement draws in elements from Smith's activities in traditional music, though it may also contain Scandinavian material. The sound is still very stark and piercing, all the more noticeable in such a sparse setting. 'Emancipation Of Dissonance', placed in the middle of the set, offers an ironic comment on Smith's agenda. 'DayDreams' and 'Memoir' appear to be spontaneously improvised. When *Reminiscence* was issued, there was a tendency to review the title and ignore the music. While Smith clearly was re-examining his past activity, he was doing so in order to see what he could do with it in future, not simply returning to successful formulae. The new album sets out agenda that the young saxophonist can develop with profit for years to come.

Misty Morning And No Time is Smith's most ambitious record to date, and to that extent takes a cue from its predecessor. The individual pieces are inspired by poet Norman McCaig, who has since died, and there is a rich poetry in the composer's responses to this most straightforward and un-literary of poets. Barker, as before, is an inspiration, tackling difficult charts as if they were familiar standards and bringing a very particular and individual sound to 'Memorial', a threnody for the poet's dead daughter, and one of the most directly emotional pieces Smith has yet to write. Arguëlles grows in stature with each record, and his interplay with Smith on 'Estuary', a dappled theme which also makes use of Barker's liquid-sounding monette (an instrument not unlike Art Farmer's flumpet), is quite exceptional in its tact and taste. At time of writing, Smith is preparing a new record (apparently to be called *Beasts Of Scotland*) with another Scottish poet, Edwin Morgan.

Willie 'The Lion' Smith (1895–1973) PIANO, VOCAL

***(*) **Willie 'The Lion' Smith 1925–1937** Classics 662
> Smith; Dave Nelson, Frankie Newton (*t*); June Clark, Jabbo Smith, Ed Allen (*c*); Jimmy Harrison (*tb*); Buster Bailey (*cl, ss, as*); Cecil Scott, Herschel Brassfield (*cl*); Prince Robinson, Robert Carroll (*ts*); Edgar Sampson (*as, vn*); Pete Brown (*as*); Buddy Christian, Gus Horsley (*bj*); Jimmy McLin (*g*); Bill Benford, Harry Hull (*tba*); Ellsworth Reynolds, John Kirby (*b*); O'Neil Spencer (*d, v*); Eric Henry (*d*); Willie Williams (*wbd*); Perry Bradford (*v*). 11/25–9/37.

**** **Willie 'The Lion' Smith And His Cubs** Timeless CBC 1-012
> As above, except omit Clark, Harrison, Robinson, Christian, Benford, Jabbo Smith, Brassfield, Sampson, Horsley and Hull. 4/35–9/37.

*** **Willie 'The Lion' Smith 1937–1938** Classics 677
> Smith; Frank Newton (*t*); Pete Brown (*as*); Buster Bailey (*cl*); Milt Herth (*org*); Jimmy McLin (*g*); Teddy Bunn (*g, v*); John Kirby (*b*); O'Neil Spencer (*d, v*). 9/37–11/38.

***(*) **Willie 'The Lion' Smith 1938–1940** Classics 692
> Smith; Sidney De Paris (*t*); Jimmy Lane, Johnny Mullins (*as*); Perry Smith (*ts*); Joe Bushkin, Jess Stacey (*p*); Bernard Addison (*g*); Richard Fullbright (*b*); George Wettling, Puss Johnson (*d*); Joe Turner, Naomi Price (*v*). 11/38–11/40.

One of the great Harlem pianists and an unrivalled raconteur, Willie Smith came into his own when an old man, reminiscing from the keyboard. But these more youthful sessions stand up very well and are surprisingly little known. Classics 662 opens with two of his very few appearances on record in the 1920s: each of the pair of sessions is by a pick-up group, both with Jimmy Harrison and one with Jabbo Smith in the front line. Typical small-group Harlem jazz of the period, with Perry Bradford shouting the odds on two titles. The remainder – and all of the Timeless CD – is devoted to sessions by Smith's Cubs, an excellent outfit: with Ed Allen, Cecil Scott and Willie Williams on washboard on the first eight titles, they can't help but sound like a Clarence Williams group, but the next three sessions include Dave Nelson (sounding better than he ever did on the King Oliver Victor records), Buster Bailey, Pete Brown and Frankie Newton, effecting a bridge between older hot music and the sharper small-band swing of the late '30s. Smith plays a lot of dextrous piano – he also has a 1934 solo, 'Finger Buster', a typical parlour show-off piece of the day – and the music has a wonderful lilt and sprightliness. The Timeless transfers are clearly superior and include a lot of alternative takes: this is the disc to get if you just want the Cubs tracks, but the other tunes on the Classics disc are also worth hearing. Classics 677 is made up mostly of tracks by Milt Herth, a Hammond organist who had Smith, Spencer and Bunn making up his group. Herth is always getting in the way, but The Lion usually pushes some decent stride piano into most of the tunes, and there are two fine 1938 solos, 'Passionette' and 'Morning Air', which show something of his penchant for rarefied 'novelty' piano of the Roy Bargy genre. Classics 692 starts with a three-piano date featuring Smith, Stacey and Bushkin, before a marathon date that produced 14 piano solos in one day: originals and show tunes, done in the manner of courteous syncopation that trade-marks Smith's style. The rest of the disc includes a rare small-band session and a pair of blues, partner-ing Smith with Joe Turner. Exemplary, although docked a notch for less-than-ideal remastering.

*** **The Lion's In Town** Vogue 11506 2
    Smith; Wallace Bishop (*d*). 12/49–1/59.
*** **Pork And Beans** Black Lion BLCD 760144
    Smith (*p, v*). 11/66.

The Lion's irrepressible showmanship often got in the way of his piano playing when it came to his later records. He loved to tell a story about every tune, and the Vogue CD starts with a 24-minute medley, 'Reminiscing The Piano Greats', 11 tunes recalled and expounded upon in his best cigar-chomping manner. The only drawback with this living history is that when he claims to demonstrate 'how that one was played', they always sound the same – like The Lion playing a stride solo. But that is pretty good entertainment, too. *The Lion's In Town* was cut on two different sessions in Paris, and Smith's own tunes are given a mercurial treatment. The sound has plenty of unwarranted scratch, but it's listenable. In Germany, in 1966, he played another 15 tunes from memory – Luckey Roberts, Eubie Blake, Irving Berlin, Fats Waller, Willie Smith. Boisterous music in good sound.

Paul Smoker (born 1941) TRUMPET

**** **Alone** sound aspects sas 018
    Smoker; Ron Rohovit (*b*); Phil Haynes (*d*). 8/86.
***(*) **Come Rain Or Come Shine** sound aspects sas 024
    As above. 8/86.
**** **Genuine Fables** hat Art CD 6126
    As above. 11/88.

Paul Smoker is a Mid-West academic who plays free-form jazz of surpassing thoughtfulness. Though by no means averse to tackling standards, he creates a lot of his own material, cleaving to quasi-classical forms which, coupled with a tight, rather correct diction, sometimes recall Don Ellis. Without a har-mony instrument, the group sound is stark and abstract. *Alone* was among the most interesting record-ings of the mid-1980s and an object-lesson in group improvisation. The dynamics (as throughout Smoker's work) are almost too self-consciously varied, with tracks seguing into one another, giving the whole a suite-like feel. Working without a harmony instrument and with only occasional stabs at pedal notes from Smoker, the rhythm section is called on to perform an unusually active function, which (as 'Mingus Amongus' seems to suggest) is reminiscent of what the great bassist did with his bands. Rohovit bows long, hold-steady notes over whispering percussion on 'Prelude' (Haynes often works at the boundaries of audibility) until Smoker enters, sounding as if his last gig was Hummel or Haydn. The standards – Armstrong's 'Cornet Chop Suey' and Ellington's 'Caravan' – are imaginatively stitched in, and the performance gives off an aura of quiet power which is wholly missing on the more eclectic and ironic charts of *Come Rain Or Come Shine*.

  Genuine Fables offers an even more challenging mixture of standards – 'St Louis Blues', 'Laura' and 'Hello, Young Lovers' – and originals. Haynes emerges as a more than competent writer, and his playing on Mingus's 'Fables Of Faubus' must have Dannie Richmond's shade looking on. A splendid, endlessly fascinating record.

  It's interesting to compare the trio version of 'Chorale And Descendance' on *Come Rain Or Come Shine* with the one recorded by Smoker's Joint Venture band on its first recorded outing. The saxophone adds nothing much to the turbulent formality of the piece, but 'Lush Life' takes on a wonderfully awkward grace, like a drunk getting the walk right just long enough to get to the other side of the bar where the girl is sitting. Beautiful, but not a patch on the sober stillness of *Alone*. Strongly recommended.

Gary Smulyan BARITONE SAXOPHONE

*** The Lure Of Beauty Criss Cross 1049
> Smulyan; Jimmy Knepper (*tb*); Mulgrew Miller (*b*); Ray Drummond (*b*); Kenny Washington (*d*). 12/90.

A staunch section-player, Smulyan worked with Woody Herman and Mel Lewis and has as good a grasp of baritone technique as any of the younger players of what's still a rare instrument. It was a smart idea to bring Jimmy Knepper to this session, a frequent associate of Pepper Adams and a player whose manner is individual enough to lift the music out of the hard-bop rut which several Criss Cross sessions have fallen into. The group work up a great head of steam on 'Canto Fiesta', the rhythm section grooving hard enough to sustain the feel over more than ten minutes, and there are a couple of pretty (if functional) ballad performances; but at 74 minutes the record could have lost a couple of items and been none the worse for it.

*** Homage Criss Cross 1068
> Smulyan; Tommy Flanagan (*p*); Ray Drummond (*b*); Kenny Washington (*d*). 12/91.

It was a pleasing notion to pay tribute to another baritone master, Pepper Adams, who wrote all eight themes here. Having Flanagan, an old Detroit friend of Adams's, along as well was another good idea. Smulyan is both similar to and different from the older player, less ornery than Adams but given to a comparable stoniness and scepticism with the tender approach: on a ballad such as 'Civilization And Its Discontents', his refusal to turn to a sanctimonious vibrato adds to the power of the improvising, even with Flanagan's featherbed chords to hand. The hard-bop lines of 'Claudette's Way' are reeled off with unassuming strength: this is a baritone man who understands the weight and gravitas of the instrument without having to insist on it. Smulyan doesn't always convince one that the tunes are that good, but it's an impressively substantial record.

*** Saxophone Mosaic Criss Cross 1092
> Smulyan; Dick Oatts (*ss, as, f*); Billy Drewes (*as, cl, f*); Ralph Lalama (*ts, cl, f*); Rich Perry (*ts*); Scott Robinson (*bs, bcl*); Mike LeDonne (*p*); Dennis Irwin (*b*); Kenny Washington (*d*). 12/93.

George Coleman's 'Apache Dance', which opens the record, features all the horns, but it's the exception. For the most part, Bob Belden's arrangements use this six-sax team for colour, and for something which Smulyan himself can bed down in. He peels off long, heated solos on every track, as if under pressure to make the baritone dominate the line-up, and it's an effective strategy. But here and there one wishes the other horns had taken a greater part, though everyone comes back in again on the closing 'Fingers'.

Jim Snidero ALTO SAXOPHONE

**(*) Mixed Bag Criss Cross Criss 1032
> Snidero; Brian Lynch (*t*); Benny Green (*p*); Peter Washington (*b*); Jeff Tain Watts (*d*). 12/87.

***(*) Blue Afternoon Criss Cross Criss 1072
> Snidero; Brian Lynch (*t*); Benny Green (*p*); Peter Washington (*b*); Marvin 'Smitty' Smith (*d*). 12/89.

*** Time Out Red R R 123228
> Snidero; Marc Cohen (*p*); Peter Washington (*b*); Victor Lewis (*d*). 7/89.

*** Storm Rising Ken 660 56 006
> Snidero; Mulgrew Miller (*p*); Peter Washington (*b*); Jeff Hirshfield (*d*). 4/90.

*** While Your Here Red 123241
> Snidero; Benny Green (*p*); Peter Washington (*b*); Tony Reedus (*d*). 1/91.

***(*) Vertigo Criss Cross CRISS 1112
> Snidero; Walt Weiskopf (*ts*); David Hazeltine (*p*); Peter Washington (*b*); Tony Reedus (*d*). 12/94.

Disclaimers and denials aside, 'mixed bag' just about says it all. Much as Lynch and Green have done elsewhere, Snidero's latter-day hard bop tries to touch too many bases too quickly and without the authority which comes with what used to be called dues-paying. The overall effect is a rather superficial self-confidence and blandness of conception. The solos, most noticeably on 'Pannonica', come by rote, and few of them are properly thought out. Snidero's introductory cadenza on 'Blood Count' is his only really distinctive moment. That having been said, this is a perfectly inoffensive set, free from false grandeur or pretentiousness, and, as far as it goes, quite enjoyable.

Blue Afternoon and *Storm Rising* are more enterprising, with nicely judged originals interspersed with modern compositions such as Wayne Shorter's 'Virgo' and Sam Rivers's 'Beatrice' on *Storm Rising*, Shorter's 'Infant Eyes' and, continuing the ophthalmic theme, Mal Waldron's 'Soul Eyes' on *Blue Afternoon*. Snidero trots out some of his Coltraneisms on the first track and thereafter leaves them well alone, concentrating on shaping well-crafted solos out of quite modest and unassuming materials.

The two Red records are poorly recorded and produced, and the repertoire is definitely more conserva-tive. *Time Out* is a festival gig, and one can see how Snidero might generate excitement without adding much enlightenment. The studio record is much better and, ironically, Snidero plays some of his best solo choruses on *While Your Here*, with back-to-back passages on 'I Can't Get Started' that suggest he's still got things to say and places to go if he can overcome the temptation to be all things to all men.

The best of the bunch and the record that begins to confirm his great potential is the latest. This time Snidero kicks off with some new material, including the excellent 'A.S.A.P', before switching to stand-ards, cracking interpretations of 'Ah-Leu-cha' and 'Skylark'. The band sounds well rehearsed and very responsive, and Washington feeds enough strong lines to make up for the rather uncertain Hazeltine.

Fredrik Soegaard GUITAR

(*) **Solo Guitar Improvisation Olufsen DOCD 5076
Soegaard (*g* solo). 8/88.
***(*) **Ballads** Olufsen DOCD 5160
Soegaard; Frank Jensen (*p, f, perc*); Ivan Roth (*b*); Lars Juul (*d*). 3/91.
Soegaard's impeccable music comes all too close to mere noodling on the solo record. Playing electric and acoustic, and without resorting to overdubs, Soegaard works delicately through his themes, with only the mildest of feedback adventures on 'Heaven Music'. As a show of soliloquizing, not bad, if scarcely a compelling listen. The ensemble record, though, provides a fine context for his interests. The interplay between the leader and Jensen has some of the exacting finesse of, say, the Ralph Towner/Gary Burton recordings, and Roth and Juul provide a shifting, elliptical plane for the others to work on. As before, the music is improvised from the most skeletal of ideas, but here the results are quietly compel-ling. Engineered with signature excellence by Jan-Erik Kongshaug.

Martial Solal (born 1927) PIANO

***(*) **The Vogue Recordings: Volume 1 – Trios And Quartet** Vogue 111514
Solal; Fats Sadi (*vib*); Jean-Marie Ingrand, Pierre Michelot, Benoît Quersin (*b*); Christian Garros, Pierre Lemarchand, Jean-Louis Viale (*d*). 5/53, 2/54, 1/56.
**** **The Vogue Recordings: Volume 2 – Trios And Solos** Vogue 111515
Solal; Joe Benjamin, Jean-Marie Ingrand (*b*); Roy Haynes, Jean-Louis Viale (*d*). 10 & 11/54, 7/56.
**** **The Vogue Recordings: Volume 3 – Trio And Big Band** Vogue 113111
Solal; Roger Guérin, Christian Bellest, Jean Garrec, Maurice Thomas, Fernand Verstraete, Bernard Hulin, Fred Gérard, Robert Fassin (*t*); Billy Byers, Luis Fuentes, Benny Vasseur, Charles Verstraete, André Paquinet, Nat Peck, Guy Destanque, Bill Tamper, Gaby Vilain (*tb*); André Fournier (*frhn*); Georges Grenu, Barney Wilen, Jean Aldegon, Lucky Thompson, Jack Ferrier, Pierre Gossez, Michael Cassez, Hubert Rostaing, William Boucaya, Georges Grenu, Teddy Hameline, Armand Migiani (*sax*); Pierre Michelot, Benoît Quersin (*b*); Kenny Clarke, Christian Garros, Jean-Louis Viale (*d*). 4/55, 5/56, 7/57, 58.
***(*) **Live 1959–1985: The Best Of Martial Solal** Flat & Sharp 239963
Solal; Roger Guérin (*t*); Lee Konitz (*as*); Stéphane Grappelli (*vn*); Niels-Henning Orsted-Pedersen, Paul Rovere, Gilbert Rovere (*b*); Charles Bellonzi, Daniel Humair (*d*). 59–85.
*** **Duo In Paris** Dreyfus Jazz Line 19016
Solal; Joachim Kühn (*p*). 10/75.
**** **Martial Solal Big Band** Verve 849 381
Solal; Roger Guérin, Eric Le Lann, Tony Russo (*t*); Jacques Bolognesi, Christian Guizien, Hamid Belhocine (*tb*); Marc Steckar (*tba*); François Jeanneau (*cl, ts, ss*); Jean-Pierre Debarbat (*ts, ss*); Jean-Louis Chautemps (*bcl, as, ss*); Pierre Gossez (*bs, cl*); Pierre Blanchard (*vn*); Hervé Derrien (*clo*); Christian Escoude (*g*); Césarius Alvim (*b*); André Ceccarelli (*d*). 6/81.
**** **Plays Hodeir** OMDCD 5008
As above, except omit Belhocine; add Bernard Marchais (*t*); Jacques Di Donato (*cl*); Philippe Mace (*vib*). 3 & 4/84.
***(*) **Martial Solal Big Band** Dreyfus Jazz Line 849230
As above, except add Patrick Artero (*t*), Hamid Belhocine, Glenn Ferris, Denis Deloup (*tb*); Patrice Petitdidier (*frhn*); Philippe Legris (*tba*); Pierre Mimran, Roger Simon, Jean-Pierre Solves (*sax, f*); Philippe Nadal (*clo*), Frédéric Sylvestre (*g*). 12/83, 5/84.

***(*) **Bluesine** Soul Note 121060
    Solal (*p* solo). 1/83.
(*) **Triptyque Adda 590067
    Solal; François Mechali (*b*); Jean-Louis Mechali (*d*); A Piacere Saxophone Quartet: Jean-Pierre
    Caens (*ss*), Jean-Marc Larché (*as*), Philippe Bouveret (*ts*); Yves Gerbelot (*bs*). 3/90.
***(*) **Solal–Lockwood** J M S 067
    Solal; Didier Lockwood (*vn*). 6/93.

Solal's reputation, such as it currently stands, rests largely on his solo and trio work (with Daniel
Humair, Jean-François Jenny-Clark and others) and on his film music; he wrote an unforgettable score
for Godard's *Au bout de souffle*. Fashion, a hint of prejudice and the economics that militate against
such ventures have conspired against wider appreciation of his genius as an arranger and big-band
leader.

The most promising initiative in the past few years has been the CD reissue on Vogue of Solal's
complete recordings for the Swing label in Paris (omitting only those made under the *nom de session*, Jo
Jaguar). Here, it's possible to examine in detail both his highly individual interpretation of blues and
jazz harmony and the Algerian's own brand of composition, which anticipates the folklore interests of
more recent players like Louis Sclavis and François Jeanneau. There is no mistaking his style at the
piano; Philippe Baudoin talks about 'Solalizing' standards, suggesting a great range of unfamiliar
harmonic embellishments, with percussive attack and a constant readiness to bring both hands into play
in both melodic and accompanying roles. Solal is able to distribute ideas across the length of the
keyboard with no obvious 'break'. That's particularly obvious on the tracks with Belgian vibist, Fats
Sadi.

It's also part and parcel of Solal's brilliant arranging skills. Perhaps the most significant materials in the
three Vogues are the big-band sessions on *Volume 3*. With the exception of three standard tunes for trio,
the whole disc is given over to Solal compositions. Most, like 'Midi 1/4' and 'Horloge Parlante', are very
short and pungent. None stretches more than a few seconds over three minutes, but all are marked by a
great richness of detail. Solal tunes are cleverly contoured to yield unexpected climaxes and conclusions,
sometimes seeming to run out of steam several bars before the end of a chorus; others, like 'Tourmente',
move into overtime.

Unfortunately, all the solo sides on *Volume 2* are standards, with the exception of the closing 'Blues For
Albert'. Most are, as usual, 'Solalized', often to the point of unrecognizability, but Solal favourites like
'Caravan' and 'Cherokee' never lose the shape of the original. Compare the version of 'Have You Met
Miss Jones' with the one on the live *Bluesine*, recorded nearly 30 years later; it's clear that Solal has
become more of a mainstream player and that some at least of his rhythmic idiosyncrasies in the past
can be put down to imperfect technique, a touch of astigmatism about bar shapes, rather than a specific
vision. The October 1954 trio with Haynes and Benjamin is very effective, but it's clear that the two
Americans are slightly puzzled by some of Solal's twists and turns.

The material on Flat & Sharp is very valuable though not specially well recorded. The personnel details
may be slightly misleading because Konitz and Grappelli are hardly featured and most of the tracks are
for trio. As a way of getting up to speed on his career, it is a useful record, but too bitty to stand on its
own.

Bluesine is a lovely record, but it's the larger ensembles of the 1980s that really stand out: the Gaumont
Big Band session of 1981 (long deleted) and the truly superb Hodeir set, recorded at Radio France three
years later. Trumpeter Roger Guérin is there of course and is, as always, striking, notably on the closing
Monk tribute, 'Comin' On The Hudson'. 'Transplantation I' is a companion-piece to 'Flautando' (not
included here) and features Debarbat's ringing tenor. 'D Or No' is for sextet and, like the full-band 'Le
Désert Recommence', highlights Solal at his most ironically Gallic. The Verve *Big Band* hinges on a
long, elaborate suite, which is similar in construction to 'Et c'était si vrai' on the more richly voiced
Dreyfus set. It is difficult to judge whether Solal is more effective with the larger unit or whether the
angular movement of his compositions sounds better with a small ensemble. Simple preference will
probably dictate future choices; both should certainly be sampled if at all possible.

Of the remainder, the duos with Lockwood are very attractive. There is something so inescapably Gallic
about the whole conception of the set that it prompts a smile with the very first violin phrases of Solal's
'Difficult Blues'. These fade to wonder with the quiet beauty of Miles's 'Solar'. 'Nuages' is fluffy and
insubstantial, but Lockwood's original 'Amusette 2' and the closing 'Some Day My Prince Will Come'
go right back to the non-European roots both men call on in this fine performance. The duos with Kühn
are less happy, shapeless and cluttered as two-piano sessions are apt to be.

Triptyque is something of an oddity, a suite of themes and solo spots with a slightly ragged saxophone
quartet. Solal has sounded very much better, and the two Mechalis are so eye-droopingly dull in their
features one wonders why they weren't re-taken or edited out.

**** Improvisie Pour France Musique JMS 18638 2CD
    Solal (*p* solo). 93–94.

These radio recitals were awesome enough when they first went out. Given the chance to study them at close quarters and with the repeat button, one is simply astonished at the range of Solal's talents. In recent years he has begun to explore specific areas of jazz piano history. His debt to Bud Powell has long been recognized (an influence symbiotically received during Bud's sojourn in France) but his take on Garner and Tatum is less expected, and the version on this disc of 'Tea For Two' merits comparison with the great man's. We do not exaggerate, nor is it possible to overestimate the sheer artistry of this astonishing record. Anyone interested in jazz piano should make it a priority.

**** Triangle JMS 18674
    Solal; Marc Johnson (*b*); Peter Erskine (*d*). 95.

There can be few better straight piano improvisers anywhere in the world at the moment, and this is a spanking trio. After this, one almost wonders if Erskine and Johnson have been wasting their time on some of their own projects, so good are they as accompanists to the Frenchman. Individual tracks are kept relatively short, still with the outline of a song-form in their structure. 'Round About Twelve' (geddit?) plays games with the chromatic scale, while 'Anatheme' (another pun on 'Theme pour Anna') alternates sour–sweet, dissonant–consonant passages in the most subtle way. Very fine indeed, and an ideal complement to *Improvisie*.

Lew Soloff (born 1944) TRUMPET, FLUGELHORN

*** Hanaley Bay Electric Brid K32Y 6032
    Soloff; Hiram Bullock (*g*); Gil Evans (*p*); Pete Levin (*syn*); Mark Egan (*b*); Kenwood Dennard,
    Adam Nussbaum (*d*); Manolo Badrena (*perc*). 3/85.
*** Yesterdays Paddle Wheel K32Y 6120
    Soloff; Mike Stern (*g*); Charnett Moffett (*b*); Elvin Jones (*d*). 9/86.
*** But Beautiful Paddle Wheel K32Y 6205
    Soloff; Kenny Kirkland (*p*); Richard Davis (*b*); Elvin Jones (*d*). 6/87.
**(*) My Romance Paddle Wheel K32Y 6278
    Soloff; Gil Goldstein (*p, syn*); Pete Levin (*syn*); Mark Egan (*b*); Dan Gottlieb (*d*); Airto Moreira
    (*perc*); Emily Mitchell Soloff (*hp*); Janis Siegel (*v*). 9/88.
***(*) Little Wing Sweet Basil 660 55 015
    Soloff; Ray Anderson (*tb*); Gil Goldstein (*p, syn, acc*); Pete Levin (*ky*); Mark Egan (*b*);
    Kenwood Dennard (*d*); Manolo Badrena (*perc*). 6/91.

New Yorker Soloff's career has been almost absurdly various. Classically trained and a featured soloist on several significant concerti, he spent his early twenties working a mainly Latin circuit before his recruitment in 1968 to the influential Blood, Sweat and Tears. Subsequently he was employed by one of the few bandleaders unembarrassed by an association with rock. Gil Evans used Soloff on mid-1970s tours to the Far East and elsewhere, on the excellent *Little Wing* (which is where the trumpeter got the idea!) and, in the 1980s, in his Monday Night Orchestra. Gil appears on the first record, playing electric piano with a calm majesty.

Evans gave his blessing – and his slightly uncertain, 'arranger's' touch on electric piano – to the 1985 *Hanaley Bay*, a less than wholly successful set that gives Soloff's virtuoso technique very little to chew on and digest. The later, smaller groups show less of Evans's influence and are more straightforwardly jazz-based. If standards remain a touchstone, the trumpeter's handling of 'All Blues' and 'Yesterdays', and of 'Speak Low' and 'Stella By Starlight' on *But Beautiful* suggest that he's more confident as a melodic improviser than on more complex modalities. Stern offers him fewer harmonic leads than Kirkland and makes little attempt to push him along, preferring to vary and embellish. Moffett's basslines are sometimes too heavy-handed, but the two rhythm sections are quite differently conceived, and each seems valid on its own terms. The fact that Jones, hyperactive as ever, sits comfortably in both is testimony to his remarkable powers of assimilation and adaptation.

Though *My Romance* is pretty feeble, the recent *Little Wing* shows what Soloff learnt from his stint with Evans. He's not merely following blindly here but adapting voicings and ideas to his own purposes. It's a mixed bag of material, with Ray Anderson's 'Alligatory Crocodile' and 'Tapajack' perhaps the outstanding originals, though there are also pieces from Egan, Dennard and Don Alias, all worthy of attention.

The best of Soloff's work still has to be sought in isolated solos on other people's records, but these do at least offer a concentrated distillation of what he is capable of, and there is more than enough good material to satisfy casual curiosity.

Alan Sondheim TROMBONE, SOPRANO SAXOPHONE, BASS RECORDER, OTHER INSTRUMENTS

** T'Other Little Tune ESP Disk ESP 1082
> Sondheim; Paul Phillips (*t*); John Emigh (*ts*); Gregert Johnson (*f, picc, syn*); June Sondheim (*p, v*); Joel Zabar (*d, tabla, syn*). 5/68.

If this were a *Stephen* Sondheim record, it would have to be *Sweeney Todd*. You look at the date and realize that in the month enshrined to revolution all over Europe and the United States, perfectly well-intentioned men and women were making the authorities rub their hands with complacent satisfaction, secure in the knowledge that, while the long-hairs still had their music, their pot and college places, jobs in government were secure.

Sondheim's music is the quintessence of a time and place and, like every perfect distillation, is colourless and completely tasteless. He fulfils to the letter Ronnie Scott's definition of a multi-instrumentalist who plays lots of horns. Badly. June Sondheim (relationship unclear) makes a pleasant sound and the trumpeter isn't bad. Otherwise, of archaeological interest only.

The Sound Of Choice Ensemble GROUP

**(*) Triple Exposure Olufsen DOCD 5185
> Jens Horsving (*t*); Hasse Poulsen (*g*); Lars Juul (*d*). 6/92.

Starting in the Miles Davis music of the early 1970s and ending up somewhere near where Blue Box do their stuff, this Danish trio tend to make heavy weather of their influences: Horsving is a strong player and his essentially conservative style isn't always appropriate for their intentions, rather obviously signposted by a title like 'Punk Boogie'. Poulsen's harmonic conversation fills in some of the gaps. The sort of thing that one can't help but call 'interesting'.

Eddie South (1904–62) VIOLIN

*** Eddie South 1923–1937 Classics 707
> South; Jimmy Wade (*c*); Williams Dover (*tb*); Clifford King (*cl, bcl, as*); Arnett Nelson (*cl, as*); Vernon Roulette (*cl, ts*); Teddy Weatherford, Antonia Spaulding (*p*); Walter Wright, Stéphane Grappelli, Michel Warlop (*vn*); Everett Barksdale (*g, bj, v*); Django Reinhardt, Mike McKendrick, Roger Chaput, Sterling Conaway (*g*); Louis Gross (*bb*); Wilson Myers, Milt Hinton, Paul Cordonnier (*b*); Edwin Jackson, Jimmy Bertrand, Jerome Burke (*d*). 12/23–11/37.

*** Eddie South DRG Disques Swing 8405
> As above, except omit Wade, Dover, Nelson, Roulette, Weatherford, Gross, Jackson and McKendrick. 3/29–11/37.

*** Eddie South 1937–1941 Classics 737
> South; Charlie Shavers (*t*); Buster Bailey (*cl*); Russell Procope (*as*); David Martin, Stanley Facey (*p*); Stéphane Grappelli (*vn*); Django Reinhardt, Isadore Langlois, Eddie Gibbs, Eugene Fields (*g*); Paul Cordonnier, Doles Dickens, Ernest Hill (*b*); Specs Powell, Tommy Benford (*d*); Ginny Sims (*v*). 11/37–3/41.

South wasn't simply one of the most accomplished of jazz violinists; he might have been one of the most well-schooled of all jazz musicians of his time, given a thorough classical grounding that, unusually, blossomed into a hot rather than a cool improviser's stance. If his reputation rests on his Paris recordings of 1937 – available on both Classics 707 and the DRG album – there are some interesting footnotes to an unfulfilled career in the other tracks listed here. The first Classics disc starts with a very rare 1923 track by Jimmy Wade's Moulin Rouge Orchestra: awful sound (it was recorded for Paramount), but South's intensely blue violin still cuts through the ensembles. His slightly later Chicago and New York sessions are well played if comparatively lightweight – on songs such as 'Nagasaki' or 'Marcheta' he sounds almost like a vaudevillian – but the three sessions with Grappelli and Reinhardt are fascinating, the guitarist driven into his best form, the violinist playing his finest solos on 'Sweet Georgia Brown' and 'Eddie's Blues', and the date culminating in the extraordinary improvisation on Bach's D Minor Concerto for two violins by South, Grappelli and Reinhardt together. A further 1938 session in Hilversum has some more strong playing by South's regular quintet, but his final titles from 1940–41 belabour the material, which seems designed to cast South as a romantic black gypsy and sends him back to vaudeville. He seldom recorded again. The two Classics discs (in the usual mixed sound – some of the earlier tracks sound too bass-heavy) are probably the best choices. The DRG disc sounds a little better, but preferable is the similar compilation, *Americans In Paris Vol. 3* (EMI Pathé 794126-2), which includes all these tracks and more.

South Frisco Jazz Band GROUP

**** Sage Hen Strut Stomp Off 1143
    Dan Comins, Leon Oakley (*c*); Jim Snyder (*tb*); Mike Baird (*cl, ss, as*); Bob Helm (*cl, as*);
    Robbie Rhodes (*p*); Vince Saunders (*bj*); Bob Rann (*tba*); Bob Raggio (*d, wbd*). 11/84.
***(*) Broken Promises Stomp Off 1180
    As above, except omit Helm. 9/87.
***(*) Got Everything Stomp Off 1240
    As above, except add Bob Helm (*cl, ss, v*), Jack Mangan (*d*). 11/89–9/91.
The South Frisco Jazz band (and by South Frisco they usually mean Los Angeles) have been playing as
a group, on and off, since 1960. Formed in the spirit of the Lu Watters and Turk Murphy groups, they
approach traditional material with a zest, flair and ingenuity that shame most British trad groups and
manage to combine a faithful feel with a certain irreverence: this isn't corny or the work of pasticheurs,
but it's very good fun. The band has made a fair number of records over the years and these three CDs
are a good representation of what the line-up can do. The two-cornet front line plays a fiercely hot lead
on most of the tunes, and they're abetted by Snyder's choleric trombone and Baird's authentically
quivering reed parts (Helm, an original Turk Murphy sideman, sits in on two of the discs). The material
is all original archaeology: when they play Jelly Roll Morton, it's 'Little Lawrence' or 'If Someone
Would Only Love Me' rather than 'Wolverine Blues', and there are tiny tributes scattered through the
discs to the likes of Roy Palmer, Richard M. Jones and Natty Dominique. There are plenty of rags, too.
Of these discs, *Sage Hen Strut* takes a very narrow lead for the choice of material and the complete
absence of vocals (not quite the group's strong point, though they don't do much singing). But all three
are excellent, and recorded with great punch and clarity.

Space Jazz Trio GROUP

*** Space Jazz Trio: Volume 1 yvp 3007
    Enrico Pieranunzi (*p*); Enzo Pietropaoli (*b*); Fabrizio Sferra (*d*). 6/86.
***(*) Space Jazz Trio: Volume 2 yvp 3015
    As above, except Alfred Kramer (*d*) replaces Sferra. 11/88.
The title conjures up the possibility of an offshoot from Sun Ra's Intergalactic Arkestra. The reality is
more earthbound, but by no means mundane. Able accompanists, having worked with Chet Baker
(posthumously name-checked on *Volume 2*) and Lee Konitz, their own material is highly intelligent,
open-minded and, yes, spacious. Pieranunzi (*q.v.*) is a solo recording artist of some standing, and it isn't
entirely clear where his eponymous trio ends and the SJT begins (they have Pietropaoli in common).
However, the bonus version of 'Autobahn' on *Volume 2* is much more demandingly coherent than that
on the pianist's 1987 *Moon Pie* (yvp 3011 CD/LP), confirming other indications that the recruitment of
Kramer has helped gel the group identity. The 'Open Events' (one to four, distributed across both sets)
are impressively improvised. The Sun Ra analogy may well be viable after all, for this is thoroughly post-
modern music, deeply eclectic and simultaneous in its choice of traditions, abstract and emotional by
turns. Recommended with only minor qualifications about the recordings, which are unflattering.

Muggsy Spanier (1906–67) CORNET

*** Muggshot ASV AJA 5102
    Spanier; Dick Fierge, Charlie Altier (*c*); Dave Klein, Max Connett, Lloyd Wallen, Ralph
    Muzillo, Frank Bruno, Leon Schwarz (*t*); George Brunies, Sam Blank, Floyd O'Brien, Vernon
    Brown, Bud Smith, Jules Fasthoff, Guy Carey, Jack Reid (*tb*); Sidney Bechet (*ss, cl*); Frank
    Teschemacher, Maurie Bercov, Irving Fazola, Jimmy Dorsey, Jim Cannon (*cl, as*); Mezz
    Mezzrow (*cl, ts*); Volly De Faut, Benny Goodman, Rod Cless (*cl*); Charles Pierce, Maurice
    Morse (*as*); Louis Martin (*as, bs*); Ralph Rudder, Nick Caizza, Hymie Wolfson, Eddie Miller,
    Lyle Smith, Coleman Hawkins (*ts*); Mel Stitzel, Dan Lipscomb, Joe Sullivan, Art Gronwall, Jack
    Russin, Joe Bushkin, Jess Stacy, Dave Bowman (*p*); Sam Shapiro, Sol Klein, Paul Lyman (*vn*);
    Marvin Saxbe (*bj, g*); Stuart Branch, Eddie Condon (*bj*); Tony Gerhardi, Carmen Masttren,
    Nappy Lamare, Ken Broadhurst, Jack Bland (*g*); Johnny Mueller (*b, bb*); Joe Gish, Jim
    Lannigan (*bb*); Jules Cassard, Al Morgan, Harry Barth, Bob Casey, Wellman Braud, Bob
    Haggart, Jack Kelleher (*b*); Don Carter, Ray Bauduc, Josh Billings, John Lucas, Bill Paley, Ben
    Pollack, Paul Kettler, Gene Krupa (*d*); Red McKenzie, Lee Wiley (*v*). 2/24–2/42.
Spanier was only seventeen when he made the earliest music here – by The Bucktown Five, in
Richmond, Indiana – but he was already a confident lead player, if less impressive as a soloist (his

chorus on 'Hot Mittens' is a well-meaning near-disaster). 'Mobile Blues' is nevertheless a thorough-going jazz performance by a young group which had absorbed many of the latest developments in the music. Thereafter, the CD follows Spanier's career through his dance-band work with Ray Miller and Ted Lewis, two tracks with Sidney Bechet and four by the Ragtime Band, along with other interesting moments from a chequered career. The real meat is to follow, but this is a useful cross-section; ASV's remastering is OK rather than outstanding.

**** **Muggsy Spanier 1931 And 1939** Jazz Classics In Digital Stereo RPCD 609
Spanier; Dave Klein (*t*); George Brunies (*tb, v*); Sam Blank (*tb*); Ted Lewis (*cl, v*); Benny Goodman (*cl, as*); Rod Kless (*cl*); Louis Martin (*as, bs*); Hymie Wolfson, Ray McKinstrey, Bernie Billings, Nick Caizza (*ts*); Fats Waller (*p, v*); George Zack, Joe Bushkin (*p*); Sam Shapiro, Sol Klein (*vn*); Tony Gerhardi, Bob Casey (*g, b*); Pat Pattison, Harry Barth (*b*); John Lucas, Marty Greenberg, Don Carter, Al Sidell (*d*). 3/31–12/39.

**** **The Great Sixteen** RCA 13039-2
Spanier; George Brunies (*tb, v*); Rod Kless (*cl*); Ray McKinstrey, Bernie Billings, Nick Caizza (*ts*); George Zack, Joe Bushkin (*p*); Bob Casey (*g, b*); Pat Pattison (*b*); Marty Greenberg, Don Carter, Al Sidell (*d*). 6–12/39.

**** **Muggsy Spanier 1939–1942** Classics 709
As above two discs, except add Ruby Weinstein, Elmer O'Brien (*t*), Ford Leary (*tb, v*), Karl Kates, Joe Forchetti, Ed Caine (*as*), Charlie Queener (*p*), Al Hammer (*d*), Dottie Reid (*v*). 7/39–6/42.

Spanier's 1939 Ragtime Band recordings are among the classic statements in the traditional-jazz idiom. Bob Crosby's Bob Cats had helped to initiate a modest vogue for small Dixieland bands in what was already a kind of revivalism at the height of the big-band era, and Spanier's group had audiences flocking to Chicago clubs, although by December, with a move to New York, they were forced to break up for lack of work. Their recordings have been dubbed 'The Great Sixteen' ever since. While there are many fine solos scattered through the sides – mostly by Spanier and the little-remembered Rod Kless – it's as an ensemble that the band impresses: allied to a boisterous rhythm section, the informal counter-point among the four horns (the tenor sax perfectly integrated, just as Eddie Miller was in The Bob Cats) swings through every performance. The repertoire re-established the norm for Dixieland bands and, even though the material goes back to Oliver and the ODJB, there's no hint of fustiness, even in the rollicking effects of 'Barnyard Blues'. 'Someday Sweetheart', with its sequence of elegant solos, is a masterpiece of cumulative tension, and Spanier himself secures two finest hours in the storming finish to 'Big Butter And Egg Man' and the wah-wah blues-playing on 'Relaxin' At The Touro', a poetic tribute to convalescence (he had been ill the previous year) the way Parker's 'Relaxin' At Camarillo' would subsequently be. His own playing is masterful throughout – the hot Chicago cornet-sound refined and seared away to sometimes the simplest but most telling of phrases.

While Robert Parker's stereo remastering may not be to all tastes, he honours the music with beautifully clear transcriptions, and as a bonus the album includes four tracks by the 1931 Ted Lewis band, with Spanier and Goodman and Fats Waller as star guests. An essential record.

The more recent RCA set, *The Great Sixteen*, includes eight alternative takes and is an intriguing alternative rather than a first choice. The Classics CD adds eight tracks to the definitive 16 by Muggsy's big band, none of them outstanding but all grist to the Spanier collector. Reproduction here is pretty good, though Parker's work remains our first choice.

James Spaulding (born 1937) ALTO SAXOPHONE, SOPRANO SAXOPHONE, FLUTES

*** **Gottabe A Better Way** Muse MCD 5413
Spaulding; Monte Croft (*vib*); Mulgrew Miller (*p*); Ralph Peterson (*d*); Ray Mantilla (*perc*). 5/88.

***(*) **Brilliant Corners** Muse MCD 5369
Spaulding; Wallace Roney (*t*); Mulgrew Miller (*p*); Ron Carter (*b*); Kenny Washington (*d*). 11/88.

***(*) **Songs Of Courage** Muse MCD 5382
Spaulding; Tyrone Jefferson (*tb*); Roland Alexander (*ts*); Kenny Barron (*p*); Ray Drummond (*b*); Louis Hayes (*d*). 10/91.

Frustratingly, Spaulding has tended to hide his considerable talent away in other people's groups. Despite a substantial recording history, taking in Sun Ra, as well Max Roach, Freddie Hubbard, Horace Silver, Stanley Turrentine and Wayne Shorter (in other words, many of the leading Blue Note artists of the classic period), he has recorded very little under his own name.

It may be that working with Sun Ra, for whom he played as a young man in the late 1950s, instilled a preference for more anonymous and collective set-ups. It's certainly still true that Spaulding functions best in larger-sized ensembles, soloing only quite sparingly and preferring to contribute to the overall texture, as he has with David Murray's Octet and even (again with Murray) as a stand-in with the World Saxophone Quartet.

Spaulding's personal diffidence is also reflected in the fact that, of the records bearing his name, two are dedicated to the work of other composers, albeit very great ones indeed. The Monk session is by far the most accomplished. Spaulding largely abandons the assortment of piccolos and bass flutes that help give *Gottabe* such a rich but unfocused sound. Playing just alto and (arguably his strongest horn) regular flute, he cuts a swath through 'Brilliant Corners', 'Little Rootie Tootie', 'I Mean You' and others with a maddening panache that leaves the listener wondering (again) why he's been so backward in coming forward before.

Roney's perhaps a little sharp to be the ideal partner – the dream ticket would have been Woody Shaw – but Miller's rich lines are exactly the kind of thing Spaulding sounds good against. It's harder to fathom his enthusiasm for the vibes, which give both the other sets a rather insubstantial, fly-away sensation. Nelson at least knows how to hold the line and accommodates himself to Walton admirably. The rather unsophisticated sound that has become a Muse staple actually serves Spaulding rather well, and better in most cases than Rudy van Gelder's more sensitive balancing act for Blue Note.

The latest of the Muses is almost a career retrospective. The association with Alexander (also a fine composer) and with Barron goes back a long way, and they use the encounter to review standard material like 'Wee', on which Spaulding delivers a scalding alto solo, and Elmo Hope's 'Minor Bertha'. Alexander's memorial to Martin Luther King Jr prompts a switch to flute for the most outstanding single performance of the session, a haunting lament that Kenny Barron answers stoically but with real emotion.

Martin Speake ALTO SAXOPHONE

*** **In Our Time** The Jazz Label TJL 005
   Speake; John Parricelli (*g*); Steve Watts (*b*); Steve Arguëlles (*d, perc*). 94.
At the time of its launch in 1994, it was hoped that The Jazz Label would provide a permanent access for young British talent which was not being picked up by more established imprints. Things have been rather quiet since a first batch of discs that included material by Colin Towns, guitarists John Etheridge and Gary Boyle, the folk-jazz Frev, and an important disc by the veteran drummer John Stevens, representing an older generation. Martin Speake's album was, of the whole bunch, the most welcome in that a young man who was widely respected and sought after as a sideman was being given a first chance to record his own material.

The only disappointment is that there hasn't been a quick sequel. Speake's writing is lively and strongly expressive, whether in the Vesala-like 'Twisted Tungo' or the darkly rhythmic tribute to 'Blackwell', the great American drummer who had recently died. Speake's alto is reminiscent of earlier British players Ray Warleigh, Stan Sulzmann and, in the freer passages, Elton Dean. The key to the group sound is the highly talented Arguëlles, a leader himself and one of the strongest musical personalities to emerge from the 'Loose Tubes generation', whatever that may be. A good strong debut. Someone pick him up, please.

Glenn Spearman (born 1947) TENOR SAXOPHONE

***(*) **Mystery Project** Black Saint 120147
   Spearman; Larry Ochs (*ts, sno*); Chris Brown (*p, D X7*); Ben Lindgren (*b*); Donald Robinson, William Winant (*d*). 8/92.
**** **Smokehouse** Black Saint 120157
   Spearman; Larry Ochs (*ts, sno*); Chris Brown (*p*); Ben Lindgren (*b*); Donald Robinson, William Winant (*d*). 11/93.
Spearman started out as a screamer in the post-Coltrane mode. A 1981 duo record with drummer Robinson was widely compared to Trane and Rashied Ali's *Interstellar Space* duets, but by that time Spearman had come under the tutelage of Frank Wright, with whom he had bunked and woodshedded in France, and it was clear that he was moving in a new direction. After recording with trumpeter Raphe Malik's sextet, Spearman founded his Double Trio.

Dedicated to Ornette Coleman (and particularly to the structured freedom of Ornette's own Double Quartet), *Mystery Project* consists of a large three-part suite, in which the direction of the music is dictated not so much by notated passages as by the distribution of personnel. As in ROVA man Larry Ochs's 'Double Image', the basic group is a palette from which various colours and shadings can be drawn. Having said that, Spearman's personal colour code would seem to be black and red. He's a fierce player, still wedded to the upper register, virtually incapable of anything less than full throttle. That it doesn't pall or sound dated is testimony to his intelligence, and that of the group. This is intense but not unsubtle music. The shifting network of instrumental sounds (with Winant and Robinson coming out of opposite channels) lends it considerable variety.

The follow-up record again makes use of doubled instruments and is organized as a long – 75-minute – suite with an intermission built in. Spearman's time in Europe opened up many interesting compositional ideas to him, but these performances are squarely in the tradition of the 1960s avant-garde, and their strength comes from his profound conviction that the ideas adumbrated at that time are far from exhausted and redundant but still constitute the *lingua franca* for improvisatory jazz today. The 'in-take' and 'out-take' of 'Axe, Beautiful Acts' exude a fierce poetry that is worthy of Cecil Taylor.

Sphere GROUP

*** **Pumpkin's Delight** Red R R 123207
  Charlie Rouse (*ts*); Kenny Barron (*p*); Buster Williams (*b*); Ben Riley (*d*). 86.
Taking its name from Thelonious Sphere Monk, Sphere was a festival supergroup for a while after the master's death, managing to sustain a repertoire based on his compositions without attempting to pastiche his sound. Barron wisely sticks to what he knows best and only very rarely throws in a direct quote; unconsciously, one suspects. Rouse's slightly adenoidal sound is always attractive, and in some respects this is his best recorded statement. Not a great record, but a thoroughly enjoyable one.

Spirit Level GROUP

*** **New Year** Future Music F M R CD 03 1290
  Tim Richards (*p, ldr*); Jerry Underwood (*ts*); Ernest Mothle (*b*); Mark Sanders (*d*). 9/90.
**** **On The Level** 33 Records 33JAZZ026
  As above, except replace Mothle with Kubryk Townshend (*b*), Sanders with Kenrick Rowe (*d*). 94.
Tim Richards's group is in the anomalous position of being better known abroad than in the United Kingdom. Richards is a strong, sometimes idiosyncratic writer, with the ability to give his musicians exactly the kind of material they need without ever sounding as though he is compromising his own vision, and being prepared to allow others to contribute as both writers and players to that vision. The group has been through a number of personnel changes over the years (a past version included Paul Dunmall on saxophones) and the process of change has continued until recently without ever seeming to affect the underlying character of a group which is more than Richards's personal vehicle. One of the authors wrote the liner-notes to *On The Level*, so our enthusiasm for it can be taken as read, and read *in situ*. The earlier record is not quite so compelling, though it shows off facets of the group – its melodism, its ability to sustain extended grooves in relatively short compass, its dynamic logic – which are slightly diffused on the more polished later disc.

The Spirits Of Rhythm GROUP

*** **The Spirits Of Rhythm, 1933–34** JSP JSPCD 307
  Teddy Bunn (*g*); Leo Watson, Wilbur Daniels, Douglas Daniels (*tipples, v*); Wilson Myers (*b*); Virgil Scroggins (*d, v*); Red McKenzie (*v*). 33–34.
The Spirits are now treasured largely for nurturing the extraordinary guitar-playing of Teddy Bunn, one of the undoubted giants of the instrument in jazz before Charlie Christian and Wes Montgomery revolutionized it, often ironically smoothing out the very features which made it different from the horns and piano. No less – and no less improbable – a personage than improviser Derek Bailey has pointed to Bunn as an early influence. The Spirits were, however, essentially a singing group, not quite a novelty act but not a million miles from it. Watson and the two Daniels boys sang jovial scat lines, accompanying themselves on tipples (jumbo ukuleles), while Bunn kept up a solid but ever-changing background. Like Freddy Guy, for whom he once depped in the Ellington band, and Freddie Green, who did a similar job for Basie, he understood the workings of a group instinctively and, despite being wholly self-taught, had the uncanny ability to anticipate even non-standard changes.

The JSP set contains material from six sessions over a single twelve-month period. There are two versions of 'I Got Rhythm', both of them featuring Bunn quite strongly; but the outstanding track is 'I'll Be Ready' on which be plays crisp melodic breaks without a single excess gesture. The last few tracks come from a September 1934 session dominated by the doubtful talents of Red McKenzie. These are eminently dispensable.

Spontaneous Music Ensemble GROUP

***(*) **Summer 1967** Emanem 4005
> Evan Parker (*ts, ss*); Peter Kowald (*b*); John Stevens (*d*). 67.

**** **Karyobin** Chronoscope CPE 2001
> Kenny Wheeler (*t, flhn*); Evan Parker (*ss*); Derek Bailey (*g*); Dave Holland (*b*); John Stevens (*d*). 2/68.

**** **Face To Face** Emanem 4003
> Trevor Watts (*as*); John Stevens (*d*). 73.

*** **Hot And Cold Heroes** Emanem 4008
> Nigel Coombes (*vn*); Roger Smith (*g*); John Stevens (*d*). 80, 91.

**** **A New Distance** Acta 8
> John Butcher (*ts, ss*); Roger Smith (*g*); John Stevens (*d*). 1 & 5/94.

Asked recently, 25 years on, to say what had been important to him about 1968, Derek Bailey made the typically perceptive and clear-sighted point that the year of revolutions had really made much less difference to the way things were, in either politics or culture, than a whole string of dates in the previous decade. For admirers of British improvised music, though, 1968 saw the emergence of the SME from the rather constricting cocoon of 'free jazz' into an approach that placed all its weight on a collectively generated, non-hierarchical sound with no preconceived structures of any sort.

As if to confirm Bailey's argument, the earliest of these goes back a half-step in time. *Summer 1967* is significant not just in documenting one of Evan Parker's earliest recordings; it also preserves his and Stevens's first meeting with a player whom both were later to credit with opening up whole new areas of improvisational language to them. Kowald is a central figure in the European free movement, a gener-ous, open-minded player who never for a moment stops listening to what is going on around him. This doesn't happen in a confrontationl-conversational way, but with a constant awareness of what is going on in what Stevens was later to describe, using an analogy from his other art-form, as 'peripheral vision', an ability to pick up fleeting clues and render them as significant as the apparent focal point. That to a degree is what the SME has always been about, whatever its exact personnel and instrumentation.

The first significant product of the SME's change in philosophy – not dictated by the group's catalyst, John Stevens, but certainly determined by changes in his philosophy and approach – was *Karyobin*, a strikingly light-toned and unaggressive exploration of group identity that lasts 49 minutes but contains within it arrays and patterns of musical sound which suggest infinity. The title is the collective name of the birds who inhabit paradise, living in harmony with one another. *Karyobin* has been a collectors' item on vinyl for many years. It transfers to CD pretty well, de-emphasizing the horns and drums slightly and letting Holland and Bailey come through with a bit more definition.

A few years further on, SME was functioning as a duo. Stevens and Watts were later to part company, somewhat acrimoniously, but for the duration of their partnership they created music of astonishing harmoniousness; 'harmony' would be the wrong word. Again, it is the delicacy of Stevens's percussion that is notable, while Watts's keening cries have an emotional pull that makes nonsense of attempts to re-label this sort of music 'abstract'. Small wonder that so many of these players were profoundly affected by the work of Samuel Beckett, in whom abstraction and the most passionate humanitarianism were wedded.

There is at this point something of a jump in the documentation, and the final two items belong to a rather later SME. If the Stevens–Parker, Stevens–Watts axes were critical to earlier incarnations, those roles have more recently been taken by another saxophonist, John Butcher, and by guitarist Roger Smith, a musician of intense focus and awareness. They appear together on *A New Distance*, the most recent of the batch, which includes two London performances just a few months apart and in the last months of Stevens's life. Butcher's playing on both occasions is exceptional, gleaming with intelligence and a wonderful reserve.

Of all the players associated with the group, the one who seems most wholly defined by the experience, and yet the one constitutionally least adjusted to its collectivist, ego-less philosophy, is Coombes. The material on *Hot And Cold Heroes*, unlike the other records, has not been available before. Despite its obvious importance, it lacks their sheer impact and should perhaps not be considered a priority find. *Karyobin* and *A New Distance* are, in our view, essential.

Jess Stacy (1904–94) PIANO

**** Jess Stacy 1935–1939 Classics 795

Stacy; Billy Butterfield (*t*); Les Jenkins (*tb*); Hank D'Amico, Irving Fazola (*cl*); Eddie Miller, Bud Freeman (*ts*); Allen Hanlon (*g*); Israel Crosby, Sid Weiss (*b*); Gene Krupa, Don Carter (*d*); Carlotta Dale (*v*). 11/35–11/39.

**** Ec-Stacy ASV AJA 5172

Stacy; Bobby Hackett, Muggsy Spanier (*c*); Charlie Teagarden, Harry James, Ziggy Elman, Chris Griffin, Yank Lawson, Lyman Vunk, Max Herman, Billy Butterfield, Pee Wee Irwin, Anthony Natoli, Nate Kazebier, Bunny Berigan, Ralph Muzillo (*t*); Floyd O'Brien, Red Ballard, Joe Harris, Murray McEachern, Elmer Smithers, Buddy Morrow, Will Bradley, Jack Satterfield (*tb*); Benny Goodman; Johnny Hodges, Pee Wee Russell, Danny Polo, Hymie Schertzer, Bill De Pew, Dick Clark, Arthur Rollini, George Koenig, Vido Musso, Bud Freeman, Dave Mathews, Noni Bernardi, Matty Matlock, Art Mendelsohn, Eddie Miller, Gil Rodin, Sal Franzella, Henry Ross, Larry Binyon, Julius Bradley, Arthur Rando (*reeds*); Nappy Lamare, Allan Reuss, Frank Worrell, Ben Heller (*g*); Israel Crosby, Sid Wess, Artie Shapiro, Harry Goodman, Bob Haggart (*b*); Specs Powell, Gene Krupa, George Wettling, Ray Bauduc, Mario Toscarelli, Buddy Schutz (*d*); Lee Wiley (*v*). 11/35–6/45.

One of the great piano masters of the 1930s gets his due at last with these two very strong compilations of his early work. There is a duplication of three of the early solo pieces, but the chronological Classics compilation concentrates on Commodore and Varsity material from 1938–9, while the ASV disc covers sideman work with Benny Goodman, Bob Crosby, Lionel Hampton, Bud Freeman and Pee Wee Russell for an exceptionally well-rounded portrait of a man who appeared in many interesting situations. His unassuming virtuosity went with a deceptively romantic streak – 'the intensity of Hines with the logic of Bix', as Vic Bellerby puts it – and his impeccable touch and undercurrent of blues feeling, even if tempered by a rather civilized irony, give him a rare position among the piano players of the era. The Classics set includes two splendid blues-based fantasies in 'Ramblin'' and 'Complainin'', the excellent solo session from 1939 and two engaging band dates, while the ASV offers several rarities, including an aircheck version of Beiderbecke's 'In A Mist', three 1944 duets with Specs Powell and the beautiful 'Down To Steamboat Tennessee' with Muggsy Spanier and Lee Wiley. Transfers are mostly very fair. Both discs are a strongly recommended portrait of a remarkable personality.

*** Stacy Still Swings Chiaroscuro CR(D) 133

Stacy (*p* solo). 7/74–7/77.

The veteran Condonite (as he later became) quit professional music in the 1950s but came back to festivals and studios very occasionally. This congenial, easy-going set of solos was among the last he made: nothing much has changed over the years except the tempos, and even then he was never exactly a tornado at the keyboard. His own tunes, such as 'Lookout Mountain Squirrels', are charming but robust; his standards are an old-fashioned choice.

Tomasz Stańko (born 1942) TRUMPET

*** Music For K Power Bros 00131

Stańko; Zbigniew Seifert (*as*); Janusz Muniak (*ts*); Bronislaw Suchanek (*b*); Janusz Stefanski (*d*). 1/70.

***(*) Balladyna ECM 1071

Stańko; Tomasz Szukalski (*ts, ss*); Dave Holland (*b*); Edward Vesala (*d*). 12/75.

Stańko's music sounds at first as if it bears closer kinship to the abstract experimentalism of the Polish avant-garde than to orthodox or even free jazz. This is deceptive, for the trumpeter is deeply versed in all the defining elements of jazz. Stańko's first big influence was Chet Baker, though subsequently Miles Davis was to become his bellwether, both as a player and for his whole-hearted dedication to life-as-art. Totally free playing has, perhaps surprisingly, never played a large part in Polish jazz. Even when the setting is ostensibly abstract, there is still an underlying jazz 'feel', expressible both as a pulse and as dimly familiar harmonies and structures.

Though the important sessions for Edward Vesala's Leo Records in Finland have not reappeared on CD, the even earlier *Music For K* has been revived and welcomed. It is a forceful, sometimes inchoate session, with as much emphasis on Seifert's raw, emotive alto (this is before the ill-fated young genius made his shift to violin) as on the leader. The rhythm section leaves something to be desired but, with no harmony instrument, they are handed a pretty hefty task. 'Cry' is the closest thing to American jazz of the time, but it is 'Music For K', dedicated to the late Krzysztof Komeda (*q.v.*), that really establishes Stańko's credentials as a composer and *auteur*. He dominates this piece entirely, even when not in the spotlight, and it points unmistakably forward to the quieter, slower conception that he shares with the Finnish percussionist, Edward Vesala (*q.v.*), who joins him on the 1974 disc.

Stańko had jammed with Vesala some time previously and shyly revealed himself as a composer. *Twet* is a collaborative project, with most of the material improvised in the studio. Nonetheless, Stańko can be heard imposing his stamp on it and the two long pieces, 'Dark Awakening' and 'Man From North', have to be heard as dialogues between trumpeter and drummer. Stańko's breakthrough album came with *Balladyna*, which used a near-identical line-up. Szukalski is a workmanlike player with, one suspects, a somewhat limited range. Stańko was fortunate in his other colleagues, however. Vesala too is cautious in his approach to free music, but Holland seems to move between freedom and structure without a blink. The collectively written 'Tale' is rather weak, but Vesala's 'Num', three more Stańko compositions, and an improvised duet with Holland give the record (which reappeared on CD in time to mark the trumpeter's thirtieth year as a musician) a sizeable impact.

*** **The Montreux Performance** ITM 1423
 Stańko; Janusz Skowron (*p, syn*); Witold E. Szczurek (*b*); Tadeusz Sudnik (*syn, elec*). 7/87.
***(*) **Tales For A Girl, 12 / A Shaky Chica** Jam CD 0891
 Stańko; Janusz Skowron (*syn*). 4 & 10/91.
Freelectronic was Stańko's regular band during the mid-1980s. Most of their work was available only on Polish vinyl labels, but *The Montreux Performance* gives a fair impression of their live act. In the absence of a percussionist, Szczurek provides much of the impetus on both string and electric basses. Skowron alternates piano and synths but places even electronic keyboards quite naturally, and the slightly treacherous atmospherics are largely down to Sudnik's switcher boards and computer-driven keys.

The weirdly titled *Tales For A Girl* actually consists of 12 fragments of musical narrative with 'A Shaky Chica' tacked on as an end-piece. The tales reflect Stańko's longstanding interest in literature and poetic language as 'codes' that can be used to shape and frame improvised performance. Skowron's freehand synth outlines are little more than notional backgrounds on which Stańko inscribes unusually terse, gnomic phrases and the occasional longer idea, like the 'Mystery Tale'. The duo clearly belongs in the same basic area as Freelectronic but is actually much more interesting. This one may be harder to track down, but it's well worth the additional effort.

***(*) **Bluish** Power Bros 00113
 Stańko; Arild Andersen (*b*); Jon Christensen (*b*). 10/91.
A marvellous record from the Rybnik-based label, which deserves the widest distribution. Paired with northern Europe's premier rhythm section (with Andersen alone on the opening 'Dialogue', a latterday version of the duet with Holland on *Balladyna*), Stańko seems content to work a long way clear of any fixed measure. The title-piece begins on a more straightforward metre but compensates with a curiously unresolved harmonic profile and breaks down into a superb solo from Christensen, heralded by hesitations and silences.

Part two of 'If You Look Enough' (it comes first for some reason) is an eerie, out-of-tempo meditation, punctuated by smears and growls. The first part (placed last in the set) features the same chordal effects, which may be processed bass, and a nagging, insect-like chitter from Christensen. The drummer creates remarkable effects with damped cymbals on the long 'Bosanetta', a tune that recalls one of Vesala's pastiches, as does the succeeding 'Third Heavy Ballad', on which Stańko plays with a quiet lyricism that will suggest Kenny Wheeler to many listeners.

*** **Caoma** Konnex KCD 5053
 Stańko; Sigi Finkel (*ts, ss, f, p*); Ed Schuller (*b*); Billy Elgart (*d*). 12/91.
Perhaps Stańko went to the well once too often in this remarkable year. This is perfectly fine on its own terms, but it comes as a bit of a disappointment after the excellence of *Bluish*. Finkel muddies the pond a bit and both Schuller and Elgart are definitely switched into a more orthodox idiom than the trumpeter, leaving the session awkwardly suspended. Enthusiasts for Stańko will doubtless find much to enjoy and to ponder; others might do well to pass for now.

**** **Bosanossa And Other Ballads** GOWI CDG 08
 Stańko; Bobo Stenson (*p*); Anders Jormin (*b*); Tony Oxley (*d, perc*). 3 & 4/93.
*** **Matka Joanna** ECM 1544
 As above. 5/94.
Stańko and another northern European rhythm section with a set of soft, quasi-harmonic themes which was one of the highlights of the 1993 Jazz Jamboree in Warsaw. Most of the material had been around for some considerable time. 'Sunia' was a staple of Freelectronic sets and is included on *The Montreux Performance*. This version is pretty well definitive, however, with Oxley's metallic patterns an integral element. The Englishman resembles Vesala in his ability to register strong metres in otherwise free settings, but he is a lighter, more abstract player and ideal for this material. It makes sense to have a piano player rather than a second horn on the session. Bobo Stenson brings an uneasy cast to

'Maldoror's Love Song' and 'Die Weisheit Von Isidore Ducasse', two pieces derived from Stańko's interest in the proto-surrealist, Lautréamont. The trumpeter uses a big, unfettered tone and long, sinuous lines that anticipate and overlap the pianist's statements by several bars. A wonderful record from a musician who deserves much wider attention.

The quartet's follow-up on ECM is something of a disappointment, to be frank. Some reviewers mistakenly assumed that this music was written as a soundtrack to Jerzy Kawalerowicz's film *Matka Joanna od Aniolow*, but this is an older work, made in 1960, and Stańko uses it only to generate 'images' for the group. Whether this turned out to be constraining rather than fruitful isn't entirely clear. Oxley is the stand-out performer, beautifully abstract but always absolutely focused. In comparison to his work on the earlier record, Stenson sounds a little uncertain, and often does little more than shadow the leader's poignant keening and wailing. A lovely record by any standard, but very much a re-run; with such creative musicians on hand, we had reason to expect a little more.

Jeremy Steig (born 1942) FLUTE, PICCOLO, ALTO FLUTE, BASS FLUTE, ELECTRONICS

**** Outlaws Enja 2098
    Steig; Eddie Gomez (*b*). 12/76.
*** Something Else LRC CDC 8512
    Steig; Jan Hammer (*electric p, gongs*); Eddie Gomez (*b*); Gene Perla (*b*); Don Alias (*d, perc*).

A virtuoso performer on all the flutes, Steig has greatly expanded the instrument's performing range by incorporating a range of unorthodox devices into his playing and writing. These include finger and pad noises, audible breathing and, in a manner reminiscent of Roland Kirk, fierce overblowing. Some of these effects were becoming part of contemporary concert music for flute (like Brian Ferneyhough's unaccompanied piece, *Unity Capsule*) and Steig has shown an interest in that genre; his third album with regular associate, Eddie Gomez, is an example of latter-day Third Stream.

Steig's interest in electronics, though, comes not so much from the avant-garde as from jazz–rock. Joachim Berendt cites his now largely forgotten 1970s band, Jeremy and the Satyrs, as an influence on the fusion movement, and there are elements of a more populist cross-over on *Something Else*. (The resemblance of title to Ornette Coleman's emphatically revolutionary *Something Else!* is quite incidental.)

Steig's duets with Gomez are very effective, utilizing extremes of sonority and sophisticated structures. The earliest, *Outlaws*, is the most obviously jazz-centred and includes two beautifully redrafted standards, 'Autumn Leaves' and 'Nardis'. Much of the rest of their work together moved in apparently irreconcilable directions, towards greater formal abstraction and towards a strict-tempo immediacy.

An adventurous and technically remarkable player, Steig has yet to break through to a wider audience. That shouldn't put anyone off.

Leni Stern GUITAR

***(*) Clairvoyant Passport PJ 88015
    Stern; Bob Berg (*ts*); Bill Frisell (*g*); Larry Willis (*p*); Harvie Swartz (*b*); Paul Motian (*d*). 12/85.
***(*) Secrets Enja 5093
    Stern; Bob Berg (*ts*); Wayne Krantz, Dave Tronzo (*g*); Lincoln Goines, Harvie Swartz (*g*);
    Dennis Chambers (*d*); Don Alias (*perc*). 9 & 10/88.
**** Closer To The Light Enja 6034
    Stern; David Sanborn (*as*); Wayne Krantz (*g*); Lincoln Goines, Paul Socolow (*b*); Dennis
    Chambers, Zachary Danziger (*d*); Don Alias (*perc*). 11 & 12/89.

Stern quickly backed out of the fusion *cul-de-sac* to create albums of subtle presence that depend on interplay rather than very sophisticated themes. Perhaps oddly (or perhaps because she rejects conventional axe-man *machismo*), she has preferred to surround herself with other, often more dominant guitarists (Frisell on *Clairvoyant* and her established duo partner, Wayne Krantz, on the excellent *Secrets*). Krantz's title-track on the latter is one of the few false notes: a busy, hectic theme that overpowers the band. Stern herself works best with easy-paced melodies and settings that leave room for delicate, spontaneous touches. Though Frisell and Motian seem admirably suited to that intention, *Clairvoyant* is slightly uneasy in execution, and Berg's contributions seem much less appropriate than on the later record. Sanborn, perhaps surprisingly, fits in much better on his two tracks on the well-balanced *Closer* (which also seems to have been released as *Phoenix*). Stern's duos with Krantz and the two-guitar quartets (with Goines and Chambers or Socolow and Danziger backing them) are the best she's committed to record so far.

** **Ten Songs** Lipstick LIP 890092
>   Stern; Bob Malach (*ts*); Billy Drewes (*ss*); Gil Goldstein (*ky*); Wayne Krantz (*g*); Alain Caron,
>   Michael Formanek, Lincoln Goines (*b*); Dennis Chambers, Rodney Homes (*d*); Donal Alias
>   (*perc*); Badal Roy (*tablas, perc*). 10/91.

Stern was a more interesting player on her earlier, bare-faced sessions, with their scrubbed-down sound.
For the Lipstick set, she's given herself a rather blowsy funk sound, with every instrument puffed up and
over-loud. The two best tunes are credited to Wayne Krantz; 'Our Man's Gone Now' sounds as if it
might be a tribute to Miles, who is (or, rather, Marcus Miller is) the main influence on the arrangements;
'If Anything' features Stern on her Spanish and slide guitars, which are consistently her most effective
instruments (only Sonny Sharrock has made a more developed use of slide guitar in a jazz context). A
rather inconsequential set that somehow reflects the slightly throwaway title.

Mike Stern (born 1954) GUITAR

*** **Time In Place** Atlantic 781840-2
>   Stern; Bob Berg, Michael Brecker (*ts*); Don Grolnick (*org*); Jim Beard (*ky*); Jeff Andrews (*b*);
>   Peter Erskine (*d*); Don Alias (*perc*). 12/87.
(*) **Jigsaw Atlantic 782027-2
>   Stern; Bob Berg (*ts*); Jim Beard (*ky*); Jeff Andrews (*b*); Peter Erskine, Dennis Chambers (*d*);
>   Manolo Badrena (*perc*). 2/89.
*** **Odds And Ends** Atlantic 82297-2
>   As above, except add Lincoln Goines, Anthony Jackson (*b*), Ben Perowsky (*d*), Don Alias
>   (*perc*), omit Andrews, Erskine and Badrena. 91.
***(*) **Standards (And Other Songs)** Atlantic 782419-2
>   Stern; Randy Brecker (*t*); Bob Berg (*ts*); Gil Goldstein (*ky*); Jay Anderson, Larry Grenadier (*b*);
>   Ben Perowsky (*d*). 92.
***(*) **Is What It Is** Atlantic 82571-2
>   Stern; Michael Brecker, Bob Malach (*ts*); Jim Beard (*ky*); Will Lee, Harvie Swartz (*b*); Ben
>   Perowsky, Dennis Chambers (*d*). 93.
*** **Between The Lines** Atlantic 82835-2
>   Stern; Bob Malach (*ts*); Jim Beard (*ky*); Lincoln Goines, Jeff Andrews (*b*); Dave Weckl, Dennis
>   Chambers (*d*). 95.

First impressions of Stern were unfortunate, since he seemed set on treating the Miles Davis group of
the early 1980s as a jazz-metal band while working out a sideman tenure. His albums for Atlantic are
much more palatable, pushing through the kind of muscular, musicianly fusion which is the standard
alternative to the wispy variety suggested by Windham Hill's roster. The problem, as usual, is the
material, which is little more than a springboard for solos – and these are tidy and intermittently
powerful (especially Berg's) on the earlier sets. Chambers and Erskine provide other interest with their
interactive parts but, while the band acquired a substantial reputation on the live circuit, it's too much a
rational and unsurprising group in the studios. *Odds And Ends* turned out to be plenty more of the same,
with a slight sharpening of focus on both material and studio sound, but the following *Standards (And
Other Songs)* recast Stern as a 'serious' improviser at the moment when he might have drifted back
towards jazz-metal. Instead, with seven standard jazz or show tunes dominating the programme, Stern
cooled off the pace without surrendering all his fire-power. His best solos here have a fluency and
resonance that might have got him his job with Davis in the first place. *Is What It Is* returns to original
themes: Jim Beard's production orchestrates the keyboards and rhythm instruments into a thick, almost
juicy, studio mix, which Stern's guitar noses through and occasionally screams over. Brecker and
Malach lend heavyweight sax support, but the fundamental text is attractively lyrical in tunes such as
'What I Meant To Say'. *Between The Lines*, again produced by Beard, follows a similar path, though
there's a sense of diminishing returns, and, while the record scores big on texture, individual parts don't
really impress beyond a surface attraction. It also goes on for too long, at 70 minutes. But 'Wing And A
Prayer' at least is among the prettiest tunes Stern has given us.

John Stevens (1940–94) DRUMS, PERCUSSION, BUGLE

*** **A Luta Continua** Konnex LC 5056
>   Stevens; Jon Corbett (*t, tb*); Alan Tomlinson (*tb*); Paul Rutherford (*tb, euph*); Robert Calvert
>   (*ts*); Trevor Watts (*as, ss*); Lol Coxhill (*ss*); Elton Dean (*saxello*); Dave Cole, Nigel Moyse,
>   Martin Holder, Tim Stone, Mark Hewins (*g*); John Martyn (*g, v*); Jeff Young (*org*); Paul
>   Rogers, Nick Stephens, Ron Herman, Andre Holmes (*b*); Francis Dixon, Richie Stevens (*perc*);
>   Pepi Lemer (*v*). 5/77, 10/79, 12/81.

*** **Mutual Benefit** Konnex LC 8718
> Stevens; Jon Corbett (*t*); Robert Calvert (*ts, ss*); Nigel Moyse, Tim Stone (*g*); Jeff Young (*p, org*); Ron Herman, Nick Stephens (*b*). 5/77, 12/78, 5/80.

*** **Touching On** Konnex KCD 5023
> Stevens; John Calvin (*sax*); Dave Cole, Allan Holdsworth, Nigel Moyse (*g*); Jeff Young (*p*); Ron Mathewson, Nick Stephens (*b*).

**** **New Cool** The Jazz Label TJL 006
> Stevens; Byron Wallen (*t*); Ed Jones (*ts*); Gary Crosby (*b*). 8/92.

Stevens was an agile and forceful drummer, a protean figure who seemed at ease in a bewildering range of musics, from hard-edged free improvisation, through semi-rock and traditional jazz, and even latterly encompassing classical composition. He was also a gifted educator, who has left his mark on a whole generation of young British players. He came from an art school background, and several CD covers bear witness to his skill as a graphic artist. Initially inspired by Phil Seamen, his most obvious stylistic debts are to Kenny Clarke's proto-bop and to Elvin Jones. His Spontaneous Music Ensemble/Orchestra (see separate entry) was one of the most influential improvising groups of the period, while other Stevens groups, Splinters, the rock-defined Away and the Dance Orchestra, were more concerned with pre-structured forms. Stevens, it has to be said, claimed never to see any difference.

As often happens, he has been better represented on record since his death than at any time since the late 1960s, an irony that probably wouldn't have troubled him in the slightest. The Dance Orchestra tracks on *A Luta Continua* (the war-cry of the Portuguese anti-fascist movement) embrace groups of very different sizes; like SME, the Orchestra was always intended to be a flexible ensemble, the only constants being Stevens, trumpeter Jon Corbett and saxophonist Trevor Watts, who was co-leader of SME. As always, and unusually in free-jazz circles, Stevens put considerable emphasis on vocals, and the October 1979 tracks that make up about half the disc even include parts by folk-rocker John Martyn. There is also an unexpected emphasis on guitar, sometimes used as a conventional harmony instrument (Stevens only rarely called on a piano player, though he liked to feature Jeff Young on organ), sometimes as on 'Birds' used quite abstractly.

Though *Mutual Benefit* is nominally an Away record, there is considerable overlap between the two, both in style and personnel (and two tracks from the same May 1977 recording session). Stevens's crisp, almost militaristic accents create passages of dissipated melody over which the other players are relatively free to improvise. The striking thing about his playing is that he was always able to give the sense – or illusion – of a regular metre or pulse, even when it was clear from the most casual listening that what Stevens was playing was anything but regular. It is easy to be seduced by parts of *Mutual Benefit* into thinking that not much is going on, but, like Ornette Coleman's experiments with electric groups, there is a great deal of complexity behind the rather one-dimensional exterior.

Touching On is a free-ish jazz–rock session that reflects Stevens's talents only inadequately. Perhaps the most interesting tracks are those featuring Allan Holdsworth, one of many artists who receive a dedication on *Mutual Benefit*. This process was far from incidental or *ex post facto* to Stevens. Almost everything he did, whether it was with long-standing colleagues like Trevor Watts or with college students, was specifically designed with individuals in mind.

To the very end of his life, Stevens continued to bring forward gifted young players. The SME evolved constantly, as its specific ethos demanded, but so too did his other groups, and *New Cool*, recorded at the Crawley Jazz Festival, is an excellent example of how seriously he took his mission to lead younger musicians at an accelerated pace through some of the major epiphanies of his own career. Of the four tracks, two are reworkings of Ornette and John Coltrane material, 'Ramblin'' and 'Lonnie's Lament' respectively. The listener doesn't need to be aware of this to enjoy or appreciate this music, which is immensely accessible, but it adds a significant dimension once the connection becomes obvious. As always, Stevens is thinking about old friends as well, in this case the two South Africans, Johnny Mbizo Dyani and Dudu Pukwana, whose own early deaths he was to echo all too soon thereafter.

Grant Stewart (born 1971) TENOR SAXOPHONE

*** **Downtown Sounds** Criss Cross CRISS 1085
> Stewart; Joe Magnarelli (*t*); Brad Mehldau (*p*); Peter Washington (*b*); Kenny Washington (*d*). 12/92.

Criss Cross Promising Young Tenor No. 47; or so it seems. Stewart is Canadian, raised in Toronto and influenced in the main by Pat LaBarbera and Bob Mover. At 21, he sounds very confident but in no hurry to force his own interpretations too hard. This is a solid repertoire session, with an interesting spin. One doesn't hear Rollins's 'Audobahn', Strayhorn's 'Smada', 'Daydream' and 'Intimacy Of The Blues', or Cole Porter's 'From This Moment On' on a young man's record. He tackles them all with modesty and some aplomb, unfazed by the twists and turns of Parker's 'Ko-Ko', but more at ease with medium tempo pieces that sit more comfortably for his relaxed, Wardell Gray-like tenor sound. A bit early to command much expressive authority, but plenty of time to work on that.

Rex Stewart (1907–67) CORNET, KAZOO, VOCALS

*** **Duke Ellington's Trumpets** Black and Blue BLE 59.231
> Stewart; Louis Bacon, Freddy Jenkins (*t*); Tricky Sam Nanton (*tb*); Barney Bigard (*cl*); Johnny Hodges (*as*); Harry Carney (*bs*); Duke Ellington (*p*); Brick Fleagle (*g*); Hayes Alvis, Billy Taylor (*b*); Sonny Greer, Jack Maisel (*d*). 7/37, 3/39.

***(*) **Rex Stewart And The Ellingtonians** Original Jazz Classics OJC 1710
> Stewart; Lawrence Brown (*tb*); Barney Bigard (*cl*); Billy Kyle (*p*); Brick Fleagle (*g*); Wellman Braud, John Levy (*b*); Cozy Cole, Dave Tough (*d*). 7/40, 46.

*** **Trumpet Jive!** Prestige PCD 24119
> Stewart; Tyree Glenn (*tb, vib*); Earl Bostic (*as*); Cecil Scott (*ts, bs*); John Dengler (*bsx, wbd, kazoo*); Wilbert Kirk (*hca, perc*); Dave Rivera (*p*); Jerome Darr, Brick Fleagle, Chauncey Westbrook (*g*); Junior Raglin (*b*); J. C. Heard, Charles Lampkin (*d*). 7/45, 3/60.

**** **Chatter Jazz** RCA 2118525
> Stewart; Dicky Wells (*tb*); John Bunch (*p*); Leonard Gaskin (*b*); Charles Master Paolo (*d*). 1/59.

The poet John Keats once wrote about the way very great artists erect a Great Wall across their respective genres, Shakespeare in the drama, Milton in the poetic epic. For trumpeters of the 1920s, Louis Armstrong fell into that category. His achievement was so primal and so pre-eminent that it was extraordinarily difficult to see a way round or over it. Rex Stewart, a self-confessed Armstrong slave (though he also loved Bix), experienced the problem more directly than most when he took over Armstrong's chair in the Fletcher Henderson orchestra.

In reaction to the inevitable but invidious comparisons, Stewart developed his distinctive 'half-valving' technique. By depressing the trumpet keys to mid-positions, he was able to generate an astonishing and sometimes surreal chromaticism which, though much imitated, has only really resurfaced with the avant-garde of the 1960s. As a maverick, Stewart was ideal for the Ellington orchestra of the mid-1930s, though the Black and Blue sessions seem, despite the august company, to step back a generation to the sound of the Hot Sevens. Stewart was never to lose that loyalty. On the Prestige, he can be heard singing in obvious (and authentic) imitation of Pops, but also taking in a good deal of what he had learnt with Henderson.

It was probably from Django Reinhardt, with whom he recorded, that Stewart first heard the Hot Club staple, 'Nagasaki'; the cornetist returned to it in 1960, as part of the *Happy Jazz* session repackaged with Wingy Manone material on Prestige. (*Trumpet Jive!* was the name of a Manone LP.)

The RCA comes pretty late in the story, but Rex had developed a seemingly effortless route round his own limitations and could still put on a show. The chemistry with Wells was spot on, and this is one of his most engaging records of any period.

Stewart's vocalized style had few imitators, though Clark Terry gave it a more contemporary slant, bridging the gap with the modernists. In later life, Stewart became one of the most persuasive writers on jazz and his *Jazz Masters of the '30s* is required reading for students of the period. His ability to give convincing demonstrations of changes in trumpet playing became a component of his act, and the later, Rudy van Gelder-recorded session on *Trumpet Jive!* is just such a date, with Stewart sending himself up on his own 'Rasputin' and 'Tell Me'.

Slam Stewart (born 1914) DOUBLE BASS, VOICE

***(*) **Slam Stewart** Black & Blue 233027
> Stewart; Milt Buckner, Wild Bill Davis (*p*); Al Casey (*g*); Jo Jones, Joe Marshall (*d*). 4/71, 6/72.

*** **Fish Scales** Black & Blue 233109
> Stewart; Wild Bill Davis, Johnny Guarnieri, Gene Rodgers (*p*); Al Casey, Jimmy Shirley (*g*); Jo Jones, Joe Marshall, Jackie Williams (*d*). 3/75, 7/72.

*** **Two Big Mice** Black & Blue 59.124
> Stewart; Major Holley (*b, v*); Hank Jones (*p*); George Duvivier (*b*); Oliver Jackson (*d*). 7/77.

*** **Shut Yo' Mouth** Delos 1024
> Stewart; Major Holley (*b, v*); Oliver Jackson (*d*).

Stewart was already a star when he appeared in the movie, *Stormy Weather*, in 1943. During the 1930s he had been a stalwart of the New York scene, playing with Art Tatum and forming an evergreen partnership (love it, hate it; it sold records) with Slim Gaillard which exploited the less serious side of

Stewart's virtuosic self-harmonizing on bass and vocals. However corny he now seems, few modern bass players have taken up the technical challenge Stewart posed (though Major Holley had a stab and joins up with his role-model on *Two Big Mice*), and the purely musical aspects of his work are of abiding value.

The very oddity of Stewart's technique is initially off-putting, but on repeated listening its complexities begin to make an impact. Best to stick to the two excellent Black & Blue CDs from the later stages of Stewart's active career. Much of the manic energy has gone, but 'The Flat Foot Floogie' (a massive hit with Gaillard; Ronald Reagan could remember the words even when he couldn't remember whether or not he'd ever met Oliver North) is as nutty as it always was, while the versions of 'On Green Dolphin Street' and 'All The Things You Are' (all three from *Slam Stewart*) are absolutely impeccable modern standards performances. Perhaps more of *Fish Scales* is given over to comedy material, but 'Willow Weep For Me' with Davis, Casey and Marshall is genuinely affecting.

It's perhaps a shame that Stewart wasn't able – or didn't choose – to record with more of the younger modern bassists. If Mingus and Pettiford are now thought to have set the instrument free, much of what they did was already implicit in Stewart's work of the 1930s. The *Two Big Mice* sessions, which include fine trio performances under Holley's name, suggest how productive such encounters could have been. (See also under Slim Gaillard.)

G. E. Stinson GUITAR

***(*) **The Same Without You** Nine Winds NWCD 0154
    Stinson; John Fumo (*t*); Steuart Liebig (*b*); Alex Cline (*d*). 2/92.
Stinson bolsters his guitar sound with a battery of effects – his favourite setting seems to be hugely reverberant sustain, washed down with a variety of fuzz tones. But hardnose improvisers like Fumo and Cline leaven any suggestion that this might be an ersatz rock record. The quartet sometimes get lost in the long, rambling structures, especially the massive 'Oklahoma Elegy', but four-way improvisations like 'Mr Spoonful' and 'Goin' For The Jar' have real substance and none of the post-mod posturings that this kind of instrumentation has recently lost out to elsewhere. Cline has never supplied a rockier beat, but he's as much a master of that as he is of jazz time.

Sonny Stitt (1924–82) ALTO, TENOR AND BARITONE SAXOPHONES

*** **Sonny Stitt / Bud Powell / J. J. Johnson** Original Jazz Classics OJC 009
    Stitt; J. J. Johnson (*tb*); Bud Powell, John Lewis (*p*); Curley Russell, Nelson Boyd (*b*); Max Roach (*d*). 10/49–1/50.
(*) **Prestige First Sessions Vol. 2 Prestige 24115
    Stitt; Al Outcalt, Matthew Gee (*tb*); Gene Ammons (*bs*); Kenny Drew, Duke Jordan, Junior Mance, Clarence Anderson (*p*); Tommy Potter, Earl May, Gene Wright (*b*); Art Blakey, Teddy Stewart, Wesley Landers, Jo Jones (*d*); Larry Townsend (*v*). 2/50–8/51.
*** **Kaleidoscope** Original Jazz Classics OJC 060
    Stitt; Bill Massey, Joe Newman (*t*); Kenny Drew, Charles Bateman, Junior Mance, John Houston (*p*); Tommy Potter, Gene Wright, Ernie Shepard (*b*); Art Blakey, Teddy Stewart, Shadow Wilson (*d*); Humberto Morales (*perc*). 2/50–2/52.
Considering the size of his discography – there are at least 100 albums under Stitt's own name – the saxophonist has relatively little left in the catalogue, although the desultory nature of many of his records suggests that perhaps it is better this way. Stitt took every opportunity to record, often with undistinguished pick-up groups, and while his impassive professionalism meant that he seldom sounded less than strong, his records need careful sifting to find him genuinely at his best. Originally, he was acclaimed as a rival to Charlie Parker, and the derivation of his style – which may have been arrived at quite independently of Bird – is a famously moot point. Whatever the case, by the time of the 1949 sessions on OJC 009, he was in complete command of the bop vocabulary and playing with quite as much skill as any man in the milieu. This disc finds him exclusively on tenor, which he plays with a rather stony tone but no lack of energy. Powell contributes some superb playing on such up-tempo pieces as 'All God's Children Got Rhythm', and the 1950 group with Johnson and Lewis, though less obviously hot, finds Stitt at his best on the urgent improvisation on 'Afternoon In Paris'. Both the Prestige collection and *Kaleidoscope* bring together bits and pieces from the early days of the label and, though some of the tracks sound foreshortened, Stitt dominates throughout both discs. He occasionally played baritone, too, and there's a surprisingly full-blooded ballad treatment of 'P.S. I Love You' on *Kaleidoscope* which suggests that his use of the bigger horn was by no means offhand. The boxy sound of the originals carries over into all the CD issues.

*** **Jazz Masters 50** Verve 527651-2

    Stitt; Lee Katzman, Jack Sheldon, Dizzy Gillespie (*t*); Frank Rosolino (*tb*); Sonny Rollins (*ts*); Amos Trice, John Lewis, Jimmy Jones, Lou Levy, Oscar Peterson, Bobby Timmons, Jimmy Rowles (*p*); Skeeter Best, Paul Weedon, Herb Ellis (*g*); Al Pollan (*tba*); George Morrow, Percy Heath, Ray Brown, Paul Chambers, Leroy Vinnegar, Edgar Willis, Buddy Clark, Tommy Bryant (*b*); Lenny McBrowne, Charli Persip, Billy James, Stan Levey, Ed Thigpen, Kenny Dennis, Lawrence Marable (*d*); strings. 1/56–2/62.

Verve's compilation series reached number 50 with this useful Stitt collection, picking a dozen tracks, no fewer than nine of which come from out-of-print Stitt albums. But all the best moments here – save perhaps for the lovely ballad-with-strings 'Time After Time', from 1961 – are from familiar records: *Sonny Side Up* with Gillespie and Rollins and *Sits In With The Oscar Peterson Trio*. Stitt's own-name dates weren't any more commanding then than his later sets for Prestige. Of course there's still much exemplary alto and tenor, and the remastering gets the most out of Sonny's impeccable tone and delivery.

***(*) **Sonny Stitt Sits In With The Oscar Peterson Trio** Verve 849396-2

    Stitt; Oscar Peterson (*p*); Herb Ellis (*g*); Ray Brown (*b*); Ed Thigpen, Stan Levey (*d*). 10/57–5/58.

A memorable meeting. Stitt plays alto and tenor here, and sounds unusually at ease with a pianist who might have brought out his most sparring side: instead, on the likes of 'Moten Swing' and 'Blues For Pres', they intermingle their respective many-noted approaches as plausibly as if this were a regular band (in fact, they never recorded together again). The CD includes three tracks from a session a year earlier, previously unreleased, with a storming 'I Know That You Know' emerging as the highlight. Excellent CD remastering.

(*) **Sonny Stitt Meets Brother Jack Original Jazz Classics OJC 703

    Stitt; Jack McDuff (*org*); Eddie Diehl (*g*); Art Taylor (*d*); Ray Barretto (*perc*). 2/62.

(*) **Autumn In New York Black Lion BLCD 760130

    Stitt; Howard McGhee (*t*); Walter Bishop (*p*); Tommy Potter (*b*); Kenny Clarke (*d*). 10/67.

*** **Soul Classics** Original Jazz Classics OJC 6003

    Stitt; Virgil Jones (*t*); Jack McDuff, Don Patterson, Gene Ludwig, Leon Spencer (*org*); Hank Jones (*p*); Pat Martino, Grant Green, Billy Butler, Melvin Sparks, Eddie Diehl (*g*); Leonard Gaskin, George Duvivier (*b*); Idris Muhammed, Art Taylor, Billy James, Randy Gillespie (*d*). 2/62–2/72.

*** **Soul People** Prestige 24127-2

    Stitt; Booker Ervin (*ts*); Grant Green, Vinnie Corrao (*g*); Don Patterson (*org*); Billy James (*d*). 8/64–9/69.

Whatever the state of jazz's declining fortunes in the 1960s, Stitt worked and recorded incessantly, if often carelessly. A lot of run-of-the-mill albums for Roulette and Cadet are currently unavailable; these Prestige dates scarcely break the mould. With McDuff in tow, Stitt strolls unblinkingly through a programme of rootless blues. *Soul People* has some natty sparring with Booker Ervin, never one to shirk some cheerful sax fisticuffs, and though the ballad medley is a bit dragging, 'Flying Home' isn't. A 1969 'Tune Up' and one track with Patterson in the chair fills up the disc. *Soul Classics* collects tracks from eight sessions over a decade and is a truthful picture of Stitt's ups and downs. Four tracks feature the saxophonist with his varitone horn, a gimmick which didn't last; but more encouraging is the tough 'Night Crawler' with Patterson and a dark blue 'Goin' Down Slow' with a surprise guest-slot by Hank Jones. The Black Lion quintet, recorded in Switzerland, is about as authentic as bebop bands get, though these four tracks spark only intermittently; the earlier tracks with an unknown group are a little more exciting.

**** **Tune-Up!** Muse MCD 5334

    Stitt; Barry Harris (*p*); Sam Jones (*b*); Alan Dawson (*d*). 2/72.

**** **Constellation** Muse MCD 5323

    As above, except Roy Brooks (*d*) replaces Dawson. 6/72.

Despite the apparently unexceptional circumstances of these records – Stitt had by now settled into a regimen of sax-and-rhythm dates that offered no deeper challenges than some familiar standards and a touch of the blues – the results were vivid and masterful examples of a great bopper at his best. The tempos are a fraction sharper, the tunes a little more interesting, the settings zestier – Harris is a quietly compelling foil, his discreetly appropriate comps and solos the earth to Stitt's skywriting, but bassist Jones is equally important, roving all over the bass with inspired aplomb. There's almost nothing to choose between these two sessions. Stitt rifles Parker's 'Constellation' with scathing abandon, and follows that with a piercingly clear-headed take on 'I Don't Stand A Ghost Of A Chance With You', alto following tenor throughout both dates, with *Constellation* having perhaps just the edge.

*** **The Champ** Muse MCD 5429
> Stitt; Joe Newman (*t*); Duke Jordan (*p*); Sam Jones (*b*); Roy Brooks (*d*). 4/73.

Stitt loved to play with Barry Harris behind him, and the pianist assists on most of his subsequent Muse dates. All are now gone from print except this one. The title-track is a smartly orchestrated feast of bop licks which sets up the session, and Stitt sounds at his creamiest on the succeeding 'Sweet And Lovely'; Jordan's scholarly touch is a nice bonus on the date.

(*) **Back To My Own Home Town Black & Blue 59574-2
> Stitt; Gerald Price (*p*); Don Mosley (*b*); Bobby Durham (*d*). 11/79.

*** **The Last Stitt Sessions** Muse MCD 6003
> Stitt; Bill Hardman (*t*); Junior Mance, Walter Davis (*p*); George Duvivier (*b*); Jimmy Cobb (*d*). 6/82.

Stitt died a few weeks after making *The Last Stitt Sessions*, but he betrayed only a few signs of failing powers. The pick-up date in France (Black & Blue) is as rote as one might imagine. The final sessions have no valedictory feel and seem more like just another capable Sonny Stitt date: Davis plays rather eccentrically on his share of duty, and the leader sounds a shade tired here and there, but the dudgeon which sustained him through so many sessions endures here, too.

Markus Stockhausen TRUMPET, FLUGELHORN, SYNTHESIZER

(*) **Cosi Lontano . . . Quasi Dentro ECM 1371
> Stockhausen; Fabrizio Ottaviucci (*p*); Gary Peacock (*b*); Zoro Babel (*d*). 3/88.

*** **Aparis** ECM 1404
> Stockhausen; Simon Stockhausen (*sax, syn*); Jo Thones (*d, electric d*). 8/89.

***(*) **Despite The Fire-Fighters' Efforts . . .** ECM 1496
> As above. 7/92.

***(*) **Possible Worlds** CMP CD 68
> Stockhausen; Fabrizio Ottaviucci (*p, v*); Rohan De Saram (*clo*); Simon Stockhausen (*syn, perc*); Ramesh Shotham (*perc*). 93–95.

*** **Sol Mestizo** Act 9222
> Stockhausen; Philip Catherine (*g*); Chano Dominguez (*p*); Simon Stockhausen (*ky, ss*); Jochen Schmidt (*b*); Enrique Diaz (*b, v*); Thomas Alkier (*d*); Filipe Mandingo (*perc*); Juanita Lascarro, Alexandra Naumann, Pia Miranda (*v*). 2/95.

Markus Stockhausen came to prominence as Michael, the main soloist in his father's opera, *Donnerstag*, the first part of the colossal *Licht* cycle, which bids fair to become the twenty-first century's *Ring*. As an improvising performer he has the same purity of tone all through the range but lacks entirely the dramatic force he draws from his father's global conception on 'Michaels Reise um die Erde'. Though the material is quite impressive, the conventional quartet set-up on *Cosi Lontano . . .* suits his approach not one bit. His solos are vague and unanchored and, without Peacock's patient figuring, it would all fall apart.

In recent years, Stockhausen has continued to experiment with his own brand of theatricality and world music. *Possible Worlds* would seem to refer to something like his father's aesthetic of cultural simultaneity and is a very strong statement. *Sol Mestizo* is a set of pieces written by the Chilean, Enrique Diaz. On the face of it a strange project for Stockhausen, it actually works very well, and his trumpet playing (minus the quarter-tone effects of the earlier record) is quite straightforward and often very upbeat, reminiscent of some early bebopper experimenting with free rhythms.

Markus and half-brother Simon have also constituted two-thirds of a group called Aparis. The eponymous record and the very impressive *Despite The Fire-Fighters' Efforts . . .* are more straightforwardly impressionistic and altogether more successful. Neo-funk tracks like 'High Ride' on the former sit rather uneasily, but Thones's acoustic and electric drums and Simon's intelligent sequencing bring a propulsive energy to even the quieter, watercoloured pieces. No clear indication why they've used a shot of Windsor Castle ablaze on the cover of the second group record, and there's a persistent avoidance of the dramatic climaxes individual pieces seem to promise, as if every piece, not just the album title, ends with a string of ellipses. Increasingly impressive, though it's hard to shake off the feeling that this is just relaxation from working in the old man's shop.

Stockholm Jazz Orchestra GROUP

*** **Dreams** Dragon DRCD 169
> Jan Kohlin, Fredrik Norén, Lars Lindgren, Stig Persson, Gustavo Bergalli (*t, flhn*); Bob

Brookmeyer (*vtb*); Mikael Råberg, Bertil Strandberg, Mats Hermansson (*tb*); Sven Larsson (*btb*); Dave Castle (*ss, as, cl*); Håkan Broström (*ss, as, f*); Ulf Andersson, Johan Alenius (*ss, ts, cl*); Hans Arktoft (*bs, bcl*); Anders Widmark (*ky*); Jan Adefeldt (*b*); Johan Dielemans (*d*). 8/88.

*** Jigsaw Dragon DRCD 213

As above, except Peter Asplund (*t, flhn*), Anders Wiborg (*tb*), Johan Hörlén (*ss, as, cl, f*), Jan Levander (*ts, cl, f*), Joakim Milder (*ts*), Jim McNeely (*p*), Martin Löfgren (*d*) replace Lindgren, Brookmeyer, Larsson, Broström, Alenius, Widmark and Dielemans. 3/91.

Originally a rehearsal band, and now an occasional enterprise under a nominal leadership from Fredrik Norén, the SJO has recorded two CDs to celebrate working with guest arrangers: *Dreams* with Bob Brookmeyer, and *Jigsaw* with Jim McNeely. While the two sessions are unalike in tone and delivery, each is rewarding. Brookmeyer, who spends much time as a resident composer with West German Radio, knows European orchestras, and his themes make the most of the prowess of the band: difficult scoring in 'Missing Monk' and 'Cats' is despatched without much effort by the group and, while the soloists take a lesser role, they're perfectly in tune with Brookmeyer's quirkily structured pieces. Some of them resemble no more than eccentrically linked episodes, but there are many striking passages – the first three tracks are an informal suite, with 'Lies' a particularly intriguing patchwork – which deserve a close listen.

Jigsaw is a more conventional record. One gets the feeling that McNeely is a more meticulous and thoroughgoing composer than Brookmeyer but a less inspirational one. The modern orchestral bop of 'Off The Cuff', for instance, or the concerto for Milder in 'The Decision' are convincing and tersely wound set-pieces, but the freewheeling demeanour of the earlier record is missed. Still, it may suit some tastes better. Both discs are excellently recorded, doing justice to a very skilful band.

Strata Institute GROUP

*** Transmigration DIW 860

Von Freeman (*ts*); Steve Coleman, Greg Osby (*as*); David Gilmore (*g*); Kenny Davis (*b*); Marvin 'Smitty' Smith (*d*). 1/91.

Not so very different in conception (or personnel) from Steve Coleman's Five Elements group or the M-Base Collective, the big plus on this is the robust tenor of Chicagoan Von Freeman, one of those figures whose recorded output suggests only a fraction of his actual significance.

He's used to showing younger guys how to do it right, and it's presumably at his behest that material like Lockjaw Davis's 'Jimdog' and Tadd Dameron's 'If You Could See Me Now' are included in the programme. His playing is unimpeachable, threading its way under the more impatient sound of the two altos; but there's a slight sense of overload around that part of the overall spectrum. Gilmore's guitar cuts through on occasion and Smith is as reliable and varied as ever. But the disc as a whole lacks character. Coleman produced and co-supervised the mix with his regular partner, Osby. Untypically, the sound's very middleish and unfocused.

Billy Strayhorn (1915–67) PIANO, COMPOSER, ARRANGER

***(*) Great Times! Original Jazz Classics OJC 108

Strayhorn; Duke Ellington (*p*); Wendell Marshall (*b*); Oscar Pettiford (*b, clo*); Lloyd Trottman (*b*); Jo Jones (*d*). 9, 10 & 11/50.

**** Lush Life Red Baron RED 472206

Strayhorn; Cat Anderson, Rolf Ericson, Herbie Jones, Cootie Williams (*t*); Clark Terrry (*t, flhn*); Lawrence Brown, Buster Cooper, Chuck Connors (*tb*); Willie Ruff (*frhn*); Russell Procope, Johnny Hodges, Jimmy Hamilton, Paul Gonsalves, Harry Carney (*reeds*); Bob Wilber (*cl, ss*); Duke Ellington (*p*); Wendell Marshall, Ernie Shepherd (*b*); Dave Bailey, Sam Woodyard (*d*); Ozzie Bailey (*v*). 1/64, 6, 7 & 8/65.

They were like two aspects of a single complex self. Where Duke Ellington was immodest, priapic and thumpingly egocentric, his longtime writing and arranging partner, Billy Strayhorn, was shy, gay and self-effacing. It's now very difficult, given the closeness of their relationship and their inevitable tendency to draw on aspects of the other's style and method, to separate which elements of an 'Ellington–Strayhorn' composition belong to each; but there is no doubt that Swee' Pea, as Ellington called him, made an immense impact on his boss's music. Even if he had done no more than write 'Lush Life' (see below) and 'Take The "A" Train', Strayhorn would still have been guaranteed a place in jazz history. Just after his painful death from cancer in 1967, Ellington recorded the tribute *And His Mother Called Him Bill* (RCA). After the session was over, but with mikes still on, the Duke sat on at the piano and played an impromptu epitaph that counts as one of the most moving farewells from one musician to another ever played.

Strayhorn was not a particularly inspiring pianist (he sounded a bit like Duke on an off-day) and wasn't, of course, an instinctive performer. There is next to nothing on record, but in fairness the 1950 *Great Times!* might be credited to Strayhorn's account. In performance terms he's overshadowed by his boss, playing much more 'correctly' and inside the key than the Duke found comfortable. It's easier to separate them on the inevitable ' "A" Train' and 'Oscalypso', when Strayhorn switches to celeste.

The later *Lush Life* begins with two live tracks, one of the Ellington band playing 'Passion Flower', the other Strayhorn singing the title-track in that soft, self-mocking way that makes so much more sense of the lyric than most latter-day Alcoholics Anonymous epics. The summer 1965 sessions feature Strayhorn at the head of a small group of musicians he particularly admired. 'Passion Flower' is taken at a very different pace and is much more spacious with the small group. 'Upper Manhattan Medical Group' and 'Chelsea Bridge' (the latter for a beautifully voiced septet) are delicate and song-like, but with a graceful, dancing lilt that the Ellington bands couldn't match. The addition of Willie Ruff's horn gave the sound a new resonance and depth of colour that clearly appealed to Strayhorn; his own playing is much richer on the later set. Ozzie Bailey's vocals are pleasant enough. The final session, from August 1965, offers further versions of 'Love Came' and 'Something To Live For', both of which had been done by the group. His playing is still attractively hesitant, but it is possible to hear him re-think the exact cadence of a phrase as he repeats it, leaning just a little harder on the middle or last beat to give it either more forward motion or else a more categorical conclusion.

(One further extraordinary tribute to Strayhorn exists on disc. In the early 1980s clarinettist Tony Scott (*q.v.*) recorded an astonishing two-volume exploration of 'Lush Life', Core COCD 9.00666/7 (see under Scott). It includes nine versions of the song, mostly solo performances on saxophones, clarinet and electric piano, but also including spin-off improvisations for duo and trio, an unaccompanied vocal version by Monica Sciacca, and, of course, Strayhorn himself on piano and vocals, establishing the Urtext.)

Frank Strazzeri (born 1930) PIANO

*** **Little Giant** Fresh Sound FSR-CD 184
    Strazzeri; Horacio Fumero (*b*); Peer Wyboris (*d*). 11/89.
*** **Wood Winds West** Jazz Mark 111
    Strazzeri; Bill Perkins (*ss, as, f, af*); Bob Cooper (*ts, cl*); Jack Nimitz (*bs, bcl*); Dave Stone (*b*);
    Paul Kreibach (*d*). 2/92.

A journeyman pianist who's worked under many a famous leader, Strazzeri's kind of jazz glides off surfaces rather than cutting deep, and these sunny, cool, rounded sessions are as close to definitive as he'll ever find himself on record. Conservative in terms of harmony and rhythm, his distinctiveness comes out in his touch: he plays with a delicacy that makes all his solos flow evenly across each chorus, with nothing struck very hard and no phrase emerging out of kilter with the others. In other situations it might result in merely dull music, but Strazzeri picks tunes like a man who's easily bored. *Little Giant* was a session organized at a few hours' notice, and the temptation to go for easy old warhorses must have been hard to resist; instead, there's scarcely anything which isn't out of the ordinary, including 'Don'cha Go 'Way Mad', Carl Perkins's 'Grooveyard', George Shearing's 'Conception' and Ellington's 'I'm Gonna Go Fishin''. Fumero and Wyboris keep spontaneously good time. The *Wood Winds West* date is more about Strazzeri's talents as an arranger for the multiple horns of Perkins, Cooper and Nimitz and, on a straight, lush theme like 'Nocturne', it can seem like an exercise in mood music rather than a jazzman's undertaking. But these old pros find serendipitous routes to many nice touches.

String Trio Of New York GROUP

*** **Common Goal** Black Saint 120058
    Billy Bang (*vn, yokobue, f*); James Emery (*g, soprano g, mand*): John Lindberg (*b*). 11/81.
***(*) **Rebirth Of A Feeling** Black Saint 120068
    As above. 11/83.
***(*) **Ascendant** Stash STCD 532
    As above; replace Bang with Charles Burnham. 6/90.
*** **Time Never Lies** Stash STCD 544
    As above.
***(*) **Intermobility** Arabesque AJ018
    As above; replace Burnham with Regina Carter. 7/92.

***(*) **Octagon** Black Saint 120131
    As above. 11/92.

In the interests of neatness it would be convenient to shorthand these albums: 'with Billy Bang – good; without – not'. Despite a general critical consensus to that effect, the reality isn't so simple. Though Bang's ducks-and-drakes approach to tonality was a vital component of the STNY's first four albums, Burnham is a perfectly adequate replacement, and it's clear that much of the impetus of the band comes from the bassist, who is also an impressive writer and emerges with a bang of his own on *Time Never Lies* with the fascinating 'Middle Eastern Essay'.

Whatever the merits of the post-Bang STNY (and they are considerable), there's no doubt that their best albums are those involving him; unfortunately, there's scarcely any of it left around to clinch the point. Of the rejigged line-ups, there is more and more to savour. *Ascendant* is certainly one of the most entertaining of the records, with a Kronos-style take on Jimi Hendrix's 'Manic Depression', some Satie and, to keep jazz credentials afloat, Monk, Charlie Parker and Jimmy Garrison. 'Ah-Leu-Cha' is tender, almost melancholic, but the title-track – credited to Coltrane's bassist – has an earthy grind. There are moments when it all sounds like one of John McLaughlin's gut-strung Mahavishnu Orchestra tracks, with Jerry Goodman's violin floating above. And none the worse for that.

The interplay of the group has reached a highly sophisticated stage with *Time Never Lies*, but here all the emphasis seems to fall on careful co-ordination of parts. Some of the anarchy that Bang inevitably brought is missing. This is the most ambitious recording yet, with an attempt to inscribe the group and its unfashionable instrumentation into the jazz tradition proper; versions of Ornette's 'Ramblin'', Coltrane's 'After The Rain', and, dipping back in time, 'Honeysuckle Rose'.

There was a further change of personnel after 1990, with Regina Carter coming in for Burnham. She's not a particularly imaginative player (certainly not when placed against someone like Britain's Sylvia Hallett), but *Intermobility* restored a little of the buzz and fire, a few of the raw edges; and *Octagon* is an ambitious record nevertheless, covering a startling range of contemporary compositions (Marty Ehrlich, Muhal Richard Abrams, Mark Helias, Leo Smith and Bobby Previte are all credited), and Carter's own 'Forever February' is one of the loveliest things they've done, which bodes well for future projects.

Reissued just before press time, *Rebirth Of A Feeling* claims the attention more than any of the later discs. Centred round Bang's 'Penguins An' Other Strange Birds' (a gloriously wacky piece) and the long, rather more brooding 'Utility Grey', which was written by Lindberg, it's a superb record which can be recommended warmly to anyone who hasn't yet encountered the STNY.

Dave Stryker (born 1957) GUITAR

***(*) **First Stryke** Someday 1011
    Stryker; Steve Slagle (*ss, as*); Marc Cohen (*p*); Ron McClure (*b*); Billy Hart (*d*). 5/89.
*** **Stryke Zone** Steeplechase SCCD 31277
    Stryker; Marc Cohen (*p*); Ron McClure (*b*); Ronnie Burrage (*d*). 10/90.
***(*) **Guitar On Top** Ken 019
    Stryker; Mulgrew Miller (*p*); Robert Hurst (*b*); Victor Lewis (*d*). 9/91.
**** **Passage** Steeplechase SCCD 31330
    Stryker; Steve Slagle (*ss, as*); Joey Calderazzo (*p*); Jay Anderson (*b*); Adam Nussbaum (*d*). 3/91.
***(*) **Blue Degrees** Steeplechase SCCD 31315
    Stryker; Rick Margitza (*ts*); Larry Goldings (*org*); Jeff Hirshfield (*d*). 4/92.
*** **Full Moon** Steeplechase SCCD 31345
    Stryker; Steve Slagle (*as, f*); Jay Anderson (*b*); Jeff Hirshfield (*d*). 10/93.

Stryker is impressive, even amidst the legion of guitar players who've staked a recent claim for attention. He did long service in the pressure-cooker atmosphere of Jack McDuff and Jimmy Smith groups, and while he prefers a slightly blurred tone over the crisp lines of many modern guitarists he has a knack for cutting through any ensemble. 'Jungle' on *Passage* is an example of how he digs into a solo – the leering bent notes and swaggering delivery are a startling display; but the fast bop lines of 'It's You Or No One' on the same record show he has the necessary language down pat. Consistently energetic and persuasive, there's little to choose between these records as regards his own playing. The debut is impressive for the sheer clout of the opening three tracks, and favourite partner Slagle is an inspiring presence. *Stryke Zone* is a shade behind for a rhythm section that doesn't quite strike best sparks, but that charge can hardly be levelled at the all-star team on *Guitar On Top*. The next two Steeplechases are the place to start, though. *Passage* is an all-round programme – there's a brief, pretty 'I Fall In Love Too Easily' as a nice change of pace – with both intensity and finesse. *Blue Degrees* is just a touch cooler – Goldings, the only organ player ever to feature on a Steeplechase date, is more of a pastel player than a bar-burner – but the undervalued Margitza is a welcome presence, and Stryker is full of ideas again.

Full Moon is perhaps a mite disappointing as the next in the sequence. Ornette Coleman's 'The Sphinx' makes a hurried, splashy opening, Coltrane's 'Wise One' is mush for flute and acoustic guitar, and not till Slagle's 'Leadbelly Sez' do they really dig in. But there's still some marvellous playing on Wayne Shorter's 'Deluge' and two slow-to-mid blues.

John Stubblefield TENOR SAXOPHONE, SOPRANO SAXOPHONE

***(*) **Confessin'** Soul Note 121095
   Stubblefield; Cecil Bridgewater (*t, flhn*); Mulgrew Miller (*p*); Rufus Reid (*b*); Eddie Gladden (*d*). 9/84.
***(*) **Bushman Song** Enja 5015
   Stubblefield; Geri Allen (*p, syn*); Charnett Moffett (*b*); Victor Lewis (*d, perc*); Mino Cinelu (*perc, v*). 4/86.
**** **Countin' The Blues** Enja 5051
   Stubblefield; Hamiet Bluiett (*bs*); Mulgrew Miller (*p*); Charnett Moffett (*b*); Victor Lewis (*d*). 5/87.
***(*) **Morning Song** Enja 8036
   Stubblefield; George Cables (*p*); Clint Houston (*b*); Victor Lewis (*d*). 5/93.

Despite a similar concern for the jazz tradition, Stubblefield has attracted far less critical attention as a solo recording artist than David Murray, for whom he has occasionally depped in the World Saxophone Quartet. The Arkansas man is a more narrowly focused player, without Murray's extraordinary fluency in almost every dialect of the jazz tradition, but he has a strongly individual voice, constructs solos with impeccable logic, and his own music has a rootsy immediacy and appeal.

Confessin' is a strongly worded testament from a player who has always clung to the notion of tenor saxophone as essentially a vocalized instrument. 'Spiral Dance' and 'Waltz For Duke Pearson' (dedicated to the now-underrated pianist) are well constructed, with something of the WSQ's emphasis on improvisation *within* the basic structure of the piece (compare some of the Art Ensemble of Chicago references on *Bushman Song*, which traces Stubblefield's engagement with a wider than usual spectrum of black music), and 'Confessin'' brings the set to a fine climax.

The more recent *Countin' The Blues* reunites Stubblefield with his WSQ colleague, Bluiett. Unlike Murray, who left the smaller horn aside in favour of tenor and bass clarinet, Stubblefield has worked steadily on soprano saxophone. Pitched 'parallel' to Bluiett's baritone, it heightens the tonal impact of both horns. Miller is excellent (as he is on *Confessin'*), but it's left to Moffett and the increasingly confident Lewis to give the arrangements the forward thrust they get on *Bushman Song* from a rock-tinged Geri Allen and from Moffett.

The most recent of the records lacks the urgency and sheer inventiveness of its predecessor. With more of the weight thrown on Stubblefield himself, it gets a shade discursive in places, particularly on the long(ish) originals. There is, though, a brilliant reading of drummer Lewis's 'Shaw Of Newark' to savour, gorgeously gruff readings of 'Blue Moon' and 'In A Sentimental Mood', Miles's 'So What' and a piece by the Afro-American composer, William Grant Still.

With David Murray albums going around in threes and catching all the plaudits, it would be easy to forget about Stubblefield. Spare him a moment.

Dick Sudhalter (born 1938) CORNET, TRUMPET, FLUGELHORN

*** **With Pleasure** Audiophile ACD-159
   Sudhalter; Dan Barrett (*tb*); Bob Reitmeier (*cl, as, ts*); Dan Levinson (*cl, ts*); Joe Muranyi (*cl*); Dave Frishberg (*p, v*); James Cirillo (*g*); Howard Alden (*g, bj*); Putter Smith (*tba, b*); Bill Crow (*b*); Eddie Locke, Dick Berk (*d*). 3/81–4/94.
*** **After Awhile** Challenge 70014
   Sudhalter; Roy Williams (*tb*); Jim Shepherd (*tb, bsx*); John R. T. Davies (*as*); Al Gay (*ts*); Keith Nichols (*p, tb*); Mick Pyne (*p*); Nevil Skrimshire, Paul Sealey (*g*); Dave Green, Jack Fallon (*b*); Allan Ganley, Jack Parnell (*d*); Chris Ellis (*v*). 5–6/94.

Sudhalter's Bixian brass stylings have tended to take a back seat to his jazz scholarship, but he is a lyrical player and a rare example of a musician-historian who can make his enthusiasms take on a personal cast when he plays. These amiable sessions make no great demands on a listener, but they're enjoyable for all that. The first reissues a 1981 date with eight extra, subsequent tracks, and it blends the echoes of a vanished Chicago with a few more modern licks: Sudhalter cuts from such ancient cloth as 'Madame Dynamite' and 'Boneyard Shuffle' and reshapes a Beiderbecke legacy such as 'Slow River' into a winsome duet with Frishberg. The Challenge album goes to the other side of the Atlantic – to the

Bull's Head in Barnes, in fact – and brings on an English team for a similarly inclined session. The material isn't quite so arcane here, but the playing probably isn't quite as vivacious either.

Idrees Sulieman (born 1923) TRUMPET, FLUGELHORN

(*) **Now Is The Time Steeplechase SCCD 31052
    Sulieman; Cedar Walton (p); Sam Jones (b); Billy Higgins (d). 2/76.
(*) **Bird's Grass Steeplechase SCCD 31202
    Sulieman; Per Goldschmidt (ts); Horace Parlan (p); Niels-Henning Orsted-Pedersen (b); Kenny Clarke (d). 12/76.
** **Groovin'** Steeplechase SCCD 31218
    Sulieman; Per Goldschmidt (ts, bs); Horace Parlan (p); Mads Vinding (b); Billy Hart (d). 8/85.
Sulieman seems destined to be a forgotten man of bebop trumpet, even though he recorded with Monk in the 1940s and appeared with many leading boppers. His subsequent career found him buried in big bands and, after decamping to Europe in the 1960s, he was spied only intermittently by an international audience. These three Steeplechase albums find him only a shadow of his former self. The articulation sounds blurred – badly so by the time of the 1985 date – and the ideas are unremarkable; he struggles at fast tempos and does no more than hold his own on ballads, though 'The Summer Knows', from *Bird's Grass*, is prettily done. Exposed on the first album, he needs Goldschmidt's support on the second, and by the third, in which the saxophonist bides his time between tenor and baritone, one feels that these are sessions best left alone by posterity.

Joe Sullivan (1906–71) PIANO

*** **Joe Sullivan 1933–1941** Classics 821
    Sullivan; Ed Anderson (t); Benny Morton (tb); Edmond Hall, Pee Wee Russell (cl); Danny Polo (ts, cl); Freddie Green (g); Billy Taylor, Henry Turner (b); Yank Porter, Zutty Singleton, Johnny Wells (d); Joe Turner, Helen Ward (v). 9/33–3/41.
This collects all of Sullivan's piano solos of the period, plus the two dates by his Café Society Orchestra and a 1941 trio date for Commodore with Pee Wee Russell and Zutty Singleton. Sullivan had a terrific left hand, and his style was a personal blend of boogie woogie and stride language, imbued with a shot of local Chicago blues. Not a great melodist, perhaps, which gives some of the dozen solos here a certain sameness, and the band tracks are nothing very special; but the intensity of Sullivan's style has weathered the years well enough and his bluff passion gives the music bite. Transfers are variable but the music survives the surface noise and boomy bass patterns.

Maxine Sullivan (1911–87) VOCAL

*** **More 1940–1941** Circle CCD-125
    Sullivan; Charlie Shavers (t); Buster Bailey (cl); Russell Procope (as); Billy Kyle (p); John Kirby (b); O'Neil Spencer (d). 10/40–11/41.
'Loch Lomond' was the novelty hit which launched Maxine Sullivan's career, part of a faintly ludicrous vogue for turning folk tunes and 'light music' into swing vehicles. The song (and 'Darling Nellie Gray', 'It Was A Lover And His Lass' and so forth) still works, though, because of Sullivan's transparent, almost ghostly singing. She didn't really swing her material so much as give it a lilting quality, floating it on phrasing that was measured and controlled without sounding excessively polite. Her version of 'St Louis Blues' sounds mousy next to a voice like Bessie Smith's, but the demure melancholy she invests it with is surprisingly compelling. Unfortunately, these early sessions seem to be in limbo at present since the Affinity collection listed in our last edition has gone.
    She went on to work with John Kirby's small band, and the Circle CD collects a series of transcriptions by the group, six of which feature Sullivan. Some of them continue the folk-towards-jazz theme, and Kirby's willowy band are perhaps all too suitable as a backing group, but the music exudes an undeniable period charm. Excellent sound, given the source.

**** **Close As Pages In A Book** Audiophile 203
    Sullivan; Bob Wilber (ss, cl); Bernie Leighton (p); George Duvivier (b); Gus Johnson Jr (d). 6/69.
*** **Shakespeare** Audiophile 250
    Sullivan; Rusty Dedrick (t, flhn); Dick Hyman (p, hpd); Bucky Pizzarelli (g); Milt Hinton (b); Don Lamond (d). 6/71.

***(*) **The Queen: Something To Remember Her By** Kenneth CKS 3406
> Sullivan; Bent Persson (*t*); Georg Vernon (*tb*); Claes Brodda (*cl, ts*); Goran Eriksson (*as*); Erik Persson (*ts, bs*); Bjorn Milder (*p*); Mikael Selander (*g*); Olle Brostedt (*g, b*); Goran Lind (*b*); Sigge Dellert (*d*). 10/78–7/84.

*** **Great Songs From The Cotton Club** Mobile Fidelity MFCD 836
> Sullivan; Keith Ingham (*p*). 11/84.

*** **Uptown** Concord CCD 4288
> Sullivan; Scott Hamilton (*ts*); John Bunch (*p*); Chris Flory (*g*); Phil Flanigan (*b*); Chuck Riggs (*d*). 1/85.

*** **Swingin' Street** Concord CCD 4351
> As above. 9/86.

(*) **Spring Isn't Everything Audiophile 229
> Sullivan; Loonis McGlohon (*p*); Jim Stack (*vib*); Terry Peoples (*b*); Bill Stowe (*d*). 7/86.

Sullivan retired in the 1950s but later returned to regular singing (she also played flugelhorn and valve-trombone) and by the 1980s was as widely admired as she had ever been. Her manner didn't change much but, as recording improved, her intimate style and meticulous delivery sounded as classic as any of the great jazz singers. In her seventies there was inevitably a decline in the strength of her voice, but careful production ensured that her albums sounded very good.

Close As Pages In A Book was long a collectors' favourite, and it makes a welcome return on CD. The dozen songs are perfectly delivered – thoughtful, graceful, introspective without being introverted, this is peerless jazz singing, and the accompaniments by Wilber and his team are as *simpatico* as one could wish. The Shakespeare collection was the last word on Sullivan's 'Elizabethan' direction, and sounds better, at least, than Cleo Laine's efforts in this field. Some other LPs for Audiophile are still awaited on CD, but the later *Spring Isn't Everything*, one of her last sessions, features a 'songbook' recital (the tracks are all by Harry Warren) which finds her still in excellent shape. Unfortunately the studio balance doesn't favour her at all. Better to turn to the two Concord dates with Hamilton's smooth neo-classic band, which do as fine a job for her as they do for Rosemary Clooney and what was an award-winning album with Keith Ingham, dedicated to tunes associated with the Cotton Club. Best of the lot, though, may be the beautiful collection on Kenneth, cut in Sweden with local players. The sessions date covers a six-year period, but Maxine sounds entirely at ease throughout, whether swinging on 'You Were Meant For Me' or strolling through 'Thanks For The Memory'. The band are very fine, too, with Brodda's Websterish tenor and Eriksson's sinuous alto particularly impressive. The recording is rather dry but otherwise sounds very good.

Stan Sulzmann (born 1948) TENOR SAXOPHONE, ALTO SAXOPHONE, SOPRANO SAXOPHONE, ALTO FLUTE

***(*) **Feudal Rabbits** Ah Um 011
> Sulzmann; Patrick Bettison, Mick Hutton (*b*); Steve Arguëlles (*d*). 12/90.

(*) **Never At All Future FMR CD 05 28193
> Sulzmann; Marc Copland (*p, syn*). 2/92.

*** **Treasure Trove** ASC CD 7
> Sulzmann; Nikki Iles (*p*); Martin Pyne (*perc*). 10/95.

A classic case of a Talent Deserving Wider Recognition who has consistently failed to break through to the audiences his ability and commitment would seem to merit. Chronically under-recorded, Sulzmann made what looked like a promising return to his late-1970s form (*Krark* was a much-underrated record) with the curiously titled *Feudal Rabbits*. In the event, it's electric bassist Bettison who steals most of the honours, heavily featured on a number of tracks and name-checked on 'Feeling Bettison'. Sulzmann's delivery is introspective and melancholic and there's hardly an up-tempo track on the afternoon. The best single piece is a version of Kenny Wheeler's delicate '3/4 In The Afternoon'. Pleasantly downbeat jazz that asks to be played late at night. One feels there ought to be a more challenging context for one of Britain's unsung instrumentalists.

Unfortunately, *Never At All* isn't it. American keyboard man Copland had worked with Sulzmann off and on for years, following a chance encounter in the 1970s. They've clearly built up a level of mutual understanding, but it tends to drain the music of tension rather than activating it. Sulzmann's flute is sharply etched over clouds of synthesizer tones on the lovely 'Phobos And Demios', but only Copland's long 'Never At All' and 'Guinevere' offer much evidence of thoughtful interchange rather than merely companionable conversation.

Pianist and composer Nikki Iles has long been recognized as an artist of special promise. She has something of Geri Allen's richness of texture and rhythmic awareness and, good as she is in a larger group setting (most notably Emanon with her husband, trumpeter Richard Iles), she comes across most formidably in settings like *Treasure Trove*. Pyne is restricted to just one number, on which Sulzmann also airs his beautifully toned alto flute, and it was a good notion not to clutter this partnership with any other guest slots. The range of Sulzmann's reeds and Iles's intelligently varied attack, in combination with fascinating material (all originals, except Paul Simon's 'I Do It For Your Love' and Bill Evans's 'Since We Met'), contribute to a thoroughly satisfying set that could perhaps have done with a bit more studio presence.

Sun Ra (1914–93) PIANO, CLAVIOLINE, CELESTE, ORGAN, SYNTHESIZER

***(*) **Sound Sun Pleasure!!** Evidence ECD 22014
 Sun Ra; Hobart Dotson, Ahktal Ebah, Art Hoyle (*t*); Bob Northern (*flhn*); Marshall Allen, Danny Davis (*as*); John Gilmore (*ts*); Charles Davis, Pat Patrick (*bs*); Danny Thompson (*reeds*); Stuff Smith (*vn*); Ronnie Boykins, Vic Sproles (*b*); Robert Barry, Nimrod Hunt, James Jackson, Clifford Jarvis (*d*); Hatty Randolph, Clyde Williams (*v*). ?53–60.

***(*) **Supersonic Jazz** Evidence ECD 22015
 Sun Ra; Art Hoyle (*t*); Julian Priester (*tb*); James Scales (*as*); Pat Patrick (*as, bs*); John Gilmore (*ts*); Charles Davis (*bs*); Wilburn Green, Victor Sproles (*b*); Robert Barry, William Cochran (*d*); Jim Herndon (*perc*). 56.

***(*) **Visits Planet Earth / Interstellar Low Ways** Evidence ECD 22039
 Sun Ra; Phil Cohran, Art Hoyle, George Hudson, Lucious Randolph, Dave Young (*t*); Julian Priester, Nate Pryor (*tb*); James Spaulding (*as*); Marshall Allen (*as, f*); Pat Patrick (*as, bs, space f, bells, solar d*); John Gilmore (*ts, bells, solar d*); Charles Davis (*bs*); Ronnie Boykins, Victor Sproles (*b*); Robert Barry, William Cochran, Edward Skinner (*d*); Jim Herndon (*perc*). 56, 58, 60.

**** **We Travel The Spaceways / Bad And Beautiful** Evidence ECD 22038
 Sun Ra; Art Hoyle, Walter Strickland (*t*); Phil Cohran (*t, space harp, perc*); Julian Priester, Nate Pryor (*tb*); James Scales, James Spaulding (*as*); Marshall Allen (*as, bells, flying saucer, perc*); John Gilmore (*ts, cosmic bells, perc*); Pat Patrick (*bs, perc*); Ronnie Boykins, Wilburn Green (*b*); Tommy Hunter (*d*); Robert Barry (*d, perc*); Edward Skinner (*perc*). 56, 58 or 59, 59 or 60, 61.

*** **Angels And Demons At Play / The Nubians Of Plutonia** Evidence ECD 22066
 Sun Ra; Bill Fielder, Lucious Randolph (*t*); Phil Cohran (*t, zither*); Bob Bailey, Julian Priester, Nate Pryor (*tb*); James Spaulding (*as*); Marshall Allen (*as, f*); Pat Patrick (*as, bs*); John Gilmore (*ts, cl, bells*); Charles Davis (*bs*); Ronnie Boykins, Wilburn Green (*b*); Robert Barry, Jon Hardy (*d*); Jim Herndon (*perc*). 56, 60.

**** **Jazz In Silhouette** Evidence ECD 22012
 Sun Ra; Hobart Dotson (*t*); Julian Priester (*tb*); Marshall Allen, James Spaulding (*as, f*); John Gilmore (*ts*); Charles Davis (*bs*); Pat Patrick (*bs, f*); Ronnie Boykins (*b*); William Cochran (*d*). 58.

A much-maligned and hugely influential figure, Sun Ra was either born in Chicago under the earth-name Herman Poole 'Sonny' Blount, as the birth-roll insists, or on Saturn, as the man himself often claimed. Uncertainty about his seriousness (and sanity) tended to divert attention from a considerable three-decade output, which included well over 100 LPs. Because much of it remained inaccessible during his lifetime, critical responses were apt to concentrate on the paraphernalia associated with his Arkestra big band, rather than on the music. Nevertheless, he was one of the most significant band-leaders of the post-war period. He drew on Ellington and Fletcher Henderson (for whom he did arrangements after the war), but also on the bop-derived avant garde, and was a pioneer of collective improvisation. Though rarely acknowledged as an instrumentalist, he developed a convincing role for the synthesizer and was a strong rather than subtle piano player. The solo recordings, some of which have been reissued (see below), are only now being appreciated.

Above all, Sun Ra maintained a solitary independence from the music industry, a principled stance that certainly cost him dear in critical and commercial terms. For the first time in many years, it's possible again to get hold of important material self-released on the El Saturn label. These discs are being reissued *in toto* by Evidence (who work out of Conshohocken, Pennsylvania), a colossal project that will presumably take several years. Sound-quality is remarkably good, given the often shaky balance of the original masters and the fact that they've been subjected to uncertain storage conditions. The original El Saturn titles have been preserved wherever possible, even when this has led to rather cumbersome doubling up. One of the drawbacks of Evidence's programme is the out-of-sequence pairing of sessions, rendering a strictly chronological review impossible. A more orderly approach or a separate chrono-logical listing might have been helpful, even though exact recording dates remain a matter of controversy.

The 1950s were in many respects a golden age for Sun Ra and the Arkestra. The music is frankly experimental (in the sense that both leaders and players are clearly working through ideas on the stand) and the sci-fi apparatus was already part and parcel of American culture through the latter half of the decade. Chants like 'We Travel The Spaceways' began to sound more artful and mannered as the years went by, but for now they manage to sound almost spontaneous. There was always a suspicion that titles like 'Rocket Number Nine Take Off For The Planet Venus' were simply a diversionary addition to a fairly conventional jazz tune.

The bands themselves are terrific, of course. The marvellous *Jazz In Silhouette* will surely some day be recognized as one of the most important jazz records since the war. The closing 'Blues At Midnight' is sheer excitement. The baritone solo on the short 'Saturn', most probably Patrick, is an extension of Sun Ra's brilliantly individual voicings. The leader makes considerable use of the baritone and flutes, but also includes a specialist flugelhorn player on *Sound Sun Pleasure!!*, and elsewhere he makes distinctive use of electric bass, tympani and log drums. The great surprise of these recordings (though presumably no surprise to those who have taken the Saturnian aesthetic fully on board) is their *timelessness*. Listening to 'Enlightenment', given an uncharacteristically straightforward reading on *Jazz In Silhouette*, it's very difficult to guess a date for the performance. As Francis Davis suggests in a useful liner-note, the *Jazz In Silhouette* 'Enlightenment' is ideal 'blindfold test' material that might have been recorded at any point from the 1940s to the late 1980s. Only the long drum passage on 'Ancient Aiethopia' and the astonishing Dotson solo and chants that follow sound unequivocally 'modern'. Inevitably, the next track, 'Hours After', is orthodox swing.

The original *Sound Sun Pleasure!!* has been filled out for CD by material from the 1950s which was released in 1973 as *Deep Purple*. The earliest material appears to come from as early as 1953, a useful round-number indicator of Sun Ra's remarkable longevity, and features violinist Stuff Smith on the lo-fi, home-recorded title-track. *Supersonic Jazz* comes from the same period. Again, it is a set of originals combining conventional harmony and orchestrations with a thoroughly individual 'voice' (conveyed in occasional devices like Wilburn Green's use of electric bass on 'Super Blonde' and the closing 'Medicine For A Nightmare') and a striking gentleness that contrast sharply with the often brutal aspect of contemporaneous hard bop. So good is Julian Priester's own brief 'Soft Talk' (the only non-Sun Ra composition) that one immediately wishes for more. All the Evidence reissues have original cover-art, crude by present standards but wildly unconventional in the late 1950s and '60s when a pretty girl with a low-IQ expression was generally considered essential to successful music marketing.

Bad And Beautiful, recorded during 1961, is thought to be the first Arkestra disc to be made in New York City. Chronologically it belongs after the last of the Chicago discs, *Fate In A Pleasant Mood*, which is discussed below. There is no doubt that the pace slackened somewhat after this point, allowing greater concentration on detail and on refining the Arkestra sound. Compare the version of Sun Ra's bluesy 'Ankh' here with a harder-edged performance on *Art Forms For Dimensions Tomorrow*, below. There are three standards on the session, the Previn/Raksin title-track, 'And This Is My Beloved' and 'Just In Time', played in a rather more mannered and deliberate style than later in his career, but with no outer-space embellishments.

(A word about personnels. There may seem a degree of redundancy in listing every player on every available Arkestra recording, except, of course, those which offer no breakdown. Despite the improbable but common misconception that Sun Ra commanded the loyalty of a single group of musicians for nearly four decades, personnels changed very rapidly. Instrumentations are also remarkably capricious. Most players doubled on percussion and vocals at some time or other; at various stages, others may be credited with a secondary instrument only: Gilmore on bass clarinet, Allen on oboe, and so on. We have tried to note these in accordance with the details given on the disc, recognizing all the while that these are often unreliable in the extreme. It is sometimes possible to hear uncredited instruments, and former Arkestra members have taken convincing issue with specific attributions. These, however, are matters for the specialist. Apart from normalizing inconsistent spelling, details above and below are as given.)

*** The Futuristic Sounds Of Sun Ra Savoy SV 0213

Sun Ra; Bernard McKinney (*tb, euph, bells*); Marshall Allen (*as, ts, bells*); John Gilmore (*ts, bcl, bells*); Pat Patrick (*bs, bells*); Ronnie Boykins (*b, bells*); Willie Jones (*d, perc*); Leah Ananda (*perc*); Ricky Murray (*v*). 61.

Not the kind of thing Savoy normally did, this is actually rather good, a piano-driven romp through now familiar themes. There's almost a barrelhouse quality to some of his playing, and anyone who evinces surprise at the 'late' turn back to the mainstream would do well to ignore track-titles like 'Space Jazz Reverie' and 'Of Wounds And Something Else', pay no mind to the bells for the time being, and just concentrate on the back line to something like 'Jet Flight' or 'What's That'. Fletcher Henderson isn't so far away.

*** Monorails And Satellites Evidence ECD 22013 2

Sun Ra (*p* solo). 66.

***(*) **Solo Piano** Improvising Artists Inc I A I 123850
    As above. 5/77.
**** **St Louis Blues** Improvising Artists Inc I A I 123858
    As above. 7/77.

Before considering the Arkestra recordings of the 1960s, it is worth interpolating a comment about the solo material. There has always been a convention that Sun Ra's 'real' instrument was the collective sound of the Arkestra itself, and while it has been contextualized with reference to the Henderson and Ellington orchestras or, looking forward, to Gil Evans and AACM, it's very rare to find the leader's piano playing contextualized in the same way.

With that in mind, it's worth noting that in the year *Monorails And Satellites* was made, Andrew Hill released *Andrew!* amd Cecil Taylor *Unit Structures* on Blue Note; Chick Corea released his debut *Tones For Joans Bones*; *Solo Monk* had appeared the year before, fellow-Chicagoan Muhal Richard Abrams' *Levels And Degrees Of Light* was still some months away. How does Sun Ra fare compared to these? The immediate and obvious response is that *Monorails And Satellites* sounds rather old-fashioned, but at a second hearing there are aspects which are entirely unprecedented: great blocks of pure sound, a tonal richness and uncertainty that suggest Scriabin rather than James P. Johnson. There are few warp-speed runs on *Monorails*; rather, a gently spacey version of 'arranger's piano' that always seems to suggest cues for an absent band. The title-track certainly sounds like a direct transcription of Arkestra charts, as does the opening 'Space Towers'. 'The Galaxy Way', though, is entirely pianistic, a remarkable perform-ance by any standards. Only one standard this time round: a surprisingly smooth version of 'East Street'.

The earlier of the two solo discs made for Paul Bley's Improvising Artists Incorporated label is rather disappointing. It is surprisingly bluesy but in a rather soft-centred way; Howard Mandel decided it was 'sentimental' and it's hard to disagree. Though recorded just two months later, *St Louis Blues* is a much tauter and more dynamic session. Sun Ra's version of the title-track, like the material on *Monorails*, may sound perfectly legitimate and conventional at first hearing, but it uncovers layers of ambiguity with each subsequent exposure. There is also greater consistency between the standards and original material, less sense of tipping different stylistic hats. *St Louis Blues* is also available as a video [Mastersession MSN 5017], a must for completists.

*** **Fate In A Pleasant Mood / When Sun Comes Out** Evidence ECD 22068
    Sun Ra; Phil Cohran, George Hudson, Walter Miller, Lucious Randolph (*t*); Teddy Nance,
    Bernhard Pettaway, Nate Pryor (*tb*); Danny Davis (*as*); Marshall Allen (*as, f, bells, perc*); John
    Gilmore (*ts*); Pat Patrick (*bs*); Ronnie Boykins (*b*); Jon Hardy (*d*); Clifford Jarvis (*d, perc*);
    Tommy Hunter (*gong, perc*); Theda Barbara (*v*). 60, 62–63.
**** **Cosmic Tones For Mental Therapy / Art Forms For Dimensions Tomorrow** Evidence ECD 22036
    Sun Ra; Manny Smith (*t*); Ali Hassan (*tb*); John Gilmore (*ts, bcl, dragon d, sky d*); Pat Patrick
    (*bs, f*); Marshall Allen (*as, ob, astro space d*); Danny Davis (*as, f*); Robert Cummings (*bcl*); James
    Jackson (*f, log d*); Ronnie Boykins, John Ore (*b*); Clifford Jarvis, C. Scoby Stroman (*d, perc*);
    Thomas Hunter (*perc*). 61–62, 63.
**** **Other Planes Of There** Evidence ECD 22037
    Sun Ra; Walter Miller (*t*); Ali Hassan, Teddy Nance (*tb*); Bernhard Pettaway (*btb*); Marshall
    Allen (*as, ob, f*); Danny Davis (*as, f*); John Gilmore (*ts*); Ronnie Cummings (*bcl*); Pat Patrick
    (*bs*); Ronnie Boykins (*b*); Roger Blank, Lex Humphries (*d*). 64.

This is where the outer-space stuff begins with a vengeance. Sun Ra briefly experimented with the Hammond, producing huge, blocky areas of sound. Curiously, it wasn't an instrument that greatly attracted him, and recorded instances are surprisingly rare; there is another on *We Travel The Spaceways*. He coaxes extraordinary percussive effects from it on 'Moon Dance', the first highlight of *Cosmic Tones*. The other, unquestionably, is John Gilmore's long solo on 'Adventure-Equation'. It's a rare outing for Gilmore on bass clarinet (duties normally assigned to Robert Cummings), the only instrument he's credited with on this album. There has to be some doubt about this, as about most of these personnel details; but there is no doubt about the quality of the solo, which is his most compelling on record until 'Body And Soul' on *Holiday For Soul Dance*, several years later.

The album is awash with echo effects and thunderous reverb, apparently devised by drummer Thomas Hunter, who claimed production and engineering credits. The 1961–2 *Art Forms* material is a good deal more straightforward in terms of pure sound, and the playing is absolutely up to standard. The band turns in a sterling performance of 'Ankh' (see *Bad And Beautiful*, above) which includes steaming solos from Patrick and trombonist Ali Hassan. Highly recommended.

Fate/Sun is a less appealing compilation but it does catch the Arkestra at a critical juncture. *Fate In A Pleasant Mood* documents the last Arkestra to be based in Chicago; it therefore strictly precedes the first of the New York sessions, *Bad And Beautiful*, which is listed above. Following a trip to Canada in the spring of 1961, a long-standing Arkestra began to break up, leaving only a rump of loyal adherents:

Gilmore, Allen, Boykins and, despite having set out on a solo course, Pat Patrick, who signed up for a second term. Sun Ra began recruiting new members, including the teenage Danny Davis, who makes a solid impact on *When Sun Comes Out*. Gilmore sounds jaded and tentative on this record, and there is little of the spark of the earlier band, less still of its inspired weirdness. The appearance of Theda Barbara on 'Circe' is a foretaste of how important singers like June Tyson were to become in years to come.

Other Planes Of There is a long-overlooked masterpiece, but certainly also an oddity in the canon. In effect, it is Sun Ra's concerto for Arkestra. His own piano introduction touches bases all the way from Bud Powell to Cecil Taylor, and there are wonderful solos from Danny Davis, Gilmore and Marshall Allen (on oboe). The rest of the record consists of shorter, jazzier segments, with another thoughtful solo from Gilmore on 'Sketch' and a more sensuous statement from Patrick on 'Pleasure'. *Other Planes* stands apart from the other recordings in this group. The instrumentation is straighter and the structures more obviously polyphonic. It shows how adaptable Sun Ra's concept still was in the mid-'60s.

**** **The Heliocentric Worlds Of Sun Ra: Volume 1** ESP Disk ESP 1014
> Sun Ra; Chris Capers (*t*); Teddy Nance (*tb*); Bernhard Pettaway (*btb*); Danny Davis (*f, as*); .
> Marshall Allen (*as, picc, bells, perc*); John Gilmore (*ts, tim*); Robert Cummings (*bcl, woodblocks*);
> Pat Patrick (*bs, perc*); Ronnie Boykins (*b*); Jimhmi Johnson (*perc, tim*). 4/65.

*** **The Heliocentric Worlds Of Sun Ra: Volume 2** ESP Disk ESP 1017
> Sun Ra; Walter Miller (*t*); Marshall Allen (*f, as, picc, perc*); John Gilmore (*ts, perc*); Pat Patrick
> (*bs, perc*); Robert Cummings (*bcl, perc*); Ronnie Boykins (*b*); Roger Blank (*d*). 11/65.

***(*) **Nothing Is** ESP Disk ESP 1045
> Sun Ra; Teddy Nance (*t*); Ali Hassan (*tb*); Marshall Allen (*as, ob*); John Gilmore (*ts*); Pat
> Patrick (*bs*); Robert Cummings (*bcl*); James Jackson (*f, log d*); Ronnie Boykins (*b, tba*); Clifford
> Jarvis (*d*); Carl Nimrod (*sun hn, gong*). 5/66.

These were the first Sun Ra recordings to receive widespread attention in Europe, attaining almost mythological status (though no great rarity) during many years out of catalogue. *Heliocentric Worlds* helped consolidate awareness of the Arkestra as a free-floating but dedicated ensemble made up of players otherwise little known on the jazz scene. Foremost among these was the ever-present John Gilmore, who was widely considered in the 1950s to be the coming man on tenor saxophone (and proved to be a potent inspiration for John Coltrane) but who chose to throw in his lot with Sun Ra and remained – along with Marshall Allen and Pat Patrick – his most significant soloist.

This was the period when Sun Ra was developing a conception of extended harmony based on the now infamous 'space chord'. He doesn't use organ on *Heliocentric Worlds*, sticking quite squarely with piano and relying on celeste, marimba and clavioline (a French-made proto-synthesizer) for more exotic effects. The range of secondary or 'space' instruments assigned to the band is more limited than on some earlier recordings, and there is less acoustic manipulation than on some of the El Saturns. The clearest expression of his interest in 'clouds' or clusters of tones is 'Nebulae' on Volume One, which has the leader alone at his piano and celeste. Otherwise the textures are sparer and more clearly etched than might be supposed and, though the emphasis at this period had shifted towards free-form sonic exploration, the structures are still as watertight as ever. Of all the Arkestra recordings, these are the only ones which strike one as essentially ensemble pieces, relying less than usual on soloing. They stand up surprisingly well to the passage of time and are still, Volume One certainly, an ideal introduction to Sun Ra's music.

Though recording quality on *Nothing Is* leaves a lot to be desired, it is probably a better bet than the rather thin second volume of *Heliocentric Worlds*. It's a joyous, dancing record, with full-throated playing from the brasses and marvellous interplay between Patrick and Gilmore.

**** **The Magic City** Evidence ECD 22069
> Sun Ra; Walter Miller (*t, perc*); Chris Capers (*t, perc*); Ali Hassan, Teddy Nance (*tb*); Bernard
> Petaway (*btb*); Marshall Allen (*as, f, picc*); Danny Davis (*as, f*); Harry Spencer (*as*); John
> Gilmore (*ts*); Pat Patrick (*bs, f*); Robert Cummings (*bcl*); Ronnie Boykins (*b*); Roger Blank,
> Jimhmi Johnson (*d*); James Jackson (*perc*). 65.

**** **Atlantis** Evidence ECD 22067
> Sun Ra; Akh Tal Ebah, Wayne Harris (*t*); Ali Hassan, Charles Stephens (*tb*); Robert Northern
> (*frhn*); Marshall Allen (*as, ob, Jupiter f, perc*); Danny Davis (*as*); John Gilmore (*ts, perc*); Robert
> Cummings (*bcl*); Pat Patrick (*bs, f, perc*); Robert Barry, Clifford Jarvis (*d, perc*); James Jackson
> (*perc*). 67, 69.

As befits its majestic programme, the 22-minute 'Atlantis' is for the biggest Arkestra yet. Only the similarly conceived 'Magic City' matches it for sheer power, but it is about a futuristic place trapped in the present, rather than a past civilization swallowed up by history. 'The Magic City' was a promotional slogan for Birmingham, Alabama, to boost it as a commercial centre. References to slavery and race in an accompanying poem are bound up with imagery borrowed from the Bible or *Paradise Lost*, suggest-

ing the rootedness of Sun Ra's fantastical vision in contemporary reality and in Afro-American tradition. The piece itself was collectively improvised, though the confident synchronization of small-group
sections within the main piece strongly suggests either an element of 'conduction' or of predetermined
sequences. This was the period of Ornette's *Free Jazz* and, more to the point, of Coltrane's huge
Ascension, and 'The Magic City' stands up remarkably well in that company.

Sun Ra himself plays (often simultaneously) both piano and clavioline. He claimed the latter gave him
the 'purest' sound he'd ever had from an electric instrument. Oddly, though economics may have had
something to do with it (the Arkestra was still a shoestring operation and busted instruments were not
always repaired or replaced), by the time of *Atlantis* he's using squeaky little keyboards like the Hohner
Clavinet or the Gibson Kalamazoo organ (a sound immortalized by Ray Manzarek of The Doors). By
this time, though, the sound is very much better, and *Atlantis* gained wider than usual currency, following reissue on the Impulse! label.

Four tracks are for Sun Ra with Gilmore, Robert Barry and Clifford Jarvis only. A fifth, 'Bimini', adds
Allen, Patrick and Jackson on percussion. These were supposed by some observers to be Sun Ra's nod
in the direction of Thelonious Monk, but Cecil Taylor seems a more likely point of reference. The main
piece starts *in media res* (just like *Paradise Lost*) and rumbles hellishly before Sun Ra kicks in with a
quite extraordinary organ solo that must count as one of his most significant instrumental passages. Ali
Hassan plays a dadaist trombone solo before the piece is turned on its head with a skittish beat and the
chant: 'Sun Ra and band from outer space have entertained you here.' It's an odd gesture, given the
emotional temperature of what goes before, but that was Sun Ra . . .

**** Outer Spaceways Incorporated Black Lion BLCD 760191
> Sun Ra; Akh Tal Ebah, Kwame Hadi (*t, d*); Ali Hassan, Teddy Nance (*tb, d*); Bernhard Pettaway
> (*tb*); Marshall Allen (*as, f, ob, d*); Danny Davis (*as, f*); Robert Cummings (*bcl*); Pat Patrick (*bs, f,
> d*); John Gilmore (*ts, d*); Ronnie Boykins (*b*); Nimrod Hunt (*d*); James Jackson (*d, f*); Clifford
> Jarvis (*perc*). 68.

The most startling thing about this 1971 release was the label it was on. Black Lion was more commonly
identified with the conservative end of mainstream, but Alan Bates (also known for his work with
Candid) was admirably open-eared and pluralistic in his tastes and came up with left-field sets like this
for the label more often than is commonly supposed.

Outer Spaceways Incorporated is notable for one of the most measured and sympathetic sleeve-notes
ever written for a Sun Ra record. Victor Schonfield had been an ardent champion of the free scene in the
United Kingdom and was instinctively drawn to the Arkestra's collectivist ethos (enlightened despotism
might be a more accurate description). His description of the leader's 'spavined piano, and the carefully
controlled clanking dissonance of the horns' is just about right, too.

Whatever the exact occasion of its recording, *Outer Spaceways Inc.* seemed to draw together aspects of
the Arkestra's music from the previous decade while simultaneously pointing forward. 'Somewhere
There' gets things going in an atmosphere of whirling chaos which gradually resolves into a semblance
of order on the title-track and the previously unreleased 'Intergalactic Motion'.

The second half of the record is very different. 'Saturn' is, as Schonfield points out, a relatively straightforward big-band piece, constructed round a timeless Gilmore solo. 'Song Of The Sparer' (a theme that
anticipates 'I Am The Alter-Destiny' on *Space Is The Place*) is hauntingly beautiful, while 'Spontaneous
Simplicity', dominated by flutes and Latin-American drum patterns, sounds like a later version of the
Arkestra's 'here to entertain you' tail-piece on *Atlantis*.

For a good many people who hadn't caught up with *Heliocentric Worlds*, this was a first introduction to
the Arkestra's music. In Britain certainly, it was for some time the best-known Sun Ra record. The
augmented CD, with Schonfield's original notes reproduced intact, is still an excellent buy.

***(*) Holiday For Soul Dance Evidence ECD 22011
> Sun Ra; Phil Corhan (*c*); Danny Davis, Akh Tal Ebah, Wayne Harris (*t*); Ali Hassan (*tb*);
> Marshall Allen, Danny Thompson (*as*); John Gilmore (*ts*); Pat Patrick (*bs, b*); Robert
> Cummings (*bcl*); Bob Barry (*d*); James Jackson, Carl Nimrod (*perc*); Ricky Murray (*v*). 68–69.

*** My Brother The Wind, Volume II Evidence ECD 22040
> Sun Ra; Akh Tal Ebah, Kwame Hadi (*t*); Marshall Allen (*as, ob, f*); Danny Davis (*as, acl, f*);
> John Gilmore (*ts, perc*); Pat Patrick, Danny Thompson (*bs, f*); James Jackson (*ob, perc*);
> Alejandro Blake (*b*); Clifford Jarvis, Lex Humphries (*d*); Nimrod Hunt (*hand d*); William
> Brister, Robert Cummings (*perc*). 69, 70.

Predictably, *My Brother The Wind, Volume II* was followed many moons later by Volume One. Sun Ra's
organ really does sound 'intergalactic' on this one, but he also checks out that ubiquitous squealer of the
late '60s, the Mini-Moog. His approach, inevitably, is heterodox in the extreme. Instead of making the
synth sound like anything else, he homes in unerringly on its 'own' sound – shrill, with loads of vibrato –
and then pushes all the buttons to get right into its uptight psyche: angry bleeps, TV shut-down hiss, off-
station crackles. The band, unfortunately, have begun to plod a bit, though the (uncredited) appearance

of June Tyson on 'Walking On The Moon' – no relation to the pop hit – marks a hitherto undocumented association that was to last until the 1990s; Tyson died shortly after Sun Ra in 1993.

Holiday is a more appealing album, largely because the band get their act together. It's entirely a standards set, but for the brief snippet of cornetist Corhan's 'Dorothy's Dance', which may have been conceived in homage to Oz. Sun Ra's opening solos on 'Holiday For Strings' and 'I Loves You, Porgy' amply confirm his *bona fides* as a 'straight' swing soloist. He shows a surprisingly light touch and gently alternates emphasis on left-and right-hand figures which again bear only a fleeting and misleading resemblance to Monk's.

Gilmore's solo on 'Body And Soul', the tenor saxophonist's proving-ground, suggests something of what Coltrane found in his work. Much less well-known, Hobart Dotson also emerges strongly as an underrated player deserving of reassessment. Boykins's unexplained absence leaves the bottom end a bit straggly. Alejandro Blake is at best only a stop-gap replacement; at several points he's audibly flummoxed by what's going on and chugs out bland ostinato figures or else – what the hell! – goes quietly mad.

***(*) Space Is The Place Evidence ECD 22070

> Sun Ra; Kwame Hadi (*t, vib, perc*); Wayne Harris (*t*); Marshall Allen (*as, f, ob, bsn, kora, perc*); Danny Davis (*as, f, acl, perc*); Larry Northington (*as, perc*); John Gilmore (*ts, perc, v*); Eloe Omoe (*bcl, perc*); Danny Thompson (*bs, perc*); Lex Humphries (*d*); Ken Moshesh (*perc*); June Tyson (*v*). 72.

In 1968, the year of upheaval in America as elsewhere, Sun Ra and the Arkestra made their first trip to the West Coast. Perhaps surprisingly, they were met with a wholly lukewarm response. Three years later, Sun Ra taught a course entitled 'The Black Man in the Cosmos' at the University of California, Berkeley, developing ideas that were to influence Anthony Braxton; Braxton wasn't on the course – but, then, hardly anyone was. Sun Ra felt rejected by the university and by California in general, and he returned east in high dudgeon. It was a repeat of the stormy Montreal trip.

However, Sun Ra had been spotted by producer Jim Newman, who suggested making a feature film loosely based on the mythology implicit in the Berkeley course. *Space Is The Place* cast Sun Ra as a cosmic equalizer, John Shaft in an even more outrageous suit, locked in combat with The Overseer, an interplanetary super-pimp who symbolizes the exploitation of the black races. As with a lot of experimental cinema of the time (a good example is Conrad Rooks's ill-fated *Chappaqua*, for which Ornette Coleman wrote the music), the soundtrack was far more interesting than the film itself. Using material from the previous few years – 'Outer Spaceways Incorporated', 'Calling Planet Earth', 'Space Is The Place' – Sun Ra compiled a brisk montage of Arkestra music. Sixteen tracks was unusually quick turnover, but it works remarkably well and the playing is tight and enigmatic. Tracks like 'Mysterious Crystal' were almost unprecedented in the Arkestra canon, combining a huge array of elements into something that simply cannot be characterized by reference to any other music.

A setting like this was tailor-made for June Tyson, who sings hypnotically on 'Blackman'. Marshall Allen switches from his occasional oboe to bassoon to suggest the creaking evil of 'The Overseer', while Danny Davis switches to alto clarinet (anticipating Hamiet Bluiett's experiments on that unfamiliar horn by many years). The movie may still be circulating in obscure art-houses. Whatever the case, the music stands up amazingly well.

**(*) Concert For The Comet Kohoutek ESP Disk ESP 3033

> Sun Ra; Randy Burns (*g*); Donald Rafael Garrett (*b*); other personnel unknown or uncertain. 12/73.

Though not quite the damp squib that Halley's 1990s return turned out to be, Kohoutek's flypast wasn't quite the apocalyptic event it was billed to be. It did, however, inspire a quite bizarre range of musical (remember Argent?), literary and artistic projects. The Arkestra did its bit at Town Hall in New York City. Mostly it's Age of Aquarius nonsense, from a seemingly unfamiliar outfit, but there are moments when the old flash and fire come through. The 'Kohoutek Theme' is subjected to various permutations and 'Journey Through The Outer Darkness' is undeniably atmospheric, even moving. They finish with – what else? – 'Space Is The Place'. Not a great record – but, according to a quick back-of-envelope calculation, it'll be several hundred years before you have to play it again, when the wanderer returns.

*** A Quiet Place In The Universe Leo CD LR 198

> Sun Ra; probably Ahmed Abdullah (*t*); Akh Tal Ebah (*t, v*); Craig Harris (*tb*); Vincent Chauncey (*frhn*); Marshall Allen (*as, picc*); Pat Patrick (*as*); John Gilmore (*ts*); Danny Thompson (*bs, f*) Luqman Ali (*d*); Atakatune, Eddie Thomas (*perc*); Eloe Omoe (*bcl, f*); James Jackson (*bsn, f, perc*); June Tyson (*v*). 76–77.

We have to declare ourselves a touch confused about this one. According to a liner-note, tracks 3–6 – 'Images', 'Love In Outer Space', 'I'll Never Be The Same' and 'Space Is The Place' – have already been released on *A Night In East Berlin*, CD LR 149. The last of these four is ubiquitous, but none of the other tracks matches, and the listed personnels differ, and the suggested dates differ, so we are in the dark. This tape was no more illuminating than usual, found with just a number but believed (by expert Chris Trent) to be 1976 or 1977. If so, and it seems likely, this fills a long gap in the current discography. The sound is murky and congested and there is considerable to-ing and fro-ing even though it does appear to be a concert documentation. 'I Pharoah' is a slice of music-theatre which homes in close on the leader and sounds to us as if it may not have been recorded at the same time or from the same position as the rest . . .? The plus, as always, is the Gilmore solo, this time on the title-track, which is unusually arranged and followed by a french horn solo from Vincent Chauncey. Some good music, then, but outstanding questions about the exact provenance.

/* Live From Soundscape D1W 388
Sun Ra; Michael Ray, Walter Miller (*t*); Charles Stephens (*tb*); Vincent Chauncey (*frhn*); Marshall Allen, John Gilmore, Danny Davis, Eloe Omoe, James Jackson, Danny Thompson (*reeds, perc*); Skeeter McFarland (*g*); Damon Choice (*vib*); Richard Williams (*b*); Luqman Ali (*d*); Atakatune (*perc*); June Tyson (*v*). 11/79.

Though the music was fairly routine, a limited edition of this disc offered an extra CD containing a 72-minute unedited lecture by Sun Ra, recorded the night before the Soundscape concert. Though it might have been more effective as a 30-minute edited lecture, it offers a unique insight into Sun Ra's thinking as it had developed since *Space Is The Place*, which was, after all, only a B-movie version of his basic mythology, heavily compromised by 'blaxploitation' clichés.

The limited edition was issued in numbers that guaranteed it would become a collectors' item, but some copies are bound to turn up second-hand. These merit four-star rating (and may well command five-star prices).

***(*) Sunrise In Different Dimensions hat Art 6099
Sun Ra; Marshall Allen (*as, ob, f*); John Gilmore (*ts, cl, f*); Noel Scott (*as, bs, f*); Danny Thompson (*bs, f*); Kenneth Williams (*ts, bs, f*); Michael Ray (*t, flhn*); Chris Henderson, Eric Walker (*d*). 2/80.

Perhaps the most valuable of the recent live issues, this was recorded in Switzerland as long ago as 1980. Sun Ra is on piano only and the relatively small band deployed spaciously – so to speak – with more emphasis on unaccompanied soloing than earlier or later. The mix of material is by now familiar, with 'Limehouse Blues', 'King Porter Stomp', 'Cocktails For Two' and a delightfully jagged ''Round Midnight' and other swing-era classics from Noble Sissle, Fletcher Henderson and Erskine Hawkins also in evidence. Entertaining and provocative.

***(*) A Night In East Berlin / My Brothers The Wind And Sun No. 9 Leo CD LR 149
Sun Ra; Michael Ray, Ahmed Abdullah (*t*); Tyrone Hill (*tb*); Pat Patrick (*as*); Marshall Allen (*as, f*); John Gilmore (*ts, perc, v*); Danny Ray Thompson (*bs, perc*); Kenny Williams (*bs*); Eloe Omoe (*as, bcl*); James Jackson (*bsn, perc*); Bruce Edwards (*g*); Billy Bang, Owen Brown Jr (*vn*); June Tyson (*vn, v*); John Ore, Rollo Redford (*b*); Luqman Ali, Earl Buster Smith (*d*); ?Pharoah Abdullah (*perc*); Art Jenkins (*v*). 6/86, 1/88 or 90.

In true Leo Records style, the origins of these tapes are shrouded in uncertainty, and the disc fades in on the opening of the East Berlin set, as if the mikes weren't on quick enough. Whatever the technical shortcomings, there's no mistaking the quality or beauty of the music. 'Mystic Prophecy' highlights two of the Arkestra's pillars, Marshall Allen and John Gilmore, and Gilmore is pressed into vocal duty with his boss in the absence of June Tyson, who seems not to have made the trip on this occasion.

The material on *My Brothers The Wind And Sun No. 9* was originally released in an extremely limited edition on an El Saturn white-label release with just a number and (in some cases) a few hand-written comments. Like the East German material, titles weren't known till later. It's thought this may have been recorded at the Knitting Factory in New York City, and there is apparently further material from that time. Good news, because this is a steamingly good band, fierce and propulsive in the slipstream of Sun Ra's synth and with the additional bonus of Billy Bang in the ensembles and soloing. Regrettably, this being *samizdat*-land, it's interrupted by the end of the tape.

The most valuable single item on the disc is the quasi-atonal 'The Shadow World', a most unexpected conception even for this most unexpected of groups. No surprise that it should again feature Allen and Gilmore.

*** Reflections In Blue Black Saint 120101
Sun Ra; Randall Murray (*t*); Tyrone Hill (*tb*); Pat Patrick (*as, cl*); Marshall Allen (*as, f, ob, picc*); Danny Ray Thompson (*as, cl, bcl*); John Gilmore, Ronald Wilson (*ts*); James Jackson (*bsn, African d*); Carl LeBlanc (*g*); Tyler Mitchell (*b*); Thomas Hunter, Earl Buster Smith (*d*).

**(*) Hours After Black Saint 120111
As above. 12/86.

*** Love In Outer Space Leo CD LR 180
Sun Ra and his Arkestra; no personnel details. 12/83.
*** Cosmo Omnibus Imaginable Illusion DIW 824
Sun Ra; Michael Ray (*t, v*); Ahmed Abdullah (*t*); Tyrone Hill (*tb*); Marshall Allen (*as*); John
Gilmore (*ts, perc*); Danny Thompson (*bs*); Leroy Taylor (*cl, bcl*); Bruce Edwards (*g*); Rollo
Rodford (*b*); Eric Walter (*b*); Earl Buster Smith (*d*); June Tyson (*v, vn*); Judith Holton (*dancer*).
8/88.
***(*) Blue Delight A & M SP 5260
Sun Ra; Ahmed Abdullah, Fred Adams, Tommy Turrentine (*t*); Tyrone Hill, Julian Priester (*tb*);
Al Evans (*flhn, frhn*); Marshall Allen (*as, f, ob, picc, cl*); Noel Scott (*as, perc*); Danny Ray
Thompson (*as, bs, f, perc*); John Gilmore (*ts, cl, perc*); Eloe Omoe (*bcl, as, contra acl, perc*);
James Jackson (*bsn, f, perc*); Bruce Edwards, Carl Leblanc (*g*); John Ore (*b*); Billy Higgins, Earl
Buster Smith (*d*); Elson Nascimento (*perc*). 12/88.
***(*) Purple Night A & M SP 5324
Sun Ra; Ahmed Abdullah, Jothan Callins, Fred Adams, Al Evans, Don Cherry (*t*); Tyrone Hill,
Julian Priester (*tb*); James Spaulding (*as, f*); Marshall Allen (*as, f, perc*); John Gilmore (*ts, perc,
v*); James Jackson (*f, d*); Reynold Scott (*bs, f*); John Ore, Rollo Radford (*b*); June Tyson (*v, vn*);
Earl Buster Smith, Eric Walker, Thomas Henderson (*d*); Elson Nascimento, Jorge Silva (*perc*).
11/89.
The 1980s were a period of steady and often unimaginative consolidation. Sun Ra's music had, at last,
become a *style*. Even so, the Arkestra were still able to create an astonishing impact in performance.
There are powerful moments on *Love In Outer Space*, which was recorded at a concert in Utrecht. The
closing 'Space Is The Place' still sounds positive and challenging, and there are outrageous versions of
'Big John's Special' and ''Round Midnight'.
Of later 1980s performances, the DIW, recorded in Tokyo, combines a suite of mythic themes with a
surprisingly straight 'Prelude To A Kiss'. Edit out the chants and some of the more self-conscious FX,
and it sounds like one of Sun Ra's most complete and convincing recordings of the last 15 years.
Reflections In Blue and, from the same sessions, *Hours After* concentrate exclusively on mainstream
composition (though the latter is punctuated by a chaotic 'Dance Of The Extra Terrestrians' and 'Love
On A Far Away Planet', which are more typical of past snippets from the Arkestra's anarchic shows).
This is broadly the pattern of *Blue Delight* and *Purple Night*, somewhat unexpectedly released on A&M.
The appearance of guest stars on both albums underlines the unusually slick, showbizzy feel, and it's
hard to avoid 'Jazz At The Philharmonic goes to Mars' jokes. Don Cherry seems a perfect choice for
other-worldly settings, but it's slightly startling to find trumpeter Tommy Turrentine in this company. As
the track-title has it: 'Your Guest Is As Good As Mine'. *Blue Delight* mixes 'Out Of Nowhere' and 'Days
Of Wine And Roses' with 'They Dwell On Other Planets'. The arrangements are tight and uncontroversial, confidently swinging, and may be a little difficult to square with the Spacemaster's joke-shop
reputation. These are neither 'way out' nor uncomfortably 'radical', nor anything but highly accomplished. So listen.

*** Second Star To The Right: Salute To Walt Disney Leo CD LR 230
Sun Ra; Michael Ray (*t, v*); Tyrone Hill, Julian Priester (*tb*); Marshall Allen (*as, cl, f*); Eloe
Omoe (*as, cl, bcl*); Noel Scott (*as, f*); James Jackson (*bsn, ob, v*); Bruce Edwards (*g*); Arthur
Joonie Booth (*b*); June Tyson (*vn, v*); Earl Buster Smith (*d*); Elson Nascimento Santos (*perc*). 4/
89.
Sun Ra plays Disney. Of course. Initially this sounds so perverse as to go all the way round to being
inevitable. A&M had done an album of Disney covers which included the Arkestra doing 'Pink
Elephants On Parade' from *Dumbo*, but this Austrian concert goes the whole hog. Marshall Allen
provides alto solos of surreal beauty in the opening chant on 'Forest Of No Return' and to the Sun Ra-
introduced 'Someday My Prince Will Come'. The leader even quotes a couple of Miles Davis tags on his
long, delicate opening, before horns, vocalists June Tyson and a falsetto Michael Ray, and then the
rhythm come in behind him. 'Frisco Fog' isn't Disney and, perversely, it's the best band track on the
date, a driving, train-time number that gets the sections properly worked out. 'I'm Wishing' is pretty
good but takes an age to get under way. The title-tune gives Hill a lot of space, and 'Hi Ho! Hi Ho!'
features Scott on alto and clarinet. Sun Ra expert seems to think 'Zip-A-Dee-Doo-Dah' is from *Sleeping
Beauty* but, apart from that, it's good to have what is effectively a private bootleg recording so fully
documented. The sound is awful; someone coughs right in the mike at one point and there is only a
rather artificial balance on some tracks. The piano is clearly audible, though, and no complaints about
the quality of the music

**** Mayan Temples Black Saint 120121
Sun Ra; Ahmed Abdullah, Michael Ray (*t, v*); Tyrone Hill (*tb*); Noel Scott (*as*); Marshall Allen
(*as, f*); John Gilmore (*ts, perc*); James Jackson (*bsn, perc*); Jothan Callins (*b*); Clifford Barbaro,

Earl Buster Smith (*d*); Ron McBee, Elson Nascimento, Jorge Silva (*perc*); June Tyson (*v*). 7/90. As Francis Davis points out in his liner-note, this studio session restores the emphasis to Sun Ra's piano playing. Illness would shortly curtail his ability to play acoustic keyboards this crisply. His introductions and leads are absolutely in the line of Ellington, and the voicings are supple, open-ended and often quietly ambiguous, leaving considerable emphasis on the soloists. As always, Gilmore is a giant and Marshall Allen's searing solo on 'Prelude To Stargazers' is a model of controlled fury. He re-records 'El Is A Sound Of Joy' (see *Supersonic Jazz*, above), a late-1950s theme that sounds completely contemporary and brings a freshness and simplicity to 'Alone Together' that is quite breathtaking. 'Discipline No. 1' is a lovely ballad, illustrating Sun Ra's ability to give simple material an unexpected rhythmic profile (Davis rightly points to the example of Mingus in this case) and the closing 'Sunset On The Night On The River Nile' is one of his very best space anthems. Few Sun Ra albums give a better sense of his extraordinary versatility; this is far preferable to the majority of recent live sets.

***(*) Live At The Hackney Empire Leo CD LR 214/215 2CD

Sun Ra; Michael Ray (*t, v*); Jothan Callins (*t*); Tyrone Hill (*tb*); Marshall Allen (*as, f, picc, ob*); Noel Scott (*as, bcl*); John Gilmore (*ts, cl, perc, v*); Charles Davis (*bs*); James Jackson (*bsn, perc*); India Cooke (*vn*); Kash Killion (*clo*); John Ore (*b*); Clifford Barbaro, Earl Buster Smith (*d*); Talvin Singh (*perc, v*); Elson Nascimento (*perc*); June Tyson (*v*). 10/90.

This concert was recorded as part of a documentary project originally for Britain's Channel 4. Originally, there was a projected backdrop and other effects, but so far the finished work – by Chris Foster and Dave Hayes – has not materialized. It has nevertheless bequeathed us some excellent music, if unsurprising in content by Arkestra standards, until the second set, at any rate. All the familiar names are present and all in good form: Gilmore, Allen (glorious on 'Prelude To A Kiss') and Tyson.

Disc two begins with a violin improvisation, before Davis, Cooke, Allen and others solo over 'Discipline 27-II'. There is then a version of 'East Of The Sun' (vocalist, Gilmore), a beautiful rendition of a Sun Ra favourite, 'Somewhere Over The Rainbow', and a rapid charge through the Sissle/Henderson anthem 'Yeah Man!' and 'Frisco Fog'. A now-familiar mixture of the strange and the traditional, this is a highly attractive set. It will be good to see the film when funds make it possible but, for now, this is recommended. One of the best later Arkestra recordings.

(***) Pleiades Leo CD LR 210/211 2CD

Sun Ra; Jothan Callins, Michael Ray (*t*); Tyrone Hill (*tb*); Marshall Allen (*as*); John Gilmore, Noel Scott (*ts*); Charles Davis (*bs*); James Jackson (*ob, d*); India Cooke (*vl*); Stephen Killion (*clo*); John Orr (*b*); Clifford Barbaro, Earl C. Smith (*d*); Elson Nascimento (*perc*); T. Singh (*tabla*); June Tyson (*v, vn*); unidentified symphony orchestra. 10/90.

It is a measure of Sun Ra's belatedly growing reputation that this concert was able to take place at all. Recorded in Paris, it features a mainly unfamiliar Arkestra and all-too-familiar repertoire (with the exception of Chopin's 'Prelude in A major'!) in an acoustic that is Jupiterian in resonance. The recording falls so far below acceptable standards that *Pleiades* seems to represent a return to the snap, crackle and pop of the old El Saturns (and of Leo's original, *samizdat* catalogue).

One wonders how good and faithful servants like Gilmore and Allen viewed the music by this stage; Tyson's enthusiasm, though, is undimmed, and it is significant that she should have survived Sun Ra by such a short time.

**(*) Friendly Galaxy Leo CD LR 188

Sun Ra Arkestra; no personnel details. 4/91.

**(*) Destination Unknown Enja 7071

Sun Ra; Ahmed Abdullah, Michael Ray (*t*); Tyrone Hill (*tb*); Marshall Allen (*as*); James Jackson (*bsn, d*); Bruce Edwards (*g*); Jothan Callins (*b*); Earl Buster Smith (*d*); Elson Nascimento, Stanley Morgan (*perc*). 3/92.

The rest should have been silence, but just as the concert appearances (and the word is used advisedly) continued to the bitter end, so too will offcuts and live sessions continue to emerge. Neither of these does Sun Ra's memory any credit. Ill and tired, he plays a largely symbolic role in the proceedings, fronting shrunken ensembles that no longer seem to have the concentration to play ensemble music. The absence of Gilmore on the last session, whatever the reason, has to be seen as symbolic.

There will be other releases, and continued debate about the enigma that was Sun Ra. As for his place in history, one must conclude that, for the moment at least . . . destination unknown.

Monty Sunshine (born 1928) CLARINET

*** **In London** Black Lion BLCD 760508

Sunshine; Alan Gresty (*t*); Eddie Blashfield (*tb*); Ken Barton (*bj, g, v*); Micky Ashman (*b*); Geoff Downes (*d*). 7/79.

(*) **Gotta Travel On Timeless TTD 570

Sunshine; Alan Gresty (*t*); John Beecham (*tb*); Barry Dew (*bj, g, v*); Tony Bagot (*b*); Geoff Downes (*d, v*). 7/91.

*** **South** Timeless CD TTD 583

As above, except Tony Scriven (*d*) replaces Downes. 8/93.

An auld licht traditionalist, Sunshine stood firm when the Chris Barber band began to shift its ground in the late 1950s to accommodate the growing vogue for skiffle and the blues. Sunshine had contributed materially to the group's success and was the featured soloist on the big hit, 'Petite Fleur'. Leaving Barber certainly punched holes in his marketability, but he has commanded a loyal following in both Britain and continental Europe throughout the past three decades.

The earlier Sunshine is well represented on Chris Barber records and on some useful trad compilations. The more recent things under his own name are also well worth having, though the solos are increasingly by the book and are perhaps even a little leg-weary on the 1991 session, which was recorded live at The Bull's Head in Barnes, London, a long-standing jazz haunt. *In London* sounds a little shrill transferred to CD and doesn't offer an entirely accurate representation of Sunshine's Bechet-influenced tone. It does, though, give a fair sense of his approach to standard material. The arrangements of 'Just A Closer Walk With Thee' and 'Careless Love' are nicely personalized. Gresty knows the stuff inside out and chips in with some forceful statements of his own on both sets.

South is a very decent set from the line-up who've stuck with Sunshine during his latter-day resurgence. Again, no great surprises or revelations, just good, strong, revivalist jazz, articulated clearly and without fuss.

Klaus Suonsaari (born 1959) DRUMS

***(*) **Reflecting Times** Storyville STCD 4157

Suonsaari; Tom Harrell (*t, flhn*); Bob Berg (*ts*); Niels Lan Doky (*p*); Ray Drummond (*b*). 3/87.

***(*) **True Colours** L + R CDLR 45080

Suonsaari; Tom Harrell (*t, flhn*); Scott Robinson (*ts, bsx*); Niels Lan Doky (*p*); Niels-Henning Orsted-Pedersen (*b*). 3/92.

*** **Inside Out** Soul Note 121274

Suonsaari; Scott Wendholt (*t, flhn*); Scott Robinson (*ts, ss, f*); Renée Rosnes (*p*); Steve Nelson (*vib*); Ray Drummond (*b*). 3/94.

A Finnish drummer who sounds not a bit like Edward Vesala (but is a physical ringer for Bill Frisell), Suonsaari led one of his country's best young jazz groups, Blue Train, before striking out as a name artist. The Storyville record obviously gains visibility from the other band members, but it is the leader's clean, unaffected swing, reminiscent of Billy Hart or Billy Higgins, that strikes even the casual listener straight away, and it has become clear that he is not just a facile time-keeper but is also a very thoughtful musician, contributing several numbers to *Inside Out*, a very polished record which is disappointing only relative to earlier promise. Something doesn't quite gel about it. One of the most intriguing aspects of the L + R set is Robinson's use of bass saxophone and a range of colours on 'Bemsha Swing' and 'Round Midnight' which one would not ordinarily expect to hear. Suonsaari will surely go from strength to strength. Despite the bright opening, we have not heard the best from him yet.

John Surman (born 1944) BARITONE SAXOPHONE, SOPRANO SAXOPHONE, BASS CLARINET, ALTO CLARINET SYNTHESIZERS, PIANO, RECORDER

*** **Westering Home** FMR CD 19

Surman (solo; various instruments). 72.

***(*) **Morning Glory** FMR CD 21

Surman; Malcolm Griffiths (*tb*); John Taylor (*p*); Terje Rypdal (*g*); Chris Laurence (*b*); John Marshall (*d*). 73.

Surman first came to notice as a member of Mike Westbrook's group. An innovative soloist, who managed to bring some of Coltrane's harmonic diversity and intensity to the baritone saxophone, but to combine it – improbably at first – with a delicate, folksy lyricism, and to synthesize advanced 'vertical' improvisation with simpler diatonic themes. As well as folk themes, Surman was drawn to church music, and there were many occasions in the lives of groups like The Trio and the later saxophone trio, SOS, when he seemed to be thinking in terms of chants, chorales and organ fugues rather than jazz.

Westering Home was a very early version of the multi-tracked solo projects that Surman was to make his staple in the 1970s and '80s. He uses a variety of horns, piano and percussion to construct an evocative collage that, despite hornpipes and pibroch elements, is almost impossible to locate geographically but which seems to belong to Surman alone.

Morning Glory was an unfortunately short-lived group that could – and perhaps should – have been allowed to develop further. Surman is very definitely both front man and chief composer. Though Rypdal is the colourist and decorator, it is the saxophonist (who had temporarily given up playing his baritone at this point, in favour of soprano and bass clarinet) who sets the mood and erects the scaffolding of each intriguing piece. Though *Westering Home* is probably now no more than a curiosity, *Morning Glory* is one of the essential works of British jazz in the 1970s; its return to the catalogue is very welcome indeed.

*** Upon Reflection ECM 1148
Surman (*ss, bs, bcl, syn*). 5/79.
***(*) The Amazing Adventures Of Simon Simon ECM 1193
Surman; Jack DeJohnette (*d, perc, p*). 1/81.
***(*) Such Winters Of Memory ECM 1254
Surman; Karin Krog (*v, ring modulator, tambura*); Pierre Favre (*d*). 12/82.
*** Withholding Pattern ECM 1295
Surman (*ss, bs, bcl, rec, p, syn*). 12/84.
**(*) Private City ECM 1366
As above. 12/87.
***(*) Road To St Ives ECM 1418
As above. 4/90.
**** Adventure Playground ECM 1463
Surman; Paul Bley (*p*); Gary Peacock (*b*); Tony Oxley (*d*). 9/91.
***(*) The Brass Project ECM 1478
Surman; Henry Lowther, Stephen Waterman, Stuart Brooks (*t*); Malcolm Griffiths, Chris Pyne (*tb*); David Stewart, Richard Edwards (*btb*); Chris Laurence (*b*); John Marshall (*d*); John Warren (*cond*). 4/92.

A rather solitary though much-admired figure who has spent a good part of his professional career outside the United Kingdom, Surman turned an absence of satisfying commissions to (creative) advantage on a series of multi-tracked solo projects on which he improvised horn lines over his own synthesizer accompaniments. In the early 1960s, he had modernized baritone saxophone playing, giving an apparently cumbersome horn an agile grace that belied its daunting bulk and adding an upper register much beyond its notional range (somewhat as Eric Dolphy had done with Surman's second instrument, the bass clarinet, and Albert Mangelsdorff with the trombone).

Upon Reflection quickly established the rather withdrawn, inward mood that became almost a vice on *Withholding Pattern* (it's hard not to read too much into the titles), but it also revived the folkish mode of Surman's solo *Westering Home*, which had mixed free passages with piano songs and even a sailor's dance on what sounds like harmonica. Surman's work of the 1980s under the aegis of ECM has updated that experiment and allied it to the stark and unadorned 'Northern' sound associated with Jan Garbarek and the better parts of Rypdal. This is at its coolest and most detached on *Secret City*, which was based on dance scores and sounds rather inconsequential outside that context.

Withholding Pattern is a curious combination of mock jauntiness ('All Cat's Whiskers And Bee's Knees') and similar untypical abstraction, with some of his best baritone playing for years, marred by bland waterdrop synthesizer patterns. 'Doxology' reflects an early interest in church music which re-emerges in the 'organ' opening to 'Tintagel' on *Road To Saint Ives*. The 1990 album isn't intended to be directly evocative of places, but it is one of Surman's warmest and most humane performances, in which the absence of 'live' accompaniment seems less constricting. Surman is a highly rhythmic player, but his multi-tracked backgrounds are often very unresponsive.

This wasn't a problem on Surman's live and studio collaborations with percussionist and keyboard player, Jack DeJohnette. *The Adventures Of Simon Simon* re-creates the quasi-narrative style of Surman's 1970s duo collaborations with the Trio drummer, Stu Martin, who died suddenly in 1980 (*Live At Woodstock Town Hall* is rare, but worth the hunt). DeJohnette's more explicit jazz background gives the music a more linear thrust, and less of the '(with)holding pattern' stasis that sometimes creeps into it, and creeps again into the otherwise excellent collaboration with singer Sheila Jordan and percussionist Pierre Favre.

Much of Surman's compositional energy in recent years has been directed towards his Brass Project, and a record was long overdue. It represented his first opportunity to work in the studio with Canadian composer-arranger John Warren since they recorded the magnificent *Tales Of The Algonquin* at the end of the 1960s. Unfortunately, comparison of the two records doesn't reflect all that positively on *The Brass Project*. Nevertheless it's a fine record; Surman's gently bucolic themes are played with just the right mixture of exuberance and reserve, and the voicings are often very subtle.

A faint sense that Surman has spent the last decade profitably marking time in an idiom that suited ECM's high-shine production had been shattered by the previous year's *Adventure Playground*, not so much a Surman album as a series of intimate collaborations in a freer mode than has been the saxophonist's norm over the past few years. The standard of playing is very high indeed (most noticeably from Bley and Oxley) and strongly suggests that Surman has still got a great deal to contribute at the sharper end of the music.

***(*) Stranger Than Fiction ECM 1534
Surman; John Taylor (*p*); Chris Laurence (*b*); John Marshall (*d*). 12/93.
This was very nearly a re-formation of the Morning Glory group. Without a second horn or Rypdal's clangorous guitar playing, the emphasis is very squarely on Surman and Taylor and on light-footed country airs with a countervailing shadow. The long 'Triptych' with which the record closes is a masterpiece of abstract invention, relieving any doubt that they are content merely to spin out uncomplicated melodies. Careful listening suggests that Laurence and Marshall are much more important to the group than appears at first sight, supplying an unshakeable foundation and a subtle hint to the frontmen that stopping to muse is tempting but ultimately insufficient.

**** Nordic Quartet ECM 1553
Surman; Vigleik Storaas (*p*); Terje Rypdal (*g*); Karin Krog (*v*). 8/94.
Surman and long-time partner Krog are a gifted team. The interesting thing about this record is how much of the emphasis is devolved to the little-known Storaas (an elegant stylist with a few forgivable Keith Jarrett touches) and to even-handed group improvisation. Krog's voice is much jazzier than the setting strictly suggests, and her phrasing imposes a certain discipline on the opening 'Traces', 'Unwritten Letter' and 'Wild Bird'. Surman often functions as her accompanist and commentator, working off the vocal line. Rypdal is, as usual, more detached and abstract but there is a compelling logic to the music that overcomes its cool detachment and draws the listener into its world.

***(*) A Biography Of The Rev. Absalom Dawe ECM 1528
Surman (solo). 10/94.
Dawe was an ancestor of Surman's and his part in this is limited to providing a certain thematic glue to a further set of solo improvisations which nowadays place less emphasis on synthesized ostinati and much more on the detailed interplay of horn lines. Adding alto clarinet to his armoury has given Surman an important new timbre and pitch, and many of these pieces seem – at first hearing and without undue thought – to be lighter and more plain-spoken than some of the earlier ECMs. It is the same mix of jazz, folk and church themes, however, the only difference lying in the more relaxed, less stressed opposition of tension and release, and in the significance accorded to individual lead-lines. Surman is now a master of this demanding craft.

Ralph Sutton (born 1922) PIANO

**(*) Live At Haywards Heath Flyright 204
Sutton (*p* solo). 11/75.
*** Trio And Quartet Storyville STCD 8210
Sutton; Lars Blach (*g*); Hugo Rasmussen (*b*); Svend-Erik Norregaard (*d*). 5/77.
*** Last Of The Whorehouse Piano Players: The Original Sessions Chiaroscuro CR(D) 206
Sutton; Jay McShann (*p*); Milt Hinton (*b*); Gus Johnson (*d*). 12/79.
***(*) Partners In Crime Sackville SKCD 2-2023
Sutton; Bob Barnard (*t*); Milt Hinton (*b*); Len Barnard (*d*). 8/83.
**** At Café Des Copains Sackville SKCD 2-2019
Sutton (*p* solo). 6/83–1/87.
***(*) More At Café Des Copains Sackville SKCD2-2036
Sutton (*p* solo). 1/88–1/89.
***(*) Eye Opener J&M CD 500
Sutton (*p* solo). 4/90.
*** Easy Street Sackville SKCD2-2040
Sutton; Bob Barnard (*t*); Len Barnard (*d*). 5/91.
Sutton has been playing top-drawer stride and swing piano for more than 50 years and shows few signs of slowing down. He is a great favourite with British audiences and two of the solo albums were cut in

England. The Flyright record finds him in relaxed, ambling form, and there is his usual mixture of romping stride and tinkling, wayward balladry, but the piano is in bad shape and the sound isn't much of an improvement on what was a rotten LP issue. Much better to go to either the Sackville or the J&M sessions. J&M recorded him (on a Steinway) at a church hall in Woking, and besides Sutton chestnuts like the title-piece (a famous piece of virtuosity) there is a charming Willard Robison medley and mothballed stride fantasies such as 'Rippling Waters' and 'Clothes Line Ballet'.

The quartet date with the Barnard brothers has a timeless feel, since the trumpeter seems wholly unselfconscious about an Armstrong influence, and their opening romp through 'Swing That Music' shows how beautifully swing repertory can turn out when delivered in the right hands. Sutton's accompaniments are as sharp as his solos: when he leans in and clears the decks, his huge two-handed manner gives the clearest impression of what stride masters such as Waller and Johnson would have sounded like if they'd been recorded on contemporary equipment. *Easy Street* is a rematch with perhaps just the slightest shine taken off: there's some handsome playing, but a vague sense of routine about some of the tunes. The solo record from Café Des Copains, drawn from a series of broadcasts over a five-year period, uses scarce material – 'Russian Lullaby', 'Laugh Clown Laugh' and a rollicking 'Somebody Stole My Gal', with its rhythms cunningly displaced – which Sutton relishes, acknowledging the melodies but steamrollering past them into areas of what might be called 'pure' stride piano. The second helping on *More* concentrates on two shows a year apart, and gets a slightly lower mark since the material is rather more familiar this time.

The 1979 date was originally issued as two LPs on ChazJazz and it also includes two previously unreleased tracks. The meeting of Sutton and McShann is the occasion for much musical backslapping and, while their styles aren't exactly complementary, Sutton tones down enough to make McShann's wry kind of blues seep through. They both sing, although Ralph sticks to Fats Waller ham on 'Truckin''. Lots of fun.

Storyville have reissued *Trio And Quartet* after several years in the vinyl scrapyard. Recorded on one of Ralph's Scandinavian tours, this is a typically amiable encounter which finds Blach, Rasmussen and Norregard as capable if not especially effective bystanders. Sutton tends to go his own way.

***(*) **Maybeck Recital Hall Vol. 30** Concord CCD 4586
    Sutton (*p* solo). 8/93.
The main point here is that Sutton gets a decent piano-sound on record, something that has eluded him many times in the past. The programme is nothing more or less than a typical Sutton beanfeast – Waller, The Lion, Bix.

Esbjorn Svensson KEYBOARDS

*** **When Everyone Has Gone** Dragon DRCD 248
    Svensson; Dan Berglund (*b, whistle*); Magnus Ostrom (*d, v*). 7–9/93.
*** **Mr And Mrs Handkerchief** Prophone PCD 028
    As above. 3/95.
Svensson tells an attractive story at the piano even if he has nothing especially new to say. The feel on *When Everyone Has Gone* is lightly impressionistic post-bop, nodding at Keith Jarrett's Standards Trio but scaling down the grand gestures to a more manageable size. The trio play together in a loose but cleanly focused way which gives a degree of relaxation to themes that might sound merely uptight. 'Mohammed Goes To New York Part Two' is a catchy piece of Scandinavian funk, much in the style of Niels Lan Doky, but Svensson's heart is probably more in the ballads: 'Waltz For The Lonely Ones' is particularly charming. He also uses the electronic keyboards with such restraint that they acquire an almost ghostly quality at the back of the music. *Mr And Mrs Handkerchief* dispenses with the electronics, but this time Svensson alternates between upright and grand pianos: the homely quality of the upright lends an oddly clattery quality to his work, an almost perverse note when one hears the delicacy of his touch on, say, 'The Day After'. Berglund, as if in compensation, plays with a degree more urgency this time.

Ewan Svensson GUITAR, GUITAR-SYNTHESIZER

*** **Present Directions** Dragon DRCD 218
    Svensson; Palle Danielsson (*b*); Magnus Gran (*d*). 9/90–6/91.
The range of settings explored by such American guitarists as John Abercrombie, John Scofield and Bill Frisell have mapped out plenty of fresh terrain for the electric instrument and, while Svensson may not be doing anything very new, he explores that ground with great skill. Across 12 compositions and over

an hour of music on *Present Directions*, he alternates between fast, neatly picked solos and broader expressive washes via the guitar-synthesizer. What makes the difference is the exacting support offered by Danielsson, as strong a bassist as one could ask for in this setting, and Gran's busy and intelligent drumming.

*** **Reflections** Dragon DRCD 239
    Svensson; Ove Ingemarsson (*ts, EWI*); Harald Svensson (*p*); Matz Nilsson (*b*); Magnus Gran (*d*). 11/92–1/93.

*** **Next Step** Dragon DRCD 284
    As above, except omit Harald Svensson. 11/94.

More mood(y) electric jazz from Svensson, this time abetted by the severe-sounding Ingemarsson, who plays the EWI with rather more sensitivity than some practitioners. The compositions are thoughtful, if rather lacking in melody, but the duet with Harald Svensson on 'Boat Trip' is very pretty, and the leader has plenty to say beyond the usual unreeling of fast licks. The subsequent *Next Step* pares the music back to a quartet, Ingemarsson sticking to straight-ahead tenor, and his bluff authority cuts through any chaff that Svensson might have been tempted by. They move very easily through the 11 tunes. Nothing special to make the record stand out from its predecessors, though.

Steve Swallow (born 1940) BASS GUITAR

***(*) **Home** ECM 1160
    Swallow; Davie Liebman (*ss, ts*); Steve Kuhn (*p*); Lyle Mays (*syn*); Bob Moses (*d*); Sheila Jordan (*d*). 9/79.

*** **Carla** XtraWatt/2
    Swallow; Carla Bley (*org*); Larry Willis (*p*); Hiram Bullock (*g*); Victor Lewis (*d*); Don Alias (*perc*); Ida Kavafian (*vn*); Ikwhan Bae (*vla*); Fred Sherry (*clo*). 86–87.

***(*) **Swallow** XtraWatt 6
    Swallow; Steve Kuhn (*p*); Carla Bley (*org*); Karen Mantler (*ky, hca*); Gary Burton (*vib*); Hiram Bullock, John Scofield (*g*); Robby Ameen (*d*); Don Alias (*perc*). 9–11/91.

*** **Real Book** XtraWatt 7
    Swallow; Tom Harrell (*t, flhn*); Joe Lovano (*ts*); Mulgrew Miller (*p*); Jack DeJohnette (*d*). 12/93.

A thin but improving trawl for one of the most accomplished bassists of recent times and certainly the most significant living exponent of the bass guitar. The writing on *Carla* barely reflects the quality of classics like 'Arise Her Eyes' and 'Hotel Hello', which represent Swallow's other main contribution to modern jazz. But for the absence of the dedicatee's abrasive melodic mannerisms, this might just as well be a Carla Bley album (which will be sufficient recommendation for Bley fans).

For *Home*, Swallow set a group of poems by Robert Creeley, tiny snapshots of ordinariness that deliver their meanings precisely and without embellishment. Much the way Swallow plays. It might be that these pieces would work better with a less developed accompaniment, perhaps just voice, bass and piano, but the scoring is never allowed to overpower the lyric.

There's a touch of sameness about the writing on the eponymous *Swallow*, but the bassist's arrangements are impeccable and he's seldom sounded better. The tunes are mostly mid-tempo Latino grooves with plenty of solo scope. Guest players Burton and Scofield don't figure all that prominently and the most arresting voice is Karen Mantler's harmonica; her brief solo on 'Slender Thread' sets the bassist up for one of his delicate, single note constructions, built up over Bley's organ chords and a soft, shuffle beat. It could do with just one ripping tune, but that isn't Swallow's forte. On its own perfectly respectable terms, this is a beauty.

Real Book is a modest adventure for an all-star (though arguably over-familiar) band of heroes. Harrell and Lovano are dependably excellent and the session has class and aplomb from moment to moment; but this kind of meeting of heavyweights isn't necessarily Swallow's best thing, and the music misses some of his most interesting quirks.

John Swana TRUMPET, FLUGELHORN

*** **Introducing John Swana** Criss Cross Jazz 1045
    Swana; Billy Pierce (*ts*); Benny Green (*p*); Peter Washington (*b*); Kenny Washington (*d*). 12/90.

*** **John Swana And Friends** Criss Cross Jazz 1055
    Swana; Tom Harrell (*t, flhn*); Billy Pierce (*ts*); Mulgrew Miller (*p*); Ira Coleman (*b*); Billy Drummond (*d*). 12/91.

***(*) **The Feeling's Mutual** Criss Cross 1090
      Swana; Chris Potter (*ts, as, f*); Dave Posmontier (*org*); Steve Giordano (*g*); Billy Drummond (*d*).
      12/93.

Swana is a staunch modern traditionalist, firmly in the mould of such bygone masters as Lee Morgan
and Kenny Dorham, and though he also cites Tom Harrell as a key influence, it's his silvery tone,
upfront attack and ready fluency that mark him out as an accomplished player. These are meaty,
enjoyable records that just miss out on indispensability: little about the first two lingers long in the mind.
Introducing pairs him with a near-perfect companion in the useful Pierce, who manages to play muscular
tenor without quite falling into muscle-bound moves. The rhythm section are characteristically full of
brio, but the material comes out sounding the same, even with such diverse composers as Wayne Shorter,
Kenny Dorham and Swana himself. *John Swana And Friends* adds Harrell to the front line, and his
arrangements of some of the jazz tunes – a tart reharmonization of 'Oleo', for instance – introduce a
fresh twist. Yet the music never quite catches fire as it might, and Harrell's lovely playing on 'Darn That
Dream' puts Swana in the shade.

    The Feeling's Mutual is a more relaxed and convincing step forward. With the estimable Potter turning
in fine support, Swana takes some of his best solos on his originals here, but more important is the way
he's organized the group: Posmontier and Giordano (friends from Philadelphia) steer well clear of
organ/guitar band clichés, and instead the music has an open, modal feel that material like Chick
Corea's 'Litha' seems tailored for. A surprising 'When Johnny Comes Marching Home' and a yearning
ballad called 'Autumn Landscape' use the same virtues for different results. A very good Criss Cross.

Harvie Swartz DOUBLE BASS

*** **Urban Earth** Gramavision GR 8503
      Swartz; Bob Mintzer (*ss*); David Sanborn (*as*); Mike Stern (*g*); Ben Aronov (*p*); Victor Lewis
      (*d*); Manolo Badrena (*perc*). 2/85.
***(*) **Smart Moves** Gramavision GR 8607
      Swartz; Charlie Mariano (*as*); John Stubblefield (*ts*); Mike Stern (*g*); Ben Aronov (*p*); Victor
      Lewis (*d*); Mino Cinelu (*perc*). 2/86.

Vigorously impressive sessions from a bass player whose recording credits include work with singer
Sheila Jordan (a duo as well as a more conventional quartet), and with fusion guitarist, Al DiMeola,
where he was paired on some tracks with an electric bass player. The fusion elements are inevitably
slightly more evident on *Urban Earth* and the material (which ends with a ropey 'Round Midnight') is
less impressive than on the later album. Swartz himself has a good line and a firm, lyrical tone that lends
itself especially to the slower tracks, though without compromising on pace for the upbeat numbers.

    Coltrane's 'Equinox' and the standard 'My Romance' give the horns something to do. The partnership
isn't quite right, but Mariano is in excellent form and produces some lovely slithers round the theme.
The sound on both albums is very sharp, though Swartz tends to get wiped out by Berg's lower register
in the ensembles. Recommended.

Duncan Swift PIANO

(*) **The Broadwood Concert Big Bear BEARCD 34
      Swift (*p* solo). 90.
(*) **The Key Of D Is Daffodil Yellow Duncan Swift Records 1
      Swift (*p* solo). 12/92–6/93.

In the somewhat rare category of British stride, Duncan Swift works as idiomatically as anyone this side of
Keith Ingham. This is an entertaining live show, with the pianist hammering through a lengthy programme
of mostly fast showcase pieces; but its impact is diminished by the lack of light and shade: the great stride
players knew when to cool off, and Swift is less convincing in the more placid moments. Contrarily, the
second album, this time on his own label, tends to linger in its quiet moments a little too much, and his
guying of 'Maple Leaf Rag' as 'Maple Leaf Tatters' (as Thelonious Monk might have played it, apparently) is too clever by half. But Swift remains a very capable and frequently engaging performer.

Jorge Sylvester ALTO AND SOPRANO SAXOPHONES

*** **MusiCollage** Postcards POST 1011
      Sylvester; Claudio Roditi (*t, flhn*); Marvin Sewell (*g*); Monte Croft (*vib*); Santi Debriano (*b*);
      Gene Jackson (*d*); Bobby Sanabria (*perc*). 7/95.

Sylvester's assertive sax playing is but one interesting element here. The opening track, 'Token', explodes off a polyrhythmic base that suggests both Latin and African pulses without neglecting an American jazz doctrine. The subsequent pieces, which rely more on Jackson than the remarkable Sanabria, are more conventionally attuned and, to that degree, are a little less exciting; but Sylvester's fierce alto and the reliable Roditi – for once content with second spot – brighten all the tracks, and substituting vibes for piano was a shrewd textural move. Not all of it's memorable, but the tracks that work offer some real excitement.

Tomas Szukalski TENOR SAXOPHONE

**** Body And Soul Polonia CD 003
> Szukalski; Artur Dutkiewicz (*p*); Andrzej Cudzich (*b*); Marek Stach (*d*). 10/91.

Szukalski would be virtually unknown in the West were it not for an excellent performance on Tomasz Stańko's recently reissued ECM disc, *Balladyna*. The Pole established a substantial reputation in his homeland when he took part in Zbigniew Namyslowski's important *Winobranie* recording. He included a Namyslowski composition, 'Taki Soble Walczyk', in this set from the 1991 Jazz Jamboree in Warsaw. It's the longest track on the disc and the most evocative of Szukalski's wild, almost gypsy-like style. Nominally he's a Ben Webster man, and his ballads are played in the low boudoir tenor Webster made famous. 'Body And Soul' itself has tinges of Lester Young, Stan Getz (an icon for Polish jazz-players) and even Warne Marsh. The band are as well drilled and uncompromising as East European groups tend to be, and Dutkiewicz plays with great presence on his own 'Taniec Wuja Toma'.

Lew Tabackin (born 1940) TENOR SAXOPHONE, FLUTE

***(*) Desert Lady Concord CCD 4411
> Tabackin; Hank Jones (*p*); Dave Holland (*b*); Victor Lewis (*d*). 12/89.
**** I'll Be Seeing You Concord CCD 4528
> Tabackin; Benny Green (*p*); Peter Washington (*b*); Lewis Nash (*d*). 4/92.
**** What A Little Moonlight Can Do Concord CCD 4617
> As above. 4/94.

Though he is best known as co-leader with his wife, Toshiko Akiyoshi, of a distinguished big band, Tabackin is a stylish and greatly underrated small-group saxophone player who inclines towards Sonny Rollins's melodic improvisation. His solos sound both expertly structured and wholly spontaneous, and he is an able and effective flautist, with an attractively orientalized tone, picked up osmotically (so he claims) from his wife.

Both sides of his playing style are evident on *Desert Lady*, on which he is supported by an absolutely first-rate rhythm section. 'Chelsea Bridge' and Strayhorn's 'Johnny Come Lately' are constructed in such a way that the melody is implicit in each phrase and the harmonic progressions, though quite daring, are impeccably logical and thought out. Tabackin's tone isn't particularly distinctive and his flute playing is often more immediately arresting. 'Desert Lady' and 'Yesterdays' are worth investigating on an album that doesn't pall on repeated hearings.

I'll Be Seeing You and *Moonlight* are almost perfectly balanced jazz records. Tabackin has rarely been heard to such advantage on disc. His solos on 'Isfahan' and 'I Surrender Dear' and 'Poinciana' and Jimmy Knepper's 'Leave Of Absinthe' are elegance personified, and the group rise to the occasion magnificently. Green carries enormous authority on his deceptively narrow shoulders, a player of great character and authority who these days sounds like no one but himself.

Richard Tabnik ALTO SAXOPHONE

***(*) Solo Journey New Artists NA 1011
> Tabnik (*as* solo). 9/90.
***(*) In The Moment New Artists NA 1015
> Tabnik; Cameron Brown (*b*); Carol Tristano (*d*). 10/92.
*** Life At The Core New Artists NA 1016
> Tabnik; Andy Fite (*g*); Calvin Hill (*b*); Roger Mancuso (*d*). 11/92.

Tabnik has a cool, slightly nervy approach, like a cross between early Lee Konitz and some of the drier avant-gardists of the 1960s. The solo record invites an obvious comparison to Braxton, and in many ways it's a perfectly valid comparison, since so many of the source players (Lester Young, Warne Marsh, Paul Desmond) are the same. At just over the hour and 40 separate cuts, *Solo Journey* palls slightly in the later stages, though the bulk of it is crisply and imaginatively done, Tabnik finding things to say in the short sound-bites as well as in the longer and more developed tracks. His attempt to re-create Pres's clarinet solo on 'Countless Blues' is an indication of how thoroughly Tabnik has scried the canon.

He does something similar *à propos* 'Shoe Shine Boy' on the trio record, and this is perhaps his most effective setting. Cameron Brown's bass is mixed up very strong and chocolatey and sometimes over-powers the speakers, but Tabnik and Carol Tristano find plenty to do across those textures. The saxo-phonist's work on the long 'Butterflies And Universes' is among his most individual, and a long way ahead of the rather prosey material on *Life At The Core*, where he seems constrained by the presence of a harmony instrument.

As on the unaccompanied record, Tabnik doesn't mind having people eavesdrop on his rough drafts (the New Artists label seems dedicated to this approach) and includes two takes of 'It's Just A Feeling' on *In The Moment*. Set side by side, they say more about this developing artist than umpteen pages of critical text. Well worth a serious listen.

Jamaaladeen Tacuma (born 1956) BASS, PERCUSSION

*** Dreamscape DIW 904
    Tacuma; Jahphar Barron (*t*); Ben Schacter (*ss, ts*); Rick Iannacone (*g, bj*); Richard Tucker, Jef Lee Johnson (*g*); Daryl Kwesi Burge, Adam Guth (*d*); Ursula Rucker (*v*). 5–6/95.
Big, tough, dense jazz-funk by one of the music's great playing stalwarts. Tacuma's earlier discs were like jumble sales of music – bits of everything stacked high on the table – and here he's focused it down to a tight band bouncing and crashing into one another, alternately pinioned by his bass grooves and bouncing right off them. None of the compositions adds up to much, and the feel is of something hastily thrown together – but it's a nice feel. None of the musicians will be making improvisation history, either, but that's not really the point. Thick, juicy, almost live sound.

Aki Takase PIANO

*** Looking For Love Enja 5075-2
    Takase; Maria Joao (*v*). 9/87.
*** Play Ballads Of Duke Ellington Tutu 888116-2
    Takase; Gunther Klatt (*ts*). 4/90.
**** Shima Shoka Enja 6062-2
    Takase (*p* solo). 6/90.
***(*) Blue Monk Enja 7039-2
    Takase; David Murray (*ts, bcl*). 4/91.
***(*) Piano Duets Live In Berlin 93/94 FMP OWN-90002
    Takase; Alex Von Schlippenbach (*p*). 3/93–12/94.
Takase rises out of jazz piano history with unique intensity and panache. Her earlier music (there are two vinyl-only releases from the beginning of the 1980s on Enja) suggested a pianist who was involving herself in earlier methods only reluctantly – most of the music leapt into the darkness of free playing at the earliest opportunity. Her five CD releases offer a somewhat lopsided view of what she can do, since three of them are off-the-cuff duet dates, but the solo record is a triumph. With Joao and Klatt, offering one programme of gentle bop-and-after standards and one of Ellingtonia, she takes second place to the other voice: Klatt's big-toned delivery of the famous melodies works rather better than Joao's some-times effortful singing, though in both cases the pianist makes telling contributions. With Murray, these are real duets: a fat, fulsome 'Ellingtonia' and a galumphing 'Body And Soul' are highlights, but four excellent declensions of Monk are the heart of the record, which is quite as strong and accomplished as any of Murray's discs with Dave Burrell.

The solo record is where Takase makes her real mark. Her own tunes number seven, and range from the Monk derivation of 'Meraviglioso' to the brief, lightning-struck 'A.V.S.'. But her covers of other com-posers are the most remarkable things here: her treatment of Carla Bley's 'Ida Lupino' is even more deliberate, weighty and substantial than a Paul Bley reading; 'Giant Steps' is complex and superbly distilled; and her treatment of Ellington's 'Rockin' In Rhythm' is the *tour de force* of the disc, a fantasy imbued with such simultaneous drive and elegance that the composer himself – as far removed as it is from any Ellington interpretation – would surely have applauded.

The record with Schlippenbach is meticulously balanced, opening with two long pieces by AVS, centred with four Monk tunes and ending with two extended variations on Takase themes. Even the two pairs of compositions share affinities: 'Na, Na, Na, Na . . . Ist Das Der Weg?' and 'Tales Of Something' both come out of overlapping, building-block figures that achieve a terse complexity, and 'The Morlocks' (recorded before the orchestral version on the FMP CD of that title) and 'Chapelure Japonaise' are whirlwinds of prepared-piano turbulence. The Monk tunes – each pianist takes one solo – are like a breathing space and Frank Zappa's 'You Are What You Is' is like a roistering encore. For catholic tastes, perhaps, but an impressive record.

Tom Talbert PIANO

*** Bix Fats Duke Modern Concepts 0001
    Talbert; Joe Wilder, Nick Travis (*t*); Jimmy Cleveland, Eddie Bert (*tb*); Jimmy Buffington (*frhn*); Joe Soldo (*as, f*); Herb Geller (*as*); Aaron Sachs (*ts, f*); Harold Goltzer (*bsn*); Danny Bank (*bs*); George Wallington (*p*); Barry Galbraith (*g*); Oscar Pettiford (*b*); Osie Johnson (*d*). 56.

**(*) Louisiana Suite Sea Breeze CDSB-107-2
    Frank Szabo, John Harner, Bob Summers, Steve Huffsteter (*t, flhn*); Bruce Paulson (*tb*); John Leys (*btb*); Joe Soldo, Andy Mackintosh, Bob Hardaway, Howard Fallman, Lee Collet (*reeds*); Joe Diorio (*g*); Harvey Newmark (*b*); Harold Jones (*d*); Jerry Steinholtz (*perc*). 10/77.

**(*) Things As They Are Sea Breeze CDSB-2038-2
    Talbert; Bob Summers (*t, flhn*); Andy Martin (*tb*); Dick Mitchell (*as*); Lee Collet (*bs*); John Leitham (*b*); Jeff Hamilton (*d*). 8/87.

**(*) The Warm Café Modern Concepts MC-0002
    As above, except add Frank Szabo, Wayne Bergeron, Steve Huffsteter (*t*), Bob Enevoldsen (*vtb*), Suzette Moriarty (*frhn*), John Leys (*btb*), Don Shelton (*as, cl, f*), Bob Efford (*ts*), Jennifer Hall, Bob Carr (*bs*), Alan Steinberger, Tom Rainier (*p*), Jack Sperling, Roy McCurdy (*d*); omit Mitchell and Hamilton. 10/91–6/92.

*** Duke's Domain Sea Breeze CDSB-2058
    As above, except add Alex Iles (*tb*), Don Shelton (*as, cl*), Gary Foster (*as, f*), Bob Hardaway (*ts*), Tom Garvin (*p*); omit Enevoldsen and Steinberger. 10/91–5/93.

Talbert has worked in Hollywood for most of his career, and his infrequent jazz records give the game away: they're musicianly, monotonous sessions. The first two Sea Breeze albums are skilful syntheses of various big-band and small-group conventions with no distinctive flavour of their own. Dick Mitchell's Woods-like alto is the saving grace on *Things As They Are*: he manages to be relaxed and piquant at the same time in his interesting solos.

The earlier record dates back to the all-star studio days of the middle '50s. The material is unusually classic for the period, with the Beiderbecke arrangements particularly rare, though Talbert's expertise again lacks any maverick touch. The players perform the scores with some panache, and there are useful moments for Wilder and Geller.

The Warm Café is another quiet and easy-going date, often so laid-back that the music hardly registers: smoothly done, but difficult to feel enthusiastic about. *Duke's Domain* is mostly Ellingtonia, with a tribute piece to start, and this time Talbert's skills shed some interesting light on a few Ducal favourites – 'Chelsea Bridge' is particularly fine. His most assured work.

Akira Tana (born 1952) DRUMS

**(*) Yours And Mine Concord CCD 4440
    Tana; Jesse Davis (*as*); Ralph Moore (*ss, ts*); Rob Schneiderman (*p*); Rufus Reid (*b*). 9/90.

*** Passing Thoughts Concord CCD 4505
    As above, except Craig Bailey (*as, f*) and Dan Faulk (*ss, ts*) replace Davis and Moore; add Guilherme Franco (*perc*). 1/92.

*** Blue Motion Paddlewheel KICJ 172
    As above, except Frank Colon (*perc*) replaces Franco. 6/93.

All three records are by TanaReid, the group co-led by drummer Tana and bassist Reid. Since neither man is an idiosyncratic stylist, the music tends to run along familiar boppish lines: it's a nice repertory band with a few new wrinkles. Schneiderman, the only other player common to all three records, is a telling presence, contributing 'Day And Night' and 'Blue Motion' (both from the Paddlewheel album) to the book, two of their best tunes. The first album is let down a little by the horns: Moore seems below par, and Davis, though he plays enthusiastically, isn't as powerful as he is on his own Concord dates. Bailey and Faulk, though both a little raw, play with a sharper focus on *Passing Thoughts*, and by *Blue Motion* they sound comfortably at home: this is the best of the three, with some well-paced originals and deft scoring for the quintet. The leaders still sound comparatively workmanlike and unwilling to draw much attention to themselves, which makes for a clean balance but smooths off some of the band's potential edge.

Horace Tapscott (born 1934) PIANO

**** The Dark Tree: 1 hat Art 6053
    Tapscott; John Carter (*cl*); Cecil McBee (*b*); Andrew Cyrille (*d*). 12/89.
***(*) The Dark Tree: 2 hat Art 6083
    As above. 12/89.
***(*) aiee! The Phantom Arabesque AJ0119
    Tapscott; Marcus Belgrave (*t*); Abraham Burton (*as*); Reggie Workman (*b*); Andrew Cyrille (*d*).
    6/95.

There was, inevitably, a darker side to the cool 'West Coast sound' and to the conventionally sunny image of California. One hardly thinks of Eric Dolphy or Charles Mingus as 'West Coast' players, yet that is what they were, and they conveyed a fundamental truth about the region's culture that is reflected in Horace Tapscott's grievously unrecognized work.

Tapscott was and is a community musician. His decision to remain in Los Angeles as a performer–activist has undoubtedly thwarted wider recognition, but so too did the fact that he conformed to no readily marketable pigeonhole; 'West Coast Hot' was considered something of a pleonasm in the business, and there was a measure of suspicion regarding Tapscott's political agenda. In 1961 he helped establish the Union of God's Musicians and Artists Ascension, out of which grew the Pan-Afrikan People's Arkestra, both attempts to find uncompromised work for talented, young, black musicians. Their work is fiercely disciplined, built up out of deceptively simple elements, but with subtle poly-chordal shadings that reflect Tapscott's solo work and his intriguing duos and trios with members of the PAPA.

Tapscott's own first inspiration was the radical West Coast bandleader and arranger, Gerald Wilson (Dolphy's gratefully acknowledged 'G. W.'), and Tapscott's recording career took off as an arranger, turning out uncharacteristically formal and gentle charts for Sonny Criss. At the same time, though, his own long-deleted *The Giant Is Awakened* took its central impetus from the angry separatism of black cultural nationalism. Perhaps as a result, Tapscott has recorded disappointingly rarely and has restricted himself in recent years largely to solo recitals on the hard-to-find Nimbus label.

Tapscott characteristically builds pieces over sustained *ostinati* in the bass clef (he features McBee very strongly in his late-1980s band), building solos out of simple but often enigmatic themes. The most obvious influence is Monk and there are clear parallels with Randy Weston and Dollar Brand (Abdullah Ibrahim), but there is also a 'correctness' of touch and development that recalls classical technique in its purest form, not a Third Stream dilution. Over this, Tapscott likes to place a freer-sounding horn, Arthur Blythe in the late 1960s and the more abstract Carter two decades later. There are now several versions of 'The Dark Tree' on record, including one on a valuable Novus compilation called *West Coast Hot*, which, sadly, is no longer available. The versions on the hat Arts (one per volume) are much cooler and more developed than the earlier recordings, but also exposing more of the piece's deceptive structure.

The second volume of *The Dark Tree* is marginally less compelling than the first (which stands quite acceptably on its own); however, first exposure to Tapscott creates an immediate appetite for more of his gloriously dissonant music. At least one of these should be in every serious collection.

Tapscott has issued a good deal of his own music on the Nimbus label, including a swath of excellent solo sessions. If you are fortunate, these can still be had on both the old and the shinier format, but they are not going to turn up in your average High Street record store. Fortunately, Arabesque have had the good sense to get the big man into the studio to record an album. The oddly named *aiee! The Phantom* is unmistakable Tapscott: big, pounding motifs, with horns punching away over the top. The long pieces, 'Mothership' and 'Drunken Mary/Mary On Sunday', stand with some of the best of *Dark Tree*, and there is no faulting this recent band. Any which includes Workman and Cyrille obviously has a lot going for it, but on balance the earlier album, with its superb sidemen, remains our favourite.

Buddy Tate (born 1915) TENOR SAXOPHONE, CLARINET

** Jumping On The West Coast Black Lion BLCD760175
    Tate; Emmett Berry, Forest Powell (*t*); Teddy Donnelly (*tb*); Charles Q. Price (*as, v*); Frank Sleet
    (*as*); Charlie Thomas (*ts*); Bill Doggett, Frank Whyte (*p*); Louis Speiginer (*g*); Benny Booker
    (*b*); Edward Smith, Chico Hamilton, Pete McShann (*d*); Jimmy Witherspoon (*v*). 4/47–5/49.

Buddy Tate is one of the greatest and most durable of swing tenormen, a major performer for over half a century and a much-loved and amiable man; but the records under his own name are perhaps a little disappointing in the light of his grand reputation, and his reticent standing as a leader may account for the reason why he's never quite secured the wider fame of some of his peers. His great records were made with Basie – whom he joined following Herschel Evans's death in 1939 – and his old friend from the band, Buck Clayton; in 1947, when the motley collection of tracks on the Black Lion CD were made, he was still with the band but did some moonlighting in an anonymous ensemble which cut 12 of the 18 tracks here (the others are by even less identifiable groups, though there's a nice early blues from Witherspoon). The music is unpretentious but forgettable jump-band music, typical of the day.

*** **Broadway** Black & Blue 590542
    Tate; François Biensan (*t*); Wild Bill Davis (*org*); Floyd Smith (*g*); Chris Colombo (*d*). 5/72.
*** **Swinging Scorpio** Black Lion BLCD760165
    Tate; Humphrey Lyttelton (*t, cl*); Bruce Turner (*cl, as*); Kathy Stobart (*cl, ts, bs*); Mick Pyne (*p*); Dave Green (*b*); Tony Mann (*d*). 7/74.
(*) **The Texas Twister New World 352
    Tate; Paul Quinichette (*ts*); Cliff Smalls (*p*); Major Holley (*b*); Jackie Williams (*d*). 75.
***(*) **Jive At Five** Storyville STCD 5010
    Tate; Doc Cheatham (*t*); Vic Dickenson (*tb, v*); Johnny Guarnieri (*p*); George Duvivier (*b*); Oliver Jackson (*d*). 7/75.

Tate's records in the 1970s have a desultory, pick-up feel to them, but there's still plenty of ingratiating music here. *Broadway* grants him the lavish support of Wild Bill Davis, whose splayed hands and continuous pumping of the mixture stop on the organ paints in all the spaces in the music. On a blues set-piece like 'Blues In My Heart' Tate's sound becomes massive, unstoppable, an Easter Island figure come to life. Over CD length it grows wearisome, though, and the bonus of four previously unreleased tracks is dubious. The sound is a little too bright, with organ and cymbals aggressively forward. Tate does some singing on *The Texas Twister*, and at least he sounds better than Zoot Sims or Phil Woods in this role. It otherwise interrupts an attractive two-tenor workout for the leads which offers a scarce glimpse of Quinichette in his later days. *Swinging Scorpio* is more of a Humphrey Lyttelton session with Tate as guest: the band are playing charts by Tate's old chum, Buck Clayton, though, and he fits snugly if a little shakily here and there into the British ensemble. The charts could use a rather more swinging rhythm section, but otherwise the music is well handled, with Humph playing the Clayton role with some aplomb. The best of these records, though, is the all-star date on *Jive At Five*, which benefits from a perfectly balanced front line: the upright, proper Cheatham, the louche Tate, the almost lascivious-sounding Dickenson. Each man's ballad feature is a treat, and Guarnieri supports and embellishes beautifully.

***(*) **The Ballad Artistry Of Buddy Tate** Sackville SKCD-3034
    Tate; Ed Bickert (*g*); Don Thompson (*b*); Terry Clarke (*d*). 6/81.
(*) **Just Jazz Reservoir RSR CD 110
    Tate; Al Grey (*tb*); Richard Wyands (*p*); Major Holley (*b, v*); Al Harewood (*d*). 4/84.

The Ballad Artistry is surely Tate's best latter-day record. By sticking mostly to slow tempos and never forcing the pace, the supporting trio provides just the right sort of intimacy and cushioning detail to let Tate relax and, though he still has his doubtful moments, most of his solos are controlled, ruminative, nicely eloquent. It's much like a vintage Ben Webster date. Bickert is in excellent form, unobtrusively filling all the harmonic space round the saxophonist, and Thompson and Clarke both play well. An immaculate 'Darn That Dream' and the pleasing choice of Ellington's 'Isfahan' provide the highlights. The Reservoir disc is a reissue of an earlier LP with a couple of alternative takes to beef up playing time. Nothing very exciting here, but dependable playing from the principals and Grey in particular taking a witty role.

Art Tatum (1910–56) PIANO, CELESTE

***(*) **Art Tatum 1932–1934** Classics 507
    Tatum (*p* solo). 3/33–10/34.
***(*) **Art Tatum 1934–1940** Classics 560
    Tatum; Lloyd Reese (*t*); Marshall Royal (*cl*); Bill Perkins (*g*); Joe Bailey (*b*); Oscar Bradley (*d*). 10/34–7/40.
**** **Classic Early Solos 1934–1937** MCA GRP 16072
    Tatum (*p* solo). 8/34–11/37.

The enormity of Tatum's achievements makes approaching him a daunting proposition even now. His very first session, cut in New York in 1933, must have astonished every piano player who heard any of the four tracks (only available on Classics 507). 'Tiger Rag', for instance, becomes transformed from a rather old-fashioned hot novelty tune into a furious series of variations, thrown off with abandon but as closely argued and formally precise as any rag or stomp at one-quarter of the tempo. If Tatum had only recorded what is on these first CDs, he would be assured of immortality; yet, like Morton's early solos, they are both achievements in their own right and sketchbooks for the great works of his later years.

There are just a few distractions in the music leading up to 1940: Adelaide Hall sings a couple of vocals on one session, and Tatum's Swingsters record one 1937 session (which also includes Tatum on celeste). The MCA disc only goes as far as the superb final session of 1937, but the Classics CDs cover everything up to 1940. The MCA disc, though, is in considerably superior sound.

**** The Standard Transcriptions Music & Arts CD-919 2CD
    Tatum (*p* solo). 35–43.
(***) Standards Black Lion BLCD 760143
    Tatumn (*p* solo). 35–43.

Tatum's transcription discs for radio were made at several sessions over a period of several years and have survived as rather indifferently stored acetates. The Music & Arts double-CD does a heroic job in getting the best out of them. They are as valuable in their way as the later sessions for Norman Granz: briefer, many solos almost casually tossed off, and some blemished by the poor recording (Tatum never finally received the kind of studio sound which his work demanded), but it's a magnificent archive, spread here over two lengthy CDs. Some of them, such as 'I Wish I Were Twins', have the melody abstracted into a monstrously fast chunk of stride piano; others, like 'The Man I Love', become tender but firm ballads, while others begin at a medium tempo before hurtling forward in double-time. Trifles such as Dvořák's 'Humoresque' are treated with Tatum's peculiar knowing gaucheness, while his treatment of such as 'I'm Gonna Sit Right Down And Write Myself A Letter' are like destructive tributes to such colleagues as Waller and Johnson: immensely superior in terms of technique, Tatum nevertheless pays them a kind of offhand homage by adopting elements of their manner to his own vast vocabulary. 'All God's Chillun Got Rhythm', meanwhile, prefigures Powell and bebop intensity. Highly recommended, and the package comes with a superb essay by Don Asher. Music & Arts have now completely remastered their edition, making the package even more desirable, though those expecting hi-fi should be warned that many of the tracks still suffer from inferior sound. This set completely supersedes the Black Lion disc, which includes 20 solos (as compared with 61 in the Music & Arts set) in inferior mastering and with what seem to be some pitching problems created by uncertain speeds.

***(*) I Got Rhythm MCA GRP 16302
    Tatum; Guy Kelly, Lloyd Reese, Joe Thomas (*t*); Marshall Royal (*cl*); Bill Perkins, John Collins, Tiny Grimes (*g*); Joe Bailey, Billy Taylor, Slam Stewart (*b*); Oscar Bradley, Eddie Dougherty (*d*). 12/35–1/44.
***(*) Art Tatum 1940–1944 Classics 800
    Tatum; Joe Thomas (*t*); Edmond Hall (*cl*); Oscar Moore, John Collins, Tiny Grimes (*g*); Billy Taylor, Slam Stewart (*b*); Eddie Dougherty, Yank Porter (*d*); Joe Turner (*v*). 7/40–44.
**** Solos MCA MCAD-42327
    Tatum (*p* solo). 2–7/40.
***(*) Complete Brunswick & Decca Recordings 1932–1941 Affinity AFS 1035 3CD
    As above discs. 8/32–6/41.
*** Art Tatum 1944 Classics 825
    Tatum; Tiny Grimes (*g*); Slam Stewart (*b*). 5–12/44.

Tatum's 1940 solos are another superb sequence: nearly all of them are on the MCA disc in bright, if occasionally rather sharp, sound. There is a first revision of 'Tiger Rag', which first appeared at his debut session, and particularly imaginative interpretations of 'Lullaby Of The Leaves', 'Moon Glow' and, improbably enough, 'Begin The Beguine'. *I Got Rhythm* sweeps up some small-band sessions, where at times (as on the 1937 date) Tatum seems to be trying to fight his way out of the situation; exhilarating, all the same. Affinity's three-disc set covers everything up to 1941, but we find the somewhat flat sound a little disappointing compared to some of the other reissues. The Classics *1940–1944* disc covers much of the same ground as GRP 16302 but goes on to take in ten trio tracks with Grimes and Stewart, a format that took up much of the pianist's time in the 1940s. It didn't so much cramp his style as push it into a formula to a degree that some will be dissatisfied by. In a sense, though, it was characteristic of the man. Grimes and Stewart were mere mortals next to the pianist, but their earthbound playing kept Tatum within reach of a paying audience. The *1944* Classics disc covers trio sessions for the Asch and Comet labels, in rather murky sound, and goes on to a single solo date for Asch – including a version of 'Sweet And Lovely', one tune he never recorded commercially again. The low-fi sound keeps this one within specialist realms.

***(*) The Art Of Tatum ASV AJA 5164
    Tatum; Oscar Pettiford (*b*); Big Sid Catlett (*d*). 8/32–10/44.

A useful collection of early Tatum solos, with a single concert track with Pettiford and Catlett to round it off. The compilers have taken a generous sample and, though some will still find ASV's remastering rather fudgy, this may appeal to any who want only a single example of the man's earlier work.

*** **The V Discs** Black Lion BLCD 760114
    Tatum; Tiny Grimes (*g*); Oscar Pettiford, Slam Stewart (*b*); Sid Catlett (*d*). 44–46.
***(*) **In Private** Fresh Sound FSR-CD 127
    Tatum (*p* solo). *c*. 48.
*** **The Complete Capitol Recordings Vol. 1** Capitol B21Y-92866
    Tatum; Everett Barksdale (*g*); Slam Stewart (*b*). 7–12/52.
*** **The Complete Capitol Recordings Vol. 2** Capitol B21Y-92867
    As above. 9–12/52.

The V Discs is an interesting supplement rather than an essential part of the Tatum discography. Mostly solos, with the other musicians sitting in on only three tracks, these sessions for American forces overseas include some typically accomplished Tatum, but the variable sound-quality – some tracks are quite clean, others are badly marked by surface noise – makes listening through the disc a sometimes jolting experience. 'Lover', 'I'm Beginning To See The Light' and a Gershwin medley are, though, top-class Tatum. *In Private* comes from a tape allegedly made at Buddy Cole's house around 1948. There are many stories of Tatum doing even more impossible things at after-hours sessions, but he must have felt he was being watched at this one, since there is nothing strikingly different from his everyday genius here. But the disc comes in unusually clean sound, there is a notably fine 'Over The Rainbow', and a couple of tunes – 'You're Driving Me Crazy' and 'Sittin' And A Rockin'' – are ones he didn't often record. The Capitol sessions date from the period when Tatum was working with a trio, but Barksdale and Stewart actually appear on only four tracks on each disc. These are mostly fine rather than great Tatum performances: from most other pianists they would be astonishing work but, ranked next to his other recordings, these are on a comparatively lower flame. There are hints of the routine which he would often settle into on particular tunes, and one or two tracks where he sounds relatively indifferent to the occasion. On others – 'Someone To Watch Over Me' or 'Somebody Loves Me', both on the first disc – he is the great Tatum. The sound has been well enough handled in the remastering.

***(*) **Masters Of Jazz Vol. 8: Art Tatum** Storyville STCD 4108
    Tatum (*p* solo). 8/32–1/46.
*** **Piano Solos 1944–48** Zeta/Jazz Archive ZET 708
    Tatum (*p* solo). 12/44–48.

The Storyville disc is a hotchpotch of solos covering the 1930s and '40s. The music is unimpeachable but it makes little sense as a chronological compilation. The source of the Zeta material isn't entirely clear, but it covers a good cross-section of Tatum solos from the mid-1940s, though nothing that one can't find in better shape on the Capitol discs.

*** **Piano Starts Here** Columbia 476546-2
    Tatum (*p* solo). 33–49.

Tatum's debut solo session turns up again here, this time as a prelude to nine solos from a 1949 Gene Norman concert. There is one unusual choice in 'The Kerry Dance'. Valuable as always, but probably for completists only, since sound is again no better than fair.

**** **The Art Tatum Solo Masterpieces Vol. 1** Pablo 2405-432
    Tatum (*p* solo). 12/53.
**** **The Art Tatum Solo Masterpieces Vol. 2** Pablo 2405-433
    Tatum (*p* solo). 12/53.
**** **The Art Tatum Solo Masterpieces Vol. 3** Pablo 2405-434
    Tatum (*p* solo). 12/53.
**** **The Art Tatum Solo Masterpieces Vol. 4** Pablo 2405-435
    Tatum (*p* solo). 4/54.
**** **The Art Tatum Solo Masterpieces Vol. 5** Pablo 2405-436
    Tatum (*p* solo). 4/54.
**** **The Art Tatum Solo Masterpieces Vol. 6** Pablo 2405-437
    Tatum (*p* solo). 1/55.
**** **The Art Tatum Solo Masterpieces Vol. 7** Pablo 2405-438
    Tatum (*p* solo). 1/55–56.
  **** **The Complete Pablo Solo Masterpieces** Pablo 4404 7CD
    As above seven discs. 12/53–1/55.

Tatum's extraordinary achievement was set down in no more than four separate sessions over the course of a little over a year. Twenty years after his first solo records, this abundance of music does in some ways show comparatively little in the way of 'progression': he had established a pattern for playing many of the tunes in his repertoire, and changes of inflexion, nuance and touch may be the only telling differences between these and earlier variations on the theme. But there are countless small revisions of this kind, enough to make each solo a fresh experience, and mostly he is more expansive (freed from playing-time restrictions, he is still comparatively brief, but there can be a major difference between a two-and-a-half-minute and a four-minute solo), and more able to provide dynamic contrast and rhythmic variation. He still chooses Broadway tunes over any kind of jazz material and seems to care little for formal emotional commitments: a ballad is just as likely to be dismantled as it is to be made to evoke tenderness, while a feeble tune such as 'Taboo' (Vol. 7) may be transformed into something that communicates with great power and urgency. Tatum's genius (these records were originally known as 'The Genius Of Art Tatum') was a peculiar combination of carelessness – even at his most daring and virtuosic he can sometimes suggest a throwaway manner – and searching commitment to his art, and those contradictory qualities (which in some ways exemplify something of the jazz artist's lot) heighten the power of these superb solos. While it is invidious to single out particular discs, we suggest that the uncommitted start with discs four and six. The boxed-set edition includes all the music, and demands a fifth star. It is tantalizing to conjecture what Tatum might have done in contemporary studios, for his whole discography is marred by inadequate recording – even these later solos are comparatively unrefined by the studio – but the CD versions are probably the best to date.

**** The Tatum Group Masterpieces Vol. 1 Pablo 2405-424
    Tatum; Benny Carter (*as*); Louie Bellson (*d*). 6/54.
***(*) The Tatum Group Masterpieces Vol. 2 Pablo 2405-425
    Tatum; Roy Eldridge (*t*); Larry Simmons (*b*); Alvin Stoller (*d*). 3/55.
***(*) The Tatum Group Masterpieces Vol. 3 Pablo 2405-426
    Tatum; Lionel Hampton (*vib*); Buddy Rich (*d*). 8/55.
***(*) The Tatum Group Masterpieces Vol. 4 Pablo 2405-427
    As above. 8/55.
***(*) The Tatum Group Masterpieces Vol. 5 Pablo 2405-428
    Tatum; Harry 'Sweets' Edison (*t*); Lionel Hampton (*vib*); Barney Kessel (*g*); Red Callender (*b*); Buddy Rich (*d*). 9/55.
**** The Tatum Group Masterpieces Vol. 6 Pablo 2405-429
    Tatum; Red Callender (*b*); Jo Jones (*d*). 1/56.
**** The Tatum Group Masterpieces Vol. 7 Pablo 2405-430
    Tatum; Buddy DeFranco (*cl*); Red Callender (*b*); Bill Douglass (*d*). 2/56.
**** The Tatum Group Masterpieces Vol. 8 Pablo 2405-431
    Tatum; Ben Webster (*ts*); Red Callender (*b*); Bill Douglass (*d*). 9/56.
**** The Complete Pablo Group Masterpieces Pablo 4401 6CD
    As above eight discs. 6/54–8/56.

Even after the awesome achievement of the solo sessions, Tatum wasn't finished yet. Norman Granz recorded him in eight different group-settings as well. The overall quality isn't so consistently intense, since Tatum's partners are sometimes either relatively incompatible or simply looking another way: the cheery Hampton and Rich, for instance, work well enough in their trio record, but it seems to lighten the music to an inappropriate degree. Yet some of this music is actually undervalued, particularly the trio session with Callender and Douglass, the group working in beautiful accord. The sextet date with Edison, Hampton and Kessel is comparatively slight, and the meeting with Eldridge, while it has moments of excitement, again sounds like two virtuosos of somewhat contrary methods in the same room. The meetings with Carter, DeFranco and Webster, though, are unqualified masterpieces: the Carter session is worth having just for the astonishing 'Blues In C', and elsewhere – as with the DeFranco session – Carter's aristocratic elegance chimes perfectly with Tatum's grand manner. The meeting with Webster might on the face of it have been unlikely, but this time the contrasts in their styles create a moving alliance, the heavy, emotional tenor floating poignantly over the surging piano below. As music to study, live with and simply enjoy, this is the most approachable of all of Tatum's series of recordings: he finds the company stimulating and manages to vary his approach on each occasion without surrendering anything of himself. All the music sounds good in this remastering.

Art Taylor (1929–94) DRUMS

*** Taylor's Wailers Original Jazz Classics OJC 094
    Taylor; Donald Byrd (*t*); Jackie McLean (*as*); John Coltrane, Charlie Rouse (*ts*); Ray Bryant, Red Garland (*p*); Wendell Marshall, Paul Chambers (*b*). 2–3/57.
***(*) Taylor's Tenors Original Jazz Classics OJC 1852
    Taylor; Charlie Rouse, Frank Foster (*ts*); Walter Davis (*p*); Sam Jones (*b*). 6/59.

Art Taylor was a prolific visitor to the studios in the 1950s, drumming for Red Garland, John Coltrane, Miles Davis and many others on countless sessions, most of them for Prestige. The company gave him this shot at a leadership date and, while it's a well-cooked hard-bop session, it doesn't go much further than that. The album is actually compiled from two sessions, one with Coltrane, who works up a patented head of steam on 'C.T.A.', and another with Rouse, whose more circumspect passions are rather well caught in his solo on 'Batland'. 'Off Minor' and 'Well You Needn't' feature in Thelonious Monk's own arrangements but the band sound no more committed here than elsewhere, with Byrd his usual, blandly confident self. The leader's own playing is authoritative, although some of his manner-isms leave him a degree short of the single-minded drive of Art Blakey.

Taylor's Tenors is a cracker. Rouse didn't often have to play two-tenor situations but he acquits himself with honour against Foster, who moves like a particularly dangerous big cat through Taylor's flashing rhythms. 'Rhythm-A-Ning' and 'Little Chico' both go off like a rocket, 'Cape Millie' and 'Straight No Chaser' cool off, but the pots are on again for 'Dacor'. Forty minutes or so of this sort of thing is enough; and this is just right.

*** **Mr A.T.** Enja 7017-2

    Taylor; Abraham Burton (*as*); Willie Williams (*ts*); Marc Cary (*p*); Tyler Mitchell (*b*). 12/91.

***(*) **Wailin' At The Vanguard** Verve 519677-2

    As above, except Jacky Terrasson (*p*) replaces Cary. 8/92.

With the demise of Art Blakey, Taylor's Wailers looked set to be one of the principal training grounds for younger players in the manner of The Messengers, but sadly the leader himself has now passed on. *Mr A.T.* premieres the final edition of the band, with Williams and Burton striking sparks in the front line on worthwhile staples such as 'Gingerbread Boy' and 'Soul Eyes': both are big, burly players and, though Taylor still has an aristocrat's touch, he kicks the group along with real gusto, even if the music is formulaic. *Wailin' At The Vanguard* is an ounce better because of the circumstances: the band is captured live at New York's Village Vanguard, probably the most authentic home hard bop ever had, and the feel of the disc (it starts with traffic noise and a walk into the club), as well as bruising interpretations of the likes of 'Dear Old Stockholm', adds a quintessential flavour. Terrasson, a dynamic new talent, also has a fine showing.

Billy Taylor (born 1921) PIANO

(*) **Cross-Section Original Jazz Classics OJC 1730

    Taylor; Earl May (*b*); Percy Brice (*d*); Charlie Smith, Jose Mangual, Ubaldo Nieto, Machito (*perc*). 5/53–7/54.

*** **The Billy Taylor Trio With Candido** Original Jazz Classics OJC 015

    Taylor; Earl May (*b*); Percy Brice (*d*); Candido (*perc*). 9/54.

(*) **Billy Taylor With Four Flutes Original Jazz Classics OJC 1830

    Taylor; Phil Bodner, Herbie Mann, Frank Wess, Jerome Richardson, Bill Slapin, Jerry Sanfino, Seldon Powell (*f*); Tom Williams (*b*); Albert 'Tootie' Heath, Dave Bailey (*d*); Chano Pozo (*perc*). 7/59.

*** **Custom Taylored** Fresh Sound FSR-CD 205

    Taylor; Henry Grimes (*b*); Ray Mosca (*d*). 3/60.

While he has become best known as one of the most experienced and respected forces in jazz education in America, Billy Taylor's talents as a piano player should be recognized more than they are. He played with everyone from Stuff Smith to Charlie Parker on *52nd Street* in the 1940s, and having worked with Machito stood him in good enough stead to make these Latin-flavoured outings sound plausible. Taylor's affinities are essentially with bop, but his sensibility is akin to Teddy Wilson's: cultivated, gentlemanly, his improvisations take a leisurely route through his surroundings, alighting only on points which are germane to the setting but managing to suggest a complete grasp of the material and task at hand. *Cross-Section* features eight tracks by his trio with May and Brice and four with Machito's rhythm section: dainty but substantial, the music is very engaging and, although the second session is transparently fixed to feature Candido – whose conga and bongo solos tend to bore when heard at length – the slow and almost luxuriant reading of 'Love For Sale' and the swinging 'Mambo Inn' suggest Taylor's careful preparation for the date. There is no dramatic sense of Latin–jazz fusion on either of these records, just a calm and logical pairing of one genre with another. *With Four Flutes* dates from five years later and counts as one of the sillier ideas of the day, given that the massed flutes on each track do little more than try to outwhistle one another. Even so, they get up a fair head of steam on 'St Thomas', and Taylor himself keeps urbane order.

The trio fly through the dozen originals on *Custom Taylored* with fine aplomb. Originally done for a radio transcription service, and curtailed in running time, the crispness and snap of these blues and riff pieces comes fizzing through. Lightweight, maybe, but one of Billy's most enjoyable sessions.

*** **You Tempt Me** Taylor-Made 1003

    Taylor; Victor Gaskin (*b*); Curtis Boyd (*d*). 6/85.

*** **White Nights And Jazz In Leningrad** Taylor-Made 1001
    Taylor; Victor Gaskin (*b*); Bobby Thomas (*d*). 88.
*** **Solo** Taylor-Made 1002
    Taylor. 8/88.
*** **Billy Taylor And The Jazzmobile All Stars** Taylor-Made 1004
    Taylor; Jimmy Owens (*t, flhn*); Frank Wess (*ss, ts, f*); Ted Dunbar (*g*); Victor Gaskin (*b*); Bobby
    Thomas (*d*). 4/89.
*** **Dr T** GRP 9692
    Taylor; Gerry Mulligan (*bs*); Victor Gaskin (*b*); Bobby Thomas (*d*). 92.
*** **It's A Matter Of Pride** GRP 9753
    Taylor; Stanley Turrentine (*ts*); Christian McBride (*b*); Marvin 'Smitty' Smith (*d*); Ray Mantilla
    (*perc*); Grady Tate (*v*). 93.
(*) **Homage GRP 9806
    Taylor; Chip Jackson (*b*); Steve Johns (*d*); Jim Saporito (*perc*); Turtle Island String Quartet. 10/
    94.

Taylor's move into education has left his back-catalogue in some disrepair, and we must await the reappearance of such as the fine *Billy Taylor At The London House* from 1956. Establishing his own label in the 1980s has, though, made Taylor more available now than for many years. Of the four discs so far released, *White Nights* is an attempt to re-create the experience of a visit to Leningrad, and the earlier *You Tempt Me* is largely made up of a sequence of themes from the pianist's suite, 'Let Us Make A Joyful Noise', intended to evoke something of the spirit of Ellington's Sacred Concerts: although the most interesting piece is his unexpected reworking of 'Take The "A" Train' which reharmonizes Strayhorn's melody at a steady, compelling gait. Both sessions are good, but the *Solo* date is a better (or at least more comprehensive) display of Taylor's powers. There are perhaps two tunes too many in a long (72 minutes) CD, but Taylor's exact, finely wrought treatments make durable new statements out of the likes of 'Old Folks' and 'More Than You Know', as well as some of his own originals.

    The sextet session is distinguished by Taylor's uncompromising choice of material: there's nothing familiar, aside perhaps from Lee Morgan's 'Ceora', and the carefully positioned features for Owens and Wess are thoughtfully handled by the hornmen.

    His first album for GRP shows no break with his recent tradition and continues Taylor's very even line. Mulligan sits in on three tracks and sounds in very healthy form on his own 'Line For Lyons', while Taylor brushes up his bebop on the familiar tunes. Nothing to shake the earth – and probably the better for it. *It's A Matter Of Pride* sets him up with quite a team: Turrentine adds some preaching tenor to three tracks, Tate does his surprising vocal piece on two others, and McBride and Smith don't seem to be coasting. Very graciously done, though the excerpts from Taylor's suite in dedication to Luther King are a bit ponderous.

    Homage mixes rap, dance and string quartet contributions, and all the extra-curricular stuff tends to obscure Taylor himself, who remains bouncily creative in his swing-to-bop way. Not one of his best, but the catalogue's looking stronger now anyway.

Cecil Taylor (born 1930) PIANO, VOICE

**** **Jazz Advance** Blue Note B21Y-84462
    Taylor; Steve Lacy (*ss*); Buell Neidlinger (*b*); Dennis Charles (*d*). 9/56.

One of the most extraordinary debuts in jazz, and for 1956 it's an incredible effort. Taylor's 1950s music is even more radical than Ornette Coleman's, though it has seldom been recognized as such, and while Coleman has acquired the plaudits, it is Taylor's achievement which now seems the most impressive and uncompromised. While there are still many nods to conventional post-bop form in this set, it already points to the freedoms which the pianist would later immerse himself in. The interpretation of 'Bemsha Swing' reveals an approach to time which makes Monk seem utterly straightforward; 'Charge 'Em' is a blues with an entirely fresh slant on the form; Ellington's 'Azure' is a searching tribute from one keyboard master to another. 'Sweet And Lovely' and 'You'd Be So Nice To Come Home To' are standards taken to the cleaners by the pianist, yet his elaborations on the melodies will fascinate any who respond to Monk's comparable treatment of the likes of 'There's Danger In Your Eyes, Cherie'. Lacy appears on two tracks and sounds amazingly comfortable for a musician who was playing Dixieland a few years earlier. And Neidlinger and Charles ensure that, contrary to what some may claim, Taylor's music swings. The CD reissue sounds very well.

***(*) **Looking Ahead!** Original Jazz Classics OJC 452
    As above, except Earl Griffith (*vib*) replaces Lacy. 6/58.

The most pensive of Taylor's early records may be the best place to start in appreciating his music. The

A minor blues of 'Luyah! The Glorious Step', Griffith's charming 'African Violet' and the remarkable fantasy on 'Take The "A" Train', 'Excursion On A Wobbly Rail', mark the pianist's transitional explorations of jazz form, while 'Toll' embarks on a new journey towards his own territory. 'Wallering', named in tribute to Fats Waller, is a wonderfully constructed improvisation on 'two improvised figures that are simultaneous', as Taylor says in the sleeve-note. Griffith combines edginess with inborn lyricism, which works surprisingly well in context, but it's Neidlinger and Charles who are again central to Taylor's search for rhythmical freedom.

**** The World Of Cecil Taylor Candid CCD 79006
As above, except Archie Shepp (*ts*) replaces Griffith. 10/60.
***(*) Air Candid CCD 79046
As above. 1/61.
**** Jumpin' Punkins Candid CCD 79013
As above, except add Clark Terry (*t*), Roswell Rudd (*tb*), Steve Lacy (*ss*), Charles Davis (*bs*), Billy Higgins (*d*). 1/61.
***(*) New York City R&B Candid CCD 79017
As above. 1/61.
***(*) Cell Walk For Celeste Candid CCD 79034
As above. 1/61.

The 1961 recordings for Candid – some of them under the nominal leadership of Neidlinger – secure a final balance between Taylor's insistent unshackling of familiar organization and his interest in standard material. *The World Of Cecil Taylor* introduced Shepp into the pianist's difficult universe, and it is a memorable encounter: Shepp's scrawling tenor battles through 'Air' with courageous determination, but it's clear that he has little real idea what's going on, and Taylor's own superbly eloquent improvisation makes the saxophonist seem like a beginner. It's even more apparent on the alternative takes of the piece (there were 18 attempts at it in the studio), many of which are on the Mosaic boxed set of this music (see Introduction) and three of which are on *Air* (a collection of alternatives which includes two different takes of 'Number One' and one of 'Port Of Call'). But the same sessions also included the lovely and (for Taylor) surprisingly impressionistic 'Lazy Afternoon' and the blues fantasy of 'O.P.'. The larger band tackles only two tunes, both by Ellington, 'Things Ain't What They Used To Be' and 'Jumpin' Punkins', though they sound more like the Monk ensembles of *Monk's Music* than any Ellington band. Finally, there are the trio pieces: 'E.B.', which approximates a sonata and includes a superb piano improvisation, and the wholly improvised yet seemingly finished 'Cindy's Main Mood' are outstanding. The original records are *The World* and *New York City R&B*, but the various collections of out-takes are equally revealing.

***(*) Unit Structures Blue Note B21Y-84237
Taylor; Gale Stevens Jr (*t*); Jimmy Lyons (*as*); Ken McIntyre (*as, bcl, ob*); Henry Grimes, Alan Silva (*b*); Andrew Cyrille (*d*). 5/66.

With the very important Café Montmartre recordings of 1962 currently out of print, there's something of a gap before this album for Blue Note. *Unit Structures* is both as mathematically complex as its title suggests and as rich in colour and sound as the ensemble proposes, with the orchestrally varied sounds of the two bassists – Grimes is a strong, elemental driving force, Silva is tonally fugitive and mysterious – while Stevens and McIntyre add other hues and Lyons, who was steadily becoming Taylor's most faithful interpreter, improvises with and against them. The title-piece is a highly refined but naturally flowing aggregation of various cells which create or propose directions for improvisation, combinations of players and tonal and rhythmical variations. Unfortunately, the equally fine *Conquistador* has been deleted. Blue Note's recording wasn't ideal for this music but it's good enough.

***(*) Akisakila Konnex KCD 5039
Taylor; Jimmy Lyons (*as*); Andrew Cyrille (*d*). 5/73.
***(*) Akisakila Vol. 2 Konnex KCD 5040
As above. 5/73.

Originally released on vinyl in Japan, this documents a titanic Tokyo concert by the trio. The group piece lasts for some 80 minutes (somewhat awkwardly spread over the two discs) and there are 30 minutes of solo piano (not quite as much as on the original LPs). 'Bulu Akisakila Kutala' is all thunder from start to finish: Lyons is sometimes lost in the mix between piano and drums, which gives his work an even more keening quality than usual. But he stands his ground. Taylor's solos reprise some of the ideas in the solo records above; but Taylor's solo work is, of course, all of a piece. Less than ideal sound.

**** Cecil Taylor Unit New World NW 201
Taylor; Raphe Malik (*t*); Jimmy Lyons (*as*); Ramsey Ameen (*vn*); Sirone (*b*); Ronald Shannon Jackson (*d*). 4/78.

**** **3 Phasis** New World NW 203
    As above. 4/78.
**** **One Too Many Salty Swift And Not Goodbye** hat Art 2-6090 2CD
    As above. 6/78.

This was a superb group, full of contrast but bursting with the spirit of Taylor's music and exultant in its ability to make it work. The two New World albums are studio recordings, but they're performed with the intensity of a live set; the hat Art set is an overwhelming concert in which conflicts with the promoters (Taylor was disallowed the use of a superior piano) seem to inspire a torrential exhibition of playing. These are colourful records: Ameen is a key member of the group, his fiddling vaguely reminiscent of Michael Sampson with Albert Ayler (a group which Jackson also played in), and there are moments (particularly the closing section of *One Too Many*) where he aspires to a very close kinship with the pianist. But textures are only one part of this music. Malik and Lyons play bright or wounded or bitingly intense lines, and they play their part in a group chemistry which sometimes has the players contrasting with one another, sometimes combining to push the music forward, sometimes providing a textured background to Taylor's own sustained flights of invention. After the ferocity of his playing and organization in the late 1960s, there is more obvious light and shade here, the freedoms more generously stated, the underlying lyricism more apparent. If there's a slight problem, it's with Jackson, who – ingenious and masterful though he is – hasn't quite the same grasp of Taylor's designs as Sunny Murray or Andrew Cyrille. The studio sessions are very well recorded, the concert rather less so; but the music transcends any problems.

***(*) **It Is In The Brewing Luminous** hat Art CD 6012
    Taylor; Jimmy Lyons (*as*); Ramsey Ameen (*vn*); Alan Silva (*b, clo*); Jerome Cooper, Sunny
    Murray (*d*). 2/80.

This must have been a crushing experience in the tiny confines of New York's Fat Tuesday club. There is a long piano solo, though, which personifies the new currents of feeling in Taylor's work: small motifs, pensive longer lines and the familiar thunder re-aligned within an accessible but uncompromised method. The balance of the recording is again slightly problematical.

*** **The Eighth** hat Art CD 6036
    Taylor; Jimmy Lyons (*as*); William Parker (*b*); Rashid Bakr (*d*). 11/81.
**** **Garden Part One** hat Art CD 6050
    Taylor (*p* solo). 11/81.
**** **Garden Part Two** hat Art CD 6051
    As above. 11/81.

The Eighth is a relatively disappointing session, with Parker and Bakr seemingly remote from the intense communication between Taylor and Lyons and a certain sourness afflicting the music. But *Garden* is a triumphant solo recording. Taylor uses an excellent Bösendorfer piano, is well recorded – two conditions which have infrequently attended his recording career – and he takes advantage of both in three long improvisations and a sequence of brief, supplementary solos which follow his latter-day habit of epigrammatic encores.

**** **Winged Serpent (Sliding Quadrants)** Soul Note SN 1089
    Taylor; Enrico Rava, Tomasz Stańko (*t*); Jimmy Lyons (*as*); Frank Wright (*ts*); John Tchicai (*ts,*
    bcl); Gunter Hampel (*bs, bcl*); Karen Borca (*bsn*); William Parker (*b*); Rashid Bakr (*d*); Andre
    Martinez (*d*). 10/84.

An important and insufficiently recognized record. Taylor's four compositions here begin from melodic cells: an eight-note motif starts 'Taht', a sort of riff (which at one point seems ready to turn into a locomotive piece, very much in an Ellingtonian tradition!) emerges in 'Womb Waters', but mainly these are exploding, brilliantly coloured ensemble improvisations where the horns (all very well caught by the recording) make superbly euphoric collective statements. As densely characterized as Taylor's music is, these musicians make their way into it with the highest courage, and the results are extraordinarily compelling.

**** **For Olim** Soul Note SN 1150
    Taylor (*p* solo). 4/86.

By now, Taylor had built an impressive discography of solo recordings, and there is nothing rote in this further addition to it. 'Olim' is the only long piece, at some 18 minutes in duration; the others are sometimes only a couple of minutes long, isolating an idea, delivering it up, and then closing it down. What emerges most clearly from such a session is the refinement of his touch, sometimes obscured by the messier live mixes he's had to contend with, the absolute integration of favourite devices – clusters, call-and-response – into a peerless mastery of the techniques available to the pianist, and his communicative abilities: nothing here does anything but speak directly to an attentive listener.

**** **Live In Bologna** Leo LR 100
    Taylor; Carlos Ward (*as, f*); Leroy Jenkins (*vn*); William Parker (*b*); Thurman Barker (*d, mar*).
    11/87.
**** **Live In Vienna** Leo LR 174
    As above. 11/87.
(***) **Chinampas** Leo LR 153
    Taylor (speech). 11/87.

Carlos Ward is hardly the man one thinks of when citing Taylor's saxophonists, and he is hardly a match
for Jimmy Lyons; but his more directly responsive and familiar lines make an agreeable change in their
way, and Jenkins is a formidable presence on both records, adding rustic colours and primeval textures
to the mix, which also includes marimba and bell sounds from Barker. These are records of two more
great concerts, recorded within days of each other, and though they are comparatively indifferently
recorded they are still enormously exhilarating experiences. Some editing has been done from the
original vinyl to fit on to single-CD release.

    Chinampas may appeal only to hardcore Taylor devotees, since there is no piano, simply the man reading
some of his poetry. It's a fascinating adjunct to a monumental body of work; but, inevitably, it's of
limited appeal.

**** **Erzulie Maketh Scent** FMP CD 18
    Taylor (*p* solo). 7/88.
**** **Pleistozaen Mit Wasser** FMP CD 16
    Taylor; Derek Bailey (*g*). 7/88.
**** **Leaf Palm Hand** FMP CD 6
    Taylor; Tony Oxley (*d*). 7/88.
**** **Spots, Circles And Fantasy** FMP CD 5
    Taylor; Han Bennink (*perc, etc*). 7/88.
**** **Regalia** FMP CD 3
    Taylor; Paul Lovens (*perc*). 7/88.
**** **Remembrance** FMP CD 4
    Taylor; Louis Moholo (*d*). 7/88.
**** **The Hearth** FMP CD 11
    Taylor; Evan Parker (*ss, ts*); Tristan Honsinger (*clo*). 7/88.
**** **Riobec** FMP CD 2
    Taylor; Gunter Sommer (*d*). 7/88.
*** **Legba Crossing** FMP CD 0
    Taylor; Heinz-Erich Godecke (*tb*); Ove Volquartz (*ss, ts, bcl*); Joachim Gies (*as*); Brigitte
    Vinkeloe (*as, ss, f*); Daniel Werts (*ob*); Sabine Kopf (*f*); Harald Kimmig (*vn*); Alexander
    Frangenheim, Uwe Martin, George Wolf (*b*); Paul Plimley (*p*); Lukas Lindenmaier, Peeter
    Uuskyla, Trudy Morse (*v*). 7/88.
**** **Alms / Tiergarten (Spree)** FMP CD 8/9.
    Taylor; Enrico Rava (*t, flhn*); Tomasz Stańko (*t*); Peter Van Bergen (*ts*); Peter Brötzmann (*as, ts*);
    Hans Koch (*ss, ts, bcl*); Evan Parker (*ss, ts*); Louis Sclavis (*ss, cl, bcl*); Hannes Bauer, Wolter
    Wierbos, Christian Radovan (*tb*); Martin Mayes (*frhn*); Gunter Hampel (*vib*); Tristan
    Honsinger (*clo*); Peter Kowald, William Parker (*b*); Han Bennink (*d*). 7/88.

This unprecedented set of records is a towering achievement, even in Taylor's work. A document of his
visit to a celebratory festival of his music in Berlin, it matches him with several of the finest European
improvisers in meetings which secure an empathy that is almost beyond belief, given the comparative
lack of formal preparation. An unparalleled inspiration to all these players, he makes almost all of them
play above themselves, and the climactic concert with the full orchestra is a monumental event, the
colossal sonic impact tempered by Taylor's own unflinching control and a grasp of dynamics and
dramatic possibility which is breathtaking. Originally issued as a single boxed set, and now available as
individual records, no collection should be without at least some of these, as examples of the expressive
power and liberating energy which this central figure has introduced into jazz and twentieth-century
music in general. We would single out the encounters with Bailey, Parker, Honsinger, Oxley and Bennink
as particularly brilliant examples of Taylor's adaptive capabilities and his partners' own contributions,
but every one of these records is both thought-provoking and individually inspiring to any listener
prepared to give themselves over to Taylor's music. Only the Workshop record, *Legba Crossing*, which
Taylor merely directs, is in any way less than essential. As a collective achievement this stands as one of
the major jazz recording projects and, were the original boxed set still available, we would have no
hesitation in awarding it a 'crown'.

**** **In East Berlin** FMP CD 13/14 2CD
    Taylor; Gunter Sommer (*perc*). 6/88.

**** **Looking (Berlin version)** FMP CD 28
    Taylor (*p* solo). 11/89.
***(*) **Looking (Berlin Version)** Corona FMP CD 31
    Taylor; Harald Kimmig (*vn*); Muneer Abdul Fataah (*clo*); William Parker (*b*); Tony Oxley (*d*).
    11/89.
**** **Looking (The Feel Trio)** FMP CD 35
    Taylor; William Parker (*b*); Tony Oxley (*d*). 11/89.
And yet more Cecil Taylor. The duets with Sommer were recorded a month prior to the Berlin sessions: thunder and lightning, light and shade, and brimful of music, even across two long CDs. The three editions of *Looking* take a *Rashomon*-style look at the same piece of music, one solo (dense, heavily contoured, lots of pedal-sustain), one trio (magnificent interplay with Parker and Oxley, who has become a frequent Taylor confrère), and one with the somewhat more awkward string stylings of Kimmig and Fataah, the latter meshing unconvincingly with Parker. The incredible richness of event continues, with barely a pause.

**** **Celebrated Blazons** FMP CD 58
    Taylor; William Parker (*b*); Tony Oxley (*d*). 6/90.
Does Taylor swing? The old litmus test comes to mind, since Taylor's ever-widening horizons sound more in touch and touched by jazz tradition than ever. Oxley's drumming is a more European flavour than anything Taylor's other regular drummers have created, yet it only serves to emphasize the huge rhythmic resources of the leader's own playing. Where Cyrille's magnificent breakers would sometimes obscure the keyboard, Oxley's playing – a unique blend of lumpen momentum and detailed percussive colour – reveals more of it. Parker, too, is coming into his own, deflecting off what the others do while speaking his own piece. Nearly an hour of music, and it swings.

**** **Double Holy House** FMP CD 55
    Taylor (*p, v, perc*). 9/90.
Taylor's quietest, most beguiling record ever is a profound meditation on some of the well-springs of what he does. It starts with a beautiful prelude at the piano before an extended recitation of poetry, accompanied by tiny splashes of percussion, and eventually a return to the piano – although the voice and percussion were actually recorded later, the act seems spontaneously whole. Eventually the accustomed intensity of Taylor in full flow breaks through, and with his accompanying cries the music searches through vocal and non-vocal tradition with a master's aptitude. Outstanding, again.

**** **Olu Iwa** Soul Note 121139-2
    Taylor; Earl McIntyre (*tb*); Peter Brötzmann (*ts, targato*); Frank Wright (*ts*); Thurman Barker
    (*mar, perc*); William Parker (*b*); Steve McCall (*d*). 4/86.
On the shelf for eight years before release, and with Wright and McCall both gone in the interim, this has the feel of history about it already. Some of the music, too, has one reflecting on Taylor's own history: the presence of Barker's marimba harks back to Earl Griffith on the ancient *Looking Ahead!*, and the small group with horns reminds of *Unit Structures*. But the two sprawling pieces here (the first is almost 50 minutes; the second, where the horns depart, is nearly 30) have moved far on from those days. Alternately hymnal, purgatorial, intensely concentrated and wildly abandoned, the first theme is a carefully organized yet unfettered piece that again disproves Taylor's isolation (it's firmly within free-jazz traditions, yet sounds like something no one else could have delivered). The second, despite the absence of the towering Brötzmann, superb in the first half, is if anything even more fervent, with the quartet – a one-time appearance for this band on record – playing at full stretch. Another great one.

*** **Iwontunwonsi – Live At Sweet Basil** Sound Hills SSCD-8065
    Taylor (*p* solo). 2/86.
Another one from the archives, and perhaps less than essential, given that Taylor's 1980s' music is relatively widespread and in circulation. Basically a piano solo of some 45 minutes, this unspools some of the master's favourite methods into a typically Byzantine exploration of the keyboard. In the heavy company of some of the above discs, though, this one's a middleweight.

John Taylor (born 1942) PIANO

***(*) **Pause, And Think Again** FMR CD 24
    Taylor; Kenny Wheeler (*t*); Chris Pyne (*tb*); Stan Sulzmann (*as*); John Surman (*ss*); Chris
    Laurence (*b*); Tony Levin (*d*); Norma Winstone (*v*). 71.
*** **Ambleside Days** Ah Um 013
    Taylor; John Surman (*ss, bs, bcl, syn*).

*** **Blue Glass** Jazz House JHCD 020
    Taylor; Mick Hutton (*b*); Steve Arguëlles (*d*). 6/91.
Much admired, Taylor is under-recorded as a leader, though one should also weigh his work with
Azimuth in the balance. He started out as an accompanist, established and sustained a reputation with
his first wife, Norma Winstone, and is still routinely described as if his gifts are best suited to a
supportive role. In fact, Taylor is a riveting solo performer and an exceptional writer. Typically, he likes
to spin out long lines of melody braced by a firm but flexible rhythmic base. He sounds effortlessly fluent
but never less than thoughtful.

    It's ironic that the most immediately arresting of these records was made a quarter of a century ago.
Anyone familiar with Azimuth will hear powerful echoes throughout *Pause, And Think Again*, particularly when Winstone and Wheeler occupy the foreground. Even more impressive than the soloing,
though, are the tightly marshalled but intriguingly open-ended ensembles, especially on the two title-
pieces, which sandwich a thing called 'White Magic'.

    The record with Surman belongs every bit as much to the saxophonist. The two men share an interest in
pastoral ideas, and it is fascinating to listen to them both steer as close as could be to mere prettiness
before pulling suddenly away with something arresting and unexpected but also entirely appropriate.
Much the same applies to the live set from Ronnie Scott's jazz club. Like 'White Magic', 'Blue Glass' is a
good example of Taylor's gifts as a sound-painter, but it is his treatment of standards – 'Spring Is Here',
'How Deep Is The Ocean' – that catches the attention first time around. There is also a new version of
'Clapperclowe' from *Ambleside Days*, cast very differently for the trio format.

    Taylor's still something of a well-guarded secret, revered by musicians, not yet as widely appreciated as
he ought to be. Any of these would do.

Martin Taylor (born 1956) GUITAR

*** **Don't Fret** Linn AKD 014
    Taylor; David Newton (*p*); Dave Green (*b*); Allan Ganley (*d*). 9/90.
*** **Change Of Heart** Linn AKD 016
    Taylor; David Newton (*p*); Brian Shiels (*b*); John Rae (*d*). 6/91.
Taylor's unassuming virtuosity is probably a match for any guitarist of today in terms of technique and
bebop feel: his lines are so cleanly articulated that there seems to be no distance between thought and
execution. That said, these aren't very exciting records, partly because the Linn studio sound is so
blemish-free and partly through the expert but uninvolving work of the rhythm sections. *Change Of
Heart* includes a blues, 'You Don't Know Me', that Taylor takes to the cleaners, but the anodyne
brilliance of his tone takes some of the pith out of the playing and certainly undermines the conviction
of the rock-orientated 'Angel's Camp'. The earlier record is more solidly in the jazz camp, thanks
mostly to Ganley's civil adaptation of Art Blakey's beat, but the more four-square Rae does no harm to
the second session. Both finally suggest, for all their undoubted pleasures, that Taylor is best positioned
with a saltier horn player to work against.

*** **Artistry** Linn AKD 020
    Taylor (*g* solo). 5/92.
Recorded with superb polish and clarity, Taylor's solo recital is beautifully finished but misses some
element of brio. Not all the tunes are ballads, yet they all seem to come out that way: sensitive,
shimmering, and rhythmically so even that the notes fold one into another with little apparent variation.
Guitarists will enjoy, and the rest may drift off after several pieces.

**** **Spirit Of Django** Linn AKD 030
    Taylor; Dave O'Higgins (*ts, ss*); John Goldie (*g*); Jack Emblow (*acc*); Alec Dankworth (*b*);
    James Taylor (*d*). 6 & 8/94.
At this point in his career, Taylor decided to set aside solo performance for a while and work with a
group again. It was a happy, productive decision, yielding this album that is as much a tribute to
Martin's natural father as it is to the creative parent name-checked in the title. Playing acoustically and
in a setting that sets Django material ('Nuages', 'Minor Swing', 'Swing 42') off against originals and
Taylor's celebrated reworking of Robert Parker's 'Johnny And Mary' theme, he sounds very different,
less busy and textured, but at bottom exactly the same, harmonically secure player. Emblow and
O'Higgins are wonderful assets and Dankworth's bass playing could hardly be improved upon for this
setting.

***(*) **Portraits** Linn AKD 048
    Taylor; Chet Atkins (*g*). 7, 11 & 12/95.
One almost wishes that Taylor could have continued the group project somewhat longer, another record

at least, except that the thought of him duetting with the legendary Atkins is so beguiling it would be worth the sacrifice. They first appear together on 'Sweet Lorraine' and one can hear at once where some of Taylor's clean picked lines come from – not from Django after all. He tries a couple of interesting overdubs, but as before it is the solo tracks where the real action lies. A version of Earl Klugh's 'Kiko' is an unexpected gem.

Claude Tchamitchian DOUBLE BASS

*** **Jeu d'Enfants** Pan PMC 1114
　　Tchamitchian (*b* solo). 9/92.
Solo bass records are a bit of a race apart, but the best of them – Guy, Phillips, Holland – can be riveting. This isn't quite in that class, but it is entirely free of cliché and there are surprisingly few longueurs in its 50-minute-odd span. The recording is wonderfully evocative, suggesting that the bassist is in the room with you rather than uncoiling from a string of digits.

John Tchicai (born 1936) ALTO SAXOPHONE, SOPRANO SAXOPHONE, TENOR SAXOPHONE, FLUTES, BASS CLARINET, ELECTRONICS

***(*) **Cadentia Nova Danica** Freedom 32JDF 179
　　Tchicai; Hugh Steinmetz (*t*); Kim Menzer (*tb*); Karsten Vogel (*as, perc*); Max Bruel (*bs, p*);
　　Stefffen Andersen (*b*); Ivan Krill, Giorgio Musoni (*perc*). 10/68.
*** **Timo's Message** Black Saint 120094
　　Tchicai; Thomas Dürst, Christian Kuntner (*b*); Timo Fleig (*d, perc*). 2/84.
*** **Satisfaction** Enja 7033
　　Tchicai; Vitold Rek (*b*). 3/91.
**** **Grandpa's Spells** Storyville STCD 4182
　　Tchicai; Misha Mengelberg (*p*); Margriet Nabrier (*syn*); Peter Danstrup (*b*); Gilbert Matthews
　　(*d*). 3/92.
***(*) **Love Is Touching** B & W BW055
　　Tchicai; Mark Oi, Michael Grandi (*g, v*); Margriet Nabrier (*p, ky, v*); Jeff Simons (*b, v*); Andrew
　　Enberg (*d, v*); Basho Fujimoto (*perc, v*). 94.
Tchicai is not, as is commonly supposed, an American exile in Scandinavia, one of the generation who sought personal and artistic sanctuary in the 1950s and '60s, but a Copenhagen-born Dano-Congolese. He moved to the United States in the early 1960s and joined Archie Shepp and Bill Dixon in the New York Contemporary Five; but he went on to lead a more significant, if less well-known, group with percussionist Milford Graves and trombonist Roswell Rudd, known as the New York Art Quartet. In the following year he played alongside fellow altoist Marion Brown (whom he somewhat resembles in approach) on John Coltrane's epic *Ascension*, before returning to Europe to work on a number of individual projects. He has worked very fruitfully with guitarist Pierre Dorge and with the late, lamented Johnny Dyani.

The 1980s saw Tchicai has now been a very significant presence in the European avant-garde for a quarter of a century. A stripped-down version of his Cadentia Nova Danica big band can be heard on a fine self-titled CD, originally recorded in 1968, released in Japan and intermittently available elsewhere. It illustrates perfectly Tchicai's attachment to large, very rhythmic *ostinati* as a basis for his high, keening saxophone sound. Though most obviously influenced by Ornette Coleman and, to a lesser extent, Eric Dolphy, Tchicai's very individual tonality has more often been likened to that of Lee Konitz, and his performing style has followed a similar trajectory, turning away from a rather cool and dry approach towards a rootsier and more forceful delivery.

The 1980s saw Tchicai shift away from alto saxophone. His tenor and soprano work was initially competent but rather anonymous and really came into its own only during the following decade, as on the excellent *Grandpa's Spells*. For the most part, the 1970s had been a time of consolidation, of teaching and of research into Eastern musics, but he returned to performance with a group called Strange Brothers, who can be heard on excellent Storyville LPs that signalled a return to full strength. Among the more recent material, there is a fine 'Stella By Starlight' on *Timo's Message*, but again the weight of interest falls largely on Tchicai's now quite varied compositional style, which included calypso and rock elements. The duos on *Satisfaction* are fascinating but unvaried, and it's not clear why Tchicai, a consummate organizer and arranger, should prefer to record in this very exposing format.

Quite why *Love Is Touching* should have been so persistently bruited as Tchicai's 'fusion' record escapes us. Though there are straightforward jazz-funk grooves in evidence, and a Gil Scott-Heron-influenced vocal on '99½ Days', this is not an undemanding canter through the discotheque but a darkly affirmative, highly contemporary session that manages to mix street gestures (and remember that Tchicai and LeRoi Jones were experimenting with rap in the mid-1960s) with some robustly avant-garde experiment. The music is credited to Tchicai and his group, The Archetypes, who are unmistakably in the same line as the earlier Strange Brothers. Were Tchicai bidding for the middle ground, he would scarcely have opened the disc with a track like 'Breath Bridge'. The wailing guitar lines on 'Salt Lips City Blues' will also suggest a rock influence, but then Tchicai comes blaring in with an utterly distinctive and in-character solo of his own. A very good set indeed, though not quite up to the pedigree of its predecessor on Storyville.

Grandpa's Spells foreshadows Tchicai's growing interest in electronics. The basic quartet is augmented with intelligently deployed sequences that give pieces like 'Community Bells' a rich, almost orchestral texture. There are two old-fashioned improvisations from the group, with Mengelberg well to the fore, a touch of the 'fusion' direction on 'Heksehyl', some folky stuff using traditional melodies ('Fran Engeland Till Skottland'), a touch of Carl Nielsen, and two Jelly Roll Morton compositions.

All this may suggest that Tchicai is heading in too many directions at once; except that he imbues everything he tackles with the same individuality and concentration. He is a very significant figure, underdocumented, all too rarely heard in Britain and the United States, and worthy of the closest and most sympathetic attention.

Jack Teagarden (1905–64) TROMBONE, VOCAL

***(*) The Indispensable Jack Teagarden 1928-1957 RCA ND 89613 2CD

Teagarden; Leonard Davis, Tommy Gott, Manny Klein, Jimmy McPartland, Ruby Weinstein, Henry 'Red' Allen, Pee Wee Irwin, Jerry Neary, Nate Kazebier, Nat Natoli, Charlie Teagarden, Harry Goldfield, Eddie Wade, Harry James, Charlie Spivak, Bunny Berigan, Sonny Dunham, Max Kaminsky, Billy Butterfield (*t*); Tommy Dorsey, Joe Harris, Jack Fulton, Bill Rank, Hal Matthews, J. C. Higginbotham (*tb*); Benny Goodman, Peanuts Hucko (*cl*); Mezz Mezzrow, Happy Caldwell, Arnold Brilhart, Alfie Evans, Gil Rodin, Larry Binyon, Albert Nicholas, Otto Hardwick, Charlie Holmes, Hymie Schertzer, Toots Mondello, Dick Clark, Arthur Rollini, Benny Bonaccio, Jack Cordaro, Charles Strickfadden, Frankie Trumbauer, Bud Freeman, Eddie Miller, Ernie Caceres (*reeds*); Red McKenzie (*kz, v*); Joe Sullivan, Vic Briedis, Arthur Schutt, Fats Waller, Frank Froeba, Roy Bargy, Bob Zurke, Dick Cary, Gene Schroeder, Johnny Guarnieri (*p*); Vincent Pirro (*acc*); Joe Venuti, Joe Raymond, Eddie Bergman, Alex Beller (*vn*); Eddie Lang, Allan Reuss, Mike Pingatore, Carl Kress, Carmen Mastren, Jack Bland, Dick Morgan, Al Casey (*g*); Eddie Condon, Will Johnson (*bj*); Arthur Campbell, Norman McPherson (*tba*); Al Morgan, Harry Goodman, Art Miller, Bob Haggart, Jack Lesberg, Al Hall, Leonard Gaskin (*b*); George Stafford, Larry Gomar, Vic Berton, Kaiser Marshall, George Wettling, Ray Bauduc, Josh Billings, Gene Krupa, Herb Quigley, Bob White, Dave Tough, Cozy Cole (*d*); Helen Ward, Ben Pollack, Johnny Mercer (*v*). 3/28–7/57.

The trombone had a difficult time of it in the 1920s and was one of the last instruments to receive rhythmic emancipation through jazz. But once Teagarden (and, to some extent, Jimmy Harrison) had begun recording, matters changed. Miff Mole had all the flexibility and technique which Teagarden had, but for all his greatness Mole's deadpan approach had less of the mellifluous flow which for Teagarden seemed as natural as his singing voice, a sleepy Texas drawl. Besides, Teagarden was an infinite master of blues playing, and his meetings with Armstrong gave Louis the front-line partner who should have been at his shoulder for longer than he was. Teagarden made a lot of records, starting as a dance-band player and working through the big-band and revivalist periods, but there are comparatively few top-drawer albums under his own name: he was a victim of his own consistency, since there are scarcely any moments when he sounds less than wonderful. This RCA compilation is a useful starting-point. His very first record, 'She's A Great Great Girl' with Roger Wolfe Kahn, is here and, although the earlier material is a bit of a hotchpotch – tracks with Paul Whiteman and Ben Pollack and a Red McKenzie session – the trombonist illuminates every appearance with either the horn or the voice. Four 1947 tracks with Tea's Big Eight, including Kaminsky and Hucko, are useful, but the final, 1957 tracks, with a band led by Bud Freeman, are as stately and authoritative as anything here, with a dolorous 'I Cover The Waterfront' defining several aspects of Tea's art.

*** I Gotta Right To Sing The Blues ASV AJA 5059

Teagarden; Leonard Davis, Red Nichols, Ray Lodwig, Manny Klein, Charlie Teagarden, Ruby Weinstein, Sterling Bose, Dave Klein, Harry Goldfield, Nat Natoli, Frank Guarente, Leo McConville, Charlie Spivak (*t*); Jack Fulton, Glenn Miller, Ralph Copsey, Bill Rank (*tb*); Benny Goodman (*cl*); Mezz Mezzrow, Arthur Rollini, Charles Strickfadden, Benny Bonaccio, John Cordaro, Chester Hazlitt, Jimmy Dorsey, Art Karle, Eddie Miller, Matty Matlock, Joe Catalyne,

Pee Wee Russell, Max Farley, Happy Caldwell, Arnold Brilhart, Bernie Day, Sid Stoneburn, Babe Russin, Larry Binyon, Gil Rodin, Irving Friedman, Adrian Rollini, Min Leibrook (*reeds*); Red McKenzie (*kz, v*); Fats Waller (*p, v*); Joe Sullivan, Jack Russin, Lennie Hayton, Arthur Schutt, Gil Bowers, Joe Moresco, Roy Bargy, Vincent Pirro, Howard Smith (*p*); Joe Venuti, Matty Malneck, Mischa Russell, Harry Struble, Walt Edelstein, Alex Beller, Ray Cohen (*vn*); Carl Kress, Jack Bland, Nappy Lamare, Eddie Lang, Dick McDonough, Perry Botkin, Mike Pingitore, George Van Eps (*g*); Treg Brown (*bj, v*); Eddie Condon (*bj*); Artie Bernstein, Art Miller, Jerry Johnson, Harry Goodman, Al Morgan (*b*); Norman McPherson (*tba*); Ray Bauduc, George Stafford, Herb Quigley, Stan King, Gene Krupa, Josh Billings, Larry Gomar (*d*). 2/29–10/34.

Another compilation, with 12 different bands and 18 tracks, which points up how easily Teagarden could make himself at home in bands of the period. One celebrated example is the treatment meted out to a waltz called 'Dancing With Tears In My Eyes', under Joe Venuti's leadership: Teagarden contravenes everything to do with the material and charges through his solo. Two early sessions under his own name have him trading retorts with Fats Waller on 'You Rascal You' and delivering his original reading of what became a greatest hit, 'A Hundred Years From Today'. Stricter jazz material such as two tracks by The Charleston Chasers is fine, but no less enjoyable are such as Ben Pollack's 'Two Tickets To Georgia', where Teagarden's swinging outburst suggests that he treated every setting as a chance to blow. One or two of the transfers are noisy, but most of the remastering is agreeably done.

*** A Hundred Years From Today Conifer 153

Teagarden; Charlie Teagarden, Claude Whiteman, Sterling Bose, Frank Guarente (*t*); Pee Wee Russell, Benny Goodman (*cl*); Chester Hazlett, Jimmy Dorsey, Rod Cless (*cl, as*); Joe Catalyne, Max Farley, Dale Skinner, Mutt Hayes (*cl, ts*); Frankie Trumbauer (*Cmel*); Bud Freeman (*ts*); Adrian Rollini (*bsx*); Casper Reardon (*hp*); Fats Waller (*p, v*); Joe Meresco, Terry Shand, Charlie LaVere (*p*); Walt Edelstein, Joe Venuti, Lou Kosloff (*vn*); Nappy Lamare (*g, v*); Dick McPartland, Perry Botkin, Frank Worrell (*g*); Artie Bernstein, Eddie Gilbert, Art Miller (*b*); Stan King, Bob Conselman, Larry Gomar, Herb Quigley (*d*). 10/31–9/34.

*** Jack Teagarden 1930–1934 Classics 698

As above, except add Gene Austin (*v*). 10/30–3/34.

*** Jack Teagarden 1934–1939 Classics 729

Teagarden; Charlie Teagarden, Charlie Spivak, Carl Garvin, Alec Fila, Lee Castaldo (*t*); Jose Gutierrez, Mark Bennett, Charles McCamish, Red Bone (*tb*); Benny Goodman (*cl*); Clint Garvin, Art St John (*cl, as*); John Van Eps, Hub Lytle (*cl, ts*); Ernie Caceres (*cl, ts, bs*); Frankie Trumbauer (*Cmel*); Terry Shand, John Anderson (*p*); Casper Reardon (*hp*); Allan Reuss (*g*); Art Miller (*b*); Herb Quigley, Cubby Teagarden (*d*); Meredith Blake, Linda Keene (*v*). 9/34–7/39.

The two Classics discs take their usual chronological survey of Teagarden's work up to the middle of 1939. The tracks by the 1931 band are mostly spirited stuff: a hot 'Tiger Rag', a couple of items in which Fats Waller and Tea swap banter – and some feeble tracks with Gene Austin singing. The 1933 date is another heated one, with a front-rank group of Chicagoans on hand, although Classics 698 ends on a couple of dreary sessions. Classics 729 opens with Casper Reardon's famous harp party-piece, 'Junk Man', before moving to the first sessions by the big band Teagarden formed after leaving Paul Whiteman. He never had much luck as a bandleader, but this wasn't a bad group: decent if second-division swing, always suddenly illuminated when the leader took a solo. The Conifer disc is a mixed bag of 17 tracks, all issued under Teagarden's leadership. Some of the tunes are more vocal than instrumental and reveal the leader's peculiar ability to swing even at indolent tempos. Adequate sound.

**(*) Jack Teagarden 1939–1940 Classics 758

Teagarden; Charlie Spivak, Carl Garvin, Lee Castle, John Fallstitch, Tom Gonsoulin, Frank Ryerson (*t*); Jose Gutierrez, Mark Bennett, Charles McCamish, Eddie Dudley, Seymour Goldfinger, Joe Ferrall (*tb*); Clint Garvin, Art St John (*cl, as*); John Van Eps, Hub Lytle (*cl, ts*); Jack Goldie, Tony Antonelli, Joe Ferdinando (*as*); Larry Walsh (*ts*); Ernie Caceres (*bs*); John Anderson, Jack Russin, Nat Jaffe (*p*); Allan Reuss, Dan Perri (*g*); Art Miller, Arnold Fishkind, Benny Pottle (*b*); Cubby Teagarden, Dave Tough, Ed Naquin (*d*); Kitty Kallen (*v*). 3/39–2/40.

*** Jack Teagarden 1940–1941 Classics 839

Teagarden; John Fallstitch, Tom Gonsoulin, Sid Feller, Pokey Carriere (*t*); Rex Stewart (*c*); Jose Gutierrez, Seymour Goldfinger, Joe Ferrall (*tb*); Art St John, Jack Goldie, Danny Polo, Tony Antonelli, Joe Ferdinando, Larry Walsh, Benny Lagasse, Art Moore, Art Beck (*reeds*); Barney Bigard (*cl*); Ben Webster (*ts*); Billy Kyle, Ernie Hughes, Nat Jaffe (*p*); Dan Perri, Brick Fleagle (*g*); Arnold Fishkind, Billy Taylor (*b*); Ed Naquin, Paul Collins, Dave Tough (*d*); Lynn Clark, David Allen, Marianne Dunne, Kitty Kallen (*v*). 2/40–1/41.

Teagarden was struggling to find success with this band. Most of the records tend towards undemanding, commercial swing, vocalists Kallen and Allen begin to dominate, and even the leader's peerless phrasing was starting to figure less. The first disc is brightened by a mere handful of instrumentals, though there is a fine 'Wolverine Blues' and 'The Blues' is vintage Tea. Classics 839 gets its stars mainly from the session by the Teagarden Big Eight, a small group which featured the trombonist sparring with Rex Stewart on four good (if hardly earthquaking) titles. The rest is pretty dreary, with the likes of 'Fatima's Drummer Boy' plumbing the depths of material. Transfers are clean but not very lively.

** **It's Time For Tea** Jass J-CD-624
> Teagarden; John Fallstitch, Pokey Carriere, Sid Feller, Truman Quigley (t); Jose Gutierrez, Joe Ferrall, Seymour Goldfinger (tb); Danny Polo, Tony Antonelli, Joe Ferdindo, Art Moore, Art Beck (reeds); Ernie Hughes (p); Arnold Fishkind (b); Paul Collins (d); David Allen, Lynn Clark, Marianne Dunne (v). 1–6/41.

Teagarden had started leading a big band in 1939, but it wasn't until 1941 – as revealed in the excellent notes here – that it achieved much commercial success. On the evidence of the 24 sides collected here, it was done at the expense of much jazz content. Most of the tracks work politely through forgettable pop material of the day, along with leaning on a fashionable penchant for jazzing the classics: there are charts for 'Anitra's Dance' and Debussy's 'Afternoon Of A Faun' here, as well as 'Casey Jones'. It isn't until 'Harlem Jump' (number 21) that we get a thoroughgoing swing performance. There are glimmers of Teagarden – who, after all, was the band's only feasible soloist apart from Polo – but not nearly enough. For collectors only, though the remastering is painstakingly done.

*** **Has Anybody Here Seen Jackson?** Jass J-CD-637
> Teagarden; Jimmy Simms, Pokey Carriere, Truman Quigley, Roy Peters, Jimmy McPartland, Chuck Tonti, Clair Jones, Val Salata, Tex Williamson, Bob McLaughlin (t); Jose Guiterrez, Joe Ferrall, Fred Keller, Wally Wells, Ray Olsen (tb); Danny Polo, Tony Antonelli, Clint Garvin, Art Moore, Art Beck, Dale Stoddard, Gish Gilbertson, Vic Rosi, Ken Harpster, Clark Crandell (reeds); Ernie Hughes, Don Seidel (p); Myron Shapler, Don Tosti (b); Paul Collins, Frank Horrington (d); David Allen, Kitty Kallen (v). 10/41–8/44.

A second volume of Standard Transcriptions. This one comes off rather better: 'Bashful Baby Blues' is a great one, 'Sherman Shout' and 'Dig The Groove' dig in, and Tea's vocals – as well as those of the ultra-smooth David Allen, an underrated band singer – sound good. Excellent remastering and fine documentation. This covers much the same material as Masters of Jazz Vol. 10 (Storyville STCD 4110 CD), but this is the superior issue.

*** **Club Hangover Broadcasts** Arbors ARCD 19150/1 2CD
> Teagarden; Jackie Coon (t); Jay St John (cl); Norma Teagarden, Lil Armstrong, Don Ewell (p); Kas Malone (b); Ray Bauduc (d). 4/54.

Four broadcasts by a Teagarden small group in San Francisco. With the big band and the Armstrong All Stars behind him, Tea sounds settled enough, though there are no vocals from him – a by-product of an old cabaret tax law. The material is all Dixieland chestnuts and the band suffers a little under Ray Bauduc's crashing drums, but there are some nice glimpses of the leader at his best, even if they are only glimpses (and often ones where Tea isn't very well miked). Clean sound, though Coon and Bauduc (and Malone) usually sound louder than everyone else. Ewell and Armstrong are the intermission pianists and get a couple of solos each.

** **Jack Teagarden And His All Stars** Jazzology 199
> Teagarden; Dick Oakley (c); Jerry Fuller (cl); Don Ewell (p); Stan Puls (b); Ronnie Greb (d). 58.

Teagarden drifted through his final years in a way that looks as careless and slipshod as some of Armstrong's later efforts: the numerous renditions of 'St James Infirmary' and 'Rockin' Chair' (both included here) eventually sound as fatigued as his perennially tired voice. The Jazzology release is a well-recorded club date, made in Cleveland in 1958, but it features a dusty band and a leader content to amble along. There is much better Teagarden from the 1950s still awaiting reissue.

Richard Teitelbaum (born 1939) PIANO, SYNTHESIZERS, ELECTRONICS

***(*) **Concerto Grosso (1985)** hat Art CD 6004
> Teitelbaum; George Lewis (tb, elec); Anthony Braxton (reeds). 5/85.

A key member of the extremely important Musica Elettronica Viva, Teitelbaum is a pioneering exponent of electro-acoustic combinations in improvised music. The performance with Zingaro is typically challenging, but ultimately rather dry, and is perhaps returned to after hearing Teitelbaum's engrossing collaboration with two other significant performers of radical 'cross-over' music. With Concerto Grosso, he takes an intriguing step back from the aggressive futurism of the avant-garde to examine the implications for improvisation of another, older tradition.

The bracketed date is partially intended as a *caveat emptor* directed at anyone who might think they're buying a 'grand ensemble' from the Baroque period; the original form differed from a solo concerto in setting a small group, known as the *concertino*, in antiphonal relation to a large ensemble of 'replenishing' *ripieni*, who play the *tutti*. Teitelbaum's full and correct title is *Concerto Grosso (1985) For Human Concertini And Robotic Ripieno*. The idea is to place instrumental improvisers in relation to a machine-generated background of deutero-instrumental effects which is nevertheless responsive to what the improvisers themselves choose to play.

Logic and the laws of thermodynamics suggest that the only possible outcome is utter chaos and entropy. However, the responses of the human *concertini* (all of whom have shown an equal commitment to 'freedom' and 'structures' elsewhere in their careers) are so intelligently disciplined that it becomes possible to discern the fleeting ghost of an orthodox thematic development, carried on at such a level of abstraction that it is never explicitly stated. Divided into 'Invenzione', 'Fantasia' and 'Capriccio', the piece has a nicely ironic current which saves it from pomposity or any suggestion of pastiche. Not by any means for every taste, but Braxton and Lewis are worth hearing, whatever the context, and Teitelbaum's contribution merits wider recognition.

Joe Temperley (born 1929) BARITONE AND SOPRANO SAXOPHONES

*** **Nightingale** Hep CD 2052
      Temperley; Brian Lemon (*p*); Dave Green (*b*); Martin Drew (*d*). 4/91.
*** **Concerto For Joe** Hep CD 2062
      As above, except add Steve Sidwell, Eddie Severn, Gerard Presencer (*t*); Gordon Campbell, Nichol Thomson (*tb*); Peter King (*as*); Duncan Lamont (*ts*); Brian Kellock (*p*); Alec Dankworth (*b*); Jack Parnell (*d*). 9/93–7/94.

Temperley has seldom figured in record sessions in the UK since his move to America and there has been very little under his own leadership, but *Nightingale* was an opportune session. A seamless, singing manner belies the difficulties of the instrument and, though his sometimes bubbly timbre at fast tempos may not be to all tastes, there's a genuineness about his improvisations. There's a beautiful Ellington rarity in 'Sunset And A Mocking Bird', in which Temperley's sound never makes one think of Harry Carney. He ends on an *a cappella* 'My Love Is Like A Red, Red Rose' that sums up the sound he can get from the horn. The weakness lies in the rhythm section: nothing very wrong, but the sheer ordinariness of the playing is unfortunate. *Concerto For Joe* is an agreeable continuation. Jimmy Deuchar's composition for Temperley is the centrepiece of the record, performed by the saxophonist with the big group, and it's a substantial if not quite deathless performance. Elsewhere there are more quartet tracks with the previous group. Temperley sounds well enough but, in the end, as with the previous disc, a certain flavour of routine militates against its acquiring essential status.

Jacky Terrasson PIANO

*** **Jacky Terrasson** Blue Note 829351-2
      Terrasson; Ugonna Okegwo (*b*); Leon Parker (*d*). 7–8/94.
*** **Reach** Blue Note 835739-2
      As above. 95.

Terrasson has been gathering much acclaim recently, and these debut records as a leader are fine and notably single-minded efforts. He never approaches a tune from any predictable point: on the first disc, there are versions of 'I Love Paris', 'My Funny Valentine' and 'Bye Bye Blackbird' which are so revisionist as to be almost unrecognizable at times. Yet he sticks to otherwise familiar paths of harmony and rhythmic patterns which call to mind influences ranging from Ahmad Jamal to Bill Evans. The problem with both discs is a slightly exasperating ingenuity which seems less at the service of the music and more about creating a sensation. Terrasson's writing has a greater showing on the second set, *Reach*, though it often sounds to be more about motifs and vamps than full-scale structures. Okegwo and Parker perform well, but theirs is a largely subsidiary role, rather than one where a true trio music is called for.

Clark Terry (born 1920) TRUMPET, FLUGELHORN

*** **Serenade To A Bus Seat** Original Jazz Classics OJC 066
      Terry; Johnny Griffin (*ts*); Wynton Kelly (*p*); Paul Chambers (*b*); Philly Joe Jones (*d*). 4/57.
Though not reducible to his 'influences', Terry hybridizes Dizzy Gillespie's hot, fluent lines and witty

abandon with Rex Stewart's distinctive half-valving and Charlie Shavers's high-register lyricism; he is also a master of the mute, an aspect of his work that had a discernible impact on Miles Davis. Miles, though, remained unconvinced by Terry's pioneering development of the flugelhorn as a solo instrument; later in his career he traded four-bar phrases with himself, holding a horn in each hand. An irrepressible showman, with a sly sense of humour, Terry often fared better when performing under other leaders. His encounter with the Oscar Peterson Trio in 1964 is often judged his best work, and it's hard to see where and when he played better. The 'early' – he was 37 – *Serenade To A Bus Seat* combines a tribute to civil-rights activist, Rosa Parks, with pungent versions of 'Stardust' and Parker's 'Donna Lee'. Terry isn't an altogether convincing bopper, but he's working with a fine, funky band, and they carry him through some slightly unresolved moments.

*** Duke With A Difference Original Jazz Classics OJC 229
> Terry; Quentin Jackson, Britt Woodman (*tb*); Tyree Glenn (*tb, vib*); Johnny Hodges (*as*); Paul Gonsalves (*ts*); Jimmy Jones, Billy Strayhorn (*p*); Luther Henderson (*cel*); Jimmy Woode (*b*); Sam Woodyard (*d*); Marion Bruce (*v*). 7 & 9/57.

In 1957 Terry was most of the way through his eight-year stint with Ellington (he'd already worked with Charlie Barnet and Count Basie and was bound for a staff job with NBC, the first black man to get his feet under that rather clubby table) and a successful partnership with trombonist Bob Brookmeyer. It's the slide brass men he cleaves to on this mildly impertinent tribute to his boss. He undercuts both Jackson and Hodges on a beautifully arranged 'In A Sentimental Mood' (which features Strayhorn on piano and Luther Henderson on celeste) and cheerfully wrecks 'Take The "A" Train' in spite of Gonsalves's best efforts to keep it hurtling along the rails. Marion Bruce's vocals are nothing to write home about, but the band is as good as the form book says it ought to be.

**** In Orbit Original Jazz Classics OJC 302
> Terry; Thelonious Monk (*p*); Sam Jones (*b*); Philly Joe Jones (*d*). 5/58.

Terry's solitary excursion on Monk's *Brilliant Corners*, a vivid 'Bemsha Swing', underlined the degree to which Monk himself still drew sustenance from swing. *In Orbit* is firmly Terry's album. If the material is less stretching, the arrangements are surprisingly demanding, and the interplay between flugelhorn (used throughout) and piano on 'One Foot In The Gutter' and the contrasting 'Moonlight Fiesta' is highly inventive.

**** Color Changes Candid CCD 79009
> Terry; Jimmy Knepper (*tb*); Yusef Lateef (*ts, f, eng hn, ob*); Seldon Powell (*ts*); Tommy Flanagan, Budd Johnson (*p*); Joe Benjamin (*b*); Ed Shaughnessy (*d*). 11/60.

Terry's best record, and ample evidence that swing was still viable on the cusp of the decade that was to see its demise as anything but an exercise in nostalgia. What is immediately striking is the extraordinary, almost kaleidoscopic variation of tone-colour through the seven tracks. Given Lateef's inventive multi-instrumentalism, Powell's doubling on flute and Terry's use of flugelhorn and his mutes, the permutations on horn voicings seem almost infinite. 'Brother Terry' opens with a deep growl from Terry, a weaving oboe theme by composer Lateef and some beautiful harmony work from Watkins (who a matter of days later was to make such a contribution to Benny Bailey's superb Candid session, *Big Brass* (9011 CD)) and who interacts imaginatively with Knepper on Terry's 'Flutin' And Fluglin''. Again arranged by Lateef, this is a straightforward exploration of the relation between their two horns; Terry has written several 'odes' to his second instrument, and this is perhaps the most inventive.

'Nahstye Blues', written by and featuring Johnson, in for the unsuitably limpid Flanagan, comes close to Horace Silver's funk. Terry is slightly disappointing, but Lateef turns in a majestic solo that turns his own cor anglais introduction completely on its head. The closing 'Chat Qui Pêche' is an all-in, solo-apiece affair that would have sounded wonderful in the Parisian *boîte* it celebrates and brings a marvellous, expertly recorded record to a powerful finish. Needless to say, it comes highly recommended.

***(*) Mellow Moods Prestige PCD 24136
> Terry; Lester Robertson (*tb*); Budd Johnson (*ts*); George Barrow (*bs*); Junior Mance (*p*); Eddie Costa (*p, vib*); Joe Benjamin, Art Davis (*b*); Charli Persip, Ed Shaughnessy (*d*). 7/61, 5/62.

Following on from the last item, this confirms that a purple patch was in progress. A calmer, less frantic record all round, it showed off Terry's abilities as a balladeer as well as a fast action man. Mance is a good accompanist on the earlier session, a quartet with just Terry and rhythm. Inevitably there is slightly less of him on the other date, but this almost-big band generates an impressive body of noise when it gets going, and the settings laid out for him on 'If I Were You' and 'It's Fun To Think' are completely irresistible.

*** Clark After Dark MPS 529 088
> Terry; Eddie Blair, Tony Fisher, Dave Hancock, Derek Watkins, Kenny Wheeler (*t*); Cliff Hardy, Dave Horler, Nat Peck, Ray Premru (*tb*); Terry Jones (*frhn*); Roy Willox (*as, f, cl*); Al

Newman (*as, bcl*); Stan Sulzmann (*ts, f, af*); Tony Coe (*ts, f, cl*); Ronnie Ross (*bs, cl*); Gordon Beck (*p*); Martin Kershaw (*g*); Chris Laurence (*b*); Tristan Fry (*d, perc*); strings. 9/77.

A first-class British band accompany Clark on an oddly autumnal stroll. No 'Autumn Leaves', but browns and deep blues for the main part. He's playing wonderfully and the engineering does all the right and tactful things for him. 'Nature Boy' and 'Willow Weep For Me' are gems.

**** Memories Of Duke Original Jazz Classics OJC 604

Terry; Joe Pass (*g*); Jack Wilson (*p*); Ray Brown (*b*); Frank Severino (*d*). 3/80.

Obvious, really, but exquisitely done. The interplay between Pass and Brown touches unsuspected areas of 'Cotton Tail' and 'Sophisticated Lady' (compare the version with Red Mitchell, below) and, though Severino might have been dispensed with for at least a couple of the softer tracks, the overall sound is excellent.

**(*) Squeeze Me Chiaroscuro CRD 309

Terry; Virgil Jones (*t*); Al Grey, Britt Woodman (*tb*); Haywood Henry, Red Holloway, Phil Woods (*reeds*); John Campbell (*p*); Marcus McLaurine (*b*); Butch Ballard (*d*).

Good arrangements but a rather knotted sound that strips some fine horn players of any real individuality. The rhythm section sounds under-rehearsed and the tempo is always either lagging behind or rushing to catch up. Disappointing.

*** Clark Terry–Red Mitchell Enja 5011

Terry; Red Mitchell (*b, p, v*). 2/86.

***(*) Jive At Five Enja 6042

As above. 7/88.

Jive At Five is the more musicianly of these rather knockabout sets by one frustrated crooner and one master of verbal salad, whose 'Hey Mr Mumbles' gets its 5,000th airing on the earlier album. As a purely musical dialogue, these have no right to work half as well as they do, but Terry is in excellent lip on the later version of 'Big'n And The Bear' and the Ellington material. Mitchell's comping skills come into their own on 'Cotton Tail' (two nicely varied takes), 'Sophisticated Lady' and 'Prelude To A Kiss'.

***(*) Portraits Chesky JD 2

Terry; Don Friedman (*p*); Victor Gaskin (*b*); Lewis Nash (*d*). 12/88.

*** Having Fun Delos DE 4021

Terry; Bunky Green (*as*); Red Holloway (*as, ts*); John Campbell (*p*); Major Holley (*b, tba*); Lewis Nash (*d*). 4/90.

By the 1980s, Terry was more than satisfied with his billing as an elder statesman and trotted out all his tricks with almost indulgent ease. The big production numbers like 'Ciribiribin' sound good on *Portraits*, but the album overall almost sounds like an audiophile test disc, so exact and limpid is the reproduction. *Having Fun* means what it says, with jokey-straight versions of the Flintstones theme (one of the most irritating melodies ever committed) and 'It's Not Easy Being Green'. Holley is a marvellous partner; a duo record, with the two men vocalizing at full throttle, would be something to hear.

***(*) Live At The Village Gate Chesky JD 49

Terry; Jimmy Heath (*ts, ss*); Paquito D'Rivera (*as*); Don Friedman (*p*); Marcus McLaurine (*b*); Kenny Washington (*d*). 11/90.

Recorded three weeks short of Terry's seventieth birthday, this is a good-natured set of uncomplicated jazz. Terry alternates his trumpet ('my driver') and flugelhorn ('putter'), favouring a soft, blurred-edge tone that in no way compromises the clarity of his bop-influenced lines. Jimmy Heath is dry without being sterile and takes a lovely solo on 'Pint Of Bitter', a dedication to the late Tubby Hayes. D'Rivera only shows up for a single track, the appealing 'Silly Samba'.

The recording is impeccably handled, with a light sound that still captures the live ambience; on 'Keep, Keep, Keep On Keepin' On', Terry has the entire audience singing along, and so he can't resist throwing them 'Hey Mr Mumbles' at the end. 'If Sylvester Stallone can make *Rocky 3, 4, 5*, I don't see why I can't make Mumbles 8, 9 and 10.'

*** What A Wonderful World Red Baron 473714

Terry; Al Grey (*tb*); Lesa Terry (*vn*); Dado Moroni (*p*); Ron Carter (*b*); Lewis Nash (*d*). 2/93.

Subtitled 'for Louis and Duke', this is Terry doing material that he probably practises in his sleep. 'Sleepy Time Down South' segued with 'Wonderful World', beginning and near end of a career, is irresistible, but so too is a long '"A" Train' and a gorgeous version of the less well-known 'Baby Clementine' by Strayhorn. Al Grey sounds in fine voice throughout the album and, though Lesa Terry's contribution is questionable, the session as a whole has a wonderfully delicate profile to which she undoubtedly contributes.

Henri Texier (born 1945) DOUBLE BASS

*** **La Companera** Label Bleu LBLC 6525
    Texier; Michael Marre (*t, flhn*); Louis Sclavis (*cl, ts*); Philippe Deschepper (*g*); Jacques Mahieux
    (*d*). 2/83.
*** **Paris–Batignolles** Label Bleu LBLC 6506
    Texier; Louis Sclavis (*ss, bcl*); Joe Lovano (*ts*); Philippe Deschepper (*g*); Jacques Mahieux (*d*). 5/
    86.
**** **Izlaz** Label Bleu LBLC 6515
    Texier; Joe Lovano (*ts, ss, cl, f, perc*); Steve Swallow (*b*); Aldo Romano (*d*). 5/88.
*** **Colonel Skopje** Label Bleu LBLC 6523
    As above, except add John Scofield (*g*). 7/88.

Texier's double bass style is a freer and lighter version of Wilbur Ware's; he eulogizes the great
Chicagoan on a Carlyne CD, *Barret/Romano/Texier*. Texier likes to work the lower end of the register,
with a throbbing, wobbling sound in ensembles that gives way to a full-voiced lyricism as a soloist. The
earliest of these sets is distinguished by some fine work from Sclavis (at that time still relatively unknown
outside France), but the band takes off only when Marre is added for two excellent quintet tracks.

Paris–Batignolles consists of swirling dance pieces and *misterioso* folk themes from a fine band, caught
live at the Amiens Jazz Festival in 1986. Sclavis and Lovano inevitably dominate, but guitarist
Deschepper makes some effective interventions. The closing 'Noises', which sounds like an encore piece,
is a delightful crowd-pleaser.

Izlaz is credited to Texier's Transatlantik Quartet. So disinclined is he to dominate it that he brings in a
second bass player, albeit a bass guitarist. Swallow's upbeat, rock-tinged swing and confident navigation
of the melody allow Texier a measure of freedom that he exploits much more fully here than on the
disappointing mixed-bag, *Colonel Skopje*. 'Ups And Downs' bears very little relation to Bud Powell's
composition of that name, but it has a nice, slightly aggrieved bounce, and the title-track is impressively
crafted, with Lovano well to the fore. The mix is rather heavy-handed, presumably to bring Texier
forward; in the event, Romano, who's always good to listen to, is simply too loud. On the later set Texier
seems determined to allow everyone his head, and the abiding impression is of disconnected solo
'features'. Scofield and Lovano play with characteristic fire and urgency, though, and the 'rhythm
section' do their stuff like they're enjoying it.

Eje Thelin (1938–90) TROMBONE

*** **Raggruppamento** Phono Suecia PSCD 56
    Jan Kohlin, Bertil Lovgren, Hakan Nyqvist (*t*); Olle Holmqvist, Nils Landgren, Jorgen
    Johansson (*tb*); Sven Larsson (*btb*); David Wilczewski, Ulf Andersson, Jan Kling, Lennart
    Aberg, Erik Nilsson (*reeds*); Bobo Stenson (*p*); Stefan Blomquist (*ky*); Goran Klinghagen (*g*);
    Per-Ake Holmlander (*tba*); Teddy Walter (*b*); Anders Kjellberg (*d*); Andre Ferrari (*perc*). 4/89.

Thelin was an important Swedish musician who worked his way from Dixieland to free playing with an
entirely plausible logic, having developed a formidable agility on the trombone early on. There is,
regrettably, nothing under his own name at present which features his playing: this concert of his
extended suite 'Raggruppamento' was his final achievement, completed when he was already ill with
cancer and unable himself to play. It's a pity in some ways that his solo parts are performed by guitarist
Klinghagen rather than one of the trombonists: Klinghagen does a decent job, but one misses the rigour
of Thelin's own playing. The Swedish Radio Jazz group is a formidable ensemble, though, and they
translate all the sonorities of Thelin's score into a shimmering whole. The 11 parts are typically catholic
in their breadth of sympathies: Thelin's interest in electronics is reflected by Blomquist's sensitive
keyboards, but the rumbustious section-work is as important as the more translucent moments. There
are also fine solos from Wilczewski, though disappointingly few from the other horns, considering the
stellar personnel. Excellent concert recording.

The Bob Thiele Collective GROUP

*** **Sunrise Sunset** Red Baron 469286
    David Murray (*ts*); John Hicks (*p*); Cecil McBee (*b*); Andrew Cyrille (*d*). 90.
*** **Louis Satchmo** Red Baron 471578
    Red Rodney (*flhn*); Joshua Redman (*ts*); Kenny Barron (*p*); Santi Debriano (*b*); Grady Tate (*d,
    v*). 11/91.

***(*) **Lion Hearted** Red Baron 474982
>   Roy Hargrove (*t*); Ray Anderson (*tb*); Gary Bartz (*as*); Ravi Coltrane, Steve Marcus (*ts*); Kenny
>   Barron (*p*); Ray Drummond (*b*); Grady Tate (*d*). 8/93.

Not so much a regularly constituted group as what the title suggests, a loose confederation of players
brought together more or less *ad hoc*. Veteran producer Thiele always favoured bringing together players
of different generations and playing personalities. An early incarnation recorded *Sunrise Sunset* and
featured David Murray, with John Hicks, Cecil McBee and Andrew Cyrille; almost inevitably it veered
towards a more exploratory and aggressive sound. In many respects, this has to be considered a David
Murray record but it merits its place here, too.

Louis Satchmo has a more obvious inter-generational structure, pitching the young Redman in alongside a wonderful sounding Rodney (on flugelhorn) and the sort of rhythm section that money can't buy.
The title-piece is a Thiele co-composition. The remaining material is expertly arranged and performed
by a group who sound as though they spent a bit of time running things down before the light went on.
The later band has more of a big-band feel with some expert arrangements and fine section playing by
an improbably constituted band which one wouldn't expect to gel. Bartz, interestingly, is the wild card,
sounding slightly sharp in places and either unable or unwilling to adjust his broad, nasal timbre to the
group. Marcus is a highly professional player who has more big-band miles under his belt than most
players see in a lifetime. He is also a fine soloist, blending and contrasting well with the more lyrical
Coltrane Junior. These are unusual, hard-to-categorize discs, but they are consistently fascinating.

Toots Thielemans (born 1922) HARMONICA, GUITAR, WHISTLING

***(*) **Man Bites Harmonica** Original Jazz Classics OJC 1738
>   Thielemans; Pepper Adams (*bs*); Kenny Drew (*p*); Wilbur Ware (*b*); Art Taylor (*d*). 12/57.

**** **Live** Polydor 831694
>   Thielemans; Wim Overgaauw, Joop Scholten (*g*); Rob Franken (*electric p*); Victor Kaihatu, Rob
>   Langereis (*b*); Bruno Castellucci (*d*); Cees Schrama (*perc*). 4/75.

*** **The Silver Collection: Toots Thielemans** Polydor 825086
>   Thielemans; Ferdinand Povel (*ts*); Rob Franken (*ky*); Wim Overgaauw, Joop Scholten (*g*);
>   Victor Kaihatu, Niels-Henning Orsted-Pedersen (*b*); Bruno Castellucci, Evert Overweg (*d*);
>   Ruud Boos Orchestra; collective personnel, other details unknown. 4/74, 4/75.

***(*) **Toots Thielemans In Tokyo** Denon DC 8551
>   Thielemans; Tsuyoshi Yamamoto (*p*); Tsutomu Okada (*b*); Fumio Watanabe (*d*). 7/79.

*** **Apple Dimple** Denon DC 8563
>   Thielemans; Masahiko Sato (*ky*); Tsunehide Matsuki (*g*); Akira Okazawa (*b*); Yuchi Togashiki
>   (*d*); Tadomi Anai (*perc*); unknown horns and strings. 11/79.

*** **Live In The Netherlands** Pablo CD 2308 233
>   Thielemans; Joe Pass (*g*); Niels-Henning Orsted-Pedersen (*b*). 7/80.

**** **Do Not Leave Me** Stash ST CD 12
>   Thielemans; Fred Hersch (*p*); Marc Johnson (*b*); Joey Baron (*d*). 6/86.

**** **Only Trust Your Heart** Concord CCD 4355
>   Thielemans; Fred Hersch (*p*); Marc Johnson, Harvie Swartz (*b*); Joey Baron (*d*). 4 & 5/88.

***(*) **Footprints** Emarcy 846650
>   Thielemans; Mulgrew Miller (*p*); Rufus Reid (*b*); Lewis Nash (*d*).

***(*) **For My Lady** Emarcy 510133
>   Thielemans; Shirley Horn (*p, v*); Charles Ables (*b*); Steve Williams (*d*). 4/91.

Thielemans frequently finds himself in the awkward and unsatisfactory position of coming first in a
category of one or consigned to 'miscellaneous instruments'. Though ubiquitous in the blues, the
harmonica has made remarkably little impact in jazz, and there are no recognized critical standards for
his extraordinary facility as a whistler. Thielemans's pop and movie work has tended further to down-
grade his very considerable jazz credentials. Surprisingly, to those who know him primarily as a performer of moodily atmospheric soundtrack pieces (*Midnight Cowboy* pre-eminently) or as composer of
the undemanding 'Bluesette' (included in *The Silver Collection*), his roots are in bebop and in the kind
of harmonically liberated improvisation associated with John Coltrane. That's perhaps most obvious in
the dark, Chicago-influenced sound of *Man Bites Harmonica* (which includes a wonderful 'Don't Blame
Me') and on *Only Trust Your Heart* and *Footprints*, which mark a considerable revival of Thielemans's
jazz playing.

Born in Belgium, he was originally an accordionist and harmonica player but was sufficiently moved by
hearing Django Reinhardt play that he added guitar to his repertoire, and he continues to play it. There
are good solo performances of 'Muskrat Ramble', 'The Mooche' and a slightly off-beam 'You're My
Blues Machine' on *The Silver Collection*, a useful sample which establishes his bop *bona fides* with 'My

Little Suede Shoes' and is marred only by a set of rather dreary band arrangements by Boos. There's no real overlap with *Live*, which appears to confirm a long-standing belief that Thielemans is not a successful studio performer but needs the resistance and charge of a live audience. There's certainly something rather overprogrammed about the Japanese sessions on *Apple Dimple*. Haunting versions of 'Harlem Nocturne' and the movie themes 'Looking For Mr Goodbar' and 'Midnight Cowboy' are marred by deep-pile arrangements and a high-tech gloss that don't suit Thielemans's honest and straightforward approach.

A studio jazz recording by Thielemans is now a rarity, but *Only Trust Your Heart* is his masterpiece. His playing, restricted on this occasion to harmonica, is superb. The choice of material (and Fred Hersch's arranging) is impeccable and challenging and the production first rate, with Thielemans front and centre and the band spread out very evenly behind him. The set kicks off with a marvellous reading of Wayne Shorter's 'Speak No Evil', includes 'Sophisticated Lady', Monk's 'Little Rootie Tootie' and Thad Jones's 'Three And One', transposed unfamiliarly high to bring it within the range of Thielemans's instrument, which takes on the slightly yodelling timbre of soprano saxophone.

It's by no means an MOR or easy-listening set. Thielemans's solo development merits the closest attention, particularly on the original 'Sarabande', the better of two duets with Hersch. The pianist's other composition, 'Rain Waltz', deserves wider distribution. Allegedly nearly all first takes, each of the dozen tracks represents Thielemans's undervalued art at its finest.

Do Not Leave Me was recorded in Brussels a year or two earlier and has all the qualities of a sentimental homecoming. The opening 'Ne Me Quitte Pas', by Jacques Brel, another native of the city, is drenched with emotion. 'Stardust' is dedicated to Benny Goodman, who had died a few days previously. It follows a long medleyed version of Miles Davis's 'All Blues' and 'Blue 'N' Green', the latter co-written with Bill Evans. Thielemans had played with the pianist in 1978, at which session he met Marc Johnson. 'Autumn Leaves' is a bass-and-drums feature, with an astonishing solo from Baron that brings up the temperature for the samba rhythms of 'Velas', which Thielemans takes on guitar. A fine set closes with 'Bluesette', which he calls his 'calling card or, better yet, social security number'. Everyone whistles along.

The recent collaboration with Shirley Horn yields an album of impeccable performances that sound completely spontaneous and uncontrived. Horn's piano playing (which in recent years has tended to take a back seat to her singing) is the ideal accompaniment, and Thielemans responds by echoing the contours of her unmistakable vocal phrasing. There are several entrances which, for a note or two, could be either of them.

Jesper Thilo (born 1941) TENOR SAXOPHONE, CLARINET

*** **Jesper Thilo Quartet With Clark Terry** Storyville STCD 8204
    Thilo; Clark Terry (*t*); Kenny Drew (*p*); Jesper Lundgaard, Mads Vinding (*b*); Svend-Erik Nørregaard, Billy Hart (*d*). 12/80.

*** **Jesper Thilo Quintet Featuring Harry Edison** Storyville STC-CD 4120
    Thilo; Harry 'Sweets' Edison (*t*); Ole Kock Hansen (*p*); Ole Ousen (*g*); Jesper Lundgaard (*b*); Svend-Erik Nørregaard (*d*). 2/86.

(*) **Shufflin' Music Mecca CD 1015 2
    Thilo; Ole Kock Hansen, Søren Kristiansen (*p*); Henrik Bay (*g*); Jesper Lundgaard, Hugo Rasmussen (*b*); Svend-Erik Nørregaard (*d*); Ann Farholt (*v*). 9/90.

***(*) **Jesper Thilo Quintet Featuring Hank Jones** Storyville STCD 4178
    Thilo; Hank Jones (*p*); Doug Raney (*g*); Hugo Rasmussen (*b*); Svend-Erik Nørregaard (*d*). 3/91.

*** **Plays Duke Ellington** Music Mecca CD 1025-2
    Thilo; Søren Kristiansen (*p*); Hugo Rasmussen (*b*); Svend-Erik Nørregaard (*d*); Ann Farholt (*v*). 4/92.

*** **Don't Count Him Out** Music Mecca CD 1035-2
    As above. 3/93.

***(*) **Movin' Out** Music Mecca 1045-2
    Thilo; Ben Besiakow (*p*); Jesper Lundgaard (*b*). 4/94.

Thilo plays the kind of straight-ahead swing that the Scandinavians have now virtually patented: he's a tenorman in the noble tradition, a plain speaker and a reliable journeyman. The early session with Terry has just returned to the catalogue, coupled with a quartet date from the same month, and though this is no more than a friendly chug through a familiar programme the front line has real class. The set with Edison would be by far the more impressive were it not for the dullness of the accompaniments; however, the trumpeter does kick-start 'There Will Never Be Another You', and there are some graceful moments on a romantic medley recorded on a later – and better – night. *Shufflin'* is very much in the same vein, a professional club set that doesn't really bear frequent repetition at home. The bebop flourishes on 'How High The Moon', with Ann Farholt's rather strained voice acting as second horn, are quite dramatic, and there are enough imaginative flourishes on a long roster of standards to sustain interest; but, again, nothing to write home about.

The more recent records count among his best, though. The meeting with Hank Jones benefits hugely from Hank's benign but slyly alert presence, whether prodding a soloist or taking a typically suave improvisation of his own. Raney, too, plays very well. The first two Music Mecca albums are focused round Ellington and Basie repertoire and, though some of the choices are a little too familiar in each case, the quintet plays them with fine enthusiasm and Thilo musters some of his sharpest improvising (his clarinet playing on 'Duke's Place' is also a neat surprise). Farholt's singing is much more assured, and the studio sound is very crisp on each record.

It seems almost cheeky to suggest that Thilo is improving. But it's hard to avoid the feeling that *Movin' Out* is his best record. The lighter feel of a drummerless trio suits him and, though he stands in a mainstream tenor tradition, he has a more airy approach to an improvisation than some masters of the style; boppish without really sounding 'modern', his solos have a fleetness which defies cliché. 'Blue Monk' turns a contemporary blues into a masterclass of the style. Besiakow is perhaps no more than a good prop, but this is a cracker of a record.

Frode Thingnaes (born 1940) TROMBONE

*** **Watch What Happens!** Gemini GMCD 85

> Thingnaes; Steffan Stokland (*btb*); Henryk Lysiak (*p*); Pete Knutsen, Jan Erik Kongshaug (*g*); Terje Gewelt (*b*); Svein Christiansen (*d*). 11/93-1/94.

A veteran Norwegian trombonist, Frode Thingnaes doesn't stint on this rare outing as a leader – overdubbing accounts for up to six horns on each track, and with his light, singing tone he gets a very pleasing sound out of his one-man section. Some of the arrangements opt for a light-music feel rather than anything more demanding, though often the sonorities are their own reward, and when he clears the decks and gives himself a straight-ahead solo he shows himself to be a capable jazzman. Genial swing-to-bop stuff.

Gary Thomas TENOR SAXOPHONE, FLUTE

*** **Seventh Quadrant** Enja 5047

> Thomas; Paul Bollenback (*g, syn*); Renée Rosnes (*p*); Anthony Cox (*b*); Jeff Tain Watts (*d*). 4/87.

(*) **Code Violations Enja 5085

> Thomas; Paul Bollenback (*g, syn*); Tim Murphy (*p, ky*); Anthony Cox, Geoff Harper (*b*); Dennis Chambers, Steve Williams (*d*). 7/88.

*** **By Any Means Necessary** JMT 834432

> Thomas; Geri Allen, Tim Murphy (*p, syn*); Anthony Cox (*b*); Dennis Chambers (*d*); Nana Vasconcelos (*perc*). 5/89.

*** **While The Gate Is Open** JMT 834439

> Thomas; Kevin Eubanks (*g*); Renée Rosnes (*p, syn*); Anthony Cox, Dave Holland (*b*); Dennis Chambers (*d*). 5/90.

(*) **The Kold Kage JMT 849151

> Thomas; Kevin Eubanks (*g*); Paul Bollenback (*g, syn*); Mulgrew Miller (*p*); Michael Cain, Tim Murphy (*p, syn*); Anthony Perkins (*syn*); Anthony Cox (*b*); Dennis Chambers (*d*); Steve Moss (*perc*); Joe Wesson (*v*). 3, 5 & 6/91.

*** **Till We Have Faces** JMT 514000

> Thomas; Pat Metheny (*g*); Tim Murphy (*p*); Anthony Cox, Ed Howard (*b*); Terri Lyne Carrington (*d*); Steve Moss (*perc*). 5/92.

Thomas comes on very much like a latter-day Wayne Shorter. He has the same acidulous tone and preference for enigmatic and occasionally gnomic phraseology, but with little of the overall structural awareness that saves funk grooves from sounding stuck. Growing up in a musical environment required to prove itself not primarily on standards, he makes an impressive fist of half a dozen well-worn themes on the untypical *While The Gate Is Open*. His work with Seventh Quadrant is more directly funk-based than Steve Coleman's with Five Elements and is inclined to lapse into dim, Miles-influenced abstractions that have none of his former boss's taste and grasp of theatricals. Purchasers of the disappointing *Kold Kage* are warned to be careful if listening to the opening 'Threshold' while driving; one suspects that this is precisely where Thomas's later recordings will have their biggest market impact, as urban-freeway soundtracks.

The original *Seventh Quadrant* suggested an imagination aligned to Shorter's quasi-mystical side (in the manner of his *Ju-Ju* and *Odyssey of Iska*), but this gave way on the poor, over-produced *Code Violations* to a programme of black urban sc-fi (titles such as 'Maxthink', 'Traf', 'Zylog', 'Sybase', 'Adax') that falls victim to its own insufficiently worked-out premises. This is the manner, too, of *Kold Kage*, in which Thomas adds raps to a flagging funk manner that is only streety in a dilettante, 33rd-floor way.

Though it's not clear whether *By Any Means Necessary* is intended to access political sensibilities not directly evident on the other records (the title was a slogan of Malcolm X), there is a directness to both conception and production that allows two keyboard players to work together effectively and without taking each other's turf. It restores the virtues of 'Foresight, Preparation And Subterfuge', 'No' and 'The Eternal Present' on the first album. Thomas's palpable hurry to touch all the bases has probably diluted his first few records, and it is still an obstacle on *Till We Have Faces*, where he even attempts a late-night 'Lush Life' with Pat Metheny, neither of them obvious contenders for this sort of material. Thomas's playing is often ragged and indifferently pitched; odd for a record that clearly wasn't dashed off in an afternoon.

*** Exile's Gate JMT 514009-2
> Thomas; Tim Murphy, Charles Covington (*org*); Paul Bollenback, Marvin Sewell (*g*); Ed Howard (*b*); Terri Lyne Carrington, Jack DeJohnette (*d*); Steve Moss (*perc*). 5/93.

**(*) Overkill JMT 514024-2
> Thomas; Ransom (*t, v*); George Colligan (*p*); Marvin Sewell (*g*); John Lamkin III (*d*); Maysa, Godfaddah, Jovanotti, Pork Chop, Barrikade, No Name, Mustapha, Lean-Nut (*v*). 5/94–8/95.

The fifth JMT outing is no stronger (or weaker) than the previous four. Thomas continues to work a tough, lean compromise between some kind of hard-bop tradition and a more freely-moving new jazz, though the introduction of hammond organ seems to be looking forward and back at the same time. Group democracy tends to quell something of the leader's intensity, and the disc could use a knockout punch.

No shortage of aggression on the subsequent *Overkill* though. This is Thomas's rap move, jazz hip-hop rhythms used as the podium for a sequence of sour diatribes from the line-up of rappers. Thomas still gets off some impressive solos, and this time the surroundings are severe enough to extend the darker side of his own playing. Production, though, can't hold a serious candle to the typical rap record, and there's a perhaps inevitable air of compromise about an interesting experiment. Exception: the gripping repetitions of 'Soulja'.

René Thomas (1927–75) GUITAR

**** Guitar Groove Original Jazz Classics OJC 1725
> Thomas; J. R. Monterose (*ts*); Hod O'Brien (*p*); Teddy Kotick (*b*); Albert 'Tootie' Heath (*d*). 9/60.

A fatal heart attack cut short a career that was already rather overshadowed by a more colourful and charismatic guitarist, Thomas's Belgian compatriot, Django Reinhardt. Though Django must have been the unavoidable comparison when Thomas moved to North America – he spent some time in Canada in addition to New York – there really wasn't very much in common between them and Thomas's modernist credentials allowed him to fit into the American scene more comfortably than his illustrious predecessor.

Guitar Groove is a fine product of his American sojourn and is one of the high points of a poorly documented career. The original 'Spontaneous Effort' combines firm boppish melody with an easy swing. Monterose is too raw-throated for 'Milestones' but slots into 'Ruby My Dear' with impressive ease. He sits out for 'Like Someone In Love' and O'Brien joins him on the bench for the duration of 'How Long Has This Been Going On'. The sound is better balanced on these tracks than when the horn is present, but overall it sounds very good indeed.

Barbara Thompson (born 1944) SAXOPHONES, FLUTES, SOPRANINO RECORDER, KEYBOARDS

*** Mother Earth VeraBra CDVBR 2005
> Thompson; Anthony Oldridge (*vn, electric vn*); Colin Dudman (*ky*); Dill Katz (*b*); Jon Hiseman (*d, perc*). 82.

*** Barbara Thompson's Special Edition VeraBra CDVBR 2017
> Thompon; Rod Argent, Clem Clempson, Colin Dudman, Steve Melling, Bill Worrall (*ky*); Dave

Ball, Dill Katz, John Mole (*b*); Rod Dorothy, Anthony Oldridge (*vn*); Jon Hiseman (*d*); Gary Kettel (*perc*). 6/85.

***(*) **Heavenly Bodies** VeraBra CDVBR 2015

Thompson; Guy Barker, Stuart Brooks, John Thirkell (*t*); Bill Geldard (*btb*); David Cullen, Pete Lemer, Steve Melling (*ky*); Paul Dunne (*g*); Dave Ball, Andy Paak (*b*); Rod Dorothy, Patrick Halling, Robin Williams (*vn*); Tony Harris (*vla*); Quentin Williams (*clo*); Jon Hiseman (*d, perc*). 8/86.

*** **A Cry From The Heart** VeraBra CDVBR 2021

Thompson; Paul Dunne (*g*); Pete Lemer (*ky*); Phil Mulford (*b*); Jon Hiseman (*d, perc*). 11/87.

***(*) **Breathless** VeraBra CDVBR 2057

Thompson; Pete Lemer (*ky*); Malcolm MacFarlane (*g*); Jon Hiseman (*d*). 90.

(*) **Songs From The Center Of The Earth Black Sun 15014

Thompson solo. 8/90.

*** **Everlasting Flame** VeraBra CDVBR 2058

Thompson; Pete Lemer (*ky*); Malcolm MacFarlane (*g*); Paul Westwood (*b*); Jon Hiseman (*d*); Hossam Ramzy (*perc*); Anna Gracey Hiseman, London Community Gospel Singers (*v*). 93.

An astonishingly talented multi-instrumentalist, Thompson encompasses straight-ahead jazz, rock and fusion but incorporates an interest in ethnic, formal and (on her atmospheric *Songs From The Center Of The Earth*) elements of ambient and 'New Age' music. She is difficult to categorize and has therefore rarely received the critical attention she merits (though in 1979 an hour-long television documentary was devoted to her and her drummer husband, Jon Hiseman, whom she met in 1965 while both were playing with the New Jazz Orchestra). Thompson is a forceful soloist who regularly introduces unusual harmonic juxtapositions by playing two instruments simultaneously.

Thompson's band, Paraphernalia, has never perhaps been as effective in the studio as in a live setting. Earlier recordings such as *Mother Earth* (originally released in Britain on her own Temple Music label) demonstrate her facility for synthesis of quite eclectic materials. It combines quite orthodox jazz structures (albeit influenced by rock) with an underlying formal 'programme' that conforms thematically to her concern with quasi-theosophical connections between human beings and the planet they inhabit. This is done most effectively on *Heavenly Bodies*, her best currently available record, in which the musical surface and the improvisational logic are both much more highly developed.

Special Edition is a rather messy compilation of live materials by three different versions of Thompson's band, one of them including rockers Clem Clempson and Rod Argent (the last of whom can at least claim to have taken rock ideas into imaginative territory). The band featured on both *Breathless* and *Everlasting Flame* also has a strong rock tinge, but it provides Thompson with a solid platform for some of her most evocative solos on record and some of her most imaginative writing. 'The Night Before Culloden' and 'Tatami' on the later disc identify how far away from orthodox jazz she has felt able to work. They also, less encouragingly, help identify the essential bittiness of the records. Paraphernalia's live performances tend to be much more focused.

At the opposite extreme from these, though drawing on the same folk and traditional materials, is the unaccompanied *Songs From The Center Of The Earth*. Recorded in the extraordinary acoustic of the Abbey de Thoronet in Provence, these 14 pieces have a meditative and almost ritual character that occasionally belies their this-worldly character. Impressive as it is, one still misses the excellent solo performances on the long-deleted *Lady Saxophone*.

Don Thompson (born 1940) VIBES

(*) **Winter Mist Jazz Alliance TJA-10004

Thompson; Reg Schwager (*g*); Pat Collins (*b*); Barry Elmes (*d*). 4/90.

A Canadian who is better known as both pianist and bassist, Thompson plays vibes exclusively on this disc, recorded at a Toronto club. The impressionism of the title and cover-art extends to the music, which is predominantly vague, not much helped by a foggy sound-quality that relegates Collins in particular to the shadows. Schwager, though, comes up with some pleasing solos and, while there's far too much music at 74 minutes, the best of it passes agreeably enough.

Gail Thompson COMPOSER

*** **Gail Force** EFZ 1005

Gerard Presencer, Martin Shaw (*t, flhn*); Winston Rollins (*tb*); Andy McIntosh (*as, ss, f*); Scott Garland, Dave O'Higgins (*ts*); Mark Lockheart (*ts, ss*); Adrian York (*ky*); Jim Mullen (*g*); Laurence Cottle (*b*); Ian Thomas (*d*); Gary Hammond (*perc*); Ian Shaw (*v*). 1/94.

The story and the significance of Thompson's omission from the *dramatis personae* is particularly sad. Having become a highly respected player, fronting her own Gail Force on baritone saxophone and co-founding the Jazz Warriors with Courtney Pine, she suffered a mysterious crisis less than 24 hours after playing with Art Blakey and was left unable to play saxophone. She has bravely continued to work in music, notably improvisation projects for inner-city youth, and to write for jazz ensembles, and this record, expertly arranged by Fayyaz Virji and Mike Hornet, is something more than a testimonial. One misses her stormy, loquacious delivery, but the presence of O'Higgins as a guest performer on 'Maybe It's Me' makes up some of the deficit. The anchor of the band is guitarist Mullen's regular quartet and they hold things together expertly. Mullen's solos on 'The Big Picture' and the ambiguously titled '16 And Ready' are models of bluesy straightforwardness, as always. The disc might look a little padded with two radio edits, but the seven main pieces hardly stint, running out at anything from 6½ to more than 11 minutes of forceful, focused music.

Lucky Thompson (born 1924) TENOR SAXOPHONE, SOPRANO SAXOPHONE

**** Accent On Tenor Sax Fresh Sound FSCD 2001
Thompson; Ernie Royal (*t*); Jimmy Hamilton (*cl*); Earl Knight, Billy Taylor (*p*); Sidney Gross (*g*); Oscar Pettiford (*b*); Osie Johnson (*d*). 54.

***(*) Tricotism Impulse! GRP 11352
Thompson; Jimmy Cleveland (*tb*); Don Abney, Hank Jones (*p*); Oscar Pettiford (*b*); Skeeter Best (*g*); Osie Johnson (*d*). 1 & 12/56.

*** Lucky Sessions Vogue 2111510
Thompson; Fred Gérard, Roger Guérin (*t*); Benny Vasseur (*tb*); Teddy Hameline (*as*); Jean-Louis Chautemps (*ts*); Michel Hausser (*vib*); Martial Solal (*p*); Jean-Pierre Sasson (*g*); Pierre Michelot, Benoît Quersin, Peter Trunk (*b*); Daniel Humair, Roger Paraboschi, Gérard Pochonnet (*d*). 3/56, 10/60.

*** Street Scenes Vogue 2115467
Thompson; Christian Bellest, Fernand Verstraete (*t*); André Paquinet, Charles Verstraete (*tb*); Jo Hrasko (*as*); Marcel Hrasko (*bs*); Martial Solal (*p*); Jean-Pierre Sasson (*g*); Benoît Quersin (*b*); Gérard Pochonnet (*d*). 4/56.

**** Lucky Strikes Original Jazz Classics OJC 194
Thompson; Hank Jones (*p*); Richard Davis (*b*); Connie Kay (*d*). 9/64.

*** Lucky Meets Tommy Fresh Sound FSRCD 199
Thompson; Tommy Flanagan (*p*); Frank Anderson (*org*); Wally Richardson (*g*); Willie Ruff (*b*); Oliver Jackson, Walter Perkins (*d*). 65.

*** Soul's Nite Out Ensayo ENYCD 3471
Thompson; Tete Montoliu (*p*); Eric Peter (*b*); Per Wyboris (*d*). 5/70.

***(*) Lucky Thompson LRC CDC 9029
Thompson; Cedar Walton (*p, electric p*); Sam Jones, Larry Ridley (*b*); Billy Higgins (*d*).
Thompson's disappearance from the jazz scene in the 1970s was only the latest (but apparently the last) of a highly intermittent career. He recorded with Charlie Parker just after the war (a rare example of that chimera, the bebop tenor player), but then returned to his native Detroit, where he became involved in R&B and publishing. Like Don Byas, whom he most resembles in tone and in his development of solos, he has a slightly oblique and uneasy stance on bop, cleaving to a kind of accelerated swing idiom with a distinctive 'snap' to his softly enunciated phrases and an advanced harmonic language that occasionally moves into areas of surprising freedom.

There is a good deal of that on the Vogue *Lucky Sessions* and *Street Scenes*, where the French groups, either Pochonnet's band or a later trio, feed him just the sort of gentle ambiguity which he seems to thrive on. The Pochonnet arrangements are uniformly interesting and well executed, and tunes like 'Undecided' are done with a good deal of imagination. The Impulse! disc brings together two LPs from the beginning and end of that same year, straddling the French trip. Much of the music was formerly available as *Dancing Sunbeam* on the same label. It finds the saxophonist at his relaxed best, working with highly sympathetic American groups and with an engineer, Creed Taylor, who knew how to get the best out of him sound-wise. Compared to the Vogues, *Tricotism* simply *sounds* right from the first few notes of 'Bo-Bi My Boy', the first of a whole set of originals. The drummerless trio with Pettiford and Best is a highly sympathetic one and is recorded in a warm, enveloping acoustic. Thompson's best performances as leader, though, are on the *Accent On Tenor Sax* and *Lucky Strikes* discs, where his partners are first rate. Thompson's rich, driving style coaxes some astonishing playing out of Jimmy Hamilton, who contributes 'Mr E-Z' to the session. Thompson's tenor has a smooth, clarinet quality on 'Where Or When', gliding over the changes with total ease. Though very far back in the mix, Pettiford and Johnson play superbly, and the bassist checks in with one fine composition, 'Kamman's A'Comin''. For the last four tracks, including a superb 'Mood Indigo', Ernie Royal comes in on trumpet and Earl Knight replaces the guesting Billy Taylor.

Lucky Strikes is tighter and more precise. In the meantime Thompson had made significant bounds in his understanding of harmonic theory, and he attempts transitions that would have been quite alien to him a decade earlier. All his characteristic virtues of tone and smooth development are in place, though. He subtly blurs the melodic surface of 'In A Sentimental Mood' (a curious opener) and adjusts his tone significantly for the intriguing 'Reminiscent', 'Midnite Oil' and 'Prey Loot'. The Swiss concert material is far more conventional, perhaps in deference to the ticket office, but more probably because the group is so stiffly unswinging. The undated and annoyingly unannotated LRC CD, which comes from a catalogue of classic material produced by Sonny Lester, develops Thompson's soprano work considerably, confirming its significance within his output. Apart from the brief opening 'Home Come'n', the overall impression is of soft, soul-tinged, late-night jazz, but there is considerable sophis-tication even on the superficially undemanding 'Tea Time' and 'Sun Out', both soprano tracks. The former gives a first taste of Cedar Walton's subtly modulated electric piano voicings (he even manages a tinkling, celeste-like opening to 'Then Soul Walked In' before switching back to an acoustic instrument).

Thompson has something of a cult following, not least in Barcelona where local fans and musicians have long regarded him as up there with the very greats. That is where *Soul's Nite Out* was recorded, on a symbolically potent May Day in 1970. Thompson concentrates very largely on soprano, as so often at this time, switching to his tenor for Duke's 'I Got It Bad' and three other numbers. The tunes are all surprisingly short and solos rarely run to more than a few choruses, but there is no mistaking the inventiveness and sophistication of his playing. Montoliu and the locally celebrated rhythm section provide a fertile base.

Even now, Thompson is still known to the average modern-jazz fan only for a walk-on role in the Parker discography. He's well worth investigating more closely.

Malachi Thompson (born 1941) TRUMPET

*** Spirit Delmark DD-442
> Thompson; Carter Jefferson (*ts*); Albert Dailey (*p*); James King (*b*); Nasar Abeday (*d*); Randy Abbott (*perc*); Leon Thomas, Arnae Burton (*v*).

*** The Jaz Life (sic.) Delmark DD-453
> Thompson; Joe Ford (*ss, as*); Carter Jefferson (*ts*); Kirk Brown (*p*); Harrison Bankhead (*b*); Nasar Abeday (*d*); Richard Lawrence (*perc*). 6/91.

*** Lift Every Voice Delmark DE-463
> Thompson; David Spencer, Kenny Anderson, Bob Griffin, Elmer Brown (*t*); Edwin Williams, Bill McFarland, Ray Ripperston (*tb*); Steve Berry (*btb*); Carter Jefferson (*ts*); Kirk Brown (*p*); Harrison Bankhead (*b*); Aureeayl Ra (*d*); Richard Lawrence, Enoch (*perc*); voices. 8/92.

*** New Standards Delmark DE-473
> Thompson; Steve Berry (*tb*); Joe Ford (*as*); Ron Bridgewater, Sonny Seals, Carter Jefferson (*ts*); Kirk Brown (*p*); Yosef Ben Israel, John Whitfield (*b*); Aureeayl Ra, Nasar Abeday (*d*); Dr Cuz (*perc*). 4/93.

*** Buddy Bolden's Rag Delmark DE-484
> Thompson; David Spencer, Kenny Anderson, Phillip Perkins, Lester Bowie, Zane Massey (*t*); Edwin Williams, Bill McFarland, Ray Riperton, Steve Berry (*tb*); Ari Brown (*ts*); Harrison Bankhead (*b*); Darryl Ervin (*d*); Richard Lawrence, Dr Cuz (*perc*). 94.

With 20 years of recording behind him and no real recognition on a world stage, Thompson has been quietly building up a catalogue of records for Delmark in his home base of Chicago. Despite a serious illness diagnosed as lymphoma in 1989, he has come back with a personal take on new Chicagoan developments which bespeaks a courageous outlook. If he is not an especially outstanding technician or a genius at innovation, his music is a skilled synthesis of several threads from the Chicagoan repertory.

That said, none of these discs really marks itself out from the others, and each has its share of disap-pointments as well as successes. *Spirit* dates from the early 1980s and is relatively sketchy, but his long association with Carter Jefferson provides a confident front line and Dailey's dignified piano parts lend extra weight. *The Jaz Life* was almost a comeback album after his illness and peaks on the splendid swagger of Thompson's arrangement of the Ray Charles chestnut, 'Drown In My Own Tears'. *Lift Every Voice* is the first album to feature his big brass ensemble, which shares duties with his regular Freebop Band, and 'Elephantine Island' and 'Old Man River' make sonorous waves. Sometimes, though, it seems as if Thompson isn't sure of what to do with the orchestra. He is back on safer ground with *New Standards*, which looks at some choice pieces of modern repertory. Freebop's slightly ragged edges are at least a change from the smart orthodoxy of most modern revivalists, but they could use a grain of extra finesse here and there. This was Jefferson's last album (he died in 1993) and his fine tenor improvisation on Booker Little's 'We Speak' is a poignant farewell.

Buddy Bolden's Rag brings back Africa Brass, with Bowie, Massey and Ari Brown as guests: Brown gets off a knockout solo on 'Harold The Great', Bowie makes some mysterious noises on a revised 'Nubian Call' and the brass play with real enthusiasm. Though one still feels that Thompson's collaring of this genre misses some of the visionary clout which Brass Fantasy has brought to this kind of big-band music, and the leader's own solos miss the ripe authority of Bowie himself, it's an entertaining set.

Claude Thornhill (1909–65) PIANO, ARRANGER

*** The 1948 Transcription Performances Hep CD 17

Thornhill; Louis Mucci, Emil Terry, Ed Zandy, Johnny Vohs, Bob Peck, Johnny Carisi, Gene Roland (*t*); Allan Langstaff, Johnny Torick, Leon Cox (*tb*); Walter Weschler, Sandy Siegelstein, Al Antonucci, Addison Collins (*frhn*); Danny Polo, Lee Konitz, Gerry Mulligan, Mickey Folus, Jerry Sanfino, Brew Moore, Jet Rollo (*reeds*); Barry Galbraith, Joe Derise (*g*); Bill Barber (*tba*); Russ Saunders, Joe Shulman (*b*); Bill Exiner (*d*); The Snowflakes (*v*). 4–10/48.

With the revival of interest in mood-music mandarins like Martin Denny and Arthur Lyman, it's not inconceivable that Thornhill's work could catch the ear of those seeking something in the classic easy-listening style. He was a pianist and arranger who formed a band in 1939, struggled with it for three years, then re-formed it after his war service. Never a striking commercial success, Thornhill's interest in a meticulousness of sound – subtle section-work, carefully filtered reed textures, the static bass harmony provided by Barber's tuba parts – resulted in little classics like his theme, 'Snowfall'. But his relationship to jazz is rather hazy, given the formalized tone of the band, and though there were major cool-school players in the orchestra and it features much of the early work of Gil Evans and Mulligan as arrangers, many of the recordings are exotically ephemeral.

The studio recordings are all out of print, but Hep have done a fine job in restoring these transcriptions in excellent sound. Highlights include Evans's immaculate score for 'Anthropology', Mulligan's first take on 'Godchild', and a number of standards relayed through the veils of sound which were Thornhill's speciality. One feels, though, that the pieces he liked best were things like 'Spanish Dance', 'Adios' and 'La Paloma', where his aspirations to have a unique-sounding group weren't troubled by any mild leanings towards bop terminology. 'Royal Garden Blues' is a jazz standard almost as Mantovani might have played it. A good souvenir of Thornhill's benign music.

Henry Threadgill (born 1944) ALTO SAXOPHONE, TENOR SAXOPHONE, CLARINET, BASS FLUTE

*** Easily Slip Into Another World Novus PD 83025

Threadgill; Rasul Siddik (*t*); Frank Lacy (*tb, flhn, frhn*); Dierdre Murray (*clo*); Fred Hopkins (*b*); Pheeroan akLaff, Reggie Nicholson (*d*); Asha Putli (*v*). 9/87.

***(*) Rag, Bush And All Novus PD 83052

Threadgill; Ted Daniels (*t, flhn*); Bill Lowe (*btb*); Dierdre Murray (*clo*); Fred Hopkins (*b*); Newman Baker, Reggie Nicholson (*d, perc*). 12/88.

***(*) Spirit Of Nuff . . . Nuff Black Saint 120134

Threadgill; Curtis Fowlkes (*tb*); Edwin Rodriguez, Marcus Rojas (*tba*); Masuhjaa, Brandon Ross (*g*); Gene Lake (*d*). 11/90.

*** Live At Koncepts Taylor Made TMR 10292

As above, except omit Fowlkes, Lake; add Mark Taylor (*frhn*), Larry Bright (*d*). 5/91.

***(*) Song Out Of My Trees Black Saint 120 154

Threadgill; Ted Daniel (*t*); Myra Melford (*p*); Amina Claudine Myers (*org, hpd*); James Emery, Ed Cherry, Brandon Ross (*g*); Dierdre Murray, Michelle Kinney (*clo*); Jerome Richardson (*b*); Gene Lake, Reggie Nicholson (*d*). 8/93.

**** Carry The Day Columbia CK 66995

Threadgill; Mark Taylor (*flhn*); Edwin Rodriguez, Marcus Roja (*tba*); Brandon Ross, Masujaa (*g*); Tony Cedras (*acc*); Jason Hwang (*vn*); Wu Man (*pipa*); Johnny Rudas, Miguel Urbina (*perc, v*); Sentienla Toy, Mossa Bildner (*v*). 94.

The free-for-all theatricality of the Art Ensemble of Chicago was out of favour in the more hidebound 1980s, subordinated to a revival of interest in form. Classically trained and an inventive composer, Threadgill did sterling service with Air, another of the Chicago groups to emerge out of the legendary AACM proving ground, and one distinguished by a strong interest in early jazz and its procedures.

In line with that, Threadgill is not an effusive soloist, putting much greater emphasis on often very unusual ensemble arrangements that have gradually eroded the conventional triumvirate of lead, harmony and rhythm instruments. Threadgill habitually uses low brasses (sometimes instead of string bass, as in the earliest jazz groups), twinned drummers (and, more recently, electric guitarists, in the manner of Ornette Coleman's Prime Time), and he has regularly used Dierdre Murray's highly effective cello.

The earliest two of the currently available albums still betray their AACM derivation. The sound is 'democratic', matted and slightly chaotic, though some of the fault for that lies in the production, since Threadgill's arrangements are admirably open-textured. It is, though, hard to imagine him working precisely in the manner of 'Bermuda Blues' or 'Black Hands Bejewelled' again. *Rag, Bush And All* still stands out as one of the finest albums of the later 1980s. Uncategorizable, but marked throughout by Threadgill's distinctive tonal, timbral and rhythmic devices, it shifts the emphasis away from smaller-scale blowing tunes to generously proportioned themes which gradually reveal, as on the opening 'Off The Rag' and the long concluding 'Sweet Holy Rag', a firm structural logic. Daniels is also a more interesting player than Siddik.

Threadgill's Very Very Circus appears to be the culmination of a cycle in his work. *Spirit of Nuff . . . Nuff* (his titles are nothing if not enigmatic) deploys the band in a way that recalls 1960s' experiments with structures and free improvisation, but with far more discipline. Threadgill's writing has been quite muted in emotional timbre and 'Unrealistic Love', in which Threadgill's solo is announced by a long guitar passage, is typical. The arrangements on 'First Church Of This' (on which he plays flute) and 'Driving You Slow And Crazy' (which opens with a fractured chorale from the brasses) are consistently inventive, but it's increasingly clear that Threadgill, like Anthony Braxton, has now almost reached the limits of what he can do with a more or less conventional jazz instrumentation. It will be interesting to see whether he is able to develop a new instrumental idiom or whether he will choose – or be forced – to remain within the conventions.

Live At Koncepts suggests that there is still considerable mileage in this transitional period. Very Very Circus sounds entirely individual, but still with some ties back into jazz. The group blends very skilfully, with three low brasses and two electric guitars ranged across the back of the mix, leaving lots of room for Threadgill's now strangely familiar saxophone to speak in its unmistakable accent. The recent *Song Out Of My Trees* is effectively a string-based session, though the title-track is played over organ (Amina in testifyin' mood) and guitar. By using soprano and alto guitars in addition, tracks like 'Crea' take on a rich harmonic coloration that is quite difficult to pin down. On the superb 'Grief', Threadgill switches to a line-up of accordion, harpsichord and two cellos, a dazzling mixture of sounds and textures. Perhaps structural concerns have been downplayed to some extent here in the search for a new timbral language. It's a fascinating process to watch at close quarters, but slightly wearying after a few listens.

Carry The Day is dizzyingly wonderful. Threadgill throws together disparate elements – African pop, salsa, Andalusian chant, tuba, *pipa*, accordion – with a master surrealist's touch, and he comes up with something that on the title-piece makes its own weird and incommunicable sense. Almost every track sounds as if poised on the brink of entropic noise yet manages (precariously on 'Growing A Big Banana') to pull it all together and save the day. Where does he come from? What does it all mean? Don't ask us, but we know what we like.

Steve Tibbetts GUITAR, MANDOLIN, SITAR, KEYBOARDS, KALIMBA

(*) **Northern Song ECM 1218
    Tibbetts; Marc Anderson (*perc*). 10/81.
*** **Bye Bye Safe Journey** ECM 1355
    Tibbetts; Bob Hughes (*b*); Marc Anderson, Steve Cochrane, Tim Wienhold (*perc*). 83.
*** **Yr** ECM 1355
    As above. 80.
*** **Exploded View** ECM 1335
    As above, except add Marcus Hughes (*perc*), Claudia Schmidt, Bruce Henry, Jan Reimer (*v*); omit Cochrane and Wienhold. 85–86.
*** **Big Map Idea** ECM 1380
    Tibbetts; Michelle Kinney (*clo*); Marc Anderson, Marcus Wise (*perc*). 87–88.
***(*) **The Fall Of Us All** ECM 1527
    As above, except add Mike Olson (*syn*); Jim Anton, Eric Anderson (*b*), Claudia Schmidt, Rhea Valentine (*v*); omit Kinney. 93.

Steve Tibbetts and Marc Anderson are Minnesota-based musicians whose methodical, dreamy patchworks of guitars and percussion are surprisingly invigorating, taken a record at a time. Tibbetts's favourite device is to lay long, skirling electric solos over a bed of congas and acoustic guitars; at its best, the music attains a genuinely mesmeric quality. While their pieces are mostly short in duration, an interview included in the notes to *Big Map Idea* reveals that many are excerpts from much longer jamming situations, and Tibbetts's self-deprecating stance – 'When I tape four hours of sound, only ten minutes have any potential, and only 30 seconds ends up being used' – is refreshing. Anderson is clearly as important an influence in the music, and his pattering, insinuating rhythms are an appealing change from the usual indiscriminate throb of world-music situations. *Bye Bye Safe Journey* is perhaps the best of the earlier albums: Tibbetts plays at his most forceful and there's very little slack in the music. 'Running', which features the ingenious use of a tape of a child running, shows how inventively Tibbetts can use found sound. *Yr* is a reissue of his first album, previously available on an independent label, and *Northern Song* is a bit too quiet and rarefied. *Big Map Idea* opens with a charming treatment of Led Zeppelin's 'Black Dog' and, although some of the tracks suggest that Tibbetts has been listening to Bill Frisell – dreaminess overtaking the rhythmic impetus at times – it is a landscape of his own.

In a way, Tibbetts and Anderson are as consistent as a hard-bop band: the differences between their records are more a matter of nuance and small variation than of any dramatic development. *Exploded View* and *Big Map Idea* continued the run of their 1980s work with patient inevitability, the tracks following one another like a sequence of snapshots or episodes from work in progress. The only striking difference was a greater interest in the use of (wordless) voices. *The Fall Of Us All*, Tibbetts's first album of the '90s, sounds bigger and more powerful than anything that went before. Rhythm is the presiding element for much of the record, Anderson playing a grander role than ever before, and the big, digital soundstage is nearly overwhelming at times. This is large-scale impressionism, and in 'Full Moon Dogs' or 'All For Nothing' Tibbetts has created some of his most imposing and vivid music.

Timeless All Stars GROUP

*** **It's Timeless** Timeless SJP 178
    Curtis Fuller (*tb*); Harold Land (*ts*); Bobby Hutcherson (*vib*); Cedar Walton (*p*); Buster Williams (*b*); Billy Higgins (*d*). 4/82.
(*) **Timeless Heart Timeless SJP 182
    As above. 4/83.
This short-lived band were All Stars indeed, and their London visit at the time of the earlier session resulted in some lovely music. The records, though, are comparatively lightweight. The standards on the first record are performed with assurance rather than intensity: Hutcherson's 'My Foolish Heart' ballad feature is, for instance, better on his own *Solo/Quartet* record, and Land and Walton play with professional elegance. The originals on the second set aren't terribly uplifting: nobody was saving their best writing for this band. In many ways the star of both records is Billy Higgins, whose commitment to swinging is as consistent as always. Not bad for when you're after something not too demanding.

Bobby Timmons (1935–74) PIANO

***(*) **This Here Is Bobby Timmons** Original Jazz Classics OJC 104
    Timmons; Sam Jones (*b*); Jimmy Cobb (*d*). 1/60.
*** **Easy Does It** Original Jazz Classics OJC 722
    As above.
**** **In Person** Original Jazz Classics OJC 364
    Timmons; Ron Carter (*b*); Albert 'Tootie' Heath (*d*).
This Here is a pun on 'Dat Dere', Timmons's second-best-known tune, to which Oscar Brown Jr subsequently added a lyric. Timmons will for ever be remembered, though, as the composer of 'Moanin'', recorded by the Jazz Messengers in 1958 on a marvellous album of that name and a staple of live performances thereafter. *This Here* was recorded two years later, just before his second stint with Art Blakey. It features both the hit tracks; as a disc, it is probably less good value than a now-deleted Milestone compilation, also called *Moanin'*, which includes material from the January 1960 session, together with excellent tracks recorded over the next three years. *Easy Does It* is slightly shop-soiled and untidy round the edges, though 'Groovin' High' is splendid. Only those who really appreciate Timmons's piano playing need consider it a priority purchase.

Timmons's characteristic style was a rolling, gospelly funk, perhaps longer on sheer energy than on harmonic sophistication. The live *In Person* is surprisingly restrained, though Timmons takes 'Autumn Leaves' and 'Softly, As In A Morning Sunrise' at an unfamiliar tempo. The drummer is probably better suited to Timmons's style than Cobb, but there's nothing between Carter and Jones. Timmons's handling of more delicate material here is rather better than expected and certainly better than on *This Here*; there, 'My Funny Valentine' (also on the Milestone *Moanin'*) and 'Prelude To A Kiss' leave a lot to be desired, and the unaccompanied 'Lush Life' (a song whose subject-matter was rather close to home) is uncomfortably slewed. Traces of Bud Powell in his approach at this time slowly disappeared over the next few years. 'Sometimes I Feel Like A Motherless Child', from an August 1963 session on the Milestone *Moanin'*, is perhaps the most typical if not the best trio performance on record. The OJCs will more than suffice, though.

Keith Tippett (born 1947) PIANO, OTHER INSTRUMENTS

**** Mujician III (August Air) FMP CD 12
    Tippett (solo). 6/87.

Though routinely likened to Cecil Taylor (he actually *sounds* much more like Jaki Byard), Tippett is unique among contemporary piano improvisers. He shows little interest in linear or thematic development, but creates huge, athematic improvisations which juxtapose darks and lights, open-textured single-note passages and huge, triple-*f ostinati* in the lowest register. On *Mujician III*, his most accomplished work, these sustained rumbles persist so long that the mind is drawn inexorably towards tiny chinks in the darkness, like points of light in a night sky.

Tippett has always insisted that listeners should not concern themselves with *how* particular sounds are made in his performances, but absorb themselves in what he clearly sees as a highly emotional and spontaneous process in which 'technique' is not separable from the more instinctual aspects of the music. In addition to now relatively conventional practices like playing 'inside', he makes use of distinctive sound-altering devices, such as laying wood blocks and metal bars on the strings, producing zither and koto effects. Though there are similarities, this is very different from John Cage's use of 'prepared piano'. Cage's effects, once installed, are immutable; Tippett's are spontaneous and flexible.

Though he is still remembered for such quixotic projects as the 50-strong Centipede band, for whom he wrote *Septober Energy*, Tippett is still best heard as a solo and duo performer. It may turn out that the three *Mujician* albums made for FMP during the 1980s (the word was his daughter's childish version of her father's vocation) will be regarded as among the most self-consistent and beautiful solo improvisations of the decade and a significant reprogramming of the language of piano. Though there are unmistakable gestures to the presence of Cecil Taylor (especially on the first album), the differences of basic conception could hardly be greater.

The long 'August Air' is one of the essential performances of the decade. It seems to complete a cycle whose development can only be experienced and intuited, not rationalized. FMP may yet transfer the original, rather sour, vinyl recordings of *Mujician* and *Mujician II* to CD; the final volume reaches tonalities and holds decays and overtones which are completely lost on its predecessors.

Cal Tjader (1925–82) VIBES, PERCUSSION, VOCAL

**(*) Mambo With Tjader Original Jazz Classics OJC 271
    Tjader; Manuel Duran (*p*); Carlos Duran (*b*); Edward Rosalies, Edward Verlardi, Bernardo Verlardi (*perc*). 9/54.
*** Los Ritmos Calientes Fantasy FCD-24712-2
    Tjader; Joe Silva (*ts*); Jerry Sanfino, Jerome Richardson (*f*); Vince Guaraldi, Richard Wyands, Manuel Duran (*p*); Al McKibbon, Bob Rodriguez, Eugene Wright (*b*); Roy Haynes, Al Torres (*d*); Willie Bobo, Armando Peraza, Luis Kant, Armando Sanchez, Mongo Santamaria, Bayardo Velarde (*perc*). 54–57.
*** Black Orchid Fantasy FCD-24730-2
    Similar to above; add Paul Horn (*f*), Luis Miranda (*perc*). 54–57.
**(*) Latin Kick Original Jazz Classics OJC 642
    Tjader; Brew Moore (*ts*); Manuel Duran (*p*); Carlos Duran (*b*); Luis Miranda, Bayardo Velarde (*perc*). 56.
**(*) Jazz At The Blackhawk Original Jazz Classics OJC 436
    Tjader; Vince Guaraldi (*p*); Gene Wright (*b*); Al Torres (*d*). 1/57.
** Latin Concert Original Jazz Classics OJC 643
    Tjader; Vince Guaraldi (*p*); Al McKibbon (*b*); Willie Bobo, Mongo Santamaria (*perc*); strings. 9/58.
*** Monterey Concerts Prestige P24026
    Tjader; Paul Horn (*f*); Lonnie Hewitt (*p*); Al McKibbon (*b*); Willie Bobo, Mongo Santamaria (*perc*). 4/59.

Cal Tjader was a great popularizer whose musical mind ran a lot deeper than some have allowed. As a vibes player, he was an able and not quite outstanding soloist, but his interest in Latin rhythms and their potential for blending with West Coast jazz was a genuine one, and his best records have a jaunty and informed atmosphere which denigrates neither side of the fusion. He made a lot of records, and many of them have been awarded reissue, which makes it difficult to choose particular winners. Tjader helped to break Willie Bobo and Mongo Santamaria to wider audiences, and the steps towards an almost pure salsa sound are documented on most of the records listed above. *Latin Kick*, which has Brew Moore guesting on tenor, is a good one, and *A Night At The Blackhawk* is a superior live session. *Jazz At The Blackhawk* is the most straight-ahead of these records and, while it's scarcely up to the level of a top-drawer Milt Jackson session, Tjader sounds at ease on standard material. *Latin Concert*, though, starts to run the formula down, and the intrusion of strings marks the inevitable move towards wallpaper which Tjader seemed shameless enough about. Two recent compilations, *Los Ritmos Calientes* and *Black Orchid*, collect the residue of Tjader's fantasy sessions from the period, and they're effectively split between authentic Latin themes (on Fantasy 24712) and Tjaderized jazz and show-tune standards (Fantasy 24730). Not bad.

*** **El Sonido Nuevo** Verve 519812-2

Tjader; Barry Rogers (*tb, perc*); Julian Priester, Jose Rodriguez, Mark Weinstein (*tb*); George Castro (*f, perc*); Jerry Dodgion (*f*); Derek Smith (*org*); Lonnie Hewitt, Chick Corea, Eddie Palmieri, Al Zulaica (*p*); unknown (*g*); Stan Appelbaum (*cel*); Bobby Rodriguez, Stan Gilbert, George Duvivier (*b*); Tommy Lopez, Manny Oquendo, Carl Burnett, Grady Tate (*d*); Armando Peraza, Ismael Quintana, Ray Barretto (*perc*). 11/63–3/67.

Held in high esteem as the album which commenced the real fusion of Latin and jazz called salsa, *El Sonido Nuevo* (here with six extra tracks, drawn from the otherwise unavailable *Breeze From The East* and *Along Comes Cal*) draws its power more from pianist Eddie Palmieri and his arrangements than anything Tjader does. The title-track illustrates the difference: Tjader embellishes the percussive onslaught below with pretty figures, then Palmieri comes in and intensifies it with his hard, percussive piano parts. Too many of the tracks are still too short, in the fashion of the day, and one longs for a decisive blast from the ensemble but, next to much of Tjader's work, it's impressive. The bonus tracks are softer and a good deal sweeter.

*** **Soul Sauce** Verve 521668-2

Tjader; Donald Byrd (*t*); Jimmy Heath (*ts*); Lonnie Hewitt (*p*); Kenny Burrell (*g*); Bob Bushnell, Richard Davis, John Hilliard (*b*); Johnny Rae, Grady Tate (*d*); Armando Peraza, Alberto Valdes, Willie Bobo (*perc*). 11/64.

*** **Jazz Masters 39** Verve 521858-2

Tjader; various studio groups arranged by Lalo Schifrin, Claus Ogerman, Bobby Bryant. 61–67.

Soul Sauce is good fun – Creed Taylor reins in any freewheeling approach Tjader might have thought about, and the situations are about as formularized as this music would ever be, but it's smart and crisp enough to remain very playable. Byrd and Heath squeeze out a bit of interest in their solo spots. The Jazz Masters disc is a useful trawl through eight Verve albums, most of them out of print, and the settings range from Schifrin-directed orchestras to small groups.

** **Amazonas** Original Jazz Classics OJC 840

Tjader; Raoul De Souza (*tb*); Hermeto Pascoal (*f*); Egberto Gismonti, Dawilli Gonga (*ky*); Aloisio Milanez (*p*); David Amaro (*g*); Lis Alves (*b*); Roberto Silva (*d*). 6/75.

(*) **La Onda Va Bien Concord CCD 4113

Tjader; Roger Glenn (*f, perc*); Mark Levine (*p*); Rob Fisher (*b*); Vince Lateano (*d*); Poncho Sanchez (*perc*). 7/79.

** **Gozame! Pero Ya . . .** Concord CCD 4133

As above, except add Mundell Lowe (*g*). 6/80.

*** **The Shining Sea** Concord CCD 4159

Tjader; Scott Hamilton (*ts*); Hank Jones (*p*); Dean Reilly (*b*); Vince Lateano (*d*). 3/81.

(*) **A Fuego Viva Concord CCD 4176

Tjader; Gary Foster (*ss, as, f*); Mark Levine (*p*); Rob Fisher (*b*); Vince Lateano (*d*); Poncho Sanchez, Ramon Banda (*perc*). 8/81.

** **Good Vibes** Concord CCD 4247

As above, except omit Banda. 83.

Tjader had something of a comeback when he joined Concord, though the music wasn't very different from what he'd been doing 20 years earlier. Cleaner, crisper recording and highly schooled musicianship put a patina of class on these records, but it still emerges as high-octane muzak from track to track. *Good Vibes* in particular is an unseemly farewell. The best things happen on *The Shining Sea* and *A Fuego Viva*: the former introduces Hamilton and Jones and can't really fail from that point, while Gary Foster's experience with Clare Fischer stands him in useful stead for the latter record. A stray, late album from the Fantasy stable is *Amazonas*: rather flimsy stuff. Too softcore for real Latin aficionados, too lightweight for a sterner jazz audience, Tjader fell between stools to the end, but, if one can take the trouble to sift through his records, there are rewards to be found.

Charles Tolliver (born 1942) TRUMPET, FLUGELHORN

**** The Ringer Black Lion BLCD 760174
> Tolliver; Stanley Cowell (*p*); Steve Novosel (*b*); Jimmy Hopps (*d*). 6/69.

***(*) Music Inc Strata East 660 51 009
> Tolliver; Larry Greenwich, Virgil Jones, Danny Moore, Richard Williams (*t*); Garnett Brown,
> Curtis Fuller, John Gordon, John Griffin (*tb*); Jimmy Heath (*ts, ss, f*); Bob Brown, Clifford
> Jordan (*ts, f*); Wilbur Brown (*reeds*); Howard Johnson (*bs, tba*); Stanley Cowell (*p*); Cecil McBee
> (*b*); Jimmy Hopps (*d*). 11/70.

***(*) Grand Max Black Lion BLCD 760145
> Tolliver; John Hicks (*p*); Reggie Workman (*b*); Alvin Queen (*d*). 8/72.

**** Impact Strata East 660 51 004
> Tolliver; Jon Faddis, Larry Greenwich, Virgil Jones, Richard Williams (*t*); Garnett Brown, John
> Gordon, Jack Jeffers, Kiane Zawadi (*tb*); Charles McPherson (*as*); James Spaulding (*as, ss, picc,*
> *f*); Harold Vick (*ts, ss, f*); Charles Davis (*bs*); Stanley Cowell (*p*); Clint Houston, Cecil McBee
> (*b*); Clifford Barbaro (*d*); Big Black, Billy Parker, Warren Smith (*perc*); strings. 1/75.

*** Compassion Strata East 660 51 007
> Tolliver; Nathan Page (*p*); Steve Novosel (*b*); Alvin Queen (*d*). 11/77.

***(*) Live In Berlin: At The Quasimodo – Volume 1 Strata East 660 51 001
> Tolliver; Alain Jean-Marie (*p*); Ugonna Ukegwo (*b*); Ralph Van Duncan (*d*). 7/88.

*** Live In Berlin: At The Quasimodo – Volume 2 Strata East 660 51 011
> As above.

The particular challenge of Tolliver's music is its dramatic simplicity. In place of the complex chord-sequences favoured by most composers of his generation, he favours very basic motifs, often consisting of only four or five notes, repeated in *ostinato*. It's very much harder to play inventively over such a background than where the chords offer endless permutations of 'changes', but Tolliver develops solo material apparently without limit in a highly lyrical mainstream style that recalls Clifford Brown. *The Ringer* is the most swingingly straightforward of the available records, though Cowell's chords are never quite orthodox and many of the leader's solos seem to float in with less support than a Mexican bank.

Nowhere is the bricks-without-straw impression more forceful than on 'Peace With Myself', one of six remarkable originals on Tolliver's 1968 solo debut, *Paper Man* on Arista, and, together with the title-track (which featured Gary Bartz), one of his finest performances. After coming to prominence with Jackie McLean, Tolliver played with Bartz in one of Max Roach's best small groups (they recorded the still-underrated *Members Don't Git Weary* for Atlantic), and the powerful, rhythmic 'Grand Max' is dedicated to the drummer. The big-band version on *Impact* is probably preferable for sheer excitement, but the brisk, live feel of the Black Lion gives a better representation of Tolliver's method. The trumpeter formed his Music Inc group with Stanley Cowell in 1969. There is an earlier (but now deleted) *Impact* on Enja with a superb version of the exciting title-track, but Tolliver's solo on the Strata East is one of his most fluid, with a pronounced Spanish tinge and a typically sophisticated internal rhythm that contrasts well with the endlessly repeated basic motif.

Spaulding, Cowell and Coleman are the main soloists on the album after Tolliver. The final 'Mournin' Variations' is a beautiful, string-led feature in double time for the tenorist. *Grand Max* seems to lack some of the bite of earlier and later albums, and it might have benefited from a saxophone player of Coleman's or Bartz's skills; but it's Tolliver who occupies the foreground, a superb technician with an utterly distinctive voice.

The Berlin dates are pretty and unaffected, authentic examples of what Tolliver could do on a club date. *Compassion* is the only weak link, four tracks of drear abstraction – even 'Impact' – redeemed only by the trumpeter's delicious phrase-making and unfailing rhythmic sense. This sort of thing used to be called 'vanity publishing' and though that is snobbish nonsense – Tolliver is an honest broker and a genuine enthusiast – every now and then it trips him up.

Tolvan Big Band GROUP

*** Colours Phono Suecia PSCD 47
> Roy Wall, Anders Gustavsson, Sten Ingel, Fredrik Davidsson, Anders Bergcrantz (*t, flhn*);
> Vincent Nilsson, Olle Tull, Ola Akerman, Stefan Wikstrom (*tb*); Bjorn Hangsel (*btb*); Helge
> Albin (*as, f*); Per Backer (*as, syn*); Cennet Jonsson (*ss, ts, syn*); Inge Petersson (*ts*); Bernt
> Sjunnesson (*bs, f*); Lars Jansson (*ky*); Anders Lindvall (*g*); Lars Danielsson (*b*); Lennart
> Gruvstedt (*d*); Bjarne Hansen (*perc*). 12/89.

Under the direction of tenorman Helge Albin, this Swedish big band has made some superb records. Albin's arrangements are highly personal and colouristic: he gets a strikingly individual sound out of the reed section in particular, with extensive use of flutes in the tonal palette and a gripping demonstration of contrast with the brass. But this is in some ways a disappointing set after three excellent albums for Dragon (all yet to appear on CD). All ten themes are by Albin and, while he's an interesting composer, it's his variations on other standards which are compelling on the earlier records. Some of these pieces fail to muster a genuine melodic weight. But there are still marvellous moments – the five-way saxophone rumpus on 'Gold Ochre', Danielsson's thoughtful bass pattern on 'Zinnober', the cut-and-thrust of 'Kobolt' – and Jansson and Petersson are worthy new members of the band. The recording is perhaps a shade too bright on CD.

***(*) **The Touch** Pep Pop PPP0415
> As above, except Christer Gustavsson (*t*), Ola Nordqvist (*tb*), Ronny Stensson (*ss, as*), Jorgen Emborg (*ky*) replace Ingel, Wikstrom, Backer, Jansson and Hansen. 2/95.

Back to their best. Albin cajoles some superlative playing from the band on these eight charts – six originals plus a terrific revitalization of Coltrane's 'Mr Syms' and an ingenious 'I Remember You' – which show off the flair and snap of the section-work as never before. There are starring solos from Bergcrantz, Lindvall, Petersson and others, but it's the responsiveness of the orchestra which impresses, and the studio mix lets one hear every element in their sound.

Giovanni Tommaso (born 1941) DOUBLE BASS

***(*) **Via G.T.** Red R R 123256
> Tommaso; Danilo Fresu (*t*); Massimo Urbani (*as*); Danilo Rea (*p*); Roberto Gatto (*d*). 86.

*** **To Chet** Red R R 123220
> As above. 88.

*** **Over The Ocean** Red R R 123256
> Tommaso; Flavio Boltro (*t*); Pietro Tonolo (*ts, ss*); Danilo Rea (*p*); Roberto Gatto (*d*); Carl Marcotulli (*v*). 1/93.

Like a good many Italian jazz players, Tommaso is a quiet iconoclast who retains a great affection for traditional values. His quintet is a highly organized and well-drilled unit, and Tommaso writes carefully tailored parts. Fresu and Boltro are assets in any group, the latter a particularly expressive player who often recalls Herb Robertson. Rea is also an entertainer, singing falsetto as he solos. The only disappointing performer is Tommaso himself. His featured spots lack muscle and originality and are certainly less compelling than the compositions from which they derive.

Of the three, the earliest is still the most innovative. The Chet Baker tribute (the trumpeter has a thriving cult in Italy) is rather run-of-the-mill, and on *Over The Ocean* Tommaso seems to have sacrificed pace for a rather stilted Buggins's turn of solo breaks which spoils the continuity of an otherwise excellent record. 'Kelly's Tune' is little more than a sequence on which Boltro and Tonolo improvise (in markedly different directions).

Pietro Tonolo SOPRANO AND TENOR SAXOPHONE

*** **Slowly** Splasc(h) 327-2
> Tonolo; Roberto Rossi (*tb, shells*); Piero Leveratto (*b*); Alfred Kramer (*d*). 5/90.

***(*) **Tresse** Splasc(h) 386-2
> Tonolo; Henri Texier (*b*); Aldo Romano (*d*). 5/92.

Tonolo's accomplished midstream tenor works a creditable contemporary groove across both these sessions. *Slowly* features tight, almost disciplined interplay between trombone and tenor, while bass and drums cut a neo-classic hard-bop groove on tunes such as 'Misterioso' and 'Introspection'. *Tresse* is a further step forward in that Tonolo (on tenor exclusively this time) creates a wide range of settings with his distinguished partners without really stepping far from familiar signposts. They are conventionally swinging on 'You're The Top', thrillingly intense on 'Gammon', airily lyrical on 'For Heaven's Sake'. Tonolo doesn't seem like a grandly ambitious spirit – several of these pieces are finished inside five minutes – but he has a hip, versatile mind.

Sumi Tonooka (born 1956) PIANO

*** **Taking Time** Candid CCD 79502
> Tonooka; Craig Handy (*ss, ts*); Rufus Reid (*b*); Akira Tana (*d*). 11/90.

*** Here Comes Kai Candid CCD 79516
    Tonooka; Rufus Reid (*b*); Lewis Nash (*d*). 3/91.

Sumi Tonooka made a couple of small-label albums in the 1980s to little response, but these Candid records are strong and intelligent statements. *Taking Time* has its impact dispersed a little by the presence of Handy, who plays well enough but who tends to distract from the trio, Tonooka's most productive setting. She has an assertive touch which lacks nothing in technique, but her interest in breaking up her phrasing into horn-like lines clears away a lot of the excess which many modern pianists can't resist. She writes good tunes, too: 'It Must Be Real' and 'In The Void', both from the second record, have their melodies integrated into arrangements which involve Reid and Nash closely enough to make this a real group at work. Reid, especially, responds with some of his most alert playing. Excellent sound, on the second session in particular.

Mel Torme (born 1925) VOCAL, DRUMS

*** The Best Of The Capitol Years Capitol 799426-2
    Torme; Red Norvo (*vib*); Howard Roberts, Tal Farlow (*g*); Peggy Lee (*v*); studio orchestras. 1/ 49–5/52.

The young Torme's voice was honey-smooth, light, limber, ineffably romantic and boyish; and it's amazing how many of those qualities he has kept, even into old age. His 1940s material for Musicraft seems to be back in the deletion racks, but this is a pleasing miscellany from his tenure with Capitol, very cleanly remastered. There are four previously unreleased tracks with Norvo and Farlow in support and a couple of duets with Peggy Lee, as well as two songs that find Mel himself at the piano. Some of the material is less than top-of-the-line, and most of the arrangements heave rather than glide, but Torme's rhythmic panache and tonal sweetness turn back the years.

*** In Hollywood MCA/Decca GRD-617
    Torme; Al Pellegrini (*cl, p*); James Dupre (*b*); Richard Shanahan (*d*). 12/54.

A typical club set that finds Torme at Hollywood's Crescendo, a few days before Christmas in 1954. He plays piano himself for much of the set (Pellegrini takes over the keyboard for the rest of the time) and the voice is creamily defined. There are some touches of kitsch that Torme would abjure in later years, and this is aimed at a supper-club rather than a jazz audience, but it's good to have an early version of his homespun classic 'County Fair'.

**** Mel Torme Swings Shubert Alley Verve 821581
    Torme; Al Porcino, Stu Williamson (*tb*); Frank Rosolino (*tb*); Vince DeRosa (*frhn*); Art Pepper (*as*); Bill Perkins (*ts*); Bill Hood (*bs*); Marty Paich (*p*); Red Callender (*tba*); Joe Mondragon (*b*); Mel Lewis (*d*). 1–2/60.

**** The Ellington & Basie Songbooks Verve 823248-2
    Torme; Jack Sheldon (*t*); Frank Rosolino, Stu Williamson (*tb*); Joe Maini (*as*); Teddy Edwards (*ts*); Bill Perkins (*bs*); Jimmy Rowles (*p*); Al Hendrickson (*g*); Joe Mondragon (*b*); Shelly Manne (*d*). 12/60–2/61.

This is arguably Torme's greatest period on record, and these capture the singer in full flight. Torme's range has grown a shade tougher since his 1940s records, but his voice is also more flexible, his phrasing infinitely assured, and the essential lightness of timbre is used to suggest a unique kind of tenderness. Marty Paich's arrangements are beautifully polished and rich-toned, the french horns lending a distinctive colour to ensembles which sound brassy without being metallic. There may be only a few spots for soloists but they're all made to count, in the West Coast manner of the day. The showstopper is *Swings Shubert Alley*, which is loaded with note-perfect scores from Paich and a coupe of pinnacles of sheer swing in 'Too Darn Hot' (a treatment Torme has kept in his set to this day) and 'Just In Time', as well as a definitive 'A Sleepin' Bee'. The Ellington/Basie set is another winner: Torme loves this material, and his own words for 'Reminiscing In Tempo' are movingly delivered, as well as the up-tempo set-pieces of the order of 'I'm Gonna Go Fishin''. Both albums were superbly recorded at the time, and the transfers are fine, if no particular improvement on the vinyl. It's a pity that Torme's Bethlehem sessions from the same period are currently out of print, since they're of a similar quality.

*** Round Midnight Stash ST-CD-4
    Torme; Pete Candoli, Don Fagerquist, Don Rader, Joe Newman, Sonny Cohn, Fip Ricard, Al Aarons (*t*); Shorty Rogers (*flhn*); Bob Enevoldsen (*vtb*); Ken Shroyer (*bt*); Henry Coker, Benny Powell, Grover Mitchell, Urbie Green, Jerry Collins, Carl Fontana, Henry Southall (*tb*); Paul Horn (*cl, as, f*); Marshall Royal, Woody Herman (*cl, as*); Bud Shank (*as, f*); Eric Dixon, Frank Wess, Frank Foster (*as, ts*); Bob Cooper, Bob Pierson, Louis Orenstein, Sal Nistico (*ts*); Arthur Herfurt, Buddy Collette (*reeds*); Bill Hood (*bcl, bsx, tba*); Tom Anastas, Charlie Fowlkes, Jack

DuLong (*bs*); Count Basie, Donn Trenner, Marty Paich, Lou Levy, Nat Pierce (*p*); Allan Reuss, Freddie Green (*g*); Verlye Mills (*hp*); Albert Pollan (*tba*); Red Mitchell, Perry Lind, Monty Budwig, Buddy Catlett, Tony Leonardi (*b*); Ronnie Zito, Sonny Payne, Mel Lewis, Larry Bunker, Benny Barth (*d*); Chester Ricord, Ralph Hansell (*perc*); Mort Lindsay Orchestra. 56–68.

Pieced together from various off-the-air recordings, this is an intriguing stroll through a dozen years of Torme's career. He plays drums with Woody Herman on 'Four Brothers', joshes through 'Lil' Darlin'' with Basie's band, and accompanies himself elsewhere on both piano and baritone ukulele. There are 27 songs here, many of them unavailable on any other Torme record, and on such as 'Don't Let That Moon Get Away' and 'Lonely Girl' the singer sounds at his most thoughtful and determined, wasting nothing in the lyrics. The sound-quality is often indifferent, and there are some merely throwaway pieces, so this might be for hardened Torme collectors rather than a casual listener; but it's hard not to enjoy such a surprising set. Admirable sleeve-notes by Will Friedwald.

*** Prelude To A Kiss Fresh Sound FSR-CD 109

Torme; Don Fagerquist (*t*); Vince DeRosa (*frhn*); Hynie Gunker (*as, cl*); Ronnie Lang (*as, bs, cl*); Bob Enevoldsen (*ts, bcl*); Stella Castellucci (*hp*); Bill Pilman (*g*); Joe Mondragon (*b*); Mel Lewis (*d*); strings.

Vinyl collectors will remember this one with some affection, issued on minor labels at budget price for several years. Originally interspersed with dialogue between Mel and an unnamed female admirer (sadly expunged from this release, though a little of it survives before the final track), the music and singing are actually pretty marvellous, arranged by Marty Paich in the style of the great Bethlehem and Verve sessions. Mel sounds terrific on the likes of 'One Morning In May' and 'I'm Getting Sentimental Over You'. Docked a notch for brevity, and for cutting the chat.

*** Sunday In New York Atlantic 780078-2

Torme; studio orchestras directed by Shorty Rogers, Dick Hazard and Johnny Williams. 12/63.
Not a classic Torme session, but it's nice that Atlantic have kept something from his tenure with them in circulation. The tunes are all to do with New York, and it's not a bad concept with 'Autumn In New York', 'Harlem Nocturne' and a charming rarity, 'There's A Broken Heart For Every Light In Broadway', in the setlist.

*** Torme A New Album Paddlewheel KICJ 128

Torme; Kenny Wheeler (*t*); Phil Woods (*as*); Barry Miles, Gordon Beck (*p*); Vic Juris (*g*); Annie Ross (*v*); strings. 6/77.

Torme went through a difficult period in the late 1960s and '70s, much like such contemporaries as Tony Bennett, searching for a niche in a market that had lost some of its taste for the virtues of their sort of singing. This album was cut in London for a small label and has been reissued on Paddlewheel with five extra tracks. The material is an awkward mix of pop and older tunes, and there are one or two clinkers such as 'New York State Of Mind'; but Torme sings with real intensity and cast-iron class.

*** Live In New York Paddlewheel KICJ 129

Torme; Mike Renzi (*p*); Jay Leonhart (*b*); Donny Osborne (*d*). 3/82.

*** An Evening With George Shearing And Mel Torme Concord CCD 4190

Torme; George Shearing (*p*); Brian Torff (*b*). 4/82.

*** Top Drawer Concord CCD 4219

Torme; George Shearing (*p*); Don Thompson (*b*). 3/83.

*** An Evening At Charlie's Concord CCD 4248

As above, except add Donny Osborne (*d*). 10/83.

**(*) Mel Torme–Rob McConnell And The Boss Brass Concord CCD 4306

Torme; Arnie Chycoski, Erich Traugott, Guido Basso, Dave Woods, John McLeod (*t, flhn*); Rob McConnell, Ian McDougall, Bob Livingston, Dave McMurdo (*tb*); Ron Hughes (*btb*); George Stimpson, Jim McDonald (*frhn*); Moe Koffman (*ss, as, cl, f*); Jerry Toth (*as, cl, f*); Eugene Amaro (*ts, f*); Rick Wilkins (*ts, cl*); Robert Leonard (*bs, bcl, f*); Jimmy Dale (*p*); Ed Bickert (*g*); Steve Wallace (*b*); Jerry Fuller (*d*); Brian Leonard (*perc*). 5/86.

*** A Vintage Year Concord CCD 4341

Torme; George Shearing (*p*); John Leitham (*b*); Donny Osborne (*d*). 8/87.

*** Reunion Concord CCD 4360

Torme; Warren Luening, Jack Sheldon (*t*); Bob Enevoldsen (*vtb*); Lou McCreary (*tb*); Gary Foster (*as*); Ken Peplowski (*ts*); Bob Efford (*bs*); Pete Jolly (*p*); Jim Self (*tba*); Chuck Berghofer (*b*); Jeff Hamilton (*d*); Joe Porcaro, Efrain Toro (*perc*). 8/88.

**(*) In Concert Tokyo Concord CCD 4382

As above, except add Dan Barrett (*tb*), Allen Farnham (*p*), John Von Ohlen (*d*), omit Jolly, Hamilton, Porcaro and Toro. 12/88.

*** **Night At The Concord Pavilion** Concord CCD 4433
  Torme; John Campbell (*p*); Bob Maize (*b*); Donny Osborne (*d*); Frank Wess Orchestra. 8/90.
*** **Fujitsu–Concord Jazz Festival 1990** Concord CCD 4481
  As above. 11/90.
** **Mel And George Do World War Two** Concord CCD 4471
  Torme; George Shearing (*p*); John Leitham (*b*). 90.

Torme's contract with Concord has given him the chance to record a long run of albums that should provide his final legacy as a singer. Even though most singers would be thinking about easing up at this stage, Torme's workload and enthusiasm both seem limitless. The voice has throttled back a little, and there is a greyness at the edges, but he still makes his way to high notes very sweetly and will sometimes cap a song with an extraordinary, long-held note that defies the rules on senior singers.

If there's a problem with these records, it's the formulaic settings which Concord tend to encourage for some of their regulars. The duo setting with Shearing is actually a good one, since both men seem to admire each other's work to the point where some of the sessions threaten to slip into mutual congratulations; and context is given to both Shearing's sometimes dinky playing and Torme's romantic sweeps. Of their records together, both *Top Drawer* and *An Evening With* are splendid, and *An Evening At Charlie's* isn't far behind; but there are too many live albums here, where Torme can slip into an ingratiating showmanship and an intrusive audience distracts from what is really a close and intimate kind of jazz singing. The World War Two disc founders on the terrible material, charmingly though the principals deal with it.

Of the other discs, the meeting with Rob McConnell's band is marred by a certain glibness on both sides; the two albums with Paich don't quite recapture their great collaborative feel of the 1950s, but *Reunion* sparkles, with a lovely 'Bossa Nova Potpourri' and a hip reading of Donald Fagen's 'The Goodbye Look'; and the two 1990 concert sessions find Torme in ebullient form, delivering a gorgeous 'Early Autumn' on *Concord Pavilion* and two equally distinctive ballads in 'Wave' and 'Star Dust' on *Fujitsu–Concord*.

The Paddlewheel album is a snapshot of Torme in action just before he started working with Concord. He is in extravagant good humour and there is probably far too much clowning on the record for all but the most dedicated Torme fans; some fine singing too, though.

** **Nothing Without You** Concord CCD 4516
  Torme; Guy Barker (*t, flhn*); Chris Smith (*tb*); John Dankworth (*ss, as, cl*); Ray Swinfield (*as, cl*); Ray Loeckle (*ts, f, bcl*); David Roach (*ts, f*); Jamie Talbot (*bs, bcl, cl*); John Colianni (*p*); Larry Koonse (*g*); John Leitham (*b*); Donny Osborne (*d*); Martyn David (*perc*); Cleo Laine (*v*). 3/91.
** **Christmas Songs** Telarc CD-83315
  Torme; John Colianni (*p*); John Leitham (*b*); Donny Osborne (*d*). 4/92.
(*) **Sing, Sing, Sing Concord CCD 4542
  Torme; Ken Peplowski (*cl*); Peter Appleyard (*vib*); John Colianni (*p*); John Leitham (*b*); Donny Osborne (*d*). 11/92.

These recent records are a disappointing set, suggesting that Torme needs a producer with some fresh ideas in the studio. *Nothing Without You* is shared with Cleo Laine, whose voice isn't quite the come-hither instrument it once was, and the mawkish atmosphere and over-cute situations make this one dispensable to all but obsessive devotees of either singer. The Christmas album is fair game for a man who wrote 'The Christmas Song' but otherwise it goes the seasonal way of all such projects. *Sing, Sing, Sing* finds Mel with two Concord regulars sitting in with his rhythm section at the 1992 Fujitsu Festival, with a 14-minute Benny Goodman medley as the centrepiece. Fair enough, but there are already plenty of live Torme albums in the catalogue and this adds little to the list.

(*) **The Great American Songbook Telarc 83328
  Torme; Bob Milikan, Ross Konikoff, John Walsh, Frank London (*t*); Tom Artin, Rich Willey, Timothy Newman (*tb*); Jack Stuckey (*as, cl, f*); Adam Brenner (*as, cl*); Jerry Weidon, Jeff Rupert (*ts, cl*); David Schumacher (*bs, bcl*); John Colianni (*p*); John Leitham (*b*); Donny Osborne (*d*). 10/92.
*** **Velvet And Brass** Concord CCD 4667
  Torme; Arnie Chycoski, Steve McDade, John MacLeod, Guido Basso, Kevin Turcotte (*t, flhn*); Alistair Kay, Bob Livingston, Jerry Johnson (*tb*); Ernie Pattison (*btb*); Rob McConnell (*vtb*); Gary Pattison, James MacDonald (*frhn*); Moe Koffman, John Johnson, Rick Wilkins, Alex Dean, Bob Leonard (*reeds*); David Restivo (*p*); Reg Schwager (*g*); Jim Vivian (*b*); Ted Warren (*d*); Brian Leonard (*perc*). 7/95.

The Telarc album is yet another live offering from Torme: he retains his usual high standards without suggesting that the record demands a place in any but the most devoted admirer's archive. There is a very fine 'Stardust', as good a version as he's ever done, but the medleys and more routine moments don't amount to much. The Concord set offers a return bout with Rob McConnell's Boss Brass, a group he loves to sing with, and this time the record is a keeper. Torme is in remarkably good shape for a 70-year-old, and though one tends to credit singers with the mere ability to keep singing at such a stage in their careers, this is a project with some challenge in it. McConnell's band play with some discernment, and several of the songs depart from convention: 'Autumn Serenade', 'High And Low' and, especially, 'If You Could See Me Now'.

Gosta Torner (1912–82) TRUMPET

*** **Trumpet Player** Phontastic PHONTCD 9301
    Torner; Arnold Johansson (*t*); Bob Henders, Georg Vernon, Miff Gorling, Nils Ahqvist, Gunnar Medberg (*tb*); Stan Hasselgård, Putte Wickman, Sven Gustafsson, Ove Lind (*cl*); Ake Blomqvist, John Bjorling (*as, cl*); Arne Domnérus, Sven Garder (*as*); Zilas Gorling, Carl-Henrik Noren, Harry Arnold, Georg Bjorklund, Lennart Kohlin (*ts*); Per-Arne Croona (*bs*); Thore Swanerud, Bob Laine, Allan Johansson, Stig Holm, Reinhold Svensson, Rolf Larsson (*p*); Folke Eriksberg, Sten Carlberg, Curt Fahgen (*g*); Thore Jederby, Jon Jandel, Simon Brehm, Hasse Tellemar, Leppe Sundevall, Gunnar Almstedt (*b*); Sven Arefeldt, Gosta Heden, Bertil Frylmark, Henry Wallin, Jack Noren, Sven Bollhem, Egil Johansen (*d*). 8/37–3/64.

The earliest track, 'Jammin'', by the Sonora Swing Swingers, is an Armstrong pastiche of modest merit. But the subtle muted solo on the next one, 'Buster's Idea', cut only four years later, shows how smartly Torner progressed. He was arguably the trumpet doyen of Sweden's mainstream community, and this cross-section of work covers 30-odd years and a dozen bands. The 13 tracks from the 1940s swing a little uncertainly between mainstream and bop and, while the likes of 'Cupol Special' and 'Bob's Idea' look towards the new direction, it's odd to find them immediately followed by a version of the already-ancient 'Ostrich Walk'. There are usually good readmen on hand – Noren, Wickman, Domnérus – and the ensembles work up the casually enjoyable swing which Swedish jazz always seems to be adept at. But Torner himself often seems uncertain of his own direction, even when turning in graceful and pleasantly hot playing. The final seven tracks come from a mainstream session of 1964 by a quintet including Ove Lind, and here Torner does sound a shade past his best. Decent remastering.

Jean Toussaint (born 1957) TENOR AND SOPRANO SAXOPHONES

*** **What Goes Around** World Circuit WCD 029
    Toussaint; Tony Remy (*g*); Julian Joseph, Jason Rebello, Bheki Mseleku (*p*); Wayne Batchelor, Alec Dankworth (*b*); Mark Mondesir, Clifford Jarvis (*d*); Cleveland Watkiss (*v*). 9/91.
(*) **Life I Want New Note NNCD 1001
    Toussaint; Dennis Rollins (*tb*); Jason Rebello (*ky*); Jean Michel Pilc, Christian Vaughan (*p*); Tony Remy, Ciyo Brown (*g*); Wayne Batchelor (*b*); Darren Abraham, Mark Mondesir, Winston Clifford (*d*); Karl Vanden Bossche, Nana Tsiboe (*perc*); Cleveland Watkiss (*v*). 95.

An ex-Jazz Messengers tenorman who now lives and works in London, Jean Toussaint's leadership debut is finally let down a little by its eclecticism. The various combinations of rhythm section – a clutch of contemporary British stars – are all worthwhile in themselves, but the three tracks with Joseph, Dankworth and Mondesir are concentrated and direct in a way that makes one wish Toussaint had stuck to this quartet for the entire record. He's generous in allotting solo space to others and, as a result, the impact of his own playing is diminished, but his firm tone and picked phrasing suggest a player not much interested in bluster. Two Monk tunes put his own original material in a poorer light, but the title-piece is a curt, nicely weighted theme that hangs in the mind, and only Watkiss's feature, 'Lower Bridge Level', sounds misplaced.

    Life I Want is also let down by lightweight material. Toussaint has assembled a crew of smart British players, but they haven't the force of character to put anything dramatic into the tunes. What comes out is a solid, enjoyable but quickly forgettable set of themes.

Ralph Towner (born 1940) GUITAR, CLASSICAL GUITAR, 12-STRING GUITAR, PIANO, FRENCH HORN, SYNTHESIZER, CORNET

***(*) **Trios / Solos** ECM 1025
    Towner solo and with Paul McCandless (*ob*); Glen Moore (*b*); Collin Walcott (*tabla*). 11/72.
**** **Diary** ECM 1032
    Towner solo. 4/73.

***(*) **Solo Concert** ECM 1173
        As above. 10/79.
(*) **Blue Sun ECM 1250
        As above. 12/82.

Towner once told the critic Joachim Berendt that he preferred to treat the guitar 'like a piano trio'. Towner's classical interest pre-dates his involvement in jazz and his work retains many of the qualities of European chamber music, but he's by no means as unswinging'as that may sound; in the same interview with Berendt he talked about his 'one-man-band approach' to solo performance.

The best measure of that philosophy is his fine *Solo Concert*, where he alternates delicate contrapuntal runs over plummy harmonics and 'Eastern' drone effects with sharp, percussive passages involving flamenco-style slaps on the sound-box. In the studio, though, as with his highly influential band, Oregon, Towner has been notably willing to use overdubs. It doesn't work on the rather perverse *Blue Sun*, Towner's least impressive record, but it succeeds admirably elsewhere. What appears to be a solitary duo on the beautiful *Trios/Solos* album actually features Moore on bass and Towner on both guitar and piano. Not usually known for playing standards or jazz repertoire, he gives a persuasive reading of Bill Evans's 'Re: Person I Knew', a tune tailor-made for his delicate approach; Miles Davis's 'Nardis', on *Solo Concert*, is also associated with Evans. On *Diary*, 'Icarus' is a highly effective overdub, but 'The Silence Of A Candle', one of the most beautiful melodies of recent times, seems to be calling out for the crisp guitar harmonics Towner brought to the piece on the Oregon album, *Music Of Another Present Era*. As a solo piano player, he is slightly thick-fingered, with too much arm-weight and not enough space round the notes, the antithesis of his qualities as a guitarist.

In solo performance, Towner has rarely attempted the level of abstraction which played a significant role on the two earliest Oregon albums and which has remained an aspect of their concert performances. 'Erg' on *Diary* is a rather brittle and glaring piece, in sharp contrast to 'Silence Of A Candle', which follows, but the most abstract and ambitious piece on *Trios/Solos* is Glen Moore's remarkable unaccompanied 'A Belt Of Asteroids'. Towner's '1×12' and 'Suite: 3×12' on the same album resemble little academic blues exercises with elements of Viennese dodecaphony thrown in. Effective, but rather slight. 'Raven's Wood' brings in McCandless for a single track, echoing the nascent Oregon sound; its nocturnal, elegiac quality looks forward to the days when the group would, once again, have to work without Collin Walcott, who guests on the opening 'Brujo'.

**** **Solstice** ECM 1060
        Towner; Jan Garbarek (*ts, ss, f*); Eberhard Weber (*b, clo*); Jon Christensen (*d, perc*). 12/74.
***(*) **Sound And Shadows** ECM 1095
        As above. 2/77.

If Oregon was never an orthodox jazz group, this (and a guest appearance on Weather Report's *I Sing The Body Electric*) placed Towner in rhythmic contexts which suggested, if not a theme-and-solos approach, then at least a more straightforwardly jazz-orientated setting. The *Solstice* band, though, was particularly attuned to Towner's conception. The rhythm section has a high degree of autonomy and, though 'Distant Hills' on the later *Sound And Shadows* is treated very differently from the Oregon version of the same composition, it's clear that Weber and Christensen don't play merely supportive roles. 'Drifting Petals' on *Solstice* illustrates a rather sentimental streak in Towner's work (and, again, his rather stiff piano style) but Weber's 'Piscean Dance' is taut and vigorous and the bassist/cellist's highly melodic playing helps give both sets a complex contrapuntal rhythm over which Garbarek floats, sometimes plaintive, sometimes hostile.

*** **Matchbook** ECM 1056
        Towner; Gary Burton (*vib*). 75.

We have already reviewed this disc under Gary Burton's name, since he is the dominant personality on the session. Towner's contribution is rather muted, and for long periods he does little more than accompany Burton's restlessly shifting melodies. Something a little more incendiary would have been welcome. There are rumours (apocryphal, very possibly) that some of the best material from the date was dropped because it was too abrasive.

***(*) **Batik** ECM 1121
        Towner; Eddie Gomez (*b*); Jack DeJohnette (*d*). 78.

This is a more obviously jazz-based setting than the previous records, though it carries over much of their delicate shading. DeJohnette chafes a little with the minimalist approach but, as he settles to a role other than orthodox time-keeping, his distinctive skills become apparent. Gomez is, as always, rock solid and highly expressive, playing low responsions to the guitar melodies and constructing a scaffolding of rhythms for the drummer to scale.

The remastered CD has Towner better balanced with the other pair, and the results are very positive indeed. A fine record that stands out a little from Towner's other work of the period.

*** Old Friends, New Friends ECM 1153
> Towner; Kenny Wheeler (*t, flhn*); David Darling (*clo*); Eddie Gomez (*b*); Michael DiPasqua (*d, perc*). 7/79.

A curiously tentative set that, but for Kenny Wheeler's tensely lyrical passages, sounds remarkably like a watered-down version of Oregon. One can see how Jan Garbarek might have fitted into Darling's slot.

*** Slide Show ECM 1306
> Towner; Gary Burton (*vib, mar*). 5/85.

Matchbook, a previous record by this pairing, was credited to Gary Burton. *Slide Show* is in every respect a comedown, lacking entirely the coherence of the earlier record. The material is certainly more sophisticated but seems to get badly snagged in the awkward textures set up by vibes and 12-string guitar. Burton sounds more convincing on marimba in this context.

** Works ECM 823268
> Towner; Kenny Wheeler (*t, flhn*); Jan Garbarek (*ts, f*); Eddie Gomez (*b*); Eberhard Weber (*b, clo*); David Darling (*clo*); Jon Christensen, Michael DiPasqua (*d, perc*). 74–82.

It's hard to see the rationale for this weird sample of Towner's ECM material. Nothing whatever from *Diary* or *Trios/Solos*; instead, two tracks from the weak and unrepresentative *Blue Sun*, a shapeless duo with cellist Darling from *Old Friends, New Friends*, plus another group track from that album and, making up the numbers, two of the more obvious cuts from the *Solstice* band. Neither musically compelling nor great value for money.

*** City Of Eyes ECM 1388
> Towner; Markus Stockhausen (*t, picc t*); Paul McCandless (*ob, eng hn*); Gary Peacock (*b*); Jerry Granelli (*d*). 90.

This is very nearly a terrific record. At several points it sounds remarkably like an unreleased Oregon set (McCandless's oboe will always have that association) but the Stockhausen trumpet moves it into a more abstract idiom. The main deficiency is Granelli, who simply isn't up to the standard of his colleagues and does little more than parrot a restricted repertoire of five or six equally boring devices.

** Open Letter ECM 1462
> Towner; Peter Erskine (*d*). 7/91.

'Volcanic' isn't a word normally applied to Ralph Towner or his playing. If the cover and title are intended as a distant echo of *Diary*, they're clearly also intended to suggest that this is a very different album. In place of the quiet seascape of the earlier album, there's a huge pall of smoky ash, dark and threatening. The addition of drums and of Towner's increasingly confident Prophet backgrounds certainly gives the music more immediate clout than the rather delicate structures of *Diary*, but repeated hearings don't tend to confirm that Towner's 'open letter' is any less inward and personal than his more private musings, and there's some evidence that Erskine's contributions were added as an afterthought; they certainly don't sound like an integral element. The turn to heaviness also begins to sound a touch contrived, with Erskine largely restricted to sombre, tymp effects (presumably using soft mallets on his tom-toms) and skitteringly unmetrical cymbal touches. Fans may regret what looks like a pointless trading-off of Towner's most distinctive qualities.

*** Lost And Found ECM 1563
> Towner; Denny Goodhew (*sno, ss, bs, bcl*); Marc Johnson (*b*); Jon Christensen (*d*). 5/95.

As he approaches a quarter-century (count 'em) of activity for the label, Towner these days comes with all the pluses and problems that accompany near-institutional status. Yes, it's all become rather formulaic and predictable, but no, nobody really wants him to change, rather resenting any variation on the formula. Goodhew is a more driving player than Garbarek, and Johnson is a wonderful narrator. This is an untypical Towner record to the extent that one remembers it as a series of snippety short stories, rather than as a row of pictures. There is a linear quality, and a briskness of delivery – 15 tracks in somewhat under an hour – that belies the guitarist's usual stately pace; it's a refreshing change of pace, and reprogramming the tracks throws up some interesting juxtapositions, especially where Johnson's and Goodhew's compositions are concerned.

Towner is, of course, unambiguously a guitarist again. Lovely as the piano playing was, it palled faster than the other stuff. He never sounds more himself than when the big 12-string is shouldered and those fulsome, arpeggiated chords start rippling out of the speakers. No one can say he hasn't been road-tested. At this stage in the game, *Lost And Found* is as good as it gets

Tino Tracanna SOPRANO, ALTO AND TENOR SAXOPHONES

*** 292 Splasc(h) H 322

Tracanna; Paolo Fresu (*t, flhn*); Massimo Colombo (*ky*); Marco Micheli (*b*); Francesco Sotgiu (*d*); Naco (*perc*); Mariapia De Vito, Marti Robertson (*v*). 6/90.

*** Arcadia Modern Times 30118

Tracanna; Paolo Fresu (*t*); Emilio Gallante (*f*); Massimo Colombo (*p*); Bebo Ferra (*g*); Paolino Dalla Porta (*b*); Francesco Petrini (*d*); Naco (*perc*). n.d.

Tracanna is another member of Italy's young jazz vanguard, and he's made two briskly entertaining albums for Splasc(h) (the first, *Mr Frankenstein Blues*, isn't yet on CD). The second record is more considered than his first and more confidently finished. Tracanna plays soprano as his first horn here, although there's a startling, helter-skelter alto solo on 'P.F.C. Concept', and his meditations on 'Argomenti Persuasivi' and the pretty ballad, 'Notti Eluse Ed Attese Deluse' (which also appears as a song, delivered by De Vito), are very well done. Fresu and Colombo are suitably challenging partners. Several of the same team reappear on *Arcadia*, which carries on the good and eclectic work, with the merest tinges of funk creeping into 'Mitologie Metropolitane' as opposed to the ECM feel of '23.5'. Tracanna himself continues to develop the soprano as his main horn and he gets a lucid, lyrical timbre out of it.

Stan Tracey (born 1926) PIANO, SYNTHESIZER

**** Under Milk Wood Blue Note CDP 789449

Tracey; Bobby Wellins (*ts*); Jeff Clyne (*b*); Jackie Dougan (*d*). 5/65.

**(*) Duets Blue Note CDP 7894502

Tracey; John Surman (*ss, bs, bcl, t rec, syn*); Keith Tippett (*p*). 12/74, 4/78.

*** Genesis Steam SJCD 114

Tracey; Guy Barker, Steve Sidwell, John Barclay, Henry Lowther, Alan Downey (*t*); Malcolm Griffiths, Geoff Perkins, Pete Smith, Pete Beechel (*tb*); Peter King, Jamie Talbot (*as*); Tony Coe (*ts, cl*); Art Themen (*ts*); Phil Todd (*bs*); Roy Babbington (*b*); Clark Tracey (*d*). 1/87, 8/89.

**** Portraits Plus Blue Note CDP 780696

Tracey; Guy Barker (*t*); Malcolm Griffiths (*tb*); Peter King (*as*); Don Weller (*ts*); Art Themen (*ts, ss*); Dave Green (*b*); Clark Tracey (*d*). 3/92.

Stan Tracey is one of Britain's few genuinely original contributions to world jazz. The persistent notion that Tracey only plays a rather second-hand, olde-worlde version of his original mentors, Duke Ellington and Thelonious Monk (or what one critic called 'white man's blues'), is completely misleading. While elements of Monk's style – the insistent, percussive left hand, the quirky melodism – and of Duke's capacious structural understanding remain components of Tracey's work in all its various forms and outlets, he has brought something entirely original to the music.

That was first seen in *Under Milk Wood*, a suite for jazz quartet inspired by Dylan Thomas's play for voices. What's immediately striking about it, certainly compared to later suites like the Ellington tribute, *We Love You Madly*, and *The Bracknell Connection*, is how spare and unadorned it all is, and yet how elaborate and evocative the whole piece becomes when listened to as a totality, as it ought to be. In a sense, the reputation of *Under Milk Wood* has been hijacked by just one track, indeed just one solo. Bobby Wellins's soft, burring tenor on 'Starless And Bible Black' is an undoubted high point, but it shouldn't be allowed to divert attention away from the rest of the record. Tracey's slowly bouncing figures on 'Llareggub' and 'A.M. Mayhem', and the lorn romanticism of 'I Lost My Step In Nantucket' are equally worthy of attention.

Tracey's absence from the first edition of the *Guide* was widely noted; his omission reflected the parlous state of his discography. In 1990 his own Steam label (on which *Milk Wood* had appeared) was in abeyance, and after nearly 50 years in the music business he still could not boast a major-label contract. That was finally rectified in 1992, with a recording for Blue Note, a label that had sometimes looked to Britain for new (*sic*!) talent during the later 1980s. For his first disc, Tracey assembled his regular Octet and a set of pieces that reflected his debt of gratitude to Duke, Monk, Sonny Rollins, Gil Evans (Tracey is also a brilliantly instinctive arranger) and others. The outstanding track was 'Mrs Clinkscales' – as Dylan Thomas-ish a name as Mrs Organ Morgan, perhaps, but in this case a real person, in fact Duke Ellington's piano teacher. Altoist Peter King's solo deserves in future to be talked about in similar tones to Wellins's of 27 years previously. There are other similar moments, like Art Themen's exotic soprano on 'Spectrum No. 2', but the essence of *Portraits Plus* is the ensemble sound, a full-throated roar one moment, a patiently detailed fabric of harmonies and overlapping rhythms the next.

One hears the same qualities on *Genesis*, the only one of Tracey's large-scale suites to be available on CD at this juncture. Unlike *Milk Wood*, which makes no obvious attempt to be programme music (a re-

recorded vocal version with a later band was signally unsuccessful), to a large extent *Genesis* is constrained by its attempt to express the Creation myth as sound. There are moments of pure invention, as on 'The Sun, Moon & Stars', with Themen and Guy Barker again to the fore, but there is something slightly plodding about the rest, and one wonders, if Tracey had simply been writing nine discontinuous pieces, with no overarching theme, whether they would not have been executed more successfully.

Tracey has now been around long enough to see his son Clark take over the drum chair in the *Portraits Plus* group, succeeding the admirable Bryan Spring. Tracey Jr's finely developed time sense holds together tracks like 'Rocky Mount', which is dedicated to Monk. It has the same nuts and bolts, slightly Heath Robinson or Rube Goldberg approach to harmony, the same limping gait and unexpected agility. Clark also produced the record, and he has given the whole band a big, wide-spectrum sound that catches something of its live impact without losing resolution in any department.

He is also responsible for giving the rather shaky sound-balance of the two *Duets* sets the sort of polish a CD audience will expect. One of the great side-benefits of the Blue Note contract is an undertaking to reissue parts of the Steam catalogue on CD. *Under Milk Wood* was only the first and most obvious of them. Its follow-up, *Duets*, completely lacks the former's timeless brilliance; indeed, it sounds uncomfortably past its sell-by date. Tracey's duos with Keith Tippett were expressively billed as T'N'T, a fairly accurate indication of their characteristic dynamic range. Unfortunately, a pairing that worked dazzlingly well in concert fails to communicate on record, even on one as scrupulously reconstructed as this. The duos with Surman, originally released as *Sonatinas*, nowadays sound desperately unfocused. Tracey's flirtation with synthesizers really adds nothing significant to his armoury, and Surman's multi-instrumentalism often stands in the path of genuine invention in this wholly improvised set.

Theo Travis TENOR SAXOPHONE

*** **2 a.m.** 33 Records 33JAZZ 011
   Travis; David Gordon (*p*); Mark Wood (*g*); Rob Statham (*b*); Ichiro Tatsuhara (*d*); Robin Jones (*perc*).
Tough contemporary jazz with a boppish edge from the young Birmingham-born saxophonist who has been winning plaudits for both his enterprise and playing skill. Apart from Duke's 'In A Mellow Tone', Travis is responsible for all the material. If the sound-world it represents is too self-consciously varied, that is probably both inevitable and forgivable on a self-produced, small-label release by a player still working on a distinctive voice.

The tunes range from the hectic clatter of 'Sex, Food, and Money (Part Two)' and 'Nightmare In New York' to the calmer lyricism of 'Shore Thing', which makes impressive use of space and silence. Travis knows his changes and seems to be able to operate in a quasi-free register as well, while hanging on to a basic tonality. Not quite a debut recording (an earlier session was tape-only) but an impressive start nevertheless.

Trio San Francisco GROUP

*** **Prisoners Of Pleasure** Bvhaast CD 9605
   Sean Bergin (*as, ts, cl, f, concertina*); Tobias Delius, Daniele D'Agaro (*ts, cl*). 4–10/94.
Saxophone quartets are a commonplace, but this trio is a rarity. They play clarinets as often as saxes, and while Bergin chops around between horns, the other two follow a more consistent path. Improvisations mingle with meticulous arrangements: there's an ingenious reduction of Dudu Pukwana's 'MRA' and a lugubrious 'Monk's Mood'. The playing is reserved rather than uproarious, powder kept dry for another occasion perhaps; and the recording, done at three concerts, is all right.

Trio Trabant A Roma GROUP

(*) **State Of Volgograd FMP CD 57
   Lindsay Cooper (*bsn, sno, p, elec*); Alfred 23 Harth (*as, ss, ts, cl, sno, bcl, p, org, syn*); Phil Minton (*v, p*). 10/91.
Appallingly recorded but interesting music from three idiosyncratic improvisers. Harth's a bit of a show-off, with more toys than anyone else, but he makes more interesting noises here than on many of his other recordings. Minton's vocals are now completely unique and unrepeatable, and his contribution to the long central 'Main Movies Et Negentropical Territories' is chilling in its intensity. No excuse for the sound-quality, but worth sampling.

Lennie Tristano (1919–78) PIANO

**** The Complete Lennie Tristano Mercury 830921-2
   Tristano; Billy Bauer (*g*); Clyde Lombardi, Bob Leininger (*b*). 10/46–5/47.
(***) Live At Birdland 1952 Jazz Records JR-1CD
   Tristano; Lee Konitz (*as*); Warne Marsh (*ts*); Billy Bauer (*g*); Arnold Fishkin (*b*); Jeff Morton
   (*d*). 45–52.
(***) Wow Jazz Records JR-9
   As above, except omit Fishkin and Morton. 50.
***(*) Live In Toronto Jazz Records JR-5
   As above, except add Peter Ind (*b*), Al Levitt (*d*). 6/52.
**** Lennie Tristano / The New Tristano Rhino/Atlantic R2 71595
   Tristano; Lee Konitz (*as*); Gene Ramey, Peter Ind (*b*); Jeff Morton, Art Taylor (*d*). 55–61.
*** Continuity Jazz JR-6
   Tristano; Lee Konitz (*as*); Warne Marsh (*ts*); Henry Grimes, Sonny Dallas (*b*); Paul Motian,
   Nick Stabulas (*d*). 10/58–6/64.
*** Note To Note Jazz Records JR-10
   Tristano; Sonny Dallas (*b*); Carol Tristano (*d*). 64–65.

If Charlie Parker can be made to seem the Schoenberg of modern jazz, then Tristano is certainly its Webern; he represents its 'difficult' phase. Whereas most horn-led post-bop delved into uncomfortable psychic regions and cultivated a scouring intensity, Tristano ruthlessly purged his music of emotion, in sharp contrast to the highly expressive playing of his disciple, Bill Evans. Perhaps because his basic instruction to his horn players – the best-known of whom were, of course, Lee Konitz and Warne Marsh – was that they should use a deliberately uninflected and neutral inflexion, concentrating instead on the structure of a solo, Tristano has remained a minority taste, and a rather intellectual one.

This is a pity, because Tristano's music is always vital and usually exciting. Though he abandoned the rhythmic eccentricities of bop in favour of an even background count, his playing is far from conventional, deploying long sequences of even semiquavers in subtly shifting time-signatures, adding sophisticated dissonances to quite basic chordal progressions. If his emphasis on structural rigour and technical (rather than emotional) virtuosity still alienates some listeners, there is a problem for the beginner in the nature of the Tristano discography, much of which involves indifferent live recordings and posthumously released private tapes. However, far from being the cerebral purist of legend, the blind Tristano was fascinated by every possibility of music-making and was a pioneer in studio overdubbing and in speeding up half-speed recordings to give them a cool, almost synthesized timbre.

That track was 'Requiem', perhaps the most striking item on the 1955 Atlantic sessions, reissued on the indispensable Rhino CD. His overdubbing and multi-tracking would influence the Bill Evans of *Conversations With Myself*. But the latter part of the album offers a rare club date with Lee Konitz: the saxophonist sounds dry and slightly prosaic on 'If I Had You' and much more like his normal self on a beautiful 'Ghost Of A Chance'. Tristano's own solos are derived, as usual, from the refined and twicedistilled code of standard material.

This is the essential Tristano CD, but the early sessions on the Mercury disc are almost as important. They catch Tristano just before bebop – specifically, Powell and Parker – had had a significant impact on his playing, so his style, refracted through Tatum and Hines, is like a mysterious, charged yet inscrutable distillation of swing piano's most elaborate settings. One is sometimes reminded of Tatum's (or Nat Cole's) trio recordings, yet Tristano's ideas, while harmonically dense, adapt bop's irresistible spontaneity better than either of those peers. Eleven of the 19 tracks are previously unreleased alternative takes, and the five versions of 'Interlude' (alias 'A Night In Tunisia') are as varied as Parker's Dials. In Bauer he had one of his most sympathetic partners: often lost to jazz history, the guitarist's lines are unfailingly apt yet fresh. Comparison between each take shows how insistent Tristano already was on making his music new from moment to moment. Some of the surviving masters were in imperfect shape, with occasional high-note distortions, but it won't trouble anyone used to music from this period.

The New Tristano was his celebrated multi-piano recording. The multiple time patterns secured on most of the tracks suggest a vertiginous, almost mathematical piano music that moves beyond its scientific sheen to a point where the ingenuities acquire their own beauty: 'I can never think and play at the same time. It's emotionally impossible.' However the conjoining of technique, interpretation and feeling may work for the listener, this is remarkable piano jazz, and the contrasting ballads of 'You Don't Know What Love Is' and 'Love Lines' suggest a world of expression which jazz has seldom looked at since.

The Jazz Records releases are from tapes kept in the Tristano family archive. Both *Live At Birdland 1952* (which also includes four early piano solos from 1945) and *Wow* are tarnished by terrible sound, the discs apparently made from wire recordings: more's the pity, since both feature the musicians in what is, even through the detritus of the flawed sound, masterful music. That becomes clearer on the considerably superior (if still imperfect) sound of the 1952 Toronto concert. Any who might doubt Tristano's ability to outswing any of the regular bebop pianists should lend an ear to the astonishing solo on the first piece, his favourite 'Lennie's Pennies'. Throughout, the group work with uncanny accord, improvisations moving seamlessly from one man to the next, yet set within a palpable groove by Ind (though he's nearly inaudible) and Levitt.

The concert fragments on *Continuity* are in much better sound. There are four pieces from 1958 with Marsh, Grimes and Motian, including an 'Everything Happens To Me' which fades after 50 tantalizing seconds, and some 24 minutes from 1964 with Marsh, Konitz, Dallas and Stabulas. The playing is of a typically high order, with a fine '317 East 32nd', but the snapshot documentation is finally rather frustrating, and the Konitz *Live At The Half Note* set on Verve, even with Bill Evans in for Tristano, may appease less specialist appetites.

The duos with Dallas date from the early 1960s. Five improvisations cover 40 minutes, and the overdubbed drums (hardly sacrilege – Carol Tristano merely centres the rhythm, never doing more than mark time) fill out an otherwise rather dry recording. Like all the Jazz releases, there's a half-finished quality: rigorous though Tristano was, such notebook survivals inevitably lack the precise brilliance of such as *The New Tristano*. But there are insights enough here to make this a valuable pendant to the other solo music.

Gianluigi Trovesi (born 1944) ALTO AND SOPRANO SAXOPHONES, ALTO AND BASS CLARINET, PICCOLO

(*) **Dances Red 181
    Trovesi; Paolo Damiani (*b, clo*); Ettore Fioravanti (*d*). 1/85.
** **Les Boites A Musique** Splasc(h) H 152
    Trovesi; Luciano Mirto (*elec*); Tiziano Tononi (*perc*). 3/88.
**** **From G To G** Soul Note 121231-2
    Trovesi; Pino Minafra (*t, flhn, didjeridoo, v*); Rodolfo Migliardi (*tb, tba*); Marco Remondrini (*clo*); Roberto Bonati, Marco Micheli (*b*); Vittorio Marinoni (*d*); Fulvio Maras (*perc*). 5/92.
Trovesi's earlier records were sometimes heavy going, and both the Splasc(h) and the Red albums suggested a racked, lugubrious stylist. Luciano Mirto is credited as 'computer operator', and he establishes harsh, jangling washes of sound which Trovesi decorates with a mirthless intensity while Tononi patters away in the background. Interesting, but the genre has been handled with better results elsewhere. *Dances* ends on the track 'Sorry I Can't Dance', which suggests a sense of humour, though the playing here seems curiously effortful – even though bass and drums employ a wide variety of rhythms.

From G To G is another matter altogether. Without sacrificing any of his intensities, Trovesi has created a colourful, unpredictable, brilliant marshalling of devices drawn from jazz and far beyond. While there are hints of Italian folk music and remote echoes of ancient masters of Italian composition, the synthesis leads inexorably to a real Italian jazz. 'Herbop' uses two themes which are split and reshaped continuously through 18 minutes of music, soloists and ensemble set in perfect balance. 'Now I Can' and 'Hercab' are satirical without being heavy-handed and without losing an underlying severity which Trovesi uses to pare off any fat in the music. But the finest piece is probably 'From G To G' itself, a long, serenely effective dirge in memory of a friend, with a memorable solo from Minafra. The brass player turns in some of his most lucid work here, Migliardi is rumbustious on tuba and urgently expressive on trombone; but it's Trovesi himself who leads from the front, his alto solos elegantly moving forward from Dolphy and Coleman into a sonority that again suggests the tradition of Italian song. Very fine indeed.

*** **Let** Splasc(h) H 429
    Trovesi; Giancarlo Schiaffini (*tb, euph, elec*); Walter Prati (*elec*); Fulvio Maras (*perc, elec*). 1/92.
This deconstructivist free-with-electronics session isn't really Trovesi's forte, and he plays more of a willing second fiddle to Sciaffini, whose short-breathed monologues and wheezing electronics (abetted by Prati) fill in most of the space. Pitched somewhere between improvisation and shapeless soundblocks, the music aspires to dialogue here and there – notably in the horn conversation of 'Allegro, Adagio, Quasi Vivo' – and climaxes in the epic 'Canzona Duodecima', which seems to reprise everything else that's happened in 11 packed minutes.

Robert Trowers TROMBONE

(*) **Synopsis Concord CCD 4545
    Trowers; Jesse Davis (*as*); Carl Ace Carter (*p*); Marcus McLaurine (*b*); Lewis Nash (*d*). 6/92.
There are a couple of giveaways here. On the cover of his debut disc, Trowers is pictured posing on a

stack of jazz biographies – Basie, Armstrong, Ellington, Mingus, Coltrane – and there's a bit of a feeling that he's done no more than fair-copy patient graduate-school résumés of classic licks. As a trombone player, of course, he starts with the benefit of a little camouflage. It's not quite possible to pin him down to an influence, except that he largely avoids the J. J. Johnson style in favour of one that's older and more brassy.

No youngster, Trowers possesses a well-filled diary and has waited some time for his first recording. There's still a feeling, though, that it's premature. Without the supporting voice of Jesse Davis, returning the favour of the trombonist's work on *his* Concord debut, the remaining tracks are really very bland. Trowers plays well, but even when he stretches out on Tadd Dameron's 'If You Could See Me Now' he sounds nervous and unsure.

Andrzej Trzaskowski PIANO

*** **Polish Jazz: Volume 2 – Andrzej Trzaskowski** Polskie Nagrania MUZA PNCD 025
    Trzaskowski; Ted Curson, Tomasz Stańko (*t*); Wlodzimierz Nahorny (*as*); Janusz Muniak (*as, ss*); Jacek Ostaszewski (*b*); Adam Jedrzejowski (*d*). 65, 66.

In 1960 Trzaskowski became the first Polish jazz musician to play with an American star, when his group accompanied Stan Getz at the Warsaw Jazz Jamboree. It was an important moment of recognition for one of the co-founders of the legendary Melomani (Krzysztof Komeda was the other), a group that perfectly encapsulated the contradictions of Polish jazz in the 1950s, poised as it was between a slightly abject traditionalism and revolutionary optimism.

Trzaskowski's own recordings of the 1960s, culminating in the wonderful 'Synopsis' and 'Cosinusoida', both of which are on this compilation, find him at a point where he is moving beyond the constraints of hard bop into something harmonically and rhythmically freer, but also more obviously structured and 'composed' (in the sense of being put together). Trzaskowski demonstrated his understanding of hard bop in the brief exercise, 'Ballad With Cadence In Horace Silver's Style'. His signposts, however, were not always directed westward. The immaculate development of 'Synopsis', a performance that featured trumpeter Tomasz Stańko, is unmistakably European in origin, though very far removed from the folksiness that crept into other Polish jazz of the period. A few months later Stańko was replaced by the American, Ted Curson, who made his name with the Charles Mingus group. The later band is even less orthodox in its translation of new jazz. Muniak's soprano wails in exotic registers that seem to baffle even Curson; Nahorny plods a little in his wake.

These are very important recordings in the development of European jazz. Like his friend and fellow-conspirator, Komeda, Trzaskowski is a major figure.

Gust William Tsilis VIBRAPHONE, MARIMBA

*** **Possibilities** Ken 660.56.009
    Tsilis; Peter Madsen (*p*); Anthony Cox (*b*); Billy Hart (*d*). 3/88.
*** **Pale Fire** Enja 5061
    Tsilis; Arthur Blythe (*as*); Allen Farnham (*ky*); Anthony Cox (*b*); Horace Arnold (*d*); Arto Tuncboyaci (*perc, v*).
***(*) **Sequestered Days** Enja 6094
    Tsilis; Joe Lovano (*ts, f*); Peter Madsen (*p*); Anthony Cox (*b*); Billy Hart (*d*). 3/91.
*** **Heritage** Ken 660.56.018
    Tsilis; Arthur Blythe (*as*); John Abercrombie (*g*); Mark Feldman (*vn*); Anthony Cox (*b*); Terri Lyne Carrington (*d*). 6/91.

Tsilis plays an unfashionable instrument as if no one had ever used it in a jazz context before. That's the most positive thing about his work: the feeling that he is inventing a language, rather than appropriating what others – Hampton, Norvo, Jackson, Hutcherson, Jamal – have already done. His touch on the first of the two Kens is not quite sure enough, but the group is consistently interesting, and Tsilis's writing is engagingly offbeat.

His Enja debut is a curious mixture of earthy modern jazz and slightly awkward, post-Weather Report atmospheric pieces that never quite took shape. His use of marimba veered towards an ironic imitation of electronic blips and waterdrops, a device that recurs on 'Not Ever Quite', one of the less dynamic tracks on the altogether better *Sequestered Days*. Even in his current fine form, Blythe is a rather one-dimensional player when compared to Lovano, who can conjure up anything from smooth swing insinuations, as on the opening 'Mahalia', to a more brittle sound over freer passages. On 'Lisa Robin', he opens on flute over Tsilis's marimba in what sounds like one of Joe Zawinul's folksier themes; the piece develops into an evocative solo from Cox, who underpins the long 'Crazy Horse'. Tsilis's vibraharp work on 'Evening In Paris' is less than wholly convincing, but elsewhere he lets the rhythm prod him towards a livelier delivery, as on 'Medger Evers', which is perhaps the best tune of the set. Its real find is the fluent Madsen, who takes over from the leader and punches out a fine, two-handed solo over Hart's clattering, swishing percussion, before handing over to Lovano in his Coltrane hat to take it out. The title-track is a strong modal theme one would like to see tackled by a much bigger band, for, as on *Pale Fire*, it's clear that Tsilis knows what he wants from his musicians; the arrangements are full of promise.

The later *Heritage* is excellent in its way, but already there are signs of recycling – which is disappointing, just four albums in. Blythe is having one of his regular off-spells and there is too much emphasis on guitar. The addition of Feldman suggests an interesting direction, and it would be good to hear Tsilis work with creative string players in a more developed context.

Mickey Tucker (born 1941) PIANO

*** **Blues In Five Dimensions** Steeplechase SCCD 31258
    Tucker; Ted Dunbar (*g*); Rufus Reid (*b*); David Jones (*d*). 6/89.
*** **Hang In There** Steeplechase SCCD 31302
    Tucker; Greg Gisbert (*t*); Donald Harrison (*as*); Javon Jackson (*ts*); Ray Drummond (*b*);
    Marvin 'Smitty' Smith (*d*). 12/91.
(*) **Getting There Steeplechase SCCD 31365
    Tucker (*p* solo). 4/94.

Tucker led a journeyman career in the 1960s and '70s with only a handful of dates under his own name. His return to leading his own sessions is celebrated on these pleasing efforts. Essentially the first album is a collaboration between Tucker and Dunbar: Reid and Jones provide pulse and flow, but the most creative thinking comes from piano and guitar, the lines intersecting and parrying each other with consummate empathy. Tucker contributes only the title-track, while Dunbar's 'A Nice Clean Machine For Pedro' makes light work of a testing piece. The fine recording serves Tucker better than any of his previous records, his subtle touch and expressive facility clear at last. These days he lives in Australia, but a 1991 trip to New York resulted in the pick-up date captured on *Hang In There*. A superb line-up is let down slightly by Gisbert, who's defeated by the superfast tempo for 'Happy'; but Harrison and Jackson are giants, Smith is utterly mercurial, and Tucker stands as tall as the rest of them. 'Hook-Turns And Hectares' is as smartly convoluted as its title. The solo album, though, is sometimes disappointing. Tucker seems to have decided to invest the occasion with some pomp and ceremony: Shorter's 'Paraphernalia' and Strayhorn's 'Lush Life' are heavy and airless, the three-part dedication to Coltrane is nothing special, and 'Jitterbug Waltz' is unnecessarily prolix. The most interesting thing by far is the straight composition by a Lebanese composer, Boghos Gelalian, given a very strong and lucid reading.

Bertram Turetzky BASS

(*) **Intersections Nine Winds NWCD 0129
    Turetzky; Vinny Golia (*reeds, f, picc*). 8–12/86.

Eleven duets – although four of them involve multiple overdubs – between Turetzky's irreproachably solemn bass and Golia's arsenal of clarinets and flutes. This is slow, grain-by-grain music, with both men insisting on the lower frequencies for much of the record and the interplay more a matter of harmonization than of line countering line. It's interesting, even compelling at times, but the weight of the music can just as often be oppressive. Hard work.

Bruce Turner (1922–93) CLARINET, ALTO SAXOPHONE

*** **That's The Blues, Dad** Lake LACD49
    Turner; Kenny Baker, Terry Brown (*t*); Keith Christie (*tb*); Wally Fawkes (*cl*); Jimmy Skidmore
    (*ts*); Harry Klein (*bs*); Dill Jones, Lennie Felix, Al Mead (*p*); Ike Isaacs, Cedric West, Fitzroy
    Coleman (*g*); Frank Clarke, Jim Bray, Major Holley, Danny Haggerty (*b*); Benny Goodman,
    Stan Greig, Don Lawson, Phil Seamen, Billy Loch (*d*). 2/55–1/58.

A pleasing memorial to the reedman who was a much-loved fixture in British trad-to-swing circles. In later years he was often more like the modernist which trad fans were afraid had been imported into the Humphrey Lyttelton band in the early '50s, but here his affection for Hodges, Carter and other masters of swing alto is more obvious. Paul Adams's meticulous compilation puts together tracks by groups co-led by Turner and Fawkes, the Jazz Today group with Kenny Baker and Keith Christie and Turner's own

Jump Band. None of these groups was destined for immortality, and Fawkes and Turner stand out like beacons of inventiveness, but they all made light, amiable work out of a small corner of the music. Adams has done his best with a mix of surviving vinyl and master tapes, and the sound is as good as one can hope for.

Joe Turner (1907–90) PIANO, VOCAL

***(*) **Sweet & Lovely** RCA Vogue 74321 11507 2
    Turner (*p* solo). 3/52.
***(*) **Stride By Stride Vol. 1** Solo Art SACD 106
    Turner (*p, v*). 12/60.
*** **Joe Turner** Black & Blue BLE 233031
    Turner; Slam Stewart (*b, v*); Jo Jones, Panama Francis (*d*). 8/71–5/74.
*** **I Understand** Black & Blue 59.153.2
    Turner (*p, v*). 10/79.

Turner was one of the least well-known of the great Harlem stride pianists, since he did very little recording in the USA and decamped for Europe in the 1940s. These albums reveal an often self-effacing, gentlemanly stylist, fond of an occasional vocal but concentrating on the keyboard, playing the tunes with a modest amount of elaboration and voicing his lines with a certain restraint: he seldom goes for the hurricane kind of stride, and when he plays something like 'Boogie' (on *Stride By Stride Vol. 1*) it's relatively perfunctory. 'Tea For Two' was one of his favourites: three takes on the Vogue disc are all different from one another, the tempo easing back as he goes on, and there's a memorable version on *Stride By Stride Vol. 1*. These are the best places to hear him: sound on the Vogue disc is superior to some of the issues in this series, and the Solo Art set (once issued on vinyl on 77, and emanating from a Swiss club session) is fine. The Black & Blue discs are good fun, though: by himself, Turner runs through everything from 'Echoes Of Spring' to 'I Left My Heart In San Francisco', in the tradition of the Harlem parlour entertainers; and with Francis, Jones and Stewart (an acquired taste, as usual) he even does 'Route 66' and 'Honey Hush'.

Mark Turner TENOR SAXOPHONE

**** **Yam Yam** Criss Cross 1094
    Turner; Seamus Blake, Terence Dean (*ts*); Brad Mehldau (*p*); Kurt Rosenwinkel (*g*); Larry
    Grenadier (*b*); Jorge Rossy (*d*). 12/94.

A superb debut. Turner's album is almost nothing like the traditional tenor/rhythm date and he has the character to make such a contrary effort almost entirely successful. It's interesting that he lists Warne Marsh as an influence, since the sinuous lines of most of his improvisations are both like and unlike that tenor master. His own tunes are off-centred, oblique, never quite going the way one expects; with the equally unpredictable Rosenwinkel as the other main horn – if one discounts the superlative Mehldau, that is – the music emerges as a seamless yet intriguingly episodic sequence. In one striking departure, the tenors of Blake and Dean join in on 'Zurich' in a remarkable, almost ghostly interweaving of saxophone sound. This must be deemed a very impressive start.

Steve Turre TROMBONE, CONCHES

***(*) **Viewpoints And Vibrations** Stash ST CD 2
    Turre; Jon Faddis, Bill Hardman (*t*); Bob Stewart (*tba*); Haywood Henry (*cl*); Junior Cook (*ts*);
    Mulgrew Miller, Hilton Ruiz (*p*); Akua Dixon (*clo*); Peter Washington, Andy Gonzales, Paul
    Brown (*b*); Idris Muhammad, Leroy Williams (*d*); Manny Oquendo, Charlie Santiago (*perc*);
    Suzanne Klewan, Timmy Shepherd (*v*). 1/86, 2/87.
**** **Fire And Ice** Stash ST CD 7
    Turre; Cedar Walton (*p*); John Blake, Gayle Dixon (*vn*); Melvyn Roundtree (*vla*); Akua Dixon
    (*clo*); Buster Williams (*b*); Billy Higgins (*d*); Jerry Gonsales (*perc*). 2/88.
***(*) **Right There** Antilles ANCD 510040
    Turre; Wynton Marsalis (*t*); Benny Golson (*ts*); Dave Valentin (*f*); John Blake (*vn*); Benny
    Green, Willie Rodriguez (*p*); Akua Dixon Turre (*clo, v*); Buster Williams (*b*); Billy Higgins (*d*);
    George Delgado, Herman Olivera, Manny Oquendo (*perc*). 3/91.

A player of formidable technique, Turre has recorded with Woody Shaw, Ralph Moore and Dizzy Gillespie, and worked in the house band at *Saturday Night Live*, a demanding gig for any musician. He is now established as a major figure on the least fashionable and most problematic of the major horns. The writing is fairly basic and most of Turre's inventive energy has gone into arranging and playing.

The two Stashes are marked by an imaginative choice of material, though on *Viewpoints And Vibrations* there's too obvious an attempt to showcase all the various aspects of his skills. It opens with devastating effectiveness on a trio interpretation of J. J. Johnson's 'Lament', continues with 'In A Sentimental Mood' and 'All Blues', and finds space for three Roland Kirk tunes at the end. *Fire And Ice* is no less varied, but here Turre has the advantage of the Walton–Williams–Higgins rhythm section for his quartet numbers, and the undeniably beautiful string-sounds of his Quartette Indigo on 'Andromeda' and 'Mood Indigo', the latter involving all the musicians. What's striking already is the trombonist's ability to put whole albums together with an eye for drama and instrumental colour.

It goes to pot a little bit at Antilles. Though he's the dominant voice on *Right There*, with a sound that recalls aspects of Curtis Fuller's best work, he allows sufficient room for the band to assert itself. Violinist Blake again makes some interesting contributions but is under-used and, but for a few solo excursions, under-recorded. Guest spots by Wynton Marsalis ('Woody And Bu', and the vocal 'Unfinished Rooms') and Benny Golson ('Woody And Bu') lend a touch of variety to the front line. No problems whatever about the rhythm section. Higgins and Williams are *huge*, and Benny Green plays out of his skin, confirming at least some of the promise as yet unfulfilled on his own projects. The two songs are interesting, so long as you concentrate on Akua Dixon Turre's voice on 'Duke's Mountain' and not on her husband's lyric. The couple perform an odd and not altogether successful duet on Ellington's 'Echoes Of Harlem'. If the idea of a jazzman playing seashells bothers you, be reassured that it's restricted to the shambolic final track and sounds perfectly in place there.

The most recent of the records deliberately highlights Turre's unique double. His conches produce a raw, exclamatory sound that is very similar to Roland Kirk's siren and multiphonic effects. It's all pushed a bit hard on *Sanctified Shells*, occupying three overlong interludes in what is presumably intended to be a suite of notionally related Third and Fourth World pieces. Dizzy Gillespie's guest appearance is a valuable imprimatur, but it doesn't take away a sense that this is not entirely successful music. Turre needs to take a step back to the imaginative work of the early records.

Stanley Turrentine (born 1934) TENOR SAXOPHONE

*** **Up At 'Minton's'** Blue Note CDP 828885 2CD
  Turrentine; Grant Green (*g*); Horace Parlan (*p*); George Tucker (*b*); Al Harewood (*d*). 2/61.
*** **Z.T.'s Blues** Blue Note B21Y 84424
  Turrentine; Grant Green (*g*); Tommy Flanagan (*p*); Paul Chambers (*b*); Art Taylor (*d*). 9/61.
*** **Never Let Me Go** Blue Note CDP 784129
  Turrentine; Shirley Scott (*org*); Sam Jones, Major Holley (*b*); Al Harewood, Clarence Johnston (*d*); Ray Barretto (*perc*). 1 & 2/63.
*** **Let It Go** Impulse! GRP 1104
  Turrentine; Shirley Scott (*org*); Ron Carter, Bob Cranshaw (*b*); Otis Finch (*d*). 66.
***(*) **The Best Of Stanley Turrentine: The Blue Note Years** Blue Note CDP 793201
  Turrentine; Blue Mitchell (*t*); Curtis Fuller, Julian Priester (*tb*); James Spaulding (*as*); Pepper Adams (*bs*); Herbie Hancock, Gene Harris, Les McCann, Horace Parlan, McCoy Tyner (*p*); Shirley Scott, Jimmy Smith (*org*); George Benson, Kenny Burrell, Grant Green (*g*); Ron Carter, Bob Cranshaw, Major Holley, Herbie Lewis, Andy Simpkins, George Tucker (*b*); Bill Dowdy, Otis Finch, Al Harewood, Clarence Johnston, Jimmy Madison, Mickey Roker, Grady Tate (*d*). 60–84.
(*) **The Best Of Mr T Fantasy 7708
  Turrentine; Freddie Hubbard (*t*); Cedar Walton (*p*); Paul Griffin, Patrice Rushen, Joe Sample (*ky*); Cornell Dupree, Eric Gale, Ray Parker Jr, Lee Ritenour (*g*); Ron Carter (*b*); Jack DeJohnette, Harvey Mason (*d*).
(*) **Wonderland Blue Note B21Y 46762
  Turrentine; Mike Miller (*g*); Ronnie Foster (*p*); Eddie Del Barrio, Don Grusin (*ky*); Stevie Wonder (*hca*); Abe Laboriel (*b*); Harvey Mason (*d*); Paulinho Da Costa (*perc*). 86.
(*) **La Place Blue Note 790261
  Turrentine; Freddie Hubbard, Michael Stewart (*t*); Bobby Lyle (*ky*); Paul Jackson Jr, Phil Upchurch, David T. Walker (*g*); Gerald Albright, Kevin Brandon, Abe Laboriel (*b*); Michael Baker, Tony Lewis (*d*); Paulinho Da Costa (*perc*); strings. 89.
** **If I Could** MusicMasters 518 444
  Turrentine; Hubert Laws (*f, picc*); Sir Roland Hanna (*p*); Gloria Agostini (*hp*); Ron Carter (*b*); Grady Tate (*d*); Steve Kroon, Vincent Leroy Evans (*perc*); strings conducted by Matthew Raimondi. 5/93.

Turrentine's bluesy soul-jazz enjoyed considerable commercial success in the 1960s and after. His forte was the mid-tempo blues, often in minor keys, played with a vibrato as broad as his grin. The set on the double CD, *Up At 'Minton's'*, gives a good sense of how Turrentine must have sounded in a club setting at that period. Here he joins in with what was effectively the house band at the famous club.

Let It Go is confusingly similar in title to an earlier Blue Note. Both feature the saxophonist's then wife, Shirley Scott, in what is probably the best available example of that vein. Turrentine has a big, slightly raw tone that sometimes is subtler than first appears. The Blue Note *Best Of* is thoroughly recommended, picking nine longish tracks (the shortest are a lovely, brief 'God Bless The Child' from the excellent *Never Let Me Go* and the previously unreleased 'Lonesome Lover', a Max Roach composition). The other 'best of' compilation, on Fantasy, relates to later, fusion-orientated work and should be avoided by all except those committed to that rather heavy-handed style.

Despite a partial return to jazz structures in subsequent decades, Turrentine appears to have moved over permanently to pop, like his collaborator on the thumping *Straight Ahead*, George Benson. An album of Stevie Wonder covers, *Wonderland* features some of his best playing (and an unmistakable guest appearance by Wonder, playing mouth harp on 'Boogie On, Reggae Woman'). *La Place* is mostly dull and too many tracks are guitar- or synth-ridden; 'Terrible T' is good, though, and 'La Place Street', significantly the only track arranged by Turrentine himself, has a fine jazz feel. *If I Could* is close to useless.

Richard Twardzik (1931–55) PIANO

(****) 1954 Improvisations New Artists NA 1006
  Twardzik; Jack Lawlor (*b*); Peter Littman (*perc*). 54.

Much cited but seldom heard, Twardzik was a precociously brilliant young player from Danvers, Massachusetts, who recorded with Serge Chaloff, Charlie Mariano and Chet Baker, and accompanied Charlie Parker on a radio broadcast before succumbing to the same problem that had stained Parker's life. Apart from 'Yellow Waltz', he left nothing behind with his name on it.

That itself justified the release after more than 30 years of these oddly haunting recordings. Do not be misled: these are not professional recordings but the results of amateur taping. There is little significant drop-out, though once or twice some slowing does seem to occur. Acoustically, though, no worse than many a treasured Bud Powell set. What compounds and complicates the problem is that Twardzik is playing a bar-room upright so out of tune (until the seventh track, 'Yesterdays', by which time the Man with the Dog has been summoned) that he almost sounds as if he's using a 'prepared' instrument.

All the same, his attention to originals like 'All The Things You Are', 'Nice Work If You Can Get It' and a wonderfully bizarre 'Get Happy' demands the closest attention, even if prolonged listening induces an effect rather like being tapped on the forehead with a spoon. Twardzik's warm-up is as interesting a piece of musicianly actuality as anything since Brownie's practice tapes were released, and track by track one can almost hear him thinking out, rejecting, revising and refining his strategy, note by thoughtful note. Jazz-piano enthusiasts will be fascinated; jazz pianists will want to give it the closest study.

Twenty-Ninth Street Saxophone Quartet GROUP

***(*) Live Red R R 123223
  Ed Jackson, Bobby Watson (*as*); Rich Rothenberg (*ts*); Jim Hartog (*bs*). 7/88.
*** Milano New York Bridge Red 123262-2
  As above. 11/92–12/93.

At once the most fun and the most coherent and self-challenging of the saxophone quartets, 29th Street was first put together at the behest of Jackson and Hartog, who both met Rich Rothenberg independently of each other and then persuaded Bobby Watson to enlist. If Watson is in many ways the key member of the group – his are the most distinctive improvisations, and his romantic streak softens the edges of some of their repertoire to beneficial effect – there's an exceptional uniformity of ideas and abilities in this band. Since they never double on other instruments, there's a special concentration on individual and collective timbre, which has been raised to a very high level, and their interaction is now so advanced that they're close to that fabled point where improvisation and structure merge into one. Yet it's a high-spirited, funky and contagiously exciting group to listen to. They like to enjoy themselves.

Live is arguably their most vivid record. While there are occasional flaws – at least by their own prodigiously high standards – the sheer exuberance of the playing is phenomenal. Hartog's 'New Moon' must be the prettiest of all their ballads, and the way Jackson's yelping alto leads into the collective barnstorming of Kevin Eubanks's 'Sundance' is enough to elicit cheers from any listener. Very close and clear recording.

They've been hurt by the deletions axe of late. *Milano New York Bridge* is a survivor, but not quite one of their best: mostly jazz standards, tightly arranged and a bit airless in parts.

Charles Tyler (1941–92) ALTO SAXOPHONE, BARITONE SAXOPHONE

**** Charles Tyler Ensemble ESP Disk ESP 1029
    Tyler; Charles Moffett (*vib*); Joel Friedman (*clo*); Henry Grimes (*b*); Ronald Shannon Jackson (*d*). 2/66.
*** Eastern Man Alone ESP Disk ESP 1059
    Tyler; David Baker (*clo*); Brent McKesson, Kent Brinkley (*b*). 1/67.

Tyler's apotheosis came with a part in Albert Ayler's *Spirits Rejoice* and the (literally) one-sided *Bells* session, both for ESP. On alto, he sounds very much like Ayler, squawky and passionate; but Tyler's musical interests were almost bizarrely varied, ranging from movie themes to the pre-Baroque. He ran his own label, Ak-Ba, for a time, but his most enduring work was done in the 1960s.

Ensemble is a storming record. Second lead is Moffett's orchestral vibraphone, which puts out an extraordinary amount of noise. The session's also valuable for further evidence of Ronald Shannon Jackson's early powers. 'Strange Uhuru' and 'Black Mysticism' bear enough of a resemblance to Jackson's later work with the Decoding Society to prompt chicken-and-egg questions.

In the absence of percussion, the strings provide a slightly rheumaticky background on *Eastern Man Alone*. Baker stays in tune and chugs away manfully but, even by the end of 'Cha-Lacy's Out East', it's starting to sound like a bit of a chore.

*** Autumn In Paris Silkheart SH 118
    Tyler; Arne Forsen (*p*); Ulf Akerheim (*b*); Gilbert Matthews (*d*). 6/88.

After the 1960s, Tyler never sounded as distinctive on anything bearing his own name as he does on Billy Bang's fine *Rainbow Gladiator*. A 1981 Storyville session called *Definite* was made slightly earlier than the seething Bang session, and Tyler comes across as uncertain in tone and unclear about his own stance on the tradition. *Autumn In Paris* is more settled in tone, but inescapably dull, with Tyler's free tonal approach significantly narrowed down; 'Legend Of The Lawman' is the specific point of comparison, its rooted, black sound considerably diluted by the European group. The later album also includes none of his fierce, Hamiet Bluiett-influenced baritone. High point of the two records is an alto–drums duet on *Definite*, 'Hip Day In L.A.'.

Chris Tyle's New Orleans Rover Boys GROUP

*** A Tribute To Benny Strickler Stomp Off CD1235
    Chris Tyle (*c, v*); David Sager (*tb*); Bob Helm (*cl, v*); Orange Kellin (*cl*); Steve Pistorius (*p*); John Gill (*bj*); Bill Carroll (*tba*); Hal Smith (*d, v*). 6/91.

More fine revivalism from the current crop of New Orleans traditionalists, this time under the nominal leadership of Tyle whose gruff, scratchy sound on the cornet is a suitable voice to pay tribute to the obscure Strickler. Born in 1917, the dedicatee was killed by tuberculosis in 1946 and left a mere four recordings. All four are covered here, along with 18 other tunes; the double-clarinet front line adds extra piquancy, since Bob Helm was actually in Strickler's original band. Tyle arranges it so that there are enough twists in the tempos and the delivery to keep the warhorses surprisingly fresh, and the rhythm section know their stuff.

McCoy Tyner (born 1938) PIANO, KOTO, FLUTE, PERCUSSION

***(*) Inception / Nights Of Ballads And Blues MCA/Impulse! 42000
    Tyner; Art Davis, Steve Davis (*b*); Elvin Jones, Lex Humphries (*d*). 1/62–3/63.
*** Today And Tomorrow GRP/Impulse! GRD-105
    Tyner; Thad Jones (*t*); Frank Strozier (*as*); John Gilmore (*ts*); Jimmy Garrison, Butch Warren (*b*); Elvin Jones, Albert 'Tootie' Heath (*d*). 6/63–2/64.
**(*) Plays Ellington MCA/Impulse! 33124
    Tyner; Jimmy Garrison (*b*); Elvin Jones (*d*); Willie Rodriguez, Johnny Pacheco (*perc*). 12/64.

Tyner was still with John Coltrane's group when he started making records under his own name, and while these early sessions add little to what he was doing with the saxophonist, they do reveal what the pianist was doing more clearly than the engine-room of the Coltrane band could allow. *Inception/Nights*

Of Ballads And Blues couples two trio sessions on to one CD, and they are among Tyner's sunniest and most lyrical efforts. He had yet to build his playing into the massive, orchestral concept which came later, and his variations on 'There Is No Greater Love' and his own 'Inception' and 'Blues For Gwen' from the first date are beautifully bright and lively. The second session is, as suggested, all ballads and blues, and Tyner responds as though it were a welcome breather from Coltrane's thunder. *Today And Tomorrow* is split between three sextet pieces and six with Garrison and Heath, three of the latter drawn from material that was originally issued on sampler albums. The sextet pieces are sometimes lamely delivered: Jones sounds mystified, Gilmore is his private self, and Strozier plays vigorous but inappropriate bebop. Better are the trio pieces, with a glittering 'Autumn Leaves' emerging as especially fine. The Ellington album is disappointing: Tyner's romanticism emerges, but his interpretative bent seems untested by the likes of 'Satin Doll', and the addition of the percussionists on four tracks seems like nothing but a gimmick.

**** The Real McCoy Blue Note B21Y-465122
    Tyner; Joe Henderson (*ts*); Ron Carter (*b*); Elvin Jones (*d*). 4/67.
A key album in Tyner's discography. On the face of it, the music might be a direct extension of the Coltrane group, with Henderson substituting for Trane. But, with Tyner calling the tunes, it sounds quite different: dynamics are much more varied, form is more finely articulated and, while the band pushes at limits of tonality and metre alike, it never quite breaches them. The opening 'Passion Dance' is a definitive Tyner composition: structured round a single key but pounding through a metre which the leader noted as 'evoking ritual and trance-like states', it gathers power through the piano and saxophone statements until it sounds ready to explode, yet the concluding regrouping and subsequent variations are resolved immaculately. 'Contemplation', 'Four By Five' and 'Search For Peace' explore this brinkmanship further, through 3/4, 4/4 and 5/4 rhythms and fragments of melody which are enough to fuel all of the band's manoeuvres. Henderson is superbly resolute in avoiding cliché, Carter and Jones work with dramatic compatibility, and Tyner's own playing exults in some of his discoveries learnt over the previous three years: his grand pedal-chords and fluttering right-hand lines establish the classic patterns of call-and-response which have dominated his manner ever since, and the sound he gets is peculiarly translucent, enabling one to hear through the clusters and follow all of his complex lines. Very highly recommended, though the CD is currently a US release only.

*** Sahara Original Jazz Classics OJC 311
    Tyner; Sonny Fortune (*ss, as, f*); Calvin Hill (*b, perc*); Alphonse Mouzon (*d, t, f*). 1/72.
Another important record for Tyner. After leaving Blue Note (the last few albums he recorded for them in the 1960s are deleted), his career floundered until he was signed by Milestone: his first release, *Sahara*, was a poll-winning record which established his course for the 1970s. Mouzon couldn't have played the way he does but for Elvin Jones, yet his choked cymbals and relentless emphasis of the beat are very different from Jones's polyrhythmic swells. Fortune plays with uproarious power and velocity, and his solo on 'Rebirth' is electrifying, but his is essentially a decorative role, while the pianist drives and dominates the music. The group acts as the opposing face to Cecil Taylor's brand of energy music: controlled by harmonic and metrical ground-rules, nobody flies for freedom, but there is a compensating jubilation in the leader's mighty utterance. 'Sahara' and 'Ebony Queen' best express that here, although the piano solo, 'A Prayer For My Family', is a useful oasis of calm. Later Tyner records would be better engineered and realized, but this one remains excitingly fresh.

*** Song For My Lady Original Jazz Classics OJC 313
    As above, except add Charles Tolliver (*flhn*), Michael White (*vn*), Mtume (*perc*). 9–11/72.
***(*) Echoes Of A Friend Original Jazz Classics OJC 650
    Tyner. 11/72.
**(*) Song Of The New World Original Jazz Classics OJC 618
    Tyner; Virgil Jones, Cecil Bridgewater, Jon Faddis (*t*); Garnett Brown, Dick Griffin (*tb*); Julius Watkins, Willie Ruff, William Warnick III (*frhn*); Hubert Laws (*picc, f*); Sonny Fortune (*ss, as, f*); Harry Smyles (*ob*); Kiane Zawadi (*euph*); Bob Stewart (*tba*); Juni Booth (*b*); Alphonse Mouzon (*d*); Sonny Morgan (*perc*); strings. 4/73.
***(*) Enlightenment Milestone MCD-55001-2
    Tyner; Azar Lawrence (*ss, ts*); Juni Booth (*b*); Alphonse Mouzon (*d*). 7/73.
***(*) Atlantis Milestone MCD-55002-2
    Tyner; Azar Lawrence (*ss, ts*); Juni Booth (*b*); Willy Fletcher (*d*); Guilherme Franco (*perc*). 8–9/74.
*** Trident Original Jazz Classics OJC 720
    Tyner; Ron Carter (*b*); Elvin Jones (*d*). 2/75.

** Fly With The Wind Original Jazz Classics OJC 699

    Tyner; Hubert Laws (*f, af*); Paul Renzi (*picc, f*); Raymond Duste (*ob*); Linda Wood (*hp*); Ron Carter (*b*); Billy Cobham (*d*); strings. 1/76.

Following the success of *Sahara*, Tyner embarked on a regular schedule of recording and found himself a popular concert draw at last. The music certainly sounded at home among 'progressive' trends in rock and beyond, although the pianist's beefy romanticism had a lot more profundity in it than most such music-making. *Song For My Lady* varied the cast of the previous disc by adding Michael White and Charles Tolliver to two open-ended pieces, but it was the lyricism of the title-track and Tyner's solo outing, 'A Silent Tear', which were most impressive. *Echoes Of A Friend* is a solo tribute to John Coltrane which resounds with all the grand exhortation which the pianist can wring from the keyboard. *Atlantis* and *Enlightenment* are two huge, sprawling concert recordings which will drain most listeners: Tyner's piano outpourings seem unstoppable, and Lawrence comes on as an even fiercer spirit than Fortune, even if both are in thrall to Coltrane. The *Enlightenment* set, cut at Montreux, is marginally superior, if only for the pile-driving 'Walk Spirit, Talk Spirit'; but *Atlantis* is still very strong, with a majestic turn through 'My One And Only Love' and another torrential group-performance on the title-piece.

It was this kind of incantatory concert form which began to make Tyner's output sound overcrowded with effort: without the ability to soar away from structure, the music could seem bloated, as if packed with steroids. His other Milestone records of the period compensate with varied settings: *Song Of The New World* adds brass and string sections, *Fly With The Wind* sets up an orchestra behind him. But the latter seems to have its energy papered over with the strings, and *Song Of The New World* uses the extra musicians to no very bountiful purpose. *Trident* reunited him with Elvin Jones, but the results were genial rather than passionate. Some fine albums from the period are currently deleted – including *Sama Layuca*, *The Greeting* and *Passion Dance* – and, though they all contain music of lesser power than *Enlightenment*, Tyner's search for strength and tenderness in equal measure remains compelling.

***(*) Supertrios Milestone MCD 55003-2

    Tyner; Ron Carter, Eddie Gomez (*b*); Tony Williams, Jack DeJohnette (*d*). 4/77.

*** Quartets 4 × 4 Milestone MCD-55007-2

    Tyner; Freddie Hubbard (*t*); Arthur Blythe (*as*); Bobby Hutcherson (*vib*); John Abercrombie (*g*); Cecil McBee (*b*); Al Foster (*d*). 3–5/80.

Shrewdly balanced between show-tunes, jazz standards and Tyner originals, the double-trio event, with Tyner meeting Gomez and DeJohnette on one date and Carter and Williams on the other, is a memorable one. Almost 15 years after his first trio records, Tyner's methods have taken on an invincible assurance, and with musicians like these he is working at his highest level. The session with Carter and Williams is slightly the more invigorating, with pianist and drummer working trenchantly through 'I Mean You' and 'A Moment's Notice' which stands out among many versions the pianist has played.

The album of quartets, with Abercrombie, Hubbard, Blythe and Hutcherson taking turns as the star guest, is pretty disappointing, given the personnel. Everyone plays politely rather than with any pressing need to communicate anything, and as a result it's perhaps the meeting with Hutcherson, most thoughtful of musicians, which comes off best.

**(*) Double Trios Denon 33CY-1128

    Tyner; Avery Sharpe, Marcus Miller (*b*); Louis Hayes, Jeff Watts (*d*); Steve Thornton (*perc*). 6/86.

*** Bon Voyage Timeless SJP 260

    Tyner; Avery Sharpe (*b*); Louis Hayes (*d*). 6/87.

**(*) Live At Sweet Basil Paddle Wheel 292E 6033

    As above, except Aaron Scott (*d*) replaces Hayes. 5/89.

**(*) Live At Sweet Basil Vol. 2 Paddle Wheel 292E 6034

    As above. 5/89.

Moving from a larger unit back to a trio as his regular working line-up stymied Tyner's progress to some degree. These records are listenable enough but there's little here which he hasn't done better on previous records, and the preponderance of concert recordings does less than complete justice to a format which, because of the leader's fondness for lots of pedal and high-density playing, is hard to record truthfully. *Double Trios* has a bewitching original in 'Dreamer' and a good 'Lover Man', but the session with the second rhythm section (Marcus Miller and Jeff Watts) is misconceived and features the leader on a tinny electric piano at one point. *Bon Voyage* features mainly standards. The Sweet Basil discs are good enough, the first volume opening with a titanic rush through Coltrane's 'Crescent', but the feeling that there's a lot of muscle for muscle's sake predominates, and the sound fails to accommodate whatever inner voicings Tyner intends to field. Sharpe, Hayes and (subsequently) Scott do what they can to shadow the great boxing presence of the leader, even if at times that seems to mean merely crashing alongside.

***(*) Uptown / Downtown Milestone M 9167

Tyner; Virgil Jones, Earl Gardner, Kamau Adilefu (*t*); Robin Eubanks (*tb*); Steve Turre (*tb, dijeridu*); John Clark (*frhn*); Joe Ford, Doug Harris (*ss, as*); Ricky Ford, Junior Cook (*ts*); Howard Johnson (*tba*); Avery Sharpe (*b*); Louis Hayes (*d*); Steve Thornton (*perc*). 11/88.

A memorable departure for Tyner, which he has built on with his recent Birdology albums. The six charts here amplify the sweep of his groups of the 1970s, and the miracle is that it comes across as expansive and uncongested. Although he hardly seems like a big-band pianist, his own solos seem able to raise the already grand sound of the orchestra to an even higher level, and the choice of horn soloists – Ford, Turre, Cook, Ford – makes for a thrillingly coloured and barnstorming effect. Five of the pieces are Tyner originals, the sixth is by Steve Turre, and nothing misfires; even the live sound is good enough to expose the few touches of under-rehearsal which slip through.

**** Revelations Blue Note B21Y-91651

Tyner (*p* solo). 10/88.

***(*) Things Ain't What They Used To Be Blue Note B21Y-935982

Tyner; George Adams (*ts*); John Scofield (*g*). 89.

Tyner has returned to Blue Note as a solo artist, and these albums are prized examples of a great player in his late prime. Turning fifty, the pianist recorded *Revelations* as a solo 'studio' recital in New York's Merkin Hall, and the excellent sound makes clear his mastery of touch and the refinement he can summon when not required to create climax after climax. While some of the standards are a shade too familiar, he approaches them all with a diligence that lends weight to the accustomed romantic flourishes. *Things Ain't What They Used To Be* is more of the same, although Scofield and Adams duet on some tracks. Again Tyner sees no reason to check his regular flow, and as a result the three pieces with Scofield sound too full, but the duet with Adams on 'My One And Only Love' is gloriously realized, and some of the solos – particularly his latest thoughts on 'Naima' – are Tyner at his finest.

*** New York Reunion Chesky JD 51

Tyner; Joe Henderson (*ts*); Ron Carter (*b*); Al Foster (*d*). 4/91.

***(*) 44th Street Suite Red Baron AK 48630

Tyner; Arthur Blythe (*as*); David Murray (*ts*); Ron Carter (*b*); Aaron Scott (*d*). 5/91.

Tyner often seems to find himself heading up all-star sessions, and these two are predictably enjoyable if not quite indispensable dates. The *New York Reunion* never quite catches fire: Henderson doesn't know how to be boring, but his occasional diffidence on such as 'What Is This Thing Called Love?' suggests he isn't fully involved, and even the duet with Tyner on 'Ask Me Now', which starts with four minutes of unaccompanied tenor, is finally more interesting as an exercise than as a piece of music one wants to return to. Blythe and Murray are as ebullient as always on the Red Baron session: there is a voluptuously rich 'Bessie's Blues'; an improvised two-part title-track, which Murray sits out, and Blythe opens by quoting 'Softly As In A Morning Sunrise', digging in harder than he almost ever has; and casual themes such as 'Blue Piano' and 'Not For Beginners' are show-off pieces that the musicians transcend through sheer force of playing. Great fun, although Bob Thiele's studio sound may strike some as artificially heavy and fat-sounding.

**** Soliloquy Blue Note CDP 796429-2

Tyner (*p* solo). 2/91.

Tyner's third solo outing for Blue Note completes a triptych that sums up his art: rushing, open-hearted, grand of gesture, ineffably romantic, muscular, florid. He still takes every chance to overplay his hand, but that is his way: 'Willow Weep For Me', for instance, is about as aggressive a version of this tune as has ever been recorded. Yet his best melodies – either written or improvised out of tunes by Powell, Coltrane and, surprisingly, Dexter Gordon – are as communicative as they are powerful. He has written for long enough to make his own choices of tune a reflection on his own dynasty: 'Effendi' dates back to his earliest Impulse! sessions, 'Espanola' – a haunting use of the Spanish tinge – is brand-new, and both are performed with fine evocative skill. The piano sound (the album was, like its predecessors, recorded at Merkin Hall in New York) is superb.

***(*) Remembering John Enja 6080-2

Tyner; Avery Sharpe (*b*); Aaron Scott (*d*). 2/91.

Tyner's latest look at Coltrane is by turns restless, impetuous and profoundly considered. He avoids most of the obvious choices: only 'Giant Steps', punched out in a relentless two minutes twenty seconds, could be called an old chestnut. 'One And Four', bounced off its bass vamp, and 'Pursuance' are Tyner at his loosest and most exciting, while 'Up 'Gainst The Wall' is a more structured but no less intense sequence. 'Good Morning Heartache' is unusually delicate. 'In Walked Bud' seems to have drifted in from another session, but no matter: it merely makes one want to hear Tyner take on Monk more often than he does. Sharpe and Scott, too, are assuming a stature of their own beyond their status as long-serving disciples.

***(*) **Warsaw Concert 1991** Fresh Sound FSR-CD 185
>   Tyner (*p* solo). 10/91.

Tyner's solo concerts are a blessed mix of the reverential and the powerhouse. He goes at 'Giant Steps' hammer and tongs, but on a charming original such as 'Lady From Caracas' he gets a melting kind of romanticism out of the keyboard. A round dozen interpretations offer Tyner, Monk, Coltrane and two standards as source material and, if everything is as expected, nothing is quite predictable. Good concert sound.

**** **The Turning Point** Birdology 513573-2
>   Tyner; Kamua Adilefu, Earl Gardner, Virgil Jones (*t*); Steve Turre, Frank Lacy (*tb*); John Clark (*frhn*); Doug Harris (*ss, f*); Joe Ford (*as*); John Stubblefield, Junior Cook (*ts*); Howard Johnson (*tba*); Avery Sharpe (*b*); Aaron Scott (*d*); Jerry Gonzalez (*perc*). 11/91.

***(*) **Journey** Birdology 519941-2
>   As above, except add Eddie Henderson (*t*), Slide Hampton (*tb*), Billy Harper (*ts*), Ronnie Cuber (*bs*), Tony Underwood (*tba*), Waltinho Anastacio (*perc*), Dianne Reeves (*v*); omit Adilefu, Cook and Johnson. 5/93.

Tyner's big band is making music that can stand with any of his mightiest records from the 1970s. *The Turning Point* packs a colossal punch, revitalizing Tyner favourites such as 'Fly With The Wind' and 'Passion Dance' with fresh arrangements – entrusted to several other hands, so leaving the leader to concentrate on leading from the front as a performer – and at least one major new piece in his Monk tribute, 'High Priest'. While most big-band work still trades heavily on nostalgia, Tyner's focus is on invigorating his own repertoire rather than recycling favourite clichés. *Journey* repeats the trick at a slightly lower voltage overall – Dianne Reeves's feature on 'You Taught My Heart To Sing' is an inappropriately sentimental gesture – but features one of the best tracks from both sessions in the tumultuous reading of 'Peresina'. A valuable development from this remarkable jazzman.

**** **Manhattan Moods** Blue Note CDP 828423-2
>   Tyner; Bobby Hutcherson (*vib, mar*). 12/93.

They've met before with auspicious results, but this encounter is pure bliss from first to last. Instead of the instruments cancelling each other out, as is often the case in this kind of situation, keyboard and vibes entwine to create textures of ecstatic beauty, limpid, resonant, revealing. Tyner allows Hutcherson centre stage for much of the time, even if the piano is slightly the more forward in the mix, and Bobby responds with some of his most rapt playing. One could complain that they might have chosen some fresher tunes to play, but the results tend to sweep aside reservations, and the closing look at 'For Heaven's Sake' is on a par with Hutcherson's superlative version with Kenny Barron (discussed under the pianist's name).

*** **Infinity** Impulse! 11712
>   Tyner; Michael Brecker (*ts*); Avery Sharpe (*b*); Aaron Scott (*d*); Waltinho Anastacio (*perc*). 94.
*** **Prelude And Sonata** Milestone MCD-9244-2
>   Tyner; Joshua Redman (*ts*); Antonio Hart (*as*); Christian McBride (*b*); Marvin 'Smitty' Smith (*d*). 11/94.

Infinity marks the return of Impulse! as a 'new' jazz label, and it's fitting that it should be Tyner who starts it off. This isn't one of his greatest: Brecker could have been the fall-guy here, cast in the Coltrane role, but he manages to sidestep too many of the comparisons without finally convincing that he needn't walk in giant steps. *Prelude And Sonata* is basically a ballad album, bookended with pieces of Chopin and Beethoven, and it's interesting to note that McBride and Smith – for all their star status – are no more an appropriate match for Tyner than the undervalued Sharpe and Scott. The saxophonists play well, but this kind of session has become a commonplace which Tyner doesn't especially respond to. He plays professionally on both records without ever getting into his top gear.

Gebhard Ullmann TENOR AND SOPRANO SAXOPHONES, BASS CLARINET, FLUTE, BASS FLUTE, ALTO FLUTE

*** **Per-Dee-Doo** Nabel 4640
>   Ullmann; Michael Rodach (*g*); Martin Lillich (*b*); Nikolas Schauble (*d*). 7/89.
*** **Suite Noire** Nabel 4649
>   Ullmann; Andreas Willers (*g*); Bob Stewart (*tba*); Marvin 'Smitty' Smith (*d*). 1–8/90.
***(*) **Basement Research** Soul Note 12171-2
>   Ullmann; Ellery Eskelin (*ts*); Drew Gress (*b*); Phil Haynes (*d*). 11/93.

Ullmann's records are fascinating essays on various aspects of tradition and the avant-garde and how they intertwine. *Per-Dee-Doo* is a revisionist look at ten jazz standards – from Miles Davis's 'Fall' all the way back to Benny Goodman's 'Seven Come Eleven' – cut up and creatively damaged by Rodach's guitar, Ullmann's woodwind arsenal and the broken rhythms of the other two. The recording sometimes gets too muddy for the good of the music, but there is much intriguing turmoil, without too much obvious desecration along the way. *Suite Noire* tracks the duo work of Ullmann and Willers over ten years of performing together. Smith is on two tracks, including a quite pulverizing 'medley' of 'Lonely Woman' and 'Double Density', while Stewart adds human-breath bass-lines to another two. Essentially, though, this is a duo record, overlapping lines and densely-coloured textures dominating the music.

The meeting with the Eskelin/Gress/Haynes trio on *Basement Research* is different again. Ullmann is stepping into a trio environment where the players already know one another well, and he's cautiously welcomed, though there's some provocative duelling for space. If Eskelin is the further out of the two players, Ullmann's primarily cool extremism is still cutting-edge, and the tracks where the two both play tenor have a splendidly combative element. A fine disc, well recorded.

James Blood Ulmer (born 1942) GUITAR, VOCALS

***(*) **Revealing** In + Out 7007
    Ulmer; George Adams (*ts, bcl*); Cecil McBee (*b*); Doug Hammond (*d, perc*). 77.
*** **Got Something Good For You** Moers 02046
    Ulmer; George Adams (*ts, v*); Amin Ali (*b*); Grant Calvin Weston (*d*). 9/85.
***(*) **Original Phalanx** DIW 8013
    Ulmer; George Adams (*ts, ss, f*); Sirone (*b*); Rashied Ali (*d*). 2/87.
***(*) **In Touch** DIW 8026
    As above. 2//88.
(*) **Blues Allnight In + Out 7005
    Ulmer; Ronnie Drayton (*g, v*); Amin Ali (*b, v*); Grant Calvin Weston (*d, v*); Winnie Leyh (*v*). 5/89.
** **Black And Blues** DIW 845 E
    Ulmer; Ronnie Drayton (*g*); Amin Ali (*b*); Grant Calvin Weston (*d*). 91.
Often described as a student of Ornette Coleman's still-unassimilated 'harmolodics' – a theory which dispenses with the normal hierarchy of 'lead' and 'rhythm' instruments, allowing free harmonic interchange at all levels of a group – Ulmer had actually started to devise similar ideas independently. In the late 1960s he played with organists Hank Marr and Big John Patton (as he did later on the great Larry Young's *Lawrence of Newark* (Perception)), promoting a harsh modern derivative of soul–jazz. His work with drummer Rashied Ali (who rejoined one of the more abstract of Ulmer's late-1980s bands, Original Phalanx/Phalanx) brought him to the attention of Ornette Coleman.

During the 1970s, the guitarist toured regularly with Coleman and played superbly on Arthur Blythe's excellent *Lenox Avenue Breakdown* (CBS). Ulmer's breakthrough album was the remarkable *Tales Of Captain Black* (Artist's House) which featured Coleman, his mallet-fisted son, Denardo Coleman, and bassist Jamaaladeen Tacuma, and included a detailed discussion of Ulmer's harmolodic approach. Whatever critics and fans thought, A&R men were none the wiser, and Ulmer found himself and his music increasingly marginalized. Partly in reaction, he turned towards the less outwardly complex, funk-based approach which is evident on most of the current releases. As with Coleman's music, this emphasized the extent to which the guitarist's 'radicalism' was based on traditional procedures. Most of Ulmer's characteristic distortions of pitch and loud riffing are part of a long-established electric blues idiom; what distinguishes Ulmer is the extremity to which he pushes such devices (to the point of tonal abstraction) and the bitter, inchoate quality of his playing.

None of the current releases matches up to the quality of *Tales* (reissued as we went to press) or the later *Are You Glad To Be In America?*. *Revealing* is by far the best of the albums with Adams, with 'Raw Groove' and 'Overtime' outstanding. The Moers is fine, but poorly recorded. *Blues Allnight* is dull funk-rock, uncharacteristically overproduced and soft-centred; *Black And Blues* is just dull.

Hans Ulrik (born 1965) TENOR AND SOPRANO SAXOPHONES

*** **Ulrik/Hess Quartet** Olufsen DOCD 5081
    Ulrik; Nikolaj Hess (*p*); Hugo Rasmussen (*b*); Aage Tanggaard (*d*); Lisbeth Diers (*perc*). 12/89.
*** **Day After Day** Storyville STCD 4189
    Ulrik; Niels Lan Doky (*p*); John Abercrombie (*g*); Gary Peacock (*b*); Adam Nussbaum (*d*); Mino Cinelu (*perc*). 12/91.
Ulrik is a big-toned, impressionistic tenorman in the new Scandinavian tradition, and both of these records will appeal to lovers of the Garbarek/Stenson quartet. The Olufsen record is very much in that

mould, although the tighter arrangements and more quickly resolved tunes suggest that Ulrik and the percussive Hess would rather wrap things up than let themselves ramble on. 'Siddharta' and 'Time Together' are familiar-sounding new tunes and there's a clever conflation of standards by Coltrane and Cedar Walton in 'Impressions Of Bolivia'.

Day After Day brings in some heavyweights from the New World, though the results are finally no more impressive than those of the homegrown quartet. Some of the tunes drift by without leaving much trace, but Abercrombie, Lan Doky and the magisterial Peacock play with as much involvement as the leader.

United Jazz + Rock Ensemble GROUP

*** **About Time, Too!** VeraBra CDVBR 2014

>Ian Carr, Ack Van Rooyen, Kenny Wheeler (*t, flhn*); Albert Mangelsdorff (*tb*); Charlie Mariano (*as*); Barbara Thompson (*as, f*); Wolfgang Dauner (*p, syn*); Steve Melling (*ky*); Volker Kriegel (*g*); Rod Dorothy (*v*); Eberhard Weber (*b*); Jon Hiseman (*d, perc*).

Founded in 1975 by keyboard player, Wolfgang Dauner, the UJ + RE began life as house band on a quietly politicized Sunday-evening German television programme directed by Werner Schretzmeier. In addition to giving airtime to young unknowns, Schretzmeier promoted his 'Band of Bandleaders' so successfully that in 1977 the group began to give live concerts. In the same year, the German contingent in the band formed Mood Records with the express intention of promoting its music. A decade later, a boxed set containing six of the group's records was released, to considerable public acclaim.

Unfortunately, *About Time, Too!*, which grafts Dorothy and Melling, members of Barbara Thompson's Paraphernalia, on to the basic UJ + RE line-up, is rather disappointing. The large-scale structures achieve a nice balance between jazz freedoms and more accessible rock reference points, but there is an uncharacteristic lack of focus and substance in the solos, and the whole set seems grossly overproduced. It may be preferable to dig out second-hand copies of *Opus Sechs* or the earlier *Break-Even Point* and *Live In Berlin*.

University Of Northern Colorado Jazz Lab Band GROUP

*** **Alive VIII** Night Life CDNLR-3005

>Paul Quist, Darryl Abrahamson, Mike Krueger, Suzanne Higinbotham, Stan Baran (*t*); David Glenn, Brad Schmidt, David Wiske, Ray Heberer, Tim Carless (*tb*); Dav Hoof, Brian Bayman, Michael Cox, Tobin Rockley, Todd Wilkinson (*saxes*); Dan Geisler (*ky*); Eric Thorin (*b*); Dave Rohlf (*d*). 88.

*** **Alive, 1989!** Sea Breeze SB 2040

>Paul Quist, Darryl Abrahamson, Todd Kelly, Suzanne Higinbotham, Dave Scott (*t*); Brad Schmidt, Mike Buckley, Dave Wiske, Dan Gauper, Tom Matta (*tb*); Dav Hoof, Rick Nelson, Michael Cox, Jill Geist, Fritz Whitney (*saxes*); Skip Wilkins (*p*); Eric Thorin (*b*); Terry Vermillion (*d*); Tom Van Schoick, Mike Packer (*perc*). 89.

There's no better indicator of the fierce standards in American college bands than the UNC Jazz Lab Band. Under director Gene Aitken, they've secured a level of expertise which seems to be consistent from year to year, even with an orchestra which must inevitably be in a state of constant flux. After seven albums of limited distribution, the band signed to the Sea Breeze/Night Life operation and have so far released two further sets of crisp, hard-hitting big-band music. The arrangements tend towards showmanship of a no-nonsense sort: some charts seem designed to give either reeds or brass a tough exercise programme, while others are based around stop-on-a-dime dynamics. As a result, the band can't help but be a little impersonal: the aesthetic has little to do with characterful timbre and, although the principal soloists – Michael Cox, Dav Hoof and Dave Scott – have space enough to let fly, their improvisations are situated rather than individual. But it would be churlish to deny the excitement the band creates at its best – as on the chase between Hoof and Cox on Wayne Shorter's 'Yes And No', from *Alive, 1989!*, the brimful arrangement of Bob Mintzer's 'Flying', on *Alive VIII*, or the convincing elaboration of Mike Stern's 'Upside, Downside' on *Alive, 1989!*. The sound on both discs is suitably bright and full.

University Of Wisconsin–Eau Claire Jazz Ensemble GROUP

** **Jazz In Clear Water** Walrus CDWR-4507

>Jeremy Miloszewicz, Pat Phalen, Dan Julson, Jamey Simmons, Todd Walker (*t*); Doug Williams, Kevin Loughney, Adam Bever, Chris Fulton, Eric Olson (*tb*); Kristin Bucholz, Jason Gillette

(*as*); Drew Disher, Donald Pashby, Chad Walker (*ts*); Chris Campbell (*bs*); Tom Benz (*g*); Michael Weiser, Matt Harris (*p*); Chris Bates, Scott Pingel (*b*); Williams Wood, Andy Algire (*d*). 3/93.

*** In Transit Sea Breeze SBV-4509

As above, except add Dennis Luginbill, Kyle Newmaster (*t*), Scott Busse (*tb*), Bill Voltz (*ts*), Adi Yeshaya (*p*), Matt Neesley (*d*); omit Phalen, Walker, Williams, Olson, Bucholz, Pashby, Harris, Bates and Wood. 94.

As usual with American college bands, standards here are set very high, with not many notes out of place. As so often, though, precision tends to steamroller flair and excitement into a somewhat flat pancake. The first disc, admittedly, is sabotaged by the soundmix: recorded live, all the pointed ensemble-work sounds indistinct, and Pingel's awful bass showcase 'Chop Suey' is a marathon the record could have done without. The succeeding studio album works out much better (even though Pingel has another tedious solo outing). Greg Hopkins's arrangement of 'What Are You Doing The Rest Of Your Life' is a properly arresting setting for Gillette's alto, the opening 'Body And Soul' finds some interesting folds in a faded bloom and, if the flag-wavers are typically overdone, they're still big on impact. Excellent sound this time.

Massimo Urbani (1957–93) ALTO SAXOPHONE

*** 360 Degrees Aeutopia Red R R 123146-2

Urbani; Ron Burton (*p*); Cameron Brown (*b*); Beaver Harris (*d*). 6/79.

***(*) Dedications To Albert Ayler And John Coltrane Red R R 123160-2

Urbani; Luigi Bonafede (*p*); Furio Di Castri (*b*); Paolo Pellegatti (*d*). 6/80.

***(*) Easy To Love Red R R 123208-2

Urbani; Luca Flores (*as*); Furio Di Castri (*b*); Roberto Gatto (*d*). 1/87.

***(*) Out Of Nowhere Splasc(h) H 336-2

Urbani; Paul Rodberg (*tb*); Giuseppe Emmanuele (*p*); Nello Toscano (*b*); Pucci Nicosia (*d*). 4/90.

**** The Blessing Red R R 123257-2

Urbani; Maurizio Urbani (*ts*); Danilo Rea (*p*); Giovanni Tommaso (*b*); Roberto Gatto (*d*). 2/93.

Urbani's senseless death – from a heroin overdose in 1993 – robbed Europe of a player whose records are a flawed testament to a bopper of enormous guts and facility. Marcello Piras describes him as a 'wastrel genius' in his notes to the Splasc(h) issue. Certainly Urbani's earlier records sometimes failed to live up to the reputation he had as a wunderkind in the 1970s, but these recent reissues still make an impressive group. The opening of the first Red album consists of an astonishing outburst of alto on 'Cherokee', at a suitably hectic tempo, and though matters cool off somewhat from that point, Urbani's grip seldom lets go. Cameron Brown is superb at the bass, but Beaver Harris's splashy drumming isn't right for the group. The *Dedications* set poses an intriguing premise, although Urbani never really tackles Ayler head on, except in some of his distortions. It's more about linking Parker and Coltrane. There is a lustrous, acerbic 'Naima' as well as one of his fighting bebop miniatures in 'Scrapple From The Apple'. *Easy To Love* is a relatively straightforward programme of standards, apart from the opening 'A Trane From The East'; Urbani burns through them.

The final offerings, both taken down almost by chance, are a memorable and even chastening last statement. The Splasc(h) record, cut at Rodberg's studio with the trombonist sitting in on two tunes, is simple, standard fare, with a very modest rhythm section, but Urbani's herculean playing comes through all the more strongly as a result, utterly tempestuous on 'There Is No Greater Love' and surprisingly lyrical on 'Alfie'. Highly recommended; but the final session for Red is even stronger. For all the glances in the direction of Coltrane, Urbani was a diehard bopper to the end; but his brother, Maurizio, looked forward in other directions, and his two appearances offer a tart contrast in styles on a pair of originals by Tommaso. Otherwise Urbani's coruscating tone and energy command all the attention, even with the impressive Rea in the group: two takes of 'What's New' are brimming with ideas, and a solo 'Blues For Bird' is an astonishing tribute to Parker.

*** Urlo Elicona 3343-2

Urbani; Carlo Atti (*ts*); Massimo Farao (*p*); Piero Leveratto (*b*); Gianni Cazzola (*d*). 10/88.

*** Round About . . . Max Sentemo SNT 30392

Urbani; Gianni Lenoci (*p*); Pasquale Gadaleat (*b*); Antonio Di Lorenzo (*d*); strings. 11/91.

Urbani's passing has made remaining documents of his work more precious, so these two otherwise unexceptional discs are welcome. *Urlo* is a brief quartet date with three originals by Farao and Leveratto balanced by three standards and a blues. Urbani coasts here and there but there is the unpredictable launching into sheer passion which makes his music so exhilarating from moment to moment. *Round About... Max* includes two tracks with a string section, along with five other standards. The recording is pretty atrocious for something made in the 1990s – the bass frequencies are negligible, and even Urbani sounds thin at times – but his outlandish solo treatment of 'Days Of Wine And Roses' is a gem, and a duet with Lenoci on 'Invitation' was worth preserving.

Michal Urbaniak (born 1943) ELECTRIC VIOLIN, SAXOPHONES

***(*) **Polish Jazz: Volume 9 – Michal Urbaniak** Polskie Nagrania MUZA PNCD 032
    Urbaniak; Adam Makowicz (*p, ky*); Wojciech Karolak (*ky*); Pawel Jarzebski (*b*); Czeslaw
    Bartkowski (*d*); Urszula Dudziak (*v, perc*). 71, 73.
*** **Take Good Care Of My Heart** Steeplechase SCCD 31195
    Urbaniak; Horace Parlan (*p*); Jesper Lundgaard (*b*); Aage Tanggaard (*d*). 8/84.
**** **Songbird** Steeplechase SCCD 31278
    Urbaniak; Kenny Barron (*p*); Peter Washington (*b*); Kenny Washington (*d*). 10/90.
*** **Live In New York** L + R 45041
    Urbaniak; Michael Gerber (*p*); Ron Carter (*b*); Lenny White (*d*). 91.

Like his tragic fellow-countryman and -instrumentalist, Zbigniew Seifert, Urbaniak began his career as a Coltrane-influenced saxophonist, concentrating increasingly on violin as he found an individual voice. He is heard on saxophone on the Polskie Nagrania compilation, on which he includes one of the Krzysztof Komeda compositions, 'Crazy Girl', he played while Komeda's saxophonist in the mid-'60s. In contrast to Seifert, who died in his early thirties in 1979, Urbaniak has shown less interest in free music than in accommodating conventional jazz structures and those folk elements which seem most adaptable to his instrument; very recently, he has been recording in a more or less straight folk idiom, though these records may be difficult to find outside Poland. In the 1970s he also showed a strong interest in electronics, experimented with the wind-generated lyricon and made a number of successful albums with his singer wife, Ursula Dudziak. One of the earliest of these, before he was taken up by the American majors, can be found on the *Polish Jazz* compilation; Adam Makowicz was also in the band, and together with Dudziak they became important symbols to Polish musicians and fans of what it was possible for non-Western musicians to achieve.

    Of the later material, the recent *Songbird* is quite the most impressive, a mature set of originals that see the violinist finally come into his own as a wholly convincing harmonic and melodic improviser. His tone on the amplified instrument is cleaner and less raw-edged than previously, but he clearly knows how to vary bow-weight and left-hand stopping in order to create a range of articulations which do not so much mimic the saxophone as raise the violin to the same expressive level in this context. The early sets are pretty much of a piece, but less coherent, and never quite attain the authority of the *Songbird* band.

    The live disc is disappointing in many regards. Urbaniak is not a standards player first and foremost, and he sounds ill at ease and unprepared for 'Softly As In A Morning Sunrise' and 'In Your Own Sweet Way'. Later in the set, more of the displaced phrasing and syncopated beats appear out of his native idiom, and as a result the whole thing becomes more convincing and expressive.

Warren Vaché Sr BASS

*** **Swingin' And Singin'** Jazzology JCD-202
    Vaché; Larry Weiss (*c*); Nick Capella (*tb*); Nick Sassone (*cl, ts*); Lou Carter (*p*); Dawes
    Thompson (*g*); Mike Burgevin (*d*). 2/90.

The senior Vaché takes an unassuming role as bassist and MD in this engaging set by a group of seasoned old-timers ('There are no kids in this band', he says proudly in the sleevenote). On the plus side is an interesting programme of material, deliberately avoiding too many Dixieland warhorses; Weiss's poised and full-toned cornet, a voice firmly in the great tradition; and the air of easy-going enjoyment that the band generates. The minuses are minor, but they would include the two vocals and tempos that occasionally get a little too restful to keep the attention. The recording is soft-focused and sometimes rather remote.

Warren Vaché (born 1951) CORNET

*** **Midtown Jazz** Concord CCD 4203
    Vaché; John Bunch (*p*); Phil Flanigan (*b*). 2/82.

*** **Easy Going** Concord CCD 4323
>   Vaché; Dan Barrett (*tb*); Howard Alden (*g*); John Harkins (*p*); Jack Lesberg (*b*); Chuck Riggs
>   (*d*). 12/86.

** **Warm Evenings** Concord CCD 4392
>   Vaché; Ben Aronov (*p*); Lincoln Milliman (*b*); Giampaolo Biagi (*d*); Beaux Arts String Quartet.
>   6/89.

A triumph of style over substance, Warren Vaché's mellifluous cornet is instantly attractive, but gall-ingly lacking in content; 'Midtown Jazz' is just about the right designation. Though jazz players value 'sound' above all else, one is always conscious of a missing element in Vaché's playing. A traditionalist in the same young-fogey vein as tenor saxophonist Scott Hamilton, with whom he has performed, Vaché harks back to the days of classic swing, but with a rather detached, 'chamber jazz' feel. The most obvious measure of his virtuosity, his ability to play extremes of pitch very quietly, is something of a mixed blessing, and can be seen to rob his music of much of its dramatic tension.

Easy Going is equally well named. Mannerly enough to be completely ignorable, it cries out for some modulation of mood and attack. The tunes are almost all brief and relatively undeveloped and, while there is no intrinsic objection to Vaché's concentration on melody ('playing the changes' can be as arid as integral serialism), he seems rather unwilling to stamp his own personality on the music. Porter's 'You'd Be So Nice To Come Home To' and the closing 'Moon Song' (significantly the longest track) suggest some willingness to put himself on the line, but not enough to save the set. Dan Barrett is an unexpected revelation.

It's as well not to dismiss *Warm Evenings* out of hand. Charlie Parker made the 'with strings' format perfectly respectable, if a trifle restrictive. Vaché chooses to be constrained by Jack Gale's arrangements, and he makes them sound more banal than they actually are; in point of fact, Gale seems to appreciate tunes like 'A Flower Is A Lovesome Thing' more thoroughly than the cornetist. The four (jazz) quartet tracks don't redeem a very dull and slightly craven album that grossly undersells Vaché's considerable talent.

Kid Thomas Valentine (1896–1987) TRUMPET

**** **Kid Thomas And His Algiers Stompers** American Music AMCD-10
>   Valentine; Bob Thomas, Harrison Barnes (*tb*); Emile Barnes (*cl*); George Guesnon (*g, bj*);
>   Joseph Phillips (*b*); George Henderson (*d*). 9/51.

*** **The Dance Hall Years** American Music AMCD-48
>   Valentine; Louis Nelson (*tb*); Emanuel Paul (*cl, ts*); Joe James, James 'Sing' Miller (*p*); Burke
>   Stevenson, Joseph Butler (*b*); Sammy Penn (*d*); 'Pa' (*v*). 59–3/64.

(*) **Kid Thomas' Dixieland Band 1960 With Emanuel Paul 504 CD33
>   Valentine; Louis Nelson (*tb*); Emanuel Paul (*ts*); Joe James (*p, v*); Joseph Butler (*b*); Sammy
>   Penn (*d, v*). 9/60.

*** **Kid Thomas And His Algiers Stompers** Original Jazz Classics OJC 1833
>   As above, except add Emile Barnes, Albert Burbank (*cl*), Homer Eugene (*p*). 8/60–1/61.

(*) **Kid Thomas And His Algiers Stompers Original Jazz Classics OJC 1845
>   As above, except omit Burbank, Eugene. 1/61.

*** **Kid Thomas And Emanuel Paul With Barry Martyn's Band** GHB BCD-257
>   Valentine; Cuff Billett (*t*); Pete Dyer (*tb*); Emanuel Paul, Bill Greenow (*ts*); Richard Simmons
>   (*p*); Terry Knight (*b*); Barry Martyn (*d*). 64.

***(*) **Kid Thomas At Moose Hall** GHB BCD-305
>   Valentine; Bill Connell (*cl*); Dick Griffith (*bj*); Dick McCarthy (*b*); Bill Bissonnette (*d*). 67.

*** **Same Old Soupbone!** Jazz Crusade JC-3001
>   Valentine; Louis Nelson (*tb*); Emanuel Paul (*ts*); Charlie Hamilton (*p*); Joe Butler (*b*); Sammy
>   Penn (*d*). 10/68.

**** **Kid Thomas In California** GHB BCD-296
>   Valentine; Bill Bissonnette (*tb, v*); Capt. John Handy (*as*); Cyril Bennett (*p*); Jim Tutunjian (*b*);
>   Sammy Penn (*d*); Carol Leigh (*v*). 2–3/69.

***(*) **Spirit Of New Orleans 4** Music Mecca 1059-2
>   Valentine; Percy Humphrey (*t*); Louis Nelson, Jim Robinson (*tb*); Orange Kellin, Albert
>   Burbank (*cl*); Emanuel Paul (*ts*); Charlie Hamilton (*p*); Ricardo Hansen (*bj*); Chester Zardis,
>   Joseph Hutler (*b*); Cie Frazier, Alonzo Stewart (*d*). 71–72.

'Kid' Thomas Valentine arrived in New Orleans rather late – in 1922. By the time he made his first records, almost 30 years later, he had led bands all over Louisiana but remained based in the city, where he continued to play for a further 35 years. He approached this awesome career with an almost Zen simplicity, reducing the New Orleans sound to its essentials and creating a lifetime's work from them. A fascinating lead-trumpeter, his methods – including a severe observance of the melody, a blunt, jabbing attack and a vibrato that sounds like an angry trill – manage to create high drama and lyrical depth alike, and though he seldom took solos he dominates every performance.

He made a lot of records during his long life and they are slowly starting to reappear on CD, mostly through George Buck's group of labels. These are the first of many planned for reissue, and they offer a fine glimpse of one of the great jazz hornmen in action. The first (1951) sessions have survived in excellent sound and find Valentine and Barnes in their first prime: there are two trombonists, since Bob Thomas had to leave after three numbers, and the changed balance of the front line tells much about the sensitivity of the New Orleans ensemble. Alden Ashforth's excellent notes chronicle the whole session in detail. The most characteristic is *The Dance Hall Years*, where Thomas plays with his regular working band (usually called The Algiers Stompers) at a couple of dance sessions, one identified only to the late '50s, the other dated precisely to March 1964. The material is familiar New Orleans stuff and a few blues. The seven earlier tracks are dustily recorded but the remainder sound good, although there seems to be no audience present. Nelson and Paul are in strong form and the band drives along with the ramshackle but perfectly appropriate rhythm that makes this music tick. The 504 CD is drawn from the Larry Borenstein archives, and this one is a less significant survival: the band sound shopworn in parts and the sound is rather dusty, though Thomas rouses them on occasion. The two OJCs are more from Riverside's *New Orleans; The Living Legends* series, and they're surprisingly disappointing in some ways. Though clearly recorded, the band sound shrill – especially the clarinets – and some of the tempos seem either too hurried or down to a crawl. OJC 1833 is the better of the two. The session with Barry Martyn and his British team is a spirited, affectionate meeting between men of vastly different backgrounds and, while Martyn anchors the pulse, his colleagues don't do so well, with Dyer especially blasting all before him to no real purpose. Thomas and Paul, though, fashion a more graceful partnership.

At Moose Hall and *In California* were both recorded by Bissonnette, a stalwart crusader for New Orleans jazz, who usually worked out of Connecticut. Forced to switch from his usual trombone to drums for the earlier session, he drafted in local hero Connell and booked Thomas to play the session, which suffers from an imperfect location sound and plenty of clinkers by the players yet still offers much great Thomas. He was obliged to play more solos than usual, which he never liked, but somehow took to the task with great relish, even though the rhythm section plays a lot faster and with more bounce than he was used to. As Bissonnette notes, there is more Kid Thomas on this one record than on two or three of his regular dates.

In California is the best available disc. Bissonnette secured a very good sound, recording mostly at Earthquake McGoon's, and the front-line partnership of Thomas and Handy strikes many sparks. 'Say Si Si' and 'Rose Room' are tunes less often encountered in the Thomas discography, and Penn's drumming is an outstanding show of maverick New Orleans timekeeping. Carol Leigh contributes two sweet-toned but convincing vocals. Highly recommended.

Jazz Crusade is Bissonnette's own label and *Same Old Soupbone!* is salvaged from a local TV appearance by Thomas's band. A good if comparatively routine Thomas date by his standard band, playing much of their usual material. The title is a favourite saying of the leader's, the sort of thing he would say to shrug off compliments or questions.

Music Mecca's compilation of two different LPs (plus four previously unreleased tracks) has Thomas sharing the billing with a Percy Humphrey-led band. The Humphrey tracks are slightly better since he is in great form, but Thomas's tunes fare well, with the Europeans Kellin and Hansen fitting in without a murmur. Bright but effective sound.

Eric Van der Westen (born 1963) BASS

***(*) **Working Dreamer** Bvhaast CD 9212

> Van Der Westen; Chris Abelen, Hans Sparla (*tb*); Erwin Vann (*ss, ts, bcl*); Paul Van Kemenade (*as*); Paul De Leest (*cl, ts*); Ge Bijvoet (*p*); Pieter Bast (*d*). n.d.

Van der Westen has been listening to David Murray's Octet – his own musters a lot of the same brio, with rollicking counterpoint and horns-answering-horns music. His 'Ballad For John Carter' is a dirge Murray would be proud of; the conflation of Mingus melodies in 'The Underdog' is prime jazz repertory; and the five-part 'Out Of Time, Out Of Space' gets the most out of a little big band. But he puts, naturally, a Europeanized spin on it, too. The record may be on Bvhaast and these might be Dutchmen at work, but it's tellingly different from a Willem Breuker band – more streamlined, less soberly comic. A nice absence of trumpets, a lot of good reeds, and a very good record.

Joe Van Enkhuizen TENOR SAXOPHONE

*** Joe Meets The Rhythm Section Timeless SJP 249
> Van Enkhuizen; Horace Parlan (*p*); Rufus Reid (*b*); Al Harewood (*d*). 7/86.
*** Ellington My Way Timeless SJP 419
> Van Enkhuizen; Frits Landesbergen (*vib*); Hein Van der Geyin (*b*); Doug Sides (*d*). 3/88–11/91.
*** Blues Ahead Timeless SJP 356
> Van Enkhuizen; Carlo Dewys (*org*); Han Bennink (*d*). 12/88–4/89.

This tenorman sounds as if he could have worked in southern R&B bands: he has the ripe, swaggering quality which makes the *Blues Ahead* organ-combo session sound entirely authentic. But he's from Holland. *Joe Meets The Rhythm Section* is hard-bop repertory enlivened by some out-of-the-way choices of material. *Blues Ahead* offers a rare glimpse of Bennink on a straight-ahead kind of session and, with Dewys enthusiastically copying Jack McDuff and Shirley Scott, the leader's fuming solos emerge with gutsy vividness. The Ellington disc was recorded at four sessions over three years, yet is all of a piece – 11 choice chunks of Ellingtonia given a bluff, no-nonsense interpretation, with the surprise choice of Landesbergen's vibes to add colour on four tracks. Van Enkhuizen's group also backs Major Holley on *Major Step* (Timeless SJP 364).

Marc Van Roon PIANO

***(*) Falling Stones Mons 874 669
> Van Roon; Dave Liebman (*ss*); Joshua Samson (*ts*); Tony Overwater (*b*); Wim Kegel (*d*); Jasper Blom (*perc*). 4/94.

Although Van Roon's name is at the top, this is dominated by Dave Liebman, who heard this rhythm section on a trip to Amsterdam and decided to record with them on his next visit. The results are splendidly forceful and imaginative and mark another fine entry from the saxophonist. Tranquil tone-poems such as the title-track mingle with all-out energy pieces such as 'Get Me Back To The Apple', and the improvising has a clarity that always lets one hear the form beneath. If he more or less has the date hijacked by Liebman, Van Roon nevertheless contributes three of the best themes. Blom sits in on two tracks, Samson on one.

Jasper Van't Hof (born 1947) PIANO, KEYBOARDS

***(*) Solo Piano Timeless SJP 286
> Van't Hof solo. 10/87.
*** Dinner For Two M.A. Music International A 803
> Van't Hof; Bob Malach (*ts*).
*** Blau ACT 9203
> Van't Hof; Bob Malach (*ts*); Wayne Krantz (*g*); Nicholas Fiszman (*b*); Philippe Allaert (*d*).
**(*) The Prague Concert P & J 102
> Van't Hof; Bob Malach (*ts*). 1/92.
*** Face To Face veraBra vBr 2063
> Van't Hof; Ernie Watts (*ts*); Bo Stief (*b*); Aldo Romano (*d*). 94.

Solo Piano shows off a side of van't Hof which for much of his career has remained buried under a rather showy, Chick Corea-derived keyboard style. The Timeless sessions include a slightly blowsy 'Prelude To A Kiss'. There's also a well-etched reading of 'Dinner For Two' which compares more than favourably with one on the duo with Malach, a performance that recalls van't Hof's work with Archie Shepp. Identified for much of his career as a fusion player given to sweeping synthesizer gestures and melancholy romanticism, the Dutchman's touch on a concert grand is suprisingly like McCoy Tyner's, with the same confident absorption of idiom.

In the mid-1970s, van't Hof led the excellent group, Pork Pie. His long association with saxophonist Charlie Mariano and guitarist Philip Catherine (the three are heard together on the romantic *Sleep, My Love*, on CMP, who have a couple of other van't Hof items in the back-catalogue) began then. What the later records suggest more than anything is that van't Hof is desperately in need of a sympathetic contract from a label with the clout to let him record with top-ranking musicians who will challenge him to get out of the rather airy-fairy rut in which he now seems firmly stuck. The 1994 album almost answers the need: a great band, politely fixated on the classic Coltrane quartet, but washed away in a slippery, whispery mix that would have had even the great man and certainly the redoubtable Watts (who hasn't usually been thought of as a Trane disciple) sounding as if he were playing in the bathroom.

Tom Varner FRENCH HORN

*** **Tom Varner Quartet** Soul Note 121017-2
   Varner; Ed Jackson (*as*); Fred Hopkins (*b*); Billy Hart (*d*). 8/80.
*** **Long Night Big Day** New World NW 80410-2
   Varner; Frank London (*t*); Steve Swell (*tb*); Ed Jackson, Thomas Chapin (*as*); Rich Rothenberg (*ts*); Lindsey Horner (*b*); Phil Haynes (*d*). 3/90..
**** **The Mystery Of Compassion** Soul Note 121217-2
   Varner; Steve Swell (*tb*); Dave Taylor (*btb*); Matt Darriau, Ed Jackson (*as*); Rich Rothenberg, Ellery Eskelin (*ts*); Jim Hartog (*bs*); Mark Feldman (*vn*); Mike Richmond (*b*); Tom Rainey (*d*). 3/92.

Varner's unassuming efforts at establishing french horn in the contemporary avant-garde have been only sporadically successful: three good but flawed earlier records have already disappeared from the catalogue. A blindfold listener might well assume that they were listening to a trombonist, given the timbre of the horn, and, as adept and agile as Varner is, he hasn't always convinced that he can make a case for the horn's merits. *Quartet* has returned on CD: basically a good if uneventful display of free bop, with Jackson a supportive partner, this depends on its satisfying solos to make an impact. The New World album was easily his most ambitious record to that point, but it's finally let down by a failure or two, despite the excellence of several pieces. The basic unit is three horns, bass and drums (London, Swell and Chapin appear only on 'Wind Trio +') and, if the earlier records were designed to display Varner's powers as an improviser, it's his sense of structure which gets tested here. 'Big Day', 'Search For Sanity' and especially 'Prince Of Jamaica (Queens)' manage to transcend their compositional complexities, while 'Wind Trio +' is a fascinatingly realized set-piece for two wind trios and percussion. But 'Arts And Leisure' is a terribly unconvincing mixture of tone rows and twelve-bar blues, and the title-piece merely rambles in search of coherence.

All doubts are dramatically purged, though, by the superb 1992 Soul Note date, *The Mystery Of Compassion*. Here, Varner's alarming juxtapositions (a watermark for new New York musicians) make coherent sense without losing their capacity to surprise, and the players involved respond with a passionate intensity that's rare even among these driven musicians. The central group is a quintet made up of Varner, Jackson, Rothenberg, Richmond and Rainey. On all-out barnstormers like 'How Does Power Work?' and '$1000 Hat' they play with terrific panache. 'The Well' is a concerto-like piece for Feldman, and 'Death At The Right Time' uses a tentet to create a bemusing recall of Coltrane's 'Ascension'. Varner's own improvising has never been better – he actually makes the instrument assert its personal qualities – and he closes the record on a sombre antiphonal piece for low brass called 'Prayer' that makes a moving coda to the rest.

Nana Vasconcelos (born 1944) BERIMBAU, PERCUSSION, VOICE

(*) **Saudades ECM 1147
   Vasconcelos solo and with Egberto Gismonti (*8-string g*); strings. 3/79.
*** **Lester** Soul Note 121157
   Vasconcelos; Antonello Salis (*g, acc, v*). 12/85.

Unlike his slightly older compatriot, Airto Moreira, who was propelled into independent stardom by a stint with Miles Davis and on the strength of his wife Flora Purim's astonishing voice, Vasconcelos has largely suffered from the old and patronizing Hollywood syndrome of 'specialist extra' recruitment: 'Six Chinees for a street scene in Kowloon!' . . . 'One Lascar and a Hottentot!' Vasconcelos has played bit-parts on countless Latin-modern sessions, bringing a distinctive range of sounds largely based on the Afro-Latin *berimbau*, a bow with a wire string plucked with a coin or stroked with a stick, its sound modified by a gourd or shell resonator pressed against the player's abdomen. Whereas Moreira was inclined to put together a rhythmic background like a pizza chef, throwing in aural ingredients with more sense of drama than of taste, Vasconcelos is a much more concentrated musician, capable of sustained performance on his own and as a full member of improvising groups; some of his best work is with guitarist Egberto Gismonti, who guests on *Saudades*, but also with Codona (*q.v.*).

The problem has been how to make Vasconcelos's intensely rhythmic but rather specialized music accessible to a Western audience. *Saudades* is, alas, not the solution. In addition to overdubbing his vocal parts (which seems completely redundant), the album places him in highly chromatic string-settings which are utterly European in conception. Vasconcelos's Tarzan cry on the opening 'O Berimbau' appears to startle the orchestral players for a moment; it certainly throws the whole set into perspective.

Lester is very much truer to the Brazilian's enormous talents, though Salis is a surprisingly passive partner, following rather than confronting. There is an interesting Antilles set, *Bush Dance*, but this is not currently available, and Vasconcelos still, regrettably, has to be sought on other leaders' albums. The three Codona sets probably remain the best bet.

Sarah Vaughan (1924–90) VOCAL, PIANO

*** It's You Or No One Musicraft 70055-2
> Vaughan; Buck Clayton, Dizzy Gillespie, Freddy Webster (*t*); Charlie Parker, Scoville Brown, Leroy Harris (*as*); Don Byas (*ts*); George James, Cecil Payne (*bs*); Al Haig, Jimmy Jones, Teddy Wilson, Bud Powell (*p*); John Collins, Remo Palmieri (*g*); Al McKibbon, Curley Russell, Billy Taylor, Ted Sturgis (*b*); Big Sid Catlett, Kenny Clarke, J. C. Heard (*d*); George Treadwell Orchestra. 46–47.

**(*) Tenderly Musicraft 70057-2
> Similar to above; omit Parker, Gillespie, Powell, Clayton, Byas. 46–47.

**(*) Time And Again Musicraft 70061-2
> Similar to above, except add Ted Dale Orchestra, Stuff Smith (*vn*), Earl Rodgers Choir, Georgie Auld Orchestra. 47–48.

***(*) The Divine Sarah Vaughan: The Columbia Years 1949–1953 Columbia 465597 2CD
> Vaughan; Miles Davis, Billy Butterfield, Taft Jordan, Andrew Ferretti, Bernie Privin, Yank Lawson, Carl Poole, Ziggy Elman (*t*); Will Bradley, Jack Satterfield, William Rausch, Benny Green, John D'Agostino, William Pritchard (*tb*); Tony Scott (*cl*); Hymie Schertzer, Art Drelinger, George Kelly, Toots Mondello, Al Klink, Bill Versaci, Richard Banzer, Bill Hitz, Budd Johnson (*saxes*); Jimmy Jones (*p*); Freddie Green, Al Caiola, Mundell Lowe (*g*); Frank Carroll, Eddie Safranski, Jack Lesberg, Billy Taylor, Bob Haggart (*b*); J. C. Heard, Terry Snyder, Norris Shawker, Bill Coles (*d*); strings; studio orchestras led by Percy Faith, Paul Weston and Norman Leyden. 1/49–1/53.

**** 16 Most Requested Songs Columbia 474399-2
> As above. 1/49–1/53.

Her vocal on the 1946 Dizzy Gillespie Sextet record of 'Lover Man' was Sarah Vaughan's banner arrival, but her sessions for Musicraft and Columbia were her first significant body of records, following her stint with the Billy Eckstine Orchestra. The three Musicraft discs are middleweight pop of the era, none of them very clearly recorded, and the presence of some star names in the jazz field is unfortunately no guarantee of great quality, though the date with Gillespie and Parker on the first disc is worth remembering. The bulk of the Columbias are scarcely jazz-orientated sessions either, with full orchestras and hefty ballads, but two sessions from May 1950 put Vaughan in front of a small band including Miles Davis, Tony Scott and Budd Johnson for eight fine tracks. Vaughan's musical insight – she was a more than capable pianist – and involvement with bop's early days gave her a hip awareness that went with a voice of vast range and power, and her early Billy Eckstine influence – both singers use vibrato to the same enormously ripe effect – makes her sound like a close relation of Eckstine on all these tracks. Far from disguising the operatic qualities of her voice, Vaughan insists on them, sometimes dispersing the sense of a lyric while luxuriating in the depth of her own voice. Luckily, the material on the Columbia sessions is good enough to withstand such indulgence, and it's a very enjoyable double set, acceptably if not outstandingly remastered. But less committed souls will prefer the useful single-disc compilation, *16 Most Requested Songs*, which luckily includes four of the tracks with the small group.

*** Perdido: Live At Birdland 1953 Natasha 4004
> Vaughan; Dizzy Gillespie (*t*); Jimmy Mordecai, John Malachi (*p*); Wild Bill Davis (*org*); Wyatt Ruther, Lou Hatton (*b*); Fats Herd, Al Jones (*d*). 51–53.

This is for Vaughan specialists, but it's a rare chance to hear her in her early prime, away from the studios. The disc collects a clutch of Birdland broadcasts: a lot of talk and announcements, the audience sing 'Happy Birthday' to her at one date, and Gillespie turns up to play some discreet backings on a few songs. There's some duplication of material, with three versions of 'Perdido' probably one too many. Vaughan's swing, timing and sense of power in reserve are marvellous, though.

**** Sarah Vaughan With Clifford Brown Emarcy 814641
> Vaughan; Clifford Brown (*t*); Paul Quinichette (*ts*); Herbie Mann (*f*); Jimmy Jones (*p*); Joe Benjamin (*b*); Roy Haynes (*d*). 12/54.

**** Swingin' Easy Emarcy 514072-2
> Vaughan; Jimmy Jones, John Malachi (*p*); Richard Davis, Joe Benjamin (*b*); Roy Haynes (d). 54–57.

The session with Clifford Brown was a glorious occasion, and one that was repeated far too infrequently during the rest of Sarah's career. A blue-chip band (even Mann doesn't disgrace himself) on a slow-burning set of standards that Vaughan lingers over and details with all the finesse of her early-mature voice: 'Lullaby Of Birdland' (with an extra take on the CD edition) is taken at a pace that suspends or lets time drift, and the very slow pace for 'Embraceable You' and 'Bill' doesn't falter into a trudge. Perhaps there could have been one or two more speedier numbers – 'It's Crazy' is about the only one – and Brown and Quinichette are perhaps not quite as commanding as they might have been. But it's still a superb set, with Jones in particular following every turn of the singer's delivery. Excellent remastering. *Swingin' Easy* isn't far behind, though. With just a rhythm section in support, Vaughan is at her freest and most good-humoured: it's worth having just for the cheeky, sublime 'Shulie A Bop', but there's also a gorgeous 'Lover Man', a shivery 'Linger Awhile'.

*** **The Rodgers And Hart Songbook** Emarcy 842864-2
     Vaughan; Hal Mooney Orchestra. 9–10/56.
*** **In The Land Of Hi-Fi** Emarcy 826454-2
     Vaughan; Hal Mooney Orchestra. 56.
*** **The George Gershwin Songbook Vol. 1** Emarcy 846895-2
     Vaughan; Hal Mooney Orchestra. 57.
*** **The George Gershwin Songbook Vol. 2** Emarcy 846896-2
     Vaughan; Hal Mooney Orchestra. 57.
***(*) **The Irving Berlin Songbook** Emarcy 822526-2
     Vaughan; Hal Mooney Orchestra; Billy Eckstine (*v*). 57.
*** **Golden Hits** Mercury 824891-2
     Vaughan; Hal Mooney Orchestra. 58.
*** **Misty** Emarcy 846488-2
     Vaughan; Zoot Sims, Jo Hrasko, William Boucaya, Marcel Hrasko (*saxes*); Ronnell Bright, Maurice Vander (*p*); Michel Hausser (*vib*); Pierre Cullaz (*g*); Richard Davis, Pierre Michelot (*b*); Kenny Clarke, Kansas Fields (*d*); strings. 7/58.
***(*) **Sings Broadway: Great Songs From Great Shows** Verve 526464-2 2CD
     As above discs. 3/54–1/56.
***(*) **Jazz Masters 42: The Jazz Sides** Verve 526817-2
     As above.

Vaughan's later Mercury sessions are sometimes a shade self-conscious – not in any sense an embarrassment to Vaughan, but in the way that she can get hung up on the sound of her own voice, the criticism most often levelled at her. Musicality and the comparative brevity of each piece usually win through, though, and while her 'songbook' collections miss some of the simple swing and infectiousness of the contemporaneous Ella Fitzgerald records in the same style, Vaughan's grandness and the lavish Mercury recording make these rich sonic experiences. Eckstine joins in on the Irving Berlin session to make matters even more resplendent. *Misty* includes Zoot Sims on a session recorded in Paris, and *In The Land Of Hi-Fi* and *Golden Hits* offer some of the best cross-sections of material, although the occasional stuffiness of the studio orchestras discourages any hint that Vaughan might use the occasions as springboards for more idiomatic jazz singing. Her coloratura tones and sweeping phrasing work instead to a different aesthetic, and one that is as individually creative.

Sings Broadway is an intelligent compilation from this era, with a 'songbook' approach to the material, and scarcely a dud track amongst it all. Some may prefer the *Jazz Masters* choice from her more jazz-directed sessions, but it's still no substitute for the four-star discs listed above.

***(*) **At Mister Kelly's** Emarcy 832791-2
     Vaughan; Jimmy Jones (*p*); Richard Davis (*b*); Roy Haynes (*d*). 57.
***(*) **Sassy Swings The Tivoli** Mercury 832788-2 2CD
     Vaughan; Kirk Stuart (*p*); Charles Williams (*b*); Georges Hughes (*d*). 7/63.
*** **Sassy Swings Again** Emarcy 814587-2
     Vaughan; Clark Terry, Charlie Shavers, Joe Newman, Freddie Hubbard (*t*); J. J. Johnson, Kai Winding (*tb*); Phil Woods (*as*); Benny Golson (*ts*); Bob James (*p*); others. 1/67.

The best of these live sessions is the earliest, *At Mister Kelly's*. Most singers can't wait to get out of clubs and into concert halls, but the 'intimacy' of the situation can be a boon, and with this excellent trio Vaughan sounds completely relaxed. Nineteen songs, some of them dashed off, but she dashes better than most. The two later dates are very good rather than great. *Tivoli* is a solid balance between the unbridled grandeur of her range and the more loose-limbed jazz-musician stance – despite the grandiloquence of her voice, most of her best records have been done with small groups rather than orchestras – and *Swings Again* sets her up with a star-studded group that she does, nevertheless, seem less happy with, and the band have a bought-in feeling too.

***(*) **Masterpieces Of Sarah Vaughan** Emarcy 846330-2
     Vaughan; various groups. 54–67.

***(*) **'Round Midnight: Sarah Vaughan** Verve 510086-2
>   As above.
***(*) **Verve Jazz Masters: Sarah Vaughan** Verve 518199-2
>   As above.

None of these compilations holds a candle to either *With Clifford Brown* or *Swingin' Easy*, even though they take tracks from both. But each has enough classics – 'Shulie A Bop', 'Lullaby Of Birdland', 'Stardust' on *Masterpieces*, 'April In Paris', 'Jim', 'Darn That Dream' on *'Round Midnight*, 'Say It Isn't So' and 'Lonely Woman' on *Jazz Masters* – to satisfy a seeker after a run-through of Sarah's Emarcy/ Mercury period.

*** **I'll Be Seeing You** Vintage Jazz Classics VJC 1015-2
>   Vaughan; Clark Terry, Willie Cook, Francis Williams, Ray Nance, Dick Vance, Sonny Cohn, Thad Jones, Joe Newman, Snooky Young (*t*); Henry Coker, Benny Powell, Al Grey, Juan Tizol, Britt Woodman, Quentin Jackson (*tb*); Woody Herman (*cl*); Jimmy Hamilton, Paul Gonsalves, Johnny Hodges, Harry Carney, Russell Procope, Willie Smith, Marshall Royal, Frank Foster, Frank Wess, Billy Mitchell, Charlie Fowlkes (*reeds*); Jimmy Jones, Ronnell Bright, Count Basie (*p*); Freddie Green (*g*); Eddie Jones, Richard Davis, Joe Benjamin (*b*); Sonny Payne, Roy Haynes, Percy Bryce (*d*); Nat Cole (*v*). 49–60.

A collection of concert rarities, a few with Ellington (in very dusty sound) and Basie (a sweet duet with Joe Williams on 'Teach Me Tonight'), but mostly trio material from 1960–61 sessions. She is in very good voice for the latter, and there are fine readings of 'All Of Me', 'Misty' and others; but this is really a supplement for Vaughan fanatics. The sound is (aside from the Ellington pieces) vivid enough, though inevitably short of the studio records.

*** **Sarah Sings Soulfully** Roulette CDP 7984452
>   Vaughan; Carmell Jones (*t*); Teddy Edwards (*ts*); Ernie Freeman (*org*); unknown *g, b*; Milt Turner (*d*). 6/63.
***(*) **The Roulette Years Vols. 1 & 2** Roulette B21Y-94983-2
>   As above, plus Count Basie Orchestra, Barney Kessel (*g*), Joe Comfort (*b*). 60–64.

Vaughan's Roulette records veer between a hypnotic beauty and a fulsome, cod-operatic extravagance. The latter trait is caught particularly on *The Roulette Years* compilation, a good-value set with 24 tracks from 11 original Roulette albums, including her collaboration with the Basie band, two from *After Hours* and its lesser-known repeat of the formula, *Sarah Plus Two*, and various arrangements by Benny Carter (a very fine 'The Man I Love'), Quincy Jones and Don Costa. *Sarah Sings Soulfully* puts the singer in front of a combo dominated by Freeman's organ, but it's not a bad session: 'Sermonette' swings brightly, and there's an impressively smouldering ''Round Midnight'. The only drawback is Milt Turner's noisy drumming.

***(*) **How Long Has This Been Going On?** Pablo 2310-821
>   Vaughan; Oscar Peterson (*p*); Joe Pass (*g*); Ray Brown (*b*); Louie Bellson (*d*). 4/78.
***(*) **Duke Ellington Song Book One** Pablo 2312-111
>   Vaughan; Waymon Reed (*t, flhn*); J. J. Johnson (*tb*); Eddie Vinson (*as, v*); Frank Wess (*ts, f*); Frank Foster, Zoot Sims (*ts*); Jimmy Rowles, Mike Wofford (*p*); Joe Pass, Bucky Pizzarelli, Pee Wee Crayton (*g*); Andy Simpkins, Bill Walker (*b*); Grady Tate, Charles Randell (*d*); big band. 8–9/79.
***(*) **Duke Ellington Song Book Two** Pablo 2312-116
>   As above. 8–9/79.
**** **Copacabana** Pablo 2312-125
>   Vaughan; Helio Delmiro (*g*); Andy Simpkins (*b*); Grady Tate (*d*) 10/79.
*** **Send In The Clowns** Pablo 2312-230
>   Vaughan; Sonny Cohn, Frank Szabo, Willie Cook, Bob Summers, Dale Carley (*t*); Booty Wood, Bill Hughes, Dennis Wilson, Grover Mitchell (*tb*); Kenny Hing, Eric Dixon, Bobby Plater, Danny Turner, Johnny Williams (*saxes*); George Gaffney (*p*); Freddie Green (*g*); Andy Simpkins (*b*); Harold Jones (*d*). 2–5/81.
**** **Crazy And Mixed Up** Pablo 2312-137
>   Vaughan; Sir Roland Hanna (*p*); Joe Pass (*g*); Andy Simpkins (*b*); Harold Jones (*d*). 3/82.

Vaughan's Pablo albums will endure as some of her most finely crafted music. *How Long Has This Been Going On?* introduced a new note of seriousness into her recording career after several years of indifferent efforts and a seemingly careless approach to the studios. The voice has never been better or more closely recorded, and the picked session players and uniformly strong material make these six albums the most consistent of her career. *How Long* has the odd flaw, but there are beautiful readings of 'I've Got The World On A String' and the title-tune, and when Vaughan takes it in turns to do a duo with each member of the band it's a marvellous display of her ability. The Ellington albums gave her – at last

– the opportunity to stamp her identity on the greatest of jazz songbooks, and while again there are a few disappointments – a second-class 'Solitude' that should have been a classic, the sometimes overbearing heft of Bill Byers's arrangements and the slightly problematical balance – there are some exceptionally bountiful treatments, of 'In A Sentimental Mood', 'I'm Just A Lucky So-And-So' and 'Chelsea Bridge' to cite three. Both discs stand as a worthy counterpoint to Fiztgerald's celebrated Ellington collaboration.

Send In The Clowns features the Basie orchestra minus Basie, and it's good – the gliding 'All The Things You Are' and a lovely 'Indian Summer' especially – the hard power of the band and Vaughan's own superhuman technique sometimes secure a coldness rather than any warmth of interpretation. *Copacabana* is the neglected album of the bunch, with the sparest of accompaniments to support the great, glowing voice, and the bossa/samba material proving unexpectedly strong material for Vaughan. Best of all, perhaps, is *Crazy And Mixed Up*, a disappointingly short (about 32 minutes) but ideally paced and delivered set of standards with the most sympathetic of accompaniments.

** **Send In The Clowns** Columbia 480682-2
    Vaughan; personnel unlisted. n.d.
*(*) **Songs Of The Beatles** Atlantic 81483-2
    Vaughan; rock instrumentation. 81.
(*) **Brazilian Romance Columbia M K 42519
    Vaughan; Marcio Montarroyos (*t, flhn*); Ernie Watts (*as*); Hubert Laws (*f*); Tom Scott (*lyricon*);
    George Duke (*ky*); Dan Huff, Dori Caymmi (*g*); Alphonso Johnson, Chuck Domanico (*b*);
    Carlos Vega (*d*); Paulinho Da Costa (*perc*); strings. 1–2/87.

Vaughan's final records are disappointing, not so much for any decline in her singing as for the dreadful production values. Flung in with rock stews, Latin soups and disco nightmares, she still sings as if she means it, though it's hard to tell why – especially on the utterly absurd Beatles album. *Send In The Clowns* is marginally better, though still feeble, while the Latin collection (produced by Sergio Mendes) at least has some decent material, even if it doesn't sound very appetizing in these noisy arrangements.

Glen Velez PERCUSSION

*** **Internal Combustion** CM P 23
    Velez; Layne Redmond (*frame d, v*). 5/85.
***(*) **Seven Heaven** CM P 30
    Velez; Steven Gorn (*bamboo f*); Layne Redmond (*perc*). 5/87.
**** **Assyrian Rose** CM P 42
    Velez; John Clark (*frhn*); Steven Gorn (*bamboo f, South American f*); Howard Levy (*hca, p*);
    Layne Redmond (*perc, v*). 6/89.
***(*) **Doctrine Of Signatures** CM P 54
    Velez; Steve Gorn (*bamboo f*); Ed Brunicardi, Eva Atsalis, Randy Crafton, Jan Hagiwara (*d*). 12/
    90.

A regular with oud player Rabih Abou-Khalil's groups, Velez favours instruments with natural resonance, accentuating their constituent materials. He will make quite different use of the small Spanish *pandero* than of a larger frame drum, the Moroccan *bendir*, and exploits metal percussion like the Caribbean steel drum (notably on 'Assyrian Rose') and a Chinese opera gong for very specific tonal and timbral effects. In performances as seamlessly produced as those on the 1989 album, the precise configuration of instruments is of only specialist interest. On *Internal Combustion*, though, and the more varied *Seven Heaven*, there is a far greater concentration on the individual characteristics of fewer instruments whose language and properties are explored at length and enshrined in self-descriptive titles like 'Bodhran' and 'Bendir' (a device also used on Don Cherry's similarly disposed *Multi Kulti* album).

All but two tracks on *Seven Heaven* are for a trio of bamboo flute, *mbira* (kalimba) and percussion that glosses the traditional jazz format of horn, piano and drums. Velez explores subtly polyrhythmic structures which often reveal surprisingly simple components, and it's the essence of his music that it resists self-serving complexity, preferring to build up colour and detail in delicate brush-strokes. *Assyrian Rose* is a masterpiece, evidence of Velez's growing confidence and originality as a writer-arranger. Clark and Levy are used with great sophistication, and co-writer Gorn's bamboo and (what sound like) ceramic flutes provide an unembellished top line of great clarity. There are moments, as at the opening of 'Assyrian Rose', when the music is more awkwardly impressionistic, like the leitmotifs of a spaghetti-Western score, but such occasions are rare, as are more rarefied and extended percussion exercises later on the album; despite Gorn's evocative flute, 'Amazonas' palls well before its nine and a half minutes are up. Though there is no doubt which of these is going to have longest shelf-life in the average collection, it's useful to hear Velez's recordings in chronological order. The most recent is certainly the most sophisticated. Some of the counter-rhythms on *Doctrine Of Signatures* are bogglingly difficult to follow. Music of this sort is something of an acquired taste, but it merits inclusion here every bit as much as Max Roach's all-percussion groups. Velez is a highly original performer, and CMP provides him with just the right combination of technical excellence and artistic freedom to follow his star unhindered.

Charlie Ventura (1916–92) TENOR SAXOPHONE

*** The Crazy Rhythms Savoy SV 0195
    Ventura; Arnold Ross (*p*); John Levy (*b*); Specs Powell (*d*). 8/45.
Trading under the slogan 'Bop For The People', Ventura purveyed a brand of modernism much adulterated by R&B and still awkwardly dependent on an initial swing influence. Ventura played with Charlie Parker at the Royal Roost, and 'How High The Moon' underlines how awkward his Hawkins-derived phrasing could sound in such company. The material on Savoy (a disc shared with fellow tenorist Charlie Kennedy) is too slight to get much of a fix on him but tends to confirm that he was very much a second-division player who tried to keep enough swing clichés floating around in a solo to satisfy those suspicious of out-and-out modernism.

Joe Venuti (1903–78) VIOLIN, PIANO

**** Joe Venuti And Eddie Lang Vol. 1 JSP 309
    Venuti; Jimmy Dorsey (*cl, as, bs*); Don Murray (*cl, bs*); Adrian Rollini (*bsx, gfs, hot fountain pen*); Arthur Schutt, Rube Bloom, Frank Signorelli (*p*); Eddie Lang (*g*); Justin Ring (*d*). 9/26–9/28.

**** Joe Venuti And Eddie Lang Vol. 2 JSP 310
    Venuti; Jimmy Dorsey (*t, cl, as, bs*); Frankie Trumbauer (*Cmel, bsn*); Pete Pumiglio (*cl, bs*); Adrian Rollini (*bsx, gfs, hot fountain pen*); Lennie Hayton (*p, cel*); Rube Bloom, Frank Signorelli, Itzy Riskin (*p*); Eddie Lang (*g*); Joe Tarto (*b*); Justin Ring, Paul Graselli (*d*); Harold Arlen (*v*). 6/28–9/31.

*** Joe Venuti And Eddie Lang Jazz Classics in Digital Stereo 644
    As above two discs, except add Tommy Dorsey (*t, tb*); Charlie Margulis, Leo McConville, Charlie Teagarden, Red Nichols (*t*); Bix Beiderbecke, Andy Secrest (*c*); Jack Teagarden (*tb, v*); Miff Mole, Bill Rank (*tb*); Benny Goodman (*cl*); Charles Strickfadden, Bobby Davis (*as*); Issy Friedman (*cl, ts*); Min Leibrook (*bsx*); Red McKenzie (*kzo, v*); Phil Ward, Fulton McGrath (*p*); Dick McDonough (*g*); Eddie Condon (*bj*); Ward Lay (*b*); Stan King, Neil Marshall, Vic Berton, Chauncey Morehouse (*d*). 11/26–5/33.

*** Stringin' The Blues Topaz TPZ 1015
    Similar to above; add Don Barrigo (*ts*), Arthur Young (*p*), Frank Victor (*g*), Doug Lees (*b*). 9/26–9/34.

***(*) Violin Jazz 1927–1934 Yazoo 1062
    Similar to above. 27–34.

*** Pretty Trix IAJRC 1003
    Venuti; Jerry Colonna (*tb*); Fulton McGrath, Joe White (*p*); Red Norvo (*xy*); Neil Marshall (*d*); Louis Prima (*v*); rest unknown. 12/34.

While there was a danger that Joe Venuti would be best remembered for his practical jokes rather than his violin playing, these marvellous reissues should allay any such fears. Venuti wasn't the only violinist to play jazz in the 1920s but he established the style for the instrument as surely as Coleman Hawkins did for the saxophone. He was a key figure on the New York session scene of the era, and appears on many dance-band records alongside Beiderbecke, Trumbauer and the Dorseys; but his most important association was with Eddie Lang, and although their partnership was curtailed by Lang's death in 1933 it was a pairing which has endured like few other jazz double-acts. The tracks they made together as a duo and as part of Venuti's Blue Four are collected on the two JSP CDs. Some of them – 'Wild Cat', 'Doin' Things' – are like spontaneous bursts of virtuosity, Venuti's reeling melody lines counterpointed by Lang's driving accompaniment and subtle variations of dynamic; others, especially the Blue Four tracks, feature oddball instruments – Trumbauer on bassoon on 'Running Ragged', Jimmy Dorsey on trumpet on 'My Honey's Lovin' Arms', Rollini on everything he plays on – to create a kind of jazz chamber music of improbable zip and bravado. There are touches of kitsch in the style, too, and the occasional indifferent vocal (even if the singer on one session was none other than Harold Arlen!), but Venuti's irascible swing makes sure that every record is an event. Flawlessly remastered, the two JSP discs honour the music, and present it in chronological order, leaving out only those sessions where Venuti headed up a bigger band called Venuti's New Yorkers (which are much more like conventional dance-band records). Robert Parker's compilation gets lower marks since it presents only a cross-section of various tracks featuring Venuti and Lang and the remastering isn't one of Parker's better efforts. The Yazoo disc is a splendid compilation and there are a few rare alternative takes – of 'Raggin' The Scale', 'Hey! Young Fella' and 'Jig-Saw Puzzle Blues' – included among the 14 tracks. Remastering leaves a lot of the surface hiss alone, but the music itself comes through very brightly. The Topaz disc is half in the 1920s and half out: useful to have some of the later Blue Six titles together, and the final session from 1934 is unusual, though some of the transfers from (British) Columbia 78s are occasionally noisy, and the overall standard is weaker than JSP's. The important 1931 session by the Venuti–Lang All Star Orchestra can be found on *BG And Big Tea In New York* (*MCA*), listed under Benny Goodman's name.

The *Pretty Trix* date is a pendant to the other records, a set of rare radio transcriptions featuring Venuti, Prima and Norvo with a 1934 band of largely unknown personnel. The playing is sometimes sloppy and the sound mixed, but Venuti's best moments have all the flash of old and it's a scarce glimpse of a musician who wouldn't have any limelight again for decades.

***(*) **Joe Venuti And Zoot Sims** Chiaroscuro CRD 142
    Venuti; Spiegel Wilcox (*tb*); Zoot Sims (*ts*); Dick Hyman, John Bunch (*p*); Bucky Pizzarelli (*g*); Milt Hinton (*b*); Cliff Leeman, Bobby Rosengarden (*d*). 5/74–5/75.
**** **Alone At The Palace** Chiaroscuro CRD 160
    Venuti; Dave McKenna (*p*). 4/77.
(*) **Joe In Chicago, 1978 Flying Fish FF-70077
    Venuti; John Young (*p*); Jethro Burns (*mand*); Mike Dowling, Steve Goodman, Curley Chalker, Eldon Shamblin (*g*); John Vany, Jim Tullio (*b*); Barrett Deems, Angie Vartas (*d*). 76–78.

Venuti's Indian summer in the studios is currently represented by only these three records. He remained in such good form to the end of his playing life that all his final records are worth hearing at least. The partnership with Zoot Sims has perhaps been a shade overrated, since Sims's bluff swing is no different from anything he plays on his own records and occasionally sounds a little glib, whereas Venuti's own playing – coloured by unexpected bursts of pizzicato, oddball kinds of bowing and resinous streams of melody that seem to go on for ever – is of a different order. *Sliding By* continued a profitable association with Dick Hyman, but it's *Alone At The Palace* which is Venuti's valedictory masterpiece. McKenna's granitic swing and authority are just the kind of bedrock the violinist loved, and whether they play 'At The Jazz Band Ball' or 'Runnin' Ragged' (almost exactly 50 years after Venuti's original version) or a slush-free 'Send In The Clowns', it's all superbly achieved. Four months later, Joe was gone. The CD reissue of the original LP includes four new tracks and three alternative takes, all equally welcome, and the sound is admirably clear. The Flying Fish session is missable, though: studio sound is amateurish, with Joe sounding like he's miles away, and the accompaniments are terribly lame. Even so, the old man jousts through two numbers from *My Fair Lady* with great finesse, and it's worth hearing for those alone.

Billy Verplanck (born 1930) TROMBONE, ARRANGER

*** **Jazz For Playgirls** Savoy SV-0209
    Verplanck; Clyde Reasinger, Joe Wilder, Phil Sunkel, Bernie Glow (*t*); Bill Harris (*tb*); Phil Woods (*as*); Seldon Powell (*ts*); Gene Allen, Sol Schlinger (*bs*); Eddie Costa (*p, vib*); George Duvivier, Wendell Marshall (*b*); Bobby Donaldson, Gus Johnson (*d*). 57.
(*) **Dancing Jazz Savoy SV-0235
    Bernie Glow, Joe Wilder, Donald Byrd (*t*); Frank Rehak (*tb*); Hal McKusick (*as, bcl*); Phil Woods (*as*); Bobby Jaspar (*ts, f*); Buzzy Brauner (*ts*); Gene Allen (*bs*); George Duvivier, Wendell Marshall (*b*); Bobby Donaldson (*d*). 57.

A strong cross-section of swing, bop and cool players on these two studio dates under the leadership of arranger Verplanck; but the results are no more than pleasant, and the aimless feel of the music says something about the Savoy label's slipshod attention to making a long-playing record something more than a collection of tracks. *Jazz For Playgirls* has some fine moments from the soloists, with Woods ripping through 'Whoo-Ee!' and reliable souls like Harris and Powell making light of their duties, and at least the charts assemble a proper head of steam. *Dancing Jazz* sounds too relaxed by half: it suits the urbane Wilder, but the tempos could use a kick and the performers trundle through it. Crisp and clean remastering.

Edward Vesala (born 1945) DRUMS, PERCUSSION, OTHER INSTRUMENTS

***(*) **Nan Madol** ECM 1077

Vesala; Kaj Backlund (*t*); Mircea Stan (*tb*); Charlie Mariano (*as, f, nagaswaram*); Juhani Aaltonen (*ts, ss, f*); Pentti Lahti (*ss, bcl*); Seppo Paakkunainen (*ss, f*); Sakari Kukko (*f*); Elisabeth Leistola (*hp*); Juhani Poutanen (*vn, alto vn*); Teppo Hauta-aho (*b*). 4/74.

**** **Lumi** ECM 1339

Vesala; Esko Heikkinen (*t, picc t*); Tom Bildo (*tb, tba*); Pentti Lahti (*as, bs, f*); Jorma Tapio (*as, cl, bcl, f*); Tapani Rinne (*ts, ss, cl, bcl*); Kari Heinilä (*ts, ss, f*); Raoul Björkenheim (*g*); Taito Vainio (*acc*); Iro Haarla (*hp*); Häkä (*b*). 6/86.

**** **Ode To The Death Of Jazz** ECM 1413

Vesala; Matti Riikonen (*t*); Jorma Tapio (*as, bcl, f*); Jouni Kannisto (*ts, f*); Pepa Päivinen (*ts, ss, bs, f, cl, bcl*); Tim Ferchen (*mar, bells*); Taito Vainio (*acc*); Iro Haarla (*p, hp, ky*); Jimi Sumen (*g*); Uffe Krokfors (*b*). 4 & 5/89.

**** **Invisible Storm** ECM 1461

Vesala; Matti Riikonen (*t*); Jorma Tapio (*as, bcl, f, bf, perc*); Jouni Kannisto (*ts, f*); Pepa Päivinen (*ts, ss, bs, f, af*); Jimi Sumen (*g*); Pekka Sarmanto (*b*); Marko Ylönen (*clo*); Mark Nauseef (*perc*).

*** **Nordic Gallery** ECM 1541

Vesala; Matti Riikonen (*t*); Tapani Rinne (*cl*); Jorma Tapio (*as, bcl, acl, bf*); Jouni Kannisto (*ts, f*); Pepa Päivinen (*ts, ss, bs, bsx, f, af, picc*); Iro Haarla (*hp, p, ky, acc, koto*); Petri Ikkela (*acc*); Jimi Sumen (*g*); Pekka Sarmanto (*b*); Kari Linsted (*clo*). 93–94.

Edward Vesala bears an uncanny physical resemblance to Richard Brautigan and weaves narratives and textures which, like the late American novelist's, are magically suffused, wry and tender by turns. Vesala is one of very few percussionists capable of sustaining interest as a solo performer (an early-1980s recording of extracts from the Finnish epic, *Kalevala*, rivets the attention despite the minimalist accompaniment and the fact that no English translation is provided); despite this, Vesala has been sparing of solo tracks on his records (the brief 'Call From The Sea' on *Nan Madol* is an exception), preferring to elevate his light, pulse-driven but often non-metrical drumming until it occupies the forefront of a piece. Recording with ECM has greatly enhanced his capacity in this regard. Vesala's groups have a unique sound, compounded of folk and popular references, but with a grasp of orchestration that, for all his commitment to themes and solos, is more typical of through-composed concert music. He favours extremes of timbre, alternating very dark themes exploiting sombre modes and tonalities with light, airy arrangements of flutes, soprano saxophones and harp; typically, though, he reverses the expressive polarity, investing light-toned pieces like 'The Wind' (on *Nan Madol*, re-recorded later) with a sinister quality, often reserving darker instrumentation for tongue-in-cheek compositions based on popular forms.

Vesala has produced one masterpiece. *Lumi* is one of the finest jazz albums of the 1980s. Even its cover, of a shrouded, Golem-like figure on an empty road under a threatening sky, suggests something of Vesala's distinctive combination of almost Gothic intensity and sheer playfulness. A re-recording of 'The Wind' shows how much he has advanced since 1974. It is spare, subtly voiced, less dependent on literal reference than its predecessor, but not a whit less evocative. 'Frozen Melody' is a superb exercise in static harmony; Vesala works variations on a descending repetition of four notes of the same pitch, gradually unpicking the rhythmic implications. 'Fingo', like 'A Glimmer Of Sepal' on *Ode To The Death Of Jazz*, is based on tango rhythms and illustrates Vesala's interest in extreme stylistic repetitions. This is evident on the later album, too, in 'Winds Of Sahara', which begins in spooky 'ethnic' mode, wobbles a bit, and then breaks into a camel-racing flag-waver of Maynard Ferguson proportions; 'Calypso Bulbosa' evokes similar incongruities.

Vesala works slowly and has not been a prolific recorder. Each of his records has been a superb balance of careful organization and arrangment and all-out freedom. Though not too much should be invested in chance resemblances and coincidences, it's interesting to note a parallel between Vesala's method on 'The Way Of . . .' (*Nan Madol*) and that of British drummer Tony Oxley on his classic, 1969 CBS album, *The Baptised Traveller*, notably the extraordinary 'Stone Garden', composed by Charlie Mariano, who appears on two tracks on Vesala's album. The descending sequences are, though, entirely characteristic of Vesala and owe no apparent debt to anyone else.

Lumi remains his most convincing marshalling of quite disparate elements, and the addition of Raoul Björkenheim's dog-howls and (on 'Camel Walk') percussive choke rhythms is probably enough to lift it a peg above the others. Vesala is not a regular tourer in the English-speaking countries and has concentrated most of his energies on the burgeoning music scene in Helsinki. He is, though, a major musical presence and deserves the widest recognition.

The opening four tracks of *Invisible Storm* represent the most powerfully dramatic work Vesala has yet to commit to record. It opens with an extraordinary recitation, 'Sheets And Shrouds', a cracked voice in an unfamiliar tongue (and Finnish has a quality that is both ancient and curiously Asian) before giving way to 'Murmuring Morning', a slow chorale highlit by Ylönen's cello, and then exploding in the thudding fury of 'Gordion's Flashes'. The fourth piece – and each is successively longer – also features a spoken vocal; 'Shadows On The Frontier' is in English but preserves the tranced quality of the opening. Though there is no explicit reason to connect them, they do seem to cohere in a way that later tracks do not. Of these, 'Somnamblues' is another of Vesala's brilliant generic parodies, and the closing 'Caccaroo Boohoo' is dryly witty. The longest single item, 'The Wedding Of All Essential Parts', and the title-track are less impressive – but only relative to Vesala's now absurdly high standard. His melodic inventiveness grows apace, concentrating on sinuously extended figures that evade conventional rhythmic resolution but underneath which there beats a powerful, even dramatic, pulse. *Lumi* remains the record of choice, but it's hard to put *Invisible Storm* lower than essential in terms of contemporary recording. Needless to say, the studio work and mastering are impeccable.

The most recent of the group is the only real disappointment. Newcomers may well still be entranced by the sheer unexpectedness of Vesala's sound-world in this series of still landscapes and wry portraits, but anyone who has followed his course over a few discs will surely find *Nordic Gallery* formulaic and repetitive, a reworking of elements rather than anything new.

Andrea Vicari PIANO, KEYBOARDS

*** **Suburban Gorillas** 33 Records 33JAZZ016
    Vicari; Simon Da Silva (*t*); Malcolm Earle Smith (*tb*); Martin Dunsdon (*ts, ss, f*); Leigh Etherington (*as, ss*); Mornington Lockett (*ts, perc*); Hilary Cameron (*ky, v*); Mark Ridout (*g*); Dorian Lockett (*b*); Simon Pearson (*d, perc*); Rony Barrak (*tabla*). 1/94.
***(*) **Lunar Spell** 33 Records 33JAZZ026
    Vicari; Mornington Lockett (*ts, ss*); Phil Robson (*g*); Dorian Lockett (*b*); Tristan Maillot (*d*). 2 & 3/95.

Born in America and raised in the United Kingdom, Vicari is a prodigally talented pianist and composer whose debut recording has enough poise and maturity to pass for the fruit of a decade rather than of just three or four years' professional music-making.

The large-scale debut reflects her ambition. It was put together to fulfil an Arts Council commission, the 'French Suite' which concludes the disc. Here Vicari allows her interest in classical harmonies and ethnic rhythms – largely Arabic, but with further hints of salsa and samba – to collide without embarrassment. The result is exhilarating on 'L'Orchestre Des Fous' and strangely moving on the more thoughtful 'Dance Verdange'.

The strength of the album lies almost entirely in the writing. Though there are impressive statements by Leigh Etherington on 'Southern Comfort', a Keith Jarrett-influenced country tune, from Malcolm Smith on 'Pegasus', and from Mornington Lockett throughout, it is the youthful, fresh-voiced ensembles that mainly catch the ear.

Opportunities for Suburban Gorillas to play live have been predictably rare, but the quintet on *Lunar Spell* has a seasoned, well-travelled feel. This record is a big step forward in performance terms. Vicari's muscular chords, almost obsessively repeated in the opening 'You're Reported', set up a powerful blowing groove for her band. Robson provides a lot of the harmonic colour, allowing her to thump away in the left hand and to spin long, attractive solo lines up in the treble. The long title-piece is hugely impressive, as are the generous contours of the Latin '¡Vay a Tomar!' Both Locketts are in sharp form, and the only question mark about Maillot's performance relates to his place in a slightly off-balance studio mix. With its monochrome cover and straight look from Ms Vicari, this is a plain-spoken declaration of independence and of intent.

Vienna Art Orchestra & Choir GROUP

***(*) **Concerto Piccolo** hat Art 6038
    Matthias Rüegg (*comp, arr*); Karl Fian (*t*); Herbert Joos (*t, flhn, double t, bhn, alphorn*); Christian Radovan (*tb*); Billy Fuchs (*tba*); Harry Sokal (*f, ts, ss*); Wolfgang Puschnig (*picc, f, as*); Roman Schwaller (*ts*); Stefan Bauer (*vib*); Uli Scherer (*p, ky*); Jürgen Wuchner (*b*); Joris Dudli (*d*); Wolfgang Reisinger (*perc*); Lauren Newton (*v*). 10/80.
*** **Suite For The Green Eighties** hat Art 6054
    As for *Concerto Piccolo*, except Woody Schabata (*vib*) replaces Bauer, Ingo Morgana (*ts*) replaces Schwaller; add Janusz Stefanski (*d, perc*). 6 & 10/81.

**** From No Time To Rag Time hat Art 6073
        Matthias Rüegg (*cond*); Karl Fian (*t*); Herbert Joos (*flhn, double t, alphorn*); Christian Radovan
        (*tb*); John Sass (*tba*); Harry Sokal (*ts, ss, f*); Roman Schwaller (*ts, cl*); Wolfgang Puschnig (*as,*
        bcl, f, picc); Uli Scherer (*p, melodica*); Woody Schabata (*mar, vib*); Jürgen Wuchner (*b*);
        Wolfgang Reisinger, Janusz Stefanski (*d, perc*); Lauren Newton (*v*). 10/82.
  **** The Minimalism Of Erik Satie hat Art 6024
        Matthias Rüegg (*p, arr*); Karl Fian, Hannes Kottek (*t, flhn*); Herbert Joos (*t, flhn, bhn, alphorn*);
        Christian Radovan (*tb*); John Sass (*tba*); Co Strieff (*as, f*); Harry Sokal (*ts, ss, f*); Roman
        Schwaller (*ts*); Woody Schabata (*vib*); Uli Scherer (*ky, perc*); Heiri Kaenzig (*b*); Wolfgang
        Reisinger (*d*); Ima (*tamboura*); Lauren Newton (*v*). 9/83 & 3/84.
***(*) A Notion In Perpetual Motion hat Art 6096
        As for *Minimalism*, except add Wolfgang Puschnig (*as, sno, f, picc*); Joris Dudli (*d, perc*). 5/85.
**** Nightride Of A Lonely Saxophoneplayer Moers 02054/5 2CD
        As for *Minimalism*, except omit Co Strieff; add Erich Dorfinger (*sound effects*); Andy Manndorff
        (*g*); Tom Nicholas (*perc*). 10/85.
*** Two Little Animals Moers 02066
        As for *Minimalism*, except omit Co Strieff; add Andy Manndorff (*g*). 10/87.
***(*) Inside Out Moers 02062/3
        As above. 11/87.
***(*) Blues For Brahms Amadeo 839105 2CD
        As for *Minimalism*, except omit Puschnig, Strieff, Schabata, Ima. 11/88.
***(*) Innocence Of Clichés Amadeo 841646 2CD
        As for *Blues For Brahms*, except add Erich Dorfinger (*sound effects*). 9/89.

Erik Satie thought that the beauty of jazz lay in how the world ignored its scream of sorrow. One of his abiding concerns was the degree of attention that was or could be directed towards music; it is not, after all, seriously possible to listen to all of his *Vexations*, 840 'very slow' repetitions of a single theme, occupying 28 hours of playing time. Whereas patrons of concert music (Satie's parodic targets) are expected to concentrate all their attention on it, jazz has had to grow up in an environment of profound inattention. With the Vienna Art Orchestra the Swiss composer and pianist, Matthias Rüegg, has attempted to square the formal demands of concert music with the freedoms of the century's most significant *musique pauvre*.

Like Willem Breuker, H. K. Gruber and the British composer, Mike Westbrook, Rüegg takes a broadly theatrical approach, drawing parallels between jazz soloing and Satie's 'face-pulling' exercises in incidental music (this is made explicit on the marvellous *Minimalism* record, still perhaps the best *entrée* into the VAO's methodology). Rüegg consistently makes reference to classic jazz, using tuba to mimic the brass bass of the New Orleans bands, rejecting strings in favour of unruly brasses and reeds. Though he also 'covers' standards in a relatively conventional way ('Cry Me A River' on *Inside Out*, 'In A Sentimental Mood' on *Innocence Of Clichés*, 'Body And Soul' on *Blues For Brahms*), Rüegg generally prefers to create large-scale pastiches of jazz and pre-jazz styles (like 'Ragtime' on *Nightride Of A Lonely Saxophoneplayer*) or curious thematic hippogriffs ('You Are The Ghost Of A Romance In June' on *Two Little Animals*, 'What Is This Thing Called Free Jazz' on *Blues For Brahms*) whose titles clearly reflect his interest in Mingus's compositional strategies. ('Jelly Roll But Mingus Rolls Better' on *Concerto Piccolo* is an explicit homage.) This intertextual approach is probably best sampled on the recently reissued *From No Time To Rag Time*, which was the VAO's finest hour until *Minimalism* came along to topple it. On the 1982 disc, Rüegg leads the group through an assortment of oblique variations on compositions by Scott Joplin, Ornette Coleman, Anthony Braxton, Roswell Rudd and the Austrian saxophonist, Hans Koller. It's a magnificent, bravura display of invention, and the most insistent parallel has to be John Zorn's reworkings of Morricone and Ornette.

Rüegg is, like Satie, deeply motivated by a sympathy for the dispossessed, and it is important not to miss the emotional underpinning of music that, unheard, might seem forbidding and excessively formal. His titles are full of references to imprisonment and oppression, characteristically expressed in puns like 'Bars & Stripes' (*Blues For Brahms*), and his attraction to Satie's 'Gnossiennes' is not so much for their formal mystery as for the fact that they express the oppression of a people (a Greek scale is used throughout) whose culture has been frozen in stone and appropriated as required, just as Western classical music has ossified, calling on jazz only where and as it suits a formal or social purpose.

The Minimalism Of Erik Satie is one of the most important recordings of recent years and, though there are excellent things on all the VAO's recordings to date, this is the one that commands attention. Most of the tracks briefly articulate Satie's original theme before proceeding to work variations on it. The orchestral voicings are bright and spare, with most of the space devoted to solo material. 'Gnossienne No. 1' has a superb sopranino solo by Puschnig that immediately recalls Lindsay Cooper's work with Mike Westbrook (*q.v.*) on his Rossini project, a vivid, snake-charming improvisation that sways up out of Satie's theme. Most remarkable of all are the three essays on 'Vexations'. These originally occupied sides 3 and 4 of the original LP set and are unusual in being for permutations of only three musicians: singer Lauren Newton in a Berberian-derived vocalise, Roman Schwaller on tenor saxophone, Wolfgang Puschnig on bass clarinet, each duetting with vibraharpist, Woody Schabata, who maintains a steady chordal pulse underneath. The final 'Vexations 2105' with Puschnig is a masterful redefinition of jazz as a sorrow song. Quite wonderful.

*** **Highlights, 1977–1990** Amadeo 513 325

As for *Blues For Brahms*, except add Joseph Bowie, Gabriele Rosenberg (*tb*); Rudi Berger (*vn*); Klaus Dickbauer, Florian Bramböck (*reeds*); Thomas Alkier (*d*). 5 & 9/89, 11/90.

By the turn of the 1990s, collecting VAO records was becoming rather an expensive hobby. *Highlights* is one that can safely be passed over. A live concert, with a couple of tracks – from *Innocence Of Clichés* and the unavailable *Chapter II* – tacked on, it covers ground that will be pretty familiar to the initiated. 'Two Little Animals', 'Blue Loop Play', 'K Wie Ikeda' and 'A Liberate Proposal' all come across strongly, but there's not much that is really arresting. Anyone looking for a quick introduction to Rüegg's world of musical fantasy should go directly to *No Time* and *Minimalism* without delay.

**** **The Original Charts** Verve 551 928

Rüegg; Thorsten Benkenstein, Matthieu Michel, Bumi Fian (*t*); Herbert Joos (*flhn*); Christian Radovan, Danilo Terenzi (*tb*); Charly Wagner (*btb*); Claudio Pontiggia (*frhn*); Harry Sokal, Klaus Dickbauer, Florian Bramböck, Andy Scherrer, Herwig Gradischnig (*reeds*); Frank Tortiller (*vib*); Uli Scherer (*p*); Heiri Kanzig (*b*); Thomas Alkier (*d*); Corin Cuschellas (*v*). 10/93.

Perfectly logical territory for Rüegg and the VAO, the masterworks of Duke Ellington and Charles Mingus, but whereas one might have expected an idiosyncratic, almost perverse spin on the proceedings, the leader has this time gone back to the original charts – or subsequent arrangements transcribed from discs – and built his concert programme from there.

Recorded live at the Five Spot in New York City, this is arguably the best representation of how rigorously but tolerantly Rüegg controls his players. The performances are bright, very together and almost always at the service of the music. Whatever order was originally followed, there is a clear logic to the progression here, from greater freedom and uncertainty (kicking off with Mingus, 'Hobo Ho', 'The Shoes of the Fisherman's Wife' and 'Don't Be Afraid, The Clown's Afraid, Too') and moving towards greater order with the Ellington material. Towards the end there are two versions of 'Anitra's Dance', Duke's version of a piece by Grieg, arranged by Strayhorn and then transcribed by Dave Berger. As Rüegg says, 'That sounds more post-modern than it really is'; though this record clearly falls into a rich new vein of tradition-bending, it is more respectfully traditional than most, more straightforwardly directed to the masters.

**** **European Songbook** Verve 527 672

Similar to above, except add Thomas Biber (*frhn*); Joris Dudli (*d*). 9/92–1/93.

This sounds exactly as post-modern as it is, and we're being gently post-modern in putting it out of chronological sequence. Whether these intriguing sessions were withheld, hesitated over, or simply not considered ready, they were released only in 1995. Essentially, they consist of arrangements of music by Verdi, Wagner and Schubert, with material by Rüegg interposed in the first pair and a rather more diffident and respectful stance on the greatest songwriter ever. The *Winterreise* arrangements are glorious; anyone steeped in this music, however hidebound and 'correct' in attitude, will be moved and, though they form part three of the record, it is as well to absorb them first before listening to the whole.

Quite clearly Wagner's music in *Tristan und Isolde* affected everything that followed. One hears intimations of atonality and its logical progression all the way through the opera, and Rüegg's 'additions' seem geared to making that lineage explicit. The Verdi material is more straightforward, a curtain-raiser on a wonderful programme. Most of it was written for George Tabori's production, *Lovers and Lunatics*, and it does seem to sit a little apart from the rest.

Our enthusiasm for the VAO should by now be obvious. It would be a pity if anyone were inclined to skip this one because of its non-jazz provenance. It's absolutely consistent with the rest of their output.

**** **From No Art To Mo(z)-Art** Moers 02002

Matthias Rüegg (*leader*); Kurt Azesberger, Maria Bayer, Renate Bochdansky, Patricia Caya, Peter Jelosits, Lis Malina, Sharon Natalie, Lauren Newton, Christof Prinz, Karen Reisner (*v*); accompanied by George Lewis, Christian Radovan (*tb*); Wolfgang Puschnig (*reeds*). 5/83.

**** **Five Old Songs** Moers 02036

As above, but accompanied by Herbert Joos (*flhn, alphorn*); George Lewis, Christian Radovan (*tb*); Wolfgang Puschnig (*reeds*); Woody Schabata (*xy, dulcimer*). 5/84.

***(*) **Swiss Swing** Moers 02060

Karl Fian (*t*); Woody Schabata (*vib*); Hans Hassler (*acc*); Uli Scherer (*ky*); Heiri Kaenzig (*b*); Wolfgang Reisinger (*d*); Elfi Aichinger, Sarah Barrett, Maria Bayer, Renate Bochdansky, Lauren Newton (*v*). 3/86.

The Vienna Art Choir was formed in 1983, broadly in accordance with the same principles as the VAO. The original *From No Art To Mo(z)-Art* is a huge syllabic fantasy which calls on a wide range of vocal technique, from the free-form vocalise Newton brought to 'Vexations' to more conventional, modern choral devices. *Five Old Songs*, like the 'Ländler für funf Stimme' on *Swiss Swing* (which is more strictly a VAO record, but may be usefully compared with the Choir's work) are more formal in conception. Accompaniments are basic but highly imaginative, and the overall impact is very powerful. Also strongly recommended.

***(*) **Plays For Jean Cocteau** Verve 529290-2
    Similar to above. 96.
Rüegg's programme, dedicated to Jean Cocteau, was originally written for the Banlieues Bleues Festival in Paris under the title *La Belle et la Bête* and was conceived as a parallel text to the director's visionary film. Corin Curschellas's voice is the key element, originally intended to be shadowed by actor Rremi Brandner, who is not heard on the CD. The music is cool, dark-toned and ambiguous.

Frank Vignola GUITAR, BANJO

*** **Appel Direct** Concord CCD 4576
    Vignola; John Goldsby (*b*); Joseph Ascione (*d, perc*). 4/93.
***(*) **Let It Happen** Concord CCD 4625
    As above, except add Ken Peplowski (*cl*); Arnie Lawrence (*as, ss*); Dave Grisman (*mand*). 4/94.
Frank is one of the latest in Concord's stable of smoothly accomplished guitar players. We'll have to take their word for it that these two sessions were recorded a year apart. The second of the pair might almost have been a guest walk-up to the first session, so seamlessly do they fit together. The guests certainly lift things. Peplowski's contribution to 'Fleche D'Or' is typically graceful, and the addition of a second stringed instrument, Grisman's mandolin, on four Latin numbers brings a further range of sounds to the date. We were less persuaded by Lawrence, except that he sits very comfortably with Vignola's unflustered armchair sound.

Eddie 'Cleanhead' Vinson (1917–88) ALTO SAXOPHONE, VOCALS

**** **Cleanhead & Cannonball** Landmark 1309
    Vinson; Julian 'Cannonball' Adderley (*as*); Nat Adderley (*c*); Joe Zawinul (*p*); Sam Jones (*b*);
    Louis Hayes (*d*). 9/61, 2/62.
*** **Kidney Stew** Black & Blue 233021
    Vinson; Al Grey (*tb*); Eddie 'Lockjaw' Davis, Hal Singer (*ts*); T-Bone Walker (*g*); Jay McShann
    (*p*); Wild Bill Davis, Bill Doggett (*org*); Floyd Smith (*g*); Milt Hinton, Roland Lobligeois (*b*);
    Paul Gunther, J. C. Heard (*d*). 3/69, 7/72.
*** **Jamming The Blues** Black Lion BLCD 760188
    Vinson; Hal Singer (*ts*); Peter Wingfield (*p*); Joe Wright (*g*); Jerome Rinson (*b*); Peter Van
    Hooke (*d*). 7/74.
*** **I Want A Little Girl** Pablo 2310866
    Vinson; Martin Banks (*t*); Rashied Jamal Ali (*ts*); Cal Green (*g*); Art Hillery (*p, org*); John
    Heard (*b*); Roy McCurdy (*d*). 2/81.
*** **Eddie Cleanhead Vinson & Roomful Of Blues** Muse MCD 5382
    Vinson; Bob Enos (*t*); Porky Cohen (*tb*); Rich Lataille (*as*); Greg Piccolo (*ts*); Doug James (*bs*);
    Ronnie Earl Horvath (*g*); Al Copley (*p*); Jimmy Wimpfheimer (*b*); John Rossi (*d*). 1/82.
A hugely entertaining singer/saxophonist, Vinson became a festival favourite in the 1970s, guesting with anyone who thought they could take his pace, playing Parker-tinged R&B with disconcerting self-possession. Some claim to find a Louis Jordan influence in Vinson's work, but this may have more to do with his performing personality than with any stylistic borrowing. 'Kidney Stew' was a major hit and, later, something of a millstone; it appears on both the Black & Blue, which brings together some interesting but unexceptional material, and the very fine Landmark, on which there's a nice balance of instrumental numbers to offset the vocals; the CD has a bonus performance of 'Vinsonology', one of the more obvious of his takes on Parker's blues style. The Montreux Festival set on *Jamming The Blues* includes a terrific 'Now's The Time' and some smoothly Parkerish solos on themes of his own and Ellington's 'C Jam Blues'.

The Pablo and *Roomful Of Blues* feature Vinson the festival personality with slightly heavy-fisted bands. *I Want A Little Girl* runs through a bag of blues numbers and contains a surprising 'Straight, No

Chaser' and an excellent version of Pettiford's 'Blues In The Closet'. Nothing quite so compelling on the Muse, which will probably appeal more to straight blues fans.

D. M. Visotzky ALTO SAXOPHONE

*** **Uncovered Memories** Black Moon 8901
    Visotzky; Ralph Kundig (*syn*); Jean-Bruno Meier (*d*). 89.
(*) **One-Eyed Cat Plainisphare 1267-37
    Visotzky; François Volpe (*vib, mar, perc, ky*). 89.
(*) **Straight Line Plainisphare 1267-56
    As above, except add Thierry Carpenter (*b*), François Bauer (*d*). 4–7/90.
*** **Instant Collusion** 4 Ears CD 307
    Visotzky; David Gattiker (*clo*); Gunter Muller (*d, elec*). 2/91.
** **The Last Leaf** 4 Ears CD 306
    Visotzky; Jacques Widmer (*d*). 11/91.

Originally from Montreal but based in Geneva, Visotzky plays free-association alto, which he tempers with a broken kind of romanticism and a taste for singing saxophone timbre. *Uncovered Memories* evokes recall of swing-band sax since Visotzky chooses to employ multiple alto overdubs on most of the tracks – unusually, he sticks to the alto alone for this as in all of his more spontaneous playing. Kundig and Meier make cameo appearances. A rather rare and refreshing counterpoint to other recent all-sax records. There is some overdubbing on *One-Eyed Cat*, too, since Visotzky and Volpe like variety, though the flat-footed funk of 'Stone Head' is ineffective. Better the pleasing melodic tang of the alto–vibes interplay on the title-track. The subsequent quartet date is marred by Bauer's inappropriate drums, but Visoztky and Volpe again shine when in conversation with each other.

The two 4 Ears discs have similarly mixed results. Two long-form duets with Widmer on *The Last Leaf* go nowhere special, the music rising and falling in predictable waves and the drummer's lack of finesse blunting whatever impact was intended. *Instant Collusion* works out much better – there's a humorous empathy at work here, with Gattiker's amplified cello tugging at the sleeves of the other two and Visotzky pulling out some of his best improvising, though studio sound isn't what it could be. Some of the titles – 'Diary Of A Crazy Man Who Drives Camels Through His Eyes' – are a bit much.

Miroslav Vitous (born 1947) DOUBLE BASS

***(*) **First Meeting** ECM 1145
    Vitous; John Surman (*ss, bcl*); Kenny Kirkland (*p*); Jon Christensen (*d*). 5/79.
**** **Journey's End** ECM 1242
    As above, except add (*bs*) to Surman; omit Kirkland; add John Taylor (*p*). 7/82.
***(*) **Emergence** ECM 1312
    Vitous solo. 9/85.

After leaving Weather Report in 1973, having recorded three classic albums (he appears only briefly on *Mysterious Traveller*, the group's fourth release), Vitous experimented with various 'lead' and 'piccolo' basses, but doesn't seem to have acquired the confidence in their use that made Stanley Clarke and a later Weather Report member, Jaco Pastorius, such charismatic figures (compare Vitous's and Pastorius's work with guitarist Bireli Lagrene, and that becomes clear). It took Vitous some time to re-establish the musical identity stamped all over his marvellous pre-Weather Report solo debut, *Infinite Search* (later re-released on Atlantic as *Mountain In The Clouds*), and there's an awkwardness to the piano and synthesizer shelters he digs for himself on *Miroslav* (currently unavailable). The ECM is far more accomplished and begins to reintegrate the classical and folk-impressionistic elements on the earlier record (tracks such as 'Concerto In E Minor' and the Zawinul-influenced 'Pictures Of Moravia') into a much more coherent performance.

No problems with the recording-quality on *Journey's End* – the sound is rich and warm. That's also true of *First Meeting*, except that Kirkland's approach doesn't seem altogether appropriate for tunes like 'Silver Lake' and 'Beautiful Place To', too obviously jazz-based and funky and lacking Taylor's floating lyricism. Surman still wasn't playing any baritone when the first record was made, and its deep rich sound is much missed. *Emergence* is both a step forward and a summation. 'Morning Lake Forever' relates back to a composition on the first Weather Report record, and there's a new solo version of 'When Face Gets Pale' from *Miroslav Vitous Group*, which still hasn't appeared on CD. It begins with an 'Epilogue', which suggests a degree of self-reassessment, and though the 'Atlantis Suite' is rather too floating in conception (like the pretentiously titled 'Concerto in Three Parts' on *First Meeting*) there is a new solidity of purpose to his playing. Originally influenced by Scott LaFaro's remarkable performances with the Bill Evans Trio, Vitous has returned to something close to those singing lines. Though *Emergence* is a triumph, Vitous's best work still has to be sought out on the albums of other leaders, notably Chick Corea and Jack DeJohnette. Vitous also features prominently on two recent discs featuring Jan Garbarek: the duo *Atmos*, and *Star*, widely hailed as the saxophonist's 'return to jazz'. Both are listed under Garbarek's name.

Urs Voerkel PIANO

***(*) **Weiss** Unit 4043
        Voerkel; Fredi Luscher (*p*). 91.
Voerkel is a charter member of the Swiss avant-garde, and this disc (there are two much earlier dates for FMP which are worth searching for) finds him taking unexpected routes to an impressive result. *Weiss* sets Voerkel in tandem with fellow pianist Luscher in a sequence of small, introspective, improbably delicate improvisations. With some of the pieces amounting to little more than a couple of gestures, the first impression is of a fragmented, perhaps dissolute set: but there is a memorable concentration about their interplay, using free-piano string-plucks and other techniques to the most sparing of ends, and the sense of surprise that pulls some of the pieces up short is evidence of real, unaffected improvisation.

Larry Vuckovich PIANO

*** **Tres Palabras** Concorc CCD 4416
        Vuckovich; Tom Harrell (*t, flhn*); Larry Grenadier (*b*); Eddie Marshall (*d*); Pete Escovedo
        (*perc*). 8/89.
We tend to operate on the basis that if Tom Harrell is on a record, it's worth listening to. No reason to abandon the principle here, except that it might mislead readers into thinking that Vuckovich *isn't* worth listening to. Nothing could be further from the truth. He resembles Hampton Hawes in many respects, a tensely lyrical solo style welded on to absolutely certain accompanying skills. Even 'Cast Your Fate To The Wind' acquires a degree of grandeur, and the Latin tracks manage to skirt banality without falling foul of it. With or without Harrell (who is, of course, magnificent), worth hearing.

Petras Vysniauskias SOPRANO SAXOPHONE, ALTO SAXOPHONE, BASS CLARINET, FLUTE

*** **Viennese Concert** Leo CDLR 172
        Vysniauskias; Vyacheslav Ganelin, Kestutis Lusas (*p, syn*); Mika Markovich (*d*); Gediminas
        Laurinavicius (*perc*). 6/89.
(*) **Lithuania ITM 1449
        Vysniauskias; Arkadij Gotesman (*d, perc*). 6/90.
Vysniauskias is a gifted young Lithuanian who demonstrates extraordinary command of all the saxophones, clarinets and flute. Like the Ganelin Trio, he favours what has been called a 'mixed composition technique', combining free improvisation with predetermined structures. In performance, he has a disconcerting habit of concentrating on the upper registers of the low-pitched instruments, and the lower register of his soprano saxophone and flute. This creates a very distinctive timbre that bears an unmistakable echo of folk music, and Vysniauskias has made a significant use of Lithuanian forms in his compositions and performances.

   Both of his available recordings suffer from considerable *longueurs* where the music doesn't seem to be going anywhere. The opening item of the *Viennese Concert* is a rather wistful soprano saxophone solo called 'Plunge' that has an inconsequential, practice-tape quality. The long – and presumably partly scored – 'Salto Mortale Op. 8' is a collage of free tonal, abstract and quasi-bop passages, all played with considerable restraint. Kestutis Lusas, who can also be heard in extended improvisation with the saxophonist on Leo's enormous eight-CD *Document* (Leo 801/8), is a much more effective collaborator than Ganelin, who has become increasingly mannered and self-conscious in settings other than those which he completely dominates. Lusas's solemn, hymnic synthesizer accompaniment to the saxophonist's distracted wailing on 'Salto Mortale' gives the piece some shape and restores interest in an album that really could have done with an early change of pace and intensity.

   The duos with Gotesman are more obviously folkish. The opening 'Sonet' is dedicated to Lithuania and includes apparent references to pre-war anthems and popular songs. Like Markovich, Gotesman is quite prepared to make use of silence and of acoustically minimal gestures, tiny fragments of sound that barely register on the hearer. Vysniauskias plays bass clarinet and flute in addition to his saxophone, following his normal practice of concentrating on extremes of pitch. Ironically, this is something he avoids on the *Viennese Concert*, where his soprano playing is strikingly reminiscent of the rather dry tonality one associates with Steve Lacy.

Interesting music, but perhaps a little too rarefied for most tastes.

Chad Wackerman DRUMS

*** **Forty Reasons** CMP CD 48
   Wackerman; Allan Holdsworth (*g*); Jim Cox (*p, org, ky*); Jimmy Johnson (*b*). 6/91.
The splendidly monikered Wackerman was anchor man in one of the late Frank Zappa's most adventurous latter-day groups. He plays with a strong rock feel but favours out-of-tempo passages and unusual sonorities that vary the diet interestingly. He also writes well.

On this debut solo venture, he's ably assisted by Johnson and by fusion wizard Holdsworth, who returns the favour of mid-'80s sessions like *Atavachron* and *Sand*. Indeed, blindfold testees may be convinced that this *is* a Holdsworth session, with Gary Husband spanking away at the kit. What gives it away as Wackerman's gig is the very eccentricity of the rhythm, which often seems to have gone completely out of control, sometimes catching up with itself only two bars ahead. The title-piece and the opening 'Holiday Insane' are worth sampling by the sceptical, but the strongest charts are for 'House On Fire' and the offbeat 'Waltzing On Jupiter', the latter betraying a well-assimilated Zappa influence.

Steve Waddell TROMBONE, VOCAL

*** **Egyptian Ella** Stomp Off CD 1230
   Waddell; Bob Pattie (*c*); Dafydd Wisner-Ellix (*cl, ss, perc, v*); Doug Rawson (*p*); John Brown
   (*bj*); Fred Clark (*tba*). 12/90–2/91.
Steve Waddell's Creole Bells come from Melbourne, Australia, and this CD offers an amiable continuation of the kind of down-under trad that Graeme Bell initiated some 40 years earlier. The absence of a drummer frees the group from the tyranny of the trad beat to some degree, although Fred Clark's gruff bass-lines are suitably ponderous. Waddell's noisy trombone and the scratchily hot solos by Pattie give the group its character, and the material is inventively chosen; on the minus side, the vocals are close to hopeless. There is nearly 70 minutes' music, and plenty of fun.

Collin Walcott (1945–84) TABLAS, SITAR, PERCUSSION INSTRUMENTS, VOICE

**** **Cloud Dance** ECM 1062
   Walcott; John Abercrombie (*g*); Dave Holland (*b*); Jack DeJohnette (*d*). 3/75.
***(*) **Grazing Dreams** ECM 1096
   Walcott; Don Cherry (*t, f, doussn'gouni*); John Abercrombie (*g, electric mand*); Palle Danielsson
   (*b*); Dom Um Romao (*perc*). 2/77.
*** **Dawn Dance** ECM 1198
   Walcott; Steve Eliovson (*g*). 1/81.
***(*) **Works** ECM 837276
   Walcott; Don Cherry (*t, f, doussn'gouni*); John Abercrombie (*g*); Palle Danielsson, Dave
   Holland, Glen Moore (*b*); Dom Um Romao (*perc*); Nana Vasconcelos (*berimbau, perc*). 75–84.
Walcott's sudden death in a road accident in East Germany robbed contemporary music of a remarkable player who, more than any other individual of his generation (except, perhaps, his friend and colleague, Don Cherry, with whom he formed the group Codona (*q.v.*)), was possessed of a genuinely global understanding. It's significant that the classically trained Walcott, who also studied tabla under Alla Rakha and sitar under Ravi Shankar, should have spent some professional time with clarinettist Tony Scott, one of the first American musicians to understand and explore the trade-off between Eastern and Western musics. What is often forgotten about Walcott is that, for all his occasionally ethereal effects, he is capable of a thumpingly compelling beat on tablas and robust bass-lines on the normally 'atmospheric' sitar. Like most musicians of his generation, Walcott was much influenced by the John Coltrane quartet. However, few have so thoroughly explored the implications of Coltrane's masterful rhythm section. Walcott was instrumental in inviting drummer Elvin Jones to collaborate on a (long-deleted) recording by Oregon, a venture which emphasized and reinforced the group's solid rhythmic foundation.

ECM's 'Works' series is only occasionally recommendable. Though it's obviously preferable to encounter Walcott's albums in their carefully modulated entirety, the posthumous sampler is a fair and honest representation of his solo work, the three Codona albums, and a late track with Oregon, recorded only a month before his death. Though *Grazing Dreams* has much to recommend it, *Cloud Dance* has a freshness and originality that sustain its appeal. 'Prancing', for just tablas and double bass, is one of the most exciting performances in the ECM catalogue and convincing evidence of Walcott's desire to extend the idiom of the Garrison/Jones rhythm section. Of the other duos, 'Padma', for sitar and guitar, works less well; but the album as a whole can quite reasonably be heard as a suite of related pieces that dance towards their thematic source in the closing title-piece. The quartet format on *Grazing Dreams* inevitably anticipates Walcott's and Cherry's work with Codona, and the long 'Song Of The Morrow' is a perfect encapsulation of the group's idiom. (All the tracks cited, with the exception of 'Cloud Dance', are included on *Works*.)

Walcott's duo record with guitarist Eliovson is undeservedly little known (the only sample on *Works* is a Walcott solo) and is well worth investigating.

Mal Waldron (born 1926) PIANO

***(*) **Update** Soul Note SN 1130

    Waldron (*p* solo). 3/86.

An immensely gifted and prolific player whose professional roots are in the raw soul-jazz of Big Nick Nicholas and Ike Quebec, Waldron typically builds up solos from relatively simple ideas (his classic, much-covered 'Soul Eyes' could hardly be less elaborate), paying great attention to colour and shading, and to space. He favours block chords rather than rapid single-note runs, a style which has lent itself equally to large ensembles and smaller blowing groups (he worked with Mingus and Coltrane in the mid-1950s and early 1960s), sensitive accompaniment (he spent more than two years with Billie Holiday), and free playing.

Though it's clear that Waldron's main influences are Bud Powell and Thelonious Monk, he has developed independently and sounds quite unlike either. Until relatively recently he has not been a prolific solo performer, and this record is by no means his best music. But it does allow closer inspection of his compositional and improvising style and it helps establish the brand identity of one of the labels which have consistently supported his work, Enja giving him a darker and more lugubrious sound, Soul Note a sunnier, clearer focus. Unfortunately, the Enja vinyl catalogue has taken a pasting and, while it may be possible to find vinyl copies like *Mingus Lives*, recorded one week after the great bassist's death, *Black Glory*, *A Touch Of The Blues*, *Hard Talk*, *One-Upmanship* and *What It Is* (all of which are reviewed in the first edition of the *Guide*), there is as yet no sign of them on compact disc.

Update is unusual in including a standard (in addition to 'Night In Tunisia', there is a very individual gloss on a Frank Loesser tune); Waldron has generally preferred to spin his own material out of dark, minor intervals and from an area in the centre of the keyboard, using extremes of pitch only for dramatic contrast and colour effects. *Update* also further adjusts Waldron's polite reserve *vis-à-vis* free playing, which he explored with the 1969 *Free At Last* trio, below. Taken together, 'Free For C. T.' and 'Variations On A Theme By Cecil Taylor' firmly underscore Waldron's rugged individualism and refusal to be colonized by what has become the most invasive of contemporary piano styles. The variations are subtly rhythmic and beautifully proportioned. This is an important album in Waldron's career, coming at a time when his group performances were also at a peak. It merits the closest attention.

*** **Mal – 1** Original Jazz Classics OJC 611

    Waldron; Idrees Sulieman (*t*); Gigi Gryce (*as*); Julian Euell (*b*); Arthur Edgehill (*d*). 11/56.

*** **Mal – 2** Original Jazz Classics OJC 671

    Waldron; Bill Hardman (*t*); Jackie McLean, Sahib Shihab (*as*); John Coltrane (*ts*); Julian Euell (*b*); Arthur Taylor, Ed Thigpen (*d*). 4 & 5/57.

*** **Mal – 3: Sounds** Original Jazz Classics OJC 1814

    Waldron; Art Farmer (*t*); Eric Dixon (*ts*); Calo Scott (*clo*); Julian Euell (*b*); Elvin Jones (*d*). 58.

***(*) **Mal – 4** Original Jazz Classics OJC 1856

    Waldron; Addison Farmer (*b*); Kenny Dennis (*d*). 9/58.

**** **Impressions** Original Jazz Classics OJC 132

    Waldron; Addison Farmer (*b*); Albert 'Tootie' Heath (*d*). 59.

*** **Left Alone** Bethlehem BET 6024-2

    Waldron; Jackie McLean (*as*); Julian Euell (*b*); Al Dreares (*d*). 2/59.

Despite Sulieman's and Gryce's bursting expressiveness, the first OJC is a low-key selection from Waldron's Prestige period, which saw the pianist concentrating on sophisticated harmonic patterns and cross-rhythms. The sound – as they used to say about serving girls – is no better than it ought to be, but, given the anonymity of the rhythm section, not much is lost. A fine 'Yesterdays' picks things up a bit at the end. All the same material can also be found on a high-gloss Coltrane on Prestige set (16 CDs for Gold Card types) and, if anything, sounds rather sharper there.

The later tracks with Coltrane and McLean are inevitably of greatest interest. Waldron made substantial strides as a composer towards the end of the 1950s and that's reflected in his solo construction, too. In 1957, Coltrane had finally decided to rid himself of a deeply rooted drug and alcohol dependency. It isn't reading too much into basically conventional performances to suggest that his solos have a new maturity, coupled with an emotional vulnerability, which McLean seems to comprehend better than the rather single-minded Shihab, but round which Waldron steals with unfailing tact and supportive ease. No classic tracks, though 'Don't Explain' (with McLean) and 'The Way You Look Tonight' (with Shihab) are a cut above the rest.

Mal – 3 already shows signs of the tremendous stresses and tensions that make *Impressions* such a darkly wonderful record; there is even a track at the beginning of the 1958 disc called 'Tension', as if to signal what's coming. There is something extremely comfortable about listening to Waldron at this period. The echos of Bud Powell are unmistakable and faintly sinister, given the breakdown in Waldron's health just a couple of years later. 'Champs Elysées' and 'With A Song In My Heart' are both outwardly sanguine but, all the way through, Waldron is inverting harmonies, throwing in minor-key variations, generally changing the emotional temper. It's a stern experience, but a rewarding and chastening one. *Mal – 4* skins the line-up back to a trio and is again rather Janus-faced in its delivery: compare the opening 'Splidium-Dow' with the subsequent 'Get Happy' (!), interestingly enough another favourite of Powell's. These are scarce and rather little-known records in their original form and deserve to be in wider currency. The Bethlehem reissue comes on like a footnote to the OJCs and is relatively slight, but collectors will welcome McLean's guest appearance on the title-piece, and there is also a spoken reminiscence from Mal regarding the then lately-deceased Billie Holiday.

***(*) Free At Last ECM 1001
Waldron; Isla Eckinger (*b*); Clarence Beckton (*d*). 11/69.

To call Waldron 'unmelodic' is a description, not a criticism. He has rarely written memorable tunes, concentrating instead on subtly coded tonal cells out of which, as his career has continued, longer and longer improvisations can be developed. *Free At Last* was a conscious attempt to come to terms with free jazz; in Waldron's own words, it represented his desire to play 'rhythmically instead of soloing on chord changes'. At the same time, Waldron utterly rejects any notion of free jazz as 'complete anarchy or disorganized sound'. At first glance, these half-dozen tracks are disappointingly constrained and modest in scope. The long 'Rat Now' (a typical Waldron pun) and 'Rock My Soul' point a way forward for extended improvisation that does not depend on chord sequences; but, interestingly, both have the same 'feel' as more conventionally harmonic music because Waldron's clusters always seem to gravitate towards specific resolutions.

A useful trivia question, especially for anyone who wields the 'ECM sound' *canard* too freely, is to ask what the label's very first release was. If one quality characterizes ECM's output, it has been a search for new principles of organization in jazz, its only constraint a rejection of anarchic disorganization. *Free At Last* was a fine send-off.

***(*) Blues For Lady Day Black Lion BLCD 760193
Waldron; Henk Haverhoek (*b*); Pierre Courbois (*d*). 2/72.

Bassist and drummer figure on only the last two tracks, recorded a few days later, down the road from Baarn in Leiden. They're interesting pieces: after the brooding intro, 'A.L.B.O.M.' (or 'A Little Bit Of Miles'), is thoroughly untypical Waldron, distributed all over the keyboard and with considerable dynamic variation; 'Here, There And Everywhere' (*not* the Beatles tune) is an arresting exercise in pace and variation, constantly speeding up and retarding the beat. He fares pretty well with the rhythm section, who seem to understand what he's about, but the meat of the record is still the solo stuff, a vintage selection of tunes associated with his one-time boss, Billie Holiday. On 'Strange Fruit' he goes off into territory darker than Billie ever trod, and his version of 'The Man I Love' is convincingly anguished.

***(*) Moods Enja 3021
Waldron solo, and with Terumasa Hino (*t*); Hermann Breuer (*tb*); Steve Lacy (*ss*); Cameron Brown (*b*); Cameron Ntoshko (*d*). 5/78.

The mid- to late 1970s was a vintage spell in Waldron's career. With perverse predictability, it's here that the biggest hole in the current discography (apart from the gap in the '60s when the pianist's health collapsed almost fatally) should occur. His improvisations were stretching out and growing more adventurous as he absorbed the lessons of free playing. In this regard, the association with Lacy was of paramount importance. Though they seem fundamentally opposed in basic aesthetics, it's clear that Lacy's dry abstraction is only a continual refinement of his Dixieland roots. He swings with absolute conviction on all these sides.

The absent *Hard Talk* remains the most compelling. *Moods* is much more varied, with an extra horn in the ensembles and a valuable sample of Waldron's rather mournful solo style; 'Soul Eyes' and 'I

Thought About You' are beautiful and serve as reminders of the pianist's contact with Coltrane; but 'Anxiety', 'Lonely', 'Thoughtful' and 'Happiness' sound like 'face-pulling' exercises; and the soft, Monkish figurations of 'Duquility' are rather too elliptical. Waldron hits the keys with uncommon firmness, perhaps unused to or unsatisfied with the piano, perhaps merely trying new levels of attack.

*** **Dedication** Soul Note 121178-2
      Waldron; David Friesen (*b*). 11/85.
Something of an oddity, but an enjoyable one. Friesen's floating, soft-edged bass-lines (played on an amplified, bodyless instrument, credited as 'Oregon bass') actually work rather well over Waldron's dark mutterings, and the set as a whole has a coherence and unity that begin to sound slightly repetitive only on subsequent hearings.

**** **Songs Of Love And Regret** Freelance FRL CD006
      Waldron; Marion Brown (*as*). 11/85.
***(*) **Much More!** Freelance FRL CD010
      As above. 11/88.
**** **Sempre Amore** Soul Note 121170-2
      Waldron; Steve Lacy (*ss*). 2/86.
***(*) **Art Of The Duo** Tutu 888106
      Waldron; Jim Pepper (*ts, ss*). 88.
For straightforward beauty these are unsurpassed in Waldron's output. Clearly there is a sharp difference between Brown's waveringly pitched emotionalism and Lacy's dry phrasing (and between either and Jim Pepper's almost folksy delivery); but in all cases the two saxophonists get inside the song, concentrating in a manner one doesn't normally associate with Waldron on developing the melody. *Sempre Amore* is dedicated to Ellington–Strayhorn material, which must have made an intriguing change from Lacy's specialized diet of Monk. The two Freelances are more eclectic, taking in 'All God's Chillun Got Rhythm' and 'Now's The Time' (*Much More!*), McCoy Tyner's 'Contemplation' and (for comparison with the Lacy set) 'A Flower Is A Lovesome Thing' (*Love And Regret*). The earlier set opens with a slightly hesitant 'Blue Monk' (the CD reissue includes a rejected take that comes in at double the length and is far superior) which is then glossed in Waldron's own 'A Cause De Monk' and Brown's own 'To The Golden Lady In Her Graham Cracker Window', a typically delicate tune. Pepper gets a hold of 'Somewhere Over The Rainbow' and gives it the kind of gruff bear-hug that he often brought to ballads. A reading of 'Ruby My Dear' is less successful, though Waldron clearly has no worries about the tonality. The originals favour the saxophonist's relaxed blues phrasing.
   A vintage selection. Not for hardened cynics.

**** **Left Alone '86** Paddle Wheel K28P 6453
      Waldron; Jackie McLean (*as*); Herbie Lewis (*b*); Eddie Moore (*d*). 9/86.
Recorded at the beginning of a vintage month for Waldron groups (see items below) in what was already a vintage year for the pianist, *Left Alone* has a searing melancholy. Basically a tribute to Billie Holiday, it consists of four tracks associated with her – 'Lover Man', 'Good Morning Heartache', 'All Of Me' and 'God Bless The Child' – interspersed with Waldron originals that are calculated to accentuate the mood of solitude and bluesy ennui Lady Day gave off in her final couple of years (when Waldron was her accompanist). McLean's alto playing has regained all its old fire; this is one his best performances of recent years.

***(*) **The Git Go** Soul Note 121118-2
      Waldron; Woody Shaw (*t, flhn*); Charlie Rouse (*ts, f*); Reggie Workman (*b*); Ed Blackwell (*d*). 9/86.
**** **The Seagulls Of Kristiansund** Soul Note 121148-2
      As above. 9/86.
Two top-flight sets from a single night of a fine week's engagement at the Village Vanguard in New York City. All six compositions are Waldron's and his playing is supremely economical, sketching in tonal centres with a minimum of elaboration, soloing on the faster tracks with a positive touch, shading beautifully on the slow 'Seagulls Of Kristiansund'. This shows a side of Waldron's work which some critics have likened to American minimalism: a slow accretion of almost subliminal harmonic and rhythmic shifts steadily pile up until the music seems ready to overbalance.
   Perhaps oddly – for subsequent releases from live or studio sessions rarely match up to the original albums – the second album is more appealing. *The Git Go* consists of no more than the title-piece and an overlong 'Status Seeking', which seems to have lost much of the terse discipline Waldron brought to it on *The Quest*.
   On the second album, Waldron kicks off 'Snake Out' with a menacing bass pulse that builds up almost unbearable tension before loosing Woody Shaw on one of his most unfettered solos. Rouse's solo is more compact and provides a taut bridge between Shaw and Waldron, who plays lyrically over a bleak

vamp. Blackwell and Workman both solo effectively, though the drummer's finest moment comes at the end of 'Judy', the middle track of the set and a tribute to Waldron's great supporter, Judy Sneed. Shaw's solo is astonishing. Blackwell shines again on 'Seagulls', producing non-metrical effects on his splash cymbal; Workman's foghorn and seabird effects are straight out of Mingus's bag.

The Git Go has some *longueurs*, but its successor is thoroughly and straightforwardly enjoyable, and should be tried for size.

**** **Our Colline's A Tresure** Soul Note 121198-2
Waldron; Leonard Jones (*b*); Sangoma Everett (*d*). 4/87.
Still on a high. Waldron's handling of 'The Git Go' is markedly different from that on the Village Vanguard sessions, tighter in conception, if not in length, and with most of the solo space inevitably restored to the composer. The opening 'Spaces' is a superb example of direct motivic improvisation and lets in Jones for the first of several fine contributions. Everett, a neighbour of Waldron's in Munich, is less well known but sounds more than competent. The title-piece (and the mis-spelt word is probably deliberate) is dedicated to a young French friend of Waldron's, who may grow up to tresure the beautiful waltz-tune better than she will the picture on the cover.

***(*) **Live At Sweet Basil** Paddle Wheel K32Y 6208
Waldron; Steve Lacy (*ss*); Reggie Workman (*b*); Eddie Moore (*d*). 8/87.
Billed as the Super Quartet, this one is far less stellar than the Village Vanguard group. The music has a drier, less varied texture and features another saxophonist whose adoration for Monk ('Evidence') came from further off but went every bit as deep as Rouse's. Lacy's tightly pinched phrases are like accents on Waldron's bold, sans-serif lettering; Moore and Workman underscore firmly, sometimes overpowering the foreground.

*** **Mal Dance And Soul** Tutu 888102
Waldron; Jim Pepper (*ts*); Ed Schuller (*b*); John Betsch (*d*). 11/87.
***(*) **Quadrologue At Utopia** Tutu 888118
As above. 10/89.
***(*) **The Git-Go At Utopia, Volume 2** Tutu 888148
As above. 10/89.
Good, mostly new material from Waldron's late-1980s band. As with Clifford Jordan, above, it is Pepper's peculiar tonality that fits him for this context. The saxophonist, who is of American Indian descent, appears only on 'Soulmates' in the 1987 session, but he is a full-blooded presence on the aptly named *Quadrologue* and is especially good on the atmospheric 'Mistral Breeze'. Though less versatile than Joe Lovano (with whom he used to work in the Paul Motian group), Pepper has an enormous emotional range and the kind of innate rhythmic sophistication that Waldron requires. The leader sounds faintly muted on 'Ticket To Utopia' but warms towards an excellent finish on 'Funny Glasses & A Moustache'.

The second volume (and as a pairing these are interestingly comparable to the 1986 Soul Notes, one of which shares the title) maintains the standard, with – if anything – a stronger showing from Waldron himself. 'The Git-Go' now sounds so well worn as to have been around for ever. Even so, the leader still finds new things to do with it, reversing the changes in a later section and transposing his own accompaniment down through the keys in weird minor intervals that suggest the whole thing is suddenly going to come apart.

*** **No More Tears (For Lady Day)** Timeless SJP 328
Waldron; Joey Cardoso (*b*); John Betsch (*d*). 11/88.
Unlike *You And The Night And The Music*, this one doesn't really get off the ground. Waldron has clearly reached a point in his career where he is prepared to re-examine a more traditional jazz repertoire, and it would be cynical to suggest that the choice of material was conditioned by his sidemen's limitations. Betsch is one of the finest European-based drummers, but Cardoso is a plodding fellow whose solo on the opening 'Yesterdays' begins to pall before he has got himself properly warmed up. This comes from a Timeless series dedicated to the preservation of the traditional piano trio (almost as if they were steam engines or an endangered species). Fortunately, Waldron does a fine conservation job on his own, injecting new life into warhorses like 'Smoke Gets In Your Eyes' and 'Alone Together', which used to be as plentiful in the catalogue as buffalo on the plains of Wisconsin but which seem to have been exploited to death and appear much more rarely on standards sets of late.

**** **Crowd Scene** Soul Note 121218
Waldron; Sonny Fortune (*as*); Ricky Ford (*ts*); Reggie Workman (*b*); Eddie Moore (*d*). 6/89.
***(*) **Where Are You?** Soul Note 121248
As above. 6/89.
'Crowd Scene' is a large-scale piece that attempts to capture the point atwhich individual elements begin

to cohere and act in unison, as a collectivity. Waldron has always liked to describe himself as a parcel of disparate elements, held together by chance, everyday necessities, good luck, rather than by any pressing philosophy, and something of that seems to underline this piece. 'Yin And Yang', the other long track, perhaps represents a more specific and settled viewpoint, but one that in no way contradicts the first. Like 'Crowd Scene', it's held together by riffs and ostinati, rather than by any single principle of development. The two saxophonists, who managed to dramatise a sense of diversity and questioning plurality in the first piece, are not so much opposites, as two sides of a single reality in the second, playing in close intervals but with markedly different timbres. The effect is very powerful and engineer Kazunori Sugiyama has done a marvellous job capturing it so accurately. For once, it's good to have Waldron in the studio. Much would have been lost in a club or concert hall.

There's a bit of padding on the second disc; only a second and longer take of 'Where Are You?' takes it up over the 50-minute mark. However, what there is is so good that no casual purchaser will feel short-changed. 'Waltz For Marianne' is gorgeous, with Workman playing a prominent role. One feels that, with a little judicious editing, an absolutely top-flight single CD could have been made out of these.

***(*) **Waldron–Haslam** Slam 305
    Waldron; George Haslam (*bs*). 2/94.
*** **Two New** Slam 306
    Waldron; George Haslam (*bs, tarogato*). 4/95.
Spells of indifferent health have slowed up Waldron's recording regimen of late. These engaging duet records with British baritone man Haslam don't have the gravitas and sheer monumentality of the best Waldron, but their friendly dialogue has its own rewards and at some moments – especially in the two improvised pieces on the first disc, 'Catch As Catch Should' and 'Motion In Order' – there is the trademark dry, lyrical intensity which is in all of the pianist's best work. Though Haslam might have been outclassed, especially in having to step into the shoes of some of Waldron's other horn partners, his light, flexible lines make an attractively serene counterpoint. Excellent recording on both discs.

Bennie Wallace (born 1946) TENOR SAXOPHONE

*** **The Fourteen Bar Blues** Enja 3029
    Wallace; Eddie Gomez (*b*); Eddie Moore (*d*). 1/78.
*** **The Free Will** Enja 3063
    Wallace; Tommy Flanagan (*p*); Eddie Gomez (*b*); Dannie Richmond (*d*). 1–2/80.
*** **The Bennie Wallace Trio And Chick Corea** Enja 4028
    As above, except Chick Corea (*p*) replaces Flanagan. 5/82.
***(*) **Plays Monk** Enja 3091
    Wallace; Jimmy Knepper (*tb*); Eddie Gomez (*b*); Dannie Richmond (*d*). 3/81.
***(*) **Big Jim's Tango** Enja 4046
    Wallace; Dave Holland (*b*); Elvin Jones (*d*). 11–12/82.
*** **Sweeping Through The City** Enja 4078
    Wallace; Ray Anderson (*tb*); Pat Conley (*p*); John Scofield (*g*); Mike Richmond, Dennis Irwin (*b*); Tom Whaley (*d*); The Wings of Song (*v*). 3/84.
A traditionalist of the best kind, Bennie Wallace has made a lot of highly entertaining records without quite finding the bigger audience his populist music might reach. His trio albums give him the space he enjoys and set up his Sonny Rollins influence to its most effective ends: the grand, swaggering rhythms and tonal exaggerations buttress an improvising style which owes much to R&B and roadhouse music, a greasiness which can distract from the intense structures which Wallace can work together. He isn't a licks player, doesn't dawdle in clichés, and the essential heartiness of his music is deceptive, for he provides greater rewards for listeners who are prepared to work with him. The first trio albums suffer just a little from a slightly awkward mix of personalities: Gomez's rubbery virtuosity doesn't always suit Wallace's moves, even if they clearly enjoy playing together, and the following *The Free Will* is also too gentlemanly, through Flanagan's characteristically professorial touch. Chick Corea's guest appearance doesn't do anything much for the trio – only Corea could contribute a tune called 'Mystic Bridge' to follow a Wallace original entitled 'The Bob Crosby Blues' – and, while Gomez follows the pianist, Richmond tends to stick with the tenorman. The Monk collection ups the ante: Wallace likes these tunes, he picks a couple of the less obvious ones, and Jimmy Knepper sits in on three tracks for a typically quizzical dialogue. The line-up for *Big Jim's Tango* is another formidable one – Wallace has never been shy of playing with his peers – and the extravagant terpsichorea of 'Big Jim Does The Tango For You' is in some ways the definitive Wallace performance. Holland and Jones are their unimpeachable selves, here and elsewhere. *Sweeping Through The City* invents some gospel roots for Bennie via the

roistering contribution of The Wings of Song on two tracks; the rest is neo-bop and blues, with Anderson and Scofield adding their own characteristic thoughts to the mixture.

***(*) **Brilliant Corners** Denon 32CY-2430

    Wallace; Yosuke Yamashita (*p*); Jay Anderson (*b*); Jeff Hirshfield (*d*). 9/86.

**** **The Art Of The Saxophone** Denon 33CY-1648

    Wallace; Oliver Lake (*as*); Jerry Bergonzi, Harold Ashby, Lew Tabackin (*ts*); John Scofield (*g*); Eddie Gomez (*b*); Dannie Richmond (*d*). 2/87.

Two outstanding and insufficiently known records. The quartet date with Yamashita leans heavily on Monk's repertoire and, with the pianist playing in a kind of overdriven-Monk manner, it's almost akin to a modernization of the quartet with Rouse (whose tonalities Wallace can occasionally evoke). Lucid, scathingly sharp, this is a bristling instance of post-bop repertory. *The Art Of The Saxophone* goes a notch better by inviting four other masters in for various duets: Tabackin and Wallace do an *a cappella* 'All Too Soon', Ashby feathers his way through 'Prelude To A Kiss', Lake tears through 'Prince Charles' and Bergonzi makes three attacking appearances. Wallace and Scofield bind the appearances together and make everybody at home.

***(*) **The Old Songs** Audioquest 1017

    Wallace; Lou Levy (*p*); Bill Huntington (*b*); Alvin Queen (*d*). 1/93.

*** **The Talk Of The Town** Enja 7091-2

    As above, except Jerry Hahn (*g*) replaces Levy. 1/93.

Left out in the cold by Blue Note, Wallace makes a welcome return with two new records for different labels (he has in the meantime been busy on film-score work). Cut live to two-track, *The Old Songs* finds Bennie rumbling through a bunch of standards with one original tune, 'At Lulu Whitte's', to keep his composing hand in. Levy appears on only three tracks and the freely spaced rhythms of Huntington and Queen give Wallace plenty of space to break the melodies open: 'When You Wish Upon A Star' is a classic revision, 'Love Letters' a vintage piece of Wallace frowsiness. The same kind of set-up prevails on *The Talk Of The Town*, though here five of the eight tunes are Wallace originals. The tenorman scrubs his way through 'The Best Things In Life Are Free' and 'I Concentrate On You', but the best moments come on his movie ballad, 'If I Lose', and the closing tribute to Lockjaw Davis, 'Blues Velvet', a screamer of a blues. If the record is a shade below par for this fine musician, it may be because Hahn isn't much of a sparring partner.

Thomas 'Fats' Waller (1904–43) PIANO, ORGAN, VOCAL

(*) **Classic Jazz From Rare Piano Rolls Biograph BCD 104

    Waller; James P. Johnson, Lawrence J. Cook (*piano rolls*). 3/23–1/29.

*** **Low Down Papa** Biograph BCD 114

    Waller; James P. Johnson (*piano rolls*). 5/23–6/31.

Thomas Waller was already deputizing for James P. Johnson and playing film and stage-show accompaniments when he started making piano-rolls for the QRS company in 1923. These two discs transfer some of his many rolls to CD. Most of the tunes are typical light blues novelties of the day, and they're played with a crisp, courtly demeanour, although individuality is to some extent suppressed by the machinery of the roll system: certainly Waller's first piano records show much more idiosyncrasy than any of these tracks. There are a couple of items with Johnson, Waller's great mentor, and one on the earlier disc which was credited to Waller but is actually by Lawrence Cook. Ebullience and good humour are persistent to the point of becoming exasperating here, and perhaps these pieces are best sampled a few at a time: there are only a few genuinely Walleresque touches such as the abrupt doubling of tempo in 'Your Time Now', on *Low Down Papa*. The rolls have been brightly recorded, although *Low Down Papa* is less glassy and generally has the better selection of themes.

*(*) **Fats At The Organ** ASV AJA 5007R

    Waller (*org*). 23–27.

A unique record, if a bizarre one. Waller made several pipe-organ solos early in his career, but this set consists of organ transcriptions of piano-roll solos: Waller is heard twice-removed. If the piano-roll discs listed above sound artificial, it's hard to hear much of Waller in here except in the merry rhythmic gait of the original rolls: all the choices of registration are made by Ronald Curtis, admittedly after studying Waller's original organ records, and any authenticity which remains comes off a second-best to whatever a 78 can produce.

(*) **Fats Waller 1922–1926 Classics 664

    Waller; Clarence Williams (*kz, v*); Clarence Todd (*kz*); Justin Ring (*perc*); Sara Martin, Alberta

Hunter, Anna Jones, Porter Grainger, Rosa Henderson, Alta Browne, Bertha Powell, Caroline Johnson (v). 10/22–4/26.

This is fantastically obscure music, 19 tracks of classic blues and vaudeville singers accompanied by Waller, plus two 1922 solos and two tracks with the Jamaica Jazzers (Clarence Williams and Clarence Todd blowing through their kazoos). Those accustomed to listening to the earliest blues reissues will know what to expect in terms of sound-quality; everyone else may be in for a shock (and even Classics themselves have apologized for it on the sleeve). On its own terms, fascinating, with the almost unknown titles by Alta Browne, Bertha Powell and Anna Jones especially interesting.

** The Complete Early Band Works 1927–29 Halcyon HDL 115

Waller; Tom Morris (c); Charlie Gaines, Henry Allen, Leonard Davis (t); Jack Teagarden, Jimmy Archey, J. C. Higginbotham (tb); Arville Harris (cl, as, ts); Albert Nicholas, Charlie Holmes (cl, as); Larry Binyon (ts); Bobbie Leecan (g); Will Johnson, Eddie Condon (bj); Pops Foster, Al Morgan (b); Eddie King, Gene Krupa, Kaiser Marshall (d); The Four Wanderers (v). 5/27–12/29.

*** Fats And His Buddies RCA Bluebird 90649

As above, except add Jabbo Smith (c), Garvin Bushell (cl, as, bsn), James P. Johnson (p). 5/27–12/29.

**(*) Fats Waller 1926–1927 Classics 674

As above discs, except add Alberta Hunter, Maude Mills (v). 11/26–6/27.

*** Fats Waller 1927–1929 Classics 689

As above discs, except add Bert Howell (vn, v), Lou Raderman, Howard Nelson (vn), David Martin (clo), Chuck Campbell (tb), J. Lapitino (hp), Gene Austin, Andy Razaf, Juanita Chappelle (v). 11/27–6/29.

***(*) Fats Waller 1929 Classics 702

As above discs. 6–12/29.

Waller doesn't sing anywhere on the first two records above (which basically duplicate each other) and, given the nightmarish vocals by The Four Wanderers on two tracks, perhaps he was numbed into silence. The seven tracks by Fats with Tom Morris's Hot Babies are a garish mismatch of pipe organ and cornet-led hot band and, since the resonances and overtones of the organ tamp down everything the other players do, it's hard to imagine how anyone could have thought that the group would work. The eight tracks by Fats Waller & His Buddies (the best of which are also included on some of the Bluebird records which follow) are merely loose-knit New York jazz of the period (1929). Where Bluebird score is in including six tracks by the Louisiana Sugar Babes, which are otherwise available under Jabbo Smith's name. The original sides have been nicely handled in the remastering on both discs.

The Classics discs go forward with Waller's 1926–7 organ solos, beautiful, lilting creations, as well as some of the Morris Hot Babies tracks and more accompaniments to Mills and Hunter. There is some very strange stuff on Classics 689 – three tearful tributes to the lately departed Florence Mills, where Waller plays respectful piano, and a version of 'Chloe' with violin, organ and piano. It ends with Gene Austin singing 'Maybe – Who Knows?'. In between, though, are several classic piano solos and 'I Ain't Got Nobody', one of the best of his organ records. Remastering on all these is mixed but quite an improvement on Classics 664. The 1929 disc offers a great run of his finest piano solos (see below): still not the best sound, but it's a strong one-disc primer on early Waller.

*** Jazz Classics: Fats Waller 1927–1934 Jazz Classics in Digital Stereo RPCD 619

As above, except add Rex Stewart, Muggsy Spanier (c); Dave Klein, Herman Autrey (t); Georg Brunies, Sam Blank, Floyd O'Brien (tb); Benny Goodman, Jimmy Lord, Mezz Mezzrow (cl); Don Redman, Benny Carter (cl, as); Louis Martin (as, bs); Coleman Hawkins, Hymie Wolfson, Pee Wee Russell (ts); Sam Shapiro, Sol Klein (vn); Tony Gerhardi, Jack Bland, Al Casey (g); Cyrus St Clair (bb); Harry Barth, Pops Foster, Billy Taylor (b); George Stafford, Zutty Singleton, John Lucas, Harry Dial (d); Billy Banks (v).

A superior handling of what was a complicated period of Waller's life, as far as studio work was concerned. He turns up here as a guest with Ted Lewis, Billy Banks's Rhythmakers and the Little Chocolate Dandies, and there are various tracks from the Hot Babies and Buddies sessions, as well as some piano solos and an organ version of 'Sugar'. Cleverly programmed, this is a disc that works as both an overview and a playable compilation, ending with an early Rhythm track and the piano solo, 'Alligator Crawl'. This was one of Robert Parker's earliest stereo remastering efforts, and the sometimes over-resonant acoustic may bother some ears, even if the originals are obviously in fine condition.

**** Piano Solos 1929-1941 RCA ND 89741 2CD

Waller. 2/27–5/41.

***(*) Piano Masterworks Vol. 1 EPM 5106

Waller. 10/22–9/29.

Musically, the RCA set is the one Waller record which should be in every collection: it collates the results of all the solo sessions he recorded for Victor. Deplorably, for a pianist of his stature, he was allowed to cut only two sessions as a soloist after 1934, so most of these tracks date from 1929 to 1934, with a solitary title, 'Blue Black Bottom', coming from 1927. Waller's inventiveness within the idiom of stride piano is astonishingly fecund, particularly in the two sessions made in August 1929: 'Valentine Stomp', 'Sweet Savannah Sue' and 'Baby Oh Where Can You Be' are among his finest statements on record, organized with sober attention to formality but graced with an inimitable energy and a delicate humour that's quite unlike the Waller of the 1930s. Almost as good are 'Smashing Thirds' and the rather cheeky miniatures of 'Clothes Line Ballet' and 'African Ripples', while the 1941 solos, culminating in a masterful treatment of James P. Johnson's 'Carolina Shout', find him reflecting on a career that was consistently directed away from such 'serious' studies. The double-CD and album includes several alternative takes, some of which – particularly those for 'I've Got A Feeling I'm Falling' and 'Love Me Or Leave Me' – show some surprising variations in manner (the LP issue omits some of these).

The latest RCA edition is a reissue of their Black & White two-LP set, which remains a little variable in terms of sound but is at least quite superior to the previous Bluebird incarnation. The EPM disc collects all the solos up to 1929, including two little-known sides for OKeh from 1922, again in rather erratic sound; but the RCA set is now clearly the one to get.

(*) You Rascal You ASV AJA 5040
> Waller; Henry 'Red' Allen, Len Davis, Bill Coleman, Herman Autrey, Charlie Gains, Charlie Teagarden, Sterling Bose (*t*); Jack Teagarden (*tb, v*); Charlie Irvis, Tommy Dorsey, J. C. Higginbotham, Charlie Green (*tb*); Arville Harris, Ben Whittet, Artie Shaw, Albert Nicholas, Larry Binyon (*cl, as*); Gene Sedric, Larry Binyon (*cl, ts*); Bud Freeman (*ts*); Al Casey, Dick McDonough (*g*); Eddie Condon (*bj*); Billy Taylor, Pops Foster, Artie Bernstein (*b*); Stan King, Kaiser Marshall, Harry Dial (*d*). 3/29–11/34.

*** **Fats Waller 1929–1934** Classics 720
> As above. 12/29–11/34.

Waller's early band sides, picked out in this cross-section of 1929–34 sessions, suggested a mercurial talent pondering on its ultimate direction. The two sides by Fats Waller's Buddies are frantic small-band New York jazz of the day (1929), with little of the slyness of the Rhythm sides represented by seven 1934 tracks, and the guest-star role he takes on a Jack Teagarden version of 'You Rascal You' offers little more than inspired mugging, entertaining as it is. A few solos, including the enchanting 'My Fate Is In Your Hands', suggest the other side of Waller's art, and the complexity of his personality. Mixed reproduction again, alas: some sides sound very dull, others are clear and strong. Much the same applies to the Classics version of this material.

*** **Fats Waller 1934–35** Classics 732
> Waller; Herman Autrey, Bill Coleman (*t*); Floyd O'Brien (*tb*); Gene Sedric (*cl, ts*); Mezz Mezzrow (*cl, as*); Al Casey (*g*); Billy Taylor, Charles Turner (*b*); Harry Dial (*d, vib*). 9/34–1/35.

***(*) **Fats Waller 1935** Classics 746
> As above, except add Rudy Powell (*cl, as*), James Smith (*g*), Arnold Bolling (*d*); omit Mezzrow and Taylor. 1/35–6/35.

***(*) **Fats Waller 1935 Vol. 2** Classics 760
> As above, except omit Coleman, Sedric, Dial. 6–8/35.

***(*) **Fats Waller 1935–1936** Classics 776
> As above, except add Benny Morton (*tb*), Emmett Matthews (*ss*), Bob Caroll, Gene Sedric (*ts*), Hank Duncan (*p*), Yank Porter (*d*); omit Powell, Smith. 11/35–2/36.

*** **Fats Waller 1936** Classics 797
> As above, except add Slick Jones (*d*); omit Morton, Matthews, Caroll, Duncan. 6–9/36.

*** **Fats Waller 1936–1937** Classics 816
> As above, except omit Bolling, Porter. 11/36–3/37.

*** **Fats Waller 1937** Classics 838
> As above, except add Bunny Berigan (*t*), Tommy Dorsey (*tb*), Dick McDonough (*g*), George Wettling (*d*). 3–6/37.

***(*) **The Middle Years Part 1 (1936–38)** Bluebird 07863 66083-2 3CD
> Waller; Herman Autrey, Paul Campbell, John Hamilton, Nat Williams (*t*); George Robinson, John Haughton (*tb*); Gene Sedric (*cl, ts*); Caughey Roberts, Lonnie Simmons, William Alsop, Alfred Skerritt, James Powell (*reeds*); Ceele Burke, Al Casey (*g*); Charles Turner, Al Morgan, Cedric Wallace (*b*); Slick Jones, Lee Young (*d, vib*); Peggy Dade (*v*). 12/36–4/38.

*** **The Middle Years Part 2 (1938–1940)** Bluebird 07863 66552-2 3CD
> Similar to above. 38–40.

Waller worked hard in the studios and, though his material has been traditionally looked down upon, he did usually make the most of it, even if the relentless clowning, yelled asides, importuning of soloists and general mayhem obscured much of what his hands were doing at the keyboard. This is knockabout music, but whenever he gets to a good melody or does one of his own better tunes – such as the 12-inch master of 'Blue Turning Grey Over You' – its underlying seriousness rises to the surface. Autrey and Sedric, the most ubiquitous yet least recognized of horn players, are always ready to heat things up. Bill Coleman's presence on a few early sessions introduces some of his elegant horn, and the almost forgotten Rudy Powell replaced Sedric on several of the 1935 dates.

Much order has been imposed on these sessions since our last edition, with both RCA and Classics embarking on comprehensive surveys of the so-called 'Middle Years'. The Classics CDs are the easiest to follow, but the RCA sets are attractively packaged and the remastering (much improved on the earlier standards of the Bluebird reissues) is generally a shade better.

Classics 732 includes four piano solos as well as the session which produced 'Serenade For A Wealthy Widow'; 'Baby Brown' is another good one. Classics 746 has 'Rosetta', 'I'm Gonna Sit Right Down And Write Myself A Letter', the outstanding 'Dinah' and 'Sweet And Slow'. Either this or the following Classics 760 might be a good one to sample: the latter includes several more of the best Rhythm tracks, with one of the best ever versions of 'Somebody Stole My Gal'. Classics 776 has the fruits of a session involving a 12-piece band, which even has a second pianist, Hank Duncan, who brings on a joshing cutting contest on 'I Got Rhythm'. Also on this disc is a particularly fine session that produced 'The Panic Is On', 'Sugar Rose' and 'West Wind'. There is still a decent quota of good music on Classics 797, but this and the next two see the Rhythm formula wearing dangerously thin and some truly dreadful material coming under assault. There are many pickings here, but they're camouflaged by a lot of nonsense. By the time the Classics sequence reaches its end, this will be a fairly monumental set, but follow the stars in the meantime for Waller's better moments.

(***) The Joint Is Jumpin' RCA Bluebird ND 86288
> Waller; Charlie Gaines, Herman Autrey, John 'Bugs' Hamilton, Bunny Berigan, Nathaniel Williams, Benny Carter (*t*); Charlie Irvis, Tommy Dorsey, George Robinson, John Haughton, Slim Moore (*tb*); Arville Harris, Rudy Powell, Gene Sedric, William Allsop, James Powell, Fred Skerritt, Lonnie Simmons, Gene Porter (*reeds*); Al Casey, John Smith, Dick McDonough, Irving Ashby (*g*); Charlie Turner, Cedric Wallace, Slam Stewart (*b*); Harry Dial, Slick Jones, George Wettling, Zutty Singleton (*d*). 3/29–1/43.

A competent choice of some of Waller's best on the Bluebird disc: hits such as 'Your Feet's Too Big', two versions of 'Honeysuckle Rose' (including one from the 1937 'Jam Session At Victor' date) and a shrewd selection of ten of his best solos, in a generous 23 tracks. But the CD is again badly let down by the remastering, which sounds bright and clear on only very few of the tracks.

*** The Definitive Fats Waller, His Rhythm, His Piano Stash ST-CD-528
> Waller; Herman Autrey (*t*); Rudy Powell (*cl, as*); Gene Sedric (*cl, ts*); Al Casey (*g*); Cedric Wallace, Charles Turner (*b*); Slick Jones, Harry Dial (*d*). 35–39.

A generous (76 minutes) helping of Waller and the Rhythm from broadcasts in 1935 and 1939. The material is staple Waller fare and the exuberance is as expected, in surprisingly good sound for the period and the sources. While the 'new' versions aren't strikingly revelatory of any different side to Waller, they confirm his ability to create happy music out of the thinnest of tunes.

*** London Sessions 1938–1939 EMI Pathé/Jazztime 251271-2
> Waller; Dave Wilkins (*t*); George Chisholm (*tb*); Alfie Kahn (*cl, ts*); Ian Sheppard (*ts, vn*); Alan Ferguson (*g*); Len Harrison (*b*); Hymie Schneider, Max Levin, Edmundo Ros (*d*); Adelaide Hall (*v*). 8/38–6/39.

Waller visited Europe twice in the late 1930s, and recorded in London on both trips. Two sessions in 1938 found him handling organ and piano with a British band, cutting six organ solos (including a surprisingly bleak and unsettling 'Deep River') and backing Adelaide Hall for two further songs. Next year, he worked alone or with drum-only support. There are six wistful miniatures, the 'London Suite', and a rather mournful 'Smoke Dreams Of You', which go to suggest the reflective side of Waller's art which rarely made it to record yet which is always touted by supporters as his shamefully overlooked inner self. Whatever the case, these are slight but charming pieces. Unfortunately the original pressings were in poor shape and remastering has done little for the later tracks, although the earlier session rings out clearly.

***(*) The Last Years 1940–1943 RCA Bluebird ND 90411 3CD
> Waller; Herman Autrey, John 'Bugs' Hamilton, Bob Williams, Joe Thomas, Nathaniel Williams, Benny Carter (*t*); George Wilson, Ray Hogan, Herb Flemming, Alton Moore (*tb*); Jimmy Powell, Dave Macrae, George James, Lawrence Fields, Gene Porter (*as*); Gene Sedric (*cl, ts*); Bob Carroll (*ts*); John Smith, Al Casey, Irving Ashby (*g*); Cedric Wallace, Slam Stewart (*b*); Slick Jones, Arthur Trappier, Zutty Singleton (*d*); Kathryn Perry, The Deep River Boys (*v*). 4/40–1/43.

*** **The Indispensable Fats Waller 1940–1943** RCA 74321 15526 2 2CD
    As above. 40–43.
If Waller was ultimately trapped by his non-stop funny-man image, the routine of his 'Fats Waller And His Rhythm' records at least helped to focus a talent that was sometimes in danger of merely running ragged. The dozens of throwaway tunes he lampooned may have had little intrinsic merit, and he often falls back on favourite lines and devices, but – like Armstrong in the same period – Waller remains an inimitable talent, and the space limitations of the records often result in performances full of compressed excitement. A little-known track such as 'You're Gonna Be Sorry' (1941) works up an explosive swing which Waller, Hamilton and Sedric turn to exciting advantage. Nor is it true to say that the Rhythm recordings declined in quality: the 1941–2 sessions include some of the finest sides the band made, and Hamilton, Sedric and Autrey, all minor figures who nevertheless played handsomely at the right moment, lend a more urgently swinging touch to the music than anything provided by, say, the Louis Jordan band (compare Waller's 'Your Socks Don't Match' or 'Don't Give Me That Jive', two very Jordanesque tunes, with any of the altoman's records – next to Jordan's calculating burlesques, Waller's wit sounds wholly spontaneous). With the disappearance of the US Bluebird complete Waller set on LP, this is the only comprehensive look at the later sessions and, given the large number of less familiar tunes, it's a surprisingly playable set, with fine sessions like the 1941 big-band date which pulled off a terrific 'Chant Of The Groove', the non-vocal Rhythm sides including 'Pantin' In The Panther Room' and the final studio date that included Benny Carter on trumpet and delivered a valedictory 'Ain't Misbehavin''. The remastering is rather better than on some other Bluebird discs, and we must recommend the set to even cautious Waller listeners. RCA have also put out a two-disc set from the same period in their Black & White/Tribune series: at mid-price, a sound purchase if one doesn't need the full survey.

Per Henrik Wallin PIANO

***(*) **Dolphins, Dolphins, Dolphins** Dragon DRCD 215
    Wallin; Mats Gustafsson (*ss, ts, bs*); Kjell Nordeson (*d*). 8/91.
Wallin's extensive discography has been seriously depleted by the disappearance of vinyl. He is a fascinating pianist, taking whatever he wants from free- and post-bop piano language: a bravado delivery, involving tumultuous climaxes and moment-by-moment contrast, makes him hard to follow or even like at times, but he is surely a European original. Hospitalized after a crippling accident in 1988, Wallin astonishingly came back with none of his power depleted. The shade most closely evoked here is Thelonious Monk, since 'Nu Nu Och Då Nu Går Då Och Nu' sounds like a perversion of ''Round Midnight', and other Monkish melodies drift through the remaining tunes. But the level of interplay here – confrontational and conspiratorial in equal proportion – goes against the impression given by much of his earlier work, that Wallin is best by himself, although his long solo 'J.W.' is a wonderfully expressive tribute to a painter friend. Gustafsson is gothically powerful and jagged, Nordeson works with military intensity, and it's all splendidly recorded.

George Wallington (1924–93) PIANO

***(*) **The George Wallington Trio** Savoy SV-0136
    Wallington; Jerry Floyd (*t*); Kai Winding (*tb*); Brew Moore (*ts*); Gerry Mulligan (*bs*); Curley Russell (*b*); Charlie Perry, Max Roach (*d*); Buddy Stewart (*v*). 5/49–11/51.
***(*) **The George Wallington Trios** Original Jazz Classics OJC 1754
    Wallington; Chuck Wayne (*mandola*); Charles Mingus, Oscar Pettiford, Curley Russell (*b*); Max Roach (*d*). 9/52–5/53.
*** **Trios** RCA Vogue 74321 11504 2
    Wallington; Pierre Michelot (*b*); Jean-Louis Viale (*d*). 9/54.
More so even than Joe Albany or Dodo Marmarosa, George Wallington is the underrated master of bebop piano: his name is still best known for his composing 'Lemon Drop' and 'Godchild'. His speed is breathtaking, his melodies unspooling in long, unbroken lines, and he writes tunes which are rather more than the customary convoluted riffs on familiar chord-changes. His touch on these early sessions – the first eight trio tracks were cut in 1951, the two bigger-band pieces and the final trio tracks dating from two years earlier – is percussive without suggesting aggression, and there's an aristocratic flavour to the writing of 'Hyacinth' and the latterly ubiquitous 'Polka Dot'. The two band-pieces are lithe shots of cool bebop, with Brew Moore superb on 'Knockout', but the trio music is the stuff to hear. A few tracks have reverberations on the piano, but the remastering is mostly good. The OJC *Trios* disc is all piano, bass and drums, and there are marvellous, flashing virtuoso pieces like the ultrafast 'Cuckoo

Around The Clock', although the elegance of 'I Married An Angel' is a harbinger of Wallington's later work. The eight tracks on the Vogue disc (there are a further six by Jimmy Jones) are cooler, more reflective treatments, including a definitive version of one of his own favourite compositions, 'Ny'. The sound here is clear enough, though bass and drums aren't served well.

*** **Live! At Café Bohemia** Original Jazz Classics OJC 1813
    Wallington; Donald Byrd (*t*); Jackie McLean (*as*); Paul Chambers (*b*); Art Taylor (*d*). 9/55.
*** **Jazz For The Carriage Trade** Original Jazz Classics OJC 1704
    As above, except Phil Woods (*as*) and Teddy Kotick (*b*) replace McLean and Chambers. 1/56.
***(*) **The New York Scene** Original Jazz Classics OJC 1805
    As above, except Nick Stabulas (*d*) replaces Taylor. 3/57.
*** **Jazz At Hotchkiss** Savoy SV-0119
    Wallington; Donald Byrd (*t*); Phil Woods (*as*); Knobby Totah (*b*); Nick Stabulas (*d*). 11/57.
Some of these are merely serviceable hard-bop entries, prosaic stuff after the fine fierceness of the earlier records; but some of the music takes exception. Wallington's playing seemed to turn inwards and his improvisations are at an altogether cooler temperature: the best piece on *Jazz At Hotchkiss*, his own theme, 'Before Dawn', is a starless ballad of surprisingly desolate feeling. Byrd muddles through the first two dates and is approaching his faceless self on the later two, yet this anonymity throws some of Wallington's own contributions into sharper relief – almost like Freddie Hubbard on some of the more outré Blue Notes of the next decade. Woods hits every note he needs to with his usual accuracy on his appearances; McLean is his customary tart mid-'50s self on the earliest date. *Café Bohemia*, *Carriage Trade* and *Hotchkiss* are tough and darting but finally straight-ahead in their demeanour; it's *The New York Scene* that looks a little further out, thanks to Wallington's material and his own solos, which have begun to skin bebop language back to something more elemental. A shame that he chose this point to quit jazz altogether.

*** **The Pleasure Of A Jazz Inspiration** VSOP 84
    Wallington (*p* solo). 8/85.
Tempted back into the studios, Wallington created this 'jazz tone poem' in eight parts. Bebop figures drift through some of the themes: 'Writing In The Sand' is very like Powell's 'Parisian Thoroughfare'. But the slower pieces are unusually dark, with the harmonies of 'Memory Of The Heart' almost impenetrably dense, and there's a hint of sourness that goes with the pleasure. Wallington sounds rusty here and there, and much of the old exhilaration has dissipated, but it's an interesting if eccentric postscript to a frustrating career.

Jack Walrath (born 1946) TRUMPET

***(*) **Wholly Trinity** Muse 600612
    Walrath; Chip Jackson (*b*); Jimmy Madison (*d*). 3 & 4/86.
**** **Out Of The Tradition** Muse MCD 5043
    Walrath; Benny Green (*p*); Larry Coryell (*g*); Anthony Cox (*b*); Ronnie Burrage (*d*). 5/90.
In a period dominated largely by the saxophone and by the muted, melted edges of Miles Davis's trumpet style, it's good to find a player who restores some of brass's authentic ring and bite. Walrath is a hugely talented player with a tough, almost percussive sound. A high-note man in several contemporary big bands (Charles Mingus's *Cumbia And Jazz Fusion* and *Three Or Four Shades Of Blues* spring immediately to mind, but he has also done sterling service with Charli Persip Superbands), Walrath has so far not made his deserved impact as a leader. Two good Blue Notes (look particularly for *Neohippus*) are currently out of the catalogue, and there is a two-volume live set on Red which is worth searching for. Of those that are left, *Wholly Trinity* is the most successful. Working without a harmony instrument or second horn is a bold stroke for a trumpeter, but Walrath sounds completely assured. A first take of 'Killer Bunnies' (Walrath is a horror-movie freak and dedicated his Blue Note debut to the *Master Of Suspense*) is better than the version on *Killer Bunnies*, an LP-only Spotlite release by Spirit Level. Compositions like 'Spherious' and 'Spontooneous', also on the Muse, point not just to Walrath's rather zany sense of humour but also to his oblique, Monk-like compositional sense, which often makes use of folk and popular elements in a highly original way.

    Those elements are in place again on *Out Of The Tradition*. Walrath opens 'Out Of This World' with a strange North African scale and non-tempered sounds blown on a detached trumpet mouthpiece. There are hints of Coltrane's version in what follows, but they are used as stepping stones, not as a final destination. Walrath has located his playing *outside* the tradition and is constantly working towards points of departure. That is dramatized in Mingus's 'So Long, Eric', on which Coryell and Green play a large part, and it comes across in the cod Bach of 'Wake Up And Wash It Off', a pun too complicated to merit unpicking here. Walrath's now regular Pops feature comes on 'Cabin In The Sky', one of his best recent performances, and he then drops back into gentler mode for 'I'm Getting Sentimental Over You'. It's done no harm to doff the cap-and-bells for a while; this is a terrific jazz album.

Cedar Walton (born 1934) PIANO

***(*) **Cedar!** Original Jazz Classics OJC 462
    Walton; Kenny Dorham (*t*); Junior Cook (*ts*); Leroy Vinnegar (*b*); Billy Higgins (*d*). 7/67.
**** **Cedar Walton Plays Cedar Walton** Original Jazz Classics OJC 6002
    As above, plus Blue Mitchell (*t*); Clifford Jordan (*ts*); Bob Cranshaw, Richard Davis (*b*); Jack DeJohnette, Mickey Roker (*d*). 7/67, 5/68, 1/69.

Walton has not yet been widely recognized as a significant jazz composer. Tunes like 'Bolivia', 'Ojos De Rojo', 'Maestro' and 'Ugetsu' rival McCoy Tyner's work for sophisticated inventiveness. During the 1970s Walton was anchoring Clifford Jordan's Magic Triangle band. They seem to have struck up an immediate rapport on these earlier sessions, made for Prestige. *Plays* contains a useful sample of the earlier quartet and quintet stuff with Dorham and Cook, but the compilation misses a fine trio, 'My Ship'. Paired with the characteristically blunt Mitchell, Jordan takes the direct route to goal, with no sign of his irritating tendency to mark time in mid-solo. 'Higgins Holler' and 'Jakes Milkshakes' also feature sterling work by DeJohnette, who still sounds rather eager to please. There's an excellent trio performance of Walton's 'Fantasy In D', 'Ugetsu', with Roker and Cranshaw. Though there's good stuff on OJC 462, the compilation has to be a better bet.

***(*) **First Set** Steeplechase SCCD 31085
    As above. 1 & 10/77.
***(*) **Second Set** Steeplechase SCCD 31113
    As above.
*** **Third Set** Steeplechase SCCD 31179
    As above.

This was a vintage period for Walton. His European gigs were models of tough contemporary bop and, though the incidence of covers is higher than one might like, the standard of performance is consistently high, and for once Steeplechase's exhaustive documentation seems justified. Berg turns in an excellent performance of Coltrane's 'Blue Train' on *Second Set*. There are several good Monk performances, but the opening 'Off Minor' on *First Set* is the most dynamic. The original 'Ojos De Rojo' appears on both *First Set* and the later of the Timeless sets. Though sounding a bit better since transfer to CD (audiophile vinyl pressings of the first two are still available), the *Third Set* is surprisingly inconsequential.

***(*) **The Maestro** Muse MCD 6008
    Walton; Bob Berg (*ts*); David Williams (*b*); Billy Higgins (*d*). 12/80.

This is the band which (with some variations in the wind section) was to become Eastern Rebellion; see above for a separate entry. It might be asked how that band differs from records issued under Walton's own name. The honest answer is: very little. However, the pianist does still tend to dominate the eponymous selections and he's notably forward and centre on this recording, which rather swamps the redoubtable Williams.

Though he isn't automatically thought of as an accompanist (as Mal Waldron or Tommy Flanagan might reasonably be), Walton has always been interested in singers and has frequently expressed an interest in having someone write lyrics to his compositions. Working with Abbey Lincoln (on four tracks here) suggests that indeed he does have a special touch for this kind of session. Lincoln is often a difficult singer to back; her inherent musicality demands a self-confident response from the band if she isn't to sound stilted. Walton does her proud, and she in turn brings something quite exquisite to 'In A Sentimental Mood'.

The quartet tracks are up to Walton's consistently high standard. Two Monk tunes dominate, but there is also a highly imaginative arrangement of a section from Ferde Grofé's *Grand Canyon Suite*. One wishes Walton had done more work in this area: an album of Americana, maybe, with Ives, Copland, Still and Ellington all represented.

***(*) **Among Friends** Evidence ECD 2023
    Walton; Bobby Hutcherson (*vib*); Buster Williams (*b*); Billy Higgins (*d*). 7/82.

Recorded during the final months of its life, the Keystone Korner in San Francisco became a regular resort for recording companies in search of cheap atmospheric recordings. In July 1982 vibist Hutcherson was there with his group, a residency documented on *Farewell Keystone*. Walton's trio was the warm-up act and was playing so well that a decision was taken to record them as well. Perhaps the most valuable part of the session is the solo medley from the pianist at the end, a rippling segue from 'Ruby My Dear' to 'My Old Flame' and 'I've Grown Accustomed To Her Face', played with great feeling and understanding. Hutcherson actually appears as a guest on only one track, the long 'My Foolish Heart', but he raises the ante considerably. Williams and Higgins are impeccable, but then, aren't they always?

***(*) **Cedar Walton–Ron Carter–Jack DeJohnette** Limetree MCD 0021
    Walton; Ron Carter (*b*); Jack DeJohnette (*d*). 12/83.
The young DeJohnette had proved his value to Walton on the 1968 Prestige sessions; 15 years made a substantial difference to the drummer's chops. In 1983 he's confident enough to play less and quieter, and all three players are intuitively musical in approach, which encourages a tight, unembellished style. Walton's own 'Rubber Man' is the outstanding track, but there are also worthwhile performances of 'Alone Together' and 'All The Things You Are', tunes which can sound thoroughly shop-soiled when accorded only routine treatment.

***(*) **Bluesville Time** Criss Cross Criss 1017
    Walton; Dale Barlow (*ts*); David Williams (*b*); Billy Higgins (*d*). 4/85.
**** **Cedar** Timeless SJP 223
    As above, except omit Barlow. 4/85.
Williams and Higgins were the ground floor of Walton's fine 1980s groups. The drummer's ability to sustain and develop a pattern became increasingly important to the pianist as he simplified and reduced his delivery. Barlow compares very favourably with the inventive Bob Berg, who had played for a time in Walton's other group, Eastern Rebellion (see above). The material is excellent – 'Naima' and 'I Remember Clifford' alongside distinctive originals like 'Rubber Man' and 'Ojos De Rojo' – but the playing, Higgins apart, isn't quite crisp enough. The drummer sounds great on *Cedar*, but the material doesn't give anyone enough to bite down on and there's too much filling for too little substance.

***(*) **The Trio: Volume 1** Red 123192
***(*) **The Trio: Volume 2** Red 123193
*** **The Trio: Volume 3** Red 123194
    Walton; David Williams (*b*); Billy Higgins (*d*). 3/85.
Recorded live in Bologna, these represent a compelling mixture of originals ('Ojos De Rojo', 'Jacob's Ladder', 'Holy Land'), standards ('Lover Man', 'Every Time We Say Goodbye') and challenging repertoire pieces (Ellington's 'Satin Doll', Fred Lacey's 'Theme For Ernie', S. R. Kyner's 'Bluesville'). Walton's brilliant phrasing and inbuilt harmonic awareness keep thematic material in view at all times, and his solos and accompaniments are always entirely logical and consistently developed. About Higgins there is very little more to add, but that he has inherited and fully deserved the mantle of Elvin Jones. Williams offers firm, unobtrusive support, but isn't a very exciting soloist.

*** **My Funny Valentine** Sweet Basil 660-55-010
    Walton; Ron Carter (*b*); Billy Higgins (*d*). 2/91.
Noisy backgrounds contribute to the prized 'live feel', but these are rather bland sessions, stringing together all the clichés in the book – rhythmic downshifts, long chromatic transitions, endless quotation – into an attractive confection that never quite rises above a drab choice of standards material. Carter and Higgins are well up to scratch, but the bassist has developed irritating harmonic mannerisms which grate after a while.

**** **Manhattan Afternoon** Criss Cross 1082
    Walton; David Williams (*b*); Billy Higgins (*d*). 12/92.
A tremendous record by the master. With just two originals tucked away in the middle of the set, Walton sticks to a programme of fairly routine standards and repertoire pieces – Monk's 'I Mean You' isn't his most played piece, though – and dispatches them all with consummate skill. His very first solo, on 'There Is No Greater Love', is replete with unexpected angles, and the soft harmonic displacements recur later on John Lewis's 'Afternoon In Paris'. Williams and Higgins fit the music like a glove. Strongly recommended.

Wanderlust GROUP

(*) **Wanderlust ABC Jazz 518650-2
    Miroslav Bukovsky (*t, flhn*); Charles Greening (*tb*); Tony Gorman (*as, cl*); Alan Dargin (*didgeridu*); Alister Spence (*ky*); Carl Orr (*g*); Adam Armstrong (*b*); Fabian Hevia (*d*); Greg Sheehan (*perc, v*). 93.
*** **Border Crossing** Rufus RF018
    As above, except Julian Gough (*ts*) replaces Gorman; add Renée Geyer (*v*); omit Sheehan and Dargin. 5/95.

Miroslav Bukovsky leads this entertaining if lightweight Australian group, working an area that blends jazz chops and solos with a setting that has more to do with a mood/world music. Spence's keyboards set up hazy harmonic backdrops for horn and percussion workouts that tend to roll amiably on without making too great a dent on the listener. The first album is more arranged and suffers from a reticent production, but the second is stronger, Greening in particular emerging as a maverick voice, tailgating his way through his surroundings. Bukovsky himself sounds like an eclectic – which does, after all, suit the music. Both records run close to 80 minutes apiece, and they could have trimmed away some of the noodling.

Carlos Ward (born 1940) ALTO SAXOPHONE, FLUTE

***(*) **Lito** Leo CD LR 166
　　　Ward; Woody Shaw (*t*); Walter Schmocker (*b*); Alex Deutsch (*d*). 7/88.
Recorded live at the North Sea Festival and sounding a little as if the sound were being sent down a pipeline, this is nevertheless a valuable documentation both of Ward and of Woody Shaw, who sounds magnificent. An atmospheric player rather than a highly virtuosic one, Ward, who was born in the Panama Canal Zone, has a piercing, keening tone that works best on short, discontinuous phrases. Long association with Dollar Brand/Abdullah Ibrahim has given his work a distinctive, almost folksy quality; but what is interesting about *Lito* is how effective a writer the saxophonist is, spinning out ideas through the long title-suite, and in three shorter tracks on the second side, best of which is a tribute to Thelonious Monk entitled 'First Love'. Ward's flute chimes sympathetically with Shaw in the middle sections of 'Lito', and the trumpeter's middle-register responses rank with his best work on record.

David S. Ware (born 1949) TENOR SAXOPHONE, SAXELLO, STRITCH

***(*) **Passage To Music** Silkheart SH 113
　　　Ware; William Parker (*b*); Marc Edwards (*b*). 4/88.
A quasi-mystic journey from 'The Ancient Formula', through 'African Secrets' and down 'The Elders Path' to the final 'Mystery' of jazz. Ware's use of the stritch and saxello (horns related to the alto saxophone; the former is closely associated with Rahsaan Roland Kirk, and it would be interesting to know whether Ware was introduced to the other as a result of Silkheart man, Dennis Gonzalez's, work with a British group that included saxello player Elton Dean) is more than a respectful nod to Kirk's ghost. Ware allows the unfamiliar tonality of the stritch in particular to suggest the ambiguities and perils of a journey through jazz history. He touches on mysterious harmonies with an almost ritual intensity and detachment. Parker is a forceful trio bassist (watch out for his sessions with Jimmy Lyons soundalike, Marco Einedi, on the limited release *Vermont – Spring 1986* (Botticelli 1001)) with a strong sense of harmony. It would have been interesting to hear him paired again with Silkheart regular Dennis Charles, as on Rob Brown's *Breath Rhyme* (Silkheart SH 122), one of the strongest rhythm-section performances of recent years.

*** **Great Bliss: Volume 1** Silkheart SHCD 127
　　　Ware; Matthew Shipp (*p*); William Parker (*b*); Marc Edwards (*d, perc*). 1/90.
***(*) **Flight Of i** DIW 856
　　　As above. 12/91.
Ware's 1960s revivalism has never been more clearly stated than on the turbulent Silkheart, first of a two-volume set. His adoption of stritch and saxello, non-standard horns with off-centre pitching, has given him a distinctive sound which is obviously related to Roland Kirk's more wayward experimentations but which, like Kirk's, is intimately bound up with an interest in primitive blues, field hollers, gospel shouts and rags. Pianist Matthew Shipp is a valuable acquisition, a patient, sober-sounding player who lacks conventional swing but creates big, throbbing pulses, often round a single key. Drummer Edwards makes dramatic use of tymps and bells, and it's unfortunate that he is conventionally disposed on the DIW.

　　The CD of *Great Bliss* has four tracks (22½ minutes of music) that are not on the LP configuration. The unaccompanied 'Saxelloscape One' would not be greatly missed, but not to have 'Angular' (saxello again) or 'Bliss Theme' (a throbbing tenor vehicle) would seriously lessen the impact of the album. Ware plays his stritch on the long, rather shapeless 'Cadenza' and his flute on the opening 'Forward Motion' and (CD only) 'Mind Time'. An exploratory album, its overall tone and approach strongly recall the 1960s avant-garde, and it may be that Ware hasn't yet worked that influence out of his system.

　　He sticks with his tenor on *Flight Of i*, cleaving to a line between Rollins and Ayler, constantly reverting to the melody (as on 'There Will Never Be Another You') despite Shipp's exciting habit of bashing the original theme into submission; it would be interesting to hear the pianist let loose on a trio session. 'Flight Of i' and the long 'Infi-Rhythms No. 1' suggest that the saxophonist has been paying attention to David Murray's long-standing rehabilitation of Ayler, building huge upper-register prayers out of very basic thematic material. The title-track is one of the most remarkably sustained saxophone performances of recent years, and the album should be heard.

*** **Third Ear Recitation** DIW 870
     Ware; Matthew Shipp (*p*); William Parker (*b*); Whit Dickey (*d*). 93.
Ware continues to grow and develop with a much more measured and self-aware record than any he has previously made. Opening with 'Autumn Leaves' was a surprise, but the real revelation was his treatment of 'East Broadway Run Down' by Sonny Rollins. Shipp has such an intuitive grasp of what's going on that he regularly anticipates Ware's shifts of rhythm. He certainly sounds more on the case than Dickey, who's a bit sleepy.

Wilbur Ware (1923–79) DOUBLE BASS

***(*) **The Chicago Sound** Original Jazz Classics OJC 1737
     Ware; John Jenkins (*as*); Johnny Griffin (*ts*); Junior Mance (*p*); Wilbur Campbell, Frank Dunlop (*d*). 10 & 11/57.
Though much of what Ware did stemmed directly from Jimmy Blanton's 'Jack The Bear', he developed into a highly individual performer whose unmistakable sound lives on in the low-register work of contemporary bassists like Charlie Haden. Ware's technique has been questioned but seems to have been a conscious development, a way of hearing the chord rather than a way of skirting his own supposed shortcomings. He could solo at speed, shifting the time-signature from bar to bar while retaining an absolutely reliable pulse. Significantly, one of his most important employers was Thelonious Monk, who valued displacements of that sort within an essentially four-square rhythm and traditional (but not European-traditional) tonality; the bassist also contributed substantially to one of Sonny Rollins's finest recordings. He grew up in the sanctified church and there is a gospely quality to 'Mamma-Daddy', a relatively rare original, on *The Chicago Sound*. The only other Ware composition on the record, '31st And State', might have come from Johnny Griffin's head; the saxophonist roars in over the beat and entirely swamps Jenkins, whose main contribution to the session is a composition credit on two good tracks.

    Though the Ware discography is huge (with numerous credits for Riverside in the 1950s), his solo technique is at its most developed on his own record. 'Lullaby Of The Leaves' is almost entirely for bass, and there are magnificent solos on 'Body And Soul' (where he sounds *huge*) and 'The Man I Love'. One wonders if a couple of alternative takes mightn't have been included on the CD. Ware's impact was enormous, and one record (albeit a fine one) seems a poor trawl.

Washboard Rhythm Kings GROUP

*** **Washboard Rhythm Kings Vol. 1** Collectors Classics COCD-17
     Dave Page (*t*); Ben Smith (*as*); Jimmy Shine (*as, v*); Carl Wade (*ts*); Eddie Miles (*p, v*); Steve Washington (*bj, g*); Teddy Bunn (*g*); Jimmy Spencer (*wbd*); Jake Fenderson, The Melody Four (*v*). 4/31–3/32.
*** **Washboard Rhythm Kings Vol. 2** Collectors Classics COCD-18
     As above, except add Taft Jordan (*t*), Wilbur Daniels (*bj*), Leo Watson, George 'Ghost' Howell (*b, v*), H. Smith (*wbd*). 32.
*** **Washboard Rhythm Kings Vol. 3** Collectors Classics COCD-19
     As above, except add Valaida Snow (*t*), John 'Shorty' Haughton (*tb*), Jerome Carrington (*as*), Bella Benson, Lavada Carter (*v*). 10/32–8/33.
There are plenty of unidentified names to add to the various personnel listed above, which gives some idea of how little is known about this group, which recorded around New York for a period of a couple of years at the beginning of the 1930s. Smith, Wade and Miles seem to have been the mainstays of the band, which otherwise fluctuated between a quartet and a group running to ten pieces. While a washboard may have been appropriate for the earlier tracks, which sounded about as downhome as a band working in New Jersey could be, by the time of the final session in August 1933 it was anachronistic for a group that was playing quite a tough and respectable small-group swing. The material is a peculiar blend of blues, jazz themes and pop tunes: 'Please Tell Me' (*Vol. 1*), for instance, is a mixture of Ellington's 'Stevedore Stomp' and Blind Blake's 'Diddy Wah Diddy'. The earlier stuff is attractively rough and unpretentious, the later tracks more ambitious; but all of it makes up a valuable backwater in the

recording of jazz at the end of the first golden age. John R. T. Davies has done the transfers on all three discs and they are from mainly superb originals.

Dinah Washington (1924–63) VOCAL

*** Mellow Mama Delmark DD 451
Washington; Karl George (*t*); Jewell Grant (*as*); Lucky Thompson (*ts*); Milt Jackson (*vib*); Wilbert Baranco (*p*); Charles Mingus (*b*); Lee Young (*d*). 12/45.

Whether or not she counts as a 'jazz singer', Washington frequently appeared in the company of the finest jazz musicians and, while she was no improviser and stood slightly apart from such contemporaries as Fitzgerald or Vaughan, she could drill through blues and ballads with a huge, sometimes slightly terrifying delivery. Her start came with the Lionel Hampton band, and after leaving him she made these dozen tracks for Apollo Records in the company of a band organized by Lucky Thompson. While Washington herself sounds comparatively raw and unformed, the jump-blues material doesn't demand a great range, and she swings through the likes of 'My Voot Is Really Vout' as well as the more traditional 'Beggin' Mama Blues'. Thompson's team sound as if they're having fun, and the remastering is quite clear.

***(*) Dinah Jams Emarcy 814639-2
Washington; Clifford Brown, Clark Terry, Maynard Ferguson (*t*); Herb Geller (*as*); Harold Land (*ts*); Junior Mance, Richie Powell (*p*); Keter Betts, George Morrow (*b*); Max Roach (*d*). 8/54.

Washington's sole 'jazz' record is fine, but not as fine as the closely contemporary Sarah Vaughan record with a similar backing group, and therein lies a tale about Washington's abilities. She claimed she could sing anything – which was probably true – but her big, bluesy voice is no more comfortable in this stratum of Tin Pan Alley than was Joe Turner's. Still, the long and luxuriant jams on 'You Go To My Head' and 'Lover Come Back To Me' are rather wonderful in their way, and there is always Clifford Brown to listen to.

***(*) For Those In Love Emarcy 514073-2
Washington; Clark Terry (*t*); Jimmy Cleveland (*tb*); Paul Quinichette (*ts*); Cecil Payne (*bs*); Wynton Kelly (*p*); Barry Galbraith (*g*); Keter Betts (*b*); Jimmy Cobb (*d*). 55.
*** Dinah! Emarcy 842139-2
Washington; Hal Mooney Orchestra. 55.
*** In The Land Of Hi-Fi Emarcy 826453-2
Washington; Hal Mooney Orchestra. 4/56.
*** The Fats Waller Songbook Emarcy 818930-2
Washington; Ernie Royal, Johnny Coles, Joe Newman, Clark Terry (*t*); Melba Liston, Julian Priester, Rod Levitt (*tb*); Eddie Chamblee, Jerome Richardson, Benny Golson, Frank Wess, Sahib Shihab (*reeds*); Jack Wilson (*p*); Freddie Green (*g*); Richard Evans (*b*); Charli Persip (*d*). 10/57.
*** The Bessie Smith Songbook Emarcy 826663-2
Washington; Blue Mitchell (*t*); Melba Liston (*tb*); Harold Ousley (*ts*); Sahib Shihab (*bs*); Wynton Kelly (*p*); Paul West (*b*); Max Roach (*d*). 7/58.
*** What A Diff'rence A Day Makes! Emarcy 818815-2
Washington; studio orchestra. 59.
*** Unforgettable Mercury 510602-2
Washington; studio orchestra. 59–1/61.
***(*) Verve Jazz Masters: Dinah Washington Verve 518200-2
As above Emarcy discs, plus Quincy Jones Orchestra. 55–61.
*** Verve Jazz Masters: Sings Standards Verve 522055-2
As above. 52–58.
*** 'Round Midnight: Dinah Washington Verve 510087
As above, except add Nook Shrier Orchestra, Eddie Chamblee Orchestra, Tab Smith Orchestra, Jimmy Cobb Orchestra. 10/46–12/61.
**** The Dinah Washington Story Mercury 514841-2 2CD
As above discs. 43–59.

Washington's studio albums for Emarcy are a good if fairly interchangeable lot: the quality of the backing doesn't much affect the calibre of her singing, and a frowsy studio orchestra is as likely to generate a great vocal as a smoking jazz ensemble. *For Those In Love* is a stand-out from this pack, since the accompaniment is as classy as that on the *Dinah Jams* session, and at least one track – a perfectly realized 'I Could Write A Book' – is a stone classic. But *The Dinah Washington Story* sweeps the board:

a 40-track double set that creams off all the most interesting songs from the period, with a few from her earliest days to round out the picture. The other compilations will do fine for anyone wanting a one-disc representation of Dinah's albums from this period.

Anyone wanting a complete Washington collection from her Mercury years is directed to the several multi-disc sets available in the US comprising *The Complete Dinah Washington On Mercury Volumes 1–7*. Each is a three-disc set, and in total they cover the period 1952–61 as comprehensively as anyone would wish.

**(*) In Love Roulette CDP 7972732
> Washington; studio orchestra. 62.

*** The Best Of Dinah Washington Roulette CDP 7991142
> Washington; studio orchestras. 62–63.

**(*) Dinah '63 Roulette 7945762
> Washington; studio orchestra. 63.

The Roulette albums merely continue what was a disappointing decline on record, even though it's hard to define exactly where the problem lies. Washington sings mightily and with no lack of attention throughout all these records, and an improvisational gleam resides at the heart of many of these songs, especially 'Do Nothin' Til You Hear From Me' (*In Love*). But the relentlessly tasteful orchestrations by Don Costa and Fred Norman turn down the heat all the way through, and Washington can sound curiously alone and friendless on a lot of the tracks. The remastering has been respectably done.

Grover Washington Jr ALTO SAXOPHONE, SOPRANO SAXOPHONE, BARITONE SAXOPHONE

*** Winelight Elektra 60338
> Washington; Paul Griffin, Richard Tee (*p*); Bill Eaton, Ed Walsh, Raymond Chew (*syn*); Eric Gale (*g*); Marcus Miller (*b*); Steve Gadd (*d*); Robert Grenidge, Ralph MacDonald (*perc*); Bill Withers, Hilda Harris, Yvonne Lewis, Ullanda McCullough (*v*). 6 & 7/80.

***(*) Come Morning Elektra 60337
> Washington; Richard Tee (*p*); Paul Griffin (*syn*); Eric Gale (*g*); Marcus Miller (*b*); Steve Gadd (*d*); Ralph MacDonald (*perc*); Grady Tate, Yvonne Lewis, Vivian Cherry, Ullanda McCullough, Frank Floyd, Zack Sanders, William Eaton (*v*). 6–9/81.

*** The Best Is Yet To Come Elektra 60215
> Washington; Jon Faddis (*t*); Frank Wess, Alex Foster (*ts*); Mona Goldman-Yoskin (*f*); Teddi Schlossman, Richard Tee (*p*); James Lloyd, Paul Griffin, Billy Childs, Dexter Wansel (*ky*); James Herb Smith, Eric Gale, Lee Ritenour, Richard Steacker (*g*); Marcus Miller, Cedric Napoleon, Abe Laboriel (*b*); Yogi Horton, Harvey Mason, Darryl Washington (*d*); Victor Feldman, Kevin Johnson, Leonard Gibbs, Ralph MacDonald (*perc*); Patti Labelle, Bobby McFerrin, Carla Benson, Evette Benton, Lucille Jones (*v*). 82.

*** Anthology Of Grover Washington Jr Elektra 60415
> Washington; no other personnel specified, but as above.

*** Time Out Of Mind Columbia 465526
> Washington; Bill Jolly (*p*); Donald Robinson, Sid Simmons, Philip Woo (*ky*); Randy Bowland, Richard Lee Steacker (*g*); Gerald Veasley (*b*); Darryl Washington (*d*); Jim Salamone (*d, perc*); Darryl Burgee, Miguel Fuentes, Dr Gibbs (*perc*); Spencer Harrison, Lawrence Newton, Tracey Alston, Paula Holloway, Phyllis Hyman (*v*). 89.

Much exploited for television signature tunes, programme stings and advertising, Washington's brand of smooth, contemporary soul-jazz has rarely won over the more sober jazz critics, who like to think he's just another pop musician. There is, however, no getting away from Washington's consummate musicianship and taste. He has a lovely, melting tone, even on the treacherous soprano, and is capable of writing simple, beautiful ballads, like the Grammy-winning 'Just The Two Of Us', which appeal to pop and jazz fans alike. The only comparable figure in the music is Sadao Watanabe.

A time-served session-man with Prestige, Washington tends to make albums the way American football is played. Players are called on for cameo performances in highly specialized roles and are then dispensed with. The sound is teased and plucked and sprayed into shape but manages, unlike most commercial pop product, to sound relatively unconfected and even, on some of the earlier discs, quite spontaneous.

The only real constant is Washington himself. He phrases a little like Cannonball Adderley, who was the main inspiration behind 1975's wonderful *Mister Magic*. There's nothing that good in the present batch, and newcomers might do worse than try out the interestingly titled *Anthology*, which, though it does cover obvious things like 'The Best Is Yet To Come', 'East River Drive' and (of course) 'Just The Two

Of Us', is also quite sensitively programmed. The man responsible for the cover art – step forward, one Scott Reynolds – should be disciplined, something like combing Kenny G's hair every morning for six months.

Sadao Watanabe (born 1933) ALTO SAXOPHONE, SOPRANINO SAXOPHONE, SOPRANO SAXOPHONE, FLUTE

*** **Bossa Nova Concert** Denon DC 8556
>Watanabe; Masabumi Kikuchi (*p*); Sadanori Nakamure (*g*); Masanaga Harada (*b*); Masahiko Togashi (*d*); strings. 7/67, 3/69.

*** **Sadao Meets Brazilian Friends** Denon DC 8557
>Watanabe; Waldir DeBaros (*t*); Jose Ferreira, Godinho Filho (*as*); Carlos Albertot Alcantara (*ss*); Aparecido Bianchi (*p, org*); Joao Carlos Pegoro (*p, vib*); Olmir Secaer (*g*); Mathias Da Silva Matos (*b*); Douglas De Oliveira (*d*). 7/68.

*** **Plays Ballads** Denori DC 8555
>As for *Bossa Nova Concert*, except add Sadanori Nakamure (*g*), Hideo Miyata (*perc*). 3/69.

***(*) **Dedicated To Charlie Parker** Denon DC 8558
>Watanabe; Terumasa Hino (*t*); Kazuo Yashior (*p*); Masanaga Harada (*b*); Fumio Watanabe (*d*). 3/69.

***(*) **Parker's Mood** Elektra 60475
>Watanabe; James Williams (*p*); Charnett Moffett (*b*); Jeff Watts (*d*). 7/85.

***(*) **Tokyo Dating** Elektra WPCP 4327
>As above. 7/85.

(*) **Good Time For Love Elektra 60945
>Watanabe; Kenji Nishiyama (*tb*); Ansel Collins, Onaje Allan Gumbs, Rob Monsey, Sohichi Noriki (*ky*); Keiichi Gotoh (*syn*); Bobby Broom, Radcliffe Bryan, Takayuki Hijikata, Tsunehide Matsuki, Jeff Mironov, Earl Smith, Tohru Tatsuki (*g*); Victor Bailey, Bertram McLean, Kenji Takamizu, Ken Watanabe (*b*); Will Lee (*b, v*); Poogie Bell, Carton Davis, Shuichi Murakami, Chris Parker, Hideo Yamaki (*d*); Mino Cinelu, Sue Evans, Sydoney Wolfe (*perc*); Eve (*v*); collective personnel. 2 & 3/86.

*** **Birds Of Passage** Elektra 60748
>Watanabe; Freddie Hubbard (*flhn*); Hubert Laws (*f*); George Duke, Russell Errante (*ky*); Dan Huff, Paul Jackson (*g*); Abraham Laboriel (*b*); Vinnie Colaiuta, John Robinson, Carlos Vega (*d*); Alex Acuna, Paulinho Da Costa (*perc*); collective personnel. 87.

*** **Elis** Elektra 60816
>Watanabe; Cesar Camargo Mariano (*ky*); Heitor Teixeira Pereira (*g*); Nico Assumpcao (*b*); Paulinho Braga (*d*); Papeti (*perc*); Toquinho (*v, g*). 2/88.

*** **Made In Coracao** Elektra WPCP 4331
>Watanabe; Toquinho (*v, g*); Amilson Godoy (*ky*); Edson Jose Alves (*g*); Ivani Sabino (*b*); William Caram (*d*); Osvaldo Batto, Papeti (*perc*). 3 & 4/88.

***(*) **Selected** Elektra WPCP 4332
>As for *Fill Up The Night, Rendezvous, Maisha, Good Time For Love, Birds Of Passage, Elis,* plus Robbie Buchanan (*ky*); Steve Erquiaga, Paul Jackson Jr (*g*); Keith Jones (*b*); Andy Narell (*steel d*); William Kennedy, Chester Thompson (*d*); Kenneth Nash (*perc*). 83–88.

Like most Japanese of his generation (the composer Toru Takemitsu tells a very similar story), Sadao Watanabe heard nothing but Japanese traditional and German martial music during his teens, and was exposed to Western popular music only through American forces radio; he also cites Norman Granz's Jazz At The Philharmonic broadcasts as a big influence. Watanabe had already largely rejected Japanese music (his father was a teacher of *biwa*, a lute-like instrument). By the time he was twenty, he was sufficiently adept on the alto saxophone to join Toshiko Akiyoshi and perform in America.

He subsequently recorded with both Chico Hamilton (who was always on the look-out for unusual tonalities) and Gary McFarland, who turned Watanabe on to the fashionable sound of *bossa nova*. Perhaps because he encountered jazz at a relatively advanced stage in its development, Watanabe seemed able to take virtually any of its stylistic variants (swing, bop, Latin, Afro and, later, fusion) on their own terms. Though his recent recordings have tended to be heavily produced, middle-market fusion, Watanabe has recorded with an impressive array of American heavyweights including (to mention only the piano players) Chick Corea, Herbie Hancock, Cedar Walton and Richard Tee. In 1967 he collaborated with Toshiko Akiyoshi's ex-husband Charlie Mariano, producing three fine albums of standards and oriental themes.

These, like most of Watanabe's output, were released only in Japan. Between 1961 and 1980, he made a total of 36 albums, some of which turn up second-hand. The best of them – *Round Trip* with Corea, *At Pit Inn* with Walton, and, one of several Parker tributes, *Bird Of Paradise* with Jones – are the more swinging, 'American' sets. Watanabe's Japanese bands have tended to be correct but rather stiff, a criticism that might be levelled at his own playing but for the surpassing beauty of his tone. *Dedicated* and *Ballads* were both apparently recorded at the same concert; the latter is smothered in strings, the former has the benefit of Hino's bright Dorham-ish trumpet, varying a rather stolid group-sound.

In recent years, following illness, Watanabe has given up flute, which he plays beautifully on the *Bossa Nova Concert* and *Round Trip*; he does, though, continue to double on sopranino, a treacherously pitched horn with an attractive, 'Eastern' quality. Watanabe is one of only a handful who have specialized on it, and his theme statement on 'My Dear Life', included on *Selected*, is his signature piece.

Of the albums with an American release, the most interesting from a straight jazz point of view are the live Parker set and subsequent studio album with Williams, Moffett and Watts. The recent Brazilian sets will appeal to Latin fans, and these probably have a sharper rhythmic edge than the drifting studio fusion of most of the others. For all but determined collectors, *Selected* should be sufficient. There is a vocal and an unreleased instrumental version of the haunting 'My Dear Life', a fine live version of 'California Shower' (the original album of that name came out in 1978) and three good examples of Watanabe sopranino work – 'Pastoral' (*Birds Of Passage*), 'Desert Ride' and 'Say When' (from the deleted *Maisha* and *Fill Up The Night* respectively). You'd never guess he'd even heard of Charlie Parker, though. Two subsequent albums for Verve Forecast offer more pretty, tuneful stuff, scarcely worth listing here.

Benny Waters (born 1902) ALTO AND TENOR SAXOPHONES, CLARINET, VOCAL

(*) Jazz A La Huchette 1972–1979 EMI Jazz Time 253622-2
    Waters; Jean Claude Naude (*t*); Daniel Barda (*tb*); Wani Hinder (*ts, bs*); Gérard Raingo (*p*); Jean-Pierre Sasson (*g*); Jean-Pierre Mulot (*b*); Guy Hayat (*d*). 5/72.

*** **Benny Waters–Freddy Randall Jazz Band** Jazzology JCD-124
    Waters; Freddy Randall (*t*); Jim Shepherd (*tb*); Stan Greig (*p*); Paul Sealey (*g, bj*); Tiny Winters, Mike Durrell (*b*); Laurie Chescoe (*d*). 12/82.

*** **Hearing Is Convincing** Muse M 5340
    Waters; Don Coates (*p*); Earl May (*b*); Ronnie Cole (*d*). 6/87.

Waters is an indomitable personality, among the oldest practising jazzmen, and though his recent records tend to be too accommodating for a man who doesn't like to act his age, there is much vigorous work on clarinet and alto. Like Benny Carter or Doc Cheatham, he sounds like a survivor from another age, raising his voice among us with few concessions to his surroundings. His tone, vibrato and delivery are antiquarian, but none of this suggests frailty, more an enduring style. The Jazz Time CD is shared with a Bill Coleman date, and Waters blows cheerfully through eight brief tunes; the French band, though, play vaudevillian Dixieland in support. The meeting with Freddy Randall and a prime British crew is good enough, though some of the rhythms plod and there's too much solo space given to the sidemen; Randall's brusquely hot solos and Waters's sometimes impish humour are the reasons to listen. As a feature session, though, the Muse disc is still the one to go for. Restlessly switching between alto, tenor and clarinet, often within the space of a single tune, Benny's improvisations have a crusty logic and resolution to them: the second tenor chorus on 'Everything Happens To Me' is a model of polished lyricism. He still phrases the saxophone in a way that players don't any more. His singing, too, is very lively indeed on 'Romance Without Finance'.

*** **Swinging Again** Jazz Point 1037
    Waters; Thilo Wagner (*p*); Jan Jankeje (*b*); Gregor Beck (*d*). 5/93.

(*) Plays Songs Of Love Jazz Point 1039
    Waters; Red Richards (*p*); Vic Juris (*g*); Johnny Williams Jr (*b*); Jackie Williams (*d*). 7/93.

In his nineties, Waters is a phenomenon. That doesn't guarantee that his records would be anything more than a novelty from someone who makes Benny Carter seem like a youngster, but *Swinging Again* is a creditable effort from any saxman, and if the support from the European rhythm section is a bit faceless, Waters has character enough to go around. Ten more tunes, three vocals. The second album is slush of a high order by what's mostly a team of oldtimers, and the material runs the gamut from 'Always' (which creaks a bit, even if Waters was born before it was written) to 'You Are The Sunshine Of My Life'.

Mitch Watkins GUITAR, GUITAR SYNTHESIZER, KEYBOARDS

(*) Underneath It All Enja 5099-2
> Watkins; Stephen Zirkel (*t, flhn*); Paul Ostermayer (*ss*); Rob Lockart (*ts, syn*); Anthony Cox (*b*); Dennis Chambers (*d*); Arto Tuncboyaci (*perc, v*). 1/89.

*** Curves Enja 6054-2
> Watkins; Bob Berg (*ts*); Jay Anderson (*b*); Dennis Chambers (*d*). 5/90.

***(*) Strings With Wings Tiptoe 888814-2
> Watkins; Bill Ginn (*ky*); Gene Elders (*vn*); Marty Muse (*pedal steel g*); Chris Maresh (*b*); Paul Glasse (*mand*); Brannen Temple, Scott Laningham (*d*); James Fenner (*perc*). 1/92.

Mitch Watkins plays in almost every guitar style one can think of, which lends inevitable identity problems to these records. He has a caseful of jazz-rock licks when the amps are turned up and the fuzzbox is on, but he's rather better served by the countrified twang that ties him to his native Texas. *Underneath It All* is an excessively modish debut that suffers from some overheated and tuneless tunes, but the sinuous line he draws out of the title-track makes up for matters like the merely silly version of 'Lester Leaps In'. *Curves* sets him up in a quartet where he plays Mike Stern to Bob Berg's Bob Berg – he does it very well, but it seems a tad pointless. The breakthrough comes with the surprisingly light and charming *Strings With Wings*, where he records with a crew of fellow Texans and comes up with a fusion of styles that makes for heartbreaking ballads such as 'One Lost Love' and simple, picturesque miniatures that let his thoughtful improvisations resonate through a clean, wiry sound-mix.

Bobby Watson (born 1953) ALTO SAXOPHONE, SOPRANO SAXOPHONE

**** Love Remains Red CD 123212
> Watson; John Hicks (*p*); Curtis Lundy (*b*); Marvin 'Smitty' Smith (*d*). 11/86.

***(*) This Little Light Of Mine Red R R 123250
> Watson (*as solo*). 93.

Few contemporary saxophonists are more instantly recognizable than the brilliant Kansan. Watson's hard, bright sound and trademark descending wail (a device that seems increasingly mannered as years go by) were first acclaimed in a vintage Jazz Messengers line-up. Watson went on to work in Charli Persip's Superband and to co-found the 29th Street Saxophone Quartet.

Though the quartet has been internationally successful, Watson's recording career has been intermittent to say the least. Most of his best work has been for the Italian Red label. With typical perversity, both his Blue Note discs with Horizon have disappeared from the catalogue. *Post-Motown Bop* has its moments, but it's a far less enterprising set than *The Inventor*, which was recorded a year before.

Most of Watson's titles from the late 1970s to mid-'80s have so far failed to make the transition to CD (the loss of *Estimated Time Of Arrival*, named after his theme-tune, and 1984's *Perpetual Groove* leaves a bit of a hole). However, his masterpiece has survived. *Love Remains* is a startlingly poised performance. From the Parker-influenced 'Mystery Of Ebop' to the solemnly funky 'Dark Days (Against Apartheid)', it has a complete unity of purpose. The title-piece, jointly credited to Bobby and Pamela Watson, is built round a three-note motif which means the same thing in any language. Hicks's solo is a perfect foil for Watson's slightly plangent second entry, while Lundy and Smitty Smith sustain a dark bass pulse. Lundy's 'Sho Thang' is the only non-Watson composition, a weak interlude before Pam Watson's 'The Love We Had Yesterday' rounds off the set. If the '80s threw up maybe a baker's dozen essential jazz albums, *Love Remains* comes in somewhere near the top.

The solo saxophone album was a challenge Watson had resisted for many years. The results are inevitably patchy, and it isn't the kind of set that makes for comfortable listening straight through. Better to concentrate on one track at a time and savour Watson's deft phrasing and sinuous developments. A few of the pieces are little more than work-outs: 'These Foolish Things', 'Body And Soul', and a quick run through the 'Giant Steps' changes. 'Misterioso', 'Donna Lee' and Joe Henderson's 'Recorda Me' are more developed, but some of the most interesting ideas emerge out of traditional material; there are two takes of Apostoloy Kaldara's 'Mes'Tou Bosporou' and the title-track is an old spiritual Watson's preacher grandfather used to sing. *This Little Light* doesn't quite take him full circle, but it sets out certain agenda that he could usefully spend the next ten years addressing.

**** Present Tense Columbia CK 52400
> Watson; Terell Stafford (*t*); Edward Simon (*p*); Essiet Essiet (*b*); Victor Lewis (*d*). 12/91.

***(*) Tailor Made Columbia CK 53416/473766-2
> As above, except omit Simon; add Jon Faddis, Melton Mustafa, Ryan Kisor (*t*); Steve Turre, Robin Eubanks, Frank Lacy, Doug Purviance (*tb*); Tom Varner (*frhn*); Bobby Porcelli, Ed Jackson, Rich Rothenberg, Bill Saxton, Patience Higgins, Jim Hartog (*reeds*); James Williams,

Danilo Perez, Eddie Martinez (*p*); Paul Socolow (*b*); Steve Berrios (*d*); Ray Mantilla (*perc*). The earlier of these sessions sounds remarkably like a bigger-budget version of the wonderful *Love Remains*. Watson re-does both the title-piece and 'The Mystery Of Ebop', but in the process loses something of the earlier album's moody lyricism. It's all a bit too pat and overmixed, though punchier tracks like 'Monk He See, Monk He Do' gain considerably.

Tailor Made is the fulfilment of Watson's ambition to record with a big band. The members of Horizon, with the brilliant Stephen Scott in for Simon, are embedded in a wish-list line-up for a session that (bravely) consists almost entirely of new stuff. Pamela Watson contributes two numbers, a tribute to 'Ms BC', Betty Carter, and 'Like It Was Before', a tune that probably requires a smaller-scale and more intimate arrangement than it gets here. All the horns are beautifully registered, and Victor Lewis, by this stage Watson's main man in the rhythm section, is well mixed up, giving the whole session a slightly hard sonority that does it no harm whatsoever. One suspects that a less sympathetic production team would have softened the edges just a little.

He switches to soprano for 'Beam Me Up' on the quintet disc, sounding unmistakably like himself, with the same attractive eccentricity of pitching, self-consistent but edgy. Neither album gives the leader particular emphasis, and it may be that Watson sees his future progress more as a composer/bandleader. That would be a loss, of course; but on this showing there are likely to be sterling gains, too.

***(*) **Midwest Shuffle** Columbia 475925

Watson; Terell Stafford (*t*); Edward Simon (*p*); Essiet Essiet (*b*); Victor Lewis (*d*). 10 & 11/93. In the old reviewer's cliché, this one 'answers a long-felt need'. Impressive as Watson is in the studio, his real skill and charm are evident only when he takes the stage, and this live album, Watson's first, documents what was by all accounts an excellent tour.

It should, like the Blue Notes, have been attributed to Watson and Horizon, since the band plays a major part in the music's success. Stafford is a fine young trumpeter who manages to steer clear of the hard-bop banalities of most young Clifford'n'Lee imitators. Though he is not yet widely recorded, he has a very identifiable sound which has clearly been moulded in rehearsal and on tour to fit in with the leader's. Their solos on the long opening 'Blues Of Hope' establish a high standard; the rest of the set merely confirms it. 'Complex Dialogue' and 'Midwest Shuffle' itself mark out the boundaries of what the group does. Tightly written and highly rhythmic, Watson's compositions don't leave too much space for long, noodling solos. It's all highly disciplined.

Inevitably, something of Watson's presence is lost, even on a live record. Smiling or nodding thoughtfully at the other members of the band, he keeps up a cat-limbed dance – which may yet become fashionable as the Midwest Shuffle – sliding his palms together like a guiro player during his colleagues' solos. Some attempt has been made to give the record as much presence and atmosphere as possible. Watson introduces the players by section on 'The Cats' and there are a couple of other brief, spoken interludes, of welcome and introduction. The set opens with the hilarious moment when one fan in the audience was so moved by the music as to stand up and tell 'Mr Watson' (this is the Mid-West after all) just how much he was enjoying it. Him, and us, too.

***(*) **Jewel** Evidence ECD 22043

Watson; Mulgrew Miller (*p*); Steve Nelson (*vib*); Curtis Lundy (*b*); Marvin 'Smitty' Smith (*d*); Dom Um Romao (*perc*). 93.

**** **Gumbo** Evidence ECD 22078

Watson; Melton Mustafa (*t, flhn*); Hamiet Bluiett (*bs*); Mulgrew Miller (*p*); Curtis Lundy (*b*); Marvin 'Smitty' Smith (*d*). 94.

A new label and a new initiative. The 1994 date with Bluiett and Mustafa is quite clearly an attempt to take his music in a darker and rootsier direction than the more familiar post-bop of *Jewel*. It now seems a trifle hackneyed, given the new languages that he is exploring under Bluiett's seeming influence. Both records are recognizably by the same artist who made *Love Remains* and *Post-Motown Bop*, but Watson has continued to absorb new influences and to work at aspects of his own compositional approach, not least his growing resistance to song-forms. These are so clearly transitional records that it is hard to get a fix on them. Watson enthusiasts will love them; others may need more persuasion.

Eric Watson PIANO

*** **The Amiens Concert** Label Bleu 6512

Watson; Steve Lacy (*ss*); John Lindberg (*b*). 11/87.

(*) **Broadway By Twilight Musidisc 500482

Watson (*p* solo). 2/92.

*** **Soundpost** Music & Arts 920
> Watson; John Lindberg (*b*). 9/90–5/95.

Watson is an interesting player, but he's hard to characterize: influences such as Monk, John Lewis and Mal Waldron seem to drift in and out of his music, and his composing favours dark, sluggish structures that mysteriously relax into moments of pure lyricism. Intriguing – but sometimes hard to take over the course of a record, and the hints of humour suggested by his titles ('New Canaan Con Man', 'Substance Abuse') never really surface. Steve Lacy seems to have been attracted by Watson's grainy intensity, and he makes a fist of the settings on this record without quite invading Watson's world. *The Amiens Concert* is a bleak, unsmiling recital, with four Watson themes and one apiece by the others: again, when Lacy absconds on 'Substance Abuse', Watson and Lindberg reach a scowling truce. The duo record *Soundpost* is just as demanding, recorded mainly in 1995 with two stray solo tracks from earlier sessions. Watson's thick left-hand sonorities allow Lindberg to roam over his instrument with no less of an impact, and when they toil implacably through the pianist's five-part 'The Twisted Suite', the players create a dense thunder of sound that can seem brutally intimidating. Stern but absorbing.

Broadway By Twilight is just on the far side of agreeable. Watson milks all the sweetness out of seven standards and leaves each one a dark, cauterized corpse. The funereal tempos and brooding development aren't very nice, though that's hardly Watson's style. Less impressive is his own kind of routine: each theme ends up sounding the same, perhaps.

Ernie Watts TENOR SAXOPHONE, ALTO SAXOPHONE, SOPRANO SAXOPHONE

***(*) **Ernie Watts Quartet** JVC 3309
> Watts; Pat Coil (*p*); Joel Di Bartolo (*b*); Bob Leatherbarrow (*d*). 12/87.
*** **Afoxé** CTI R2 79479
> Watts; Kenny Kirkland (*p*); Robert Sadin, Dunn Pearson (*ky*); Jack DeJohnette (*ky, d*); Marlon Graves, Romero Lubambo (*g*); Mark Egan, Eddie Gomez, Victor Bailey, Marcus Miller (*b*); Ray Bardani, Frank Colón, Cafe, Manolo Badrena, Mino Cinélu, Tony Mola (*perc*); Sharon Bryant (*v*); Gilberto Gil (*v, g*). 91.
**** **Reaching Up** JVC 2031
> Watts; Arturo Sandoval (*t*); Mulgrew Miller (*p*); Charles Fambrough (*b*); Jack DeJohnette (*d*). 93.

One of the real delights of Charlie Haden's largely unsung Quartet West was Watts's tender-muscular sax and synth patterns, looming and shimmering out of Haden's Angelean fogs. Watts's solo career has been slow in getting under way, but the last few years have seen some interesting activity. The eponymous *Quartet* features his rawer-sounding alto and positively desolate soprano (which might have sounded good in Quartet West) in a broadly romantic set of themes. The rhythm section are nothing to write home about and Watts is left with most of the work on 'Body And Soul', but as a package it's very accomplished.

Afoxé is an odd record, part-jazz, part-soul, part-New Age / world music / environmental-concern manifesto. Gil's monologues about Brazil (the Portuguese, African and Japanese diaspora) are actually very listenable and Watts's soprano playing fits the bill admirably. However, the singing is deplorable and often poorly registered, so it's a treat to turn to *Reaching Up*, unambiguously a jazz album, albeit with other inputs hovering round the edges. DeJohnette had contributed to *Afoxé*, playing drums and keyboard kalimba. Here, he provides the fuel for a driving, energetic work-out that highlights the leader's solo construction perfectly. Arturo Sandoval turns up on two tracks, bringing his usual fierce integrity, but the stage is Watts's and he uses it to the full.

Jeff Tain Watts DRUMS

*** **Megawatts** Sunnyside SSC 1055D
> Watts; Kenny Kirkland (*p*); Charles Fambrough (*b*). 7/91.

Watts emerged as one of the leading drummers of his time when he worked in the first Wynton Marsalis Quintet, and this debut set under his own name reunites the original rhythm section from that band. His two original tunes have no special interest: Watts makes noise as a player, not as a composer, and his favourite devices – thumping interpolations on the toms, crash-cymbal strokes that seem to linger in their own time, and an iron-faced swing – are well in evidence here. Kirkland is gregariously on top of the material. It's a good record, if rather charmless: there is some light and shade, but the trio are really interested only when they have the burners up full.

Trevor Watts (born 1939) ALTO SAXOPHONE, SOPRANO SAXOPHONE

*** A Wider Embrace ECM 1449

> Watts; Colin McKenzie (*b*); Nana Tsiboe, Nee-Daku Patato, Jojo Yates, Nana Appiah, Paapa J. Mensah (*perc*). 4/93.

***(*) Moiré Intakt CD 039

> Watts; Colin McKenzie (*b*); Paapa J. Mensah (*d, perc, v*); 3/95.

A stalwart of the British free-jazz scene, Watts has to some extent turned his back entirely on abstract music in order to explore the strongly rhythmic, non-European language of his two main groups of the 1980s, the Drum Orchestra and (as on the first record) Moiré Music. The word 'moiré' refers to the shimmering patterns one sees in watered silk, and what Watts was trying to do was to create such patterns musically by overlaying rhythmic patterns and textures in live performance.

Moiré Music performances have tended to be either entrancing or dull. The ECM album inclines to the latter but is still eminently listenable, and techno buffs can marvel at the way engineer Gary Thomas and Steve Lake at ECM managed to get so many drums sounding good. Watts's studies in African percussion music have occasionally resulted in illustrated lectures. While there is a wealth of ethnomusicological detail attached to this recording, it is altogether more flowing, and Watts is playing singingly and with passion. Unfashionable he may be, even as a negative example, but this is territory opened up by Ginger Baker in the years after Cream. Though some aspects of the music have still not been thought through, it's a significant performance.

The tight, fierce trio on the Intakt disc gives a better sense of how his current work relates back to British free-movement projects like Amalgam. Mensah is a big presence, bringing a pungent vocal attack as well as wild percussion, and McKenzie's bass lines weave to and fro like oiled rope.

Weather Report GROUP

*** Weather Report Columbia 468212

> Joe Zawinul (*ky*); Wayne Shorter (*ts, ss*); Miroslav Vitous (*b*); Alphonse Mouzon (*d*); Airto Moreira (*perc*). 71.

**** I Sing The Body Electric Columbia 468207

> Joe Zawinul (*ky*); Wayne Shorter (*ts, ss*); Miroslav Vitous (*b*); Eric Gravátt (*d*); Dom Um Romao (*perc*); with Ralph Towner (*g*); Wilmer Wise (*t, picc t*); Hubert Laws (*f*); Andrew White (*eng hn*); Joshie Armstrong, Yolande Bavan, Chapman Roberts (*v*). 72.

**** Mysterious Traveller Columbia 487931

> Joe Zawinul (*ky*); Wayne Shorter (*ts, ss*); Miroslav Vitous (*b*); Ismael Wilburn (*d*); Dom Um Romao (*perc*). 73–74.

*** Tale Spinnin' Columbia 476907

> As above, except Alphonso Johnson (*b*) replaces Vitous; omit Romao, Wilburn; add Leon Ndugu Chancler (*d*), Alyrio Lima (*perc*). 74.

***(*) Black Market Columbia 468210

> Joe Zawinul (*ky*); Wayne Shorter (*ts, ss*); Alphonso Johnson, Jaco Pastorius (*b*); Chester Thompson, Narada Michael Walden (*d*); Alejandro Neciosup Acuna, Don Alias (*perc*). 76.

***(*) Heavy Weather Columbia 468209

> Joe Zawinul (*ky*); Wayne Shorter (*ts, ss*); Jaco Pastorius (*b*); Alejandro Neciosup Acuna (*d, perc*); Manolo Badrena (*perc*). 76.

*** Mr Gone Columbia 468208

> Joe Zawinul (*ky*); Wayne Shorter (*ts, ss*); Jaco Pastorius (*b*); Tony Williams, Steve Gadd, Pete Erskine (*d*); Manolo Badrena (*perc*); Denice Williams, Jon Lucien (*v*). 78.

*** Night Passage Columbia 468211

> Joe Zawinul (*ky*); Wayne Shorter (*ts, ss*); Jaco Pastorius (*b*); Peter Erskine (*d*); Robert Thomas Jr (*perc*). 80.

*** Domino Theory Columbia 25839

> Joe Zawinul (*ky*); Wayne Shorter (*ss, ts*); Victor Bailey (*b*); Omar Hakim (*d*); Jose Rossy (*perc*). 84.

Weather Report are one of the great contemporary jazz groups. 'Birdland' on *Heavy Weather* is one of only a tiny handful of contemporary jazz tunes that everyone seems to have heard. Though it has tended to overshadow the rest of the group's output, it encapsulates perfectly the formula that has made the group so successful: solid part-writing from Joe Zawinul, Wayne Shorter's enigmatic saxophone sound, a free-floating personnel round the Zawinul–Shorter cadre, and great product marketing (Weather Report covers have been consistently eye-catching and aesthetically pleasing). In 1990 Columbia withdrew the whole Weather Report catalogue on vinyl and embarked on a programme of CD reissues. That programme has been very welcome, though the packaging leaves something to be desired; in line with other Columbia reissues, newcomers have to look long and hard to sort out personnels, which are given as printed above. Reprinting old liner-notes and running self-serving and misleading puffs in place of clear and straightforward information is something of a dereliction (though absolutely in line with CBS's famously cavalier attitude to musicians and fans alike).

From its inception until its demise in 1986, Weather Report was a flexible ensemble. After the first album, it was unmistakably Zawinul's flexible ensemble. From that point, Zawinul claimed the majority of composition credits (though Shorter, Pastorius and others chipped in) and steered the band's increasingly rhythm-orientated conception. Zawinul compositions are typically riff-centred bass-clef ideas built up in layers by the rest of the band. Those who had followed Shorter's developing career were alternately baffled and horrified by the exiguous squeaks and tonal smears that suddenly were passing for solos (solos, it had been pointed out, were not the Weather Report way; 'we always solo and we never solo'). The first album was a set of fey acrylic sketches, clearly derived from the pastel side of the 1969–70 Miles Davis band (in which both Zawinul and Shorter saw service) but much rawer in tone. The opening 'Milky Way' is a pleased-with-itself set of FX on electric piano and soprano saxophone; 'it has to do with overtones and the way one uses the piano pedals?' Yeah? That's great, man. Most of the rest is in similar vein. Many years later, Vitous rejigged his folksy 'Morning Lake' and made something of it. The recording is thin and erratic, which is a shame, for Shorter's closing 'Eurydice' introduces some promise.

Everything about *I Sing The Body Electric* was very 1972: the title lifted from Whitman via Ray Bradbury, the brilliant sci-fi artwork (an overdue hand, please, for Ed Lee, Jack Trompetter and Fred Swanson), the psychobabble liner-note ('There is flow. There is selflessness'). There was also a band on the brink of premature extinction. Side one is more or less an extension of the debut album. The (presumably) anti-war 'Unknown Soldier' is almost prettified. The only thing that redeems it from banality is a tense cymbal pulse that on the live second side erupts into some of the most torrential and threatening percussion of the period. Zawinul is on record as thinking that Gravátt was the finest drummer the group ever had. On 'Vertical Invader' he plays with a clubbing hostility that somehow intensifies the impression that the group was heading off in four or five (Dom Um Romao was only a part-timer) directions at once. These days, Gravátt works as a prison guard. *Plus ça change.*

Mysterious Traveller is still perhaps the most sheerly beautiful of the records, from the wild joy of 'Nubian Sundance' with its synthed crowd noises to the quietness of 'Blackthorn Rose', a lyrical, delicate piece of music that suggests this may have been the point of maximum closeness between the band's onlie begetters, Zawinul and Shorter.

Ever afterwards, Weather Report albums were inclined to look like audition sessions for new drummers. Steve Gadd, Tony Williams and Peter Erskine all played on *Mr Gone*, suggesting (in that correctly) a band that was going in too many directions at once. The syndrome also afflicted *Sweetnighter*, *Mysterious Traveller* and *Tale Spinnin'*. These have been available intermittently, but not in every territory, and not all at the same time. *Black Market* seems to combine their virtues (atmospheric tone-poetry, thudding, joyous rhythms) in the first unambiguously satisfying Weather Report album. With Pastorius arriving in time to cut the funky 'Barbary Coast', Zawinul has the engine-room tuned to his obvious satisfaction. 'Black Market' is a wonderful, thunderous tune that completely blows out Shorter's rather wimpy 'Three Clowns' and utterly wimpy lyricon figures; galling, because on 'Cannon Ball', dedicated to Julian Cannonball Adderley, for whom Zawinul played and wrote 'Country Preacher' and 'Mercy, Mercy, Mercy', Shorter signs in again with some chunky tenor.

Heavy Weather was the breakthrough album in market terms. It allegedly shifted in excess of 400,000, largely on the strength of 'Birdland', a whistleable, riffy tune dedicated to the New York jazz club. No one had ever danced to 'Orange Lady' or 'Surucucú'; suddenly, Weather Report were big, a fact that comfortably disguised the detail that, 'Birdland' and 'A Remark You Made' apart, *Heavy Weather* was nothing much. Onstage, the band went decidedly *nouveau riche*, tossing around techno-nonsense, indulging in pointless virtuosity.

All except Shorter. He is widely taken to be *Mr Gone* (at high school, they'd called him 'Mr Weird'), but he shows his taste, maintaining virtual silence on the band's worst record, lower than which it took them some time to dive. *Night Passage* was better, but it was already obvious that a decade was more than enough, the band had done its best work; the rest was for the fans and for CBS, not for the players, and that makes an important and unhappy difference. *Domino Theory* has one signature Zawinul piece, 'The Peasant', which earns the stars, but that's about it.

Chick Webb (1909–39) DRUMS

**** Chick Webb 1929–1934 Classics 502
    Webb; Ward Pinkett, Louis Bacon, Taft Jordan (*t, v*); Edwin Swayzee, Mario Bauza, Reunald

Jones, Bobby Stark, Shelton Hemphill, Louis Hunt (*t*); Robert Horton, Jimmy Harrison, Sandy
Williams, Ferdinand Arbello, Claude Jones (*tb*); Hilton Jefferson, Louis Jordan, Benny Carter
(*cl, as*); Pete Clark, Edgar Sampson (*as*); Elmer Williams (*cl, ts*); Wayman Carver (*ts, f*); Don
Kirkpatrick, Joe Steele (*p*); John Trueheart (*bj, g*); Elmer James (*bb, b*); John Kirby (*b*); Chuck
Richards, Charles Linton (*v*). 6/29–11/34.

***(*) Rhythm Man 1931–1934 Hep CD 1023

As above. 31–34.

***(*) Chick Webb 1935–1938 Classics 517

As above, except add Nat Story, George Matthews (*tb*), Chauncey Houghton (*cl, as*), Ted
McRae (*ts*), Tommy Fulford (*p*), Bill Thomas, Beverley Peer (*b*); omit Bacon, Swayzee, Jones,
Hemphill, Hunt, Horton, Harrison, Arbello, Carter, Kirkpatrick, Richards, Linton. 6/35–8/38.

**** Spinnin' The Webb MCA GRP 16352

As above two discs, except add Dick Vance (*t*). 6/29–2/39.

Between them, these CDs include all of Webb's studio recordings aside from those with vocals by Ella
Fitzgerald, which Classics have released under her name. The two tracks by The Jungle Band of 1929
sound almost primitive in comparison to the ensuing sessions, driven as much by Trueheart's machine-
like banjo strumming as by Webb, but its use of the reeds and Webb's already exciting playing point a
way out of the 1920s and, by the time of the 1931 session – which includes a memorable arrangement by
Benny Carter of his own 'Blues In My Heart' and a valedictory appearance by Jimmy Harrison, who
died not long afterwards – Webb was running a great band, which eventually (in 1933) won him a long-
running residency at Harlem's Savoy Ballroom. Edgar Sampson handled some of the best of the earlier
arrangements, and the leader could boast fine soloists in Taft Jordan (later to join Ellington), Sandy
Williams, Bobby Stark and Elmer Williams, as well as a rhythm section that was almost unrivalled for
attack and swing. Webb's own mastery of an enormous drum-kit allowed him to pack a whole range of
percussive effects into breaks and solos which never disjointed the momentum of the band. His distance
from the showmanship of Gene Krupa, who would far surpass him in acclaim, was complete. Some of
the best examples of what he could do are on the second disc, including the terrific drive of 'Go Harlem'
and the breaks in 'Clap Hands! Here Comes Charley'. Once Fitzgerald had started singing with the
band and began to secure a wider fame, though, some of the zip went out of their playing and, although
the worst material is confined to the Fitzgerald CDs, the closing tracks on Classics 517 show them
cooling off.

Choosing among these discs is a matter of individual taste. The two Classics CDs offer uninterrupted
coverage, but their reproduction, though quite listenable, is second-best to both the Hep disc and the
MCA compilation. Hep's excellent survey covers only the period 1931–4 and misses many of the best
tracks but is still a fine set in excellent sound. MCA's cross-section covers the whole era, includes most
of the best tracks, and sounds clean: as a one-disc survey, this gets first choice.

***(*) Chick Webb And His Savoy Ballroom Orchestra 1939 Tax 3706-2

Webb; Dick Vance, Bobby Stark, Taft Jordan (*t*); Sandy Williams, Nat Story, George Matthews
(*tb*); Garvin Bushell, Hilton Jefferson (*cl, as*); Wayman Carver (*ts, f*); Ted McRae (*ts*); Tommy
Fulford (*p*); Bobby Johnson (*g*); Beverley Peer (*b*); Ella Fitzgerald (*v*). 1–5/39.

The swing which Webb and the orchestra generate on these broadcasts, made not long before Webb's
death later in 1939, belie any hint on the studio records that the band was getting fatigued. Twenty-two
tracks from two sessions, the first with Fitzgerald absent, find all concerned in top form. Stark, Jordan
and Williams are again the outstanding soloists, but Webb's own playing is certainly the most powerful
thing on the second date, where he combines with the excellent Peer to turn unlikely tunes such as 'My
Wild Irish Rose' into battlegrounds. The slightly superior sound gives it an advantage over the first
session, but both are very listenable, and the treatment of Count Basie's showcase 'One O'Clock Jump'
on the earlier set reminds that Webb managed to defeat Basie's orchestra in a 'battle of the bands' at the
Savoy almost exactly a year before.

Eberhard Weber (born 1940) BASS, CELLO, OCARINA, KEYBOARDS

***(*) The Colours Of Chloe ECM 1042

Weber; Ack Van Rooyen (*flhn*); Rainer Bruninghaus (*ky*); Peter Giger, Ralf Hubner (*d*); strings.
12/73.

Having played straight-ahead jazz bass through the 1960s, Weber delivered this uncannily beautiful
album to Manfred Eicher's ECM operation and won himself an award or two. If some passages now
suggest a cooler version of *Tubular Bells*, with the overlapping themes of 'No Motion Picture' hinting at
the tranquillizing pomposity of progressive rock, the singular beauty of the textures and Weber's
discovery of a new world based around massed cellos and subtle electronic treatments remains insidi-

ously affecting. While the improvisational content is carefully rationed against the measure of the themes, Bruninghaus and Weber himself emerge as thoughtful and surprisingly vigorous virtuosos. While the CD offers few improvements over the excellent original vinyl edition, the recording itself still sounds splendid.

**** **Yellow Fields** ECM 1066
    Weber; Charlie Mariano (*ss, shenai*); Rainer Bruninghaus (*ky*); Jon Christensen (*d*). 9/75.
Weber's masterpiece is essentially a period piece which will surely outface time. The sound of it seems almost absurdly opulent: bass passages and swimming keyboard textures that reverberate from the speakers, chords that seem to hum with huge overtones. The keyboard textures in particular are of a kind that will probably never be heard on record again. But there's little prolixity or meandering in this music. Weber builds very keenly around riffs and rhythmical figures, and solos – Mariano sounding piercingly exotic on the shenai, heartbreakingly intense on soprano – are perfectly ensconced within the sound-field. The key element, though, is the inspirational series of cross-rhythms and accents which Christensen delivers, rising to an extraordinary crescendo towards the close of 'Sand-Glass', a sprawling performance built from simple materials. And the leader's own bass never sounded better.

** **The Following Morning** ECM 1084
    Weber; Rainer Bruninghaus (*ky*); Oslo Philharmonic Orchestra. 8/76.
*** **Silent Feet** ECM 1107
    Weber; Charlie Mariano (*ss, shenai*); Rainer Bruninghaus (*ky*); John Marshall (*d*). 11/77.
(*) **Fluid / Rustle ECM 1137
    Weber; Gary Burton (*vib, mar*); Bill Frisell (*g, bal*); Bonnie Herman, Norma Winstone (*v*). 1/79.
The anchorless drifting of *The Following Morning* was a disappointing continuation, rhythmically dead and texturally thin, with Weber and Bruninghaus circling dolefully through their material and badly missing a drummer. *Silent Feet* introduced John Marshall, formerly of Soft Machine, into the Colours band which Weber was touring with and, while his stiffer virtuosity wasn't the same thing as Christensen's sober flair, he restored some of the punch to Weber's music. The record hasn't the memorable tunes and perfect empathy of the earlier discs, though. Nor is *Fluid/Rustle* much more than enervating, with Burton's blandly effortful playing and Frisell's as-yet-unfocused contributions adding little to Weber's pretty but uninvolving pieces.

(*) **Later That Evening ECM 1231
    Weber; Paul McCandless (*ss, cor, ob, bcl*); Lyle Mays (*p*); Bill Frisell (*g*); Michael DiPasqua (*d*). 3/82.
Two new bands provided Weber with better results. *Little Movements* was his best since *Yellow Fields*, the intricacies of 'A Dark Spell' and Bruninghaus's 'Bali' fielded with no problems, and Marshall growing into a resilient timekeeper for the band, but unfortunately it has still to appear on CD and Weberites will have to search for remaining vinyl copies. *Later That Evening* isn't quite as good, with Mays a poor substitute for Bruninghaus and McCandless missing Mariano's acute sense of context, but it has its moments.

(*) **Chorus ECM 1288
    Weber; Jan Garbarek (*ss, ts*); Manfred Hoffbauer (*cl, f*); Martin Kunstner (*ob, cor*); Ralf Hubner (*d*). 9/84.
*** **Orchestra** ECM 1374
    Weber; Herbert Joos, Anton Jillich, Wolfgang Czelusta, Andreas Richter (*tb*); Winfried Rapp (*btb*); Rudolf Diebetsberger, Thomas Hauschild (*frhn*); Franz Stagl (*tba*). 5–8/88.
Weber has lacked a valuable context in recent years: having patented one of the most gorgeous of bass sounds, he doesn't seem to have much else to say with it. *Chorus* is heavy on the brooding-spirit element, with Garbarek delivering some of his most stentorian commentaries on what are less than riveting themes, as Weber and Hubner toil away in the background. As a sequence of mood-music cameos, it may appeal strongly to some, but it's a depressing listen over the course of an entire record. *Orchestra* will disappoint any who've attended Weber's highly entertaining solo concerts. He splits the album between bass soliloquies and counterpoint with a chilly brass section, yet the prettiest piece on the disc is the synthesizer tune, 'On A Summer's Evening'.

**** **Pendulum** ECM 1518
    Weber (*b* solo).
Weber's second solo record is all bass this time and finds much of the beguiling and unexpectedly light-hearted feel of his one-man concerts. Ironically, it is much more studio-orientated: where *Orchestra* was overdub-free and essentially live, *Pendulum*, while remaining a solo meditation, is carefully edited for maximum effect. Weber's bass remains a unique sound in the music, and here he finds an almost perfect balance between the mixed blessing of bass opulence and the sing-song quality of his best melodies.

Overlapping riffs or vamps counter the steady onward flow of the improviser's ideas, and in 'Street Scenes', 'Children's Song No. 1' or 'Pendulum' itself he secures a marvellous, patient equilibrium. His sleeve-notes are remarkably self-aware and offer some useful signposts for working through this encounter with 'my life-long preoccupation – also my old adversary'. Weber's best for many years.

*** **Works** ECM 825429-2
A solid selection of Weber highlights, all but one of the pieces dating back to his music from the 1970s, with the memorable 'Touch' from *Yellow Fields* and 'Sand' from Ralph Towner's *Solstice* album particularly fine.

Ben Webster (1909–73) TENOR SAXOPHONE

*** **The Horn** Progressive PCD-7001
> Webster; Hot Lips Page (*t*); Clyde Hart (*p*); Charlie Drayton (*b*); Denzil Best (*d*). 2/44.

**** **King Of The Tenors** Verve 519806-2
> Webster; Harry 'Sweets' Edison (*t*); Benny Carter (*as*); Oscar Peterson (*p*); Barney Kessel, Herb Ellis (*g*); Ray Brown (*b*); Alvin Stoller, J. C. Heard (*d*). 5–12/53.

**** **Soulville** Verve 833551-2
> Webster; Oscar Peterson (*p*); Barney Kessel, Herb Ellis (*g*); Ray Brown (*b*); J. C. Heard, Stan Levey (*d*). 5/53–10/57.

**** **Ben Webster Meets Oscar Peterson** Verve 829167-2
> Webster; Oscar Peterson (*p*); Ray Brown (*b*); Ed Thigpen (*d*). 59.

The best-loved of all saxophonists, perhaps of all jazz musicians, Ben Webster created a style which is the most personal and immediately identifiable sound in all of the music. As he got older and less partial to any tempo above a very slow lope, he pared his manner back to essentials which still, no matter how often one hears them, remain uniquely affecting. The best of his early work is with Duke Ellington – he remained, along with Paul Gonsalves, one of only two tenormen to make a genuine impression on Ducal history – but his records as a solo player, from the early 1950s onwards, are a formidable legacy. *The Horn* is a collection of WBC transcriptions featuring Ben as nominal leader of a quintet with Hot Lips Page: the flow of the music is somewhat jolted by the programme, which includes various false starts and alternatives for the sake of completeness, and Lips Page takes a subsidiary role; but Webster's playing is already graceful and creating its own time and space. The remastering is occasionally cloudy but mostly good. There are some beautifully bleary sessions with strings from the 1950s which have yet to make their way to domestic CD release, but all three of the Verve discs find Ben in terrific form, and the remastering catches his sound at its ripest. *King Of The Tenors* blends a date with Oscar Peterson plus rhythm section with another where Edison and Carter sit in too, though the spotlight is always on Webster. 'Tenderly' has never been more tender, 'That's All' is sheer heaven, but 'Jive At Six' is a good piece of studio knockabout. Peterson may seem an unlikely partner but, just as Webster played superbly next to Art Tatum, so he mastered the potentially open floodgates of Peterson's playing. On *Soulville*, there are lustrous ballads in 'Where Are You' and an eerily desolate 'Ill Wind', while 'Boogie Woogie' brings out the raucous side of the tenorman. Three previously unissued tracks from the sessions are also included on the CD. *Meets Oscar Peterson* is just as fine, with two melting ballads in 'The Touch Of Your Lips' and 'In The Wee Small Hours Of The Morning' and a lissom 'This Can't Be Love'.

**** **Music For Loving** Verve 527774-2 2CD
> Webster; Harry Carney (*bs*); Teddy Wilson, Billy Strayhorn, Leroy Lovett (*p*); Billy Bauer (*g*); Ray Brown, George Duvivier, Wendell Marshall (*b*); Jo Jones, Osie Johnson, Louie Bellson (*d*); horns and strings. 3/54–9/55.

**** **The Soul Of Ben Webster** Verve 527475-2 2CD
> Webster; Art Farmer, Harry 'Sweets' Edison, Roy Eldridge (*t*); Vic Dickenson (*tb*); Johnny Hodges (*as*); Harold Ashby (*ts*); Jimmy Jones, Oscar Peterson, Billy Strayhorn (*p*); Mundell Lowe, Barney Kessel, Herb Ellis (*g*); Milt Hinton, Ray Brown, Jimmy Woode (*b*); Dave Bailey, Alvin Stoller, Sam Woodyard (*d*). 3/57–7/58.

Impeccably prepared, these two-disc reissues are among Webster's best records. The strings sessions, mostly arranged by Ralph Burns, may sound a little thin to ears used to digital grandeur, but the writing is beguiling and Webster sweeps through what must have been an ideal setting for him. Hidden away at the end of the package, almost as a bonus, is the rare album which Harry Carney recorded with strings, a fine date in its own right.

The Soul Of Ben Webster puts together three original LPs: the title album, Harry Edison's *Gee Baby Ain't I Good To You*, and Johnny Hodges's *Blues A-Plenty*. With three superb bands on hand, the music is a blueprint for small-group swing, and Webster contributes some of his most rounded and accomplished playing: the mesmerizing drift through 'Chelsea Bridge', for instance. His own date featured Ashby as second tenor, and there's a palpable camaraderie. Some of the Hodges titles are a bit slight, but this is altogether an indispensable issue.

***(*) **Verve Jazz Masters 43: Ben Webster** Verve 525431-2
    As Verve records above, except add Ella Fitzgerald (*v*), Johnny Otis Orchestra. 12/51–11/59.
A choice selection from Webster's Verve years. Besides some of the staples from the albums listed above, there's Ella doing 'In A Mellow Tone' from the *Ellington Songbook* sessions and a 1951 version of 'Star Dust' with Johnny Otis that seems to float skyward, star-dusted indeed.

*** **At The Renaissance** Original Jazz Classics OJC 390
    Webster; Jimmy Rowles (*p*); Jim Hall (*g*); Red Mitchell (*b*); Frank Butler (*d*). 10/60.
***(*) **Ben And 'Sweets'** Columbia 460613-2
    Webster; Harry 'Sweets' Edison (*t*); Hank Jones (*p*); George Duvivier (*b*); Clarence Johnston (*d*). 6/62.
Among friends and feeling fine. Nobody ever played 'My Romance' like Ben, and the version on *Ben And 'Sweets'* is very close to definitive, a chorus of melody and another of improvisation which unfold with unerring logic. His treatment of melody remains a compulsory point of study for aspiring improvisers: he respects every part of each measure, yet makes it his own by eliminating a note, adding another, or taking breaths at moments when no one else would think of pausing, lest the momentum fall down. Webster's inner clock never fails him. Edison, the wryest of sidekicks, noodles alongside in his happiest lazybones manner, and Jones takes a handful of princely solos. The remastering will sound a bit lifeless to those who've heard the original vinyl. *At The Renaissance* finds Webster in unusual company and, while Rowles reads him like a good book, the others sometimes sound a little too smartly present and correct. 'Gone With The Wind', though, is a beauty.

(*) **Live At Pio's Enja 2038
    Webster; Junior Mance (*p*); Bob Cranshaw (*b*); Mickey Roker (*d*). 63.
(*) **Live! Providence, Rhode Island, 1963 Storyville STCD 8237
    Webster; Mike Renzi (*p*); Bob Petterutti (*b*); Joe Veletri (*d*). 12/63.
*** **Soulmates** Original Jazz Classics OJC 390
    Webster; Thad Jones (*c*); Joe Zawinul (*p*); Richard Davis (*b*); Philly Joe Jones (*d*). 9–10/63.
Ben was already settling into a favourite repertory of tunes when he made the live album: 'Sunday', 'How Long Has This Been Going On?' and 'Gone With The Wind' were three of them. Docked a notch for imperfect live sound and Mance's tiresome clichés at the piano, but Webster sounds well enough. He enjoyed himself in Providence, too: 'My Romance', 'Embraceable You', 'Danny Boy'. The local rhythm section plays respectfully but the sound is from an average, amateur tape. *Soulmates* offered a strange pairing with the young Joe Zawinul, with Jones sitting in on four tracks, although Webster was happy with any pianist who stood his ground. Highlights include a poignant reflection on Billie Holiday's 'Trav'lin' Light' and the title-blues.

***(*) **Stormy Weather** Black Lion BLCD 760108
    Webster; Kenny Drew (*p*); Niels-Henning Orsted-Pedersen (*b*); Alex Riel (*d*). 1/65.
***(*) **Gone With The Wind** Black Lion BLCD 760125
    As above. 1/65.
Recorded on a single long, long night at Copenhagen's Café Montmartre, these glorious records commemorate the start of Webster's lengthy European sojourn. Drew's scholarly blend of blues and bop phrasing lends gentlemanly support, while the two local youngsters on bass and drums behave respectfully without losing their enthusiasm. All, though, rests with Webster's now inimitable tone and delivery. Close to the microphone, he's often content barely to enunciate the melody in an exhalation which feathers down to a pitchless vibration as often as it hits an actual note. Up-tempo pieces tend to be throwaway bundles of phrases, but anything slower becomes a carefully orchestrated set-piece. Sometimes the pace becomes almost too stolid, and perhaps the records are best heard a few tracks at a time, but it's enormously characterful jazz.

*** **There Is No Greater Love** Black Lion BLCD 760151
    As above. 9/65.
*** **The Jeep Is Jumping** Black Lion BLCD 760147
    Webster; Arnvid Mayer (*t*); John Darville (*tb*); Niels Jorgen Steen (*p*); Henrik Hartmann, Hugo Rasmussen (*b*); Hans Nymand (*d*). 9/65.
Webster back at the Montmartre in September, with an only marginally less engaging set, including his latest thoughts on 'I Got It Bad And That Ain't Good'. The session with Arnvid Mayer's band hems the saxophonist in a little more, with the group plodding at points, although Webster himself is again serenely in charge.

*** Big Ben Time! Philips 814410-2
    Webster; Dick Katz (*p*); Alan Haven (*org*); Spike Heatley (*b*); Tony Crombie (*d*). 1/67.
**(*) Ben Webster Meets Bill Coleman Black Lion BLCD 760141
    Webster; Bill Coleman (*t, flhn, v*); Fred Hunt (*p*); Jim Douglas (*g*); Ronnie Rae (*b*); Lennie
    Hastings (*d*). 4/67.

Big Ben Time! found Webster with a British rhythm section on a London visit. This isn't absolutely
prime Webster, but admirers will relish 'How Deep Is The Ocean?', 'Where Or When?' and some
characteristic musings on a few choices cuts of Ellington. The other date is a bit disappointing. Webster
and Coleman were both in London (as was Buck Clayton, scheduled for the date but, in the event,
indisposed) and they cut this session with Alex Welsh's rhythm section in support. It's pleasing enough,
but something tired seems to have crept into the music: the tempos plod a little too much, holding back
both hornmen – and, considering the quality of Webster's playing on 'For Max' (dedicated to Max
Jones) and 'For All We Know', it's a shame.

*** Ben And Buck Storyville STCD 8245
    Webster; Buck Clayton (*t*); Camille De Ceunyck (*p*); Tony Vaes (*b*); Charlie Pauvels (*d*). 6/67.
Webster and Clayton could have been a dream team, but they actually don't play together all that much
here. Most of the set is a feature for one or other of them and, when they do work together, it's usually at
the kind of tempo Webster didn't like (anything over slow). Still, the individual features are often
wonderful, and it's a shame that the inadequate sound doesn't catch the range of Clayton's lovely tone.

*** Masters Of Jazz Vol. 5: Ben Webster Storyville 4105
    Webster; Palle Mikkelborg, Perry Knudsen, Palle Bolvig, Allan Botschinsky (*t*); Per Espersen,
    Torolf Moolgaard, Axel Windfeld, Ole Kurt Jensen (*tb*); Uffe Karskov, Jesper Thilo, Dexter
    Gordon, Sahib Shihab, Bent Nielsen (*reeds*); Ole Kock Hansen, Kenny Drew (*p*); Ole Molin (*g*);
    Niels-Henning Orsted-Pedersen, Hugo Rasmussen (*b*); Ole Steenberg, Albert 'Tootie' Heath,
    Bjarne Rostvold (*d*); strings. 68–70.
*** Plays Ballads Storyville STCD 4118
    As above, except add Erling Christensen, Flemming Madsen (*reeds*), William Schiopffe (*d*),
    John Steffensen (*perc*). 7/67–11/71.
**(*) Live At The Haarlemse Jazz Club Limetree MCD 0040
    Webster; Tete Montoliu (*p*); Rob Langereis (*b*); Tony Inzalaco (*d*). 5/72.
*** Gentle Ben Ensayo ENY-CD 3433
    Webster; Tete Montoliu (*p*); Eric Peter (*b*); Peer Wyboris (*d*). 11/72.
**(*) My Man Steeplechase SCCD 31008
    Webster; Ole Kock Hansen (*p*); Bo Stief (*b*); Alex Riel (*d*). 4/73.

Webster's final years found him based in Copenhagen, and his manner was by now so *sui generis* that it's
tempting to view the later work as a single, lachrymose meditation on the same handful of favourite
ballads and Ellington tunes. But Ben's own subtle variations on himself create absorbing differences
between each stately rendition of 'Prelude To A Kiss' or 'Old Folks'. He was lucky in his accompanists:
while several of the rhythm sections sound anonymous in themselves, Webster's knack of helping them
raise their game elicits some exceptionally sympathetic playing from almost everybody. The two
Storyville albums collect scatterings from several sessions over a five-year period, including dates with
strings, some heavenly ballads, and a couple of dates with Teddy Wilson at the piano: both mixed bags,
but plenty of vintage Webster. *My Man* is a middling session, recorded on a typical late night at the Café
Montmartre and a bit too relaxed. Sound on the Haarlemse club date is pretty dusty but there is a lovely
'Star Dust' to enjoy, and only Inzalaco's enthusiasms sometimes get the better of the music. Montoliu is
on hand again for the Barcelona studio date, *Gentle Ben*, which catches Ben's sound beautifully. Peter
and Wyboris are less than ideal, but otherwise this is a bountiful example of late Webster. Anyone who
loves the sound of Ben Webster will find something to enjoy in all these records.

Tad Weed PIANO

***(*) Soloing 9 Winds NWCD 0148
    Weed; Ken Filiano (*b*); Joe LaBarbera, Billy Mintz (*d*). 7/90–5/91.
Weed's broad stylistic range, sureness of touch and carefully controlled quirkiness give this record a real
unaffected sparkle. Despite the title, only five of the 11 tracks are done as solos: his version of Gerry
Niewood's flimsy 'Joy' lends the melody unexpected strength by introducing dark, thoughtful voicings
without losing the sprightliness of the tune. Clifford Brown's 'Joyspring' is fast without sounding hectic,
yet Weed has it down coolly enough to introduce some deft rhythmical risks. The trio pieces benefit from
LaBarbera's excellent drumming (Mintz sits in on only two tracks), and in over an hour of music there
are only a very few dull moments. The piano-sound is a little dry, though few will find it troubling.

George Wein (born 1925) PIANO

*** **Jazz At The Modern** Bethlehem BET 6025-2
>   Wein; Shorty Baker (*t*); Tyree Glenn (*tb*); Pee Wee Russell (*cl*); Bill Crow (*b*); Mickey Sheen (*d*).
>   60.

*** **The Magic Horn** RCA Victor 74321 13038 2
>   Wein; Ruby Braff (*t*); Jimmy McPartland (*c*); Vic Dickenson (*tb*); Bill Stegmeyer, Peanuts
>   Hucko (*cl*); Ernie Caceres (*bs*); Danny Barker (*bj*); Milt Hinton (*b*); Buzzy Drootin (*d*). 5/56.

(*) **Swing That Music Columbia 474048-2
>   Wein; Clark Terry (*t*); Warren Vaché (*c*); Al Grey (*tb*); Illinois Jacquet, Flip Phillips (*ts*);
>   Howard Alden (*g*); Eddie Jones (*b*); Kenny Washington (*d*). 8/93.

Wein's place in jazz history is as an impresario, the Newport Festival founder and a man with a hand in many other jazz projects. But he's a capable pianist in the mould of the Chicago mainstream, and a scattering of recording dates down the years has left him with a modest, entertaining discography. *The Magic Horn* was really the soundtrack to a TV show, but it's a rousing Dixieland date with Braff, Dickenson and the others in excellent form. Sometimes overly frantic in the manner of such occasions – 'Sugar' goes about a mile over the top – but good fun; and McPartland turns up for a cutting contest with Braff on 'Dippermouth Blues'. The Bethlehem session comes from an open-air show at the Museum of Modern Art, and it sounds like it, too: a lot of the time the music seems to be blowing away on the breeze, and whatever subtleties the players may have been looking for, they're lost. Still, it's an intriguing front line – Glenn especially making a solid foil for Russell's usual waywardness.

The recent all-star date organized around Wein for Columbia is disappointing. Most of these old-stagers know each other only too well, and they've trotted out this kind of thing many times before. Nothing much happens beyond the nice duet between Alden and Flip Phillips on a couple of Django tunes. The rest is mere backslapping, contentedly done.

Walt Weiskopf (born 1959) TENOR SAXOPHONE

*** **Exact Science** Iris ICD-1002
>   Weiskopf; Joel Weiskopf (*p*); Jay Anderson (*b*); Jeff Hirshfield (*d*). 89.

***(*) **Mindwalking** Iris ICD-1003
>   As above. 6–9/90.

**** **Simplicity** Criss Cross Jazz 1075
>   Weiskopf; Conrad Herwig (*tb*); Andy Fusco (*as*); Joel Weiskopf (*p*); Peter Washington (*b*); Billy
>   Drummond (*d*). 12/92.

*** **A World Away** Criss Cross 1100
>   Weiskopf; Larry Goldings (*org*); Peter Bernstein (*g*); Bill Stewart (*d*). 12/93.

Weiskopf is an experienced section-player (with Buddy Rich and Toshiko Akiyoshi), but these records are a lot more ambitious than the usual sideman-steps-out date. *Exact Science* is a carefully weighted set of tunes that place as much emphasis on the writing as on the improvising: Weiskopf's lean, slightly querulous tone might sound like Coltrane-lite, but his phrasing is scrupulously thoughtful and personal. Some of the themes are intriguingly paced – 'Mr Golyadkin' might have come off a Jan Garbarek/Bobo Stenson date – and others don't quite come off, while the sound of the record has a sometimes unflattering timbre. *Mindwalking* is better still, with a superior mix and scarcely a dud moment. The brevity of several tracks shows how little waste there is in Weiskopf's music, improvisations always in balance with themes, and the prevailing feel of intellectual surprise sets him quite apart from the midstream of modern hard bop. Yet the one standard, Alec Wilder's 'Blackberry Winter', is as deeply felt and fully achieved as any more obvious tenor rhapsody.

Both discs lead naturally to the splendid *Simplicity*. More than ever, Weiskopf chooses to assert his writing over his playing, with his own solos relatively discreet and deferential. The brimming, complex melodies of 'Subordination', the artfully overlapping horns of 'Brazilia' and the wholly original revision of 'Lazy Afternoon' are among the most interesting moments, but there's nothing here to disappoint. Fusco and Herwig are modest personalities too, but their relative mildness lets the calibre of Weiskopf's writing come through, and his rhythm section, ably led by brother Joel, is keenly alert.

A World Away puts the emphasis more keenly on Weiskopf's own playing, and for once the setting doesn't seem just right for him. Goldings, Bernstein and Stewart are old hands at the organ–guitar groove and, though clichés are displaced by the leader's typically penetrating writing, the music misses the firm centre of the previous discs. One compensation is another ingenious standard choice, 'The Long Hot Summer'.

Michael Weiss (born 1958) PIANO

**(*) Presenting Michael Weiss Criss Cross Jazz Criss 1022
> Weiss; Tom Kirkpatrick (*t*); Ralph Lalama (*ts*); Ray Drummond (*b*); Kenny Washington (*d*). 4/86.

This debut set is very much in the house style: no-frills contemporary bebop on a handful of jazz standards and a couple of originals. Nothing amiss, but not much excitement unless you're playing in the band. Kirkpatrick, a vaguely irascible trumpeter, is the most striking player here, given that Drummond and Washington seem to be watching the clock for once, and Weiss is a perfectly accomplished and uninteresting leader.

Bobby Wellins (born 1936) TENOR SAXOPHONE

***(*) Nomad Hot House HHCD 1008
> Wellins; Jonathan Gee (*p*); Thad Kelly (*b*); Spike Wells (*d*); Claire Martin (*v*). 4/92.

Despite the sleeve-notes' maundering attempts at Britjazz nostalgia, Wellins remains a singular saxophone voice, one of the more intriguing players to emerge in Britain's modest wave of post-bop. His phrasing has taken on a faintly tired demeanour that lends a bittersweet lyricism to his solos, but he still tackles unusual or difficult themes, as on this standards-based programme: Monk's 'Little Rootie Tootie', Hank Mobley's 'This I Dig Of You', Clifford Brown's 'Sandu'. There are three original songs with lyrics delivered by Claire Martin, and Bobby's obbligatos on 'Remember Me' are quite remarkable. Gee, Kelly and Wells play well, if sometimes in the bloodless way of the British rhythm section, but it's Wellins's idiosyncratic take on the tenor tradition that sustains the record.

Bill Wells (born 1955) DOUBLE BASS

*** Live '93–'94 Loathsome Reels LR 001
> Wells; Robert Henderson (*t*); John Burgess, John Longbotham (*as*); Phil Bancroft, Russell Cowieson (*ts*); Allon Beauvoisin (*bs*); Steve Kettley (*ss*); Lindsay Cooper, Oren Marshall (*tba*); Nigel Clark, Kevin Mackenzie (*g*); Tom Bancroft, Iain Copeland (*d*); Josefina Cupido (*perc*). 3/93–7/94.

Wells is a resourceful Scot with a well-defined musical personality, writing charts which occasionally recall fellow-bassist Charles Mingus. His Octet performs only somewhat rarely, but Wells has taken the trouble to record the group (and an even more rarely convened big band) on home-produced cassette and on this debut CD.

The performances usefully reflect the quality of young players on the contemporary scene in Scotland – Henderson, Mackenzie, Cowieson and the Bancroft brothers most obviously – but the laurels go to the leader himself for some finely crafted and consistently intelligent charts. 'Corduroy Road' is an atmospheric opener, but it is the two 'Loathsome Reels' and the wry closing 'Elongated Cat Theme' which offer the best measure of (as the polls say) a Talent Deserving Wider Recognition.

Dick Wellstood (1927–90) PIANO

*** The Blue Three At Hanratty's Chaz Jazz CJ 109
> Wellstood; Kenny Davern (*ss, cl*); Bob Rosengarden (*d*). 81.

*** Dick Wellstood And His Famous Orchestra Featuring Kenny Davern Chiaroscuro CRD 128
> As above, except omit Rosengarden.

*** Dick Wellstood And His All-Star Orchestra Featuring Kenny Davern Chiaroscuro CRD 129
> As above. 81.

A jobbing musician who was content to play supper-club dates, parties and tribute recordings to great predecessors like Waller, James P. Johnson and Art Tatum, Dick Wellstood is easily underestimated. Always up for a gig though he may have been, he was also a practising lawyer, and his easy, engaging stride approach masks a steel-trap understanding of every wrinkle of piano jazz, an eclecticism that allows him to play in virtually every idiom from early ragtime to quasi-modal compositions from the shores opposite bop. He has a decent touch with a Monk tune, as he shows on the third of the discs above. Regrettably, much of his work has bloomed and faded in highly unappreciative settings and company, and he is not well represented in the current catalogue. There is a distinct shortage of CD material for so active and undemanding a player.

At the keyboard, he sounds most like a younger version of James P. Johnson, setting up big and forceful alternations in the left hand against a characteristic tremolo in the melody line. He favours huge, raw bass-figures and counters their jagged outlines with wonderfully subtle fills and footnotes. The personnels above are not incomplete, despite the titles. The 'orchestra' business is one of Wellstood's jokes, as are originals like 'Fat As A Bastard'. In his late fifties he tempered his approach slightly, enough to admit an occasional ballad, though often in very improbable keys. Wellstood is something of an acquired taste.

Alex Welsh (1929–82) CORNET, VOCALS

***(*) **Classic Concert** Black Lion BLCD 760503
> Welsh; Roy Williams (*tb, v*); John Barnes (*cl, as, bs, f, v*); Fred Hunt (*p*); Jim Douglas (*bj, g*); Harvey Weston (*b*); Lennie Hastings (*d*). 10/71.

*** **Doggin' Around** Black Lion BLCD 760510
> Welsh; Roy Williams (*tb*); Johnny Barnes (*as, bs, cl, f*); Jim Douglas (*g*); Fred Hunt (*p*); Harvey Weston (*b*); Roger Nobes (*d*). 7 & 8/73.

Despite the surname, Welsh was a Scot. A taut wee man with a gammy leg, he didn't entirely look the part but was nevertheless a fine cornetist, influenced by Wild Bill Davison (though he emphatically denied this). When he died in 1982, Humphrey Lyttelton described the Welsh band's impact as a combination of 'romanticism and rage', a near-perfect characterization of its leader's buttoned-up ferocity.

The band changed markedly in approach during the 1960s, a period during which the once teetotal Welsh acquired a famous thirst for vodka, moving away from the ragged, Chicagoan 'Condon style' towards a more orthodox swing approach. The band's enormous success at Antibes in 1967 and at later American festivals seemed to do no more than reinforce internal divisions. The cupboard is looking slightly bare since the Dormouse label went into limbo. At the moment, the only period of Welsh's career preserved on CD is the early 1970s, a period of relatively undemonstrative consolidation for the band. Though less limber than the 1960 front line of Roy Crimmins and the wounded Archie Semple, the 1971 line-up of Williams and the multi-talented Barnes was still capable of performing powerfully. Side by side, 'Sleepy Time Down South' and 'Maple Leaf Rag' confirm something of Lyttelton's description; set alongside the 'Clark And Randolph Blues', a previously unissued version of the Art Hodes tune on the Lake compilation, they're slightly wan. Welsh himself sounds tired but plays with great straightforwardness and a lovely tone.

The slightly later record is no less enjoyable, but there is something amiss with the sound-balance, which has everyone ricocheting around in what sounds like an aircraft hangar. Barnes is a great asset on his baritone sax and Roy Williams maintains his form on trombone, but a lot of the spark has gone out of the group, along with about 85 per cent of the rage. 'You Are The Sunshine Of My Life' has all the romantic urgency of a brisk handshake, and it's only on up-tempo traditional numbers like 'Limehouse Blues' that Welsh sounds at all committed to the gig.

Scott Wendholt TRUMPET, FLUGELHORN

*** **The Scheme Of Things** Criss Cross Jazz 1078
> Wendholt; Vincent Herring (*ss, as*); Kevin Hays (*p*); Dwayne Burno (*b*); Billy Drummond (*d*). 1/93.

*** **Through The Shadows** Criss Cross 1101
> Wendholt; Don Braden (*ts, f*); Bruce Barth (*p*); Ira Coleman (*b*); Billy Drummond (*d*). 12/94.

Wendholt is a young musician of great skill, though it's hard to spot interesting distinctions in his playing. In almost 70 minutes of good, substantial post-bop on *The Scheme Of Things* there is plenty to enjoy yet not much to remember. The most striking thing is the contrast between Herring (who has a working quintet with the trumpeter) and Wendholt: the saxophonist's sour, blue playing is a piquant alternative to the polished, processional manner of some of Wendholt's solos. The leader isn't terribly well served by the recording, and he sounds a bit thin on Freddie Hubbard's 'Birdlike', the sort of tune where a trumpeter should stand tall. But there is some impressive improvising, and his favourite device, a fast trill, comes in for clever use.

The writing on *Through The Shadows* is one point of advance; the other is the band, which, man for man, is arguably no stronger than the first but seems a more purposeful group for Wendholt's ideas. 'Totem' and the title-piece are especially strong, and the mid-tempo for Duke Pearson's 'You Know I Care' elicits a solo of real finesse and control by Wendholt. Overall, still short of a major statement, but this is a fine set.

Jens Wendleboe TROMBONE

**(*) 'Lone Attic NOPA 2905
    Wendleboe; Christian Beck, Fred Noddelund, Bernt Steen, Ole Antonsen (*t*); Tore Nilsen,
    Harald Halvorsen, Dag Eriksen, Oivind Westby (*tb*); Johan Bergli, Arild Stav (*as*); Knut
    Riisnaes, Odd Riisnaes (*ts*); Vidar Johansen (*bs*); Helge Iberg (*ky*); Frode Alnaes (*g*); Tom
    Antonsen (*b*); Svein Christiansen (*d*). 85.
***(*) Big Crazy Energy Band NOPA/NRK NN 1001-2
    Wendleboe; David Zalud, Petter Kateraas, Svein Gjermundrod, Jens Petter Antonsen (*t, flhn*);
    Anders Stengard, Harald Halvorsen, Helge Sunde, Oivind Westby (*tb*); Daniel Wilensky, Johan
    Bergli, Georg Reiss, Knut Riisnaes, Vidar Johansen, Rolf Malm (*reeds*); Bugge Wesseltoft (*ky*);
    Asbjorn Ruud (*g*); Bjorn Holta (*b*); Erik Smith (*d*); Frank Jakobsen (*perc*); Elisabeth Moberg
    (*v*). 4–5/91.

Wendleboe is a Norwegian trombonist/arranger who loves to push his big bands through hair-raising
charts that bounce between jazz, rock and anything else he can think of: kindred spirits might be Loose
Tubes, Ornicar Big Band, Either/Orchestra. But Wendleboe never quite lets go as he might, and *'Lone
Attic* in particular sounds stiff when it should really be taking off. Part of the problem is a penchant for
tongue-in-cheek rock and disco rhythms that tie the band down to a tyrannical beat. Despite having
such skilful improvisers in the earlier band as the Riisnaes brothers, Wendleboe also finds it difficult to
frame soloists to their best advantage. But *Big Crazy Energy Band* is a major improvement. They belt
through the opening 'The Night Of The 1990's' with stunning aplomb, and the ensuing 'Fanfare And
Punk' and Wesseltoft's rippling Hammond organ transformation of 'Abide With Me' are tremendous
set-pieces. It isn't quite sustained at that level, and Moberg's vocals are an unnecessary addition; but
there's enough fine music to merit a strong rating.

Peter Weniger SOPRANO AND TENOR SAXOPHONES

**(*) Hymn To Gobro Jazzline JL 11132-2
    Weniger; Conrad Herwig (*tb*); Hubert Nuss (*p*); Ingmar Heller (*b*); Hardy Fischotter (*d*). 11/89.
*** Private Concert Mons 1878
    Weniger; Hubert Nuss (*p*). 4/90.
*** The Point Of Presence Mons 1889
    As above, except add Conrad Herwig (*tb*). 5/91.
*** Key Of The Moment Mons 1901
    Weniger; David Liebman (*ss*); John Abercrombie (*g*); Rufus Reid (*b*); Adam Nussbaum (*d*). 2/
    93.

Weniger's approach to improvising is a conscientious balancing of traditional and nearly free form. The
duo concert with Nuss is based round standards and three originals, but the wide-ranging interpretations of 'Stella By Starlight' and Dave Liebman's 'What It Is' alike suggest that both men – though
Weniger especially – like the minimum of signposts for their playing. Weniger's full-bodied tone on both
tenor and soprano seldom breaks into anything like a false register: he likes to stretch melody lines and
structural experiments off into infinity as his way of being free.

    The Point Of Presence is marginally superior, since Herwig's enlistment was an inspired piece of casting.
He goes an inch further than Weniger by blowing chords on the horn and adapting other avant-garde
techniques, but he also likes to stay within relatively contained boundaries. On the soprano/trombone
duet piece, 'Blue Beauty', or the multifarious directions of 'The Point Of Presence' itself, the music
acquires refinement and detail without losing spontaneity. The earlier quintet session is much more
straightforward, a light, easy-going and not unpleasing group of originals – Herwig's 'Opalescent' is
particularly engaging – and two jazz standards, with a capable if anonymous rhythm section.

    Key Of The Moment directs Weniger towards more mainstream modernism. Liebman appears on only
one track, 'Flatbush', where the two sopranos trade licks; the rest is polished, literate jazz of a high if
not especially distinctive order. No reason to deny it three stars, but the best of Weniger is with Nuss.

Kenny Werner PIANO

**(*) Introducing The Trio Sunnyside SSC 1038D
    Werner; Ratzo Harris (*b*); Tom Rainey (*d*). 3/89.
*** Uncovered Heart Sunnyside SSC 1048D
    Werner; Randy Brecker (*t, flhn*); Joe Lovano (*ss, ts*); Eddie Gomez (*b*); John Riley (*d*). 90.

***(*) **Press Enter** Sunnyside SSC 1056D
>   Werner; Ratzo Harris (*b*); Tom Rainey (*d*). 8/91.

Werner is a beguiling player, perfectly at home in either a solo, trio or rhythm-and-horns date, and if he often seems a little too becalmed in his playing it does gradually draw an attentive listener in. *Uncovered Heart* includes some good originals, and if the horns perform with mundane expertise, Werner himself stands up as a leader worthy of respect. The first trio album seems a little undercooked, with nods to Bill Evans that sometimes turn into slavish imitation; but the second, *Press Enter*, is beautifully handled and suggests a much stronger empathy among the three players. Werner's long out-of-tempo introduction to a very thoughtful 'Blue In Green' sets one of the keynotes for the record, an exploration of shifting rhythms, and Rainey's almost pointillistic stickwork is ideally directed. Certainly the best place to start listening to Werner.

(*) **Meditations Steeplechase SCCD 31327
>   Werner (*p* solo). 12/92.

Not bad, but Werner's return to the solo recital (there is a forgettable Enja record in the deletion pile) is prettily nondescript. There are three numbered 'Meditations' and a 'Contemplation Suite', all leaves from the same tree, judiciously played, charmingly articulated, but rhythmically and melodically mundane. The best interpretation is a dense revision of 'Giant Steps': Aki Takase and Dick Wellstood have done it, but piano-solo treatments are comparatively rare, and this one's a vivid nod to Coltrane. Monk and Debussy are mistakenly alluded to in the sleeve-notes: Werner is not in their league, but he's worth hearing.

*** **Copenhagen Calypso** Steeplechase SCCD 31346
>   Werner (*p* solo). 10/93.
*** **Maybeck Recital Hall Vol. 34** Concord CCD 4622
>   Werner (*p* solo). 2/94.

Two more solo dates, and not so much mixed successes as unexceptional recitals. The Copenhagen set has a vague air of Coltrane hovering around it, with 'Ballad For Trane' and 'Naima' in the programme, while the Maybeck set – in impeccable sound as always – mixes various strands of post-bop piano on a sequence of familiar pieces, along with another 'Naima' – though it must be said that Werner distils a very attractive lyricism out of the tune. Sound efforts, but it would be good to have Werner get back to his own writing, which has rather more character than he often invests in other people's works.

Fred Wesley TROMBONE

(*) **New Friends Minor Music 801016
>   Wesley; Stanton Davis (*t, flhn*); Steve Turre, Robin Eubanks (*tb*); Maceo Parker (*as, perc*); Tim
>   Green (*ts, perc*); Geri Allen (*ky*); Anthony Cox (*b*); Bill Stewart (*d*); Carmen Lundy (*v*). 90.
(*) **Comme Ci Comme Ça Minor Music 801020
>   Wesley; Hugh Ragin (*t, flhn*); Maceo Parker (*as*); Karl Denson (*ss, ts, f*); Peter Madsen (*p*);
>   Rodney Jones (*g*); Anthony Cox (*b*); Bill Stewart (*d*); Teresa Carroll (*v*). 8/91.
*** **Swing And Be Funky** Minor Music MM 801027
>   As above, except Dwayne Dolphin (*b, v*) replaces Cox, Bruce Cox (*d, v*) replaces Stewart; omit
>   Parker. 5/92.

Wesley and his frequent collaborator, Maceo Parker, are James Brown cohorts whose credentials in funky soul music are unimpeachable. Deprived of a groove – Stewart and Cox are good drummers, but they're coming from a hard-bop experience, not James Brown – they tend to falter on long solos and group interplay. The jazz set-pieces on the first record include 'Rockin' In Rhythm' and two Monk tunes, but they're no more than passable efforts, and the intended trombone summit meeting on 'For The Elders' isn't any more profound than a Kai Winding 'bone extravaganza. *Comme Ci Comme Ça* is an ounce weightier, with the unexpected appearance of Ragin adding bite to the front line. The original material is lightweight – anything called 'Love In L.A.' sounds a sure candidate for oblivion – but the band work hard and the studio sound is bigger and sharper. *Swing And Be Funky* catches the band on a live show, which is probably the best place to hear it, but, as with so many hot live groups, much is lost in the transfer, and the closing 'Bop To The Boogie' is a useless piece of exhortation. Wesley himself is an adept and rather sonorous player, eschewing the horn's rasp in favour of fluency and sweetness, but he's scarcely a major figure on the instrument.

Frank Wess (born 1922) TENOR SAXOPHONE, FLUTE

*** **North, East, South . . . Wess** Savoy S V 0139
> Wess; Frank Foster (*ts*); Henry Coker, Bennie Powell (*tb*); Kenny Burrell (*g*); Eddie Jones (*b*); Kenny Clarke (*d*). 3/56.

*** **Opus In Swing** Savoy S V 0144
> Wess; Kenny Burrell, Freddie Green (*g*); Eddie Jones (*b*); Kenny Clarke (*d*). 6/56.

*** **Trombones And Flute** Savoy S V 0190
> Wess; Bennie Powell, Henry Coker, Jimmy Cleveland, Bill Hughes (*tb*); Ronnell Bright (*p*); Eddie Jones (*b*); Freddie Green (*g*); Kenny Clarke (*d*). 7/56.

*** **Jazz For Playboys** Savoy S V 0191
> Wess; Joe Newman (*t*); Ed Thigpen (*d*). 12/56.

*** **Opus De Blues** Savoy S V 0137
> Wess; Thad Jones (*t*); Curtis Fuller (*tb*); Charlie Fowlkes (*bs*); Hank Jones (*p*); Eddie Jones (*b*); Gus Johnson (*d*). 12/59.

***(*) **Dear Mr Basie** Concord CCD 4420
> Wess; Joe Newman, Harry 'Sweets' Edison, Al Aarons, Snooky Young, Raymond Brown (*t*); Al Grey, Grover Mitchell, Benny Powell, Michael Grey (*tb*); Marshall Royal, Curtis Peagler (*as*); Billy Mitchell (*ts*); Bill Ramsay (*bs*); Ted Dunbar (*g*); Eddie Jones (*b*); Gregg Field (*d*). 11/89.

**** **Live At The 1990 Concord Jazz Festival: Second Set** Concord CCD 4452
> Wess; Pete Minger (*flhn*); Marshall Royal (*as*); Rick Wilkins (*ts*); Gerry Wiggins (*p*); Lynn Seaton (*b, v*); Harold Jones (*d*). 8/90.

***(*) **Entre Nous** Concord CCD 4456
> Wess; Ron Tooley, Snooky Young (*t*); Joe Newman (*t, v*); Pete Minger (*t, flhn*); Art Baron, Grover Mitchell, Doug Purviance, Dennis Wilson (*tb*); Curtis Peagler, Bill Ramsay (*as*); Billy Mitchell (*ts*); Arthur Clarke (*bs*); Tee Carson (*p*); Ted Dunbar (*g*); Eddie Jones (*b*); Dennis Mackrel (*d*). 11/90.

Inseparable in most people's minds from Frank Foster, with whom he replaced Herschel Evans and Lester Young in the Basie band, Wess's main claim to fame is his pioneering use of flute as a solo instrument in jazz. A forthright swing soloist, virtually unmarked by bop, Wess is probably less distinctive than Foster on the saxophone (the original *NESW* liner-note helpfully identified individual contributions); their highly successful quintet was probably most listenable when they exploited 'alternate' horns. *Opus De Jazz* was a bold and well-intentioned effort that didn't quite come off and sounds rather stiff and remote in places, chamber jazz that never gets up enough body heat to compel interest. Those that followed with similar names in that great mid-'50s flurry of activity for Savoy sustain a little more jazz activity and signal the slow emergence of Wess as a fully fledged soloist, something that took surprisingly long, despite his pedigree and training. There is still a curious experimentalism, as in the *Trombones And Flute* disc, which unveils Wess's 'other' (and, even at this period, possibly better) horn against a rich brass background, a formation not often tried since.

Wess's flute solo on the custom-built 'Entre Nous', title-piece of the fine 1990 concert album, recorded in Japan, shows off his burnished and now supremely confident tone to the utmost. Ironically, the live recording displays it better than the earlier Savoys, which are close-miked and rather brittle in sound. The twinned horns of *North, East, South . . . Wess* are only occasionally effective. There really isn't enough between Coker and Powell to give their contributions much in the way of dramatic differentiation. It's Foster who shines, with a superb solo on 'Dancing On The Ceiling'.

Wess capitalized on his long tenure in the Basie band with his own large ensemble. *Dear Mr Basie* is probably the more exciting of the two records and it represents a wholly successful homage to the great man, but it is *Entre Nous* that catches at the throat with moments of sheer beauty; and it is on the other Concord, recorded at the label's August 1990 showcase event, that Wess demonstrates that he has lost nothing of the sparky intelligence which made those early records as fascinating as they can be maddening.

*** **Surprise! Surprise!** Gemini GMCD 84
> Wess; Norman Simmons (*p*); Joe Cohn (*g*); Lynn Seaton (*b*); Jackie Williams (*d*). 8/93.

**** **Tryin' To Make My Blues Turn Green** Concord 4596
> Wess; Cecil Bridgewater, Greg Gisbert (*t*); Steve Turre (*tb, shells*); Scott Robinson (*ts, acl*); Richard Wyands (*p*); Lyn Seaton (*b*); Gregory Hutchinson (*d*). 9/93.

Recent times have seen Wess working more comfortably in small-group settings and these, recorded within a month of one another during the man's 71st summer, are a good example of how he has turned a serviceable band style into an expressive and very personal voice. The Gemini disc was recorded at Oslo's Rainbow Studio and engineered by Jan Erik Kongshaug, who is responsible for most of ECM's output. Predictably, it sounds as good as they get, even though on this occasion the band Wess assembled has some creaking elements. It would be unfair to point to individuals, beyond saying that the rhythm section don't sound so much unrehearsed as rather stiff and unswinging. Wess switches to flute for the brand-new 'Equal Parts' but for once fails to convince, and it is his tenor solo on Ettore Stratta's 'Forget The Woman' which takes the laurels. Joe Cohn, son of saxophonist Al, wins credit for his elegant soloing and solid accompaniment.

The Concord disc is a very different kettle of fish, much more confected. Teamed with players of the class of Turre, Bridgewater and the developing Gisbert, Wess has to go some to assert his leadership, but it's evident in the richness of the textures and in the overall configuration of the set, which is masterful. Seaton will be a revelation to some, a flawless timekeeper who solos persuasively, both pizzicato and with the bow.

Mike Westbrook (born 1936) COMPOSER, PIANO, TUBA

*** **For The Record** Transatlantic/Line TACD 9.00785
> Westbrook; Phil Minton (*t, v*); Kate Westbrook (*thn, picc, v*); Dave Chambers (*reeds, v*); Paul Rutherford (*tb, euph, v*). 10/75.

***(*) **Love / Dream And Variations** Transatlantic/Line TACD 9.00788
> Westbrook; George Chisholm, Paul Cosh, Alan Downey, Henry Lowther (*t*); Malcolm Griffiths, Geoff Perkins, Paul Rutherford (*tb*); Dave Chambers, John Holbrooke, Mike Page, John Warren (*reeds*); Dave MacRae (*p*); Brian Godding (*g*); John Mitchell (*vib, perc*); Chris Laurence (*b*); Alan Jackson (*d, perc*). 2/76.

***(*) **The Westbrook Blake: Bright As Fire** Impetus IMP 18013
> Westbrook; Mike Davies, Dave Hancock, Henry Lowther (*t*); Phil Minton (*t, v*); Malcolm Griffiths (*tb*); Alan Sinclair (*tba*); Kate Westbrook (*thn, picc, v*); Chris Biscoe, Alan Wakeman (*reeds*); Georgie Born (*clo*); Chris Laurence (*b*); Dave Barry (*d*). 80.

**** **The Cortège** Enja 7087 2CD
> Westbrook; Phil Minton (*t, v*); Guy Barker, Dave Pearce, Dave Plews (*t, flhn*); Malcolm Griffiths (*tb, btb*); Kate Westbrook (*thn, bamboo f, picc, v*); Alan Sinclair, Dave Powell (*tba*); Chris Hunter (*as, ss, ts, f*); Phil Todd (*ts, ss, as, cl, af*); Lindsay Cooper (*bsn, ob, sno*); Chris Biscoe (*bs, as, ss, acl, f*); Brian Godding (*g*); Georgie Born (*clo*); Steve Cook (*b*); Dave Barry (*d, perc*). 3–4/82.

**** **On Duke's Birthday** hat Art 6021
> Westbrook; Kate Westbrook (*thn, picc, bamboo f, v*); Phil Minton (*t, v*); Stuart Brooks (*t, flhn*); Danilo Terenzi (*tb*); Chris Biscoe (*as, ss, bs, picc, acl*); Brian Godding (*g*); Dominique Pifarély (*vn*); Georgie Born (*clo*); Steve Cook (*b*); Tony Marsh (*d*). 5/84.

***(*) **Love For Sale** hat Art 6061
> Westbrook; Kate Westbrook (*thn, picc, bamboo f, v*); Chris Biscoe (*as, ss, bs, acl*). 12/85.

***(*) **Pierides** Core/Line COCD 9.00377
> Westbrook; Kate Westbrook (*thn, picc, v*); Peter Whyman (*as, cl*); Brian Godding (*g, g syn*). 3/86.

***(*) **Westbrook–Rossini** hat Art 6002
> Westbrook; Kate Westbrook (*thn, picc, v*); Paul Nieman (*tb*); Andy Grappy (*tba*); Lindsay Cooper (*sno*); Peter Whyman (*as*); Peter Fairclough (*d*). 86.

**** **Westbrook–Rossini** hat Art CD 6152 2CD
> As above. 11/86.

***(*) **Off Abbey Road** TipToe 888805
> Westbrook; Kate Westbrook (*thn, v*); Phil Minton (*t, v*); Alan Wakeman (*ss, ts*); Peter Whyman (*as*); Andy Grappy (*tba*); Brian Godding (*g*); Peter Fairclough (*d*). 8/89.

It's tempting to suggest that were Mike Westbrook American or German rather than English his career might already have been garlanded with the praise it so conspicuously deserves. Britain's neglect of one of its most distinguished contemporary composers amounts to a national disgrace. Westbrook's regular groups – the early Concert Band, which included John Surman, the mixed-media Cosmic Circus, which paved the way for much of his later theatrical work, the jazz-rock Solid Gold Cadillac, and most recently the Brass Band (which is responsible for the slightly disappointing *For The Record*) – have drawn from a startling range of musical and performance backgrounds. In a very real sense, Westbrook is not a jazz musician at all but a musical magpie; Rossini's 'La Gazza Ladra' and the '*Lone Ranger*' theme may have touched a chord of self-awareness (great artists thieve, after all, and Westbrook is certainly a masked loner).

If he is also an improviser, and there is no doubt that he is, it is not as an instrumentalist. Instead, he improvises with genre and with the boundaries of genre. Purely musical influences like Ellington (who lies behind all the early and mid-period big-band compositions, such as *Metropolis* and *Citadell/Room 315* and whose 'Creole Love Call' is covered on the excellent *Love/Dream And Variations*) and

Thelonious Monk are tempered by an interest in the boundaries of music and verse, theatre, the plastic arts and agit-prop, which has led Westbrook to reconsider the work of Brecht and Weill and The Beatles.

Together with the former Kate Barnard, Westbrook has since devised a remarkable series of performances/entertainments which blend elements of jazz, popular song, verse and theatre. The finest of these are *The Cortège* and its dark thematic twin, *London Bridge Is Broken Down* (which represents the same drama of life-in-death-in-life but is currently out of circulation). *The Cortège* is a major composition by any standards. First performed at the Bracknell Jazz Festival in 1979 and released subsequently on Original Records, it has been a hole in Westbrook's discography for some time. Modelled loosely on a New Orleans funeral procession, it has the same fast-slow-fast rhythm. Westbrook has used the number '3' as the basic structural principle of the piece, which is full of three-note melodies and nine-note patterns raised on very small harmonic intervals with similarly invariant bass-lines. The texts are drawn from Lorca, Rimbaud, Hesse and elsewhere. Perhaps the most forceful integration of words and music occurs at the start of Rimbaud's '*Démocratie*', where Kate Westbrook sings over cello and bassoon, before the orchestra gradually enters and the piece builds towards the climactic '*En avant, route!*'. 'Erme Estuary', by contrast, is a threnody for Westbrook's father, who instilled in him a love of music and the theatre.

If *The Cortège* is the most dramatic of the large-scale suites, perhaps the purest and most straight-forward is the trio, *Love For Sale*, which weaves a remarkable range of sources (including an old Westbrook touchstone, William Blake, and a range of standard and traditional tunes) into a coherent performance that balances social anger, sentiment and purely formal control. The unifying factor, as in many of Westbrook's pieces, is Kate Westbrook's remarkable, if rather mannered, voice. 'England Have My Bones' features it at its most Grand Guignol, but she is equally capable of a whisky-and-nicotine romanticism, as with 'Lush Life', and of a husky purity which is reminiscent of the classical contralto Kathleen Ferrier. Westbrook contributes simple, thought-out piano and tuba accompaniments, and most of the embellishments derive from Biscoe's generous array of horns. The vocal and instrumental recipe works nearly as well on *Pierides*, where Godding's guitar adds a further dimension to music that was originally conceived as a dance/theatre piece known as *Pier Rides*, a wry Anglicization of the collective name of the Greek Muses; it's also (to give a sense of the serendipitous way Westbrook's imagination seems to work) the name given to the nine Thessalian maidens who, having challenged the Muses to a singing contest and lost, are turned into magpies.

Westbrook's later orchestral works have been tighter and less detailed than the beautiful abstract impressionism of *Metropolis*, or the free-Ellingtonian style of *Citadell/Room 315*, which, along with the classic early *Marching Song*, is his best non-vocal work. Two of the later pieces afford an interesting comparative exercise. Unlike *Westbrook–Rossini*, which treats the 'Thieving Magpie' theme (one lent a curiously threatening resonance by its use in Stanley Kubrick's *A Clockwork Orange*) and other tunes almost as if they were show-tune standards for solo improvisations, *On Duke's Birthday* is a set of original scores which reflect the spirit of Ellington's compositions and arrangements, but which refer to them only subliminally. Neither approach is that of a *pasticheur*. Westbrook's arrangements are clean-limbed and his big bands have a simplicity and directness of detail very little different from the vocal trios and quartets. The studio CD of *Westbrook–Rossini* replaced an earlier double live album of the same material, which has now been restored on CD. Some of the studio solos, Lindsay Cooper's snake-charmer sopranino in particular, lack the spontaneity of the live set and, though the sound is very much better, the double concert set is miles better value for money.

Westbrook belongs to a long-standing English musical tradition one associates (though Westbrook is from semi-rural High Wycombe) with the Lancashire Catholic background out of which John Lennon emerged (and to which novelist/composer Anthony Burgess has paid tribute). Underneath its wry whimsicality there is a dark thread of social romanticism (particularly important on the Blake settings) and protest that breaks the surface weave more or less often, depending on how serious or angry the piece in question happens to be. The Beatles arrangements are mostly light in touch but highly ambiguous in import; 'Maxwell's Silver Hammer', 'She Came In Through The Bathroom Window' and 'Come Together' all make an impact out of reasonable proportion to their actual content, and even 'Mean Mr Mustard' and 'Polythene Pam' demand further hearings.

Randy Weston (born 1926) PIANO

***(*) **Jazz A La Bohemia** Original Jazz Classics OJC 1747
    Weston; Cecil Payne (*bs*); Ahmed Abdul-Malik (*b*); Al Dreares (*d*). 10/56.
***(*) **Monterey '66** Verve 519 698
    Weston; Ray Copeland (*t, flhn*); Booker Ervin (*ts*); Cecil Payne (*bs*); Bill Wood (*b*); Lenny McBrowne (*d*); Big Black (*perc*). 9/66.

*** **Nuit Africaine** Enja ENJ 2086
    Weston (*p* solo). 8/74.
*** **Perspective** Denon DC 8554
    Weston; Vishnu Wood (*b*). 12/76.

Six-foot something-ridiculous in his bare feet, Weston cuts such an impressive figure that his rather marginal critical standing remains an enigma. Though dozens of players every year turn to the joyous 'Hi-Fly' theme, few of them seem to have probed any deeper into Weston's output, which is considerable and impressive. Like many players of his generation, his main initial influence was Thelonious Monk. In later years, though, Weston was to explore African and Caribbean musics, somewhat in the manner of Dollar Brand/Abdullah Ibrahim and Andrew Hill, and to attempt larger-scale structures of a sort pioneered by James P. Johnson and Duke Ellington. Though a ruggedly beautiful performer, it is as a composer that he is most seriously underrated.

It's clear that he was already attracted to African musics before he ever set foot on the continent. The 1966 Monterey sextet (Ervin was a guest artist) was well ahead of its time, extending the ideas of both Duke Ellington, who appeared on the same bill at Monterey, and Dizzy Gillespie. Weston had been working on a jazz programme in the public school system, and there is a didactic undercurrent to the music, even in a festival context. Big Black's drumming is of considerable significance and is much underrated relative to people like Chano Pozo and the later modernists like Sunny Murray and Andrew Cyrille. This was actually the sextet's last appearance; it sounds like a band that has been together for some time. In these days, Weston was a rather diffident pianist, generally playing only accompaniments to the horns and concentrating on the shape of his compositions, of which the most important here is 'African Cookbook' at a sprawling 25 minutes. Almost all of Weston's later music and most of his important themes ('Little Niles' included) are already present in this period, and most of his later music draws directly on it.

For the clearest sense of what Weston gained – harmonically, rhythmically, spiritually – from his trip to Africa, it's necessary only to compare the excellent *Carnival* (currently deleted) with the much earlier *Jazz A La Bohemia*. It isn't the case that Weston passively 'discovered' African rhythms and tonalities on one of his early-1960s study trips. Art is seldom the product of accidents. As one can clearly hear from the Africanized inflexions of the 1950s Riverside sessions, Weston went in search of confirmation for what he was already doing. 'You Go To My Head' has a quality quite unlike the average standards performance of the time, and Payne's rather solemn-sounding baritone on the other tracks can almost suggest the buzz and thump of Central African drones. Among younger-generation players, probably only Billy Harper had the right combination of traditionalism and modernist, post-bop technique, though later Weston was to record successfully with the new avant-traditionalist of tenor saxophone, David Murray.

Though very well played in their way, the duos with Wood are a bit of an oddity. Weston isn't the most exciting pianist to listen to in this context, and he seems intent on delivering familiar themes – 'Body And Soul', 'Hi-Fly', 'African Cookbook' – with a minimum of additives. What it lacks, fatally, is colour and spice.

**** **Tanjah** Verve 527 778
    Weston; Ray Copeland, Jon Faddis, Ernie Royal (*t, flhn*); Al Grey (*tb*); Jack Jeffers (*btb*); Julius Watkins (*frhn*); Norris Turney (*as, picc*); Billy Harper (*ts, f*); Budd Johnson (*ts, ss, cl*); Danny Bank (*bs, bcl, f*); Ahmed Abdul-Malik (*oud, v*); Ron Carter (*b*); Rudy Collins (*d*); Azzedin Weston, Candido Camero, Earl Williams (*perc*); Delores Ivory Davies (*v*). 5/73.

This was the natural extension of Ellington's multi-cultural experiments, a band that overlapped with the Duke's last years and spun out his vision in a new direction. Melba Liston's arrangements are the key to these astonishing tracks and, if the CD seems a little padded with two alternative takes of 'Sweet Meat', then check out Norris Turney's three solos; not a repetitive lick in earshot. It's a salty, not at all saccharine, township song, the sort of things the guys whistle behind your sister as she sways down the street. The opening 'Hi-Fly' is one of the most exhilarating big-band moments of that decade, a vintage performance of a classic piece, and the closing 'Little Niles' has to run some of the solo performances close for sheer expressive beauty.

*** **Portraits Of Duke Ellington / Caravan** Verve 841 312
    Weston; Jamil Nasser (*b*); Idris Muhammad (*d*); Eric Asante (*perc*). 6/89.
***(*) **Portraits Of Thelonious Monk / Well You Needn't** Verve 814 313
    As above. 6/89.
*** **Self Portraits** Verve 814 314
    As above. 6/89.
*** **Marrakech In The Cool Of The Evening** Verve 521 588
    Weston (*p* solo). 9/92.

Recorded over a three-day stretch on a magnificently resonant Bösendorfer Imperial in Paris, these were meant to set Weston's work in the context of his ancestors in a slightly more personalized sense than the larger group sessions, below. It had always been obvious that Duke and Monk played a part in his thinking and in his development as a player. It's extraordinary how close to Duke's own playing, simple melody lines and abstract accompaniments, he gets on 'Caravan' and 'Sepia Panorama' in particular. Tackling Monk, he sounds like no one but himself. 'Misterioso' and 'Well You Needn't' are not very assured, but the long take of 'Functional' must be one of the most searching performances of Weston's whole career, taking him off into unfamiliar harmonic tangles out of which he lifts himself with impressive ease.

The *Self Portraits* disc is more straightforward. It sounds very much as though Weston has deliberately tried to exclude echoes of the other two from this session, bar a few explicit quotes on 'African Night' and 'Berkshire Blues'. As before, Nasser and Muhammad are with him every step of the way. *Marrakech* more or less completes this cycle. A beautiful, laid-back disc, recorded on a hotel balcony in Morocco, it includes tributes to Nat Cole, Billie Holiday, Dizzy, Fats Waller and Billy Strayhorn, with Weston's own 'Blues For Five Reasons' and 'Two Different Ways To Play The Blues' and some other things wedged in alongside. It's the least exploratory of the four records, but it may well be the most immediately appealing, despite a rather distant sound.

***(*) **The Spirit Of Our Ancestors** Verve 511857 2CD
> Weston; Idrees Sulieman (*t*); Benny Powell (*tb*); Talib Kibwe (*af*); Billy Harper, Dewey Redman (*ts*); Pharoah Sanders (*ts, gaita*); Alex Blake, Jamil Nasser (*b*); Idris Muhammad (*d*); Yassir Chadly (*karkaba*); Azzedin Weston, Big Black (*perc*). 5/91.

Though the spring of compositional ideas had largely dried up, Weston continued to rework earlier themes with great imagination in the 1990s, bringing a quiet, evangelical fervour to the music, perhaps recognizing (though completely without rancour) the extent to which he had been overlooked as a composer. The double-CD *Spirit Of Our Ancestors* updates at least three of his most important works: 'The Healers' and 'African Village Bedford-Stuyvesant' (with Billy Harper and Dewey Redman) and 'African Cookbook' (with Big Black still doing his stuff). Weston also does solo versions of 'African Village' and 'A Prayer For Us All', but again his playing is of less interest than the shape of the pieces themselves and the interpretations of them by soloists like Harper, Redman and Pharoah Sanders. Why Abdullah Ibrahim should have attracted so much more positive critical attention than Weston is a constant surprise.

***(*) **Volcano Blues** Verve 519 269
> Weston; Wallace Roney (*t*); Benny Powell (*tb*); Talib Kibwe (*as, ss, f*); Teddy Edwards (*ts*); Hamiet Bluiett (*bs*); Ted Dunbar (*g*); Jamil Nasser (*b*); Charli Persip (*d*); Obo Addy, Neil Clarke (*perc*); Johnny Copeland (*v, g*). 2/93.

This disc immediately suggests what was lacking on *Spirits*: a firm hand in the arranging department. Veteran Melba Liston takes control, rightly gaining a joint authorship credit for herself in the process. After an opening blues vocal by Johnny Copeland, who accompanies himself on guitar, Weston solos with the band on all the remaining tracks. It's a more varied programme (though what would Liston have done to 'Hi-Fly'?) and includes tunes by Basie ('Volcano', 'Harvard Blues') and Guy Warren. Like *Spirits*, though, much of the spotlight falls on other soloists. Wallace Roney, Benny Powell, Teddy Edwards and Ted Dunbar all stand out, and Charli Persip's intro on the closing track is wonderfully solid. This is by no means a typical Weston record, and it's slightly difficult to locate *vis-à-vis* the rest. That shouldn't stop anyone sampling it, however.

***(*) **Saga** Verve 529 237
> Weston; Benny Powell (*tb*); Talib Kibwe (*as, f*); Billy Harper (*ts*); Alex Blake (*b*); Billy Higgins (*d*); Neil Clarke (*perc*). 4/95.

This is a great *group* record, perhaps less wholly Weston's than any of the above, but none the worse for a touch of diversity and a more even-handed sharing out of solo duties to the African Rhythms. Powell is in excellent form and his solo, behind Weston's, on 'F.E.W. Blues', dedicated to the pianist's dad, is very moving. As usual, there is another of his club tunes, this one 'Saucer Eyes', a slightly raucous remembrance of a beautiful barmaid from years gone by. *Saga* is both lyrical and narrative. It opens with a clear statement of resolve on 'The Beauty Of It All'; this is one of Weston's loveliest conceptions in years and Billy Harper's solo is a tender mixture of gospel chant and deep song.

Ian Wheeler CLARINET, ALTO SAXOPHONE, HARMONICA

(*) **At Farnham Maltings Lake LACD 32
> Wheeler; Rod Mason (*c, v*); Ole 'Fessor' Lindgreen (*tb*); Ray Foxley (*p*); Vic Pitt (*b*); Colin Bowden (*d*). 4/93.

A stalwart of the Chris Barber band, Wheeler is an accomplished and sometimes rather sly clarinet player: on 'Higher Ground', for instance, he has George Lewis down to a faintly cruel t. But it also tends to mean that, as a leader at least, he doesn't impose a particularly individual stamp. Mason makes a suitable front-line partner with his Armstrong licks, but the excellent Lindgreen outplays both of them. They play it safe with the material and Mason's singing is ill-advised, but that is the norm for British trad records. In context, Ray Foxley's solo run through his own 'Liberia Rag' is rather charming. Strong and clean sound.

Kenny Wheeler (born 1930) TRUMPET, FLUGELHORN

***(*) **Gnu High** ECM 1069
  Wheeler; Keith Jarrett (p); Dave Holland (b); Jack DeJohnette (d). 6/75.
**** **Deer Wan** ECM 1102
  Wheeler; Jan Garbarek (ts, ss); John Abercrombie (g, electric mand); Ralph Towner (12-string g); Dave Holland (b); Jack DeJohnette (d). 7/77.
***(*) **Double, Double You** ECM 1262
  Wheeler; Michael Brecker (ts); John Taylor (p); Dave Holland (b); Jack DeJohnette (d). 5/83.
***(*) **Welcome** Soul Note 121171
  Wheeler; Claudio Fasoli (t, flhn); Jean-François Jenny-Clark (b); Daniel Humair (d). 3/86.
*** **Flutter By, Butterfly** Soul Note 121146
  Wheeler; Stan Sulzmann (ss, ts, f); John Taylor (p); Billy Elgart (d). 5/87.
**** **Music For Large And Small Ensembles** ECM 1415/6 2CD/2LP
  Wheeler; Alan Downey, Ian Hamer, Henry Lowther, Derek Watkins (t); Hugh Fraser, Dave Horler, Chris Pyne, Paul Rutherford (tb); Julian Arguëlles, Duncan Lamont, Evan Parker, Ray Warleigh (sax); Stan Sulzmann (ts, f); John Taylor (p); John Abercrombie (g); Dave Holland (b); Peter Erskine (d); Norma Winstone (v). 1/90.
**** **The Widow In The Window** ECM 1417
  Wheeler; John Abercrombie (g); John Taylor (p); Dave Holland (b); Peter Erskine (d). 2/90.
*** **California Daydream** Musidisc 50029
  Wheeler; Jeff Gardner (p); Hein Van De Geyn (b); André Ceccarelli (d). 12/91.
(**) **Kayak Ah Um 012
  Wheeler; Dave Horler, Chris Pyne (tb); Dave Stewart (btb, tba); John Rook (frhn); Stan Sulzmann (ss, ts, f); Julian Arguëlles (ss, ts); John Horler, John Taylor (p); Chris Laurence (b); Peter Erskine (d). 5/92.

Kenny Wheeler's sixtieth birthday in 1990 was treated in many quarters with a kind of suspicious amazement, as if he'd been lying about his age down the years. Wheeler has been a fixture on the British jazz scene since 1952, when he emigrated from his native Canada and did section work with some of the best bandleaders of the time, joining John Dankworth in 1959 and staying until the mid-1960s. Initially influenced by the bop trumpet of Fats Navarro and his equally short-lived descendant, Booker Little, Wheeler also took on board the clipped abstractions and parched romanticism of trumpeter and flugelhorn player Art Farmer. Under this combination of interests, Wheeler turned towards free playing, joining John Stevens's influential Spontaneous Music Ensemble, Alexander von Schlippenbach's Globe Unity Orchestra and Anthony Braxton's superb early-1970s quartet. More recently, Wheeler has played with Norma Winstone and her pianist husband, John Taylor, in the impressionistic Azimuth, and he became the latest permanent recruit to the United Jazz + Rock Ensemble in 1979.

It was possible in 1990 to wonder at Wheeler's threescore years because he became a leader only rather late in his career. Famously self-critical, the trumpeter seemed to lack the basic ego-count required to front a working band. Association with Manfred Eicher's musician-friendly ECM made an enormous difference to Wheeler's self-perception, and since 1975 he has regularly recorded for the label whose painstaking technical virtues match his own. With ECM, Wheeler has also made enormous strides as a composer; standards are now very rare in his recorded work and the Dietz/Schwartz 'By Myself' on ECM 1416 seems a significant exception. 'Ana', on The Widow In The Window, had already been given a notable reading by the Berlin Contemporary Jazz Orchestra (ECM 1409 CD/LP). Music For Large And Small Ensembles contains some of Wheeler's most distinctive scores and is, perhaps, the best place to gain an understanding of how Wheeler's particular grasp of tonality and instrumental colour works in a mixture of scored and improvised settings. As in Azimuth, he uses Norma Winstone's voice to increase the chromaticism of his arrangements and further humanize unwontedly personal and self-revealing pieces, full of folk echoes and deeply embedded North American themes (the 'Opening' to 'Sweet Time Suite' sounds like a variant on a cowboy tune, and there's a wide-open quality to the voicings that can be heard in fellow-Canadian, Leonard Cohen's, eclectic jazz–buckskin–musette–rock syntheses).

The trios that conclude disc two (there are also three duets which do not involve Wheeler as a player) are closer to his free-abstract work than to the thematic improvisations on his best-known ECM records. Significantly, the most abstract of the albums he has made for the label, *Around 6*, is currently deleted. The best of those that remain is undoubtedly *Deer Wan*. It includes Wheeler's most atmospheric brass effects and some of his most unfettered playing. The opening 'Peace For Five' is a straightforward blowing theme, with fine solos by each of the players. The three remaining tracks are more elliptical but no less impressive, and only the relatively brief '3/4 In The Afternoon', featuring one of Ralph Towner's off-the-peg 12-string spots, is a mild disappointment.

Deer Wan's predecessor on ECM is distinguished by being Keith Jarrett's last session as a sideman. There is some evidence that the pianist was less than happy with the music, but he produces three startling performances that are matched by Wheeler's distinctive phraseology and impeccable tone. An important album for the trumpeter, it's still marked by a degree of diffidence which persists through the later work. The two Soul Notes suffer from a flatter acoustic, which seems to rob Wheeler's higher-register passages of their ringing strength. Musically, they're well up to scratch; 'Everybody's Song But My Own' (*Flutter By*) and 'Invisible Sound' and 'Emptiness' (*Silence*) utilize the softly falling figures one has heard in Wheeler's work from the outset but which increasingly play a structural role in the composition. The recent *Widow In The Window* recaptures – but for Garbarek – the sound of *Deer Wan*, while adding a new solidity of conception. Taken in conjunction with the contemporaneous *Music For Large And Small Ensembles*, it signals Wheeler's emergence as a major jazz composer. Late in the day by some standards, but none the less welcome.

Kayak is marred by oddly balanced sound, but is musically fascinating. The latter part of the set is taken up with a suite loosely centred on C: 'See Horse', the impressionistic 'Sea Lady' (with a fine flute solo from Sulzmann), 'C Man' (dedicated to bassist Laurence, who introduces the solos), and 'C. C. Signor!' (a rollicking tribute to Chick Corea that brings the album to a very effective close).

Wheeler distributes the solo space very even-handedly, concentrating exclusively on flugelhorn for his carefully crafted explorations. The writing is consistently excellent, mixing older material like '5 4 6' and 'Gentle Piece – Old Ballad', the latter strongly recalling the Wheeler of *Deer Wan*. Despite reservations about the production, strongly recommended.

The Musidisc is a live session, recorded in Paris. Gardner and Van De Geyn chip in with two pieces each, but they're so unsophisticated alongside Wheeler's 'The Imminent Immigrant' and 'Bethan' (which, quite properly, start and finish the set) that it's ridiculous. Sound is a bit echoey and overfull, but it's a nice record and one that Wheeler fans will definitely want to have.

Jiggs Whigham (born 1943) TROMBONE, TROMBONIUM

**(*) The Jiggs Up Capri 74024-2

Whigham; Bud Shank (*as*); George Cables (*p*); John Clayton (*b*); Jeff Hamilton (*d*). 7/89.

*(*) Hope Mons 1888

Whigham; Ferdinand Povel (*ss, as, ts, f*); Rob Franken (*ky*); Niels-Henning Orsted-Pedersen (*b*); Grady Tate (*d*). 1/76.

Whigham has lived and worked in Cologne since going there in the mid-1960s to join Kurt Edelhagen's big band, although this set was recorded on one of his return visits to the USA. He has a smooth-as-chocolate sound on the trombone, entirely unblemished by tonal exaggerations, and while this can lead to blandness he has an agility on the horn which is nearly the match of Bill Watrous, a player of similar style. *Hope* is a belated release of a 1976 session which should be heard only by the curious: Whigham uses ancient technology like the multivider, plays a trombonium, and does very little of interest with either. The band play with gutless competence. *The Jiggs Up*, recorded in concert, is an enjoyable blow for all involved: Shank sounds in happy mood, although some of his solos take on an aggressively opposing stance to his former, more controlled manner, and it doesn't always suit him. Cables, Clayton and Hamilton play with professional class. The best moments come with the ballads, especially Whigham's charming 'For Someone Never Known'. Unfortunately the recording is less impressive: Shank in particular frequently drifts off-mike, and the rhythm section sound distant.

Brian White CLARINET

*** Muggsy Remembered Vol. 1 Jazzology JCD-116

White; Alan Gresty (*t*); Geoff Cole (*tb*); Goff Dubber (*ss, ts*); Alan Root, Jonathan Vinten (*p*); Tony Bagot (*b*); Ian Castle (*d*). 4/88–10/93.

*** **Muggsy Remembered Vol. 2** Jazzology JCD-200
    As above, except omit Vinten. 4/44–4/89.
*** **Pleasure Mad** Jazzology JCD-178
    White; Ben Cohen (*t, v*); Geoff Cole (*tb*); Alan Thomas (*p*); Joe Becket, Gordon Davis (*b*); Ian
    Castle (*d*).
*** **Really The Blues** GHB BCD-303
    White; Alan Elsdon (*t*); Goff Dubber (*ss, cl, v*); Neville Dickie, John Clarke (*p*); Malcolm
    Harrison (*g*); Gordon Davis (*b*); Colin Miller (*d*). 5–8/90.
*** **C'est Magnafique** Jazzology JCD-248
    White; Ben Cohen (*c*); Geoff Cole (*tb*); Jonathan Vinten (*p*); Richard Lyons (*b*); Colin Miller
    (*d*). 12/92.

The English clarinettist White takes repertory to a near-fanatical state on these affectionate, punctilious
re-creations of bygone jazz. The Spanier albums mix Muggsy's 'Great Sixteen' tunes with a handful of
other variations on the Ragtime Band style and, while there is some ingenious counterfeiting here, they
do tend to make one long to hear the originals. Problematically, while the band try stretching out on a
few of the previously 78-length arrangements, they add nothing of consequence. Gresty does a com-
mendable job of ghosting for the original, but his nearly note-perfect takes on Muggsy's superb
'Someday Sweetheart' improvisation or the climactic 'I Want A Big Butter And Egg Man' hardly
compete with the master. Volume One was actually reissued after Volume Two, and is enhanced by four
tracks from 1993, recorded partly in tribute to pianist Root, who died earlier that year.

    The re-creations of the King Jazz sessions on *Really The Blues* are rather more effective, but finally not
much different in impact. Dubber and White make a more obviously compatible team than Bechet and
Mezzrow, and they sound the more personal for it; but Elsdon's trumpet parts are merely derivative, and
the rhythm section secure a somewhat hollow bounce. *Pleasure Mad* casts a wider net and reels in Hot
Five tunes and '1919 March', among others. This set is by White's Magna Jazz Band, which he's led
since 1951, and *C'est Magnafique* continues their tradition. It's some comment on the group's resilience
that this is as good a disc as any they've made. The 16 tracks include an intelligent choice of rarities –
from the books of Bechet, Don Redman, Jimmy Blythe and others – and all are despatched with an
enthusiasm that sounds to be second nature by now. Good, clean recording on all these discs.

Chip White DRUMS

*** **Harlem Sunset** Postcards POST1006
    White; Claudio Roditi (*t, flhn*); Robin Eubanks (*tb*); Gary Bartz (*ss, as*); Steve Nelson (*vib*);
    Buster Williams (*b*). 6/94.

Beautiful playing, though the music tends to stand revealed after a single play: pleasing as White's tunes
are, familiarity doesn't reveal any great profundities. He's a busy but not overpowering drummer,
pushing the tunes along in straightforward time, embellished by deft use of the sticks, and he gets a light,
sometimes haunting sound out of the horns, cushioned on Nelson's vibes which give a resonance to the
chords that a piano might have dulled. 'Circle Dance' and 'Excuse Me Now' are particularly attractive.
There's a nice contrast between Roditi's brimming style and Eubanks's more sober virtuosity, while
Bartz is his usual strong self, if at a rather lower wattage than normal.

David White GUITAR

*** **All Stories Are True** Cadence CJR 1057
    White; Valery Ponomarev (*t*); Tom Armacost (*ts*); Calvin Hill (*b*); Victor Jones (*d*). 5/93.

Likeable, oddball neo-bop, but not without its problems. White's muffled, sometimes bluesy sound is a
refreshing change from the standard Montgomery/Scofield options, and he has a Tristano-like sense of
selflessness: some of his solos sound completely 'inside'. He takes on some interesting structures, too,
such as the various metres of 'Iconoclasts' and the contrary 'Hot Issues In An Open House'. Ponomarev
and Armacost come up with some strong improvisations in support. But the rhythm section often seem
unaware of what's going on and where everybody's headed. Hill, especially, is very busy yet oblivious to
the rest of the music, and both he and Jones are given an unpleasant studio sound. A mixed result.

Tim Whitehead (born 1950) TENOR SAXOPHONE

*** **Authentic** Ronnie Scott's Jazz House JHCD 017
    Whitehead; Pete Jacobsen (*p, syn*); Arnie Somogyi (*b*); Dave Barry (*d*). 2/91.

A nimble writer and improviser, Whitehead garnered considerable praise from visiting Americans for this stint at Ronnie Scott's Soho club. The band is tight, workmanlike and often quite provocative, anchored on Jacobsen's briskly unpredictable chordal patterns and Somogyi's (still to be more widely acknowledged) bass playing. Playing spot-the-influence is pretty redundant with the leader, who has already devised his own voice, but another Jazz House artist, George Coleman, is in there somewhere, beefy but not unsubtle, harmonically adventurous but with a sharp ear for a melody line as well.

Weslia Whitfield VOCAL

(*) **Lucky To Be Me Landmark LCD-1524-2
    Whitfield; Mike Greensill (*p*); Dean Reilly (*b*). 11/89.
(*) **Live In San Francisco Landmark LCD-1531-2
    As above. 4/91.
*** **Seeker Of Wisdom And Truth** Cabaret CACD 5012
    As above, except add John Goldsby (*b*), Tim Horner (*d*); omit Reilly. 11/93.
*** **Nice Work . . .** Landmark LCD-1544-2
    As above, except add Gene Bertoncini (*g*), Michael Moore (*b*); omit Reilly. 12/94.
Whitfield's clear, strong voice and concern for lyrics should make for a distinguished member of the classic school of jazz singers, but her first albums tend to linger on the least appealing aspects of her work. Her intonation seems unintentionally mannered and, while she uses scarcely any vibrato, a certain plumminess blemishes too many lines. *Lucky To Be Me* is a pleasing mixture of comfortable standards and some genuine Tin Pan Alley rarities, but the consistently slow tempos lend a monotonal feel that makes it hard to differentiate one tune from the next. The live album, taken down at her home base in San Francisco, is beautifully recorded, yet again lacks the inventive edge that would take Whitfield into the top echelon. All that said, however, the best moments on both records – 'Glad To Be Unhappy' on the first record and an exceptional 'I Didn't Know About You' on the live set – are very satisfying.

    Seeker Of Wisdom And Truth is a notch better – the Astaire medley is delightful, 'The Boy Next Door' has a nice ambiguity about it, and 'I Want To Talk About You' is very fine – and *Nice Work . . .* is surely her best yet, even though some of the songs still don't seem to suit her style at all. 'I'm An Errand Girl For Rhythm' doesn't work even as irony: Ms Whitfield is not really a swinging singer. Where she excels is in bringing a new light to a familiar work: 'Bewitched, Bothered And Bewildered', though at first phrased at what seems to be an odd tempo, is done brilliantly, 'I'm Gonna Laugh You Out Of My Life' is a perfect example of controlled sadness. She likes to sing the verses; she also likes to hold a long note without any vibrato, which can be a devastating effect in an otherwise restrained interpretation. Greensill accompanies deftly. A step away from a classic, perhaps.

Sebastian Whittaker DRUMS

*** **First Outing** Justice JR 0201
    Whittaker; Dennis Dotson (*t, flhn*); James Lakey (*tb*); Shelley Carrol, John Gordon (*ts*); Stefan Karlsson (*p*); David Craig (*b*). 90.
*** **Searchin' For The Truth** Justice JR 0202
    Whittaker; Barry Lee Hall (*t*); James Lakey (*tb*); Jesse Davis (*as*); Stefan Karlsson (*p*); David Craig (*b*). 91.
Whittaker is a young man who has overcome considerable personal difficulties to become a musician. Sightless piano players are relatively common, but drumming requires a very different spatial sense and orientation, and this Whittaker seems to have acquired. His label goes out under the Green-ish slogan 'Recycle Paper, Not Music'; but there is a persistent sense that much of the Justice catalogue is recycled hard bop. Whittaker is a more honest practitioner than most, and the combination of his Blakey-derived technique (with rather individual bass accents) and a misty analogue sound frequently conjures up the impression that one is listening to some obscure corner of the late-'50s Blue Note catalogue.

    First Outing is probably the better of the two discs by a whisker, though the appearance of Jesse Davis on *Searchin' For The Truth* in place of two barely individuated tenors is a step in the right direction. The first album offers a fine, abrupt arrangement of John Coltrane's 'Impressions', a blues theme which sometimes tempts young players into evening-long meanderings but which Whittaker handles quite briskly. It's somehow suggestive that he insists on calling individual numbers 'songs'; that's very much how he handles them. There's no sense that either he or The Creators are short on ideas, merely that he sees no virtue in scales and modal exercises.

    Pianist Karlsson, also a Justice recording artist, is an important influence, though surprisingly it's Lakey and Craig who between them dominate the writing credits on *First Outing*. Whittaker's own stuff is pretty basic, and only 'Searchin' For The Truth' (the longest track on either disc) overstretches itself. Whittaker isn't an altogether inspiring soloist, preferring to concentrate on small areas of sound before moving on to something else. Like the rest of the music, it's very focused, but in a relaxed, almost consciously undramatic way.

Dick Whittington PIANO

*** In New York Concord CCD 4498
    Whittington; Steve Gilmore (*b*); Bill Goodwin (*d*). 10/86.
Since this set was recorded (it wasn't released until 1992), Whittington has perhaps become more renowned as the voice introducing each of Concord's Maybeck Recital Hall series; he's the owner of the venue. But he's no slouch as a piano player himself, owing something to Hampton Hawes and Red Garland in style. With even-handed support from Gilmore and Goodwin, erstwhile members of Phil Woods' rhythm section, he goes through ten pieces with great bounce and vigour: 'Manteca' is taken at a very fast clip, and Ahmad Jamal's 'New Rhumba' surrenders nothing to the composer's versions of the tune. While there are many such mainstream-into-post-bop dates, this one's as solidly entertaining as any.

Tommy Whittle (born 1926) TENOR SAXOPHONE

**(*) Warm Glow Teejay 103
    Whittle; Brian Dee (*p*); Len Skeat (*b*); Bobby Orr (*d*). 2/92.
This veteran tenorman has spent much of his time ensconced in various kinds of studio band, but he still does a good Websterish ballad and a cordial mid-tempo stroll. The title of the record sums it up, although there's a little more heat on a blues and 'Fascinating Rhythm'.

Putte Wickman (born 1924) CLARINET

*** Young, Searching And Swinging Phontastic CD 9304
    Wickman; Gosta Torner (*t*); Georg Vernon (*tb*); Arne Domnérus, S. Gustafsson (*as*); G. Bjorklund, Gosta Theselius (*ts*); Charlie Norman, Bob Laine, Reinhold Svensson, Gunnar Svensson (*p*); Johan Adolfsson (*acc*); Fred Eriksberg, Stefan Carlberg, Kalle Lohr, Rolf Berg, Rune Gustafsson (*g*); Sune Svensson, Bo Kallstrom (*vib*); Thore Jederby, Simon Brehm, Roland Bengtsson, Yngve Akerberg, Hans Burman (*b*); Ake Brandes, B. Frylmark, Georg Oddner, Jack Noren, S. Bollhem, Robert Edman, Sture Kallin (*d*). 3/45–2/55.
*** Bewitched Bluebell ABCD 051
    Wickman; Claes Crona (*p*); Mads Vinding, Ove Stenberg (*b*); Bjarne Rostvold, Nils-Erik Slorner (*d*). 9/80–7/82.
*** Desire / Mr Clarinet Four Leaf FLC-CD 101
    Wickman; Lars Samuelsson (*t*); Bjorn J-Son Lindh (*ky, f*); Janne Schaffer (*g*); Teddy Walter (*b*); Magnus Persson, Per Lindvall (*d*). 4/84–6/85.
***(*) The Very Thought Of You Dragon DRCD 161
    Wickman; Red Mitchell (*b*). 12/87–1/88.
**** Some O' This And Some O' That Dragon DRCD 187
    Wickman; Roger Kellaway (*p*); Red Mitchell (*b*). 6/89.
***(*) Putte Wickman In Trombones Phontastic NCD 8826
    Wickman; Olle Holmqvist, Bertil Strandberg, Anders Wiborg, Urban Wiborg, Nils Landgren (*tb*); Gosta Rundqvist (*p*); Sture Akerberg, Christian Spering (*b*); Peter Ostlund (*d*). 5–6/92.
*** In Silhouette Phontastic NCD 8848
    Wickman; Butch Lacy (*p*); Rune Gustafsson (*g*); Jesper Lundgaard (*b*); Arne Tangaard (*d*). 6/94.
Putte Wickman is still, after five decades, completely at home among Sweden's jazz masters. An impeccable swing player who followed cool developments in the 1950s, Wickman has spent time away from jazz but seems fully aware of every kind of development in the music. Some of his earlier recordings have been restored to circulation by *Young, Searching And Swinging*, which compiles 22 tracks from various playing situations – though all small groups – over his first ten years in the studio. Many are with pianist Reinhold Svensson, who partnered the clarinettist in a quartet for several years. The format doesn't move far beyond the small-band sides by Goodman and Shaw, and could even seem anachronistic at a time when bop had taken a grip, but Wickman's essentially cool stance allowed wrinkles of

modernism to sidle into the music. By the time of the final sextet tracks that persona is firmly in place. Some of the earlier tracks sound a little grey, but remastering is mostly good.

From here, the current discography jumps straight into the 1980s. *Bewitched* covers two trio sessions – Crona plays on both – in which Putte investigates two sets of standards. The 1980 session is better by a whisker: Stenberg plays with real drive and there's an interesting version of Bernie Senensky's 'Another Gift' which makes one wish that Wickman would look at contemporary tunes more often. The music tends to be sleepy on melody statements, then gradually wakes up when the leader probes his way through a solo. The Four Leaf CD reissues a pair of albums where the clarinettist works in a soft-fusion setting: it's slight stuff, the playing vitiated a little by the context, but Wickman finds things to say, and the music remains disarmingly pretty.

The two Dragons find Wickman in splendid fettle. The duo set with Mitchell is momentarily troubled by the bassist's capricious streak: his fascination with the lowest register sometimes strays into indulgence, and the huffing momentum won't be to all tastes. But Wickman goes on spinning out memorable improvisations, and they devise some unexpected variations on the (standard) material: Basie's 'Topsy' becomes rather intense and brooding, and the Ellington themes have no sniff of routine in them. When Kellaway joins in, the music spreads itself out (eight pieces take 72 minutes here, whereas there are 13 in 68 minutes on the duo record), and Kellaway's extravagant imagination is perfectly checked by Wickman's insidious, wily lines. They all play very hard. The recording is sometimes a little flat, since both discs were made in Red Mitchell's apartment rather than a studio, but it suits the intimacy of the music.

Putte likes trombones: they make a sound he 'can pull over himself like a comforting down quilt'. *In Trombones* is a little reminiscent of an oddball West Coast date of 40 years earlier, but the excellent charts – Strandberg, Rundqvist, Bo Sylven – create a leaner tone on some tracks; others have the clarinet bedding down in deep-pile trombone luxury. Wickman still sounds brilliantly zestful and alert: the clarinet solos on 'Ebony Dance' remind that, even when some have been talking about the clarinet finding its modern feet via Braxton and Byron, Putte Wickman's been here all the time.

In Silhouette is a mixed bag where Wickman again does his best work on the originals, and the relatively pale interpretations of some of the standards suggest that he should always be given fresh challenges. Gustafsson, another wily veteran by now, has his own ideas and gets just enough space to sneak them in.

Widespread Depression Orchestra GROUP

*** **Downtown Uproar / Boogie In The Barnyard** Stash ST-CD-540
   Jordan Sandke (*t*); Tim Atherton (*tb*); Michael Hashim (*as*); Dean Nicyper (*ts*); David Lillie
   (*bs*); Michael LeDonne (*p*); Jonny Holtzman (*vib, v*); Phil Flanigan (*b*); John Ellis (*d*). 79–80.
Though they subsequently called themselves 'Widespread Jazz Orchestra', presumably to avoid using misery as a label, the two albums coupled on one CD here were by the WDO, which sets out to revivify midstream swing material in the classic manner: as if the Lu Watters Band had been reincarnated as a crew of New England youngsters, which is what most of the musicians were when they started out in 1972. For all the spirit and interpretative elegance of the players, this is a genre exercise, and the fact that they include plenty of collectors'-item tunes (Coleman Hawkins's 'Hollywood Stampede', for instance, or Brick Fleagle's 'Zaza' or Ellington's 'Downtown Uproar') only adds to the inky-fingered aura which surrounds the music. But it's plenty of fun taken a few tracks at a time (the 76 minutes here are perhaps rather too many), and no doubting the calibre of the soloists, especially Michael Hashim's Hodges-inspired alto.

Gerald Wiggins (born 1922) PIANO

** **Music From Around The World In Eighty Days In Modern Jazz** Original Jazz Classics OJC 1761
   Wiggins; Eugene Wright (*b*); Bill Douglass (*d*).
Gerry Wiggins began with swing big bands, but he has pursued much of his career as an accompanist, originally with Lena Horne. On his own, with an appropriate rhythm section, he plays light, undemanding but beguiling swing-to-cool piano, rarely challenging the listener and preferring to make a few well-chosen remarks rather than refashioning a tune. The *Eighty Days* material is typical of many records that were worked up from popular contemporary film and show material and, while it's not bad, it sounds as perfunctory as most such genre entries. The superior *Relax And Enjoy It!* has yet to make it to CD.

*** **Wig Is Here** Black & Blue 590692
   Wiggins; Major Holley (*b*); Ed Thigpen, Oliver Jackson (*d*). 5/74–2/77.

Wiggins caught in two trio settings in Paris, with Holley present on both occasions. Little has changed since the OJC albums and, although he is now playing Stevie Wonder as well as 'The Lady Is A Tramp', the same reliable, tension-free swing is at hand.

***(*) **Live At Maybeck Recital Hall Volume Eight** Concord CCD 4450
Wiggins. 8/90.

Wig's entry in this splendid ongoing series is arguably his best-ever record. On a good piano, with impeccable sound, the quality which Jimmy Rowles – very much a kindred stylistic spirit – refers to in his sleeve-note as 'natural relaxation' emerges in full bloom. It's not so much a matter of taking his time, since none of the pieces here runs to much more than five minutes in length, more a point of shaping a performance to precisely the right tempo and dynamic in order to set down the thoughts the pianist has in mind. Here, for instance, he treats 'I Should Care' as a kind of slow stride interpretation, and Ahmad Jamal's 'Night Mist Blues' has a rocking steadiness which even the composer has never quite realized. He doesn't dawdle over ballads, but nothing's played at any kind of a fast tempo either. Some of the tunes are perhaps over-familiar, even to Wig himself, who has little of significance to add to 'Take The "A" Train' or 'Body And Soul', but that is the privilege of senior status. The recording is as truthful as usual in this fine sequence of records.

Johnny Wiggs (1899–1977) CORNET

*** **Sounds Of New Orleans Vol. 2: Johnny Wiggs** Storyville STCD 6009
Wiggs; Tom Brown, Jack Delaney (tb); Harry Shields, Raymond Burke (cl); Stanley Mendelson, Armand Hug (p); Edmond 'Doc' Souchon (g, v); Joe Capraro (g); Sherwood Mangiapane, Arnold 'Deacon' Loyacano, Phil Darois (b); Roger Johnston, Ray Bauduc (d). 50–55.

Johnny Wiggs played in the classic New Orleans style, but the distinctiveness of his sound goes to prove the breadth and variety of New Orleans jazz, even within the over-familiar repertoire here. Wiggs heard King Oliver in 1916, according to Chris Albertson's notes, and his use of a firmly placed terminal vibrato suggests a close kinship with the King; but 'I'm Coming Virginia', played as a duet with Armand Hug, shows how closely he listened to Bix Beiderbecke, too. These recordings date from the period of Wiggs's first 'comeback' – he had been a teacher for some 20 years before returning in the height of the N.O. revival – and feature two unusually assertive bands, with splendid clarinet from both Shields and Burke and a rare glimpse of the somewhat legendary trombonist Tom Brown. Some of the tracks are more like informal jams, Wiggs blowing with just a rhythm section on five tracks; and even where the material is dusty, there's genuine spirit in all the playing: 'Congo Square' and 'King Zulu Parade March', both from the earliest session, suggest that Wiggs was a useful composer, too. Lifted from private tapes, the sound is inevitably less than perfect but it won't trouble anyone interested in this fascinating area of the music.

*** **Penn–Wiggs New Orleans All Stars Concert Volume One** GHB BCD-301
Wiggs; Louis Nelson (tb); George Lewis (cl); Charlie Hamilton (p); Joseph Butler (b, v); Sammy Penn (d, v). 12/66.
*** **Penn–Wiggs New Orleans All Stars Concert Volume Two** GHB BCD-302
As above. 12/66.

Wiggs and Penn co-led this aggregation of home-town masters for a brief period, and George Buck recorded a concert in Columbia, S.C., which appears on these two CDs (in excellent sound). The relaxed occasion led to the group stretching out more than usual on most of the tunes, and this adds a rising intensity to such as 'Make Me A Pallet On The Floor'. Lewis was in unusually good spirits and plays very well, but the self-effacing Nelson found the demands of being a soloist a bit much, and Wiggs isn't really up to the fast tempo for 'Dipper Mouth Blues'. The rhythm section, though, creates a lilting beat throughout.

Bob Wilber (born 1928) SOPRANO, ALTO AND TENOR SAXOPHONES, CLARINET

*** **At Thatchers** J&M 501
Wilber; Kenny Davern (ss, cl); Dave Cliff (g); Peter Ind (b); Lennie Hastings (d). 10/76.
***(*) **Soprano Summit In Concert** Concord CCD 4029
Wilber; Kenny Davern (ss, cl); Marty Grosz (g); Ray Brown (b); Jake Hanna (d). 7/76.
*** **Soprano Summit Live At Concord '77** Concord CCD 4052
As above, except Monty Budwig (b) replaces Brown. 77.

*** **Bob Wilber And The Scott Hamilton Quartet** Chiaroscuro CR(D) 171
 Wilber; Scott Hamilton (*ts*); Chris Flory (*g*); Phil Flanigan (*b*); Chuck Riggs (*d*). 6–7/77.
***(*) **On The Road** Jazzology JCD-214
 Wilber; Glenn Zottola (*t*); Mark Sahne (*p*); Mike Peters (*g, bj*); Len Skeat (*b*); Butch Miles (*d*).
 11/81.
*** **The Duet** Progressive PCD 7080
 Wilber; Dick Wellstood (*p*). 3/84.
*** **Bechet Legacy** Challenge CHR 70018
 Wilber; Randy Sandke (*t*); Mike Peters (*g*); John Goldsby (*b*). 1/84.
**** **Dancing On A Rainbow** Circle CCD-159
 Wilber; Wallace Davenport (*t*); Dave Sager (*tb*); Clarence Ford (*cl, ts, bs*); Dave Bodenhouse (*p*);
 Danny Barker (*g*); Dewey Sampson (*b*); Freddie Kohlman (*d*); Joanne 'Pug' Horton (*v*). 12/89.
***(*) **Summit Reunion** Chiaroscuro CR(D) 311
 Wilber; Kenny Davern (*cl*); Dick Hyman (*p*); Bucky Pizzarelli (*g*); Milt Hinton (*b*); Bobby
 Rosengarden (*d*). 5/90.
*** **Summit Reunion – Jazz Im Amerika Haus Vol. 5** Nagel-Heyer 015
 Wilber; Kenny Davern (*cl*); Dave Cliff (*g*); Dave Green (*b*); Bobby Worth (*d*). 9/94.
***(*) **Moments Like This** Phontastic NCD 8811
 Wilber; Antti Sarpila (*ss, ts, cl*); Ulf Johansson (*tb, p, v*); Sture Akerberg (*b*); Ronnie Gardiner
 (*d*). 5/91.

Once upon a time everyone tried to play soprano sax like Sidney Bechet. Now that everyone tries to play soprano like either Coltrane or Steve Lacy, Bob Wilber seems like something of a throwback. Since he actually played with Bechet and has done more than anyone to keep that master's music in circulation, there's no 'authenticity' problem here. Wilber still seeks the wide, singing tone of his mentor, but he long since became his own man, and even where there is a specific homage – as in *On The Road*, which was made by his band Bechet Legacy – he still sounds like himself. This is an impressive run of records. The *Soprano Summit* discs are by a popular double-act with Davern, who has since reverted to clarinet only (which is what he plays on the *Summit Reunion* disc). Both Concord albums were recorded live and they suffer from a tad too much showmanship here and there, but the brimming energy of the up-tempo pieces is a marvel, and Wilber always knows when to cool things off: his gorgeous treatment of 'The Golden Rooster' on *In Concert* is as good as any Hodges showcase. Their reunion album is another fine set, the more piquant since there's a regular contrast between the horns rather than a doppelgänger effect. The J&M disc is another live one, with a so-so British rhythm section. The group carries on into the '90s, though the latest concert set from the Amerika Haus is a potboiler – Wilber and Davern seem to be jogging through this one rather than striking sparks.

Wilber's other projects are rather more interesting. *On The Road* is a very fine salute to Bechet, uncovering many rarities in the material and with top-notch support from Zottola in particular. The CD remastering is a bit bright. *Bechet Legacy* puts similar material into a concert situation and, though Sandke isn't much like Muggsy Spanier, the instrumentation inevitably evokes the Bechet–Spanier small group. Another astute piece of revivalism. Better still, though, is *Dancing On A Rainbow*. This is an exemplary mainstream outfit, with Sager's quirky trombone and Ford's ripe gallery of reeds lending character as well as precision, and Wilber's Ellington archaeology is spot-on: it was a shrewd idea to bring back 'Love In My Heart' and 'Charlie The Chulo'; but all the material turns out well. The 1977 album with Scott Hamilton is merely OK mainstream, with the tenorman still in his copycat phase, but the recent *Moments Like This* sets up Wilber with another young disciple, the Swedish reedsman, Sarpila. Johansson does his usual trick of doubling trombone and piano, and it sounds like a happy occasion.

The 1984 duets with Dick Wellstood have made a welcome transition to CD. Wellstood's slightly macabre imagination might not be to all tastes, as in his transformation of 'I've Got You Under My Skin' into a stride showcase, but he was a thinking player and had the executive powers to match. Wilber, more of a literalist, makes a nice balance, and the disc has some superb moments.

*** **Horns A-Plenty** Arbors ARCD 19135
 Wilber; Johnny Varro (*p*); Phil Flanigan (*b*); Ed Metz Jr (*d*). 3/94.
***(*) **Bean** Arbors ARCD 19144
 Wilber; Harry Allen, Tommy Whittle, Antti Sarpila (*ts*); Mick Pyne (*p*); Dave Green (*b*); Clark
 Tracey (*d*). 10/94.
(*) **Nostalgia Arbors ARCD 19145
 Wilber; Ralph Sutton (*p*); Bucky Pizzarelli (*g*); Bob Haggart (*b*); Butch Miles (*d*). 3/95.

His consistency is such that it's hard to imagine Wilber cutting a bad record. That said, his recent excursions into repertory are a mixed lot. *Horns A-Plenty* finds him switching between clarinet and four saxes on a typically arcane set of tunes, with a few lightweight originals floating in amongst the likes of

'Just A Rose In A Garden Of Weeds'. Not bad, but the music's pleasantries tend to leave no impression. *Bean* puts a four-man tenor team through their paces on a tribute to Coleman Hawkins. Wilber concentrates on Hawk's music from the 1930s and early '40s, and there are some ingenious reductions and embellishments on what are in several cases neglected originals. The team are recorded in a dry but very effective acoustic, and some of the unison passages are wonderfully played, with Wilber and Whittle emerging as the most Hawk-like. *Nostalgia* is mostly ballads and tunes from bygone albums. If Wilber were British, he might have thought twice about doing 'The Lambeth Walk' here; and a couple of the classical pieces recall the days of Rudy Wiedoft. Stately stuff. If Wellstood were still alive, he might have lent a Machiavellian touch at the piano, but Sutton, admirable though he is, is no such ironist.

Joe Wilder (born 1922) TRUMPET, FLUGELHORN

*** Wilder 'N' Wilder Savoy SV-0131

Wilder; Hank Jones (*p*); Wendell Marshall (*b*); Kenny Clarke (*d*). 1/56.

A rare outing as a leader for this much-travelled sideman and studio player. Although he emerged at the time of bop – he was with Dizzy Gillespie in the Les Hite band – Joe was a sweeter, more temperate player. The title is a misnomer: there's nothing very wild about the playing here, although 'Six Bit Blues', a 3/4 walking blues, features some growl trumpet which the leader evidently enjoys. 'Cherokee' is taken at a light medium tempo and strolls on for 10 minutes, while most of the others stand as ballads. Wilder's broad tone and lightly shimmering vibrato are set against Jones's customarily civilized playing to maximum effect. The remastering is clear and well focused.

***(*) Alone With Just My Dreams Evening Star ES-101

Wilder; James Williams (*p*); Remo Palmieri (*g*); Jay Leonhart (*b*); Sherman Ferguson (*d*). 8/91.

The bittersweet title is perfectly appropriate for this autumnal recital by a great hornman. Joe's command has faded a little, but his choice of notes and august delivery are more than moving. On 'Struttin' With Some Barbecue' he evokes memories of a lost generation of hot trumpet players, but it's the ballads which are quietly affecting, and the final reading of 'What A Wonderful World' will melt hearts of stone. The supporting players were very well cast.

Barney Wilen (1937–96) SOPRANO, ALTO, TENOR AND BARITONE SAXOPHONES

*** Un Temoin Dans La Ville / Jazz Sur Seine Fontana 832658-2

Wilen; Kenny Dorham (*t*); Duke Jordan, Milt Jackson (*p*); Paul Rovere, Percy Heath (*b*); Kenny Clarke (*d*); Gana M'Bow (*perc*). 58–59.

*** Newport '59 Fresh Sound FSR-CD 165

Wilen; Clark Terry (*t*); Toshiko Akiyoshi, Bud Powell, Ewald Heidepriem (*p*); Tommy Bryant, Eric Peter, Karl Theodor Geier (*b*); Roy Haynes, Kenny Clarke, Eberhardt Stengl (*d*). 59.

Basically a tenor player, Wilen made his name when Miles Davis chose him to play in a group he was fronting in Europe in 1957. But Wilen had already garnered a reputation with visiting Americans for a considerably accomplished technique and a real mastery of hard-bop forms. The Fontana album is an early one, combining two film soundtrack scores: *Un Temoin* is curtailed to fit the purposes of the film, and the group never really get going, but Wilen and Dorham have a few nice moments. *Jazz Sur Seine* is more like a regular quartet date, with Jackson (on piano for once), Heath and Clarke. Most of the tunes are French jazz staples – a thoughtful 'Nuages', a bright 'Swing 39', and they finish on Monk's 'Epistrophy'.

Wilen's subsequent visit to play at Newport in 1959 is commemorated by the Fresh Sound CD, although there's only 20 minutes of music from that occasion: Akiyoshi plays exuberant bebop piano in support and Wilen's even, supple tenor works patiently and impressively through 'Passport' and 'Barney's Tune', with what was then a rare appearance of the soprano on ''Round Midnight', in which his tonal control is impressive. Two other tracks of unclear date find him with Powell (very subdued), Terry and Clarke; Wilen's solo on 'No Problem' is typically artful – since the recording is subject to some vagaries of balance, he seems to emerge from the shadows here. There is also another ''Round Midnight' with a German rhythm section. The sound is very mixed throughout but it's listenable enough.

**(*) La Note Bleue IDA 010

Wilen; Alain Jean-Marie (*p, org*); Philippe Petit (*g*); Riccardo Del Frà (*b*); Sangoma Everett (*d*). 12/86.

*** **French Ballads** IDA 014
> Wilen; Michel Graillier (*p*); Riccardo Del Frà (*b*); Sangoma Everett (*d*). 87.

**** **Wild Dogs Of The Ruwenzori** IDA 020
> Wilen; Alain Jean-Marie (*ky*); Riccardo Del Frà (*b*); Sangoma Everett (*d*); Henri Guedon (*perc*). 11/88.

**** **Sanctuary** IDA 029
> Wilen; Philip Catherine (*g*); Palle Danielsson (*b*). 1/91.

Wilen's contract for IDA helped create a comeback for a fine musician. In the 1980s he tinkered with jazz–rock and African rhythms (he went to live in Africa in the late 1960s) and his return to a bop-inflected style has something of the full-circle maturity which Stan Getz came to in his later work; Wilen's tenor sound does, indeed, have something of the magisterial sweep which Getz delivered, but the main character of his playing continues to lie in his even trajectory. His solos have a serene assurance which eschews dynamic shifts in favour of a single flowing line. With his tone still exceptionally bright and refined, it grants his playing a rare, persuasive power.

La Note Bleue was a disappointing start, though, because the record is so bitty: what seem to be little fragments and codas from longer pieces are made into whole tracks, the material is dryly over-familiar, and the pieces are cut short before the group can get going. With Wilen perfectly adept at long solos, this foreshortening sounds wrong. *French Ballads* is better, although some of the playing again seems proscribed, and Wilen despatches a few of the themes with a too casual finesse. *Wild Dogs Of The Ruwenzori* finally establishes his second wind: it's beautifully programmed, with straight-ahead swingers, hints of calypso rhythm and a few deftly understated fusion pulses setting a delightful variation in tempos. The title-tune and 'Pauline Extended' bond Wilen's solos into a tight electronic framework, but his latest reflections on Rollins in 'Little Lu' and the two versions of 'Oh Johnny' are flawlessly paced and delivered. The rhythm section does well on all three records.

Sanctuary continued Wilen's good run. Catherine switches between acoustic and electric instruments and Wilen chooses classical rapture or firm, propulsive lines depending on the tempo. Danielsson's third voice is immensely rich and apposite. One might pick out the absolutely lovely reading of 'How Deep Is The Ocean', but there's scarcely a weak moment on the record.

***(*) **Movie Themes From France** Timeless SJP 335
> Wilen; Mal Waldron (*p*); Stafford James (*b*); Eddie Moore (*d*). 10/90.

Wilen is still in great voice here. Perhaps Waldron isn't an ideal choice, since his usual impassive stance dries out some of these romantic melodies to the point of desiccation: 'Les Parapluies De Cherbourg' sounds like a dirge at the start. But it pays off over the long haul, with a powerful 'Autumn Leaves' and a still, serene, ominous treatment of two of the 'Lift to the Scaffold' themes. The saxophonist breaks new melodies and ideas out of all this material and, though he sounds tired at some points, it adds to his gravitas.

*** **Dream Time** Deux Z 84108
> Wilen; Alain Jean-Marie (*p*). 3/91.

*** **New York Romance** Sunnyside SSC 1067
> Wilen; Kenny Barron (*p*); Ira Coleman (*b*); Lewis Nash (*d*). 6/94.

A certain waywardness crept into Wilen's playing; while it subverts some of the sax-meets-rhythm expectations, it isn't always comfortable. The duet with Jean-Marie comes from a 1991 festival appearance: Wilen sounds rusty on 'Latin Alley' and the exposed format doesn't always suit him, but the long, serpentine lines of 'No Problem' and 'Afternoon In Paris' have all his old mastery. His tone on tenor is taking on a foggy side which sounds even more pronounced on the rare baritone outing on 'Blues Walk' from *New York Romance*. This is one of several albums Wilen has recorded for the Japanese Venus label, this one then being licensed to Sunnyside. Compared to the supersharp rhythm section, Barney sounds a little bleary here and there, and his imprecision isn't always beneficial: the rather taut and wound-up 'You'd Be So Nice To Come Home To' is disappointing. But the desolate soprano outing on 'Cry Me A River', with its wide dynamic contrasts, and an unexpectedly slow and bleak 'Mack The Knife' show his powers as yet undimmed. His passing in 1996 was another sad loss.

Buster Williams DOUBLE BASS

***(*) **Toku Do** Denon DC 8549
> Williams; Kenny Barron (*p*); Ben Riley (*d*). 1/78.

**** **Something More** In and Out 7004
> Williams; Shunzo Ono (*t*); Wayne Shorter (*ts, ss*); Herbie Hancock (*p*); Al Foster (*d*). 3/89.

You're a bassist. You don't get to record under your own name too often. So when you *do* get the chance, out comes the wish-list and you call in a couple of favours. The most encouraging things about these discs are the quality of Williams's writing and the quality of playing all round. The first is still largely unrecognized, even by fellow players. Williams, like Sam Jones before him, has a great sense of melody. 'Toku Do' is only the most memorable. The album bearing its name has a good, even-handed feel, and one has the feeling that when any member of the group is improvising, the others are responding to him rather than simply marking time. The interplay on 'Some Day My Prince Will Come' is breathtaking.

Wayne Shorter had been in serious eclipse in the 1980s but is absolutely sterling on *Something More*, step for step with Williams's involved themes. Apart from a dispensable piccolo bass solo on 'Sophisticated Lady', most of the leader's energies are directed to group playing; he favours a dark sonority (which is why the Ellington piece is irritatingly unrepresentative) which falls somewhere between Wilbur Ware and Jimmy Garrison, varying quite simple lines with passing notes and soft, left-hand strums. What a band, though!

Clarence Williams (1893–1965) PIANO, JUG, VOCAL

*** **Complete Sessions Vol. 1 1923** EPM/Hot 'N Sweet FDC 5107
Williams; Thomas Morris (*c*); Charlie Irvis, John Mayfield (*tb*); Sidney Bechet (*cl, ss*); Buddy Christian (*bj*); Sara Martin, Eva Taylor, Lawrence Lomax, Rosetta Crawford, Mamie Smith, Margaret Johnson (*v*). 7–11/23.

***(*) **Complete Sessions Vol. 2 1923–1925** EPM/Hot 'N Sweet FDC 5109
As above, except add Louis Armstrong, Bubber Miley (*c*); Aaron Thompson (*tb*); Buster Bailey, Lorenzo Tio (*cl, ss*); Don Redman (*as*); Virginia Liston, Maureen Englin, Sippie Wallace (*v*); omit Martin, Lomax, Crawford and Smith. 11/23–3/25.

(*) **Clarence Williams 1921–1924 Classics 679
Similar to above two discs. 10/21–11/24.

*** **Complete Sessions Vol. 3 1925–26** EPM/Hot 'N Sweet 15122
As above, except add Johnny Dunn, Big Charlie Thomas, Edward Allen (*c*); Joe 'Tricky Sam' Nanton, Jimmy Harrison, Jake Frazier (*tb*); Bob Fuller (*cl*); Coleman Hawkins (*cl, ts, bs*); Leroy Harris (*bj*); Cyrus St Clair (*tba*); Clarence Todd (*v*); omit Thompson, Tio, Liston, Englin, Wallace. 7/25–4/26.

*** **Clarence Williams 1924–1926** Classics 695
Similar to above. 12/24–1/26.

*** **Clarence Williams 1926–27** Classics 718
Williams; Tommy Ladnier, Jabbo Smith, Ed Allen, Bubber Miley, Tom Morris, Louis Metcalf (*c*); Jimmy Harrison, Joe Nanton (*tb*); Buster Bailey (*cl*); Arville Harris, Don Redman (*cl, as*); Coleman Hawkins (*ts*); Fats Waller (*p*); Leroy Harris (*bj*); Cyrus St Clair (*bb*); Eva Taylor (*v*). 3/26–4/27.

*** **Clarence Williams 1927** Classics 736
Williams; Ed Allen (*c*); Henry Allen, Ed Anderson (*t*); Charlie Irvis (*tb*); Buster Bailey (*ss, cl*); Carmelo Jari, Arville Harris, Ben Whittet, Albert Soccaras (*cl, as*); Leroy Harris (*bj*); Cyrus St Clair (*bb*); Floyd Casey (*wbd*); Clarence Lee, Evelyn Preer (*v*). 3–9/27.

Williams ran a publishing business and was A&R man on countless record dates during the 1920s and early '30s. He wasn't a great pianist, handled vocals with clumsy enthusiasm and often resorted to blowing a jug on his Jug Band records; but he was a brilliant hustler and a master at making record dates come together. At his very first session, on the first CD listed above, he secured the services of Sidney Bechet (also making his debut), and in fact Bechet appears on every track on this disc. Later sessions brought in Armstrong alongside Bechet, Bubber Miley, Lorenzo Tio and others. The material was mostly novelty tunes ('Who'll Chop Your Suey When I'm Gone?') or vaudeville blues, with the occasional tougher piece – such as Sippie Wallace's two tracks on Volume 2 – and some instrumentals by Clarence Williams's Blue Five.

Both Classics and Hot 'N Sweet have undertaken complete series, but the latter seems to have come to a halt. The Classics discs got off to an indifferent start with the first two discs, which had very mixed reproduction, although Classics 718 and 736 are more consistent and quite lively. Musically, the later sides are hotter, though Bechet makes a striking impact throughout the first disc, and his partnership with Armstrong on 'Cake Walking Babies From Home', 'Mandy Make Up Your Mind' and a few others is exhilarating enough to cut through the acoustic recording. Hot 'N Sweet's Volume 2 is perhaps the best disc to sample; but the third volume introduces cornetist Ed Allen, Williams's most loyal sideman, who seldom recorded elsewhere, and it includes some rollicking band sides. The first Classics disc starts off with some ancient 1921 material in which Williams is basically a band singer on six tracks, historical curios more than anything. Classics 718 has several tracks where Williams and The Blue Five are accompanying the sweet-voiced Eva Taylor, but there is more jazz on Classics 736: three different versions of Williams's hit, 'Cushion Foot Stomp', the knockabout 'Old Folks Shuffle', a Brunswick date with Henry Allen and Ed Anderson as a two-trumpet front line, and two versions of another Williams favourite, 'Shootin' The Pistol'.

*** Clarence Williams 1927–1928 Classics 752
Williams; Ed Allen, King Oliver (*c*); Ed Cuffee (*tb*); Arville Harris, Benny Waters, Albert Soccaras, Buster Bailey (*cl, as*); Coleman Hawkins (*ts*); James P. Johnson (*p*); Leroy Harris (*bj*); Cyrus St Clair (*tba*); Floyd Casey (*d, wbd*). 10/27–8/28.

***(*) Clarence Williams 1928–1929 Classics 771
As above, except add Ed Anderson (*c*), Ben Whittet (*cl, as*), Ernest Elliott (*cl*), Claude Hopkins (*p*), Charlie Dixon (*bj*), Kaiser Marshall (*d*); omit Hawkins, Johnson. 8/28–1/29.

*** Clarence Williams 1929 Classics 791
As above, except add James P. Johnson (p), Russell Procope (*cl, as*); omit Anderson, Elliott, Hopkins, Dixon, Marshall. 1/29–5/29.

***(*) Clarence Williams 1929–1930 Classics 810
As above, except add Ed Anderson, Charlie Gaines, Leonard Davis, Henry 'Red' Allen (*t*); Geechie Fields (*tb*), Frank Robinson (*bsx, hca, v*), Prince Robinson (*cl, ts*). 6/29–4/30.

*** Clarence Williams 1930–1931 Classics 832
Williams; Ed Allen, Bill Dillard, Ward Pinkett, Henry Allen, Charlie Gaines (*t*); Jimmy Archey (*tb*); Albert Soccaras (*cl, as, f*); Henry Jones (*as*); Arville Harris, Prince Robinson, Bingie Madison (*cl, ts*); Fred Skerritt (*bs, as*); Gene Rodgers, Herman Chittison (*p*); Lonnie Johnson (*g*); Goldie Lucas (*g, bj*); Ikey Robinson, Leroy Harris (*bj*); Cyrus St Clair (*tba*); Richard Fullbright (*b*); Bill Beason (*d*); Floyd Casey (*wbd*); Eva Taylor, Clarence Todd (*v*). 5/30–2/31.

*** Clarence Williams 1933 Classics 845
Williams; Ed Allen (*c*); Albert Nicholas, Cecil Scott (*cl*); Herman Chittison, Willie 'The Lion' Smith (*p*); Ikey Robinson (*bj, g*); Cyrus St Clair (*tba*); Willie Williams, Floyd Casey (*d, wbd*); Eva Taylor, Clarence Todd (*v*). 5–11/33.

Classics have pursued their Williams series almost to completion, which is probably a first as far as reissue goes (and certainly in the CD era). Williams's music doesn't have any great variety in it: his basic configurations were the Washboard and Jug bands, the Jazz Kings sides, a few stray piano solos, the occasional vocal where he's accompanied by another (James P. Johnson on one occasion) and some ensemble dates which are simply credited to the Williams Orchestra. The more knockabout material was reserved for the jug or washboard situations, but some of these also have a gentleness about them and, though Casey's irresistible beat and St Clair's parping lines provide a steady momentum, Williams could often find unexpected subtleties in some of his line-ups – pairing reeds together, or providing space for the faithful Ed Allen to play one of his tight, incisive solos. Allen is the unsung hero of most of these dates, unfailingly consistent and interesting, and though a few star names turn up here and there – notably King Oliver, Eddie Lang and James P. – it's Williams's repertory cast that make most of the music: Allen, Harris, St Clair, Casey, Whittet and a few others. Because the playing is fun and unpretentious, these tracks have often been undervalued over the years, but at the same time it's hard to pick out special highlights. The later material is better recorded, but by the time of the 1933 disc a rather forlorn and dated air has started to creep into the playing: this was ancient-sounding stuff at a time when the swing era was only heartbeats away. We award a token extra notch for Classics 771 (some excellent individual tracks) and Classics 810 (a particularly nice variety of bands and approaches), but if you enjoy one of these discs, you'll enjoy them all. The transfers (from unlisted sources, as usual) vary almost from track to track, and some sound very sludgy, but the music shines through on the best of them.

***(*) Clarence Williams 1927 To 1934 Jazz Classics In Digital Stereo RPCD 633
As above discs. 1/27–7/34.

***(*) Clarence Williams Vol. 1 Collectors Classics COCD-19
As above discs. 27–28.

***(*) Clarence Williams Vol. 2 Collectors Classics COCD-20
As above discs. 28.

No single compilation of Williams stands out as essential, though these three all sound better than the Classics sequence. Parker's Digital Stereo disc is handsomely done, but so are the two Collectors Classics sets, remastered by John R. T. Davies. Serious collectors should check the track listings – on the other hand, they will probably want the complete edition anyway.

Cootie Williams (1910–85) TRUMPET

**** Duke Ellington's Trumpets Black & Blue BLE 59.231
Williams; Joe 'Tricky Sam' Nanton (*tb*); Barney Bigard (*cl*); Johnny Hodges (*as, ss*); Otto

Hardwick (*as, bsx*); Harry Carney (*bs*); Duke Ellington, Billy Strayhorn (*p*); Billy Taylor (*b*);
Sonny Greer (*d*). 3/37–2/40.

*** **Echoes Of Harlem** Topaz TPZ 1042
As above and below, except add Lawrence Brown, Juan Tizol (*tb*); Benny Goodman, Mezz
Mezzrow (*cl*); Georgie Auld (*ts*); Count Basie, Tommy Fulford, Jess Stacy (*p*); Bernard
Addison, Allan Reuss (*g*); Hayes Alvis, Jimmy Blanton John Kirby (*b*); Cozy Cole, Lionel
Hampton, Harry Jaeger, Chick Webb (*d*). 12/36–8/44.

***(*) **Cootie Williams, 1941-1944** Classics 827
Williams; Milton Fraser, Joe Guy, Harold Money Johnson, Ermit V. Perry, George Treadwell
(*t*); Louis Bacon (*t, v*); Ed Burke, Jonas Walker, Robert Horton, George Stevenson, Sandy
Williams, Lou McGarity (*tb*); Charlie Holmes, Les Robinson (*as*); Eddie Cleanhead Vinson (*as,
v*); Eddie 'Lockjaw' Davis, Bob Dorsey, Lee Pope, Greely Walters (*ts*); John Williams (*bs*);
Skippy Martin, Eddie De Verteuil (bs); Johnny Guarnieri, Kenny Kersey, Bud Powell (*p*); Artie
Bernstein, Norman Keenan (*b*); Butch Ballard, Jo Jones, Vess Payne (*d*); Pearl Bailey (*v*). 5/41–8/
44.

(*) **The Big Challenge Fresh Sound FSRCD 77
Williams; Rex Stewart (*c*); Bud Freeman, Coleman Hawkins (*ts*); Lawrence Brown, J. C.
Higginbotham (*tb*); Hank Jones (*p*); Milt Hinton (*b*); Gus Johnson (*d*). 4 & 5/57.

Ellington wrote 'Do Nothing Till You Hear From Me' as a 'Concerto For Cootie', a feature for the
young growler he recruited at nineteen as a replacement for Bubber Miley. During the 1930s Williams
showed himself (as the sessions collected on Black & Blue prove) of all the Ellingtonians the one most
capable of sustaining an independent career. His high, bright trumpet was to be replaced by even more
agile players, but no one with the sheer musical intelligence of Cootie. The material here is all excellent
and, though much of it is already quite well known, it is good to have it on the one disc. (The set also
includes some tracks by Rex Stewart's pre-war bands.)

The Topaz and Classics compilations have a certain amount of overlap in the later sessions but, as per
usual, the French strict-constructionists do not include material recorded under any other leader, so the
tracks with Hamp's band or Barney Bigard's Jazzopators are not included on Classics. As so often in
this very valuable and clearly documented series, one is apt to be distracted from the leader's achievement by early sightings of soon-to-be important players. Bud Powell's appearance with the Williams
Orchestra marked an important phase in his career, and the band also made the first recordings of two
Thelonious Monk compositions, 'Fly Right' (aka 'Epistrophy') and 'Round Midnight', the latter from
the August 1944 date covered on both discs.

Cootie's own contributions go their growling, alternately chipper and sombre, way. Topaz usefully
includes 'Concerto' and a 'Royal Garden Blues' with Benny Goodman's Sextet and, in terms of roundness and representativeness, this is by far the better option unless much of the material is owned already.
Some will undoubtedly favour the Orchestra sides with Vinson playing and singing, and Lockjaw
beginning to make his move. These are delightful recordings and even the rather muddy Classics sound
can't blunt their appeal.

By the late 1950s, when *The Big Challenge* was set up (and set up is the operative term), Williams was
working with a rock-and-roll group, a drab routine that had significantly blunted the edge of his tough,
brassy sound. Much of his most effective playing on the set seems to derive from the man in the opposite
corner. He reduplicates Rex Stewart's half-valved style and gruff swoops authentically but also rather
redundantly, because the cornetist is in excellent, pungent form. Williams plays most convincingly on
'Walkin' My Baby Back Home', where he throws in a muted solo even the Duke would have liked. The
two tenors compare more straightforwardly, trading choruses on 'Alphonse And Gaston' with the polite
brutality of a Larry Holmes fight. The closing 'I Knew You When' is a carefully matched head arrangement that allows Williams and Stewart to slug it out to a finish. Not altogether inspiring stuff and a
sorry reminder of the way in which Williams's independent career, thwarted by the draft and the
recording ban, was short-circuited into blandly commercial sessions that offered little scope for his
towering talent.

James Williams (born 1951) PIANO

*** **Progress Report** Sunnyside SSC 1012D
Williams; Bill Easley (*as*); Bill Pierce (*ts*); Kevin Eubanks (*g*); Rufus Reid (*b*); Tony Reedus (*d*);
Jerry Gonzalez (*perc*). 85.

*** **I Remember Clifford** DIW 601
Williams; Richard Davis (*b*); Ronnie Burrage (*d*).

*** **Meets The Saxophone Masters** DIW 868

> Williams; George Coleman, Billy Pierce, Joe Henderson (*ts*); James Genus (*b*); Tony Reedus (*d*). 9/91.

Williams, who comes from Memphis, made his first major mark with The Jazz Messengers, and the Sunnyside session – there are earlier discs for Concord which are out of print – certainly keeps Blakey's faith, with a typically muscular but lyrical approach. The horns, though, do little but go through well-practised motions: it's a workmanlike, intermittently sparking record.

Williams is finally just a touch too diffident to characterize these otherwise pleasing records as best he might. There is authoritative leadership but not quite the last ounce of personal brio which might have taken these discs into the front rank. That said, the interplay on *I Remember Clifford* is admirable, with Davis in shining form and the studio sound glistening with class, and the two dates with Blakey, Brown and Jones are predictably grandmasterly. Moffett and Watts are a little more uppity and needle Williams a little here and there, but his inner calm is finally unaffected.

He's strongly challenged on the *Saxophone Masters* disc but holds his own, despite often losing out in sheer volume to a crowded front line. It might have been better to have broken up the band a bit. Henderson is so obviously out in front of the other two on this occasion that one wants to hear more of him and a bit less of the other two, who come lumbering out of left and right channels like hungry linebackers.

Jeff Williams (born 1950) DRUMS

***(*) **Coalescence** Steeplechase SCCD 31308

> Williams; Tim Ries (*ts, f*); Pat Zimmerli (*ts, bcl*); Kevin Hays (*p*); Doug Weiss (*b*). 5/91.

Williams has been very busy as a sideman since the early 1970s, but his leadership debut shows no sign of fatigue or routine. The eight themes here are resoundingly free of hard-bop cliché or empty rhetoric, and the decidedly unstarry band – Ries and Zimmerli have thus far had little limelight – makes light of a demanding occasion. The two-tenor pieces which open and close show the horns as darkly complementary rather than combative and, throughout, Williams works to make the music unpredictable: the sequence of duets in 'Dialogue', the timeless quality of 'Autonomy'. There are small flaws: the outward-bound bass clarinet and soprano of 'Skulduggery' is unconvincing, and 'Wondering' studies too hard on sounding gloomy. But Weiss and Williams make a fascinating rhythm section, and sometimes one listens past the others and into their endlessly inventive time. Excellent sound.

Joe Williams (born 1918) VOCAL

** **Joe Williams Sings** Savoy SV-0199

> Williams; Sonny Sohn, King Kolax (*t*); Bennie Green (*tb*); Riley Hampton (*as*); Leon Washington, Dick Davis (*ts*); McKinley Easton (*bs*); Earl Washington, Prentice McCarey (*p*); Ike Perkins (*g*); Walt Champion, Cowboy Martin (*b*); Red Saunders, Kansas Fields (*d*). 50–51.

*** **A Swingin' Night In Birdland** Roulette B21Y-95335-2

> Williams; Harry 'Sweets' Edison (*t*); Jimmy Forrest (*ts*); Hugh Lawson (*p*); Ike Isaacs (*b*); Clarence Johnston (*d*). 6/62.

*** **Jump For Joy** Bluebird 07863 52713 2

> Williams; Clark Terry, Bernie Glow, Thad Jones, Snooky Young (*t*); Urbie Green, Quentin Jackson, Jimmy Cleveland (*tb*); Phil Woods, Robert Ashton, Danny Banks, Phil Bodner, Jerome Richardson, Romeo Penque, Walt Levinsky, George Dorsey (*reeds*); Hank Jones, Herbie Hancock, Bernie Leighton (*p*); Kenny Burrell, Jim Hall (*g*); Milt Hinton, Wendell Marshall (*b*); Osie Johnson, Sol Grubin (*d*). 3/63.

*** **Newport '63** RCA Victor 21831-2

> Williams; Clark Terry, Howard McGhee (*t*); Coleman Hawkins, Zoot Sims (*ts*); Junior Mance (*p*); Bob Cranshaw (*b*); Mickey Roker (*d*). 7/63.

*** **Me And The Blues** RCA 21823-2

> Williams; Clark Terry (*t*); Jimmy Cleveland, Urbie Green (*tb*); Phil Woods (*as*); Jerome Richardson (*ts, f, bs*); Danny Banks (*bs*); Phil Bodner (*ts, f*); Ben Webster, Seldon Powell (*ts*); Bernie Leighton, Hank Jones, Junior Mance (*p*); Kenny Burrell, Barry Galbraith (*g*); Milt Hinton, Bob Cranshaw (*b*); Osie Johnson, Sol Grubin (*d*). 2–12/63.

Williams followed on from Billy Eckstine in bringing in a new sophistication to the black male singer's stance. Though he made his name singing blues with Count Basie (and their albums together are classics), Williams preferred superior standards and original material. *Joe Williams Sings* collects some early tracks for Savoy: the great, mellifluous baritone is already there, but the backings are shambolic and mock Williams's efforts. The Birdland date sounds a bit scrappy, with Edison's group lowering rather than raising the tone, but Williams is in fine voice (and Sweets gets in a couple of smart solos). *Jump For Joy* has big, gleaming arrangements by Oliver Nelson and Jimmy Jones, and Williams relaxes on the orchestral cushion. Some of the material is rather obscure, although the huge baritone voice has a way of making any unfamiliarity seem trivial: 'I Went Out Of My Way Today' sounds like something he was just handed on the day, yet he makes it work.

Joe was in great heart at Newport in 1963, and the all-star band serve him well, but some of the songs are put away too quickly, as if he was under time pressure: there could have been half as many, more relaxed and expansive performances. *Me And The Blues* is as elegant as ever, though some of Jimmy Jones's arrangements do little for the singer, and again some of the material seems treated cursorily.

***(*) **Ballad And Blues Master** Verve 511354-2
    Williams; Norman Simmons (*p*); Henry Johnson (*g*); Bob Badgley (*b*); Gerryck King (*d*). 87.
***(*) **Live At Vine Street** Verve 833236-2
    As above. 87.
*** **In Good Company** Verve 837932-2
    As above, except add Shirley Horn (*p*); Charles Ables (*b*), Steve Williams (*d*); orchestra. 89.
*** **That Holiday Feelin'** Verve 843956-2
    Williams; Clark Terry, Joe Wilder (*t*); Al Grey (*tb*); Frank Wess (*f*); Bob Cranshaw (*b*); Dennis Mackrel (*d*). 90.
(*) **Joe Williams With The Count Basie Orchestra Telarc CD-83329
    Williams; Frank Foster (*ts*); Count Basie Orchestra. 11/92.
**** **Every Day – The Best Of The Verve Years** Verve 519813-2 2CD
    Williams; various groups. 55–90.

Williams has endured marvellously well, even into his seventies. The top end has lost much of its old limber power and there might be a shake where once all was honey-smooth, but he still phrases with the assurance of a singer who knows where the pulse is all the time and he can hit a note with the same regal potency. The two albums recorded at a Vine Street engagement are a notch ahead for the sense of fun Joe has with the group: he even enjoys the blues medley at the end of *Ballad And Blues Master*, and Simmons is no slouch. *In Good Company* varies between that rhythm section and Shirley Horn's group. *That Holiday Feelin'* is a Christmas album, and Joe does as well as anybody with this material; the trumpet players help a little. *Every Day* is the wrap-up choice, since it skims off the best of Joe's tracks with Basie from the 1950s on the first disc and covers all the best of the latter-day material on the second.

His appearance with the Foster/Basie ensemble is a nostalgic one, and he handles himself with dignity and an almost Zen calm on the slower ones. But at 74, the voice is sounding frayed.

*** **Here's To Life** Telarc 83357
    Williams; strings conducted by Robert Farnon. 8/93.

Farnon's limousine of an orchestra is the most gorgeous thistledown for Joe to get comfortable in. He gives himself a few tough ones, several surprising high notes here and there, and generally makes a go of a situation that most singers approaching his age wouldn't even think about.

Mary Lou Williams (1910–81) PIANO

***(*) **Mary Lou Williams, 1927–40** Classics 630
    Williams; Harold Baker, Henry McCord, Earl Thompson (*t*); Bradley Bullett, Ted Donnelly (*tb*); Edward Inge (*cl*); Earl Buddy Miller (*cl, as*); Dick Wilson (*ts*); John Williams (*as, bsx*); Ted Robinson, Floyd Smith (*g*); Joe Williams (*bj*); Booker Collins (*b*); Robert Price, Ben Thigpen (*d*). 1/27–11/40.
***(*) **Key Moments** Topaz TPZ 1016
    Similar to above. 29–40.
**** **Mary Lou Williams, 1944** Classics 814
    Williams; Bill Coleman (*t, v*); Frankie Newton, Charlie Shavers, Dick Vance (*t*); Vic Dickenson, Trummy Young (*tb*); Claude Greene, Edmond Hall (*cl*); Remo Palmieri (*g*); Al Hall, Al Lucas (*b*); Jack Parker, Specs Powell (*d*); Nora Lee King (*v*). 2–11/44.
***(*) **The Zodiac Suite** Smithsonian Folkways SF CD 40810
    Williams; unidentified big band, featuring Ben Webster (*ts*); New York Philharmonic Orchestra. 12/45.
***(*) **On Vogue** Vogue 111505
    Williams; Don Byas (*ts*); Buddy Banks (*b*); Gérard Pochonnet (*d*). 12/53.

**** **Zoning** Smithsonian Folkways S F CD 40811
     Williams (*p* solo). 74.
**** **Free Spirits** Steeplechase SCCD 31043
     Williams; Buster Williams (*b*); Mickey Roker (*d*). 7/75.
***(*) **Live At The Cookery** Chiaroscuro CRD 146
     Williams; Brian Torff (*b*). 11/75.

Duke Ellington described her as 'perpetually contemporary'. Mary Lou Williams's career encompassed weary days of travel with Andy Kirk's Clouds of Joy band (she began as a part-time arranger and only grudgingly won recognition as a piano player), staff arranging for Ellington, and band-leading. Having divorced John Williams, who had taken her on the road with Kirk, she married trumpeter Harold Baker and co-led a group with him.

The earlier Classics *Chronological* compilation covers some intriguing early stuff, including sides made with Jeanette's Synco Jazzers as Mary Leo Burley (her step-father's name) when she was only sixteen, and two good solo sides recorded for the Brunswick label in Chicago in 1930. There are also two useful solos from rather later; 'Mary's Special' from April 1936 has her doubling on celeste, and there's a fine 'Little Joe From Chicago', recorded for Columbia in October 1939. The next decade saw Mary move out as an artist in her own right, and the Classics compilation (1944) includes much of the best of that material, including 'Little Joe From Chicago', 'Roll 'Em' and a piece from a jam session organized by the photographer and film-maker, Gjon Mili. The disc includes some excellent solos as well as forgettable work accompanying singer Nora Lee King.

In 1946 Williams gave a remarkable performance of her *Zodiac Suite* with the New York Philharmonic at Town Hall. It's a sequence of dedications to fellow-musicians (identified by their astrological characteristics) and combines straight orchestral writing of a slightly bland, film-soundtrack sort with jazz interpolations and occasional sections ('Taurus' and 'Gemini', significantly) where the two seem to coincide. Wiliams had been profoundly dissatisfied with a partial reading of the music, recorded in 1957 for Norman Granz's Verve label, and the rediscovery of the 'lost' tapes from the Town Hall concert is a significant addition to Williams's still thin discography. The sound isn't always very reliable, with occasional crackles and some loss of resolution in the string parts, but Williams is caught in close-up.

There followed a period away from the United States, living in France (where she recorded for Vogue), and then away from music altogether, during which time she worked with drug addicts. Renewed activity from the late 1950s onwards included lecture-recitals on the history of jazz, large-scale sacred compositions – *Mary Lou's Mass* and *Black Christ Of The Andes* – reflecting her conversion, and stormy contact with the new avant-garde, as on her remarkable collaboration with Cecil Taylor. *Embraced* gives off little sense of the hostilities behind the scenes, but it underlines her ability to play from almost any stance within the black music tradition: gospel, blues, swing, bop, free. Typical of much of her extensive output, it's currently unavailable, though her legacy continues to spread in tunes like 'What's Your Story, Morning Glory', which is increasingly being covered by other musicians.

Williams was treated dismissively by male colleagues for much of her career (Kirk finds room for only half a dozen references in his autobiography, and his acknowledgement of her 'tremendous influence' seems rather *pro forma*). In the 1970s she was releasing material on her own label, Mary Records, including the superb *Zoning* (since reissued on Smithsonian Folkways) and the huge *Mary Lou's Mass*. A valuable *Solo Recital* from Montreux in 1978 has also disappeared. Williams's formal and historical concerns turned almost every performance at this time into a lecture on the roots of black American music, and there's a rather programmatic feel to the sequence of tracks. But it's an important piece of work, all the more valuable for the present scarcity of alternatives. The rather earlier *Live At The Cookery* is a better bet. Jon Bates has done an excellent job of bringing the sound up to current standards and there's a minimum of distortion and extraneous noise ('I'm recording. If you talk too loud, it'll be on the record'). It's not clear why she tolerated Brian Torff thudding away relentlessly in her left ear, but Williams had always tended to be a right-sided player and, here more than ever, concentrates on a middle and upper register. Her playing is superb throughout and there are vintage performances of 'Roll 'Em', 'The Surrey With The Fringe On Top' (an odd favourite of hers), 'The Man I Love' and Johnny Hodges's 'The Jeep Is Jumping'.

As a straightforward performance, *Free Spirits* is very much better. Williams's health was still robust (it began to break down towards the end of the 1970s) and her playing is much sharper and surer, also more relaxed and swinging. Typically, she mixes standards ('Temptation', 'Surrey With The Fringe On Top') with jazz staples (Miles's 'All Blues', Bobby Timmons's gospel-tinged 'Dat Dere') and her own work, 'Ode To Saint Cecilie', 'Gloria', 'Blues For Timme', unexpectedly adding two John Stubblefield compositions (two takes each of 'Baby Man' and 'Free Spirits') and a promising 'Pale Blue' by bassist Buster Williams, who provides a perfect complement to her light left hand.

Perhaps inevitably, she rejected the term 'jazz', not so much because it was a white construct but because it was a fundamentally reductive one. However swinging and jazz-based her solo and small-group output, Williams transcended the conventional bounds of jazz composition and performance. With the rediscovery of *Zodiac Suite*, it may at last be possible to attempt a comprehensive reassessment of one of the most significant figures in black American music and one of its great teachers.

Rod Williams PIANO

*** **Hanging In The Balance** Muse MCD 5380
> Williams; Graham Haynes (*c, t*); Marty Ehrlich (*ss, as, f*); Kevin Bruce Harris (*b*); Tani Tabbal (*d*); Sadiq (*perc*). 5/89.

***(*) **Destiny Express** Muse MCD 5412
> Williams; Rasul Siddik (*t*); Marty Ehrlich (*ss, as, cl, bcl, f*); Junko Ohasi (*koto*); Jaribu Shahid (*b*); Tani Tabbal (*d*); Cassandra Wilson (*v*). 7/90.

Williams made a name as Cassandra Wilson's pianist – she sings only on 'False Face', a tune allegedly dedicated to her, on *Destiny Express* – but he has much to say beyond the boundaries of being an accompanist. Both records make an expressive and impressive point of shifting what are basic hard-bop configurations through unexpected harmonic and rhythmic twists. Where some of Williams's contemporaries go the whole hog with impossible time-signatures and tongue-twisting melodies, the pianist prefers just enough of a displacement to intrigue the ear without losing it. Ehrlich, the best kind of in-to-out player, is crucial to the success of both records, and Haynes is useful on the first; but it's the sax-and-rhythm quartet at the heart of *Destiny Express*, which sat on the unreleased shelves for three years, that makes the most telling music. Although Henry Threadgill contributes 'Blanche's Wedding', the most effective pieces come from Williams himself, with 'Closet Romantics' and 'Middle Way' emerging as fascinating themes that Ehrlich improvises on with superb aplomb. There's also a brief, exceptional piano solo in 'Edge' that makes one eager to hear more of Williams by himself.

Roy Williams (born 1937) TROMBONE

*** **Gruesome Twosome** Black Lion BLCD 760507
> Williams; John Barnes (*ss, bs*); Brian Lemon (*p*); Len Skeat (*b*); Stan Bourke (*d*). 7/80.

*** **Royal Trombone** Phontastic 7556
> Williams; John Mclevy (*t*); Arne Domnérus (*as, cl*); Putte Wickman (*cl*); Nisse Sandstrom (*ts*); Bengt Hallberg (*p*); Rune Gustafsson (*g*); Len Skeat, Georg Riedel (*b*); Rune Carlsson (*d*). 12/83.

Williams emerged as a second-eleven man in British trad, but his stay with the Alex Welsh band of the 1960s (and, subsequently, with Humphrey Lyttelton) revealed a much more accomplished and versatile performer than anything most of his colleagues could aspire to. He has a lovely, creamy sound on the trombone which, with its relatively quiet dynamic and effortless delivery, has drawn comparisons with Jack Teagarden that are surprisingly near the mark. These albums are typically relaxed, almost indolent on the Black Lion date, but inimitably Williams. The trombonist and John Mclevy were visiting Sweden for the Phontastic sessions and teamed up with an all-star group of locals. Standards make up most of the menu, although Hallberg pens a crafty twist on 'Exactly Like You' called 'Accurately Like You', and there's a lot of variation in voicings and instrumentations: 'I'm Old Fashioned' is a duet for trombone and piano. Wickman aces out Williams from time to time and has a serene 'I Remember Clifford' to himself, but the guest leader plays admirably throughout. The CD issue adds some tracks to the original LP release but leaves out some that were on the matching album, *Again!*. The meeting with John Barnes on *Gruesome Twosome* is marked by British diffidence: the rhythm section scarcely rouse themselves above ticking off the time. But the two horns have some delicious moments: Barnes plays baritone for the most part, and some of the interplay with Williams is much like that between Mulligan and Brookmeyer at their best, with 'People Will Say We're In Love' particularly enjoyable.

Tom Williams (born 1962) TRUMPET, FLUGELHORN

*** **Introducing Tom Williams** Criss Cross CRISS 1064
> Williams; Javon Jackson (*ts*); Kenny Barron (*p*); Peter Washington (*b*); Kenny Washington (*d*). 12/91.

**** **Straight Street** Criss Cross CRISS 1091
> Williams; Gary Thomas (*ts, ss*); Kevin Hays (*p*); Peter Washington (*b*); Kenny Washington (*d*). 12/93.

Williams is a fine young trumpeter from Baltimore whose main avowed influence is Kenny Dorham, a connection that rightly suggests richly melodic phrasing, subtle tone coloration and a deceptive simplicity of line. Other influences include Clifford Brown and (particularly) Woody Shaw, and Williams is unusual among younger-generation horn players in not being unduly tinged by Miles.

His debut recording followed a period with the Ellington orchestra under Mercer Ellington and regular gigs with such senior players as Hank Jones, Charlie Rouse and Jackie McLean. It's an unfussy start. As on the follow-up album, a Dorham composition 'Windmill' (on *Straight Street* 'Short Story') occupies an important position just past mid-way. His opening shot is the original 'Thursday The Twelfth', a slightly derivative piece that serves very well as a calling card; Barron's solo steals the show. 'The Pursuit Of Happiness' is a long, thoughtful piece with a curious, militaristic quality that perhaps reflects his day job in US Army bands. He also does Horace Silver's 'Peace' as a companion work, which may confirm the point.

Straight Street brings together a very similar band. If Barron is missed, Thomas seems a more than acceptable substitute for the dark-toned and often lugubrious Jackson. The set opens with Woody Shaw's lyrical 'If', given a bright, more contemporary sound than the slightly routine bebop aspect of its predecessor. No Williams compositions this time round. Coltrane's 'Straight Street' is given a Latin treatment. 'Jitterbug Waltz' follows and tees up highly impressive renditions of Mingus's 'Duke Ellington's Sound Of Love' and then, played rather less straight, Wayne Shorter's 'Nefertiti', a challenging piece at the best of times.

Williams doubles on flugelhorn second time round, and he makes telling use of the bigger, fatter tone. This is an immensely impressive record, conscious of its own limitations but bold enough to ignore them when the pace heats up and Thomas calls for a more abrasive approach.

Tony Williams (born 1945) DRUMS

***(*) **Spring** Blue Note B21Y 46135
    Williams; Sam Rivers, Wayne Shorter (*ts*); Herbie Hancock (*p*); Gary Peacock (*b*). 8/65.
(**) **Emergency! Polydor 849 068
    Williams; John McLaughlin (*g*); Larry Young (*org*). 5/69.
***(*) **Foreign Intrigue** Blue Note B21Y 46289
    Williams; Wallace Roney (*t*); Donald Harrison (*as*); Bobby Hutcherson (*vib*); Mulgrew Miller
    (*p*); Ron Carter (*b*). 8/85.
*** **The Story Of Neptune** Blue Note CDP 798169
    As above, except Ira Coleman (*b*) replaces Moffett. 11 & 12/91.

Williams had his baptism of fire with Miles Davis at seventeen, anchoring one of the legendary rhythm sections in one of the finest jazz groups of all time. After leaving Davis, for whom he created a matrix of rhythmic cues so encompassing as to allow the trumpeter to angle a phrase or an entire solo any way he chose, Williams formed the thunderous Lifetime, a group consisting of guitarist John McLaughlin, organist Larry Young and, more briefly, bassist/singer Jack Bruce, which was a seminal influence on the development of jazz–rock. *Emergency!* always sounded horrible (the reissue includes a disclaimer from Phil Schapp who produced/rescued it), but there is a huge, surging energy underneath all the buzz and fuzz, and it remains undeniably exciting. Young's thudding bass pedal lines have a teetering momentum that drives every track relentlessly forward, freeing Williams to work all over his kit, often with scant regard for metre or even pulse. McLaughlin suffered most from the deficiencies of the original tapes, but he comes across no worse than Jimi Hendrix on some of his most sanctified recordings.

It's quite interesting to go back to Williams's early Blue Notes after the whirlwind of Lifetime. They're intense, sometimes rather inward-looking explorations of the rhythmic possibilities opened up by bebop. Working with Jackie McLean, whose advances on Parker's idiom are still not fully appreciated, gave him ample opportunity to break down the basic 4/4 into complex counter-patterns and asymmetrical rhythms. Rivers's angular approach probably suited the drummer's sound better than any other horn player around at the time (though the apotheosis of Williams's early career was, of course, his work with Hutcherson and Davis on Eric Dolphy's *Out To Lunch!*). The addition of Shorter on *Spring* gives the music an enigmatic, brooding quality, but this, too, was an inspired piece of casting. *Foreign Intrigue* has a touch of passion that lifts it above the rather mechanical forcefulness of the later sessions. Roney's bright, diamond-cut lines are completely in keeping with Williams's splintery execution, and Hutcherson gives the rhythmic profile an intriguing, multi-dimensional character, but the later sets (actually most of them now deleted) are foggy by comparison, with no obvious explanation as to why.

Though *The Story Of Neptune* restores some of the rough edges, it does so in the context of one of Williams's most ambitious projects, a suite of connected pieces round the Neptune theme. Williams simplifies his own sound again, moving back to something like the sound of the mid-'60s records, and one wonders if the inspiration for this disc isn't the Shorter and Hancock Blue Notes of that period, with their mixture of soulful grooves and advanced harmonics. Williams clearly still has the chops and one wonders what he might have done had he recruited different players for each of these sessions, rather than relying on a stable band.

Willie Williams TENOR SAXOPHONE, SOPRANO SAXOPHONE

*** **Spirit Willie** Enja 7045-2
　　Williams; Geoff Keezer (*p*); Christian McBride (*b*); Victor Lewis (*d*). 3/92.
The Philadelphia saxophonist's one major recording credit in the late 1980s was with Bobby Watson's Horizon, on the Blue Note session, *The Inventor*. Having made a promising debut with *House Calls*, Williams seemed to slip from view for a while. He reappeared around the turn of the '90s, working with Gary Bartz and holding down a chair in Clifford Jordan's big band.

However he spent those missing years, the break did him some good. Willie could always groove like King Curtis (an early influence) but now he has taken on some of Watson's harmonic shapes, evident on the cover 'After All This Time', and has begun to make them work for him in solos. Like almost every other tenorman from Philly, he's inexorably drawn by the example of John Coltrane, but he hasn't been drawn into slavish imitation. 'Song For Me' is a deceptively familiar variant on the *Giant Steps* changes. Brief though it is, it brings out probably the best solo of the whole session.

McBride's poise is ridiculous for a nineteen-year-old. He gives the session a low, unshakeable centre of gravity, allowing both Keezer and the imaginative Lewis to move with considerable freedom. On 'Quittin' Time', a Jordan composition and an ideal closer, it's the bassist who alone keeps the rhythm together. Williams still has room for growth and he is still rather apt to sound like a different saxophonist on every cut, but he's marked out highly competitive territory and might well have the chops to defend it.

Larry Willis (born 1940) PIANO

*** **Just In Time** Steeplechase SCCD 31251
　　Willis; Bob Cranshaw (*b*); Kenny Washington (*d*). 7/89.
*** **Heavy Blue** Steeplechase SCCD 31269
　　Willis; Jerry Gonzalez (*t, flhn*); Joe Ford (*ss, as*); Don Pate (*b*); Jeff Watts (*d*). 12/89.
*** **Let's Play** Steeplechase SCCD 31283
　　Willis; Santi Debriano (*b*); Victor Lewis (*d*). 1/91.
*** **Steal Away** Audioquest AQ-CD1009
　　Willis; Gary Bartz (*as*); Cecil McBee (*b*). 12/91.
***(*) **How Do You Keep The Music Playing?** Steeplechase SCCD 31312
　　Willis; David Williams (*b*); Lewis Nash (*d*). 4/92.
(*) **Unforgettable Steeplechase SCCD 31318
　　Willis (*p* solo). 5/92.
*** **Solo Spirit** Mapleshade 1432
　　Willis (*p* solo). 4/92.
***(*) **A Tribute To Someone** Audioquest AQ 1022
　　Willis; Tom Williams (*t*); Curtis Fuller (*tb*); John Stubblefield (*ss, ts*); David Williams (*b*); Ben Riley (*d*). 7/93.
Something of a journeyman, whose stints with Blood Sweat And Tears and numerous high-profile leaders have kept him involved but out of the spotlight, Willis has come into his own with the fine series of Steeplechases. He plays at the gentler end of hard-bop piano, writes tunes that often wind up somewhere near the blues, and often picks other compositions that have been neglected by others. *Just In Time* is a solid start, but *Heavy Blue* is a more interesting date for the contrasting horns: Gonzalez sounds handsomely lyrical on flugelhorn and is countered by Joe Ford's bruising alto solos, which are always bursting into double-time runs. Willis's five originals here are all worthwhile. The next two piano-trio albums, *Let's Play* and *How Do You Keep The Music Playing?*, are probably the best places to hear Willis's own playing. The first has lovely readings of 'Who Can I Turn To?' and 'Bess, You Is My Woman Now', and Lewis is in fine form, though Debriano is a bit overbearing at times. *How Do You Keep The Music Playing?* finds Willis distilling the lightest of tones out of Wayne Shorter's usually impenetrable 'Dance Cadaverous'; he throws in some gentlemanly funk on 'Slick Rick' and even makes 'Ezekiel Saw The Wheel' fit the programme. Williams and Nash are a near-perfect team. The trio with Bartz and McBee sounds a little too off-the-cuff, as if the participants were surprised to walk into the studio together, and the bassist can't always find the spaces between Bartz and Willis, except on his beloved 'D Bass-ic Blues'; but Bartz continues his renaissance, and it would be good to hear him with Willis and a full rhythm section. The only disappointment in this stack is the Steeplechase solo disc,

dedicated to Nat Cole ballads and, finally, a bit soporific. By himself, Willis expands his voicings and makes some of these tunes sound too weighty and formal, though there are still some pleasing variations. He seems much more at home, though, with the programme of gospel and sanctified themes on *Solo Spirit*. Some of the pieces are perhaps a bit heavy on the reverence – nine themes run to nearly 80 minutes – and Ellington's 'Come Sunday' suits him better than 'Take My Hand, Precious Lord'. But he sustains it as a contemplative solo recital.

The dedicatee of *A Tribute To Someone* is Herbie Hancock, who penned the title-tune and two others in the programme. It's agreeable to find a record with this instrumentation that doesn't sound too much like a Jazz Messengers date, and Willis's distinguished touch rubs off on his team: these are notably elegant group performances. The title-piece is done with both panache and power in reserve, and the trio number, 'Sensei', is a lovely tune, given a perfect reading by Willis, Williams and Riley. The only false notes are struck by Stubblefield, whose noisy playing sounds merely coarse here instead of exciting.

Bert Wilson ALTO AND TENOR SAXOPHONES

*** **Live At The Zoo** Nine Winds 0138
Wilson; Nancy Curtis (*f*); Allen Youngblood (*p*); Chuck Metcalf (*b*); Bob Meyer (*d*). 8/88.
*** **Further Adventures In Jazz** FMO 004
Wilson; Syd Potter (*t*); Nancy Curtis (*f*); Craig Hoyer (*p*); Peter Vinikow (*b*); Bob Meyer (*d*); Michael Olson (*perc*); Greta Matassa (*v*). 1/92.

Bert Wilson and his band, Rebirth, make cheerful, passionate jazz that is as life-affirming as it is questing. The leader's alto and tenor style is an extravagant symposium of hard-bop licks and wildly expressive effects, trademarked by a big, whinnying vibrato that harks back to classic free jazz without really planting its flag there: he prefers quite tight structures and a careful sifting of group sounds, as peppery as the group can become. The earlier record (several LPs are in vinyl heaven) documents a fine edition of Rebirth, marked out as much by the intelligent work of the rhythm section as by Wilson's howling solos and Curtis's less freewheeling but still interesting flute work. *Further Adventures In Jazz* offers a new line-up, though Curtis and Meyer continue, with guest spots for Potter and Matassa on two tracks apiece. Wilson's affection for hard-bop virtuosity is often worn on his sleeve: he describes 'Happy Pretty' as '12 keys in 12 bars in 12 seconds, though we play it somewhat faster here'. Some of the tunes on both records are a bit scrappy or ragged, even for such a roistering group, and a little more finesse in the production would have helped; but both are entertaining sessions of great character.

Cassandra Wilson (born 1955) VOICE

*** **Point Of View** JMT 834404-2
Wilson; Grachan Moncur III (*tb*); Steve Coleman (*as, perc*); Jean-Paul Bourelly (*g*); Lonnie Plaxico (*b*); Mark Johnson (*d*). 12/85.
(*) **Days Aweigh JMT 834412-2
Wilson; Steve Coleman (*as*); Rod Williams (*ky*); Jean-Paul Bourelly (*g*); Kevin Bruce Harris, Kenneth Davis (*b*); Mark Johnson (*d*). 5/87.
***(*) **Blue Skies** JMT 834419-2
Wilson; Mulgrew Miller (*p*); Lonnie Plaxico (*b*); Terri Lyne Carrington (*d*). 2/88.
** **Jumpworld** JMT 834434-2
Wilson; Graham Haynes (*t*); Robin Eubanks (*tb*); Steve Coleman (*as*); Rod Williams (*ky*); David Gilmore (*g*); Kevin Bruce Harris, Lonnie Plaxico (*b*); Mark Johnson (*d*); James Moore (*v*). 7–8/89.
*** **She Who Weeps** JMT 834443-2
Wilson; Rod Williams (*p*); Jean-Paul Bourelly (*g, g-syn*); Kevin Bruce Harris, Herman Fowlkes, Reggie Washington (*b*); Mark Johnson, Tani Tabbal (*d*). 11–12/90.
*** **Live** JMT 849149-2
Wilson; James Weidman (*ky*); Kevin Bruce Harris (*b*); Mark Johnson (*d*). 90.
*** **After The Beginning Again** JMT 514001-2
Wilson; James Weidman (*ky*); Kevin Bruce Harris (*b*); Mark Johnson (*d*); Jeff Haynes (*perc*). 91.
** **Dance To The Drums Again** DIW/Columbia 472972-2
As above, except add Jean-Paul Bourelly (*g*), Rod Williams (*ky*), Kevin Johnson, Bill McClellan (*d*). n.d.

Wilson is among the most interesting of singers to appear in recent years, and her association with such musicians as Coleman and Bourelly has given her an acknowledged place in the so-called M-BASE movement of New York players. But her records are often rather awkward compromises between a more traditional jazz singing role and the funk and rap influences which dominate today's black music. Her own compositions are flavourless vehicles for her style, marked by rambling melodies, vaguely prescriptive lyrics and rhythmical staggers; the early records (up to *Blue Skies*) are an occasionally exciting but often unfocused attempt at finding a balance. She shows a marked Betty Carter influence rhythmically, but the timbre of her voice is cloudier, and it can throw an interesting spin on otherwise familiar songs. *Blue Skies* is the least typical but easily the best of her JMT records: though made up entirely of standards with a conventional rhythm section, the recital finds Wilson investing the likes of 'Shall We Dance?' with a wholly unfamiliar range of inflexions and melodic extensions which is captivating. Her third-person version of 'Sweet Lorraine' is peculiarly dark and compelling and, while some of the songs drift a little too far off base, it's a remarkable record, and it makes the ensuing *Jumpworld*, a return to self-consciously 'modern' music, sound all the more contrived. *She Who Weeps* takes a middle ground, with a mostly acoustic backing and a programme which includes an overlong 'Body And Soul' and a wordless and rather effective 'Chelsea Bridge'. The live session confirms that Wilson can sustain a concert set which is essentially a seamless, ongoing vocal improvisation, but the slipshod attention to quality-control, as far as the material is concerned, is a point which seems to afflict most of what she does. *After The Beginning Again* is one of her strongest studio dates – 'There She Goes' is a haunting tune, built round Wilson's yearning tag-line, and there's a memorably downcast treatment of 'Baubles, Bangles And Beads' – but *Dance To The Drums Again* sounds flat and tired, leaving Wilson apparently stranded in a creative impasse.

*** **Blue Light 'Til Dawn** Blue Note CDP 781357-2

Wilson; Olu Dara (*c*); Don Byron (*cl*); Tony Cedras (*acc*); Charles Burnham (*vn*); Gib Wharton (*steel g*); Brandon Ross, Chris Whitley (*g*); Lonnie Plaxico, Kenny Davis (*b*); Lance Carter, Bill McClellan (*d*); Cyro Baptista, Jeff Haynes, Kevin Johnson, Vinx (*perc*). n.d.

Wilson's debut for Blue Note was hailed in many quarters (mostly by rock critics) as a masterpiece, and it's certainly a clear step forward from her recent records: Brandon Ross's production clarifies all the colours of her voice for the first time, and the inventive textures involving Dara, Byron, Burnham and Baptista create digital fantasies on country blues and string-band forms. Yet Wilson again makes peculiar labour out of some of the songs: Joni Mitchell and Robert Johnson tunes stagger under her mannerisms, and it's on the simpler, more straightforward arrangements, such as a lovely glide through Van Morrison's 'Tupelo Honey', that it all comes together.

*** **New Moon Daughter** Blue Note 837183-2

As above, except add Graham Haynes, Butch Morris (*c*), Gary Breit (*org*), Kevin Breit (*g*), Mark Anthony Peterson (*b*), Dougie Bowne (*d*); omit Dara, Byron, Davis, Carter, McClellan, Johnson, Vinx. 95.

The same again, only more polished, a shade more inventive, as well as a fraction more arch: 'Last Train To Clarksville' was a cute idea for a cover, and Wilson takes it over, but her improvisation on the fade suggests that she doesn't really know what to do with it. 'Strange Fruit' is harrowing in a deadpan, designerish way, and the Robert Johnson tunes again don't fit. Where she really puts her mark on the music is in her own writing: the calm, serenely pretty 'Until' is outstanding, and so are 'Memphis' and 'Find Him'. Jazz as art-song, and pretty damn accomplished.

Gerald Wilson (born 1918) TRUMPET, BANDLEADER

**** **Portraits** Pacific Jazz CDP 7934142

Wilson; Jules Chaikin, Freddie Hall, Carmell Jones, Nat Meeks, Al Porcino, Ray Triscari (*t*); Bob Edmondson, Bob Ewing, Lew McCreary, Lester Robinson, Don Switzer (*tb*); Bud Shank (*f*); Joe Maini, Jimmy Woods (*as*); Teddy Edwards, Harold Land (*ts*); Jack Nimitz (*bs*); Jack Wilson (*p*); Joe Pass (*g*); Dave Dyson, Leroy Vinnegar (*b*); Chuck Carter (*d*); Modesto Duran (*perc*). 63.

**** **State Street Sweet** Mama MMF 1010

Wilson; Snooky Young, Ron Barrows, Bob Clark, Frank Szabo, George Graham, Tony Lujan, Bobby Shew (*t*); Charlie Loper, Ira Nepus, Thurman Green, Alex Iles (*tb*); Maurice Spears (*btb*); John Stephens, Randall Willis (*as*); Plas Johnson, Carl Randall, Louis Taylor (*ts*); Jack Nimitz (*bs*); Brian O'Rourke (*p*); Eric Otis, Anthony Wilson (*g*); Trey Henry (*b*); Mel Lee (*d*).

After cutting his teeth with the Jimmie Lunceford Orchestra, where he replaced another trumpeter, Sy Oliver, as staff arranger, Wilson formed his own band and has continued to lead and write ever since, preferring the warmth of California to the more cut-throat East Coast scene. Wilson favours heavy block chord figures that have the rhythmic immediacy and insistence of small-group jazz, but he frequently writes in multi-part harmony, as with the middle passages of the beautiful 'Ay-Ee-En' on *Love*

You Madly, a combination of Ellington tunes and originals that features Wilson's 'Orchestra of the '80s'. Unfortunately, this one has drifted out of catalogue at present.

Comparing it with work recorded two decades earlier reveals that Wilson's successful formula has changed very little over the years, other than to incorporate elements of rock rhythm and occasional (very effective) use of electric guitar and keyboards. Wilson's earliest West Coast bands were, however, notably modern in their use of unusual harmonies, and Eric Dolphy, for one, was deeply influenced by his ability to work highly inventive variations on very basic tonalities and dedicated an early composition, 'G.W.', to the bandleader. Wilson's best work is finely wrought and never sounds like a mere run-down or head arrangement. For that reason, it's best assimilated quite slowly, paying some attention to the layers of sound that build up over the course of an arrangement. Look, as a single instance, at what he does to Miles Davis's battle-scarred 'So What' on *Portraits*, first of a series of sensitive *hommages*. Wilson's reading has all the delicacy and precision of the *Birth Of The Cool* sessions, but with all the contained power that comes from a full brass and reeds line-up. Perhaps only Mulligan creates the same balance of delicacy and strength.

Though *Portraits* is the most interesting of the early sessions, Wilson's work is in some respects all of a piece and, in equally important regards, so varied that only a track-by-track analysis would reveal his particular genius. Of the much later albums, *Jenna* was the one to go for before *State Street Sweet* came along (there's also a fine session on Trend, *Calafia* (TRCD 537 CD), which is worth finding).

Wilson's work covers an immense range of modern jazz and blues. Heavily marked by the blues, it nevertheless also touches on bebop, rock and modern 'straight' techniques, using devices from each in a quite unselfconscious and integral fashion. One of the great orchestrators in jazz, Wilson's reputation, always solid among players and in California, has begun to extend more widely. Thanks to the Mama Foundation – the title comes from Music Archives, but is also a nod to president Gene Czerwinski's late wife and partner – the latest Wilson band has been been given an airing on *State Street Sweet*. The voicings and arrangements are as good as ever and there are excellent solos from band member Willis (on the title-piece), Bobby Shew (on 'The Serpent') and guest Plas Johnson on 'Come Back To Sorrento'. A storming, elegantly crafted record, it may not be the easiest thing to find, but it will certainly repay big-band fans' efforts many times over.

Glenn Wilson BARITONE SAXOPHONE, BASS CLARINET, ALTO FLUTE

**(*) Elusive Sunnyside 1030
    Wilson; Jim Powell (*t, flhn*); Bob Belden (*ts*); Harold Danko (*p*); Dennis Irwin (*b*); Adam
    Nussbaum (*d*). 12/87.
*** Bittersweet Sunnyside SSC 1057D
    Wilson; Rory Stuart (*g*). 6/90–9/92.

Although, like so many baritone specialists, Wilson seems doomed to recording mainly as a section sideman, he plays with fine gusto and thoughtful intelligence on the records made under his own leadership. *Elusive* is perhaps a little too civilized: the baritone blow-out on 'McCoy's Passion' is excitingly realized, 'Outformation' is a surprising on-the-spot four-way improvisation, and 'Adams Park' a well-sustained threnody for Pepper Adams. But the tracks where Wilson is joined by Belden and Powell emerge as routine post-bop, and the soft-edged production lacks the impact the music needs to collar attention. *Bittersweet* is an engaging duo album with the adept guitar of Stuart keeping Wilson company. Standing thus exposed holds few terrors for the saxophonist, whose melody lines seem to grow longer, more even, with individual notes softened by his delivery. A couple of pieces feature overdubbed bass clarinet and alto flute, which varies the pace a little: perhaps it's impossible to avoid a certain monotony in this situation. The material is all jazz themes, aside from 'Without A Song', and both men find much to say, even on blues material by Sam Jones and Oliver Nelson.

Steve Wilson ALTO SAXOPHONE

***(*) New York Summit Criss Cross Criss 1062
    Wilson; Tom Williams (*t*); Mulgrew Miller (*p*); James Genus (*b*); Carl Allen (*d*). 12/91.
*** Blues For Marcus Criss Cross Criss 1073
    Wilson; Steve Nelson (*vib*); Bruce Barth (*p*); James Genus (*b*); Lewis Nash (*d*). 1/93.

Wilson first surfaced in the mid-'80s with Out of the Blue, a group dedicated to the classic Blue Note sound. With a sound reminiscent of former Messenger Bobby Watson (a stylistic link confirmed by his sound-alike duets with vibraphonist Nelson on *Blues For Marcus*), the young Virginian acquitted himself more than respectably.

Wilson is by no means an uncritical retro hard bopper. His first two CDs as leader demonstrate impressive if marginally over-ambitious skills as a composer ('Diaspora' on the second record gets rather hung up on complex time-signatures) but also an instinct for unusual repertoire. The first record opens with Ted Curson's lovely 'Reava's Waltz' and includes material by Ron Carter, Duke Ellington, Eddie Harris, Thelonious Monk, Joe Sample and Bobby Timmons ('Damned If I Know', rather than the ubiquitous 'Moanin'') alongside a single original. By 1993, Wilson's confidence in his own work is more evident, but there is still room for Ornette Coleman's 'Jayne', Joe Chambers's 'Patterns' and Roland Kirk's 'The Haunted Melody'.

Wilson hasn't as yet quite put together the band that suits his approach. Tom Williams is a competent rather than exciting trumpeter in the Freddie Hubbard mould; he sounds clean and orderly in ensembles but lacks pep in his solos. An outing on the Wilson original, 'Ujima', is little more than a warm-up effort. Ironically, he's missed on the second album, which is rather light in sound. Barth contributes an original, 'Cornerstone', but as a player he lacks Mulgrew Miller's firmly anchored chords and easy switches of register. Genus is the only common element. He may have slipped the engineers a sawbuck before the later sessions, for he's much more clearly audible than on *Summit*.

*** **Step Lively** Criss Cross Criss 1096

Wilson; Cyrus Chestnut (*p*); Freddie Bryant (*g*); Dennis Irwin (*b*); Gregory Hutchinson (*d*); Daniel Sadownick (*perc*). 12/93.

Wilson's third Criss Cross is not so much a progression as an affirmation of the sound impression of the previous two. His lean, unsentimental tone on the alto blends with a rather good-humoured approach, which makes for a somewhat unusual blend of lightness and intensity. He restricts himself to two self-penned originals, the complex blues of the title-track and the jaunty 'The Epicurean', and the presence of the admirable Chestnut lends further muscle. In the end, perhaps no more than another solid Criss Cross date, but there are plenty of rewarding things, and Wilson deserves attention.

Teddy Wilson (1912–86) PIANO

***(*) **Teddy Wilson 1934–35** Classics CL 508

Wilson; Roy Eldridge, Dick Clark (*t*); Benny Morton (*tb*); Tom Macey, Benny Goodman, Cecil Scott (*cl*); Hilton Jefferson, Johnny Hodges (*as*); Chu Berry, Ben Webster (*ts*); John Trueheart, Lawrence Lucie, Dave Barbour (*g*); John Kirby, Grachan Moncur (*b*); Cozy Cole (*d*); Billie Holiday (*v*). 5/34–12/35.

***(*) **Teddy Wilson Vol. 1: Too Hot For Words** Hep 1012

As above. 1–10/35.

Few jazz records have endured quite as well as Teddy Wilson's 1930s music. Wilson arrived in New York as, on the basis of the four solo titles which open the first Classics CD, an enthusiastic young stride pianist, already under the spell of Earl Hines and of Art Tatum, with whom he worked as a two-man piano team. But even here there are the signs of an individual whose meticulous, dapper delivery and subtle reading of harmony would be hugely influential. Amazingly, everything is in place by the time of the first band session in July 1935: the initial line-up includes Eldridge, Goodman and Webster, and the singer is Billie Holiday, who would feature as vocalist on most of Wilson's pre-war records. Two classics were made immediately – 'What A Little Moonlight Can Do' and 'Miss Brown To You' – and the style was set: a band chorus, a vocal, and another chorus for the band, with solos and obbligatos in perfect accord with every other note and accent. All the others seem to take their cue from the leader's own poise, and even potentially unruly spirits such as Eldridge and Webster behave. The first of Classics' comprehensive seven-disc series includes 11 piano solos and 12 band sides, and it's a delight from start to finish, even though there was better to come.

The reissue of these records has been complicated by Holiday's presence, for all of her tracks with Wilson are now also available on discs under her own name. Collectors will have to follow their own tastes, but we would opine that, of all the various transfers of this material, the Hep discs – which follow the Classics discs fairly closely in sequencing, if finally not quite so generous in the number of tracks on each disc – have the most truthful sound. Even so, the Classics CD, above, is consistently clean and enjoyable in sonic terms.

***(*) **Teddy Wilson 1935–36** Classics CL 511

Wilson; Dick Clark, Gordon Griffin, Frank Newton, Roy Eldridge, Jonah Jones (*t*); Benny Morton (*tb*); Benny Goodman, Buster Bailey, Rudy Powell, Tom Macey (*cl*); Jerry Blake (*cl, as*); Vido Musso (*cl, ts*); Harry Carney (*cl, bs*); Johnny Hodges (*as*); Ted McRae, Chu Berry (*ts*); Dave Barbour, John Trueheart, Allan Reuss, Bob Lessey, Lawrence Lucie (*g*); Lionel Hampton (*vib*); Israel Crosby, Harry Goodman, Leemie Stanfield, Grachan Moncur, John Kirby (*b*); Gene Krupa, Big Sid Catlett, Cozy Cole (*d*); Helen Ward, Ella Fitzgerald, Red Harper, Billie Holiday (*v*). 12/35–8/36.

**** **Teddy Wilson Vol. 2: Warmin' Up** Hep 1014
    As above. 12/35–6/36.
*** **Teddy Wilson 1936–37** Classics 521
    Wilson; Gordon Griffin, Irving Randolph, Henry Allen, Jonah Jones, Buck Clayton, Cootie
    Williams (*t*); Cecil Scott (*cl, as, ts*); Vido Musso (*cl, ts*); Harry Carney (*cl, bs*); Benny Goodman
    (*cl*); Johnny Hodges (*as*); Ben Webster, Prince Robinson, Lester Young (*ts*); Allan Reuss,
    Freddie Green, James McLin (*g*); Harry Goodman, Milt Hinton, Walter Page, John Kirby (*b*);
    Cozy Cole, Jo Jones, Gene Krupa (*d*); Billie Holiday, Midge Williams, Red Harper (*v*). 8/36–3/
    37.
**** **Teddy Wilson Vol. 3: Of Thee I Swing** Hep 1020
    Largely as above. 8/36–2/37.
Wilson hit his stride as this long series of sessions proceeded. The next two Classics CDs are laden with
fine music, and Billie Holiday's contributions assume greatness: the 16 tracks she sings on Classics 521
number among her finest records, and the mixed quality of the material seems to make no difference to
her. Just as Lionel Hampton began pilfering men from local big bands for his Victor sessions, so Wilson
organized similar contingents for his records, and some of these bands are drawn from either the
Goodman or the Basie orchestra, although one offbeat session features Henry Allen, Cecil Scott and
Prince Robinson. The spotlight is off Wilson to some extent, but one of the major reasons for the
success of these dates is the light, singing fluency of the rhythm section, and the pianist's unemphatic
but decisive lead is the prime reason for that. Ella Fitzgerald sings on one session on Classics 511 and
Midge Williams, Helen Ward and Red Harper take their turns at the microphone, but it's Holiday one
remembers. Lester Young's association with the singer also starts here, but his solos are really no more
memorable than the offerings by Buck Clayton, Benny Goodman or Roy Eldridge. Those collecting the
Classics CDs may be dismayed by the erratic sound-quality on Classics 521 in particular, and once
again we prefer the Hep series.

**** **Teddy Wilson 1937** Classics 531
    Wilson; Cootie Williams, Harry James, Buck Clayton (*t*); Buster Bailey, Benny Goodman,
    Archie Rosati (*cl*); Harry Carney (*cl, bs*); Johnny Hodges (*as*); Vido Musso, Lester Young (*ts*);
    Red Norvo (*xy*); Allan Reuss, Freddie Green (*g*); John Kirby, John Simmons, Harry Goodman,
    Artie Bernstein, Walter Page (*b*); Cozy Cole, Jo Jones, Gene Krupa (*d*); Helen Ward, Billie
    Holiday, Frances Hunt, Boots Castle (*v*). 3–8/37.
**** **Teddy Wilson Vol. 4: Fine & Dandy** Hep 1029
    Largely as above. 3–7/37.
***(*) **Teddy Wilson 1937–1938** Classics 548
    Wilson; Harry James, Buck Clayton (*t*); Bobby Hackett (*c*); Benny Morton (*tb*); Pee Wee
    Russell, Prince Robinson (*cl*); Johnny Hodges, Tab Smith (*as*); Gene Sedric, Lester Young, Chu
    Berry, Vido Musso (*ts*); Red Norvo (*xy*); Allan Reuss, Freddie Green (*g*); Walter Page, Al Hall,
    John Simmons (*b*); Johnny Blowers, Jo Jones, Cozy Cole (*d*); Billie Holiday, Nan Wynn (*v*). 9/
    37–4/38.
**** **Teddy Wilson Vol. 5: Blue Mood** Hep 1035
    As above. 8/37–1/38.
**** **Teddy Wilson 1938** Classics 556
    Wilson; Jonah Jones, Harry James (*t*); Bobby Hackett (*c*); Trummy Young, Benny Morton (*tb*);
    Pee Wee Russell (*cl*); Benny Carter, Johnny Hodges, Toots Mondello, Ted Buckner, Edgar
    Sampson (*as*); Lester Young, Herschel Evans, Bud Freeman, Chu Berry, Ben Webster (*ts*); Allan
    Reuss, Al Casey (*g*); Al Hall, John Kirby, Milt Hinton, Walter Page (*b*); Johnny Blowers, Cozy
    Cole, Jo Jones (*d*); Billie Holiday, Nan Wynn (*v*). 4–11/38.
**** **Moments Like This** Hep CD 1043
    As above, except add Roy Eldridge (*t*), Ernie Powell (*c*). 3/38–1/39.
This is jazz of such a consistently high level that it seems churlish to offer criticism. The Classics CDs
are mainly in pretty good, clean sound, with the occasional track sounding a little starchier: the Hep
transfers continue to be our first recommendation, though the Classics 'uniform' editions may appeal
more to some collectors. The first 1937 CD is magnificent, the first five sessions as strong in material as
they are in performances: 'Mean To Me', 'I'll Get By', 'How Am I To Know?' and more. These are also
among Holiday's greatest records. The 1937–8 disc includes the September 1937 session which included
the memorable two-part 'Just A Mood' quartet with Harry James and Red Norvo, as well as a previously rejected date. The 1938 set sees Bobby Hackett arriving to play lead, as well as six solos originally
made for the 'Teddy Wilson School For Pianists'. Wilson's mixture of lyricism and vigour is almost
unique in the jazz of the period and it suggests a path which jazz doctrine has seldom explored since.

*** **Teddy Wilson 1939** Classics 571
    Wilson; Roy Eldridge, Karl George, Harold Baker (*t*); Floyd Brady (*tb*); Pete Clark (*cl, as, bs*);

Rudy Powell (*cl, as*); Benny Carter (*as, ts*); Ben Webster, George Irish (*ts*); Danny Barker, Al Casey (*g*); Al Hall, Milt Hinton (*b*); Cozy Cole, J. C. Heard (*d*); Billie Holiday, Thelma Carpenter, Jean Eldridge (*v*). 1–9/39.

Inevitably, Wilson went on to lead his own big band, and musicians were more than impressed by its secure power and purposeful clarity of tone, a direct extension of Wilson's own manner. But it failed commercially, and its records don't quite match its reputation, largely through charts that are only so-so but which may have come alive in person. The 1939 sides are collected here, along with four more Wilson solos, including a sparkling 'China Boy'.

*** Teddy Wilson 1939–1941 Classics 620

Similar to above, except add Doc Cheatham, Bill Coleman (*t*), Floyd Brady, Benny Morton (*tb*), Jimmy Hamilton (*cl*), George James (*bs*); Eddie Gibbs (*g*), Yank Porter (*d*), Helen Ward (*v*), omit Eldridge, Powell, Barker, Carter, Hinton, Cole, Carpenter, Holiday and Jean Eldridge. 12/39–4/41.

After two more sessions with the big band, Wilson returned to small groups and then a trio as his last sessions for Columbia. Still not quite up to the impeccable calibre of the earlier dates, but a 1940 date with Bill Coleman and Benny Morton in the front line is fine, and Wilson's solos-with-rhythm maintain his own fierce standards.

*** Central Avenue Blues VJC 1013

Wilson; Charlie Shavers (*t*); Benny Morton (*tb*); Joe Thomas (*reeds*); Ed Hall (*cl*); Red Norvo (*vib*); Remo Palmieri (*g*); Big Sid Catlett (*d*); Paul Baron Orchestra. *c.* 48.

Central Avenue Blues is a collection of V-Disc masters in excellently refurbished sound: Shavers will sound as overbearing as usual to some ears, but the more considered methods of Hall and Norvo should counterbalance that, and Wilson is Wilson.

*** And Then They Wrote . . . Columbia 476524-2

Wilson; Major Holley (*b*); Bert Dale (*d*). 59.

An interesting date from an otherwise quiet period in Wilson's working life. He tackles a dozen pieces by 12 different jazz pianists, and it's intriguing to hear him handle Monk, Brubeck and Shearing. The 'old' tunes are predictable enough, but his spare yet bright version of 'Round Midnight' and the unabashed lyricism of 'The Duke' make this a useful departure. Holley and Dale aren't assets, but they don't make too much trouble.

** Air Mail Special Black Lion BLCD 760115

Wilson; Dave Shepherd (*cl*); Ronnie Gleaves (*vib*); Peter Chapman (*b*); Johnny Richardson (*d*). 6/67.

**(*) The Dutch Swing College Band Meet Teddy Wilson Timeless CDTTD 525

Wilson; Ray Kaart (*t*); Bert De Kort (*c*); Dick Kaart (*tb*); Bob Kaper (*cl*); Peter Schilperoot (*cl, ts, bs, p*); Arie Ligthart (*g*); Henk Bosch Van Drakestein, Bob Van Oven, Fred Pronk (*b*); Huub Janssen, Louis De Lussanet (*d*). 2/64–10/73.

** Teddy Wilson Meets Eiji Kitamura Storyville 4152

Wilson; Eiji Kitamura (*cl*); Ichiro Masuda (*vib*); Masanaga Harada (*b*); Buffalo Bill Robinson (*d*). 10/70.

*** With Billie In Mind Chiaroscuro CRD III

Wilson. 5/72.

*** Runnin' Wild Black Lion BLCD 760184

Wilson; Dave Shepherd (*cl*); Kenny Baldock (*b*); Johnny Richardson (*d*). 7/73.

**(*) Blues For Thomas Waller Black Lion BLCD 760131

Wilson (*p* solo). 1/74.

*** Three Little Words Black & Blue 233 094

Wilson; Milt Hinton (*b*); Oliver Jackson (*d*). 7/76.

Wilson's later music is frequently disappointing in the light of his earlier achievements. Lacking any commitment from a major label, he seemed to wander from session to session with a sometimes cynical approach to the occasion, careless of the company and relying on an inner light which had long since burned down to a routine. Only when a sympathetic producer was on hand did Wilson raise his game, and the solo records listed above include some of the best music of his later albums. *With Billie In Mind* is devoted to material he had recorded with Holiday in the 1930s, and its graceful, characteristic atmosphere makes for a special occasion. Six titles are added to the original LP issue. The Waller collection is less happy; the mature Wilson was a very different pianist from Waller, and his brand of sober gaiety isn't well attuned to the bumptious themes here, although 'Black And Blue' is more like the familiar Wilson. *Three Little Words* is a fine trio date, Wilson very much at home with players he trusts. *Runnin' Wild* was recorded at the 1973 Montreux Festival and is an unusually muscular and hard-hitting occasion: Wilson almost storms into 'One O'Clock Jump', plays 'Mood Indigo' with something like abandon and seems to enjoy sparring with Shepherd on 'Runnin' Wild' itself. An interesting change of pace, and the recording is rather aggressive too.

The other records are eminently missable. *Air Mail Special* features dreary British mainstream, and Wilson doesn't bother to disguise his boredom. Eiji Kitamura and his companions do marginally better, but the music is mostly second-hand swing. The Dutch Swing College Band play with their customary zeal and Wilson sounds in good spirits on 'Limehouse Blues' in particular; but there's little to remark on, other than pleasant mainstream noodling (the tracks from the 1960s don't feature Wilson).

*** **Masters Of Jazz Vol. 11: Teddy Wilson** Storyville 4111
> Wilson; Jesper Lundgaard, Niels-Henning Orsted-Pedersen (*b*); Bjarne Rostvold, Ed Thigpen (*d*). 12/68–6/80.

*** **Alone** Storyville STCD 8211
> Wilson (*p* solo). 5/83.

Wilson carried on working into the 1980s, and these are among his final recordings. He still sounds much as he did nearly 50 years before. The material on the *Masters Of Jazz* disc – drawn from two trio dates 12 years apart – is still heavily reliant on the 1930s standards which Wilson always stood by. As good as anything he recorded later in life. *Alone* was cut at a Danish concert. The normally taciturn pianist talks between some of the tunes, and he sounds in amiable spirits on some of his favourites, though the location sound and the piano itself seem no more than adequate.

Lem Winchester VIBES

** **Winchester Special** Original Jazz Classics OJC 1719
> Winchester; Benny Golson (*ts*); Tommy Flanagan (*p*); Wendell Marshall (*b*); Art Taylor (*d*). 9/59.

** **Lem's Beat** Original Jazz Classics OJC 1785
> Winchester; Curtis Peagler (*as*); Oliver Nelson (*ts*); Billy Brown (*g*); Roy Johnson (*p*); Wendell Marshall (*b*); Art Taylor (*d*). 60.

(*) **Another Opus Original Jazz Classics OJC 1816
> Winchester; Frank Wess (*f*); Hank Jones (*p*); Johnny Hammond Smith (*org*); Eddie McFadden (*g*); Eddie Jones, Wendell Marshall (*b*); Bill Erskine, Gus Johnson (*d*). 6 & 10/60.

Winchester's vibes playing is vigorous enough, if sometimes flat-footed, but he is one of those players who tends to be comprehensively upstaged by his sidemen. Golson's gruff, argumentative tenor on the first record and Nelson's loamy sound on the second create most of the interest, and Wess is as interesting as always on *Another Opus*, a vastly underrated exponent of the flute. The rhythm section on *Lem's Beat* and the bonus 'Lid Flippin'' on the third record hint at some of the forthcoming extroversions of soul-jazz without quite leaving hard-bop routine behind. It's a little hard to be excited about Winchester. His moment seems more likely to have passed than still to be coming, and these records will probably sustain interest only among collectors of the subsidiary personnel.

Kai Winding (1922–83) TROMBONE, TROMBONIUM

***(*) **Jive At Five** Status DSTS 1012
> Winding; Carl Fontana, Wayne Andre (*tb, trombonium*); Dick Lieb (*btb, trombonium*); Roy Frazee (*p*); Kenny O'Brien (*b*); Tom Montgomery (*d*). 6/57.

The success of Jay & Kai was, in the end, not altogether equitably shared. J. J. Johnson's unchallenged dominance on the trombone as a bop voice was always questionable. Where J. J. brought a saxophone-like articulation to the instrument, it was the Danish-born Winding who showed how it could follow the woodwind players' fast vibrato and percussive attack and still retain its distinctive character. While with the Kenton band, Winding worked out ways of producing a very tight vibrato with the lip rather than using the slide, and this had a marked impact on a younger generation of players.

A lot of the suriving Winding material is on discs also featuring J. J., Bennie Green and others. The above is under his sole leadership. Winding's stint with Kenton had convinced him that massed trombones made the noise closest to the angels and he persisted with the choral approach. Here it works very well indeed and, though some will be put off by what might be thought to be Kentonisms, they should be assured that the idiom and the arrangements are Winding's own. The key tracks are an original blues and a thoroughly wonderful version of 'In A Sentimental Mood' in which the voicings could hardly be bettered. There remains, to be sure, something a little cold about Winding's work. Certainly, compared to J. J., he couldn't give a ballad more than a gruff expressiveness, but that was not his forte. What he did, he did well, and he deserves more credit for it.

Norma Winstone (born 1941) VOCALS

***(*) **Somewhere Called Home** ECM 1337
Winstone; Tony Coe (*cl, ts*); John Taylor (*p*). 7/86.
***(*) **Well Kept Secret** Hot House HHCD 1015
Winstone; Stacy Rowles (*flhn*); Jimmy Rowles (*p*); George Mraz (*b*); Joe LaBarbera (*d*). 10/93.

Winstone's first entry on Mike Westbrook's remarkable road-movie of an album, *Metropolis*, is one of the most breathtaking in contemporary jazz, a pure, reed-like tone that suddenly rises up out of the growling 'male' horns. Very powerful. One of the things that makes Winstone so exceptional as a singer is her equal confidence with pure abstraction (as in much of her work with Azimuth) and the most straightforward vocal line; she has talked of a 'Radio 2' side to her work but has often proved to be a sensitive lyricist as well as a standards singer.

In the absence of the now-rare *Edge Of Time* (released by Deram in 1971) *Somewhere Called Home* is a more-than-acceptable sample of Winstone's atmospheric approach. It takes a certain amount of brass neck to include 'Hi Lili Hi Lo' and 'Tea For Two' on a set like this. Coe and Taylor (Mr Winstone when off duty) are able and sensitive partners, but one wonders whether it wouldn't have come off better with just Taylor's thoughtful acompaniments.

The title of *Well Kept Secret* just about says it all. This finds Winstone where she should be (no disrespect to Taylor *et al.*), working with an international musician of Rowles's quality. They don't do 'Peacocks', which Jeri Brown seems to have nabbed, but 'A Timeless Place' is gorgeous, with its Winstone lyric, and 'A Flower Is A Lovesome Thing' is fragile and delicate without giving any sense that it will be easy to pull apart. An excellent vocal record. Why has it not been noised about since its release?

Jens Winther (born 1960) TRUMPET, FLUGELHORN

(*) **Looking Through Storyville STCD 4127
Winther; Tomas Franck (*ts*); Thomas Clausen (*p*); Jesper Lundgaard (*b*); Alex Riel (*d*). 4/88.
***(*) **Scorpio Dance** Storyville STCD 4179
Winther; Tomas Franck (*ts*); Ben Besiakow (*p*); Lennart Ginman (*b*); Al Foster (*d*). 3/91.

A Danishman with plenty of international experience, Winther has the confidence to play either tight, modern, hard bop or a more free-thinking, if fundamentally conservative, kind of improvisation. He can sustain long solos, but his ballad statements or flugelhorn lead on the likes of 'Ubataba', on the first record, are just as revealing. The earlier session is solid Danish jazz, but it could have lost a couple of tracks and been the better for it: Lundgaard and Riel don't sound terribly interested for once, and Clausen's frequent use of a Fender Rhodes electric piano lends a somewhat dated feel to the sound. *Scorpio Dance* is sharper all round. The sound is crisper, if a little dry, and Foster's presence (at Winther's own invitation) is inspirational, with the drummer on tirelessly inventive form. The two long tracks, 'Scorpio Dance' and 'Tree Of Life', bring out terrific solos from Winther, and there is a probing trumpet–drums duet performance on 'Intimy'. Ginman is lost in the mix, but otherwise the group sound very alert, and Besiakow sensibly takes much more of a back seat than Clausen did on the earlier record.

Mike Wofford PIANO

*** **At Maybeck Volume Eighteen** Concord CCD 4514
Wofford (*p* solo). 9/91.

With all his albums for Revelation wiped off the racks, Wofford is served only by this solo session in Concord's Maybeck series. It's a good one, although the pianist's oblique manner won't be to all tastes. A funky theme like Ray Bryant's 'Tonk' is ingeniously broken down, but the results aren't exactly funky. Jazz standards such as 'Stablemates' and 'Main Stem' are run through an elaborate series of variations and, while some of them are intriguing, there are moments when it seems as if the journey is going to sound interesting only to the man who's creating it. He is perhaps at his best on the briefest track, 'Too Marvellous For Words', where the melody is referred to only periodically and the improvisation is tautly conceived. Excellent sound as usual in this series.

Rickey Woodard (born 1956) TENOR AND ALTO SAXOPHONES

*** **The Frank Capp Trio Presents Rickey Woodard** Concord CCD 4469
Woodard; Tom Ranier (*p*); Chuck Berghofer (*b*); Frank Capp (*d*).

*** **California Cooking!** Candid CCD 79509
> Woodard; Dwight Dickerson (*p*); Tony Dumas (*b*); Harold Mason (*d*). 2/91.

***(*) **The Tokyo Express** Candid CCD 79527
> Woodard; James Williams (*p*); Christian McBride (*b*); Joe Chambers (*d*). 6/92.

***(*) **Yazoo** Concord CCD 4629
> Woodard; Ray Brown (*t*); Cedar Walton (*p*); Jeff Littleton (*b*); Ralph Penland (*d*). 94.

At last, a young(ish) tenorman who isn't in thrall to either Coltrane or Rollins. Woodard is actually from Nashville but works in Los Angeles, and there's a flavour of West Coast sunshine about the music, which has a burnished, easy-going lilt to it without sacrificing anything in energy. Zoot Sims, surprisingly, is the stylist whose manner Woodard most closely resembles, but his tone is as close to unique as a tenorman's can be in an age of a thousand tenor players: lean but hard, with a dusky timbre that he sustains through all the registers. His alto playing is more in hock to soul–bop sax playing, but there's the same fluency and bite. Dickerson and the others keep up and take occasional solos, but everything here is down to Woodard, and he completely dominates the 66 minutes which include fine readings of Hank Mobley's 'This I Dig Of You' and Duke Pearson's rare 'Jeannine'. The piano sounds a fraction recessed, but the sound is otherwise excellent.

The Tokyo Express, like so many of Candid's recent discs recorded live at Birdland in New York, is a significant step forward. Increased visibility means a better response-rate on the phone calls, and here Woodard has a first-rate band behind him. The leader's approach to standards grows more confident with every session and his solo on 'Polka Dots And Moonbeams' touches all sorts of unexpected bases, including an unmistakable quote from Paul Desmond, a player not always fully acknowledged by musicians of Woodard's generation. The sound is very good, letting the rhythm section come through truly and with good definition.

Woodard can also be heard with Frank Capp's trio on a showcase record designed to show off the young player. The problem here is that the rhythm section comes through like a Sherman tank, leaving Woodard sounding as if he was playing in a goods yard.

Yazoo is tantalizingly close to being something really special. Trumpeter Brown sits out two tracks and allows Woodard to try things that the more detailed arrangements rule out. His solo on 'September In The Rain' and 'Portrait Of Jennie' are exemplary, but the real stars of the disc are Walton and his composition 'Holy Land', a truly lovely thing that should be in everybody's band-book.

Phil Woods (born 1931) ALTO AND SOPRANO SAXOPHONE, CLARINET, BASS CLARINET, VOCAL

(**) **Bird's Eyes** Philology W 57-2
> Woods; Hal Serra (*p*); Joe Raich (*vib*); Sal Salvador (*g*); Chuck Andrews (*b*); Joe Morello (*d, v*).

*** **Woodlore** Original Jazz Classics OJC 052
> Woods; John Williams (*p*); Teddy Kotick (*b*); Nick Stabulas (*d*). 11/55.

*** **Pairing Off** Original Jazz Classics OJC 092
> Woods; Donald Byrd, Kenny Dorham (*t*); Gene Quill (*as*); Tommy Flanagan (*p*); Doug Watkins (*b*); Philly Joe Jones (*d*). 6/56.

** **The Young Bloods** Original Jazz Classics OJC 1732
> Woods; Donald Byrd (*t*); Al Haig (*p*); Teddy Kotick (*b*); Charli Persip (*d*). 11/56.

(*) **Four Altos Original Jazz Classics OJC 1734
> Woods; Gene Quill, Sahib Shihab, Hal Stein (*as*); Mal Waldron (*p*); Tommy Potter (*b*); Louis Hayes (*d*). 2/57.

***(*) **Phil & Quill** Original Jazz Classics OJC 215
> Woods; Gene Quill (*as*); George Syran (*p*); Teddy Kotick (*b*); Nick Stabulas (*d*). 3/57.

(*) **Bird's Night Savoy CV-0143
> Woods; Frank Socolow (*as, ts*); Cecil Payne (*bs*); Duke Jordan (*p*); Wendell Marshall (*b*); Art Taylor (*d*). 8/57.

Phil Woods sprang into jazz recording with a fully formed style: tone, speed of execution and ideas were all first-hand borrowings from bebop and, inevitably, Parker, but he sounded like a mature player from the first. The 1947 recordings must be discounted, since they're from private acetates and the fidelity is almost as poor as some of the worst Charlie Parker airshots. Yet the bristling insistence of the sixteen-year-old Woods is already astonishingly in evidence, assuming the date is accurate (there are some 30 minutes of music by this band on the CD; the rest continues the series of live Parker recordings). *Woodlore* is a relatively quiet business, considering that Woods thrived on blowing-session shoot-outs at the time, and it's the prettiness of his sound which impresses on 'Be My Love' and 'Falling In Love All Over Again'; but 'Get Happy' is a burner. The rhythm section, with Williams sometimes barely in touch, is less impressive. *Pairing Off* and *Four Altos* milk the jam-session format which was beloved by Prestige at the time, and both dates come off better than most. *Pairing Off* features a couple of crackerjack blues in the title-tune and 'Stanley The Steamer', and only Byrd's relative greenness lets the side down; Philly Joe is superbly inventive at the kit. *Four Altos* is an idea that ought to pall quickly, but the enthusiasm of Woods and Quill in particular elevates the makeshift charts into something worthwhile. They made a very fine team: *Phil & Quill* doesn't have an ounce of spare fat in the solos, and the spanking delivery on, say, 'A Night At St Nick's' is as compelling as anything Prestige were recording at the period. Quill's duskier tone and more extreme intensities are barely a beat behind Woods's in terms of quality of thought (they also have two tracks on the subsequent compilation, *Bird Feathers*, OJC 1735 CD). *The Young Bloods*, although interesting for a rare 1950s appearance by Al Haig, is beset by the familiar problem of Byrd's lack of authority, and sparks never fly between the horns the way Woods would probably have wished. All five discs are remastered to the customary high standards of OJC. *Bird's Night* resurrects a live broadcast from New York's Five Spot: four jams on Parker tunes, the kind of thing Woods played every day and had the measure of from the beginning. Nothing said here that one can't find on any of the studio dates.

*** **Rights Of Swing** Candid CCD79016
    Woods; Benny Bailey (*t*); Curtis Fuller, Willie Dennis (*tb*); Julius Watkins (*frhn*); Sahib Shihab (*bs*); Tommy Flanagan (*p*); Buddy Catlett (*b*); Osie Johnson, Mickey Roker (*d*). 1–2/61.
Something of a one-off in the Woods lexicon, since he has seldom fronted self-composed arrangements for a larger group. The music rather self-consciously negotiates a five-part 'symphonic' structure and, perhaps inevitably, takes its real life from the improvising, which the leader blows through with his usual gumption.

**** **Integrity** Red 123177-2 2CD
    Woods; Tom Harrell (*t, flhn*); Hal Galper (*p*); Steve Gilmore (*b*); Bill Goodwin (*d*). 4/84.
This became a firm line-up, and any who heard the group in concert will surely want this live record, for it's a fine souvenir of one of the great touring bands of the 1980s. Harrell had worked for some years as a freelance in search of a context, and with Woods he secured a precise focus: the material here is a connoisseur's choice of jazz themes – including Neal Hefti's 'Repetition', Ellington's 'Azure', Wayne Shorter's 'Infant Eyes' and Sam Rivers's '222' – mediated through a very clear-headed approach to modern bop playing. Harrell's lucid tone and nimble, carefully sifted lines are as piquant a contrast with Woods as one could wish, without creating any clashes of temperament. Galper's pensiveness is occasionally a fraction too laid back, but he moves as one with bass and drums. Woods himself assumes a role both paternal and sporting, stating themes and directions with unswerving authority but still taking risky routes to resolving an idea: his solo on Charlie Mariano's 'Blue Walls', for instance, is rhythmically as daring as any of his early work. Good in-concert recording.

*** **Gratitude** Denon 33CY-1316
    As above. 6/86.
***(*) **Bop Stew** Concord CCD 4345
    As above. 11/87.
***(*) **Bouquet** Concord CCD 4377
    As above. 11/87.
**** **Flash** Concord CCD 4408
    As above, except add Hal Crook (*tb*). 4/89.
As consistent a series of records as any in this period. Woods's facility seems ageless and, if his parameters remain tied to orthodox bop language, he has developed it as inventively as a player can, making the most of dynamic contrast and colour and granting each member of the band his own space. *Bop Stew* and *Bouquet* are from a fine Japanese concert. *Gratitude* is docked one star for the studio sound which seems rather distant and unfocused, although the playing time runs for a more-than-generous 70 minutes. *Flash*, the final album with Harrell (who has since been replaced by Hal Crook as the front-line horn), has the edge of some outstanding composing by the trumpeter – 'Weaver' and 'Rado' are particularly sound vehicles – and Crook's extra tones on a few tracks.

*** **All Bird's Children** Concord CCD 4441
    As above, except omit Harrell. 6/90.
As good as Crook is, with a sparkling fluency as a soloist and a canny arranger's ear, it's hard to avoid the feeling that Harrell will be missed by the band. In other respects, it's another assured session by the Woods band. Highlight: the lush 'Gotham Serenade' by Galper, who has also since departed the group.

*** **Evolution** Concord CCD 4361
    As above, except add Nelson Hill (*ts*); Nick Brignola (*bs*). 5/88.

***(*) **Real Life** Chesky JD 47
    As above, except Jim McNeely (*p*) replaces Galper. 9/90.
*** **Here's To My Lady** Chesky JD 3
    Woods; Tommy Flanagan (*p*); George Mraz (*b*); Kenny Washington (*d*). 12/88.
Woods's Little Big Band builds on the virtues of the quintet with smart logic. Arrangements by Galper,
Woods, Harrell and Crook leave the group without a specific identity, allowing it to shape a vocabulary
through the charisma of the leader and the pro's pro feel of the ensemble. *Real Life* is the bigger and
more confident record, with a couple of lovely ballad features for Woods and a burning memorial to his
old sparring partner, 'Quill', in which Brignola takes the second alto part; but the somewhat eccentric
Chesky studio sound, an attempt to secure analogue warmth and presence on digital equipment, may
not be to all tastes. Similar remarks apply to the quartet Chesky session, although the blue-chip rhythm
section are so apposite to Woods's needs that it makes one wish he would take a vacation from his usual
band a little more often. The mood here is rather more languid than usual, with nothing breaking into a
gallop, and it's a useful appendix to his more full-blooded work in the 1980s.

*** **Embraceable You** Philology 214 W 25
    Woods; Marco Tamburini, Flavio Boltro, Paolo Fresu (*t, flhn*); Danilo Terenzi, Hal Crook,
    Roberto Rossi (*tb*); Giancarlo Maurino (*ss, as*); Mario Raja (*ss, ts*); Maurizio Giammarco (*ts*);
    Roberto Ottini (*bs*); Danilo Rea (*ky*); Enzo Pietropaoli (*b*); Roberto Gatto (*d*). 7/88.
A passionate mess. Nothing wrong with the calibre of the band – these are some of Italy's finest. Woods,
too, is in strong form and occasionally reaches exalted heights: the reading of 'Embraceable You',
characterized with the purplest of prose in the sleeve-notes, is almost as good as the producer makes
out. But Mario Raja's arrangements are cumbersome, the band seem under-rehearsed, and the studio
sound is hopelessly ill-focused: Paolo Piangiarelli may be a great fan, but he should entrust production
duties to someone else.

*** **Phil On Etna** Philology W 38/39 2CD
    Woods; Giovanni La Ferlita, Mario Cavallaro, Giuseppe Privitera, Enzo Gulizia (*t*); Camillo
    Pavone, Paul Zelig Rodberg, Benvenuto Ramaci (*tb*); Salvo Di Stefano (*btb*); Carlo Cattano,
    Umberto Di Pietro (*as*); Salvo Famiani, Ercole Tringale (*ts*); Antonio Russo (*bs*); Giuseppe
    Emmanuele (*p*); Nello Toscano (*b*); Pucci Nicosia (*d*); Antonella Consolo (*v*). 3/89.
Another extravagant set from Philology, compiling 100 minutes of music from a concert with the
Catania City Brass Orkestra, a young big band following up a week's tuition under Woods's direction.
They're eager to please, and Woods himself plays with astonishing commitment as featured soloist
throughout: several of the improvisations here rank with anything he's recorded in recent years. But the
band lack any notable finesse and, faced with a demanding chart such as 'Pink Sunrise', they're audibly
struggling. The few other soloists play with the trepidation of keen but bashful students. Good live
sound, though.

*** **Flowers For Hodges** Concord CCD 4485
    Woods; Jim McNeely (*ky*). 6/91.
*** **Elsa** Philology W 206-2
    Woods; Enrico Pieranunzi (*p*). 7/91.
Woods in two very different duo situations. He plays all his collection of reeds on the Concord album,
which pairs him with McNeely on a set of tunes associated with Johnny Hodges. Soprano aside, it might
have been more appropriate to have stuck to the alto, and McNeely's occasional synthesizer introduces a
watery taste that Hodges might not have approved of; the familiar prickly romanticism endures, nevertheless. *Elsa* is from an Italian concert. While Pieranunzi listens and follows intently, Woods goes his
own way, so the interactive elements are all in one direction. Philology's warts-and-all presentation,
intent on capturing every note, also lets the impact of the music falter, since 78 minutes is really too
much of a good thing in less than perfect sound. But there is still much vivid and inimitable playing: the
title-tune and the following shift into 'Some Day My Prince Will Come' are full of great alto playing.

*** **Phil's Mood** Philology W 207-2
    Woods; Enrico Pieranunzi (*p*); Enzo Pietropaoli (*b*); Alfred Kramer (*d*). 90.
(*) **Live At The Corridonia Jazz Festival Philology W 211-2
    As above, except Roberto Gatto (*d*) replaces Kramer. 7/91.
Woods's partnership with Pieranunzi is a fruitful new step for him. The studio album, *Phil's Mood*, uses
some of the same material as the live disc and, since there are also multiple takes – four altogether of
'New Lands' – they cover the ground with scrupulous intensity. A wider choice of material would have
made the earlier record stronger, but it still stands as a persuasive Woods session, the rhythm section
responding to his customary plangency. The live album is again blemished by too much material and
indifferent sound: more festival versions of 'Lover Man' and 'Anthropology' are hardly the best way to
encounter Woods on record today.

(*) A Jazz Life Philology W 74-2
>   Woods; wide-ranging personnel, including Dizzy Gillespie orchestra, Lee Konitz (*as*), North
>   Texas State Lab Band, Big Bang Orchestra, European Rhythm Machine. 56–88.

A hotchpotch of bits and pieces from a full and varied career. There are some routine off-cuts, a nice duel with Konitz on a 1977 'Donna Lee', an extended trawl through 'Body And Soul' and much else, with the sound inevitably very mixed in quality. For fanatics only.

*** **Full House** Milestone 9196
>   Woods; Hal Crook (*tb*); Jim McNeely (*p*); Steve Gilmore (*b*); Bill Goodwin (*d*). 2/91.

Cut live at Hollywood's Catalina, this latest live set shows no sign of energy flagging, though there's no special felicities – just a top band going through its sure-footed paces.

Reggie Workman (born 1937) DOUBLE BASS

***(*) **Synthesis** Leo CDLR 131
>   Workman; Oliver Lake (*reeds*); Marilyn Crispell (*p*); Andrew Cyrille (*d*). 6/86.
*** **Images** Music & Arts CD 634
>   Workman; Don Byron (*cl*); Michele Navazio (*g*); Marilyn Crispell (*p*); Gerry Hemingway (*d*);
>   Jeanne Lee (*v*). 1 & 7/89.
***(*) **Altered Spaces** Leo CDLR 183
>   As above, except omit Navazio, add Jason Hwang (*vn*). 2/92.

As befits the name, Workman has clocked up an astonishing number and range of sideman credits: with Coltrane (*Olé*, the 1961 European tour, the *Africa/Brass* sessions) and with Wayne Shorter, Mal Waldron, Art Blakey, Archie Shepp and David Murray. Workman is also a forceful leader who has moved on to explore areas of musical freedom influenced by African idioms and frequently resembling the trance music of the *griots*. Of the available albums, *Synthesis*, a live performance from The Painted Bride in Philadelphia, is the most convincing. Workman bows, triple-stops and produces unreliably pitched sounds (presumably from below the bridge), leaving it to Crispell, as on *Images*, to give the performance its undoubted sense of coherence. Of the six tracks on *Synthesis*, it is her 'Chant' which sounds most like a fully articulated composition. Workman's ideas are developed less completely and, while they often lead to more adventurous solo excursions from the individual performers, they rarely do much more than peter out. 'Jus' Ole Mae' on *Synthesis* is '(Revisited)' on the later album, a brighter and more evocative performance but one that lacks the sheer daring and adventurous seat-of-the-pants logic of the Philadelphia version.

Altered Spaces is the most ambitious work the Ensemble has yet tackled. The long suite, 'Apart', explores territory very close to Don Byron's chilling *Tuskegee Experiments* yet seems closer in spirit to the revolutionary stoicism of Brecht's *Mother Courage*, which Jeanne Lee's vocal explicitly quotes. The bass-and-violin prelude serves as an introduction to Jason Hwang, author of the controversial play, *M. Butterfly*, and of the libretto for Philip Glass's *1000 Airplanes On The Roof*. A new member of the Ensemble, Hwang brings an oriental calm that takes the music ever further away from 'jazz'. Oddly, on this occasion it is Crispell who sounds locked into a formulaic sound that seems to be pushing for resolutions that the two string players' long lines and Hemingway's open-ended patters serve to resist. Impressive, all the same, for its sheer cross-grainedness.

**** **Summit Conference** Postcards POST1003
>   Workman; Julian Priester (*tb*); Sam Rivers (*ts, ss*); Andrew Hill (*p*); Pheeroan akLaff (*d*). 12/93.
**** **Cerebral Caverns** Postcards POST1010
>   Workman; Julian Priester (*tb*); Sam Rivers (*ts, ss, f*); Elizabeth Panzer (*hp*); (Geri Allen (*p*);
>   Gerry Hemingway (*d, elec*); Al Foster (*d*); Tapan Modak (*tablas*).

Wow! Whatever vitamin supplements Workman has been taking over the last couple of years should be made widely available to all practising musicians. These are cracking records, made by top-flight players. The *Summit Conference* group has a wish-list quality and delivers from the very start. Rivers and Priester are in boilingly good form, and the younger akLaff keeps the pace up. Slight quibbles about Hill's audibility; he isn't a delicate player and it worried us that he didn't seem to be coming through. Though the bulk of the session is up-tempo, often in fractured metres, there's still room for a heart-on-sleeve ballad, Rivers's 'Solace', introduced by trombone, piano and sax (in that order) before the composer goes up a gear and delivers his most magisterial solo for years. Priester's 'Breath' is pitched in a distant, sharp-ridden key that would have most players twitching; this group brings it on exactly on the button and without a hesitant moment.

Almost inevitably, *Cerebral Caverns* (now isn't that an off-putting title?) doesn't quite match up, but it's hard to mark it down, given the quality of performances. Allen is always better on other people's dates, and here she's called on to do the sort of high-intensity stuff that Marilyn Crispell brought to previous

Workman groups. She's featured in two trios with Workman, one with Hemingway (superb), one with harp (fascinating, but not quite there). 'Fast Forward' reunites the earlier group, without piano, and with the more experienced but no less passionate Foster on drums. The title-piece is the most ambitious in terms of sound, with harp again, flute, and Hemingway's electronically triggered drum-pads contributing to a complex mix of textures. All praise to Postcards producer, Ralph Simon, who might just look at the way he mikes and mixes piano. Otherwise A1.

World Saxophone Quartet GROUP

***(*) **Point Of No Return** Moers 01034
    Hamiet Bluiett (*bs, f, af, acl*); Julius Hemphill (*f, ss, as*); Oliver Lake (*ss, ts, as, f*); David Murray (*ts, bcl*). 6/77.
*** **Steppin'** Black Saint 120027
    As above. 12/78.
**** **W.S.Q.** Black Saint 120046
    As above. 3/80.
***(*) **Revue** Black Saint 120056
    As above. 10/80.
*** **Live In Zurich** Black Saint 120077
    As above. 11/81.
***(*) **Plays Duke Ellington** Elektra Musician 979137
    As above. 4/86.
**** **Dances And Ballads** Elektra Musician 979164
    As above. 4/87.
***(*) **Rhythm And Blues** Elektra Musician 60864
    As above. 11/88.

Market-leaders in the now well-attested saxophone-quartet format, the WSQ were founded in 1977. The debut album was not particularly well recorded but it helped establish the group's identity as adventurous composer-improvisers who could offer great swinging ensembles (not quite as hokey as those of the 29th Street Saxophone Quartet) and remarkable duo and trio divisions of the basic instrumentation. On *Point Of No Return* the armoury of reeds is pretty modest, but increasingly after 1978 all four members began to 'double' on more exotic specimens, with Bluiett's alto clarinet (rarely used in a jazz context) and Murray's bass clarinet both lending significant variations of tonality and texture. 'Scared Sheetless' from the first album gives a fair impression of its not altogether serious appropriation of free-jazz devices. 'R & B' on the second album plays with genre in a friendlier and more ironic way.

The best of the earlier records, *W.S.Q.*, is dominated by a long suite that blends jazz and popular elements with considerable ingenuity and real improvisational fire. 'The Key' and 'Ballad For Eddie Jefferson' (dedicated to the inventor of jazz vocalese) are perhaps the most interesting elements, but the closing 'Fast Life' is as fine a curtain-piece as the group has recorded. With *Revue* (a significant pun), the centre of gravity shifts slightly towards rising star Murray and towards what looks like a reassessment of the group's development. Murray's 'Ming' is well known from his own records but has never been played with such fierce beauty.

The Ellington album marks a gentle, middle-market turn that has done the group no harm at all. Opening and closing with 'Take The "A" Train', they check out 'Sophisticated Lady' and 'I Let A Song Go Out Of My Heart', do a wonderful 'Come Sunday', and add a raw lyricism to 'Lush Life' and 'Prelude To A Kiss'. The sound is better than usual, with no congestion round about the middle, as on some of the earlier sets. There's a broader big-band sound to *Dances And Ballads*, achieved without the addition of outsiders as on *Metamorphosis*, below, which seems to draw something from the Ellington set. Hemphill contributes only two tracks, but there's a fine version of David Murray's Prez tribute 'For Lester' (later to appear on his octet, *HopeScope*), and Oliver Lake's 'West African Snap', 'Belly Up' and 'Adjacent' are among the best of his recorded compositions. The soul staples covered on *Rhythm And Blues* – including 'Let's Get It On', '(Sittin' On) The Dock Of The Bay', and, unforgettably, 'Try A Little Tenderness', with Murray's tenor going places Otis Redding never heard of – are done with absolute conviction and seriousness. Only *Steppin'* and the rather rough *Live In Zurich* are disappointments, though the latter has a fine reading of 'Steppin'' itself.

All four members have developed highly individual careers apart, Murray most of all; along with Hemphill, he is the most distinctive and flexible composer. The durability of the group lay in the degree to which personal strengths were encouraged and exploited rather than subordinated. With so many instrumental permutations and the possibility of internal subdivisions, the WSQ's exploratory sound has never settled into a manner.

*** **Metamorphosis** Elektra Nonesuch 979258
> Oliver Lake (*as, ss, f*); David Murray (*ts, bcl*); Hamiet Bluiett (*bs*); Arthur Blythe (*as*); Melvin
> Gibbs (*b*); Chief Bey, Mar Gueye, Mor Thiam (*perc*). 4/90.

The departure of Julius Hemphill and arrival of Arthur Blythe couldn't have looked altogether propi-
tious, given (a) Hemphill's importance as a writer for the group, and (b) Blythe's stuttering fortunes in
recent years. The title-track, though, is given over to the new boy and he fills the outgoing man's shoes
with impressive confidence, checking in with a powerful contrapuntal weave that is lifted a notch by the
(initially disturbing; the WSQ used always to go it alone) presence of the three African drummers. In
the event, they add a great deal more than bassist Gibbs, who clocks on for three tracks only and might
as well not have bothered. Murray's 'Ballad For The Black Man' is very much an individual feature and
easily the most coherent single track; Lake's 'Love Like Sisters' has tremendous potential but might well
sound better tackled by a more conventional horn-plus-inventive-rhythm outfit. A new departure? Or a
rearguard action? Time will tell.

***(*) **Moving Right Along** Black Saint 120127
> Oliver Lake, Eric Person (*as, ss*); James Spaulding (*as*); David Murray (*ts, bcl*); Hamiet Bluiett
> (*bs, acl*). 10/93.

First indications are that the WSQ are going to be feeling their way around for some time. *Moving Right
Along* sees the first recording of the group with Eric Person, who also contributes a fresh original,
'Antithesis'. He fits in immediately and well, and sounds closer to the group's overall conception than
Spaulding.

There are few long blowing tracks. The emphasis this time is on sharp, tight arrangements. 'Giant Steps'
is dispatched in less than three minutes and there is a superb two-part arrangement of 'Amazing Grace'
by Bluiett, who also contributes 'N.T.', a hard-edged portrait of the Black insurrectionist. Bluiett's
'Astral Travels' are less convincing, but his alto clarinet has become an integral component of the group
sound; opening up the lower registers previously led to the more romantically inclined Murray on his
second horn.

This is a typically accomplished record, but it leaves a great deal of room for future development in a
number of directions. It's still difficult to read the signs.

Frank Wright (1935–90) TENOR SAXOPHONE

***(*) **Frank Wright Trio** ESP Disk ESP 1023
> Wright; Henry Grimes (*b*); Tom Price (*d*). 11/65.

*** **Your Prayer** ESP Disk ESP 1053
> Wright; Jacques Coursil (*t*); Arthur Jones (*as*); Steve Tintweiss (*b*); Muhammad Ali (*d*). 5/67.

Nicknamed 'The Reverend', Wright belonged to the Broad Church of Euro-American free music.
Though he left America for good in 1969 to live in France, even his freest playing retained the intense
preaching sound which he had taken from Albert Ayler (who persuaded Wright to abandon the double
bass for saxophone).

The later of the two ESPs is certainly an attempt to capture the Ayler sound. It succeeds only very
partially. Coursil has little to offer this music and often substitutes unsubtle dynamics for improvisational ideas. The second saxophonist only muddies the water. The earlier trio brings out the best in
Wright; three vestigial themes – 'The Earth', 'Jerry', 'The Moon' – which open up into long, fearsome
blows with excellent input from both Grimes and the little-known Price, whose recording history seems
to have been limited to ESP.

Richard Wyands (born 1928) PIANO

*** **The Arrival** DIW 611
> Wyands; Lisle Atkinson (*b*); Leroy Williams (*d*). 6/92.

Oakland-born Wyands is a considerably underrated composer (though not a prolific one) with a keyboard style that falls around the romantic end of Red Garland's far broader spectrum. Atkinson has
recorded with him before, and he makes a very important contribution to the success of this expertly
produced disc. 'Dee's Den' is the sole original here, but Wyands has a talent for getting inside tunes and
re-inventing significant aspects of the left-hand parts. He does so with 'Warm Valley' and Gene
DePaul's too rarely played 'Teach Me Tonight'. Wyands's Storyville recordings have slipped from view.
It would be good to have more from him in this polished vein.

Albert Wynn (1907–73) TROMBONE

*** Albert Wynn And His Gutbucket Seven Original Jazz Classics OJC 1826
>   Wynn; Bill Martin (*t, v*); Darnell Howard (*cl*); Bus Moten, Blind John Davis (*p*); Mike
>   McKendrick (*g, bj*); Robert Wilson (*b*); Booker Washington (*d*). 9/61.

Wynn is on a fair number of Chicago records from the 1920s, but he was something of a forgotten man
by the time he made this entry in Riverside's *Living Legends* series. His solos are rather careful and
circumspect, which leaves the main limelight to the formidable Howard, whose bustling work leans
towards the gaspipe manner at some points but is undeniably exciting. Martin's rather mannered trumpet is a nice balance, and the only time-wasting is from bluesman Davis, whose two vocals are dispensable. Wilson and Washington keep unobtrusive time. A worthwhile survival.

Yosuke Yamashita PIANO

***(*) It Don't Mean A Thing DIW 810
>   Yamashita (*p* solo). 2/84.
**** Kurdish Dance Verve 517708-2
>   Yamashita; Joe Lovano (*ts*); Cecil McBee (*b*); Pheeroan AkLaff (*d*). 92.

An intriguing stylist with a highly individual take on the modern-jazz tradition, Yamashita has explored
bop and swing staples like those on *It Don't Mean A Thing*, and classic ballads like ''Round Midnight',
but has also delved into the turbulent sound-world of Albert Ayler, in the company of his compatriot,
Sakata. With a sharp but curiously delicate touch, Yamashita prefers to play in short, apparently
discontinuous blocks of sound that often do not connect in accordance with accepted harmonic or even
rhythmic logic. His piano–shakuhachi duets with Hozan Yamamoto (one of a group of deleted Enjas)
are particularly unusual in their approach to rhythm, and it's often the flute that holds a basic pulse
while Yamashita ranges more freely.

   Though much of his more experimental work is now past history, it does have a bearing on what he does
with Joe Lovano, normally a very foursquare player, on *Kurdish Dance*, in which the saxophonist guests
with Yamashita's New York Trio. It's a very compelling record, full of surprises and puzzling moments
that make perfect sense in the context of the piece. Much the same is true of the solo performances on *It
Don't Mean A Thing*, from which one takes away a sense of having heard something very original
without being able to specify exactly how and why. Yamashita is an original who repays close attention.

*** Asian Games Verve Forecast 518344-2
>   Yamashita; Ryuchi Sakamoto, Nicky Skopelitis (*ky*); Bill Laswell (*b*); Aiyb Dieng (*perc*). 88.
***(*) Dazzling Days Verve 521303-2
>   Yamashita; Joe Lovano (*ts*); Cecil McBee (*b*); Pheeroan akLaff (*d*). 5/93.

The *Asian Games* sessions were released outside Japan somewhat belatedly in 1994. The music is a
typically off-centre Bill Laswell production, with Yamashita enthusiastically centring the whirling textures and for once sounding like the straight man of the team. A notebook of ideas rather than a fully
fledged album, perhaps, but some intriguing music comes out. The return match with Lovano and his
New York band is another exciting encounter: nothing quite as outstanding as the title-track on *Kurdish
Dance* maybe, but 'Dazzling Cradle' is pretty stunning, and the extraordinary treatment of 'My
Grandfather's Clock' would make anyone sit up.

**** Ways Of Time Verve 523841-2
>   As above, except add Tim Berne (*as, bs*). 5–6/94.
***(*) Spider Verve 531271-2
>   As above, except omit Lovano and Berne. 6/95.

Continuing an excellent and unreasonably little-known sequence of records, *Ways Of Time* is almost
equally split between trio tracks, a sequence with Lovano, and three with the peripatetic Berne (the
saxmen play together on the march-like 'Acupuntura' to superb effect). The result is arguably
Yamashita's most absorbing, intelligently varied and accomplished record. Try the way the group moves
from in to out and back again on the intriguing 'Picasso', the stuttering ingenuities of 'Chiasma' or the
signature blend of rhythmic complexity and fine melodic fabric on 'Music Land'. If *Spider* seems
comparatively the lesser record, it's only because Yamashita interacts so well with a horn player that an
all-trio date is to that extent lacking in something. His inventiveness and imagination remain at a peak,
and McBee and akLaff are in complete accord.

Hajime Yoshizawa (born 1963) PIANO

*** **Hajime** ah um 008
     Yoshizawa; Bob Mintzer (*ts*); John Abercrombie (*g*); Marc Johnson (*b*); Peter Erskine (*d*). 12/
     90.
Like a lot of Japanese, Yoshizawa sounds remarkably like Bill Evans; there's an obvious converse, but on this occasion the influence seems to be there. The presence of Marc Johnson on the date cements the connection, and it's Johnson who brings much-needed definition to what might otherwise have been a rather wispy and soft-centred project. Attractive as Yoshizawa is both in his playing and in his composition, there's nothing immediately arresting about him, and he may require more patience than most listeners are willing to devote. 'Bless Me With Your Breath', a poem to his father, is too softly enunciated to come first on the record. Better, surely, to have kicked off with one of the tracks featuring the button-holing Mintzer?

George Young TENOR, ALTO AND SOPRANO SAXOPHONES, CLARINET

*** **Burgundy** Paddle Wheel K 28P 6449
     Young; Toots Thielemans (*hca*); Warren Bernhardt (*p*); Ron Carter (*b*); Al Foster (*d*). 10/86.
*** **Oleo** Paddle Wheel K 28P 6481
     Young; Warren Bernhardt (*p*); Dave Holland (*b*); Jack DeJohnette (*d*). 11/87.
** **Yesterday And Today** Paddle Wheel 292 E 6028
     Young; Gil Goldstein (*p*); Chip Jackson (*b*); Dave Weckl (*d*). 3/89.
*** **Spring Fever** Paddle Wheel 660.55.009
     Young; Peter Philips (*tb*); Ron Feuer (*p*); Tony Marino (*b*); Jamey Haddad (*d*). 10/89.
Lacking any special characteristic to make him stand out from the ranks of modern tenors, Young is nevertheless a musician who can muster convincingly exciting music at will. A listener's reaction, as with the many records Young has made with the Manhattan Jazz Quintet, may depend on whether he or she is prepared to listen through the session-man gloss which tends to varnish over this kind of jazz and to appreciate the ideas within. At times, as with most of *Yesterday And Today*, the music burnishes inspiration down to a matter of professional pride, and it's difficult to feel involved in what's going on. But with *Oleo*, where the accompanying trio are too good to be boringly excellent, Young's thesis on the achievements of Rollins and Coltrane takes on some stature of its own. *Burgundy* is enlivened by the appearance of Toots Thielemans on one track. *Spring Fever* has him bringing out his alto and clarinet: there is a very ripe 'Imagination' on the former horn, but the clarinet sounds terribly bland.

John Young (born 1922) PIANO

*** **Serenata** Delmark DD 403
     Young; Victor Sproles (*b*); Phil Thomas (*d*). 2/59.
A local legend in Chicago, where he has worked and played his whole life, John Young has done little to put his name in the history books or discographies. This short, enjoyable session – three alternative takes take it just past the 40-minute mark – makes no case for immortality, but this is a fine example of how the music is succoured by the craftsmanship of such an accomplished player. Young hits a soulful groove on some tunes, abetted by the alert but quite sopacious rhythms of Sproles and Young, and his naturally dancing, infectious manner has enough of the blues in it to make his swing and bebop stylings stay close to the tradition. 'Cubana Chant' is as good as any Ray Bryant or Red Garland fingersnapper, and the title-piece has an unfussy lyricism which is very attractive. Excellent remastering for CD issue.

Larry Young (1940–79) ORGAN

***(*) **Testifying** Original Jazz Classics OJC 1793
     Young; Thornel Schwartz (*g*); Jimmie Smith (*d*).
***(*) **Young Blues** Original Jazz Classics OJC 1831
     Young; Thornel Schwartz (*g*); Wendell Marshall (*b*); Jimmie Smith (*d*). 9/60.
*** **Groove Street** Original Jazz Classics OJC 1853
     Young; Bill Leslie (*ts*); Thornel Schwartz (*g*); Jimmie Smith (*d*). 2/62.
Larry Young – later known as Khalid Yasin – was the first Hammond player to shake off the pervasive influence of Jimmy Smith (not to be confused with the drummer on these records) and begin the assimilation of John Coltrane's harmonics to the disputed border territory between jazz and nascent

rock. Young's best-known work was with Tony Williams's Lifetime band, for whom he created great billowing sheets of sound, doubling until Jack Bruce's arrival as a (pedal) bass player. He can also be heard on John McLaughlin's *Devotion*, prominent on such fire-eating numbers as 'Don't Let The Dragon Eat Your Mother'. Significantly, he also played a part in Miles Davis's epochal *Bitches Brew*.

It's profoundly unfortunate, though, that so little of his already small but highly significant output should remain available. *Testifying* and *Young Blues* are early recordings, still rather stuck in the soul-jazz, Jimmy McGriff mould, out of which Young was fledging by the session (Schwartz, it should be noted, also worked for McGriff) but already showing some signs of the tonal sophistication of later work. James Blood Ulmer fans would sense an ancestral influence on tracks like 'Exercise For Chihuahuas', 'Some Thorny Blues' and the title-number. The sound is a bit shimmery and harsh, but adequate.

The reappearance of *Groove Street*, a broodingly funky organ/guitar/saxophone workout is very welcome, but it hardly makes up for the seeming absence of *Unity*, the best of the Blue Notes and one of the finest jazz records of modern times.

Lester Young (1909–59) TENOR SAXOPHONE, CLARINET, VOCAL

*** **Lester – Amadeus!** Phontastic CD 7639
  Young; Buck Clayton, Ed Lewis, Bobby Moore, Harry 'Sweets' Edison, Carl Smith (*t*); George Hunt, Dan Minor, Dicky Wells, Benny Morton (*tb*); Earl Warren (*as, bs*); Herschel Evans (*ts*); Jack Washington (*bs*); Count Basie (*p*); Eddie Durham, Freddie Green (*g*); Walter Page (*b*); Jo Jones (*d*); Helen Humes (*v*). 36–38.
***(*) **The MasterTouch** Savoy SV 0113
  Young; Jesse Drakes (*t*); Jerry Elliott (*tb*); Count Basie, Junior Mance (*p*); Freddie Green (*g*); Leroy Jackson, Rodney Richardson (*b*); Roy Haynes, Shadow Wilson (*d*). 5/44, 6/49.
***(*) **Lester Young & The Piano Giants** Verve 835316
  Young; Harry 'Sweets' Edison, Roy Eldridge (*t*); Vic Dickenson (*tb*); Nat Cole, Hank Jones, John Lewis, Oscar Peterson, Teddy Wilson (*p*); Herb Ellis, Freddie Green (*g*); Ray Brown, Gene Ramey, Joe Shulman (*b*); Bill Clark, Jo Jones, Buddy Rich (*d*). 3/46–1/56.
*** **Lester Young Trio** Verve 521 650
  Young; Harry 'Sweets' Edison (*t*); Dexter Gordon (*ts*); Nat Cole (*p*); Red Callender (*b*); Juicy Owens, Buddy Rich (*d*). 43, 4/46.
*** **Blue Lester** Savoy SV 0112
  Young; Billy Butterfield, Jesse Drakes, Harry 'Sweets' Edison (*t*); Jerry Elliott (*tb*); Hank D'Amico (*cl*); Johnny Guarnieri, Count Basie, Clyde Hart, Junior Mance (*p*); Dexter Hall, Freddie Green (*g*); Billy Taylor, Rodney Richardson, Leroy Jackson (*b*); Cozy Cole, Shadow Wilson, Roy Haynes (*d*). 44–49.
*** **Prez Conferences** Jass J CD 18
  Young; Buck Clayton (*t*); Coleman Hawkins (*ts*); Mike Caluccio, Nat Cole, Kenny Kersey, Nat Pierce, Bill Potts, Sinclair Raney (*p*); Irving Ashby, Oscar Moore, Mary Osborne (*g*); Billy Hadnott, Johnny Miller, Gene Ramey, Doug Watkins, Norman Williams (*b*); Jim Lucht, Buddy Rich, Willie Jones, Specs Powell, Shadow Wilson (*d*). 46–58.
*** **Jazz Immortal Series: The Pres** Savoy SV 0180
  Young; Jesse Drakes (*t*); other personnel unknown. 4/50.
*** **Masters Of Jazz: Lester Young** Storyville STCD 4107
  Young; Jesse Drakes, Idrees Sulieman (*t*); John Lewis, Bill Potts, Horace Silver (*p*); Aaron Bell, Gene Ramey, Franklin Skeete, Norman Williams (*b*); Jo Jones, Connie Kay, Abram Lee, Jim Lucht (*d*). 5/51–12/56.
***(*) **The President Plays** Verve 831 670
  Young; Oscar Peterson (*p*); Barney Kessel (*g*); Ray Brown (*b*); J. C. Heard (*d*). 11/52.
*** **Pres & Sweets** Verve 849391
  Young; Harry 'Sweets' Edison (*t*); Oscar Peterson (*p*); Herb Ellis (*g*); Ray Brown (*b*); Buddy Rich (*d*). 12/55.
*** **Pres & Teddy** Verve 831270
  Young; Teddy Wilson (*p*); Gene Ramey (*b*); Jo Jones (*d*). 1/56.
*** **Lester Young In Washington, D.C. 1956: Volume 1** Original Jazz Classics OJC 782
  Young; Bill Potts (*p*); Norman Williams (*b*); Jim Lucht (*d*). 12/56.
*** **Lester Young In Washington, D.C. 1956: Volume 2** Pablo Live 2308225
  As above. 12/56.

*** **The Best Of Lester Young** Pablo 2405420
   As above.

For every ten jazz fans who can whistle 'Goodbye, Pork Pie Hat', there's probably only one who can claim any real knowledge of Lester Young's music. Universally acknowledged as a major influence on the bop and post-bop schools, Young's own output is neglected and frequently misunderstood. Serious appraisal of his work is complicated by an irreconcilable controversy about the quality of Young's post-war work, from which virtually all the above recordings are drawn.

Young grew up in the jazz heartland near New Orleans and served a nomadic apprenticeship with Art Bronson's Bostonians, Walter Page's Blue Devils (and later the Thirteen Original Blue Devils), moving to Minneapolis in 1931. A year or so later, he had an encounter with Charlie Christian that must count as one of the significant episodes in the pre-history of bebop. In 1933 he joined the Bennie Moten band, before signing up with Count Basie the following year on the strength of an impassioned postcard he had written to the bandleader he later christened 'The Holy Main'.

Young made his name in the Basie band, but only after an unhappy sojourn in Fletcher Henderson's orchestra, where the saxophone section ganged up on his unconventional approach and unusual sound. After brief stints with Andy Kirk and a tough spell as a 'single' in Kansas City, he returned to the Basie band. Young quickly became a major soloist, using a delivery that was the precise opposite of the dominant Coleman Hawkins style; they can be heard together on three 1946 shots recorded in Hollywood on the rather drab Jass compilation. Where Hawkins was bluff, aggressive and sensual, Young developed a sound that was dry, precise and almost delicate. Some of its curiosities of tone are traceable to the example of Jimmy Dorsey, a greatly underrated saxophonist who had created a vocabulary of alternate fingerings and low, almost unpitched breath-sounds through the horn. The only other predecessor to influence Young was Bix's sidekick, Frank Trumbauer, though less for his sound (Trumbauer favoured a C-melody saxophone) than for his distinctive habit of building solos up out of brief thematic and melodic units which he subjected to seamless variation and augmentation, building up solos of great formal control which, coupled with his unmistakable sound, represent the single most important advance in saxophone improvisation until the advent of Charlie Parker. Unlike Hawkins, Young was little concerned with playing on harmonic changes.

Versions of what followed vary – and the precise emphasis matters significantly – but in 1944 Young was drafted and began a year-long nightmare in the US Army. Some accounts suggest that he was conscripted after being spotted smoking marijuana by a plain-clothes military whipper-in scouring the clubs for able-bodied men. Other sources suggest that Young's drug (and later alcohol) problems began *in reaction to* the repressive horrors of army life. A convenient mythology suggests that the army destroyed Young as a man and an artist and that the post-war recordings are sad dregs from a once-fine musician. Another tendency suggests that Young's later recordings are actually much more experimental and exploratory as he attempts to come to terms with the rise of bebop (a music he is credited with having influenced).

Listeners who have heard Young's classic solos – the 1936 'Lady Be Good' with Jo Jones and Carson Smith, 'Jumpin' At The Woodside' and the later 'Lester Leaps In' with Basie – will have to judge how much of a falling-off is evident in the material on the Savoy sessions, which are marked by flashes of brilliance but not distributed consistently enough. The truth is that Young's best work was nearly all done for others.

Immediately after the war there was evidence of some of the less desirable traits that crept into his 1950s work (a formulaic repetition and a self-conscious and histrionic distortion of tone and phrasing akin to his friend Billie Holiday's around the same time); it's clear that he is trying to rethink harmonic progression. A new device, much noted, is his use of an arpeggiated tonic triad in first inversion (i.e. with the third rather than the root in lowest position) which, whatever its technical niceties, smoothed out chordal progression from ever shorter phrases.

It's patent nonsense to suggest that the 1950s Young was merely a broken hack, mawkishly and, as often as not, drunkenly rehashing old solos, hanging behind the beat as he tried to keep one step ahead of a failing technique. However chastened, the 1950s recordings preserved a good deal of the original genius, but placed it in a new and unfamiliar, and therefore challenging, context. The 1952 session for Norman Granz (now believed to have been made in November, not in August) includes the slightly bizarre sound of Young lewdly singing the lyric to 'It Takes Two To Tango': 'Drop your drawers, take them off. . .' It's a curiosity, but the rest of the session is very good indeed. The Verve compilation includes some excellent material, recorded in January 1956, with Roy Eldridge, another stylistic bridge-builder, and Teddy Wilson, together with a 1950 version of 'Up'N'Adam' with Hank Jones. The Nat Cole material is available separately on the *Trio* album. The 1956 Pablos (one of which is now on OJC) further confound the notion of a man who had given up on life and art; though drastically reconceived and hardly abetted by Potts's backward-looking accompaniments (it was often Prez's sidemen who wanted to play in the 'old style' about which he became so painfully ambivalent), 'Lester Leaps In' and 'These Foolish Things' (both on the better Volume 2) are major jazz performances. Right to the very end, Young was capable of quite extraordinary things. 'There Will Never Be Another You', with Kenny Clarke, Jimmy Gourley, Harold Kauffman and Jean-Marie Ingrand (with one exception, not the company he deserved) was recorded within a fortnight of his death and still sounds vital, moving and full of musical intelligence.

Young's later years have been unhelpfully coloured by too many sorry anecdotes (about his drinking, world-weariness, and increasingly restricted conversational code) and, more recently, by Bertrand Tavernier's composite anti-hero Dale Turner in *Round Midnight*, a character who is truer in spirit to the declining Bud Powell. Powell felt safe in the past and retreated into re-creations of his best work. Throughout his life, Young had been brutally cut off from his own past; by its end the only direction he knew was uneasily forward.

Bobby Zankel ALTO SAXOPHONE

*** Seeking Spirit Cadence CJR 1050
      Zankel; Stan Slotter (*t, f*); Johnny Coles (*t*); Odean Pope (*ts*); Ray Wright (*bs*); Sumi Tonooka, Uri Caine (*p*); Tyrone Brown (*b*); Craig McIver, David Gibson (*d*). 3/91–1/92.
**(*) Emerging From The Earth Cadence CJR 1059
      As above, except add John Blake (*vn*), Ralph Peterson Jr (*d*), Ron Howerton (*perc*), omit Coles, Pope, Wright, Tonooka, McIver, Gibson. 3/94.
**(*) Human Flowers CIMP 103
      Zankel; Marilyn Crispell (*p*); Newman Baker (*d*). 11/95.
The Philadelphia-based Zankel is a talented player-composer and it's a pity that his debut album is let down by some unwarranted flaws. The record is evenly split between sessions for quartet and octet: the former blaze along on the back of Gibson's explosive drumming, and some clever touches in the writing – the layered rhythms of 'Something Up Her Sleeve', for instance – help to concentrate the intensity of the playing. The five octet pieces are a shade more ambitious, but the sometimes ragged ensembles distract from thoughtful improvising by Pope, Coles and Tonooka. The leader's own alto works off a strangulated tone and impassioned delivery, but he's badly served by the production, which should have him much nearer the front. *Emerging From The Earth* is an ambitious continuation, involving the septet in all eight pieces, but there are again disappointing aspects. Even as Zankel crowds his compositions with incident, the sound of the group seems awry – Blake's violin doesn't really fit in, and some of the ensembles demand a coherence which eludes them – while the sound is again a drawback: too often the instruments sound like a muddle, and the rhythm section in particular is made to seem chaotic by the mix.

The trio session, *Human Flowers*, is entirely different. Performed as a continuous three-way conversation, with few changes in dynamics, this is rather wearying stuff over the long haul, and when Zankel's ingenuities are tested to the full he comes up a bit short at times. The CIMP philosophy of releasing unmixed live digital sound doesn't work very well here: piano and drums both sound too thin to give the music sufficient impact.

Joe Zawinul (born 1932) PIANO, KEYBOARDS

*** And The Austrian All Stars / His Majesty Swinging Nephews, 1954–1957 RST 91549
      Zawinul; Dick Murphy (*t*); Hans Salomon (*as, ts*); Karl Drewo (*ts*); Johnny Fischer, Rudolf Hansen (*b*); Viktor Plasil (*d*). 10/54–3/57.
*** The Beginning Fresh Sound FSRCD 142
      Zawinul; George Tucker (*b*); Frankie Dunlop (*d*); Ray Barretto (*perc*). 9/59.
*** The Rise And Fall Of The Third Stream / Money In The Pocket Rhino R2 71675
      Zawinul; Blue Mitchell, Jimmy Owens (*t*); William Fischer, Joe Henderson, Clifford Jordan (*ts*); Pepper Adams (*bs*); Bob Cranshaw, Richard Davis, Sam Jones (*b*); Louis Hayes, Roy McCurdy, Freddie Waits (*d*); Warren Smith (*perc*). 4/66, 10 & 12/67.
***(*) Zawinul Atlantic 7567 81375
      Zawinul; Jimmy Owens, Woody Shaw (*t*); Wayne Shorter, Earl Turbinton (*ss*); Hubert Laws, George Davis (*f*); Herbie Hancock (*p*); Walter Booker, Miroslav Vitous (*b*); Joe Chambers, Billy Hart, David Lee (*d*); Jack DeJohnette (*mca, perc*). 70.
For a long time, it was perhaps only those who'd spotted Zawinul peeping out from behind Cannonball Adderley in the festival location sequences in the Clint Eastwood film, *Play Misty for Me*, who were aware that he'd had much of a career before Weather Report. Fans of a half a generation earlier, of course, recognized him as the writer of 'Mercy, Mercy, Mercy', one of Cannonball's most effective recordings. It has taken quite some time, and the demise of Weather Report and its disappointing later cognates, for Zawinul's long career to take on some perspective.

The young pianist left his native Austria for the United States in 1959, so the items above have to be seen as before and after samples, two distinct phases of that career. Studying in Vienna, Zawinul was bound for the concert platform as a classical player before the jazz bug bit. During his student years he had various top-up jobs with dance bands and as house accompanist at Polydor, and through these he came into contact with Friedrich Gulda, a catalytic figure in contemporary music in the city. Having been forcibly discouraged (let's say) during the Nazi era, jazz in Greater Germany (as they used to call it) underwent an accelerated development and modernization during the period of reconstruction. The RST disc documents what was probably the most advanced Austrian group of its time, formed in 1954 and sounding, blindfold, pretty much on a par with any similarly-aged and -inclined group from the United States. Originally recorded for Turicaphon's Elite Special label, it's a fascinating session for a first glimpse of Zawinul as jazz composer. Even this early, 'Mekka' is unmistakably his, a forceful pounding left hand holding the whole conception together, exotic intervals and resolutions consigned to the top line. Elsewhere, Zawinul takes the least likely harmonic path, occasionally leaving the otherwise excellent Salomon and the slightly less adept Drewo at the starting gate.

By 1957, a trio with Fischer and Plasil, it's clear that he needs broader horizons for his playing. The move to America seemed inevitable. There, he gigged with Maynard Ferguson and Dinah Washington before falling in with Adderley and making a record, still to be found in the second-hand trays, with Ben Webster. The Fresh Sound – misleadingly titled, unless one really does think of the Stateside move as the beginning of his career – was made very soon after his arrival, testimony to the substantial word-of-mouth reputation Zawinul built up on an already overcrowded scene. In what was then, mercifully, not the parlance, he really goes for it, obviously trying to make an impact with a set of lyrical standards. Given the instincts of Tucker and Dunlop, the pace is generally medium to up, but there are affecting ballad performances as well; 'My One And Only Love' is beautiful, only slightly marred by Barretto's intrusive percussion.

The big shift towards fusion, inspired by Miles Davis, was a year or two away. *Third Stream/Money In The Pocket* is very much of its time, a mixture of funky soul-jazz on the slightly earlier *Money* and then-fashionable classical/non-European crossovers on the autumn–winter 1967 sessions. As a concept, 'Third Stream' is currently undergoing a certain revival, or at least is no longer the risibly pretentious nonsense it has often seemed. The very opening track, 'Baptismal', neatly underlines one very legitimate objection. A brooding cello solo with viola just behind (anticipating the tonality of later tone-poems like 'His Last Journey' on *Zawinul*) gives way to a medium-pace jazz tune, which bears only the slightest relation to the introduction. The setting of the two-part 'Soul Of A Village' would seem, on the face of it, to be far to the east of Tyrol (China, possibly), and the embellishments are a little intrusive. Extraordinarily, then, these are not Zawinul compositions at all; with the exception of 'From Vienna, With Love', a Gulda tune, everything is credited to William Fischer. (We take leave to doubt this; though Fischer certainly did the arrangements, surely at least some of these ideas are Zawinul's? If not, then the resemblance is uncanny.)

The jazzier *Money* session is nicely done; Joel Dorn's hand at the controls was something of a guarantee of quality at this time, and where he sounds a bit heavy-fisted in capturing the strings on *Third Stream*, the horn arrangements on the remaining tracks are brightly, spaciously registered, with lots of room for Adams's rich tone, and a clear vantage for the underrated Mitchell. Zawinul here shares the credits with Henderson (the thoughtful 'If') and two tunes by another musician who always gets the foundations right before he does the curlicues, bassist Sam Jones. It isn't a classic session, but whenever the horns give ground to Zawinul and the rhythm section, as on the closing 'Del Sasser', his playing is absolutely riveting.

The eponymous Atlantic album was made in the year that Weather Report was formed, and a year after Zawinul took part in Miles Davis's epochal – or, at very least, transitional – *In A Silent Way*, for which the Austrian wrote the title-track, also included here. *Zawinul* is a lovely, lovely record. Rather pretentiously subtitled 'music for two electric pianos, jazz flute, trumpet, soprano saxophone, two contrabasses and percussion', it nods backwards in the direction of his conservatory past almost as much as it anticipates the coming experiments in fusion music. Woody Shaw's echoplexed trumpet strongly recalls Miles but, with Vitous handling one of the bass parts and Shorter replacing the little-known Earl Turbinton on 'Double Image', the original Weather Report is already in place. *I Sing The Body Electric*, the group's second disc, was to include a live-in-Japan version of 'Doctor Honoris Causa', a tribute to his keyboard twin, Herbie Hancock. Here it gets a much more measured reading, less frenetic and intense, more floating and indefinite, as in 'His Last Journey', where the electric piano's ability to imitate tolling bells is exploited very effectively.

Not just because Shorter is present, 'Double Image' is the track that most clearly points forward. The brief 'Arrival In New York' is an aural impression of the immigrant wharfs; not far removed from Mingus's 'Foggy Day' on *Pithecanthropus Erectus*, it underlines how important sheer sound was to Zawinul and his group. With its strangely haunting cover photograph, a close-up portrait of an unsmiling, Slavic-looking Zawinul, this has acquired the status of a minor modern classic. On their day,

Weather Report were more dynamic, more intense and certainly much riskier; they were seldom more uncomplicatedly beautiful.

Denny Zeitlin (born 1937) PIANO

*** **Time Remembers One Time Once** ECM 1239
    Zeitlin; Charlie Haden (*b*). 7/81.
(*) **In Concert ITM Pacific 970068
    Zeitlin; David Friesen (*b*). 92.
**** **Maybeck Hall Recital Series: Volume 27** Concord CCD 4572
    Zeitlin (*p* solo). 10/92.
If only Iannis Xenakis did solo jazz recitals, Concord would have a full alphabetical set. They're certainly not scraping the barrel with Zeitlin, who's been a consistently under-praised performer for many years and might reasonably expect a larger entry than this. The duo with Haden (Zeitlin seems to relish this format) gives a measure of his particular balance of skills: delicacy of touch married to firmness of conception, a subtle blend of funk and classical grace. He plays the blues with lots of passing notes and unusual chord-sequences, and his approach to a standard like 'How High The Moon' challenges even Haden.

The other duo is less interesting because Friesen is such a bitty and inconsistent player; but 'Speak No Evil' and 'My Funny Valentine' are both as inventive as anything on the roughly contemporary Maybeck recital. This is well up to scratch for a now thoroughly distinguished series. Like most of the players before him, Zeitlin sticks mainly to standards, but his own 'Country Fair' will suggest how much he has, as a composer, in common with Chick Corea and the younger Keith Jarrett, without garnering a tithe of their critical reputation. Time, perhaps, to put that right.

Hannes Zerbe (born 1941) PIANO

*** **Rondo A La Fried** Bvhaast CD 9207
    Zerbe; Jochen Gleichmann (*t, flhn*); Andreas Altenfelder, Harry Kuhn (*t*); Jorg Huke (*tb*);
    Gundolf Nandico, Wolfgang Stahl (*frhn*); Jurgen Kupke (*cl*); Willem Breuker (*ss, as, bs, bcl*);
    Manfred Hering (*as*); Helmut Forsthoff (*ts*); Gerhard Kubach (*b*); Wolfram Dix (*d*). 3/92.
Zerbe has led his Brass Band since 1979, but this is a rare appearance on record. Although they start with a piece by Eisler, the bulk of the disc features Zerbe's naggingly memorable title-piece, setting a poem by Erich Fried, and the 'Suite In Sieben Sätzen Aus Konig K', which starts with an oom-pah march and goes through progressive disintegrations. The music stands squarely in the Euro improv tradition – beer-hall music laced with composerly flourishes, goosed up with a free-form freak-out here and there – which makes Breuker's sponsorship (and guest appearance) logical. But it's all done with great gusto, and there is some terrific playing, though the sound-mix is rather harsh on the brass.

James Zitro DRUMS

*** **James Zitro** ESP Disk ESP 1052
    Zitro; Warren Gale (*t*); Allan Praskin (*as*); Bert Wilson (*ts*); Michael Cohen (*p*); Bruce Gale (*b*).
    4/67.
Having given the world Milford Graves and Sunny Murray, it was unlikely that ESP Disk was going to score three of a kind with another master drummer. Zitro is very much a man of his time. Which is not to say he lacks interest, just that he may not have much to say across the years, even in the antagonistic Esperanto of this music. The rest of the group, with the exception of Gale, have joined him in oblivion.

Attila Zoller (born 1927) GUITAR, BASS

*** **The Horizon Beyond** Act 9211
    Zoller; Don Friedman (*p*); Barre Phillips (*b*); Daniel Humair (*d*). 3/65.
*** **Common Cause** Enja ENJ 3043
    Zoller; Ron Carter (*b*); Joe Chambers (*d*). 5 & 10/79.
***(*) **The K & K In New York** L+R 40009
    Zoller; Hans Koller (*ts, sno*); George Mraz (*b*). 6/79.

***(*) **Memories Of Pannonia** Enja ENJ 5027
    Zoller; Michael Formanek (*b*); Daniel Humair (*d*). 6/86.
*** **Overcome** Enja ENJ 5055
    As above, except add Kirk Lightsey (*p*). 11/86.

Like many quiet and understated players, Zoller has rarely received his fair share of critical attention. Among fellow players, though, his stock remains very high. Recognized as a fine, romantic accompanist, he is also highly regarded as a solo player and small-group leader who has been part of the modern scene in Europe since the end of the war. Zoller sounds slightly overpowered by a drummer and the elegant counterpoint of the 1979 reunion with Koller (who tries out a reflective sopranino saxophone in addition to his smooth tenor) is a new departure. Mraz's melodic lines are featured on a fine duet, 'The Clown Down And Upstairs', with Koller, who rather steals the album.

The 1986 trio is one of Zoller's best records, graced with a lovely reading of 'Sophisticated Lady', which catches his restrained lyricism perfectly. The addition of Lightsey was a happy thought, and the two get on famously, intelligent musicians engaged in discussion of above-average sophistication. The record was made at the Leverkusen Festival and there are some technical deficiencies as well as a rather ponderous pace which diminishes its impact and calls for more work than most listeners will consider worth the investment.

John Zorn (born 1954) ALTO SAXOPHONE, DUCK CALLS

***(*) **Cobra** hat Art CD 2034
    Zorn; Jim Staley (*tb*); Carol Emmanuel, Zeena Parkins (*hp*); Bill Frisell (*g*); Elliott Sharp (*g, b*); Arto Lindsay (*g, v*); Anthony Coleman, Wayne Horvitz (*p, ky*); David Weinstein (*ky*); David Klucevsek (*acc*); Bob James (*tapes*); Christian Marclay (*turntables*); J. A. Deane (*tb synthesizer, elec*); Bobby Previte (*perc*). 10/85, 5/86.

Listening to John Zorn is like flicking through a stack of comic books or watching endless Hanna–Barbera and Fred Quimby re-runs on a TV set whose brightness and contrast have been jacked up to migraine level. Zorn is not the first but is certainly the most thorough and considered post-modernist thrown up by jazz, and there's a certain appropriateness to his alphabetical position. More than any other individual musician, he appears to mark the point of transition between a period of high-value technical virtuosity and a new synthesis of art that does not presume to raise itself above the throwaway, five-minute, all-tastes-are-equal, recyclable culture. He is, when he chooses to be, a fine boppish saxophonist, using duck calls as ironic punctuations, much in the way that Rahsaan Roland Kirk, another underrated player and expert surrealist, used to end solos with raucous siren blasts. It's not surprising to find Zorn turning, as he does in *Spy Vs Spy*, below, to the music of Ornette Coleman, whose reconstitution of melody in jazz is probably the most significant technical advance since the advent of bebop. However, Zorn's fundamental premises are in many regards the opposite of Coleman's. In so far as he belongs to any creative tendency, Zorn is a 'free' player whose hectic collage-ism is only a populist version of the invent-your-own-language gestures of the free movement. An aficionado of game systems (and of other, more traditional aspects of Japanese culture and art: two-dimensionality, false perspective, simultaneity, violence-as-aesthetics), Zorn has frequently drawn on games and sports. Earlier works such as *Archery* (Parachute), *The Classic Guide To Strategy* (Lumina) and the marvellous *Yankees* (a Celluloid release with Derek Bailey and George Lewis; the instrumentation has been revived in the Lulu project, below) drew heavily on game-theory as a matrix for 'free' (but no longer abjectly free) improvisation. The remarkable *Cobra* is perhaps the most developed example of this strand in Zorn's work and, with Butch Morris's 'conduction' (Zorn played on Morris's *Current Trends In Racism In Modern America*), is perhaps the most radical recent attempt to restructure improvisation without imposing structures on it.

Cobra was inspired by the war-game of that name, and the title carries a suggestion of unpredictability which suits Zorn's purpose (it may also suggest the snake-charming illusion by which he conjures players up out of a pre-informational 'basket'). Zorn stands in relation to *Cobra* as a game-programmer, not as a composer. His only sleeve credit is as a 'prompter'. Though unfettered by a notated score, players respond to his hand-signals, as in Morris's work, interpreting them pretty much according to their own lights. The result is by no means inchoate. Zorn attaches Italian tempo markings – 'Allegro', 'Violento', 'Lento/Misterioso' – and quasi-generic names – 'Fantasia', 'Capriccio' – to each of the movements, giving them an ironic formality. The music is often serendipitously beautiful, but Zorn typically refuses to allow any dalliance on lyrical or promisingly rhythmic passages, constantly changing the on-screen image like a station-zapping teenager. The juxtaposition of two versions of the game-piece is perhaps a nudging comment on the fetishization of 'live' performance in both jazz and rock. The live sections (recorded first) tend to be longer, but no more structurally developed.

Though sharply alienating in impact, *Cobra* remains the best point of entry into Zorn's intriguing sound-world. The only element missing is the appealing squawk and bite of his saxophone.

***(*) **Locus Solus** Eva/Wave WWCX 2035

Zorn; Wayne Horvitz (*ky*); Arto Lindsay (*g*); Anton Fier, Mark Miller, Ikue Mori (*d*); Christian Marclay (*turntables*); Whiz Kid (*scratching*); Peter Blegvad (*v*). 83.

Only very recently reissued on CD, this is one of the sacred texts of '80s New York improv, a fierce, scrabbly set of associations that draw heavily on the power-trio aesthetic of rock bands like Hüsker Dü. Zorn favours the short, sharp shock approach to improvisation, steering sessions that are remarkably reminiscent of Billy Jenkins's 12 × 3-minute-round 'Big Fights', but for the fact that one player is always refereeing and sometimes even normalizing the music. Noted out of chronological sequence here, *Locus Solus* is one of those records that, in one respect very much of its time, also seems to float freely without obvious stylistic or fashion anchors. It's impressively compact but sometimes rather too abrupt.

**** **The Big Gundown** Elektra Nonesuch 979139

Zorn; Jim Staley (*tb, btb*); Tim Berne (*as*); Vicki Bodner (*ob, eng hn*); Bill Frisell, Fred Frith, Jody Harris, Robert Quine, Vernon Reid (*g*); Arto Lindsay, Anthony Coleman (*p, ky*); Wayne Horvitz (*p*); Big John Patton (*org*); Orvin Acquart (*hca*); Toots Thielemans (*hca, whistling*); Ned Rothenburg (*shakuhachi, etc.*); Michihiro Sato (*shamisen*); Guy Klucevsek (*acc*); Carol Emanuel (*hp*); Polly Bradfield (*vn*); Melvin Gibbs (*b*); Anton Fier (*d*); Mark Miller, Bobby Previte (*d, perc*); Cyro Baptista, Reinaldo Fernandes, Duduka Fonseca, Claudio Silva, Jorge Silva (*perc*); David Weinstein (*elec*); Bob James (*tapes*); Christian Marclay (*turntables*); Laura Biscotto, Diamanda Galas, Shelley Hirsch (*v*). 9/84–9/85.

Utterly remarkable in every way and one of the essential records of the 1980s. Ennio Morricone's soundtrack scores – to movies by Pontecorvo, Lelouch, Bertolucci, Petri and, most memorably, Sergio Leone – are among the most significant artistic collaborations of recent times, a simultaneous confirmation and dismantling of the *auteur* myth. Zorn appears to have been influenced every bit as much by Leone's weird pans, sustained close-ups and frozen poses (where a fly or a melting harmonica note on the soundtrack might command more attention than the actor), followed by bouts of violence which are ritualized rather than choreographed (as they would be in a Peckinpah movie).

Zorn assembles musicians with his usual puppet-master care, bringing on harmonica player Toots Thielemans to whistle plangently on 'Poverty' from *Once Upon A Time In America*, organist Big John Patton to grind out the 'Erotico' line from *The Burglars*, Diamanda Galas and Vernon Reid to lash up a storm on 'Metamorfosi', a theme from Petri's *La Classe Operaia Va In Paradiso*. Zorn's political concerns are engaged to the extent of his determination to raise preterite music to the gates of heaven, thereby overcoming what he considers the 'racist' compartmentalization of high and low, black and white, formal and improvised styles on which the music industry depends.

The Big Gundown establishes the pattern for much of Zorn's subsequent music. It is very much a 'studio' record, an artefact, and Zorn himself has adduced the example of George Martin and the Beatles, or the earlier works of another enormous, alphabetically and stylistically late-coming influence, Frank Zappa. Like Zappa, Zorn appears to trash the very musics he seems to be setting up as icons. The result is ambivalent, unsettling and utterly contemporary.

**** **Spillane** Elektra Nonesuch 79172

Zorn; Jim Staley (*tb*); Anthony Coleman, Wayne Horvitz (*p, ky*); Big John Patton (*org*); Dave Weinstein (*ky*); Carol Emanuel (*hp*); Albert Collins, Bill Frisell (*g*); Melvin Gibbs (*b*); David Hofstra (*b, tba*); Bob James (*tapes, CDs*); Ronald Shannon Jackson (*d*); Bobby Previte (*d, perc*); Christian Marclay (*turntables*); Kronos Quartet: David Harrington, John Sherba (*vn*); Hank Dutt (*vla*); Joan Jeanrenaud (*clo*); Ohta Hiromi (*v*). 8/86, 6 & 9/87.

Zorn's own liner-notes to *Spillane* offer immensely valuable insights into his work and philosophy: his interest in Carl Stalling, composer of Bugs Bunny and other cartoon soundtracks; his Japan obsession (reflected here in 'Forbidden Fruit' for voice and string quartet); his conceptual-collage, file-card approach to 'Spillane' itself; the need for longer durations to accommodate Albert Collins's blues lines on 'Two-Lane Highway'; his overall conviction that 'the era of the composer as autonomous musical mind has just about come to an end'.

For all their apparent serendipity, Zorn's groups are selected with very great care. He approaches instrumental coloration much as a graphic artist might use a 'paintbox' package on a computer graphics screen, trying possibilities consecutively or even simultaneously, but making his gestures in a very precise, hard-edged way. 'Spillane' is a sequence of tiny sound-bites, evocative not so much of Mickey Spillane's fictional world (in the sense of dim bars, lonely roads, chalked outlines on the pavement) as of his language, which is notably fragmentary, clipped and elided, poised between literalism and the purest self-reference. Zorn has pointed to the fact that Schoenberg's earliest atonal works were given unity only by use of texts; and it's clear that Zorn's imagery works in much the same way, with Mickey Spillane's voices soundtracking the music rather than vice versa.

'Two-Lane Highway' follows a more systematic and structured groove, a concerto for bluesman and improvising orchestra, with Collins's guitar, voice, mere *presence* taking the part of the solo instrument. The final part, 'Forbidden Fruit', is actually more conventional and is by far the dullest thing Zorn has done on record, reminiscent of Ennio Morricone's non-film, squeaky-door compositions.

**** **Spy Vs Spy** Elektra Musician 960844
     Zorn; Tim Berne (*as*); Mark Dresser (*b*); Joey Baron, Michael Vatcher (*d*).
In some respects a more straightforward tribute than the Morricone set, Zorn's take on the music of Ornette Coleman is a headlong, hardcore thrash that approaches levels of sheer intensity never attempted by Coleman's own Prime Time band. Only one of the first dozen tracks is over three minutes in length. 'Chronology', from Coleman's classic Atlantic album, *The Shape Of Jazz To Come*, lasts exactly 68 seconds, and half a dozen others, drawn from Coleman's output between 1958 and the 1980s, occupy no more than 15 minutes between them. It is these, rather than the more measured performances, which seem most faithful to the originals. The twinned altos, sharply separated by channel, scribble all over the white-noise drumming, brutal graffito effects which almost miraculously preserve Coleman's melodic outlines.

***(*) **News For Lulu** hat Art CD 6005
     Zorn; George Lewis (*tb*); Bill Frisell (*g*). 8/87.
**** **More News For Lulu** hat Art CD 6055
As above. 1/89.
Named after a composition by Sonny Clark, a reviving reputation among bop piano players, *News For Lulu* and its live sequel offer the best-recorded instances of Zorn as bop saxophonist. (Zorn has also fronted a 'Sonny Clark Memorial Quintet', recording the pianist's compositions on an excellent Black Saint album, *Voodoo* (BSR 1019 CD/LP), which is not currently in the catalogue.) Lewis is the ideal partner, poised midway between total freedom and a more structured melodic/harmonic approach. Frisell takes a relatively modest role, painting backgrounds rather than the foreground figures but keeping his more extravagant washes and treatments in reserve for Zorn's thrash-core Naked City project. There are versions of Kenny Dorham's 'K.D.'s Motion', 'Lotus Blossom' and 'Windmill', Hank Mobley's 'Funk In Deep Freeze' and the title-piece on both; two studio cuts of Clark's 'Blue Minor' are supplemented by two more, better still, from the Paris concert.

More also features material by Freddie Redd, also the focus of some revisionist attention, and an original piece by Misha Mengelberg. The live sound is a bit flat and unresponsive, but the performances are a shade more vivid; read what you will into that.

**** **Filmworks: 1986–1990** Elektra Nonesuch 979270
     Zorn; Jim Staley (*tb*); Tom Varner (*frhn*); Vicki Bodner (*ob*); Marty Ehrlich (*ts, cl*); Ned
     Rothenberg (*bcl*); Bill Frisell, Robert Quine (*g*); Arto Lindsay (*g, v*); Anthony Coleman, Wayne
     Horvitz, David Weinstein (*ky*); Carol Emanuel (*hp*); Mark Dresser, Fred Frith, Melvin Gibbs,
     David Hofstra (*b*); Anton Fier (*d*); Bobby Previte (*d, mar, perc, v*); Cyro Baptista, Nana
     Vasconcelos (*perc*); David Shea (*turntables, v*); Shelley Hirsch (*v*). 6/86–5/90.
Much to his disappointment, Hollywood didn't a beat a path to Zorn's door after the Spillane and Morricone tributes. Independent movie-maker Rob Schwebber did, however, commission a soundtrack for his short *White And Lazy*, and Zorn put together a name band of downtown eclectics capable of the jump-cut style-switching that Zorn demands. The same sort of thing goes on in a score for Raul Ruiz's *The Golden Boat*. This is a more developed sequence of stylistic bites, with Zorn's saxophone on 'Jazz I' sounding uncannily like Ornette Coleman for a few bars, more rockabilly, a touch of 'Horror Organ' and some Bernard Hermann harmonies. *She Must Be Seeing Things*, by Sheila McLaughlin, is a story of lesbian love and jealousy, and Zorn's music, scored for saxophones, horns and keyboards, has a threatening, polymorphous quality that fits the movie's emotional temper very well. The long 'Seduction' is an extraordinary mood-swing blues, by far the most coherent thing Zorn has done in this idiom. There's one additional track. 'The Good, The Bad And The Ugly' was a try-out for a Camel cigarettes campaign for South East Asia (!). Zorn's submission, a typical cut-up, was close, but no cigar. So to speak.

   Lighter and less compelling than the earlier film materials, this is a thoroughly entertaining and often provocative insight into the working methods of perhaps the most distinctive 'composer' (if he'd accept the term) in jazz music today. It's also beautifully recorded, with a big rock mix that demands to be turned up higher and higher.

**** **Masada: Alef** DIW 888
     Zorn; Dave Douglas (*t*); Greg Cohen (*b*); Joey Baron (*d*). 95.
***(*) **Masada: Beit** DIW 889
     As above.

*** **Masada: Gimel** DIW 890
    As above.
*** **Masada: 5** DIW 891
    As above.
*** **Masada: 6** DIW 892
    As above.

By the mid-'90s, the Zorn discography has become unmanageable. There is in preparation a 100-CD set, marketed in Japan, where Zorn is something of a cult hero. Even a project like this one, in which the saxophonist often movingly explores aspects of his Judaism, raises questions about opportunism. Why was his interest in Hebrew culture not made known sooner? A desire for privacy? A slow awakening to his cultural roots? Or a more cynical reason?

   There seems no reason to take the third course in approaching these records. They are beautifully played, folk themes with a contemporary cutting edge, performed by a razor-sharp band whose stylistic reach is almost unbelievably capacious. The first three, named after the A-B-C of the Hebrew alphabet, are almost required listening, but thereafter the series becomes almost indistinguishably repetitive, an impression reinforced by near-identical covers. Number four is not listed because it was issued only as a free record for those who had bought earlier CDs. As always, and even when ostensibly drawing his inspiration from the notorious mass suicide of the Zealots at Masada, a key moment in Jewish history, Zorn has an eye to the market strategy. He has become an ambiguous superstar of the avant-garde; the only artist one might compare him to is Laurie Anderson, except that he has never sought her brand of middle-market appeal. An astonishing musician, as these records confirm, his place in the music is no more clear-cut than before.

Zubop GROUP

*** **Freewheeling** 33 Records 33JAZZ015
    Will Wisbling (*t, vtb, v*); Ricky Edwards (*as, f, v*); Jon Petter (*ts, cl, darbouka, perc, v*); Philip
    Clouts (*p, ky*); Duncan Noble (*b*); Sean Randle (*d*); Gary Hammond (*perc*). 8/93.

This follow-up sustains the velocipede metaphor of Zubop's debut, *Cycle City*, which we have not had an opportunity to review (it may still be available). Recorded in hot weather, *Freewheeling* communicates a breezy exhilaration and an unexpected, occasionally dark side, as in parts of the long centrepiece, '20,000 Leagues Above Peckham'. Individual musicianship is less significant than group values and these are generally very consistent, though one feels a certain spontaneity has been sacrificed in the rehearsal room. The writing and arrangements are very professional, if a little too 'eclectic', and the recording is handled by the redoubtable Dill Katz, which speaks for itself. We look forward to catching up with *Cycle City*.

Axel Zwingenberger PIANO, CELESTE

*** **Boogie Woogie Live** Vagabond VR 8.85007
    Zwingenberger (*p* solo).
*** **Boogie Woogie Breakdown** Vagabond VRCD 8.78013
    As above. 8 & 9/76.
(*) **Let's Boogie All Night Long Vagabond VRCD 8.79012
    Zwingenberger; Big Joe Turner (*v*); Torsten Zwingenberger (*d*). 5/78.
(*) **Powerhouse Boogie Vagabond VRCD 8.80011
    Zwingenberger; Roy Dyke (*d*). 11/79.
(*) **Boogie Woogie Jubilee Vagabond VR 8.81010
    Zwingenberger; Big Joe Turner (*v*); other personnel unknown. 81.
***(*) **Axel Zwingenberger & The Friends Of Boogie Woogie: Volume 6** Vagabond VR 8.85005
    Zwingenberger; Joe Newman (*t*); Lloyd Glenn (*p*); Torsten Zwingenberger (*d*); Big Joe Turner
    (*v*). 5/81, 1/82.
***(*) **The Boogie Woogie Album** Vagabond VR 8.88008
    Zwingenberger; Lionel Hampton (*vib*); Barry Reis, Johnny Walker (*t*); Tom Chapin, Yoshi
    Malta (*as*); Arnett Cobb, Ricky Ford, Illinois Jacquet, George Kelly (*ts*); Ralph Hamperian,
    Arvell Shaw (*b*); Panama Francis (*d*); other personnel unknown. 1/82.
*** **Axel Zwingenberger And The Friends Of Boogie Woogie: Volume 4 – The Blues Of Mama Yancey**
Vagabond VRCD 8.8009
    Zwingenberger; Estella Yancey (*v*). 10/82, 8/83.

** **Sippie Wallace / Axel Zwingenberger And The Friends Of Boogie Woogie** Vagabond VRCD 8.84002
    Zwingenberger; Sippie Wallace (*v*). 8/83.

** **An Evening With Sippie Wallace** Vagabond VRCD 8.86006
    As above. 10/84.

*** **Boogie Woogie Bros** Vagabond VR 8.89015
    Zwingenberger; Torsten Zwingenberger (*d*). 2/88.

*** **Axel Zwingenberger & The Friends Of Boogie Woogie: Volume 6** Vagabond VR 8.90016
    Zwingenberger; Torsten Zwingenberger (*d*); Champion Jack Dupree (*v*). 2/88.

** **Axel Zwingerberger And The Friends Of Boogie Woogie: Volume 7 – Champion Jack Dupree Sings Blues Classics** Vagabond VRCD 8.92018
    Zwingenberger; Mogens Seidlin (*b*); Michael Strasser (*d*); Champion Jack Dupree (*v*). 9/90.

Boogie and, furthermore, woogie. Good-natured nonsense from a dedicated revivalist with a solo technique that would sit comfortably alongside all the great boogie-woogie players. Zwingenberger has something of Pinetop Smith's ability to vary 'the sixteens' in the bass, and his right-hand figures, which seem to combine Smith with Meade Lux Lewis, are impressively modulated. His concentration of energy is genuinely impressive and the music a great deal more varied than might ever have been expected. The sessions with Newman and the rejuvenated Hampton are predictably the best, but the duos with brother Torsten are rousing (try the splendidly entitled 'Two Eels Walking On An Icecake'); only the vocal sides tend to pall rather quickly. The recordings are excellent. It helps having a label all to yourself. We hope that all these are still out there somewhere!

Index